M. M.
décembre 1958

A HISTORY OF WESTERN ART

A HISTORY

WESTERN

OF

ART

JOHN IVES SEWALL

HENRY HOLT AND COMPANY New York

PRINTED IN THE UNITED STATES OF AMERICA
LIBRARY OF CONGRESS CATALOG CARD NUMBER: 52-13904

INTRODUCTION

This book is an attempt to provide the reader with an introduction to the study of the visual arts. The chief problem has been one of space. How, in a few hundred pages, can one cover a field with a present literature so vast that no single scholar can be physically capable of reading it all? There are two possible methods: to say a very little about everything, or to select. I have chosen the latter.

There is perhaps no principle of selection with which everybody would agree. No matter what an author may do, he is bound at many points to disappoint himself and the reader. In the main, I have assigned or denied space by reference to two criteria.

First and most important, I have asked myself not what the reader might find easiest to assimilate or be entertained to know (or what I might most enjoy writing about), but what the reader ought to know *first*. I have tried, that is, to determine when, how, why, and where the definitive decisions were made in the history of art. I have attempted to identify the crucial monuments, if such are still in existence, or at least monuments illustrative of the main course of events. Everything else I have omitted.

Secondly, I have expanded or contracted my text by reference to the comparative availability of other reading. I have construed availability as meaning the existence of books written in English — books, furthermore, which one might reasonably expect to find in every college and public library above the medium size.

The result of such selection will be evident from the Table of Contents. Chapter 9, on the Early Middle Ages, is the longest in the book; but where else can the general reader find a connected narrative covering that very difficult but vitally important field which has for fifty years been perhaps the most active of all with respect to research? It will at first seem strange, to cite another chapter, that the Baroque and Rococo are compressed into only 37 pages with a virtual omission of the Dutch, English, and Spanish painters. The immense amount of art produced during that era — and its familiarity to American readers — is nevertheless not a governing consideration. It can all be understood in terms of what went before; and space had to be saved for detailed explanation of the major developments which came afterward.

In many places the reader will, however, find passages of the briefest and barest summary. Worthless if they had to stand alone, such paragraphs will nevertheless prove a guide for future study. They are designed to make a connection between the present text and the important ramifications which are regretfully but necessarily left out. By consulting the index, the reader will find it possible to establish numerous other relationships not directly treated herewith.

In addition to tracing the main outline of the history of western art, I have undertaken to face up to the problem of aesthetic judgment. Numerous critical terms which lack, as yet, any strict and accepted usage will be found indexed and defined. I have endeavored to keep my own use of them constant. It would be impertinent to claim that my definitions are final; but I hope that, with the help of the index, it will be possible to understand what I have intended to say. In spelling such words, and all others, I have preferred to Anglicize everything whenever a choice was permissible. That custom often violates linguistic consistency; but it corresponds to the way we talk.

Any writer worth his salt has strong opinions; and I can hardly demand that every friend and colleague agree with mine. When undertaking interpretation or when setting forth an estimate of worth, I have done my best to be fair. The context, if it is as I have tried to make it, ought to show where statement of fact ends and where criticism begins. I hope that no one will feel that he has been tricked into agreeing with anything; and I hope that every man will find that he has at least had a plain statement of whatever he does not want to believe. For the sake of brevity and clarity, many such statements appear to be more dogmatic than they are; and I hope that the reader will remember throughout that the greatness in great art is no simple matter. Not only are two, three, and even four points of view possible; all may actually be on the road toward truth.

There is no such thing as an adequately illustrated volume on the history of art; one could always use more and more plates. In selecting those which appear here, I have done my utmost to secure examples of the best modern photography. Wherever possible, I have put in a fresh view. Many items appear for the first time. A few photographs were specially taken; and except for a small number otherwise credited, the architectural drawings are entirely original.

It is earnestly to be hoped that the plates are a proper compromise between the incompatible requirements of number and size. It is also hoped that the arrangement, pagination, and numbering will (with the aid of the tapes bound in as bookmarkers) be convenient, minimizing the ever-tedious annoyance of having to turn over pages.

The index is unusually complete; but no index can be entirely satisfactory. Appreciating that many persons will not care to read the entire book but may wish to consult it for material upon a topic of special interest, I felt compelled to supplement the index with numerous cross-references included within the body of the text. I believe that such will be welcomed by readers who look something up only to find themselves bogged down, as it were, in a moving train of unfamiliar thought. The cross-references mar the appearance of the pages and break the cursive quality of many a sentence. I am sorry for it; but I hope those who enjoy the beatitude of total recall will be gracious enough merely to close their eyes.

Most parts of the text are easy enough, but some substantial sections are undeniably hard. Presumably the reader will often find it an onerous task to follow and to understand; but he must accept the necessity. It is a gross error to assume that an introductory volume should be or can be simpler than the subject with which it deals. It is not the erudite refinements of knowledge that challenge the mind, but the fundamental elements thereof. Learned men, if we tell the truth of it, are seldom called upon to perform the feats of comprehension we daily assign to freshmen. Having taught the latter annually for more than 20 years (and in three widely separated parts of the country) I can say that there is nothing in the book which is beyond them. I have made it a rule to start every matter from the very beginning; and that, in my experience, is all that will be asked by the ingenious youngsters with which this land is so generously blessed.

AUXILIARY REFERENCES

While the text is complete in itself, it must be assumed that the reader has access to or will find his way to a collection of photographs. Such collections now constitute a standard section of a college or departmental library, and are available in most museums and at many public libraries. "Picture books" too numerous for citation have in recent years multiplied in number until, today, they offer a comparatively inexpensive substitute for mounted photographs. It is merely necessary to discriminate between the small and inexpensive plates (useful for reminder of what one already knows) and the finer reproductions suitable for primary study.

Where no definition is supplied herein, Webster may be assumed to govern whenever a question of denotation comes up.

For serious exploration of matters all too briefly covered, the standard reference books must be consulted; the earnest student will, with the help of the librarian, be able to find his own way. For succinct articles of the kind needed to clarify a point instantly, the *Columbia Encyclopedia* is unexcelled; but one should also have at hand Webster's *Biographical Dictionary* and W. L. Langer's *Encyclopedia of World History*.

No one can learn very much about the history of art without appreciating the necessity for geographical information. Unfortunately, however, the best and latest American atlases give better coverage on Indiana than on France and Italy. Places like Cluny — the center of the world during the 12th Century — are unlisted and perhaps all but uninhabited. European atlases are better for the purpose; but the best are none too good. A big atlas of any kind is, moreover, a major investment.

What we need is an art historical atlas; but none exists. There are various " classical " and " historical " atlases, of course; but not one of them, or all together, supply the want. They all went out of print years ago, anyway, and are only to be obtained when one is lucky enough to make a find on the second-hand counter.

I have therefore tried at every point to indicate the location of important sites by distance and direction from some modern city. With that much information, the reader will be prepared to search out further details in the excellent guidebooks of Baedeker, Hachette, Muirehead, and others. It is further recommended that he purchase for himself a set of the excellent maps available at nominal cost from the National Geographic Society in Washington.

ACKNOWLEDGEMENTS

In this as in every other book, considerations of space sternly curtail what may be said under the heading above. Indeed, whenever a reader sees this heading, he has learned to expect nothing more than a list of names and a few flourishes of rhetoric. I doubt whether I can do better; but that is not how I feel.

This book has been in preparation for seven years. During that time, I have bothered and badgered people with innumerable inquiries both large and small. Many such have been addressed to my friends, upon whom I had at least some claim; but in the nature of the case, and in a correspondence extending from Honolulu to Constantinople and Tel Aviv, I have perforce frequently imposed upon the good nature of persons to whom I was a complete stranger. The response? Kindliness, generosity, trouble straightway undertaken and without stint, cordial encouragement in my task, and the best of good wishes.

When I reflect that more than one of those to whom I refer was but lately an enemy in war, I take renewed confidence in the worth of the visual arts and I feel new hope for the whole world.

It is obviously impossible to mention by name everybody who has helped me. I can only refer to those who were most intimately concerned and most constantly appealed to. I am sure that all the others will know that the memory of their assistance is very much alive, and will be content.

Almost all the architectural drawings (and they constitute a major contribution) are the work of Dr. W. D. Richmond of Boston. Few persons possess his technical training as both architect and art historian. His experience as a teacher will be obvious to all who have themselves taught. I would make it emphatically plain that the ingenuity displayed is his own, and not mine.

Most of the photographs used as copy for the illustrations were sought out abroad by Flaminia Guerrini and Barbara Ives Beyer. Unless he has tried it, the reader can have no idea of the tedious complexity of such an enterprise, or of the unremitting demands upon knowledge and taste. I think that the illustrations are very good; but I can claim little credit for it. Had it not been for the devoted aid of the two ladies mentioned, the plates would have been pedestrian indeed — or at least I fear so.

Whenever a photograph came from a private or commerical photographer, that fact is indicated by the signature which appears with the plate. Material obtained direct from a museum bears no signature; in such cases, the reader will understand that the work of staff photographers is represented. The several directors, curators, and trustees, appreciating the desirability of brevity in the captions, have been most cooperative in waiving the necessity for lengthy and repetitious statements of acknowledgement. For that, as well as for the permission to reproduce, my publishers join me in expressing cordial thanks. The List of Illustrations at the front of the volume contains detailed citation for all the plates borrowed from other publications; for permission to use those, I am grateful to the respective publishers.

The generosity to which I have referred in general terms at the beginning of this section demands specific attention in three further instances. Professor Clarence Kennedy of Smith College took an immense amount of trouble to furnish me with prints from a number of his incomparable negatives. Professor Clarence Ward of Oberlin was equally openhanded in letting me use many of his unique and remarkable photographs of the Gothic; these were taken especially for his own use in a projected work on medieval architecture. The new Brogi photographs of statuary by Donatello were intended first to appear in a new monograph being prepared by Professor H. W. Janson of

New York University. All three gentlemen instantly released the material when asked. The reader will have gathered that their action was typical of my general experience, but I am not one whit the less heartily in their debt.

In writing the text, I have enjoyed the continuous support and encouragement of Julian Park, Dean of the College of Arts & Sciences at the University of Buffalo. I first undertook the work in response to the urging (perhaps better stated as the demand) of my friend the late Philip Wickser; I hope it is worthy of his all too generous expectations. Professor Ulrich Middledorf of Chicago was kind enough to read several of the early chapters in first draft, and he encouraged me to continue. My dependence upon my sometime teachers Karl Weston, C. R. Morey, Arthur Pope, Chandler Post, P. J. Sachs, Kingsley Porter, G. H. Edgell, and George Chase will be evident to all who know their work — but none of them has had a chance at me for twenty years, and none may be blamed for anything.

On matters of historical information and upon matters of critical estimate, I have been much advantaged by day to day advice from my colleagues Mrs. Beyer (already mentioned), Edgar C. Schenck, and Patrick J. Kelleher — the two latter being Director and Curator, respectively, at the Albright Art Gallery. How could a man write without someone to answer queries over the phone? If I have bothered these people once, I have bothered them ten thousand times apiece. Their immense knowledge of the field has saved me from more mistakes than I should like to acknowledge.

Professors Sumner Crosby and S. L. Faison, Jr., generously read through the penultimate draft of Chapter 12, and gave me the benefit of their criticism. Chapter 19 is the end result of protracted conference and argument between myself, Mr. Wickser, and my quondam colleague Professor William C. Seitz. In saying that I am grateful to these persons, and to those mentioned in the paragraph above, I make no suggestion that they endorse what I have written in its entirety. In fact, they have done no such thing; but I see no more reason for agreeing with them than they with me. By learning, logic, and wit, however, they have sharpened up many a point and forced me to clarify my own position. That is what I am grateful for.

Even the shortest book involves an author in bibliographical problems quite beyond his ken. A long book full of illustrations presents a multiplication of perplexities, some of them seemingly hopeless. But just as I used to do in student days, I always asked Miss Louise Lucas, the distinguished librarian of the Fogg Museum in Cambridge. And just as she did then, Miss Lucas produced the answer without fail and in almost no time, often when others had confessed themselves stumped. All librarians are patient and kind; but was ever one more learned in her craft?

The quotations from classical authors come mostly from the Loeb Library translations. If better than that, they are the work of my colleague Professor Edward Schauroth; if worse, my own. For quotations from Plato, I have relied upon the Jowett translation; and for Plotinus, I have borrowed from W. R. Inge and Grace Turnbull. Other direct quotations are acknowledged where they appear.

J. I. S.

The University of Buffalo
March 1953

CONTENTS

List of Illustrations

PHOTOGRAPHERS REPRESENTED

Because they cannot, in the ordinary course, supply material, the names of several private photographers have been omitted from the list.

Aero-Photo, 19 Rue de Sévigné, Paris 4
Alinari, Via Nazionale 8, Florence; U.S. agent: Art Reference Bureau, 225 5th Ave., N.Y.
D. Anderson, Via Salaria 7, Rome
Wayne Andrews, 110 Remsen St., Brooklyn 2, N.Y.
Archives Photographiques, 229 Galerie Montpensier, Paris 1
Bibliothèque Nationale, 58 Rue de Richlieu, Paris 2
Braun & Cie., 18 Rue Louis-le-Grand, Paris 2; U.S. agent E. S. Herrmann Inc., 385 Madison Ave., N.Y.
Brogi di Laurati, Corso dei Tintori 13, Florence
Bulloz, 21 Rue Bonaparte, Paris 6
Country Life, 2 Tavistock St., Covent Garden, London W.C. 2
F. H. Crossley, 19 Shavington Avenue, Chester, England
Crown Copyright: H. M. Stationery Office, 429 Oxford St., London, W.I.
Deutscher Kunstverlag, Zentralinstitut für Kunstgeschichte, Arcisstrasse 10, Munich
French Government Tourist Office, 610 5th Ave., N.Y.
Gabinetto Fotografico Nazionale, Via in Miranda 5, Rome
Giraudon, 9 Rue des Beaux Arts, Paris 6
Professor Walter Hege, Breddestrasse 19, Gelsenkirchen-Buer, Germany
Charles Hurault, 9 Rue de Metz, St. Germain-en-Laye, Seine-et-Oise, France
F. Kaufmann, Luisentstrasse 27, Munich
Professor Clarence Kennedy, Smith College, Northampton, Mass.
Foto-Marburg, Marburg/Lahn, Germany
T. H. Mason, 5 Dame St., Dublin
National Buildings Record, 37 Onslow Gardens, London S.W. I
Nellys, 19 East 57th St., N.Y.
Jean Roubier, 18 Rue de Liège, Paris 9
Foto-Sabah, Istiklal Caddesi 289, Istanbul, Turkey
R. Sansaini, Via Monte Santo 10, Rome
F. Stoedtner, Graf Adolf Strasse 10, Dusseldorf; U.S. agent: Dr. Konrad Prothmann, 7 Soper Ave., Baldwin, L.I., N.Y.
Tel, 3 Rue de Grenelle, Paris 6
Raphael Tuck & Sons, Spencer Factory, Countess Rd., St. James, Northampton, England
C. B. van Weelderen, Rooseveltweg 116, Utrecht, Holland
Vizzavona, 2 Rue Saint-Simon, Paris 7
Professor Clarence Ward, Oberlin, Ohio
Professor S. S. Weinberg, University of Missouri, Columbia, Mo.
F. R. Winstone, 23 Hyland Grove, Henbury Hill, Bristol, England

*

1

THE STUDY OF ART

THE SEVERAL DIVISIONS OF THE SUBJECT

Let us begin by defining our field.

The history of art as conceived today in the American university is an all-embracing subject; the name means much more than the words say. In a strict and narrow sense art history is merely a department of all history; and the first duty of the art historian is to explain the monuments of architecture, sculpture, and painting in so far as they stand as records of the past. As such, works of art are often more accurate than any other indication about the state of affairs at some remote but crucial juncture in the progress of humanity. When men speak or write, they are often guarded and devious. But when they build or paint, they are usually perfectly open about what they want. By studying the visual arts from any society, we can usually tell what the people lived for and for what they might be willing to die.

As just defined, the history of art is surely a legitimate and rewarding field of knowledge, but no one could possibly accept the limitations implied by what we have so far said. Over and above the attractions of political, military, and social history, art history has the special advantage of dealing with material that tends to expand the personality, refine the emotions, and increase the domain where the sympathies are at home. Art is a product of man's creative impulse. It is as old as the race. A society without artistic taste and standards is a society forever yearning and confused. For reasons like these, art history merges by imperceptible degrees with philosophy, psychology, and religious impulse. We find ourselves constantly involved with ideals and aspirations, and with questions of hope, pride, tragedy, exaltation, and a host of other experiences having to do with the soul's welfare or defeat. Only in part are we concerned with the problem of beauty, although we must labor hard over it. The fundamental concept with which we should begin is this: the visual arts are a means of communication and record; they open straight into the heart and mind of all humanity both living and dead.

The matters just mentioned are not susceptible of measurement on any numerical scale, but art history, like all other modern studies, nevertheless depends for its validity upon a solid foundation of fact. Except for the research of countless scholars, a book like this one would be an impossibility. It is important for the reader to have some picture of the process by which our knowledge has been built up and of the present state of the subject. In general, it may be said that scholarly activity has tended to divide itself into various specialties, each making an essential contribution to the field as a whole.

Archaelogy is the field work of art history. Its business is to recover objects preserved from earlier times. *Anthropology* does the same thing; but as ordinarily understood, it implies research into remote and primitive mankind while archaeology deals with material from periods of high civilization. Both activities result in the accumulation of *artifacts* (objects worked by the hand of man) and *monuments* (artifacts construable as cultural expression) in our museums.

Archaeological scholarship, as distinct from field work, is the further study of the monuments we possess with the purpose of establishing relations of cause and effect between the earlier monuments and the later. Such scholarship deals indiscriminately with objects unearthed yesterday, and with monuments that have never been out of sight. Ostensibly its purpose is narrowly historical and facts are its object; but we must not overlook the insight it offers into the creative process. The most original artist is incapable of total creation; all are necessarily creatures of their own past and their own present. We can tell much from the work of art alone, but it is folly to overlook the connotations and overtones opened up for our understanding by apposite if collateral evidence.

Whenever he can locate it, the archaeological scholar depends upon evidence external to the work of art itself. The ideal thing to have, of course, is a receipted bill from someone like Titian saying in unmistakable language that he has, on a certain date, received payment for such and such a Madonna. Sadly for the scholar, elaborate bookkeeping is a very recent addition to our civilization, and efficient filing systems are still largely unknown and unpopular except in the United States of America and in Germany. Neat and conclusive proof in documentary form is rare indeed when artistic monuments are being traced to their source. As a general statement, it is probably fair to say that, for any period earlier than the 16th Century, such documents exist only by the merest chance. After that, one can usually locate something or other if he hunts long enough.

The *archivist* is the man who makes a specialty of finding such papers. With respect to getting covered with dirt, his daily task is not unlike that of the archaeologist in the field; and his patience must be even greater because there is less drama in his life. Devoted men and women are nevertheless at work every day in the libraries of Europe and in the repositories where public and private records are stored, usually in indescribable lack of order. The archivist must not only be an expert linguist in the ordinary sense; he also has to know tricks of script and abbreviation with which most of us are never concerned. Once in a while, he finds himself reading words that settle once and for all a question long vigorously debated.

An immense amount of work remains to be done in the archives, but conceivably at some future time we shall have assembled all the apposite documents on earth. In the meanwhile, life goes on and decisions must be made about works of art about which we know nothing except what we may properly infer by inspecting the object itself; or, to put it in technical language, we have to base our judgment upon *internal* or *stylistic evidence.*

The situation will be clear if we attempt to visualize the problem of a museum director who is considering the purchase of a painting for the collection under his care. Works of art are unique; the opportunity to purchase may never come again. The art market is also unique; and the price of a painting depends upon a number of things extraneous to its absolute value as a picture, but most of all upon its authenticity as the work of a great master. If public funds in a large amount are to be disbursed, a heavy responsibility rests upon the man who must decide whether to purchase or whether to let the offer go.

Because there are all kinds of pictures, no individual can possibly be intimately familiar with every class and variety. It is customary, therefore, to seek the advice of some scholar known to be an expert, or *connoisseur,* of the particular category in which the contemplated purchase falls.

Connoisseurship is that branch of archaeological study which deals entirely with the single work of art, and depends altogether upon stylistic evidence. As before, the purpose is to establish the *provenance* (place of origin), the date, and the authorship of a given picture or statue. After thorough study, the professional connoisseur signs an affirmation of authenticity or the opposite. This amounts to an assertion that he risks his reputation upon his belief that the work of art is truly what he says it is.

Every once in a while, the public prints burst forth with an announcement that the connoisseurs have been fooled. A great museum pays $100,000 for a marble tomb; it turns out to have been made, not in the 15th Century and at Florence as confidently supposed, but a year or two ago by a forger in Milan. Paintings celebrated as newly discovered examples by a great Dutch master are presently found to be nothing but a psychopath's pitiful attempt to gain recognition.

Such news makes exciting headlines, and at times even good reading. As ordinarily presented in the papers, however, it is all too commonly false in emphasis and interpretation, if not in fact.

It is conceivable that a forger might so perfectly imitate the work of an earlier great master as to fool everyone forever. If so, his work would be as " good " as that of the great master even if discovery of the fraud destroyed its value on the market. In effect, the forger would actually have brought about a resurrection of the dead master's personality; we would be dealing with the work of the same mind once again set into motion. Such a thing is certainly difficult to credit; but no one can prove it has never happened. Most indications suggest that genius sufficient for success in so devious and unrewarding an enterprise ordinarily finds a more direct and legitimate outlet.

It should be noted, moreover, that in the several instances where important forgeries have recently been detected, the fraud has come to light within a year or two — certainly no very great interval of time. If we look behind the scenes, we can appreciate that even the curator of a public collection may at times feel compelled to take a chance: to buy something, that is, without waiting for the report of a connoisseur who might need several months to arrive at his opinion. It takes great courage to announce that one has been fooled, but such announcements are the rule rather than the exception.

The reader must realize that any attribution based only upon internal evidence is necessarily a statement of probability. General confidence in the authenticity of an undocumented work of art is established only over a substantial period of time. Things that stand up for years to the repeated inspection of experts are either genuine or miraculous in their power to deceive.

Connoisseurship, it must also be understood, cannot be undertaken effectively except by direct contact with the originals. Photographic reproductions are among the tools of the trade, of course, but they merely aid the memory in matters of comparative study. A sound attribution on stylistic evidence demands that the eye be close to the surface of the picture. Chemical tests, X-ray, and other laboratory techniques extend one's power to observe, but to date nothing has the scope and reliability of the trained eye aided, perhaps, by a simple magnifier.

There is nothing occult about the method. Everyone who recognizes a signature on a check is to that extent a connoisseur. In general it is believed that authenticity is best indicated by the minute physical characteristics of the picture. The master under review might, for instance, have had a favorite sort of brush with hairs that left a special kind of mark. Small details of every kind tend to be handled in the same way by the same man: as, for example, a routine trick for drawing the corner of the eye or a favorite contour for the finger nails.

Obviously such indications of manual usage are often so insignificant that the painter himself might not recognize them as his own. All indications point to the likelihood that such data are all the more reliable for the very reason of their being the product of unconscious habit.

By its very nature, connoisseurship is intensively specialized. The professional is ordinarily compelled to limit himself to the work of a single school, or even to the work of one or two masters within a school. And because he must deal with the minutiae of so narrow a field, the connoisseur is hardly ever a reliable guide on the broader and more philosophical aspects of art history and criticism.

Once the work of art is installed in a museum — by purchase, by gift, by bequest, or however else it got there — its worth to the community may or may not be instantly self-evident. Before accepting anything as an important cultural monument, people require to know something about it. What does the picture represent? Is it beautiful, or is it important and moving in some other way? Such questions bring us to still other departments of our general field.

Iconography (from *icon* or *ikon,* an image or representation) is the study of the subject matter of the visual arts. Except for modern art of the so-called nonobjective sort, almost every picture and statue has content. It was produced, that is to say, for the purpose of expressing something or communicating something. Narrative subject matter is only the most obvious type of content. Pictures that tell no story may possess great devotional significance. Upon occasion, abstract design carries a symbolic meaning for those who know the key. Inasmuch as many things that once were common knowledge are now obscure, an immense effort of research has been required and still goes on with the simple purpose of enabling us to make sense of what we we see.

It has been fashionable for the past thirty years or so to declare that an interest in iconography is beneath the dignity of the true art critic. He should, we are told, confine his attention to the problem of beauty which, according to this school of thought, is to be sought solely in the abstract organization of mass, line, light and dark, and color. Such study is of course both legitimate and necessary, to say nothing of its fascination. The error in the view just summarized is in what it denies, not in what it asserts.

Under the name *aesthetics,* philosophers have long recognized that art criticism formed part of their responsibility. By analogy to such absolutes as good and evil, it has been presumed that beauty might be isolated from other and extraneous elements, and contemplated, defined, and understood by and for itself. This study deals primarily with the professional competence of the artist; not with what he does, but with how well he does it. Its ultimate achievement would be to explain why some artists are great, some merely good, and some not worthwhile.

As generally understood, aesthetics aims to solve the problem of beauty on a universal basis. If successful, it would presently furnish us with an explanation of the quality common to Greek temples, Gothic cathedrals, Renaissance paintings, and all good art from whatever place or time. As distinct from this grand approach, we shall find it convenient to limit our objectives now and again, and think in terms of *historical criticism.* Making no attempt to find the common denominator between Greek and Gothic beauty, the historical critic undertakes to explain both styles by reference to their own internal logic. He takes either as a law unto itself, and tries to show how things must work so long as we accept the Greek or Gothic premises and follow them out to the end.

The *theory of art,* sometimes called the *theory of design,* is another important department of aesthetics which attempts to make tangible progress by similar limitation of its field of inquiry. The facts of the visual universe are the beginning of all artistic theory. The second level of its foundation rests in the physiology and psychology of sight. Beyond that, theory studies the tools and materials of the artist, their special powers and limitations, and the consequences of such. By studying what the great artists have done with their materials, one builds up an idea of what is artistically appropriate, what can be done, and what had best be avoided.

Linear perspective, worked out once and for all at Florence during the early part of the 15th Century, is the most familiar part of artistic theory. Without some fairly clear notion of its laws, one cannot draw anything. Another branch of theory studies the properties of color, and of light and dark, both as they act in nature and as they may legitimately be applied in painting. From such fundamental beginnings, the further study of theory involves the arrangement of pictorial materials into *compositions,* an investigation involving the interrelation of masses, lines, colors, statics and dynamics, and all the harmonies, rhythms, balances, tensions, and compensations that may enter into the exhaustive effort of a great artist as he struggles to produce a perfect thing. It is important to understand that theory proceeds inductively; it deals not with artistic law, but with the actual practice of artists and with the phenomena of nature.

Art criticism is the process of arriving at a just estimate of the cultural value of artistic monuments. If he is to command respect, the critic must be vigilantly alert to the implications of anything and everything that may shed light upon the work of art under review; he cannot afford to neglect any department of art study as we have described it above. Walter Pater's estimate of Leonardo is considerably weakened today, for example, because we know that Pater accepted as genuine paintings which have not stood the test of connoisseurship. Romanesque sculpture was once considered barbarous, and the very name *Gothic* originated as a term of contempt; today, on the basis of comparative study and historical criticism, both are recognized at what is probably their true and permanent worth. During the early centuries of Christendom when the Roman polity was crumbling, there was no place for artistic theory and little for technical skill. We nevertheless can make out a very strong case for Early Christian sculpture as a human and historical document of priceless value. And in the same voice, we may admire the dazzling accomplishment of many a Baroque artist while deploring the essential vulgarity of the display. In short, it is not the business of the critic to further the popularity of any particular style or kind of art at the expense of any other kind. His obligation lies, rather, in the direction of exhausting all resources in an effort to be fair.

THE STATE OF THE SUBJECT

Modern art history is almost exactly two centuries old. It commenced with the work of the German scholar J. J. Winckelmann who published his *Geschichte der Kunst des Altertums* (*History of the Art of Ancient Times*) in 1764. At that time, factual knowledge was in an appalling state. Winckelmann's statements about date and authorship are often wrong almost beyond belief. His critical estimates, however, have become part of our folklore; the man in the street who never heard of Winckelmann will nevertheless quote him if asked to express an opinion about art. No other art historian has had a comparable influence upon European taste.

Since Winckelmann, our factual knowledge has steadily increased. Under his inspiration, classical art was the first field to be systematically worked. The Italian Renaissance next claimed attention; and during the second half of the 19th Century, the art of the Middle Ages, hitherto the province of a few independent thinkers who refused to accept the notion that an era of darkness separated the enlightenment of Rome from the felicity of modern times, came strongly into its own.

As things stand today, the narrative chronicle of European art history will probably remain forever much as we find it set forth. The important buildings are known. Most of the great pictures and statues have gravitated into the public domain, and are generally accessible in museums or otherwise. Debate still takes place about matters of historical probability; but the contention has to do with particulars and details rather than with fundamentals: the major historical forces have been identified, and the main trend of their operation is clear to all.

Two things combined to forward the grand program of research. Both were impossible until the Industrial Revolution had done its work. Western Europe became crisscrossed with a network of railways. Photography was invented. Travel for the first time became safe, fast, and inexpensive. Photography made it possible to make trustworthy records of what one had seen, and gradually to accumulate a reference file of reproductions. The net result was to open art history to any one who might be interested.

The efficiency of the study has also been tremendously improved. It is still necessary for the specialist to inspect the originals no matter how far he must travel to see them, but he can prepare himself for the experience by the study of photographs and thus make his first-hand investigation more intelligently. Even more important than that, comparisons are now conveniently made which, for Winckelmann, would have required the expenditure of tremendous energy. At Harvard, at Princeton, in the Frick Library, in Sir Robert Witt's library, or in the files of Marburg University one can have a look at almost anything merely by consulting the card catalogue. The required photograph awaits him in its proper place in a drawer that runs on wheels. Valid conclusions on most matters are as easily made in Chicago as in Vienna or Rome.

What remains to be done?

There is probably more classical art underground than we have yet dug up. One of the great outstanding issues in medieval archaeology, to name another possibility, is the likelihood that the Near East in some way furnished the inspiration for the architectural styles common in Western Europe during the later Middle Age; but only a few competent persons have toured the back country of Syria where Christian cities existed until the Arab conquest of the 7th Century. Almost nobody has seen the lands between the Black and Caspian Seas, to say nothing of the Oxus River valley further east and the Altai region still further on to the north and east. And yet important secrets are to be solved by anyone who can look at visible monuments with a trained eye. Where travel is difficult and dangerous, art history hangs fire.

But that does not mean that new information can be acquired only by heroic methods. Spain and Portugal still offer the chance for significant achievement, as distinct from refining what has already been done. Latin America contains much important art of which we are all but ignorant. The papers of more than one major artist of the 19th Century merely await the arrival of the student who has the skill, the time, and the patience.

Even so, it would seem that the opportunity to make a further contribution to factual knowledge looms small by comparison with the vistas that beckon in aesthetics, theory, and criticism. These matters have occasionally received the attention of some of the greatest men in our intellectual history, but none of them possessed anything like our facilities for arriving at sound judgments. It seems hard on Plato, for instance, to search his words for statements that might be definitive with regard to the Gothic cathedral at Amiens — Plato died in 347 B.C., or about 1,600 years before the church was built, and never saw anything remotely like it. On the other hand, both Plato and Aristotle have left us remarks that stand as a capital instance of historical criticism: about the Greek style with which both were familiar, they speak with clarity and authority. What would such men have been able to say if, like ourselves, the whole history of European art was spread out before them?

In the field of theory, progress of the most obvious and practical kind may be expected within the next generation, for it is here that scholar, scientist, and artist meet on common ground. Painters no longer need to learn their art in the narrow channel of the local school to which they happen to belong; the museums, of which there were none before the 19th Century and no good ones until the last part of that period, offer all the wisdom of the past to the young artist trying to work out his own mode of expression. The ultimate historical position of Paul Cézanne (died 1906), the founder of modern art, will probably rest upon the intelligent use he made of such sources, and also upon the fact that most of his painting, like that of Matisse, is a record of theoretical research. Had Cézanne chosen to write down his ideas, we might have been closer to a theory of art which would compare in utility and profundity to the theoretical understanding of music that is now accepted as essential for all well-educated musicians.

In the publications of D. W. Ross and Arthur Pope, we already have a color theory which has now stood the test of about fifty years of practical application to the problems of painting. The same theory, because of its simplicity and substantial accuracy, is at this date gaining increasing popularity among scientists.

The theory of architecture is being pursued even more enthusiastically. Eminent practitioners of the art, like M. le Corbusier and Mr. Frank Lloyd

Wright, feel obliged to explain their buildings; each new project is accompanied by a statement of the philosophy behind it — one need not agree with what is said in order to appreciate the profound sense of responsibility felt by the architect. In this general effort, the writings of social thinkers, like Mr. Lewis Mumford and Mr. Sigfried Giedion, supplement the utterances of the active designers.

The end result of artistic theory should be twofold. All those who look to art for wisdom and for aesthetic nourishment need a more reliable method of procedure. The artist — and all 19th-Century Romanticism to the contrary, for the creative process is as much rational as intuitive — should find a mature artistic theory extremely useful; it would set forth the possibilities and the limitations, and save much trial and error.

Fig. 2.1 Altamira. Drawing to show the arrangement of animal paintings on the ceiling of the cave.

Fig. 2.2 Bison. Incized on the roof of a cave.

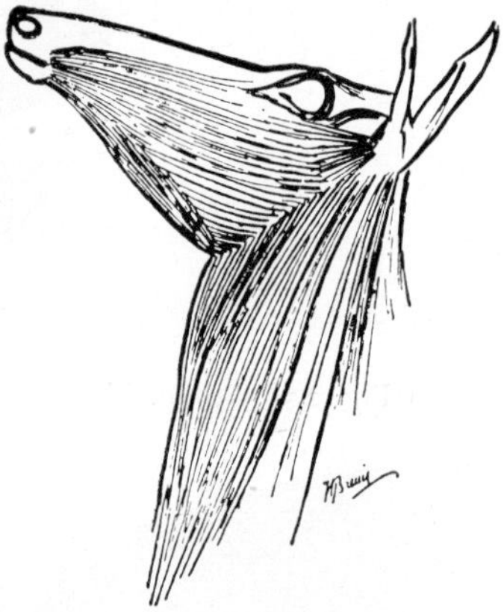

Fig. 2.3 Altamira. Deer's head.

Fig. 2.4 Altamira. Wild Boar.

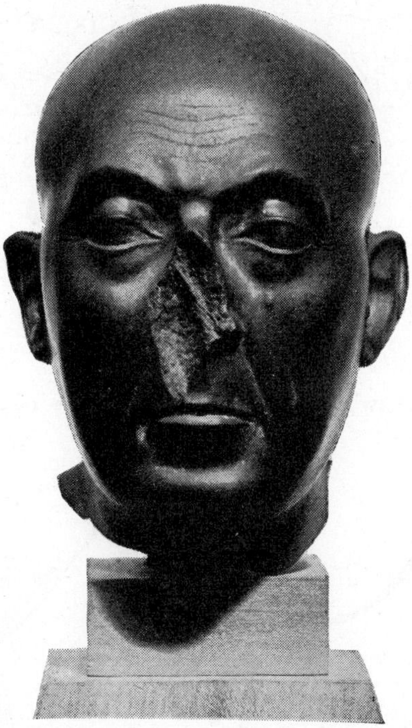

Fig. 2.5 Boston. Museum of Fine Arts. Head of a priest. Basalt.

Figs. 2.6–7 Berlin. Staatliche Museum. Head of Nofretite. PHOTOGRAPHS TAKEN FOR THE U. S. MILITARY GOVERNMENT.

Fig. 2.8 Boston. Museum of Fine Arts. Mycerinus and his Queen.

Fig. 2.9 Boston. Museum of Fine Arts. Relief from the Mastaba of Ptah-Sekhem-Ankh.

Fig. 2.10 Williamstown, Mass. Lawrence Museum. Ashurnasirpal the 2nd.

Fig. 2.11 New York. Metropolitan Museum. Five-legged gateway monster from the Palace of Ashurnasirpal the 2nd at Nimrud. First half of the 9th Century B.C.

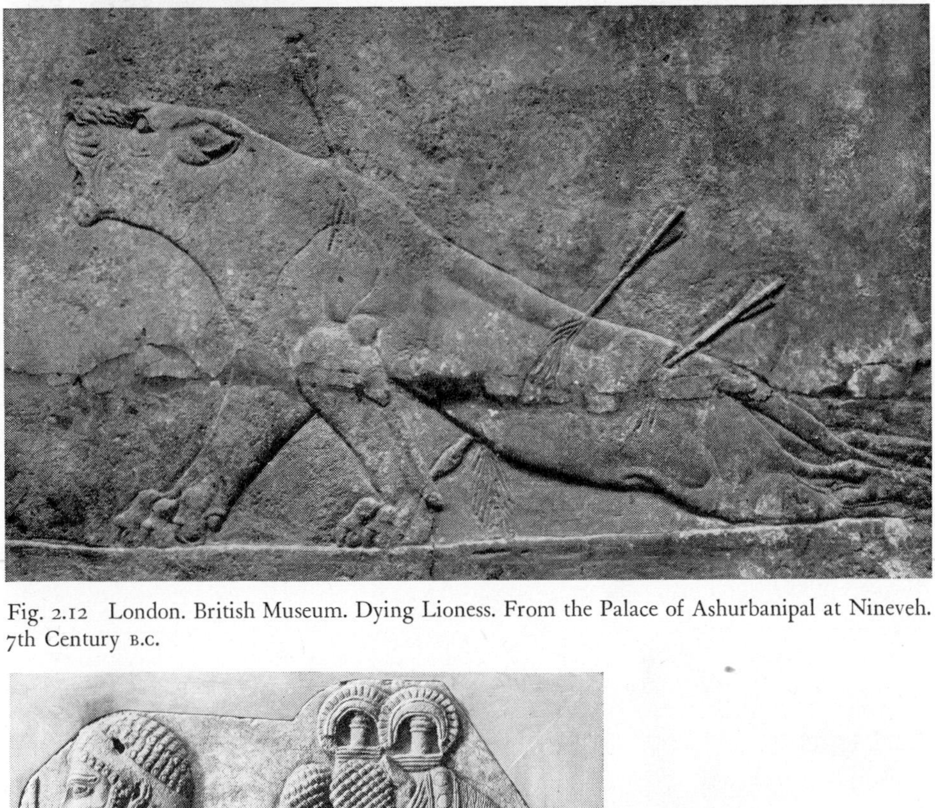

Fig. 2.12 London. British Museum. Dying Lioness. From the Palace of Ashurbanipal at Nineveh. 7th Century B.C.

Fig. 2.13 New York. Metropolitan Museum. A Median leading two horses. 8th Century B.C.

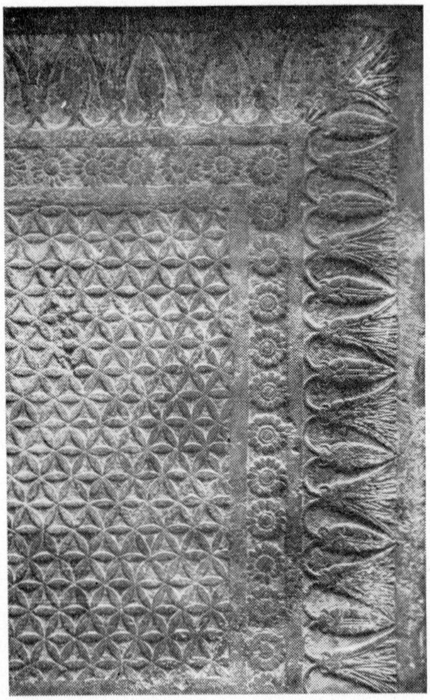

Fig. 2.14 London. British Museum. Fragment of pavement from Nineveh. About 700 B.C.

STOEDTNER

Fig. 2.15 Berlin. Glazed tiles from the Palace of Nebuchadnezzar at Babylon.

RICHARD W. DWIGHT

Fig. 2.16 Granada. The Alhambra. Court of the Myrtles. 13th Century A.D.

*

2

FORERUNNERS OF THE WESTERN TRADITION

PALEOLITHIC, EGYPTIAN, AND MESOPOTAMIAN ART

THE PALEOLITHIC CAVE PAINTINGS

The extreme antiquity of the visual arts was dramatically demonstrated in 1880 by the announcement that paintings of Paleolithic date had been discovered on the roof of the cave of Altamira near Santander on the Biscay coast of Spain. In 1879, a gentleman named Sautuola had explored the cave in company with his small daughter. The child was the first to discern the pictures on the ceiling above her, and delightedly shouted out to her father, "Toros! Toros!" — having mistaken some ancient bisons for modern bulls.

Sautuola's discovery naturally stimulated interest in the exploration of other caves. In all, about fifty are now known which contain important paintings. They lie mostly in the general region of southwest France and the northeasterly section of Spain. A great many bits of bone and ivory, some of them carved or incised with drawings, have been unearthed from strata of Paleolithic date. We thus possess a considerable body of material from that remote era.

The assertion that any artistic material whatever falls between 20,000 B.C. and 40,000 B.C. is not one to be accepted lightly; but as a matter of fact, it rests upon data considerably more sound than the evidence we often depend upon to set the period of objects only a few centuries old. Some of the animals represented are extinct, but are known to have been native to the region before the last glacier. Many of the caves, moreover, were closed by gravel deposits

laid down as the glacier retreated, thus furnishing proof that the cavern behind had not been entered since.

Because we know nothing of the people who painted the pictures and because the pictures themselves came to light so recently, Paleolithic art hardly forms part of the European tradition. Certain general conclusions may be drawn from the paintings, however; and these are perhaps more cogent for the very reason that historical continuity is not involved.

In the first place, it is interesting to see that the Paleolithic artists knew all the fundamental techniques of drawing and painting. In one place or another, we may find instances of pure *delineation*, of *form drawing* (line plus modeling in monotone), of *line and local tone* (line plus flat washes of color), and of complete painting (Figs. 2.2–4).

In the manipulation of all techniques, moreover, these early and forgotten artists reached a level of skill which must be described as superb. They understood how to vary the character of their line to express the sleek grace of the antelope and the bumpy stance of the buffalo; for a similar demonstration we must look to the great painters of China and Japan. Their modeling is equally subtle. They grade their tones from light to dark in a way that defines contour in no uncertain fashion. More than that, they manage to work the brush in such a way as to suggest textures without actually describing them; few artists of our era have been capable of a similar performance.

Splendid as they were in the rendering of single animals, these remote artists appear to have had no notion of the artistic possibilities inherent in the arrangement of several figures in relation to each other and in relation also to a setting. The art of *composition,* that is to say, seems not yet to have been conceived. Many of the best animal figures overlap others, and a general view of any large number together furnishes us with a definition for the term *helter-skelter* (Fig. 2.1). Composition aside, however, Paleolithic painting stands as irrefutable proof that the history of art is by no means equivalent to an upward evolution of technique. As more than one competent critic has felt impelled to declare, these artists were as skilful as anybody since. One cannot paint better; he can only paint differently.

EGYPTIAN ART

The Pyramids are the most conspicuous and famous of all Egyptian monuments. The three biggest stand at Giza on the western bank of the Nile a short distance upstream from modern Cairo. In the old days, a prodigious and romantic antiquity was assigned to these imposing piles, but more modern research has sobered our estimate. Reasoning largely from astronomical events recorded in the written history of Egypt, scholars have found it possible to fix the chronology within broad but sure limits. It is now generally believed that King Khufu, or Cheops, who dedicated the biggest pyramid, reigned about 3000 B.C.

The monument he left us remains to this day the largest of man-made structures. It is the largest, that is, ever raised from a level footing as distinct from the application of masonry to a hill or mound. Originally it measured approximately 755 feet square on the base, rose to an apex 481 feet above the ground, and defined a volume of about 85,000,000 cubic feet. It has been estimated that 2,300,000 blocks of cut stone went into its construction, each weighing two and a half tons or thereabouts.

The mere act of raising such a structure bespeaks a prosperous and highly organized society, but the devotion of so much labor upon a single monument also declares the existence of a compelling motive in any society whatever, no matter how rich. The accurate orientation of the pyramids, each with its sides facing the cardinal points of the compass, has suggested to some that astronomical observations might have been part of the intention. But accurate surveying was commonplace in Egypt, having developed early because landmarks were so often washed away by the inundations of the Nile. Casting aside this and other suggestions of an equally ingenious kind, we come back in the end to the traditional explanation; namely, that the pyramids were no more and no less than royal tombs.

As such, they reflect several aspects of the Egyptian character. More than power and social leadership was centered in the person of the Pharaoh. He was believed to be something very close to a deity on earth; and yet, by a paradox, he was mortal enough to make it of supreme importance that his immortality be guaranteed by a tremendous effort devoted to the permanent preservation of his body. The body itself was elaborately embalmed, and the great mass of the pyramid did no more than secrete and shelter it.

The student of social history might well pause at this point to consider the implications of so immense an investment for such a purpose, but it is our present business to learn artistic lessons from the pyramids. In some ways they are peculiarly useful simply because they are extreme. They illustrate better than any other monuments, in fact, the three-part nature of architecture. Because we must look at it, architecture is an art of form, like sculpture. Because we must build it, architecture is a department of mechanics and may be assessed as good or bad merely by reference to the efficiency with which physical problems are solved. And because we must use it, any building is a device devoted to the functions of human life. Every structure on earth represents a balance of some kind between these three elements.

The designers of the pyramids chose to emphasize form at the expense of engineering and utility. Their construction, while simple in principle, was wasteful of material to an almost unbelievable degree. No buildings on earth contain a smaller useful volume of space in proportion to their bulk; and for the special function of safeguarding the royal mummy, the pyramids proved a complete failure — every tomb-chamber was rifled at an early date. But over against these faults, we must list the tremendous effect of a simple, lucid shape rendered on the colossal scale. Geometric beauty has never been made more impressive.

In addition to that virtue, we must mention still another that might at first escape attention: the virtue of permanence. In some form and to some degree, every great artist has always intended that his work should last forever. Indeed, it may be questioned whether greatness is a psychological possibility without the sobering discipline of a beckoning eternity. In any case, it is an obvious probability that the pyramids will remain in plain sight long after every other work of our race has passed into nothingness, for in durability those great landmarks surpass anything and everything else in the history of art.

Even so, the pyramids remain an historical curiosity. As an architectural type, they did not survive the so-called Old Kingdom (about 2980–2475 B.C.), and except for the three big ones at Giza, there are no others of general interest or importance. Thus even in Egypt, these celebrated buildings must be thought of as a passing episode in art history.

The Egyptians built houses, palaces, and public buildings, but their temples are the only other type of building where the urge for permanence governed the design and construction. As an architectural type, the Egyptian temple is of local interest only, and we need not delay over it. It nevertheless had its importance in history for several reasons.

At some very early date and for reasons impossible to explain, the Egyptians decided to engineer their temples on the post-and-lintel system. (See Chapter 7, Structural Principles.) They were perfectly familiar with the arch, which in many ways is a better method for spanning the gap between vertical supports; but with characteristic fixity of mind, they made a convention of the lintel and used nothing else for the next 4,000 years. Greek architecture, as we shall presently see, maintains exactly the same convention during the course of its shorter but much more important development.

The peculiar form given the post and the lintel by the Egyptians may also have served as an example to Greece. The typical Egyptian post is a column, which is to say a vertical supporting member with a circular, or nearly circular, cross-section; and the typical Egyptian lintel finishes off at the top with an overhanging member, or *cornice*. Columns were destined to be habitual in Greece, although direct adaptations of the several Egyptian types are almost unknown. All Greek architecture uses the cornice; and here and there, especially during the Hellenistic Period, one may find reflections of the *cavetto cornice,* sometimes called the *Egyptian gorge,* which was native to the Nile Valley.

Egypt produced an immense amount of sculpture. The motive was religious. It had to do with the belief that survival of the soul depended upon preservation of the body, and statuary furnished a method of providing the soul with extra bodies in the shape of portrait figures. Sometimes these were duplicated and reduplicated in job lots in the apparent hope that at least one might survive.

Accurate portraiture was the prime desideratum for such a purpose, and it developed early and remained a distinctive feature of Egyptian art throughout its long history. It is notable that the bodies and legs of Egyptian statues are often rendered in perfunctory fashion, and that attached to these rather nondescript torsos we find heads modeled with such subtlety that they seem literally to be alive. The Egyptian sculptors thus furnish us with the first demonstration of the artistic philosophy we may recognize as *objective realism.*

The objective realist starts out by subjecting some living model to minute scrutiny. He then attempts in straightforward, honest fashion to describe that human being without permitting either prejudice or preference to guide his hand. Because neither sculpture nor painting can reproduce the conditions of nature, a strict copy of the model may not be attempted and never results in any normal studio. But within the simple limitations of his medium, the artist sticks to the facts as best he can.

The strength of objective realism is the same as the strength of science. In those few periods where it has flourished, the greater artists were in fact scientists engaged in the investigation of optical phenomena. The weakness of objective realism is made all too apparent, however, by the general run of Egyptian portraiture. As a philosophy, it tends to chain the artist to the particular person or object he is attempting to describe and record. He is unlikely to permit the intrusion of ideas, much less to make positive suggestions of an idealistic sort. The net result is all too likely to be no more than a mere statement of fact, without discrimination between the importance of facts.

For our better understanding of objective realism, it is necessary to remark that the word *realism* (without the adjective) has attained a special meaning through its frequent application to the work of artists and authors who deliberately select unlovely and even sordid subject matter. Without suggesting that their philosophy lacks a legitimate place in art, we must recognize that they employ the unlovely or the morbid for reasons of their own which have to do with the expression of particular ideas — and not with the reality of the visual world. Nature, so far as we can tell, is impartial. The rain falls on the just and unjust alike, and both beauty and the hideous are brought into being in equal measure. As objective realists, the Egyptian portrait sculptors were as neutral as nature herself. Given an elderly and wrinkled sitter (Fig. 2.5), they turned out many a portrait head which can hardly be described as handsome. Such work bristles with artistic integrity nevertheless. And when confronted with the fact of beauty, these artists proceeded in the same honest fashion, as we may see in the well-known bust of *Queen Nofretite* (Figs. 2.6–7). Too often photographed in what the lady herself might have described as a favorable light, the piece is generally thought to be an example of idealism. When it came under the jurisdiction of the American Fine Arts officers at Wiesbaden in 1945, those gentlemen were impressed with the fact that Nofretite was well past her girlhood at the time she sat for this portrait. A series of new photographs were taken, from two of which our book plates come. When lighted with the deliberate intention of showing every modulation of surface, the bust tells us of a woman just beginning to lose the smooth contours that go with youth. Her beauty remains, but it depends upon the fundamental structure of the skull. It would have been easy for the sculptor to smooth over the nascent wrinkles, or to alter the angle and proportion of the oddly elongated neck. Obviously, his philosophy forbade such tampering with visual fact, and the lady we see in the bust is the lady who actually lived in Egypt 3,400 years ago.

In accordance with the Egyptian habit of repeatedly solving the same problem in the same way, the sculptors of the Nile Valley settled very early upon a certain list of conventions, and maintained them without change for nearly 4,000 years. Far from unfortunate in themselves, these conventions have much merit.

Almost every material that might be made into a statue was used at some time or other: metal, wood, pottery, stone. But the favorite and standard medium for full-size statuary remained one of the harder stones like basalt or diorite. The motive, as usual, was permanence; and as a by-product, it results that most Egyptian sculpture is dark in color — a fact responsible for a considerable part of its distinctive character and effect.

When statues were carved out in the round, certain other measures were taken to insure their durability. It was customary, for example, to leave part of the original block in the shape of a slab attached to the back of the figure (Fig. 2.8). The familiar way of dressing the hair in the form of a long, wide bob is not reflective of contemporary fashion, but signifies the artist's desire to brace the head against being broken off at the neck. The wisdom of these arrangements is attested by the fact that most Egyptian figures have survived in almost perfect condition — a statement that cannot be made about any other school of sculpture.

For the pose of standing and seated figures rendered in the round, the Egyptians almost without exception adhered to the anatomical arrangement we know as *the convention of frontality*, also illustrated by Fig. 2.8. The expression means that a vertical line drawn from the middle of the forehead to the ground will approximately bisect the statue. It follows that the body must be stiffly erect. It is impossible to maintain this pose and represent any action more complicated than putting one foot slightly forward from the other; and by the same token, the expression of content or feeling through physical movement is foreclosed. A certain degree of ceremonial dignity is nevertheless realized. It is doubtless for that reason that these superb technicians felt it appropriate to continue a feature often unconsciously produced in the sculpture of children and other genuinely primitive artists.

In addition to portrait statues in the round, the Egyptians covered vast areas of wall space with narrative paintings or with sculpture in relief. The necessity for rendering the human body (a three-dimensional form) on a flat surface demanded some systematic method of representation. As accomplished geometers, the Egyptians were perfectly familiar with our modern perspective projection, and minor or incidental figures were occasionally drawn with ease and accuracy even in complex and difficult poses. But for major art, which is to say wherever the artist became self-conscious about matters like dignity, *the convention of broadest aspect* was applied (Fig. 2.9).

A figure drawn according to this convention exhibits the following peculiarities: The head is seen in profile; but within the profile of the face, the eye is presented in full-face view. The torso is also presented in full-face view. To it are attached the arms and legs, both rendered in profile. All parts are hooked together without any indication of the muscular contortion that would have to take place were the pose attempted by a living model.

Because children tend to draw this way, it seems likely that the convention reflects an original state of technical ignorance, but we cannot dispose of it so lightly. For very good reasons, Picasso and other modern artists occasionally revert to broadest aspect or something very near it. Among the things that recommend the idea to the mature mind are such concepts as these.

Our modern convention of perspective and foreshortening permits us only the view of a man as he might appear across our line of sight at a particular and passing instant of time. The merit of this convention inheres in its correspondence with visual experience; but far from being sacred, visual experience of an instantaneous kind is often extremely unsatisfactory. When asked to examine a house, a tree, or a statue we instinctively take more than one look. We walk around the object in an effort to observe each part to the best advantage. We do not remember what we have seen as we saw it at any single moment; we recall, rather, each part of the whole at the time that part impressed us the most. If asked to write a description of what we saw, it is a virtual certainty that we will set down the facts not according to the convention of perspective and foreshortening, but in a manner very close to the convention of broadest aspect.

It will be appreciated, therefore, that the difference between this ancient convention and our own is not a difference between truth and untruth, but merely the question of whether we wish art to correspond with ocular experience or with the procedure we in fact follow when comprehending a set of visual data and remembering them. From the standpoint of completeness, the advantage is with the convention of broadest aspect. It gives emphasis to the significant, disregards the nonessential, and leaves nothing to luck. Outlandish though it may seem until we become accustomed to it, there is no denying that the method is rational, and no escaping the conclusion that it opens up the possibility of a more considered analysis of whatever truth may be communicated by way of the visual arts.

MESOPOTAMIAN ART
The Tradition of Savagery

Two ethnic groups composed the ancient population of Mesopotamia, the Babylonians and the Assyrians. The greatest cities of the region were Babylon on the Euphrates and Nineveh on the Tigris, the latter being the Assyrian capital. These two races remained separate to an unusual degree and hated each other. The political history of the region is an account of shifting ascendancy, first one race being on top and then the other. Warfare was developed almost to its logical conclusion. The so-called Palace of Sargon at Khorsabad remains the most imposing fort ever built. It contained about 700 rooms, some of them immense, and it rose from the ground on a platform over 50 feet high, about 1,100 feet long, and about 950 wide. The exterior walls were 28 feet thick, and their continuity was broken by a sophisticated arrangement of salient towers designed to permit cross-fire from archers stationed on the battlements. The need for such a structure, and one aspect of the nature of the people, may be inferred from the action of the Babylonians in 612 B.C. In that year they captured Nineveh, killed most of the inhabitants, and did their utmost to destroy the city. Xenophon, who passed that way in 401 B.C. as a member of the ill-fated army of Cyrus the Younger, merely noted (*Anabasis* Bk. III) the existence of a vast and totally uninhabited ruin. He estimated the circuit of the place as about twenty miles, recorded that the walls rose to a hundred feet at some places, and called the site Mespila.

These things are important because one of Mesopotamia's chief contributions to later art is a tradition of savagery. The ceremonial portraits of Mesopotamian kings present an appalling class of humanity (Fig. 2.10). Prodigious strength, described all too unmistakably by the method of broadest aspect, is vested in the person of a monarch whose face, while intelligent, is both fierce and pitiless. Reliefs with more personal and intimate subject matter have also been found in large numbers. Some of these give us vignettes into the daily life of the time, but those in which both artist and patron obviously took the greatest satisfaction are devoted to the most sanguinary kind of hunting scene. The king always seems to be in the very act of killing. Some of the animal portraits, if considered merely as demonstrations of representative skill, are rendered with a delicate hand guided by sensitive observation — an impression which is all but reversed by the cruelty of their content (Fig. 2.12).

Among the various monuments that emphasize the savage aspect of Mesopotamian character, we should make special mention of the imaginary monsters. These exist in various sizes and in the round as well as in relief. Best known, simply because they are immense and therefore conspicuous, are the five-legged beasts, half-bull and half-human, habitually set up to either side of a palace gateway (Fig. 2.11). It is from this general category, including dragons and griffins as well as fanciful combinations of more ordinary anatomy, that we get, by a vague and devious route presently to be explained (page 293), the gargoyles and other grotesques of Western medieval art.

The Matter of Artistic Style, and the Three Fundamental Styles of European Art

An even more cogent and far-reaching contribution made by Mesopotamia was the invention and perfection of the mode of artistic expression we have come to recognize as the *Style of the Near East*, often loosely and conveniently referred to as "the Oriental Style." Before attempting a definition and analysis, we must digress for a brief account of recent events in art history.

C. R. Morey's most important contribution to scholarship was contained in a short but profound article which appeared in the *Art Bulletin* (Vol. 7,

No. 2) for December 1924. At the moment, Mr. Morey was attempting to produce an explanation which would bring order out of the chaos in which he found the archaeology of the Early Middle Ages. He succeeded in that objective, but in so doing, he wrote down some of the most penetrating, fundamental, and illuminating observations that have ever been put forward by an art historian. His judicious view encompassed a broader horizon than any heretofore vouchsafed; and he saw that his immediate problem was no local and temporary mix-up. It was, rather, a single instance in the operation of the broad forces which account for the entire history of European art.

His great idea was to realize that the apparent confusion of the Western tradition in art might be explained much as we explain the history of the several spoken languages, namely, by reference to the history, operation, and amalgamation of only three fundamental styles — each of which had at one time and in its native region existed in a comparatively pure and unadulterated form. The styles Morey recognized were: the *Style of the Near East,* the *Classical Style* which originated in Greece, and the *Northern Style* which was introduced by the barbarian races who destroyed the Roman Empire.

We shall deal immediately with the Style of the Near East, and with the other two in due season. In approaching all three, it is necessary to remember that we are speaking in broad generalizations. As over against the truth of such generalizations, numerous exceptions bear no weight. The reader should neglect them. Still a hypothesis, Morey's theory has so far stood the test of nearly a generation, and when his *Medieval Art* appeared in 1942, the theory was republished virtually as first stated.

Once the main tenor of Morey's thought is accepted, it follows that every later work of art may to a large extent be explained by reference to the cross-breeding that has taken place between the elements that form its heritage. Artists, that is to say, find their personal expression through an artistic language they inherit. They do not invent the language, although a single great career may serve to modify it. They use artistic styles as naturally and unconsciously as we speak English — a native tongue which is a historical accident for each of us, and a tool we turn to our own purpose without complaining that we did not choose it.

It is necessary at this point to give a more formal definition to the word *style* than has hitherto been required. It is a mistake to use the word as a term of praise or to confuse it with passing fashion. We shall be wiser if we reserve it for cases where we discern an established artistic usage. Things that happen only once are not styles. The term becomes appropriate only when we can see a familiar set of visual facts in a familiar coordination.

What facts do we look for, and what coordination? If distinguishing between the numerous assistants who worked for Rubens and produced the paintings Rubens signed, we must deal with the minutiae which separate collaborators in the same enterprise. But in the present situation, where we are merely attempting to explain the broadest and most general kind of difference, a few coarse and obvious criteria will serve us better. In approaching this matter, the reader must remember that all styles tend to make themselves universal, tend to dictate the design of every man-made object from the cathedral to the punctuation point. At the same time, every known style has been flexible enough to permit a broad scope of individual expression.

The first way in which we can distinguish one style from another is by reference to its *favorite medium.* We cannot tell the reason, but we can nevertheless note the fact that whenever and wherever a number of artists may be thought of as a school or related group, all members share the tacit assumption that some particular art is the fundamental art. During the 19th Century, it was painting. It was architecture in Gothic France, and sculpture in Greece. Modes of expression natural and appropriate for the favorite medium invariably affect everything else, and sometimes appear in strange applications.

The stylistic psychology of any artistic school is perhaps even more intimately affected by the *aesthetic means* appropriate to its favorite medium. The sculptor thinks always of mass and contour, and the painter who imitates the sculptor will do the same thing. Draftsmen express themselves by using the line, and keep doing it when they paint. The rug-maker and the weaver are inevitably self-conscious about color and texture; if such a man becomes a sculptor, his carving will betray his background.

Subject matter is a third element to which we may refer when defining an artistic style or when contrasting it with another. History shows that the preference for one kind of subject has at times been virtually exclusive — as, for example, the Greek preoccupation with the human figure and the northern genius for the grotesque.

Fourthly and finally, we may know a style by the principles to which it habitually appeals when arranging the component parts of a painting or building into an artistic composition, as, for example, the Greek use of geometry and the dynamics of the Baroque. Once set, the same compositional system will be used innumerable times for works of art which differ radically in scale and purpose, and even in effect upon our sensibilities.

The Style of the Near East

Keeping in mind the nature of style as such, and the four bare essentials just mentioned, we may now define and characterize the Style of the Near

East which, in all essentials, originated in ancient Mesopotamia and was brought to perfection there.

Everyone knows that the Near East produces most of the world's finest rugs and carpets, and that was so during Antiquity also. Every object of Mesopotamian art bears the imprint of a mind that conceived rug-weaving as the fundamental art. Whenever men are made into statues, the Mesopotamian sculptor dwells with infinite care upon the rendering of textures in whatever garments constitute the costume. Hair and beard rarely appear as they would on the living model; the opportunity is taken, rather, to work them into patterns of the kind appropriate to a fine stuff. Fig. 2.13 shows an example in which the special taste of the artist for carpet-textures is obvious.

As to subject matter and in spite of the numerous instances during Antiquity where outright and descriptive representation takes place, the artists of the Near East preferred to use only decorative patterns of the kind still familiar on modern Persian rugs. As time went on, the preference for abstract design grew into something very close to a phobia — if we look ahead to the start of the Christian era, we shall see a Near East which abhorred the representation of humanity and found visual expression only in decorative patterns composed of motives originally derived from plants and flowers and other natural forms but so conventionalized as to make specific recognition impossible.

We have no rugs from ancient Mesopotamia, but we know just what they looked like. The stone slabs of palace pavements (Fig. 2.14) were often carved in very low relief to imitate carpets, and we have some of the slabs. Even better for our purpose are the colored tiles used as exterior finish on walls made from sun-dried brick. An unusually interesting bit of this work is preserved at Berlin; originally it decorated Nebuchadnezzar's palace at Babylon (Fig. 2.15). This single specimen is in itself a demonstration of the Oriental means of expression and of the principles used for composition, both self-evidently derivative from practices suitable for the design of textiles. The power of the textile tradition may be gauged by the very fact that an aesthetic preference of so specialized a type could be deliberately carried over into the manufacture of building materials.

The patterned tile now brought under review exists like a rug as a flat surface. There is no relief of any kind. No graded shadows suggest convexity or concavity of form. The technique is a pure case of line and flat tone; and while any skilful artist can manipulate line and flat tone in such a way that contours are suggested but not described, even that expedient was deliberately avoided. Each separate and conventionalized floral motive asserts its visual existence solely as a spot of color in contrast with the background. Contrasts of color, or light and dark, or both together, constitute the ultimate means of aesthetic expression to which the Near Eastern artist instinctively turns.

As a whole, the work of art may be described as a succession of spots of light-on-dark, and in understanding the system according to which these are composed, two points need explanation. They are: *rhythm* and *indefinite extension.*

Rhythm depends upon the existence of accents. In music, the accented note is struck louder, more sharply, or otherwise given distinction among the rest. The rhythm of poetry depends upon the accented syllable, and the rhythm of dancing depends upon the accentuation of certain motions. But accents alone cannot produce a rhythm; the important thing is to make the accents come according to a system. The system may be utterly simple or unbelievably complex, but without a schedule for the appearance and reappearance of accents, there is no rhythm.

In the visual arts, the rhythmic sensation may be evoked in numerous ways. Undulations of drapery often produce the effect, as do the rise and fall of arches in an arcade. Human figures represented as in rhythmic motion can have a similar influence upon our sensibilities. The essential thing in talking about any particular instance of rhythm is to name the means by which accent is called into being: in the present case we are looking at a rhythm established by spots of light against a dark ground. Each spot gives the eye a kind of shock, and the shocks come at systematic intervals.

Within the field covered by our book plate, we see three different bands of spots across the surface. They differ in the shape and scale of the single motives which are brought out in accent, and they differ in the schedule that governs the arrangement of accents. The phenomenon before us is familiar in music; namely, the experience of comprehending several rhythms simultaneously.

Rhythm, in itself, has no limits. The internal logic of our detail from the brick frieze once at Babylon tells us nothing about where the frieze began or where it will end. It might be a few yards long, or extend from Babylon to Boston without self-contradiction. Conceivably, the composition might spread indefinitely in all four directions until it covered the universe. There is no necessary beginning, middle, or end; no frame and no boundaries.

But what could be better common sense if one is in the business of designing textiles? Can the weaver predict how we will cut up his bolt of cloth, or the rug-maker tell what sections of his rug we may choose to obscure with furniture? Such men are wise if, as in the present case, they restrict themselves to the compositional method studio jargon knows as the "all-over pattern," an expression meaning that every section of the area covered is quite as interesting as every other section, and that our attention is evenly distributed all over the surface. Color, in short, is the means and rhythm is the method for producing the desired result of indefinite extension.

In assessing the value and determining the propriety of the compositional method of the Near East, we must never forget that it was invented for the design of cloth and is useful wherever a more or less indefinite area must be covered with decoration — extensive wall paintings, for example, and continuous friezes of any kind (Fig. 2.16). We must not confuse these peculiar and special advantages with artistic excellence arrived at by other methods and for different purposes. Artistic unity, which we often hear mentioned as an essential element of all aesthetic goodness, is absent by the very nature of the Near Eastern method. Unity was, in fact, exactly what they did not want. It is here, we shall find (page 64), that the Oriental mind comes most radically into contrast with the Greeks.

*

3

GREEK ART TO 450 B.C.

OUR KNOWLEDGE OF GREEK ART— ITS LIMITS AND ITS IMPORTANCE

Our knowledge of Greek art is more limited than we sometimes permit ourselves to suppose.

The subject has been under assiduous investigation, almost without pause, since Winckelmann published his famous *History of Ancient Art* in 1764. It is impossible to exaggerate the amount of scholarly effort expended upon digging and other forms of archaeological activity. It is similarly difficult to find words to describe in any adequate way the intelligence and the patience brought to focus on every tiniest bit of evidence; everything we possess has been worked to the limit in the hope of shedding all possible light on problems that still remain uncertain.

As a result of this prolonged effort we have assembled a substantial collection of Greek art, and we have established with something close to certainty the main outlines of its evolution. We can trace its development in orderly fashion from primitive beginnings to the so-called " Great Age " of the 5th and 4th Centuries B.C. Somewhat less neatly but still with reasonable assurance, we can explain how Greek influence spread with the conquests of Alexander and how outside influences affected Greece. Still later, it is clearly established that Rome, the political mistress of the Mediterranean world, was in her art a later derivative from Greece. Finally, we can describe in a general way how the Classical Style passed out of existence as Antiquity failed and the Middle Ages began.

With respect to monuments, we are most fortunate in the field of architecture. There are enough well-preserved temple ruins to give us a completely accurate knowledge of the best Greek religious buildings. We can also be con-

Fig. 3.1 Buffalo. Albright Art Gallery. *Cycladic Idol.* About 3000 B.C. 13½ inches high.

Fig. 3.2 Boston. Museum of Fine Arts. *Snake Goddess.* Gold & Ivory. 7 inches high.

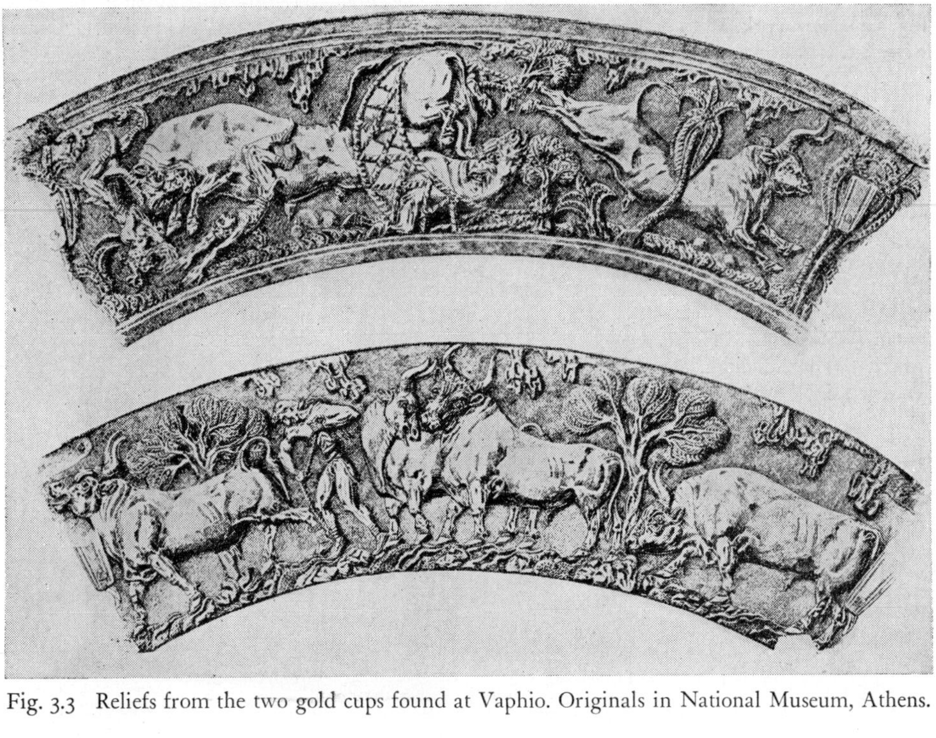

Fig. 3.3 Reliefs from the two gold cups found at Vaphio. Originals in National Museum, Athens.

Fig. 3.4 New York. Metropolitan Museum. *Dipylon Vase*. 8th Century B.C.

Fig. 3.6 Boston. Museum of Fine Arts. Vase from "the period of Oriental Influence." 7th Century B.C.

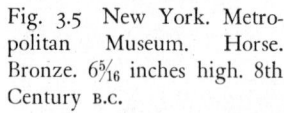

Fig. 3.5 New York. Metropolitan Museum. Horse. Bronze. $6\frac{5}{16}$ inches high. 8th Century B.C.

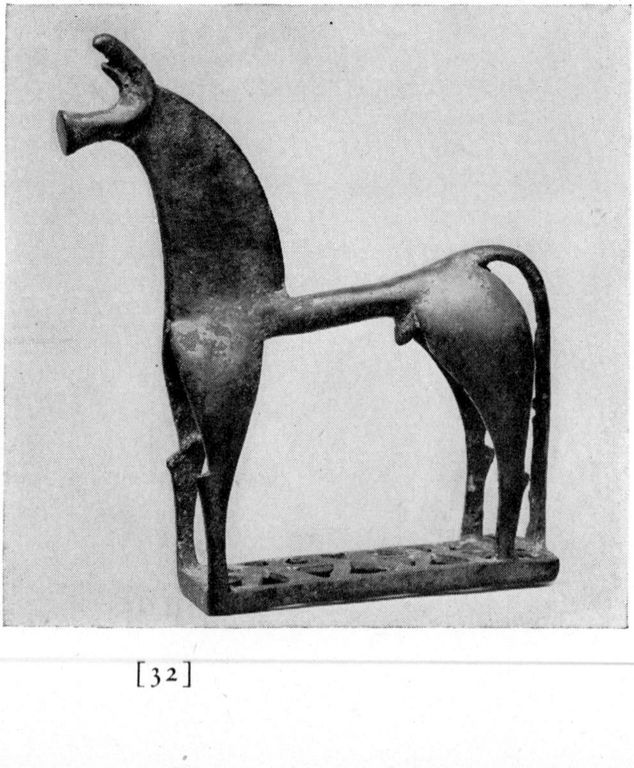

ALINARI

Fig. 3.7 Paris. Louvre. The Nikandra Statue.

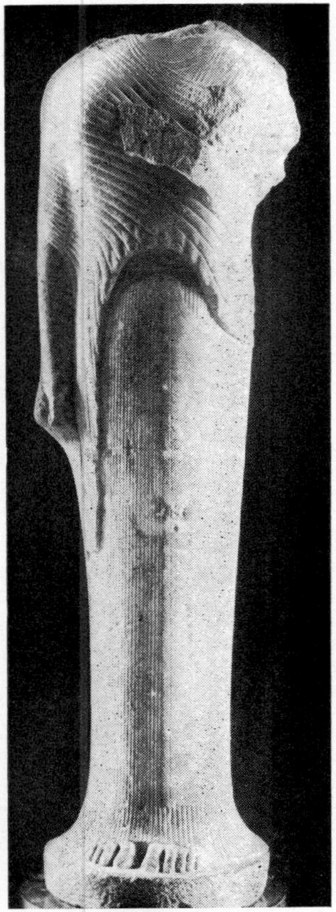

ARCHIVES PHOTOGRAPHIQUES

Fig. 3.8 Paris. Louvre. *The Hera from Samos.*

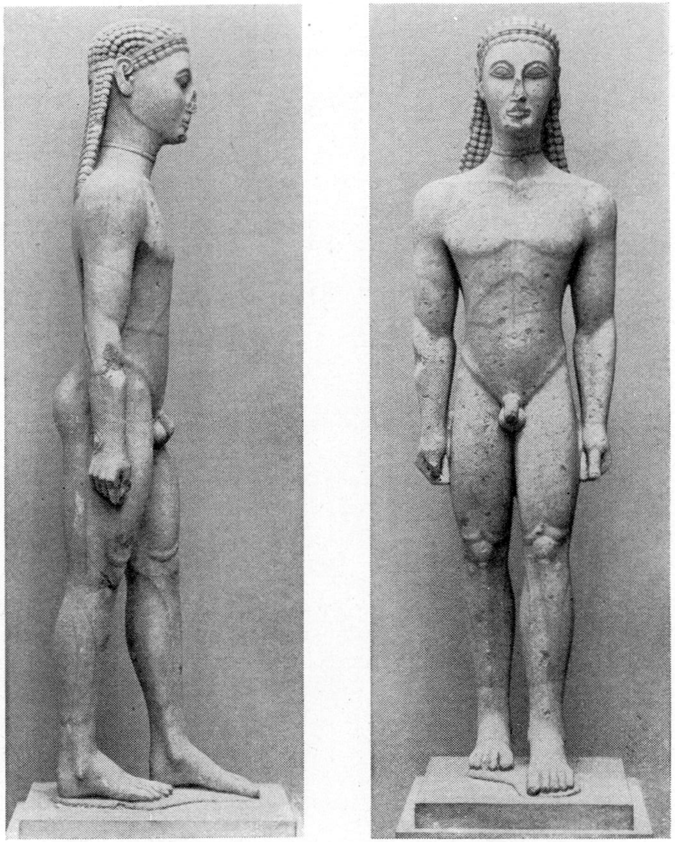

Fig. 3.9 New York. Metropolitan Museum. Statue of a young man.

ALINARI

Fig. 3.10 Athens. National Museum. Stele of Aristion. Detail.

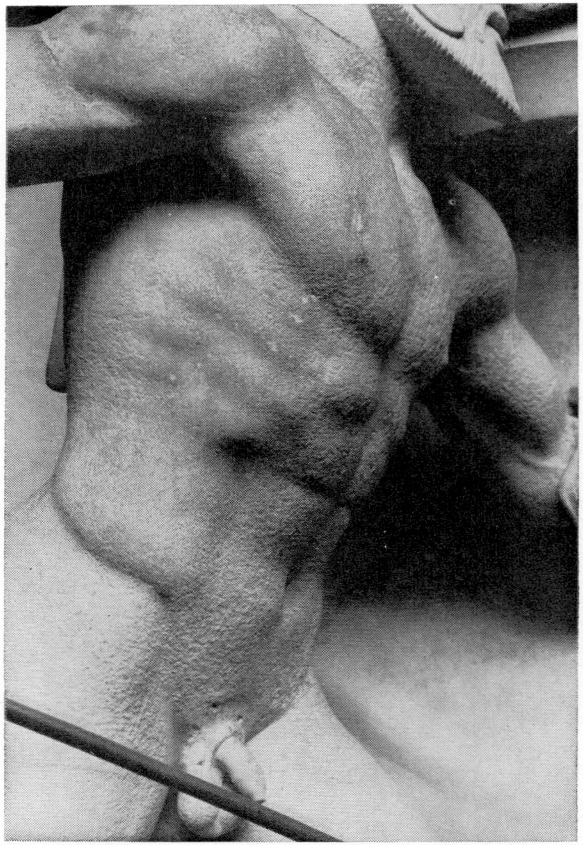

CLARENCE KENNEDY

Fig. 3.11 Torso of a warrior from the pedimental sculpture of the Temple of Aphaia at Aegina.

ANDERSON

Fig. 3.12 Rome. Terme Museum. *Birth of Aphrodite*. Central panel from the so-called "Ludovisi Throne." About 480–470 B.C.

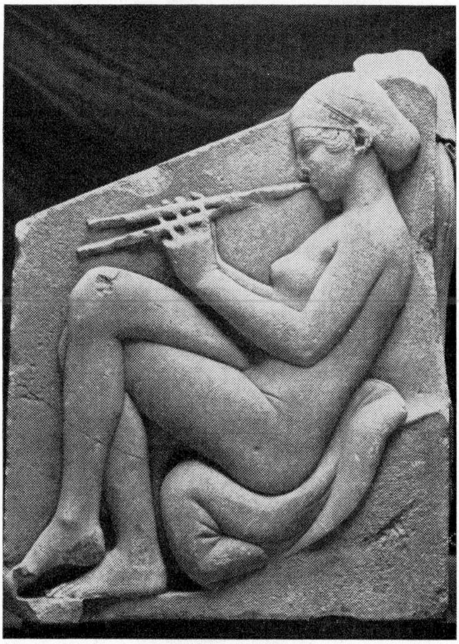

ANDERSON

Fig. 3.13 One of the side panels from the "Ludovisi Throne."

ALINARI

Fig. 3.14 Paris. Louvre. Metope of *Heracles and the Cretan Bull* from the Temple of Zeus at Olympia. About 475–465 B.C.

Fig. 3.15–16 The Pedimental Compositions of the Temple of Zeus at Olympia as reconstructed in the models at the Altes Museum, Berlin. From photographs by Walter Hege; retouched. Above: the moment before the chariot race between Pelops and Oenomaos (Eastern pediment). Below: the battle between the Greeks and the Centaurs (Western pediment).

ALINARI

Figs. 3.17–18–19 Delphi. Museum. *The Charioteer from Delphi.*

ALINARI

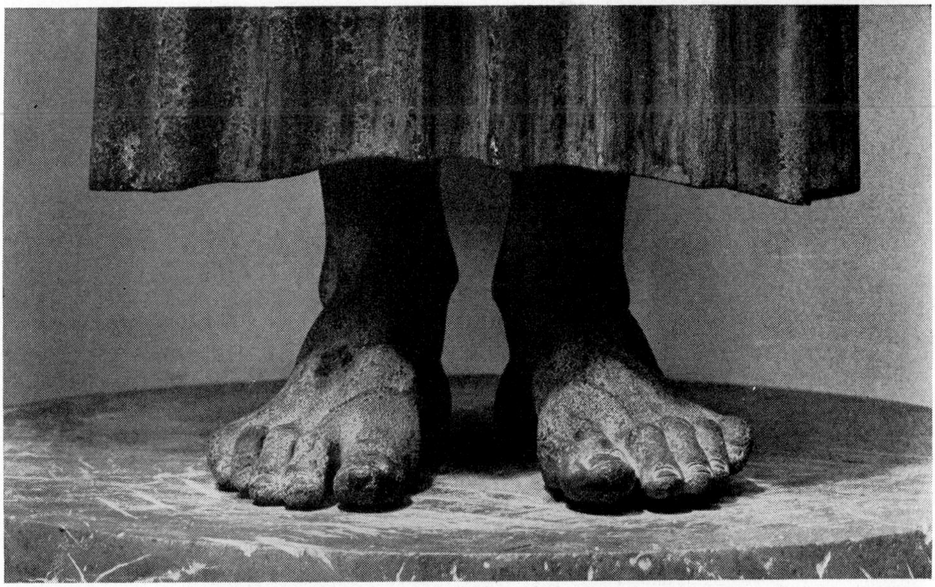

CLARENCE KENNEDY

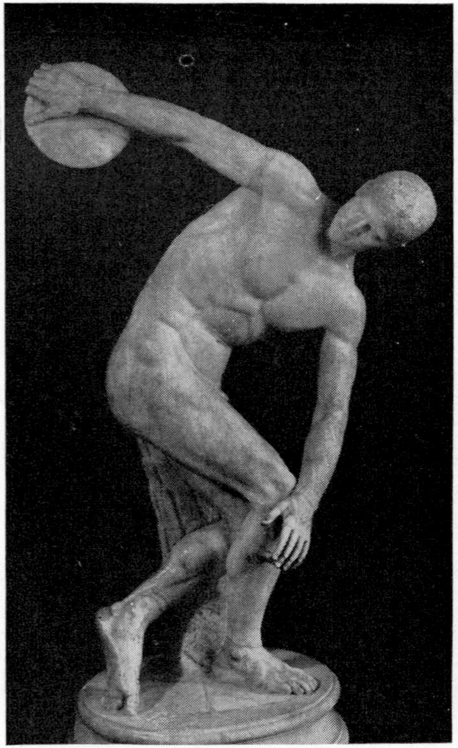

GAB. FOT. NAZ.

Fig. 3.20 Rome. Borghese Gallery (formerly in the Lancellotti Palace). *The Discobolos.* Marble. 5 feet high.

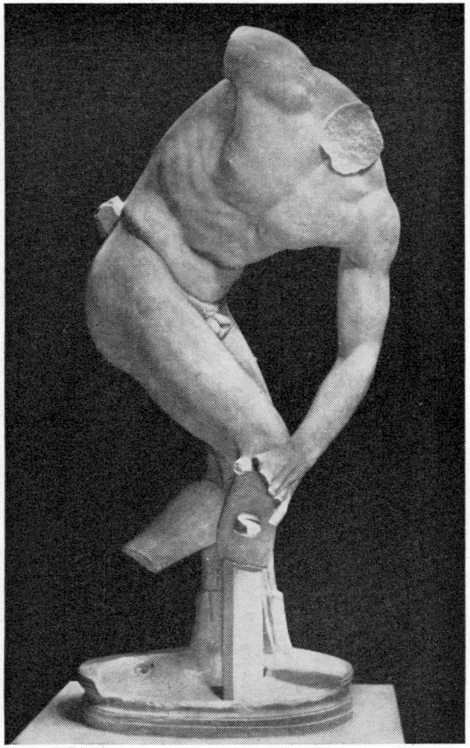

ALINARI

Fig. 3.21 Rome. Terme Museum. *The Discobolos.* Found at Castel Porziano.

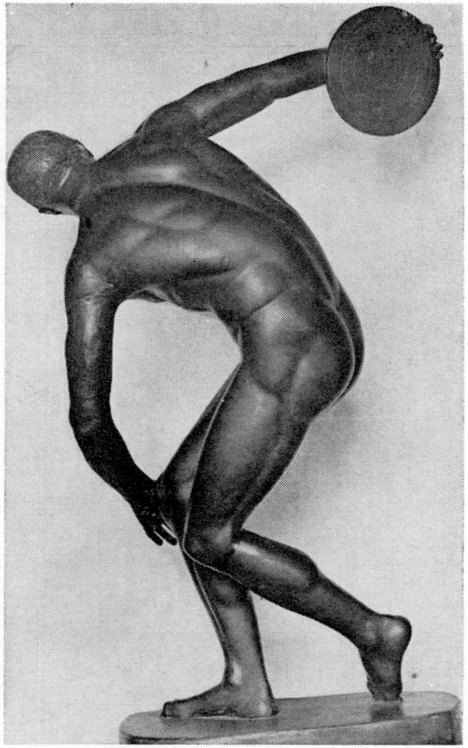

STOEDTNER

Fig. 3.22 *The Discobolos.* Reconstruction combining the features of several Roman copies.

fident with regard to the Greek theatre. But we know next to nothing about any other class of Greek building.

We have an excellent collection of originals from the Archaic and Transitional Periods of Greek sculpture (about 1100–450 B.C.), and we are well off for monuments from the Hellenistic and Roman Periods (323 B.C. to about 300 A.D.). For the Great Age (about 450–325 B.C.), our monumental evidence is pitiful: we have only one putative original from the hand of a sculptor who commanded fame and prestige in ancient times. Our picture of Greek sculpture at its best, that is to say, is a mere archaeological reconstruction based upon literary evidence, analogies, and monumental evidence of the second, third, and fourth level of excellence. We nevertheless have a clear and probably a very accurate account of what happened.

We know that Greek painting was important. There is some reason to think, indeed, that the Greeks themselves ranked their painters as being greater artists, on the whole, or at least more definitive artists than their sculptors. When writing *The Poetics,* Aristotle mentioned a painter almost every time he wanted to make an analogy with the visual arts, and he hardly refers to sculpture. We may assume that the painters came most easily to mind simply because they had made a greater impression upon him.

But beyond repeating the names he mentions (Polygnotus, Zeuxis, Pauson, Dionysos) we have almost nothing to say. At times famous paintings were rather freely copied by the commercial artists employed in the decoration of Greek pottery, and we are lucky enough to have inherited a substantial number of their vases. In Greece, even those humbler artists were uncommonly fine, and Greek vase painting constitutes one of the most charming byways of art history. It would be unfair to describe it in stronger terms; and as for gaining any satisfactory visualization of the great lost paintings, many of us have studied the vase pictures without success.

In the face of this somewhat discouraging situation, it is undeniable that there is magic in Greek art. It has laid hold on the European imagination as no other art has ever done. It is always there as an influence tending to mold the shape of other modes and manners, and Greek standards are forever asserting themselves as the plane of reference to which other art should be referred.

An important and recurring phenomenon of art history is the likelihood that the Greek style in surprisingly pure form may flare up anywhere. It never completely died out in Italy, even during the Middle Ages. It strongly affected the architecture of the Romanesque cathedral at Autun, and it modified the style of the Gothic sculptors of Reims. Giotto's later compositions are according to the Greek system, and Greece is the underlying ideal of the entire High Renaissance. During the 19th Century, David, Ingres, and the other

French Neo-Classicists sought in the literal sense of the word to bring Greek art back to life — an enterprise that came close to success in the so-called Greek Revival architecture of America. We are correctly reminded of the Greek in many paintings by Picasso.

Nothing else in art history has the same importance.

HISTORICAL CONSIDERATIONS

Our Western civilization, including its artistic tradition, started with Greece, but it is necessary to make it plain what *Greece* means in this connection.

We refer to *Classical Greece,* or to the culture and civilization which achieved its special and definitive character about the time of the poet Homer, who seems to have lived in Ionia (Asia Minor) during the 9th Century B.C.

The people we call the Greeks were an amalgam of several races. So far as we can tell, the population of the area sprang from the mixture of its aborigines with the peoples who entered the region in at least three successive waves of invasion and migration, each separated from the last by an interval of centuries. The aborigines appear to have had their centers among the islands called the Cyclades which stretch like a chain southeasterly from the coast near Athens. Of these people we know nothing more than we can deduce from their art, but even that is significant.

About 3000 B.C. another civilization became dominant. It centered on the Island of Crete, with the capital at Knossos. Knossos and other sites on the island have been actively excavated from the first years of the 20th Century, and the discoveries have been analyzed from time to time in the voluminous reports of Sir Arthur Evans. The ruins of an immense palace have been laid bare at Knossos. Everything points to a civilization notable for refinement of life and justifiable pride of culture. Sea power was evidently the source of its security, for Knossos was without fortification. The Cretan civilization is referred to by various names, most of them intended to be noncommittal. Sir Arthur Evans wisely prefers to call it *Minoan,* a pretty word which has at least the endorsement of later mythology, for King Minos, proprietor of the terrible Minotaur, lived on Crete. *Minotaur* means merely "Minos's bull," and both the frescoes and carvings of this race show that the bullfight was a favorite sport.

About 1400 B.C. Crete was invaded and Knossos destroyed by fire. We are probably justified in calling the conquerors Achaeans. Their centers were on the mainland at Mycenae and Tiryns, both places being near the head of the Gulf of Argolis. These sites were excavated with astonishing success by

Heinrich Schliemann (1822–1890), who worked at Mycenae in 1876 and at Tiryns in 1884.

Schliemann's finds were rich beyond comparison. At Mycenae, he recovered 701 decorated gold discs in one grave alone. The style of the decoration of these, and of pottery and frescoes from the same era, is similar to the style of the material found on Crete, but stiffer and less accomplished. From this and other indications, most scholars draw the conclusion that the Achaeans were culturally more rude than the Minoans, but wise enough to absorb what they could of the earlier civilization.

About 1100 B.C. the Achaeans were overwhelmed by a vigorous race we call the Dorians. Their culture was strong in those elements that make for survival and dominion; they brought the use of iron with them, all earlier inhabitants having been limited to bronze. It now seems that the Dorians were less outrageously barbaric than we used to be told, but it is still obvious their taste lacked the amenities which were characteristic of both the Minoans and the Achaeans.

The history of the next 400 years is unusually obscure. The period is often called the Greek Dark Ages, but there must have been some merit in the situation because the classical Greeks emerged at the end of it. Sculpture and painting in the earliest version of the Classical Style begin about 700 B.C. The first full-size statues appear to date about 50 or 75 years after that.

It will be noted that Homer's career falls in the middle of the period just summarized. His poems are notably disparaging whenever reference is made to the culture of his own time. Our best guess is that his narratives recount actual events in the heroic Achaean past, which he saw as a bygone age of gold.

It would not serve our central purpose to take space for a connected and detailed account of Cycladic, Minoan, Achaean, and Doric art. Certain elements from this past nevertheless survived as the classical heritage, and some aspects of later Greek art are difficult to understand without reference to earlier tastes and customs. A few comments are therefore in order.

ART OF THE GREEK AREA PREVIOUS TO THE CLASSICAL ERA

The Cycladic Idols (Before 3000 B.C.)

A number of stone statuettes, all fairly consistent in style, have been recovered on the Cyclades from strata which, from other evidence, we can place before 3000 B.C. For lack of a better name, the statuettes are known as the *Cycladic Idols.* The British Museum has a number, and there are a good many in the Louvre. A particularly fine example was acquired in 1940 for the collection of the Albright Art Gallery in Buffalo (Fig. 3.1).

The critics of past generations could see nothing but ignorance and crudity in the *Cycladic Idols*. Today we are inclined to be more respectful. *Primitive art* used to carry a strong connotation that the artist was unenlightened and knew no better, but that the speaker did. Serious and sympathetic study of earlier civilizations, or those isolated from European influence, has inclined our more recent opinion to caution. Mature reflection very often suggests that the so-called " primitive " peoples were in fact extremely sophisticated, and that their apparent crudity often denotes profound wisdom expressed with devastating directness. In the case of the *Cylcadic Idols*, there is much to sustain such a view.

Those monuments testify to the existence of a school of sculptors with extraordinary powers for *abstraction*.

As a critical term for use in discussing the visual arts, we may define *abstraction* as the act of summarizing the appearance of a man, a scene, or an object, as contrasted to attempting a complete and detailed description thereof. All art is to some degree an abstraction simply because the artist's tools and materials cannot accomplish minute visual description no matter how hard he tries. But as a useful word, we had best reserve *abstraction* for monuments where the artist declines to employ all the descriptive techniques at hand, and insists upon summarizing so radically that he obviously abbreviates.

Abbreviation, by its very nature, tends to deny us something we might wish to see, but it has the virtue of enabling the artist to select the important and eliminate the extraneous. Obviously, the process can either go a little way, or so far that all resemblance to the original subject is lost. The sculptors who did the *Cycladic Idols* abstracted perhaps as much as might be possible without causing us to wonder whether human beings are represented. What is left?

The folded arms and erect pose suggest presence at some solemn ceremony. The thighs, torso, and shoulders are described only enough to tell us that the body is in excellent tone, that the muscles carry it with ease. The head is held high, and even though the face is blank except for the prominent nose, there is a plain statement of racial and family pride. The whole carriage, in fact, suggests an aristocracy and a code of manners where grace might shift instantly into arrogance. However brief his methods, it is difficult to miss the sculptor's intent.

It is an oddity that the art of the Greek area should have commenced with so extreme a style. While it is impossible to make any direct historical connections between the *Cycladic Idols* and later Greek work, it is by no means unreasonable to suggest that the artistic theory behind them formed part of the

Greek heritage and left a taste for abstraction capable of coming into the open at any time. It is notable in this connection that the great sculpture of the 5th Century, while predominantly naturalistic, nevertheless stands as a substantial simplication of natural fact which partakes strongly of the tendency to abstract.

Minoan and Mycenaean Art (About 3000 to 1100 B.C.)

In treating the human figure, Minoan art is by no means lacking in abstraction, but exhibits at the same time a direct delight in the actual appearance of people, animals, plants, flowers, fish, and seaweeds. Almost every piece is eloquent of a happy life and a pleasant relation between man and his environment. Among the notable objects from this era, we may cite the following.

A beehive tomb was excavated in 1889 at a site beside the Eurotas River about five miles south of Sparta. The place is known as Vaphio, and the objects found there were sent to the National Museum of Athens. Among them were two remarkable gold cups generally agreed to be of Cretan provenance, and doubtless imported thence and preserved on the mainland (Fig. 3.3).

Both cups are decorated with miniature compositions in high relief, executed by the *repoussé* process (i.e., the metal being worked or beaten into a mould from behind). The technique is so delicate and yet so vigorous as to belie the scale. Nothing in all art history is more thoroughly lively. One cup shows domesticated bulls enjoying themselves in a pasture. The other shows several Minoans risking life and limb to capture some wild bulls by catching them in nets. The laws of anatomy are blithely defied with consequent gain to the spirit of the occasion.

The Museum of Fine Arts in Boston has a little *Snake Goddess* of gold and ivory, also almost certainly of Minoan workmanship (Fig.3.2). There is considerable abstraction in the body, particularly about the waist, which duplicates in conventional fashion the waist of many another Minoan figure, but both the posture and the face are eloquent of portraiture. Whoever the young lady may have been, her person and her personality remain herself, never seen before and never duplicated again. The tiny figure can be magnified almost indefinitely without loss of refinement; indeed it rather gains from a substantial increase in size, as on the lecture screen.

Minoan painting and sculpture went dead with the Achaean invasion. Objects associated with the era of Mycenae and Tiryns are obviously derivative from the style which had centered in Crete. They are not lacking in daintiness, but they have nothing like the life typical of the best production of the period before the destruction of Knossos. We may therefore pass over such material entirely in the present narrative.

Without going into detail, it is nevertheless necessary to record that the type of building we know as the Greek temple seems to have achieved its definitive form during the Mycenaean age. A conspicuous feature of the plan of the citadel at Tiryns is the rectangular outline of a building which, during the classical era, would have been known as a *templum in antis* — the standard plan for small temples at all times, and the central element of the plan of the largest and most elaborate buildings put up in the Greek world. Because the history of all Greek architecture is summed up in the refinement of this single type of building, we may reserve discussion until we come to the time of the greatest temples of all, those put up on the Acropolis at Athens during the latter half of the 5th Century B.C.

The Geometric Style (About 1100 to 700 B.C.)

The art that came in with the Dorians is generally known as the *Geometric Style,* and its monuments consist of small bronze statuettes and pictures painted on vases. In general, these are even more radically abstracted than the *Cycladic Idols.* The curves natural to human bodies and to animals are hardened into angular shapes or reduced to circular arcs. Such shapes are connected together to suggest a man or beast as the case may be. Decorative patterns show a similar severity; for the most part they amount to the repetition of the simplest geometric forms like the chevron, the meander, the checkerboard, and simple stripes or hatchings.

It was extremely difficult for the earlier critics to find anything good to say about the Geometric Style except that it came to an end in the space of about 400 years. The modern student has the advantage of broader standards of comparison, and he will reason much as we have already done with respect to the *Cycladic Idols.*

The best Geometric painting is found on the so-called *Dipylon Vases.* These are some very large pieces of pottery used as grave monuments in the Dipylon Cemetery at Athens, from which they take their name. They are not made to hold water, and might be called funnels rather than vases — where we put flowers on the grave, it was the humane custom of that time to refresh the deceased by pouring wine down to him (Fig. 3.4).

If we can accept the abstraction, and it is admittedly harsh, some of the scenes on the *Dipylon Vases* are entertaining and even exciting. The funeral procession is a favorite subject, as the purpose of the vase might suggest, but other scenes often appear. Of these, naval battles form a notable category. Some of them unmistakably reflect a memory of whole fleets in combat, and tell us that naval warfare was highly developed and that great battles took place in that now forgotten time.

None of the Geometric vase paintings have anything like the quality of the best bronzes from the same era. Of these, a notable example in almost perfect preservation is the miniature horse now in the Metropolitan Museum (Fig. 3.5). Somewhat puzzling to adults who have formed their taste solely upon representation, the merit of the little statue is attested by its great popularity among children. They are almost invariably delighted with it, and they have no difficulty in seeing that the sculptor meant to record the proud stance, the alert ears, the sensitive distension of the the nostrils, and the sleek strong thighs. If they worry about the anatomy of the knees, they do not worry long: the artist merely meant to say the knee is bumpy.

The 7th Century B.C., *or "The Period of Oriental Influence"*

During the 7th Century B.C., Greek taste seems to have shifted away from the severity of the Geometric Style. For reasons not entirely clear, but suggested by the establishment of Greek colonies on the Nile delta and by the spread of Phoenician commerce, the Dorian population had its eyes opened to the richer and gentler art of the Near East. The entire century is sometimes referred to, therefore, as "The Period of Oriental Influence." As before, the record of such influence is found almost exclusively in vase painting.

Geometric abstraction did not entirely die out, but the typical vase of the 7th Century is decorated with rosettes, confronted birds, grotesque monsters, and various more or less natural but rather schematized animals. Human figures are very rare (Fig. 3.6).

A strange immobility marks even the most naturalistic items in this catalogue of decoration. Running figures get nowhere. Roaring dragons make no noise. Nothing happens even though action ostensibly is represented.

The reason is not far to seek. The various decorative motives taken up by the Greek workmen come directly from the tradition of the Near East, where since the world began those with artistic inclination have turned most naturally to designing carpets and other textiles. Textile designers are forced by the nature of their medium to work toward a composition characterized by an even spread of interest over the entire surface (page 27), and it follows that any bird, flower, or animal appeals to the designer not as a factor in a narrative to be told, but merely as a spot of color against the background. He therefore arranges them without much regard for dramatic content, and his primary purpose is to produce a succession of rhythmic accents.

CHRONOLOGY OF THE CLASSICAL ERA OF GREEK ART

Such was the background when the classical era began in Greece. Each element of the heritage seems to have left something of itself in the Greek genius, and the separate parts of the heredity appear alone or in recognizable combination at odd times and places: the intellectual severity of abstraction, delight in natural fact, a certain love for rich decoration.

At some indefinite time during the latter part of the obscure period we have been covering, a new element came into the artistic philosophy of Greece. There is absolutely no way to explain how or why the decision was made, but it remains one of the most important in European cultural history. The Greeks chose to adopt the human figure as the chief and virtually the exclusive subject of their artistic endeavor. From the 7th Century onward, their sculptors made practically nothing else, and their painters seem to have done much the same.

It has long been customary to recognize five periods in the evolution of Greek art during its classical phase. These coincide with significant political and social mutations; but as stylistic divisions, the separate periods correspond most closely with the development of sculpture, and only in a general way with architecture and painting. Greek sculpture therefore stands out as a peculiarly perfect case where the history of art gives a record of the contemporary state of mind.

The earliest statues of large size date somewhere this side of 650 B.C., and the period from that moment until about 500 B.C. is known by the name *Archaic*. Statues from the Archaic Period exhibit major technical faults; namely, gross anatomical errors, timid technique, obvious lack of control over facial expression.

The Persian Wars were over by 479 B.C.; and as war so often does, they stimulated the Greek mind and forced rapid development. The first half of the 5th Century B.C. is generally called the *Transitional Period*, a somewhat unfortunate term, but one which at least suggests progress. The course of the progress was always in the direction of complete technical mastery over both the medium and the subtleties of the human anatomy. Sculpture was still somewhat clumsy at the beginning of the half-century. At the end, the Greek artists had perfect control and were thenceforth limited only by the boundaries of their own imagination. A few lingering minor errors of anatomy (such as failure to overlap the eyelid, or an almost imperceptible stiffness of pose) linger to indicate a date earlier than 450.

The " Great Age," as it is called, extends from the Age of Pericles to the death of Alexander, or from about 450 B.C to 323 B.C. The Great Age is subdivided into the *Greek Fifth Century* (450–400 B.C.) and the *Greek Fourth Century* (400–323 B.C.), and those terms are used in the special sense indicated.

The Great Age is by common consent the period of supreme and definitive accomplishment, not only in art but in philosophy, culture, and ideals. Great civic monuments are the characteristic sculpture of the Fifth Century, usually representing the major gods. The two periods are separated by the tragedy of the Peloponnesian War, from which the political genius of Greece never recovered. Work from the Fourth Century is usually on a smaller, more personal scale. Subject matter is neither so grand nor so stirring, but more gracefully presented. The whole spirit of the century is contemplative and introspective.

Alexander's conquests spread Greek influence eastward, and exposed Greece to influences from outside. The results are both inspiring and confusing. Most of the fixed conventions of Greek art went by the board in favor of variety and experiment. Some of the greatest monuments were brought into being and some of the very worst. To distinguish the age from earlier times we call it *Hellenistic* (Greek-like, or cultivating Greek ways) as contrasted to *Hellenic* (true Greek).

The kingdoms established by Alexander's heirs survived more or less independently until the Mediterranean world came under Roman dominion. The year 146 B.C., when Mummius took Corinth and erased the last claim of Greek independence, is sometimes cited as the end of the Hellenistic Period. However significant in political history, the event marks no important cultural or stylistic change. Roman art hardly exists before contact with Greece and constitutes a further development of the Hellenistic.

THE ARCHAIC PERIOD (About 650 B.C. to about 480 B.C.)

We may skip lightly over developments during the Archaic Period. Its principal contribution was to lay technical foundation for what was to come. Its sculptural output may be classified under four simple types of figures: a nondescript seated type, flying figures, and standing figures both male and female — the male being nude in most examples and the female always draped. Only the two latter categories are of general interest.

Our very earliest statue — at least most of us believe it to be so — is a draped female figure of Naxian marble, now in the Louvre (Fig. 3.7). An inscription says it was dedicated by Nikandra in honor of Artemis. The statue is shallow and flat, a fact which some have taken to indicate earlier wooden prototypes made from heavy planks. On the whole, it seems more likely that the sculptor, as most beginners still do, merely failed to appreciate how much space he needed for the third dimension.

The Nikandra figure has two features which in all probability reflect some contact with Egyptian work: the hair is spread broadly to either side, as though in a long bob, in an effort to brace the neck against possible breakage; and the pose exhibits the familiar convention of frontality. Both of these features had been habitual in Egypt from the earliest times.

The crudity of Nikandra's dedication did not last long in Greece, and we may next turn our attention to the *Hera from Samos,* of some uncertain later date and also in the Louvre (Fig. 3.8). This statue is almost cylindrical in cross-section, a circumstance which has often been interpreted as indicating technical crudity. One sometimes hears the explanation that the primitive sculptor was translating into stone an early and inarticulate class of figure half-formed from the trunk of a tree. Because we know that naturalism was the coming thing in Greek art, it is deceptively easy to dismiss the *Hera* as an inadequate essay in that direction, but any such notion comes into contradiction with the obvious skill with which certain passages are handled. The differentiation of textures as between the silk of the skirt and the wool of the jacket is a capital instance of unmistakable suggestion without any labored attempt at complete visual description. The same may be said for the truly adequate swell of the bust and the protruding toes. In the end we find it extremely difficult to maintain the thought that ignorance of any kind may be adduced to explain what we see. It is more reasonable to recognize this grandly columnar figure as virtually the final expression of the strong tradition of abstraction in force when the Archaic Period began.

We have a great many standing male figures from the Archaic Period. It used to be customary to refer to the lot of them as "the Apollos," but since there is little reason to believe that the god was represented, the somewhat more accurate and noncommittal word *kouros* is becoming popular. It is nothing more than a transliteration of the Greek for *young man* (Fig. 3.9).

As a class, the *kouroi* suggest very strongly that the idea of large sculpture was suggested to the Greeks because such art had been popular in Egypt. As though by convention, frontality is maintained almost to the very end of the Archaic era. Another duplication of Egyptian custom is the habit of putting the left foot forward, a nonessential feature that might well have been borrowed more or less unconsciously while trying to emulate a model.

A great gulf of difference separates the crudest Greek work from the Egyptian, however. The most important change of all is the mere fact that the

Greek statues are nude. In the first instance, this custom may have started with nothing more profound than the observation that clothes get in the way when one is exercising. As a national institution, the Olympic Games appear to date from the first recorded victories of 776 B.C., a year not overly far removed from the class of statue now under review. But however simple its beginnings, the introduction of the nude figure is one of the most important events in the history of art. The simple possibility of using the entire surface of the body opened up broader horizons almost beyond measure.

The artistic worth of the human nude derives from its superiority over the draped figure as a vehicle for communicating content. The state of the emotions and even the state of the soul makes itself manifest not in the face alone, but in every muscle. When the body is concealed by cloth, the artist simply has less area to work with and greater difficulty in making himself plain.

The nude may or may not be erotic. It is an untruth to say it never is, but it is a fair statement that such intention is absent in the overwhelming majority of the many thousand nudes in the history of European art.

During the Archaic Period itself, the Greek artists did not get very far ahead with the exploitation of the nude as a vehicle for subtle or important content. Their effort seems to have been consumed in attempting to master the complex mechanics of the human body, and to gain control over pose and expression. They succeeded only indifferently well.

Almost every example of the *kouros* class is much too wide across the shoulders. Evidently, the full width of the block was assigned for the upper part of the body, with the resultant necessity of making the hips too narrow in order to have enough material for the wrists and hands. It was customary to put the ear out of place, usually too high; and to let the eyeballs protrude like marbles from the forehead. Facial expressions usually demonstrate ludicrous lack of control. If serious, they appear to be either stupid or surly; and if a smile is intended, we see the smirk of an idiot.

Toward the end of the Archaic Period, say from about 550 B.C. onward, most critics feel the presence of two divergent tendencies of style, the Dorian and the Ionic.

The Dorian is associated with the Peloponnesus where the military and athletic regimen was most rigorously cultivated. Scientific anatomy, or any honest attempt to approach toward it, is identified with this group of sculptors. Their figure-style runs to a stocky canon of proportions, a more or less cubical head, grim facial expression, and musculature that imparts a feeling of genuine force even when it is grossly incorrect in detail. The twin *kouroi* in the museum at Delphi illustrate this trend of style in an early form.

The Ionic division of Archaic sculpture was gay. It ran to fancy clothes, elaborate coiffures, and lively faces. The male muscles are often emphasized as much as by the Dorian sculptors, but they seem merely bulky. This lighthearted style, if we may call it that, seems to have centered at Athens and coincides in date with a considerable immigration of artists from Ionia. They fled, it would seem, from the expansion of Persian power — it was in 546 that Cyrus the Great overwhelmed the Greek kingdom of Lydia, captured King Croesus, sacked Sardis, and subdued all the other Ionian cities except Miletos. To the exiled artists, generous hospital was offered by the court of Peisistratos, then tyrant at Athens.

The Ionizing sculpture of Athens during the next generation has been preserved in good quantity largely because Athens suffered disaster during the campaign of 480. In that year, the Persians, marching south from Thermopylae to their ultimate defeat at Salamis and Plataea, paused to sack and destroy the city. A great many statues stood on the Acropolis. They were all overturned, but not utterly broken. The returning Greeks did not bother to repair them; they simply buried them there. Hence we possess in remarkably fresh condition a considerable number of late Archaic monuments, mostly female figures in richly pleated costumes and with elaborately curled hair.

As a class, these female figures are called the *Acropolis Maidens*. For our purposes the Ionic tendency will be even better illustrated by a male counterpart, the grave monument known as the *Stele of Aristion* (Fig. 3.10). Dated at about 510 B.C. by the type of lettering used for its inscription, this relief shows a Greek dandy dressed to the limit in natty but abbreviated costume. The sculptor appears to have attempted to combine strength and elegance in his rendering of the arms and legs. He did not entirely fail in the latter intention.

Because sobered by its scientific bent, the Dorian tendency was capable of greater discipline and progress along the predetermined line of sculptural development. This fact is splendidly illustrated by the *Aegina Marbles*, the last important sculpture we must classify as archaic.

The figures come from the pediments of the Temple of Aphaia on the island of Aegina, south of Athens (page 83). The date of the sculpture hinges upon the style of the architecture, which is Doric just before its final perfection at Olympia and on the Acropolis of Athens. If we make the necessary allowance for a cessation of artistic progress during the period of the Persian Wars (499–479 B.C.), it seems likely that the right moment is somewhere close to 500 B.C. or a little later.

The archaeological value of the sculpture from this temple is somewhat discredited by a series of unfortunate manipulations during the 19th Century. The site was excavated by a group of young gentlemen, English and German, who had come to Athens as students. They lacked professional qualifications; but in those easy-going times, they were able to organize an expedition, proceed to the island, and dig. They unearthed the pedimental figures, took them off, and sold them to Ludwig of Bavaria.

Before putting them on exhibition in Munich, Ludwig engaged Bertel Thorwaldsen (1770–1844), then a leader of the Neo-Classical movement (page 844 ff), to repair and refinish the statues.

Because the excavators kept no strict records, it is impossible today to be completely certain that we have each statue assigned to its proper place in the pediment, or even to the correct end of the building. Because Thorwaldsen did a substantial amount of work and was equally vague about what he had done, it is likewise impossible to be absolutely sure we are looking at surfaces carved by Greek hands. In spite of the reservations it is necessary to make, however, the figures from Aegina stand out from all other Archaic work with an unmistakably dynamic quality (Fig. 3.11). Minor inaccuracies will strike the eye of the skilled anatomist, and it must be conceded that the sculptor's drive toward expression still outruns his technical resources. At the same time, the chunky little bodies have more snap and life than anything ever seen before.

The most important single element of the achievement at Aegina is the fact that the artist depends hardly at all upon the face to carry his meaning. One of the fallen warriors may or may not express pain upon the countenance; it is possible to contend that an accident of lighting produces the effect. Otherwise the case is clear: the faces are very nearly neutral, and almost unnecessary.

THE TRANSITIONAL PERIOD (About 480 B.C. to about 450 B.C.)

The Persian Wars ended with the battle of Plataea in 479 B.C., and the Persian menace was a thing of the past. No other political or military event has anything like the same importance for the history of Europe; it may be said, indeed, that Western civilization acquired by the fact of that victory its best and most distinctive qualities.

The Persian Wars brought spiritual values into issue as no other conflict has ever done. The westward expansion of Persia was politically normal; and, within the contemporary frame of reference, ethical. The Greek decision to resist was hardly wise if judged in relation to military probability. The Persian army was the most potent force on earth. It had a record of complete success. The Greeks had no rational evidence for expecting anything but annihilation. To resist under those circumstances amounted to an assertion of the superiority of certain ideals over every other consideration including survival.

When the unbelievable happened and it emerged as fact that the Greeks had won the war, ideals as such assumed a new and different aspect. No longer a figment of the imagination, idealism was plainly worthwhile as a basis for practical policy, and the particular ideals of the Greeks seemed obviously more potent than any others. The whole population experienced a driving sense of uplift; no danger on earth could conceivably be worse than the danger so recently faced and conquered.

Under these circumstances, it is not remarkable that the Greeks as a people found themselves looking out upon the universe from a new and more lofty plateau. Their famous tendency to judge all things in terms of man doubtless derived from the consciousness that men seemed for the moment not mere chattels of fate, but intelligent beings capable of controlling the environment. Human dignity, a concept that had scarcely existed before, entered the philosophy of Europe at this point in history — ever to remain as the chief distinction of Western culture.

The progress of Greek sculpture is perhaps our most vivid record of the general state of mind after the Persian Wars.

Returning to find their cities in ruins and their most sacred shrines desecrated and despoiled, the Greeks seem not for a moment to have looked backward. They did not pause to repair even the monuments which might easily have been put back into good order. They simply started on a program of replacing the lot with something new and incomparably better.

Technical advance went forward with incredible rapidity. In the thirty years between the Persian Wars and the middle of the 5th Century B.C., more was learned and mastered than during the past two centuries. By about 450 Greece had the most accomplished school of sculptors, and presumably of painters as well, that the world had ever seen.

The Ludovisi Throne and the Boston Reliefs

In a period of general advance along a known course of development, we are almost certainly justified in dating monuments on style. Assuming, therefore, that those exhibiting less accurate anatomy come earlier, we may begin the Transitional Period with the marble panels of relief known as the *Ludovisi Throne* (Figs. 3.12–13) and the *Boston Reliefs.*

The two are companion pieces. Each consists of three faces of relief, one large and two small. The panels now in Boston have been separated. Originally they probably were in much the same state as those of the *Ludovisi Throne,* which is a single large block of marble hollowed out on one side to form what first was taken to be a bench of some kind.

The main panel of the *Ludovisi Throne* appears to represent the birth of Aphrodite. The main panel of the Boston set seems to show Aphrodite and

Persephone with a well-grown Cupid between them holding a set of scales. Presumably there is some reference to the story of Adonis.

The four smaller panels have caused considerable puzzlement. Each of the four has a single figure: a nude boy and a nude girl playing musical instruments, an enigmatic young priestess, and an elderly woman with bobbed hair. Because these figures are presented in a curiously intimate way, they are out of character with reference to almost all other full-size Greek sculpture. Analogous figures may be found in the minor arts, however — vase painting, statuettes, and so forth. The explanation is probably something like this: that most of the sculpture we possess is ceremonial sculpture intended for public display, and that the monuments now under view are exceptional because commissioned by a private patron. Presumably there were numerous others of the same kind which have not survived.

The *Birth of Aphrodite* is the most important panel of the six. According to the myth, the Goddess was born a full-grown young woman. She emerged from the foam of the Aegean Sea and came ashore on the Isle of Cythera, just off the southeastern tip of the Peloponnesus. Apparently we see her being assisted from the water.

Anatomical inaccuracy is evident in the figure of Aphrodite. The breasts are placed too far on either side, and are seen almost in the three-quarter view. Some indication of muscular strain would be necessary for an accurate description of a neck twisted a full ninety degrees; but none is indicated. The eye is also inconsistent with the position of the head; it is insufficiently foreshortened and presents too broad an aspect.

Such matters pale into insignificance in view of the radiant look of the Goddess as she awakens to life. No praise can be too high, moreover, for the composition; it is still unexcelled.

The arrangement depends upon the interaction of directional impulses from the sides toward the middle, and from the center out toward the sides. The two attendant figures furnish the former; both must have been looking eagerly down toward the face of Aphrodite. The Goddess's arms swing in a parabolic arc outward to right and left; and the relation between middle and sides is reinforced by the folds of the sheet of drapery below, and the arms from which it hangs.

The over-all effect is to produce a situation where every part not only fits with the next, but is connected to it by some linear device. Within the composition, coherence is tight and unmistakable, and no frame is needed to declare the integrity and unity of the whole.

If we are correct in feeling that the *Ludovisi Throne* was made during the decade between 480 and 470 B.C., it is evident that a considerable and systematic study of formal composition must have taken place even before the Persian Wars. As restored, the Aegina pediments are arranged on much the same system we find here, but for the reasons stated at the time (page 50), we cannot fairly use them as evidence for the state of Greek composition.

In addition to its excellent composition, the Ludovisi *Birth of Aphrodite* is notable in any company for the subtle linear patterns it presents to the eye. Two kinds of line are used, the zigzag and the graded curve. Angles are played off against swings, and the swings themselves vary in the speed of curvature without departing into another category of curve altogether.

On the principle that the eye will follow the bony structure of any figure down through the spine and supporting leg to the ground, we may for the sake of analysis forget that human females are represented and say that the Goddess's two assistants tell abstractly as rather sharp zigzags to either side.

These angular and somewhat staccato boundaries are connected by the swing of easy curves all of which conform fairly closely to the scheme of the parabola. Aphrodite's arms describe such an arc, and the folds of the drapery below show similar arcs, each of parabolic character, but becoming tighter step by step.

By keeping to the parabolic type of curve, the sculptor furnishes us with what we may call a *linear harmony.*

Harmony, as a critical term, is best reserved in the visual arts to indicate the existence of similarity, repetition, or reminiscence. The sense of harmony may be evoked by precise duplication; or, as here, by a more subtle method involving orderly variation upon a theme already familiar. Obviously, artistic harmony is no absolute; it may be definite and emphatic, or suggested by the merest echo of what has gone before.

It is still further necessary to stipulate that an assertion that harmony is observed must in every instance be accompanied by some statement of the terms in which the harmony is expressed. In the present instance, we have a harmony *of line.* If we were dealing with red repeated here and there, or any other color, we would have a harmony *of hue.* A row of small ivory elephants would confront us with a harmony of hue plus a harmony of shape.

In architectural decoration and in the design of cloth, harmony is often built by the repetition of identical motives. White polkadots on a blue ground are a simple example, and the Doric triglyph another. In almost every instance, the idea of harmony goes hand in hand with rhythm as it does in the case of the triglyphs (page 102) or in the colors of a Persian rug.

The application of so abstract a principle to representative art usually involves the artist, as it does in the *Birth of Aphrodite,* in even greater complexity. The parabolic curves he has so carefully worked into the folds of his drapery are not alike; they vary from comparatively flat to a tighter and more rapid curvature. The variation is not capricious, but proceeds by orderly steps. We shall find it convenient to describe such a situation as involving not only simple harmony and simple variation, but the idea of *progression* as well.

The Charioteer of Delphi

The justly famous *Charioteer of Delphi* (Fig. 3.17) is the only full-size bronze we have inherited from Greek Antiquity in anything like a good state of preservation. It probably formed part of a complete group that originally included both horses and vehicle; some fragments of the horses' legs were found with it when unearthed in 1896. The style of the statue and some words on its original pedestal seem to settle the date as close to 470 B.C.

The frontal pose seems for an instant to suggest an earlier period, but it probably reflects nothing more than the military posture assumed when receiving the prize awarded in honor of the victory commemorated by the statue. In most other respects, the anatomy is easy and accurate, and the only significant sign of archaism is seen in the hair.

Except for a few locks about the ears, the hair scarcely exists in any substantial form. Chariot racers presumably would dislike long hair, but the presence of an abstract linear pattern around the upper part of the cranium says quite plainly that the artist wants us to read the texture of hair and not a shaved head.

The explanation of this situation is to be sought in the difficulties of casting bronze. Large statues must of necessity be cast hollow; the weight and the cost of the material preclude any other expedient. As readers of Benvenuto Cellini know from his narrative of casting the *Perseus,* it is a tricky and dangerous process to turn out anything so complicated in its shape as a statue. It should also be mentioned that no industrial castings in general use today put anything like the same demands upon the skill of the men in the foundry. Inasmuch as hair involves multitudinous tiny projections and hollows, it is perhaps the most difficult part of the figure to cast successfully. Complete freedom in modeling the hair was therefore the very last technical problem to be solved, a state of fact which surely is understandable.

A further study of the *Charioteer* tends to increase the validity of our recognizing a Transitional Period in Greek sculpture. The monument gives evidence of the intense struggle for mastery over the anatomy — the chief artistic effort of the immediate past. It also predicts the future by suggesting the idealism that was presently to become an inflexible convention of the Greek style.

A number of things indicate that the sculptor was, at least in part, committed to the philosophy of objective realism. (See above, page 20.) Without supposing that they were actually observed in the physique of the young man who posed as model, we find it extremely difficult to explain the wispy side-burns, the peculiar curve of the mouth, and the gathering of the drapery in back — the latter being in adventitious folds of a sort that might be produced by accident in tightening the ribbon that held the gown against the chest and prevented it from ballooning in the wind. The matter is clinched if we examine the feet (Fig. 3.19). Nothing of the kind was ever committed to bronze except by direct study of the living model.

The sculptor's involvement with the coming cult of idealization is manifest in the forehead and nose (Fig. 3.18).

As an artistic philosophy, *idealism* starts, as do most other theories about art, with the appearance of a human being or some other object seen in the natural world. In contrast to the realist, the idealist does not accept visual fact as his artistic law. He does not try to describe what he has observed, but from the very first tries to represent things as they might be rather than as they are.

So understood, *idealism* involves no more than *idea*. A gargoyle may be called *idealistic* in this strict and simple sense of the term, simply because it departs from natural fact in the direction of the artist's concept of the grotesque and hideous.

Most of the time, however, we find ourselves saying *idealism* with the intention of suggesting that the artist represented things not only as they might be, but also as they should be. The word in this special and somewhat colloquial sense therefore takes on overtones. It suggests beauty greater than we are likely to find on earth. It connotes lofty thoughts, and it involves us in hope and aspiration.

As a practical proposition for use in the studio, the idealistic point of view almost automatically results in a certain degree of abstraction. The artist eliminates the accidental bump or wrinkle which detracts from the beauty of a face. He does not copy the actual outline of the eyelid, but smoothes it into a graceful curve. In the act of beautifying, he also tends to simplify and to regularize. In the end, he usually has something handsomer than his model, but much less personal.

In the case of the Delphi *Charioteer*, the contour of the forehead has been simplified into a shape closely approaching a cylindrical curve. The sinuses are radically abstracted; each is an unbroken flat surface over the eye, and meets the forehead in a sharp and altogether non-natural edge.

The nose is rather long and its bridge is straight. Seen in profile, there is almost no break in the line where the nose joins the forehead. A straight-edge, that is to say, placed tangent to the bridge of the nose would also be very nearly tangent to the surface of the forehead.

It is this peculiar arrangement of the features that became popular to the exclusion of all others. Only by special exception was any other type of head used at any time between the Transitional Period and the Hellenistic age, and it has truly been said that all Greek statues look enough alike to be cousins. It is useful to have a name for so fixed a convention. We may refer to heads with this appearance as having *the classical profile.*

We must emphasize that the classical profile was invented in the studio. It is an artistic abstraction peculiarly appropriate to sculpture — an art that lends itself to expression by means of the simplified mass. The skulls found in Greek burials have no such characteristic, and when by chance such a profile actually occurs in life, it seems hardly so handsome in flesh and blood as in marble or bronze.

The Olympia Marbles

The most important architectural sculpture of the Transitional Period comes from the Temple of Zeus at Olympia. As was customary with Greek temples (see below, pages 81–86), the building itself had but one purpose: to serve as a shrine housing an important cult image, in this instance the famous seated *Zeus* of gold and ivory by Phidias himself. It was customary, however, to decorate so important a building with a substantial amount of sculpture designed not so much for its own sake or as an end in itself, but as a subordinate enhancement of the architecture. Both *pediments* (Figs. 3.15–16) at Olympia carried full-scale marble statuary rendered in the round and arranged in narrative compositions. The *metopes* (Fig. 3.14) were also decorated, but in high relief.

The temple must have been complete in 457 B.C., because Pausanius (V.10.4) says that a golden shield was put at the apex of the eastern pediment to commemorate the battle of Tanagra which took place that year. In view of the imposing size of the building (about 210 feet by 91 feet) we must assume as much as a decade for construction. The *Olympia Marbles* therefore date from about 465.

The temple seems to have stood intact until the 6th Century A.D., when it was thrown down by two severe earthquakes. Landslides confused the site, and the rivers Kladeos and Alpheios periodically changed course and covered the place with sand. A French expedition worked there in 1829, taking its finds to the Louvre. Much more was accomplished by the German dig between 1875 and 1881, which brought to light the pedimental figures and the remaining metopes. All of this last material remains in the museum at Olympia.

As a source of information about the Greek figure-style, the sculptures from Olympia must be appreciated for what they are. The Doric columns of the temple stood a little more than 34 feet high, and the entablature (Fig. 4.17) must have taken up another ten feet odd. Thus, the pediments were more than 45 feet above the ground. In order to look at them comfortably, one would have to walk to a station some little distance from the temple. This being so, delicacy was hardly appropriate. Simplicity and boldness, even coarse work, was requisite in order to make the statues carry the necessary distance. The sculptors therefore carved out only the main masses. For the hair and other details, it seems certain they relied on the application of color to make the distinction between adjacent contours. Excellent for their purpose, these very features make the *Olympia Marbles* somewhat misleading as examples for close study.

It is also necessary to remember that none of the eminent sculptors of Greece could possibly have found time to work at first hand on statuary intended merely for architectural decoration. Had time been available, the matter of prestige must be reckoned with. It was the Phidian *Zeus* which shed glory on the site, not the building that contained it.

It seems likely, on the other hand, that a master of exalted standing would take care to exert supervision over the design of architectural decoration, and would then exercise general oversight as the carving proceeded. Pausanius says that Paeonius and Alkamenes were responsible respectively for the eastern and western pediments. Our stylistic evidence, such as it is, makes it likely he was wrong; but in spirit, he probably was right. The *composition* of the pediments and metopes was probably worked out by some great artist. In studying the *Olympia Marbles,* therefore, it seems wise to concentrate our attention upon the principles of their design. For such a study, they are the most perfect demonstration of Greek art we possess.

The eastern pediment from Olympia (Fig. 3.15) shows us Pelops and Oenomäos at what is apparently the moment before their celebrated chariot race.

Oenomäos was king of the southern peninsula of Greece. He had a beautiful daughter named Hippodameia, and her loveliness attracted many suitors for her hand. This, however, did not please the monarch because he had been told by an oracle that he would meet death at the hand of his son-in-law. He therefore undertook to postpone the acquisition of a son-in-law. To the successive candidates, he had formed the habit of making a sporting proposition. "I will race you for it," he would say. "If you win, you get the girl and half the kingdom. If I win, you get executed." Inasmuch as the king maintained the best stables in Greece, he experienced little trouble in deferring his daughter's marriage. Then came the hero Pelops. Realizing he could not possibly beat the king in a fair race, he bribed a groom to remove the pins that served to hold the chariot wheels onto their axles. As Oenomäos swung into the first turn, the wheels came off, the chariot overturned, and the king broke his neck. Pelops married Hippodameia, took the entire kingdom, and gave his name to the area ever since known as the Peloponnesus.

The modern sportsman must look askance at Pelops's methods, but he was remembered among the Greeks as the heroic prototype of all victors in the Olympic games. As such, his story was specially appropriate for the Temple of Zeus around which took place the sacrificial ceremonies which were the central and most solemn feature of the Olympic festival.

In handling the subject, the designers of the pediment were subject to certain limitations. Some of these were physical, some were arbitrarily imposed by the increasingly rigid conventions of Greek art, and some represent universal and permanent artistic problems.

During the Transitional Period, Greek taste had found itself, and public opinion was sufficiently definite to govern the mode in which an artist might express himself. The most conspicuous dictate of the sort was the stipulation that subject matter must be restricted to the human figure. This convention was even narrower than it sounds because it also stipulated the kind of human figure that might be used: men and women between 25 and 35, which is to say at full maturity of mind and body and still without blemish from time's attrition. Animals were sometimes permitted if the narrative required it; but in general, no other subject matter was seriously attempted before the Hellenistic Period.

One odd result of the exclusively anthropomorphic idiom is the total elimination of setting. Landscape detail and stage properties simply are not there. We see no indication of locality, and we may describe the standard Greek setting as completely neutral if not altogether abstract.

Because narrative subject matter often demanded some statement of the place where the events happened, the Greeks ingeniously adopted the habit of personification. The two young men lolling about at the extreme corners of the eastern pediment are probably meant for the river gods Kladeos and Alpheios, the two streams that run through the town of Olympia. Like every other kind of allegory, personification can become a dangerous habit. We may entertain doubts of its adequacy in the present instance, but it is at least illustrative of the logical consistency with which the Greeks were willing to follow their ideas out to the end.

Architectural limitations may originally have suggested the idea of the neutral setting. At any rate, they made such a setting seem proper and almost natural. The pedimental space provides a shelf on which the statues may stand. Immediately behind them runs a stone wall. There is room for only one kind of arrangement: the figures must be placed one at a time in a single row. Movement, and indeed every sort of directional impulse, must go right or left; it cannot go backward, forward, or diagonally.

It is historically very important, in this connection, to remember that the pedimental background is *impenetrable*. It does more than curtail movement. It denies the extension of space into the indefinite distance — a point that will assume considerable importance presently.

In addition to the physical restrictions within which he had to compose, and the human figure which formed his only means of expression, the Greek artist was subject also to a convention that governed his presentation of subject matter. We refer to *the unity of time,* which also may be designated as *the instantaneous mode of presentation.*

Because most readers have been brought up with this convention and accept it without thought, it is necessary to emphasize that there are several other ways of communicating visual subject matter, and that the instantaneous mode is actually arrived at not by the operation of natural law, but by conscious selection on the part of the artist. We shall address ourselves to the other modes of presentation in due time (pages 295; 327).

The unity of time, as applied to the visual arts, amounts to the tacit assumption that everything represented in a picture is taking place simultaneously, and that the action presented to the eye represents the position of every figure, the conditions of light and every other phenomenon in view, just as they were at a special instant in the past.

It follows that a long narrative can be covered only by a series of compositions, one scene to one frame, each adding but one event to the sequence.

The effect of this convention at Olympia and everywhere else it has been used is to demand that the designer choose a *point of time,* or a moment when the characters involved in the story would appear in some situation peculiarly vital to the narrative as a whole, or at least characteristic of it. Obviously much depends upon the right selection. It is a matter of artistic strategy; a mistake can hardly be corrected by any expedient of technique.

The static nature of painting and sculpture compels the artist to assume (or to hope) that the memory and imagination of the observer will function to supply all that the work of art omits. Literature and music have a certain progress in time, as do the other modes of presenting visual data, but nothing of the sort is available to the man who works under the rule now being reviewed.

Because the sculptors at Olympia could not lay in the atmosphere created by previous events or describe what happened afterward, they were fortunate in being able to feel that everybody knew the story of Pelops. Today we have to repeat it *in extenso* or we do not get the point. It is perhaps part of our duty as beneficiaries under the artistic transaction to perform the necessary labor of research; but it is worth remarking that one attribute of the very greatest works of art is subject matter that transcends the local and temporary — a thought to which we shall often return.

In selecting his point of time, the designer of the eastern pediment, whoever he may have been, was apparently most self-conscious with respect to his medium, and much influenced thereby in his choice of the narrative moment.

Speed is the reason for chariot races; they are no good without it. But one may entertain legitimate objections to the direct description of violent movement in a medium which, like stone, is principally characterized by inertia. Marble statues rendered in the full round must be heavy. Statues, moreover, cannot move. Some of the most skilful sculptors in history have nevertheless tried to impart the impression of fast movement. It is difficult to name an instance where the result has proven entirely satisfactory — if successful in producing the illusion, the work invariably calls undue attention to the tour de force of technique called up for the special purpose of making a sensation. Many persons therefore take the extreme position of saying that because statues must forever remain static, no sculptor should attempt to represent active figures — also that the best sculpture finds its expression in terms of what can be done with motionless and almost immovable masses.

Without endorsing that view in its literal entirety, it is nevertheless evident that there is much to be said for it whenever sculpture is used to decorate buildings. The architecture being static, an element of harmony results when the statues also are still. Certainly some such consideration must have been in the mind of the artist of the eastern pediment. We therefore find him picking the moment just before the two contestants stepped into their chariots to run the race — a moment, that is, which predicts action but escapes the necessity of describing it.

Having made his decision, the sculptor was then confronted with the necessity of arranging his adult human figures within the frame of the pedimental triangle. This presents a very tricky problem. Adult human beings come in various sizes, to be sure, but there isn't much difference between the big ones and the little ones. The height of the pediment, on the other hand, shows a radical variation from central apex to corners.

The resolution of the conflict at Olympia can best be understood by reference to the example itself. The middle portion of the eastern pediment is filled by a group of five persons. They are symmetrically arranged. In the center stands a tall male figure. A nude male, slightly smaller, comes to either side; and beyond each of these males, there comes a clothed female figure. The central statue probably represents Zeus; he is present to oversee the race about to be run off. The others are presumably Pelops and Hippodameia to one side, and Oenomäos and his queen on the other.

The arrangement produces a neat fit in the frame, and the physical fit is achieved in a manner that makes no trespass against one's sense of the plausible. Gods are probably larger than men, and men taller than women. An arrangement of one god, two men, and two women will produce an upper silhouette sloping gently downward to either side from an apex in the middle.

A similar propriety inheres in the fit between the frame and the sloping profile presented by the horses with their chariots behind them. After that, however, the resources of the designer seems to have failed him. There is nothing in the story of Pelops to account for the figures who are made to kneel in front of each team of horses, and there is a similar lack of dramatic motivation for the seated people who fill the difficult space farther on toward the corner. The river gods lying on their stomachs at the extreme ends of the composition may perhaps be explained by reference to the small responsibility and lazy habits of minor deities as a class, but their presence seems gratuitous at best.

It will be necessary to return to the eastern pediment presently in order to discuss the way unity of the whole is achieved; but since that is best illustrated by comparison, let us shift our attention to the arrangement of the western pediment.

The subject of the western pediment (Fig. 3.16) is the battle between the Lapiths (Greeks) and the centaurs. This took place at the wedding party of Perithöos. The centaurs, who were cousins of the bride, were invited for the reasons that usually apply in such cases. Like bride's cousins the world over, they took too much to drink, became intoxicated, and became an embarrassment to their hostess. In accordance with the dash of those early and vigorous times, the embarrassment took the form of an organized attempt to abduct all the bridesmaids. A terrific fight ensued, and it is at the height of the battle that the Greek designer has put his point of time.

In the center stands Apollo, a calm, assured figure. To either side of him are figures in violent action. A close look will show that they are arranged in groups of two or three, each group being balanced by its symmetrical counterpart on the opposite side of the center.

On the whole, the triangular space is filled more effectively than that of the eastern pediment. Violent combat makes any posture likely; thus there is rational causation for varying the height of the figures by making some stand, showing some halfway down, and still others flat on the floor. The subject is almost a ready-made solution for the problem of putting adult human figures into the pediment.

The coherence between adjacent figures and adjacent groups is surely more emphatic than in the eastern pediment, if not absolutely better. The fact of combat furnishes an ideological relationship between figure and figure. As though this were not enough, every motion, every glance, and every gesture directs us to look on almost immediately to the next figure or next group as the case may be.

It will also be observed that directional impulses of every kind go outward from the middle toward the ends, and inward from either corner toward the middle. The dynamics of the violent narrative are thus brought under discipline and control, and the struggling figures form a tightly knit, intensely coherent, almost aggressively unified whole. By comparison, the arrangement of the other pediment, while unified by much the same system of directional forces, seems a collection of separate statues, each an artistic integer. But both pediments, or either, serve as an emphatic demonstration of the internal logic demanded by the Greek mind, a logic so inexorable that the entire architectural enframement may be dispensed with and still we find each composition almost a universe unto itself.

Excellent though the formal design of the western pediment may be, the reader might be pardoned for harboring a lingering query about the propriety of the subject. Why select so disgraceful an episode for commemoration in the sculpture of a great temple?

The answer is suggested by the difference between the faces of the Greeks and the centaurs. The latter show a complete lack of restraint; almost every countenance is hideous with drink and lust. The Greeks, by contrast, remain calm. This is true even of the girls most violently set upon; all of them maintain a certain serenity of expression.

Obviously, the sculptor did not intend to record a drunken brawl, but to draw a moral from the contrast between the dignity of the Greeks and the bestiality of the centaurs. It was the Greek custom to read in the myths an earlier portent of recent events, and it is probably correct to assume that this particular subject was understood as a prototype for the Persian Wars in which the Greek nation, by superior virtue, had emerged victorious. So long as the Great Age lasted, it remained the fixed custom never to represent current history in the subject matter of public and ceremonial art, pediments or otherwise. Personified abstractions like *Victory* were acceptable to public taste, as were events from the far long ago and from the myths. The Greek convention inaugurated a habit of the Western imagination; we may name it *the heroic tradition*.

The heroic tradition deals with abstractions and remote events because such material is never subject to the venal pressure of contemporary issues; the more remote, the more that is true. If the person or event is chosen as an instance of virtue or of heroism, it is easy to construe it as inspirational with respect to present conduct. Excellence suggests goodness and heroism begets gallantry. This reasoning continued to govern the major art of Antiquity until Rome passed away. It suffered a partial eclipse during the Middle Ages, only to emerge in greater force than ever as the Renaissance reached full flower. Heroic art enjoyed still another period of popularity during the earlier half of the 19th Century, when it was revived in an effort to celebrate the advent of democratic government in France and America. No concept is more important in art history, and none has been a more cogent mother of genius: it is to this idea that we owe the very few works of art which in fact arrive at the epic level.

Still more needs to be said about the serene countenance as such. Announced, as it were, at Olympia, it became still another convention governing Greek art, and lasted until the Hellenistic Period. Such faces are far from expressionless. In fact, they are highly provocative, but it is difficult to find verbal equivalents for what they tell us. We shall not be far wrong, however, if we take it as the Greek intention to express an aloofness from environment, even a superiority to it — much the same intention that dictated the neutral setting for the pedimental composition as a whole, and indicative of a desire to rise above the particular and incidental toward the kind of truth that is contained in universal principles. These ideas received philosophical expression in Socrates and Plato, but it would appear from the indications of art that they existed in the Greek mind at this comparatively early date.

The metopes of the Temple of Zeus at Olympia were devoted to the labors of Heracles. Some are preserved only in fragments; but the most stirring one of all, *Heracles Taming the Cretan Bull,* is fortunately almost complete in all its vital parts (Fig. 3.14).

The metopes are a subdivision of the frieze of a temple of the Doric Order (see below, Figs. 4.17, 20–21), and each metope stands between two triglyphs. Because the latter are working members of the fabric, carrying the weight of the roof, all action must be confined within the boundaries delimited by the frame if we are to avoid an apparent threat to the stability of the building. At the same time, violent movement is specially desirable even within so confined a space because the architecture is heavy and static, and needs to be relieved by an element of contrast.

The design of this metope could scarcely be improved upon for the purpose. Heracles yanks one way. The bull pulls the other way. For the moment, the two figures are at a standstill, the momentum of one canceling out the opposite movement of the other. Action was taking place an instant back. Movement will commence an instant hence. But at the precise point of time chosen, there is equilibrium, and no residual forces are left over to endanger the integrity of the frame.

The scheme used here became still another convention of Greek art. It was almost invariably employed whenever strong movement needed to be represented in major sculpture. The theory involved is merely to pick a point of time when the direction of the motion is about to reverse itself. At such a point in the sequence of any action, there is in fact an instant when things come to a complete stop. For the reasons stated elsewhere (page 61), such an instant gives a pose peculiarly appropriate to full-size sculpture in a ponderous medium, but it is also important to note that no sacrifice of expression is involved. Because the eye sees active figures most plainly at just those brief moments when motion is turned back upon itself, the memory becomes involved. We recall as characteristic of the action itself the poses of the body we saw most clearly.

Over and above its other virtues, the metope of *Heracles and the Bull* furnishes us with a capital example of an interior arrangement in subtle harmony with the shape of its frame.

In this instance, the frame is very nearly a square. The lines defining the circumference come to mind first, whenever a square is mentioned, as being characteristic of the shape. But in thinking of any rectangle whatever, thought of the circumference is promptly followed by consideration of the diagonals. By placing both Heracles and the bull in positions that correspond approximately with the run of the diagnoals, the designer has given us what amounts to the theme of the frame expressed in its first variation.

The Organic Theory of Artistic Composition

The system developed by the Greeks for arranging figures in a pediment is merely an extension of the method used for simpler compositions like the *Birth of Aphrodite* from the *Ludovisi Throne*. There is every reason to believe that this very same system reflects precisely the Greek point of view toward artistic compositions of every kind. It is no accident that the matter was eventually set down in writing, and thus we find it pretty well summed up by Aristotle, who did his work approximately a hundred years after the Transitional Period of Greek sculpture.

In the *Nichomachean Ethics* (II.6), we find him dropping a passing remark, as though everyone knew it, that in a good work of art " it is not possible either to take away anything or to add anything." And in the *Poetics* (23), he comes out for " a single action, one that is a complete whole in itself with a beginning, middle, and end, so as to enable the work to produce its proper pleasure with all the organic unity of a living creature."

Although he happened to be dealing with poetry and drama at the time, Aristotle might equally well have been referring to the pediments of the Parthenon or those of Olympia. His last allusion springs in part, doubtless, from the circumstance that he was a doctor's son and himself a formidable biologist, but he would never have put the idea forward so easily and confidently had he suspected any one might disagree. Obviously, he had heard it bruited about everywhere that there was an analogy between the structure of an artistic composition and the anatomy of a living thing. By putting the idea so succinctly into words, he succeeded in crystallizing one of the important aesthetic theories. We may call it *the organic theory of composition.*

Nothing is more completely characteristic of the Greek mind. *Organic composition* is, in fact, the most cogent and far-reaching contribution of the Greeks to the future history of art. No other theory of composition had any show in the Mediterranean world until northern and Near Eastern influences intruded as Rome declined. The Greek system of composing was revived by Giotto in the early 14th Century, was dropped again only to be taken up by Leonardo about 1475. In general, it has been the dominant idea of artistic composition ever since. Something very like it, moreover, constitutes the essence of the structural aesthetic which is today the most popular rationale for Gothic architecture.

Certain writers have rather recently formed the habit of using the adjective *architectural* as a term of praise designating a composition in painting or sculpture distinguished by clarity and logical arrangement. They would use that word where we have used *organic,* and there is merit in their idea to the extent that the process of composing involves the painter or sculptor in " building up " his arrangement of figures. *Architectural* in so esoteric a sense has proven, however, a very confusing term. It attributes a false glory to architecture, an art often very badly practiced. The analogy, moreover, between a building and a painting, while perhaps clear enough to the scholar, is likely to impress the layman as unusually farfetched.

THE GREAT SCULPTORS OF GREECE

Six sculptors were celebrated during Antiquity as the very greatest who ever practiced the art. They were: Myron, Phidias, Polycleitos, Praxiteles, Scopas, and Lysippos. Myron's career falls within the limits of the Transitional Period, and the others proceed in the order named until the time of Alexander the Great, for whom Lysippos seems to have been court sculptor.

Time and luck have been devastatingly hard on these famous men. We have nothing whatever from their hands with the possible exception of the *Hermes* of Praxiteles, and even that is suspect in responsible quarters. Scholars have nevertheless expended an incredible amount of ingenuity trying to form some idea of their art. Every resource of historical detection has been exhausted. Over and above direct excavation (which yet may yield epoch-making finds), we have been compelled to rely upon two main sources of information known respectively as *the monumental evidence* and *the literary evidence.* Neither source is in the least satisfactory, but there is nowhere else to turn.

The literary evidence is the testimony of ancient literature. Acting on the assumption that writers who lived before the fall of Rome would in the normal course of life become reasonably well-informed about Greek art, scholars have searched every sentence of every known Greek and Latin text. Every statement about art and every allusion to it has been noted out, and its meaning pondered.

From the literary evidence, we have been able to assemble a fragmentary list of the bare names of the statues that once existed, with assignment of each to its author. In many instances, we possess sufficient descriptive material to be able to identify the statues, or copies of them, should they ever be found.

The ideal monumental evidence, of course, would be an original statue of known authorship. In the absence of that, we are compelled to make the best of anything that may in some way or other reflect its appearance. Because the ancients, like ourselves, reproduced famous monuments on coins, in vase painting, or made small models of them for sale as souvenirs, we can sometimes form a surprisingly satisfactory notion of an otherwise lost masterpiece.

Our corpus of monumental evidence is immensely increased because full-size reproductions of famous Greek statues were long in demand on the Roman market. The more famous the statue, the more likely it was to be copied, and in a few instances we possess a really substantial number of copies after the same Greek masterpiece. By judicious interpretation of these, we can get closer to the original than might otherwise be possible.

MYRON

The period of Myron's activity is closely fixed by unusually reliable evidence. In 446 B.C., his son signed the pedestal of a statue at the entrance to the Propylaeum at Athens. The inscription is preserved, but the statue is gone. The son must have had a considerable reputation to have enjoyed so important a commission; presumably he was 35 years old at least. In round numbers, almost any father will be thirty years older than his son; and thus Myron would have been 65 in 446 B.C., and approaching the end of his active career.

The literary sources tell us he was notable as a sculptor of athletes in action and as a sculptor of animals. The latter specialty was presently destined to be squeezed almost out of respectability by the increasing tendency of Greek taste to insist upon expression exclusively in terms of the human figure, but Myron's *Cow* was nevertheless the most popular statue at Athens. Bulls made love to that celebrated bronze beast, calves tried to suckle, and lions tried to eat it up. Or at least so it is said. Whatever else we may conclude, it is evident that technical difficulties were completely under control by the date of Myron's maturity.

Myron's famous statues are impossible of visual recovery on the basis of any evidence we now have, but for his *Discobolos*, a minor work, we are more fortunate. In the eighteenth chapter of the *Philopseudes*, Lucian (2nd Century A.D.) makes one of his characters say he saw the statue in the entrance hall of the home of "Eucrates the Magnificent." The *Philopseudes* ("The Lover of Lies") is one of Lucian's satirical dialogues, but his allusion to Eucrates' collection of statuary has nothing to do with the satire — the citation is there simply to give an impression of the atmosphere of the great house. As translated by A. M. Harmon, the passage reads:

> "Statue," said I, "what do you mean?"
>
> "Have you not observed on coming in," said he, "a very fine statue set up in the hall, the work of Demetrius the maker of portrait statues?"
>
> "Do you mean the discus thrower," said I, "the one bent over in the position of the throw, with his head turned back toward the hand that holds the discus, with one leg slightly bent, looking as if he would spring up all at once with the cast?"
>
> "Not that one," said he, "for that is one of Myron's works, the discus thrower you speak of. Neither do I mean the one beside it, the one binding his head with the fillet, the handsome lad, for that is Polycleitos' work. Never mind those to the right as you come in, among which stand the tyrant-slayers modeled by Critias and Nesiotes; but if you noticed one beside the fountain, pot-bellied, bald on the forehead, half bared by the hang of his coat, with some of the hairs of his beard wind-blown, that is the one I mean; he is thought to be Pellichus, the Corinthian general."

It will be seen that Lucian, in this single passage, gives us data about several important statues. We have recognized in Roman copies the *Tyrannicides* of which he speaks, also the *Diadumenos* of Polycleitos, a statue with which we shall presently be concerned. As for the *Discobolos* of Myron, Lucian's description is sufficiently circumstantial to make confusion with any other statue unlikely. More than that, his attribution to Myron is unusually reliable for two important reasons: Lucian lived at Athens where such information was most likely to be available, and he himself had been trained as a sculptor. We rarely get literary evidence from a man who was in the right place to know, and who also had the professional qualifications entitling him to an opinion.

According to the most recent list (prepared at Rome for inclusion in the catalogue of the *Second National Exhibition of Works of Art Recovered from Germany*) there are no less than seven full-size statues which were certainly made and sold as copies of the *Discobolos*. In addition, there are six statuettes, four separate heads, two hands, one arm, and one leg. Over and above those 21 items, we can recognize reflections of the statue on engraved gems.

These copies violate the description in matters of detail only. The British Museum *Discobolos* and that in the Vatican now carry heads of a later date wrongly attached to make the athlete look away from the discus, not toward it. An otherwise interesting statuette in Munich is compositionally correct, but shows an attempt to bring Myron up to date by using the softer modeling of a later era. An inspection of the various copies will also reveal substantial differences in quality, doubtless reflecting the standards of the shops from which they came and the price the patron was prepared to pay. Such being the case, it is probably fair to assume that the most subtle and sensitive work is closest to the master so long as we are careful to accept nothing out of line with going custom at the time of Myron's career.

A damaged marble torso found on the shore near Castel Porziano, near Ostia, and now in the Museo delle Terme at Rome, is substantially finer than any of the others (Fig. 3.21). The only copy that preserves the head in its proper position is the one formerly in the Lancellotti Palace and now in the Borghese Gallery (Fig. 3.20). By applying the Lancellotti head to the Castel Porziano torso and fitting the latter out with arms and legs, it is obvious we would be fetching closer to the original than before.

But still another step in reconstruction is necessary before we have done the best we can. Like all other marble copies after bronze originals, the Castel Porziano *Discobolos* carries the unpleasant addition of a tree stump intended to reinforce, in this brittle material, the dangerous fragility of the legs. If we eliminate the tree stump and paint the cast with bronze, we arrive at something like Fig 3.22, which is as close as we can get to Myron.

It is rare that the work of archaeological detection proceeds in so orderly a fashion to arrive at a positive result. The very neatness with which we have solved our problem is deceptive. It lures us on to the notion we have actually rediscovered Myron himself, but the fact is we have not recovered the work of Myron at all. We merely have a Roman copy thereof which if compared with an original from the hand, say, of Donatello or Michaelangelo, will infallibly impress us as inferior. We do not begin to know Myron, in short, unless we can supply from our knowledge and imagination the snap and life which has escaped the copyist.

Having stated that most necessary word of caution, we need not despond: our composite Roman copy of the *Discobolos* surely preserves much of Myron, and we can form a much better idea of his work than we might get of Jefferson's, for example, from the reflection of Monticello on our five-cent piece.

In the matter of technique, the only remaining hint of archaism is in the hair, which is still kept close to the skull. Otherwise, it is abundantly plain that anatomy is completely at the artist's disposal. By using so complex and difficult a pose, he seems in fact almost to parade his accomplishment; and the same may be said for the modeling of the muscles, which are rendered with hard, clean detail as though the master were still conscious of how recently such a performance had become possible. From all of this, and still allowing for the fact that our visual evidence forbids subtle reasoning about matters of surface quality, we may conclude that Myron's style was direct, chaste, and that its appeal came through the beauty of line and contour as contrasted to delicacy of texture and refinements of facial expression.

For analysis of composition, our evidence admits of definite conclusions. All the copies are almost exactly alike with respect to the pose, and are probably very reliable reproductions of Myron's arrangement in all essential particulars. They make it possible to say flatly that the world has never seen a better man when it comes to the manipulation of the single figure.

Very few statues are designed to have an omnifacial composition; and although the *Discobolos* holds up well from almost any angle of view, the effect is best from a station almost directly in front with the eye high enough to see the figure approximately as it appears in Fig. 3.21.

In accordance with the over-all Greek theory that the work of art must be complete in itself, Myron has been at pains to declare an enframement even though none exists in physical fact. By making the eye run around the curve of the two arms, he starts it off on an elliptical path, sufficient momentum being accumulated in the process to make it a certainty that we will follow the figure around through space and complete the oval where it would join the farther hand. One of the troubles with the falsely restored copies in London and at the Vatican is the breaking of the suggested ellipse by putting on a head that stares outward and thus destroys the flow of the curve. The original head, on the other hand, tends to reinforce the integrity of the boundary by keeping severely within it.

Having guaranteed the unity of the composition by establishing the concept of an enclosing curve, Myron then runs the body across the oval figure with a strong zigzag movement, and pierces the zigzag, as it were, with the intense straight line suggested by the glance of the eye. Simple enough in principle, the resulting contrast is inexpressibly bold and subtle in execution. There has never been a better artistic demonstration of the famous Greek maxim of neither too much nor too little. After 2,400 years of further experiment with the human figure the *Discobolos* — which we know only at an archaeological remove — must still be listed as one of the greatest statues of all time.

*

4

GREEK ARCHITECTURE

The entire history of architecture has been influenced by the Greek style. The Greeks lavished almost 100 percent of their architectural thought upon the temple. They needed houses and public buildings, of course; but none of those were designed to endure. Our knowledge of civil and domestic architecture is therefore limited to what we can infer from evidence that is altogether inadequate; general conclusions of any kind are inappropriate. But the reverse is true of the temple. Its plan and columnar character were established as early as 1600 B.C., if we are correct in our reading of the data unearthed at Tiryns. In the useful list of monuments published as an appendix to his *Greek and Roman Architecture,* Mr. D. S. Robertson names no fewer than 133 temple ruins dating from the 10th Century B.C. onward to about the year 150 A.D. It is rare to find any single class of monument represented by so many examples, all of which support the flat statement that the Greek temple stands as one of the finest achievements of the race in any field of endeavor, physical or otherwise.

The fundamental form of the temple seems to have given satisfaction from the very beginning. Its long history is merely an account of increasing refinement. By common consent, the best and most typical temples were those built at Athens during the second half of the Fifth Century B.C. By concentrating our attention upon those alone, we can learn almost all there is to know about Greek architecture.

The Acropolis at Athens

The Persian Wars came to an end in 479 B.C., and the Athenians returned to find their city in ruins. Their first efforts were naturally devoted to housing and to military architecture, also to political matters such as the organization

HERMAN WAGNER

HERMAN WAGNER

Figs. 4.1–2 Athens. The Parthenon. 447–432 B.C. Approximately 228 by 104 feet. Columns 34 feet high.

S. S. WEINBERG

Fig. 4.3 Athens. The Parthenon. Southwest corner.

S. S. WEINBERG

Fig. 4.4 Athens. The Parthenon. View in the ambulatory.

WALTER HEGE

Fig. 4.5 Athens. The Parthenon. View at the west end, showing a portion of the inner frieze.

Figs. 4.6–7 Paris. Bibliothèque Nationale. The western pediment of the Parthenon as recorded in the "Carrey drawings" made in 1674.

Fig. 4.8 Schematic drawing of a typical Greek temple of the Doric Order, showing the cult statue in place.

ALINARI

Fig. 4.9 Athens. Temple of Athena Nike.

CLARENCE KENNEDY

WALTER HEGE

Figs. 4.10–11 Athens. The Erectheum. Above: View from the south Left: The "Honeysuckle Band." Detail.

WALTER HEGE

Fig. 4.12 Athens. Acropolis. A Doric capital from the Parthenon.

WALTER HEGE

Fig. 4.13 Athens. Propylaeum. Ionic capital of the passageway.

ALINARI

Fig. 4.14 Athens. National Museum. Corinthian capital from the Tholos at Epidauros.

of the Delian League, an alliance intended to make further aggression impossible. Activities of this kind took the better part of a generation.

In 461 B.C., Pericles emerged as the civic leader of Athens. He held power until his death in 429. After devoting some time to other affairs, he turned his immense abilities to the cultural development of the city, with such brilliant success that the entire era is often and correctly referred to as the Age of Pericles. The principal artistic enterprise undertaken by him was the embellishment of the Acropolis with four new buildings, to replace those destroyed when the Persians occupied the town.

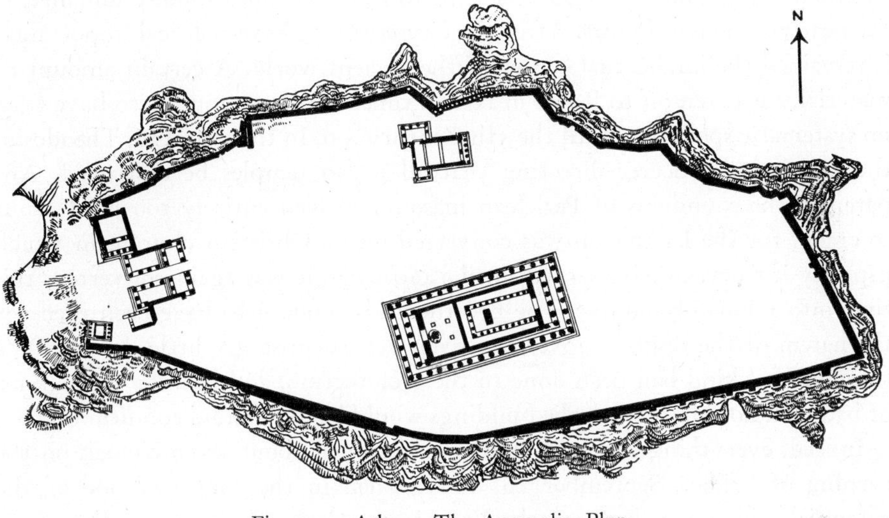

Fig. 4.15 Athens. The Acropolis. Plan.

The Acropolis (Fig. 4.15) is a hill rising abruptly from the land around it. Its rocky sides are almost vertical, and access is convenient only at the west end. The place has been fortified since time immemorial, and at the period of which we speak, the top had long ago been leveled off to a more or less even surface about 1,000 feet long by about 500 feet at its widest point. Upon the site thus prepared, Pericles caused four notable buildings to be put up: the *Parthenon* (447–438; lower center), the *Propylaeum* (437–432; upper left), the *Temple of Athena Nike* (during the 430's; extreme lower left), and the *Erectheum* (begun at an uncertain date after 438, finished about 404; upper center). The Parthenon is the only one of the four which might be described as large, and a total of four buildings is a short list. Periclean architecture nevertheless holds its place unchallenged. The reason is quality.

The man personally responsible for the excellence of the work was Pericles's friend Phidias. His reputation had been made as a sculptor; it was for his

Athena Parthenos that the Parthenon was built. But as general superintendent or *master of the works,* as he might have been called at a later period, Phidias made a contribution that is unique. Artists of the first rank must have assembled at Athens by the score. Over this assembly of creative persons, unparalleled in world history, Phidias appears to have been able to exert a certain organizing force that was more like inspiration than direction. Every man seems to have outdone himself, and every detail of the vast project finds a common denominator in the Phidian dignity.

The buildings on the Acropolis seem to have remained almost undamaged for nearly a thousand years. After the city ceased to have political importance, it remained the intellectual center of the ancient world. A certain amount of material was taken off to Rome in Nero's time, but there appears to have been no systematic spoliation until the 5th Century A.D. In the year 426, Theodosius the 2nd issued a decree directing that all pagan temples be destroyed. Apparently the soundness of Periclean masonry proved entirely too hard a nut to crack, for the Parthenon was converted into a Christian church, in which capacity it seems to have served until 1460 when it was again converted, this time into a Turkish mosque. The Erectheum is thought to have been used for the harem of the resident governor. Even yet, surprisingly little damage of a fundamental kind had been done to the architecture, and had the worst kind of bad luck not intervened, the buildings would be in splendid condition today.

Indeed, everything survived almost intact until about seven o'clock on the evening of Friday, September 26, 1687, when in the course of one of the perennial minor wars between the Venetians and the Turks, an artillery lieutenant succeeded in dropping an explosive shell square in the middle of the Parthenon. The Turks had stored their powder there, and the entire middle portion of the temple was blown to pieces in an instant. Of an inferior building, it is probable nothing whatever would be left today.

Fortunately and by the merest chance, the Marquis de Nointel had visited the city in 1674, and was interested enough in the Parthenon to set his hack artist to work making the so-called " Carrey drawings " preserved today in the Bibliothèque Nationale (Figs. 4.6–7). These insensitive sketches constitute our only pictorial record of the building as it stood before the explosion, and our only other pictorial record of any kind is contained in *The Antiquities of Athens,* published in London in 1760 by James Stuart and Nicholas Revett and containing a number of quaint views of the stately classical ruins emerging through and above a hodgepodge of nondescript medieval building, domestic and otherwise. Unbelievable though it seems to the modern reader, Stuart and Revett's book had great value as news when it appeared. Athens had all but passed out of the Western memory; people were startled to know that important monuments were still there, visible to the naked eye.

It was in 1801 that Lord Elgin succeeded in removing to London most of the remaining sculptures of the Parthenon; they are visible today in the British Museum. But even yet, Greek work was hardly available for study. Photographs dating from the 1890's show the Acropolis still invested with third-rate works of medieval military engineering. Only for a very few years has it been possible to see the buildings in proper fashion, or to publish good plates like those which accompany the present chapter.

THE GREEK TEMPLE AS AN ARCHITECTURAL TYPE

The excellence of the Greek temple has so often been celebrated that an effort is required to take a balanced view of the whole subject of Greek architecture. We must attempt to see the building as it is, for what it is, and certainly as no more or less than it is.

The Greek temple is a distinct form or genus in the history of architecture. It illustrates both the strength and the weakness of specialization; it is an extreme type. In order to appreciate what this means, we must understand the purpose for which the building was built. Nothing could be more simple, more direct. The temple was designed to house a single large religious statue (Fig. 4.8). It had no other function. There was no demand, as there is in a Christian church, for a large auditorium where several hundred persons might meet. There was no need to divide the enclosed space into a series of special rooms devoted to one or another of the particular purposes essential to the modern concept of efficiency. If the interior provided a single room (called the *cella*) large enough to house and display the cult statue, the Greeks were satisfied. The most elaborate and expensive temples add to this only one other room, usually called a *treasury* and presumably devoted to the storage of paraphernalia.

One can hardly exaggerate the degree to which this extreme elimination simplified the designer's problems. It was possible for him to avoid hundreds of compromises, each in itself a minor artistic disappointment, and he was saved the vexation of difficult engineering.

Seen in ground plan (Fig. 4.16) the Greek temple is a simple oblong. There was considerable experimentation with the proportions of this oblong. The evolution ran from a comparatively long and narrow shape to the proportion used for the Parthenon, this being not far from the ratio of four-to-nine.

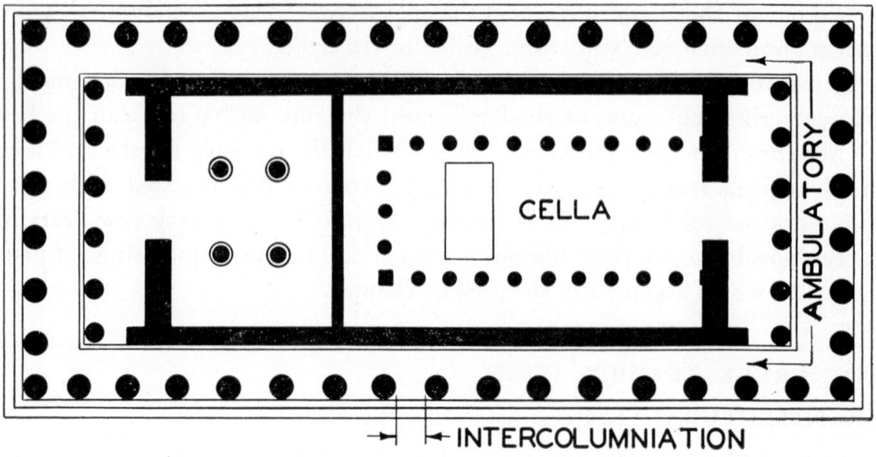

Fig. 4.16 Athens. The Parthenon. Plan.

The increased width was probably suggested by a desire to gain space for the better display of the statue.

Seen in elevation (Fig. 4.17), the Greek temple rises from a low and horizontal platform which serves as a base or pedestal. Traditionally, the platform is made up of three shallow steps; and the top step is known as the *stylobate.* Occasionally, we shall find it convenient to extend the meaning of stylobate to suggest the entire upper surface of the platform. It should be noted, also, that the custom of using three steps had to do with the Greek theory of proportion, not with utility. On a large temple, the risers would be too high for

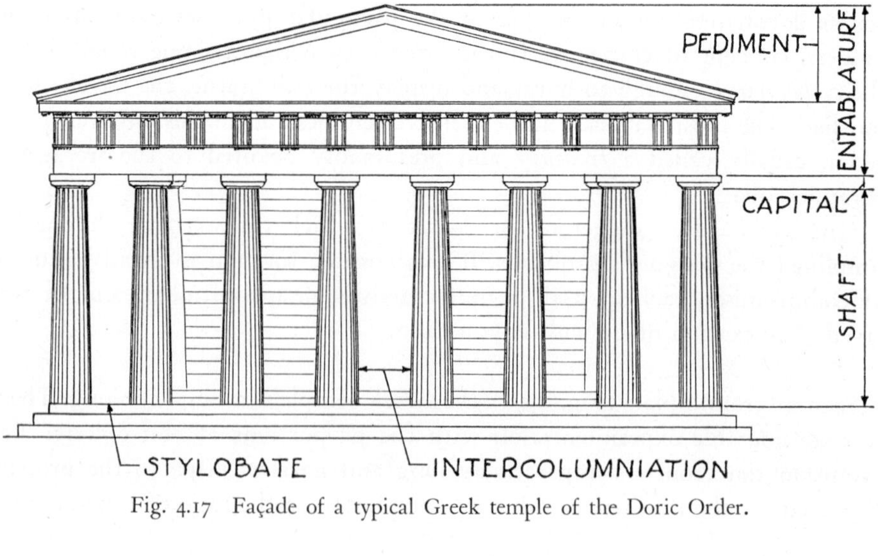

Fig. 4.17 Façade of a typical Greek temple of the Doric Order.

practical purposes, and a set of smaller steps had to be supplied to let people enter.

Around the outer edge of the stylobate there runs a range of free-standing columns known as the *peristyle*.

Between the peristyle and the cella wall, there is an open passageway known as the *ambulatory* (Fig. 4.4).

Figs. 4.1–2 give a good idea of the temple as it appears in three-dimensional actuality. They show that the general shape of the building is defined by the conjunction of two simple geometric solids. The body of the temple is a rectangular oblong solid, and the roof is a solid with triangular cross-section. Fig. 4.18 is an attempt to summarize this situation visually.

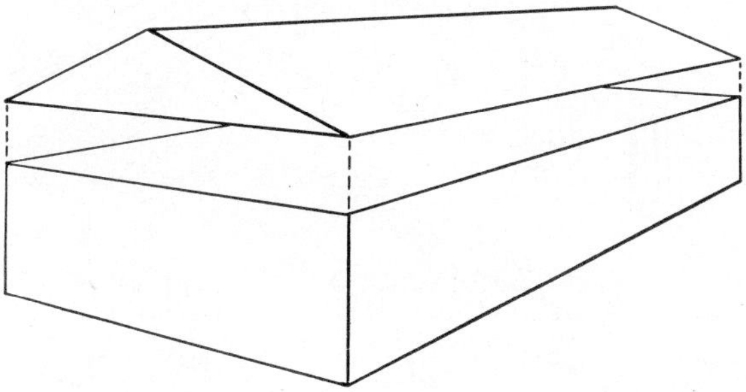

Fig. 4.18 Schematic drawing to demonstrate the shape of a Greek temple.

The appearance of the roof as shown by Fig. 4.18 was doubtless complicated in some instances by the installation of skylights; but the general shape (as indicated by representations on coins) remained that of the single, simple triangular form, with the ridge running strictly horizontally.

As seen from either narrow end, or *façade*, the roof makes a triangular gable. The Greek gable is a distinct type in architectural history; we separate it from all others by the special name *pediment*. The most important feature of the pediment is the obtuse angle at the ridge pole. In good Greek work, this ordinarily is on the order of 150°, but in many modern adaptations, a more acute intersection is employed — usually because the Greek temple-front is being applied to a block of utilitarian building out behind, and more height is desirable. The expedient is rarely satisfactory.

We have already dealt at some length with the compositional problems forced upon the sculptors first by the odd shape of the pedimental surface, and secondly by the Greek convention that it must be filled with figures representing adult human beings. (See above, page 59.)

Strong boundaries enframe the two solids that compose the Greek temple.

They function to give the building a definite, unbroken, completely closed silhouette. Aesthetically, the boundaries seem to declare that the composition is altogether self-contained, depends upon its own internal logic, and exists almost as a small universe unto itself. No other type of building asserts a more intense unity. It follows, of course, that all reference to anything outside the boundaries is suppressed, and we must recognize that the unity of the Greek temple involves a certain element of negation. It is something alone and apart, separate from the rest of the world. In general, we find that this is typical of all works of art executed in the Classical Style.

Fig. 4.19 Schematic drawing to illustrate the possibility that the Greek Doric forms had their genesis in wooden construction.

Structurally, the Greek temple is an example of the most elementary kind of engineering. At some very early date and probably as the result of contact with Egyptian customs, the convention became established that all temples should be constructed on the *post-and-lintel system*. Vertical supports (the posts) were set up at intervals, with horizontal beams (the lintels) making the span across the openings between them. The Greeks were fully informed about the arch; and they surely realized that the post-and-lintel method, while simple enough in theory, is expensive and even dangerous for the construction of good-sized buildings. Once in force, convention seems never to have been challenged, and the entire history of Greek architecture amounts to an effort to perfect the post and the lintel. (For structural details, the reader is referred to Chapter 7.)

For the wider span of the roof, stone proved too heavy and too brittle. No temple roof has survived, but it is certain that the lintels for this considerable

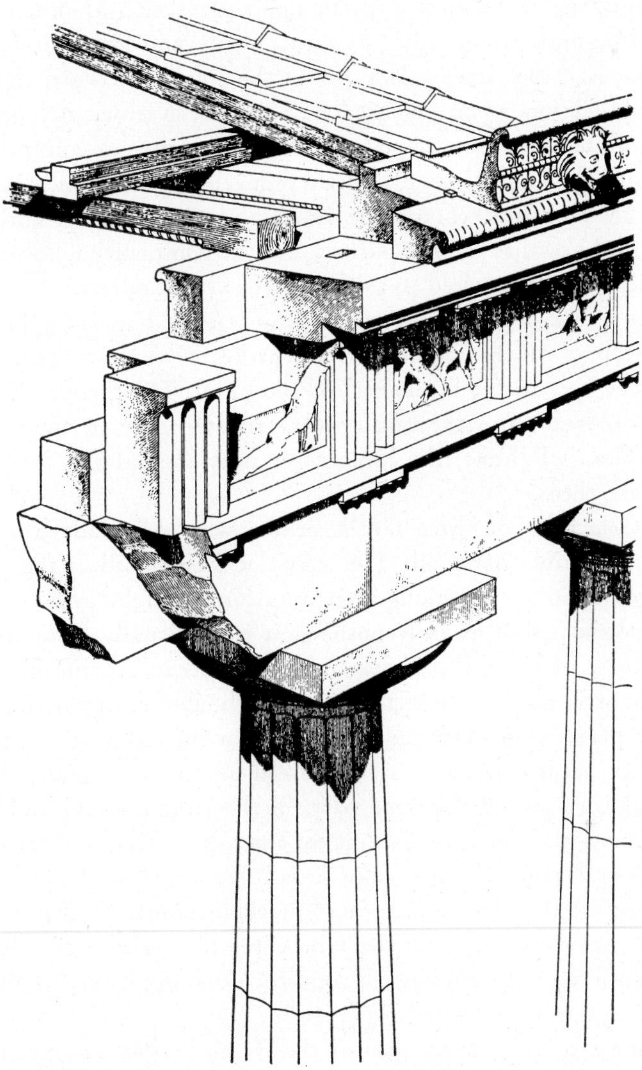

Fig. 4.20 Schematic drawing to illustrate the construction of a typical Greek entablature in the Doric Order.

span must have been of wood, doubtless assembled into a framework of the sort known as a *truss* (Fig. 9.56). An important objection to wood as a structural material is its liability to both rot and fire; otherwise it is excellent, being stronger for its weight than anything else available even today.

Having committed themselves to it, the Greek architects carried the post-and-lintel system to an unexcelled level of refinement. The merit of their work depends, in fact, almost entirely upon perfection of detail, and its excellence can be understood only by minute study and long familiarity.

For their posts, the Greeks always used the *column,* a word that suggests a circular cross-section whenever used in a technical sense; any other kind of post is a *pier*. The Greeks developed three different types of column (the Doric, the Ionic, and the Corinthian), and they developed two kinds of lintel (one for the Doric and another for the Ionic and Corinthian). Either kind of Greek lintel is known as an *entablature,* and the complete ensemble of columns and lintel together is referred to as one of the Greek *orders.*

The three Greek orders are most conveniently told apart by looking at the *capital,* that part of the column which makes a visual transition from the vertical of the post to the horizontal of the lintel. The three orders differ also in matters of detail, and they differ very substantially in their proportions. The Corinthian is lightest, the Ionic a bit heavier, and the Doric much the heaviest of the three.

It is possible that all three Greek orders were originally worked out in temples built entirely of wood (Fig. 4.19). Often stated as fact, this notion actually rests upon an ingenious interpretation of slight evidence. There are those who doubt it, but as an hypothesis, it is admittedly attractive.

In the course of time, the Greek orders tended to become lighter in their over-all proportions; this is especially true of the Doric. But within the system of whatever proportion happened to be in use at the moment, the parts typical of each order became severely standardized at an early date. The ensemble consists, that is to say, of the same parts in the same number and in the same relative size and placement. An immense amount of trial and error went into the formula so developed; early ruins, it is to be noted, often look clumsy. By the beginning of the 5th Century B.C. or thereabouts, further improvement was almost inconceivable, and the Greek temple became established as the single known historical case where a rigid formula might repeatedly be applied successfully in the realm of artistic creation.

Because used so often, every part of the Greek temple was given a name. In the recital to follow and in labeling the text figures, we have confined ourselves to the more important details and to vocabulary that will prove generally useful.

ELEMENTS OF THE DORIC ORDER

The Doric column is, by comparison to almost all other columns, a very heavy one (Fig. 4.17). Early examples actually show a ratio between height and diameter of close to four-to-one — that is, the greatest diameter multiplied by four will be equal to the total height of the column from its base to the upper surface of the capital. The columns of the Parthenon, generally considered the happiest proportion ever arrived at for the medium of marble, average about 5.78 diameters to the height. The general trend of the style was to grow lighter, and there are late examples that show a proportion of about eight and one-half diameters to the height.

These proportions were worked out for buildings made of stone. There is pretty general agreement that, in the Doric Order, any substantial departure from a proportion as heavy as about five and one-half diameters to the height results in a "brittle looking" column. The columns in much American Colonial architecture are lighter than this, and they do not look brittle. The American columns are made of wood, however; and the instance is an illustration of the inseparable relation of medium to design. The ponderous proportion of the Greek Doric is in splendid harmony with the ponderous nature of stone.

It is notable, however, that people are of one mind in finding these massive columns wonderfully graceful. There is no argument on the point, and it contradicts the ordinary assumption that grace is necessarily associated with delicacy. The beauty of the Doric columns undoubtedly derives in part from the harmony of proportion and material; much of their loveliness must also be ascribed to a list of refinements which will appear in the course of our discussion.

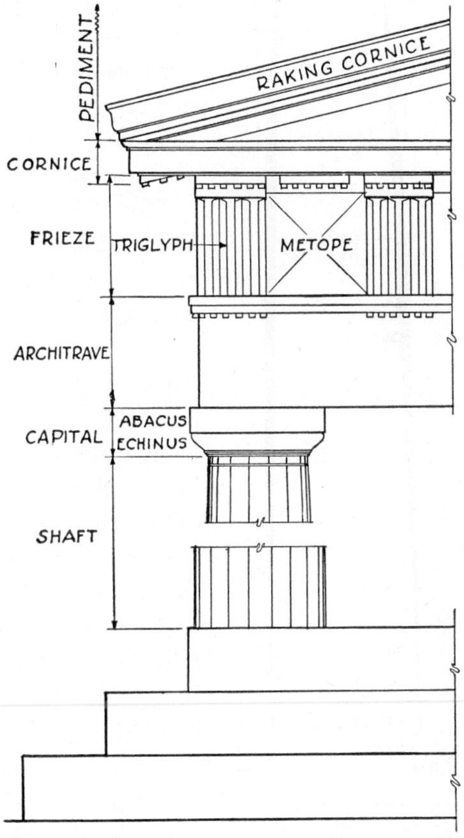

Fig. 4.21 Component parts of the Doric Order.

The Doric *shaft* (Fig. 4.21) rests flat upon the stylobate. There is no transitional moulding, or base. The shaft tapers moderately, being widest at the bottom. In the best Greek examples, the silhouette of the shaft, moreover, is not bounded by straight lines but by curves, giving it a bulge called the *entasis* (Fig. 4.22). The amount of bulge is very slight indeed, and the curves used are of a character more subtle than the arc of a circle.

It is impossible in a written statement to give an explanation of the delicacy of judgment imposed by the use of entasis. The amount of extension beyond a straight line, the spot chosen for the high-point of the curve, the speed of curvature to either side of this apex, and the pitch of the curve as a whole with respect to the axis of the column — these are some of the variables involved. The difficulty of resolving them is demonstrated by any number of columns, both ancient and modern, which are spoiled by some minor fault of the entasis.

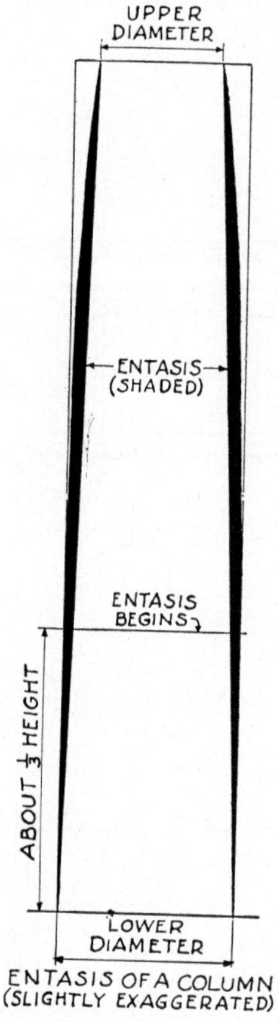

Fig. 4.22 Schematic drawing to illustrate the entasis of a Doric shaft.

Most Greek columns are *fluted*. The fluting of the Doric Order (Fig. 4.23), which differs somewhat from that used for Ionic and Corinthian (Fig. 4.24), usually consists of some twenty *channels*. The peculiar character of Doric fluting is the result of two things. The adjacent channels meet in sharp edges, each known as an *arris*, and the curvature of each channel is shallow, being a short arc of a circle of long radius. The resulting combination of crisp line and soft shadow is one of the chief beauties of the Doric Order, and gives an emphasis to the texture of fine marble not achieved by the slightly different fluting of the other orders.

Over and above the special advantages which pertain to the Doric system of fluting, there are several things that recommend the practice of fluting in general. In the first place, a column is a vertical supporting member. The force it sustains is a force of compression. The axis of each channel of fluting is in line with the direction of that force, and the total effect of some twenty channels is to give emphasis to the fundamental dynamics of the structural forces present.

The arrises extend up and down to form crisp lines, each of which is an unmistakable repeat of the entasis of the shaft. When facing the column, we see one-half its circumference, or ten lines, and thus we observe the entasis in every aspect from full-face to profile. The difference between the lines as so seen illustrates *variety* as we understand it in art criticism, and the similarity comes close to defining what we mean by artistic *harmony*. The complex elegance of the pattern actually presented to the eye is more evident in Doric than in the other orders because the Doric entasis is ordinarily more pronounced.

It is sometimes suggested that the ample proportions of the shaft combine with the grace of the entasis to produce an impression that the column does its work with ease. This is really equivalent to contending that we experience a feeling of *empathy* (identification of ourselves with what we see in art) when we look at the Doric Order, and it is true that there is a resemblance between the bulge of the entasis and the bulge of muscles bearing weight. Without accepting the idea as literally true, it offers a profitable train of thought.

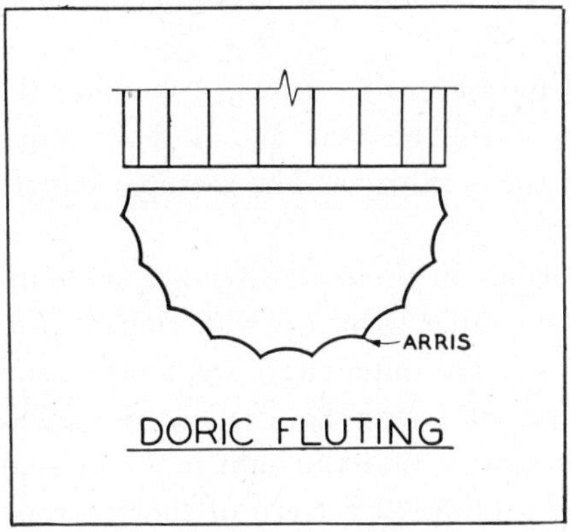

Fig. 4.23 Fluting of a Doric shaft.

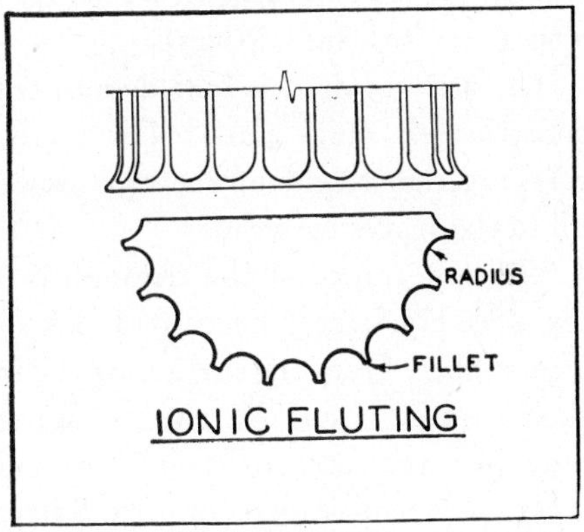

Fig. 4.24 Fluting of an Ionic shaft.

The Doric capital consists of two parts, the *abacus* and the *echinus*. The echinus is the lower part; it is a circular member flaring upward as though to cushion the abacus above. The abacus is a shallow square of stone placed directly underneath the lintel.

This is a very simple capital. It depends for its beauty upon the profile of the echinus and upon the contrast between that curvature of surface and the squared face of the abacus. In good Greek work, the curve used for an echinus is always a *graded curve*. The rate of curvature is not constant as in a circle, but accelerates as the curve goes upward. Careful analysis of a number of examples seems to establish a Greek preference for hyperbolic arcs in Doric echini. Such may have been drawn freehand, but it seems certain the Greeks possessed some sort of analytical geometry. In any case, it seems likely that the capitals were turned on a gigantic lathe, probably operated by horsepower.

The complete Greek lintel, or *entablature*, consists of three parts; the three-part division obtains no matter which order is in use. These are: the *architrave*, the *frieze*, and the *cornice* — each being a horizontal section stretching the length of the entablature.

The architrave is the lowest of the three. In Doric, it is an undecorated beam of stone resting directly on the abaci.

The cornice is the upper and overhanging member. It extends out from the face of the frieze a distance equal to about one-half the height of the architrave. The cornice may have been invented to keep the drip of the rain away from the joining between roof and wall, but its principal function is aesthetic. It tells as a line, and it casts a heavy shadow, thus forming one of the boundaries that close in the silhouette of the temple.

The frieze is the horizontal division between architrave and cornice. In Doric, it is subdivided into *triglyphs* (τρείγλυφος, triple groove) and *metopes* (μετόπαι, interspaces).

The arrangement is best demonstrated by a cutaway drawing showing the construction (Fig. 4.20). The triglyphs, it will be seen, act as short posts, carrying the weight of the roof down to the architrave. The metopes merely fill in the spaces between.

The appearance of the triglyph is important in the total effect of the temple. (See Fig. 4.17.) Each is a block of stone, taller than it is wide, which projects slightly from the surface of the building. The outer edges are beveled, and their surface is cut by two strong grooves of triangular cross-section. The triglyphs, as a result of their form and placement, take the light in a way that gives a vigorous impression of solidity, and produces a pattern of short, strong vertical lines. The over-all arrangement of the triglyphs to compose the frieze as a whole is one of the refinements of the Greek temple, to be discussed in detail later. At this point, suffice it to say there is a triglyph over every column and a triglyph over every *intercolumniation,* or space between adjacent columns — surely the longest word ever invented to signify nothing at all.

The metopes are slightly wider than their height, and they offer a surface that invites decoration. The Parthenon originally had a full set of 92 decorated metopes, each containing an original composition in high relief. Combat subjects were popular for these spaces because they offered a chance of adding movement to the ponderous statics of the temple itself; but as explained above (page 64), the stop-in-action pose was ordinarily adopted to keep the represented action within strict limits, thus avoiding an apparent threat to the stability of the triglyphs and the structure of the building.

ELEMENTS OF THE IONIC ORDER

Many features of the Doric temple are standard, also, in the Ionic Order and need no further explanation. The fundamental shape and arrangement of the building is the same, and yet the general aspect of an Ionic temple differs from the Doric to a surprising degree. The contrast is probably the result of the more delicate proportions which govern individual parts of the building, and of the difference in texture that derives from the generous use of ornamental detail.

All parts of an Ionic temple (Fig. 4.25) are lighter than they would be in Doric buildings of the same overall dimensions. The proportions of the column will furnish an index to the general scheme of proportions in general. Ionic columns run from about eight to about ten diameters to the height, the individual cases tending to vary more than Doric custom permitted.

The Ionic column always has a base. This consists of an arrangement of concave and convex mouldings, there being no rule to govern either the scale, the form, the sequence, or the number of the mouldings. Frequently, there is a plinth (a shallow rectangular block like the Doric abacus) underneath the mouldings of the base. Occasionally one sees a statement which attempts to read regional or chronological significance into the arrangement of the Ionic base, but it seems safer to assume merely that custom encouraged innovations in this instance and that the bases therefore simply differ from building to building.

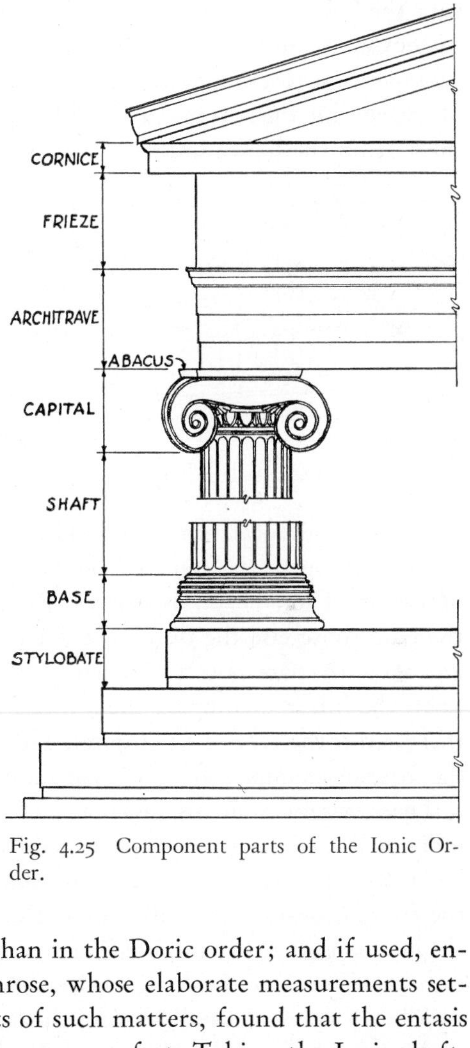

Fig. 4.25 Component parts of the Ionic Order.

The use of entasis is less common than in the Doric order; and if used, entasis is much more delicate. F. C. Penrose, whose elaborate measurements settled once and for all the physical facts of such matters, found that the entasis of the Parthenon's Doric shafts measures 0.057 feet. Taking the Ionic shafts of the Erectheum's North Porch as a standard and adjusting these to the same height, Penrose demonstrated that the maximum entasis for Ionic would, at that moment in Greek history, come to only 0.029 feet — roughly half as much. A great many modern architects have given an Ionic shaft more bulge than this, but always with baleful effect.

Ionic fluting (Fig. 4.24) differs from the Doric (Fig. 4.23). Normally there are 24 channels around the circumference of the shaft, and the adjacent channels are separated by narrow strips, or *fillets,* left from the original surface. The channels have a shorter radius of curvature than the Doric, and thus the hollows are narrow and deep. The steeper side of the channel results, of course, in a much darker shadow within: a shadow, moreover, in immediate juxtaposition to the narrow band of full light produced when the direct rays of the sun hit the surface of the fillets. This is different from the way a Doric shaft takes the light, and the sharp alternation of brightness and dark probably accounts more than anything else for the habit we have of describing the Ionic as " more lively " than the Doric.

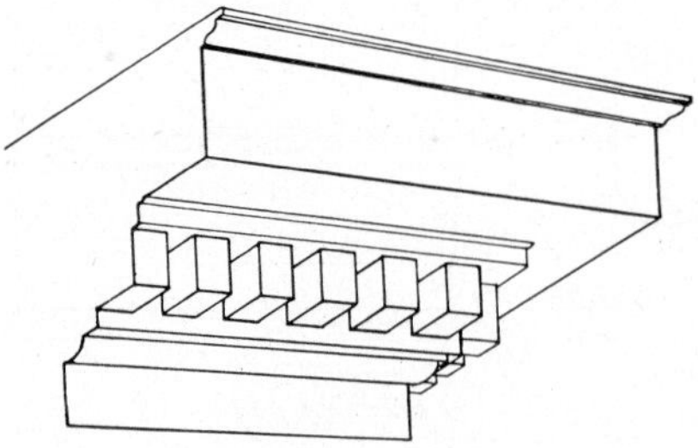

Fig. 4.26 A dentil range.

The distinctive feature of the Ionic Order is its capital (Fig. 4.13). Appearing at first glance to be completely different from the Doric, it is really remarkably similar. A close look will show that the echinus and abacus are still there, with their shape somewhat obscured by decorative carving. The real difference between the two capitals is the addition to the Ionic of the two spiral whirls called *volutes.* Inspection of a series of Ionic capitals (Greek, Roman, and Modern) will illustrate better than anything else the difference between curves that are graceful and alive, and those that are not. The merit of an Ionic capital depends almost entirely upon the linear quality of the volutes themselves and the sweep connecting them across the face of the capital. The best examples elicit ready admiration; the inferior examples are very bad indeed.

There was a certain amount of freedom in the design of the entablature for individual Ionic temples. The general spirit of the three-part division into architrave, frieze, and cornice was maintained; but in a number of examples, the frieze proper is omitted and its place taken by ornamental mouldings.

One such ornamental moulding occurs frequently enough to demand mention as a feature of the Ionic Order. This is the *dentil range* (Fig. 4.26). The dentils are a row of small rectangular blocks placed up under the cornice and sticking out beyond the plane of the architrave about one-half the total overhang of the cornice itself. The name *dentil* comes, it is said, from their resemblance to teeth, and they do indeed look like the teeth of a jack-o'-lantern.

In Ionic, when the frieze is included, the dentil range often is omitted. In

Ionic, the frieze is never subdivided, and runs without a break for its entire length. At times, the Greeks used the frieze to introduce color contrasts; an example is the blue limestone frieze of the Erectheum (Fig. 4.10). A very fine temple would have its frieze decorated with a continuous composition in relief sculpture — hence the use of the word for any long, narrow, continuous band of decoration.

The only feature of the Ionic entablature which is strictly standard is the architrave. This is not plain as in Doric, but is subdivided into three bands or steps, the projection of each step being very slight indeed, with the result that the shadow it casts is narrow and crisp to a degree. In some examples, there is a graduation in the width, or depth, of the three steps, the highest usually being the widest. In other examples, the steps are of uniform height.

A discussion of the Ionic Order would be incomplete without a brief reference to the problem presented by the corner capitals of an Ionic peristyle. The Ionic capital lacks an *omnifacial composition* — that is, it cannot like the Doric capital be viewed from all sides with similar satisfaction. The Greek solution is illustrated by the corner capitals of the Nike Temple on the Acropolis at Athens (Fig. 4.9). The capital is given a face on each side of the building, and the volute at the corner is bent out so that its axis bisects the right angle made by the front and side coming together. An odd and clumsy shape is made almost necessary at the inside corner opposite the bent volute, but that hardly matters because it is out of sight from any normal station of the observer.

ELEMENTS OF THE CORINTHIAN ORDER

The Corinthian Order scarcely differs from the Ionic except for its capital, the ostentatious appearance of which made it overly popular with the Romans while restricting its use by the Greeks to a very few examples.

The Corinthian capital (Figs. 4.14 and 8.5) is taller than the others, which accounts for the apparent extra delicacy of buildings where it is used. It is simpler than it looks, and its composition follows a rather mechanical routine. There are two fundamental parts: a bell-shaped core, with an abacus on top. The Corinthian abacus is ordinarily concave on the sides, and the profile of its vertical surfaces is often given a delicate reverse curve. The general shape is often called *campaniform,* a Latin derivative meaning no more and no less than bell-shaped.

Foliage in high relief decorates the surface of the bell-shaped core. Leaves of many kinds have been used, first and last, and sometimes more than one variety of leaf appears on a single capital. The Corinthian capital found at the

Tholos of Epidauros (Fig. 4.14) may be taken as a standard example. The leaves there used are a regularized form of the *acanthus*, a free-growing plant familiar in Greece, and they are arranged in systematic fashion. There are two rows of leaves, one above the other. The axis of each leaf is vertical; and the two rows are placed at equal and alternate intervals around the circumference. Usually there are eight leaves to a row.

On each face of the capital, ornaments resembling fern fronds rise from beneath the acanthus to swing up and meet those from the adjacent faces in miniature volutes formed under the four corners of the abacus. Smaller ornaments of the same kind sweep up toward the top and middle of each face of the core, filling in an area that would otherwise remain blank.

GREEK REFINEMENTS: THE PARTHENON AT ATHENS

The details of Greek architecture instantly impress the layman with their refinement, and years of study tend to reinforce the first impression. It is even more remarkable that a similar and much less obvious perfection is discernible in the design of the temple as a whole. The great fabric is conceived as an entity; and a number of physical facts, some of them demanding the utmost subtlety from the builders, are not to be understood unless we have some grasp of the artistic scheme governing the whole.

The idea of giving an entire building a refinement equal to that of its most delicate part was carried to the limit in the design and construction of the Parthenon. Similar refinements have been noted in other temples, but none compare with the Parthenon in the thoroughness with which perfection was demanded and sought.

There can be no doubt about the physical facts. The building was measured with minute accuracy by F. C. Penrose, who published his findings as *An Investigation into the Principles of Athenian Architecture* in 1851. Penrose worked with instruments compensated for variations in the temperature, and he rounded off his dimensions at the third decimal place of a foot. His accuracy has never been questioned, and greater precision would obviously be pointless.

While there can be no doubt about the facts, there is considerable difference between the theories which attempt to explain the intention of the architects. We had best proceed by reciting the facts first, and undertaking to explain them later.

The platform of the Parthenon is not a level plane surface. It rises toward the center in a way Mr. D. S. Robertson has neatly compared to the appearance of a carpet nailed down at the four corners only, and suddenly lifted from the floor by a blast of wind. The curvature of the upper surface as a whole produces a curvature in each of the "horizontal" lines that bound the stylobate on its four sides. On the short ends of the Parthenon, the rise amounts to 2⅗ inches, and to 4¼ inches on the long sides. These curves are repeated in the entablature with slightly less rise.

The columns of the Parthenon are not vertical, but incline inward at a very slight angle. We might compare the building to the base of an extremely tall, narrow pyramid. If we imagine the axes of all the columns projected indefinitely into the air, they would meet at an apex a little more than a mile above the earth. Our statement simplifies slightly the conditions measured by Penrose. The columns along the sides incline inward only and those at the corners alone have a compound inclination. The figure described is therefore not precisely pyramidal, a fact which need not disturb us. Figure 4.27 is an attempt to visualize the situation.

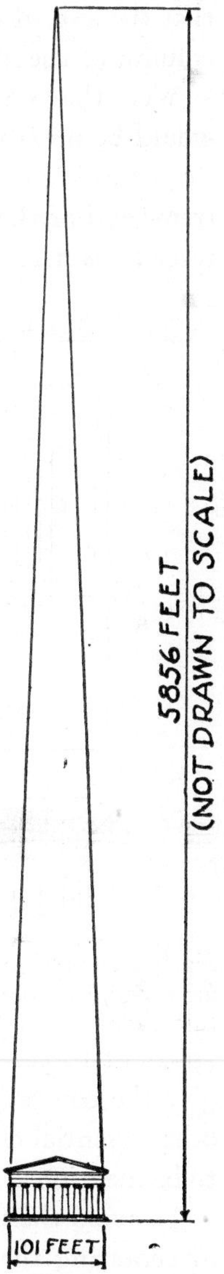

Fig. 4.27 Schematic drawing to illustrate the inclination of the columns of the Parthenon.

The columns of the Parthenon are not alone in their inclination. The walls of the cella are also made to incline slightly inward while all minor wall surfaces incline the opposite way. The entablature, for instance, has an outward pitch, and the upper edge overhangs the lower slightly but noticeably.

The distance between the Parthenon's columns is not uniform. There is, on the contrary, a clearly discernible difference in their spacing. Those at the corners are slightly more than six feet from their neighbors, while those along the front and sides are just over eight feet apart.

Measurement of the corner columns shows, moreover, that they are slightly heavier than all the others. The increase in diameter amounts to about 1.7 inches, or slightly more than a fortieth part of the diameter of a standard column.

A glance at the building will demonstrate, also, that there is more to the arrangement of the triglyphs than might at first be supposed. As stated earlier, there is one triglyph for every column and one for every intercolumniation. It is perhaps natural to suppose that the axis of each triglyph ought to correspond with the center line of its column or the middle of its intercolumniation, but such is not the case.

Were that system used, mechanical order would of course result, and there would be no trouble if we never arrived at a corner. But the triglyph being shaped as it is, centering one over the corner column would leave at the extreme end of the frieze a blank space which for lack of a better name we may refer to as half-a-metope. The corner of the building would lack weight and

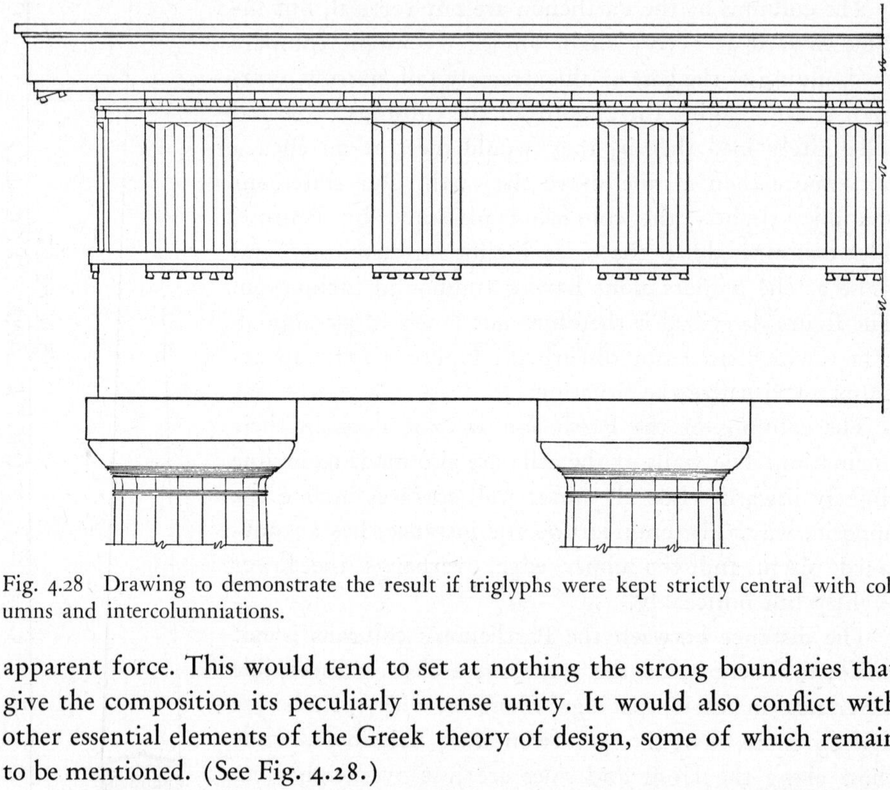

Fig. 4.28 Drawing to demonstrate the result if triglyphs were kept strictly central with columns and intercolumniations.

apparent force. This would tend to set at nothing the strong boundaries that give the composition its peculiarly intense unity. It would also conflict with other essential elements of the Greek theory of design, some of which remain to be mentioned. (See Fig. 4.28.)

To avoid the situation just outlined, the Greek architects gave up the notion of centering the triglyphs over column and intercolumniation. Instead they brought the pair on adjacent sides of the temple together at the corner (Fig. 4.3). They put the middle triglyph of the frieze centrally over the middle intercolumniation of the peristyle. The others were placed off-center in an amount that increases as we approach the corners of the building.

Such are the most important facts of curvature, position, and inclination which go to make up the so-called refinements of the Parthenon. We must now attempt an explanation. As stated, there is much difference of opinion about the matter. It is worthwhile to summarize the most popular and important theories, after which a new and, it is hoped, a more satisfying idea will be put forward.

It is often suggested that the curves of the Parthenon are a matter of chance. It is pointed out in this connection that irregularities are common in medieval buildings, and we are induced to believe that similar irregularities are inevitable in any fairly large fabric. Other Greek temples, moreover, lack perfect regularity.

This suggestion can hardly be entertained for long. The curves of the Parthenon are symmetrically repeated on opposite sides of the structure. Irregularity might be accepted as the result of chance; systematic and symmetrical correspondence of the strictest kind has never yet happened by coincidence.

A second suggestion, not altogether different from the last, is the supposition that the builders anticipated settling and sinking of the fabric, and that the curves were intended to disappear after a certain period of time. This notion involves two separate presumptions: that the Parthenon has not subsided as expected, and that the Greek builders wanted straight lines. Neither idea will stand analysis.

It is true that many buildings, ancient and modern alike, distort by amounts greater than the curvature of the Parthenon. There are two reasons for it: poor foundations and inferior construction. Unlike the mudbank upon which London lies, the Parthenon rests on bed rock which has not subsided or become compressed by any significant amount during the past 2,500 years. Furthermore, no modern building has anything like the quality of construction put into the Parthenon by builders with something like a thousand years of experience in temple architecture. Greece is wealthy in marble, and the stones used here were of uncommon soundness. The fitting of the masonry is uniquely elegant. No mortar was used. Every joint is the conjunction of two perfectly squared and polished surfaces, and the blocks were brought tight together by methods that need not concern us except to say they virtually preclude the possibility of further movement. It is thus inappropriate to reason by analogy to inferior buildings where, in return for cheap work, we accept as inevitable shrinkage in the materials, squeezing at the joints, and the twisting that comes from a poor substratum, inadequate foundations, or both.

The assumption that the Greek builders wanted straight lines, and intended to get them when the building settled, is similarly out of order. It is true that the modern contractor works on straight lines, but his reason for doing so bears no relation to aesthetic theory. He merely knows that the plumb and level reduce the cost by saving an immense amount of time making checks and measurements of every imaginable sort. There is no legitimate reason for comparing such work with the work that went into the Parthenon.

The builders of that great temple belong to quite another guild and class. The nearest modern parallel is to be sought in the shipyard. Anyone who has worked there will instantly appreciate the curves of the Parthenon. To establish the wonderful lines that were built into the marble and remain, what a world of patient labor in the drafting room and on the lofting floor! What infinite skill and care in cutting the innumerable perfect and subtle bevels that fit so perfectly together and produce the unparalleled loveliness!

More popular than either of these suggestions is the theory endorsed by Penrose, who seems to have elaborated upon a somewhat cryptic passage in Vitruvius.

Vitruvius was a Roman builder of the 1st Century A.D. He wrote a treatise on architecture, a copy of which was discovered at Saint Gall in Switzerland by the Florentine humanist Poggio who came that way in 1416. Nothing else survives from the pen of any man who was himself a classical architect, and Vitruvius has therefore occupied a unique position of authority ever since.

In Book III, Chapter IV, Mr. M. H. Morgan translates his text as follows:

> "The level of the stylobate must be increased along the middle by the *scamilli impares;* for if it is laid perfectly level, it will look to the eye as though it were hollowed a little. At the end of the book a figure will be found, with a description showing how the *scamilli* may be made to suit this purpose."

The drawing Vitruvius mentions did not survive with his text, but the *scamilli impares*, or something very like them, survive in the building trades. As explained in a learned note by Mr. H. L. Warren, added as an appendix to Morgan's *Vitruvius*, the *scamilli* are a set of little blocks of varying height. By setting them up at carefully measured intervals and sighting along them, the builder can adjust a stylobate to any curve he wants.

There can be little doubt that Vitruvius knew how to construct such curves, and there can be little doubt, also, that his remarks reflect a general custom bruited about among Roman builders; namely, that a good and proper temple ought to have curvature and inclination something like that of the Parthenon. Further confirmation is supplied by a passing word or two in Cicero (*In Verrem* II, 1, 51) where that famous trial lawyer impeaches a witness by suggesting the man is so ignorant as to suppose that pillars should be made to stand exactly plumb.

Building upon such classical tradition and extending its implications in a manner that is admittedly plausible, Penrose asserted that the curves and inclinations of the Parthenon were intended to compensate for optical illusions. Without such adjustments from the plumb and level, he declared that the stylobate would "seem to sag, the entablature would seem to recede, and the angle columns look thin against the sky."

Penrose's suggestion is often illustrated by drawings; a typical set appears among the superb and indispensable set of plates in Sir Bannister Fletcher's *History of Architecture*. Such drawings may not, however, be taken as rational evidence. By no means do they represent the actual conditions obtaining in a view of the Parthenon, but an exaggeration thereof. We must dismiss them as caricature.

In scrutinizing Penrose's theory, we must first of all disabuse ourselves of the prestige it has acquired by a hundred years of repetition. Often stated as fact, it still remains merely a suggestion like any other.

First of all, it is well to examine Penrose's ancient authority.

Any reader of Vitruvius is bound to observe that, Roman builder though he was, Vitruvius was hardly an educated man. His Latin was inelegant, and his powers of expression were poor. The latter undoubtedly reflect something more serious than an absence of ease and grace; the truth is that Vitruvius was neither a well-informed man nor a clear-headed man. Whenever he alludes to anything that demands close reasoning and subtle knowledge (Polycleitos's canon of proportion for the human figure, for example) he gets mixed up and gives us a garbled account. It is plain enough he knew that curvature and inclination were the going custom, and it seems likely he knew a practical method for building them into a temple. It by no means follows that he understood the aesthetic theories of the Greek architects who first invented the refinements. In that connection, we must remind ourselves, moreover, that Vitruvius was no contemporary observer. He lived about 600 years after the Parthenon was built.

Cicero was a person of different stripe. It seems probable that he might have been able to give us a succinct account of the theory involved; but, like Vitruvius, he doesn't. He merely refers to it in quite another connection, and passes on.

In sum, we must accept the fact that we have no ancient mandate one way or the other, and the idea that the refinements compensate for optical illusions, if true, must rest on modern deduction.

One way to check Penrose's assertions is to examine modern buildings known to be plumb and level. The examination must be made, of course, under conditions of diffused light and by persons trained in accurate, objective visual inspection — we cannot take a majority vote to decide the matter because the unskilled observer can so easily be persuaded that he sees what he is told to see. When plumb and level buildings are so examined, the optical illusions predicted by Penrose do not appear unless some extraneous factor is introduced. Again, we must beware of the familiar tricky drawings which do in truth deceive the eye, but which bear no fair analogy to conditions at the Parthenon.

Penrose's assertions overlook another fact of importance. They contain the tacit suggestion that the curves are not perceptible with the naked eye, and that the building impresses the observer as being plumb and level. The reverse is true. When a considerable overlay of medieval rubble was removed in 1837 to put the whole stylobate in plain sight for the first time during our era, the curves were at once noted. Three observers actually published the fact, and Penrose's research was undertaken in the first place to verify such statements. Any number of modern observers who have visited the site repeat the testimony of those who first inspected the temple: the curves are there to be seen with the naked eye. Any good-size photograph also shows them up plainly and accurately (Figs. 4.1–2).

We are thus compelled to believe that compensation for optical illusions offers no satisfactory explanation for the situation we know to obtain. In structures without such adjustments, the optical illusions do not take place, and at the Parthenon the refinements do not produce the plumb and level appearance.

The modern student, accustomed to the best engineering the world has ever seen, will also want to know whether the Parthenon's refinements perform some practical service, but this possibility must also be discarded as unimportant. Drainage is improved by making any floor convex rather than flat, but drainage can be taken care of equally well by some method less heroically expensive and difficult. The increased diameter of the corner columns and the pitch of all columns doubtless tends to increase the stability of the fabric when subjected to shock or vibration of any kind — an earthquake or an explosion, for instance. But in neither case is the adjustment of the right order of magnitude to make any significant difference, and the Doric temple, with its ponderous columns and slight superstructure, is an extremely stable building to begin with.

It would appear that the only avenue offering any hope of explaining the Parthenon's refinements is the assumption that the Greek designers were compelled by some deeply felt aesthetic necessity. The idea that aesthetic satisfaction might seem so important may not immediately impress the reader as plausible, but the facts point that way.

The artists who assembled at Athens to work under Phidias had the greatest opportunity ever afforded in the entire history of the ancient world. Because Athens controlled the Delian League, unlimited funds were available. It would have been easy to build larger buildings or more buildings. Instead, the money was expended and fabulous labor devoted to the attainment of quality.

Insofar as we can recapture the Greek state of mind and thus understand the exhaustive perfection of the Parthenon, the following considerations are apposite.

As we have seen from our study of Greek pedimental arrangement and other instances of design applied to sculpture and painting (see above, pages 56–66), the Greeks who lived and worked in Periclean Athens were possessed of and committed to a particular and excellent theory of artistic order which we have named *the organic composition*. Of this, the chief elements are the establishment of an intensive and assertive unity for the whole (usually brought about by firm boundaries, either visible or suggested), and, within the frame, the maintenance of coherence between part and part and between part and whole (usually by some logical and unmistakable suggestion). When drawing plans for their greatest temple, would the Greeks suddenly embark upon some new and untried theory of design? That is certainly possible. In one instance, it seems even to have happened (see below, page 347), but everything combines to indicate that the Parthenon is simply the largest, and also the most subtle instance of the theory of design so succinctly stated by Aristotle and cited in the last chapter. To understand the building, we merely need apply to architecture what we already know to be true of sculpture. Everything then falls into a reasonable pattern.

All architecture begins with the site. There is perhaps no such thing as a good building as such; we must ask where it is to go and in what surroundings it will come into view. In accordance with classical custom, the site of the Parthenon had been leveled off into a horizontal plane surface.

The upward curve of the stylobate is in physical juxtaposition to the horizontal ground line beneath it. If projected slightly at either end, the curve would have an origin in the ground a short distance from the façade of the building. Thence it would rise to its apex, and swing downward to an ending at a point in the ground an equal and opposite distance beyond the temple's far end.

Given the character of the curve and its reference to the horizontal beneath, any smallest arc of it tells the story. By its own internal logic it says that the middle of the building must come at such and such a point, and that its end must also come at a definite distance farther on. There is no room for doubt;

but a straight and horizontal stylobate would make no similar reference to the ground. There is nothing within a straight line to tell us where it begins, ends, or has a middle; it might stop anywhere or go on forever.

The inclination of the columns makes sense by reference to the same theory. The effect is to make the building the base of a pyramidal figure; and as a general proposition, it may be stated that once the notion of symmetry has been evoked in the feelings of the observer, inclination of any sort whatever will demand its equal and opposite.

The increased diameter of the corner columns and their closer spacing both contribute to the same scheme. They strengthen the enframement and emphasize the limits of the composition. The same may be said of the triglyphs which join at the corners of the frieze, but there is more to be discussed before we are through with the so-called " triglyph problem."

The arrangement of the triglyphs has traditionally been presented as an almost intolerable irregularity of the Doric temple which the Greek designers were clever enough to ameliorate by a kind of artistic counter-irritant so subtly applied as to escape attention. Such a view must have had its genesis in the notion that the rhythm of the triglyphs ought to be geared to the rhythm of the columns — a concept that might apply to a machine, but one which is unnecessary when dealing with a work of art.

Because of its projection, its distinctive shape, and the way it takes the light, each triglyph is of course an accent. They do not come at precisely even intervals, but that need cause us no more than a moment's difficulty. The spacing changes in a rational manner. There is order, that is to say, in the rate of change. We are perfectly familiar with that type of order in music, and we merely see it here in visual terms. It is probably an excellent thing rather than a fault to have the columns come in one rhythm and the triglyphs in another. The experience of simultaneous rhythm is also familiar enough, and we may summarize by saying that the triglyphs constitute an element of variety in the decoration of a building which tends on the whole to be overly regular.

We have been speaking of the composition of the Parthenon as though it were self-evidently a good thing. To an extent, that is true. As the supreme demonstration of organic composition, the great building is unexcelled. It is a celebration of the Greek capacity for formulating clear, consistent ideas and making practical affairs conform to an order directed by the mind. All men must admire such a quality in a people. We must nevertheless be prepared to compare the Greek achievement with others — as, for example, with the Style of the Near East which lacks (but for excellent reasons) the Aristotelean beginning, middle, and end. Before proceeding, it behooves us to pause for a few remarks that may still further explain the character of Greek art.

The various refinements of the Parthenon combine to produce an extraordinary sense of integration, completeness, and fulfillment. By its very nature, the organic theory of composition seems to proceed toward that result with a beautiful inevitability. It is necessary to appreciate, however, that such a result is achieved at a cost. A work of art which exists in such a state that nothing may be added or taken away is not only static, it is inflexible. Nothing is left to do; indeed nothing more can be done. When they built the Parthenon, the Greeks had arrived at the end of a road. A great many temples were built in later generations, some of them larger and more elaborate. But what is there to be said about them?

Greek excellence was achieved by the method of setting limits. Every one of the refinements of the Parthenon contributes to the establishment of boundaries for the composition. It would appear that the Greek mind sought boundaries because limitation makes it possible to understand, to control, and to excel. But the very same feeling was also a negation: the Greeks may fairly be described as harboring a terror of the indefinite. In art and in all forms of thought, their accomplishment was bought by rigorous restriction of the field of attention, and by stern exclusion of everything beyond the problem in hand.

Thus the Greek temple makes no reference to the universe around it. Its clarity and integration is unparalleled, but it comes at the cost of dealing only with the finite.

The Sculpture of the Parthenon

Not satisfied with refinement of an architectural nature, the Athenians gave the Parthenon a prodigious wealth of sculpture. In addition to the two pedimental compositions, all 92 metopes were decorated with individual compositions in high relief; and in addition to the metopes, there was an extra and unique feature in the form of an inner frieze in low relief, 3 feet and 4 inches high, placed at the very top of the exterior wall of the cella and immediately under the ceiling of the ambulatory. The frieze ran all the way around the cella, and originally measured a full 524 feet long (Fig. 4.5).

In the absence of originals by the great masters of the Fifth Century, a special importance attaches to the marbles from the Parthenon. As architectural sculpture goes, the work is unusually fine, but can we legitimately associate it with the personal style of Phidias? Opinions vary. Some critics want to believe he designed everything; others contend that he designed nothing. On the whole, the latter seems more likely, unwelcome though it is. In view of his immense responsibilities at the time, he must have been compelled to delegate even so important a task as this. From Phidias or some other personality, however, there surely emanated a certain unity both of style and spirit. All the sculpture from the Parthenon is tinged with a lofty sobriety that separates it even from the rest of the Greek output.

The subject matter of the metopes was, as usual, drawn from mythological combat. On the east we might have seen the gods fighting the giants, on the west the Greeks against the Amazons, and on the south the Lapiths and the Centaurs. Only the southern metopes are sufficiently well preserved to make study worthwhile; those from the north side were so badly damaged that even their subject is a matter of debate. On the whole, the metopes are somewhat less satisfactory than the rest of the sculpture. A few of them might even be called crude. The reason is not far to seek: the structural procedure demanded that the metopes be finished early and dropped permanently into place long before it was necessary to carve anything for the pediments or for the inner frieze. Because a very large number of sculptors were required to get the work done in any reasonable time, it is probably a good guess that the carving of the metopes took place at a period of organization during which it was necessary to accept compromises. By the time that first enterprise was complete, the corps of sculptors was capable of working together as a unit, and would by then have become familiar with the conceptions and standards at which Phidias aimed. At any rate, the metopes — taking them as a collection — exhibit unhappy variations in quality.

For its eastern pediment, the Parthenon had the *Birth of Athena,* a subject involving the emergence of that goddess from the forehead of her father Zeus. Inasmuch as she came into the world full-grown and wearing a suit of armor, the delivery was incontestably the greatest obstetrical miracle in history. One would like to know how the sculptors handled it, but except for a very doubtful reflection on a marble well-head in Madrid (showing the situation after it was all over), we have no guidance. The vital central portion of this pediment was destroyed to make room for the apse when the temple was converted into a church during the 5th Century. The rest of the composition was memorialized in one of the " Carrey drawings," and the preserved figures are on view in London. The reclining male nude known as " Theseus " has often been suggested as our best source on Phidian figure-style. The rhythmical drapery of the so-called " Three Fates " is something of a tour de force, although much admired. Best of all, however, are the figures which localize the event in the heavens and name the time as dawn: at the left-hand corner, the horses of

Helios (the Sun) rise from the sea puffing with energy; and at the right, the tired horses of Selene (the Moon) sink beneath the waves.

The western pediment had the *Contest between Athena and Poseidon for the Land of Attica.* We know the arrangement of the central portion only through the "Carrey drawing" of 1674 (Figs. 4.6–7). Poseidon's horses were lost in a clumsy attempt to lower them with the object of carrying them off to Venice when the Venetians evacuated the city in 1688 — Morosini, their leader, had descended from the Morosini who brought home from Constantinople the four bronze horses which now stand over the principal entrance to Saint Mark's.

While it is difficult to reason from so poor a source, the drawing is good enough to suggest that the subtlety of pedimental composition had advanced since Olympia. Instead of posing each figure flat against the background, many of the statues are seen in the three-quarter view, thus calling into operation a very moderate sense of space forward and back in the horizontal plane and producing a more varied pattern of shadow. The chief feature of the design, however, is the elimination of the single standing figure placed on the central axis; at Olympia and probably at Aegina also, the presence of such a figure inevitably suggested a division of the whole into halves. Here at the Parthenon, the middle of the pediment was filled with a criss-cross of diagonals. It is a fair guess that an even more intensive unity was thereby arrived at, but it is admittedly hard to tell from the source we are compelled to rely upon.

The Parthenon was first opened to the public on the occasion of the Panathenaic Festival of 438 B.C. Appropriately enough, the subject matter of its lengthy interior frieze was an idealized version of the procession that took place as its final and culminating ceremony. The Panathenaea was originally no more than a local custom. Peisistratus had undertaken to magnify its importance, and by the time of which we speak, the affair had become a national celebration scheduled every fourth year and involving games, musical contests, and oratorical performances. The procession was a great and major spectacle of old men and maidens and a cavalry escort. Forming in the town, it filed up onto the Acropolis. There was performed the focal ceremony of the whole affair: putting a new saffron-colored robe (*peplos*) on a venerable wooden statue of Athena.

The Parthenon is so placed that the visitor approaches it from the southwest corner, and it is there that the design begins. The western section of the frieze still remains in place (Fig. 4.5), and there we see preparations in progress, with some of the horsemen already in motion toward our left. The procession splits, as it were, to follow both sides of the temple; and it comes together again at the middle of the eastern front of the building, where some gods are seated waiting for the arrival of the *peplos.* The arrangement is natural enough, and makes it impossible to inspect the composition backwards.

Although the frieze is ostensibly continuous, the Greek sense of artistic propriety made it necessary that some account be taken of the corners of the temple. Rapid motion was therefore confined to the long sides of the building. Near the corners, we see the movement slowed down, with marshalls there to direct the marchers. This is approximately what we might expect in the light of what we already know about Greek art; certain other features, however, require special mention.

Placed up under the roof and shielded by the entablature, the inner frieze received almost all its light by reflection from the ambulatory floor and the ground outside. By comparison to the intensity of the light outside, the frieze existed in comparative gloom. Dark shadows of any kind had to be avoided at all costs; otherwise, it would literally be impossible to make out what one was looking at. Relief was therefore kept exceedingly low; and the upper parts were modeled out with slightly more depth than the lower. At the top, the relief rises about 2¼ inches above the background, and at the bottom, about 1¼ inches. In order to avoid greater projection and cast shadows, some radical distortions were introduced: to accommodate the legs of the riders without bringing them out too far from the background, the sculptors simply caved in the rib-cages of the dainty little horses to get the necessary hollow. Still other distortions were employed for similarly rational reasons. Scale is violated, for example, to keep all the heads at the same height, thus repeating the architectural line which forms the upper boundary: men on foot come to the same level as men on horseback, and the horses themselves are on a smaller scale than the men.

In matters of detail, it is probably impossible to find an equally extended design that maintains the same high quality of sensibility. By exception in Greek sculpture, rapid motion is represented; the usual method is to confront the eye with a figure that would be unstable unless we understand that dynamics enter into the situation. Almost every variety of rhythm known to sculpture is to be noted at some place or other in the immense length of the frieze. The manual skill of the sculptors remains unexcelled; where can one find greater brilliance of line, or more sensitive modeling?

It is nevertheless impossible to say whether this inner frieze was a success. There is much to make one doubt it. However excellent in itself, its placement was such as to render comfortable inspection impossible. Because the eye adjusts to the brightest illumination within the field of vision, not the dimmest, did the frieze attract its fair share of attention in the bright Mediterranean climate? Or was it lost in the dark as details are lost in paintings by Caravaggio and Rembrandt? Now that the roof is gone, it is difficult to guess at these things. As seen on the building, in the British Museum, and in every available photograph, the cast shadows fall downward, which is the reverse of the way they were intended to fall. Even if this were corrected by artificial light within the museum, outdoor conditions would scarcely be duplicated. In their original condition, moreover, the panels must have been most subtly finished on the surface to take the light in the best manner; but it is hopeless to attempt to restore that surface. In the end we are left in a quandary, with a number of important worries unresolved.

THE ERECTHEUM

The conventional nature of most Greek architecture is pointed up with emphasis by the very existence of the Erectheum at Athens (Fig. 4.10). The building was designed by Mnesicles, who must be ranked high among those capable of original acts of genius.

Instead of leveling off the site as classical architects almost invariably did, Mnesicles accepted the footing as he found it. He built the structure on two levels that differ by about 10½ feet, and he provided two separate façades, one at the east end and the other at the northwest corner. Doubtless there were religious as well as physical reasons for the arrangement. It is said that Athena's olive tree and Poseidon's salt spring both were to be seen at this very spot; and while nothing has been established with certainty, it is likely that the building was intended to incorporate several shrines, one of which had to do with Erectheus — hence the name. The interior arrangements have been altogether erased, but it seems most likely that the Erectheum was a double temple, with a partition at some point separating the east end from the west.

Because the building is assymetrical, critics have invariably pictured Mnesicles as a much put upon man. We are told that he was a clever person, who tried to beguile us away from fundamental imperfection (i.e., absence of geometric order) by elegant details and by surprises like the famous *Porch of the Maidens* attached to the southwest corner on the side facing the Parthenon. On the assumption that no Greek in his right mind would willingly design the building as it stands, we are often asked to excuse Mnesicles on the ground that he hoped to set things right someday by adding an entire wing out toward the west, an expedient which would "balance" the composition by making it symmetrical to an axis through the middle of the Porch of the Maidens.

There is no archaeological evidence that compels us to believe Mnesicles intended any such thing. Neither is there any reason to apologize for the Erectheum as it stands. Everything in view is susceptible of explanation by reference to well-established principles of design.

As always, we must first consider the building in relation to its setting. It stands about fifty yards north of the Parthenon, and at a slight angle thereto. It is doubtful whether we would think so highly of the Parthenon were it not for its juxtaposition to the irregular and delicate Erectheum. The two go together, the daintiness of the one setting off the strength of the other (Fig. 4.15). The modern observer, accustomed as he is to the mechanical planning that derives from Rome, might interpret the absence of parallelism as an indication no such relation was intended, but he would be mistaken. By pitching the two axes differently, the Greek designers made certain that the two buildings would take the light differently, thus avoiding the monotonous pattern of shadows which results from putting every surface in line with every other.

The matter becomes even more interesting if we consider the Erectheum by itself. The south face, toward the Parthenon, is the one that best illustrates the principles in operation (Fig. 4.10). It is necessary, of course, to supply in imagination the missing parts of the entablature, and the vanished roof.

Seen from this point of view, the composition presents us with an extensive area of blank wall stretching off to the east and right. At the lower left-hand corner, we see the Porch of the Maidens which is small in scale, but an artistic tour de force: young ladies carrying an entablature on their heads. Empathy does not operate to make us feel fatigue even though they have stood there some 2,400 years; the architect gets away with it because his sculptor chose a very adequate canon of proportions and was supremely skilful in posing the figures, especially around the head and neck, so that they appear to do their work with complete ease, even with freedom.

The composition is in perfect balance. It is merely necessary to realize that for the purposes of a work of art, balance is not a mechanical matter but a question of the observer's psychology. We may balance mass off against mass, much as we balance weight against weight when using a simple set of scales. Up to this point, we have found it unnecessary to refer to any other kind of balance, but the Erectheum demands an extension of our understanding. It confronts us with the phenomenon of the small item which is intensely interesting (the Porch of the Maidens) placed far off center, but establishing by the very fact of its interest an equilibrium as over against a large bulk of comparatively neutral material (the blank wall). In its present condition without either entablature or roof, the composition is out of order because the Porch of the Maidens exerts a disproportionate appeal to one's attention.

Were the Erectheum the only instance of its kind, we might put it down as an historical eccentricity, and pass on. The very same arrangement, however, appears to have been used in ancient painting, returned to popularity at Venice during the 16th Century (see below, pages 762–763), and has been used so many times since that we may recognize it as a standard artistic form. As indicated, the essential principle is to balance a bulk of inert material against a small item of intense interest. As seen in painting, the latter is almost invariably a vista into the distance. The vista, performing for the picture the same function as the Porch of the Maidens on the Erectheum, will usually be found at the upper right-hand corner, or the upper left. It may be anywhere else so long as it does its work properly, and we need not be confused simply because the Porch of the Maidens comes at a lower corner rather than an upper.

If our present explanation be accepted — and it seems to give more satisfaction than any other — our admiration for the Greek genius is increased, and our comments about the limitations of the Greek mind are softened somewhat. Sadly enough, however, the principles illustrated by the Erectheum never took hold during Antiquity, and the building remains the single instance of their employment by any classical architect.

THE INFLUENCE OF GREEK ARCHITECTURE UPON LATER STYLES

The influence of the Greek style upon the subsequent history of architecture is a matter of common knowledge. The beauty of the Greek orders has been as cogent, perhaps, as any other single factor in maintaining the cultural prestige of Antiquity. As decorative detail, the orders (or reminiscences of them) appear in wholesale quantities on Roman buildings, Byzantine buildings, Renaissance buildings, Baroque buildings, Rococo buildings, and indeed almost everywhere except in Romanesque and Gothic. This is the literal and mechanical aspect of the Greek influence.

Far more important are the tendencies which derive from the inward spirit of the Greek style. These have to do with the shape and the subtleties of shape given to individual members, and with the way parts combine into an orderly scheme conceived in terms of geometry. In the Greek temple, those impulses combined to produce a building which is, in the last analysis, a gigantic piece of geometric sculpture.

The basic psychology that derives from such a conception of architecture has had a far-reaching effect. It has been the dominant factor in architectural thought since the start of the Renaissance, and it was the dominant factor in the architectural thought of the Romans.

An architect who holds the Greek point of view experiences his first conception of the building in a sculptor's terms. His initial effort to visualize the completed building creates in his mind's eye a picture of the *outside* of the building. He sees a set of masses. Each one will be a familiar geometric solid, pierced perhaps by doors and windows arranged at equal intervals, or according to some other scheme of easily-comprehended regularity. The more the mass of the building conforms to the simplicity and unity of the Greek temple, the more closely will it suit the taste of its architect.

Provision has to be made for the human activities that must go on inside the structure and round about it. In point of time, this consideration arrives in the mind of the architect only after he has already formed a preference for an exterior of a particular shape. The truth is that he packs in the practical details much as we pack a suitcase, and the volume of space originally chosen almost always is too much or too little. To use a bit of legitimate jargon, the architect who feels as the Greeks felt "designs from the outside inward."

The process almost invariably produces buildings that yearn for the condition of the Greek temple. Adjustments and additions are difficult to make, and the expense is usually higher than it otherwise might be. Neatness and order are almost sure to be arrived at, however; and no other procedure is so likely to produce formal beauty. As Alberti was so eloquently to point out during the Renaissance, formal beauty is no mere luxury. It has to do with the dignity of man, and is necessary if his soul is to be fed.

ALINARI

SANSAINI

Fig. 5.2 (above) Rome. Terme Museum. Red jasper gem signed by Aspasios. Early 1st Century A.D. Both are believed to reflect the appearance of the Athena Parthenos by Phidias.

Fig. 5.1 (left) Athens. National Museum. The "Varvakeion Statue" of Athena. Marble. 39 inches high.

Fig. 5.3 Paris. Bibliothèque Nationale. Coin of Olympia. About 360 B.C.

Figs. 5.4–5 Coins of Elis. Period of Hadrian (117–138 A.D.).

Believed to reflect the appearance of the Olympian Zeus by Phidias. From casts in the Metropolitan Museum, New York.

Figs. 5.6–8 Bologna. Museo Cirico. *The Athena Lemnia.* Believed to be a Roman copy of unusually fine quality after an original by Phidias. PHOTOGRAPHS BY CLARENCE KENNEDY.

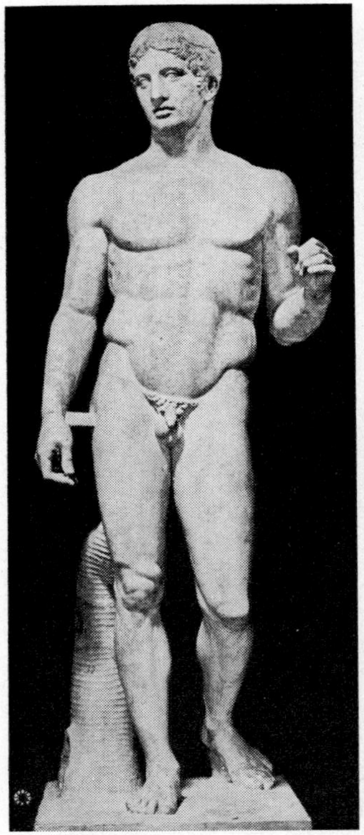

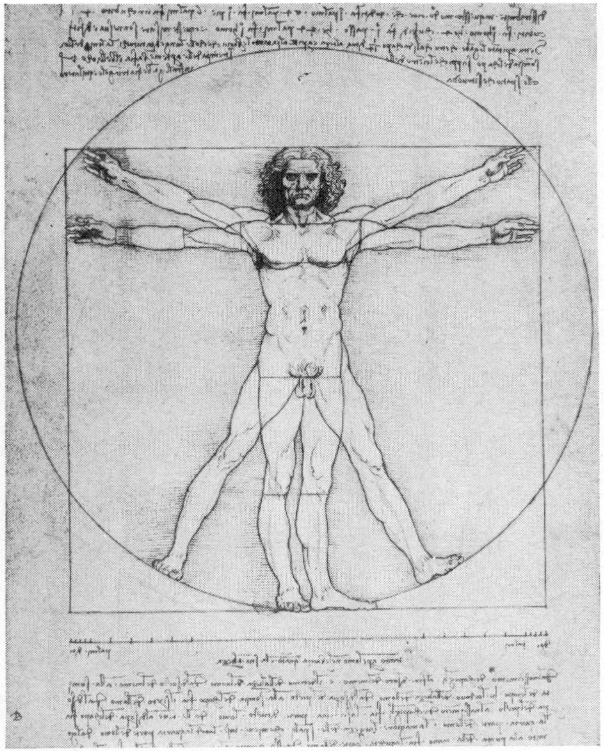

ALINARI

Fig. 5.9 (left) Naples. National Museum. Roman copy believed to reflect the appearance of the *Doryphoros* by Polycleitos. Marble. About 7 feet high. Fig. 5.10 (middle) New York. Metropolitan Museum. Terracotta statuette believed to reflect the appearance of the *Diadumenos* by Polycleitos. Fig. 5.11 (right) A page from one of Leonardo's notebooks; an attempt to visualize the Polycleitan scheme for human proportions. Venice. Academy.

ALINARI

Figs. 5.12–13 Praxiteles. *Hermes*. Olympia. Middle 4th Century B.C. Parian marble. 6 feet, 11 inches high. PHOTOGRAPHS BY WALTER HEGE.

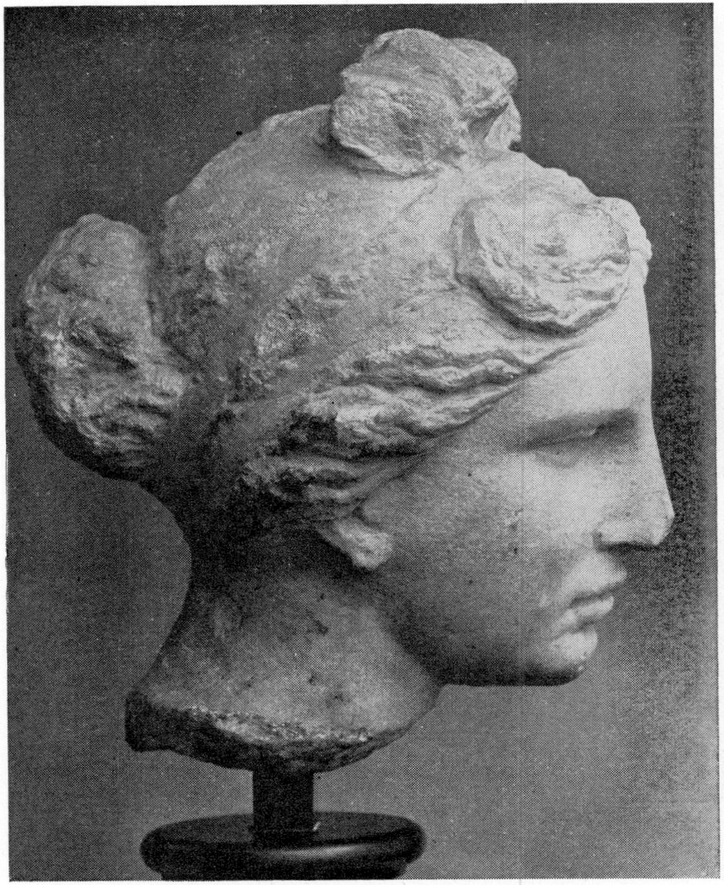

Figs. 5.14–15 Boston. Museum of Fine Arts. The Bartlett Aphrodite. PHOTOGRAPHS BY CLARENCE KENNEDY.

Figs. 5.16 Cambridge, Massachusetts. Fogg Museum. *The Harvard Meleager*. Believed to reflect the appearance of a statue by Scopas.

FROM A CAST IN THE METROPOLITAN MUSEUM.

ALINARI

Figs. 5.17–18 Heads from the pedimental sculptures of the Temple of Athena Alea at Tegea.

ALINARI

Fig. 5.19 Rome. Vatican. Roman copy believed to reflect the appearance of the *Apoxyomenos* by Lysippos.

Fig. 5.20 (below) Constantinople. Ottoman Museum. *The Alexander Sarcophagus.*

SABAH

*

5

GREEK SCULPTORS OF THE GREAT AGE

ABOUT 450 TO ABOUT 300 B.C.

PHIDIAS

The opinion of the ancients, as expressed in their literary records, gives the unmistakable impression that Phidias was the greatest artist of Greece. Because we possess so much of it in good condition we are likely to think of the building program on the Acropolis as his greatest achievement, but it would appear that we are mistaken. His fame during Antiquity derived from his authorship of the two greatest cult statues of the peninsula: the *Athena Parthenos* for which the Parthenon itself was built, and the seated *Zeus* in the Temple of Zeus at Olympia. For the Greeks these two statues had immense religious significance, and as objects of pilgrimage and devotion meant as much or more than the shrine of Santiago at Compostella was destined to mean in the days of medieval Christianity. Phidias's role, in short, was to furnish Greece with its visual imagery for the great Gods. The testimony of our literary records is practically unanimous in praising his supreme success in that profoundly difficult and immensely important enterprise.

Both the *Zeus* and the *Athena Parthenos* were of colossal size, standing about forty feet high. Because the *Zeus* was a seated figure, the scale was even larger.

Both were *chryselephantine,* which is to say made of gold and ivory. A complex wooden frame supported the statue; and over this, ivory plates were laid for the flesh surfaces, with gold for drapery and accessories. Precious stones were added to some extent. Because of the scale, various surfaces not ordinarily available for such use were employed as fields for subordinate decoration in narrative relief. The soles of Athena's sandals, for example, were deep enough to carry a *Battle of Lapiths and Centaurs,* and her shield had a *Battle of the Greeks and Amazons* into which Phidias is said to have introduced portraits of himself and Pericles. There can be no doubt that these subordinate decorations added much to the interest of both statues, and made each, in effect, a museum of Phidias's art.

It is impossible to say with any certainty which statue was the earlier; and, as a matter of fact, our visual evidence is so slight as to make such a question utterly academic. The only fixed date in the sculptor's entire career is 438 B.C., when the *Athena Parthenos* was dedicated. Either before that or after it, he went to Olympia. There is a record that he got into trouble over an alleged theft of some of the gold used for the *Zeus*, and may even have died in prison. Greek politics being what they were, it looks as though his association with Pericles were the real reason behind the rumor; probably some of his enemies got him after Pericles died in 429. At any rate, we may make the guess Phidias was born about 490, and that his activity extended to 430 or a little longer.

Pausanius, that Baedeker of the Ancient World, was in Greece during the 2nd Century A.D., and saw the *Athena Parthenos*. In his *Description of Greece* (I.24.5), he says:

> On the middle of the helmet rests a sphinx and on either side of the helmet griffins are represented. The statue of Athena stands erect and wears a tunic reaching to the feet. On its breast is represented in ivory the head of Medusa, and a *Victory* about four cubits in height stands on one of its hands, while in the other it holds a spear. At its feet rests a shield, and close to the shield is a serpent which no doubt represents Erichthonios. On the base of the statue, the *Birth of Pandora* is represented in relief.

It is from Pliny (*Natural History* XXXVI.18) that we get the further information that "on the shield was wrought in relief the *Battle of the Amazons* on the convex surface, and the *Combat of the Gods and Giants* on the concave side, while on the sandals was represented those of the *Lapiths and Centaurs*."

Plutarch (*Pericles* XXXI.4) completes such description as we have with the remark that on the shield Phidias included " a figure of himself as a bald old man lifting up a stone in both hands, and a very fine portrait of Pericles fighting an Amazon." Pericles, he further indicates, was shown with one arm across his face.

Suffering a certain amount of attrition, the original statue still stood in the cella as late as 375 A.D. After that time, accounts vary. There was a fire during the 5th Century A.D. in which the *Athena* may have perished; at any rate, it seems to have been gone by about 485. One bit of evidence suggests it was at Constantinople during the 10th Century, but we can by no means be certain what actually happened to it. As usual, we are left to do the best we can with what we have.

The *Strangford Shield* in the British Museum is probably a copy after the shield of the *Athena Parthenos,* and seems to show Phidias and Pericles as we might expect to find them from Plutarch's citation. If so, this monument is the nearest thing we have to a self-portrait by any ancient artist, and is in itself evidence for the sculptor's age at the date of the statue.

Other monumental evidence is discouraging to a degree. The so-called *Varvakeion Copy* (Fig. 5.1) is the only complete statue that comes anywhere near fitting the stipulations of the literary evidence. One wishes it had never been found; it is lifeless, stupid, vulgar. About all that may properly be deduced from it is a summary notion of Phidias's figure-style as of that particular moment: a stocky canon of proportions and a head characterized by considerable breadth in the region of the mouth and chin. The *Lenormant Statuette* is a bit pleasanter than the *Varvakeion Copy,* but suffers from poor workmanship and bad condition.

A head in the Staatliche Museum of Berlin is of better quality, as are reflections appearing on Athenian coins. The only reflection of the great Athena which in and of itself has any finesse, however, is a carved gem by Aspasios, now in the Terme Museum at Rome (Fig. 5.2). But even that is florid, and we are forced to the conclusion that visual recovery of the *Athena Parthenos* is today impossible. Unless further evidence comes our way, we must abandon hope of having any adequate idea what it looked like.

For the *Olympian Zeus,* we are a little better off. The general appearance of the statue we know by following much the same method as before. It was seated on a throne. The upper half of the body was nude. The majesty of the expression was softened by kindness.

The ensemble is reflected on later coins of Elis, the district in which Olympia is situated, and in a rather empty fresco of Roman date discovered at Eleusis. A full-size marble head at Boston corresponds generally to the heads appearing on the coins, but its expression overdoes the element of kindness to the complete exclusion of the force for which the original was famous.

If this were all, we would once again have to abandon hope of spiritual or aesthetic satisfaction; but among the various coins which presumably reflect the appearance of the *Zeus,* there is one that rings true (Fig. 5.5). A mass-produced article in the first place, dulled by usage, preserved by the merest chance, reproduced in the form of a plaster cast, and reproduced again for our book plate, this tiny monument is enough to establish the calibre of its original and the authenticity of the reverence in which it was held.

"When you stand before this statue," says Dion Chrysostomos (*Orat.* XII.14), "you forget every misfortune of our earthly life, even though you have been broken by adversities and grief, and sleep shuns your eyes. . . ." In other places, we hear that the fame of the *Zeus* went through all lands, that it was the unrivaled statue, and stood as the symbol and guardian of Hellas.

Like the *Athena Parthenos,* the *Zeus* remained in position for nearly a thousand years. In 426 A.D., the Emperor Theodosius the 2nd issued his decree calling for the destruction of all remaining pagan temples. That order seems actually to have been carried out at Olympia at least to the extent of putting the torch to the wooden roof and other inflammable parts of the building. It may be that the *Zeus* perished in the fire, but there is a rumor it was taken off to Constantinople, where it burned with the palace in which it stood about 475 A.D.

Left as we are with nothing but a coin and a gem to give us any adequate notion of Phidias's major works, it is tempting to make as much as we can of the architectural sculptures from the Parthenon. Opinions vary as to the extent they may be used as an indication of his personal style. They are certainly unusually fine for the purpose to which they were put, but the whole weight of probability warns us that Phidias can have had very little to do with them at first hand, and perhaps nothing. Any interpretation which connects them with himself must be put forward with the utmost reserve — and is thus useful only for the most general and superficial kind of analysis.

That being so, is there any hope of recovering one of the less celebrated monuments? The wish to do so amounts to strong pressure on every student of archaeology, and the hope for a positive result begets a tendency among the best of men to stretch every item of evidence to the limit. Such an instance is Adolf Furtwängler's reconstruction of the *Athena Lemnia,* conducted in 1891 and described in his *Masterpieces of Greek Sculpture* which appeared under the Scribner imprint in 1895.

The *Athena Lemnia,* we know from literature, was a bronze statue that stood on the Acropolis. It seems to have been dedicated between 451 and 448 by some Athenians who were leaving their native city to establish a colony on the Island of Lemnos. Pausanius (I.28.2) declares it to have been Phidias's most remarkable work. His statement might be discounted were it not for the fact that Lucian (*Images,* 4) once said he preferred it to all the other works of Phidias. Lucian was a good critic, and his opinion is repeated by every other critic. The *Lemnia* was preferred by some to Praxiteles's *Aphrodite of Knidos,* the most famous female nude in history, and there is good reason to believe that the *Lemnia* is the statue habitually referred to as " the Beautiful." If such opinions were entertained by competent men who knew the great chryselephantine cult statues, it is obvious there must have been something exquisite about the *Athena Lemnia.*

We need not take space for a detailed recapitulation of Furtwängler's argument. Suffice it to say that the head shown in our Figs. 5.6–8 is of a type known in several marble copies, and on a gem. In several museums there existed some draped bodies recognizable as Athenas because they wore the *aegis*, but all these bodies either had been restored with heads that did not belong, or lacked heads altogether.

Two of the bodies were at Dresden. In 1891, it was decided to correct the erroneous modern repairs. In the course of that work, it occurred to Furtwängler to try the experiment of fitting a cast of the *Bologna Head* into one of the statues at Dresden. "The Bologna bust fitted into the hollowed torso," he says, "as exactly as if it had been made for it, hardly a millimetre of alteration being necessary." He later observed that head and body were carved from the same marble.

The *Bologna Head* had not previously been recognized as an Athena; but under the circumstances just set forth, no other conclusion seemed reasonable. The identification of the newly reconstructed statue as reflective of the *Athena Lemnia* depends upon the oddity that, of all the Athenas famous in Antiquity, the *Lemnia* was the only one without a helmet. "Phidias substituted beauty for the helmet" in this instance — or at least so runs one of the epigrams.

The *Bologna Head,* presuming it to be of Roman workmanship, is in a class by itself among marble copies. Nothing we possess so nicely fulfills our hope of Phidias in his gentler, more lyrical moments. Nothing so charming has ever been so chaste, nor anything so strong half so winsome. These circumstances lure us into sympathy with Furtwängler's hypothesis even while sober judgment tells us to hold back. The fact is that the identification rests on descriptive evidence of the very slightest kind, and the mechanical fit of the *Bologna Head* into the torso at Dresden may mean nothing more than the custom of a particular Roman shop. Many another head might, if we pursued the matter to the end, be found to drop quite as neatly into the same cavity.

Whatever else we may think of it, the *Bologna Head* of *Furtwängler's Athena Lemnia* (as we must call it if we are going to be cautious) is equal to Greek work in quality, and a splendid demonstration of the developed style of the Greek Fifth Century.

The delicacy of the subject and the taste of the workmanship tend to obscure our realization of the stylistic facts. The severity of the classical profile has, it is true, been softened somewhat by subtler contours and by the gentle texture of the lovely marble from which it is carved. The cylindrical forehead is still there, however, and the hard clean edge where the sinuses meet its contour. The hair, while more free than in earlier work, is in fact a sculptor's abstraction intended merely to suggest softness rather than represent it. The contour of every surface, moreover, is made to take a smooth, true curve which necessarily eliminates the lines, convexities, hollows, and the innumerable other irregularities inevitably present on the body of any living model. The subdivisions of the head are very nearly in symmetrical balance as well, each curve having its equal and opposite with a precision of balance never seen in nature.

Because most educated adults have been accustomed to Greek sculpture since childhood, these peculiarities of style are usually accepted without comment, or not even noted as peculiarities. It is therefore necessary to give strong emphasis to the fact that the *Athena Lemnia* may not properly be described as realistic, or even by the more general term of *naturalism*. It retains enough resemblance to the human female to preclude our confusing it with anything else, but it is actually at several removes from representative art. Had the process of abstracting and idealizing been carried only a little further, Fifth Century sculpture would have arrived at something very close to modern Cubism.

In drawing conclusions from all that has gone before, it is evident that *as an artist* we know almost nothing about Phidias. As an idea, the reverse is true. The Phidian imagery for the Great Gods continued throughout Antiquity. It went on over into the Christian tradition almost without change. Michaelangelo's paintings of the Almighty differ only in detail from the *Olympian Zeus;* no one has ever suggested the conception was unwise or unworthy. In the whole tradition of Western art, we may, in fact, recognize the constant force of a Phidian ideal, for it is he rather than any other artist who best personifies Greece.

POLYCLEITOS

Polycleitos flourished at the same time as Phidias. He was a citizen of Argos, and did the great chryselephantine *Hera* for the Temple of Hera at Argos, to replace an earlier cult image destroyed by fire in 422 B.C. For the most part, however, he worked on athletic statues. A number of signed bases were found at Olympia, and we may guess that Polycleitos, true to his southern origin, carried forward into the Great Age the Dorian tradition noted during the Archaic Period.

Inadequate reflections of the *Hera* appear on coins. We can also recognize in several Roman copies a reflection of that very *Diadumenos* (Fig. 5.10) Lucian places in the collection of Eucrates the Magnificent. Neither of these monuments have anything like the interest and importance of another which we find reflected in a full-size marble copy at Naples, a fine bronze bust in the same place, and on a grave relief in the National Museum at Athens.

We refer to the so-called *Doryphoros* (Fig. 5.9) which Pliny (*Natural History* XXXIV.55) describes as "a boy of manly form bearing a lance, called *The Canon* by artists who draw from it the rudiments of art as from a code, so that Polycleitos is held to be the only man who has embodied art itself in a work of art."

The last part of Pliny's statement gives us the key to Polycleitos's position in the history of art. In addition to being much respected as a sculptor, he was the chief aesthetic philosopher of Greece, and from his theories others were eager to learn. Lysippos himself declared that Polycleitos's work had been his "school," and there are others who say the same thing.

Polycleitos evidently made a specialty of Olympic victors (the *Doryphoros* almost certainly falls in that category) because such subject matter gave him an unparalleled opportunity for life-long study of superior human bodies. At the height of his career, he published a theory of proportion as applied to the body. It may or may not be true that the *Doryphoros* is the particular statue executed to demonstrate the rules; but if not, we have small cause for worry. Polycleitos, according to all accounts, worked for refinement along a single theme, and the less discriminating members of the ancient community sometimes complained that all his statues were very much alike.

Polycleitos's Canon of Proportions

A number of ancient writers refer more or less definitely to Polycleitos's theory of proportions. "Chrysippos holds beauty to consist in the proportions not of the elements but of the parts," says Galen (*De Plac. Hipp. et Plat.* 5). "That is to say, of finger to finger and of all the fingers to the palm and the wrist, and of all these to the forearm, and of the forearm to the upper arm, and of all parts to each other, as they are set forth in the canon of Polycleitos." Obviously, he is merely (and probably correctly) attaching Polycleitos's name to the sentiment expressed by Plato in the *Timaeus* (31): "And the fairest bond is that which makes the most complete fusion of itself and the things which it combines; and proportion is best adapted to effect such a union. For whenever in any three numbers, whether cube or square, there is a mean, which is to the last term what the first is to it; and again, when the mean is to the first term as the last term is to the mean — then the mean becoming first and last and the first and last both becoming means, they will all of them of necessity come to the same, and having become the same with one another will all be one."

While suggestive, those statements are difficult; and the reader may be forgiven if he fails to see how they might be applied to art. He will be happy to turn to Vitruvius, the only extant text that attempts to supply the data which might enable an artist to apply such ideas to the practical problems of the studio. In the first chapter of Book III, he tries to tell us what fraction of a man's total height ought to be allotted to the different parts of the body. The length of the foot should be $\frac{1}{6}$ of the height, he says; and $\frac{1}{10}$ the height should be the measure of the distance from the wrist to the tip of the middle finger. After mentioning some other proportions, he suggests a more general proposition; namely, that if we take the navel as a center and describe a circle, the extended arms and feet will fall on its circumference. This latter notion has been honored more than once by some of our greatest artists, who have drawn up figures to illustrate it. One may doubt whether such proved useful, for the truth is that Vitruvius was badly mixed up and did not understand the subject he purported to explain. He says just enough, in fact, to drive one crazy.

His garbled statements have nevertheless been sufficient to make the recovery of Polycleitos's system one of the major endeavors of modern scholarship. In 1416 or 1417, the Florentine humanist Poggio took a walking trip in quest of classical manuscripts. In the neglected library at the remote monastery of Saint Gall in Switzerland, he found a copy of Vitruvius, and thus set the whole research into motion. The first effort at recovery was attempted by no less a genius than Leon Battista Alberti. Piero della Francesca thought it worth his while to investigate proportion. The mathematician Luca Pacioli published a *Divina Proportione* in 1509. Similar studies were undertaken at about the same time by both Leonardo da Vinci (Fig. 5.11) and Albrecht Dürer. The quest still goes on. Mr. Jay Hambidge's *Dynamic Symmetry* and Miss Irma Richter's *Rhythmic Form* all derive from the Polycleitan tradition. Each author works with what he happens to fancy as *the golden section,* which is the magic-making name for Polycleitos's mathematics, whatever they were.

The several publications mentioned will prove interesting for every reader and fascinating for those adept with figures and diagrams. There is unmistakable merit in every point of view yet put forward, but we must recognize that we are not yet close to Polycleitos. Neither have we yet produced a practical formula for use by the artist. From the general welter of perplexity, a few helpful ideas nevertheless emerge and deserve to be stated.

All the authors seem to agree that beauty — at least as understood by Polycleitos — was no simple quality of an object. It had to do with the fact of relation and interrelation. " Nothing simple and devoid of parts can be beautiful," said Plotinus (*Enneads,* I.IV.i), " only a composite."

Another feature of the theory, and one upon which the ancients set great store, appears to have been the idea of making all magnitudes commensurate. A fundamental unit, or *module,* was chosen. Every dimension of the body then had to be expressible in even multiples of the module. Polycleitos's module remains to be identified. There are those who think it was a unit of volume, not a unit of linear measure. The chief purpose of the module, it also ought to be mentioned, may have been utilitarian rather than aesthetic: uniform standards of linear measure were not established as they now are, and it was often necessary to establish a new unit for each job that came to hand.

It seems clear, also, that Polycleitos derived his theory by some sort of statistical procedure. Living models, it seems, were measured one after another for a very long period of time. The measurements were then combined somehow, and the result was set forth as a table. Because Vitruvius, Alberti, and many others have interpreted the process as a systematic effort to determine nature's true and sacred intention (she being visualized as the Goddess of Art), it is important to appreciate that Polycleitos probably realized as well as we do that nature is impartial as between the beautiful and ugly, producing both with an even hand. In this connection, we might remember the words of an Athenian who was very hard to fool. "When you want to represent beautiful figures," said Socrates to the painter Parrhasios (*Memorabilia,* III.8), "since it is not easy to find one person with every part perfect, do you not select out of many the most beautiful parts of each, and thus represent figures beautiful in every part?" "We do so," said the painter. Polycleitos's method, in short, aimed at no average result; he stacked the cards in favor of his own intuitive concept of the beautiful.

What started Polycleitos on his research? What keeps the research going? The answer is to be sought in the intellectual atmosphere of 5th-Century Greece; and if we look there, it is plain enough. However indirectly all such thinking derives from the theory of numbers which was the chief contribution of Pythagoras (latter half of the 6th Century B.C.). This theory asserts that numbers have a real and objective existence, and are fundamental in the universe. The idea sounds cold and narrow at first, but no utterance of the human mind has proven more profound. Every modern theory of matter and all theories of wave-motion relate to it. Even in Antiquity, it inspired some transcendent researches.

One of these, and doubtless the one that set Polycleitos on his way, was the Pythagorean theory of music. Pythagoras and his associates investigated the vibration of taut strings and demonstrated that such were lawful: the number of vibrations varies inversely according to the length of the string. With this information in hand, it was possible to define the intervals of the scale.

The concept of universal law is the inspiring part of the discovery — even more inspiring to the Greeks, perhaps, than to ourselves for we lack their complete faith in conceptual thinking. How wonderfully beautiful must be the supersensory laws by which we can explain music, the primeval art, the most natural and widely felt, the least definite but most connotative! If music be lawful, it ought to be possible for painters, sculptors, and architects to discover analogous laws, principles which have always existed and always have been true. The whole idea still fills the imagination with life, and doubtless was the vision that moved Polycleitos to his great effort.

Not knowing Polycleitos's theory, we cannot say whether he actually produced an analysis of art comparable to the precise definitions and distinctions long established within the field of music. In attempting to appreciate what he was about, it is of the essence to realize that the musical scale analyzed by Pythagoras, and the bodily proportions studied by Polycleitos, were both in general use and giving satisfaction before the researchers began their work. As to whether such matters may or may not be orderly, we do well to remind ourselves of a sage remark once set down by Alberti: " It is a common error of ignorance," said he, " to maintain that what one does not know does not exist."

The proportions of the *Doryphoros* are naturally of special interest, but at first seem strange to the modern observer. The head compares to the height in the ratio of 1 to 6.84, a numeral that has more decimal places than significant figures. The general aspect of the body has often been characterized as " square "; and by all ordinary standards, it is indeed very stocky.

At least two reasons may be adduced to account for the popularity of so ponderous a figure-style. Hand-to-hand fighting with the short sword was the fundamental of Greek warfare; when such work was afoot, the *Doryphoros* would be a better man to follow than to face. Sculpture being an art of mass, moreover, weight is the chief means by which the artist can evoke an impression of force and power, and it is notable that heavy proportions have almost always been employed by those sculptors whom we think of as taking a special interest in the theory of sculpture as such.

Whether the modern reader finds Polycleitos's method congenial or not, all the ancient evidence says that the greatest Greek artists found his Canon useful. We must therefore take it seriously; and it is a pity that so important a theory should have its chief visual demonstration in the Naples copy of the *Doryphoros* (Fig. 5.9), which is admittedly the product of a Roman copy factory of the second or third rank. By making a strong effort of the imagination we can, however, gain some notion of the original.

The Naples copy suffers from being executed in marble. In the original bronze, one would not be annoyed by the adventitious value contrasts resulting from the dark shadows cast by the overhang of every muscular contour. In bronze, these abrupt and almost linear boundaries would be almost necessary as an aid for reading the modeling.

According to all ancient testimony, the work of Polycleitos was distinguished even in that great era for unusual subtlety of technique. His enigmatic remark to the effect that the labor was hardest when the surface came "under the nail" probably refers to the infinite pains he devoted to the modeling of the wax surface of the form from which he cast his bronzes. But beauty of surface, sadly enough, is distinguished largely by its absence in the Naples marble copy, and we can only do our best to imagine what that statue might look like had the copyist been Desiderio or Verrocchio. The bronze bust also in Naples and signed by Apollonious helps in that endeavor, but not much. Unless some new copy comes out of the earth, the celebrated refinement of Polycleitos has gone with the wind.

In the end we are as usual put into the position of having to be content with general conclusions of the kind we may legitimately draw from the inferior monumental evidence available. Nothing could be harder on Polycleitos. Both the literature and the Roman copies say the same thing; namely, that he was an artist incapable of ostentation. The excellence of his statues was the excellence of superb technique devoted not to superficial appeal, but to the service of profound convictions in the matter of design. With that in mind, we may perhaps open our eyes to greater beauty in the *Doryphoros* than at first seemed possible.

Knowing it as we must at an archaeological remove, the great remaining merit of the statue is in the pose. The *Doryphoros* is presented as walking slowly forward with the poise and rhythm of the athlete who is also a dancer. By comparison, the familiar stop-in-action pose used by Myron and others seems lacking in finesse. Movement is here actually represented, but the overall ease of attitude and the relaxation of the pace cancel out any worry that might be suggested by the inertia of the medium.

The statics of the *Doryphoros* are hardly less interesting. The body is given a slight twist to our left. The supporting leg is on the side of the arm that hangs slack, and the tensed arm above the leg that is eased. The arrangement gives the torso a delicate, sinuous curvature. It also makes it necessary that some muscles be slightly stretched while others are compressed, a situation that produces an infinitely varied modulation of contour.

It is evident the ancients were not mistaken in their estimate of Polycleitos. He had neither Myron's dash nor Phidias's majesty, but his grasp of formal relationships was perhaps deeper and more subtle than theirs. His place in ancient art is comparable to the station later occupied by Verrocchio, the greatest teacher of great masters that the modern world has known.

THE FOURTH CENTURY

Differences of a fundamental nature separate the Greek Fourth Century from the era before it. The whole land had suffered terribly during the Peloponnesian War (431–404) and the plagues which accompanied it. The new century thus started with treasuries low and with the population decreased. The effects of the long drawn out war were accentuated by prolonged instability in political life. The Spartan hegemony, the Athenian League against Sparta, the period of Theban control, and finally the rise of Macedon complete the century.

For art history, the most conspicuous result of these conditions is the abandonment of large public buildings. In Ionia, it is true, several big temples went up — notably that of Artemis at Ephesus (after 356) and the *Didyma* near Miletus (about 330); but on the Greek peninsula, the absence of important buildings seems to reflect a general loss of confidence in civic enterprise.

The Greek genius was by no means asleep, however. With Plato (429–347) and Aristotle (384–321), philosophy attained a new and nobler eminence. The century also produced its great artists, as already listed above, but their art was of a new and more introspective kind.

Because there were no important temples to call great cult statues into being, certain changes took place in the general run of subject matter. The Great Gods had been the typical subject of the Fifth Century; the Fourth turned appropriately away from these toward material of a more intimate nature. Gods, when they appear in Fourth Century art, are the lesser divinities. Even these divinities are softened, humanized, and presented not at moments from the heroic past, but in activities evocative of charm, grace, and elegance. Epic glory is the business of the Fifth Century; lyrical loveliness belongs to the Fourth.

Personal portraits, hitherto conceived and executed as public monuments when done at all, became for the first time an important part of the artist's business. All too few originals have survived, but it is obvious that considerable realism must have been wanted. Lysippos, for example, is said to have used casts taken from the model as an aid in the studio, but a statement of Aristotle's (*Poetics* 15) shows that idealism was far from being out of fashion. The " good portrait painters," he takes it for granted, " reproduce the distinctive features of a man, and without losing the likeness, make him handsomer than he is." Doubtless those who followed that advice prospered then as now.

Allegory also became a very popular category of subject matter. The mythological narratives used for pedimental sculpture had always been allegorically understood, to be sure; but the pediments, if properly interpreted, had a plain purpose of a social and ethical nature. The new allegories were of another kind. Lysippos did a famous and typical one, his statue of *Opportunity*. It carried a razor to encourage keenness. It flew on the wings of the wind. The back of the head was kept shaven as smooth as a billiard ball to prevent any grabbing by those who saw it only as it went by. Assuming that our notices are correct, any statue capable of giving so complex an impression was a clever piece of work, but the allegory comes close to existing by and for itself. We may infer that the patrons of the Fourth Century were sometimes more interested in refining the process of thought than in drawing important conclusions.

The general tendency of Greek life to change from a heroic to a more humane experience is also well illustrated by the growth of the sanctuary of Asklepios at Epidauros (near Mycenae). Asklepios was the god of healing. Although his shrine was an old one, it had never been in big business before the Fourth Century, but by 350 or thereabout, the traffic of patients and visitors justified the construction of a temple to the God, a large gymnasium, a 180-room hotel built around four courtyards, and the finest of all Greek theatres. So far as we can tell, every kind of Greek medicine from the worst to the best was available there; and the place remained a popular resort throughout Antiquity.

Such was the atmosphere in which Fourth Century art flourished. Its definitive master was Praxiteles.

PRAXITELES

Pausanius was at Olympia some time during the latter half of the 2nd Century A.D. In addition to what he had to say about the important things to be noted there by future visitors, he set down a passing note (V.17.3) which recounts without comment, "In later times other offerings were dedicated in the Heraion. Among these was a *Hermes* of marble, bearing the infant Dionysos, the work of Praxiteles."

On May 8, 1877, a marble statue came to light as the earth was cleared from the floor of the temple (Figs. 5.12–13). It was obviously a Hermes carrying an infant, and the style was in perfect correspondence with everything hitherto known or inferred about the work of Praxiteles. The piece was immediately attributed to him, and remains the only statue which can possibly be an original from the hand of any artist whom the Greeks themselves recognized as a great master.

The remarkable condition of the monument is accountable, paradoxically enough, to the unusually poor construction of the Temple of Hera in which it stood. The Heraion was a very old temple, perhaps the oldest we have, and its cella walls were made from sun-dried brick. After the roof was gone, the rain gradually converted the bricks back into clay. When the statue was overthrown, presumably by the earthquakes of the 6th Century A.D., there seems already to have been a deep, soft bed of mud ready to receive it. Thus we have it intact except for the two legs below the knee, the right forearm, and both arms of the child.

Hermes is presented as in the act of taking the baby Dionysos to the Nymphs of Mount Nysa, by which ladies he was brought up. The god is apparently in no hurry and perhaps even a bit bored with his assignment. He stops for a moment to ease the muscles of the left side by resting his elbow on a convenient tree stump, and he whiles away the time by amusing the youngster with something held high in the right hand, possibly a bunch of grapes.

While very weighty by modern standards, the canon of proportions is more slender than that used by Phidias or Polycleitos. The greater length of the body invites experiment with curvature, and the action taken throws the whole form into a pronounced S-curve. The pose is no different in principle from that of the *Doryphoros,* but the desire for elegance is more obvious and certainly far more overt. Curvature of this order of magnitude, it should be noted, was not peculiar to Praxiteles but is characteristic of all Fourth Century masters. The personal factor is the cultivation of grace for its own sake, and the winsome but nostalgic mood.

Aside from the more slender canon of proportions and the pronounced curve of the pose, the most conspicuous element of style has to do with the textures. These are differentiated with a new and almost incredible subtlety. The story is told that the statue was set upright and photographed as soon as found, and copies of the prints went posthaste to Berlin. One of the experts called in to see them complained, it is said, at the stupidity of photographing the *Hermes* in such haste. Someone, said he, should have taken the trouble to remove the cloth from the tree stump.

Unimportant in itself, the anecdote suggests much about Praxiteles. The bold summary modeling of the Fifth Century has been replaced by discrimination carried to its ultimate conclusion. Whereas Fifth Century sculptors aimed to make a clear, unmistakable, and heroic statement, Praxiteles wants to miss no least nuance of beauty. The contours of the body are lovingly rendered in modulations so subtle as to defy resolution by the eye alone; the hands must feel the surface if we are to comprehend in any adequate fashion the full measure of the author's skill.

The more detailed modeling and the greater variation between textures has an effect rather startling by comparison to Fifth Century sculpture. One feels a vivid impression of actuality and human warmth. At first this may be mistaken for realism, but it is such only in a limited and comparative sense. *Hermes'* hair is modeled freely, for example; and its surface is very different from the areas of flesh. At the same time the hair is abstracted into bunches or locks, as we may care to call them. From a little distance, these take the light rather as hair does, but closely inspected each will be seen to be a small mass defined by orderly contours and twisted in a spiral fashion. The eyes, the lips, and the nostrils show a similar tendency to regularize every curve and make it graceful. The fact is that the *Hermes* is a humanization of an ideal type, not an idealization from the living model.

While the general opinion accepts the *Hermes* almost without question as a Praxitelean original, it is all too seldom stated that the attribution rests upon what is believed to be the probability, not upon what can objectively be shown as a certainty. Although the majority view is probably correct, it is important to furnish the reader with some of the outstanding reservations which make it possible to entertain reasonable doubts of the statue's authenticity.

The only external evidence for Praxiteles's authorship is Pausanius's passing statement; the value of that may be impeached. In the first place Pausanius was not a contemporary critic; he visited Olympia some six centuries after Praxiteles. He was a visitor, moreover, and not a citizen of the place. Like all tourists, he may have got his information about the authorship from some ignorant and irresponsible guide of the sort all too familiar today. Unlike Lucian, Pausanius was hardly enough of a connoisseur to make or to suspect attributions on the basis of his own observation.

The style of the *Hermes* fits perfectly with everything we believe to be typical of Praxiteles, but this internal evidence is a bit deceptive also. In the absence of any other original, " what we believe to be typical of Praxiteles " is a very general idea indeed. As compared to the visual data available for the study of most modern masters, we have next to nothing to go on. Connoisseurship in the ordinary sense of minute comparison is impossible.

It means rather little, in any case, to find a statue of Praxitelean style. The great Fourth Century Praxiteles was the most popular artist of the ancient world. His style was imitated everywhere and anywhere for a very long time, as Raphael's style was to be later. Conceivably, the *Hermes* might have been executed by some Hellenistic artist trained to imitate Praxiteles.

The circumstances just cited are made the more cogent by the fact that Praxiteles, while not now a common name, was more or less frequent in Greece. We know of other artists called Praxiteles. Some of them seem to have been descendants. Doubtless these would feel a strong temptation to capitalize upon the genius of the founder of their house by perpetuating his style as long as possible.

Loopholes in the evidence must be conceded to exist. It has even been suggested that the marble *Hermes* Pausanius says he saw was a marble replica put there by way of consolation and penance by the collector lucky enough to acquire an original *Hermes* of bronze; if so, Pausanius cannot be relied upon to know the difference.

Against such a view, the chief argument is the superior workmanship of the *Hermes,* which all concede to have set a new and higher standard. The statue is superior in that respect to anything of comparable date, though not better than a number of Hellenistic items which, while equal from the standpoint of technique, hardly measure up in content and spirit.

Having done our duty by telling the reader both sides, we may conclude by saying that the attribution is still accepted in most quarters.

Praxiteles' most famous statue was the *Aphrodite of Knidos.* The goddess was represented as nude, with one hand in front of her. There are reflections on Knidian coins of Roman date, and these show her standing beside a large urn over which she has dropped her drapery — and with the folded surface thereof, her smooth body must have made a vivid contrast.

All the ancient authors unite in celebrating her charm. Pliny (*Natural History* XXXVI.20) flatly says she was the finest statue in the world. Lucian (*Images* 6) speaks specifically of the " finely penciled eyebrows " and the " melting gaze of the eyes with their bright and joyous expression."

A good many other pieces of sculpture were accumulated by the citizens of Knidos, but the *Aphrodite* outshone them all. In 84 B.C., Sulla laid heavy levies upon Knidos; and King Nikomedes of Bythinia offered to defray the entire public debt, enormous as it was, in return for the statue. But, says Pliny, the Knidians preferred " to undergo the worst "; and presumably their *Aphrodite* continued to stand there in her open shrine lending fame and loveliness to the island.

No replicas of acceptable quality have been found. The best known is a Roman copy in the Vatican, which reproduces the pose as shown on the coins. After knowing the *Hermes,* it is very hard to reconcile oneself to that coarse statue. The *Von Kaufmann Head* in Berlin is a little better, and casts are sometimes made with this head upon the Vatican body. The resulting statue is still a great disappointment. We must unhappily admit that the wonderful original is still very far off.

The *Bartlett Aphrodite* in the Boston Museum (Figs. 5.14–15) goes far, however, to ameliorate the situation just outlined. It may one day be established as a Praxitelean original. The chief argument against it is the fact that the skull structure is less massive than most Fourth Century work. The chief arguments for it are the workmanship, which is as good as the *Hermes*, and the inexpressible charm which almost spells out the name Praxiteles.

Because the mood is more pensive than joyous, it seems likely that we have here another *Aphrodite*, and not the one from Knidos. The dreamy loveliness of the gentle face is intensely feminine, not in itself emotional but extending the strongest appeal to emotion.

In producing such an effect, the sculptor must necessarily allow his hand to be guided largely by feeling and intuition, but calculation enters into the method to a very great extent nevertheless. For the general understanding of the Fourth Century style, and its differences from that of Phidias and Polycleitos, the *Bartlett Aphrodite* must be compared in some detail with the *Athena Lemnia*.

The expressive power of the *Lemnia* (Figs. 5.6–8) is produced almost exclusively by plastic means. We may define *plastic* as referring to tangible masses, and to the shape thereof. Sculpture is often called " the plastic art " because the sculptor either carves stone or wood into the desired shape, builds the shape up with clay, or casts the shape in bronze. In the end, he depends upon the shape of his statue for whatever merit it may have.

From the standpoint of the observer, sculpture of a perfectly plastic kind is susceptible of inspection by the sense of touch. A blind man in a completely darkened room would not, for instance, find it overly difficult to form a very good notion of the *Lemnia* merely by feeling it with his fingers. It follows that in the complicated psychological process by which we make ourselves familiar with works of art, those which depend upon plastic means necessarily excite the sense of touch. If we feel stimulation of that sense, we say that the work has *tactile value*. It should be understood, also, that while tactile values are primarily the province of the sculptor, it is possible for painters (Giotto, for example) to define mass vigorously and explicitly, thus getting much the same effect.

A detailed look at the *Bartlett Aphrodite* will show that while subtly plastic over some fields, the Fourth Century sculptor was using quite another method for certain passages.

If we look at the flesh surfaces alone, the Bartlett head is for the most part quite as plastic as the *Athena Lemnia.* The obvious difference can be explained without referring to any other mode of expression. The contours of *Lemnia* are simplified in summary fashion, and the transitions are bold and abrupt. The contours of the *Aphrodite* are a study in the nuances of modulation, and the various surfaces flow into each other.

It is in the hair that we see the most obvious departure from means that may be interpreted as plastic. The hair of the *Lemnia,* as we were at pains to point out at the time, communicates the idea of texture by an actual modeling of the marble; we could understand it by feeling it. The hair of the Bartlett head extends deeper into the third dimension and seems much less of a mere surface treatment, but the very qualities which at first may be thought to depend upon modeling actually depend upon the play of light and dark. It is not the marble surface of the hair which gives the impression of soft bulk and texture, but the shadows produced by undercutting the larger locks and roughening the surface in general. The effect depends, in short, upon the existence of normal light conditions rather than upon the manipulation of mass.

What is true of the hair is also true of the facial expression. The sculptor has broadened the bridge of the nose near the forehead, and has sunk eyes abnormally deep into the skull. The eyeballs do not protrude as anatomy says they must, and the eyelids are reduced in thickness. The result is to lose the eye, as it were, in a dark shadow, and we read the result as facial expression of a certain kind. It is doubtful whether the fingertips of a blind man would, by going over the surface, impart anything like the same impression, if indeed he could make sense of the Bartlett head at all.

Some critics have used the word *coloristic* whenever sculpture depends upon light and dark rather than modeling. Others would apply the adjective *pictorial* to situations like the one just reviewed, their reason being that pictures demand the use of the eye and that the eye is also needed to pick up any effect in sculpture which depends upon light and dark as distinct from shape. It seems unwise to use either term in such a way. *Coloristic* has always been a tricky word, and *pictorial* is better reserved for reliefs that attempt spatial representation, like those of the Romans and like those of Ghiberti. For a manipulation of light and dark of the sort seen on the Bartlett head, no accepted name exists, and it is merely necessary to explain in each instance that shadows do the work.

It is obvious from all that has gone before that Praxiteles was at his best when doing statues of women, and that his finely-drawn style was actually inappropriate for subject matter that demanded heroics. His special gift was to open the eyes of Greece to daintiness, grace, and charm; he is, in fact, the very first artist in the history of the world who made charm a primary aim. The possible weakness of such an art is obvious, but if we may judge by the *Bartlett Aphrodite,* no artist has ever offered us a more perfect appreciation of the peculiar loveliness that belongs only to lovely women.

Although we have lost the *Aphrodite of Knidos,* that statue in itself was enough to give Praxiteles an unchallenged place in the history of European art. Knowing very little about the original, it is impossible to say precisely what the sculptor's intention may have been. Did he have it in mind to celebrate the goddess Aphrodite in her aspect as a religious figure? Was he merely indulging his great endowments in the matter of texture and modeling to produce something of surpassing physical beauty? Or was the statue popular because of erotic overtones?

At one time or another, each and every possibility of the female nude, including those just listed, has since been exploited to the full by countless painters and sculptors. No other figure has been so popular in art, but before Praxiteles, the subject hardly occurred. It is he, therefore, who introduced it to the history of art and made it part of our cultural idiom.

SCOPAS

The art of Scopas is still unknown unless we take the liberty of drawing conclusions from sparse evidence of an admittedly shaky kind. Literary sources make the man out to have been a wanderer. He worked in the Peloponnesus, and in Ionia. He seems to have been an architect as well as a sculptor, and from the date of the buildings with which the authors associate him, he must have been at the height of his career about the middle of the 4th Century B.C.

The only line of inquiry that has led directly to sculpture in what may be the Scopasian manner stems from Pausanius. When noting down his impressions of a visit to the Temple of Athena Alea at Tegea, about 25 miles north of Sparta, Pausanius (VIII.45.4 & 46.1) says, "I was told the architect was Scopas of Paros, who was the sculptor of many statues in different parts of Greece proper and also in Ionia and Karia." It will be noted that Pausanius assumes no responsibility for the fact; he merely says he was told.

The temple at Tegea was a Doric edifice of peculiar beauty, or at least so it is said. It replaced an older temple that burned in 395 B.C., but the style of the architecture, with columns six diameters high and an echinus profile so tense as to approach a straight line, suggests a dating of about 360 to 350 — which would be consistent with Scopas's presence there.

The temple stood for about 700 years, and was destroyed by Alaric the

Goth during the 4th Century A.D. The vandalism must have been unusually savage. Four separate efforts at excavation, beginning in 1879 and extending to 1913, have yielded only fragmentary remains. From the pediments in particular, we have only a few battered heads. The rest of the statuary must have been broken up at considerable effort, possibly for reduction to lime.

Battered as they are, these poor fragments nevertheless exhibit a figure-style that is markedly different from the general run of Greek sculpture. It is necessary to assume the work, or at least the direction, of some powerful personality with ideas of his own. If he was eminent both as sculptor and architect, we may fairly hazard a guess that Scopas would be inclined to exert a more detailed supervision over the sculpture for one of his temples than might be the case with the ordinary run of architects. And if that is so, then probably the original and individual style of these heads is his.

Seen either in full face or in profile, the heads from Tegea (Figs. 5.17–18) make a strangely " square " impression, and would in fact fit neatly into a cubical box. The vertical dimension is relatively less than any other Greek heads, and the nose is shorter. The Tegean fragments retain enough of the neck to show that the head had a strong twist on the body, and that the gaze was directed slightly upward. The eye is put back into shadow by sinking it deep into the skull, but the method is applied vigorously rather than with finesse: the sinuses overhang the eye-sockets in great rolls of muscle. The nostrils are slightly dilated, and the mouth is opened a little — both latter features suggesting a stronger breathing appropriate to action or excitement.

The subject matter of the eastern pediment had been the *Calydonian Boar Hunt*. The hero of that event was Meleager, who had been one of the Argonauts. When Artemis became angry at his father, the King of Calydon, and sent an immense wild boar to ravage the land, Meleager assembled a band of heroes and killed the beast. He gave its head to the virgin huntress Atalanta, whom he loved, and thus set into motion the series of jealous events which resulted in his death.

Now boar hunting always has been and remains the sport of kings. The wild boar is native in Europe and North Africa, and the domestic pig will, if permitted to run wild, revert to type in a few generations. No other European animal is half so dangerous to the hunter, and yet boars may be killed in comparative safety by men who have the nerve and skill. Traditionally, they are run with dogs, brought to bay, and dispatched with a heavy spear. The risk comes when a ferocious boar charges, for the hunter then will have no second chance if he fails to drive the spear home.

We have several marble statues of a youth who appears to carry a boar spear; sometimes there is a dog beside him. Meleager was, of course, the heroic prototype of all boar hunters, and the Meleager-subject suggests Scopas. Most of these statues show enough resemblance to the Tegean heads to make an association plausible.

The several statues in European collections have the usual coarseness of the routine Roman copy, but the *Harvard Meleager* (Fig. 5.16) is noticeably better. The modeling is sensitive, the anatomy full of vigor, and the pose dignified. If we are correct in associating the heads from Tegea with Scopas, this statue brings us closer to knowing him than any other we now possess.

The writers say that Scopas went off to Ionia, where he worked on the *Mausoleum* at Halicarnassos and on the Temple of Diana at Ephesos. Both buildings fall approximately in the middle of the 4th Century, and both included much sculpture. It is difficult to associate Scopas with the material preserved from these two places, but his influence may be felt in a very general way. Insofar as we have any right to particularize, a train of thought is suggested by the tradition that one of his famous statues was a *Raving Maenad*, possibly reflected in a very battered statue in Dresden. The Maenads were the mad women who accompanied Dionysos, and something can be made of the fact that Scopas was willing to undertake such a work.

The essence of the Maenad-subject is loss of control: the Maenads were traditionally supposed not only to be possessed, but were habitually in a violent state of intoxication. They flung themselves about in the wildest manner, half in ecstasy and half in torment. Obviously such material could not be handled within the limitations of conventional Greek sculpture. The statics hitherto thought appropriate for major statuary necessarily were tossed aside, and the direct representation of fast movement was accepted.

Even more important are the emotional and spiritual implications. Phidias had presented man as a creature of lofty calm for whom environment was a mere abstraction. Praxiteles made man conscious of his surroundings, but easy in his mind about them. Scopas admits conflict between humanity and the universe; his people feel and struggle.

Whether Scopasian or not, the reliefs from the frieze of the *Mausoleum*, now preserved in London, are surely in line with the general tendency just suggested. The narrative subject is the *Battle Between the Greeks and the Amazons*, and that combat is described in a manner well along the road toward realistic representation. Formal considerations (as, for example, the desirability of putting all heads on one level to maintain unbroken the architectural lines, as on the Parthenon frieze) are forgotten. The figures stand or fall, thrust and parry much as they might in actual hand-to-hand combat. The effect is spirited to a degree, but Greek dignity has gone by the board.

It was the mission of Scopas, if we have made him out correctly, to extend the subject matter of Greek art to include passion and action. By the same act, he destroyed the foundation of restraint which had hitherto kept sculpture moving straight down a predetermined road to greater and greater achievement.

LYSIPPOS

The career of Lysippos parallels that of Alexander the Great. Lysippos must have been born about 370 or earlier, because he began making portraits of the conqueror when the latter was a small boy. No other sculptor, it is said, could satisfy Alexander, who in the end forbade portraits by anyone else. The others capitalized the celebrated and almost effeminate beauty of his person; Lysippos alone was able to combine this with an impression of courage, intelligence, and power.

Of Lysippos's famous allegory *Opportunity,* we have already spoken. Among his other celebrated works was a *Heracles Epitrapezios,* so called because it was designed as a table decoration — it was a bronze statuette about a foot high, the hero being seated on a rock with a wine cup in one hand and his club in the other. By all accounts this tiny object conveyed an extraordinary sense of monumentality. " In how small a space," says Statius (*Silvae,* IV.6), " what illusion of great size! " The *Heracles* was a much sought-after collectors' item; it is said to have been owned successively by Alexander himself, by Hannibal, and by Sulla. Although we have more than one statuette of Heracles sitting on a rock, both style and details of the composition differ from the descriptions, and it is only on worn coins that we see anything suggestive of the original.

Lysippos apparently made his greatest reputation by doing monumental groups of figures in violent action. In this line, he appears to have anticipated an art form often cited as an innovation of the Hellenistic Period. One group showed about 25 Macedonians of the king's guard sacrificing themselves in a gallant defensive action. Another showed a troop of Alexander's horse, and still another included several four-horse chariots. Hunting scenes sometimes furnished a pretext for these elaborate works of art. Lysippos did a *Lion Hunt* for King Krateros, which was set up at Delphi, and he did at least one hunting scene which included a portrait of Alexander.

It is impossible to say whether Lysippos arranged his grandiose compositions in the form of a frieze, or as free-standing sculpture in omnifacial composition. The latter is more probable, judging by the *Laocöon,* the *Farnese Bull,* and other Hellenistic groups.

A fascinating possibility was opened up, however, when some seventeen marble sarcophagi were discovered in an underground tomb at Sidon in the year 1887. They are now preserved in the Ottoman Museum at Constantinople. One of them, the so-called *Alexander Sarcophagus* (Fig. 5.20), is of peculiar interest in the present connection. No one doubts that it is Greek work, and there is general agreement that it comes from the last quarter of the 4th Century — or within the possible lifetime of Lysippos. The practical limitations of sarcophagus-design preclude free-standing sculpture; friezes are the only arrangement possible. In shape, the *Alexander Sarcophagus* is like a miniature temple. On one long side and one short side, it shows Alexander hunting the lion and the leopard respectively. The other two sides show Alexander in battle with the Persians.

While no evidence now in our possession would permit a direct attribution to Lysippos, an association with him is almost unavoidable. The reliefs have dash and spirit of the sort required. The rendering of details is very finely executed, another thing the authors describe as characteristic, and more than one of the heads is unmistakably a portrait. If not specifically Lysippic, surely these reliefs are illustrative of the trend of style to which Lysippos himself belonged.

The trend itself is important, regardless of personalities. At this point in their history, it is evident that the Greek artists had made an end of the conventions with which the Great Age began. Their art had not ceased to be heroic, but abstraction of every kind was all but abandoned, and epic events were about to be represented as physical occurrences. Obviously, artistic taste was feeling an ever-stronger impulse toward actuality, one aspect of which is vividly illustrated by the sarcophagus under review.

The violent motion represented continues to be directed to the right and left only, in parallel with the background. The separate figures often overlap each other, however; and one feels that the sculptor is yearning for an art which permits the representation of space-in-depth. Such an impression is strongly enhanced by the fact that most of the figures were in color, and still retain their color. Faded as they are, the scenes look from a slight distance very much like painting. Under these circumstances, we find ourselves tending to read the blank marble of the background not as a neutral and impenetrable denial of space (which it had been in the pedimental compositions of the Fifth Century), but as the sky. From here, it will take only another move or two to arrive at an art which directly undertakes to represent space, to depict scenery, and to show the figure within a natural setting. That result was actually attained during the Hellenistic age, and a similar rendering has of course been habitual in European art since the Renaissance.

For Lysippos's figure-style, the evidence is discouraging. By the usual methods, but with something less than the usual weight of probability, two male statues can be associated with his name. They are the *Apoxyomenos* in the Vatican (Fig. 5.19) and the portrait of an athlete named *Agias,* apparently a Greek original of inferior quality, found at Delphi and now in the museum there.

It is hard to accept both statues as originating with the same sculptor. The differences have been rationalized in various ways: that both are portraits and reflect the personal appearance of two men who did not look alike; that the *Agias* is a contemporary derivative (a most unlikely assumption at this date) and differs from the other simply because the *Apoxyomenos* is a later Roman copy; or that the differences exist because one statue was an early Lysippos and the other done late in his career.

On the whole, it seems most likely that neither is within reaching distance of the master's personal work, but that both — to whatever extent they are alike — are " Lysippic " in the sense of reflecting his very great influence upon his sculptural successors for the remainder of Antiquity. Standing thus on thin ice, we may be forgiven for attempting to recognize in these two dull statues the elements of a new style.

The first thing to be noted is a new canon of proportions. Pliny (*Natural History,* XXXIV.65) attempts to give an account of Lysippos's theory, but his words betray a mixture of fact and hearsay. It is probably a waste of time to attempt making anything of them except in a very approximate way. If we do that, it appears that Lysippos used a more slender figure with a smaller head. It also appears that he was much concerned to give the onlooker a strong impression of the actuality of his figures: ". . . he represented them as they appeared to the eye," says Pliny in an otherwise confusing sentence.

The head of the *Apoxyomenos* measures about one-eighth the total height of the figure, a substantial difference from the Polycleitan proportion of one to seven or a little less. These measurements, moreover, are inseparably related to certain features of the pose. The longer legs invite more expressive movement of the entire body; and while not active, the figure gives the impression of muscles that have not yet relaxed after exercise. One has a feeling of tense nerves which express their condition in occasional shifts of the body, and the transfer of weight from one leg to the other.

Unquestionably these expedients result in making us feel that the sculptor intended to represent something alive, but much has been sacrificed to gain that end. Lysippos's athletes are neither gods nor heroes. They are simply young men, and tired young men at that. In the face of the *Apoxyomenos* there is a peculiar vulgarity hitherto utterly foreign to Greek art; it seems evident that the statue reflects the appearance of a particular man whose face was no better than it should be.

It is important to realize, in addition to all of this, that Lysippos is giving us an individual person as he appeared at a single instant of time — in contrast to the things we might remember as significant aspects of the sitter's personality or his character. The position taken by the artist is, in effect, a negation of both generalization and idealism. In scenes of action like those on the *Alexander Sarcophagus* (Fig. 5.20), the instantaneous view (probably what Pliny meant by " as they appeared to the eye ") is almost necessary and may pass unnoticed; in static figures like these, it thrusts itself forward as an artistic philosophy.

As such, it amounts to the artist's accepting visual experience as equivalent to artistic law. The work of art — within the practical limits of the medium in use — is required to maintain a one-to-one relationship with something the artist saw in nature. This, of course, is the position of the objective realist, and it would appear that Lysippos had gone very far in that direction. Because realism of all kinds, objective and otherwise, was destined to flourish during the Hellenistic Period, it is evident that the thinking of this last of the great masters had a far-reaching effect.

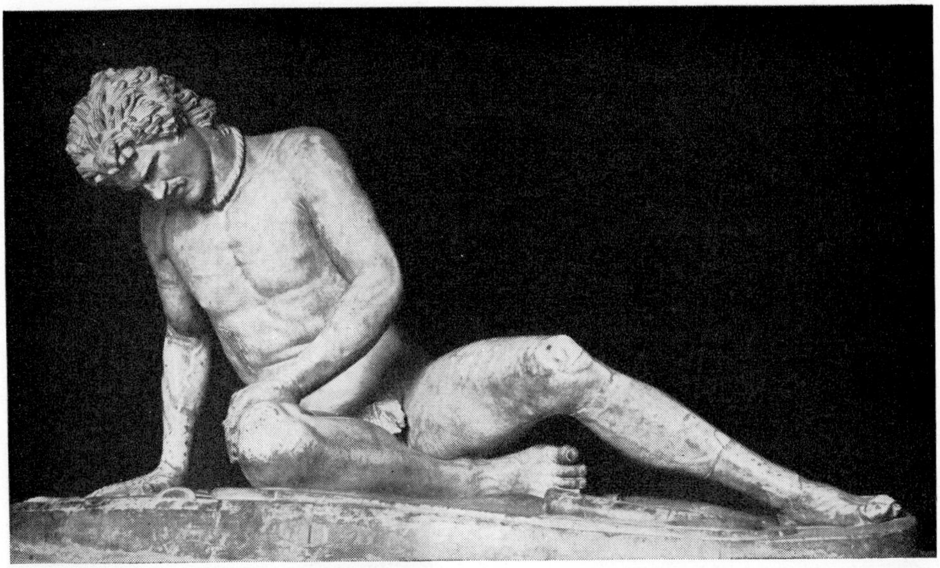

ANDERSON Fig. 6.1 Rome. Capitoline Museum. *The Dying Gaul.*

Fig. 6.2 New York. Metropolitan Museum. Old Woman going to Market.

GAB. FOT. NAZ.
Fig. 6.3 Rome. Lateran Museum. Rose Pillar.

Fig. 6.4 DEUTSCHEN ARCHAEOLOGISCHEN INSTITUT. Rome. Torlonia Museum. King Euthydemos of Bactria.

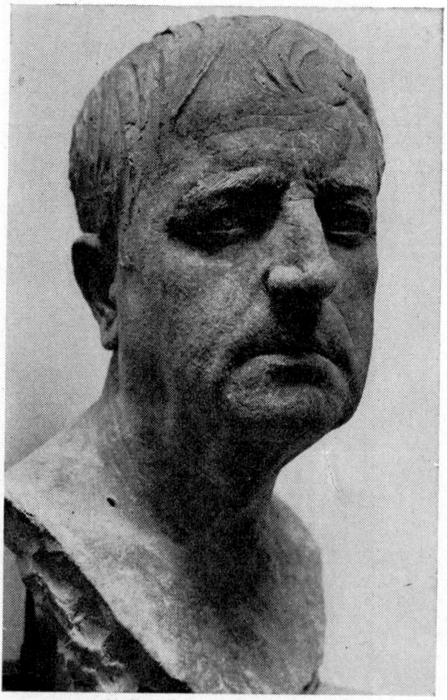

Fig. 6.5 Boston. Museum of Fine Arts. Portrait of a Roman. 1st Century B.C.

CLARENCE KENNEDY

Fig. 6.6 Athens. National Museum. Portrait of a Roman girl.

KAUFMAN

Fig. 6.7 Munich. Glyptothek. Peasant taking a bull to market. Marble. 11 inches high.

ANDERSON

Fig. 6.8 Florence. Uffizi. *Earth, Air, and Water*. From the *Ara Pacis Augustae* (13–9 B.C.).

ARCHIVES PHOTOGRAPHIQUES

Fig. 6.9 Paris. Louvre. *The Judgment of Paris*. Mosaic. Found at Antioch.

Fig. 6.10 Rome. Vatican Library. Pal. Grec. 431–IV. *The Joshua Roll*. Illustration for *Joshua* 5: 13–15.

GIRAUDON
Fig. 6.11 Paris. Bibliothèque Nationale. Grec. 139. Folio I verso. *David Playing the Harp.*

GAB. FOT. NAZ.
Fig. 6.13 Rome. Terme Museum. Putto on a ladder. Fresco. 1st Century A.D.

ANDERSON
Fig. 6.12 Rome. Arch of Titus. 81 A.D. The spoils of Jerusalem carried in triumphal procession.

Figs. 6.14–15 Rome. Vatican. Two scenes from Book 10 of the *Odyssey*. The Lastrygonians rushing to attack (above); and destroying the Greek flotilla (below). PHOTOGRAPHS BY ALINARI.

ARCHIVES PHOTOGRAPHIQUES

Fig. 6.16 Paris. Louvre. *The Nike from Samothrace.*

Fig. 6.17 Paris. Bibliothèque Nationale. Coin of Demetrios Poliorcetes, showing a Nike something like the *Nike from Samothrace*. Shortly after 306 B.C.

DEUTSCHER KUNSTVERLAG

Fig. 6.18 Berlin. Pergamon Museum. Detail from the frieze of *The Great Altar of Pergamon:* Athena killing a giant.

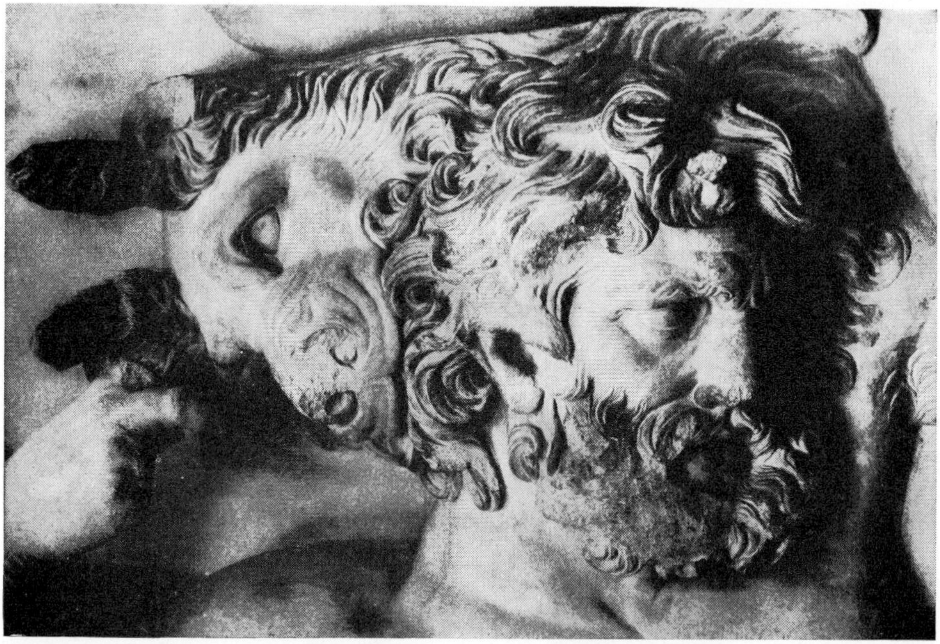

STOEDTNER
Fig. 6.19 Berlin. Pergamon Museum. Detail from the frieze of *The Great Altar of Pergamon.*

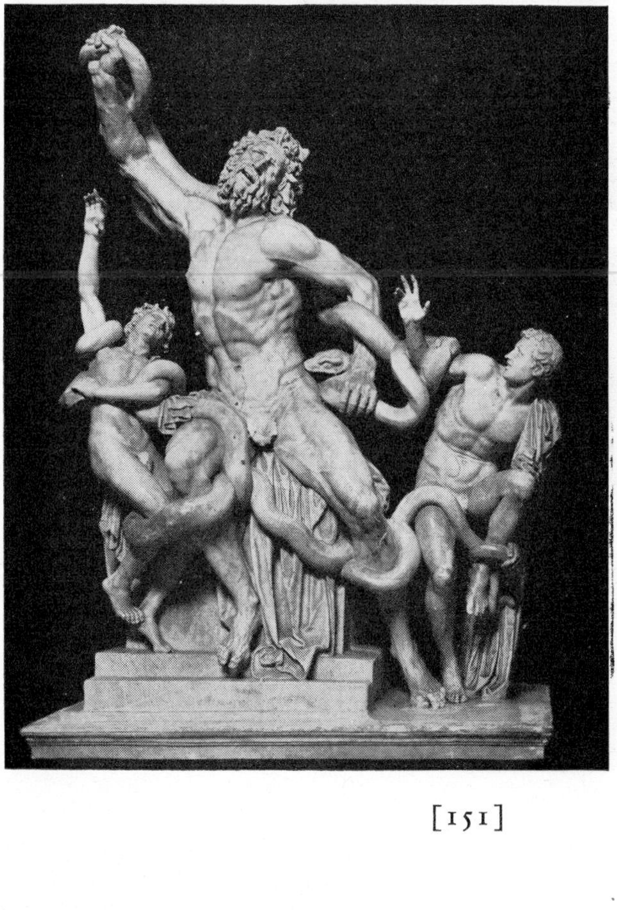

ANDERSON
Fig. 6.20 Rome. Vatican. *The Laocöon Group.* About 50 B.C.

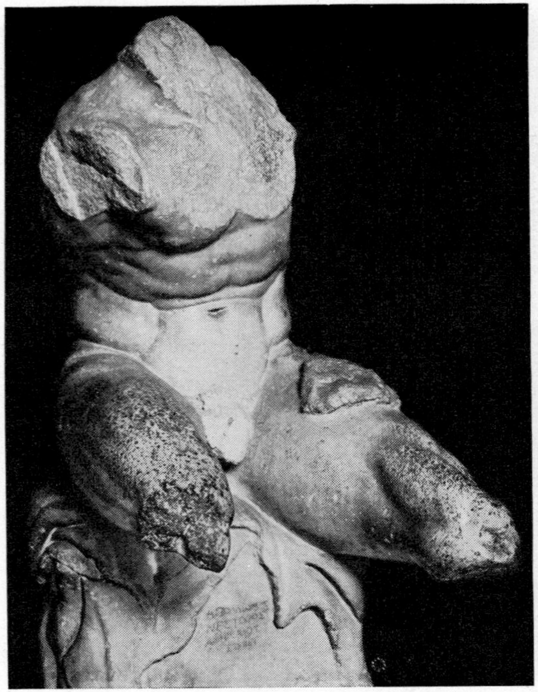

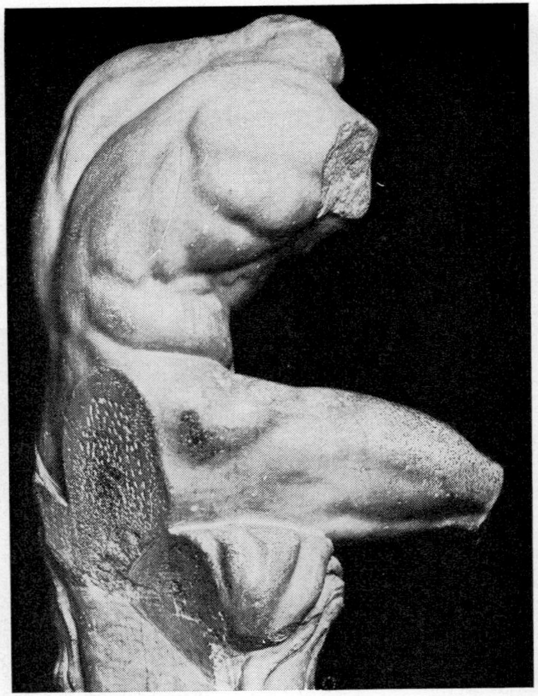

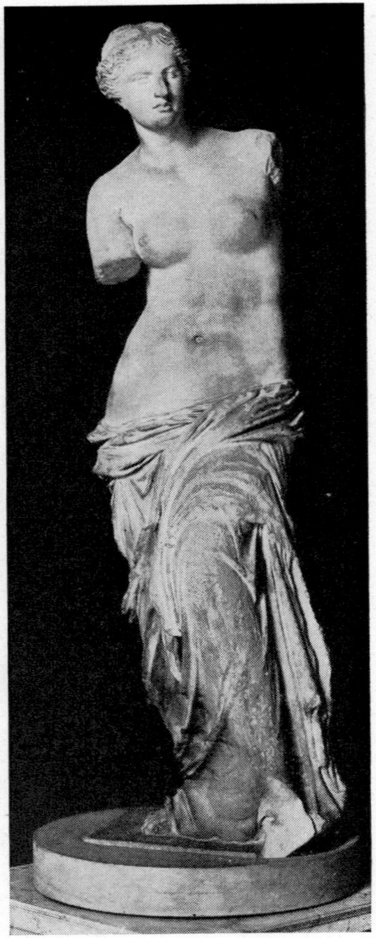

Figs. 6.21–22 Rome. Vatican. *The Belvedere Torso* (ANDERSON).

Fig. 6.23 (right) Paris. Louvre. *The Aphrodite from Melos* (ARCHIVES PHOTOGRAPHIQUES).

Figs. 6.24–25
Rome. Vatican. *The Apollo Belvedere* (ANDERSON).

*

6

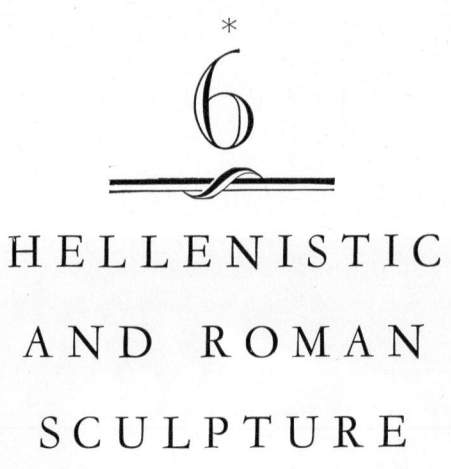

HELLENISTIC AND ROMAN SCULPTURE

WITH SOME MENTION OF PAINTING

INTRODUCTORY

In dealing with the history of art from the death of Alexander until the end of Antiquity, we must set aside our habit of outlining by reference to political changes and military events. It has long been customary to recognize a Hellenistic Period (323–146 B.C.), a Graeco-Roman era (146 B.C. to about 1 A.D.), and a Roman Period (about 1 A.D. to 476 A.D.). These divisions correspond approximately to the heyday of the kingdoms governed by Alexander's heirs, to the period when the Romans were absorbing Greek culture, and to the era of the Roman Empire.

On the whole, the evidence of the monuments argues against so elaborate a subdivision. It is true that Mummius took Corinth in 146 B.C., and it is fair enough for the historian of politics to use that date as signalizing the end of Greek independence and the beginning of Roman dominion. It is also legitimate to point out that Roman art as such did not start until the reign of Augustus (27 B.C.–14 A.D.); but it is contrary to fact to suppose that these happenings altered the direct and predetermined course of cultural history. We should begin our new study, therefore, with the concept that Hellenistic and Roman art are part of the Greek tradition; not different in kind, but a normal evolution from what went before, a natural extension over a wider area of a familiar artistic philosophy.

Except for Alexander, Greece would be remembered as an historical curiosity. Because of him, Greek modes of thought and Greek values run Western civilization. The effect of his conquests was to spread Greek ideas; so many people were favorably impressed that it became virtually a certainty that the Greek spirit would somehow survive. Culturally speaking, Rome is but another Alexander. Without a strong art or literature of their own, the Romans attempted to adopt what they found in Greece. In so doing, they themselves became captured by the tradition they attempted to possess, and they transmitted it to the medieval world and even more directly to the Renaissance.

The latter-day ancients had no feeling that the world had crossed a great divide with the death of Alexander (323 B.C.); the recorded achievements of the following 500 years give the lie to any such notion. In fact, from the outlook of the men then alive, it must have appeared that civilization was constantly and rapidly improving until the Roman polity began to work badly during the 3rd Century A.D.

Immediately after the death of Alexander, new cities began to be important. Alexandria, Antioch, Pergamon, and Rhodes were in their heyday larger, richer, and busier than anything ever known before. They totally eclipsed the familiar centers of Greece proper. Commerce became more ramified and sophisticated. Trade went forward over longer routes and in greater bulk, involving practices of credit and banking thought to be very modern indeed. Immense wealth accumulated, permitting those who held it to live more easily, more comfortably, and more beautifully. By comparison, the customs of the 4th and 5th Centuries B.C. must have seemed crude and cheerless.

As Mr. Benjamin Farrington has so ably set forth in his *Greek Science,* the Hellenistic age saw accomplishments in research on a par with anything that happened in modern Europe prior to the Industrial Revolution. Pure mathematics embraced a usable trigonometry which enabled astronomers to observe such refinements of celestial motion as the precession of the equinoxes. Knowing the earth to be a globe, they measured its diameter within 14 percent of the truth; some say much less. The coordinates of latitude and longitude were established, and the latitude of particular points was measured almost as accurately as we can do it today: the recorded figures put the Pharos (lighthouse) in the harbor of Alexandria out by only 16 minutes of arc, a figure the modern navigator will instantly recognize as the semidiameter of the sun's disc. All sorts of mechanical principles were known, and numerous pieces of machinery were actually built: clocks, water organs, engines for siege and defense. Medicine was within an ace of Harvey's theory of the circulation of the blood. All of this learning, moreover, was organized on a system very much like the system of modern scholarship. Libraries and museums first became important public institutions during the Hellenistic age, and the duty of scholarly publication was widely observed with the intention of making findings accessible to later generations.

To the modern student, it seems almost incredible that the Industrial Revolution did not start during the Hellenistic Period. About the middle of the 3rd Century B.C., Ctesbius of Alexandria had already invented a force pump and a pneumatic gun. He knew, that is to say, the principle of the piston and was in approximately the same position of intellectual advantage as James Watt when the latter undertook to invent a practical steam engine. What deterred the sophisticated businessmen of the time from embracing an opportunity to acquire fabulous wealth? The answer is necessarily a matter for speculation, but opinion centers upon two factors, each functioning as a mental block in the psychology of those who controlled society.

The first suggestion is that slaves were altogether too cheap and plentiful, and even at times and in places where this was not true, the ancient imagination was chained to the indispensability of slave labor. In a larger sense, we may say that the absence of modern notions of humanity closed the ancient mind to the desirability of seeking a substitute for the pain and degradation of those persons who were born to bondage. We must not be hasty in our judgment of that narrowness. Saint Augustine (354–430 A.D.) accepted slavery as God's penalty for original sin, and the whole social structure of the medieval world was hampered by the stultifying notion that theory was honorable, but that its application in the form of labor was to be despised even if the laborer happened to be a free man. The artists of the Renaissance, as we shall see, had to fight a battle to prove themselves gentlemen even though they worked with their hands.

Ancient religion also operated to restrain the practical application of science. Heraclides of Pontus knew that the universe was heliocentric as early as 300 B.C., and various astronomers noted the eccentricities of motion which prove that the orbits are not circular. The general adoption of such ideas was foreclosed by the fixed notion that the heavens were sacred, that circles were the only perfect curves, and that the earth was the center of things. It is not surprising that a society committed to such thoughts would, when descending to the lower realms of science, view the whole field of mechanics simply as an opportunity to manufacture artificial miracles for the greater conviction of the ignorant. In fact, except for war machines and a fire engine built by Ctesbius, it is hard to name many useful applications of the data compiled. Ancient research was pure to the extent of being sterile.

The controlling members of society, innocent though they were of concepts which to us seem fundamental, had reason to congratulate themselves. Anywhere one looked, there was evidence that the human mind continued to be fertile and productive. In one important area of life, however, there was cause for gloom: in the art of government, the later Greeks have left a ghastly record. Many of their rulers were men of capacity; brilliance, even genius, occurred about as often as it did during the Italian Renaissance. But from the society as a whole, teeming as it was with thought and possessed of unprecedented potential, there emerged no constitutional scheme capable of producing a decent sort of political order. The polity of the Hellenistic kingdoms defies analysis or description. Each consisted of a hundred different relationships between government and the governed, involving every degree of absolutism and independence. It was truly a world of catch as catch can, and the happiest men of all were mercenary generals, who enjoyed to the limit the luxury of having no loyalties.

But even the political troubles of the ancient world were solved with the advent of Rome. The *Pax Romanum* was harsh in its original application, but it was the only protracted period of unbroken peace ever enjoyed by the European peoples. It may be said to have lasted approximately from the start of the Christian era to the end of the 2nd Century A.D., at which time both economic and governmental regularity began to fail.

Before we are ready to consider Hellenistic and Roman art, we must mention the two new systems of thought which were called into being during the Hellenistic Period: that of the Stoics, and that of Epicurus.

The latter advises us to forget the riddle of existence — the implication being that if an answer to the same exists, the human mind lacks the capacity to comprehend it. Such being the case, we had best make the most of the only life we are sure of. Often vulgarized into "the pleasure principle," the recommendations of Epicurus actually make an identity between personal satisfaction and a way of life which, by any standard, is both prudent and praiseworthy. If followed literally and honestly, his philosophy would make a good citizen out of any man.

The Stoics likewise defaulted from wrestling with the ultimates. Our problem, according to them, is to adjust to the world as it is. The chances, moreover, greatly favor our finding the world a bad place to be. Every man's daily routine puts him through toil and often through pain. Whatever plans we make, it is more than likely our hopes will finish in frustration and disappointment. No one can or will help another man much. Each person's resource is within himself alone, but by resolute action of the will, the self can be strengthened sufficiently to withstand the worst. No matter what happens, one need not play the part of the coward. A man can learn to face his fate with dignity.

Men capable of these ideas obviously were not the Greeks as they were during the age of Pericles. Both the Epicureans and the Stoics were engaged in finding some way to face a situation too confusing to be understood and circumstances too difficult to be controlled. The relationship between humanity and the environment has, if we believe what these men said, been changed. Man's weakness is to be accepted as a fact. The power of events is to be accepted as irresistible. Only blind luck can avert inevitable defeat. Fortitude and virtue remain intelligible as concepts; but their practical application can accomplish only a little: in the case of the Epicureans, grace; in the case of the Stoics, dignity. The history of art seems to show that both grace and dignity endured as long as the ancient world, and when we encounter monuments that lack both, we shall know we are in the Middle Ages.

Until very recently, it was customary to present Hellenistic art as an art of display, indulgence, and decline. Roman art fared even worse at the hands of the historian; it is still difficult for the student to find an adequate and clear-headed summary of the subject. Admittedly neither Hellenistic Greece nor Rome produced a single artist of the same order of creative originality as Phidias, Polycleitos, or Praxiteles. We may therefore summarize, speaking of general tendencies where before a considerable effort of analysis was obligatory. But we may not perpetuate the notion that everything that departs from the conventions of the Greek Fifth and Fourth Centuries is an offense against the artistic right.

The obvious differences between the art of later Antiquity and that of the Great Age are to be explained in quite another way. The expansion of every other horizon had its counterpart in a great broadening of the artist's horizon. In the following chapters, we shall have occasion to see that the simple Greek temple no longer contained the imagination of architects; new structural methods were explored and perfected, new decorative themes were tried, and a great variety of types — religious, civil, and domestic — emerged. In sculpture, the most conspicuous development is an immense expansion of the catalogue of subject matter. The Hellenistic and Roman sculptors refused to limit themselves to figures of idealized young adults. Like artists of our own day, they used any subject that pleased or interested them. With respect to style, all artists of this later era depend rather obviously upon Greece, but there is no Hellenistic or Roman style as such. Separate schools and even individual artists determined style to suit themselves, and radically different methods were used in the same place at the same time in accordance with individual preference.

In sum, all of this means that Hellenistic and Roman art present an historical picture more complex and difficult than anything we have yet encountered. At the same time, Hellenistic and Roman archaeology are today in far worse case than the archaeology of earlier sections of the classical era. We are by no means certain about the location of important centers of production. By chance, we know a few artists by name, but we can make very little from it. Chronology has yet to be worked out; some of the most important monuments are still dated more by opinion than by evidence — and competent men often want to place the same statue a couple of hundred years apart. Except for passing mention of dates, we shall therefore abandon any attempt at chronological arrangement of the text. Instead, we shall endeavor to explain things by reference to the several major artistic tendencies which first make their appearance in history after the death of Alexander.

THE TASTE FOR COLOSSI

The vigor of Hellenistic life expressed itself in many an overt gesture. Nothing is more typical of the time than the arrival of a taste for colossal statues, a taste most unrestrainedly asserted by the inhabitants of Rhodes. It is said no less than a hundred immense figures were once on view there, of which the most famous was the celebrated *Colossus of Rhodes,* put up about 280 B.C. by Chares of Lindus, thought to have been a pupil of Lysippos. Antipater of Sidon (2nd Century B.C.), who compiled the earliest known list of "the seven wonders of the world," included the *Colossus* among them. It is a great pity we have no substantial evidence which might help us to visualize so conspicuous a monument, but it is worth making an effort with what we possess. The subject was said to have been *Helios,* the god of the sun. The statue was of bronze purchased with the money realized from the war machines left behind by Demetrios Poliorcetes when he abandoned his unsuccessful siege of the island. It stood about 105 feet high, or 45 feet less than the *Statue of Liberty.* There was a winding staircase inside, and "glasses" for looking at distant shores and ships. Contrary to popular legend, the figure did not stand astride the channel leading into the harbor, and the idea that ships sailed between its legs is out of the question except in the case of small boats. As a matter of fact, the exact site is unknown; we merely know it was adjacent to the harbor. The *Colossus* endured only a short while. An earthquake occurred in 224 B.C., apparently breaking the figure in two. The ruin remained in plain sight until 672 A.D., when the incumbent Saracen governor sold it to a merchant of Edessa. Nine hundred camel loads of scrap were taken away, it is said; and its value, according to an 18th-Century authority, came to the then equivalent of 36,000 pounds sterling.

Another famous colossus was the one Nero set up in the courtyard of his Golden House at Rome, an extravagantly gorgeous palace built after the city burned in 64 A.D. That was also a sun-god, but Nero himself had posed as the model. The statue stood about 118 feet high, and showed the emperor with rays around his head. It was still standing as late as 354 A.D., and was the subject of the baleful prophecy: "While stands the *Colossus*, stands Rome. When falls the *Colossus*, Rome falls; and when Rome falls, with it shall fall the whole world." It is thought the prophecy originated with pilgrims to the Eternal City, and there are versions of it datable back to the 7th Century of our era. Because it was near the *Colossus*, everyone has always called the Flavian Amphitheatre the *Colosseum*.

Big statues retained their popularity until the very end. The Conservatori Museum at Rome has a bronze head of good workmanship and about six feet high; it is usually labelled *Constantius* — one of Constantine's sons. A seated statue of Constantine himself (regnal dates 306–337 A.D.) was placed in the central apse of the immense Basilica of Constantine at Rome. Some fragments of the arms and lower legs survive in the courtyard of the Conservatori, together with the head (Fig. 9.5), the latter being no less than eight feet high.

THE REALISTIC TENDENCY

In our study of Lysippos, we had occasion to observe that idealism was already on the wane at the end of the 4th Century B.C., and that an increasing consciousness of actuality seemed to be taking its place in the mind of the Greek artist. The process appears to have gone rapidly toward its logical conclusion, and presently the unparalleled resources of Hellenistic technique were devoted to reproducing the appearance of nature — or at least giving a vivid impression thereof. Within the general scope of the realistic movement, we will find it convenient to recognize two divisions. The first has to do with realism as applied to the single figure or to any other object that is best presented in close-up by plastic methods. The second has to do with realism as applied to the representation not of figures and objects, but of entire scenes in broader view, with figures and stage properties placed within the represented space.

The *Dying Gaul*, now in the Capitoline Museum at Rome (Fig. 6.1), marks the final abandonment of idealistic pretensions, and the complete acceptance of objective realism. The figure is a marble replica from a bronze original, one of a set believed to have been dedicated to commemorate the victory in 230 B.C. of King Attalus the 1st of Pergamon in Asia Minor. Attalus gained the gratitude of all Greece by soundly defeating the army of these folk who were already forcing their way into the Mediterranean world. It seems extraordinary that an ancient victor should do his enemy so much honor, but Attalus is said to have admired the way the Gauls fought and the way they died.

As evidence of the contemporary orientation between man and the world, the statue is shocking in view of the conceptions entertained at an earlier date. The outright expression of terrible pain would have been unthinkable during the Great Age. So would the very idea of making a defeated man, even an enemy, the subject of a public monument. Some vestige of former outlook survives in the dignity with which the man dies, and the *Dying Gaul* may be remembered as an excellent illustration of the then popular retreat into Stoicism.

Realism is not always severe. Its gentler, more homely applications are known as *genre:* subjects from everyday life, neither beautiful nor inspiring, but presented because they recall familiar experience. The *Boy Struggling with a Goose* of the Munich Museum is an example, and the *Old Market Woman* in the Metropolitan Museum (Fig. 6.2) is another. The latter is of special interest as an instance of the expansion of subject matter. Most of the human beings heretofore seen in Greek art have been handsome, healthy, intelligent, and even noble. Even the evildoers (centaurs, for example) have at least been vigorous. But here we have the study of humble humanity at a time of life when the body becomes increasingly frail and unlovely with every passing year. Such a theme might well have invited the sculptor's sense of tragedy; in such a case, the statue would have been made the vehicle for expressions of sadness, futility, resentment, and despair. One of the things that makes it genre is the complete absence of connotative overtones; the realism is straightforward, but the feeling is gentle.

Whenever and wherever art tends to be realistic, there is big business in the portrait trade, and personal portraits begin to be an important art form with the start of the Hellenistic Period. We must distinguish between two types of portrait, both of which we have inherited in quantity. Public men naturally ordered monuments; and this created a demand for such ceremonial portraits as the *Augustus from Prima Porta,* now in the Vatican — a standing figure in the tradition of Polycleitos, with attributes recalling the mythical generation of the Julian line from Venus herself, and surmounted by a flattering rendering of the imperial countenance. Much more interesting are the portraits ostensibly ordered for private consumption; in these latter, objective realism seems to have reached its logical fulfilment. Portraits of this less pretentious class are usually busts of an abbreviated type, showing head and neck only.

Because so many of them — and their number is legion — stand in plain sight in the museums of Italy, we are all too often told that the realistic portrait is strictly an Italian phenomenon invented by the Romans for their own use, but that is hardly true. Realism of the most uncompromising kind is to be found in later Greek work, long before the Roman market opened up. A particularly striking instance, probably dating from about 230 B.C., is the head of *King Euthydemus of Bactria,* in the Torlonia Museum of Rome (Fig. 6.4). No Roman face is more incisively and unsparingly rendered; few are so severe. It is true, however, that realism suited the Roman respect for facts; and for that reason, the market for realistic portraits was greatly stimulated as soon as the Romans started to order.

The range of Roman work is well illustrated by the contrast between the Boston terra-cotta head of an unknown Roman (Fig. 6.5) and the head of an equally unknown girl (Fig. 6.6) in the National Museum at Athens. Both show that objective realism at times has the awful finality of an accounting. Nature makes most young girls pretty, but gives them little else. Moderately successful men are bound to think overly well of themselves at sixty. The facts are frozen for all time; and the realistic artist, by the logic of his own philosophy, must take them as they come.

The same cast of mind, when turned to the study of flowers and shrubs, produced some of the finest floral sculpture the world has ever seen. From this class of work, a typical and favorite example is the relief known as the *Rose Pillar from the Tomb of the Haterii,* preserved in the Lateran Museum at Rome (Fig. 6.3). Monuments like this give us a new point of view toward realism; one aspect of that philosophy involves a communion between man and nature, a response of the senses to the grandeur of the world and also to the great wonder of nature in her more delicate manifestations.

Indeed, if we compare the *Rose Pillar* with the *Honeysuckle Band* of the Erectheum (Fig. 4.11), we have before us the difference between sense perception and conceptual thinking. The Greek feels compelled to make nature conform to axioms which, to him, seem luminously true. He therefore idealizes his floral ornament, reduces its forms to the plastic shapes he likes to use, and arranges the successive items according to the rules of a rhythm selected for the occasion. The Roman believes his eyes. Not denying the existence of general principles (in terms of which nature may have some ultimate order), he nevertheless declines to discredit the testimony of appearance — and the appearance of nature is very far from orderly. The Roman sculptor therefore gives his rose vine no more regularity than we might expect to see in any well-tended garden, and he includes innumerable accidental irregularities.

Love of nature is commonplace in the modern world, and the expression of it in Roman floral sculpture is unlikely to impress the reader as historically notable unless we warn him. The history of art contains no evidence that anyone ever loved nature before the Romans did, with the single exception of the Minoan Greeks who had passed out of history with precious little legacy behind them. The beauty and kindness of nature left European culture, moreover, with the death of Antiquity; such feelings were utterly absent from the medieval temperament until the High Gothic of the 13th Century A.D. At that moment, nature in its original unspoiled disorder once again rather timidly entered the vocabulary of art as a modest prelude to the modern passion for natural beauty, the latter dating not earlier than the 15th Century.

THE PICTORIAL RELIEFS

The realistic enterprise did not stop with the study of the plastic facts of the human figure and other objects in nature. The research extended into every aspect of actuality including the representation of space and the placement of things forward and back within the setting called into being by the techniques of the artist. The enterprise is often referred to as *illusionism,* a word with somewhat unfortunate connotations but one which may apply if a work of art is, in fact or in fancy, momentarily mistaken for a view into the real vista. If used at all, *illusionism* should be reserved for spatial representation; its inventor, Professor Wickhoff, often extended the meaning to include anything whatever that might evoke a vivid impression of existence.

The representation of space depends upon a knowledge of perspective, a subject which seems first to have been investigated at Alexandria during the 3rd Century B.C., apparently with about the same results that were once again arrived at in Florence during the 15th Century A.D. Painters and sculptors share two principal methods for representing space: *linear perspective* and *atmospheric perspective.*

Linear perspective is the studio term for descriptive geometry, or the science of projection. It governs the outline of objects as they appear in drawing and painting, and is easiest to explain when architectural masses — or any other rectangular masses — are projected onto a flat surface like that of the canvas. When that is done, all lines which are parallel on the surface of the mass must, on the surface of the picture, be made to converge in systematic fashion toward one or more *vanishing points.* The same principles apply for the projection of irregular masses (the human body, for example), but the explanation is more tedious and the phenomenon less obvious to the layman's eye. *Foreshortening* is a word used as a near-synonym for linear perspective whenever one wishes to say that some mass (for example, an arm represented as being extended at right angles to the picture-plane, as though directly toward the eye of the observer) is presented in bold close-up. From the logic of linear perspective, it follows that more and more distant objects subtend increasingly small arcs of the field of vision; thus small things in the foreground take up more room on the canvas than immense things far off.

If we may judge by the general run of preserved monuments, linear perspective was understood only fairly well by the ancient artists; they used it in a rule-of-thumb way and by no means so scientifically as the masters of the Renaissance. Atmospheric perspective, on the other hand, seems to have been very well handled indeed. It results from the curtain of dust and mist which almost always hangs in the air, softening the outlines of distant objects, obscuring details, and neutralizing their color. As a means of estimating distance in nature or representing it in art, atmospheric perspective is of greater psychological importance than the geometry of projection. Whenever conditions are abnormal or unfamiliar (as in some parts of the American west where there is little dust and mist), the ordinary man is prone to make gross errors when he tries to say how far off anything may be.

The painter is able to simulate all the conditions of both linear and atmospheric perspective. When carving a relief, the sculptor can of course make use of the principle of the vanishing point. He can also make his relief lower and his modeling less distinct in order to avail himself of atmospheric perspective, but he lacks the ability to " place " objects within the represented space by modulating the color relationships. Offhand, it would sound as though the sculptor had most of the available methods at his command, but the reverse is true. The one technique he lacks is the most important of all. It is by way of the color sensation that we habitually make most of our judgments about distance.

Within the broad category of spatial representation, we have recently come to recognize two classes of work which seem distinct in theory and separate in historical origin, although the two often merge together in particular monuments. One is the so-called *Alexandrian Style,* and the other is the Roman or *Latin Style.*

Typical of the Alexandrian Style is the tiny marble panel in Munich showing a peasant leading his bull to market (Fig. 6.7). It belongs to a class of small marble reliefs found in various places. Presumably they originated at some common center. The identification of Alexandria as that center is probable, but conjectural. It rests upon two lines of evidence, the first being the likelihood that pictorial reliefs would originate where the study of perspective started. The second reason has to do with subject matter.

With reasonable consistency, the Alexandrian reliefs deal with pastoral and bucolic themes. An analogy therefore suggests itself: there had been no pastoral poetry earlier than the Hellenistic Period; it was called into being by the crowded life of the teeming Hellenistic cities, probably as a nostalgic remembrance of simpler days. Theocritus was the father of pastoral poetry. He spent most of his active career at Alexandria, arriving there about 276 B.C. Although there are critics who believe that not one of the reliefs now brought under review may be dated before the Roman era, the affinities with Theocritus and the generally Greek tone make the Alexandrian association far from irrational.

Regardless of their archaeological source, we can recognize a category of monuments alike in subject matter, and even more uniform in the method of presenting subject matter. In fact, the arrangement amounts to a formula; and the scheme was used so often and so long we may conveniently name it the *Alexandrian Formula,* thus dignifying it for what it is: a distinct and useful pictorial scheme adaptable to the purposes of any artist who wants to show a few figures out-of-doors.

One and all, these pictorial renderings are like Theocritus in calling up sentimentally lovely Greek figures who people with easy grace an outdoor setting that celebrates, in similarly sentimental mood, the softer and more generous aspects of nature. It is hardly true, however, to say that the figures are within their setting. On the contrary, they are brought forward as though to the edge of a stage. In that position, they loom large, fill a substantial proportion of the available area within the frame, and obscure the landscape behind them. It is evident that Greek art was not yet ready to abandon humanity as its chief vehicle of expression, and to the Greek hate for the indefinite, we may assign the peculiarity of the extreme caution with which artists of this school employ their space.

We tend, of course, to read the blank upper background as the sky; but almost without exception, compositions of the Alexandrian category seem deliberately arranged to prevent the eye from searching off into the unlimited distance. Nowhere is it possible to enter the scene, as it were, at the foreground and continue straight back into space without interruption. Rows of people, landscape details, and stage properties of every kind stand in the way. If it be desired to detain our attention within measurable bounds, nothing could be a stronger deterrent to an imagination likely to soar off into the infinite.

Although scholars are probably correct in assuming that any object fitting this general description belongs either directly or indirectly to the eastern part of the Mediterranean world, it is obvious from the monuments that pictures and reliefs of the Alexandrian type had a wide vogue and extended at least into Roman Italy. What we have said of the *Peasant and Bull* may also be said of the so-called "Tellus panel" from the *Ara Pacis Augustae* (Fig. 6.8), erected at Rome between 13 and 9 B.C., and in which we see a personified Lady Earth attended by Air and Water — all three celebrating the boost to agricultural productivity alleged to have resulted when Augustus assumed the purple. Many of the mosaics uncovered recently at Antioch conform to the Alexandrian scheme, notably the splendid *Judgment of Paris* (Fig. 6.9) now in the Louvre; the same thing may be said of perhaps two thirds of the pictures recovered at Pompeii.

The popularity of the Alexandrian Formula decidedly did not cease with the decay of ancient civilization and the gradual dissolution of almost everything else that was classical. This scheme for the arrangement of a picture proved as useful for Christian subject matter as it had for pagan, and was carried over directly into the art of the early Middle Ages. Some of the mosaics in the churches and tombs at Ravenna are stylistically close to the Greek and Roman monuments just cited, particularly the *Christ as Good Shepherd* in the Mausoleum of Galla Placidia. Even purer examples of the formula were produced at a much later date by miniature painters employed in the important medieval industry of manuscript illumination. Because every classical or Christian text was necessarily a copy and because the very desire for a copy involves the sense of authenticity, only the most independent artists dared undertake any deliberate and significant departure from either the words or the illustrations set before them. There are, of course, numerous instances of technical incompetence resulting in the inability to execute adequate copies of older pictures, but whenever a skilful man was put to work, the ancient style enjoyed a momentary revival. To some such circumstance we must assign the miniatures of the so-called "Joshua Roll" of the Vatican; and in Fig. 6.10, we see the event described in Joshua 5:13–15, where Joshua encountered the angel sent as Captain of the Host of the Lord. According to the best guess we can now make, these pictures were done about 700 A.D., perhaps at Constantinople, and were either copied or closely adapted from an original of three or four hundred years earlier. An even earlier original probably accounts for the better miniatures among the fourteen that illustrate the so-called "Paris Psalter." The *David Playing the Harp* (Fig. 6.11) might easily and properly be mistaken for a classical picture. The manuscript is almost completely innocent, in fact, of anything that is necessarily Christian; and the purity of its classical imagery, obvious enough in a general way, is made unmistakable by some precise resemblances. Our picture shows David with Melody seated beside him, while Echo pops her head in from the upper right. The pretty Melody, as Mr. Morey has pointed out, is all but a duplicate of an Io in one of the Pompeian frescoes. The label "Bethlehem," moreover, hardly suffices as a Christian conversion for the lazy God at the lower right-hand corner who is present to localize the scene by the time-honored pagan method of personification. To complete the history, it should be pointed out that the Alexandrian Formula was fastened upon and used again by the artists of the Renaissance. It was especially popular at Venice, and a general description of numerous easel paintings by Titian and others would serve equally well as a description of any of the ancient works of art covered in this section.

As the name implies, the Latin Style was almost certainly an Italian innovation of Roman date. It differs from the Alexandrian in the vital matter of spatial manipulation: there is no attempt to control or curtail the represented space; it is always unlimited and sometimes emphatically so. The Latin Style also embodies a relaxation of the emphasis traditionally given the human figure in all classical art to date. Even when figures are placed up in the foreground, we are given clearly to understand that they are *within* the represented space, not out in front of it. In the monuments which seem best to illustrate the intention of the Latin School, the human actors are made small in scale; they do not overshadow the setting, but have their being as details of a broader picture.

Two large and imposing panels of relief line the passageway through the Arch of Titus in the Forum Romanum (Fig. 6.12). Both are badly damaged. The heads of the figures in the front row were originally executed in the round, or near it, and these have been knocked off. In spite of the mutilation, the several subtle gradations from sculpture in the round toward sculpture in low relief are entirely adequate to convey a sense of atmospheric perspective. The effect is unmistakable, and we instinctively read the blank background as the blue sky.

For an adequate demonstration of the Latin Style in full force, we must turn to Roman painting — of which a great many examples have survived, almost all of them the work of hack artists in the employ of interior decorators. The subject matter of such painting is frequently idyllic and reminiscent of the Alexandrian, but the handling is significantly different. In radical contrast to the shallow stage used in the Alexandrian Formula, the Latin setting opens up from the very edge of the picture and continues out into the far distance. Nothing impedes the eye. Figures and other details are placed far apart, and there is room, as it were, to go between them. Within the represented space, we see human beings and animals, but they are tiny in relation to the picture as a whole.

There is also a substantial difference in the definition of detail. As a general rule, the persons who appear in pictures of the Alexandrian type seem to have been conceived as animated statues; contours are smooth and precisely defined. By contrast, practitioners of the Latin Style tend to be *impressionists.*

The word *impressionism* as applied to Roman painting may cause momentary confusion. The very same word is today current as the name for a school of French painters (Manet, Monet, Degas, Renoir, et al.) who flourished during the last generation of the 19th Century. It would be better if we always referred to that school as the *French Impressionists,* never forgetting to apply the adjective. They were certainly impressionists in every sense of the term, but they were a great deal more than that, as we shall see in due time.

Impressionism as such is as old as Rome and probably as old as painting. It has no necessary or essential connection with spatial representation, or with any particular formula for the arrangement of a picture. As an artistic theory, impressionism has to do merely with the handling of the brush and the rendering of detail. The laboratory case of the impressionist painter would be a man with only one brush, and that brush a large one. He would find it impractical to work out in minute particularity the arrangement of lights and colors which might, in nature, be noted by the unaided eye on the surface of a single white button. The impressionist would merely slap down a spot of white, and let it stand as a suggestion for the button. In its purely technical aspect, impressionism is a kind of private conspiracy whereby the painter agrees with himself to describe detail only when it is comparatively large in scale. He has a lower limit of size beyond which he will not go. That lower limit, it must be emphasized, is not set by tools and materials. It is a matter of deliberate choice; the impressionist painter consciously refrains from using the more delicate methods which are available to him.

As compared with a more detailed and plastic rendering, impressionism is closer to the visual experience of the average man. Most of us go through life without ever having occasion to make a minute inspection of anything whatever. We do not examine the human figure, or anything else, with the intense vision of a Greek sculptor. Most of our seeing is hasty. Our visual images are vague and incomplete — in a word, impressions. The impressionist painter therefore has the considerable advantage of offering an artistic experience almost precisely parallel to the visual experience of daily life. The danger is that his art will be no more profound than daily life, but it must enthusiastically be conceded that the good examples of impressionism have a snap and reality more vivid than any other kind of painting.

The snap and reality to which we refer suffer not at all from the fact that impressionism is superior to any other mode of rendering with respect to the internal logic of a liquid or viscous vehicle applied with the brush. In the nature of the case, it invites strong, racy strokes and demands a certain measure of bold abstraction. When well done, the life of the painting is tremendously enhanced by a clear record of the muscular activity of the painter as he worked. Impressionism gives the observer a keen feeling for the pressure and motion of the brush. There is, so to speak, a sense of participation denied by smoother and ostensibly more elegant methods.

To all of this we may add that there is some virtue in the very fact that the impressionist theory forecloses the artist from complete description of objects. The observer's imagination must supply the imagery that is lacking — an act sometimes referred to as "the re-creative function," and an experience the value of which is not to be denied. Would we feel inclined to change the little *Putto on a Ladder* (Fig. 6.13) for a more tightly modeled rendering of the same subject?

The originators of the Latin Style, whoever they were, deserve to be remembered as the men who conquered the traditional classical fear of the infinite, and opened ancient eyes to the emotional grandeur of vast distances. The pictures that seem most typical of the Latin Style are those where the represented space itself assumes the importance of subject matter. None are better than the so-called *Odyssey Landscapes* (Figs. 6.14–15), found about 1850 in a house on the Esquiline, apparently of the 1st Century A.D.

The series of pictures, today incomplete, was conceived as having a continuous landscape. The separate subjects were divided by painting in Ionic pilasters at regular intervals. The narrative comes from Books 10 and 11 of *The Odyssey*, covering the adventures of Odysseus among the Laestrygonians, with Circe, and his expedition to the lower world. We see his men meeting the stately but immense daughter of King Antiphates who, as all the world knows, promptly stirred up a peck of trouble. The savage, gigantic Laestrygonians went into a fury, gathered great rocks (Fig. 6.14), and, rushing to the harbor, dashed to pieces all the ships but one (Fig. 6.15) — also harpooning the men of the crew, whom they carried off for supper. But the wily Odysseus had moored his own vessel outside the cove; he cut the mooring line with his sword, ordered his crew to row for their lives, and got safely out to sea.

The *Odyssey Landscapes* are among the first pictures where the space itself attains anything that might be described as grandeur. Every vista opens straight out toward a remote horizon. Within such settings, the human actors assume something like the actual proportion of man in relation to the natural world. They move violently about, often darting in directions diagonal to the picture-plane, thus making it necessary for us to postulate the reality of the volume in which they move. But all their strength and action fails to dominate the greater drama of hills, ocean, and the air.

It remains to add a word about the further history and influence of the Latin Style. Like the Alexandrian Style, the Latin survived Antiquity because pictures rendered in that formula were copied along with the classical and biblical texts they happened to illustrate. The best of the miniatures of the so-called *First Vatican Vergil* (4th Century A.D.) are rather slavish copies after originals executed according to this formula. Once in a while, however, the task of copying a manuscript happened to fall into the hands of a scribe who was himself a great master. Such was the case during the 9th Century A.D. when some now vanished Book of Psalms, illustrated with pictures in the Latin Style, was sent for copying to a man greatly accomplished in the linear technique which came into European art with the Barbarian invaders of the Roman world. (See Chapter 9.) The result was the *Utrecht Psalter* (Figs. 9.45–46), perhaps the greatest of medieval manuscripts, recently published in full-scale facsimile by Mr. Ernest De Wald. But we are not even yet through with the inspirational power of the Latin Style. It played its part during the Renaissance also. Where else are we to turn for the classical inspiration of Ghiberti (Figs. 15.27–28), the greatest pictorial sculptor of all time?

The advent of spatial representation raises one of the perennial questions of modern art criticism. The painter obviously has the requisite techniques ready at hand, but is the sculptor wise to undertake an enterprise in which he is bound to come off second best? Ancient critics, and those of the Renaissance, were less sensitive to the internal logic of medium than we are; but at the very least, it may be pointed out that sculptors who represent space abandon expression by means of the mass. They cast aside the unique asset of their own business. The effect of that act cannot be understood or assessed by studying photographs; reproductions of every kind are themselves pictures, and not trustworthy as evidence on this special point. Suffice it to say that pictorial relief, when seen in three dimensions and under light conditions that fall short of the best, is often unsuccessful. The gradations of height in the relief prove difficult to construe as an indication of atmospheric perspective, and the texture of the background makes it an implausible suggestion for the sky.

THE SECOND SCHOOL OF PERGAMON, AND ASSOCIATED MONUMENTS

At the very start of the Hellenistic Period, Greek sculptors — taking them as a class — were in possession of the most accomplished tradition of the human figure that the world has ever seen. They also lived in a society still committed to the human figure as its chief, indeed almost its exclusive vehicle for artistic expression. It might not at first be supposed that this combination of circumstances created an artistic problem, but such seems to have been the situation. One of the very few generalizations that applies to every period and school in the history of art is the tendency of the creative mind to seek some enterprise offering the zest of discovery. But what (after Praxiteles, Scopas, and Lysippos) was there to discover about the human figure? Nothing of an essential nature, to be sure. But it was still possible to experiment with the pose, which could be made more complicated, elegant, and stirring than ever before. It was also possible to seek new effects by novel manipulations of the muscles and drapery, with the end result of arriving at more spectacular drama, if not more profound.

From some such ferment as this — and our guess is unlikely to be far from the truth — there emerged one of the distinctive new movements of Hellenistic and Roman art. The most famous single demonstration of the tendency now under review was the *Great Altar of Pergamon,* set up by King Eumenes the 2nd to commemorate his successful repulse (with Roman help) of an invasion threatened by Antiochus of Syria. The *Great Altar* now exists in fragments which were taken to Berlin and there arranged for exhibition in partial restoration. The work probably began shortly after 188 B.C., which is the only fixed point in the history we are now tracing. For that reason, it is fair to label all associated monuments as belonging to a Pergamene tradition, but some of the most important of them surely date before the 2nd Century B.C.

The *Nike from Samothrace* (Fig. 6.16) was discovered in 1863. Samothrace is an island situated about forty miles northwesterly from the entrance to the Dardanelles. From the very earliest times, the place was important as a religious center, and remained so throughout Greek history. The royal house of Macedon took a special interest in the cult that grew up on this remote, almost inaccessible spot. In the course of time, a number of memorials were set up there, of which this appears to be one.

Because her pedestal consists of the prow of a moving vessel, it is obvious the *Nike* commemorates a naval victory, but we are by no means certain what victory. Much can be made of the fact that a *Nike* similar in pose and drapery appears on a coin (Fig. 6.17) issued by Demetrios Poliorcetes, one of the most brilliant and dissolute figures of the period, who ruled for a time as tyrant at Athens, and, in 306 B.C., won a smashing naval victory over Ptolemy 1st off Cyprus.

The *Victory* on the coin is shown in profile view, riding the prow of a ship and blowing a big horn. The muscles of the statue in Paris seem to require a different position for the arms, but that may perhaps be explained away by the suggestion that the designer of the coin was merely making small changes appropriate to the composition of a metallic disc. He therefore used the profile view to get the broadest aspect, whereas the statue itself composes best from in front or when seen on a moderate diagonal. He also arranged the arms differently in order to adapt the upper silhouette to the circular shape of the coin.

If we are correct in associating the statue with the coin, we have a date of around 300 B.C., but several critics have felt that the differences are sufficient to impeach the evidence offered by the coin. By various arguments, they have persuaded themselves that several other dates are more probable. The chief suggestions have been: the middle of the 3rd Century, the latter half of the 2nd, and both the beginning and the end of the 1st Century B.C. The reader may judge for himself the truth of our general dictum that Hellenistic archaeology is confused.

As to the statue itself, there can be no question that it is, and probably always will remain, the supreme example of personification. The ample and magnificent figure alights in perfect poise on the forepeak of the fast moving galley. Common sense simply fails to register against the inspiration of the imagery; it seems thrillingly true that Victory is a Goddess who brings fortune to her own.

The concept, in itself, is an index to Hellenistic taste. The master's success, whoever he may have been, is neither here nor there when it comes to recognizing his purpose for what it is; namely, outright theatricals of a kind hitherto not indulged in by Greek artists engaged in the production of public monuments. No one can quarrel with the effect when it is so fine as we see it here, but hell beckons for the artist, musician, or author who makes a business of providing thrills.

Although some of his methods are abstract, the sculptor gets his effect by evoking a strong sense of reality. The drapery, for example, is a superb instance of rhythmic line and contour, and utterly unlike the folds into which actual cloth might fall. It would even be impossible deliberately to arrange cloth in such a fashion unless the stuff is made into a sculptor's material by the addition of paste or glue. The impression created by the plastic manipulation of the drapery is an impression of the actual forward movement of the body through the resistant air. Or, in more general terms, we are compelled to postulate the physical materials of the environment in order to make sense of what we see.

It is interesting in this connection to recall that the statue was at first set up in the Louvre without the base. It enjoyed small popularity, but when the base was unearthed in 1875 and added to the ensemble, the *Nike* almost immediately became celebrated as one of the chief treasures of that great museum. The setting, in short, is not an accessory but an indispensable element — a situation not to be complained of, but one that signifies a considerable alteration in the Greek philosophy of art.

The figure-style is typical of the entire Pergamene tradition. Vigorous monumentality is the aim. The canon of proportions approaches the gigantic. Youth, daintiness, even grace are sacrificed, and the compensation is an amplitude of adult beauty which in itself conveys a sense of adequacy and permanence. For public monuments of a patriotic sort, there have been worse conceptions.

The pose evolves directly from the tradition begun by Polycleitos and continued by Praxiteles and Scopas, but every tendency there to be discerned is here carried very far indeed. The legs are stretched wide apart, and the great torso twists at the waist with a compound rotary movement to throw the bust forward and bring one shoulder lower than the other. The muscular conformation becomes an indescribable complexity of surfaces, some flat, some tense, some soft and bulging. Nothing so complicated had been undertaken during the Great Age, and the technique required for such a performance, while superb, inevitably attracts attention to itself for that very reason. We may list parade of skill as another feature new with the times.

The *Great Altar of Pergamon* was a grandiose architectural rectangle surrounding the altar proper. A monumental staircase opened on one side. Around the other three sides, there ran a roofed colonnade raised high on a basement story, and around the entire outer surface of the basement story, there ran a continuous frieze in high relief almost eight feet high and no less than 400 feet long. The subject was the *Battle Between the Gods and the Giants* (Figs. 6.18–19).

No earlier display of sculpture could compare with this for sheer, dazzling extent, and the magnitude of the work was matched by an unequalled parade of technique. As though that were not enough, the enormous number of figures demanded that every ramification of the subject be explored. Giants appear in every known form, including some with legs like serpents. There are some monsters believed to be totally original, to say nothing of lesser deities who almost never appear in art because there is rarely room to work them in. As a display of erudition, the composition may be compared with Raphael's later frescoes (see Chapter 16), but, unlike Raphael, the Pergamene sculptors helped us by inscribing the name of every figure.

In point of style, the Second School of Pergamon falls in line with tendencies already recognized and established. The element of novelty consists in a vigorous exaggeration of almost everything. The figure-canon recalls the *Nike from Samothrace,* but the bodies are not only big, they are bigger. The poses are more than complicated; they are bizarre. Realistic treatment of the muscles has passed far beyond the objective stage; the treatment signifies, in fact, the birth of a new and differently directed idealism. Where the sculptors of the Fifth Century had eliminated and simplified, those of Pergamon stress every detail. Every twisting torso seems to confine living tissue under intense compression; the muscles bulge out as though they would burst the skin. The precedent set here proved historically productive, and we may henceforth list a taste for overt musculature among the several separate departments of Hellenistic imagery.

Philosophically, the Pergamene frieze is a disturbing monument. What are we to make of the religion of an age capable of visualizing, for the purpose of a public monument, its major Gods as involved in combat and having a very bad time of it? The extravagant display seems, when considered in the light of these implications, to be in itself evidence of spiritual insecurity already well-nigh incurable.

The *Laocöon Group* (Fig. 6.20) was discovered at Rome in 1506 on the site of the Baths of Trajan. In 1531, a restoration was undertaken by a sculptor named Montorsoli, who in all likelihood restored Laocöon's right arm with insufficient curvature back toward the head. The unfortunate Laocöon was a Trojan priest who tried to warn his fellow citizens against the wooden horse. He met his death at some later time while walking on the beach with his sons; savage serpents appeared, attacked the three men, and strangled them.

Because of its early discovery and because the Roman Renaissance was at that very moment in full flower, the group attracted immediate attention and extravagant praise — a circumstance which may be assigned, in some degree at least, to the unusual size of the piece and to the contemporary habit of praising everything of classical origin. In much the same mood, Lessing wrote his famous essay called *The Laocöon* (1766), in which he compared the sculptor's handling of the Laocöon theme with the same subject matter as rendered by Vergil — attempting therefrom to deduce general principles about the nature and limitations of both poetry and the visual arts. Lessing's essay, taking it as a whole, is now out of date, but it still contains words of wisdom.

Not one modern critic would agree with the high estimates just cited. The *Laocöon,* today, is perhaps the most unpopular piece of sculpture in the history of Greek art. Undeniably a superb technical demonstration, it seems, by comparison with more sober statuary, to be somewhat offensive for that very reason: the sculptors (there were three of them) have tried to overwhelm us with a flow of skill. The fundamental trouble with the performance, however, has to do with an inadequate conception of tragedy. The death of Laocöon is a trivial detail in history; it illustrates no important principle of character or conduct, was neither the cause of a significant result nor the result of a significant cause. A broader plane of reference being absent, the group remains a morbid thriller, a roller-coaster terror, about which one refuses to become distressed.

The monument nevertheless stands as a kind of historical milestone. It is the first instance among preserved statuary where a major work of art has been devoted to the subject of despair. Where is human dignity when such a thing can happen? And yet, if we are right in accepting the now-popular but by no means certain dating of about 50 B.C., Antiquity had a long course yet to run.

The *Belvedere Torso* (Figs. 6.21–22) is known to have belonged to the Colonna family at Rome as early as 1430 or thereabouts; and it came to the Vatican with Clement the 7th (regnal dates 1523–1534), who set it up in the court called the Belvedere — hence its name. If the paw attached to the skin on which the figure sits were that of a lion, we might call it a Hercules, but because the paw is almost surely that of a panther, we probably have the fragments of a faun. Considerably less spectacular than some other monuments of the Pergamene tradition, the torso has a special place in history: Michaelangelo derived his later figure-style from it, as any student of the ceiling of the Sistine Chapel can verify by inspection. That greatest of all modern sculptors even went so far as to refer to the battered figure as his " school."

The *Aphrodite from Melos,* or *Venus de Milo* (Fig. 6.23), was found by a peasant on that island in 1820, and sold to the French ambassador at Constantinople. The statue therefore went to Paris at a psychologically advantageous moment. The Greek War for Independence (1821–1830) was just under way; it stirred up an immense amount of sympathy in western Europe. The citizenry, especially the French, were also in precisely the right mood to rejoice over the acquisition of a notable antiquity — the Neo-Classicism of David and Ingres had recently established itself as the most enlightened form of aesthetics, and the Romantic Revolt had not yet begun to do its work. It is therefore no wonder that the statue soon became famous, and it has remained so ever since by virtue of its central placement in the principal museum of the greatest tourist center in the modern world.

Although the serious student is bound to feel some annoyance over extravagant praise in any form, the public has made no error in thinking highly of the *Aphrodite;* the only mistake is the supposition that it is better than some less-advertised pieces of Greek work which happen to be just as good. Any sober view of the thing itself is sure to give it a top rank among Hellenistic monuments.

There has been a great deal of debate over the dating, some of it motivated by a desire to enhance the prestige of the work by putting it in the Greek Fifth or Fourth Century. A pedestal found nearby carried an inscription which might settle the affair, but the pedestal cannot be firmly associated with the statue. Thus the date must rest upon one's deductions from the syle, and on that basis, most of the recent authorities are agreed in putting the figure about 100 B.C. The chief arguments for that date have to do with the content and with the pose. The content seems to be an attempt to combine the sensual charm of Praxiteles with the cold serenity of the Fifth Century. On an opulent torso, we find a strangely Phidian head which is nevertheless modeled to give some sort of expression, one hardly knows what. The pose, while less overtly vigorous than some others in the general tradition of Pergamon, is extravagantly manipulated. Head and shoulders are given a strong lift up and to the statue's left. The right hip swings outward to the right so far that the word *contortion* may legitimately be applied, and the left thigh thrusts strongly out in front. The upsurge of the torso at the top is offset by the droop of the drapery below. The precarious hang of the drapery, moreover, is in itself a theatrical touch, combining with everything else to suggest a period of much sophistication and a rather academic inclination to sample every kind of taste at once.

THE CULT OF ELEGANCE

The coexistence during the Hellenistic age of every kind of taste is well pointed up by the contrast between the tradition that stemmed from Pergamon and the cult of elegance now to be discussed. Of the latter, the prime and central monument is the famous *Apollo Belvedere* (Figs. 6.24–25), so called because it has always stood in the Belvedere at the Vatican. Discovered at some early date, it has been viewed by visitors to Rome from the 15th Century onward. The notion persists that the marble statue now in Rome is a copy, itself from the 1st Century B.C., after a Greek bronze by Leochares, a sculptor of the late 4th Century. Because we have no adequate way to form any notion of Leochares's style and because the *Apollo* is an extreme demonstration by any standards, it seems wiser to accept it as predominantly an original creation from its own period.

The artistic philosophy of its author may be inferred from the incongruity between the subject and its style. A certain lady named Niobe had seven sons and seven daughters. She was careless enough to boast of her many children to Leto, a lady who had only two, and Leto's feelings were hurt. But Leto's two were Apollo and Artemis, who took immediate action to put Niobe in her place. They took their hunting bows, sought out the prolific family, and shot all fourteen children full of arrows while their helpless mother looked on. The myth is one of the most brutal in the history of Greek literature; were it to be committed to sculpture at all, one would think it might have attracted the interest of some morbid realist capable of rendering the heartless brother and sister as the dangerous animals they had for the moment become.

Instead of that, we see Apollo in the very act of letting off an arrow, his pose as self-consciously graceful as a dancing master, his face vacant of expression, his hair and drapery a definition of the careful carelessness that has ever been the special province of the dandy. The rendering of the nude anatomy is even more important. The stylistic intention appears to be almost opposite to the musculature cultivated by the Pergamene tradition. Instead of emphasizing and exaggerating the bulge and number of the muscles, a systematic effort has been made to simplify the surface into the smallest feasible number of contours. Each contour was then polished to a smooth, gentle curvature. That elegance and even grace result, no one can deny; but a certain weakness — especially inappropriate for so robustly callous an action — is all too apparent.

Like the *Belvedere Torso,* the *Apollo Belvedere* had historical influence thrust upon it. When, during the period of the French Revolution and the days that followed, it fell to the painter David (see Chapter 18) to bring Neo-Classical art into being, he and other members of the movement fastened upon the figure-style represented by the Apollo, and made it their own. They believed they were working from Greek sculpture at its purest and best, an archaeological error made possible only by the lack of better examples from the classical period — most of the good ones, as set forth above, having become accessible only after it was already too late to change the temper of Neo-Classicism.

*

7

STRUCTURAL PRINCIPLES

In most architecture prior to that of the Romans, the structural principles employed are so simple and straightforward as to require little explanation and small effort of understanding. The historical role of the Romans was to appreciate the possibilities of the arch and vault — long known in principle, but never applied on a significant scale. By exploiting, developing, and refining the arch and the vault, the Romans brought engineering forward as far as it ever advanced before the Industrial Revolution of the 19th Century A.D. They made structure an integral part of the aesthetic transaction; without an adequate knowledge of the forces at work and the members designed to withstand and sustain them, it becomes quite impossible to make any rational estimate of the merit of a Roman building. Because the same principles the Romans used were also employed in later styles, we shall find it convenient to review the entire problem of structure as such without restricting ourselves to Roman applications.

The primary purpose of architecture is to enclose useful space, thus permitting human beings to keep themselves warm, dry, and nourished. Without buildings of some kind, life could not be maintained on this planet except in the most favored climates. In most places where people live, rather elaborate and expensive buildings are necessary because of the severity of the weather. Until the time of the Romans, appreciation of useful space was for the most part limited to the provision of physical necessities. The aesthetic possibilities of interior architecture were explored only in the most elementary way. It is to the eternal credit of the Romans that they opened up this fundamental realm of art, and, in their best buildings, produced great masterpieces of interior design. Without intimate knowledge of the arch and vault, nothing of the sort would have been possible.

ANDERSON

Fig. 7.1 Rome. The Pantheon. From an engraving.

ARCHIVES PHOTOGRAPHIQUES

Fig. 7.2 The abutment of a tunnel vault by means of two continuous half-tunnel vaults. From a model of Notre Dame du Port at Clermont-Ferrand.

ARCHIVES PHOTOGRAPHIQUES

Fig. 7.3 Toulouse. Saint Sernin. View in the nave.

Fig. 7.4 Salient pier buttresses arranged to take the thrust of a ribbed tunnel vault. From a restoration of the Abbey Church at Cluny.

STOEDTNER

ARCHIVES PHOTOGRAPHIQUES

Fig. 7.5 A view underneath the wooden roof superimposed to keep the weather from the tunnel vaulting of a French church of the Romanesque Period.

Fig. 7.6 The cross vaults of the Cathedral at Chartres as they appeared after the burning of the wooden roof in 1836.

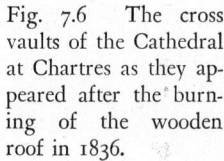

ARCHIVES PHOTOGRAPHIQUES

For the sake of completeness, we must mention that all building begins with the foundation. Because the foundations are out of sight below the ground, we may omit detailed consideration here; it is one of the few instances where engineering may legitimately be separated from art, and relegated to another department of study. Even so, it is worth remarking that very few of the world's great buildings stand on firm rock. The ledge comes close to the surface at Athens, providing an ideal substructure for the Parthenon and other temples, but the entire city of London, probably the most densely populated area in the world, rests on wet mud. It is a considerable problem to build any large building there. Skyscrapers are nonexistent in spite of the high land values in the city and elsewhere. It is probable that the foundations of some of the great buildings in the British capital actually represent more intelligence and judgment than the superstructure which interests the art critic. Recording that truth, let us pass on.

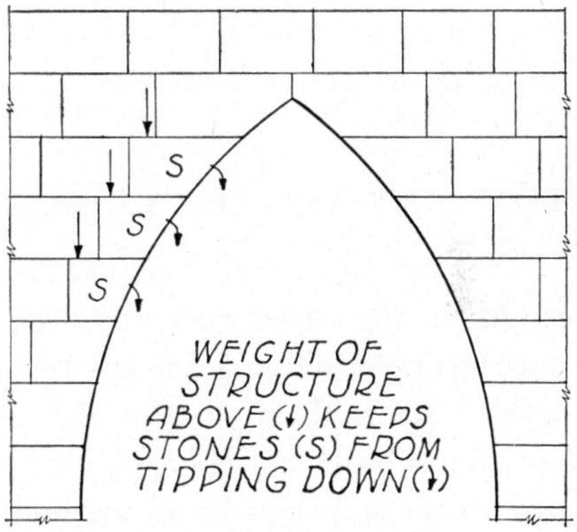

Fig. 7.7 The corbelled arch.

Foundations having been provided and vertical supports having been set up in the form of columns, piers, or parallel walls, the problem of enclosing space resolves itself into spanning the opening between supports. The methods for doing so are few in number and involve physical principles of an elementary kind; it is their application which is tricky, expensive, and dangerous. In application, moreover, the several methods for spanning a gap are severely limited by the materials available.

Until structural steel and glass became available in large sizes and at low cost, construction was limited to wood and masonry. Metal and glass were known, of course, but came only in little pieces — enough for a window or a hinge. The architect had to think of them as accessory rather than fundamental. Limited to wood and stone, he could span an opening by (*a*) using a *beam* or *truss,* both of which fall under the generic term of *lintel;* or by (*b*) using the *true arch.* A third method, the *corbelled arch* (Fig. 7.7), might be listed for the sake of completeness; it has seldom been used except in Mycenaean Greece and for some of the buildings put up in Central and South America before the arrival of the Europeans.

The word *arch* is ordinarily reserved for a door or window which happens to illustrate the arch principle. When precisely the same theory is extended to the construction of a masonry roof, we speak of a *vault.* Vaulting was the only fireproof roofing available until very recent times. There are several kinds, none perfect. We shall describe presently the three types of vault which have gained an important place in architectural history, either because they were mechanically convenient or especially good-looking.

When steel became available in large pieces at low cost, and could also be fabricated in other ways, two further principles opened up for the architect. Both had been known since time immemorial, but neither had ever before been practical in the requisite size and strength. The new principles are: (*c*) the *cantilever,* and (*d*) *suspension.* Neither has yet been sufficiently seasoned to have its mature effect upon design; it is nevertheless a safe prediction that the appearance of our future buildings will be radically different from anything we are now used to.

THE POST-AND-LINTEL SYSTEM

The post-and-lintel system of construction has already been covered at some length in the chapter about Greek architecture. Every child has invented it once again for himself. He sets two of his blocks endwise on the floor, and lays a third across them to span the gap. The vertical blocks are *posts,* and the horizontal block is the *lintel.* However simple in theory and elegant in application, the post-and-lintel method presents some serious practical difficulties (or did until steel became available) whenever applied to a building any larger than a shed.

Because stone is brittle, lintels of that material will crack of their own weight unless the span between posts is kept very narrow; and even then, no stone lintel may safely be loaded with any great amount of weight — as, for example, the upper stories of a high building. Large blocks of stone present serious problems, moreover, in the matter of procurement. Few quarries furnish sound material in big sizes, and even where available, great lintels of stone demand either an excellent system of roads, conveniently located rivers and harbors, or a system of canals — before the railroad, they could not otherwise be transported from the quarry to the site of the building. It is only in Roman times and our own that the necessary transport has been feasible; in other periods, some other method had to be used if big buildings were to be constructed at all.

Whenever columns or piers are placed close together, the floor space is inconveniently curtailed and the vista of the interior crowded. For that reason alone, the Romans had a strong motive for developing the vaulted roof; but whenever and wherever it was necessary to span a gap that amounted to anything without resort to the principle of the arch, the wooden lintel was the only member that could serve. Simple wooden lintels of large size demand primeval forests; they are unknown in most of Europe. Instead, wide spans were bridged by some form of *truss* (Fig. 9.56). We may define the truss as an open-work lintel made from a number of short lengths of material bolted together. The object is to arrange the pieces so that they cooperate in stiffening the member as a whole. The truss is known in a variety of patterns. All look complicated, but the system behind the arrangement can always be resolved by reference to the triangle — a form that cannot be made to change its shape unless one or more of its legs be broken. The most intricate truss usually amounts to a number of small triangles, each defying distortion. Because it can be made from small parts, the truss offers no special problem of transport. It is also an exceedingly efficient device mechanically, but very rarely is it good-looking. In first-class buildings, therefore, the trusses of the roof are usually concealed by a ceiling, a custom to which the only notable exception is the English *hammer beam* truss of the late medieval period (Fig. 12.27).

Like every other wooden member, the wooden truss is subject to rot, fire, and destruction by insects. One might jump to the plausible notion that all these faults were corrected when steel trusses became available, but unhappily such is only half the truth. Steel is fireproof only in the sense that it will not feed the flames. The material loses strength rapidly at elevated temperatures, and buildings framed in steel do not enjoy a high rating with the underwriters. Most steels so far put into use, moreover, are subject to rust. They are subject also to the phenomenon known as the fatigue of metals, a gradual and unpredictable loss of strength culminating in sudden failure. For all these reasons, structural steel — in spite of its great strength and the easy solution it offers for many a vexing structural problem — is no panacea even though it is the greatest boon of modern architecture.

PRINCIPLES OF THE ARCH

The practical application of the arch principle is of great antiquity, but to this day there exist no reliable formulas for predicting within close limits the carrying capacity of a particular arch or the various forces it will generate. The statements made below may be taken as a summary of the time-honored assumptions to which engineers refer when they design arches and vaults, but the reader has a right to know that a certain school of thought has lately developed in France — exemplified principally by the writings of Pol Abraham — which challenges our standard theory as overly intellectual and entirely too cautious. As yet, these new suggestions have gained more currency among art historians than among the men who have to take the responsibility for actual construction. Allusions will nevertheless be made from time to time, pointing out where the conventional analysis may in fact need revision.

The principles of the so-called *true arch* can best be explained by reference to Fig. 7.8, which shows, in several views, a semicircular arch built of cut stone. Arches of any other shape may be constructed at the option of the builder

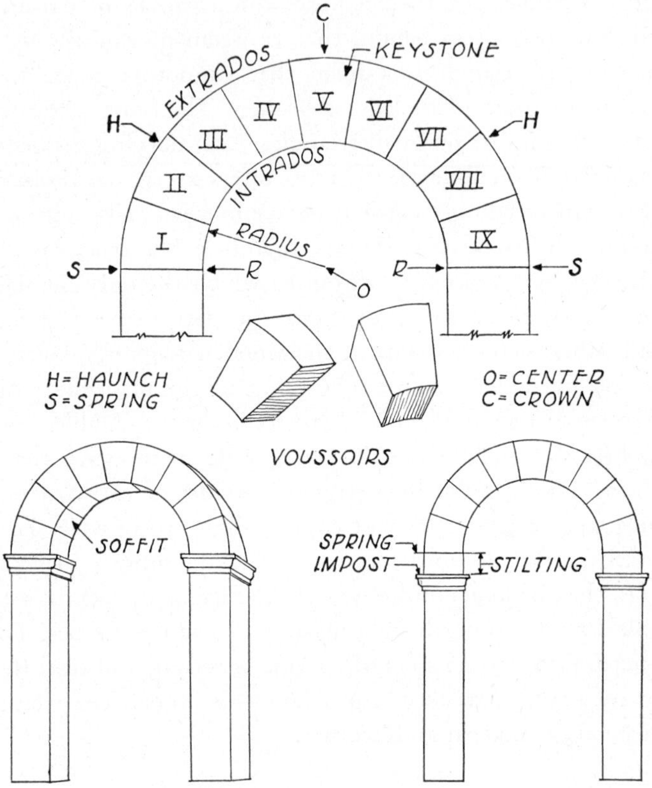

Fig. 7.8 Elements of the true arch.

without any change in the fundamental procedure, and with little more difficulty than it takes to produce this simple shape. Fig. 7.9 shows some of the shapes that have gained currency at one time or another.

A great many arches are not built of cut stone like the one shown in Fig. 7.8. Concrete, either pure or reinforced, is often used, in which case the arch becomes virtually monolithic as soon as the cement has set. It is nevertheless assumed in practice that the action of a concrete arch will duplicate that of an arch built from cut stone. The same provision is therefore made for the safety of the structure; and for purposes of explanation, we may assume that all arches are similar in principle to the one shown in the figure.

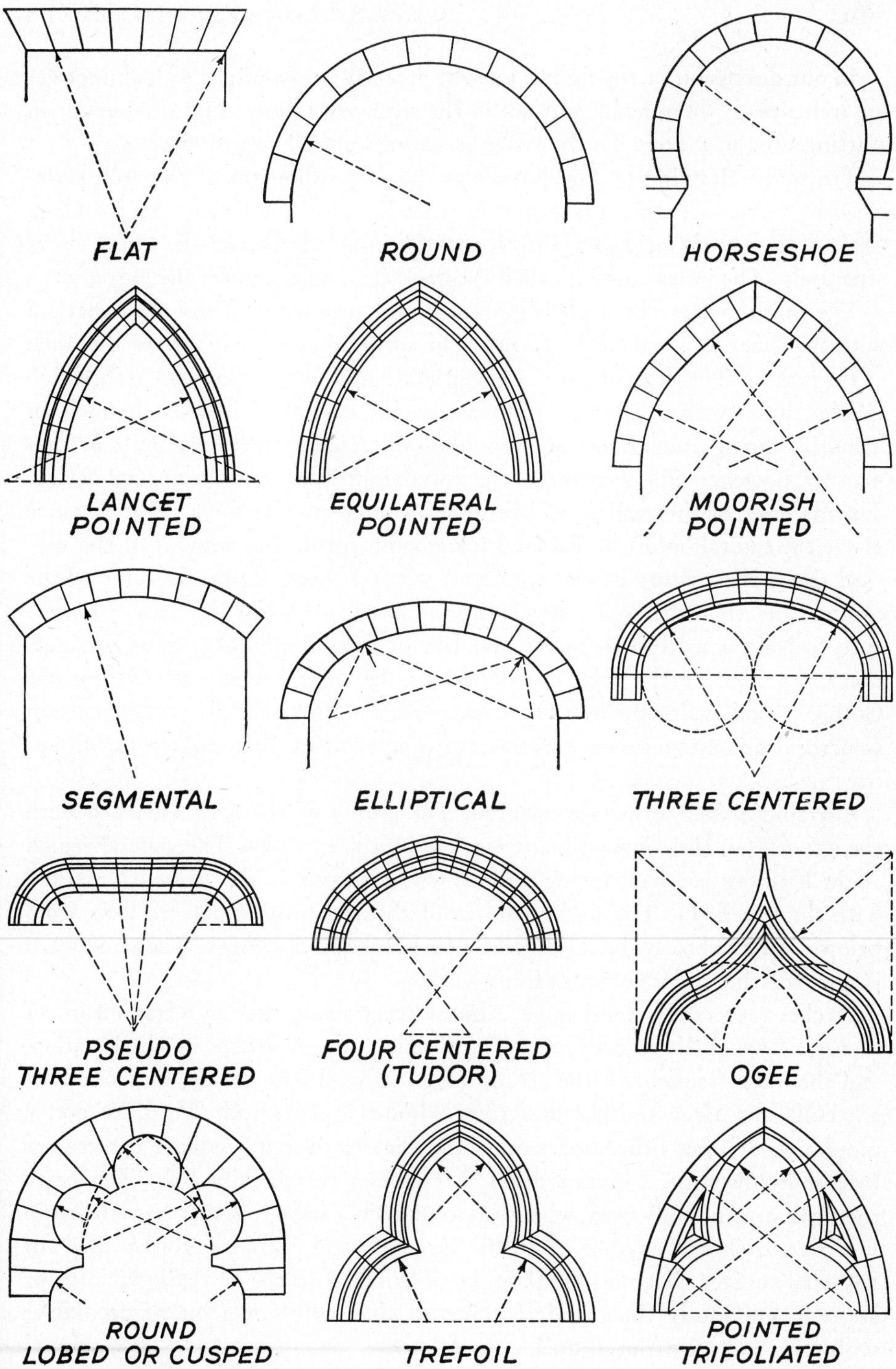

Fig. 7.9 Drawing to illustrate the great variety of openings to which the principle of the true arch lends itself.

In our discussion of the figure, we will proceed as one might in looking over an arch already completed, and not in the sequence followed by the builder in putting up a new arch. To the latter concern, we shall return later.

The upper drawing of Fig. 7.8 shows that the silhouette of the arch is defined by two concentric arcs struck in from the center marked with the letter O. It is frequently necessary to refer to the inner curve and the outer curve separately. The inner curve is called the *intrados*, and the outer the *extrados*.

The point where the arch begins to curve upward and inward (marked with the letter S) is called the *spring*. The spring may or may not be the same as the *impost*. The drawing in the lower left-hand corner shows an arch which springs directly from the upper surface of the capital of its pier; in such an instance, spring and impost are synonymous. Arches are rarely built in that manner, however. The drawing to the lower right illustrates the normal design. The masonry of the arch, it will be noted, rises vertically for a slight distance above the capital before actual curvature commences. The amount of the vertical rise is the *stilting* of the arch, and where stilting exists, we refer to the capital beneath as the impost, reserving the word *spring* for the start of curvature. Stilting is used in the great majority of cases simply because it enhances the appearance of the arch in relation to the piers beneath it. During the Gothic period, stilting was used in extreme amounts in order to get certain structural advantages. We may reserve discussion of that matter for Chapter 12.

Certain further terms are essential. The *crown* of the arch (marked with the letter *C*) is the topmost point reached by the extrados. The general region about halfway between spring and crown is known as the *haunch* (marked with the letter *H*). The under surface of the arch into which we look from below is referred to as the *soffit* (see lower left-hand drawing). The same word is used for the under surface of any vault.

Arches very rarely stand alone. Almost every vault rests on a framework of arches, as we shall see presently. The simplest use of arches in combination, and the most frequent, is the arcade (Fig. 7.16). In an arcade, similar arches are built one after another in a row. Almost every arcade has a cornice, a moulding, or some other horizontal immediately over it, clearing the crowns by a short distance, a juxtaposition that gives a certain visual significance to the small area of wall space where adjacent arches melt together. As labeled in Fig. 7.16, such wall space is called the *spandrel;* and the same word is used for any wall surface that may be thought of as being in the aesthetic vicinity of an arch. Obviously the spandrels offer an ideal field for a bit of decorative sculpture, and are often so used.

The arch drawn at the top of Fig. 7.8 is made up of nine separate pieces of stone, each labeled with a Roman numeral. Each piece is in the shape of a wedge, and the technical term for any one of these wedges is a *voussoir*. Two voussoirs are drawn in perspective at the middle of Fig. 7.8. There is of course nothing sacred about the number nine. Most arches actually have more than nine voussoirs, but there is no use in complicating our drawing and making it hard to read. Whatever the number chosen, it is usual to make it an odd number, for reasons that will appear in a moment. As drawn, each of the nine voussoirs subtends an angle of twenty degrees measured at the center of the arch. The central and highest voussoir is known as the *keystone* (No. V on our drawing), a distinction that has a certain practical reason behind it, as we shall see.

Consideration of the data so far presented will show why the arch is usually preferable to the post-and-lintel system. A very large arch can be built from small stones; indeed some of the greatest medieval cathedrals contain hardly a stone that could not be lifted into place by a gang of twenty or thirty men aided by the block and tackle, the inclined plane, and other simple devices. In Roman work, spans of forty or fifty feet pass unnoticed, and the dome of the Pantheon (in effect an arch; see Fig. 7.18) swings no less than 142 feet between supports. Such heroic dimensions are impossible in masonry by any other known method of building. It is worth noting in this connection that a wooden truss can be built with a wide span. The hammer-beam roof of Westminster Hall in London (about 92 feet between walls) long had the reputation of being the greatest span ever achieved in wood; but during World War II, improved methods of fastening timbers together were developed in response to the shortage of steel — resulting in some tremendous trusses bridging even wider gaps.

A well-constructed arch can be loaded with an almost unbelievable amount of weight, which is a vital consideration in a large building or a high building where several thousand tons of masonry may have to be carried by a spanning member. Inspection of Fig. 7.8 will show, however, that any increase of weight above the crown will result in squeezing the voussoirs more and more tightly together. No matter how intense, the strain on each voussoir is compression, a force that good stone is well able to endure. Twisting and bending strains, which stone cannot sustain, are altogether avoided.

We must now turn our attention to the faults of the arch, which are two in number and both serious. For assembly, every arch requires *centering;* and when built, every arch requires *abutment* or it is unsafe.

Centering is the technical name for the wooden form over which the arch must be constructed. As indicated by Fig. 7.10, the form must remain in

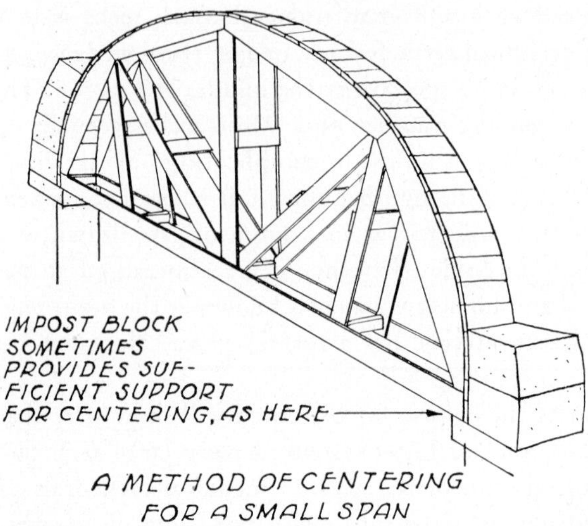

Fig. 7.10 An arch under construction, illustrating the use of wooden centering.

place until the keystone is dropped into position; otherwise there would be nothing to prevent the voussoirs from falling to the ground. The essential feature of any piece of centering is that its upper surface correspond precisely with the true shape of the soffit of the arch, and obviously it must be strong enough to hold this shape without any distortion whatever against the very considerable weight of all the voussoirs. It is no easy matter to build such a form. Excellent design and much sound timber are requisite. Timber being

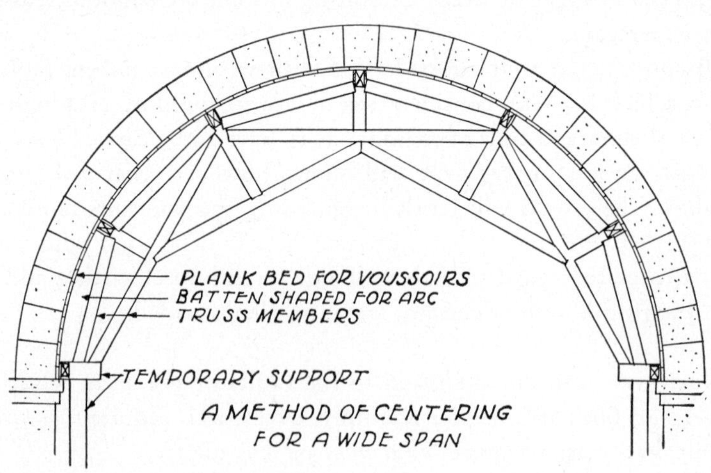

Fig. 7.11 An arch completed, with centering yet to be removed, illustrating an economy of material as compared to Fig. 7.10.

scarce and expensive, all sorts of stratagems have been employed from time to time to reduce the cost of centering. Fig. 7.11 shows one method of building the form with slightly less timber than Fig. 7.10 would require.

Abutment is made necessary by the *thrust* of the arch. Thrust results from the fact that every voussoir is a wedge, and acts like any other wedge. For purposes of understanding the principles involved, we may concentrate our attention upon the keystone only, and postulate extreme conditions. Let us assume that a giant with an immense hammer strikes a blow vertically downward, hitting the keystone plumb in the middle. Fig. 7.12 is an attempt to visualize what would happen if the keystone was driven downward, the other voussoirs failing to slide over each other: the arch would expand beyond its original boundaries as represented by the dotted lines. The slow force of weight tends constantly and inexorably to accomplish the same results as the giant's hammer. Any arch bearing a considerable burden is constantly trying to bulge outward along the extrados. This is the force we call *thrust*. Fig. 7.12 was drawn merely to introduce the conception of thrust; it oversimplifies the action of that force in actual cases. Fig. 7.13 comes nearer to illustrating what happens when an arch fails. Assuming that the spring is held in place, the first breaks will occur in the region of the haunch. In practice, abutment of one kind or another is usually brought to bear against both spring and haunch; in which case, the arch is assumed to be safe.

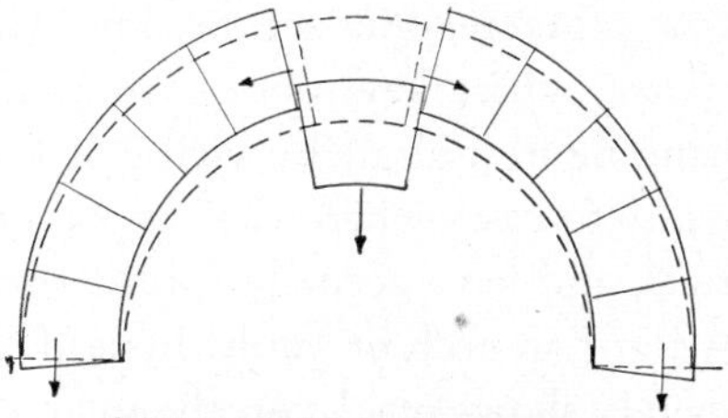

Fig. 7.12 Schematic drawing to illustrate the phenomenon of thrust.

It will be noted that both Fig. 7.12 and Fig. 7.13 make sense only if we assume that the voussoirs can slide over each other, and such has been the as-

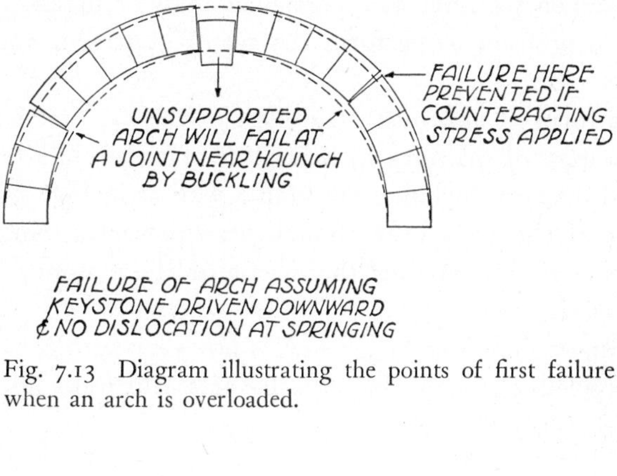

Fig. 7.13 Diagram illustrating the points of first failure when an arch is overloaded.

sumption upon which we have been proceeding in our entire discussion of thrust. Everything that we have said would be literally true if, in the laboratory, we made some voussoirs of polished steel, oiled them, and put them together to form an arch. But no one builds that way, and it is here that the recent critics of our conventional theory of thrust get their ammunition. They point out that stones under compression can scarcely be made to slide at all, that stones joined with mortar tend to stick together as though glued, and that concrete, once set, becomes virtually monolithic. They bring forward instances where keystones have been removed, leaving the two sides of an arch hanging in mid-air by virtue of the adhesive quality of the mortar. They also point to cases where the supporting piers have sunk, departed from the vertical, and have actually spread further apart at the top — thus stretching the span of an arch or vault. Instead of falling in, the much abused arch or vault merely shows cracks on the soffit.

As indicated earlier, none of these arguments have as yet impressed the engineer. All of them depend upon the assertion, direct or tacit, that masonry may safely be subjected to twisting and bending strains, any and all of which produce tension somewhere or other. Masonry will sometimes endure a moderate amount of tension for a very long time; there are instances where masonry has endured it for centuries. It is nevertheless a fundamental principle of structural design that no brittle material shall ever be deliberately subjected to tension. There is no way to tell when it may crack and collapse.

Methods of Abutment

There is no way to keep an arch from changing shape and collapsing except to provide a compression force opposite in direction to the thrust and equal to it. The act of doing this is denoted by the verb *to abut,* from which we derive the generic noun *abutment*. The noun *buttress* and the verb *to buttress* are near-synonyms. If there is any difference in meaning, usage seems to prefer *buttress* when we refer to a particular mass of masonry of specialized design, placed in position to perform the act of abutment for an individual arch.

The simplest form of abutment (simplest in theory, that is; often hardest to provide) is a mass of masonry to either side of the arch, a familiar instance being an arched doorway opening through a wall as in Fig. 7.14A. In such a case, the thrust of the arch, even though very powerful, would almost certainly be insufficient to overcome the inertia of the masonry, and no movement can take place.

The arrangement shown in Fig. 7.14A is not very subtle. It demands only the vaguest knowledge of how thrust really acts. But quite apart from its rationale, abutment by a mass of masonry to the right and left of an arch, opposing the thrust by sheer weight, is altogether impractical if not downright impossible in the majority of buildings. If, for instance, an arch springs from a point a hundred feet above the ground (and that is not uncommon), an extravagantly ponderous substructure would be required to support the neces-

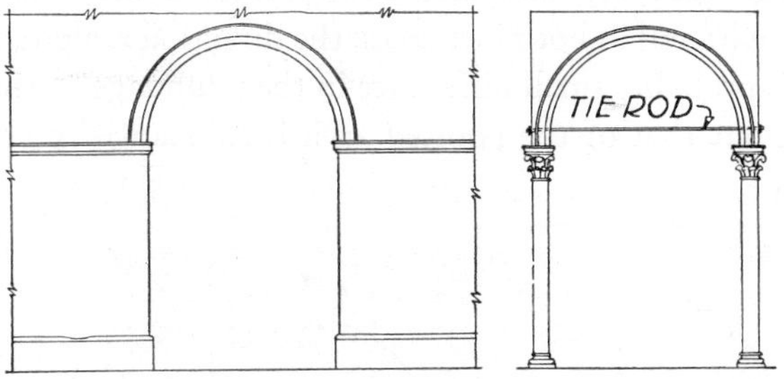

Fig. 7.14A–B A. Arch opening through the thickness of a wall. B. Arch buttressed by a tie rod.

sary material. The cost would be prohibitive, the cubic measure of masonry being a rough indication of expense. The appearance and utility of the lower parts of the building would be ruined.

In order to escape this necessity, architects have resorted to all sorts of arrangements, all intended to reduce the amount of buttressing. Individual applications vary in appearance, but the most important principles to be borne in mind are the following:

To reduce the thrust of the arch: This can be accomplished in two different ways: (*a*) by reducing the weight of all parts of the building, thus reducing the pressure upon the arch and hence its capacity to generate thrust; (*b*) by

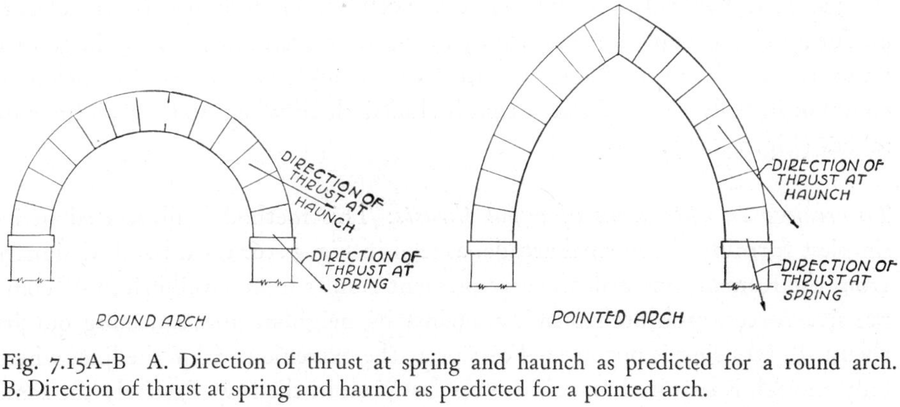

Fig. 7.15A–B A. Direction of thrust at spring and haunch as predicted for a round arch. B. Direction of thrust at spring and haunch as predicted for a pointed arch.

changing the shape of the arch until a form is found that thrusts less for a given load over a given span. In general, the flatter the arch the more it thrusts. Steeply pointed arches thrust least of all. To understand the last statement, refer to Fig. 7.15A which shows the familiar semicircular or " round " arch in contrast to a pointed arch approximately like those used in the French Gothic cathedrals. In each case, arrows indicate the predicted direction of the thrust at spring and haunch; and in both instances, the direction is along a downward diagonal. There is probably small difference in the poundage of the thrust exerted by either arch, but that of the pointed arch is substantially closer to the ver-

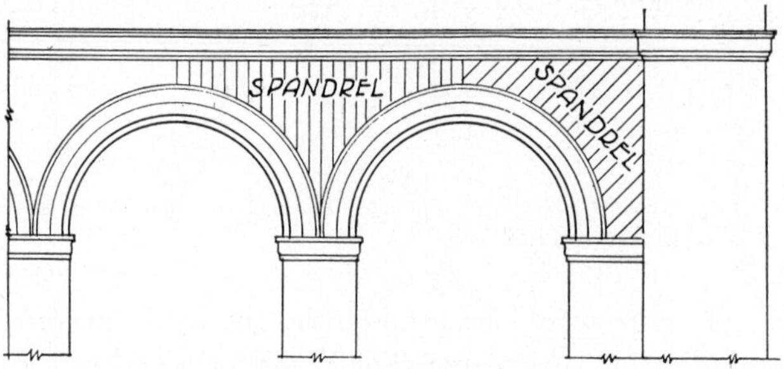

Fig. 7.16 An arcade.

tical — or as the physicist would put it, its horizontal component is less. Less masonry is therefore demanded to prevent it from spreading sidewise.

To introduce a tension member in the fabric of the arch: The so-called " tie rods " familiar in Italian work of the Gothic and Renaissance periods illustrate this method (Fig. 7.14B). The tie rod binds the arch together across the spring, thrust to the right pulling against thrust to the left with equilibrium resulting. Made of wood or iron, the tie rods are quite able to sustain the tension; and mechanically, the expedient is excellent. Tie rods are also the cheapest form of abutment, but everybody agrees they are hideous. They introduce an extraneous line into the composition of the arch but were nevertheless so common in Italy that painters often included them when making pictures of arches (Fig. 15.31).

To arrange an opposition of equal thrusts: This method is illustrated in its simplest form by the normal arcade, as seen in Fig. 7.16. Used by all designers from the Romans onward, the arrangement results in an equilibrium of compressive forces, each arch pushing against its neighbor and canceling out its thrust. Buttressing is not needed except at the extreme ends of the line, where only enough is required to stabilize the last arch in the row. Precisely the same principle, but in more complex application, was employed to contain the thrust of the largest Roman and medieval vaults. See below, pages 201 ff.

To group arches of comparable size together in such a way that thrusts are concentrated at a few predetermined points: Similar in principle to the method just cited, this technique is primarily a solution to the problems of vaulting where many arches may be thrusting in several directions. We shall postpone further explanation until we discuss the cross vault. See pages 203 ff.

To refine the shape and placement of the buttress, thus making it possible to reduce its size: The flying buttresses of the French Gothic are the best example. See Figs. 12.18,46. These delicate members contain the thrust of some very large vaults. Nothing of the sort could have been possible except for the supreme knowledge of the amount and direction of thrust available to the French master builder during the 13th Century. No other abutment has been equally daring. It is important to emphasize that the knowledge to which we have just referred was not arrived at by mathematical calculation; in fact, mathematical analysis of the arch remained completely impossible until the development of the Calculus during the 17th Century. Practical builders learned by trial and failure, and passed their knowledge on to favorite apprentices by word of mouth. Often they were very close-mouthed indeed; hence the frequency with which the " mysteries " of one craft or another are mentioned. In the absence of anything resembling our modern formulas and building codes, hideous accidents were common.

PRINCIPLES OF THE VAULT

The Motive for Vaulting

The construction of any sizeable vault is obviously an immensely expensive, laborious, and dangerous operation, but there is still no better way to enclose a reasonable volume of space beneath a fireproof roof. The modern reader cannot possibly feel the fear of fire as the ancient and medieval builders felt it. Fire protection is now so efficient that every insurance company, as a matter of conservative financial practice, assumes risks many times its total assets. The only serious conflagrations within recent memory are those which resulted from bombing during World War II. Conditions were bad enough during Antiquity, and much worse during the Middle Ages. A few examples will perhaps suffice to show that the risk of fire is enough to account for the tremendous energies expended in the development of vaulting; we need seek no other motive.

In 1120, an inflammable church at Vézelay, the predecessor of the present Madeleine, burned up with a loss of 1,127 lives. In 1134, the basilican cathedral at Chartres was totally destroyed, an event that accounts for the start of the present church on the same site. During the single year 1188, the cities of Rouen, Troyes, Beauvais, Provins, and Moissac were all laid waste by fire. In 1194, a second blaze swept the cathedral at Chartres; the loss of life is not accurately known, but all records say it was terrific. During the first 25 years of the 13th Century, Rouen burned six times.

All of these fires are believed to have been accidental. To see the risk as the medieval builders saw it, we must add to this partial citation from the awful total all of the burning deliberately set during wars, disorders, and punitive measures. An inspection of the pictures by Hieronymus Bosch and Peter Brueghel will furnish visual evidence enough; the backgrounds contain many a burning farm and village, the work of Margaret of Parma or the Duke of Alba as the case may be.

Those who have read descriptions of the great fire of London in 1666 can form for themselves an impression of the fire risk in a medieval city. What could be done when inflammable buildings were conglomerated along miles of narrow, crooked alleyways? In the complete absence of adequate organization and equipment, such a place, once well alight, would burn until there was no more fuel for the flames.

The designer of a building was thus compelled, at any period prior to our own, to assume that the town around his church, cathedral, or temple would be entirely consumed by fire not once or twice during the life of his edifice, but many times.

By use of the vault, however, it was possible to make almost certain that the major buildings would endure. They are in plain sight to this day all over Europe. The grand old Pantheon at Rome has lasted for more than eighteen centuries without significant repair. Churches more than 500 years old are in daily use in almost every city. Indeed we may say that well-designed vaulted buildings will, with any reasonable care, resist the attrition of nature indefinitely. Their chief enemy is man — either the peasants coming to purloin ready-cut building stone, or the government deliberately removing a monument as the French did with the old abbey at Cluny toward the end of the 18th Century.

It is necessary, of course, to surmount almost every vault with a peaked roof of wood, the function of which is merely to protect the masonry from rain and snow (Fig. 7.5). These wooden rain-sheds are inflammable, but they can burn with surprisingly little effect upon the masonry below. The wooden roof over the vaults of Chartres burned in 1836. A drawing made after clearing the debris shows the fabric of the church almost undamaged (Fig. 7.6). In 1914, the cathedral at Reims was subjected to shelling; and its wooden superstructure burned with the same comparatively innocuous result — the damage done to the church at that time was almost entirely the work of explosion, not fire.

The Dome

The *dome* can best be described as a vault whose shape is generated by rotating a simple arch around its vertical axis, much as we generate an ellipsoid by rotating an ellipse around its long axis.

Fig. 7.17 shows a dome, about half finished, being built of cut stone. It will be noted that each voussoir is beveled in two planes, vertically and horizontally. As a result, the dome consists of a series of rings, or *courses*, of masonry. Each course is self-sustaining as soon as its last voussoir is dropped into place. There is no necessity for a keystone at the top; and, more than half the time, this space is left open to help solve the difficult problem of lighting the interior. If completely open, as it is in the Pantheon (Figs. 7.1,18) at Rome, we call the hole an *oculus*. If covered with an openwork tower as it is in most Renaissance and Baroque examples (Fig. 17.9) the word *lantern* is used — for opening, for tower, or for both as convenient.

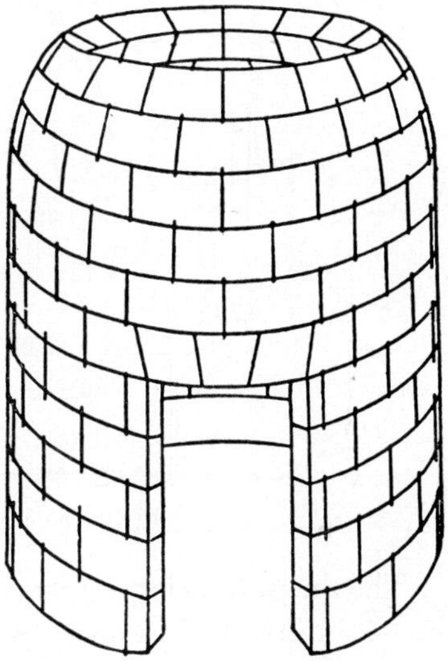

Fig. 7.17 A dome constructed from cut stone.

Very few large domes have been constructed of beveled voussoirs as shown in Fig. 7.17. The dome of the Pantheon at Rome seems to have been built by pouring concrete around a framework of brick arches. That of Hagia Sophia in Constantinople (Figs. 10.1–4) is believed to depend upon a similar skeleton, special care having been taken to make the work as light as possible. During the Middle Ages, only a few domes were built in Western Europe. The best, and one of the finest compositions in the history of architecture, is the dome over the Old Cathedral at Salamanca (Fig. 11.32). It is supported by a system of ribs, salient ribs being the usual thing for all medieval vaulting. When Brunelleschi designed the dome over the crossing of the Cathedral at Florence, he also used ribs to do the work, but in accordance with Renaissance feeling for form as contrasted to function, he tried to smooth up the surface by concealing the working members. The same thing applied to the great domes of Saint Peter's in Rome (Fig. 17.9) and Saint Paul's in London. Regardless of the chosen method of construction, it is assumed in practice, and rightly so, that all domes will act like the one shown in Fig. 7.17: there will be a continuous pressure of thrust all the way around the circle, extending upward as high as the haunch.

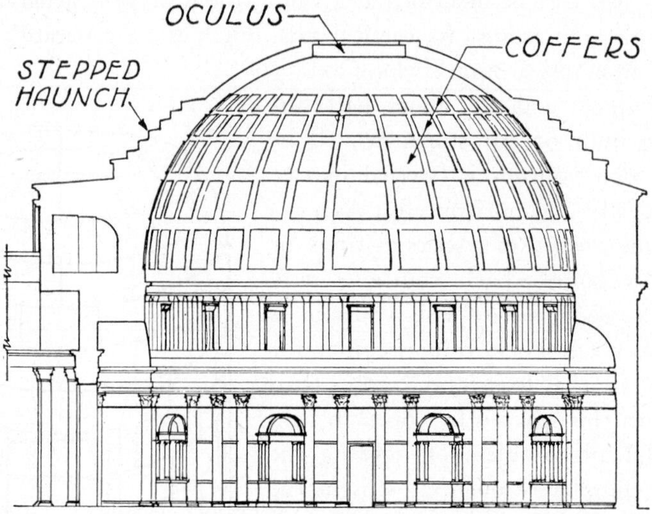

Fig. 7.18 Rome. The Pantheon. Cross section.

The thrust of a dome puts the architect upon the horns of a dilemma. If adequately buttressed by inert masonry as in Fig. 7.18, the exterior silhouette is almost entirely concealed. If lifted into the air where its majestic form can show up, chances must be taken with the abutment — a fact attested by more than one disastrous collapse. The dome of Hagia Sophia (about 107 feet in diameter) has collapsed either in whole or in part at least three times: in 558 A.D., 567, and 987.

Accepting the risk, the designers of the largest domes built during the past 500 years have deliberately raised their domes high in the air, setting them up on a circular ring of masonry technically known as a *drum* (Fig. 17.9). In such a situation, abutment must be provided by tension. Several great wooden rings, or *chains*, hold in these domes as a belt holds in the belly. Thus the handsome appearance of the exterior is bought at a steep price: when they fail, tension members fail suddenly; and there is no way to ascertain their future endurance within reasonable limits. Because no one can give utter assurance that such a dome may not one day fall down, the use of tension for abutment has never gained absolute approval. It is possible that wire rope woven from some superior and noncorrosive material may one day nullify these reservations.

The Dome over a Rectangular Ground Plan: Squinches and Pendentives

Another consideration militating against the frequent use of the dome is the fact that its shape does not make an easy fit with any ground plan convenient for ordinary use. The Pantheon has a circular ground plan (Fig. 7.1). Its substructure may properly be described as an immense drum, artistically harmonious with the dome above. But a circular room lends itself only to a few purposes; for most functions, a worse shape cannot be found. Most furniture and most human work fit better into a rectangular room.

It is also necessary to point out that almost every service and ceremony entails a focus of attention by an audience or congregation, which is the same thing as saying that many eyes should be directed along a horizontal line of sight toward a speaker, an altar, or whatever. But the dome, by its very shape, insists that we give attention to the vertical axis around which it is generated, the effect being to emphasize a spot on the floor. Excellent for tombs, baptistries, and other small and specialized buildings, the centralizing effect is often undesirable, as any picture taken inside Saint Peter's or Saint Paul's will show. The drum of the dome opens up a hole in the ceiling; one wonders what in the world can be up there — an innocent revery in itself, but not identical to reverent attention upon the altar. In spite of all this, the exterior beauty of the dome has dictated its choice in many instances. In almost every case, the dome has been raised over a rectangular room for the reasons stated; and in almost all cases, also, the dome is supported by four piers describing the corners of a square.

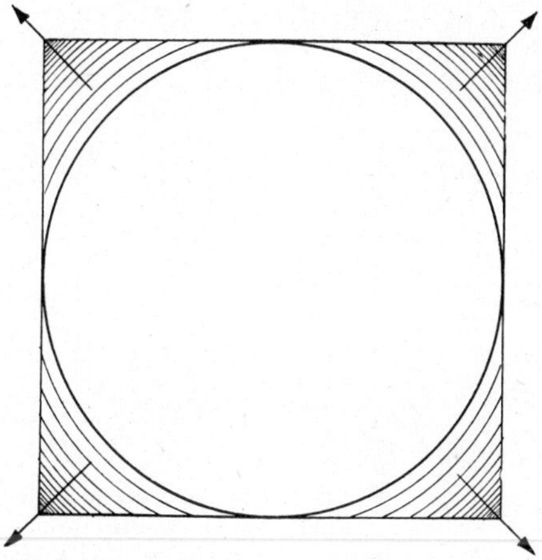

Fig. 7.19 Schematic drawing in plan view to illustrate the necessity for transitional members whenever a dome is placed over a rectangular ground plan.

Figs. 7.19 and 7.20 are intended as an aid in visualizing the situation. A dome raised over a square ground plan may have a diameter shorter than the length of one side of the square. Many domes do. But, plainly, no dome may have a diameter longer than the length of a single side of the square, and geometry tells us that the diagonal of any square must be longer than one of its sides. A square amounts to two right triangles, each being subject to the law that the square on the hypotenuse is equal to the sum of the squares on the other two sides — hence if the square shown in our figures is 50 feet on a side, its diagonals must measure 70.71 feet. No matter how we try to get out of it, the circular dome above will not cover all the floor space described by

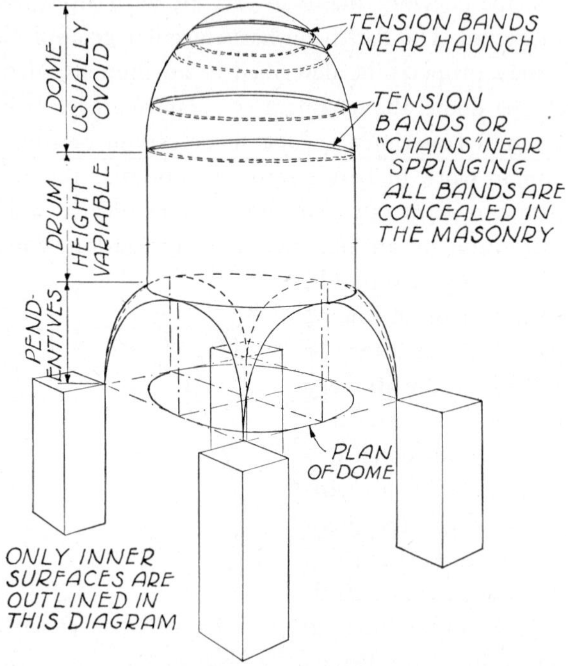

Fig. 7.20 Schematic drawing illustrating the component parts of an architectural fabric involving a dome raised on a drum above pendentives.

the square beneath. We are left with four vacant spaces at the corners as shown in Fig. 7.19; and we must fill them up with transitional members as shown in Fig. 7.20. The problem, of course, is to design a transitional member which will modulate the shape of the square into the circular shape from which the dome can spring, and which will be, at the same time, both structurally sound and aesthetically acceptable. Various devices have been tried; two, the *pendentive* and the *squinch,* have excelled all others in popularity.

The Pendentive

Generally considered the more elegant of the two popular solutions to the problem just outlined, the pendentive was selected to support the dome at Hagia Sophia in Constantinople, for Saint Peter's at Rome, and for Saint

Paul's in London — to say nothing of almost every other domed building where prestige was a special desideratum.

The early history of the pendentive is obscure. The Romans evidently did not know it, but they surely came close to it in some of their buildings. The complete mastery of the pendentive evident at Hagia Sophia (532–537 A.D.) has never been adequately explained. It must have been reasonably familiar to the architects; otherwise they would hardly have dared use it for the support of one of the largest domes ever built, about 107 feet in diameter. Among art historians, the general belief is that the pendentive was invented and developed in the Near East, perhaps as far away as Armenia. The date of the invention seems to be somewhere between 300 A.D. and the beginning of the 6th Century.

A *pendentive* (Fig. 7.21) is a spherical triangle. Four are needed. One must spring from each pier, spreading upward and inward to meet the others. A circular base is thus provided from which the dome can spring. In most cases, the radius used for each pendentive is approximately equal to one-half the length of the diagonal of the square below. But this is by no means necessary. By using a longer radius, the pendentives can be made to sweep further inward over the floor, meeting in a smaller circle, and providing a base for a smaller dome.

Fig. 7.21 Pendentives as seen from below.

The shape of a pendentive is handsome. By using it in connection with the dome, the architect opens up for himself the whole realm of curvature, an area scarcely entered as yet except for the brief period of the Byzantine 6th Century. Because our modern ferro-concrete lends itself to curves more conveniently than any earlier building material, we may perhaps look forward, when modernism becomes mature, to seeing parabolic and hyperbolic contours where we now see angles and unrelieved straight lines.

But like everything else, the pendentive is not without its drawbacks. Because it partakes of the nature of an arch, a pendentive exerts thrust, and the pressure of the thrust will be distributed, more or less, over its entire outer surface. The direction of the thrust will, moreover, be along the diagonals of the square beneath the dome. Logical abutment can be provided by a substantial mass of masonry with its own axis along the same diagonal; or, on the principal of vector diagrams, the diagonal force may be subdivided into its components and buttresses built to suit. A neat and perfect solution to this special problem of abutment has not to date appeared in the history of architecture; even Hagia Sophia, the queen of domed buildings, leaves much to be desired in this respect.

The Squinch

Used mostly for the smaller and less famous monuments of Byzantine and other medieval architecture, the squinch has more to recommend it than one might at first suppose. Various shapes have been used. In principle, they all boil down to the typical form shown in Fig. 7.22. Arches are thrown across the gap between the four piers as before, giving support to a square wall surface. Across each corner of the square thus established, smaller arches are thrown, converting the square into an octagon. Because the octagon approaches the shape of a circle, the dome may be allowed to spring from it if care is taken to adjust each course of masonry in or out a bit as the case may be. The fit is not perfect, but it is good enough.

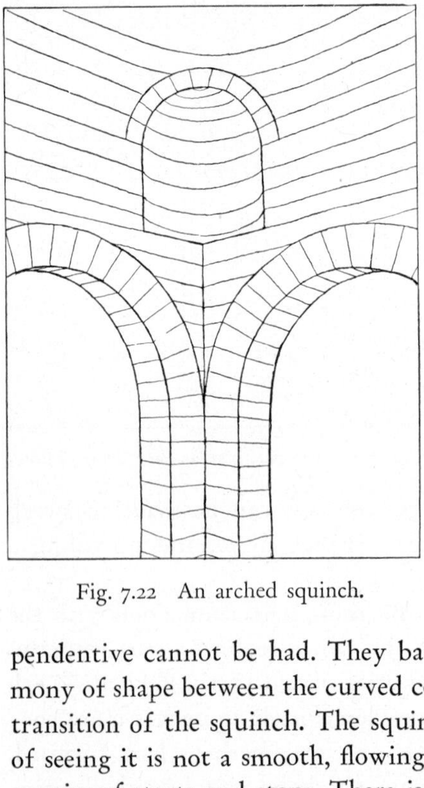

Fig. 7.22 An arched squinch.

Most writers seem to suggest that the squinch is something to be pitied — a makeshift to be tolerated when the pendentive cannot be had. They base their feeling upon the obvious disharmony of shape between the curved contour of the dome and the rather abrupt transition of the squinch. The squinch does give a bump to the eye: the act of seeing it is not a smooth, flowing motion as it is with the pendentive, but a series of starts and stops. There is more to design than harmony, however. Contrast is just as useful: for example, the juxtaposition of dissimilar shapes which squinches provide. While pendentives are admittedly more suave, squinches are rugged and direct. Incontestably, one can take solid satisfaction in the looks of them.

The Tunnel Vault

Considerably more adaptable to general utility, the *tunnel vault* (often called the *barrel vault*) has a shape as simple and lucid as the dome. The shape can be described as that of a simple arch indefinitely extended in the horizontal direction (Fig. 7.23). The tunnel vault has the very great advantage of making a natural fit with a rectangular ground plan. Its shape also tends to produce a strong emphasis on the longer horizontal axis of an interior, an emphasis corresponding with the ceremonial requirements of churches, law courts, and other public buildings.

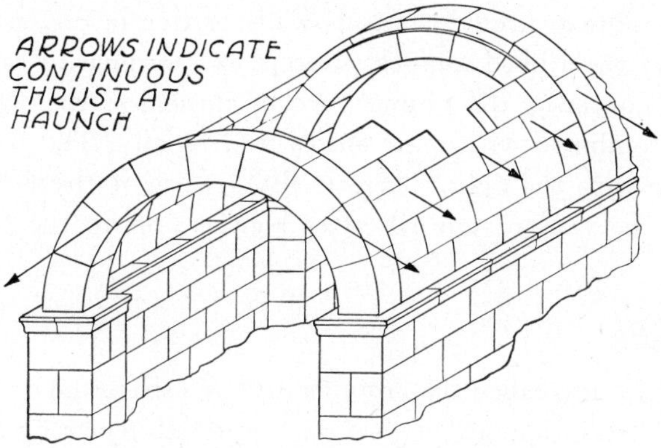

Fig. 7.23 A ribbed tunnel vault.

But in spite of its pleasant form, the tunnel vault shares certain faults with the dome. Abutment is required along every foot of its length, as shown in Fig. 7.23. Such abutment is automatically supplied in the New York subway system, but is difficult and expensive to provide whenever a tunnel vault is raised high in the air. Unless lighted by electricity, the tunnel vault is also almost certain to be gloomy because it is unwise to place windows higher than the spring. Windows often appear there, but it is impossible to guarantee the stability of any vault if pierced above the spring.

Like the dome, many tunnel vaults are finished smooth or have the soffit decorated with some surface pattern. In a number of excellent examples, however, the problem of continuous thrust was ameliorated by the use of ribs. The Romans did this when vaulting the so-called Baths of Diana at Nîmes, and the ribbed system was popular in the Romanesque architecture of the 12th Century (Fig. 7.3). A series of duplicate arches were first swung transversely across the rectangular chamber below. A single piece of centering doubtless sufficed for all, being moved on to the next station as each arch was completed. The vault was then in frame, and the primary ribs divided the whole into compartments, or cells. Each cell was then filled in with much lighter masonry as suggested in Fig. 7.23. Every cell of masonry between a pair of rib-arches became, in effect, a short section of tunnel vaulting, but because of its light weight, logic could be cast aside and its thrust neglected. For all practical purposes, the stability of a ribbed tunnel vault can be insured by placing buttresses against each of the main ribs. In effect, a division of the total thrust had been brought about, with pressures localized at a series of points along the sides of the building. Usually such buttresses take the form of salient piers standing against the outside walls, as seen in Fig. 7.4.

Aesthetically, the ribbed tunnel vault is extraordinarily satisfactory. By repetition, the curves of the primary arches emphasize the character of the shape. Line is combined with mass simply and lucidly. The shadows cast by the ribs change with the light. There is also a sense of rhythmic progression established by the view of one rib after another, off to the far end of the building.

The Cross Vault

The *cross vault,* also called the *groin vault,* has a shape too complex for convenient verbal description, although it may be worth repeating the loose statement that the form would result if two tunnel vaults were built intersecting each other at right angles. Such vaults may be constructed from beveled voussoirs, but most of those in existence depend upon a framework of six arches with the cells between closed in by light material. Fig. 7.24 shows the framework of a single ensemble, or *bay,* of cross vaulting, and Fig. 12.12 gives a good idea of the appearance of a number of bays joined together to cover the oblong nave of a great church. In medieval vaulting, the ribs of the frame are almost invariably left in plain sight. Roman and Renaissance architects almost always used a frame similar to that shown, but concealed it in some way or other in order to produce a smooth soffit.

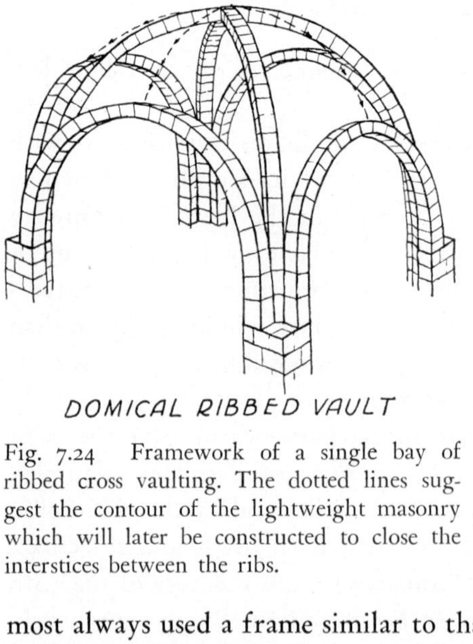

Fig. 7.24 Framework of a single bay of ribbed cross vaulting. The dotted lines suggest the contour of the lightweight masonry which will later be constructed to close the interstices between the ribs.

The two special advantages of the cross vault are these: For covering a long, narrow interior like the nave of a church, no other vault can be buttressed so easily or so cheaply, and the shape of the vault automatically provides spaces for large windows at a very high level. It is natural that such considerations would appeal to the engineer. We have, however, been subjected to a plethora of quasi-aesthetic praise based on the untenable notion that anything that is efficient must also be lovely. The truth of it is that unless very well designed indeed, the cross vault produces a chaos of line and contour. On purely formal grounds, the best of them are none too good.

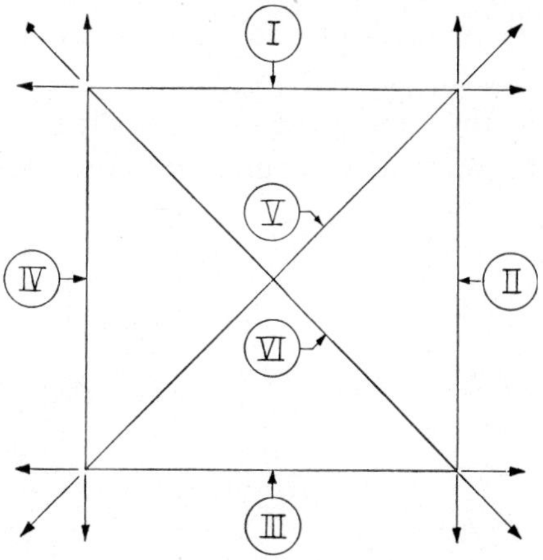

Fig. 7.25 Thrust pattern of a single bay of cross vaulting as seen in the plan view.

Fig. 7.25 shows Fig. 7.24 in plan view, the six arches of the frame being symbolized by straight lines on the paper. Each of the six arches will be exerting thrust both ways in the normal manner, as indicated by the three arrows drawn at each corner. Obviously, the thrust pattern is so complex that it would be a great nuisance to provide abutment for a single bay of cross vaulting. A single bay, in fact, is no good at all, and is never used. The real merit of the system begins to appear only when several bays of such vaulting are

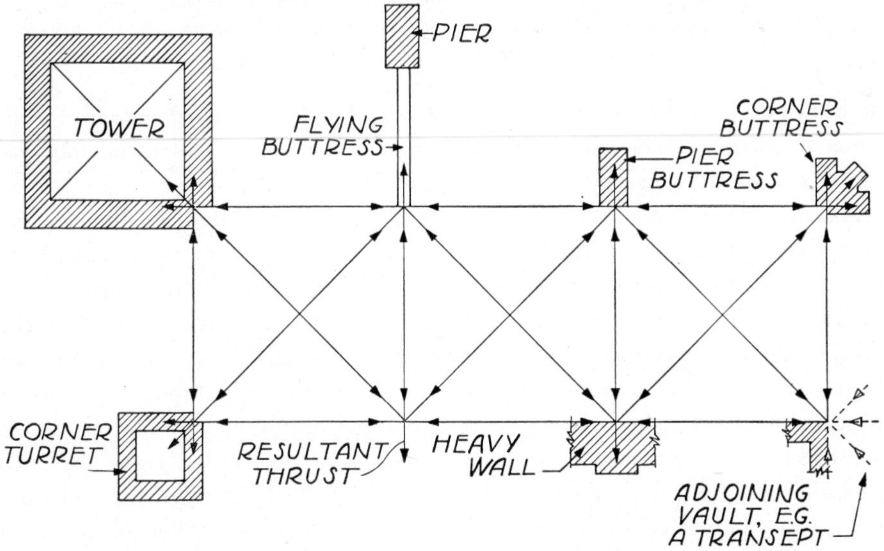

Fig. 7.26 Schematic drawing of several bays of cross vaulting arranged as they would be to cover the nave of a church, with indications of various methods for abutment.

grouped together in sequence as in Fig. 12.12 and as indicated in the schematic plan presented in Fig. 7.26.

Rather complicated at first glance, Fig. 7.26 will gradually make sense as we proceed. Overlooking its details for the moment, let us give the separate ribs the names they ordinarily bear in such an ensemble. The arches which lie in the same plane as the walls of the building are called the *wall ribs.* The arches that swing directly across the interior at right angles to the long axis of

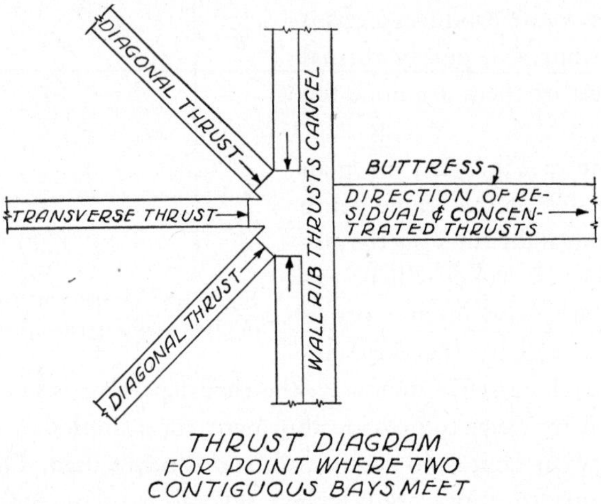

Fig. 7.27 Diagram to illustrate the interaction of thrusts where two contiguous bays of cross vaulting come together at a common corner.

the building are called the *transverse arches.* Those that go diagonally from corner to corner, intersecting at the crown of each bay, are called the *diagonal ribs,* or simply the *diagonals.*

The notable properties of the cross vault become manifest when we consider what happens to the thrust pattern every time a pair of contiguous bays come together at a common corner. Fig. 7.27 is an attempt to illustrate the situation; its intelligibility depends upon the reader's capacity to visualize the several arches rising up toward him, each being indicated here only by lines on the flat surface of the paper. The two wall ribs act like any duplicate arches in an ordinary arcade; their thrust being equal and opposite, they merely cancel each other out. The transverse ribs necessarily press outward at right angles to the building. There is nothing in the frame itself to hold them in, and buttresses must be placed to contain them. The two diagonals press against each other, and combine to produce a resultant thrust also at right angles to the wall of the building. We might prove this by vector diagrams, but the principle will be plain if the reader will merely put his palms together with the forearms diagonally behind them. By exerting an equal pressure on each palm, he will force his hands directly forward in the manner of the diagonal ribs of the vault. It follows that the thrust of the diagonals simply has the effect of in-

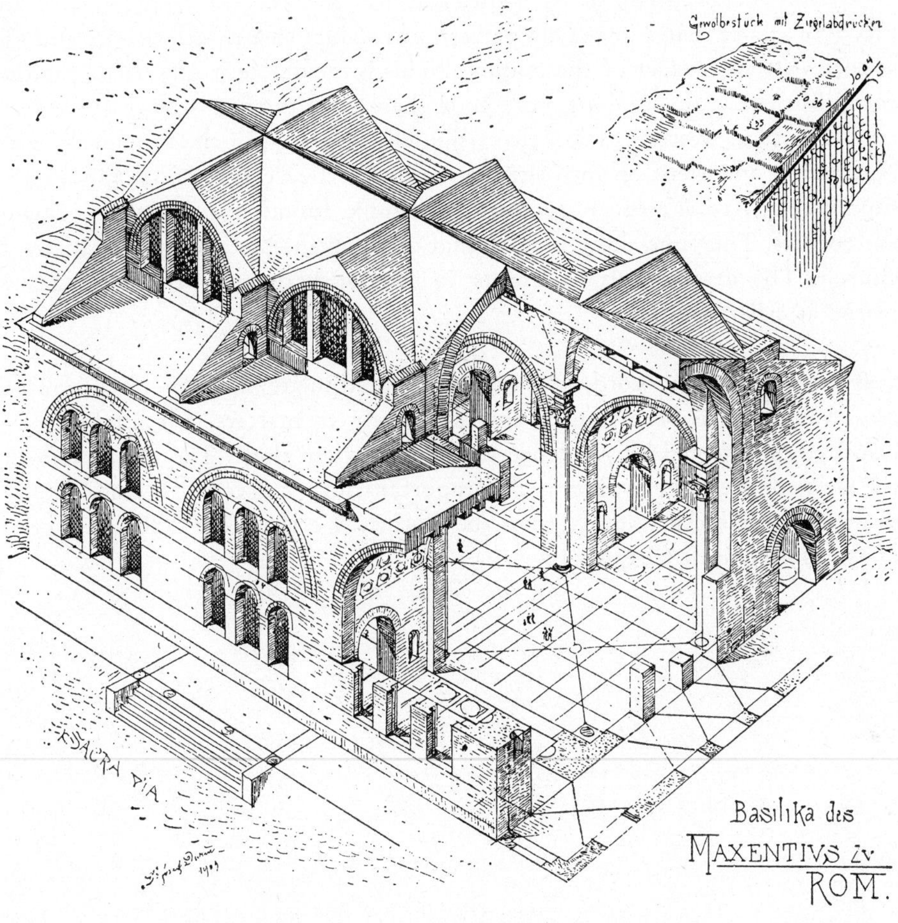

Fig. 7.28 Rome. Basilica of Constantine. Reconstruction.

creasing the thrust already exerted by the transverse ribs. Both may be stabilized by the same buttress made a little heavier.

Various shapes and kinds of buttresses have been used from time to time to provide abutment for cross vaulting. Fig. 7.28 shows a reconstruction of a great Roman building with cross vaults. In its original condition, the interior looked very much like the main concourse of the Pennsylvania Station in New York, that building being a self-conscious derivative. The immense windows and small buttresses are impressive testimony to the efficiency of the mechanics of the cross vault. The dainty flying buttresses of the French Gothic cathedrals (Fig. 12.18) stand as the ultimate refinement in the art and science of abutment.

Another detail needs to be mentioned for the sake of completeness. In Fig. 7.26 we see that a mixed-up pattern of residual thrusts is left outstanding at each extreme corner of the building. This is inevitable in the nature of the form, but the fault has done more good than harm in the history of architecture. The twin western towers that originally appeared in the Romanesque of Normandy and went on into the Gothic of the Ile de France, in appearance superb (Figs. 11.16; 12.7), perform the simple function of weighting down the corners. The same thing may be said of the transepts and apse of many a church. The drawing also attempts to suggest various types of buttresses placed at other points.

By way of a final word, it is necessary to stipulate that our discussion of cross vaulting has been limited almost entirely to matters that might be illustrated or inferred by reference to the plan view alone. The interaction of the arches as seen in elevation is also important, but it does not become vitally so in any architecture earlier than the Gothic. We therefore defer treatment of the matter until Chapter 12.

JULIAN HUXLEY

Fig. 8.1 Petra. The Khazna.

ALINARI

Fig. 8.2 Cori. The Doric Temple.

Fig. 8.3 Baalbek. The Round Temple. After an engraving.

RICHARD W. DWIGHT

Fig. 8.4 Nîmes. Pont du Gard. 175 feet high.

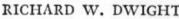

ARCHIVES PHOTOGRAPHIQUES

Fig. 8.5 Nîmes. Maison Carée. Early 1st Century A.D. 87 by 45 feet. Columns 29 feet high.

ALINARI

Fig. 8.6 Rome. The Arch of Constantine. 312 A.D.

*

8

HELLENISTIC AND ROMAN ARCHITECTURE

The history of architecture during the Hellenistic age and under the Roman Empire bears a striking resemblance to developments during the latter part of the Gothic era, and also to what happened as the Renaissance moved on into its Baroque and Rococo phase. In all three instances, even the ordinary architect was erudite in the manipulation of the current style. Professional opportunities, moreover, were many and generous, but nothing had happened to change the world enough to create a demand for the discard of the style to which people were then accustomed, and the invention of a new one. Every problem presented by the inner logic of the incumbent style had been solved long ago; there was no great or fundamental challenge to the imagination. In its absence, designers tried to get to what satisfaction they might from sophisticated variations on familiar themes. It is all too easy for the historian to dismiss such work with a passing word; some of it is very fine indeed, and all of it is entertaining. It is true, however, that the reader is already well equipped to understand the architecture of late Antiquity, and we may legitimately save space by confining ourselves to a few broad generalizations.

The first of these is the existence of an obvious parallel between the architecture of late Antiquity and its contemporary sculpture, the latter already reviewed in Chapter 6. Amid the confusion of many separate tendencies of style, we may discern at least three distinct trends of architectural thought. Most conspicuous and most fertile of monuments was the tendency to complicate design and proliferate ornament, as exemplified by the round temple at Baalbek (Fig. 8.3) and by the rock-cut tomb façades of Petra (Fig. 8.1). Keeping always within the classical idiom and yet contorting it, such architecture arrives at compositions so spectacular as to be hardly classical at all — the natural counterpart of sculpture in the Pergamene tradition. Over against this strident urge for display, we may note a certain lesser number of designs which, like sculpture in the class of the *Apollo Belvedere*, are distinguished by overt chastity. Among them the small Doric temple at Cori (Fig. 8.2), about 35 miles southeast of Rome, is a conspicuous example. Its shafts are no less than 8⅔ diameters in height, its abaci virtually straight-sided, and its total effect so neat and sanitary that the Parthenon seems by comparison somewhat immodest. In addition to the two trends of taste just cited, the realistic point of view, so productive in the field of sculpture, made itself felt in architecture also. Its operation is manifest in the appearance of a great variety of specialized buildings, some frankly and completely utilitarian: markets, law courts, theatres and amphitheatres, race courses and grandstands, fora, aqueducts, libraries, lighthouses, sidewalks protected by roofs and colonnades, gateways, bathing establishments, and so on. We are dealing, in short, with the architecture of an increasingly refined civilization, with complexities disturbingly like our own.

The fondness for colossal dimensions, which to ancient eyes must have seemed the most conspicuous feature of Hellenistic statuary, was far exceeded in the field of architecture. It commenced almost before the Hellenistic Period began. The two greatest temples of the 4th Century B.C. — that of Artemis at Ephesos (begun in 356) and that of Apollo Didymaeus at Miletus (335–320) — have linear measurements approximately twice those of the Parthenon, and on the basis of cubic measurement (a better criterion for comparison of size) work out to be about eight times as big.

But even the Hellenistic Greeks must take a place far behind the Romans whenever scale enters our calculations. The Colosseum is an oval some 620 feet long, 500 feet wide, and a little more than 157 feet high; it seated about 40,000 persons. The Pont du Gard at Nîmes (Fig. 8.4) rises 157 feet above the stream it spans. The rotunda of the Pantheon at Rome (Fig. 7.1) is 142 feet in diameter and 142 feet high. The main hall of the Basilica of Constantine was 226 feet long by 82 feet wide, and its cross vaults swung 114 feet above the floor. These measurements were approximately duplicated in the so-called *tepidaria*, or central concourse, of the Baths of Caracalla and those of Diocletian. Those immense rooms, very much the same as the main concourse of the Pennsylvania Station in New York, are all but lost in the ground plan of the entire establishment (Fig. 8.10) which, as a whole, amounted to a veritable district set up on a platform 1,080 feet on a side.

In assessing the cumulative effect of the architecture of later Antiquity, it is not enough to emphasize its geographical extent or the large number of buildings put up. We must also take account of size; and in so doing, must prod ourselves with the realization that our own sensitivity to scale has become somewhat jaded by the performances of the 20th Century. To the medieval man, even the Gothic man, the size of Roman buildings represented something quite out of the question by reference to any techniques he knew or could imagine as practical. His topography was marked with Roman ruins, and he could explain their colossal dimensions only by assuming that Roman times were grander than his own. To the man of the Renaissance, Roman scale stood as a challenge, a test of whether he was worthy to recapture the power and scope of the ancient world. It is significant the test was met only two or three times: the Cathedral of Florence, Saint Peter's at Rome, and Saint Paul's in London. Otherwise, for scale like the Roman the world had to wait for the Industrial Revolution, and it is no wonder the uniquely beautiful buildings at Athens tended to become forgotten amid a wealth of larger and more assertively gorgeous monuments.

In a world teeming with builders hard at work, it was inevitable that a certain amount of progress should take place even though no fundamental change of view came to the architectural philosophy established during the Great Age of Greece. A few important experiments were tried. Some of these proved successful; and in the ensuing discussion, we shall confine ourselves to Hellenistic and Roman developments important enough to have exerted a substantial influence on the future.

Standards of Construction During Late Antiquity

It is possible to read in a hundred books that standards of construction became inferior as soon as the Great Age of Greek art passed into memory. The comparison is hardly fair. It rests upon the presumption that the marble of Periclean Athens may be taken as typical of "Greek work," in comparison to which we may in the same breath express our scorn for the masonry of the average workaday Roman contractors. The buildings on the Acropolis are of course a special case, uniquely fine and typical of nothing; the Greeks did a great deal of work that is worse, some of it even worse than the dead average of later Antiquity.

However inevitable, such comparisons furnish a poor start toward an appreciation of Hellenistic and Roman construction. We should commence, rather, by attempting to visualize the problems that opened up for the architect as the Greek horizon expanded after the death of Alexander and again as Rome organized the civilization of the whole European world. The assignment, if we may call it that, was bigger than the task of lending beauty and dignity to a single part of a single city. It amounted to nothing less than the construction of entire cities in all kinds of places, some with building materials in good supply near at hand and others remote from essential resources. The explanation for the Hellenistic and Roman outlook lies waiting for the reader if he will turn to one of the several translations of Vitruvius.

A mere perusal of the headings will suffice to indicate what is meant. Vitruvius felt under the necessity of writing a section giving people advice about the selection of a site for a city. Throughout his text, he returns again and again to consequences of the choice, and ramifications thereof. Streets, he warned, ought to have their direction determined by that of the prevailing winds. He wrote at some length about finding water, storing water, and distributing water around the town. He pointed out that domestic architecture must vary in style with the climate, and had something to say about the exposure desirable for rooms of one kind and another. He also put forward suggestions for adapting one's house to the site available, and he cited considerations to be kept in mind when selecting a place to build the various public buildings considered necessary in that age of ramified economy and government.

His statement of general desiderata is accompanied throughout with rather specific instructions for the handling of materials. Brick, sand, lime, stone, stucco, timber, and paints found their place in his book at one point or another. Before he let himself go with respect to architecture as a cultural manifestation, he took time, moreover, to write down a few home-truths about foundations and substructures. Indeed, it is only when he forsakes the practical and ventures into the history, philosophy, and psychology of art that he gets beyond his depth and ceases to carry conviction.

Space prevents our trespassing further upon what the reader may find for himself in Vitruvius, but it is important to give special emphasis to the great single development in the materials of architecture, a development that first became important in Hellenistic days and emerged in Roman times as supremely important. We refer to concrete.

Even the best cement is less attractive than good cut stone; less attractive, even, than the best of bricks. At the same time, no rational person can overlook the tremendous advantages offered by the material. Because concrete can be mixed by unskilled workmen from ingredients obtainable almost everywhere, and poured by them, it is possible for a few educated architects to direct the labor of an immense number of men — and thus construct buildings more cheaply than would otherwise be possible. Concrete may be used clear, adulterated with nondescript rubble, or reinforced. In good Roman work, the latter was usually the case. As in the dome of the Pantheon, the cement would fill the interstices of a logical lace-work of brick arches. The strength and endurance of a wall or vault so constructed is beyond calculation; suffice it to say that if permanence is all we have in mind, Roman concrete is the best building material the world has yet seen. The Roman dominion made its excellence a matter of common knowledge, with the result that concrete remained the builder's chief reliance throughout the Middle Ages and Renaissance. Today when machinery has replaced the unskilled labor of earlier centuries and iron is available for reinforcement, concrete has more than ever come into its own. Its introduction during late Antiquity must be classed as a major event in the history of architecture.

The Roman Temple

There is no important Roman architecture from the Republican period. Augustus himself is quoted as saying, "I found Rome a city of bricks, and I shall leave it a city of marble." He got the idea from contact with the architecture of Hellenistic Greece, and his policy is but an illustration of the extraordinary capacity of Rome to assimilate good things wherever they might be found. At that time, the Greek architectural tradition was the most accomplished the world had yet seen, and the Romans felt no impulse to invent another. Their temples, therefore, conform to the Greek type with certain historically significant changes.

One of the very best is the so-called *Maison Carée* at Nîmes (Fig. 8.5), originally dedicated to two grandsons of Augustus and dating from the very first years of the Christian era. As compared to the Greek temple, the most important difference is the introduction of a pedestal, or *podium,* which raises the entire building half a story above the ground. The podium provides useful space below the floor of the cella, and by increasing the total height, tends to increase the temple's value as a landmark. The use of a podium makes it necessary to provide a staircase by which one may climb up to the cella level, and we see such a staircase attached to one short end of the building, which thus attains a certain emphasis as the principal front or façade. It is important to note that the capacity of the stairway is far greater than that of the door to which it leads; it can accommodate more people than we can imagine wanting to enter or leave the building at any one moment. The purposes of such a stairway is not functional, but aesthetic: it is a grandiose piece of geometric sculpture, worthwhile for its varied mass, for the play of line it provides, and for the way it takes the light at different times of day. If of practical dimensions, it would have no such merit of appearance.

The Romans rarely used the free-standing peristyle of the Greek temple because they disliked the waste of interior space inevitable whenever an ambulatory is included on the plan. They therefore brought the cella walls out to the edge of the podium, and ran a peristyle of *engaged columns* (i.e., columns in contact with the wall) around. As a further means of dignifying the main front, it was customary to keep the cella fairly short, leaving several columns free-standing to form an entrance porch at the top of the stairway.

It is the Roman adaptation of the Greek temple, and not the Greek temple itself, which has dictated the design of so much modern building in the several classicizing styles. The deep portico at the entrance end is the " temple front " we find attached to innumerable blocks of utilitarian construction. The elevation of the Roman temple has also proven historically important. It established a sequence of elements: podium, order, entablature, roof — which we may find repeated in all proportions on thousands of exteriors all over the world.

The Maison Carée, like most other Roman columnar buildings, was built in the Corinthian Order. The entablature is much the same as the Greek Ionic except for the addition of small scroll-like brackets under the cornice. These are called *modillions*. They have an historical importance because they were borrowed in later times by Renaissance and Baroque designers, who used them (often in exaggerated sizes) to soften the linear transition presented to the eye when two parts of a building must come together at a right angle. It will also be observed that the Roman pediment is commonly built with an angle slightly more acute than the Greek. The change may be good to whatever extent it tends to balance the podium, but most critics dislike the proportions it dictates for the pedimental triangle.

The Question of Etruscan Influence on Roman Art

A great many scholars feel dissatisfied with any historical treatment of Roman art that does not include some allusion to Etruscan influence. The Etruscans, it will be remembered, were the strongest contenders against Rome in the early days when Rome was still attempting to establish her rule over the peninsula. They lived in the district we now call Tuscany, and in the end they were so thoroughly chastened and absorbed by the Romans as to render Etruscan archaeology a most difficult subject.

According to Vitruvius, the standard Roman temple, as described in the last section, conforms in the details of its arrangement to Etruscan temples. Having got the general idea of the temple shape from the Greeks, the Etruscans supposedly modified the type to the extent of making the cella wider, as just described, and adding the entrance porch. As drawn by Vitruvius, a typical Etruscan temple is almost square in plan (Fig. 8.7). Undoubtedly, Vitruvius correctly reflects the current belief among Roman architects that these

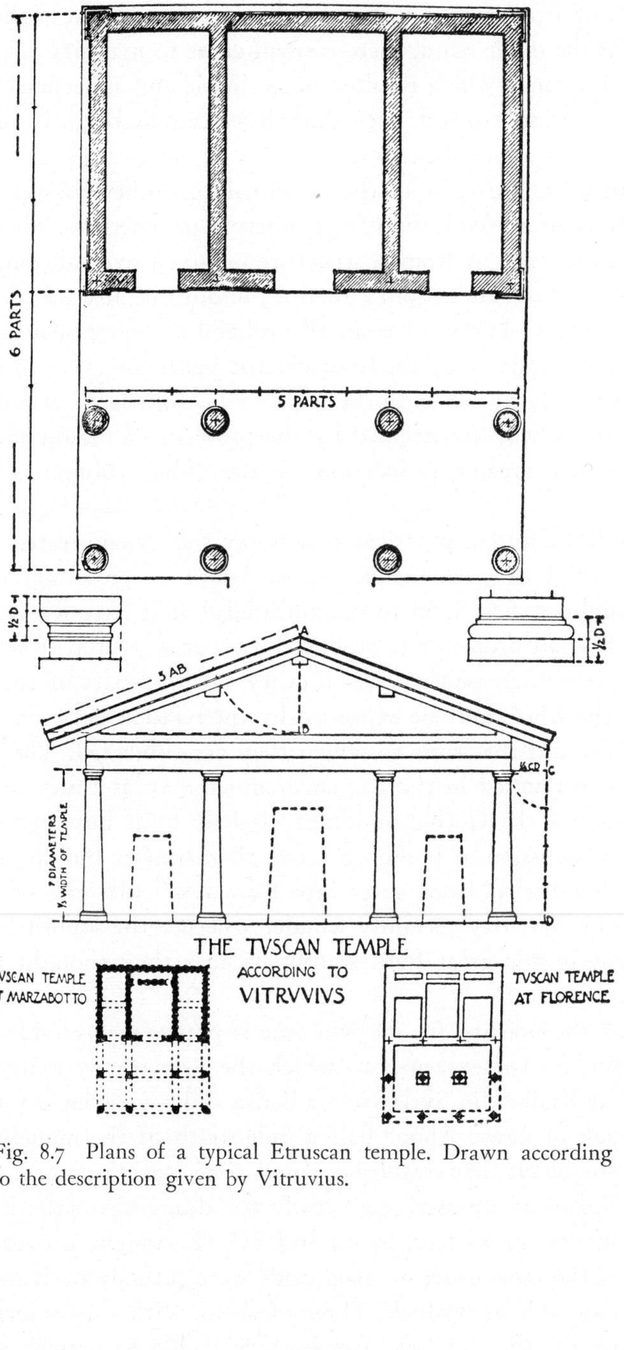

Fig. 8.7 Plans of a typical Etruscan temple. Drawn according to the description given by Vitruvius.

features were of Etruscan origin, and there is no reason to challenge his archaeology. On the other hand, there is small cause to magnify the importance of an artistic influence which resulted in so simple and superficial an effect.

There is some reason to feel, even though we cannot begin to prove it, that Etruscan precedent affected the whole history of art in Italy in a more subtle and profound way. We refer to the perennial and otherwise inexplicable recurrence in Italy of a predilection for ponderous proportions. This is first seen in Roman architecture. A Roman structure of given over-all dimensions will contain a greater bulk of masonry than a building in any other style except the Egyptian. The Colosseum has, in all probability, more openings than any other building ever put up by the Romans; and yet in any view of the exterior, the eye is met mostly by solids. In the Arch of Titus, where the designer's sense of form was in no way constrained by the problem of permitting crowds to circulate, a much greater proportion of the cubic volume is assigned to masonry.

It is difficult to find a practical reason for such exaggerated weight and solidity. The ideal of permanence — that common possession of all great builders — might at first seem to be indicated, but it is really very doubtful whether the Roman proportions produced a superior factor of safety. To increase weight is to increase the load on every working part of the fabric, and the safety of the whole may be expressed by the relation between the strength of the members and the stress to which they are subjected. The very inertia of buildings constructed in the Roman manner may at times be dangerous: during World War II, Gothic buildings (lightly built but logically braced) sustained the concussion of bombing better than heavier buildings of the Roman type. Explosives did not enter into Roman calculations, of course; but earthquakes did. We may certainly wonder whether the sophisticated Roman engineers went in for great bulk simply because they thought it might be stronger.

The love of the massive for its own sake is pretty well established as their motive, in fact, by the extremes to which the Romans went upon occasion. The quarries at Baalbek in Syria yield a dense and somewhat crystalline stone notable for lack of flaws. About half a mile south of the modern town, one may still see the block that establishes an all-time world's record. Called "the trlithon," it lies tilted up as though ready for dragging to the building site. The measurements are 70 feet, by 14 and 13. The weight is over a thousand tons. Stones of the same order of magnitude were actually built into the walls of the great ensemble at Baalbek. Three of them, with a cross section 14 feet by 11, measure 64, 63, and 62½ feet long. Such blocks present an herculean problem for the builder, and there is no special good in them if we are merely interested in sound construction. Split into smaller pieces, any one of them would furnish material for a house 60 feet by 60 on ground plan, 40 feet high, and with walls a foot thick. For such a performance, some reason other than the structural must be sought.

The heavy Roman proportions seem much more likely to have had their genesis in the plastic sense which so strongly dominated all classical taste. A strong tactile interest begets an interest in mass. An interest in mass breeds a desire for greater mass, which is to say for ponderous proportions. In view of the fact that the Romans carried this process much further than the Greeks and, unlike the Greeks, failed to work out an elegant system of proportional relations, we must call the tendency Roman or find some other source for it.

If a source exists, it is probably Etruscan. There are two main reasons for believing this. An Etruscan arch still stands in the ancient city walls of Perugia, known as the Arch of Augustus because part of the frieze above dates from that reign. It is a semicircular arch and terrifically, even inchoately heavy. The same may be said of other remains of Etruscan work, few though they are at this date. Some Etruscan paintings survive, and these tell the same story. The figure-style is bulky to a degree. There is reason, simply because the Romans lived in the same part of the world as the Etruscans, to believe that Etruscan precedent established the love of bulk. If so, the Etruscan temperament demonstrated an extraordinary power for survival. There are those who believe it lay dormant among Italians for an incredible number of centuries, coming sporadically out into the open to produce the ponderous figure-style of such artists as Giotto, Signorelli, and Michaelangelo. Were some other suggestion conveniently at hand to explain the phenomena just cited, the notion of recurrent Etruscan taste would be preposterous, but nothing else seems so satisfactory as a cause for otherwise capricious happenings. Pending findings of a very substantial kind, however, the whole question of Etruscan influence must be labeled a possibility, not a fact; and suggestions like these must be accepted as inferential.

Combinations of the Arch and the Orders

The Greek prejudice against the arch was strong enough to last a very long time, and seems to have relaxed only under the Roman Empire. As soon, however, as the arch became artistically acceptable, designers began to work with compositions in which it was combined with the orders. Arches were made to spring from columns in long arcades in the justly famous colonnaded streets of Palmyra, in certain parts of the small town known as Diocletian's Palace at Spalato, and elsewhere. Experiments of various sorts and kinds were tried, and two particular ensembles of arch and order achieved historical importance.

The first is well illustrated by the façade of the Temple at Termessus (Fig. 8.8), a place on the banks of the Catarrhactes River in southern Asia Minor and about 23 miles north from the coast. It is this very same arrangement that Brunelleschi adopted for the Pazzi Chapel façade (Fig. 15.23) when, as one of the leaders of the new Italian Renaissance, he conceived a re-

Fig. 8.8 Termessus. Façade of the temple.

vival of classical architecture. The point of the arrangement is to dignify the intercolumniation which leads to the cella door, and with that purpose in view, the entablature is broken in the middle and a handsome arch opens up the pediment above. Once the theme became established, variations on it were tried. Of these, the most significant is that illustrated by the entrance portico at Baalbek (Fig. 8.9). There the entablature is broken, to be sure, but less abruptly. Conceived as a great moulding, the ensemble of architrave, frieze, and cornice is carried clear around the curve of the arch, to continue in its usual horizontal form on the far side. Much the same use was made of the curved entablature for the entranceway leading from the forecourt of Diocletian's Palace at Spalato, but in that application, the arched opening is central in an ensemble of only three intercolumniations. To either side of it, there is a square-headed opening of the usual Greek kind. Taken together, the three amount to the architectural motive which became famous during the High Renaissance under the name *Palladian Window*.

For the combinations of arch and order just cited, there is no generally accepted name, probably because each instance differs slightly from the last. The

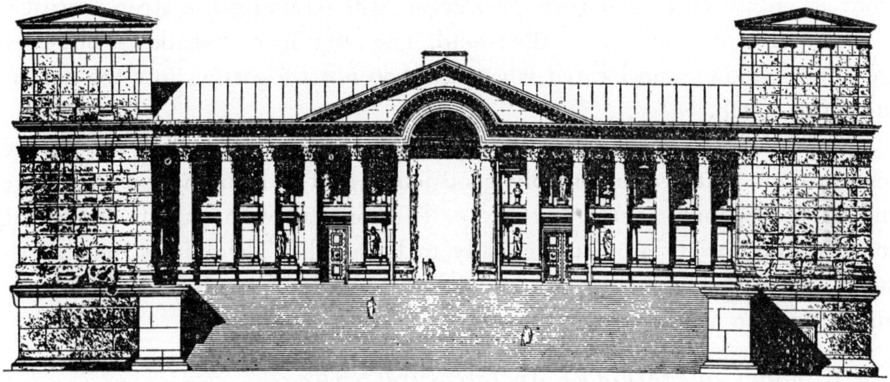

Fig. 8.9 Baalbek. The entrance portico.

so-called *Roman Arch Order* became sufficiently standardized to become a recognized item in the architectural vocabulary of Europe. The motive is seen in its simplest form on the numerous triumphal arches of Rome, each a memorial gateway put up in honor of some military conquest or equally important event in political history. The Arch of Titus is a good example. It was erected in 81 A.D. to commemorate the capture of Jerusalem, an event that had taken place a decade earlier. The structural parts consist of two substantial piers with an arch spanning the opening between them. Above the arch there rises a block of masonry half a story high, technically known as an *attic*, and offering a useful surface for inscriptions. The Greek orders are applied to the surface of the structure just described; they do no work and have no value except that they are handsome. As distinguished from other combinations of the same elements, the Roman Arch Order puts the columns to either side of the arch, and runs the entablature *above* its crown. Once established, this simple motive may be repeated any number of times. It is used three times on each face of the Arches of Constantine and Septimus Severus, and it is continuously repeated on each of the three lower stories of the Colosseum, all the way round the entire circumference of that immense pile.

As used on the Arches of Titus, Constantine, and Septimius Severus, the applied entablature shows a characteristic that has become a standard resource of the architect. We refer to the use of ressaults — a *ressault* being a block or chunk of entablature that rests directly on the capital of a column. As seen on the Arch of Constantine (Fig. 8.6), there is a ressault over each column, but between the columns, the entablature is made to recede almost to the surface of the wall. The columns and their separate ressaults, to put it another way, are in the round, while the rest of the entablature is in low relief. The purpose of the expedient is to eliminate the cast shadow which would fall from an entablature of normal projection, still retaining the strong vertical that results from a column in the round. The ressaults cast shadows, but they are small shadows, and located where they do not trespass against the curvature of the arch.

By combining the arch with the orders, the Romans were able to produce compositions that are undeniably good-looking. The combination of square and curved openings is the opposite of harmony as we have defined it, but contrast and variety are often equally to be sought. There are strong arguments, nevertheless, against this and other Roman habits of design; they are summarized in a later section.

The Roman Conception of Architectural Space

Space is part of the architectural medium. The painter can represent space, and thus make some use of it in his art. A few modern sculptors have attempted to make reference to space by devices calculated to direct the attention of the observer toward it, but for the most part, sculpture as we have known it must resist space. Only the architect has an actual volume of air at his disposal. It was the greatest single architectural achievement of the Romans to arrive at this conception, and to explore in a particular way its aesthetic possibilities. The Egyptian notion of interior design had approached absolute zero; the most sacred part of their temples was a cramped sanctuary notable for its absolute blackness. The Greek cella was better than that, but we may legitimately wonder whether it offered an amplitude in keeping with the dignity of the statues housed there. The majestic volume enclosed by the dome of the Pantheon (Fig. 7.1) may not be mentioned in the same breath.

The Roman interior, vast though it may be, represents a logical extension of the principles laid down for all classical art. It is, in its fundamental character, as plastic as any Greek statue — an apparent paradox we must make haste to explain. Taking the Pantheon as an example, it is fair to say we are dealing with a work of art where the solids are more important than the voids. The masonry of the dome dominates a large portion of our consciousness. It is the act of less than an instant to recognize its shape as hemispherical, and we remain permanently impressed with the shape. The hollow squares of *coffering* sunk into its surface serve not only to enhance the texture, but to make more keen one's feeling for the thickness of the ceiling — and hence its tangible solidity. The interior of the Pantheon is, in short, as truly a piece of geometric sculpture as the exterior of a Greek temple. There is no difference in principle; we have merely exchanged the convex for the concave, and are inside the sculpture rather than outside.

The same interior demonstrates also that unity-through-separation which characterizes all classical art. No windows permit us to discern or recall anything outside the building; wherever the eye may look, so long as the line of sight is kept within normal limits, the vista is closed. To enter is to enter the world-that-is-the-Pantheon. No other extant interior separates the occupant from the rest of the universe in the same degree, and it is interesting to see that the oculus left open at the crown militates not at all against that impression. It opens at a remote and inaccessible spot upon a void foreign to our experience. It is doubtful whether the high-set windows of other Roman interiors functioned differently.

It would be incorrect to conclude from this that the Roman version of interior design constitutes a negation of space. The designers of the Pantheon were far from negligent with respect to the emotional implications of the magnificent cubic-footage enclosed by their building, but like all classical artists, they assigned to the tactile sense a reality more vital and essential than any other sense. This led them to feel that air itself was a sculptor's material, to be sequestered and moulded into a predetermined contour — in this instance, that of a cylinder surmounted by half a sphere. Their position on the matter was by no means untenable. Indeed, there is perhaps no better way to deal with the problem of interior design, and certainly none more appropriate to the disciplines of the Classical Style. As a matter of historical fact, moreover, the Roman and plastic conception of enclosed space remains one of the two (and only two) approaches to the matter yet to appear in the whole history of architecture — the other being most perfectly realized in the French Gothic of the 13th Century A.D. and in some of our most modern buildings of steel and glass.

Roman Symmetrical Planning

A great many Roman architectural designs involve more than one building. Artistic order, that is to say, was imposed upon an extensive area, with single buildings conceived as mere parts in a grander composition. The idea did not originate with the Romans; but while they undertook to organize the civilized world, examples of such design multiplied and their scale became grander than ever before. It is the Roman system of composition rather than any other which has, for better or worse, set the pattern for the greater number of similar enterprises ever since.

Excellent examples of Roman practice in the layout of such group-design are the Forum of Trajan at Rome, the ensemble of temple and forum at Baalbek in Syria, and the gigantic Baths built at Rome by Caracalla and Diocle-

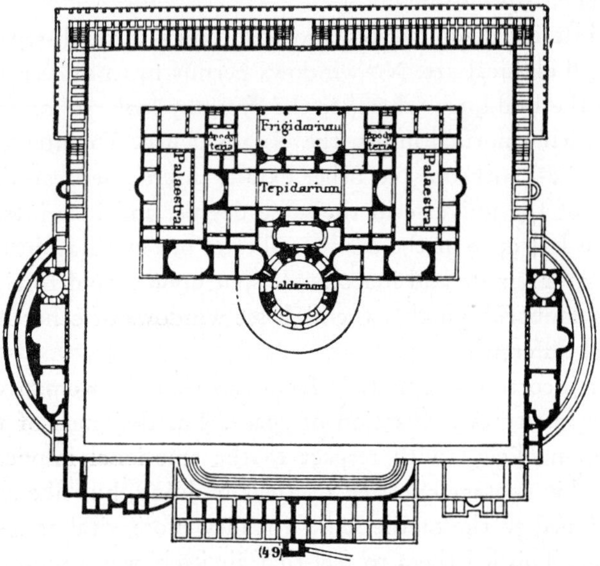

Fig. 8.10 Rome. The Baths of Caracalla. Plan. Restored.

tian (Fig. 8.10). In each of these instances, a certain amount of reconstruction is necessary in matters of detail, but the evidence is sufficient to make our generalizations reliable.

The Roman procedure in arranging such a composition was as follows: First, the surface of the site was leveled off to a plane. Second, through the center of the available area, or through some other convenient point, two axes were drawn at right angles to each other. At this juncture the governing conditions of the plan were set. All subsequent designing, whatever its apparent variety and complexity, proceeds with direct and simple reference to the plane and level surface, and to the axes drawn across it. The third step was to lay out in ground plan the various buildings to be included in the ensemble; and the fourth to arrange the subdivisions within the plan of each building. The plan of the Baths of Caracalla gives an instantaneous summary of the Roman mental machine and its functioning in work of this kind.

Everything is arranged symmetrically. It is often impractical to maintain absolute symmetry with both axes. One axis is therefore chosen as the *main axis;* and to this, symmetry is perfect. All possible symmetry with the subordinate axis is also maintained, it will be noted. The main axis may be either the long one or the short one; that is a mere detail.

Symmetrical planning, especially when the plan embraces an extended area, requires explanation. Its reason for existence is far from obvious. Symmetry has no relation whatever to practical considerations. Such plans demand the plane and level site beneath them; otherwise the symmetry is rendered less intelligible. The duplication of rooms at equal and opposite distances either side of an axis often makes it necessary to tolerate a substantial increase in the cubic bulk of the building. Both these features of the symmetrical system represent cost over and above provision for daily use — an oval room is often a pleasant change from the rectangular, but what conceivable human need can be adduced to suggest an economic justification for oval rooms in symmetrical pairs, as seen in the Baths of Caracalla? Neither economy nor efficiency entered into the account, and we must accept the fact that Roman symmetrical planning took place in response to some deeply felt psychological need.

The need was not for beauty. Most Roman plans make pretty drawings when seen in India ink on white paper. But the niceties of arrangement thus revealed were destined to be concealed by the roof; and, in the absence of airplanes, were never contemplated by anybody once the building was complete. We ordinarily see architecture in elevation, along a horizontal line of sight; and the materials of the draftsman differ from those of the builder. For the Romans, symmetry appears to have had an almost religious power, nevertheless. They served it with devotion worthy of a better cause. Their true reason? *Order!* We cannot repeat too often that symmetry is not a principle of beauty, but a way of imposing regularity. As such it appealed to a race of military men and administrators, but as compared to the disorder with which the buildings on the Acropolis are arranged, symmetry is a tedious business.

Outstanding Reservations About Roman Architecture

Every serious critic feels some sense of reservation with respect to Roman architecture; and in addition to the matters already covered, it is important to mention certain further and broader implications of Roman practice — because, on the whole, most modern builders have approached their problems with the same attitude as the Romans. Some of the time-honored objections to Roman work are cogent; some will not bear analysis — but in the end material for a negative critique exists.

Something is always said about the Roman habit of using the Greek orders decoratively, applying them as surface embellishment to buildings engineered on the principle of the arch. The column, so this argument goes, had been invented as a structural member. In the average Greek temple, it was not otherwise used; every column actually carried considerable compression from the weight above it. As applied decoratively by the Romans, the orders carry no load, or so little it doesn't matter. At this point in the usual statement of the argument, a tacit appeal is made to the supposed dignity of labor as contrasted with idleness, the latter by plain implication being an evil. The upshot is to assign the structural act a value higher than the decorative act. Before the reader knows it, he finds himself entertaining the notion that diverting into decoration a member hitherto put to work is a form of prostitution. Without entering the difficult question of the respective influence of labor and idleness upon human charactei, it is possible for us to see that structure is not work in the human sense. Even more emphatically, it is plain that decoration bears no resemblance to idleness. Its artistic value is of the highest; those who insist upon disapproving of it must sternly turn their back upon the *Elgin Marbles* and all the statuary of Reims and Amiens. It may also be pointed out that the Greek column, while used structurally by the Greeks, is in effect a piece of abstract sculpture; as a mechanical device, it leaves much to be desired.

The real complaint against the Roman use of the orders has nothing to do with their alleged structural chastity or violation thereof. It has to do with the confusion of the Roman mind with respect to architecture and engineering. They evidently separated the two arts as we moderns have so often and so disastrously done. After the engineers left, the decorators arrived to conceal Roman concrete with a surface overlay (i.e., a *veneer*) of marble, and to apply the orders, statues, or whatever. The separation of the two arts naturally resulted in a failure to integrate structural parts and decorative parts, and it may be said that Roman work in this respect is inferior both to the Greek and to the best we have from the Middle Ages.

The point is strongly brought home by the contrast between the more elaborate examples of the triumphal arch and the several great aqueducts which still survive: the Claudian, that at Segovia in Spain, and the famous Pont du Gard near Nîmes (Fig. 8.4). Because the aqueducts were considered purely utilitarian, they were left altogether without decoration. But while decoration may enhance beauty, it never makes it. The unadorned structure must depend upon its fundamental shape and line. The Roman aqueducts are universally admired for their scale, and for the powerful rhythmic swing of their great arches. It would appear, however, that these virtues were arrived at almost by chance. What did the Romans do to find handsome curves for the arches, to adjust proportions nicely, to arrive at a good surface texture? Let the reader compare the Pont du Gard with the nave arcade of Amiens (Fig. 12.13), with arcades designed by Brunelleschi (Fig. 15.22), with the Ponte Santa Trinità at Florence; the difference is hardly one of more or less decoration, but of greater sensitivity in design. As Roebling was to demonstrate so conclusively at the end of the 19th Century, the elementary mechanical parts of an utterly plain bridge can have the highest elegance. In the work of a master, the borderline between architecture and engineering does not exist.

We have no right to complain, however, because the Roman builders failed to exploit the aesthetic pattern existing in the interplay of structural forces in the fabric of a great building — a realization which forms an essential part of the Gothic genius. All classical art, Roman architecture included, was an art of form, and the genius of Roman engineers was devoted to the production of handsome shapes and pleasing surfaces. If well done, there can be no objection to architecture of that kind, but the false separation of structure from beauty seems often to have lured the Romans into shoddy applications of their own philosophy. Decoration is detestable unless very fine indeed, and the general run of Roman decoration is poor stuff. Roman mouldings resolve themselves into dull circular arcs, as contrasted with the tense curves typical of good Greek work (Fig. 4.11); Roman capitals are often poorly shaped and coarsely carved, with the Corinthian the predominant choice. Luxuriance and display are the result, rather than beauty, and it was not for nothing that the poet Poe wrote *glory* when he thought of Greece, and *grandeur* for Rome.

*

9

THE ART OF THE EARLY MIDDLE AGES IN WESTERN EUROPE

FROM THE DECLINE OF THE ROMAN EMPIRE TO ABOUT 1000 A.D.

INTRODUCTORY: A STATEMENT OF COVERAGE

No period in European history is more confusing than the span of years that starts with Rome's decline; and no part of that history is more confused than the history of art. We deal with the physical legacy of a world in flux. Military operations, large and small, succeeded and failed. Races corroded each other by contact, or merged imperceptibly. A major religious change was in progress; and other cultural and social changes succeeded each other rapidly, or existed side by side, leaving the historian baffled to know what is cause and what effect. Political and economic conditions were bad, as everyone knows; and that fact contributes heavily to the burdens of the art historian — for in bad times the artist is usually forced to confine himself to small enterprises. A small enterprise ordinarily means a portable work of art; and thus, a manuscript found today in the library of a castle in Carinthia may have originated at Reims or in Syria — and no one knows when, for meticulous accession records were unheard-of before the 19th Century.

No other period challenges the art historian as this one does; but the very difficulty of the problems, many of them permanently insoluble, has served to attract the vigorous interest of some of the best scholars in Europe and America. Their findings are still largely hypothetical, and depend upon archaeological argument of the most abstruse kind. Insofar as such can be reduced to an

Fig. 9.1 Buffalo. Albright Art Gallery. Roman sarcophagus with putti personifying the Four Seasons. About 200 A.D.

STOEDTNER

Fig. 9.2 Rome. Arch of Constantine. Panel from the contemporary frieze. 312 A.D. For the entire arch, see Fig. 8.6.

ALINARI

Fig. 9.3 Naples. National Museum. Caracalla (Regnal dates: 211–217 A.D.).

ALINARI

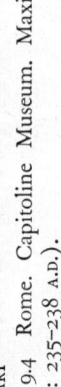

Fig. 9.4 Rome. Capitoline Museum. Maximin (Regnal dates: 235–238 A.D.).

ANDERSON

Fig. 9.5 Rome. Conservatori Museum. Constantine (Regnal dates: 306–337 A.D.). 8 feet high.

ANDERSON

Fig. 9.6 Barletta. An unidentified emperor. Early 5th Century? Bronze. 14 feet high.

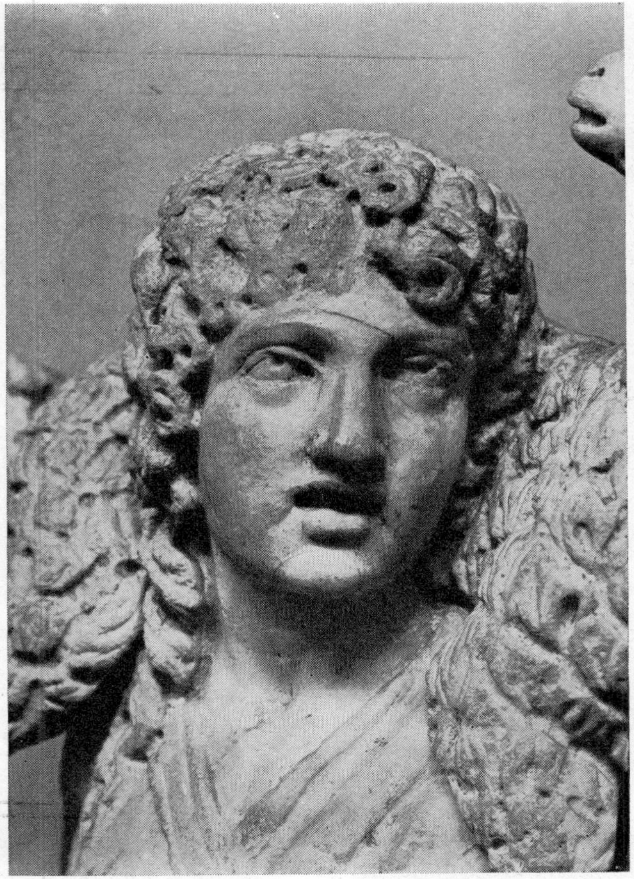

SANSAINI

SANSAINI

Figs. 9.7–8 Rome. Lateran Museum. Christ as Good Shepherd. 3rd Century? Marble 37½ inches high.

SABAH

Fig. 9.9 Constantinople. Ottoman Museum. *The Sarcophagus from Sidamara.* About 150 A.D.

MARBURG

Fig. 9.10 Berlin. Staatliche Museum. *The Frieze from Mschatta.* Detail.

Fig. 9.11 London. British Museum. The Archangel Michael. 4th Century. Ivory. About 16 inches high.

ALINARI

Fig. 9.12 Rome. Santa Maria Maggiore. Mosaic in the triforium. Not later than 400 A.D. *Abraham Parting from Lot.*

Fig. 9.13 Berlin. Kaiser Friedrich Museum. Fragment of a sarcophagus from Sulu Monastir in Constantinople, showing Christ with two Apostles. About 400 A.D.

Fig. 9.14 Paris. Bibliothèque Nationale. Diptych of the Consul Anastasius. 517 A.D.

Fig. 9.15 (below) Ravenna. Palace of the Archbishop. Detail from the so-called "Throne of Maximianus," showing four Apostles. About 500 A.D. Ivory panels on a wooden frame. ANDERSON

ANDERSON

ALINARI

Figs. 9.16–17 Ravenna. San Vitale. Mosaic of the Emperor Justinian and his Courtiers. About 547 A.D.

Fig. 9.18 Ravenna. Sant' Apollinare in Classe. Sarcophagus of the Archbishop Theodore. 5th Century A.D.

ALINARI

ANDERSON

Fig. 9.19 Rome. Santa Sabina. Cypress wood doors. 432 A.D. or shortly after. Detail: *The Crucifixion*.

ANDERSON

Fig. 9.20 Rome. Lateran Museum. The Jonah Sarcophagus.

ANDERSON

Fig. 9.21 Rome. Vatican. Museo Petriano. Model of Old Saint Peter's. Destroyed at the end of the 15th Century to make way for the present edifice.

ALINARI Fig. 9.22 Ravenna. Sant' Appolinare in Classe. View from the East.

ALINARI

Fig. 9.23 Ravenna. Sant' Apollinare Nuovo. Diagonal view from aisle, showing mosaics in the triforium.

ANDERSON

Fig. 9.24 Ravenna. Sant' Apollinare in Classe. Mosaics of the apse and arch. On the arch: Christ with the Signs of the Evangelists, and the twelve Apostles in the guise of lambs. In the apse: the Transfiguration on Mount Tabor (above) and Saint Apollinaris in Paradise (below).

ANDERSON Fig. 9.25 Rome. Santa Pudenziana. Mosaic in the apse. Christ enthroned with the twelve Apostles. About 400 A.D.

ALINARI Fig. 9.26 Rome. San Paolo fuori le Mura. Founded 386 A.D. Rebuilt during the 19th Century. Diagonal view across the nave.

Fig. 9.27 (left above) Oxford. Ashmolean Museum. Graeco-Persian Gem. 5th Century B.C.
Fig. 9.28 (right above) Chicago. Oriental Institute. Detail from a Persian plaque. Probably used as a trial piece for making jewelry. 5th–4th Centuries B.C.

Fig. 9.29 Leningrad. Hermitage Museum. Gold buckle found in Siberia. About 5¼ inches long.

Fig. 9.30 Line drawing after an animal in *The Book of Lindesfarne*. Irish. Early 8th Century A.D. FRANÇOISE HENRY.

Fig. 9.31 (left) Glendalough. County Wicklow. Round Tower (110 feet high) and "Saint Kevin's Kitchen" (25 by 15 feet). Fig. 9.32 (right) Monasterboice. County Louth. Cross of Muiredach. South side. 19 feet high. PHOTOGRAPHS BY T. H. MASON.

Figs. 9.33–34 Dublin. Trinity College. *The Book of Durrow*. Late 7th Century A.D. Page of interlace at the beginning of Saint John's Gospel (left), and Portrait of Saint Matthew (right).

Figs. 9.35–36 London. British Museum. *The Book of Lindesfarne.* (Left) Folio 26 verso. "The Cross Page." (Right) Folio 25 verso. Portrait of Saint Matthew.

Fig. 9.37 Dublin. Trinity College. *The Book of Kells*. Folio 34 recto. "The Monogram Page." Shortly after 800 A.D.

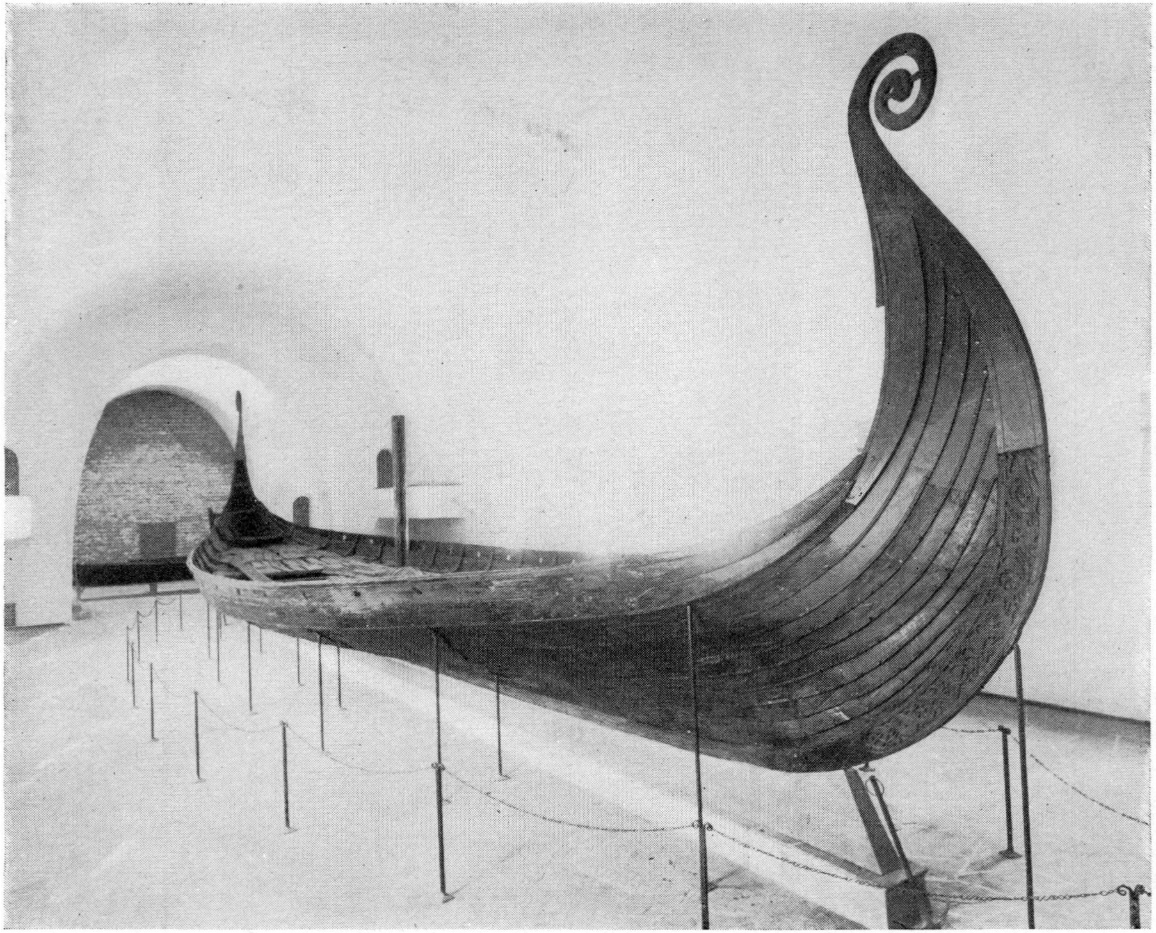

Fig. 9.38 Oslo. University Museum. *The Oseberg Ship*. 64 feet long, 16½ feet extreme beam.

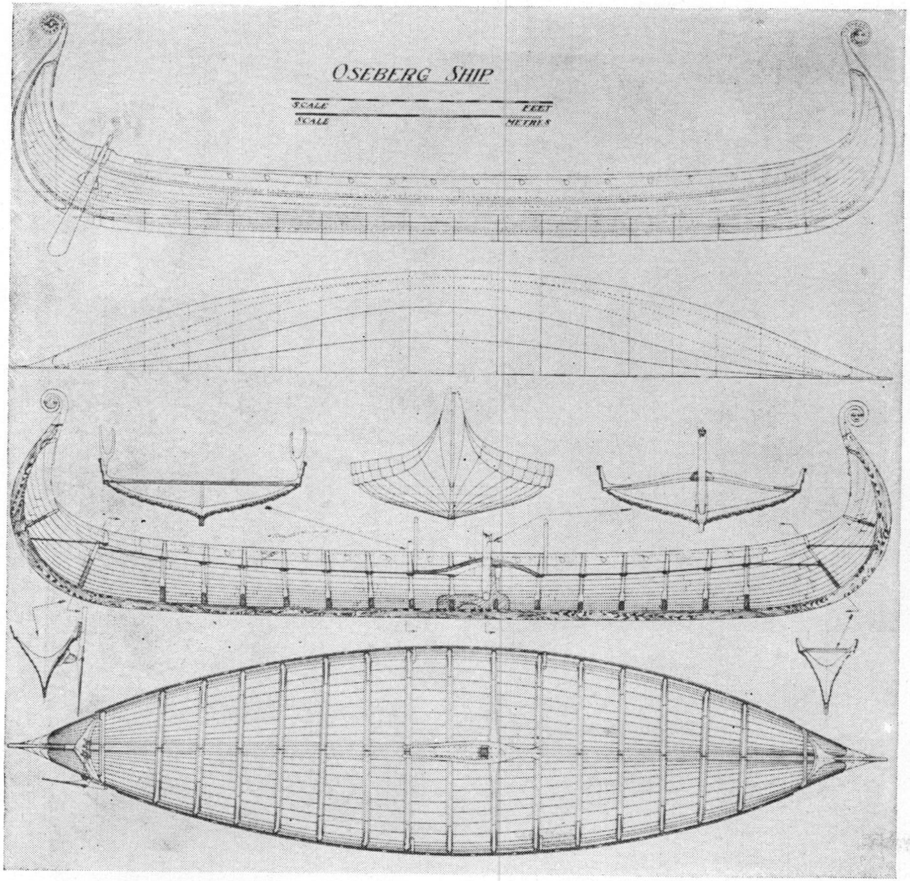

Fig. 9.39 *The Oseberg Ship*. Profile, water lines, and cross sections as drawn by Uffa Fox.

Fig. 9.40 Oslo. University Museum. *The Gokstad Ship*.

Figs. 9.41–42 Naranco. Santa Maria. 848 A.D. 40 feet long, 12 feet wide. PHOTOGRAPHS BY STOEDTNER.

MARBURG

Fig. 9.43 Lorsch. The Basilican Gate. About 800 A.D.

STOEDTNER

Fig. 9.44 Munich. Staatsbibliothek. *Codex Aureus* from Saint Emmeram at Regensburg. *The Four and Twenty Elders before the Throne.*

Fig. 9.45 Utrecht. University Library. *The Utrecht Psalter.* Folio 1 verso. Illustration for the 1st Psalm.

The upper register shows the righteous man opposite the ungodly man, who appears to the right as a prince accompanied by soldiers. An angel stands behind the righteous man, who has the law book of the Lord on the lectern before him; he meditates thereon day and night, as indicated by the sun and moon in the sky above. In the middle, two persons are seen discussing these men. The lower register shows, at the left, the tree planted beside the river of waters, with the river emerging from an urn held by a reclining demigod. In the middle, the face of the wind appears, blowing at a group of the ungodly. At the right, demons are casting more of the ungodly into the pit of hell.

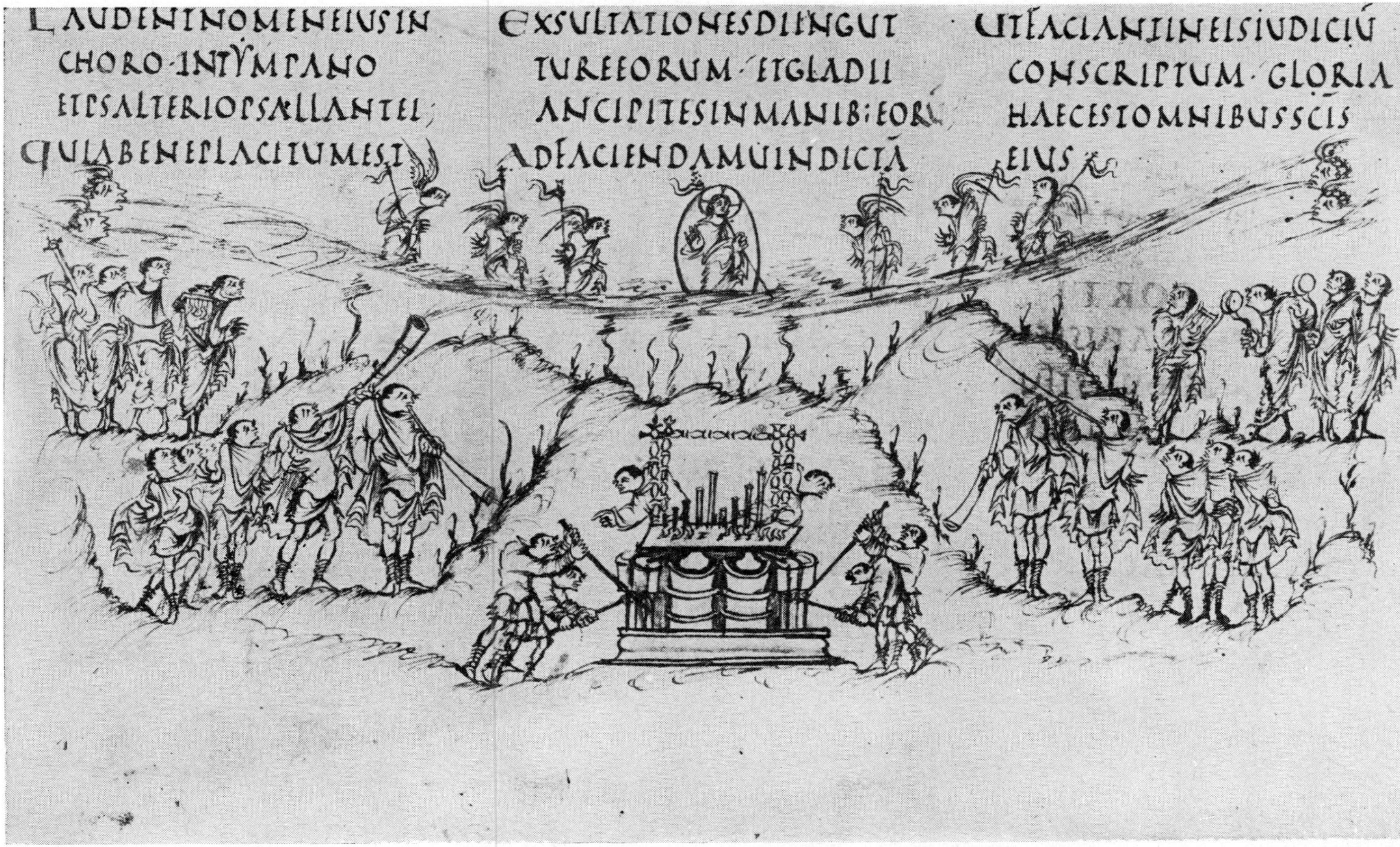
LAUDENTNOMENEIUSIN
CHORO·INTYMPANO
ETPSALTERIOPSALLANTEI
QUIABENEPLACITUMEST
EXSULTATIONESDIINGUT
TUREEORUM·ETGLADII
ANCIPITESINMANIB;EOR
ADFACIENDAMUINDICTA
UTFACIANTINEISIUDICIU
CONSCRIPTUM·GLORIA
HAECESTOMNIBUSSCIS
EIUS

C. B. VAN WEELDEREN

Fig. 9.46 *The Utrecht Psalter*. Folio 83 recto. Illustration for the 150th Psalm.

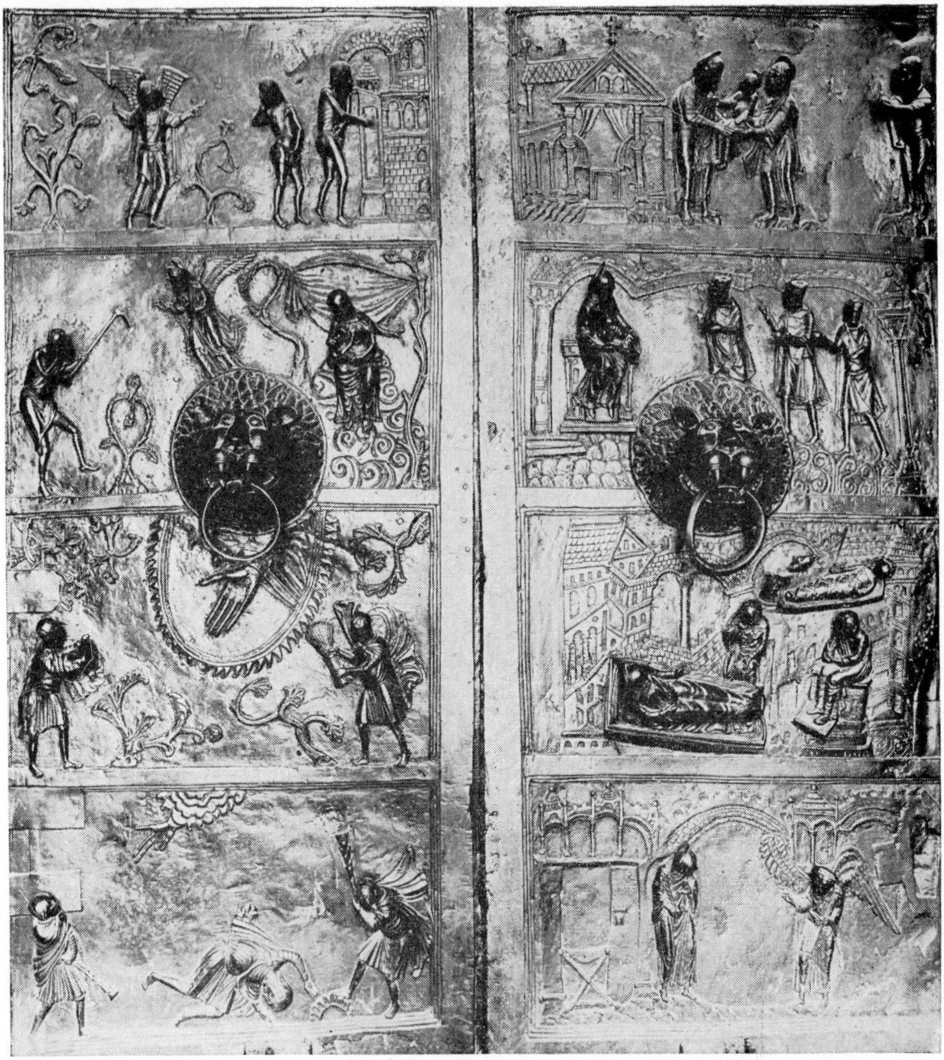

STOEDTNER

Fig. 9.47 Hildesheim. Cathedral. Bronze Doors, lower half. 1007–1015 A.D.

Left side, reading down: Expulsion from the Garden of Eden, Labors of Adam and Eve, Offerings of Cain and Abel, Murder of Abel.

Right side, reading up: The Annunciation, The Nativity, Adoration of the Magi, Presentation in the Temple.

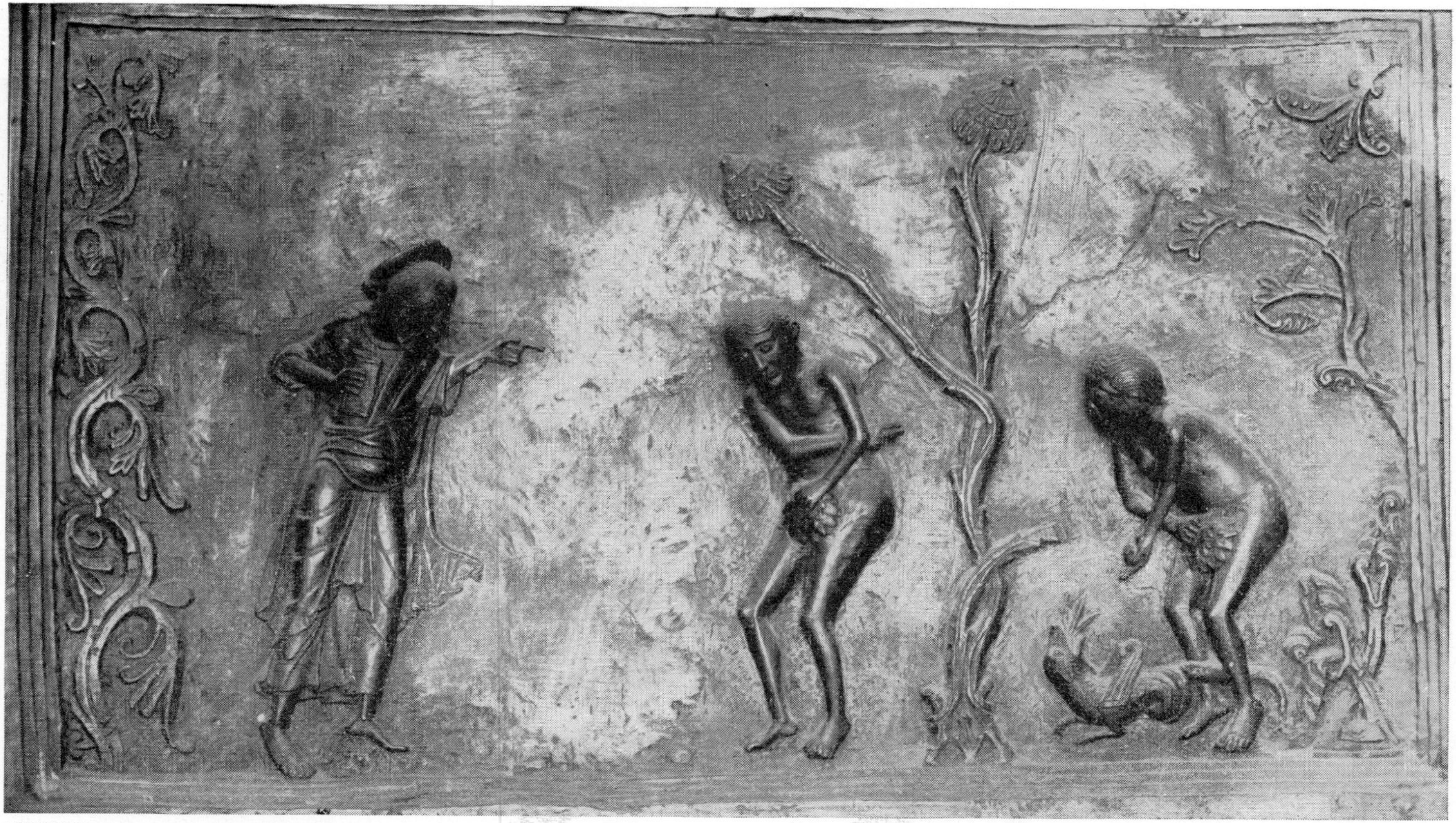

MARBURG

Fig. 9.48 Hildesheim. Cathedral. Bronze Doors. Detail. God passing judgment on Adam and Eve.

F. REECE WINSTONE

Fig. 9.49 Earl's Barton. The Saxon Tower. Early 11th Century. 68 feet, 8 inches tall. 24 feet wide.

NATIONAL BUILDINGS RECORD

Fig. 9.50 Bradford-on-Avon. Saint Laurence's. About 700 A.D.

GIRAUDON

Figs. 9.51–52 Bayeux. Cathedral Museum. The Bayeux Tapestry. (Above) The Norman fleet crossing the Channel. (Below) The Battle of Hastings.

over-all statement, the attempt will be made herewith; but at best, our chapter cannot be more orderly than the data it tries to set forth. Let us begin by making a statement of the coverage at which we shall aim.

In point of time, we begin at an indefinite moment: with the decline of Rome and the advent of Christianity. We terminate with the start of the Romanesque Period, in round numbers about 1000 A.D.; and we shall use the term *Early Middle Ages* to denote the whole of this era and to make a distinction between this period and the *High Middle Age* (1000–1400) which produced the Romanesque and the Gothic.

Geographically, we have several areas to consider. The Roman world was artistically more or less of a unit until the 6th Century A.D., which is the approximate time when the separation between Rome and Constantinople became artistically apparent with the maturing of the so-called *Byzantine Style*. After the 6th Century, we deal — in regions that were formerly classical — with Italy alone. We shall use the name *Early Christian* to denote the art of the entire Mediterranean world prior to the 6th Century, and that of Italy until the year 1000.

We must then proceed to consider certain artistic movements widely separated from each other and connected to Italy only by the common tie of Christianity. First and most important is the art of the barbarian peoples who destroyed the Roman Empire. The *Barbarian Style* is the third of the fundamental styles recognized by Mr. Morey (see above, pages 24–26); and it flourished only where the Romans had never been: in Ireland and in Scandinavia. We next must deal with certain small but important churches in Spain, especially those in the Asturias, the only part of the land that never came under the Moorish dominion. The art of the so-called "Carolingian Renaissance," the period of the empire established by Charles the Great, requires attention even though space prohibits any substantial consideration of its archaeological problems. Finally, the pre-Norman monuments of England, obscure though they are, may not be omitted if the later art of England is to be understood. And last of all, there must be a word or two about the incomparable *Bayeux Tapestry*, the greatest secular monument of the earlier Middle Ages. For reasons already made plain, the reader must not expect a smooth or even a connected narrative, but he may look forward to making the acquaintance of some very great works of art.

THE END OF ANTIQUITY

Most of us learn in school that the Roman Empire ended in 476 A.D. That date is significant only in the barest legal sense. It was the year in which Romulus Augustulus, the last man holding a *pro forma* claim to the imperium by right of succession from the Caesars, resigned. He did so at the request of Odoacer, a Goth, who thereupon established a kingdom in Italy.

Everyone knows that things did not happen so suddenly. The event of 476 merely symbolizes the reality of a disintegration that had long been in the making. The *Pax Romana* had lasted for about 200 years, or from the reign of Augustus to the end of the first generation of the 3rd Century A.D. By that time, barbarian pressure (always a fact of Roman life) had ceased to be geographically remote. Actual invasions of Italy were in prospect, and began to take place on a substantial scale by the middle of the century. The state, in short, proved unable to perform the first office of government; namely, the physical protection of its citizens.

Under such conditions, no arm of society has anything like the importance of the army. No individual compares in prestige with the man who controls the soldiers. It was only natural to find that the office of emperor became synonymous with military authority, and eventually one of its perquisites. It is conceivable, of course, that a great personality might have saved the situation by combining in himself soldierly skill, statesmanship, and a magnanimous philosophy. No such personality appeared at the time of the emergency; and there were, between 235 and 285, twenty-six so-called "soldier emperors," none of them able to hold office for long, and each of them gaining it in the first place by intrigue. It has been suggested that such a situation was inevitable because the Roman army had become almost entirely professional (e.g., mercenary), and was largely recruited from border populations with no special loyalty to Italy. Other hypotheses have been put forward: as, for example, the suggestion that Christianity, with its emphasis on the spirit rather than the world, and upon gentleness rather than power, proved corrosive to the imperial ideal of military dictatorship. Whatever the reason (and no one is satisfied that he knows it), this fact is evident: by the close of the 3rd Century A.D., Roman civilization was in an advanced stage of decay.

Toward the end of the 3rd Century, two leaders emerged who, however unsuccessful their efforts may have been, had sufficient courage and imagination to take steps of a nature as radical as the situation itself. In 286, the Emperor Diocletian relinquished the theory that central government could be maintained. He partitioned the Empire, and divided the imperial authority with colleagues. In 330, his successor Constantine made an even more pessimistic decision. He defaulted from the attempt to maintain physical control over the entire Roman territory, abandoned the western half of the empire, and moved his capital to the city of Byzantium, since known as Constantinople.

This expedient resulted in a political and cultural separation between East and West which has lasted 1,600 years, and may well be permanent. It was successful from Constantine's point of view, because it enabled him to retain the eastern empire intact. Popularly known as the *Byzantine Empire,* the government established by him in 330 endured until the Turkish conquest of 1453. Its history and art, largely separate from the western tradition, do not concern us here. We deal with them at length in Chapter 10 below.

Political events of the first magnitude, stated so briefly, seem as abstract as the planetary motions. Nor do we help ourselves greatly by remarking that "ruinous" taxation was required to keep up the military machine, with resulting disaster to "agriculture" and "commerce." Suicide, we hear, was on the increase, but the idea has a certain sanitary distance from our own sensibilities. It is necessary, indeed, to make a special effort to comprehend the devastation that took place. In 410, the Visigoths under Alaric sacked Rome itself; and in 452, Attila the Hun came to the gates of Rome and then retired — traditionally because rebuked by Pope Leo the 1st, but probably because well paid. In 455, Gaiseric and his Vandals sacked the city; the wanton thoroughness of their destruction accounts for the stigma ever since attached to the name *vandal.* These events were no more than significant instances in a general process. According to one estimate, the population of metropolitan Rome amounted to about 1,500,000 at the start of the 2nd Century A.D. By about 400, the population was somewhere around 500,000 people, and after the events just described, not more than 5,000. On several occasions and for various short periods, it is believed the entire population fled, leaving the Eternal City totally vacant. A spiritual pall descended, it would seem; and the Campagna, that vast and fertile plain which surrounds Rome and originally gave it prosperity, remained almost uninhabited and little cultivated until the end of the 19th Century. Even today, the city is less extensive than it was, and truck gardening goes on amid the ruins in areas once densely populated. It must be emphasized, moreover, that outrages decidedly did not cease with the 5th Century. They continued throughout the earlier Middle Age and later. Rome was sacked again by Totila the Ostrogoth in 546; and once again by the Saracens in 846 — they by that time having made the Mediterranean into a Moslem lake.

While this colossal decay went inexorably on, what of the population? Unable to find a solution in fact, they sought surcease in games and celebrations, a condition commemorated by a class of ivory carvings known as the *Consular Diptychs* (Fig. 9.14), of which a great many are preserved from the end of the 5th Century and later. Upon assuming the somewhat hollow title of consul, the politicians of this distressing period were accustomed to order a number of ivories, each with the donor's portrait, and hand them around as gifts to important friends. Almost invariably the newly appointed public figure was shown in the act of tossing out a money bag as the signal for the start of a horse race. As Karl Federn quotes a certain Roman of the time, " It is as though the Roman people had eaten the herbs of Sardinia and were forced to break out in a disease of laughter. *Moritur et ridet* — it laughs and dies! "

No chapter in history is better illustrated by art than the disastrous and fateful decline of the only world-order the genius of mankind has yet produced. It takes no technical knowledge to read the course of events in any series of dated monuments; one has only to look, and he sees Antiquity fade before his eyes.

The most obvious sign of decadence is in technique. Signs of weakness are apparent at the end of the 2nd Century; and by the middle of the 3rd, most monuments are conspicuously poor by comparison to earlier standards. Many are manifestly incompetent, but we must always remember that something produced at the very same moment by an artist more fortunately situated may, upon occasion, be excellently well done. The good work is sporadic, however; and the passage of time generally spelled out a further loss of skill. The trend is well illustrated by the following comparison.

A marble sarcophagus now in Buffalo (Fig. 9.1) is thought to have been produced at Rome about 200 A.D. The four nude *putti* personify the seasons. Reading from the left, we see Winter, Spring, Summer, and Autumn — each with a vase filled with appropriate fruits and flowers. In the middle beneath the portrait medallion, there is a figure of Mother Earth; originally, she probably held a cornucopia. As so often happened, this sarcophagus was used more than once, and some subsequent lady-owner had the portrait bust done over in a later style. Because marble sarcophagi were popular at the time, the idea suggests itself that we have here an example of commercial rather than fine art; but in estimating the technical standards of the day, we may remind ourselves that the best Greek vase paintings were the commercial art of an earlier period. The sculptor of these figures appears, on the whole, to have been as competent as contemporary portrait artists; and it is patent he knew his business none too well. His carving of fruit and flowers lacks the snap and life characteristic of Augustan floral ornament, and his handling of anatomy and drapery is somewhat less than knowledgeable. But a strange haunting loveliness still emanates from the monument; one is reminded of the fragrance of a dying flower. In such marble tombs, as Mr. Morey once remarked, the latter-day Romans buried the last of Greek beauty along with themselves.

If we pass on to the beginning of the 4th Century, it becomes impossible any longer to maintain that the classical spirit was still alive. The Arch of

Constantine (Fig. 8.6) was erected to commemorate his victory over Maxentius in 312 A.D. It is generously decorated with sculpture, and would appear at first glance to testify that good artists were still working at Rome. Scholarly inspection of the various reliefs has proven that the reverse was true. Almost all the sculpture was secondhand. The only work surely of Constantinian date is found in the two narrow friezes at a level just above the crowns of the smaller archways (Fig. 9.2). Of considerable interest to historians because they furnish us with an early instance of the impingement of Orientalism upon classical art (see below, pages 261–268), there can be no question that the sculptor of these panels was grievously short on skill. The dumpy little figures are inarticulate, almost dead. Workmanship is perfunctory in general, and occasionally the work is scamped. Because an observer looking up from the ground level would find his view partially obscured by the moulding below, the man did not bother to carve feet on a great many of his figures. Other examples might be cited, but this one is enough evidence for the conclusion we must necessarily draw. Conditions were bad indeed if Constantine, with all the facilities of imperial authority at his command, felt compelled to borrow sculpture, and for new work could find no one better than the author of this mean and niggardly frieze.

More poignant than the decadence of technique is the course of the decline as we see it reflected in the faces of individual Romans whom we know through their portraits. Had we no other source on Roman history, its general outline might be surmised from this evidence alone. Until the end of the 2nd Century, Roman portraiture depicts a vigorous and competent population. Vespasian, who ruled from 69 to 79 A.D., has the countenance of a man who might today be at the head of a great and prosperous industry — an appearance entirely consistent with his magnificent capacity and substantial success in the business of government. Marcus Aurelius (161–180 A.D.) had a face so confident that it is completely composed, as though pressure and hurry had been civilized out of existence — which is remarkable in view of the facts of his reign: earthquakes, pestilence, military campaigns of the most tedious and uninspiring kind. It is no wonder his *Meditations* betray a great weariness, and it is natural that Stoicism (a philosophy calculated to make patient endurance tolerable, as contrasted with the production of positive good) should have appealed to him with religious power. The important thing is to realize that (for the ostensible purposes of portraiture, at any rate) Marcus Aurelius felt able to maintain the theory that man still had within himself the capacity to rise above the confusion and mischance of environment.

The downward trend commenced, perhaps, with Caracalla (regnal dates 211–217). That monarch, as we know him in the familiar bust portrait now in Naples, seems almost the type of the man who succeeds by expending energy faster than he can ever take it in. His face has power and intelligence, but his nervous pose betrays him. As the 3rd Century went on, outright neurosis becomes evident even to the casual observer (Figs. 9.3–4).

To illustrate the end of the appalling story, we have two imperial portraits, both of great size. One is the immense head of Constantine, already mentioned in another connection (page 160). Its eight feet of height, and its grim exposure to the weather in the courtyard of the Conservatori, make it all the more devastating as a document of bad times — for the face is the face of a man who has seen a ghost (Fig. 9.5).

In Barletta, a town on the Adriatic coast of South Italy, there exists a baleful standing figure fourteen feet high (Fig. 9.6). People say that it came from the wreck of a Venetian ship which met disaster there in 1204, presumably on the way home from Constantinople. After lying neglected on the shore for 250 years, it was set up in its present position with slight restorations to the legs and hands. Sometimes it is called a portrait of Valentinian the 1st (late 4th Century), but the truth is no one knows just who may be represented. The costume is that of a Roman general; and the exhausted eyes look out at us from features that show a certain strength of character, but betoken even more clearly coarseness and vulgarity — a devastating revelation of an insensitive personality broken by circumstances more brutal than itself.

Horrible as must have been the state of mind of those who watched the end approaching, there is tragedy also in the popular viewpoint. The man in the street saw much to indicate that civilization was strong. Diocletian, the very monarch who provided himself with a personal fort, also dedicated a bathing establishment as big and as elaborate as Caracalla's. Maxentius, the man who competed with Constantine and lost, raised the great basilica (Fig. 7.28) which his rival took over and renamed for himself just as he was about to abandon Rome to its fate. These are among the largest and most grandiose of Roman buildings, demanding for their construction the highest order of engineering and organization. Such things illustrate the paradoxical nature of human affairs. Like a floating ice cake in the spring, the Roman polity retained much of its outward form and much of its strength, but it was ready to melt away faster than seems possible.

CHRISTIANITY AND ITS EFFECT UPON CLASSICAL SCULPTURE AND PAINTING

Amid the tragic decadence of late Antiquity, Christianity gained momentum because it offered hope — making sense out of a world in confusion by stating that the world itself was temporary, nonessential, and possessed of meaning only by reference to the higher reality of heaven.

Such a view of life is in substantial contrast to the imperial ideal. As a result, Christianity was unpopular with the Roman government — never more so, in fact, than during the reign of Marcus Aurelius. Noted as a humanitarian, this man is also remembered as a philosopher. It was therefore plain to him that the Christian allegiance to a God beyond and above the empire could not, either in theory or in practice, be reconciled with what he considered the political necessities. He therefore undertook to suppress the new religion by methods today considered inhuman. Few Roman emperors had the same grasp of philosophical implications, however; and for the most part, Christianity was tolerated if the Christians themselves eschewed any action calculated to attract attention or to acquire power for themselves.

By the end of the 3rd Century, the new faith had become so important in the Roman polity that it was no longer feasible to restrict it. In the year 313, Constantine therefore promulgated the Edict of Milan, which removed the legal restraints hitherto curtailing Christian activity. Subsequently, he embraced the new faith himself, and it presently emerged as the official religion of the entire empire.

There is ample evidence to prove that Christian art was produced prior to the Edict of Milan. Certain paintings in the catacombs at Rome almost certainly were executed earlier than 313; but for all practical purposes, it may be assumed that any important or conspicuous monument of Christian art necessarily comes later. It seems equally certain that the Edict of Milan was the signal for a prolific output of Christian art of all kinds. Much of this was probably the direct result of Constantine's personal interest. He himself caused many a church to be founded, of which few survive except in name.

The acceptance of Christianity had almost no immediate effect upon artistic style. Just as Christian authors wrote in the classical languages, the first Christian artists used the idiom of late classical art. The earliest depictions of Christ, to cite the most conspicuous subject of all, show him in the guise of a young and rather handsome Greek youth; and thus we see him in the justly famous statue of the *Good Shepherd* (Figs. 9.7–8) in the Lateran collection at Rome. The latter is very nearly a duplicate of numerous pagan statues of Hermes carrying a ram or some other sacrificial animal, the most famous being the *Calf-Bearer,* one of the Archaic monuments recovered from the Persian debris on the Acropolis at Athens. As contrasted with the Roman statues from which it derives, the Lateran *Good Shepherd* seems pathetically to aim at spiritual content far beyond the technical skill of its sculptor; there is perhaps no nobler example of profound meaning that seeks expression through crass material.

Substantial changes in style were destined to come, but the process was gradual rather than sudden. With respect to the Early Christian art of the Mediterranean basin, the most important changes of style reflect the fact that Christianity is a religion that came from the Near East. It not only started there, but flourished there to an extent unknown in the West until much later. A church building at Edessa in northern Syria was referred to as " old " in the year 202. One at Arbela in Mesopotamia is said to have been built in 123. Of the church polities still surviving, the oldest of all is the Armenian. It will be recalled, moreover, that the Epistles of Paul were addressed to Christian communities in the Near East. The most splendid churches of the early centuries stand in parts of Syria which today are inaccessible. They were abandoned as a result of the Arab conquest of the 7th Century; but even in ruins, they are architecturally superior to any pre-Romanesque church in Italy or Western Europe. The importance of the Near East is still further emphasized by the choice Constantine made: unable to keep all, he chose the more valuable half of his empire and moved his government eastward. It must still further be remembered that Christianity was not the only Eastern religion in vogue during late Antiquity; the Olympian Gods were competing also with Mithras, with Atys and Cybele, and with Osiris. As religions, the others suffer by comparison with Christianity and were destined to drop out of sight; but at the time, all channels were effective in converting the Roman mind to Eastern culture. The general absorption of Eastern points of view had its effect upon art, and, as time went on, made an end of the Classical Style.

The Influence of Oriental Art upon the Classical Style: Flattening, and Loss of Plasticity

It is difficult to imagine two styles more different than the Greek and the Oriental (see above, pages 24–26). A crossbreed between the two was and is irrational, but that is precisely what happened. We can review the evolution by considering a series of monuments which, if not dated exactly, are dated well enough to fall into sequence. The general effect, as we shall see, was to " flatten " classical art until, ultimately, its plastic character was destroyed and all but forgotten. The end product was the *Byzantine Style,* which arrived at its permanent peculiarities about the middle of the 6th Century A.D.

Let us start with the *Sarcophagus from Sidamara* (Fig. 9.9). It was found at the place of that name in western Asia Minor; and because of its great weight, may be presumed to have been made there. At first glance, one might assume it to be something from the Greek Fourth Century, and the mistake would be a natural one. The figures, considered individually, are not unlike those of Praxiteles and Lysippos. They are worked in the full round, and it should specially be noted that they bend gracefully toward us and away — the pose thus being used to emphasize the existence of the third dimension and the spatial displacement required for the statue. Better on the whole than most of the Roman copies which so greatly influence our visualization of Greek work, the actual date of these figures is probably about 150 A.D.; and they constitute a vivid demonstration of the extraordinary power of Greek art to survive in places where survival was favored by tradition and circumstance.

The setting is also reminiscent of the Greek. The statues stand on a shallow platform. The background is immediately behind them. It is embellished with architectural detail, but it shares with the Greek pediment the quality of being solid and impenetrable. Every suggestion of movement is necessarily to the right or left, and never to any significant extent in or out. The arrangement amounts, as we have been at pains to note in other instances, to an artistic formula; and because it was used often over a long period of time, we shall find it convenient to give the formula a name. The name *Neo-Attic* has gained some currency among American scholars. We shall use it here, but a cautionary word is necessary because the very same term is often applied to a group of Greek sculptors who worked in Italy during the 1st Century B.C. — they signed " Athenaios." The important thing to remember about the Neo-Attic Formula, as here designated, is its impenetrable background. Almost anything may be substituted for the architecture seen on the *Sidamara Sarcophagus* providing it carries the conviction of impenetrability: the purple vellum of a manuscript page will do, and a blank background of pure gold proves perhaps most effective of all.

The Oriental influence which hardly affected the figure-style of the Sidamara statues made itself more than manifest in the architectural detail. A comparison with any typical piece of Greek or Roman ornament will show that a change has taken place. Greek and Roman detail tends to be plastic, but the Sidamara designer is working toward expression on a flat surface. Every smallest item of floral ornament tends to be brought forward into the same plane as all the others, and every detail is silhouetted sharply by deep undercutting of its edges. Such work takes the light very differently from its classical counterpart. Graded shadows are almost absent, and the total effect resolves itself into a pattern of bright whites sharply juxtaposed to black darks. A rhythmic alternation of light and dark results, and it is the rhythm which attracts and hold one's attention. Shapes, outlines, and other visual facts which, under other circumstances, might exert an appeal tend here to be overlooked altogether.

Architectural detail of the sort just described constitutes the closest approach that can be made in marble, and with sculptor's tools, to the color rhythms so characteristic of Oriental textiles. In good examples, the effect is rich and excellent, something new under the sun. It was destined to become extremely popular in Early Christian, Byzantine, and Moslem decoration.

Because of their ability to annoy, the desert tribes who lived in the Arabian desert east of the district of Moab, which itself is the land east of the Dead Sea, were able to extract subsidies and other concessions from the Romans, the Persians, and everyone else who ever wished to live quietly in Syria proper. Where the grazing was good, the leaders of these tribes were accustomed to spend a great part of the year at the edge of the desert; and when they became wealthy from the sources just cited, some of them built elaborate stone palaces there. Mschatta was such a palace, and its ruins are still in view. One feature was a gorgeous enclosing wall about fifteen feet high decorated with a lace-like frieze of ornament. Parts of the frieze are now in Berlin, and our Fig. 9.10 illustrates a detail thereof but fails to demonstrate the strong rhythm established by repeats in chevron-pattern of the great V's, and fails also to bring out in proper emphasis the large rosettes which also recur as strong accents.

It would be hard to name a monument which more perfectly demonstrates the merging of classical and Oriental taste during the period when Antiquity was on the wane and the Middle Ages were beginning. There is enough plasticity in the mouldings, and even in the representative forms, to make us remember Greece, and yet the subject matter itself and the dominant glitter of black and white are plainly from the Near East. The date has never been settled. Some authorities want to put it earlier, but most are noncommittal and set limits at the 4th and 7th Centuries A.D.

With respect to architectural ornament, the end result of the Orientalizing process may be illustrated by the decorative carving of capitals and other surfaces in Hagia Sophia (Fig. 10.1–4). Classical forms as seen there amount to a faint memory. Insofar as possible, the carving has achieved the state of surface decoration on the flat, with two dimensions only — an effect obviously beyond the reach of architecture, but one closely approached in this instance. When we have arrived at this point in the evolution, we have the mature Byzantine Style before us.

We return now to the flattening process as applied to the human figure — which, as stated, was more resistant than ornament to the Oriental influence. Among preserved monuments, the one which illustrates the next step after the figures on the *Sidamara Sarcophagus* is a splendid ivory of the *Archangel Michael,* now in the British Museum (Fig. 9.11). Its extraordinary size (about 16 inches high) would make it notable in any case, but the great dignity of the figure lends truth to the often repeated comment that no other ivory carving compares with this — it is rare that we may call small things noble. Probably executed somewhere in the Christian East, probably in some region where Greek art remained unusually vital, and probably not later than the 4th Century of our era, it gives a first impression of roundness and plasticity. Closer inspection reveals that the expression takes place only in part through the manipulation of contours. The pose approaches the frontal, with both legs brought almost into the same plane as the torso. Only the head retains any vigorous suggestion of roundness, and it will be noted that the feet hang down over the steps as though the sculptor no longer cared about foreshortening and even less about giving expression to the mechanical action of carrying weight. The format is a typical instance of the Neo-Attic, and it has been suggested that the archway with steps derives from the proscenium of the Roman theatre which had similar doorways for the entrance of actors onto the stage.

With respect to plastic qualities, monuments rendered according to the Alexandrian Formula fared much the same. The mosaic pictures which decorate the triforium space to either side of the nave of Santa Maria Maggiore at Rome are illustrative in this respect. Of uncertain date, they can hardly come later than 400 A.D., and in the *Abraham Parting from Lot* (Fig. 9.12), we may see how Orientalism has dealt with spatial representation. The two old gentlemen in the foreground still seem to have weight and volume, but it is only by habit that we read distance into the setting beyond them. By the logic of the situation, we are required to suppose that six or eight persons stand behind each of the principal actors, which would require a stage about ten feet deep. Nothing of the sort is made clear either by the drawing or by the color relationships, however; and the truth is that the latter reach out, as it were, toward the ideal of Oriental flat pattern.

In Berlin, there is a fragment from a fine sarcophagus of the Sidamara type, also probably of about 400 A.D., with an interesting figure of Christ, represented, as usual in early monuments, without the beard (Fig. 9.13). The statue is carved very nearly in the round, but in no sense was the sculptor sympathetic to statues in the round. The figure faces square front; and, as compared to the *Angel* of the British Museum, a peculiar importance has been given to what we may call its front face, or façade. The operative carving of both anatomy and drapery is confined to a near-plane surface roughly parallel to the background. We feel no impulse to investigate how the figure might appear from one side or the other; it is perfectly certain there is nothing interesting around the corner. All of this is antithetical to the nature of true classical art, and the effect arrived at here is approximately what we might expect to see were a Greek statue compressed from behind against a sheet of plate glass.

The next and very nearly the last step in the evolution toward flatness is to be seen in the *Consular Diptychs* (Fig. 9.14), a class of ivory carving already cited in another connection (see above, page 256). Some of the earlier diptychs have truly plastic qualities, but those that come after 500 impart small sense of contour — an effect, it must be pointed out, that has nothing to do with the fact the relief is low. An accomplished sculptor can use perspective and foreshortening, and thus make the lowest relief give a forceful expression of mass and space. At this point in the general evolution, the desire to do so was absent. It is characteristic in the *Consular Diptychs* to see feet that collapse downward like the flappers of a duck, and even the floor beneath them begins to be tipped upward for its better functioning as an item of flat pattern. The Roman toga, moreover, has given way to vestments heavy with Oriental embroidery, vestments that are necessarily stiff and hang flat, thus contributing to the general impression.

In point of date, the *Consular Diptychs* have brought us into the 6th Century. Well along the road toward the Byzantine Style, they nevertheless lack some of its essential features. More had to happen before that style emerged in its own name and right. It is reasonably clear that the critical changes took place at Constantinople during the first half of the 6th Century, but it is difficult and perhaps impossible to trace the development in detail. An immense destruction of art took place all over the Byzantine Empire during the period of Iconoclasm (726–843). A number of frescoes and mosaics are still obscured by Turkish whitewash. Because almost nothing remains at the capital, we are forced to depend upon examples in the provinces. Supposedly, such examples are inferior to those that once existed at Constantinople.

Insofar as we may safely describe what happened, the following narrative, inferential though it is, probably does not distort history much. In the first place, both the Alexandrian Formula and its derivative the Latin Style passed virtually out of use except for occasional copies in manuscript illustration. In view of the instinct of the Oriental artist to seek expression on the flat surface, spatial representation of any kind had a very doubtful chance for survival in the art of a society increasingly Near Eastern in its culture and outlook. But since Christian narrative demanded human actors, an altogether abstract art was out of the question. The Neo-Attic Formula was the only thing in sight which offered an acceptable compromise. Its indefinite settings were especially attractive, we may assume, to a population given over to a mystic and non-material religion, and it is noteworthy that most Byzantine artists tried to make the setting more abstract than ever before. The architectural backgrounds common in earlier works executed according to the Neo-Attic scheme were generally discontinued in favor of blank areas of gold. Even the ground line at the bottom of a scene was commonly omitted, probably with deliberate intent to deny or forget the physical truth of gravitation. To these statements a few exceptions must necessarily be made. Certain subjects — the *Nativity*, for example — would be unintelligible without a few stage properties. Although such were of course included in the pictures, their number was reduced to a minimum; and the rendering was brought so close to line and flat tone as to deny the observer any significant suggestion of spatial displacement beyond and behind the plane of the picture-surface.

The process just described produced works of art like the mosaic picture of *Justinian and His Courtiers* in the choir of San Vitale at Ravenna (Figs. 9.16–17). The church was dedicated in 547. Presumably the mosaic dates from about the same time. It is one of a pair, the other showing *Theodora and Her Ladies*. For all practical purposes, we may remember these pictures as the first major-scale monuments which illustrate Byzantine art in the sense of a new style centering at Constantinople and radiating into Italy and Sicily.

As a derivative from the Neo-Attic Formula (and ultimately from Greek pedimental compositions), the general format of the picture has already been sufficiently discussed: we look up at a single row of figures silhouetted against a blank ground of gold. Important changes in the figure-style and rendering now need to be described. Let us begin with the distortion of the human figure. Because important political personages were represented — people who wished to be recognized by name whenever anyone looked at the picture — the heads remain in normal proportion, except for a considerable enlargement of the eye (Fig. 9.17). Legs and torso, however, have been elongated, and the effect of their abnormal length has been enhanced by the repetition of verticals in the drapery. By actual measurement, the average Byzantine head comes out at $\frac{1}{9}$, $\frac{1}{10}$, or an even smaller fraction of the total height; it is often impossible to be definite, because, as here, we commonly lack a firm ground line to take as a base. It seems likely that the vertical distortion had to do with ideas of dignity; it is merely an exaggeration of the erect posture considered appropriate for important persons on ceremonial occasions. If our memories of classical art and our modern habits of thought make it difficult to accept the distortion, we must sharply remind ourselves that we are dealing with the Middle Ages and with the work of men who had no such reverence for the body as we do. As a matter of fact, the extra length of the Byzantine figure is moderate by comparison to the very slender ladies who appear in fashion magazines.

The emperor and his men are clad in rich vestments which stretch from neck to ankle and totally conceal the mechanism of the body. These clothes are so stiff and heavy that only one pose is possible: the static figure standing erect. Movement, if attempted at all, must be very moderate indeed. As a vehicle for artistic communication the human body — that essential of all classical art — was necessarily made almost useless; and it is important to appreciate that Byzantine artists rarely relied upon the body to carry any substantial part of their content.

Instead, they relied on the broad flat areas of color made possible by applying the Near Eastern temperament to what once had been the undulating folds of Greek drapery. The robes seen here are modeled, to be sure, in light, half light, and dark, but that old and familiar sequence of tones is no longer gradual. Instead, the eye is confronted by abrupt shifts (white, gray, black) which amount almost to stripes. The representative function of the stripes is easy enough to understand in the present example; in many later Byzantine pictures, drapery is in fact reduced to completely flat pattern.

We may sum up by saying that the Byzantine Style is a hybrid. Its Greek heritage remains in the form of human actors in a narrative, and in the formula according to which the picture is composed. But insofar as such a thing is physically possible, Greek art has been converted into Oriental pattern: Justinian and his companions tell as a near-approach to color-accents on the flat surface, arranged in a simple rhythm.

The virtues of the new style may at first escape the reader. Its aim was hieratic solemnity, an atmosphere perhaps uncongenial to the modern American. It is nevertheless a pictorial record of a very considerable era in our history. From the 6th Century to the 15th, Constantinople was the center of the Western world. Its court and its church presented a spectacle of opulence almost impossible to believe. Contemporary descriptions of its stately ceremonies seem to be hyperbole, but are probably factual. No city in history has left a more resplendent memory.

We must also remember the placement for which such mosaic pictures were designed, and the circumstances under which people looked at them. As a relief from the overabundant sunlight, most churches in the Mediterranean area have small windows. Some are dark enough to make candles appropriate at noon. In dim light, the reflective quality of mosaic makes it the best of all media. Mosaic pictures have the power to carry with undiminished clarity over distances impossible for paintings in any other medium.

With the arrival of the Byzantine Style we have something new, and an art capable of effects which, if no better than those possible in either of the styles from which it had derived, were certainly different. The long and further history of this style concerns us no more in the present chapter; we shall summarize it in Chapter 10 below. Enough has been said, however, to inform the reader about the evolution that was going on during the Early Christian centuries, and to prepare him for monuments in any stage of transition.

Early Christian Asceticism and the Negation of Classical Beauty

An idealized and excellent anatomy had since the Greek Fifth Century retained its standing as an artistic desideratum. Beauty of that particular kind had a value, it would seem, as self-evident as one of Euclid's luminous axioms. It continued to have the same value in certain parts of the empire. These regions are geographically vague, but are presumed to be localities in the Greek area more or less insulated from the general course of change, thus permitting the Greek formulas for physical loveliness to survive as Elizabethan English survives in the mountain communities of Tennessee and Kentucky. The British Museum's ivory carving of the Archangel Michael (Fig. 9.11) may be presumed to have come from some such place.

But in other places and probably most, physical beauty in general and the Greek formula for it in particular got themselves into bad company. It was inevitable, perhaps, that Greek art would be associated with paganism in much the same way that the Rococo was associated with the decapitated French aristocracy in 1789 and later. It was natural that there would be a tendency to discard and dislike any art tending to remind people of distasteful things.

There was, however, a much more positive reason for the negation of Greek beauty. It was much more common in the earlier centuries than it is now to translate into extreme action those aspects of the Christian theory which have to do with a contempt for the world, for material things, and for the flesh. Christianity is in part a religion of renunciation, and one way to renounce the world was to become a hermit. Hermitage of one sort or another was common enough in the early centuries to be described as popular. It was often indulged in with spectacular austerity. Saint Simeon Stylites, who died about 460 after spending 35 years on top of a tall column, is no isolated example of religious athleticism. He had many colleagues. The modern reader must thoroughly understand that such men were not considered eccentric. They were considered holy, and their holiness received tribute in the most tangible and expensive fashion. One of the noblest Syrian ruins is the monastery of Saint Simeon Stylites at Kalat Seman, about halfway between Antioch and Aleppo. An octagonal enclosure was erected around the base of his column, and four large churches stretched out from that octagon like the arms of a Greek cross.

People who treat their bodies as Saint Simeon treated his rarely conform in their appearance to the norm of Greek statuary, but Simeon and others like him constituted the closest possible approach to the Christian ideal. It is no wonder, therefore, that people began to read spiritual significance into the ravagement characteristic of their bodies. Some such feeling must account for the advent of what amounts to a cult of emaciation. A good instance would be the five male figures (Fig. 9.15) across the front of the elaborate ivory cathedra traditionally, but probably not correctly, known as the *Throne of Maximianus*. The throne has been at Ravenna from a very early date, but probably originated somewhere in the Christian East before the end of the 5th Century. Emaciation, it is important to understand, is not realism in the direct and simple sense of the word. There is nothing objective about monuments like the one now under review; they came into being because a deliberate choice was made with the purpose of getting a certain reaction from the observer. Extreme physical types were sought out in the hope that their unusual appearance would evoke an equally unusual strength of feeling in the heart of the Christian onlooker. Such an attempt partakes of the philosophy often called *expressionism* (see below, pages 624; 933 ff). It should be noticed that part of the method is to direct the eye of the figure in such a way that it seems to search one's soul and make a demand. When enlarged, as they so often are in Byzantine art, such eyes assert the dogma in inescapable fashion.

THE SUBJECT MATTER OF EARLY CHRISTIAN ART

In handling the Christian themes, the early artists used two different methods: allegory and symbol, and historical narrative represented in the usual way. The use of symbolism suggests secrecy, but it is hard to know what the motive for secrecy may have been. We must not be too ready to accept the usual suggestion that the Christians communicated with each other in cryptic ways because they dared not be open during the three centuries when their religion existed under the ban of the law. The Roman police were entirely too competent to have been fooled by so simple a ruse. As a criterion for date, symbolism in itself indicates little; we cannot say there were no historical subjects before 313 A.D.; and there were innumerable symbolic subjects later than that.

A good example of allegory is the subject of the sheep. Whenever we see a sheep in Early Christian art, we must depend upon the context to tell us whether we are to read it as a symbol for Christ himself, or one of the Christians. " Behold the Lamb of God," said Saint John (I:29), and the word has ever since been a synonym for Jesus. But there are also a great many passages in the Bible which refer to members of the Christian community as sheep (Matthew 15:24; Luke 15:4–5; John 10:1–27 & 21:15–17).

If Christians are sheep, Christ is their shepherd — as so beautifully set forth in the 23rd Psalm and in the *Good Shepherd* statue of the Lateran (Figs. 9.7–8). The name *Good Shepherd* must be of very early origin; at any rate, Mr. Walter Lowrie (*Monuments of the Early Church*, page 218) found it in an early prayer for the dead: " Let us pray God that the deceased carried on the shoulders of the Good Shepherd, may enjoy the fellowship of the Saints." The prayer comes from the Sacramentary associated with Saint Gelasius, who was Pope from 492 to 496. It is interesting that the iconography for this subject, so perfect an instance of Christian sentiment, should have been taken over bodily from pagan precedent, as already described (see above, page 260).

The prime case of outright symbolism is furnished by the frequent appearance of a fish more or less realistically depicted. If juxtaposed to loaves of bread, the fish may merely refer to the miracle of the loaves and fishes; and by extension, that event may be construed as a prefigurement in cryptic form of the Last Supper. More often, however, the fish appears all alone. If so, we are to read *Christ*. The association depends upon an acrostic pun. The Greek word for fish is ἰχθύς (ICHTHUS); and the five letters of ἰχθύς may be arranged as the initials of an expression as follows:

’Ιησοῦς	Χρίστος	Θέου	ὕιος	Σώτηρ
Jesus	Christ	of God	the Son	Savior

The vine was another popular symbol for Christ, being derived from the expression " I am the vine and you are the branches " (John 15:5). If associated directly with wine-making, as it is in some of the mosaics of Santa Costanza at Rome, a reference to the Last Supper may be assumed. Very frequently several symbolic subjects appear together in a single composition. That is true of the well-known *Sarcophagus of Theodore*, preserved at Ravenna, where we find the vine and the grapes intimately juxtaposed to a medallion and two peacocks (Fig. 9.18).

The peacocks symbolize immortality. Apparently they had carried some such connotation even in pagan art. The association seems to have been threefold. In the first place, the peacock was confused with the phoenix bird, which was reborn every 500 years after consuming itself in a bonfire. Secondly, the periodic renewal of the peacock's splendid feathers came to be associated with the idea of resurrection; but even more convincing than these notions was the belief, shared by so great an authority as Saint Augustine himself, that the flesh of this bird would never putrefy no matter how long it might be kept.

But lest the reader imagine that early symbolism was governed by strict rules, it would be well to mention some other meanings at times attached to the peacock. Mr. G. G. Coulton (in Chapter 14 and Appendix 18 of his *Art and the Reformation*) cites a 14th-Century compilation which would appear to be an attempt to catalogue every symbolic reference to the peacock up to that time — some of the meanings undoubtedly very old. Because the hideous voice of the bird was supposed to frighten snakes and because the cock sometimes protects the peahen, the few actual virtues of this gaudy fowl were at times exaggerated to make him symbolize goodness, justice, and perfect religion. And on the other side of the balance, the well-known vices of the peacock made him now and then the symbol for pride, vanity, envy, avarice, secretive methods, persecution, and the shame that follows transitory beauty. In addition, his serpentine neck and fiendish call made him occasionally stand for the devil, while his polygamy epitomized lust — but since polygamy must contain some measure of gallantry, the very same vice was at times associated with charity.

The medallions which occur on the main face of the *Sarcophagus of Theodore* and three times on the cover are the medallions of Jesus Christ. The Greek letters X (chi) and P (rho) for the *Chr* of *Christos* are combined with the initial and terminal letters of the Greek alphabet, the A (alpha) and ω (omega) of Revelations 1:8, "I am Alpha and Omega, the beginning and the ending, saith the Lord. . . ." The circular shield upon which the letters are inscribed may be a mere carry-over from the art of coinage. Or it may reflect the religious confusion of Constantine, who is said to have confounded Christianity in some way with the worship of the Sun. It is also likely that the monogram was thought of as a sign of triumph; for that reason, it has been suggested, it was rarely used after the Gothic invasions of Italy during the 5th Century.

The monogram of Christ seems to have been construed as a near-symbol for the cross, to which it bears a farfetched resemblance. However that may be, it is notable that the very earliest Christian art contains no reference to the Crucifixion. Even as a symbol, the subject seems to have been quarantined from the visual arts until the time of Constantine; and if we may be guided by the examples coming down to us, representations of the event — even in restrained form — are considerably later. The reason for this may not be immediately clear to the modern reader, within whose experience no other symbol has anything like the prestige and nobility of the cross. But that was decidedly not so in the earliest period of the Church.

In late Antiquity, crucifixion was a very familiar thing. It was the punishment meted out to criminals of a loathsome and contemptible kind, who were thus put slowly to death in a manner excruciating enough to reduce the fortitude of the most stoical victim, leaving him at the last an example of complete degradation. As Cicero indicates in the *Verres*, the penalty was not suitable for Roman citizens. Hence we hear that Paul was beheaded, while Peter and the others were crucified. In Jewish custom, moreover, a curse attached to men whose bodies were hung from trees. Crucifixion amounted to the same thing.

All of these ideas combined to make the manner of Jesus' death anything but an advantage to the missionary effort of the new religion. In First Corinthians 1:23, Paul says so in plain words: ". . . we preach Christ Crucified — unto the Jews a stumbling block, and unto the Greeks foolishness." Even though Christ had upon several occasions, as in Matthew 10:38, spoken of "taking up the Cross," we may wonder whether he intended any more than to emphasize by an extreme figure of speech the great difficulty facing himself and his followers, and the degree of loyalty demanded. In any event, we may be sure that everyone within hearing was familiar with the sight of the condemned carrying the cross-bar (not the entire cross, as so often represented) while being marched to the spot where sentence would be inflicted.

It took time to bring about a reversal in the significance of the Crucifixion, but it is plain that the process was well under way during the lifetime of Paul. At a number of places in his Epistles, we find him giving emphasis to the spiritual meaning of the event. Thus, in Galatians 6:14, he declares, " But far be it from me to glory, save in the Cross of our Lord Jesus Christ." And in the sixth Chapter of Romans, he goes on to explain what he means in a discourse that makes the cross an instrument whereby man, through mortal death, is freed from sin and finds the way open to resurrection and heavenly immortality.

Paul's ideas seem to have been generally accepted within the Christian brotherhood — not promptly, perhaps, but within a space of time. Tertulian of Carthage (about 160–230) speaks of the gesture still known as " making the sign of the Cross." He described it as habitual, and obviously assumes that the procedure will be perfectly familiar to his readers.

Nevertheless, we must remember that it was still illegal to be a Christian, and the going opinion of the Roman world can be gauged from the character of what seems to be our earliest representation of the *Crucifixion*, dating from the end of the 2nd Century. This is a *graffito* (drawing scratched on a wall with a stilus) now preserved in the Terme Museum at Rome (Fig. 9.53). It originally came from the so-called *paedogogium*, supposedly the page-boys' room, in one of the palace ruins on the Palatine Hill. The picture shows a figure with an ass's head, attached to the cross. Underneath, a Greek inscription reads, " Alexaminos adores his God " — probably a cruel dig at the feelings of some young Christian.

We may make a shrewd guess that it required Constantine's famous vision of the Cross in the Sky to give the symbol any honor with the Roman world at large. He used the cross, mostly in monogram form, on coins and on military standards. But coins and standards hardly engage the attention of important artists. It is impossible to tell how quickly the imperial endorsement may have been able to bring the cross or the Crucifixion into use as a standard subject in the fine arts. The earliest preserved examples of any significant size date long after Constantine.

For the cross as a symbol in its present meaning, the first monument is believed to be the mosaic picture filling the apse of Santa Pudenziana at Rome

Fig. 9.53 Rome. Terme Museum. Satyrical Crucifixion. Originally in a palace on the Palatine Hill.

(Fig. 9.25), where we find a jeweled cross rising grandly against the background sky. We shall return at some length to this important picture presently. Its date probably falls shortly before the year 400.

At about the same time, it seems that actual pictures of the Crucifixion became common — representations, that is, describing the event itself in some detail. Of these, the earliest we have was carved on one of the 18 extant panels (from an original 28) of the cypress-wood doors of Santa Sabina at Rome (Fig. 9.19). The church was dedicated in 432; and the doors must come from the same time, and are little affected by repair and restoration. In the panel of the *Crucifixion,* the three crosses are shown against the background of a city wall, apparently to tell us that the execution took place outside Jerusalem. The posture of the figures is hardly as we are now accustomed to see it. They do not hang from the arms as usually represented, but are crucified with the arms held sidewise. The attitude corresponds with the position then customary for prayer, a matter to which we must now turn our attention.

A figure who stands erect and prays with arms upraised is technically known as an *orant,* or *orans.* The imagery derives from the classical attitude for prayer which was still in use during the early centuries, but was going out of vogue to be replaced by the postures of Near Eastern derivation familiar today.

In Mark 14:35, we are told that Jesus went forward a little, and *fell on the ground* to pray. His action closely resembles the etiquette of a subject abasing himself before an Eastern potentate, and reflects a similarly Eastern concept of the proper relations between man and God. This idea is reinforced by Matthew 6:5, where Jesus is quoted as denouncing hypocrites. He mentions in passing that they pray standing up. Certainly the posture assumed for prayer makes no difference one way or the other in relation to the un-ethics of hypocrisy; unless the erect position offended Jesus's sense of propriety, it is hard to see why he bothered to mention it. But in religion as well as in art, an intuitive taste was operating to make an end of classical Antiquity.

But classical Antiquity did not die in a day, and what was left of it endorsed the standing posture. In Homer, men " lift up their hands and pray aloud " (*Iliad* III.275). They do the same in Vergil (III.263–4): old Anchises stands on the shore with outstretched hands, invoking the great divinities. Praying figures are so represented by pagan artists — for example, the bronze *Praying Boy* of the Lateran.

Jewish custom also permitted the standing position, and there is evidence to prove that some Early Christians prayed sitting or kneeling. Christ's resort to the prostrate position — presumably as a gesture of special urgency and sincerity — must reflect a very doctrinaire Orientalism, not yet accepted by everyone. This is certainly what one would gather from the frequent appearance of the *orant* in catacomb painting and in the relief sculpture on sarcophagi.

But it is one thing to suggest a derivation for the *orant,* and another to tell its precise meaning as understood by the Early Christians. It seems likely that several significations were current, none of them necessarily excluding the others.

The simplest explanation is that the *orant* represents the soul of the deceased who, having arrived in the realm of blessedness, prays for his loved ones left on earth. By playing up the connotations of this spirit-portrait, it is possible to contend that the *orant* might upon occasion mean much more. Prayer postulates *faith,* a virtue upon which Christianity hinges. In the absence of any other specific symbol for faith, the *orant* may have that meaning. And since faith, when construed generically, is the amalgam giving unity to the Church, we often find ourselves referring almost interchangeably to " the Faith " and "the Church." By the same token, the *orant* may stand for "the Church." On some of the Catacomb ceilings, this is very probably the true interpretation, because the *orant* appears there in complete separation from the idea of individual portraiture — often in compositional relationship to the Good Shepherd. The likelihood of this meaning is enhanced by the fact that such *orants* are female, a custom in grammatical agreement with *ecclesia,* a feminine noun.

For an example of narrative subject matter, we may turn to the well-known *Jonah Sarcophagus,* now in the Lateran Museum, and so-called not from its occupant but from the subject that takes up most of the space (Fig. 9.20). We see Jonah thrown overboard into the mouth of the whale, spewed up on shore, and finally taking his ease under a tree. Other scenes are there also: the raising of Lazarus, Moses striking water from the rock, and a jack-in-the-box who stands for Noah in his ark. It will be noted that a single train of thought is dominant in the choice of these subjects. Each one amounts to an instance in which the faithful escape destruction through the direct and physical intervention of God himself. In Early Christian days preoccupation with deliverance was not confined to art; it is reflected also in many early prayers, a parallel noted by several scholars. One prayer quoted by Mr. Walter Lowrie (*Monuments of the Early Church,* pages 198–199) is sometimes still used to commend the soul to God in the hour of death. It reads:

> Receive, O Lord, thy servant into the place of salvation which he may hope of thy mercy. Deliver, O Lord, thy servant from the pains of Hell. . . . Deliver, O Lord, his soul as thou didst deliver Enoch and Elijah from the common death of the world. Deliver, O Lord, his soul as thou didst deliver Noah from the deluge. Deliver, O Lord, his soul as thou didst deliver Isaac from sacrifice at the hand of his father Abraham.

And in this and other prayers, we find much the same formula repeated to cite the precedents established by the delivery of Daniel from the lions, the three children from the fiery furnace, Abraham from Ur of the Chaldees, Job from his sufferings, Moses from Pharaoh, Susanna from false accusation, David from Saul and from Goliath, Peter and Paul from prison, Thecla from torture, and Jonah from the belly of the whale.

The intent behind such a prayer is pathetically clear. Helpless in the disaster of Roman disintegration, these people could not, in any worldly terms, imagine a solution for their troubles. God alone might help them. Indeed the hope of his help was the only hope available, and the citation of precedent the only reassurance.

Such, then, were the themes of Early Christian sculpture and painting. It is remarkable how, at this remote date, we can feel their meaning. As communicators of content, no artists have ever been more successful — a fact that emerges with ever greater clarity as we pursue the history of religious art from century to century. Some of the best technicians in the world, working under conditions infinitely more propitious to success, have aimed at the sublime and have arrived at bombast. But in these early monuments, often badly executed, where do we find a real failure?

"The Bible of the Poor"

The value of visual aids to education is appreciated today as never before, and the reader will naturally be curious to know to what extent sacred statues and pictures were used in teaching the early doctrine. In any number of places, one can read that every bit of carved stone told a story, that the medieval ideal was to present a complete religious program by way of the visual arts, and that the fully developed cathedral was in fact "the Bible of the Poor." Such notions have not become diminished by repetition, and more than one writer has found in them sufficient inspiration for language that is undeniably graceful. The entire matter, however, requires examination.

There can be no doubt whatever that the officials of the church repeatedly entertained the idea of a system of visual education. Pope Gregory the Great (regnal dates 590–604) in a letter primarily concerned with idolatry disposed of that danger by remarking that ". . . for what writing is to them that can read, a picture is to them that cannot read but only look, since in it even the ignorant can see what they should follow." Upon returning to England from one of his several journeys to Rome, Benedict Biscop (628–690) brought back with him a series of pictures painted on boards, and it is a matter of record that he intended to use them for teaching. Fear of idols was not easily overcome, however; and the entire Iconoclastic Controversy (726–843), which shook the Byzantine Empire to its foundations and resulted in wholesale destruction of religious art, had its genesis in suspicion of representative art as such, and prejudice against its use for religious purposes. Even a finding in favor of pictures and images by the Second Council of Nicaea (787) failed to end the trouble. The immense production of sacred art during the Romanesque and Gothic periods, and throughout the entire Renaissance, seems on the face of it to betoken a purpose more serious than the mere embellishment of churches; and it is a fact that the churchmen who met at the Council of Trent (1545–63) regarded art as one of the best weapons of the Counter Reformation.

In spite of all this, the weight of the evidence is strongly against the concept that religious art functioned as an educational system, and there is scarcely a possibility that it ever served as a substitute for literacy. Statues and pictures doubtless helped to recall, for those who knew them already, favorite stories from the Bible and the lore of the Saints; but in the pages above and often in those to come, the reader cannot fail to be impressed with the recondite nature of most medieval art. Nothing so complicated and erudite could be any use at all for the instruction of ignorant persons. To think otherwise is to imagine the medieval serf as being edified by imagery so subtle in its mysticism as often to escape the grasp of the most astute intellects of the present day. Medieval religion had great power, to be sure, but we can hardly believe it provided an unlettered population with supernatural penetration and incredible acumen. The proof of the matter is to be found in the routine utterances of the churchmen themselves. A good preacher might make a very telling point by referring to a storied capital in the nave arcade, or to a mosaic on the triforium; but after reading an immense number of medieval sermons, Mr. G. G. Coulton (*Art and the Reformation,* page 317) testifies that such things almost never happened. He reached the over-all conclusion that a large part of the imagery was never generally understood, and that much of it was rapidly forgotten even by the clergy. The late Mr. Kingsley Porter was of practically the same opinion. This is not to assert that art was never so used. Occasionally, the artist himself has left a record of didactic intention — that was done by Giselbertus, the author of the *Last Judgment* of Autun (see below, pages 422–423), who inscribed the words "Let this horror appall those bound by earthly sin!" But such instances of direct appeal to the public were the exceptions which have all too often been construed as the rule. The truth seems to be that most religious art was commissioned by the learned and remained the affair of the learned.

THE EARLY CHRISTIAN BASILICA

The great architectural achievement of the Early Christian Period was the invention of the *basilican church.*

This set the type for all subsequent church architecture. A great many changes of style have since taken place, but their effect upon design has been restricted to construction and surface appearance. With the exception of odd and experimental buildings, the standard Christian church has retained the plan, the orientation, the parts and the arrangement of parts much as they were first established in the basilicas built in the days of Constantine.

Basilican churches existed at one time all over the Roman world. Fragmentary ruins may be seen to this day as far afield as England and Armenia.

For basilicas in good repair, the modern student must turn the focus of his attention to Rome and Ravenna. In these two cities numerous very early churches are still in daily use.

But even those are unfortunately not in anything like their original condition. Renaissance and Baroque additions in the form of altars, ceilings, and decorative pictures mar the interiors. Out-of-doors, pretentious portals, if not entire façades, belie the character of the buildings. It is not so much that these later embellishments are gorgeous; the disharmony has to do with a gross incongruence of style. For, as we shall see, Early Christian architecture is distinguished by an unusual directness and simplicity, particularly in its structural methods. The High Renaissance and the Baroque have their own virtues, but not these.

It is nevertheless important to understand — since the contrary impression is widely entertained — that the early churches were not necessarily of a dull, ascetic appearance.

This is well demonstrated in the writings of Sollius Apollinaris Sidonius, a set of documents that guide us in a remarkably vivid way over the bridge between Antiquity and the Middle Ages. Sidonius was a Gallo-Roman of an old and honorable family, long resident in the region we now know as Auvergne. He was born at Lyons about 431, and died at Clermont in 489.

In or about the year 470, this man wrote a letter to his friend Hesperius, including a poetical description of the basilica recently built at Lyons by Bishop Patiens. He speaks of the impression made by the external scale of the building, and of its excellent site between the highway and the river Saône. He compares the numerous columns to the forest trees, and praises the dignity of the porticoes that gave access to atrium and narthex. Of the interior, he says that it shone with light, the ceiling being of gilded coffers, the floor and walls brilliant with colored marbles and mosaic pictures. The church he describes was destroyed by the Huguenots in 1562. The description is enough, however, to correct any false impressions about the effect considered appropriate by the Early Christians themselves: far from a negation of architectural beauty, it was as gorgeous and expensive as circumstances might permit.

No one knows why the early Christian churches are called *basilicas*. The same word is familiar, of course, in Latin usage, where it meant a courthouse. A similar mystery surrounds the derivation of the building. Transitional and experimental monuments are usually at hand to explain the evolution of a new and original type, but these are lacking in the case of the basilican church. The ruins of some pagan basilicas (notably the Basilica Julia in the Roman Forum) demonstrate a certain analogy to the basilican churches. But the parallel features are features that do not count. The things that make the Christian basilicas worthwhile seem absent from the Roman ruins.

No other great architects ever worked under handicaps comparable with those which impeded the Early Christian builders. The modern reader can only marvel at the momentum of a civilization which enabled them, in such a situation, to construct not only numerous churches but some of the largest and noblest ever built. For the atmosphere in which they worked, we may perhaps turn again to Sidonius. He was fully aware of the political and mili-

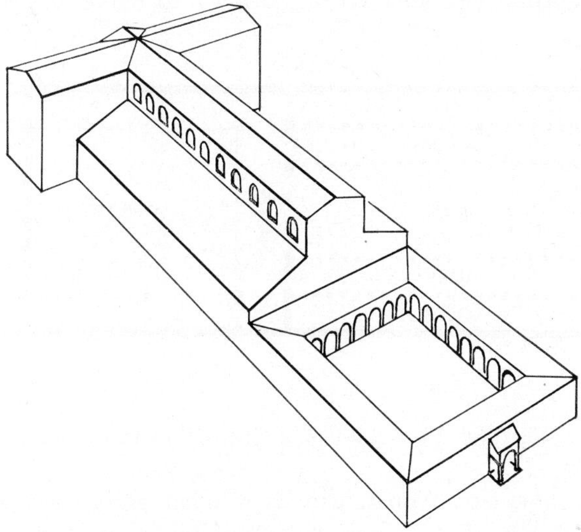

Fig. 9.54 Schematic drawing of an Early Christian Basilica.

tary exigencies, and distinguished himself in combat against the barbarian invaders. But the most impressive fact emerging from his letters is the expectation that he would continue, allowing for interruptions, to lead the elaborately pleasant life of a Roman country gentleman, cultivating and improving his estate near Clermont.

One aspect of the decline must be listed as a substantial asset to Early Christian architecture. The subsidence of paganism proved more than a spiritual blessing. Pagan temples were on the market, and fine building materials could be had secondhand and ready-made. Almost every range of columns built into an Early Christian church once decorated some heathen shrine, now dismantled. Indeed, cases exist where columns, lintels, and other parts must have originated at several different Roman temples — and we find them all put together in more or less informal fashion to make one Christian church.

It is hard to know what the Early Christian builders might have done had this classical material not been at hand. Inevitably, Roman columns and capitals (usually tending to err on the side of display) seem incongruous and flamboyant in buildings distinguished chiefly by virtues of a more transcendental kind. The reader must attempt to discount this mischance of history as he discounts the adventitious alterations to which we have already referred.

A large and notable basilica was the original church of Saint Peter at Rome, commonly referred to as " Old Saint Peter's." Founded by Constantine, that venerable building lasted for twelve centuries, and was torn down at the end of the 15th Century (see Chapter 16, below) to make way for the present

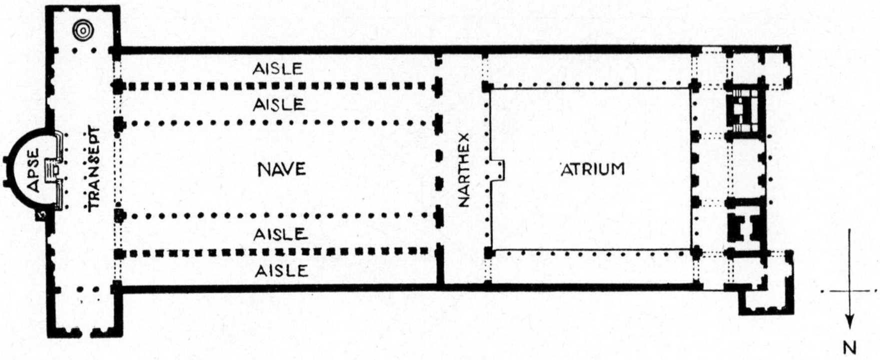

Fig. 9.55 Plan of a typical Early Christian Basilica.

church on the same site. Apparently its wooden parts were rotten, and the difficulty of replacing them (some of the beams were more than 75 feet long) doubtless contributed to the decision to rebuild on a different design. Our records are sufficiently accurate, however, to enable us to make drawings of the church. No existing example will serve quite so well to illustrate the features of the type. Fig. 9.21, taken from the model in the Museo Petriano at the Vatican, shows the fine old building much as it probably looked in the 15th Century. Fig. 9.22 gives a view of another typical basilica as seen from the other end, and Fig. 9.54 is intended to illustrate the essential scheme of the type without any of the details which confuse the appearance of actual monuments.

As seen in ground plan (Fig. 9.55) the Early Christian basilica has the general shape of an oblong. By convention, the long axis is oriented east and west. The altar is placed at the eastern end, and the entrance doors and façade at the west end. Local conditions occasionally make the usual orientation undesirable (as they happen to do at Saint Peter's itself), but in speaking of any church it is common to say " west end " when we mean the entrance front, and " east end " when we mean the rear of the building, regardless of what the actual directions may be.

Proceeding from west to east, and using the bird's-eye view of the church as a supplement to the ground plan, we find that the structure is divided into the following parts:

An open courtyard (called the *atrium*) precedes the church building, or basilica proper. This is surrounded by an arcaded walk. The effect is precisely similar to that of the cloister, so familiar in the later Middle Ages, and the Early Christian atrium is undoubtedly the architectural ancestor of the cloister. Most extant basilicas have lost their atria — an unfortunate deletion, especially in a teeming city like Rome, for the atrium provided a most desirable transition from the activity of the street to the quiet of the church. The baptismal font was usually placed in the middle of the atrium. There is some reason to believe that noncommunicants were excluded from the church itself, but were permitted to enter the atrium. However that may be, it is certainly plain that the designers conceived the building as becoming progressively more sanctified as one goes from west to east. (See below, pages 284–289.)

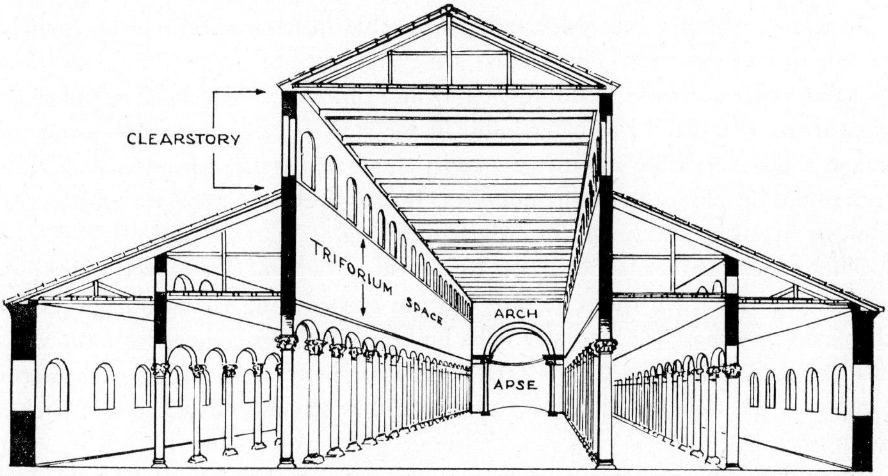

Fig. 9.56 Perspective cross section of an Early Christian Basilica, with component parts labeled.

At the east end of the atrium is the *narthex*. The arrangement of the narthex differs in different buildings. For our purposes, it is enough to say that the narthex is the vestibule of the church, and usually consists of an aisle or corridor running in the north-and-south direction.

The main body of the basilica — and here the reader should use the vertical cross section (Fig. 9.56) in conjunction with the other drawings — is divided into five *aisles*. The middle aisle, known as the *nave*, is the widest. In smaller churches we will usually find only one aisle to either side of the nave, but the division of the plan into nave-and-side-aisles is an almost inflexible convention of church design.

We will do well to concentrate our attention for a moment upon the fact just stated. Other arrangements have been tried. Some of them are admittedly successful. They have not, however, become popular. The Early Christian decision to use this particular arrangement is, therefore, one of the crucial decisions in the history of architecture. We cannot help asking ourselves whether any good, either practical or aesthetic, was realized as a result. The answer tends to increase one's respect for the designers of the basilica.

In a large church, side aisles make it possible to have a number of chapels, each with its own altar. The chapels are extremely useful for the smaller and more intimate services: weddings, baptisms, funerals, and others attended by a gathering that would be utterly lost in the vast space of the nave — and for whom it is nevertheless a comfort to participate in the associations which cluster around an old and famous building. It is entirely practical to hold several such services simultaneously in different chapels.

The modern reader, accustomed to a great variety of specialized buildings, needs to be reminded that churches did not exist during the Middle Ages for the performance of services only. The buildings were in constant use for various community purposes, and even served as shelters where pilgrims might camp out. The separation of nave and aisles has obvious advantages in such a situation.

In addition to these practical reasons the division into nave and aisles had aesthetic value as well. To that matter we shall turn presently; but at the moment we must, in all fairness, point out that the basilican arrangement confronts the designers with structural difficulties of a very serious kind. The structural history of medieval architecture can be summed up, in fact, by saying that it is an attempt to reach a satisfactory solution to the problem imposed by nave and aisles; and to that problem, we shall find ourselves coming back a great many times.

Returning to the plan, we find that nave and aisles open, at their eastern end, into the *transept.* In effect, the transept is still another aisle, running north and south, and extending outward from the east-to-west walls of the building. In height, the transept often rises, as it did at Old Saint Peter's, to the full elevation of the nave, and maintains that level for its entire length north and south. As a result, it becomes a conspicuous feature of the exterior, as seen in the bird's-eye view of Saint Peter's. The word *transept* is often used in the plural (*transepts*) if the context suggests it. If small and inconspicuous, as it sometimes is in Early Christian churches, the transept is occasionally called a *bema.*

At the extreme eastern end of the basilica, and centered on its long axis, is the *apse*. This is a recess, semicircular in plan, and usually covered with a semidome. The high altar was ordinarily placed just in front of it, and the bishop, in cathedral churches, has his *cathedra* (throne) centered against the eastern wall of the apse.

Turning now with greater particularity to the vertical cross section of the basilica (Fig. 9.56) we find:

The roofing is divided into three parts, each of which may be considered as a unit.

Over the columns of the nave arcade, vertical walls are built. These rise to a considerable height, and are topped off by a gabled roof.

Each side aisle is covered by a roof of the lean-to type. At their highest, these aisle roofs reach a level that is: (*a*) considerably higher than the top of the nave arcade, and (*b*) considerably lower than the spring of the gabled roof over the nave.

The vertical wall rising over the nave arcade is thus subdivided into two parts. These are: (1) the *triforium area,* extending from the top of the nave arcade to the level at which the aisle roof abuts the side of the building; and (2) the *clearstory* (sometimes spelled *clerestory*), which rises from this point to the spring of the gabled roof over the nave. The effect of this arrangement of the roofing is to give the impression that the middle part, or nave portion, of the building lifts bodily upward above the rest.

Almost every clearstory in history, and the device is as old as Egypt, has been pierced by windows. Excellent lighting results. So much light is admitted, in fact, that clear glass is undesirable. Stained glass was the natural answer; and various other expedients, all tending to reduce the glare, have been used.

Clearstory lighting is one of the great merits in the design of the Early Christian basilica. It comes, unhappily enough, at a price. The designer, if he is to use it, has his choice between (*a*) a wooden roof, which is subject to the risk of fire; and (*b*) a vaulted roof, which is much more expensive to build because abutment is necessary. The second choice was one from which the Early Christians were foreclosed by economic conditions; but in the long-term view of the church, the fire risk loomed large indeed. As a result, architects wrestled with the problem for centuries, until they were able, by Gothic methods, to produce at reasonable cost a fireproof building with clearstory lighting, and the traditional basilican arrangement of the plan.

Such, in bald fact, are the physical features of the Early Christian basilica. It would be a great mistake to round-off the discussion at this point, leaving the reader with the impression that those early monuments are of interest only for historical and sentimental reasons, and represent, as works of art, the mere best that might be expected under bad conditions. The reverse is true. No excuse is needed. Properly interpreted, the Early Christian basilica is a radical advance over any previous building. It symbolizes, in fact, the advent of a broader concept of architecture. For sheer originality, it is unexcelled.

In the design of the basilica, the Early Christian architect focused his attention upon the interior. In this, he continued what had become almost standard practice among the Romans. But in his treatment of the interior the Early Christian designer worked toward new ends. These are: (*a*) progression and focus; and (*b*) an architecture conceived in terms of voids rather than solids. It is possible, even though delicate argument is involved, to read into each of these ideas a peculiarly Christian meaning.

The idea of progression and focus is best appreciated as one enters the church from the west end, and faces the altar. The effect of progression derives from the sequence of the columns. One sees a column beyond a column beyond a column. Ultimately, the eye arrives at the altar. There is no impulse to think of the columns as individual objects; one does not count them. The thing comprehended is the process of moving step-by-step toward a destination.

The effect of focus is a function of the architectural horizontals. It is most easily explained by reference to a drawing or photograph, but operates as plainly in the actual building. If in a photograph of any basilican interior, a straight edge is placed along any horizontal (for example, the line formed by the bases of the nave colonnade, or the line formed where the clearstory meets the ceiling), it will be found that these lines intersect at a vanishing point which is very close to the position of the altar.

These two arrangements acting in unison make it almost impossible for one to avoid a concentration of attention toward the east end of the church in general and the altar in particular. The effect of such concentration, naturally, is to suggest that the east end of the church symbolizes a goal, result, or condition of peculiar sanctity, toward which it behooves one to move. No earlier architecture provided so meaningful an interior.

It is interesting to see that the pictorial decoration of the church was arranged in general consistency with this idea. The available monuments show considerable variety, making it difficult to suggest that any fixed scheme of arrangement was ever arrived at in Early Christian times. It nevertheless appears that the subject matter ordinarily chosen for the triforium and clearstory space was historical in character, and that the subject matter chosen for the apse was transcendental. For the *arch* (i.e., the wall space between the walls and ceiling of the nave, and the actual arch of the apse-opening), it seems to have been customary to choose scenes midway between the two — historical and yet divine.

Thus, in Santa Maria Maggiore at Rome, we find the available wall spaces of the nave decorated with mosaic pictures depicting events in the careers of Abraham, Jacob, Moses, and Joshua. Fig. 9.12, already mentioned in another connection, is one of the series.

Even better known, perhaps, are the nave mosaics of Sant' Apollinare Nuovo at Ravenna (Fig. 9.23). There are three series of pictures, each at a different level: (*a*) at the very top, above the clearstory windows, there are scenes from the life and passion of Our Lord; (*b*) between the windows there appear single male figures, probably representing prophets and apostles; (*c*) below these, on the walls of the triforium proper, there are two long processions of crown-bearing martyrs. The female martyrs are represented as proceeding from the town of Classis toward an enthroned Madonna and Child. The male martyrs proceed from Ravenna toward an enthroned figure of Christ. There is an interesting fusion here of history and symbolism. Another noteworthy detail is the fact that Christ, as he appears in various places throughout the ensemble of decoration, sometimes wears the beard, and sometimes does not. It is questionable whether that has any chronological significance, even though there is some reason to suppose that the mosaics were started about 510 A.D., and were not complete until about 560.

A good example of an elaborately decorated arch is that of Santa Maria Maggiore at Rome. Unfortunately, the pictures do not show up at all well in the best available photographs, but a list of the subjects will perhaps suffice to illustrate our point.

Across the crown of the arch is the Throne of the Apocalypse; to either side of it are Peter and Paul and the Symbols of the Evangelists (see below, page 286); below it, is the signature of Pope Sixtus the 3rd, who had to do with a remodeling of the basilica about the middle of the 5th Century.

On the left side of the arch, reading downward, we may see: *The Annunciation,* including an angel who reassures Joseph with respect to the miraculous pregnancy of Mary; *The Adoration of the Magi; the Massacre of the Innocents;* and *Jerusalem.*

On the right hand side of the arch, also reading down, there are: *The Presentation of Christ in the Temple;* a scene sometimes identified as Christ disputing with the doctors, and again as the arrival of the Holy Family at the court of King Aphrodisius of Egypt — whose idols fell down when they approached; *The Magi before Herod;* and *Bethlehem.*

Most of the material, it will be observed, involves the operation of divine forces in events which are historical in the sense that they happened on earth, thus fulfilling the stipulation that the arch suggests a transition from worldly to heavenly things.

The arch of Sant' Apollinare in Classe (Fig. 9.24) is far less pretentious and much more quaint. In the lower register, around the extrados of the apse, are the twelve apostles symbolized as sheep. Above, we see a bust portrait of Christ; and to either side of him, four strange creatures rise in half length from the clouds. These are the *Symbols of the Evangelists,* destined to have a long history in the art of Europe. They also appear in the apse of Santa Pudenziana (Fig. 9.25), and we must do our best to explain them without further delay — merely noting, as we pass on, that by symbolic means, this arch also conforms to the general principle of subject matter from the lifetime of Jesus.

The man stands for Matthew, the lion for Mark, the ox for Luke, and the eagle for John. It is not at all certain how or why these monsters came to be associated with the Evangelists, but the symbolism is generally thought to derive from Ezekiel's vision as set forth in his first chapter. In their present meaning, the symbols appear to date from Jerome's commentary on Ezekiel (end of the 4th Century), but other interpretations were current in the early days.

The story usually told to account for the individual assignment of the symbols is this one: The man goes to Matthew because he dwells on the human generation of Jesus Christ, and sets considerable store upon the fact of his incarnation. The lion goes to Mark for several reasons. The lion is the king of beasts, and Mark is held to stress the royal dignity of Christ. Baby lions, according to a myth, were born dead. After three days, they came to life when the sire roared — a procedure construed as an allegory for the Resurrection, of which Mark is the principal historian. Mark's Gospel, moreover, begins with "the voice of one crying in the wilderness" and ends with "he that believeth not shall be damned." Roaring and cursing, it was said, tend to be habitual with the lion.

Luke has the ox because he dwelt upon the priesthood and sacrifice of the Savior, the ox having for centuries been the typical sacrificial animal. The eagle belongs to John, we are told, because his imagination soared upward like the vertical flight of the eagle to arrive at an actual contemplation of the divinity of Christ.

For the apse, it was apparently considered appropriate to select a scene that demanded a setting beyond and above the time and circumstance that curtail all earthly activity. It is probable that some such intention dominated the thought of the now unknown architect of the noblest apse of all, that of Santa Pudenziana at Rome (Fig. 9.25). Various suggestions have been put forward with regard to the date, ranging from the 2nd to the 8th Century, and the question remains vexed. The majority opinion would put the picture at about 400 A.D.

The theme is probably that of Christ and the Apostolic College, but there has been considerable argument over the identification of the setting, and to find some reason for the presence in the picture of two ladies.

If we are correct in believing that a heavenly setting was usually wanted for the apse mosaic of a basilican church, we would be required to read this as the Heavenly City. In that case, the two ladies conveniently become the *Ecclesia ex Circumcisione* and the *Ecclesia ex Gentibus*, an interpretation suggested by the identity of the male figures over whose heads they hold wreaths. Peter, who was conceived as head of the Jewish element in the church, is always depicted as wearing a square-cut white beard. Paul, the Apostle of the Gentiles, always as a lanky, bald-headed man with a long, pointed brown beard. The uniformity of the iconography makes it likely that this is how the men actually looked in life.

A much less lofty but no less imaginative idea of the matter denies all holy content whatever. The setting, we are told, is Rome, and the district the part of Rome where Pudens, the donor of the church, lived. The persons represented become, in this interpretation, nothing but Pudens and his family engaged in the ceremony of foundation; and the two ladies are his daughters Praxed and Pudenziana.

A third suggestion, spiritually midway between the other two, says that the city is Jerusalem. Thus the mound on which the cross is set becomes Golgotha. The small domed building to left of center becomes the Holy Sepulchre, and the immediate foreground would be the atrium of the Constantinian basilica of the same name where, on Good Fridays, the bishop was accustomed to set his throne before a cross, reading passages from the Gospel while surrounded by his Presbyters. Unfortunately, the buildings needed to make this identification positive have long since vanished; they went, so far as we know, during the Arab invasion of the 7th Century.

Various other things about the picture are notable. As pointed out above (page 273), this is probably the first monument of major importance where the cross appears in its modern connotation as a symbol for sacrifice and glory. If we are correct in calling the central figure Christ, we have also the earliest instance of the now-familiar Syrian and bearded Jesus of modern imagery. In addition, we must remember this mosaic when the time comes to study the great ceremonial pictures of the High Renaissance (Chapter 16). Lacking the historical perspective which we of today so conveniently acquire, the men of the 15th and 16th Centuries often made the mistake of thinking that the

Early Christian basilicas were classical temples converted to Christian use, or at least were "Roman churches." Mosaics like the one now under discussion were therefore construed as examples of classical art, and played a formative role in the great effort of that period to make the world over again on ancient models.

It is rare that so many associations cluster around a single work of art; and it is a tragedy that the apse of Santa Pudenziana has been badly handled in the course of history. There is reason to believe it was modified somewhat during the 8th Century. We know it was cut down at the sides in the 16th Century, and at the bottom during the Baroque era. Finally, in 1831–32, considerable restoration took place on the right-hand side. The monument is nevertheless archaeologically reliable for conclusions of the sort mentioned above.

The apse mosaic of Sant' Apollinare in Classe (Fig. 9.24) lacks the same grandeur, but is infinitely more quaint and charming. Two subjects merge together in the picture, and an explanation is required before it can be understood.

At the crown of the arch, the hand of the Almighty is seen to issue from the clouds. The central and upper field beneath is filled by a jewelled cross enclosed in a circular glory studded with stars. A small bust portrait of Christ may be seen at the center of the cross. To either side, there are half-length male figures rising from the clouds.

The lower part of the picture seems to be the ground beneath the very same sky in which the cross is seen. It is a garden setting, and a bearded saint stands in the center foreground, his arms uplifted in the position of the *orans.* A dozen sheep stand on the same level as the saint, and there are three more sheep in the middle distance. These latter seem to be giving their attention to the cross in the sky.

The probable explanation of this obscure composition is as follows:

The upper section is to be understood as a symbolic rendering of the Transfiguration on Mount Tabor (Matthew 17; Mark 9; Luke 9). We are to read the cross as *Christ,* an interpretation driven home by the juxtaposition of the cross to the words ΙΧΘΥΣ and *Salus Mundi,* and to the letters Alpha and Omega. The half-length male figures to either side are Moses and Elias, who came into view upon that occasion. The three lambs immediately below stand for Peter, James, and John, the witnesses to the event.

It is doubtful whether the lower part of the picture has any narrative content whatever. The saint is labeled as Apollinaris himself. The twelve lambs are the apostles. The setting is probably paradise — the word being construed in its original Graeco-Persian sense: a park, or a garden.

The total effect of the two-part composition comes closer to unity, in the emotional sense, than one might at first suppose. The Transfiguration amounts to an occasion when persons resident on earth were given, in physical fact, a glimpse of heaven; while in the lower scene, we find heaven actually represented. It was visualized, apparently, as a permanent state of salubrious climate where Apollinaris, the apostle of Ravenna, enjoys an appropriate reward.

The date of the mosaic is fixed with fair assurance in the second quarter of the 6th Century, and the style is a good instance of a halfway station between classical and Byzantine art. The author was of two minds. He still loved the bucolic charm of the outdoor setting as it was habitually made to appear in Hellenistic and Roman painting. On the other hand, he felt impelled toward the consideration of objects for their value as flat areas of color, adaptable to rhythmic arrangements like those seen in Oriental textiles. Unable to do one thing or the other, he handles the figures of Moses and Elias in plastic fashion, and he preserves to a moderate degree the conventions of spatial relationship: it is at least clear that we are supposed to understand that the lower edge of the picture is nearer than the upper edge, but it is notable that there is no overlapping of silhouettes, every object standing clear from every other. Each item, moreover, is taken in broadest aspect and laid flat, as it were, against a comparatively blank and neutral ground.

The meaning of *an architecture conceived in terms of voids rather than solids* can best be comprehended if one takes up a station in the outer aisle of any large basilica, and looks diagonally across the building (Fig. 9.26). From this point of view, the basilica confronts us with an arch beyond an arch beyond an arch. The area of the openings is greater out of all proportion than the area of the solids. The thing that counts is the existence of the openings. The columns and arches signify only because they outline the openings, defining them, as it were, for our visual apprehension. In such architecture, any comment is almost necessarily directed to the character of the opening, and rarely to the solid members performing the act of enframement.

The psychological effect of the basilican interior is, as a result of the preponderance of voids, almost opposite to the effect produced by a Roman interior like that of the Pantheon, where, as set forth above (pages 220–221), the solids mean much and the voids little.

Openings have a certain suggestive power. It is possible in physical fact to walk through an opening. This possibility is noted and felt even though we have no immediate intention of doing it. The result may be described as a *sense of exit*, or of potential exit. Roman interiors, and the innumerable modern interiors deriving more or less directly from Rome, achieve their unity and completeness by denying the sense of exit. They exist, as it were, each as a small universe unto itself.

In a building like the basilica, however, there is unity of an entirely different kind. The sense of exit is unintelligible unless we understand that there is somewhere for us to go; e.g., that the universe is not contained by the building in which one happens to be. Thus, as we look through the nearest archway, we see another beyond it, and another still beyond that — until, whether it happens to be in view or not, we are bound to arrive at an opening which will reveal the world. There is, in a word, a chain of suggestion connecting the interior to the out-of-doors. The train of thought thus set into motion is likely to lead one on toward consideration of the world as a whole, and finally of the infinite. The artistic " unity " of the Early Christian church results, in short, from its integration with all else. This is in radical contrast to the unity of classical buildings, which, excellent though they are, depend for artistic oneness upon separation from all else.

Our interpretation of the basilican church is one that invites direct association with Christianity. Such an association makes of the church building an analogue for the world as conceived by the Christian.

A casual inspection of either the world or the basilica is likely to result in a sense of confusion. Details make sense only when construed as steps in a progress that leads to where we would be. Motivation is lacking unless one focuses his attention and directs his movement toward an ideal — of which the altar is the visible and earthly symbol.

The unity of the immediate and particular with the general and infinite has always been a central concept in Christian teaching, which in this respect appears to go somewhat beyond Plato in asserting not only that the fact and the principle are connected, but that the two are at one. The basilican designers, in their use of openings, appear to have acted in correspondence with that principle.

Such suggestions are derived from a reading of the buildings themselves. Documentary proof is lacking. In its absence, it is possible to construe the intentions of the designers differently. It is difficult to believe, however, that those men were not conversant with the implications of Christian thought, or that they did not desire to design buildings which (within the inevitable limitations of the architectural medium) would correspond with Christian ideas. More than one modern architect has, by his own say-so, been motivated by considerations equally abstract and perhaps less worthy, and we probably take no liberty in assuming that the earliest Christian churches were meant to have meaning as well as utility.

The exterior appearance of the basilica — as illustrated by the few examples we are lucky enough to have on view today — was nondescript. This fact has long been a puzzle to critics. In the absence of definitive evidence, several interpretations are equally attractive.

There may be symbolic meaning in the radical contrast between the glowing interior and the ascetically chaste exterior view. Is this an architectural parallel for the character of the ideal Christian? Have we here an abstract but eloquent statement that what counts is inner and spiritual beauty, and that alone? Such an explanation is anything but farfetched, and it has satisfied some very learned scholars.

Another contention, based upon the subsequent history of architecture and upon compositional facts, must also be entertained. The nondescript character of the basilican exterior results to some extent from the absence of decorative detail, but it could not be corrected by supplying that lack. The buildings look like great sheds because the shape of the building-mass is that of a shed. The ridge-pole of the nave roof lies gaunt against the sky. Its axial power has the same force out of doors as inside, but it does not make the same sense: there is no altar to which the eye is guided. Similarly, on purely artistic grounds, it may be said that the length of the church has no rational beginning, middle, or end.

It is entirely possible that the Early Christian builders, either through necessity or by a conscious rejection of classical formalism, adopted a theory of architecture almost identical to 20th Century Functionalism. They surely focused their attention almost exclusively upon the interior arrangements which, in a purely functional sense, remain unexcelled for the performance of Christian services. They conceived the walls and roof to be no more than an envelope enclosing the desired facilities, and let them assume whatever shape they might.

If so, the parallel to modern times is enlightening, especially in view of what happened in the centuries to follow. It seems obvious that people were dissatisfied with the basilican exterior, and that neither the symbolic argument nor the functional argument sufficed to explain away the evidence of the eyes. Byzantine architecture is, among other things, an attempt to combine the basilican nave and aisles with a good external composition. Similarly, the many towers of the Romanesque and Gothic, integrated by a great variety of stratagems with the basilican mass, were hardly undertaken merely to ring bells.

Imperfect though it is, the Early Christian basilica is nevertheless a mighty landmark in the cultural history of Europe. No other type of building has had anything like the same influence upon the history of architecture. No other building advances, with reference to its immediate past, further ahead into realms as yet unexplored by the architect. And yet no architects ever received less from the economy and polity within which they found themselves. Thus, in terms of absolute achievement, it is difficult indeed to cite a parallel.

The Central Church

The Early Christians did possess a type of building not subject to the particular criticism just leveled against the basilica. This is the *central type,* a term

Fig. 9.57 Plan and cross section of a typical Early Christian church of the central type.

deriving from the symmetry of the structure to its central vertical axis. Such buildings were built with a Greek Cross (arms of equal length) for the ground plan, like the Mausoleum of Galla Placidia at Ravenna. More commonly, however, they were either circular or octagonal, as respectively illustrated by Santa Costanza at Rome (Fig. 9.57) and San Vitale at Ravenna.

In all central buildings, the symmetrical emphasis upon the vertical axis produces a powerful focus upon a point in the middle of the floor. Appropriate for a tomb or baptistry (where font or sarcophagus, as the case may be, can be put at that precise point), such a focus is ill adapted to the great majority of Christian ceremonies. In a word, the interior of a central church is impractical.

But the clearstory of a central building, whether covered by a dome or not, rises like a squat tower in the middle of the mass. It gives unity to the exterior design much as the hub of a wheel provides a point of common reference for the spokes and rim. The exterior composition of a central church is *omnifacial* — that is, it looks equally well from any point of view. Such buildings are naturally better landmarks than the basilicas, with more artistic interest and dignity. Nevertheless, the fundamental fault just cited foreclosed the central type from any great popularity. It was used for a few rather small, rather specialized buildings.

THE BARBARIANS AND THEIR ART

The Sources of the Barbarian Style

For the early history of the barbarians, we have nothing like the comparatively systematic sources that enable us to make a reasonably connected narrative of Greek and Roman history. Thus the origin of the Barbarian Style in art is a matter for debate and falls within the province of the anthropologist rather than the historian. Insofar as a definite statement can be made, the evidence seems to permit the following.

At the time when the Romans penetrated into the regions north and west of Italy, those areas were populated by tribes who had come from somewhere else, presumably from an easterly direction and for reasons at present unknown. The general tendency to migrate from east to west continued well into the classical period, a notable instance thereof being the Gallic pressure upon Pergamon during the 3rd Century B.C. — which resulted, as we have seen (pages 160–161) in the erection by Attalus the 1st of a commemorative monument to which the *Dying Gaul* (Fig. 6.1) belonged. It is surprising how little the Gaul resembles typical members of the modern Latin races, and how very like he is to many an Irishman or Scandinavian.

In their effort to trace the Barbarian Style in art, scholars tend to reason in this way: A conspicuous feature of all art that is barbarian or derives therefrom is the frequent and habitual use of animal subject matter, usually grotesque and more often than not demonstrating a fondness for the invention of plausible but highly imaginary monsters. Now animals had been very common in the art of ancient Mesopotamia, and the Persian empire had, in due course, fallen heir to the artistic tradition originally centered in the region of the Tigris and Euphrates. From Persia, the same tradition was transmitted to the region north and east of the Black Sea. It seems to have been brought there by some people called the Scyths, and the whole region, indefinite in area, has ever since been referred to as Scythia. As to whether the Scyths were wandering barbarians who merely came in contact with Persia or were related to the Persians, no one cares to state in any arbitrary fashion. There is merely a tradition that they had been there and left, presumably because driven out, and probably about the 7th Century B.C. As so many other barbarian nations did, the Scythians gradually lost their ethnic identity; at the start of the Christian era, their name no longer meant anything. But the art they once practiced had spread far to the west and far to the east as well.

The narrative as given above appears to be corroborated by the history of language, and the monumental evidence for it is a great collection of small objects found in barbarian burials. There is an unmistakable resemblance between objects found at widely separated points. Two examples may be cited, merely as an illustration of the method.

A Greek gem, now in the Ashmolean Museum at Oxford (Fig. 9.27) shows the figure of a prancing hybrid monster best described as a lion-griffin. He belongs to the genealogy of the fantastic five-legged beasts that once frowned down from either side of certain Mesopotamian gateways (compare Fig. 2.11), but the workmanship is probably Greek. The object belongs to a class of gem known as the Graeco-Persian, and it is supposed that such things were made by Greek artists resident in Persia, or made in Greece for export to markets in Persia. This particular piece was found near Pantacapaeum, a Greek city on the Crimean peninsula not far from the so-called Cimmerian Bosphorus, the straits which lead into the Sea of Azov. As to how it got there, or why, one cannot say; it may or may not be significant that lion-griffins of a similar kind were sometimes struck on the coins of Pantacapaeum.

A belt buckle found in Siberia also has a lion-griffin on it (Fig. 9.29). The beast is not a duplicate of the other, but the resemblance is so close that a connection must be assumed. The object belongs to a recognizable category of Siberian finds, of which it is an unusually definitive example. As compared with the beast on the gem at Oxford, this one illustrates even more convincingly the survival of the cult of savagery which formed so important an aspect of ancient Mesopotamian art. Some very important stylistic innovations are also to be noted. The Siberian buckles reflect a self-conscious cultivation of the asymmetrical: most of them are substantially higher and heavier on one side than the other. There is no suggestion of a governing enframement; the animals themselves form the silhouette, which is substantially irregular and much complicated. In handling the bodies of beasts, the author of this design, whoever he may have been, is like all other barbarian artists in caring nothing whatever for anatomical fact. He twists and contorts things in a strange way, as though driven by an inward force to seek an elusive pattern that remains forever beyond him. At this stage, the animals retain much plastic quality; but if their bodies were elongated, made thin, and abstracted into a linear interlace, this very subject might appear in one of the Irish manuscripts, where it would pass unnoticed. (Compare Figs. 9.28,29,30.)

If we knew more about the objects found in Siberian burials, the genealogy just set forth would be more dependable, or would be corrected, as the case may be. But almost nothing is certainly known about that class of material beyond the fact that its style must derive from Scythia and its date must fall within the period covered by the present chapter. We may rest the matter by saying that such art was widely dispersed in Northern and Western Europe by the time the Roman empire began to expand into those regions. It was temporarily submerged wherever the Roman role was imposed, but it remained latent in the population as an artistic instinct nevertheless — ultimately to spring to life once more at the start of the Gothic period. Only two parts of Europe escaped the Roman and classical culture: Ireland and Scandinavia. In both of those regions, the Barbarian Style flourished in the period between the fall of Rome and the start of the Romanesque.

Essential Features of the Barbarian Style

The dominating characteristic of the Barbarian Style is the fact it is dynamic. Because dynamism can take many forms, it is hard to find one or two examples which sum up in themselves all the important qualities of barbarian art. There can be no more typical monuments, however, than the *Cross Page* from the *Book of Lindesfarne* (Fig. 9.35) and the *Monogram Page* from the *Book of Kells* (Fig. 9.37).

The observer's first impression of either is one of complexity, and he is right. Unlike classical art which finds expression through compositions involving only a few large parts, the northern and barbarian instinct is to use a myriad of tiny details. The sense of infinite number is never absent from our feeling about its monuments.

Because humanity lacks the power to comprehend infinite number in any sudden or rapid fashion, it is impossible for barbarian work to take effect upon the sensibilities except by the passage of time. Comprehension is gained by repeated acts of partial inspection, each added to each, until we begin to assimilate what we see. Complete familiarity, even with the single composition, arrives only after a series of separate visual experiences until in the end we possess ourselves of the whole.

Northern art follows a procedure of visual communication fundamentally different from the classical. Classical compositions, as we have seen (see above, pages 59–61), tend for the most part to have their effect as a single, instantaneous vision of the whole. We therefore found it convenient to name the classical system *the instantaneous, or simultaneous, mode of presentation.* We shall refer to the northern method — in which time and memory play so large a part — as *the cumulative mode of presentation.*

The force of what has just been said is much enhanced by the northern habit of defining every detail, however minute, with a precision so intense as to be passionate. The component parts of any full page of Irish illumination are as the sands of the sea. It is nevertheless self-evident that every minute element received in its turn the fierce focus of the master's complete concentration — which lives forever in the surpassing clarity of every line and boundary. We often hear it suggested that too much attention to detail is dangerous; it may militate against unity of the whole — and in other artistic styles, details may legitimately be suppressed or slurred over for that very purpose. Northern art neither seeks nor wants unity of that particular kind, as we shall see when we get further on.

Imaginary monsters were the only subject matter natural to barbarian art; nothing else is ever represented except through necessity or under outside influence — the human anatomy and plant forms are specially foreign to the instinct of the style. Even the monsters are abstracted in an extreme degree (Figs. 9.29,30,33); otherwise they are not typical.

The nature of the abstraction is plain enough from our illustrations: regardless of what he started with, the northern artist invariably reduced it to pure line. Pure line was his chief aesthetic reliance, and so far as possible the only system of expression he used. The line served him in two different ways.

The *Cross Page* of the *Book of Lindesfarne* (Fig. 9.35) shows us the first of the two. Whenever the barbarian artist wanted to fill up a space, he resorted to patterns of linear interlace. Confronted for the first time with an example, one is likely to dismiss it as nothing but another case of the braid, but that is an error. Frequently, the interlacing conforms to a geometric system or something like it; but just as we make up our minds that we understand the rhythm of over-and-under, the line will suddenly take a twist or curve that could not possibly have been predicted by all the logic of what has gone before. In small matters, we may describe the habit as capricious; in important affairs, the qualities indicated are invention and a certain fundamental flexibility and adaptability of which both classical and Near Eastern art are completely incapable.

The three large letters on the *Monogram Page* of the *Book of Kells* (Fig. 9.37) are the Greek *chi*, *rho*, and *iota* which transliterate as the *Chri* of Christ. If from the rest of the decoration we take out the great *chi* and let it stand alone as in Fig. 9.58, we have a good illustration of the other way in which the northern artists put line to use. The letter starts from a point of origin at the intersection of its several legs. Thence, the four legs sweep away in powerful, moving curves to dissolve in sharp points at the end. Except for using a center from which to start, the arrangement contains not a single element that can be understood, described, or discussed in the vocabulary of geometry. The four parts of the letter are uneven in length and weight. They are unlike in curvature. Symmetry is not only absent; it evidently was disliked and eschewed. There is no balance whatever; in fact, the Barbarian Style feels no need for the " repose " so often praised in classical art.

The life that is in the line itself is what gives compositional validity to barbarian art, and makes it intelligible. As we look at this magnificent monogram, the eye moves fast with an urgent force. Gathering momentum as it goes, it

Fig. 9.58 The letter *Chi* from the Monogram Page of the Book of Kells.

sweeps through the curves and is cast off into space at the end — to move still further along a path predicated by the character of the curvature. Presently, one recovers, and returns to the composition. So vital is the experience that we begin to read the movement into the work of art, thus endowing it with life. That is true even of static things like manuscript pages. For the full measure of the living quality of barbarian line, we must turn our attention presently to works of art designed to move. We have some in the several Viking ships preserved by the lucky chance of local burial customs and the occasional existence of clay peculiarly favorable for the preservation of wood (Figs. 9.38–40).

As distinguished from the organic compositions of the Greeks and the rhythmic compositions of the Near East, we may call the barbarian organization *eccentric*. It will be observed that the eccentric theory begets asymmetry, as already pointed out. It also brings about the silhouette characteristic of and peculiar to northern art. Instead of the plainly defined boundaries and compact unity of the Greek temple, any northern design will have what we may call the *dissolving silhouette,* characterized in initial letters and otherwise by a multiplication of small projections pointing outward in all directions, and in the architecture which presently came from the barbarian tradition by towers and spires pointing up into the air to produce the broken skyline typical of most medieval buildings.

IRISH ART DURING THE EARLY MIDDLE AGES

In 431, Patrick, then at Auxerre, was consecrated bishop and at once set forth for Ireland. His missionary success was immediate and extraordinary. When he died thirty years later, he left behind him a Christian land, and he had set into motion a cultural development that stands out like a light in the general rudeness of the Early Middle Ages.

We need not quibble by pointing out that Patrick could not personally and alone have converted the entire population. He built, rather, upon a foundation of already-present Christianity, but this fact means almost nothing in understanding the Golden Age about to begin. Our deeper insight must find its terms in the imponderables of the Irish character, which depends, to a great extent, upon the racial background of the Irish.

Insofar as any ethnic group may at any time be called "pure," the 5th Century inhabitants of Ireland were Celts. They had come there from the continent perhaps as early as the 6th Century B.C., and probably more or less continuously for some time thereafter. Because of their position on a remote island — and one not particularly alluring to the Romans — the Irish Celts were permitted to maintain their native habits free from the opposite if excellent genius by which classicism had been imposed upon continental Europe.

The same remoteness operated to insulate Ireland from the Roman disintegration. The full effect of that disaster landed elsewhere. Thus, while France, Spain, and Italy were backward-looking and at times in despair, the atmosphere of Ireland was vital and creative. In the interval permitted by history, the Irish produced an immense body of Gaelic literature and the most celebrated early monuments of the Barbarian Style.

As to the nature of the Celts and of Celtic art, we can find food for thought in the comments of Julius Caesar. That most rational of the rational Romans came into contact with Celtic populations during his campaigns in Gaul. He was principally impressed with their instability, restlessness, and the comparative ease with which they could be incited to undertake important enterprises upon which no Roman would embark without elaborate survey of the ramifications and consequences. Nevertheless, he found much to praise. He admired the depth of feeling of which the Celts were capable, especially when put in the service of liberty and against the servile. He also conceded a native ingenuity.

In appreciating Caesar's remarks, we must of course allow for the incapacity of the Roman mind to evaluate a nature so opposite to itself. For the same reason but to a lesser degree, we must not take literally the remarks of modern scholars about Gaelic poetry. Where is the linguist who did not learn Latin and Greek as a schoolboy? Nevertheless, like Caesar, these gentlemen can help us to understand Irish art.

In Irish poetry, the decorum of the Ancients is replaced by vanity and truculence, often by outright ferocity. Men act like beasts. Irish heroes, moreover, seem incapable of steady, calculating purpose. Starting out to do one thing, they arrive doing something else or nothing at all. They do not present their accounts and wind up their business in orderly fashion. Compositionally speaking, narratives of which this is true lack the sacred beginning, middle, and end essential to every classical and classicizing expression.

Even more bothersome to the classical taste, and indeed to the scientific spirit, is the Irish indifference to credulity. The Greeks, the Romans, and all European masters from the Renaissance on — painters and authors alike — have felt an obligation to fact, even to probability. Physical possibility stood as a boundary line beyond which no man might go. Artistic prudence (as distinct from the law) set likelihood as a limit. Mere plausibility has never been acceptable to the classical taste unless advertised in the title by such words as farce, fantasy, extravaganza, burlesque.

We must thoroughly understand that the Irish poets and artists neither knew that code nor subscribed to it. For them, natural fact was a restriction pertaining to the physical world alone. Surges of feeling, audacity of imagination, or both together could easily carry art and poetry completely beyond such limits. The position has much in common with that of the 20th-Century Surrealists, from whom the medieval Irish differ not so much in philosophy as in immediate background.

The Surrealists derive from the intellectual sophistication of modern times; their art deals with the fearful unknown of the mind. The poets and artists with whom we now concern ourselves were likewise confronted with a fearful unknown in the shape of a confusing and apparently capricious world. Or perhaps it might be more accurate to say that by the time of Saint Patrick, the population was in a nether world between fear and understanding.

There is good reason to believe that the abstract patterns common in Irish art derive from representations and symbols originally invented to propitiate and placate the forces of nature. The interlace, for instance, may mean flowing water; as such, it can be connected with fertility and purification. Snakes mean earth, the key-pattern fire, and birds signify the air.

Christianity undoubtedly softened the relationship between man and the environment. When these symbols appear, for instance, in the *Book of Kells*, we are probably justified in assuming that most of the dark magic had gone out of them, but also that they were still understood as declarative statements. In minor passages of the same set of illuminations, the prevailing abstraction is tempered by a friendly study direct from nature.

Similarly, in *The Deer's Cry*, a poem traditionally said to be the work of Saint Patrick himself, we hear God praised for the sensuous beauty of the sun, the moonlight, and the firmness of the earth. But in the very same breath, the good Saint asks protection from snares laid by devils, and spells set against him by women, smiths, and wizards. For the naturalism, one looks ahead to Saint Francis, for the magic, back into the shades of the forest.

It will be seen that the Irish were somewhat short of thorough civilization in the 5th Century, but they had the audacity to embrace a new religion at once and with great depth of feeling. One indication of their sincerity is the notable tendency to combine both political and religious authority in the person of the same man. The Irish establishments were primarily monastic. The monasteries seem often to have derived from the pattern of the clans, and in some cases to have taken over the social function and significance of the clan. The abbot-bishop commonly felt like a chief or even a king, and acted like one — perpetuating old feuds as vigorously as he pursued the religious life. Irish culture of this period presents us with many a paradox; infinite refinement of mind and taste and the strongest moral impulses are seen to coexist with barbarity, sometimes in the character of the same person.

If one great figure may be allowed to stand for all the rest, we may profitably cite the name of Saint Columba (about 520–597), better known as Colum Kille. According to reliable tradition, this man early dedicated himself to the religious life. He was nevertheless found guilty in the matter known as the Judgment of Tara, perhaps the earliest copyright suit on record. By stealth, Colum Kille had made himself a copy of a Gospel book belonging to a friend. The owner registered a complaint with King Dermot at Tara. The King ruled with simple logic: To every cow her calf, and to every book its son-book. Whether subsequent events represent the Saint's revenge for this humiliation, we cannot possibly find out at this date. But at any rate, it seems that Colum Kille belonged to a clan with a long-standing grievance against Dermot, and that Colum Kille was at the bottom of the plot which resulted in a bloody battle and Dermot's death. One story has it that his fellow churchmen drove him out of Ireland for his part in the affair; but, whatever the reason, Colum Kille left Ireland in 563, and went to Hy (now Iona), one of the Western Isles of Scotland. He there founded a monastery from which he made excursions all the rest of his life, establishing other foundations and undertaking the general conversion of Scotland. He thus began a great tradition.

Other Irish churchmen followed in his footsteps, and for a brief period Celtic Christianity bade fair to wrest primacy from Rome. Saint Columban (543–615), also called Columbanus, went to the Vosges region to found the monastery of Luxeuil and to draw up a monastic rule widely used elsewhere. From Luxeuil, he went on to found Bobbio in the Apennines. Another Irishman who penetrated into Italy was Saint Cathaldus, a 7th-Century Bishop of Tarentum. It was from Iona, moreover, that Saint Aidan went in 635 to found Lindesfarne, long one of the most important religious centers of Northumbria.

It remains to mention one more feature of Irish culture: its direct connection with the Near East. Sufficient evidence survives to prove that such interchange took place in significant measure — if, indeed, it was not actually lively. Various things contributed to bring it about.

In the first place, the Irish foundations were primarily teaching institutions. Most of the instruction seems to have been oral and fewer books were written than we could wish; opinions therefore legitimately vary with regard to the temper and quality of Irish intellectual life. It was certainly as good as anything else available to the student during the Early Middle Ages, probably better. Young men therefore made their way to Ireland from all parts of the Christian world.

It will be observed, also, that the period of Irish ascendancy coincides with the period when Arab pressure was driving Christianity out of the eastern Mediterranean. In the nature of the case, a proportion of the emigrants would find their way to Ireland. Indeed there may have been an attraction in the fact that by going there one got as far as possible from the Moslems. In various literary records, therefore, we naturally find mention of monks who came from Egypt and of a bishop who came from Armenia.

The Near Easterners carried their artistic traditions with them either in feeling and memory, or in the form of portable artifacts like manuscript books. The Irish monuments were thereby affected, and illustrate vividly how little right we have to be surprised at anything that may happen in the history of art. The Eastern influence may be noted in certain architectural details, and in manuscript painting.

Some of the Irish churches (and some of the earliest churches in England also) have two projecting chambers, usually flanking the apse and usually of rectangular plan, technically known as the *Prothesis* and the *Diaconicon.* At first glance, one might mistake the feature for a transept; but there is a distinction: Transepts open into nave as widely and with as little architectural impediment as structural necessity permits. The Prothesis and the Diaconicon, on the contrary, are shut off by walls and entered through narrow doors. The weight of the evidence seems to say that this particular feature of the plan remained popular in Syria, Asia Minor, and North Africa after having been abandoned in Italy and continental Europe as early as 400 A.D.

In manuscript painting, the Eastern affinities were invited, as it were, by the complete lack of any barbarian method for representing the human figure. When called upon to produce Gospel books, the Irish artist inevitably had certain challenges thrown up to him. By time-honored custom, each Evangelist was entitled to a portrait as frontispiece for his Gospel. Pictures of the Madonna and Child were desirable, also narrative events from sacred history. The best the Irish could do was to follow the models that happened to be available. It is obvious what those would be: when they migrated westward, the Eastern Christian refugees must have carried some of their best books with them, and they probably took pains to advertise in Ireland the excellence of what they brought. For that reason, the figure-style of the great Irish manuscripts is a naïve adaptation of Mediterranean types only half understood and rather incongruously surrounded by abstract decoration of incredible refinement.

A few of the most important instances of such adaptation are as follows:

The *Portrait of Matthew* in the *Book of Lindesfarne* (Fig. 9.36) has long been recognized as following an Eastern model. The general scheme is in the ancient Greek tradition: large figures presented in comparative close-up, a shallow stage-like setting, a blank background. The Saint himself is a bearded philosopher reminiscent of the dignified gentleman who sits in the central position on the *Sidamara Sarcophagus* (Fig. 9.9). An entertaining detail is the second old gentleman who pokes his head out from behind the curtain. Because Matthew, according to one tradition, was more immediately inspired by God than the other Evangelists, the suggestion has been made that we have here an early attempt to visualize the Deity. The artistic genealogy is plain enough whatever the content may be; it seems probable the Irish artist worked from a model that included a Muse put there to maintain the inspiration of the writer. (Compare Fig. 6.11.)

The *Book of Kells,* on Folio 7 verso, has a picture of the Madonna and Child, rendered in a coarse but powerful style that seems to look ahead to the monumental frescoes of the Romanesque period. Among the sources that might have been available to Irish artists at the time, one stands out from all the rest: Coptic Egypt. In general terms, the resemblance has been understood for some time. Miss Françoise Henry has recently made it specific; she found a very similar Madonna in one of the Coptic manuscripts now in the Morgan Library.

While it lasted, the monastic culture of Ireland could boast with good reason that Armagh was the capital of the world and " multitudinous Glendalough " the Western Rome. For six or seven generations, subtle minds could flourish there, threatened only by such personal violence as we can imagine to be reflected in the law that made killing a scribe equal to killing a bishop. The top of the curve was approached about 650 A.D., and maintained throughout the entire 8th Century.

Disaster then struck. The Vikings came. Their first recorded raid dates from 795. For about thirty years, occasional but destructive incursions were frequent. These, however, were a mere probing of the field. A crescendo may then be noted. A veritable tempest of destruction ensued, lasting until approximately 880, by which time Ireland was permanently ruined as an artistically important center. Its further history is a record of battles between the remaining Irish patriots and the Norse monarchs established at Dublin, Limerick, Waterford, and elsewhere, or between the monarchs themselves. Indeed there is little more to be said except that Ireland was ultimately annexed to the British Crown by Henry the 2nd in 1171.

The Viking destruction was unbelievably thorough. In most places where monasteries once stood, there is literally nothing left to see. We are compelled to identify the site itself by searching the literary records for indications of locality. In one place or another, fortunately, fragments survive. There are enough of them so that we can visualize fairly well what an Irish establishment must have looked like.

Irish Architecture

The general nature of all northern architecture, including the Irish, is suggested by a puzzled statement in the sixteenth chapter of Tacitus's *Germania*. " There is in German towns," he says, " neither contiguity nor contact with one another of the houses which make up their settlements. Each lives apart wherever a spring, a meadow, or the forest attracts him. There he sets his dwelling, which is made of clay, either to avoid fire or because of his little knowledge of architecture. . . ."

Tacitus was certainly right in thinking that Roman masonry was a superior material; but with respect to our immediate interest, his remarks are valuable because of his instinctive recognition of a difference in style which reflected a different scheme of values. He could not accommodate himself to an architecture not arranged in accordance with some geometric plan; and knowing what he was used to, we may assume that the contiguity and contact of which he speaks referred to Roman regularity — the level site, the axes, and the symmetry. By contrast, the Irish and most other medieval builders used the site as they found it, fitting their buildings to the existing irregularities, and often to good advantage.

The Irish had no interest in monumental architecture. Perhaps because they believed small buildings were artistically effective, they simply added extra churches as their establishments enlarged. There were at least seven at Glendalough, an instance which appears to be typical.

The little buildings themselves had racy lines. In plan, most of them were a simple oblong; and in elevation, the average proportions dictated about five feet of height against every four feet of width. The distinctive feature was an extremely high peaked roof. The gable-angle usually measures about sixty degrees, and the sloping surfaces of the roof account for approximately three fifths of the total height. Like the walls, the roofing is entirely of stone laid in horizontal courses. Each successive course extends slightly inward beyond the one below. This process is continued as the roof rises upward until the two sides meet near the ridge. Taken as a unit, the roof may be described as an eccentric type of corbelled vault.

These simple conventions produced an architecture at once quaint and saucy, retaining its daintiness and life through all the centuries of attrition. In Ireland an important example is Saint Kevin's Kitchen at Glendalough (Fig. 9.31). For a slightly more elaborate building of similar shape, the reader is referred ahead to Saint Laurence's, Bradford-on-Avon (Fig. 9.50).

The members of the monastery lived in huts grouped in casual fashion in the general vicinity of the more important buildings. Few of the huts were constructed of permanent materials; in fact, the half dozen beehive dwellings of stone that still survive on the island of Skellig Michael, off the Kerry coast, probably represent something more elaborate than the ordinary.

Both churches and huts were innocent of decoration, but the lack was made up by a number of *High Crosses* (Fig. 9.32) almost completely invested with sculpture carved in strong relief. As the name implies, the Irish High Cross was raised well into the air by a tapered rectangular shaft. The cross proper is similar in shape to the Maltese type, and is ordinarily superimposed upon a circle of stone. Apparently each cross was dedicated to a saint, or at least named for one. The form provided ample area for sculpture, both abstract and narrative. The iconography is peculiar; apparently much of it has to do with now-forgotten events in Ireland. A conspicuous exception to the general rule that sculpture is rare before the year 1000, the Irish Crosses remain a subject for scholarly debate. As yet, the most fundamental questions of date and subject matter are undecided. The medieval popularity of this kind of monument may be inferred, however, from the legend which assigns to Iona the amazing total of 360 crosses — doubtless an exaggeration, but still descriptive of the spirit of the times.

The *Round Tower* (Fig. 9.31), many of them still standing, was another striking feature of the Irish monasteries. No one fully understands what they were for. If used for bells, the bell must have been struck because there is no room for it to swing. It is possible the towers were built as places of refuge for the duration of the more temporary Viking raids. The placement of the doorways at a great height above the ground suggests a defensive use, but if so, the exaggerated slenderness of the shaft most unreasonably reduced the space of the interior. A suggestion rarely made is that the Irish built towers for the same reason we provide our churches with steeples: namely, they look fine against the sky.

The Irish Manuscripts

Manuscript illumination was the chief artistic specialty of Ireland. It must not be dismissed as a minor art merely because the scale is small. Irish calligraphy is one of the great traditions of art history, and its leading men take their place among our greatest artists.

In order to account for the quality of the examples we have, it is necessary to postulate something more than personal talent. We must imagine a system of art education with a discipline more thorough and refined than we have seen recently in Europe or America. In order to perform the manual feats demanded by the fastidious complexity of the style, gifted pupils must have spent years driving themselves through endless repetitions of practice until the muscles would respond and coordinate perfectly. Chinese artists are trained in such a way, as are musicians all over the world.

From the great corpus of manuscripts that once existed, we have inherited about forty examples of significant interest. Among these three books stand out as great monuments: *The Book of Durrow, The Book of Lindesfarne,* and *The Book of Kells.*

The *Book of Lindesfarne* can be dated with assurance in the first quarter of the 8th Century. Because the *Book of Durrow* is done in a coarser, stronger style, most scholars place it at least a generation earlier. By the same criterion, the more flamboyant calligraphy of the *Book of Kells* suggests a later date, perhaps slightly beyond 800.

While generally accepted, these dates involve a tacit assumption to which attention should be directed. Greek sculpture began with a direct and " primitive " phase, and evolved toward a final and Hellenistic phase marked by superb technique and effete design. Gothic architecture similarly proceeded from the straightforward into the flamboyant. In like manner the Renaissance ended in the Baroque and Rococo. Do these three histories establish a principle applicable to all art history? Are we justified in assuming that conditions in early Ireland were similar, and that human nature governs the evolution of human expression always in the same way?

The *Book of Durrow* (Figs. 9.33–34) takes its name from the monastery of Durrow near Tullamore in County Offaly. It was there when the monasteries were dissolved, and passed into the hands of an owner named MacGeoghegan. It is said he used it for veterinary purposes, curing sick cattle with doses of water run over the manuscript. The book came to Trinity College in Dublin with the library of its 17th Century chancellor, Henry Jones. The text is the Four Gospels according to the rendering of Saint Jerome in the Vulgate. Because the Vulgate was unknown in the British Isles until Benedict Biscop introduced it into Northumbria about 650 (Saint Patrick having used the so-called " Old Latin " version) the work can hardly date before the end of the 7th Century.

The illuminations of the *Book of Durrow* have a massive power, a curious strength and finality. It is difficult to realize that the pages are only 9½ by 6½ inches, allowing about forty square inches of working space inside the necessary margins. The comparative sobriety of style may perhaps be explained by the suggestion that the layout for each page derives from the mosaic pavements common in Roman Britain, and by the likelihood that the Durrow artist had worked in one of the shops where enamels were produced. At any rate, he refused to be lured into the virtuosity which the pen invites. The easy sweeps, neat reversals, and clever crossings are absent. Instead, the curves are bold. Changes of direction come like bumps, and the eye is often brought to a dead stop.

The reader must not construe such things as indicating imperfections of technique, for the hand of this artist was utterly sure; a close study of the pages will show that he pursued his way with an almost musical accomplishment. Holding back from any tour de force which might challenge the resolving power of the eye, he made the intricate rhythm of the Celtic interlace plain and clear.

His immense artistic refinement stood, it would seem, in strange relation to a spirit without sentiment, untamed, even wild. This we may feel whenever he turns his essentially abstract art in the direction of representation. Compelled by the growing strength of Christian convention to consider including portraits of the Evangelists, he appears to have paid small attention to the refinements of the East Christian models supposedly available to him. For Mark, he used a monster more savage than any lion, he gave John an eagle boldly abstracted into flat pattern, and Luke got a cow. Matthew alone was granted a portrait (Fig. 9.34). The history of art hardly contains a more unabashed abstraction from the human figure. We are reminded of the menhirs that stand gaunt and bold in many places in the lands that border the northern ocean. More like a Druid than a Saint, the outlandish face is decidedly not without intellectual subtlety.

The *Book of Lindesfarne* (Figs. 9.30, 35, 36) is a magnificent volume consisting of 258 leaves of vellum approximately 13½ by 9⅞ inches. The text is Latin, with an interlinear gloss in Anglo Saxon added during the 10th Century by a priest named Aldred. The same Aldred also wrote in a *colophon,* or terminal note, which gives us the date of the manuscript. It was done, he says, by Aedfrith and bound by his successor Ethilwald. The veracity of the statement has been challenged, but unsuccessfully. Aedfrith was otherwise an undistinguished figure about whom Aldred had no motive for boasting. He was bishop from 698 to 721; as to whether he was the artist or the patron, we cannot say. Tradition has it that the book was one of the objects carried about with the miracle-working remains of Saint Cuthbert. Like some other manuscripts, it had a reputation for being proof against the dangers of the sea. Lost overboard, it was recovered at low tide on the shores of the Solway Firth, and was thereafter carried on the Lindesfarne inventory as "Liber S. Cuthberti qui demersus erat in mare." With the dissolution of the monasteries, the book apparently passed into secular hands. Robert Bowyer had it during the reign of James the 1st. Bowyer sold it to Robert Cotton, and it came to the British Museum with the Cotton Library.

The date of the *Book of Lindesfarne* falls at a critical moment in religious history. It was just at this time that the Roman and Mediterranean church was beginning to absorb and submerge the Irish. Lindesfarne was an Irish monastery, founded in 635 by Saint Aidan who came from Iona in response to the invitation of King Oswald, but the Irish church was already juxtaposed to the Roman as represented by Saint Augustine, the first Archbishop of Canterbury, who arrived there in 597 with forty monks, having been sent direct from Rome by Gregory the Great. The two currents met in Northumbria. The official date for the victory of the Roman church over the Celtic is 664, when the outstanding liturgical arguments were settled at the Synod of Whitby. The Irishmen did not submit gracefully. Indeed, they did not submit at all. Saint Colman and a group of intransigeants abandoned Lindesfarne for Iona, and the Irish remained stubbornly independent; but by so doing, they abandoned the main course of development. Under Theodore of Tarsus, a Greek who served as Archbishop of Canterbury from 669 to 680, the ecclesiastical polity of England was organized on the Roman pattern.

Because it was produced during a period when the English imagination was turned toward Rome, more than one scholar has tried to interpret the *Book of Lindesfarne* as a monument of the English Roman church, as distinct from the Irish. A few features undoubtedly derive from Mediterranean models. The text is Latin, and includes a tabulation of feast days according to the usage of Naples. Similarly, the Evangelist portraits, as demonstrated a few pages back, were adapted from East Christian models. There is no denying, moreover, that the composition of many pages shows a feeling for Roman sobriety. The *Cross Page* (Fig. 9.35) is axial in pattern, for instance, and symmetrically arranged.

The artist's insistence upon equilibrium was by no means limited to balance between areas of ornament and the resolution of motive forces. It was applied, also, to the color relationships. The important hues are red, yellow, apple green, blue, and violet. Chemical analysis has shown that while some of the pigment materials were locally available, others came from the ends of the earth. The ultramarine blue, it is believed, found its way to Northumbria by some tedious route from farther Asia. It is evident that an effort was made to realize the highest possible intensity of each pigment material. Fading must have ensued to some extent, but it is difficult to imagine the colors as brighter and fresher than they now are. Because of its complete investiture with ornament, the *Cross Page* (Fig. 9.35) is the most gorgeous of all. Each of the hues mentioned recurs at more or less regular intervals. Although the spots of color are small, the precise outlines of the interlace prevent them from losing their identity; there is a complete absence of the blurring, blending, and mixing of tones as in French Impressionist painting. Neither does any single hue gain dominance to produce a tonality in the manner of Venetian painting. The principle at work is the idea of balance between contrasting colors. From any reasonable distance, every spot is easily resolved by the eye, and seems to attract to itself only its just proportion of attention.

None of these things, nor all of them together, make a Roman monument of the book. It remains obvious at a glance that the overwhelming interest of the artist was to find expression in the linear idiom of northern style. As such, the work is less powerful than the *Book of Durrow* and less gorgeous than the *Book of Kells,* but there is a special beauty not to be found in either of the others. The pages have a remarkable integration of design; one may not separate the ornament from the text, or either from the empty spaces. Without resorting to geometry except as noted, the designer has arrived at organic composition by a method different from the classical. It simply seems that each item makes the next necessary, and there is a certain asymmetrical inevitability in the relation between part and whole.

The ornament is an impeccable demonstration of draftsmanship. For precision, it is the ultimate; in dexterity, stupendous but restrained. The pages are filled with an endless melody of graceful evolution, but in all the innumerable variations, there is never hesitation or experiment. The hand of the artist moved like the hand of a dancer. It swung with the curves, bore down to lend weight to the line, and lifted like a song.

In the illumination of the *Book of Kells* (Fig. 9.37), Irish art came to the full realization of its own genius. The volume is a Gospel book of thick vellum. There are now 339 leaves, but there must originally have been more. The book suffered mutilation on at least two occasions. In 1007, it was stolen for the value of the cover, and found buried under a sod. About 1800 or a little later, a new binding was put on, and the binder barbarously cropped the pages to their present size of about 13 by 9½ inches, spoiling the placement of the ornament on the pages and actually cutting into some of the compositions. The history of the manuscript is well known. When the monastery at Kells was surrendered to the Crown in 1539, the book was there and Richard Plunkett was abbot. We hear of it next in the hands of one Gerald Plunkett of Dublin, who wrote some notes in it; and from this later Plunkett, the book went to a man named Ussher. Ussher's entire library came to Trinity College in 1621.

We can hardly be so definite about the authorship and place where the work was done. Miss Françoise Henry has come to the conclusion that there were at least four responsible masters plus a number of assistants. Often a single page demonstrates the work of several different hands. In itself, the situation would suggest a long period of production and several interruptions.

Miss Henry has pointed out several circumstances which unmistakably suggest Scotland. Some of the animals are like those rendered by the Picts, and there is substantial identity between the ornament carved on one of the crosses at Iona and the passages enclosed within the right-hand upper fork of the letter *chi* on the *Monogram Page* (Fig. 9.37). Certainty being denied us, the most likely guess is that the work started at Iona about 760 or so, and dragged on until Iona was abandoned after the Viking sack of 801. The fleeing monks went to Kells. Presumably, they had the book with them, and the rest of the work ensued. This version of the probabilities is consistent with the text, which is a mixed Irish version differing substantially from the Vulgate — the kind of thing one might expect to find at Iona, a center of Irish nonacceptance of Roman Christianity as represented by the findings of the Synod of Whitby.

We have alluded above to Miss Henry's demonstration that the monumental Madonna of Folio 7 verso derives from a Coptic model, and it is similarly worthy of remark that the *Book of Kells* contains a number of symmetrical compositions enclosed within firm borders. Anglo-Roman classicism was unmistakably in the air, but everything that counts about the manuscript is triumphantly Irish, Celtic, and barbarian.

Nowhere is this more dramatically true than on the famous *Monogram Page* (Fig. 9.37). It comes at the eighteenth verse of the first chapter of Matthew. After a statistical citation covering fourteen generations of forebears, the Evangelist finds himself ready for the great climactic announcement: "Now the birth of Jesus Christ was on this wise. . . ." — and in the *Book of Kells,* we find the Nativity celebrated by a burst of illumination more inspired than any other in history. The master pushed aside every provincial limitation. His line sweeps across space in magnificent open curves that cannot be contained by frames or borders. He left symmetry behind, and every other rule of static stability. The demonstration shoves all but one word of text onto the next page. We find ourselves in a new dimension like that of flight. The words that apply are *ahead, speed, transcendency,* and the rules in force are those of dynamics. Northern line broke free at this point in history; and the instinct then set loose ultimately sent mighty spires towering into the sky.

Our interest in its finest page must not close our eyes to certain less conspicuous excellencies of the manuscript. No verbal description can possibly forewarn the reader of what awaits his eye in the original, in the magnificent facsimile edition published in 1950 by the Board of Trinity College, or in the more modest but very useful plates in Sir Edward Sullivan's monograph. The array of initial letters is beyond belief; every verse of every chapter in all four Gospels has its own initial, an original and unique work of art in itself. A statistical count claims to have isolated more than 800 variations of the Irish interlace. A more bewildering display of accomplishment would be hard to cite.

Another notable detail is the occasional appearance of naturalistic subject matter. The lower central part of the *Monogram Page* shows us two cats and four mice. A bit to the right, there is a black otter with a fish in his mouth. Obviously one of the men must have laughed off the formulas drilled into him as an apprentice; these animals are alive and studied direct from nature. Analogous items can be found on the sculptured crosses, but in the main the performance is exceptional. It would seem that the lyric love of nature, so conspicuous in Irish poetry, was rather thoroughly quarantined from the visual arts.

THE VIKING SHIPS

The Viking raids began immediately prior to the year 800 A.D. Until then the history of the north is nearly a blank. We cannot even be definite about the pressures and impulses which set events into motion. Some modern historians fancy that polygamy among the upper orders had produced in Norway a superfluity of persons accustomed to privilege. Finding it impossible to maintain their preferment at home, such men went adventuring over the western horizon.

For about fifty years, the Vikings contented themselves with plunder and the sport of piracy. After that they began to take over the land. Within the next two or three generations, we find them permanently established as the aristocracy at Novgorod in Russia, in Iceland, Greenland, Ireland, England, and Normandy. But the expansive drive was not satisfied even yet. The Russian Vikings extended their power southward to the Black Sea. Beginning with a raid of two hundred ships in the year 860, they continuously threatened Constantinople for the next two centuries. Sometimes they were fought off, more often bought off. Similarly, the Norman Conquests of England (1066) and of Sicily (1072–1091) must be regarded as mature instances of the policy that began when the first ship sailed out of the fiords. But even those great and far-reaching events lack the romance of the Viking expeditions to North America.

There is no longer the slightest doubt that Norse mariners reached America about the year 1000, and were familiar with the eastern shores of this continent. Half a dozen sections of the land are mentioned by name in the sagas and elsewhere, but most of them cannot be definitely located. An exception is *Vineland*, which must have been in the region of the Chesapeake Bay. We can make this assertion by reference to Liev Erikson's observations of the sun: he could not possibly have seen what he says he saw any further north than the 37th parallel.

Opinion varies as to whether the Vikings established substantial, permanent colonies here or whether they simply came and went on hunting and fishing expeditions. So far, the search for Viking monuments has proven disappointing. Nevertheless, there are two items worthy of mention.

The only building even alleged to be Norse is the *Old Stone Mill* in Touro Park at Newport, Rhode Island. Most recent writers have thought it safer to say that the structure was a windmill of 17th-Century construction, but the evidence for that is shaky. Certain peculiarities of the design are incongruous and even dangerous in a windmill, but correspond to features found in Norwegian churches. Although conclusive proof is lacking, a good case can be made out for reconstructing the old ruin as the arcade and clearstory of a central church.

More startling if less pretentious is the monument known as the *Kensington Stone,* found in Northwestern Minnesota, and bearing a runic inscription that records the presence of 8 Goths and 22 Norwegians at that place in the year 1362. Often denounced as a forgery, the inscription is now accepted as genuine by the majority of scholars.

The Viking era was bound to leave its mark upon the history of European art. Its destructive effect has long been obvious. The invasions made an end of the Celtic tradition in Ireland and England, and brought the Carolingian Renaissance to a similar termination. On the positive side, we may cite the immense contribution that stemmed out from Normandy. By adding the Norman strain to the European population, the Vikings supplied the yeast in the lump. Gothic art might well have evolved from the Romanesque without the help of the Normans, but it would not look like the Gothic we know. To this narrative we must presently return. In the meantime, what of the art of the Vikings themselves?

From Viking burials we have an immense number of objects, mostly household utensils, arms, and articles of personal adornment. Wood carving may be cited as the chief decorative art of the Vikings. In general, its patterns are analogous to the Irish interlace but bolder, choppier, and without the cursive manoeuvres so gracefully achieved by the master-penmen. In the so-called Jellinge Style, the Ringerike Style, and the Urnes Style, the evolution of this art may be traced well into the High Middle Age.

But if we look at Viking civilization as a whole, it is plain that calligraphy never captured the imagination of the best men as it had done in Ireland. The Norse were interested in the actuality of speed and motion. Their great and dominating art was naval architecture; and their outstanding achievement was the design of the Viking ship. Few historians have as yet appreciated either the art or the science represented by those vessels. For their efficiency and for their beauty, no praise can be too high.

Numerous literary records testify to the sometime existence of very large Viking ships. Size is usually indicated by reference to the number of rowing benches in the vessel. A 34-seater owned by Olav Trygvasson probably represents the largest that was in any way usual; her length would work out at about 180 feet, or larger than most of the vessels in common use prior to the 19th Century.

In all the north, it was customary for persons of standing to be buried in their ships. Often the barrows were prepared with immense care, the ship being sealed airtight within a tumulus of peat overlaid with clay. With luck, wood can endure almost indefinitely under such conditions, and we are fortunate in possessing nearly a score of ships in more or less fragmentary form. The most important are the following:

The *Nydam Boat* was found in the mosses of Schleswig in 1863. She was 77 feet long, 10 feet, 10 inches wide, and very shallow. Her extreme narrowness indicates she was intended purely as a fast rowing vessel that would carry no sails. Shortly before World War II, a German firm built a replica for use in an historical motion picture.

The *Gokstad Ship* (Fig. 9.40) was discovered beside the Oslo Fiord in 1880. She is 72 feet long, 16 feet wide, and would draw perhaps 4 feet when loaded. She probably is a good example of the vessels used by the Norse for amphibious warfare: burdensome enough to carry a moderate cargo, stable enough to carry sail, narrow and sharp enough to row easily, shallow enough to enter any harbor or river, and of a shape that passes almost silently through the water. A replica of this vessel was built in 1893, and sailed from Norway to the Columbian Exposition held in Chicago that year. Her captain, Magnus Andersen, compiled a substantial account of the trip (*Vikingsfaerden 1893*), available only in the Norwegian. He states that the vessel reached a maximum speed of eleven knots. There are handsome and accurate models of the Gokstad Ship in the Science Museum, South Kensington, London; in the Glasgow Art Gallery; in the Musée Naval, Paris; and in the Deutsches Museum, Munich.

An even more beautiful and highly developed vessel was the *Oseberg Ship* (Figs. 9.38–39) discovered in 1903 on the western bank of the Oslo Fiord a bit to the north of modern Tönsberg. Unfortunately, this superb design has not yet attracted the modern builder, but she obviously represents the ideal of her type, and we may single her out presently for special mention.

The *Gokstad Ship* probably was, as stated, an example of the vessels used for raiding. The *Oseberg Ship* was a royal yacht. Both were intended above all to be fast, and neither could carry a bulky cargo. Readers who wish to visualize the boats that made the long trip to Iceland and the longer trip to America will do well to inspect the Viking model made by Mr. James Robertson Jack when he was head of the Department of Naval Architecture at Massachusetts Institute of Technology, now in the Francis R. Hart Museum at that institution. She is coarser in shape than the others and would be much slower, but she would carry a profitable cargo.

Before proceeding with specific comment, we would be well advised to correct certain misapprehensions which the reader may entertain if he happens to be a landsman. The first of these has to do with seaworthiness. Seaworthiness has nothing to do with size; it is a function of buoyancy, which is in turn a function of good construction and proper design. The great waves do not hit little boats hard; they merely lift them and move them along. Thus the fearful crest which inflicts a terrific impact upon some giant liner is likely to do no worse than shake up the occupants of a small vessel; their experience may be strenuous and unpleasant, but cannot be described as lethally dangerous.

Many writers have carelessly described the Viking ships as " open boats " — the implication being that the vessels would fill with water in anything worse than a fresh breeze, and were thus unsafe at sea. For safety, there must of course be a tight deck. The model at M.I.T. is completely decked over, and it will be noted that both the Oseberg and Gokstad examples have decks at a lower level, but still sufficient to prevent water from filling the hull. These are not open boats, and it is hardly to be supposed that the incomparable sailors who manned them did not understand why. Uncomfortable though such vessels undoubtedly were, we have no good reason to be surprised at the distances they covered. There was nothing on the deep water to stop them.

Another popular misconception gives rise to the often repeated statement that the Viking ships could not sail to windward " because they had nothing but square sails." Readers of the sagas will remember numerous references to fleets that waited for fair winds. That does not mean the ships could not work to windward, but merely that it pays to seek a following wind when bound 500 miles beyond the horizon. Tacking into a harbor or out around a headland is quite another matter, and there is plenty of evidence the Northmen did it every day.

An apposite passage will be found in the *Saga of Saint Olaf*. On one occasion when the Saint had landed on the Finnish shore to plunder some villages, he met more determined resistance than expected. The Finns drove him back to his boats with heavy losses, and there was nothing to do but get out. At this point the saga says that " the Finlanders conjured by their witchcraft a dreadful storm and bad weather at sea. But the king ordered the anchors to be weighed and sail hoisted, and beat off all night to the outside of the land. The king's luck prevailed more than the Finlanders' witchcraft, for he had the luck to beat around Baalagaard's side in the night, and so got out to sea."

It matters very little whether Olaf's activities are correctly reported. The important thing is that the manoeuvre of beating to windward is referred to as something perfectly well understood by the reader. It is also interesting to see that the " Russian Finns " had a reputation for black magic even at this remote date.

It should be understood that the square sail, even if less efficient than the same area set fore and aft, can be trimmed for windward sailing, and that all square-rigged ships of the seagoing nations have always been fitted with the proper gear. One simply swings the yard around until it approaches correspondence with the center line of the vessel, and flattens down the sail by sheeting in (i.e., pulling down with a rope) both lower corners, or *clews*.

The *Oseberg Ship* (Figs. 9.38–39) was designed and built as a royal yacht, and the owner was a remarkable lady. Her name was Asa. She was the daughter of King Harald Redbeard, and wife to King Gudrod the Magnificent. When about eighteen or twenty years old, she received and declined Gudrod's proposal of marriage — which so infuriated the king that he came in force, killed her father and her brothers, and carried the lady off to be his queen. As a mature and powerful man, already once widowed, Gudrod doubtless thought he was disciplining a child. He was mistaken.

About two years later on a night when the king got very drunk, Asa simply ordered one of her servants to stick a spear into him. She never denied responsibility for the murder. Her son, Halvdan the Black, was about one year old at the time; the queen ruled in his name until he grew up. She died about 850, probably in her thirties. Her grandson was Harald Hairfair, who brought all Norway under his rule.

The Oseberg barrow proved to be an archaeological discovery of almost unbelievable munificence. In addition to the ship herself, the burial included a voluminous number of fascinating objects. The barest inventory would take up too much space, and we must refer the reader to the magnificent publication *Osebergfundet,* of which Professor A. W. Brøgger was the senior author. Even so, it is worthwhile to mention here an anchor resembling the modern Herreshoff design and considerably better than most of those now in use, a little wagon, and a small sled. The latter two items are richly carved and might well have appeared in a fairy tale. In fact, everything in the burial was of the finest. Queen Asa obviously had been a collector and connoisseur. But her initiative and discrimination went far beyond mere decorative refinements like the beautiful carving with which the stem, stern, and tiller-head of her ship were adorned. That lady must have known very well how to choose a naval architect and how to judge whether he had done his work well.

It would be interesting to know what procedure the designer may have followed when making plans for this vessel. Her shape demonstrates a knowledge both profound and subtle, and we may assume that highly developed methods were familiar in 9th-Century Norway. Today, most ship-designers are trained in engineering schools, and they prefer to work by making a number of drawings which define the shape of the vessel. But the formulas available to the modern engineer are still decidedly inadequate for so refined a problem, and the leading naval architects are still primarily artists. The best of them all, the late Mr. Nathaniel G. Herreshoff, an accomplished mathematician and one of the greatest engineers of the last generation, designed his ships as a sculptor carves statues. He carved a model out of pine wood, doing the creative work freehand and determining by eye alone the more subtle and important factors in the design of a Cup Defender or fast torpedo boat. A staff of assistants was available to check his judgment by such calculations as he thought desirable, but more often than not, he did not bother to have the check made. Some of Mr. Herreshoff's models are in the Francis R. Hart Museum of the Massachusetts Institute of Technology. His methods will explain how it was possible for the Viking shipbuilders, completely innocent of all but the simplest mathematics, to produce some of the best vessels that ever sailed.

Considered without relation to her function and purely as an exercise in formal design, it is evident at a glance that the *Oseberg Ship* belongs to the same school as the Irish manuscripts. There is a plain resemblance between her decorative carving and the interlacing patterns so conspicuous in the art of the illuminators, but we hardly refer to such details. The fundamental form of the vessel is generated by a series of lines, and the lines themselves are much the same as those drawn for another purpose in Ireland. The extreme height of bow and stern exists merely to dissolve the silhouette with a linear flourish at either end; this feature has no functional value. The skin of the ship consists of planks laid fore and aft over frames which define each cross-section, and it will be noted that each strake of planking overlaps the one beneath. The construction is still used today. Known as *clinker built,* it is slightly stronger for the same weight than smooth planking; but its chief advantage has to do with appearance: it emphasizes the lines of the vessel by the method of repeating them, producing a splendid and varied linear rhythm. It is no accident that sailors only occasionally speak of a ship's shape, but often of her " lines."

The *Oseberg Ship* attains a maximum *beam,* or width, of 16½ feet, and she is 64 feet long. Had she been intended for rowing only, she would have been made narrower. The extra beam is explained by the mast and rigging found with her: it gave sufficient stability to carry a press of sail. A notable feature of the design is the extreme skill of the designer in combining this feature with other and conflicting desiderata. Wide at the middle, the ship is beautifully sharp where she enters the water and fine again to let it close easily behind her. A look at the cross sections in Fig. 9.39 will demonstrate further that she would never put her full breadth down onto the water until heeled over under sail. As between her extreme beam and her width on the waterline while floating upright, there is a difference of no less than six feet.

The purpose of the refinement was to reduce to the minimum the total area in contact with the water, or *wetted surface* as it is often called. As a general principle, the more wetted surface, the more friction with the water as the vessel moves through it — and the slower she will be. It is interesting that a designer so studiously aware of that fact should add a long keel projecting some distance down from the body of the ship. A shallower keel would have been sufficient to protect the bottom when grounding, and the deep keel adds much drag. It is to be explained only because without it she would slide bodily sidewise when sailing, and never go to windward.

Inasmuch as a ship is better than a raft only because she can go, speed is of the essence in the design of any vessel. Like many other peoples, the Vikings had the habit of recording distances by reference to the time consumed, and not to the linear measurement between places. The run from Norway to Iceland was commonly classed as a seven day trip, and works out to an average of about 3½ knots, or the same speed we might expect today under sail and allowing for unfavorable conditions along with the good. There are records which indicate that the same run occasionally was made twice as fast. When comparing vessels for speed, however, we must take account of their maximum speed when full power, engines or sails as the case may be, has been applied. We must also take account of the size.

As a general rule, the speed of ships varies in a certain relation to the square root of their length. If we measure the length in feet and express the speed in terms of knots — or nautical miles (6,080 feet) per hour — the best possible speed will be about 1.5 times the square root of the length. Thus, a ship a hundred feet long may now and then attain 15 knots — but only when the wind is strong, the water smooth, and only if her design is of the best. Since all these conditions rarely occur together, maximum speed under sail is a memorable event. The 11 knots recorded for the 1893 replica of the Gokstad vessel approaches the theoretical maximum for her size. The Oseberg design is more refined, and would surely be faster. With a strong breeze over the quarter, one would expect her to log 12 knots or even more if the water were smooth. In a note to the author, Mr. Francis Herreshoff has expressed an opinion that may be taken as authoritative; namely, that a strong crew could row this vessel at 10 knots for long enough to escape from a tight place. It is questionable whether a better type has yet been developed for amphibious warfare. We should also note that the best modern yachts, which would be no good for war, can sail no faster even though they are considerably handier. For a length on the order of a thousand feet, the 28 knots of the great Atlantic liners is a snail's pace, and to be explained only by considerations of economy: higher speeds are mechanically feasible, but bigger engines cost more to run.

Enough has been said to show that the Viking ships, too long neglected as part of the subject matter of art history, are among the most refined and highly developed products of the medieval mind. Certainly no other works of art had so great and immediate an effect upon political and social history. Except for the remarkable qualities of their vessels, the Vikings would never have come to Ireland, there would have been no Normans and no Norman Conquest, and no Norman kingdom in Sicily.

PRE-ROMANESQUE CHURCHES IN SPAIN

Some of the most interesting monuments of the Early Middle Ages exist in Spain. Small in size and not immediately impressive, these buildings are important both artistically and historically. Nothing so good was built anywhere else in Western Europe at anything like the same date. Some of the archaeological connections are fascinating. Here we may mention only two of the most important churches; for a more complete treatment, the reader is referred to an admirably compact monograph by the late Professor Georgiana Goddard King (*Pre-Romanesque Churches of Spain*, Bryn Mawr Notes and Monographs, Vol. 7, 1924).

At Baños de Cerrato in Palencia, near modern Valladolid, there is a little basilica dedicated to San Juan Bautista. An inscription says that the church was founded in 661 A.D. by Receswinth, a Visigothic king. Suffering from the stone, he had come to Baños to take the waters, and was cured — a miracle indeed if the chemical content was then the same as now. Except at the east end, the building appears to be without substantial alteration. It is unusually good for its period, and it has two features which stir up considerable archaeological wonderment.

We ordinarily associate the horseshoe arch with Moslem architecture, but there is no example of it in any Moslem monument that can with certainty be dated earlier than 711, when the Moors first crossed the Straits of Gibraltar to invade Spain. The arches used at San Juan Bautista are, however, a moderate example of the horseshoe type; and, as just stated, they were built fifty years before the Moors arrived. A suspicion thus arises that the Moslems got the motive from the Visigoths; but against that suggestion, small differences between the Visigothic horseshoe and the Mohammedan must be listed. The arches at San Juan are stilted a little; and there is a slight difference between the curve of the intrados and the curves of the extrados. The horns of the arch, moreover, project inward only a very little, the curve of the intrados hardly being projected beyond its horizontal diameter. Moslem arches (those at the Mosque of Cordova, for example) usually have extrados and intrados parallel, they are rarely stilted, and the inward extension of the horns is pronounced. The whole matter is still further complicated — as historical questions almost always are in the Early Middle Ages — by the existence in Spain of a horseshoe arch of Roman date and by the existence of similar arches in Armenia.

The other peculiarity of the building has to do with the plan. The arrangement of the east end has now been changed; but its original outline can be discerned with virtual certainty. This shows that the church, as first built, had a transept or bema of reasonable projection from which there opened three apses, each rectangular in plan. Contemporary Italian basilicas almost invariably had the familiar semicircular apse. In fact, no other European church of similar date has this peculiar arrangement for the east end. Parallels exist, however, in Armenia.

Of immense technical importance to the ultimate understanding of medieval history, these matters have great illustrative value even for the general reader. The archaeological darkness surrounding San Juan Bautista at Baños is typical of the period rather than exceptional. At the same time, there is evidence enough to open up vistas of knowledge which, if it ever becomes amplified and provable, may entirely readjust our present picture of contact with the East at this early date.

A special interest attaches to the architecture of the Asturias, the only region in Spain never held by the Moors. While it would be sentimental to assume that political independence always works in favor of architectural originality, it is certainly a fact that in this small territory where the Christians maintained their sovereignty, some extraordinary work was done. For logic and intelligence of design, there is nothing to compare with it in all Western Europe between the fall of the Roman empire and the 12th Century A.D.

Perhaps the best of all the Asturian churches is Santa Maria at Naranco, near modern Oviedo (Figs. 9.41–42). There has been debate as to whether the building was originally a church or a palace; obviously it formed part of an ensemble constructed by King Ramiro the 1st, and the ensemble appears to have included both a church and a palace. An inscription fixes the date at 848 A.D.

The little building is approximately forty feet long and a dozen feet wide, but its architect was correctly described by Miss King as a man " of great and hardy invention." He designed one of the very few fireproof buildings put up in Europe during the entire period between the fall of Rome and the start of the Romanesque. The church is covered by a ribbed tunnel vault. The separate thrusts are contained by a system of salient pier buttresses against the outside walls. On the interior, a blind arcade runs down either side wall, and it is important to notice that each rib of the vault is centered directly over the crown of one of its arches, or over one of the engaged columns, as the case may be. For an earlier parallel, one first recalls the Baths of Diana at Nîmes, but an even closer parallel to this construction is to be found at Shaqqa in Syria, where a similar articulation was given a long hall built early in the 3rd Century A.D.

The structural logic of Santa Maria at Naranco is, however, somewhat more overt; in fact, for a tunnel-vaulted nave with salient ribs and no aisles, the engineering is nearly impeccable. For the first time in our study of architectural history, we are confronted with the work of a man whose whole theory of design stemmed from the concept that structural forces themselves might suggest the shape and arrangement of the component parts of the fabric. The so-called "structural aesthetic" — destined to be one of the prime forces governing the design of the later Romanesque and Gothic — was evidently very well understood in the Asturias during the 9th Century. Before attention was focused on these long-forgotten little churches, it was commonly taken for granted that no such idea had ever entered the European mind prior to the late 11th and 12th Centuries. When the existence of the Spanish buildings became a matter of general knowledge, scholars at first refused to accept the dating, but it may now be said that no good reason to doubt it has emerged. The Asturias has always been a comparatively remote region, however; and its churches were too small to become famous. Thus ideas which might have advanced architecture by as much as two centuries never saw the light. We shall find ourselves returning to them, and at no small length, in Chapter 11.

THE ART OF THE CAROLINGIAN ERA

For convenience, we shall use the adjective *Carolingian* to indicate the cultural movement set into motion by the career of Charles the Great (regnal dates 771–814). A more detailed survey would demand our making a distinction between the lifetime and immediate influence of Charles, and the separate movements that took place in France and Germany after his death. It will be sufficient for our purposes, however, to think of the whole affair as one, and we shall use *Carolingian* as though it included the art sometimes catalogued under the headings *West Frankish* and *Ottonian*. In point of time, the period under review stretches forward at least as far as the reign in Germany of Henry the 2nd, who died in 1024.

Charles was the only monarch of the earlier Middle Ages who proved able to organize a central government in Western Europe. His power depended to an unfortunate extent upon his personal capacity rather than upon well-conceived and durable institutions of government, but at the height of his success he held, in name at least, everything from the Pyrenees to a line drawn between Denmark and Dalmatia, including Italy as far south as Rome.

On Christmas Day of the year 800, Charles attended services in the old basilican church of Saint Peter at Rome. On that occasion the Pope, under circumstances that have never been entirely clear, crowned him Roman emperor. The papal act raised serious questions of jurisdiction, and proved in future a perennial subject of friction between Church and State. There can be no question, however, that Charles conceived himself as heir to the Caesars, and his imperial program as an effort to restore Roman order.

Personally preoccupied with military enterprises and with the political organization, Charles nevertheless did an immense amount to initiate and foster cultural revival. He delegated authority to various able men, of whom the most important was Alcuin of York (735–804). There is a tradition that Alcuin's handwriting became the model for the script used all over Europe. However that may be, the " schools " organized by Alcuin at Aachen, Tours, Reims, and elsewhere actually produced a monumental amount of learning, with the result that we often hear the whole era described as " the Carolingian Renaissance " — an exaggerated term, but an indicative one nevertheless.

Had Charlemagne's empire been kept intact after his death, the effect upon both history and art would probably have been beneficial to an extent appreciable only in our own time. But imperial unity apparently appealed to the 9th-Century mind as a principle far less important than the right of the individual heir to inherit his proportional share of a decedent's estate. At the Treaty of Verdun in 843, the empire was divided among the claimants. The division took cognizance — probably for administrative convenience at the moment — of language differences and other situations conducive to separatism rather than unity. Louis the German took everything east of the Rhine. Charles the Bald took the west. Lothair took what was then called " the middle kingdom," part of which still bears the name Lorraine, a softening of Lothair Regnum. Modern France and modern Germany, indeed nationalism itself, started with this division — and with it the turmoil of the 20th Century.

It is extremely hard to interpret the artistic monuments we have inherited from the Carolingian era. Indeed it would be an error to build our picture of those times on the basis of the physical relics still in existence: a considerable corpus of illuminated manuscripts, a number of statuettes, a certain amount of jewelry, and some rather discouraging architecture. Fortunately, there is reasonably adequate information about material we no longer have.

Carolingian Architecture

At Ingelheim and at Aachen, it is possible to discern the general outline of palaces built by Charlemagne himself. The gates of the palace at Aachen were standing, it is said, as late as the 14th Century. Literary evidence supplements the meager remains, and we read of terraced gardens, banqueting halls, and of river views commanded by upper windows and balconies. Obviously such facilities were not called into being except in response to a certain standard of dignity and refinement in the life of the court, but all the palaces were built of wood and other impermanent materials — a fact we modern historians are likely to weigh too heavily. We also hear of a fort at Merliacum that literally towered over the plain, and had a moat and drawbridge. It would appear that the design of defensive fortification improved greatly during this era for the simple reason that the central government could not protect its citizens from the Viking raiders. The strong tower intended as a place of refuge probably dates from Carolingian days; it was good enough to serve against the Vikings because they usually went away promptly and long before the garrison could be starved out.

Perhaps the most interesting single bit of evidence is a plan found at Saint Gall (Fig. 9.59), showing the arrangement of a monastic establishment. Often presented as reflecting actual construction, it is now generally conceded to be an imaginative layout for an ideal monastery. The geometric regularity of the composition suggests that the monks had studied the precious copy of Vitruvius which lay waiting in their library for another 500 years before its existence was announced to the modern world (see above, page 98). The plan is proof enough that men of this era thought in terms of a complex and highly developed community. It would be difficult for the production manager of a modern factory to arrange better for the various functions and services requisite to a self-contained and self-sustaining community. In addition to a church and dormitories, barns, stables, storage cellars, and workshops, there is provision for a hospital, a guest house, and a library.

The standard type of church in Carolingian days was the basilica. In the absence of classical columns in ready supply as in Italy, most of the Carolingian basilicas carried their wooden roofs on coarse piers capped by clumsy columns. Among existing examples, the small, severe *Basseoeuvre* at Beauvais (the nave to which the great Gothic transepts, choir, and apse are now attached) is as illustrative as any. At the little town of Lorsch near Worms, however, there still stands a set of three arches (Fig. 9.43) known as *The Basilican Gate*. Traditionally, and probably correctly, the monument is supposed to be all that is left from the narthex of a substantial basilican church. The date falls at the

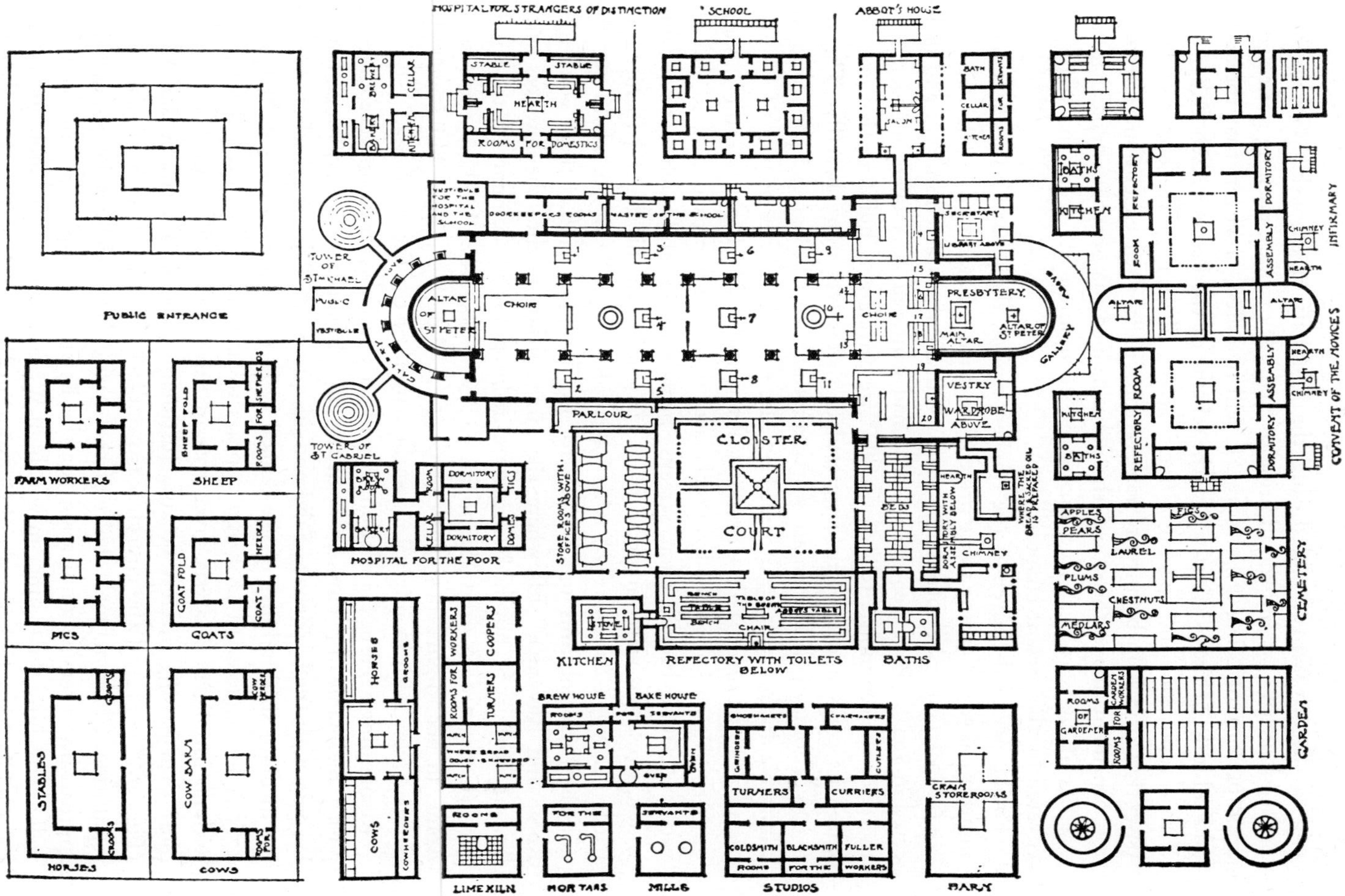

Fig. 9.59 Plan of an ideal monastery. Redrawn on the basis of a manuscript of Carolingian date found at Saint Gall.

end of the 8th Century, or during the first half of the 9th. With its high peaked modern roof and the addition of a couple of apses, nothing at first gives an impression of being less classical. It will be noted, however, that the arches and columns of the lower story fit the scheme of the Roman Arch Order even if the proportions and spacing differ. The ten pilasters of the upper story are patently Corinthian by intent, however provincial their execution. The chevron ornament above them and the polychromed masonry are typical incongruities of the sort that lend quaintness to monuments from the whole era covered by the present chapter.

For his personal church at the Aachen capital, the great Charles was determined to have something more pretentious than the standard basilica. His *Palace Chapel* (now the rotunda of the cathedral) was started in 796, and dedicated in 804 by Pope Leo the 3rd who had wintered at Aachen in order to be there for the ceremony. It is doubtful if we can name a building that ever inspired its contemporaries to congratulate themselves more heartily. The remarks of some of these men are worth quoting; we take our excerpts from the admirable documentation included by Mr. Kingsley Porter as part of his *Medieval Architecture* (Yale University Press, 1909. Vol. I, pages 170 ff). Various writers mention the de luxe ecclesiastical furniture provided: gold and silver candelabra, bronze choir screens, bronze doors, and such — to execute which, workmen were imported from far places. On this general theme, Einhardt (*Life of Charlemagne*) adds for emphasis that " since he could not obtain elsewhere columns and marbles for this building, he had them sent from Rome and Ravenna." Elsewhere the same author credits the builders with " wonderful art "; but he is moderate in his praise by comparison to Angilbert (*Carmen de Carolo Magno* iii, 94) who declares: " Where the second Rome, in her mighty new flower rises great aloft . . . some build well the temple lovely with its mighty mass, the temple of the Eternal King."

Resounding even in translation, Angilbert's periods earned him the contemporary nickname of " Homer "; but the church he praises is very much out of keeping with the hyperbole. Solid and adequate, the Palace Chapel at Aachen is a medium-size building of the central type, covered by a dome a little over 47 feet in diameter. The design appears to have been borrowed direct, and without intelligent analysis, from that of San Vitale at Ravenna — a fact of more than passing interest because Justinian's portrait appears at San Vitale (Figs. 9.16–17) and the church was peculiarly associated with his name and reputation. Charlemagne's choice of that particular model betokens something approaching a servile admiration for the Byzantine empire and illustrates as well as anything the manner in which all Western Europe, throughout the entire Middle Ages, looked toward Constantinople as modern men look to Paris,

London, and New York. It was the great and gilded metropolis, the center of the world. Conditions in the West may be inferred from the fact that Charlemagne had to import his skilled workmen, had to get his classical columns second-hand, and astonished his contemporaries with what amounts to a coarse and modest church. It is nevertheless the sober truth that his chapel was the most important building constructed in northern Europe between the fall of Rome and the late 11th Century.

Carolingian Manuscripts

Books were the great preoccupation of the Carolingian era. The brains and energies of its best men were directed to the acquisition and preservation of books, and to the production of copies. A great number of illuminated manuscripts survive from the period. Stylistically, they furnish us with a bewildering tangle of problems. There were apparently a number of centers at which the work went on. Within the limits of human patience and with occasional interpolations by the scribe, the copies were turned out with reasonable strictness insofar as the written text was concerned. With respect to the illustrations, it was apparently customary to copy more freely. Sometimes, indeed, the Carolingian illuminator lacked the skill to copy any other way. Thus any particular miniature may represent a style and composition of very complicated genealogy. In every instance, one has to visualize the style and composition of the manuscript used as a model — which may itself have had an involved derivation. One then must interpret what he sees with reference to the technical training of the illuminator who did the work. Of great historical interest, the detailed pursuit of such questions is hardly appropriate to the present work. Suffice it to say that the questions exist, and that there is to date no general agreement on such fundamentals as the number and location of the various Carolingian centers.

The dead average of Carolingian illumination is artistically inferior. The illuminators, or most of them at any rate, worked under conditions scarcely conducive to originality. Their business was to reproduce, not to create; but even under that system — closer to the factory than the studio — some of them rose to greatness. The occasional excellence of a single figure was now and again surpassed by an equally brilliant imagery embracing an entire scene. For an instance, we may turn our attention to a justly celebrated miniature from the *Codex Aureus* from Saint Emmeram at Regensburg, now in the Staatsbibliothek in Munich (Fig. 9.44).

The narrative comes from the Apocalypse (Revelations 4:10–11), where the four and twenty elders cast their crowns before the throne, saying, " Thou art worthy, O Lord, to receive glory and honor and power, for thou has created all things, and for thy pleasure they are and were created." Christ is symbolized by the Lamb, and we see the elders grouped before him in a great hemicycle. Stylistically, the work might be understandable by reference to the Neo-Attic branch of Hellenistic art, and perhaps the artist was in the habit of working from models that put Greek figures in front of a neutral background. It is quite impossible to explain the content, however, by any conceivable derivation from the classical. The imagery itself is transcendental, and the surcharge of feeling is as wild and exalted as the Apocalypse itself. This is perhaps the first monument we have reviewed which indicates that the medieval temperament — as distinct from the classical and the modern — was at long last beginning to find itself, and means for its expression.

Every other Carolingian monument, or all of them together, may be dismissed as insignificant by comparison to the *Utrecht Psalter* (Figs. 9.45–46). That incomparable manuscript fortunately lends itself to reproduction, and it is now available to the whole world in Mr. Ernest de Wald's recent monograph (*The Utrecht Psalter,* Princeton University Press, 1932). The book consists of 108 vellum leaves. It contains the 150 Psalms, the canticles (liturgical songs from the Old Testament), the Te Deum, Gloria in Excelsis, Pater Noster, Apostles Creed, Fides Catholica, and the so-called " Apocryphal Psalm." The miniatures are line drawings in brown ink, and there is a picture to illustrate every bit of the text that lends itself to visual expression. In addition to this terrific volume of material, the artist had the energy to include an enormous amount of contemporary detail: birds, animals, tools and apparatus, men at work, landscape, and virtually everything else that came under his eye. The book was in England during the later Middle Ages, and was copied there more than once. Sir Robert Cotton owned it during the early part of the 17th Century, but it left his library for that of a Dutchman who presented it to the University at Utrecht in 1718.

The whole history of art hardly contains a parallel example of freedom on the part of an artist. We have to make an effort to appreciate that the miniatures preserve some resemblance to an earlier model. In fact, it can be said the book is " a copy " only by pointing out that most of the drawings seem to adhere to an original border; and that the trees, the hills, and the half-hidden buildings here and there recall similar items in the Joshua Roll and Paris Psalter. The model must, however, have contained pictures less like the Alexandrian and more like the *Odyssey Landscapes* (Figs. 6.14–15), because we see little figures moving fast within the represented space of great landscapes of infinite extension out into the distance. As an equivalent for the impressionism of Roman painting, the artist avoided the cursive outline, and drew his figures by making the pen zig-zag in a brilliant but nervous fashion. All of these phenomena are best explained by the assumption that the master, whoever he was, was an accomplished manipulator of the Celtic linear technique, and of sufficient prestige to adapt the style of his model as he chose. Such a happening was rare indeed during the Carolingian era.

The northern temperament is made manifest by matters more important than a mere preference for line. In response to his classicizing model, the artist gave many of his pictures a certain measure of geometric order, but he obviously cared little for it. The schemes that came most naturally to him eschewed both rhythm and balance. The compositions hold together and make sense only through the fact of an all-pervading animation and vitality. The narration is according to the so-called " continuous method " familiar in much Roman work (the reliefs on the Column of Trajan, for example). Episodes which happened at different moments, that is to say, are included within the same picture without separation by frames or any other visual barriers. So strong is the common bond of action, however, that one does not care even if he bothers to know. The psychology of the observer's comprehension, it is still further to be noted, is not instantaneous as in classical art, but cumulative. The total impression is built up by the successive impact of innumerable visual experiences, each intense — a fact which makes the manuscript belong to the north even though its original came from the Mediterranean.

Details are better studied by reference to the captions under our book plates, which in this instance are appropriately extended. Certain general conclusions of an extremely significant kind can be drawn from what we may call the pictorial policy of the artist. When he read in the first Psalm that the righteous man delights in the law of the Lord, and meditates upon it day and night, this formidably imaginative master felt compelled to visualize the event as physical fact (Fig. 9.45). In like fashion, the illustration that goes with Psalm 150 (Fig. 9.46) actually shows us the musical instruments which the psalm requires, including a pipe organ even to the detail of a musician raging at the organ boys to give him more wind.

We may pass over the naïveté that permitted so profound a mind to visualize in 9th-Century French terms events described by a Jewish writer of a remote epoch. The crucial realization is this: he conceived the Scriptures as a record of human experience within the confines of this earth — for even his deities differ from men only by having the power to neglect gravitation. Unusual in its own day, this is the philosophy which was destined to dominate European thought in the end, and to produce the so-called " realistic convention " of modern art. (See below, Chapter 13.)

There is no voice to challenge the assertion that the *Utrecht Psalter* belongs among the very greatest monuments of pictorial art, or that its unknown author deserves to have his name mentioned in any company. There was no man of equal calibre to carry the style forward, however, and found a school. There are of course a good many items which are obvious derivatives, but they all make the same impression as a watered drink.

To the last statement, there is a single notable exception which, if we wish to be strict about it, falls in the Ottonian period as distinct from the Carolingian.

In 1019, when Saint Bernward was bishop at Hildesheim, a set of bronze doors were installed at the Church of Saint Michael (Figs. 9.47–48). The doors have since been removed to the cathedral. They consist of sixteen panels of relief, embracing selected scenes from Genesis and from the life of Christ. Most of the scenes have a single row of figures against the background, but it is more than plain that the master strenuously intended to represent actual distance as distinguished from the backdrop of a stage. His little figures move with the same nervous vitality as those in the *Utrecht Psalter;* most of them break loose, as it were, from the panel behind. Unskillful and unscientific in the matter of anatomy, this artist was magnificent in the department of vigorous gesture; small though they are, his people move with an epic finality. Their extraordinary power is not in the least diminished by the harsh and masterly realism of the faces.

With the doors of Hildesheim, spatial representation ceased to play an important part in painting and sculpture for some time. By the logic of their subject matter, a number of popular scenes required some kind of setting, but anything so adequate and convincing as this demonstration remained all but unheard of until the realistic movement of the 15th Century had done its work.

PRE-ROMANESQUE MONUMENTS IN ENGLAND

England was a poor country until the 18th Century and the influx of wealth from overseas. That economic handicap has contributed generously to archaeology, since it predisposed the English to keep and preserve their old buildings. All over the island, the traveler will find material dating earlier than 1066, but it is very rare to find a complete building. The Pre-Norman remains usually amount to a tower, a crypt, or a doorway now built into masonry of later date. Quaint and lovable, these venerable fragments have the greatest possible appeal to the sentiments, and we must resist the temptation to dwell upon them at length. For what we cannot say here, the reader may refer to the ample and delightful volumes by the late G. Baldwin Brown. Matters of principle will be illustrated if we confine ourselves to only two buildings.

At Earl's Barton, about eight miles east of Northampton, there still stands the finest of Saxon towers (Fig. 9.49), now attached to a later church. Squat and square-headed, the proportions of the Saxon tower were also destined to endure as an essentially English motive in the architecture of the later Middle Ages. The coarse surface decoration and balustered windows seen here were, in subsequent examples, replaced by the plate and bar tracery of the later medieval styles, but the mass and silhouette of the English tower have never changed in any significant respect. Similar towers were common in Normandy during the 12th Century (Fig. 11.16) and from there were passed on into the Gothic of the Ile de France (Fig. 12.7). There is a possibility that every church tower on earth was originally intended to carry a spire. Occasionally some modern draftsman restores the Earl's Barton tower on paper, drawing in the allegedly missing feature. Consistent perhaps with the intention of the designers in some cases, spires are usually out of keeping with the flavor of English architecture. Most English towers never had them, and look better without.

At Bradford-on-Avon, about twenty miles southeast of Bristol, there exists the little church of Saint Laurence (Fig. 9.50). The original foundation dates from Saint Aldhelm, who died in 709. It seems unlikely that the entire present fabric is so early, but it is equally improbable that any significant part, including the blind arcading on the exterior walls, dates later than the Norman Conquest.

The small size of the church is typical of the Saxon period, an interesting circumstance when one reflects that most of the great cathedral foundations date from the generation after 1066 — the Normans, like the Romans, using architecture to impress the inhabitants with the superiority of their administration. The total interior length, including the eastern chapel, is only 42 feet; and the nave measures only 25 by 13 feet, 8 inches. The proportions are extremely high and narrow, the same nave being all of 25 feet high. Entrance is by way of the extended transepts (one missing as of now), but instead of opening broad into the nave, these give only through a narrow door in a manner reminiscent of the Syrian prothesis and diaconicon (see above, page 302).

As a demonstration of certain permanent tendencies of all medieval design and of the British in particular, Saint Laurence's could hardly be improved upon. Throughout the sequence of styles that was destined to take place, the semicircular apse remained rare and exceptional in England; and the square east end, as here, was a perennial favorite. The broad and pronounced extension of the transepts is as notable a feature at Salisbury (Fig. 12.22) as it is at Bradford-on-Avon. In addition, it should be noted that the little building, taking it as a whole, amounts to an ensemble of no less than four distinct units: the nave, the apse, and the two transepts. The size and placement of each unit was governed by functional considerations, physical or ceremonial as the case might be. The composition of the whole is the antithesis of Greek unity, and a splendid demonstration of the cumulative method of medieval art — flexibility having taken the place of strict logic of design.

THE BAYEUX TAPESTRY

The *Bayeux Tapestry* (Figs. 9.51–52) has often been presented as an historical curiosity, largely because modern eyes have long been habituated to "correct" drawing and "accurate" anatomy. The truth is that no other monument from the period of the Norman Conquest is half so important as a work of art. The tapestry is in fact an embroidery in eight colors of wool on a ground of coarse linen. Originally there were 76 scenes, of which we retain 72. The narrative begins with the decision of Edward the Confessor to assign the English succession to Duke William, and with his dispatch of Harold to make the arrangements. Considerable space is assigned to Harold's exploits and adventures in France, and the story concludes with William's amphibious expedition and the battle at Hastings. The width is 20 inches, and the length 231 feet — in the space of which we see over 600 human figures, more than 500 animals, 37 ships, and a great deal of scenery. A gallant but incorrect tradition says that the work was done by the Norman queen and her ladies, hence the name "La Tapisserie de la Reine Mathilde" — a designation that seems to have originated during the early 19th Century. The weight of evidence suggests that the actual patron was Odo, Bishop of Bayeux and half-brother to the Conqueror.

It is easy to make the mistake of associating the tapestry with manuscript illumination, but the true analogies are with mural painting — of which we have much from the 12th Century and rather little from this period. The designer obviously carried over into his drawings the habits and techniques he was accustomed to use for the execution of big frescoes intended to be seen from a considerable remove. There is no laboring of detail. Eyes, noses, and mouths are rendered by broad harsh lines. There is a minimum of modeling; most of the representation is in line and flat tone, with strong contrast of hue. In physical fact, there is a resemblance to the cultivated boldness characteristic of some 20th-Century painters (see below, pages 917–920), but the master of the *Bayeux Tapestry* was able to carry conviction as none of the modern primitivists can do: he was himself a member of a violent society with rough ways, and his coarse methods were as natural and authentic as breathing.

The power and brutality of combat, and the undeniable fascination of war, have perhaps never been dealt with so well in the history of the visual arts. Meissonier's painfully descriptive paintings of Napoleon's army are worthless by comparison, and even Goya must take second place. Not one of the combat artists of World War II was able to achieve a like power. Where can one find a better picture of a well-organized fleet at sea? (Fig. 9.51.) Is there anywhere on earth another battle scene with even a fraction of the same clash and rhythm? (Fig. 9.52.) As visual description, the pictures are grossly incomplete, but nothing important has been left out. Every single thing is unquestionably true, and the total effect is literally vested with authority.

Like so many other monuments from the earlier Middle Ages, the *Bayeux Tapestry* seems hardly to have started the artistic tradition which its excellent qualities justify. The prestige of miniature pictures in manuscripts appears to have been too great; and the power of both Romanesque sculpture and Romanesque painting (see Chapter 11), if any criticism of it is appropriate, was unfortunately diluted by complexities and refinements more in keeping with the work of the master penman. The grand simplicity of the tapestry was hardly ever arrived at again.

GENERAL CONCLUSIONS WITH REGARD TO THE ART OF THE EARLY MIDDLE AGES

In view of the evidence cited in this chapter alone, it is hardly possible to maintain the old-fashioned view that we may properly use the words "Dark Ages" when referring to the period of history between Rome and the 12th Century. The development of the basilican church, the perfection of the Viking ships, the Irish manuscripts, the *Utrecht Psalter*, and the *Bayeux Tapestry* require no defense. They simply take their own place among the great artistic monuments. It is thus plain that we may not dispose lightly of the culture of the Early Middle Ages. Indeed, what other era witnessed so many decisions which were to prove historically determinative and perhaps final?

We may not, on the other hand, indulge in overestimate. Most of the time, the art historian cites his examples from plenty. He mentions one work by Donatello, or writes about the Parthenon. The reader is supposed to assume that the citations are typical of a class — which is to say that there are many others of the same kind, and what he learns will prove useful when he sees them. During the period covered by the present chapter, that is not so. The examples that have been cited hardly amount to the total, but the chapter is still no survey. Almost every work of the first rank has been referred to at least by allusion. It is altogether plain that the 500 years, more or less, which have passed under review did not compare in rate of production with various other areas of art history.

From this we may learn much about the life of the time. Conditions obviously militated against a superior level of culture. The preserved physical remains are inexpensive except for the small amount of jeweler's work that still exists. The artifacts most characteristic of the time are small to the point of being conveniently portable. The remarkable, indeed the amazing thing is that so poor an era produced so much — and, even more incredible, that so many of the survivals remain among the memorable instances of human achievement.

MARBURG

Fig. 10.1 Constantinople. Hagia Sophia. 532–537 A.D. Minarets: 15th–16th Centuries. 247 feet long, 231 feet wide, 184 feet high.

Figs. 10.2–3 Constantinople. Hagia Sophia. General view of the nave from the west (left), and diagonal view from the south aisle. MARBURG PHOTOGRAPHS.

SABAH

Fig. 10.4 View upward in one of the exedrae opening at the corners of the nave of Hagia Sophia.

Fig. 10.5 London. Victoria and Albert Museum. Ivory casket from Veroli. *The Rape of Europa*. Middle 9th Century?

NELLYS

Fig. 10.6 Athens. The Little Metropolis. About 1150. 38 by 25½ feet. Interior height to crown of dome: 36 feet.

MARBURG

Fig. 10.7 Mistra. Saint Theodore. Late 13th Century.

MARBURG

Fig. 10.8 Hosios Loukas. Small Church. Early 11th Century

PROF. CESARE FASOLA

ALINARI

Figs. 10.9–10 Daphni. Monastery Church. Late 11th Century. View into the dome, showing mosaic picture of Christ as *Pantocrator* (above) and mosaic of the *Crucifixion*.

Fig. 10.11 (left) Utrecht. Archiepiscopal Museum. Ivory Madonna. 11th Century.

Fig. 10.12 (right) New York. Metropolitan Museum. Ivory Crucifixion. 11th Century.

Fig. 10.13 Manassia. Church. 1407 A.D.

SABAH

Fig. 10.14 Constantinople. Killissé Djami. *The Magi Following the Star,* and *The Magi before Herod*. Mosaic. Early 14th Century.

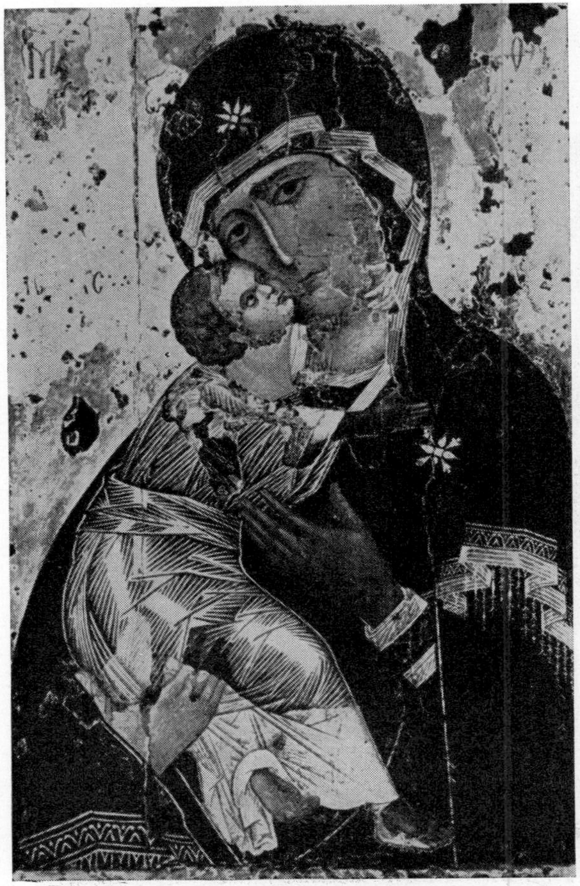

Fig. 10.15 Moscow. Historical Museum. *The Ikon of Vladimir.*

ANDERSON

Fig. 10.16 Torcello. Cathedral. Mosaics of the apse and arch. 11th Century.

ALINARI

ANDERSON

Fig. 10.17 King William the 2nd offering a church to the Madonna. Mosaic. 12th Century.

Fig. 10.18 (right) Duccio. Head of Saint Agnes. Detail from *The Madonna in Majesty.* 1308–11. Siena. Cathedral Museum.

Fig. 10.19 Duccio. Triptych with Madonna and Saints. London. National Gallery.

ANDERSON

Fig. 10.20 Simone Martini. *The Sant' Ansano Annunciation*. Florence. Uffizi. 1333.

ANDERSON

Fig. 10.21 (above) Simone Martini. Guidoriccio Fogliani. Siena. Palazzo Pubblico. 1328.

Fig. 10.22 (left) Pietro Lorenzetti. *Madonna with Saint John and Saint Francis.* Church of Saint Francis, Assissi.

ANDERSON

*

10

BYZANTINE ART

WITH SOME MENTION OF THE ITALO-BYZANTINE SCHOOL AND THE 14TH-CENTURY SCHOOL OF SIENA

Byzantine art is the art of the Eastern Roman Empire, centering at Constantinople. It is an oddity of history that the name is taken from the original title for the city, for Byzantium was a word already 200 years out of date by the middle of the 6th Century when the style became clearly defined. (See above, pages 261–268.)

Byzantine art is one of the most important cultural phenomena in European history. It lasted longer than any other style. Its geographical coverage was immense, and it long furnished innumerable persons with the idiom of their visual imagery. Strange and foreign to the American eye, often carelessly explained and misunderstood, the Byzantine is by no means to be thought of as an exotic taste. It has a peculiar beauty and grandeur. It appeals to emotions which are different, and therefore new. It offers satisfactions not to be found elsewhere.

As compared to other areas of art history, Byzantine archaeology remains in a formative stage. A reliable synthesis is probably impossible at this date. The literature of the subject is still dispersed in the files of learned periodicals, in occasional monographs, and in several languages. In spite of the immense efforts of Strzygowski, Millet, and Dalton, and with all honor for the valuable papers that occasionally emerge from Dumbarton Oaks, the only comprehensive and comprehensible summary that exists today is Charles Diehl's *Manuel d'art byzantin* — which bears the date 1925, was largely compiled about fifteen years earlier, and has long been out of print and hard to buy. It is extraordinarily difficult, in fact, even to accumulate a reasonable number of photographs of Byzantine monuments; those that appear herewith are the product of an unusually strenuous correspondence.

The reason for all this is not far to seek. Byzantine territory began to fall into Moslem hands as early as the 7th Century, and the capture of Constantinople by the Turks in 1453 merely concluded the process. Innumerable examples of pictorial art have of course vanished forever, and as many more remain obscured by Turkish whitewash. Travel in the more remote parts of what was once the Christian East has been slow and difficult, often unsafe. There are a great many towns that have not seen a visitor from Western Europe within the memory of the oldest inhabitant.

It is entirely likely, however, that the next twenty to thirty years may resolve the confused situation. Relations between Turkey and the West have become increasingly cordial. The attitude of the incumbent Turkish government is liberal and enlightened — as conspicuously evidenced by the secularization of Hagia Sophia and the program for cleaning its mosaics. Warning the reader, therefore, that a much better and more adequate chapter will doubtless be possible before this book is many years old, we shall content ourselves with the conventional outline and confine our statements to a brevity altogether out of keeping with the importance of the field.

The Byzantine style has three chronological divisions, each commonly referred to as a *Golden Age*. The First Golden Age commenced with the reign of Justinian (527–565), and lasted until the outbreak of *Iconoclasm* in 726. The Second Golden Age is dated from the end of Iconoclasm in 843 to the year 1204 when the Fourth Crusade was diverted to the capture of Constantinople. The Third Golden Age covered the period from the end of the Latin Monarchy established by the Crusaders to the final fall of the city, or from 1261 to 1453. These dates refer, of course, to eras of substantial production of art in what we may properly call Byzantine territory. They do not apply with the same accuracy to the various provincial schools in Sicily, Russia, and elsewhere. To the latter, we shall have occasion to make passing reference as the historical connections come up.

THE FIRST GOLDEN AGE

The most important enterprise of the First Golden Age was the design and construction of Hagia Sophia at Constantinople (Figs. 10.1–4,23). The present edifice is the fourth church of the same name on the same site, the third having been destroyed in the course of the so-called *Nika* riots of 532. Work appears to have commenced at once on the new building, and it was dedicated by Justinian himself in December of 537. The name *Hagia Sophia* is a transliteration from the Greek; it means " Holy Wisdom."

Justinian's church was designed by Anthemios of Tralles and Isodoros of Miletos. Both, it will be noted, hailed from Asia Minor. The choice of Eastern architects for this immensely important commission is highly significant. It indicates that the best thought was then to be found at the eastern end of the

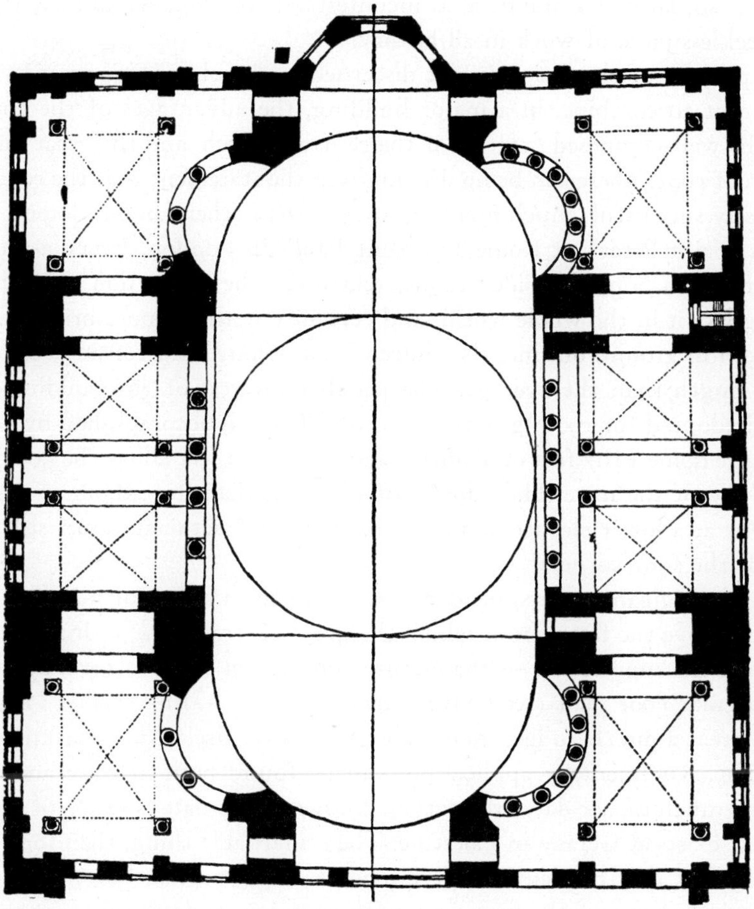

Fig. 10.23 Constantinople. Hagia Sophia. Plan. Left half at ground story level. Right half at gallery level.

Mediterranean rather than at Rome, and tends to corroborate still further the supposition that Constantine abandoned the West because he considered it the less valuable part of the empire.

The historical sources for Hagia Sophia are obscure. An immense amount of polemical argument has taken place, but as yet no one has adduced a dated series of smaller monuments, either around Rome or in the East, which form anything like an acceptable genealogical chain culminating in the great church at Constantinople. In the case of so large a building, such a circumstance is extremely rare, but it surely begins to look as though Hagia Sophia itself were an experimental fabric. Certain imperfections in the design and the occurrence of serious accidents during and after construction all lend color to such an idea which, if so, labels the building as incontestably the boldest and perhaps the most reckless piece of work in all history.

The purpose of the design is best discerned in the plan (Fig. 10.23). It was an attempt to combine, in a major building, the advantages of the basilican nave, the well-composed exterior of the central church, and the great merit of a fireproof roof. There can be no dissent from the statement that the result was immensely successful; much more so, in fact, than other famous domed buildings like Saint Peter's at Rome and Saint Paul's in London. Every aspect and vista of Hagia Sophia, inside or out, reinforces the conviction that there is nothing like it in the whole world, and certainly nothing more brilliant.

As seen in ground outline, the church is an oblong, and considerably wider for its length than the average. The peculiar interest of the building is the method adopted for roofing over the nave. That was accomplished by centering a large dome (107 feet in diameter and rising 180 feet above the floor) over the middle of the nave. Half domes of the same diameter adjoin to east and west, but at a lower elevation, and there are four fractional domes still lower down at the four corners.

From four gigantic piers, pendentives rise to form a ring of masonry about 130 feet above the floor, from which the great central dome springs. It is this feature of the engineering — the mature and perfect solution for a dome over a rectangular floor plan (see above, pages 197–200) — that makes Hagia Sophia so great a puzzle to historians. The pendentive itself had been known for some time. Rudimentary applications can be found both in Italy and in the East at a much earlier date; the earliest known, if its date is really of the 2nd Century, exists at Gerasia in Palestine. The remarkable thing, therefore, is not the mere fact that pendentives were used at Hagia Sophia, but the fact they were used, perhaps for the first time, with complete understanding of the possibilities of the form, and to full advantage.

No other great interior presents anything like the same number of varied vistas (Fig. 10.3), and none has ever been more perfectly integrated (Fig. 10.2). Much of the power and fascination of the building derives from the sense of magnificent space — very like in effect to the sense of nobility, and enhanced by the use of innumerable columns and other members of the normal size. The wonderful dome, pierced by forty windows around its base, rests as lightly as a cloud above the floor. The eye sweeps upward through the subordinate vaults into the dome, and down again toward the apse. It would be a mistake to say the curves flow into one another, for they do not. As contrasted with modern streamlining, where the individual contour means nothing and the flow of the whole means everything, each vault surface retains its own shape and identity. We can see and feel it for itself, that is to say, and also with reference to the entirety.

Most of this the reader must regrettably accept on faith, for reasons of psychology rather than optics. A great many photographs are available which purport to show the interior as a whole; and it is geometrically true that they do so. But no single negative embracing everything from top to bottom can be satisfactory even though the exposure be made through the best lens in the world. The human eye embraces an angle of vision of about 120 degrees, of which a central cone of perhaps 65 degrees is alone in good focus. Visual inspection of such an interior demands, therefore, a succession of acts. The attention is first directed here, then there — an experience difficult or impossible to reproduce on paper.

Color, moreover — rich, deep, and glowing — was an essential feature of the design which can hardly be duplicated until the ultimate perfection of the colored motion picture. The walls and arches were constructed of brick and mortar, but the entire Mediterranean world was ransacked for columns and other marbles of unheard-of variety. There is Phrygian white marble with rose-colored stripes, green marble from Laconia, blue from Lybia, black Celtic marble with white veins, and white marble from the Bosphorus region with black veins, Egyptian starred granite, and Saitic porphyry. Eight immense purple columns were brought from Rome, having come originally from Baalbek, and there are eight green ones that once were thought to have come from Ephesos. To this display, we must add the superb mosaic pictures which have been out of view since the 15th Century; originally, they covered every important wall surface, the most important being a Madonna in the apse, an Apocalyptic Christ in the dome, and four seraphim on the pendentives. We can only imagine the church as it will be when the cleaning begun in 1934 is at length complete.

The inexhaustible excellencies of the interior are scarcely equaled by the exterior view — which is, nevertheless, one of the most interesting in history. As seen from a distance, the great church is a landmark never to be forgotten: superb, serene, modest. Its imperfections become apparent only in comparative close-up, and upon analysis.

We must discount, of course, the nondescript buildings which cluster around the base; they are an accretion of the years and no part of the original plan. The same thing may be said of the varicolored striping which mars the exterior. The four minarets are a Turkish addition, to be sure; but on the whole, they improve the composition. Making such allowances, it is still difficult to feel that Hagia Sophia stands as more than an experimental essay toward a new theory of architectural design.

The extreme haste of the construction was to say the least unfortunate. Trouble seems to have been experienced before the building was half done. Piers sank in differential fashion, splayed out of vertical, and allowed arches to drop between. The foundations and substructure of the immense fabric have, in fact, been a constant worry from the beginning. The present dome is the second, or even the third, to cover the nave. The first collapsed completely in 558. Rebuilding proceeded under the direction of Isodoros the Younger, a nephew of one of the original designers; and it is believed he used a steeper pitch for the new dome, an expedient that somewhat marred the unity of the interior ceilings, but produced less thrust. An ambiguous record seems to say that the dome fell again in 567, but whether partially or completely, one cannot be sure. Part of it certainly fell in during the year 987. To this catalogue of disaster, we must add the fact that the four great supporting piers, as originally designed, proved too light; they were strengthened by Isodoros the Younger, and apparently remain as he left them — their greater bulk choking the aisles.

The abutment of the vaults, all too often explained in sentences more systematic than the facts, was surely more daring than prudent. Piercing the main dome with forty windows at its very spring was an aesthetic inspiration of the first order, but no one can call the expedient cautious. There is a certain merit in the placement of the two large semidomes to the east and west of the main dome. In that position, they tend to contain its thrust, but it must be conceded that they are hardly high enough to act as efficient buttresses. To the north and south, there seems originally to have been no equivalent provision for the containment of the great central dome. The unsightly masses of masonry which inefficiently perform that office today were added entire, or at least greatly increased in size, as late as the 13th Century. For the diagonal thrust of the four immense pendentives, there seems never to have been any well-conceived scheme of abutment.

It would appear to be a mistake, therefore, to suggest that the abutment of Hagia Sophia depends upon a system of thrust and counterthrust comparable to the scheme later developed in France for the Gothic cathedrals. On the face of it, we are justified in making the guess that neither Anthemios nor Isodoros had anything of the sort in mind. We know, for example, that they went to great pains to reduce the weight of their vaults by using hollow tile and other very light material. Also, that they attempted to cement everything together.

As contrasted to a logical system of buttresses, the aim seems to have been to eliminate thrust altogether by producing homogeneous and even monolithic vaults which would exert no more thrust than a teacup once the mortar had set hard. That, it would appear, is the reason the domes stand today.

Admitting all these faults, it is nevertheless impossible not to feel deeply that an important theory of exterior design is implicit in the appearance of Hagia Sophia. Except for the architecture of the First Golden Age and its derivatives, the builder's art has traditionally been an art of angles and flat surfaces. Here the design was governed by the nature of the convex curve — as seen in the contour of the main dome, and in the swing of the subordinate domes which build up toward it. While different from modern streamlining as already set forth above, the effect is closer to that recent theory of design than anything which has come and gone between the 6th Century and our own era. Modern ferroconcrete lends itself to such manipulation. Materials available before the Industrial Revolution do not. One might well hazard the guess that the true modern architecture, when it arrives, will be an art of curves, and more like the Byzantine than we have perhaps supposed.

Because they are larger and more conspicuous than the later Byzantine churches, the monuments of the First Golden Age — of which Hagia Sophia is merely the prime example — are the monuments which were emulated elsewhere. San Vitale at Ravenna, almost precisely contemporary to Hagia Sophia, was an attempt to imitate, in a region at that time provincial, the style of the metropolis. Charlemagne's Palace Chapel at Aachen (see above, page 324) was an imitation of San Vitale in a part of the world more provincial yet. Saint Mark's at Venice (begun 1063; disregard the addition of the conspicuous false domes) took its Greek cross plan, and its five domes on pendentives, direct from Justinian's Church of the Holy Apostles which stood at Constantinople until torn down in 1463. Exactly the same plan was popular in the 12th-Century Romanesque of Aquitaine. Saint Front at Perigueux is the prime example, and there are others much like it in the same district. Even more important than these West Christian borrowings is the little-appreciated fact that the domed architecture of the Moslem world, indeed much of the architecture of the whole Orient, came into being only after contact with the great buildings at Constantinople. The Taj Mahal at Agra is a plain case in point.

THE PERIOD OF ICONOCLASM

The First Golden Age of Byzantine art was brought to a disastrous end by the Iconoclastic Controversy. In a technical sense, the period of the controversy began with a decree against images issued in 726 by the Emperor Leo the Isaurian. It ended with the restoration of images by a later Theodora in the year 843. With respect to bitterness of feeling and ruthless action, the entire affair must be ranged as the greatest and longest of the many altercations that shook the foundations of early Christendom. Ostensibly having its genesis in a difference of view about modes of worship, the struggle came to involve issues of almost every other kind: geographical, racial, social, political, and military — a web so complex and interwoven as to tax the re-creative powers of the best historians, and to render a true picture of the situation quite beyond the scope of our present purpose. It is important, however, to take note of the fact that Iconoclasm was coincident in date with the beginning of the split that has since separated the Eastern and Orthodox communion from the Roman and Catholic.

With respect to the history of art, Iconoclasm (literally, the smashing of *ikons* or images) stands as a matter of major importance because it almost completely eliminated any chance we might have had of studying the best Byzantine painting and mosaic of the First Golden Age. The religious issue involved was the age-old conflict between monotheism and polytheism, and the fear of idolatry. The complaint of the Iconoclasts was that the various saints had become, through the agency of idols (i.e., representative art), objects of worship roughly analogous to the numerous minor gods of the pagan hierarchy. They alleged still further that works of art on display in churches (viz., pictures and statues in their capacity as mere objects) were often worshipped for themselves, as distinguished from worshipping the person or ideal the picture was intended to recall or symbolize.

The Iconoclasts held political control at the capital for more than a hundred years. Their purpose, however deeply felt, was ruthless, and their actions efficient and devastating. Religious art of all kinds was systematically destroyed in wholesale fashion. Of the wealth of material that once existed at the capital, we have virtually nothing. It is possible, of course, that something of importance may still appear at Hagia Sophia and elsewhere, but we shall be fortunate if much turns up that dates from the First Golden Age.

For the reasons just cited, we shall omit any attempt to survey the subject. Indeed, insofar as any conception of 6th, 7th, and 8th Century work may be reconstructed, the reader cannot do better than refer back to our citation of mosaics at Ravenna (pages 265–267), or refer ahead to the section within the present chapter where we deal with the Italo-Byzantine school as such (pages 364–369).

While Iconoclasm must be regarded as a cultural tragedy for which there is no repair, the darkness of its effect is mitigated by one pale ray of happy light.

The Iconoclasts focused their animosity upon religious art. They did not have the same objection to secular art. It is therefore generally supposed that artists sought employment in the production of objects of a nonreligious kind; and for models, they turned to the two rich sources available to them: classical sculpture and oriental textiles.

A typical product of that tendency is a small ivory casket, formerly in the Cathedral at Veroli, a place about fifty miles to the east and south of Rome, and now in the Victoria and Albert Museum of London (Fig. 10.5). The general aspect of the principal panel of relief cannot fail to evoke a sense of reminiscence in persons who are familiar with later classical art. At the same time, the heavy borders consist of scrolls and rosettes deriving from motives familiar in Near Eastern work, these items alternating with bust-portraits that recall Roman coins and gems. In itself a distinctly minor work, the Veroli casket illustrates a healthy tendency: it comes from a new inspiration even if its sources are old, and it is lively. As such, it helps us to see how Iconoclasm, however accidentally and unintentionally, brought about a desirable relaxation of the hieratic standards at which Byzantine art — if we may judge from such instances as the mosaics at San Vitale — had evidently arrived. The effect upon the art of the Second Golden Age was excellent, as we shall presently have cause to note.

THE SECOND GOLDEN AGE

The Four-column Church

The churches of the Second Golden Age are distinguished not by size but by smallness. The largest of them are very modest with respect to dimensions, and the little ones are tiny. The architects of the period nevertheless displayed a remarkable sense for three-dimensional composition, and they developed a distinctive type of building that is without a peer in that respect.

All too often obscured by ill-arranged additions to the fabric of the church proper, the elements of the new type are best studied by reference to schematic drawings such as our Figs. 10.24 and 25. Three levels, or stories, are involved. The ground outline is a square, from which walls rise vertically for some distance to form what we may call the first story. The second story consists of four short sections of tunnel vaulting arranged symmetrically around the central dome to form the arms of a Greek cross. The tiny dome, set high on a drum, rises from the center of the cross to form the third level of the composition.

The typical system of construction is indicated by Fig. 10.25. Well within the larger square of the ground plan, four piers are set up to define the corners of a smaller and interior square. The piers carry the inner ends of the second story vaulting, and the dome above. As shown on both drawings, small saucer-shaped domes were often added over the otherwise vacant corners of the ground story; during the period now under review, these four extra and subordinate domes were usually very low indeed. In most examples, they are completely concealed under the lean-to roofing of the exterior, a situation indicated at one corner of Fig. 10.24.

Fig. 10.24 Schematic drawing showing exterior composition of a typical four-column church of the Second Golden Age.

As a new and distinct architectural type, such churches deserve a name; we might call them *the four-column churches of the Second Golden Age*. Experiments with the several elements of the form can be traced in the early architecture of Armenia and Asia Minor, but the scheme in its entirety seems first to have been worked out in the so-called " new church " of Basil the 1st, usually called *La Nea*. It must have been complete when that emperor died in 886; and, although long since vanished, it ought to be remembered as the pilot model for the entire era.

At Constantinople, perhaps the best extant example of the new type is the building now called the *Kilissé Djami* (formerly Saint Theodore Trio), a structure extremely difficult to illustrate photographically. For a free-standing building, we may turn to the Little Metropolis at Athens (Fig. 10.6). It differs in some details from the typical as we have described it, but the differences are not in view on the exterior. Most churches of the period were varied in their mass by salient apses, and their texture was enriched by elaborately pattened brickwork. A capital example is the church of Saint Theodore at Mistra (Fig. 10.7), that remarkable ruined town a few miles west of Sparta.

Interior views of the four-columned churches are difficult to obtain. Fig. 10.8 is probably the best available. It shows the interior of the smaller of the two churches at the monastery of Hosios Loukas, dedicated to Saint Luke Stirites who died there in 946, and located a short way to the east of the modern hamlet of Stiris, which lies near the sea on the north shore of the Gulf of Corinth. The walls and ceilings have rather recently been done over in a delicate Rococo fashion, a fact we may disregard because of the good light and because the usual clutter of ecclesiastical furniture is happily absent.

In summarizing our remarks about the churches of the Second Golden Age, we may pass over such matters as the homely and comfortable excellence of their texture (a considerable relief at times from the slick surface of classical marble). We may also defer attention to the special refinement of door and window openings: the period was approximately contemporary with the Romanesque of western Europe, and we may save space by referring the reader ahead to the appropriate chapter (pages 391–396), where he will find that similar openings were the common property of East and West at this moment in history. The great and special distinction of the four-column churches resides in the almost infallible excellence of their exterior composition.

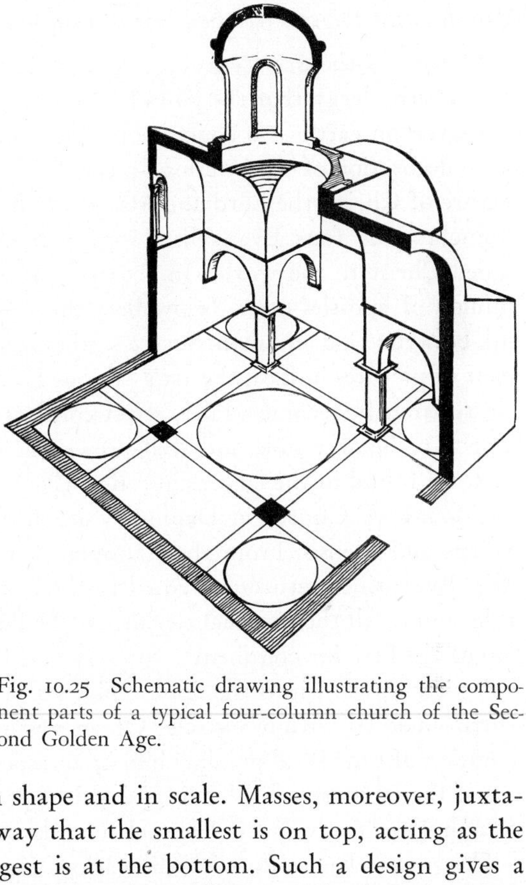

Fig. 10.25 Schematic drawing illustrating the component parts of a typical four-column church of the Second Golden Age.

They compose in masses. We may think of the ground story as a great square solid. Each arm of the Greek cross above is, in broad terms, a mass something like a Greek temple if it happens to have gables, or a cylindrical shape if the roofing corresponds to the vault below. The dome and its drum ordinarily amount to an octagon surmounted by a hemisphere. The composition, in a word, is an arrangement of no less than seven masses which vary in shape and in scale. Masses, moreover, juxtaposed to one another in such a way that the smallest is on top, acting as the hub of the system, and the biggest is at the bottom. Such a design gives a powerful effect of solidity and stability. The build-up to the dome proceeds as though by inevitability, and the order is sure. The words necessary to describe such a composition, it will have been noted, have a curious familiarity for the modern reader: they sound very like the several aphorisms from Cézanne which only yesterday were cited as the sanction for cubism, and today furnish the chief authority for abstract art of every kind.

The churches of the Second Golden Age have a monumentality quite beyond anything that might be predicted for little buildings. It seems impossible that the Little Metropolis measures only 25 feet across the façade; and that its dome has a diameter of no more than nine. As though to emphasize its distinction as the smallest cathedral in the world, the blocks of masonry — most of them from classical ruins — were not reduced in proportion, but remain of normal size. And yet where can we find a design that betokens a broader view of architecture, or is more strong and competent?

Mosaics and Ivories of the Second Golden Age

As early as the 8th Century, the idea seems to have been prevalent among the Eastern clergy that the church building was to be understood as a symbol of heaven on earth — a conception that found its best expression in the pictorial decoration of the interior. In the dome, it was customary to put a mosaic picture of Christ, the Lord and Master of the universe. On the pendentives or squinches, the four Evangelists appeared; they were the men who had revealed Christ to the world. In the apse, Mary found her place, with a communion of apostles often below her; these were the persons who formed the link between God and man. Such a system seems to have governed the arrangement of pictures in Basil the 1st's famous *La Nea;* and by the 11th Century, it had apparently become a fairly strict convention. Among the monuments that happen to be accessible and well-preserved, the most complete mosaic cycles are to be found in the larger church of the monastery at Hosios Loukas and in the Monastery Church at Daphni, a site on the ancient Sacred Way between Athens and Eleusis. From the standpoint of quality, it may be said that no other Byzantine pictures are equal to those at Daphni; they reflect the Greek style, and recall the spiritual elegance of Hellenic idealism. We may select only two of the best for comment.

A view upward into the dome (Fig. 10.9) shows a bust-length portrait of Christ enclosed within a circle. Of an awful solemnity, this majestic representation of Our Lord presents him in an aspect unfamiliar to the average citizen of the Western world. His strength approaches the brutal. His expression is harsh. How can we reconcile such a rendering with the gentle Saviour?

The answer has to do with the various functions for which Christ may be imagined to be responsible in the operation of the religious polity. We see him here in the role of *Pantokrator* (literally, all-ruler), which means his executive and judicial capacity as governor of the universe, whose inhabitants he will one day bring to the ultimate reckoning of the Last Judgment. It is in this guise that most Christians thought of him and visualized him until the popular imagery was revised by the movement of sentiment and affection — which we can see reflected in art not much earlier than the West Porch at Chartres (about 1145; Fig. 12.5), and of which the prime exemplar was Saint Francis.

It is in the *Crucifixion* (Fig. 10.10) that we may see most clearly the influence from classical Greece. Neglecting the figure-style for the moment, the formula for the picture might be described as follows.

Against a neutral and impenetrable background, human figures appear in a single row as though on a shallow stage. The people are rather large, and are presented in comparative close-up. The composition is arranged on the principle of bilateral symmetry, the figure of Mary balancing that of Saint John at an equal and opposite distance from the central vertical axis. Mary and John, furthermore, direct their gestures inward and upward; their action serves to close the composition on either side, and to establish the triangularity of the arrangement.

All of these points might with equal accuracy be cited as characteristic of the formula used for the Greek pediments (see above, pages 57–66), and there can be no question that we see here an instance — in a different medium and very different in superficial appearance — of the traditional organic composition first developed by the ancient Greeks. Indeed, the only departure from an almost Phidian restraint is the inclusion of a mere indication of setting. At the foot of the cross, we see a small mound of earth and a skull; these signify Golgotha.

The figure of Saint John is Hellenic to a degree. The vertical dimension of the body is scarcely exaggerated. The pose has the chiastic twist familiar in Greek art from Polycleitos onward (see above, pages 123–142). The head has the classical profile, and the expression is more than reminiscent of Praxiteles's melting sweetness. The drapery also is very Greek. Indeed it is only when we look closely at the anatomical details that we can find a substantial divergence from ancient standards, but it is true that the chest is sunken, and lacks that athletic convexity which was a Greek convention. The hands are exaggerated and their structure neglected; likewise the toes. The mechanical action of wrists and ankles is misunderstood.

Further evidence of Greek feeling is to be noted in the graded curves into which the artist has abstracted the Saviour's torso, and the graceful bend given the spurt of blood from his side. Otherwise the figure is a good example of the small store set upon anatomical accuracy during the Middle Ages.

Such matters are not even remembered, however, when one considers the content. As a historical narrative, a sequence of physical events, the death of Christ on the cross could be contemplated in detail only by persons having a legitimate interest in its medical aspects, by morbid persons, or by people without sensibilities. A colored motion picture of the Crucifixion would be beyond endurance. No subject can be named which better illustrates the limited usefulness of art that aims merely to represent.

The reality of Christ's death has its existence in the realm of ideas and the emotions. It is important as the prime symbol for the very essence of generosity and personal sacrifice — in the name of which it exerts an ennobling influence upon all human motivation. The subject presents the artist, in short, not with a narrative problem, but with a demand for interpretive power of a high order. It is fortunate, therefore, that the Byzantine artist working at Daphni had the benefit of the renewed classical inspiration brought about by Iconoclasm, also that he lived within walking distance of Athens. In all history, the Greeks are pre-eminent for their ability to extract from sordid and physical facts lessons that are divine; that capacity was the great legacy of the Greek genius to the Christian world. Upon the artist of the Daphni *Crucifixion* it had the effect of inducing order, clarity, elegance, and restraint.

He therefore kept his picture completely free from distracting details. The three persons who appear are the three most intimately connected with the tragedy; no others are necessary to convey its meaning. The fact of the Saviour's passing is indicated only by the pathetic relaxation of his body; the agony is over. Mary's erect pose betokens a state of shock; but even in shock, she holds herself with dignity. It is her figure, indeed, which carries most of the meaning, for her entire attitude is one of comprehension rather than panic. Our view of the Madonna is at once touching and heroic, both intimate and royal; surely there is no more adequate picture of Mary than this.

In accordance with its Eastern heritage, Constantinople never produced any significant amount of large statuary, but there was no prejudice against ivory carvings, and such were never more exquisite than during the Second Golden Age.

For our immediate purposes, the best example for special attention is the single figure of the Madonna (Fig. 10.11) now in the Archepiscopal Museum of Utrecht. There is no more typical instance of what we may call the standard Byzantine Madonna — an artistic type which became virtually a convention, and is important because it furnished all Europe with its visual imagery for Mary over a period totalling nearly 700 years.

The proportions of such a figure are elongated. Precise measurements always involve a certain amount of interpretation with regard to the limits between which we measure, but it may be said that the figure now under review is at least ten heads to the height. The impression of tallness is greatly enhanced by unusually narrow shoulders; also by an extraordinary and abnormal length of calf and thigh — putting the waistline very far above the usual.

The child is customarily held on the left arm. It is rather difficult to understand the mechanics of the costume, but it seems we may infer the existence of two garments: a dress or gown gathered up at the waist; and a loose mantle or jacket worn over this, swung up over the head to form the familiar female headdress. The skirt falls to the ground; one knee pokes slightly forward to make a convexity; and on the other side, the folds are arranged in a radiating pattern reminiscent of a partly opened fan.

The head and its covering demand special attention. The upper silhouette of the cranium is rounded like a bullet, and the distance between the eyes and the extreme top of the figure as we see it is so great that there must be a special reason. Little as the Byzantines cared for anatomy, the likeliest guess seems to be that some form of stiff hat was worn under the mantle to give this appearance. Seen in full-face or in profile, the shape of the head is a delicate oval. The mouth is small, the nose long, and the eyes large and almond-shaped. The length of the cheek, from mouth to eye, is peculiarly great, and the total effect of the face is strange in the sense that an overbred animal is always exotically attractive. Often loosely described as "Oriental," this type of head is merely a refined exaggeration of a shape that occurs rather often among the populations of the eastern Mediterranean. The purpose of so finely drawn a figure was to suggest not nature and ordinary life, but an ethereal state of being from which the holy persons look out upon us, their own thoughts turned inward and their eyes demanding a recognition of their significance.

The standard Byzantine type for the Madonna remained constant in East Christian art for a very long time. With minor variations, it is the same as the Madonna who appears in the art of western Europe also. The peculiar fixity of a particular visualization requires a word of explanation.

In recent centuries, it has been more or less taken for granted that artists should have almost unlimited freedom to invent imagery for whatever subject they might undertake to represent. The physical appearance of the Madonna, that is to say — or the arrangement of figures and stage properties for a Nativity — are commonly thought to be within the jurisdiction of the individual. We even compare modern artists by reference to their fertility of imagination in this respect. Without suggesting that we are wrong in doing so, it is necessary to understand that medieval custom was radically different.

The imagery for any sacred character, and the iconography for any narrative scene, became established at a very early date; thereafter, the arrangement was governed by strict and specific rules. The authority of such rules, indeed their very existence, has often been denounced by recent writers as an intolerable repression of the creative imagination. There can be no doubt that it often was, but there was more reason for the rules than one might at first suppose.

The rules were intended to make pictures correspond with historical truth.

Saint Peter, as we have already mentioned (see above, page 287) always appeared with a square-cut white beard because people believed he wore one. Similarly, Saint Paul was always shown as a lanky man with a bald pate and a long, pointed brown beard. For the imagery of the Madonna, there was similar circumstantial evidence.

According to a persistent tradition, Saint Luke himself had painted a portrait of the Virgin. During the 5th Century, the Empress Eudocia acquired a panel at Antioch, and brought it home to Constantinople; she believed, and others believed, that the picture was the very same one painted from life by the Evangelist. It was set up at a crossroad, doubtless enclosed in some kind of shrine, and it acquired the nickname *Hodegetria,* loosely " she who points the way." It is impossible for us to know exactly what the *Hodegetria* looked like. Much less can we assert that the contemporary connoisseurs were correct in identifying the hand of the painter Luke. But the facts make less difference than what was accepted as truth in 5th-Century Constantinople, and it is a fair guess that the standard Byzantine Madonna does not differ radically from the *Hodegetria.* That being understood, it is easy to see why public opinion would compel every artist to stick very close to the original type, and would consider any meddling an impious outrage.

In histories of Italian painting, the word *Byzantine* has so often been used in an unfortunate sense that it behooves us to correct the impression — an impression gained from provincial and more or less inadequate work in Italy, and one which is altogether erroneous when applied to the production of the best Byzantine masters. The excellence of the latter was never better demonstrated than in a series of miniature ivory altar pieces, some of them literally of pocket size, related in style and coming mostly from the 11th Century. The most elaborate of the class is the well-known *Harbaville Triptych* in the Louvre. On the main face, it shows an enthroned Christ with more than a dozen other figures; and on the reverse we see still other saints flanking a central panel of uncommon beauty which perhaps represents the Triumph of the Cross in the Garden of Eden. While heavily vested in the usual stiff costumes, the figures of the saints are obviously studied from nature and vigorously individualized. The central panel, seeming at first to be a more or less mechanical rendering of Near Eastern motives, is actually as fresh and lively as a manuscript page by Jean Pucelle.

Even more exquisite, if such a thing is possible, is a tiny *Crucifixion* (Fig. 10.12). The quaint iconography is explained thus: the cross springs from the body of Adam (according to a widely held belief it had actually done so), while above are the soldiers who cast lots for the Saviour's clothing.

The End of the Second Golden Age

The Second Golden Age of Byzantine art was brought to an end by the Fourth Crusade. In the entire history of Christendom, no other scandal compares with it. Assembling at Venice with the intention of going to the Holy Land in Venetian ships, the Crusaders were persuaded to act as mercenaries in the service of Venice. In that capacity, they captured and sacked Zara in Dalmatia. Encouraged still further by the Venetians, they next proceeded against Constantinople. In 1204, they entered the city. There they behaved in a manner shocking even to the sensibilities of a world that took excess for granted as the inevitable privilege of conquerors. Dividing the spoils with the Venetians, the Crusaders gave up any idea of fighting the infidel. They simply settled down in the region of the Bosphorus, establishing a loose feudal government known as the Latin Monarchy. Never accepted as *de jure* by the population, the actual power of that government was maintained always on a most adventurous basis. Except for the capital and a few strong points here and there along the coast, it was no government at all. In the year 1261, under the leadership of the distinguished Paleologos family, the western rulers were expelled; and the Byzantine Empire re-established.

During the period of the Latin Monarchy, Constantinople was rendered sterile as a market for art. Architects and artists left the city. Many of them found employment in the Balkans and in Russia, regions already well disposed toward the Byzantine style. The dispersion of artists at this particular juncture in history is probably the reason why Byzantine art, given up long since elsewhere, survives to this day as the national style of Russia.

Seen against the broader canvas of world history, the Fourth Crusade and Latin Monarchy mark the final, and as yet irreparable schism between Greek and Roman Christianity. The differences of doctrine are of course important each to its respective clergy, but the popular basis for the separation springs from a lingering resentment against the brutality and debauchery of the Crusaders, of which the best that can be said is to pronounce it a blasphemy. This sadly natural reaction of the Byzantine population also had the effect of making Moslem civilization seem on the whole better than that of the Christian West, thus tending to diminish the will to resist the Arab invasion when it finally came.

THE THIRD GOLDEN AGE

The best examples of Third Golden Age architecture are to be found in the Balkans rather than in the region of Constantinople. Excellent monuments to illustrate the character of the style are the Church of the Holy Apostles at Saloniki (1315), and the Serbian churches of Ravanitsa (1381) and Manassia (Fig. 10.13), which dates from 1407.

In plan the usual church of the Third Golden Age does not differ from the four-column buildings of the previous era: there is the same Greek cross inscribed within a square, the same central dome and the same subordinate domes in the corners. In elevation, however, there is a substantial change. The proportions of the lower square, or first story, are exaggerated vertically; and the vertical dimension is often emphasized by attaching slender engaged shafts to the exterior wall surface. The four corner and subordinate domes, usually concealed entirely during the Second Golden Age, were commonly raised high on drums. They act as towers, and complicate the sky line. The over-all effect has often been characterized as "the Byzantine Gothic" — a term that undoubtedly has historical validity because the western Gothic was at its height just as the Third Golden Age began.

For the purpose of understanding the changes that gave new flavor to the pictures of the Third Golden Age, it is wise to begin with an example which dates considerably earlier than the Fourth Crusade, but one which nevertheless signalizes the trend of the future. The painting referred to is the celebrated *Ikon of Vladimir,* a half-length panel picture of the Madonna and Child (Fig. 10.15). It almost certainly was painted at Constantinople before the end of the 11th Century, and it was exported thence to Russia. It there acquired an immense reputation as a picture with almost miraculous religious power. In 1395, for instance, it was brought to Moscow with the idea that it might help in repelling the armies of Tamarlane.

Generally similar to the standard Madonna in figure-style and costume, the *Ikon of Vladimir* is nevertheless strikingly different from the stately empress familiar in earlier work. The contrast has little to do with style; it is a matter of content. In the Vladimir Madonna, the baby has his arm around his mother's neck; he pulls himself toward her in a warm embrace. Mary inclines her head downward, holding her cheek against his, and she pulls the child to her in a gesture like his own. The picture is full of maternal desire. It has the tone of personal experience — experience, moreover, in which the observer shares because no man alive has failed to participate in similar acts and feelings at some time.

The qualities just cited are the very qualities that have long been cited as the special contribution of the humanistic philosophy which we conventionally suppose to have been unknown in Europe earlier than the Italian Renaissance. (See below, pages 619–621.) As knowledge of later Byzantine art becomes more complete and more accessible, it is obvious that a number of notions may have to be revised.

A number of important frescoes and mosaics are preserved from the Third Golden Age. Of these, perhaps the most notable are the mosaics of Kahrie Djami at Constantinople, from which we reproduce only one (Fig. 10.14). By comparison to the general run of modern representative painting, these pictures of the very early 14th Century may very well make the impression of being stiff and conventional. But by comparison to the mosaics at Daphni, they reflect a radical change in point of view. The artist of Daphni was a mystic. His purpose was devotional. His pictures stand as symbols for values of a transcendental kind. The artists of the Third Golden Age, on the other hand, seem to have thought of themselves as dramatists. Their purpose was to tell the sacred narrative in such a way that it would carry conviction; and in their view, there was nothing more convincing than a sense of actuality.

The most obvious index to this new conception may be discerned in the setting. Buildings and landscape appear in an intelligible relationship with the human actors. As for the latter, no one can doubt that the artist intended to show something that was alive, moving, and surrounded by air and space.

Here again, we find that East Christian artists appear to have anticipated those of the West. Techniques of accurate representation, in particular, have long been claimed as the special and original contribution of modern Western art, and even as artistic evidence for the superiority of the Western view of life and the world. (See below, pages 539–542.) The truth is that the mosaic painter of Kahrie Djami had little to apologize for in this respect, even to his great Florentine contemporary Giotto.

THE END OF THE BYZANTINE EMPIRE

In 1439, the Emperor John Paleologos journeyed to Italy to participate in the Council of Florence, the purpose of which was to reconcile the Roman church with the Greek. The concessions he was willing to make might actually have done so had they proven acceptable in the East; but the reverse was true — the attempt simply infuriated the population, and is reckoned actually to have facilitated the Turkish conquest which was about to come.

The intelligent face of John Paleologos is commemorated on a medal by Pisanello (Fig. 13.18). His visit to Italy did a great cultural service even though his prime objective was not realized. In his train, he brought several distinguished Greek scholars. The bearing of these men in public debate and private conversation fascinated the Italians, and it is at this date that the study of Greek in addition to Latin achieved its traditional importance in

Western education. In particular, the Greeks knew Plato, a philosopher almost forgotten in the West since the time of Saint Augustine. According to the testimony of contemporaries, the great Cosimo Medici, head of the famous Florentine house, immediately determined to set up at Florence an Academy for Platonic studies. Thus commenced the so-called Neo-Platonic movement which so profoundly affected art history by moulding the spirit of Botticelli and by furnishing the philosophy by which Michaelangelo lived. (See below, pages 649–654 ff.)

The emperor's progress from town to town was marked by an inflated bombast of elaborate and expensive ceremonies. At the moment, such were probably mistaken for grandeur; it seems doubtful whether anyone appreciated that the empire had only fifteen years more to live.

In February 1453, Mohammed the Conqueror laid siege to the city of Constantinople. The defenders were able to hold out some time because of the excellent system of defensive walls; but on May 29, the Turks forced an entrance, and the Byzantine empire came to an end after more than a thousand years of existence.

ITALO-BYZANTINE ART

From the time of Justinian in the 6th Century to the time of Giotto at the beginning of the 14th, Italy was an artistic province of Byzantium. To this statement, we must make only the exception of the great Nicola Pisano (see below, pages 545–546), who dedicated his famous classical pulpit at Pisa in 1260. In the previous chapter (pages 265–267), we have already dealt with the mosaics of Ravenna, a place where there was little production subsequent to the 6th Century. In other regions, however, work in the Byzantine Style continued to be turned out in quantity until the end of the 14th Century and later. The chief centers were at Venice and on the island of Sicily.

Always more than half eastern in its taste and culture, Venice kept to the Byzantine style longer than any other Italian city. The mosaic decoration of Saint Mark's began as soon as the walls were ready, and the building is today a museum of every change in style that has come since. Like so much provincial work, the work at Saint Mark's lacks the elegance and refinement to be expected at the artistic capital. Occasionally, however, the Italo-Byzantine artists rose to a very high level; this we may see in the stately Madonna which occupies the semidome of the apse at Torcello, an island near Venice (Fig. 10.16). With the usual row of apostles beneath her and sustained, as it were, by a flood of glowing and sombre color, she seems in her person to embody the most solemn and majestic concepts of religion.

During the 12th Century, an immense amount of Byzantine art was turned out in Sicily. Some of it, if we may judge by a fondness for Greek inscriptions, must be the work of artists who came from the Near East. The chief monuments are the great cathedral churches at Monreale and Cefalù, and the smaller but even more gorgeous chapels of the Palace and the Martorana at Palermo. Accessible to the modern traveler and surviving in wholesale quantity, the Sicilian mosaics furnish our best opportunity to have visual experience of the Byzantine interior as the Byzantine designers wished it to be. The two chapels mentioned are literally invested with mosaic. Virtually every surface confronts the eye with the rich color and jewel-like texture of that most gorgeous medium.

Superb though the general effect may be, the same can hardly be said for the merit of individual pictures. A typical example is the *King William the 2nd Offering a Church to the Virgin* (Fig. 10.17). Here we may indeed sympathize with the critics who have praised Giotto for turning his back upon the Byzantine style, thus making himself the father of modern art. Among other obvious defects, we may merely cite the drapery of the Madonna. Neither the major convolutions nor the minor folds preserve any reasonable relationship to the human form we are asked to read into the figure. It seems obvious that the Byzantine manner, at least as manipulated by the second-rate artists in the provinces, had been feeding too long upon its own conventions. The only remedy yet located for such an art is to have the artists return again to the direct study of nature.

The School of Siena

By bold steps and leaving much unsaid, we have brought ourselves to a point where it is appropriate to consider the artistic situation in Italy at the end of the 13th Century — the period which witnessed the self-assertion of numerous new and vital city schools of painting, and, through the agency of the 14th-Century School of Siena, a new and (as it was to turn out) final flowering of Byzantine art.

The force and prestige of the Byzantine conventions had been considerably weakened by the attrition of time and the advent of new ideas. The art that began about 1300 differed from that of earlier periods principally in the fact that the artist enjoyed a much wider margin of choice than before. At Rome, Pietro Cavallini at first cautiously departed from Byzantine models, and then attempted to recover some measure of Roman naturalism. At Florence, as we shall see in Chapter 13, the great Giotto struck out for himself along untried lines. But at Siena, the most conservative city in the world, it seemed natural to attempt to pump new life into the time-honored formulas.

Duccio (active 1279; died 1319) was the founder of the new Sienese School. In 1311, he finished an immense altarpiece for the cathedral of that city. The main face showed a large Byzantine Madonna enthroned among saints. The reverse of the great panel carried 26 rectangular panels of narrative painting, covering significant events from the Passion of Christ. In addition to these 26, there were originally still more subordinate panels in the *predella* (i.e., the lower border) and in the Gothic pinnacles across the top. In all, it has been reckoned that there were originally no fewer than 91 compositions in addition to the *Madonna in Majesty* of the main front. Long since dismantled and removed from its place in the cathedral, most of the preserved material is on view today in the cathedral museum nearby. A few panels have wandered into other hands; one of them is the *Temptation on the Mountain* in the Frick Gallery of New York.

The head of Saint Agnes (Fig. 10.18), one of the saints standing to the right of the Madonna on the main face, is in itself an epitome of Duccio's painting. The physical type is already familiar; the painter's special contribution has been to infuse the old formula with a warmer life, even with personality. Much of the meaning, moreover, is carried by the slow winding of the infinitely graceful lines, some of them brought out in pure gold against a darker ground. As the eye follows these curves, the mood of the painting is induced.

Duccio's line requires special comment. There is no other line like it in western Europe, even in Gothic France which was contemporary and where linear calligraphy had been carried to a high level of accomplishment. The nearest true parallel is to be found no closer than China, where the Sung painters had used pure line with similar purpose and effect. We must either postulate an alchemy of circumstances which somehow caused Duccio to develop the same aesthetic means, or we must suppose that he had seen some Chinese painting. The latter hypothesis is more likely. It has long been entertained by scholars, almost all of whom have failed to summon the courage to make an actual assertion in the absence of objective evidence. The likelihood that Chinese paintings were now and then on view at Siena puts no strain on the imagination, however.

We learn in school that Vasco da Gama rounded the Cape, went to the Orient, and returned on his great voyage of 1497–99. We also hear that Columbus discovered America by mistake, having intended also to reach the Far East. We forget, or we never hear, that the Middle East was not actually sealed off until the end of the 14th Century, at which time the western Tartars embraced Islam, the Seljuk Turks advanced, and the Mongol dynasty was overthrown in China. Until then, the routes were open. Marco Polo (about 1254–

1324) had been to China and back, as all the world knows. A Roman Catholic bishop established a diocese at Pekin at the end of the 13th Century. During the 14th, Francesco Pegolotti, a member of the Bardi bank at Florence, was enough impressed with the traffic to write a set of directions covering the route to Pekin. It was safe all the way, he said, if one merely took reasonable precautions.

In view of these facts, it would be remarkable if a few Chinese paintings failed to find their way west. Doubly so, in fact, if we stop to remember that the favorite pictorial form of China was the roll, the most conveniently portable kind of pictorial art, and the kind least likely to be accidentally damaged. The real puzzle is not that Duccio shows Oriental affinities, but why he is the only Western painter who does so.

Duccio stayed continuously at home, where he had the reputation of getting into trouble with his friends and neighbors. The other great Sienese painter of the 14th Century, Simone Martini (1285?–1344), was not only a widely traveled man of the world, but a distinguished gentleman. Well-born and himself a knight, he associated on terms of personal friendship with the highest in the land. He was, in fact, one of the very first artists to do so — a matter to which we shall allude at some length in a later chapter (see below, pages 532–533). After important commissions all over Italy, he was called in 1339 to the Papal Court, then resident at Avignon. He died there in 1344. Petrarch, also at Avignon, knew him well; in two of his sonnets, he speaks appreciatively of Simone's portrait of Laura, a picture unhappily lost. The presence of this eminent Sienese painter at Avignon had wide repercussions upon the history of art, for Avignon (see below, pages 531–539) proved to be the focus of origin for the so-called International Style, a type of Late Gothic painting of unusual charm.

Like Duccio (Fig. 10.19), Simone turned out a number of altarpieces of the kind that were virtually standard with the Sienese painters. The painting was done in tempera on prepared wooden panels. The background was invariably blank and of pure gold. The central subject was always a Madonna (for Siena considered herself to be under the special protection of the Virgin). Customarily, the Madonna was dressed in a gown and headdress of the usual Byzantine mode, the color being ultramarine blue. Such paintings were sumptuous and expensive; the blue pigment alone, made from powdered lapis lazuli, often cost a staggering sum and a good deal more than the gold, which cost enough. The Fenway Court Museum of Boston has a fine altarpiece by Simone, a Madonna with four saints. There one should look, also, at the little single Madonna by Lippo Memmi, Simone's closest follower; it is in better condition of the two. The museum visitor must remember, also, that Sienese paintings suffer when taken out of context. They were designed to carry the length of the nave in dark churches, lit only by candles on the altar. Very few of them remain in position, a rare exception being Pietro Lorenzetti's panel on the high altar of the Pieve at Arezzo.

The pictures for which Simone is best remembered, however, are those in which to some extent he breaks away from the Byzantine manner and becomes a man of modern times. Like all members of the upper orders during the High Middle Age, he was literally fascinated with the theory of social hierarchy. Anyone who inspects with a sharp eye his frescoes of the life of Saint Martin, in the church of Saint Francis at Assisi, will receive a lesson in stratification that scarcely seems possible. As a native son who had acquired a broader horizon, he looked with good-natured satire upon the provincial solemnities of his own small city, an attitude we can see plainly demonstrated in his portrait of Guidoriccio Fogliani (Fig. 10.21), a mercenary general whose small services were thus commemorated on the wall of a principal chamber in the Palazzo Pubblico. Across a grand landscape panorama, dotted with hill towns and showing a military encampment over which flies the incomparable black and white banner of Siena, the silly little fat man rides his magnificent horse, taking himself seriously.

The drapery of the general's horse has often been hailed as the most gorgeous linear symphony in European art. Certainly a notable demonstration, it suffers by comparison with Duccio. Duccio's quiet conceals his daring; he often relies upon a single strand of gold to carry an entire field. For a full understanding of the multiplication and complexity in which Simone indulges here and elsewhere, we must refer the reader ahead to the most florid of the Late Gothic, a movement in which he was actually an early participant.

The Gothic affinities just suggested come out even more plainly in the famous *Sant' Ansano Annunciation* of 1333 (Fig. 10.20). All too often cited as the quintessence of both Simone and the entire Sienese School, it is better described as half Byzantine and half French; the Madonna's gown, for instance, duplicates French costumes of the very same date. It doubtless came from Paris, which even then occupied its familiar position as the fashion center of the west.

The workmanship is consummately fine, but Simone's *Annunciation* remains a curiously shallow picture. He participates, like Duccio, in Oriental methods, and here attempts to characterize persons and describe their emotions by the use of line. Every curve of Gabriel's body, wings, and drapery is suave, flowing, and urbanely pressing forward. By contrast, Mary shrinks back, startled and even annoyed; this being indicated by her receding silhouette, and by the sharper twists and angular junctions within the drapery. Without challenging the success of these devices, we may still have reservations about an imagery which conceived so holy an event as occurring in a Late Gothic palace, the Virgin being a Sienese débutante disturbed while snatching a moment of reading between engagements.

When Simone left for Avignon, the leadership of the Sienese school passed into the hands of the brothers Pietro and Ambrogio Lorenzetti, both of whom seem to have died in the Black Death of 1348. In spite of the important commissions entrusted to them by an enthusiastic clientele, neither brother had anything like the distinction of Duccio or Simone. Ambrogio's large frescoes of *Good and Bad Government*, executed for the Palazzo Pubblico between 1337 and 1339, are a tedious imitation of Giotto (who had by that time made his reputation); nothing could provide a stronger warning against the dangers of allegory. On one occasion, however, Pietro outdid the ordinary standards of the firm. We refer to his *Madonna with Francis and John* in the left transept of the lower church at Assisi (Fig. 10.22). The Mary is a poignantly appealing figure; mystic yearning survives in sufficient force to guarantee dignity, yet the effect is emotional to a degree beyond anything yet cited in the present chapter. The painting may be described, in fact, as very forward looking for its date in the 1330's; it actually foreshadows the famous Madonnas of Donatello. (See below, pages 619–621.)

The later history of the Sienese school is of general importance only in broad outline. Excellent paintings continued to be produced there well into the 15th Century, but no new masters of significant originality appeared. True to the extreme conservatism of the city, each successive man did his best to provide sensitive but minor variations upon the formulas of Duccio or Simone Martini. In a remarkable way, all of these masters kept alive the essential and peculiar spirit of Siena long after the rest of the world had gone modern. For special students and connoisseurs, the field is a paradise, but we must pass on.

11

ROMANESQUE ART

The name *Romanesque* refers to the new style of art which appeared in western Europe about 1000 A.D., and went out of use with the great sweep of Gothic taste that spread like wildfire during the second half of the 12th Century. The great merit of the Romanesque monuments is today an accepted fact among art historians, but appreciation of the period came late. It is still possible to read in too many places that the Romanesque was some kind of humble and countrified derivative from Rome, or that it amounts to a cloddish period of fumbling, of interest only to patient historians, out of which at long last the Gothic evolved. Neither view is in the least fair or accurate.

The truth is that the era now introduced was one of the greatest in the history of art. For abundant variety and teeming originality, no other period compares with it; major inspiration seems to have been almost a daily occurrence in every district of Europe. To the 11th Century goes the credit for reviving the art of monumental sculpture, virtually tabu for 500 years, and restoring it to its ancient and present status as an essential department of human expression. To the architects of the time goes the credit for recovering the ability to vault over large interiors, also a skill lost in the west since the decline of Rome. Confronted by problems and necessities unknown to the ancient Romans, they conceived and brought to near perfection the fundamental concepts that have ever since governed the thought of engineers — ideas even more alive and productive today than when first presented to the world. It is impossible to relegate such achievement to the status of historical subordination, and we therefore give the Romanesque more space and emphasis than it has sometimes received.

The Name Romanesque

The word *Romanesque* requires considerable explanation. The meaning is the same as *romance* — that is, " from the Roman." The word seems to have had its origin in a superficial resemblance between Romanesque architecture

Figs. 11.1–2 Pisa. The Cathedral (1063–1100) and The Leaning Tower (1174–1350). Cathedral. 312 feet long. Tower: 179 feet high. Below: Detail of the blind arcade on the south side, showing irregularity in the height and span of the arches. PHOTOGRAPHS BY BROGI.

ALINARI

Fig. 11.3 Arezzo. Santa Maria della Pieve. Apse, showing dog-leg colonnette.

ANDERSON

Fig. 11.4 Modena. Cathedral. 1099–1106.

ALINARI

Figs. 11.5-6 Milan. Sant' Ambrogio. 11th Century? Diagonal view across the nave, and detail showing one bay of the nave arcade. Length of nave: about 210 feet. Width between main piers: about 37 feet. Height to underside of vault: about 62 feet.

MARBURG

Fig. 11.7 Aulnay. Saint Pierre. South transept portal. 12th Century.

ARCHIVES PHOTOGRAPHIQUES

Fig. 11.8 Arles. Saint Trophime. Main portal.

ARCHIVES PHOTOGRAPHIQUES

Fig. 11.9 Saint Nectaire Church. 11th Century. View from the southeast.

ARCHIVES PHOTOGRAPHIQUES

Fig. 11.10 Poitiers. Notre Dame la Grande.

ARCHIVES PHOTOGRAPHIQUES

Fig. 11.11 Autun. Saint Lazare. Narthex.

HURAULT

Fig. 11.12 Autun. Saint Lazare. Tympanum of the main portal. *The Last Judgment*. About 1132.

MARBURG Fig. 11.13 Autun. Saint Lazare.

ARCHIVES PHOTOGRAPHIQUES Fig. 11.14 Jumièges. Abbey Church. 1067.

DEUTSCHER KUNSTVERLAG

Fig. 11.15 Worms. Cathedral. 11th–12th Centuries largely; west choir 13th Century.

ARCHIVES PHOTOGRAPHIQUES

Fig. 11.16 (left) Caen. La Trinité. ("Abbaye aux Dames") Width of façade: 79 feet.

Fig. 11.17 (right) Souilliac. Notre Dame. *The Prophet Isaiah.*

ARCHIVES PHOTOGRAPHIQUES

ARCHIVES PHOTOGRAPHIQUES

Fig. 11.18 Conques. Saint Foy. Tympanum of *The Last Judgment.* Detail: Devils tossing the damned into the mouth of Hell.

Fig. 11.19 Vézelay. Museum. A Romanesque Capital.

ARCHIVES PHOTOGRAPHIQUES

ARCHIVES PHOTOGRAPHIQUES

Fig. 11.20 Moissac. Saint Pierre. Tympanum with *Christ enthroned among the Four and Twenty Elders*. From a cast.

ARCHIVES PHOTOGRAPHIQUES

Fig. 11.21 Detail of Fig. 11.20.

ARCHIVES PHOTOGRAPHIQUES

Fig. 11.22 Vézelay. Church of the Madeleine. Tympanum: *Pentecost.* From a cast.

Fig. 11.23 (left) Detail of Fig. 11.22.

ARCHIVES PHOTOGRAPHIQUES

and that of ancient Rome. The Romans habitually had used the round arch, the engaged shaft, and ponderous proportions. Because the same elements might be observed in the 11th- and 12th-Century architecture of regions which once had been contained within the western half of the Roman Empire, it seemed self-evident to certain early and careless critics that the later style must inevitably have derived from the earlier. There can be no doubt that a connection exists, but the general trend of research gives us cause to minimize the direct influence from Rome. General statements are still premature, but there are certainly a number of questions which cannot be answered by reference to anything Roman.

Why is it that the peculiar arrangement of twin towers on the façade of the 12th-Century cathedrals at Monreale and Cefalù, the chief churches of Sicily, is not to be found elsewhere in Europe while almost the same arrangement existed in the now-ruined church at Tourmanin in a remote part of Syria? A notable feature of the famous cathedral at Pisa is the graceful blind arcade running down either side of the building (Fig. 11.1). What are we to say about the fact that no other known arcade of earlier date is so much like it as the arcade in a similar position on the cathedral at Ani in Armenia? Similarities like these may, on first reading, impress the layman as being of a rather mechanical sort, and hardly significant enough to invite historical conclusions, but the reverse opinion is entertained by professional scholars. The important thing to understand is not so much that a few precise duplications have been noted, but that in all the imponderable elements which give flavor and atmosphere to a building, the western Romanesque closely resembles eastern prototypes, and is very much less like anything Roman than its name implies. If, for example, we hastily glance at a photograph of an arch from the Colosseum and then at one from the octagon of Saint Simeon Stylites in Syria, it is the latter we might instinctively confuse with French or Italian design of the 11th or 12th Century.

The name *Romanesque* offers still other objections of an historical kind. It completely fails to take into account the heritage of the Northern and Barbarian Style (see above, pages 295–298) which so plainly exerted a definitive influence upon several essential features of the 11th- and 12th-Century art. An association with Rome also overlooks the peculiarities of the sculpture and painting produced in such abundance during the period about to be reviewed; both in style and content, nothing could possibly be at a further remove from anything classical. Romanesque engineering, moreover, was completely different from the Roman; social conditions were in radical contrast to those of Antiquity and it was impossible to organize large armies of workmen, or to transport and handle ponderous materials. For these handicaps, the builders of the era compensated by a boldness and creative ingenuity different from and superior to anything Roman.

In addition to these points, there are persons who claim that the teeming variety of the 11th and 12th Centuries spells confusion of style, not unity — and that any single and inclusive title is therefore inappropriate. With that view it is not necessary to agree, as the pages to follow will demonstrate. But surely we have said enough to convince the reader some other name might have been a wiser choice than *Romanesque:* a pretty word, to be sure, and now time-honored. No one intends to give it up.

The Direct Causes of the Romanesque Style

The emergence of the Romanesque Style was visible evidence that western Europe had at last recovered from the classical disaster and from the political and economic uncertainties of the Early Middle Age. Insofar as the development may be connected with any system of secular politics, it seems to have derived from the relative safety and prosperity provided by the feudal system, then fully developed; and to have been furthered by the existence of the many towns and cities which were in those years beginning to assert a measure of social self-consciousness.

The numerous regional styles into which we must divide the Romanesque as a whole (see below, pages 398–408) constitute, in fact, a straightforward reflection of the political geography of Europe as it then existed. The hurdle to understanding is merely our modern habit of thinking in terms of a nationalism which did not signify during the era covered by this chapter. The culture of Europe did not divide itself between England, France, Germany, Italy, and Spain, but according to much smaller units which survive today merely as words with an aura of the romantic past: Normandy, Burgundy, the Auvergne, Provence, Lombardy, Tuscany, and so on. Of these, it is enough to say that most of them correspond with the sometime existence of a *grand seigneur.*

While preserving a hope of central government, with all officials deriving their authority by delegation from the king, the feudal system was altogether different in practical application. Effective power tended to fall into the hands of the men who found themselves best able to make their power felt by those around them. In view of the economy, which was agricultural and based on the theory of small self-sufficient units — also in view of the unbelievably bad roads and consequent dangers and delays in communication — the largest region that could be administered efficiently corresponded in size to the modern county. The count or the duke thereof could get around fast enough to keep track of affairs and make his will felt; he paid only lip-service to the king whom he rarely saw. Hardly logical enough to suit the modern taste, the government so provided was sufficiently good to permit immense investments in architecture.

The advent of the Romanesque signifies still more than political and economic recovery; it is tangible proof that the Roman Catholic Church had become a very efficient organization. For the modern reader who lives in a secular world, an effort of the imagination is required even to conceive the situation as it then existed. The separation between the temporal and spiritual, which we take for granted, hardly had come into the European mind even as a theory. It was impossible to go through life without repeatedly coming into contact with the authority and rulings of the church. Not only did the institution collect taxes (tithes) in its own name and right, but also the church courts held jurisdiction over more than half the matters in which the normal citizen might sooner or later be involved. They ruled on everything of which clerics might complain or be accused, by virtue of their membership in the hierarchy. On certain subjects, by virtue of their impingement upon religion and ceremony, the church ruled no matter who was involved: marriage, widows and orphans, wills and inheritance.

The Catholic polity was something more, it will be seen, than an organization offering religious services at stated intervals. It was an engine of government. People were more frequently and more keenly conscious of it than of the civil authority. If one were devout — and the universal piety of the Middle Ages has at times been overstated — its communion was essential. If one were less than devout, the discipline of the church might at any moment be applied to render life intolerable if not actually impossible. Men under its ban found themselves cut off not only from the sacraments; they were shunned under pain of a similar fate by every human being, and the ordinary transactions essential to life were foreclosed of performance. The most powerful prince ruled in fear of ecclesiastical rebuke. The humblest person could not follow his obscure way of life except in relation to the clergy. Under such conditions, inclusion within the membership assumed an exigence unknown today.

In visualizing the church as it then existed, the modern reader must still further adjust his ideas to the fact that monasticism was immensely important during the Romanesque Period — as indicated by the preponderance of churches referred to in the pages below as " abbey churches." Today we have only casual contact with monks and nuns; but during the Middle Ages, the secular clergy (those who do the work of the church among the people) comprised only part, and at times the weaker part of the hierarchy. The regular clergy (from the Latin *regula*, for " rule," and applied to monks and nuns because they lived according to rules laid down by their order) were numerous, rich, well-organized, and powerful. The greatest abbey of all was that at Cluny (see below, page 404), the central foundation of an order that owned and controlled over 300 major establishments, all of which were subordinate to a discipline as strict as the Jesuit. Western monasticism may be said to have gained full headway when Saint Benedict established the abbey at Monte Cassino (520 A.D.); but its heyday began when Cluny was founded in 910, and its attainment of immense proportions coincides with the period of Romanesque art.

It is evident from what we have said that there was cause enough for the exclusively religious cast of Romanesque art. A certain number of civil, domestic, and military buildings survive from the era, and there are a few instances of painting and sculpture of a secular kind. By comparison, however, those exceptions do not count, and we shall find no space to deal with them. Even so, the reader must not imagine that the government of the church had yet reached its ultimate perfection; that was delayed until the 13th Century, as we shall describe in the appropriate place. The divergence and separatism of the Romanesque Style correctly records a large measure of local authority, even variety of doctrine, during the 11th Century and the 12th.

Each of the causes so far cited, and all of them together, were of gradual application. Something further is required in order to account for the rather sudden start of a pan-European building effort — for it is a fact that substantial, permanent churches dating before 1000 are scarce as can be, while almost every locality can point to at least one Romanesque building still in good condition and daily use. The missing bit of motivation (the final impulse that brought action, so to speak) was very probably the safe passage of the year 1000 itself.

Although a number of scholars have been at some pains to scout the whole theory, there is certainly a great deal of evidence that large segments of the population dreaded the end of the world in that year. In understanding the remarks about to be made, the reader must appreciate that it never entered the medieval mind to construe the words of the Bible as plain language. Far from meaning what they said, the sacred writings were generally thought to be guarded and cryptic to a degree, their true purport to be fathomed only by a great effort of interpretation. So approached, and digested and redigested with devious intelligence, passages and combinations of passages often attained, in the imagination of medieval readers, some very surprising implications.

The idea of the Sabbath (Genesis 2:3) was combined with "the thousand years in thy sight" of Psalm 90:4 to create the notion that world history must proceed according to units of a thousand years, vaguely as the days of the week. Six millennia of toil were to be succeeded by a millennium of rest, and there were many dark hints in the scriptures as to what must happen before the glorious days might commence. The " wars and rumours of wars " mentioned in Matthew 24:6 and Mark 13:7 would (according to the parallel passage in Luke 21:11) be announced to the world by great earthquakes, famines, pestilences, and " fearful sights and great signs . . . from heaven." To these passages, we may add the twentieth chapter of Revelations; for an imagination already whetted to expect the worst, its wild metaphor could easily seem to announce the end.

The church itself never endorsed such an interpretation; indeed, the obvious danger of social paralysis caused the Abbot of Fleury (about 995) to speak out in very strong terms: as a young man, he said, he had believed and preached that the Antichrist would come when a thousand years were finished, but now opposed the notion with all his force.

Other churchmen of perhaps equal authority took another view. About the middle of the 10th Century, Bernhardt of Thuringia had written a visionary treatise on the Apocalypse, expressing the opinion that the end of the world was presently at hand. The study of early English sermons has unearthed a number of items indicating that the Danish and Viking raids were there thought to be the very troubles predicted in the Bible. Wulfstan, Archbishop of York from 1003 until his death twenty years later and a former Bishop of London, gained much of his substantial reputation by writing homilies which hinted at the end of the world. In his 12th Homily, he says in part ". . . for the greatest evil shall come upon mankind when the Antichrist himself shall come . . . and it seems to us that it is very close to that time. . . ." Wulfstan's contemporary Aelfric, a monk who ranks as the greatest of Anglo-Saxon prose writers because he made a specialty of translating homilies from the Latin, accounts for his activity in one place by saying that he did it " for the sake of unlearned men who, especially at this time when the end is near, need to be fortified against tribulation."

It is obvious that a certain proportion of the great and powerful were by no means easy in their minds; and where such is the case, the ignorant and superstitious may always be expected to make a contribution. People were seeing things all the time and everywhere, including a whale the size of an island. Raoul Glaber, a monk who died at Cluny about 1044, has left a chronicle of events that must have disturbed even the most sanguine men.

During the decade 990–1000, a great many worrisome things happened. That ten years was marked by five successive seasons of crop failure; the famine was so bad that cannibalism was widely reported among the population insane for food. Fires, the perennial curse of medieval life, were unusually frequent and devastating in France and Italy. One such fire at Rome ignited the roof of Old Saint Peter's. The helpless people called out in a mighty voice, challenging Saint Peter on threat of their curse to take care of his own — which he did, for the fire went promptly out. The plague known as Saint Anthony's Fire became epidemic. Serious heresies arose, one in France and one in Italy. Mount Vesuvius, as though to predict the whole course of events, had erupted in 993 with a hideous emission of noxious gases.

"So on the threshold of the aforesaid year, some two or three years after it," writes Glaber (as translated by G. G. Coulton, *Life in the Middle Ages*, page 3), "it befel almost throughout the world but especially in Italy and Gaul, that the fabrics of churches were rebuilt, although many of these were still seemly and needed no such care; but every nation of Christendom rivaled with the other, which should worship in the seemliest buildings. So it was as though the very world had shaken herself and cast off her old age, and were clothing herself with a white garment of churches. Then indeed the faithful rebuilt and bettered almost all the cathedral churches, and other monasteries dedicated to divers saints, and smaller parish churches. . . ."

It is unnecessary to exaggerate Glaber's testimony in order to draw the conclusion that he believed the year 1000 to have been a signal for the commencement of building activity. As a matter of statistical fact, however, the overwhelming number of important Romanesque monuments seem to have been started at least a generation after Glaber died, and most of those that survive today were completed well after 1100. Hence the frequency with which one hears the Romanesque referred to as a "12th-Century style." For all practical purposes, we may say that its elements were worked out during its first hundred years, and that most of its production took place during the next century.

THE ELEMENTS OF THE ROMANESQUE STYLE IN ARCHITECTURE

The Romanesque was the most diverse style in history. No two examples are alike; every building seems to reflect in some measure a novel conception. It is nevertheless possible to draw up a list of features which, by their repeated appearance all over Europe, furnish a kind of common denominator for all monuments. The diversity explains itself largely by reference to geography, each region having its peculiar type of church, built of the local materials and with an arrangement of towers, apses, and transepts found nowhere else. The features possessed in common by all regions are a series of special motives (doors, windows, mouldings, piers, capitals, etc.) scarcely predicted by any earlier style, and for all practical purposes the contribution of the Romanesque. To these we shall now turn our attention, leaving a brief treatment of the regional differences for the next section.

Before we proceed, it is necessary to warn the reader what to expect. Familiarity with classical art may be a positive handicap in attempting to comprehend the Romanesque. No abstractions governed the designers of the 11th and 12th Centuries. Geometric order, either in plan or elevation, did not preoccupy them for a moment; they used such order or left it alone as they chose at the time. There is no system of proportions to which they adhered; their style encompasses some of the most delicate and some of the most ponderous building known in Europe. Because bulk transport over long distances passed beyond the realm of feasibility when Rome fell, we may expect to see any of the typical Romanesque motives executed in cheap brick, local limestone, exquisite marble, or whatever else may have been at hand. Almost every color available in masonry occurs at one place or another, and the textures may be as slick as silk or of a homely coarseness like tweed. The thing that counts, if we are to grasp the essential unity of the style as a whole, is to be able to recognize the typical motives no matter how they may be varied or on what part of the building they may appear.

Towers

It is difficult for us to imagine a time when towers and steeples were rare; and we are thus likely to overlook the most conspicuous novelty of the Romanesque. Towers had always been used for military purposes and other purposes; but the now-familiar identity of towers with church architecture dates from the period covered by the present chapter. We shall not at the moment take space to discuss the innumerable variations of the tower, with or without a spire to top it off, that were invented in the several districts of Europe. Suffice it to say that the Italians usually built the tower free-standing and separate from the body of their churches. The English and the Normans continued to use the tower of Saxon times (Fig. 9.49), square in plan and square of head. In the Rhineland, round towers with sharp spires were the going thing, while the people of Aquitaine developed a stumpy, bossy little spire very much like a pine cone (Fig. 11.10). The great contribution of the Spanish Romanesque was the invention of the so-called "Salamantine Lantern" (Fig. 11.32) — neither spire nor dome but partaking of both, and one of the most inspired combinations of simple elements in all architectural history.

It is difficult to account for all the Romanesque towers by reference to considerations that are practical in nature. We think of a church tower as a place to hang a bell, and it is true that the association of churches and bells is at least as old as the traditional " invention " of church bells by Saint Paulinus of Nola (died 431). A certain symbolical intention may also have operated to increase the popularity of towers. Towers over the crossing may have evolved from the domes of the *martyria* (tombs raised over the graves of martyrs, or the relics thereof), a more or less familiar kind of building in the Near East. The incorporation of towers in the western façade (very rare in Italy, common elsewhere) may have been suggested by the notion that the emperor, God's vicar for secular matters, ought to be honored by a conspicuous feature — balancing the sacred apse, as it were — on the part of the church that faced the world. Either of these ideas might suggest the construction of a single tower, but both together hardly account for the multiplication of towers which so evidently was the Romanesque ideal. The notion of the tower obviously struck a very sympathetic chord in the aesthetic sensibilities of the people. In other words, they felt a powerful stylistic impulse. Among the influences available to them, the obvious one is the Northern and Barbarian Style. We may assume that the Romanesque builders, whatever they may have thought about the iconographical significance of their towers, felt inclined to build them for the same reasons that the Irish illuminators had, during an earlier era, rung infinite changes upon the complicated silhouettes of their initial letters, and for the same reason that the Viking shipbuilders used to extend stem and stern strongly upward into the air. Towers, in a word, give Romanesque churches the dissolving silhouette of northern art.

Ever since the Romanesque period, it has been habitual to think of the spire as a Christian symbol. For many persons, a church without a steeple is no church. The vertical momentum imparted to the eye by a tower is intimately expressive; it is impossible to challenge the propriety of an association with the aspiring element in Christianity. But before people might make the association, they had to have towers to look at — and the introduction of towers would seem to have antedated the modern symbolism.

In every architectural style, much and sometimes everything depends upon the particular kind of door or window which may be characteristic of the style as a whole. The standard Romanesque opening, as already indicated in other connections, was the round arch, but the round arch was rarely used in a plain and simple form. The Romanesque gets its flavor from a series of typical openings — each a distinct artistic motive in its own right — produced by rather simple manipulations and combinations of the round arch. The most important combinations are five in number: the splayed opening, the Lombard porch, the compound arch, the wheel window, and the Tuscan door.

The Splayed Opening

No better example of the splayed opening exists than the south transept portal of the Abbey Church at Aulnay in Saintonge (Fig. 11.7), a place a little more than fifty miles southeast of Poitiers. As the name implies, the splayed door is beveled in the plan view, and flares out toward one through the thickness of the wall. No other kind of opening seems to fulfill so well the several purposes of a doorway. In a crude and mechanical sense, doors merely permit circulation through walls, while protecting the interior from the weather. Artistically, a door is far more important than that. It is the barrier between outdoors and indoors, a psychological boundary that may be gentle or abrupt, which can invite or forbid. The splayed door softens the transition. It brings the actual opening into special focus; and by walking under its overhang, one finds himself halfway in while still outside — without further effort of the will, he may pass into the building.

The splayed door, in a word, extends a welcome peculiarly in keeping with a church building, and it was no accident that we find the idea of splaying brought to perfection in the Gothic churches of the 13th Century — all other types of doorway being virtually abandoned.

Both in the Romanesque and the later Gothic, the splayed doorway was made up of several concentric arches, at Aulnay four of them. The extrados of the inmost arch is identical, that is to say, with the intrados of the next one — and so on, until the outer surface of the wall is reached. Each of the four arches that make up the doorway at Aulnay may be described as an *order;* and the entire ensemble can conveniently be designated as *a splayed arch in four orders.*

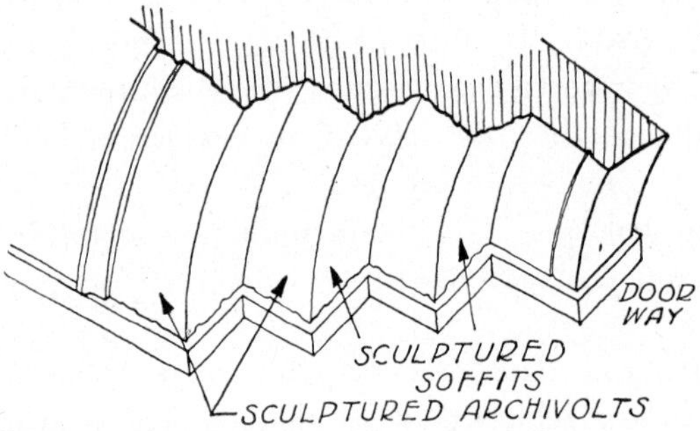

Fig. 11.24 Perspective cross section through the four orders of a typical Romanesque splayed arch.

The arches used at Aulnay are the typical round arches of the Romanesque Style. While used for the majority of Romanesque churches — with an equal preponderance of the pointed arch in Gothic — it is by no means enough to distinguish one style from the other merely by reference to its favorite shape of arch. Round arches occur in the fully developed Gothic (Orvieto), and pointed arches are by no means uncommon in the Romanesque (e.g., at Autun and in Sicily). The real difference has to do with the comparative simplicity of the Romanesque, as contrasted with the elegant complication of the Gothic. Fig. 11.24 is an attempt to illustrate this point insofar as the Romanesque usage goes; it is a schematic cross section taken through a splayed door like that at Aulnay, at a level a little above the spring.

It will be noted that each of the four concentric orders has a simple rectangular cross section, within the limits of which even the sculptural decoration is severely compressed. There are, moreover, only four orders; and the end of each is as plain as the beginning of the next. Other Romanesque doorways of the splayed type use a round rather than a rectangular face for each order, but the criterion of simple shape, clear division, and a limited number of parts persists. By comparison, the Gothic will present the eye with a bewildering refinement.

The Compounding of Supports: the Theory of Structural Logic

The three outer orders of the splayed arch at Aulnay come down, it will still further be observed, each on its separate colonnette, with a section of wall acting as support for the fourth order (Fig. 11.25). Such an articulation of supports is of the essence in the new theory of structural logic which first captured the imagination of Europe during the Romanesque Period, and from which all modern engineering stems. Although the theory is discussed at length in the next section but one (pages 409–416), we must for the sake of clarity now make a brief statement of what is involved.

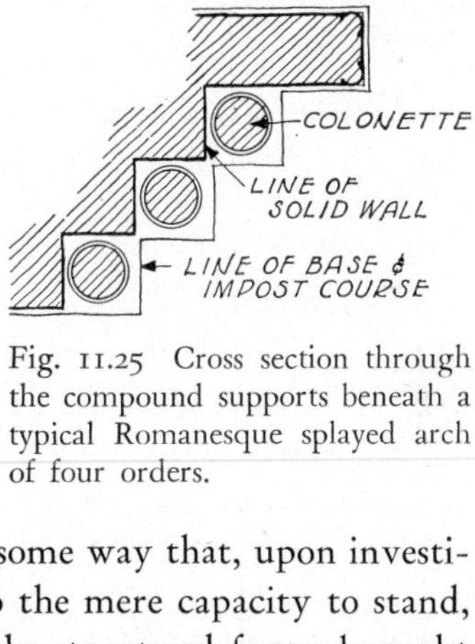

Fig. 11.25 Cross section through the compound supports beneath a typical Romanesque splayed arch of four orders.

Much earlier architecture is structurally logical in the sense that it has endured. It may be said, indeed, that nothing will stand even for a moment unless the force of gravity is opposed in some way that, upon investigation, proves to be logical. We refer here not to the mere capacity to stand, but to a theory of design that had its genesis in the structural forces brought into play by the mechanism of a building, and in the work done by each component part. There are four parts in the splayed arch at Aulnay; therefore, we find four members in the support beneath. A one-to-one correspondence exists between the work done and the shape of the members that do it.

In getting at the last point, it may be helpful to think of the Aulnay door as having been produced in an attempt to eliminate (more strictly, to omit) unnecessary masonry. Such a theory works toward the ideal of making the least material do the maximum amount of work. Structures so designed depend for their safety upon an accurate analysis of forces, and a precision in the placement of parts. It follows that designers, as they become more and more familiar with a particular structural problem, will begin to give every part a shape best adapted to the work it must do. The procedure may or may not produce beauty; when form follows function, we sometimes arrive at the hideous — as we shall point out here and there in the chapters to follow.

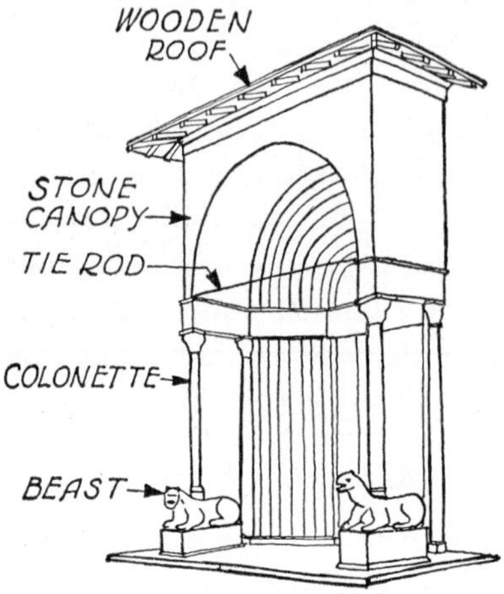

Fig. 11.26 Schematic drawing to show the principal parts of a typical Lombard porch.

Thought of collectively, the ensemble of shafts under either side of the arch at Aulnay would be referred to as a *compound support*. As an architectural unit, the compound support is more often encountered in the form of a *compound pier*, which is merely a free-standing post with a cross section determined by whatever it carries. The compound piers of Saint Sernin (Fig. 7.3) are comparatively simple because they carry little, while those of Sant' Ambrogio at Milan (Figs. 11.5,6,37) are complicated because they carry a number of arches.

The Lombard Porch

The Lombard Porch, indicated schematically by Fig. 11.26 and well-illustrated by the main portal of the Cathedral of Modena in Lombardy (Fig. 11.4) is made up of the following elements. The builder starts with two stone beasts sitting on pedestals. Lions are the most common, but other preferences (griffins on the transept portals of Modena, elephants at Bari) may be accommodated. From the back of each beast, there springs a slender colonnette, and from the colonnettes, the arches of a delicate canopy. At Modena, a second story is provided to shelter a tomb; most Lombard porches have only one story.

The Compound Arch

The façade of Modena shows us still another very common Romanesque opening, the compound arch. Never used as a door, it is often employed for

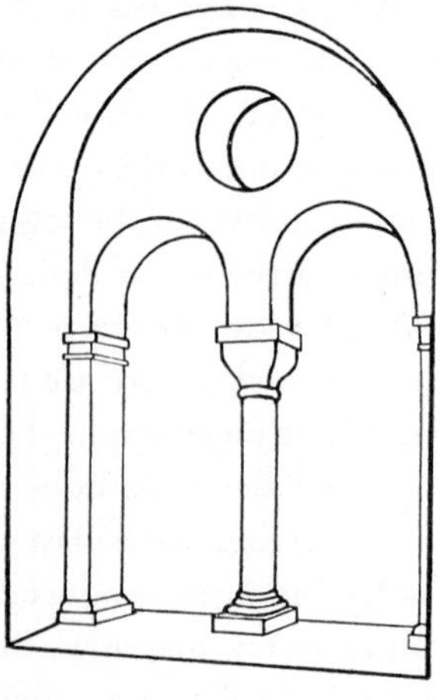

Fig. 11.27 The compound arch.

gallery openings, tower windows, or as we see it here, to form an open gallery in the thickness of the wall. The compound arch in its simplest essentials is shown in Fig. 11.27. It amounts to a side-by-side arrangement of little arches which spring from a colonnette and are enclosed within the frame of a big arch. The same motive was common in Byzantine architecture of the Second Golden Age, was passed on from the Romanesque into the Gothic (the pointed arch being substituted for the round), and occurs in a few examples of the Early Renaissance (classical mouldings and classical columns taking the place of the medieval). Surprisingly simple in its form, the compound arch enriches any building with an intricate and delightful variety of line and surface, and an ever-changing pattern of light and shadow.

Fig. 11.28 A typical Romanesque wheel window.

The Wheel Window

The conspicuous circular window above the central entrance at Modena is still another typically Romanesque motive. The complex of stone mullions within it is called *tracery*. As it happens, the tracery at Modena appears to have been restored during the Gothic era, as one can tell from the pointing of the arches. A more usual form during the Romanesque would be like Fig. 11.28, where the arches are cusped but rounded. A wheel window is often called a *rose window*. There can be no strict differentiation between the terms. If the tracery impresses one as the spokes of a wheel, use the former; if as the petals of a flower, use the latter.

The Tuscan Door

The Tuscan Door appears in Fig. 11.29; and in a somewhat unusual form on the main front of the Cathedral at Pisa (Fig. 11.1). In typical examples, two fat Corinthian pilasters form the door jambs, with a lintel spanning the opening and a relieving arch above the lintel. Lions' heads, or other grotesques, mark the impost blocks at the spring of the relieving arch, within the *lunette* (sometimes called *tympanum;* Fig. 11.29) of which one often finds a panel of relief or perhaps a painting protected by glass.

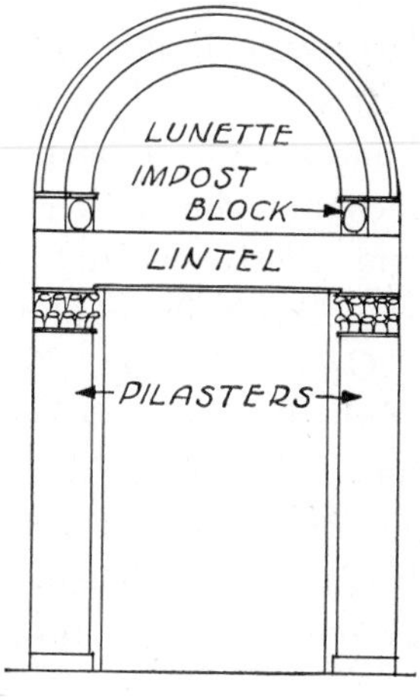

Fig. 11.29 Schematic drawing to illustrate the principal parts of a typical Tuscan portal.

Motives for the Decoration of Wall Surfaces

Whatever their practical utility as doors and windows, the several Romanesque motives so far cited serve the aesthetic purpose of lending an extraordinary interest to the wall surfaces of the Romanesque church. No other designers were so clever and inventive — when it came to that particular department of architecture — as those of the 11th and 12th Centuries. Among the many minor and decorative devices developed for such a purpose, we may mention the following.

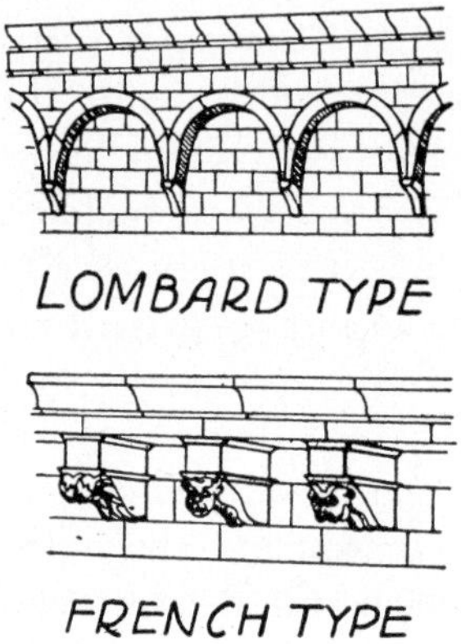

Fig. 11.30 Corbel tables.

In innumerable instances, an otherwise blank wall will be found subdivided by delicate horizontal mouldings which project but slightly from the surface, and cast a narrow, crisp shadow. Such are known as *string courses.*

A string course will often be strengthened in its effect by the addition of *corbels,* sometimes called *corbel tables.* Two kinds are shown in Fig. 11.30. The Lombard corbels are tiny arcades that hang in mid-air. The French are little brackets, sometimes with gargoyles, projecting at right angles to the wall. While in general true, the implied geographical distinction must not be construed as restrictive.

The *blind arcade* (Fig. 11.31) is found on a very large scale at Pisa, where it stands the full height of the aisle walls and runs completely around the building. On a smaller scale, and with compartments of almost every imaginable proportion, the same motive will be seen everywhere the Romanesque was built, and both indoors and out.

Fig. 11.31 A typical blind arcade of the Romanesque period.

Geometric shapes formed still another resource of the Romanesque architect. At Pisa, we see them used as hollow coffers sunk in the wall, as indicated also by Fig. 11.2. Elsewhere, and especially in Lombardy, crosses, diamonds, triangles, and other simple forms were used whenever an architect felt inclined to design an odd kind of window.

The Eccentricity of the Style

To the list of typically Romanesque motives so far cited, we must add another element which is underlying and fundamental to the whole style, but by no means susceptible of easy definition. We refer to what may be called the eccentricity of the Romanesque — a factor which is in part spontaneous, and in part the product of calculated intention.

Any perusal of a dozen or more measured drawings which faithfully reflect the actual condition of as many Romanesque churches will surprise if not shock the modern reader. Walls are often slightly out of parallel. Bays of vaulting are defined by " squares " which are not strictly rectangular, but have one or more angles askew. The arches of an arcade, as in the blind arches of the ground story on the south side of the Cathedral at Pisa (Fig. 11.2) rise to different levels at the crown, differ somewhat in curvature and span.

Such things reflect methods of building which were easygoing to a degree. Medieval society was completely incapable of the strict discipline familiar in Roman times and today. Without impeaching the nobility of the chivalric code which emerged during the later Middle Age and ameliorated the realities of conflict, in theory at least, with a few intrusions of decency, the fact remains that the medieval armies were perhaps the most inefficient and ineffective in history, size for size. The great numbers of workmen necessary for a large building project were similarly loose in their organization. Plans in the modern sense of complete and accurate scaled drawings, appear to have been unknown, although small models of the intended fabric seem to have been common. As a result, there was nothing like the modern regularity of procedure. Much was left to the improvisation of the moment. The case of the Cathedral at Florence — a Gothic building, but perfectly illustrative of the point before us — may be mentioned as typical. Dissatisfied with the conventional arrangement of transepts and apse, the original designers gave the church an immense octagonal crossing a full 138 feet across. They hadn't the slightest idea how to build the dome with which they intended to cover that part of the building. The last dome of similar scale had been designed 600 years before by Anthemios and Isodoros, for Hagia Sophia. Construction can hardly be said to have progressed at Florence; it dragged on for over a hundred years before the octagon was ready for its dome — with the method of building the dome still to be thought up. It was necessary to advertise and to hold a competition in order to get suggestions. Brunelleschi (see below, pages 631–638) won, and he made his reputation with a brilliant and daring design.

Such methods of building — and they obtained throughout the entire Middle Ages, not applying to Romanesque alone — were not economical. A great many churches fell down, altogether or in part. On the other hand, not one critic in the whole world would trade medieval irregularity for the sterile precision of modern and Roman methods. In a much more informal way and often capriciously, the effect arrived at is similar in nature to the curvature of the Parthenon. There is life in the stones. The buildings are quaint, picturesque, and lovable.

Deliberate eccentricity often formed part of the Romanesque intention. It was not by chance, but by design, that the fifth column from the left in the open arcade at Arezzo (Fig. 11.3) was given a dog-leg twist in the middle. The famous Leaning Tower of Pisa (Fig. 11.1) is another instance of whimsy let loose in the field of architecture. It was by no means unique; there were other leaning towers, including two at Bologna. Objective proof of the designers' intentions is lacking in this particular instance; but although the contrary statement has often been categorically made, the weight of the evidence attests that the lean was planned from the beginning. The foundations have subsided somewhat, it is true; but not enough to account for the phenomenon.

For Romanesque eccentricity, the reader must not look for a rational explanation; the thing itself is not of the mind. Let him instead turn back and review the pages in which he was first introduced to the northern and barbarian temperament as expressed in art (see above, pages 298–301). The leaning tower and other deliberate violations of common sense are to be explained as the Irishman — a member of an ancient tradition, as we are able to know — explained jumping through the plate-glass window: he couldn't say why he had done it, but could certify that the idea seemed good at the time.

THE REGIONAL STYLES OF THE ROMANESQUE

Although it was the most varied style in history, the Romanesque tended to assume a certain amount of uniformity in different parts of Europe. Within the limits of the style as a whole, it is customary to recognize a number of regional subdivisions. Each one is an artistic pattern in its own right, a special field of study not to be dismissed as mere local history. Limitations of space permit us here only the briefest passing description of the more conspicuous features by which the taste of the several regions may be recognized when seen, and the regional styles mentioned below are merely the most important and by no means all that exist. So rapid a summary is bound to be bare. Unavoidably, it fails to convey the richness of local culture which still survives in Europe. Even so, it opens up a vista that is all too often overlooked.

The simplest scheme of classification that is free from misleading implications is as follows. In Italy, the styles of Lombardy and Tuscany require special mention. In France, no less than five districts must be cited as producing distinct types of Romanesque architecture: Provence, Auvergne, Languedoc, Aquitaine, Burgundy, and Normandy. In addition to these seven divisions, the most superficial kind of completeness requires at least an allusion or two to the derivative schools of England, Germany, Spain, South Italy, and Sicily.

Tuscany

The churches of Tuscany are beyond compare the loveliest and most graceful of all. Often built almost entirely from the superb local marble and unique in their attempt to make every part delicate rather than ponderous, these buildings present the eye with a pattern of line and color that has often and correctly been compared to the effect of a ship under sail. The Cathedral at Pisa (Figs. 11.1,2) is the largest and most famous monument of the district. A number of smaller churches are equally worth knowing: at nearby Lucca, the Cathedral, San Michele, and San Giusto; at Florence, San Miniato; the Pieve at Arezzo (Fig. 11.3); and the several churches at Toscanella, of which San Pietro is the most notable.

In a period characterized by a ferment of structural ingenuity, the architects of Tuscany were distinguished for a complete lack of interest in engineering. Except for the presence of Romanesque details, Pisa might accurately be described as an Early Christian Basilica. Because there was no vaulting, no problems of abutment hampered the provision of large clearstory windows, with the result that the interior is full of light — the effect thereof being enhanced by the color and texture of the marble walls. As to the latter, photographs are grievously deceptive. Stripes of soft blue limestone run at intervals through the courses of marble. Because blue tends to reproduce as black in a photograph, the contrast becomes unpleasantly exaggerated; but in fact, it is rather pleasant.

In matters of detail, the most striking feature of the Tuscan style is the profusion of open galleries, always in the form of miniature arcades supported by delicate colonnettes. Ideally, an entire building would be enveloped with such arcades, a result nearly achieved in the Leaning Tower at Pisa — with an almost Oriental enrichment of the texture. Blind arcades, supported either by engaged columns or by slender pilasters, were used for almost all wall surfaces where the open arcade was not wanted. In addition to these features, the Tuscan designers made considerable use of geometric shapes, either as inlays in several colors or in the form of hollow coffers sunk into the masonry.

Lombardy

It was the Lombards who first gave mature and logical expression to the structural aesthetic which was certainly the most original, and probably the greatest single contribution of the Romanesque period to architectural design. Their prowess in that respect forms the subject of the next section of this chapter. We shall postpone discussion at this point, and concentrate upon the decorative charm of the Lombard churches — a matter some authors have passed over in their enthusiasm for Lombard engineering.

Modena may stand as a typical example for the region (Fig. 11.4). It has all the characteristic features except that its façade conforms to the basilican cross section, a shape used only about half the time in Lombardy. Numerous other churches make the façade into a kind of screen, with a single very broad gable at the top; for instances, see San Michele at Pavia and the Cathedral of Parma.

In the texture and color of their masonry, the important Lombard churches are less dazzling than the marble buildings of Tuscany, but they have a quiet elegance even so. The individual blocks are small, neatly cut, and closely joined, with a smooth rather than a polished surface. There is a certain crispness in edges and lines.

It was customary in Lombardy to unify the composition of the façade by strong verticals, usually in the form of continuous pilaster strips as at Modena. Where corbels appear, the Lombard type was usual, as we might expect, and the favorite doorway was the Lombard Porch. Open arcades composed of compound arches are as common here as the simple arcade in Tuscany. Lombardy developed, moreover, one of the important local schools of Romanesque sculpture. When human figures were involved, Lombard sculpture has a solid and plastic character not usually found in relief. Where grotesques and animals appear, the local artists took a delight in savagery unusual even in a period famous for that specialty. As we may judge from the panels that appear on the façade at Modena, the Lombards failed to work out any coherent theory of the interaction between sculpture and architecture by which each art can be made to help the other.

South Italy and Sicily

It is perhaps a mistake to refer to the 11th- and 12th-Century churches of " the two Sicilies " as Romanesque. Successively controlled by the Greeks, the Romans, the Byzantines, the Saracens, and from approximately 1100 on by a Norman dynasty with connections developing in Italy and Spain, it is difficult to imagine a region where a greater variety of inspiration might affect the decisions of an artist. Of those cited, almost all influences seem to have been in active operation during the Romanesque era; and to the offerings from the historical past, we must add the direct imitation of the contemporary Romanesque of other districts. In fact the only thing available that seems not to have been directly copied at one time or another is the Greek architecture of the region — for well-preserved temples remain in good repair at Paestum, south of Naples, and at Segesta and Agrigentum on the island of Sicily.

All of this being so, it comes as no surprise to find that the similar cathedral churches at Monreale and Cefalù, near Palermo (see above, pages 364–365), amount to large basilicas, with arcades of pointed arches in the Saracen form, their interiors ablaze with Byzantine mosaics, and their outside walls decorated with Oriental patterning. The general hodgepodge of inheritance did not, however, prevent the construction of some buildings which, if imitative rather than original, are among the finest we have. Such a one is the Cathedral at Troia, about sixty miles northeast of Naples. The body of the church is like Pisa; but the flavor of the design is changed by the addition of some superb Lombard detail.

Provence

The two most important churches of the Provençal Romanesque are Saint Trophime at Arles (Fig. 11.8), and Saint Gilles nearby. The special feature of these is the splendor of their western portals. The entrance to Saint Gilles, the more elaborate of the two, remains one of the noblest entrances in existence. Distinctively Romanesque in detail, both façades emanate a monumental calm not always associated with the period. Since both date later than 1150, that characteristic may reflect the advent of the Gothic point of view; but to an even greater degree, the atmosphere of weighty quiet probably derives from the unparalleled wealth of classical material still standing at Arles, at Nîmes, and throughout Provence.

Because of the substantial difference in proportions, the resemblance at first escapes attention, but it is a fact that both portals reflect the standard scheme for a Roman triumphal arch: the podium at the bottom, and then the familiar sequence of order and entablature. The capitals do not deviate far from the Corinthian silhouette, and the larger statues possess a dignity which has aptly been described as "senatorial."

Auvergne

The churches of Auvergne are at once the most ponderous and picturesque of all the French Romanesque; they also happen to be, as a group, the oldest. Notre Dame du Port at Clermont-Ferrand, the central monument of the region, dates from the middle of the 11th Century. Because that church is hemmed about with other buildings, it can scarcely be photographed as a unit. We therefore illustrate the type by Fig. 11.9, which shows Saint-Nectaire, about fifteen miles south of Clermont, a free-standing church splendidly set on top of a hill.

Seen in plan, the average church of the Auvergne is more complex than most other Romanesque types. The transepts extend a considerable distance out from the nave. The arm of the cross between the transept and the apse is elongated to form a *choir;* and six or eight columns were commonly arranged in a semicircle at the eastern end of the choir to make a kind of open apse with an ambulatory behind it. Opening off the ambulatory, we often find a series of miniature chapels, each circular in form. These are called *absidioles,* and they ordinarily are arranged radially, like the petals of a flower. The effect is to produce a ground outline at the east end strikingly similar in plan to that of the High Gothic.

To the architects of the Auvergne must also go the credit for intelligent experiment with vaults, and for the invention of the system of abutment illustrated by Fig. 7.2, where the thrust of a tunnel vault over the nave is contained by continuous half tunnel vaults over the galleries to either side. From Auvergne, the arrangement went to several other districts, as we shall note in due time.

Excellent as an insurance of structural stability, no arrangement could have been much worse when it came to providing light for the interior. In an effort to ameliorate that fault, the local architects resorted to a bold adjustment in the elevation of the building. At the crossing, they raised a rectangular attic with a north and south dimension corresponding to the width of the nave. Above the attic, they built an octagonal tower, usually only two stories in height, topped off by a squat spire. Clearstory windows were thus provided at an ideal height but hardly in an ideal relation to the long axis of the church.

As seen from the east, however, the Auvergnat churches are among the most interesting ever designed. The various masses present the eye with harmonies and contrasts of size and shape. Absidioles, apse, and attic arrange themselves in a graduated and ascending sequence, culminating in the tower. The total effect is both solid and lively, and there are analogies to the best examples of modern abstract painting and sculpture.

Languedoc

Toulouse is the principal city of Languedoc, and its central monument is the Church of Saint Sernin (Fig. 7.3). The Romanesque churches of that region — to be visualized roughly as the southwest corner of France — are very much like those of Auvergne. While the western façade of Saint Sernin is without special distinction, the view from the east is imposing. The apse is flanked by absidioles radially arranged; and while the attic familiar in Auvergne was here omitted and the transepts extended, there is an unmistakable attempt to build the masses up into a composition culminating in an octagonal tower — which in this instance runs a full five stories high.

The ribbed tunnel vault of the building, and its abutment, have already been adequately dealt with in Chapter 7 (see pages 201–202); from the standpoint of structural logic, this particular form of vault has rarely been better handled.

A special interest must always attach to Saint Sernin, because at Compostella, at the extreme northwest corner of Spain, there stands the church of Santiago which is — except in matters of detail — a duplicate of Saint Sernin. The resemblance is almost certainly to be explained by reference to the medieval custom of going on pilgrimages.

The body of Saint James, after transportation from the Near East by ship, had supposedly been laid at rest at Compostella. That remote place presently assumed an immense importance. It eclipsed all other destinations in attraction to pilgrims. While details remain obscure, it seems almost certain that the pilgrims followed routes that were well-defined, and it is believed that the church must have maintained a considerable organization to provide for their welfare. If so, we may infer that a number of buildings were put up. Being under one administration, those would naturally tend to assume a definite and single style. Inasmuch as Toulouse was an important stopping point on "the way of Saint James," the virtual identity between the two churches is probably thus to be explained.

Aquitaine

We have already had occasion to refer to the Romanesque of Aquitaine (see above, page 351), because the builders of that region so often paid homage to Constantinople by vaulting over their churches with multiple domes on pendentives (Fig. 7.21). Saint Front at Perigueux is usually cited as the most important monument of the region. It is surely unexcelled in the unique and delicate complexity of its skyline, but it is an individual and special, rather than a typical building. The Cathedral at Angoulême has a more usual plan in the shape of a Latin rather than a Greek cross, and it shares with Notre Dame la Grande at Poitiers (Fig. 11.10) the distinction of an excellent and typical façade.

Roughly derivative from the basilican cross section, the central portion of the façade is flanked by two low towers, each of which may be described as a grandiose compound pier (see below, page 394) topped off by the characteristic pine cone spire of Aquitaine. Horizontally, the composition is likewise divided into three parts, the lines of demarcation being established by heavy string courses over a set of corbels that combine both the Lombard and the French types. Constructed of smooth masonry, this façade might be quite without merit. As it stands, it is one of the best ever done in the Romanesque style. The profusion of sculpture combines with the coarse tiles to impart an over-all sense of rough and kindly texture which has, on the whole, been improved rather than harmed by centuries of weathering.

Burgundy

The Abbey Church at Cluny (Fig. 7.4) was the central monument of the Burgundian Romanesque and the administrative focus of the vast and powerful Cluniac Order, the most cogent subdivision ever developed within the Roman Catholic hierarchy. The church proper had a double set of transepts, five aisles, and no less than fifteen absidioles opening off transepts and ambulatory. Its length approached 500 feet, to which we must add the length of a monumental narthex, itself another nave, extending westward five bays more. Largely the work of the middle 12th Century, the magnificent building survived until the time of the French Revolution. By then neglected and in disrepair, it was destroyed with blasting powder, and the rubble sold for cheap building stone — a succinct and terrible illustration of the extreme modernity of what we may call the historical sense. The architecture of Cluny is known to us through the archaeological reconstruction conducted by Mr. Kenneth Conant, and a few pieces of decorative sculpture have been preserved. Their quality establishes the presumption that the excellence of the immense fabric was as notable as its size.

Cluny being gone, we must form our impression of the Burgundian Romanesque by reference to smaller monuments. The style is on the whole well represented by the Abbey Church (La Madeleine) at Vézelay, and by the Cathedral (Saint Lazare) at Autun (Figs. 11.11–13). At both Vézelay and Autun, a good sized narthex precedes the nave; and above the great doorway leading therefrom into the church, there is a semicircular lunette, or *tympanum,* with a major composition in relief sculpture (see below, pages 420–423). Aside from the narthex, which is more elaborately developed here than elsewhere, the churches of Burgundy remind us in their architectural features of Auvergne and Languedoc. The distinctively Burgundian contribution has little to do, in fact, with either the form or the major component parts of the building. It inheres, rather, in a special precision and finesse, even a richness and luxury, notable in every detail of the fabric. Not only is there much more sculpture here than elsewhere, but every bit of carving, even the smallest moulding, is of an unequaled delicacy. In addition, an imponderable flavor from the Antique imbues everything Burgundian: the fluted pilasters at Autun seem spiritually more classical than many a bit of work from the Italian Renaissance — a circumstance less surprising than it seems when we remind ourselves that fragments of a temple to Apollo may still be seen at Autun, and that the Porte Saint André once formed part of the Roman walls.

Normandy

Because of its connection with England and because it made so direct a contribution to the French Gothic, the Norman Romanesque seems in many ways to be the culmination of the style. No church is more typically Norman than the gaunt and ruined Abbey at Jumièges (Fig. 11.14) standing within a great meander of the Seine about ten miles, as the crow flies, due west from Rouen. At the date of its consecration in 1067, it was the grandest building produced in the west since the Early Christian period and the architectural symbol of a great and learned monastery.

Jumièges might be called a basilica transformed by the Romanesque. In plan and general disposition of parts, it conforms to the traditional arrangement, and it carried a timber roof. But in every aspect of appearance and atmosphere, it was a new thing in a sense the Tuscan churches were not. It is important as one of the very earliest major buildings where a frank and thoroughgoing attempt was made to emphasize the vertical dimension. In accordance with what became standard Norman practice, the western façade embodied twin towers integral with the central section; but even by Norman and Gothic standards, the proportions employed at Jumièges were uncommonly narrow, and the angle at the gable of the nave roof acute beyond precedent. At the crossing still another tower soared into the air; of that, only a fragment remains.

The body of the church was divided into the usual nave and aisles, with an unusually high gallery at the triforium level. For the supports, simple circular columns alternated with compound piers. On the inner side of each compound pier a pilaster strip was placed, with a slender shaft engaged on its face; shaft and pilaster ran the full height of the nave from floor to ceiling. It is supposed that the main beams of the roof crossed the nave at the points of support thus provided; and the entire arrangement betokens the presence of a nice sense for the structural proprieties. It may also be cited as a linear method for emphasizing the height of the interior; and as such, it is an early indication of the movement of taste in the direction of the Gothic.

The two abbey churches at Caen, La Trinité (Abbaye aux Dames) and Saint Étienne (Abbaye aux Hommes) were founded by William the Conqueror and his queen. Students of the period disagree as to whether they were intended from the first to carry cross vaulting, or were converted during the 12th Century from wooden ceilings. Certainly the present vaults are clumsy in appearance, seemingly experimental in design, and hardly in harmony with the refinement of the parts below. However primitive the engineering, the Church of the Trinity occupies a unique place in history because the architect who designed its vaulting appears to have been the man who invented the flying buttress (see below, page 416). The same church furnishes us with an almost perfect Norman façade (Fig. 11.16). It is this façade that went directly into the French Gothic, and became the formula for the western front of all the great cathedrals of the Ile de France.

Taking them as a class, the Norman churches are notable for severity in matters of detail. There is some sculpture, but not much. There are a few ornamental mouldings and an occasional indulgence in geometric pattern; but again, not a great deal. Jumièges may be taken as the extreme with respect to restraint; and La Trinité is actually ornate by comparison with many others. There seems to have been some sympathy for decoration that might be contrived from strictly architectural motives in simple combinations. Blind arcades of various sorts and sizes were used to relieve otherwise blank surfaces; and an arcade of narrow compartments — with tiny arches on top of lengthy colonnettes — was a special favorite of the district.

The apparent promise of the Norman style came to an end early in the 12th Century, after which very few churches were built. There was trouble within the Norman clergy, friction between the Norman king and the Roman hierarchy, and a general tendency on the part of vigorous and imaginative Normans to seek their fortune in England. By the time those difficulties were resolved, the taste of all Europe had changed, and the Normans, like everybody else, found themselves building in the Gothic style.

Romanesque Architecture in England, Spain, and Germany

Architecture was a prime and immediate interest of the Norman monarchy in England. A long list of famous cathedrals date their foundation within a generation of the Conquest, and furnish us with a tangible record of the superb administrative judgment of the new government. By forwarding the construction of cathedrals, they both propitiated the bishops and kept them at a distance from London. The crown was advertised as cooperative with the church, and interested in the betterment of local conditions. It was no accident that the Romanesque of England ran to exaggerated size.

Unfortunately, none of the great English churches survive in their original Norman form. Neither have any of them entirely lost it. With a paradoxical love for both the old and the new, it was for centuries the British habit to do over small parts of a building in whatever happened to be the going style of the moment. Thus almost every monument became a kind of historical museum illustrating all the architectural fads and fashions of the centuries.

Few medieval buildings survived the fire which devastated London in September 1666. Saint John's Chapel in the Tower, grim in its severity, and

Saint Bartholomew's, Smithfield, are the principal Romanesque monuments still to be seen in the capital.

The Cathedral at Durham, even though its towers and windows are partly Gothic, comes as close as any building to furnishing us with what we may visualize as the Anglo-Norman Romanesque exterior. Standing grandly above the river Wear, the great church is one of the finest sights in the world; indeed it is a truism to say that no other race of men has ever possessed a fraction of the English genius for composing architecture in relation to landscape and foliage — an art of which some continental architects appear to have been totally unaware. The interior of Durham has suffered to an unusual extent from the 19th-Century enthusiasm for restoration; in their overconfidence, the restorers reduced the nave to an uncommon, historically erroneous, and cold simplicity. The north transept of Winchester (the nave having been done over in Late Gothic) probably gives us today our best impression of a large Norman interior.

The Romanesque of Spain was in general derivative from that of southwestern France. Certain distinctively Iberian characteristics are notable, however. Because of their immediate association with a large Moorish population, and because authentically Oriental architecture was in plain sight at Cordova and Granada (Fig. 2.16), it was inevitable that Spanish artists should attempt to combine the Western forms with Near Eastern decorative motives. Cusped arches and horseshoe arches appear in arrangements that are otherwise typically Romanesque. Rhythmic patterning of wall surfaces (for example, the brick work of San Lorenzo at Sahagun) was common. In addition, fountains — always included by the Moors wherever possible — are numerous in Spain while rather rare elsewhere. As noted above, the great contribution of Spain during this period was the Salamantine Lantern (Fig. 11.32), a squat tower with turrets at its four corners and gabled niches on the four sides, with a historical derivation that seems to draw upon a mixture of suggestion from Normandy and Aquitaine. Because of its late date, the Old Cathedral at Salamanca is sometimes classified as Proto-Gothic.

There are a great many Romanesque churches in Germany. In fact, the style so perfectly fitted the national taste that it has never died out there, and is often used today for new buildings. A number of the German churches are basilican; Saint Godehard's at Hildesheim is a good example. In matters of detail, Lombard influence is evident; likewise a Byzantine flavor (the result of direct contact through royal marriages) lingers like an aftertaste in all the medieval art of Germany.

Fig. 11.32 Salamanca. Old Cathedral. Lantern.

More spectacular and more famous are the great vaulted minsters of the Rhine: those at Cologne, and the magnificent cathedrals at Mainz, Speyer, and Worms (Fig. 11.15). Late in date and derivative in detail from Lombardy, these large buildings are somewhat behind their time with respect to structure, but no reservations need deter our admiration for their exterior appearance. Worms in particular is a noble pile. Its immense size indicated by the multiplication of normal parts, its powerful masses seem endowed with life; it rises rather than stands above the lesser things around.

ROMANESQUE ENGINEERING: THE DEVELOPMENT OF THE STRUCTURAL AESTHETIC

With respect to felicity of design, the best Romanesque churches are those that carry the wooden roof. By comparison, most of the vaulted buildings are dark, overbearing, stern, and often outright clumsy. It was nevertheless these latter that looked toward the future, and make it necessary for us to recognize the Romanesque mind as a powerful force, capable of great new inspirations and major accomplishment.

Romanesque society was a society emerging from several centuries of disorder. People were prompted by a strong, immediate, and perhaps personal memory of destruction. They felt impelled to sacrifice something, and at times almost everything, for the permanence of vaulting. It was reserved for the Gothic to solve in final fashion the age-old problem of ecclesiastical architecture: how to design a well-lighted building of the traditional basilican form, but covered by a fireproof roof. The Romanesque period was the era of experiment leading forward to that desideratum, and some of the experiments were ingenious and original to a degree.

Fig. 11.33 Loches. Saint Ours. Schematic drawing to illustrate the peculiarities of the vaulting.

Some of the most eccentric vault forms ever conceived came into being in an effort to find a shape that would require little centering, exert small thrust, and which above all might be constructed from comparatively small stones. Although it seems at first to be outright bizarre, the roofing of Saint Ours at Loches (Fig. 11.33) is extremely clever and entirely practical. The nave was covered over by a series of steeples, each in effect a hollow pyramid. It is probable that little or no centering was required, and the pyramids exert no substantial thrust horizontally. The only complaint against the expedient is aesthetic: the unity of the ceiling necessarily breaks up into a series of separate items between which no visual coherence exists. Otherwise, the system might have become popular.

A system of even greater merit was tried at Saint Philibert in Tournus (Fig. 11.34). It was perhaps not entirely the invention of the Romanesque builders, because a similar arrangement formed part of the substructure of Hadrian's villa at Tivoli; but the tricky problem of abutment has never been better solved, and good lighting was easy to provide. The vaulting of the nave was simply subdivided into five transverse compartments, each one being covered by a small tunnel vault with its axis at right angles to the nave. A clearstory window opened at either end of each compartment. The construction is perfectly safe. Each bay cancels out the thrust of its neighbors, and the total abutment required was only enough to hold in the last bay at either end of the series. Mechanically, there could hardly be anything more efficient, but the arrangement proved aesthetically intolerable; not only did it break the ceiling up into separate parts without artistic relation to each other, but the elements themselves (each section, that is, of tunnel vaulting) ran contrary to the long axis, or most important directional force, of the nave.

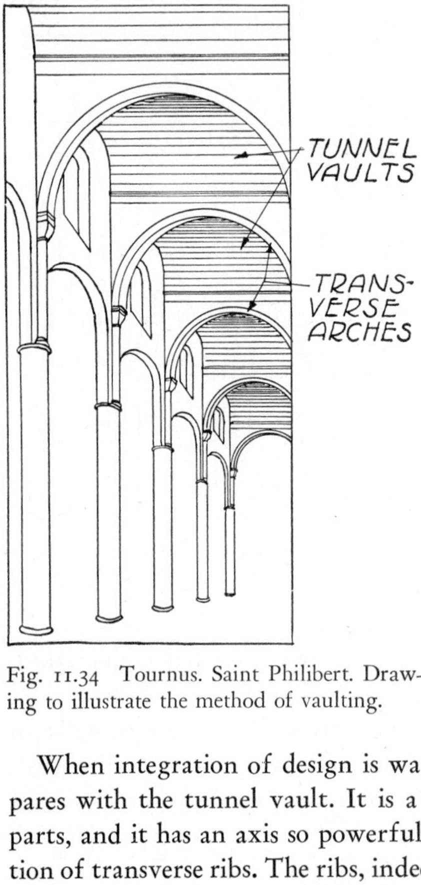

Fig. 11.34 Tournus. Saint Philibert. Drawing to illustrate the method of vaulting.

The domed churches of Aquitaine have already been cited in another connection. They were fireproof, to be sure; but they were ill-lighted and, from the standpoint of an aesthetic unity of the ceiling, perhaps even worse than either of the two systems just reviewed.

When integration of design is wanted for an interior, no other vault compares with the tunnel vault. It is a natural unit rather than an assembly of parts, and it has an axis so powerful that its force is not harmed by the addition of transverse ribs. The ribs, indeed, may be said to emphasize the length by providing a step by step progression toward the apse. Cluny had such a vault; and among those preserved, the finest are at Autun, Saint Sernin at Toulouse, and at Compostella (Figs. 7.3 and 11.13).

It seems logical to suppose that the thrusts of a ribbed tunnel vault would concentrate themselves almost entirely at the ribs. The system seems to invite the use of small separate buttresses properly located to contain each individual rib. Either because they did not believe this or because they had not yet comprehended all that might be accomplished by utilizing such concentration, it was common Romanesque practice to buttress such a nave by some form of gallery vault at a high level, more or less as shown in Fig. 7.2. Because the arrangement renders clearstory windows inexpedient, such a nave was almost certain to be gloomy. Inexpedient or not, windows were sometimes provided (Fig. 11.13). In such instances, the stability of the vault must depend upon the inertia of its own weight (i.e., wasteful bulk of masonry), and upon the tensile strength of the mortar — for it can hardly be buttressed in any neat or logical fashion.

It seems a pity the ribbed tunnel vault passed out of popularity with the 12th Century. Had the full force of medieval genius been turned to the development and perfection of that pleasant form, the subsequent history of ecclesiastical architecture might have been favorably affected. That did not happen because the ribbed cross vault captured the imagination of architects. There is no denying it offered the easiest solution to their perennial problems; and it therefore became the only kind of vault ever used by the Gothic builders. While it is impossible to withhold admiration for the brilliant engineering ensuing upon its general adoption, there is no escaping the truth that a bay of cross vaulting, ribbed or otherwise, presents the eye with a confusion of line and contour. As an artistic form, the thing itself leaves much to be desired.

Sant' Ambrogio at Milan: Organic Architecture

Experimental cross vaults were common in Romanesque architecture. Usually, however, the nature of the form was incompletely understood, and its special advantage exploited only in part. By common consent, the earliest logical and mature use of the cross vault occurred when the plans were drawn for the nave of Sant' Ambrogio at Milan (Figs. 11.5–6,35–39). The precise date of the design remains to be firmly established. Some parts of the church are very old; it was rebuilt several times, and the records are not clear about which period of rebuilding included the vaulted portions we are interested in. Italian scholars, perhaps overly anxious to claim priority for their own nation, used to contend that the entire fabric dated from the 9th Century; but they reasoned too boldly from an ambiguous inscription. It seems likely that the important elements of the vault system were designed, and perhaps built, during the pontificate of a certain Guido (1046–1071); but they may date from still another period of activity around 1129. In 1196 major repairs were necessary. French critics, likewise moved more by patriotism than evidence, have tried upon occasion to reduce the historical importance of Sant' Ambrogio by suggesting that the repair of 1196 was in fact a complete redesign and reconstruction according to French models — which by then had in truth surpassed the primitive structural logic of the church at Milan. And there the question rests.

Sant' Ambrogio has no transepts. The plan shows a three-aisled church, with the nave divided into four bays. We are concerned only with the western three, because the one nearest the apse is covered by a cupola. For some reason best known to themselves (there being no advantage one way or the other) Italian architects have traditionally preferred to use square bays of vaulting, and at Sant' Ambrogio the aisles were therefore made half as wide as the nave, with the result that two small bays exist in the aisle beside each big bay in the nave. Fig. 11.35 illustrates the relationship. Because a pier was necessary to take

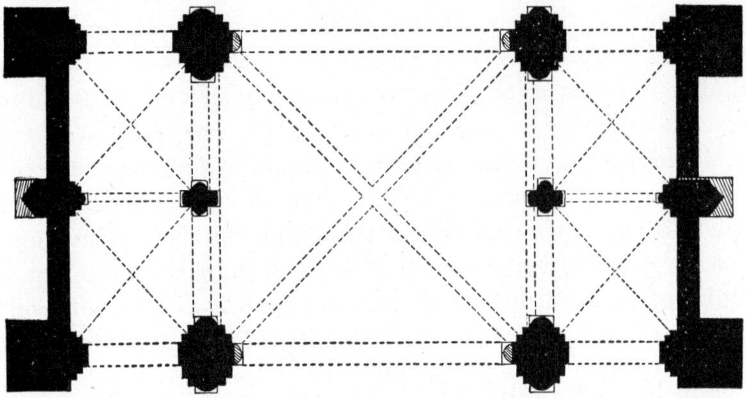

Fig. 11.35 Milan. Sant' Ambrogio. A detail from the plan, showing the relationship between the nave bays and the aisle bays, and illustrating the reason for an alternating system of supports.

the spring of every transverse rib in the aisles, the total number of piers was determined not by the nave vaulting, but by the number of bays in the aisle. But since some piers carried much and some little, the size and shape of any particular pier was adjusted accordingly. Hence the alternation of big complicated piers and small simple piers as shown by Fig. 11.6. Any church with such an arrangement of supports is said to have " the alternating system," as contrasted with " the uniform system " which was common in France.

Fig. 11.36 is an attempt to show in schematic fashion the complicated skeleton of ribs which forms the fabric of Sant' Ambrogio. The great vaults, as will be seen, were buttressed in adequate if not perfect fashion by smaller cross vaulting at the triforium level. A study of this drawing will make plain better than words the extent to which the entire design, from its first conception, was governed by a penetrating sensitivity for structural fact; and while inspecting the photographic plates, the reader should take care to note that questions ordinarily decided by artistic intuition (and for the sake of appearance only) were here settled by reference to structural logic. Every capital, for example, was placed at a level determined by the impost of the arch it carries. Capitals bearing diagonal ribs have a diagonal orientation. The shafts from which the great nave ribs rise are unbroken verticals; they cut boldly through all subordinate material.

The intimate and functional relationship between part and part bears some analogy to the skeletal structure of a living thing. The attractiveness of the

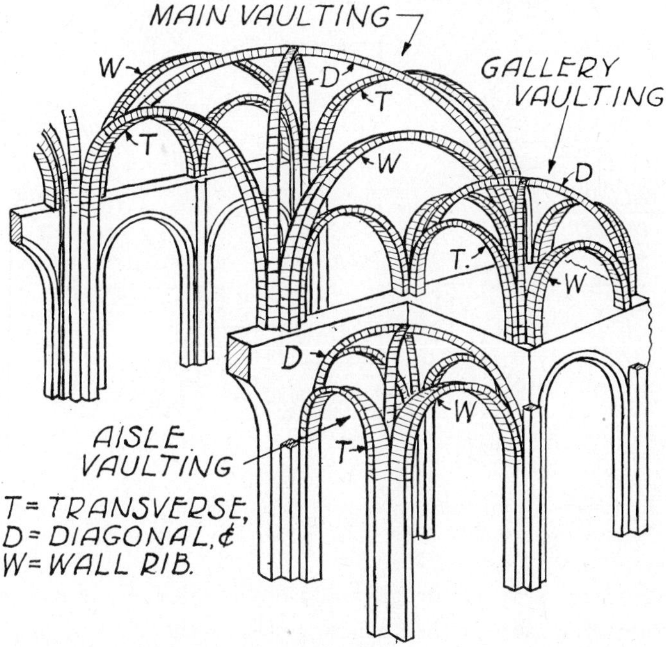

Fig. 11.36 Milan. Sant' Ambrogio. Schematic drawing to illustrate the arrangement of the more important parts of the fabric.

analogy is increased by the notion that there is life in the arches of the framework. Subjected to compression and exerting thrust, they seem to be undergoing an actual experience of a muscular kind.

The remarks just made will suggest a train of thought which has been popular among architectural critics for the past three generations and more. It has been usual to refer to a fabric like that of Sant' Ambrogio as *organic*, a term that entered the American vocabulary through the eloquent teaching and persuasive writing of the late Charles H. Moore. We have used the same word to name the system of composition invented and perfected by the Greeks and used by others (see above, page 65). There is no reason why the term may not prove useful, and perhaps helpful, in both applications, but a word of caution is requisite. *Organic* implies alive, and we think of life as good. *Inor-*

ganic, a word Mr. Moore used too often, seems by the same token to say dead. Moore applied it to any building that did not happen to be vaulted and to demonstrate in its design, moreover, a lively interest in the structural aesthetic outlined herewith.

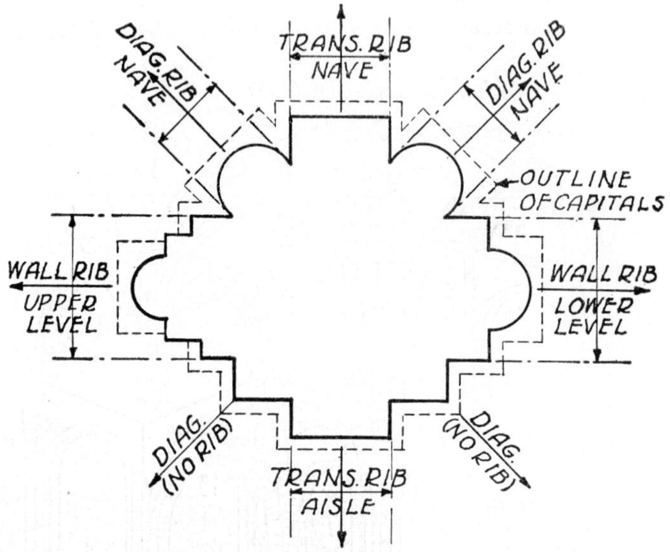

Fig. 11.37 Milan. Sant' Ambrogio. Cross section through one of the larger compound piers.

By any standard, Sant' Ambrogio was a notable design and a highly articulate expression of what was then a new aesthetic theory, and one which has since proven wonderfully productive. It seems a shame that justice requires us to call attention to some serious faults. The abutment, as already suggested, was far from a final solution of the problem; the high gallery condemns the

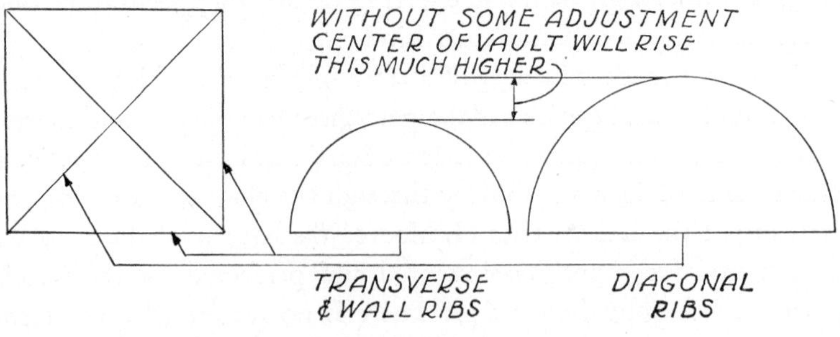

Fig. 11.38 Schematic drawing to demonstrate why the cross vaults of Sant' Ambrogio are of a domical shape.

nave to gloom. The doctrinaire application of structural logic to the piers (one part in the pier for every rib in the vault) made it necessary to accept a pier of great bulk and tedious complexity. Fig. 11.37 shows a cross section; impeccably logical, it is hardly a lucid expression.

The chief and major defect of the building is schematically indicated by Figs. 11.38–39. It appears never to have occurred to the Lombard designers to stilt the ribs of their vaults (as the Gothic architects were later to do) with the purpose of governing the height to which the crown of each rib might

Fig. 11.39 Milan. Sant' Ambrogio. Longitudinal cross section to demonstrate the rise of the domical vaults.

rise. They simply used the half circle for the shape of every arch they built. The bays being square, it followed that the diagonals had to rise higher than the other ribs; and because of that, each bay of cross vaulting was forced into a shape much closer to the dome than we might at first suppose. All of those things being settled, there was no chance left for getting a ceiling that might compose as an artistic unit. Instead, the nave of Sant' Ambrogio confronts the eye with three great gloomy and separate hollows. Its designers had nevertheless grasped most of the principles employed during the 13th Century. In order to arrive at the perfected Gothic, it was only necessary to draw a few conclusions from the suggestions implicit in the construction of this 11th-Century building. Men can be forgiven for a great deal of crudity when they are 200 years before their time.

Buttresses of the Abbaye aux Dames at Caen

Of all the faults listed at Sant' Ambrogio, clumsy abutment is perhaps the worst; but before a remedy could be found, it was necessary to wait for the invention of a new and neater type of buttress — the *flying buttress* which forms so conspicuous a feature of the Gothic. As suggested above (page 406) the principle of the thing seems first to have been conceived at Caen, and by the man who designed the vaults for the Church of the Trinity.

That church has no gallery. Instead, the triforium space is occupied by a frieze of blind arcading only a few feet high. There is a lean-to roof behind the triforium and over the aisles. Under that roof and opposite each impost where the ribs of the nave vault gather to concentrate the thrusts, we find a series of segmental arches pitched steeply downward to meet the outer walls. These half arches act as compression members, transmitting the thrust of the nave vaults. Above the triforium, clearstory windows open into the nave. The interior is one of the pleasantest in Europe.

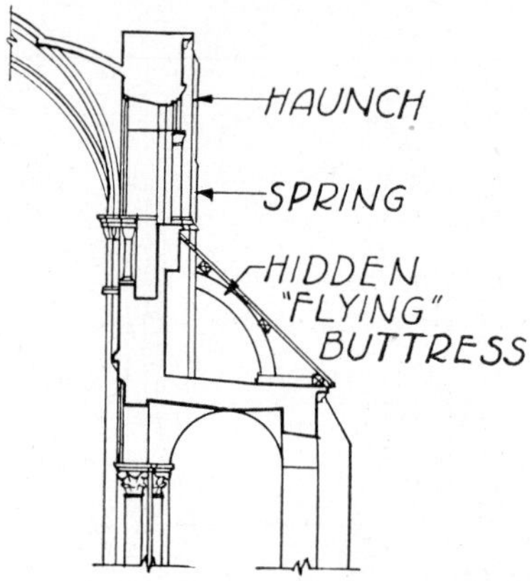

Fig. 11.40 Caen. La Trinité (Abbaye aux Dames). Drawing to illustrate the placement of the buttresses.

Each of the segmental arches referred to is in truth a flying buttress; they merely are not permitted to fly. All that remained to produce the ultimate solution of the problem of the fireproof and well-lighted church was to remove the aisle roof, bring the buttresses outdoors, and raise them up to a position where they might act efficiently. For, as Fig. 11.40 shows, the ones at Caen are far too low to do their work well, and the stability of the vault depends much upon its own inertia and the weight of the walls.

ROMANESQUE SCULPTURE AND PAINTING

The Romanesque period witnessed the revival of monumental sculpture and painting. Since Early Christian times, the art of painting had been largely limited to the production of miniature illustrations designed to be bound up in books. Of full scale sculpture, Europe had seen almost none since pagan Antiquity.

It is not easy to account for the revival at this particular moment in history. We may suppose that the same forces which called Romanesque architecture into being also account for its adornment. It is also clear that the strength had gone out of the distaste for sculpture which Europe had imported from the Near East along with Christianity. But whatever the causation, the artists of the 11th and 12th Centuries produced a prodigious harvest of material; so much, indeed, that a whole lifetime of study would hardly be enough to make one intimately familiar with all the monuments. To save space, we shall confine our attention to Romanesque sculpture alone, and to certain French monuments which, by common consent, may fairly be called the definitive examples of the style as a whole. Of Romanesque painting, we must content ourselves with the mere remark that its stylistic features are similar, and that its study has of late years occupied the attention of some excellent scholars. A few examples are on view in American museums, notably the paintings that originally decorated the apse of Santa Maria de Mur, now in Boston.

The best way to approach Romanesque sculpture is to attempt to visualize the practical problems faced by the sculptors themselves. Confronted with the necessity of reviving an art that had been out of use for 500 years, what were they to do? Where could they look for guidance?

In the first place, all patronage came from the hierarchy of the church. Secular subject matter seems hardly to have been forbidden, but there was so little of it that it did not signify. In radical contrast with our modern view of the matter, neither painting nor sculpture seems to have been so much as conceived in the light of an independent art. Both were considered merely as an extension of architecture; the business of sculptor and painter was to increase the merit of churches by adding suitable embellishment.

It must be conceded, moreover, that Romanesque architects were almost invariably somewhat arbitrary and even rather stupid when it came to making proper provision for the work of the sculptors and painters. During the Gothic era, suitable arrangements for the display of sculpture were thought a necessity; niches and pedestals of the right sort were integral with the design of the church itself — and sculpture has never been better shown (see below, pages 464–467). But during the period now under review, the reverse was true. Major compositions had to be crowded into spaces that appear at times actually to have been left over. Narrative subject matter of a briefer kind was often ordered as a replacement for the acanthus leaves on the capitals of columns and piers, most of which remind us in a general way of the Corinthian. Single figures of major saints were specified at points and in places where no one would now dream of putting them.

All of these things combined to produce an art at first extremely confusing to the modern student. Distortions are commonplace, often simply for the purpose of adjusting things to the space assigned. Miniature figures are juxtaposed with oversize figures, in defiance of normal relations of scale. Compositions teem with item after item, as though a tempestuous spirit were being cramped within the containment of the frame.

Architectural limitations and impositions account for much that we see, but what of the other sources that produced this uniquely fascinating art which has the power to lure us quickly away from the classical and Renaissance standards of modern society? Like all other artists, the Romanesque sculptors were men, not Gods. Lacking the power of total creation, they could create only by borrowing from the work of earlier artists, and producing a new synthesis of their own. And when — and rather suddenly, it would seem — the order came for them to start a new artistic period, their first impulse was to copy. What was there for them to look at?

It is probably no exaggeration to say that the complete catalogue of Romanesque sculpture reflects somewhere the appearance of almost everything that might have been on view in the medieval world. At one extreme, we find such instances as the tympanum of the church at Dinton in Wiltshire, for all practical purposes a barbarian drawing committed to stone. At the other, we find the archaeologically self-conscious sculpture of South Italy, a local and premature Renaissance, which produced marble busts that might easily and properly be mistaken for classical sculpture. Most of the time, however, the Romanesque sculptor found his model in the works of art his ecclesiastical patrons already owned and were used to, namely, the illustrations of Christian manuscripts. It was this fact that accounts for much that is complex and strange in the whole period. Not only were there available manuscripts of a great many kinds, but the sculptors themselves, primitive in their own craft, were yet deriving their style from an extremely sophisticated tradition in another medium.

Occasionally, it is possible to identify the particular miniature which served as model for a capital or lunette. More often, the style itself is a self-evident indication that some such transaction took place, and we can usually make a fairly good guess about the particular class of manuscript from which the sculptor worked. Within the great variety of style, or styles, thus brought into the total catalogue of the period, it is fair to say that most work in what we may call the main current of the Romanesque derived from manuscripts of two kinds.

For animals, grotesques, and devils the whole barbarian tradition furnished sources of incomparable virtuosity. We may imagine frequent reference to such manuscripts as the *Book of Kells* (see above, pages 305–310); but in order to account for the more plausible but still fantastic creatures to be seen on the face of the outer order of the splayed arch at Aulnay (Fig. 11.7), we must refer also to the *bestiaries,* a peculiar kind of book that had become immensely popular.

A bestiary purported to furnish information about the appearance and nature of living creatures. A large one might include descriptions of as many as 200 animals, from whose habits the text would draw religious lessons. As a class, the bestiaries may be traced back into pagan times, and some of the entries reflect classical fables. The zoological metaphor in which the Bible abounds also stimulated the medieval imagination, and if we look for them we may see lambs of God, lions of the House of Judah, and even the deaf adder that stoppeth up her ears. The influence of the bestiaries did much to make Romanesque sculpture into an art " splendidly free from the fetters of realism " — for most of the beasts in the bestiaries are imaginary.

Drawing upon the northern tradition as expanded by the bestiaries, Romanesque artists brought into being a class of sculpture in which the wildest and strangest visions of the mind were reduced to tangible representation and made permanent in stone (Fig. 11.18). The entire society of the period was peculiarly congenial to such material. No account could possibly be long enough to describe in detail the manifold variations of the Romanesque excursion into the supernatural, and we must be content with only an instance or two to illustrate the temper and trend of the time.

The story of the Devil's endeavor to tempt Christ seems, for example, to have furnished a precedent for innumerable personal appearances by the Black Master and his demons to humbler Christians. Raoul Glaber, quoted above (page 389) in quite another connection, says that the Devil bothered him on at least three occasions. " He was of small stature. He had a protruding belly, and a low forehead. His large mouth revealed a denture like that of a dog. His hair stood on end, and his movements were convulsive." It is one of the innumerable contributions of M. Emile Mâle to have recognized that Glaber's description conforms very closely with the Devil who appears several times on the capitals of Vézelay (Fig. 11.19).

For subject matter demanding the presence of the human figure, the leading Romanesque sculptors (in France, at any rate) seem to have relied for their models upon manuscripts either produced by the Carolingian School of Reims (see above, pages 326–328), or deriving from one of the traditions set in motion by that school. Their preference is profoundly indicative of the direction in which European taste was moving, for it had been the great achievement of the Reims illuminators to have adapted northern line to the rendering of the human figure. In suggesting the work of Reims as a favorite source during the period covered by the present chapter, it is necessary to stipulate that we refer to figure-style only; the spatial representation so competently handled by the Reims painters formed no part of the Romanesque borrowing.

The handling of the single figure is epitomized by the *Prophet Isaiah* of the Abbey Church at Souillac (Fig. 11.17). The slender canon of proportions, the extravagant pose, the action of the body in the region of the hips — all remind us of manuscripts from Reims. The surcharge of feeling, in which the artist so plainly participated, could have come from nowhere else. With incredible skill, the sculptor rendered in stone the swirling curves of some master penman. In several places, he has resorted to under-cutting in order to produce shadows which recall to some extent the darker areas of paintings. Purists will raise objections that such a tour de force, however accomplished in the technical sense, forms no part of the proper business of the sculptor. There is much to be said on their side; surely nothing could be more out of place in stone carving than the meander pattern below the figure, which is rendered in perspective because perspective had been necessary in the picture that was used for a model. Such reservations tend to be forgotten, however, when one considers the total effect of the whole work: where or when has religious ecstasy been more adequately demonstrated in visual terms?

For the modern student to whom the beauty and dignity of the body seems axiomatic, this and other Romanesque figures nevertheless require considerable apology and explanation. The emaciated, unhealthy, unlovely, and incorrect anatomy of the *Isaiah* do violence to our taste and habits of thought. It must be remembered that the Romanesque artists lived in a world into which the modern scientific point of view had not yet intruded, and in a religious atmosphere that held the body in contempt. Its creation in the divine image was minimized, and its capacity as an instrument of temptation and evil was reinforced by constant warning. The point was not to celebrate humanity, but to visualize states of the spirit. So appreciated, the Romanesque figure-style becomes entirely comprehensible.

Having thus characterized the Romanesque style in sculpture, we may turn our attention to its most notable major monuments. From the wealth of available material, it is difficult to choose; but there are few who would quarrel with the statement that the three grandest compositions of the period are the great tympana of Moissac, Vézelay, and Autun.

The subject of the tympanum at Moissac (Figs. 11.20–21) is taken from the fourth chapter of Revelations, where Saint John describes his vision of God's throne. A gate opened into heaven, revealing the Almighty surrounded by four-and-twenty elders who wore crowns of gold, and by the four beasts we know as the Symbols of the Evangelists (see above, pages 286–287). In his hand, God held a book sealed with seven seals, and there was " a strong angel proclaiming in a loud voice, ' Who is worthy to open the book, and to loose the seals thereof? ' " The artist has supplied a second angel, but that is no liberty, since many of them were there, continuously singing.

Crowded and confusing at first glance, the composition becomes vivid and clear as one gathers familiarity: like all other art related in any way with the Northern Style, the total effect arrives only after a cumulative process of comprehension. Once one knows the tympanum well, the realization emerges that no style bound by the rules of natural fact could possibly compete with the Romanesque in the field of Apocalyptic imagery. Transcendental visions demand an art that surges quite beyond the limits of all possible experience on earth.

For the student who becomes interested in problems of stylistic derivation, the Moissac tympanum offers an added interest. Professor Mâle (*L'art religieuse en France du XIIe siècle,* Chapter I) believes that he has identified the very manuscripts (or some so like them it makes no difference) which were used as models by the Moissac sculptor. The four-and-twenty elders with their peculiar musical instruments appear in an illustration preserved in the Bibliothèque Nationale, in a copy of the commentary on the Apocalypse written by Beatus of Liebana, a Spanish monk. For the figure of Christ, M. Mâle finds a likely source in a miniature now in the library of the Cathedral at Auxerre.

Although other explanations have been suggested, it seems almost certain that the tympanum of Vézelay (Fig. 11.22–23) was intended to represent Pentecost. The bare description of the event as given in the second chapter of The Acts has been considerably elaborated and built upon by the imagination of the artist. In the middle, there is a Christ enclosed in an elliptical glory (full length halo). To either side of him, a bit of cloud serves as an indication of his heavenly location. We are intended to suppose that his body is the radiating center through which the heavenly spirit passes, thence being transmitted to the Apostles below by means of rays emanating from his fingertips. The agitated draperies indicate the sculptor's attempt to depict the " rushing mighty wind " that swept down from heaven and filled the house.

Different scholars have advanced different views about the identity of the numerous figures across the lintel below the main scene, and those contained in the compartments which run above and around it. While it is far from easy to decide the matter, a probable explanation is as follows:

During the Middle Ages, Pentecost was understood to signify more than the gift of tongues; it was a mandate to carry the Gospel to all humanity. That idea furnishes a reason for the otherwise incomprehensible variety of people who crowd every available space. A detailed study will reveal many of the wonders of the 12th-Century ethnography. Many of the figures, it seems, were intended to represent the various heathen to whom the word would be taken. Of special interest are the Cynocephaloi, a dog-headed tribe believed to live in India; and the Panotii, with immense ears, who were then to be found in South Russia — or at least so it was said. In the semicircle around the whole, in little circular compartments, are the *Signs of the Zodiac* and the *Labors of the Months,* subjects which remained in high favor as long as the Middle Age lasted. Over and above their interest as genre, it seems plausible to suppose that the monthly cycle of activities would suggest the passage of time on earth. The astronomical symbols seem similarly related to the vaster concept of the universe, and of eternity.

The tympanum of Saint Lazare at Autun is a *Last Judgment* (Figs. 11.11–12). It is signed by the sculptor Giselbertus, who states his purposes plainly: *Terreat quos terreus alligat error* — "Let this horror appall those bound by earthly sin!"

In the lower register, the dead are rising from their graves. Two of them, just to left of center, carry musette bags, one with the mark of the cross and the other with a conch shell, the badge of pilgrims to Jerusalem and Compostella respectively. In the middle of the lunette above, there is a gigantic figure of Christ. The inscription around the border of his glory announces the business of the occasion: to the blessed he will award crowns; the evil he will send to perdition. The tympanum, judged barbarous by the canons of the church, was covered with a brick facing in 1766 — a mistake which probably saved it from complete destruction during the revolution, but one that accounts for the mutilation of the Christ and other figures. The head of the Christ was identified, however, in 1949; and it is back in place today.

To the Saviour's right, in the top register, we see the virgin; and to his left, Saint John the Evangelist. Both are there to act as intercessors for the souls who come to judgment. Beyond them, and in several other places, are angels with trumpets, blowing the blast that will one day announce the end of the world. To Christ's right and a bit below, Saint Peter stands with his immense key; he is surrounded by angels who help him chaperon the souls of the blessed into the heavenly city. On the other side, Saint Michael superintends the weighing of the souls. The ethics of the Devil and his minions may be inferred by their eagerness to pull the scales down on their side. Those who have failed the test are tossed into the flaming mouth of hell, which opens like a hopper at the extreme right.

Living long after the Greeks and long before the Italian Renaissance, Giselbertus was not bothered by artistic theories which inevitably influence our thought today. Among those theories, we must make special mention of the notion that there is an inevitable association of art with beauty — an idea that we inherit from the Italian artists, who in turn had inherited it from Antiquity. Beauty was obviously quite the opposite of Giselbertus's intention when he executed his famous *Last Judgment* — which is probably the most terrible and hideous work of art on record. It is immensely important to appreciate, however, that his philosophy was different from the Greek idealists not in kind, but in direction. Where the Greeks picked, chose, elided, and in general corrected the works of nature to fit their peculiar ideas of the noble and beautiful, this 12th-Century sculptor (also starting from things he had seen in the world) used his imagination to produce the worst devils in history. His point of view was not far different from that of the modern Surrealists (see below, pages 936 ff.). They derive their subject matter from the little known reaches of the mind, often with shocking effect. He drew his from the visualizations evoked by the more extreme and terrible suggestions contained within the Bible, and he arrived at the most extreme and radical art the world has yet to see.

*

12

GOTHIC ARCHITECTURE

Gothic art began to assume its characteristic forms during the first generation of the 12th Century. As though by manifesto, the existence of a new style was announced in the year 1140, when the Abbot Suger approved the plans and caused work to commence upon a new church for the royal abbey at Saint Denis, about 2½ miles outside the northern walls of Paris, and on the site where the martyred first bishop of the city had been buried — after walking, it is said, all the way from his decapitation on Montmartre, carrying his head in his hands. Unfortunately, Suger's church was almost completely obliterated by a reconstruction undertaken in 1231, the new work being done in the then dominant High Gothic style. From what is left and from what may legitimately be inferred, Saint Denis was the first large and important church in which all parts were fully articulated to produce the skeletal structure henceforth typical of the Gothic.

It would be a mistake to suggest that the design of Suger's Saint Denis came into being by way of a single act of inspiration. The truth is that every essential of the new system had been in plain sight somewhere or other among the manifold variations of the Romanesque. The novelty lay in an original synthesis of well-tried features; and for the synthesis itself, earlier and humbler churches in the vicinity had pioneered the way.

Saint Denis is to be remembered not only as the signal for the arrival of the Gothic style, but also as the monument which marks the assumption by France of the cultural leadership of the whole Western world. The France to which we refer is not the extensive modern political unit, but the medieval France, more exactly known as the *Ile de France,* which was the traditional name in feudal times for the district reserved by the king as his personal domain. The name is often rather loosely applied, and the area designated differed from time to time. For our purposes, we may visualize it as the region around Paris. Chartres, Amiens, Reims, and Bourges may be thought of as suggesting its artistic if not its political boundaries.

Figs. 12.1–2 Laon. Cathedral. Started about 1165. Overall length 397 feet; 178 feet across transepts. Towers 187 feet high. Width across nave 67 feet. Height of vaults 78 feet. PHOTOGRAPHS BY CLARENCE WARD.

ROUBIER

Fig. 12.3 Chartres. Cathedral. The three western doorways, together with their sculpture, originally formed part of an earlier church and date from about 1145. Most of the fabric, including the north tower, is of the first half of the 13th Century. The spire on the south tower was added in 1510.

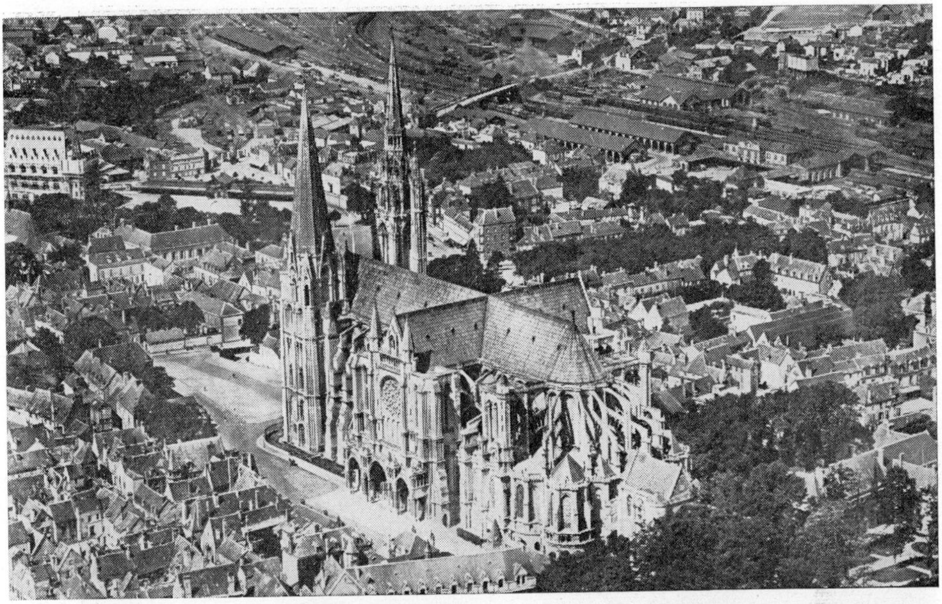

AERO-PHOTO

Fig. 12.4 (above) Chartres. Cathedral.

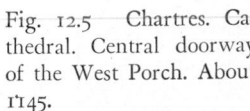

Fig. 12.5 Chartres. Cathedral. Central doorway of the West Porch. About 1145.

ARCHIVES PHOTOGRAPHIQUES

TEL

Fig. 12.6 Chartres. Cathedral. Statue of Melchisidek, on trumeau of the central door of the North Porch.

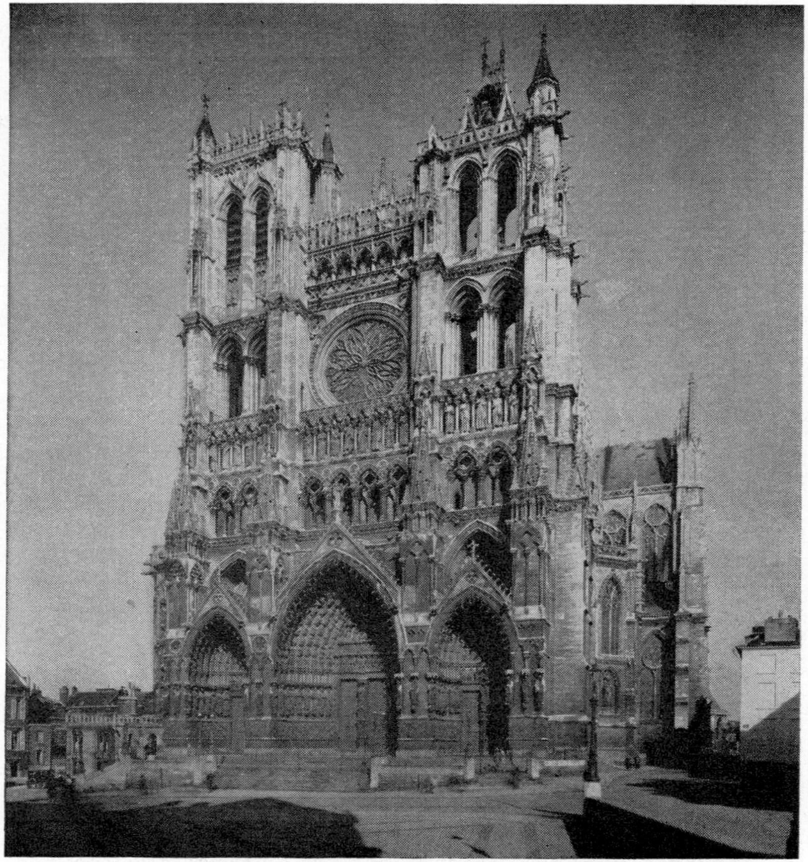

CLARENCE WARD

Fig. 12.7 Amiens. Cathedral. Started 1220. Height of north tower: 216 feet.

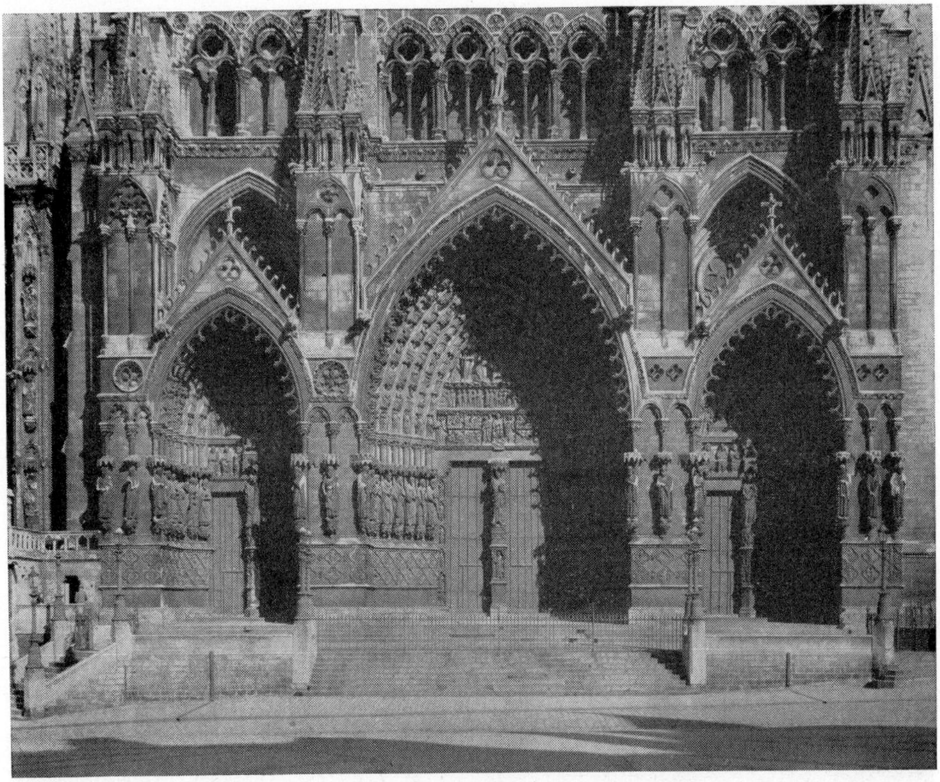

CLARENCE WARD

Fig. 12.8 Amiens. Western doors. Width across façade: about 130 feet.

GIRAUDON

Fig. 12.9 Amiens. View from the south. Height to ridge of the roof: 200 feet. To tip of flèche: 370 feet. Length: about 475 feet.

Fig. 12.10 (left) Amiens. North door on the West front, with statue of Saint Firmin on the trumeau. CLARENCE WARD. Fig. 12.11 (above) Trumeau of the central door, with "Le Beau Dieu." ROUBIER.

CLARENCE WARD

Fig. 12.12 Amiens. View into the vaults of the choir and apse. Height to underside of vaulting: about 139 feet.

CLARENCE WARD

Fig. 12.13 Amiens. View of the nave from the gallery of the south transept. Width of nave: about 46 feet. Extreme width of church from wall to wall: about 150 feet. Height to underside of vaulting: 139 feet.

CLARENCE WARD

Fig. 12.14 Reims. Cathedral.

Figs. 12.15–16 Reims. Main portal of the western façade. Left: *The Presentation in the Temple.* Right: *The Annunciation* and *The Visitation.* PHOTOGRAPHS BY ROUBIER.

ARCHIVES PHOTOGRAPHIQUES

Fig. 12.17 LeMans. Cathedral. The chevet. End of the 13th Century.

CLARENCE WARD

Fig. 12.18 Beauvais. The choir as rebuilt after the collapse of the vaults in 1284.

ANDERSON

Fig. 12.19 Florence. Santa Croce. Started 1294.

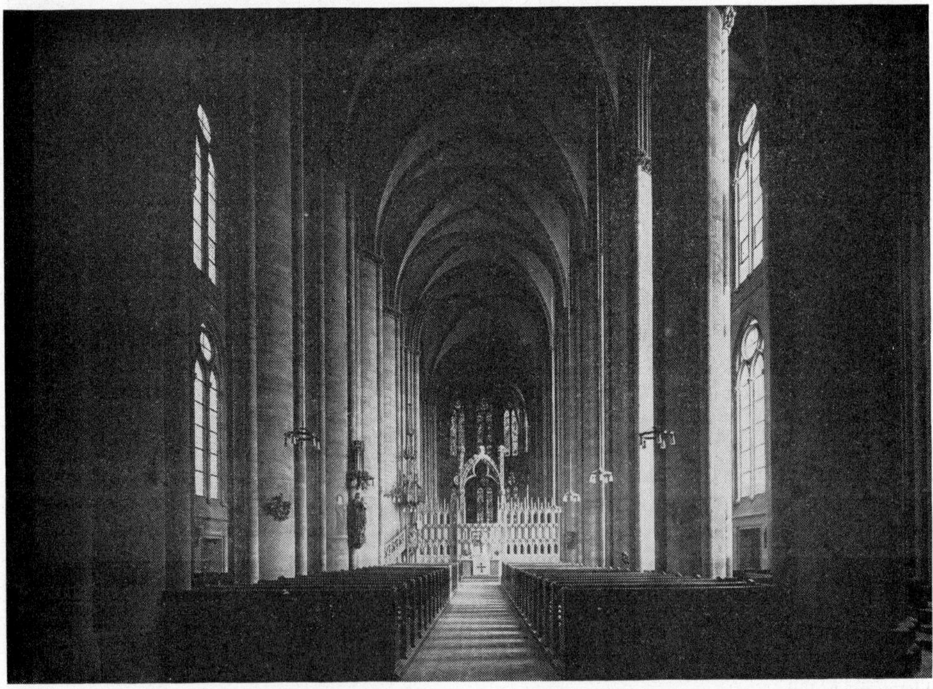

MARBURG

Fig. 12.20 Marburg. Saint Elizabeth's. Started 1235.

DEUTSCHER KUNSTVERLAG

Fig. 12.21 Ulm. Cathedral.

NATIONAL BUILDINGS RECORD

Fig. 12.22 Salisbury. Cathedral.

CROSSLEY

Fig. 12.23 Exeter. Cathedral. Vaulting of the Nave. 14th Century.

COUNTRY LIFE

Fig. 12.24 Cambridge. King's College Chapel. 1446 to about 1535.

NATIONAL BUILDINGS RECORD

Figs. 12.25–26 London. Westminster Abbey. Chapel of Henry the 7th. 1502–1520. View from the southeast (above) and view of the vaulting (below).

CROWN COPYRIGHT

Fig. 12.27 London. Westminster Hall. Hammerbeam roof. 1398. Span: 68 feet.

TUCK

WAYNE ANDREWS

Fig. 12.28 (above) Topsfield, Massachusetts. The Parson Capen House. 1683.

Fig. 12.29 (left) Cottage at Kingsbury Green, Middlesex.

M. S. BRIGGS

BROGI

ALINARI

Fig. 12.30 Milan. Cathedral. 1386–1500.
Fig. 12.31 (right) Siena. Palazzo Pubblico. 1287–1305. Tower. 1338–1405.

Figs. 12.32–33 Valladolid. College of San Gregorio. 1488. PHOTOGRAPHS BY RICHARD W. DWIGHT.

STOEDTNER

Fig. 12.34 Salamanca. University. Detail of façade.

MARBURG

Fig. 12.35 (left) Coutances. Saint Pierre. Finished 1494.

ARCHIVES PHOTOGRAPHIQUES

Fig. 12.36 Bourg. The Church of Brou. Tomb of Marguerite of Austria (died 1530).

FRENCH GOVERNMENT TOURIST OFFICE

Fig. 12.37 Chambord. Chateau. 1526–44. View from the air.

Once the internal logic of the new style had been made manifest at Saint Denis, development went on apace within the Ile de France. Perfection succeeded development, and refinement perfection. Word of the new advances went outward from the Ile de France to all parts of Christendom, attracting ready interest. As the 13th Century opened, almost every region was prepared to abandon its local Romanesque for the novel French manner — which was more or less perfectly understood, as later pages will demonstrate. And as he reads the text below, let the reader often remind himself that where the Gothic went, everything else that was French came with it. French books, French clothes and manners, French schools and procedures, French customs and institutions — all were a pattern for the rest of the Christian world. It is a simple statement of fact to say that the heart of Gothic Europe lay in Paris.

Reasons for the Cultural Primacy of France During the Gothic Era

Artistic styles do not emerge from nothing. The reader will naturally be curious to know what causes combined to produce the Gothic in the Ile de France at the particular juncture when it appeared, and to maintain northern France, moreover, as the vital and creative center of the style for better than 150 years.

The primacy of France depended upon more than the presence in that area of the cleverest architects; it derived from a great combination of things. In the first place, the power of the French kings, hitherto nominal, had been strengthened into the best centralized and best administered civil authority in Europe. Philip Augustus (reigned 1180–1223) was the creative genius who performed the final act of solidifying the royal power; superb in both diplomacy and force, he looms as a personality of brutal grandeur.

A much more attractive figure was Philip's grandson, Louis the 9th, who came to the throne in 1226. With the Pope, he had a *modus vivendi* which was positively cordial by contrast to the relations between the pontiff and other rulers. While both Germany and England were disrupted by civil wars, he managed to maintain comparative peace in France. He understood very well the value of court display as an adjunct to the royal dignity; but at the same time, and with the insight of an artist, he discerned the meaning of restraint in dress, and of gentleness and consideration in relations with others. His lifetime coincides with the general acceptance of the ennobling code of chivalry, which has ever since remained the European philosophy of manners. The contrast, indeed, between his court and that of his mighty grandfather has caused more than one historian to declare that there were absolutely no gentlemen in western Europe before the 13th Century. Profoundly religious, Louis injured his health by ascetic practices. An accomplished knight, he went on two Crusades; he died in North Africa on the second, in the year 1270. All the virtues of medieval society seem to have been concentrated in the person of this king. He was canonized in 1297, and he is usually known as Saint Louis.

In addition to being the seat of a monarchy both strong and good, the Ile de France had certain material reasons to aid her assumption of leadership. A glance at the map will show that the area was uncommonly well situated to participate in the general expansion of trade which took place all over Europe during the Gothic era. The celebrated and circulating *Fairs of Champaigne,* the most highly developed system of marketing since Rome, were conveniently at hand. The district was also ideally placed to profit by the traffic along several great river highways. Prosperity ensued, and must not be forgotten as a necessary pre-condition for the construction of great cathedrals.

By comparison to the rest of Europe, the Ile de France had, when considered as a likely center for a new era in human culture, the immense additional advantage of being the seat of the greatest of medieval universities. After existing informally for a generation and more, the University of Paris assumed its corporate identity shortly after 1150. It set a new standard for all the others, and it remains one of the best. No other institution has ever had teachers remotely comparable to the series of great men who taught there. Abelard and Peter Lombard were among its earlier professors, to be followed by Albertus Magnus and Saint Thomas Aquinas.

The university had started as a place where advanced students might receive instruction in the art of dialectic; and the earliest curriculum, if it may be called that, set the pattern for future policy. By importation from Spain and the Near East, Western scholars had gradually come into possession of better and more complete texts of Aristotle. They put their improved knowledge to work in a full-scale attempt to create a distinctively Christian philosophy which has ever since been known as the *Scholastic* — the name is not an attempt to describe their ideas; it merely means they taught in schools. The great single monument of Scholasticism is the *Summa Theologica* of Saint Thomas, a work that concerns us deeply because it bears intimate analogies with Gothic art.

Saint Thomas's great idea was to prove the truth of the Christian dogma by reference to data we see about us in the world. His ultimate aim was to present a consistent picture of the universe by showing that every item and object fitted into the divine scheme. The final conclusion to which his thinking leads us is the concept that there is no difference between the finite and the infinite, but that one is simply an extension of the other.

So brief a summary does severe injustice to a work almost as large in bulk as it is in intellectual grandeur; let the reader seek the original for himself. We have said enough, however, to make our present point, namely, that the colossal scale of Thomas's inquiry made brilliant powers of arrangement necessary. Thousands of ideas had to be marshalled in an effective system of heading and subheading. His success may be judged by the numerous ways in which one may hear it said that everything in the *Summa* fits into a place. Its minute parts fit not only one another, but make sense in relation to the general scheme. Word for word, the same statement is precisely true of the French Gothic cathedral.

It is not suggested that all the master builders were philosophers with university training, but it would not be surprising to find proof one day that some of them were. The important thing to appreciate is the certainty that Scholasticism had a much broader and more popular base than we might at first imagine. The artists of that period breathed in a deep respect for sustained intellectual activity. That, without doubt, was the reason why everything Gothic — over and above its other excellencies — had to stand logical analysis and satisfy the rational faculty. In comprehending the force and color of what has just been said, we must attempt to see that the Gothic mind felt no need to separate the idea of divinity from the physical world. To the builder of the period, it probably seemed plain common sense to regard the stones of his church as details in God's universal order. Thrust and abutment, for one in the same state of mind, were less brute forces, and more a department of celestial physics. Building (so viewed) became more than a skill; to understand it was to possess an essential constituent of the knowledge by which men might come to a Christian understanding of their world.

Such seem to have been the reasons for the superior ingenuity which distinguishes the Gothic of northern France from all the rest of Gothic, making it at once more scientific, more elegant, and more abstract. But still another reason — a final item to remind us that history does not always proceed along avenues laid out on the grand scale — must be adduced to show why the Ile de France became the birthplace of the new day. The simple fact of the matter is that the region had not been prosperous during the Romanesque period. Its monuments from that time are small and few. There thus existed the plainest possible reason for architectural activity: in Paris and the towns around it, there was a serious lack of adequate churches.

The Name Gothic

Before attempting to deal with the monuments, it is requisite that we pause briefly to explain how the new French style came to be called *Gothic*. The word is a misnomer, and in general use today only through habit. In no sense was it contemporary with the art it designates, and it originated as a taunt. The first persons to use it were men of the later Renaissance who wanted to give trenchant expression to their contempt for everything medieval. A more catholic taste would have corrected their criticism. A more precise knowledge of history would have corrected their language. There were no Goths left in Europe during the 12th Century; they had disappeared as a distinct ethnic group about 600 years earlier. It is strange that men of the highest mental powers could have entertained such views or made so gross an error, but we must remember that the modern historical perspective by which we profit dates only from the 19th Century.

Gothic retained its opprobrious connotation until the latter part of the 18th Century. Its use in any kindly sense was probably unknown until the time of Horace Walpole; but from that point onward, the word has gained an ever-increasing aura of prestige. Medieval art actually vied with the classical during the 19th Century as a field for art-historical research; the greatest monument from that movement is the still indispensable *Dictionaire raisonné de l'architecture francaise du XIe au XVIe siècle,* which was complete in 1868. The author was Viollet-le-Duc, and his ten handy volumes constitute a gold mine of lucid architectural drawings, some of which we reproduce here. It is also to be remembered that the Romantic movement of the same period (see below, pages 852–861) was largely inspired by sympathy for the medieval values. The result was that *Gothic* began to emerge as a term of praise.

Once established as such, it followed inevitably that an attempt would be made to refine its meaning. One of the most cogent thinkers along that line was the late Charles H. Moore, the first curator of the Fogg Museum at Harvard University. We have already referred to his organic theory of architecture (see above, pages 411–416). With respect to the name Gothic, Moore's intention was to reserve its use for monuments of demonstrable superiority — which to his mind meant only the most organic of all. Moore asserted that the essence of the Gothic style (and therefore the meaning of the name) was to be found in a peculiar structural system which depended for stability not upon inert mass ". . . but upon a logical adjustment of parts, whose opposing forces neutralize each other and produce a perfect equilibrium." All other buildings, however much they looked like Gothic, were relegated by Moore to the category of " pointed " architecture.

Moore learned his theory from Viollet-le-Duc, but his central position at the oldest and then the only great university in America lent his words a special influence which still continues. His assertions always had an unusual power to convince; and as a teacher of teachers, he has probably been more precisely remembered and explicitly quoted than any other critic of art.

Moore was correct in most of what he asserted but gravely wrong in what he denied. His strictures would deny the name Gothic to everything from the era except the architecture of northern France. In construing Gothic solely as architecture, he forgot the sculpture, the stained glass, the manuscripts, the furniture, the jewelry, and all the other arts that are truly Gothic — and to which, as a matter of fact, he alluded often in his writings. In presenting the development of Gothic architecture solely as a mechanical evolution brought about by a gradual refinement of engineering, he left out the crucial truth that there would have been no Gothic except for the presence in Europe of the Northern and Barbarian Style — of which, as we shall see presently, Gothic was the mature and ultimate expression.

Even today, there is substantial difference of opinion about the meaning and interpretation of the Gothic; scholars who are otherwise friends argue and contradict with feelings that tend to become aroused. How can the same visual data evoke such difference of reaction? The answer is that Gothic is at once a supremely emotional and a supremely rational art, a situation sometimes described by reference to a union of reason with faith. Characterized by infinite detail and strict rules of organization, it is also characterized by an extraordinary immediacy of appeal to the feelings. It dazzles the casual passer-by; and it furnishes the most rational and objective student with an experience that is very close to mysticism. Every expression of sincere opinion about so ramified and subtle an art is bound to contain much truth, and every attempt at explanation is equally bound to leave something unsaid.

Gothic as a Product of the Northern and Barbarian Style

As set forth in the last chapter, the Romanesque period signalized the emergence of the medieval mind from a keen and helpless sense of inferiority to Rome. The Gothic period marks the arrival of the European population upon a new plateau of existence: they were then ready to express themselves in terms of their own. They respected Rome, but they did not feel inferior. Dante's choice of the vernacular was one result of the new cast of mind. Gothic art was another.

It would be extreme to say that Roman influence was completely absent from the Gothic. Its presence in matters of detail is often plain enough; and it may be argued that Gothic engineering derived from a logical power ultimately traceable to the Romans. But however casual the inspection, it is manifestly clear that the effect of any work of art in the Gothic style is completely different from anything classical. The intention was not in the least the same, and the artistic idiom is impossible to explain by reference to the Antique.

Gothic is linear. At Ulm or Amiens or Toledo, wherever the eye falls, it finds itself on a line along which it is impelled to move. Gothic architects went to an immense amount of trouble to produce such an effect. In one way or another, almost everything they did had some relation to the production and multiplication of lines. They reduced the bulk of working members to the limit of safety — an excellent structural expedient, to be sure, but also a process which reduces the possibility that a pier or a buttress might impress us as a mass. The narrower and thinner anything becomes, the greater the likelihood that it will tell as a line.

The linear predilection is specially conspicuous in Gothic mouldings. If the splayed doorways of Amiens (Fig. 12.8) are compared with the Romanesque door at Aulnay (Fig. 11.7), the increased complexity of line will be instantly apparent. The cross section of any typical Gothic moulding (Fig. 12.10), to state it another way, is exceedingly subdivided and subtle by comparison to its simple Romanesque counterpart (Fig. 11.24). Indeed, it seems to be a fact that the ultimate ideal of every Gothic architect was to reduce his aesthetic means to unadulterated line. In a few extreme examples of the later Gothic (Figs. 12.24,26,30) that end was very nearly arrived at. Nothing built of stone could possibly be less plastic; and to become more linear, one would have to resort to structural steel and wire rope.

The instinct of every Gothic artist to multiply lines was part and parcel of a general stylistic desire to multiply parts. Every Gothic object, whether a manuscript page (Fig. 13.11) or a cathedral (Figs. 12.1–23) consists of an infinite number of small details, each intensively defined. Standing in the nave of Amiens (Figs. 12.12–13), who can count the parts? But when we walk into the Pantheon at Rome (Fig. 7.1), we see only two things: the cylindrical rotunda beneath, and the hemisphere above.

In their methods of composition, the Gothic artists felt no need of geometric order. Symmetry like that of the western front of the Cathedral at Paris is rare rather than common, and even there is far from strict. The situation at Chartres (Fig. 12.3) is much closer to the normal for Gothic. The two western towers are radically different; but the eccentric arrangement is not only more interesting, but more true to the nature of the style.

By contrast to the classical artist whose instinct was to enclose his compositions within actual frames of a simple geometric outline, or to suggest in some subtle but unmistakable way the existence of an unseen but very present boundary line (see above, pages 70, 83, 109), the Gothic artist invariably attempts to produce a silhouette distinguished by innumerable sharp projections and innumerable deep indentations. His smallest punctuation mark (Fig. 13.7) thrusts its little spiny points out into the space around it. Wherever statues are comparatively free from the restrictions ordinarily imposed by architecture, they are given a very complicated outline (Fig. 13.13). In architecture, a broken outline was feasible only at the top — which suggests the genesis of the vertical emphasis for which the Gothic church is noted. It being impossible to throw the eye off in all four directions, the decision was made to emphasize the easiest and most practical direction: upward. All lines lead up until they converge at the tip of a spire. Momentum then carries the eye out into the sky (Fig. 12.38).

But even on the skyline, a dissolving silhouette was by no means easy to provide. A few odd situations made such an outline almost natural if not automatic; Mont Saint Michel was perhaps the most fortunate site of all from that special point of view. Otherwise, it was requisite to build unusually tall steeples, as at Salisbury (Fig. 12.22), or to multiply miniature finials in prodigal fashion as at Milan (Fig. 12.30).

Such are the major elements of a more abstract kind that go to make up the Gothic style: the linear idiom, the myriad detail, the dynamic and eccentric composition which demands the broken silhouette. To these we must add a minor element that has to do with content: whenever the Gothic artist undertook representation, he demonstrated a powerful taste for the grotesque. When rendering the human body, he did not hesitate to distort whenever it helped or convenienced him.

All of these factors in combination can signify only one thing: Gothic was a product of the Northern and Barbarian Style. (See above, pages 295–298.) No other artistic source can possibly explain it except for superficial details. By comparison with earlier monuments in the same style, Gothic was disciplined by civilization and inspired by Christianity, but it was nevertheless the product of a deep and long dormant yearning for an authentically northern art — which made itself manifest just before the middle of the 12th Century, swept all before it, and came forward in full force in 13th-Century France.

Chronology

We shall find it convenient to recognize three subdivisions within the Gothic era: the *Early Gothic*, the *High Gothic*, and the *Late Gothic*.

Taking Saint Denis as the initial monument in the new style, a general overview of the second half of the 12th Century will show that a number of buildings may be grouped together as forming a stylistic group. A distinct departure from the Romanesque, these churches differ from those of the next century in the matter of proportions. They are heavier; and their effect is quieter. The term *transitional* is sometimes applied to them, but its unfortunate connotations make it better to refer to the group as Early Gothic.

The great Gothic century was the 13th; it is to work of that time we refer

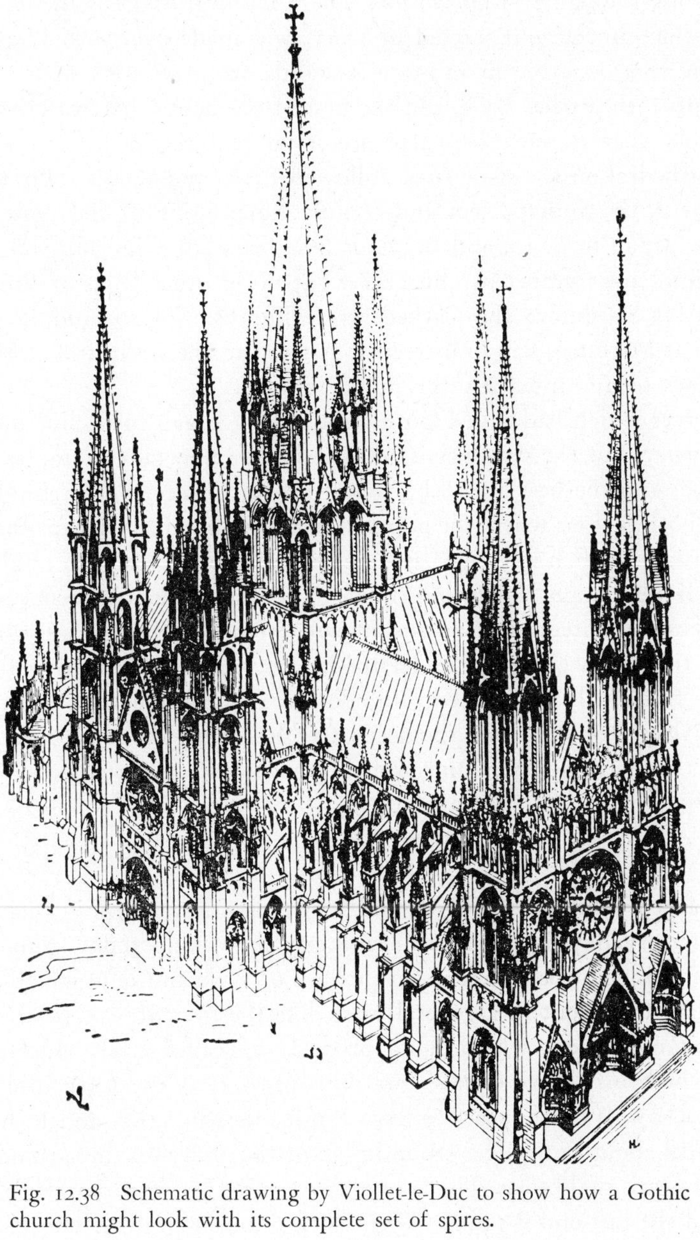

Fig. 12.38 Schematic drawing by Viollet-le-Duc to show how a Gothic church might look with its complete set of spires.

when we use the name High Gothic. The Cathedral of Paris, designed as an Early Gothic church and started in 1163, was made over into High Gothic after a fire that occurred in 1235; as it stands, we may think of it as the last monument in the earlier style, and the first of the new. Chartres (the body of the church, that is, not the parts preserved and retained from the Early Gothic cathedral on the same site) followed Paris, and Reims followed Chartres. Amiens, the most perfect and complete expression of the 13th Century style, was begun in 1220, and Beauvais five years later. During the same period, an immense number of churches went up in other parts of Europe: the Cathedral at Salisbury; the Cathedrals at Burgos, Toledo, and Leon; Saint Elizabeth at Marburg; San Francesco at Assisi, and the Cathedral at Siena. Europe has not seen so much church building since.

The forces which had called Gothic into being began to decline during the 14th Century, but the style persisted. The latest important examples fall well after 1500, and the best are to be found not in France, but in England and Spain — both regions where the population was reluctant to accept the taste of the Renaissance which was, by that time, at full flood in Italy. In High Gothic, as we shall see, design had found much of its motivation in structural facts, but the later architects felt no inspiration from the engineering which had for some time been generally understood. They understood it so well, indeed, that they frequently performed tours de force of construction. Most of their imaginative energy went into the decorative aspects of the style, a department in which they have not been and probably never will be surpassed.

THE EARLY GOTHIC

The Cathedrals at Sens, Noyon, and Senlis must have been, in their original condition, very like Suger's Saint Denis. As they stand today, somewhat altered and changed, they present perplexities of style and date which foreclose an adequate treatment in a general work like the present.

The last monument which could properly be called Early Gothic (and a church which may have equals, but no superiors) is the Cathedral at Laon (Figs. 12.1–2). Work appears to have commenced in 1165, and to have continued until about 1225. The ground plan of the church is unusual among the large cathedrals of France. The transepts extend further from the nave than usual, and the east end is square. Both features occur in other churches of the same diocese, and both are typical of England. Perhaps the matter is to be explained by the fact that an Englishman held the see during the early part of the 12th Century.

Laon is also highly distinctive in elevation. It has five towers: two for the western façade, as in Norman Romanesque; two flanking the nave westward of the transepts; and another over the crossing. It was intended that there should be two more, or seven in all. The remarkable thing is not the number of towers included in the plan, for the Gothic went even further than the Romanesque in the matter of the broken skyline, but that as many as five were actually put up. Most other churches never received the full complement of towers originally visualized by the builder. The towers themselves are magnificent. Poking their heads out at different levels are statues of oxen, in memory of the beasts who hauled the stone up the precipitous hill on which the town and its cathedral stand. "I have been in many countries," wrote Villard of Honnecourt (the only Gothic architect from whom we inherit a word; see below, pages 459–461), "but I have never seen such other towers." Aside from the special magic of Laon, what are the differences that separate the Early Gothic from the Romanesque? The façade of the Church of the Trinity at Caen (Fig. 11.16) will give us a closely analogous composition in the earlier style, and comparison will bring out the following differences.

The Romanesque building, for all its splayed doors and blind arcades, is fundamentally a plastic expression. One is impressed with the stone: its weight, its shape, and the solidity of the masses into which it is built. It can hardly be said that Laon is without plastic interest, but something has been added. One is first impressed, perhaps, with the play of surfaces in and out. The splayed doors are much deeper. The wheel window is set well into the thickness of the wall. Going higher, we find that the western towers are not simple units of shape as they were at Caen, but consist of many smaller parts cleverly coordinated with each other to make an integral whole. There is so much openwork that the voids begin to do as much work upon our sensibilities as the solids.

Whatever else it may be, the total effect of Laon is considerably more complicated than that of any Romanesque building. There is a greater articulation of parts, and there are more parts. Perhaps the most important aspect of the result is the creation of spatial relationships more subtle and ramified than any to be found in all the earlier styles of architecture. Space penetrates the masonry in numerous places, and at new and unexpected angles.

The spatial expectations raised by the exterior are not belied indoors (Fig. 12.2). The actual area of openwork has been made relatively much greater than ever before, and the masonry correspondingly reduced in bulk. The difference from Romanesque will be made plain if we once again avail ourselves of a comparison. Fig. 12.39 shows the nave arcade, the clearstory, and part of the cross vaulting of the Old Cathedral at Salamanca, a design that is Gothic in every sense except that the hand and heart of its architect remained Romanesque. The archways and the windows scarcely impress one. The mass and shape of the masonry tell the whole story. Without suggesting better or worse, it is evident that the builder of Laon had possessed himself of a different architectural vocabulary.

Turning with more particularity to the details of the fabric, it will be noted that there are four horizontal divisions in the nave system. The triforium space, that is to say, is subdivided; over a high gallery of compound arches, there is a smaller and shallower gallery in bays of three simple arches carried by colonnettes. The four-part arrangement had the advantage of gaining height, a dimension that was put to very good use on the exterior of the church. The lower buttresses, meeting the nave vaults at the spring, are supported directly by the gallery vaults, and there is a heavy and somewhat primitive flying buttress above each of these, impinging upon the nave arches approximately at the haunch. The same four-part arrangement was characteristic of all the Early Gothic churches.

Fig. 12.39 Salamanca. Old Cathedral. Drawing of two bays of the nave.

The cross vaults of the nave are of the six-part type. An extra transverse rib is run across the nave through the intersection of each pair of diagonals, thus dividing each bay of vaulting into six cells rather than the usual four. Six-part vaulting was popular in France both during the Romanesque period and for the Early Gothic. It is difficult to say why. The extra rib helps very little in the matter of reducing thrusts at the fundamental points of concentration, and the extra cells of the vault complicate an overly complicated form still further. But as compared with the best Romanesque vaulting, the vaults at Laon reflect a major advance. For a detailed discussion, we refer the reader ahead to pages 472–480. At this point, it will suffice to say that a more thorough understanding of the cross vault had made excellent clearstory lighting both safe and convenient, and that the age-old problems of church architecture were very close to a final solution at this time.

One cannot look at Laon or any other Gothic building without being impressed by an elegance heretofore unknown in the history of medieval architecture. Simple by comparison with later Gothic, the mouldings used at Laon are delicate and subtle by comparison with the Romanesque. Not only has the absolute bulk of each part been cut down, but there was also evidently a serious preoccupation with proportions and relative proportions. One instance of that is the graduation in the weight and thickness of parts as the fabric rises; the nave arcade is heavy, the triforium light, and the clearstory lighter still. Still another indication of the new aesthetic sense is to be seen in the clever equilibrium between horizontal and vertical lines, both dimensions being emphasized and both equally so. Finally, it is significant that structural logic has been tempered with a nice feeling for form. The engaged shafts which correspond to the ribs of the vaulting come down only to the nave capitals, and there they stop, permitting the lower piers to be unencumbered and neat.

THE HIGH GOTHIC: THE CATHEDRAL AT AMIENS

It is customary to think of the 13th-Century cathedrals of northern France as representing the Gothic in its best and most typical form. Considerations of chronological priority do not enter into the verdict, because the French churches are almost exactly contemporary to those of other lands. The preeminence of the Gothic of the Ile de France rests, rather, upon considerations of design. As a group, the churches of that region are more uniform in appearance than those of any other region. In their construction, they conform more thoroughly to what we may call the disciplines of the style. In matters of detail, they demonstrate a richness and polish — and yet a harmonious simplicity — not duplicated elsewhere, or at any other time.

Among the French churches, Amiens (Figs. 12.7–13) is the one that demonstrates the greatest over-all elegance and coherence. In the evolution of Gothic, it came at the perfect moment when all the subtleties of the style were understood, and before any tendency toward elaboration had started to assert itself.

Like most other cathedral churches in France, Amiens was dedicated to the Virgin Mary. Dedications to the Virgin had been frequent enough in other times, but during the 13th Century there were so many that we almost forget all the other saints. The reason is not far to seek: at this time, the inner quality of French society was coming to full flower in the code we call Chivalry. In sum, that code assigned to the female the staggering responsibility for maintaining on earth almost every kind of idealism. Her task began with personal loveliness, and ended only with the attainment of transcendent virtue. Her person was sacred, and her mere presence was enough to enforce better behavior than men considered suitable as between themselves. The thought of her was an ethical power extending outward to the ends of the earth; in distant lands, it inspired her true knight to valor altogether beyond his ordinary capacity. Only the Madonna might conceivably fulfill every detail of so amazing an obligation. Hence the cult of the Madonna in Gothic art, the innumerable churches dedicated to her, the countless pictures and statues. She was the ultimate fulfillment of womanhood, and a queen who owned the hearts as well as the allegiance of all mankind.

Amiens owes much of its excellence to the fortunate circumstance of having been built to a single set of plans, and by a single continuous building effort long enough to complete most of the fabric. The present edifice replaces an earlier church which had been struck by lightning in 1218 and badly damaged by fire. Work on the new cathedral apparently commenced immediately. An inscription in the pavement (now removed) may be translated as follows:

> In the year of grace 1220 this work was first begun. Evrard of blessed memory was then bishop of this diocese and Louis son of Philip the Wise was king of France. He who was master builder was Master Robert and surnamed de Lusarches. Master Thomas de Cormont succeeded him, and afterwards his son Master Regnault who caused this inscription to be placed here in the year 1288.*

It appears that the choir of the old church was still usable. Therefore the builders of Amiens started their work with the façade, a reversal of the usual custom. By 1228, they had raised the nave to the clearstory level, and the nave was vaulted over by 1236. The façade was by then complete up to the level of the string course just above the rose window. Sixteen years had sufficed for an immense amount of construction.

From that point on, things progressed more slowly. By 1247, the choir was finished up to the level of the triforium string course. Rather little seems to have been accomplished during the next decade. A severe fire during the year 1258 did a good deal of damage at the east end of the building. In 1279, with considerable ceremony, relics were translated to the new sanctuary, an event which probably signalizes the final completion of the choir and apse.

But like most other Gothic buildings, Amiens was destined to become venerable but never complete. Between 1366 and 1402, the two western towers were carried to their present height. There is no knowing whether they were meant to be left square-headed or to have spires. Over the crossing, probably

* As translated by A. K. Porter, *Medieval Architecture,* Vol. 2, page 304.

in accordance with the intention of the original designer, a delicate spire was raised. Such a spire in such a place is referred to as a *flèche;* the same word had long been used to denote a dart or an arrow. The present flèche is a reconstruction of 1529, and a good example of Late Gothic openwork. The gallery between the western towers was the last substantial addition; it dates from the 19th Century, and Viollet-le-Duc was the designer.

Fig. 12.40 Paris. Bibliothèque Nationale. Album of Villard de Honnecourt. Folio 10 verso. The Towers of Laon.

The Builders of Amiens

The name of Robert de Luzarches introduces us to the idea of the master builder. It also plunges us into one of the major mysteries of medieval history. Who built the great cathedrals? On that important question, our sources are almost silent, and we shall never have a satisfactory answer unless it be found one day in some paper that still lies hidden.

The suggestion has repeatedly been put forward that each community built its own cathedral. In order to bolster up that notion, reference is frequently made to hysterical demonstrations of religious enthusiasm which now and again found expression in parades. A notable instance occurred at Chartres in 1144; and at about the same time, the Abbot Suger wrote of events at Saint Denis: "How often did both our own people and our very devoted neighbors, nobles and serfs together, tie about their arms, their chests, their shoulders, the rope attached to columns to drag them up the hill! Thus instead of beasts of burden, they did the labor." *

The popularity of that particular form of religious exercise did not last long. In 1194, an attempt seems to have been made at Chartres to duplicate the per-

* As translated by A. K. Porter, *Medieval Architecture,* Vol. 2, pages 150 ff.

formance of 1144, but without success. The whole affair appears to have been a 12th-Century phenomenon, and the instances recorded smack of the remarkable rather than the customary. We may therefore doubt whether any significant bulk of building material was ever transported by the device of religious parades.

It is conspicuous, moreover, that the records mention only the transport of raw materials. They do not say that members of the community were permitted to shape and assemble the stones. It is one thing to work off enthusiasm by pulling a cart, and quite another to cut the voussoirs for an arch that will stand 140 feet in the air. The theory of popular and spontaneous construction is attractive because it is both romantic and democratic, but we dare not believe it. The Gothic church is too large, too complex, too elegant, and too closely reasoned a piece of work — something, in short, utterly beyond the capacity of amateurs.

Fig. 12.41 Paris. Bibliothèque Nationale. Album of Villard de Honnecourt. Folio 18 verso. Cubist studies of various figures.

It is certain, in fact, that experts were employed. Most of them seem to have been laymen. In addition to Robert de Lusarches and his successors at Amiens, we know a good many others by name: Jean le Loup, Peter Parler, William of Sens, Ingebram, Walter of Melun, Villard of Honnecourt — merely to list a few. But when the medieval documents mention these men, they simply cite a forgotten name and say no more. To us such treatment is amazing in view of the responsibilities entrusted to them by their contemporaries, and especially so when compared with the wealth of biographical detail about second- and even third-rate artists of the Renaissance. Anonymity on the part of the great is one of the pieces of evidence that separates the Middle Ages from the modern world. People simply did not set the same value upon fame. The Abbot Suger, to cite the most conspicuous instance of them all, was so much impressed with his new Saint Denis that he wrote a substantial account of the building procedure — but he fails to say one word about the master builder he was privileged to employ.

As to the building procedures, we know surprisingly little. We can get some idea of what the ordinary 13th-Century architectural drawing looked like from the notebook of Villard of Honnecourt, today preserved in the Bibliothèque Nationale (Figs. 12.40–42). It contains numerous drawings. The rendering is strictly linear, and the obvious intention was merely to show the mechanical relationship between part and part. Far from precise, Villard's drawings are nevertheless wonderfully direct and purposeful. Such drawings were almost certainly supplemented and reinforced by a small model of the building. We have an occasional reference to such models, though none have survived.

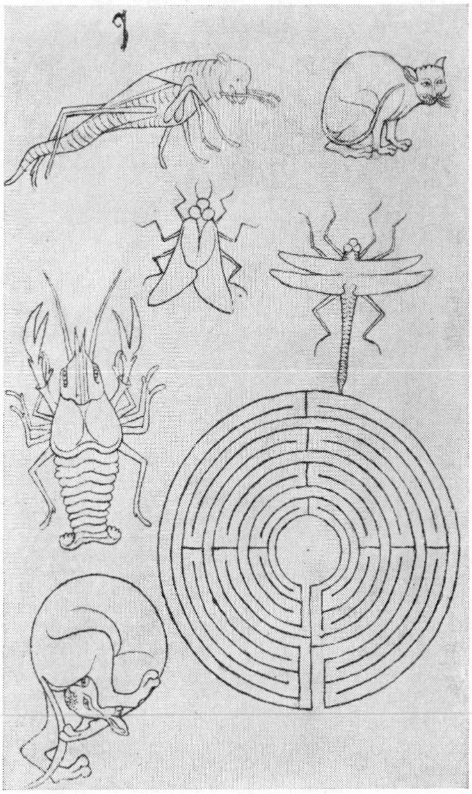

Fig. 12.42 Paris. Bibliothèque Nationale. Album of Villard de Honnecourt. Folio 7 verso. Animals and a maze.

When plans and model, such as they were, had been approved, what did the master builder do next? Suger speaks of summoning skilled modelers and sculptors; but whom did he summon, how did he know they were skilful, and from where? The matter is an almost complete mystery, and any supposition we may make must be speculative.

Because a great many men of special training were needed, it is obvious that the required number could not have been found at Amiens and could never have supported themselves there except during a period of work on a very large building. If they did not come from Amiens, they must have come from somewhere else, and it seems necessary to suppose that they came together. We may guess, in short, at the existence of some sort of corporation. If so, what rules did they have, what by-laws? Was Master Robert an elected officer, or an employer?

The theory of migrant communities of artists and builders is supported to some extent by the congruence of style in some of the sculpture at Reims, Bamberg, and Strasbourg, making it seem likely that the same men worked at all three places at different times. But staggering though it is to the imagination, great numbers of these men — comparable in creative power to the famous artists of Greece and the Renaissance — have literally vanished from the face of the earth without leaving a hint of their personal or corporate identity. We have their art; but of themselves, we know nothing.

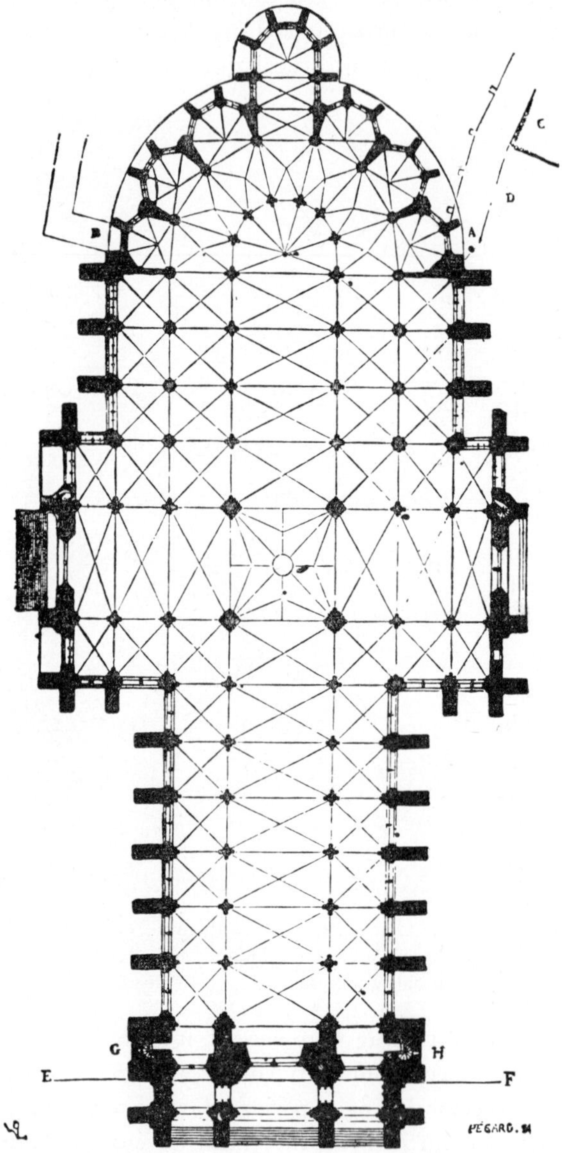

Fig. 12.43 Amiens. Cathedral. Plan.

The Plan

An outline drawing of the ground plan of Amiens (Fig. 12.43) has a deceptively stubby proportion which is altogether obliterated in the building itself by the articulation of the elevation. Such a drawing shows us a cruciform church, with transepts of very moderate projection, and a very long choir. The three western doorways open directly into the nave and side aisles. West of the crossing, the space which might have been used for a second set of aisles is subdivided by lateral partitions into chapels. The transepts have three aisles, and a five-aisle arrangement is used for the length of the choir. An ambulatory of one aisle runs around the semicircle of the apse, opening into a set of seven radial chapels.

By contrast to the square bays which were popular in some Romanesque schools, the main vaults of Amiens are arranged in a series of narrow oblongs, with the long axis of each oblong at right angles to that of the nave. Such was the usual scheme for Gothic. By adjusting the proportions of the oblongs, it was perfectly convenient to make them correspond with any desired intercolumniation and to any rational arrangement of the aisle vaults. The need for an alternating system of supports was thus eliminated. In order to achieve this new freedom in plan, it was necessary for the Gothic designers to invent a radically ingenious arrangement of the vault-ribs, a matter to which we shall return in due course.

But there is more to be discerned in the plan of Amiens than this. A great many persons testify that French Gothic plans bring up memories of lace or of flowers. The impression is far from superficial. We must expect to understand Gothic in terms of lines and open spaces. It is only occasionally an art of surfaces, and rarely an art of mass. Of that general condition, there is more than a suggestion in the ground plan. As indicated on the plan by the inked-in sections, the total area of masonry is minute by comparison to the total space enclosed by the boundaries of the building. It may be said, indeed, that the Gothic church has no walls. In the traditional sense of the wall as a structural member under compression, that is literally true. In Gothic, the weight of the building is carried on a framework of arches which spring from a series of isolated and separate supports. The interior is protected from the weather by immense windows.

The Elevation

Most of the French cathedrals are city churches. Most of them face on city squares. For that reason and in some contrast with the Gothic of England and Germany, the French churches were designed on the assumption that the western façade — considered as a composition in its own right — was more important than the appearance of the whole building as seen from some other angle. The façades of Amiens and Chartres (Figs. 12.7,3) give a good idea of the grace and power with which such churches loom above their surroundings. Of the two, Amiens is the more typical, for Chartres had a checkered history to which we shall allude from time to time.

As the prime illustration of a special type in the history of architecture, the façade of Amiens deserves special attention. The fundamentals of the composition come directly from the Norman Romanesque (see above, pages 405–406), but during the 13th Century certain Gothic features became standard. Upon occasion, these latter might be large or small, and placed high or low, but there seems to have been a feeling that all ought to be there.

The façade is divided into three parts both vertically and horizontally. The two towers and their smaller doors correspond to the side aisles. The large central door opens into the nave. Strong vertical buttresses which, though continuous, exhibit an extraordinary variety of form at different levels, mark these three vertical divisions. The verticals have enough relief so that they always take the sun, and stand out as axial elements unifying the façade. Most photographs have been taken in a diffused light, but the French façade is at its best when bold dark shadows are cast to the right or left.

The horizontal boundary lines are plainly visible, though considerably less vigorous. An elaborate moulding runs across the façade at the height of the gable over the central doorway. The next horizontal division is itself subdivided. It consists of an open gallery of delicate, pointed compound arches, and a " row of kings " — a series of male statues in niches. The notion that they represent either kings of France or kings of Judah may have a basis in fact, but probably has an even stronger basis in fancy. Above the row of kings, we find the rose window with its curvilinear tracery, and the two towers which, at this level, are pierced with arches.

The thing that counts about the tripartite horizontal division is not the mere fact of its existence, but the relation maintained between solids and voids. In the lowest section, there is scarcely any open work at all. In the middle section, the voids and the solids are approximately equal. In the upper part, the openings occupy more area than the masonry. There is reason behind such a graduation. The lowest and heaviest part of the façade corresponds closely in height with the nave arcade, the heaviest section within. The middle part of the façade fits with the triforium level, and the more open upper section has its interior counterpart in the clearstory. The designers, we may guess, felt driven to prove the unity of the whole building by demonstrating in this way the intimate harmony of its parts. It is by such insistence upon relationships that they show themselves to work with artistic problems in very much the same way that the Scholastic philosophers worked with religion.

A similar instinct for order and relationship made itself felt in the disposition of the numerous statues on the façade and throughout the church. Because each cathedral was in this respect an individual proposition, we must avoid any suggestion that the Gothic designers followed a book of rules. It is true, however, that they recognized certain general principles of hierarchy, and arranged their sculpture with a nice sense for precedence. It will be understood in what follows that we are concerned here not with the statues as such (which is the business of the next chapter), but only with the architectural implications of the sculpture.

On the *trumeau* of the central doorway (the place of highest honor) we usually find, as at Amiens (Fig. 12.11), a statue of Christ. In a similar position on the trumeaux of the lateral doorways, are statues of the Virgin and of Saint Firmin, the first bishop of Amiens who died a martyr's death in the year 289 (Fig. 12.10). In the central tympanum over the Savior, we find the event for which the universal church had engaged to prepare mankind: the Last Judgment. In that position it catches the final glow of the setting sun which one day will set on the last evening of the world. In the splay of the central doorway, statues of the Apostles flank that of the Christ. Saint Firmin is accompanied by other saints of whom the cathedral possessed relics, and Mary is accompanied by figures recalling the story of her life.

The principal statues of the façade thus took account of sacred personages and events of both general and local importance; and, in a similar manner of having a reason for everything, it was more or less customary to put Old Testament subject matter on the façade of the northern transept because the northern dark and cold seemed analogous to unenlightenment. New Testament material was common for the southern façade, facing the region of warmth and light.

In controlling the style of their statues, the Gothic architects were less unreasonable than the Romanesque (see above, page 417), but they were rigorous. No matter how sacred the subject, the statue was thought of as an embellishment of the building and subject to architectural rules. Because Gothic was fundamentally a linear art, that general proposition was construed as meaning that statues should be used to lend variety and interest to architectural lines. On the façade of Amiens, we find them used for almost nothing else.

A straightedge placed along the axis of one of the great verticals bisects not only the buttress it follows, but several statues as well. The little statuettes that decorate the separate orders of the splayed doors are arranged to conform with the curvature of the arch — not with the rules of representation, for some of them appear to be in the act of defying gravity. It will be further observed that each of the large statues in the door jambs below is placed in such a way that its axis, if projected, carries into the curve of an order in the archway above.

The relationship between architecture and sculpture, as just described, seems to have been well-understood as early as Saint Denis. Like many another logical system, it was more severely and literally applied when new. Thus, the statues on the West Porch at Chartres (Fig. 12.5), which dates from about 1145 and formed part of the Early Gothic church replaced by the present one, are uncompromising in their architectural reference. In order to make certain that each figure would tell as a line, the vertical dimension was radically exaggerated, and the poses were made to conform with the principle of frontality (see above, page 22).

The 13th Century was slightly less doctrinaire. The *Beau Dieu* of Amiens (Fig. 12.11) was designed with a primary regard for its architectural purpose. The proportions of the body were governed by the dimensions of the trumeau to which it was to be attached. The pose is strictly vertical, and the elbows are held in contact with the sides. The right hand, raised in benediction, projects straight up. Only in the drapery is there a suggestion of the diagonal. But as Fig. 12.11 indicates, there is much naturalism in the anatomy and much plasticity in the modeling.

If we study the façade still further, it will be unmistakably clear that its designer went to a great deal of trouble to provide a proper place for every statue. A great many figures stand in niches. For others, corbels project from the wall, and there are canopies overhead. The design of the building, it may even be said, demands a statue wherever we see one: sculpture is literally incorporated into the surface of the walls.

So quickly stated and reviewed, the Gothic theory of sculptural decoration sounds rigid and unfeeling, but no such impression can be entertained when we judge by the results. An amazing number of statues were accommodated by these methods. Reims is said to have about 2,000 in all, of which 530 appear on the western front alone. Yet no taint of excess mars its beauty.

A Gothic artist would doubtless have declared that the purpose of decoration was to increase the beauty of the thing decorated — the meaning of which we may comprehend by walking away from a Gothic church until we reach the distance where the eye can no longer resolve small details. The statuary then begins to tell as a flicker of light and dark enlivening the fundamental lines of the church. At a very great distance when even that much may not be accurately discerned, one is still conscious of an opulence of texture never to be observed where sculpture is lacking.

The transepts, which scarcely show up at all in the ground plan, were given during the 13th Century a development only less imposing than the western front. They rise as high as the nave (Fig. 12.4), and each has a considerable façade of its own.

It must be confessed, however, that the French architects never arrived at an adequate handling of the great volumes imposed by the dimensions of the interior. Such becomes distinctly and disturbingly apparent whenever one takes a station to the north or south, and sees the cathedral in full broad-side (Fig. 12.9). The western towers, so imposing from the front, seem to shrink and lose their power. The elaborate transepts lack the strength, and the flêche lacks the scale to adjust the composition. The long, level ridge of the roof obtrudes itself as the most conspicuous feature in sight; and the dissolving silhouette — that essential of all northern art — is destroyed. Feeling that the level ridge is "out of style," every historian has made the most of each bit of evidence that might indicate an original intention on the part of the Gothic architects to multiply towers and otherwise adjust the situation. Some have even gone to the trouble of preparing drawings to show what the ideal cathedral ought to look like — as, for example, the drawing by Viollet-le-Duc reproduced in our Fig. 12.38.

The eastern aspect of a French Gothic church is, however, almost as grand as the façade. From that point of view, the flying buttresses show up to the best advantage. They meet the vault ribs at points of concentration, and swing through the air carrying the thrusts to the vertical pier buttresses which are placed at intervals around the semicircle of the apse. The entire assembly (apse, radial chapels, and buttresses) is known as the *chevet*. The chevet of Amiens is not the best, so we substitute for it that of Le Mans (Fig. 12.17), perhaps the most powerful and ascending composition of them all.

The Interior

The nave of Amiens (Fig. 12.13) has long been recognized as the supreme achievement of 13th-Century architecture. The nave proper consists of seven oblong bays of four-part ribbed vaulting, carried on compound piers. A square bay covers the crossing; its ribs are arranged in the pattern of a four-pointed star. Beyond the crossing, the choir extends in four more oblong bays to the apse. The principal difference between the nave and the choir is the fact that in the choir, in keeping with the somewhat later date, both triforium and clearstory were glazed.

The problem of the basilican church with fireproof roof and good, even generous clearstory lighting had been solved with the Early Gothic. The special excellence of Amiens depends not so much on any fundamental advance over immediately previous church design, but upon a perfect fulfillment of everything good in the Gothic style. In a period noted for grace, the architectural details drawn by Robert de Lusarches stand nearly alone in their elegance. Every line and contour has a modest beauty, and in no other Gothic church was so nice a standard maintained throughout the entire fabric. But perfection of detail would not be enough to justify the assertion that Amiens is the best of the Gothic churches. The building is notable for the success with which the possibilities of scale and proportion have been realized, and it is our best illustration of the Gothic concept of spatial composition.

Although the Gothic architect did everything he could to reduce the volume of his masonry, he still had to use a great deal of it. And even though the voids are more important than the solids, the scale and proportion of the stonework at Amiens was nevertheless a vital matter. As with all Gothic buildings, the whole is an ensemble of small parts — a northern infinity of detail. In a large cathedral interior, the effect was to produce in an exaggerated form the experience noted at Hagia Sophia (see above, page 348). We construct our concept of the size of the whole by adding up, as it were, the sum of the parts. When one considers that the apse is about 125 yards from a man who has just come in through the western doors, and the vaulting about 135 feet above the level of his eyes, it becomes evident that even the best photograph in the world can convey very little of the real impression of scale. In the original condition of the building, all of the windows were presumably of stained glass. The dim and colored light must have exaggerated, as though by atmospheric perspective, the actual distances and sizes.

In addition to the effect of absolute size, established as described, the vertical and horizontal dimensions received direct and unmistakable emphasis. The nave is more than three times as high as its width. The pointed arches point up, a fact often lost sight of by those critics who cannot pause in their haste to explain that thrust is reduced when an arch is pointed. Verticality was also emphasized by an almost infinite repetition of vertical lines.

It is easy, of course, to stress one dimension at the expense of another; but as compared with the other Gothic cathedrals, the interior of Amiens is remarkable for the reconcilement between the vertical and horizontal. A good many things contribute to the power of the long axis. First, the rhythmic repeat of the bays, which produces a sense of progression toward the apse and altar. Then there are three linear horizontals which lead the eye toward the far end of the church: the successive capitals of the nave arcade form one such line; the floral moulding at the lower boundary of the triforium is another; and the string course along the base of the clearstory is a third.

To a great extent, the wonderful harmony of height and length was made possible by a relaxation of the theory of structural logic. Although the excellence of the French cathedrals has often been cited as *prima facie* proof of the organic dogma, the fact is that detail for detail Amiens is less precise than Sant' Ambrogio at Milan (see above, page 413) when it comes to furnishing us with an illustration of form governed by structural principles. At Amiens, the shafts that correspond to the wall ribs are radically reduced in diameter, and are carried down only to the triforium level. The shafts corresponding to the diagonals are only slightly larger, and they terminate on the abaci of the nave capitals. The only verticals of any substantial size are those under the transverse arches. They alone go to the floor, and only they are permitted to cross over a horizontal line. It is important to point out in passing that there is no mechanical basis for the diameter assigned to each of the clustered vertical ribs. Their size is not in proportion to what they carry; if the wall rib is adequate to bear the weight upon it, the shaft under the transverse arch is altogether too big. The dainty order of the graduated sizes simply softens the boundary between the wall surface and the verticals engaged upon it. They rise gently from their background, and blend gently back into it.

A sober succession of declarative sentences may with good luck describe all the details we have mentioned, but more poetical language is needed if we are to give any hint of their effect when brought into complete and simultaneous view. Almost every writer who has commented upon the nave of Amiens has resorted to the vocabulary of flight, for no other physical sensation so well combines the vertical and the horizontal as we see them architecturally combined at Amiens. When we speak of the " soaring effect " of this interior, we are telling the truth, but it is important to understand also that we are recognizing a new quality in the linear idiom of northern art. Celtic line has risen above its original impetuous movement, and come to maturity. The jerk and yank of Romanesque sculpture have likewise given way to a serenity of motion. Amiens is dynamic art at its best, full of poise and elegance, full of grace and dignity.

Any man who has climbed a mountain and looked at the view is conversant with the emotional appeal of space. Among the arts, architecture alone offers an opportunity for the manipulation of space which exists in fact. With the exception of a few 20th-Century pieces which may be said to have a spatial reference or implication, sculpture is form surrounded by space and isolated from it. Painting exists on a plane surface; and although some of its most profound effects have been achieved by representing space, the painter is nevertheless subject to some severe handicaps. He must select an eye point; and in spite of the claims sometimes advanced for certain recent experiments, painters have to date been able to deal successfully with space from only one aspect at a time. Only the architect may use actual space as part of his medium.

In the history of architecture, it is possible to recognize three schools of thought with respect to the handling of space. The first is represented by the Greeks and the Egyptians; it is doubtful whether the designers of the Parthenon gave a thought to voids except to use them as a set-off for their admittedly superb solids. It was the great single achievement of Roman architecture to advance beyond such negation of space; but true to the classical habit of mind, the Romans construed space as a material for sculptural manipulation: their vast buildings isolated a block of space, if we may use the expression, and modeled it. By so doing, they separated the interior from the world outside and controlled the space within — both operations being consistent with the classical fear of the indefinite. It was no accident that Roman windows were set high and at inaccessible points where one could not conceivably use them as exits.

The Early Christian basilicas marked a great new conception with regard to the handling of enclosed space, not necessarily better in itself but certainly different from anything earlier. Handicapped by a tottering government and a ruined economy, the architects of that time were foreclosed from following out the logic of their inspiration; the projects they dreamed of remain in the realm of speculation. Certain elements of their enlightened thinking are nevertheless indisputably plain in their work. As we noted in Chapter 4 (pages 289–290), those men assigned to space a new artistic dignity. They gave it the same importance as masonry. They seem to have appreciated that air was a gas. Instead of shaping chunks of it, they let it flow through passageways and interistices. But beyond and above all of that, their feeling was not curtailed by the classical dread of the infinite. The occupants of an Early Christian basilica are not imprisoned by walls as they would be inside the Pantheon. Doors and windows are numerous, fairly large, and above all accessible. The light and air of the interior is not part of a constricted artistic unity, but an extension of the light and air of the whole world.

With respect to the handling of space, nothing built between about 500 A.D. and the start of the Gothic period can be cited as any considerable improvement over the Early Christian basilica. Hagia Sophia (see above, pages 348–349) has perhaps the best interior ever designed, but the theory behind it is eclectic rather than original — half Roman, half Early Christian. Some Romanesque churches follow the Roman theory of space; in others and especially in the more organic buildings, structural problems so preoccupied the designers as to exclude any significant manipulation of space for artistic effect. But by about 1200, the mechanics of church architecture were a matter of common knowledge and no longer an end in themselves. It was then possible to make a significant advance.

The Gothic architects invented no new theory of space; they simply had the techniques which made it possible to follow out the implications of the Early Christian system. Many of the items mentioned in the paragraphs immediately above contribute to the spatial composition. The innumerable small parts, each a unit of measure, perform their function as readily with reference to the enclosed volume as with reference to length and height. The soaring effect produced by the various linear elements may also be thought of as a spatial concept; to suggest flight is to suggest an unlimited volume of air opening from the foreground into the remote distance.

The practical exigencies of construction forced the Gothic church, in its aspect as a mechanical fabric, to approach completeness and self-sufficiency (see below, pages 472–480); and for that reason, a number of critics have sincerely put forward the idea that, in the end, the Gothic principle and the classical principle are the same. To whatever extent they meant to say that Gothic compositions have the same protective unity as the Greek and Roman, they spoke too soon. The truth is that the Gothic mind found it unthinkable to establish in a work of art a miniature cosmos with rules of its own.

In fact, Gothic architects went to the greatest pains to declare the unity of the cathedral not as of itself and for itself, but with the whole universe around. Out-of-doors, that purpose was made plain by the broken skyline — the very last thing, incidentally, to be given up during the period when the Late Gothic was being abandoned for the style of the Renaissance. Within the church, the same intention was expressed by the size and placement of passageways, doors, and windows.

A diagonal view across the nave of Amiens (Fig. 12.13) gives us in a more refined and perfect form the same experience noted when one takes up a similar station in one of the Early Christian basilicas (Fig. 9.26). Beyond the archway in the immediate foreground, there is another, and beyond that, openings succeed each other until a window or door is arrived at. As an approximate statement, it is fair to say that every line of sight ends in an accessible opening, and that no other kind of terminal was permitted if the architect could possibly help it. The extent to which that custom amounted almost to a rule may be assessed if we recall that one end of the long axis of each of the French churches ends in the windows of the apse, and that the opposite vista is not closed, as we usually say, but opens up into the great rose of the western façade. The square east end that was standard in England invited exploitation of this stirring effect; and in extreme instances, the entire eastern wall was glazed — a notable example being the immense perpendicular window at Gloucester.

As seen at the end of a vista, the large and accessible Gothic windows have an important effect. Unlike masonry, glass does not shut the world away; it lets it in. Light and air interpenetrate the architecture. Similarly, the windows provide no barrier for the mind. Either in thought or in actuality, it is easy to make the transition from indoors to the immensity of the universe outside. It may be said, indeed, that Gothic space is a continuation of universal space, and part of it — differing from the Early Christian only in the greater degree of artistic success with which the effect is made. These facts, it must be added, contribute powerfully to the truth of the idea that Gothic architecture forms a physical record of Christian aspiration. Through the medium of space, it is made clear that nothing exists alone; even the mighty fabric of the cathedral relates itself to the divine order, and occupies an appointed place.

The experience of Gothic space is one of the most profound the visual arts provide; but for the fullness of its effect, another element, not so far mentioned, must be present. That is the stained glass, which still exists in anything like the original amount and condition only at Chartres in France and at Leon in Spain.

As a major art, stained glass painting became feasible as soon as Gothic engineering eliminated the structural handicaps which in every earlier style had curtailed the size of window openings. From the standpoint of adequate illumination only, most Gothic windows are in fact too large; and unless the glass is colored, the interior is likely to suffer on bright days from an unpleasant glare. But by flooding the whole church with colored light, the Gothic artists introduced a new element.

While it is possible to prepare a useful rationale for color (see below, pages 564–578), it was true in the 13th Century and it is true today that the effect of color upon us is one of the great emotional mysteries. Upon entering Chartres, all persons experience a surge of feeling that goes altogether beyond understanding. It is easy, and certainly very appropriate, to associate that experience with the superrational or transcendental component of religion. Color, it might be said, is the physical attribute of mysticism. By comparison with churches that lack stained glass, Chartres calls up an experience which is much more intimate: no other monument brings one so close to fulfilment, or so nearly satisfies the soul's yearning for union with the infinite.

GOTHIC ENGINEERING

The stylistic and spiritual intentions which brought Gothic into being have been sufficiently well-summarized above to suggest that Gothic engineering, however wonderful its accomplishments, was a resource to which the Christian society of that time turned for the aesthetic expression of their religion. In no sense was engineering the cause of Gothic or the motive for it, as Mr. Moore and others believed — even though they were indubitably correct in pointing out that the development of Gothic coincides in time with a rapid advance in structural sophistication. It is hardly too much to say, in fact, that a serious student might comprehend the true if not the full meaning of the style without once bothering his head about the complex of ribs, buttresses, shafts, and other working members which make the lofty vaults and great windows practical. But for anybody in the least mechanically inclined, such an omission would be impossible and intolerable.

Engineering has correctly been defined as the art of making the findings of pure science available for human use; but when we apply the word to anything medieval, the reader must understand the obvious difference between the *ad hoc* experiments of the 11th and 12th Centuries, and the methods of the modern laboratory. In all the medieval world, there was no mathematics capable of dealing with subtle mechanical problems of any kind whatever. There never was, in fact, until the development of the calculus during the 17th Century; even Leonardo da Vinci, the greatest scientist of the High Renaissance, was unable to comprehend variation in terms of the square or cube — problems we assign to school boys today. When he took the responsibility for designing Amiens, Robert de Lusarches nevertheless had at his command an immense and certain knowledge about the construction of vaulted churches. Even now no one knows any more than he knew; but the data then in his possession were nothing like our modern formulas. He could calculate not at all, but he carried in his memory a tremendous record of reckless trial and disastrous error — and he knew how. His outlook, moreover, was not stultified by the disastrous modern distinction between art and engineering — a separation as wretched from the mechanical point of view as from the aesthetic. One of the chief glories of Gothic architecture is the truth that for once in all history, structure and beauty were everywhere and always the same. There was literally no difference between the two, and we have no right to separate them except for convenience in discussion.

In attempting to understand the superb mechanics of Amiens and other cathedrals, it is well to begin with a brief list of considerations that were fixed, and questions which were no longer outstanding. The basilican type of church was as firmly established as Catholicism itself. Another kind of building might have served the ritual as well and been easier to build, but probably nobody gave a moment's consideration to such a change of custom. The ribbed cross vault was, by 1220, almost as firmly established as the basilican form for the church. The master builders knew that it would work, and they knew that they could trust their supervisors and workmen to build it. As shrewd country builders still observe about one thing and another, it was "the proper way."

Masonry, moreover, was the only fire resistant material available. One cannot help wondering what the Gothic builders would have done with structural steel, but they never heard of it. In considering their masonry, there are several special points to remember. A good deal of cement went into the fabric of every Gothic building, but the use of concrete as a fundamental material (as the Romans had done) seems to have died with Antiquity. The point just made is one with which some scholars disagree; and on their side, it must be conceded that here and there one encounters a very ingenious application of mortar and rubble. Nevertheless, for purposes of general understanding, it is fair to say that the Gothic architects did their thinking in terms of cut stone, and that their structural system contemplates the action of cut stone under compression, and provides for it.

Fig. 12.44 Amiens Cathedral. Perspective cross section.

Gothic architecture was an architecture of small stones. The point cannot be too strongly or too often emphasized, for much of the atmosphere of the whole style derives from it. The gigantic monoliths of the Romans are absent both in fact and in spirit. Most of the stones laid during the Gothic era were small enough so that half a dozen men could pick them up and put them in place. A great many blocks were bigger than that; but it is rare to see one that could not be pulled along an ordinary country road by a yoke of oxen harnessed to a sledge. The miserable facilities at hand most certainly provided the necessity that was the mother of Gothic invention.

Keeping these points in mind, we may now refer to the several structural drawings of Amiens (Figs. 12.44–46). It will be evident at a glance that the designer was keenly alive to the aesthetic difficulties imposed by the thrust of arches. Most of what he did may be interpreted as an effort to minimize that factor. He found ways to reduce the absolute thrust of every arch in the fabric, and he found ways to prevent the abutment from spoiling the beauty of the church.

Of the various stratagems resorted to, none has anything like the importance of the extreme delicacy of construction characteristic of the High Gothic. No other medieval invention compares with that one in mechanical excellence. Every component part was reduced in scale to a proportion approaching the danger point. The result was an architecture that made the most efficient use of materials on record — with the possible exception of the best, but not all, of the bridges designed by Mr. Roebling at the turn of the last century. No other architecture used less masonry (an approximate index for cost) in relation to the cubic content enclosed. But above all, the bold reduction in weight radically reduced the capacity of the arches and vaults to exert thrust.

Fig. 12.45 Amiens. Cathedral. Longitudinal cross section to illustrate the very moderate undulation of the vault surface along the axis of the ceiling.

The daring of Gothic construction is no figure of speech. It can hardly be exaggerated, and the venturesome spirit of the period may be emphasized by pointing out what happened at Beauvais (Fig. 12.18). Started only five years after Amiens, with vaults only a few feet higher and with parts only a little lighter, the choir was finished and put into use in 1272. In 1284, the vaults came crashing down. The original design for the choir had called for four-part vaults; as now reconstructed, each of the bays was divided into two by adding an extra pier, and an extra rib was added to make the vaults six-part. The work dragged, and the transepts were not complete until 1500. Instead of starting to erect the nave, the canons then elected (in 1548) to build themselves a tower over the crossing. It was a shade over 500 feet high; and it must have been a sight to startle the world. In 1573, the tower tumbled down. There are various possible explanations both for the collapse of the choir vaults and for the crash of the tower. We need not go into the matter, but anybody has a right to remark that the builders had overreached themselves. It is also worth pointing out that our modern building codes (admittedly erring far on the side of caution) would condemn as in flagrant violation a great many Gothic churches that have stood for 600 years.

Fig. 12.46 Amiens. Cathedral. One of the flying buttresses of the nave.

A second innovation that helped to control thrust was adoption of the pointed arch. As set forth in Chapter 7 (pages 190–193) the advantage of the pointed arch is not that its thrust, measured in pounds, is less; but simply that the thrust is directed at a steeper angle toward the ground. Or to put it another way, the horizontal component of the thrust is less — a consideration of the utmost importance in view of the lofty placement and delicate proportions of the fully perfected flying buttresses. It should be noted, however, that round arches often occur in the Gothic, especially in Italy.

As to the flying buttress, it was made necessary by the basilican form of the cathedrals. It was almost never used except on churches with a clearstory rising above side aisles. The Sainte Chapelle at Paris, for example, needed no aisles because of its special purpose, and its abutment is by pier buttresses only, engaged to the outside walls. But where vaults were high and clearstory windows large, it was imperative to find a form of buttress that would cast the least possible shadow across the stained glass. Hence the segmental arches we call flying buttresses (Fig. 12.46), which meet the nave vaults at points where the thrusts are concentrated, take the compression, and swing it over to pier buttresses arranged along the outer borders of the church. It will be noted that the extrados of each flying buttress is loaded with masonry, a clever way of making it bear a little harder against the thrust of the vault — a small consideration that indicates the narrow margin between stability and danger in Gothic construction. The diagonal inclination of the buttresses serves also to indicate in graphic and jaunty fashion the direction of the thrust.

There has been a certain amount of debate recently as to the actual function of the flying buttresses in the Gothic fabric. When buttresses happen to get destroyed, as by bombardment, the vaults do not always collapse as the rule book says they ought to do. Generalizing from altogether too few such instances, some writers have even gone so far as to say that once the cement has hardened, Gothic vaults exert no thrust and the buttresses do no work. There is just enough basis for their belief to create sincere perplexity.

Mortar is an adhesive. It tends to glue all the voussoirs of an arch or vault together. So long as the mortar holds, the vault is nearly in the condition of a monolith; and it probably exerts little or no thrust unless something happens to break the joints open. But mortar is not a strong or even a good adhesive. With luck, it may upon occasion hold in surprising fashion, but one cannot safely rely upon it. A designer must always expect the worst — which in vaulted architecture means that no reliance can be placed upon the holding power of cement, and everything must be arranged on the assumption that every stone might some time try to slide over the next. It is from that point of view that the following paragraphs are written.

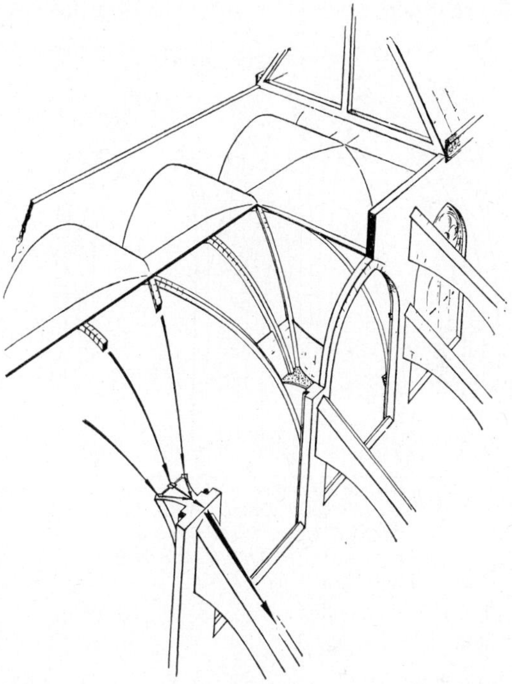

Fig. 12.47 Schematic drawing to illustrate the concentration of thrusts achieved by the special system of cross vaulting developed in France during the High Gothic era.

The flying buttresses of the High Gothic are extraordinarily slight for the work they do, but they were used with confidence all over northern France. No such performance would have been possible except for the development of a new and special form of the cross vault — a vault with a peculiar shape which brought the thrusts of all ribs into a single force focused upon a very narrow area at either side of the church. Because the direction of that force was known, it was feasible to counteract it by putting a flying buttress in exactly the right place, and pitching it at precisely the right angle.

As stated in Chapter 7 (page 206), an adequate comprehension of the thrust pattern of cross vaulting can ordinarily be gained by reference to the plan view only. When, however, we deal with the more clever and more subtle elements of Gothic vaulting, the thrusts as seen in plan retain the same importance, but we must be prepared to give simultaneous consideration to the grouping of arches and shafts as they appear in vertical elevation (Fig. 12.47).

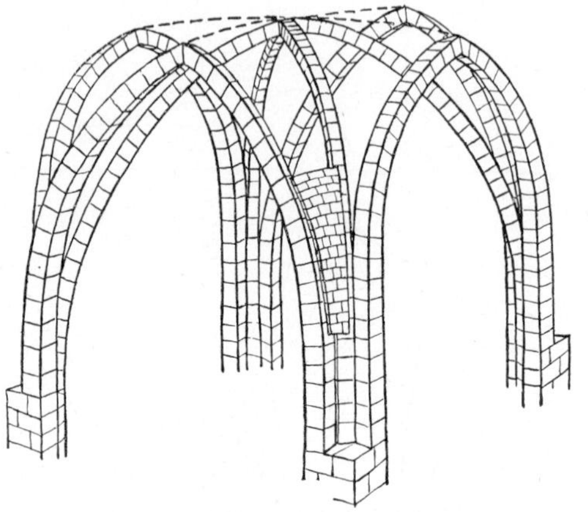

Fig. 12.48 Drawing of the developed Gothic vault.

Referring again to our discussion of the domical vaults at Sant' Ambrogio (pages 414–415), and comparing Fig. 11.36 with Fig. 12.48, the notable superiority of Gothic vaulting becomes apparent. Every bay at Amiens, as seen in plan (Fig. 12.43), is a narrow oblong. By comparison with the square, an oblong plan makes the diagonals span a distance relatively much greater, and the wall ribs receive a span exaggeratedly shorter by comparison. One might jump to the conclusion that an even worse shape than that of Sant' Ambrogio's dark hollows would have to be accepted, but it was one of the great Gothic inventions to find a way to make each of the six arches of the vault frame rise to an equal height (Fig. 12.49). The transverse arches were merely pointed a little more, which brought their crowns to the same level as the diagonals. The wall ribs were given a steeper pointing still; and they were

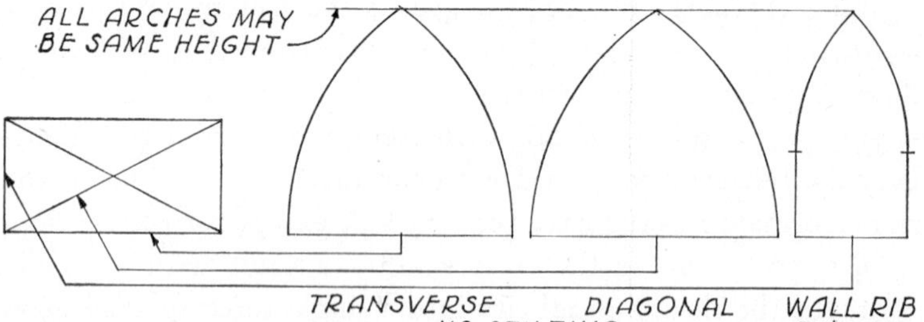

Fig. 12.49 Schematic drawing to illustrate the Gothic method for bringing all arches of the vault frame to the same height regardless of their great or short span.

stilted in radical fashion, so that they spring from a level many feet higher than the diagonals — but they come to just about the same elevation at the crown.

One excellent result of the arrangement is illustrated by Fig. 12.45. Instead of rising up in great concaves, the vaulting of Amiens undulates only slightly. The bays have, in colloquial language, a fairly "level crown." The advantage of the level crown is apparent in any view of the nave. The use of cross vaulting made it necessary to divide the ceiling into a number of separate bays, each a form artistically separate from the next. Perfect unity of the entirety was impossible so long as that kind of vault was used, but the level crown permits a reasonable coherence between bay and bay, and a reasonable continuity in the long axis of the ceiling.

About the stilting of the wall rib, there is much more to be said. The structural brilliance of that expedient has, to this point, hardly been touched upon. A glance at Fig. 12.12 will show that the transverse arches which designate the boundary between each pair of contiguous bays may be said to belong to each bay equally. Because we know that the thrust of the transverse arch is at right angles to the nave, and directly in line with the buttresses, we may from here on take it for granted, and neglect it in our explanation. It contributes nothing to the subtleties of our problem. Let us instead concentrate our attention upon the diamond-shaped areas of vaulting which spread upwards from each pier, being bounded by the diagonals.

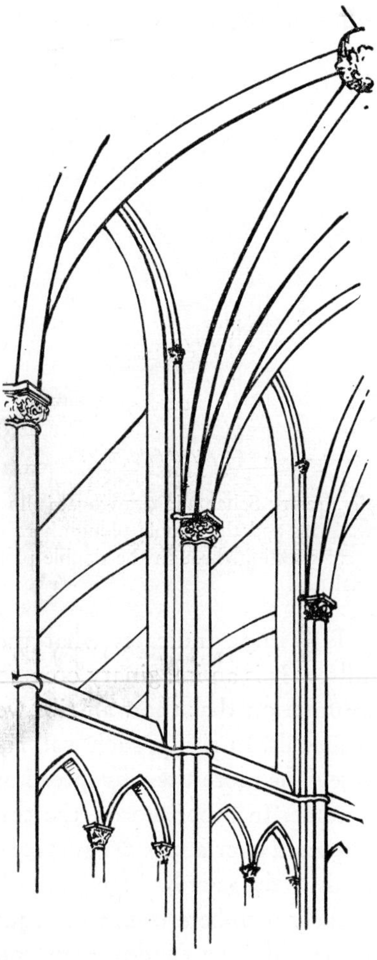

Fig. 12.50 Schematic drawing to illustrate the impingement of flying buttresses against the double ploughshare solids of French vaulting. The proportions are approximately standard for the period of the High Gothic.

Fig. 12.13 and Fig. 12.50 show the same diamond-shaped parts of the vaulting from another angle, and we should observe that there rises from each pier a three-dimensional solid of masonry of peculiar shape.

We need a name for it. Sometimes referred to as the *Gothic vault conoid* it might better be called *the double ploughshare solid* of Gothic vaulting. If we imagine one of these solids to be cut by a horizontal plane at a level near the haunch, its cross section will approximate that shown in Fig. 12.51. Such a cross section indicates the tremendous advantage (from the standpoint of focussing all thrusts upon a narrow area) obtained as a result of stilting the wall ribs. Figs. 12.12–13,18,46–47,50, all indicate how closely the thrusts are squeezed together to bear upon the narrow inner face of each flying buttress.

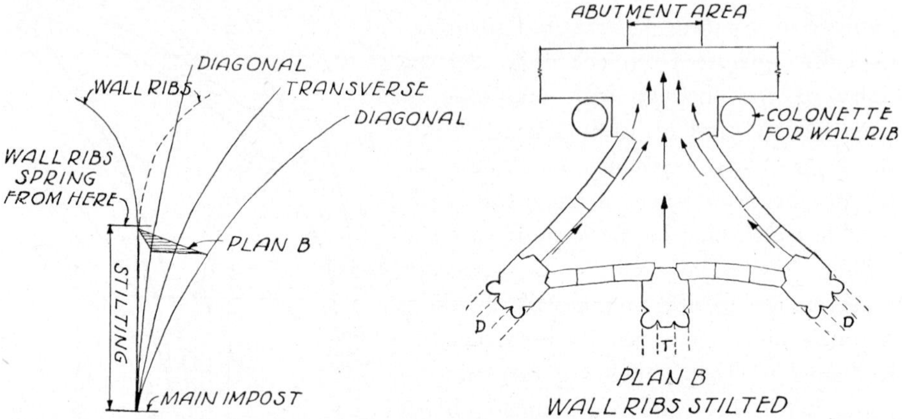

Fig. 12.51 Schematic drawing to illustrate the focus of thrusts made possible by the stilted wall ribs and the double ploughshare solid. Left: the various ribs seen in perspective. Right: a cross section through the double ploughshare solid at the level of the haunch of the diagonal ribs.

Fig. 12.52 indicates what the situation would be were the wall ribs not stilted. It is an imaginary cross section, similar to Fig. 12.51, but drawn on the assumption that the wall ribs were made to spring from the same level as the diagonals. In rising, such wall ribs would of course spread apart as fast as they rose. The more the ribs spread apart, the wider the area between them would become. In other words, the compressive force of the vault-thrust would be dispersed over a broader surface — a surface which could not possibly be covered by the narrow inner face of a delicate flying buttress. Ponderous and unshapely members would be required instead, if safe and proper abutment was to be had. The window area, moreover, would be considerably reduced.

The description just completed will give the reader an introduction to the major achievements of Gothic engineering. Detailed inspection of the monuments will reward him with an almost infinite number of structural refinements in which the builders themselves obviously took the keenest pleasure.

Wall ribs, for example, usually have capitals at the level of their own springing. The tiny spires placed as finials for the pier buttresses (Fig. 12.46) almost always appear at the outside edge of the buttress, where their small weight aids the abutment by squeezing the outer joints of the masonry more tightly together. Once generally understood, moreover, the flying buttress itself was used in a great variety of dispositions; no two churches have them arranged in just the same way.

Another sidelight on Gothic engineering is the fact that those great design-

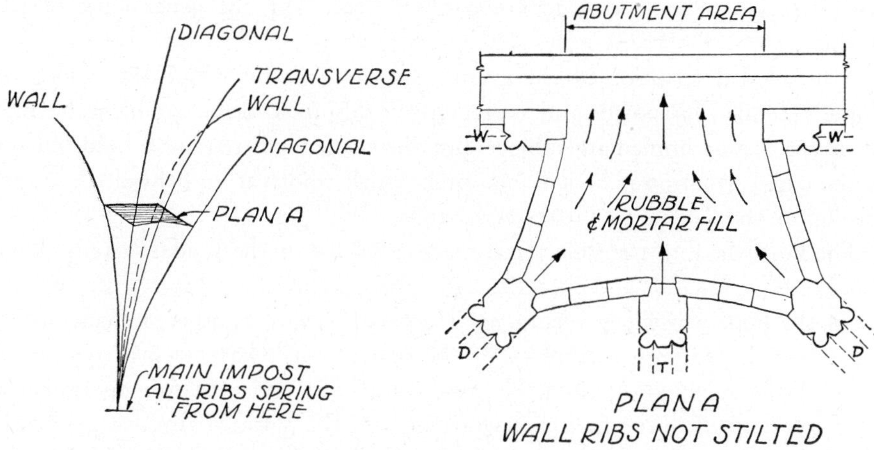

Fig. 12.52 Schematic drawing to be compared with Fig. 12.51: the thrust pattern of a ribbed cross vault without stilted wall ribs.

ers refused to be enslaved by their own structural theory. For example, the upper tier of flying buttresses at Reims ostensibly impinges upon the vaulting at the haunch, but when the roof burned off after the bombardment of 1914, it was revealed (to the great surprise of people not intimately familiar with the church) that those buttresses came nowhere near the haunch. They were too high, and they had been pushing against each other through horizontal beams for nearly 700 years. From that instance alone, we may observe that the Gothic architects, although more concerned than any earlier school with mechanical excellence, were not immune to the charm of form.

THE 13TH-CENTURY CHURCH, AND THE SPREAD OF THE GOTHIC STYLE

The 13th Century was a heyday of church building, and everywhere the style was Gothic. Over and above the unique prestige of the Ile de France, there must have been other strong reasons for the adoption of a single and universal style — a considerable contrast with the previous diversity. The strongest reason of all is doubtless to be sought in the character of the 13th-Century church.

The difference between Gothic Christianity and Romanesque Christianity was not a matter of the comparative level of individual piety. It had to do, rather, with church government. The relative separatism of the ecclesiastical polity during the two Romanesque centuries is well evidenced by the numerous local subdivisions we are compelled to recognize within that style. The centralization of authority at Rome was reflected by the general use of the Gothic.

A detailed description of the events and methods by which the Bishop of Rome extended his power and perfected his administration would be beyond the scope of our immediate subject, but the reader will require a bold outline of the papal situation if he is to comprehend the motivation behind the transmission of the Gothic to all western Europe.

The Popes had, in the first place, made good use of the feudal system. They held lands personally; and over a considerable part of central Italy, the authority of the Pope was the government. They had vassals, as other monarchs did; and while the *de facto* authority of the pontiff must have seemed remote in some of the regions of which he was technically the overlord, an immense prestige attached to the fact that whoever held the Vatican also was acknowledged feudal lord of Sicily, Aragon, England, Ireland, and the Latin monarchy established after 1204 at Constantinople. At any moment and upon any pretext of his own choosing, the Pope could and did assert his right to interfere in the practical affairs of the populations mentioned.

In addition to the powers just cited, which belonged to the Pope in his capacity as a property holder, there were other recognized powers which derived from the moral and spiritual status of the Vatican; often these proved even more cogent when the church wished to sway the imagination and, in some measure, direct the impulses of men. From the moment when Leo the 3rd crowned Charlemagne, the Popes had claimed the right to crown, or not to crown, the elected successors of Charlemagne. Endless friction and conflict ensued; but in the period immediately before the 13th Century, the papacy had enjoyed better than average success in asserting the superiority of the spiritual leadership over the temporal. The Popes thus started the Gothic period in a position of great political influence.

Upon the daily affairs of all persons, the church continued, as before, to exercise an ever-present effect unknown today; but more and more, policy and even specific direction tended to come from Rome. The collection of church revenues was perfected into a complex system of taxation which gave the church a share in almost every profitable enterprise, and fetched into the Vatican treasury an enormous sum annually. Canon law, which previously had lacked unity and system, was brought into uniformity, largely as the result of Gratian's *Decretum* — a compilation of documents, plus a treatise in which the learned author attempted to solve their contradictions and arrive at a coherent juridical system. Brought together about 1148, Gratian's work, although not a set of statutes, presently began to acquire the effective authority we recognize today in the writings of Blackstone and Coke.

In addition to the jurisdiction the church claimed as its own, its function in the medieval world was made even more effective and indispensable by conditions which, for the time, played into its hands. The feudal monarchies, even that of France, were loose and ineffective to a degree almost impossible to comprehend today; they simply did not perform many of the duties necessary for the operation of society. Into the vacuum stepped the church with an organization so perfect it may rightly be compared with that of the Roman Empire. The papal prerogative to appoint bishops (a power long disputed) had become absolute early in the 12th Century. By the start of the 13th, its technique had been refined into a system of patronage and discipline rarely equalled in the history of human institutions. In every community of the Western world, the Roman authority was represented by direct appointees of the Pope, most of them able and much respected men. It was the exception rather than the rule for promising young churchmen to remain in one place; most of them had served the church in many lands before they could be called mature and prominent. With them they took their medieval Latin, in which language all church business was conducted. Inelegant by comparison with the classical, it was nevertheless the closest thing to the gift of Pentecost yet seen on earth. It furnished a channel for the passage of information and ideas unknown before the perfection of the Catholic polity, and unknown since. Where there is unity of tongue, there is likely to be unity of taste, and the Gothic style in art seems to have traveled the obvious route.

But none of these things, nor all of them together, furnish us with an adequate explanation either for the imposing powers of the 13th Century church or for the completeness with which Gothic art was devoted to the service of religion. Lusty and often barbarously cruel, Gothic society was genuinely religious in a sense for which history has no parallel. The people believed what the church taught. Their membership in a common religion was everywhere symbolized by the building of churches in a common style.

THE HIGH GOTHIC IN SPAIN, ITALY, GERMANY, AND ENGLAND

The largest and most famous French cathedrals are not earlier, but approximately contemporary to those of the rest of Europe. Salisbury was begun the same year as Amiens. The cathedrals at Burgos and Toledo were started in 1221 and 1227 respectively. The church of Saint Francis at Assisi dates from 1228, and that of Saint Elizabeth at Marburg from 1223. The figures make it unmistakable that the actual transmission of the style from the Ile de France outward must have taken place before 1200 or thereabouts. In trying to understand the operation of the French influence, it would therefore be a mistake to give a great deal of weight to the highly perfected work of the 13th Century. While no simple statement can be entirely true, it appears to be generally so that the foreign architects, insofar as they depended directly upon French models, remembered as they worked, not the High Gothic of Amiens, but the Early Gothic — and often in a less developed state than Leon.

Few of the foreign churches carry out the logic of the style as it was understood in northern France at the time Amiens was designed. As machines, most of them lack the precision and polish common in French work. Flying buttresses, if used at all, tend to have a clumsy shape, and often are neither placed nor pitched ideally. Mouldings are simpler. Most parts tend to be heavier.

Spain

During the 13th Century, Spain was an artistic province of France. It is possible to recognize a bit of authentic local flavor in the tracery of the rose and in the cusped arches of the triforium openings at Burgos, but much of the surface embellishment that gives character to the interior is, like the lantern and western spires, Late Gothic. The mouldings and piers of Toledo are very French. The western façade of Leon derives directly from the unique lateral porches of Chartres; Leon is, in fact, a watered version of a French church.

Italy

Italian Gothic is one of the anomalies of art history. It is like a bird that cannot fly. Nothing but the overwhelming prestige of France could have brought a northern style into the very dooryard of classical art, and the outland manner was never fully understood or accepted. The vaulted cathedrals at Florence, Siena, and Orvieto are the most famous, perhaps; but they give a false impression of the typical form taken by Gothic architecture in Italy. For that purpose, Santa Croce at Florence (Fig. 12.19) will serve us better.

It may be described as a wooden roofed basilica built with pointed arches. The piers, capitals, and mouldings betray in their form an extreme reluctance to render more than lip service to the prevailing French fashion, a condition in general true everywhere on the peninsula. The plan of Santa Croce is peculiar to Italy, and typical of the average Italian Gothic church (Fig. 12.53). The apse and choir amount to a separate chapel, narrower than the nave. To the north and south, a series of smaller chapels open through the eastern wall; in two of them on the south side, Giotto (see below, pages 550–563) did cycles of frescoes, and the church contains an amazing collection of monuments by famous artists of the Renaissance.

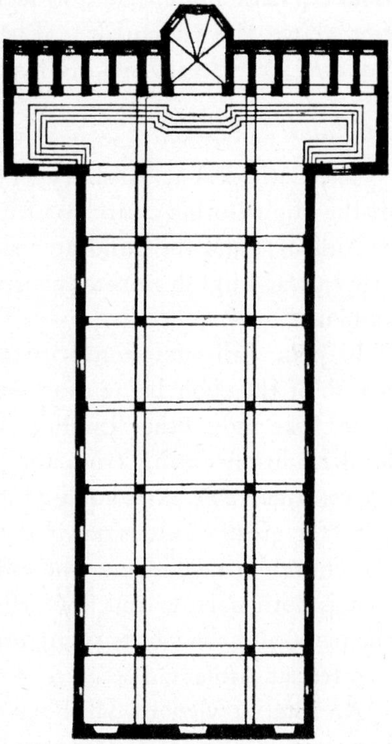

Fig. 12.53 Florence. Santa Croce. Plan.

Germany

It has often been said that the Romanesque style was more congenial to the German temperament than the Gothic, and that buildings like the cathedral of Cologne (a direct derivative from Amiens) reflect no more than a temporary affectation for something French. Such statements are half true, to be sure, but they overlook at least two excellent contributions to the Gothic which appear to have originated in Germany.

In the arrangement of the interior, the Germans made an interesting departure from the traditional cross section of the basilica. Saint Elizabeth's at Marburg (Fig. 12.20) is an example. The nave and the side aisles are of equal height, eliminating the conventional triforium and clearstory. The effect is to open up the interior from wall to wall, and to unify rather than subdivide the space it contains. As a type such buildings are known as *hall churches.* Rather than a chevet, Saint Elizabeth's has a trefoil arrangement at the east end.

In the composition of the exterior, the Germans also proved inventive. The cathedral at Freiburg in Breisgau will illustrate their contribution in this department. Instead of the twin towers characteristic of France and common all over Europe, the western front was given a single tower of monumental dimensions. Because the German nave was usually much lower than that of a comparable French church (the interior height at Freiburg is about 89 feet, and the tower stands a full 380 feet high) such towers dominate the composition and make a diagonal view of the building as good as its eastern or western aspect. The principle involved was carried to its logical conclusion in the Late Gothic cathedral at Ulm (Fig. 12.21). The over-all length at ground level is a little more than 400 feet. The spire soars into the air to an apex 528 feet above the pavement (Washington Monument: 555 feet; Woolworth Building: 750 feet), making it the highest church tower in the world.

England

The Cathedral at Salisbury (Fig. 12.22) is stylistically the most consistent of the High Gothic churches of England. Work began in 1220 (the same year as Amiens), and the building was substantially complete forty years later. No other great English minster ever went up in so prompt and straightforward a fashion.

In plan, Salisbury conforms to the shape of an archiepiscopal cross, the length of the choir being exaggerated to accommodate the second set of transepts. Like most other English churches, the apse is square, maintaining the local tradition dating from the very earliest years of the Middle Ages (see above, page 329). As compared to Amiens, the plan seems long and rambling, with far greater extension of the transepts; but in terms of feet and inches, the church is no longer. The effect of length depends, rather, upon a nave that is both narrow and low. Salisbury measures only 32 or 33 feet between the piers, and the vaults swing only 82 feet above the floor — as compared to 139 feet at Amiens.

An interior view of Salisbury can hardly be expected to please people who have learned their taste at Amiens and Laon. The English were never much interested in the organic theory of architectural design; and there is neither the refinement, the logic, or the coherence between part and part which so distinguishes the French cathedrals.

All of that is forgiven if not forgotten when one goes out of doors. Like most other English churches, Salisbury stands in a park. The lawns and trees around it have received competent and sensitive care for generation after generation; and the church, taken together with its setting, forms a picture incomparably better than anything to be seen on the continent — where noble buildings are usually in immediate juxtaposition to all the bustle and squalor of commercial life within a crowded city. It is no accident that the medieval architecture of England has formed one of the traditional subjects for painting, as the reader may see for himself in the numerous portraits of this very cathedral by no less a master than John Constable.

The church itself could hardly be better designed for the situation in which we find it. From any angle and every angle of view, its silhouette is rich and various. The grand central tower, 404 feet high and the loftiest in England, dominates and centralizes the composition, and gives the mass of the building an omnifacial organization in sharp contrast to the unfortunate appearance of Amiens when seen from the side.

The façade of Salisbury is very moderate by comparison with the west front of either Lincoln or Peterborough, but it conforms to a general English custom of designing the entrance front as though it were an independent screen without any necessary or essential relationship to the building behind. The artistic philosophy involved is not far different from that which became popular during the Italian Renaissance (see below, pages 634–635); both then and now, most critics feel some sense of reservation about it — especially when the screen, as a screen, leaves something to be desired in harmony and coherence of line and texture.

As the reader may have reflected when considering the comparatively moderate height of the nave, the design of Salisbury is but one instance indicating that the Gothic architects of England remained ultra-conservative in matters of structure. By 1220, anyone who cared to learn might have acquired without great trouble an adequate knowledge of abutment by means of the flying buttress, but such buttresses are conspicuous by their absence at Salisbury and on most other English churches. The walls are thick; and with the addition of small pier buttresses at appropriate points, enough inertia is provided to contain the thrusts. It may be questioned whether Salisbury is thereby rendered safer against earthquake, bomb concussion, or other destructive accidents: during World War II, it was the delicate but well-braced Gothic of France that stood punishment best of all.

LATE GOTHIC ARCHITECTURE

The forces which had made Gothic did not outlast the 13th Century. By comparison with that inspired era, the 14th Century is horrible to contemplate.

It was the century of the Hundred Years' War. Northern and western France were subjected to pillage and ruin. From the standpoint of the population, it made little difference whether French or English armies passed over the land; the result was the same. As the creative center of European life, France was through.

The so-called Babylonian Captivity of the Papacy began in 1305. The Popes removed to Avignon, where they remained until 1378. The Babylonian Captivity was followed by the Great Schism. In legal technicality, the schism came to an end in 1415 when the Council of Constance elected Martin the 5th, deposed one of the competing Popes, and persuaded the other to resign. But the harm was done. The whole of Europe had resented the sojourn at Avignon, and the general state of mind was not in the least mollified by the sumptuous court maintained there by the pontiffs. The position of the Pope was forever compromised. Church government ceased to be what it had been. Discipline was difficult, and in some places impossible to enforce. Many of the clergy became notorious for their corruption.

Certain controversies in the matter of doctrine still further tended to undermine the unity of Christendom. Bitter differences of opinion, it must be remembered, had been perennial within the Catholic church, but those who lost the argument never got away with it before the 14th Century. During the 13th Century, for example, Roger Bacon had been silenced; the Emperor Frederick the 2nd of Sicily and all his line had been eliminated; and the Albigensian heresy had been crushed out of existence with a barbarity as sincere as it was terrible. But during this new era, John Wyclyffe rose up in England to claim that the Bishop of Rome had usurped his extraordinary powers, thus paving the way for the ultimate secession of the English church. Unlike earlier heretics, Wyclyffe died in his bed, the Papacy being without power to get at him. Some of Wyclyffe's students at Oxford returned to their native Bohemia with the ideas they had learned in England. The upshot was the heresy of John Huss, at whom the church could get. Huss was burned at the stake, but under circumstances that impressed innumerable persons as grossly unjust. An irresistible groundswell of feeling began to make itself felt — presently to become a tidal wave sweeping on toward the Renaissance, the Reformation, and modern times.

Heart-rending enough to this point, the narrative of the 14th Century is still incomplete. In 1348, all Europe was swept by the plague. Known in England as the Black Death, that epidemic was the worst on record. It is difficult to make a sound guess as to the mortality, but most authorities feel that about half the population of Europe died of it.

In the face of such a historical summary, it is difficult to see how cultural progress of any kind was possible, and it must be conceded that unified Christendom suffered a blow that has proven as yet irreparable. At the same time, the current of tragedy did not sweep with equal force everywhere. It left islands where humane accomplishment remained feasible: this is the century that produced Chaucer, Dante, Petrarch, Giotto (see below, pages 550–563), and the Late Gothic.

Origins and Causes of the Late Gothic

Modern art history has not yet done its work on the Late Gothic. Historians may perhaps be forgiven for taking more interest in the origin of styles than in their maturity, but the fact is that some of the finest expressions of the whole Gothic era fall well after the 13th Century. Insofar as we can now interpret the evidence, it seems likely that England took the lead in this further development of the style. Building ceased almost completely in France; and when churches were built there again (and not many of them then), the style had changed. By comparison, the English churches went up at more regular intervals, and seem to show a more orderly movement toward the later and more ornate stages of development. Beginning with the " Early English " of Salisbury, it is possible to follow a kind of evolution in the tracery of windows and in the increasingly elaborate patterns assumed by the ribs of the vaulting. A " Geometrical Decorated " stage and a " Curvilinear Decorated " stage are said to lead the way toward the " Perpendicular " which was popular during the 15th Century and the " Tudor " of the 16th. Easy enough to put down on paper, such a classification is at times very, very hard to apply to the monuments with any real assurance, and it is fair to hazard a guess that during the whole Late Gothic episode in England and everywhere else, rather little depended upon the precise state of a centralized style, and much upon the taste and judgment of the individual architect. We shall therefore give up any attempt to arrange our examples to fit some logical scheme; but for convenience, we shall group them according to the modern national divisions.

England

The Cathedral at Exeter (Fig. 12.23) is our best example of the Late Gothic in its first stage. The towers adjacent to the transepts are Norman, and a few fragments of masonry are thought to date from Saxon times. Most of the present fabric was built under six different bishops between 1257 and 1394. In spite of its protracted and heterodox history, Exeter has an over-all harmony and oneness unsurpassed among medieval churches. A certain uniformity of scale and texture was maintained as each successive addition was made, with the happy result that the various forms blend together.

The general effect is more opulent than that of any High Gothic church, but the particular feature to which we should turn our attention is the vaulting of the nave. The crown is almost perfectly level, and a continuous ridge rib follows the axis of the ceiling. From each main impost on either side, no fewer than eleven ribs spring upward and outward in a radial pattern. Some of these meet each other at the ridge rib, and others meet their opposites at various points along the transverse arches. All ribs are the same size, and the familiar appearance of cross vaulting is quite done away with, but may be traced if one makes the effort.

The aesthetic purpose of the new rib system at Exeter can hardly be explained in terms of simple and single intention. It certainly indicates a desire to elaborate upon the decorative aspect of a style that no longer offered any important opportunity for structural improvement; and while opinions differ, there can be no denying that the somewhat confusing contours of cross vaulting are lost in a rich new complexity of line and texture — and the ceiling pulled into a better unity thereby.

The addition of subordinate ribs makes it necessary to introduce two new terms. An extra rib that springs from a pier is named a *tierceron*. Tiercerons are to be distinguished from *liernes*, because liernes run between two main ribs, springing from one and terminating on another without coming into any contact with a pier.

The tracery of the windows at Exeter would fall into the category of "Curvilinear Decorated," and there is a distinct difference between the Late Gothic as we find it there, and the ultimate or "Perpendicular" stage of the style. Insofar as the transition was orderly, it may be studied at Winchester and Gloucester, both originally Norman churches and both remodeled during the 14th Century to fit contemporary fashion. For the Perpendicular in full flower, we must turn to King's College Chapel at Cambridge (Fig. 12.24) and to the Chapel of Henry 7th, attached to Westminster Abbey at its extreme east end (Figs. 12.25–26).

The exterior of King's College Chapel is unimpressive; it amounts to a rectangular framework of piers and arches, with the skyline rather weakly broken by a number of small spires. The interior, however, is surely one of the best ever designed. The walls, if we may still call them that, consist of 25 immense stained glass windows. The windows are so big, in fact, that the supremely delicate stonework functions, in an almost literal sense, as a mere frame of reference for the light and color that flood the space within. The arches used for the window heads and the transverse ribs are good examples of the four-centered "Tudor" arch (see also Fig. 7.9); they are "pointed" only in a very strict sense of the term. The name *Perpendicular* comes from the tracery of the windows. Curvilinear work is restricted to the extreme upper part; and about halfway up, the vertical mullions are intersected by a horizontal mullion, or *transom bar*. These particular windows are unusual in having but one transom bar; others of the same class have many.

A geometrical description of the so-called "fan vaulting" of the chapel would be tediously long and artistically insignificant. Those familiar with the *double ploughshare solid* of the High Gothic will have no trouble in recognizing the heredity, but it is worth remarking that at this point the ploughshare solids are true conoids with a semicircular cross section. The vaults were built of cut stone voussoirs; they do not depend upon the ribs for support. Because the latter — once " working members " — now became a mere enrichment of the surface texture, fan vaulting has been unpopular with those who attach moral significance to the revelation of structure.

The circular nature of the fans made it awkward to adapt such vaulting to a rectangular plan because an empty space inevitably appeared in the middle of each bay. At Cambridge, those spaces were glossed over by carved pendants decorated with heraldry. In successive bays, the Beaufort portcullis alternates with the Tudor rose.

The Chapel of Henry the 7th (Figs. 12.25–26) represents the Late Gothic in an extreme form. Built at the time architectural stonecutting had reached its quintessential perfection all over Europe, the vaulting is a tour de force of daring. The voussoirs are a triumph of applied geometry; depending on their bevel alone, the architect has suspended in mid-air large pendants of stone.

The exterior is only less remarkable. It was one of the very few instances where the nature and logic of perpendicular tracery had full rein. The pattern of window lights, transom bars, and mullions was carried in low relief right around the vertical piers and other areas of masonry. Even through the soot of innumerable London winters, this supremely neat working of the surface carries unhindered; in the deepest and most smoke-laden fog, to see this building is to see something chaste and gay.

All Gothic, early or late, was predominantly a vaulted architecture, but we must not omit mention of certain notable developments in wood. Because English society was and remains (all London notwithstanding) rural and agricultural by preference, that country has always raised trees and entertained an uncommon liking for wood. Because, also, men from every part of the island have traditionally gone to sea, at no time has there been a village that lacked at least one man with something better than a passing acquaintance with boat building. Wood is the age-old medium of boat builders, ever princes among craftsmen: their work is subtle, complex, and expert beyond anything within the capacity of the cabinetmaker. It was no wonder, then, that England bred a race of connoisseurs in the working of wood. During the Late Gothic era, when elaboration was the order of the day, that taste came out in a great number of superb wooden ceilings of different kinds. Among them, the most famous type was the *hammer-beam roof,* evolved at the end of the 14th Century.

A hammer beam is a bracket, or *cantilever.* Its simplest form is shown in Fig. 12.54, and its function is to carry a vertical strut on the upper and outer corner. The strut, in turn, connects with an inclined rafter, and helps stiffen it. The rafters may therefore be longer than would otherwise be feasible, and the span between wall and wall (and hence the area of floor free from supports) greater.

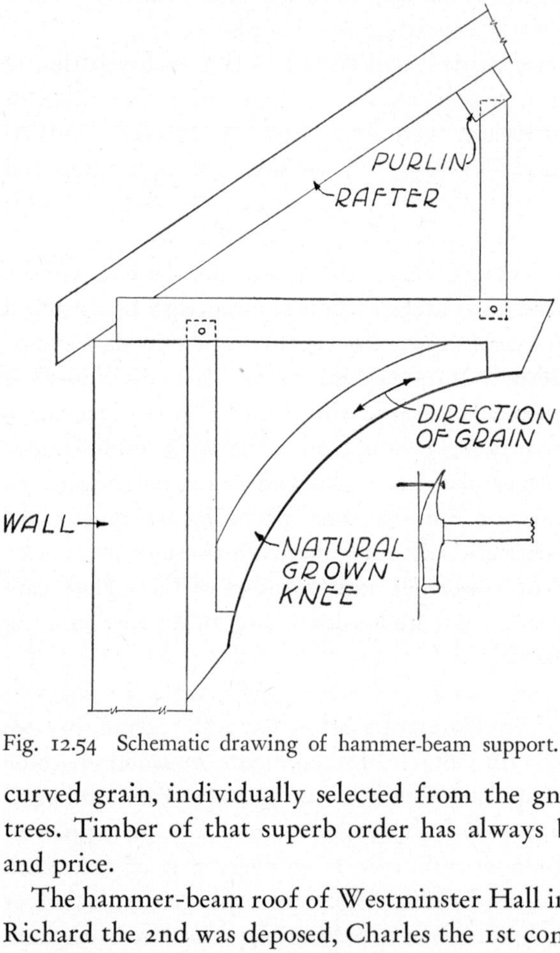

Fig. 12.54 Schematic drawing of hammer-beam support.

We may doubt whether such structural considerations dictated the choice of hammer beams in many instances. A great many hammer-beam roofs are so complex and elegant that almost any kind of vault would have been cheaper. That fact will be apparent if we note how very often curved pieces of wood were included in the innumerable variations of the form, especially for the hypotenuse leg of the triangle. Such pieces, if they were to hold their shape indefinitely, had to be *knees* of curved grain, individually selected from the gnarled limbs of the finest oak trees. Timber of that superb order has always been a matter of great pride and price.

The hammer-beam roof of Westminster Hall in London (Fig. 12.27), where Richard the 2nd was deposed, Charles the 1st condemned to death, and Cromwell proclaimed Lord Protector, has a span of 68 feet, one of the very widest ever attempted in wood prior to the invention of new fastening methods during World War II. The northern nature of Gothic has certainly never been more emphatically expressed; the shape of the hammer beams might have been suggested by a bit of Irish jewelry.

It should be mentioned, lest our enthusiasm for marvellous craftsmanship carry us away, that the hammer-beam roof is hardly admirable as a structural device. Without tie beams to take tension and hold the lower ends of the rafters at a predetermined distance from each other, such a roof exerts thrust. In most cases, no system of buttresses was provided, but the roof was light and the walls thick enough to stand such thrust as there was. Fortunately, there is little snow in England to load the roofs of buildings, but serious trouble has been experienced with this and similar construction in other countries.

Every man who reads or speaks English has a special place in his heart for the domestic architecture of the Tudor period. These are the houses in which the English raised country life to the artistic level. These are the rooms where the greatest poets and the greatest wits did their thinking, their writing, and their talking. The stupendous adventurers who went to the New World, moreover, remembered Tudor villages when they thought of home.

It is generally conceded that English homes of the Late Gothic era represent a considerable improvement over anything earlier in date. From Hampton Court Palace to the smallest house in the Cotswolds, the design of such buildings proceeded on much the same theory. The required rooms were laid out as seemed best by owner and builder. Many plans conform roughly to the shape of a square, an H, or an L, but geometry did not in the least detain or preoccupy the men who put up these houses. They concerned themselves with the means and the practical needs of the family, with the conformation of the site, the direction of prevailing winds, and the view from the windows. Then they enclosed their rooms with walls and roofing. The method, it will be seen, is identical in theory to the procedure advocated by all the talk and writing of our most advanced architects today. It is true that " modern " houses look different from Tudor houses, but the resemblance would be surprising if the gabled roof were added to many a " radical " 20th-Century dwelling.

A small Tudor cottage (Fig. 12.29) is sometimes vaguely reminiscent of the Greek temple form; but because a wide span between walls was difficult to handle, such houses are always narrower; the gable has the steep Gothic angle; and the skyline tends to be more or less broken by chimneys and chimney pots. The second story often has an overhang which adds slightly to the floor area above — and which also invites the attachment of decorative pendants similar in nature if not so refined as the pendants that hang from the vaults of Henry the 7th's Chapel. Narrow clapboards were common in England, but just as common and much more conspicuous was the construction known as *half-timbered*. The timbers of the framework, that is to say, were left in plain sight, and the interstices between them were filled in with plaster. Timbers or clapboards as the case might be, the result was a Gothic complexity of line.

The temple-like unity of typical Tudor cottages reflects the comparative simplicity of the life lived by those with modest means. As soon as any family bettered itself, its home ceased to be so simple in form. Additional rooms of any size and any shape, and running in any convenient direction, were simply added on. Thus any old or large Tudor dwelling is likely to be long, low, rambling, and possessed of a markedly irregular sky line. Nothing could be more unlike the classical, or more consistent with the nature of northern art.

The High Renaissance was almost over in Italy before any important change took place in the artistic taste of the English people. It has often been a matter for remark, indeed, that England has always remained Gothic. Where else, for example, is the government conducted in buildings of that style? The very same point may be illustrated by reference to the earliest permanent architecture of the English colonies in America.

Few of the early colonists had any claim to aristocracy, which meant that few of them had any personal taste for the Italianate details modestly added to great houses from the time of Henry the 8th onward. Although their great-grandsons were to study, admire, and import such ideas, it is probable that hardly a man in the colonies had ever taken so much as a serious look at the work of Inigo Jones, John Webb, or Sir Christopher Wren. Naturally and without self-consciousness, the Americans of the 17th Century simply put up homes of the kind they were used to (Fig. 12.28).

Thus while Italy and France were Baroque, America was still in the Gothic phase; but for that fact, no hint of apology is required. Only a few of the earliest houses survive, but there is much to be said in favor of those that do. Designed for a domestic economy that did not contemplate servants, such homes provided a comfort and efficiency excelled not by all, but only by the very best houses of our modern day. The kitchen fireplace was the only source of heat, to be sure; but if a small fire was maintained at all times (thus keeping the great mass of brickwork warm) a surprising amount of comfort was possible even in zero weather — and with much less fuel than one might suppose. Gas, electricity, running water, and even the iron stove were lacking, but anyone who has inspected a large number of colonial gadgets and implements can testify that labor-saving devices were conspicuously plentiful. Contrary to what we tend to take for granted nowadays, life under such conditions was neither without the essentials nor the amenities. Above all, the kitchen and the living room were identical in the 17th-Century American home. By that simple expedient of arrangement, the colonial housewife saved the steps that her 20th-Century sister can save only if she is lucky enough to have a streamlined modern dwelling.

Germany

The Cathedral of Ulm, already cited above (page 486, and Fig. 12.21) was surely the most conspicuous achievement of the Late Gothic in Germany; but that land is rich in smaller and less pretentious monuments which have exerted a much broader influence than most of us realize. One thinks especially of the old houses in Nuremburg, and of the great city squares so common in Germany, with civil and commercial buildings crowded around them. Congestion combined with prosperity to produce multistoried houses with immense gabled roofs high enough to contain within themselves an extra floor or two of rooms. The type of architecture referred to often appears in the background of plates by Albrecht Dürer (Figs. 16.47–50), and it has contributed greatly to the appearance of the average American city. In order to understand why, one must recall the years before 1914, when Germany was as much admired in America as Hitler's Reich was later detested.

A particular development in ecclesiastical architecture that ought to be singled out for special mention was the celebrated brick Gothic of Germany. The Frauenkirche of Munich, with its onion spires, is a well-known example; but as a class, the brick churches (mostly of the 15th Century) were more characteristic of the Baltic provinces. Their warm color and pleasant texture offer a refreshing variation from the limestone of most Gothic, which when weathered all too often becomes tediously gray.

Italy

The Cathedral at Milan (Fig. 12.30) was begun in 1386 and all but finished by 1500. The western façade was not entirely complete until the time of Napoleon; it was then given some Baroque doors and windows. The general shape of the building is unusual; it seems to have been suggested by that type of Lombard Romanesque (see above, page 400) characterized by a single, continuous, and very broad western gable. In accordance with Italian custom, moreover, no bell towers were incorporated into the mass of the church itself.

Milan was intended to outdo all existing cathedral churches. No architects in Italy had sufficient reputation to command confidence for the project in view. Various masters from France and Germany were therefore called in; two of them had worked on the Cathedral at Ulm. No one can say that these men were negligent in their attempt to dazzle the world. The church is immensely big. The masonry is fine marble, itself a symbol of elegance and luxury unusual in Gothic architecture. There are said to be 2,300 statues (mostly modern). The nave capitals themselves were transformed into pedestals for statuary. The vaulting is not vaulting at all, but a dreamy lacework of open tracery.

Milan is unquestionably the most sumptuous church in the world, but it does not stand comparison with other works of the Late Gothic. The gorgeous detail, so wonderful at first glance, is in truth only complicated and expensive. The carving that covers so many surfaces, including the flying buttresses, lacks the sensitivity of Henry the 7th's Chapel at Westminster. The statuary is empty of content, and the innumerable little pinnacles that break the skyline are individually dull — their repetition becomes tiresome on acquaintance. The interior, which seems grand when one first enters, is in fact merely grandiose; there is nothing to remind us of the proportions or the spatial understanding of Amiens. As an engineering proposition, Milan is stupid. Tie rods were required to absorb thrusts not properly provided for by the placement of the buttresses.

Italy is full of less bizarre monuments dating from the Late Gothic period: at Venice, the Palace of the Doges; at Florence, the Palazzo Vecchio and the Bargello; at Siena, numerous private palaces still occupied by the families that built them, and the Palazzo Pubblico. Except for the use of pointed arches for the window openings, most of these buildings are hardly Gothic at all. Deriving mostly from military architecture and marked by the expediency always associated with such a source, it would not be overly harsh to say that numerous well-known Italian buildings of this era have no style at all. But from age and use they have taken on an appealing patina, and the sternest critic finds it hard to judge them with impartiality. The clemency of the Mediterranean climate, the charm of the Italian scenery, and the incomparable richness of historical association all combine to make one sentimental. But if an attempt at objectivity is made, we shall find ourselves arriving at the conclusion that the only great and definitive work of architecture produced in Italy during the period now under review was the so-called "Mangia Tower" rising over the eastern end of the Palazzo Pubblico at Siena (Fig. 12.31).

The general form of the Mangia upsets all the ordinary proprieties of tower designing. It is slender and delicate at the bottom, heavy and wide at the top. Presented with a table of dimensions or even with a description in words, almost anyone would feel inclined to make a flat statement that the design was certain to prove a failure; yet the truth is that no other tower so perfectly fulfills the Gothic ideal of flight, and by implication the Gothic ideal of infinite space. An adequate analysis of the reasons remains to be written, but there is no voice to contradict the universal admiration. It is obvious, of course, that the use of a lighter color at the top contributes in some measure to the effect by calling up unconscious reminiscences of plant forms; but beyond that suggestion, our present aesthetics seems curiously unable to grapple with the problem.

Spain

An immense amount of work went on in Spain during the Late Gothic era, but the larger and more prominent enterprises of that time are curiously dry and disappointing. The 15th-Century lantern and the western spires of Burgos were built by Germans; they are florid, and cloy quickly. The Cathedral at Seville, begun in 1403, has the distinction, for whatever it is worth, of enclosing the second largest floor area of any Christian church. The dimensions seem to have been suggested by those of the mosque which once occupied the same site. The *Giralda,* a bell tower that is pretty and has an even prettier name, stands at one corner. Originally the minaret of the mosque, its lower portions are Moorish and of the 12th Century, while the present spire and belfry are additions of the 16th. If such monuments represented the best Spanish work of the later Middle Ages, we might well omit the present section entirely; but if we turn to smaller and less famous examples, there is a different story to tell.

Spain presents us with the phenomenon of a population that might with equal reason express itself artistically in the idiom of the Near East (Fig. 2.16) or the northern and linear style that flowered in the Gothic. The earlier history of Spanish art demonstrates for the most part a tendency to do one or the other, with provincial dependence upon the French or Moorish source as the case might be. But during the 15th Century, the Near Eastern heritage amalgamated with the northern for the first time in the so-called " Plateresque " style. The name is from *platero,* a silversmith; and it is an attempt to characterize both the opulence of the decoration and the lovely precision with which its tiny details were rendered.

Two façades at Valladolid illustrate the Plateresque in its most perfect form. They are San Pablo and San Gregorio (Figs. 12.32–33). The immediate impact of the two is more Oriental than Gothic. A very casual glance might lead one to confuse them with examples from the earliest part of the Middle Ages, when the Oriental form-will was working the Classical Style over into the Byzantine (see above, pages 261–269). The Gothic component of the design comes out, however, in the arrangement of the sculpture and its subject matter, in the continuous buttresses and the broken skyline, and in the elaborate variety of novel variations on the pointed arch.

The Plateresque survived the Late Gothic era, and the very same name is often used to designate work like that shown in Fig. 12.34, where the architectural forms are plainly derived from the earlier phase of the Italian Renaissance. The shift from Late Gothic is likely, however, to pass almost unnoticed. It is not the architecture that governs, but the texture and quality of the immensely fertile decoration which came into its own at this time in Spain. Indeed, it may truly be said that from the Late Gothic onward, Spanish architecture (while running through the standard cycle of Early Renaissance, High Renaissance, Baroque, and Rococo) continued to be dominated by an Oriental enrichment of surface unparalleled for sheer richness and virtuosity.

France

During most of the Late Gothic era, Frenchmen were compelled to limit their architecture to comparatively small buildings, or to finishing up churches of earlier date. Most of the Late Gothic monuments of France are of the latter class: towers, porches, choir screens, rose windows, tombs (Fig. 12.36), and similar items. By a kind of tacit understanding, the original plans (if they still existed) were cast aside, and the work to be done was freely designed to fit the fashion of its own date. Thus we find that the transept façades of Beauvais do not correspond with the Gothic of the choir, but to the Gothic as it was in the early 16th Century. The same thing may be said of the new western front of Rouen, and the façade of Troyes. In every instance, it would seem, when new work was added to old, the junction between the two was handled cleverly. Now that several centuries of weathering have intervened to blend all the masonry into a common color, it is often difficult to recognize the precise place where the later additions begin. Such being the case, the casual observer may be forgiven for thinking that everything in view comes from the same period; if so, he forms the mistaken notion that the High Gothic — really a rather chaste style — was very fancy indeed. The northern and later spire of Chartres is an instance in point (Fig. 12.3).

About the middle of the 15th Century, conditions became more propitious in France, and some notable work was done. The Late Gothic choir and apse of Mont Saint Michel were begun in 1450. Hard and perhaps impossible to photograph in any adequate fashion, nothing could better illustrate the Late Gothic at its flamboyant and exquisite best. The so-called "Butter Tower" at Rouen dates from 1487. One may have a preference for something less elaborate or a good reason for wanting something more simple, but it would be a stubborn purist indeed who dared level any serious argument against it.

As the 16th Century drew near, there was a reaction in France against the extremes at which the Late Gothic had arrived. A certain number of buildings, therefore, were designed with the idea of using flamboyant carving not as an over-all investiture of architectural form, but as a foil played off against plain and neutral surfaces. The nave of Saint Pierre at Coutances (Fig. 12.35) is a case in point, and the Church of Brou, put up at Bourg by Margaret of

Austria, is another. It would not be hard to contend that both represent the best, not of the Late Gothic alone, but of all Gothic. Wonderfully gentle and lovely, this final flower of the medieval style seems to sum up all the indefinable qualities of France. At no other time has there been so perfect a combination of chastity and finesse.

Transition from the Gothic to the Renaissance: the Chateaux

Readers with a sense for the schedule of history must have realized long ago that a great many of the Late Gothic monuments fall much beyond the date we ordinarily use to mark the beginning of the Renaissance, but the Renaissance (in the simple sense of a style consciously derived from the classical) was at least a hundred years old in Italy before it had much influence north of the Alps. It first attracted the attention of influential Frenchmen in the course of the Italian campaigns of Charles the 9th and Louis the 12th, who invaded Italy twice during the decade 1494–1504. Those monarchs were so charmed by the new Italian style, especially its northern variation, that they undertook to import it when they returned home. The first effect of the foreign taste and the transition from one style to another is marked by the existence of a number of monumental residences, mostly in the Loire Valley where, for a span, the aristocracy made a vogue of elegant country life in the charming atmosphere of Touraine.

For our immediate purpose, the best example to study is the Chateau at Chambord (Fig. 12.37). The general conception was borrowed from military architecture, and conforms fairly well to the type known as a *concentric castle.* The essential feature of such a castle is that it shall have one wall within another, permitting the outer defenses to be sacrificed gradually while the garrison retreats in good order to an impregnable central unit variously known as the tower, the donjon, or the keep. The main block of building at Chambord, containing the important halls and chambers, is a reminiscence of the donjon. The turrets are circular in plan because that shape more easily resisted the impact of the battering ram, and they project from the wall in the manner of towers intended to restrain an enemy from scaling by permitting cross-fire from above. But as a military building, Chambord was grossly out of date: during the 15th Century it had been made abundantly plain that any commander who understood the crude artillery of the era might expect to take the strongest castle in a matter of days. Reflection upon these points will suggest a certain artificiality in the design of all the chateaux. For perhaps the first time in our study we encounter a sentimental harking back to forms that had once been useful, but at the date of building had little to offer beyond atmosphere.

While all its elements are medieval, even to the broken skyline, a Roman spirit governed the disposition of parts at Chambord (see above, pages 221–223). The plan was kept perfectly symmetrical to its short axis, and approaches symmetry to the long. In elevation, mass was made to balance mass according to the classical, and not the Gothic rule. The windows, moreover, were made square-headed, and strong horizontals predict the coming revival of entablatures. Such things also meant that the Gothic was about to end.

MARBURG

Fig. 13.1 Bamberg. Cathedral. Detail from the screen of Saint George's Choir. *Jonas*. About 1230.

MARBURG

Fig. 13.2 Strassbourg. Cathedral. *The Synagogue*. About 1250.

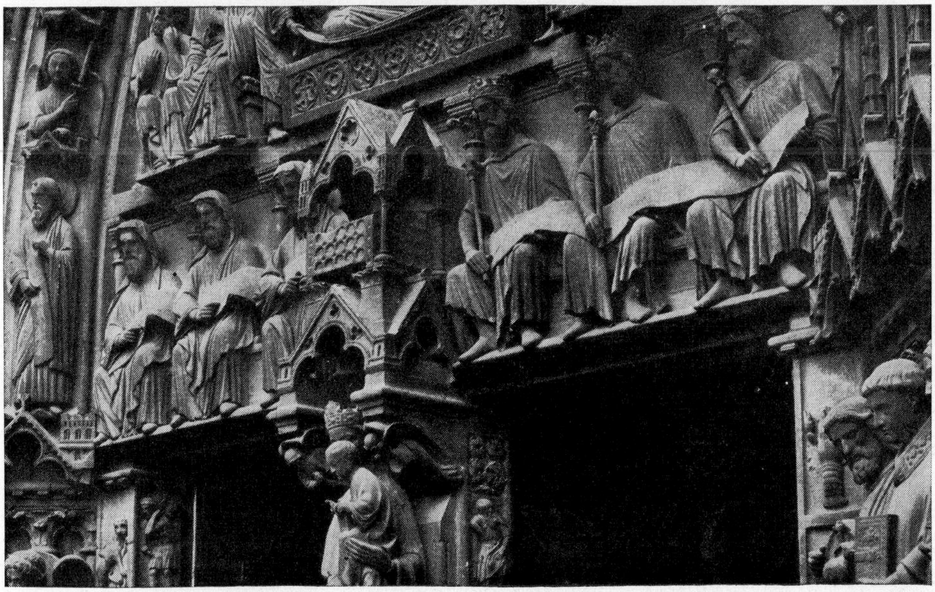

TEL Fig. 13.3 Paris. Cathedral. North door of the west front. Detail of the tympanum, showing six Royal Prophets. About 1230.

ALINARI

Fig. 13.4 Paris. Cathedral. Madonna on the trumeau of the north transept portal. Shortly after 1250.

BULLOZ

Fig. 13.5 Amiens. Cathedral. Madonna on the trumeau of the south transept portal. "La Vierge d'Orée." 1280–1300. From a cast.

ALINARI

Fig. 13.6 Paris. Cathedral. "Notre Dame de Paris." 1330.

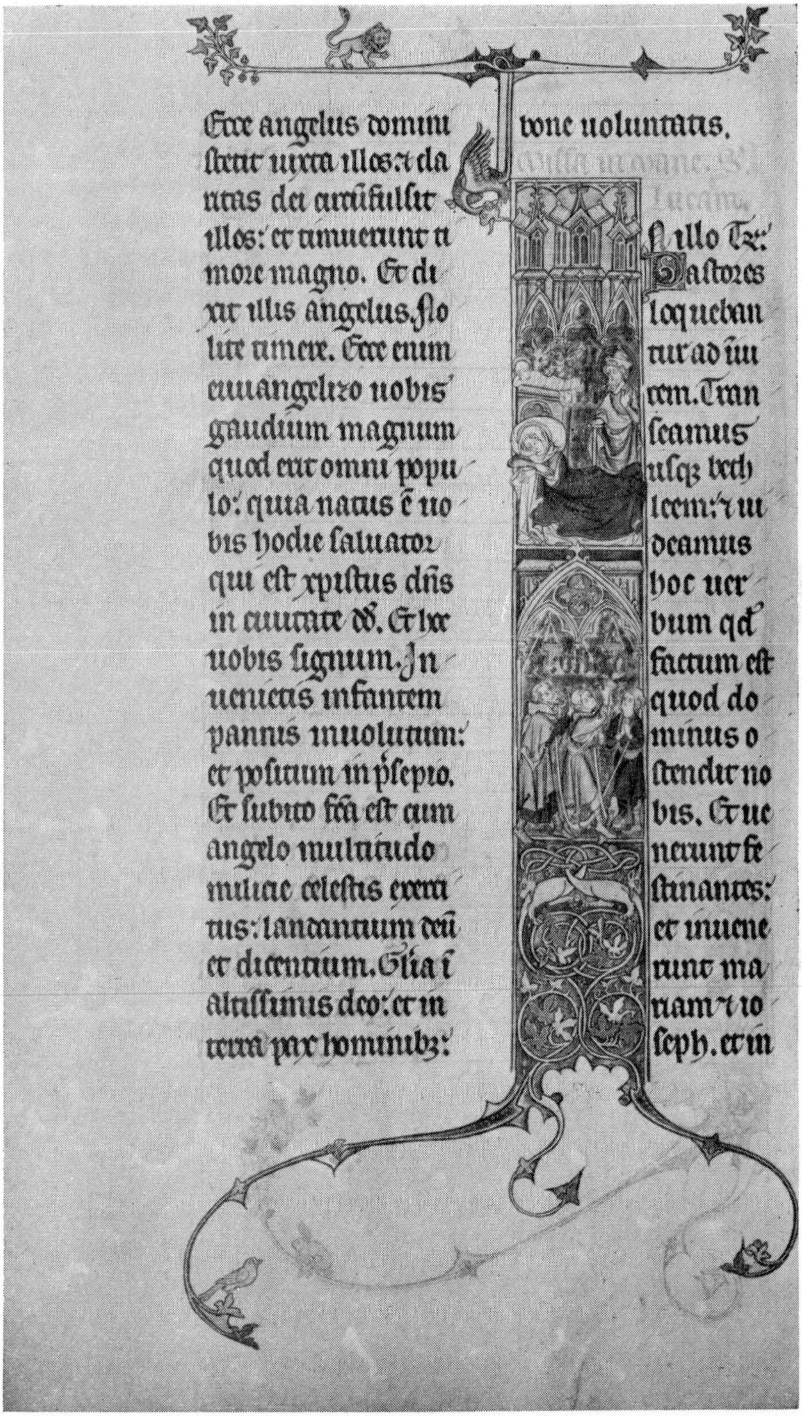

Fig. 13.7 London. British Museum. Additional Manuscript No. 17341. Folio 10 verso. A French Gospel Lectionary of the 13th Century.

Fig. 13.8 Pompey quitting Rome. A miniature from a French manuscript of the 13th Century.

ARCHIVES PHOTOGRAPHIQUES

Fig. 13.9 Paris. Bibliothèque Nationale. Lat. 14284. Scene from the life of David.

Fig. 13.10 Paris. Bibliothèque Nationale. *The Breviary of Belleville.* Folio 118. The murder of Thomas à Becket.

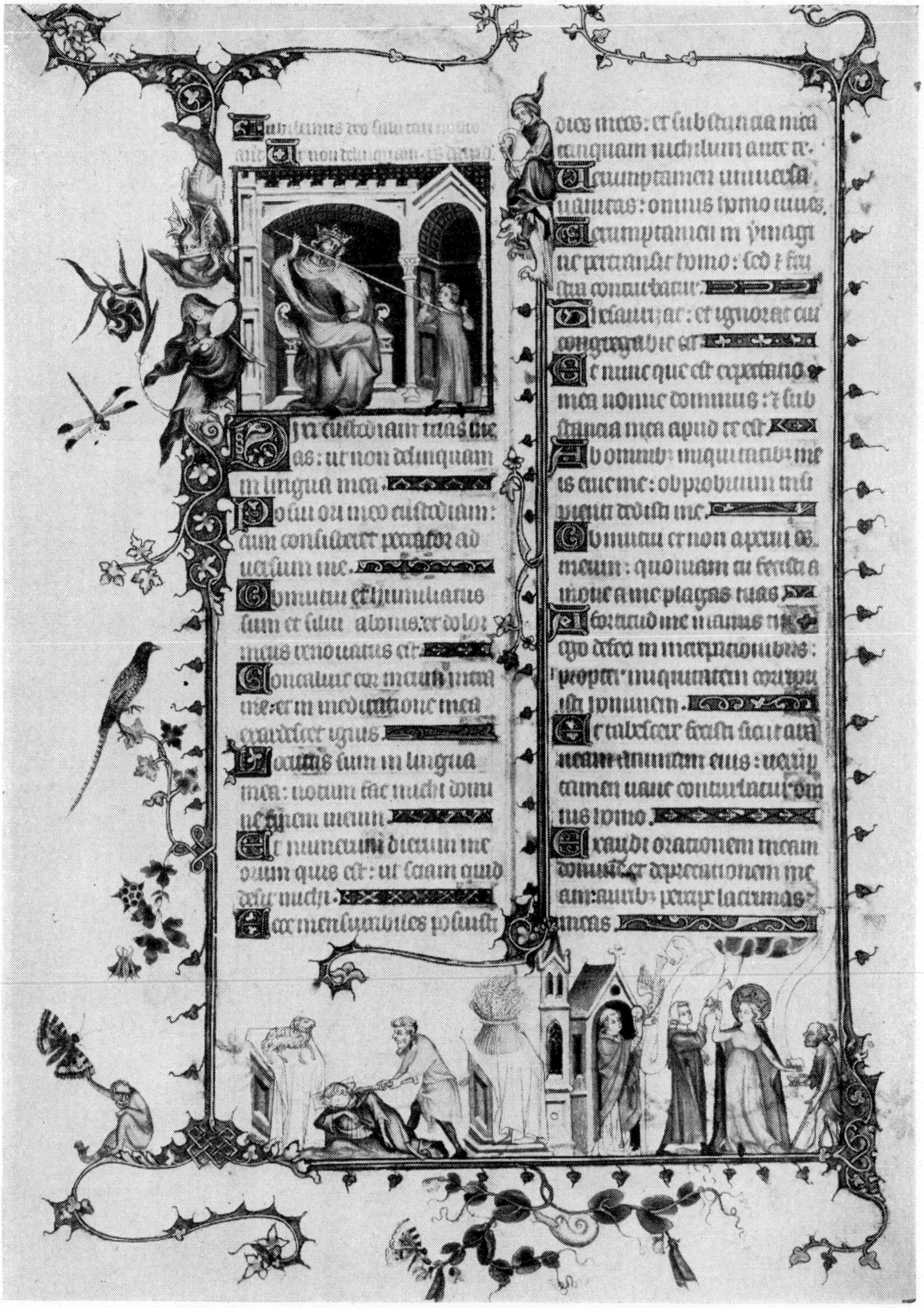

Fig. 13.11 Paris. Bibliothèque Nationale. Lat. 10483. *The Breviary of Belleville.* Folio 24 verso. Saul throwing a spear at David (upper left), the murder of Abel (lower left), and figures symbolizing the Eucharist and Charity. From the shop of Jean Pucelle.

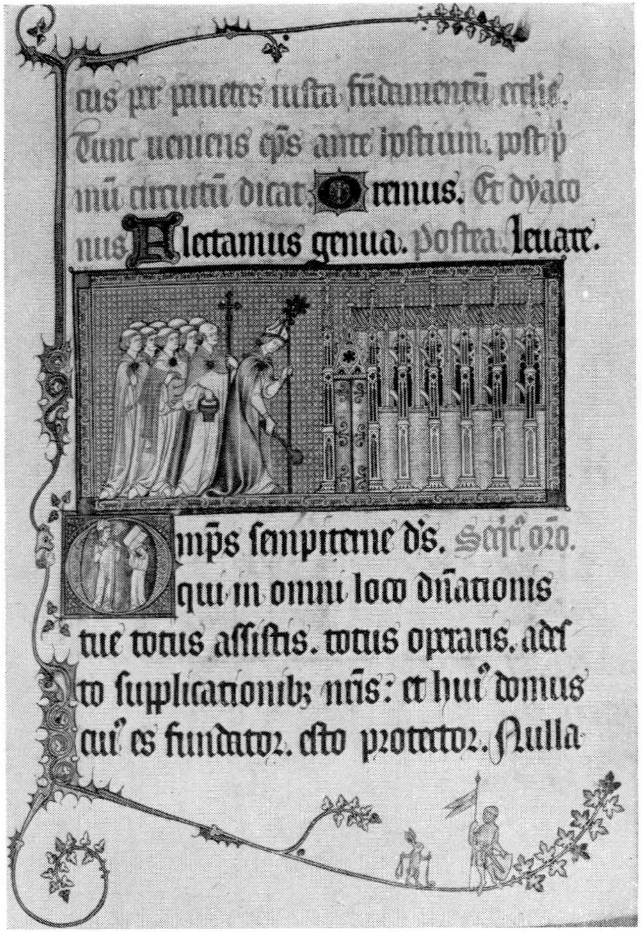

Fig. 13.12 (left) Cambridge, England. Fitzwilliam Museum. *The Pontifical of Metz*. First half of the 14th Century. A bishop sprinkling holy water during the ceremony of dedicating a church; and (below) parody of David and Goliath.

Fig. 13.13 (right) Paris. Louvre. Silver statuette of the Madonna. 1339.

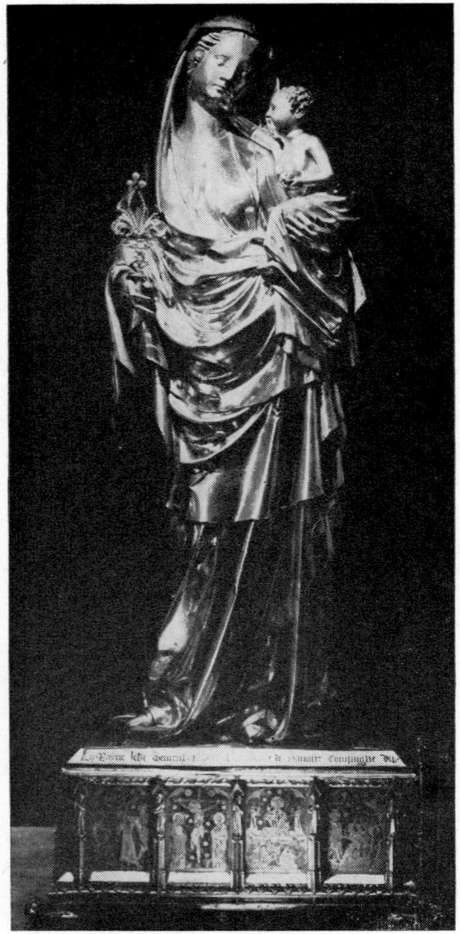

ARCHIVES PHOTOGRAPHIQUES

Figs. 13.14–15 The Brothers Limbourg. Two miniatures from the *Très Riches Heures*. *February* (left); and *August*, with the château of Étampes in the background.
PHOTOGRAPHS BY GIRAUDON

Fig. 13.16 (left) Stefan Lochner. *Madonna with a Violet*. Cologne. Archiepiscopal Palace.

Fig. 13.17 (right) Bernardo Martorell ("The Master of Saint George"). *Saint George and the Dragon*. Chicago. Art Institute. Tempera on panel. 38 x 56 inches.

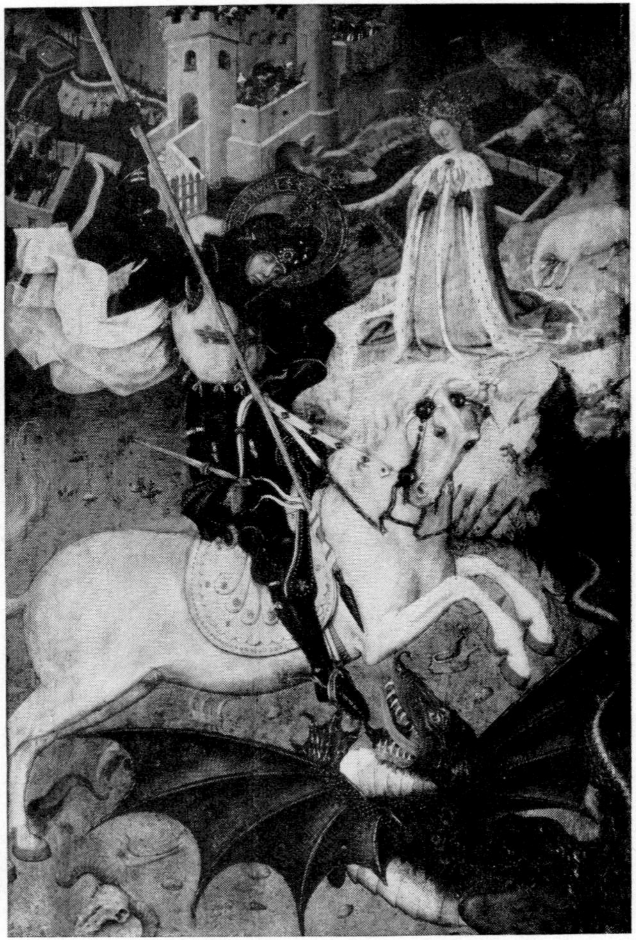

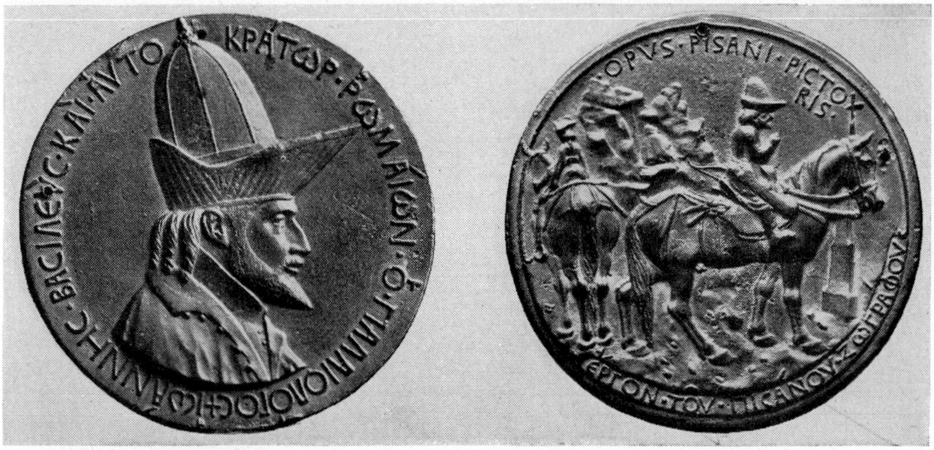

ANDERSON

Fig. 13.18 Pisanello. Medal of John Paleologos, commemorating that Emperor's visit to Italy in 1438–39. Florence. Bargello. Obverse: portrait of the Emperor. Reverse: the Emperor stopping at a roadside shrine while on his way to the Council of Florence.

Fig. 13.19 Pisanello. *Saint Eustace's Vision of Christ in the Form of a Stag*. 1436. London. National Gallery.

ANDERSON

Figs. 13.20–21 Gentile da Fabriano. Above: *Nativity*. Predella panel to *The Adoration of the Magi*. 1423. Florence. Uffizi. *Madonna* (right). New Haven. Yale University Art Gallery.

Fig. 13.22 (below) Uccello. *The Battle of San Romano*. 1432. London. National Gallery. Tempera on panel. 6 feet high.

GIRAUDON

Fig. 13.23 Portrait of Charles the 5th. Detail of the *Parement de Narbonne*. 1374–1378. Paris. Louvre.

ARCHIVES PHOTOGRAPHIQUES

Fig. 13.24 Statue of Charles the 5th. About 1378. Paris. Louvre.

ARCHIVES PHOTOGRAPHIQUES

Figs. 13.25–26 Saint Denis. Tomb of Bertrand du Guesclin. Died 1380.

ARCHIVES PHOTOGRAPHIQUES

Figs. 13.27–28 Claus Sluter. *The Moses Well*. 1395–1406. Dijon. Chartreuse de Champmol. Height 10½ feet. Detail above: Isaiah.

Figs. 13.29–30 Two miniatures painted on leaves of the manuscript originally known as the *Très Belles Heures*. Above: William of Bavaria landing at Veere, from the so-called "Turin Hours" lost in 1903. Below: Baptism of Christ from the so-called "Milan Hours" now in the Museo Civico, Turin.

Figs. 13.31–33 Rome. Vatican Library. Pal. Lat. 1071. The *De Arte Venandi cum Avibus*. Birds on folio 11 verso, portrait of Frederick the 2nd on folio 1 verso, and falconers on folio 103 recto.

ANDERSON

Figs. 13.34–35 Capua. Museum. Colossal heads of personified Capua and Pier delle Vigne. First half of the 13th Century.

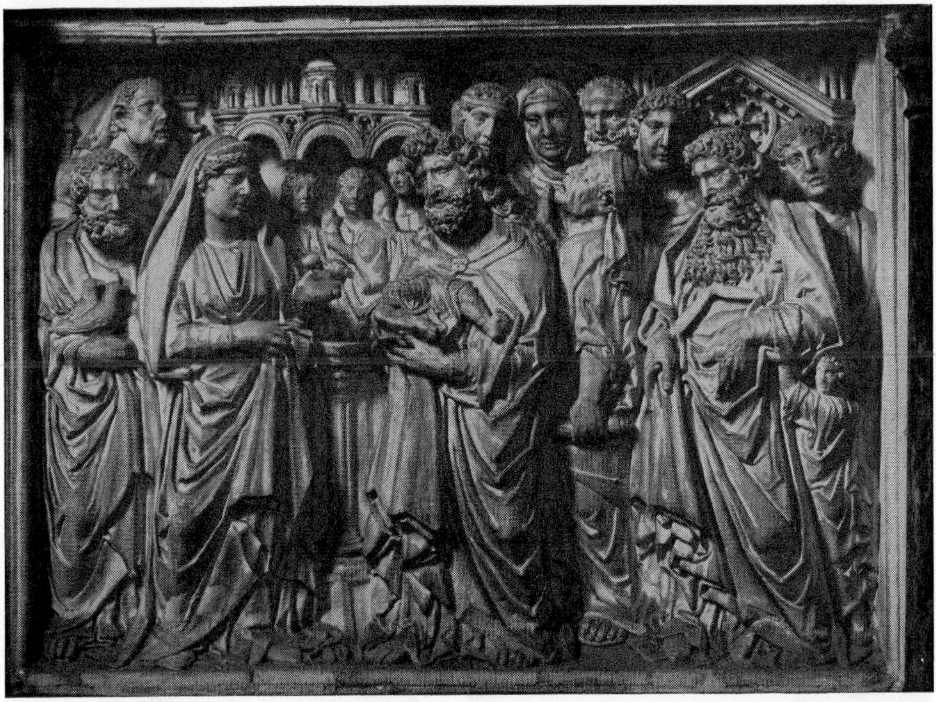

ALINARI

Fig. 13.36 Nicola Pisano. One panel from the pulpit of the Baptistry of Pisa. *The Presentation in the Temple.* 1260.

ANDERSON Fig. 13.37 Giovanni Pisano. *The Crucifixion*. From the pulpit completed in 1310 for the Cathedral of Pisa.

ANDERSON

Fig. 13.38 Giovanni Pisano. Madonna. Pisa. Campo Santo.

CLARENCE KENNEDY

Fig. 13.39 Verona. Tomb of Can' Grande della Scala. Died 1329.

ANDERSON — Fig. 13.40 Orvieto. Cathedral. Scenes from Genesis on the pilasters of the west front. Early 14th Century. Probably by Lorenzo Maitani.

ARCHIVES PHOTOGRAPHIQUES — Fig. 13.41 Paris. Cathedral. Tympanum over the so-called "Red Door." About 1270.

Figs. 13.42–43 Giotto. Frescoes in the nave of the Upper Church of Saint Francis at Assisi. About 1296. *Saint Francis Renouncing His Father* (left) and *Saint Francis's Sermon to the Birds.* ANDERSON

Figs. 13.44–45 Giotto. Frescoes at the Arena Chapel in Padua. 1303–05. *The Meeting at the Golden Gate* (above) and a detail from *The Nativity*. ANDERSON

ANDERSON

Fig. 13.46 Giotto. *The Flight into Egypt.* Padua. Arena Chapel. 1303–05.

ANDERSON

Fig. 13.47 Giotto. *The Death of Saint Francis.* Florence. Santa Croce. Between 1318 and 1322.

*

13

SCULPTURE AND PAINTING DURING THE GOTHIC PERIOD

Introductory: Statement of Coverage

The business of the present chapter is twofold. It is in the first place an attempt to acquaint the reader with the most important monuments of statuary and painting produced during the Gothic period. But over and above their worth as an essential department of Gothic art, those same monuments offer us perspective upon the manner and process by which the Middle Ages came to an end and the world of the Renaissance began. Before proceeding with our narrative, it behooves us, therefore, to give the reader warning as to the course of events. He may then know what to look for.

In the north of Europe, there was no precise break between medieval and Renaissance culture. The Renaissance art of France, Flanders, and Germany came into being by a gradual and even orderly evolution from the Gothic. Things were different in Italy, where the population had never entirely accepted the Gothic nor forgotten the Classical. Ideas and expressions in the key of the Renaissance were more overt in Italy, but it is impossible to maintain the conventional notion that the entire movement originated there. The very earliest examples of northern Gothic sculpture contain within themselves a prediction of the future — and hence of the values which have governed European motivation from the 15th Century onward to our own time.

The first thing to watch for is this: as the narrative proceeds, the reader will note how art history (as the dates get later) finds its frame of reference less and less in the great ecclesiastical tradition, and in the immense cathedrals which survive as the principal monuments of the medieval church. Almost unconsciously, we shall find our attention directed toward single statues and pictures — works of comparatively small size, executed by individual artists. More and more, as we go along, our powers of observation will tend to focus themselves upon the people who are represented. The single human figure, we shall presently realize, ultimately became the prime factor in all art, the irreducible and indispensable unit thereof.

The stage of development just described was arrived at in Italy before the end of the 13th Century, and its advent was sudden and dramatic. In the more prosaic north, the process was less spectacular and the evolution more regular in its movement; but in all Europe, it was during the 14th and 15th Centuries that the human individual asserted himself and took his place as the essential element in society. *Humanism* became the faith of the world, and it has furnished the foundation for all philosophical speculation these past 500 years. Of both individualism and humanism, we shall have much to say at a number of points. For our immediate purpose, it will suffice to mention the following.

The word *humanism* has been used in a variety of senses, some of them entirely arbitrary. We use it here to designate the philosophy which starts from the concept that the individual has dignity — worth, that is to say, in and of himself and during his brief and mortal life. Such a view conduces to a picture of reality as an equation between the race and the environment, and such was in fact the outlook that became general as the Renaissance arrived.

Nothing could be at a farther remove from the philosophy typical of the Middle Ages. The medieval mind had seen life as an equation between man and God. If the notion of personal worth asserted itself at all, the assertion was submerged in the need for grace. We all know, of course, that innumerable persons during the Middle Ages did not live up to such idealism. Many of them were drunkards, libertines, and worse. Undoubtedly, they derived from their activities as much worldly pleasure as may be so derived at any period in history, but we must distinguish between ideals and behavior. Insofar as the accepted dogma of society governed, the suggestion that either a good or a complete life might be possible on earth had been outlawed. All hope had been fastened on heaven. If we were able to name the moment when Western civilization passed into the Renaissance, it would be the instant when a majority accepted in their hearts the idea of this world's respectability.

Acceptance of the world made it necessary that art should become realistic; also that art should in some degree become expressive of interest and satisfaction in worldly things. In Gothic art a single monument might, and often did, combine both those elements; but to an unusual extent, the two purposes remained distinct and separate.

As early as the middle of the 13th Century, we can recognize a tendency we shall designate as *Gothic Realism.* It is exemplified by such vivid statues as the *Jonas* at Bamberg (Fig. 13.1). The artists who belonged to the realistic movement specialized in statues and pictures primarily motivated by the belief that the appearance of things in nature, including all the unlovely accidents, amounted to the law of art. Some of them restricted their attention to increasingly accurate and severe studies of anatomy. Others became specialists in representing the figure within the environment. Both groups entertained a theory of art in no way different from the objective realism of Antiquity. As things turned out, Gothic Realism was the art of the future; its advent marked the beginning of the *Representative Convention* (see below, pages 539–542) which governed all European art until the end of the 19th Century.

In substantial contrast to the Gothic Realists, and contemporary with them, were other artists whom we may name the *Gothic Mannerists.* The general nature of their work is indicated by the figure of the personified *Synagogue* at Strasbourg (Fig. 13.2). Such men were comparatively indifferent to accuracy of representation, although most of them knew enough about it at any given time to avoid obvious mistakes that would label their work as out of date. Their art was the perfect counterpart for the more luxurious kind of Late Gothic architecture. Their purpose was to emphasize grace and elegance in the figure and to capitalize upon fine clothes for people, fine trappings for animals, and the lovelier aspects of scenery and the climate.

Gothic Mannerism had nothing like so long a history, nor so important an influence as Gothic Realism. It continued as a strong style only while the feudal aristocracy devoted itself to making life a florid and gorgeous pageant vaguely based upon the ideals of chivalry. The last flower of Gothic Mannerism was the so-called " International Style " which dominated much of European art from about 1350 onward (see below, pages 531–539). By about 1450, only the most conservative artists still showed elements of mannerism, and after that the whole theory was dead.

In our survey of Gothic sculpture and painting up to the end of the 13th Century, we need merely to remember that both realism and mannerism were present as tendencies; the style of a particular piece of work sometimes swung one way, sometimes the other. About the beginning of the 14th Century, however, the two tendencies became divergent movements, each represented by a school of specialists. At that point we shall find it convenient to trace each movement separately.

EARLY GOTHIC SCULPTURE: THE WEST PORCH OF CHARTRES

The three western doorways of the present Cathedral of Chartres were preserved from an earlier fabric. The statues probably date shortly before 1150, at which time they were the last word in modernity. We usually cite them as the earliest preserved examples in an authentically Gothic style, but the reader should make a mental note that the work at Chartres was probably derivative from slightly earlier and similar statuary executed for Suger's Saint Denis.

The statues at Chartres (Fig. 12.5) were the work of men to whom the Gothic theory of architectural sculpture (see above, pages 464–466) was a new thing, to be implemented in the most exact and specific manner. Because Gothic is linear, the figures were radically distorted in the vertical direction. Each statue is so tall that its plastic values are all but lost in its function as an enriched architectural line; and for the same reason, all the poses were kept frontal and stiff.

And yet there is much here that will please the most ardent humanist. Each face is unique and personal. Hundreds of visitors have demanded to know the names of the sitters. The old folk are characters and the young people are charming. Only one or two of the girls and women are pretty, but all are winsome and dainty — an emphasis upon femininity new in European art at this time, and reflecting, no doubt, the arrival of the chivalric code of manners.

HIGH GOTHIC SCULPTURE: PARIS, THE LATER WORK AT CHARTRES, AMIENS, REIMS

During the 13th Century, architectural dictates were enforced upon the sculptor, but much less severely. When a given figure was meant to run with an architectural line, it was incumbent upon the sculptor to minimize diagonal impulses of the sort produced by extended arms and crosswise drapery, but no one asked him to make the figure itself into a kind of line. Excellent niches and brackets were designed as an integral part of the architecture, with the result that statuary has never been more advantageously displayed. Within reasonable limits of cooperation, the sculptors could thus do about as they pleased. With a nice sense for the implications of their own medium, the best men conceived and executed all the larger statues as free-standing figures rendered plastically and in the round, and the " architectural restrictions " may be written off as having done no harm. There was, for instance, no particular reason for distortion; and while less precise than the laboriously accurate anatomy of the 15th Century, most 13th Century sculpture is approximately correct.

The content of 13th Century work was, like the style, both restricted and free. There seems to have been a common understanding that all religious art must aim at a lofty and spiritual tone, but within that policy considerable variation was permitted. Thus we find that High Gothic sculpture, while recognizably uniform in style, presents a much greater range of emotion than we found true of Greek art of the Great Age. Each city, in fact, seems to have given its statues something of its own special character.

The *Saint Firmin* of Amiens (Fig. 12.10) was one of the solid men of that guild-governed town, a monument to all the people who do the world's work. In some contrast are the six royal prophets (Fig. 13.3) who sit across the lower register of the north, or *Virgin Portal* on the west front of Paris. A continuous scroll runs over their knees; it probably signifies philosophical agreement. In their faces we may recognize a quality not often seen except in university towns — the plain but indefinable mark of the scholar. Or we may go again to Chartres, where the statues of the two transept porches (Fig. 12.6) were gradually assembled from perhaps 1210 to as late as 1275. Easier in pose and realized more plastically than those of the West Porch, these later figures maintain the same lyric and even mystic charm. One tends to think of them as transfigured rustic types; the male countenances in particular have a gentleness almost never seen except in quiet rural places.

The monuments just mentioned are typical of the High Gothic at its best. As statues in their own right: above criticism. As architectural decoration: unexcelled in the whole history of art. As an expression of the Gothic ideal: a gracious moderation of earlier severity in the direction of human warmth. To such remarks, a more complete demonstration than we can undertake in the present text would add a staggering variety of lesser sculpture including in its subject matter an exhaustive survey of almost every creature on earth or imagined — an encyclopedic catalogue of all things included within the divine scheme.

But at a very early date, High Gothic statues began to exhibit certain qualities which predicted the decline of the medieval synthesis to the same degree that they predicted the future course of art. Shortly after the middle of the 13th Century, for example, the two transept portals of the Cathedral of Paris were finished up complete with sculpture. It would not be hard to contend that the doorway of the northern transept with its beautiful Madonna on the trumeau (Fig. 13.4) is the most perfect bit of Gothic that we have. It is strong without being coarse, delicate without a hint of weakness, mature but not yet overblown, and the very definition of elegance. But if we take a closer look at the figure of the Madonna, we may sense all that was good in the 13th Century, and yet feel a certain departure from its religious motivation.

The model chosen for the Madonna was a woman of about 35. Her body is heavier and more robust than a girl's, but her pose is lithe and fluent. She stands with the weight on the left foot. The right leg is held slack, with the foot slightly back and the knee gently forward to make a convexity in the drapery. The baby (now lost) was originally present to balance the composition. The costume is of peculiar interest, for it was during the 13th Century that Paris became the world capital for female fashions. The waist is high, and the upper parts of the dress, including the sleeves, are closely fitted around shoulders and bust. The skirt, by contrast, contains a voluminous amount of cloth which necessarily falls in great undulating folds. In order to walk, or merely to free the feet for an easy standing posture, such a skirt must be caught up (as here) by a hand — a gesture that produces a diagonal cascade of drapery to one side or the other.

There is no possibility of a contention against the statement that this Madonna is utterly charming; but at the same time, she signalizes the discard of Gothic conventions. The curvilinear pose and diagonal drapery, although moderate at this point in the evolution, signify the intention of sculptors to break completely away from the subordination of sculpture to architecture. What was to be gained in freedom for their own art was, in equal measure, to be a sacrifice of integration for all the arts. In the matter of content, we may be happy to welcome the arrival of that peculiar department of charm — something both less and more than beauty — which makes the Frenchwoman an adornment of the race, but at the same moment we embrace standards that are less spiritual than those of a generation earlier.

The sacrifice at first seems trivial until we turn our attention to the next step in the process which we shall find well illustrated by the famous *Vierge d'Orée* attached to the south transept portal at Amiens (Fig. 13.5). Because the portal as a whole had a complicated building history, the precise date is not agreed upon, but we may safely assume that this particular figure falls between 1280 and 1300.

In the matter of style, the tendencies remarked upon above are more pronounced and less decorous. Pose and costume alike have been made extreme. There is no longer any possibility of considering the statue as a desirable enhancement of architecture either by harmony or by contrast. It is simply a jarring and conflicting note. As to content, no defensible aspect of humanism will excuse it; for the Queen of Heaven, we are asked to accept a smirking middle-class woman who learned her manners as a shop girl. It is worth noting before we pass on that the figure is called golden because it was in fact gilded when installed.

Both the Madonnas just cited illustrate very well how a prediction of the coming realism and a prediction of the coming mannerism often coexisted within the same work of art. For the first demonstration of mannerism as such, and in strong measure, we must turn to the west front of Reims (Figs. 12.14–16). The design of the whole façade was a grandiose attempt to secure greater luxuriance and refinement than elsewhere; but because Reims was under construction for ninety years and in view of the large number of statues, a sweeping statement is bound to have exceptions. Almost every tendency known during the entire 13th Century is illustrated somewhere in the ensemble.

Two of the best-known and best-loved statues are the Mary and Elizabeth of the *Visitation* (Luke 1:39–45), to the right of the central doorway (Fig. 12.16). In their general appearance, they bring back memories of certain classical marbles, particularly the *Demeter of Cnidos* now in the British Museum, but a closer inspection shows that the types are Teutonic. The Elizabeth, in fact, is very like an Elizabeth on the Cathedral at Bamberg.

For these two particular statues, it is impossible to question the religious content. Where can we go for a more perfect rendering of Saint Elizabeth's mature tenderness toward Mary? Or for Mary's joy in her approaching motherhood, made grave by the weight of her holy mission? And yet, are not these emotions very conscious and highly drawn? And what of the guess amounting to conviction, that the style actually was drawn from several sources; are we not there somewhere near the border where creative power passes over into aesthetic discernment?

Once again, our impulse to reservation may seem altogether too ready, especially when applied to the *Visitation* group. The phrase *mannered elegance* hits straight home, however, with respect to various other statues at Reims. Among those, the most famous are two angels (Fig. 12.16) originally intended as a symmetrical pair and rearranged to make one of them the Gabriel of the *Annunciation* (Luke 1:26–35). Both seem to have been the work of a master who came to Reims about 1260.

For the bodies, he used a very slender, tall proportion, with an unusually small head. For the pose, he used the strong S-curve that was the vogue of the moment. The combination produced sinuous and even serpentine figures, an impression fortified by the exaggerated grace with which the head is poised. The inner lines of the drapery and the silhouette of the wings have a similarly self-conscious refinement; their curvature is more feline than human. On the faces, there is a smile that has attained a notoriety almost equal to that of the

Mona Lisa. Doubtless the sculptor intended it for the sublime, but he produced the epicene. In connection with his attempt, it is worth remarking that innumerable others have failed in the same endeavor. In the entire history of art, there are perhaps eight or ten monuments capable of inspiring an observer with emotions authentically transcendental.

Because angels do not live on earth, the strictures just listed might be dismissed as a mere misunderstanding of something supernatural, but the same escape clause is hardly available in those instances when the Reims sculptors undertook to represent people. If we turn our attention to other figures by the same hand, the Joseph, for instance, and the lady who attends Mary (sometimes called the Prophetess Anne) of the *Presentation* (Luke 2:25–35; Fig. 12.15) we are likely to experience much the same puzzlement as that evoked by certain monuments of Greek sculpture during its Hellenistic phase. The statues are either better than anything that came before, or shallow and cheap, or both at the same time. One's first impulse is to say of the Joseph, " What a wonderful face! How gentle, how cultured, how refined! " And of the lady, " How dainty she is, and yet how intelligent! " But reservations and qualifications thrust themselves forward. The lady's hair and dress, to say nothing of Joseph's handsome whiskers, occupy too prominent a place in our attention. The sculptor used much skill in elaborating those details, but the elaboration seems to have been something extra — a kind of overlay obscuring the contour and meaning of the mass beneath. Once started, such a train of thought suggests the suspicion that we have here the work of a master who judged by surface appearances, and whose philosophy tended uneasily toward the frivolous.

FRENCH MANUSCRIPT ILLUMINATION TO ABOUT 1400 A.D.

An immense number of books survive from the Gothic period, but they have not been given their proper place in art history. All too often, we find such material dismissed with a mere allusion which seems to hint that serious authors have no time for pretty little things. The truth is that book designing reached its high point during the 13th Century, and has never been so good since. As to the art of decorating pages, there has never been anything finer, and the little pictures which are worked in here and there are, except for their tiny size, as worthy as any other class of painting (Fig. 13.8). In addition to their absolute value as works of art, the Gothic manuscripts have a peculiar importance historically. During the 13th Century, the art of bookmaking became more and more closely centered at Paris until it approached a near-monopoly, and was referred to as such by Dante. The influence of French taste upon the rest of Europe may in large measure be accounted for by the continuous export of those portable works of art.

For a typical piece of work corresponding in date and spirit to the great cathedrals, we may turn to a page from a Gospel Lectionary (book of readings) now in the library of the British Museum (Fig. 13.7). It has often been said that every element and quality of the Gothic style shows up somewhere on every page of Gothic illumination, and the statement is scarcely an exaggeration. This particular page, for example, has a composition closely analogous to that of the cathedrals. There is the same absence of symmetry, the same dynamic use of line to achieve an eccentric type of unity, the same intimate organization of details into a complex whole. The text and the pictures and the decorations all form essential parts of a single and coherent visual scheme. Just as the Gothic architect designed suitable niches for the accommodation of statuary, the Gothic book designer provided an enframement of much the same sort for the pictures. His choice of architectural forms for the purpose was no matter of chance, it appears to have been a uniform custom by which we are reminded of the cathedral, and reminded, also, that no work of Gothic art ever exists alone. It will be noted still further that every letter and punctuation mark was given the intense definition typical of all northern detail; also, that each one is in itself a miniature demonstration of Gothic composition and outline. There could be no more thoroughgoing manifesto of the universal nature of the Gothic style, or of the determination of every Gothic artist, whatever his medium, to make his work a reflection of the idea that the universe is complicated, and can be made intelligible only by a supreme act of logical organization.

Certain other features peculiar to Gothic illumination and more or less constant in its practice are worth mentioning. The space below the lower picture is filled with a 13th-Century version of the Irish interlace. The floral spray sweeping across the top and bottom of the page also takes a Celtic swing; and it will be noted that its upper branch is, by all the laws of anatomy, the foliate double tail of a little dragon. But the vocabulary of these artists was not limited to the grotesque. At the top of the page, there is a very good lion; and at the bottom, an excellent bird.

All of these items tend to attract our attention one by one, and to delay comprehension of the fact that the two little paintings, taking them as a pair, depict *The Adoration of the Magi.* Here again we see how very Gothic is the work of the Gothic illuminator. The effect of the page is not instantaneous, as in classical and Renaissance art. We proceed cumulatively, noticing one thing at a time, and ultimately construct for ourselves an organic whole.

In strict logic, we should probably reserve the word *illumination* to describe pages like the one just reviewed, and to signify that the painter accepted a scheme of subordination in which the picture (a part) was made intelligible by its decorative relation to the page (a whole). So understood, the little *Adoration* bears the same relation to the entire composition as the *Beau Dieu* (Fig. 12.11) bears to the Cathedral of Amiens. Such a conception of the function of pictures continued until about the middle of the 13th Century, up to which time the full-page *illustrations* (i.e., separate pictures that belong to books merely because they are bound in) were rare even in very handsome manuscripts.

It was only natural, however, that the Gothic painters would, like the sculptors, find themselves working away from standards which, while excellent, tended to curtail the independence of individual artists. The first stage in the process is well illustrated in the work of Jean Pucelle (Figs. 13.10–11), an artist who attained special prominence as early as 1320, and ran the best shop in Paris for about 25 years. The word *pucelle* was then used for a dragon-fly, and the master used to sign with that insect. His assistant Chevrier, for a similar reason, signed with the bagpiper.

In the matter of style, Pucelle maintained an approximation to the Gothic ideal of page composition as outlined above, but he gave the pictures much more room and prominence. He and his men devoted their delicate technique to butterflies, squirrels, birds, plants, grasses—all of which appear like embroidery in the margins. The tiny things in nature have never seemed more joyous, nor more joyously drawn; and the demonstration, if florid, is altogether beguiling.

As time went on, it appears that the internal logic of painting asserted itself more and more. Pictures tended to break away from the text, and the end result was to make the full page illustration the standard thing rather than the exception. That state of affairs was achieved by the end of the 14th Century, at which time the easel pictures (ever since the most popular and prevalent European art form) began to appear in ever larger numbers. To illustrate the transition at its halfway mark, we cannot do better than inspect the illustrations of the *Pontifical of Metz,* one of which we reproduce in Fig. 13.12. The book is a volume of services to be read by a bishop, or pontiff, and we find it open at the pages which give the order for the dedication of a church. By comparison to our earlier examples, the size of the main picture has been considerably enlarged. A proportional enlargement of the lettering enables the latter to keep its visual importance in the composition, but the spray and other details necessarily remain about their former size. The art of painting had, in short, stolen the show, and illumination no longer existed in its 13th-Century sense.

A notable minor feature of this and innumerable other Gothic pages is the addition of an element of humor. In the present instance, it amounts to no more than a caprice of the imagination; but on other pages of the same manuscript, there are examples of impudent grotesques who indulge in outright satires of the principal scene.

While the figures in the dedication scene are, if considered singly, good examples of moderate mannerism, the scene in which they appear shows an effort at realism when taken as a whole. There seems to have been some intention of representing space, and indicating the relative placement of different persons within it. At the date when this work was done, there was probably not a single master in France who could have carried the enterprise off successfully. The requisite techniques of drawing and of tone relations were not yet understood; but the die had been cast, and the next great effort in the history of painting was destined to gain mastery of those very skills.

THE LATER HISTORY OF GOTHIC MANNERISM, AND THE ARRIVAL OF THE INTERNATIONAL STYLE

The first half of the 14th Century witnessed the complete divorce of sculpture from its previous inseparable relation to architecture. Free-standing statues became common. The most popular subject was the Madonna and Child, and the new fashion seems to have appeared at about the same time in both France and Italy (see below, pages 546–547). Of the numerous French examples, the most famous is the so-called " Notre Dame de Paris " (Fig. 13.6), a figure which happens to have been set up in the choir of the cathedral in the year 1330. Its sobriquet explains the content: the statue has always been rather loosely construed as a symbol for the city, the more superficial aspects of which it so perfectly personifies. No one ever thought of it as being religious except in the most technical way; and it survived intact the wholesale destruction of religious art that took place during the French Revolution. It is notable that the costume is almost identical with the gown of the Virgin Annunciate painted three years later by Simone Martini (Fig. 10.20), and the exaggerated pose and canon of proportions are likewise much the same — illustrating once again how literally French taste was accepted all over Europe.

Although there are a great many of them, full-size stone statues were not the typical product of 14th-Century mannerism. The Madonnas that best sum up the spirit of the period are the exquisite little statuettes done in gold, silver, or ivory (Fig. 13.13). Such things, it is important to mention, were never intended for public exhibition. They were made for private patrons — a class of person hitherto rare, but beginning in the 14th Century to assume a controlling position with relation to art of all kinds. Because the little figures were intended for private devotions, the artists who did them worked away from the solemnity typical of High Gothic cathedral sculpture. They sought to establish between onlooker and statue a relationship more personal and intimate than might be appropriate for public monuments. In that endeavor, they enjoyed varying degrees of success. Some statuettes are no better than cute; others seem lovely and satisfactory beyond description.

The Popes came to Avignon in 1305, and the papal court soon became a cultural center. Artists and men of letters came there from all points, sojourned, and returned home stimulated and refreshed by intercourse with their peers from other lands. Petrarch, the reputed inventor of the sonnet, made his first trip to Avignon in 1326. In 1339, his friend Simone Martini (see above, pages 367–369) also came. Giotto having died three years before (see below, pages 550–563), Simone was at that moment the most prominent Italian artist alive, but his special ability to influence the style of other artists rested upon grounds that were ulterior to painting.

Siena, from which he came, was and still remains the most self-consciously aristocratic city in Europe. Simone, who was himself a knight, appears to have moved in the upper circles of Sienese society. No northern artist earlier than John Van Eyck (died 1440) had anything like the same social position. In order to assess the importance of that fact, certain medieval prejudices must be recalled.

Medieval society was obsessed with the notion of propriety. Certain functions and activities were honorable. Others were venal. In the former, an aristocrat was proud to engage; the latter he would not touch. As applied to our special interest and the matter of Simone's influence at Avignon, we must deal with a particular ramification of such conventions. The *liberal arts,* in their original Greek meaning, had been the arts open to free men who were free in the sense that they might depend upon the work of slaves to provide them with all the necessities of life. During the Middle Ages, the list of liberal arts was frozen; only seven studies were so recognized: grammar, logic, rhetoric, arithmetic, geometry, music, and astronomy. Those arts were "liberal" because the mind of the student was "free" to go where it would in the realm of pure reason, without being impeded by the recalcitrance of matter. Carpentry, by contrast, was not liberal; it was *adulterine* because the thoughts of the carpenter were adulterated by the necessity of using his hands to force his tools against the stubborn wood. Artists, because they worked with their hands and used tools, had traditionally been classed as laborers. There was noticeable discrimination against them for that reason long after the period now under consideration. Michaelangelo himself once felt compelled, for example, to ask a correspondent to address letters to him by his surname Buonarroti — if addressed to Michaelangelo the Sculptor, communications might suggest to careless people that he belonged with the bricklayers. It was, however, true that the prejudice referred to had been substantially undermined in Italy early in the 14th Century. We may remember Simone as the man who introduced northern Europe to the concept of the artist as a gentleman, and we cannot exaggerate the added effect it gave his influence.

Simone stayed at Avignon five years, and died there. He did a good deal of painting, almost all of it irrevocably lost. He brought to Avignon the peculiar linear genius of Siena, and he found in France a Gothic linear predilection almost as accomplished as his own. As to whether he was the teacher or the collaborator, we need not argue; the fact is that the style of Sienese painting combined at Avignon to produce a new version of the Late Gothic which was enthusiastically received by every lord and lady in Europe. From Avignon, artists returned home. The result was that schools sprang up in numerous places and that the style was much the same everywhere. Hence the name *International Style* for the delicate art of the people who move through the pages of Sir John Froissart — the society that crossed the great divide at Agincourt in 1415.

The greatest monument of the International Style is the manuscript known as the *Très Riches Heures* (Figs. 13.14–15). For a reasonable comprehension of that most sumptuous book, the reader is referred to the good colored plates published as a separate monograph in *Verve* for April–July 1940 (Vol. 2, No. 7). The work was done for John, Duke of Berry, the younger brother of Charles the 5th of France. The political and social theories of the Duke of Berry are shocking by modern standards; no one was more savage in reducing those who opposed him, or more merciless in bleeding those whom he had in his grip. But the fabulous wealth thus accumulated made it possible for him to spend most of his 76 years in unceasing patronage of the arts. Toward the end of his life, he conceived the project of making himself the owner of the handsomest book ever produced by the hand of man.

He first commissioned a Book of Hours known today by the popular name of the *Très Belles Heures de Notre Dame,* but he became dissatisfied before the work was finished; and about 1412, he disposed of the leaves which were divided, as we shall recount in the next section (page 541). The reason for his change of plan seems to have been his discovery of some artists known today as The Brothers Limbourg, who had come to France from Gelderland, south of the Zuider Zee. He set them to work on a new manuscript, the *Très Riches Heures;* and they ceased work when the Duke died in 1416. By that time the Limbourgs had completed 39 of the larger pictures, two of medium size, and 34 little ones. Between 1485 and 1489, the manuscript was completed with the addition of 61 more pictures by an artist named Jean Colombe.

It will be evident that the *Très Riches Heures* is not a monument in the ordinary sense; it is a major museum in portable form, and a treasure trove for anyone who wants a glimpse of the world as it was 500 years ago. The name *book of hours* derives from the *hours canonical,* the schedule used by monasteries for the daily routine of religious exercises. As ordinarily used, the phrase describes a book of readings intended for a similar round of private devotions on the part of a lay owner. For his convenience, extra material was often bound up with the religious sections: a calendar, for example, and tables for finding the date of Easter. Because services devoted to the Virgin were popular, the illustrations often included some very lovely Late Gothic Madonnas.

In the case of the *Très Riches Heures,* the most interesting pictures are the full-page illustrations for the calendar, each arranged with a semicircular tabulation of dates immediately above a rectangular picture showing a scene typical of that time of year. In each instance, the vista includes a castle owned by the Duke, or one of his favorite views. A great favorite is the page devoted to February (Fig. 13.14) which represents a farmyard in winter. The sheep are crowded in their fold, the beehives are covered by a light fall of snow, a two-wheeled cart lies idle, the casks are upended to keep them clear. Indoors, a man and two women are warming themselves before a fire. Another person comes shivering across the yard. In the middle distance, a man is cutting wood, and another man leads a donkey off toward a village. Nothing could be more quaint or pleasing, but the work is almost as clumsy from a representational point of view as the execution is delicate. The artists had only the vaguest knowledge of either anatomy or perspective, and their attempt at *genre* has often been characterized as "realism without any science." The little picture is nevertheless notable as one of the very first which completely excludes religious subject matter or ecclesiastical overtones of any kind.

If we turn to the miniature for August (Fig. 13.15), the chill of winter is long forgotten, and so is the damp green of early summer. The grass has reached its honey-colored stage; and in the middle distance before the castle of Étampes, peasants are busy haying. Some of them have taken time off to go swimming. Across the foreground, a cavalcade of ladies and gentlemen come by, bound for a leisurely afternoon of hawking. They wear clothes in the extreme of later Gothic elegance; and lest the jewel-like elegance of the rendering beguile us, it would be well to inspect the anatomy with a critical eye. The figures of the nobility have been elongated to fit contemporary notions of grace, in the name of which some preposterous distortion has been indulged. The lady riding pillion on the darker horse to the right furnishes a conspicuous instance. Her head and neck are within the realm of possibility, but her bust, waist, abdomen, and thighs are bizarre — an excellent lesson in the extremes to which the mannerists were prepared to go.

It is important to remember that the illustrations of the *Très Riches Heures* — to us quaint and naïve — were more than up to date in 1416. The novelty at that time lay not so much in the degree of representative accuracy attained as in the content. The pictures are evidence of a kind of awakening. People were beginning to open their eyes to the face of nature. They found the earth surpassingly full of wonder and delight, and they felt no need to interpret at all. What landscapes make a more direct appeal to the senses than these? Where can one find pictures more adequate to evoke the feeling of temperature and the seasonal differences in the texture of the air? The smell of the ground at various times of year is also called to mind, and the experience of muscular activity all the way from heavy labor to easy promenade.

The International Style appealed to the families favored by the feudal system, and there is much nostalgia as we look back upon the lords and ladies who moved through daily life with a cadence and gentility comparable to the dance. But in the light of events they shine with the lustre of an overblown rose, and their pageantry was in truth a sublimation of the coarse realities of the past. The sun of chivalry had already set, and the color of their display was the iridescence of its afterglow. We cannot survey in detail the numerous local schools of the International movement, and we must be content with a few statements that will prove useful in other applications.

At Cologne, the greatest Internationalist was Stefan Lochner (1400–1451), who made a specialty of painting ingénue Madonnas with corn-colored hair (Fig. 13.16), usually in a setting of roses or violets. By making Mary into a sweet child asking our love and protection, he brought her closer, perhaps, to humanity, but he opened the door to a reduction of her status.

At Barcelona, a certain Master of Saint George (he may have been named Martorell) was at work from about 1430 to about 1450. His title is taken from a large altarpiece showing *Saint George and the Dragon* (Fig. 13.17) which combines within itself all the good and all the weakness of the entire movement to which it belongs. As representation, it is too insistently naïve. As danger, bravery, combat, and deliverance, it is closer to the dance floor than to

Robert the Bruce at Bannockburn or the sound of the Campbell pipes at Lucknow. Nevertheless there is much that brings back to life for a moment the authentic beauty that once attached to the profession of arms. The saint swings his horse and poises the lance with a wonderful inevitability, the superb motion of a connoisseur in dynamics to whom violence itself was subject matter for artistic cadence and timing.

In Italy, the International movement was somewhat more strongly affected by local conditions. During the 14th and 15th Centuries, Italian painting tended to form itself on the basis of local schools identified with one of the provinces of the peninsula, or with a single city. Each of the Italian schools started with painting of the International kind, and rapidly matured as the Renaissance itself went forward. The painters cited here might well find a more comfortable place in Chapter 15, but it is important to point out the extent to which Late Gothic Mannerism survived in spirit for a very long time even in Italy.

In Lombardy, Pisanello of Verona (Figs. 13.18–19) was the most important master, his activity extending from about 1430 to 1455. He was the greatest medalist who ever lived and the only sculptor to produce first-class work within the general limits of the International Style. His medals were not intended to be worn at the end of a ribbon, but were conceived as relief sculpture in portable size — a class of art object all too little cultivated, and especially appropriate for personal presentation. Most of Pisanello's medals are discs of bronze about four inches in diameter, with an extreme thickness of about a quarter of an inch. The obverse usually has a profile portrait in bust length; and on the reverse, there is ordinarily a symbolical, historical, or mythological scene related in some way to the sitter. Pisanello did not strike his medals from a die as we do today. He preferred to cast them, a process that permitted him to bring out all the gentler qualities of the bronze, including the marvelous lettering which is so soft and yet so sharp.

As a painter and draftsman, Pisanello (in keeping with the somewhat later period of his career and his residence in Italy) was an immensely competent technician, but his outlook remained as direct and enjoyable as the Limbourgs. The most notable drawings form a series of animal studies in which Gothic Mannerism is strengthened by an acute observation. It was his custom to depend upon the notebooks for material to be combined into paintings, and such an example is the *Saint Eustace* (Fig. 13.19). The narrative, in which the saint while hunting saw a vision of Christ in the form of a stag, was highly congenial to Pisanello; but while sharing his delight in the beasts he so lovingly shows us, we may politely wonder whether he was equally interested in the conversion of Eustace as a result of his strange experience.

Gentile da Fabriano (about 1360–1427), the first notable painter born in Umbria, was an artist of much greater importance than one might suppose. Luck has been unkind to him, and most of his bigger commissions have perished. The pictures that remain are distinguished by gentleness and sweet reverence, a quality which endeared him to Michaelangelo and caused that most unsparing of critics to write a cogent appreciation of Gentile's work. He loved him for the softness of his touch and for his sweet and reflective content, both qualities being almost the opposite of the turbulent force which marks almost everything Michaelangelo himself touched or did.

Most people remember Gentile for the good-sized *Adoration of the Magi* now in the Uffizi, finished in 1423, but the picture is, as a matter of fact, one of his rare failures. The composition is ruined by an unsuccessful attempt to swing the interest to the left, where the Madonna sits; and the whole show is stolen by a crowded plethora of fancy costumes and trappings. Even so, nobody has ever managed to dislike the picture.

As an artistic achievement, there is much more to excite our serious interest in a little panel from the predella of the same *Adoration*, showing the barnyard of the inn at Bethlehem (Fig. 13.20). It is the middle of the night, and the friendly beasts lie out behind, shifting a bit in half wakefulness as animals do in the dark. Saint Joseph sits in deep sleep at the right. In the middle foreground, Mary kneels in adoration over the Christ child, from whose person there comes a gentle but brilliant light, transfiguring her maternity. There is reason to believe that the little picture may be the first nocturne in modern painting, and its existence establishes Gentile, conservative though his idiom may be, as one of the leading experimental artists of his generation.

The general average of his work, insofar as we can assess it from existing examples, is well summed up in a series of small Madonnas in which Mary appears alone with the child. Most are in half length, and it would seem that Gentile borrowed his formula from the Sienese School of the 14th Century (see above, pages 365–369), but disregarded the Byzantine characteristics thereof. He substituted a sublimated Italian femininity, as seen in Fig. 13.21.

We ordinarily associate influence with extroversion, and we therefore tend to overlook the far-reaching effect of Gentile's career. He was a man of reputation, and his work was in demand all over Italy. About 1409, he went to Venice, where he spent five years doing some frescoes in the Ducal Palace. He then worked at Florence and Orvieto and was subsequently called to Rome by Martin the 5th, who was anxious to restore the dignity of that city after the interim at Avignon. Fire destroyed the frescoes at Venice and also those in Saint John's Lateran at Rome, but we can nevertheless make an excellent guess that Gentile's Venetian sojourn accounts for the atmosphere of the great Venetian School of High Renaissance painting. Jacopo Bellini (1400–1474) was the first Venetian painter of consequence; his half-length Madonnas are very like Gentile's. Giovanni Bellini (about 1430–1516), his son, might be described as a High Renaissance Gentile (Fig. 16.31). The style of Venice pursued, of course, the usual evolution from the earlier Renaissance to the later Baroque; but stray as they might into other channels, the great Venetians habitually returned to the soft tempo and lyric gentleness suggested by the work of this early master.

Gentile was the last Italian master who might properly be classed as an actual member of the International Style, but the spirit of Late Gothic Mannerism decidedly did not cease with his generation. We shall therefore find it convenient to mention at this point several other artists whose work has some times been misunderstood. The men to whom we refer belonged to the Renaissance in the sense of understanding and using its broader and more realistically accurate techniques. The aspect that is often overlooked is the equally important fact that the content of their work differed very little from that typical of the International Style.

The sculptor Ghiberti (see below, pages 638–643) stands in history as one of the research artists who discovered our modern methods for representing infinite vistas of space, but his figure-style and spirit are the most elegant kind of Gothic. Ghiberti's assistant Benozzo Gozzoli (1420–1497), also a superb technician, is notable largely because neither his taste nor his ideas had advanced in the least beyond the light and easy content we associate with painters like the Master of Saint George. His *Journey of the Magi* (Fig. 14.3) seems, in fact, to be nothing more profound than an excellent record of one of the pageants that took place in Medici Florence. Fra Angelico (1387–1455) belongs more thoroughly to the Renaissance, and thus finds a place in our treatment of that era. It should never be forgotten, however, that the Gabriel of his celebrated *Annunciation* (Fig. 15.31) might actually replace one of the smiling angels of Reims without attracting any comment whatever.

Paolo Uccello (1397–1475), a painter whom nobody entirely understands, has often and carelessly been dismissed with the comment that his place in history was earned by his investigation into the geometry of sight and the principles of linear perspective. Such a view is not entirely incorrect, but it is surely incomplete. Uccello's battle pieces in the Uffizi and in London (Fig. 13.22) are among the most vigorously decorative paintings ever executed. In every particular of subject matter, they fit the style that started at Avignon, with the simple but profound difference that sure technical knowledge and a measure of classical monumentality have fetched the International manner up onto an entirely new plateau. The perspective for which Uccello was noted, he employed, moreover, to simplify contours in a manner that comes very close to the strong abstraction of analytical cubism (see below, pages 925–928). A fair and final estimate of this fascinating artist must, it would seem, make him at once a conservative and a radical — and certainly an immense success.

THE LATER HISTORY OF GOTHIC REALISM AND THE ESTABLISHMENT OF THE REPRESENTATIVE CONVENTION

While Late Gothic Mannerism was running its course as outlined above, the artists who were interested in realism continued their work. By 1350, or thereabouts, they had set in motion the convention which was destined to govern European art, almost with the force of law, from the beginning of the 15th Century to our own day. We refer to the *Representative Convention,* by which we mean that something very close to the philosophy of objective realism (page 20) became the fixed and only theory of art acceptable to the public.

The representative convention has amounted to a tacit understanding by all parties that the human figure, when it appears in painting and sculpture, must conform closely to the proportions that are normal for the average living model. The convention assumes also that details of anatomy will be scientifically accurate within very narrow limits of tolerance. It further assumes that linear perspective must approximate very closely the actual geometry of sight, and it assumes in addition that the tonal relations employed for atmospheric perspective ought similarly to correspond with the colors observed in nature.

Every artist has trespassed against the rules of the representative convention, and every competent historian and critic knows it. The truth is that strict adherence to the convention is technically quite impractical, but the liberties taken have always been cautious minor infringements calculated to escape casual attention. The experts, that is to say, have conspired to cheat the system, but always with the sure knowledge that the public would get angry enough to fight if confronted with anything in art not instantly recognizable as "true to life." The widespread distaste for 20th-Century painting and sculpture has had its genesis in the fact that the leading artists have refused any longer to be governed by representation. The public, on the other hand, continues to insist that the convention be respected.

The advent of the representative convention may be associated with the personality of King Charles the 5th of France (1337–1380), sometimes called

Charles the Wise. With greater particularity, it may even be thought of as having to do with that monarch's nose, a large one with a distinctive shape. Hardly a handsome feature, the royal proboscis might graciously have been altered a bit in the interest of Gothic grace; but with the arrival of the then new convention which has now lasted so long, every fact of appearance put an obligation upon the conscience of the artist even if it happened to be an unfortunate accident. For that reason, the various portraits of Charles (Figs. 13.23–24) are handled with a realism approaching the brutal.

The words *portrait* and *representation* seem first to have come into common use during the second half of the 14th Century. The two were used as near-synonyms, and were most often applied to the tomb monuments which became increasingly popular at the time. The purpose in view was to give people a more personal immortality than they hitherto had asked, a hope which by its very existence betokens the waning of the Middle Ages. To illustrate the severe enthusiasm with which realistic truth was insisted upon, we may turn to the tomb of Bertrand du Guesclin (Figs. 13.25–26). After a long and brilliant military career in the service of France, and after gaining the profound respect of friend and foe as much for his character as for valor, that superb gentleman spent the last decade of his life as Constable of France. The 14th Century produced no greater hero, but his tomb portrait is true to life in the sense of telling us merely that his person was insignificant.

With respect to the representation of anatomy, it is likely that the credit for the earliest achievement of complete competence must go to the sculptors of Burgundy, and probably to Claus Sluter, who died in 1406. His greatest monument was the so-called *Moses Well* in the Carthusian monastery of Champmol near Dijon. More accurately described as a well-head, the composition originally consisted of a hollow pedestal surmounted by a Crucifix. The general conformation of the pedestal itself (Fig. 13.27) appears to be a conscious reflection of the classical Corinthian capital. Around a hexagonal core, six male statues are arranged under an overhanging abacus, with angels bending out under its corners in place of the familiar volutes. The larger statues all depict elderly gentlemen; they are prophets (Fig. 13.28), and supposedly they are engaged in explaining the necessity of atonement for the sacrifice of Jesus. All of them are notable figures, but the Moses is the most impressive of all — hence the name of the well. As Michaelangelo was later to do, Sluter followed an incorrect translation of the Bible which describes Moses as having horns on his head after his long sojourn with God on Mount Sinai.

Earlier realists had been quite as unsparing as Sluter in the matter of anatomy. The extra power of his work derives from a more incisive rendering of momentary poses. The most trivial and even the most ill-advised gestures and expressions were made permanent in his sculpture, as the unlovely little angels under the abacus amply demonstrate. The accuracy of such figures is precise; no artist needs to know any more about anatomy than Sluter did. In only one particular was he still the prisoner of medieval conventions: he still conceived sculpture to be an art of drapery, and he lost the action of torso and legs (and hence the expressive power of the body's complete surface) beneath a superfluity of cloth. Voluminous drapery became, in fact, a special feature of Burgundian sculpture, and it was destined, as we shall see, to have an overly long history in all northern painting as well.

For the establishment of the representative convention in painting, we must return to the manuscript called the *Très Belles Heures,* discarded by the magnificent Duke of Berry in 1412, as mentioned on page 533. The scribes had done their work and a number of the miniatures had been painted in the going Franco-Flemish-Gothic style when the Duke made up his mind to start again with the Limbourgs. The leaves were never bound up as a book and were soon divided. Some of them, complete with the pictures just mentioned, ultimately found their way into the Rothschild collection; they are known as "The Hours of Paris." Some of the unfinished pages, complete only as to text and foliate borders, were bought by William of Bavaria, Count of Holland, who was the Duke's nephew. Part of them ended up in the library at Turin, where they were lost in the fire of 1903. Fortunately photographs had been made in 1902, and a handsome monograph was published by the French scholar Paul Durrieux, under the title *Heures de Turin.* Several other pages from Duke William's part of the book eventually arrived in the library of Prince Trivulzio at Milan. Those latter leaves are usually referred to as "The Hours of Milan"; but they rather recently passed to the library at Turin — a destination that hardly simplifies a nomenclature already vexing enough.

Why did William want to buy the unfinished leaves of the manuscript? The best guess seems to be that he wanted to commission a piece of work by a particular artist. If so, his judgment was more than good. The small number of miniatures done before his death in 1417 rank among the chief wonders of European art.

One of the pictures shows Duke William landing on the beach at Veere in Holland (Fig. 13.29). The date was June 1416. The Duke had been to England to assist in making peace after the campaign of Agincourt, and he had sailed home in the remarkable time of twenty hours. The picture shows his happy daughter Jacqueline there to meet him. She was then seventeen years old, but within a year was destined to lose both her father and her husband

and to spend the rest of her life in an unequal struggle with betrayal and intrigue.

On another page Duke William had his artist paint a *Birth of Saint John the Baptist* at the top; and across the bottom, he had a river view put in (Fig. 13.30). The stream is placid; it goes past a castle in the middle distance, and curves off around a tree-grown bluff. Far away, we can see some magnificent hills. In the immediate foreground, Saint John is performing the baptism, a ceremony that goes almost unnoticed against such scenery.

When the historian looks at these tiny pictures and reflects that they were done before 1417, he loses his breath. He loses it every time, no matter how often he has seen them. It takes no expert to know at once that they are the work of a man who knew things completely beyond the imagination of the Limbourgs. This artist diminished the size of distant objects systematically, and he did it with marvelous precision. He handled shadows and atmosphere with a similar ease. He understood, moreover, how to make his space convincing by providing a linear continuity from the foreground into the distance. In the *Baptism,* for example, the eye picks up the shore line at the lower left-hand corner, and follows the river bank into the far away. A similar device was used for the beach at Veere.

The effect of all this was to produce pictures where the space, air, and light strike one with the force of physical experience. One feels the puffy northwest breeze blowing over the Dutch estuary; and in the Baptism, one almost expects to hear the sounds that carry so far in the still air of a perfect day at sunset. By comparison, the landscapes of the Limbourgs seem reduced to mere backdrops. Duke William's painter knew how to put things *in* the space he represented.

We need to remind ourselves that his work was done at the very moment when the Limbourgs were considered the best artists in northern Europe, and were enjoying the most lucrative commission; but the contrast between their work and his is the difference between ingenuous trial and the ease of learned mastery. We are confronted, in short, with the arrival of a phenomenal genius who was able, in one act of creation, to lift medieval painting to the Renaissance level. His name has naturally been sought with every resource of scholarship, but conclusive proof of his identity is sadly lacking. Without entering into argument about the evidence, let us simply say that the master was probably Hubert Van Eyck, who died at Ghent in 1426. His younger brother John Van Eyck (see below, pages 609–615) was the first major painter of Flanders and the founder of the northern Renaissance.

THE SCULPTURE AND PAINTING OF ITALY DURING THE GOTHIC ERA: THE PROTO-RENAISSANCE

Italian Gothic was always a reluctantly imported fashion; and like the architecture of the same period, Italy's sculpture and painting was often Gothic more in date than in style. The classic tradition never entirely died out, and neither did the Byzantine. Humanism did not appear earlier in Italy than in the north; but it hit harder and moved faster. It filled the familiar Byzantine and Gothic figures with life, and made them vibrate in a new key. Individualism — if we can conceive it as separate from humanism — was more pronounced among the Italian population, and became overt at an early date. Most French and Flemish artists retained the outlook and attitude of craftsmen until well after 1400; but Nicola Pisano's marble pulpit (see below, page 545), the very first work of art conceived as the personal expression of a great man, dates from the year 1260. It begins, moreover, a section of art history destined to last more than four centuries, the whole of it being for the most part an account of the activities of single artists as distinct from schools and movements. All of these considerations have led certain writers to designate the art of Italy during the era about to be reviewed as *Proto-Renaissance,* by which they mean that the style might still be Byzantine or Gothic, but that the content was often distinctly modern.

Art in South Italy and Sicily at the Time of Frederick the 2nd

The Proto-Renaissance began during the first half of the 13th Century. The locale was South Italy and Sicily, and the moving spirit was the Emperor Frederick the 2nd, who had been born of a Norman mother and a German father in 1194, and who died in 1250. Medieval history contains no more brilliant figure. With an almost diabolical genius, Frederick's every impulse and virtue impelled him toward attitudes radically modern, but intolerable and monstrous to the medieval mind. Instead of faith, he openly professed audacious doubt, and actively pursued investigations in search of objective evidence. As a king whose principal city was Naples, he was more concerned with the Church-as-a-state than with the Church-as-a-mystery, and his agnosticism was supplemented by political opposition to the Vatican. Naturally, such a man was more than the Popes could endure. A less powerful personage would have been snuffed out at once, but Frederick maintained himself and his throne in spite of several excommunications. After he died, the Papacy made short work of his heirs and did to death the kind of art he had started.

Frederick made two different moves toward the Renaissance, each immensely important in its own way and all too little known. His patronage brought into being the first modern sculpture and architecture in a truly classical style; and the earliest massive and lasting enterprise of representative art is to be found in the illustrations, about a thousand in number, for Frederick's own treatise on falconry — itself an unsurpassed piece of biological research.

The antiquarian phase of the enterprise seems to have centered on the South Italian mainland. There are a good many monuments in the general vicinity of Naples. At Salerno, there is a stone pulpit veneered with colored marbles, but surmounted by a robust classical head very much in the style of the Greek 5th Century B.C. In 1234, Frederick undertook the sculptural decoration of a now-ruined building at Capua, perhaps a fort of some kind. The principal feature was a gateway like a Roman triumphal arch. The gate carried a good many statues. The list included a portrait of the emperor dressed in a senatorial toga, busts of his ministers (Fig. 13.34), and a fine head personifying the city of Capua (Fig. 13.35). It was remarkable that anyone then alive had the independence of taste to conduct so frank a negation of the current artistic style, and it was even more remarkable that artists could be found to do it so very well. Their work is sensitive and alive, nothing like the clodden carving of men who try to copy something classical without having the vaguest idea what it means.

Still another monument, and in surprisingly good repair, is the Castel Santa Maria del Monte, dating from 1240, on a bare and rocky hill about a dozen miles south of Barletta. It was the main building of what today we would call a breeding and research station, one of the several centers where Frederick conducted his passionate exploration of ornithology in general and the falcon in particular. The main block of the building is a pentagon; and it has a fine doorway that might momentarily be mistaken for work of the High Renaissance.

In projecting a treatise on falconry, the emperor was acting not only as an ardent sportsman, but as a responsible monarch. The reader must make an attempt to recapture the idea of game as a reliable staple of food. Old gentlemen still live who can tell of clouds of ducks and other water fowl, and the quail in whistling millions. Medieval Italy must have presented something like the same opportunity, but Frederick's endeavor took on a more intense modernity, hardly to be explained by reference to practical problems alone. The scope of his inquiry was exhaustive. He wanted to know and include everything, and to refine his understanding of what he had found out. He wanted to pass his knowledge on to the whole world. His impulses, in short, were identical to those of pure science; and for his achievement, no excuses are necessary.

Known generally by its Latin title, the *De Arte Venandi cum Avibus* (The Art of Hunting with Birds) exists today in some sixteen manuscript copies, which vary considerably in the quality of their illustrations. The best one is in the Vatican Library (Cod. Pal. Lat. 1071). Written in splendid Italian Gothic script, the text is illustrated by marginal illustrations covering the subject of falconry in general. In all, more than 900 birds appear.

It would be hard to exaggerate the acumen with which the birds are painted (Fig. 13.31). Many of them appear in flight; they are so vivid and convincing that we must postulate a corps of artists specially trained in the technique of instantaneous vision and in the most precise kind of visual memory. Modern photographs do not reveal the essentials half so well; and Audubon's pictures, mostly painted at leisure from specimens he shot and hung up, are hopelessly inferior.

The manuscript is interesting, also, as an illustration of the way convention operates during a period when the forces of transition are active. The birds, as stated, were freshly studied from the life. The servants and huntsmen are less satisfactory than the birds (Fig. 13.33) but there can be no doubt the artist meant to depict something alive. Whenever a member of the court appears (Fig. 13.32), the style relapses into Byzantine slavery.

The Pisanesque Tradition in Sculpture

The first man of modern times to use art as the vehicle for expressing his own character, ideas, and feelings was Nicola Pisano (about 1205–1278). During the period of his important achievements, he made his home at Pisa, and was probably a citizen there. It seems likely that he was born and trained in South Italy and in the classicizing school of sculptors established by Frederick the 2nd. For that reason, many scholars prefer to call him Nicola d'Apulia.

His greatest monument is the marble pulpit still in use in the Baptistry at Pisa. The pulpit is a hexagonal box raised on top of Corinthian columns, with a stairway up from the floor. Every other column comes down on the back of a lion, and cusped arches swing from capital to capital to make a little arcade. The pulpit was completed in the year 1260.

Five panels of high relief form its walls, of which we reproduce the one illustrating Luke 3:22–28, ordinarily entitled *The Presentation of Christ in the Temple,* and sometimes *The Circumcision* (Fig. 13.36). Certain defects impress themselves immediately. In the first place, no photographs at present available give an adequate impression of the superb technique and finish; the reader must defer judgment until he can study the original. As in so many other reliefs of medieval date, the composition is painfully crowded, and the excellence of the artist makes itself manifest only in the single figure, or in a couple of figures seen together — which the observer must separate out by making a special effort, much as one isolates an aphorism from the text around it. If we make that compromise with Nicola Pisano, he emerges as a sculptor of unexcelled force.

The figure of Saint Simeon will serve to illustrate the point. Like several other figures on the pulpit, its classical source has been specifically identified. It is an adaptation of the Bacchus on an ancient marble vase decorated with a scene showing that god in company with the Maenads. Perhaps no figure in art history ever received an equal adjustment of spiritual status in the upward direction, but Nicola's Simeon differs from its classical source as the alpha of civilization contrasts with its omega. The personal force of the artist seems to have entered with explosive pressure into the marble, and the figure inspires an admiration not untinged by fear. The same epic and even wrathful quality was destined to occur again in Italian art; Jacopo della Quercia had it, and so did Michaelangelo. To neither sculptor was Nicola inferior, and we may confidently give this early master a place in that select company of artists who have in fact achieved the heroic.

Nicola Pisano started a tradition in sculpture which lasted until the beginning of the 15th Century, at which time it was rather suddenly replaced by the style associated with Donatello (see below, pages 617–626). Historians have formed the habit of referring to all such sculpture as *Pisanesque*, but the designation is somewhat misleading. Except in a very general way, few of the sculptors involved followed Nicola's style.

The most important of them was Giovanni Pisano (about 1250–after 1317), Nicola's son. The importance of the commissions entrusted to him has strangely escaped the emphasis of many writers. He designed the Campo Santo at Pisa, and the façade of the Cathedral at Siena; those are perhaps the finest bits of Gothic in Italy. In 1305, he was called upon to supply a standing Madonna for the altar of the Arena Chapel at Padua (see below, pages 555–558). Giotto, as all the world knows, probably designed the building, and painted therein the greatest cycle of religious frescoes Christendom had seen up to that time. It seems obvious that Giotto considered Giovanni the best sculptor in Italy.

In the course of art history, Giovanni's special importance is the fact that he nipped his father's classical renaissance in the bud. He had in all probability sojourned in France between 1266 and 1277, which is to say at the moment when elegant statues like the north portal Madonna of Paris (Fig. 13.4) were the very latest thing. Giovanni was so impressed with the type that he took it back to Italy with him — standing Madonnas having been rare on the peninsula up to that time. Of his many versions of the subject — one of which we show in Fig. 13.38 — it may be said that he avoided the linear virtuosity of his French models, and made the expression more plastic. He also eschewed the *chic* of Paris, substituting for it a serenity both human and classical, of which only an Italian could have been capable. It should also be noted before we pass on that these sweet and stately figures are among the earliest modern statues conceived as semiportable sculpture, complete in itself and without necessary reference to an architectural composition.

Like his father, Giovanni was fond of marble pulpits, and did several. The most elaborate was done for the Cathedral of Pisa, and completed in 1310. Damaged by fire late in the 16th Century, it is no longer in use, but part of the sculpture is preserved at Pisa, and part in Berlin. The *Crucifixion* panel (Fig. 13.37) illustrates exceedingly well Giovanni's radical departure from the style of his father. He seems to have been affected not only by the French Gothic, but by such Romanesque tympana as that at Autun (Figs. 11.11–12), where the figure-style is different, but the crowded composition and the surcharge of feeling much the same. It is impossible, in fact, to cite a more emotional *Crucifixion* than this one. Restraint is almost literally absent. In order to carry the import or religious passion at fever heat, the artist has resorted to startling devices. Many of the figures exhibit a pathological emaciation, and distortion has been freely used to bring out the macabre details. Attitudes and gestures are violent, only to be explained by hysteria. The total effect can hardly be called tragedy; it is close to abandonment and despair. Highly subjective on the part of the artist and demanding the intimate participation of the observer (as distinct from his contemplation and reflection), it establishes its author as an important exponent of the philosophy of Expressionism (see above, pages 624; 933 ff). Nothing could be more different from the serenity of his Madonnas, and it may fairly be said that Giovanni's emotional range was outstanding not only during the 14th Century, but for all time.

The higher incidence of individualism in Italy even during the Gothic period is well demonstrated by the special type of tomb which suited the taste of the della Scala family of Verona, whom Dante immortalized in the 17th Canto of the *Paradise*. For several generations, the Scaligers, as they are often called, amused themselves by erecting fanciful Gothic canopies high into the air over their sarcophagi; and on top of the canopies, they perched humorous equestrian statues of the respective decedents, each as he had appeared in life (Fig. 13.39). The whole proposition was witty in the extreme, and made the best use of both mannerism and realism to achieve results that fit none of the conventional patterns of Gothic or any other art.

Still another special and notable Italian achievement of the earlier 14th

Century was the design by Lorenzo Maitani of Siena (about 1275–1330) for the façade of the Cathedral of Orvieto. Wide pilasters decorated in low relief separate the three western portals, and mosaic pictures fill the gables and upper wall spaces. Seen from a moderate distance, Orvieto is one of the finest sights in Europe. There is reason to think that Maitani himself carved some of the scenes from the narrative of Genesis (Fig. 13.40), which are remarkable as an early and not altogether unsuccessful attempt to recover the Roman art of pictorial sculpture (see above, pages 163–170). More startling still, when we remember the date, was the use made of the nude.

It is an untruth to say that the nude went out of use during the Middle Ages; there are plenty of them even in Romanesque sculpture. But in medieval society, the nude was not liked. Nakedness was a state of shame. As a form of penance, it was sometimes imposed in extreme cases when all other discipline had failed, and it was by intention that most of the nude figures in medieval art appear as the damned in the *Last Judgment,* the blessed usually being handsomely dressed. The seminudity of Christ in the *Crucifixion* was, according to medieval sentiment, a statement that he had suffered the ultimate insult when the Roman soldiers stripped him.

Maitani's sculpture was startlingly radical in its day; he was perhaps the very first artist to reverse the medieval point of view, and to offer aesthetic pleasure in the human body. The soft texture and smooth grace of his figures would have been charming at any period; but during an era when voluminous drapery was the regular thing, it is amazing that his designs were not suppressed. Except in Italy, they probably would have been.

The Career of Saint Francis

The start of the superb Italian tradition in painting was closely connected with the great and modern religious impulse inspired by Saint Francis of Assisi (about 1182–1226). Biographies of that wonderful man are available everywhere, varying in tone from careful history to sloppy appreciation; but one and all, they tell of a personality full of love for God, for nature, and for humanity, and loved by all people in return. It is necessary to point out that Francis looked out upon nature with eyes different from those of the later humanists. He enjoyed it because it was related to God; they enjoyed it more directly, and because it was beautiful. Even so, Francis was the first man of definitive influence to declare an identity between the worship of God and joy on earth. " Praised be my Lord and God," he sang in his glorious *Canticle of the Sun,* " for Mother Earth who governs and sustains us, who gives birth to all the many fruits and colored flowers."

It is doubtful whether any other human being had a like capacity for profound affection. Francis loved God, and he loved everybody and everything with a passion and openness only less intense. His point of view was typical of the complete reorientation between man and God then in progress, and may even have caused it. The *Pantocrators* of Byzantine art, and the *Last Judgments* so popular in the Romanesque and Gothic, had reflected an authoritarian church. Such art was spiritually elevating in the sense stating the just claims of religion, and the consequences of delinquency. The method implicit in Francis's teaching was different. He asked people to serve the Lord because the Lord loved them, and they could learn to love him. Our entire concept of the fatherhood and kindness of the Almighty seems to have been extraordinarily rare if not altogether unknown before the balance was swung by Francis's point of view on the matter. It is obvious that God and man would be brought closer together by such thinking; but in order to understand the practical effect upon art, we must say more.

One tendency of the Franciscan doctrine was to increase the respectability of representative art by endorsing the legitimacy of joy in the natural world. That was immensely important at the time, but the new idea of love for God proved even more important. Francis established the idea that the love of man for God, and of God for man, was similar to the affection felt by one person for another. More profound and important, to be sure, but the identical emotion in different degree. The important point to grasp is the assertion that God himself has feelings like our own; it is the essential concept in the humanizing process by which art was about to be transformed, and the saints to become better understood.

What was accepted as true of love, it seemed to follow, might be true of the other emotions. Granting that much, people found the Holy Family and all the saints endowed with sensibilities like their own. It began to be possible to understand the sacred narrative as a series of events illustrative, in principle at least, of certain types of experience, both exalted and terrible. What had happened before was bound to happen again and again, and the great men of the church became important not because they were unique and remote, but because they too were human. While susceptible of cheap misunderstanding, the effect of such concepts was on the whole good: one had some chance of emulating persons like himself, and none of following in the footsteps of those who were supernatural.

It is the presence of such ideas that makes the great difference between northern art of the later Middle Age and the Italian. Homely realism was incipient in the north at the very period we are discussing, but neither the French nor the Flemish artists were capable of revealing the grander mysteries of faith in the language of common feeling. They possessed accuracy of representation, but they lacked the emotional authenticity which made it possible for certain Italians to express all the power of religious conviction with the warmth of an event occurring at home.

"Let the brethren have care," wrote Francis in one of his colloquies, "not on any account to accept churches or dwellings that may be built for them unless they are in accordance with the rule of Holy Poverty." In another place, he visualized the proper Franciscan buildings as poor little churches, preferably abandoned by others. The negation of property was central to his rule, and he must have been aware that great monastic orders had, more than once in the past, made architectural and artistic investments during periods of spiritual laxity. But the admonitions of the founder were destined to have only a moderate effect upon the policy of the order.

The grandiose double church of Saint Francis at Assisi, really two Gothic naves built one over the other on the side of a hill, was started in 1228. Because of the excessive Italian sunlight, the builders walled up most of the space available for windows, leaving only a moderate area for glass. By the same act, they provided an excellent field for fresco painting. Toward the end of the 13th Century, painters began to come to Assisi to decorate those walls. In the course of time, virtually every important master had a commission there until there was no space left. There was extra reason for hurrying such work along during the final years of the 13th Century. The year 1330 was a Jubilee year; and the monks wanted to make their church attractive to the pilgrims who would inevitably stream through the town on their way to and from Rome. About 1295, therefore, a cycle of 28 frescoes from the life of Francis was commissioned for the Upper Church. The series runs all the way around the nave, constituting its lowest and most advantageously placed tier of pictorial decoration. The incidents depicted were apparently drawn from Saint Bonaventura's life of Francis, then a new book dating from 1261. The handling of the subject matter is completely different from anything of earlier date; plainly, a number of the pictures reflect the operation of a mind with an exceedingly forward looking approach to human problems. Although no one cares to assign all 28 frescoes to him, although no impeccable evidence even places him at Assisi at the time, and although certain prominent modern critics are convinced he was never there, tradition is probably correct that the painter was Giotto.

Giotto

Giotto was probably born in 1266. Vasari, whose *Lives of the Most Eminent Painters, Sculptors, and Architects* first came out in 1550, wrote the date ten years later, but he was almost certainly wrong. Giotto, according to tradition, was apprenticed to Cimabue, a strong master in the Italo-Byzantine Style and the leading painter at Florence. Assuming that the boy went into the shop when he was about twelve or thirteen, and served his seven years, he would have left Cimabue's employment at the age of nineteen or twenty. It would then be customary for him to spend several years as a *journeyman.*

Journeymen were the graduate students of art. They went from town to town doing odd jobs. When a journeyman-painter walked into a town, he called upon the first master-painter whose shop he came upon. The master was under obligation to give him work if he had it, to help him get work with someone else, or to furnish him with food and money for the trip to the next place. After several years as a journeyman, the young man would settle down somewhere, but he was not permitted to do business in his own name and right until he had gained admittance to the local guild. Admittance was granted upon the presentation of a painting or a statue which the masters of the guild were willing to endorse as sound work; hence the word *masterpiece,* which now has a slightly different meaning. After acceptance of his masterpiece, the new member's name was recorded in the archives of the guild, and he was ready to accept commissions.

The guild not only protected his interests from that point on, but exercised a positive discipline designed to protect the quality and dignity of art itself. The only tools, materials, and methods an artist might use were those formally endorsed by the guild. In matters of dispute as between patron and painter, the guild acted as judge, and was often as ready to punish an erring member as to tell off the other party to the bargain. Admittedly such a system was likely to restrain experiment and to freeze art in a pattern of one kind or another. That actually happened in Flanders during the 15th Century (see below, pages 615–616), but the greater independence of Italian artists minimized such an effect in their part of the world. The virtue of control by the guild is all too seldom stated: it actually succeeded in quarantining the world from really bad art.

No one knows for certain where Giotto went during his *wanderjahre;* but from various indications, we can make a shrewd guess. Everything in his mature life describes him as a man who liked travel, was stimulated by new places, and went whenever he got the chance. Are we to imagine he stayed home when he was twenty? Or did he slip his collar and dash off to see the world? And what part of the world would draw like a magnet upon the curiosity of a young artist from Italy — a place which had not yet begun to make the reputation it built up during the centuries to follow? The answer is France, which was still the cultural capital of the Western world. The chances are that Giotto made the best of his way in that direction, and it is in France that the sources of his new style will be discovered if it ever becomes possible to identify them specifically.

The view just put forward contradicts the traditional assumption that Giotto knew no art except the Italian. It means nothing, of course, that there are no notices of him before his arrival at Assisi; graduate students leave no mark in the places they sojourn. The important thing to remember is that he had time enough to cover all Europe on foot during the years that remain unaccounted for. There would be nothing unusual in his having done so, for travellers were at all times in movement on the roads and along the rivers.

Giotto's style was a complete negation of the Italo-Byzantine manner which had dominated Italian painting for 700 years, and in which tradition he must have been educated by Cimabue. On the assumption that Giotto never left Italy, it has been conventional to explain his work by reference to Giovanni Pisano's sculpture, to some frescoes painted at Rome by a master named Cavallini who is himself a shadowy figure, and by further reference to the special powers with which men of genius are endowed. Inasmuch as it is very hard to conjure up Giotto from either Giovanni Pisano, Cavallini, or both, an unreasonable function must be assigned to his creative powers unless some other factor may be introduced.

The suggestion of a sojourn in France is provocative, to say the least. It makes sense of elements in Giotto's art that otherwise remain unexplained. He painted heavy, thick-set people dressed in extremely simple clothes. The principal feature of his technique was a vivid and meticulous definition of contour — a declaration, as it were, that no fact of the natural world is more important than the existence of mass (see below, pages 558–560). The sculpturesque nature of his figures has long been recognized, but few writers have attempted to draw the obvious conclusion that Giotto, a painter, was imitating statues. It is obvious from his mature work that his taste predisposed him toward the monumental and permanent, and away from the finesse and virtuosity for which the French miniature painters were justly noted. We may therefore hazard the guess that the kind of thing which most interested him in France was the latest French sculpture, some of which included narrative groups in very high relief. An example is the tympanum of the so-called "Red Door" of the Cathedral at Paris (Fig. 13.41). By comparison with the people who appear in any painting by Giotto, the actors in that little scene are without the spark of life, but it does not take great art to put ideas into the head of a great artist. It would not be too farfetched to imagine that when Giotto went back to Italy, he undertook to adapt such compositions to the ample wall spaces that were so rare in France and so plentiful and so empty in Italy.

Giotto must have been nearly thirty years old when he arrived to start work at Assisi, and it seems unreasonable to think he had prolonged his wanderings that long. It is equally unlikely that he spent his time doing something totally divorced from painting; and in that connection, it is important to remember that artists of his day did not specialize as more recent artists have done. They stood ready to design buildings, carve statues, paint pictures, make furniture and weapons, weave textiles, or cooperate in the production of pageants and plays. Men with special talents naturally received more commissions of one kind than another, but the watertight compartmentation of the profession, as we see it today, simply did not exist.

The theatre looks like the place where Giotto worked as a young man. His special power, as will appear below, was to make the entire figure expressive. It is not the face, the hands, or the pose, but the absolute totality of the person that he filled with meaning. In part, we may assign his rare ability to the operation of genius, but it has all too often been explained by reference to his "study direct from nature." About study from nature, it should be pointed out that the anatomy of the average human being is not an expressive vehicle. Giotto might have watched ordinary citizens move and gesture for years without learning a single useful thing. It is necessary to believe he studied the more lucid action of experts. Had he studied dancers, it seems likely he might have learned to represent motion much better than he did on the few occasions he tried it. Thus the theatre — of which there was a great deal in both France and Italy — remains the obvious place where he learned how to paint human beings utterly perfect for the parts they play, and to compose them into pictures that strike home with a truth and vitality not only beyond the capacity of any earlier artist, but beyond that of all other artists to date. To the hypothesis of a long experience in acting and production, we may add a minor point of corroboration. How else to explain the miniature architecture that appears as background in so many of his pictures, often odd and impractical in design and so unreasonably out of scale with the people? As portable stage scenery, intended merely to symbolize the existence of buildings, such constructions not only make perfect sense, but are known to have been used in the medieval drama.

The best-known picture at Assisi is the *Saint Francis Preaching to the Birds* (Fig. 13.43). Francis was one of those persons to whom all sorts of animals respond with complete trust. The tale is told that one Sunday morning, he called some birds to him, and they sat quite still while he preached them a sermon. Delicate sentiment is somewhat outside the realm of Giotto's usual interest; but it is significant to see that when he undertook it, he produced a painting not only popular but worthwhile. The daring of the performance can hardly be overstated. Success depended upon the willingness of the public to accept the picture in the spirit of a little child. In such matters, there is no middle ground; success is absolute, or failure is maudlin — and there can be no excuse for the artist.

The *Saint Francis Renouncing His Father* (Fig. 13.42) shows Giotto in the field where he stands alone. The narrative behind the painting runs as follows: After he had returned home from military imprisonment at Perugia, Francis indulged in religious activities of an evangelical kind. His acts and utterances seemed in bad taste, and proved embarrassing to his parents — especially his newly formed theories against property. Presently an open break occurred. Relations went from bad to worse, culminating in the shocking incident chosen by Giotto for his point of time. The enraged father has undertaken to beat his grown son. The son has run for sanctuary to the cathedral, only to be overtaken and publicly denounced on the steps outside. The father has just issued a demand for obedience by virtue of the material support hitherto provided by his money, including the very clothes on Francis's back. In response to that reasoning, Francis immediately stripped himself naked, and made a statement of renunciation covering both his earthly father and the clothing.

The picture is remarkable for the states of mind and shades of emotion contained within a single frame. The father, a much put-upon man according to the best of his own judgment, may even be said to be pleading for the best interest of his son. Most youthful evangelists are merely disturbed and unstable young men; who could then have predicted that Francis would be remembered as a saint in glory? As Giotto understands him, this parent is to blame for nothing.

Another kind of feeling is being experienced by the Bishop of Assisi, who covers the boy's middle with his own robe, and mutters instructions to an assistant. As all Bishops must, his task was to compromise with Mammon so that the work of God on earth might proceed. An intransigeant rebuke to an influential citizen can at times be the only course; but as an administrative technique, it has always been strong medicine. Bishops ever hope to find another way first; but at the same time, could this Bishop on this occasion deny his protection to a church member coming hotfoot to claim it as a right, and declaring in a loud voice the precise sentiments the church publicly recommends to all? Surely there has never been a more expressive picture of a man who wishes he could be somewhere else.

As a foil to the important figures, Giotto provided us with the minor actors so typically present at embarrassing moments. We see the tensely impassive faces of those who dare not commit themselves one way or the other. There is also the fool who thinks his whisper can't be overheard, and who passes a snide remark. There are the inevitable children who don't know whether it would be safe and interesting to throw stones, or better to seek associates more in their line.

Almost every critic has commented adversely upon the composition, which is divided. It is of course fair to contend that the division corresponds with the gulf of misunderstanding between the parties represented, and may therefore be justified on dramatic grounds. Still another guess, and one that seems most likely of all, is simply that Giotto came to Assisi comparatively fresh from the theatre. Scenes of confrontation are common on the stage, and very forceful. But the play moves on, as pictures do not, and what is appropriate on the boards may be less so in the more static and permanent art of wall painting.

Giotto's greatest surviving monument is the fresco cycle in the Arena Chapel at Padua. The name comes from the ruins of a Roman arena, still visible on the site. The donor was Enrico Scrovegno, who had been anxious to atone in some measure for the evil memory of his father, a notorious usurer whom Dante (Purgatorio, Canto 17) places in the seventh circle of Hell. Circumstances make it look as though Giotto himself designed the building. Architecturally, it is a mere brick shed about 95 feet long, but the tunnel vaulted interior, with a perfectly flat expanse of wall surface and carefully arranged windows, offered the best field for fresco painting ever provided an Italian painter. Work began in 1303, and the consecration took place on March 16, 1305. It is evident that Giotto had made himself the head of an exceedingly well-organized shop. There was some restoration in 1869, but the work was well done, and for all practical purposes the pictures may be cited as originals.

Both side walls were covered with narrative frescoes, rising in three registers of rectangular pictures over a lower row of personsified Virtues and Vices. A Last Judgment fills the space over the entrance doorway, and there are still more pictures on the arch. It is instantly apparent upon entrance that the numerous paintings were planned from the beginning to go together in a grand scheme.

Color is perhaps the most expressive element of the synthesis. No photographs yet available even suggest it. Most of the black-and-white negatives were made before modern films and color filters were invented. Thus generations of students, educated on plates like those reproduced here, have formed the impression that Giotto worked in severe gray monotones as depressing as the winter sky. Nothing could falsify the reality more unkindly. The experience of seeing the chapel for the first time may be compared to entering a greenhouse full of spring flowers. Only the very best of our present colored reproductions give a hint of the truth.

A guiding thought runs through the subject matter of all the pictures. Giotto's purpose was to give us a meditative exposition of the mysteries of Incarnation and Redemption as demonstrated by events in the life of Mary, and of Jesus. The narrative commences with the experiences of Joachim and Anne, the parents of Mary, largely as set forth in the *Protevangelion,* or *Book of James,* from the *New Testament Apocrypha,* with the help of which the student may follow the earlier part of the history. The series then carries on through the earthly career of Mary and the Saviour, and culminates in the *Last Judgment.*

An unbroken flow of narrative was no more available to Giotto than to any other painter. Narrative painting must of necessity be episodic unless one is willing to abandon the simultaneous mode of presentation (see above, pages 59–65). The significance of the episodes chosen thus becomes the first test of artistic judgment, and the matter was one in which Giotto did not demonstrate uniform success. A full-scale study of the chapel would perforce include a few rather dull and superfluous pictures; but if we restrict our attention to the best, as we must in so short an account, we shall find ourselves dealing with drama of supreme range and penetration.

It is hard, for example, to see how the dignity and beauty of faith might be better expressed than we find it in the *Meeting at the Golden Gate* (Fig. 13.44). Joachim and Anne had been weighed down with grief because they had arrived at old age without children. Some days before the event depicted, Joachim had taken himself off on a lonely trip to visit his shepherds in the mountains. An angel came to both the elderly husband and his wife, to say that a child would be born. Joachim hurried home, and Anne went out to meet him. Half a dozen bystanders appear with the principle actors; they gossip as they pass along, giving only a casual glance at the old couple who kiss as they meet. But Giotto's power to tell a tale with the briefest means is summed up in those two crucial figures. They move with the deliberation of age. Their stance remains unchanged, and their embrace is a bending from the waist only. The whole tempo of the scene reflects the peaceful masculine and feminine of the long married. Transfigured by the divine grace and lost in the privacy of their special knowledge, they express their joy not overtly as children might, but in quiet confidence.

The *Nativity* is likewise a picture where Giotto made supreme use of the single figure. Most of the surface is occupied by inert material intended merely to supply the necessary quiet of midnight: the sleepy donkeys, a somnolent Saint Joseph, the quiet shepherds with their sheep, and some angels flying with muted wings in the sky above. At the extreme left (Fig. 13.45) we see the Virgin. She rises slightly on her elbows, and obviously with some pain, to receive her baby from a gentle nurse. It is doubtful whether an equal force of passion has ever been communicated to the world by so small an area of painting. The imagery is almost painfully vivid — so real, indeed, as to banish from memory every other version of this popular subject. Not only did Giotto paint the *Nativity;* he painted maternity itself.

For the *Flight into Egypt* (Fig. 13.46) Giotto chose to set the event in a rocky pass of the mountains. Cliffs hem the Holy Family in. Movement is curtailed in every direction except forward, and the urgency of the situation is heightened by the impenetrable, massive, material limits to action. An angel in the sky gestures angrily for more speed. Mary sits stiff, erect, tense on the back of the donkey; she can only hold her child and await the outcome now beyond remedy, for nothing more can be done. More in frustration than hope, Joseph turns to urge the driver to go faster, and the man pulls forward on the halter. But it does no good. The donkey merely cocks his ears the other way. Thus in a picture that strains the human spirit with anxiety almost beyond endurance, we are given to understand that the fate of Christendom once hinged upon the intractable temperament of an ass.

Another very penetrating picture is the *Judas Receiving the Thirty Pieces of Silver.* As so often happens, the Biblical narrative is very brief, and most of it is left to be inferred. The conventional understanding of the affair puts all the blame on Judas. He was a monster, that is, motivated by avarice, and he sold his loyalty for a price. But Giotto, with an insight worthy of Rousseau, fastens upon the greater complexity of the truth, and the broader implications of the story.

He makes Judas a sensitive, handsome man tempted by a devil real enough to be seen in the picture, thus bringing up the mature ethical concept of a necessary relationship between the offense and the pressure upon the offender. Upon the High Priests, Giotto also turned the awful eye of a man who could not be fooled. It was they who had manipulated the situation with conscious policy. They picked the right time for Jesus' arrest, and made the arrangements for inciting the rabble who ultimately came " with swords and staves." They provided the bribe calculated to impell an unstable personality toward a deed too risky for themselves. It is manifest that they do not even like to appear in the picture, and would not if they dared trust each other. An instant hence, once sure that events have been put in course, they will separate, each rushing off in a different direction.

But Giotto was not ruthless even in his treatment of the High Priests. Such men exist in numbers in every society. Many are pillars of the State, the

Church, the armed services, and every other sort of institution. Publicly, they elucidate high principles with real eloquence; and in practice, they do the right rather than the wrong almost all the time. But every so often, such men find their position and interest really threatened. Then they stoop to crime, but they move secretly, put nothing on paper, get someone else to assume the onus of initiative. Giotto knew the High Priests were swine, but he realized that there will always be some of them in every community.

Enough has been said to illustrate Giotto's ability to interpret human experience as an illustration of permanent truth; no one compares with him in that respect. The same cannot be said of the personified *Virtues* and *Vices* of the lowest, or dado register of the chapel. They are dull and inadequate to a degree, which seems extraordinary when one considers his manipulation of the single figure elsewhere. One might expect him to handle allegory not worse than other painters, but better. Possibly he was unsympathetic to the subject matter, and turned it over to one of the many assistants he brought with him to Padua.

The same guess may account for the occurrence of good and bad compositions in approximately equal measure throughout the series of frescoes. The pictures representing the birth, courtship, and marriage of the Virgin may be cited among the perfunctory and even careless arrangements, while the *Flight into Egypt* is one of the most distinguished essays in formal design to antedate the High Renaissance. Pictorial means were used to integrate that picture. It needs no frame to define its beginning, middle, and end. The limits are established by the three persons entering from the left, and by Joseph's backward and inward gesture on the right. The Madonna fits into a stable and lucid triangular space, and provides a powerful central axis. The rocks behind have a pyramidal shape, harmonious to the triangle just mentioned.

Arrangements so subtle and complex do not occur by chance. We must assume that Giotto had turned his attention to the problem of composition, and had given the matter much thought. The method he arrived at is identical to the one we have elsewhere named the *Greek organic composition* (see above, pages 65–66), and it is probable that Giotto had seen and studied enough classical work to have deduced the principle once again. If the reader will turn back, however, and compare his work with such examples as the pediments of Olympia (Figs. 3.15–16), it will be evident that he had carried the art of arrangement further forward than the Greeks — or at least further forward than we see it in any preserved work from Greece.

As compared with all earlier pictures and with most paintings of any period whatever, the whole power of Giotto's art may be summed up in the statement that one is instantly convinced that everything he painted was true. No one has ever had a moment's doubt that he vigorously intended to depict something real. The objects are actual, and the people are solidly alive. What is the special secret of Giotto's method?

In the first few pages of his *Florentine Painters* (first published in 1896), Mr. Bernard Berenson gave an answer which has given satisfaction for over fifty years. He said that Giotto painted in such a way that retinal impressions attained *tactile values.*

That is to say, he painted his figures as though they occupied space in three dimensions. No earlier painter had attached anything like the same importance to the spatial displacement of masses. In order to get the effect desired, Giotto had to paint as though his figures existed in an ample but diffused light. By grading his shadows with precision as they modeled from light into dark, he described the surface of every contour accurately. So exact are the specifications of convexity and concavity that a competent sculptor might with ease translate one of Giotto's people into stone; there would never be any doubt about how the carving should be done. Giotto's painting is intensely plastic, that is to say; and the effect is enhanced in no small measure by his original choice of a ponderous canon of proportions and his grand taste for simplicity.

With a psychological penetration considerably in advance of the time, Mr. Berenson correctly declared that Giotto's figures, although inspected through the eye, caused the observer to experience a powerful excitement of the sense of touch. He contended further that a representative painter is always wisest when he concentrates upon tactile imagery. If the observer can be convinced that the painted figure has tangibility, his imagination will supply all other necessary phenomena: space within which to stand, ground to stand on, the action of gravity, air to breathe, and light to see with. The tactile values, he concluded, are what make Giotto's pictures seem so real that memory sometimes plays tricks, leaving us with the impression we have witnessed actual events.

Mr. Berenson may have erred in concentrating his argument too exclusively upon the plastic element in Giotto's work, but there is no doubt that tactile values are a powerfully operative factor in the result. It is interesting to realize that Berenson's essay came out at the very time when Cézanne was turning his back upon French Impressionism (see below, page 912), and directing the course of modern art back toward the very definition of mass that Giotto had inaugurated five centuries before.

The reader must not make the mistake of assuming that Giotto's technique was derived from natural fact. Like most other medieval and many Renaissance painters, Giotto painted in the *Mode of Relief*, for which an analysis will be found in the next chapter. It will suffice here to point out that the method entails certain purely arbitrary assumptions about the action of light as it falls upon the masses of the human figure and its setting. The lighting of form as seen in the paintings is almost never duplicated on any shapes we are in the habit of seeing; and the whole scheme, while intelligent and perfectly lucid, is in fact an abstraction.

The world has produced an immense amount of painting since 1305, but Giotto's work at the Arena Chapel remains unsurpassed by any subsequent monument of Western civilization. During the 14th Century, there was nothing with which it might even be compared. Giotto was a famous man and a first citizen. Opportunities beckoned wherever he looked. In addition to notices that place him off and on in his native Florence, we know that he worked on important commissions in Rome, at Rimini, at Verona, at Ferrara, and perhaps also in Avignon. About 1318, he was again working at Florence, doing wall paintings in the Bardi and Peruzzi chapels of Santa Croce. The two commissions occupied most of his time for about four years.

Pictures from both chapels are often reproduced with the label " Giotto "; but we can accept them as such only in a very restricted sense. Like every other early artist, Giotto lost his reputation during the High Renaissance, and never regained it again until the general historical research of the 19th Century brought his work out in the open once more, with resulting comparisons. At some unknown date, the frescoes at Santa Croce were covered with a coat of whitewash. They were then quite forgotten. In 1841, they were rediscovered, but the date was still too early. The pictures were of course dilapidated, and a painter named Bianchi was engaged to renovate them. He did more harm than the whitewash. His over-painting looks more like a 19th-Century German greeting card than it looks like Giotto; but even if the hand is no longer his, the compositions must be.

Restored as they are, the paintings are still adequate to justify several statements about the course of Giotto's thought and art during the period of his full maturity. By comparison to the work at Padua, the psychological climate is less intense, the tempo grander, the intention less actual and more majestic. There is a breadth of view and a dignity of arrangement hitherto not observed. The pictures are not equally successful; and as before, we may take the liberty of citing only the best, which is undoubtedly the justly celebrated *Death of Saint Francis* (Fig. 13.47).

To students familiar with the later history of Italian painting, no picture could possibly be more full of suggestion. Giotto's later work may in general be said to foreshadow " the Grand Style " of the High Renaissance; and in this instance, he has produced a formal design not only as good as 16th Century work, but equal to the best of Raphael or Leonardo.

The point of time is the moment of death. Across the middle of the picture, the ponderous corpse of the saint lies in utter stillness. All eyes are directed toward the dead man except for one brother who is granted a vision of the soul's ascension. In wonder too sudden for ecstasy, he looks upward toward the sky, where angels may be seen lifting the immortal element heavenward. Dramatically speaking, we may say that the picture eloquently compares the static incubus of death with the freedom and transcendency of the eternal.

The formal means used by Giotto to present this unforgettably stately spectacle depend fundamentally upon a slow harmony of ponderous verticals and horizontals, upon the contrast of these with diagonals, and upon the dynamic and directional power inherent in the glance of the eye.

The composition is framed in on either hand by several figures who stand like statues, all of them motionless but intent upon the dead man. The verticality of those figures is echoed in the paneling of the wall behind; but even that emphasis is insufficient to overbear the predominating motive of stability and the horizontal.

The grouping opens up in the middle to bring the bier into full view. It is notable that the recumbent figure is very large, and the bier very long. Across the top of the enclosing wall runs the most powerful linear device in the picture, likewise horizontal.

Across the rectilinear elements just outlined, we may discern the existence of a superimposed triangular figure. To the right, one leg thereof is established by the inclined shaft of the cross and banner. To the left, by following the line of sight of the monk who sees the vision, we construct the other side of the figure. Both lead the eye to the celestial incident above, and thus serve to integrate an arrangement which otherwise would exist in separate registers.

Bare statements like those just made must not be construed by the reader as an adequate description of Giotto's composition. At best, plain language can only suggest the visual activity by which one comprehends pictorial form, and it is legitimate for an author to point up his meaning by occasional resort to superlatives. The *Death of Francis*, repainted as it is, remains one of the very greatest essays in formal design. It is as lucid as any known composition by the Greeks, and there is no extant Greek work of the same complexity. It is free from the erudition which so often lured even the best painters of the High Renaissance into sophisticated display. At the date when Giotto finished it, there had been no one since the fall of Rome who could even have attempted a similar performance; and after his death, there was, for about a hundred years, no one who so much as comprehended the secrets of his method.

Giotto died in January 1337. He had been once more to Assisi after finishing his work at Santa Croce. He had executed a fresco commission in the Bargello at Florence, which contains the familiar portrait of Dante, restored by an insensitive hand after having been damaged in a fire. Giotto did work also at Milan, and he spent three years at Naples, where in 1330 he was named a "familiar" of the court of King Robert — an incident of some significance because it illustrates the comparatively early date when Italians began to feel disposed to accord artists high social standing by virtue of their achievements in art. In 1334, Giotto was named chief architect to the city of Florence; and in that capacity, he made plans for the bell tower of the Cathedral which is still called "Giotto's tower."

Such were the honors heaped upon a man whose merit and scope give him rank as a world figure. It would not be difficult to contend that Giotto had the most profound intelligence yet to express itself in art. His work is marked throughout by an absence of mysticism and morbid ecstasy. He applied robust good sense to the sacred story, and everything he did demonstrates a determination to realize the objects of faith as facts. Subtleties and details never delayed him, even the detail of beauty. His people are without intellectual or physical distinction. They are often unlovely, and sometimes vulgar, but no contemporary had to walk even outside his own door to imagine the setting and atmosphere where Giotto made the great events occur: they occurred at home.

After Giotto's death, Italy produced no artist of the first rank until the 15th Century. Every year continued to produce a substantial amount of painting, however; and to fill in the history, a paragraph or two may be justified.

The School of Siena (see above, pages 365–369) continued to maintain a good over-all level of quality, and kept its special character throughout the 14th Century. At Florence, painting took two different directions. One group of men, of whom Bernardo Daddi and Spinello Aretino were exemplars, tried to combine the style of Giotto with that of Siena. They painted mostly on panel, and their formula was to clothe one of Giotto's large and plastic figures in ultramarine blue, and silhouette it against a blank ground of gold. The other group at Florence made an attempt to extend to panoramic proportions the narrative techniques that had made Giotto famous. The *Allegory of Church and State* in the Spanish Chapel at Santa Maria Novella in Florence, probably by Francesco Traini, is a good instance of their work. As wall decoration, such frescoes delight the eye with color, but not one of the Giotteschi appears to have had the slightest notion of the elements that made Giotto great.

With a certain naïve realism, things are presented in all the confusion of their original disorder and without a bit of the lucidity which enabled the master to tell the truth. Unpopular for centuries, such painting nevertheless had enough merit to serve as the principal source for the style of the modern Mexican artists Rivera and Orozco.

*

14

COLOR THEORY AND THE MODES OF PAINTING

Giotto's career stands as a historical landmark in more ways than one. Over and above the merit of his work, he holds the distinction of having been the first *painter* to achieve the rank of a world figure; but since his time, great painters have been common. It may be stated, in fact, that with Giotto, painting became the primary vehicle for artistic expression in Europe. The history of art for the past five centuries is predominantly a history of painting. We do not mean to imply that there has been a lack of great sculptors or of great architects, much less that the best of them occupy a position secondary to the painters. We merely mean to say that the majority of men capable of significant creation have turned, for reasons that defy analysis, to the production of pictures. The phenomenon has been so obvious that it usually escapes comment, but it is nevertheless an important matter to note the readiness with which the average citizen of today (unless we take pains to warn him otherwise) understands us to mean *painter* whenever we use the word *artist.*

Inasmuch as the chapters to come will be very much concerned with pictures, it is wise at this point to forget historical narrative for a space, and turn to certain physical and theoretical considerations that govern all painting of whatever place and date.

Let us first consider the fundamental differences which put any painter in a situation quite unlike that of the architect or sculptor. An architect might build a good building (though certainly not a great one) merely by drawing up a brief list of practical requirements, and making common-sense use of the materials and labor at hand. A sculptor might carve a satisfactory portrait bust simply by measuring the sitter's head with calipers, recording the dimensions, and reproducing them in wood or stone. None of the great artists, of course,

ALINARI

Fig. 14.1 Andrea del Castagno. *The Last Supper*. Florence. Sant' Apollonia. 1445–50. An interior painted in the Mode of Relief.

Fig. 14.2 Emmanuel de Witte. Interior of a church at Amsterdam during a sermon. 1686. Detroit. Institute of Arts. An interior scene painted in the Mode of the Total Visual Effect.

Fig. 14.3 Detail from Benozzo Gozzoli's *Journey of the Magi* in the chapel of the Medici Palace, Florence. 1459. A landscape painted in the Mode of Relief.

ALINARI

Fig. 14.4 Van der Heyden (1637–1712). *A Street in Cologne*. London. National Gallery. An outdoor scene painted in the Mode of the Total Visual Effect.

Fig. 14.5 Crivelli. Detail from a Madonna in the National Gallery, London. 1476. Still life painted in the Mode of Relief.

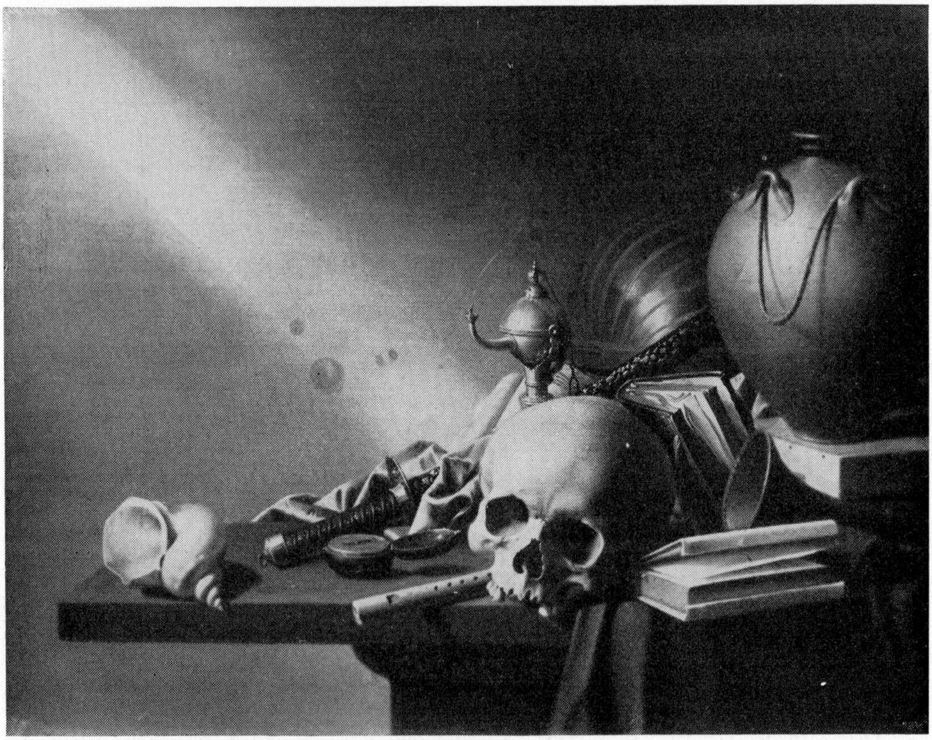

Fig. 14.6 Steenwyck (1612–after 1656). Still life. London. National Gallery. Still life painted in the Mode of the Total Visual Effect.

Fig. 14.7 Vermeer (1632–1675). *Young Lady at the Virginals.* London. National Gallery. The human figure painted in the Mode of the Total Visual Effect.

Fig. 14.8 Carlo Crivelli. Detail from a Madonna in the National Gallery, London. 1476. The human figure painted in the Mode of Relief.

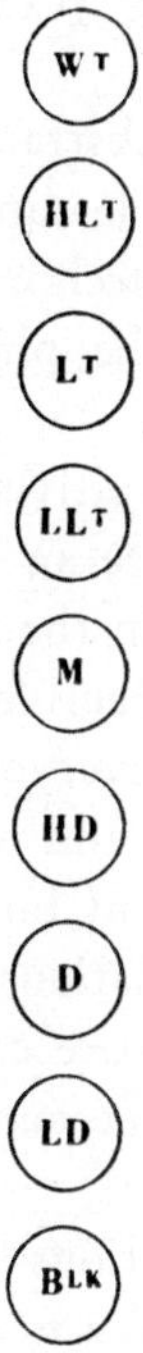

Fig. 14.9 The Value Scale.

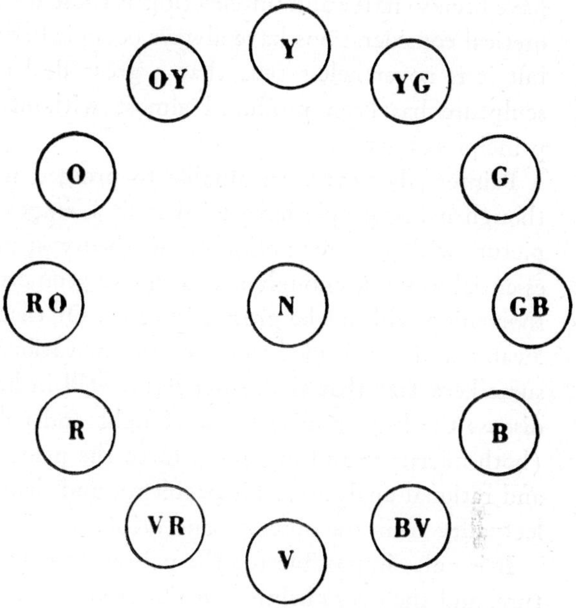

Fig. 14.10 The Scale of Hues.

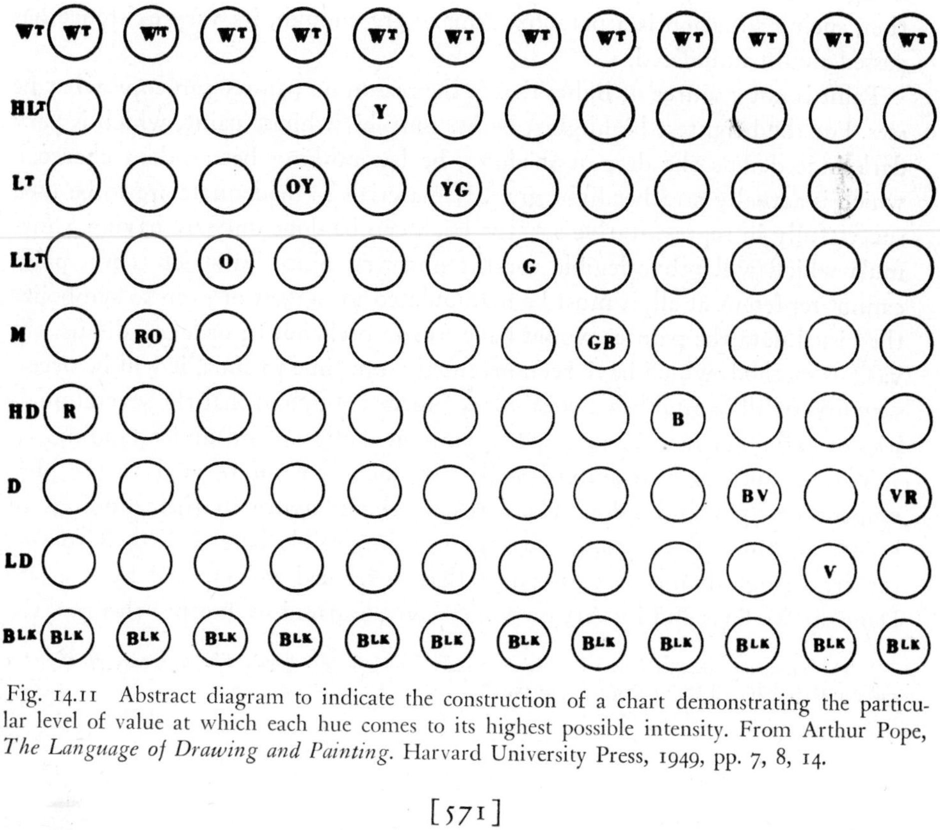

Fig. 14.11 Abstract diagram to indicate the construction of a chart demonstrating the particular level of value at which each hue comes to its highest possible intensity. From Arthur Pope, *The Language of Drawing and Painting.* Harvard University Press, 1949, pp. 7, 8, 14.

have been so naïve and unreflecting as those we suggest here. Abstract and theoretical considerations have always occupied the minds of the leading masters, but it is nevertheless true that a great deal of acceptable architecture and sculpture has been produced almost without thought of the philosophical principles of art.

Painters, however, are unable to proceed in the same intuitive way. Although many people have tried it, it is impossible to produce an acceptable picture without some notion of the theory of painting. It is, in the first place, essential to know enough of descriptive geometry so that perspective and foreshortening will not be grossly in error. Of that fact, almost everyone is fully aware; we have alluded to the matter at various points above, and we shall assume hereafter that the reader has it well in hand. Our present business is to discuss the less familiar topic of light and color, the modulations of which (both in nature and in paint) force the painter to make a more complicated and rational analysis of his problems, and demand a higher measure of intellectuality from the observer and critic.

It is quite impossible for the painter to copy the tonal relations seen in nature, and the overwhelming majority of pictures demonstrate a manipulation of light and color altogether out of correspondence with the modulations existing in the visual world. In a society committed to the representative convention, such a situation is a paradox. Amazingly enough, its very existence has passed almost unnoticed.

Paint is not a source of light; that is the reason no painter can copy what he sees. For the brightest highlights, he has only his whitest paint, which is very dark indeed. For the deepest shadows, he has nothing better than charcoal, which is actually a rather light gray. If materials so inadequate are to be used successfully in representative art, the trick can be done only by having a formula which will prove legible for the observer. Since, in strict truth, paint cannot represent at all, it must be manipulated to suggest or even to symbolize the visual data the painter would have us comprehend. In order to discuss the various methods which have been invented from time to time, it will be necessary first of all to establish a vocabulary precise enough so that the several qualities of any color may be referred to without danger of misunderstanding.

Various authors have published books which attempt to analyze the phenomena of light and color. There is enough difference in their findings to render anything like a complete summary impossible here. We shall follow, rather, a single point of view only: that developed at Harvard by the late Denman W. Ross and by Arthur Pope.* As compared with other theories, the

* The latest and most complete exposition will be found in Mr. Pope's *The Language of Drawing and Painting*. Harvard University Press, 1949.

system of Ross and Pope is lacking in certain refinements which may upon occasion be of interest to the scientist; but, for our purposes, it has the incomparable advantage of simplicity and practical accuracy. Both Ross and Pope were themselves accomplished painters. Their thinking originated with the actual problems of the medium, and the structure of their analysis fits the needs of those who wish either to paint or to understand pictures. Furthermore, and in substantial contrast with other authors, Ross and Pope proceeded to apply their theory of color to definitive examples from the work of the greatest masters of painting, with the result that such may now be explained in a way that renders all other explanations inadequate and capricious.

The most important concept entertained by Ross and Pope was the idea that the facts established by optical physics were, within the field of artistic expression, decidedly secondary to the facts of human psychology as they operate whenever one sees and reacts to a color. The reader should appreciate at the start, therefore, that every assertion made below depends for its validity not upon measurements made with instruments in the laboratory (none of which as yet approach the subtle accuracy of the well-trained eye) but upon the considered judgment of men with an incomparable experience of color in its most accomplished practical application.

THE THEORY OF COLOR

Proceeding upon the basis indicated, Ross and Pope worked out the following vocabulary. It was unfortunate that some of the words they decided upon were and remain in common use with quite another meaning, but it would be inappropriate to attempt a correction here. If each term is accepted in the technical sense given below, and if the reader will make an effort to forget for the moment all contrary senses together with their connotations, he will find himself in possession of some very efficient tools of thought.

The word *color,* although all of us continue to employ it conversationally in a more particular sense, had best be understood generically. It is the name for the study which embodies and contains all the phenomena mentioned herewith. The word *tone* is often convenient as a near-synonym.

The different " colors " like red, blue, green, yellow, and violet are best referred to as *hues*. The difference between red and blue, for example, is a contrast of hue; and the similarity between blue-violet and red-violet is a harmony of hue.

Grays are tones which we recognize as being more or less light or dark, but which lack any recognizable hue. For that reason, grays are usually referred to as *neutrals*. The darkest neutral is named *black,* and the lightest neutral *white*.

The difference between white and black is referred to as a contrast of *value*, and we shall presently find it convenient to construct a *value scale* in even steps between black and white which will enable us to name particular *value levels* with the expectation of being understood.

In addition to possessing hue, any tone that gives us the sensation of red, green, orange, etc., obviously possesses the quality of value also. If we wish to name a particular tone approximately, we simply call it a " dark red " or a " light green " as the case may be. If we want to name it exactly, we must name the precise hue, the precise value level, and the degree to which the hue is in contrast with the neutral gray at the same level of value. The latter quality — the amount of contrast with the neutral of equivalent value — is referred to as the *intensity* of the hue.

To recapitulate: *We may name any tone by naming its hue, its value, and the degree of its intensity.*

It is obvious that intensity varies in much the same manner as value. It is possible to imagine that every conceivable hue might be produced at every conceivable level of value, and in all degrees of intensity at each level. Possibly painters may find that true in heaven. On earth, they have to accommodate themselves to the action of pigment materials. One of the most important limitations thereof is the tendency of any paint to lose its hue (i.e., to neutralize) the minute one attempts to darken it or make it lighter. To put it another way, for every recognizable hue, there is but one value level where we may have that particular hue at its maximum intensity, usually referred to as the *highest possible* intensity. Yellow, for example, can be had at highest possible intensity only when the tone is very close at the value level of white. Absolute violet, neither reddish or bluish, is most intense only when nearly as dark as black — a fact upon which the technique of the French Impressionists depends (see below, pages 866–874). Red-orange comes to highest possible intensity at about the middle value, and the other hues behave as indicated diagrammatically by Fig. 14.11.

Hues at their highest possible intensity were, as a matter of historical fact, very rarely used in painting at any date earlier than about 1870, when the French Impressionists assumed the identity of a school and style. It therefore becomes a matter of interest to have an expression which indicates the degree of intensity of any hue at whatever value level we care to name. If we want to use red-orange (which comes to highest possible intensity at about the middle value) at a value level halfway between middle and black, the strongest intensity *available at that particular value* is best called *full intensity;* but the term *full intensity* is meaningless unless we simultaneously name the value level to which we refer. At any given level of value, a tone may of course be used, and often is, at considerably less than full intensity. As convenience indicates, we then refer to it as " half neutralized " or " at half intensity " — or any other degree of intensity or neutralization — as the facts demand.

Naming the Values

We can save much laborious explanation in the pages to come if at this point we establish a system for naming a reasonable number of values between black and white. Fig. 14.9 indicates in abstract fashion how such a scale may be constructed. The reader may rightly wonder why the diagram does not appear in successive stages of gray, but it is still unfortunately true that only the most painstaking work of the best printers (at an expense prohibitive for a book of this sort) can accomplish anything better than approximate reproduction of the tones as they might appear in a carefully executed water color or oil. Let the reader, therefore, take his own box of paints, and proceed as directed below. If he has an instructor to help him, so much the better; and if not, he is bound to learn much if he is willing to be severe with himself and use his eyes.

Nine levels of value will prove sufficient for all practical requirements. If using water color, one begins by laying successive coats of charcoal black over the lowest circle in the diagram until it becomes as dark as the pigments in use permit. The top circle may be left without paint, the white of the paper standing for white.

The next thing to do is to establish the middle value. Upon the manner of doing it, one's entire understanding of color depends, and the next few sentences have a special importance.

The middle value is defined as the value which contrasts equally with both white and black. We must find a gray, that is, which compares to black precisely as it compares with white. As indicated earlier, the judgment must be made with the eye. It is a subjective judgment, but experienced observers working with the same pigment materials tend to arrive at identical results. In any case, we must remember that paintings are never sent to the physics laboratory for analysis. They are hung on the wall for people to look at.

Once the middle value has been satisfactorily arrived at, the rest of the scale may be constructed by following the same method. *Dark* is defined as the value which compares to middle precisely as it compares with black. *Light* has a similar station between middle and white. *High light, low light, high dark,* and *low dark* must likewise contrast equally with the grays immediately above and below them. In theory, an infinite number of steps might be worked out; but, as stated, nine are sufficient.

The reader doubtless has already been bothered by the thought that a value scale executed in water color, as suggested, would not and could not demonstrate the full range of values available in all the pigment materials on earth. Black enamel, for example, is much darker than any black we can produce with water color, but the circumstance is of no artistic importance whatever. One does not shift from water color to enamel in the course of painting a single picture. For the artist, the important thing is to know the range that is possible within the limits of his chosen medium. Thus, the useful chart is the chart that is consistent with itself, and which demonstrates what can be done with the materials in hand.

The value scale, while laborious to construct and tedious to read about, is vitally important because it demonstrates in conclusive and unmistakable fashion the chief reason why the painter cannot possibly copy what he sees. As it appears on these pages, the diagram measures about three inches from black to white. Were we to symbolize the value relationships of nature in the same way, using vertical length to indicate the difference between black and white, we would require a scale as high as a house. The blackest darks of a sunlit scene, that is to say, contrast with the brightest lights so violently that the difference between white paint and black paint is insignificant by comparison. If the painter is to describe such a scene at all, he obviously must have a well-conceived system for making the feeble medium of paint suggest, symbolize, hint at, or otherwise recall to the observer the imagery of the natural world. The chief technical endeavor of the past 500 years has been addressed to the problem just stated; and a major part of our effort hereafter will be to trace the several solutions attempted, and to assess the merit of each.

Naming the Hues

The desirability of a systematic way for naming the hues is suggested by the annual crop of tricky names invented in the dress trade and for the colors of motor cars: Sahara yellow, rose beige, Glengarry green, *Endeavor* blue, safari brown, faded denim, acqua — and the list goes endlessly on. Admittedly, some of the names are attractive and a few may even be poetical, but the serious student will require something more reliable.

The hues are best named by laying them out on a circular diagram like Fig. 14.10, usually called the *color circle,* or the *color wheel.* Such diagrams have often been published without much explanation, and perhaps with small understanding of the method of construction or the significance of the result. The principles involved are the same used for the construction of the value scale; namely, the governing conception is to maintain an equal contrast between each hue and the two on either side of it.

The circular diagram permits us to range the so-called " warm colors " on one side, and the " cool colors " on the other. In order to maintain mutual consistency between our diagrams, it is worthwhile to keep the graduations of the color circle in step with the value scale, an operation that demands slight departures here and there from theoretical accuracy but one that involves no practical inconvenience. All hues are produced at the highest possible intensity. Yellow and violet fall on the central vertical axis because yellow comes to full intensity at high light, and violet at low dark. The contrast between them is not only a contrast of hue, but the strongest value contrast available as between any two hues. In order to define yellow and violet, we resort to the familiar notion of the warm and cool colors. Absolute yellow must not contain a hint of orange or a hint of green. Absolute violet is the hue that tends neither toward blue nor toward red.

When actually constructing the twelve-hue color circle indicated in Fig. 14.10, one does not establish yellow and violet first. In order to avail ourselves of the principle of equal contrasts, and at the same time to produce a color circle that corresponds with the value scale, we start out by laying in yellow, red, and blue — which fall at equal angular intervals around the circumference and are defined as having equal contrasts, each with the other two. Violet, orange, and green then fall in place, each once more being defined as the hue in equal contrast to the two on either side of it. Orange-yellow, yellow-green, green-blue, blue-violet, red-violet, and red-orange may then be put in as intermediaries between the hues already located.

It takes skill to construct a reasonably accurate, self-consistent color circle. The beginner will continuously be vexed by mistakes and adjustments; but if he perseveres, he will be in a position to make on his own authority some very cogent observations about the operation of colors. Perhaps the most important of these is the interaction of value and hue, as set forth above and as indicated by Fig. 14.11. It will also be found that the color circle has a beneficial and sharpening effect upon one's colloquial vocabulary. Almost every "red" in common use is in fact a red-orange. Practically all the "browns" are neutralized oranges. Most of the "pinks" are tints of red-violet.

It will still further be noted that every hue, as laid out on the color circle, falls on the same diameter as its *complementary*, which we define as the color that gives the maximum possible contrast with respect to hue. From physics we know that pigment materials obtain their capacity to exert the force of hue because they act like filters when light falls upon them. A blue pigment, for example, absorbs every part of white light except for the blue rays, and an orange pigment releases only the orange rays. Theoretically, blue and orange (or any other two complementaries) ought to cancel each other out if mixed, producing a neutral as indicated by the small circle labelled *N* in the middle of the color wheel. That matter requires considerable explanation, however, because mixtures of paint do not produce the same results as mixtures of colored light (see below, page 870). It will suffice here to point out that the hues at opposite ends of each diameter in the color circle may be thought of as approximate *pigment complementaries.* When mixed, any two give a gray. The diagram seems also to suggest that every neutral formed by the mixture of any two complementaries will also be a neutral at the middle value. Such, however, is hardly the truth. Paints are capricious more often than not. No one can predict within narrow limits what any two pigments will do when mixed. Trial and error is the only way to learn.

Another defect of the color circle also requires mention. By direction and definition, each hue on the circumference is at its highest possible intensity; but as laid out on the diagram, each hue is also equidistant from the center, which is to say from neutral. The inference would seem to be legitimate that every hue makes an equal contrast with its neutral gray of equivalent value. The notion is contrary to fact. In general, all the warm tones seem to differ from neutral more than the cool tones; and every hue in the lighter ranges strikes the eye as being less like gray than any of the darker colors.

For ordinary purposes of making ourselves understood, it is extremely important to have command of the principles outlined above; but only occasionally does one find it necessary to name a tone with the precision suggested. Once one has comprehended the idea of hue, value, and intensity (and considerable training of the eye is requisite before one can be sure of himself), approximate language is often plain enough for the needs of the moment. In that connection, it is well to mention several words which will prove especially convenient.

For all hues above the middle value, *tint* is an expressive designation. Everything darker than that is a *shade* of orange, violet, blue, or green, or whatever else the hue may happen to be.

Two other terms are similarly useful. A *field* is any area within a painting which constitutes a natural unit of a single hue. A grass plot, for example, would form a field of yellow-green. A red dress would be a field of red, smaller in area; and a sapphire set in a finger ring would be a tiny field of blue. In each instance, the yellow-green, the red, or the blue would be designated as the *local tone* of its field.

THE MODES OF PAINTING

Having provided ourselves with a vocabulary that permits intelligible discussion of the tonal relations in painting, it becomes possible to deal with the relation between the painter and his subject matter. From the advent of the representative convention onward, European painting has ostensibly been an attempt to find expression of one kind and another by means of pictures which purport to show visual facts in plausible fashion. But what is visual truth?

The reality of the visual world is by no means easy to define. Certain phenomena are variable; sunlight and darkness, for example, alter the world on a daily cycle that is never quite the same. Hills that look soft as pillows when seen from an aircraft prove viciously hard when we slip on the ice and fall flat. We comprehend nature, moreover, not by the eye alone, but with all the senses. The action of the senses, to make matters still more difficult, is not uniform. When out hunting pheasants, a man does well to observe every bush and grass plot with alert intensity, but he may be forgiven for savouring a more easy and general flavor of the same landscape as he sits on the porch smoking his pipe after supper. Certain details impress us about people and things as well as scenes; such remain vivid in the memory when all the rest is forgotten.

We have said enough to indicate that painting a picture amounts to much more than the direct application of technical skill to something the artist wants to paint. Confronted with subject matter, he cannot proceed unthinkingly even if he wants. The complexity of the human spirit forces choice upon him; and he must decide what he is driving at before he begins. Numerous styles have come and gone since the time of Giotto, and innumerable personalities have left their mark on the history of art. Insofar, however, as painting stands as a reflection of a relationship between the artist and the visual world, virtually every picture in the immense catalogue conforms in its technique to one of four fundamental systems, known as the *Modes of Painting*.

It was the greatest achievement of Messrs. Ross and Pope to draw the sweeping conclusion just stated. The validity of their findings has been attested by a significant absence of challenge. The modes they recognized are as follows: The Mode of Line and Flat Tone, the Mode of the Total Visual Effect, the Mode of Relief, and the Venetian Mode. We shall discuss the first three herewith. The Venetian Mode — in which, as a matter of fact, the great majority of paintings have been and still are executed — we shall postpone until Chapter 16.

The Mode of Line and Flat Tone

The Mode of Line and Flat Tone was mentioned in connection with Paleolithic painting (page 17) and needs little additional explanation here. The silhouette of each field is indicated by delineation, and the local tone of the area is then painted in without any attempt to indicate modeling by means of graded shadows. The technique is simple; children often paint that way because they do not understand how to model. Good results (if adequate representation is a desideratum) depend upon skill in the use of line. In that specialty, artists of the Far East, taking them as a class, have been the best the world has ever seen, and they produced in this mode some of the greatest painting ever executed. They appear to have taken pride, in fact, in using line so well that other and less elegant means were superfluous. Except for Antiquity and a few occasions when Western art came under Eastern influence, Line and Flat Tone has been rare in European painting.

The Mode of the Total Visual Effect

As indicated in the captions, the illustrations for the present chapter are an attempt to juxtapose examples of painting in the Mode of Relief (those bearing odd numbers) with comparable examples executed in the Mode of the Total Visual Effect (the even numbers). The series includes typical instances in each mode of an interior, a landscape, still life, and figure painting. Because most of the statements made below are generalizations which apply with almost equal weight to all the plates, we shall only occasionally make specific reference.

There was no painting in the Mode of the Total Visual Effect until the Flemish oil technique was perfected by the Brothers Van Eyck, as described below on pages 613–614. Up to the beginning of the 15th Century, that is to say, most European painting, including that of Giotto, had been in the Mode of Relief. Ease of explanation dictates the present order of discussion; for while earlier in date, the Mode of Relief is harder to comprehend.

With respect to tonal relations, any painter who uses the Mode of the Total Visual Effect puts himself in the position of the objective realist (see above, pages 20–21). As the name of the mode indicates, he accepts the light and color of nature in the same spirit which makes the realistic sculptor accept the structure of the human body. Whatever he sees, he construes as an artistic rule, and the first thing to look for in pictures that conform to this mode is a specific indication of the source or direction from which the light comes. Something of the kind is almost always included, as though to tell us the painter has obeyed the rules.

Objects and parts of objects are made to cast their shadows in a fashion that is orderly and consistent with the light source indicated, but a word of caution is necessary lest the reader apply that criterion too literally. Reflected light sometimes plays hob with what seems at first to be the simple logic of illumination, often reversing the shadow pattern that might be predicted for a particular field. The principle involved is nevertheless as stated.

Examination of the human form, or any other object of complex shape, when seen in a good light, will reveal that the normal eye under normal conditions does not, and indeed cannot, see everything that is there. It is difficult or impossible to follow the contours within the areas of shadow; and if we are honest with ourselves, we must admit that our knowledge of shape within the darks rests more upon inference than upon perception. The effect just mentioned is somewhat enhanced by the instinctive tendency of the eye to accommodate itself not to the darkest areas in view, but to the brightest. Pictures executed in the Mode of the Total Visual Effect take account of the phenomenon just described. In the darker areas, detail is made increasingly vague, and sometimes blacked out altogether.

Because of the pitifully short value range available in paint, it is obvious that some rational way had to be discovered for rendering the tonal relations of nature on the surface of the canvas or panel. Those painters who have made best use of the Mode of the Total Visual Effect seem to have looked upon the contrast between the natural value scale and the painter's not as a disaster, but as a proportion. Unable to make direct use of the former, they could nevertheless transpose it into paint by an act of just and systematic compression. Thus, the pigments in the pictures do not and cannot contrast with each other as the local tones do in nature, but it was possible to maintain their lesser contrasts in much the same relation. To see what is meant, the reader should examine the reproductions illustrating this chapter. It will be noticed that when modeling a field of white, the painters did not allow themselves the full range of values, but kept the darker shadows of the field up as high as the middle value, or thereabouts. Conversely, when modeling a black drapery, the convexities of the folds (which receive the strongest and most direct illumination) hardly go above the middle value unless, in a special situation, a bright highlight needs to be indicated as reflecting from an otherwise dark surface.

It is necessary to stipulate that the remarks just made apply with strict literalism only to the greatest exemplars of the mode now under review: to Van Eyck, to Vermeer, to Antonello of Messina, and to various Dutchmen of the 17th Century who deserve to be more famous than they are. A great many pictures which otherwise follow the same rules do not exhibit anything like the same fastidious care in maintaining a just proportion between the value scale of nature and that of paint.

Take the case of Vermeer, for instance (Fig. 14.7). What separates his work from that of the other " little masters " of Holland who painted pictures that look very much like his, but never give the same satisfaction? The answer is that Vermeer modeled each field in accordance with its own internal logic, but he also made every field bear a precise relation to every other area of color, well-lighted or not, in both the near and the distant parts of the picture. Many of the other masters allow themselves the full range of the available value scale for modeling every field, light or dark though the local tone may be. They accordingly fail to achieve the extraordinary effect of genuine daylight which makes Vermeer's technique a marvel.

With respect to the modulation of hue, pictures in the Mode of the Total Visual Effect are consistent with the action of colors as observed in nature. The paints are brought to strongest intensity where the illumination is strongest, and the shadows are made gradually more neutral as they become darker. That particular detail of technique has a representational usefulness more important than might be supposed. One hears a great deal, especially in the art schools, of colors that " come forward " and colors that " recede." It is surely true that certain tones are more useful than others for the indication of spatial displacement forward and back, but it is suggested that intensity has failed to receive its proper recognition as an operative factor in the representational scheme. In the opinion of the author, it is the more intense tones (regardless of hue) which are most useful to the painter when he wants us to read one part of a mass as nearer than another.

It will be seen that the Mode of the Total Visual Effect depends upon an unbroken chain of logic through which the mechanics of a painting may be referred back to the data of visual experience. It is the only kind of painting which even attempts to maintain a one-to-one relationship between the picture and what the eye actually sees in nature. As such, it is representative painting *par excellence.*

Such being the case, it will perhaps surprise the reader that there has been very little of it. Only a handful of the best masters have used it, and pictures so rendered are something close to a rarity. Admittedly it is the one and only straightforwardly " natural " way to paint, but any attempt to render the total visual effect necessarily binds painting to a number of rules which, if true of the actual world, need not be true of painting. The greater popularity of the other modes has doubtless been due to the fact that, while sufficiently accurate to satisfy the taste for representation, they offer much greater freedom in the realm of emotional expression.

The Mode of Relief

Berenson was profoundly right in recognizing the sculpturesque quality of Giotto's painting (see above, pages 559–560), and his vivid phraseology has served to make almost everybody conversant with the matter. It is important for the reader to understand, however, that Giotto's system of painting was not unique. His work is simply a vigorous application of the method Messrs. Ross and Pope have designated as the Mode of Relief. Almost every medieval painter used that mode, and it continued as the standard scheme in Italian Renaissance painting until the very end of the 15th Century. Even later than that, Michaelangelo painted his superb pictures in much the same way, although it may be helpful to think of his work as painting having affinities not so much with relief as with sculpture in the full round.

The key to the Mode of Relief is its special system for handling light and color. We must understand at the start that the scheme disregards some of the observed facts of nature as comprehended through the eye, and actually reverses some others. These matters will become clear if we inspect Andrea del Castagno's *Last Supper* (Fig. 14.1).

Ostensibly, the light in the picture comes from two windows pierced through the wall to our right. If so, the persons near the windows ought (in nature) to be more strongly illuminated than the figures remote from the windows. Similarly, the figures located toward the source of light should cast shadows on those next removed. A general darkness, moreover, would necessarily obscure everything underneath the table.

But none of those things are true of the painting. The lower extremities of the figures, which we might expect to find lost in a great shadow, are revealed beneath the table in exactly as much light as everything else. There are no cast shadows anywhere; and all the way across the scene, each person is illuminated as generously as those right next to the windows. In a word, the light is the same everywhere, a condition possible in nature only under the rarest circumstances. Even then, Castagno's uniform diffusion is approached, not duplicated.

Such a painting cannot be a transcription of a scene the painter saw, for it is impossible to see anything of the kind. What we have, rather, is a synthesis of many separate observations, each detail and each field of drapery having been studied under selected conditions of light. It goes without saying that the principle of selection depended upon the accurate revelation of shape and form. The light that suited best was the light that made most conspicuous the convexities and hollows which give us the most positive sensation of mass. The system is abstract and arbitrary, but it has the special virtue of permitting the greatest possible emphasis upon tactile values.

In their desire to realize figures and objects as entities displacing three-dimensional or cubic space, many Italian painters deliberately overlooked the effect of atmosphere, which even on a clear day and even over moderate distances tends to soften outlines and reduce contrasts of hue. A glance at our detail from Benozzo Gozzoli's fresco (Fig. 14.3) will illustrate the point. Distant buildings are diminished in size more or less accurately according to the rules of linear perspective, but each and every one is modeled out with almost the same vigor and precision as figures in the foreground.

The central purpose of the Mode of Relief is illustrated perhaps even more vividly by Figs. 14.5–8, which undertake to compare typical examples of still life and figure painting with cognate examples executed according to the rules of Total Visual Effect. Instead of darkening the shadows in accordance with the action of shadows in nature, the lighting of Figs. 14.5 and 8 is maintained at a level sufficient to reveal the precise curvature of every contour in which the painter is interested. No amount of rationalization will explain, in terms of actuality, the light effect used by Crivelli to model the head of the Madonna shown in Fig. 14.8; it is obvious that the artist cared nothing for the visual laws of nature, and everything for the expressive power of shape.

The Mode of Relief probably originated as an attempt by painters to imitate the work of sculptors. Giotto, if our surmise is correct, got his figure-style either from French Gothic sculpture, or from Giovanni Pisano, or both. The sculptor Donatello (see below, pages 617–626) was the creative leader for the entire Italian 15th Century, and the same Benozzo Gozzoli we have just mentioned learned his trade as assistant to the sculptor Ghiberti (see below, pages 638–643). In addition to such direct influence from another medium, the availability of pigment materials played a very important part in establishing and maintaining this particular way of painting.

The oil vehicle was not available anywhere until invented in Flanders about 1400, and it remained almost unknown in Italy for another 75 years after that. Before oil came into general use, wall paintings were executed in fresco, and panels were done in tempera. As compared with oil, both vehicles are subject to a very sharp loss of intensity whenever darkened in the least. Any attempt, therefore, to neutralize the shadows when modeling (as in the Mode of Total Visual Effect) was bound to result in broad areas of gray. The darker the local tones, the greater the proportion of neutral — which is to say that the picture would be almost without the appeal of color.

It became habitual, therefore, with workers in the Mode of Relief, to put the full strength of the hues wherever a dark tone was required. From there, they modeled up toward white. Sometimes they merely added more and more white to the original pigment. Sometimes they shifted first to a lighter hue, and then to one still lighter, arriving somewhere near white only at the very end of the gradation. Value-wise, the sequence conforms to the arrangement of tones in nature by putting the tints on the convexities of drapery, and the shades down in the hollows. But with respect to intensities, the system quite reverses the order we observe in the world around us; and the legibility of such pictures depends not upon tonal relations, but upon the drawing.

The system of modeling just described has some advantages that deserve emphasis. With vehicles incapable of producing vivid color at low values, it made possible the production of pictures which if not opulent in hue, are at least blonde and gleaming. A more subtle matter has to do with the spatial implications of intense and neutral tones. In paintings of the sort we now discuss, the drawing of drapery and other details demands that we read certain parts as being farther away than others, but the intense hues are seen in just those places. Our habit of feeling that intense colors " come forward " tends, that is to say, to soften the indications given by the drawing. But what at first might seem to be a method of design at war with itself turns out to provide an added charm. The net result is to emphasize the flat surface of the painting, an effect in distinct harmony with the truth that all paintings exist in fact upon a vertical plane.

Lest the reader mistakenly construe the Mode of Relief as primitive (and the Mode of the Total Visual Effect as a more enlightened way to paint), we may well conclude with some additional remarks to reinforce what has already been said in our discussion of Giotto.

By disregarding some of nature's optical laws, the Mode of Relief did not curtail the expressive power of painting; it increased it. In that connection, it is worthwhile to list some of the disadvantages and inadequacies of human vision. Even the keenest eye gets a muzzy view of things; and if the reader will look ahead to Chapter 18, he may see for himself that French Impressionism (which took its philosophy from the physical experience of vision) ended up by producing some very clever and very insubstantial paintings. Instantaneous vision, moreover, is bound to suffer from the faults inherent with any procedure that is done in a hurry. If painters choose to make a law of that brief kind of view, they may boast that their work is " true to life," but one may complain that their notion of life is slight.

Visual observation is one thing, visual experience is another, and comprehension of both is something yet again. The person seeking a full measure of comprehension can never be satisfied with the single and rapid view of a human model or landscape vista in which he may happen to be interested. His examination involves one observation after another. He discovers something every time; and in the end, he knows the thing he has studied.

Among other lessons, he has learned that light conditions are never the same twice, and that colors change with them. The silhouette of a mass changes, also, with each new station taken up by the observer, but the identity of the mass remains constant. It is that element of permanence which has repeatedly drawn European painters back to methods of painting in which the definition of mass is the central purpose. One goes too far if he contends that only mass is true and real, simply because mass alone abides. It is nevertheless easy to see how many excellent artists came to believe that unique and special virtue inhered in the sensation of mass, and it is such a belief that accounts for the existence of the Mode of Relief.

GIRAUDON

STOEDTNER

Figs. 15.1–3 John Van Eyck. *The Madonna with Chancellor Rolin* (to the right and above). Paris. Louvre. Upper right: *Santa Barbara.* Antwerp.

GIRAUDON

Figs. 15.4–5 John Van Eyck. *John Arnolfini and His Wife*. 1434. London. National Gallery.

Figs. 15.6–7 Desiderio da Settignano. *A Princess of Urbino*. Berlin. Kaiser Friedrich Museum. CLARENCE KENNEDY

CLARENCE KENNEDY

Fig. 15.8 Desiderio da Settignano. *Madonna and Child*. Turin. Pinacoteca.

Fig. 15.9 Donatello. Detail from a Madonna in the Victoria and Albert Museum, London.

BROGI Figs. 15.10–11 Donatello. Details from *Lo Zuccone*. Florence. Giotto's Tower.

Figs. 15.12–14 Donatello. Upper left: *The Head of John the Baptist Being Presented to Herodias*. Siena. Baptistry. ANDERSON. Upper right: Detail from the frame of *The Annunciation*. Florence. Santa Croce. About 1433. BROGI. Below: Detail from *Christ Presenting the Keys to Saint Peter*. London. Victoria and Albert Museum.

BROGI

ANDERSON

Figs. 15.15–16 Donatello. *Gattamelata*. Padua. Piazza Sant' Antonio. 1446–1453. Height of horse and rider about 9 feet.

ANDERSON

Fig. 15.17 Donatello. *Saint John the Baptist.* Florence. Bargello.

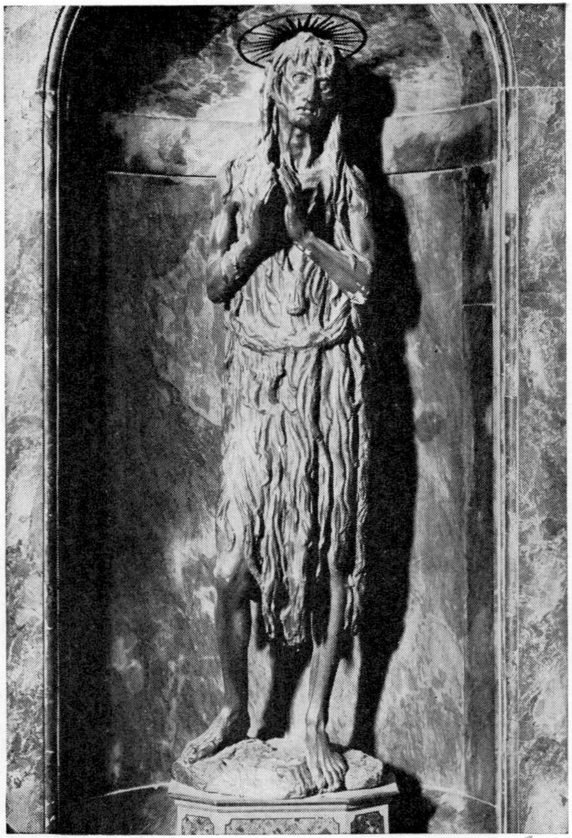

BROGI

Fig. 15.18 Donatello. *Repentant Magdalen.* Florence. Baptistry.

ALINARI

Fig. 15.19 Masaccio. *Expulsion of Adam and Eve from the Garden of Eden.* Florence. Church of the Carmine. About 1427.

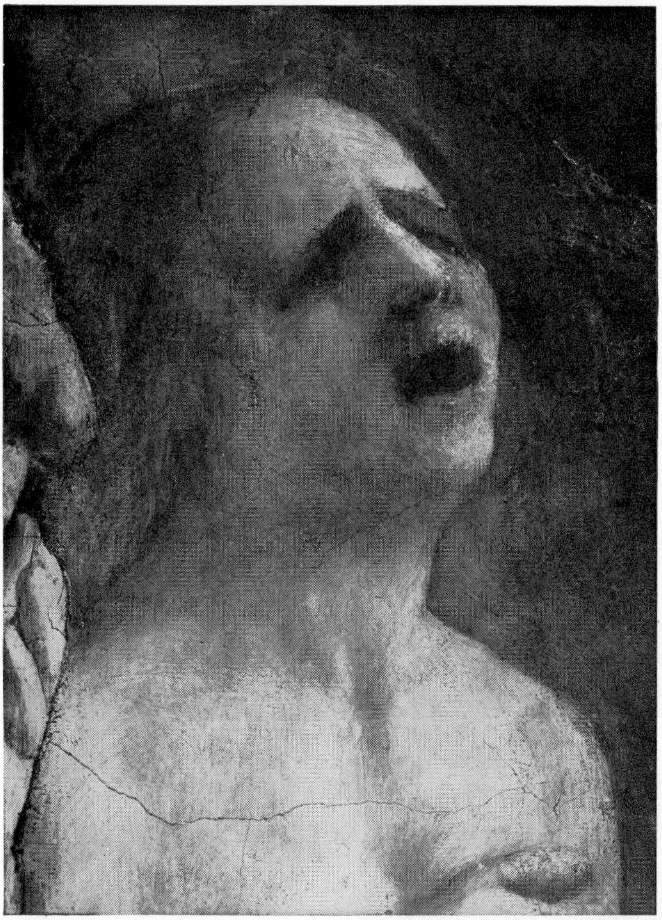

ALINARI

Fig. 15.20 Masaccio. Head of Eve. Detail of Fig. 15.19.

ANDERSON

Fig. 15.21 Masaccio. *The Tribute Money*. Florence. Church of the Carmine. About 1427. Figures life-size.

ANDERSON

ALINARI

Figs. 15.22–23 Brunelleschi. Florence. The Foundling Hospital (above). Started in 1421. The Pazzi Chapel (below). About 1430.

ALINARI

Fig. 15.24 Florence. Pazzi Chapel. Detail of Fig. 15.23.

Figs. 15.25–26 Panels submitted in the competition of 1401 by Brunelleschi (left) and by Ghiberti. Florence. National Museum. ALINARI

Figs. 15.27–28 Ghiberti. Eastern Doors of the Baptistry at Florence. 1425–1452. Panel with *The Sacrifice of Isaac* (left) and detail showing *The Creation of Eve*. BROGI.

BROGI

Fig. 15.29 Jacopo della Quericia. *Creation of Eve.* 1425–1438. Bologna. San Petronio.

ANDERSON

Fig. 15.30 Fra Angelico. Detail from *Death and Assumption of the Virgin.* Before 1430. Boston. Isabella Stewart Gardner Museum.

Fig. 15.31 Fra Angelico. *The Annunciation.* About 1440. Florence. San Marco. Fresco. 7½ by 9¾ feet.

ANDERSON

Fig. 15.32 Fra Filippo Lippi. Madonna. About 1455. Florence. Uffizi. Tempera on panel 25 by 36¼ inches.

ANDERSON

Fig. 15.33 Antonio Pollaiuolo. *Hercules and the Hydra*. Florence. Uffizi. 4¾ by 6 11/16 inches.

ALINARI

Fig. 15.34 Botticelli. *Madonna of the Eucharist*. 1470–1474. Boston. Isabella Stewart Gardner Museum. Tempera on panel 24¾ by 33 inches.

ALINARI

Fig. 15.35 Botticelli. *Allegory of Spring.* Florence. Uffizi. About 1478. Tempera on panel 6 feet, 8 inches high.

ALINARI

Fig. 15.36 Botticelli. *The Birth of Venus.* Florence. Uffizi. About 1485. Tempera on canvas 8 feet, 11 inches by 5 feet, 3¼ inches.

ANDERSON

Fig. 15.37 Botticelli. *The Birth of Venus.* Detail. Head of Venus. Florence. Uffizi.

ANDERSON

Fig. 15.38 Botticelli. Illustration for Dante's *Inferno*. Canto 9. Rome. Vatican Library. Pen and ink on parchment.
"Where in a moment saw I swift uprisen the three infernal Furies stained with blood, who had the limbs of women and their mein, and with the greenest hydras were begirt; small serpents and cerastes were their tresses, wherewith their horrid temples were entwined."

*

15

THE EARLY RENAISSANCE

The start of the Renaissance marked the beginning of modern civilization. The new era may be said to have arrived by 1400, or shortly thereafter; and we shall find it convenient to recognize two subdivisions: the 15th Century is appropriately known as the *Early Renaissance,* and the 16th as the *High Renaissance.*

The cause of the Renaissance was not the revival of classical studies; the ferment of classical enthusiasm which so dominated the imagination of several generations did not, as a matter of fact, commence until all the decisive philosophical decisions had been made and all the modern values generally accepted. The Renaissance, in short, was not what the name seems to say: a mere rebirth of classical culture. It was a fundamental change in human nature. All society joined in the belief that certain specific things were worth working for, worth having, and worth defending. The very same things have been central in our motivation ever since, and give a specious validity to the old saw that " human nature is the same everywhere." Grossly wrong if applied to all humanity and all history, the notion is approximately accurate if we limit its application to the inhabitants of Western Europe during the past 500 years.

As demonstrated in Chapter 13, the new point of view did not come as a sudden burst of light; there were signs of it as early as the West Porch at Chartres (pages 522–524). The actuality of the Renaissance did not depend upon the existence of its fundamental concepts in a few minds, however; it was a matter of the universal acceptance of those concepts as self-evidently true. The ideas to which we refer are summed up in the words *humanism* and *individualism,* and in the phrase *belief in the value of the world.* Because all the art we are still to survey amounts, in spite of its great variety, to a single celebration of the beliefs just named, it is time to explore the philosophy of the Renaissance more thoroughly than we have yet done.

The emergence of human nature in its modern form coincided with the period when the medieval church was declining from its former position of dominance in European society. While outright paganism was conspicuous in the behavior of certain individuals, it would be a mistake to infer that religion lost all its meaning, or even most of its meaning. Many of the most brilliant leaders of the period, the very men whom we remember as actual builders of the modern world, were profoundly sincere in their faith: Pico of Mirandola, for example, and Marsilio Ficino. The change should be thought of less in terms of a negation of the religious values, and more as an awakening to the worth of things of which the medieval mind had been comparatively unconscious, or of which medieval society had been taught to be ashamed.

More was involved than the mere act we attempt to describe as the opening of eyes to the wonder and beauty of the world. Even more was involved than the actual placement of hope and belief in our life here as mortals. The Western world crossed the great divide, it would seem, when people began to feel confidence in the possibility of human achievement. The thing that best characterizes the attitude typical of the Renaissance is the feeling that one holds a map in his hand which shows the road to fulfilment of the heart's desire. Seeing life as an equation between himself and the environment, Western man has undertaken to subdue nature and make it work for him. The actual exploration of the globe coincides with the period we now study — also, the beginnings of modern science. Since the 15th Century, the resources of the planet have been mapped in circumstantial detail, and the physical laws of nature have been codified by methods increasingly and stupendously precise and refined.

The artistic counterpart to the age of exploration and research was an increased realism. With respect to the human anatomy, the realists of the Renaissance cast off every vestige of medieval prejudice. Nudity lost its connotation of shame. Anatomical investigation of the entire body became a routine part of artistic training. Dissection presently extended the knowledge of artists beyond the limits of surface examination. As an artistic vehicle, the nude regained something like its ancient usefulness; but as distinguished both from the classical nude and from Gothic realism, the anatomy in the average Renaissance statue or picture is more intensive in its correctness. More than adequate for their immediate purpose of carrying content, such figures might often be mistaken for biological studies — which in fact they are.

With respect to the representation of space, a working knowledge of perspective and foreshortening was replaced by stricter standards. The convergence of lines to a vanishing point, and consistency therein with regard to every object in the picture, was insisted upon in art as severely as it might be demanded today in an engineering school. The result was to call into being standards of draftsmanship the like of which the world had never seen before. The second- and third-rate artists of the Renaissance, if we may for the moment judge them only by their capacity to represent accurately, had a technique beyond praise. As for the great men, we need merely to recall that Michaelangelo felt he might sneer at Titian because "Venetians cannot draw." Everyone, then and now, concedes that the remark was his privilege, but no one else can have the same privilege.

Atmospheric perspective was hardly susceptible of the same reduction to rules; conditions of light and atmosphere permit too many variations. Although often disregarded as superfluous by artists who preferred to paint in the Mode of Relief (pages 582–586), the subject nevertheless received thorough investigation. When precise linear perspective was combined with a scheme of tones calculated to induce the sensation of space and distance, representative painting attained an unprecedented power to convince. Pictures began to assume a verisimilitude that is often startling even today when the world has had a long time to get used to it.

The convention of exact representation was only one way by which art reflected an acceptance of the world. The cognate idea of man's place within the environment found an outlet in various manifestations which, in one way or another and from this angle and that, expressed and recorded a new consciousness of the self. We have summed up that new consciousness with the phrase *human dignity,* which is an abstraction. Without denying that the grand abstractions run the show at all times, what of the particular notions which served during the Renaissance as impulses to govern action — including the creation of the works of art which stand as monuments to the hope and belief of that time?

Power is one of the values that came in with the Renaissance. Beginning with the 15th Century, a certain measure of personal power, hitherto reserved only for the great, began to be looked upon as a human right. Since that time, every man might be counted upon to seek at every opportunity an increase in the power he already possessed. In the overwhelming majority of instances, the forces of public order have compelled people to seek power in the milder form we call wealth, and to use it with varying degrees of moderation. The forces of public order have never in themselves reflected a disbelief in the value of power, even though they have restrained it. They represent, rather, the collective effort of lesser individuals to protect their own sphere of anarchy. To restrain individualism, that is, in the interest of human dignity.

The urge to power has often been in conflict with human dignity, since power so commonly implies the subjection of others to a single will. The coexistence in the same mind of the divergent impulses is one of the paradoxes of modern civilization, but the two ideas have nevertheless often functioned as one, with results propitious to the culture of the race and especially to its art.

In order to live as befits his dignity, the individual must have power to regulate the circumstances of his daily routine. During the Renaissance, countless persons began to ask for more than mere protection from the elements and a diet sufficient to keep them alive. They felt entitled to comfort and to health. Having that, it was taken for granted that a man would strive for still further improvement of his lot on earth: for a house that provided beauty in addition to comfort; for food that was pleasurable as well as nourishing; for clothes that were handsome over and above being adequate; for tools, utensils, and weapons which were articles of choice; and for a code of behavior that lent ceremony to the conduct of business both at home and abroad. Carried to an extreme, the process described results in display, a vice all too often illustrated in the history of art. In a more genial form, the combination of power and dignity has demonstrated elements of nobility, and has certainly affected art for the better.

In order to understand the art we are to study, we must appreciate that it most often expresses the feelings of persons who believed that man can realize his highest good by being true to himself. That, essentially, is an artistic concept. Everything hinges upon the individual's confidence that his body, his mind, and his personality constitute an artistic medium, potentially responsive to the creative imagination. The activities of his life are, by extension, a work of art also. His home and possessions logically become a setting. As a doctrine consciously held, the concept of life as a work of art awaited overt expression until the High Renaissance, when it was stated in words as plainly as we state it here (page 713). The incipient force of the thought may be discerned, however, much earlier. How else are we to account for the more vital quality of personality, as imponderable and as actual as an electric shock, which literally stares out at us from even the slightest objects of Renaissance art (Figs. 15.6–7)?

Success in the humanistic endeavor, as just described, has never been universal; but whenever a man of special powers extended himself to the full potential of his personality, the event was conspicuous and the man became famous. Because fame, coming soon or late, almost always arrived for those who approached the common ideal, humanity leapt to the assumption, perhaps an illogical one, that fame itself was a reward and a fulfilment. Even power came to be thought of as a mere steppingstone to the higher good of fame; few men have been content with the reality of the former if denied the prominence that ordinarily goes with it.

Fame has probably been the closest thing to an absolute known in the workaday world. " In my mind's eye," once wrote Lord Nelson, " I ever saw a radiant orb suspended which beckoned me onward to renown! " The same statement might have been made by any other successful man during the past five centuries; and in saying what he did, the great admiral gave expression to the point of view the modern world has substituted for the medieval beatitude of salvation. Unable to live very long, people have projected themselves toward eternity by doing something to get remembered by. As death approached, how many a man has laid down with comparative equanimity all that he ever had in the comfortable thought of leaving a reputation behind him!

The general acceptance of fame as a desideratum has been amply reflected in the history of art. The remarkable thing to contemplate is the complete success enjoyed by those wise enough to employ first-rate artists for the purpose of making their names and personalities immortal. The reader needs merely to page through the earlier illustrations of this book to find numerous examples of men and women who would be totally forgotten except for the existence of statues and pictures; and in the periods to be covered below, let him note the increasing incidence of personal monuments. We refer not only to portraits, but to the identification of great enterprises with personalities, culminating in the colossal extravagance of Versailles (Fig. 17.1) built by Louis the 14th because his minister Colbert shrewdly propounded the policy that " a king is known by his monuments."

Another aspect of the belief in fame was the way in which works of art gradually became something more than a reflection of the desires of the patron, however great he might be. Giotto's frescoes are not remembered in the name of the donor Scrovegno; we think of them as the personal monument of the artist. Giotto was an early instance of what has been commonplace since. In this chapter, we embark upon an era when artists insisted upon signing, recording, and even boasting of their artistic achievements. Recognition has been necessary or they could not breathe.

In that latter connection, it is important for the reader to understand that most of the good artists got prompt and generous recognition. Giotto and Simone Martini, we have already mentioned; both lived and died as esteemed citizens of Italy and the world. Fra Angelico (pages 645–649) found it difficult to keep free from the unsought honors and responsibilities which were thrust upon him. When Raphael died in 1520 and when Michaelangelo died in 1564, the whole world mourned and the bodies lay in state like those of emperors. Rubens (pages 815–817), remembered by us as a painter, was esteemed in his own time almost as much for his sagacity as a diplomat. Sir Joshua Reynolds (1723–1792) associated on terms of friendship with royalty, and with the intellectual élite around Dr. Johnson. He also accumulated a very large fortune.

For something over 400 years, the profession of artist held out to ambitious young men a glittering hope for the future. The artists cited in the paragraph above were typical; any number of others might be named to draw the same illustration. It is important to appreciate that in every instance, the foundation of fame and fortune was neither birth nor luck, but good art; and it is specially important before we turn to specific matters to realize that the situation just summarized changed radically for the worse during the 19th Century. Not until then, did any good artist find himself compelled to sacrifice a single comfort or decency of life as the cost of doing the work he wanted to do. Not until a hundred years ago, more or less, did any great artist lack for money and friends. Because neither the present author, the present reader, nor any living artist has witnessed anything like the conditions of art during the Renaissance and later, the human tendency to judge from our own experience must be sternly governed.

As he considers what we have set forth above, the reader must be forcefully reminded that wherever we have referred to *man* we have meant not the human race, but the population of Western Europe and its derivatives in North and South America. The philosophy of humanism was peculiarly a European product. It was often debased into materialism, and has acted in that form as a sanction for the worst kind of behavior. In innumerable instances, however, humanism has brought about the results visualized by its most ardent advocates.

During the past few centuries, European culture has been permitted to maintain an autochthonous growth. The products and the customs of Europe have often moved outward to affect other regions; but there has been little influence, and until World War II certainly no impact, from the other direction. The present indications, if we may be permitted a guess, are that the Renaissance ended in 1914. Certainly 20th Century art betokens a change in the standards described above; but to that matter, we must return in Chapter 19.

FLEMISH PAINTING DURING THE EARLY RENAISSANCE

Realism was the most important feature of all European art during the 15th Century. There were two main centers of production, Flanders and Italy.

Donatello (pages 617–626) was the dominant figure at Florence, and that city was by far the most important center on the peninsula. Almost exactly contemporary with him was John Van Eyck (about 1380–1441), who with his brother Hubert founded the Flemish School and set the style for all the art north of the Alps. Because his work continues without a break the tradition of Late Gothic Realism (pages 539–542) we shall deal with it first.

The most famous monument connected with the name Van Eyck is the altarpiece of *The Adoration of the Lamb,* colloquially known as *The Ghent Altarpiece,* set in place in the church of Saint John (now Saint Bavon's) at Ghent during the month of May 1432. The work is a very large triptych, with two side panels hinged to open out in panoramic fashion, or to close from either hand and thus cover the middle section. Paintings appear on both sides; and, depending on how we count them, some twenty subjects or more are depicted. It will be seen that the monument is not a picture, but a collection of pictures. For that reason, and because the handling of detail is meticulous and minute, the illustrations so often published in books of normal size are intolerable. Large colored plates are necessary in order to give any notion of the whole, and numerous details at full size are requisite if the student is to construct an adequate visualization of the original. Such being impractical in this volume, we refer the reader to several monographs where he will find them.* Herewith, we will merely set down a few directions which will tell him what to look for.

The main face of the *Ghent Altarpiece* is an arrangement of panels in two registers. The upper register consists of seven separate panels, of which five are tightly filled, each by a large single figure seen in close-up. It is doubtful whether the upper seven panels were ever intended to go together, and much more unlikely that they were meant to be shown in their present juxtaposition to the single panoramic composition in the lower register.

The lower register consists of five panels; but, as indicated, a landscape background runs continuously across all five. In considerable contrast to the paintings above, the lower composition shows a great many small figures within a deep space. How are we to account for its incongruous and unfortunate position in relation to pictures which, if equally good of their kind, are patently quite a different and incompatible type of painting?

* Leo van Puyvelde, *The Holy Lamb,* Paris and Brussels: Marion Press, 1947.

Ludwig Baldass, *Jan Van Eyck,* Phaidon, 1952.

Emile Renders, *Jean Van Eyck,* Brussels, 1950.

See also a forthcoming work by Erwin Panofsky, presently to be published by the Harvard University Press.

Life Magazine, Vol. 26 No. 16 (April 18, 1949), has a short explanatory article accompanied by good colored plates.

On the assumption that the original designer intended to have the pictures as we now see them, the suggestion has been made that the upper register may be considered as heaven. Thus, the bearded Christ who fills its center panel can be understood as sitting directly above the lamb of the lower register, which would be his symbol on earth. Such an idea smacks of borrowing from Raphael's *Disputà* (pages 730–731), and imputes to an accomplished master an unusual lack of taste in the matter of artistic harmony.

The simplest explanation is probably the true one. According to tradition and to an inscription on the original frame, the work was begun by Hubert Van Eyck (pages 541–542) and finished by his younger brother John. Hubert appears to have died at Ghent in September 1426, at which time John was in Spain on a mission for the Duke of Burgundy. Upon his return, John was probably pressed by the donor, Jodoc Vydt, to complete the commission as best he could, but his official duties prevented his giving the matter full-time attention. We may therefore make the further guess that John finished up whatever panels he happened to find in his brother's shop, and assembled them into an arrangement that has a certain iconographical coherence. He probably realized as well as we do that artistic unity was lacking, but he also knew perhaps better than ourselves that he was giving the donor a small museum of the finest representative painting in the world.

The iconography of the picture in the lower register is of special interest, and requires explanation. There is no agreement among scholars as to particulars; but the imagery certainly has something to do with the following sources. Some of it apparently reflects John I:29, and the 7th, 14th, and 19th Chapters of the Book of Revelation. It seems also to have been influenced by Jacobus de Voragine's *Golden Legend;* and the reader will do well to peruse his chapter on the Feast of All Saints, where he describes a vision seen by the sacristan of Saint Peter's. Certain details thereof appear to be reflected in the picture.

Insofar as the meaning may be summed up briefly, the theme has to do with the idea of redemption through the Blood of the Lamb. An altar and a fountain are placed on the central axis of the main panel. The Lamb stands on the altar. From his breast, a stream of blood flows into a chalice; this, presumably, becomes (by a mystic process) the water issuing from the fountain below, upon the base of which we find an inscription adapted from the 22nd Book of Revelation: "This is the water of the river of life proceeding out of the throne of God and of the Lamb."

Angels kneel on the grass around the altar; some swing censers and others carry the instruments of the Passion. Four processions converge toward the sacred area. From the left come Prophets and Gentiles, followed by Knights of Christ and Just Judges. From the right, Apostles and Confessors, followed by

Hermits and Pilgrims. A group of Virgin Martyrs is seen approaching from the right-hand middle distance; and a group of male martyrs from the left. Out behind, a superb landscape opens up into the vastness of the sky, the horizon line being broken by fanciful buildings in the Late Gothic style.

Among the seven pictures of the upper register, the *Adam* and *Eve* are the most important. Neither is in the least a pleasant figure, but either or both may be said to constitute a historical landmark of the greatest importance. For the first time since Antiquity, the public found itself confronted with two human nudes rendered on a large scale with meticulous accuracy by an artist who was technically competent to do it. It may be contended that neither figure demonstrates any significant use of the revealed muscles as a vehicle for the communication of an emotion or state of being (as the Greeks had done, and as the Italians were almost immediately to do), but no one can quarrel with Sir Martin Conway's passing remark that the work literally bristles with intelligence.

The special flavor of John Van Eyck's work is best discerned in his single panels of simpler iconography, of which the *Madonna and Chancellor Rolin* (Figs. 15.1–2) may be taken as typical. The figure of the Madonna is somewhat heavier than average, but is otherwise typical of the type that remained popular in Flanders for a hundred years thereafter. The peculiar arrangement of the hair (tight across the head and caught back from the ears, but hanging free in a long bob over the shoulders) remained constant for a very long time. Likewise the high-waisted costume, with a voluminous over-mantle which spreads out over the floor and gives the whole figure a more or less triangular silhouette.

The two most important features of the Flemish style are well illustrated by Fig. 15.2. It was apparently a matter of pride to describe every detail with an intensity which recalls the Irish manuscripts (pages 305–310) and fits the northern tradition in general. The smallest wrinkle in the skin, even the stubble of the beard, received an analysis reserved by most painters for the tonal modulations of a mountain or a valley. The work must have been done with the aid of a lens, and we may therefore name the Flemish convention in that matter as *microscopic*. For the equally meticulous description of distant landscape, the Flemish custom is more expressively referred to as *telescopic*. As technical terms, both words will be found useful whenever we wish to have an antonym for *impressionism* (page 168). Call it microscopic or telescopic as the case demands, the more closely we examine detail in Flemish paintings, the more we see.

For the rendering of space, the Van Eycks originated a color convention that remained standard in northern painting for a century and more. Most of the pictures have natural boundaries which divide the setting into a well-defined foreground, middle ground, and distance. Warm tones and strong contrasts of hue are reserved for the foreground. The middle ground usually contains a mixture of warm and cool tones; but in the distance, warm tones are avoided, and everything is pulled into a common tonality of rather strong blue-green. Often stated to be in accordance with the observed arrangement of color in nature, the sequence described appears in actual landscape only under special conditions. In particular, the intense blue-green of the distance is rarely observed except when the sun is obscured by pure white clouds immediately after a rain storm. In New England and New York, especially during the months when leaves are on the trees, the effect may be noted at such times, but only for a brief period before blue sky emerges again.

No one can say whether the tradition is correct which names the Brothers Van Eyck as the inventors of oil painting, but they were surely the first important masters to use that vehicle extensively and explore its possibilities to the full. The precise nature of their medium still defies analysis, although several modern researchers have arrived at similar results. The process was nothing like the linseed oil painting in common use today, for which reason a brief summary of the method will prove illuminating.

Most Flemish paintings are on wooden panels. First, the surface of the panel was covered with a ground of fine cement (called *gesso*), which gave a smooth surface to paint on. The entire picture was then drawn in ink, and the modeling carried out in neutral monotone. The appearance at that stage would be very much as we see it in the little *Saint Barbara* (Fig. 15.3).

The next step was to apply color. Most of the Flemish paints were transparent; properly, they should be referred to as *varnishes*, or *glazes*. They were apparently used not in a liquid state, but thick and stiff like glue. After each field had received its glaze, the viscosity of the latter permitted prolonged work with the brush. The glaze could be made thinner here and thicker there simply by stroking it with the bristles in the right way, and the result would be to refine the tonal modulations already established by the monotone painting below.

The system was very long drawn out. Today, when there has been so much recent emphasis upon the value of spontaneity, the Flemish oil technique often seems unbelievably tedious, but it had certain virtues that deserve emphasis. It produced pictures which still gleam like jewels; the problem of preserving them is not a problem of preserving the paint, but a problem of maintaining the wooden panels. Correction, which is so easy and so much abused when painters use opaque pigments and linseed oil, was so difficult as to be impractical; that fact made it necessary for the painter to visualize the completed picture in minute detail before he began. As compared with methods which permit him to be more easygoing, the Flemish procedure was admittedly severe, but it induced a thoroughness and maturity of consideration which makes the pictures seem " right " in a way that is all too rare. For those technically interested, moreover, there is a special beauty in the precision with which every surface, however small, is intimately expressive of the master's intention.

In addition to the virtues just cited, Flemish oil offered still another quality of the utmost interest to painters and patrons who were literally inspired by the idea of representation. With respect to making strong intensities of hue available at low values, the new vehicle was and remains second only to mosaic and enamel. When using oil, it was no longer necessary to reverse the tonal sequence of nature (page 584) in order to get pictures that were colorful. The properties of the medium seem to have invited painting in the Mode of the Total Visual Effect (pages 580–582); and John Van Eyck, if not inventor of that mode, was the first great master to make full use of it.

The picture which most perfectly exemplifies his accomplishment in such endeavor is the *Portrait of John Arnolfini and His Wife* (Figs. 15.4–5). There was no earlier and there still is no more remarkable demonstration of the proportional compression of nature's value scale into that of paint. The subject was extensive. Many fields were involved, each with its special relation to the source of light. The play of light was greatly complicated by reflections, and by the capacity of various surfaces to reflect. The technical problem was, in fact, too ramified and difficult to permit adequate description in words; but even as seen in our small book plates, it is immediately plain that the subtlest variations of value and hue were rendered with an unbelievable consistency and accuracy. The figures and objects seen in the picture give no suggestion of colored sculpture. There is also no suggestion of light controlled in some unnatural way. The picture stands as perhaps the first instance in the history of the world where a painter was able to arrive at a complete realization of existence in air and space.

At the moment when this is written, most of our leading artists have set aside the principles of realism. Their reasons form part of the business of Chapter 19, but the publicity attendant upon their effort has brought about in art circles something resembling a bias against the kind of painting upon which John Van Eyck expended so prodigious an amount of energy, intelligence, and technique. What merit and value did he see in representative painting? What made him undertake the effort?

It is hardly enough to point out that representation challenged artists during the 15th Century because so few of them could do it. It is true that the creative mind thrives on the zest of a new thing; but experiment for its own sake, while stimulating to the technical imagination, has never in and of itself produced any great art.

Certainly the Arnolfini portrait cannot be called great because of its subject matter. Arnolfini was the Medici agent at Bruges. Presumably he was financially shrewd or he would not have held that position; but it would be hard to find a more hateful face, figure, or spirit in the entire history of art. His young wife, about to have her first child, is insignificant. There is, in short, no nobility or profundity of character to be interpreted or expressed; and the value of the picture, if any, must be sought on some basis completely different from the approach which leads us, for example, to an explanation of Giotto.

Perhaps the best way to suggest the greatness of John Van Eyck is to point out that he lived at a time when modern science was just beginning, and when there was as yet no distinction between the painter, the philosopher, and the scientist. He devoted himself to visual observation in all its ramifications because it seemed to offer one road toward understanding the environment, a desideratum which in that generation looked identical with wisdom and meaning. His northern background suggested that such investigation must be intense, omitting no detail, for all northern art from the beginning had been conceived as a synthesis of infinite detail. But lest the student dismiss such work with the epithet "photographic" and lest he imagine that the painter was a bore who got that way because he tried to tell everything, let him stop and consider the exhaustive nature of Van Eyck's accomplishment. Such painting is completely beyond the capacity of any ordinary realist. It reflects an investigation so thorough and intelligent as to transcend the mere facts of appearance; it sprang from a knowledge of light and color (and of methods for recording knowledge in paint) which partakes not of ordinary life, but of celestial physics. A realist of that magnitude may be said to have lived on a lofty plateau. It is true that Van Eyck denied himself personal and even human expression, but his exposition of visual truth betokens a singular and reverent humility. If his unlovely pictures have beauty, they have the beauty of infinite law.

Followers of the Van Eycks

The work of the Van Eycks started a tradition that lasted over a hundred years. Important not only in Flanders but everywhere else, their style may be said to have dominated the taste of Europe until the end of the 15th Century, and in some places even longer. Only in Italy was there enough independence of mind to produce artists who did not attempt to imitate the Flemish style; but even there, future research is likely to reveal more influence from the north than we commonly suppose.

The endurance of the style established by the Van Eycks was to a great extent a function of the guild system (pages 550–552), which was more strict and efficient in Flanders than elsewhere. It prevented the production of bad pictures for a century, but one has to concede that as a monument of the human intellect, the work of the founders stands alone.

The most important master in the period immediately following the Van Eycks was Roger van der Weyden (about 1400–1464), sometimes called Rogier de la Pasture. A more introspective painter than the Van Eycks, he was peculiarly concerned with the element of tragedy in the Christian story, and with interpretive portraiture.

Hans Memling (about 1433–1494) and Hugo van der Goes (about 1430–1482) stood out as leaders in the next generation. The latter has a special if fortuitous distinction because he was the author of the *Portinari Altarpiece,* a large panel depicting the *Adoration of the Shepherds,* now in the Uffizi. As the name implies, it was done for an Italian patron. He shipped it to Florence, probably about 1477. One sometimes hears it said that its arrival converted the Italians to oil painting, a statement which is untrue by about one generation. It is no exaggeration, however, to mention that the wonderful Flemish colors, to say nothing of the magnificent way in which space was represented, made a sensation in the town which was then the cultural capital of the world. For the next two generations, the student-painters in Italy studied Hugo van der Goes with almost the same care they accorded to the work of their own Masaccio.

The latest master who can be described as a Van Eyck derivative was Gerard David (about 1460–1523). If we take any earlier Madonna from the Flemish School and compare it with his *Rest on the Flight into Egypt,* now in the National Gallery at Washington, it will be easy to draw up a long list of similarities. There are a few differences, but they are not immediately obvious.

It was not until the arrival of Hieronymous Bosch (about 1462–1516) that the north produced a master of sufficient force to make a significant change in the style set by the Van Eycks. His work is dealt with in the next chapter.

Between the art of 15th-Century Flanders and that of Germany, there existed the most obvious parallels. The sculptors Veit Stoss, Adam Kraft, and Tilman Riemenschneider all used a figure-style similar to the Flemish painters. The same thing may be said of Conrad Witz, a remarkable painter of light and space, who worked at Geneva and Basel. Because there is some doubt about direct contact between Switzerland and Flanders, Witz's career serves to strengthen the probability that 15th-Century realism rose like the tide, being caused by no man. Martin Schongauer, who did his best work in black and white prints, continued the Van Eyck tradition until the very end of the 15th Century. He spent most of his life at Colmar.

France, during the 15th Century, was likewise an artistic province of Flanders. Nicholas Froment, Enguerrand Charenton, and the unknown Master of Moulins can be distinguished by the expert as French; but the learned often overlook the obvious: in all essentials, those masters were provincial Flemings. The anonymous artist who painted the famous *Pietà of Villeneuve-les-Avignon*, now in the Louvre, and the painter Jean Fouquet were men of a different stripe. Their Flemish affinities are evident, but both were capable of strong abstraction in a startlingly modern manner.

The recent researches of Chandler Post have furnished the world for the first time with an authoritative and reasonably complete catalogue of Spanish painting of the 15th Century. From that great effort of scholarship, one of the most extensive ever undertaken singlehanded, the most important conclusion to be drawn is that Spain, like France and Germany, was largely dependent upon Flanders for the style of its painting. John Van Eyck had been there in 1428–29. He came not to paint, but to negotiate for a royal marriage; but his visit established the prestige of Flemish art in Spain. Paintings and tapestries from the Low Countries were continuously imported; and even Isabella, an enthusiastic collector of Roger van der Weyden, preferred to hire Flemings rather than Spaniards. It was no accident, therefore, that native masters like Fernando Gallego and Bartolommeo Bermejo, both active toward the middle of the century, imitated the northern style.

THE EARLY RENAISSANCE IN ITALY

Donatello and the Style of the Early Renaissance

Realism was as strong in Italy as in the north during the 15th Century. To a surprising degree, any attempt to characterize Italian realism of that period tends to evoke the very same words and phrases we have already used in our treatment of the Flemish masters, but every person of ordinary emotional sensibility feels and knows that there was a great difference between John Van Eyck and Donatello. The difference is not easy to locate or describe; but if the reader will make a general examination of the work of both schools, it is likely he will arrive at the conclusion that humanism and individualism were more vital in Italy. Donatello's *Zuccone* (Figs. 15.10–11) is not the statue of a handsome man. Indeed, the sitter was quite as homely as Van Eyck's Arnolfini (Fig. 15.4). But the Italian figure seems far less to be the subject, and much less the victim of the world. Every muscle is instinct with life and power; and if the face is wrinkled with the struggle of an intense life, one feels that the effort still goes on. The difference between the Italians and the northerners seems to be that the Italians expected to get somewhere. Progress was the standard assumption, and victory was freely entertained as likely.

In the matter of style — and let us consider it for the moment merely in its mechanical and physical aspect — there was also considerable difference between Italy and Flanders. Flemish realism originated with painters, and the Flemish artists explored in thoroughgoing fashion the tonal relations of nature and the representative possibilities of paint. The Italian painters, as briefly indicated in Chapter 14, continued to use the Mode of Relief throughout the whole 15th Century and in some individual instances much later. The reason is not far to seek.

In Italy during the first generation of the 15th Century, we may recognize two distinct styles: that of the sculptor Donatello and that of the painter Masaccio. Masaccio, while always revered, had little direct and practical influence on art until the High Renaissance, when his epic manner came into its own. It was Donatello who fathered the style that became typical of Italy during the Early Renaissance. It may have been a mere matter of chance that he happened to be a sculptor. Or his choice of medium may itself have been an instance of emulating the ancients, for it is a fact that most of the visible ancient monuments which represented the human figure were pieces of sculpture and not paintings. At any rate, Donatello was the artist who, more than any other man in his generation, had the peculiar power of impressing himself upon his contemporaries. Where he led, the other artists followed. Although demonstrated some forty years ago by Chandler Post and Arthur Pope, and although the fact has been and is known to every art historian, the priority of Donatello, and its effect on Italian art, have rarely been emphasized with the proper vigor.

From the standpoint of one who wants to understand, the crux of the matter is to appreciate that the Italians of the 15th Century considered sculpture and painting as being interchangeable. Recent criticism has been concerned, and probably too much so, with the internal logic of the several media. One reads much of the inherent possibilities of painting, from which sculpture is foreclosed, and vice versa. Discussion of that type seems not to have interested or delayed the artists we now consider. The reason seems to have been the existence of a general belief, perhaps a belief inculcated by the classicism that always hung in the Italian air, that mass and the shape of mass constituted the ultimate and permanent reality of visual truth. Consciously or not, sculpture was therefore assigned a philosophical priority over painting. The result was the production of innumerable pictures, excellent of their kind and excellent with reference to any other kind of painting, where the artist's chief purpose was to make the paint simulate the plastic modeling with which sculptors dealt directly.

The style of Italy during the Early Renaissance is epitomized in the numerous half-length Madonnas of Donatello. Introduced by him at an early date in his long career, the conception became a formula repeated with minor variations by almost every artist in Italy, sculptor and painter alike. Fig. 15.9 shows a detail from one of Donatello's own Madonnas of the type mentioned; but in order to illustrate his influence upon others and because Professor Kennedy's peculiarly sensitive photograph is available, we choose to summarize the features of the type from Fig. 15.8, a Madonna in similar style by Donatello's close follower, Desiderio da Settignano.

Whether we find it in sculpture, painting, or architecture, the style of the Early Renaissance was always conceived as low relief. We possess, of course, many free-standing busts and statues; but even upon those, details of every kind were rendered with a minimum of projection and often by what amounts to a linear method (Figs. 15.6–7). The work, that is to say, was felt as an interplay of line and surface, with very little movement in and out, and with a careful avoidance of broad, dark shadows. As expressed in sculpture, the delicate modeling characteristic of the period often became a tour de force of slightness. In Desiderio's Madonna and in some of Donatello's pictorial relief (Fig. 15.14), the subtlety of surface is prodigious. Ideal conditions of light are necessary even for a decent reading of such modeling, a truth indicated by the extreme rarity of satisfactory photographs thereof.

More than one writer has correctly declared that the world was young in Italy during the 15th Century, and there could be no better proof of it than the figure-style to which painters and sculptors habitually turned when left to their own devices. The typical Madonna of the period was always a girl. Sometimes, they made her as young as seventeen; and until the time of Leonardo (pages 722–725), it is surely hard to name any Mary who might possibly be older than twenty-five. The canon of proportions was tall and slender. Such women might stand 5 feet, 6 inches tall, and weigh 110 pounds. Lithe rather than thin, the type is an active one; flesh and muscles were always shown in good training, and the texture of the skin, while often delicate, suggests the natural bloom of youth rather than any special effort to idealize.

Donatello and his followers gave these youthful Madonnas contemporary costumes. It is very evident that 15th-Century realism governed even the sweetest subject, for the artists were mechanically accurate in the representation of clothing. One can always tell what garments were being worn, how they were made, and where they buttoned or tied. This is worth mentioning for later contrast with the customs of the High Renaissance, when clothing of the ordinary kind gave place to generalized undulations of drapery.

It is notable, also, that the favorite costumes of the 15th Century seem to have been of rather light, soft material. Most artists rendered them with innumerable small hollows and ridges, much as lighter and looser stuffs tend to wrinkle. Perhaps a concession to realistic accuracy, the effect is often far from rhythmic and in some instances unpleasantly busy.

Such were the physical conventions of the style of the Early Renaissance in Italy. Gentler than sculpture in the round, low relief gave greater relative clarity to linear passages in the hair, the drapery, and elsewhere. It also invited the most dainty differentiation of surface texture. It therefore lent itself, as a style, to a sensitive kind of painting in the Mode of Relief, which depends quite as much upon linear expression as upon color and modeling. Thus, a long series of pictures by a great many artists are, in effect, the painter's version of a sculptor's style (Figs. 15.32,34).

With remarkable uniformity, a long series of artists adhered to the formula described above; but within the limits thereof, a great variety of personal expression was possible. The high intellectuality of Donatello's Madonnas (Fig. 15.9) was peculiar to him. So was the intensity with which he so often imbued them, as though the whole tragic narrative were foreknown and too distressful to bear. Other artists, while producing Madonnas substantially the same in every physical particular, ran through an immense range of spiritual content or the lack of it. Filippo Lippi (Fig. 15.32) makes the Virgin a lyrically pretty girl who turns out, upon long acquaintance with the picture, to be nothing else. Mino of Fiesole virtually defined the word *dainty,* and Desiderio (Fig. 15.8) the word *winsome.* The learned and introspective Botticelli (Fig. 15.34) penetrated to the truth like Donatello, but made it a holy mystery rather than a human tragedy.

It is necessary to add a word about a common quality of content which remained constant in Italian art during the entire Early Renaissance, regardless of the shallowness or profundity of the individual master. 15th-Century Italian art was *intimate.* Pictures, statues, and reliefs were almost never above life size; most of them are comparatively small. Almost all were designed to be shown at the eye level. When looking at them, the natural impulse is to walk up within three or four feet, and often to come closer for the inspection of special areas. The persons seen in painting and relief are brought forward in the frame, as it were, on that assumption, and the statues are similarly easy to construe as persons in the same room with us. Attitudes, postures, costumes, and facial expressions lack self-consciousness; the guarded dignity of a ceremonial appearance is absent. The cumulative effect of all these things is to give the impression that one has come into personal relation, and has been permitted to share the private feelings of the sitter for a portrait, the Madonna, a saint, or anyone else who may have appeared in the art of the period. Such an experience is peculiarly endearing, and it is no wonder that the Early Renaissance in Italy is specially popular with American students, themselves born with a taste for informality. As a historical phenomenon, the quality just reviewed should be kept in mind as an element of contrast between the work of the Early and that of the High Renaissance.

Donatello was born about 1385 and died in 1466. His accomplishments were greater and more varied than those of any other 15th-Century artist. Only by a stern reduction to categories is it possible to convey within the available space an idea of the art of such a man. Leaving much to the future studies of the reader, we shall have to content ourselves with a few examples selected to illustrate the numerous ramifications of his work.

Like the Brothers Van Eyck, Donatello was a prime mover in establishing the representative convention, but it would appear that classical inspiration of a special kind, absent in the north of Europe, helped him on his way. As a youngster, he took a trip to Rome with Brunelleschi (pages 631–638); and there, at a formative period in his life, he was confronted with the achievements of Roman realism. That proved to be the most cogent inspiration he received, for realism runs like a guiding theme through all his immensely varied production. No one ever explored the subject more thoroughly or completely. His catalogue includes at least one example of everything that might be related to the term.

In the ordinary use of the word, his realism is perhaps best illustrated by the *Zuccone* (Figs. 15.10–11), one of several statues made to fit available niches on Giotto's Tower. Probably intended for a Job or a Habbakuk, its official title has never been used. The Florentines simply called it "pumpkin head," and so it is known. As mentioned above, the penetrating glance, the terrific arms, and the muscles tensed in readiness for the mind's next order all separate the statue from the workaday figures of Roman portraiture, and from the northern art of its own period. Physically speaking, the representation could hardly be more unsparing; but a concern with spiritual meaning — frequent in all Florentine art — permits the most unlovely body to participate in God's image.

The range of Donatello's subject matter is well demonstrated by the contrast between the *Zuccone* and a number of other works equally scientific in physical fact, but radically various in content. The well-known *Saint George,* in a niche on Or San Michele, is one of the world's best expositions of man in his twenties, the time maturity asserts itself just as the body is strongest and most responsive. Dating from 1416, it may be cited as the first modern work of art to demonstrate complete mastery over the body as an artistic vehicle. No one else could have done it at the same moment, and few would even have understood the method.

Some years later in date, but equally original from the standpoint of anatomical research, is the sandstone *Annunciation* in Santa Croce. The Mary is a feminine counterpart for the Saint George, but even more particular attention should be directed to the infants who stand as acroteria above the pedimental frame (Fig. 15.12). They are among the very first to be accurately rendered since Antiquity; and they are devastating when compared to the sublimated children of some other artists — Sir Joshua Reynolds, for example — which fact suggests that the truth can charm as cogently as it sometimes chides. The architectural frame of the *Annunciation* is notable in itself. All the details are of classical origin, but their relative size and combination is original and free, a situation generally characteristic of the period.

Not satisfied with studies of the single figure, Donatello extended his researches to embrace the entire field of pictorial sculpture. An early and important example is the relief showing *Saint George and the Dragon,* originally the predella for the statue of Saint George. Now sadly weathered, its date of 1416 certifies Donatello as Ghiberti's peer in the specialty upon which Ghiberti's entire reputation rests (pages 638–642).

Better for study, because better preserved, is the *Salome at Herod's Feast* (Fig. 15.13), a rectangular bronze panel attached to the font in the Baptistry at Siena. The monument is specially interesting as an instance of representative strategy. The displacement of things into the distance is rendered by four stages in the lowering of the relief, each stage being assigned a particular remove from the foreground. Architectural barriers separate the several vertical planes suggested by the arrangement, making the spatial relationships not only legible, but also inevitably convincing.

The *Saint Peter Receiving the Keys* (Fig. 15.14) may be cited as typical of the master's more mature and confident productions in the field of spatial representation; but as stated, the modulations of surface, upon which the legibility of the subject matter depends, are so elaborately cunning that the work is a failure unless given the benefit of special lighting.

Monumental works of art were, as already mentioned, rare during the 15th

Century, but there were a few. It was natural and even inevitable that Donatello, the world's leading sculptor, should have received the commission for the most ambitious undertaking contemplated during the entire period. We refer to the *Gattamelata* (Figs. 15.15–16), the first full-scale bronze equestrian statue since Roman Antiquity, and still the greatest on earth. The statue is at first very puzzling, for it lacks the great crashing drama which, in work of the High Renaissance and the Baroque, seems to lift us toward the sublime. Although it is a very large statue indeed, the whole method and purpose fit the wonderful perception of the Italian Early Renaissance rather than the heroics characteristic of the so-called " Grand Style " of the next century.

It may even be said that the *Gattamelata*, when seen for the first time, is not even impressive. Everybody begins by wondering why a man on so high a horse cannot put on a better show; but by that erroneous first impression, we gain an insight into the mind of the author. It presently becomes evident that the significance hinges upon the incongruity of scale between horse and rider; and that the apparent absence of any performance by either is in fact the meaningful situation with which we are presented. The general sits his mount with a stiff grace, a lifetime of military horsemanship behind him. Obviously his pose was merely habitual, and he himself unconscious of it. The bridle rein lies slack from the left hand, while the right raises the baton in a quiet, conventional gesture. The great horse underneath is tense with nervous power, a volcano of energy ready to explode into terrific action at any instant.

By what authority does the man sit so calmly in the saddle, directing, controlling, and containing strength so much greater than his own? A look at the face will give the answer. It is full of rational intelligence: the memory, the experience, and the judgment the horse lacks and no animal can have. In general terms, the statue may be described as a profound demonstration of humanism; but with greater particularity, we should point out that the content is neither formal, idealized, nor ceremonial. It would be hard to find a more public place than the Paduan square where the pedestal is raised; but even so, almost as doctors are admitted into the affairs of their patients, we are shown the private, inward character of a man.

The work so far considered will give the reader a sample of Donatello's realism in its more judicial and naturalistic aspect. Differing as they do in detail, all the examples cited above show us the artist more or less governed by the normal manifestations of anatomy and scenery. But from time to time throughout his extended career, Donatello projected his theories far beyond the ordinary limitations. In a number of his most powerful productions, he extended realism well past anything that may be construed as objective analysis either of character or of form. As distinct from his rational faculty and his judgment, he permitted his feelings to enter into the act of creation. He crossed, that is to say, the vague boundary line which separates realism, or any other type of art, from *expressionism.*

Two statues of the youthful *Saint John,* both of them now in the Bargello and one shown in Fig. 15.17, are among the milder demonstrations of the tendency just described. Both are emaciated. How are we to reconcile such things with the fact that it was Donatello himself, and nobody else, who started the Renaissance tradition of the human body emerging in glory from its medieval mortification? And yet these are on the whole popular statues; the average observer finds himself fascinated by them along with the expert.

The explanation of their exotic appeal may perhaps be found in reasons that account for the state of the anatomy. Spiritual energy often drives high-minded men to exertion utterly beyond physically prudent limits. Such exertions leave their mark. A similar idealism, although a less lofty one, is part of the American fashion at the present moment; an absence of soft flesh is cultivated by male and female alike, presumably because an equation is rightly or wrongly drawn between a spare body and a good character. The reader will also recognize in this class of work by Donatello the principal inspiration for the cult of emaciation in modern sculpture, of which Lembruck (Fig. 19.27) is the leading exponent.

The two Saint Johns are but a halfway station on the road Donatello traveled. At some indefinite date toward the end of his life, he carved the *Repentant Magdalen* (Fig. 15.18), a wooden statue in the Baptistry at Florence. It is impossible to deal with that piece of work in moderate terms. Beauty, in any ordinary denotation, is a word quite out of place. For the casual observer who usually associates art with relaxation and entertainment, a view of the *Magdalen* is equivalent to the whip of an insult. Even the serious student is likely to find the imagery shocking. The work is not genre. The intention is foreign to the grotesque. All the familiar formulas fail to explain it, including the one which makes realism a research enterprise. Try as we will to escape facing the question, the savage fascination of the statue forces us to account for the legitimacy of the hideous in art. Without suggesting that the following words solve so vexed a question, they may at least be helpful.

An artist of Donatello's experience must have been conversant with the nature of his medium. He would appreciate, for instance, that the poet asks the reader to supply most of the images, and that the reader may escape the poet by choosing his own psychical distance when threatened with shock and offense. It is, on the other hand, the privilege of the sculptor to choose his own imagery, and his medium delivers it to the eye of the public in the most tangible manner available. For that very reason, Lessing urged in the *Laocoön* that sculptors apply the whip gently and discreetly, with a courtly regard for the sensibilities of human beings. Why then did Donatello smash down all the standards of artistic decorum? Successful, honored, and admired — and knowing we cannot escape — what vengeance did he seek? Why does he make us look, holding us there with all his power, disgusted as we are and in pain? For it is evident that the model for the *Magdalen* was a female cadaver, and that with a technique few sculptors could equal, Donatello chose to confront us with a walking death apparently capable of question, answer, and ethical responsibility.

In searching for the truth within the revolting spectacle, we may make something of the fact that the *Magdalen* was chosen for placement in the Baptistry. It was there that infants were first admitted to society, to begin the career inevitably ending in physical decadence and death, and quite as certainly including the crucifixion of sin and repentance. There is a certain propriety, as it were, in predicting the end at the beginning, and a spiritual realism in so grim a reminder at the ceremony where all is innocence and joy.

But the desperate extreme of the *Magdalen* was not unique in Donatello's later work, and some more general motive must be sought for what amounted to a policy of getting after us to inflict upon hearts and nerves a ruthless exacerbation. If a satisfactory explanation is ever forthcoming, the reasons will probably be found in the subconsciousness only now being revealed by psychological research. Among those findings is the proposition that the will to die, like the more familiar will to survive, is latent in the population. Suicide, it has been suggested, results not from impulse but from a pattern of desires traceable far back into the childhood and heredity of an unfortunate minority. Viewed in the light of such ideas, it becomes evident, pending a definite explanation, that Donatello's *Magdalen* may be assigned to needs more profound than morbid. Once again, it would appear that we have an example of artistic insight penetrating centuries ahead of science, and finding an expression beyond present understanding.

After such a citation of major achievement, short though it is in relation to the subject, a summary of Donatello's standing in history would seem redundant. It is nevertheless true that certain important aspects of his genius are inconspicuous and need to be remarked upon.

First, our sense for dates must be kept unusually on the alert or we shall forget that, in point of historical fact, Donatello was a " primitive " artist. His original efforts, that is to say, had to begin with technical problems. To appreciate the state of Florentine sculpture during Donatello's youth, the reader will have to investigate archaeological byways ordinarily entered only by specialists in the field. Suffice it to say that ignorance is hardly too strong a word for describing Donatello's starting point. In the presence of supreme skill, as shown in the incomparable *Gattamelata,* it is almost impossible to believe that the competence before us commenced with primary research into such elementary matters as anatomy.

We expect a certain crudity in the work of pioneers, but its absence in Donatello is hardly so great a wonder as the variety of his output. He worked on every scale. He used every technique and material in which sculpture can be executed. He had no style in the usual sense of the term (i.e., the repetition of some personal formula or mode of expression, however good). Instead, he varied and adapted different human models to suit his immediate purpose. His freedom of selection in that respect remains unapproached by any other artist in history, and the shifts in technique are of equal variety. Similarly, there is no habitual tone, spirit, or content to which we can tie him down; his work puts the student through almost every kind of response the art of sculpture might conceivably call up.

Indeed, the only constants in the art of that great man were his intellect and his restraint. A high seriousness emanates even from his prettiest things. A great modesty enabled him to avoid parade.

Masaccio

Masaccio, the first great painter of the Renaissance in Italy, was one of the most remarkable characters in history. Born in 1401, he was killed at the age of twenty-seven. As a master in his own right, he painted for approximately five years. On technical grounds, it is possible to associate his hand with about twenty pictures, but there are critics who will challenge some of those. In any case, only three or four are useful in their entirety as a demonstration of the powers that make Masaccio significant.

An infinite number of men have left a larger corpus of material behind them, only to pass into oblivion as soon as they died, but Masaccio instantly became a historical figure. His present reputation is greater than ever, having been enhanced by the sober methods of modern history. The reason for all of this is that his painting contained within it the germ of almost everything realized by the full tide of the High Renaissance. Masaccio, to put it colloquially, was virtually the inventor of the "Grand Style." Inasmuch as the "Grand Style" has remained the tacitly accepted ideal and criterion of all European art, regardless of excursions in other directions, until the advent of Post Impressionism (pages 908 ff), it may be said that Masaccio's ideas remained implicit in European taste until 1900 or thereabouts. But the reader must not confuse such long-term influence upon history with an immediate effect like that achieved by Donatello. It was the latter, as explained above, who set the pace for most 15th-Century work; but the personality of Masaccio was always brooding over Florence, waiting for the day when the humane and intelligent art of the Early Renaissance should give way to conceptions more God-like and sublime.

Masaccio's greatest work was done during the period of his association with the fresco decoration of the Brancacci Chapel at the Church of the Carmine in Florence. There is an unfortunate amount of confusion about the authorship of the pictures there. The original contract was set in motion by Brancacci's will in the year 1422. The commission was apparently awarded to Masolino, a master who painted in a late version of the International Style (pages 531–539). Probably he was the head of the shop in which the youthful Masaccio worked. Before the work at Florence can possibly have been completed, Masolino was at Buda in Hungary, working on another contract. Was Masaccio left in charge at Florence? Did he take the contract over in his own name? How much work had been completed when the direction shifted? Who did what? What are we to look for in the pictures? When he visits Florence, the reader can spend a profitable day attempting to answer those questions for himself by studying the originals. What we want here is the mature work of Masaccio, uninhibited and undiluted. We very probably have it in two frescoes: the *Expulsion from the Garden of Eden* and the *Tribute Money.*

The *Expulsion* (Figs. 15.19–20) is ostensibly a simple picture, but one can exhaust his knowledge and judgment before he really understands it. Traditionally, the subject had been popular because it gave artists a socially acceptable reason for studying the nude. Masaccio, as we shall see, examined into the visual reality of the figures, but his primary purpose had little to do with facts. His overwhelming concern was with the initial act of original sin. Hopeless remorse is personified by his Adam. The convulsive Eve sums up every cry of shame and despair utterable by a woman. Over Earth's disillusionment, the severe and pitying angel flies on sublime wings. The picture embodies a higher drama than any other work of art we have had occasion to survey since the chapters on Greece. The event itself was crucial in the moral history of the race; and the action, as shown, has heroic overtones. It was such a subject, and such a treatment of the subject that separated Masaccio from his contemporaries of the Early Renaissance. When successful, the "Grand Style" at which he aimed achieved epic status.

Having perhaps gained some entrance into the august and gloomy spirit of the painter, we must turn to a list of technical matters of great importance to the serious student. Masaccio originated his own theory of art, which produced pictures seemingly less attractive than those we think of as typically Florentine and of the period. There are no pretty costumes, no jewels, no pleasant furniture. There is none of the linear calligraphy we love to see in the hair, and none of the smooth, youthful contours of the body. The pretty white light that so softly and so certainly illuminates everything has given way to broad, dark shadows; and the shadows in turn have taken away the bright colors, so that a sombre tonality dominates the whole.

Masaccio, as all those things indicate, was the first important Italian painter to turn away from the Mode of Relief (pages 582–586). While his technique departed therefrom in the direction of the Mode of the Total Visual Effect (pages 580–582) he never went all the way down the line to that result. His work may be understood as a halfway station between, partaking of both modes.

When we move close to the paintings, to examine them minutely (Fig. 15.20) we find none of the usual finesse. Details are absent. The construction of the bodies is declared largely by an arrangement of shadows; and as shadows, those painted by Masaccio lack the elegant gradations other artists cultivated. One may be forgiven, at first, for thinking him a slovenly painter.

The matter is to be explained by reference to the way in which the eye actually receives visual data. Unlike his contemporaries, Masaccio refused to employ an artificial lighting. He also declined the use of the telescope to reveal the distance and the microscope to bring up local details. He appears to have accepted as artistically valid a process of seeing that is in some ways less satisfying, but which is correct with reference to human experience: his painting corresponds very closely with the fuzzy imperfection of the single view, as it is actually available to the unaided eye, from a single station at a specified remove from the object of sight. It has sometimes been suggested that his philosophy of vision remained standard in all European painting until driven into the ground by the French Impressionists (pages 863–874), but such is hardly the case. Certain schools of painting followed his precept; others did not.

When he chose to take the human optical powers, limited as they are, as the first frame of reference for his art, Masaccio did not by that act deny the validity of tactile values or turn his back on the Mode of Relief. He merely added a new and complicating element, the physiology of sight. It was that which seems to have made him blend the forms insensibly into one another, fogging the definition of contours, and denying linear edges to the silhouettes. But the shapes and masses are nevertheless forcefully described, as though that were what he would have us see through the screen. The comparative difficulty with which we perceive them does not militate against the artist's belief in their special validity. Qualified though they are, tactile values remain the operative factor in Masaccio's painting.

Even so, an important difference separates Masaccio's version of the Mode of Relief from that of his Italian contemporaries. Most of the latter took their idiom from the delicate low relief of Donatello. Masaccio's painting, with its more generous range of shadow, finds its natural counterpart with sculpture in the round. It is entirely probable that the amplitude and darkness of his shading reflects a synthesis of observations direct from nature, but the forms he represents by that method still unmistakably suggest sculpture. The particular kind of sculpture they recall, moreover, is the grander and more serious material among the monuments of ancient art; and the question suggests itself: was there in Masaccio's background some ancient monument, as yet unidentified, that inspired him as the *Belvedere Torso* (Figs. 6.21–22) was later to inspire Michaelangelo?

Years ago, when the history of Italian painting was all too often presented as an evolution in representative technique, Masaccio was labeled as the man who invented atmospheric perspective. No one takes so limited a view today, but it is still necessary to point out that he used that device more obviously and with greater effect than any other Italian painter of the 15th Century. By dimming the tones and outlines of the angel in the upper background of the *Expulsion,* he succeeded in making us read that figure as behind the Adam and Eve. It is worth noting that the ordinary effect of atmosphere was exaggerated for the purpose; only a bad London fog can curtail details to such a degree within the space of two or three yards. The boldness of the manipulation suggests not mere representation, but drama. Adam and Eve attract attention because they alone are rendered in something like a full range of values; the focus upon them seems to suggest an intention to contrast the all too present nature of worldly pain against the dim way in which we discern the divine justice of events.

The *Tribute Money* (Fig. 15.21) was a much more ambitious undertaking. Immediately recognized as Masaccio's testament, it received the minute study of every young artist who lived or sojourned at Florence for the next hundred years and more.

The subject comes from Matthew 17:24–27. Having arrived at Capernäum, the Holy Company was asked to pay a small tax; but they were without funds. Acting on instructions from Jesus, Peter went to the shore, caught a fish, found a coin in its mouth, and handed the coin over to the collector. The Gospel gives that narrative, together with a certain amount of dialogue between Jesus and Peter. The meaning and intent of the talk is extraordinarily vague, however;

and it is difficult to make anything important from it. As for specific information, Masaccio's picture adds little to what we can read in the Bible.

Perhaps under the influence of some Roman monument, he arranged the picture according to the continuous method of narration. Three successive events are combined within the same composition. In the middle, we see the collector accosting the Holy Company. At the extreme left, Peter takes the coin from the fish's mouth. At the extreme right, he hands it over to the same collector. Obviously, the impressive monumentality of the painting can scarcely derive from so trivial a set of events; to explain it, we must venture boldly forward into the mysterious realm of the imponderables.

It would seem that Masaccio here took up the problem of mural painting where Giotto left off at Santa Croce in the 1320's (pages 560–561). Large figures are accommodated in an ample setting, in juxtaposition with architecture in scale with themselves. The governing principles of the composition are the same as Giotto's, and the atmosphere is one that seems to be reaching out toward grandeur.

Masaccio's use of space is probably the most important single element contributory to the majesty and solemnity of the conception. Prodigious mountains loom up in the distance, more cogent in their venerable dignity because far away. In that setting, we find a race of men equally prodigious. Their bodies are Herculean, their strength gigantic. Their faces betoken vast intellect, and their mood is fierce with righteous purpose. Even their clothing has the heave of the mountains in every fold. No one else even attempted such pictures at the same date. Although many have tried to do so since, Masaccio's is one of the very few authentically heroic styles in the history of art. Who else can so convince us that he deals not with people, but with men whom God intends shall subdue and possess the earth?

Had Masaccio been able to continue his career, the High Renaissance would very probably have arrived earlier, with consequent changes in the schedule of Italian painting and the entire history of European art. But in 1428, he abandoned the unfinished commission at the Carmine. The work was brought to an inconclusive completion fifty years later by the younger Lippi. Masaccio went off to Rome, probably as much to escape creditors as to seek glory. He got into trouble there. He died either from poison, or from a knife wound received in a drunken brawl; there is gossip both ways. He left no school behind him to establish a tradition. He simply stepped off the stage, having achieved eminence in the space of a single scene. No other artist so overwhelms the observer. His power is unadorned, uncomplicated, sheer.

Brunelleschi

Daring was the outstanding characteristic in the personality of Brunelleschi, the first great architect of the Italian Renaissance. But that impetuous virtue was remarkably combined with a capacity for precise calculation, and with austerity of taste rarely associated with an unbridled imagination.

Brunelleschi at first intended to be a sculptor; and he achieved sufficient success in that line to be Ghiberti's closest competitor in the famous contest of 1401, to the winner of which the Florentines awarded the commission for the new bronze doors of the Baptistry (see below, pages 638–639). Disgusted with his failure to excel, Brunelleschi took himself off to Rome in company with the youthful Donatello (page 621), and never thereafter engaged seriously in the sculptor's art. In 1418, he was back in Florence; and in that year, he won a competition — this time, the commission for the design and construction of the great dome over the crossing of the Cathedral at Florence. He had no reputation as an architect at that date, and certainly none as an engineer. His temerity in entering the competition was exceeded by the courage of those who put the project in his hands. The situation was one where both parties to the bargain overreached themselves; and although it is a famous monument, Brunelleschi's dome leaves much to be desired. For details, we may refer the reader to the appropriate chapter in General Parson's excellent work,* commenting here only as follows.

The city of Florence had voted the new cathedral as early as 1294. The original plans are said to have been made by Arnolfo di Cambio, who died in 1302. The church as it now stands is one of the biggest in Europe. Not satisfied with scale alone, the citizens projected an architectural novelty. Instead of using the conventional Gothic east end, they decided to open up the crossing into an immense octagon. Presumably, a dome was visualized from the beginning to cover that area. There was some conference about details in 1366, and the present walls of the octagon must have been approximately complete by 1405 or so.

It is here that the modern reader must pause in wide-eyed amazement: no one on earth had any definite idea how to build the required dome. The span measured about 150 feet. The last dome of that scale had been the dome of Hagia Sophia (pages 346–351). Brunelleschi was thus undertaking a task unparalleled for eight centuries, and from that we may judge the spirit of the times and the temper of the man.

The winning design got the prize, it is said, because Brunelleschi had figured

* W. B. Parsons, *Engineers and Engineering in the Renaissance*, Baltimore: Williams and Wilkins, 1939.

out a way to build the dome with a bare minimum of centering (pages 187–189); he made the pitch so steep that the sides approach the vertical. Historically speaking, the design is important because it amounted to something like a manifesto of the philosophy of Renaissance architecture. In order to get the most benefit from the shape, the architect abandoned inert abutment and made the dome spring from the top of a high drum. The thrust is of course contained by chains under tension, as described in Chapter 7. Practically every other dome built during the Renaissance, and since, has conformed to the same general type, the popularity of which signifies a belief in the value of pure form even at the expense of risky construction.

The construction decided upon was Gothic rather than classical in method. Eight large segmental arches were raised like ribs, converging at the oculus. The eight main ribs formed the guiding lines for a network of smaller ribs and connecting arches, very much in the manner of Gothic tracery but in a different application. The smooth surfaces visible within and without are superficial covering. They exist to serve the Renaissance ideal of form, and it will be noted that Brunelleschi, when he decided to conceal the working framework beneath, indulged thereby in a complete negation of the Gothic theory that structural fact might be made to suggest aesthetic design (pages 411 ff, 472 ff).

The dome soars 308 feet into the air, and it is a mighty landmark. The curve of the exterior silhouette, however, is weak and uninteresting. The interior appearance amounts to a most unfortunate hole in the ceiling, something that harms rather than aids the effect of the nave. For such reasons as those, we may turn with some relief to the smaller churches in the design of which Brunelleschi established himself among the immortals.

The façade of the Foundling Hospital (Fig. 15.22) was probably designed in 1418. Its most conspicuous feature was an open loggia of nine delicate arches springing from slender Corinthian columns, and approached by a broad flight of shallow steps, also nine in number. Above the arcade, we see a subtle entablature, and above that, a second story pierced at intervals by windows, each centered over an arch. Circular medallions in terra cotta, the work of the Della Robbia shop, fill the spandrels.

How rare it is that a notable work of art can be described in so few words! But the hand of this designer was sure. His brief expression was perfect, like an Elizabethan lyric. Everything fits everything else, but still remains pure and separate. The entire composition is like a creation of springtime, a new life, an indication that the world was young.

Of the styles antedating the 15th Century, one instinctively recalls the Greek as the closest to Brunelleschi's work, but there is almost no chance he had ever looked at anything we would call Greek today. His inspiration probably came from a combination of sources. He had, of course, been to Rome; and the separate parts of his architecture are classical in form but a great deal lighter in proportion. He also retained much of the feeling of the Romanesque of Tuscany, as exemplified by Sant Miniato, a church in plain sight on a hill over Florence, and by the grander buildings at Pisa (Figs. 11.1–2). And yet there seems to be more in the superb elegance of his style than we may account for by referring to Roman and Romanesque inspiration. We cannot prove that he had visited Paris and Amiens; neither can we prove he did not. It seems likely, however, that in some way he formed a taste for the high Gothic of France, and if we are to characterize his work in a phrase, we would not be far wrong to call it Latin handled with a French accent.

In blending and fusing those disparate elements, Brunelleschi was evidently extremely conscious of the taste for low relief by which contemporary painters and sculptors were governed. His architectural style was primarily an expression in terms of line and surface. The entablature, the window frames, and the mouldings might well be described as more drawn than modeled. Their relief is radically slight; were it less, the individual parts would be indistinct. It is obvious that the designer was deliberately avoiding the plastic mass characteristic of Roman work; at the same time, by keeping every projection close in, he narrowed the cast shadows and prevented them from interfering with the flow of artistically invaluable lines.

But over against all the specific and physical sources he so marvellously made into a new style, it is plain that Brunelleschi understood and accepted certain classical principles of design. Viewed as a whole, the façade of the Foundling Hospital is a horizontal rectangle enclosed by substantial architectural boundaries. Symmetry governs the arrangement of parts, even though the symmetry is not paraded as it was in most Greek and Roman composition. Each part, moreover, is an artistic unit, a small composition which conceivably might stand alone. The system in use is plainly the organic scheme of composition, which originated with the Greeks (pages 65–66).

While we must repeat again that it seems very unlikely that Brunelleschi had ever studied any Greek art, his work has one virtue common in Greek design and almost invariably absent from the Roman. We refer to the employment of blank spaces, often called " functional voids " in the composition. His interest in that device seems to have invited its use with daring liberality. The proportion of empty wall is altogether out of the ordinary. Each fastidious motive is widely set off from its neighbor, compelled to stand on its own chaste merits like a theme stated by one instrument. It is the ostensibly vacant areas which give the whole façade its unexcelled gentleness, its perfect grace and quiet tempo. We ordinarily do not associate risk and daring with tranquility, but the extreme simplicity of the design was almost preposterously bold. A single error, even a hint of imperfection in the smallest detail, would have been enough to ruin the whole.

The Pazzi Chapel (Figs. 15.23–24) seems to have been started in 1429. The date of completion is less definite; it is generally believed that some of the work, at least, went on after Brunelleschi's death in 1446. For that reason, some scholars have worried as to whether the present edifice is purely his, or not. Dodging such argument and assuming that the original architect dictated the major dispositions, the little building is of peculiar interest because it gave the designer an opportunity to demonstrate whatever theories he may have entertained. The functional need was uncomplicated. The scale was miniature. There were, in short, almost none of the usual considerations which interfere with impulses that are purely artistic.

The little church has only three component parts: a handsome tunnel-vaulted loggia across the western and entrance front; a nave chamber running parallel to that, with its long axis north and south; and a dome centered over the nave. The type seems to have been borrowed in a free way, as was to be the case with many another Renaissance church, from the four-column central churches of the Byzantine Second Golden Age (pages 353–356).

For the entrance front, Brunelleschi seems to have wanted a monumental façade on the miniature scale. He drew up what amounts to a screen of low-relief architecture carried by six columns with an entablature over them. He broke the entablature in the middle to raise an arch over the entranceway, much in the manner of certain Hellenistic and Roman temples (Figs. 8.8–9). To the right and left of the central arch, he put sections of paneling enframed by paired pilasters. The entire composition was closed in at the top by a second entablature.

Having thus completed the composition for the façade — and, in effect, it amounts to one classical temple on top of another — Brunelleschi seems to have felt no need to relate the western screen to the mass of the building behind. As we see it today, the front elevation of the chapel seems, artistically speaking, to break in two. Behind and above the exquisite screen, there rises the dome over the nave. The latter was made high, in order to produce the proportions desired for the interior. The screen could not conveniently be made higher because the horizontal nature of classical architecture (pages 82–83) had already been strained to the limit. Thus, there was no good way to make a connection between the façade in front and the building behind it. With his usual boldness, Brunelleschi simply accepted that fact. He made the exterior of the dome as plain and inconspicuous as possible, and he put a stilted lean-to roof over the vault of the loggia, where it hardly fills the gap very well.

It is unreasonable to suppose that what we see was the result of carelessness or improvisation; Brunelleschi was the last man to be easygoing. The lack of coherence between part and part, to say nothing of an absence of definite relation between every part and the whole, must have had its genesis in a philosophy of design. It seems evident that Brunelleschi considered it enough to make each element, taken by itself, a perfect thing in terms of its own internal logic. As to making every part fit the next, and as for maintaining throughout all parts a consistent sense for the entirety, we must assume he thought it not worthwhile. It is difficult to accept his point of view, especially when one considers the innumerable buildings since constructed, as the wag said, "with a Queen Anne front and a Mary Anne behind."

As to the interior of the Pazzi Chapel, the walls and ceiling admirably carry out the principles of expression by line and surface already characterized above. The atmosphere is therefore much less ponderous than that of a Roman interior, but it will be noted that the world is shut away as definitely as it was in the Pantheon (Fig. 7.1). Brunelleschi had discarded, that is to say, the Gothic theory of interior design (pages 469–472), and he had returned to the modeling of air and space which had been popular during classical Antiquity (pages 220–221). The choice was of course but another instance of the resurgence of Roman taste in Italy at the time. It is also important because the taste reflected has, on the whole, been dominant in the design of interiors from that moment until steel and glass became available during the latter half of the 19th Century.

Brunelleschi was one of the men who searched for the secret of classical art, and who believed they would find it by mathematical analysis. Although remembered as an architect, it was he — or so many scholars are coming to think — who was largely responsible for working out the theory of perspective which so greatly advanced the art of representation. He also researched into the mystery of proportion, having doubtless been influenced by the cryptic remarks of the recently recovered Vitruvius (pages 124–127). In his later work, he seems to have made an attempt to apply such conclusions as he was able to draw.

He had occasion to design two basilican churches at Florence, San Lorenzo in 1419 and Santo Spirito in 1435. The choice of the basilican type was in itself significant, because the Early Christian basilicas (pages 277–292) were then thought of as classical churches. Both the buildings mentioned show Brunelleschi's free classical detail at its superb best, but we need not reiterate praise that has already been given. Our chief concern here is with the serene spatial expression at which he arrived, particularly in the interior design of Santo Spirito. Difficult to comprehend by way of drawings and photographs, the effect is almost tangible when one enters the building. If not able to reproduce the experience by describing it, we can at least suggest in part the method the architect himself seems to have followed. Like the Greek sculptor Poly-

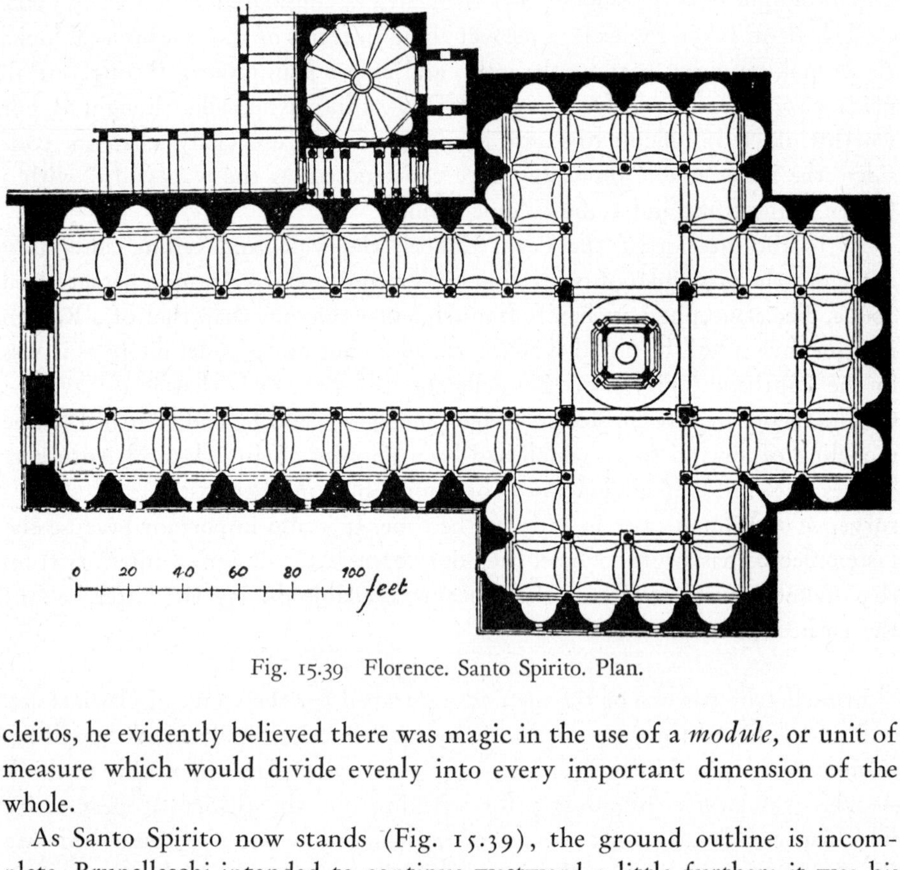

Fig. 15.39 Florence. Santo Spirito. Plan.

cleitos, he evidently believed there was magic in the use of a *module,* or unit of measure which would divide evenly into every important dimension of the whole.

As Santo Spirito now stands (Fig. 15.39), the ground outline is incomplete. Brunelleschi intended to continue westward a little further; it was his purpose to run the aisle entirely around the building without a break at the façade, thus providing a narthex at the entrance and a western range of interior columns reminiscent of certain pagan basilicas, like the Basilica Julia in the Forum Romanum.

The design of the east end was also an innovation. Discarding the time honored semicircular apse, he opened up the crossing into what we may call three arms of a Greek Cross. The arrangement seems to yearn for the condition of the central church, one of which Brunelleschi had actually designed in 1434.

It was to have been known as Santa Maria degli Angeli, but construction was abandoned before the building was halfway up. We know it today from the ground outline and some apparently reliable engravings. The central church may be associated in a curious way with humanism (pages 704–706); and as a type, it was destined to have a strong span of popularity later in the Renaissance. Indeed, it looked for a time as though the basilica would pass out of use altogether.

With the unaided eye, it is easy to see that the plan of Santo Spirito depends upon a harmony of commensurate elements. The apse duplicates either transept. The open floor inside the columns is a square, and the nave consists of four and a half such squares — or an even five had the designer's intention been carried out. All the items mentioned are in turn reduceable to multiples of the intercolumniation, as one may prove with the help of dividers.

Were drawings of the elevation available, it would be possible to show that the principle of commensuration was applied in similar fashion to the vertical dimensions; and if one appreciates that the linear dimensions merely define cubic modules of space, it seems plain that some rather complex and definite formula was being applied. While serious doubts must assail the man who cares to assert that strict multiples of the same unit make good proportions, or indeed that any proportion is inevitably better than any other, there can be little question that Brunelleschi was experimenting along such lines. Let the reader decide for himself whether the great architect thereby explained the secret of his own success.

Brunelleschi's style established the norm for the Early Renaissance architecture of Italy. At Florence, other architects used detail similar to his, especially for the arcaded courtyards in the great palace-forts, each a hollow square, which they built for the powerful families of the city. In Florentine painting, especially in the work of Fra Angelico (pages 645–649), we find buildings of a similar type. The remarkable truth of the matter is, however, that not one other architect was able to rival the spiritual authority of the man who originated the style. The Palazzo del Consiglio at Verona might at first seem a brilliant exception to that statement, but familiarity will soon settle the question. The distinction of Brunelleschi's gifts may also be estimated by the caution with which his manner has been used in modern times. Even in America during the 19th Century, when every kind of historical imitation was being drawn up helter-skelter, most firms steered clear. Only McKim, Mead, and White — an office peculiarly anxious to establish its artistic superiority over all others — made any serious attempt to emulate Brunelleschi. They had comparative success with the Morgan Library in New York, and with the Art

Museum at Bowdoin College. Both structures are graceful enough, but no one wants a watered drink from the fountain of youth. As yet, Brunelleschi stands alone.

Ghiberti

Ghiberti's signal importance in the art of the Early Renaissance has already been attested by the various times we have found it necessary to mention his name. He first became famous when he won the competition of 1401; and as the prize for winning, was awarded the commission for the new and second set of bronze doors of the venerable Baptistry of Florence. It is important to understand that the Baptistry already had the finest bronze doors in the world, the work of Andrea Pisano, a sculptor strongly influenced by Giotto and the best of the Giotteschi. The building had three entrances, so perhaps three sets of doors were in order, but it was typical of the time and the place to want something better than the best, to expect to get it, and to be willing to pay for it.

Some interesting rules governed the competition. It was stipulated that the competing works of art should be in relief, and that they should conform in size and shape with the Gothic medallions that made up Andrea Pisano's doors. The subject matter was likewise specified. It was *The Sacrifice of Isaac,* a story demanding the use of landscape, animals, and human figures both clothed and nude. Inasmuch as the rules must have reflected an attempt to embody the latest taste, it is evident that the representative convention was taken for granted.

Ghiberti's nearest competitor was Brunelleschi (page 630), and the two competing reliefs are preserved (Figs. 15.25–26). Few modern critics would disagree with the verdict. The composition of Brunelleschi's panel is inferior. He appears to have conceived the area of the frame as a plane surface, to be covered by figures and objects much as checkers lie flat on the board. The arrangement seems marked by something close to hysteria, as though the artist were filling in a modern tax form and felt obliged to put something in every part of the difficult medallion shape. The important figures he merely put in the middle, and the rest of the area received here a detail of setting, there a figure. The broad side of a donkey takes up most of the lower register, while the subordinate persons of the drama thrust their elbows and butt their posteriors across the boundary lines.

Ghiberti's superior performance is patent at first glance. With respect to composition, he felt as much at home in the third (and represented) dimension as he did with the length and breadth of the panel. As though to declare the existence of air and room, he deliberately made his foreground figures overlap those further removed, and he gave the anatomy an elegant *contrapposto,* so that each pair of shoulders became, in effect, an axis diagonal to the plane of the background. In the right arm of the Abraham and in the entire body of the angel, we see a formidable demonstration of foreshortening.

Taken as a whole, Ghiberti's drama was infinitely more skilful than Brunelleschi's. The operative group of Abraham and Isaac, he placed high and to the right, its intensity being balanced by a bulk of more quiet material filling all the remaining (and larger) area of the frame. Attention was directed toward the crucial action by directional impulses from the left.

It would be hard to overstate the extent to which such a composition was forward-looking at the very beginning of the 15th Century, although a similar interest in the formalities of arrangement became common enough during the High Renaissance. As already mentioned above (page 538), Ghiberti's ordinary figure-style, although scientific with respect to anatomical structure, continued the physical types and the costumes typical of Late Gothic Mannerism. His practice in that respect has dimmed many an eye to the truly classical nature, also rare and advanced for the date, of some other figures. The nude Isaac was taken directly from a classical torso, still preserved in the Uffizi and at the time in Ghiberti's personal possession. Taken by itself, it might well be confused with Hellenistic work of unusually high quality, and it was perhaps the first figure in modern art to demonstrate an obvious honor for the body.

The very urbanity of the performance has betrayed many writers into an understatement of Ghiberti's immense originality. The genuinely Gothic elements of his style are so familiar from earlier art that one tends to overlook the profound — and at that time new — knowledge of representative science. The interpretation of the subject tends to corroborate the same impression. Brunelleschi made Isaac writhe in an agony of physical fear; the angel of a supposedly kind and omnipotent Lord is seen to arrive in a hurry, making it only just in time. But Ghiberti's classical Isaac shows in every placid muscle a truly Gothic confidence in the complete wisdom, mercy, and competence of God. What are we to say of such a combination of things? Was Ghiberti a paradoxical character, looking backwards and forwards like the Roman deity Janus? The true answer, rather, seems to be that he was the ideal conservative. We use the appellation to mean what its derivation says; namely, a man with something worth guarding and preserving. He kept what he thought good in the Gothic style and in the Christianity of Gothic times. To suggest that he therefore opposed progress would be preposterous.

Having received the formal commission for the new bronze doors, Ghiberti devoted the next twenty-one years of his life to the project. The general character of those doors is well suggested by the competition panel; they consist of small scenes in pictorial relief, enclosed in the same Gothic medallions. So well did the work satisfy the Florentines that they immediately commissioned Ghiberti to do another set of doors. When the latter were finally hung in the main portal of the Baptistry, facing the cathedral, the date was 1452. The doors of 1403–24 went to the south entrance, where they still are; and Andrea Pisano's had already been placed in the northern one, where they also still are. It is doubtful whether any municipal government ever expended more money for sculpture, or made a better investment. There are those who still claim that Andrea's reliefs are the best of the lot; and there is certainly no building on earth where first rank sculpture is on view in equal concentration.

The present east doors of the Baptistry (the second set by Ghiberti, and for the building the third) fulfil in rich measure the promise of the artist's earlier career. He abandoned the scheme of Gothic medallions used before, and he laid out a plan consisting of only ten large rectangular panels surrounded by an elaborate border of foliate ornament interspersed with tiny human busts and exquisite statuettes in niches. For the door jambs, he composed a pattern of fruits and flowers modeled in full relief. The principal panels contain stories from the Old Testament, presented according to the continuous mode of narration (page 630). The little busts and statuettes ostensibly comprise sybils, Hebrew worthies, and notables of the past in general; but from the sharply individualized faces, we may guess that contemporary portraiture was involved.

The ten large panels of which one is shown in Fig. 15.27 present the sacred narrative at a tempered pace which is still not without dramatic moments. The figure-style, as seen in the detail given by Fig. 15.28, is more wonderful than ever before; it combines the acme of Gothic grace with an ease of anatomical science most uncommon at an earlier period. Over all and everything, we feel the magic spell of an unequivocal desire for beauty which was in part the gift of the classical revival, in part a heritage from the Late Gothic, and in part Ghiberti's own. But none of those excellencies, nor all of them together, constitute the central interest of the work; at that time and in history, Ghiberti's great accomplishment was the sculptural conquest of space.

In his earlier sculpture he had, to be sure, undertaken to represent depth, but he had been cautious about it. An inspection of the competition panel (Fig. 15.26) and of the earlier doors will show that he generally brought his figures up front, with a setting behind them, more or less in the manner of the Alexandrian division of ancient pictorial art (pages 164–167). Displacement out into the beyond was indicated clearly enough in such earlier work, but the vistas were often closed by architecture or landscape, and successive steps further away were commonly marked by some barrier or hurdle of setting. The infinite and unlimited sky rarely was permitted to occupy any substantial part of the available area.

The reliefs of 1425–52 (Fig. 15.27) were incomparably more bold. There was no further suggestion of action near the front of the stage. The represented space does not begin, in fact, at the lower border of the panels; it seems to start some yards this side of it. The nearest figures stand, that is to say, in the middle ground; and the atmosphere sweeps out into the furthest limits of the firmament. In several panels, architecture was required to fulfil the requirements of a setting within city limits; but even then, one has no sensation of masonry presented broadside to announce definite vertical planes of spatial removal. The perspective is both precise and elegant, making the buildings fade off gradually. The living air, moreover, seems to pass freely in and out the windows and doors. There are, in truth, no conventions or rules we need keep in mind to understand the sculptor's purpose; it is emphatically plain he meant to furnish us with an illusion so perfect that we would read the scenes as real.

The inspiration for so magnificent a demonstration is probably to be sought in a variety of places. Maitani's reliefs at Orvieto (pages 547–548) come to mind at once as predicting what Ghiberti achieved with the aid of science unknown a century before. In addition, it seems probable that he had studied some examples of Roman painting, and the cognate relief, of the general type we have elsewhere named the Latin Style (pages 167–170); a general description of one of the *Odyssey Landscapes* will duplicate in circumstantial fashion a general description of one of Ghiberti's panels.

Those ancient sources seem to have combined with a concept of space that is distinctly more Gothic than Roman. As an accomplished composer, Ghiberti must have been familiar with every trick for establishing visual coherence between figures and details within a panel; but by comparison to the Greeks, to Giotto, and to his own earlier work, the compositions of 1425–52 are remarkable for an absence of directional gestures as between figure and figure, and for an absence of geometrical methods in general. The great over-all principle of coherence was the represented space itself. The air penetrates everywhere and envelopes everything. Space is the pervasive fact which makes it seem reasonable for Ghiberti to have abandoned the Graeco-modern convention of the unity of time (page 60); we accept the continuous method as natural because the space goes on and on, including and containing the successive events. The artistic unity to which the reliefs appeal is not the self-contained internal economy made familiar by Greek art and so often described as organic (page 65).

It is the vaster unity of the infinite to which the particular thing is connected by the continuity of space (page 469). So conceived, each panel is a glimpse and a beginning, and there is no necessary end.

Ghiberti's reliefs, if we had nothing else to prove it, are evidence enough to demonstrate that the Italian artists of the Early Renaissance wasted very little energy over certain questions with which modern criticism has been strenuously concerned. We refer in particular to the idea that there is an intimate relationship between medium and design. The tools and the stuff with which the artist works, that is to say, are held to possess a special nature, distinct from the nature of other tools and other raw materials. It follows, if we choose to accept such a theory, that whenever a man decides to become a sculptor, he should reconcile himself to the internal logic of sculpture. He should strive only for the kind of expression of which sculpture is capable, and he should eschew any attempt to cultivate effects that are not directly in line with the nature of his chosen medium.

On the basis of such thinking, Ghiberti has been made the target for some of the best-calculated derogatory comment in the annals of art criticism. The contention against him is that he endeavored to accomplish with sculpture that representation of distance which painting, with its modulations of tone (pages 612–613), represents so easily, so directly, and so adequately. That Ghiberti had superb technique, no one dares to deny; but technique, or so says the argument, is beside the point. Or, if not beside the point, is there not an actual complaint that Ghiberti had to make a parade of his skill in order to succeed, thus attracting more attention to the manipulation than to his meaning?

The cogency of the contentions just mentioned is to some extent substantiated by the greater satisfaction one gets from Ghiberti when single figures are seen in close up, as in Fig. 15.28. Such a view brings out the plastic merit of the shapes (i.e., the quality " natural " for sculpture). A more distant station, far enough away to include an entire panel within the frame of sight, denies the eye a chance to follow the minute graduations of contour by means of which the beauty of forms and of draperies may be communicated and received.

Without attempting to settle the argument, it is necessary to point out a further fact. The critics who object to Ghiberti's panels base their objection upon experience of the originals. Most students find it difficult to sympathize with their point of view. The reason is that students usually know the panels only through photographs, and the photographs appear to sustain Ghiberti. As a matter of fact, they sustain those who complain against him.

Any photograph is necessarily a picture, and subject to pictorial imperatives analogous to the imperatives allegedly imposed upon sculpture by its own nature. In studying a photograph after Ghiberti, our knowledge of spatial representation depends little upon qualities inherent in the relief itself, and much upon the light and dark that belongs solely to the picture. Every photograph clear enough to be published was taken under special conditions of light; but at another moment of the day, or on a different kind of day, the pictorial qualities of the bronze may not show up nearly so well. In truth, they usually do not. Cast shadows fall the wrong way. Value relationships become confused. Textures are more obtrusive. All too often, it must be confessed in spite of our admiration, we find ourselves reading solid plate metal where Ghiberti intended us to read the soft blue sky.

Jacopo della Quercia

Circumstances have conspired to cloud our estimate of Jacopo della Quercia (about 1374–1438); but even though we have little from his hand, it is plain that his contemporary reputation was well founded.

The *Tomb of Ilaria del Carretto,* in the Cathedral at Lucca, has long been attributed to him by word of mouth tradition. Unquestionably it is one of the loveliest monuments from the entire Renaissance. No other work of art so perfectly demonstrates the capacity of the Italian temperament to understand everything in terms of beauty: death seems merely to have given that exquisite lady a more perfect sleep. Because the poetic quality there expressed seems very different from the tone and content of Quercia's documented works, serious doubt has been cast upon the authenticity of the attribution, but the inconsistency involved in accepting it is hardly so great as the contrasts included within the sure work of Donatello. Without attempting to settle the question, it may be observed that the burden of proof is upon those who doubt.

Quercia's most important commission was for the *Fonte Gaia* at Siena, a sculptural ensemble involving numerous figures in the round, and some panels of narrative relief. Only battered fragments remain, now stored for safe keeping in the Palazzo Pubblico.

We are fortunate enough to have one important commission in a good state of preservation. In 1425, Quercia began a series of reliefs for the jambs of the main portal at San Petronio in Bologna. They go together with some statues of the Virgin and the Saints, and comprise subject matter from Genesis and from the infancy of Christ. From the standpoint of style, the panels (Fig. 15.29) fulfil almost to the letter the recommendations of those who would quarrel with Ghiberti. Landscape settings were used; but where Ghiberti tried to include everything, Quercia could hardly eliminate another detail without canceling the pictorial effect entirely. With a similar severity of purpose, he eschewed the crowds of people cultivated by both Donatello and Ghiberti, and he handled the narrative with only two or three figures to a panel. The latter were rendered in much bolder relief than was common at the time, and they fill the foreground.

It is evident that Quercia adjusted the balance of elements very differently from Ghiberti. Instead of making represented space the operative component, he depended almost entirely upon the figures. His formula corresponded closely with the Alexandrian division of Hellenistic art (pages 164–167). Without much doubt, the derivation was direct and intentional, but the figure-style incorporated within that familiar scheme of composition could hardly be more different from the elegant weaklings who people those bucolic yearnings from waning Antiquity. Quercia's people belong to the recurrent tradition of central Italy, a taste which appears to stretch back and back into the remote Etruscan past, accounting for the repeated appearance — without proximate cause — of an anatomy heavy enough to be called gigantic. Giotto and Masaccio belonged to the same tradition, which passed on from the earlier Renaissance into the work of Signorelli and Michaelangelo.

There is much in Quercia to recall, also, numerous sources closer in date. The passion with which he imbued both face and body finds its closest resemblance in the work of Nicola Pisano (pages 546–547). The hip-shot poses recall the S-curve that was popular in French Gothic art of the mannerist persuasion (pages 531–539), but he employed the device as an expression of heaving power rather than of grace.

To his heritage from the past, we must add the items which were new, personal, or both. The burning actuality of his narrative might be duplicated in the work of Donatello, but narrative of that special kind was new with the 15th Century and peculiarly Italian. Quercia's endorsement of the nude was more absolute and emphatic than that even of Donatello. The fierce power, potentially dangerous and devastating, which he literally breathed into his figures, was personal; it proved to be the strongest single influence upon Michaelangelo during his formative period (page 737).

While there were good artists in every Italian town during the first half of the 15th Century, Quercia was unique among the great originators in not having been a Florentine. Incongruously, he was a citizen of Siena. His monumentally plastic art was the direct opposite of the local tradition (pages 365–369), and it is interesting to note that Francesco di Giorgio, who projected Siena's mystic and delicate painting right through the 15th Century, was not born until the year after Quercia died. In view of those facts, it is legitimate to understand Quercia's art as self-expression. That his personal choices and purposes were generally respected even by the extremely conservative society of his native city is a circumstance that speaks volumes for the atmosphere of the times.

Fra Angelico

Fra Angelico was a nickname. The painter universally so called was christened Guido, and took the religious name Fra Giovanni of Fiesole when he entered the Dominican order at the age of twenty. He came to be called Angelico in affectionate recognition of the pretty angelic types (Fig. 15.30) that fill his earlier pictures.

As a painter and a personality, he has been secure in the affections of scholar and public alike for several centuries. It therefore requires an act of stern historical self-discipline to say that he was an artist of the second rank, separated from the Donatellos and the Masaccios by a demonstrable difference. Theirs was stupendous genius, big enough to open up a new era. Angelico's gifts and capacities may be summed up by saying that he combined the best of the old with a sound grasp of the new, and originated neither. But even in a century opulent with greatness, that was enough to make him a considerable figure.

In a book where space is necessarily curtailed, the introduction of such an artist is necessary in order to round out the contemporary picture. Everything we know of Angelico makes him out as a thoughtful, intelligent man. As he calculated his chances for success in art, he may well have estimated that Donatello and Masaccio represented the speculative wing of the profession. Their work was of interest to forward looking patrons who were willing to take a chance. The volume of established business was going elsewhere. Angelico's formative years coincided with the latter part of the maturity of Gentile da Fabriano (pages 537–538), who died in 1427. At Florence, moreover, there was still a great deal of painting in the same Late Gothic and International Style of which Gentile was merely the most famous Italian exemplar. The most prominent Florentine artist of the kind was named Lorenzo Monaco (about 1370–1425). He ran one of the largest establishments in the city, with numerous apprentices and assistants. Angelico may have been one of them.

Monaco's art was intelligently eclectic. Probably born at Siena, he surely was trained by some enthusiastic follower of Simone Martini (pages 367–369). Coming to Florence, he picked up a thing or two from the later Giotteschi (pages 562–563). At the time Angelico knew him, he had an International Style tinged with Florentine monumentality. Florid and poetical in about equal measure, his pictures were notable for prodigies of linear calligraphy. On the basis of proven performance, general popularity, and financial record, Monaco's art was the safer thing.

Still other thoughts must have gone through Angelico's mind as he chose his road. In an age distinguished for the rapid decline of the religious sanctions and the onset of actual corruption within the Catholic polity, Angelico was a sincere Christian. He did not enter the monastery by chance or under duress, but freely as a young man who must already have been able to support himself well in his profession. When Angelico made his choice of a style, the classical revival in art had not yet become associated in any direct way with the neopaganism of the Renaissance, although such an association was made later in the century (pages 662–663). His choice, then, was in no sense a negation of the trend of the times. He probably felt that Gothic art, which had never been used for anything else but Christian subject matter, was the art of the church. He seems to have accepted the style as loyally as he embraced the dogma. For that reason, as cited on page 538, his earlier work belongs plainly to the International Style.

The Death and Assumption of the Virgin, of which Fig. 15.30 shows a detail, is ample illustration of Angelico's earlier style. It is one of four panels done for the account of a single patron; the other three are in the Angelico collection now housed at San Marco in Florence. The casual observer might be forgiven for dating such pictures a hundred years before their actual time.

The frames are florid Gothic. The figure-style and costume are about the same as those seen in Gothic manuscripts (Figs 13.10–11). The average angel painted by Angelico at this period of his career looks, indeed, like a miniature rendition of one of the smiling angels at Reims (Figs. 12.15–16). There is much gold, and the colors are dainty and glitter like jewelry. Everything at first seems like a mystic's view of heaven, but a closer examination shows that the world had been discovered. The anatomy is too well constructed to date earlier than the 15th Century, and there are other indications that the painter understood very well the disciplines of the new representative science.

From that point on, the general development of Angelico's art shows a judicious absorption of the findings of his contemporaries at Florence. The *Madonna of the Linen Guild,* dating from 1433, was given no Gothic frame, but one in the form of a simple round arch, and the gentle Mary was more plastically described than before. Two pictures of the *Coronation of the Virgin* also come from the middle 1430's. The one in the Uffizi has its setting in a blaze of glory, and the one at the Louvre provides a raised dais of solid steps. Both of them, however, demonstrate a regard for the mechanical realities familiar on earth: gravitation, the displacement of bodies in space, anatomical construction, and so on. And yet none of this may properly be construed as an acceptance by Angelico of the worldly values discovered in his time and accepted as governing principles by so many artists of his era. We probably come close to the truth when we say that he attempted to harness realism to religious expression, and that from his point of view accurate representation was worthwhile only as a technique for demonstrating the reality of Christian truth mystically apprehended.

The suggestions set down above are well borne out by the greatest commission of the painter's career, which we are lucky enough to possess almost in its entirety. We refer to the extensive fresco decoration of the convent of San Marco at Florence. The monks went into residence there in 1436. Most of Angelico's painting dates between 1439 and 1445. The property had been given to the order by Cosimo de Medici. The architecture is a hodgepodge of Italian Gothic, but extensive rebuilding, alteration, and some additions were put in progress. The architect in charge was Michelozzo, a man who collaborated for a period with Donatello and who ranks second only to Brunelleschi as a designer in the style of the Early Renaissance. Within the convent, Angelico and his shop executed nearly half a hundred frescoes. Some were very large, and others were as small as panel pictures, being painted on the walls of the individual cells. With notable exceptions such as the badly repainted *Crucifixion,* one of the largest of them all and once a great painting, the general state of preservation is excellent.

Among the larger pictures is the familiar *Annunciation* (Fig. 15.31) which for generations has been a favorite monument of Italian art. It came as the culmination of a long period of rehearsal. Angelico had made a specialty of the subject. He always used the same figures in approximately the same costumes and poses. We must point to his cautious development of a single theme as one of the differences separating him from the prime movers of the Renaissance; but at the same time, few paintings embody so many elements of diverse interest. It is all but impossible to put down everything that the reader might legitimately demand to be told about it.

In response to the nature of wall painting, Angelico changed his style substantially. The tiny glittering details so appropriate for little panels (which presume an intimate inspection by eyes only a foot or two away) are absent. Instead, we see wider, simpler, stronger areas of tone. Linear calligraphy is still much in evidence, but it is disposed in big swings of line, as contrasted with the elegant complexity of the painter's earlier rhythms. The composition as a whole has been opened up; there is more distance between the figures, more room everywhere, and a convincing amplitude of air. All of those measures combine to produce a painting suitably viewed from a station across the room; and one capable of giving the broader effect generally wanted for architectural decoration.

Certain aspects of the setting have a special significance. The garden, as such, was in the direct tradition of the International Style; but there is good reason to believe that Angelico meant it to refer to the imagery of the 4th Chapter in the Song of Solomon, where a lady is metaphorically referred to as " a garden enclosed . . . a spring shut up, a fountain sealed." The passage was peculiarly appropriate in association with the Annunciation because it had often been construed as a symbolic prediction of Mary's perpetual virginity.

The patch of ground opening up to the left is of course a mere detail in a more important subject; but a closer view will reveal a side of Angelico's personality for which the reader is unlikely to be prepared. We might expect a gentle, lovable painter to excel at painting flowers; but exactly where, at this date, can we find blossoms, leaves, and grasses like these? The representation is incisive, penetrating, authentic — in the strictest sense, the work of a scientist. Botany has never been served by a higher talent.

The little loggia is another feature we might dismiss as nothing remarkable, a standard bit of setting unconsciously included by the painter. The reverse is actually the case. At the moment of painting, such an arcade was the last word in Renaissance architecture. In fact, it would be more accurate to call it the prediction of the next move; a study published some years ago by Langton Douglas makes it seem highly likely that the architects learned more from Angelico than he from them. Only a man with a professional interest would experiment with the capitals as he did here. The demonstration as a whole is beyond the capacity of the casual student, and it compels us to believe that the painter, old-fashioned though he was in some respects, was completely familiar with every detail of the classical revival.

The figure-style is yet another thing that becomes more profound than we expect. Ostensibly a mere reliance on old formulas and repeated by Angelico rather monotonously from picture to picture, it nevertheless was something unique. He actually produced a Madonna both holy and humane. The ethereal face is at once actual and ideal; the personality that of a saint, but a saint possessed of personality. It is obvious that neither humanism nor individualism had passed this painter by; and once again, we are made to realize that hardly any man of the era was more completely informed about the progress of the times.

The literal sense in which the last statement is true makes it necessary to pass on from the *Annunciation* to an accomplishment not demonstrable within the limits of the imagery of a closed garden. Angelico was a magnificently competent landscape painter, conversant in every detail with the skills developed by Masaccio, Donatello, and Ghiberti. A great many of his pictures have deep landscape backgrounds, of which the *Deposition from the*

Cross at San Marco (probably finished in 1440) may serve as an instance. It is doubtful whether any other painter except the dead Masaccio could have equaled the performance at the same date.

The work at San Marco was a great success, and Angelico found himself pressed with important commissions thereafter. Two of them took him to Rome, once in 1445 and again in 1447. The first was for Eugenius the 4th. It involved a series of scenes from the life of Christ; by an act of extraordinary obtuseness, the paintings were destroyed during the 16th Century by Paul the 3rd. The second Roman commission was for Nicholas the 5th, and it survives.

The pictures give various scenes from the life of Saints Stephen and Lawrence. For the settings, Angelico painted rich and ponderous complexities of heavier Renaissance architecture, and he filled them with dignified figures solidly rendered. No one who has felt the sweetness of his earlier painting can possibly be happy about the change, but the change in itself signalized an important transition in Italian art. Firstly, it may be remembered as the complete end of anything that even looked back to the Gothic. Secondly, the new pictures were well ahead on the main road; although dating only in the middle of the century, they predicted the end of the Early Renaissance.

The difference, if we may anticipate for a moment, had more to do with content than with style. The frescoes in the chapel of Nicholas the 5th are formal and ceremonial pictures; and through the medium of ceremony, Angelico was apparently reaching out for greater solemnity. The desire for it came as the result of deeper ruminations about the nature of man and his dignity. Such ideas were to be made generally manifest fifty years later (pages 711–715), and it is plain Angelico felt them only vaguely — certainly by no means clearly enough to paint them. Primitive and tentative as they are, the reader might nevertheless do well to remember his last works as an essay toward the High Renaissance.

FLORENTINE NEO-PLATONISM, AND ITS INFLUENCE UPON THE ART OF THE RENAISSANCE

When, in a general way, we want to contrast the art of the Early Renaissance with that of the High, we find ourselves saying that the 15th Century was a century of realism, and the 16th one of idealism. The distinction is coarsely made and too briefly stated to be true, but the statement is on the right track. The cause of the change is to be sought in the intellectual life of Florence, and it can be localized in the thought of a circle of erudite and powerful men. We refer to the members of the so-called "Florentine Academy," sometimes referred to as the *Platonic Academy*, and more strictly described as the *Neo-Platonic Academy*.

The Academy was considerably less institutional than its name might suggest. Actually it amounted to a circle of intellectuals under Medici sponsorship. At the period of our present interest, the group was more or less dependent upon the philosopher Marsilio Ficino (1433–99). The organization, if we may call it that, had grown up rather naturally as the result of Cosimo de Medici's personal interest in Plato.

That avocation, so far as we know, dated from the Council of Florence and Ferrara (1438–39), to which John Paleologus (pages 363–364) had come from Constantinople, bringing in his train a number of distinguished Greek scholars. In their arguments at the Council and in private discourse, those latter opened the eyes of Italy to the importance of Plato, a philosopher who had been out of use in the West since the time of Saint Augustine.

According to the testimony of younger contemporaries, Cosimo soon conceived the idea of a Florentine academy devoted to Platonic studies. An obvious part of the program was to make Plato accessible to Italian readers. Because only a small portion of the material existed in any language an Italian could easily handle, a full-scale effort at translation was requisite. For that, Cosimo made some long-headed plans. He apparently picked at once Marsilio Ficino, then seven years old, and arranged for his education. In 1462, he set the young man up in a villa at Careggi, a spot in the hills a couple of miles north of town. From that event, we may date the only formal organization the Academy ever had.

For the next generation, the villa at Careggi was the spiritual home of the most brilliant men alive. Ficino had a most endearing personality. His greatest pleasure was to call his friends around him, and they would sit listening while the master expounded the dialogues. In addition to direct contact with every leader of thought who lived at Florence or might pass through, Ficino maintained a large correspondence. His letters, friendly in tone but prepared as though for publication, circulated all over Europe; a few we happen to know about were received in France, Germany, Poland, Hungary, and the Low Countries, to say nothing of all the cities in Italy.

As a translator, Ficino finished his work with Plato in 1477, and committed it to print in 1482. Hardly comparable to our modern renderings, his text nevertheless remained in wide use until superseded during the past century. He then turned his attention to Plotinus, and finished a translation of the *Enneads* in 1492. That second effort of scholarship proved to be immensely important. It colored Ficino's interpretation of Plato; and thus, it slanted his influence upon art and poetry. Plato died in 347 B.C. Plotinus was born about

205 A.D. The dates give modern students a signal to look for differences, but Ficino got no such signal. Thus the distinction between Platonism as of Plato and the Neo-Platonism represented by Plotinus largely escaped him. Having recorded that circumstance, which will explain why the academy should be called Neo-Platonic, we need pursue the matter no further at the moment. Our concern is with the influence of the Academy upon the history of art, especially as it is reflected in the work of Botticelli (pages 654–663) and Michaelangelo (pages 734–750). We shall try, that is, to recapture the environment and to understand art by reference to the spiritual food of the artist. That will involve us in much that may first seem far removed from painting and sculpture, but we shall connect it up in the end.

As the central figure of the Florentine Academy and the acknowledged first philosopher of the century, Ficino put his mark on every educated Italian for a hundred years. By so doing, he placed himself at the focus of the immense influence Italy exerted upon world culture. The Platonism of Spenser and Goethe came to them by way of Florence; and we can follow the effect right on into the 19th Century in the writings of Wordsworth, Emerson, and Thoreau — to mention only a few names at random. Every student of history must pause in reverence at so bountiful a harvest, but every student of ideas must at the same time feel a strong sense of paradox in the phenomenon. Ficino, if we compare him with the great men of philosophy, makes a poor showing. Of original and creative material, he gave us little that is first class. His energy seems to have been consumed trying to understand and explain ancient ideas, and even those were modified more than he knew himself by the society of which he was a member. The world, however, was hungry for the kind of food he had to offer; and he was there in the act of offering it. Because of that historical chance, a thinker of the second order opened the eyes of great artists and set them on their way.

Among the various theories developed by the Florentine Academy, two had a direct and unmistakable effect upon art. The first was the theory of creation, by reference to which the work of Michaelangelo becomes intelligible; and the second was the theory of love and beauty, which tends to explain certain artistic developments which first became important in the painting of Botticelli.*

The Florentine theory of creation had perforce to take account of the existence of the Christian Church. Ficino's central purpose, indeed, was to reconcile the traditional European religion with the classics. He himself became a priest in 1473, and canon of the Cathedral in 1487. Appalled by the irresistible tide of the new civilization, he hoped that Plato would prove a means, as Aris-

* See P. O. Kristeller, *The Philosophy of Marsilio Ficino.* Columbia University Press, 1943.

totle had for Saint Thomas, of saving the world for the Church. For a time, he even sympathized with Savonarola when that great and bigoted preacher took over Florence in the name of ideas that damned Ficino's Medici sponsors, and would have done his own work to death had they permanently prevailed.

Ficino's confusion with Plotinus helped him to reconcile Christianity with the ancient standards, for much of that philosopher's thinking had already been absorbed into our dogma by such early fathers as Augustine. Plotinus followed Plato in his general conception of the creation, and man's present situation. The difference may perhaps be summarized as a greater readiness to invoke the supernatural. According to the narrative as understood by Ficino, mankind had originally lived in glory. In some primeval disaster, man got separated from the divine. We need not investigate how such a thing happened; the significant fact is that people now find themselves in a condition somewhere between the unhappy and the intolerable. Obviously, the strongest human instinct must be to seek reunion with the glory from which we have been banished; to do otherwise would be to declare one's self insane.

A course of self-purification was recommended as the best procedure, and it was part of the psychology of the Renaissance to assume that much might be accomplished even during a mortal lifetime. It will be seen that the idea is cognate to what we have elsewhere (page 696) referred to as the artistic concept of life, and the effect was to add a Christian sanction to the ideals of humanism and individualism. By directing and refining the impulses already very evident within themselves, men might hope, even during life, for temporary reunion, a state defined as *ecstasy* — literally to stand outside one's self. Perhaps Thoreau meant somewhat the same thing when he spoke of drifting on Walden Pond, and experiencing moments when he "ceased to live and began to be."

We may now turn to the idea of beauty as it came to be understood at Florence under the spell of the Neo-Platonic studies. Beauty, as those men conceived it, was a component of creation. When men had lived in glory, they also had lived in beauty. For that reason, the notion became current that people knew beauty whenever they saw it. They simply remembered it. The yearning for beauty, it will be seen, was thus given a meaning closely equivalent to the soul's yearning for reunion with the divine. Not only did the idea make it a permissible thing to want beauty; it virtually labeled the desire as a religious impulse.

The reader may also have observed that the definition of beauty, as given above, was more noble than distinct. It assigned to beauty a function that had to do with the more elevated and spiritual impulses of mankind, but it made beauty a matter of intuition nevertheless. At the practical level of ordinary life, the definition furnished small guidance. In fact, it invited men to settle such questions their own way, and to name as beautiful anything they happened to fancy. To the particular kind of beauty which in fact proved favorite among the men of the Renaissance, we shall presently turn our attention. The matter was inseparable from the Neo-Platonic theory of love, which we must now review.

Love had been made necessary by man's fall from grace. It was understood to be the instinct which impelled him to seek reunion with the divine. In instances where that had actually been accomplished (the saints in heaven, for example) love had served its purpose. There could be no more desire, nor any intelligible reason for desire. The state of glory would presumably be the state of complete fulfilment and continuous satisfaction into eternity.

In order to make such ideas useful, it was necessary to place love and beauty on earth. That was done by saying that beauty emanates from its locus in heaven, permeating nature and dwelling in many places. It was therefore made reasonable to find beauty in trees, rocks, bodies, and for pictures and statues to be beautiful. They all got their beauty from above. Much, indeed, as the lines of force from a mighty magnet give life to iron filings, and pull them toward itself.

As Plotinus put it in the 5th part of the 3rd *Ennead,* "Everyone recognizes that the emotional state for which we make love responsible rises in souls aspiring to be knit in closest union with some beautiful object; and it is sound, I think, to find the primal source of love in a tendency toward pure beauty, in a recognition of it, and a kinship with it." On a cognate theme, Ficino himself wrote, "Love unites the mind more quickly, more closely, and more stably with God than does knowledge, because the force of knowledge consists more in distinction, that of love more in union." In plain words, the Florentines believed that love started to operate whenever beauty was noted, and that love, when it came, was to be welcomed because it moved one toward God.

The Neo-Platonic theory of both love and beauty was wonderfully popular with the Italians. Ficino's friends were doubtless competent philosophers, and as such they would be interested in following out the Platonic machinery into the more and more abstract levels of idealism. The citizenry at large wasted no energy on so impersonal and impractical an endeavor. They thought they knew what Ficino's words meant, and they thought they knew what to do about them. With chivalry (page 458) in the immediate background and still a living thing, it seemed obvious that nobody would have been crazy enough to put forward at Florence a philosophy suggesting that ladies step down from their pedestal. The Florentines were delighted to have all kinds of beauty made thoroughly respectable, but the kind that came most often to mind was the beauty of women. Ficino was understood to say that the experience of this beauty, and the consequent onset of love, amounted to a discipline for the soul, virtually an act of worship. His conscientious attempts to distinguish between higher and lower forms of love, and beauties greater and less, were construed in gallant applications. Men saw visions of fair women, but fair women now symbolized the yearning of the soul toward eternity, and the pathos of man's separation from the divine.

As we look back upon what happened, it is evident that Florentine Neo-Platonism opened every eye to the complexity of the human emotional system, and to the advisability of its refinement. First in Italy and then elsewhere, a considerable literature of love and beauty came into being. Ridiculous popularizations of course occurred, but it is remarkable how strongly Ficino's subtle and elevated teaching resisted the intrusion of vulgarity. Even the publications intended to guide ladies in beauty culture at least suggested that beauty was a subject not to be understood without a reasonable effort at discrimination. For some of the more important documents, no praise can be too high. There is no more eloquent discourse than the speech of the Cardinal Bembo, to be found toward the end of Baldassare Castiglione's *The Courtier* (1528), where the reader will find the tradition of chivalry most gracefully combined with the sentiments of Plato's *Symposium*. The same might be said for Spenser's *An Hymne in Honour of Love* and his *An Hymne in Honour of Beautie*, both marvels of much in small compass, and both derivative from Ficino.

Botticelli

The painter Botticelli (1444–1510) was the first important artist to be deeply affected by Neo-Platonism. His profound and baffling nature may not immediately make itself apparent. No artist ever made sentiment more lyric in its soft loveliness. He appeals by being winsome and wistful at the same time. It is easy to think one loves his pictures; but after some little acquaintance with them, there comes a consciousness of the conflict and frustration that existed within him, strangely like the conflicts and frustrations of our own day.

We must understand at the outset that the inner beauties of Botticelli's art are not for everybody. Even in 15th-Century Florence, he was not a popular artist in the sense of appealing to the public at large. He worked for a small circle of erudite persons who had the knowledge and taste to appreciate his exotic genius. Most of them were directly associated with the Florentine Academy, as indeed the painter himself may have been. It was his special role in history to create the visual imagery that expressed and commemorated the idealism newly introduced to Italy by the Neo-Platonic movement. His career also included an episode connected with the conflict between the life of the Renaissance and the views of the Church; of that, we shall say a word at the end.

With respect to style, Botticelli need cause us no problems. To the day of his death, and long after the manner of the High Renaissance had been introduced to the world by Leonardo and others (pages 722–726), he continued to paint in the low relief manner inaugurated by Donatello at the very beginning of the 15th Century (pages 617–621). He got his fundamental training in the shop of Filippo Lippi (1406–69). A comparison between Fig. 15.32 and Fig. 15.34 will show how much the pupil owed to the master. It will also indicate the radical difference in the nature of the two men.

Lippi, like many another man of strong appetites and coarse behavior, maintained throughout his spectacular career an almost reverent taste for the daintier, more virginal aspects of feminine beauty. In his picture, we get little else; but in Botticelli's version of the same subject, we instantly feel overtones and connotations. The sentiment is of the same kind, but of loftier order. The faces are more finely drawn. The youthful muscles of cheek, eye, and mouth have already been stretched and modeled by thought and feeling. The grapes and the wheat, symbols of the Last Supper, drive the meaning home. Botticelli's picture is both an idyl and a tragedy.

As a young man, Botticelli worked for a time with the sculptor and painter Antonio Pollaiuolo (1429–98). Pollaiuolo was a famous anatomist; and as an artist, he made a specialty of putting the human body into unusual and even contorted positions. What he liked best was a powerful figure in violent action (Fig. 15.33). His studies were at times academic; but in all cases, they were saved by the zest of the man. Everything he touched is vital. In his detailed demonstrations of nature's complex and ingenious machinery, one feels the intellectual joy of fruitful research; and at the same time, there is an animal fulfilment of action for its own sake.

Violence in any form, even the harmless vigor of athletics, was foreign to Botticelli's temperament, but his art nevertheless owed much to Pollaiuolo. It was that second master from whom he learned how to make his figures move, something which many artists of the time could do passably well but not one with the same superb authenticity.

Botticelli's two most famous pictures are the *Primavera* of 1478 (Fig. 15.35) and the *Birth of Venus* of some six or seven years later (Figs. 15.36–37). It is certain that both were done for Medici patronage, but there is a minor confusion as to which Medici gave the order. In 1503, the two were in a villa at

Castello, a house owned by the illegitimate branch of the family. It seems likely, therefore, that the original owner was Lorenzo di Pier Francesco Medici, natural second cousin to Lorenzo the Magnificent.

In part, both paintings constitute a direct attempt to bring Antiquity back to life. As we shall see, the painter knew that certain Greek artists had painted similar subject matter, and that certain classical poets had used similar imagery. A more proximate cause, however, was the Neo-Platonic theory of love and beauty (pages 651–654), which was enough in itself to account for the choice of Venus as the central figure and for the ethereal idealization of the feminine which forms so striking a feature of both works.

The *Primavera* (Fig. 15.35) consists of nine figures seen against the background of an orange grove. Spring flowers thrust themselves up in delicate profusion from the earth. In the middle, and removed slightly toward the background, stands a lady whom we may identify as Venus herself. A blind Cupid is in the air above her.

At the extreme left, a male figure reaches upward with a wand, apparently engaged in dispersing a cloudlet. Behind him, three girls move in the rhythm of a slow dance. Each wears but a single garment of the most diaphanous white, and their femininity is the more apparent therefore.

On the other side, we see two females figures and a flying male. The one in front is dressed in an elaborately flowered gown. She tosses flowers from a bunch held in the fold of her skirt. The girl behind wears a gauze drapery like that of the dancing figures, but her costume is in disorder. She appears to be running as best she may from the flying male who grabs for her with outstretched hands and puffed-up cheeks.

As a demonstration of formal design, the composition is notable. One is at first conscious of the color, now sadly dimmed by time and by treatment of the panel to rid it of worms. If less bold than they were, the tones are still exciting to the sensibilities. The effect may be compared to tapestry, except that where tapestry is rich the painting is keen and dainty. Warm spots vie with cool for possession of our feelings, and tints with shades. As between one category and another, there is little to choose. The principle in use is that of tonal balance, and the result is to spread color interest almost evenly over the whole surface. In the matter of using intense hues to reestablish the flatness of the panel (page 585), Botticelli was an expert. Although space is represented to the depth of thirty feet or more, the picture surface gives one a peculiar sense of smoothness, a characteristic extremely attractive in paintings intended (as this one probably was) for permanent incorporation in the paneling of a wall.

As to the content, the spirit is Platonic, but the details of iconography have proven elusive. A small literature exists on the subject, from which we shall draw only a few of the more obvious bits of analysis. The picture appears to be a great mixture of allusions, all of which were undoubtedly instantly recognizable by the learned gentlemen for whom the painting was intended.

The general theme seems to come from the *De Rerum Natura* of Lucretius (1st Century B.C.). Venus, in the ancient world, had also been Goddess of Gardens; and in his opening invocation, Lucretius hailed her as the great generative force of the world. Such a notion was carried out by Botticelli in almost every detail of his painting. The earth produces flowers. The trees give fruit. Each woman is carrying a child. Cupid shoots his arrows every which way. The time of year may have been suggested by another passage in Lucretius. "Spring comes," wrote he in his 5th Book, "and Venus. . . ."

As to the Flora at the right, strewing flowers, she also appeared in the *De Rerum Natura,* but the lascivious puffing Zephyr seems to have been taken from a passage in the work of Poliziano, a contemporary Florentine poet. We may also set down that Horace spoke of spring as the time when Venus led forth her band, and of the naked Graces dancing with measured tread before Mercury, who would presumably be the young man at the left.

For reasons made obvious by the paragraphs just above, strictures have often been leveled at Botticelli for being the originator (as he very nearly was) of the fanciful picture derived from literature. The practice, it is contended, tends to put the art of the painter in a secondary position. At best, or so we are told, the picture becomes a mere extension of the book; and at worst, a slavish illustration thereof. In either case, the painting would necessarily derive whatever merit it might possess, not from itself, but from the authority of the literary source.

There is much weight in the argument, and it can be applied with damning effect at various points in the history of art. It cannot, however, be used successfully against Botticelli. Living in an atmosphere of enthusiastic classicism, he took his inspiration where he found it. The crucial point is that the inspiration was genuine, by which we mean to say that the literary sources (none of which he followed closely, much less mechanically) merely set in motion feelings that were the painter's own. His affinities with the poets were real and deep, but he shared rather than borrowed their imagery.

Nothing we have yet said even begins to account for the sadness which fills the soft air of the picture. That nostalgic overtone, which lingers more in the memory than any other quality of the work, probably derived from contemporary persons and events, of which the reader will now require a recitation.

In 1469, Marco Vespucci had brought his bride home to Florence. She was Simonetta Cattaneo, a Genoese, sixteen years old; and so sweet and charming, said a contemporary, that all men praised her and no woman blamed her. In no time at all, the girl became the acknowledged belle of Florence. Giuliano Medici, the younger brother of the Magnificent Lorenzo, was specially her friend. It is a waste of time to speculate whether she was also his mistress; it can make no difference now, one way or the other. The important fact was that she was affectionately included within the intimate life of the Medici circle. In 1475, she was Queen of Beauty in a great tournament held in Giuliano's honor. That publicly established her, in a ceremonial sense at any rate, as the lady to whom Giuliano pledged his knightly devotion.

In 1476, Simonetta died after a short illness. Lorenzo the Magnificent, then absent at Pisa, kept his personal physicians in charge. He insisted upon daily bulletins. On the evening of her death, he went walking with a friend. Pointing up to a star of special beauty, he suggested that it might be a new star and "the soul of that most gentle lady."

Simonetta died in April. She went to her tomb with face uncovered in the sunlight. There was much remark, it is said, about the flowers that covered the earth like a blanket; always lovely in the Italian spring, they must have been specially so that year. The death of one so young amid so much beauty made dignified citizens cry in the streets of Florence. Everyone was reminded that spring cannot last.

In 1478, the Pazzi conspirators murdered Giuliano Medici. By coincidence, the date was April 26, the second anniversary of Simonetta's passing.

Those events, so brief in the statement, cast a pall over the intellectual life of Florence. Contrary to what we hear of domestic relations in some other families, the Medici brothers had been unselfishly devoted. Lorenzo was the older and more respected, Giuliano the more handsome and charming. The affection between Giuliano and Simonetta appears to have been a living symbol of the love and beauty which, for older and more serious persons, necessarily remained an intellectual ideal. It has long been a tradition that the *Primavera* was intended as a memorial for the two. With respect to Simonetta, that is probably true. Part of the tradition has it that the six female figures, all alike enough to be sisters, are each and all portraits of her. The Mercury at the far left is similarly suggested as a portrait of Giuliano; but if a memory of him was also involved, the timing was very close indeed.

Unhappily, the facts cannot be determined. Several portraits of the right kind and period have been labeled with Simonetta's name, but they depict several different women. None of them correspond satisfactorily with the women of the picture, or with the Venus in the *Birth of Venus,* which is even more likely to be Simonetta. Lack of positive evidence is no good reason, however, for denying the tradition.

The nature of Florentine Neo-Platonism, and its close involvement with the Medici family, make it seem likely that Simonetta was in fact Botticelli's model. Her reputation gives us a woman of fragile beauty, strangely powerful in physical allure. Her temperament must have been, if we read the signs correctly, an appealing mixture of the mind and the intuition. Such women do not attract the common man, but their singular wisdom keeps the wiser male in constant wonderment. Simonetta alive had been the darling of her erudite friends, a walking example of femininity raised to a higher order. Simonetta dead easily became, it would seem, almost the definition of pure beauty. Happily, the supernal image was not nameless, but warm and personal. What better instance could there have been of the ideal within the thing? Of earthly loveliness as an emanation from heaven? Of the way in which the beauty of women might, upon occasion, turn the soul toward God?

The *Birth of Venus* (Figs. 15.36–37) was ostensibly a direct attempt at classical revival, a veritable school figure for the literal definition of the Renaissance. The imagery derived originally from Homer, who described the newborn goddess as being blown ashore from the Aegean Sea by the soft breath of the zephyrs, while the Hours waited to spread a star-strewn robe over her white body, and countless flowers sprang from the grass her feet would tread.

The very same imagery had been used for one of the most famous paintings of the ancient world, as Botticelli well knew. That was the *Aphrodite Rising from the Sea* by Apelles, the most famous painter of the Greek Fourth Century B.C. and a figure closely associated with the court of Alexander. Apelles did his famous *Aphrodite* for the temple of Asklepios on the Island of Kos. Augustus brought the picture to Rome, and put it on exhibition in the temple of the Divine Julius in the Forum. The beauty of the nude figure, especially the flesh tones in contrast with the cooler hues of the water, was the subject of much admiring remark. The supreme skill of Apelles was negatively made plain during a later reign when the painting was damaged in its lower parts, and no Roman artist could perform a restoration.

Like many another popular masterpiece, Apelles's *Aphrodite* had inspired imitations, of which a good many were statues more or less closely reproducing the appearance of the central figure in the painting. By chance, one of the latter was at Florence: the Hellenistic *Medici Venus,* today on view at the Uffizi. Rightly or wrongly, people then thought it close to the style of Apelles, and Botticelli used it for the pose but not the form of his own Venus.

So much for the sources from which Botticelli worked. It would be hard to imagine a more straightforward, pedestrian narrative; but fortunately, we have only reached the point where Botticelli came in.

Rather than confuse the right-hand side of the composition, he used only one personified Hour where the poets had mentioned three. In the matter of color, however, he was wisely governed by the reputation of his model; he tried to emulate what he knew of Apelles. The cool hues of the water modulate through the pearly tints of the shell, and transpose into the pink flesh tones. The sequence from cool toward warm culminates in the hair, which is a field of golden bronze. The highlights are brought out in pure gold, a circumstance that lends the event a supernatural aura and, incidentally, makes the painting unsuitable for hanging in a direct light.

It is doubtful whether Apelles, or anyone else, ever handled colors with greater delicacy. Surely no Greek ever used line better than Botticelli. Always sensitive to the movement of light and delicate things, his line here became a celebration, as it were, of the soft breeze over the ocean. With a sure cool strength, it lifts the draperies and moves the goddess's hair, and it blows her floating figure surely and gently toward the land.

According to the ancient sources, Apelles's *Aphrodite* derived her loveliness from a living model. Two ladies, Phryne and Pankaspe, survive in name because one or both posed for the great Greek painter. It is difficult to know whether Botticelli may have been cognizant of the story or not; if so, he had classical authority for deriving an ideal figure from a mortal woman.

We have a special reason for making a shrewd guess that Simonetta was the model. She had been born at Porto Venere, the little harbor at the very tip of the peninsula closing the Gulf of Spezia on the west. The place gets its name from the Roman tradition that Venus stepped ashore there — and not on the Island of Cythera, as the Greek myth tells it. There was material for a pretty compliment in the circumstance, and it is inconceivable that the gentlemen of Florence would have missed so obvious an opportunity to combine the chivalric tradition with classical lore.

It is a pity that Simonetta's association with Botticelli has been marred by an appalling narrative widely credited in English-speaking lands; namely, that the chaste Simonetta, for love of art and beauty, sacrificed her modesty to pose in the nude for this painting, her protection from Botticelli's potential lust being solely the abstract harmonies observable in her form. With those, we are told, the artist instantly became so engrossed as to preclude indelicacy. There is no early record to sustain such a story. It appears first to have been printed by Ruskin as a footnote to his *Ariadne Fiorentina.*

Ruskin's suggestion demonstrated an unpardonable tendency to read the Victorian proprieties into a situation where they could not possibly be made to apply, but Ruskin was nevertheless a great critic. Often narrow, frequently mistaken in matters of detail, he was never without penetration and depth. No matter what he said, there is usually truth to be found in it somewhere and in some measure. In this instance, he made a fundamental observation about Botticelli's Venus, even if he advanced the wrong reasons for it.

Her nudity is an unusual and special case. Ruskin was wrong in attributing it to the hysteria of violated convention, but he was right in knowing that Botticelli's Venus feels the touch of our eyes. Others have been equally mistaken in suggesting that we see a holdover from the medieval sense of shame; at the date of painting, the nude no longer had that connotation. Neither does Botticelli predict the coming of the High Renaissance; there is simply no suggestion of the refined sensuality so greatly cultivated in the art of that period. Similarly, the very sense of nudity separates the figure from every classical nude, because freedom from consciousness of the body had been the prime appeal and chief lesson of naked figures in Greek art. We must look further, evidently, in order to understand what we see. The following hypothesis may offer a line of thought, and help toward an explanation.

Whether he knew her intimately or not, Simonetta's death must have made a permanent impression upon the painter. To understand the Venus for which she served as an inspiration, we must interpret the incident of her passing as an illustration of more general principles. The beauty of her body had proven transitory, as physical beauties must be. Even the love directed toward her complete personality, body and soul together, was now denied an immediate object; such is the inevitable fate of all love that is personal. Forgetting Simonetta as a woman and realizing that she merely furnished the starting point for a sublimated figure, we may think of Venus much as Lucretius did. The love Venus brought to the earth was the gift of life, but life is hard to explain. As a great generative force, it carries forward toward eternity. Inexorably, the race survives and increases, but the individual men and women suffer loss, sadness, heartbreak, and death. For them, there is no permanence and no deliverance on earth. Such thoughts are full of pathos; they suggest why Botticelli gave Venus no joy in her birth, and why he filled her face with compassion.

Late in his career, Botticelli undertook to do one hundred drawings to illustrate a copy of Dante which was projected by one of the Medici. Most of the drawings survive; there are eighty-five in Berlin and eleven in the Vatican Library. As they now stand, all but a few of them are totally innocent of both hue and shading. Everything was rendered by unaided line. Fig. 15.38 was selected for reproduction not because it is essentially more attractive or important than any of the others (which, in fact, it is not) but because it offers a great variety of material: fire, water, stone, figures nude and figures clothed, things in the foreground, and things further away.

Technique, as such, rarely interests us in the history of art; we merely take excellence for granted. But Botticelli's linear accomplishment transcends all ordinary standards. Considered merely as demonstrations in the field of representation, the Dante drawings constitute a great monument. The texture, weight, and shape of objects were specified as precisely as a sculptor could do it. Within the represented space, the relative placement of things forward, right, left, and back was stated as unmistakably as any painter might indicate with the full resources of hue, value, and intensity. Botticelli's descriptive powers were so highly developed that he had a linear device for every situation; the most esoteric necessities seem scarcely to have delayed his pen. He painted in the Mode of Relief (pages 582–586), but the Dante drawings illustrate the often-repeated statement that all color and all modeling might be subtracted from the paintings while still retaining perhaps three quarters of their expressive value.

Insofar as insubstantial words can describe an artistic experience, we may say that as the eye follows the movement of Botticelli's hand, the line itself comes alive. It swings, sparkles, and dashes. It sleeps and wakens. It becomes sad, or lifts like a song. Similar in nature to Far-Eastern calligraphy, Botticelli's line nevertheless belongs to the representative tradition of the west. As in Chinese work, every smallest mark is an angle or curve of abstract beauty; but where the Eastern artist sought also to find an abstract motive which would still be legible as representation, Botticelli kept to what we may, for the moment, call the *working line*. His touch was everywhere governed by the structure of the object described, and his special merit was to raise such line above its office of physical description. He made it also an expressive vehicle; and so understood, it will bear close comparison with the tones of music.

The most complete exposure of Botticelli's introspective sensitivity was furnished by his connection with the Savonarola episode. That affair had its start in a variety of matters; but in a broad way, we may interpret it as the violent reaction of the popular mind to the neopaganism of the Medici era.

When the great Lorenzo died in 1492, he left sons who lacked his ability. Their incapacity soon ended in disgrace, the occasion thereof being the investiture of Florence by the French in the course of their expedition of 1494. All Italy was humiliated, and the Florentines were ready to mend their ways.

Girolamo Savonarola was prior at San Marco. He was a man of extraordinary force and dignity, and of completely independent mind. He had made it a practice to preach against the new worldliness; and in 1494, he pointed to the excesses of the Medici as the direct cause of his country's mortification at the hands of Charles the 8th of France. He presently assumed dictatorial power at Florence. His enemies, not the least of whom was the notorious Borgia Pope Alexander the 6th, at once began to intrigue against him. At length he was brought to trial, repeatedly tortured, and finally condemned. Sentence was carried out by hanging and burning in front of the Palazzo Vecchio on May 28, 1498.

There is a strong tradition that Botticelli came under the influence of the great Dominican preacher. He is said to have abandoned his Renaissance ways in a passion of guilt and remorse. He is further said to have assisted Savonarola's agents in collecting his own classical nudes for the Burning of the Vanities, a perverted ceremony of religious carnival staged in 1497 and again in 1498.

Some critics, probably with more caution than judgment, claim that the evidence sustains no such positive assertions. It is surely true, however, that a marked alteration in both the subject matter and spirit of Botticelli's painting coincides with the period of Savonarola, and it is perfectly plain from his latest work that his nervous stability had suffered a traumatic strain. Among the works that reflect the tumultuous state of his being, we may cite first the *Mystical Nativity* (1500) in the National Gallery of London, which has a Greek inscription referring to the Apocalypse and to the troubles in Italy.

An even more desperate expression is the violent *Crucifixion* now in the Fogg Museum. A Magdalen fiercely embraces the foot of the cross. An avenging angel holds by its left hind leg the heraldic lion of Florence, and whips it with a rod. Smoke and flame fill the right background, while to the left we see Florence lying under a sinister light. Admittedly obscure and possibly without specific denotation, the picture has with some justice been interpreted as predicting the doom of the city in punishment for Savonarola's death.

Botticelli was the last artist who belonged to the Early Renaissance, and the extreme conservatism of his style may be assessed if we make a comparison of dates. Botticelli was actually forty years younger than Leon Battista Alberti (1404–72), whose career marked a new phase in the history of European culture. In fact, it was Alberti whose thought laid the foundation not only for the art, but for the entire outlook of the 16th Century. With the introduction of his name, we appropriately pass on to the next chapter.

*

16

THE HIGH RENAISSANCE

LEON BATTISTA ALBERTI

Leon Battista Alberti, the founder of the High Renaissance, was born as early as 1404. By the time of his death in 1472, the new movement was underway; and by about 1500, both its style and its philosophy were generally accepted.

Alberti was born at Genoa, the illegitimate son of a very notable Florentine family then banished to the north after losing a political fight at home. The Alberti were rich, and their ample funds made natural and easy the best education available, an opportunity which the young man followed up with incredible brilliance and acumen. His Latin was good enough to enable him, during student days, to write a comedy that was mistaken for the work of Terence. He was also an accomplished musician. After graduating in canon law at Bologna, he later spent two years in the same place learning all there then was to know about natural science.

His name was enough to make him welcome anywhere; and that circumstance, in combination with personal charm and extraordinary ability, opened up splendid opportunities when funds failed at the death of his father. In 1428, he went to France and Germany as secretary to Cardinal Albergati (of whom there is a picture by John Van Eyck). In 1431 he was invited to Rome as Cardinal Moulin's secretary. From there he went to a position on the learned staff of the Vatican. His routine duties left him plenty of time to acquire an expert knowledge of the antiquities, and for creative work. On several occasions, he accompanied the reigning pontiff on diplomatic journeys. He was with Eugene the 4th at Florence, for example, in 1434, and with Pius the 2nd at Mantua in 1459. The trip first mentioned brought him into contact with Brunelleschi, Donatello, and other great Florentines, and the second resulted

Fig. 16.1 Alberti. Self Portrait. Washington. National Gallery. (Previously in the Dreyfus and the Kress Collections.) Bronze. 7 29/32 inches high by 5 11/32 inches wide.

ALINARI

Fig. 16.2 Rimini. San Francesco. South side, as remodeled 1446–1455 according to plans by Alberti.

Figs. 16.3–4 Mantua. Sant' Andrea. Built from plans drawn by Alberti. Started 1472.

ANDERSON

ALINARI

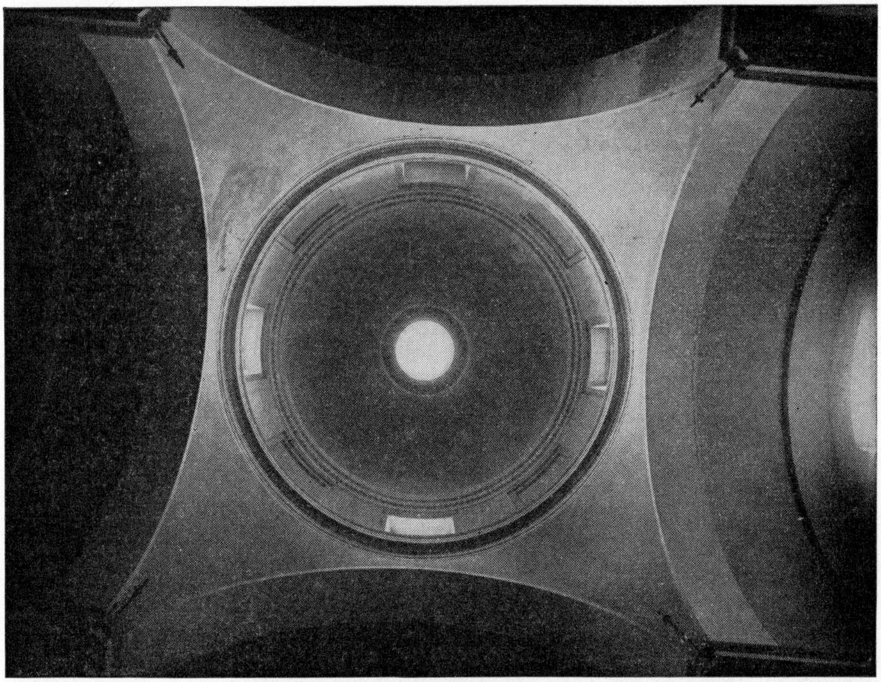

GAB. FOT. NAZ.

Fig. 16.5 (above) Rome. Sant' Eligio degli Orefici. 1509. Designed by Raphael.

Fig. 16.6 Todi. Santa Maria della Consolazione. Church 1508–1524; dome 1606. Height about 165 feet. Width about 145 feet.

ALINARI

Figs. 16.7–9 Verrocchio. *Boy with Dolphin*. Florence. Palazzo Vecchio. 1465. Bronze. PHOTOGRAPHS BY BROGI.

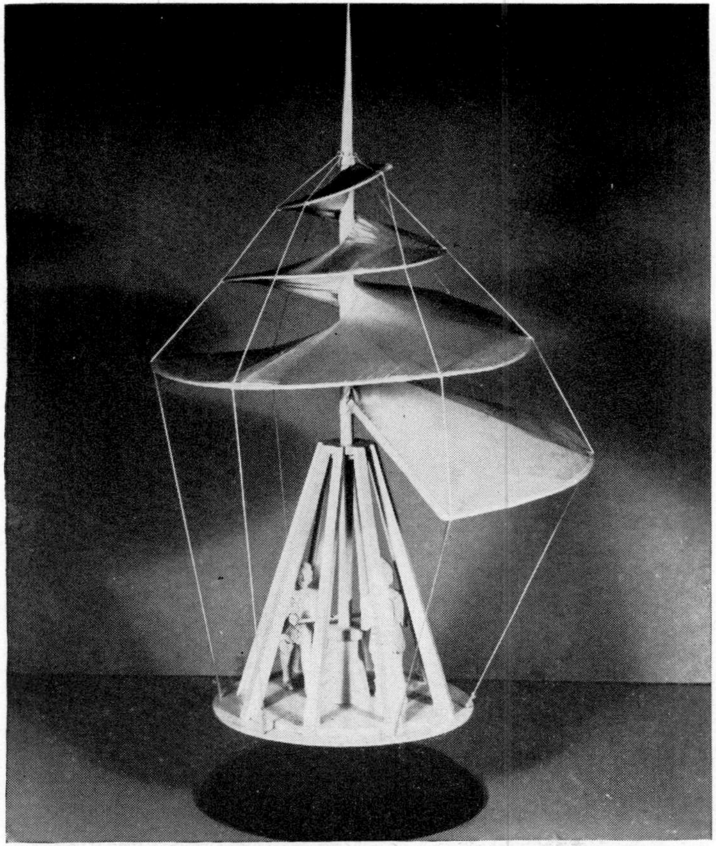

Figs. 16.10–12 Leonardo da Vinci. Helicopter, Fieldpiece with 36 Barrels, and Variable Speed Drive. Collection of the International Business Machines Corporation.

ALINARI

GIRAUDON

Figs. 16.13–14 Leonardo da Vinci. *Madonna of the Rocks.* About 1482. Paris. Louvre. Oil on wood, transferred to canvas. 6 feet, 6½ inches high.

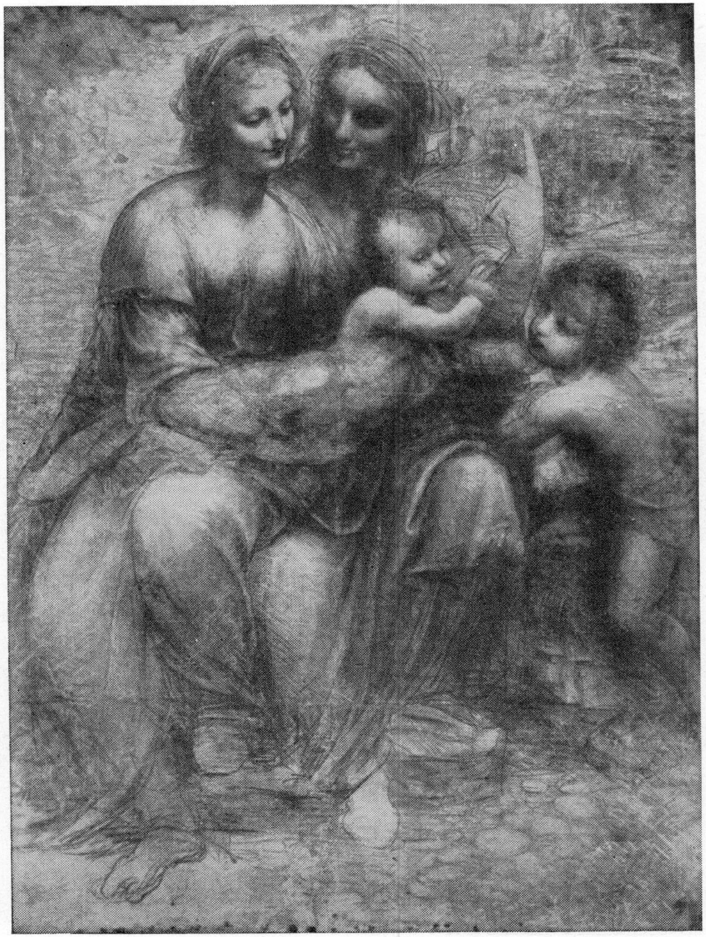

ALINARI

Fig. 16.16 Raphael. *Madonna of the Goldfinch*. 1507. Florence. Uffizi. Fig. 16.15 (left) Leonardo da Vinci. Cartoon for a painting of the Madonna and Child with Saint Anne. London. Burlington House. Museum of the Royal Academy.

ANDERSON

Fig. 16.17 Raphael. *The Disputà*. Rome. Vatican.

Fig. 16.18 (opposite page) Diagram to indicate the identity of the various persons shown in *The Disputà*.

The composition is arranged in three registers. At the top, we see God the Father (27) raising his hand in benediction and holding the globe. To either side of him (23–26, 4–6) are angels and cherubim. In the middle register are Christ with Mary and John the Baptist (1–3) silhouetted against a glory; Christ raises his hands to show the stigmata, which are symbols of redemption. Immediately below (13–16) are four small angels, each with a Gospel Book, and the Holy Spirit descending in the form of a dove. The twelve figures to right and left are prophets, apostles, and confessors; note that representatives of the old dispensation alternate with representatives of the new. Reading from

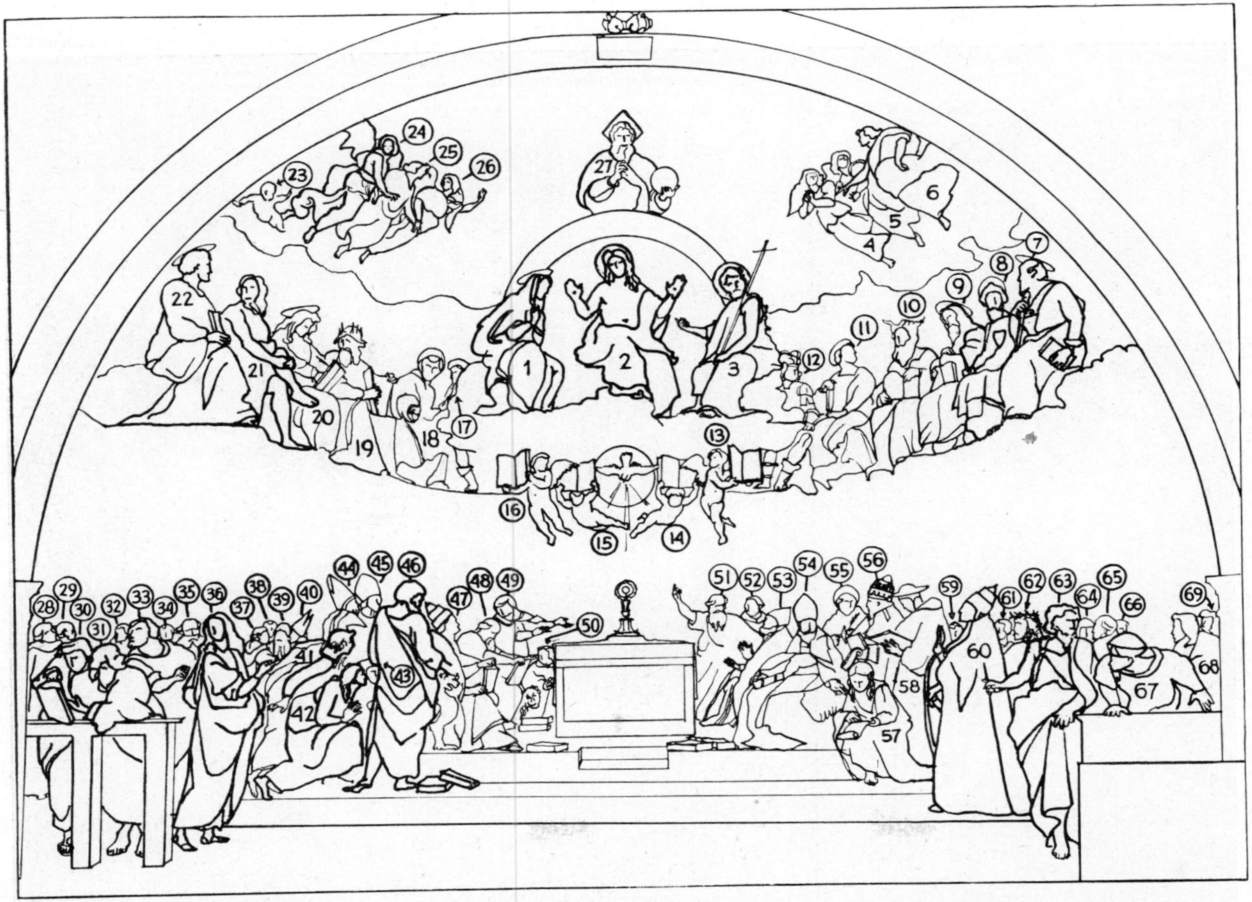

the left: Peter (22), Adam (21), John the Evangelist writing the *Revelation* (20), David playing the harp (19), Stephen or perhaps Laurence (18), Jeremiah or perhaps Martin of Tours (17). Reading from the right: Paul (7), Abraham (8), Moses with the Tablets (9), James the Greater (10), Laurence (11), George or perhaps Judas Maccabeus (12). The bottom register has an altar in the center, with the Host exhibited in a monstrance. The persons round about cannot all be identified; predominantly, they appear to be Christian writers who presumably find a common ground in faith. To the left of the altar is Gregory the Great (47) holding his treatise on Job and looking heavenward. Next to him is Jerome (48) meditating on the Scriptures. To the right are Ambrose (53), Augustine dictating *The City of God* (54), Thomas Aquinas (55), Innocent the 3rd (56), Bonaventura (58), Sixtus the 4th (60); Dante (62), and Savonarola (63). At the extreme left are portraits of Fra Angelico (30) and of Bramante (31).

ANDERSON

Fig. 16.19 Raphael. *The School of Athens.* Rome. Vatican.

Fig. 16.20 (opposite page) Diagram to indicate the identity of the persons who appear in *The School of Athens.*

On the platform, in the middle, stand Plato (1) and Aristotle (2). To the left of them we see Socrates (49) and some of his famous pupils. Xenophon (48) leans against the pilaster. Alcibiades (45) is the young man in armor. The old man (46) listening so intently is probably one of the artisans with whom Socrates loved to talk because their minds were not cluttered with false ideas. From the far left, a young man (42) comes running in, eager to join the discussion. He is delayed by a Sophist (43), while Aeschines (44), the sausage seller who later became a famous orator, raises his arm in protest. The figures to the immediate right of Plato and Aristotle are difficult to identify. Further on, there are some Eclectic philosophers. One of them (13) is busy taking notes, while a Stoic (15) looks at them in contempt. Alone on the steps is Diogenes (28), and to the left Heracleitos (29) and a

fied as Anaxagoras or Xenocrates. The old man writing (33) is Pythagoras. A pupil kneels beside him with the harmonic tables. The man crowded in behind Pythagoras (34) may be Terpander, who had also investigated musical scales. The Arab (35) is probably Averrhoës, who wrote a famous commentary on Aristotle. The jovial man with a wreath around his head (37) is probably Plotinus, to whom an old man (40) brings a pupil (39). At the lower right, we see Bramante (23) playing the part of Archimedes. Ptolemy (21) and Zoroaster (22) stand holding globes. The two young men at the extreme right are Raphael himself (19) and his colleague Sodoma (20). The statues in niches to the upper right and left (not shown in the diagram) are Athena and Apollo. Several contemporary portraits were included, more or less gratuitously with respect to the subject and probably by order of the pope. The boy behind Plotinus (36) has been identified as Frederick of Mantua, who was brought up at the court of Julius the 2nd. The handsome young man (31) is said to be Francesco Maria della Rovere, Duke of Urbino.

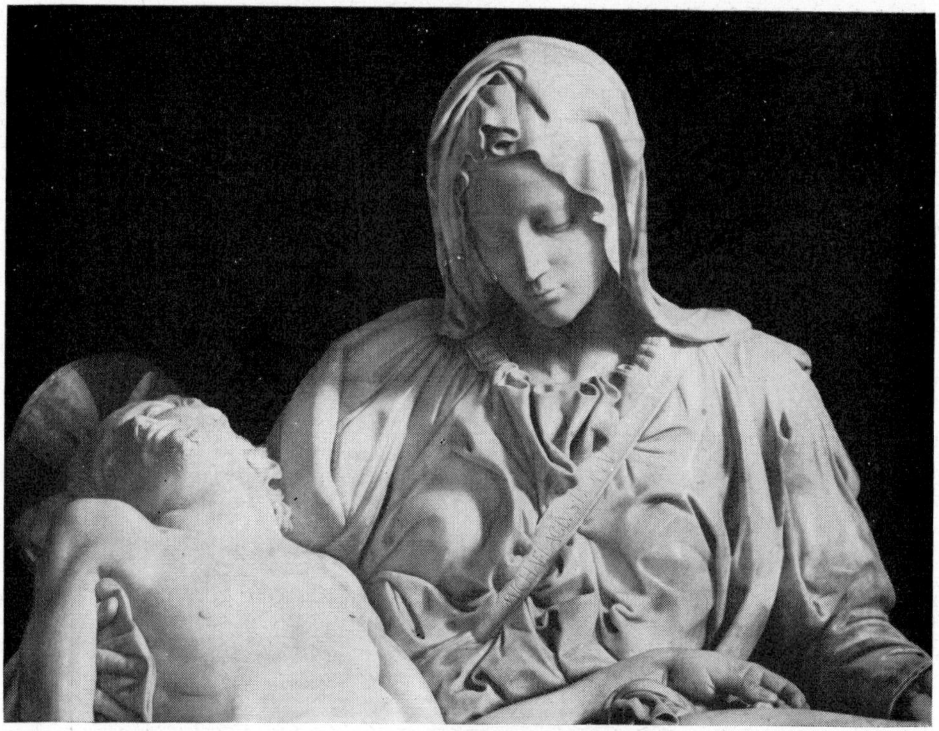

ALINARI Fig. 16.21 Michaelangelo. *Pietà*. Detail. Rome. Saint Peter's. Before 1500.

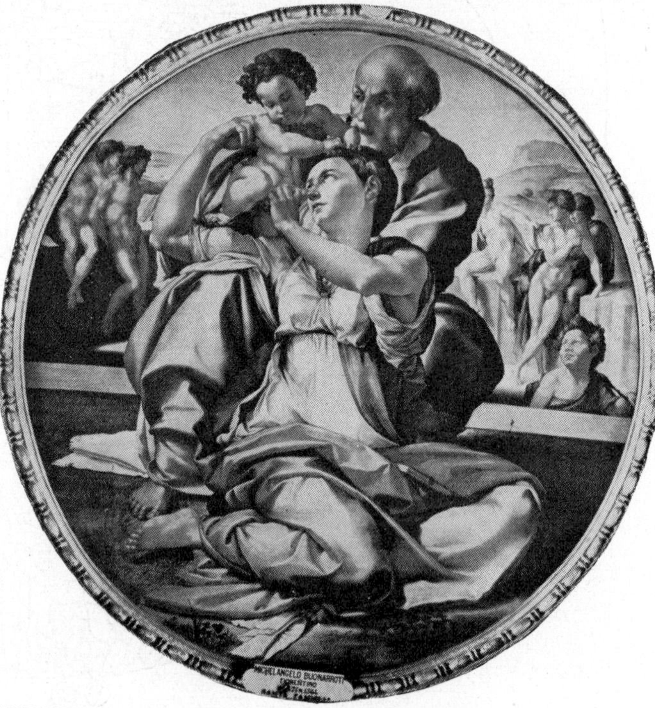

Fig. 16.22 Michaelangelo. *Holy Family*. Florence. Uffizi. About 1505.

ANDERSON

Fig. 16.23 The Tomb of Julius the 2nd as reconstructed by Erwin Panofsky: an attempt to visualize Michaelangelo's original plan.

Figs. 16.24–25 (right) Figures intended for the Tomb of Julius the 2nd.

Paris. Louvre CLARENCE KENNEDY

Florence. Academy ANDERSON

ANDERSON

Figs. 16.26–27 Michaelangelo. Frescoes on the ceiling of the Sistine Chapel in the Vatican. 1508–1512. *Creation of the Sun and Moon,* and *Creation of Adam.*

ANDERSON

Fig. 16.28 Michaelangelo. Tomb of Giuliano Medici, Duke of Nemours. Florence. San Lorenzo. New Sacristy. About 1523 to about 1533. Marble. Approximately 20 feet high.

ANDERSON

Fig. 16.29 Rome. Palace of the Senate. Designed by Michaelangelo. Begun 1538.

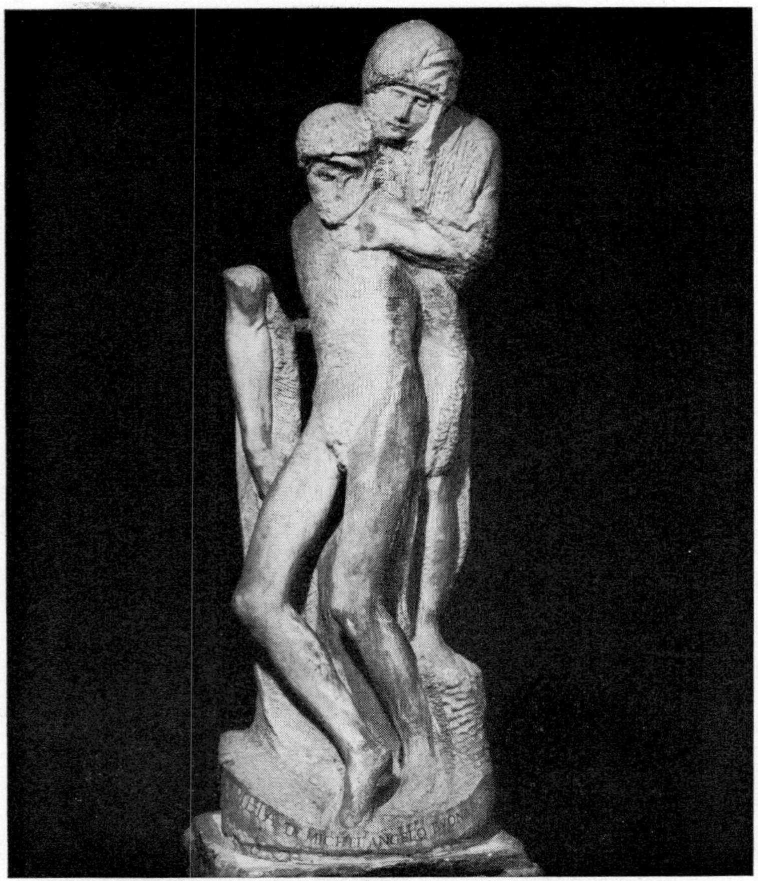

ANDERSON

Fig. 16.30 Michaelangelo. *Pietà.* Rome. Palazzo Rondanini.

Fig. 16.31 Giovanni Bellini. *Madonna and Child.* Cambridge, Massachusetts. Fogg Museum.

ALINARI

Fig. 16.32 Giorgione. *The Sleeping Venus*. Dresden. Gallery. Oil on canvas. 5 feet, 10 inches long by 3 feet, 7 inches high.

ANDERSON

Fig. 16.33 Giorgione. *The Concert*. Florence. Pitti Palace. About 1510. Oil on canvas. 3 feet 6½ inches high.

ANDERSON

Fig. 16.34 Titian. *Sacred and Profane Love*. Rome. Borghese Gallery. About 1514. Oil on canvas. 8 feet, 7 inches long by 3 feet, 6 inches high.

Figs. 16.35–36 Titian. *Bacchus and Ariadne.* London. National Gallery. 1523. Oil on canvas. 5 feet, 9 inches high.

ANDERSON

Fig. 16.37 Titian. *Charles the 5th.* Madrid. Prado. 1548. Oil on canvas. 10 feet, 10¾ inches high.

Fig. 16.38 (below) Titian. *The Deposition.* Venice. Academy. 1573–76.

ANDERSON

Fig. 16.39 (above) Tintoretto. *The Presentation of the Virgin*. Venice. Santa Maria del Orto. 1552–56.

Fig. 16.40 Tintoretto. Detail from *The Miracle of Saint Mark*. Venice. Academy. 1548.

ANDERSON

ANDERSON

Fig. 16.41 Tintoretto. *The Last Supper*. Venice. San Giorgio Maggiore. 1594.

GIRAUDON

Fig. 16.42 Veronese. *The Marriage at Cana*. Paris. Louvre. 1563. Oil on canvas. 32 feet, 5 inches wide by 21 feet, 10 inches high.

Fig. 16.43 Jan Gossaert, called Mabuse. *Adam and Eve*. Berlin. Kaiser Friedrich Museum.

Fig. 16.44 (below) Bosch. *Christ before Pilate*. Princeton University Museum.

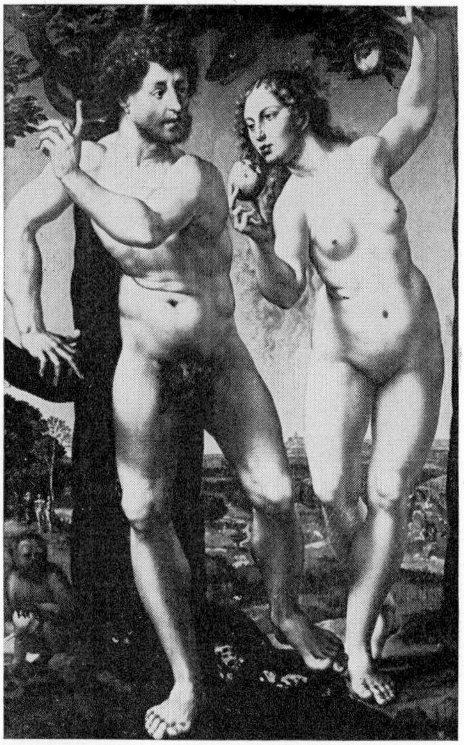

STOEDTNER

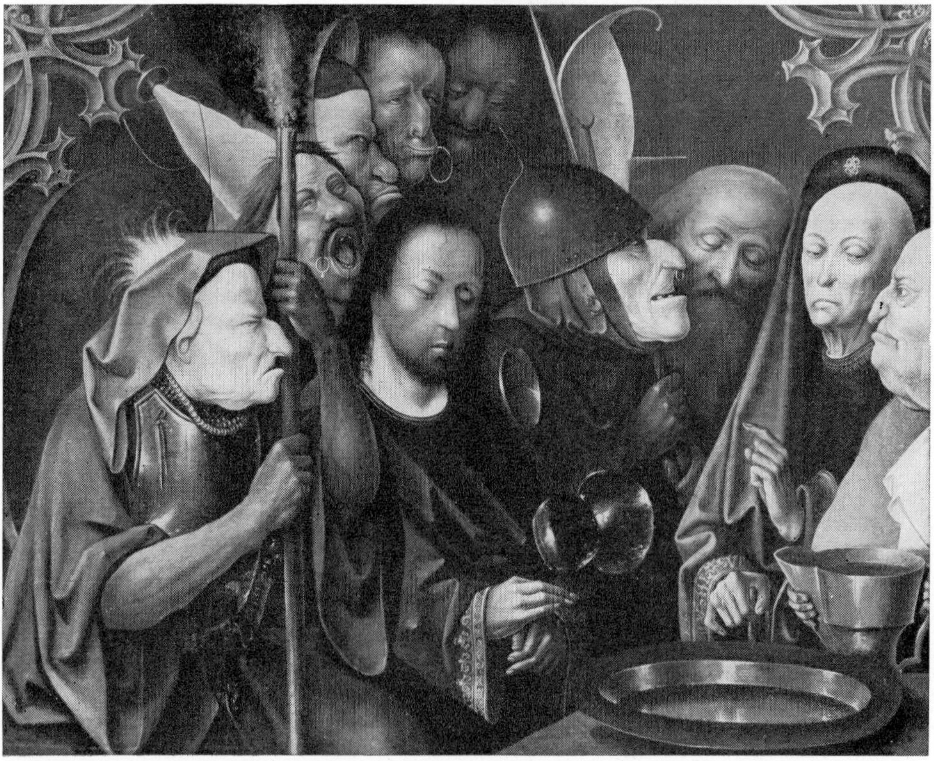

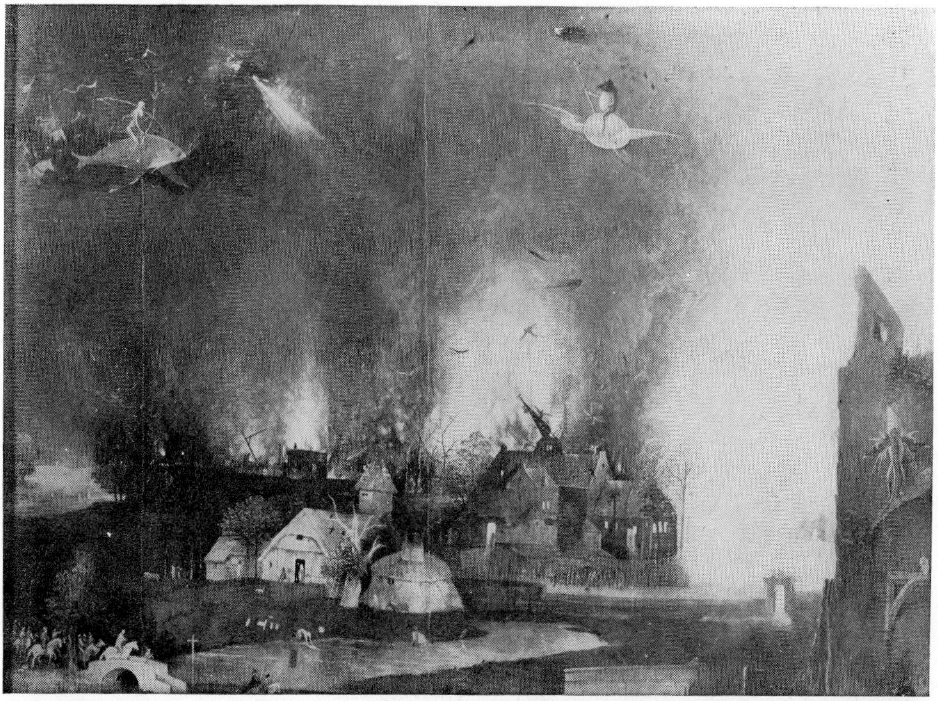

GIRAUDON

BULLOZ

Figs. 16.45–46 Bosch. Details from *The Temptation of Saint Anthony*. Lisbon. National Fine Arts Museum.

Fig. 16.47 Dürer. *Knight, Death, and the Devil*. Engraving. 9¾ by 7¼ inches. 1513. New York. Metropolitan Museum.

Fig. 16.48 Dürer. *Melancholia I*. 1514. New York. Metropolitan Museum.

Fig. 16.49 Dürer. *Saint Jerome in his Study*. Engraving. New York. Metropolitan Museum. 1514.

Fig. 16.50 Dürer. *Saint Anthony*. Engraving. New York. Metropolitan Museum. 1519.

ANDERSON

Fig. 16.51 Brueghel. *The Blind Leading the Blind*. Naples. National Museum. 1568.

Fig. 16.52 Brueghel. Detail from *The Wedding Dance*. Detroit. Institute of Arts. 1566.

BRAUN

Fig. 16.53 Brueghel. *The Way to Golgotha.* Vienna. Kunsthistorisches Museum. 1564. Oil on panel. 66¾ inches wide by 48¾ inches high.

BULLOZ Fig. 16.54 Brueghel. *The Magpie on the Gibbet*. Darmstadt. Museum. 1568.

GIRAUDON Fig. 16.55 Brueghel. *The Big Fish Eat the Little Fish*. Vienna. Albertina.

in his drawing plans for Sant' Andrea at Mantua (Figs. 16.3–4), an extraordinarily important church.

Alberti's presence on the papal staff made the papal visits themselves memorable. The high regard in which he was held at Rome was excelled only by the impression he made everywhere else. His physical attributes did much to make him conspicuous, and thus enhanced the brilliance of his mind. Unbelievable tales are told of his feats of strength and skill. Without repeating them, we can say that much is indicated by this: in an age entirely dependent upon the horse, he was a world-famous horseman. His advice about training and breeding, moreover, was sought far and wide. All in all, he seems to have been the complete embodiment of the Renaissance ideal: the perfect body, the mind of universal genius.

Alberti's Writings

Although usually mentioned as an architect, Alberti often spoke of himself as a painter and sculptor. He surely had a right to, if we may judge from the incisive self-portrait (which exists in three slightly variant versions) done in low relief on a medal (Fig. 16.1). Unfortunately, it is the only thing of the kind from his hand. The buildings he designed all date from his middle age or later, and they number but a handful. It is evident that his original works of art were simply too few to account for the immense respect the man commanded during one of the most brilliant periods of Western civilization. The fact of the matter is that Alberti spent most of his time writing. He wrote poems and plays. He wrote essays on ethics and sociology. But the great work of his life was a monumental exposition of artistic theory. It consists of three parts: the *Della Pittura* (On Painting) of 1435–36, with a dedication to Brunelleschi; the *De Statua* (On Sculpture), which dates from 1464; and the *De Re Aedificatoria* (On the Matter of Architecture), which appears to have been in hand from 1450 to 1472, and was posthumously printed in 1485.

As compared with the works of others who have from time to time written on the subject of art, Alberti's three books were uniquely successful. They are unique in being the words of a man who was himself a great artist — of a man, moreover, who lived in one of the great productive periods, and who knew numerous other artists of world reputation, what they did, how they did it, and what they thought. The value of practical experience has sometimes been overstated, but all highly trained technicians recognize by a kind of instinct the voice of a man who knows what he is talking about. Few of the greater philosophers have had the slightest influence upon the history of art, but Alberti stands as the paramount influence for the entire period between the middle 15th Century and 1900.

Insofar as the artists of the Renaissance were concerned, the most important thing of all was that he purported to furnish them with a philosophy. Artists had never been admitted to the upper orders during the Middle Age (pages 532–533); and with significant exceptions, they still deeply felt the need of a theory to which they might refer. Alberti seemed to explain what they wanted to have made clear; namely, that the manual work they did was directed, not by mere craft rules, but by principles comprehensible only through the intellect. In order to understand how they felt, the reader must try to imagine a society where conceptual thinking was given an altogether arbitrary, but very effective prestige. Respectability itself hinged upon the difference between the liberal and the adulterine — on whether, that is, a man's activities were honorable or menial.

We cannot follow Alberti's thought in detail within the space of the present volume; let the student read over for himself the material so well selected and so well translated in Mrs. Holt's convenient publication.* Those who do may be disconcerted, for Alberti's theoretical writings are by no means so lucid as they ought to be. In perusing any book of an earlier day, one expects to be delayed from time to time by terms which now have a different usage or even a different meaning; but with Alberti, the reader will find himself puzzled by more than vocabulary. As a literary man, he lacked the compositional power he displayed as an architect. As a philosopher, he often did not perceive the inevitable implications of his own ideas. The meat of his thought comes in small pieces, surrounded by a dressing of manners and replete with allusions to matters that are no longer interesting. Nevertheless, anyone who wants to understand the Renaissance will find illumination on every page. Many of the ideas illustrate verbatim borrowing from the classical. Others attack problems that have been in the air since Alberti's time, and still are. Sooner or later, there is an explicit statement of almost every belief, hope, and desire which made the Renaissance operate.

Perhaps the most important idea put forward by Alberti was the notion that beauty was a philosophical reality beyond the reach of taste and fancy. Throughout his writing, that seems to be the electricity which made the motor turn, the invisible power that kept the whole enterprise going. The thought was not far out of line with the Neo-Platonism presently to become popular at Florence (pages 649–654), a fact which gave it an extra chance for survival. Carried to its logical conclusion, such a concept might well have led Alberti in the end to a philosophy not unlike that of modern cubism. As it was, his favorite art was architecture, the nearest thing to complete abstraction socially acceptable in a world committed to representation.

* Elizabeth Gilmore Holt, *Literary Sources of Art History,* Princeton University Press, 1947.

It was imperative, of course, for him to reconcile his highly abstracted theories of beauty with the practical problems of art as he found it. It would have been useless to urge artists to abandon the representative convention (page 539), and ridiculous to suggest that a humanistic society find expression by way of some artistic vehicle other than the human figure (page 522). We do not say that Alberti ever wanted to bring about either; we merely say that the logic of his own philosophy would have forced him in that direction had he followed it out. As a matter of fact, his personal taste was altogether in keeping with that of his contemporaries, and not with his theories. Nature was his goddess. He loved her, and could blame her for nothing. He broke into tears at the sight of a noble tree or pleasant field; and once when sick, he cured himself by looking at a beautiful landscape. We cannot doubt the intensity or the sincerity of his feelings. They were an expression of the most profound faith imaginable, but they surely imposed upon him the necessity of resolving a conflict between his heart and his head.

The task was to find a way to make abstract beauty seem a natural thing. In doing it, he was helped by the recently recovered text of Vitruvius; as stated in an earlier chapter (page 125) it was Alberti who put on the first full-powered effort to arrive once again at the lost canon of proportions of the Greek sculptor Polycleitos. " We have taken the trouble," he said, " to set down the principal measurements of a man. We did not, however, choose this or that single body; but as far as possible, we tried to note and set down in writing the highest beauty scattered, as if in calculated portions, among many bodies. . . . We have chosen a number of bodies considered by the skillful to be the most beautiful, and we have taken the dimensions of each of these. These we compared together, and leaving aside the extreme measurements which were below or above certain limits, we chose out those which the agreement of many cases showed to be the average."

In the end, Alberti compiled a table of dimensions, but the passage just quoted is indeed a tricky one. Every idea in it is slippery. Obviously it says that the *type* is more important than the single manifestation, but what reason was there (except for an apparent classical precedent) to imagine that the arithmetical average would be identical to pure beauty? Such worries did not delay the research, however. Alberti simply declared that his system enabled us to discover nature's intention. He did not raise the question as to whether nature was, or was not, attempting to produce ideal beauty; he simply assumed that such must be the case. Apparently, it did not bother him, either, that calling in " the skillful " betrayed a disloyal bit of doubt on his own part with respect to the infallibility of nature's judgment. But what did not embarrass Alberti disturbed no one else. One by one, Italian painters and sculptors went down the line, and the result was to give High Renaissance art an idealized figure-style (page 714) in considerable contrast with the realism which had remained standard almost until the end of the 15th Century.

Alberti's interest in ideal anatomy was a typical manifestation of his general belief in the perfectibility of mankind, a subject upon which his personal endowments foreordained an exceedingly optimistic view. Nowhere can we read more eloquent and emphatic statements as to what might be accomplished. It was axiomatic in his thinking that man must be impelled upward by the power of his own humanity. With the will for a driving force, he urged men to work upon the raw material of themselves. Because natural gifts are unevenly distributed, he told every man to assess his own, to perfect the good qualities, and restrain the others. Having done that, he told men to live. And what would be the end of such a life? As much, said he, as a man might want to achieve.

Those ideas, if we apply them to the history of the past five centuries, have an endlessly ramified significance. No social force has been more powerful than the belief (essentially an artistic one) that mankind can be improved. Temporary, and perhaps peculiar to the era of the Renaissance and to Italy, was the further belief that important results might be expected within the span of a lifetime. Boundless enthusiasm for boundless achievement was the engine that made Alberti go; and he, more than any other figure of the time, personified the impulse for the innumerable beautified bodies destined to appear in Italian art. He also gave voice to the motive behind countless ensembles of architecture the world over, their cost incalculable, and their purpose to provide a setting for man.

It was the last-mentioned topic — the alteration of the environment for the better — that furnished the pretext for Alberti's book on architecture, which was intended as the crowning achievement of his career. It circulated widely in manuscript before being printed in 1485, or only about twenty years after the very first press had been set up in Italy. In its pages we may read one statement after another having to do with the general theme of the dignity of man.

With an unusual insight into what makes people want to live, Alberti, in the 2nd chapter of Book VI, set forth certain ideas about beauty which deserve wider credence. Beauty, he said, is a great power in society. Not a luxury, not merely worth its cost, but an essential food for the good life. Alberti praised the Greeks and Romans for insisting upon beauty in their laws, their ceremonies, and even their military affairs. He fastened on architecture as the most conspicuous of the arts, indeed the only art whose imagery we cannot escape, and he correctly pointed out that beauty was not an adornment of a building, but a necessity. Without beauty, he declared, the deepest resentments are fomented, and all classes of men get stirred up. There was an irony in his entertaining such a view at such a time, for in spite of the fact that beautiful buildings were continuously going up all over Italy, Italian society could hardly have been more continuously stirred to acts of private and public cruelty and violence. We must remember, however, that Alberti was thinking of the ultimate effect upon mankind of an environment completely made over by the creative achievements of art. His ideas have a curiously familiar ring, because we so often hear exactly the same kind of thing today — and with hardly less irony — whenever housing, city planning, or any other aspect of human welfare may be mentioned.

Alberti's architectural imagination followed out his train of thought into conceptions of epic grandeur. He never forgot the importance of refinement in matters of detail, but his greater vision embraced whole cities. He visualized a metropolis composed according to artistic principles, with each handsome structure an harmonious element in the general design. The government, he thought, should have buildings of the most imposing kind (a conception that looked forward to Versailles and every modern capital). He counseled the leading citizens to maintain establishments proper for their station, warning them at the same time to avoid overt display.

While his background and personality were aristocratic and while he plainly thought society depended upon a creative minority, he had the kindness and consistency to realize that the less gifted majority must also participate in the dignity of man. He carried that idea to its logical conclusion. Hospitals should be provided, he said, to keep cripples and beggars off the street. The relief of suffering, it would seem, was but a secondary motive; the central purpose was to save such persons from a degradation of their human dignity, and to prevent the sight of them from offending others. Going still further, he spoke strongly against contemporary prisons. Conceding that society must confine criminals, he declared that even the vicious were entitled to decent jails.

Sociological preoccupations of the kind just described inevitably suggest that buildings ought to be useful, a point to which Alberti closed the eyes and ears of many readers by his strong emphasis on the value of beauty. It cannot be said, however, that he was guilty of anything worse than faulty weighting of the subject matter. In a number of places, and in different ways, he made it plain that he had no patience with an inconvenient building, or with one that cost more than it ought. His error was to think that practical requirements were easily fulfilled. "The having satisfied necessity," he says in Book VI, Chapter 2, "is a very small matter. . . ." Elsewhere, he urges the architect always to focus his attention on beauty, merely keeping function somewhere in the back of his mind. That thousands have followed this advice is all too evident; but as we have seen, the difference between Alberti's theories and those of the 20th Century is far less than one might suppose.

One of the features which made Alberti's writings acceptable to artists was the fact that he never failed to point out how aesthetic theory might be applied to practical problems. With respect to the creation of an architecture suitable to the dignity of the race, he thought he had an infallible formula. He depended upon Vitruvius. The inelegance of the Vitruvian Latin was doubtless a matter for regret to a man who was himself a stylist in that language, but every word nevertheless seemed golden. Where other classical authors made allusions to art, Vitruvius told how he personally had gone about putting up Roman temples, and gave directions for doing the same. If we consider the temper of the times, it is no wonder Alberti thought he was reading the word of God. At any rate, it would seem that he never discerned a significant difference between the architecture Vitruvius described and the perfect beauty for which his heart yearned.

In addition to what he could glean from Vitruvius, Alberti had expended an immense amount of his own time studying the classical monuments. His observations must not be confused with the mere contemplation of scenery which happened to be enhanced by Roman ruins; it amounted to a thorough course of self-discipline. He examined classical architecture by measuring it, and the data he took home would have enabled a good workman to build the like anywhere. With utter confidence, therefore, he furnished his readers with precise specifications for the classical orders.

When he published his tables for the classical orders, Alberti threw the door open to a more literal interpretation of classicism, to the implications of which we must now turn our attention. The reader will keep in mind, of course, that as explained in another connection (pages 847 ff) a classical revival of any kind is never a simple matter of cause and effect. Because classical Antiquity was no single thing, it is always necessary to know what department of ancient art was, in any particular instance, operating as a guide for the modern artists. We also need to know how thoroughly they understood it, and how strictly they were attempting to copy.

In the case of Alberti, it was the orders as used by the Romans for which he furnished dimensions. He knew nothing of Greek architecture. Neither did anyone else. The entire Renaissance went its way and ran its course, in fact, largely upon inspiration from Rome.

Neither were Alberti's findings final. His book proved to be merely the first in a very long series of similar publications. With respect to the orders, it was actually superseded rather soon by an even more minute analysis published in 1563 by Giacomo Vignola, who also worked for the popes at Rome. Nor was Vignola alone. In 1573, Andrea Palladio, whose country houses in northern Italy set the model for similar houses in England and America, published his monumental *Four Books on Architecture*. These books and others like them set an Italian and Renaissance precedent for similar publication in other countries. Fig. 17.14 is a plate from a typical English volume of the early 18th Century. The names cited are merely suggestive of many others, and the important thing to understand is that each and every one of the architects involved purported to furnish new and better information about classical architecture, plus the very latest ideas about how it might be adapted to the necessities of modern building. Penrose's work at Athens (pages 94–100) merely capped the climax of the custom initiated by Alberti. The origin of the custom, it ought to be added, was Alberti's belief that the good architect must also be a scholar. The extraordinary number of publications resulting is but another index to the fact that his ideas prevailed and endured.

But the full meaning of Alberti's classical research has not even yet been made plain. In the first place, he did not question the authority of the ancients. He assumed that their architecture represented perfection arrived at by centuries of intelligent trial and error. On the face of it, a modern architect would be a fool to repeat their drudgery when he might quite as easily capitalize on their findings, and take up where they left off. His attitude toward the Romans was still further colored by considerations of an imponderable but cogent kind. His classicism, like every other brand of classicism, depended upon the existence of a sincere belief that the ancient world and the men in it were better than the modern world may reasonably expect to be within the measurable future. It is to that faith we refer whenever we speak of classical authority, and it was Alberti who made classical authority all too accessible.

His tables made it easy to copy the Roman orders. In itself, doing so might have been an innocent activity had not the very same tables tacitly labeled as ridiculous any further experiment with the orders. It would hardly be too much to say that they laid the dead hand of the past on architecture itself, stifled the creative imagination, and begot the dullest five centuries in the history of the art. From here on, the reader may look for no more Brunelleschis —or at least not until after the Industrial Revolution of the 19th Century.

Alberti's Buildings

Alberti's travels on Vatican business took him now and again into north Italy, and it was there that he received the commissions for his most important architecture. His relation to the buildings was new and different from what had been customary before. In part, the matter may have been decided by his responsibilities at Rome and by the impossibility of his remaining away for indefinite periods; but his procedure nevertheless reflected a modified conception of the function of the architect. Alberti merely drew the plans. He had a good knowledge of practical construction; but having furnished the design, he left the work to be carried out by others. His custom in that respect has remained the standard usage in Europe and America; and as a philosophical proposition, it will be noted that the net effect was to minimize the adulterine element in building (page 532) and to maximize architecture's role as a liberal art.

At Rimini, Alberti worked for Sigismondo Malatesta. It appears not to have concerned him that the man was the quintessence of Renaissance paganism, or that the commission was to remodel a church originally dedicated to Saint Francis but now intended as a kind of shrine in honor of Sigismondo's mistress Isotta. The fabric of the building was Gothic. Alberti merely undertook to conceal it with an overlay of Renaissance forms. The plans were carried out only in part; and the renovation remains incomplete today. In its day, it was — with reference to the future progress of style — well ahead of its time.

Across the façade, Alberti put a Roman Arch Order (page 219), the first of its kind in modern architecture. Instead of pilasters, he used columns, and he rendered the entablature in ressault (page 220). The heavier proportions and greater relief of the members constituted an important indication of the way Renaissance art was to develop. The remark applies not only to architecture, but to sculpture and painting as well; for where the 15th Century artists tended to deal in line and surface, those of the High Renaissance worked with the mass.

Down the sides of the building (Fig. 16.2), Alberti designed a powerful arcade running the length of the nave. The arches are round. The soffits are very deep. Each arch might be described as a short bay of tunnel vaulting. The supporting verticals are substantial piers of masonry, with rectangular cross-section. The design appears to be derivative from the fabric of the Colosseum at Rome, but the proportions were more carefully studied, and the detail more elegant.

Under each arch, Alberti placed a sarcophagus. Sigismondo and Isotta were to have been similarly entombed on the façade, and these lateral arrangements were meant to accommodate illustrious members of their spectacular court. The custom of putting a sarcophagus under an arch in the thickness of a wall was a very old one, but Alberti's design opened up new vistas in mortuary architecture. His means for expression were completely abstract: mass, line, proportion, light, shadow. Yet he was able to convey an impression as clearly and specifically as it might have been done in words, or by representative art. It is impossible to think of the sarcophagi he designed as coffins where lie the worn out bodies of more or less forgotten dead men. The place was built for heroes; indeed, it is a cenotaph for the concept of greatness.

Sant' Andrea at Mantua was Alberti's most characteristic and influential design (Figs. 16.3–4). He drew the plans for Ludovico Gonzaga, then head of

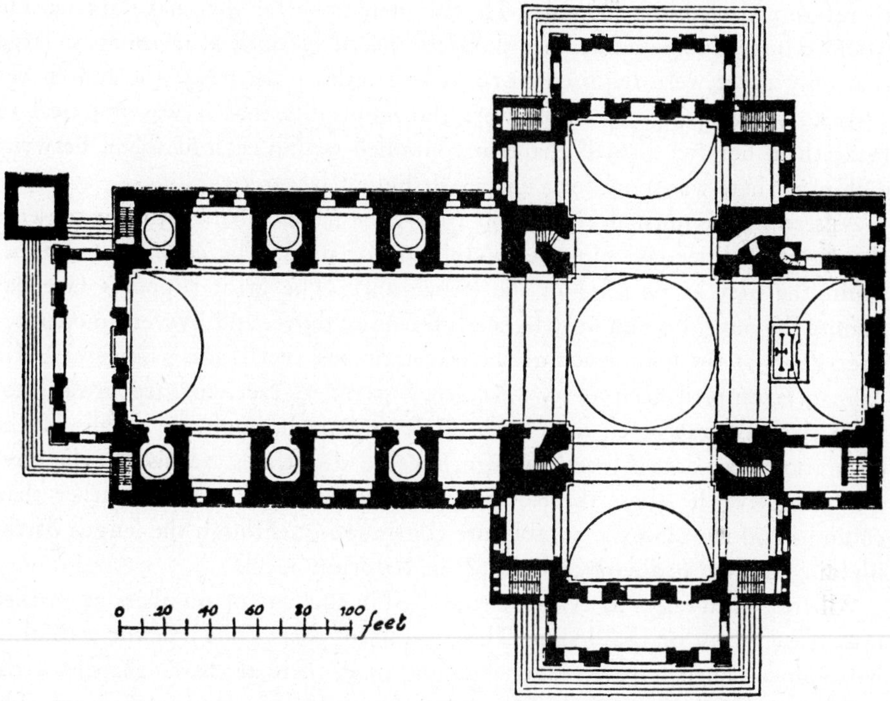

Fig. 16.56 Mantua. Sant' Andrea. Plan.

Mantua's greatest family, and he left the construction to be carried out by the local court architect. Most of the work was done after Alberti's death in 1472. The surface decoration of the interior, typical North Italian work of the period, was not designed by him; it is neither good nor bad. The arrangement of windows in the drum of the dome over the crossing was likewise no plan of his. Otherwise, the church is much as he intended it to be.

The plan (Fig. 16.56) had been predicted by Brunelleschi's Santo Spirito at Florence (Fig. 15.39), and also by the arrangement of several North Italian churches. Sant' Andrea is nevertheless the key monument. It brought earlier experiments to fruition; and while it conforms in a general way to the basilican scheme, it departs therefrom in significant respects. The departure was enough to make it a new type, and the first really successful modification of the traditional Christian church.

Alberti's manifest purpose was to give full expression to the plastic impulse already strong in his earlier work. He wanted a more emphatic modeling for the masonry, and a greater gravity of effect. He also wanted a more definite, more simple, and more lucid moulding of the spatial volume enclosed. For such results, the traditional division of nave and aisles was unsuitable. He therefore canceled out the aisles. He eliminated the familiar nave arcade. He specified instead some immense and closely spaced verticals of masonry, so large that only three were required to run the length of the nave; the fourth belongs to the crossing. So ample were those uprights that it was practical to make them hollow; a small chapel is contained within each of them. Between each pair, there was room for a chapel of slightly larger area.

As seen in the normal view (Fig. 16.4), the nave of Sant' Andrea presents the eye with little else but the modulation of mass. The ceiling is a tunnel vault, the first of its kind in the Renaissance. The great supports face flat against the nave, broken only by a small oculus above, and by very moderate-sized doors at the floor. Each of the larger chapels recalls the passageway of a Roman triumphal arch (Fig. 8.6); they seem, in fact, to face inward toward the nave rather than to open off from it. Although the details of the decoration post-date Alberti's design, the broad outlines are his. As the governing motive, he chose the Roman Arch Order, using pilasters rather than columns and running the entablature continuously through the length of the building at what ordinarily would be the triforium level.

Alberti's study of Vitruvius was reflected in the play of numbers he worked into the rhythm of the design. Three great supports (odd) define a total of half a dozen chapels (even). At the same time, there are three chapels of the small size, and three of the larger (a harmony in terms of odd numbers). The three piers on either side of the nave come into contrast with the four verticals under the crossing; and the total of six piers in the nave is commensurate with four by reference to the module two. Without asserting that such numerical relationships account for Alberti's success, it is evident he was interested in them.

It would be difficult to name another interior so complicated as that of Sant' Andrea which has anything like an equal lucidity of arrangement. By using large members, Alberti was able to use very few of them. When one enters the western doors, the furthest piers stand out almost as clearly as the nearest. The plastic shape of the enclosed space is clear to a degree; and the same may be said of the carved masonry. Such features bespeak the inner spirit of classicism, so perfectly a part of the architect's nature as to be the material of his intuitions. No amount of archaeological learning can tell one how to produce forms like those he designed. The argument from classical authority (furnished by Alberti to lesser men, and for them a narcotic poison) seems for himself to have been an aesthetic food. It would be incorrect to say that Sant' Andrea marked the recapture of Roman architecture. It follows Roman principles, to be sure, but there were never any architects at Rome good enough to design it.

The façade of Sant' Andrea (Fig. 16.3) was hardly less important than the interior. Much criticized because its height does not correspond with the height of the church behind, it is in reality a porch. As such, its function may be understood as simply to dignify the entranceway, and its artistic business is with the man in front, not with the nave behind. Within the limitations of such a scheme, Alberti's design may be considered a notable contribution in the vexed matter of adapting the classical orders to modern buildings (page 109). Originally worked out for temples of one story only, the orders fit nothing else perfectly. Modern architecture, however, almost invariably demands several floors.

Alberti's purpose seems to have been to give the world an academic demonstration to show how those disparate elements might be combined. Somewhat gratuitously (for there is no such division within), he gave himself three stories, and marked them with the aisle doors, and with windows at two levels above. Each window, it will be noted, rises from a horizontal that was kept low in relief. The central entrance is a tunnel vault. Its height is the same as the higher windows to either side, and its shape is marked on the front by a pair of pilasters and a classical moulding around the arch.

Above, around, and through the items of the ensemble, he ran the members of a complete temple front, also rendered in low relief. A pediment and entablature frame in the top of the façade. Beneath are four great Corinthian pilasters running unbroken to the ground. Those latter are of the proper classical proportion for their height. They are thus large in relation to every detail with which they are juxtaposed. Nothing is big enough to compete in any serious way with their vertical strength. They pass upward regardless of the delicate horizontals, and they pull everything together and tie the composition into one.

Any order that runs through several stories is technically described as a *colossal order*. The term has no reference to absolute size, and would be used for the colonnettes of a fireplace if the same fulfilled the condition of running through two or more horizontal divisions. By giving the weight of his authority to the colossal order, Alberti unquestionably furnished Renaissance architecture with a useful compositional resource. Almost any collection of sculpture, openings, and what not can be brought into unity if a colossal order of sufficient strength is merely superimposed. But like everything else that is easy, the device has too often been relied upon to correct mistakes which never should have been made in the first place.

Sant' Andrea was too radical a building to become immediately popular; but in the long run, it exerted a great influence upon Renaissance architecture. Alberti was connected with the Vatican when Nicholas the 5th (regnal dates 1447–55) decided not to repair the ailing Early Christian church of Saint Peter (Fig. 9.21), but to tear it down and build anew. We may fairly infer that Alberti had much to do with swinging the decision against sentiment for the past, and forward toward a grander modern Rome. When at length, Bramante's first plans for the new building were approved by Julius the 2nd (1503), they were plans calling for a church more than a little like Sant' Andrea. Bramante died in 1514, leaving the work only begun. After various false starts with other architects, Michaelangelo was finally put in charge in the year 1546. He revised Bramante's plans to make the immense structure even more like Sant' Andrea (page 747). The example set at Saint Peter's laid down the style for almost all of the smaller churches built in Rome from that date forward. The Church of the Gésu, designed by Vignola and begun in 1568, may be taken as the typical example. The churches of Rome in turn set the type for Baroque and Rococo churches everywhere else. It may fairly be said, in fact, that Alberti's elimination of the nave arcade, with evident improvement in the floor space, very substantially modified the basilican tradition (pages 277–292) to which Europe had so long been unswervingly loyal.

Alberti, Bramante, and the Central Church

Alberti also drew plans for another and less celebrated church at Mantua, and the type he chose for that second building has a special significance. We refer to San Sebastiano, probably designed in 1460. Because Brunelleschi's Santa Maria degli Angeli had never been finished (page 636), San Sebastiano was the first good-sized modern church to be completed on the central plan. Experimentation with the central plan might seem to indicate nothing more than one more revival in an age given to revivals; but knowing what happened afterward, we can see that a considerable movement was underway, with Alberti among the leaders. The difficulty of adapting the central form to the ritual was no less than it ever had been (page 292). What, then, was the appeal?

The answer seems to be twofold. In the first place, as Mr. Nikolaus Pevsner has so well put it in his brief but profound history of architecture, the central building seemed to be the perfect architectural expression of Renaissance individualism.

By standing precisely at the floor's middle point, a man identifies his own body with the axis of the design. He and he alone — for only one man can be there at a time — becomes for the present the creature to whom the governing symmetry refers, the central integer that brings it significance. No other kind or type of artistic composition puts the single personality in a similar position. For the moment, one exists as the absolute focus of everything in view. If the church has nobility of design, the sensation is glorious. If the church is enormous as well, the personality gains scale in proportion with the architecture.

The basilican interior invited no such feelings. Because it embodied the ideas of progression and focus (pages 284–289), it always and inevitably suggested realities beyond the observer's immediate compass. By doing that, the basilica was likely to induce thoughts of man's insignificant stature and philosophical incompleteness — ideas which men like Alberti doubtless recognized as valid, but upon which they did not care to dwell. They preferred, rather, an architecture which corroborated man's confidence in himself. As to what that indicated about the then relations between man and God we need not explain; but as an expression of monarchy over the environment, nothing could excel the central building.

The second reason for the rather sudden popularity of central churches during the Renaissance had to do with a recrudesence of age-old ideas about the symbolic meaning of the domical shape. As made plain by evidence recently brought together and made accessible in Mr. E. Baldwin Smith's monograph on the dome, such notions may be traced back almost as far as the race. The precise symbolism has changed from time to time, but no race has ever become quite so controlled by its head as to disassociate itself completely from the impression that domes, as such, are animate with holy power. As soon as Florentine Neo-Platonism (pages 749–754) started to do its work in Italy, the dome began to be specifically identified with the heaven from which mankind had been banished, and toward which it aspired to climb back. Neo-Platonism also contributed the concept that beauty, especially the beauty of the primeval state of grace and glory, was an abstract and inaccessible ideal.

At any other time in the history of art, such difficult ideas might have received very indifferent treatment in the visual arts, but Italy was then literally full of artists who were thoroughly familiar with the expression of sublime concepts. A number of domes were designed with the deliberate intention of making the appearance, as seen on the interior, suggest heaven in all its transcendent, ineffable, and utter beauty. As a class, the domes of the period are distinguished by a deliberate separation of the dome from the drum (by one method or another) and of the drum from the pendentives beneath — in obvious parallelism with the Platonic scheme of an existence arranged in graded categories, each higher and better than the one beneath. Without doubt, the most perfect realization of such ideas was the dome of Sant' Eligio degli Orifici (Fig. 16.5), which has the same ineluctable fascination as a crystal ball. It was designed by Raphael (pages 727 ff).

Alberti's endorsement of the central type set in motion a whole series of designs. Among the designers involved in the tendency, Bramante was the most important man; and among the centralizing churches he designed, we may mention the so-called " Tempietto " at San Pietro in Montorio, Rome, and Santa Maria della Consolazione at Todi (Fig. 16.6). When Bramante took charge of the works at Saint Peter's, he firmly intended to make the great new building a central church on the Greek cross scheme. When Michaelangelo succeeded Bramante, he had his own ideas about details, but he had no intention of changing the fundamental arrangement of the composition. He died, in fact, without ever imagining that Saint Peter's would not be a central church.

While all that was going on at the capital, sizable central churches were going up in the provinces, of which we may mention San Biagio at Montepulciano, designed by the elder San Gallo and dating from 1518–37. It looked, indeed, as though the basilica had been superseded and as though the central type would be remembered as the chief contribution of High Renaissance architecture.

The popularity of the scheme might, indeed, have endured a very long time had it not been for the Protestant Reformation. That movement, seemingly nonarchitectural in its implications, raised the question as to whether the ideals of the Renaissance had not been responsible, in part at least, for the Protestant defection. The general tenor of opinion at the Council of Trent, which sat from 1545 to 1563 and which was called to start the Counter Reformation, held that the Church should turn its eyes and methods back to the usage of earlier generations. Among those usages was the traditional basilican plan for churches, the appeal of which was strong enough to dictate a fundamental alteration in Saint Peter's itself. Carlo Maderna was therefore employed to ruin Michaelangelo's composition by adding the present extended nave (Fig. 17.9). The work dates from 1606–26; and with it, the central type crossed the great divide into oblivion.

THE ARRIVAL OF THE HIGH RENAISSANCE

While it is hardly possible to exaggerate Alberti's part in starting the High Renaissance, there was a substantial interval between the time his ideas were made public and the time they took effect. We may think of him as a prime mover in calling the new era into being, but the fact is that he was dead before we can note any considerable frequency in the phenomena which marked the arrival of another cultural climate. The actual transition from the Early Renaissance to the High took place during the last quarter of the 15th Century, and we may pause here to note a few of the events and tendencies which made themselves felt, attracted approval, and finally changed the entire scheme of things.

For the art historian, the most conspicuous fact of all was the shift of the cultural capital of Italy from Florence to Rome. That had doubtless been inevitable from the moment when Nicholas the 5th (page 704) decided to build a gigantic new Saint Peter's, but various other happenings predicted the turn of the tide.

Among them was the construction of a new chapel at the Vatican, known as the Sistine Chapel. Aesthetically undistinguished, the room was nevertheless notable for being bigger than almost any other private or semiprivate chamber designed up to that time. It is a tunnel-vaulted oblong measuring 133 feet long, 43 feet wide, and 85 feet high. It was designed with high windows and large areas of wall, doubtless with the idea of providing space for mural painting. The chapel was ready in 1481; and there being no competent painters at Rome, the Pope summoned prominent masters from Umbria and Florence. They painted the pictures which are still there on the side walls, but not one of them had the breadth of style requisite for the task. Botticelli, for example, did three frescoes which are curiously busy with delicate passages, and utterly empty of the monumentality which was needed. Perugino's *Christ Presenting the Keys to Saint Peter* came closest to success; but it, too, merely reached toward the " Grand Style." Obviously, the habits of visualization peculiar to the Early Renaissance were out of keeping with the taste of the incoming era. A new and larger imagery was requisite to fit the scale of the big pictures which alone were appropriate in a more pretentious setting. The men who had grown up in the tradition of 15th Century realism were unable to make the change; but by a kind of instinct, the members of the next artistic generation knew just what to do.

The reign of Julius the 2nd (1505–1513) coincides with the actual achievement of artistic primacy at Rome. That energetic pontiff pushed forward the procrastinated project for the new Saint Peter's. It was he who appointed Bramante architect, with the result that construction commenced in 1506. He was the man who summoned Michaelangelo to Rome to design and build for him a tomb (pages 740–744) which, had it been completed, would have outdone the Mausoleum at Halicarnassus. It was he, also, who commissioned the frescoes of the Sistine Chapel ceiling (pages 744–747). While Michaelangelo was working on that stupendous task, Julius kept Raphael simultaneously at work on the frescoes of the Vatican Stanze, the paintings which forever guarantee their author's place in history (pages 729–734).

The activity just described is to be put in contrast with the handful of commissions which had emanated from the Vatican during the previous two generations. When at length the popes had become artistically self-conscious, there was, as noted, scarcely an artist at Rome with calibre enough to undertake a major enterprise; but at the turn of the century, outsiders came there not to sojourn but to stay. Bramante, Raphael, and Michaelangelo are the most famous men who did that, but innumerable artists of lesser imagination but excellent capacity were also resident. Raphael, for example, constantly maintained a staff of at least fifty first-class technicians to assist him; without their help, he could hardly have begun to accomplish the work now known by his name. The men were recruited from all over Italy, and the very fact that competent persons could be found in numerous places is significant. It means that the local schools, always existing almost everywhere on the peninsula, had now become mature, and were closing the lead hitherto maintained by Florence.

The centralization of the Renaissance at Rome was concomitant with the spread of the Renaissance to the rest of Europe — for it was during the early 16th Century that Italy began to furnish the modern world with a cultural leadership similar and comparable to that exerted by Athens during later Antiquity. As indicated by Ficino's immense correspondence (page 650), there already existed a considerable tendency for northern intellectuals to turn their faces toward Italy; but, as compared with the 15th Century, the era of the High Renaissance is chiefly different for the appearance all over Europe of men who not only equalled the learning and genius of the Italians, but thought in just the same way and belonged to the same culture. The Dutchman Erasmus (1466?–1536), who published the first modern edition of Aristotle and worked on more accurate translations of the scriptures, has been remembered ever since as epitomizing in his person everything that was good in the humanism of the period. Copernicus (1473–1543), a Pole who knew Rome well but spent most of his life in East Prussia, may be cited as the author of the most influential publication of the entire era. His *De revolutionibus orbium colestium* (1543) settled once and for all the perennially disputed question of whether the sun was or was not the center of the universe. Contemporary with such men and upon terms of personal friendship with them were men of similar calibre and similar interests in other lands — Thomas More and John Colet, for example, merely to mention two names which will be familiar to the English-speaking student. By pursuing the subject further, we would rapidly find ourselves building up a picture of a Europe which more and more subscribed to a common philosophy of life with its creative center in Italy. For the matter of our present interest, it is necessary to add that Italian standards in art followed Italian standards of every other kind: the 16th Century was the period when almost all of the European world consciously cast off the Late Gothic and adopted the style of the Renaissance.

The first half of the 16th Century is the only time when Germany produced artists of world importance. The best of them retained a certain measure of northern taste, but all were strongly conscious of the Renaissance. As compared with the great Italians, Albrecht Dürer (pages 774–779) and Peter Brueghel (pages 779–785) stand out in history as men of similar mind and equal calibre.

France deliberately imported the Italian style as a result of the military expeditions into Italy, beginning with the invasion of 1494 (page 662). The wing added to the château of Blois in 1503 by Louis the 12th is generally mentioned as the first French monument in the new manner; but actually, it amounts merely to a sobering of the later Gothic. The same can be said with similar force for the more elaborate additions put up by Francis the 1st between 1505 and 1519, but it was that very same Francis who invited Leonardo to France (page 709). The great man died there in 1519 without having accomplished much, but his coming was reflective of a conscious policy. Francis imported other Italians, mostly second-string men, and some of them stayed. From that beginning sprang the exotic School of Fontainebleau, a conscious negation of the native and northern tradition.

Spain, like the rest of continental Europe, embraced the Renaissance during the first generation of the 16th Century. Her painters had hitherto been stylistically dependent upon Flanders (page 617). They now cultivated generalized forms and triangular compositions like those of Raphael (Fig. 16.16), and retained that habit until the coming of the Baroque. Even the exuberant Plateresque architecture, one of the great achievements of the Late Gothic, modulated its details toward the classical, and sobered down (Figs. 12.32–34).

Only in England did the tide of the Renaissance fail to sweep all before it. Henry the 8th (regnal dates 1509–1547) is frequently nominated as the first Renaissance king of England, but that is more nearly correct with respect to his orientation and outlook than it is of English art. Hampton Court (1515–40) and other buildings often catalogued as "English Renaissance" fit the characterization in date rather than style.

Thus in England — and especially in England because of the greater vitality with which native taste survived — we may note a major oddity of modern culture: the coexistence in the same society of a native and vulgar tradition beside an elegant and imported one. In Italy, the contrast is unknown, and its tensions never felt. Peasant and scholar alike inherit direct from Latinity. But in all northern countries, we are constantly confronted by a double standard. Chaucer on the one hand, and Milton on the other. Or Hogarth's truculent assertion of a British art resistant to continental standards as exemplified by Sir Anthony Van Dyck (page 764) and his followers.

The impression made upon Alberti by his long residence at Rome was symptomatic of the impression Rome now made on everybody. Florence had begun its artistic tradition with Giotto, and Florentine artists had continued in the progressive spirit, with an eye always on the future and a reputation yet to make. The shift to Rome was a shift to another world. Rome was and is overwhelmingly a city of the past. Ancient ruins of immense size loom up in every vista. To this day, no one can point to their equal; and the world hardly offers a similarly wholesale demonstration of scale combined with permanence. It was inevitable that artists would be affected by the spectacle. In subtle ways, their motivation changed from originality to emulation. A number of single incidents, none crucial or definitive in itself, contributed each in its own way to the state of mind described.

In 1506, the celebrated *Laocoön* group (Fig. 6.20) was dug up. Michelangelo himself examined it with minute care. His admiration was boundless. The experience doubtless turned his attention to the Pergamene division of ancient art (pages 170–176 ff) from which he drew the inspiration for his later figure-style. The *Belvedere Torso* (Figs. 6.21–22), a less conspicuous example of the same kind, had been in the possession of the Colonna family as early as the 1430's, but first came to public attention when Clement the 7th (regnal dates 1523–34) brought it to the Vatican. To those monuments, it is perhaps worthwhile to add the name of the *Farnese Hercules,* which came to light in 1540.

Archaeological activity is always interesting; but in the flamboyant musculature of those particular antiquities, Italian artists sensed something lacking in their own art. Apparently they felt that the statues revealed man's most complete and perfect physical development. All artists with a taste for force and power were impelled toward experiments along the same line. Even those, like Leonardo and Raphael, who had no special liking for power as such, became profoundly interested in the elaborate twisting of the body, the contrapposto, which has become almost a synonym for the figure-style of the

High Renaissance — as, indeed, it had been a synonym for the particular class of ancient statue then brought so much to the fore.

If, in our imagination, we add the news of lesser finds to such famous bits of excavation, it is easy to see that the recovery of Antiquity was a lively topic at Rome, and kept on as a lively topic for a long while. Other things that were going on also contributed to the same effect, and gave men added reason to be conscious of Roman greatness.

When, for instance, it was desired to move the Vatican Obelisk from the Circus of Nero, where it stood, to its present position in the middle of the Piazza San Pietro, no one knew how to do it. A conference of experts was summoned from all over Italy. They talked for weeks. Finally, the scheme presented by Domenico Fontana was adopted. After impressively elaborate preparations, he brought the job off in 1586. An immense amount of public interest came to a focus as the work went on. Everyone who watched was doubtless impressed by the fact that the Roman engineers, acting under orders from Caligula, had in 41 A.D. brought the very same obelisk all the way from Heliopolis on the Nile Delta, across the sea, up the Tiber, and into its place about 250 yards from the spot to which Fontana had now moved it.

The events mentioned are but incidents in history. They will nevertheless suggest why so many artists of the highest personal accomplishment were willing to accept classical art as a guide. Some were even willing to accept it as a book of wise and just rules which, if faithfully followed, might be counted upon to yield success. Alberti had suggested such a course when he published his tables for the ancient orders (page 698), and the general nature of architecture made it easy for builders to follow his advice — especially those who wished to play safe. Painters and sculptors inevitably had problems which precluded so direct and precise a following of ancient rules, but they too became as classical as it was practical for them to be. In fact, one of the great over-all differences which signalized the advent of the High Renaissance was a turning away from nature, and a yearning for an idealized art comparable to that of Antiquity.

The increased classicism of the High Renaissance, cogent though it was, did not exist in its own right, but as an expression of certain spiritual needs which had become better understood and more openly asserted. The whole era had its genesis in a severe and more profound belief in the dignity of man. For that, the thought and writing of Alberti had prepared the way, but society had started early to move in the direction he seemed to indicate.

In spite of Alberti's generous concern for the masses of the population, one can scarcely find a page in his work which does not in some way or other suggest aristocracy. For leadership, safety, and progress, it seems implicit in what he said that mankind must rely not upon all the people, but upon certain selected persons of superior powers.

During the second half of the 15th Century, Italian society had in fact tended to become more and more a court society — royal, noble, or ecclesiastical as the local conditions might require. In general, what was true in Italy was true everywhere; the famous Italian families merely furnished a pattern of life that was copied in other lands. The net result was to concentrate significance within the upper social orders, and the tendency to do so invited the expenditure of a prodigious amount of thought upon the general subject of superiority. What qualities gave a man a right to membership in the privileged circle? What behavior was appropriate for the members thereof as between themselves, and in their contacts with the world outside?

Machiavelli's *The Prince* (1514) was an attempt to set forth a political method. Baldassare Castiglione's *The Courtier* (1527) was the most notable among a great many books which attempted to explore the question of how responsible persons ought to act in social situations. Alberti himself, it will be remembered, had raised the question of propriety with respect to architecture (page 697) and other physical surroundings. Palladio's writings and his architectural practice were an even more thoroughgoing application of the same ideas. In every instance, it was not the generality to whom the discussion was directed, but the better man, supposedly in a position to make far-reaching choices.

The aristocratic mode of life in Italy became identical with the ideal of dignity, and produced the standards of decorum which have been stereotyped in Western Europe and all its cultural derivatives. Solemnity was the emotion essential to the new era; people began to take themselves and the progress of their lives with high seriousness. Movement of the body, if acceptable under the new system, was thought best and wisest when it partook of the cadence of a slow dance. The vocabulary, it came to be thought, ought to be carefully chosen, and the voice used like a musical instrument.

Above all, the new manners called for an impregnable adequacy on the part and in the person of the lady and gentleman. Grace of voice and of posture should, it was thought, be achieved without apparent effort. Ideally, such attributes existed within the character, were unconsciously possessed and employed, might even be instinctive. Overt elegance, either in dress, in bearing, or in one's belongings, logically became an offense; but the worst offense of all would be to prove inadequate to a situation, to be compelled to scramble for control of self and environment and thus to transgress the rhythm and tempo of the gracious life.

The Neo-Platonic elements in the new concept of the dignity of man will be evident without specific citation; the ideal man of the High Renaissance would be the man who had completed the course of self-improvement recommended by Alberti and Ficino. A few persons, in the opinion of their contemporaries, actually exemplified the ideal in their own persons. Alberti was such a man, Leonardo and Raphael were others; but the person most often mentioned as the quintessential gentleman of the era was Frederick of Montefeltro, Duke of Urbino, of whom there is a fine portrait by Piero della Francesca. It is notable, however, that the praise directed toward Frederick makes an identity between the excellence of the man and the consistency with which his actions might be explained by reference to a code of behavior. It would be unintelligible, of course, to suggest a code of behavior unless it be assumed that the innumerable situations arising in life are known, can be classified according to type, and the best action prescribed for each. Once that truth is comprehended, the causal connection between Neo-Platonism and the High Renaissance becomes obvious.

Unquestionably the people of the High Renaissance had good reason for self-respect. Equally without cavil, we must concede that they had a philosophy which moved the population of Europe far on the road toward achievement of humanity, and added much to Western civilization. But as reflected in the history of art, the increasingly elevated concepts entertained by the controlling members of society resulted in the elimination of certain points of view hitherto notable as fonts of creation. Direct delight in nature, the chief inspiration of 15th-Century art, tended to pass out of the emotional pattern. The visual facts of the world no longer evoked the same response, and shortly ceased to furnish an adequate reason for painting and sculpture. At first thought, Leonardo's notebooks (pages 716–720) might seem to contradict the statement just made; but in fact they sustain it: they were and remained entirely private; the work that made his reputation was typical of the new era.

Subject matter took on an increasing depth of significance as the High Renaissance developed and came into its own. Any theme that might be used for a picture, it presently appeared, had to be a theme of cosmic importance. An excellent example was Raphael's misnamed *Disputà* (Fig. 16.17), where the painter undertook no less than a visual demonstration of the truth of Transubstantiation, opened heaven before our eyes, and made Christ above the pictorial counterpart of the host on the altar below. It was a remarkable thing that such paintings were even attempted. Even more amazing is the fact that conceptions of similar magnitude were repeatedly and successfully brought off during the Italian 16th Century. Most incredible of all was the magnificent clarity, both visual and intellectual, with which stupendous themes were presented. In the case of the Raphael just mentioned, it takes no wit to draw the inference that the wafer of bread is indeed Christ's body, and that the miracle of the Incarnation is repeated every time we perform the sacrament.

The grandeur of view which permeated contemporary society challenged and extended the artistic genius with which Italy was so generously endowed at the time. In the character of the 16th-Century Italian artist, nicety of distinction may be said to have supplied something like the motivation furnished by realism a century before. Having once chosen a theme with judicious consideration of its suitability and import, artists and patrons alike put forth a terrific effort toward the analysis and understanding of every detail. Within the drama and meaning of the subject, they sought to recognize the significant facts and actions. To the limit of practical possibility, artistic emphasis was reserved for such; and by the same logic, everything extraneous to the grand import of the matter in hand was sternly suppressed, even eliminated entirely, regardless of its truth in fact. The end product of the process was an iconography more complicated and elaborate than ever before. Easel pictures containing two or three figures are often inexplicable unless one has at his finger tips a great fund of erudite lore. As for the large wall paintings of the High Renaissance, it usually takes half a day merely to identify the characters depicted, and relate each in the briefest way to the central theme.

The tendency just described lent a lofty abstraction even to the smallest works of High Renaissance art (Fig. 16.22). As for the large ones, they often reached the level of the cosmic and sublime. The very same tendency was intimately operative in changing the figure-style, a topic we shall presently consider in detail, but certain general aspects of which are apposite for mention here. With respect to the human figure, Italian art, as of 1475 and after, found itself in much the same position as the art of Greece during the generation when the Transitional Period became the Great Age. Realistic studies were, of course, no longer an end in themselves. Personality was less interesting than certain more universal qualities of which the figure might be made expressive. Both realism and personality were therefore eliminated even in portraiture. Instead, the figure was refined, idealized, and generalized into a superior type. Nor was the idealization concerned with the body alone; almost every human being who appears in 16th-Century Italian art seems to be thinking an important thought, or to be under the spell of profound insight. For the expression of such content (and in keeping with the contemporary taste for codifying everything under the sun) an entire system of pose and gesture was built up for the use of painters and sculptors, and presently became very nearly standardized. As was bound to happen, a writer ultimately appeared to set the matter forth in print. In 1593, a man named Cesare Ripa published a book called *Iconologia* — in effect, a quasi-official catalogue purporting to furnish artists with the right imagery for a great variety of situations and subjects. The headings were arranged alphabetically; and if the reader cares to spend an hour paging through, he will find brief articles, each illustrated by a clumsy woodcut showing an appropriate personification for *Ambition, Benignity, Confidence, Fecundity, Infelicity, Penitence, Tragedy,* and several hundred other rather abstract conceptions. It seems odd that such a volume, to our notions both dull and presumptuous, could have enjoyed any currency among creative artists of the first rank; but it appears to have proved useful. Otherwise, why were there a number of editions, published in several different places?

The increased formality in behavior and the more analytical study of classical art also and inevitably evoked extreme formalism in the arrangement of works of art. Except for instances here and there and noted from time to time in the chapters above, composition as such had received very little systematic study at any period prior to the later 15th Century. It then became a matter of general interest. By 1550 or thereabouts, the subject was as well understood as it ever has been, and nobody has added much to what was then a matter of general knowledge in Italy.

In keeping with their classical heritage (pages 109–110), the 16th-Century artists relied upon geometry as the governing principle of design. Buildings were almost always given a symmetrical plan on the Roman model (page 222). Pictures and groups of sculpture were universally composed according to the organic system of the Greeks (pages 65–66). As in Greek design, the geometry was (so long as the High Renaissance lasted) kept simple and lucid. Small paintings were generally arranged with reference to the vertical plane of the canvas only. Most of them compose on a triangular pattern (Figs. 16.13,15–16). The circle and half circle came next in popularity (Fig. 16.22), followed in statistical frequency by arrangements of an elliptical nature. The immense wall paintings which were popular during the 16th Century often included a very large number of figures. Space had to be represented in order to accommodate them, and the problem of arrangement was complicated thereby. The typical solution is once again illustrated by Raphael's *Disputà* (Fig. 16.17). It was geometrical and organic; but the governing geometrical figures — in that instance, half circles — lie in the horizontal plane rather than the vertical, and refer more to the space of the picture than to its surface.

LEONARDO DA VINCI

Leonardo da Vinci (1452–1519) was the man who created the style of the High Renaissance as applied to painting and sculpture. His relation to the new period was analogous to the service performed by Donatello for the artists of the 15th Century; but in spite of his great influence upon European art, it is a mistake to think of him as an artist. He spent only a small part of his time painting, and the catalogue of his surviving pictures, according to Mr. Berenson's latest list, numbers only nineteen examples, some of which are challenged by other critics and several of which are not entirely by Leonardo's hand. A more accurate and fairer view of this great man's career would make it necessary for us to describe him as a scientist and engineer. Inasmuch as our business is with his art, we cannot explore his other achievements in detail. The reader will find them well described in General Parsons' book (page 631), the only one so far published by an author competent to follow Leonardo's scientific thought. A summary is appropriate here, however; indeed, without it, we could have no notion of the tremendous mentality behind the pictures.

In all its endless ramifications, Leonardo's genius seems to have derived from a single magnificent act of the imagination: he adopted, if indeed he did not invent, the experimental point of view. "If we doubt the certainty of everything that comes to us through the senses," we find him saying in his notes, "how much more should we doubt those things that cannot be tested by the senses. . . ." That position was probably unique at the time. It was not generally understood in a society devoted to the authority of the Classics, a fact which made some of the humanists consider Leonardo ill-educated, giving rise to a rather resentful note which says, "Although I may not, like them, be able to quote other authors, I rely on that which is much greater and more worthy: on experience, the mistress of their masters." Leonardo, that is to say, would accept nothing as fact until proved right by rigid experiment or sustained observation of a more general sort. In all his writings, the underlying thought was the existence of fixed and demonstrable law which, if known, would permit man to conduct his affairs according to sure rules.

Proceeding on such assumptions, he spent his life accumulating evidence. His powers of observation were perhaps the greatest ever vested in a human being, and his acumen was unbelievable. It was his habit to note things down, with or without illustrative drawings, and we have inherited a substantial part of his records in the form of the so-called *Notebooks*. They amount to about 5,300 pages, and more may well turn up when, if ever, the libraries and archives of Europe are adequately catalogued.

Considerable mystery of an artificial kind surrounds his methods for recording what he observed. Being more or less ambidextrous like any good painter, and naturally left-handed, he preferred to write backwards. The cypher can be resolved merely by reversing the text in the mirror, and by understanding the abbreviations systematically used. Some of the latter, it must be conceded, still defy the student, and many passages remain unintelligible. With the help of the drawings, however, we can be sure of enough to establish him as a man about two centuries ahead of his time.

In the field of physics, he understood the pull toward the earth's center which Newton later reduced to a formula and introduced as the Law of Gravity. He investigated the acceleration of falling bodies, the trajectory of projectiles, and centrifugal force. He was familiar with the theory of the conservation of energy, and he put down what we know as the formula for work. His thoughts embraced molecular attraction and the idea of the vacuum, and looked forward to the atom and the electron.

As a painter, Leonardo naturally took a special interest in optics. Discarding the fantastic theory of sight entertained from the remote time of Pythagoras, he correctly reasoned that vision amounted to a triple play between the eye, the object under view, and the light source. He established the law that the angle of incidence of a light ray is equal to the angle of reflection, understood stereoscopic vision and the other geometric aspects of seeing, and was close to the theory of wave-motion by which today we explain both light and sound.

His investigations of color, undertaken along with linear perspective as a basis for a projected *Treatise on Painting*, led him into direct spectral investigation. He made himself a spectroscope, and hoped to develop from his findings something like a scientific basis for the art of representation. He got far enough with the project to note down some minute directions for the control of graded-shadows in painting. In connection with his anatomical investigations (he dissected the human eye, and recognized the function of its parts), he discovered the so-called *negative afterimage*, now believed to be a photochemical reaction of the eye, and the phenomenon used as the starting point for all color-theories deriving from the idea of complementaries.

As a geologist, Leonardo understood the difference between the earth's geographical center and its center of gravity. He recognized the stratification of the surface, the existence of fossils, and the general alteration of topography by erosion and deposit. From this, he was able to correct the contemporary notion that the world was about 5,000 years old.

As to whether he came into personal contact with Copernicus during the latter's sojourn at Rome and in North Italy, we cannot say, but the notes make it plain he understood and accepted the Copernican theory of a helio-central universe. He knew, moreover, that the earth's orbit was an ellipse and that its axis was inclined to the plane of its revolution. Although the telescope is commonly believed a Dutch invention of about 1608, we find in Leonardo's notes a singular and unexplained reference to making " glasses to see the Moon magnified."

His botany was, if anything, more remarkable still. He discovered the relation between tree-rings and the passage of the years, and noted their variation in response to annual tricks and changes in the weather. He also observed and explained the phenomenon known as phylotaxis, that spiralling of branches and leaves which so simply and marvelously arranges for the sunning and ventilation of each leaf, and the systematic delivery of rain drops from leaf to leaf all the way down.

Most of the findings so far mentioned have now been more adequately explored or left behind; but the same statement cannot be made with regard to Leonardo's anatomical drawings. They date a full generation earlier than the eminent anatomist Vesalius, and are the first accurate and competent illustrations of their kind. As the only ones ever made in quantity by an artist who ranks with the great, they are still among the best. It is a matter of record that Leonardo frequented the hospitals and performed autopsies. In the course of such work, he recognized hardening of the arteries and was very close to Harvey's ultimate explanation of the circulatory system. His greatest anatomical researches, however, would appear to be those of a mechanical nature: he was the first to explore and explain the true location of various bones and muscles, and the tensions and leverages of movement.

In these modern days, the impracticality of the pure scientist often furnishes the theme for humorous anecdote; few such men have the least idea how to make their findings of any use at all. By exception to what seems a rule of the game, Leonardo was both pure scientist and engineer.

He instinctively recognized the vital importance of bulk transport, thus anticipating the ideas of Admiral Mahan and Sir Halford Mackinder. Much of his active life, therefore, was devoted to the development of canals — until the railroad the one and only economical way to move freight across country. While working for the Sforzas he made a study of the hydraulic problems of the Lombard plane. He later did hydraulic engineering in the Arno valley, and one strong reason for his being called to France in 1516 was the hope that he might construct a canal to connect Tours, Amboise, and Lyon. He did not invent (as has been claimed) the lock, but he did improve it. Many locks in daily use today are mechanically inferior to those we see in his drawings.

As a mechanical engineer, Leonardo designed a great many machines. Most of them are the same in principle as modern machines, and many are better than anything put into service at any date previous to the later 19th Century. It must be understood that many of them were built and operated, although most seem never to have got beyond the paper plans. A particularly interesting series are the rolling-mills. Leonardo appears to have designed them to roll out long iron bars which he then welded together to make barrels for cannon, a process necessary because of the unreliability of large castings. We have drawings for one of them. It was driven by a horizontal water turbine through worm reduction gears, one of two stages and one of three, thus giving a differential motion to rolls and bar. The notes say that this particular machine is his twenty-second of the same kind, and give formulas for determining the power required — the latter, he says, having been worked out after thirteen machines had been tried.

Smaller guns he was accustomed to cast, and developed new ways for keeping the bore central with the circumference of the barrel. His designs for firearms include multibarrelled weapons (Fig.16.11), elevation screws, field pieces on wheels, and breach loaders. Mechanically, most of them are greatly superior to everything in general use up to the time of the American Civil War, and better than most in use then. A mere machinist never made a good piece, and those accustomed to weapons will recognize in Leonardo's work the touch of the master.

The drawings show that he was not only interested in the guns themselves, but in the long-term implications of gunpowder. The multibarrelled field pieces indicate a grasp of the principle of fire-power. There are drawings illustrating barrage fire, and plans for forts which include cushioning material for the walls — a principle used by Japanese engineeers in World War II, and one that proved vexing for the American artillery.

Most famous of all are Leonardo's plans for an airplane. There can be no doubt that he would have been the first man to fly if, like the Wright brothers, he had possessed the gasoline engine. Less well known but equally ingenious are the drawings for a helicopter (Fig. 16.10) and several essays in the field of naval architecture. One of the latter is specially brilliant: a streamlined boat, shaped very nearly in accordance with William Froude's 19th-Century findings which established the principle that each following square foot of wetted surface causes less resistance than the one immediately ahead of it — hence the exaggerated length of our modern liners.

In attempting to comprehend the meaning of all this research, probably the greatest total of original work ever accomplished by one man, it is important to appreciate that Leonardo's methods were instinctive, direct, and by rule of thumb. He tried many times to settle upon formulas covering such matters as the strength of beams, the capacity of columns, the breaking strength of wire and rope, and the pressure of water upon the surface of a lock gate. But in all such determination he was foreclosed from success by primitive mathematics. He could not figure out such comparatively simple variations, for instance, as those which come in terms of the square and the cube. That, perhaps, is one of the reasons why his immense and brilliant labors proved almost totally unproductive.

It is obvious that he contemplated a certain number of publications. For one of them, the *Treatise on Painting*, we have some parts that look like fair copy, but an incredible disorder is the only arrangement discernible in most of the material. The painful conclusion is forced upon us that Leonardo either lacked the inclination or the capacity to bring his work into a state of synthesis.

He kept the notebooks with him as long as he lived. No one knows how many there may have been originally; a man who called on him at Amboise in 1517 describes them as "an endless number of volumes." When Leonardo died in 1519, his will directed that all his papers go to Francesco Melzi, a friend and associate. Melzi took them to Milan, and cherished them until he himself died in 1570. Melzi's heirs had no notion of their value. After making one or two ineffectual attempts to realize small sums for them, the later Melzi consigned the collection to the attic, and gave individual volumes away to friends and acquaintances who happened to be interested. Thus the great collection of papers became divided. Many must have been lost. Those that remain are scattered among the various museums and libraries of the world, some private and some public.

Had Leonardo's findings become even moderately well known in the early 16th Century, world history would differ from the story we know. Among other things, it seems almost impossible that the Industrial Revolution would have delayed its arrival until the 19th Century. But although the value of the papers became recognized early enough for Napoleon to order some of them transferred from the Ambrosiana at Milan to the Bibliothèque Nationale, and for the Italians to demand them back in 1815, almost everybody who saw the material looked upon it as a curiosity — hardly art and hardly science. The stupendous nature of the research has been generally understood only very recently; and, tragically enough, only after the bulk of it had been repeated by successful but more plodding men.

With respect to his artistic education, Leonardo could scarcely have been more fortunate. He was apprenticed to Andrea Verrocchio (1435–88). Although enrolled in the painter's guild under his own name in 1472, Leonardo appears to have remained as a member of Verrocchio's establishment until at least as late as 1477.

Verrocchio's personality is known to us mostly by inference, but the inferences are unusually strong and clear. Only a few works can with certainty be attached to his name, but those few are among the best that ever came out of Italy. Most famous, of course, is the bronze equestrian statue of *Bartolommeo Colleoni* at Venice, on which the master was at work from about 1481 until his death. It is surely one of the two best equestrian monuments in the history of art, excelling the *Gattamelata* in force, dash, and drama while remaining inferior to it in connotations and overtones. The bronze *David* (1476) in the Bargello is another important example. Where can one go to find a better treatment of youth in all its unformed beauty, its lithe grace, and its gawky strength-wasting movements?

From the standpoint of stylistic evolution, an even more important and revealing work is the *Boy with a Dolphin* (Figs. 16.7–9), the diminutive fountain figure which for a very long time has impressed its gaiety upon the ponderous architecture of the courtyard of the Palazzo Vecchio. The little statue might be said to put its small foot squarely on the divide between the 15th Century and the High Renaissance. Nothing could be more definitively typical of the earlier period than so realistic an appreciation of the infant and his direct methods for enjoying life. At the same time, both the design and the technique exhibit a self-conscious, calculating aesthetics rare at the date of the statue, but altogether typical of the 16th Century.

The nature of the medium had evidently been much explored; the peculiar virtues of bronze have, in fact, been exploited with the utmost sagacity. The capacity of the material to render textures was worked to the limit. Its tensile strength permitted the artist to poise the tiny figure upon a single delicate support, and invited him to indulge in a tour de force of projections which, in a more brittle material, would have been folly.

More remarkable still is the composition. The pose, seemingly so innocent and spontaneous, is in fact a contrapposto no less studied and elaborate than that of the *Nike of Samothrace* (Fig. 6.16) and quite worthy of Michaelangelo. More interesting still is the fact that the figure, unlike the great majority of statues both ancient and modern, was designed not to be viewed from one angle only, but omnifacially. As our three views indicate, one may walk round and round it without finding a single station from which it does not compose with a subtle rhythm of statics and dynamics.

The entire performance explains why Verrocchio was at once the most admired and best loved master at Florence, and why his home was like a club for the leading artists and thinkers of the city. With respect to our present business of historical transition, the central point to be grasped is the academic nature of his outlook. To the direct and natural enjoyment of content and expression, he added a new interest: the aesthetics of method. In addition to all its other virtues, his *Boy with a Dolphin* is a learned experiment, an attempt to explore still further the possibilities of what can and what may not be done with sculpture, and to demonstrate whatever findings the artist was able to make. The conception of the work of art as a problem to be solved, and of its permanent value in terms of such solution, was new at the time. It has been commonplace since.

Leonardo's debt to his eminent master was immense. It was nevertheless reserved for the pupil to realize and declare, as it were, the style of the High Renaissance. For convenience of explanation, we may discuss his contribution under two headings, taking easel pictures as one department of activity and mural painting as another.

Among the easel pictures, the first that belongs unequivocally to the High Renaissance is the *Virgin of the Rocks* (Fig. 16.13). The painting exists in two versions. The one in Paris probably belonged to Francis the 1st, and is listed in an early catalogue of the pictures at Fontainebleau. The one in London came to England in 1796 as the property of Gavin Hamilton. Superficially in better condition and more attractive, the latter is considerably less refined in the matter of drawing. The supposition is that the London picture was executed by members of Leonardo's staff, probably to replace the one now in the Louvre, which the master seems to have taken with him to France in 1516.

The classical precedent used by Leonardo and other High Renaissance painters has too rarely been pointed out. It was the so-called Alexandrian formula (pages 164–167), one of the two recognizable divisions of Hellenistic pictorial art. The distinguishing feature was to bring the human figures forward on the stage, putting them in front of the landscape background, as it were, rather than within it.

Among the extant examples of classical painting, not one shows anything like the command over composition demonstrated by Leonardo. As seen on the surface of the panel, the figure group falls within a triangular outline. If we become conscious of the represented space, we begin to feel the design as pyramidal. In either instance, the principle of order is geometrical, and the form chosen, simple, lucid, symmetrical, and stable.

The lucidity of the arrangement is perhaps better than that achieved by any other method of design, but it comes at a price. The four figures shown form a compact, self-contained, organic group; attention is so thoroughly concentrated within its area that the setting seldom receives its fair share of inspection. But the setting is important. We may not dismiss it as a mere memory of some young mother resting out the heat of the day in a cool spot. As usual with High Renaissance art, everything seen in the picture has a meaning.

In the opinion of Mr. Edgar Wind, the gloomy rocks, suggestive as they are of caves and dark chambers, stand for the rock of the Holy Sepulchre, and thus for the sacrifice of Christ. If that is so, we can make something of the gestures. The infant John can be thought of as symbolizing the human race for whom Christ gave his life. The Virgin's caressing him with her right hand endorses the sacrifice; her left hand, held like a halo over the baby Jesus, blesses him. The pointing finger of the angel to the right drives home the lesson.

The adult figures in the *Virgin of the Rocks* realize the standards of the High Renaissance less perfectly than some Leonardo painted later, which we shall discuss presently; but a comparison of the babies with those of Donatello (Fig. 15.13), or with Verrocchio's fountain figure (Figs. 16.7–9) will prove in itself a complete survey of the difference between the two periods. Both of Leonardo's children take poses indicative of mature religious feeling. John kneels in transfigured adoration. The little Christ is as full of authority as he is soft and young. He raises his right hand in a gesture of blessing of which the Pope himself might be proud. The motions represented are, in fact, utterly unlike the impulsive actions normal among children. So are the poses. The Savior, for instance, rests on his left hand, turns at the waist, and raises the right with an utter completeness of nervous and physical adequacy. On earth, we witness such things only when some great athlete has taken holy orders and risen to high office in the hierarchy. The ceremonial nature of High Renaissance art could hardly be exemplified better.

The *Virgin of the Rocks,* like the *Mona Lisa,* is overlaid with much dirt and varnish. Hence, we experience a submarine effect where a more brilliant luminosity once reigned; and for that reason, any remarks about Leonardo's employment of light and shadow must be made and accepted with extreme caution. It is safe enough to say, however, that he felt inclined to depart somewhat from the Mode of Relief (pages 582–586) typical of earlier Italian painting. He was among the first in Italy to shift over to the oil vehicle, which as we have seen (page 614) invited broader and darker shadows. As one of the most accurate observers of natural fact who ever lived, he must have been even more aware than we are that contemporary methods of painting did not in the least correspond with the action of light in the visible world; but it is difficult to entertain the notion that he intended either to abandon expression through mass and form, or to work toward the Mode of the Total Visual Effect (pages 580–582).

Leonardo's interest in light and shadow, we may fairly guess, was primarily emotional: he perceived that shadowy areas were in themselves mysterious, and illuminated areas revealing. In addition, he doubtless felt inclined toward the broader rhythms which could be developed with stronger contrasts. His method made each individual field of light (or dark) larger in relation to the total surface of the picture. Thus as convexities took the light and hollows fell into shadow (node or accent as the case might be) the alternation gained a scale and authority rarely encountered before. The eye was delayed longer by each successive obscurity and illumination, and the tempo of the rhythm was slowed down. In contrast with the dancing lights and darks common in 15th Century painting, the impression given was of something more splendid and imposing.

The lighting of any mass, human or otherwise, is of course inseparable from its modeling. Insofar as the new style depended upon the realization of mass, its idiom was mass in the full round. Left to his own devices, the architect of the High Renaissance expressed himself by plastic means, as we have seen (page 702). The sculptors of the same period turned as naturally to statuary in the round, rather than to the low relief of Donatello and his followers (page 619). Leonardo did the same. When we speak conversationally of " the broader effect " he cultivated, we mean not only the rhythm of the values as described in the last paragraph, but the sense that the figures are stipulated to exist free-standing in space.

All of the elements just cited came into synthesis in Leonardo's *Virgin and Child with Saint Anne* (Fig. 16.15). Not a finished painting, but a *cartoon* (a monochrome drawing prepared as a rehearsal for a painting), the work might at first seem unsuitable as a basis for generalization; but on second thought, the reader will see that nothing could be more useful for our purpose. The drawing doubtless put forward whatever the artist himself considered essential; and when he made it, he gave himself no chance to become distracted by secondary thoughts and accessory notions.

The cartoon is extraordinarily useful as a demonstration of the figure-style which was to become generally typical of the age. The two adult women are shown in the fullness of maturity. One would put Mary's age at 35 or older, and her weight at 140 pounds. A substantial layer of soft flesh underlies the delicate complexion; beneath its ample contours, the angularity of the skeleton is lost. The shoulders are large, and the bust deep.

Neither youthful nor active, such a woman would be incapable of sustained physical exertion, and yet her body is vividly alive. With the studied ease of a dancer, she twists at the waist, slightly lifts the left knee, and bends the torso gently forward. If not full of action, the pose is certainly full of grace. We may rightly infer that the picture presents the Madonna as a lady of standing. Her life, unless appearances deceive, would be a judiciously tasteful routine, and a certain cadence and repose would mark every procedure in which she might engage.

To render the clothing of such a figure with the curious particularity of a century earlier would have been impertinent. The artist's intention in that matter is made more baldly plain in the drawing than it might be in a completed painting, but the trend of the style is obvious. Details are completely lost in the darks; and by contrast to the busy little folds so usual in Early Renaissance art, we are given nothing but the grander undulations of the drapery. As to the nature of the costume, one can say only that it must have been made of heavy material. The cloth responds to the movement of the limbs, but remains static until the wearer alters position again. There is no indication as to the construction of the garments, or how they were buttoned, tied, or otherwise held in place. As compared to earlier work, the difference is once again as between specificity and generalization.

The much celebrated *Last Supper* in the refectory of Santa Maria delle Grazie at Milan was unquestionably Leonardo's greatest achievement in the field of art, and the earliest complete and perfect realization of High Renaissance painting. Such pictures reflect better than anything else the ideals of the period. They were grand in size, grand in style, and grand in conception.

The work started, so far as we can tell, in 1495. Luca Pacioli, in a publication dating from February 1498, spoke of it as though it were complete. From that date onward, its history is sad in the telling. Because he was philosophically unable to accept the bold finality of fresco painting, Leonardo wanted a medium that might be worked and reworked. Most unwisely, he attempted to employ an experimental technique for this important commission. He tried to waterproof the wall behind the painting, and he then proceeded to work in some combination of tempera, oil, and varnish. The experiment proved a disastrous failure. As early as 1517, the picture was already in a ruinous condition. Vasari saw it in 1566, by which time it was a muddle of blotches. Some eighty years later, a visitor noted that one could not even make out the subject. Numerous restorations have taken place; there were at least four during the 18th Century alone. A cleaning of 1908 helped somewhat; but during World War II, the roof suffered bomb damage, and the picture was exposed to the elements. The harm then done can scarcely be a matter for mourning because every speck of paint in view was of the 18th Century at the earliest.

In spite of all such misfortunes and mischances, the great picture continues to haunt the Western imagination. By reference to drawings by Leonardo and his staff, Mr. Edgar Wind and others have been able to visualize the original to some extent. We may not retrace their studies here; suffice it to say that the over-all effect of their findings has been to refine the drawing and to correct the facial expression of individual heads — both items being intolerably bad in all extant reproductions after "the original." It will be obvious that the painting is unsuitable for appearance in any book plate of practical size. In the remarks below we shall confine ourselves, therefore, to comment of the sort which will prove useful for understanding the theory which governed the great wall paintings of the period.

The setting was indoors, with the table of the Last Supper parallel to the picture plane. Christ sat in the center, with the Apostles on either hand. Emphasis upon the central figure was insured in two ways. First, the head of the Savior was put in silhouette against an open doorway at the far end of the chamber. Secondly, his head was placed at the vanishing point, and the location of the vanishing point was emphatically pointed out by an extra measure of beams in the ceiling, and other architectural lines. The scheme of the composition, it will be seen, had more to do with the arrangement of things on the horizontal plane of the stage plan than with the vertical surface of the painting — a condition that was destined to become typical of every large picture.

As usual in High Renaissance art, Leonardo made a masterly choice of the point of time. He chose the instant when Christ said, "Verily, verily, I say unto you that one of you shall betray me!" At that moment, shock was made to run outward from the center of the table, being felt less and less violently by the disciples further away until the farthest of them felt the need to gesture back inward toward the center as though to make certain of what they thought they had heard. Judas alone did not gesticulate. Not isolated on the opposite side of the table as had been usual in earlier versions of the subject (Fig. 14.1), he was isolated by his guilty knowledge. Leonardo showed him as sitting in studied calm, almost with unconcern, dissimulating by a simple refusal to become excited.

The method of the composition also became strictly usual during the High Renaissance. It was the Greek organic method (pages 65–66); but no other demonstration thereof, either ancient or modern, more perfectly realized all the possibilities of that excellent system. The diversity was great, and the unity intense. The physical arrangement was complete in itself and inseparable from the drama by reference to which it had cause and effect.

RAPHAEL

The brilliance of Raphael's career is manifest from its brevity. He was born at Urbino in 1483, worked at Perugia from 1500 to 1504, at Florence from 1504 to 1508, and at Rome from 1508 until his death in 1520.

When he left Urbino, he was a boyishly charming provincial painter. The *Dream of a Knight,* now in the National Gallery in London, comes from that time. At Perugia, he worked on the staff of Perugino, a master the world had already passed by. It was nevertheless no small achievement for the youthful Raphael to gain, almost at once and almost without effort, a complete command over Perugino's methods for representing deep vistas of space, and Perugino's quiet excellence in the figure-style of the 15th Century. From that second period of Raphael's career come the *Marriage of the Virgin* in the Brera Gallery at Milan and the *Colonna Altarpiece* in New York.

Realizing that Perugia was also a small town. Raphael went to Florence at the age of twenty-one. He arrived just at the moment when Leonardo and Michaelangelo simultaneously put on public exhibition the full-scale cartoons that were intended to eventuate in some great frescoes for the council chamber of the Palazzo Vecchio. Lost, and known to us only by indirect evidence, each was to commemorate a battle in which Florentine arms had gained memorable distinction. All indications characterize the two battle pieces, singly and together, as a veritable apotheosis of what the High Renaissance had to offer: dazzling technique, epic subject matter, force and power communicated with dramatic clarity hitherto unheard of.

Raphael's natural gifts were lyric. Grandeur had to date been foreign to his art; but once again, he performed a spectacular act of assimilation. He set out to master the "Grand Style." By doing so, he illustrated both his genius and such weakness as can be urged against him. The willingness to make the change indicated a certain flexibility of temperament common among popular artists, and alien to the character of figures like Giotto, Donatello, and Michaelangelo. Raphael's error can best be illustrated by such pictures as the *Entombment* of the Borghese collection at Rome. He labored infinitely, it is said, over the composition, the gesticulation, and the musculature of the figures; but in the end, he produced a watered drink.

While admittedly requisite for certain themes, violence of action and feeling did not suit his temperament. Distinguished in his private life for lovableness and gentle manners, he was at his best when painting in a softer vein. It was fortunate, therefore, that he made easel pictures of the Madonna a specialty while at Florence. His work immediately became popular, and he had a great number of orders. As a result, he produced a whole class of paintings which are known collectively as the *Florentine Madonnas;* one of them appears in Fig. 16.16. A description of one fits them all, though no two are alike. In fact, no other painter has ever maintained better standards of freshness and variety while continuing to manipulate a set formula.

The setting is usually out of doors. Neither cold nor heat obtrude themselves upon our attention. The air is still and salubrious. Nature, as Raphael presented her, was a tranquil, compassionate power offering much to love and nothing to fear. Landscapes of the same kind had been Perugino's special stock in trade, but the figure-style and the pyramidal composition came from Leonardo. Raphael made both his own; they became so thoroughly his own, in fact, that he rather than Leonardo is usually cited as the definitive painter of the period.

The *Florentine Madonnas* were the best-liked paintings of their generation, and they remain the best-known and most popular Madonnas in existence. It is not too much to say that most of the European family gets its visual image of the Madonna from those pictures. It is nevertheless common to hear serious and responsible critics attack the reputation of the whole class, and of Raphael. Objection cannot be maintained if it takes off from a technical platform, or from considerations of abstract design: Raphael was superb in both departments. There is legitimate complaint, however, about the way he manipulated the theme. He made a questionable appeal when he decided to surmount an opulent Leonardesque anatomy with the face of a simple, childish girl. While it is also to be supposed that the Madonna was young, healthy, gentle, modest, and that her maternal passion expressed itself in a decorous way, paintings which celebrate those qualities alone neglect history and close out innumerable connotations. The character of Mary is hardly a fit subject for light and sentimental treatment. Her career was tragic and supreme. To make it anything else is to deprive her of meaning. One suspects Raphael, in fact, of a studied policy calculated never to displease.

When Julius the 2nd called Raphael to Rome in 1508, the great Vatican program of artistic investment was already well under way. Michaelangelo was at work on the frescoes of the Sistine Chapel ceiling (pages 744 ff), and Bramante had made significant progress on the new Saint Peter's. Raphael, at that point, was merely a successful young artist who had yet to be awarded a single major commission. Bramante, it is believed, recommended him to the Pope; no matter what predictions he made when doing so, they fell radically short of the truth the immediate future was to open up. There is no parallel for Raphael's success at Rome. The Pope already had numerous artists on the ground. Most of them were men of standing. Some were men of fame. Within an unbelievably short time, almost all were summarily dismissed, or made subordinate to Raphael. Much of their completed work was ripped from the walls, and instructions were issued Raphael to fill the spaces with work of his own. Bramante and Michaelangelo were the only important men to survive the purge. The latter was perennially suspicious and hostile, but there is almost nothing to suggest that Raphael had conducted a malicious campaign for preferment. The amazing thing is the cordial regard which surrounded his name. His superior abilities seem simply to have been conceded by men who might have been his enemies, and his genius in human relations made it possible for him to organize and direct the work of a great corps of mature artists who normally would have been competitors. Such developments seem specially remarkable in view of Raphael's appearance. His face, even during his thirties, remained adolescent and unformed. He had the uncertain stance of a delicate boy. He nevertheless seems to have made upon everyone who knew or saw him an impression of prodigious ability. There was no limit to his resources of energy, patience, and creation. Everything he touched went fast and wonderfully well, and he did it all with such ease that there seemed to be no limit to what he could undertake.

His most important commission and greatest success at Rome began when the Pope assigned him the task of decorating the so-called "Vatican Stanze," a series of connecting rooms on an upper floor of one wing in the Vatican complex. The plan was to maintain a certain degree of system in the choice of subject matter. In general, the theme was High Renaissance Christianity as made manifest by significant instances in the ancient and modern history of the Roman Church and by the flowering of humanistic culture.

Raphael's first-hand contribution was largely limited to the *Stanza della Segnatura*, so called because the room was often used for the ceremonial signing of documents and for meetings of the *Segnatura di Grazia*, a papal court of justice. The chamber is architecturally undistinguished. It has a vaulted ceiling and measures about 30 by 35 feet on the floor. On the ceiling, Raphael put four round medallions containing personifications of *Theology*, *Poetry*, *Philosophy*, and *Jurisprudence*. Corresponding to them on the four walls below are: the *Disputà* (Fig. 16.17) beneath *Theology*, *The School of Athens* (Fig. 16.19) beneath *Philosophy*, the *Parnassus* under *Poetry*, and under *Jurisprudence*, the personified virtues associated with the operation of justice: *Force*, *Prudence*, and *Moderation*.

Labored in the telling, ponderous and perhaps even tedious in fact, the iconography just summarized becomes a clear statement if we reflect upon it. Necessarily expressed in broadest generalization, does it not come close to being a succinct declaration of the conceptions which have controlled European culture since the Renaissance? A notable point in the ensemble is the even treatment, pictorially and otherwise, given to each subject. The others are in no manner subordinated to *Theology,* and we may conclude that the papal court of the moment felt that the world had arrived on a new plateau. Traditional religion, it would appear, was expected to remain as a great and essential part of the modern orientation; but the resources of secular philosophy and the richness of classical learning were also thought essential. To such, obvious necessity demanded the addition of a decent measure of social regularity as summed up in the institution of the law.

By universal consent, the *Disputà* and *The School of Athens* stand not only as Raphael's greatest pictures, but as the most felicitous expression ever attained in the style of the High Renaissance. The *Disputà* (Fig. 16.17) was the earlier of the two. The name is a mistake. It seems to have come into colloquial use during some period when the complexities of the iconography were not understood, and because certain gestures are similar to those used in debate. As indicated by our previous citation of the picture (page 713) there is no debate at all. In fact, the very idea of debate is opposite to the whole affair, the intention of which was to make people see the truth of the dogma of Transubstantiation.

There can be no doubt that each of the many figures was intended to represent a particular personage, but accurate records do not exist to certify every identity beyond a reasonable doubt. Our diagram (Fig. 16.18) gives the probable identities, some of which are suggested by familiar physical types standard for certain characters and others by attributes like David's harp and Jerome's lion. It will be understood that variant readings exist, but they all indicate that the persons seen in heaven with Christ come from Biblical history, while those on earth around the altar come from the annals of the medieval church.

Although painting on a flat field in a square room, Raphael chose to make the picture simulate the semidome of an Early Christian apse (page 287). His doing so is but another indication that the members of the Renaissance thought that the basilicas were classical monuments. It will be noted also that the resemblance does not stop with the familiar appearance; the theme involves a glimpse into heaven and thus repeats the supernatural setting standard in those earliest days of the faith.

While we can have no doubt that Raphael had it in mind to emulate the solemn dignity of such apses as that of Santa Pudenziana (Fig. 9.25), he had learned his lesson well from Leonardo, and he had at his disposal an art of composition unknown during the Middle Ages. As seen in black and white, the three horizontal registers appear more separate than they are in fact; the apparent fault is corrected in the original by color harmonies. By the date of this painting, Leonardo's resort to the vanishing point was the common property of all artists; everybody was using it as he had done to focus attention where desired. No one ever applied the principle more boldly, however, than Raphael did when working out this particular composition. By putting the wafer in its monstrance precisely at the spot of convergence, he succeeded in centralizing the entire ensemble around an exceedingly small area on the surface of the picture. The history of painting contains no parallel for the performance, but there was a good reason for resorting to extreme measures. The bits of bread consumed in the ceremony of the Eucharist are small and ordinary and do not, as a matter of fact, change in texture or taste in the course of the service. The only thing that makes them important is the miracle which is believed to occur: the attributes of the wafer remain constant, but its substance has become divine. It takes great faith to comprehend what has happened, and it took great art for Raphael to present a visual demonstration of so beautiful and so intangible a reality.

In *The School of Athens* (Figs. 16.19–20) Raphael painted the picture which is probably the greatest produced during the Renaissance. The quality of greatness derives from a combination of things. The pictorial mechanics are superb. The iconography is of an intellectual profundity that can be appreciated only by the serious student, and only then after study. The physical relationships of the figures to each other, and of all the figures to the setting, complies in miraculous fashion with the correspondence or contrast in the concepts and systems for which they, as persons, stand. Emotionally the content is mature and elevated beyond almost all else in the history of Western painting; if it is possible to comprehend philosophy through the feelings, one can do it by a study of *The School of Athens.*

So complicated a work of art demands a small explanatory volume of its own. As with the *Disputà,* much depends upon the identity of this figure and that, and there are many questions outstanding. The best brief essay available will be found in Baedeker's *Handbook for Rome.* A longer and better treatment was included by Eugène Müntz in his great work on the Renaissance, now all too seldom remembered. As this is written, Mr. Edgar Wind has in preparation a monograph which will summarize all the important suggestions in something like final form. Referring the reader to our own diagram (Fig. 16.20) for details, we shall confine ourselves below to such generalization as seems reliable and just.

Philosophy is the subject of the picture; but the word meant more in 1509 than it does now. It included everything taught in the universities, and it also included every science, every art, and every other activity that brought the rational faculty into operation. The subject matter is correctly understood, therefore, as a celebration of the earthly accomplishments of man: his physical productions and his perfection of himself.

Lucretius had spoken of "the temples raised by philosophy," an idea which doubtless suggested to Raphael the use of architecture for a setting. In primitive times, building had been the art of shelter; but in periods of high civilization, architecture meant what Alberti had so grandly imagined that it might and ought to be: it was the better environment for a race that knew dignity, the majestic symbol of man's reasoned control over the hostile forces of nature.

Because of Raphael's friendship with Bramante, it has often been suggested that the building we see here is Saint Peter's as Bramante would have built it. That is probable; but it is equally probable that Bramante got his ideas from Raphael. Why else would the latter have been appointed as superintendent of the works after Bramante died in 1514? All such matters are speculative, and however we fancy to work them out, the church in Raphael's painting is a better church than the overbearing one actually built by Michaelangelo. Scale, in Raphael's design, was rendered easy by grace, and the oppressive weight of the vaulting was lightened by glimpses into the sky. The magnificent space of the nave was made more inspiring by the openings out into the air; the interior atmosphere thus gained the light, life, and movement of all outdoors.

It is hardly possible to say too much or to think too much about the setting as Raphael designed it, for the setting carries more meaning than the figures. No one can hesitate in ascribing pre-eminence to the two who stand at the vanishing point, centered on the stage in such a place. The elderly Plato is one (the face is perhaps an idealized portrait of Leonardo); he carries a copy of the *Timaeus,* and he points upward to indicate the locus and source of wisdom. Aristotle is the other man. He is appropriately represented in vigorous middle age; he carries a copy of his *Ethics,* and gestures in dignified remonstrance toward the world of men where all the daily choices must be made and the practical decisions taken.

Representatives of the abstract and practical sciences fall into an easy elliptical arrangement outward and downward on either hand. Except for a few contemporary portraits, every character is classical. There also seems to have been a governing sense of history in the arrangement. Pythagoras (6th Century B.C.) is at the lower left, and Archimedes (died 212 B.C.) at the lower right; apparently those two were thought of as the beginning and the end of the Greek School.

It will also be noted from the diagram that the men famous for practical achievements are in general placed on the lower levels, and that we tend to climb upward before reaching the men who symbolize pure reason. But there are subtle distinctions over and above that obvious one. Old Socrates, it will be seen, still feels he must argue his point, while Plato's gesture is above and beyond contention: having produced the most perfect synthesis yet achieved by the human intellect, he merely expounds his doctrine.

Certain recent critics have refused to believe that Raphael was personally responsible for the philosophical erudition demonstrated in *The School of Athens*. The notion is even current that good artists, taking them as a class, never have been, and never ought to be interested in such matters. Such a view is mistaken, and derives from several sources, all rather recent.

The 19th-Century movement known as Romanticism (pages 852–863) was in part an attempt to discredit the rational faculty altogether. Those who are under its spell find it peculiarly distasteful to have art connected in any way with learning. They reassure themselves by pointing to the occasional instances when worthwhile work has in fact been produced by men of little education, but they go too far when they suggest that knowledge is like poison to the creative imagination. As applied to Raphael, such thoughts are without contemporary documentation; indeed every bit of 16th-Century evidence tends flatly to contradict the whole idea.

During the early years of the present century, furthermore, the British critic Roger Fry (pages 909; 923) promulgated the doctrine that subject matter of any kind had no legitimate place in the artistic transaction. Because his theories offered a sanction for modern abstraction, they have been popular. If applied to *The School of Athens*, Fry's dogma would tell the student to neglect the iconography entirely. It would even warn him to resist any impulse to become interested in the content of the painting — on pain of losing his capacity for " aesthetic " experience. Is it not impertinent, however, for a modern theorist to refuse to pay attention to aspects of Raphael's art which Raphael himself obviously considered worth the expenditure of an immense amount of labor?

We may sum up by saying that there is no reason whatever to question Raphael's total responsibility for *The School of Athens*. He doubtless had the benefit of much conference with the best scholars of the age. It is unreasonable to suppose that he did not draw upon their learning, but it is even more unreasonable to imagine that he could have made such magnificent pictorial use of ideas that he did not thoroughly understand. He was not only associated with scholars; he was a scholar himself. To his other endowments, therefore, we must add the final accolade: that his mind was also one of the greatest of the Renaissance.

During the twelve years he spent at Rome, every imaginable honor was heaped upon Raphael and every sort of enterprise placed under his control. In addition to the artistic and architectural responsibilities already mentioned, there were numerous other commissions of an important kind. Because of his affability and because he seemed to accomplish every assignment with grace and ease, the Vatican asked him to do more and more. He was put in charge, for instance, of an archaeological survey of Rome, out of which was supposed eventually to emerge an elaborate new map of the area. Obviously, Raphael soon ceased to be an artist; like Phidias he became a statesman of art. Presently, the limit was reached. In 1520, at the age of 37, he caught an acute infection, lacked the strength to rally, and died after an illness of less than a fortnight. He was buried in the Pantheon.

MICHAELANGELO

Michaelangelo died in 1564 at the age of eighty-nine. He had been an important master before reaching his twentieth year. He left behind him a series of stupendous monuments: Saint Peter's church at Rome, the frescoes of the Sistine Chapel ceiling, and the noblest sculpture since Greece. Recognized as one of the world's leading citizens, he was mourned like an emperor. Everyone knew that he had been an ornament of Western civilization.

And yet no other human being so thoroughly exemplifies the tragedy of mortal endeavor. Unhappy as a child, this very great man became increasingly downcast as mature insight clarified for him the meaning of things. He died in complete discouragement after a career marked by the most dazzling success in all the history of art. Before attempting to review his productions, we must do what we can to explain a temperament apparently so far out of keeping with the lesson of the facts.

Michaelangelo was born into a distinguished family, the Buonarroti of Florence. His aptitude for sculpture asserted itself strongly and at once, but brought down upon him the wrath of his relatives: the medieval prejudice against manual labor (page 532) was still strong enough to have effect.

Physically, Michaelangelo was small and misshapen, a circumstance that contributed to morbid reaction in a personality endowed with a supreme passion for beauty and strength. Affairs were not improved by the passage of time. As a youth, he received a severe beating in a fist fight and carried the mark of it the rest of his life in a badly smashed nose. As an adult, he several times yielded to cowardice when threatened by physical danger, a form of behavior in mortifying contrast to his heroic ideals.

Raphael's gift in human relations found its opposite in Michaelangelo. He disliked and distrusted everybody. He could not get a block of marble out of the quarry without quarrelling with the workmen, and he never found more than a handful of assistants whose presence in the shop he could abide. For his incapacity as an executive, he compensated by a prodigious expenditure of energy and by a rapidity of execution that passes belief, even in the face of the incontrovertible facts.

Having few normal friendships and small outlet for the affections, he found it all the harder that bad luck frustrated every project he undertook. He was compelled to leave every one of them a mere fragment and suggestion of the nobler conception with which he had commenced. In all fairness, it must be stated that his imagination knew no limits. He lacked the most elementary grasp of costs, labor, and materials. He was obtuse in his judgment of those who employed him, and seems to have expected, as though by right, patronage with patience and single-mindedness never found anywhere in this world.

Powerful men were ready, it is true, to invest vast sums in art. Individual genius was never more highly respected. Personal capacity was never less restrained by the social order. Most educated persons, moreover, shared a common culture. The Italian 16th Century was nevertheless the very worst period and the very worst place into which Michaelangelo could possibly have been born.

Modern nationalism was the chief product of the 16th Century. England, France, and Spain each had a dynasty, and the Spanish Hapsburgs maintained a personal union with the German imperium. Each one of those nations was openly embarked upon a program of imperial aggrandizement. In such company, the Italian people were hopelessly outclassed. From the start of the Middle Age the peninsula had been the home of small city-states, intense local loyalties, implacable feuds and hatreds. Most Italians of Michaelangelo's generation were quite incapable of comprehending even the notion of national interest, and the Italian despots literally invited (as Ludovico Sforza invited Charles the 8th in 1494) the great powers to invade Italy to interfere in Italian affairs. From that period onward, Italy was a battleground where foreign rivalries were fought out, only to flame up again from new sources and in new combinations. Mercenary armies marched wherever they wanted to go, and often did as they pleased. The crowning infamy occurred on May 6, 1527, when the Spanish and German troops of Charles the 5th sacked Rome. The details of the outrage are too revolting to repeat; in the roster of Christian disgrace, the event is second only to the Fourth Crusade. Thus during Michaelangelo's adult life and by one of the great paradoxes, Italy was being degraded at the very moment when Italian culture was teaching the rest of the world how to live. It is impossible to exaggerate the degree to which political humiliation depressed the Italian spirit. The nation remained supine until the time of Garibaldi.

But even the political situation can hardly have borne down upon Michaelangelo so heavily as the religious events simultaneously in progress. The first generation of the 16th Century marks the nadir of Roman Catholicism. For some time the Chair of Saint Peter had been occupied by popes occasionally marked by energy, often by intellectual distinction, always by culture, but never by religious pre-eminence. The evil side of Roman living became an international scandal in the behavior of some of these men. The details are scarcely fit for print, but may be read by the student in a number of places. All of the popes mentioned operated the Church as though it were merely another State in the general competition between governments. On the whole, the Papacy was competent and alert with respect to its temporal advantage, but none of the popes of the period fulfilled the obligation of spiritual leadership. Feeling began to run high in many places. Resentment became more bitter and more open; but with an incredible conceit, a whole series of pontiffs neglected the matter. They did not even try to find ways to correct the situation. The great and final break came with Luther's Reformation of 1517, followed by the Act of Supremacy (1534) which separated the English church from Rome.

Confronted at last with overt action of unmistakable cogency, the Papacy took measures of its own. The Society of Jesus was founded in 1540. The Universal Inquisition was established in 1542. With the avowed hope of finding a generally acceptable mode for reorganizing the Catholic polity, the Council of Trent held its first assembly in 1545, and met off and on until 1564. Among the dignitaries who attended the council, there was real difference of opinion with respect to the methods that might be used to heal the Reformation. In the end, the Church emerged with a program more intransigeant and authoritarian than ever before. However helpful in guaranteeing discipline within the Catholic organization itself, the so-called Counter Reformation then undertaken proved a ghastly failure. The Inquisition left a heritage of implacable hatred wherever it attempted to operate. In Germany and the Low Countries, the Hapsburgs identified their own political aims with the interests of Catholicism; although they staged a reign of terror more dreadful than anything known until the infamies of Hitler, they merely succeeded in making the population hate both the church and themselves. The same Hapsburgs sent the Spanish Armada against England in 1588, with much the same purpose; and again, they succeeded only in making patriotism synonymous with freedom from Rome.

Michaelangelo's state of mind during those times can be imagined only if we fully appreciate that his Christianity was appropriate for a saint. The 13th Century might have been more congenial for him than the 16th. His writings are replete with spiritual reflections, usually expressed in a tone of despair. His ultimate discouragement was the worse, moreover, because he was one of those who advocated a more moderate method for dealing with the Protestants.

Michaelangelo's artistic education need not delay us long, but contains certain points of interest. In 1489, he entered the atelier of Domenico Ghirlandaio (1449–1494), a society painter notable for philosophical insignificance. The man nevertheless had technical methods greater artists would have been wise to copy. The work went through his shop fast. It came out with scarcely a blemish. It has endured in splendid condition. No school could have been better for a youthful genius than one which taught him decision, dispatch, and the virtue of bringing work to a conclusion — it is on those very points that Leonardo was weak, and Michaelangelo strong.

After a short time, Michaelangelo moved on to become the pupil of the elderly sculptor Bertoldo, a man who had actually worked with Donatello and who conducted a kind of museum in the Medici gardens. The relationship brought the young man into contact with the Classical style, and the immediate result was his rather youthful but powerful relief now in the Casa Buonarroti, showing a *Battle of the Centaurs.*

An even more significant incident was a sojourn of several months in Bologna. Having fled Florence in terror during a political crisis in 1494, Michaelangelo stopped in just the place where he might be affected by the work of Jacopo della Quercia (Fig. 15.29). He remained long enough to carve a small marble saint to fill a vacant station on the elaborate *Shrine of Saint Domenic.* Vigorously personal like all his work, this statue still bears an obvious resemblance to one of the figures Quercia placed in the lunette over the doorway at San Petronio. From that point on, the terrible force of Quercia's style became part of Michaelangelo's own and remained with him the rest of his life.

The first work of permanent significance is the *Pietà* now placed in one of the side chapels at Saint Peter's (Fig. 16.21). Generally given the date 1498–1500, it may be earlier. The style is an interesting combination of elements from the Early Renaissance, the 16th Century, and the personal proclivities of the artist.

The composition is a Leonardesque pyramid, and one of the very first instances where that figure had been used in sculpture. We have already commented upon the capacity of the triangle to concentrate interest within itself (page 722), for which reason the form is perhaps more appropriate for sculpture than for painting. By making the work of art emphatically complete as a visual unit, there is no necessity for association with a niche or any other kind of architectural background. From that circumstance alone we might guess that the young artist was already asserting his famous, complete, and belligerent independence.

Some authors have attempted to see a topical reference in the content. Does it refer to Savonarola's martyrdom? Or to the new crucifixion of Christ in the form of the infamous Borgia pope, Alexander the 6th, who was then in office? Without suggesting that such things failed to affect the spirit of the sculptor, a more general interpretation is in order. It is first of all evident that Michaelangelo made the Madonna draw into herself, bearing her sorrow much as he had been compelled by the contemporary world to shut his personality away. Only the gesture of her left hand seems in any way to be addressed outward. That much is obvious. Less easy to account for is the distortion in which he freely indulged.

The distortion is of several kinds. In the first place, the Madonna is on a larger scale than the Christ; such a woman would be nine feet high if she stood up. Secondly, her dress contains a preposterous amount of cloth. These physical improbabilities and impossibilities are even less radical than a distortion of historical and biological fact. It is possible for a girl of eighteen to be a mother, but it is not possible for her to have a child thirty years old, as Christ was when he died.

Michaelangelo himself explained the last point: a woman of perfect purity, he said, would keep her youth forever. As to the others, we are left to work out our own reasons. By exaggerating the Madonna's size, it was possible to make her handle an adult Christ as easily as a normal mother handles a baby; the entire group thus was made plausible. The extra bulk of drapery contributed to a broad, stable base for the statue, a less exalted purpose but an artistically important one. But we have not yet got to the bottom of the matter.

In the first place, no one can deny that the distortions, both physical and historical, constitute instances of emotional truth, but are quite untrue as facts. Seen in historical perspective, the resort to such methods signifies a potent attack by Michaelangelo, even at the beginning of his career, against the whole philosophy of the representative convention (pages 539 ff). It took nearly four centuries for his point of view to gain a controlling position; but as this is written, the world's best artists, as stated in Chapter 19, take the position that representation is actually unimportant by comparison with the efficiency of art as an expressive vehicle.

It is obvious that Michaelangelo's methods partake of the nature of expressionism (page 933 ff), but his particular application of that theory included a new element: Renaissance individualism in its most extreme form. He was the first artist who dared to take the view that his art was his own. Raphael's *School of Athens*, to cite a recent comparison, was less Raphael's picture than a celebration of the culture of the age. In everything that Michaelangelo touched, the balance was adjusted radically in the opposite direction. He was often under pressure from his patrons, who tried to push him in one direction or another; but regardless of who paid the bill or what he had ordered, the emerging work of art belonged to the artist. The reader may well be amazed that such a thing could be brought off. As to how it was possible, we can adduce two cogent reasons. In the first place, genius as such was privileged in Italy during the High Renaissance. In the second place, the power of Michaelangelo's personality was unique. It is recorded that the most powerful men of the era actually felt fear when in his presence, and were glad enough to leave him alone.

The extent to which Michaelangelo went in the matter of expressing his personal opinions is well illustrated by the marble *David*, commissioned in 1501. Because David was a slayer of tyrants, the subject was an incongruous choice for a civic monument at a moment in Florentine history when the question of tyranny was likely to stir up action as well as feeling. The net result, however, was to establish the young sculptor as one of the world's most admired artists. A trivial circumstance has lent the *David* an adventitious fame. Michaelangelo carved it free-hand from a block of marble which had been badly mauled by a sculptor named Baccellino about thirty-five years earlier. Traces of Baccellino's chisel may still be seen on the back and on the top of the head. The incident is of course merely an illustration of the superior power of visualization common among professional artists. Set up in 1504, the *David* was taken to the Academy in 1873, to protect it from further weathering. Well displayed there, its gigantic size (height 18 feet) renders the best possible indoor setting inadequate.

In 1505, Michaelangelo received from Agnolo Doni (who had his portrait done by Raphael that same year) what is believed to be his first commission as a painter: the circular *Holy Family* (Fig. 16.22) now in the Uffizi. The work introduces us to a new class of Renaissance art, although it was hardly the first of its kind. We refer to the so-called " devotional picture," which derived from Neo-Platonic concepts and requires, if it is to be understood, a frame of reference utterly separate from that which applies to narrative painting.

The devotional picture has no story to tell. The artist may pose the figures as he wants; he is not governed by the necessity of making them do some particular thing. There is no point of time to bring up memories of the past, or to suggest future expectations. No local facts dictate the setting. All the factors which ordinarily control the imagination are removed; but by the same token, the artist is deprived of all those which ordinarily help him in the act of visualization. He is left free to perform the appalling task of presenting us with absolute beauty.

It was natural for any 16th-Century master to assume that absolute beauty would find its best expression in the language of the human body, and specially natural for Michaelangelo to find the body's greatest beauty in its shape and movement. Beyond that, the picture may be said to be abstract. The lighting has no parallel on earth. In a magnificent manipulation of the Mode of Relief (pages 582–586 ff), Michaelangelo modeled the figures as no one else could possibly have done, and we see the Holy Family as though in a vision. " Had my soul not been created God-like," wrote the artist himself in a passage which is surely apposite, " it would seek no more than outward beauty, the delight of the eyes. But since that fades so fast, my soul soars beyond, to the eternal form." The statement is enigmatic without such a picture to illustrate it, and needs in any case the supplement of another aphorism from the same source, namely, that " the heart is slow to love what the eye cannot see."

With such evidence in hand, we may justly infer that Michaelangelo considered it his artistic destiny to find visual imagery adequate to suggest, and perhaps even to portray the most exalted concepts permitted to the human consciousness. The " eternal form " mentioned by him is probably to be understood in at least two ways: as a synonym for the glory of God from which humanity was banished at the time of creation (page 652); and as an artist's name for the divine quality felt whenever beauty is discerned in the shape of things on earth (page 653). " The wise," he said in still another statement, " believe all lovely things we see on earth approach more closely than anything else to that font from which we all derive."

In 1505, Michaelangelo went back to Rome to discuss with Julius the 2nd plans for a tomb suitable to the station, character, and taste of that most vigorous pontiff. The commission was in every way congenial, and the ideas of the Pope appear to have corresponded remarkably with those of the artist. Between the two, they projected the most remarkable tomb in the history of the world. It appears to have disturbed neither of them that their plans were fantastically impractical.

The original plan called for a small temple (Fig. 16.23) intended to stand inside the new Saint Peter's. Julius had no intention of appearing in effigy as mortal, recumbent, and dead. Instead, we were to look up at his figure in the very act of entering heaven, into which place he intended to go seated bolt upright on his papal throne, riding on a catafalque carried by two angels, with his hand raised in the gesture of benediction and his eyes looking fearlessly forward into eternity.

No fewer than 47 full-scale marble statues were to be included in the composition, plus six panels of bronze relief. Except for the reliefs, which were to commemorate biographical episodes in the life of the Pope, the subject matter was to be a grandiose demonstration of the recondite iconography so satisfying to the taste of the period. Different scholars have developed different explanations, but we shall not be far wrong if we understand the tomb as an artistic parallel for Ficino's *Theologica Platonica.*

The elevation of the tomb was arranged in three levels. The purpose was to use the physically high and low to demonstrate the extremes of heaven and earth, and a stage of comparative grace between.

Around the exterior of the lowest story, there were to be series of niches, with a *Victory* in each niche. On both sides of every *Victory,* nude and writhing *Captives* were to appear, each lashed to a slab (Figs. 16.24–25). Long recognized as reflecting to some extent the state of their author's own spirit, the *Captives* were intended (in the official iconography of the tomb) to typify the Neo-Platonic concept of the immortal soul disgraced by imprisonment within the body, and struggling against the slavery of man's lower nature. In the same way, the *Victories* would also have an ethical meaning; they would stand for instances where reason had conquered the base emotions, giving man a taste of freedom and glory even here on earth.

On the second level, which corresponds to the top of the ground story, there were to be only four large statues, one at each corner, and all free-standing. The characters to be depicted were Rachel and Leah, Moses and Paul. Moses and Paul had a special following at the time; they were often cited as men who had actually attained a synthesis of thought and action, thus enjoying spiritual grace during life. Leah and Rachel fell into a similar category. They symbolized the active and the contemplative life, both being considered necessary for the soul in its struggle back toward God.

As indicated above, the gates of heaven itself were to be the setting for the third and top level, occupied by the Pope and his angels. One of the latter, it is said, was to have a face full of rapture that so good a man should receive his reward. The other was to be in tears, because the world had lost him.

Very little work was actually completed in preparation for the tomb. Michaelangelo spent an immense amount of time and disbursed tremendous sums accumulating a great stock of marble for the purpose, and the Pope himself lost interest as costs added up with little to show for it. In 1508, he diverted Michaelangelo to painting the Sistine Chapel ceiling, originally intended as an interim project. In 1513, Julius died, and with him all hope of completing the plans.

After an enormous amount of delay and a tedious succession of revisions, the heirs, between 1542 and 1545, finally put together a simple wall tomb, using completed details intended for the full-scale project. The great Pope, as everybody knew, intended to rest in his magnificent new Saint Peter's of the Vatican; but by a maliciously ingenious reading of his will, the name *San Pietro* was construed in a generic way. He was therefore put in San Pietro in Vincoli, a small basilica on a side street.

The *Moses*, the only completed statue of the four projected for the second level of the tomb as planned, appears as the central figure in the arrangement at San Pietro in Vincoli. It is on the floor level, where it is probably even more awe-compelling than if placed as intended. To many, the force of the statue seems identified with rebuke, and the suggestion is made that Moses is shown as in Exodus 22:19. That is to say, we see him just as he is about to shatter the tablets of the law by casting them down in his wrath as he witnesses the celebration around the Golden Calf. An eccentric detail tends to substantiate such an interpretation. An erroneous translation of the scripture was then current which said that horns sprouted from Moses' head on that occasion.

The moral dignity of the statue is inconsistent with Moses' somewhat childish behavior on the occasion mentioned; and on the whole, it seems likely that Michaelangelo, as usual, intended to transcend historical narrative. If that be so, we may read the figures as a more general study of the Moses character, in which connection the last few verses of Exodus 24 seem apposite. They tell how Moses' face shone with light during and after his conversations with God. The Israelites were frightened thereby, and Moses had to put on a veil. It also seems likely that the statue was an attempt to depict the supernatural excitement known to all good students of Plato when, for an instant, the truth comes clear. In the words of Ficino, it " petrifies and almost kills the body while it enraptures the soul."

Among the other statues that were finished, or brought well along, are the *Victory* now in the Palazzo Vecchio, and some of the statues (Figs. 16.24–25) already cited as belonging to the lowest register of the arrangement as first planned. As a group, the *Captives* are colloquially known as " the Slaves." Two figures are in the Louvre, and four are in the Academy at Florence. The latter are believed to come from an abortive revision of 1532, which involved discarding all the work completed to date. They are larger than the statues in Paris, also more extreme. Their tortured bodies actually writhe back and forth in depth a greater distance than the total width across the shoulders.

Taking them as a set, " the Slaves " offer much provocation to anyone with a zeal for interpretation. Who can say what they mean? A number of suggestions have been put forward, all plausible. Perhaps they do not represent captives as previously stated, but the arts and sciences reduced to impotence by the death of so generous a patron. Another idea has it that they personify the political mortification of Italy, or even that they personify the foreign powers then reducing Italy, and show what Michaelangelo wanted done with them. There can actually be no sure right or wrong in the matter of interpretation. Neither do the various suggestions necessarily exclude one another; on the contrary, all may be true.

The truth of the matter is that, except for the use of the human body in recognizable form, " the Slaves " are abstract. Every man must infer what he can from the pose of the statue and the state of the muscles; even facial expression, of which there is close to none, fails to offer its usual help. It is fair to stipulate, however, that every honest interpretation must limit itself to generic words. Most of the meaning cannot be described; it belongs in the realm of the undefined emotions.

In the latter connection, it is of peculiar interest that several of the figures remain unfinished. Their condition may not easily be disposed of by reference to the sculptor's crowded schedule. Such a suggestion is out of character because of Michaelangelo's pre-eminence among artists for instant decision in matters of design, and for terrific speed in pushing work to a conclusion. Why should he have left something unfinished when he could have completed it with very little further labor? We must conclude that he intended to leave things as we see them.

What was the power that might be destroyed had he carried each statue further? The answer must in some way relate to the special strength of the cogent but indefinite statement — a resource familiar in literature. Such statements set the reader or the observer, as the case may be, off on his own. The artist names the train of thought even though he does not map its course. So conceived, it seems that the unfinished marbles, which in artistic fact are form emerging from matter, have something to do with humanity's struggle against the material incubus, and the beatitude vouchsafed when man realizes his humanity and later his salvation.

Michaelangelo was at Florence when Julius sent for him to paint the ceiling of the Sistine Chapel. Having small taste for painting, and suspicious that Bramante and Raphael were at the bottom of the scheme (i.e., hoping to discredit him), he flatly refused to come back to Rome. After prolonged negotiations, Julius — a man not accustomed to negotiate with anybody — appealed to the government of Florence, asking that the artist be brought by force. "You have tried a bout with the Pope," said one of the Florentine officials, "on which the king of France would not have ventured. . . ." Nothing daunted, and realizing that Christendom would not be big enough to hold him, Michaelangelo declared he would take refuge with the sultan of Turkey. Then presently he gave in.

At that time, the ceiling of the chapel was a mere field of decorator's work, blue and studded with stars. The Pope asked only that the twelve apostles be painted on the vault, but Michaelangelo would have none of it. Disliking the task as he did, and with every reason to get it over with fast, he detested little plans even more. The scheme became increasingly big, and emerged as an attempt to provide an Old Testament foundation for the narrative frescoes painted on the walls of the chapel thirty years before (page 707). The main theme may be described as the Creation, God's subsequent wrath with mankind, and the survival of humanity by virtue of Noah's immunity. The narrative pictures are reinforced by seven Prophets and five sybils, thus recalling how one event foretold another, and putting classical mythology openly on a par with Christian history. In addition, there are innumerable subordinate figures of purely artistic utility; they are disposed for compositional purposes, to enframe units of narrative, or to lead the eye onward. The total area covered measures about 700 square yards. Michaelangelo is believed to have executed almost every inch of it personally, and his sustained expenditure of energy during the herculean performance is without a parallel in the history of art, or in any other history. He paused only when exhausted. In his creative fury, he neglected the simplest and most obvious routines of health and comfort. Forgetting to remove his shoes for a period of weeks, for instance, he pulled the skin off with them when finally persuaded to change his clothes. He worked almost entirely flat on his back; and as a result, he suffered serious ocular maladjustment for some time after completing the commission and resuming once again the normal posture.

Although individual pictures on the ceiling are among the greatest known on earth, the project as a whole could hardly have been more unwise. It being nearly impossible to bring the entire field into view at once, the surface had to be subdivided into panels, with scenes coming seriatim. The contour of the vault was no proper field for painting. It was often poorly lighted; and under the best of conditions, the height (about 85 feet) and the vertical angle of sight made inspection of the paintings uncomfortable at all times, and often impossible. It is notable, in that connection, that few of them are genuine ceiling pictures in any case; most were designed as though to be viewed horizontally, like normal paintings.

After finishing the panels that told the story of Noah, Michaelangelo apparently removed the scaffolding and studied the work from the floor. As a result, he very considerably simplified the compositions which dealt with the Creation, two of which we show in Figs. 16.26–27. He reduced the setting to the lowest limit possible with any remaining correspondence to the narrative. The meaning is carried almost exclusively by the human figures. The latter were also reduced in number until there could be no fewer. Each was painted in the strongest possible application of the Mode of Relief (pages 582 ff); sometimes they make the impression of having been hewed from the block rather than painted.

The figure-style shows the full effect upon Michaelangelo of the Pergamene division of Hellenistic art (pages 170 & 710) with which he had recently become fascinated by way of the few decadent manifestations thereof visible at Rome. But his skill and judgment in posing the body were incomparably better than either the *Laocoön* (Fig. 6.20) or the *Belvedere Torso* (Figs. 6.21–22). Starting with such flamboyant and empty sources, he arrived once again at standards of excellence comparable to those of the Greek Great Age.

His iconography was at once grand and pathetic, a truth best demonstrated by the *Creation of Adam* (Fig. 16:27). For a sincere Christian, the gift of life was no gift at all in Italy during the 16th Century; and we therefore see Adam accepting it reluctantly, and God giving it, divine fire though it is, with sympathy and anxiety. It is also to be noted that Adam is placed on earth (from which he came) and near God (whose image he was to bear). The juxtaposition suggests a remark in Pico della Mirandola's *Oration on Human Dignity;* namely, that Adam had the right to choose: he might abase himself to the brutes, or become divine. The numerous figures enclosed within God's mantle amplify the meaning further. The lovely girl encircled by his arm must be Eve, whom God would presently give to Adam. It is significant that she is younger here than in the panel showing her own incarnation, and she looks out with fear and wonder upon the miracle of birth which she was destined so often to repeat upon the earth. The numerous babies suggest the descendants of Adam and Eve, but it will be observed that one of them is singled out from the rest. The fingers of the Almighty rest with painful weight on his shoulder, and the child feels the burden. He must be meant for the Christ child, and it would seem that the Almighty felt need of him at this significant moment.

The next important commission, and the first in Michaelangelo's career to involve a substantial amount of architecture, was the *New Sacristy* attached to San Lorenzo at Florence, often called the *Medici Chapel* because it was undertaken to provide a family mausoleum. Work began in 1521, and the project was abandoned unfinished in 1534.

The architecture Michaelangelo designed as a setting for the several tombs throws a new light on his personality. Uncompromisingly proud and completely aware of his own genius, it was his habit to respond to the opinions of others with intolerable arrogance. He was nevertheless capable of humility, and was occasionally more than gracious in his appreciation of other artists. Those he admired most seem to have been those opposite to himself: Gentile da Fabriano, for example, and Fra Angelico. On this occasion, he paid Brunelleschi the compliment of emulating his style. Michaelangelo's handling of the decorative orders, and his employment of line and surface, echo the architecture of the modest and elegant nave just a few steps back through the entrance passageway. But at the same time, a master habituated to plastic expression and accustomed to make himself emphatic could not be Brunelleschi over again. Everywhere we look, therefore, we can feel the stronger relief and the greater weight of the High Renaissance.

Lorenzo the Magnificent and his murdered brother lie in a plain sarcophagus along the entrance wall; a more elaborate tomb for them was part of the original plan. The famous "Medici Tombs," one of which appears in Fig. 16.28 (the other is almost the same in design), house two later and lesser Medici: Giuliano, Duke of Nemours, and Lorenzo, Duke of Urbino, who had died in 1516 and 1519 respectively. Into the iconography of those monuments we need not go in detail. Suffice it to say that it conformed to yet another scheme of Neo-Platonic categories. Taken together, the two tombs were intended to set forth the dual concept of the active and the contemplative life, and into that theme was woven the notion of mortality and time, the latter being suggested by the recumbent statues of *Night, Day, Dawn,* and *Dusk* which lie so uncomfortably inclined upon the lids of the two sarcophagi. About the design, much is to be said.

Michaelangelo was the founder of the Baroque (Chapter 17) in the same sense that Alberti founded the High Renaissance. As they stand, the two

Medici Tombs are incomplete. Both were to include a pair of river gods, probably reclining on the floor at angles opposite to the statues which now lie on the sarcophagi. The addition of those intended figures would tend to tighten the composition; but even as they stand, the tombs have an extraordinary finality of design. They are, in fact, the earliest demonstration of the principles by which Baroque art was to be governed. As such, they belong to the next chapter rather than to this, and it is appropriate to defer discussion until that time. Equally a prediction of the Baroque was the immense *Last Judgment* on the eastern wall of the Sistine Chapel, upon which Michaelangelo was at work from 1534 to 1541.

The *Last Judgment* proved to be his final important commission in either painting or sculpture. In 1535, Paul the 3rd asked him to become superintendent of the Vatican buildings, a position that did not mean much at the moment, but one which eventuated in his taking over the construction of Saint Peter's (1546), the completion of the Farnese Palace, and the design of a piazza and a group of buildings around it for the Capitol Hill — that venerable site being still without suitable embellishment.

When Michaelangelo took over Saint Peter's, he found the fabric much as Bramante had left it in 1514 (page 706). The various interim architects had made a number of paper plans and a number of small wooden models, but they had accomplished little construction. It is difficult to say to what extent his decisions were dictated by circumstances over which he had no control. At any rate, he designed a central church around the existing piers at the crossing, with arms so short and a plan so compact that the body of the building would tell (much as it does today in the apse view) as a pedestal for the immense dome. The dome itself was a refinement of the one Brunelleschi had designed at Florence (page 631). There is no telling whether its present elliptical silhouette was designed by Michaelangelo or by Della Porta, who took over after his death, at which time the work was complete to the top of the drum.

There can be no question that Saint Peter's would be a better building had Michaelangelo's central plan remained. The extended nave ruined the composition; any normal view including the present façade gives the church an unfortunately disjointed look. When all is said and done, the chief present interest of the design has to do with Michaelangelo's manipulation of scale, a matter in which he made a significant historical contribution.

He took the fundamental shape of the nave from Alberti's Sant' Andrea at Mantua (Fig. 16.4), but he had a special problem because the building at Rome was intended to be immensely bigger. In making the adaptation, he proceeded in a bold new way. He discarded the idea of multiplying the conventional classical members. Instead, he merely gave the new church the usual number of parts by the method of increasing the size of each part in proportion with the gigantic scale of the whole.

Upon entering, one's sensibilities are affected in peculiar fashion. There is no chance to form a notion of size by the familiar method of counting parts, as we do at Hagia Sophia (Figs. 10.2–3) and at Amiens (Figs. 12.12–13). In fact, the exaggerated scale of familiar mouldings and orders may at first pass unnoticed. Presently, however, the unusual surroundings begin to impart a feeling of their own size. The feet seem to wear seven-league boots, and every other capacity of the person becomes, for the present, enlarged in the imagination. Merely amusing at its inception, the sensation gradually becomes an idea seriously entertained. It is hardly too much to say that the end result is to impart a sense of personal grandeur to every man and woman within.

For the ensemble on the Capitol Hill (Fig. 16.29) Michaelangelo prepared a design that is surely one of the best in history. A bronze equestrian statue of Marcus Aurelius, unique among classical antiquities, was chosen as the focus for the entire composition. Around it extends the pavement of the small piazza, bounded on three sides by palaces and opening on the fourth upon a tremendous stairway down the steep side of the hill. The Palace of the Senate closes the vista established by the axis of the stairs. It is a larger, slightly more ornate building than its flanking palaces. The latter are identical duplicates, and they lie at a moderate angle to each other.

Precedent for such an arrangement was not lacking; indeed, the inspiration may have come from a somewhat similar grouping at Pienza. But no earlier plan accomplished in the same measure an aesthetic coherence as between several buildings in a group. Michaelangelo's success on this occasion inaugurated the modern tradition of working with units of architecture much as the painter manipulates single items within a composition. As compared with other essays along the same line, his design is perhaps still the very best.

Aesthetic emphasis was produced by the size and central placement of the largest building, and yet the others have scale enough to stand in their own right, and not as mere outbuildings. Of particular interest is Michaelangelo's care for the fall of the light. It was natural for him to approach architectural design from a sculptor's point of view, and it is said he would never permit construction until he had made and studied a model of the proposed building. In this instance, he demonstrated extraordinary judgment in the placement and projection of parts, with the result that cast shadows aid rather than harm the forms: the absence of parallelism in the plan guarantees that no two of the buildings will ever take the sun in the same way at the same time.

Considered separately, the Palace of the Senate can justly be hailed as the best, and probably the final solution of the Renaissance problem of combining the aesthetic qualities of classical architecture with the demands of modern utilitarian buildings, most of which must have several stories. As such, it proved to be the model for so many derivative buildings in Europe, America, and elsewhere that it would be futile even to guess at the number; there are probably a thousand new ones under construction as this is written.

As a class, the Palace of the Senate and all derivatives take their original guidance from the Roman variation of the Greek temple (Fig. 8.5). Its three divisions (podium, order, entablature) are obvious on the façade, but Michaelangelo's design called for a podium considerably higher and a colossal order much shorter than classical rules would suggest. In all such designs, it is essential to give the order (pilasters or columns as the case may be) sufficient vertical power to unify the elevation. It is correspondingly important to minimize the horizontality of the several levels of floor, a result which was aided in this instance by a clever variation in the size and shape of the windows.

At the top of the building, Michaelangelo found himself in the perennial trouble that besets every man who tries to adapt the classical orders to modern work. An entablature in proportion with the order would be too small to operate as a proper enframement for the whole building, while an entablature big enough to fit the height of the building would dwarf the order immediately beneath. Michaelangelo's solution has been the standard one ever since: he added a decorative balustrade, by means of which he gained height without overbearing weight.

The great man was seventy-two years old when he redesigned Saint Peter's, and the colossal spirit of that church remains as a testament to the regard in which he was held in Rome. His later years were more and more unhappy, however, and his isolation, seemingly grand, was in fact desperate. He could neither approve nor disapprove the policies of the Counter Reformation, a fact which increased his personal turmoil. Certain minor aspects thereof even proved a direct embarrassment to him.

One of the matters to which the Catholic reformers turned their attention was the question of decorum. In view of the flamboyant sensuality marking the immediate Italian past, their concern was appropriate, but it led them into some artistically ridiculous notions. Nudity as such became suspect; and Michaelangelo himself, the most admired artist in the world, was accused of impropriety because his *Last Judgment* contained many naked figures. Paul the 4th actually had Daniele da Volterra (1555–59) paint shorts on some of the offending bodies. It was even suggested that the painting be removed entirely.

Before Michaelangelo was dead, both Catholics and Protestants were indulging in some of the worst cruelties known in the Western world. The excesses of the religious wars may be thought of as an outward and vulgar counterpart for the spiritual stress within his own soul. His later writings are replete with passages expressing a sense of utter futility. " Lord, what shall I do unless thou visit me with thine ineffable grace? " he says in one place. And again, " I have let the vanities of the world rob me of the time I had for the contemplation of God."

Among his later drawings many approach complete dematerialization, but perhaps the best and most intimate record from his old age is to be found in the medium he loved best. Only three sculptural groups survive from those years. All three deal with the entombment of Christ. All three utterly renounce the pagan ideals of beauty and strength with which he had amazed the world in earlier days, and still does. Fig. 16.30 is perhaps the most pathetic of them all, but let the student also consult the grander group originally intended for his own tomb and now appropriately placed behind the high altar in the Cathedral at Florence. It stands all alone there, the last and by no means the least statement from the small, unhappy Florentine gentleman in whose person all the greatness of Italy was concentrated.

VENETIAN PAINTING DURING THE HIGH RENAISSANCE

The Renaissance came late at Venice, the reason being more or less evident in the character of the city. It is hardly accurate to think of Venice as Italian; in fact the place never has been so until rather recent times. From its foundation during the 6th Century, the town was a maritime power and is still one of the busiest ports in Europe. The natural line of intercourse was with the Germanies by way of the Brenner Pass, and with the Levant by way of the Mediterranean. The important Venetian families had relatives resident at Constantinople, Saloniki, Tyre, Alexandria, and a host of other places. For the same reason of trade, colonies of Greeks, Arabs, Slavs, Syrians, Turks, and Germans lived at Venice to handle their end of the immense transshipment which flowed continuously through the city, leaving wealth in its train. It was natural enough that commercial considerations loomed much larger in the Venetian mind than philosophical or religious questions, and inevitable that materialism would assert itself strongly in the local culture. The cosmopolitan atmosphere of the place involved much more than mere trade, however. From the beginning of the 13th Century onward, Venice held political and military control over many of the eastern islands, and over substantial portions of the mainland as far afield as the shores of the Black Sea. Except for a series of conflicts with Genoa, her only rival on the sea, Venice remained not so much aloof as unconcerned with Italian politics and Italian culture. Her interests lay over the horizon.

To identify one's self with Venice, moreover, was to call up visual imagery unique in all the earth. The reality of the place is like a dream. No other city was ever built on so irrational a site, with canals for thoroughfares and gondolas for transport. Venetian architecture is as fantastic as the idea of the town itself. Great palaces rise like lace out of the water, and all the ordinary customs seem replaced by farfetched romance. Nature has done her part to enhance the spectacle. The sea and clouds take on colors that are extravagant even for the Mediterranean. The very air often glows with golden light, bathing the colored marbles with bizarre opalescence.

It would be unreasonable to ask the inhabitants of such a place to spend their time wrestling with the severe abstractions of architecture, or to be content with the monotones of sculpture. Everywhere they looked, the view whipped them up to a lust for color. Their art may well have been delayed, in fact, by the lack of the right medium. Mosaic was too sombre for the spirit of the times. Both tempera and fresco had proven fugitive in the damp atmosphere. The start of the school coincided, in fact, with a visit by Antonello da Messina (page 581) who came there in 1475 to paint a large *Madonna Enthroned,* now broken up and preserved only in part. Antonello, it will be remembered, was one of the very few Italians who ever painted in the Mode of the Total Visual Effect, one of the earliest who habitually used oil, and one of the very few men then alive who understood its properties.

The Venetians adopted oil instantly, and made it their own. The best artists of the place have invariably been painters, and the historical contribution of the school depends upon their surpassing judgment in the development and perfection of methods for painting with oil. Most writers have erred by stating the matter too gingerly. They may perhaps be forgiven, because the truth of Venetian achievement and influence is so sweeping as to challenge the credulity of the reader.

As to the achievement of the Venetian masters, it may be said that their research was exhaustive and very nearly final. Except for the special and somewhat limited contribution made by the French Impressionists (pages 863–874), there has been nothing new in the way of technique since. It will be understood, of course, that the expression of mature men is ramified beyond description, and that when we state that such and such an artist painted by Venetian methods, we make no suggestion that his pictures look anything like Titian or Tintoretto. We merely mean that he accomplished his own purpose with the same tools and the same materials used in similar fashion. That being plain, we can make a very brief statement of the breadth of Venetian influence.

Through the agency of El Greco (about 1548–1614), who had learned his trade in Titian's shop before going to Toledo, the Venetian oil technique was transmitted to Spain. Every Iberian artist since might justly be called a Venetian derivative.

Through the agency of Rubens (1577–1640), who spent a full eight years in Italy and made many copies after Titian, the Venetian manner went to the entire north of Europe. Flemish, French, and much Dutch painting has ever since been Venetian in method. Rubens's distinguished pupil Van Dyck (1599–1641) took the same technique to England, and every British painter and all American painters have employed it since.

The influence so broadly described above has not yet lost momentum. As with most other instances of cultural invention and borrowing, the Venetian method was widely adopted because artists thought it better and more convenient; they instinctively recognized its theory as being fundamentally in keeping with the art of painting, and as opening up more complete possibilities of expression. Most of the technical stratagems in the work of Cézanne (pages 908–917) — all too often put forward as original inventions of his own — were matters of common knowledge at Venice during the 16th Century, and he learned them from Venetian paintings he had studied in the museums. What was true of Cézanne is equally true of the followers of Cézanne. The retrospective exhibition of Matisse, held in New York in the autumn of 1951, showed that supposedly radical and modern master to be an immensely skilful painter indeed; but although the problems he had set himself were special and even new, his tactics in solving them were Venetian.

The Venetian Mode

The Venetian Mode, sometimes called the Pictorial Mode of the Later Renaissance, was the fourth and last theory of painting to be promulgated successfully in the history of European art. It derived from the Mode of the Total Visual Effect (pages 580 ff); in some respects, the two are often so nearly alike as to be difficult to distinguish. As the reader has doubtless inferred from what has gone before, the principal advantage of the Venetian Mode over its predecessors was the fact that it offered greater flexibility to the art of painting. While producing pictures of acceptable verisimilitude, the new system set the painter free from the artistic lock-step which must be accepted as the inevitable consequence of maintaining a strict one-to-one relationship between the facts of the painting and the facts of nature.

It will be understood, of course, that the Venetian departure from nature was partial, and not complete. In Venetian pictures, the human anatomy is reasonably strict. Linear perspective is likewise correct. But in every department having to do with tonal relations, the Venetians did as they pleased with only the slightest regard for the rules of light and color which John Van Eyck (pages 614 ff) had investigated so thoroughly and mastered so well.

Having cast aside natural fact as the law of art, they were able to make direct and arbitrary use of value, hue, and intensity in several ways from which painters had hitherto been foreclosed. Upon occasion, representation itself (especially the placement of objects forward and back within the represented space) was made easier by calculated contrasts between the tone of the near thing and the tone of the far thing. By an equally arbitrary manipulation of the tone, the Venetian painters threw the light, so to speak, upon a person in the act of doing something crucial in the drama of the picture. By a cognate use of shadow, they relegated other figures to subordinate status. Sometimes shadow has the opposite effect, and directs attention to a particular face by the simple power of our curiosity to explore the undefined.

The two routines just described (the use of tone to aid representation, and the use of tone for emphasis and suppression) were the techniques which made the Venetian Mode popular with other schools. Somewhat more local to Venice was a special and additional preoccupation with grand schemes of interior decoration, into which single paintings had to fit as details in the larger design. Such taste begot the habit of planning the hues of a painting in harmony with each other, so that the final composition, considered as a whole and as an area on the wall, would fall in the general region of some chosen hue — or, in technical language, would possess a definite *tonality*. In very large paintings, it was almost equally important to make the rhythm of the picture, as established by accents of value and hue, correspond well with the architectural rhythm of the chamber in which it was to hang. Because good artists, especially schools of them, usually come close to accomplishing what they set out to do, the Venetians made pictures that were more decorative than any the world had seen before. At the same time, it must be conceded that their strong interest in beauty tended rather often to result in beauty alone, and we shall look in vain for the intellectual and spiritual qualities characteristic of all art that stemmed from Florence.

All of the Venetian painters used the Venetian Mode; but for the purpose of explanation by reference to black and white plates on a scale practical for the present volume, we shall find the plainest examples in the work of Tintoretto. Giorgione and Titian used the same methods, but they were less obvious about it. In keeping with the more strident nature of his art, which looked forward toward the coming Baroque (Chapter 17), Tintoretto did not even attempt to be restrained about the methods he used. His theory of painting, in spite of all we have had to say by way of preparation, was baldly simple and direct: it was the same theory which brought the spotlight into general use in the theatre, where nobody worries about the naturalism of the effect.

An excellent instance of a comparatively simple painting in the Venetian Mode is Tintoretto's *Presentation of the Virgin* (Fig. 16.39). It will occur to the reader to compare it with Giotto's version of the same subject at Padua, from which much can be deduced with respect to what Venice wanted from her painters. But forgetting the spirit of the picture, let us note how he used the light.

One's attention is arrested at once by the oval flood of brilliance which carries up the stairs and stops at the small figure of the Virgin. Dramatically, what could be in more perfect order than the idea that a radiance as of divine grace followed her up the steps that day? And yet what could be more inconsistent with the logic of illumination as we observe it on earth? A single field here and there models, with reference to itself alone, in rational fashion; but the same cannot be said of the broader areas of light and shadow which form so essential a feature of the composition. Why does the light fall only where it does? How does it happen that the child herself merely leads the light up the stone stairs, and receives almost none of it? Why is there so exaggerated a contrast of value between the illuminated areas, which seem to get the full sun, and the shaded areas, which seem almost like nocturnes? What is there to say about the brightness of the amazed old man at the lower left? And what of the fact that the canvas divides into almost equal halves of light and dark along the diagonal?

So long as we insist upon finding a natural or mechanical cause for everything we see in the picture, it must remain an outlandish engima. Immediately we accept the artistic propriety of using paint without reference to the facts of visual experience, the entire Venetian theory of painting opens up. Because painting is in many respects more flexible than nature and much more under the control of the artist, it becomes feasible — once we accept as legitimate a substantial departure from the tone relations of nature — to create a pictorial world with effects of light and color which otherwise would remain quite out of the question. Out of the question, it is worth remarking, even in the modern theatre with its battery of lights. The imagery of art, to put it briefly, can be different, more extended, and more responsive to the creative imagination than the imagery of sight.

In his well-known *Miracle of Saint Mark,* Tintoretto arbitrarily bathed some of the figures in light and some in shadow, and he thereby achieved emphasis and subordination as described above. Our Fig. 16.40 reproduces a section from the upper right-hand corner of the composition, and the purpose of the selection is to illustrate a modest instance of the Venetian habit of using contrasts of value, hue, intensity, or all three, as a method for making us read certain masses as being forward or back from certain others within the represented space of the painting. The detail shows one figure entire, and part of another. The two lie approximately in the same vertical plane, and it was necessary for the painter to make both " come forward " from a background he wished to " place " about twenty yards away. Neither the drawing of the figures nor the drawing of the background would, in itself, furnish sufficient indication of the spatial relation he wanted us to comprehend. With respect to the two arms of the man at the lower left, he was aided in the representation by atmospheric perspective, and even more by the sharp contrast between the high value of the white gateway and the arms sihouetted against it. No such fortunate arrangement of contrasts existed to " place " the old gentleman at the upper right in the same manner, and he resorted to an arbitrary expedient.

Around the upper silhouette of the figure, he ran a ribbon of tint very near to white in value. Depending upon the variation in local contrast between the figure and its background, the whitish ribbon was made narrower or wider as circumstances required. The result, as seen either in the original or in a good photograph, was to make the figure " snap forward " into the desired position.

Technically, the trick is known as *disconnection.* Mr. Arthur Pope called attention long ago to the fact that the device was common to both Venetian and Chinese painting. It is impossible to know whether the Venetians performed an act of total invention, or whether they adopted methods observed in pictures that somehow found their way to the head of the Adriatic in the course of Eastern trade. Either may have happened. At any rate, most painters ever since have freely resorted to arbitrary modulations of tone, to calculated contrasts of local hue, and to any other convenient manipulation of pigments whenever such would serve to supplement other indications of spatial displacement as between objects seen in the picture. It is in this department of art where Cézanne, in particular, owed so much to the Venetians.

Although Venetian paintings purported to be representative and were often stirringly dramatic, the going taste at Venice demanded, as already stated, that pictures be something more than a vehicle for expression. There was an almost equal interest in paintings as an integral part of the interior decoration. In theory, any colors might have been chosen, or a great variety of colors; but the 16th-Century Venetian fashion called for paneling in rich brown woods, with decorative accents occasionally brought out in gold. With exceptions, furniture and hangings were chosen with an eye more to harmony than to contrast, and the same principle applied to the color scheme for paintings.

While a quick look at a Venetian picture gives one the impression of experiencing all the hues in more or less vivid state, a more sober and systematic analysis (especially if it involves putting the Venetian example into contrast with some other) corrects the original hasty reaction. If catalogued, diagrammatically or otherwise, all the hues within the Venetian painting will fall on the color circle in the general region of red-orange; and the painting, considered as a unit of area, will tell as a spot or section of that hue. Such a statement seemingly contradicts the unmistakable evidence of our eyes; but the fields which tell as bright blue in Titian's *Europa* at Fenway Court — simply to name an example accessible to American students — actually are neutralized blue-grays. They tell as intense blue only through the agency of contrast; they are cooler and bluer, that is, than the tones with which they are juxtaposed. Because there is nothing to contrast in any serious fashion with the dominance of red-orange, the totality of the picture gleams with that hue, and has the effect so often colloquially referred to as " the Venetian glow."

In keeping with the tendencies of the High Renaissance, a great many Venetian paintings were very large indeed, often covering an entire wall. In such extended compositions, there was an obvious argument against a strong localization of interest; and the even continuation of decorative appeal, similar in principle to the rhythmic and unlimited composition appropriate for an upholstery or hanging (pages 26–29), offered a suitable solution to the problem. The prime desideratum (regardless of the subject matter depicted) was to make the painting an area of rhythmic decoration, a kind of tapestry on canvas within which the eye finds interesting hues and values everywhere. The desired happy effect would be difficult or impossible if the artist felt obliged to put a shadow everywhere nature might put one.

In the bigger Venetian pictures, the alternations of tone were generally governed by the decorative scheme, which was followed whether it happened to be consistent with visual fact or not, and without much regard for making the right-hand half of the painting conform with the left in the matter of illumination. Tintoretto's immense *Crucifixion* in San Rocco is a capital example, but it reproduces abominably in black and white. Veronese's *Marriage at Cana* (Fig. 16.42) will illustrate the point as well as it can be done in a photograph. If studied according to the theory of the Total Visual Effect, its arrangement in value and color is irrational, but it is full of merit and wisdom if we understand that the painter intended in arbitrary fashion to carry a decorative rhythm across a broad panorama of figures and architecture. Lights succeed darks. Dark appears against light, and light against dark. The shadows are cast, or omitted, according to the rules of pattern and not according to the rules of nature. What was true of the large paintings was in general true of the small ones. Tintoretto's *Miracle of Saint Mark,* taking it as a whole, is a good example of rhythmic spotting over a more limited area; and Giorgione's *The Concert* (Fig. 16.33) illustrates how the principles of tonal rhythm may be applied even to a small, portable painting.

By giving painters a sanction for modulations of color not to be justified by reference to nature, but acceptable by reference to their expressive power, the Venetian Mode extended an invitation to attempt bizarre effects. In later years, Tintoretto in particular carried boldness to the point of violence, thus suggesting to the Venetian-trained El Greco the eerie wildness so appropriate in the fervidly Catholic art produced by that Greek master after he took up residence at Toledo in Spain. Tintoretto's *Last Supper* in San Giorgio Maggiore (Fig. 16.41) will illustrate what is meant.

The Bellini

Jacopo Bellini (about 1400–1470) was the earliest important master native to Venice. Little of his painting survives, but his sketch books now in the Louvre show him as a member of the International Style (pages 531–539). His immediate inspiration came from Gentile da Fabriano, and like Gentile (Figs. 13.20–21), he made a specialty of sweet Madonnas in half-length.

Jacopo had two sons, Gentile and Giovanni. Gentile Bellini (1429–1507) was an able but uninspired painter. He devoted his entire career to pictures of Venetian life, and specialized in panoramic canvases recording the innumerable processions and ceremonies which seem to have been the chief joy of the official calendar in that picturesque city. Gentile may be said, in fact, to have established Venice as one of the perennial subjects of Western art. He was followed in that vein by Carpaccio (about 1455–1522), and by a long line of native painters culminating in Canaletto (1697–1768) and Guardi (1712–1793). Once started, the tradition of the Venetian view attracted painters from elsewhere. Claude Lorrain (1600–82) did a number of harbor scenes suggested by the imagery of the canals. Turner (1775–1851) chose Venice for the setting of one impressionistic tour de force after another. The fantastic light and color of the place will probably never cease to excite the skilled technician, and for that reason some of the very best luminist experiments by both Manet and Monet (pages 863–874) are pictures of Venice.

Giovanni Bellini (1430–1516) was emotionally more profound than either his brother or his father, and was much affected by contact with his brother-in-law, Andrea Mantegna (1431–1506), the most powerful personality in

Lombardy and Donatello's heir at Padua. Giovanni emerged in his own name about 1475, and from that date onward, paintings in large numbers came from his studio every year. Young painters were glad to work there — among them, Giorgione and Titian.

From the first, Giovanni's art belonged to the High Renaissance. A weaker man would have felt inclined to lean upon Mantegna, who was distinguished for his theoretical powers and marked in his work by a realism as passionate as the 15th Century ever produced. Giovanni's gifts were gentler, however. His most characteristic painting might be described as visual poetry; it must be felt through the intuitions, or it will have no meaning at all.

As though by unanimous consent, Giovanni got the best commissions at Venice for thirty years and more. He did a number of large pictures. The *Frari Madonna* and the *Madonna Enthroned* of San Zaccharia, may stand as examples of his work in religious art; and we may refer to his *Feast of the Gods,* the subject of a monograph by Mr. Edgar Wind, to show his capacity in handling the classical themes.

Excellent though they are, the ceremonial pictures in public places hardly spell Giovanni Bellini for those who care most about him. The pictures which reveal his nature best are the half-length Madonnas he turned out in large numbers. Fig. 16.31 shows a typical example. All of them are arranged according to the same formula. The Madonna is seen behind a low wall, on which the child stands. A narrow screen is placed a couple of feet behind her. To either side, we get glimpses of the sky and sometimes of foliage. If the latter, the leafage is always of early summer, and the light and air are soft and still. The mood is as moderate and as unforgettable as that perfect time of year. Often the Madonna looks softly down. Sometimes her eyes open out toward us. In every instance, the expression is completely innocent of any effort to appeal or to impress. The affinity with Gentile da Fabriano (Fig. 13.21) is obvious at a glance; in fact, Giovanni's Madonnas might well be thought of as the International Style brought up to date. His paintings remain unexcelled whenever and wherever a sentimental treatment of the Madonna subject might be appropriate. As compared with Raphael's Florentine Madonnas (Fig. 16.16), they maintain a level of dignity sadly lacking there. It is amazing that a single artist could so often repeat the same simple arrangement without precise duplication. It is even more remarkable that the content, which is delicate to the point of making each picture a serious aesthetic risk, never once fails or cloys.

Giorgione

Giorgione of Castelfranco (about 1475–1510) was an even more lyrical painter than Giovanni Bellini, in whose shop he worked with Titian and was his intimate friend. Unlike modern oil paintings, Venetian pictures were very slow in production; often a canvas would be turned to the wall after each stage of underpainting, and allowed to lie idle for months at a time until the paint became utterly dry. It is not surprising, therefore, that a number of pictures were only half finished when Giorgione suddenly died in 1510. Titian took them over and finished them. An immense effort of connoisseurship has failed to separate the hands; and for the purist, there is a group of paintings known as " the Giorgione-Titians " — of which Fig. 16.33 shows one.

We have already spoken of the design (page 757). The meaning can be inferred from the faces of the three performers. The young face at the left has the shallow look of the singer who can use his voice, but knows neither how he does it or what the music says. The man to the right is merely a good workman. Between the two, we see the face and hands of one whom we may judge to be the leader of the group. Obviously the only real musician of the lot, he turns as though in appeal for some sign that the others share even a little of his learning and his emotions. The loneliness of the exceptional man, if so elusive a thing can be put in words, is the subject of the painting.

In the art of the modern world, it fell to Giorgione to perform the role of Praxiteles (page 136) and to establish the female nude as a subject in its own right, to be accepted as though out of obligation by Titian, Rubens, Rembrandt, Velasquez, Goya, Canova, Ingres, Bouguereau, Cabanel, and a host of others. The painting which set the tradition in motion was the well-known *Sleeping Venus* shown in Fig. 16.32.

Any honest discussion of the picture involves the English-speaking critic in problems of the greatest social delicacy. The Victorian tradition is still strong enough to make some recent writers insist that sexual allure formed no part of Giorgione's expression. The same can hardly be said of the chaste Botticelli, who was steeped in a lofty Platonism. Much less can it be said of a painter who was popular at Venice during the 16th Century, when that city included within its catalogue of luxuries a mature and refined taste for the sensual. It is irrational to suggest that Giorgione felt a distaste for matters which were the subject of direct and open interest among his friends and contemporaries, and it is fantastic to entertain the thought that the painting constitutes a kind of prophecy of the manners and customs of England and America during the 19th Century.

The attempt to expurgate the picture is not only a failure; it is highly improper. It is far better to appreciate the painting for what it is, namely, a declaration of that physical attraction by which men are drawn to women and become devoted to them. The theme is presented tranquilly, without excitement. The fact of sleep, it will be noted, exerts a generalizing power over the warm appeal of the body. The essence of the matter, indeed, is a complete absence of narrative. Because no story is suggested, it is possible to contemplate the permanent reality of the universal desire to which all must respond in some measure. The subject of physical love thus attains the spiritual overtones without which desire itself remains incomplete, immature, and certainly no blessing.

Titian

Titian (1477–1576) enjoyed the longest career ever permitted a European artist. He was one of the world's best technicians before he finished his training under Giovanni Bellini; and when he died a few months before his hundredth birthday, he was not only still active, but capable of work that justifies the factual use of the adjective *phenomenal.* No other painter ever had the opportunity to acquire an equal measure of experience. No other was ever more fortunate — from the standpoint of technique — in the place he lived or the period he lived there, and certainly no other was better qualified by temperament and talent to advance in his chosen field. The reader will not be surprised, therefore, to be told that Titian had a broader influence upon subsequent painting than any other artist of the High Renaissance. His work, more than that of any other man, has set the standard and remained as the ideal and the norm for nearly 400 years.

In view of the length of his career, the development of Titian's style holds an unusual interest. An excellent example of his early manner is the *Sacred and Profane Love* (Fig. 16.34) in the Borghese Gallery at Rome. The odd name under which it has long been known is surely a mistake; but in spite of considerable effort scholars have not yet found an explanation that gives complete satisfaction. We can get some feeling for the content from the probability that the sarcophagus was intended for that of Adonis, whose murder by the jealous Mars appears in relief on its face. If so, the nude woman is Venus, and the baby Cupid. A recent opinion would have us identify the clothed girl as Polia, a character who appeared in the *Hypnerotomachia Poliphili,* a collection of allegorical and antiquarian love stories published at Venice in 1499. Polia was in the habit of frequenting a fountain which was kept filled with water from Adonis's stone coffin. If that is correct, Venus must be urging her to take a lover she has so far rejected.

As compared with the painter's later work, the modeling is strongly plastic, and the point of view not radically different from the Mode of Relief (pages 582–586). The masses, both in foreground and distance, seem to assert their three-dimensionality by repelling the atmosphere around them. As time went on, Titian became less and less interested in sculpturesque definition, and more and more interested in the softening and blending of things much as they actually appear on the retina of the eye.

His output during middle life was immense. It included important commissions of every kind: religious, classical, portraits. Every writer has so many favorite paintings that he cannot choose one or two for discussion without doing violence to his own feelings, let alone the preferences of his colleagues. If, however, the citation of a "typical Titian" be required, there can certainly be no quarrel with the statement that it is the *Bacchus and Ariadne* of the National Gallery in London (Figs. 16.35–36).

The picture belongs to a famous chapter in High Renaissance taste. It was commissioned by Alfonso d'Este, Duke of Ferrara, who vied with his sister Isabella in the patronage of works of art intended to explore and make manifest the ramifications of the then-popular philosophy of love (pages 653–654). Between them, the two scholarly aristocrats called into being a substantial corpus of refined erotica, most of it with classical subject matter. For the whole story, we may refer the reader again to Mr. Wind's monograph (page 758), merely placing the Bacchus in the series by saying that it seems to deal with the frustrative aspect of the relations between male and female.

Mr. Wind pointed out that the imagery corresponds reasonably well with lines 505–508 in the *Fasti* III of Ovid, and he believes the scene is meant for the final encounter between the two lovers. Ariadne had long since been abandoned by the faithless God. One day as she was walking on the beach bemoaning her condition and hoping for death, she suddenly found herself pursued by Bacchus. He was passing by in the course of his triumphant return from a trip to India. The presence of the Corona Borealis in the sky above Ariadne's head seems enough in itself to identify the moment, because the jewels of her crown became stars in heaven only as she died in Bacchus's arms on that occasion.

Strangely enough, the literary source for the painting had, since the 17th Century, been cited as a passage from Catullus (*Carmina* LXIV), which does not fit nearly so well in the matter of imagery, and tells, moreover, of the first and not the last meeting of the two. How could it have happened that the narrative content of so famous and so accessible a painting was mistakenly interpreted for so long? Why was there no expression of dissatisfaction, no searching for a better answer? Are we to suppose that otherwise energetic scholars used no common sense? Or is it more likely that they simply did not bother with subject matter because subject matter is rarely worth bothering about in Titian?

Before embarking upon a statement, it is fair that the reader should be warned that, with respect to Titian's content, sincere students of the subject take variant views. The opinion presented here is one the author has found no reason to change for some years, but one with which others strongly disagree.

Here, and elsewhere, it seems that Titian indulged his interest in visual aesthetics even to the brink of contradicting what he purported to represent. The painting states that Bacchus has just jumped clean out of his chariot in a crazy dive toward Ariadne, but Bacchus is in fact a static figure. The same may be said of every other. The postures are those ordinarily assumed only under exertion; but there is no strain and nobody moves. We are reminded of the event Keats described on the Grecian urn: nothing is going to happen, and the future is the same as the present. The story was taken, that is to say, at a point when all its visual imagery fell into composition, and the artist's concern was less with the passion and tragedy of the narrative, and more with the inspired decorative surface Titian was better able to produce than any other man.

Accepting his scheme for what it appears to have been, no praise can be too high. The painting contains within it almost every expedient of design known to the art. No analysis in words can possibly do more than hint at the complexity and perfection of its organization.

The broader elements of the composition, for example, can scarcely be comprehended at all unless we analyze the arrangement in at least three different ways. As usual, the Venetian rhythm of value alternations (page 756) carries the interest evenly over the entire surface in every direction. At the same time, a low triangular figure may be discerned, with Bacchus's head at the top; a moving Bacchus, it is worth remarking, would scarcely be appropriate at the apex of so inflexible a form. Either of the two systems mentioned (the rhythmic or the geometrical) would have been sufficient to give the painting order and intelligibility, but both coexist with a third scheme of composition which, because of its immense popularity since, requires special emphasis.

The system of arrangement was at least as old as the composition of the south front of the Erectheum at Athens (page 108). The balance, that is to say, depends upon an assymetrical grouping of objects within the represented space. The principle involved was to work out a psychologically satisfactory equilibrium by producing an equation of subject matter. The method is in considerable contrast with balance obtained through the stability of a geometric figure (Fig. 16.13), with balance established by an equilibrium of forces (Fig. 3.14), and also with balance which depends upon the leverage of avoirdupois in symmetrical groups (Figs. 3.15–16).

Within the limits of the scheme, innumerable variations are possible, but the one Titian used here (which he appears to have worked out with Giorgione, who had used it for his *Sleeping Venus*) occurs most often. It has been popular enough, in fact, to account for the composition of more than half the paintings since produced in Europe and America.

The eye, it will be noted, can reach out into the distance only at the upper left-hand corner of the picture. The opposite side is screened off from top to bottom by barriers which are very nearly impenetrable, and the foreground extends broad across the canvas from the bottom edge of the frame upward for about half its height.

The form depends for success upon our intense curiosity about what may be discovered in the far distance. That appeal for attention registers upon the consciousness even though we may believe and declare that we look at nothing and care for nothing but the subject matter in the foreground.

In pulling an explanation out of the semiconsciousness as we do, we indulge in a method of argument admittedly susceptible of abuse. It may help, therefore, to point out that the pictorial function of a deep vista may escape the awareness of an observer for several reasons. The distance may seem, for example, to be neutral with respect to narrative, but inspection of a hundred paintings will show that the landscape chosen for each is ordinarily of a character likely to enhance the mood of the foreground content. Just as the sustaining instruments in the orchestra escape direct analysis, but are necessary, so the small areas of distance are not only vital to this particular form of pictorial composition, but powerful enough in their attraction to balance an immense weight of active subject matter on the opposite side of the painting. In the instance under review, it will be observed that Titian took pains to make certain the vista he used would have ample power to attract attention. Bacchus and his companions enter from the upper right, and proceed over the ground in an arc that is roughly circular. The eye is led from left to right along one thing and another until Ariadne's right arm points directly out into the beyond; and the bluffs on the shore continue back and back in an unbroken curve.

Because the reader is destined to see similar compositions constantly as he studies the further history of painting, and because the scheme of arrangement analyzed here actually attained sufficient currency to make it a pictorial form comparable to one of the recognized musical or poetical forms, it will be useful to give it a name. We may refer to it as *the composition dependent upon a balance of mass against distance,* or more accurately as an arrangement of *mass against interest.* Although the small area of distance is usually at one upper corner or another, it obviously may be placed in the middle or anywhere else; the essential thing is to arrive at an equilibrium of appeal to the observer's attention. Distance, moreover, is merely the most usual subject matter employed for that purpose. Anything else which is comparatively small in scale but intense in the power to attract will do as well.

The intricate perfection of the composition of the *Bacchus and Ariadne* is matched by an equally accomplished handling of its most minute details. Throughout the painting, there runs a theme of harmony with respect to line and shape which is identical in physical fact with a great variety in the matter of hue and value.

The cloud above Ariadne, for example, has a silhouette that echoes her own, while the branch over Bacchus is an approximate repeat of his flying fold of drapery, but of opposite outline and in dark rather than light. The spaniel dog, on a smaller scale, has much the same outline as the leopard harnessed to the chariot; but once again, the value of its original is reversed. Repetitions of a V-shaped figure run all through the painting, sometimes flat on the plane of the picture, sometimes at an angle to it. The legs of the infant satyr may be said to announce the motive, which is symmetrically reflected by the front outline of the little dog and by the ears of the calf's head on the ground behind. Thence the V's go out to either side in the legs and arms of almost everybody else.

However honestly and thoroughly we make lists of such matters when we see them, the intricate visual perfection of those interacting elements cannot be carried over into verbal description; it is merely hoped that the latter will aid the eye of the reader. Taking the history of painting as a whole, however, there are few who would quarrel with the assertion that Titian's mastery of the pictorial art was not only more facile and ramified than that of any earlier artist, but plainly more accomplished. To date, it must be added, no other painter has demonstrated a comparable fertility of imagination in those abstract inventions which he so easily incorporated into the design of something that many persons have taken as no more than an unusually skilful performance in the field of representative painting.

Portraits formed a minor but constant part of Titian's business. It may be questioned whether portraiture, as such, ever has or ever can open up vistas leading toward the full greatness of art; and were it not for Titian's paramount influence upon all future paintings of that class, we might skip the department altogether. Titian worked out a certain portrait-formula, however. Rubens took it up, and passed it on both to the court painters of France, and to Van Dyck. Van Dyck's spectacular success in London established the same formula in England, and no other was used by Hogarth, Reynolds, Romney, Raeburn, or any of the other British portrait painters down through Sir Thomas Lawrence, who died in 1830. In details of style, portrait painting changed several times during the 19th Century, but the original Titianesque formula is still often used for the arrangement. Mr. Wyndham Lewis used it once again, for example, when painting a portrait of Chancellor Capen (1937) for the University of Buffalo — a picture that is otherwise radically modern, being Byzantine in figure-style and cubistic in modeling.

Among the many available examples, none is better as a general demonstration than the *Charles the 5th* (Fig. 16.37). We may note in passing that the handling shows, by comparison to earlier work, considerably less plasticity and substantially more blending of the masses into the environment; but with respect to the formula now under review, the first point to be considered is the size of the canvas, which is grandiose for so simple a picture. Next, it should be observed that we find our line of sight directed upward toward the magnificently competent emperor, who wears his gorgeous armor as unconsciously as a peasant might wear a smock. The environment is appropriate to the majesty of the sitter: he rides not through wild country, but over the lawns of a great park. The occasion for the painting, moreover, was a significant moment in the history of the Hapsburgs and of Europe; Charles's army had just beaten the troops of the Elector of Saxony at Muhlberg, thus scoring heavily for the Catholic cause in the Counter Reformation.

What went for the king, went also for the king's men, and official portraiture has ever since been much as Titian established it. The paintings, that is to say, have been in the Venetian Mode. They have been made as large as possible, with the line of sight arranged to make it necessary to hang them abnormally high. Whatever the facts, the pictures have uniformly described the sitter as a person of superior physical, moral, and intellectual power, with the inevitable suggestion that he thought in large terms and was dependable in the world of great affairs. Aristocracy has been the true subject matter of all such portraiture, to which the average man must incline his eyes upward from a remove as though to admire his betters.

And yet it is always politic to remind the commons that however nobly the lords conform to the ideal of nobility, the lords are human and humane. It therefore became customary to include some object indicative of the sitter's private interests, or to show him doing something he liked to do. Scholars look up from a book. Scientists have an instrument in hand, or beside them. Sportsmen stand beside a fine horse. But best of all, from the standpoint of eliciting the ordinary man's sincere admiration, was an opportunity to show the sitter performing some everyday act in which he excelled. Titian set the fashion when he chose to put the emperor on a horse and make him hold a lance in his hand. Everyone who saw the painting was thereby reminded of a boastful complaint that had become a byword in Charles's armies, namely, that affairs of state had robbed them of the best cavalry commander in Europe — presumably to the disappointment of the monarch also.

In 1545, Titian went to Rome. He stayed there eight months. It is difficult, as indicated, to know the inward heart of such a man, or to tell how profoundly he was capable of being affected by an experience; but we may certainly note a substantial change in his painting which seems to date from approximately that time.

The Rome Titian saw was Rome at the start of the Counter Reformation, and the same Rome in which Michaelangelo was spending the latter part of his career. It is evident from the later pictures that Titian felt some necessity for responding to what looked like a ground swell in European art and culture. Like Michaelangelo, he moved in a direction that predicted the Baroque. Perhaps under the influence of the *Laocoön* (Fig. 6.20) and the other Hellenistic pieces by which Michaelangelo himself was being influenced (page 745), he made his later figure-style more ponderous, and began to employ poses eloquent of true muscular strain. We may note the same new stridency in both his religious and his mythological painting, and we may assume that he was attempting to supply the fervid excitement which, foreign though it was to his temperament as we have known it to date, was to be of the essence in the art of the 17th Century.

The *Rape of Europa* (1559), one of many classical subjects painted for Philip the 2nd of Spain and now in Fenway Court in Boston, is typical of the later mythologies and unquestionably the best Titian in America. The experience of inspecting the picture is a strain on the eyes. To the right, the figure group performs a slashing diagonal across the vertical surface. The distance opens up on the left in no gentle fashion; the vista is a breakneck rush out into space. The color by no means diminishes the general commotion; it is bold in the foreground and alive with fire over the mountains. Tricks of perspective add a disquieting sense of the supernatural. We see Europa and the bull along the horizontal line of sight, but look down from a great height into the landscape far behind and beyond them. Presumably we are up in the air with no platform to stand on, and we look two ways at once as we sometimes do in dreams.

Needless to say, the balance of such a composition is precarious, and the total effect of the painting strenuous rather than reposeful. The whole affair illustrates not only the trend of the times, but still further the odd relation between Titian and his subject matter. Why did he open up with such thunder about an abduction that amounts to a fairy tale?

Among the later religious paintings, we can do no better than study the last of them all, the *Pietà* (Fig. 16.38) Titian intended for his own tomb. The design dates from 1573, and the execution was not quite complete when the master died in 1576.

In the matter of style, the picture carries almost to a conclusion the predictions inherent in his later development. The technique bears no further relationship to the Mode of Relief (pages 582–586), by which — whatever its merits — the art of painting had for so long taken its lessons from sculpture. The plastic reality of figures and objects was, in this last phase of his style, submerged in a vaporous harmony of atmosphere. Only by a conscious effort, in fact, can the eye separate out any particular shape for special inspection. Titian's control over tonal relations was more subtle and more profound than ever before. The tones themselves have the quiet of an elderly man. A soft golden light is reflected from the apse; it plays over the figures in this direction and that, bathing everything in gentle melancholy. The brushwork, which might be described as moderately impressionistic, is hardly that if the term connotes incomplete description; the technique is so magnificently competent that the slightest flick of the brush told its tale to the full. There is, as a matter of fact, almost no paint on the surface, and the grain of the canvas shows through.

The content, unfortunately, was slightly marred by the increasingly operatic taste of the later 16th Century. What place has a pirouetting angel of the Cupid type in this quiet scene? Why is the Magdalen presented to us in a state of shock, yelling? Aside from those incongruous details, the scene is among the most dignified in the history of sepulchral art. Titian himself appears in the role of Saint Joseph of Arimathea. It is a notable characterization. The old gentleman kneels with courtly tenderness to assist the Madonna, accepting the inevitable tragedy as quietly as he accepted the certainty of his own early death.

Tintoretto

Jacopo Robusti (1518–94), universally known as Tintoretto, was the last of the great figures in the Venetian School, and except for Caravaggio (pages 806–808) the last Italian artist who, in the long view of history, may be styled as a creative genius of the first order.

He was apprenticed to Titian, but Titian disliked him and dismissed him from the shop before his time was up. An early account of the affair imputes jealousy as Titian's motive, which is incredible because of the position he then occupied at Venice. The probable truth of the matter lies in their personal differences. Tintoretto's style derived from Titian's, but his taste and temperament were of a kind admirably calculated to offend the older master. Paradoxically enough, the offensive element was an early demonstration of the very qualities Titian himself tried to incorporate in his own later work. Tintoretto reacted vigorously and at times flamboyantly to his subject matter.

His most characteristic pictures are full of urgency and action. He seemed to consider it important to whip up the observer's emotions by every devise of technique and content. To study even his more moderate paintings (Fig. 16.39) is to become conscious of a certain heightening in the atmosphere.

The broader principles of his art have been set forth in our discussion of the Venetian Mode (pages 752–757). It now remains to summarize the innovations to which we have just referred.

No earlier painter employed directional forces with an equal prodigality. His first consideration was to find an angle of sight so new, so odd, and so unfamiliar as to be startling in its own right. An upward angle of vision had been used before, but hardly with the same temerity. It is one thing to ask the observer to raise his eyes (Fig. 16.37) and another thing to put the central actors of the pictorial drama at the top of a near vertical incline going off diagonally from the surface of the picture (Fig. 16.39).

Having found an angle of vision sufficiently novel to meet his taste, Tintoretto would then figure out ways to enforce movement into the represented space. Every imaginable directional impulse was used in one picture or another: the gesture, the figure in motion, the glance of a startled eye, spectacular foreshortening, powerful perspectives of architecture — and the list has only begun. Because he almost invariably forced the movement inward, or somewhere near it, certain important and novel results were obtained. The space represented by the picture tended to impress the observer as a continuation of the volume within which he himself was standing at the moment, and the effect of that was to evoke a sense of personal involvement with the events already so strongly described. In extreme instances, Tintoretto may be said to blast his way into our sensibilities. However vivid, the experience is not without pain.

By historical chance, it was Tintoretto rather than any other man who first became synonymous in the European mind with everything suave, elegant, desirable, and Italian in the artistic manipulation of the human figure. The popular mystery of El Greco's art can be explained, for example, if we merely appreciate that his earliest imagery came from the late Byzantine pictures he saw on the Island of Crete, that he cross-bred that style with Tintoretto, and moved on to Spain to use it for paintings which are either lofty or morbid in their mysticism, or both.

Tintoretto had a slogan lettered on his wall, to which he often called attention. It read: *The color of Titian and the drawing of Michaelangelo.* In trying to make out his meaning, we should probably construe the word *color* very broadly indeed. In addition to its strict denotation in terms of hue, tint, and shade, he doubtless meant to call up a total impression of those ways in which Titian differed from Michaelangelo: the absence of intellectual severity and the presence of sensuous and even sensual beauty. The aim was very nearly achieved. His women are unusually large, unusually soft of flesh, and unusually delicate in complexion. His men are fit mates for them. Both sexes commonly were made to sit or stand in exaggerated contrapposto; and in accordance with his habit, he usually presented both from some unusual angle of view. However insignificant for the narrative in hand, every figure was made to move like a dancer (Fig. 16.41, lower right) and was made to seem in itself a thing of absolute beauty.

Without impeaching the authenticity of Tintoretto's art, we must recognize that his deliberate combination of two recent successful styles differed from the normal assimilation by a younger artist of elements in the art of his elders. He was not trying to create a new thing, but to play safe by combining two known values in the hope of losing neither and profiting by both. His point of view bore a subtle but all-important contrast to the outlook entertained by Giotto, Donatello, Michaelangelo and other men upon whose work the history of art depends. His was a philosophy of derivation. The concept of creative synthesis, the life-giving element in all the greatest art, was lacking.

In the case of Tintoretto, the reader may well complain that we bear down too heavily upon a distinction that made small difference. In the world-view, however, the very existence of the distinction proved prophetic. The day Tintoretto put his slogan on the wall was the day Italian art crossed a great divide. The results were at first hardly perceptible, but in the end Italy ceased to be the center of European art and culture.

Tintoretto's career, especially his endorsement of amazement as a value in its own right, proved to be a signal that a new era in Renaissance culture was about to open up and swallow all within it. Not only does he mark the end of his era and the beginning of the Baroque; with him, the importance of the Venetian School ceased. Venice continued to have good painters right up to the Napoleonic era; but between Canaletto, Guardi, Tiepolo, and Longhi on the one hand, and Titian on the other, everyone must accept a difference in calibre. One cause seems to have been the loss by Venice of the special advantages which had formed the foundation of her materialistic philosophy. The discovery of the direct route to the Far East around the Cape of Good Hope (1498) opened that trade to shipping from northern Europe, and gradually subtracted from the importance of the Mediterranean. The opening of the New World had a similar effect. To this day, the city maintains her local pride and a substantial prosperity; but her pre-eminence lies in the past.

NORTHERN ARTISTS OF THE HIGH RENAISSANCE

As set forth in Chapters 13 and 15, the north of Europe had developed its realistic tradition direct from the Gothic; and whatever its content and however scientific its representational techniques, northern art remained Gothic in form throughout the 15th Century. Only here and there do we find a detail or two to suggest direct influence either from Italy or the Antique: for example, the architecture in *The Madonna with Chancellor Rolin* (Fig. 15.1) makes one wonder if the painter had been south of the Alps.

By about 1500, however, the situation was different. It was no longer possible for anybody to escape consciousness of an artistic garden, blooming with a new and gracious fragrance, stretching from the Piedmont to Naples, and full of beguiling southern flowers. As one might expect, a good many northern artists who otherwise might have continued in their own tradition made tours of Italy and tried as best they might to assimilate the lovely Italian style. Such men were most numerous in court circles or at metropolitan centers: at Fontainebleau, for example, and also at Antwerp, which by then had assumed its modern character of the greatest port in Europe, with an active trade leading to Italy and everywhere else.

As typical of the many Flemish artists who cultivated an Italian style, we may name Jan Gossaert, called Mabuse (1470–1541); Bernard van Orley (1493–1542); Jan Sanders, called Hemessen (1504–63); and Fran Floris (1516–70). Fig. 16.43 may be taken as characteristic of their work.

By the time such men felt its influence, the Italian Renaissance had passed into the grander and more idealized phase represented by the later work of Raphael (Figs. 16.16–20) and his contemporaries. Not one of the Flemings mentioned was strongly creative in his own right; it may be doubted whether any of them, if born in Italy, would have made a reputation there. All of them were too easily influenced and, worse than that, too quick to assume they understood the purpose and method of the great Italians. It is difficult to explain the immense difference between authentic Italian art and the work of such Italianizing northerners, since the physical facts are so much the same. The complaint against the Flemings is not their inability to paint, for they painted well. It is the truth that the "Grand Style," whenever the epic mind was lacking, has invariably proven the very worst art known to man. Unable to think or feel in heroic terms, the artists now under review considered their problem to be merely one of adaptation, not complete change. Instead of approaching the matter philosophically, they merely smoothed up the customary anatomy of 15th-Century Flemish realism, and made it more ample and more sensual. The net result was a vulgar, uncomfortable, hybrid art with the faults of both its sources.

The painters just dealt with were popular. Without doubt they pictured themselves as leaders if not creators of taste, in the act of opening new vistas for the northern imagination. But seen in historical perspective, they were faddish men who had nothing to do with the true worth of northern art during the High Renaissance. The latter depended upon the existence of several masters of grand scope and magnificent personality who, although very well informed about the Italian style, remained steadfastly Gothic in their idiom while demonstrating an imaginative drive and expressive power equal to the best of the Italians. We refer to Hieronymus Bosch, Albrecht Dürer, and Peter Brueghel.

Hieronymus Bosch

Hieronymus Bosch (about 1450–1516) was probably born at Aachen. He painted a good many pictures of the conventional Flemish kind, of which his *Adoration of the Magi,* a three-paneled folding altarpiece now in Madrid, may serve as an example. His special reputation depends, however, on work of quite another sort.

One of the most famous is a large triptych in the Museum of Fine Arts at Lisbon. The subject is a highly imaginative rendering of the *Temptations of Saint Anthony*. The Saint to whom we refer was the one born at Alexandria in the 4th Century. He was a celebrated hermit. Even by the strenuous standards of that time and place, his asceticism attracted unusual interest and made him a special target for the schemes of the Devil. First, that Black Master undertook to torment the Saint with all kinds of seductive thoughts calculated to drive him mad by filling his mind with images of the comforts and pleasures he might enjoy by a mere relaxation of the will. When that failed, the Devil resorted to physical methods. Delicious foods and drinks were set out to lure Anthony from his unimaginably austere diet. Lovely courtesans were sent to assail his chastity. When those measures also failed, the Devil lost his temper and sent demons and monsters to give the Saint a brutal beating.

Bosch handled the subject with an intensity of detail typical of all northern art (page 296). Although the panels are large, items appear in such multiplicity as to render the whole painting unsuitable for reproduction on a small scale, and in Figs. 16.45–46 we accordingly show two typical sections in close-up. Seen as a whole, the painting shows Anthony seated before a Crucifix in a cell opening toward us in the middle of a castle ruin which fills the central part of the main panel; Bosch probably derived the idea from the tradition that Anthony lived in a cave. The courtesans disport themselves at table on a stone terrace outside. Around the ruin, there may be seen an unrivalled collection of real and imaginary monsters (Fig. 16.46), all of the most sinister aspect. Every one of them seems himself to be tortured, morbid, or both, and every gesture is surcharged with ghastly menace.

The terrific scene is presented against a landscape which runs continuously through all three panels. The wings open up to a view of sea and harbor; doomed ships are there, either wrecked or sinking. A burning village (Fig. 16.45) appears in the background of the main panel, with a party of armed men traversing a bridge.

It goes without saying that Bosch worked in the region later to be entered by William Blake (1757–1827) and still later by Chirico, Dali, and the other Surrealists of the present day. As explained above (page 423), Surrealism abandons a setting in the world, and finds a locus elsewhere. Its method is always the same: to depict with devastating specificity the most radical concepts of the visual imagination. A generation ago, it was customary to explain Bosch's diabolism as an excursion of the fancy, usually intended to amuse. Whenever, in a particular instance, the appeal to humor failed to satisfy, the notion of satire came forward; and when that too seemed incongruous in the face of the painter's self-evident earnestness, one heard the phrase ". . . foolish superstition which the world has now outgrown." All such notions now seem like nonsense. Anticipating psychiatry by about 450 years, Bosch did his greatest work in the nether reaches of the mind, that realm more-real and yet not-real, before whose gateway all men pause in dread.

The subject matter with which Bosch dealt was different from the psychological malaise with which we are immediately familiar. He lived among a population largely illiterate, during an era when the Church was losing its power to soothe and reassure. Terrible imaginings came to the surface, more dreadful than any we moderns can comprehend because there was no way to explain them, and no hope of therapy.

Those who have traced northern art from its beginnings (pages 295 ff) will of course recognize the pedigree of Bosch's grotesques; the genus is as old as the barbarian invasions of the ancient world. One effect of Christianity, however, had been to hold under control the violence of the northern temperament and, by the same token, its tendency to radically fantastic imagery. In general, that restraining influence was remarkably effective during the entire Middle Age, with the ever-existent turbulence of the barbarian taste breaking through only occasionally as in the Utrecht Psalter (Figs. 9.45–46) and the more extreme Romanesque tympana (Fig. 11.12). Bosch appeared just when the discipline of the Church was becoming less effective as a social reality. He was therefore free to roam where he pleased in an area hitherto quarantined. He appeared, also, at a time and place almost ideal for the purpose: in the Flemish region when it was impossible to be a painter at all without possessing an exhaustive knowledge of representative accuracy and the best techniques for achieving it. Without realism, Surrealism is impossible; its power to convince depends upon its capacity to say that the outlandish is actual.

Again capitalizing upon the achievements of northern realism, Bosch may be said to have been the founder of the modern tradition of *vulgar genre,* an aspect of northern art destined to survive long after the patrician taste of the Renaissance had submerged every other remnant of Gothic feeling. The so-called *Prodigal Son,* formerly in the Figdor collection at Vienna, is perhaps the best-known painting of the class. Fig. 16.44, important for other reasons also, will likewise illustrate what is involved. As a general category, vulgar genre finds interest in the stable and the drunken party, and displays a liking for the company of farmhands, peddlers, tramps, whores, and bums. Bosch was simply the first of a notable line of northern artists, among whom we may name Adrian Brouwer (1605–85), Adriaen van Ostade (1610–85), David Teniers the Younger (1610–90), the 17th-Century French painters called Le Nain, and the British Hogarth (1697–1764), who was the last of the great Gothic artists. To a man, such painters used all the skills of the Renaissance to assert the reality and validity of the unthinking majority who owned nothing, hoped for nothing, and worked with their hands. Their philosophy was opposite to the classical and Italian bent for selection by reference to some theory of beauty or edification. In the presence of their art, the heartbeat of Renaissance decorum inexorably slows and misses time. What are the deep racial instincts which pull us toward surroundings and behavior from which we are foreclosed by every tenet in the code of manners that all the world learned from Italy during the 16th Century?

Bosch seems less to participate in his own vulgar genre than to tell its story with an overtone of heartbreak. Subtle and perhaps imperceptible in many paintings, his deep bitterness comes out plainly in the great *Christ before Pilate,* at Princeton (Fig. 16.44). The use of gross persons as actors in the sacred drama was in itself a shocking thing, but the device has to do with a judicious realism of thought as applied to Christianity. The meaning of the picture hinges upon the physical and even the mental contrast between Christ and the persons around him. In a world where shrewd officials train and control professionally brutal men to keep the mob in hand, is it intelligent to expect much from a little preacher who, as history tells us, got himself hopelessly caught? Although rarely stated so baldly then or now, there is much evidence, pictorial and otherwise, to indicate that more than one prominent person of the 16th Century entertained the specific belief that Christianity had failed. Michaelangelo certainly squared up to that possibility, even if he did not accept it (pages 745–750). Peter Brueghel, as we shall see, seems to have abandoned hope like Bosch.

Albrecht Dürer

In the history of German culture, Albrecht Dürer (1471–1528) occupies a position comparable to the one held by Leonardo with reference to Italy. He had immense prestige among his contemporaries, prestige which rested only in part upon his accomplishments as an artist. He wrote a book on geometry with special reference to its application in art. Another book dealt with fortification, and still another with anatomy and the human proportions. He was an intelligent and profound scholar in almost every field of learning then available, a fact which greatly enhanced the contemporary authority of his art. He was, in addition, a friendly man.

Dürer has traditionally been introduced to students as a painter. His career in that medium may be evaluated by reference to the portrait of his father (1490), now in Florence, and to the three self-portraits — in the Louvre (1493), the Prado (1498), and the Alte Pinakothek at Munich (1500?). Supplementary reference should also be made to such religious paintings as the *Landauer Altarpiece,* an *Adoration of the Magi* (1511), now in Vienna; and to the *Four Apostles* (1526) in the Alte Pinakothek. An honest estimate of such work is bound to suggest that we must hold Dürer's painting in less esteem than we hold the man. The technique was superb, but the style was an unsuccessful attempt to combine an exceptionally florid Late Gothic taste with the measured idealism of the Italian High Renaissance.

It is a mere affectation, however, to think of painting as a " major art " and print making as a " minor art "; the truth about Dürer is that he ought to be approached by way of his engraving, and judged by it. He had a personal taste for the medium, evidencing thereby the German genius for mechanics and for metal work in general. The unparalleled precision of the graver made a virtue, in fact, rather than a fault of the Gothic instinct for intensive detail. In Dürer's case, that was unusually fortunate and necessary, because he seems to have had an unlimited faith in the power of elaboration. As an architect, he would have been weak and tedious. As a painter, he was prolix. But with his own tools, he turned out a wealth of work which defies the faultfinder. Not only was he the greatest engraver who ever lived; engraving was par excellence the ideal medium for making the most of German taste at that period.

It is possible to have a personal fondness for almost every plate Dürer ever did. On the basis of technical perfection and on the basis also of spiritual profundity, three particular prints stand out from all the others. They are the *Knight, Death, and Devil* (1513) (Fig. 16.47) and the two plates from the next year, *Saint Jerome in His Study* and the *Melancholia*. The three are about of the same size, and were evidently intended as a set. They were not meant to be shown as a single composition; the unity of the set depends, rather, upon an organic relation of content. The *Knight* typifies the Christian faced with the problems of the daily world in which he must decide, act, and persevere. The *Saint Jerome* stands for the Christian scholar who secludes himself to make contemplation possible. The *Melancholia* refers to the creative faculty of mankind; it suggests that humanity is there closest to the divine, and yet sadly ineffective. The iconography of all three is complex; we can only suggest it here and refer the reader to the excellent account in Mr. Edwin Panofsky's *Dürer*.

It is probable that Dürer had been in north Italy in 1494. He must inevitably have seen Donatello's *Gattamelata* at Padua (Figs. 15.15–16), and he must also have studied Verrocchio's *Colleoni* at Venice (page 721), which had been set up on its marble pedestal only a year or two before. In addition to those notable monuments, all the world knew that Leonardo himself was then at Milan, and had declared his intention of making himself the author of an even greater equestrian group. His notebooks contain many sketches which we now relate to the *Francesco Sforza* upon which the great Florentine did intermittent work from 1483 to 1493, in which latter year he was ready to put a full-size model on exhibition — presumably the same model that stood in the courtyard of the Castello when the French entered Milan in October 1494 (page 709) and put an end to the project by destroying both the model and the house of Sforza. It seems inescapable that Dürer's interest in an equestrian composition must have been stimulated if not suggested by his Italian tour, and scholars have amused themselves ever since by finding resemblances between the *Knight*, the two completed statues in Italy, and the drawings of Leonardo, with which Dürer must in some way have become familiar. The rhythm of his engraved horse seems to be Donatello's, but the conformation of the animal and the armor of the rider are more like Verrocchio. It is worth remarking as we pass that the triangular composition of the figure and its setting in a rocky pass are reminiscent of Giotto's *Flight into Egypt* (Fig. 13.46), a painting Dürer must have seen even though 16th-Century artists, taking them as a class, were snobbish in their attitude toward " the primitives."

The content is both very ancient and very new. We see the knight riding across the picture, presumably making his way toward a beautiful city set high on a peak and appearing against the sky in the far distance. Death on a tired horse speaks to him, and brandishes an hourglass. The Devil, half pig and half wolf, apparently also has tried to get a hearing, but the rider has already gone by. A big dog, something like our modern golden retriever, runs along intent on some errand outside the picture.

The image of the Christian as a warrior goes back to Saint Paul, whose epistles are often spiced with the military vocabulary. Dürer also inherited the idea from the Crusades; and even more directly from Erasmus, who had used *Christian Soldier* in the title of one of his early essays.

For any well-informed German, the " breastplate of righteousness " was no mere figure of speech in 1513. The religious situation was volcanic. Violence was to be expected, and Erasmus tried to exert a moderating influence. In effect, it was his hope to bring about harmony by persuading both clergy and laity to embrace a better understanding of both Christianity and humanism. Sin, he contended, was not only prohibited by God, but beneath the dignity of man. If that much could be generally accepted, it followed that temptations would lose their power, and no one need fear them. Such, probably, was Dürer's reason for showing fiends as mere spooks. The Christian knight simply overlooks them, and the Christian dog doesn't even bother to sniff their scent.

The *Saint Jerome in His Study* (Fig. 16.49) can hardly be excelled as a celebration of the *vita contemplativa.* Although spatial realization had been a northern specialty for more than a hundred years, Dürer's elegant perspective — the work of an accomplished mathematician — opens up the room before us in extraordinary fashion. It is hard to believe we are inspecting a small picture; it seems much more as though we had actually looked in upon the fine old gentleman and saw him as friends might who had just come in the door. His lion looks sleepily up as Saint Bernard dogs do when familiars arrive; in a moment, the saint will finish his paragraph and look up also. In the meantime, we can envy the order and simple comfort possible only for bachelors: a few pieces of good furniture, and all one's gear ready at hand without any crowding. The windows face the south; and from the shadows, we may judge it is the middle of the morning on a fine day. No painter and no photographer could possibly rival the beauty of the light; not only does the engraver have sharper contrasts to work with, but also he can stipple and make the sun flicker with life in a manner from which even the French Impressionists were foreclosed by the coarse tools they used.

From the *Saint Jerome,* in which the artist himself obviously took so much simple, genial pleasure, it is a disquieting experience to turn to the *Melancholia*

(Fig. 16.48). If we may judge from the shadow cast by an hourglass hung on the wall above the head of the central figure, the setting is in moonlight. A comet blazes across the sky, and it is chilly enough to make the half-fed dog curl up. The personified Melancholy crowds herself heavily into the right foreground. Her face is sensitive, tired, and distraught. Her hair and her dress are in a mess, the result of long, concentrated effort. She has wings, but the idea of flight is ridiculous because they are too small for so gross a body. She sits in front of a partially finished building, with some fine tools in disorder around her. In her hand, she holds a beautiful pair of dividers, and there is a discarded book on her knee. A baby, perched uncomfortably on the rim of a grinding wheel, digs busily into a slate with an iron spike, doubtless making horrid squeaks as he does it.

The mood of the *Melancholia* is plain enough at a glance. Its more profound meaning involves an immensely complex excursion into medieval lore. The main features may, however, be explained without reference to details.

In its ultimate heritage, the theme goes back to the classical tradition which held that the nature of mankind might be explained by reference to four humors: the sanguine, the choleric, the phlegmatic, and the melancholic. Each humor responded to a physical cause in the form of a vital fluid supposedly contained within the system. Ideally, all four fluids ought to be in what sounds like physical and chemical balance. Since they usually were not, individual men had to submit to a more or less warped temperament.

The four humors were also thought to have an astrological significance. The planet Saturn had come to be identified with the melancholic cast of mind; hence the adjective *saturnine*. Because Saturn was an earth god who had much influence over agriculture, he was conceived as having a special and necessary interest in quantitative measure of all kinds. In particular, he was thought to hold jurisdiction over the survey of land. From that, it was no step at all to making Saturn God of Geometry. The magic square on the wall at the upper right was, as a matter of fact, a talisman in sixteen compartments calculated to divert the gloomy influence of Saturn into constructive channels.

Among the 16th-Century intellectuals, of whom Dürer was one, both melancholy and geometry had recently acquired new life and meaning. The entire representative convention (pages 539–542) owed much of its prestige to the sanction from geometry as reflected in the 15th-Century research into the principles of linear perspective. As the Early Renaissance passed on into the High, a further attempt had been made (page 722) to satisfy the aesthetic sense by geometric compositions which, it had been hoped, would provide art with the finality and completeness of the Antique.

Already connected with art through Saturn and geometry, the melancholic temperament had lately become identified with the creative imagination by another and yet stronger chain of reasoning. Marsilio Ficino (pages 649 ff) had, among his other contributions, popularized a bit of Aristotle's mistaken but unbelievably accurate dogmatism. Aristotle (384–322 B.C.) noted that creative persons tend to be abstracted, that they exhaust themselves with effort, and that they often get downhearted. Neglecting the more exalted moments of the creative cycle, he flatly declared that every superior man is necessarily a melancholic. The amusing discovery that Plato himself had been born under the sign of Saturn added a further thought that did nothing to diminish the popularity of that idea. To this day, intellectual snobs the world over cultivate melancholy, and creative persons often give the impression of it.

With such information to help us, Dürer's obscure plate may be understood. The little baby with his slate signifies the optimism of naïve and misdirected effort. The frustrated goddess symbolizes the incapacity of the mature mind to realize meaningful achievement. There is some reason to think that the geometrical apparatus, disposed in most ungeometrical arrangement, reflects Dürer's personal discouragement with geometry as such. The history of his critical writings indicates that he had first hoped to locate beauty by increasingly subtle geometric reasoning. After a great deal of work, he gave the idea up as impractical. In the absence of better mathematics, it would seem that he identified geometry with the rational faculty. The trouble with the rational faculty, as Dürer seems to have found out, is our inability to reason beyond what we can measure and count. In a word, every man must be enough of a mystic to know that the mind cannot keep pace with the imagination. It must be some such feeling that accounts for the inadequate wings Dürer gave his goddess and for her apparent realization that her keys would open nothing.

Inasmuch, also, as all three of the plates under review date from a time when religious issues were tense and grave, and when Dürer himself was in agony over which way to turn, it is possible to interpret the *Melancholia* as an expression of doubt with respect to the Renaissance itself. Humanism, particularly humanism as represented by such men as Alberti, inevitably involved some measure of departure from religion as the hope of grace, and an equivalent assumption by the self of the burden for achieving happiness on earth and ultimate salvation. The rational faculty was the principal tool to be employed in the process. Faith in the rational faculty was the essence of the new era; but Dürer, like Botticelli (page 662) and Michaelangelo (page 750), had evidently started to doubt.

However discouraged he may have become with them as a method for solving the problem of existence, Dürer's geometrical investigations led him into trains of thought of peculiar interest to students of 20th-Century art. His engraving of *Saint Anthony* (Fig. 16.50) stands as one of the most accomplished fusions of representative drawing with geometrical abstraction. The figure of the saint would fit almost precisely into a hollow cone. The pile of buildings rising behind him has much the same structure we can see in eroded lava of the columnar type. Dürer's work, at this particular moment in his career, was governed by a theory identical with the early Corot and the architectural pictures of Cézanne. From that position, it is scarcely a step and we arrive at Analytical Cubism (pages 925–928). A pen drawing, also dated 1519, shows two heads abstracted into a series of plane surfaces that intersect each other like the facets of a diamond. Dürer certainly had no intention of using so extreme an idiom in a finished painting. His drawing must be recognized as something he put down as it passed through his mind, but his train of thought was nevertheless indistinguishable from the one that led Cézanne toward cubism, and Picasso and Braque (building on Cézanne) right on into it.

Peter Brueghel

Peter Brueghel the Elder (about 1528–69) took his name from the place where he was born. Of the various villages available under that name or something like it, the one near Bois-le-Duc seems most likely. Because Bosch came from the same locality, his powerful influence upon Brueghel is conveniently explained. The artist himself omitted the *h* upon occasion, making the name Bruegel; but for the spelling with the German diphthong *eu* there is no authority even though his descendants sometimes use it.

Because of his low taste, English speaking critics have been slow to recognize Brueghel's greatness. The pictures so offensive to their delicacy are the numerous examples of vulgar genre, in which department of art he heartily outdid Bosch and everyone else who ever tried it. Examples are the *Peasant Dance*, the *Peasant Wedding*, and the *Parable of the Bird's Nest* in Vienna; also the *Peasant Dance* in Detroit, from which we show a detail (Fig. 16.52). In addition, there are numerous single figures depicting the same class of people. From the standpoint of the genteel, the enormity resides in the painter's apparent failure to feel distaste for such subject matter, and from the historical knowledge that he personally participated in similar revelries, did it habitually, and enjoyed it.

Some decorous critics, compelled nevertheless to admire, have tried to find a way out by interpreting Brueghel's vulgar paintings in much the same way we are supposed to get the point of the Neo-Classical tracts (Figs. 18.2–3) later produced by Jacques Louis David; i.e., as containing an edifying suggestion. In a few instances, like the *Blind Leading the Blind* (Fig. 16.51), there appears actually to have been a text (Matthew 15:14); but in other instances, if text there be, the sentiment expressed can hardly recommend the painter to the bourgeoisie. The parable of the bird's nest, for example, contains the disquieting conclusion that "He who knows where the nest is has the knowledge; he who steals it has the nest."

Without suggesting that Brueghel's wit is uniformly suitable for the drawing room, it must be conceded his offenses against daintiness are about the same as those of the poet Chaucer. In disposing of him as negligible because he was coarse, the Victorians overlooked some of the greatest painting ever done in Europe. It is now necessary to take another point of view.

In 1552–53, Brueghel made a tour of Italy, apparently going as far south as Naples. He seems to have journeyed down by way of the Rhone Valley, and to have returned over the Brenner Pass. The things he saw furnished him with new and grander subject matter for his painting and had a remarkable effect upon his artistic methods. In astonishing contrast with almost every other northerner who went to Italy, he remained completely his own man. Instead of being led around by the nose, as it were, and beguiled into imitation, he paid no attention to the superficial attractions of Italian art. At the same time, he was profoundly affected by its underlying fundamentals.

From Michaelangelo, he learned how to pose a ponderous anatomy in complex and accomplished contrapposto; but he showed no interest in a classically idealized figure-style. From Raphael and the Umbrians in general, he learned how to make space carry meaning. In fact, he seems at once to have understood the special power of Tintoretto's enforcement of movement into the represented space (page 768), and many of his landscape compositions are laid out on an inward diagonal (Fig. 16.54). The most unusual circumstance of all, considering how much he gained from Italy, is the extreme rarity of instances where we can discern a one-to-one relationship with any specific Italian masterpiece. In fact, almost the only sure case of the sort is a drawing in Hamburg, in which the figure of a northern peasant is posed exactly like one of the incidental nudes on the ceiling of the Sistine Chapel.

As a landscape painter, Brueghel has few equals and no superiors. Several of his best pictures record the winter scenery of the Low Countries; they are hardly to be surpassed for the excellence with which they communicate the damp, the cold, and the *gemütlichkeit* nowhere else to be found in the same combination at the same season of the year. The human figure, as rendered by him in such a setting, tends to take on the aspect of line and flat tone that forms actually take in nature when seen against ice and snow. By the outline alone, he was able to define mass and describe action. He demonstrated a genius for the silhouette, in fact, unknown elsewhere except in the Far East.

His true greatness had its genesis, however, in the Italian journey which brought him into contact with mountain scenery of a grandeur unknown in the Netherlands and which he employed in a series of magnificent paintings. The most famous are five which date from the two years 1565–66. They are: *The Hunters in the Snow, The Dark Day,* and *The Return of the Herd,* all in Vienna; *The Hay Harvest,* formerly in the collection of Count Lobkowitz at Raudnitz; and *The Corn Harvest,* now in the Metropolitan Museum. As distinguished from most other landscape paintings, either earlier or later, the pictures mentioned are important for the successful use of vast distances: not vistas of a mile or two, that is, but stupendous extensions of space as seen from an elevated station high in the hills, and imparting much the same sense of exaltation.

The space unaided would scarcely have carried its meaning, but it came to life under Brueghel's miraculous power to make us feel the very essence of the atmosphere at different times of the year and under various conditions of weather. His method was similar to that of the Venetians. He did not depend, that is to say, upon a systematic translation into paint of the natural phenomena. He worked, rather, through the direct appeal of tones to the emotions, and he appears to have made his choice upon that basis, whether in selecting local hues or in modeling a field.

In the familiar *Hunters in the Snow,* for example, he rendered every object within the limits of a very narrow range of tones. In addition to white for the snow, he used tints of green and of red-orange neutralized almost to the limit. A few spots of black must be mentioned for completeness, and the painting as a whole may be described roughly as gray-green pointed up here and there with the merest hint of warmth. Such are not necessarily the actual colors of winter, but they have the mood of winter in them, and no other painting concerned with that cold season carries the same conviction. By similar methods, the *Corn Harvest* is full of the golden air of autumn.

Had he lived in a happy world, Brueghel perhaps could have spent his life composing landscapes that were serene, noble, poetical, or intimate as inspiration might from time to time suggest. His career had its setting, however, amid horrors which until the time of Hitler were generally considered the worst ever perpetrated by an educated and Christian population. The Protestant Reformation had started in 1517. Because it was popular in the Netherlands, and because the Netherlands were also important for their wealth, the Catholic emperors Charles the 5th (Fig. 16.37) and his son Philip the 2nd made Brueghel's homeland the special object of their most resolute policy. Bosch had lived through some of their activity. Brueghel's maturity coincided with repressive measures of the utmost inhumanity. For the narrative at length, the reader should turn to J. L. Motley's *Rise of the Dutch Republic*. It is important to recall here that the 16th Century was the period when the Spanish Empire was attempting to solidify its power not only in the New World but in England and on the continent. Events in Flanders and Holland, where most of the important churchmen, governors, and soldiers were Spaniards, formed merely part of the larger picture.

Protestant defection in the Low Countries had brought the Inquisition into vigorous activity. The infamous memory in which it is held springs from two sources. Its methods were diametrically opposed to everything summed up in the common law of England and America, or any other law possessed of a just procedure. Its sentences, moreover, were considered barbarous even during the 16th Century. For so slight an offense as the oral discussion of theological matters, the average man was almost certain to suffer death if accused. His only hope was to establish repentance, in which case he would be hanged rather than burned.

In 1567, lesser measures having failed, Philip the 2nd sent the Duke of Alba into the Netherlands with the double purpose of suppressing heresy and crushing the liberty of the towns. Alba was one of the most competent Spaniards of the century. He came with a well-disciplined army. His sincerity cannot be questioned. His methods, however, remain a byword for inhumanity and in the end failed to accomplish the calculated result. In the course of his administration, Alba brought about the torture, maiming, hanging, burying alive, and burning of innumerable individuals. He himself estimated one batch of executions at 18,000 — a figure which must be interpreted in relation to the then population. He also mercilessly exacted ruinous taxation, and he missed no opportunity to subject both cities and citizens alike to calculated humiliation. He remained in the north six years, and returned in honor to Spain, where he died in 1583.

Brueghel's most definite description of the Spanish outrages is a drawing in the Royal Library at Brussels. It was used as copy for an engraving known as the *Justicia*, in which the details are reversed mirror-wise and seem strangely less immediate than in the original. In the middle, the Blind Goddess stands on a slab labeled with her name. A trial is being held over at the left. The space at the lower right is taken up by the figure of a man stretched on the wrack. Simultaneously he is also receiving the water cure; his abdomen is already horribly distended, and men are pouring another jar full into his mouth through a funnel. The middle ground and distance give us a catalogue of punishments which were favorite at the time: a beheading, the crushing of a right hand, a flogging, a man suspended head and heels by a rope, tall poles surmounted by cart wheels to which men are trussed, half a dozen hangings, and a burning at the stake.

Among the major paintings which deal with the same sort of thing, two stand out from all the others: *The Massacre of the Innocents* and *The Way to Golgotha.* The former is conceived as an event in a Flemish village. The savagery and pathos of the action are brought into contrast with the magnificent discipline of the Spanish cavalry; a whole company of them remain in formation while the nasty work goes on.

As a picture, *The Way to Golgotha* (Fig. 16.53) is more complicated. Its implications are likewise more sweeping. It is set in barren ground. In some particulars, the spot may recall a site near one of the Lowland cities, but a pinnacle rock like those around Le Puy suggests a memory of the painter's route to Italy. The crucifixion will take place at the upper right-hand corner, where a great circle of spectators has already formed, in the manner of the time, around the two crosses already set up. A hole in the ground awaits the shaft of the third.

Christ may be found near the center of the middle ground. The point of time is the moment when he has collapsed under the weight of the cross. A bit to the left, a press gang has taken Simon of Cyrene, to make him help with the work. Simon's desperate wife protests, and a soldier callously repels her with a spear. The other peasants run away.

The Holy Mourners occupy the lower right-hand corner of the composition; they look like a group by Roger van der Weyden (page 616). The rest of the picture is filled with Spaniards on their fine horses, yokels on their way to the show, and the detritus of yesterday's executions. The two thieves may be picked out as the men tied up and riding in a cart.

To understand the picture, it is first of all necessary to appreciate that Brueghel's dramatic method was fundamentally different from that of the Italian "Grand Style." An Italian artist, in handling the same subject, would have approached his problem very much as a Greek might have done. To him, the human figure would have seemed the artistic vehicle par excellence. The unity of time (page 60) would have been his primary artistic obligation. The unity of words, his procedure would have been to simplify the drama as much as possible by selecting the principal actors and eliminating the others, and then to pose the essential figures in such a way that the full meaning of their action would come into the field of attention instantly.

Brueghel, however, was a northern artist, and one of the very few who ever attempted to use the northern and cumulative method of presenting subject matter (page 295) in an epic painting. He had no awe for the human figure, and he did not accept the classical theory of selection, elimination, and simplification. Indeed, we cannot find Christ himself without hunting for him; he is an obscure person in a crowd which itself is a mere part of the setting. Many things are going on at once. The eye must resolve them one by one, turning to the next thing in due time. Memory plays a part in the process. Comprehension is gradual, and the effect is built up piece by piece and item by item until we finally possess ourselves of the picture, total and complete.

Realizing that we cannot come into visual possession of the picture by a single act of inspection, and understanding also that its meaning is compound rather than simple, we can see that there is significance even in the bare mechanics of the method. Brueghel makes the world a vast universe of space, the human population a detail, and the single person insignificant. Jesus is by no means obvious in such a place; and even when he has been found, it is patent that he influences the behavior of almost nobody. In fact, he is abused. Some such intention must also have suggested rendering the Holy Mourners in a style then a hundred years out of date, i.e., that conventional expressions of Christian regret do not moderate the march of contemporary events.

The analogy between the Crucifixion of Christ and the 16th-Century crucifixion of Flanders is obvious. Every historian has wondered how Brueghel managed to get away with it. None of the simple explanations fit the case. He was well known. His pictures did not remain hidden. No powerful patron protected him. The religious titles would not in themselves have fooled anybody. The Spaniards were the opposite of tolerant and liberal, and none of them admired good art enough to excuse the unflattering part the painter made them play on his stage. There can be no chance of our mistaking the intent, for we have Brueghel's own word for it. As he lay dying, he ordered his young wife to destroy a great many of the paintings then in stock for fear they would get her into trouble with the authorities. In view of what we still possess, it is appalling to imagine the content of those Martha Brueghel burned up.

The modern reader, who thinks of self-expression as a right, perforce has difficulty in accommodating himself to the conditions of the 16th Century, when it was wiser for a man to keep his deeper thoughts to himself. For the most part, Brueghel did that; except in his scenes of vulgar genre, he seems usually to have remained aloof, an observer and recorder rather than a participant in the drama. One or two pictures survive, however, which tend to supplement what we already know of his more private feelings.

In the great and terrible *Dance under the Gallows* (Fig. 16.54) he juxtaposed inhumanity and natural beauty. He made rough peasants dance under the gibbet, apparently without appreciating that it symbolized their mortality and humiliation. We may infer that, for the painter, *carpe diem* was more than a poet's conceit; in that generation, it was a crass necessity, the best that might be expected in a ghastly world.

In a drawing at Vienna (Fig. 16.55) he was even more specific and, empirically speaking, more inclusive. Here we see an immense fish stranded on the beach. Men are cutting his belly open. A vomit of little fish floods from his mouth. The little fish regurgitate fishes smaller still. On the shore, some of the little ones hang from a tree; past them goes a larger fish endowed with the legs of a man, making haste toward the safety of the distance.

On the knife, we see an astronomical symbol that stands for earth, i.e., so go earthly affairs. Grandeur gets stranded by its own size. The little scoundrels hang while the bigger scoundrels get clear. Dean Swift would have liked the picture had he known it. By paraphrasing a line or two from that author, we may perhaps summarize Brueghel's outlook on a terrible world.

> The big fish eat the little fish
> And chew on them and bite 'em.
> The little fish eat littler fish
> And so *ad infinitum*.

*

17

THE BAROQUE AND THE ROCOCO

In all probability, history will show that the Renaissance ended in 1914, for until that fateful year, nothing happened to bring about a cultural change comparable to the difference between the Gothic and the Renaissance. The fundamental concepts which were first asserted at Florence shortly after 1400, and which were modified and developed a century later to make the philosophy of the High Renaissance, have governed. The ideas which then went out from Italy to the rest of Europe still furnish most of the world with its values, its customs, and its way of life.

It is true that great events have changed the outlook. Nationalism, which had never been an important factor in European life at any time anterior to the High Renaissance, emerged during the 17th Century as the only political fact worth talking about. The national monarchies were in due course superseded by the national democracies, and democracy — a theory which at first seemed patently absurd — today is so firmly established as an ideal that no dictator has as yet dared assert he disbelieves in it. Science has come into its own; and for the first time in history, the economy has become geared not to agriculture, but to industry. The Americas have been settled and civilized. Western ideas have extended themselves to the Orient, with results which cannot be foretold. The church has ceased to exist as the primary patron of cultural enterprises, to be succeeded by the government, the wealthy person, and even the public at large. But not one of the things mentioned has been big enough to modify the foundation of Western civilization.

Art history bears out that truth perhaps better than any other record of the era. The period since 1600 has been immensely productive. The 17th Century alone witnessed the first important school of artists in Spain, the only Dutch art of any significance in history, the start of British painting, and the assumption by France of the artistic leadership of the world. Most of the buildings,

Fig. 17.1 Versailles. COURTESY OF THE FRENCH GOVERNMENT TOURIST OFFICE. NEW YORK.

ANDERSON

Fig. 17.2 Caravaggio. *The Calling of Saint Matthew*. Rome. San Luigi de' Francesi. 1597–98.

GIRAUDON

Fig. 17.3 Caravaggio. *The Death of the Virgin*. Paris. Louvre.

Figs. 17.4–6 Bernini. *The Ecstasy of Santa Theresa* (center) and (left and right) members of the Cornaro family. Rome. Santa Maria della Vittoria. 1646. ANDERSON

ALINARI Fig. 17.7 Bernini. Elephant and Obelisk. Rome. Piazza della Minerva. 1667.

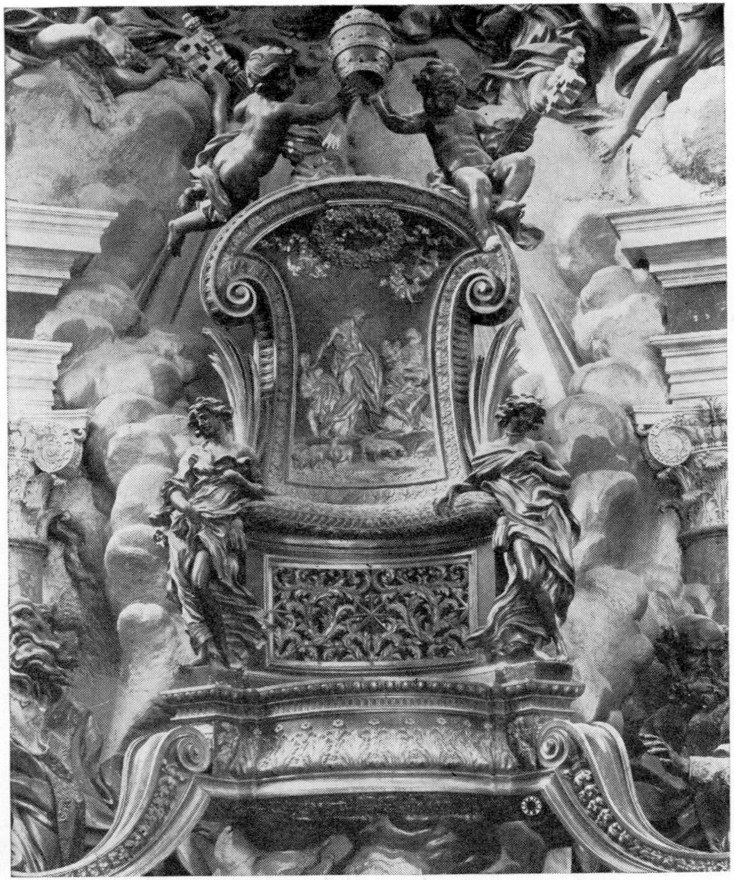

ANDERSON Fig. 17.8 Bernini. Shrine for the Chair of Saint Peter. Rome. Saint Peter's.

Fig. 17.9 Rome. Saint Peter's. Saint Peter's was originally designed as a central church by Bramante and begun in 1506. After work had dragged under a series of architects, Michaelangelo took charge in 1547; by the time of his death in 1564, the drum under the dome was complete as redesigned by him. Giacomo della Porta built the dome (1588–1592), using a steeper pitch than Michaelangelo had intended. Carlo Maderna was employed (1606–1626) to extend the nave and to build the façade. The great colonnades are the work of Bernini and date from 1656–1663.
PHOTOGRAPH BY ALINARI

ANDERSON

Fig. 17.10 Rome. Sant' Ignazio. Central portion of the ceiling painted by Andrea Pozzo, 1691–94. *Saint Ignatius in Heaven.* Sometimes called *The Glorification of the Company of Jesus.* The complete picture includes a full story of architecture beneath what we see here. The personifications of "The Four Parts of the World" appear below the portion shown.

Figs. 17.11–12 Rome. Perspective Gallery in the Palazzo Spada (left) and the cloister of San Carlino alle Quattro Fontane. Both designed by Borromini. PHOTOGRAPHS BY ALINARI

ALINARI Fig. 17.13 Rome. Sant' Agnese in Piazza Navona. Designed by Borromini. 1652.

Fig. 17.14 London. Saint Martin's in the Fields. Designed by James Gibbs. 1721.

Fig. 17.15 Rubens. *Lion Hunt*. Munich. Alte Pinakothek. About 1617.

Fig. 17.16 Rubens. *Rape of the Daughters of Leucippus*. Munich. Alte Pinakothek. About 1619.

GIRAUDON

Fig. 17.17 Watteau. *Jupiter and Antiope*. Paris. Louvre.

PIERPONT MORGAN LIBRARY

BRITISH MUSEUM

Figs. 17.18–19 Drawings by Watteau.

Fig. 17.20 Watteau. Les Champs Élysées. London. Wallace Collection. Between 1717 and 1721. 16⅜ by 12½ inches.

Fig. 17.21 Engraving by Gabriel Huquier, after a drawing by Watteau. New York. Cooper Union.

ARCHIVES PHOTOGRAPHIQUES

Fig. 17.22 Versailles. Apartment of Louis the 15th.

Fig. 17.23 (left) Dresden. The Zwinger Palace. Entrance of the northwest wing. 1711–1722. PHOTOGRAPH BY MARBURG

Fig. 17.24 (right) Boucher. *Cupid as Captive*. London. Wallace Collection. 1754.

Fig. 17.25 Fragonard. *The Swing*. London. Wallace Collection. Probably 1766.

pictures, and statues in sight date from the last 350 years, as do most of the artists we know by name. But however loudly we hear the cry of originality, European culture has remained much the same. With respect to European art, all the crucial decisions were taken before Michaelangelo died, all the definitive influences were at work; and every artist since then has been, in sober fact, a Renaissance artist. There have been interesting departures from the style of the High Renaissance; but regardless of what may be claimed, every single development is easily understood as an extension of the Renaissance expression.

The circumstances just outlined pose an insoluble problem for the author of an introductory volume. No solution exists that will not do violence to some sentiment, some interest, some favorite material of both the reader and the writer. But if we are to hew to the line originally chosen, we must apply to the last three and a half centuries exactly the same perspective we applied to every earlier era. We must rigorously decline to be lured into a detailed treatment of artists and schools that loom large only because luck has intervened to put them in our immediate historical foreground. We must accept the fact that the world has just passed through a dozen generations bearing to Italy the same relation that the Hellenistic Period bore to Athens, and we must assign to the art of those years only the amount of space it deserves in view of its absolute importance.

The art of the 17th and 18th Centuries forms a unit of style with a recognizable difference reflected in the custom of referring to the 17th Century as *The Baroque*, and to the 18th as *The Rococo*. *Baroque* may come from the Portuguese *barroco*, an irregular pearl. Supposedly the sheen and curvature of the pearl correspond to similar qualities in the art of the period. *Rococo* appears to be a fanciful construction on the stem *roc*, and its application to art is said to derive from a resemblance between the motives used in French interior decoration and the waterworn shells seen in the elaborate rock gardens then popular. Neither derivation is certain, and neither word has any certainty in usage.

Both terms still carry an unfortunate connotation of reproach. While both styles developed in orderly fashion from the High Renaissance, both differed therefrom in the direction of elaboration and display. In such differences, earlier critics could see nothing but a welter of indulgence. Readers and students were advised, on pain of bad taste, to experience feelings of disgust whenever confronted with a work of art dating after 1600. That impression has been corrected by the development of art history as a university discipline. There is much merit in the Baroque and the Rococo. It is not difficult to demonstrate the merit to any fair-minded person, and it is only in careless parlance that either word still suggests any hint of blame.

While the two styles were really one, as stated, and while there are innumerable instances where one name applies as fairly as the other, there was sufficient development during the two hundred years of their coverage to justify the separation with respect to title.

The Baroque stemmed directly from Italy. In particular, it was the work of Rubens and Bernini, both of whom took off from the plane of reference furnished by the later art of Michaelangelo, Titian, and Tintoretto. The Baroque was the going style when the church decided to make use of art as one of the weapons of the Counter Reformation; because of that historical circumstance, Baroque art was the last art affected in any fundamental fashion by Roman Catholicism, or even by religion. Simultaneous with that final period of church patronage, the world witnessed (in the person of Louis the 14th of France) the earliest large-scale disbursement of public funds for art intended to glorify a modern government. As might be imagined from its sources and the purposes to which it was directed, Baroque art was characterized by power and strength, and its intention was to call up profound and even violent sensations.

The construction of Versailles (Fig. 17.1) marked more than the commencement of the modern governmental custom of making major investments in architecture; it may conveniently be remembered, also, as the monument which commemorates the shift of the artistic capital from Rome to Paris. Ever since, the history of art has been very nearly synonymous with the history of French art.

The Rococo, which was simply a later and more delicate Baroque, was French. It was primarily secular and aristocratic, and is the best record we have of the beauty of life among the upper orders before democracy and the French Revolution. Using much the same stylistic devices as the Baroque, the Rococo directed itself toward the exquisite in both form and content. Its movement is gentle and graceful and its purpose to charm and delight.

RENAISSANCE MANNERISM

Michaelangelo, Titian, and Tintoretto belonged to the High Renaissance, and were so presented in the last chapter. The reader will recall, however, that we were more than once at pains to suggest that those artists did not remain single-minded and assured. Especially as their activity drew toward a close, all three lost, now and again, the decorum of their era. More and more frequently they broke over into expression marked by an absence of emotional control. Whenever they did so, they predicted the Baroque.

An increasing number of critics have begun to make more and more of the aberrations just cited. They claim that more was involved than the simple transition between two major styles. They contend that we must recognize an interim period between the High Renaissance and the Baroque — another style which would itself be a natural unit in the history of art — to which they give the name *Mannerism.*

The monumental evidence for their contention is to be found in the work of a number of artists, some of them as early as the first generation of the 16th Century, who do not fit the standards of the High Renaissance and who have heretofore been relegated to secondary rank. We refer to such men as: Giulio Romano (1492–1564), Raphael's chief assistant; Primaticcio (1504–70), the chief founder of the School of Fontainebleau (page 709); Pontormo (1494–1557) and Bronzino (1503–73), both Florentines; and Parmagianino (1503–40), a very strange master who has recently attracted serious attention.

It is evident at a glance that all of the artists mentioned fed upon their more famous contemporaries and upon the past. That had always been done; the new element was to do it self-consciously, systematically, and in more literal fashion. Our statement is no mere conclusion from the evidence; it was openly expressed as the wisest, and indeed the only practical artistic philosophy as early as 1550, in which year Giorgio Vasari published the first edition of his invaluable *Lives of the Most Eminent Architects, Painters, and Sculptors.*

Vasari's work paved the way for the founding at Bologna in 1585 of an institution which included in its name the significant word *Academy.* The founders were a family of cousins named Carracci; and they made themselves the first faculty to offer a formal curriculum in the theory and practice of art. Their theory was the eclectic one just described. Though it has often been damned as evil in itself, the program was in fact very intelligent. No system of training, it must be pointed out, can teach greatness. The fair test of education is whether it equips men to make something of themselves, and upon that score, it must be conceded that the pupils of the Carracci were excellent technicians.

While he must be prepared for allusions to the development just summarized, the reader will be wise to steer clear of argument until he feels able to weigh the evidence on his own authority. As of this date, Mannerism remains a hypothesis which may or may not become defined as a separate artistic style with a distinct philosophy. In any case, should such a style become defined — and considerable research and publication is still required on the matter — its chief elements will be approximately what one might infer from the remarks already made, and the remarks about to be made, concerning Michaelangelo, Titian, and Tintoretto in their capacity as forerunners and creators of the Baroque.

In any case, a better name should be sought by those who wish to establish the existence of an interim style. *Mannerism* is a descriptive and even provocative word with two meanings: (1) *mannered*, as we have used it in Chapter 13, to signify the self-conscious cultivation of artificial grace, and (2) *in the manner of*, to signify eclectic borrowing without performing once again the act of creative synthesis. Neither applies to the totality of the questions raised herewith; and while it is convenient to add another meaning to a familiar term, it is never permissible to do so when, as in the present instance, the new sense must necessarily destroy the old.

FORM AND CONTENT IN THE BAROQUE

Almost every convention and technical expedient of the Baroque existed in principle somewhere in the work of Michaelangelo, and we shall find ourselves alluding constantly to that master in the summary to follow. His first and most fundamental legacy to the 17th Century was the habit of making stupendous plans. Versailles would never have come to mind had it not been for his vaunting imagination in proposing such projects as the tomb of Julius the 2nd, and in realizing such achievements as Saint Peter's. Having spread from Rome to France, the fashion he set went to every other land and affected the plan and appearance of innumerable cities — the river front of Paris, for example, and the layout of Washington.

If stupendous plans were out of place for reasons of cost, need, or otherwise, the Baroque artists settled for the kindred effect of the amazing. By one method or another, they undertook to move the observer to the depths, and to move him fast. They aimed, as it were, directly at his emotional vitals, and the successful work of art was conceived as the one that provided an almost painful heightening of the sensibilities and the most vivid imaginable awareness of the experience of the moment. There are so many ways to startle, dazzle, and amaze that we can only suggest the possibilities and leave the reader braced, as it were, for the remaining broadsides in the battery of Baroque art.

The simplest method of all was to play a trick. Opera and the theatre were under intensive development during the 17th Century, and the borderline between monumental art and stage scenery seems often to have been non-existent. The greatest artists of the period did not hesitate to present misleading visual data to the eye whenever it suited their convenience. In the sense of dishonesty, there was no conspiracy to deceive; the members of the public were sophisticated in artistic matters, and could be counted upon to enjoy the demonstration of skill.

Among the various devices that fall under the heading of tricks, none was more entertaining than the constructed perspective. Theatre sets (most of them permanent rather than movable, as now) were usually designed that way; and the same sort of thing often added a fillip to the sobriety of formal architecture. A capital instance is shown in Fig. 17.11, where the illusion is so perfect that one might pass by without realizing the truth unless warned. Ostensibly, we look down a long gallery and see a life-size statue about a hundred feet away. The actual distance is less than twenty feet.

Tours de force of technique went hand-in-hand with the cult of tricks and illusions. With the entire Renaissance behind them, the artists of the 17th Century were in possession of more skill than any others who can be named as a class or group; in comparing even the simplest objects from the period with examples from any other, the soberest critic cannot withhold his admiration for standards of craftsmanship beyond praise.

Because painting lends itself more easily than any other art to spectacular effects, the Baroque painters may perhaps be singled out to illustrate the point under discussion; among the painters, we may focus our attention upon the ceiling painters. Ceiling painting was not new. Mantegna had done some illusionistic paintings of that kind at Mantua as early as 1474. Correggio's *Assumption of the Virgin* (1524), painted on the underside of the dome of the Cathedral at Parma, remains one of the unsurpassed technical demonstrations. But such things, when done at all, had been a special effort. They now became a standard performance. Among the notable examples, we may mention Guercino's *Aurora* in the Casino of the Villa Ludovisi (1621–23), Pietro da Cortona's *Triumph of Divine Providence* in the Barberini Palace (1633–39), and Andrea Pozzo's *Glorification of the Company of Jesus* (Fig. 17.10). It seems almost impossible that technique could become more magnificent than we see it in the three ceilings mentioned, but such proved to be the case. All other ceiling painters pale by comparison to the complete master of the business, Giovanni Battista Tiepolo (1696–1770) of Venice. Aided by the trend of taste toward the Rococo, he sought lighter and gentler effects; thus he covered the overhead of a great many rooms with compositions as charming as they are spectacular.

Baroque ceiling painting opens up some interesting critical questions. In approaching these, we must stipulate that in every typical instance, the eye is cleverly led upward into the represented space of the picture by some transitional passage between the walls of the chamber and the surface of the ceiling. The favorite method was to put the sky in the middle of the overhead and paint a border of architecture around it. The painted architecture carried down to the eye of the observer as another story or two piled on top of the walls below. The picture on the ceiling was conceived, to put it another way, as an indefinite upward extension of the volume defined by the walls.

To the purist in architecture, such a performance is hateful. "It blows the roof off!" he will declare; but surely it is legitimate for us to inquire whether beams and masonry are in fact sacred. Why must we forbid the architect to avail himself of the painter's help? No one can deny that pictures are useful for interior decoration, or that it is difficult to design an interior which offers a sense of the fullness of space. Conceding that every technique contains within itself the germs of its own defeat, what can be wrong with an architectural design which, from the beginning, includes the conception of a ceiling picture to add upward volume?

Over and above such theories of design — in which they were intensely interested — the Baroque artists of Italy and other Catholic lands had a sober reason for adopting the optical illusion as a standard resource of their trade. It was a crucial need of the Counter Reformation to convince the public that transcendental things were real. Artists had the skill to call another world into being, and they could make people see the things the Church wished them to believe.

The philosophical legitimacy of using art for such a purpose cannot, as a theory, be attacked, but the advent of such ideas during the Baroque called into being an immense corpus of religious art which requires explanation. We must continually remind ourselves that the program of the Counter Reformation was a program directed at the mass of the population. The narrative subject matter for religious art was chosen accordingly. It almost never appealed to the mind; it almost always appealed to the sentiments, the emotions, and to the sheer credulity of people who not only could be swayed by the bizarre but enjoyed the sensation. It follows that cultivated persons, and above all intellectually inclined persons, find Catholic Baroque art uncongenial and even offensive. To such, the Church has always been inclined to say: beware of pride.

Caravaggio

Dazzling views into heaven formed only one department of the Catholic art to which we have just referred. Another branch of the same program embraced the simpler and more familiar stories from religious history, and such were generally rendered with a verisimilitude so intense that we must include a super-realism among the achievements of the Baroque. Among the masters who engaged in that effort, Caravaggio and Bernini have a magnitude beyond all the others and require individual attention.

Michelangelo Merisi (1573–1610) was known as Caravaggio from the town in north Italy where he was born. He fits into no pattern yet established by the history of art unless it be the one we suggest here. He was a revolutionary personality. He cared nothing for the conventions of respectable life, and was often in trouble with the law. He openly resented the aesthetic theories upon which all High Renaissance culture had been founded, and his painting seems to have been deliberately intended to insult persons who wanted decorum in life and dignity in art. His method of insulting them was the most offensive and infallible of all. He simply did his utmost to tell the truth.

Even in Italy vulgar genre had long been sufficiently familiar so that such material, of itself, carried no offense. An occasional tavern scene was relished by the best of men; but it was quite another thing to choose a tavern for the setting of a sacred picture. In a series of paintings done for San Luigi dei Francesi, Caravaggio did exactly that; we find Christ summoning Saint Matthew (Fig. 17.2) from a group who sit around a table gambling. Sacred history was of course on the painter's side. Our Lord had described himself as often having to do with publicans and sinners, but neither the contemporary church nor the contemporary public had much stomach for visualizing his words. Had the painter not been a very dangerous man, he might well have found himself in serious trouble.

As a matter of fact, he did experience the refusal of several of his greatest pictures, notably the *Death of the Virgin* (Fig. 17.3), which impressed the authorities as so ignoble as to be indecent. Being somewhat less preoccupied with notions about the dignity of man, we may take a different view. Unquestionably, the painting is one of the most moving in the history of art, and few others carry the same weight of conviction. The actuality it evokes is in itself formidable, but the thing we feel even more is the strength of the painter's devotion to the humble circumstances of Mary's life and death.

The shock of Caravaggio's subject matter might have been softened had he been willing to communicate the material in a conventionally elegant manner of painting. Instead of doing that, he developed a new and personal style distinguished by devastating professional competence and aggressive treatment of the observer. The most striking feature of his method was to evoke sensation by violent contrasts of light and dark. The idea doubtless came from his contact with Venetian painting (page 753); but his scheme was more systematic and his purpose philosophical rather than decorative.

The end in view was to focus attention more vividly than ever before upon the dramatically operative areas of the canvas by bringing them strongly up into the light. At the same time, other areas were deprived of their power to attract attention by making them subside into the dark. As contrasted with earlier manipulations of value for the sake of emphasis and suppression, Caravaggio's work was radical because he confined the light to a very small section of the picture surface. The important figure, or even the important part of a figure, was thereby given a stridency sufficient to stun the sensibilities for a moment.

His style, as indicated, derived from the Venetian Mode, but it corresponds more closely with the actualities of sight than we might suppose. When viewing any scene whatever, the eye adjusts itself for the brightest light. Conscious readjustment is necessary to inspect material contained within the darks. Our visual world, therefore, is more like Caravaggio's painting than our habits of thought permit us to realize; his methods, while hardly naturalistic, bear a strong relation to reality as we see it.

His procedure has long been known as "crowding the darks." The expression describes the technique very well. Everything on the posed model or contained within the natural scene was crowded down into the darker shades of paint if in fact its local tone was fairly dark. By the same token, the modeling of face, hands, etc., was immeasurably emphasized because a disproportionate length of the value scale became available for that purpose. Because strong contrasts were possible within, and only within, such lighter fields, mass and shape came out vividly there. The special merit of the system becomes plain when we reflect that the most expressive parts of the body are the areas which fall above the middle value.

Because of his personality and tastes, to say nothing of his theories, Caravaggio no more founded a school than belonged to one. It is still impossible to trace his influence in detail, but his rejection of the High Renaissance, however unwelcome at Rome, proved inspiring to any number of younger and later artists. The Brothers le Nain, already cited in another connection (page 773), derive from him both in subject and in style. Much the same can be said of the Spaniard Ribera (1588–1656) and of the early period in the career of his greater compatriot, Velasquez (1599–1660). Rembrandt (1606–69), the greatest of the Dutch masters, is hardly conceivable without Caravaggio as a spiritual forefather. At first glance it might appear that this unusual man had influence everywhere except in his own country. The personal features of his art did not, as a matter of fact, affect many Italian painters. It is notable, however, that Baroque architects and sculptors soon began to cultivate stratagems calculated to produce Caravaggesque effects of light and dark.

Bernini

The new realism inaugurated by Caravaggio lent itself particularly well to the depiction of miracles, and it was of the essence in the program of the

Counter Reformation to establish and fortify a literal belief in the truth thereof. Because the continued and present reality of divine intervention was an important issue of the moment, recent miracles were often chosen as subject matter in preference to miracles of greater fame but more distant date. In presenting such material, the 17th-Century artists outdid themselves in developing methods for getting after the observer and making him feel a party to the event depicted. It was Bernini (1598–1680) who, in his capacity as the most prominent artist at Rome, embraced such enterprises in the most enthusiastic fashion and carried them through without compromise or relief.

In the whole history of art, there is no experience at all equivalent to one's first view of Bernini's *Ecstasy of Santa Theresa* (Fig. 17.5) over the main altar of the small Baroque church of Santa Maria della Vittoria. Upon entering the nave, attention is pulled toward the main subject by a magnificent architectural enframement rendered in dark marbles in combination with surfaces of gold, amber, and pinker tones. The broken pediment above (in itself a manifesto of the Baroque) swells out toward us, and then recedes as though in homage to the niche it encloses. Within the niche, we see the saint accompanied by an angel. The marble figures are carved with a relentless realism, but with a skill so exquisite as to defy belief. A golden light bathes the scene. It comes through a yellow pane of glass concealed above, and its power to convince is by no means diminished by a set of gilt rods arranged radially behind, to simulate heavenly rays.

The saint is represented as a young and comely woman. She falls back and yet rises in voluptuous transport, swooning and losing consciousness of the earth, her body undulating with effort, pain, and delight. Above stands the angel. In compassion and understanding, he is about to thrust through her heart the dart of heavenly love which, by Theresa's own testimony, tore her breast whenever she had union with the divine.

So intense is the experience of viewing the central group that it is only afterward one becomes conscious of the bystanders; but they are present. On the walls to right and left, there are other niches unmistakably like boxes at the opera (Figs. 17.4,6). In them sit the donors — in poses too casual by half — watching the show.

Such performances raise serious questions with respect to the propriety of much 17th-Century religious art. Above all, we may challenge the use made of the subject matter. Santa Theresa (1515–82) was a nobly born woman of Castile. She became a Carmelite nun in 1535, and she distinguished herself both as a mystic and as an executive of capacity and foresight. Her writings are excellent examples of the literary craft. In easy, elegant Spanish she set forth the difficult philosophy of direct religious experience, and her various publications proved among the most effective available for the Counter Reformation. She brought about a revision of the Carmelite rule and founded about a dozen new convents. Every memorial speaks of her common sense and good humor. Bernini's figure bears small resemblance to the chubby and somewhat jolly person of the saint herself, and the most ardent religionist should be given pause by the particular imagery he chose to evoke in his attempt to convince the public of her union with God.

Although his name is a virtual synonym for all that was extravagant and bombastic in the Baroque, the very same Bernini could be thoroughly delightful when he turned his hand to less pompous material. He designed a great many fountains, which remain among the best on earth. In an occasional minor work, moreover, he devoted every resource of his formidable technique to fanciful themes. For an instance, let the reader turn to the *Elephant and Obelisk* (Fig. 17.7).

The official iconography, as analyzed by W. S. Heckscher in *The Art Bulletin* for September 1947 (Vol. 29, No. 3) is recondite to a degree. The little obelisk was an ancient one, dug up in 1665. Originally it had belonged to a temple of Isis and Serapis near the same site. Because it pointed upward and because the Egyptians had associated such monuments with the sun, 17th-Century iconologists construed the Egyptian understanding as a pre-figurement of Christianity and made the obelisk into a symbol for Divine Wisdom. The elephant was chosen as caryatid for a great variety of reasons. Historically, elephants had often been used as emblems of strength and fortitude. The well known intelligence of the great beasts had served, moreover, to build up a veritable cult of admiration. People even believed them to be capable of such concepts as chastity. The animals were actually credited with a capacity for the religious impulse. Because Pliny had said that elephants courteously piloted lost wanderers out of the desert, the elephant was occasionally associated with the Savior himself.

There was thus a great deal of reason for Bernini to make a marble elephant when he wanted a support for an obelisk; but to all this old-time lore we must add something new. Every once in a while, a real live elephant had been imported into Europe, apparently to the delight of young and old, the same as now. There was all kinds of gossip about the tricks they could learn. One elephant, for example, who had taken up his residence in Holland, had actually learned to enjoy his pipe of tobacco daily! So for all its ostensibly serious and ceremonial character, it is evident that Bernini took the same direct and delighted pleasure in the subject as a child. Only the hard of heart can think of a word to say against it.

Almost everything we have so far said contributes to the general conclusion that the Baroque aimed at the smashing effect calculated to throw the observer's emotions out of control and make him yield to the purpose of the artist. That terrific drive must not, however, be confused with spontaneous methods of artistic production, much less with improvisation or lack of restraint. Most Baroque artists were farsighted. They knew excitement doesn't last. They appreciated the necessity for confirming the first and immediate impression by offering within the work of art material for rational analysis and material for contemplation. However rapid the first onslaught, every major monument from the period is completely logical with respect to iconography and composition.

With respect to iconography, the 17th-Century artists proceeded upon the policy inaugurated by the larger compositions of Raphael and Michaelangelo. The ideal Baroque picture, that is to say, was an immense ensemble of persons governed by the terms of some extended allegory. As compared with the High Renaissance (Figs. 16.17–20) the difference is not one of kind, but one of relative complexity. The great pictures of the 16th Century had been distinguished by a general lucidity no matter how many significant details they contained. In marching forward along the same road, the Baroque masters usually left lucidity far behind; but their most complicated productions continued, nevertheless, to be governed by ice-cold logic. Many of them were so minutely calculated as to have earned and to deserve the sobriquet " machines."

The spirit of the times is epitomized by Andrea Pozzo's ceiling at Sant' Ignazio, already cited in another connection. Fig. 17.10, for the sake of illustration on a legible scale, shows only the central portion of that immense composition. Around the area covered by our bookplate there is a full story of Baroque architecture painted in bold foreshortening, and conveying the illusion that the actual walls of the building rise continuously upward without a break to their ultimate opening into the sky.

At the vanishing point, where all lines of the architectural perspective converge, we find the Holy Trinity in the form of God the Father, Christ with his Cross, and a Dove. Saint Ignatius is seen in ecstasy immediately below, rising heavenward on a cloud. Rays of light proceed from the Savior to the Saint. From the Saint the same rays fan outward in four directions, ultimately coming to rest upon four figures (not seen in the book plate) who personify the " Four Parts of the World ": Europe, Asia, Africa, and America. As with all similar compositions, there is but one station on the floor from which an observer can look up and see all parts of the perspective in perfect order. The spot is indicated by a small circle of marble.

The more obvious meaning of the picture is indicated in a letter from the painter to Prince Lichtenstein. It has to do with the missionary enterprise of the Jesuit Order, to which Pozzo himself belonged. The imagery was suggested by Luke 12:49: "I am come to send fire on the earth. . . ." The fire referred to meant (to the painter) the fire of faith; and along with his personifications of the four continents, he included portraits of missionary saints who had distinguished themselves each in his separate region.

A deeper and more subtle symbolism lay beneath the surface of the iconography. Pozzo was the author of a definitive work on perspective, which first appeared in 1693. It contains 100 magnificent plates, including several which illustrate his system for laying out the perspective grid on this particular ceiling. The author's foreword is addressed "To the Lovers of Perspective" and concludes with the admonition, "Therefore, Reader, my advice is that you cheerfully begin your work with a resolution to draw all the points thereof to that true point, the Glory of God; and I dare predict and promise you good success in so honorable an undertaking." The art of perspective, as conceived by Pozzo, was the artistic vehicle whereby one might make people see the direct and systematic connection between the Deity in heaven and each single and separate human being on earth. With that in mind, it is permissible to read a specifically Jesuit symbolism into the mark on the floor which tells one where to stand — an innovation of Pozzo's, lacking in similar and earlier situations where it would have been just as useful. The mark may be construed as an order, and the man who obeys may be thought of as submitting himself to the discipline of the perspective much as the artist had accepted the rule of the Society of Jesus. The inference is obvious that only those who so submit can hope to comprehend the divine scheme with clarity and truth; all others must accept a distorted view. The device itself (namely, the central placement of an observer) had been used during the High Renaissance (page 705), but with an almost opposite meaning.

It is impossible to deny that the arrangement just described bespeaks for its author a high order of intellectual power, a profound grasp of theology, and a magnificent imagination. At the same time, none of those qualities carry over to the observer from the painting itself. Without suggesting that one may arrive at a mature understanding of any important matter, including a work of art, without knowledge and study, most critics would agree that painters go too far when their pictures are virtually unintelligible without the help of a guide book and schematic diagram. Only to a certain extent do we read paintings as we read literature. It is the business of artists to find forms and figures which communicate the meaning, or most of it, to any man who is willing to use his eyes. It is appropriate to ask that the eyes be made keen by education, but another thing entirely to substitute erudition for visual perception.

The intense drama of the Baroque belies the conservative nature of the principles of design which governed the composition of its major monuments. The methods are as old as Greece. Geometry furnished the order. Symmetry furnished the system. The Greek organic method (pages 65–66) furnished the coherence and the unity. In applying such classical sanctions, the men of the 17th Century developed some extraordinarily original manipulations to which we must now turn our attention. Some of them were mere novelties. Others constitute significant innovations.

Precarious equilibrium was one of the devices that became popular in Baroque times. It was peculiarly useful for making the observer keenly conscious of the present experience. Michaelangelo had been the first artist to use it boldly and openly. When called upon to design a new pedestal for the equestrian Marcus Aurelius (page 748) used as the pivotal element in his architectural composition on top of the Capitol Hill (Fig. 16.29), he chose to put the ponderous statue on top of an unusually delicate pedestal. Similarly, when designing the Medici Tombs (Fig. 16.28), he put supports under the sarcophagi which neither look adequate nor are adequate, and he designed the lids in such a way that the recumbent figures thereon lie at the limiting angle of repose. In both instances, he evoked a sense not only of potential movement, but of potentially disastrous movement. The expedient would have been anathema to the Greeks or to Raphael, but it got certain results desired by the Baroque. To see such manipulation is to feel a charge go into the nervous system; willingly or not, one is prepared thereby for the upheaval the artist intends.

Single elements in precarious equilibrium were, in Baroque art, habitually regimented within symmetrical arrangements controlled by a literal application of the Greek organic system of composition. The Medici Tombs (Fig. 16.28) compose on that principle, but their balance is by no means at peace with itself. The figure to the right is equal and opposite to its converse on the left; but something more than equivalence is involved. The recumbent *Night*, *Day*, *Dawn*, and *Dusk* writhe with inner compulsion. Locomotion is denied them; but they struggle agonizingly to have it. Should their energy get an outlet, they would heave up and destroy the composition.

The balance, to put it in other words, is an opposition between forces that strain away from each other, between emphatic opposites mutually frustratory and bent upon canceling each other out. The over-all impression is that great power has been imprisoned within a rigorous system and that content is struggling to be free from its form. The state of mind just suggested was one the Baroque artists made a habit of evoking, and the method was always the same: tumultuous expression compressed within conventional order.

Innumerable applications of the same scheme might be adduced in the architecture, sculpture, and painting of the 17th and 18th Centuries. Let the largest monument of all tell the story for the rest: Versailles (Fig. 17.1). Its fabulous area of palace and gardens is without parallel or equal. But everything conforms to a regimentation predetermined by the stipulation that there should be a main axis brought to a focus upon the bedchamber of the King of France, and from that severe and central purpose, not a single bush was permitted to deviate.

Baroque art, the reader will already have surmised, was in the grip of an immense paradox. Its content was irreconcilable with its form. We may assume that the Baroque artists were even more aware than we are of their ambivalent position, and their difficulties were not diminished by the contemporary taste for elaboration which dictated that all expression depend upon small parts in infinite number — a strange and as yet unexplained analogue with the Gothic (page 451). Their effort, taken in its totality, may be described as an attempt to make riotous, teeming complexity seem a rational thing capable of statement by a simple grammar of rules. Nothing illustrates the trend of their thought better than the peculiar relationship which came to be typical as between the Baroque whole and the Baroque detail.

The point at issue can best be explained by asking the reader to imagine his sensations if, by chance, the *Night, Day, Dawn,* or *Dusk* were removed from its place in the Medici Chapel (Fig. 16.28) and set up alone in some museum. It would be unmistakably a fragment. Is it possible to imagine anything that would seem more radically homeless, more distressingly in need of the surroundings for which it was designed? Very much the same statement might be made of either subordinate palace in the group on the Capitol Hill (Fig. 16.29); without the other two buildings, our sensibilities would grope for an aesthetic answer much as they grope for the completion of an unresolved chord.

We may summarize by saying that the complexity and violence of Baroque art demanded heroic measures for discipline and control. Otherwise, coherence between part and part might be lost, and the relation of the part to the whole would become confused. The measure most often taken was the one invented by Michaelangelo, namely, to design parts which, taken alone, seem grievously distorted, but which make perfect sense when placed in context. To some extent, systematic interdependence had been an essential of organic composition from the very beginning; the Baroque innovation was to force the theory of coherence out to the very end.

Our analysis of Baroque coherence must not be mistaken for an effort to indicate a tendency. The system as described was habitually applied in an absolute and literal way. It is conspicuous in the composition of every Baroque façade, obvious as the governing principle in every Baroque and Rococo staircase, and is best seen on the grand scale in the colonnades Bernini designed to enclose the piazza before Saint Peter's (Fig. 17.9). The doctrinaire way in which the system was often applied is illustrated even better by some of Bernini's smaller monuments. He went the limit, for example, when he designed the shrine for Saint Peter's chair which stands at the extreme east end of the church (Fig. 17.8). Display reached its apogee the day that monument went on view. Its luxury of colors, textures, and details goes further than to defy description: it defies inspection. But where there seems to be so much life, why is the entirety dead? One can only conclude that the end result of Baroque coherence is to kill.

The potential excellence of the concept has nevertheless made itself manifest in innumerable ways ever since, and most conspicuously in the field of architectural design, landscape architecture, and city planning. It would be incorrect to say that those arts date from the Baroque period, but it is emphatically true that when previously asserted at all, they had remained in the realm of enlightened speculation (page 697) and sporadic experiment (page 748). Ever since, the reverse has been true. The universal habit of undertaking large projects has, in the main, been governed by a broader and more inclusive notion of the artistic unit. Whenever new buildings, streets, bridges, and parks have been projected, there has always been some consciousness that their nature and arrangement ought to fit into an all-embracing scheme which could be cited as artistically respectable.

Rubens

But no building or statue can possibly epitomize the spirit of the Baroque so well as the painting of Peter Paul Rubens (1577–1640). In the whole history of art, he was the only man possessed of sheer power in the same measure as Michaelangelo; but there is an important difference between the two. Michaelangelo almost invariably presented us with figures struggling to move but denied motion (Fig. 16.25). Their energy, that is to say, was kept in explosive reserve. Rubens unleashed his people and let them go.

His figure-style was even heavier than Michaelangelo's, and by representing such persons in violent action, he gave us the best available demonstration of still another vital element of the Baroque. Even in the abstract art of architecture, movement was of the essence, and Baroque movement was always the motion of heavy masses. Such movement might be fast, as it usually was in the work of Rubens, or it might be slow; but invariably, Baroque movement was strong.

Rubens made something of a hobby of doing hunting pictures (Fig. 17.15).

In most of them, nude men and armed men are seen at intimate quarters with tigers, crocodiles, lions, hippopotami, and similar beasts. Both sides are invariably raised to fury, and fight with indescribable hate and desperation. Such scenes certainly illustrate the importance of dynamics in Baroque art; but it is all too seldom pointed out that even Rubens never let his action run wild.

Men and beasts alike weave their violence into an excellent Venetian rhythm (page 756) of light and dark. The headlong combat seems impossible of containment within a frame; but an analysis of the composition quickly indicates that the action is turned and made to curtail and contain itself by the direction in which it goes. Rubens's geometry was never strict like Raphael's, but we seldom lose assurance that the fighting figures mill about within the limits of an elliptical or circular figure. Sometimes the limiting outline appears flat on the picture plane. More often it lies diagonally thereto, and frequently at a compound inclination as in Fig. 17.15. But in every instance the principle is the same, and no different from the one Little Black Sambo invoked when he persuaded the tigers to chase each other around and around in a circle until they all turned to butter.

Because of its comparative simplicity, the *Rape of the Daughters of Leucippus* (Fig. 17.16) is specially useful for the study of the points just made. Ponderous bodies are in violent motion within the confines of an enclosing outline. The darks and the lights make a spectacular pattern of contrasts across the surface. The differentiation of textures, a technique which Rubens had learned well from Titian (page 752), is glitteringly skilful and luxuriant to a degree. Still further, the painting makes manifest another fundamental feature of the Baroque which has been in evidence all along, though not yet singled out for direct comment.

Insofar as such a thing was practical, the Baroque avoided straight lines. By the same token, flat surfaces were eliminated whenever possible, and the same taste dictated that artists refrain from angularity of any kind. The curve was the irreducible unit of the Baroque idiom, and the favorite kind of curve was the one which defined the contour of a substantial mass, human or otherwise. In the work of Rubens, which may be taken as typical, most compositions are curvilinear even though his frames were conventional and rectangular. What was true of major facts of arrangement was equally true of details. The assertive convexity of his female nudes may be regarded as a case in point.

As stated in the last chapter (page 699) architecture had ceased with the coming of the High Renaissance to be the prime mover among the arts. Although there was an immense amount of building during the 17th Century, the architects of that period were derivative from its sculptors and painters in both style and spirit. The paradox of Baroque form and Baroque content pressed down upon them, in fact, with an insuperable weight, and presented them with a problem which was literally insoluble.

Public taste, as the preceding pages indicate, had changed strongly in the direction of novelty and sensation; but artistic doctrine, as publicly understood and accepted, had failed to keep pace. Classicism commanded just as much respect as ever, and those who ordered buildings insisted just as specifically as ever that the style be classical. For painters and sculptors, classicism was a relatively flexible thing; but for architects, classicism was what Alberti and others had said it was when they froze the style (page 711) by invoking the argument from Roman authority. Sadly for the architects' peace of mind, the same patrons who wanted classical buildings declared in the very same voice that each new building should provide the same surprise, thrill, and dazzlement as a picture by Rubens.

All over Europe, architects began a concerted effort to see what might be done. Using no detail which was not self-evidently of classical derivation, and ignorant, in all probability, of the more extreme examples of Hellenistic date, (Fig. 8.1), they produced an architecture which may be criticized for elaboration, but may not so much as be frowned upon with reference to the elegance, originality, and essential interest of its details.

In general, the fundamental principles of Baroque design were applied as literally to buildings as to any other art; we need not repeat the demonstration here. Confining ourselves, rather, to the novelties which have specially to do with architecture, we may say that the idea of curvature and the idea of movement were the principal innovations of the period.

Curves are difficult and expensive to build in masonry; nevertheless, we may discern in Baroque structures the same preference for strong contour that we noted in the work of Rubens. In Rome a whole series of small churches, by various designers, were given an oval plan; some of them were covered with domical vaulting to fit.

Borromini

Francesco Borromini (1599–1677) was more daring and ingenious than any other Italian architect. His design for San Carlino alle Quattro Fontane was one of the most original of the Baroque or any other period, and the tiny building relates to its whole era much as the Pazzi Chapel (page 634) relates to the Renaissance. The body of the church dates from 1633. The present façade was Borromini's last design; it was added the year of his death.

For the plan of the nave, he took the shape of a cartouche in delicate, extended quatrefoil. The ground outline comprises curves, both concave and convex, flowing into each other with slight breaks and joinings which seem so natural as to be foreordained. When projected upward as wall surfaces, the curves of the plan present the eye with rhythmic undulations hitherto unapproached in subtlety, and with modulations of light and shadow more delicate and various than any yet seen.

It is a pity that the tiny nave, in many ways the most exquisite designed during the 17th Century, should have been marred by maladjustments. The curvature of the interior walls is somewhat obscured by the weight of a peristyle of Corinthian columns which, although engaged, project a full three quarters of their diameter. The façade is similarly encrusted with ornament. Each item considered alone could hardly be better, for Borromini had the most fertile decorative imagination in modern history; but by a special caprice of the great Baroque paradox, his drive toward expression actually challenged the governing principles of the design. Perhaps his best and most perfect bit of work is the miniature cloister for the same church (Fig. 17.12). Stark and even cold as it looks in the photograph, nothing from the 17th Century will more richly repay serious inspection.

Sant' Agnese in Piazza Navona (Fig. 17.13) is illustrative of his practice in buildings of greater size and may be taken as typical of Baroque ecclesiastical architecture in general. There isn't a work of art in all the world which so thoroughly sets the critic against himself and prevents him from arriving at an opinion. An inspection of the details (including the cupolas which Borromini contributed by an indirect route to colonial America) delights the eye with a succession of elegant motives then completely new. It is probable, for example, that no other building exhibits a like variety of door and window openings, all excellent. At the same time, novelty succeeds novelty at a very rapid pace; we can scarcely see anything because something else is forever already in the corner of the eye. It disturbs one to withhold approbation where there is so much to praise and admire; but what shall we say of a composition where the detail tends to steal the show?

Sir Christopher Wren

The reader will have judged for himself that Baroque architecture demonstrated an immense vitality within the scheme of its restrictions; but certainly — from the standpoint of facing up to the impossible — the greatest achievement of the century was that of Sir Christopher Wren. In 1666, a disastrous fire swept what is now the eastern section (called " the city ") of London. In keeping with the tendency of the times, it was decided that the rebuilding should proceed according to a master plan. The plan was drawn by Wren, but it unfortunately conflicted with local traditions and interests and was never properly carried out. The precedent set proved important nevertheless. On a smaller scale, some of Wren's ideas were carried out at Bath (1754 ff), in the New Quarter of Nancy (1753–57), and in the plan for Washington (drawn 1791).

Our present interest, however, is not concerned with Wren's plan as a whole, but with the numerous parish churches he was called upon to design to replace those that had been lost. It was his first intention to give them the appearance of classical temples; but England (page 709) had not ceased, and has not yet ceased, to be a Gothic country. Both the clergy and the congregations, most of whom seem to have thought of the spire as a Christian symbol (page 391), were determined to have steeples on their churches no matter what the going architectural style happened to be. The spire, of course, was a northern, linear, and Gothic form, primarily vertical and of dissolving silhouette. The temple was a classical form one story high, predominantly horizontal, and with an outline severely enclosed by cornices (page 83). To pile one temple on top of another; to destroy the horizontal divisions intended by the Greeks to stop the eye; to lead us upward within a light, airy silhouette to a sharp point; and to do this with forms that are classical in appearance and plastic in nature—such were the elements explaining Wren's success. Everyone has been gasping at his temerity ever since.

Because most of the London parishes were poor, the little city churches Wren designed were cheap and undistinguished buildings except for the lovely spire each raised against the sky. For illustration, therefore, we reproduce Saint Martin's in the Fields (Fig. 17.14), then on the outskirts of town and now facing Trafalgar Square. The building is representative of a distinct type in ecclesiastical architecture: a church modeled as closely as possible upon the classical temple, with a temple front and a spire of the sort Wren had been the first to design. Our illustration comes from a book of plans, which will explain how easily the type was imported to America and thus became the standard model for all colonial churches.

THE ROCOCO

Although we Americans will always have a special place in our hearts for it, the 18th Century was not a century of great art. It nevertheless put its mark on everything it touched, and its special contribution was to touch everything. There were no artists capable of major creation, but their absence was compensated for by universal good taste which applied itself to the refinement and perfection of almost every man-made object. There is no ready explanation for the phenomenon, but it is a fact that gunsmiths in Pennsylvania demonstrated quite as nice an aesthetic sense as painters in Paris, and worked in the same style.

The Rococo was, in fact, the last style to which all Western civilization subscribed. Most of the furniture, silverware, china, cloth, and wallpaper in use today was actually designed during the 18th Century, to say nothing of most of the architecture. It has been truly said that the era embodied every advance made since the fall of Rome, including a great many more of the so-called mechanical conveniences than we might suppose.

The Rococo developed directly from the Baroque, and as a distinct variation thereof, it may first be recognized in Paris during the last few years of the reign of Louis the 14th. Neither the king nor the court had anything to do with it; they remained resident at Versailles until the more than timely demise of the monarch in 1715. In the meantime, the Rococo had been getting under way. The artist who best illustrates every important feature of the style was Antoine Watteau (1684–1721), a painter of Flemish origin who arrived at the capital in 1715. He first supported himself by doing hack work. Presently he built up a patronage among the rich folk of the city. Many of them were newly rich; some had actually returned to Europe after making fortunes in the new world. All of them seem to have been specially endowed with the aesthetic intelligence so common at the time, and instinctively, all seem to have appreciated that Watteau was the man who could make the Baroque over into a pleasanter, less bombastic idiom, suitable for the home as contrasted with the palace. In bringing about the required modification of the style, Watteau not only worked for and with the gentlemen who paid his bills, but with their wives as well. The emergence of the Rococo marks, in fact, the first important operation of feminine taste as a definitive factor in the history of art.

The difference between the Baroque and the Rococo is epitomized by the comparison between Figs. 17.16 and 17.17, and the reader will find it helpful to supplement the latter by reference to Figs. 17.18 and 17.19. Watteau's painting derived directly from Rubens. That fact comes out much more plainly in full color than in photographs, but the resemblance is clear enough in the latter nevertheless. Watteau had a daintier figure-style than Rubens; it would be incorrect, however, to say that his canon was delicate. The poses he habitually used are much closer to Rubens than seems at first evident. As Rubens had done, Watteau conceived the anatomy to be an ensemble of several related masses. He almost always gave the figure a pronounced turn at the waist. He pitched the torso at an angle to the hips. He turned the head on the neck; and he lifted or depressed the chin. Such habits almost invariably made it necessary to present at least one part of the body in bold foreshortening, with consequent enhancement, on the part of the observer, of a sense of thrust in the shoulders, hips, bust, head, or elbows as the case might be. Watteau's dynamics, in short, were much the same as Rubens'; the important difference between the two artists had less to do with style than with content.

In sum, we may say that like the Baroque, the Rococo was an art of movement; but the movement was slower and gentler. The masses set in motion, moreover, were lighter; the comparison between the two styles was as the difference between power and grace. What applied to movement applied to everything else. The lighting was similar, but softer. The contours were convex, but less emphatically so. The textures were luxuriant, but more modest. And above all, the favorite subject matter, narrative or otherwise, was mild, charming, and for the most part inconsequential. Impact had been the most obvious effect of the Baroque upon the emotions; the Rococo merely sought to delight.

Watteau was, in fact, one of the very few authentically lyric painters in the whole history of art, and he made his reputation by painting a goodly number of pictures like Fig. 17.20. As a class, they are known as *fêtes galantes;* the formula for one was the formula for all. The setting is always out of doors, usually in a Baroque garden. The time of day is always dusk, or thereabouts. The time of year is always early summer, and the fresh foliage is shown as growing half wild, with consequent amelioration of the severity of such architecture and sculpture as may be in view. Ladies and gentlemen sit on the grass or stroll through the groves, making love to each other or simply enjoying that perfect time of day and year. There is no sense of hurry; but neither is there a hint of lassitude. The technique itself is peculiarly in keeping with such a mood; it is a moderate impressionism (page 167) which describes everything adequately and pleasantly.

The remarkable thing was that Watteau could successfully multiply pictures of the same kind. He did not hesitate to use the same figure again and again in successive compositions; in fact, the same figure sometimes occurs more than once in the same composition (Figs. 17.17 and 17.20). His methods of work were systematic and rational to a degree; and yet he never failed to evoke the elusive, indefinable, precious poetry which we think of as characteristic of Giovanni Bellini (page 757), Giorgione (page 758), and almost no one else.

As indicated above, the Rococo was an all-inclusive style. Paintings like those just reviewed were never intended to exist independently. All of the Rococo artists were prepared to design entire schemes of interior decoration, and their pictures, however excellent in themselves, were meant to fit in. Watteau's position as prime mover in that new fashion has all too seldom been emphasized; Fig. 17.21 shows one of his designs — the kind of drawing which might eventuate in a painting, an overmantel carved in wood, a panel of stone sculpture, or a tapestry back for a sofa.

With respect to the subject matter, it is much as we might expect to find it, but certain details of the style demand our attention because they are essential to an understanding of the Rococo as it expressed itself in architecture, furniture, silverware, and all the other arts which are relatively abstract and deal in solid materials. Like the Baroque, the individual forms were largely of classical derivation, and there is a similar sense of curvature and movement in and out. Every proportion was made radically lighter, however — lighter to such a degree, indeed, that the style remained only slightly plastic, and tended to become linear.

At whatever point the artist himself began to feel that he was expressing himself in line, certain new possibilities opened up before him. He made a study of curvature, with the result that the Rococo contains the greatest variety of graceful curves known to the history of art. In combining one curve with another, Watteau was meticulous to preserve the identity of both. Instead of making one flow into another, as in modern streamlining, he employed the principle of tangency. The drawing under review contains a great many examples. In most instances, two curves of contrary direction are brought into contact, with the result that the motion of the eye is arrested and gently reversed at every point of tangency.

The style Watteau had made popular was promptly taken up by the court and nobility as soon as Louis the 14th died. For that reason, we often hear the Rococo referred to colloquially as "Louis Quinze." Because the existence of Versailles made further building superfluous (and also because the population felt strongly about the late king's depletion of the treasury for that purpose), there was almost no major construction in France for the rest of the century. A few sections of Versailles were subdivided, however, on a more intimate scale, and these were entirely redecorated and refurnished in the Rococo manner. Fig. 17.22 shows a characteristic example.

In Germany, however, the situation was reversed. The French language, French clothes, and French customs of every kind were immensely popular among the privileged classes there during the 18th Century. As a result, the numerous noblemen who, as a loose federation, provided Germany with a collective government, each and all yearned to emulate Versailles on such scale as they could afford. Frederick the Great himself built a Rococo palace at Potsdam and named it *Sanssouci.* As an instance of style, we shall be better served, however, by Fig. 17.23, which shows the Baroque just at the stage when it might first be called Rococo.

In France, Watteau had two immediate followers, Lancret and Pater. Their principal function in history was to demonstrate the excellence of their master, for both failed every time as inevitably as Watteau succeeded. The reader may amuse himself at leisure by trying to ascertain why; the answer is by no means easy or certain — a painting by either man looks, in fact, enough like a painting by Watteau to be carelessly mistaken for one.

The Rococo continued to dominate French taste, and the taste of the world, until the Revolution of 1789. Francois Boucher (1703–70) was its most prominent practitioner during his long career. As the favorite painter of Madame Pompadour, he made a business of erotica which, though superbly conceived and executed, were so cold as to remain innocuous (Fig. 17.24).

In due course, Fragonard (1732–1806) succeeded Boucher as the leading artist of France. He made a tour of Italy, and to that experience we owe a number of superb and sensitive landscape pictures, mostly of the Baroque gardens taken over by trees and shrubs which, by that time, were all of a century old. His French patrons were interested in horticulture, however, only insofar as it furnished a setting for human dalliance; and Fragonard delightedly supplied their demand. He became the prince among painters of naughty gallantry (Fig. 17.25). It is doubtful, in fact, whether he ever painted a single scene which represented love in its aspect as an honorable emotion. The lovers who meet in his pictures seem always to be meeting clandestinely, and he was unable even to permit a lady to receive a note without making her look furtively up as though it contained a sentiment she had no right to read.

Because both Boucher and Fragonard worked for the French aristocracy and summed up in their painting all its elegance and irresponsibility, the end result of their art was to make the Rococo identical with everything the French Revolution was against. When at length the explosion took place, it was in the natural course of events for the new government to frown upon the Rococo as a style. Fragonard survived the Revolution. No one had anything against him personally; but during the later years of his life, he was unable to get work and existed in near poverty. The Rococo had in the meantime been replaced by Neo-Classicism, to which we turn our attention in the next chapter.

*

18

THE 19TH CENTURY

We are still too close to the 19th Century to see it in adequate perspective. We all too often hear that the world experienced vast and significant changes during those hundred years — changes that were more radical than at any other time, and faster moving. There is truth behind such assertions, but it is easy to exaggerate. No other period except the 20th Century puts an equal obligation upon the historian, art historian or any other kind, to tread lightly. In the nature of the case, every judgment must be more than usually subjective, and even though the principal phenomena of the period are known, today's estimate of cause and effect may have to be revised tomorrow.

So far as we can now tell from the indications of the history of art, the 19th Century was the twilight of the Renaissance. The era started in normal fashion, and for something more than its first generation, artistic tendencies and developments are easily understandable by reference to points of view established during the 16th Century. We then begin to find ourselves confused by situations for which there had been no earlier parallel.

The great single fact of 19th-Century art was the exclusive importance of France, and within France the exclusive importance of painting. Nothing else counted. Even men so great as Turner (1775–1851) were off the main track. The Italian sculptor Canova (Fig. 18.1) might for a time have been considered the most prominent living artist, but the decisive history of the Neo-Classical movement to which he belonged was written in France and conducted by painters. The French sculptor Rodin (1840–1917) likewise had a great vogue in his day; but he was a follower of the painters rather than a leader, and played no important part in bringing about the several major shifts of style by which the century was marked.

Within the history of French painting we may recognize three such shifts during the century, to each of which a section of the present chapter is devoted. The *Neo-Classical Style* was called into being by the French Revolution, and in the hands of the French Academy it dominated both art and the

ANDERSON Fig. 18.1 Canova. *Pauline Bonaparte as Venus*. Rome. Borghese. Gallery. Finished 1808. Marble. Life size.

Fig. 18.2 David. *The Lictors Bring Back to Brutus the Bodies of His Sons*. Hartford. Wadsworth Athenaeum. (There is another version in the Louvre, slightly larger.) Oil on canvas. 36 by 27½ inches.

Figs. 18.3–4 David. *The Sabine Women*. Paris. Louvre. 1799.
GIRAUDON

Fig. 18.5 Ingres. *The Stamaty Family*. Paris. Louvre. 1808.

Fig. 18.6 (below) Ingres. *The Apotheosis of Homer*. Paris. Louvre. 1827.

GIRAUDON

GIRAUDON

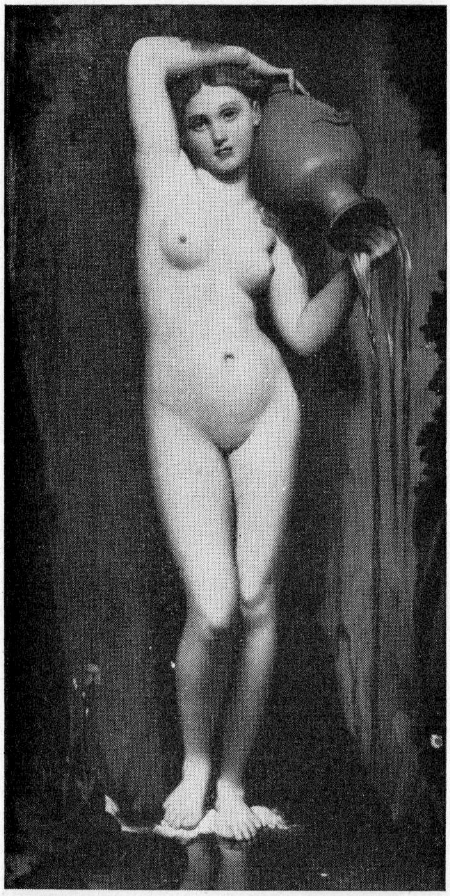

GIRAUDON

Fig. 18.7 (left) Ingres. *La Source*. Paris. Louvre. 1856. Oil on canvas. 5 feet, 5 inches high.

Fig. 18.8 Couture. *The Romans of the Decadence*. Paris. Louvre. 1847. Oil on canvas. 15 feet, 3½ inches high.

ALINARI

ARCHIVES PHOTOGRAPHIQUES

Fig. 18.9 Bouguereau. *Birth of Venus*. Paris. Luxembourg. 1879.

GIRAUDON

Fig. 18.10 Cabanel. *Birth of Venus*. Paris. Luxembourg.

ARCHIVES PHOTOGRAPHIQUES

Fig. 18.11 Collin. *Floreal*. 1886. Paris. Luxembourg.

Fig. 18.12 John Constable. Detail from *The Hay Wain*. Shown in London 1821; in Paris 1824. London. National Gallery.

Fig. 18.13 Delacroix. *The Lion Hunt.* Chicago. Art Institute. 1861.

GIRAUDON Fig. 18.14 Delacroix. *Death of Sardanapalus.* Paris. Louvre. 1827.

Fig. 18.15 Courbet. *The Sleeping Bather*. Detroit. Institute of Arts. 1845.

Fig. 18.16 (below) Manet. *Olympia*. Paris. Louvre. 1863.

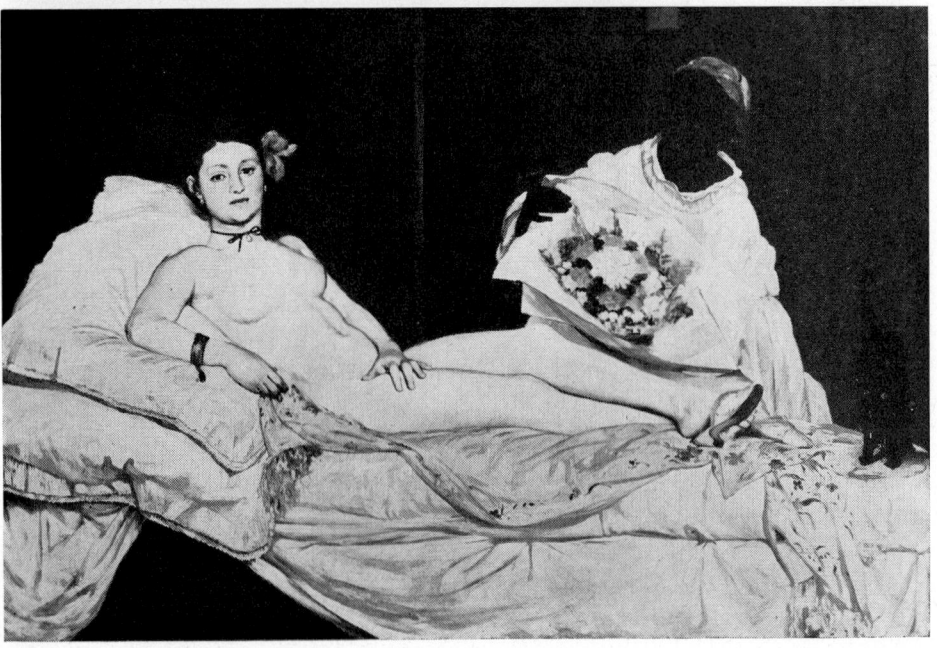

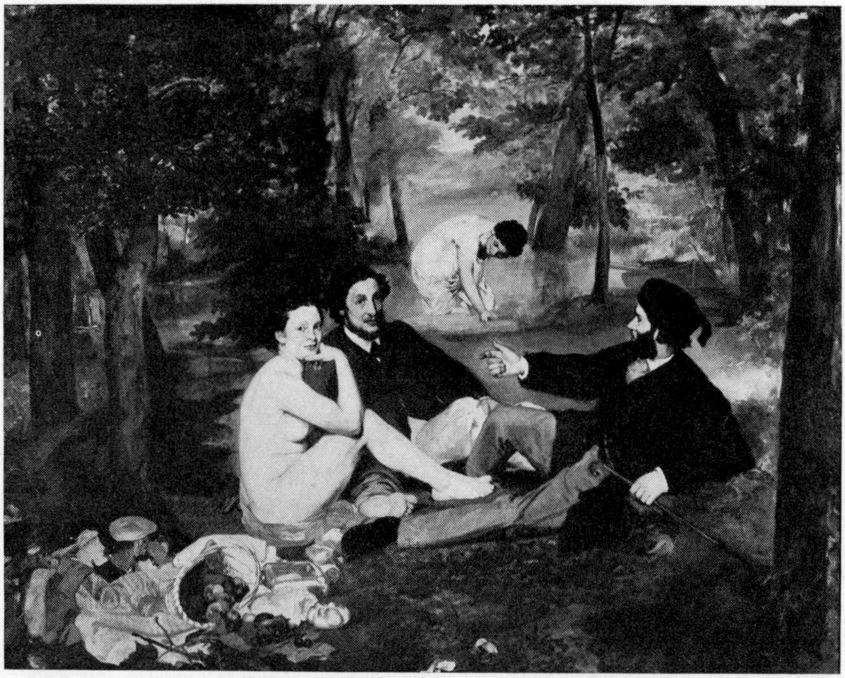

GIRAUDON Fig. 18.17 Manet. *The Picnic on the Grass*. Paris. Louvre. 1863.

Fig. 18.18 Manet. *The Folkstone Boat*. Philadelphia. Collection of Mr. Carroll S. Tyson, Jr.

BULLOZ Fig. 18.19 Degas. *The Pedicure*. Paris. Louvre. 1873.

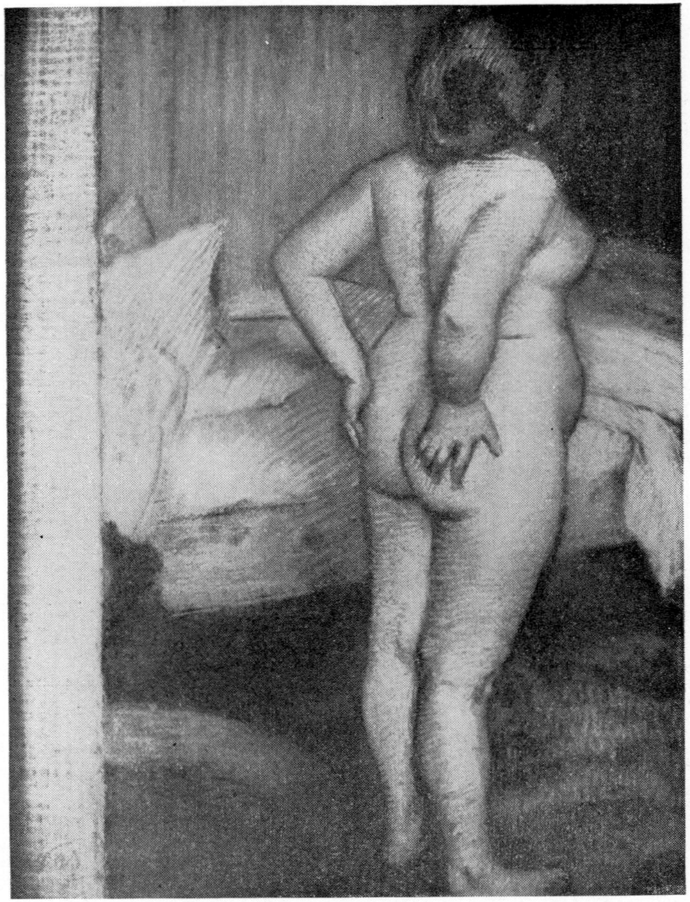

BULLOZ Fig. 18.20 Degas. *Woman Stretching Herself*.

BULLOZ

Fig. 18.21 Degas. *The Cotton Exchange at New Orleans.* Pau. Museum. 1873.

VIZZAVONA Fig. 18.22 Monet. *The Breakfast Table.* Paris. Luxembourg.

VIZZAVONA Fig. 18.23 Monet. *The Houses of Parliament.*

Fig. 18.24 Monet. *Argenteuil-sur-Seine.* Chicago. Art Institute.

Fig. 18.25 Seurat. *Le Chahut.* First version, 1889. Buffalo. Albright Art Gallery.

education of artists until the middle of the century. It has not yet ceased to function, but as the central fact of French art, it was succeeded by the variegated work we may classify loosely under the name *Romanticism*. A philosophy rather than a style, the Romantic Movement started about 1820, gained momentum during the next two decades, and finally attained general acceptance about the middle of the century. Romanticism was, indeed, the very last artistic philosophy ever to enlist the cordial sympathy of the public at large. To this day, most people still subscribe to that theory of art; thus the *French Impressionists,* who became identifiable as a school about 1870, had always to work against an onus of unpopularity, and still do. A more complete outline might list the so-called " Realism " of Courbet, which is better understood as an eccentric excursion within the Romantic Movement. The century ended, and modern art began, with Paul Cézanne (1838–1906), who started out as an Impressionist, turned his back on both the style and its theory, and promulgated the statements which gave a sanction for 20th Century abstract art.

There are various remarkable sidelights to the narrative just summarized so briefly. One of them is the apparent lack of connection between 19th-Century art and the ostensible course of 19th-Century life. One may study the political, social, military, and economic history of all nations during that era without gleaning an iota of useful information about its art. Except for the French Revolution which, as stated, left an artistic record in the Neo-Classical Style, the various wars, shifts of government, social advances, and even the Industrial Revolution itself seem to have arrived and passed on without doing more than to supply incidental subject matter for artists.

As the century proceeded, a significant change took place with respect to the position of artists in society. During every earlier period (page 609), fame and fortune were the prompt reward of every successful artist. The 19th Century also had its successful artists. Some of them received generous patronage and made huge sums of money. But none of the men who enjoyed the approbation of the world a hundred years ago remains in honor today. Most of them have gained the contempt of every serious scholar. The great painters of the period (those whose pictures hang in the Louvre and the Luxembourg and in the major museums of England and America) had to wait a generation or more for the most rudimentary kind of fair treatment. Even today they are far from popular with most citizens.

The phenomenon of the great artist unable to make a dignified living from his art will probably prove in the end to be more significant than any other event, and perhaps more significant than all other events of the 19th Century. While the causes are still obscure, we can trace the gradual separation of the artist from other men. Merely troublesome at the beginning, the misunderstanding proved devastating in the end. A chasm opened up between the creative mind and society. By the time of the Impressionists, the barrier had become impassable. By then, the average solid citizen frankly disliked the creative art of his own day and was all too willing to express his antagonism. Instead of beckoning with opportunity, the career of the artist became synonymous with renunciation. By 1900, artists as a class had lost any rational and workable connection with the economic system. Most of them lived as they could, and those who elected to make peace with the going order were stigmatized as "commercial artists."

It is not pleasant to contemplate a world that lacks the fundamental need of expression by way of the visual arts; but it is true that the 19th Century drove artists into a world of their own. That will be the chief lesson of the present chapter. As to the elusive cause, it is still up in the historical air. No one has come forward with a provable analysis of why things happened which we know did happen. The best we can do is to sketch the main outlines of the general picture as it affected art, suggesting reasons where we can.

THE FRENCH ACADEMY

When Louis the 14th built Versailles (Fig. 17.1), he thereby moved the artistic capital of the world from Rome to Paris (page 802); but even the grandiose scale of his new palace would not, in itself, have been enough to account for the maintenance by France of artistic leadership ever since. The operative factor in the situation (and a factor which did not become central until the time of the Revolution) was the long-term policy of the French people, a permanent and popular state of mind expressing itself in action at the highest levels of government.

In other lands, the cultural and intellectual life of the population has, with exceptions, remained a private affair and no concern of the political authorities. Conditions in France have been different. Ever since the time of Louis the 14th, the French have considered such matters to be a national responsibility. In addition to its political appointments, the government has systematically maintained boards of eminent men charged with the responsibility of defining and safeguarding the excellence of the French language, the soundness of French science, and the superiority of French taste in the visual arts.

The great enterprise began in 1635 with the establishment of the Academy of Literature. The Academy of Painting and Sculpture followed in 1648, that of Science in 1666, and that of Architecture in 1671. The first important administrative reorganization took place as early as 1663, when Colbert consolidated the existing academies under one ruling body. Since then, the corporate complexion and the official title have changed several times. A detailed history would not aid us in our immediate purpose; we may therefore take the liberty of resorting to popular parlance and refer to the entire official personnel so designated by the government simply as "The French Academy." Let the reader visualize it as a board of gentlemen publicly declared by the government to be *grands seigneurs* of literature, science, and art, and empowered by the government to speak and to act in the name of France.

Once established, the academic principle survived and still does. Usually representative of the conservative point of view, the members of the Academy have always demonstrated a remarkable political agility, and the organization has been able to adapt its chosen formulae to every successive situation since. We may say, in fact, that the existence of the Academy remained the rock around which every artistic current has swirled for more than two hundred years, and a great many things make no sense at all unless we remember that the Academy was always there to reward its own and to undermine the prestige of outsiders.

Art has for so long been identified with freedom that the reader may be forgiven if he has not taken the last few sentences seriously. In order to appreciate that they mean even more than they say, he will require amplification. To belong to the Academy was to be something more than the holder of an honorary degree; it meant that a man belonged to an organization which had the legal power to control French art. Such control was implemented largely in two ways: control of exhibition, and control of education.

Members of the academy were permitted to exhibit their work in public only at the official exhibitions sponsored by the Academy. Artists not associated with the Academy were forbidden by law to exhibit at all. Shows of paintings had begun to assume great importance from the beginning of the 18th Century onward. The "Salons," as they were called, were first held at Paris only every other year; but from 1737 onward, they were annual. As time went on, more and more people came, and painting began to reflect the taste and needs of the middle class as well as the nobility. Finally the king himself, once the sole arbiter of taste, became merely the greatest among a large number of patrons.

The members of the Academy did not hesitate to exercise their control for their own benefit. An indicative statistic is the following: the Salon of 1789 was the last held under the monarchy; only 350 pictures were hung. The Revolution forced, for the time being, a more liberal policy. The degree of previous restriction may be gauged from the fact that there were more than 800 paintings in the show of the next year, more than 1,000 in 1793 (the year of the Terror), and over 3,000 in 1795. The restrictive policy was not, however, brought to an end by the Revolution. Throughout the 19th Century, the Academicians found ways to control the exhibitions; and at every opportunity and upon a variety of pretexts, they denied a showing to persons, styles, and subjects of which they disapproved. In 1863, for example, they excluded more than 4,000 pictures, causing a national scandal. Even then the fight was not over; however, we need not pursue the narrative further. Enough has been said to illustrate the nature of the operation.

Cynical self-interest surely formed part of the Academic motivation in the behavior described, but it would be most unfair to conclude that nothing else was involved. From the beginning, the Academy had assumed not only the right but the competence and responsibility for fostering art of the sort France ought to have — which meant choosing and endorsing certain kinds of art and discouraging other kinds. At the moment when the Academy was founded, nobody entertained any serious doubt as to what the best sort of art might be: it was the "Grand Style" created by Italy during the High Renaissance (page 725) and imported tentatively by Francis the 1st (page 709) and in thoroughgoing fashion by Louis the 14th, who had even gone so far as to employ Bernini himself for a period.

In the course of time, pictures executed in the "Grand Style" came to be known as "history paintings," since most of them contained subject matter which impinged in one way or another upon heroic tradition. The superior merit of such painting seemed obvious: it was edifying. "Art is a lever of instruction," wrote Antoine Quatremaire de Quincy in 1791. "It educates both the mind and the character when it records important historical events, when it depicts great or noble deeds, and when it represents the beauty of the human body. Who does not know the force of example? The statue of a hero is an object lesson in courage, and that of a wise man a treatise on morals." It is significant that the writer of those lines became permanent secretary of the Beaux Arts (page 842) in 1816; his statement may be taken as an epitome of the Academic purpose, namely, that the right kind of subject for the serious artist must be a historical incident illustrative in some way of the enduring qualities of the good man and the good citizen.

Recent criticism contains so many polemical denunciations of the ideas just stated that a notion is widely current today to the effect that the visual arts are and always have been dead wrong whenever they attempted to teach. We are told that art may entertain, contribute to our comfort, appeal to our feelings, and elevate our aesthetic sense — providing such may be accomplished by abstract methods. All such statements, it is necessary to warn the reader, are opinions; and while the reader as a free man is at liberty to dislike didactic art, he may not, if he wishes to be well informed, overlook the sincerity with which didactic art has been advocated at various times in the past, including the period now under review. It is essential to realize that the Academicians were not venal, but for the most part were acting from a sense of responsibility. None of them was ever more high-minded than Ingres (pages 850-852), upon whom the mantle of David (pages 844–850) had fallen; and his belief in the validity of the Academic program may be assessed from the following incident.

In 1851, Delacroix (pages 854–857) had come up for election to the Academy. He had been denied admittance several times before; and to a correspondent who asked for Ingres' support when the matter came to a vote, Ingres wrote, " Although I am much obliged to you for your kind letter, I must even so express my regret on learning that you uphold certain doctrines and certain tendencies which, in my opinion, are dangerous — in the person of an artist whose talent, honorable character, and distinguished personality I otherwise fully acknowledge."

If France was to have the right kind of art, France had to provide itself with the right kind of artists; and from the very first, art education was conceived as a primary function of the Academy. The effectiveness of the whole organization, in fact, has largely depended upon its continued dominance over the several channels through which instruction might proceed.

An *École Academique* was founded in 1648. In 1793, its name was changed to the presently familiar form, the *École des Beaux Arts,* colloquially known simply as " the Beaux Arts." Now free to both men and women between fifteen and thirty upon passing an entrance examination, the institution from its inception made available formal instruction under established masters. Attendance there has always been the easiest and most natural way for young artists to put themselves (usually for a fee) under the personal tutelage of some leading figure of the day.

In 1666, the Academy extended the facilities of its school by creating the French Academy at Rome and by establishing the famous *Prix de Rome,* which both Fragonard and David in due course held. Every promising student was encouraged to compete for that prize. Several years of carefree existence in the fabulous and eternal city awaited the candidate deemed worthy. Obviously, the system conduced to docility on the part of the student, but the most rambunctiously independent young man would have been a fool not to ponder the advantages of winning the scholarship. Who could not learn much at Rome? Who had the right to be so proud as to overlook the professional preferment beckoning in later years for those so honored in youth? And over and above such prestige as it might confer merely through its official label as the best, no one could deny that the training offered by the Academy was in many ways excellent.

Beginning with the foundation of its Roman branch, the Academic curriculum had veered more and more away from the study of Renaissance and Baroque models. The set was increasingly toward the study of classical models, which began to assume the authority of primary historical sources. Inasmuch as the only important classical models available were pieces of marble sculpture, the net effect was to focus study not upon painting, which most of the students intended to practice, but upon sculpture, an art in which few of them had any direct interest.

The developed curriculum of the Academy is so familiar as scarcely to require description; it still exists in conservative art schools all over the world. Beginners started by drawing with charcoal from ancient marble statues. Because statues cannot move and might be left in position for weeks or even months at a time, such instruction offered an opportunity for a protracted refinement of the drawing. Because shadows show up well on white, and because light conditions in the studio might easily be controlled and kept constant, a similar exercise in the modeling of contour was feasible.

Because not every student was able to sojourn at Rome, it became necessary to bring Rome to every studio. That was done by importing a collection of plaster casts after famous classical statues. In point of fact, the overwhelming majority of students studied not from the originals, but from casts; hence the phrase " cast drawing " as a title for courses of the kind described. Because the original purpose of cast drawing has been almost totally forgotten even where such work still goes on every day in the year, it is necessary to point out that the regimen was first conceived as a functional part of a well planned curriculum. By drawing from the cast, the student perforce made himself intimately familiar with the style of classical sculpture; that was the first purpose and first step in his training.

Because the style of classical sculpture, like any other style, is merely a habitual and satisfactory way of expressing oneself, the students who learned from the cast formed habits which were considered eminently desirable. Consciously and unconsciously, they might be counted upon to pose the figure in similar fashion and to idealize its contours and texture. By that time they were ready for the living model, and they entered what has since been known as " life class " or merely as " life." Because the model could hold a pose only so long, and because a particular pose could never be duplicated precisely, speedy execution replaced the deliberation appropriate for cast drawing. Otherwise studies from the living model were merely an extension of the same pedagogy.

Insofar as it might be convenient, the schools employed models who looked like classical statues; but when that was not possible, every student who had learned well from the casts knew exactly what to do. He corrected nature's oversight by abstracting the model's appearance in the general direction of Greek idealism.

Those who were able to draw or paint one figure could, it was assumed, be counted upon to paint two, three, four, or even twenty figures. The end product of the curriculum was to be — or so people hoped — the artist who would then furnish the world with one edifying " history " after another. Nothing of the kind actually happened, as we shall see in due time.

DAVID AND THE NEO-CLASSICAL STYLE

Destruction of the old regime was important to the purposes of the revolutionary government, and that intention accounts for the abrupt end of the Rococo. Even more important was the positive program of the new era. The vision and wisdom of the men then in control cannot be overstated. The end in view was the creation of a new world order. History contains no equivalent demonstration of the creative imagination exercised at the highest levels of government; the French and American democracies constitute the most complete fulfilment of beliefs like those of Alberti (page 696) with respect to the perfectibility of the race.

The political events of the late 18th Century were epic events, and everybody knew it. As Frenchmen of education and culture, the republican leaders felt a manifest necessity for having a new art capable of commemorating the great things which had just happened and the better life to come.

The Academy was ready-made for calling such an art into being. It had immense prestige, and its prestige was identified in the public mind with France rather than with discarded royalty. The Academy's procedures and techniques, hitherto devoted to the Baroque and Rococo, might as effectively be turned to furthering the purpose in view. An artistic executive of the first order of skill — a man who looked like a man of genius and destiny — was on the ground, moreover; and he had a plan which offered every political advantage, was congenial both to the learned and the ignorant, and then looked so perfect it must have seemed God given.

The man to whom we refer was Jacques Louis David (1748–1825), a painter. We may skip the details of the royal patronage he had received shortly before the Revolution, of his personal connection with the revolt, and of his brilliant and unscrupulous shifts of loyalty as one faction succeeded another in the years after 1789. Suffice it to say that no matter what he had done in the immediate past and no matter how black it looked, he was always able to turn it to his personal advantage whenever a change took place. History, it would seem, was rolling in his favor with loaded dice, and every tide he picked led on to fortune. His greatest single achievement was to convince himself and everybody else that the particular kind of art in which he happened to be interested was and always had been a moral expression identical with the morals of the new order.

At the time of which we speak, David was a conspicuous exemplar of the Neo-Classical movement to which we alluded in the last section and which had been in progress for a generation. As a young painter, he had started in the Rococo style. In 1776 he won the Prix de Rome, and after four years there had scored a great success at the Paris Salon with his *Date obolum Belisario,* the painting which secured his election to the Academy. During the next seven years, he followed up his advantage with *The Oath of the Horatii, Andromache Mourning the Death of Hector, The Death of Socrates, The Lictors Bringing Back to Brutus the Bodies of His Sons* (Fig. 18.2), and *Paris and Helen.* Several of those pictures had been purchased by Louis the 16th. Not all of them were susceptible of an edifying political interpretation, but most of them were. As compared with the work of Fragonard or Boucher, the style was much simpler and the content more calm.

At a time when resentment was mounting against the aristocracy and the court, it was easy to popularize any contrast with the Rococo. David's simplicity became " nobility " and his calmness became " great." Almost every government on record has represented itself as subscribing to both those abstractions; but there was a special reason of a more logical sort for drawing an identity between Neo-Classicism and democracy.

While all students of government recognize important constitutional differences between the French and American democracies and the republics of the ancient world, the notion was nevertheless prevalent that the new system had been drawn up in sagacious disregard for about eighteen centuries of error. The citizens thought they had jumped back over all of that, and they believed that their new tradition invoked sound principles originally established and proven in the city republics of Greece and the awesome republic of Rome. It is a waste of time to analyze their error with respect to technicalities. The possibility of making a direct association between the new era and classical times was enough to swing the artistic decision.

One of the great original intentions of the Renaissance had, of course, been to recapture the civilization of Antiquity. In the pages above, we have taken note how data accumulated and how practicing artists felt increasingly obliged to provide themselves with a more and more precise acquaintance with the facts of classical art. From the middle of the 18th Century onward, however, a series of events had served to redouble classical enthusiasm all over Europe and to make all previous archaeology seem inadequate, erroneous, and out of date.

In 1757, the modern excavations had commenced at Pompeii and Herculaneum. Everybody who could read was delighted and fascinated by the news. An ancient city preserved in fairly good repair, even to the bodies of some incinerated citizens, was a new kind of archaeology, much more lively than the usual battered and depressing ruins.

In 1760, there appeared in London a book called *The Antiquities of Athens*, the work of two young Englishmen named Stuart and Revett. The volume contained some fine big plates showing the Parthenon and the other temples still encumbered with nondescript medieval buildings, but standing nobly forth nevertheless. Athens had been a very inaccessible place for a very long time, and even the existence of such a treasure-trove came as a surprise to most western Europeans. The book had a wide effect in a world which hitherto had possessed only the foggiest notion of Greece as something separate from Rome and perhaps finer, and its publication doubtless paved the way for Lord Elgin's operations of 1801–1810, which resulted in the shipment to London of most of the remaining sculpture on the Parthenon (page 81), and its ultimate assignment to the British Museum.

But the event that really made the difference was the publication in 1764 of Winckelmann's *History of Ancient Art*, with which we have already had to deal in an earlier connection (page 7). Winckelmann's great success was due only in part to the fact that he addressed a public already well disposed. His intellect was of an order to command respect, and his expression, in great contrast with most other writers on similar subjects, was clear and carried conviction. His greatest single contribution was his exposition, which then had the force of a thrilling announcement, that classical art had two divisions — Greek and Roman — and that the Greek was better. " Causes . . . of the superiority of Greek art beyond that of other nations " we may read in his very first chapter heading. The statement opened up an entirely new perspective.

His fundamental thesis was reinforced by corroborating analyses of a newly definite and newly rational kind. Let those who wish to understand David read some of the other chapter headings: *The essential point in art: the drawing of the nude figure based on beauty; Ideal beauty formed from beautiful parts of individuals; The conformation and beauty of the male deities and heroes; The conformation and beauty of the female deities and heroines; The expression of beauty in features and action; Beauty of the individual parts of the body.*

Such words sound trite because we have so often heard them paraphrased, and still do whenever artistic taste is discussed. It was Winckelmann, however, who first set down on paper the Neo-Classical theory which today survives in good measure. Contemporary aesthetics is colored by it, and so are the press notices which celebrate the " conformation and beauty " of such female deities and heroines as we are permitted to view in the cinema. Mistaken though he may have been in matters of detail, the merit of Winckelmann was the merit of being right: he had a just estimate of the methods by which the Greek artists had arrived at their high idealism, and his recommendations were practical. How fortunate, from the standpoint of David and the Academy, to be able to claim such a man as their philosopher!

It was David who brought to perfection the Beaux Arts system of training for young artists, and he also who most vigorously and specifically looked forward to a great new democratic, and French, era in art. It may be doubted whether any enterprise in the history of culture was better planned or seemed more certain of magnificent success than that program. The monumental subject matter was at hand. A style was ready which was not only popular, but combined present advantage with an aura of history. The need was there and was expressing itself as an insistent demand. And yet Neo-Classicism, which started out with high hopes, was destined to end in tragic and even miserable failure. What was wrong?

A satisfactory answer to that question remains to be found, but certain facts are obvious. One such circumstance was the lack of good ancient art upon which to build a Neo-Classical Style. Let the reader peruse again Chapters 3 & 5. He will be more than ever impressed with the newness of most of our data; it is not too much to say, in fact, that by Thanksgiving holiday, the average freshman knows more about classical art than either Winckelmann or David could possibly have known. The archaeological knowledge available to them was not far better than the statement made long before by Alfonse du Fresnoy in his *De Arte Graphica* (1668), namely, that ancient art ". . . is that which has been made from the time of Alexander the Great to the time of Phocas." Obviously du Fresnoy didn't know what he was talking about, for Phocas was a Byzantine emperor of bad character who ruled at Constantinople between 602 and 610 A.D. Historical mistakes of that order can have an important practical effect. In the case of David, the result was to lead him into a gross error when he selected, from the numerous classical monuments available, the model for his own figure-style.

The model he selected was the *Apollo Belvedere* (page 177), which he sincerely believed to be an example of the best Greek art. It was a dangerous move in any case for a painter to adopt a statue for his model; but the choice was not made blindly, as some writers seem to suggest. The cold and static nature of classical marbles appealed to David as desirable. The white monotone of the surface seemed to him expressive of purity. The absence of movement signified, by a similar train of thought, stability, permanence, strength, and inexorable dignity. His attitude toward sculpture as such seems to have been similar to that which, during the Renaissance, had expressed itself in the Mode of Relief (pages 582–586).

With respect to the particular department of ancient sculpture from which he elected to choose, nothing could have been more unfortunate. The *Apollo Belvedere* and cognate pieces are not popular today, but they must be conceded a certain elegance and grace. Neither elegance nor grace may be overlooked as artistic desiderata; but when those qualities are sought to the exclusion of others, art becomes a vehicle foreclosed from certain types of expression. As pointed out in various other references (page 49), the nude human figure is artistically useful only because the muscles can be manipulated to indicate innumerable states of emotion. Statues like the *Apollo Belvedere* are distinguished, however, by a refined absence of musculature, and by a chaste refusal to display feeling. Neither element can have been overlooked by so astute a man as David; both must have been misinterpreted as expressing lofty detachment or some kindred content. But the fact remains that when the die had been cast, Neo-Classicism found itself enslaved by the very kind of ancient model least capable of carrying epic subject matter or any other meaning which might be strongly and deeply felt. Another choice, even from among the monuments then available for choice (and we still lack a sufficient number to make a Neo-Classical enterprise feasible) might have brought more fortunate results. As it was, Neo-Classical painting, which sprang from a bloody revolution, was condemned from the beginning to be a bloodless art.

The miscalculations which are now so easy to discern did not appear as such to David and his contemporaries. With a genuinely classical faith in the superior dignity of events from remote history (page 63), the doctrine was promulgated that Greek and Roman literature contained somewhere every subject worthy of serious artistic treatment. Such a notion — which had the effect of supplying a substitute for the Bible — fell in with the anticlerical program of the Revolution. Almost any classical subject was virtually certified as acceptable, and David himself was not above painting a few that were distinctly racy. The kind of subject to be taken seriously, however, was epitomized in the *Brutus* (Fig. 18.2).

The Brutus of the picture was Lucius Junius Brutus, nephew to Tarquinius

Superbus, the last king of Rome. In 510 B.C., the Tarquins were expelled and Rome became a republic, with Brutus as one of the two first consuls. His sons, however, became involved in a conspiracy to restore the dynasty, which would have meant the end of the new republic. Brutus ordered the execution of the young men as impartially as he might have directed that of any other young men; the painting shows him sitting shattered, broken hearted, and alone, having lost not only his dead sons but also his living womenfolk, who shriek with horror as the bodies are brought home.

The moral of such a painting was too obvious to escape the dullest citizen. The incident depicted was an example of conflicting loyalties: private loyalty on the one hand, civic loyalty on the other. The strength of the picture derived in large part from its honesty; the cost of putting the state above self and family was made ghastly plain, while the intangible reward of heroism was left to the imagination.

David's developed style is better exemplified by the painting he himself is said to have considered his best, the *Sabine Women* (Figs. 18.3–4) of 1799. Not only was the picture concerned with the civic welfare; to a certain extent, it was even a civic project. David had announced that he intended to paint the subject, but indicated that he could hardly do it justice without the help of models of both beauty and character. His male friends were cooperative, of course, and we have an index to the high seriousness with which his art was regarded when we read that their wives and daughters were equally ready to pose. Ladies appeared in a concourse, it is said, to undrape their forms before him, and he was able to choose as he wished.

The employment of living models doubtless accounts in some measure for the disquieting element of personality in figures otherwise as smooth as marble. The news that such had been the procedure contributed, equally without doubt, to the popularity of the painting — which was unprecedented. David put it on view as a commercial exhibition. He promised his staff and pupils a dinner should the take exceed 24,000 francs; but even at the then substantial admission of 1 franc 80, three times that amount, and over, was realized. The delighted pupils demanded three dinners, for which the delighted master paid. With the balance he bought himself a country estate, and although well pleased with himself, he did not try the same trick again. The critics got after him, suggesting motives that were less lofty than the obvious lesson of the painting.

The latter, it is necessary to add, applied to the internecine strife within the government, which by that time had become the Directoire. The Rape of the Sabines, said the picture, gave just cause for grievance; but the Sabine women were right when, as shown, they came between their avenging kinsmen and the Romans, thus saving irreparable bloodshed.

Like many another revolutionary, David became an admirer of Napoleon. By still another act of the formidable rationalization at which he had so often proven expert, he converted to the glory of that despot the very art which he had first brought into being as a celebration of democracy and freedom. When the Bourbons returned in 1816 he was exiled because as a member of the Convention he had voted for the death of the king when that matter came up in January 1793. He spent his last years in Brussels.

Because academic art of every kind is unpopular at this date, the reader should be warned to inspect David's work more closely than he might feel inclined to do. His portraits in particular deserve attention; they are not only keen, but fresh and lovely. It is within our province to disagree with his theory of art; but no one knows so much about painting as to be above learning from his technique. There was none finer during the 19th Century, and there has been none finer since.

The Decadence of Academic Art

Academic art was decadent even before the Neo-Classical enterprise got well under way. Classical literature contains a number of episodes which, instructive though they may be, are unlikely to edify. David's early *Paris and Helen* had been one such example; his later *Cupid and Psyche* was an unmistakably salacious picture. The power of ancient authority is well illustrated by the fact that such a work, in every way antithetical to 19th-Century mores, proved not scandalous, but acceptable.

David left Paris forever in 1816. His position as the semiofficial dean of French art was presently assumed by his former pupil Jean Auguste Dominique Ingres (1780–1867), who had won the Prix de Rome in 1801, had been unable to depart for Italy until 1806 but had spent the next fourteen years at Rome and the following four at Florence, and had arrived back in Paris in 1824. The technique of Ingres sums up everything that was good in the Beaux Arts system. No one ever knew how to draw better. Of his painting, Delacroix wrote in 1855, " After examining the Homer picture [Fig. 18.6] I am bound to say I have never seen anything approaching the way it is executed. . . ." The skill to which we refer is best illustrated in a long series of pencil portraits like Fig. 18.5, which Ingres used rapidly to run off during his stay in Italy.

Upon his return to France, he became almost ashamed of them, and refused to do more. Slamming the door in the face of a lady who inquired, " Is this the place where the gentleman lives who does little pencil portraits? " he declaimed, " No, Madam! This is the place where a history painter lives! "

As to his history painting, it is all summed up in his greatest single effort, the *Apotheosis of Homer* (Fig. 18.6), where we see Homer being crowned by

Victory, with the personified Iliad and Odyssey at his feet, and in the presence of a carefully selected group of the world's great from ancient to modern times — Shakespeare and Goethe being excluded from the delegation as being insufficiently classical. It is doubtful whether an equal measure of intelligence and skill was ever expended upon so complete an absurdity, for in addition to its conceits of content, the painting was intended as a ceiling decoration for one of the galleries of the Louvre. It is now hung vertically.

Ingres had it in mind to emulate and even to surpass Raphael's *School of Athens* (Fig. 16.19). The essential folly of the Academic theory is well demonstrated by his complete failure to evoke anything like the same sensations. The reason would appear to be his sole reliance upon the human figure as a vehicle of communication, and the absence of the space (page 732) which Raphael had used so well.

It will be noted, also, that the theme was laboriously contrived, and was not, in strict truth, classical history. Obviously it was intended to elevate; but the conception lacked the epic proportions to which the painter pretended. The whole affair is illustrative of another serious error in the Academic dogma. The classical literatures simply failed to contain the inexhaustible supply of inspiring subjects which, as an article of faith, the Neo-Classicists had loudly claimed were there, ready and waiting.

Other painters began to do what Ingres had done. They tried to make up, that is, stories and situations which were classical only in the sense of including classical characters, showing them in actions that were plausible. A prime example was Couture's *Romans of the Decadence* (Fig. 18.8). The picture was famous in its day and immensely popular, especially in New England, where it was understood as proof positive that wine and women would be fast poison for any civilization. No one stopped to figure that those corrosive agents had taken all of 476 years to ruin Rome, but doubtless some characters were stiffened by a perusal of the original or one of the prints after it. In passing, the author nevertheless begs leave to wonder whether, while fishing for smelts through the ice or shivering in the duck blind, his Quaker and Congregational forefathers (who had nothing against fast horses, and habitually used Jamaica Rum in quantities appropriate to the temperature) did not entertain an occasional sneaking reflection upon the merit of sin in a warm country, as so fascinatingly illustrated by Couture.

Large and complicated paintings continued to be the Academic stock in trade and to have the best hanging at the annual Salons. Because there was no private market for ceremonial art of that size and kind, many of them were bought by the nation and may be seen today in the provincial museums of France — where, presumably, they fit the taste of persons insufficiently knowledgeable to appreciate the better pictures shown in Paris. But in order to appeal to the individual buyer, the Academic painters provided, almost from the first, a class of smaller and simpler pictures including only a couple of figures, or perhaps only one. Some such actually had classical subject matter: the *Oedipus and the Sphinx* (1808) of Ingres, for example. More often, however, the classicism was farfetched, as illustrated also by Ingres in his *Bather* of the same year. The latter shows a single nude female, seen from behind on a slight diagonal and seated by the edge of a sunken bath. The allusion to Praxiteles (page 133) was obvious; but it is significant that no one ever refers to the painting as an Aphrodite. It is representative, rather, of a whole class of Academic nudes known as " studies " — demonstrations by mature masters, that is to say, of the single-figure pictures which formed an essential part of the Neo-Classical curriculum for students. Many such are extremely lovely; Ingres' *La Source* (Fig. 18.7) is perhaps the favorite work of the kind.

It is very difficult to understand how it was possible for such paintings to maintain the approval of 19th-Century society; but such was the case. As time went on, the display became more and more daring, as seen in Figs. 18.9 and 10. Ultimately, even the custom of idealizing the model was forgotten in what amounted, as Mr. Mather once said, to a cult of the " heroic altogether," and the pictures became no more than pretty girls posed undressed on the model stand, with incidental landscape painted in later (Fig. 18.11). It is interesting that certain classes of patronage, innocent in all probability of Neo-Classical theory, understood perfectly what such pictures implied. Before the First World War, canvases of the sort referred to found an appropriate hanging behind the bottles and above the gleaming mirror of the " gentleman's bar " in many an old-time saloon.

ROMANTICISM

It was inevitable that there would be a reaction to the activities of the Academy; and it came in the form of the so-called " Romantic Revolt," the start of which we may date from the Salon of 1819.

In that year, Théodore Géricault (1791–1824) exhibited *The Raft of the Medusa.* The painting would never have been hung except that, under a technicality in the rules, the artist had the right to by-pass the jury. As it was, it was exhibited as " A Nautical Scene "; but the equivocal title fooled nobody. All the world knew that a French naval vessel named *Medusa* had been sent to sea in questionable condition, had been badly navigated and run ashore on the sands off Cape Bon on the west coast of Africa, that the officers had not acted properly, that the surviving enlisted personnel had drifted in agony on a raft until rescued by a British corvette, and that the Admiralty intended to cover up the whole affair. It was likewise a matter of common knowledge that Géricault had been incensed by the whole business, had dug out the truth, and had painted his picture on the basis of firsthand conferences with the men who still lived. In addition to all of that, it was an immense canvas which by virtue of size alone asserted the same demand for serious attention as any Neo-Classical history.

The modern reader will find it difficult to understand why the painting stirred up so violent a reaction in Paris, not only among artists, but from everybody else as well. It is necessary, once again, to emphasize the strength of faith behind the Academic program; that alone can explain why Géricault's art impressed so many persons as dangerous and hateful. The style, it is important to stipulate, was reasonably sculpturesque, and except for the use of darker and broader shadows could not in itself have been particularly offensive. It was the content that mattered. Instead of an incident dignified by history, it depicted an event still classified as topical. The question raised by the event, moreover, had not yet been settled; there was burning difference of opinion on the matter. In addition to that, the painter took sides, and the painting attacked the integrity of an armed service. It was impossible, under such circumstances, to maintain even for a moment the judicial type of contemplation which, according to the Neo-Classicists, was equivalent to artistic propriety. As though that were not enough, by representing human beings in helpless agony, the artist attacked all established conventions with respect to the dignity of man.

It has been truly said that the French Academy never slept peacefully again. Its entire program had been challenged, and with some success, by another program so thoroughly opposite that the two could not possibly live and let live. Géricault had in effect issued a manifesto which denied the right of the Academy to direct French art, and which, in the same breath, asserted the right of the artist to make art whatever he pleased. Géricault's position was peculiarly strong because it contained the magic word *freedom*, which was something the Academy dared not openly oppose. In understanding the situation, however, it is extremely important for the reader to recognize that historical chance was also playing its part at the moment.

There was no essential connection between the content Géricault chose to paint and the personal freedom of artists. He wished to be free to paint subject matter which he found greatly exciting as well as profoundly moving. The Academy was then insisting upon a calculated subject matter which appealed more to the mind than to the feelings. As of 1819, individual freedom was identified, that is to say, with the emotional values, and civic pressure was identified with the intellectual values. Today the tables are turned. Romanticism in due course undermined the Academy, and a habitually Romantic public is today shocked by art that fails to enlist its feelings. Picasso, Braque, and others (page 923) are demanding personal freedom as vehemently as ever Géricault did; but they want to exercise it for an art more highly rational, colder, and more elaborately calculated than anything the Academy ever advocated.

The epoch-making picture of 1819 was Géricault's greatest work, but it was a sombre, ponderous composition and not at all a standard example of his expression. With an ingenuity that, to the Academy, must have seemed perverse, he collected material which, though morbidly interesting, was nevertheless bound to fascinate: the faces of mad men, the heads of dead men, stallions fighting. His interest in horses is suggested by the last item, and as one of the most competent painters thereof on record, he was once again sure to be successful in a world where every intelligent man had to be concerned with the subject. He was not interested in the horse as a philosophical expression, but in the horse as a means for action and speed. His best pictures defied the statics of Academic art by showing splendid animals and daring riders engaged in stirring feats which could not help but thrill anyone who had ever been in the saddle. He himself owned stallions and rode them with marvellous abandon, and his untimely death came as the result of complications following injuries received in a heavy fall.

When Géricault died, the leadership of the Romantic Revolt devolved upon his good friend Eugène Delacroix (1798–1863), an equally brilliant and much sounder character. From the standpoint of the Academy, it was unfortunate that Delacroix was born into a distinguished family. Throughout his life, he had powerful friends who were able to steer good commissions his way in spite of all contrary influence. From earliest childhood, his manner of life, like Géricault's, was the opposite of safe and sane. The affairs of his family were habitually conducted in an impulsive way, and his becoming a professional rather than an amateur artist was decided only in 1819, when he suddenly found himself without funds upon the demise of his mother. Reckless and careless at all times, he managed during a single year of his boyhood to get poisoned, to experience suffocation, to set fire to his bed and nearly burn alive, to hang himself — not in attempted suicide but while demonstrating the details of a case that had been in the news — and to be rescued at the last minute from drowning in the sea. It was no wonder that he grew up without great awe for convention and without fear of anything or anybody.

His first important painting was the *Dante and Vergil in Hell,* shown in the Salon in 1822. The subject would not seem radical today, but the notion of finding merit in a 14th-Century poet was equivalent, in the Neo-Classical mind, to absurdity; the picture was vilified by such persons as exaggerated and detestable. For the first adjective there was in fact some justification because the damned souls represented as swimming in the water of the River Styx were in fact adaptations from the figures Michaelangelo had used on the Medici Tombs (Fig. 16.28). The modeling was nevertheless reasonably plastic.

Delacroix seems to have found his way to his developed style as the result of an incident of 1824; this constitutes one of the very rare occasions upon which the course of French art was affected in any profound fashion by outside influence during the entire 19th Century. In that year the British painter John Constable (1776–1837) sent over to the Salon his *Hay Wain,* a detail of which appears in Fig. 18.12. Constable was a gentle painter of the gentle landscape around Salisbury, but he had developed a technique which often is not recognized as dazzling simply because he devoted it to quiet themes. Most of the elements of French Impressionism (pages 863–874) are there. Delacroix was not the only Frenchman to be enthusiastic over the brilliant play of light and color Constable had found ways to make possible. It seemed warm, hearty, and welcome as a change from the cautious tinting the Neo-Classicists had been using in their attempt to combine the appeal of the living nude with the appearance of marble statuary. He therefore took himself off to England in 1825, and he returned a moderate impressionist with an addiction to brighter colors.

The direct inspiration of Constable seems to have brought Delacroix's temperament into a state of synthesis. He had an early taste for Venetian painting and for Rubens, and for the rest of his life he seems to have been engaged in bringing Rubens back again by handling the paint in the manner originally suggested to him by Constable. His industry may be judged from the corpus of material that still survives: about 800 major paintings, about 1,000 small and minor ones, and some 6,000 drawings. The most notable feature of that immense catalogue is the catholicity of its subject coverage. Classical and religious paintings are there, also material from Dante, Shakespeare, from new and unproven authors like Byron and Scott, and from contemporary events like the Greek War of Independence and the Revolution of 1830.

A particular category of content stands out from all the rest as specially significant with relation to the developing philosophy of the Romantic movement. In 1832, Delacroix had made a trip to North Africa as member of a diplomatic mission. He never went again, but the experience added Near Eastern subjects to his repertoire (Fig. 18.13), and he kept on painting them the rest of his life. More was involved than a tourist's memory of the sights he had seen. More was involved than the impulse which, three centuries before, had sent men exploring the New World. More, also, was involved than the peculiar satisfaction such material gave to Delacroix personally.

Whether he appreciated it or not, he had found expression for a great unsatisfied — and until that date undefined — yearning in the European heart. We refer to the desire for escape, which has ever since been of the essence in Romanticism, and which crops out in strange ways and in strange places. That such a desire should be most keenly felt by the creative minority within the population is an important and disturbing phenomenon. To say that the grass is greener in the next field is to say that the grass is not green enough where one is. One does not depart to improve his lot unless unhappy with the present situation. We must face up to the probability that Romanticism, insofar as it involved the idea of escape, amounted to nothing less than a philosophical negation of Western civilization which, in Delacroix's day, was already rapidly being transformed by the materialism resultant upon the Industrial Revolution.

As expressed in art, the desire for escape has so far found two avenues for making itself articulate. Both are represented in the work of Delacroix.

One may escape by going somewhere else, as he had done when he went to Africa. It is not easy to account for the satisfaction he took in the experience. For the Arabs and Moors who lived there, North Africa was a dull place, and still is; but for the highly educated Frenchman, it was full of fascination and worth not to be had at home. It becomes still harder to account for the impulse to go when we reflect that artists by the hundreds have annually come to France from other lands to find the inspiration Delacroix left France to get. When Gauguin abandoned France for Tahiti in 1891, he merely felt the same yearning and sought the same surcease.

Those who cannot escape in physical fact must escape into the realm of the imagination, which is feasible in art and literature simply by choosing a setting in some era different from one's own. Delacroix did that frequently. He did it when he painted two versions of the *Abduction of Rebecca,* both with the Castle of Torquilstone burning in the background while the wicked Sir Bryan de Bois Gilbert swings the fainting maiden onto his war horse. He did it once again when he painted *The Crusaders Entering Constantinople in 1204* (page 361); but he outdid himself when he painted *The Death of Sardanapalus* (Fig. 18.14). Better known as Ashurbanipal, King of Assyria, that monarch had lost his life when the Babylonians destroyed Nineveh in 612 B.C. Having decided that the city was doomed, the fierce king ordered all his dogs, horses, and women killed in his presence. He ordered the palace set on fire; the smoke may be seen already rolling in. He then calmly slit the veins of his wrists.

The painting is illustrative not only of the Romantic escape, but of certain other tendencies destined to become operative whenever and wherever the Romantic impulse took effect. Delacroix's crusade, as we have seen, was for the value of emotion in art. Emotional satisfaction is surely a good thing in art and in life, and it had admittedly been absent from Academic art. No one needs to be told, however, that emotion is unreliable and at times unsafe. It sometimes directs the judgment properly and provides the fuel for good action, but it also tends to feed upon itself. Excellent though it was in its aspect as a necessary readjustment in French art at the time, Romanticism exemplified one of its chief faults in works of art like the *Sardanapalus*. By making excitement his measure of value, Delacroix — unwittingly, we may suppose — opened the door to the assumption that where some excitement was good, more would be better. The best picture, according to such reasoning, would be the picture which contained excitement in the greatest variety and in the highest degree.

The same train of thought inevitably was applied to the technical process by which pictures were painted. Exciting subject matter, that is to say, seemed to demand exciting technique; and exciting technique came to be identified in the public mind with visual evidence that the artist had been excited while he worked. The excitement of the artist as he worked came, by another step of the process, to be classified as a supernatural condition, often colloquially referred to as a " divine passion."

The notion was not invented during the 19th Century; it had the specific sanction of the most honorable authority. In the *Phaedrus*, Plato had spoken of ". . . the madness of those who are possessed by the Muses," and likened the creative impulse to " inspiring frenzy." In the *Ion* he had elaborated more specifically upon the same theme. " For the poet," said he, " is a light and winged and holy thing; and there is no invention in him until he has been inspired and is out of his senses, and the mind is no longer in him. When he has not attained to that state, he is powerless, and is unable to utter his oracles." As for those who had " no touch of the Muses's madness," Plato by direction and indirection wrote them off as incapable of significant creation, no matter how hard they tried or how clever they might be. The same thing, we may infer from what he said, would apply to the potentially creative personality at all times except when possessed by the Muse.

Plato has always been in the European air, and as Mr. Santayana once remarked, a great many people are Platonists who don't in the least realize it. While it is still too early to speak dogmatically about the philosophical basis for the Romantic movement, there is serious reason to believe that Plato's notion of the psychology of creation was supplemented in the mind of the 19th

Century by certain vulgarized excerpts from the ethical theory of Immanuel Kant (1724–1804) and borrowings from the social theory of Jean Jacques Rousseau (1712–68).

According to Kant, for a perfectly rational being who was also completely informed, there was no choice except to do the right thing. Upon such a being, as it is usually explained, the ethical problem was no problem at all; the correct action was a categorical imperative. A moment's reflection will show that Kant's theory is scarcely susceptible of general application in day to day living, for who except the Deity can ever expect to be perfectly rational and completely informed? The 19th-Century public was not delayed, however, by such refinements of thought. Ordinary men were sufficiently sure of themselves to resent any suggestion that they might be ignorant or unreasonable. Kant was generally understood to say that each man had within himself an infallible and automatic mechanism for deciding matters of right and wrong. By letting one's " conscience " be the guide, as it was colloquially put, a man could decide things for himself. Originally intended for application to moral questions, it was easy enough to apply the same technique of decision to artistic questions; and the artistic good or bad presently became, or so it was contended, not a matter for social judgment but a matter for personal judgment.

Rousseau had been the first philosopher to challenge in any fundamental fashion the essential righteousness of Western civilization. Although his vast influence is still grossly underestimated, we may not take space to pursue his ideas in detail. The concept that interests us in connection with Romanticism was his assertion that people, if left in a state of innocence, would be good. Evil, he contended, was to be accounted for by the pressure of social institutions upon the individual. Here again, a simple transference to the problems of art gave Rousseau's dicta the force of saying that artists, if not put upon by others, would turn out good art.

By pondering the ideas just summarized, the reader can put himself in a position to account for much that has occurred in the history of art since the start of the Romantic Revolt. By following Plato out to the end, works of art would inevitably be removed from the reach of the intellect. Such never actually came to be the case; but in the words of the late Irving Babbitt, Romanticism did in fact become a systematic conspiracy to discredit the rational faculty.

As part of the creed they were prepared to assert and defend, Romantic artists began militantly to impeach all criticism. From Rousseau they had it that critics were the agents of society; because social pressure forced the individual toward evil, criticism was to be resisted and resented. From Plato, even the artist was foreclosed from criticizing his own work; for how, when in his normal state of mind, could he deal with the products of divine madness?

It was such thinking that soon began to affect the technical process by which pictures were painted. In the painting of Géricault and Delacroix, the change was for the better; as compared with the tightness of Academic technique, their brush work was alive and even thrilling. But as the century wore on and the internal logic of Romanticism became more and more literally to be asserted and applied, the appearance of the average European painting was substantially altered for the worse.

With respect to design as well as technique, calculation of any kind was disqualified. Spontaneity was made the essential thing. Taking a broad view of all painting since 1850 or thereabouts, the result of such doctrine has been conspicuous in at least three ways: it has dictated the medium used, it has changed the fashion with respect to pictorial composition, and it has made coarse impressionism the going method for handling details.

As to the medium, protracted procedures of any kind similar to those used in Flanders (page 613) or at Venice (page 759) were inconsistent with the Romantic concept of artistic creation. Ideally, the right kind of paint was the kind that gave the desired tones at once, which covered in a single coat, and which would permit every field within a painting to be executed at a sitting. Complicated pictures could not be and never have been turned out so rapidly, but the impulse to do so was always present. Whatever their merits, paintings from the last hundred years certainly lack the finish hitherto characteristic of European art.

Equally conspicuous was a decline of interest in the art of formal arrangement. Judging by their work and what we know of their methods, rather few artists of the later 19th Century even attempted to visualize in minute detail the completed canvas before they began. Instead, they improvised. With respect to the arrangement of masses, of colors, of value contrasts, and directional impulses, the average painting from the period under review lacks the well considered composition which had become standard during the High Renaissance (page 762). Instead of inspiring us with the feeling that everything to be seen has an inevitable place and necessary function in the whole, the compositional relationships often seem haphazard and frequently are sloppy. Undeniably, however, the work was spontaneous in the sense that the authors thereof were studiously innocent of scheming.

Worship of spontaneity had still another result which first made itself manifest in the work of Delacroix, became increasingly overt toward the end of the century, and today constitutes an extreme defect of modern painting. Because periods of intense inspiration were necessarily brief, fast work was essential. Otherwise, the Muses might loosen their grip upon the painter and go away before he could finish. Fast work meant bold work. Bold work meant coarse work, which in a way was excellent because there was nothing like it for making the observer experience in empathetic fashion the actual sensations felt by the painter in his muscles as he held and moved the brush, turned it, put pressure on the bristles, and let the hand rise again. There is no denying that this particular tenet of Romanticism produced some very lively painting. "Sir, you do not paint," Cézanne said one day to Van Gogh, "you *attack the canvas!*" As to the merits and defects of the doctrine, the work of Van Gogh is intimately illustrative. His best brush strokes are inspired, similar to the Chinese and as good. His impetuous methods betrayed him into his worst work, also; of that, the less said the better.

It took about a generation for Romanticism to gain public support, and its ultimate victory over the Academy may perhaps be dated in round numbers from Delacroix's final election to that body in 1857. In attempting to understand why and how such a theory won the hearts of the population, we must first remember that while at their inception both the democratic revolution and the Neo-Classical Style had started with high civic idealism, the Napoleonic Wars left Frenchmen disillusioned and ready for some philosophy which might give meaning to individual existence by reference to something warmer and more immediate than one's sense of membership in society.

The appeal of Romanticism is still further not to be understood without reference to the personalities of the artists and poets who were its leaders. To a man, they were as charming as they were dashing and brilliant, and very easy men to love. Because they claimed to be abused, and because they were fighting a brave battle against odds, they became, as a class, the first artists in history who, in their professional capacity as painters and poets, were heroes.

Because the history of art inevitably tends to become a history of styles, it is specially important to emphasize that Romantic art was never a style. Because of its individualistic platform, Romanticism could not, without self-contradiction, influence artists in the matter of style, and it was therefore impossible for the movement to bring about sufficient uniformity to make the word style intelligible in connection with the art it called into being. The reverse, in fact, has been true. Romanticism brought about complete artistic freedom; and it was the latter, more than any other influence upon European life, which in turn brought about the clamoring chaos which has dominated Western taste for some time.

Even more important, and indeed the most far-reaching of all phenomena resultant upon the general acceptance of the Romantic doctrine, was a fundamental alteration of attitude with respect to the function of art in Western civilization. With the significant exception of Michaelangelo (page 739) it is fair to say that, before the outbreak of the Romantic Revolt, no artist had presumed to work for himself alone. For generations, in fact, it had been a point of honor among established masters to offer the patron, when the picture he had ordered was ready, an opportunity to refuse delivery, and to refuse payment as well unless perfectly satisfied.

By virtue of its emphasis upon the self, Romanticism made art into self-expression. How very rare it is at this date to hear the worth of a picture estimated by reference to the satisfaction it gives the owner. How equally seldom do we hear any significant emphasis upon the picture in its capacity as a visual synthesis for some important truth or inspiring idea. And how commonly are we told, both directly and by implication, that the crucial question, from beginning to end, is whether the work of art gave satisfaction to its creator.

The general acceptance of Romanticism, it is necessary to add by way of a final word, must be understood by the reader in a broad rather than a literal way. The movement was not a movement within the world of art alone; it was a system of ideas which, if accepted, would in the end alter one's whole orientation to the world. As with most other philosophies, it has functioned as an influence and not as a set of rules. Its literal application has never been attempted except in extreme cases, but its influence goes on, and tends to account for much that is otherwise inexplicable in the motivation of Western society.

Courbet's " Realism "

The capricious nature of 19th-Century taste is well illustrated by the cycle which began to make itself apparent as soon as the Romantic movement was well under way. Throughout the century, every new thing in art had its genesis not in and of itself, but as a resentful reaction to some established situation. As an illustration of what we mean, we cannot do better than to give the reader a brief account of the career of the painter Gustave Courbet (1819–77), who had arrived in Paris as a youth of twenty and who came prominently into the public eye in connection with his rejection by the jury in his early years there, and the hanging of two paintings in the Salon of 1849.

Romanticism had not brought about the discontinuance of Academic art. Both had plenty of life and force in them. Courbet declared that the one was arrogantly abstract and the other exotic. He wanted no truck with either; and in the name of what he called " Realism " he announced his intention of painting " things as they are." " Show me a Goddess," he said, " and I will paint her."

Those who have read the earlier chapters of the present work will appreciate that he was announcing a policy which was impossible. It is not easy to say what a thing is. Complex questions, both philosophical and technical, confront every artist who attempts to paint visual truth. Realistic art is not a straightforward business, but a problem.

In a superficial way, however, Courbet did succeed in being photographic. Although his artistic instincts often betrayed him into excellent compositions, he cultivated chance arrangements, especially with regard to the broader areas of light and shadow. As shown in Fig. 18.15, he was perhaps the first artist of all time to accept the accident of a cast shadow falling across the face of a nude model. As the same picture shows, he systematically refused to idealize the human figure in any way whatever.

His most famous painting, and the only one that even approaches greatness, was the *Funeral at Ornans*, which he was able to hang in the Salon of 1850 as a matter of right, by virtue of having won a prize the year before. The picture is grim, but straightforward. The setting is in the gloomy district of the Jura Mountains, from which the painter had come. There is an open grave, unrelieved by flowers. Around it stand the friends and family of the deceased; they are working people dressed in their miserable best. A priest whose face is equally common and whose vestments seem shabbily elaborate, reads the service. A bird dog is among the mourners.

The painting did much to give the word realism its modern connotation of having to do only with the poorer and coarser classes within the community, with the overt description of brutal and depressing facts, and with the studied avoidance of gentle feeling, noble thoughts, and heroism. Because of such usage, we have been under the necessity in earlier chapters of qualifying the word and giving a special application to the phrase *objective realism* (pages 20, 623).

As a defiance of both the Academy and the Romantics, Courbet's picture had considerable success, and the success got him into serious trouble. No one knows whether he had it in mind to stir up sympathy for the underprivileged classes, but it was so assumed. His painting was hailed as the art of socialism. More conceited than shrewd, he adopted that doctrine, parading his sincerity and increasing his vogue by refusing the Legion of Honor when Napoleon the 3rd offered it to him. In 1871 he took part in the Commune, was elected to the Chamber of Deputies, and became President of the Commission on Fine Arts. In that capacity he had something to do with the destruction of the column in the Place Vendome, and after the suppression of the Commune, his enemies fastened the responsibility for that act upon him. He was sent to jail for six months and ordered to restore the monument personally at an impossible cost. He therefore fled the country, and died in Switzerland a few years later.

Courbet's " Realism " is less interesting for itself than as a ramification of the Romantic impulse. Contrary to what he thought, his contentions did not militate against the fundamental tenets of the Romantic faith; in fact, they had the opposite effect. He endorsed the validity of emotion with the same emphasis as Delacroix. He merely denied that such satisfaction must be sought in the strange and the remote. His real contribution, and it was a great one, was to assert the truth that the stimuli for significant emotions lie all around us. The end result was to establish the dignity of humble things, and to free art from the formal preconceptions of the High Renaissance (pages 711–715).

FRENCH IMPRESSIONISM

The Impressionists became a force in French art about 1870, and the history of their doctrine followed the usual 19th-Century cycle. Denounced as radical and dangerous in the beginning, the kind of painting they advocated gained grudging acceptance by about 1890 and is today the conservative way to paint.

The Impressionists remain the last artists who can by any legitimate reasoning be grouped together as a school. The name is a mistake, and it gained currency more by accident than design. In 1874, Manet and a group of artists who had come into association with him held an exhibition at Nadar's Gallery to show a number of their paintings, some of which had previously been turned down at the Salons for several years back. Manet's catalogue mentioned the possibility that the purpose of a picture might be to render " an impression." The word *impression* appeared in the titles given to several paintings: *An Impression: the Sun Rising, Impression of a Cat Going for a Walk, Impression of a Saucepan.* The critic Jules Claretie, when writing up the show, called it the " Salon des Impressionistes," and the name stuck.

Luminism would be a better and more descriptive title, because — while painting for the most part in the Venetian Mode (pages 752 ff) — the common interest of these Frenchmen was to find a technique which, for the first time, would give in art the experience of seeing bright sunlight in nature. Impressionism in the strict sense of refusing to define small details was part of their method, but it was only a cog in the machine.

The study of French Impressionism will teach the reader to beware of what artists say and to note with a narrow eye what they do. As we shall make clear in due course, the aesthetic doctrine of the Impressionists was one thing as stated and another thing as carried out. Insofar as they themselves ever put it into words, their theory was susceptible of the very briefest statement, namely, that *the dullest object on earth becomes a thing of beauty when transfigured by the light.* The idea obviously was derived from Courbet's " Realism," and there was thus more connection between Impressionism and the Romantic movement than most authors have allowed.

In order to implement their doctrine, they invented a new and brilliant technique for symbolizing in paint the action and life of the sun as seen in nature; but their art was never understood by the public, much less sympathized with. We already have sufficient perspective on the period to declare dogmatically that no other artists then alive compared in creative capacity with the leaders of the Impressionist movement; but not one of them could gain either fame or fortune from his painting. The reason, or reasons, are as yet far from plain; it is important, however, to mention those which now seem clear.

Laboratory science had come a long way by 1870; and most educated persons had, by that time, accepted as valid the scientific method of reaching a finding by means of an objective study conducted under controlled conditions. The French Impressionist painters claimed to be doing the same kind of thing within the field of representative art. Their pictures, said they, were to be understood as problems in research, and the particular research upon which they, as a group, were engaged (i.e., luminism) was, according to them, reason enough for their work and explanation enough for their art.

Matters of technique had been of intense interest at all periods in the previous history of art, but no responsible group of persons had ever before put forward even a suggestion that technique was in and of itself enough to command the kind of respect to which major artists were entitled. It is worthwhile to point out at this juncture that the Impressionists never did exactly what they claimed they were doing; but, as understood by the public, they were denying the necessity for content in art, and in extreme instances, even its existence.

The technique they developed by their research impressed most persons as sensational to the point of vulgarity — an accusation not always without some basis in fact. The explanation of the said technique, when explanation could be elicited at all, proved to be a rather difficult intellectual exercise. The age was an age of formulae, to be sure, but the momentum of the Romantic movement was sufficient to make most persons suspect that a formula, or any other distinctly rational activity, had no rightful place in art or in the artistic transaction. To the extent that it was of the mind, it may be said that Impressionism compromised its chance for popular success.

In addition to the items mentioned — all of which tended to puzzle and annoy — there was the fact that the Impressionists seemed to be lying about their subject matter. The movement had got off to a bad start with the public when its elder statesman Edouard Manet (1832–83) had put on exhibition two extremely offensive paintings, the *Olympia* (Fig. 18.16) and the *Picnic on the Grass* (Fig. 18.17). Both seem perfectly understandable and decidedly healthy today when seen for what they were, namely, a proper dressing down for persons who misinterpreted as interest in art their taste for the girl shows provided by Bouguereau and Cabanel (Figs. 18.9 and 10). The *Olympia* was a naked strumpet who looked out of the painting not with the sweet allure that so often went with the title Venus, but as bold as brass; the same might be said of the healthy young woman in the other picture. It was the latter, strangely enough, which aroused the stronger reaction. The close juxtaposition of clothed male figures with the feminine nude was, people declared, not to be accounted for except as an elaborately contrived insult to public morals. The suggestion was seriously advanced that the painting would undermine the French home. A similar grouping of male and female figures had long been on view at the Louvre without having had that result, but it was by Giorgione, who had lived more than two centuries before and in another country.

As long as the leading Impressionists lived, they continued to paint pictures which in one way or another needled the accepted taste of the time. The outburst against Manet, which had assumed sinister proportions, was never repeated in the same measure, but annoyance and even disgust was a habitual reaction among solid citizens. Degas (1834–1917) not only appeared to go out of his way to find material that seemed unfit for major painting (Fig. 18.19); there can be no question that he actually did pick his subjects with the intention of offending. In a great many pictures of the female nude, for example, there is perhaps not one figure which could possibly have appealed to any one as the form of a lovely woman (Fig. 18.20). Monet (1840–1926) could rarely be called positively insolent, but he unquestionably made a studied habit of painting inconsequential material in haphazard arrangements (Fig. 18.22).

Inquiries as to the meaning and purpose of such painting were inevitable and frequent. The standard explanation, as received either from the painters or from persons who assumed the right to speak for them, was baffling. The inquirer was told, in effect, to understand or get out. He was directed to discontinue his age-old habits of observation, interest, and appreciation. Nobody but the ignorant and naïve, he was assured, would make the mistake of assuming that the subject matter of an Impressionist painting was identical with the objects represented therein. The objects made no difference one way or the other; if such a thing as content was any longer a matter for legitimate interest, the content was the light. And therefore, the lesson concluded, let men learn to look at this new art by using their eyes in a completely new and different way. Let them learn enough about technique to be able to look at painting by methods different from the way they looked at anything else, and get therefrom a satisfaction unknown in any other department of human life. No earlier school of artists had ever made the same distinction between the aesthetically educated and the ordinary citizen, a gesture which was resented. Quite aside from the fact that such explanations were overly rational, they were also believed to be partially untrue.

All too little emphasis has been placed upon the aspect of the Impressionist operation to which we have just alluded. The important truth which emerges from the story is this: as extremely able men to whom society had given the cold shoulder, the Impressionist painters, as a unit, turned upon society. We can deplore the false taste of the period and the blindness of its citizens. We may be excused for sympathizing with the feelings of the painters, but we must be appalled by the outcome. The breach which opened between society in general and its artistically creative minority widened. The parting of the ways became a positive misunderstanding, and the misunderstanding turned to mutual dislike. Dislike, in turn, all too often became hate; and it is from the last third of the 19th Century that we must date the psychological maladjustment which today constitutes an almost insuperable barrier to the progress of modern art.

It is obviously very important to have a competent knowledge of the main principles of the French Impressionist technique, but there is an immense amount of misunderstanding about the matter. Innumerable writers have stated it as fact that the Impressionist methods were developed in direct response to recent scientific discoveries in the field of physics and optical physiology. The names of prominent scientists like Rood, Chevreul, and Helmholz are sometimes appended to such statements, and we are told that this painter and that had the writings of such men in his library.

As to the use the Impressionists made of the information they gleaned therefrom, we are usually told something like this: since the spectral colors result from the disintegration of white light and may be reintegrated once again into white light, the painter can produce an illusion of white light if he lays on the canvas a full selection of spectral tones in a pure, unmixed state. When seen by the eye, it is asserted, such tones will be mixed on the retina, with the desired result. To the points already listed, almost every writer who fancies this particular rationale for Impressionism has added a word or two about complementaries, with a hint here and a hint there that the complementary relationship between tones was of the greatest practical use in the technique he purports to analyze. Still further, mention is usually made of recent psychological investigation, and we are reminded of the photo-chemical reactions of the eye (page 717), the familiar optical illusions, and the color top.

The reader may make what he can of the ideas just summarized. He will certainly be able to assure himself that there was considerable interchange as between artists and scientists. The artists bought the scientific reports and read them. The scientists were interested in the possibility of making a contribution to art. Chevreul, who was a chemist, published in 1838 a paper on contrasting colors, for example, and while director of the Gobelin tapestry works made some practical experiments.

If he pursues the matter very far, however, the reader will be impressed with the dogmatism of the view which wants to make Impressionism a department of physics. While allusions are made both to science and psychology, detailed proof (i.e., point by point reference to a particular painting on the one hand, and to science on the other) is conspicuous by its absence. After some years of attempting detailed proof, the author arrived at the opinion that a one-to-one connection between optical physics and French Impressionism was a will-o'-the-wisp. Some simpler and more workmanlike theory seemed necessary to explain what one actually saw with his eyes in the pictures. The following paragraphs, originally suggested by conversations with Mr. Arthur Pope, are put forward as a substitute for the sanction-from-science usually offered to students. Without suggesting that he is laying down the final law on the subject, the author is in a position to point out that he has inspected a great number of Impressionist paintings during the past twenty-odd years and remains satisfied with the analysis given below.

Like every other kind of art, French Impressionism had its foundation in a set of philosophical assumptions about the reality of our visual world. The visual experience of the race is no single thing. Circumstances alter not only what we see, but what we are able to see, and we change our techniques to suit the occasion. When, for instance, we study biology, we inspect the specimens continuously for a considerable period of time. Such vision is always under the constant direction of the mind. It is purposeful. It is, moreover, a process involving consecutive acts of sight. Let such work be compared to a vista which suddenly comes into view through the window of a moving train, and as suddenly is taken away. Of the latter, one lacks a *knowledge,* but he may retain a most vivid *impression.*

The strength of the Impressionist theory resided in a statistical argument, namely, that controlled, systematic, and intellectually directed inspection of objects (as in the laboratory) is rare. So rare, indeed, as not to be part of daily life at all. The instantaneous view, passively received as from the train window, sums up — or so they alleged — so great a part of our visual life that, for the practical purposes of art, it may properly be taken as the totality.

That much being accepted, it followed that the painter's problem was first of all to make certain of what went on in the mind and in the feelings during such moments of instantaneous, simultaneous, and summary vision. Various statements have been made which purport to be descriptive of our sensations at such times; all contain a measure of truth, and all are as yet inaccurate in the sense of being incomplete and inconclusive. Every single suggestion, however, has this much in common with every other, namely, that we almost never see the view clearly. The Mode of the Total Visual Effect (pages 580–582), that is to say, presents things as they might be seen by the perfect eye directed by the perfect mind, a situation not to be hoped for on earth. The Mode of Relief (pages 582–586) depends upon an assumption about the superior reality of mass; that assumption, according to the Impressionist doctrine, is an abstraction contrary to experience.

From such reasoning, it followed that the French Impressionists would, as a matter of principle, be impressionists (page 167) indeed; they would perforce describe objects in the same fuzzy way that the eye received them during moments of instantaneous vision.

Further analysis of passive and momentary vision suggested that its most cogent effects depended upon the state of the light at the instant when sight took place. Inasmuch as light works upon the local hue of the objects within the field of view, the psychology of the situation is often colloquially described by the statement " the eye sees nothing but color." Strictly applied, the statement is dangerously misleading, but it is true when understood as a description of the Impressionist method.

Masses in the typical Impressionist painting (Fig. 18.23) were rendered as areas of tone in contrast with the sky behind, or whatever else the background might be. The logical conclusion to such a train of thought would be to produce paintings in the Mode of Line and Flat Tone, an eventuality which actually came to pass in the work of Matisse (Fig. 19.10). Certain other aspects of the 19th Century formula precluded so extreme a result, however, and in the painting referred to, Monet gave some indication of the major relations of light and dark which, within the silhouette, might be read as modeling.

There is no one who would quarrel with the statement that by insisting upon the validity of instantaneous vision, the Impressionists opened up for painting an entire area of human experience — and a very large and important area — into which no earlier school had ventured. Such pictures need no defense. They deal with something that happens, and the immediacy of the reaction they evoke is apology enough. In that very strength, however, there was a serious weakness which in the end made Cézanne feel obliged to turn his back upon Impressionism (pages 908 ff) with the result that the school came to an end. Postponing discussion of his action, let us turn our attention to certain difficulties which became urgently apparent the moment the Impressionists decided to discard analytical and consecutive vision, and to cultivate the momentary kind.

When they decided that the action of light must govern painting, the Impressionists put themselves under a very unstable government. Light conditions are forever changing. The dogma that objects, dull and otherwise, were transfigured by the light, put the painters under an obligation to record and celebrate an infinite number of transfigurations. They did not shirk. Monet, in particular, faced up to the task and met it with an industry as immense as the problem itself. It is difficult to know just how many pictures he painted of the façade of Rouen Cathedral, but a series of no less than twenty were run off, it is said, during 1874 alone. The principal difference between them is merely that the light has changed — not much, it must be understood, but only enough to make a distinction for a connoisseur of light.

The reader will have noted that the doctrine of momentary vision had much in common with the Romantic belief in the value of spontaneity (page 859); but in the hands of the Impressionists, spontaneity itself began to assume a different character. The idea of spontaneity in the sense of emotional response was lost, as it were, in the rush. The spontaneous momentary view was the accidental view, and in order to make sure that no one would accuse him of contriving, the average Impressionist painter felt obliged to furnish visual evidence of his innocence in that respect. The expedient resorted to most often was to refrain from pictorial composition or, in extreme instances, to defy formal design by arrangements which were deliberately put in disorder.

The necessity for recording fleeting instants of visual experience imposed upon the artists, moreover, a pressure more intense than ever before to work fast. The element of their theory which had to do with the rendering of detail invited such work in any case. Strong insistence upon spontaneity undermined still further any belief in the value of deliberate methods; and it is not surprising to read that whenever they exhibited their pictures, the Impressionists were accused not only of sensationalism, but of hasty, careless, sloppy, inferior workmanship. While such words were and still are fighting words, they were all too close to the truth. The door had been opened to the assumption, which today is often belligerently asserted as a fact, that one might be very clumsy with his hands and still be a first-class painter.

While carried further toward a logical conclusion than any earlier theories about the nature of ordinary vision (page 168), the several elements of 19th-Century French Impressionism, as so far surveyed, were not new in kind. The techniques then developed for rendering the effect of sunlight were new, however, and now demand analysis. Four essential factors were involved: new pigment materials, the additive mixing of hues, a method for symbolizing the flicker of light, and a system of modeling which in large measure compensated for the short value scale available in paint.

Although much has been written about a possible connection between Impressionism and physics, it is rare to read anything which suggests the debt of the movement to chemistry; but there is no question that developments in the latter field furnished painters with some very powerful pigments. The first chemical pigment is generally believed to have been Prussian blue, discovered by Dresbach in 1704; but that was a comparatively isolated incident. The real harvest of new pigments began to come in toward the end of the 18th Century. Zinc white, chrome green, cobalt green, and cobalt blue all date from around 1800. In 1826 Guimet discovered how to make artificial ultramarine blue, thus replacing the genuine ultramarine which had to be made from powdered lapis lazuli brought all the way from the Far East. Cadmium yellow appeared in 1846. The years 1859–61 produced mauve (the first coal-tar color), cobalt yellow, and magenta. Several new reds arrived during the late 1850's, and from then on there seems literally to have been a deluge of chemical pigments. Many of the new pigments proved fugitive and have since dropped out of the artist's palette; but many proved good and remain. It would be going rather far to say that the old organic and mineral colors dropped out of use, but let the reader judge the upshot for himself.* When walking quickly in a museum from a room of earlier pictures into a room where the Impressionists are hung, one experiences a stimulating sense that the color has been heightened, not a little but a very great deal. The new and brighter paints were used, moreover, at highest possible intensity (page 574), by a method next to be described.

When we take some blue paint and stir it up in a pot with some yellow paint in the usual way, we indulge in *subtractive mixing*. Constable (page 855) was one of the very earliest artists to attempt mixtures of any other kind, and his motive for experimenting was the fact that subtractive mixing is almost invariably a disappointment. Different pigments and different vehicles combine capriciously, and it is impossible to lay down a general rule about what to expect. The subtractive mixture, however, will usually be both darker and less intense than either of the colors which were combined to make it.

Additive mixing, in the literal meaning of the term, is possible only with the

* For most of this information I am indebted to E. P. Richardson of The Detroit Institute of Arts. See also F. W. Weber, *Artists' Pigments*, New York. Van Nostrand. 1923.

aid of equipment which enables us to blend two or more beams of colored light. Such mixing is a daily routine in the theatre, but it is hardly available to those who must use paint. A near substitute for true additive mixing had been used in the textile industry for hundreds of years, however, and the French Impressionist painters took it over and made it their own. Most gray tweed, for example, is woven not from thread of a uniform gray, but from whiter and blacker threads in a predetermined proportion. When one looks down at the sleeve of his jacket, the separate strands are in plain sight; but when one looks at the same jacket from twenty feet away, the eye can no longer resolve details so small. The dark tones tend to lower the value of the field. The lighter tones tend to raise it. When asked to name the local tone of the whole, the observer deals neither with the light or the darker threads, but with the tone produced by the blend of them as seen from his particular station. The principle involved can be applied to any other mixture of values or hues; the essential thing is the juxtaposition of one color with another, and the blurring of small spots as seen in the distant view.

It will be obvious from what we have said that the effect of green can be had by a judicious spotting of a surface with blue and yellow, or that a red can be made into an orange by arranging flecks of red and flecks of yellow in much the same way. The reader will find it amusing to prove it with his own paints. He will doubtless find it disciplinary as well, for it takes an immensely subtle judgment to produce the tone one wants to see. Such experiments carried a bit further will also illustrate how a tint of any hue can be produced (and a very lively tint, too) by spotting in more or less pure white. As for the production of shades, the matter is not so simple, as we shall presently explain.

Various names have been given to the Impressionist technique which brought about the additive mixing of the hues. "Broken brush work" and "divisionism" are expressive. "Pointilism" (i.e., *pointillisme,* but the word should be Anglicized) is the most common designation; strictly it applies to doctrinaire applications of the theory as seen in the work of Signac and Seurat (Fig. 18.25), where the definition is brought about by nothing else but spots of paint.

As a matter of fact, the various Impressionist painters were alike merely in using the broken color technique most of the time. There was no standard or accepted size or shape for the single touch of the brush or palette knife. Comma strokes, mosaic squares, and dabs of every sort were used. Monet now and then approached the spirit of mosaic almost as closely as Seurat; at other times he simply cross-hatched or flecked with the several hues he wished to mix, maintaining no uniformity of size, shape, or direction, and varying the pressure upon the brush as judgment indicated. Van Gogh often used serpentine strokes, leaving stripes of paint a quarter of an inch wide or more and as long as he pleased. Renoir, in much of his work, was apparently averse to anything that might deny the liquidity of the vehicle; his colors, while broken, seem to flow against each other, and to be in hydraulic rather than mechanical juxtaposition.

Every author who has attempted to describe the broken color technique has stressed too heavily the phenomenon of the blurring of the juxtaposed spots whenever Impressionist pictures are seen from a normal remove. Our own paragraphs on the subject are no exception; and we must now qualify what we have said. In every typical painting of the kind, the individual spots or flecks of color are significantly large. When seen from any distance short of a hundred feet or so (which surely is farther away than one would stand to look at a painting) they do not blend completely together. Each spot retains a certain measure of its own identity. Additive mixing takes place, to be sure; and one is conscious of the new tone thereby built up. But the additive mixing remains incomplete at the same time, and one is almost equally sensitive to the several hues which go to make up the mix. The latter phenomenon is almost as important as the first.

Because it was part of the Impressionist system to use every pigment at highest possible intensity, the contrast between any two contiguous spots of paint was perforce (and intentionally) the maximum contrast possible as between those two hues. The surface of an Impressionist painting might accurately be described as an infinite number of such contrasts, tiny in size but violent with respect to the clash of colors. The psychological effect upon the observer has often been described as "vibratory." Purists in the language may protest that no vibration exists, but thousands of persons have felt that sensation under the circumstances we mention.

This was, in fact, one of the most vital achievements of the Impressionist technique. The response of the optical system is not only similar, but may very well be the same response that we experience whenever we see the leaves of a tree flicker as they move in the sunlight, or whenever we see reflections on clear and rippling water. As a reinforcement to the other representative aspects of the painting, we instinctively read the vibratory effect as indicative not only of the living sunlight, but also of movement in the air.

As set forth in Chapter 14, the principal handicap of all representative painting derives from the infinitely short contrast between black paint and white paint, as compared to the immense contrast in nature between the darkest shadows and the brightest high lights. It was the greatest merit of the Impressionists to develop and perfect the best artistic compromise yet known for dealing with that inexorable fact.

The most familiar and conspicuous consequence of their method was the bright purple which they painted into the darkest parts of their pictures. We often hear it said that they were " the first artists to realize that shadows are in fact purple," but nothing of the sort is true. Purple shadows are familiar in nature under certain conditions, and unknown under other conditions. Shadows of every other hue occur as often as purple shadows. The use of purple by the Impressionists did not result from naturalistic motives, but from a well-calculated artistic scheme.

Their theory in that respect was extremely simple for so excellent a stratagem, and it may be stated briefly. Pissarro followed the formula more literally and consistently than most of the others, and the reader will find in his work a number of paintings which might be classified as laboratory demonstrations. The rest of the school conformed more to the spirit than to the letter of the rule; but if the principle is understood, the reader will be prepared for variations and approximations in practice.

The crux of the whole matter was to substitute violent contrasts of hue (which were available in paint) for the terrific value contrasts of nature (which could not be duplicated by paint).

Let us assume that a single field contains both the darkest shadows and the brightest high lights within the entire picture. In modeling such a field, the doctrinaire Impressionist would paint purple at highest possible intensity into the darkest areas. He would reserve his brightest yellow for the areas in full illumination, and white for the high lights. In grading from the dark up toward the light, the painter would then shift from hue to hue around either the warm side or the cold side of the color circle (Fig. 14.10). In doing so, he would use every hue at highest possible intensity. A " warm field " would thus go from absolute purple through red-violet and the reds, and thence into the oranges up to yellow. A " cold field " would follow a similar sequence of shifts by way of the blues and greens.

It will be understood, of course, that it is extremely rare to be confronted with the necessity for modeling a single field which, within itself, contains both the brightest and the darkest areas of the picture. Yellow and purple, as we noted in Chapter 14, lie on the vertical axis of the color circle simply because they happen to be the two hues which, when at highest possible intensity, give the maximum contrast with respect to value. For any hue other than yellow, the maximum possible contrast is not obtained from purple, but by using the complementary. If he inspects Impressionist paintings with care, the reader will find numerous instances where that fact, also, was employed for modeling fields where the full range of value was either inappropriate or not desired. The lighter complementary, that is to say, would go in the lights, and the darker complementary, whatever it happened to be, in the shadows. In similar fashion, spots of the complementary were often introduced by the pointilist method whenever it was desirable to " gray " a particular area.

If the reader is at a loss to understand why Impressionist painting was at first so very unpopular, he has much of the answer in the paragraphs immediately above. To an eye and a taste habituated to suave color harmonies as in Venetian painting (page 756) and to the cautious use of contrast as in Constable and Delacroix, the employment of maximum contrasts with respect to hue seemed blatant, sensational, and crass; a defiance, in short, of the decorum to which art had been the servant since the 16th Century. There was something in such an opinion, for it is possible to want a kind of painting not included within the repertoire of the Impressionists. Taking a longer view, however, it must be conceded that the Impressionist system of modeling was overwhelmingly successful. It accomplished the desired result, and for the first time in the history of European art, brought the sun out from under the clouds.

As to the ultimate value of French Impressionism, it is very hard to take a position at this date. The weakness of the movement lay in its worship of natural accident. Its strength, it would seem, derived not from the creation of beauty, but from the recognition of it. In the personal view of the author, the best Impressionist paintings are those that record vivid, perfect moments of intense vision (Figs. 18.18,21,24). Visual situations, that is to say, where nature and luck have become the artists, and the painter the recording secretary.

STOEDTNER

Fig. 19.1 Mies van der Rohe. Model for a skyscraper with walls of glass.

WAYNE ANDREWS

Fig. 19.2 Racine. Johnson Wax Building. Designed by Frank Lloyd Wright.

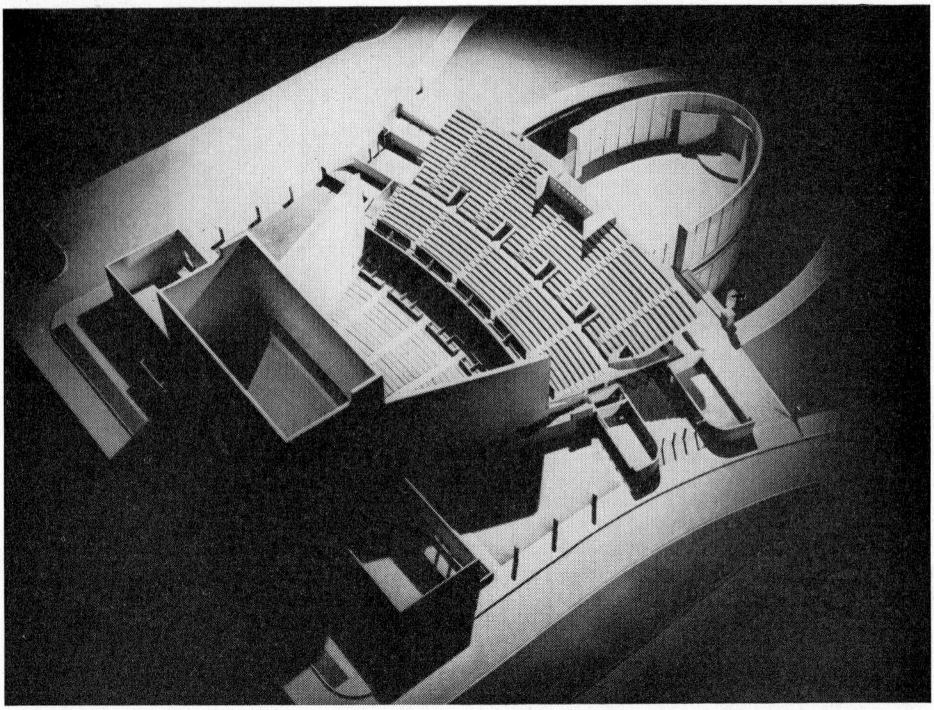

Fig. 19.3 Buffalo. The Kleinhans Music Hall. Architect's Model. Designed by Eliel Saarinen.

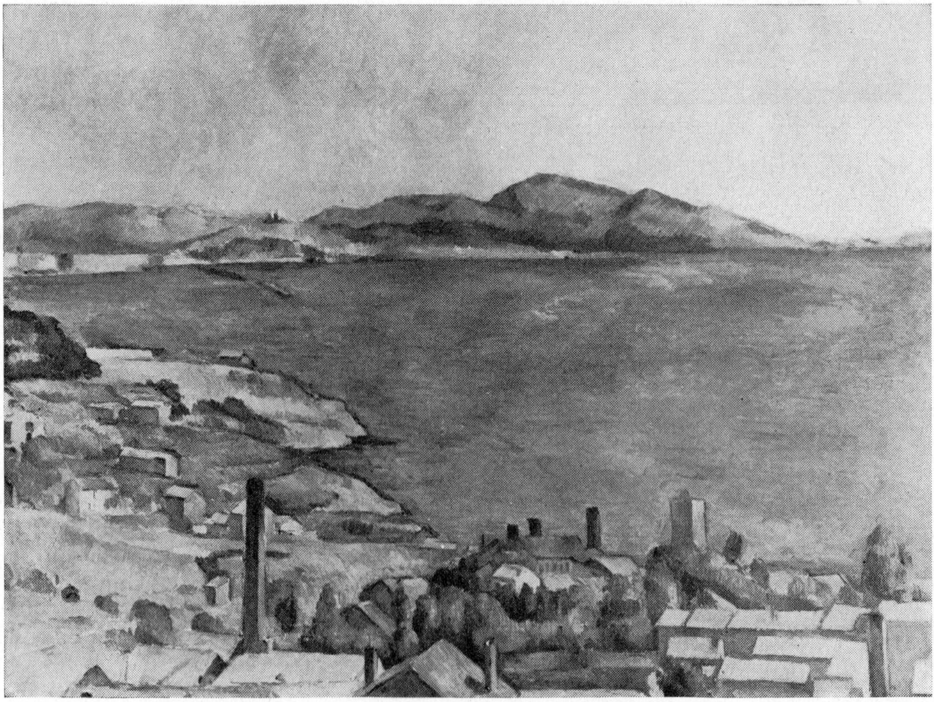

Fig. 19.4 Cézanne. *L'Estaque and the Bay of Marseilles.* New York. Metropolitan Museum.

BULLOZ

Fig. 19.5 Cézanne. *The Card Players.* New York. Collection of Mr. Stephen C. Clark.

BULLOZ Fig. 19.6 Cézanne. *View at Le Jas de Bouffon.* Hamburg. Von Bewmann Collection.

Fig. 19.7 (above) Cézanne. *View of Mont Saint Victoire.* Washington. Phillips Memorial Gallery.

Fig. 19.8 Cézanne. *View of Gardanne.* Harrison, N.Y. Collection of Dr. F. A. Hirschland.

Fig. 19.9 Cézanne. *Morning in Provence*. Buffalo. Albright Art Gallery. 1900–06.

Fig. 19.10 Matisse. *La Musique*. Buffalo. Albright Art Gallery. 1939.

Fig. 19.11 Demuth. *View in Lancaster, Pennsylvania.* Buffalo. Albright Art Gallery. 1921.

Fig. 19.12 (below) Feininger. *The Glorious Victory of the Sloop Maria.* Saint Louis. City Art Museum.

Fig. 19.13 Picasso. *Woman's Head*. Buffalo. Albright Art Gallery. About 1909.

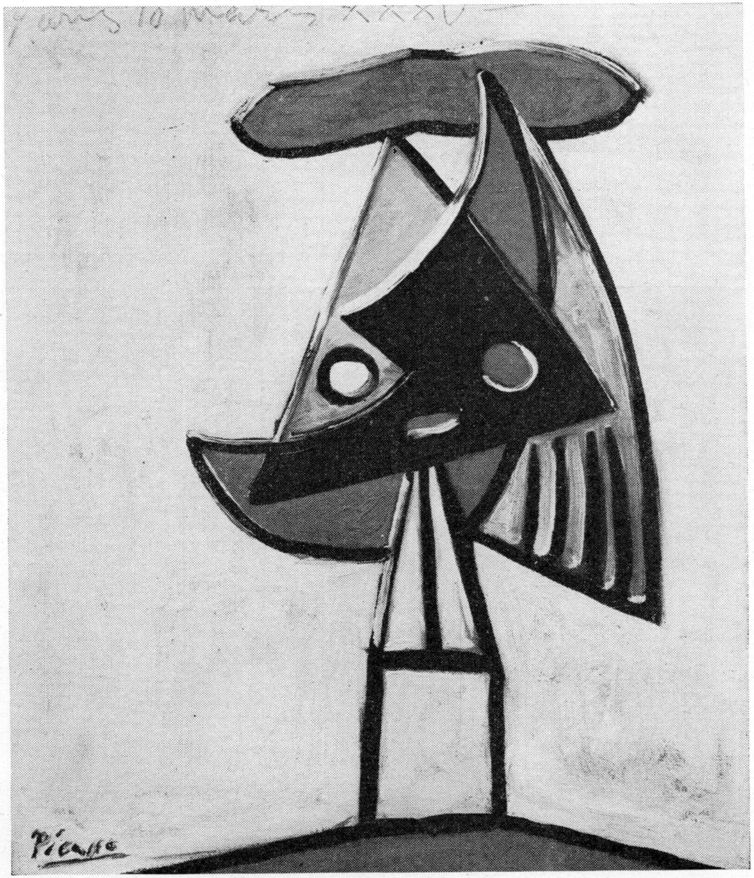

Fig. 19.14 Picasso. *Harlequin: Project for a Monument*. Buffalo. Albright Art Gallery. 1935

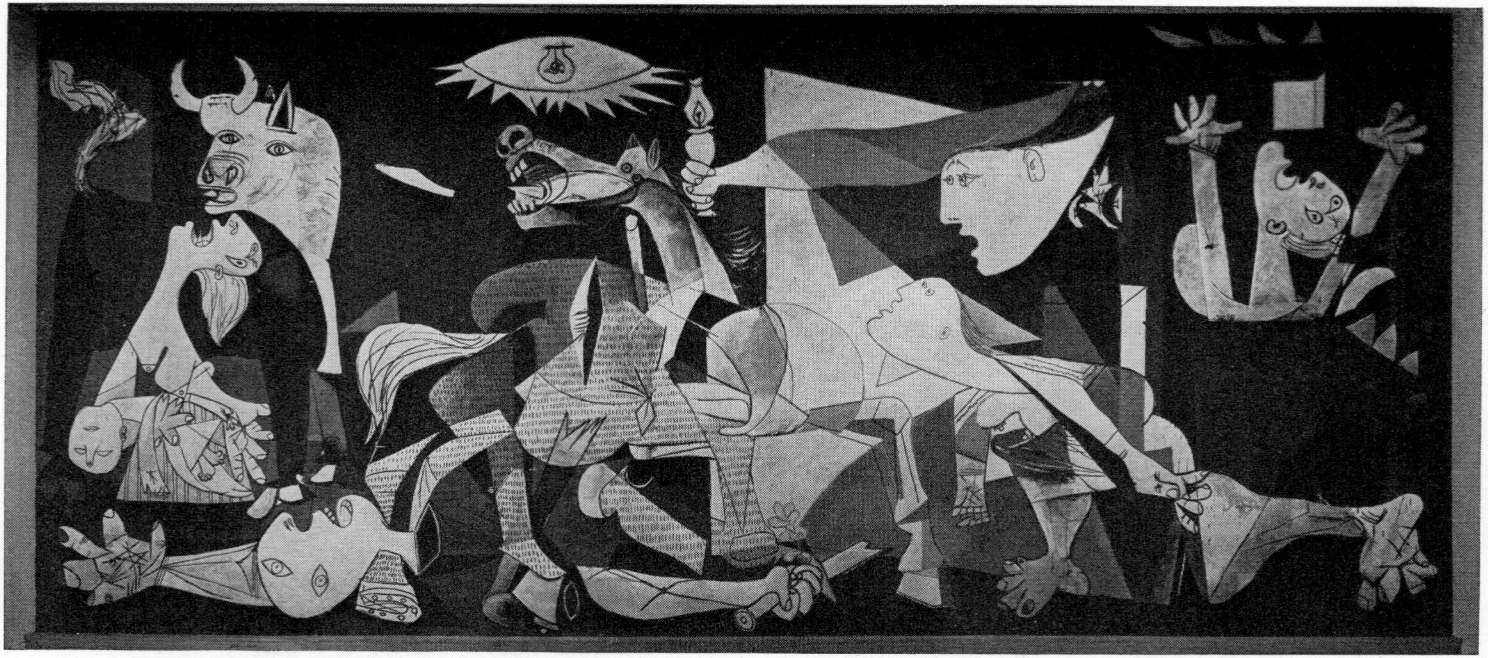

Fig. 19.15 Picasso. *Guernica.* New York. Museum of Modern Art. Owned by the artist. 1937. 25 feet, 8 inches wide; 11 feet, 6 inches high.

Fig. 19.16 Lipchitz. *Sailor*. Buffalo. Albright Art Gallery. 1914.

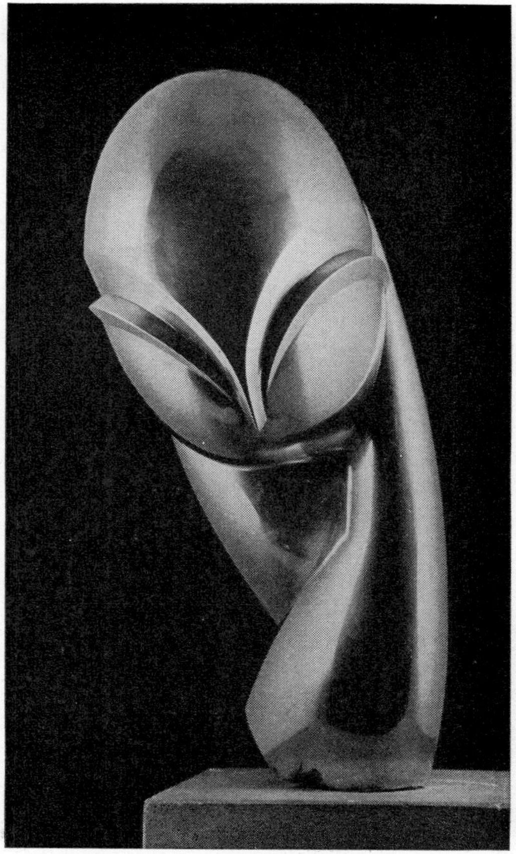

Fig. 19.17 Brancusi. *Mademoiselle Pogany*. Buffalo. Albright Art Gallery. 1920.

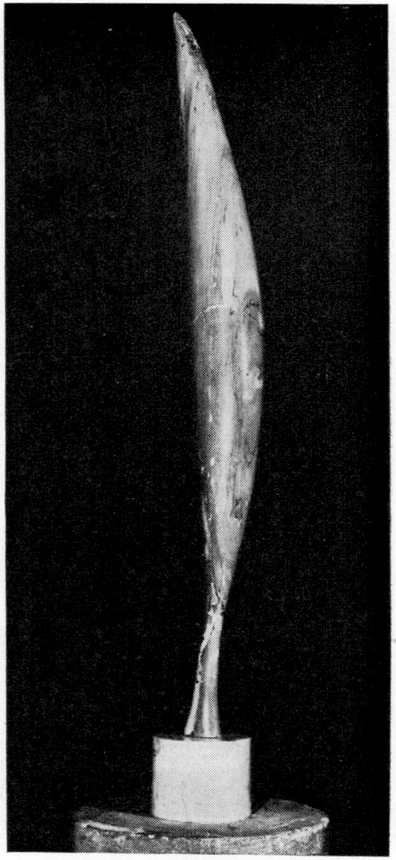

Fig. 19.18 Brancusi. *Yellow Bird*. Philadelphia Museum of Art. The Louise and Walter Arensberg Collection. About 1922–24.

Fig. 19.19 Archipenko. *Boxers*. 1913.

Fig. 19.20 Duchamp. *Nude Descending a Staircase*. Philadelphia Museum of Art. The Louise and Walter Arensberg Collection. 1912.

Fig. 19.21 Braque. *Violin and Pipe*. Philadelphia Museum of Art. The Louise and Walter Arensberg Collection. 1920–21.

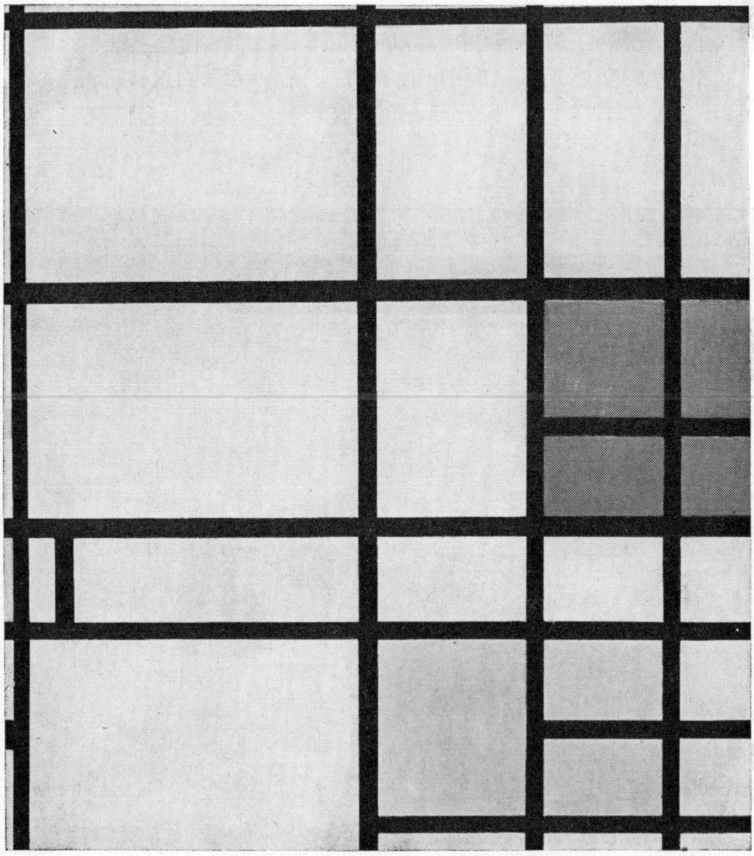

Fig. 19.22 Piet Mondrian. *Composition*. Buffalo. Albright Art Gallery. 1940–42.

Fig. 19.23 Maillol. *Night*. Buffalo. Albright Art Gallery. Cast in lead in 1939 from a statue executed between 1902 and 1909.

Fig. 19.24 Carl Hallsthammer. *Venus in Red Cherry*.

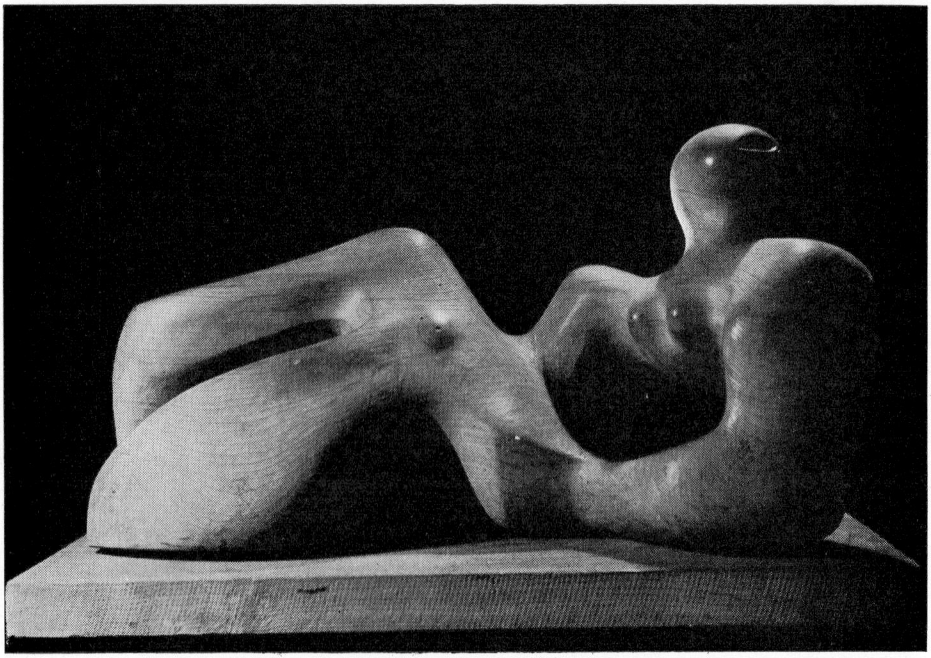

Fig. 19.25 Henry Moore. *Reclining Figure*. Buffalo. Albright Art Gallery. 1935.

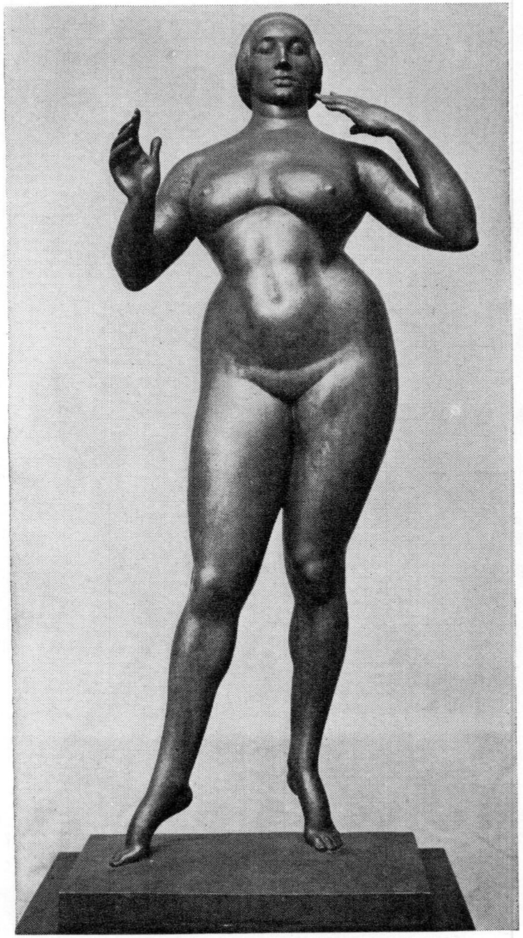

Fig. 19.26 (left) Gaston Lachaise. *Standing Woman*. Buffalo. Albright Art Gallery. Cast in 1927 from a statue begun in 1912.

Fig. 19.27 (right) Lehmbruck. *Kneeling Woman*. Buffalo. Albright Art Gallery. 1911.

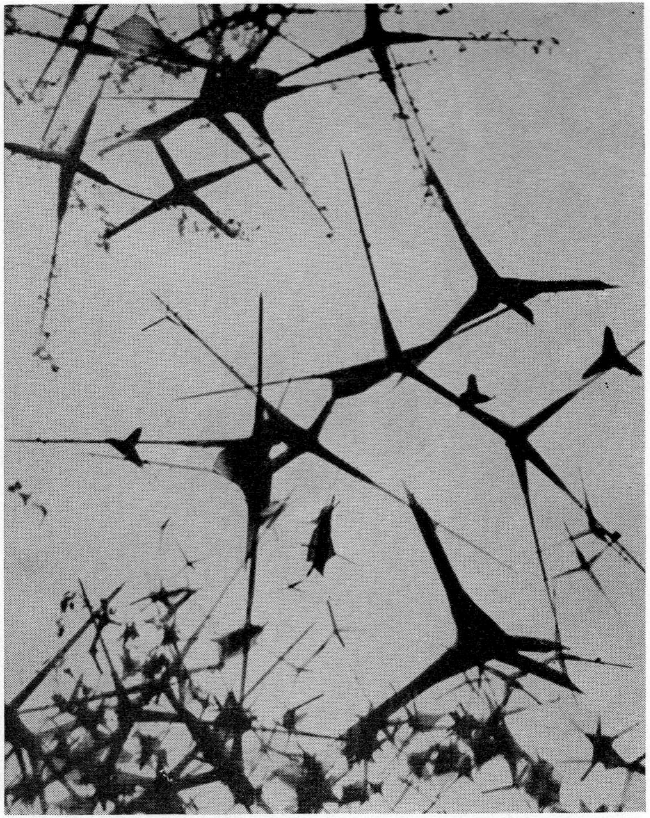

Fig. 19.28 a. Kandinsky. *Small Worlds*. New York. Metropolitan Museum.
b. Microphotograph of zinc oxide magnified 50,000 diameters.

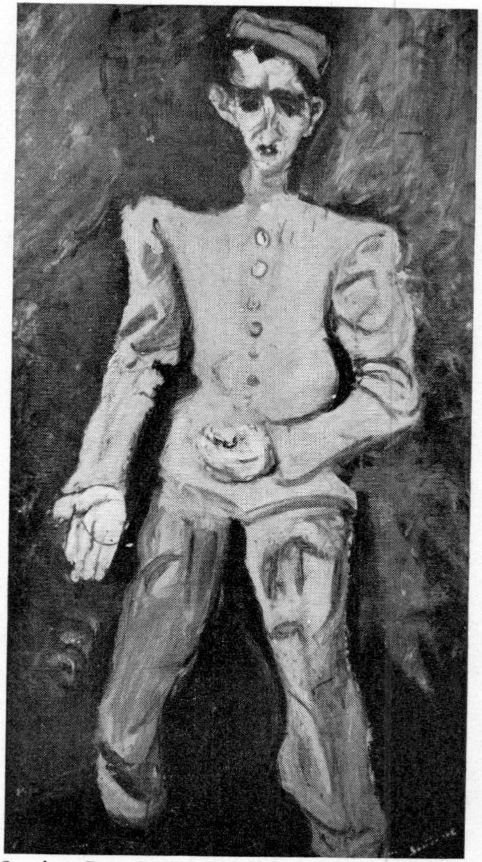

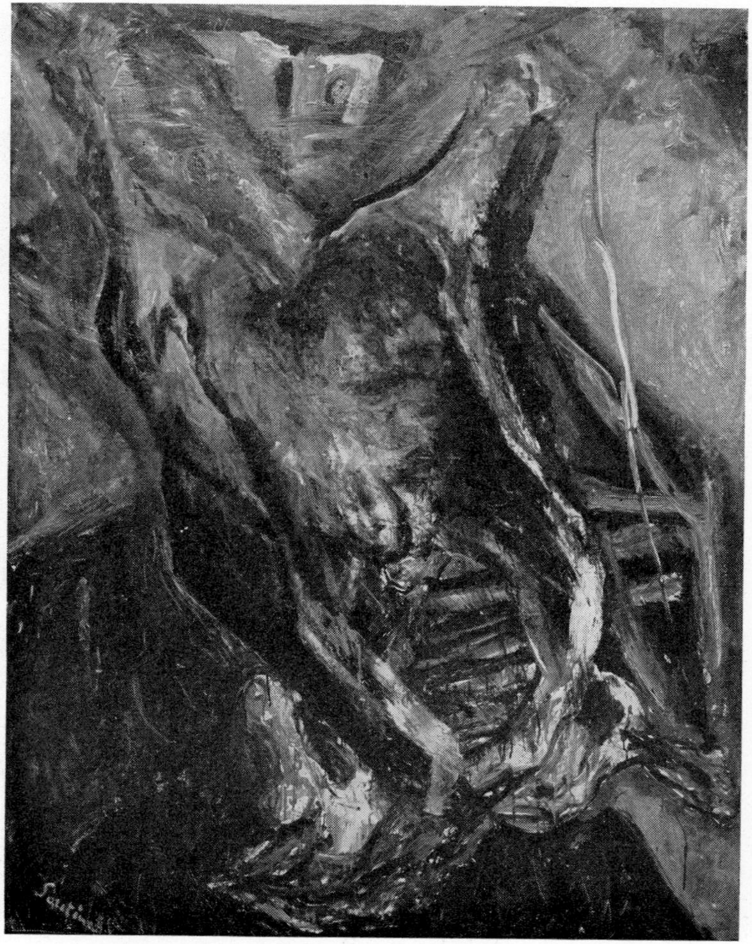

Fig. 19.29 Soutine. *Page Boy at Maxim's*. Buffalo. Albright Art Gallery. 1927.
Fig. 19.30 Soutine. (right) *Side of Beef*. Buffalo. Albright Art Gallery.

Fig. 19.31 Salvador Dali. *Soft Construction with Boiled Beans: Premonition of Civil War*. Philadelphia Museum of Art. The Louise and Walter Arensberg Collection. 1936.

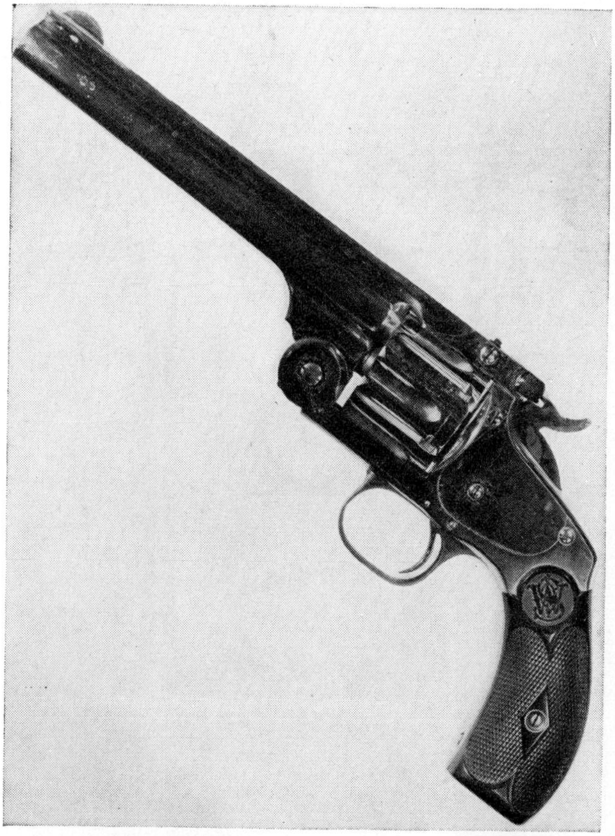

Fig. 19.32 The "Russian Model" Revolver. 1870.

Fig. 19.33 Double-barrelled shotgun. Model 21. 1930.

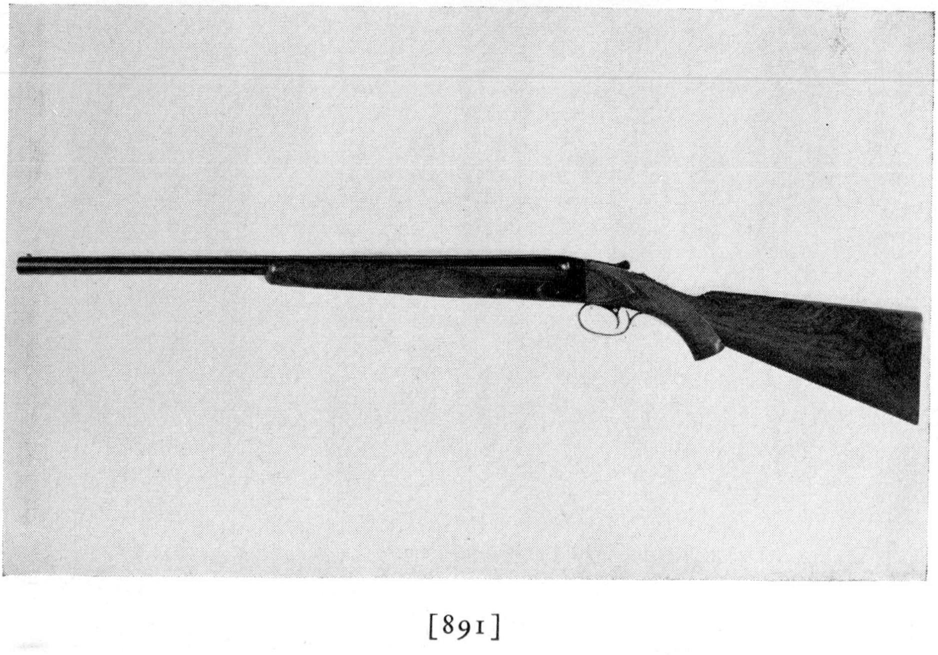

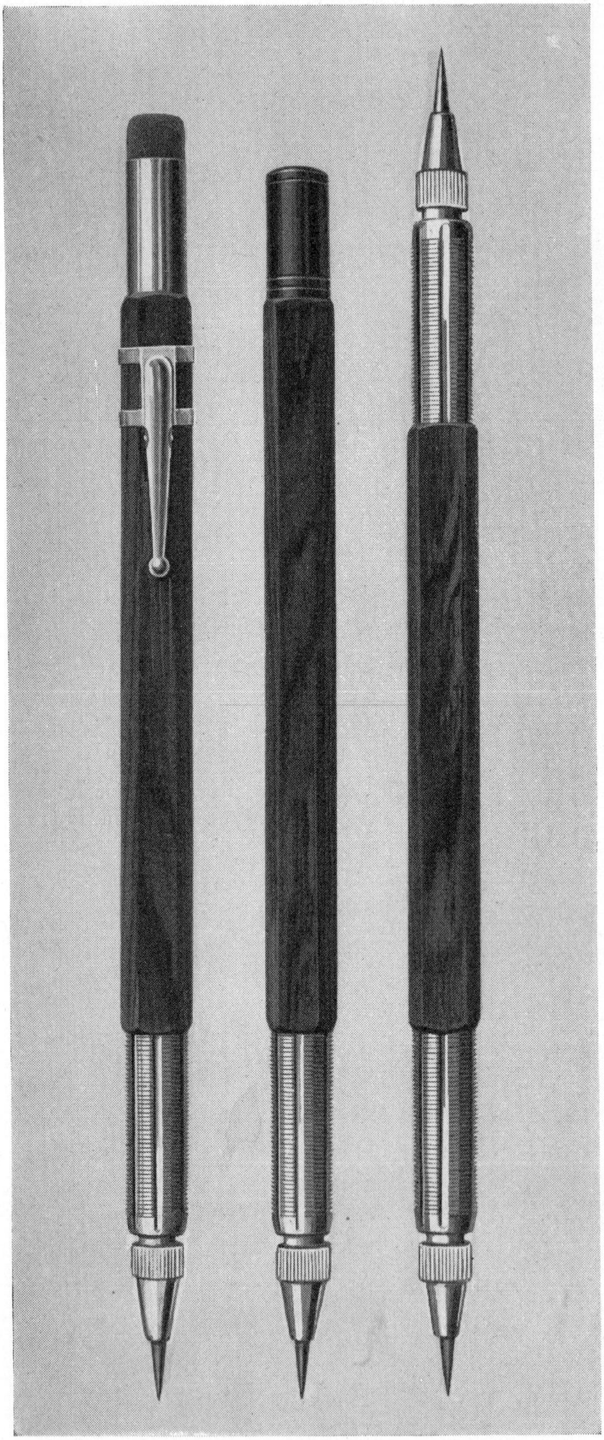

Fig. 19.34 Pencil for artists and draftsmen.

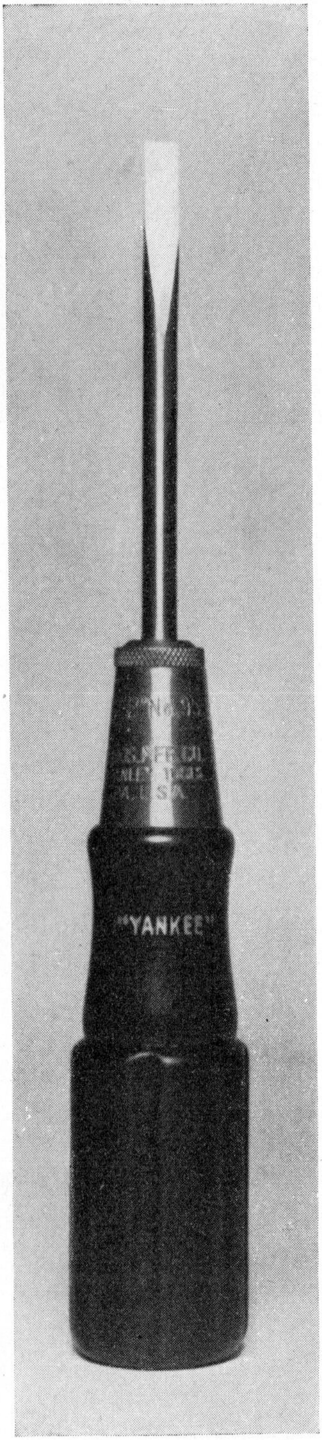

Fig. 19.35 Screw driver.

*

19

CONTEMPORARY ART

Modern art is confusing, and has yet to stand the test of time. We cannot estimate the stature of Picasso and Matisse with the same assurance we use in describing the greatness of Giotto. Certain things are nevertheless as clear today as they ever will be; there is no reason for the critic to retreat to an agnostic position, and certainly there is no excuse that will condone a refusal to put forward hypotheses and make predictions. All men must do that whenever contemporary affairs are under discussion. The risk of error must be assumed.

In approaching the subject, we must first take account of the critical situation as it now stands with respect to contemporary art, and we must offer the reader some guidance through the immense amount of printed matter which already exists, and which purports to deal in one way or another with the latest developments. The literature falls into two distinct and widely separated classes.

Because modern art is by no means popular, one is bound to encounter statements to that effect. Some of them have been eloquent; but since it stands to reason that those most familiar with the history of art are the least likely to be startled by something new, the reader should always inquire into the professional qualifications of the persons who damn things out of hand. He should also ask himself whether the particular statement under review is in fact an aesthetic analysis having to do with works of art, or whether it is merely an exposition of the writer's feelings. If the latter, there is little to be learned.

The negative bias to which we have just referred did not result from any desire on the part of these writers to be unkind or unfair; it merely reflects the feeling that modern art, like all past art, ought to give satisfaction. The second category of critical writing is devoted to the ideal that public sympathy will follow close upon knowledge. It therefore endeavors to expound and explain what modern artists are driving at, and for the most part consists of exhibition catalogues and monographs. Taking them as a class, the authors thereof are much better educated for the task than those who express dislike of modernism; but it is impossible to read very far without realizing that they are also invariably on the side of the artists about whom they write. In a sense we should not be surprised. Exhibitions are always arranged to demonstrate something worthwhile, and the attendant publicity properly stresses the positive. In similar fashion, no one writes a book about an artist unless he believes the artist deserves a place in the sun. The writers of monographs may therefore be forgiven if they too have erred, though on the side of praise.

The author of a general work is not entitled to the same privileges. His obligation is to give every period even treatment, and in the case of 20th-Century art, to place it in context and to see it in proportion. It is not the business of the present chapter, therefore, to urge the reader to approve or disapprove, much less to wear his heart on his sleeve. Dissatisfaction with the old styles exists, and that in itself is a good reason for seeking a new style. But it is a question of fact whether a new style has yet come into being. If it is here, its worth is not to be measured by the enthusiasm of those who cheer for it, but by whether it does or does not give satisfaction. The satisfaction mentioned, moreover, must cover the complete artistic transaction: it must be that of the artist on the one hand, and that of some significant section of the community on the other.

The above will explain why the author refuses to be an advocate for modern art, modern artists, or indeed for the modern world. In writing what follows, it has been his intention to furnish a fair and balanced estimate. No one believes more firmly that there never has been, nor can there ever be, a good society without a strong art; but that belief does not imply a personal capacity to find order and meaning where none may exist. Much less does the author feel in a position to assure his readers that everything is coming out all right in the end, as it does in a fairy tale. In fact, some of the best features of modern art are those which both the author and the reader must like the least. We live in a cruel world where the artist is as worried as any other man. His business is not to beguile us with sweet nothings, and if he cannot find the silver lining, he may at least tell the truth as he sees it. Artists are, of course, liable to error; but history shows they are less so than most of us. It is therefore of the utmost importance that we try to ascertain the meaning of modern art. It cannot be dismissed as an accessory or peripheral part of our civilization; on the contrary, there is no other vehicle which offers a more penetrating and central perspective upon the course of events.

Modern art is much more traditional than it is usually thought to be. Like Cézanne (pages 908 ff), most recent artists have learned from the museums. Instead of a single contemporary fashion, we therefore are confronted with the greatest variety of styles and manners ever to be exhibited contemporaneously. More often than not, the very things that seem like offensive novelties reflect the direct influence upon the contemporary artist of some mode, technique, or stratagem observed in the work of an earlier period. As a general statement, it is possible, in fact, to declare that no style in use today is without precedent. Persons inclined to set up the judgment of their own taste as against the rationale behind recent work had better tread lightly; embarrassment may ensue when one learns the name of the authority he has just defied.

At the same time, modern art is a break with the past. Insofar as we are now able to judge, the break signifies the end of the Renaissance and the commencement of another era as different from the last as the Renaissance was different from the Middle Ages. Modern pictures usually look very different from traditional pictures, and modern artists, more often than not, have a point of view equally different. The average citizen who came to maturity before the First World War is ill equipped by his background to make the necessary adjustment of taste. Those who came to maturity before the Second World War are in better case, but not much.

A rereading of Chapter 18 may help to explain why. Inheriting from the High Renaissance, the Neo-Classical movement taught us that art should exist on the sublime or epic level. Beauty was the language of art, according to the same doctrine, and the purpose of art was to edify. The Romantics taught that art should evoke feelings of thrill achievable less through simple beauty than by way of dash, glamor, and distinction. Insofar as Impressionism ever succeeded in teaching anything, its lesson was to associate art with aesthetic sophistication.

It should be emphasized that such presuppositions, which usually coexist in the taste of the same individual regardless of the fact that they tend to be mutually exclusive, are of very recent vintage and cannot be applied to about nine tenths of the art in our six thousand years of recorded history. Inconsistent medley that they are, the notions mentioned die hard, or perhaps will not die at all. For persons whose artistic standards are already fixed, modern art has nothing to offer but trouble. For those still able to change, it can offer the increase of wisdom which always results from serious aesthetic experience.

THE CONTEMPORARY TREND IN ARCHITECTURE

The history of architecture from about 1750, where we left it in Chapter 17, to about 1900 can be described in one word. It was predominantly eclectic. The authority assigned by Alberti (page 699) to the classical style was presently assigned to every other style. The Beaux Arts remained the principal agency of instruction for architects of all nations, and although the slant of the curriculum there remained predominantly classical, it presently came — along with the curricula of other schools founded in imitation of the Beaux Arts — to include the discipline known as " the historical styles."

Every style was assumed to have possessed an internal logic which might be reduced to a set of rules. The presumption was historically incorrect; but it was nevertheless possible to construct a practical system for any style by a selective process. That is to say, the " best " monuments from every period were measured, taken out of context, and published in books of plans. They were thus made available for study in London, Berlin, Boston, Natchez, and Milwaukee as conveniently as casts might be obtained for studio work.

When offered a commission, the typical eclectic architect would first ask the patron to specify the style he happened to fancy. The building, whatever it might be, was designed accordingly. Some incongruous adaptations of course resulted; but in the main, it is remarkable how good eclectic architecture was. The best men, like H. H. Richardson, Stanford White, and Bertram Goodhue, so thoroughly mastered the styles in which they were interested as to make them their own.

Running quickly through the most important adaptations which still make the American city a kind of museum of reproductions, and following the historical order rather than the confused order of 19th-Century appearance, the sights described below will be familiar to all readers.

The Assyrian ziggurat gained a brief revival as the first response to the zoning laws of New York and Chicago, which required a " setback " for every rise of so many stories. The so-called " Greek Revival," which lasted until the Civil War, might as well be described as a Doric revival, because that order — hitherto almost never used — became popular for structures which otherwise fitted into the scheme of the High Renaissance. Most Classical detail continued, however, to be Roman, as indeed did most ground plans. The Harvard Stadium, the Yale Bowl, and the numerous other football theatres copied Rome precisely, and for the same purpose. Except for a few fine synagogues, the Byzantine style has had little vogue, but the Romanesque became positively a fashion under the inspiration of Richardson. His adaptation of the Salamantine Lantern for Trinity Church in Boston was excellent; but of the railway stations and libraries either designed by him or derivative from him, the less said the better. Goodhue had a similar gift for the Gothic; but although that style was popular for churches — especially for steeples, most of which resemble the south tower of Chartres — almost no one else understood it. Thomas Jefferson not only used the style of the High Renaissance but was in fact an authentic High Renaissance architect, and one of the best. The " Georgian

Colonial," as such work came to be called in this country, is still in general use. Because white columns and red brick are attractive, many clumsy manipulations make a passable impression if not studied closely. The full Baroque and Rococo were never appealing to the chaste taste of America, but a whole series of curvilinear staircases attests to the ability of known and unknown architects to clean up the latter style and make it simple.

Although still taught in the conservative schools of architecture, eclecticism is today extremely unpopular with art historians and with progressive architects. The reasons are not necessarily those usually given. It is, in the first place, unwise to attempt a damnation of eclectic architecture by reference to physical quality; the imitations have been too clever and too good. It is equally unwise to attack the historical styles as impractical for modern use. It is extremely difficult, for example, to make any significant improvement upon a Gothic church, and there is probably no improvement possible in the football stadia, where the modern problem is identical with the Roman. It might seem that the office building, being a distinctively recent phenomenon, would fetch to the surface the inadequacies of past styles; but sadly for the advocates of "modern architecture" some of the "Romanesque" and "Gothic" skyscrapers have made an annual profit, while many of the "modern" ones have not.

The most cogent complaint against eclecticism is philosophical, namely, that the spiritual motives which called each of the historical styles into being are absent from our society. Therefore, no building newly designed to look Greek or Gothic can possibly give the same satisfaction it gave during the 5th Century B.C. or the 13th Century A.D. Neither can it give us the same satisfaction we get from an authentic historical monument of either period. It is not easy to say why the latter may be true; but it is. The difference is as the difference between stage scenery and reality.

The obvious remedy is to bring about a new architectural style having the same autochthonous relation to our age as the historical styles had, each to its own period. No cultural enterprise now in view enjoys anything like the same popular support. Everybody is asking for "modern architecture"; architects who offer plans for a Gothic gymnasium, as actually happened at a certain college recently, find themselves on the defensive. The main outlines of the contemporary demand, while all too often expressed in hortatory imperatives, are clear.

The modern style must make an end of imitation; its buildings must have a new appearance, unlike anything earlier. The modern style must be "functional" — not an easy word to define narrowly, as we shall see. It must be expressive of the modern world. The modern style must find itself by casting off ancient materials and techniques, and by following out the logic of new materials and techniques. All such stipulations are mixed up together in the public mind. The ramifications are rarely appreciated, and the implications rarely accepted; but the general insistence cannot be overlooked. It amounts to a cultural ground swell, and it must now be our business to inquire how much has been accomplished.

The Industrial Revolution provided architecture with two new media, steel and glass. At any date prior to the American Civil War, metal of every kind had been a luxury item necessarily reserved for nails, screws, hinges, locks, and the like. During the latter half of the 19th Century, it became available in large pieces and at low cost. The principal use of the material to date has been in one of three forms: as wire rope, as reinforcement for concrete, and in beams.

Glass in significantly large plates had been literally unknown before. Big windows, when made at all, were necessarily assembled from many small panes. Larger panels appeared long before 1900, but the very large ones which are commonplace today were still a special item before the First World War. At this writing, glass is actually a raw material for architecture.

In the whole history of all the arts, there had never been a comparable situation. Even the arrival of the oil vehicle (page 613) did not change the conditions of painting to the extent that steel and glass altered the architectural outlook. Any estimate of modern architecture must therefore take into account the necessity for experiments on the lowest level of primitive groping — the kind of trial and error which results from blank ignorance and which, for every other known architectural medium, took place so long ago as to have escaped history. We have no right to be surprised, therefore, if some experiments turn out very badly indeed, as some have done. An immense number of failures must be accepted as the cost of ultimate success.

It is still too early to say what the ultimate effect will be. To whatever extent the modern style of architecture has arrived, the novel appearance of the latest buildings seems to key in with a more and more complete understanding of the internal logic of steel and glass. Up to date, steel has been the dominant medium; but a shift of emphasis toward glass is apparently now in progress. The most important monuments of modern architecture have so far been called into being by commerce (office buildings) or by the transportation system (bridges), and the principal effect to be noted is a vast increase in scale. Bridges span openings hitherto undreamed of. Single buildings of immense volume and dizzy height, notable in any earlier era merely for their size, are today a routine performance all over the Western world.

The mechanical principles of modern steel construction are not new. Some of the most spectacular modern forms are, as forms, of primeval antiquity. The important advances made during the past century were easy enough to figure out in the imagination, but hitherto were forbidden in practice simply for the lack of the right material. From the standpoint of its absolute capacity to carry out any plan the architect can visualize, the special qualities of steel opened up a new world, and made architecture more literally a liberal art than ever before.

As noted in Chapter 7, the fire-resistant properties of steel are exaggerated in the public imagination; nevertheless the material has certain great advantages. As compared with stone, the principal difference is that steel may be put under tension. A host of compact and efficient assemblies are therefore practical which were completely out of the question so long as architecture remained an art of masonry.

As compared with wood, which is still the lightest known material for a given strength, steel members may be fastened together more compactly and more securely. The assembly shown in Fig. 19.44, for example, would be impractical with wood. The ends of the beams would split open, and triangular bracing would be required to secure the assembly against any stress which might give either member a tendency to turn over the other with the joint as a center. The point is well illustrated by what usually happens when an abandoned barn finally collapses; the beams and uprights rotate at the joints, and the building subsides one way or the other.

The modern bridge has assumed four different forms, as illustrated by Figs. 19.36–39. The choice has depended upon the footing available, and similar considerations having to do with the site and sometimes with the special purpose of a particular bridge. The so-called steel and concrete " arches " shown

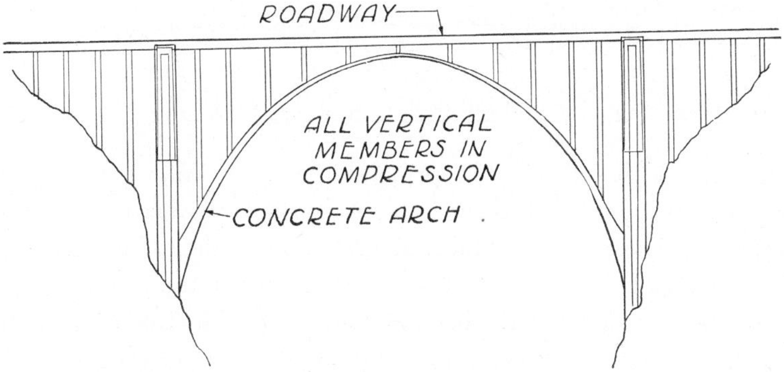

Fig. 19.36 Bridge supported by a modern arch of ferroconcrete.

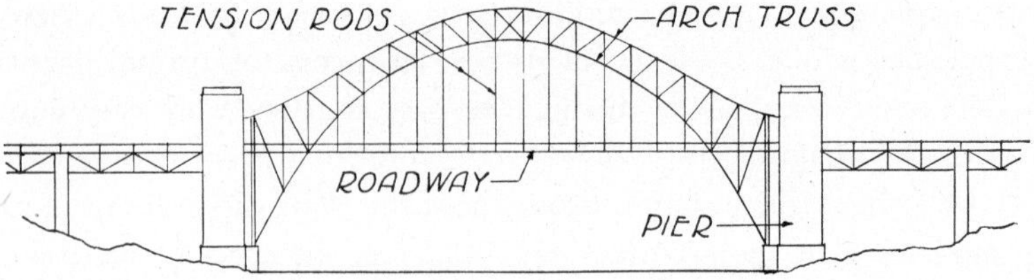

Fig. 19.37 Bridge carried by a steel truss in the form of an arch.

in Figs. 19.36–37 are not in fact arches (pages 183 ff) but trusses hogged up in the middle to resemble the profile of a true arch. If loaded heavily enough, either might exert a slight thrust, as would any member of the same shape; but the triangular bracing, which is visible in Fig. 19.37 and concealed by the cement in Fig. 19.36 makes both forms very stiff indeed.

The cantilever bridge is merely a pair of big steel brackets which stick out over the river to be spanned, and meet in the middle. As drawn in Fig. 19.38,

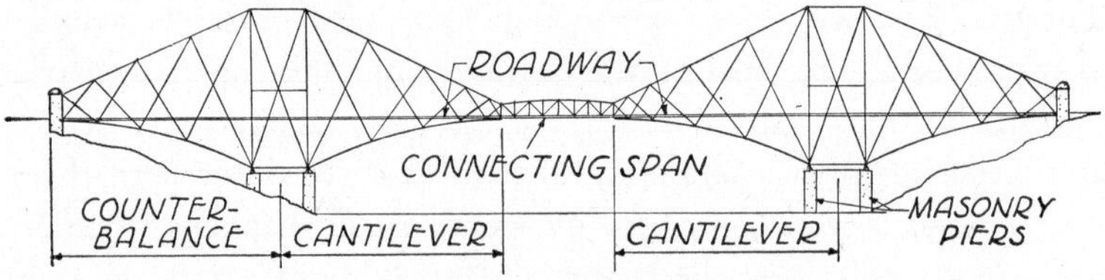

Fig. 19.38 The principle of the cantilever bridge.

the bridge might be called a balanced cantilever, because each extension has its equal and opposite to the other side of the fulcrum.

The suspension bridge (Fig. 19.39) has a power over the imagination not

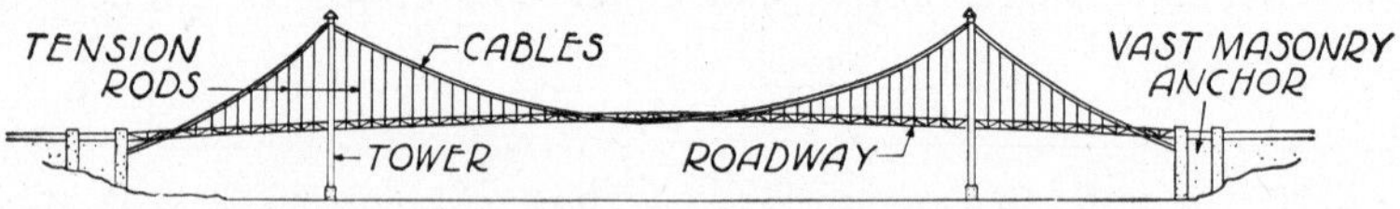

Fig. 19.39 The principle of the suspension bridge.

even suggested by the others. The principle has been known as long as men have known anything, and there is a primordial satisfaction in our final achievement of the capacity to build the form as it ought to be built. All other methods of bridge building seem wasteful of material and clumsy in appearance by comparison. Some of the bridges designed by Mr. Roebling at the turn of the century were, in fact, the very quintessence of engineering. The suspension bridge has one fault, however, and it is a bad one: like its primitive prototype made of grass rope in the jungle, the modern suspension bridge can swing and sway. In a few instances (apparently when the wind sets up a vibration in key with the period of the wires) dangerous conditions result, and traffic has to be suspended.

By comparison with the bridges, the construction of steel frame buildings seems prosaic; but there can be no question of its utilitarian virtues. The availability of large steel beams made feasible the now familiar " bird cage " system of framing, as illustrated by Fig. 19.40. With respect to the problem of spanning openings between vertical supports, the method is simply a special application of the post and lintel system (page 182), longer spans being permitted because steel beams may be given a cross-section which makes for stiffness. It is important to note, however, that the whole pattern of the fabric has been immensely simplified as a result of the compact joining of members possible only when metal components are used. The beams cross the columns at a right angle. Triangular bracing of any sort is conspicuous by its absence. Such a fabric, moreover, forms a structural integer in a sense hitherto unknown. It may even be bolted down to bedrock like a flagpole, and, in theory at least, will be damaged by waving in the wind or by earthquake shock no more than will a fishing rod. The expedient mentioned has been tried innumerable times in the case of water towers, windmills, and other comparatively small structures. As yet, all large buildings depend for stability upon their own weight. As construction gets lighter (for it is now a possibility that various extremely light alloys may presently replace steel), it is actually conceivable that one day a skyscraper may be blown over by the wind. Doubtless bolting down will then become popular; as it is, to feel our present buildings sway as the squalls hit is to feel a bit like the giant Antaeus when Hercules hoisted him off the ground.

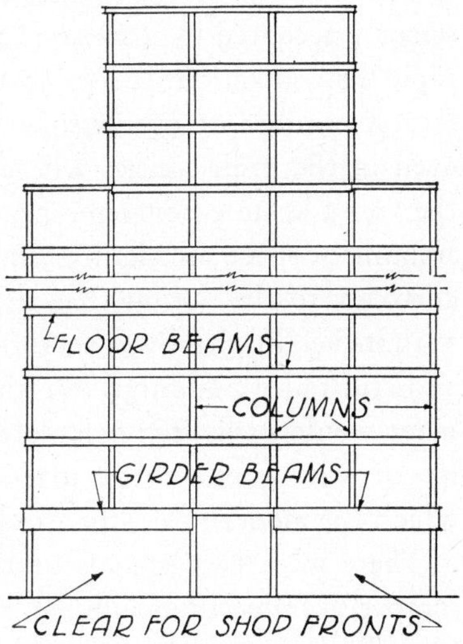

Fig. 19.40 Modern steel construction.

William LeBaron Jenney (1832–1907) is believed to have designed the first building in the world in which both the floors and the exterior masonry (which merely kept out the weather) were supported by a bird cage of steel beams bolted to steel columns. It was the Home Insurance Building in Chicago, opened in 1883, and ten stories high. Louis Sullivan (1856–1924), who had worked in Jenney's office, became the first articulate philosopher of modern architecture. His Wainwright Building in Chicago (1890) was the earliest design which made any significant or successful attempt to work out an aesthetic theory by reference to the mechanics of steel construction — much as the medieval builders had worked out a theory (page 411) on the basis of the stone arch. The Guaranty (now Prudential) Building in Buffalo, of 1896, was perhaps Sullivan's best design; in the opinion of the author, it remains the handsomest of all steel frame buildings.

The work of Sullivan and others was illustrative of a trend almost unconsciously accepted by architects and public alike. Business was in the process of rapid centralization. It seemed to be a prime desideratum to accommodate the largest number of businessmen within the smallest possible area. Pronounced even in the prairie cities where horizontal movement was the natural thing, the trend assumed extreme proportions in New York because of the limited amount of space on Manhattan Island. Architecturally, the result was to give currency to the notion that the efficiency of an office building was identical with its height. Steel was therefore devoted to the construction of taller, taller, and still taller buildings. We should mention in passing that such a development would have been completely out of the question except for the availability of wire rope — that marvellous and little celebrated material without which the modern elevator would be impossible.

There were two schools of thought with regard to the aesthetics of skyscraper architecture. Sullivan represented one. He, and those who followed him, did everything they could to multiply vertical lines on the exterior. They also did whatever needed to be done to suppress horizontal lines. Sullivan had used a cornice to top off the Prudential Building in Buffalo, but other designers, notably Raymond Hood, borrowed Gothic detail for the skyline, and with some reason. Gradually, the prejudice against eclecticism forbade even that, but the emphasis on verticality remained. The end result of the linear school of thought may be seen in Rockefeller Center.

Another group of designers became impressed with the cubic capacity of the immense new buildings. They were also impressed with the possibility that aesthetic guidance might be found in the zoning laws and their requirement of a " setback " after every rise of so many stories. Taking inspiration from the ziggurat, they drew up a number of boxy buildings composed, as we were told, " in volumes." The Hotel Shelton on Lexington Avenue was one of the best. While such architecture formed a logical counterpart for the cubist movement in painting and sculpture, the certain knowledge that its great blocks were thin and hollow took the power out of them.

If the reader will reflect upon what has gone before, he will see that most designers of skyscrapers have even to the present day been very much preoccupied with the matter of exterior appearance. Their point of view was actually the same as the formalism of the High Renaissance (page 696) even though the resulting architecture looked different.

A certain reaction presently set in. The idea became current that the building should be designed not " from the outside in " but " from the inside out." The accommodations provided indoors, said this newer theory, were paramount. Good accommodations often demanded a serious compromise with respect to exterior design; but, continued the argument, we can't have everything. If a choice had to be made, the human element was more important than the aesthetic conceit of " expressing the medium " or " expressing the vertical dimension."

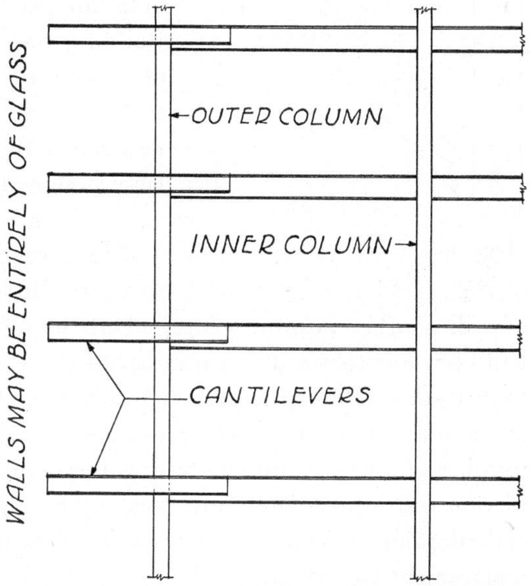

Fig. 19.41 Use of internal columns and extending cantilevers in modern steel construction.

So far, the result of such thinking has been to make glass the primary medium, and to make steel the servant of glass. The idea was anything but new. Some of the very first " modern " buildings, like the Crystal Palace in London (1851) had walls almost entirely of glass. Every small town in America, moreover, possessed at least one greenhouse, the special virtues of which were a matter of common knowledge. The application of glass walls to the tall office building was first suggested, it is believed, by Mies van der Rohe, and the possibilities were demonstrated by his model shown in Fig. 19.1.

Steel frame construction makes it possible to locate the vertical supports of a building in a number of different ways. In Fig. 19.41 we see the columns placed well in from the outer surface. The floors are then extended out for a considerable distance beyond the columns. The latter do not cast shadows across the windows as they must when used to make vertical lines on the exterior, as Sullivan had used them. In theory, the entire wall might be made of glass. Such an arrangement is feasible because the steel beams may be extended outward from the columns for a reasonable distance, in which case they are known as *cantilevers.*

Figs. 19.42–44 demonstrate the principle of the cantilever. A cantilever is a bracket. A bracket is a cantilever. The mechanical principle is the same whether we use wood or metal, and whether the cantilever holds up a kitchen shelf or a directors' meeting. As applied to the floors of a building, where the loading is light in proportion to stiffness, steel cantilevers have the merit of being extremely compact. They take up no useful room. The McGraw-Hill Building was one of the first to make frank use of the cantilever method, which now appears to be the currently popular construction. The new Lever Brothers Building (1952) was similarly designed.

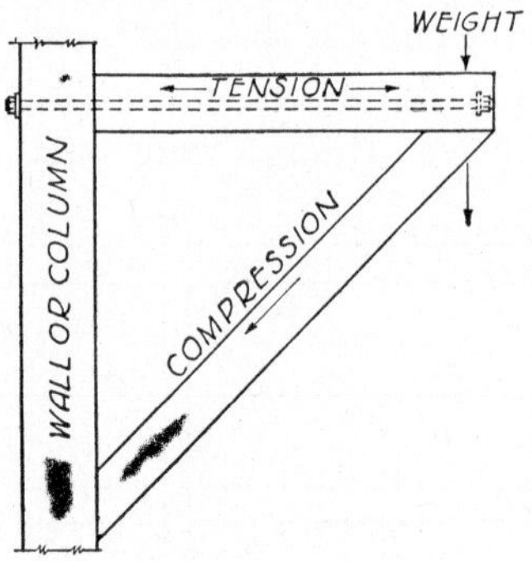

Fig. 19.42 The principle of the cantilever.

The Lever Brothers Building is believed also to be the first large fabric to take advantage of still another possibility opened up by steel frame construction. The idea had been put forward in a number of drawings and in several houses actually built to the plans of the French architect Le Corbusier: the bulk of the building was set up on stilts. The ground story, that is to say, was eliminated. The number of vertical columns was reduced to a minimum, and the intercolumniation was appropriately increased. One may walk at will underneath. A general adoption of such a scheme — which would not at all involve a complete replacement of existing architecture — may in time prove to be the cure for the infamous congestion in New York.

The great office buildings of New York and Chicago have furnished modern architecture with its focus and certainly with its most conspicuous monuments. The reader, like the author, would doubtless be happy to shift attention to the matter of the modern house. It is regrettably impossible to tell him what he wants to hear.

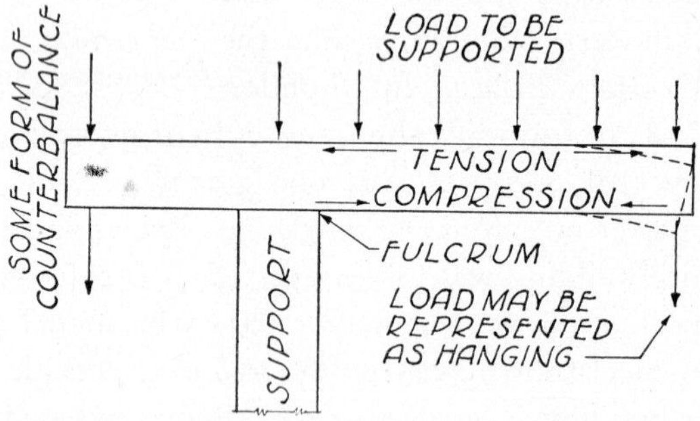

Fig. 19.43 Forces upon a steel beam used as a cantilever.

The use of modern materials has so far been largely restricted to big buildings where nothing else will do, and to the work of contractors who have made an immense investment in the ponderous machinery required. Steel beams are still too expensive for the lighter loads imposed by domestic buildings. Concrete reinforced with steel rods is likewise dear; it requires expensive moulds. A number of houses have been built from one or both materials, however, but at high cost in relation to the accommodation provided. Future developments, both economic and mechanical, may render the house carpenter obsolete; but he is still more efficient than all the machinery on earth if he knows his job and if the job is within his capacity.

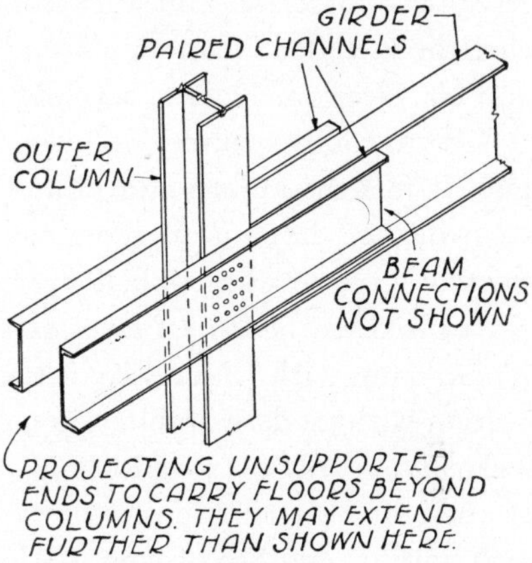

Fig. 19.44 A method of using steel beams as cantilevers.

Many owners have nevertheless insisted upon having a modernistic home even if compelled to use conventional materials. The author has inspected a number of them. He has yet to see an example which can be described as better than the same arrangement of rooms enclosed within a traditional exterior; and in every instance recalled, serious faults have been noted. It is not easy to improve upon the folkways of the house builder. The forms he is accustomed to build did not result from aesthetic fancy. They are expressive of the virtues, and defensive with respect to the faults, of wood and masonry. When the old-time mechanic says, "This is the proper way," the university-trained engineer had better listen.

The word *functional* has been the battle cry of the modern movement in architecture; but more often than not, it would seem that the adjective has been used as a vague term of praise, and with small understanding of what was meant. It is by no means an easy word to define.

The skyscrapers were functional in the sense that their design called for a clever use of material to accomplish something previously impossible, but from the standpoint of human values, they are among the worst buildings ever built. No conceivable system of transportation can fill and empty such monsters at the beginning and the end of the working day, and the wonders of the New York subway system are canceled out by its offense to decency. Williwaws worse than those which blow down from the heights above the Straits of Magellan are familiar in the manufactured canyons of New York; and the pedestrian, delayed by elevators but supposedly free to enjoy the beatitude of being within walking distance of everything, is often the victim of dirt and germs carried in stinging barrage on the wings of the squall. It now appears, in fact, that our teachers were mistaken when they told us thirty years ago that the skyscrapers were the modern architecture for which the world was waiting. Too little weight was then given to the special conditions on Manhattan; high buildings have fortunately never become popular elsewhere. From the beginning they were much more of an aesthetic exercise than we first permitted ourselves to appreciate. Our very confusion of mind about them makes it plain that the so-called " functionalism " of modern architecture needs examination and clarification. Does it actually exist? Is it an intelligible aesthetic theory?

" Form follows function," we are told. The statement is attractively rhythmic. It fills the mouth and pleases the ear. It seems vigorously in line with a scientific age. Even though we never hear a demonstration that the words tell the truth, we all want to believe them; but what do they mean?

Reduced to the lowest level of survival, the statement would appear to be synonymous with " Necessity is the mother of invention "; but as used in connection with modern architecture, there is always a plain implication that *form* means *beauty*. If so, a number of perplexities lie in our path — also a number of outright contradictions. *Function,* unfortunately, has many shades of sense, each with its own set of connotations.

Does function mean *efficiency* in the performance of some mechanical service? Why, then, is the Thompson submachine gun not handsomer than the duelling pistol? And why is the atomic bomb not prettier than both? What is the trouble with the liner *United States* that she is a poor thing, aesthetically speaking, by comparison with the tea clipper *Cutty Sark?* Does anyone really want to cast out the Parthenon because it scarcely had any utility at all?

Does *function* mean *economy?* If so, the function of human comfort and convenience is often at war with the monetary function. The reader does not need to have it pointed out to him that when one saves money, he usually takes it out of his hide. The cheap house is the " best " house only by reference to the account book; the proportion of cheap buildings that are even attractive in appearance is low.

If economy and mechancial efficiency be set up as our prime desiderata in architecture or any other art, what gives us the impression that fulfilment of either or both is to be sought along the lines of modernistic style? Why take a chance on modern chairs when Rococo designs are not only better looking but much more comfortable? Why purchase a coffeepot shaped like a bullet which neither fits the hand nor hits the mark when the shops are full of 18th-Century designs that do both? Why streamline a refrigerator which will never feel the resistance of a fluid medium while in motion?

The answers to such questions, and a host of similar questions, must give pause to readers who entertain the popular assumption that the forms of modern architecture are in some way governed by functional requirements. Progressive architects have been overly ready to permit that impression to grow, but responsible critics have no business keeping it alive. The truth is that modernistic architecture is aesthetically self-conscious to a degree; if considered merely as exercises in abstract sculpture, many of the modern buildings are splendid (Fig. 19.2).

As to whether they are also more economical and efficient than traditional buildings, and as to whether any particular bulge or hollow has some mechanical purpose, it is extraordinarily difficult to say. No one can tell from a couple of photographs; financial information is usually kept secret, and complete plans are rarely released. In the absence of such information, the question with regard to any particular building must remain open. Numerous reports which have reached the author by direct channels suggest, however, that claims of superior efficiency be accepted with reserve. Owners too often describe modern houses by famous architects as worse rather than better than others. Office buildings of fascinatingly modern appearance can be arranged on the inside with incredible stupidity; some of them demand a wasteful expenditure for air conditioning during the hot months, and the superb modern windows sometimes leak.

Insofar as a general statement is permissible, it is the opinion of the author that functional requirements have furnished guidance toward good form in modern architecture only when the function was simple and direct. Roebling's bridges have already been mentioned as a case in point. The Kleinhans Music Hall in Buffalo (Fig. 19.3) may be cited as illustrative of modern architecture devoted to a more complex function, but still a well-defined one. The plan and elevation of its two auditoria were determined by acoustical principles. Except for the color of the walls and ceiling, there is no interior decoration whatever to compete for attention against the music. For that reason, the interior is almost painfully without meaning whenever empty, but suddenly comes to life when put in use. There is not another place on earth where concerts may be presented and heard with such ease and advantage. The circulation of the large audience upon arrival and departure is notably easy and comfortable. The same is true of the provision for automobile traffic, a most important matter in so bad a climate. In appearance, both inside and out, the building must be regarded as experimental and forward looking, not as beautiful.

It is the further opinion of the author that the word *functional* as applied to modern architecture does not mean exactly what it says, no matter how we ramify the sense. Elimination has been the principal symptom of functionalism to date: the omission and removal, that is to say, of temple fronts, pilasters, mouldings, and historical detail of every kind until even the face of one's watch becomes purified by the absence of the pretty Arabic numerals. The tendency described seems to be the expression of a deep but inchoate yearning, the nature of which is not yet plain and the meaning of which we can only guess.

One guess is that it is part of the evidence which spells the end of the Renaissance. The stern elimination of " unnecessary " detail looks like a strong negation of the artistic concept of life which began with Alberti (page 696). As we pointed out at the time, the Renaissance ideal did not apply to all mankind, but presupposed the control of society by a superior group of persons. That theory of social organization did not exclude the average citizen. It furnished him, rather, with an ideal toward which he might aim, and every generation had its roster of men who had started at the bottom, demonstrated superiority, and gained membership in the upper orders. Such men were entitled to think of buildings as a setting for themselves.

Is the contemporary interest in functionalism a sign of disillusionment with that ideal? Do men no longer think they can accomplish as much as they can imagine? Must we accept what we can get from life, and be content with architecture at the subsistence level, which is what some of the most articulate proponents of modernism seem to be telling us? Or are we witnessing a shift in the control of society, which to date has always resided wherever the direction of artistic taste might be found? Is it the art of the court alone that is going? Are we actually about to achieve the true art of democracy?

THE CONTEMPORARY TREND IN SCULPTURE AND PAINTING: THE PRIMACY OF CÉZANNE

Paul Cézanne (1839–1906) is well established as the occupant of a historically pivotal position. His art brought French Impressionism to a dead stop and opened the door upon a new era. No small man could have had so important an effect. We may be misled, however, when we accept at face value the assertion that authority for almost everything that has happened since may be found somewhere either in the painting or in the utterances of Cézanne. Such a conclusion by no means follows from the fact that his career proved to be a turning point. Neither does it follow from the merit or demerit of his art. Contemporary painting and sculpture have many branches and numerous ramifications; it is exceedingly difficult, if not impossible, to establish a one-to-one connection between Cézanne and many of the recent movements in art. The sanction-from-Cézanne should therefore be scrutinized narrowly in every instance.

Cézanne started out as an Impressionist. He got most of his early inspiration from Pissarro. He became dissatisfied with Impressionism and turned his back upon it. From about 1877 onward, he isolated himself and lived in seclusion at Aix-en-Provence, where he had been born. He painted continuously, but he never attempted to sell pictures. A niggardly weekly allowance enabled him to subsist until the death of his father; after that, he was modestly well off. Because he was almost forgotten by the world, the potential influence of his art remained in abeyance. In 1895 Vollard gave him a one-man show. In 1900 he had three works at the centennial exhibition. In 1904 he had a whole room at the autumn salon; and in 1906, the year of his death, there was a retrospective exhibition. His emergence as a major figure seems to date from the last two exhibitions mentioned, and his great influence upon Picasso, Braque, and others started at about that time.

The professional artists who saw his paintings on exhibit in Paris presumably absorbed the influence directly, but even they must have gained assurance from the fact of Cézanne's acquisition of a champion in the person of Roger Fry (page 733). Fry spent the rest of his life writing on aesthetic matters, and his writings are notable for the dogged reiteration of a central theme: namely, that Cézanne's art was no passing phase, that every touch of his brush carried great and absolute authority, and that the man belonged to the ages.

Largely as a result of Fry's sincerity and eloquence, Cézanne today occupies a unique position among artists. He is the only recent master anyone dares mention in the same breath with Giotto, Donatello, Leonardo, Michaelangelo, and Titian. His admirers are firm in their faith as they are firm about nothing else. It may fairly be said, indeed, that he has become a myth and a cult, a modern dogma not lightly to be challenged. Unfortunately, an adequate explanation of his wisdom and profundity (if it can be made) is so difficult to locate that it may be described as nonexistent. Fry's writings, persuasive though they have proved to be, offer no such thing, and the same may be said of the polemical and even more stimulating essays by the American collector and critic Albert Barnes. Our business here is not to take sides, but to inquire and find out. If Cézanne was a great master, the bare elements of his greatness ought not to elude us. Even though greatness must forever remain imponderable in some measure, its existence has always been indicated by obvious facts.

The first such fact is that Cézanne acquired his artistic education in a new way. "I have wanted," he said late in life, "to make of Impressionism something as solid and durable as the art of the museums." The statement sounds almost like a platitude today; but it was a new idea during the period of Cézanne's formative years. The public museum of art was then a novelty, one of the democratic developments. The Louvre, as an art museum, dates only from the time of Napoleon. The National Gallery in London was founded in 1824. The Metropolitan Museum in New York was incorporated in 1870. If we allow for the length of time it ordinarily takes for a museum to gain momentum, it will be seen that Cézanne availed himself of an advantage hitherto not conveniently at hand. In earlier generations, the training of artists had proceeded according to a straight-line tradition; one learned from a master, who had in turn learned from his master. Artists of originality borrowed where they pleased at all periods, of course, but the sweep of the particular movement to which they belonged was far more important as a formative pressure. Cézanne's break with Impressionism, therefore, was more than a mere exercise of personal taste. It was a step so strongly independent as to be almost unprecedented.

By taking that step, Cézanne probably set the modern pattern, for it is today literally a physical impossibility not to be influenced by the works of art on exhibit in museums — which is to say that artists will henceforth learn from the whole history of art, as contrasted to the closed channel of stylistic transmission which previously held sway. Cézanne learned a great deal in the museums, as we shall indicate from time to time in the paragraphs below. It is the opinion of the author that most of his so-called "inventions" were not new, but reflect the benefit of intelligent study and assimilation. Much is still to be learned along those lines, but readers with an interest in technique will find common sense in a preliminary paper by Mr. James M. Carpenter (*Art Bulletin,* Vol. 33. No. 3, September 1951).

Although he left the Impressionist movement, Cézanne took many of its essential doctrines with him. His coarse handling of the paint, and the rough surface peculiar to Impressionist pictures, remained with him the rest of his life, although he devoted them to different ends. The Impressionist concept of art as research (page 864) was fundamental in his whole career. He remained so steadfast in that faith that both his art and his manner of life stand out as the extreme illustration of the experimental method. Except for what he might discover, he had literally no interest in his own paintings. When convinced that a particular project was sterile, he dropped it at once. When successful, he cared almost as little for the vehicle of his success. Madame Cézanne had to tag after him, picking up canvases he abandoned in the woods. He let children amuse themselves by cutting holes with knives where he had painted doors and windows. The cook cleaned the stove with some of his work when rags were in short supply. Inevitably a great many paintings were preserved in an unfinished state. A large number of those still in existence must have been thought failures by the artist himself, but today they possess a gratuitous sanctity. The extra difficulty of arriving at a sound estimate of his stature will be obvious. The truth is that we cannot even be utterly certain about his intentions.

It is clear from the evidence at hand that Cézanne looked forward to giving the world a full-scale theory of painting. He once alluded to his isolation as the result of a decision to remain silent until " the time I felt myself capable of defending theoretically the result of my efforts." In later years he wrote, " I am too old. I have not realized, and shall not realize now. I remain the primitive of the method I have discovered." Provocative as such statements are, they seem to have been passing statements, even chance statements. We have no right to weigh every word as we might weigh the words of the formal exposition the painter never wrote. We can nevertheless make out the drift of what he had in mind.

It is plain that Cézanne had forgotten Romanticism; for him, painting was an exceedingly deliberate activity to be directed by the mind. It is also plain that his preoccupation with technique was an immense preoccupation; but other things make us see that he had passed beyond the Impressionist notion that technique might in itself be the purpose of art. While his paintings are a better index than his remarks, there is some guidance in the enigmatic conversations quoted from memory by such friends as Émile Bernard and Maurice Denis. Even though the material comes to us decidedly secondhand, two ideas stand out as central simply because Cézanne mentioned them so often. The first is that art ought to become " classic " again, and the second is the firm stipulation that art must proceed according to nature even while in the act of becoming classic. Frequent allusions to the name of Poussin suggest that, for Cézanne, pictures by Poussin came close to epitomizing what he visualized as " classic."

Taken in conjunction with his work, such remarks would seem to tell us that Cézanne retained from Impressionism a faith that art ought to remain in gear with natural phenomena, and that he refused to create a well composed world straight out of the imagination, as Poussin had done.

The same statements seem also to say that he expected to find something in nature not yet properly understood by mankind or portrayed by painting. His departure from the Impressionists apparently took place because he could no longer stomach their doctrine that visual happenstance (pages 867 ff) was equivalent to reality. As to the significance he sought, there is much to ponder in his use of the word *solid* in immediate connection with the word *durable.*

The juxtaposition may be construed as a statement that he considered permanence to be the paramount value, and that he felt permanence might find its best imagery in the tactile quality of mass. Philosophically, his position was highly similar to that of Giotto (page 559). Undoubtedly his studies had made him familiar with the Mode of Relief (pages 582 ff), but his experience with the Impressionist technique apparently suggested to him that an even better way might be found to accomplish the expression intended.

The statement that he wanted to paint " like Poussin " invites still another inference. Nicholas Poussin (1594–1665) was a Frenchman who spent most of his life in Italy. Baroque in date but not Baroque in spirit, he carried on into the 17th Century the more sober and classical elements of the style of the High Renaissance. If he can be characterized in a word, he was the heir of Raphael; in a great series of landscape paintings, he carried even further forward the implications inherent in the design of such pictures as *The School of Athens* (Fig. 16.19). Cézanne's reference to Poussin seems tacitly to say that he expected to find in nature not only intelligibility and order, but a grand formal design.

As it had been with the Impressionists, color was the prime reliance in the system of painting he worked out; but instead of devoting color to the representation of light, Cézanne devoted it to the plastic description of mass, and to the description of the placement of masses within the space represented by the painting. The reader is bound to encounter a number of essays which leave the impression that his research brought about a new science of representation, dependent almost exclusively upon hue, the implication always being that he discovered certain hitherto unknown " principles " having to do with local tones, the action of tones in modeling, and with complementaries. In the opinion of the author, such allegations are largely misguided.

His representative techniques are best explained as a new combination derived on the one hand from French Impressionism and on the other from his study of Venetian painting. His methods included everything listed as typical of the Venetian Mode (pages 752 ff), a fact which has often escaped attention simply because his handling of the paint was coarsely impressionistic, the colors he used were different, and his subject matter altogether unlike. Allowing for those points of contrast, he might fairly be described as a close follower of Tintoretto.

Any estimate of Cézanne as a representative artist must take into account, moreover, the factor of his drawing. One does not read objects seen in his pictures as being near or far merely because they are set off from each other by contrasts of tone. Common sense and linear perspective play their usual part.

Objects placed in front of other objects by the drawing, and more or less plastically described, make it imperative to understand that the painter meant to indicate placement forward and away within the space represented.

In typical pictures by Cézanne (Figs. 19.4–5) the existence of space, miles or inches as the case may demand, is declared not only by color, but by mechanical barriers or "fences." Cézanne appears to have preferred in most cases to run his "fences" parallel with the plane of the canvas, or nearly so. The method was the method of a cautious man, and one is reminded of early investigations by Donatello (page 622). In order to indicate the distance between the thing in front and the thing behind, he used the device of disconnection (page 755). He strengthened the upper edge of the near silhouette by an arbitrary shift of value or of intensity, or he changed the hue entirely. It is the author's opinion that such useful modulations of tone were not governed by a strict theory consistently applied. Scrutiny indicates, rather, that any particular instance was a matter of convenience, and that the painter's choice of the trick to be used was improvised at the moment.

Nothing that has been said above is to be construed as suggesting that color relationships were not extremely important in Cézanne's representation; but had they possessed the total function sometimes claimed for them, black and white photographs of his work would be unintelligible. Interestingly enough that is true of a certain number of his sketches, notably the sketch in oils, one of his very last pieces of work, known as *Morning in Provence* (Fig. 19.9). In everything which might be considered a finished painting, however, Cézanne seems to have maintained an almost conventional reliance upon drawing.

In attempting to apply the foregoing to various paintings, the reader must be prepared for occasional perplexity. Over and above the inevitability of seeing pictures that did not come off and which have survived more or less against the painter's own better judgment, it must be realized that Cézanne was not a great technician. He was not even a first class technician; he never gained the control over his hands which would have permitted him to show his competence as Giotto did the day he drew the famous circle. We thus find ourselves rather often in the extraordinary position of giving him credit for what we believe he aimed to do, and not, to use his own word, for what he realized.

There is no other painter, in fact, whose work permits a like variety of understanding and misunderstanding. It is not uncommon for two different persons to entertain different readings of what they see while standing together in the same room looking at the same picture. We refer not to estimates of aesthetic worth, but to the mundane function of the colors and brush strokes as they perform, or fail to accomplish, the humble service of representative description. Some people testify that whenever Cézanne painted the human figure, he gave it solidity and weight; others fail to get that impression. To some people his houses and rocks seem flat and light; others declare them monumental. The simple objects in his still life pictures seem to some admirers literally animate with power; others, even when they want to feel that sensation, simply do not.

Surely we have said enough so that the reader can not possibly be ignorant of the difficulties. What can we now say to sum up the essential worth of Cézanne's art?

As a designer, Cézanne was a paradox, at once reactionary and radical. The pictorial forms he used were more often than not strictly conventional. His *Card Players* (Fig. 19.5) and the so-called " Large Bathers," now in Philadelphia, reflect a literal borrowing from the triangular compositions first introduced by Leonardo (page 722) and popularized by Raphael. For landscapes he made routine use of the composition which depends upon a balance between mass and distance (page 763). Sometimes he put the distant vista in one upper corner (Fig. 19.4), and sometimes he put it in the middle (Fig. 19.7) in the manner of Poussin and Claude Lorrain.

In a certain number of paintings, he seems deliberately to have set himself technical problems of extreme difficulty. Typical examples are the landscapes where the entire background is closed by solid material, and where almost no space at all is assigned to the sky. In such compositions, Cézanne seems to have attempted to describe the placement of things within his represented space not by the drawing, as usual, but entirely by means of tonal relations. Black and white reproductions can give only the most inadequate indication of what is meant. Fig. 19.9 shows such a painting, however; it is an especially interesting and very perplexing example because the tour de force of representation just missed, and the composition accordingly did not quite come off. Fig. 19.6 may give a better suggestion of the point at issue.

Throughout his mature career, Cézanne was also notable for introducing abstract rhythms and harmonies (pages 28 & 54) into his work. Doubtless he got the idea from Titian (page 764), but the resemblance is one of principle and not one of visual fact. His handling of the paint was usually in bigger and broader touches than had been common even with the Impressionists; and in any particular canvas, he seemed to prefer to maintain a substantial uniformity in both the scale, the proportions, and the direction of the single stroke — a technique that seems at first to be plodding, but ultimately evokes a sense of ponderous and even lofty harmony. No modern painter was more sensitive to the repetition and the contrast observable in both the shape, the color, and the outline of forms in nature, or in the works of man. The blocky houses in Figs. 19.4&8 are a case in point, and in Fig. 19.6 we see similar blocks of architecture brought into contrast with the crotches of the trees.

In view of his claim to be interested in painting " after nature," some of the things that Cézanne did are exceedingly hard to explain. The most obvious was his cavalier disregard for the facts of human anatomy. The man who sits in the middle of Fig. 19.5 is, for example, a mechanical impossibility; how are we to imagine that his knees hook up with his torso? And what kind of body would account for the bulk and silhouette of the man at the right?

The popular explanation is that the artist indulged in " distortion for the sake of design." The phrase is a weak one. To design is to plan. To plan is to foresee. To foresee competently is to provide for every situation that may arise. A farsighted designer would therefore plan to distort, or he would plan not to distort; and he would carry out his plans. He would never be caught in a jam, and he would never have to violate any convention he cared about in order to produce good compositions.

Although he is familiar with the contrary opinion of certain other critics, it is the author's guess that Cézanne rarely if ever designed his pictures in the sense of visualizing them in minute detail before he started to work. On the contrary, the evidence of the paintings seems to suggest a continuous process of improvisation as he went along. Distortion of the human anatomy was often a convenient way to fetch an arrangement into composition. It was similarly easy to make table tops, furniture, or anything else take up more or less room on the canvas by throwing them out of drawing — the device which so often was equivalent to shifting the apparent eye point of the observer. It is a mistake to praise Cézanne as a great composer because he did such things. The truth is that his compositions are not in the least better than those of many other painters, most of whom did not distort.

We may therefore pass over the compositional utility of Cézanne's distortions; the point is trivial. His free resort to distortion was nevertheless tremendously important. It is to be considered not in relation to design, but with reference to his total career, and in special connection with his negation of Impressionism and his departure into solitude at Aix.

The French Impressionists had been sophisticated city men. Most of their canvases show scenes in Paris or the suburbs. Whenever the views are bucolic or at the seaside, it is unmistakable that the artist looked through metropolitan eyes and felt with the feelings of a visitor, not the feelings of a resident. For Monet (Fig. 18.24) the banks of the Seine were places to enjoy, not places to work. Manet's interest in the channel steamer (Fig. 18.18) was a passenger's interest, and his picture does not even remotely suggest the attitude and outlook of the captain who made the run every day.

It would be incorrect to say that Cézanne retired from such a life into the existence of a peasant, but it is evident that he expected to find reality and permanence in coarser, simpler things. No one has yet stated what he found, if he found it, but his numerous pictures of Mount Saint Victoire, and a few of the compositions that contain architecture, furnish us with an inkling. In his hands, extraneous details were sternly eliminated; his paintings are extraordinarily free from trivia of every kind. Such acts of suppression made it possible for him to clarify his description of the fundamental elements in view. The procedure always seemed to result in endowing the contours of a hill, the curve of a road, or the angles of a house with energy. His mountains seem animate with geologic power. His buildings are kinesthetic phenomena. Even a peach or an apple, as seen in his still life, becomes a shape full of potential grandeur.

The real advantage gained for him by distortion is suggested in the lines of the last paragraph. Meticulous adherence to the convention of accurate drawing and accurate anatomy would have delayed him. Resort to distortion not only speeded up his progress toward what he wanted, but also was sometimes useful as a means for giving special emphasis to a figure, an object, or to part of either. Any understanding of Cézanne's distortion must be predicated upon the idea that he was working his way toward the expression of certain elemental facts in our visual experience — truths which he himself understood only in part, but felt deeply.

In that connection, the important thing to see is not that he chose to distort, but that he didn't care. He could not have omitted to care unless he had already arrived at a new orientation. What narratives do his pictures tell? What insight do they offer into character? Into personality? Have they to do with religion? With patriotism? With hope, joy, or despair? Do they thrill us? Do they even entertain us?

Cézanne's ultimate and final place in history will depend upon the answers to such questions. No man is today in a position to give the verdict. A prediction may nevertheless be made. Judging by what he did, and by what has happened since, it would appear that Cézanne was the first important master to set aside the representative convention (page 539) by which art had been governed since the 15th Century. Still further, he completed a process begun by the Romantics. Géricault had hinted that modern man might be defeated by the environment. Courbet had demonstrated that the majority of men were neither noble nor beautiful. The Impressionists as a group had moved the human figure out of its previously central position in art. Degas seems frankly to have disliked people. Cézanne painted any number of human figures, but it may be questioned whether he ever painted a human being. By doing that, he finally canceled out the humane subject altogether. It is likely that he thereby gave the signal for the end of humanism as a guiding philosophy (page 522). It is likely, too, that future generations will point to him as the first artist who belonged wholly to a new era, and not at all to the Renaissance.

STANDARDS OF TECHNIQUE IN CONTEMPORARY ART

Traditionally and properly, the art object has been an article of choice. The artist has always worked with his hands, but the word *artist* has in every previous generation denoted a person endowed with manual skill quite beyond the physical capacity of lesser craftsmen. Similarly, the phrase *work of art* has been taken to denote an object brought close to physical perfection by the devoted labor of a man who had such skill to use.

Intellectual and moral qualities were involved in those definitions. Manual skill of the highest order demands much more than physical coordination. The cunning hand must be directed by knowledge and judgment. The time and labor needed to make a perfect thing are immensely greater than the time and labor required to make a very good thing. No one can be induced to put forth so generous and seemingly so extravagant an effort unless driven from within by ideals. Physical quality, in the artistic sense, is the logical conclusion one would reach by the ultimate application of honesty and intelligence in craftsmanship.

Until very recent years, the superior quality of the work of art was obvious to everybody. It took no special insight, much less any technical knowledge, to tell the difference between the product of the masters and the product of the amateurs. However, the ideals summarized in the last two paragraphs no longer apply. " Technique? Of no importance! Color? Put it anywhere! " said the painter Braque in a recent interview. Anyone who has studied Braque's work will appreciate that he hardly meant what he seemed to say; but from the standpoint of the average citizen, there is an imposing corpus of evidence which suggests that Braque intended to be understood literally.

We waste time if we do not admit that mere sketches, often roughed out in the hastiest fashion, frequently go on public exhibition with the same hanging as Michaelangelo. We waste more time if we do not also concede that juries no longer demand high technical standards. At a recent exhibition in England, for example, there was a picture cited in the press as " a fine specimen of modernism." Whatever else may have been true of it, the technique lacked nothing in dash; for the author, who turned out to be six years of age, had merely spilled a saucer of pigment materials, sat therein, invited his cat to walk across, and let things ride. If such tales were exceptional, we might have nothing to worry about. Unfortunately, similar anecdotes (rarely untrue or even exaggerated) are commonplace. An explanation is required, perhaps an apology. The question is whether we must cite a debased technique as one of the conspicuous features of modern painting and sculpture.

The first question to answer in that connection is whether the more radical modern masters have significant skill to call upon if they want it. The answer is an emphatic yes. If the reader will take the time to review the entire catalogue of work by any of the famous contemporaries, he will find a number of conventional paintings splendidly executed. The question is therefore more complicated than it seemed: not whether good technique exists (for it does), but why those who possess it do not bother to avail themselves of their full range of resources. Why is the artist satisfied with something less than he might have done? What right has he to ask us to be satisfied with it? Is it possible to demonstrate that he created value by refraining from the exercise of part of his available talent? Did he protect something that might have been destroyed by a more complete application of his skill?

Regardless of the interpretation we may ultimately place upon the incumbent condition of technique, the history of 19th-Century art furnishes an explanation which is at least rational. We are merely witnessing the logical conclusion of tendencies set in motion by Romanticism and by French Impressionism, both of which still operate cogently within the psychology of the modern artist.

The Romantic insistence upon the supreme value of excitement (page 857) in the end became a dogma. Spontaneity is often cited as the special value of coarse, rapidly painted pictures. In place of the worth that inheres in completeness and finish, we are offered (so the argument goes) the natural expression of a creative personality caught, if we may use the word, at a moment of intense focus and high inspiration. We get, if the picture is a success, the pure thing uncorrupted by extraneous influences, a direct penetration to the heart of the problem in hand. We get also the value of brevity, for it is possible in art as in every other kind of communication, to dwell upon the same point too long. Such pictures, the argument concludes, offer no hiding place for inadequacy, and test the power of an artist more mercilessly than any others in history.

Another explanation derives from the experimental point of view first put forward by the French Impressionists (page 864) and continued by Cézanne. The concept of the artist as a research man invited the concept of the single picture as a mere step in some program of investigation. If we accept that idea, we put ourselves under an obligation to look at the picture not for itself, but with reference to the light it may shed upon the problem the artist set himself. Thus, one painting may be thought of as a preliminary note. A second might stand as the solution of the first point in the program. A third carries the matter another stage further; and so on, until we reach the artist's final report on the whole program. Matisse's so-called " Pink Nude " exists, for instance, in approximately twenty states.

One can easily see why an artist might not care to waste time on meticulous or finely finished work when he was merely interested in a particular problem. What is the use of a beautifully glazed surface when one simply wants to explore two or three color relationships? Why bother with the strict geometry of perspective when the immediate issue is to discover a way to make the brush strokes impart a sense of motion? It is such narrowing down of the function of the single picture into the solution of a single pictorial problem, or part of one, which accounts for what often looks like grossly careless execution.

Demonstrations which at first seem outlandish often make perfect sense if one can merely identify the problem the artist set himself. The rest of the chapter will largely concern itself with such problems, which are now so numerous and so various that no list can be complete. The work of Matisse, however, will furnish us with an immediate example of the kind of thing to which we have referred.

Unlike a number of other masters, Matisse (born 1869) has retained an interest in representation and in decorative painting. In its representative aspect, his work can be described as a most successful attempt to handle the Venetian Mode (pages 752 ff) strictly in terms of line and flat tone. The placement of objects within the represented space, that is to say, is accomplished solely by the contrast between the local tone of a near field and the color of the background. Fig. 19.10 shows an example where the effect carries over unusually well in black and white; but such an instance is exceptional. In most paintings by Matisse, the adjustments of hue are prodigiously delicate — so utterly precise, in fact, that the general run of colored reproductions are even less intelligible than ordinary photographs. When a normal amount of fading takes place over the next century, it is a question whether even the originals will remain legible.

In its decorative aspect, the very same work is most often a tour de force of tonal rhythm and balance, also ultimately to be derived from the practice of the Venetians (page 762). From the Impressionists, Matisse took the habit of using intense hues. He scarcely ever has aimed at a tonality comparable with the " Venetian glow "; most often he has worked toward a balance between the various hues. Those which tend to attract attention most, for example, he used sparingly and placed carefully in order to make sure they would not pull the eye more strongly than he wished.

It is obvious that tonal relations of the kind described demand a profound knowledge of the painter's business. Among contemporaries Matisse is conspicuous, however, for concealing his skill from the common man by indulging in elaborately erudite sloppiness as the colors are laid on. The question still assails us: why?

In part, the reason is again to be found in the 19th Century. Dropped from the economic system, without an invitation to significant social responsibility, without honor, artists as a class still live in the secret garden to which they then retreated. There can be no doubt that many of them are deliberate in their choice of a style which is likely to puzzle and antagonize everybody except those with special knowledge. Such a situation is, of course, abnormal. So far, it has been sterile as well.

The present abandonment of traditional standards in the matter of design and finish may also have an even deeper and more general significance. Heritage though it is, it seems also to be an intimately accurate reflection of contemporary manners. In what earlier generation would a President begin a document with " Dear Alben," or refer to a trusted assistant as " Tommy the Cork "? Why do public men use *damn* and *hell* not only in conversation, but in political speeches and when interviewed by the press? Why are ceremonies of every kind, including those of the church, much shorter and brisker than they were fifty years ago? We are an increasingly brash people, for whom a brash art is the natural thing. When our entire society is moving away from the decorum of the High Renaissance (pages 711 ff), are we to be surprised that art abandons the decorum of technique?

PAINTING AND SCULPTURE SINCE CÉZANNE

Half the 20th Century is already over, and its painting and sculpture, seen in broad outline, appear to have four distinct divisions. The representative convention has continued with real strength, but for better or worse has become closely identified with popular rather than serious art. Abstraction in two forms, the analytical and the psychological, has so far proven to be the most original movement of the period; but there is fear it is now hoist with its own petard. Expressionism in one form or another (page 624) is almost as important as abstraction, with which it sometimes overlaps. The so-called " Industrial Arts " got well under way before the century began, and attained a high level of merit which has not been maintained. They seem, however, to offer the chief hope of the future. We shall discuss each of the four topics in the order named.

Popular Art

The popular school is more numerous than members of the public seem to realize. It would be literally impossible to mention all the names, but the following persons have been turning out every year, and year after year, an immense number of pictures which belong to the representative tradition and are in every respect " normal."

Norman Rockwell is famous for his magazine illustrations. Usually they deal with some quaint aspect of American life. They have charm, humor, and genuine sentiment.

Shortly after the First World War, regional schools began to announce their existence in various parts of America, mostly under the leadership of artists with European training who then returned home. Charles Burchfield, an extremely competent water colorist, is identified with upstate New York and particularly with the Niagara Frontier. His pictures will stand as an authentic document of the region in our time: the decaying Victorian houses, the smoke, the trains, the ruts in the snow, the wonderful opulence of summer and fall. Grant Wood, Thomas Benton, and John Steuart Curry are the most important painters who have emerged in the Middle West. Identified respectively with Iowa, Missouri, and Kansas, those men represent in art the new cultural self-confidence of that region, which has ceased to feel inferior to the Atlantic seaboard, upon which it has turned its back, and which now looks to the Pacific Coast and to the Orient rather than eastward toward Europe. The various regional schools to date have suffered from the limitations of their subject matter. Epic content can probably be found in American history; but however much we may dislike to admit it, our country as of this day has lost the zest and color of pioneer times and has yet to achieve a culture comparable to Siena, Chartres, and Canterbury. The regional schools, especially those of the Middle West, have tended to err on the side of special pleading.

We must also recognize a whole class of artists who, in one way or another, have undertaken to celebrate the modern sports which undeniably occupy as big a place in our life as those of ancient Greece. Marin-Marie, the French yachtsman, is perhaps the best of the artists who devote themselves to the sea. His sincerity and knowledge are attested by two crossings of the Atlantic singlehanded, and no one has done better at painting the authentic majesty of great liners like the old *Mauretania*. Rockwell Kent is the most overt and powerful personality among popular painters. His strong oils of the Maine coast in winter and his woodcuts of Labrador and the Straits of Magellan deserve serious attention. In addition, there are any number of artists who deal with fishing and gunning, among them Lynne Bogue Hunt. The American sporting prints which illustrate the several " outdoor " magazines are, as works of art and as works of reproduction, so very good that nobody who cares about art can afford to neglect them; and they appeal greatly to a public which knows guns, rods, dogs, and horses so very well that the " imitators " of whom Plato complained (page 924) are fortunate not to be here.

In sum, it is a fact that a very large section of modern art celebrates the familiar, the pleasant, and the good in modern life. For every instance of cubism or Surrealism, there surely are at least two Scottie dogs by Marguerite Kirmse and a view of the yachts at Larchmont by Tore Asplund. A man who feels superior to such work is a man whose taste for Matisse and Braque will bear watching; one wonders whether he reacts to visual stimuli or to the vogue in certain circles. For it is a fact that much modern popular art is, as art, competent to a degree. Why is it, then, that so few scholars and so few museums take such work seriously? The answer is all too seldom stated.

The popular artist is guided by the existing taste of the public. He bewares of offending it. He eschews the controversial subject. He studies our preferences with meticulous care; indeed, they may be precisely the same as his own. If not, he changes his own. By a combination of calculation and intuition, he finds out what we like, and paints it. If such an artist is both intelligent and sensitive, as many are, it is not surprising that he pleases a great many persons and may even make a great deal of money.

The objection to following popular taste is that popular taste is largely a habit. People are much less progressive than they say they are. There are few who welcome edifying or even pleasurable experience of a new kind. Most prefer to repeat the routine of an experience known to have been satisfactory before.

At certain periods (the Greek 5th Century and the French 13th Century, for example) the current of public thought and the current of social and artistic progress have run together in a strong, creative movement. In the 20th Century, that is not so. Our habits of taste are radically out of place in a society which, if we may judge from two World Wars, is in a process of change and adjustment.

The difference between popular art today and serious art, now or any time, has to do with the values sought, and especially with the value of getting at the truth. The truth is often harsh and cruel; but the serious artist is not concerned with congratulating people upon the ideas they already entertain. We must remember that this is either the greatest century since the 15th, or the worst since the 3rd. Art is no geisha girl to help us pass the time, and we have more to worry about than pretty girls, quail shooting, and school days during the 90's.

The Abstract Movement in Contemporary Art

Abstraction is one of the constants of modern art. It is rare to see a picture or statue which does not indulge in it to some extent, and there is probably not a single contemporary artist who eschews it altogether. To a very slight extent, abstraction and distortion are the same thing; but if carried out to the end, the two tendencies are discrete. Distortion exaggerates fact. Abstraction denies that art need maintain a connection with anything observable in the world by the normal and accurate eye.

Cézanne is ordinarily cited as the father of recent abstraction in art, and Roger Fry, the chief expositor of Cézanne, has done the most to make the movement acceptable to contemporary taste. Cézanne once wrote in a letter that all aspects of nature are contained in "the cylinder, the sphere, and the cone." It is uncertain what he meant, but the remark smacks of Plato; one is particularly reminded of the *Philebus* 51-52, where Plato said:

> My meaning is certainly not obvious, and I will endeavor to be plainer. I do not mean by the beauty of form such beauty as that of animals or pictures — which many would suppose to be my meaning; but . . . understand me to mean straight lines and circles, and the plane or solid figures which are formed out of them by turning lathes and rulers and measurers of angles. For those I affirm to be not only relatively beautiful like other things, but they are eternally and absolutely beautiful. They have peculiar pleasures, quite unlike the pleasure of scratching. And there are colors which are of the same character, and have similar pleasures. Now do you understand my meaning?

Because Platonism is ever present in the European mind and heart, it makes no difference whether Cézanne happened to know the passage quoted, or whether (in the act of abstracting) Picasso, Braque, Mondrian, and Lipchitz derive their impulse directly from Plato, from Plato as endorsed by Cézanne, from Cézanne as explained by Roger Fry, or whether they are completely unconscious of all those names. The abstract movement in modern art — popularly believed to be not only radical, but close to the lunatic fringe — has a solid foundation in the most ancient and honorable authority, and it reflects the contemporary artist's endeavor to participate in humanity's eternal effort to reach an understanding of fundamentals. It is a pity that the Platonic origin of the movement is so rarely pointed out.

As a matter of fact, it was Plato himself who wrote what is still the most vigorous damnation of representative art to be found anywhere. Let the reader refer once again to the 10th Book of *The Republic,* where that eminent thinker really got down to work. He refers to all such artists as " imitators," and takes some trouble to make sure we thoroughly understand that the designation has an unflattering overtone. He compares the activities of imitative artists to the results one might get by looking at reflections in a mirror. He suggests that the ability to represent is tantamount to an infection with the virus of bluff and fraud. What else is to be expected, he suggests, from an art that enables men to make pictures of objects and activities they do not in the least understand — the resulting paintings being good enough only for those who know no more than the artist does, " and judge only by colors and figures "?

He adds a few words about the essential limitations of representative art. How can the artist investigate anything thoroughly when he must take up his station at some single vantage point? What can he hope to see except the mere appearance of his subject matter? And in addition to being mere appearance, whatever he sees is not even the whole appearance of the object, but only a single aspect of appearance. No wise man, he plainly indicates, could possibly be content with anything so incomplete and superficial.

Doubtless Plato had known some artists who were fools, as indeed we all have. It is hard to imagine that he would have thought John Van Eyck a fool (pages 609 ff); but if he could have believed representation bankrupt in the 4th Century B.C., how much more reason there is for the 20th-Century artist, looking back over 500 years of nothing else, to feel that the further exploration of representative technique no longer offers the hope of growth and increase which is the end result of all great and serious art!

Most people seem to have got their notion of contemporary abstraction not direct from Plato, but from the derivative writings of Roger Fry, which consist of a series of separate essays extending over some years and without systematic connection one with the other. Fry never worked his aesthetics through to a clear-cut theory; but insofar as a single statement may be made, we can say that he tried to explain the worth of Cézanne, and the good in all good art, by adducing a doctrine summed up by the phrase *significant form.*

Borrowing his investigative technique from the laboratory, Fry tried to isolate the aesthetic element in art by a process of elimination. His idea was to cast out everything which was not strictly aesthetic, thus narrowing the field more and more until nothing might remain under attention except that single element in the work of art which furnished the stimulus for aesthetic experience. He therefore advised a stern divorcement of one's interest from all collateral and extraneous material. He was particularly suspicious of subject matter. Narrative subject matter of any kind was, he felt, almost fatally dangerous because of the probability (which he considered a certainty) that it would lure one away from the aesthetic values by suggesting other feelings and other trains of thought. It followed that the ideal painting must be a painting without content in any accepted meaning of that term. Everything else being gone, significant form would remain in a pure state.

Fry furnished no proof of his theory. His assertions about the psychology of the aesthetic experience were conspicuously dogmatic, and, to the author, seem incorrect. The negations he suggested — and the suggestion seemed to many like an invitation to faith — have been cordially embraced by any number of artists, museum directors, critics, and scholars. As a result, abstract art is unquestionably one of the most important phenomena of the middle 20th Century. It is no overstatement to say that more than half of the most earnest and intelligent artists have turned their back upon representation, which they believe to be worn out and sterile. It is beside the point whether the author, the reader, or anyone else likes or dislikes contemporary abstractions; the necessary thing is to have some understanding of the rationale which accounts for them. In general, two main trends may be discerned. One has to do with the analysis of visual phenomena. The other has to do with the analysis of visual imagery as it passes through the consciousness. The former is sometimes called "Analytical Cubism," and the latter, with less justification, "Synthetic Cubism."

"You're either a round-head or a square-head," the author was told one day. "Everything else about your head is an accident!" The speaker was Mr. Hooton, the anthropologist. No doubt he was correct; but had he been lecturing on art, he could hardly have made a more succinct statement about the theory of analytical abstraction. The movement derives from Plato's conception of the universe as an arrangement of scaled categories (page 290) going from the single and unimportant instance upward toward the general principle, with each upper level closer to fundamental truth than the one immediately below it.

The artist who wishes to indulge in analytical abstraction begins with some object or with some scene as it exists in nature. Contrary to what one might guess, such artists have nothing against representation; they merely use it as they think best, to describe whatever they decide is important. They act upon the assumption that everything they see is a composite of (a) accidental facts of appearance which have no bearing upon visual truth, and (b) a basic or fundamental shape not peculiar to the single object, but belonging to a universal category of objects. In accordance with the Platonic dogma that conceptual thinking is superior to daily experience, it is assumed that the artist does well to eliminate from his picture or statue every single detail except those details which tend to describe and clarify the fundamental shape to which the object belongs. In other words, the steps in the technical process are to simplify, then to simplify more, and then to simplify still more and more and more.

At some point in the process of elimination and simplification, the essential form of the object should, in theory at least, emerge and become plain. Again in theory only, the appearance of the fundamental shape ought to be automatic. It should result from the character of the object under analysis. There should be no possibility of a mistake; if the analysis has been correctly carried out, the artist should arrive at the right result with utter inevitability. There is no room in the theory for his having any choice in the matter.

At this second point in their routine, the founders of the analytical movement did, however, interpose their own ideas. They forgot about the curvilinear forms mentioned in Cézanne's quasi-dictum of the cone, the sphere, and the cylinder. With an enthusiasm that was geologically naïve, to say the least, they seem to have fastened upon the notion that crystals were a natural demonstration of the irreducibly fundamental form. Because crystals shiver into prismatic fragments bounded by flat surfaces, straight lines, and angles, the analytical branch of abstract art soon became a veritable cult of the angular.

In 1908 Matisse looked in at an exhibition of such work by Braque and Picasso. Apparently he thought they had overdone it, for he exclaimed with good-natured derision, " Oh! See the little cubes! " The name stuck; and the word *cubism*, although strictly applicable only where it obviously applies, is today in colloquial use for abstraction of all kinds.

The cubists were of course mistaken in assigning to angular forms a reality and prestige beyond any other kind of shape. From the standpoint of public sympathy, no decision could have been more unfortunate. The word went round that " curves are going out "; and the application of the cubist formula to the human body caused an outburst of empathetic furore. No one liked the idea of being squeezed into so uncomfortable a mould, and the whole thing seemed to have something to do with electricity and the nasty shocks therefrom. It was small use trying to explain that no sinister conspiracy was involved. Neo-Classicism was still sufficiently alive to make people remember the soft contours of alluring Academic nudes. Romanticism still survived in sufficient force to maintain a demand for art that gave one an emotional kick. The total effect was to make abstraction unpopular and to discredit still further the whole thought of art as an intellectual activity.

At some point in the analytical procedure, the artist must, as previously explained, decide that he has gone far enough. The data then remaining must be organized into pictorial composition so that they may become intelligible for the observer. The whole affair has been described as " backing further and further away from nature " — with the stopping point always a matter of choice and degree.

Charles Demuth (Fig. 19.11) and Lyonel Feininger (Fig. 19.12) are artists who stand just beyond Cézanne in the abstracting process. One may at first be conscious only of a broad, clear style; but it soon becomes plain that innumerable details have been canceled out, and that a considerable simplification of shapes has taken place. Both artists seem to have participated in the crystalline theory to the extent of " splitting the image " as in prismatic vision.

A great many paintings by Picasso, and occasional pieces of sculpture (Fig. 19.13), demonstrate in excellent fashion the resolution of natural contours into angular facets; but it should be mentioned that so severe and doctrinaire a method did not appeal to all artists. Lipchitz (Fig. 19.16) used curves or angles as he pleased, and Brancusi (Figs. 19.17–18) rarely used the angular system at all.

The work of Brancusi brings up an aspect of the abstract movement which is rarely identified for what it actually is, namely, the importation of certain literary devices into painting and sculpture. Readers who, as school boys, may have found Sir Walter Scott on the required list know the terrors of complete description. They are in a position to commend those writers who have a genius for finding two or three words that are just right for the situation, that tell what needs to be told and tell it fast, that get the matter over with and get on with the tale. Yet the visual arts, through all history, have been accustomed to describe in infinite and often tedious detail. Brancusi is conspicuous among modern artists for experimenting, and with no small success, with the brief, striking statement which gets to the point at once. " The girl's head was a delicate oval, and her eyebrows sweeping curves," he seems to say (Fig. 19.17). " And the bird was a flash of gold! " (Fig. 19.18).

If carried far enough, the analytical process inevitably produces objects which are completely unlike anything ever seen on earth. In such instances, the genesis in nature is no longer obvious. Titles are required. Lucid, succinct titles (Figs. 19.19) are legitimate and welcome, as they always have been. They set one off on the right train of thought without any puttering about. But it is worth remarking, before we pass on, that titles have tended to become more and more representative as art has become increasingly abstract.

Against titles which are not only descriptive but also provocative, no warning can be too strong. If, in addition, the title seems recherché, or invites ridiculous ambiguity, the case is lost from the beginning. Fig. 19.20, for example, shows a figure in several positions. The figure-style is an instance of analytical abstraction rather far advanced. The several views are intended to represent the same figure in successive positions as it comes down the stairway, and the analysis of the action is similar to that furnished by a cinema in slow motion, or by the multi-flash photograph. The purpose was experimental: to see whether it was possible for painting to break through the restrictions inherent in the Greek unity of time (page 60). Technically, the work is excellent; and the picture has much to recommend it as an intellectual exercise. But the title could hardly have been more unwise. In an unenviable sense, the *Nude Descending the Staircase* is the most famous picture of our century. In clubs, Pullman cars, and at dinner parties the world over, it has been adduced a million times as prima facie evidence that the modern artist is crazy. Neo-Classicism — which in a mysterious way had made sensuality permissive in respectable circles — had taught people to expect, from such a title, something like an action portrait of *La Source* (Fig. 18.7). The average citizen becomes enraged when asked to settle for a painting which is explained to him as an attempt to deal visually with the continuum of space and time, plus a rarefication of the human nude in the direction of its fundamental shape. Certainly the artist, as a free man, had the right to do as he thought best; but he also took his risks, and must pay his price. In a democratic society, the public is also free, and will accept or reject what it pleases.

"Synthetic Cubism" is an inaccurate name for the second great division of modern abstract art. It is cubistic only to such extent as it may occasionally duplicate the methods of analytical cubism; and it is synthetic only in a special sense to be described later. Its central purpose is psychoanalytical. It attempts to deal with the visual imagery which passes through the stream of consciousness. The same thing might be attempted by a strictly representative art, and in some instances has been undertaken, but it appears to be a fact that most of our visual imagery is fragmentary. The mind's eye does not see things whole, or in full relation with a natural setting. They come, rather, in snatches. The literary counterpart for such art is to be sought in the writing of James Joyce and Gertrude Stein, and a notable feature of both the art and the literature is that ideas and images are presented in what appears to be an original disorder.

The last statement seems to suggest that the artist exerts no art; but that is not true. He exerts his art in another way. Traditionally, all artists and all authors have arranged their material in some sort of logical sequence. The order thereby established is imposed upon the data, and is no characteristic of the data as originally obtained. On the whole, the act of organizing raw data conduces to convenience in presentation, convenience in comprehension, and ease of understanding.

The synthetic cubists do not attempt any such thing, although every one of them would doubtless concede the superior lucidity of compositions by Raphael (Figs. 16.16–19). Their art, they would contend, corresponds with the realities of our visual existence; for lack of neatness and order, it endeavors to compensate by being truthful. We don't see things singly, the argument would continue, nor even coherently. Even when staring hard at a particular view, the mind remains full of fancies and memories which flit across the screen of consciousness. Subjectively speaking, such visions are as actual as any others, including whatever objects may be in plain sight at the time.

Typical paintings of the kind (Fig. 19.21) are best understood as a collection of memories. Every object is presented on the canvas not in its entirety or as it exists; rather only those parts of it and such aspects thereof are presented as may come to mind when the visual impression is recalled. The method bears a strong analogy to the Egyptian convention of broadest aspect (page 22), but it differs therefrom in omitting to hook everything up in any fashion which might be construed as natural. Nothing has any necessary relation, in fact, to anything else. The only connection existing is the presumption that everything in view passed through a single mentality.

As compared with abstraction of the analytical kind, there is usually a marked difference of style. Analytical cubism, taking it as a whole, maintained a central interest in mass, and was therefore a strongly plastic art. Synthetic cubism has often been called "flat pattern cubism"; and there is a good reason for it. As in the design of textiles, the mode aspires toward line and flat tone (page 27). For the purpose in view, the customs of the textile designer are peculiarly apt. Textile patterns have no necessary boundaries or limits; they can go on and on, or be cut off anywhere, just like our visual consciousness. Our visual life, moreover, is not a series of pictures, each organically complete in itself (page 65), but a rhythmic alternation of small vignettes, often vaguely defined like the semi-abstract motives of the Near East.

We may now discuss the propriety of using the word *synthesis* in connection with abstractions which purport to deal with the stream of consciousness. The term may apply in at least two ways. The best painters compose their pictures extremely well; this is an apparent contradiction of their own doctrine, but it is necessary for intelligibility. By giving good pictorial form to imagery which, by definition, is formless, they perform an act of synthesis.

The word *synthesis* may also have a bearing upon the ultimate state of mind of the observer when he finally puts himself in possession of the work of art. Such paintings impose unusual demands. Contemplation of the ordinary kind is inadequate. The observer remains helpless unless he attempts to *participate* in the picture even to the extent of forcing himself through a course of stimuli and reactions which are emphatically and intimately his own. Obviously the value of the experience is to be measured by the calibre of the artist, and its authenticity by the artist's skill in presenting the most difficult subject matter yet attempted in the history of art. The worth of good examples may be assessed from the extreme difficulty of attempting to imitate either Picasso or Braque. Amateur painters try everything else, but they soon learn to leave synthetic cubism alone.

Of all the theories now operating in contemporary art, synthetic cubism seems most likely to eventuate in a great modern tradition. As yet, it must be conceded that most examples, while furnishing an authentic experience, lack scale: the experience is a small one. The trouble is that the theory itself invites the artist to let his mind wander and to let his art drift. It is interesting, however, that the single essay toward a "Grand Style" of modern abstract art falls squarely within the category now under review.

We refer to Picasso's *Guernica* (Fig. 19.15), where there is no drifting. The painting refers to a particular event in the course of the Spanish Civil War. A town called Guernica was bombed out of existence by the German Air Force. The military advantage to be gained was not at all in proportion with the resultant slaughter and destruction. On the contrary, it is believed that the action was ordered by the German command in a spirit of experiment: they wanted to know what their bombers could do. There is no need to mention the ethical implications of such an act. Time alone can tell whether Picasso was adequate to the solemnity and intensity of the idea; but there is no question that his estimate of the Spanish War was correct: the bell was tolling indeed.

Conceding that the *Guernica* is, in the scale of its conception, the most important painting of our time, all critics also concede that it is a very difficult picture. Picasso has never fully explained it, but he has intimated that many of the objects therein are symbolic. The nature of visual symbolism has been discussed above (pages 269 ff), and it has not changed. The fact is that without a rule book to name the denotation of each symbol, we must either guess or remain quite ignorant. Largely abstracted though they are, the things seen in the *Guernica* are nevertheless described with enough realism to be highly suggestive. The whole question of symbolism in modern art brings up, however, a situation which cannot be regarded as a happy one.

There exist a great many modern abstractions which lack titles. As pointed out a few paragraphs back, titles are often useful; without a title the abstraction may fail in its purpose of providing insight. We must never forget what happens when an artist begins to abstract. His pictures become less and less specifically descriptive, get further and further away from anything one is likely to recognize, and become increasingly obscure. At some point in the routine of backing away from nature, the train of thought may become fatally lost. The observer is then left helpless; he cannot even tell whether the artist worked in the service of psychological exposition, to analyze form, or something else.

The end result is summed up in some recent abstractions by Picasso (Fig. 19.14) and in work by Léger, Malevich, Pevsner, Van Doesburg, and others. The apogee is to be found in the abstractions of Piet Mondrian (Fig. 19.22). It is believed that he belongs more to the analytical than to the psychological cult. It is even said that he was accustomed to start with the appearance of steel frame buildings in New York. If so, the association is no longer sufficiently plain to impose upon anybody the necessity of believing it or caring about it.

The statement just made did not originate with the author. A number of artists have recognized the condition. Some of them have decided to make good use of it. As a class, such pictures seem to be the final result of the search for significant form. If so, what is to prevent one from getting right after significant form from the start? Why bother to derive it by going through a laborious analysis either of the mind or of some object? The artists who have adopted the philosophy just described like to call themselves " non-objective " — meaning that their work neither starts with nature nor attempts to maintain any relationship with it.

Non-objective art raises serious questions. It is unfortunate that such work is so often justified by reference to problems of design, although it is true that most of the non-objective artists are excellent and even distinguished designers. It is the author's guess, in fact, that Piet Mondrian was one of the best in the history of art; but his achievements in that department did not derive from his interest in abstraction, much less from his extreme use of it. He could have designed just as well without ever leaving the confines of representative painting. He did not design in the slightest degree better than Titian. Good design is no novelty; it is merely to be expected. Nothing can be made for or against any movement in art on that basis.

The crux of the matter is not whether non-objective art is handsome — which it is — but whether such work has meaning. In that connection, one encounters an unfortunate tendency to intellectual conceit. There is plenty of innuendo to the effect that such art is not for everybody, but only for the educated. We are reminded that classical literature, music, and higher mathematics demand a soul-trying apprenticeship before they pay off; but the analogy is false. Anybody can learn Greek, counterpoint, or calculus if he wants to, but there is no resource in education that will ever enable him to penetrate the shell of privacy that encloses both the thought and the heart of those who paint secret abstractions. If such have significant form, what do they signify?

The above, brief though it is, will give the reader an accurate notion of the various departments into which modern abstraction divides itself. It remains to estimate the worth of the movement as a whole; and in that connection, the author takes a pessimistic view.

However much we may sympathize with the lot of the artist and no matter how hopeful we may be for a great modern art, it is time we bit the bullet. Contemporary abstraction has become occult. Badly navigated, it is hard aground and helpless to move down the channel of communication. But what else could we expect from a movement that cultivated the abstruse? What reason is there for supposing that solipsism, sterile everywhere else, might yield a harvest when let loose in art? So far, the function of the whole movement has been to make absolute the tragic separation of the artist from society.

The Expressionist Movement in Contemporary Art

Because of its novelty and because it challenges the intelligence, the abstract movement in contemporary art has received the lion's share of publicity and attention. Critics and historians have published a veritable corpus of literature about it. Exhibitions have featured abstractions somewhat at the expense of representative art. The result has been to create a disproportion of interest and emphasis which now requires adjustment.

A number of the most serious and skilful artists have refrained from subscribing to abstraction as a central theory. Its dangers and disadvantages (particularly with respect to intelligibility, and as a vehicle for communication) have proven a deterrent even though every well informed person, and especially every well informed artist, has been willing to accept and employ a certain measure of abstraction whenever convenient and suitable. For the most part, the artists to whom we refer may be described as expressionists, and *expressionism* requires recognition as a modern phenomenon equal in importance to abstraction, and with an approximately equal volume of production.

Expressionism is no new thing (pages 547 & 624). It begins whenever an artist chooses to abandon the position of expositor and interpreter, and himself becomes a participant in the emotional content of his work. But expressionism must do more than begin if it is to get anywhere. A second element is necessary in the situation to give it life and fire: the artist must also make an effective demand for emotional participation on the part of the observer.

The debt of Expressionism to the Romantic movement of the 19th Century (pages 852 ff) will be obvious; that second stipulation, however, explains much about our present situation which is not in plain sight on the surface. By its very nature, emotionalism was a danger to the Romantic artist; but for the expressionist of today, it has become an ever-present peril.

The reason is this: it is always the artist (and never the observer) who names the emotion. If the observer is already sympathetic, expressionism is just what he wants, and it goes like wildfire. If not, resistance occurs. In our confused century, serious artists cannot, in honesty, continuously furnish us with things we want to see. Thus, the expressionist movement has become associated with imagery most persons do not like. In order to make them look at it, the expressionist artists must apply forceful methods, with the result that expressionism as such often seems synonymous with violent color, radical distortion of forms, shock, and hysteria. It often tries to do too much too fast. The public simply retires behind a psychical barrier, and the art becomes as ineffective as the most unintelligible abstraction.

In the last paragraph we have referred, it will be understood, to baleful possibilities inherent in the expressionist tendency, not to general practice. Expressionism, it must always be remembered, is a point of view. It is not a style. Neither is it a special sort of content. The works of art it has called into being are various to a degree. Some of them are altogether moderate and restrained, and at first rather hard to associate with a theory which has produced so much art of quite another kind.

Modern expressionism even has a formal division composed of artists primarily devoted to the further exploration of medium and its relation to design. The sculptor Maillol (born 1861) is the most famous member of the group to which we refer. No artist has ever been more sensitive to the qualities of the stuff with which he worked and the capacity of the tools he used. In good examples (Fig. 19.23) there is an amplitude of form which is grandly appropriate to sculpture as an art of mass. The simple but not summary description of textures and of details is likewise in keeping with the restraints imposed by so coarse a medium. The heavy proportions give local strength to the individual parts of the body, which are in turn connected with each other in a system of bracing that would do credit to the designer of a bridge. It is likely that Maillol's statuary will enjoy a greater permanence than most other art of recent years. Could there be a better or more thorough expression not only of what sculpture is, but of what sculpture ought to be?

Carl Hallsthammar's *Venus in Red Cherry* (Fig. 19.24) is a tour de force of representative technique which at the same time is intimately expressive of the grain of the wood. From so ostensibly conservative a demonstration, it may seem a far cry to the advanced abstraction of Henry Moore; but both artists appear to share with Maillol a common technical procedure which, in theory at least, takes off from the internal logic of the material in hand. Fig. 19.25 is a piece of Surrealistic imagery (page 772), but the imagery was developed from the flow of curves in the elm, which in turn defined the contours, much as contour lines drawn on a map describe the roll of the hills. Moore's Surrealism is bound to strike a sympathetic note, for it recalls one of the deeply satisfactory experiences of childhood, when the eye traced patterns in boards and rocks and found another world. Still further, Moore's work has an elemental strength not always to be found in similar essays: his chisels and gouges have brought out the shape which would probably have appeared in due time had the block been exposed to prolonged weathering and to the abrasive action of wind-blown sand.

From 19th-Century Romanticism, modern expressionism inherited a taste for the unusual (page 856); but in accordance with a general tendency to explore every heritage further, interest in the unusual has today become a cult of the exotic. Gaston Lachaise was an artist who shared with Maillol a love for the internal logic of the stuff in which he worked; where better than in Fig. 19.26 are we to find an objective demonstration of the tensile strength of bronze, its superb capacity in the matter of textures, plus the most elegant appreciation of the simplicity appropriate to large statuary? But over and above such values, the statue is full of strange overtones as rare and unknown as the Sirens' singing.

The sculptor Lehmbruck (Fig. 19.27) may be taken as typical of the cult of the exotic in its pure state, virtually uncomplicated by technical considerations. He derives from Donatello (page 624). He also illustrates very well the freedom with which modern artists distort for effect, a habit which corresponds precisely with an exaggerated tone of voice in conversation and with the literary use of hyperbole.

A good many pictures which look like exotic imaginings are, however, nothing of the kind. Strangely enough, there is a whole class of expressionistic art which is odd and even wild-appearing, but which depends squarely upon the sober contributions of science. The microscopic examination of minute structures has become a daily routine in our high schools and colleges, but our vision has been extended even beyond the range of the microscope. By a combination of reasoning and the imagination, it is now possible to describe the atom and the parts of the atom in visual terms. It would be an inconceivable oversight for artists to refrain from investigating what amounts to a newly won empire.

A picture by Piet Mondrian in the Museum of Modern Art seems to show nothing but a great many little crosses on a blank background; it may very likely have been suggested by the sight of a culture under the microscope—a guess that seems all the more likely because the field is circular and fades around the edges. Kandinsky's debt to a similar source is made unmistakable by Fig. 19.28. Much of Joan Miro's painting apparently springs from the same inspiration.

Sociological questions have assailed our generation almost as rapidly as science has changed our economy and way of life. Incredible though it may seem, there has been strong opinion to the effect that artists have no business venturing away from the standards established during the High Renaissance, but such inhibitions have had small restraining effect. Perhaps half of the paintings that fall within the general category of expressionism relate in some way or other to the issues and pressures which make the ceremonial concept of the good life (page 712) seem like a passing notion gone with the wind.

Soutine is one of the artists who has been conspicuous for paintings with a sociological impact. As a resident of the city where two of his most important canvases hang, and as professor of art in its university, the author has special knowledge with respect to Soutine. It seems impossible that any artist could be more unpopular. His bell-hop (Fig. 19.29) is despised because it shows a human being who is literally despicable, and it only makes matters worse to point out that the picture puts society to the question. Have the cards been stacked, or have they not been stacked, so that some people cannot play with a fair hand? Does the great tradition of Washington and Jefferson also belong to an unhealthy scroop of a person dependent for his dinner upon the base custom of the tip? And how unpleasant to realize that we dress such creatures in suits of strident red, like so many monkeys, and expect them to fawn as animals do!

The *Side of Beef* (Fig. 19.30) by the same painter is considerably more accomplished as a technical demonstration. By reference to the abstract elements of its design, one can make out a good case for calling it a beautiful picture. By reference to its content, which records the impact of the sudden sight of food upon one who has known hunger, we can show that it is a humane and tragic picture. By reference to history, we can show that it is in no way a radical subject, for Rembrandt did the same. None of those arguments have sufficed even to get a hearing, much less to carry conviction. It would be impossible to reproduce on these pages the anger, the frustration, the derision, and the venom of the voices which have been raised in comment. One is told the painter had no right to paint it in the first place, that the director had no right to buy it and should be dismissed, that it ought not to be put on public display, but should remain in the cellar.

Apparently, Soutine's sin was the failure to repeat the formula that humanity was made in God's image, with males handsome, strong, and brave and females refined and beautiful. Worse than that, he did not reiterate the text that by intelligence and moral strength humanity would rise above its problems, control the environment, and live the beautiful life contemplated by Alberti (page 696). His damnation — with respect to popularity — was the absence of some ray of hope, some suggestion of glamor even in the sordid.

Sociological expressionism is sometimes almost indistinguishable from the modern version of Surrealism (page 423) which attempts to explore the nether regions of the mind. Chirico has done a good many pictures of that kind, but the name of Salvador Dali has, in later years, come to be almost a synonym for the entire movement. Dali has now and again made statements about his own art; in sum, they say that he is attempting to portray with intense and vivid realism the visual imagery of an irrational intellect, perhaps an unbalanced one (Fig. 19.31). As for the significance of what he paints, he can sometimes make suggestions, but in the main he knows no more about it than we do.

Pending the further discoveries of psychology, it is probably impossible to interpret Dali's Surrealism in specific fashion; but there is no reason to doubt the authenticity of his effort. It is obvious that his canvases — so facile and urbane with respect to technique — record part of the mental torment which is indubitably an outstanding characteristic of our time. If the pictures are morbid, is not the world also morbid to a frightening degree? How can we ask every artist to lull us to sleep with a beauty that is not here?

THE INDUSTRIAL ARTS

James Watt got his patent for the steam engine in 1769. Its first practical application was to pump water out of a coal mine. The installation was set up in 1776, and this event may prove to have been a more important turning point than the American Declaration of Independence that same year. The mechanical power introduced by Watt has changed the economy of the whole world, and today, our life has its center of gravity not on the farm, as before, but in the factory.

The impression is current that works of art ought to be produced by the very same industry which produces everything else. The idea is good; in fact, there is no suggestion in sight which seems more likely to correct the unfortunate situation of the artist in society, or to bring about the great modern democratic tradition for which the whole world has been yearning since the French Revolution (pages 844 ff).

There is any amount of proof, moreover, that the project is practical. Much of Raphael's immediate rise to international fame resulted from the sale of prints taken from his paintings. During the 18th Century, the Englishman Hogarth realized that the artist must ally himself with the printing press; most of his mature work was designed from the beginning with mechanical reproduction in mind. During the 19th Century, the Frenchman Daumier raised the newspaper cartoon to the level of great art, and the American firm of Currier & Ives sold innumerable colored prints which, if not great pictures, are at least collector's items today.

As a demonstration of what might be done, however, the chief credit must go to several firms of American gunsmiths who undertook the mass production of small arms and made the names Winchester, Colt, Remington, and Smith & Wesson known to every child alive. All four firms, and some others that have passed out of the picture, soon were producing weapons as good as those previously turned out by individual craftsmen. The price of an excellent gun was reduced from a hundred dollars odd to a third or even a quarter of that amount. Because the mechanical merit of a gun is easily and frequently tested, the firms mentioned appear never to have considered even so much as an experiment with inferior materials. Workmanship has been uniformly first class on the cheaper models, and superb on the more expensive. It is also too seldom pointed out that design was often equally good.

In the department of aesthetic sense, the Smith & Wesson company has always held a lead over the others. It seems incredible that its so-called " Russian " model (Fig. 19.32) was first sold in 1870, at the very moment when American taste in almost every other class of object could scarcely have been worse. The fundamental design, moreover, has never been surpassed, and remains better than most others since, including those of the same company. The reader may or may not be interested in firearms, but there is no denying that the piece is an object of choice. Considered as a demonstration in ab-tract design, it is physically as fine as any sculpture by Brancusi (Figs. 19.17–18) or Archipenko (Fig. 19.19).

Our facilities for refined production have been immensely extended since the end of the 19th Century. The modern foundry can produce casts of a complexity no one dared attempt even thirty years ago, as evidenced by the cylinder blocks of the latest gasoline engines. Machine work of every kind has attained an unbelievable precision. Chemistry has furnished inks, paints, and enamels of impressive quality. Yet it cannot be said that industrial design has maintained the momentum it had fifty years ago, or lived up to its apparent promise at that time.

As yet, modern industrial design is bad design. The author makes the statement with regret after having had the opportunity to inspect a veritable host of objects produced by factories here and abroad. The list includes everything from entire steamships and locomotives through Diesel engines, furnaces, furniture, typewriters, instruments, clocks and watches, down to kitchen knives and olive forks. Very few concerns stand out in the memory as fulfilling the excellence which our productive machinery holds out to us like a promise. It is rare, in fact, that the so-called " modern design " is better than the traditional thing. All too often, indeed, some essential feature has been omitted or streamlined out of existence.

Wonderfully fine things nevertheless are to be found on the market. Without suggesting that other firms have not done equally well on occasion, the author would cite the following items merely as examples of excellence.

The latest Bausch & Lomb binoculars are prettier, lighter, stronger, more nearly dust and moisture proof, and more efficient at transmitting the light than anything available twenty years ago. The Winchester firm has introduced a series of inexpensive and increasingly better rifles and shotguns, and at the same time, in addition to producing target rifles which are the world's standard for extreme accuracy, has undertaken the most exacting task of all, the double-barrelled gun. Their Model 21 (Fig. 19.33) was introduced in 1930. It is equal in beauty and workmanship to the best products of the famous London, Belgian, and Austrian makers; it is equal, also, in the indefinable quality of " feel " which makes all the difference between a hit and a miss. As an example of engineering, it is superior to any other double gun in the world. The price, while high, is something like one fourth the cost of a similar gun handmade.

Guns and binoculars are rather expensive and complicated articles, and as a general rule it may be said that it is much easier to improve a complex assembly than a simple one. What has our industry done for us in that latter category? On the whole, not a great deal as yet; but there are some brilliant exceptions.

To the Revere firm goes the credit for harnessing science to the cooking pot. Their line of stainless steel vessels, with copper bottoms welded on, is so much better than anything ever known before that there is no comparison whatever: infinitely stronger and more durable, about three times as easy to keep immaculate, and handsomer than most silverware.

The modern steel-shafted golf club, as made by several firms, is another instance of superb design; but lest the reader suppose that all good modern items must shine with chromium, let us turn to humbler things. One hammer, for instance, looks very much like any other hammer; but if you read Maydole on the label, you know that the power will flow smoothly into the head as you swing and that you will presumably hit the nail square and true. One might suppose, to cite another example likely to escape attention, that nothing could be done in our generation to improve the simple screw driver; but that is not so. Fig. 19.35 shows an example from the Yankee line; similar tools are made in a variety of sizes. The maker's name has long been synonymous with quality and with ingenious design, but the author doubts whether any of the more pretentious items actually received the time and thought which obviously were expended upon this simple one. In all sizes, the handles are of the right scale to give an elegant balance. The handles are also painted with a special enamel which is not in the slightest degree abrasive, but which at the same time does not slip, even though the hand be wet with perspiration. The grooving of the handle, moreover, permits the application of a powerful torque, but it does not hurt the hand. The knurling of the ferrule, finally, is just right for starting the screw with thumb and forefinger.

Pencils, to add still another illustration of what is possible today, have been long in use; and it might seem a waste of time to attempt improving upon so ancient and so elementary an instrument. The author probably owns and has owned as many of them as the next man; and in the main, one is as good as another. Fig. 19.34, however, is the great exception. The size and the balance are just right. The fingers fall naturally onto a grip which is grooved in two directions. The chuck is easy to operate and holds the lead perfectly; its length below the grip, moreover, seems ideal. There are no rough surfaces or sharp corners to irritate the fingers. All in all, the tool is without equal if one has any special interest in precise control of the point; and like the hammer and screw driver just mentioned, it may be cited as an instance where every apposite and available technique has been applied in an effort to create a perfect thing. The makers are the Messrs. Theodore Alteneder of Philadelphia.

Surely the articles listed above are worthy of the name art; but why do they stand out as remarkable exceptions? Why isn't every manufactured article equally good? What is the matter? Why can we find so little to cheer about when circumstances seem to say we should have so much? The reasons can only be surmised; but the following offers food for thought.

Our entire system of production and distribution is speculative. Very few articles originate with an order placed by the consumer direct with the producer. Most, including those we have praised so highly, are made at the factory, pass through the hands of middlemen, and arrive to wait on the retail counter. A buyer may or may not come. When he does appear, the salesman's problem is to persuade him to accept the item in stock: and from the standpoint of making the sale, it is beside the point whether the article is precisely what the purchaser wants. The system is an excellent one, nevertheless, whenever the wants of many buyers can be ascertained within reasonable limits, and whenever, also, a multitude of buyers can be counted upon to want the same thing at something like the same time. Is it possible that the stipulations mentioned could ever apply to the art market? Is it conceivable, that is to say, that both the expressive needs of the artist and the aesthetic needs of the buyer can ever be made to coincide, thus making standardization and mass production feasible?

The history of art tells us that standardization of the sort described is not only possible, but in the past has been the normal thing. During the Greek 5th Century B.C., during the Gothic period, and even during the Renaissance it would have been a sound business venture to manufacture statues and paintings. People knew what they wanted, agreed that they wanted very much the same kind of thing, and were more concerned with common beliefs and with shared values than with self-expression. A reverse situation presently obtains, and to an extreme degree. There is no unanimity of taste today, and at the moment, management has reason to default from the risk of industrialized art.

The chaotic nature of public taste has often combined with economic pressures to defeat enterprises which might otherwise have eventuated in an aesthetically important alliance between art and industry — the Disney studio, for example. Although it is an organization of talented men under a responsible head in whose name everything is issued — and no different in that way from the Raphael firm, the Rubens firm, or the Sir Joshua Reynolds portrait industry — its work has been restrained by fear of the box office. Serious questions are conspicuously absent from its films, although entertainment is certainly there.

The same thing applies to the newspaper cartoon. Milton Caniff may stand for all the rest. Technically speaking, his work is superb, and it is amazing to see what excellence can be carried over from the drawing board into the cheap medium of newsprint. But when he introduced the subject of death (i.e., the death of Raven Sherman) editorials were published about the event. The artist, we were told, had broken an unwritten law. He had spat in the face of an American tabu. He might suffer for it. It is good to realize that he did not; but it is unreasonable to expect great art to emerge wherever maturity is inappropriate or unacceptable.

Various firms of "industrial designers" have been in existence for some years, and a notable recent development is the tendency to include their names in the advertisements for the product. While they too offer hope for a period of first class industrial art, the day is not yet. Those who have designed automobiles may serve to explain the situation.

In the first place, they have not designed the automobiles at all. The modern car in an assembly of disparate elements. The engine comes from one source, the chassis from another, and the "designers" mentioned usually have no say about anything but the appearance of the body. The division of responsibility is inimical to good results. In some ways the machine is a mechanical marvel; however, there is not one car on the market which does not exhibit some atrocious bits of engineering. As for the bodies, few of them have been comfortable, and most are a Cubisto-Romantic phantasm in sheet metal, chrome, red lights, and costume jewelry. The element that is lacking is faith that the good thing will outsell the bad thing, and that the best thing will survive the good. Perhaps it is true that the manufacturers are not aesthetically housebroken, but can we assert that the public knows or wants anything better?

As to the artists, have they been any wiser than their potential patrons in industry? Unfortunately not; or so it would appear. Most of them remain helplessly resentful of the Industrial Revolution, and demand to do business as it was done during the 18th Century when the single work of art was executed to the order of the individual patron. The size of the average statue or painting is in itself an indication. There might be an outlet for statues a foot high or less, and weighing not more than 25 pounds; but our sculptors insist on a scale suitable for the grounds of Blenheim Palace. With most of the world living in small quarters, paintings have not contracted to correspond. Most of those presented to the jury at our various local exhibitions run a dozen square feet at the minimum and sometimes are six feet high. Our printing establishments, moreover, are ever so much better than those available to the famous print makers of Japan; but so far, our artists have defaulted from the opportunity to design prints. Thus the printing industry, by selling reproductions from masterpieces of the past, is in competition rather than cooperation.

The reader will find happy exceptions to the story of frustration and failure outlined above; but in sum, it is as stated. An equally hardheaded realism demands the mention, however, of certain important indications that another situation may obtain fifty years hence.

Most important of all is a better understanding of the good life. Economic success is meaningless except for what it will buy; and the entire population has, within the span of the author's lifetime and observation, become steadily and increasingly conscious of its aesthetic needs. So long as those remain unsatisfied, there is no happiness and no prosperity within any permissible construction of the term. Art is today a standard part of the educational curriculum, from nursery school to graduate school. Museums of art have been founded here, there, and everywhere. The question of beauty begins to impinge upon everything from shampooing the hair to the plan of a city. One lesson of history is that the people get what they want in the end. If they want a great modern art, they will get it.

Against all the cynical arguments to the contrary, we may cite the history of music during the past fifty years. As clear as yesterday, the author remembers the general opinion that the phonograph, while ingenious, would kill music in the American home. Why sing when one could crank up Caruso? Then again, the radio was going to be sure death to the sale of records — for who would buy them when the same might be had by turning the dial? We need not summarize the present condition of music; it speaks for itself. The lesson to be learned, apparently, is that the good thing will indeed flourish if it is only made accessible.

INDEX

NOTE ON THE USE OF THE INDEX

The Index is supplementary to the Table of Contents; consult the latter for a list of the major styles, periods, and topics covered by the text.

Because technical terms are defined and discussed at some length in the body of the text, the Index undertakes to perform the function of a Glossary. Page references to definitions and definitive passages are printed in **bold face.**

References to illustrations appear in *italics.*

References to buildings and museums are indexed according to the city, then alphabetically by name. Unless otherwise indicated, the reader may assume that the principal museum of the place is indicated. References to illustrations of works of art housed within museums, churches, etc., simply give the page number in *italics* and omit the figure numbers.

Whenever custom has made a prefix part of a proper name (i.e., *de, della, le, van, von, etc.*), the name is indexed according to the initial letter of the prefix. Because surnames became universal only within recent centuries, a number of artists are indexed by reference to the initial letter of the first word of the Christian name.

There is no established usage which might offer guidance for the indexing of the numerous aesthetic, critical, and philosophical topics to which the text from time to time refers. These have been indexed, therefore, in accordance with the author's best guess as to what might be in the mind of a reader searching for information, seeking to refresh the memory, or on the prowl for argument. If all such readers will be kind enough to run the eye down the columns, perhaps they may find what they want!

The Oxford
American Writer's Thesaurus

The Oxford American Writer's Thesaurus

COMPILED BY
Christine A. Lindberg

OXFORD
UNIVERSITY PRESS

2004

Oxford University Press

Oxford New York
Auckland Bangkok Buenos Aires Cape Town Chennai
Dar es Salaam Delhi Hong Kong Istanbul Karachi Kolkata
Kuala Lumpur Madrid Melbourne Mexico City Mumbai
Nairobi São Paulo Shanghai Taipei Tokyo Toronto

Published by Oxford University Press, Inc.
198 Madison Avenue, New York, New York, 10016
http://www.oup.com/us

Library of Congress Cataloging-in-Publication Data is available
ISBN 0-19-517076-8

In Search of the Exact Word, by Richard Goodman, originally appeared in The Writer's Chronicle (http://www.awpwriter.org).
Bryan Garner's usage notes were adapted with permission from Garner's Modern American Usage, second edition

Design by T. Kellers, STUDIO TWELVE 3.

Printing number: 9 8 7 6 5 4 3 2 1

Printed in the United States of America
on acid-free paper

Contents

Oxford U.S. Dictionaries Staff

Erin McKean, *Editor in Chief*
Constance Baboukis, *Managing Editor*
Christine A. Lindberg, *Editor*
Grant Barrett, *Assistant Editor*
Carol Braham, Orin Hargraves, Enid Pearson, *Special Features Editors*
Alan Hartley, Jessica Lasak, Georgia Maas, Marina Padakis,
Kathy Sietsema, *Proofreaders*
David Bowers, *Editorial Assistant*

Contributing Editors

David Auburn received the 2001 Pulitzer Prize, Tony Award, and New York Drama Critics Circle Award for Best American Play for *Proof.* His most recent work is the stage adaptation of *The Journals of Mihail Sebastian.* His plays have also been published in *Harper's* and *The New England Review.* A former Guggenheim Fellow, he lives in New York City.

Michael Dirda, a longtime staff writer and editor for the *Washington Post Book World*, received the 1993 Pulitzer Prize for criticism and is the author of *Readings: Essays and Literary Entertainments* (2000), the memoir *An Open Book* (2003), and *Bound to Please* (2004), a collection of essays about great writers and their work.

David Lehman is the author of five books of poems, most recently *The Daily Mirror* (2000) and *The Evening Sun* (2002), and five nonfiction books, including *Signs of the Times: Deconstruction and the Fall of Paul de Man* (1991) and *The Last Avant-Garde: The Making of the New York School of Poets* (1998). He is now undertaking a new edition of *The Oxford Book of American Poetry.*

Stephin Merritt writes and performs music in the Magnetic Fields, the 6ths, the Gothic Archies, and Future Bible Heroes. He also records theme songs for children's audiobooks from best-selling authors Lemony Snicket and Neil Gaiman, and writes musical scores for film and theater. Merritt's albums are available on Nonesuch (Warner Bros.) and Merge Records.

Francine Prose is the author of many works, including *The Lives of the Muses* (2002), *Bigfoot Dreams* (1986), *Household Saints* (1981), *Guided Tours of Hell* (1997), and *Blue Angel* (2000), a National Book Award finalist. Her most recent book for Oxford University Press was *Gluttony* (2003). She is a contributing editor at *Harper's* and writes regularly on art for the *Wall Street Journal.*

Zadie Smith's *White Teeth* (2000) won many awards, including the Whitbread Award for a First Novel, the *Guardian* First Book Award, and the Black Memorial Prize for Fiction. Her second novel, *The Autograph Man,* was published in October 2002 and won the *Jewish Quarterly* fiction prize. She recently spent a year as a visiting lecturer at Harvard University.

Jean Strouse, the author of *Morgan, American Financier* (1999) and *Alice James, A Biography* (1980), is director of the Dorothy and Lewis B. Cullman Center for Scholars and Writers at the New York Public Library. She has received a MacArthur Foundation fellowship and several other awards.

Simon Winchester is an author, journalist, and broadcaster and has worked as a foreign correspondent. His best-selling books include *The Professor and the Madman* (1999), and *Krakatoa, The Day the World Exploded: August 27, 1883* (2003). His most recent book for Oxford is *The Meaning of Everything: The Story of the Oxford English Dictionary* (2003).

David Foster Wallace is the Roy Edward Disney Professor in Creative Writing at Pomona College in California and the author of several books, including *Infinite Jest* (1996), *Brief Interviews with Hideous Men* (1999), *A Supposedly Fun Thing I'll Never Do Again: Essays and Arguments* (1997), *Everything and More: A Compact History of Infinity* (2003) and *Oblivion: Stories* (2004). He was the recipient of a MacArthur Foundation fellowship.

See pages xx–xxii for a complete list of the contributors' word notes.

Preface

Every writer dreads that niggling, haunting suspicion that the word she has chosen is not quite the word she wants. (Did I mean *niggling,* really? Or did I mean *irritating*?) Precious minutes, hours, and days of writing time can be eaten up by taking out one word and putting in another, and another, and another, until that feeling of doubt has been assuaged, or at least worn out.

The *Oxford American Writer's Thesaurus* is intended to be a panacea for those "is this the right word?" doubts. With more than 300,000 synonyms (and 10,000 antonyms), it guides you, by means of useful example sentences and core synonyms, to just the right group of synonyms, so you can choose the one that makes you think "yes!" instead of mumble "maybe ...." Special features, such as our word spectrums and word banks, show you even more possibilities, while usage notes and the word notes from our Contributing Editors explain tricky nuances.

Make the *Oxford American Writer's Thesaurus* an essential tool in your work—it's a compass, setting your writing on its true course; a level, keeping your writing from tilting too much one way or another; and a ruler, letting you measure your writing against the marks set by our Contributing Editors. Keep it by you and you'll never worry about having the right word again—or at least, not for long.

Erin McKean
Editor in Chief
U.S. Dictionaries
Oxford University Press

In Search of the Exact Word

Richard Goodman

The exact word. *Le mot juste*, in French, is how it's expressed. *Mot* meaning "word," and *juste* meaning "exact." Most everyone I've ever talked to, or have read, attributes this phrase to Gustave Flaubert, the celebrated nineteenth-century French perfectionist author of *Madame Bovary* and *Sentimental Education*. Sven Birkerts, for example, writes in *The American Scholar,* "Like many would-be writers, I had been deeply influenced by stories of Flaubert's grail-quest for *le mot juste,* the exact word, which of course translated into the idea of the perfect sentence, paragraph, chapter . . . book."[1] I've read the two-volume edition of Flaubert's letters, translated so wonderfully by Francis Steegmuller, at least seven or eight times, and I couldn't find the phrase. So I went to the Web. I found "Le Mot Juste Translation Service," "Le Mot Juste Communications," an e-zine named "Le Mot Juste," and an online dictionary with that name. I'm surprised I didn't find "Le Mot Juste Escort Service."

There were lots of references to Flaubert and *le mot juste*, but none told me *where* to find it. I finally did find what I wanted in a book in French by Charles Carlut, *La Correspondance de Flaubert; étude et répertoire critique*. It's an inventory of topics in Flaubert's letters with, God be praised, an excellent index. (It should be noted that Steegmuller did not translate all of Flaubert's letters.) I found Flaubert uses the expression just twice. He writes the critic Sainte-Beuve, "If I put 'blue' after 'stones,' it's because 'blue' is *le mot juste*, believe me."[2] In the other instance, he says there has to be a rapport between *le mot juste* and *le mot musical*, that is, between the meaning and the music of a word.[3] That's it, at least as far as I can determine.

Flaubert also uses the expression *le mot propre*, "the proper word." That didn't seem to catch on.

Flaubert does say, though, that, "all talent for writing consists after all of nothing more than choosing words. It's precision that gives writing power."[4] He also says that, "perfection has everywhere the same characteristic: that's precision, exactness."[5] He says he spends hours looking for a word. He expresses the struggle this way: "I am the obscure and patient pearl-fisher, who dives deep and comes up empty-handed and blue in the face."[6] And at another point, he writes a friend that he spent three days making two corrections and five days writing one sentence. Practically anything Flaubert says about writing and art is interesting, even if you totally disagree with him, though you are constantly reminded, as Henry James points out, that he felt nothing about writing but the agony of it.

However many times he actually says *le mot juste*, Flaubert represents the relentless search for artistic perfection, whatever the issue. Ernest Hemingway—who admired Flaubert's discipline—actually uses the phrase "the exact word." He called Flaubert "our most respected, honored master."[7] In his memoir about Paris, *A Moveable Feast,* Hemingway talks about Ezra Pound, saying, "here was the man I liked and trusted the most as a critic then, the man who believed in the *mot juste*—the one and only correct word to use—the man who had taught me to distrust adjectives as I would later learn to distrust certain people in certain situations...."[8] Hemingway was profoundly good at finding the exact word. It's all there for you to see, this learning, in Hemingway's writing. "This was a man to whom words mattered," Joan Didion wrote. "He worked at them, he understood them, he got inside them."[9] I'm a huge Hemingway fan just for his deep understanding of words alone.

Mark Twain was memorably good at seizing the exact word, too. Most humorists are. (Had Twain read Flaubert? I don't know. I would love to hear from a Twain scholar on this.) Their humor often depends on a choice of word; in fact the whole laugh can rest on a single word choice. When someone interviewed Evelyn Waugh for the *Paris Review,* they asked him about the process of creating a character. He said something to the effect, "I'm more interested in what word I want to use." If you read the books of the comic writers—S. J. Perelman, Thurber, Twain, Waugh, even Woody Allen—with this idea in mind you'll see how often the laugh comes from a single, well-chosen word placed exactly where it's liable to generate the loudest laugh. Twain wrote perhaps the most famous line about this particular topic ever written, "The difference between any word and the 'right' word is the difference between the lightning bug and the lightning."

Writers don't normally lack for reasons to be depressed or jealous, but in case you get low on fuel one day, think of this: Three of the best at this *mot juste* game did not speak or write English as their mother tongue: Joseph Conrad, Isak Dinesen, and Vladimir Nabokov. For Conrad, who grew up speaking Polish, it wasn't even his *second* language—French was. Dinesen's first language was Danish, Nabokov's Russian.

What *is* the exact word? I think what we usually mean by that is a word that not only conveys precisely what you, the writer, want to say, but also does it in an unforgettable way, a dramatic way, either because of its juxtaposition to its surrounding words or because it's employed in a fresh way, or both. Something else, too, I think: when it surprises, it's usually a surprise that doesn't come out of a vacuum. It communicates resoundingly, because somehow the reader understands the word well enough to appreciate its use.

So many things go into a writer's selection of a word. There's meaning, of course. The word has to mean what it is you want to say. Flaubert repeatedly says that if you really know what it is you want to say, then you'll find the right word. But what *is* meaning? Is it the dictionary meaning? Obviously, you can't use "blue" if you mean "red." That sounds pretty elementary, but believe me, I've put down words that don't mean what I *thought* they meant. It was only after I looked them up that I realized I was wrong. Take the word *livid.* What do you think it means? Now, look it up. Please get back to me with your results.

But isn't meaning more complex? Doesn't it include music, drama, and mood? Doesn't it include physical appearance? Doesn't it include surprise and context? Otherwise, why choose "crimson" over "red"? Or "furious" over "angry"? There are shades of differences in their meanings, to be sure, but there are other more prominent differences between these words. Not only does "crimson" sound different than "red"—and we do hear words when we read them, don't we?—it *looks* different. How a word looks on the page can be important; it can be pleasing or annoying. That's part of its meaning, isn't it?

I would say it includes something else, something as important if not more so—the "secret strength" of the word, as Milan Kundera expressed it. By that, he means its roots and derivation, its history. I couldn't agree more. Which is why I dote on the dictionary and lean on it like a cane as I go hobbling through my process of composition. I love the dictionary—not every single dictionary, but those at the top of the lexicographic ladder: the *New Oxford American Dictionary, Webster's Third International*, the *Random House Unabridged,* the *American Heritage Dictionary* and, of course, the vast *Oxford English*

Dictionary, the *OED*. These are fat books—in the *OED's* case, truly overweight—devoted entirely to words. There are no favorites in the dictionary; it's the ultimate nondiscriminatory book. At least, mostly. That's why you can have "slut" right next to "slushy," "barfly" just before "bargain," and "steal" on the tail of "steak set." True, the dictionary has taken more to using epithets such as "vulgar slang," "derogatory," and "offensive," but in the end these apply to very few words, and I for one don't always agree with the dictionary's opinions and often ignore them.

That's a lot to consider. But the fact is, some choices take more thinking about than others. Some thinking takes longer than other thinking as regards the selection of a word. You can spend ten seconds choosing a word or twenty minutes—or days, if you're as driven as M. Flaubert. And everything in between and beyond. There are many pains in writing, but one of its most narcotic joys is putting down a word you believe does the job extraordinarily well. It's just right. It's *juste*. When you see it there, on the page, grinning out at you in all its handsome self, you know it's been worth the effort. And when you return to it, it will still be just as handsome.

One thing about words is that some of them have developed an association specific to one gender. Words such as "pretty," "giggly," "flirtatious." If you did an informal poll and asked, for example, what gender do you think of—*quick*—when you hear the word "pretty," what would it be? By the same token, if you took the words "crude," "killer," and "ravenous," what gender would spring to mind? These words inherently don't belong to any gender. I think a writer should always keep his or her peripheral vision attuned to use one of these pigeonholed words for the unexpected gender, sort of like cross-dressing when you're writing. Boswell, in his life of Samuel Johnson, describes a scene in which Johnson berates a poor servant girl: "You blockhead!" Dr. Johnson says. Boswell, in an aside, says that at first he thought it strange to call a *woman* a blockhead but, after thinking about it, there was really no reason why you shouldn't. This role reversal is one reason why the name "Pretty Boy Floyd" is so memorable. It's also one of the reasons the word "handsome" catches the eye when applied to a woman.

Another area that has not nearly been mined comes from the definition of the words themselves. In an essay about—who else?—Samuel Johnson, T. S. Eliot writes, "Nowadays we use words so loosely that a writer's meaning may sometimes be concealed from us, simply because he has said exactly what he meant."[10] In my experience, this usually means the writer is using the word in a sense that is older than the one in current use. In *A Moveable Feast*, Hemingway describes eating some oysters in a café:

"I began my second dozen of the flat oysters, picking them from their bed of crushed ice on the silver plate, watching their unbelievably delicate brown edges react and cringe as I squeezed lemon juice on them and separated the holding muscle from the shell and lifted them to chew them carefully."[11]

The edges *cringed*. We associate that word now mainly with fear, but that's not its earliest meaning, which is, according to the *OED*, "to draw in or contract the muscles of the body involuntarily." The word comes from the Old English *cringan*, "to draw oneself together spasmodically." It's not that we don't understand Hemingway, it's that we might be taken slightly aback. What did he mean—that the oysters were *afraid*? But somehow we know exactly what he means, and we see how aptly he has employed the word, and we see those delicate edges retracting when the lemon juice is squeezed on them. Hemingway, as we know, liked simple words, basic, strong words. Because of that, when he uses a more complicated word instead, it gets your attention. For example, he often uses "commence" instead of "begin" or "start." He says that when he first started writing, he "commenced with the basic things—birth, death, love." Mark Twain has Huck Finn use that word, too.

Here's an example from *Out of Africa,* a book even Holden Caulfield liked. Dinesen writes about shooting an iguana:

"In the Reserve I have sometimes come upon the Iguana, the big lizards, as they were sunning themselves upon a flat stone in a river-bed. They are not pretty in shape, but nothing can be imagined more beautiful than their colouring. They shine like a heap of precious stones or like a pane cut out of an old church window. When, as you approach, they swish away, there is a flash of azure, green and purple over the stones, the colour seems to be standing behind them in the air, like a comet's luminous tail.

"Once I shot an Iguana. I thought that I should be able to make some pretty things from its skin. A strange thing happened then, that I have never afterwards forgotten. As I went up to him, where he was lying dead upon his stone, and actually while I was walking the few steps, he faded and grew pale, all colour died out of him as in one long sigh, and by the time that I touched him he was grey and dull like a lump of concrete. It was the live impetuous blood pulsating within the animal, which had radiated out all that glow and splendour. Now that the flame was put out, and the soul had flown, the Iguana was dead as a sandbag."[12]

The word I want to point out is "impetuous," but "sigh" is a beauty, too. The color dying "out of him as in one long sigh." The word itself is like a soft exhale, and we can feel the life emptying from the animal then and there. The use of "azure" here is effective, too, in "a flash of azure." Exotic, like the animal. And flashlike in its saying.

Then there's the "live impetuous" blood. What does she mean by that? Well, in the *OED,* the first definition of "impetuous" includes, "moving with great force or violence, or characterized by violent motion." The word comes from the Latin *impetus,* meaning "attack, assault." She's emphasizing the force of the blood thrusting through the system. I think we have a tacit understanding of what she's saying, even if we aren't familiar with this particular meaning of the word, simply because of the word's *music,* the four, nearly-equal syllables, beating out time like a pump. Also, the word, because it's a bit unusual, and therefore prominent, makes us concentrate on the animal's aliveness.

I don't know if you would agree that this is the exact word, but I can tell you I've never forgotten it.

I saw a production of Oscar Wilde's *Salomé* on Broadway, starring Al Pacino, Marisa Tomei, and Dianne Wiest. It was fascinating. Pacino played Herod. Marisa Tomei was mesmerizing as Salomé. I was struck by what she kept saying to the stern, rebuking John the Baptist, "I will kiss your mouth, Jokanaan." She—or Wilde—doesn't say, "I will kiss your lips, Jokanaan" or, "I will kiss you, Jokanaan." She says, "I will kiss your *mouth.*" Boy, does that go straight to the groin. Especially when Marisa Tomei says it. Thomas Hardy understood the power of the word "mouth," too. He uses it in *The Return of the Native* when he describes Eustacia Vye: "On Egdon, coldest and meanest kisses were at famine prices; and where was a mouth matching hers to be found?"[13] Your inclination might be to think "lips" is sexier, especially when "mouth" is often associated with "loud" and dental hygiene. But "lips" isn't sexier; "mouth" is. And you know it when you see it, or read it. This is one of the great pleasures of reading: that communication between you and the writer—almost a complicity—where you both understand precisely what's going on here. In this case, it's how sexual these mouths are, how mortally sexual. So, I would say, trust the word, and not necessarily what it's become accepted to mean or to imply.

The complicated word, or complex word, can be the right one, too. Here's one I like from Gilbert White's lovely book *The Natural History of Selborne.* White was a parson who lived in England in the mid-eighteenth century, and his book, really a series of letters, was first published in 1789. He describes a mouse's nest as "this wonderful procreant cradle."[14] *Procreant.* I may be putting a bit too much into this, but it seems to me the word has a bit of a gentle sag in the middle, like a hammock, where someone might nestle. (As it turns out, I found that White had taken the expression "procreant cradle" from *Macbeth.* Well, he knew a good phrase when he saw one.)

No writer came at words from such oblique angles, and put them to better use, than Marianne Moore. If you haven't read her prose, especially her essay on writing, "Humility, Concentration and Gusto," I urge you to. She knew more than a thing or two about good writing, and I can't for the life of me understand why she isn't referred to more in the new legion of books about writing. She says of style, for example, "Originality is, any case, a byproduct of sincerity."[15] But the example I want is when she says, "If the emotion is strong enough, the words are unambiguous."[16] What a deft way of using that word, *unambiguous.* I think what makes this so emphatic is that what she wants to say about the words is contained in one word, instead of two. Instead of saying "the words are not ambiguous," she economizes and, in a single word, gives us an example of precisely what she means. "Not ambiguous" somehow implies the possibility of ambiguity. What an insight to see that difference! Now, I don't think you arrive at this kind of choice quickly, or easily. Our instincts, I believe, would be *not* to choose "unambiguous." (Am I doing exactly the opposite of what I prescribe here?) That's why I think reading is so important. It will show you things you didn't think could be done (or you didn't think you could do) and that can be done. (Moore, by the way, was one of the least snobbish writers when she wrote about writing. She quoted from any and every source—even from a Treasury Department memo.)

One final so-called complex word, from John Cheever's splendid, moving book, *Falconer.* He speaks of "the utter poverty of erotic reasonableness."[17] That word "reasonableness" affixed to "erotic" for me summons up all the cold patterned sex one has experienced and the lack of hope found there. Cheever knew a lot about that. It's hard to read his journals and read about his having to barter with his wife for sex—his offering to buy something for her if, as he wrote, "she would let me have my way with her." Reason and Eros side by side. Where can you find a more unhappy couple?

Sometimes writers use words to describe something that couldn't happen, but nevertheless they *make* it happen. Truman Capote is describing a ride on horseback in his book *Breakfast at Tiffany's*:

"Very gently the horses began to trot, waves of wind splashed us, spanked our faces, we plunged in and out of sun and shadow pools, and joy, a glad-to-be-alive exhilaration jolted through me like a jigger of nitrogen."[18]

Now, very few of us have downed a jigger of nitrogen, but that doesn't matter, does it? We know what Capote means. I love the word "jigger," too. It's a word that immediately evokes one quick lethal shot of firewater thrown back and shooting through the system. The word takes you directly to your hand picking up a short glass.

You probably don't get to "jigger" on the first try. Maybe you *need* a jigger to get to it. But it's out there, waiting, and Capote has reassured you it is.

How can a little preposition be a candidate for the exact word? I think the answer is in Lincoln's "Gettysburg Address." Lincoln was, truly, a marvelous writer, and all you have to do is read his letters to prove it. In any case, at the end of his speech Lincoln says the words we all know:

"It is rather for us to be here dedicated to the great task before us—that from these honored dead we take increased devotion to that cause for which they gave the last full measure of devotion—that we here highly resolve that these dead shall not have died in vain—that this nation, under God, shall have a new birth of freedom—and that government of the people, by the people, for the people, shall not perish from the earth."

Of the people *by* the people *for* the people.

Of, by, for. The preposition that really hits home for me is "of." That government *of* the people. Not *from. Of.* That our democracy flows out *of* who we are. As if it's…inalienable.

It's not only the first meaning of words we should be aware of, but what's inside them. We should be aware of words' anatomies, what makes them stand up and have life. And they do have life! What did Ralph Waldo Emerson write about the American vernacular—"Cut these words & they would bleed." The etymology rests inside the word like a kernel inside a seed, and it has the same genealogical potency as a seed's kernel. A seed has within it the whole history of its species. So does a word. This is its secret power. As Kundera writes in *The Unbearable Lightness of Being,* "The secret strength of [a word's] etymology floods the word with another light and gives it a broader meaning."[19]

I think that can be a reason, maybe a subtle reason, for choosing one word over another—or at least a contributing factor. Let's say you were choosing between "mystery" and "enigma." Should it be "Her carefree behavior following her beloved husband's death was a mystery" or "Her carefree behavior following her beloved husband's death was an enigma"?

Of course you have to consider the definitions. A "mystery," the *New Oxford American Dictionary* says, is "something that is difficult or impossible to understand or explain." An "enigma" is "a person or thing that is mysterious, puzzling, or difficult to understand." But let's go to the secret meanings. "Mystery" goes back to the Greek *mystos,* which means, "to initiate into religious rites," which in turn comes from the Greek word *myein*, "to close the lips or eyes." "Enigma" is also from a Greek word, *ainigma,* which means, "to speak in riddles," which in turn is derived from the Greek *ainos*, "tale or fable."

So, what about it? Do we go with "close the lips or eyes"? Or with "speaking in riddles"? Will it be: "Her carefree behavior following her beloved husband's death was a mystery"? Or: "Her carefree behavior following her beloved husband's death was an enigma"? I really do believe this counts in trying to find the exact word, and sometimes can even be the deciding factor. It doesn't always play a significant role, but I think it's important to know what rests inside the word, because that's a lot of history, energy, and creativity lurking. A lot of concentrated power. Why not use it?

Finding the exact word is often a hunt, like looking for the Holy Grail, as Birkerts says, which, in legend, always seems to be over the next ridge. Sometimes, you have to follow your leads down all the tributaries and dead ends until you get what you want. I like to look up the definition of a word, even if I think I know it, because usually I don't know it as well as I think I do. Then I like to look at the synonyms, because though I'm sure in general what I want to say, I'm not sure exactly *how* I want to say it. Here are the shades of meanings, one word emphasizing one aspect of the idea, another word another. I usually look up the *synonyms,* too, because I probably don't know them as well as I think I do, and, besides, there might be something, some word, in the definition that might be what I'm looking for. It's impossible for me to carry all this in my head, so I have to go through this. Even Stephen Sondheim uses a rhyming dictionary.

As a reader, it's pure pleasure seeing a writer come up with a word you just *know* is as good as it gets. Like Mark Twain at the beginning of *Huckleberry Finn.* Poor Huck is grousing about living with the stern Widow Douglas. He says,

"The Widow Douglas, she took me for her son, and allowed she would sivilize me; but it was rough living in the house all the time, considering how dismal regular and decent the widow was in all her ways."

"Dismal regular and decent."

The word this laugh turns on is "dismal" modifying "decent." I laugh every time.

In the end, is it worth it? Well, we know the answer. But I want to go back to the master, Gustave Flaubert. Here's what he wrote someone about working on *Madame Bovary*, the book that gave him so much pain:

"Last Wednesday I had to get up and fetch my handkerchief; tears were streaming down my face. I had been moved by my own writing: the emotion I had conceived, the phrase that rendered it, and the satisfaction of having found the phrase—all were causing me the most exquisite pleasure."[20]

NOTES

[1] Sven Birkerts, "Flaubert's Anatomy." *The American Scholar* (Washington, DC, Winter 2004): 138.

[2] Charles Carlut, *La Correspondance de Flaubert, étude et répetoire critique* (Paris, A. G. Nizet, 1968), 421. All translations, save for those from Steegmuller's book, are Richard Goodman's.

[3] Ibid., 415.

[4] Ibid., 421.

[5] Ibid., 421.

[6] *The Letters of Gustave Flaubert, 1830–1857*, Francis Steegmuller, trans. (Cambridge, MA, Harvard University Press, 1980), 83.

[7] *Ernest Hemingway, Selected Letters,* Carlos Baker, ed. (New York, Scribner's, 1981), 624.

[8] Ernest Hemingway, *A Moveable Feast* (New York, Collier Books, 1964), 134.

[9] Joan Didion, "Last Words," *The New Yorker* (November 9, 1998), 76.

[10] T. S. Eliot, "Johnson As Critic and Poet." in *On Poetry and Poets* (New York, Farrar, Straus and Cudahy), 195.

[11] *A Moveable Feast,* 126.

[12] Karen Blixen (Isak Dinesen), *Out of Africa* (London, The Folio Society, 1980), 198.

[13] Thomas Hardy, *The Return of the Native* (New York, New American Library, 1959), 75.

[14] Gilbert White, *The Natural History of Selborne* (London, Oxford University Press, 1974), 46.

[15] Marianne Moore, "Interview With Donald Hall," *A Marianne Moore Reader* (New York, Viking, 1974), 271.

[16] Ibid., 271.

[17] John Cheever, *Falconer* (New York, Knopf, 1977).

[18] Truman Capote, *Breakfast at Tiffany's* (New York, Random House, 1958), 87.

[19] Milan Kundera, *The Unbearable Lightness of Being* (New York, HarperPerennial, 1991), 20.

[20] *The Letters of Gustave Flaubert,* 158.

Richard Goodman is the author of *French Dirt: The Story of a Garden in the South of France.* He worked as an assistant editor in the Reference Division at Random House and contributed extensively to *The Mavens' Word of the Day Collection.* He presently teaches creative nonfiction at Spalding University's brief-residency Master of Fine Arts in Writing Program.

Using This Thesaurus

ENTRIES

The synonyms in each entry are grouped in numbered sets. Major synonym sets correspond roughly to different senses of the word in a dictionary, and are identifiable by example phrases or sentences. Many sets also contain finer distinctions, which are signaled by semicolons.

The synonyms in each set that are closest in meaning to the entry word are given first, usually starting with a "core synonym" in SMALL CAPITALS. Some sets have more than one core synonym if two synonyms are very close to the entry word but neither covers the whole sense; for example, at *audience*, both *spectators* and *listeners* are given as core synonyms. Two different core synonyms may also emphasize slightly different aspects of the meaning of the entry word. For example, at *prosperous,* the first core synonym given is *thriving,* followed by a group of words closely related to that aspect of its meaning, such as *flourishing* and *successful.* Then, after a semicolon, a second core synonym, *affluent,* is given, with an allied group of synonyms such as *wealthy* and *rich.*

Phrases and idiomatic expressions are provided in bold form at the end of the entry for their principal word. For example, *make do* and *make off with* can be found with their synonyms at the end of the entry for *make.*

Most of the synonyms are standard English, but some are suitable only in certain contexts. These are grouped at the end of their synonym set and are given identifying labels, for example:

informal, e.g., *rile, flatline, flabbergast.*
literary, e.g., *beholder, afire, sylvan.*
archaic, e.g., *knave, remit.*
historical, e.g., *trencher, balladeer;* still used today, but only to refer to something that is no longer part of the modern world.
rare, e.g., *inspirit, cenobium.*
derogatory, e.g., *poetaster, guttersnipe.*
euphemistic, e.g., *physically challenged, adult.*

Antonyms are given for most entries, and many of these antonyms have entries of their own where a wider selection of words can be found.

FEATURES

Included in this thesaurus are many special features to help you distinguish just the word you need.

Word Notes

The nearly 250 word notes written by our Contributing Editors are intended to give you a working writer's perspective on a particular word or usage. Conversational, opinionated, and idiomatic, these notes are an opportunity to eavesdrop on these writers as they choose their words.

The Right Word

These notes show fine distinctions in meaning among closely related synonyms, with expanded definitions and additional examples to help distinguish the right word from the list of synonyms.

Easily Confused Words

These notes clear up confusion between close pairs, such as *censor* and *censure* or *founder* and *flounder.*

Usage Notes

Additional guidance on the finer points of English usage, including fifty notes from Bryan Garner, the author of *Garner's Modern American Usage.*

Word Spectrums

These show shadings of meaning between two polar opposites, such as *success* and *failure* and *rude* and *polite.*

Word Banks

These are tables organized by category, covering a wide range of topics (including *Hairstyles, Amphibians,* and *Gods and Goddesses*), and are a valuable source of terminology and other information for those seeking to add detail to their writing.

AN IMPORTANT NOTE

Using an unfamiliar word simply because it is listed in a thesaurus can be a disaster. To avoid inappropriate collocations or embarrassing malapropisms, users should look up unfamiliar words in a dictionary before employing them. It is important to understand the connotations of *inveigle,* for instance, before using it as a synonym for *persuade.* Although the entries in the *Oxford American Writer's Thesaurus* have been organized to make choosing the right word simpler, users should always have a good dictionary within reach.

Headword

Part of speech

Numbered senses when a word has more than one meaning

chair noun **1** *he sat down on a chair* SEAT. See table.

2 *the chair of the committee.* See CHAIRMAN.

Cross reference

Additional part of speech

▸ verb *she chairs the economic committee* PRESIDE OVER, take the chair of; lead, direct, run, manage, control, be in charge of.

Special Word Bank features show types, kinds, and proper nouns to enrich your writing

CHAIRS

Adirondack chair	high chair
armchair	ladder-back (chair)
barber chair	lawn chair
Barcalounger™	lounge chair
barstool	Morris chair
Boston rocker	press-back
butterfly chair	recliner
cane chair	rocker
captain's chair	rocking chair
dentist's chair	sidechair
dining chair	stacking chair
chaise longue	stool
deck chair	straight-backed chair
director's chair	swivel chair
easy chair	task chair
fiddleback (chair)	Windsor chair
fighting chair	wing chair
folding chair	

See also table at SOFA.

Cross reference to related feature

Homonym number distinguishes words that have the same spelling but different origins

minute[1] noun **1** *it'll only take a minute* MOMENT, short time, little while, second, instant; *informal* sec, jiff, jiffy, flash.

Sample sentences make it easier to find the right sense

The core synonym

2 *at that minute, Tony walked in* POINT, point in time, moment, instant, juncture.

3 (**minutes**) *their objection was noted in the minutes* RECORD(S), proceedings, log, notes; transcript, summary, résumé. PHRASES: **in a minute** *the biscuits will be done in a minute* VERY SOON, in a moment, in a second, in an instant, in a trice, shortly, any minute (now), in a short time, in (less than) no time, before long, momentarily; *informal* anon, in two shakes, in a snap; *literary* ere long. **this minute** *you get in here this minute!* AT ONCE, immediately, directly, this second, instantly, straightaway, right now, right away, forthwith; *informal* pronto, straight off, right off, tout de suite. **up-to-the-minute** *stay tuned for up-to-the-minute fashion tips* LATEST, newest, up-to-date, modern, fashionable, smart, chic, stylish, all the rage, in vogue, hip; *informal* trendy, with it, in, styling, phat. **wait a minute** *if you'll just wait a minute, I'm sure we can get to the bottom of this* BE PATIENT, wait a moment/second, hold on; *informal* hang on, hold your horses.

The form of the headword for which these synonyms can be used

Labels mark special uses

Semicolon separates groups of synonyms—in this case, standard from informal

Phrases

minute[2] adjective **1** *minute particles.* See MINUSCULE.

2 *a minute chance of success* NEGLIGIBLE, slight, infinitesimal, minimal, insignificant, inappreciable. ANTONYM significant.

3 *minute detail* EXHAUSTIVE, painstaking, meticulous, rigorous, scrupulous, punctilious, detailed, precise, accurate. ANTONYM cursory.

Antonym

testify verb **1** *you may be required to testify in court* GIVE EVIDENCE, bear witness, be a witness, give one's testimony, attest; *Law* make a deposition.

2 *he testified that he had been threatened by a fellow officer* ATTEST, swear, state on oath, state, declare, assert, affirm; allege, submit, claim; *Law* depose.

3 *the exhibits* ***testify to*** *the talents of the local sculptors* BE EVIDENCE/PROOF OF, attest to, confirm, prove, corroborate, substantiate, bear out; show, demonstrate, bear witness to, speak to, indicate, reveal, bespeak.

The full phrase for which these synonyms can be used

Label for specialized vocabulary

Word Notes

DAVID AUBURN

aghast
bleary
desultory
druthers (at PREFERENCE)
elegant
feckless
fervent
fixing to (at ABOUT)
galoot (at KLUTZ)
hacker
lurid
murderous
phlegmatic
pulchritude (at BEAUTY)
quirky
remarkable
saucy
stunning
swift
torpid
traipse (at WALK)
whipper
woo

MICHAEL DIRDA

boring
brave
class
crapulous (at DRUNK)
dawn
depressed
Faulknerian
feisty
female (at WOMAN)
I
like
limn (at DESCRIBE)
literate
naturally
patriotic
politically correct (at UNPREJUDICED)
postmodern
said (at say)
sexy
stippled (at SPOTTED)
style
subtext
very
whilst (at ALTHOUGH)

DAVID LEHMAN

avant-garde
blue-collar
"Commencement" (at SENIOR)
credo
dead cat bounce
"The Difference Between Brutality and Cruelty" (at CRUELTY)
edgy, hip
ekphrastic
existentialism
foundation garments
freaky
haiku
jeans
"Made in the USA" (at UNITED STATES)
"One Day at a Time" (at CLICHÉ)
poetry
postmodernism
romantic, romance
rose
"Sooner or Later" (at SOONER)
special
swell
synergy
unconscious

ERIN MCKEAN

bathos
classy
clothes horse
cordial
effete
fortnight
grandiose
grumpy
ham-fisted (at HAM-HANDED)
inordinate
kempt (at UNKEMPT)
lackadaisical
lagniappe (at BONUS)
lone
mollycoddle
novel
obdurate
old-time
paralipsis, proslepsis
saturnine
shiny
slack

smush (at CRUSH)
sordid
stilted
triage (at PRIORITIZE)
unconscionable

STEPHIN MERRITT

album
dance
drum
echo
experimental
fatigue
genre
love
lover
music
opera
rhyme
romance
sing
suburb
synthesizer
tacky
tan
tinnitus
verse
warm
world
xylophone

FRANCINE PROSE

adult
artiste (at PERFORMER)
bovine
comprise
crippled
Darwinian (at COMPETITIVE)
decency
ectoplasm (at SPIRIT)
edifying
elitist (at SNOBBISH)
hapless, unfortunate
jealousy
jingoism
longueur (at TEDIUM)
prescience
rumpus
schadenfreude
scud
share
spinster (at MAIDEN)
storied (at MYTHICAL)
taqueria
tired
tolerance

ZADIE SMITH

auricular (at EAR)
bourgeois
cernuous (at DROOPY)
ensorcell (at ENCHANT)
exilient (at EXULTANT)
fornent, fornenst (at FACING[2])
fulvous (at RED)
mentalist (at MANIAC)
motley
nullipara (at BARREN)
orbs
plash (at SPLASH)
pleonexia (at GREED)
prochronism (at DATE)
pulvinate, pulvinated (at PLUMP)
pyrotechnical (at SHOWY)
salto (at GAMBLE)
sciurine (at SQUIRREL)
setaceous (at BRISTLY)
sexercise (at EXERCISE)
stillicide (at DROP)
tabagie (at SMOKE)
thole (at ENDURE)
vagitus (at CRY)
yump

JEAN STROUSE

achingly (at ACHE)
aren't
batty (at MAD)
bloviate (at ORATE)
cheeky
chimera
clueless (at OBLIVIOUS)
deft
filch (at STEAL)
flummox
hook up, hookup (at PAIR)
hornswoggler (at CHEAT)
issues
jeremiad (at COMPLAINT)
lugubrious
orchidaceous (at EXOTIC)
parameter
problematize
quite
sanction
shirty (at IRRITABLE)
so
whinge (at WHINE)
whup (at THRASH)

DAVID FOSTER WALLACE

all of
beg
bland
critique
dialogue
dysphesia
effete
feckless
fervent

focus
hairy
if
impossibly
individual
loan
mucous
myriad
noma (at CANKER)
privilege
puchritude (at BEAUTY)
that
toward, as
unique
utilize

SIMON WINCHESTER

adumbrate (at FORESHADOW)
baroque (at ROCOCO)
chrism (at CREAM)
disinterested, uninterested
enfeoff (at BARGAIN)
fulsome
haruspex (at SOOTHSAYER)
indiction (at TAX)
Jew
Levant
mallemaroking (at CAROUSE)
négligé
niggardly
periphrastic
portmanteau (at SUITCASE)
putonghua
raspberry (at CATCALL)
Rechabite (at TEETOTAL)
rococo
set
über (at ULTRA-)
ur (at ULTRA-)
Yggdrasil

USAGE NOTES FROM BRYAN GARNER

a
aggravate
ain't
a lot
and
anxious
as
ass
but
care
chaste
chauvinism
chomp
clearly
continual
cue
cupola
dare
dastardly
data
deprecate
derring-do
despoliation
disembodied
disinterested
edification
facile
faze
fey
flaunt
frog legs
golf
historic
hopefully
ignoramus
impact
infer
it
jodhpur
less
lie[2]
media
Meritage
misnomer
myself
Native American
nimrod
octopus
odorous
palpable
penultimate
photographer
plethora
principal
reason
rebut
recant
recoup
refute
regard
rein
rhetoric
rift
sailor
scar
stratagem
successful
there
till[3]
timpani
titmouse
unique
up
who
y'all

Word Banks

Accents and Diacritical Marks (at ACCENT)
Amphibians (at AMPHIBIAN)
Apartments (at APARTMENT)
Apples, Varieties of (at APPLE)
Architectural Styles (at ARCHITECTURE)
Art Techniques and Media (at ART)
Ballet Steps (at BALLET)
Beans and Peas (at BEAN)
Bears (at BEAR[2])
Beers (at BEER)
Berries (at BERRY)
Bible, Books of the (at BIBLE)
Birds of North America (at BIRD)
Birds of Prey (at RAPTOR)
Blankets (at BLANKET)
Boats (at BOAT)
Bread and Rolls (at BREAD)
Bridges, Types of (at BRIDGE)
Butterflies (at BUTTERFLY)
Cakes, Puddings, and Other Desserts (at CAKE)
Candy and Other Sweets (at CANDY)
Card Games (at CARD)
Car, Types of (at CAR)
Cats (at CAT)
Cattle (at CATTLE)
Cereal Grains and Products (at CEREAL)
Chairs (at CHAIR)
Cheeses (at CHEESE)
Chickens and Other Ground Birds (at CHICKEN)
Clouds (at CLOUD)
Coats and Jackets (at COAT)
Cocktails and Other Mixed Drinks (at COCKTAIL)
Coffees (at COFFEE)
Constellations, The Eighty-Eight (at CONSTELLATION)
Cooking Methods and Food Preparation (at COOK)
Cookies (at COOKIE)
Cooking, Types of (at COOKING)
Crustaceans (at CRUSTACEAN)
Dances (at DANCE)
Deer (at DEER)
Dinosaurs (at DINOSAUR)
Doctors (at DOCTOR)
Dogs (at DOG)
Doughnuts & Deep-Fried Sweets (at DOUGHNUT)
Dresses (at DRESS)
Engineering, Branches of (at ENGINEER)
Fabrics (at FABRIC)
Figure Skating Terms (at FIGURE SKATING)
Fish (at FISH)
Fruits (at FRUIT)
Games (at GAME)
Gemstones (at GEM)
Geography, Branches of (at GEOGRAPHY)
Gloves and Mitts (at GLOVE)
Gods and Goddesses (at GOD)
Golf Terms (at GOLF)
Gymnastic Events (at GYM)
Hairstyles (at HAIRSTYLE)
Hats and Headcoverings (at HAT)
Herbs (at HERB)
Horse-Drawn Carriages, Carts, and Wagons (at CARRIAGE)
Horses (at HORSE)
Houses (at HOUSE)
Insects (at INSECT)
Jazz, Types of (at JAZZ)
Jewelry (at JEWELRY)
Kitchen Gadgets and Appliances (at APPLIANCE)
Knitting and Crocheting Terms (at KNIT)
Knives and Daggers (at KNIFE)
Layers of the Earth's Atmosphere (at ATMOSPHERE)
Leather, Types of (at LEATHER)
Letters, Types of (at LETTER)
Liquors and Liqueurs (at LIQUOR)
Marsupials (at MARSUPIAL)
Mathematics, Branches of (at MATHEMATICAL)
Meals, Types of (at MEAL)
Meats (at MEAT)
Medication, Forms of (at MEDICINAL)
Medicine, Branches of (at MEDICINE)
Metals and Alloys (at METAL)
Meteor Showers (at METEOR)
Mollusks (at MOLLUSK)
Monsters and Creatures (at MONSTER)
Months of the Year (at MONTH)
Moths (at MOTH)
Muses, The Nine (at MUSE)
Music (at MUSIC)
Musical Instruments (at INSTRUMENT)
Noodles (at NOODLE)
Nuts and Seeds (at NUT)
Oaths and Curses (at OATH)
Orchestral Instruments (at ORCHESTRA)
Paint, Types of (at PAINT)
Pants and Trousers (at PANTS)
Parties and Social Events (at PARTY)
Parts of Flowers (at FLOWER)

Word Spectrums

Word spectrums are chains of near-synonyms intended to show the shades of meaning available from a word to its opposite.

The Oxford
American Writer's Thesaurus

A

a, an See note below.

USAGE NOTE a, an

The indefinite article *a* is used before words beginning with a consonant sound, including /y/ and /w/ sounds. The other form, *an*, is used before words beginning with a vowel sound. Since the sound rather than the letter controls, it's not unusual to find *a* before a vowel or *an* before a consonant. Hence: *a European country*, *a one-year term*, *an FBI agent*, *an MBA degree*.

The distinction between *a* and *an* was not solidified until the nineteenth century. Up to that time, *an* preceded most words beginning with a vowel, regardless of how the first syllable sounded. The U.S. Constitution, for example, reads: "The Congress shall have Power . . . [t]o establish an uniform Rule of Naturalization." But that is no excuse for a twenty-first-century writer.

People worry about whether the correct article is *a* or *an* with *historian*, *historic*, and a few other words. Most authorities have supported *a* over *an*. The traditional rule is that if the *h*- is sounded, then *a* is the proper form. So people who aspirate their *h*'s and follow that rule would say *a historian* and *a historic*. This is not a new "rule." Even the venerated language authority H. W. Fowler, in the England of 1926, advocated *a* before *historic*, *historical*, and *humble*.

A, in the distributive sense (*ten hours a day*), has traditionally been considered preferable to *per*, which originated in commercialese and legalese. But *per* has muscled its way into idiomatic English in phrases such as *60 miles per hour* and *one golf cart per couple*. Although *an* could be substituted for *per* in the first of those phrases, *a* wouldn't work well in the second. **—BG**

aback PHRASE: **take someone aback** *everyone in the church was taken aback when the groom's ex-wife stood up and objected to the marriage* SURPRISE, shock, stun, stagger, astound, astonish, startle, take by surprise; dumbfound, stop someone in their tracks; shake (up), jolt, throw, unnerve, disconcert, unsettle, bewilder; *informal* flabbergast, floor, bowl over.

abandon verb **1** *the party abandoned policies that made it unelectable* RENOUNCE, relinquish, dispense with, disclaim, forgo disown, disavow, discard, wash one's hands of; give up, withdraw, drop, jettison, do away with; *informal* ax, ditch, dump, scrap, scrub, junk, deep-six; *formal* forswear, abjure. See note at RELINQUISH. ANTONYMS keep, retain.

2 *by that time, she had abandoned painting* GIVE UP, stop, cease, drop, forgo, desist from, dispense with, have done with, abstain from, discontinue, break off, refrain from, set aside; *informal* cut out, kick, pack in, quit. ANTONYMS take up, continue.

3 *he abandoned his wife and children* DESERT, leave, leave high and dry, turn one's back on, cast aside, break (up) with; jilt, strand, leave stranded, leave in the lurch, throw over; *informal* walk out on, run out on, dump, ditch; *literary* forsake.

4 *the skipper gave the order to abandon ship* VACATE, leave, depart from, withdraw from, quit, evacuate.

5 *a vast expanse of territory was abandoned to the invaders* RELINQUISH, surrender, give up, cede, yield, leave. ANTONYMS keep, claim.

6 *she* ***abandoned herself to*** *the sensuousness of the music* INDULGE IN, give way to, give oneself up to, yield to, lose oneself to/in. ANTONYM control oneself.

▸ noun *at age sixty he had no less abandon than when he was twenty* UNINHIBITEDNESS, recklessness, lack of restraint, lack of inhibition, wildness, impulsiveness, impetuosity, immoderation, wantonness. ANTONYM self-control.

abandoned adjective **1** *an abandoned child* DESERTED, forsaken, cast aside/off; jilted, stranded, rejected; *informal* dumped, ditched.

2 *an abandoned tin mine* UNUSED, disused, neglected, idle; deserted, unoccupied, uninhabited, empty.

3 *an abandoned dance* UNINHIBITED, reckless, unrestrained, wild, unbridled, impulsive, impetuous; immoderate, wanton.

abase verb **1** *Dunlap had a reputation for openly abasing his employees* HUMBLE, humiliate, belittle, demean, lower, degrade, debase, cheapen, discredit, bring low. See note at HUMBLE.

2 *I'd rather lose my job than continue to* ***abase myself*** grovel, kowtow, bow and scrape, toady, fawn; *informal* crawl, suck up to someone, lick someone's boots.

abasement noun *only a fiend delights in the abasement of his children* HUMILIATION, humbling, belittlement, lowering, degradation, debasement. ANTONYM pride.

abashed adjective *Iris was positively abashed when she* *rose only to realize another nominee had won the award* EMBARRASSED, ashamed, shamefaced, remorseful, conscience-stricken, mortified, humiliated, humbled, chagrined, crestfallen, sheepish, red-faced, blushing, put out of countenance, with one's tail between one's legs; taken aback, disconcerted, discomfited, fazed, disturbed; *informal* floored.

abate verb **1** *the storm had abated* SUBSIDE, die down/away/out, lessen, ease (off), let up, decrease, diminish, moderate, decline, fade, dwindle, recede, tail off, peter out, taper off, wane, ebb, weaken, come to an end; *archaic* remit. See note at ALLEVIATE. ANTONYM intensify.

2 *nothing abated his crusading zeal* DECREASE, lessen, diminish, reduce, moderate, ease, soothe, dampen, calm, tone down, allay, temper. ANTONYM increase.

abatement noun **1** *the storm rages with no sign of abatement* SUBSIDING, dying down/away/out, lessening, easing (off), letup, decrease, moderation, decline, ebb.

2 *noise abatement* DECREASE, reduction, lowering.

abattoir noun *refrigerated trucks pulled up to the abattoir at about 10:30 every night* SLAUGHTERHOUSE; *Brit.* butchery; *archaic* shambles.

abbey noun *the brothers had been hiding refugees in the abbey's catacombs* MONASTERY, CONVENT, priory, cloister, friary, nunnery; *historical* charterhouse; *rare* cenobium.

abbreviate verb *please abbreviate your essays to a length of no more than two pages* SHORTEN, reduce, cut, contract, condense, compress, abridge, truncate, pare down, prune, shrink, telescope; summarize, abstract, précis, synopsize, digest, edit. ANTONYMS lengthen, expand, elongate.

abbreviated adjective *an abbreviated version of the story* SHORTENED, reduced, cut, condensed, abridged, concise, compact, succinct; summary, thumbnail, capsule, synoptic; *formal* compendious. ANTONYMS expanded, long.

abbreviation noun **1** *the abbreviation for 'teaspoon' is 'tsp.' or just 't.'* SHORTENED FORM, short form, contraction, acronym, initialism, symbol, diminutive; elision. ANTONYM full form.

2 *'Desi Arnaz' was an abbreviation of the bandleader's full name, 'Desiderio Alberto Arnaz y de Acha III'* SHORTENING, reduction, cutting, contraction, condensation, abridgment, truncation, cropping, paring down. ANTONYM expansion.

abdicate verb **1** *the king abdicated in 1936* RESIGN, retire, stand down, step down, bow out, renounce the throne; *archaic* demit. ANTONYM be crowned.

2 *Ferdinand abdicated the throne* RESIGN FROM, relinquish, renounce, give up, surrender, vacate, cede; *Law* disclaim; *formal* abjure. ANTONYM accede to.

3 *the state abdicated all responsibility for their welfare* DISOWN, reject, renounce, give up, refuse, relinquish, repudiate, abandon, turn one's back on, wash one's hands of; forgo, waive; *formal* abjure; *literary* forsake. ANTONYMS accept, take on.

abdication noun **1** *Edward VIII's abdication* RESIGNATION, retirement; relinquishment, renunciation, surrender; *formal* abjuration; *archaic* demission. ANTONYM coronation

2 *an abdication of responsibility* DISOWNING, renunciation, rejection, refusal, relinquishment, repudiation, abandonment. ANTONYM acceptance

abdomen noun *a firm abdomen* STOMACH, belly, gut, middle, intestines; *informal* tummy, insides, guts, maw, breadbasket, pot, paunch.

abdominal adjective *abdominal pains* GASTRIC, intestinal, stomach, stomachic, enteric, duodenal, visceral, celiac, ventral.

abduct verb *police were tipped off that Kiley was planning to abduct the congressman's wife* KIDNAP, carry off, seize, capture, run away/off with, make off with, spirit away; *informal* snatch, shanghai.

aberrant adjective *eating on the floor with the dogs is just one example of his aberrant behavior* DEVIANT, deviating, divergent, abnormal, atypical, anomalous, irregular; nonconformist, rogue; strange, odd, peculiar, uncommon, freakish, quirky; twisted, warped, perverted. ANTONYMS normal, typical.

aberration noun *a statistical aberration* ANOMALY, deviation, departure from the norm, divergence, abnormality, irregularity, variation, digression, freak, rogue, rarity, oddity, peculiarity, curiosity, quirk; mistake.

abet verb *I refused to abet the neighbors in their scheme to sabotage the construction site* ASSIST, aid, help, lend a hand to, support, back, encourage; cooperate with, collaborate with, work with, connive with, collude with, go along with, be in collusion with, be hand in glove with, side with; second, endorse, sanction; promote, incite, champion, further, expedite. ANTONYM hinder.

abeyance noun *expansion plans for the middle school are* ***in abeyance*** IN SUSPENSION, in a state of suspension, in a state of dormancy, in a state of uncertainty, in remission; pending, suspended, deferred, postponed, put off, put to one side, unresolved, up in the air; *informal* in cold storage, on ice, on the back burner. See note at LATENT.

abhor verb *I abhor the taste of liver* DETEST, hate, loathe, despise, execrate, regard with disgust, shrink from, recoil from, shudder at; *formal* abominate. See note at DESPISE. ANTONYMS love, admire.

abhorrence noun *the sight of drug dealers on his street fills him with abhorrence* HATRED, loathing, detestation, execration, revulsion, abomination, disgust, repugnance, horror, odium, aversion.

abhorrent adjective *that slasher film was just one abhorrent scene after another* DETESTABLE, hateful, loathsome, despicable, abominable, execrable, repellent, repugnant, repulsive, revolting, disgusting, distasteful, horrible, horrid, horrifying, awful, heinous, reprehensible, obnoxious, odious, nauseating, offensive, contemptible. See note at OFFENSIVE. ANTONYM admirable.

abide verb **1** *he expected everybody to* ***abide by*** *the rules* COMPLY WITH, obey, observe, follow, keep to, hold to, conform to, adhere to, stick to, stand by, act in accordance with, uphold, heed, accept, go along with, acknowledge, respect, defer to. ANTONYMS flout, disobey.

2 *informal* *I can't abide the smell of cigarettes* TOLERATE, bear, stand, put up with, endure, take, countenance; *informal* stomach; *formal* brook; *archaic* suffer. ANTONYMS enjoy, relish.

3 *the memory of our parting will abide* CONTINUE, remain, survive, last, persist, stay, live on. ANTONYMS fade, disappear.

abiding adjective *theirs is an abiding friendship* ENDURING, lasting, persisting, long-lasting, lifelong, continuing, remaining, surviving, standing, durable, everlasting, perpetual, eternal, unending, constant, permanent, unchanging, steadfast, immutable. ANTONYMS short-lived, ephemeral.

ability noun 1 *the ability to read and write* CAPACITY, capability, potential, potentiality, power, faculty, aptness, facility; wherewithal, means.

2 *the president's leadership ability* TALENT, skill, expertise, adeptness, aptitude, skillfulness, savoir faire, prowess, mastery, accomplishment; competence, proficiency; dexterity, adroitness, deftness, cleverness, flair, finesse, gift, knack, genius; qualification, resources; *informal* know-how.

abject adjective 1 *abject poverty* WRETCHED, miserable, hopeless, pathetic, pitiful, pitiable, piteous, sorry, woeful, lamentable, degrading, appalling, atrocious, awful.

2 *an abject sinner* CONTEMPTIBLE, base, low, vile, worthless, debased, degraded, despicable, ignominious, mean, unworthy, ignoble.

3 *an abject apology* OBSEQUIOUS, groveling, fawning, toadyish, servile, cringing, sycophantic, submissive, craven.

abjure verb *formal she has abjured the doctrines of her parents' faith* RENOUNCE, relinquish, reject, forgo, disavow, abandon, deny, repudiate, give up, wash one's hands of; eschew, abstain from, refrain from; *informal* kick, pack in; *Law* disaffirm; *literary* forsake; *formal* forswear, abnegate.

ablaze adjective 1 *several vehicles were ablaze* ON FIRE, alight, aflame, in flames, flaming, burning, fiery, blazing; *literary* afire, igneous.

2 *every window was ablaze with light* LIT UP, alight, gleaming, glowing, aglow, illuminated, bright, shining, radiant, shimmering, sparkling, flashing, dazzling, luminous, incandescent.

3 *his eyes were ablaze with fury* PASSIONATE, impassioned, aroused, excited, adrenalized, stimulated, eager, animated, intense, ardent, fiery, fervent, frenzied.

able adjective 1 *he will soon be able to resume his duties* CAPABLE OF, competent to, equal to, up to, fit to, prepared to, qualified to; allowed to, free to, in a position to. ANTONYM incapable.

2 *an able student* INTELLIGENT, clever, talented, skillful, skilled, accomplished, gifted; proficient, apt, good, adroit, adept; capable, competent, efficient, effective. ANTONYM incompetent.

able-bodied adjective *we'll need at least six able-bodied men and women for the expedition* HEALTHY, FIT, in good health, robust, strong, sound, sturdy, vigorous, hardy, hale and hearty, athletic, muscular, strapping, burly, brawny, lusty; in good shape, in good trim, in fine fettle, fighting fit, as fit as a fiddle; *informal* husky; *dated* stalwart. ANTONYMS infirm, frail, disabled.

abnegation noun *formal* 1 *a serious abnegation of their responsibilities* RENUNCIATION, rejection, refusal, abandonment, abdication, surrender, relinquishment, repudiation, denial; *formal* abjuration. ANTONYM acceptance.

2 *people capable of abnegation and unselfishness* SELF-DENIAL, self-sacrifice, abstinence, temperance, continence, asceticism, austerity, abstemiousness. ANTONYM self-indulgence.

abnormal adjective *an increased appetite during pregnancy is not abnormal | she speaks Spanish with a Swedish accent, which is pretty abnormal* UNUSUAL, uncommon, atypical, untypical, nontypical, unrepresentative, rare, isolated, irregular, anomalous, deviant, divergent, aberrant, freak, freakish; STRANGE, odd, peculiar, curious, bizarre, weird, queer; eccentric, idiosyncratic, quirky; unexpected, unfamiliar, unconventional, surprising, unorthodox, singular, exceptional, extraordinary, out of the ordinary, out of the way; unnatural, perverse, perverted, twisted, warped, unhealthy, distorted; *informal* freaky. ANTONYMS normal, typical, common.

abnormality noun 1 *born with a heart abnormality* MALFORMATION, deformity, irregularity, flaw, defect, anomaly.

2 *the abnormality of such behavior* UNUSUALNESS, uncommonness, atypicality, irregularity, anomalousness, deviation, divergence, aberrance, aberration, freakishness; strangeness, oddness, peculiarity, unexpectedness, singularity.

abode noun *welcome to my humble abode* HOME, house, place of residence, accommodations; quarters, lodgings, domicile, rooms; address; *informal* pad, digs; *formal* dwelling, dwelling place, residence, habitation.

abolish verb *the governor never fulfilled his promise to abolish the state income tax* PUT AN END TO, get rid of, scrap, end, stop, terminate, ax, eradicate, eliminate, exterminate, destroy, annihilate, stamp out, obliterate, wipe out, extinguish, quash, expunge, extirpate; annul, cancel, invalidate, negate, nullify, void, dissolve; rescind, repeal, revoke, overturn; discontinue, remove, excise, drop, jettison; *informal* do away with, ditch, junk, scrub, dump; *formal* abrogate. ANTONYMS retain, create.

abolition noun *the abolition of slavery did not guarantee equality* SCRAPPING, ending, termination, eradication, elimination, extermination, abolishment, destruction, annihilation, obliteration, extirpation; annulment, cancellation, invalidation, nullification, dissolution; revocation, repeal, discontinuation, removal; *formal* abrogation.

abominable adjective *Caligula was among the most abominable figures in history* LOATHSOME, detestable, hateful, odious, obnoxious, despicable, contemptible, damnable, diabolical; disgusting, revolting, repellent, repulsive, offensive, repugnant, abhorrent, reprehensible, atrocious, horrifying, execrable, foul, vile, wretched, base, horrible, awful, dreadful, appalling, nauseating; horrid, nasty, disagreeable, unpleasant, distasteful; *informal* terrible, shocking, godawful; beastly; *dated* cursed, accursed. See note at OFFENSIVE. ANTONYMS good, admirable.

abominate verb *formal I truly abominate her use of coarse language* DETEST, loathe, hate, abhor, despise, execrate, shudder at, recoil from, shrink from, be repelled by. ANTONYMS like, love.

abomination noun 1 *in both wars, internment was an abomination* ATROCITY, disgrace, horror, obscenity, outrage, evil, crime, monstrosity, anathema, bane.

2 *she looked upon his kitschy decor with abomination* DETESTATION, loathing, hatred, aversion, antipathy, revulsion, repugnance, abhorrence, odium, execration, disgust, horror, hostility. ANTONYMS liking, love.

aboriginal adjective 1 *the area's aboriginal inhabitants* INDIGENOUS, native; original, earliest, first; ancient, primitive, primeval, primordial; *rare* autochthonous.

2 *Aboriginal soldiers serving in the Canadian forces* NA-

TIVE, indigenous, First Nations, Indian, Inuit, Metis. See note at NATIVE.

▸ noun *the social structure of the aboriginals* NATIVE, aborigine, original inhabitant; *rare* autochthon, indigene.

abort verb *the crew aborted the takeoff* HALT, stop, end, ax, call off, cut short, discontinue, terminate, arrest, cancel, scrub; *informal* pull the plug on.

abortion noun *her first pregnancy resulted in a spontaneous abortion* TERMINATION, miscarriage.

abortive adjective *the abortive coup was crushed after two days of fighting* UNSUCCESSFUL, failed, vain, thwarted, futile, useless, worthless, ineffective, ineffectual, to no effect, inefficacious, fruitless, unproductive, unavailing, to no avail, sterile, nugatory; *archaic* bootless. ANTONYMS successful, fruitful.

abound verb **1** *cafés and bars abound in the narrow streets* BE PLENTIFUL, be abundant, be numerous, proliferate, superabound, be thick on the ground; *informal* grow on trees.

2 *the stream* ***abounds with*** *trout and eels* BE FULL OF, overflow with, teem with, be packed with, be crowded with, be thronged with; be alive with, be crawling with, be overrun by/with, swarm with, bristle with, be infested with, be thick with; *informal* be stuffed with, be jam-packed with, be chockablock with, be chock-full of.

abounding adjective *abounding energy* ABUNDANT, plentiful, superabundant, considerable, copious, ample, lavish, luxuriant, profuse, boundless, prolific, inexhaustible, generous; galore; *literary* plenteous. ANTONYMS meager, scanty.

about preposition **1** *a book about needlecraft* REGARDING, concerning, with reference to, referring to, with regard to, with respect to, respecting, relating to, on, touching on, dealing with, relevant to, connected with, in connection with, on the subject of, in the matter of, apropos, re.

2 *two hundred people were milling about the room* AROUND, round, throughout, over, through, on every side of.

▸ adverb **1** *there were babies crawling about in the grass* AROUND, here and there, to and fro, back and forth, from place to place, hither and thither, in all directions.

2 *I knew he was somewhere about* NEAR, nearby, around, hereabouts, not far (off/away), close by, in the vicinity, in the neighborhood.

3 *the explosion caused about $15,000 worth of damage* APPROXIMATELY, roughly, around, round about, in the region of, circa, of the order of, something like; or so, or thereabouts, there or thereabouts, more or less, give or take a few, not far off; *informal* in the ballpark of.

4 *there's a lot of gossip about* AROUND, in circulation, in existence, current, going on, prevailing, prevalent, happening, in the air, abroad.

PHRASE: **about to** *I'm about to leave* (JUST) GOING TO, ready to, all set to, preparing to, getting ready to, intending to, soon to; on the point of, on the verge of, on the brink of, *informal* fixing to.

WORD NOTE **fixing to**

If you grew up in the South, you used this word a lot, and no other synonymous phrase—not *preparing to,* not *getting ready to* or *about to*—quite conveys the combination of determined intent with a hint of threat, as in, "Look out, I'm fixing to come over there . . . "—**DA**

about-face noun **1** *he saluted and did an about-face* TURNAROUND, turnabout, volte-face, U-turn; *informal* U-ey, one-eighty.

2 *the government was forced to make an about-face* U-TURN, volte-face, reversal, retraction, backtracking, swing, swerve; change of heart, change of mind, sea change.

above preposition **1** *a tiny window above the door* OVER, higher (up) than; on top of, atop, on, upon. ANTONYMS below, under, beneath.

2 *those above the rank of colonel* SUPERIOR TO, senior to, over, higher (up) than, more powerful than; in charge of, commanding. ANTONYMS below, junior to.

3 *you must be above suspicion* BEYOND, not liable to, not open to, not vulnerable to, out of reach of; immune to, exempt from.

4 *the Chinese valued pearls above gold* MORE THAN, over, before, rather than, in preference to, instead of.

5 *an increase above the rate of inflation* GREATER THAN, more than, higher than, exceeding, in excess of, over, over and above, beyond, surpassing, upwards of. ANTONYMS below, less than.

▸ adverb **1** *in the darkness above, something moved* OVERHEAD, on/at the top, high up, on high, up above, (up) in the sky, high above one's head, aloft.

2 *the two cases described above* EARLIER, previously, before, formerly.

▸ adjective *the above example* PRECEDING, previous, earlier, former, foregoing, prior, above-stated, above-mentioned, aforementioned, aforesaid.

PHRASE: **above all** *above all, deactivate the alarm before attempting to open the door* MOST IMPORTANTLY, before everything, beyond everything, first of all, most of all, chiefly, primarily, in the first place, first and foremost, mainly, principally, predominantly, especially, essentially, basically, in essence, at bottom; *informal* at the end of the day, when all is said and done.

aboveboard adjective *the proceedings were completely aboveboard* LEGITIMATE, lawful, legal, licit, honest, fair, open, frank, straight, overt, candid, forthright, unconcealed, trustworthy, unequivocal; *informal* legit, kosher, by the book, street legal, fair and square, square, on the level, on the up and up, upfront. ANTONYMS dishonest, shady.

abrade verb *the paint had been abraded by years of harsh weather* WEAR AWAY, wear down, erode, scrape away, corrode, eat away at, gnaw away at.

abrasion noun **1** *his knees were marked up with abrasions* GRAZE, cut, scrape, scratch, gash, laceration, injury, contusion; sore, ulcer.

2 *the metal is resistant to abrasion* EROSION, wearing away/down, corrosion, scraping, scouring.

abrasive adjective **1** *abrasive cleanser* CORROSIVE, corroding, erosive; caustic, harsh, scratching, coarse. ANTONYM gentle.

2 *her abrasive manner* CAUSTIC, cutting, biting, acerbic; rough, harsh, hard, tough, sharp, grating, curt, brusque, stern, severe; wounding, nasty, cruel, callous, insensitive, unfeeling, unsympathetic, inconsiderate. ANTONYMS kind, gentle.

abreast adverb **1** *they walked three abreast* IN A ROW, side by side, alongside, level, beside each other, shoulder to shoulder.

2 *try to keep **abreast of** current affairs* UP TO DATE WITH, up with, in touch with, informed about, acquainted with, knowledgeable about, conversant with, familiar with, au courant with, au fait with.

abridge verb *she was hired to abridge the works of Shakespeare for a children's book club* SHORTEN, cut, cut short, cut down, curtail, truncate, trim, crop, clip, pare down, prune; abbreviate, condense, contract, compress, reduce, decrease, shrink; summarize, sum up, abstract, précis, synopsize, give a digest of, put in a nutshell, edit; *rare* epitomize. ANTONYM lengthen.

abridged adjective *an abridged edition of the college dictionary* SHORTENED, cut, cut down, concise, condensed, abbreviated; summary, outline, thumbnail; bowdlerized, censored, expurgated.

abridgment noun *an abridgment of the full report* SUMMARY, abstract, synopsis, précis, outline, résumé, sketch, compendium, digest.

abroad adverb 1 *he regularly travels abroad* OVERSEAS, out of the country, to/in foreign parts, to/in a foreign country, to/in a foreign land.

2 *rumors were abroad* IN CIRCULATION, circulating, widely current, everywhere, in the air, 'here, there, and everywhere'; about, around; at large.

abrogate verb *formal the time has come to formally abrogate this outdated agreement* REPEAL, revoke, rescind, repudiate, overturn, annul, *Law* disallow, cancel, invalidate, nullify, void, negate, dissolve, countermand, declare null and void, discontinue; reverse, retract, remove, withdraw, abolish, put an end to, do away with, get rid of, end, stop, quash, scrap; *Law* disaffirm. See note at VOID. ANTONYMS institute, introduce.

abrogation noun *formal such a defense system would require amendment or abrogation of the 1972 antiballistic missile treaty* REPEAL, revocation, repudiation, rescinding, overturning, annulment, overruling, cancellation, invalidation, nullification, negation, dissolution, discontinuation; reversal, retraction, removal, withdrawal, abolition; *formal* rescission; *rare* deracination.

abrupt adjective 1 *an abrupt halt | an abrupt change of subject* SUDDEN, unexpected, without warning, unanticipated, unforeseen, precipitate, precipitous, surprising, startling; quick, swift, rapid, hurried, hasty, immediate, instantaneous. ANTONYMS gradual, unhurried.

2 *an abrupt manner* CURT, brusque, blunt, short, sharp, terse, crisp, gruff, rude, discourteous, uncivil, snappish, unceremonious, offhand, rough, harsh; bluff, no-nonsense, to the point; *informal* snappy. ANTONYMS friendly, expansive.

3 *abrupt, epigrammatic paragraphs* DISJOINTED, jerky, uneven, disconnected, inelegant. ANTONYMS smooth, flowing.

4 *an abrupt slope* STEEP, sheer, precipitous, bluff, sharp, sudden; perpendicular, vertical, dizzy, vertiginous. ANTONYMS gradual, gentle.

abscess noun *the abscess is what's causing the pain* ULCER, ulceration, cyst, boil, blister, sore, pustule, carbuncle, pimple, wen, whitlow, canker; inflammation, infection, eruption.

abscond verb *it seems that the one they entrusted with their stolen goods has absconded* RUN AWAY, escape, bolt, flee, make off, take flight, take off, decamp; make a break for it, take to one's heels, make a quick getaway, beat a hasty retreat, run for it, make a run for it; disappear, vanish, slip away, split, steal away, sneak away; clear out, duck out; *informal* cut and run, skedaddle, skip, skip town, head for the hills, do a disappearing act, fly the coop, take French leave, vamoose, take a powder.

absence noun 1 *what excuse has he given for his absence this time? | an extended absence* NONATTENDANCE, nonappearance, absenteeism; TRUANCY, playing truant; leave, holiday, vacation, sabbatical. ANTONYMS presence, attendance.

2 *the absence of suitable candidates* LACK, want, nonexistence, unavailability, deficiency, dearth; need. See note at LACK. ANTONYMS presence, availability.

absent adjective 1 *she was absent from work | an absent parent* AWAY, off, out, nonattending, truant; off duty, on holiday, on leave; gone, missing, unavailable, nonexistent; *informal* AWOL, playing hooky. See word spectrum on page 6. ANTONYM present.

2 *an absent look* DISTRACTED, preoccupied, inattentive, vague, absorbed, abstracted, unheeding, oblivious, distrait, absentminded, dreamy, far away, in a world of one's own, lost in thought, in a brown study; blank, empty, vacant; *informal* miles away. ANTONYMS attentive, alert.

▸ verb (**absent oneself**) *Rose absented herself from the occasion* STAY AWAY, be absent, withdraw, retire, take one's leave, remove oneself.

absentminded adjective *I tend to be most absentminded in school* FORGETFUL, distracted, preoccupied, inattentive, vague, abstracted, daydreaming, unheeding, oblivious, distrait, in a brown study; lost in thought, moony, pensive, thoughtful, brooding; *informal* scatterbrained, out of it, out to lunch, miles away, having a mind/memory like a sieve, spacey. ANTONYMS alert, observant.

absolute adjective 1 *absolute silence | an absolute disgrace* COMPLETE, total, utter, out-and-out, outright, entire, perfect, pure, decided; thorough, thoroughgoing, undivided, unqualified, unadulterated, unalloyed, unmodified, unreserved, downright, undiluted, consummate, unmitigated, sheer, arrant, rank, dyed-in-the-wool. ANTONYMS partial, qualified.

2 *the absolute truth* DEFINITE, certain, positive, unconditional, categorical, unquestionable, incontrovertible, undoubted, unequivocal, decisive, conclusive, confirmed, infallible. ANTONYMS partial, qualified.

3 *absolute power* UNLIMITED, unrestricted, unrestrained, unbounded, boundless, infinite, ultimate, total, supreme, unconditional. ANTONYMS limited, conditional.

4 *an absolute monarch* AUTOCRATIC, despotic, dictatorial, tyrannical, tyrannous, absolutist, authoritarian, arbitrary, autonomous, sovereign, autarchic, autarchical, omnipotent. ANTONYM constitutional.

5 *absolute moral standards* UNIVERSAL, fixed, independent, nonrelative, nonvariable, absolutist. ANTONYMS relative, flexible.

absolutely adverb *you're absolutely right* COMPLETELY, totally, utterly, perfectly, entirely, wholly, fully, quite, thoroughly, unreservedly; definitely, certainly, positively, unconditionally, categorically, unquestionably, undoubtedly, without (a) doubt, without question, surely,

absent
distrait
oblivious
preoccupied
vague
blank
empty
vacant
vacuous
absorbed
unheeding
abstracted
distracted
inattentive
absentminded
lost in thought
in a brown study
in a world of one's own
not with us
somewhere else
with one's head in the clouds
miles away
far away
dreamy
dreaming
wool-gathering
daydreaming
musing
thinking
thoughtful
noticing
aware
attending
interested
all ears
on the ball
awake
wideawake
not missing a trick
alert
watchful
beady-eyed
concentrating
focused
intent
absorbed
observant
heedful
mindful
on guard
vigilant
acute
engrossed
regardful
perceptive
percipient
present

unequivocally; exactly, precisely, decisively, conclusively, manifestly, in every way, in every respect, one hundred percent, every inch, to the hilt; *informal* dead. ANTONYMS partially, in no way.

▸ exclamation *informal "Have I made myself clear?" "Absolutely!"* YES, indeed, of course, definitely, certainly, quite, without (a) doubt, without question, unquestionably; affirmative, by all means. ANTONYM by no means.

absolution noun *Christianity Father, I am a sinful man in need of absolution* FORGIVENESS, pardon, exoneration, remission, dispensation, indulgence, clemency, mercy; discharge, acquittal; freedom, deliverance, release; vindication; *formal* exculpation; *archaic* shrift. ANTONYMS punishment, condemnation.

absolve verb **1** *this fact does not absolve you from responsibility* EXONERATE, discharge, acquit, vindicate; release, relieve, liberate, free, deliver, clear, exempt, let off; *formal* exculpate. ANTONYMS blame, condemn.

2 *Christianity I **absolve** you **of** your sins* FORGIVE, pardon. ANTONYMS punish, condemn.

THE RIGHT WORD

To varying degrees, all of these words mean to free from guilt or blame, and some are most frequently heard in a legal or political context. **Absolve** is the most general term, meaning to set free or release—not only from guilt or blame, but from a duty or obligation (*absolved from her promise to serve on the committee*) or from the penalties for their violation. **Pardon** is usually associated with the actions of a government or military official (*President Gerald Ford pardoned Richard Nixon following his resignation in the wake of the Watergate scandal*) and specifically refers to a release from prosecution or punishment. It is usually a legal official who decides to **acquit**, or release someone from a specific and formal accusation of wrongdoing (*the court acquitted the accused due to lack of evidence*). **Exonerate** suggests relief (its origin suggests the lifting of a burden), often in a moral sense, from a definite charge so that not even the suspicion of wrongdoing remains (*completely exonerated from the accusation of cheating*). A person who is **vindicated** is also off the hook, usually due to the examination of evidence (*she vindicated herself by producing the missing documents*). **Exempt** has less to do with guilt and punishment and more to do with duty and obligation (*exempt from paying taxes*). To **forgive**, however, is the most magnanimous act of all: It implies not only giving up on the idea that an offense should be punished, but also relinquishing any feelings of resentment or vengefulness (*"To err is human; to forgive divine"*).

absorb verb **1** *a spongelike material that absorbs water* SOAK UP, suck up, draw up/in, take up/in, blot up, mop up, sop up. ANTONYM exude.

2 *she absorbed the information in silence* ASSIMILATE, digest, take in.

3 *the company was absorbed into the new concern* INCORPORATE, assimilate, integrate, take, appropriate, subsume, include, co-opt, swallow up.

4 *these roles absorb most of his time and energy* USE (UP), consume, take (up), occupy.

5 *she was totally **absorbed in** her book* ENGROSS IN, captivate by, occupy with, preoccupy with, engage in, rivet by, grip by, hold by, interest in, intrigue by/with, immerse in, involve in, enthrall by, spellbind by, fascinate by/with.

absorbent adjective *absorbent towels* POROUS, spongy, spongelike, permeable, pervious, absorptive; *technical* spongiform. ANTONYM waterproof.

absorbing adjective *an absorbing spy novel* FASCINATING, interesting, captivating, gripping, engrossing, compelling, compulsive, enthralling, riveting, spellbinding, consuming, intriguing, thrilling, exciting; *informal* unputdownable. ANTONYMS boring, uninteresting.

absorption noun **1** *the absorption of water* SOAKING UP, sucking up; *technical* osmosis.

2 *by 1543, Scottish fears of absorption by England were allayed* INCORPORATION, assimilation, integration, appropriation, inclusion.

3 *her total **absorption in** the music* INVOLVEMENT IN, immersion in, raptness in, engrossment in, occupation with, preoccupation with, engagement in, captivation with, fascination with, enthrallment with.

abstain verb 1 *Benjamin* ***abstained from*** *wine* REFRAIN FROM, desist from, hold back from, forbear; give up, renounce, avoid, shun, eschew, forgo, go without, do without; refuse, decline; *informal* cut out; *formal* abjure. ANTONYM indulge in.

2 *pregnant women are encouraged to abstain* NOT DRINK, be teetotal, take the pledge; *informal* be on the wagon. ANTONYM drink.

3 *262 voted against, 38 abstained* NOT VOTE, decline to vote. ANTONYM vote.

abstemious adjective *the monks here have willingly chosen this abstemious life* SELF-DENYING, temperate, abstinent, moderate, self-disciplined, restrained, self-restrained, sober, austere, ascetic, puritanical, spartan, hair-shirt. ANTONYM self-indulgent.

abstinence noun 1 *AA endorses a path of abstinence* TEETOTALISM, temperance, sobriety, abstemiousness, abstention; *rare* nephalism.

2 *of course abstinence is the most effective form of birth control, but is it the most realistic?* CELIBACY, chastity, virginity, self-restraint, self-denial. ANTONYM promiscuity.

3 *three days of* ***abstinence from*** *solid food* REFRAINING FROM, desisting from, holding back from, withholding; RENUNCIATION OF, refusal of, declining, avoidance of, eschewal of, abjuration of; forgoing, shunning, going without, doing without. ANTONYM indulgence.

THE RIGHT WORD

Abstinence implies voluntary self-denial and is usually associated with the non-indulgence of an appetite (*total abstinence from cigarettes and alcohol*). **Abstemiousness** is the quality or habit of being abstinent; an abstemious person would be one who is moderate when it comes to eating and drinking. **Continence**, **temperance**, and **moderation** all imply various forms of self-restraint or self-denial: *moderation* is the avoidance of extremes or excesses (*he drank in moderation*); *temperance* is habitual moderation, or even total abstinence, particularly with regard to alcohol (*the nineteenth-century temperance movement*); and *continence* (in this regard) refers to self-restraint with regard to sexual activity. **Forbearance** is self-control, the patient endurance that characterizes deliberately holding back from action or response. **Abnegation** is the rejection or renunciation of something that is generally held in high esteem (*abnegation of the Christian Church*), although it can also mean to refuse or deny oneself a particular right, claim, or convenience (*abnegation of worldly goods*).

abstract adjective 1 *abstract concepts* THEORETICAL, conceptual, notional, intellectual, metaphysical, ideal, philosophical, academic; *rare* ideational. ANTONYMS actual, concrete.

2 *abstract art* NONREPRESENTATIONAL, nonpictorial. ANTONYM representational.

▸ verb 1 *we'll be abstracting material for an online database* SUMMARIZE, précis, abridge, condense, compress, shorten, cut down, abbreviate, synopsize; *rare* epitomize.

2 *he abstracted the art of tragedy from its context* EXTRACT, isolate, separate, detach.

▸ noun *an abstract of her speech* SUMMARY, synopsis, précis, résumé, outline, abridgment, digest, summation; wrap-up.

abstracted adjective *I apologize for being so abstracted when you were talking* ABSENTMINDED, distracted, preoccupied, in a world of one's own, with one's head in the clouds, daydreaming, dreamy, inattentive, thoughtful, pensive, lost in thought, deep in thought, immersed in thought, in a brown study, musing, brooding, absent, oblivious, moony, distrait; *informal* miles away, out to lunch. ANTONYM attentive.

abstraction noun 1 *philosophical abstractions* CONCEPT, idea, notion, thought, theory, hypothesis.

2 *she sensed his momentary abstraction* ABSENTMINDEDNESS, distraction, preoccupation, dreaminess, inattentiveness, inattention, woolgathering; thoughtfulness, pensiveness.

3 *the abstraction of metal from ore* EXTRACTION, removal, separation.

abstruse adjective *her abstruse arguments were hard to follow* OBSCURE, arcane, esoteric, little known, recherché, rarefied, recondite, difficult, hard, puzzling, perplexing, cryptic, enigmatic, Delphic, complex, complicated, involved, over/above one's head, incomprehensible, unfathomable, impenetrable, mysterious. See note at OBSCURE.

absurd adjective *what an absurd idea!* PREPOSTEROUS, ridiculous, ludicrous, farcical, laughable, risible, idiotic, stupid, foolish, silly, inane, imbecilic, insane, harebrained, cockamamie; unreasonable, irrational, illogical, nonsensical, incongruous, pointless, senseless; *informal* crazy, daft. ANTONYMS reasonable, sensible.

THE RIGHT WORD

We call something **absurd** when it is utterly inconsistent with what common sense or experience tells us (*she found herself in the absurd position of having to defend the intelligence of a cockroach*). **Ludicrous** applies to whatever is so incongruous that it provokes laughter or scorn (*a ludicrous suggestion that he might escape unnoticed if he dressed up as a woman*), and **ridiculous** implies that ridicule or mockery is the only appropriate response (*she tried to look younger, but succeeded only in making herself look ridiculous*). **Foolish** behavior shows a lack of intelligence or good judgment (*it was foolish to keep that much money under a mattress*), while **unreasonable** behavior implies that the person has intentionally acted contrary to good sense (*his response was totally unreasonable in view of the fact that he'd asked for their honest opinion*). **Preposterous** should be reserved for those acts or situations that are glaringly absurd or ludicrous. For example, it might be *unreasonable* to judge an entire nation on the basis of one tourist's experience and *foolish* to turn down an opportunity to visit that country on those grounds alone, but it would be *preposterous* to suggest that everyone who comes to the United States will be robbed at gunpoint.

absurdity noun *Milosevic spurned the evidence linking him to countless atrocities, calling the charges a supreme absurdity* PREPOSTEROUSNESS, ridiculousness, ludicrousness, incongruity, inappropriateness, risibility, idiocy, stupidity, foolishness, folly, silliness, inanity, insanity; unreasonableness, irrationality, illogicality, pointlessness, senselessness; *informal* craziness.

abundance noun *the abundance of donated funds was completely unexpected* PROFUSION, plentifulness, profuseness, copiousness, amplitude, lavishness, bountifulness, bounty; host, cornucopia, riot; plenty, quantities, scores, multitude; *informal* millions, sea, ocean(s), wealth, lot(s), heap(s), mass(es), stack(s), pile(s), load(s), bags, mountain(s), ton(s), slew, scads, oodles, gobs; *formal* plenitude. ANTONYMS lack, scarcity.

abundant adjective *an abundant supply of food* PLENTIFUL, copious, ample, profuse, rich, lavish, abounding, liberal, generous, bountiful, large, huge, great, bumper, overflowing, prolific, teeming; in plenty, in abundance; *informal* galore; *literary* plenteous, bounteous. See note at PREVALENT. ANTONYMS scarce, sparse.

abuse verb **1** *the judge abused his power* MISUSE, misapply, misemploy; exploit, take advantage of.

2 *he was accused of abusing children* MISTREAT, maltreat, ill-treat, treat badly; molest, interfere with, indecently assault, sexually abuse, sexually assault; injure, hurt, harm, damage. ANTONYMS look after, nurture.

3 *the referee was abused by players from both teams* INSULT, be rude to, swear at, curse, call someone names, taunt, badmouth, dis, shout at, revile, inveigh against, bawl out, vilify, slander, cast aspersions on. ANTONYMS compliment, flatter.

▸ noun **1** *the abuse of power* MISUSE, misapplication, misemployment; exploitation.

2 *the abuse of children* MISTREATMENT, maltreatment, ill-treatment; molestation, interference, indecent assault, sexual abuse, sexual assault; injury, hurt, harm, damage. ANTONYMS care, nurturing.

3 *the scheme is open to administrative abuse* CORRUPTION, injustice, wrongdoing, wrong, misconduct, misdeed(s), offense(s), crime(s), sin(s).

4 *torrents of abuse* INSULTS, curses, jibes, expletives, swear words; swearing, cursing, name-calling; invective, vilification, vituperation, slander; *informal* trash talk; *archaic* contumely. ANTONYMS compliments, flattery.

5 *alcohol abuse* ADDICTION, dependency, overuse, misuse, problems.

abusive adjective *such abusive language will not be tolerated in this workplace* INSULTING, rude, vulgar, offensive, disparaging, belittling, derogatory, opprobrious, disrespectful, denigratory, uncomplimentary, censorious, pejorative, vituperative; defamatory, slanderous, libelous, scurrilous, blasphemous; *informal* bitchy; *archaic* contumelious.

abut verb *two rows of forsythia abut one another where the driveway meets the sidewalk* ADJOIN, be adjacent to, butt against, border, neighbor, join, touch, meet, reach, be contiguous with.

abysmal adjective *informal some of the teaching was abysmal* VERY BAD, dreadful, awful, terrible, frightful, atrocious, disgraceful, deplorable, shameful, hopeless, lamentable; *informal* rotten, appalling, crummy, pathetic, pitiful, woeful, useless, lousy, dire, the pits.

abyss noun *a recurring nightmare in which he falls into an abyss* CHASM, gorge, ravine, canyon, fissure, rift, crevasse, hole, gulf, pit, cavity, void, bottomless pit.

academic adjective **1** *an academic institution* EDUCATIONAL, scholastic, instructional, pedagogical.

2 *his academic turn of mind* SCHOLARLY, studious, literary, well-read, intellectual, clever, erudite, learned, educated, cultured, bookish, highbrow, pedantic, donnish, cerebral; *informal* brainy, inkhorn; *dated* lettered.

3 *the debate has been largely academic* THEORETICAL, conceptual, notional, philosophical, hypothetical, speculative, conjectural, suppositional; impractical, unrealistic, ivory-tower.

▸ noun *a group of Russian academics* SCHOLAR, lecturer, teacher, tutor, professor, fellow, man/woman of letters, don, bluestocking; *informal* egghead, bookworm; *formal* pedagogue.

academy noun **1** *studied at the academy for two years* EDUCATIONAL INSTITUTION, school, college, university, institute, seminary, conservatory, conservatoire.

2 *ideas pooh-poohed by the academy* ACADEMIA, academe, the academic world.

accede verb *formal* **1** *he **acceded to** the government's demands* AGREE TO, consent to, accept, assent to, acquiesce in, comply with, go along with, concur with, surrender to, yield to, give in to, give way to, defer to.

2 *Elizabeth I **acceded to** the throne in 1558* SUCCEED TO, come to, assume, inherit, take.

3 *Albania **acceded to** the IMF in 1990* JOIN, become a member of, sign on to, sign up for.

accelerate verb **1** *the car accelerated down the hill* SPEED UP, go faster, gain momentum, increase speed, pick up speed, gather speed, put on a spurt. ANTONYMS decelerate, slow down.

2 *inflation started to accelerate* INCREASE, rise, go up, leap up, surge, escalate, spiral. ANTONYMS slow down, drop.

3 *the university accelerated the planning process* HASTEN, expedite, precipitate, speed up, quicken, make faster, step up, advance, further, forward, promote, give a boost to, stimulate, spur on; *informal* crank up, fast-track. ANTONYMS slow down, delay.

acceleration noun **1** *the acceleration of the industrial process* HASTENING, precipitation, speeding up, quickening, stepping up, advancement, furtherance, boost, stimulation, spur.

2 *an acceleration in the divorce rate* INCREASE, rise, leap, surge, escalation.

accent noun **1** *a Bronx accent* PRONUNCIATION, intonation, enunciation, articulation, inflection, tone, modulation, cadence, timbre, manner of speaking, delivery; brogue, burr, drawl, twang.

2 *the accent is on the first syllable* STRESS, emphasis, accentuation, force, prominence; beat; *technical* ictus.

3 *the accent is on comfort* EMPHASIS, stress, priority; importance, prominence.

4 *an acute accent* MARK, diacritic, diacritical mark. See table.

▸ verb *fabrics that accent the background colors in the room* FOCUS ATTENTION ON, draw attention to, point up, underline, underscore, accentuate, highlight, spotlight, foreground, feature, play up, bring to the fore, heighten, stress, emphasize.

ACCENTS AND DIACRITICAL MARKS

acute (´)
breve (˘)
cedilla (¸)
circumflex (^)
dieresis (¨)
grave (`)
macron (¯)
ogonek (˛)
tilde (˜)

accentuate verb *a haircut that accentuates your cheekbones* FOCUS ATTENTION ON, draw attention to, point up, underline, underscore, accent, highlight, spotlight, foreground, feature, play up, bring to the fore, heighten, stress, emphasize.

accept verb **1** *she accepted a pen as a present* RECEIVE, take, get, gain, obtain, acquire. ANTONYMS refuse, reject.

2 *he accepted the job immediately* TAKE ON, undertake, assume, take responsibility for. ANTONYMS turn down, refuse.

3 *she accepted an invitation to lunch* SAY YES TO, agree to. ANTONYMS turn down, refuse.

4 *she was accepted as one of the family* WELCOME, greet, receive, receive favorably, embrace, adopt. ANTONYM reject.

5 *he accepted Ellen's explanation* BELIEVE, regard as true, give credence to, credit, trust; *informal* buy, swallow. ANTONYMS reject, doubt.

6 *we have agreed to accept his decision* GO ALONG WITH, agree to, consent to, acquiesce in, concur with, assent to, acknowledge, comply with, abide by, follow, adhere to, act in accordance with, defer to, yield to, surrender to, bow to, give in to, submit to, respect; *formal* accede to. ANTONYMS defy, go against.

7 *she will just have to accept the consequences* TOLERATE, endure, put up with, bear, take, submit to, stomach, swallow; reconcile oneself to, resign oneself to, get used to, adjust to, learn to live with, make the best of; face up to.

acceptable adjective **1** *an acceptable standard of living* SATISFACTORY, adequate, reasonable, quite good, fair, decent, good enough, sufficient, sufficiently good, fine, not bad, all right, average, tolerable, passable, middling, moderate; *informal* OK, jake, so-so, 'comme ci, comme ça', fair-to-middling.

2 *the risk had seemed acceptable at the time* BEARABLE, tolerable, allowable, admissible, sustainable, justifiable, defensible.

acceptance noun **1** *the acceptance of an award* RECEIPT, receiving, taking, obtaining.

2 *the acceptance of responsibility* UNDERTAKING, assumption.

3 *acceptances to an invitation* YES, affirmative reply, confirmation.

4 *her acceptance into the group* WELCOME, favorable reception, adoption.

5 *his* ***acceptance of*** *Thom's promise* BELIEF IN, trust in, faith in, confidence in, credence in, giving of credence to.

6 *their* ***acceptance of*** *the ruling* COMPLIANCE WITH, acquiescence in, agreement with, consent to, concurrence with, assent to, acknowledgment of, adherence to, deference to, surrender to, submission to, respect for, adoption of, buy-in to.

7 *the acceptance of pain* TOLERATION, endurance, forbearance, sufferance.

accepted adjective *newspaper ads from the 1700s show that, even in New England, the brokering of slaves was an accepted practice* RECOGNIZED, acknowledged, established, traditional, orthodox, sanctioned; usual, customary, habitual, common, current, normal, general, prevailing, accustomed, familiar, wonted, popular, expected, routine, standard, stock.

access noun **1** *the building has a side access* ENTRANCE, entry, way in, means of entry; approach, means of approach.

2 *they were denied access to the stadium* ADMISSION, admittance, entry, entrée, ingress, right of entry.

3 *students have* ***access to*** *a photocopier* (THE) USE OF, permission to use/visit.

▸ verb **1** *the program is used to access data* RETRIEVE, gain access to, obtain; read.

2 *you access the building from the south side* ENTER, approach, gain entry to.

USAGE NOTE **access**

Although the verb **access** is standard and common in computing and related terminology, the word is primarily a noun. Outside computing contexts, its use as a verb in the sense of 'approach or enter a place' is often regarded as nonstandard (*You must use a password to access the account*). Even weaker is its use in an abstract sense (*access the American dream*). It is usually clear enough to say 'enter' or 'gain access to.'

accessible adjective **1** *the village is accessible only on foot* | *an easily accessible reference tool* REACHABLE, attainable, approachable; obtainable, available; *informal* get-at-able.

2 *his accessible style of writing* UNDERSTANDABLE, comprehensible, easy to understand, intelligible; *formal* exoteric.

3 *Professor Cooper is very accessible* APPROACHABLE, friendly, agreeable, obliging, congenial, affable, cordial, welcoming, easygoing, pleasant.

accession noun **1** *the Queen's* ***accession to*** *the throne* SUCCESSION TO, assumption of, inheritance of.

2 *accession to the Treaty of Rome was effected in 1971* ASSENT TO, consent to, agreement to; acceptance of, acquiescence in, compliance with, concurrence with.

3 *recent museum accessions* ADDITION, acquisition, new item, gift, purchase.

accessorize verb *accessorize a simple dress with a colorful sash* | *more and more fashion mavens are accessorizing with designer eyewear* COMPLEMENT, enhance, set off, show off; go with, accompany; decorate, adorn, ornament, trim.

accessory noun **1** *camera accessories such as tripods* ATTACHMENT, extra, addition, add-on, adjunct, appendage, appurtenance, fitment, supplement.

2 *fashion accessories* ADORNMENT, embellishment, ornament, ornamentation, decoration; frills, trimmings.

3 *two days after the murder, she was charged as an accessory* ACCOMPLICE, partner in crime, associate, collaborator, abettor, fellow conspirator, co-conspirator; henchman.

▸ adjective *an accessory gearbox* ADDITIONAL, extra, supplementary, supplemental, auxiliary, ancillary, secondary, subsidiary, reserve, add-on.

accident noun **1** *an accident at work* MISHAP, misadventure, unfortunate incident, mischance, misfortune, disaster, tragedy, catastrophe, calamity; *technical* casualty.

2 *she was injured in a highway accident* CRASH, collision, smash, bump, car crash; wreck; *informal* smash-up, pileup, fender bender.

3 *it is no accident that there is a similarity between them*

(MERE) CHANCE, coincidence, twist of fate, freak; fluke, bit of luck, serendipity; fate, fortuity, fortune, providence, happenstance.

accidental adjective **1** *an accidental meeting* FORTUITOUS, chance, adventitious, fluky, coincidental, casual, serendipitous, random; unexpected, unforeseen, unanticipated, unlooked-for, unintentional, unintended, inadvertent, unplanned, unpremeditated, unthinking, unwitting. ANTONYM intentional.

2 *the location is accidental and contributes nothing to the poem* INCIDENTAL, unimportant, by the way, by the by, supplementary, subsidiary, subordinate, secondary, accessory, peripheral, tangential, extraneous, extrinsic, irrelevant, nonessential, inessential. ANTONYM deliberate.

THE RIGHT WORD

Things don't always go as planned, but there are many ways to describe the role that chance plays. **Accidental** applies to events that occur entirely by chance (*an accidental encounter with the candidate outside the men's room*); but it is so strongly influenced by the noun "accident" that it carries connotations of undesirable or possibly disastrous results (*an accidental miscalculation of the distance he had to jump*). A **casual** act or event is one that is random or unpremeditated (*a casual conversation with her son's teacher in the grocery store*), in which the role that chance plays is not always clear. Something that is **incidental** may or may not involve chance; it typically refers to what is secondary or nonessential (*incidental expenses in the budget*) or what occurs without design or regularity (*incidental lighting throughout the garden*). **Adventitious** also implies the lack of an essential relationship, referring to something that is a mere random occurrence (*adventitious circumstances that led to victory*). In contrast, **contingent** points to something that is entirely dependent on an uncertain event for its existence or occurrence (*travel plans that are contingent upon the weather*). **Fortuitous** refers to chance events of a fortunate nature; it is about as far as one can get from *accidental* (*a fortuitous meeting with the candidate outside the men's room just before the press conference*).

accident-prone adjective *the machine shop is no place for accident-prone employees* CLUMSY, bumbling, butterfingered, like a bull in a china shop, all thumbs.

acclaim verb *the booklet has been widely acclaimed by teachers* PRAISE, applaud, cheer, commend, approve, welcome, pay tribute to, speak highly of, eulogize, compliment, celebrate, sing the praises of, rave about, heap praise on/upon, wax lyrical about, lionize, exalt, admire, hail, extol, honor, hymn; *informal* ballyhoo; *formal* laud. See note at PRAISE. ANTONYM criticize.

▸ noun *she has won acclaim for her commitment to democracy* PRAISE, applause, cheers, ovation, tribute, accolade, acclamation, salutes, plaudits, bouquets; approval, approbation, admiration, congratulations, commendation, kudos, welcome, homage; compliment, a pat on the back. ANTONYM criticism.

acclaimed adjective *the most acclaimed film director of his time* CELEBRATED, admired, highly rated, lionized, honored, esteemed, exalted, well-thought-of, well received, acknowledged; eminent, great, renowned, distinguished, prestigious, illustrious, preeminent.

acclamation noun *the proposal was received with considerable acclamation* PRAISE, applause, cheers, ovation, tribute, accolade, acclaim, salutes, plaudits, bouquets; approval, admiration, approbation, congratulations, commendation, homage; compliment, a pat on the back. ANTONYM criticism.

PHRASE: **by acclamation** *she won reelection by acclamation* BY ORAL VOTE, by a verbal vote, without a ballot, by nonballot; *Canadian* without opposition, as the only candidate.

acclimatize verb *the panda Ling Ling will acclimatize to the environment in Mexico before choosing a mate* ADJUST, acclimate, adapt, accustom, accommodate, habituate, acculturate, assimilate, attune; get used, become inured, reconcile oneself, resign oneself; familiarize oneself; get one's bearings, become seasoned, become naturalized.

accolade noun **1** *he received the accolade of knighthood* HONOR, privilege, award, gift, title; prize, laurels, bays, palm(s).

2 *the hotel won a top accolade from the inspectors* TRIBUTE, commendation, praise, testimonial, compliment, pat on the back; salute(s), plaudits, congratulations, bouquets, kudos; *informal* raves.

accommodate verb **1** *refugees were accommodated in army camps* LODGE, house, put up, billet, quarter, board, take in, shelter, give someone a roof over their head; harbor.

2 *each cottage accommodates up to six people* HOLD, take, have room for.

3 *our staff will make every effort to accommodate you* HELP, assist, aid, oblige; meet the needs/wants of, satisfy.

4 *she tried to* ***accommodate herself to*** *her new situation* ADJUST TO, adapt to, accustom oneself to, habituate oneself to, acclimatize (oneself) to, acclimate (oneself) to, acculturate to, get (oneself) accustomed to, get used to, come to terms with.

5 *the bank would be glad to accommodate you with a loan* PROVIDE, supply, furnish, grant.

accommodating adjective *her in-laws were far more accomodating than her own parents* OBLIGING, cooperative, helpful, eager to help, adaptable, amenable, considerate, unselfish, inclusionary, generous, willing, compliant, kindly, hospitable, neighborly, kind, friendly, pleasant, agreeable.

accommodation noun **1** (**accommodations**) *temporary accommodationss* HOUSING, lodging(s), living quarters, quarters, rooms; place to stay, billet; shelter, roof over one's head; *informal* digs, pad; *formal* abode, residence, place of residence, dwelling, dwelling place, habitation.

2 *lifeboat accommodations for 1,178 people* SPACE, room, seating; places.

3 *an accommodation between the two parties was reached* ARRANGEMENT, understanding, settlement, accord, deal, bargain, compromise.

4 *their accommodations to changing economic circumstances* ADJUSTMENT, adaptation, habituation, acclimatization, acclimation, acculturation; inurement.

accompaniment noun **1** *a musical accompaniment* BACKING, support, background, backup, soundtrack.

2 *the wine makes a superb accompaniment to cheese* COMPLEMENT, supplement, addition, adjunct, appendage, companion, accessory.

accompany verb **1** *I accompanied my brother to the audition* GO WITH, travel with, keep someone company, tag along with, hang out with; partner, escort, chaperone, attend, show, see, usher, conduct.

2 *the illness* ***is*** *often* ***accompanied by*** *nausea* OCCUR WITH, co-occur with, coexist with, go with, go together with, go hand in hand with, appear with, be attended by.

3 *he accompanied the choir on the piano* BACK, play with, play for, support.

accomplice noun *police have reason to believe that Johnson had two accomplices, possibly his wife and brother* PARTNER IN CRIME, associate, accessory, abettor, confederate, collaborator, fellow conspirator, co-conspirator; henchman; *informal* sidekick.

accomplish verb *the planes accomplished their mission* FULFILL, achieve, succeed in, realize, attain, manage, bring about/off, carry out/through, execute, effect, perform, do, discharge, complete, finish, consummate, conclude; *informal* pull off, nail; *formal* effectuate.

accomplished adjective *an accomplished bassoonist* EXPERT, skilled, skillful, masterly, successful, virtuoso, master, consummate, complete, proficient, talented, gifted, adept, adroit, deft, dexterous, able, good, competent, capable, efficient, experienced, seasoned, trained, practiced, professional, polished, ready, apt; *informal* great, mean, nifty, crack, ace, wizard; *informal* crackerjack.

accomplishment noun 1 *the reduction of inflation was a remarkable accomplishment* ACHIEVEMENT, act, deed, exploit, performance, attainment, effort, feat, move, coup.

2 *a poet of considerable accomplishment* EXPERTISE, skill, skillfulness, talent, adeptness, adroitness, deftness, dexterity, ability, prowess, mastery, competence, capability, proficiency, aptitude, artistry, art; *informal* know-how.

accord verb 1 *the national assembly accorded him more power* GIVE, grant, present, award, vouchsafe; confer on, bestow on, vest in, invest with. ANTONYM withhold.

2 *his views* ***accorded with*** *mine* CORRESPOND TO, agree with, match up with, concur with, be consistent with, harmonize with, be in harmony with, be compatible with, chime in with, be in tune with, correlate with, dovetail with; conform to; suit, fit, parallel, match; *informal* square with, jibe with. ANTONYMS disagree, contrast.

▸ noun 1 *a peace accord* PACT, treaty, agreement, settlement, deal, entente, concordat, protocol, contract, convention.

2 *the two sides failed to reach accord* AGREEMENT, consensus, unanimity, harmony, unison, unity; *formal* concord.

PHRASES: **of one's own accord** *Nels offered to fix the gate of his own accord* VOLUNTARILY, of one's own free will, of one's own volition, by choice; willingly, freely, readily. **with one accord** *the committee decided with one accord to approve the drainage plans* UNANIMOUSLY, in complete agreement, with one mind, without exception, as one, of one voice, to a man.

accordance noun *a ballot held* ***in accordance with*** *union rules* IN AGREEMENT WITH, in conformity with, in line with, true to, in the spirit of, observing, following, heeding.

according adjective 1 *she had a narrow escape,* ***according to*** *the doctors* AS STATED BY, as claimed by, on the authority of, in the opinion of.

2 *cook the rice* ***according to*** *the instructions* AS SPECIFIED BY, as per, in accordance with, in compliance with, in agreement with.

3 *salary will be fixed* ***according to*** *experience* IN PROPORTION TO, proportional to, commensurate with, in relation to, relative to, in line with, corresponding to.

accordingly adverb 1 *they appreciated the danger and acted accordingly* APPROPRIATELY, correspondingly, suitably.

2 *accordingly, he returned home to Kingston* THEREFORE, for that reason, consequently, so, as a result, as a consequence, in consequence, hence, thus, that being the case, ergo.

accordion noun *the auction purported to have one of Lawrence Welk's accordions* SQUEEZEBOX, concertina, melodeon.

accost verb *police accosted him in the street* CONFRONT, call to, shout to, hail, address, speak to; approach, detain, stop, waylay; *informal* buttonhole, collar, bend someone's ear.

account noun 1 *an account of the extraordinary events* DESCRIPTION, report, version, story, narration, narrative, statement, explanation, exposition, delineation, portrayal, tale; chronicle, history, record, log; view, impression.

2 *the firm's quarterly accounts* FINANCIAL RECORD, ledger, balance sheet, financial statement; (**accounts**) books.

3 *I pay the account off in full each month* BILL, invoice, tally; debt, charges; *informal* tab.

4 *his background is of no account* IMPORTANCE, import, significance, consequence, substance, note; *formal* moment.

5 *efforts to keep our most important accounts happy* CLIENT, customer.

▸ verb *her visit could not be accounted a success* CONSIDER, regard as, reckon, hold to be, think, look on as, view as, see as, judge, adjudge, count, deem, rate.

PHRASES: **account for** 1 *they must account for the delay* EXPLAIN, answer for, give reasons for, rationalize, justify. 2 *taxes account for much of the price of gasoline* CONSTITUTE, make up, form, compose, represent. **on account of** *I was invited on account of my friendship with her parents* BECAUSE OF, owing to, due to, as a consequence of, thanks to, by/in virtue of, in view of. **on no account** *on no account sign a document without reading it* NEVER, under no circumstances, not for any reason.

accountability noun *there must be accountability for the expenditure of every public cent* RESPONSIBILITY, liability, answerability.

accountable adjective 1 *the government was held accountable for the food shortage* RESPONSIBLE, liable, answerable; to blame. See note at RESPONSIBLE.

2 *the game's popularity is barely accountable* EXPLICABLE, explainable; understandable, comprehensible.

accountant noun *a good accountant is up on all the new tax laws* BOOKKEEPER, CPA, certified public accountant, comptroller; *informal* bean counter.

accoutrements plural noun *the new system will provide East Timor with all the communications accoutrements of a more developed economy* EQUIPMENT, paraphernalia, stuff, things, apparatus, tackle, implements, material(s), rig, outfit, regalia, appurtenances, impedimenta, odds and ends, bits and pieces, trappings, accessories.

accredited adjective *an accredited preschool* OFFICIAL, appointed, recognized, authorized, approved, certified, licensed.

accretion noun **1** *the accretion of sediments* ACCUMULATION, formation, collecting, cumulation, buildup, accrual; growth, increase.

2 *architectural accretions* ADDITION, extension, appendage, add-on, supplement.

accrue verb **1** *financial benefits will* ***accrue from*** *restructuring* RESULT FROM, arise from, follow from, ensue from; be caused by, attend.

2 *interest is added to the account as it accrues* ACCUMULATE, collect, build up, mount up, grow, increase.

accumulate verb *he has accumulated thousands of frequent-flier miles | mother whales transfer chemicals accumulated in their tissue to their offspring during gestation* GATHER, collect, assemble; amass, stockpile, pile up, heap up, store (up), hoard, cumulate, lay in/up; increase, mass, multiply, accrue, snowball; run up; *informal* stash (away). ANTONYM dissipate

accumulation noun *the accumulation of illegal funds | an accumulation of debris* BUILDUP, mass, pile, heap, stack, collection, stock, store, stockpile, reserve, hoard; amassing, gathering, cumulation, accrual, accretion.

accuracy noun *the accuracy of their lead story is being questioned* CORRECTNESS, precision, preciseness, exactness, exactitude; factuality, literalness, fidelity, faithfulness, truth, truthfulness, veracity, closeness, authenticity, realism, verisimilitude.

accurate adjective **1** *accurate information | an accurate representation of the situation* CORRECT, precise, exact, right, error-free, perfect; FACTUAL, fact-based, literal, faithful, true, truthful, true to life, authentic, realistic; *informal* on the mark, bang on, on the money, on the button; *formal* veracious.

2 *an accurate shot* WELL-AIMED, on target, unerring, deadly, lethal, sure, true, on the mark.

accursed adjective *dated* **1** *that accursed woman* HATEFUL, detestable, loathsome, foul, abominable, damnable, odious, obnoxious, despicable, horrible, horrid, ghastly, awful, dreadful, terrible; annoying, irritating, vile, infuriating, exasperating; *informal* damned, damn, blasted, pesky, pestilential, infernal, beastly. ANTONYM pleasant.

2 *literary he and his line are accursed* CURSED, damned, doomed, condemned, ill-fated, ill-omened, jinxed. ANTONYM blessed.

accusation noun *the Rwandan bishop has denied accusations of genocide* ALLEGATION, charge, claim, assertion, imputation; indictment, arraignment, incrimination, recrimination, inculpation; suit, lawsuit, impeachment; *informal* rap.

accuse verb **1** *four people were* ***accused of*** *assault* CHARGE WITH, indict for, arraign for; summons for, cite for, prefer charges against for; impeach for. ANTONYMS absolve, exonerate.

2 *the companies were* ***accused of*** *causing job losses* BLAME FOR, lay/pin the blame on for, hold responsible for, inculpate for, hold accountable for; condemn for, criticize for, denounce for; *informal* point the finger at for. ANTONYMS defend, hold blameless.

accustom verb *she couldn't* ***accustom herself to*** *city life* ADAPT TO, adjust to, acclimatize to, acclimate to, habituate oneself to, accommodate oneself to, acculturate to; reconcile oneself to, become reconciled to, get used to, come to terms with, learn to live with, become inured to.

accustomed adjective **1** *his accustomed lifestyle* CUSTOMARY, usual, normal, habitual, regular, routine, ordinary, typical, traditional, established, common, general; *literary* wonted.

2 *she's* ***accustomed to*** *hard work* USED TO, habituated to, acclimatized to, no stranger to, familiar with, acquainted with, in the habit of, experienced in. ANTONYM unfamiliar.

ace *informal* noun *a snowboarding ace* EXPERT, master, genius, virtuoso, maestro, adept, past master, doyen, champion, star; *informal* demon, hotshot, wizard, pro, whiz; *informal* maven, crackerjack. ANTONYMS amateur, beginner.

▸ adjective *an ace tennis player* EXCELLENT, first-rate, first-class, marvelous, wonderful, magnificent, outstanding, superlative, formidable, virtuoso, masterly, expert, champion, consummate, skillful, adept; great, terrific, tremendous, superb, fantastic, sensational, fabulous; *informal* fab, crack, hotshot, A1, mean, demon, awesome, magic, tiptop, top-notch; killer, blue-ribbon, blue-chip, brilliant, wicked. ANTONYM mediocre.

acerbic adjective *soaring melodies built around acerbic lyrics* SHARP, sarcastic, sardonic, mordant, trenchant, cutting, razor-edged, biting, piercing, stinging, searing, scathing, caustic, bitter, acrimonious, astringent, abrasive, harsh, wounding, hurtful, unkind, cruel, virulent, vitriolic, venomous, malicious, vicious; *informal* bitchy; *rare* acidulous, mordacious. ANTONYMS mild, kind.

ache noun **1** *a stomachache* PAIN, cramp, twinge, pang; gnawing, stabbing, stinging, smarting; soreness, tenderness, irritation, discomfort.

2 *the ache in her heart* SORROW, sadness, misery, grief, anguish, suffering, pain, agony, torture, hurt.

▸ verb **1** *my legs were aching* HURT, be sore, be painful, be in pain, pain, throb, pound, twinge; smart, burn.

2 *her heart ached for poor Philippa* GRIEVE, sorrow, be in distress, be miserable, be in anguish, bleed.

3 ***I ached for*** *her affection* LONG FOR, yearn for, hunger for, thirst for, hanker for, pine for, itch for; crave, desire, covet.

WORD NOTE **achingly**

Is a sunset *achingly* beautiful? Can a movie be *achingly* funny? Who's doing the aching here? Not the sunset or the beauty or the movie or its wit. An adverb modifies an adjective or a verb. Someone who says *The sunset was achingly beautiful* means "It was so beautiful it made my heart ache." He can't, without being pathetically fallacious, ascribe his own ache to the quality of the beauty. However, his belly might be achingly full after Thanksgiving dinner, because *achingly* modifies the adjective *full,* and he ought to know. **—JS**

achieve verb *the legal resources are inadequate to achieve our public health objectives* ATTAIN, reach, arrive at; realize, bring off/about, pull off, accomplish, carry off/out/through, fulfill, execute, perform, engineer, conclude, complete, finish, consummate; earn, win, gain, acquire, obtain, score, come by, get, secure, clinch, net; *informal* wrap up, wangle, swing; *formal* effectuate.

achievement noun 1 *the achievement of a high rate of economic growth* ATTAINMENT, realization, accomplishment, fulfillment, implementation, execution, performance; conclusion, completion, close, consummation.

2 *they felt justifiably proud of their achievement* ACCOMPLISHMENT, attainment, feat, performance, undertaking, act, action, deed, effort, exploit, success, triumph; work, handiwork.

Achilles heel noun *the report predicted an impact near Columbia's left main landing gear—a well-known Achilles heel for shuttles* WEAK SPOT, weak point, weak link, weakness, soft underbelly, shortcoming, failing, imperfection, flaw, defect, chink in one's armor; nemesis. ANTONYM strength.

acid adjective 1 *a slightly acid flavor* ACIDIC, SOUR, tart, bitter, sharp, acrid, pungent, acerbic, vinegary, acetic, acetous. ANTONYM sweet.

2 *acid remarks* ACERBIC, sarcastic, sharp, sardonic, scathing, cutting, razor-edged, biting, stinging, caustic, trenchant, mordant, bitter, acrimonious, astringent, harsh, abrasive, wounding, hurtful, unkind, vitriolic, venomous, waspish, spiteful, malicious; *informal* bitchy, catty; snarky. ANTONYM pleasant.

acknowledge verb 1 *the government acknowledged the need to begin talks* ADMIT, accept, grant, allow, concede, accede to, confess, own, recognize. ANTONYMS reject, deny.

2 *he did not acknowledge Colin, but hurried past* GREET, salute, address; nod to, wave to, raise one's hat to, say hello to. ANTONYM ignore.

3 *Douglas was glad to acknowledge her help* EXPRESS GRATITUDE FOR, show appreciation for, thank someone for.

4 *nobody acknowledged my letters* ANSWER, reply to, respond to. ANTONYM overlook.

acknowledged adjective *the acknowledged leader of the Turkish community* RECOGNIZED, accepted, approved, accredited, confirmed, declared, confessed, avowed.

acknowledgment noun 1 *acknowledgment of the need to take new initiatives* ACCEPTANCE, recognition, admission, concession, confession.

2 *a smile of acknowledgment* GREETING, welcome, salutation.

3 *she left without a word of acknowledgment* THANKS, gratitude, appreciation, recognition.

4 *I sent off the form, but there was no acknowledgment* ANSWER, reply, response.

acme noun *the acme of her career* PEAK, pinnacle, zenith, height, high point, crown, crest, summit, top, apex, apogee; climax, culmination. ANTONYM nadir.

acolyte noun *surrounded by eager acolytes* ASSISTANT, helper, attendant, aide, minion, underling, lackey, henchman; follower, disciple, supporter, votary; *informal* sidekick, groupie, hanger-on.

acquaint verb *this exercise will **acquaint** you **with** the food groups* FAMILIARIZE WITH, make familiar with, make aware of, inform of, advise of, apprise of, let know, get up to date on; brief on, prime on; *informal* fill in on, clue in on.

acquaintance noun 1 *a business acquaintance | friends and acquaintances* CONTACT, associate, ally, connection, colleague.

2 *my acquaintance with George* ASSOCIATION, relationship, contact; fellowship, companionship.

3 *the students had little **acquaintance with** the language* FAMILIARITY WITH, knowledge of, experience with/of, awareness of, understanding of, comprehension of, grasp of.

acquiesce verb *Bush wants to ensure that Beijing will **acquiesce in** a possible American war against Iraq* ACCEPT, consent to, agree to, allow, concede, assent to, concur with, give the nod to; comply with, cooperate with, give in to, bow to, yield to, submit to; *informal* go along with.

acquiescence noun *militia excesses were conducted with the acquiescence of the Indonesian police* CONSENT, agreement, acceptance, concurrence, assent, leave; compliance, concession, cooperation, buy-in; submission.

acquiescent adjective *the apolitical and acquiescent masses* COMPLIANT, complying, consenting, cooperative, willing, obliging, agreeable, amenable, tractable, persuadable, pliant, flexible, unprotesting; SUBMISSIVE, servile, subservient, obsequious, self-effacing, unassertive, yielding, biddable, docile, deferential; *rare* obeisant, longanimous.

acquire verb *the library's goal is to acquire eight new or upgraded computers in this fiscal year* OBTAIN, come by, get, receive, gain, earn, win, come into, be given; buy, purchase, procure, possess oneself of, secure, pick up, adopt; *informal* get one's hands on, get hold of, land, bag, cop, score. See note at GET. ANTONYMS lose, get rid of.

acquisition noun 1 *the boat is a new acquisition* PURCHASE, buy, gain, accession, addition, investment, possession.

2 *the acquisition of funds* OBTAINING, acquirement, gaining, earning, winning, procurement, collection.

acquisitive adjective *his acquisitive wife has left him for a Denver architect* GREEDY, covetous, avaricious, possessive, grasping, grabbing, predatory, avid, rapacious, mercenary, materialistic; *informal* money-grubbing. See note at GREEDY.

acquisitiveness noun *their three children seem to possess none of the acquisitiveness so typical of Hollywood brats* GREED, greediness, covetousness, cupidity, possessiveness, avarice, avidity, rapaciousness, rapacity, materialism; *informal* affluenza.

acquit verb 1 *the jury acquitted her* CLEAR, exonerate, find innocent, absolve; discharge, release, free, set free; *informal* let off (the hook); *formal* exculpate. See note at ABSOLVE. ANTONYM convict.

2 *the boys **acquitted themselves** well* BEHAVE (ONESELF), conduct oneself, perform, act; *formal* comport oneself.

acquittal noun *the acquittal of the defendants* CLEARING, exoneration, absolution; discharge, release, freeing; *formal* exculpation. ANTONYM conviction.

acrid adjective *the fruit's acrid taste was a bad surprise* PUNGENT, bitter, sharp, sour, tart, caustic, harsh, irritating, acid, acidic, vinegary, acetic, acetous; stinging, burning.

acrimonious adjective *a heated and acrimonious discussion* BITTER, angry, rancorous, caustic, acerbic, scathing, sarcastic, acid, harsh, sharp, cutting; virulent, spiteful, vicious, vitriolic, hostile, venomous, nasty, bad-tempered, ill-natured, mean, malign, malicious, malignant, waspish; *informal* bitchy, catty.

acrimony noun *the meeting ended with acrimony on both sides* BITTERNESS, anger, rancor, resentment, ill feeling, ill will, bad blood, animosity, hostility, enmity, antagonism, waspishness, spleen, malice, spite, spitefulness, peevishness, venom. ANTONYM goodwill.

acrobat noun *he toured as an acrobat for the Cirque du Soleil* GYMNAST, tumbler, tightrope walker, trapeze artist, aerialist; *rare* funambulist.

acrobatics plural noun **1** *staggering feats of acrobatics* GYMNASTICS, tumbling; agility; *rare* funambulism.

2 *the acrobatics required to negotiate an international contract* MENTAL AGILITY, skill, quick thinking, fancy footwork, alertness, inventiveness.

act verb **1** *the government must act to remedy the situation* TAKE ACTION, take steps, take measures, move, react.

2 *he was* ***acting on*** *the orders of the party leader* FOLLOW, act in accordance with, obey, heed, comply with; fulfill, meet, discharge.

3 *a real estate agent* ***acting for*** *a prospective buyer* REPRESENT, act on behalf of; stand in for, fill in for, deputize for, take the place of.

4 *Alison began to act oddly* BEHAVE, conduct oneself, react; *formal* comport oneself.

5 *the scents act as a powerful aphrodisiac* OPERATE, work, function, serve.

6 *the drug* ***acted*** *directly* ***on*** *the blood vessels* AFFECT, have an effect on, work on; have an impact on, impact on, influence.

7 *he acted in a highly successful film* PERFORM, play a part, play-act, take part, appear; *informal* tread the boards, ham it up.

8 *we laughed, but most of us were just acting* PRETEND, play-act, put it on, fake it, feign it, dissemble, dissimulate.

▸ noun **1** *acts of kindness* | *a criminal act* DEED, action, feat, exploit, move, gesture, performance, undertaking, stunt, operation; achievement, accomplishment.

2 *the act raised the tax on tobacco* LAW, decree, statute, bill, act of Congress, enactment, resolution, edict, dictum, ruling, measure; ordinance.

3 *the first act of the play* DIVISION, section, subsection, part, segment.

4 *a music hall act* PERFORMANCE, routine, number, sketch, skit, shtick, turn.

5 *it was all just an act* PRETENSE, show, front, facade, masquerade, charade, posture, pose, affectation, sham, fake; *informal* put-on.

PHRASE: **act up** *informal* **1** *all children act up from time to time* MISBEHAVE, behave badly, be up to mischief, become unruly. **2** *the engine was acting up* MALFUNCTION, go wrong, be defective, be faulty; *informal* be on the blink, be on the fritz.

acting noun *the theory and practice of acting* DRAMA, the theater, the stage, the performing arts, thespianism, dramatics, dramaturgy, stagecraft, theatricals; *informal* treading the boards.

▸ adjective *the bank's acting governor* TEMPORARY, interim, caretaker, pro tem, pro tempore, provisional, stopgap; deputy, stand-in, fill-in; *informal* pinch-hitting. ANTONYM permanent.

action noun **1** *there can be no excuse for their actions* DEED, act, move, undertaking, exploit, maneuver, endeavor, effort, exertion; behavior, conduct, activity.

2 *the need for local community action* MEASURES, steps, activity, movement, work, operation.

3 *a man of action* ENERGY, vitality, vigor, forcefulness, drive, initiative, spirit, liveliness, vim, pep; activity; *informal* get-up-and-go.

4 *the action of hormones on the pancreas* EFFECT, influence, working; power.

5 *he missed all the action while he was away* EXCITEMENT, activity, happenings, events, incidents; *informal* goings-on.

6 *twenty-nine men died in the action* FIGHTING, hostilities, battle, conflict, combat, warfare; engagement, clash, encounter, skirmish.

7 *a civil action for damages* LAWSUIT, legal action, suit, case, prosecution, litigation, proceedings.

activate verb *the alarm system can be activated remotely* OPERATE, switch on, turn on, start (up), set going, trigger (off), set in motion, initiate, actuate, energize; trip.

active adjective **1** *despite her illness she remained active* ENERGETIC, lively, sprightly, spry, mobile, vigorous, vital, dynamic, sporty; busy, occupied; *informal* on the go. ANTONYM listless.

2 *an active member of the union* HARD-WORKING, busy, industrious, diligent, tireless, contributing, effective, enterprising, involved, enthusiastic, keen, committed, devoted, zealous. ANTONYMS passive, indifferent.

3 *the mill was active until 1960* OPERATIVE, working, functioning, functional, operating, operational, in action, in operation, running; live; *informal* up and running. ANTONYM inoperative.

activist noun *a human-rights activist* MILITANT, zealot, protester; radical, extremist.

activity noun **1** *there was a lot of activity in the area* BUSTLE, hustle and bustle, busyness, action, liveliness, movement, life, stir, flurry; happenings, occurrences, proceedings, events, incidents; *informal* toing and froing, comings and goings.

2 *a wide range of activities* PURSUIT, occupation, interest, hobby, pastime, recreation, diversion; venture, undertaking, enterprise, project, scheme, business, entertainment; act, action, deed, exploit.

actor, actress noun *daily bus tours take you past the homes of your favorite Hollywood actors and actresses* PERFORMER, player, thespian, trouper; film star, star, starlet, matinee idol; *informal* ham; lead, leading man, leading lady, stand-in.

actual adjective *be honest—how much of this wild story is actual?* REAL, true, genuine, authentic, verified, attested, confirmed, definite, hard, plain, veritable; existing, existent, manifest, substantial, factual, de facto, bona fide; *informal* honest-to-goodness, real live. See note at GENUINE. ANTONYM notional.

actuality noun *it's hard to tell actuality from fiction* REALITY, fact, truth, real life.

PHRASE: **in actuality** *in actuality, she's not my daughter—she's my wife* IN (ACTUAL) FACT, actually, really, in reality, in point of fact, in truth, if truth be told, to tell the truth; as a matter of fact; *archaic* in sooth.

actually adverb *believe it or not, George actually remembered our anniversary* REALLY, in (actual) fact, in point of fact, as a matter of fact, in reality, in actuality, in truth, if truth be told, to tell the truth; literally; truly, indeed; *archaic* in sooth.

acumen noun *noted for her business acumen* ASTUTENESS, shrewdness, acuity, sharpness, sharp-wittedness, cleverness, smartness, brains; judgment, understanding, awareness, sense, common sense, canniness, discernment, wisdom, wit, sagacity, perspicacity, insight, perception, penetration; savvy, know-how, horse sense, smarts, street smarts.

acute adjective **1** *acute food shortages* SEVERE, critical, drastic, dire, dreadful, terrible, awful, grave, bad, serious, desperate, dangerous. See note at CRUCIAL. ANTONYM negligible.

2 *acute stomach pains* SHARP, severe, stabbing, piercing, excruciating, agonizing, racking, keen, shooting, searing. See note at KEEN. ANTONYMS mild, dull.

3 *an acute mind* ASTUTE, shrewd, sharp, sharp-witted, razor-sharp, rapierlike, quick, quick-witted, agile, nimble, clever, intelligent, brilliant, keen, smart, canny, discerning, perceptive, perspicacious, penetrating, insightful, incisive, piercing, discriminating, sagacious, wise, judicious; *informal* on the ball, quick off the mark, quick on the uptake, streetwise, savvy. ANTONYM slow-witted.

4 *an acute sense of smell* KEEN, sharp, good, penetrating, discerning, sensitive. ANTONYMS poor, weak.

acutely adverb *our trust in you has become acutely shaken* EXTREMELY, exceedingly, very, markedly, severely, intensely, deeply, profoundly, keenly, painfully, desperately, tremendously, enormously, thoroughly, heartily; *informal* awfully, terribly; *slang* majorly. ANTONYM slightly.

adage noun *I should have remembered the old adage 'look before you leap'* SAYING, maxim, axiom, proverb, aphorism, saw, dictum, byword, precept, motto, truism, platitude, cliché, apophthegm, commonplace. See note at SAYING.

adamant adjective *he begged his mother to let him try out for the football team, but she was adamant* UNSHAKABLE, immovable, inflexible, unwavering, unswerving, uncompromising, insistent, resolute, resolved, determined, firm, steadfast; stubborn, unrelenting, diehard, unyielding, unbending, rigid, obdurate, inexorable, intransigent, (dead) set.

adapt verb **1** *we've adapted the procedures to suit their needs* MODIFY, alter, change, adjust, readjust, convert, redesign, restyle, refashion, remodel, reshape, revamp, rework, rejig, redo, reconstruct, reorganize; customize, tailor; improve, amend, refine, tweak.

2 *he has **adapted** well **to** his new home* ADJUST TO, acclimatize oneself to, acclimate to, accommodate oneself to, attune to, conform to, habituate oneself to, become habituated to, get used to, orient oneself in, reconcile oneself to, come to terms with, get one's bearings in, find one's feet in, acculturate to, assimilate to, blend in to, fit in to.

EASILY CONFUSED WORDS **adapt, adopt**

Avoid confusing **adapt** with **adopt**. Trouble sometimes arises because in *adapting* to new conditions, an animal or plant can be said to *adopt* something, such as a new color or behavior pattern.

adaptable adjective **1** *competent and adaptable staff* FLEXIBLE, versatile, cooperative, accommodating, amenable.

2 *an adaptable piece of furniture* VERSATILE, modifiable, convertible, alterable, adjustable, changeable; multipurpose, all-purpose.

adaptation noun **1** *an adaptation of a Scandinavian folk tale* ALTERATION, modification, redesign, remodeling, revamping, reworking, reconstruction, conversion.

2 *the cubs' adaptation to the zoo environment* ADJUSTMENT, acclimatization, acclimation, accommodations, habituation, acculturation, assimilation, integration.

add verb **1** *the back room was added in 1971 | add more sugar to the mix* ATTACH, build on, join, append, affix, connect, annex; include, incorporate, throw in, toss in; admix. ANTONYM remove.

2 *they added all the numbers* TOTAL, add up, count, count up, compute, calculate, reckon, tally; *dated* cast up. ANTONYM subtract.

3 *the subsidies **added up to** $1,700* AMOUNT TO, come to, run to, make, total, equal, number.

4 *it all **adds up to** a deepening crisis* AMOUNT TO, constitute; signify, signal, mean, indicate, denote, point to, be evidence of, be symptomatic of; *informal* spell.

5 *her decision just **added to** his woe* INCREASE, magnify, amplify, augment, intensify, heighten, deepen; compound, reinforce; add fuel to the fire of, fan the flames of, rub salt on the wound of.

6 *she added that she had every confidence in Laura* GO ON TO SAY, state further, continue, carry on.

PHRASE: **add up** *informal the situation just didn't add up* MAKE SENSE, stand to reason, hold up, hold water, ring true, be convincing.

addendum noun *we can add the list of sponsors as an addendum to the program* APPENDIX, codicil, postscript, afterword, tailpiece, rider, coda, supplement, *Law* adhesion; adjunct, appendage, addition, add-on, attachment.

addict noun **1** *stealing money for your next high, just like the addicts out in the street a barbiturate addict* ABUSER, user, drug addict; *informal* junkie, druggie, -head, -freak, pill-popper, dope fiend.

2 *informal skiing addicts* ENTHUSIAST, fan, lover, devotee, aficionado; *informal* freak, buff, nut, fiend, bum, junkie, fanatic, maniac.

addicted adjective **1** *he was addicted to tranquilizers* DEPENDENT ON; *informal* hooked on, strung out on.

2 *she became **addicted to** the theater* DEVOTED TO, obsessed with, fixated on, dedicated to, fanatical about, passionate about, enamored of, a slave to; *informal* hooked on, wild about, mad about, crazy about, nuts about. ANTONYM indifferent

addiction noun **1** *his heroin addiction* DEPENDENCY, dependence, habit, problem.

2 *a slavish **addiction to** fashion* DEVOTION TO, dedication to, obsession with, infatuation with, passion for, love of, mania for, enslavement to.

addictive adjective *an addictive prescription drug* HABIT-FORMING, addicting; causing dependency.

addition noun **1** *the soil is improved by the addition of compost* ADDING, incorporation, inclusion, introduction.

2 *an addition to the existing regulations* SUPPLEMENT, adjunct, addendum, adhesion, appendage, add-on, extra, attachment; rider, appurtenance. PHRASE: **in addition 1** *the wind was frigid and, in addition, the sky threatened rain* ADDITIONALLY, as well, what's more, furthermore, moreover, also, into the bargain, to boot, likewise. **2** *three presidential hopefuls* ***in addition to*** *the vice president* BESIDES, as well as, along with, other than, apart from, on top of, plus, over and above, not to mention, to say nothing of.

additional adjective *six additional tables will be necessary to accommodate the entire crew* EXTRA, added, supplementary, supplemental, further, auxiliary, ancillary; more, other, another, new, fresh; *informal* bonus.

additionally adverb *additionally, there will be live entertainment every Thursday* ALSO, in addition, as well, too, besides, on top (of that), moreover, further, furthermore, what's more, over and above that, into the bargain, to boot, likewise; *archaic* withal.

additive noun *our flours have no additives* ADDED INGREDIENT, addition; preservative, coloring.

addled adjective *Patricia was noticeably addled after Pete suddenly stormed out* MUDDLED, confused, muzzy, fuddled, befuddled, dazed, disoriented, disorientated, fuzzy; *informal* woozy.

address noun **1** *the address on the envelope* inscription, superscription; directions, number.

2 *our officers arrived at the address* HOUSE, apartment, home; *formal* residence, dwelling, dwelling place, habitation, abode, domicile.

3 *her address to the board members* SPEECH, lecture, talk, monologue, dissertation, discourse, oration, peroration; *slang* spiel, chalk talk; sermon, homily, lesson; harangue.

▸ verb **1** *I addressed the envelope by hand* inscribe, superscribe.

2 *Rev. Lally addressed a crowded congregation* TALK TO, give a talk to, speak to, make a speech to, give a lecture to, lecture, hold forth to; PREACH TO, give a sermon to; *informal* buttonhole, collar.

3 *the question of how to address one's parents-in-law* CALL, name, designate; speak to; *formal* denominate.

4 *correspondence should be addressed to the Personnel Department* DIRECT, send, forward, communicate, convey, route, remit.

5 *the selectmen failed to address the issue of subsidies* ATTEND TO, apply oneself to, tackle, see to, deal with, confront, come to grips with, get down to, turn one's hand to, take in hand, undertake, concentrate on, focus on, devote oneself to.

adduce verb *evidence adduced to support their argument* CITE, quote, name, mention, instance, point out, refer to; put forward, present, offer, advance, propose, proffer.

adept adjective *an adept negotiator* EXPERT, proficient, accomplished, skillful, talented, masterly, masterful, consummate, virtuoso; adroit, dexterous, deft, artful; brilliant, splendid, marvelous, formidable, outstanding, first-rate, first-class, excellent, fine; *informal* great, topnotch, tip-top, A1, ace, mean, hotshot, crack, nifty, deadly; *informal* crackerjack. ANTONYM inept.

▸ ***adept***

genius
Wunderkind
grandmaster
virtuoso
maestro
prodigy
artist
wizard
master
cognoscente
maven
savant
Admirable Crichton
pantologist
authority
pro(fessional)
expert
wiz/whizz
demon
hotshot
ace
veteran
jack of all trades
dab hand
old hand
connoisseur
doyen(ne)
aficionado
devotee
buff

fan

layman
layperson
enthusiast
nonspecialist
amateur
dabbler
dilettante
trifler
dingbat
looby
nincompoop
lurdan
gilly-gawpus
klutz
schlemiel
schmuck
schmendrick
blunderer
bumbler
fumbler
duffer
stumblebum
prat
lubber
swab
clown
wally
clod
jackass
butcher
hack
jackleg
jobber
quack

bungler ◂

▸ noun *figure-skating adepts* EXPERT, past master, master, genius, maestro, doyen, virtuoso; *informal* wizard, demon, ace, hotshot, whiz, maven, crackerjack. ANTONYM amateur.

adequacy noun **1** *the adequacy of the existing services* SATISFACTORINESS, acceptability, acceptableness; sufficiency.

2 *he had deep misgivings about his own adequacy* CAPABILITY, competence, ability, aptitude, suitability; effectiveness, fitness; *formal* efficacy.

adequate adjective **1** *he lacked adequate financial resources* SUFFICIENT, enough, requisite.

2 *the company provides an adequate service* ACCEPTABLE, passable, reasonable, satisfactory, tolerable, fair, decent, quite good, pretty good, moderate, unexceptional, unremarkable, undistinguished, ordinary, average, not bad, all right, middling; *informal* OK, so-so, 'comme ci, comme ça,' fair-to-middling, nothing to write home about.

3 *the workstations were small but seemed* ***adequate to*** *the task* EQUAL TO, up to, capable of, suitable for, able to do, fit for, sufficient for.

adhere verb **1** *a dollop of cream adhered to her nose* STICK (FAST), cohere, cling, bond, attach; be stuck, be fixed, be glued, be cemented.

2 *they* ***adhere to*** *Judaic law* ABIDE BY, stick to, hold to, comply with, act in accordance with, conform to, submit to, hew to; follow, obey, heed, observe, respect, uphold, fulfill. ANTONYMS flout, ignore.

adherent noun *adherents of the Catholic faith* FOLLOWER, supporter, upholder, defender, advocate, disciple, votary, devotee, partisan, member, friend, stalwart; believer, true believer, worshiper; *rare* sectary. ANTONYM opponent.

adhesion noun *the adhesion of the gum strip to the paper fibers* STICKING, adherence.

adhesive noun *a spray adhesive* GLUE, fixative, gum, paste, cement, mucilage; *informal* stickum.

▸ adjective *adhesive paper* STICKY, tacky, gluey, gummed, stick-on, self-stick, gooey; viscous, viscid; *technical* adherent.

adieu noun & exclamation *with a cheery "adieu," they were gone* GOODBYE, farewell, until we meet again; bye-bye, bye, cheers, ciao, au revoir, adios, sayonara, so long, ta-ta, cheerio, toodle-oo.

ad infinitum adverb *this story will be told and retold, ad infinitum* FOREVER, for ever and ever, evermore, always, for all time, until the end of time, in perpetuity, until hell freezes over; perpetually, eternally, endlessly, interminably, unceasingly, unendingly, forevermore; *informal* until the cows come home, until kingdom come; *archaic* for aye.

adjacent adjective *adjacent angles* | *a patio* ***adjacent to*** *the greenhouse* ADJOINING, neighboring, next-door, abutting, contiguous, proximate; **(adjacent to)** close to, near, next to, by, by the side of, bordering on, beside, alongside, attached to, touching, cheek by jowl with.

adjoin verb *the kitchen adjoins the dining room* BE NEXT TO, be adjacent to, border (on), abut, be contiguous with, communicate with, extend to; join, conjoin, connect with, touch, meet.

adjoining adjective *adjoining hotel rooms* CONNECTING, connected, interconnecting, adjacent, ensuite, neighboring, bordering, next-door; contiguous, proximate; attached, touching.

adjourn verb **1** *the meeting was adjourned for lunch* SUSPEND, break off, discontinue, interrupt, prorogue, stay, recess.

2 *sentencing was adjourned until June 9* POSTPONE, put off, put back, defer, delay, hold over, shelve. See note at POSTPONE.

3 *they adjourned to the sitting room for liqueurs* WITHDRAW, retire, retreat, take oneself; *formal* repair, remove; *literary* betake oneself.

adjournment noun *if not now signed into law, the legislation will die with the adjournment of this Congress* SUSPENSION, discontinuation, interruption, postponement, deferment, deferral, stay, prorogation; break, pause, recess.

adjudge verb *the court adjudges and decrees that the company's conduct violates Sections 1 and 2 of the Sherman Act* JUDGE, deem, find, pronounce, proclaim, rule, hold, determine; consider, think, rate, reckon, perceive, believe.

adjudicate verb *this court cannot proceed to* ***adjudicate on*** *a matter when the accused does not have a counsel* JUDGE, try, hear, examine, arbitrate, referee, umpire; pronounce on, give a ruling on, pass judgment on, decide, determine, settle, resolve.

adjudication noun *some newspapers do not publish the names of defendants in such cases until adjudication* JUDGMENT, decision, pronouncement, ruling, settlement, resolution, arbitration, finding, verdict, sentence; *Law* determination.

adjudicator noun *the adjudicators must agree before any decision is final* JUDGE, arbitrator, arbiter; referee, umpire.

adjunct noun *the oral medication is used as an adjunct to the insulin* SUPPLEMENT, addition, extra, add-on, accessory, accompaniment, complement, appurtenance; attachment, appendage, addendum.

▸ adjective *an adjunct professor of entomology* SUBORDINATE, auxiliary, assistant; temporary, provisional.

adjust verb **1** *Nanfeldt never quite* ***adjusted to*** *military life* ADAPT TO, become accustomed to, get used to, accommodate oneself to, acclimatize to, acclimate to, orient oneself to, reconcile oneself to, habituate oneself to, assimilate to, familiarize oneself with; come to terms with, fit in with, find one's feet in.

2 *he adjusted the harness* MODIFY, alter, regulate, tune, fine-tune, calibrate, balance; adapt, arrange, rearrange, change, rejig, rework, revamp, remodel, reshape, convert, tailor, improve, enhance, customize; repair, fix, correct, rectify, overhaul, put right; *informal* tweak.

adjustable adjective *adjustable seats* ALTERABLE, adaptable, modifiable, convertible, changeable, variable, multiway, versatile.

adjustment noun **1** *a period of adjustment* ADAPTATION, accommodations, acclimatization, acclimation, habituation, acculturation, naturalization, assimilation.

2 *they had to make some adjustments to their strategy* MODIFICATION, alteration, regulation, adaptation, rearrangement, change, reconstruction, customization, refinement; repair, correction, amendment, overhaul, improvement.

ad lib verb *halfway through the speech, she started ad libbing* IMPROVISE, extemporize, speak impromptu, play it by ear, make it up as one goes along, wing it.

▸ adverb *she spoke ad lib* IMPROMPTU, extempore, without preparation, without rehearsal, extemporaneously; *informal* off the cuff, off the top of one's head; ad libitum.

▸ adjective *a live, ad lib commentary* IMPROMPTU, extempore, extemporaneous, extemporary, improvised, unprepared, unrehearsed, unscripted; *informal* off-the-cuff, spur-of-the-moment. ANTONYM rehearsed.

administer verb **1** *the union is administered by a central executive | Leighton administers an entire department* MANAGE, direct, control, operate, regulate, conduct, handle, run, organize, supervise, superintend, oversee, preside over, govern, rule, lead, head, steer; be in control of, be in charge of, be responsible for, be at the helm of; *informal* head up.

2 *the lifeboat crew administered first aid* DISPENSE, issue, give, provide, apply, allot, distribute, hand out, dole out, disburse.

3 *a gym shoe was used to administer punishment* INFLICT, mete out, deal out, deliver.

administration noun **1** *the day-to-day administration of the company* MANAGEMENT, direction, control, command, charge, conduct, operation, running, leadership, government, governing, superintendence, supervision, regulation, overseeing.

2 *the previous administration left a legacy of reckless spending* GOVERNMENT, cabinet, ministry, regime, executive, authority, directorate, council, leadership, management; parliament, congress, senate; rule, term of office, incumbency.

3 *the administration of anti-inflammatory drugs* PROVISION, issuing, issuance, application, dispensing, dispensation, distribution, disbursement.

administrative adjective *strong administrative skills* MANAGERIAL, management, directorial, executive, organizational, bureaucratic, supervisory, regulatory.

administrator noun *he became the team's top administrator in 1973* MANAGER, director, executive, controller, head, chief, leader, governor, superintendent, supervisor; *informal* boss.

admirable adjective *having done an admirable job of teaching preschoolers* COMMENDABLE, praiseworthy, laudable, estimable, meritorious, creditable, exemplary, honorable, worthy, deserving, respectable, worthwhile, good, sterling, fine, masterly, great. ANTONYM deplorable.

admiration noun *it is with much admiration that we dedicate tonight's concert to Dr. Woods* RESPECT, appreciation, (high) regard, esteem, veneration; commendation, acclaim, applause, praise, compliments, tributes, accolades, plaudits. ANTONYM scorn.

admire verb **1** *I admire your courage* ESTEEM, approve of, respect, think highly of, rate highly, hold in high regard, applaud, praise, commend, acclaim. ANTONYMS despise, disapprove of. See notes at ESTEEM, REVERE.

2 *we're just admiring your garden* DELIGHT IN, appreciate, take pleasure in.

admirer noun *a great admirer of William Finn* FAN, devotee, enthusiast, aficionado; supporter, adherent, follower, disciple.

admissible adjective *an admissible claim for damages* VALID, allowable, allowed, permissible, permitted, acceptable, satisfactory, justifiable, defensible, supportable, appropriate, well-founded, tenable, sound; legitimate, lawful, legal, licit; *informal* OK, legit, kosher.

admission noun **1** *membership entitles you to free admission* ADMITTANCE, entry, entrance, right of entry, access, right of access, ingress; entrée.

2 *the admission was $8* ENTRANCE FEE, entry charge, cover (charge), ticket.

3 *a written admission of guilt* CONFESSION, acknowledgment, mea culpa, acceptance, concession, disclosure, divulgence.

EASILY CONFUSED WORDS **admission, admittance**

Admission traditionally referred to the price paid for entry or the right to enter: *Admission was $5.* **Admittance** more often referred to physical entry: *we were denied admittance by a large man with a forbidding scowl.* In the sense of 'permission or right to enter,' these words have become almost interchangeable, although *admittance* is more formal and technical.

admit verb **1** *he unlocked the door to admit her* LET IN, allow entry, permit entry, take in, usher in, show in, receive, welcome. ANTONYM exclude.

2 *she was admitted to law school* ACCEPT TO/INTO, receive into, enroll in, enlist into, register into. ANTONYM expel.

3 *Paul admitted that he was angry* CONFESS, acknowledge, own, concede, grant, accept, allow; reveal, disclose, divulge; plead guilty. ANTONYM deny.

admittance noun *no one is granted admittance without a pass* ENTRY, right of entry, admission, entrance, access, right of access, ingress; entrée. See note at ADMISSION. ANTONYM exclusion.

admonish verb **1** *he was severely admonished by his father* REPRIMAND, rebuke, scold, reprove, reproach, upbraid, chastise, chide, berate, criticize, take to task, read the riot act to, rake/haul over the coals; dress down, bawl out, rap over the knuckles, give someone hell; chew out; *formal* castigate; *rare* reprehend. See note at REBUKE.

2 *she admonished him to drink less* ADVISE, recommend, counsel, urge, exhort, bid, enjoin; caution, warn; *formal* adjure.

adolescence noun *the lack of adequate sleep in adolescence is a growing health problem largely ignored by the public school system* TEENAGE YEARS, teens, youth; pubescence, puberty; *rare* juvenescence, juvenility.

adolescent noun *an awkward adolescent* TEENAGER, youngster, young person, youth, boy, girl; juvenile, minor; *informal* teen, teeny-bopper.

▸ adjective **1** *an adolescent boy* TEENAGE, pubescent, young; juvenile; *informal* teen.

2 *adolescent silliness* IMMATURE, childish, juvenile, infantile, puerile, jejune. See note at YOUTHFUL. ANTONYMS adult, mature.

adopt verb **1** *we adopted Sasha in 1996* TAKE AS ONE'S CHILD, be adoptive parents to, take in, take care of. ANTONYM abandon.

2 *they adopted local customs* ESPOUSE, take on/up, embrace, assume; appropriate, arrogate. ANTONYMS abandon, reject.

3 *the people adopted him as their patron saint* CHOOSE, select, pick, vote for, elect, settle on, decide on, opt for; name, nominate, appoint. See note at ADAPT. ANTONYM reject.

adorable adjective *adorable little kittens* LOVABLE, appealing, charming, cute, cuddly, sweet, enchanting, bewitching, captivating, engaging, endearing, dear, darling, delightful, lovely, beautiful, attractive, gorgeous, winsome, winning, fetching; *Scottish* bonny. ANTONYMS repulsive, hateful.

adoration noun **1** *the girl gazed at him with adoration* LOVE, devotion, care, fondness; admiration, high regard, awe, idolization, worship, hero-worship, adulation.

2 *our day of prayer and adoration* WORSHIP, glory, glorification, praise, thanksgiving, homage, exaltation, veneration, reverence.

adore verb **1** *he adored his mother* LOVE DEARLY, love, be devoted to, dote on, hold dear, cherish, treasure, prize, think the world of; admire, hold in high regard, look up to, idolize, worship; *informal* put on a pedestal. ANTONYMS hate, detest.

2 *we adore thee, Lord God* WORSHIP, glorify, praise, revere, reverence, exalt, extol, venerate, pay homage to; *formal* laud; *archaic* magnify. See note at REVERE.

3 *informal I adore oysters* LIKE, love, be very fond of, be very keen on, be partial to, have a weakness for; delight in, relish, savor; *informal* be crazy about, be wild about, have a thing about/for/with, be hooked on. ANTONYMS hate, detest.

adorn verb *we'll adorn the hall with tiny lights and ropes of pine* DECORATE, embellish, ornament, enhance; beautify, prettify, grace, bedeck, deck (out), dress (up), trim, swathe, wreathe, festoon, garland, array, emblazon, titivate. ANTONYM disfigure.

adornment noun *why all the adornment just for a casual dinner party? | we purchased way more adornments than we could ever use* DECORATION, embellishment, ornamentation, ornament, enhancement; beautification, prettification; frill, accessory, doodad, fandangle, frippery; trimmings, finishing touches.

adrift adjective **1** *their empty boat was spotted adrift* DRIFTING, unmoored, unanchored.

2 *adrift in a strange country* LOST, off course; disoriented, confused, at sea; drifting, rootless, unsettled, directionless, aimless, purposeless, without purpose.

adroit adjective *an adroit politician | adroit social commentary* SKILLFUL, adept, dexterous, deft, nimble, able, capable, skilled, expert, masterly, masterful, master, practiced, handy, polished, slick, proficient, accomplished, gifted, talented; quick-witted, quick-thinking, clever, smart, sharp, cunning, wily, resourceful, astute, shrewd, canny; *informal* nifty, crack, mean, ace, A1, clueful, on the ball, savvy, crackerjack. ANTONYMS inept, clumsy.

adroitness noun *there is an undeniable adroitness in his economic plan* SKILL, skillfulness, prowess, expertise, adeptness, dexterity, deftness, nimbleness, ability, capability, mastery, proficiency, accomplishment, artistry, art, facility, aptitude, flair, finesse, talent; quick-wittedness, cleverness, sharpness, cunning, astuteness, shrewdness, resourcefulness, savoir faire; *informal* know-how, savvy.

adulation noun *unspoiled by all the adulation he's received* HERO-WORSHIP, worship, idolization, adoration, admiration, veneration, awe, devotion, glorification, praise, flattery, blandishments.

adulatory adjective *he spoke of Leslie in adulatory terms* FLATTERING, complimentary, highly favorable, enthusiastic, glowing, rhapsodic, eulogistic, laudatory; fulsome, honeyed. ANTONYM disparaging.

adult adjective **1** *an adult woman* MATURE, grown-up, fully grown, full-grown, fully developed, of age, of legal age.

2 *an adult movie* SEXUALLY EXPLICIT, pornographic, obscene, smutty, dirty, rude, erotic, sexy, suggestive, titillating; porn, porno, naughty, blue, X-rated.

WORD NOTE adult

Somewhere along the line, this word has, so to speak, outgrown its limited association with biological age *(the adult fruit fly)* and psychological maturity. *(Despite the rancorous divorce, they behaved like adults.)* And it's come to mean sex in general, and pornography in particular. *Adult entertainment. Adult videos.* I assume that's supposed to mean that such forms of recreation, like sex itself, are the sole province of adults, and should be of no interest to children. Or perhaps it's meant as a warning to children—keep out, stay away—another example of language doing the opposite of what's intended. Otherwise, how to explain the conversation I overheard recently, in which a man explained that his two young sons had, unbeknownst to him, squandered a small fortune on adult pay TV? —**FP**

adulterate verb *some of the drinks had been adulterated with tranquilizers* MAKE IMPURE, degrade, debase, spoil, taint, contaminate; doctor, tamper with, dilute, water down, weaken; bastardize, corrupt; *informal* cut, spike, lace, dope. See note at POLLUTE. ANTONYM purify.

adulterer noun *why would you want to marry a known adulterer?* CHEAT, cheater, two-timer.

adulterous adjective *an adulterous husband | her adulterous affair* UNFAITHFUL, disloyal, untrue, inconstant, false, deceiving, deceitful, treacherous, illicit; extramarital; cheating, two-timing; extracurricular. ANTONYM faithful.

adultery noun *his adultery finally caught up with him* INFIDELITY, unfaithfulness, falseness, disloyalty, cuckoldry, extramarital sex; affair, liaison, fling, amour; *informal* carrying-on, hanky-panky, two-timing, a bit on the side, fooling around, playing around. ANTONYM fidelity.

advance verb **1** *the battalion advanced rapidly* MOVE FORWARD, proceed, press on, push on, push forward, make progress, make headway, gain ground, approach, come closer, draw nearer, near. ANTONYM retreat.

2 *the court may advance the date of the hearing* BRING FORWARD, put forward, move forward. ANTONYM postpone.

3 *the move advanced his career* PROMOTE, further, help, aid, assist, boost, strengthen, improve, benefit, foster. ANTONYMS impede, hinder.

4 *our technology has advanced in the last few years* PROGRESS, make progress, make headway, develop, evolve, make strides, move forward (in leaps and bounds), move ahead; improve, thrive, flourish, prosper. ANTONYM stagnate.

5 *the hypothesis I wish to advance in this article* PUT FOR-

WARD, present, submit, suggest, propose, introduce, offer, adduce, moot. ANTONYM retract.

6 *a relative advanced him some money* LEND, loan, put up, come up with. ANTONYM borrow.

▸ noun **1** *the advance of the aggressors* PROGRESS, forward movement; approach.

2 *a significant medical advance* BREAKTHROUGH, development, step forward, step in the right direction, (quantum) leap; find, finding, discovery, invention.

3 *share prices showed significant advances* INCREASE, rise, upturn, upsurge, upswing, growth; *informal* hike.

4 *the writer is going to be given a huge advance* DOWN PAYMENT, retainer, prepayment, deposit, front money, money up front.

5 *unwelcome sexual advances* PASS, proposition.

▸ adjective **1** *an advance party of settlers* PRELIMINARY, sent (on) ahead, first, exploratory; pilot, test, trial.

2 *advance warning* EARLY, prior, beforehand.

PHRASE: **in advance** *rental skis and boots can be reserved in advance* BEFOREHAND, before, ahead of time, earlier, previously; in readiness.

advanced adjective **1** *advanced manufacturing techniques* STATE-OF-THE-ART, new, modern, developed, cutting-edge, leading-edge, up-to-date, up-to-the-minute, the newest, the latest; progressive, avant-garde, ahead of the times, pioneering, innovative, sophisticated.

2 *advanced further-education courses* HIGHER-LEVEL, higher. ANTONYM primitive.

advancement noun **1** *the advancement of computer technology* DEVELOPMENT, progress, evolution, growth, improvement, advance, furtherance; headway.

2 *employees must be offered opportunities for advancement* PROMOTION, preferment, career development, upgrading, a step up the ladder, progress, improvement, betterment, growth.

advantage noun **1** *the advantages of belonging to a union* BENEFIT, value, good point, strong point, asset, plus, bonus, boon, blessing, virtue; attraction, beauty, usefulness, helpfulness, convenience, advantageousness, profit. ANTONYMS disadvantage, drawback.

2 *they appeared to be gaining the advantage over their opponents* UPPER HAND, edge, lead, whip hand, trump card; superiority, dominance, ascendancy, supremacy, power, mastery; *informal* inside track, catbird seat.

3 *there is no advantage to be gained from delaying the process* BENEFIT, profit, gain, good; *informal* mileage. ANTONYM detriment.

advantageous adjective **1** *an advantageous position* SUPERIOR, dominant, powerful; good, fortunate, lucky, favorable. ANTONYM inferior.

2 *the arrangement is advantageous to both sides* BENEFICIAL, of benefit, helpful, of assistance, useful, of use, of value, of service, profitable, fruitful; convenient, expedient. ANTONYM detrimental.

advent noun *the advent of a new school year* ARRIVAL, appearance, emergence, materialization, occurrence, dawn, birth, rise, development; approach, coming. ANTONYM disappearance.

adventitious adjective *he felt that the conversation was not entirely adventitious* UNPLANNED, unpremeditated, accidental, chance, fortuitous, serendipitous, coincidental, casual, random. See note at ACCIDENTAL. ANTONYM premeditated.

adventure noun **1** *they set off in search of adventure* EXCITEMENT, thrill, stimulation; risk, danger, hazard, peril, uncertainty, precariousness.

2 *her recent adventures in Italy* EXPLOIT, escapade, deed, feat, experience.

adventurer noun *an adventurer of the high seas* DAREDEVIL, hero, heroine, thrill-seeker; swashbuckler.

adventurous adjective **1** *an adventurous traveler* DARING, daredevil, intrepid, venturesome, bold, fearless, brave, unafraid, unshrinking, dauntless; *informal* gutsy, spunky. ANTONYM cautious.

2 *adventurous activities* RISKY, dangerous, perilous, hazardous, precarious, uncertain; exciting, thrilling. ANTONYM tame.

adversary noun *once his devoted comrade at West Point, Arthur was now his adversary at Bull Run* OPPONENT, rival, enemy, antagonist, combatant, challenger, contender, competitor, opposer; opposition, competition, foe. ANTONYMS ally, supporter.

adverse adjective **1** *adverse weather conditions* UNFAVORABLE, disadvantageous, inauspicious, unpropitious, unfortunate, unlucky, untimely, untoward. ANTONYMS favorable, auspicious.

2 *the drug's adverse side effects* HARMFUL, dangerous, injurious, detrimental, hurtful, negative, deleterious. ANTONYM beneficial.

3 *an adverse response from the public* HOSTILE, UNFAVORABLE, antagonistic, unfriendly, ill-disposed, negative. ANTONYMS positive, friendly. See note at HOSTILE.

EASILY CONFUSED WORDS **adverse, averse**

Adverse means 'hostile, unfavorable, opposed,' and is usually applied to situations, conditions, or events—not to people: *steering control is maintained even under adverse driving conditions.* **Averse** is related in origin and also has the sense of 'opposed,' but is usually employed to describe a person's attitude: *I would not be averse to making the repairs myself.*

adversity noun *the studio made sure the public saw only the manufactured glamour and none of the real adversity of her private life* MISFORTUNE, ill luck, bad luck, trouble, difficulty, hardship, distress, disaster, suffering, affliction, sorrow, misery, tribulation, woe, pain, trauma; mishap, misadventure, accident, upset, reverse, setback, crisis, catastrophe, tragedy, calamity, trial, cross, burden, blow; hard times, trials and tribulations; *informal* ill wind.

advertise verb *you should advertise the contest on your local radio station* PUBLICIZE, make public, make known, announce, broadcast, proclaim, trumpet, call attention to, bill, promulgate; promote, market, beat/bang the drum for, huckster; *informal* push, plug, hype, boost; ballyhoo, flack.

advertisement noun *it looked like the phone bill, but it was just an advertisement* AD, announcement, notice; commercial, infomercial, promotion, endorsement, blurb, write-up; poster, leaflet, pamphlet, flyer, bill, handbill, handout, fact sheet, circular, bulletin, brochure, sign, placard, junk mail; *informal* plug.

advice noun *they give excellent advice on running a small* *business* GUIDANCE, counseling, counsel, help, direction; information, recommendations, guidelines, suggestions, hints, tips, pointers, ideas, opinions, views, input, words of wisdom.

advisable adjective *it is advisable to book a table in advance* JUDICIOUS, desirable, preferable, well, best, sensible, prudent, proper, appropriate, apt, suitable, fitting, wise, recommended, suggested; expedient, politic, advantageous, beneficial, profitable, in one's (best) interest.

advise verb **1** *her grandmother advised her about marriage* COUNSEL, give guidance, guide, offer suggestions, give hints, give tips, give pointers.

2 *he advised caution* ADVOCATE, recommend, suggest, urge, encourage, enjoin.

3 *you will be **advised of** the requirements* INFORM OF, notify about/of, give notice of, apprise of, warn of, forewarn of; acquaint with, make familiar with, keep posted about, update about/on; *informal* fill in on.

adviser, advisor noun *the senator has been preparing to run for president in 2004, according to his advisers* COUNSELOR, mentor, guide, consultant, confidant, confidante, aide; coach, trainer, teacher, tutor, guru; *informal* main man.

advisory adjective *she agreed to serve in an advisory role* CONSULTATIVE, advising. ANTONYM executive.

advocacy noun *his **advocacy of** animal rights* SUPPORT FOR, backing of, promotion of, championing of; argument for, push for; *informal* boosterism of.

advocate noun *an advocate of children's rights* CHAMPION, upholder, supporter, backer, promoter, proponent, exponent, spokesman, spokeswoman, spokesperson, campaigner, fighter, crusader; propagandist, apostle, apologist, booster, flag-bearer; *informal* libber. ANTONYM critic.

▸ verb *heart specialists advocate a diet low in cholesterol* RECOMMEND, prescribe, advise, urge; support, back, favor, espouse, endorse, uphold, subscribe to, champion, campaign on behalf of, speak for, argue for, lobby for, promote.

aegis noun *they had wrongly assumed that Lincoln Beach fell under the aegis of the Parks Department* PROTECTION, backing, support, patronage, sponsorship, charge, care, guidance, control, guardianship, trusteeship, agency, safeguarding, shelter, umbrella, aid, assistance; auspices.

aesthetic adjective *several aesthetic gardens radiate from the fountain in the square* ARTISTIC, tasteful, in good taste; graceful, elegant, exquisite, beautiful, attractive, pleasing, lovely.

affable adjective *he would have us believe that his sexual advances were merely the charming excesses of an affable rogue* FRIENDLY, amiable, genial, congenial, cordial, warm, pleasant, nice, likable, personable, charming, agreeable, sympathetic, simpatico, good-humored, good-natured, jolly, kindly, kind, courteous, civil, gracious, approachable, accessible, amenable, sociable, hail-fellow-well-met, outgoing, gregarious, neighborly. ANTONYM unfriendly.

affair noun **1** *what you do is your own affair* BUSINESS, concern, matter, responsibility, province, preserve; problem, worry.

2 (**affairs**) *his financial affairs* TRANSACTIONS, concerns, matters, activities, dealings, undertakings, ventures, business.

3 *the board admitted responsibility for the affair* EVENT, incident, happening, occurrence, eventuality, episode; case, matter, business.

4 *his affair with Monica was over* RELATIONSHIP, love affair, affaire de coeur, romance, fling, flirtation, dalliance, liaison, involvement, intrigue, amour; *informal* hanky-panky.

affect[1] verb **1** *this development may have affected the judge's decision* HAVE AN EFFECT ON, influence, act on, work on, have an impact on, impact; change, alter, modify, transform, form, shape, sway, bias.

2 *he was visibly affected by the experience* MOVE, touch, make an impression on, hit (hard), tug at someone's heartstrings; UPSET, trouble, distress, disturb, agitate, shake (up).

3 *the disease affected his lungs* ATTACK, infect; hit, strike. See note at EMOTION.

EASILY CONFUSED WORDS **affect, effect**

Both **affect** and **effect** are both verbs and nouns, but only **effect** is common as a noun, usually meaning 'a result, consequence, impression, etc.': *my father's warnings had no effect on my adventurousness.* (The noun *affect* is restricted almost entirely to psychology.) As verbs, they are used differently.

Affect means 'to produce an effect upon': *what you eat can affect your mood.* The verb **affect**, except when used in contexts involving feelings, often serves as a vague substitute for more exact verbs and should therefore be used sparingly. **Effect** means 'to bring about': *the negotiators effected an agreement despite many difficulties.*

affect[2] verb **1** *he deliberately affected a Republican stance* ASSUME, take on, adopt, embrace, espouse.

2 *Paul affected an air of injured innocence* PRETEND, feign, fake, simulate, make a show of, make a pretense of, sham; *informal* put on, make like.

affectation noun **1** *the affectations of a prima donna* PRETENSION, pretentiousness, affectedness, artificiality, posturing, posing; airs (and graces).

2 *an affectation of calm* FACADE, front, show, appearance, pretense, simulation, posture, pose.

affected adjective *that affected voice of his really grates on me* PRETENTIOUS, artificial, contrived, unnatural, stagy, studied, mannered, ostentatious; insincere, unconvincing, feigned, false, fake, sham, simulated; *informal* la-di-da, phony, pretend, put on. ANTONYMS natural, unpretentious, genuine.

affecting adjective *an affecting piece of music* TOUCHING, moving, emotive, emotional; stirring, soul-stirring, heartwarming; poignant, pathetic, pitiful, piteous, tear-jerking, heart-rending, gut-wrenching, heartbreaking, disturbing, distressing, upsetting, sad, haunting. See note at MOVING.

affection noun *the affection they share is obvious* FONDNESS, love, liking, tenderness, warmth, devotion, endearment, care, caring, attachment, friendship; warm feelings.

affectionate adjective *an affectionate handshake | golden retrievers are known for being affectionate* LOVING, fond, adoring, devoted, caring, doting, tender, warm, warmhearted, softhearted, friendly; demonstrative, cuddly; *informal* touchy-feely, lovey-dovey. ANTONYM cold.

affiliate verb *the college is **affiliated with** the University of Wisconsin* ASSOCIATE WITH, unite with, combine with, join (up) with, link up with, team up with, ally with, align with, band together with, federate with, amalgamate with, merge with; attach to, annex to, incorporate into, integrate into.

▸ noun *Conklin Textiles is their largest Midwest affiliate* PARTNER, branch, offshoot, subsidiary.

affiliated adjective *tests on eight people affiliated with Dyess Air Force Base have come back negative for SARS | our two affiliated companies in Tipton* ASSOCIATED, allied, related, integrated, incorporated, federated, confederated, amalgamated, unified, connected, linked, joined; in league, in partnership.

affiliation noun *the project's **affiliation with** the town's welfare department | the newspaper's obvious **affiliation to** the Republican party* ASSOCIATION WITH, connection with/to, alliance with/to, alignment with, link with/to, attachment to, tie with/to, relationship with/to, fellowship with, partnership with, coalition with, union with; amalgamation with, incorporation into, integration into, federation with, confederation with.

affinity noun **1** *her **affinity with** animals and birds | an **affinity for** opera* EMPATHY FOR, rapport with, sympathy for, accord with, harmony with, relationship with, bond with, fellow feeling for, closeness with/to, understanding of/for; liking of/for, fondness of/for; *informal* chemistry with. ANTONYMS aversion, dislike.

2 *the semantic affinity between the two words* SIMILARITY, resemblance, likeness, kinship, relationship, association, link, analogy, similitude, correspondence. See note at LIKENESS. ANTONYMS dissimilitude, dissimilarity.

affirm verb **1** *he affirmed that they would lend military assistance* DECLARE, state, assert, proclaim, pronounce, attest, swear, avow, guarantee, pledge, give an undertaking; *formal* aver. ANTONYM deny.

2 *the referendum affirmed the republic's right to secede* UPHOLD, support, confirm, ratify, endorse, sanction.

affirmation noun **1** *an affirmation of faith* DECLARATION, statement, assertion, proclamation, pronouncement, attestation; oath, avowal, guarantee, pledge; deposition; *formal* averment, asseveration. ANTONYM denial.

2 *the poem ends with an affirmation of pastoral values* CONFIRMATION, ratification, endorsement.

affirmative adjective *an affirmative answer* POSITIVE, assenting, consenting, corroborative, favorable. ANTONYM negative.

▸ noun *she took his grunt as an affirmative* AGREEMENT, acceptance, assent, acquiescence, concurrence; OK, yes, thumbs-up. ANTONYM disagreement.

affix verb **1** *he affixed a stamp to the envelope* STICK, glue, paste, gum; attach, fasten, fix; clip, tack, pin; tape. ANTONYM detach.

2 *formal affix your signature to the document* APPEND, add, attach.

afflict verb *arthritis can afflict people of all ages* TROUBLE, burden, distress, cause suffering to, beset, harass, worry, oppress; torment, pester, plague, blight, bedevil, rack, smite, curse; *archaic* ail.

affliction noun **1** *a common herb reputed to cure a variety of afflictions* DISORDER, disease, malady, complaint, ailment, illness, indisposition, handicap; scourge, plague, trouble.

2 *he bore his affliction with great dignity* SUFFERING, distress, pain, trouble, misery, wretchedness, hardship, misfortune, adversity, sorrow, torment, tribulation, woe.

affluent adjective *the affluent families of Newport* WEALTHY, rich, prosperous, well off, moneyed, well-to-do; propertied, substantial, of means, of substance, plutocratic; *informal* well-heeled, rolling in it, made of money, filthy rich, stinking rich, loaded, on easy street; upper-class, upscale. See note at WEALTHY. ANTONYMS poor, impoverished.

afford verb **1** *I can't afford a new car* PAY FOR, bear the expense of, have the money for, spare the price of.

2 *it took more time than he could afford* SPARE, allow (oneself).

3 *the rooftop terrace affords beautiful views* PROVIDE, supply, furnish, offer, give, make available, yield. See note at GIVE.

affront noun *an affront to public morality* INSULT, offense, indignity, slight, snub, put-down, provocation, injury; outrage, atrocity, scandal; *informal* slap in the face, kick in the teeth.

▸ verb *she was affronted by his familiarity* INSULT, offend, mortify, provoke, pique, wound, hurt; put out, irk, displease, bother, rankle, vex, gall; outrage, scandalize, disgust; *informal* put someone's back up, needle.

aficionado noun *an aficionado of classical music* CONNOISSEUR, expert, authority, specialist, pundit; enthusiast, devotee; *informal* fan, buff, freak, nut, fiend, maniac, fanatic, addict, junkie.

aflame adjective *just moments after the lightning struck, the building was aflame* BURNING, ablaze, alight, on fire, in flames, blazing; *literary* afire.

afloat adjective & adverb *the raft was still afloat | a swimmer fighting to stay afloat* BUOYANT, floating, buoyed up, on/above the surface, (keeping one's head) above water.

afoot adjective & adverb *evil plans are afoot* GOING ON, happening, around, about, abroad, stirring, circulating, in circulation, at large, in the air/wind; brewing, looming, in the offing, on the horizon.

aforesaid adjective *the policy insures the aforesaid items* PREVIOUSLY MENTIONED, aforementioned, aforenamed; foregoing, preceding, earlier, previous; above.

afraid adjective **1** *they ran away because they were afraid* FRIGHTENED, scared, terrified, fearful, petrified, scared witless, scared to death, terror-stricken, terror-struck, frightened out of one's wits, scared out of one's wits, shaking in one's shoes, shaking like a leaf; intimidated, alarmed, panicky; faint-hearted, cowardly; *informal* scared stiff, in a cold sweat, spooked; chicken; *archaic* afeared, affrighted. ANTONYMS brave, confident.

2 *don't be afraid to ask questions* RELUCTANT, hesitant, unwilling, disinclined, loath, slow, chary, shy. ANTONYM confident.

3 *I'm afraid that your daughter is ill* SORRY, sad, distressed, regretful, apologetic. ANTONYM pleased.

afresh adverb *let's start afresh* ANEW, again, over again, once again, once more, another time.

after preposition **1** *she made a speech after the performance* FOLLOWING, subsequent to, at the close/end of, in the wake of; *formal* posterior to. ANTONYMS before, preceding.

2 *Guy shut the door after them* BEHIND, following. ANTONYM in front of.

3 *after the way he treated my sister, I never want to speak to him again* BECAUSE OF, as a result of, as a consequence of, in view of, owing to, on account of.

4 *is he still going to marry her, after all that's happened?* DESPITE, in spite of, regardless of, notwithstanding.

5 *the policeman ran after him* IN PURSUIT OF, in someone's direction, following. ANTONYMS away from, in front of.

6 *I'm after information, and I'm willing to pay for it* IN SEARCH OF, in quest of, in pursuit of, trying to find, looking for, hunting for; desirous of, wanting.

7 *they asked after Dad* ABOUT, concerning, regarding, with regard to, with respect to, with reference to.

8 *the village was named after a Roman officer* IN HONOR OF, as a tribute to.

▸ adverb **1** *the week after, we went to Madrid* LATER, afterward, after this/that, subsequently. ANTONYMS previously, before.

2 *porters were following on after with their bags* BEHIND, in the rear, at the back, in someone's wake. ANTONYMS ahead, in front.

PHRASE: **after all** *I couldn't stay mad—after all, we're best friends* ABOVE ALL, most important, most importantly, beyond everything, ultimately; *informal* when all is said and done, at the end of the day, when push comes to shove.

aftereffect noun *the aftereffects of the injury included a headache and blurred vision* REPERCUSSION, aftermath, consequence; *Medicine* sequela.

afterlife noun *they shared their personal beliefs about **the afterlife*** LIFE AFTER DEATH, the next world, the hereafter, the afterworld, eternity, kingdom come; immortality.

aftermath noun *the Red Cross is a prominent presence in the aftermath of last week's earthquake* REPERCUSSIONS, aftereffects, consequences, effects, results, fruits; wake.

afterthought noun *the few words he had added as an afterthought were the ones that would be most quoted after his death* SECOND THOUGHT, parenthesis, postscript.

afterward, afterwards adverb *afterward, we stopped for coffee* LATER, later on, subsequently, then, next, after this/that, thereafter; at a later time/date, in due course.

again adverb **1** *her spirits lifted again* ONCE MORE, another time, afresh, anew.

2 *this can add half as much again to the price* EXTRA, in addition, additionally, on top.

3 *again, evidence was not always consistent* ALSO, furthermore; moreover, besides. PHRASE: **again and again** *I've warned you again and again about that loose step* REPEATEDLY, over and over (again), time and (time) again, many times, many a time; often, frequently, continually, constantly.

against preposition **1** *a number of delegates were against the motion* OPPOSED TO, in opposition to, hostile to, averse to, antagonistic toward, inimical to, unsympathetic to, resistant to, at odds with, in disagreement with, dead set against; *informal* anti. ANTONYMS in favor of, pro.

2 *he was swimming against the tide* IN OPPOSITION TO, counter to, contrary to, in the opposite direction to. ANTONYM with.

3 *his age is against him* DISADVANTAGEOUS TO, unfavorable to, damaging to, detrimental to, prejudicial to, deleterious to, harmful to, injurious to, a drawback for. ANTONYM advantageous to.

4 *she leaned against the wall* TOUCHING, in contact with, up against, on, adjacent to.

age noun **1** *he is 35 years of age his wife is the same age* NUMBER OF YEARS, length of life; stage of life, generation, age group.

2 *her hearing had deteriorated with age* ELDERLINESS, old age, oldness, senescence, dotage, seniority, maturity; one's advancing/advanced/declining years; *literary* eld; *archaic* caducity.

3 *the Elizabethan age* ERA, epoch, period, time, eon.

4 *informal* **(ages)** *you haven't been in touch with me for ages* A LONG TIME, days/months/years on end, an eternity, an eon; *informal* ages and ages, donkey's years, a coon's age, a month of Sundays, forever.

▸ verb **1** *Cabernet Sauvignon ages well* MATURE, mellow, ripen, season.

2 *Leila has aged a lot since the last time I saw her* GROW/BECOME/GET OLD, mature, (cause to) decline, weather, fade; grow up, come of age. See note at MATURE.

aged adjective *an aged relative* ELDERLY, old, mature, older, senior, hoary, ancient, senescent, advanced in years, in one's dotage, long in the tooth, as old as the hills, past one's prime, not as young as one used to be, getting on, over the hill, no spring chicken. See note at OLD. ANTONYM young.

agency noun **1** *an advertising agency* BUSINESS, organization, company, firm, office, bureau.

2 *the infection is caused by the agency of insects* ACTION, activity, means, effect, influence, force, power, vehicle, medium.

3 *regional policy was introduced through the agency of the Board of Trade* INTERVENTION, intercession, involvement, good offices; auspices, aegis.

agenda noun **1** *the next topic on the agenda* LIST OF ITEMS, schedule, program, timetable, itinerary, lineup, list, plan.

2 *their hidden agenda* PLAN, scheme, motive.

agent noun **1** *the sale was arranged through an agent* REPRESENTATIVE, emissary, envoy, go-between, proxy, negotiator, broker, liaison, spokesperson, spokesman, spokeswoman; *informal* rep.

2 *a travel agent* AGENCY, business, organization, company, firm, bureau.

3 *a CIA agent* SPY, secret agent, undercover agent, operative, fifth columnist, mole, Mata Hari; *informal* G-man.

4 *the agents of destruction* PERFORMER, author, executor, perpetrator, producer, instrument, catalyst.

5 *a cleansing agent* MEDIUM, means, instrument, vehicle.

aggravate verb **1** *the new law could aggravate the situation* WORSEN, make worse, exacerbate, inflame, compound; add fuel to the fire/flames, add insult to injury, rub salt in the wound. ANTONYMS alleviate, improve.

2 *informal* *you don't have to aggravate people to get what you want* ANNOY, irritate, exasperate, bother, put out, nettle, provoke, antagonize, get on someone's nerves, ruffle (someone's feathers), try someone's patience; *informal* peeve, needle, bug, miff, get under someone's skin; tick off. ANTONYMS calm, conciliate.

USAGE NOTE **aggravate, aggravation**

Though documented as existing since the 1600s, *aggravate* for *annoy* or *irritate* has never gained the approval of stylists and should be avoided in formal writing. Strictly speaking, *aggravate* means "make worse; exacerbate": *writing a second apology might just aggravate the problem*. Even the eloquent American jurist Oliver Wendell Holmes, Jr., nodded once, using *aggravate* for *irritate* in a letter penned in 1895: "Our two countries aggravate each other from time to time."

In some contexts, it's genuinely difficult to tell whether the word *aggravating* is a present participle or an adjective—e.g.: "The City of Washington is notorious for aggravating allergies, and Mr. Clinton said he expected his to be more severe there than in Arkansas." (*New York Times*; Oct. 14, 1996.) The second half of that compound sentence suggests that the writer is using *aggravating* correctly. But taken alone, the phrase in the first half of the sentence ("Washington is notorious for aggravating allergies") could refer to either (1) making allergies worse (the preferred usage), or (2) allergies that are irritating or frustrating.

The confusion also occurs between the noun forms—e.g.: "Rush Limbaugh . . . has an extra tone of aggravation [read *irritation*] as he denounces the unyielding poll leads of 'the Schlickmeister' and 'noted hetero fun-seeker,' President Clinton." (*New York Times*; Sept. 25, 1996.)

Perhaps *exasperate* contributes to the misuse of *aggravate* (which sounds a bit like *exasperate*) in the sense of *irritate* (which is close in meaning to *exasperate*). Also, when *aggravate* is used in this sense it often implies something more intense than merely *irritate*. It is closer in meaning to *exasperate*. —**BG**

aggravation noun **1** *the recession led to the aggravation of unemployment problems* WORSENING, exacerbation, compounding.

2 *informal it's not worth the aggravation* NUISANCE, annoyance, irritation, hassle, headache, trouble, difficulty, inconvenience, bother, pain, distress.

aggregate noun **1** *the specimen is an aggregate of rock and mineral fragments* COLLECTION, mass, agglomeration, conglomerate, assemblage; mixture, mix, combination, blend, accumulation; compound, alloy, amalgam.

2 *he won with an aggregate of 325* TOTAL, sum total, sum, grand total.

▸ adjective *an aggregate score* TOTAL, combined, gross, overall, composite.

aggression noun **1** *an act of aggression* HOSTILITY, aggressiveness, belligerence, bellicosity, force, violence; pugnacity, pugnaciousness, militancy, warmongering; attack, assault.

2 *he played the game with unceasing aggression* CONFIDENCE, self-confidence, boldness, determination, forcefulness, vigor, energy, zeal.

aggressive adjective **1** *aggressive behavior* HOSTILE, belligerent, bellicose, antagonistic, truculent; pugnacious, combative, two-fisted, violent; macho; confrontational; quarrelsome, argumentative. ANTONYMS meek, friendly.

2 *aggressive foreign policy* WARMONGERING, warlike, warring, belligerent, bellicose, hawkish, militaristic; offensive, expansionist. ANTONYMS peaceable, peaceful.

3 *an aggressive promotional drive* ASSERTIVE, pushy, forceful, vigorous, energetic, dynamic; bold, audacious; *informal* in-your-face, feisty. See note at BOLD. ANTONYMS submissive, diffident.

aggressor noun *England was the aggressor in a succession of wars* ATTACKER, assaulter, assailant; invader, instigator, warmonger.

aggrieved adjective **1** *the manager looked aggrieved at the suggestion* RESENTFUL, affronted, indignant, disgruntled, discontented, upset, offended, piqued, riled, nettled, vexed, irked, irritated, annoyed, put out, chagrined; *informal* peeved, miffed, in a huff, sore, steamed. ANTONYM pleased.

2 *the aggrieved party* WRONGED, injured, mistreated, ill-treated, abused, harmed.

aghast adjective *eyewitnesses to the explosion were aghast* HORRIFIED, appalled, dismayed, thunderstruck, stunned, shocked, staggered; *informal* flabbergasted.

WORD NOTE **aghast**

Nothing conveys a horrified reaction better, because the whispery, gasping sound of the word personalizes it, seems to locate the horror in the victim's frozen, ghost-pale face, in their paralyzing intake of breath. —**DA**

agile adjective **1** *she was as agile as a monkey* NIMBLE, lithe, supple, limber, acrobatic, fleet-footed, light-footed, light on one's feet; *literary* fleet, lightsome. ANTONYMS clumsy, stiff.

2 *an agile mind* ALERT, sharp, acute, shrewd, astute, perceptive, quick-witted. ANTONYMS slow, dull.

agitate verb **1** *any mention of Clare agitates my grandmother* UPSET, perturb, fluster, ruffle, disconcert, unnerve, disquiet, disturb, distress, unsettle, unhinge; *informal* rattle, faze; discombobulate.

2 *she agitated for the appointment of more women* CAMPAIGN, strive, battle, fight, struggle, push, press.

3 *agitate the water to disperse the oil* STIR, whisk, churn, beat.

agitated adjective *she became increasingly agitated during the inquest* UPSET, perturbed, flustered, ruffled, disconcerted, unnerved, unstrung, disquieted, disturbed, distressed, unsettled; nervous, jumpy, on edge, tense, keyed up; *informal* rattled, fazed, in a dither, in a flap, in a state, in a lather, steamed up, jittery, in a tizzy, discombobulated. ANTONYMS calm, relaxed.

agitator noun *tell your band of agitators that my generals are heavily armed and most unsympathetic* TROUBLEMAKER, rabble-rouser, agent provocateur, demagogue, incendiary; revolutionary, firebrand, rebel, insurgent, subversive; *informal* disturber.

agnostic noun *Darrow was an avowed agnostic, legendary defense attorney, and Scopes's counsel* SKEPTIC, doubter, doubting Thomas, cynic; unbeliever, nonbeliever, rationalist; *rare* nullifidian. ANTONYMS believer, theist.

ago adverb *years ago, on this very site, was a small stone cottage* IN THE PAST, before, earlier, back, since, previously; *formal* heretofore.

agog adverb *tell us what happened—we're all agog!* EAGER, excited, impatient, keen, anxious, avid, in suspense, on tenterhooks, on the edge of one's seat, on pins and needles, waiting with bated breath.

agonize verb *he agonized about the impending layoffs* WORRY, fret, fuss, brood, upset oneself, rack one's brains, wrestle with oneself, be worried, be anxious, feel uneasy, exercise oneself; *informal* stew.

agonizing adjective *agonizing pain* EXCRUCIATING, harrowing, racking, searing, extremely painful, acute, severe, torturous, tormenting, piercing; *informal* hellish.

agony noun *the agony was both mental and physical* PAIN, hurt, suffering, torture, torment, anguish, affliction, trauma; pangs, throes.

agrarian adjective *Jefferson's vision of an agrarian society* AGRICULTURAL, rural, rustic, pastoral, countryside, farming; *literary* georgic, sylvan, Arcadian.

agree verb **1** *I agree with you* CONCUR, be of the same mind/opinion, see eye to eye, be in sympathy, be united, be as one man. ANTONYM differ.

2 *they had **agreed to** a cease-fire* CONSENT TO, assent to, acquiesce to, accept, approve, say yes to, give one's approval to, give the nod to; *informal* OK; *formal* accede to. ANTONYM reject.

3 *the plan and the drawing do not agree with each other* MATCH (UP), jibe, accord, correspond, chime in, conform, coincide, fit, tally, be in harmony/agreement, harmonize, be consistent/equivalent; *informal* square. ANTONYMS differ, contradict.

4 *they **agreed on** a price* SETTLE ON, decide on, arrive at, work out, negotiate, reach an agreement on, come to terms on, strike a bargain on, make a deal on, shake hands on.

agreeable adjective **1** *an agreeable atmosphere of rural tranquility* PLEASANT, pleasing, enjoyable, pleasurable, nice, to one's liking, appealing, charming, delightful. See note at PLEASANT. ANTONYM unpleasant.

2 *an agreeable fellow* LIKABLE, charming, amiable, affable, pleasant, nice, friendly, good-natured, sociable, genial, congenial, simpatico. ANTONYM unpleasant.

3 *we should get together for a talk, if you're agreeable* WILLING, amenable, in accord/agreement, compliant, consenting. ANTONYM unwilling.

agreement noun **1** *all heads nodded in agreement* ACCORD, concurrence, consensus; assent, acceptance, consent, acquiescence, endorsement, like-mindedness.

2 *an agreement on military cooperation* CONTRACT, compact, treaty, covenant, pact, accord, concordat, protocol.

3 *there is some agreement between my view and that of the author* CORRESPONDENCE, consistency, compatibility, accord; similarity, resemblance, likeness, similitude. ANTONYM discord.

agricultural adjective **1** *an agricultural laborer* FARM, farming, agrarian; rural, rustic, pastoral, countryside; *literary* georgic, sylvan, Arcadian. ANTONYM urban.

2 *agricultural land* FARMED, farm, agrarian, cultivated, tilled, horticultural. ANTONYMS wild, uncultivated.

agriculture noun *the mechanization of agriculture* FARMING, cultivation, tillage, tilling, husbandry, land/farm management, horticulture; agribusiness, agronomy.

aground adverb & adjective *the ship was aground when we spotted it* GROUNDED, ashore, beached, stuck, shipwrecked, high and dry, on the rocks, on the ground/bottom.

ahead adverb **1** *he peered ahead, but could see nothing* FORWARD, toward the front, frontward, onward, along. ANTONYM behind.

2 *he had ridden on ahead* IN FRONT, at the head, in the lead, at the fore, in the vanguard, in advance. ANTONYMS behind, at the back.

3 *she was preparing herself for what lay ahead* IN THE FUTURE, in time, in time to come, in the fullness of time, at a later date, after this, henceforth, later on, in due course, next. ANTONYM in the past.

4 *they are ahead by six points* LEADING, winning, in the lead, (out) in front, first, coming first. ANTONYMS trailing, losing.

PHRASE: **ahead of 1** *Blanche went ahead of the others* IN FRONT OF, before. **2** *we have a demanding trip ahead of us* IN STORE FOR, waiting for. **3** *two months ahead of schedule* IN ADVANCE OF, before, earlier than.

aid noun **1** *with the aid of his colleagues he prepared a manifesto* ASSISTANCE, support, help, backing, cooperation; a helping hand. ANTONYM hindrance.

2 *humanitarian aid* RELIEF, charity, financial assistance, donations, contributions, subsidies, handouts, subvention, succor; *historical* alms.

▸ verb **1** *he provided an army to aid the King of England* HELP, assist, abet, come to someone's aid, give assistance, lend a hand, be of service; avail, succor, sustain. ANTONYM hinder.

2 *certain teas can aid restful sleep* FACILITATE, promote, encourage, help, further, boost; speed up, hasten, accelerate, expedite. ANTONYMS discourage, hinder.

aide noun *an aide to the supervisor* ASSISTANT, helper, adviser, right-hand man, man/girl Friday, adjutant, deputy, second-in-command, second; subordinate, junior, underling, acolyte.

ailing adjective **1** *his ailing mother* ILL, sick, unwell, sickly, poorly, weak, indisposed, in poor/bad health, infirm, debilitated, diseased, delicate, valetudinarian, below par, bedridden; *informal* laid up, under the weather. ANTONYM healthy.

2 *the country's ailing economy* FAILING, in poor condition, weak, poor, deficient. ANTONYM strong.

ailment noun *a common stomach ailment* ILLNESS, disease, sickness, disorder, condition, affliction, malady, complaint, infirmity; *informal* bug, virus.

aim verb **1** *he aimed the rifle* POINT, direct, train, sight, line up.

2 *she **aimed at** the target* TAKE AIM AT, fix on, zero in on, draw a bead on.

3 *undergraduates **aiming for** a degree* WORK TOWARD, be after, set one's sights on, try for, strive for, aspire to, endeavor to achieve; *formal* essay for.

4 *this system is **aimed at** the home entertainment market* TARGET AT, intend for, destine for, direct at, design for, tailor for, market to, pitch to/at.

5 *we aim to give you the best possible service* INTEND, mean, have in mind/view; plan, resolve, propose, design. See note at INTEND.

▸ noun *our aim is to develop gymnasts to the top level* OBJECTIVE, object, goal, end, target, design, desire, desired result, intention, intent, plan, purpose, object of the exercise; ambition, aspiration, wish, dream, hope, raison d'être.

aimless adjective **1** *Flavia set out on an aimless walk* PURPOSELESS, goalless, without purpose, haphazard, wandering, without goal, desultory. ANTONYM purposeful.

2 *aimless men standing outside the bars* UNOCCUPIED, idle, at a loose end; purposeless, undirected. ANTONYM determined.

ain't See note below.

USAGE NOTE ain't

Is this word used orally in most parts of the country by cultivated speakers? In 1961, *Webster's Third New International Dictionary of the English Language* (W3) said it was, provoking a firestorm of protests from journalists and academics. W3's assessment was quite a change from that of W2 (the second edition, published in 1934), which had given it a tag: "Dial. or Illit." The editor of W3, Philip Gove, explained the change by conceding that he had no large files of empirical evidence: "Knowledge of some kind of language behavior comes through contact with its observers and is not always documented because there seems to be no reason to collect additional evidence." If that's the method, then one can confidently say that W3's treatment was flawed in its incompleteness. In 1962, the year after W3 was published, an apt cartoon appeared in *The New Yorker*. A man is standing in the reception area of G. & C. Merriam Co., Dictionary Division, as the receptionist says to him, "Sorry. Dr. Gove ain't in." Yes, *ain't* is used by cultivated speakers, but almost always for either of two reasons: (1) to be tongue-in-cheek, or (2) to flaunt their reverse snobbery. For most people, it remains a shibboleth of poor usage. **—BG**

air noun **1** *hundreds of birds hovered in the air* SKY, atmosphere; heavens, ether.

2 *open the windows to get some air into the room* BREEZE, draft, wind; breath/blast of air, gust of wind.

3 *an air of defiance* EXPRESSION, appearance, look, impression, aspect, aura, mien, countenance, manner, bearing, tone.

4 **(airs)** *putting on airs* AFFECTATIONS, pretension, pretentiousness, affectedness, posturing, airs and graces.

5 *a traditional Scottish air* TUNE, melody, song; *literary* lay.

▸ verb **1** *a chance to air your views* EXPRESS, voice, make public, ventilate, articulate, state, declare, give expression/voice to; have one's say about.

2 *the windows were opened to air the room* VENTILATE, freshen, refresh, cool.

3 *the film was aired nationwide* BROADCAST, transmit, screen, show, televise, telecast.

airborne adjective *he served with an airborne unit* FLYING, in flight, in the air, on the wing.

aircraft noun *this early aircraft is on display at the Smithsonian* airplane, jet, helicopter, balloon, glider.

airily adverb *the sparrow hopped airily along* | *the composer meant for the piece to be played airily* LIGHTLY, breezily, flippantly, casually, nonchalantly, heedlessly, without consideration. ANTONYM seriously.

airplane noun *the airplane took off* AIRCRAFT, plane, airliner, jet, jumbo jet, jetliner, bush plane, float plane, seaplane, crop duster; *dated* flying machine.

airport noun *directions to the airport* airfield, landing strip, airstrip, air terminal.

airtight adjective **1** *an airtight container* SEALED, hermetically sealed, closed tight, shut tight.

2 *an airtight alibi* INDISPUTABLE, unquestionable, incontrovertible, undeniable, incontestable, irrefutable, watertight, beyond dispute, beyond question, beyond doubt.

airy adjective **1** *the conservatory is light and airy* WELL VENTILATED, fresh; spacious, uncluttered; light, bright. ANTONYM stuffy.

2 *an airy gesture* NONCHALANT, casual, breezy, flippant, insouciant, heedless. ANTONYM serious.

3 *airy clouds* DELICATE, soft, fine, feathery, insubstantial. ANTONYMS heavy, dense.

airy-fairy adjective *chiefly Brit. informal* *an airy-fairy perspective on love* IMPRACTICAL, unrealistic, idealistic, fanciful, blue-sky. ANTONYM practical.

aisle noun *there is no sitting allowed in the aisle* PASSAGE, passageway, gangway, walkway, corridor.

ajar adjective & adverb *with shutters ajar, we got only a glimpse of the morning sun* | *use the flatiron to keep the door ajar* SLIGHTLY OPEN, half open. ANTONYMS closed, wide open.

akin adjective *much of the vegetation here is akin to that of southern California* SIMILAR, related, close, near, corresponding, comparable, equivalent; connected, alike, analogous. ANTONYM unlike.

alacrity noun *I am confident that Liberia is going to move forward now with alacrity at the peace table* EAGERNESS, willingness, readiness; enthusiasm, ardor, avidity, fervor, keenness; promptness, haste, swiftness, dispatch, speed.

alarm noun **1** *we spun around in alarm* FEAR, anxiety, apprehension, trepidation, nervousness, unease, distress, agitation, consternation, disquiet, perturbation, fright, panic. ANTONYMS calmness, composure.

2 *sound the alarm a smoke alarm* WARNING, alert, distress signal; SIREN, bell, horn, whistle; *archaic* tocsin.

▸ verb *the news had alarmed her* FRIGHTEN, scare, panic, unnerve, distress, agitate, upset, disconcert, shock, dismay, disturb; *informal* rattle, spook, scare the living daylights out of. ANTONYMS calm, reassure.

alarming adjective *the latest statistics on deaths from AIDS are more than just a little alarming* FRIGHTENING, unnerving, shocking; distressing, upsetting, disconcerting, perturbing, worrisome, worrying, dismaying, disquieting, startling, disturbing; *informal* scary. ANTONYM reassuring.

alarmist noun *until I saw the map and radar photos of the hurricane, I thought he was being an alarmist* SCAREMONGER, doomster, doomsayer, Cassandra, Chicken Little. ANTONYM optimist.

album noun **1** SCRAPBOOK, register, collection, treasury.

2 RECORD, CD, recording, disc; LP, vinyl.

WORD NOTE album

Variations in the format of recorded music: *single* (typically two songs), *maxisingle* (a long single), *EP* (for "extended play"), *twelve-inch* (a vinyl maxisingle), *long-player* (at least 25 minutes in the 1960s, at least 40 minutes today), *box set* (two or more records packaged together). A collection on CD is still an *album,* a *record,* and a *long-player* (but not an LP, that's a category of vinyl). Till the 1950s, an *album* was a batch of 78-rpm records sold in a book that looked like a photo album. The playback medium has always influenced the length of albums: for example, today's 40-minute minimum is to ensure that two albums won't fit on one CD. When the medium is as large as the Internet itself, the album will have to find its own length, if it survives at all. —**SM**

---

alchemy noun *immortality through alchemy* CHEMISTRY; magic, sorcery, witchcraft.

alcohol noun *the doctor told him to avoid alcohol* LIQUOR, intoxicating drink/beverage(s), strong drink, alcoholic drink/beverage(s), drink, spirits; *informal* booze, hooch, the hard stuff, firewater, rotgut, moonshine, white lightning, grog, the demon rum, the bottle, the sauce; *technical* ethyl alcohol, ethanol. See tables at LIQUOR, COCKTAIL.

alcoholic adjective *alcoholic drinks* INTOXICATING, inebriating, containing alcohol, fermented; strong, hard, stiff; *formal* spirituous.

▸ noun *he is an alcoholic* DIPSOMANIAC, drunk, drunkard, heavy/hard/serious drinker, problem drinker, alcohol abuser, person with a drinking problem; tippler, sot, inebriate; *informal* boozer, lush, alky, boozehound, dipso, juicer, wino, barfly.

alcove noun *nestled on a cushion in the alcove, reading a book* RECESS, niche, nook, bay; arbor, bower.

alert adjective **1** *police have asked neighbors to stay alert* VIGILANT, watchful, attentive, observant, wide awake, circumspect; on the lookout, on one's guard, on one's toes, on the qui vive; *informal* heads-up, keeping one's eyes open/peeled, bright-eyed and bushy-tailed. See note at VIGILANT. ANTONYM inattentive.

2 *mentally alert* QUICK-WITTED, sharp, bright, quick, keen, perceptive, wide awake, on one's toes; *informal* on the ball, quick on the uptake, all there, with it. ANTONYMS inattentive, slow-witted.

▸ noun **1** *a state of alert* VIGILANCE, watchfulness, attentiveness, alertness, circumspection.

2 *a flood alert* WARNING, notification, notice; siren, alarm, signal, danger signal, distress signal.

▸ verb *police were alerted by a phone call* WARN, notify, apprise, forewarn, put on one's guard, put on the qui vive; *informal* tip off, clue in.

alias noun *he is known under several aliases* ASSUMED NAME, false name, pseudonym, sobriquet, incognito; pen name, stage name, nom de plume, nom de guerre; *rare* allonym, anonym.

▸ adverb *Lester Gillis, alias Baby Face Nelson* ALSO KNOWN AS, aka, also called, otherwise known as.

alibi noun *we've both got a good alibi for last night* DEFENSE, justification, explanation, reason; *informal* story, line.

alien adjective **1** *an alien landscape* UNFAMILIAR, unknown, strange, peculiar; exotic, foreign. ANTONYM familiar.

2 *a vicious role* ***alien to*** *his nature* INCOMPATIBLE WITH, unusual for, opposed to, conflicting with, contrary to, in conflict with, at variance with, out of step with; *rare* oppugnant to. ANTONYM familiar.

3 *alien beings* EXTRATERRESTRIAL, unearthly, otherworldly; Martian, Jovian, Venutian. ANTONYM earthly.

▸ noun **1** *an illegal alien* FOREIGNER, nonnative, immigrant, emigrant, émigré.

2 *the alien's spaceship* EXTRATERRESTRIAL, ET; Martian, Jovian, Venutian; *informal* little green man.

alienate verb *was it the dispute over the inheritance that has alienated these two brothers?* ESTRANGE, divide, distance, put at a distance, isolate, cut off; set against, turn away, turn off, drive apart, marginalize, disunite, set at variance/odds, drive a wedge between.

alienation verb *my deep sense of alienation* ISOLATION, detachment, estrangement, distance, separation, division; cutting off, turning away. See note at SOLITUDE.

alight[1] verb **1** *he* ***alighted from*** *the train* GET OFF, step off, disembark from, pile out of; detrain, deplane; dismount. ANTONYMS get on, board.

2 *a swallow alighted on a branch* LAND, come to rest, settle, perch, light. ANTONYM fly off.

alight[2] adjective **1** *the bales of hay were alight* BURNING, ablaze, aflame, on fire, in flames, blazing; *literary* afire.

2 *her face was alight with laughter* LIT UP, gleaming, glowing, aglow, ablaze, bright, shining, resplendent, radiant.

align verb **1** *the desks are aligned in straight rows* LINE UP, put in order, put in rows/columns, straighten, place, position, situate, set, range.

2 *he* ***aligned himself*** *with the workers* ALLY ONESELF, affiliate oneself, associate oneself, join, side, unite, combine oneself, join forces, form an alliance, team up, band together, throw in one's lot, make common cause.

alike adjective *all the doors looked alike* SIMILAR, (much) the same, indistinguishable, identical, uniform, interchangeable, cut from the same cloth; *informal* like (two) peas in a pod, like Tweedledum and Tweedledee, much of a muchness. ANTONYM different.

▸ adverb *great minds think alike* SIMILARLY, (just) the same, in the same way/manner/fashion, equally, likewise, identically.

alimony noun *he has failed to pay alimony for more than two years* FINANCIAL SUPPORT, maintenance, support; child support.

alive adjective **1** *he was last seen alive on Labor Day | when mastodons were alive* LIVING, live; breathing, vital, functioning; animate, sentient; existing; *informal* alive and kicking, in the land of the living, among the living; *archaic* quick. ANTONYMS dead, inanimate, extinct.

2 *the association has kept her dream alive* IN EXISTENCE, existing, active, existent, extant, ongoing, abiding, functioning, in operation; current, contemporary; *informal* on the map. ANTONYMS inactive, obsolete.

3 *it was Judith's great love that made Marty so alive* ANIMATED, lively, full of life, alert, active, energetic, vigorous, spry, sprightly, vital, vivacious, buoyant, exuberant, ebullient, zestful, spirited; *informal* full of beans, bright-eyed and bushy-tailed, chirpy, chipper, peppy, full of vim and vigor. ANTONYMS listless, lethargic.

4 *the place was alive with mice* TEEMING, swarming, overrun, bristling, infested; crowded, packed; *informal* crawling, lousy; *rare* pullulating.

THE RIGHT WORD

Dead is dead, but one can be **alive** to varying degrees The broadest of these terms describing what has life or shows signs of having it, *alive* can refer to what barely exists (*he was unconscious but still alive when they found him*) as well as to what is bursting with (literal or figurative) life (*her face was alive with excitement and anticipation*). **Living**, on the other hand, is more limited in scope and implies the condition of not being dead (*at 92, she was the oldest living member of the family*) or a state of continued existence or activity (*America's greatest living historian*). **Animate** has fewer connotations than *living* or *alive*; though rare, it is used to distinguish living organisms as opposed to dead ones (*one of the few animate creatures after the devastating explosion*). **Animated**, on the other hand, is used to describe inanimate things to which life or the appearance of life has been given (*an animated cartoon*), or things that are vigorous and lively (*an animated debate on the death penalty*). Anything that is essential to life is **vital** (*vital functions; vital organs*), but it can also be used to describe the energy, activity, and alertness of living things (*an aging but vital member of the historical society*).

all adjective **1** *all the children went home* | *all creatures need sleep* EACH OF, each one of, every one of, every single one of; every (single), each and every. ANTONYMS no, none of.

2 *the sun shone all week* THE WHOLE OF THE, every bit of the, the complete, the entire. ANTONYM none of.

3 *in all honesty* | *with all speed* COMPLETE, entire, total, full; greatest (possible), maximum. ANTONYMS no, little.

▸ pronoun **1** *all are welcome* EVERYONE, everybody, each person, every person. ANTONYMS none, nobody.

2 *all of the cups were broken* EACH ONE, the sum, the total, the whole lot. ANTONYM none.

3 *they took all of it* EVERYTHING, every part, the whole amount, the (whole) lot, the entirety. ANTONYMS none, nothing.

▸ adverb *he was dressed all in black* COMPLETELY, fully, entirely, totally, wholly, absolutely, utterly; in every respect, in all respects, without reservation, without exception. ANTONYM partly.

WORD NOTE **all of**

Other than as an ironic idiom for "no more than" (e.g., *Sex with Edgar lasts all of twenty seconds*), does *all of* have any legit uses? The answer is a qualified, complicated, and personally embarrassed yes. Here's the story. An irksome habit of many student writers is to just automatically stick an *of* between *all* and any noun that follows—*All of the firemen posed for the calendar; She gave the disease to all of her friends*—and I have spent nearly a decade telling undergrads to abjure this habit, for two reasons. The first is that an excess of *of's* is one of the surest signs of flabby or maladroit writing, and the second is that the usage is often wrong. Over and over, in conference and class, I have promulgated the following rule: Except for the ironic-idiom case, the only time it's correct to use *all of* is when the adjective phrase is followed by a pronoun—*All of them got pink-eye; I wanted Edgar to have all of me*—unless, however, the relevant pronoun is possessive, in which case you must again omit the *of*, as in *All my relatives despise Edgar.* Only a few weeks ago, however, I learned (from a bright student who had gotten annoyed enough at my constant hectoring to start poring over usage guides in the hope of finding something I'd been wrong about that she could raise her hand at just the right moment in class and embarrass me with . . . which she did, and I was, and deserved it—there's nothing worse than a pedant who's wrong) that there's actually one more complication to the first part of the rule. With *all* plus a noun, it turns out that a medial *of* is required if the noun is possessive, as in *All of Edgar's problems stem from his childhood* or *All of Dave's bombast came back to haunt him that day.* I doubt now I'll ever forget this. —**DFW**

allay verb *nothing would allay his fears* REDUCE, diminish, decrease, lessen, assuage, alleviate, ease, relieve, soothe, soften, calm, take the edge off. See note at ALLEVIATE. ANTONYMS increase, intensify.

allegation noun *not one of the allegations against my client has been substantiated* CLAIM, assertion, charge, accusation, declaration, statement, contention, deposition, argument, affirmation, attestation, grievance; *formal* averment.

allege verb *both children allege that the babysitter had left them alone for hours at a time* CLAIM, assert, charge, accuse, declare, state, contend, argue, affirm, maintain, attest, testify, swear; *formal* aver.

alleged adjective *did Mr. Ramirez tell you what time this alleged crime took place?* SUPPOSED, so-called, claimed, professed, purported, ostensible, putative, unproven.

allegedly adverb *he allegedly went AWOL* REPORTEDLY, supposedly, reputedly, purportedly, ostensibly, apparently, putatively, by all accounts, so the story goes.

allegiance noun *allegiance to the queen* LOYALTY, faithfulness, fidelity, obedience, homage, devotion; *historical* fealty; *formal* troth. ANTONYMS disloyalty, treachery.

allegorical adjective *an allegorical painting* SYMBOLIC, metaphorical, figurative, representative, emblematic.

allegory noun *Saramago's latest novel is an allegory of social disintegration* PARABLE, analogy, metaphor, symbol, emblem.

allergy noun **1** *an allergy to feathers* HYPERSENSITIVITY, sensitivity, allergic reaction; anaphylaxis.

2 *informal their allergy to free enterprise* AVERSION, antipathy, opposition, hostility, antagonism, dislike, distaste.

alleviate verb *use ice to alleviate the swelling* REDUCE, ease, relieve, take the edge off, deaden, dull, diminish, lessen, weaken, lighten, attenuate, mitigate, allay, assuage, palliate, damp, soothe, help, soften, temper. ANTONYM aggravate.

THE RIGHT WORD

To **alleviate** is to make something easier to endure (*alleviate the pain following surgery*); **allay** is often used interchangeably, but it also means to put to rest, to quiet or calm (*to allay their suspicions*). **Assuage** and *allay* both suggest the calming or satisfying of a desire or appetite, but *assuage* implies a more complete or permanent satisfaction (*we allay our hunger by nibbling hors d'oeuvres, but a huge dinner assuages our appetite*). To **relieve** implies reducing the misery or discomfort to the point where something is bearable (*relieve the monotony of the cross-country bus trip*) and **mitigate**, which comes from a Latin word meaning to soften, usually means to lessen in force or intensity (*mitigate the storm's impact*). **Abate** suggests a progressive lessening in degree or intensity (*her fever was abating*). To **temper** is to soften or moderate (*to temper justice with mercy*), but it can also mean the exact opposite: to harden or toughen something (*tempering steel; a body tempered by lifting weights*).

alley noun *he disappeared down an alley on his motorbike* PASSAGE, passageway, alleyway, back alley, back lane, laneway, backstreet, lane, path, pathway, walk, allée.

alliance noun **1** *a defense alliance* ASSOCIATION, union, league, confederation, federation, confederacy, coalition, consortium, affiliation, partnership.

2 *an alliance between medicine and morality* RELATIONSHIP, affinity, association, connection.

allied adjective **1** *a group of allied nations* FEDERATED, confederated, associated, in alliance, in league, in partnership; unified, united, integrated. ANTONYM hostile.

2 *agricultural and allied industries* ASSOCIATED, related, connected, interconnected, linked; similar, like, comparable, equivalent. ANTONYMS dissimilar, unrelated.

all-important adjective *the town's all-important tourist industry* VITAL, essential, indispensable, crucial, key, vitally important, of the utmost importance; critical, life-and-death, paramount, preeminent, high-priority; urgent, pressing, burning. ANTONYM inessential.

allocate verb *how funds will be allocated is dependent on which budget gets approved* ALLOT, assign, distribute, apportion, share out, portion out, dispense, deal out, dole out, give out, dish out, parcel out, ration out, divide up/out; *informal* divvy up.

allocation noun **1** *the efficient allocation of resources* ALLOTMENT, assignment, distribution, apportionment, sharing out, handing out, dealing out, doling out, giving out, dishing out, parceling out, rationing out, dividing up/out; *informal* divvying up.

2 *our annual allocation of funds* ALLOWANCE, allotment, quota, share, ration, portion, grant, slice; *informal* cut.

allot verb *Councilwoman Crane has asked why so much tax revenue was* ***allotted to*** *park restoration* ALLOCATE TO, assign to, apportion to, distribute to, issue to, grant to; earmark for, designate for, set aside for; hand out to/for, deal out to/for, dish out to/for, dole out to/for, give out to/for; *informal* divvy up for.

allotment noun **1** *the allotment of shares by a company* ALLOCATION, assignment, distribution, apportionment, issuing, sharing out, handing out, dealing out, doling out, giving out, dishing out, parceling out, rationing out, dividing up/out; *informal* divvying up.

2 *each member received an allotment of new shares* QUOTA, share, ration, grant, allocation, allowance, slice; *informal* cut.

all out adverb *I'm working all out to finish my novel* STRENUOUSLY, energetically, vigorously, hard, with all one's might (and main), at full speed, in high gear, eagerly, enthusiastically, industriously, diligently, assiduously, sedulously, indefatigably; *informal* like mad, like crazy. ANTONYM lackadaisically.

▸ adjective *an all-out attack* STRENUOUS, energetic, vigorous, forceful, forcible; spirited, mettlesome, plucky, determined, resolute, wholehearted, unrestrained, aggressive, eager, keen, enthusiastic, zealous, ardent, fervent. ANTONYM halfhearted.

allow verb **1** *we don't allow open fires at this campground* PERMIT, let, authorize, give permission for, give authorization for, sanction, license, enable, entitle; consent to, assent to, give one's consent to/for, give one's assent to/for, give one's blessing to/for, give the nod to, acquiesce to, agree to, approve; tolerate, brook; *informal* give the go-ahead to/for, give the thumbs up to/for, OK, give the OK to/for, give the green light to/for; *formal* accede to. ANTONYMS prevent, forbid.

2 *allow an hour or so for driving* SET ASIDE, allocate, allot, earmark, designate, assign, leave.

3 *she allowed that all people had their funny little ways* ADMIT, acknowledge, recognize, agree, accept, concede, grant. ANTONYM deny.

allowable adjective *the maximum allowable number of users* PERMISSIBLE, permitted, allowed, admissible, acceptable, legal, lawful, legitimate, licit, authorized, sanctioned, approved, in order; *informal* OK, legit. ANTONYM forbidden.

allowance noun **1** *your baggage allowance* PERMITTED AMOUNT/QUANTITY, allocation, allotment, quota, share, ration, grant, limit, portion, slice.

2 *she spent her allowance on paperbacks* PAYMENT, pocket money, sum of money, contribution, grant, subsidy, stipend, maintenance, remittance, financial support, per diem.

3 *a tax allowance* CONCESSION, reduction, decrease, discount.

PHRASE: **make allowance(s) for 1** *you must make allowances for delays* TAKE INTO CONSIDERATION, take into account, bear in mind, have regard to, provide for, plan for, make plans for, get ready for, allow for, make provision for, make preparations for, prepare for. **2** *she made allowances for his faults* EXCUSE, make excuses for, forgive, pardon, overlook.

alloy noun *modern pewter is an alloy of tin, copper, and antimony* MIXTURE, mix, amalgam, fusion, meld, blend, compound, combination, composite, union; *technical* admixture.

all-powerful adjective *an all-powerful military leadership* OMNIPOTENT, almighty, supreme, preeminent; dictatorial, despotic, totalitarian, autocratic. ANTONYM powerless.

all right adjective **1** *the tea was all right* SATISFACTORY, acceptable, adequate, fairly good, passable, reasonable; *informal* so-so, 'comme ci, comme ça,' OK, jake. ANTONYM unsatisfactory.

2 *are you all right?* UNHURT, uninjured, unharmed, unscathed, in one piece, safe, safe and sound; well, fine, alive and well, OK. ANTONYMS hurt, in danger.

3 *it's all right for you to go now* PERMISSIBLE, permitted, allowed, allowable, admissible, acceptable, legal, lawful, legitimate, licit, authorized, sanctioned, approved, in order, OK, legit. ANTONYM forbidden.

▸ adverb **1** *the system works all right* SATISFACTORILY, adequately, fairly well, passably, acceptably, reasonably; OK. ANTONYM unsatisfactorily.

2 *it's him all right* DEFINITELY, certainly, unquestionably, undoubtedly, indubitably, undeniably, assuredly, for sure, without (a) doubt, beyond (any) doubt, beyond the shadow of a doubt; *archaic* in sooth, verily. ANTONYM possibly.

▸ exclamation *all right, I'll go* VERY WELL (THEN), fine, good, yes, agreed, right (then); *informal* OK, okey-dokey, roger, wilco. ANTONYM no.

allude verb *the prosecutor* ***alluded to*** *Dixon's past* REFER TO, touch on, suggest, hint at, imply, mention (in passing), make an allusion to; *formal* advert to.

allure noun *the allure of Paris* ATTRACTION, lure, draw, pull, appeal, allurement, enticement, temptation, charm, seduction, fascination. ANTONYM repulsion.

▸ verb *will sponsors be allured by such opportunities?* ATTRACT, lure, entice, tempt, appeal to, captivate, draw, win over, charm, seduce, inveigle, beguile, fascinate, whet the appetite of, make someone's mouth water. See note at TEMPT. ANTONYM repel.

alluring adjective *an alluring hostess* ENTICING, tempting, attractive, appealing, inviting, captivating, fetching, seductive; enchanting, charming, fascinating; *informal* come-hither.

allusion noun *the town's name is an **allusion to** its founding family* REFERENCE TO, mention of, suggestion of, hint to, intimation of, comment on, remark on.

ally noun *close political allies* ASSOCIATE, colleague, friend, confederate, partner, supporter. ANTONYMS enemy, opponent.

▸ verb **1** *he allied his racing experience with business acumen* COMBINE, marry, couple, merge, amalgamate, join, fuse. ANTONYM split.

2 *the Catholic powers allied with Philip II* UNITE, combine, join (up), join forces, band together, team up, collaborate, side, align oneself, form an alliance, throw in one's lot, make common cause. ANTONYM split.

almanac noun *we consult the almanac for planting times* YEARBOOK, calendar, register, annual; manual, handbook.

almighty adjective **1** *I swear by almighty God* ALL-POWERFUL, omnipotent, supreme, preeminent. ANTONYM powerless.

2 *informal an almighty explosion* VERY GREAT, huge, enormous, immense, colossal, massive, prodigious, stupendous, tremendous, monumental, mammoth, vast, gigantic, giant, mighty, Herculean, epic; very loud, deafening, ear-splitting, ear-piercing, booming, thundering, thunderous; *informal* whopping, thumping, astronomical, mega, monster, humongous, jumbo, ginormous. ANTONYM insignificant.

almost adverb *we're almost done with the attic* NEARLY, (just) about, more or less, practically, virtually, all but, as good as, close to, near, not quite, roughly, not far from, for all intents and purposes; approaching, bordering on, verging on; *informal* pretty near, pretty nearly, pretty much, pretty well; *literary* well-nigh, nigh on.

alms plural noun (chiefly **historical**) *alms for the poor* GIFT(S), donation(s), handout(s), offering(s), charity, baksheesh, largesse.

aloft adjective & adverb *they held the banner aloft* UPWARD, up, high, in(to) the air, in(to) the sky, skyward, on high, overhead, heavenward, high up, up (above). ANTONYM down.

alone adjective & adverb **1** *she lived alone | he came to the party alone* BY ONESELF, on one's own, all alone, solitary, single, singly, solo, solus; unescorted, unaccompanied, partnerless, companionless, by one's lonesome. ANTONYMS with others, accompanied.

2 *he managed the store alone* UNAIDED, unassisted, without help, without assistance, single-handedly, solo, on one's own. ANTONYM with help.

3 *Klein felt terribly alone* LONELY, isolated, solitary, deserted, abandoned, forsaken, forlorn, friendless. ANTONYMS loved, wanted, among friends.

4 *a house standing alone* APART, by itself/oneself, separate, detached, isolated. ANTONYM among others.

5 *you alone inspire me* ONLY, solely, just; and no one else, and nothing else, and no one but, and nothing but.

along preposition **1** *she walked along the corridor* DOWN, from one end of —— to the other.

2 *trees grew along the river bank* BESIDE, by the side of, on the edge of, alongside.

3 *they'll stop along the way* ON, at a point on, in the course of.

▸ adverb **1** *Maurice moved along past the other exhibits* ONWARD, on, ahead, forward, forth.

2 *I invited a friend along* AS COMPANY, with one, to accompany one, as a partner.

PHRASE: **along with** *he backpacked, along with Kate and Sean, across northern Vermont* TOGETHER WITH, accompanying, accompanied by; at the same time as; as well as, in addition to, plus, besides.

aloof adjective *part of their strategy is to remain aloof during the first stages of negotiation* DISTANT, detached, unfriendly, antisocial, unsociable, remote, unapproachable, formal, stiff, withdrawn, reserved, unforthcoming, uncommunicative, unsympathetic; *informal* standoffish. ANTONYMS familiar, friendly.

a lot See note below.

USAGE NOTE **a lot, alot**

A lot (= many) is the standard spelling. *Alot* is a nonstandard form—e.g.:

- "Alot [read *A lot*] of people have noticed that the two teams playing in the World Series have one very important thing in common." (*Boston Globe*; Oct. 22, 2000.)
- "Dalmatians are active and require alot [read *a lot*] of exercise and attention." (*Sarasota Herald-Tribune*; Dec. 2, 2000.) **—BG**

aloud adverb *please don't read aloud* AUDIBLY, out loud, for all to hear. ANTONYM silently.

alphabet noun *recite the alphabet* ABCs, letters, writing system, syllabary.

already adverb **1** *Anna had already suffered a great deal* BY THIS/THAT TIME, by now/then, thus/so far, before now/then, until now/then, up to now/then.

2 *is it 3 o'clock already?* AS EARLY AS THIS/THAT, as soon as this/that, so soon.

also adverb *she plays basketball also | gummy bears, candy corn, and also licorice whips* TOO, as well, besides, in addition, additionally, furthermore, further, moreover, into the bargain, on top (of that), what's more, to boot, equally; *informal* and all, likewise; *archaic* withal.

alter verb **1** *Eliot was persuaded to alter the opening passage to his sermon* CHANGE, make changes to, make different, make alterations to, adjust, make adjustments to, adapt, amend, modify, revise, revamp, rework, redo, refine, vary, transform; *informal* tweak; *technical* permute. ANTONYM preserve.

2 *the state of affairs has altered* CHANGE, become different, undergo a change, undergo a sea change, adjust, adapt, transform, evolve. ANTONYM stay the same.

alteration noun *the library was lovely, but they had not anticipated such extensive alterations* CHANGE, adjustment, adaptation, modification, variation, revision, amendment; rearrangement, reordering, restyling, rejigging, reworking, revamping; sea change, transformation; *humorous* transmogrification.

altercation noun *an unruly passenger got into an altercation with the flight crew* ARGUMENT, quarrel, squabble, fight, shouting match, disagreement, contretemps, difference of opinion, falling-out, dispute, disputation, clash, fracas, wrangle, blowup, skirmish, run-in, war of words, donnybrook; *informal* tiff, scrap, spat, row, rhubarb. See note at QUARREL.

alternate verb **1** *rows of trees alternate with dense shrub* BE INTERSPERSED, occur in turn, rotate, follow one another; take turns, take it in turns, work/act in sequence; oscillate, fluctuate.

2 *we could alternate the groups so that no one feels left out* GIVE TURNS TO, take in turn, rotate, take in rotation; swap, exchange, interchange.

▸ adjective **1** *she attended on alternate days* EVERY OTHER, every second.

2 *place the leeks and noodles in alternate layers* ALTERNATING, interchanging, following in sequence, sequential, occurring in turns.

3 *just in case, let's come up with a couple of alternate plans | an alternate crossing guard* ALTERNATIVE, other, another, second, different, substitute, replacement, deputy, relief, proxy, surrogate, cover, fill-in, stand-in, standby, emergency, reserve, backup, auxiliary, fallback; *informal* pinch-hitting.

alternative adjective **1** *an alternative route* DIFFERENT, other, another, second, possible, substitute, replacement, alternate; standby, emergency, reserve, backup, auxiliary, fallback.

2 *an alternative lifestyle* UNORTHODOX, unconventional, nonstandard, unusual, uncommon, out of the ordinary, radical, revolutionary, nonconformist, avant-garde; *informal* off the wall, oddball, offbeat, way-out.

▸ noun *we have no alternative* OPTION, choice, other possibility; substitute, replacement.

alternatively adverb *alternatively, you can build your own barbecue* ON THE OTHER HAND, as an alternative, or; otherwise, instead, if not, then again, alternately.

although conjunction *although I'm not a fan of country music, I thoroughly enjoyed Vince Gill's performance* IN SPITE OF THE FACT THAT, despite the fact that, notwithstanding (the fact) that, even though/if, for all that, while, whilst.

WORD NOTE **whilst**

Whilst is hardly ever used in American writing (it's still relatively common in Britain), and copyeditors will always change it to *while.* But this is too bad. *Whilst* shares with certain other nearly archaic words—*relict* and *whilom,* for example—an attractive period flavor. It calls to mind keepsake albums, rose bowers, and afternoon tea. Forgotten Edwardian novels might well open with sentences like "Whilst Lady Gwendolen . . . "—and the modern reader can immediately descry, if ever so faintly, the red velvet settee upon which the pouting young girl reclines, quietly sulking because Reginald is late again with the landau. Certainly every good writer should strive to keep alive at least a few odd and endangered words like *whilst.* —**MD**

altitude noun *clouds are classified according to form and altitude* HEIGHT, elevation, distance above the sea/ground; loftiness.

altogether adverb **1** *he wasn't altogether happy* COMPLETELY, totally, entirely, absolutely, wholly, fully, thoroughly, utterly, perfectly, one hundred percent, in all respects.

2 *we have five offices altogether* IN ALL, all told, in toto.

3 *altogether it was a great evening* ON THE WHOLE, overall, all in all, all things considered, on balance, on average, for the most part, in the main, in general, generally, by and large.

altruistic adjective *a team of altruistic doctors who left their lucrative practices to open a clinic in Zambia* UNSELFISH, selfless, compassionate, kind, public-spirited; charitable, benevolent, beneficent, philanthropic, humanitarian; *literary* bounteous.

always adverb **1** *he's always late* EVERY TIME, each time, at all times, all the time, without fail, consistently, invariably, regularly, habitually, unfailingly. ANTONYMS never, seldom, sometimes.

2 *she's always complaining* CONTINUALLY, continuously, constantly, forever, perpetually, incessantly, ceaselessly, unceasingly, endlessly, the entire time; *informal* 24-7. ANTONYMS never, on and off.

3 *the place will always be dear to me* FOREVER, for always, for good (and all), forevermore, for ever and ever, until the end of time, eternally, for eternity, until hell freezes over; *informal* for keeps, until the cows come home; *archaic* for aye. ANTONYM never.

4 *you can always take it back to the shop* AS A LAST RESORT, no matter what, in any event, in any case, come what may.

amalgamate verb *the two departments were amalgamated | various companies amalgamated* COMBINE, merge, unite, fuse, blend, meld; join (together), join forces, band (together), link (up), team up, go into partnership; *literary* commingle. ANTONYM separate.

amalgamation noun *the amalgamation of Gleich Sanitation and Air-Sentry is now official* COMBINATION, union, blend, mixture, fusion, coalescence, synthesis, composite, amalgam.

amass verb *the squirrels have amassed a huge quantity of acorns* GATHER, collect, assemble; accumulate, aggregate, stockpile, store (up), pile up, heap, cumulate, accrue, lay in/up, garner; *informal* stash (away). ANTONYM dissipate.

amateur noun **1** *the crew were all amateurs* NONPROFESSIONAL, nonspecialist, layman, layperson; dilettante; *informal* greenhorn. ANTONYM professional.

2 *what a bunch of amateurs* BUNGLER, incompetent, bumbler. ANTONYM expert.

▸ adjective **1** *an amateur sportsman* NONPROFESSIONAL, nonspecialist, lay; dilettante.

2 *their amateur efforts* INCOMPETENT, inept, unskillful, inexpert, amateurish, clumsy, maladroit, bumbling.

amatory adjective *his amatory advances were uninvited* SEXUAL, amorous, romantic, sensual, passionate, erotic, sexy; *informal* randy, naughty.

amaze verb *this shy, gawky teenager gets on the stage and amazes everyone with the best Elvis impersonation of the* *evening* ASTONISH, astound, surprise, stun, stagger, shock, stupefy, awe, stop someone in their tracks, leave open-mouthed, leave aghast, take someone's breath away, dumbfound; *informal* bowl over, flabbergast, blow away.

amazed adjective *her magic tricks were surprisingly original—I was truly amazed* ASTONISHED, thunderstruck, speechless, at a loss for words, dumbstruck; aghast, taken aback; *informal* bowled over, flabbergasted, blown away.

amazement noun *we watched in amazement as Yvonne took her first steps since the accident* ASTONISHMENT, surprise, shock, stupefaction, incredulity, disbelief, speechlessness, awe, wonder, wonderment.

amazing adjective *the interactive exhibit at the planetarium was truly amazing* ASTONISHING, astounding, surprising, stunning, staggering, shocking, startling, stupefying, breathtaking; awesome, awe-inspiring, sensational, remarkable, spectacular, stupendous, phenomenal, extraordinary, incredible, unbelievable; *informal* mind-blowing, jaw-dropping; *literary* wondrous.

ambassador noun **1** *the American ambassador* ENVOY, plenipotentiary, emissary, (papal) nuncio, representative, high commissioner, consul, consul general, diplomat; *archaic* legate.

2 *a great ambassador for the sport* CAMPAIGNER, representative, promoter, champion, supporter, backer, booster.

ambience noun *candlelight creates a certain ambience | a faded colonial ambience still pervades both capitals* ATMOSPHERE, air, aura, climate, mood, feel, feeling, character, quality, impression, complexion, flavor, look, tone, tenor; SETTING, milieu, background, backdrop, element; environment, conditions, situation; *informal* vibe(s).

ambiguity noun *the ambiguity of the rule made it impossible to follow* VAGUENESS, obscurity, abstruseness, doubtfulness, uncertainty; *formal* dubiety; ambivalence, equivocation, double meaning.

ambiguous adjective *an ambiguous explanation* EQUIVOCAL, ambivalent, open to debate/argument, arguable, debatable; obscure, unclear, imprecise, vague, abstruse, doubtful, dubious, uncertain. See note at DOUBTFUL. ANTONYM clear.

ambit noun *an issue that falls within the ambit of this council* SCOPE, extent, range, breadth, width, reach, sweep; terms of reference, field of reference, jurisdiction; area, sphere, field, realm, domain, compass.

ambition noun **1** *young people with ambition* DRIVE, determination, enterprise, initiative, eagerness, motivation, resolve, enthusiasm, zeal, hunger, commitment, a sense of purpose; *informal* get-up-and-go.

2 *her ambition was to become a diplomat* ASPIRATION, intention, goal, aim, objective, object, purpose, intent, plan, desire, wish, design, target, dream.

ambitious adjective **1** *an energetic and ambitious politician* ASPIRING, determined, forceful, pushy, enterprising, motivated, enthusiastic, energetic, zealous, committed, purposeful, power-hungry; *informal* go-getting, go-ahead. ANTONYMS lazy, laid-back.

2 *he was ambitious to make it to the top* EAGER, determined, enthusiastic, anxious, hungry, impatient, striving.

3 *an ambitious task* DIFFICULT, exacting, demanding, formidable, challenging, hard, arduous, onerous, tough; *archaic* toilsome. ANTONYM easy.

ambivalent adjective *the need to relocate has made her ambivalent about the promotion* EQUIVOCAL, uncertain, unsure, doubtful, indecisive, inconclusive, irresolute, of two minds, undecided, torn, in a quandary, on the fence, hesitating, wavering, vacillating, equivocating, blowing/running hot and cold; *informal* iffy. ANTONYMS unequivocal, certain.

amble verb *ambling through the park* STROLL, saunter, wander, ramble, promenade, walk, go for a walk, take a walk; *informal* mosey, toddle, tootle; *formal* perambulate.

ambush noun *the soldiers were killed in an ambush* SURPRISE ATTACK, trap; *archaic* ambuscade.

▸ verb *twenty youths ambushed the patrol car* ATTACK BY SURPRISE, surprise, pounce on, fall upon, lay a trap for, set an ambush for, lie in wait for, waylay, bushwhack; *archaic* ambuscade.

ameliorate verb *measures taken to ameliorate the situation* IMPROVE, make better, better, make improvements to, enhance, help, benefit, boost, amend; relieve, ease, mitigate; *informal* tweak, patch up. ANTONYM worsen.

amenable adjective **1** *an amenable child* COOPERATIVE, acquiescent, compliant, accommodating, obliging, biddable, manageable, controllable, governable, persuadable, tractable, responsive, pliant, malleable, complaisant, easily handled; *rare* persuasible. ANTONYM uncooperative.

2 *many cancers are amenable to treatment* SUSCEPTIBLE, receptive, responsive; *archaic* susceptive. ANTONYMS unresponsive, resistant.

amend verb *the membership application was recently amended* REVISE, alter, change, modify, qualify, adapt, adjust; edit, copyedit, rewrite, redraft, rephrase, reword, rework, revamp.

amends plural noun PHRASES: **make amends** *after all the pain I've caused, is it possible to make amends? | he's obviously trying to make amends for what he's done* MAKE GOOD, atone, make up, indemnify, expiate **make amends to** *it's up to you to make amends to those you've hurt* COMPENSATE, recompense, redress, indemnify, make it up to.

amenity noun *basic amenities* FACILITY, service, convenience, resource, appliance, aid, comfort, benefit, feature, advantage.

amiable adjective *you'll find that the folks in this department are genuinely amiable* FRIENDLY, affable, amicable, cordial; warm, warmhearted, good-natured, nice, pleasant, agreeable, likable, genial, good-humored, charming, easy to get along with, companionable, sociable, personable; *informal* chummy, simpatico. ANTONYMS unfriendly, disagreeable.

amicable adjective *the relationship between the kids and their stepfather is an amicable one* FRIENDLY, good-natured, cordial, easy, easygoing, neighborly, harmonious, cooperative, civilized. ANTONYM unfriendly.

amid preposition **1** *the jeep was concealed amid pine trees* IN THE MIDDLE OF, surrounded by, among, amongst; *literary* amidst, in the midst of.

2 *the truce collapsed amid fears of a revolt* AT A TIME OF, in an atmosphere of, against a background of; as a result of.

amiss adjective *an inspection revealed nothing amiss* WRONG, awry, faulty, out of order, defective, flawed, unsatisfactory, incorrect, not right; inappropriate, improper. ANTONYMS right, in order.

PHRASE: **take something amiss** *we were only kidding, but I think he took it amiss* BE OFFENDED, take offense, be upset.

amity noun *this will bring greater amity between our peoples* FRIENDSHIP, friendliness, harmony, harmoniousness, understanding, accord, cooperation, companionship, amicableness, goodwill, cordiality, warmth; *formal* concord. ANTONYMS animosity, enmity.

ammunition noun *police seized arms and ammunition* BULLETS, shells, projectiles, missiles, rounds, shot, slugs, cartridges, munitions; *informal* ammo.

amnesty noun *the governor has granted amnesty to seven of the prisoners* PARDON, pardoning, reprieve; grace; release, discharge.

amok PHRASE: **run amok** *the robot is running amok in Sector B* GO BERSERK, get out of control, rampage, riot, run riot, go on the rampage, behave like a maniac, behave wildly, behave uncontrollably, become violent, become destructive; *informal* raise hell, go postal.

among, amongst preposition **1** *you're among friends* SURROUNDED BY, in the company of, amid, in the middle of, with; *literary* amidst, in the midst of.

2 *a child was among the injured* INCLUDED IN, one/some of, in the group/number of.

3 *he distributed the proceeds among his creditors* BETWEEN, to each of.

4 *decide **among yourselves*** JOINTLY, mutually, together, with one another.

amoral adjective *are we rearing an amoral generation, spoon-fed on trash TV and violent video games?* UNPRINCIPLED, without standards, without morals, without scruples, unscrupulous, Machiavellian, unethical.See note at IMMORAL. ANTONYM principled.

amorous adjective *amorous advances* ROMANTIC, lustful, sexual, erotic, amatory, ardent, passionate, impassioned; in love, enamored, lovesick; *informal* lovey-dovey, kissy, smoochy, hot.

amorphous adjective *an amorphous lump of clay* SHAPELESS, formless, structureless, indeterminate; vague, nebulous, indefinite.

amount noun *a fair amount of roast beef | we sold a comparable amount in the second quarter* QUANTITY, number, total, aggregate, sum, quota, group, size, mass, weight, volume, bulk, lot, quantum.

PHRASES: **the full amount** *we can't make a payment schedule until we know the full amount* THE GRAND TOTAL, the total, the aggregate; *informal* the whole kit and caboodle, the whole shebang, the whole nine yards. **amount to 1** *the bill amounted to $50* ADD UP TO, come to, run (to), be, total. **2** *a result that amounted to complete failure* CONSTITUTE, be tantamount to, come down to, boil down to; signify, signal, mean, indicate, suggest, denote, point to, be evidence of, be symptomatic of; *literary* betoken. **3** *her relationships had never amounted to anything significant* BECOME, develop into, develop into, prove to be, turn out to be.

amphibian noun. See table on page 34.

amity
accord
concord
comity
peace
peacefulness
peaceableness
harmony
harmoniousness
affinity
rapport
camaraderie
fellowship
fellow feeling
fraternity
brotherhood
brotherliness
closeness
mutual affection
friendship
friendliness
comradeship
companionship
concurrence
cordiality
warmth
geniality
cordial relations
goodwill
cooperation
understanding
amicableness
tolerance
patience
composure
coolness
unfriendliness
unkindness
ill feeling
bad feeling
opposition
aggression
aggressiveness
militancy
antagonism
belligerence
bellicosity
pugnaciousness
aversion
bitterness
resentment
antipathy
animosity
hostility
animus
truculence
spitefulness
spite
rancor
malevolence
ill-will
malice
venom
anger
wrath
hatred
warlikeness
inimicalness
emnity

AMPHIBIANS

axolotl	narrow-mouthed frog
barking frog	natterjack (toad)
bell toad	newt
blind salamander	Olympic salamander
bullfrog	painted salamander
caecilian	pickerel frog
cane toad	purple salamander
cave salamander	red-backed salamander
chorus frog	red-legged frog
congo eel	red salamander
cricket frog	robber frog
dusky salamander	salamander
eft	siren
flying frog	slimy salamander
four-toed salamander	spadefoot toad
frog	spotted frog
giant salamander	spotted salamander
giant toad	spring peeper
gopher frog	tadpole
green frog	tailed toad
green salamander	Texas salamander
hellbender	tiger salamander
horned toad	toad
hyla	tree frog
Jefferson salamander	tree salamander
leopard frog	tree toad
long-tailed salamander	two-lined salamander
marbled salamander	waterdog
marine toad	whistling frog
midwife toad	white-lipped frog
mudpuppy	wood frog
mud siren	worm salamander

ample adjective **1** *there is ample time for discussion* ENOUGH, sufficient, adequate, plenty of, more than enough, enough and to spare. ANTONYM insufficient.

2 *an ample supply of wine* PLENTIFUL, abundant, copious, profuse, rich, lavish, liberal, generous, bountiful, bounteous, large, huge, great, bumper; *literary* plenteous. ANTONYM meager.

amplify verb **1** *the sound from an electric guitar was meant to be amplified* MAKE LOUDER, louden, turn up, magnify, intensify, increase, boost, step up, raise. ANTONYM quieten.

2 *these notes amplify our statement* EXPAND, enlarge upon, elaborate on, add to, supplement, develop, flesh out, add detail to, go into detail about. ANTONYM condense.

amplitude noun *the amplitude of the wave* MAGNITUDE, size, volume; extent, range, compass; breadth, width.

amputate verb *doctors had to amputate two fingers* CUT OFF, sever, remove (surgically), dismember, saw/chop off.

amulet noun *she wore an amulet that had supposedly given her grandmother mystical powers of intuition* LUCKY CHARM, charm, talisman, mojo, churinga, phylactery, fetish, totem, idol, juju; *archaic* periapt.

amuse verb **1** *the ugliest dog contest amused him* ENTERTAIN, make laugh, delight, divert, cheer (up), please, charm, tickle; *informal* tickle pink, crack up. ANTONYMS bore, depress.

2 *he amused himself by writing poetry* OCCUPY, engage, busy, employ, distract, absorb, engross; interest, entertain, divert.

amusement noun **1** *we looked with amusement at the cartoon* MIRTH, merriment, lightheartedness, hilarity, glee, delight, gaiety, joviality, fun; enjoyment, pleasure, high spirits, cheerfulness.

2 *I read the book for amusement* ENTERTAINMENT, pleasure, leisure, relaxation, fun, enjoyment, interest, diversion; *informal* R and R; *archaic* disport.

3 *a wide range of amusements* ACTIVITY, entertainment, diversion; game, sport.

amusement park noun *the rides at the amusement park* THEME PARK, fun park, exhibition, carnival, midway.

amusing adjective *an amusing story* ENTERTAINING, funny, comical, humorous, lighthearted, jocular, witty, mirthful, hilarious, droll, diverting; laughable; *informal* wacky, side-splitting, rib-tickling. ANTONYMS boring, solemn.

analogous adjective *their lab results were analogous* COMPARABLE, parallel, similar, like, akin, corresponding, related, kindred, equivalent. ANTONYM unrelated.

analogy noun *there's a thinly veiled analogy between his fiction and his real life* SIMILARITY, parallel, correspondence, likeness, resemblance, correlation, relation, kinship, equivalence, similitude, metaphor, simile. See note at LIKENESS. ANTONYM dissimilarity.

analysis noun *an interesting analysis of England's tax laws* EXAMINATION, investigation, inspection, survey, study, scrutiny; exploration, probe, research, review, evaluation, interpretation, dissection.

analyst noun *his analyst has recommended a rehabilitation facility* PSYCHOANALYST, psychiatrist, psychologist, psychotherapist, therapist; *informal* shrink.

analytical, analytic adjective *Dr. Uhlrich takes a much more analytical approach to the question of creationism* SYSTEMATIC, logical, scientific, methodical, left-brained, (well) organized, ordered, orderly, meticulous, rigorous; diagnostic. ANTONYM unsystematic.

analyze verb *chemists are analyzing the substance* EXAMINE, inspect, survey, study, scrutinize, look over; investigate, explore, probe, research, go over (with a fine-tooth comb), review, evaluate, break down, dissect, anatomize.

anarchic adjective *an anarchic society has replaced the despotism* LAWLESS, without law and order, in disorder, in turmoil, unruly, disordered, disorganized, chaotic, turbulent; mutinous, rebellious.

anarchist noun *police said they arrested 10 self-styled anarchists* NIHILIST, insurgent, agitator, subversive, terrorist, revolutionary, revolutionist, insurrectionist.

anarchy noun *conditions are dangerously ripe for anarchy* LAWLESSNESS, nihilism, mobocracy, revolution, insurrection, disorder, chaos, mayhem, tumult, turmoil. ANTONYMS government, order.

anathema noun *a nation viewed as a sponsor of terrorism, which is anathema in the West* AN ABOMINATION, an outrage, an abhorrence, a disgrace, an evil, a bane, a bugbear, a bête noire; *adjectives*ABHORRENT, hateful, repugnant, odious, repellent, offensive.

anatomy noun *the anatomy of a frog* BODILY STRUCTURE, makeup, composition, constitution, form, structure.

ancestor noun **1** *he could trace his ancestors back to colonial Boston* FOREBEAR, forefather, predecessor, antecedent, progenitor, primogenitor. ANTONYMS descendant, successor.

2 *the instrument is an ancestor of the lute* FORERUNNER, precursor, predecessor.

ancestral adjective *their ancestral hunting grounds* INHERITED, hereditary, familial; *rare* lineal.

ancestry noun *our Polish ancestry* ANCESTORS, forebears, forefathers, progenitors, antecedents; family tree; lineage, parentage, genealogy, descent, roots, stock, line.

anchor noun 1 *the anchor of the new coalition* MAINSTAY, cornerstone, linchpin, bulwark, foundation.

2 *a TV news anchor* PRESENTER, announcer, anchorman, anchorwoman, broadcaster.

▸ verb 1 *the ship was anchored in the bay* MOOR, berth, be at anchor; *dated* harbor.

2 *the fish anchors itself to the coral* SECURE, fasten, attach, affix, fix.

ancient adjective 1 *in ancient times* OF LONG AGO, early, prehistoric, primeval, primordial, primitive; *literary* of yore; *archaic* foregone. ANTONYMS recent, contemporary.

2 *an ancient custom* OLD, very old, age-old, archaic, time-worn, time-honored, venerable. See note at OLD. ANTONYMS recent, new, modern.

3 *informal I feel positively ancient* OLD, aged, elderly, antiquated, decrepit, antediluvian, in one's dotage; old-fashioned, out of date, outmoded, obsolete, passé, démodé; *informal* horse-and-buggy. ANTONYMS youthful, up to date.

ancillary adjective *the Administrative Procedures Act and ancillary documents* ADDITIONAL, auxiliary, supporting, helping, extra, supplementary, supplemental, accessory, attendant; subsidiary, secondary; *Medicine* adjuvant; *rare* adminicular.

and conjunction *coffee and a scone* TOGETHER WITH, along with, with, as well as, in addition to, also; besides, furthermore; *informal* plus.

USAGE NOTE and

It is rank superstition that this coordinating conjunction cannot properly begin a sentence:

• "Another stumbling-block to a certain type of academic mind is the conjunction *and*. It is often laid down as a rigid rule that a sentence should never begin with *and*. This was a point on which my own schoolmaster was inflexible. And quite recently a training college student whom I asked to comment on a passage from Malory condemned him for using 'the objectionable conjunction *and*.' And printers have an ugly trick of emasculating my meaning by turning my periods into commas because they happen to be followed by *and*. Taking down my Bible and opening it at random, I find that the eighth chapter of Exodus contains thirty-two sentences, twenty-five of which begin with *and*." (Philip Boswood Ballard, *Teaching and Testing English*; 1939.)

• "Many years ago schoolteachers insisted that it was improper to begin a sentence with *and*, but this convention is now outmoded. Innumerable respected writers use *and* at the beginning of a sentence." (William Morris and Mary Morris, *Harper Dictionary of Contemporary Usage*, 2d ed.; 1985.)

• "And the idea that *and* must not begin a sentence, or even a paragraph, is an empty superstition. The same goes for *but*. Indeed either word can give unimprovably early warning of the sort of thing that is to follow." (Kingsley Amis, *The King's English*; 1997.).

Schoolteachers may have laid down a prohibition against the initial *and* to counteract elementary-school students' tendency to begin every sentence with *and*. The same superstition has plagued *but* (see note at BUT). But the very best writers find occasion to begin sentences with *and*—e.g.: "And one had better make use of whatever beauty, elegance, riches the translator's language possesses, and hope that something emotionally, intellectually, aesthetically equivalent will emerge." (John Simon, *The Sheep from the Goats*; 1989.)

Oddly, *and* is frequently misused for *or* where a singular noun, or one of two nouns, is called for—e.g.: "While third-party candidates have mounted serious challenges for senator and governor in almost two dozen states this year, building an effective third-party apparatus is rare." (*New York Times*; Oct. 5, 1994.) The phrase should be "senator *or* governor"; as written, the sentence says that in each of almost 24 states, third-party candidates were running for *both* senator *and* governor—an idea belied by the context of the article.

Some writers have a tendency, especially in long enumerations, to omit *and* before the final element. To do so is often infelicitous: the reader is jarred by the abrupt period ending the sentence and may even wonder whether something has been omitted. One may occasionally omit *and* before the final element in an enumeration with a particular nuance in mind. Without *and*, the implication is that the series is incomplete—rhetoricians call this construction "asyndeton." With *and*, the implication is that the series is complete. This shade in meaning is increasingly subtle in modern prose. **—BG**

---

android noun *a space station run by androids* ROBOT, automaton, cyborg, droid, bot.

anecdote noun *amusing anecdotes* STORY, tale, narrative, incident; urban myth/legend; *informal* yarn.

anemic adjective 1 *his anemic face* COLORLESS, bloodless, pale, pallid, wan, ashen, gray, sallow, pasty-faced, whey-faced, peaked, sickly, etiolated.

2 *an anemic description of her feelings* FEEBLE, weak, insipid, wishy-washy, vapid, bland; lame, tame, lackluster, spiritless, languid, lifeless, ineffective, ineffectual, etiolated; *informal* pathetic.

anew adverb *may we please begin anew?* AGAIN, afresh, another time, once more/again, over again.

angel noun 1 *an angel appeared in the heavens* MESSENGER OF GOD, divine/heavenly messenger, divine being. ANTONYMS devil, demon.

2 *she's an absolute angel* SAINT, paragon of virtue; gem, treasure, darling, dear; *informal* star.

3 *informal a financial angel* BACKER, sponsor, benefactor, fairy godmother, promoter, patron; *rare* Maecenas.

angelic adjective 1 *angelic beings* DIVINE, heavenly, celestial, holy, seraphic, cherubic; spiritual. ANTONYMS demonic, infernal.

2 *Sophie's angelic appearance* INNOCENT, pure, virtuous, good, saintly, wholesome; beautiful.

anger noun *his face was livid with anger* RAGE, vexation, exasperation, displeasure, crossness, irritation, irritability, indignation, pique; annoyance, fury, wrath, ire, outrage, irascibility, ill temper/humor; *informal* slow burn, aggravation; *literary* choler. ANTONYMS pleasure, good humor.

▸ verb *she was angered by his terse reply* INFURIATE, irritate, exasperate, irk, vex, peeve, madden, put out; enrage, incense, annoy; rub the wrong way; *informal* make someone's blood boil, get someone's back up, make someone see red, get someone's dander up, rattle someone's cage, make someone's hackles rise; aggravate, get someone, rile, tick off, tee off, burn up. ANTONYMS pacify, placate.

angle noun **1** *the wall is sloping at an angle of 33°* GRADIENT, slant, inclination.

2 *the angle of the roof* CORNER, intersection, point, apex.

3 *consider the problem from a different angle* PERSPECTIVE, point of view, viewpoint, standpoint, position, aspect, slant, direction.

▸ verb **1** *Anna angled her camera toward the tree* TILT, slant, direct, turn.

2 *angle your answer so that it is relevant* PRESENT, slant, orient, twist, bias.

3 *he was angling for an invitation* TRY TO GET, seek to obtain, fish for, hope for, be after.

angry adjective **1** *Vivienne got angry* IRATE, mad, annoyed, cross, vexed, irritated, indignant, irked; furious, enraged, infuriated, in a temper, incensed, raging, fuming, seething, beside oneself, choleric, outraged; livid, apoplectic; *informal* hot under the collar, up in arms, in high dudgeon, foaming at the mouth, doing a slow burn, steamed up, in a lather, fit to be tied, seeing red; sore, bent out of shape, ticked off, teed off, PO'd; *literary* wrathful; *archaic* wroth. ANTONYM pleased.

2 *an angry debate* HEATED, passionate, stormy, "lively"; bad-tempered, ill-tempered, ill-natured, acrimonious, bitter. ANTONYM good-humored.

PHRASE: **get angry** *my father almost never gets angry* LOSE ONE'S TEMPER, become enraged, go into a rage, go berserk, flare up; *informal* go crazy, go bananas, hit the roof, go through the roof, go up the wall, see red, go off the deep end, fly off the handle, blow one's top, blow a fuse/gasket, flip out, have a fit, foam at the mouth, explode, go ballistic, go postal, flip one's wig, blow one's stack, have a conniption.

angst noun *business leaders expressed their angst over war and recession* ANXIETY, fear, apprehension, worry, foreboding, trepidation, malaise, disquiet, disquietude, unease, uneasiness.

anguish noun *the anguish of the hostages' families* AGONY, pain, torment, torture, suffering, distress, angst, misery, sorrow, grief, heartache, desolation, despair; *literary* dolor. ANTONYM happiness.

angular adjective **1** *an angular shape* SHARP-CORNERED, pointed, V-shaped, Y-shaped. ANTONYMS rounded, curving.

2 *an angular face* BONY, rawboned, lean, spare, thin, skinny, gaunt. ANTONYMS plump, curvy.

animal noun **1** *endangered animals* CREATURE, beast, living thing; *informal* critter, beastie; **(animals)** wildlife, fauna.

2 *the man was an animal* BRUTE, beast, monster, devil, demon, fiend; *informal* swine, bastard, pig.

▸ adjective *a grunt of animal passion* CARNAL, fleshly, bodily, physical; brutish, beastly, bestial, unrefined, uncultured, coarse.

animate verb *a sense of excitement animated the whole school* ENLIVEN, vitalize, breathe (new) life into, energize, invigorate, revive, vivify, liven up; inspire, inspirit, exhilarate, thrill, excite, fire, arouse, rouse, quicken, stir; light a fire under. See note at QUICKEN. ANTONYM depress.

▸ ***angry***
livid
choleric
wroth
wrathful
ranting and raving
foaming at the mouth
seething
enraged
furious
irate
raging
incandescent
outraged
in high dudgeon
hopping mad
seeing red
boiling
hot under the collar
doing a slow burn
fuming
fit to be tied
mad
indignant
aggrieved
vexed
cross
riled
provoked
galled
irritated
aggravated
pissed/teed off
annoyed
irked
piqued
displeased
impassive
dispassionate
phlegmatic
equable
even-tempered
equanimous
unruffled
unperturbed
undisturbed
unfazed
unmoved
cool
collected
laid-back
content(ed)
satisfied
complacent
smug
gratified
grateful
thankful
glad
delighted
as pleased as Punch
happy
over the moon
tickled pink
on cloud nine
thrilled
elated
pleased ◂

▸ adjective *an animate being* LIVING, alive, live, breathing; *archaic* quick. See note at ALIVE. ANTONYM inanimate.

animated adjective *an animated discussion | his animated walk* LIVELY, spirited, high-spirited, energetic, adrenalized, full of life, excited, enthusiastic, eager, alive, active, vigorous, vibrant, vital, vivacious, buoyant, exuberant, ebullient, effervescent, bouncy, bubbly, perky; *informal* bright-eyed and bushy-tailed, bright and breezy, chirpy, chipper, peppy; heated. See note at ALIVE. ANTONYMS lethargic, lifeless.

animosity noun *the betrayal would cause eternal animosity between two friends* ANTIPATHY, hostility, friction, antagonism, acrimony, enmity, animus, bitterness, rancor, resentment, dislike, ill feeling/will, bad blood, hatred, hate, loathing; malice, spite, spitefulness. ANTONYMS goodwill, friendship.

annals plural noun *the annals of the town's history* RECORDS, archives, chronicles, accounts, registers; *Law* muniments.

annex verb **1** *Charlemagne annexed northern Italy* TAKE OVER, take possession of, appropriate, seize, conquer, occupy.

2 *ten amendments were annexed to the constitution* ADD, append, attach, tack on, tag on.

▸ noun *the new annex will house four classrooms and a computer lab* EXTENSION, addition; wing; ell.

annexation noun *the annexation of Latvia* SEIZURE, occupation, invasion, conquest, takeover, appropriation.

annihilate verb *an ungodly tornado touched down, annihilating everything in its path* DESTROY, wipe out, obliterate, wipe off the face of the earth; eliminate, liquidate, defeat. See note at DESTROY. ANTONYM create.

annotate verb *annotate the text in Chapters 4 and 5* COMMENT ON, add notes/footnotes to, gloss, interpret, mark up.

annotation noun *the teacher's copy has annotations in the margins* NOTE, notation, comment, gloss, footnote; commentary, explanation, interpretation.

announce verb **1** *their financial results were announced* MAKE PUBLIC, make known, report, declare, divulge, state, give out, notify, publicize, broadcast, publish, advertise, circulate, proclaim, blazon.

2 *Victor announced the guests* INTRODUCE, present, name.

3 *strains of music announced her arrival* SIGNAL, indicate, give notice of, herald, proclaim; *literary* betoken.

THE RIGHT WORD

When you **announce** something, you communicate it in a formal and public manner, often for the first time (*to announce the arrival of the guest of honor*). But just how you go about announcing something depends on what you're trying to convey. If you want to make sure no one misses your message, use **blazon** (*signs along the highway blazoned the local farmers' complaints*). If you plan to make your views known to the general public through the medium of writing, use **publish** (*to publish a story on drunk driving in the local newspaper*). Use **proclaim** if you have something of great importance that you want to announce very formally and officially (*proclaim a national day of mourning*). Although **declare** also implies a very formal announcement (*declare war*), it can refer to any clear and explicit statement (*declare one's love*). **Promulgate** is usually associated with the communication of a creed, doctrine, or law (*promulgate the views of the Democratic Party*).

announcement noun **1** *an announcement by the dean* STATEMENT, report, declaration, proclamation, pronouncement, rescript; bulletin, communiqué.

2 *the announcement of the decision* DECLARATION, notification, reporting, publishing, broadcasting, proclamation; *archaic* annunciation.

announcer noun *the announcer's voice sounds familiar* PRESENTER, anchorman, anchorwoman, anchor, anchorperson; news reader, newscaster, broadcaster; host, master of ceremonies; *informal* MC, emcee.

annoy verb *their barking dog annoys me | where the movie attempts to amuse, it only annoys* IRRITATE, vex, make angry/cross, anger, exasperate, irk, gall, pique, put out, antagonize, get on someone's nerves, get to, ruffle someone's feathers, make someone's hackles rise, nettle; rub the wrong way; *informal* aggravate, peeve, hassle, miff, rile, needle, frost, bug, get someone's goat, get someone's back up, get in someone's hair, give someone the gears, drive mad/crazy/bananas, drive around the bend, drive up the wall, tee off, tick off, burn up, rankle. See note at AGGRAVATE. ANTONYMS please, gratify.

annoyance noun **1** *much to his annoyance, Louise didn't even notice* IRRITATION, exasperation, vexation, indignation, anger, displeasure, chagrin; *informal* aggravation.

2 *they found him an annoyance* NUISANCE, pest, bother, irritant, inconvenience, palaver; *informal* pain, pain in the neck/butt/ass, hassle; nudnik, burr under someone's saddle.

annoyed adjective *the debate moderator was clearly annoyed* IRRITATED, cross, angry, vexed, exasperated, irked, piqued, displeased, put out, disgruntled, chagrined, nettled, in a bad mood, in a temper; *informal* aggravated, peeved, miffed, riled; teed off, ticked off, sore, bent out of shape.

annoying adjective *what are these annoying little insects?* IRRITATING, infuriating, exasperating, maddening, trying, tiresome, troublesome, bothersome, nettlesome, obnoxious, irksome, vexing, cursed, vexatious, galling; *informal* aggravating, pesky; *informal, dated* cursed.

annual adjective **1** *the annual company picnic* YEARLY, once-a-year, every twelve months; year-end.

2 *an annual subscription to the alumni newsletter* YEARLONG, twelve-month

annually adverb *we renew our membership annually* YEARLY, once a year, each year, per annum, per year; every year.

annul verb *their parents wanted to get the marriage annulled* DECLARE INVALID, declare null and void, nullify, invalidate, void, disallow; repeal, reverse, rescind, revoke; *Law* vacate; *formal* abrogate; recall. See note at VOID. ANTONYMS restore, enact.

anoint verb *he was anointed and crowned* CONSECRATE, bless, ordain; *formal* hallow.

anomalous adjective *it's an anomalous birthmark* ABNORMAL, atypical, irregular, aberrant, heteroclite, exceptional, freak, freakish, odd, bizarre, peculiar, unusual, out of the ordinary; deviant, mutant. ANTONYMS normal, typical.

anomaly noun *the growth on the duck's bill is a harmless anomaly* ODDITY, peculiarity, abnormality, irregularity, inconsistency, incongruity, aberration, quirk, rarity.

anonymous adjective 1 *an anonymous donor* UNNAMED, of unknown name, nameless, incognito, unidentified, unknown, secret. ANTONYMS known, identified.

2 *an anonymous letter* UNSIGNED, unattributed. ANTONYM signed.

3 *an anonymous housing development* CHARACTERLESS, nondescript, impersonal, faceless.

another adjective *have another drink* ONE MORE, a further, an additional.

answer noun 1 *her answer was unequivocal* REPLY, response, rejoinder, reaction; retort, riposte; *informal* comeback. ANTONYM question.

2 *a new filter is the answer* SOLUTION, remedy, key.

▸ verb 1 *Steve was about to answer* REPLY, respond, make a rejoinder, rejoin; retort, riposte, return.

2 *she has yet to answer the charges* REBUT, defend oneself against.

3 *a man answering this description* MATCH, fit, correspond to, be similar to.

4 *we're trying to answer the needs of our audience* SATISFY, meet, fulfill, fill, measure up to.

5 ***I answer to** the commissioner* REPORT TO, work for/under, be subordinate to, be accountable to, be answerable to, be responsible to.

6 *he will answer for his crime* PAY, be punished, suffer; make amends, make reparation, atone.

7 *the government has a lot to answer for* BE ACCOUNTABLE, be responsible, be liable, take the blame; *informal* take the rap.

answerable adjective *the ensign is answerable to the captain* ACCOUNTABLE, responsible, liable; subject. See note at RESPONSIBLE.

antagonism noun *a long history of antagonism between the two nations* HOSTILITY, friction, enmity, antipathy, animus, opposition, dissension, rivalry; acrimony, bitterness, rancor, resentment, animosity, aversion, dislike, ill feeling, ill will, bad blood. ANTONYMS rapport, friendship.

antagonist noun *only in our political life are we antagonists* ADVERSARY, opponent, enemy, foe, rival, competitor; **(antagonists)** opposition, competition. ANTONYM ally.

antagonistic adjective 1 *he was **antagonistic to** the reforms* HOSTILE TO, against, (dead) set against, opposed to, inimical to, antipathetic to, ill-disposed to, resistant to, in disagreement with; *informal* anti. ANTONYMS sympathetic, pro.

2 *an antagonistic group of bystanders* HOSTILE, aggressive, belligerent, bellicose, pugnacious; *rare* oppugnant.

antagonize verb *have I done something to antagonize you?* AROUSE HOSTILITY IN, alienate; anger, annoy, provoke, vex, irritate; rub the wrong way; *informal* aggravate, rile, needle, rattle someone's cage, get someone's back up. ANTONYMS pacify, placate.

antecedent adjective *antecedent events* PREVIOUS, earlier, prior, preceding, precursory, former, foregoing; *formal* anterior. ANTONYMS subsequent, later.

▸ noun 1 *her antecedents have been traced* ANCESTOR, forefather, forebear, progenitor, primogenitor; **(antecedents)** ancestry, family tree, lineage, genealogy, roots. ANTONYM descendant.

2 *the guitar's antecedent* PRECURSOR, forerunner, predecessor. ANTONYM descendant.

antedate verb *a civilization that antedates the Roman Empire* PRECEDE, predate, come/go before, be earlier than.

antediluvian adjective *her antediluvian attitudes* OUT OF DATE, outdated, outmoded, old-fashioned, antiquated, behind the times, passé. See note at OLD.

anteroom noun *guests will be met in the anteroom* ANTECHAMBER, vestibule, lobby, foyer, outer room; *Architecture* narthex.

anthem noun *a patriotic anthem* HYMN, song, chorale, psalm, paean.

anthology noun *an anthology of American poetry* COLLECTION, selection, compendium, treasury, miscellany; *archaic* garland.

anticipate verb 1 *we don't anticipate any trouble* EXPECT, foresee, predict, be prepared for, bargain on, reckon on; *informal* figure on.

2 *the defender must anticipate the attacker's moves* PREEMPT, forestall, second-guess; *informal* beat someone to the punch.

3 *we enthusiastically anticipate your arrival* LOOK FORWARD TO, await, count the days until; *informal* lick one's lips over.

anticipation noun *her eyes sparkled with anticipation* EXPECTANCY, expectation, excitement, suspense. PHRASE: **in anticipation of** *we bought plenty of food in anticipation of holiday visitors* IN THE EXPECTATION OF, in preparation for, in case of, ready for.

anticlimactic adjective *an anticlimatic twist in the plot* BATHETIC, disappointing, dissatisfying.

anticlimax noun *for me, the anticlimax is when Reggie—for no apparent purpose to the plot—suddenly decides to quit school* LETDOWN, disappointment, comedown, nonevent; bathos.

antics plural noun *someday you'll be too old to get away with such antics* CAPERS, pranks, larks, hijinks, frolicking, skylarking, foolery, tomfoolery.

antidote noun 1 *the antidote to this poison* ANTITOXIN, antiserum, antivenin.

2 *laughter is a good antidote to stress* REMEDY, cure, nostrum.

antipathetic adjective *we were taught to be **antipathetic to** all foreigners* HOSTILE TO, against, (dead) set against, opposed to, antagonistic to/toward, ill-disposed to, unsympathetic to/toward; *informal* anti, down on. ANTONYM pro.

antipathy noun *I never encountered racial antipathy until I went to college* HOSTILITY, antagonism, animosity, aversion, animus, enmity, dislike, distaste, hatred, hate, abhorrence, loathing. ANTONYMS liking, affinity.

antiquated adjective *his views on single parenthood are antiquated* OUTDATED, out of date, outmoded, outworn, old, stale, behind the times, old-fashioned, anachronistic, old-fangled, antique, antediluvian, passé, démodé, obsolete; *informal* out of the ark, moldy, horse-and-buggy. See note at OLD. ANTONYMS modern, up to date.

antique noun *the zither is a lovely antique* COLLECTOR'S ITEM, period piece, antiquity, heirloom.

▸ adjective 1 *antique furniture* OLD, antiquarian, collectable, old-fashioned. ANTONYMS modern, new.

2 *statues of antique gods* ANCIENT, of long ago; *literary* of yore.

3 *antique work practices.* See ANTIQUATED. ANTONYMS modern, current.

antiquity noun 1 *the civilizations of antiquity* ANCIENT TIMES, the ancient past, classical times, the distant past.

2 *Islamic antiquities* ANTIQUE, period piece, collector's item.

antiseptic adjective 1 *an antiseptic substance* DISINFECTANT, germicidal, bactericidal, antibacterial, antibiotic.

2 *antiseptic bandages* STERILE, aseptic, germ-free, uncontaminated, disinfected. See note at SANITARY. ANTONYM contaminated.

3 *their antiseptic surroundings* CHARACTERLESS, colorless, soulless; clinical, institutional; dispassionate, detached. ANTONYM colorful.

▸ noun DISINFECTANT, germicide, bactericide.

antisocial adjective 1 *worrisome antisocial behavior* SOCIOPATHIC, distasteful, disruptive, rebellious, misanthropic, asocial.

2 *I'm feeling a bit antisocial* UNSOCIABLE, unfriendly, uncommunicative, reclusive, withdrawn; standoffish. See note at UNSOCIABLE.

antithesis noun *friends of the actress say she is quite the antithesis of her giddy and frivolous character* (COMPLETE) OPPOSITE, converse, contrary, reverse, inverse, obverse, other side of the coin; *informal* flip side.

antithetical adjective *your theories are* ***antithetical to*** *mine* (DIRECTLY) OPPOSED TO, contrasting with, contrary to, contradictory to, conflicting with, incompatible with, irreconcilable with, inconsistent with, at variance with, at odds with. See note at OPPOSITE. ANTONYMS identical, like.

antsy adjective *informal one week before the primary, New Hampshire voters are getting antsy* AGITATED, anxious, fidgety, jumpy, fretful, restless, stir-crazy, wired.

anxiety noun 1 *his anxiety grew* WORRY, concern, apprehension, apprehensiveness, uneasiness, unease, fearfulness, fear, disquiet, disquietude, inquietude, perturbation, agitation, angst, misgiving, nervousness, nerves, tension, tenseness; *informal* heebie-jeebies, butterflies (in one's stomach), jitteriness, the jitters, twitchiness. ANTONYMS calmness, serenity.

2 *an anxiety to please* EAGERNESS, keenness, desire.

anxious adjective 1 *her fever has us all a little anxious* WORRIED, concerned, uneasy, apprehensive, fearful, perturbed, troubled, bothered, disturbed, distressed, disquieted, fretful, agitated, nervous, edgy, antsy, unquiet, on edge, tense, overwrought, worked up, keyed up, jumpy, worried sick, with one's stomach in knots, with one's heart in one's mouth; *informal* uptight, on tenterhooks, with butterflies in one's stomach, jittery, twitchy, in a dither, in a lather, in a tizzy, het up; strung out, having kittens; antsy, spooked, squirrelly. ANTONYMS carefree, unconcerned.

2 *she was anxious for news* EAGER, keen, desirous, impatient.

USAGE NOTE **anxious**

The word *anxious* has a range of meaning. As the adjective corresponding to *anxiety*, it has long meant "uneasy, disquieted." In the most unimpeachable uses, the word stays close to that association—e.g.: "The latest holdup is the EPA's final approval of the companies' plans to test for lead at the 150 homes . . . . Some residents are getting anxious." (*Atlanta Journal Constitution*; Sept. 13, 2002.)

Today the word typically encompasses both worry and anticipation—e.g.: "Creator and anchorman Brian Lamb, the prince of un-chic, tirelessly fields the remarks of obnoxious callers, preening journalists, and anxious authors." (*National Review*; Mar. 24, 1997.)

The word carries a sense of expectation, as when discussing a major life change. But when no sense of uneasiness is attached to the situation, *anxious* isn't the best word. In those instances, it displaces a word that might traditionally have been considered its opposite—namely, eager—e.g.: "Three years ago, the Latin music industry was caught up in crossover mania, anxious [read *eager*] to ride the popularity of singers such as Ricky Martin and Enrique Iglesias by selling their English-language albums to the American mainstream." (*Sun-Sentinel* [Fort Lauderdale]; Sept. 13, 2002.) **—BG**

any adjective 1 *is there any cake left?* SOME, a piece of, a part of, a bit of.

2 *it doesn't make any difference* THE SLIGHTEST BIT OF, a scrap of, a shred of, a whit of, a particle of, an iota of, a jot of.

3 *any job will do* WHICHEVER, no matter which, never mind which; *informal* any old.

▸ pronoun 1 *you don't know any of my friends* A SINGLE ONE, one, even one.

2 *we no longer give to any, unless they represent one of our top five charities* ANYONE, anybody, any individual/person; any group

▸ adverb *is your father any better?* AT ALL, in the least, to any extent, in/to any degree.

anyhow adverb 1 *anyhow, it doesn't really matter.* See ANYWAY.

2 *her clothes were strewn about anyhow* HAPHAZARDLY, carelessly, heedlessly, negligently, in a muddle; *informal* all over the place, every which way.

anyway adverb *anyway, let's at least get together on Saturday* ANYHOW, in any case, in any event, at any rate; however, be that as it may, regardless; *informal* still and all, anyways.

apace adverb *literary the wagon moved apace across the prairie* QUICKLY, fast, swiftly, rapidly, speedily, briskly, without delay, posthaste, expeditiously. ANTONYM slowly.

apart adverb 1 *the villages are two miles apart* AWAY FROM EACH OTHER, distant from each other.

2 *Isabel stood apart* TO ONE SIDE, aside, separately, alone, by oneself/itself.

3 *his parents are living apart* SEPARATELY, independently, on one's own.

4 *the car was blown apart* TO PIECES, to bits, up; *literary* asunder. PHRASE: **apart from** *apart from the broken headlight, the car seems to be OK* EXCEPT FOR, but for, aside from, with the exception of, excepting, excluding, bar, barring, besides, other than; *informal* outside of; *formal* save.

apartment noun 1 *a rented apartment* See table on page 40.

2 *the royal apartments* SUITE (OF ROOMS), rooms, living quarters, accommodations.

APARTMENTS

- bachelor
- bachelorette
- bed-sitting room
- efficiency unit
- flat
- garden apartment
- in-law suite
- loft
- maisonette
- nanny suite
- penthouse
- pied-à-terre
- studio apartment
- suite
- walk-up

apathetic adjective *an apathetic workforce* UNINTERESTED, INDIFFERENT, unconcerned, unmoved, uninvolved, disinterested, unemotional, emotionless, dispassionate, lukewarm, unmotivated, halfhearted; *informal* couldn't-care-less; *rare* Laodicean.See note at CARE.

apathy noun *widespread apathy among the voters* INDIFFERENCE, lack of interest, lack of enthusiasm, lack of concern, unconcern, uninterestedness, unresponsiveness, impassivity, dispassion, lethargy, languor, ennui; *rare* acedia.

ape noun PRIMATE, simian; monkey; *technical* anthropoid. See table at PRIMATE.

▸ verb *he aped Barbara's accent* IMITATE, mimic, copy, parrot, do an impression of, parody, mock; *informal* take off, send up. See note at IMITATE.

aperture noun *adjusting the aperture of the camera* OPENING, hole, gap, slit, slot, vent, crevice, chink, crack, interstice; *technical* orifice, foramen.

apex noun **1** *the apex of a pyramid* TIP, peak, summit, pinnacle, top, vertex. ANTONYM bottom.

2 *the apex of his career* CLIMAX, culmination; peak, top, pinnacle, zenith, acme, apogee, high(est) point, capstone. ANTONYM nadir.

aphorism noun *she was a fount of Orwellian aphorisms* SAYING, maxim, axiom, adage, epigram, dictum, gnome, proverb, saw, tag; *rare* apophthegm. See note at SAYING.

aphrodisiac noun LOVE POTION, philter; *informal* passion potion.

apiece adverb *the caps are $10 apiece* EACH, respectively, per item, individually; *informal* a pop, a throw, per; *formal* severally.

aplenty adjective *we have fresh corn aplenty* IN ABUNDANCE, in profusion, galore, in large quantities, in large numbers, by the dozen; *informal* by the truckload.

aplomb noun *the judges were especially impressed by her aplomb* POISE, self-assurance, self-confidence, calmness, composure, collectedness, levelheadedness, sangfroid, equilibrium, equanimity; *informal* unflappability.

apocalyptic adjective *we sailed into a storm of apocalyptic proportion* DOOMSDAY, doom-laden, ominous, portentous; catastrophic, momentous.

apocryphal adjective *an apocryphal account of Jesus' childhood* FICTITIOUS, made-up, untrue, fabricated, false, spurious; unverified, unauthenticated, unsubstantiated; bogus. See note at SPURIOUS. ANTONYM authentic.

apologetic adjective *the students who defaced the lockers seemed truly apologetic* REGRETFUL, sorry, contrite, remorseful, rueful, penitent, repentant; conscience-stricken, compunctious, shamefaced, ashamed. ANTONYM unrepentant.

apologia noun *if you're expecting an apologia for the historical inaccuracies in his films, forget it* DEFENSE, justification, vindication, explanation; argument, case.

apologist noun *one of Eisenhower's better-known apologists* DEFENDER, supporter, upholder, advocate, proponent, exponent, propagandist, champion, campaigner; *informal* cheerleader. ANTONYM critic.

apologize verb *please allow me to apologize for my wrongful accusations* SAY (ONE IS) SORRY, express regret, be apologetic, make an apology, ask forgiveness, ask for pardon; *informal* eat one's words, eat humble pie.

apology noun **1** *I owe you an apology* EXPRESSION OF REGRET, one's regrets.

2 *an* ***apology for*** *capitalism* DEFENSE OF, explanation of, justification of, vindication of, apologia for.

apostate noun *after 50 years as an apostate, he returned to the faith* DISSENTER, defector, deserter, traitor, backslider, turncoat; nonconformist; schismatic; *archaic* heretic; *rare* recusant, recreant, tergiversator. ANTONYM follower.

apostle noun **1** *the twelve apostles* DISCIPLE, follower.

2 *the apostles of the Slavs* MISSIONARY, evangelist, proselytizer.

3 *an apostle of capitalism* ADVOCATE, apologist, proponent, exponent, promoter, supporter, upholder, champion, booster.

appall verb *it doesn't take much to appall her* HORRIFY, shock, dismay, distress, outrage, scandalize; disgust, repel, revolt, sicken, nauseate, offend, make someone's blood run cold.

appalling adjective **1** *an appalling crime* SHOCKING, horrific, horrifying, horrible, terrible, awful, dreadful, ghastly, hideous, horrendous, frightful, atrocious, abominable, abhorrent, outrageous, gruesome, grisly, monstrous, heinous, egregious.

2 *informal your schoolwork is appalling* BAD, dreadful, awful, terrible, frightful, atrocious, disgraceful, deplorable, hopeless, lamentable; *informal* rotten, crummy, pathetic, pitiful, woeful, useless, lousy, abysmal, dire.

apparatus noun **1** *laboratory apparatus* EQUIPMENT, gear, rig, tackle, gadgetry; appliance, instrument, machine, mechanism, device, contraption, gadget, gizmo, doohickey. See note at TOOL.

2 *the apparatus of government* STRUCTURE, system, framework, organization, network.

apparel noun *formal the senator is noted for her snazzy apparel* CLOTHES, clothing, garments, dress, attire, wear, garb, getup; *informal* gear, togs, duds, threads; *archaic* raiment, habit, habiliments.

apparent adjective **1** *their relief was all too apparent* EVIDENT, plain, obvious, clear, manifest, visible, discernible, perceptible; unmistakable, crystal clear, palpable, patent, blatant, writ large; *informal* as plain as the nose on one's face, written all over one's face. See note at OSTENSIBLE. ANTONYMS unclear, obscure.

2 *his apparent lack of concern* SEEMING, ostensible, outward, superficial; supposed, alleged, professed. ANTONYM genuine.

apparently adverb *apparently, no one had ever told him that he had a half-sister in San Diego* SEEMINGLY, evidently, it seems (that), it appears (that), it would seem (that), it would appear (that), as far as one knows, by all accounts; ostensibly, outwardly, supposedly, on the face of it, so the story goes, so I'm told; allegedly, reputedly.

apparition noun *a monstrous apparition* GHOST, phantom, specter, spirit, wraith; vision, hallucination; *informal* spook, chimera; *literary* phantasm, revenant, shade, visitant; *rare* eidolon.

appeal verb **1** *police are appealing for information* ASK URGENTLY/EARNESTLY, make an urgent/earnest request, call, make a plea, plead.

2 *Stuart **appealed to** me to help them* IMPLORE, beg, entreat, call on, plead with, exhort, ask, request, petition; *formal* adjure; *literary* beseech.

3 *the idea of traveling **appealed to** me* ATTRACT, be attractive to, interest, take someone's fancy, fascinate, tempt, entice, allure, lure, draw, whet someone's appetite.

▸ noun **1** *an appeal for help* PLEA, urgent/earnest request, entreaty, cry, call, petition, supplication, cri de coeur.

2 *the cultural appeal of the island* ATTRACTION, attractiveness, allure, charm; fascination, magnetism, drawing power, pull.

3 *the court allowed the appeal* RETRIAL, reexamination.

appealing adjective *an appealing portrait of Frances* ATTRACTIVE, engaging, alluring, enchanting, captivating, bewitching, fascinating, tempting, enticing, seductive, irresistible, winning, winsome, charming, desirable. ANTONYMS disagreeable, off-putting.

appear verb **1** *a cloud of dust appeared on the horizon* BECOME VISIBLE, come into view, come into sight, materialize, pop up. ANTONYM vanish.

2 *fundamental differences were beginning to appear* BE REVEALED, emerge, surface, manifest itself, become apparent, become evident, come to light; arise, crop up.

3 *informal* *Bill still hadn't appeared* ARRIVE, turn up, put in an appearance, come, get here/there; *informal* show (up), roll in, blow in.

4 *they **appear to be** completely devoted* SEEM TO BE, look to be, give the impression of being, come across as being, strike someone as being.

5 *the paperback edition didn't appear for two years* BECOME AVAILABLE, come on the market, go on sale, come out, be published, be produced.

6 *she appeared on Broadway* PERFORM, play, act.

appearance noun **1** *her disheveled appearance* LOOK(S), air, aspect, mien.

2 *they tried to maintain a respectable appearance* IMPRESSION, air, image, show, outward show; semblance, facade, veneer, front, pretense.

3 *the sudden appearance of her daughter* ARRIVAL, advent, coming, emergence, materialization.

4 *the appearance of these symptoms* OCCURRENCE, manifestation, development.

appease verb **1** *an attempt to appease his critics* CONCILIATE, placate, pacify, mollify, propitiate, reconcile, win over. See note at PACIFY. ANTONYMS provoke, inflame.

2 *I'd wasted a lot of money to appease my vanity* SATISFY, fulfill, gratify, indulge; assuage, relieve.

appeasement noun *a policy of appeasement* CONCILIATION, placation, concession, pacification, propitiation, reconciliation; fence-mending. ANTONYM provocation.

appellation noun *formal* *"the Eternal City" is an appellation for Rome* NAME, title, designation, tag, sobriquet, byname, nickname, cognomen; *informal* moniker, handle; *formal* denomination.

append verb *the teacher may append comments to the final report* ADD, attach, affix, tack on, tag on; *formal* subjoin.

appendage noun **1** *I am not just an appendage to the family* ADDITION, attachment, adjunct, addendum, appurtenance, accessory.

2 *a pair of feathery appendages* PROTUBERANCE, projection; *technical* process.

appendix noun *there is a windchill table in the appendix* SUPPLEMENT, addendum, postscript, codicil; coda, epilogue, afterword, tailpiece, back matter; attachment.

appertain PHRASE: **appertain to** *how do these articles appertain to the topic of our discussion?* PERTAIN TO, be pertinent to, apply to, relate to, concern, be concerned with, have to do with, be relevant to, have reference to, have a bearing on, bear on; regard.

appetite noun **1** *a walk sharpens the appetite* HUNGER, ravenousness, hungriness; taste, palate.

2 *my appetite for learning* CRAVING, longing, yearning, hankering, hunger, thirst, passion; enthusiasm, keenness, eagerness, desire; *informal* yen.

appetizer noun *tonight's featured appetizer is a dish of grilled oysters and roasted mushrooms* STARTER, first course, hors d'oeuvre, antipasto, amuse-gueule.

appetizing adjective **1** *an appetizing lunch* MOUTHWATERING, inviting, tempting; tasty, delicious, flavorful, toothsome, delectable, succulent; *informal* scrumptious, yummy, delish, lip-smacking. ANTONYMS bland, off-putting.

2 *the least appetizing part of election campaigns* APPEALING, attractive, inviting, alluring. ANTONYM unappealing.

applaud verb **1** *the audience applauded* CLAP, give a standing ovation, put one's hands together; show one's appreciation; *informal* give someone a big hand. ANTONYM boo.

2 *police have applauded the decision* PRAISE, commend, acclaim, salute, welcome, hail, celebrate, express admiration for, express approval of, look on with favor at, approve of, sing the praises of, pay tribute to, speak highly of, take one's hat off to, express respect for. ANTONYM criticize.

applause noun **1** *a massive round of applause* CLAPPING, hand clapping, (standing) ovation; acclamation.

2 *the museum's design won general applause* PRAISE, acclaim, acclamation, admiration, commendation, adulation, favor, approbation, approval, respect; compliments, accolades, tributes; *informal* props.

apple noun. See table on page 42.

VARIETIES OF APPLES

Ambrosia	Liberty
Baldwin	Lodi
Braeburn	Macoun
Cameo	McIntosh
Cortland	Monarch
crab apple	Mutsu
Crispin	Northern Spy
Criterion	Paula Red
Delicious	Pearmain
Discovery	Pink Lady
Empire	pippin
Fortune	Red Delicious
Fuji	Rome
Gala	russet
Ginger Gold	Spartan
Golden Delicious	Stayman
Golden Russet	Sturmer (pippin)
Granny Smith	sugar apple
Gravenstein	Sundowner
Greening	Sunrise
Honeycrisp	sweetsop
Ida Red	Tydeman
Jerseymac	Winesap
Jonagold	Winter Banana
Jonamac	Yellow Transparent
Jonathan	York
Lady	

appliance noun *domestic appliances* DEVICE, machine, instrument, gadget, contraption, apparatus, utensil, implement, tool, mechanism, contrivance, labor-saving device; *informal* gizmo. See table. See also note at TOOL.

KITCHEN GADGETS AND APPLIANCES

blender	meat slicer
can opener	microwave (oven)
coffee maker	mixer
convection oven	Mixmaster™
Crockpot™	pastry blender
deep fryer	percolator
dicer	pressure cooker
dishwasher	range
double boiler	refrigerator
egg beater	salad spinner
fondue pot	slow cooker
food processor	spatula
garbage disposal	steamer
garlic press	stove
grater	toaster
griddle	toaster oven
hot plate	trash compactor
icemaker	waffle iron
juicer	whisk
knife sharpener	

applicable adjective *the laws applicable to the dispute* RELEVANT, appropriate, pertinent, appurtenant, apposite, germane, material, significant, related, connected; fitting, suitable, apt, befitting, useful, helpful. ANTONYMS inappropriate, irrelevant.

applicant noun *first-time applicants must have an appointment* CANDIDATE, interviewee, competitor, contestant, contender, entrant; claimant, suppliant, supplicant, petitioner, postulant; prospective student, prospective employee, job-seeker, job-hunter, auditioner.

application noun **1** *an application for a loan* REQUEST, appeal, petition, entreaty, plea, solicitation, supplication, requisition, suit, approach, claim, demand.

2 *the application of antiinflation policies* IMPLEMENTATION, use, exercise, employment, utilization, practice, applying, discharge, execution, prosecution, enactment; *formal* praxis.

3 *the argument is clearest in its application to the theater* RELEVANCE, relevancy, bearing, significance, pertinence, aptness, appositeness, germaneness, importance.

4 *the application of makeup* PUTTING ON, rubbing in, applying.

5 *a smelly application to relieve muscle pain* OINTMENT, lotion, cream, rub, salve, emollient, preparation, liniment, embrocation, balm, unguent, poultice.

6 *a vector graphics application* PROGRAM, software, routine.

apply verb **1** *more than 300 people* ***applied for*** *the job* PUT IN AN APPLICATION FOR, put in for, try (out) for, bid for, appeal for, petition for, sue for, register for, audition for; request, seek, solicit (for), claim, ask for, try to obtain.

2 *the third paragraph applies only to returning students* BE RELEVANT, have relevance, have a bearing, appertain, pertain, relate, concern, affect, involve, cover, deal with, touch; be pertinent, be appropriate, be significant.

3 *she applied some ointment* PUT ON, rub in, work in, spread, smear.

4 *a steady pressure should be applied* EXERT, administer, implement, use, exercise, employ, utilize, bring to bear.

PHRASE: **apply oneself** *if Palermo applies himself, he has an excellent shot at the scholarship* BE DILIGENT, be industrious, be assiduous, show commitment, show dedication; work hard, exert oneself, make an effort, try hard, do one's best, give one's all, put one's shoulder to the wheel, put one's nose to the grindstone; strive, endeavor, struggle, labor, toil; pay attention, commit oneself, devote oneself; persevere, persist; *informal* put one's back into it, knuckle down, buckle down, hunker down.

appoint verb **1** *he was appointed chairman* NOMINATE, name, designate, install as, commission, engage, co-opt; select, choose, elect, vote in; *Military* detail. ANTONYM reject.

2 *the arbitrator shall appoint a date for the meeting* SPECIFY, determine, assign, designate, allot, set, fix, arrange, choose, decide on, establish, settle, ordain, prescribe, decree.

appointed adjective **1** *at the appointed time* SCHEDULED, arranged, prearranged, specified, decided, agreed, determined, assigned, designated, allotted, set, fixed, chosen, established, settled, preordained, ordained, prescribed, decreed.

2 *a well-appointed room* FURNISHED, decorated, outfitted, fitted out, provided, supplied.

appointment noun **1** *a six o'clock appointment* MEETING, engagement, interview, arrangement, consultation, session; date, rendezvous, assignation; commitment, fixture.

2 *the appointment of directors* NOMINATION, naming, designation, installation, commissioning, engagement, cooption; selection, choosing, election, voting in; *Military* detailing.

3 *he held an appointment at the university* JOB, post, position, situation, employment, place, office; *dated* station.

apportion verb *the proceeds from the sale of the restaurant will be apportioned equally among the siblings* SHARE, divide, allocate, distribute, allot, assign, give out, hand out, mete out, deal out, dish out, dole out, parcel out, prorate; ration, measure out; split; *informal* divvy up.

apposite adjective *an apposite caption accompanies each photo* APPROPRIATE, suitable, fitting, apt, befitting; relevant, pertinent, appurtenant, to the point, applicable, germane, material, congruous, felicitous; *formal* ad rem. ANTONYM inappropriate.

appraisal noun **1** *an objective appraisal of the book* ASSESSMENT, evaluation, estimation, judgment, rating, gauging, sizing up, summing-up, consideration.

2 *a free insurance appraisal* VALUATION, estimate, estimation, quotation, pricing; survey.

appraise verb **1** *they appraised their handiwork* ASSESS, evaluate, judge, rate, gauge, review, consider; *informal* size up.

2 *the goods were appraised at $1,800* VALUE, price, estimate, quote; survey.

appreciable adjective *there is an appreciable amount of sugar in the lemonade* CONSIDERABLE, substantial, significant, sizable, goodly, fair, reasonable, marked; perceptible, noticeable, visible, discernible; *informal* tidy. See note at TANGIBLE. ANTONYM negligible.

appreciate verb **1** *I'd appreciate your advice* BE GRATEFUL FOR, be thankful for, be obliged for, be indebted for, be in your debt for, be appreciative of. ANTONYM disparage.

2 *the college appreciated her greatly* VALUE, treasure, admire, respect, hold in high regard, think highly of, think much of. See note at ESTEEM.

3 *we appreciate your difficulty* RECOGNIZE, acknowledge, realize, know, be aware of, be conscious of, be sensitive to, understand, comprehend, grasp, fathom; *informal* be wise to.

4 *a home that will appreciate in value* INCREASE, gain, grow, rise, go up, escalate, soar, rocket. ANTONYMS depreciate, decrease.

appreciation noun **1** *he showed his appreciation* GRATITUDE, thanks, gratefulness, thankfulness, recognition, sense of obligation. ANTONYM ingratitude.

2 *her appreciation of literature* VALUING, treasuring, admiration, respect, regard, esteem, high opinion.

3 *an appreciation of the difficulties involved* ACKNOWLEDGMENT, recognition, realization, knowledge, awareness, consciousness, understanding, comprehension. ANTONYM unawareness.

4 *a critical appreciation of the professor's work* REVIEW, critique, criticism, critical analysis, assessment, evaluation, judgment, rating.

appreciative adjective **1** *we are* ***appreciative of*** *all your efforts* GRATEFUL FOR, thankful for, obliged for, indebted for, in someone's debt for. ANTONYM ungrateful.

2 *an appreciative audience* SUPPORTIVE, encouraging, sympathetic, responsive; enthusiastic, admiring, approving, complimentary.

apprehend verb **1** *the thieves were quickly apprehended* ARREST, catch, capture, seize; take prisoner, take into custody, detain, put in jail, put behind bars, imprison, incarcerate; *informal* bag, collar, nab, nail, run in, bust, pick up, pull in.

2 *they are slow to apprehend danger* APPRECIATE, recognize, discern, perceive, make out, take in, realize, grasp, understand, comprehend; *informal* get the picture.

apprehension noun **1** *he was filled with apprehension* ANXIETY, worry, unease, nervousness, nerves, misgivings, disquiet, concern, tension, trepidation, perturbation, consternation, angst, dread, alarm, fear, foreboding; *informal* butterflies, jitters, the willies, the creeps, the shivers, the heebie-jeebies. ANTONYM confidence.

2 *the apprehension of a perpetrator* ARREST, capture, seizure; detention, imprisonment, incarceration; *informal* collar, nabbing, bagging, busting.

apprehensive adjective *dentists know that many of their patients are apprehensive* ANXIOUS, worried, uneasy, nervous, concerned, agitated, tense, afraid, scared, frightened, fearful; *informal* on tenterhooks. ANTONYM confident.

apprentice noun *she worked with the great violin maker as his apprentice* TRAINEE, learner, probationer, novice, beginner, starter, cadet, tenderfoot; pupil, student; *informal* rookie, newbie, greenhorn. See note at NOVICE. ANTONYM veteran.

apprise verb *we'll apprise you of any changes in your husband's condition* INFORM, tell, notify, advise, brief, make aware, enlighten, update, keep posted; *informal* clue in, fill in, bring up to speed.

approach verb **1** *she approached the altar* MOVE TOWARD, come/go toward, advance toward, inch toward, go/come/draw/move nearer, go/come/draw/move closer, near; close in, gain on; reach, arrive at. ANTONYM leave.

2 *the trade deficit is approaching $20 million* BORDER ON, verge on, approximate, touch, nudge, near, come near to, come close to.

3 *she approached him about leaving his job* SPEAK TO, talk to; make advances to, make overtures to, make a proposal to, sound out, proposition.

4 *he approached the problem in the best way* TACKLE, set about, address oneself to, undertake, get down to, launch into, embark on, go about, come to grips with.

▸ noun **1** *a typical male approach* METHOD, procedure, technique, modus operandi, MO, style, way, manner; strategy, tactic, system, means.

2 *the dog barked at the approach of any intruder* ADVANCE, coming, nearing; arrival, appearance; advent.

3 *the approach to the castle* DRIVEWAY, drive, access road, road, avenue; way.

approachable adjective **1** *students found the staff approachable* FRIENDLY, welcoming, pleasant, agreeable, congenial, affable, cordial; obliging, communicative, helpful. ANTONYM aloof.

2 *the south landing is approachable by boat* ACCESSIBLE, attainable, reachable; *informal* get-at-able. ANTONYM inaccessible.

approbation noun *at age 45, he was still seeking his parents' approbation* APPROVAL, acceptance, endorsement, appreciation, respect, admiration, commendation, praise, congratulations, acclaim, esteem, applause; consent; *rare* laudation. ANTONYM criticism.

appropriate adjective *this isn't the appropriate time* SUITABLE, proper, fitting, apt, right; relevant, pertinent, apposite; convenient, opportune; seemly, befitting; *formal* ad rem; *archaic* meet. ANTONYM unsuitable.

▸ verb **1** *the barons appropriated church lands* SEIZE, commandeer, expropriate, annex, arrogate, sequestrate, sequester, take over, hijack; steal, take; *informal* swipe, nab, bag, pinch.

2 *his images have been appropriated by advertisers* PLAGIARIZE, copy; poach, steal, borrow; *informal* rip off.

3 *we are appropriating funds for these expenses* ALLOCATE, assign, allot, earmark, set aside, devote, apportion.

approval noun 1 *their proposals went to the board for approval* ACCEPTANCE, agreement, consent, assent, permission, leave; sanction, endorsement, ratification, authorization, validation; support, backing; *informal* the go-ahead, the green light, the nod, the rubber stamp, the OK, the say-so, the thumbs up. ANTONYM refusal.

2 *Lily looked at him with approval* APPROBATION, appreciation, favor, liking, admiration, regard, esteem, respect, praise. ANTONYM dislike.

approve verb 1 *his boss doesn't* ***approve of*** *his lifestyle* AGREE WITH, endorse, support, back, uphold, subscribe to, recommend, advocate, be in favor of, favor, think well of, like, appreciate, go for, hold with, take kindly to; be pleased with, admire, applaud, praise. ANTONYMS condemn, disapprove.

2 *the government approved the proposals* ACCEPT, agree to, consent to, assent to, give one's blessing to, bless, rubber-stamp; ratify, sanction, endorse, authorize, validate, pass; support, back; *informal* give the nod to, give the go-ahead to, give the green light to, give the OK to, give the thumbs-up to. ANTONYM refuse.

THE RIGHT WORD

There are a number of ways to show your support for something. The most general way is to **approve** it, a term that covers everything from simple, technical agreement (*to approve the plan*) to enthusiastic support (*she was quick to approve her son's decision to marry*). **Endorse** implies a more public and official expression of support and is used primarily in reference to things that require promotion or publicity (*endorse a political candidate*), while **commend** is to make a formal and usually public statement of approval or congratulation (*he was commended for his heroism*). **Sanction**, **certify**, and **ratify** imply that approval is not only official but that it makes something legal. To *sanction* is not only to *approve* but to authorize (*school authorities would not sanction the wearing of hats in class*), while *certify* implies conformity with certain standards (*certified to teach in the State of New York*). *Ratify* is usually confined to only the most official and authoritative settings. For example, an employer might *sanction* the idea of hiring a woman to perform a job that only men have performed in the past, and the woman in question might have to *certify* that she possesses the necessary training and qualifications. But to *ratify* a constitutional amendment granting equal rights to women requires a lengthy set of legislative procedures.

approximate adjective *approximate dimensions* ESTIMATED, rough, imprecise, inexact, indefinite, broad, loose; *informal* ballpark. ANTONYM precise.

▸ verb *the sound approximates that of a cow* RESEMBLE, be similar to, be not unlike; be/come close to, be/come near to, approach, border on, verge on.

approximately adverb *there are approximately 24 children per classroom* ROUGHLY, about, around, circa, more or less, in the neighborhood of, in the region of, on the order of, something like, around/round about, give or take (a few); near to, close to, nearly, almost, approaching; *informal* pushing, in the ballpark of. ANTONYM precisely.

approximation noun 1 *the figure is only an approximation* ESTIMATE, estimation, guess, rough calculation; *informal* guesstimate, ballpark figure.

2 *an approximation to the truth* SEMBLANCE, resemblance, likeness, similarity, correspondence.

appurtenances plural noun *artist's studio with appurtenances for rent* ACCESSORIES, trappings, appendages, accoutrements, equipment, paraphernalia, impedimenta, bits and pieces, things; *informal* stuff.

a priori adjective *a priori reasoning* THEORETICAL, deduced, deductive, inferred, postulated, suppositional. ANTONYMS empirical, a posteriori.

▸ adverb *the results cannot be predicted a priori* THEORETICALLY, deductively, scientifically.

apron noun PINAFORE, smock, overall, bib, bib apron; butcher's apron, cobbler's apron, cobbler's smock.

apropos preposition *he was asked a question apropos his resignation* WITH REFERENCE TO, with regard to, with respect to, regarding, concerning, on the subject of, connected with, about, re.

▸ adjective *the word "conglomerate" was decidedly apropos* APPROPRIATE, pertinent, relevant, apposite, apt, applicable, suitable, germane, fitting, befitting, material; right on. ANTONYM inappropriate.

PHRASE: **apropos of nothing** *apropos of nothing, she started speaking only in rhyme* IRRELEVANTLY, arbitrarily, at random, for no reason, illogically.

apt adjective 1 *a very apt description of how I felt* SUITABLE, fitting, appropriate, befitting, relevant, germane, applicable, apposite. ANTONYM inappropriate.

2 *they're apt to get a bit sloppy* INCLINED, given, likely, liable, disposed, predisposed, prone. ANTONYM unlikely.

3 *an apt pupil* CLEVER, quick, bright, sharp, smart, intelligent, able, gifted, adept, astute. ANTONYM slow.

aptitude noun *an aptitude for higher mathematics* TALENT, gift, flair, bent, skill, knack, facility, ability, proficiency, capability, potential, capacity, faculty, genius.

aquatic adjective *seals and other aquatic mammals* MARINE, water, saltwater, freshwater, seawater, sea, oceanic, river; *technical* pelagic, thalassic.

aqueduct noun *our paper boats went through the aqueduct* CONDUIT, race, channel, chute, watercourse, sluice, sluiceway, spillway.

aquiline adjective *an aquiline nose* HOOKED, curved, bent, angular, Roman; beaklike, beaky.

arable adjective *arable soil* FARMABLE, cultivable; fertile, productive.

arachnid noun. See table at SPIDER.

arbiter noun 1 *an arbiter between Moscow and Washington.* See ARBITRATOR.

2 *the great arbiter of fashion* AUTHORITY, judge, controller, director; master, expert, pundit.

arbitrary adjective 1 *an arbitrary decision* CAPRICIOUS, whimsical, random, chance, unpredictable; casual, wanton, unmotivated, motiveless, unreasoned, unsupported, irrational, illogical, groundless, unjustified; personal, discretionary, subjective. ANTONYMS reasoned, rational.

2 *the arbitrary power of the prince* AUTOCRATIC, dictatorial, autarchic, undemocratic, despotic, tyrannical, au-

thoritarian, high-handed; absolute, uncontrolled, unlimited, unrestrained. ANTONYM democratic.

arbitrate verb *a third and disinterested party was brought in to arbitrate* ADJUDICATE, judge, referee, umpire; mediate, conciliate, intervene, intercede; settle, decide, resolve, pass judgment.

arbitration noun *the council called for arbitration to settle the dispute* ADJUDICATION, judgment, arbitrament; mediation, mediatorship, conciliation, settlement, intervention.

arbitrator noun *the litigants met with a court-appointed arbitrator* ADJUDICATOR, arbiter, judge, referee, umpire; mediator, conciliator, intervenor, intercessor, go-between.

arbor noun *the arbor was overgrown with wisteria and bittersweet* BOWER, pergola; alcove, grotto, recess; gazebo.

arc noun *the arc of a circle* CURVE, arch, crescent, semicircle, half-moon; curvature, convexity.

▸ verb *I sent the ball arcing out over the river* CURL, curve; arch.

arcade noun **1** *a classical arcade* COLONNADE, gallery, cloister, loggia, portico, peristyle, stoa.

2 *playing hooky at the arcade* VIDEO ARCADE, midway.

arcane adjective *processes as old and arcane as the language of the law* MYSTERIOUS, secret; enigmatic, esoteric, cryptic, obscure, abstruse, recondite, recherché, impenetrable, opaque.

arch[1] noun **1** *a stone arch* ARCHWAY, vault, span, dome.

2 *the arch of his spine* CURVE, bow, bend, arc, curvature, convexity; hunch, crook.

▸ verb *she arched her eyebrows* CURVE, arc.

arch[2] adjective *an arch grin* MISCHIEVOUS, teasing, saucy, knowing, playful, roguish, impish, cheeky, tongue-in-cheek.

arch- combining form *his archenemy* CHIEF, principal, foremost, leading, main, major, prime, premier, greatest; *informal* number-one, numero uno. ANTONYM minor.

archaic adjective *archaic conventions* OBSOLETE, out of date, old-fashioned, outmoded, behind the times, bygone, anachronistic, antiquated, superannuated, antediluvian, old world, old-fangled; ancient, old, extinct, defunct; prehistoric; *literary* of yore. See note at OLD. ANTONYM modern.

archetypal adjective *he's the archetypal matinee idol* QUINTESSENTIAL, classic, most typical, representative, model, exemplary, textbook; stock, stereotypical, prototypical. ANTONYM atypical.

archetype noun *the archetype of Southern hospitality* QUINTESSENCE, essence, representative, model, embodiment, prototype, stereotype; original, pattern, standard, paradigm. See note at MODEL.

architect noun **1** *the architect of St. Mary's Cathedral* DESIGNER, planner, draftsman.

2 *Andrew was the architect of the plan* ORIGINATOR, author, creator, founder, father, founding father; engineer, inventor, mastermind; *literary* begetter.

architecture noun **1** *modern architecture* BUILDING DESIGN, building style, planning, building, construction; *formal* architectonics. See table.

2 *the architecture of a computer system* STRUCTURE, construction, organization, layout, design, build, anatomy, makeup; *informal* setup.

ARCHITECTURAL STYLES

Art Deco	Ionic
Art Nouveau	Islamic
baroque	Jacobean
Bauhaus	medieval
beaux-arts	mission
brutalist	modernist
Byzantine	Moorish
Carolingian	Moresque
Château style	Mozarabic
Churrigueresque	neoclassical
cinquecento	neo-Gothic
classical	Norman
colonial	Palladian
Corinthian	Perpendicular
Decorated	postmodernist
Doric	Prairie Style
Early Christian	quattrocento
Early English	Queen Anne
Early Renaissance	Regency
Edwardian	Renaissance
Elizabethan	rococo
Empire	Roman
flamboyant	Romanesque
functional	Saxon
Georgian	Spanish-Colonial
Gothic	Spanish-Mission
Gothic Revival	Tudor
Greco-Roman	Tudorbethan
Grecian	Tuscan
Greek Revival	vernacular
International Style	Victorian Gothic

archive noun **1** *she delved into the family archives* RECORDS, annals, chronicles, accounts; papers, documents, files; history; *Law* muniments.

2 *the national archive* RECORD OFFICE, registry, repository, depository, museum, chancery.

▸ verb *the videos are archived for future use* FILE, log, catalog, document, record, register; store, cache.

arctic adjective **1** **(Arctic)** *Arctic waters* POLAR, far northern, boreal; *literary* hyperborean.

2 *arctic weather conditions* (BITTERLY) COLD, wintry, freezing, frozen, icy, glacial, hypothermic, gelid, subzero, polar, Siberian, bone-chilling. ANTONYMS Antarctic, tropical.

▸ noun **(the Arctic)** *a research station in the Arctic* FAR NORTH, High Arctic, North Pole, Arctic Circle, North of Sixty. ANTONYM Antarctic.

ardent adjective *an ardent soccer fan* PASSIONATE, fervent, zealous, fervid, wholehearted, vehement, intense, fierce, fiery; enthusiastic, keen, eager, avid, committed, dedicated; *literary* perfervid. See note at EAGER. ANTONYM apathetic.

ardor noun *approaching the project with ardor* PASSION, fervor, zeal, vehemence, intensity, verve, fire, emotion; enthusiasm, eagerness, avidity, gusto, keenness, dedication.

arduous adjective *an arduous journey* ONEROUS, taxing, difficult, hard, heavy, laborious, burdensome, strenuous, vigorous, back-breaking; demanding, tough, challenging, formidable; exhausting, tiring, punishing, grueling; uphill, steep; *informal* killing; toilsome. See note at HARD. ANTONYM easy.

area noun **1** *an inner-city area* DISTRICT, region, zone, sector, quarter, precinct; locality, locale, neighborhood, parish, patch; tract, belt; *informal* neck of the woods, turf.

2 *specific areas of scientific knowledge* FIELD, sphere, discipline, realm, domain, sector, province, territory, line.

3 *the dining area* SECTION, space; place, room.

4 *the area of a circle* EXPANSE, extent, size, scope, compass; dimensions, proportions.

arena noun 1 *a hockey arena* STADIUM; amphitheater, coliseum; sportsplex; field, ring, court; bowl, park, ground; rink, ice rink; *historical* circus.

2 *the political arena* SCENE, sphere, realm, province, domain, sector, forum, territory, world.

aren't See note below.

WORD NOTE aren't

Which of the following is incorrect? a) *Aren't the Red Sox going to lose?* b) *Aren't you clever?* c) *Aren't I tall enough?* Turn the questions into statements. The Red Sox are (or aren't) going to lose. You are (or aren't) clever. But I am (or am not) tall enough, so the question with contraction would be *amn't I?* and a better idea would be *I'm tall enough, don't you think?*—**JS**

argot noun *the argot of the theater* JARGON, slang, idiom, cant, parlance, vernacular, patois; dialect, speech, language; *informal* lingo. See note at DIALECT.

arguable adjective 1 *he had an arguable claim for asylum* TENABLE, defendable, defensible, supportable, sustainable, plausible, able to hold water; reasonable, viable, acceptable. ANTONYM untenable.

2 *it is arguable whether these routes are worthwhile* DEBATABLE, questionable, open to question, controversial, contentious, doubtful, uncertain, moot. ANTONYM certain.

arguably adverb *this is arguably the best Broadway musical in ten years* POSSIBLY, conceivably, feasibly, plausibly, probably, maybe, perhaps.

argue verb 1 *they argued that the government was to blame* CONTEND, assert, maintain, insist, hold, claim, reason, allege; *formal* aver, represent, opine.

2 *the children are always arguing* QUARREL, disagree, squabble, bicker, fight, wrangle, dispute, feud, have words, cross swords, lock horns, be at each other's throats; *informal* spat.

3 *it is hard to argue the point* DISPUTE, debate, discuss, controvert, deny, question.

argument noun 1 *he had an argument with Tony* QUARREL, disagreement, squabble, fight, dispute, wrangle, clash, altercation, feud, contretemps, disputation, falling-out; *informal* tiff, row, blowup, rhubarb.

2 *arguments for the existence of God* REASONING, justification, explanation, rationalization; case, defense, vindication; evidence, reasons, grounds.

3 *the argument of the book* THEME, topic, subject matter; summary, synopsis, précis, gist, outline.

argumentative adjective *the futility of dealing with argumentative people* QUARRELSOME, disputatious, captious, contrary, cantankerous, contentious; belligerent, bellicose, combative, antagonistic, truculent, pugnacious.

arid adjective 1 *an arid landscape* DRY, dried up, bone-dry, waterless, moistureless, parched, scorched, baked, thirsty, droughty, desert; BARREN, infertile. See note at DRY. ANTONYMS wet, fertile.

2 *this town has an arid, empty feel* DREARY, dull, drab, dry, sterile, colorless, unstimulating, uninspiring, flat, boring, uninteresting, lifeless, emotionless, plain-vanilla. ANTONYM vibrant.

arise verb 1 *many problems arose* COME TO LIGHT, become apparent, appear, emerge, crop up, turn up, surface, spring up; occur; *literary* befall, come to pass.

2 *injuries arising from defective products* RESULT, proceed, follow, ensue, derive, stem, originate; be caused by.

3 *the beast arose* STAND UP, rise, get to one's feet, get up.

aristocracy noun *she was quite at home with the aristocracy* NOBILITY, peerage, gentry, gentility, upper class, ruling class, elite, high society, establishment, haut monde; aristocrats, lords, ladies, peers, peers of the realm, nobles, noblemen, noblewomen; *informal* upper crust, top drawer, aristos. ANTONYM working class.

aristocrat noun *the son of aristocrats* NOBLEMAN, noblewoman, lord, lady, peer, peeress, peer of the realm, patrician, grandee; blue blood; *informal* aristo. ANTONYM commoner.

aristocratic adjective 1 *an aristocratic family* NOBLE, titled, upper-class, blue-blooded, high-born, well-born, elite; *informal* upper-crust, top-drawer. ANTONYM working-class.

2 *an aristocratic manner* REFINED, polished, courtly, dignified, posh, decorous, gracious, fine; haughty, proud. ANTONYM vulgar.

arm noun 1 *an arm of the sea* INLET, creek, cove, fjord, bay; estuary, strait(s), sound, channel.

2 *the political arm of the group* BRANCH, section, department, division, wing, sector, detachment, offshoot, extension.

3 *the long arm of the law* REACH, power, authority, influence.

▸ verb *he armed himself with a revolver* EQUIP, provide, supply, furnish, issue, outfit, fit out.

armada noun *the world's largest armada of warships* FLEET, flotilla, squadron, navy.

armaments plural noun *a shortage of armaments* ARMS, weapons, weaponry, firearms, guns, ordnance, artillery, munitions, matériel, hardware.

armful noun *an armful of groceries* ARMLOAD, bunch, load.

armistice noun *the armistice was declared on November 11* TRUCE, cease-fire, peace, suspension of hostilities.

armor noun *a suit of armor | protected by his armor* PROTECTIVE COVERING, armor plate, shield; chain mail, coat of mail, panoply; carapace.

armored adjective *armored tanks* ARMOR-PLATED, steel-plated, ironclad; bulletproof, bombproof; reinforced, toughened.

armory noun *a Civil War exhibition at the old armory* ARSENAL, arms depot, arms cache, ordnance depot, magazine, ammunition dump.

arms plural noun 1 *the illegal export of arms* WEAPONS, weaponry, firearms, guns, ordnance, artillery, armaments, munitions, matériel.

2 *the family arms* CREST, emblem, coat of arms, heraldic device, insignia, escutcheon, shield.

army noun 1 *the invading army* ARMED FORCE, military

force, land force, military, soldiery, infantry, militia; troops, soldiers; *archaic* host.

2 *an army of tourists* CROWD, swarm, multitude, horde, mob, gang, throng, mass, flock, herd, pack.

aroma noun *the wonderful aroma of warm bread* SCENT, fragrance, perfume, smell, bouquet, balm, nose, odor, whiff; *literary* redolence. See note at SMELL.

aromatic adjective *aromatic wood chips* FRAGRANT, scented, perfumed, fragranced, odorous; *literary* redolent.

around adverb 1 *there were houses scattered around* ON EVERY SIDE, on all sides, throughout, all over (the place), everywhere; about, here and there.

2 *he turned around* IN THE OPPOSITE DIRECTION, to face the other way, backward, to the rear.

3 *there was no one around* NEARBY, near, about, close by, close, close at hand, at hand, in the vicinity, at close range.

▸ preposition 1 *the palazzo is built around a courtyard* ON ALL SIDES OF, about, encircling, surrounding, enclosing.

2 *they drove around town* ABOUT, all over, in/to all parts of.

3 *around three miles* APPROXIMATELY, about, around/round about, circa, roughly, something like, more or less, in the region of, in the neighborhood of, give or take (a few); nearly, close to, approaching; getting on for; *informal* in the ballpark of.

PHRASE: **around the clock** 1 *we're working around the clock* DAY AND NIGHT, night and day, round the clock, all the time, [morning, noon, and night], continuously, nonstop, steadily, unremittingly; *informal* 24-7. 2 *around-the-clock supervision* CONTINUOUS, round-the-clock, constant, nonstop, continual, uninterrupted.

arouse verb 1 *they had aroused his suspicion* INDUCE, prompt, trigger, stir up, bring out, kindle, fire, spark off, provoke, engender, cause, foster; *literary* enkindle. ANTONYM allay.

2 *his ability to arouse the masses* STIR UP, rouse, galvanize, excite, electrify, stimulate, inspire, inspirit, move, fire up, whip up, get going, inflame, agitate, goad, incite; *rare* inspirit. See note at INCITE. ANTONYM pacify.

3 *his touch aroused her* EXCITE, stimulate, titillate; *informal* turn on, get going, give a thrill to, light someone's fire. ANTONYM turn off.

4 *she was aroused from her sleep* WAKE (UP), awaken, bring to, rouse; *literary* waken.

arraign verb 1 *he was **arraigned for** murder* INDICT FOR, prosecute for, put on trial for, bring to trial for, take to court for, lay/file/prefer charges against for, summons for, cite for; accuse of, charge with, incriminate with; *archaic* inculpate for. ANTONYM acquit.

2 *they bitterly arraigned the government* CRITICIZE, censure, impugn, attack, condemn, chastise, lambaste, rebuke, admonish, remonstrate with, take to task, berate, reproach; *informal* knock, slam, blast, lay into; castigate, excoriate. ANTONYM praise.

arrange verb 1 *she arranged the flowers* ORDER, set out, lay out, array, position, dispose, present, display, exhibit; group, sort, organize, tidy.

2 *they hoped to arrange a meeting* ORGANIZE, fix (up), plan, schedule, pencil in, contrive, settle on, decide, determine, agree.

3 *he arranged the piece for a full orchestra* ADAPT, set, score, orchestrate, transcribe, instrument.

arrangement noun 1 *the arrangement of the furniture* POSITIONING, disposition, order, presentation, display; grouping, organization, alignment.

2 (**arrangements**) *the arrangements for my trip* PREPARATIONS, plan(s), provision(s); planning, groundwork.

3 *we had an arrangement* AGREEMENT, deal, understanding, bargain, settlement, pact, modus vivendi.

4 *an arrangement of Beethoven's symphonies* ADAPTATION, orchestration, instrumentation.

arrant adjective *what arrant nonsense!* UTTER, complete, total, absolute, downright, outright, thorough, out-and-out, sheer, pure, unmitigated, unqualified; blatant, flagrant.

array noun 1 *a huge array of cars* RANGE, collection, selection, assortment, diversity, variety; arrangement, assemblage, lineup, formation; display, exhibition, exposition.

2 *she arrived in silken array* DRESS, attire, clothing, garb, garments; finery, apparel.

▸ verb 1 *a buffet was arrayed on the table* ARRANGE, assemble, group, order, place, position, set out, exhibit, lay out, dispose; display.

2 *he was arrayed in gray flannel* DRESS, attire, clothe, garb, deck (out), outfit, get up, turn out; *archaic* apparel.

arrears plural noun *rent arrears* MONEY OWING, outstanding payment(s), debt(s), liabilities, dues. ANTONYM credit.

PHRASE: **in arrears** *the personal accounts are fine, but the business is in arrears* BEHIND, behindhand, late, overdue, in the red, in debt.

arrest verb 1 *police arrested him for murder* APPREHEND, take into custody, take prisoner, imprison, incarcerate, detain, jail, put in jail; *informal* pick up, pull in, run in, pinch, bust, nab, collar. ANTONYM release.

2 *the spread of the disease can be arrested* STOP, halt, check, block, hinder, restrict, limit, inhibit, impede, curb; prevent, obstruct; *literary* stay.

3 *she tried to arrest his attention* ATTRACT, capture, catch, hold, engage; absorb, occupy, engross.

▸ noun 1 *a warrant for your arrest* DETENTION, apprehension, seizure, capture, takedown.

2 *a cardiac arrest* STOPPAGE, halt, interruption.

arresting adjective *an arresting image* STRIKING, eye-catching, conspicuous, engaging, engrossing, fascinating, impressive, imposing, spectacular, dramatic, breathtaking, dazzling, stunning, awe-inspiring; remarkable, outstanding, distinctive. ANTONYM inconspicuous.

arrival noun 1 *they awaited Ruth's arrival* COMING, appearance, entrance, entry, approach. ANTONYM departure.

2 *staff greeted the late arrivals* COMER, entrant, incomer; visitor, caller, guest.

arrive verb 1 *more police arrived* COME, turn up, get here/there, make it, appear, enter, present oneself, come along, materialize; *informal* show (up), roll in/up, blow in, show one's face. ANTONYM depart.

2 *we **arrived at** his house* REACH, get to, come to, make it to, end up at; *informal* wind up at. ANTONYM leave.

3 *they **arrived at** an agreement* REACH, achieve, attain,

gain, accomplish; work out, draw up, put together, strike, settle on; *informal* clinch.

4 *the wedding finally arrived* HAPPEN, occur, take place, come about; present itself, crop up; *literary* come to pass.

5 *CD-ROMs arrived in the late eighties* EMERGE, appear, surface, come on the scene, dawn, be born, come into being, arise.

6 *informal their Rolls Royce proved that they had arrived* SUCCEED, be a success, do well, reach the top, make good, prosper, thrive; *informal* make it, make one's mark, do all right for oneself.

arrogant adjective *success has made him arrogant* HAUGHTY, conceited, self-important, egotistic, full of oneself, superior; overbearing, pompous, bumptious, presumptuous, imperious, overweening; proud, immodest; *informal* high and mighty, too big for one's britches, too big for one's boots, bigheaded, puffed-up; *rare* hubristic. See note at PRIDE. ANTONYM modest.

arrogate verb *the Church* ***arrogated to itself*** *the power to create kings* ASSUME, take, claim, appropriate, seize, expropriate, wrest, usurp, commandeer.

arrow noun **1** *a bow and arrow* SHAFT, bolt, dart; *historical* quarrel.

2 *the arrow pointed right* POINTER, indicator, marker, needle.

arsenal noun **1** *Britain's nuclear arsenal* WEAPONS, weaponry, arms, armaments.

2 *mutineers broke into the arsenal* ARMORY, arms depot, arms cache, ordnance depot, magazine, ammunition dump.

arson noun *the fire is being treated as arson* PYROMANIA, incendiarism; *informal* torching.

arsonist noun *police suspect this latest fire is the work of an arsonist* INCENDIARY, pyromaniac; *informal* firebug, pyro, torch.

art noun **1** *he studied art* FINE ART, artwork. See table.

2 *the art of writing* SKILL, craft, technique, knack, facility, ability, know-how.

3 *she uses art to achieve her aims* CUNNING, artfulness, slyness, craftiness, guile; deceit, duplicity, artifice, wiles.

artful adjective **1** *artful politicians* SLY, crafty, cunning, wily, scheming, devious, Machiavellian, sneaky, tricky, conniving, designing, calculating; canny, shrewd; deceitful, duplicitous, disingenuous, underhanded; *informal* foxy, shifty; *archaic* subtle. ANTONYM ingenuous.

2 *artful precision* SKILLFUL, clever, adept, adroit, skilled, expert.

article noun **1** *small household articles* ITEM, thing, object, artifact, commodity, product.

2 *an article in the paper* REPORT, account, story, write-up, feature, item, piece, column, review, commentary.

3 *the crucial article of the treaty* CLAUSE, section, subsection, point, item, paragraph, division, subdivision, part, portion.

articulate adjective *an articulate speaker* ELOQUENT, fluent, effective, persuasive, lucid, expressive, silver-tongued; intelligible, comprehensible, understandable. ANTONYM unintelligible.

▸ verb *they were unable to articulate their emotions* EXPRESS, voice, vocalize, put in words, communicate, state; air, ventilate, vent, pour out; utter, say, speak, enunciate, pronounce; *informal* come out with.

articulated adjective *an articulated bus | articulated shells* HINGED, jointed, segmented; coupled, attached, interlocked; *technical* articulate.

artifact noun *hundreds of unidentified artifacts are stored in numerous rooms beneath the museum* RELIC, article; handiwork.

artifice noun *in our trade, artifice is an asset* TRICKERY, deceit, deception, duplicity, guile, cunning, artfulness, wiliness, craftiness, slyness, chicanery; fraud, fraudulence.

artificial adjective **1** *artificial flowers* SYNTHETIC, fake, imitation, mock, ersatz, faux, substitute, replica, reproduction; man-made, manufactured, fabricated, inorganic; plastic; *informal* pretend, phony. See note at SPURIOUS. ANTONYM natural.

2 *an artificial smile* INSINCERE, feigned, false, unnatural, contrived, put-on, exaggerated, forced, labored, strained, hollow; *informal* pretend, phony, bogus. ANTONYM genuine.

artillery noun *the relentless sound of artillery* ORDNANCE, (big) guns, cannon(s); battery.

artisan noun *artisans from around North America will demonstrate their crafts* CRAFTSMAN, craftswoman, craftsperson; skilled worker, technician; smith, wright, journeyman; *archaic* artificer.

artist noun **1** *a mural artist* DESIGNER, creator, originator, producer; old master.

2 *the surgeon is an artist with the knife* EXPERT, master, maestro, past master, virtuoso, genius; *informal* pro, ace. ANTONYM novice.

artistic adjective **1** *he's very artistic* CREATIVE, imaginative, inventive, expressive; sensitive, perceptive, discerning; *informal* artsy. ANTONYM unimaginative.

ART TECHNIQUES AND MEDIA

acrylic painting	lost wax
action painting	marbling
airbrushing	marquetry
aquatint	mezzotint
batik	montage
brass rubbing	mosaic
calligraphy	mural painting
cartooning	oil painting
ceramics	painting
cire perdue	pastel
cloisonné	photography
collage	photogravure
conté	photomontage
distemper	pointillism
decoupage	screen printing
drawing	sculpture
dry point	scumbling
enameling	sgraffito
encaustic	silk-screen printing
engraving	sketching
etching	stained glass
fresco	stonecutting
gouache	tachism
grisaille	tempera
illumination	trompe l'oeil
impasto	watercolor
intaglio	wood carving
intarsia	woodcutting
linocut	wood engraving
lithography	

2 *artistic touches* AESTHETIC, aesthetically pleasing, beautiful, attractive, fine; decorative, ornamental; tasteful, stylish, elegant, exquisite. ANTONYM inelegant.

artistry noun *one immediately notices the sheer artistry in her music* CREATIVE SKILL, creativity, art, skill, talent, genius, brilliance, flair, proficiency, virtuosity, finesse, style; craftsmanship, workmanship.

artless adjective *there is a no-nonsense, artless flavor to his memoirs* NATURAL, ingenuous, naive, simple, innocent, childlike, guileless; candid, open, sincere, unaffected. ANTONYM scheming.

as conjunction **1** *she looked up as he entered the room* WHILE, just as, even as, (just) when, at the time that, at the moment that.

2 *we all felt as Frank did* IN THE (SAME) WAY THAT, the (same) way; *informal* like.

3 *do as you're told* WHAT, that which.

4 *they were free, as the case had not been proved* BECAUSE, since, seeing that/as, in view of the fact that, owing to the fact that; *informal* on account of; *literary* for.See note at TOWARD.

5 *try as she did, she couldn't smile* THOUGH, although, even though, in spite of the fact that, despite the fact that, notwithstanding that, for all that, albeit, however.

6 *relatively short distances, as Hartford to New Haven* SUCH AS, like, for instance, e.g., for example.

7 *I'm away a lot, as you know* WHICH, a fact which.

▸ preposition **1** *he was dressed as a policeman* LIKE, in the guise of, so as to appear to be.

2 *I'm speaking to you as your friend* IN THE ROLE OF, being, acting as.

PHRASES: **as for/as to** *as for interior paint, I prefer a semi-gloss latex* CONCERNING, with respect to, on the subject of, in the matter of, as regards, with regard to, regarding, with reference to, re, in re, apropos to, vis-à-vis. **as it were** *the guests were chosen, as it were, by an almost random process* SO TO SPEAK, in a manner of speaking, to some extent, so to say; *informal* sort of. **as yet** *there is no sign of them as yet* SO FAR, thus far, yet, still, up till now, up to now.

USAGE NOTE as to

First, it must be said that *as to* is an all-purpose preposition to be avoided whenever a more specific preposition will do. But *as to* isn't always indefensible. The phrase is most justifiable when introducing something previously mentioned only cursorily: "As to concerns the fair might lose on-track business if it offered its signal to the OTBs, [Dun said]: 'I figured we were going to lose the handle either way.' (*Portland Press Herald* [ME]; Sept. 7, 1997.) In beginning sentences this way, *as to* is equivalent to the more colloquial *as for*. In effect, the phrase is a passable shorthand form of *regarding*, *with regard to*, or *on the question of*.

The phrase is also (minimally) defensible when used for *about*, but that word is stylistically preferable in most contexts. *As to* smells of jargon—e.g.: "The bill carries no presumptions as to [read *about*] the effect of incorporation." (*News & Observer* [Raleigh]; Mar. 17, 1997.)

The main problem with *as to* is that it doesn't clearly establish syntactic or conceptual relationships, so it can hamper comprehensibility. In each of the following examples, another preposition would more directly and forcefully express the thought:

• "There's no rule as to [read *about*] how long you have to wait before you can enjoy your creation." (*Florida Times-Union*; Aug. 14, 1997.)

• "It is always possible that your neighbor is not aware of how disturbing his or her behavior is and that he or she can be more sensitive to your concerns, or you can agree as to [read *on*] certain time parameters or (if music is the culprit) what is an acceptable volume level." (*San Diego Union-Tribune*; Aug. 24, 1997.)

• "The same is true as to [read *of*] other cases finding for leaders by applying the regulation." (*Bankruptcy Court Decisions*; Mar. 24, 1994.)

• "There is no change in the prior IRA rules with regard to an individual's participation in other qualifying retirement plans. As such, the rules remain the same as to [read *for*] the maximum amount of adjusted gross income a taxpayer can have before the IRA deduction begins to phase out." (*Gazette-Telegraph* [Colorado Springs]; Mar. 12, 1997.)

• "Some people are a little surprised as to [read *by* or *at*] how quickly Veniard has gotten to his present level." (*Florida Times-Union*; June 28, 1999.).

•"During a trip to the Mars Pathfinder Mission Control Center in Pasadena this summer, House Aeronautics and Space Subcommittee member Sheila Jackson-Lee, D-Texas, inquired as to [read *into*] whether the Pathfinder Mission had taken pictures of the American flag planted by Neil Armstrong in 1969." (*San Francisco Chronicle*; Sept. 15, 1997.) (In this case, the better rewording of "inquired as to whether" would have been "asked whether.") **—BG**

---

ascend verb *ascending the stairs | we watched the missiles ascend* CLIMB, go up/upward, move up/upward, rise (up), clamber (up); mount, scale, conquer; take to the air, take off; rocket. ANTONYM descend.

ascendancy noun *the ascendancy of good over evil* DOMINANCE, domination, supremacy, superiority, paramountcy, predominance, primacy, dominion, hegemony, authority, control, command, power, rule, sovereignty, lordship, leadership, influence. ANTONYM subordination.

ascendant adjective *never has freedom been more ascendant in the world* RISING (IN POWER), on the rise, on the way up, up-and-coming, flourishing, prospering, burgeoning. ANTONYM declining.

ascent noun **1** *the first ascent of the Matterhorn* CLIMB, scaling, conquest. ANTONYM descent.

2 *a balloon ascent* RISE, climb, launch, takeoff, liftoff, blastoff.

3 *the ascent grew steeper* (UPWARD) SLOPE, incline, rise, upward gradient, inclination. ANTONYMS descent, drop.

ascertain verb *first let's ascertain when it was that you last saw Vince* FIND OUT, discover, get to know, work out, make out, fathom, learn, deduce, divine, discern, see, understand, comprehend; establish, determine, verify, confirm; figure out.

ascetic adjective *an ascetic life* AUSTERE, self-denying, abstinent, abstemious, self-disciplined, self-abnegating; simple, puritanical, monastic; reclusive, eremitic, hermitic; celibate, chaste. See note at SEVERE. ANTONYM sybaritic.

▸ noun *a desert ascetic* ABSTAINER, puritan, recluse, hermit, anchorite, solitary; fakir, Sufi, dervish, sadhu; *archaic* eremite. ANTONYM sybarite.

ascribe verb *much of our success can be* ***ascribed to*** *the generosity of the Fords* ATTRIBUTE TO, assign to, put down to, accredit to, credit to, chalk up to, impute to; blame on, lay at the door of; connect with, associate with.

ash noun *a pile of ash* CINDERS, ashes, embers.

ashamed adjective *I was too ashamed to return her call* SORRY, shamefaced, abashed, sheepish, guilty, contrite, remorseful, repentant, penitent, regretful, rueful, apologetic; EMBARRASSED, mortified, humiliated, chagrined, discomfited; *rare* compunctious. ANTONYMS proud, unabashed.

ashen adjective *an ashen complexion* PALE, wan, pasty, gray, ashy, colorless, sallow, pallid, anemic, white, waxen, ghostly, pale-faced, bloodless; *rare* etiolated, lymphatic. See note at PALE.

ashore adverb *passengers may now go ashore* ON TO (THE) LAND, on to the shore, aground; shoreward, landward; on the shore, on (dry) land.

aside adverb **1** *they stood aside* TO ONE SIDE, to the side, on one side; apart, away, separately.

2 *that aside, he seemed a nice man* APART, notwithstanding.

▸ noun *"Her parents died," he said in an aside* WHISPERED REMARK, confidential remark, stage whisper; digression, incidental remark, obiter dictum.

PHRASE: **aside from** *aside from the mess in the garage, this place is looking good* APART FROM, besides, in addition to, not counting, barring, other than, but (for), excluding, not including, except (for), excepting, leaving out, save (for).

asinine adjective *an asinine stunt* STUPID, foolish, brainless, mindless, senseless, idiotic, imbecilic, ridiculous, ludicrous, absurd, nonsensical, fatuous, silly, inane, witless, empty-headed; *informal* halfwitted, dimwitted, dumb, moronic. See note at STUPID. ANTONYMS intelligent, sensible.

ask verb **1** *he asked what time we opened* INQUIRE, query, want to know; question, interrogate, quiz. ANTONYM answer.

2 *they want to ask a few questions* PUT FORWARD, pose, raise, submit. ANTONYM answer.

3 *don't be afraid to* ***ask for*** *advice* REQUEST, demand; solicit, seek, crave, apply for, petition for, call for, appeal for, beg (for), sue for.

4 *let's ask them to dinner* INVITE, bid, summon, have someone over/around.

askance adverb *they look askance at anything foreign* SUSPICIOUSLY, skeptically, cynically, mistrustfully, distrustfully, doubtfully, dubiously; disapprovingly, contemptuously, scornfully, disdainfully. ANTONYM approvingly.

askew adjective *the pictures are askew* CROOKED, lopsided, tilted, angled, at an angle, skew, skewed, slanted, aslant, awry, oblique, out of true, to/on one side, uneven, off-center, asymmetrical; *informal* cockeyed, wonky. ANTONYM straight.

asleep adjective **1** *she was asleep in bed* SLEEPING, in a deep sleep, napping, catnapping, dozing, drowsing; *informal* snoozing, catching some Zs, zonked, hibernating, dead to the world, comatose, in the land of Nod, in the arms of Morpheus; *literary* slumbering. ANTONYM awake.

2 *my leg's asleep* NUMB, with no feeling, numbed, benumbed, dead, insensible; *rare* torpefied.

aspect noun **1** *the photos depict every aspect of life* FEATURE, facet, side, characteristic, particular, detail; angle, slant.

2 *his face had a sinister aspect* APPEARANCE, look, air, cast, mien, demeanor, expression; atmosphere, mood, quality, ambience, feeling.

asperity noun *he replied with some asperity in his tone* HARSHNESS, sharpness, abrasiveness, roughness, severity, acerbity, astringency, tartness, sarcasm.

aspersions PHRASE: **cast aspersions on** *in saying this, I do not mean to cast aspersions on Senator Scofield* VILIFY, disparage, denigrate, defame, run down, impugn, belittle, criticize, condemn, decry, denounce, pillory; malign, slander, libel, discredit; *informal* pull apart, throw mud at, knock, badmouth, dis.

asphalt noun *a fresh layer of asphalt* TAR, pitch, paving, blacktop, tarmac.

asphyxiate verb *they were nearly asphyxiated from the fumes* CHOKE (TO DEATH), suffocate, smother, stifle; throttle, strangle.

aspiration noun *his greatest aspiration is to win an Olympic gold medal* DESIRE, hope, dream, wish, longing, yearning; aim, ambition, expectation, goal, target.

aspire verb *Jen* ***aspires to*** *a career in veterinary medicine* DESIRE, hope for, dream of, long for, yearn for, set one's heart on, wish for, want, be desirous of; aim for, seek, pursue, set one's sights on.

aspiring adjective *an aspiring journalist* WOULD-BE, aspirant, hopeful, budding; potential, prospective, future; ambitious, determined, upwardly mobile; *informal* wannabe.

ass noun **1** *he rode on an ass* DONKEY, jackass, jenny; burro.

2 *informal don't be a silly ass* FOOL, idiot, dolt, simpleton, imbecile; dimwit, halfwit, dummy, dum-dum, loon, jackass, cretin, jerk, fathead, blockhead, jughead, boob, bozo, buffoon, numbskull, numbnuts, lummox, dunce, moron, meatball, doofus, ninny, nincompoop, dipstick, lamebrain, chump, peabrain, thickhead, dumb-ass, woodenhead, pinhead, airhead, birdbrain; nitwit, twit, turkey, goofball, putz; *dated* tomfool, muttonhead.

3 See BUTTOCKS.

USAGE NOTE ass, arse

Arse is the spelling of the British slang term—in the anatomical sense, that is, not in the horse sense. In American English, *ass* is the spelling for both meanings. There's a story behind this. Today *ass* means both (1) "donkey" and (2) "a person's bottom." Sense 1 is the historical one; sense 2 originated in the mid-eighteenth century as the result of a phonological change, as *arse* and *ass* became homophones. By the early nineteenth century, it was possible to engage in wordplay between the words—as in an 1802 cartoon ("Neddy [a donkey] Paces at Tunbridge Wells [in Kent, England]"), in which one female rider says to another, "I'll show my Ass against any Lady's at Wells." **—BG**

assail verb **1** *the army moved in to assail the enemy* ATTACK, assault, pounce on, set upon/about, fall on, charge, rush, storm; *informal* lay into, tear into, pitch into. See note at ATTACK.

2 *she was assailed by doubts* PLAGUE, torment, rack, beset, dog, trouble, disturb, worry, bedevil, nag, vex.

3 *critics assailed the policy* CRITICIZE, censure, attack, condemn, pillory, revile; *informal* knock, slam.

assailant noun *he recognized his assailant* ATTACKER, mugger, assaulter.

assassin noun *the presumed assassin, Oswald, was gunned down* MURDERER, killer, gunman; executioner; *informal* hit man, hired gun; *dated* homicide.

assassinate verb *a plot to assassinate the premier* MURDER, kill, slaughter; eliminate, execute; liquidate; *informal* hit, terminate, knock off; *literary* slay. See note at KILL.

assassination noun *the assassination of President Garfield* MURDER, killing, slaughter, homicide; political execution, elimination; *informal* hit; *literary* slaying.

assault verb **1** *he assaulted a police officer* ATTACK, hit, strike, punch, beat up, thump; pummel, pound, batter; *informal* clout, wallop, belt, clobber, hammer, bop, sock, deck, slug, plug, lay into, do over, rough up; *literary* smite.

2 *they regrouped to assault the hill* ATTACK, assail, pounce on, set upon, strike, fall on, swoop on, rush, storm, besiege. See note at ATTACK.

3 *he has no memory of assaulting the victim* RAPE, sexually assault, molest.

▸ noun **1** *he was charged with assault* BATTERY, violence; sexual assault, rape.

2 *an assault on the city* ATTACK, strike, onslaught, offensive, charge, push, thrust, invasion, bombardment, sortie, incursion, raid, blitz, campaign.

assay noun *this brand of herbal supplement will undergo independent assay* EVALUATION, assessment, appraisal, analysis, examination, test/tests, testing, inspection, scrutiny.

▸ verb *gold is assayed to determine its purity* EVALUATE, assess, appraise, analyze, examine, test, inspect, scrutinize, probe.

assemblage noun *an assemblage of protestors* COLLECTION, accumulation, conglomeration, gathering, group, grouping, cluster, aggregation, mass, number; assortment, selection, array, miscellany.

assemble verb **1** *a crowd had assembled* GATHER, collect, get together, congregate, convene, meet, muster, rally. See note at GATHER. ANTONYM disperse.

2 *he assembled the suspects* BRING TOGETHER, call together, gather, collect, round up, marshal, muster, summon; *formal* convoke. ANTONYM disperse.

3 *how to assemble the kite* CONSTRUCT, build, fabricate, manufacture, erect, set up, put together, piece together, connect, join. ANTONYM dismantle.

assembly noun **1** *an assembly of civil servants* GATHERING, meeting, congregation, convention, rally, convocation, assemblage, group, body, crowd, throng, company; *informal* get-together.

2 *the labor needed in car assembly* CONSTRUCTION, manufacture, building, fabrication, erection.

assent noun *they are likely to give their assent* AGREEMENT, acceptance, approval, approbation, consent, acquiescence, compliance, concurrence; sanction, endorsement, confirmation; permission, leave, blessing; *informal* the go-ahead, the nod, the green light, the OK, the thumbs up. ANTONYMS dissent, refusal.

▸ verb *he **assented to** the change* AGREE TO, accept, approve, consent to, acquiesce in, concur in, give one's blessing to; sanction, endorse, confirm; *informal* give the go-ahead to, give the nod to, give the green light to, give the OK to, OK, give the thumbs up to; *formal* accede to. ANTONYM refuse.

assert verb **1** *they asserted that all aboard were safe* DECLARE, maintain, contend, argue, state, claim, propound, proclaim, announce, pronounce, swear, insist, avow; *formal* aver, opine; *rare* asseverate.

2 *we find it difficult to assert our rights* INSIST ON, stand up for, uphold, defend, contend, establish, press for, push for, stress. PHRASE: **assert oneself** *these abused spouses have lost the nerve to assert themselves in even the smallest of ways* BEHAVE CONFIDENTLY, SPEAK CONFIDENTLY, be assertive, put oneself forward, take a stand, make one's presence felt; *informal* put one's foot down.

assertion noun **1** *I questioned his assertion* DECLARATION, contention, statement, claim, opinion, proclamation, announcement, pronouncement, protestation, avowal; *formal* averment; *rare* asseveration.

2 *an **assertion of** the right to march* DEFENSE OF, upholding of; insistence on.

assertive adjective *an assertive sales team* CONFIDENT, self-confident, bold, decisive, assured, self-assured, self-possessed, forthright, firm, emphatic; authoritative, strong-willed, forceful, insistent, determined, commanding; *informal* feisty, pushy. ANTONYM timid.

assess verb **1** *we need more time to assess the situation* EVALUATE, judge, gauge, rate, estimate, appraise, consider, get the measure of, determine, analyze; *informal* size up.

2 *the damage was assessed at $5 million* VALUE, calculate, work out, determine, fix, cost, price, estimate.

assessment noun **1** *a teacher's assessment of the student's abilities* EVALUATION, judgment, rating, estimation, appraisal, analysis, opinion.

2 *some assessments valued the estate at $2 million* VALUATION, appraisal, calculation, costing, pricing, estimate.

asset noun **1** *he sees his age as an asset* BENEFIT, advantage, blessing, good point, strong point, selling point, strength, forte, virtue, recommendation, attraction, resource, boon, merit, bonus, plus, pro. ANTONYMS liability, handicap.

2 **(assets)** *the seizure of all their assets* PROPERTY, resources, estate, holdings, possessions, effects, goods, valuables, belongings, chattels. ANTONYM liability.

assiduous adjective *she was assiduous in pointing out every feature* DILIGENT, careful, meticulous, thorough, sedulous, attentive, conscientious, punctilious, painstaking, rigorous, particular; persevering. See note at BUSY.

assign verb **1** *a young doctor was assigned the task* ALLOCATE, allot, give, set to; charge with, entrust with.

2 *she was **assigned to** a new post* APPOINT TO, promote to, delegate to, commission to, post to, co-opt to; select for, choose for, install in; *Military* detail to.

3 *we **assign** large sums of money **to** travel budgets* EARMARK FOR, designate for, set aside for, reserve for, appropriate for, allot to/for, allocate for, apportion for.

4 *he **assigned** the opinion **to** the prince* ASCRIBE TO, attribute to, put down to, accredit to, credit to, chalk up to, impute to; pin on, lay at the door of.

5 *he may assign the money to a third party* TRANSFER, make over, give, pass, hand over, hand down, convey, consign.

assignation noun *their secret assignation* RENDEZVOUS, date, appointment, meeting; *literary* tryst.

assignment noun 1 *I'm going to finish this assignment tonight* TASK, piece of work, job, duty, chore, mission, errand, undertaking, exercise, business, endeavor, enterprise; project, homework.

2 *the assignment of tasks* ALLOCATION, allotment, issuance, designation; sharing out, apportionment, distribution, handing out, dispensation.

3 *the assignment of property* TRANSFER, making over, giving, hand down, consignment; *Law* conveyance, devise, attornment.

assimilate verb 1 *the amount of information he can assimilate* ABSORB, take in, acquire, soak up, pick up, grasp, comprehend, understand, learn, master; digest, ingest.

2 *many tribes were assimilated by Turkic peoples* SUBSUME, incorporate, integrate, absorb, engulf, acculturate; co-opt, adopt, embrace, admit.

3 *after arriving, it took us some time to assimilate* INTEGRATE, blend in.

assist verb 1 *I spend my time assisting the chef* HELP, aid, lend a (helping) hand to, oblige, accommodate, serve; collaborate with, work with; support, back (up), second; abet; *informal* pitch in with. ANTONYM hinder.

2 *the exchange rates assisted the firm's expansion* FACILITATE, aid, ease, expedite, spur, promote, boost, benefit, foster, encourage, stimulate, precipitate, accelerate, advance, further, forward. ANTONYM impede.

assistance noun *the governor has requested federal assistance* HELP, aid, support, backing, reinforcement, succor, relief, TLC, intervention, cooperation, collaboration; a (helping) hand, a good turn; social security, benefits; *informal* a break, a leg up; the dole. ANTONYM hindrance.

assistant noun *a photographer's assistant* HELPER, deputy, second-in-command, second, number two, right-hand man/woman, aide, attendant, mate, apprentice, junior, auxiliary, subordinate; hired hand, hired help, man/girl Friday; *informal* sidekick, gofer.

associate verb 1 *the colors that we associate with fire* LINK, connect, relate, identify, equate, bracket, set side by side.

2 *I was forced to associate with them* MIX, keep company, mingle, socialize, go around, rub shoulders, rub elbows, fraternize, consort, have dealings; *informal* hobnob, hang out/around.

3 *the firm is associated with a local charity* AFFILIATE, align, connect, join, attach, team up, be in league, ally; merge, integrate, confederate.

▸ noun *his business associate* PARTNER, colleague, coworker, workmate, comrade, ally, affiliate, confederate; connection, contact, acquaintance; collaborator; *informal* crony.

associated adjective *salaries and associated costs* RELATED, connected, linked, correlated, corresponding; attendant, accompanying, incidental. ANTONYM unrelated.

association noun 1 *a trade association* ALLIANCE, consortium, coalition, union, league, guild, syndicate, federation, confederation, confederacy, conglomerate, cooperative, partnership, affiliation, organization; club, society, congress.

2 *the association between language and nationalism* RELATIONSHIP, relation, interrelation, connection, interconnection, link, bond, union, tie, attachment, interdependence, affiliation.

assorted adjective *the ribbons are available in assorted colors* VARIOUS, miscellaneous, mixed, varied, heterogeneous, varying, diverse, eclectic, multifarious, sundry; *literary* divers.

assortment noun *an assortment of antique buttons* MIXTURE, variety, array, mixed bag, mix, miscellany, selection, medley, diversity, hodgepodge, mishmash, potpourri, salmagundi, farrago, gallimaufry, omnium gatherum.

assuage verb 1 *a pain that could never be assuaged* RELIEVE, ease, alleviate, soothe, mitigate, allay, palliate, abate, suppress, subdue; moderate, lessen, diminish, reduce. See note at ALLEVIATE. ANTONYM aggravate.

2 *her hunger was quickly assuaged* SATISFY, gratify, appease, fulfill, indulge, relieve, slake, sate, satiate, quench, check. ANTONYM intensify.

assume verb 1 *I assumed he wanted me to keep the book* PRESUME, suppose, take it (as given), take for granted, take as read, conjecture, surmise, conclude, deduce, infer, reckon, reason, think, fancy, believe, understand, gather, figure.

2 *he assumed a Southern accent* AFFECT, adopt, impersonate, put on, simulate, feign, fake.

3 *the disease may assume epidemic proportions* ACQUIRE, take on, come to have.

4 *they are to assume more responsibility* ACCEPT, shoulder, bear, undertake, take on/up, manage, handle, deal with.

5 *he assumed control of their finances* SEIZE, take (over), appropriate, commandeer, expropriate, hijack, wrest, arrogate, usurp.

assumed adjective *an assumed name* FALSE, fictitious, invented, made-up, fake, bogus, sham, spurious, make-believe, improvised, adopted; *informal* pretend, phony. ANTONYM genuine.

assumption noun 1 *an informed assumption* SUPPOSITION, presumption, belief, expectation, conjecture, speculation, surmise, guess, premise, hypothesis; conclusion, deduction, inference; *rare* illation, notion, impression.

2 *the assumption of power by revolutionaries* SEIZURE, arrogation, appropriation, expropriation, commandeering, confiscation, hijacking, wresting.

3 *the early assumption of community obligation* ACCEPTANCE, shouldering, tackling, undertaking.

assurance noun 1 *her calm assurance* SELF-CONFIDENCE, confidence, self-assurance, self-possession, nerve, poise, aplomb, levelheadedness; calmness, composure, sangfroid, equanimity; *informal* cool, unflappability. ANTONYM self-doubt.

2 *you have my assurance* WORD OF HONOR, word, promise, pledge, vow, avowal, oath, bond, undertaking, guarantee, commitment.

3 *there is no assurance of getting one's money back* GUARANTEE, certainty, certitude, surety, confidence, expectation. ANTONYM uncertainty.

assure verb 1 *we must assure him of our loyal support* REASSURE, convince, satisfy, persuade, guarantee, promise, tell; affirm, pledge, swear, vow.

2 *he wants to assure a favorable vote* ENSURE, secure, guarantee, seal, clinch, confirm; *informal* sew up.

assured adjective 1 *an assured demeanor* CONFIDENT, self-confident, self-assured, self-possessed, poised, phlegmatic, levelheaded; calm, composed, equanimous, imperturbable, unruffled; *informal* unflappable, together. ANTONYM doubtful.

2 *an assured supply of weapons* GUARANTEED, certain, sure, secure, reliable, dependable, sound; infallible, unfailing; *informal* sure-fire. ANTONYM uncertain.

astonish verb *the NYPD astonished many with the success of its aggressive crime-fighting tactics* AMAZE, astound, stagger, surprise, startle, stun, confound, dumbfound, strike dumb, boggle, stupefy, daze, shock, take aback, leave open-mouthed, leave aghast; *informal* flabbergast, blow away, bowl over, floor.

astonished adjective *reports of the galaxy's unexpected behavior were announced by astonished astronomers* AMAZED, astounded, staggered, surprised, startled, stunned, thunderstruck, aghast, taken aback, dumbfounded, dumbstruck, stupefied, dazed, awestruck; *informal* flabbergasted, floored, blown away.

astonishing adjective *she's read an astonishing number of books* AMAZING, astounding, staggering, surprising, breathtaking; remarkable, extraordinary, incredible, unbelievable, phenomenal; *informal* mind-boggling.

astonishment noun *we stared in astonishment* AMAZEMENT, surprise, stupefaction, incredulity, disbelief, speechlessness, awe, wonder, wonderment.

astound verb *the dogs' tricks will astound you* AMAZE, astonish, stagger, surprise, startle, stun, confound, dumbfound, boggle, stupefy, shock, daze, take aback, leave open-mouthed, leave aghast; *informal* flabbergast, blow away, bowl over, floor.

astounding adjective *his speed and fitness were astounding* AMAZING, astonishing, staggering, surprising, breathtaking, remarkable, extraordinary, incredible, unbelievable, phenomenal; *informal* mind-boggling.

astray adverb 1 *the shots went astray* OFF TARGET, wide of the mark, awry, off course; amiss.

2 *the older boys led him astray* INTO WRONGDOING, into error, into sin, into iniquity, away from the straight and narrow, off the right course.

astringent adjective 1 *the lotion has an astringent effect on pores* CONSTRICTING, constrictive, contracting; styptic.

2 *her astringent words* SEVERE, sharp, stern, harsh, acerbic, acidulous, caustic, mordant, trenchant; scathing, spiteful, cutting, incisive, waspish.

astrology noun HOROSCOPY; horoscopes.

astronaut noun SPACEMAN, SPACEWOMAN, cosmonaut, space traveler, space cadet.

astronomical adjective 1 *astronomical alignments* PLANETARY, stellar; celestial, astral.

2 *informal the sums he has paid are astronomical* HUGE, enormous, very large, prodigious, monumental, colossal, vast, gigantic, massive; substantial, considerable, sizable, hefty; inordinate; *informal* astronomic, whopping, humongous, ginormous. ANTONYM tiny.

astute adjective *an astute investor* SHREWD, sharp, acute, adroit, quick, clever, crafty, intelligent, bright, smart, canny, intuitive, perceptive, insightful, incisive, sagacious, wise; *informal* on the ball, quick on the uptake, savvy; heads-up. See note at KEEN. ANTONYM stupid.

asunder adverb *literary the fabric of society may be torn asunder* APART, up, in two; to pieces, to shreds, to bits.

asylum noun 1 *he appealed for political asylum* REFUGE, sanctuary, shelter, safety, protection, security, immunity; a safe haven.

2 *he was confined to an asylum* PSYCHIATRIC HOSPITAL, mental hospital, mental institution, mental asylum; *informal* madhouse, loony bin, funny farm, nuthouse, bughouse; *dated* lunatic asylum; *archaic* bedlam.

asymmetrical adjective *the quilt pattern is asymmetrical* LOPSIDED, unsymmetrical, uneven, unbalanced, crooked, awry, askew, skew, misaligned; disproportionate, unequal, irregular; *informal* cockeyed, wonky.

atelier noun *Kohl and Norton rent an atelier in Greenwich Village* WORKSHOP, studio, workroom.

atheism noun *atheism was not freely discussed in his community* NONBELIEF, disbelief, unbelief, irreligion, skepticism, doubt, agnosticism; nihilism.

atheist noun *why is it often assumed that a man of science is probably an atheist?* NONBELIEVER, disbeliever, unbeliever, skeptic, doubter, doubting Thomas, agnostic; nihilist. ANTONYM believer.

athlete noun *the school's top athletes* SPORTSMAN, sportswoman, sportsperson; jock; Olympian; runner.

athletic adjective 1 *his athletic physique* MUSCULAR, muscly, sturdy, strapping, well-built, strong, powerful, robust, able-bodied, vigorous, hardy, lusty, hearty, brawny, burly, broad-shouldered, Herculean; FIT, in good shape, in trim; *informal* sporty, husky, hunky, beefy; *literary* thewy. ANTONYM puny.

2 *athletic events* SPORTING, sports; Olympic. See table at TRACK AND FIELD.

athletics plural noun SPORTS, sporting events, games, races; track and field events, track; contests; working out, exercising.

atmosphere noun 1 *the gases present in the atmosphere* AIR, aerospace; sky; *literary* heavens, firmament, blue, azure, ether. See table.

2 *the hotel has a relaxed atmosphere* AMBIENCE, air, mood, feel, feeling, character, tone, tenor, aura, quality, undercurrent, flavor; *informal* vibe.

LAYERS OF THE EARTH'S ATMOSPHERE

exosphere
ionosphere
mesosphere
ozone layer
stratosphere
thermosphere
troposphere

atom noun 1 *they build tiny circuits atom by atom* PARTICLE, molecule, bit, piece, fragment, fraction. See table at PARTICLE.

2 *there wasn't an atom of truth in the allegations* GRAIN, iota, jot, whit, mite, scrap, shred, ounce, scintilla, trace, smidgen, modicum.

atone verb *how shall I **atone for** my mistakes?* MAKE AMENDS FOR, make reparation for, make restitution for, make up for, compensate for, pay for, recompense for, expiate, redress, make good, offset; do penance for.

atrocious adjective **1** *atrocious cruelties* BRUTAL, barbaric, barbarous, savage, vicious, beastly; wicked, cruel, nasty, heinous, monstrous, vile, inhuman, black-hearted, fiendish, ghastly, horrible; abominable, outrageous, hateful, disgusting, despicable, contemptible, loathsome, odious, abhorrent, sickening, horrifying, unspeakable, execrable, egregious. ANTONYMS admirable, kindly.

2 *the weather was atrocious* APPALLING, dreadful, terrible, very bad, unpleasant, miserable; *informal* abysmal, dire, rotten, lousy, godawful. ANTONYM superb.

atrocity noun *European ministers were appalled by scenes of alleged Kosovo atrocities* ABOMINATION, cruelty, enormity, outrage, horror, monstrosity, obscenity, violation, crime, abuse; barbarity, barbarism, brutality, savagery, inhumanity, wickedness, evil, iniquity.

atrophy verb *muscles atrophy in microgravity* WASTE AWAY, become emaciated, wither, shrivel (up), shrink; decay, decline, deteriorate, degenerate, weaken. ANTONYMS strengthen, flourish.

▸ noun *muscular atrophy* WASTING, emaciation, withering, shriveling, shrinking; decay, decline, deterioration, degeneration, weakening, debilitation, enfeeblement. ANTONYM strengthening.

attach verb **1** *a lead weight is attached to the cord* FASTEN, fix, affix, join, connect, link, couple, secure, make fast, tie, bind, chain; stick, adhere, glue, fuse; append. ANTONYM detach.

2 *they attached importance to research* ASCRIBE, assign, attribute, accredit, impute.

3 *the medical officer attached to HQ* ASSIGN, appoint, allocate, second; *Military* detail.

attached adjective **1** *I'm not interested in you—I'm attached* SPOKEN FOR, married, engaged, promised in marriage; going out, involved, seeing someone; *informal* hitched, spliced, shackled, going steady; *dated* betrothed; *formal* wed, wedded; *literary* affianced; *archaic* espoused. ANTONYM single.

2 *she was very **attached to** her brother* FOND OF, devoted to; *informal* mad about, crazy about.

attachment noun **1** *he has a strong **attachment to** his mother* BOND WITH, closeness to/with, devotion to, loyalty to; fondness for, love for, affection for, feeling for; relationship with.

2 *the shower had a massage attachment* ACCESSORY, fitting, extension, add-on, appendage.

3 *the attachment of safety restraints* FIXING, fastening, linking, coupling, connection.

attack verb **1** *Chris had been brutally attacked* ASSAULT, assail, set upon, beat up; batter, pummel, punch; *informal* do over, work over, rough up.

2 *they attacked along a 10-mile front* STRIKE, charge, pounce; bombard, shell, blitz, strafe, fire, besiege. ANTONYM defend.

3 *the clergy attacked government policies* CRITICIZE, censure, condemn, pillory, savage, revile, vilify; *informal* knock, slam, blast, bash, lay into. ANTONYM praise.

4 *they have to attack the problem soon* ADDRESS, attend to, deal with, confront, apply oneself to, get to work on, undertake, embark on; *informal* get cracking on.

▸ noun **1** *the attack began at dawn* ASSAULT, onslaught, offensive, strike, blitz, raid, charge, rush, invasion, incursion.

2 *she wrote a hostile attack against him* CRITICISM, censure, rebuke, admonishment, reprimand; condemnation, denunciation, vilification; tirade, diatribe, polemic; *informal* roasting, caning, hatchet job. ANTONYMS defense, commendation.

3 *an asthmatic attack* FIT, seizure, spasm, convulsion, paroxysm, outburst, bout.

THE RIGHT WORD

There is no shortage of "fighting words." **Attack** is the most general verb, meaning to set upon someone or something in a violent, forceful, or aggressive way (*the rebels attacked at dawn*); but it can also be used figuratively (*attack the government's policy*). **Assault** implies a greater degree of violence or viciousness and the infliction of more damage. As part of the legal term "assault and battery," it suggests an attempt or threat to injure someone physically. **Molest** is another word meaning to *attack* and is used today almost exclusively of sexual molestation (*she had been molested as a child*). **Charge** and **storm** are primarily military words, both suggesting a forceful assault on a fixed position. To *charge* is to make a violent onslaught (*the infantry charged the enemy camp*) and is often used as a command (*"Charge!" the general cried*). To *storm* means to take by force, with all the momentum and fury of a storm (*after days of planning, the soldiers stormed the castle*), but there is often the suggestion of a last-ditch, all-out effort to end a long siege or avoid defeat. To **assail** is to attack with repeated thrusts or blows, implying that victory depends not so much on force as on persistence. To **bombard** is to assail continuously with bombs or shells (*they bombarded the city without mercy for days*). **Besiege** means to surround with an armed force (*to besiege the capital city*). When used figuratively, its meaning comes close to that of *assail*, but with an emphasis on being hemmed in and enclosed rather than punished repeatedly (*besieged with fears*). **Beset** also means to attack on all sides (*beset by enemies*), but it is also used frequently in other contexts to mean set or placed upon (*a bracelet beset with diamonds*).

attacker noun *the attacker escaped with her purse* ASSAILANT, assaulter, aggressor; mugger, rapist, killer, murderer.

attain verb *attempts to attain a promotion* ACHIEVE, accomplish, reach, obtain, gain, procure, secure, get, hook, net, win, earn, acquire; realize, fulfill; *informal* clinch, bag, snag, wrap up. See note at GET.

attainable adjective *a challenging but attainable target* ACHIEVABLE, obtainable, accessible, within reach, securable, realizable; practicable, workable, realistic, reasonable, viable, feasible, possible; *informal* doable, get-at-able.

attempt verb *I attempted to answer the question* TRY, strive, aim, venture, endeavor, seek, undertake, make an effort; have a go at, try one's hand at; *informal* go all out, bend over backwards, bust a gut, hazard; *formal* essay; *archaic* assay.

▸ noun *an attempt to improve the economy* EFFORT, endeavor, try, venture, trial; *informal* crack, go, bid, shot, stab; *formal* essay; *archaic* assay.

attend verb **1** *they attended a carol service* BE PRESENT AT, sit in on, take part in; appear at, present oneself at, turn up at, visit, go to; *informal* show up at, show one's face at. ANTONYM miss.

2 *he had not* ***attended to*** *the regulations* PAY ATTENTION TO, pay heed to, be attentive to, listen to; concentrate on, take note of, bear in mind, take into consideration, heed, observe, mark. ANTONYMS disregard, ignore.

3 *the wounded were* ***attended to*** *nearby* CARE FOR, look after, minister to, see to; tend (to), treat, nurse, help, aid, assist, succor; *informal* doctor.

4 *he* ***attended to*** *the boy's education* DEAL WITH, see to, manage, organize, sort out, handle, take care of, take charge of, take in hand, tackle. ANTONYM neglect.

5 *the princess was attended by an usher* ESCORT, accompany, chaperone, squire, guide, lead, conduct, usher, shepherd; assist, help, serve, wait on.

6 *her weakness* ***was attended with*** *a fever* BE ACCOMPANIED BY, occur with, coexist with, be associated with, connected with, be linked with; be produced by, originate from/in, stem from, result from, arise from.

attendance noun 1 *please confirm your attendance* PRESENCE, appearance.

2 *the attendance was dismal* TURNOUT, audience, house, gate, box office; crowd, congregation, gathering. ANTONYM absence.

PHRASE: **in attendance** *three doctors are in attendance* PRESENT, here, there, at hand, available; assisting.

attendant noun *your attendant will be Edward* STEWARD, waiter, waitress, garçon, porter, servant, waitperson, stewardess; escort, companion, retainer, aide, lady-in-waiting, equerry, chaperone; manservant, valet, butler, maidservant, maid, footman; busboy, houseman; lackey.

▸ adjective *new discoveries and the attendant excitement* ACCOMPANYING, associated, related, connected, concomitant, coincident; resultant, resulting, consequent.

attention noun 1 *the issue needs further attention* CONSIDERATION, contemplation, deliberation, thought, study, observation, scrutiny, investigation, action.

2 *he tried to attract the attention of a policeman* AWARENESS, notice, observation, heed, regard, scrutiny, surveillance.

3 *adequate medical attention* CARE, treatment, ministration, succor, relief, aid, help, assistance.

4 **(attentions)** *he was effusive in his attentions* OVERTURES, approaches, suit, wooing, courting; compliments, flattery; courtesy, politeness.

attentive adjective 1 *a bright and attentive scholar* PERCEPTIVE, observant, alert, acute, aware, heedful, vigilant; intent, focused, committed, studious, diligent, conscientious, earnest; wary, watchful; *informal* not missing a trick, on the ball.

2 *the most attentive of husbands* CONSCIENTIOUS, considerate, thoughtful, kind, caring, solicitous, understanding, sympathetic, obliging, accommodating, courteous, gallant, chivalrous; dutiful, responsible. ANTONYM inconsiderate.

attenuated adjective 1 *attenuated fingers* THIN, slender, narrow, slim, skinny, spindly, bony; *rare* attenuate. ANTONYMS plump, broad.

2 *his muscle activity was much attenuated* WEAKENED, reduced, lessened, decreased, diminished, impaired. ANTONYM strengthened.

attest verb *I can* ***attest to*** *her fitness as a mother* CERTIFY, corroborate, confirm, verify, substantiate, authenticate, evidence, demonstrate, show, prove; endorse, support, affirm, bear out, give credence to, vouch for; *formal* evince. ANTONYM disprove.

attic noun *the Christmas lights are in the attic* LOFT, garret.

attire noun *Thomas preferred formal attire* CLOTHING, clothes, garments, dress, wear, outfits, garb, costume; *informal* gear, duds, getup, threads; *formal* apparel; *archaic* raiment, habiliments.

▸ verb *she was attired in black crepe* DRESS, dress up, clothe, garb, robe, array, costume, swathe, deck, deck out, turn out, fit out, trick out; *archaic* apparel, invest, habit.

attitude noun 1 *you seem ambivalent in your attitude* VIEW, viewpoint, outlook, perspective, stance, standpoint, position, inclination, temper, orientation, approach, reaction; opinion, ideas, convictions, feelings, thinking.

2 *an attitude of prayer* POSITION, posture, pose, stance, bearing.

3 *their music is hard rock with plenty of attitude* HOSTILITY, anger, venom, vitriol, rancor, spunk, spirit; *informal* 'tude.

attorney noun LAWYER, counsel, legal practitioner, legal professional, legal representative, member of the bar, advocate; *chiefly Brit.* solicitor, barrister; *informal* mouthpiece, ambulance chaser.

attract verb 1 *positive ions are attracted to the negatively charged terminal* DRAW, pull; magnetize. ANTONYM repel.

2 *he was attracted by her smile* ENTICE, allure, lure, tempt, charm, win over, woo, engage, enthrall, enchant, entrance, captivate, beguile, bewitch, seduce. See word spectrum on page 56. ANTONYM repel.

attraction noun 1 *the stars are held together by gravitational attraction* PULL, draw; magnetism. ANTONYM repulsion.

2 *she had lost whatever attraction she once had* APPEAL, attractiveness, desirability, seductiveness, seduction, allure, animal magnetism; charisma, charm, beauty, good looks, eye-appeal. ANTONYM repulsion.

3 *the fair offers sideshows and other attractions* ENTERTAINMENT, activity, diversion, interest.

attractive adjective 1 *a more attractive career* APPEALING, inviting, tempting, irresistible; agreeable, pleasing, interesting. See note at PLEASANT. ANTONYM uninviting.

2 *she has no idea how attractive she is* GOOD-LOOKING, beautiful, pretty, handsome, lovely, stunning, striking, arresting, gorgeous, prepossessing, fetching, captivating, bewitching, beguiling, engaging, charming, enchanting, enticing, appealing, delightful, winning, photogenic, telegenic; sexy, seductive, alluring, tantalizing, irresistible, ravishing, desirable; *informal* drop-dead gorgeous, foxy; *literary* beauteous; *archaic* comely, fair. ANTONYM ugly.

attribute verb *they* ***attributed*** *their success* ***to*** *him* ASCRIBE TO, assign to, accredit to, credit to, impute to; put down to, chalk up to; hold responsible for, blame on, pin on; connect with, associate with.

▸ noun 1 *he has all the attributes of a top player* QUALITY, characteristic, trait, feature, element, aspect, property, sign, hallmark, mark, distinction.

attract
entice
lure
seduce
captivate
bewitch
spellbind
beguile
enthral
mesmerize
hypnotize
enchant
entrance
tempt
tantalize
titillate
dazzle
charm
arouse
woo
fascinate
rivet
inveigle
excite
turn on
stimulate
absorb
engage
lead on
win over
tickle someone's fancy
light someone's fire
float someone's boat
make someone's mouth water
interest
catch someone's attention
surprise
startle
disquiet
put off
turn off
give someone the heebie-jeebies
give someone the creeps
make someone's flesh creep
make someone's skin crawl
make someone's gorge rise
gross out
make someone feel sick
turn someone's stomach
make someone want to throw up
make shudder
offend
repulse
disgust
sicken
nauseate
revolt
horrify
repel

2 *the hourglass is the attribute of Father Time* SYMBOL, mark, sign, hallmark, trademark. See note at EMBLEM.

attrition noun **1** *the battle would result in further attrition of their already lame naval force* WEARING DOWN, WEARING AWAY, weakening, debilitation, enfeebling, sapping, attenuation; gradual loss.

2 *the skull shows attrition of the teeth* ABRASION, friction, erosion, corrosion, corroding, grinding; wearing away, deterioration; *rare* detrition.

attune verb *we are finally attuned to city life* ACCUSTOM, adjust, adapt, acclimatize, condition, accommodate, assimilate; acclimate.

atypical adjective *requiring only three hours of sleep a night is atypical* UNUSUAL, untypical, uncommon, unconventional, unorthodox, irregular, abnormal, anomalous, aberrant, deviant, unrepresentative; strange, odd, peculiar, bizarre, weird, queer, freakish, eccentric; exceptional, singular, unique, rare, out of the ordinary, extraordinary; *informal* funny, freaky. ANTONYM normal.

auburn adjective *auburn hair* REDDISH-BROWN, red-brown, Titian (red), tawny, russet, chestnut, copper, coppery, rufous, rust.

au courant adjective ***au courant with*** *the music scene* UP TO DATE WITH, au fait with, in touch with, familiar with, at home with, acquainted with, conversant with; abreast of, apprised of, in the know of, well-informed of, knowledgeable of, well versed in, enlightened of; *informal* clued in on, wise to, hip to.

audacious adjective **1** *an audacious remark* IMPUDENT, impertinent, insolent, presumptuous, cheeky, irreverent, discourteous, disrespectful, insubordinate, ill-mannered, unmannerly, rude, brazen, shameless, pert, defiant, cocky, bold (as brass); *informal* fresh, lippy, mouthy, saucy, sassy, nervy, ballsy; *archaic* contumelious. ANTONYM polite.

2 *his audacious exploits* BOLD, daring, fearless, intrepid, brave, courageous, valiant, heroic, plucky; daredevil, devil-may-care, reckless, madcap; venturesome, mettlesome; *informal* gutsy, spunky, ballsy; *literary* temerarious. See note at BOLD. ANTONYM timid.

audacity noun **1** *he had the audacity to contradict me* IMPUDENCE, impertinence, insolence, presumption, cheek, bad manners, effrontery, nerve, gall, defiance, temerity; *informal* chutzpah, sass. See note at TEMERITY.

2 *a traveler of extraordinary audacity* BOLDNESS, daring, fearlessness, intrepidity, bravery, courage, heroism, pluck, grit; recklessness; spirit, mettle; *informal* guts, gutsiness, spunk, moxie.

audible adjective *the radio is barely audible* HEARABLE, perceptible, discernible, detectable, appreciable; clear, distinct, loud. ANTONYM faint.

audience noun **1** *the audience applauded* SPECTATORS, LISTENERS, viewers, onlookers, patrons; crowd, throng, congregation, turnout; house, gallery.

2 *the radio station has a teenage audience* MARKET, PUBLIC, following, fans; listenership, viewership.

3 *an audience with the Pope* MEETING, consultation, conference, hearing, reception, interview; *informal* meet-and-greet.

audit noun *an audit of the party accounts* INSPECTION, examination, verification, scrutiny, probe, investigation, assessment, appraisal, evaluation, review, analysis; *informal* going-over, once-over.

▸ verb *we audited their books* INSPECT, examine, survey, go through, scrutinize, check, probe, vet, investigate, inquire into, assess, verify, appraise, evaluate, review, analyze, study; *informal* give something a/the once-over, give something a going-over.

audition noun *auditions for a new musical* TRYOUT, trial.

auditor noun *an auditor for the IRS* ACCOUNTANT, bookkeeper, inspector.

auditorium noun *orientation will be held in the auditorium* THEATER, hall, concert hall, playhouse, assembly room; chamber, room, arena, stadium, gymnasium.

augment verb *moonlighting helps augment her income* INCREASE, add to, supplement, build up, enlarge, expand, extend, raise, multiply, swell, grow; magnify, amplify, escalate; improve, boost; *informal* up, jack up, hike up, bump up. ANTONYM decrease.

augur verb *Quebec's election on Monday may augur sovereignty sentiment* BODE, portend, herald, be a sign of, warn of, forewarn of, foreshadow, be an omen of, presage, indicate, signify, signal, promise, threaten, spell, denote; predict, prophesy; *literary* betoken, foretoken, forebode. See note at PREDICT.

augury noun *you draw very blurry lines between what is coincidence and what is augury* OMEN, portent, sign, foretoken. See note at SIGN.

august adjective *our august guests* DISTINGUISHED, respected, eminent, venerable, hallowed, illustrious, prestigious, renowned, celebrated, honored, acclaimed, esteemed, exalted; great, important, lofty, noble; imposing, impressive, awe-inspiring, stately, grand, dignified.

aura noun *an aura of sophistication* ATMOSPHERE, ambience, air, quality, character, mood, feeling, feel, flavor, tone, tenor; emanation; *informal* vibe.

auspices plural noun *talks were to be held under the auspices of the UN* PATRONAGE, aegis, umbrella, protection, keeping, care; support, backing, guardianship, trusteeship, guidance, supervision.

auspicious adjective *thanks for joining us on this auspicious occasion* FAVORABLE, propitious, promising, rosy, good, encouraging; opportune, timely, lucky, fortunate, providential, felicitous, advantageous. See note at OPPORTUNE.

austere adjective **1** *an outwardly austere man* SEVERE, stern, strict, harsh, steely, flinty, dour, grim, cold, frosty, unemotional, unfriendly; formal, stiff, reserved, aloof, forbidding; grave, solemn, serious, unsmiling, unsympathetic, unforgiving; hard, unyielding, unbending, inflexible; *informal* hard-boiled. See note at SEVERE. ANTONYM genial.

2 *an austere life* ASCETIC, self-denying, self-disciplined, nonindulgent, frugal, spartan, puritanical, abstemious, abstinent, self-sacrificing, strict, temperate, sober, simple, restrained; celibate, chaste. ANTONYM immoderate.

3 *the buildings were austere* PLAIN, simple, basic, functional, modest, unadorned, unembellished, unfussy, restrained; stark, bleak, bare, clinical, spartan, ascetic; *informal* no-frills, bare-bones. ANTONYM ornate.

austerity noun *the austerity of the decor | budgetary restrictions demand that we observe strict measures of austerity* SEVERITY, strictness, seriousness, solemnity, gravity; frugality, thrift, economy, asceticism; self-discipline, abstinence, sobriety, restraint, chastity; starkness.

authentic adjective **1** *an authentic document* GENUINE, real, bona fide, true, veritable; legitimate, lawful, legal, valid; *informal* the real McCoy, the real thing, kosher. See note at GENUINE. ANTONYM fake.

2 *an authentic depiction of the situation* RELIABLE, dependable, trustworthy, authoritative, honest, faithful; accurate, factual, true, truthful; *formal* veridical, veracious. ANTONYM unreliable.

authenticate verb **1** *the evidence will authenticate his claim* VERIFY, validate, prove, substantiate, corroborate, confirm, support, back up, attest to, give credence to.

2 *a mandate authenticated by the popular vote* VALIDATE, ratify, confirm, seal, sanction, endorse.

authenticity noun **1** *the authenticity of the painting* GENUINENESS, bona fides; legitimacy, legality, validity.

2 *the authenticity of this account* RELIABILITY, dependability, trustworthiness, credibility; accuracy, truth, veracity, fidelity.

author noun **1** *modern Latin American authors* WRITER; novelist, playwright, poet, essayist, biographer; columnist, reporter; wordsmith; bard; *informal* scribe, scribbler.

2 *the author of the peace plan* ORIGINATOR, creator, instigator, founder, father, architect, designer, deviser, producer; cause, agent.

authoritarian adjective *his authoritarian manner* AUTOCRATIC, dictatorial, despotic, tyrannical, draconian, oppressive, repressive, illiberal, undemocratic; disciplinarian, domineering, overbearing, high-handed, peremptory, imperious, strict, rigid, inflexible; *informal* bossy, iron-fisted. ANTONYMS democratic, liberal.

▸ noun *the army is dominated by authoritarians* AUTOCRAT, despot, dictator, tyrant; disciplinarian, martinet.

authoritative adjective **1** *authoritative information* RELIABLE, dependable, trustworthy, sound, authentic, valid, attested, verifiable; accurate. ANTONYM unreliable.

2 *the authoritative edition* DEFINITIVE, most reliable, best; authorized, accredited, recognized, accepted, approved, standard, canonical.

3 *his authoritative manner* ASSURED, confident, assertive; commanding, masterful, lordly; domineering, imperious, overbearing, authoritarian; *informal* bossy. ANTONYMS diffident, timid.

authority noun **1** *a rebellion against those in authority* POWER, jurisdiction, command, control, charge, dominance, rule, sovereignty, supremacy; influence; *informal* clout. See note at JURISDICTION.

2 *the authority to arrest drug traffickers* AUTHORIZATION, right, power, mandate, prerogative, license, permission.

3 **(authorities)** *they failed to report the theft to the authorities* OFFICIALS, officialdom; government, administration, establishment; police; *informal* the powers that be.

4 *an authority on the stock market* EXPERT, specialist, aficionado, pundit, guru, sage.

5 *on good authority* EVIDENCE, testimony, witness, attestation, word, avowal; *Law* deposition.

authorization noun *proof of authorization* PERMISSION, consent, leave, sanction, license, dispensation, clearance; assent, agreement, approval, endorsement; authority, right, power, mandate; *informal* the go-ahead, the nod, the thumbs up, the OK, the green light. ANTONYM refusal.

authorize verb **1** *they authorized further action* SANCTION, permit, allow, approve, consent to, assent to; ratify, endorse, validate; *informal* give the green light to, give the go-ahead to, OK, give the thumbs up to. ANTONYM forbid.

2 *the troops were authorized to fire* EMPOWER, mandate, commission; entitle.

authorized adjective *an authorized biography* APPROVED, recognized, sanctioned; accredited, licensed, certified; official, lawful, legal, legitimate. ANTONYM unofficial.

autobiography noun *Nixon's autobiography* MEMOIRS, life story, personal history.

autocracy noun *most of East Asia is emerging from a long period of autocracy* ABSOLUTISM, totalitarianism, dictatorship, despotism, tyranny, monocracy, autarchy. ANTONYM democracy.

autocrat noun *the former autocrat could be banned from traveling abroad while the investigation proceeds* ABSOLUTE RULER, dictator, despot, tyrant.

autocratic adjective *autocratic governments* DESPOTIC, tyrannical, dictatorial, totalitarian, autarchic; undemocratic, one-party, monocratic; domineering, draconian, overbearing, high-handed, peremptory, imperious; harsh, rigid, inflexible, illiberal, oppressive, iron-fisted.

autograph noun *fans pestered him for his autograph* SIGNATURE; *informal* John Hancock.

▸ verb *Jack autographed copies of his book* SIGN, sign one's name to.

automatic adjective **1** *automatic garage doors* MECHANIZED, mechanical, automated, computerized, electronic, robotic; self-activating. ANTONYM manual.

2 *an automatic reaction* INSTINCTIVE, involuntary, unconscious, reflex, knee-jerk, instinctual, subconscious; spontaneous, impulsive, unthinking; mechanical; *informal* gut. ANTONYMS conscious, deliberate.

3 *he is the automatic choice for the team* INEVITABLE, unavoidable, inescapable, mandatory, compulsory; certain, definite, undoubted, assured.

automaton noun *assembly-line automatons* ROBOT, android, cyborg, droid, bot.

automobile noun *used automoblies* CAR, auto; *informal* wheels; jalopy, lemon, clunker, Tin Lizzie, rustbucket; *dated* or *Brit.* motorcar. See table at CAR.

autonomous adjective *an autonomous republic* SELF-GOVERNING, self-ruling, self-determining, independent, sovereign, free.

autonomy noun *Filipinos voted on Muslim autonomy* SELF-GOVERNMENT, self-rule, home rule, self-determination, independence, sovereignty, freedom.

autopsy noun *a state-ordered autopsy* POSTMORTEM, PM, necropsy.

auxiliary adjective **1** *an auxiliary power source* ADDITIONAL, supplementary, supplemental, extra, spare, reserve, backup, emergency, fallback, other.

2 *auxiliary staff* ANCILLARY, assistant, support.

▸ noun *a nursing auxiliary* ASSISTANT, helper, ancillary.

avail verb **1** *guests can **avail themselves of** the facilities* USE, take advantage of, utilize, employ.

2 *his arguments cannot avail him* HELP, aid, assist, benefit, profit, be of service to. PHRASE: **to no avail** *we searched all night to no avail* IN VAIN, without success, unsuccessfully, fruitlessly, for nothing.

available adjective **1** *refreshments will be available | don't worry ladies, Bryan is still available* OBTAINABLE, accessible, at hand, at one's disposal, handy, convenient; on sale, procurable; untaken, unengaged, unused; *informal* up for grabs, on tap, gettable.

2 *I'll see if he's available* FREE, unoccupied; present, in attendance; contactable; unattached, single. ANTONYMS busy, engaged.

avalanche noun **1** SNOWSLIDE.

2 *an avalanche of press comment* BARRAGE, volley, flood, deluge, torrent, tide, shower, wave.

avant-garde adjective *this year's avant-garde fashion statement* INNOVATIVE, original, experimental, left-field, inventive, ahead of the times, cutting/leading/bleeding edge, new, modern, innovatory, advanced, forward-looking, state-of-the-art, trend-setting, pioneering, progressive, Bohemian, groundbreaking, trailblazing, revolutionary; unfamiliar, unorthodox, unconventional; *informal* offbeat, way-out. ANTONYM conservative.

WORD NOTE **avant-garde**

I met a traveler from a modern land
who said: I used to think I knew
what *avant-garde* meant, it meant
new art so advanced you can't understand
it, like a chic perfume without a scent.

An avant-garde poem was abstract you
could get rid of commas and capital letters
forget making sense dreams were better
irony mandatory and meaning arbitrary
like poker with blanks instead of cards.

It was intimidating and I remained leery
until I met A. and his avant-garde smile:
"Just do the opposite of whatever's in style,"
he said with a wink when he won an award.
"You see, it isn't so hard to be avant-garde."
—DL

avarice noun *the job had become less about integrity and more about avarice* GREED, greediness, acquisitiveness, cupidity, covetousness, rapacity, materialism, mercenariness; *rare* pleonexia; *informal* money-grubbing, affluenza. See note at GREEDY. ANTONYM generosity.

avenge verb *they vowed to avenge his murder* REQUITE, punish, repay, pay back, revenge, take revenge for, take vengeance for, exact retribution for, get even for, retaliate for.

avenue noun **1** *tree-lined avenues* ROAD, street, drive, parade, boulevard, broadway, thoroughfare.

2 *possible avenues of research* LINE, path; method, approach.

average noun *the price is above the national average* MEAN, median, mode; norm, standard, rule, par.

▸ adjective **1** *the average temperature in May* MEAN, median, modal.

2 *a woman of average height* ORDINARY, standard, normal, typical, regular. See note at NORMAL.

3 *a very average director* MEDIOCRE, second-rate, undistinguished, ordinary, middle-of-the-road, unexceptional, unexciting, unremarkable, unmemorable, indifferent, pedestrian, lackluster, forgettable, amateurish; *informal* OK, so-so, 'comme ci, comme ça,' fair-to-middling, no great shakes, underwhelming, plain-vanilla. ANTONYMS outstanding, exceptional.

PHRASE: **on average** *on average, we get about two million visitors each year* NORMALLY, usually, ordinarily, generally, in general, for the most part, as a rule, typically; overall, by and large, on the whole.

averse adjective *why are you so **averse to** being hospitalized?* OPPOSED TO, against, antipathetic to, hostile to, ill-disposed to, resistant to; disinclined to, reluctant to, unwilling to, loath to; *informal* anti. See note at ADVERSE. ANTONYM keen.

aversion noun *an **aversion to** the use of force* DISLIKE OF, antipathy for, distaste for, abhorrence of, hatred of, odium of, loathing of, detestation of, hostility toward; reluctance toward, unwillingness for, disinclination toward. ANTONYM liking.

avert verb **1** *she averted her head* TURN ASIDE, turn away.

2 *an attempt to avert political chaos* PREVENT, avoid, stave off, ward off, forestall, preclude.

aviation noun *the history of aviation* FLIGHT, air travel, piloting.

aviator noun *dated* *Lindbergh, the most celebrated aviator of the century* PILOT, airman, airwoman, flyer, flyboy, aviatrix, barnstormer.

avid adjective *an avid reader of science fiction* KEEN, eager, enthusiastic, ardent, passionate, zealous, hardcore; devoted, dedicated, wholehearted, earnest. See note at EAGER. ANTONYM apathetic.

avoid verb **1** *I avoid situations that stress me out* KEEP AWAY FROM, STAY AWAY FROM, steer clear of, give a wide berth to, fight shy of. ANTONYM confront.

2 *he is trying to avoid responsibility* EVADE, dodge, sidestep, escape, run away from; *informal* duck, wriggle out of, get out of, cop out of. ANTONYM face up to.

3 *he jerked back to avoid a wild pitch* DODGE, duck, get out of the way of.

4 *you've been avoiding me all evening* SHUN, stay away from, evade, keep one's distance from, elude, hide from; ignore, give the cold shoulder. ANTONYM seek out.

5 *he should avoid drinking alcohol* REFRAIN FROM, abstain from, desist from, eschew. ANTONYM indulge in.

avoidable adjective *an avoidable mishap* PREVENTABLE, stoppable; needless, unnecessary; escapable. ANTONYM inescapable.

avow verb *in previous testimony, you avowed that you were at home all evening* ASSERT, declare, state, maintain, swear, affirm, vow, insist; admit, confess, acknowledge; *formal* aver.

avowed adjective *an avowed Marxist* SELF-CONFESSED, self-declared, acknowledged, admitted; open, overt.

await verb **1** *Peter was awaiting news* WAIT FOR, expect, anticipate.

2 *many dangers await them* BE IN STORE FOR, lie ahead of, lie in wait for, be waiting for.

awake verb **1** *she awoke the following morning* WAKE (UP), awaken, stir, come to, come around; *literary* waken.

2 *the alarm awoke her at 7:30* WAKE (UP), awaken, rouse, arouse.

3 *it awoke our interest.* See AWAKEN sense 2.

4 *they finally **awoke to** the extent of the problem* REALIZE, become aware of, become conscious of; *informal* clue in to, get wise to.

▸ adjective **1** *she was still awake at 2:00* WAKEFUL, sleepless, restless, restive; *archaic* watchful. ANTONYM asleep.

2 *stay awake at all times* VIGILANT, alert, watchful, attentive, on guard. ANTONYM inattentive.

3 *too few are **awake to** the dangers* AWARE OF, conscious of, mindful of, alert to; *formal* cognizant of; *informal* clued in to; *archaic* ware of. ANTONYMS unaware, oblivious.

awaken verb **1** *I awakened early | the jolt awakened her.* See AWAKE senses 1, 2.

2 *he had awakened strong emotions in her* AROUSE, rouse, bring out, engender, evoke, incite, trigger, provoke, stir up, stimulate, animate, quicken, kindle; revive; *literary* enkindle.

award verb *the society awarded him a silver medal* GIVE, grant, accord, assign; confer on, bestow on, present to, endow with, decorate with. See note at GIVE.

▸ noun **1** *an award for high-quality service* PRIZE, trophy, medal, decoration; reward.

2 *a libel award* PAYMENT, settlement, compensation.

3 *the Arts Council gave him an award of $1,500* GRANT, scholarship, endowment; bursary.

aware adjective **1** *she is **aware of** the dangers* CONSCIOUS OF, mindful of, informed about, acquainted with, familiar with, alive to, alert to; *informal* clued in to, wise to, in the know about, hip to; *formal* cognizant of; *archaic* ware of. ANTONYMS ignorant, oblivious.

2 *we need to be more environmentally aware* KNOWLEDGEABLE, enlightened, well-informed, au fait; *informal* clued in, tuned in, plugged in. ANTONYM ignorant.

awareness noun *the level of public awareness is questionable* CONSCIOUSNESS, recognition, realization; understanding, grasp, appreciation, knowledge, insight; familiarity; *formal* cognizance.

awash adjective **1** *the road was awash* FLOODED, under water, submerged, submersed.

2 *the city was **awash with** journalists* INUNDATED WITH, flooded with, swamped with, teeming with, overflowing with, overrun with; *informal* knee-deep in, crawling with.

away adverb **1** *she began to walk away* OFF, from here, from there.

2 *stay away from the trouble* AT A DISTANCE FROM, apart from.

▸ ***awake***
insomnolent
restless
restive
tossing and turning
watchful
sleepless
wakeful
wide awake
conscious
resting
reposing
drowsing
dozing
napping
catnapping
slumbering
sleeping
fast asleep
sound asleep
in a deep sleep
snoozing
in the land of Nod
dead to the world
flat out
comatose
dormant
out like a light
in the arms of Morpheus
asleep ◂

3 *Bernice pushed him away* ASIDE, off, to one side.

4 *we'll be away for two weeks* ELSEWHERE, abroad; gone, absent; on vacation; *chiefly Brit.* on holiday.

awe noun *we watched in awe* WONDER, wonderment; admiration, reverence, respect, esteem; dread, fear.

awed adjective *he spoke in an awed whisper* FILLED WITH WONDER, wonderstruck, awestruck, amazed, astonished, lost for words, open-mouthed; reverential.

awe-inspiring adjective. See AWESOME.

awesome adjective *the Grand Canyon is as awesome as they say it is* BREATHTAKING, awe-inspiring, magnificent, wonderful, amazing, stunning, staggering, imposing, stirring, impressive; formidable, fearsome, dreaded; *informal* mind-boggling, mind-blowing, jaw-dropping, excellent, marvelous; *literary* wondrous; *archaic* awful. ANTONYM unimpressive.

awestruck adjective *too awestruck to speak* AWED, wonderstruck, amazed, lost for words, open-mouthed; reverential, star-struck; terrified, afraid, fearful.

awful adjective 1 *the place smelled awful* DISGUSTING, horrible, terrible, dreadful, ghastly, nasty, vile, foul, revolting, repulsive, repugnant, odious, sickening, nauseating; *informal* yucky, gross, beastly. ANTONYMS wonderful, lovely.

2 *an awful book* TERRIBLE, atrocious, dreadful, frightful, execrable, abominable; inadequate, inferior, substandard, lamentable; *informal* crummy, pathetic, rotten, woeful, lousy, appalling, abysmal. ANTONYMS good, excellent.

3 *an awful accident* SERIOUS, dreadful, grave, terrible, bad, critical ANTONYM minor.

4 *you look awful—go lie down* ILL, unwell, sick, queasy, nauseous; poorly; *informal* lousy, rotten, terrible, dreadful.

5 *I felt awful for getting so angry* REMORSEFUL, guilty, ashamed, contrite, sorry, regretful, repentant.

6 *archaic* *the awful sights of nature* AWE-INSPIRING, awesome, impressive; dread, fearful.

awfully adverb 1 *informal* *an awfully nice man* VERY, extremely, really, immensely, exceedingly, thoroughly, exceptionally, remarkably, extraordinarily; *informal* terrifically, terribly, seriously, majorly, real, mighty, awful; *informal, dated* frightfully; *archaic* exceeding.

2 *we played awfully* VERY BADLY, terribly, poorly, dreadfully, atrociously, appallingly, execrably; *informal* abysmally, pitifully, diabolically; *rare* egregiously.

awhile adverb *please wait just awhile* FOR A MOMENT, for a (little) while, for a short time; *informal* for a bit.

awkward adjective 1 *the box was awkward to carry* DIFFICULT, tricky; cumbersome, unwieldy. ANTONYM easy.

2 *an awkward time* INCONVENIENT, inappropriate, inopportune, unseasonable, difficult. ANTONYM convenient.

3 *he put her in a very awkward position* EMBARRASSING, uncomfortable, unpleasant, delicate, tricky, problematic, troublesome, thorny; humiliating, compromising; *informal* sticky, dicey, hairy.

4 *she felt awkward alone with him* UNCOMFORTABLE, uneasy, tense, nervous, edgy, unquiet; self-conscious, embarrassed. ANTONYMS relaxed, at ease.

5 *his awkward movements* CLUMSY, ungainly, uncoordinated, graceless, inelegant, gauche, gawky, wooden, stiff; unskillful, maladroit, inept, blundering; *informal* clodhopping, ham-fisted, ham-handed, heavy-handed; *informal* all thumbs. ANTONYMS adroit, graceful.

awkwardness noun 1 *the gesture betrayed his momentary awkwardness* EMBARRASSMENT, self-consciousness, discomfort, discomfiture, uneasiness, edginess, tension, nervousness.

2 *the adolescent awkwardness of his angular body* UNGAINLINESS, clumsiness, lack of coordination, gracelessness, inelegance, ineptness, gaucheness, gawkiness.

awning noun *the familiar striped awning outside the Food Center* CANOPY, shade, marquee, sunshade, shelter, cover; blind.

awry adjective 1 *something was awry* AMISS, wrong; *informal* up.

2 *his wig looked awry* ASKEW, crooked, lopsided, tilted, skewed, skew, to one side, off-center, uneven; *informal* cockeyed, wonky. ANTONYMS straight, symmetrical.

ax, axe noun *a woodsman's ax* HATCHET, cleaver, tomahawk, adze, poleax, broadax; *historical* battle-ax, twibill.

▸ verb 1 *the show was axed* CANCEL, withdraw, drop, scrap, discontinue, terminate, end; *informal* ditch, dump, pull the plug on.

2 *500 employees were axed* DISMISS, fire, lay off, let go, discharge, get rid of; *informal* sack, give the sack, give marching orders, pink-slip.

axiom noun *he came to regret his belief in the axiom that there's no such thing as bad publicity* ACCEPTED TRUTH, general truth, dictum, truism, principle; maxim, adage, aphorism; *rare* apophthegm, gnome.

axis noun 1 *the earth revolves on its axis* CENTER LINE, vertical, horizontal.

2 *the Anglo-American axis* ALLIANCE, coalition, bloc, union, confederation, confederacy, league.

axle noun *the wagon's rear axle* SHAFT, spindle, rod, arbor, mandrel, pivot.

azure adjective *she wears contacts that make her eyes azure* SKY-BLUE, bright blue, blue; *literary* cerulean.

B

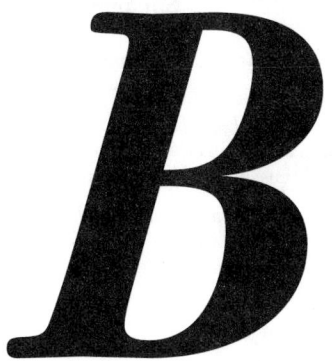

babble verb **1** *Betty babbled about the stupidest things* PRATTLE, rattle on, chatter, jabber, twitter, go on, run on, prate, ramble, burble, blather; *informal* gab, yap, yak, yabber, yatter, yammer, blabber, jaw, gas, shoot one's mouth off, run off at the mouth.

2 *a brook babbled gently* BURBLE, murmur, gurgle, tinkle; *literary* plash.

▸ noun *his inarticulate babble* PRATTLE, chatter, jabber, prating, rambling, blather; *informal* gab, yabbering, yatter.

babe noun **1** *literary a babe in arms.* See BABY noun sense 1.

2 *informal what a babe!* BEAUTY; *informal* hottie, looker, bombshell, heartthrob, knockout, fox, (piece of) arm candy, eye-catcher, dish, boy toy, hunk.

babel noun *I can't hear you above this babel* CLAMOR, din, racket, confused noise, tumult, uproar, hubbub; babble, babbling, shouting, yelling, screaming; *informal* hullabaloo.

baby noun **1** *a newborn baby* INFANT, newborn, child, tot, little one; *informal* rug rat; *Scottish* bairn; *literary* babe, babe in arms, suckling; papoose; *technical* neonate.

2 *don't be such a baby* SISSY, wimp, wuss, milquetoast; pantywaist.

▸ adjective *baby carrots* MINIATURE, mini, little, small, small-scale, scaled-down, toy, pocket, vest-pocket, midget, dwarf; *informal* teeny, teeny-weeny, teensy, teensy-weensy, itsy-bitsy, itty-bitty, little-bitty, bite-sized. ANTONYM large.

▸ verb *her aunt babied her* PAMPER, mollycoddle, spoil, cosset, coddle, indulge, overindulge, nanny, pander to.

baby carriage noun *a baby carriage for twins* STROLLER, baby buggy, pram.

babyish adjective *she hated the babyish remarks he would make about her friends* CHILDISH, immature, infantile, juvenile, puerile, adolescent. ANTONYM mature.

back noun **1** *she's broken her back* SPINE, backbone, spinal column, vertebral column.

2 *the back of the house* REAR, rear side, other side; *Nautical* stern. ANTONYM front.

3 *the back of the line* END, tail end, rear end, rear, tail, tag end. ANTONYMS front, head.

4 *the back of a postcard* REVERSE, other side, underside; verso; *informal* flip side. ANTONYMS front, face.

▸ adverb **1** *he pushed his chair back* BACKWARD, behind one, to one's rear, rearward; away, off. ANTONYM forward.

2 *a few months back* AGO, earlier, previously, before, in the past.

▸ verb **1** *the government backed the initiative with $4 million* SPONSOR, finance, put up the money for, fund, subsidize, underwrite, be a patron of, act as guarantor of; *informal* foot the bill for, pick up the tab for; bankroll, stake.

2 *most people backed the idea* SUPPORT, endorse, sanction, approve of, give one's blessing to, smile on, favor, advocate, promote, uphold, champion; vote for, ally oneself with, stand behind, stick by, side with, be on the side of, defend, take up the cudgels for; second; *informal* throw one's weight behind. ANTONYM oppose.

3 *he backed the horse at 33–1* BET ON, gamble on, stake money on.

4 *he backed out of the garage* REVERSE, draw back, step back, move backward, back off, pull back, retreat, withdraw, give ground, backtrack, retrace one's steps, recede. ANTONYMS move forward, advance.

▸ adjective **1** *the back seats* REAR, rearmost, backmost, hind, hindmost, hinder, posterior. ANTONYM front.

2 *a back copy* PAST, old, previous, earlier, former, out of date. ANTONYM future.

PHRASES: **back away** *there's no need to back away—he's a very gentle dog* DRAW BACK, step back, move away, withdraw, retreat, pull back, give ground; shrink back, cower, quail, quake. **back down** *all your begging is useless because I am not going to back down* GIVE IN, concede defeat, surrender, yield, submit, climb down, concede, reconsider; backtrack, backpedal. **back out of** *Charlie's backed out of the original agreement* RENEGE ON, go back on, withdraw from, pull out of, retreat from, fail to honor, abandon, default on, repudiate, backpedal on. **back someone up** *I was surprised when it turned out to be Dina who backed me up* SUPPORT, stand by, give one's support to, side with, be on someone's side, take someone's side, take someone's part; vouch for. **back something up** *can you back up that statement with any real evidence?* SUBSTANTIATE, corroborate, confirm, support, bear out, endorse, bolster, reinforce, lend weight to. **behind someone's back** *the takeover was planned behind the plant manager's back* SECRETLY, without someone's knowledge, on the sly, slyly, sneakily, covertly, surreptitiously, furtively.

backbiting noun *the backbiting between Democrats and Republicans has become tiresome* MALICIOUS TALK, spiteful talk, slander, libel, defamation, abuse, character assassination, disparagement, denigration, vilification, vituperation, calumny; slurs, aspersions; *informal* bitching, bitchiness, cattiness, mudslinging, bad-mouthing, dissing.

backbone noun **1** *an injured backbone* SPINE, spinal column, vertebral column, vertebrae; back; *Anatomy* dorsum, rachis.

2 *the infantry is the backbone of our army* MAINSTAY, cornerstone, foundation, chief support, buttress, pillar, tower of strength.

3 *he has enough backbone to see us through* STRENGTH OF CHARACTER, strength of will, firmness, resolution, resolve, determination, fortitude, pluck, pluckiness, nerve, courage, mettle, spirit, moral fiber; *informal* guts, spunk, grit, true grit.

back-breaking adjective *shoveling wet snow is back-breaking work* GRUELING, arduous, strenuous, onerous, punishing, crushing, demanding, exacting, taxing, exhausting, draining; *informal* killing; *archaic* toilsome. ANTONYM easy.

backer noun **1** *the backers of the proposition* SUPPORTER, defender, advocate, promoter, proponent; seconder; booster.

2 *$3 million was provided by the project's backers* SPONSOR, investor, underwriter, financier, patron, benefactor, benefactress; *informal* angel.

backfire verb *Bernard's plan backfired* REBOUND, boomerang, come back; fail, miscarry, go wrong; *informal* blow up in someone's face.

background noun **1** *a background of palm trees* BACKDROP, backcloth, surrounding(s), setting, scene.

2 *students from many different backgrounds* SOCIAL CIRCUMSTANCES, family circumstances; environment, class, culture, tradition; upbringing.

3 *her nursing background* EXPERIENCE, record, history, past, training, education, grounding, knowledge; backstory.

4 *the political background* CIRCUMSTANCES, context, conditions, situation, environment, milieu, scene, scenario.

PHRASE: **in the background** *maybe there was a sugar daddy in the background* BEHIND THE SCENES, out of the public eye, out of the spotlight, out of the limelight, backstage; inconspicuous, unobtrusive, unnoticed.

backhanded adjective *a backhanded compliment* INDIRECT, ambiguous, oblique, equivocal; double-edged, two-edged, left-handed; tongue-in-cheek. ANTONYM direct.

backing noun **1** *he has the backing of his colleagues* SUPPORT, help, assistance, aid; approval, endorsement, sanction, blessing.

2 *financial backing* SPONSORSHIP, funding, patronage; money, investment, funds, finance; grant, contribution, subsidy.

3 *musical backing* ACCOMPANIMENT; harmony, obbligato.

backlash noun *the move provoked a backlash from union leaders* ADVERSE REACTION, adverse response, counterblast, comeback, repercussion; retaliation, reprisal.

backlog noun *Stella's been gone for one day and there's already a backlog of messages* ACCUMULATION, logjam, pileup, pile, mountain.

backpack noun KNAPSACK, rucksack; school bag, book bag.

backpedal verb *they agreed to the peace initiative, but soon after they backpedaled* CHANGE ONE'S MIND, backtrack, back down, climb down, (do an) about-face, reverse course, do a U-turn, renege, go back (on), back out (of), fail to honor something, withdraw, default (on).

backslide verb *many things can cause dieters to backslide* RELAPSE, lapse, regress, weaken, lose one's resolve, give in to temptation, go astray, leave the straight and narrow, fall off the wagon. ANTONYM persevere.

backslider noun *I'll have no backslider like you in my family* RECIDIVIST, regressor; defector, deserter, turncoat, apostate, fallen angel.

backtalk noun *your backtalk is an embarrassment to us all* IMPUDENCE, impertinence, cheek, cheekiness, effrontery, insolence, rudeness; answering back, talking back; *informal* mouth, lip, sass, guff; *rare* contumely.

backtrack verb *Callahan backtracked when the poll results were released* BACKPEDAL, change one's mind, back down, reverse course, about-face, climb down.

backup noun *never enter an unsecured area without backup* HELP, support, assistance, aid; reinforcements, reserves, additional resources.

backward adjective **1** *a backward look* REARWARD, to/toward the rear, to/toward the back, behind one, reverse. ANTONYM forward.

2 *the decision was a backward step* RETROGRADE, retrogressive, regressive, for the worse, in the wrong direction, downhill, negative. ANTONYM progressive.

3 *an economically backward country* UNDERDEVELOPED, undeveloped; primitive, unsophisticated, benighted. ANTONYMS advanced, sophisticated.

4 *he was not backward in displaying his talents* HESITANT, reticent, reluctant; shy, diffident, bashful, timid; unwilling, afraid, loath, averse. ANTONYMS bold, confident.

▸ adverb (also **backwards**) **1** *Penny glanced backward* TOWARD THE REAR, rearward, behind one. ANTONYM forward.

2 *count backward from twenty to ten* IN REVERSE, in reverse order; *informal* ass-backward, bass-ackward. ANTONYM forward.

USAGE NOTE **backward, backwards**

In British English, the spelling **backwards** is more common than **backward**. In American English, the adverb form is sometimes spelled **backwards** (*the ladder fell backwards*), but the adjective is almost always **backward** (*a backward glance*). Directional words using the suffix *-ward* tend to have no *s* ending in American English, although **backwards** is more common than *afterwards*, *towards*, or *forwards*. The *s* ending often (but not always) appears in the phrases *backwards and forwards* and *bending over backwards*.

---

backwash noun **1** *a ship's backwash* WAKE, wash, slipstream.

2 *the backwash of the Cuban missile crisis* REPERCUSSIONS, reverberations, aftereffects, aftermath, fallout.

backwoods plural noun *they're bringing cable TV to the backwoods* BACK OF BEYOND, remote areas, wilds, bush, bush country, bushland, hinterlands, backwater; backcountry, backlands; middle of nowhere; *informal* sticks, boondocks, boonies, tall timbers.

bacteria plural noun *a different strain of bacteria* MICROORGANISMS, microbes, germs, bacilli, pathogens, prokaryotes; *informal* bugs.

bad adjective **1** *bad workmanship* SUBSTANDARD, poor, inferior, second-rate, second-class, unsatisfactory, inadequate, unacceptable, not up to scratch, not up to par, deficient, imperfect, defective, faulty, shoddy, amateurish, careless, negligent, miserable, sorry; incompetent, inept, inexpert, ineffectual; awful, atrocious, appalling, execrable, deplorable, terrible, abysmal, godawful; *informal* crummy, rotten, pathetic, useless, woeful, bum, lousy, not up to snuff. ANTONYMS good, excellent, skilled.

2 *the alcohol had a really bad effect on me* HARMFUL, damaging, detrimental, injurious, hurtful, inimical, destructive, ruinous, deleterious; unhealthy, unwholesome. ANTONYMS good, beneficial.

3 *the bad guys* WICKED, evil, sinful, immoral, morally wrong, corrupt, base, black-hearted, reprobate, amoral; criminal, villainous, nefarious, iniquitous, dishonest, dishonorable, unscrupulous, unprincipled; *informal* crooked, dirty; *dated* dastardly. ANTONYM virtuous.

4 *you bad girl!* BADLY BEHAVED, naughty, ill-behaved, disobedient, wayward, willful, self-willed, defiant, unruly, insubordinate, undisciplined. ANTONYM well-behaved.

5 *bad news* UNPLEASANT, disagreeable, unwelcome; unfortunate, unlucky, unfavorable; terrible, dreadful, awful, grim, distressing. ANTONYM good.

6 *a bad time to arrive* INAUSPICIOUS, unfavorable, inopportune, unpropitious, unfortunate, disadvantageous, adverse, inappropriate, unsuitable, untoward. ANTONYMS good, auspicious.

7 *a bad accident* SEVERE, serious, grave, critical, acute; *formal* grievous. ANTONYMS minor, slight.

8 *the meat's bad* ROTTEN, decayed, decomposed, decomposing, putrid, putrefied, off, moldy; sour, spoiled, rancid, rank, unfit for human consumption; (of an egg) addled, (of beer) skunky. ANTONYM fresh.

9 *if you still feel bad, stay in bed.* See ILL adjective sense 1.

10 *a bad knee* INJURED, wounded, diseased; *dated* game.

11 *I felt bad about leaving them* GUILTY, conscience-stricken, remorseful, guilt-ridden, ashamed, contrite, sorry, full of regret, regretful, shamefaced. ANTONYM unrepentant.

12 *a bad check* INVALID, worthless; counterfeit, fake, false, bogus, fraudulent; *informal* phony, dud. ANTONYM valid.

13 *bad language* OFFENSIVE, vulgar, crude, foul, obscene, rude, coarse, smutty, dirty, filthy, indecent, indecorous; blasphemous, profane.

PHRASE: **not bad** *hey, this curried octopus is not bad | the movie's not bad, but the book's much better* ALL RIGHT, adequate, good enough, pretty good, reasonable, fair, decent, average, tolerable, acceptable, passable, middling, moderate, fine; *informal* OK, so-so, 'comme ci, comme ça,' fair-to-middling, satisfactory.

badge noun **1** *the badge on her jacket was earned in combat* pin, brooch, button, emblem, crest.

2 *a badge of success* SIGN, symbol, indication, signal, mark; hallmark, trademark.

badger verb *stop badgering us* PESTER, harass, bother, plague, torment, hound, nag, harry, tease, go on at; *informal* hassle, bug, get on someone's case.

badly adverb **1** *the job had been very badly done* POORLY, incompetently, ineptly, inexpertly, inefficiently, imperfectly, deficiently, defectively, unsatisfactorily, inadequately, incorrectly, faultily, shoddily, amateurishly, carelessly, negligently; abominably; *informal* crummily, pitifully, woefully. ANTONYM well.

2 *try not to think badly of me* UNFAVORABLY, ill, critically, disapprovingly.

3 *stop behaving badly* NAUGHTILY, disobediently, willfully, reprehensibly, mischievously.

4 *he had been badly treated* CRUELLY, wickedly, unkindly, harshly, shamefully; unfairly, unjustly, wrongly, improperly.

5 *it turned out badly* UNSUCCESSFULLY, unfavorably, adversely, unfortunately, unhappily, unluckily.

6 *some of the victims are badly hurt* SEVERELY, seriously, gravely, acutely, critically; *formal* grievously. ANTONYM slightly.

7 *she badly needs help* DESPERATELY, sorely, intensely, seriously, very much, greatly, exceedingly.

bad-tempered adjective See IRRITABLE.

baffle verb *his explanations baffle the class* PERPLEX, puzzle, bewilder, mystify, bemuse, confuse, confound, disconcert; *informal* flummox, faze, stump, make someone scratch their head, be all Greek to, floor, discombobulate. See note at THWART. ANTONYM enlighten.

baffling adjective *the thief left behind some baffling clues* PUZZLING, BEWILDERING, perplexing, mystifying, bemusing, confusing, unclear; inexplicable, incomprehensible, impenetrable, cryptic, opaque. ANTONYMS clear, comprehensible.

bag noun **1** *I dug around in my bag for a lipstick* HANDBAG, purse, shoulder bag, clutch bag/purse, minaudière; sack, pouch; *historical* reticule.

2 *she began to unpack her bags* SUITCASE, case, valise, portmanteau, grip, overnighter; backpack, rucksack, knapsack, haversack, carryall, kit bag, duffel bag; satchel; **(bags)** luggage, baggage.

3 *informal mystery novels just aren't my bag* INTEREST, preoccupation, concern; *informal* thing.

▸ verb **1** *locals bagged the most fish* CATCH, land, capture, trap, snare, ensnare; kill, shoot.

2 *he bagged seven medals* GET, secure, obtain, acquire, pick up; win, achieve, attain; commandeer, grab, appropriate, take; *informal* get one's hands on, land, net.

baggage noun *leave your baggage with the inspectors* LUGGAGE, suitcases, cases, bags.

baggy adjective *baggy pants* LOOSE-FITTING, loose, roomy, full, ample, voluminous, billowing; oversized, shapeless, ill-fitting, tentlike, sacklike. ANTONYMS tight, form-fitting.

bail noun *he was released on bail* SURETY, security, assurance, indemnity, indemnification; bond, guarantee, pledge; *archaic* gage.

PHRASES: **bail out** *the pilot bailed out* EJECT, parachute to safety; desert, get out, escape. **bail someone/something out** *the state was called in to bail out the foundering housing project* RESCUE, save, relieve; finance, help (out), assist, aid; *informal* save someone's bacon/neck/skin.

bait noun **1** *the fish let go of the bait* LURE, decoy, fly, troll, jig, plug.

2 *was she the bait to lure him into a trap?* ENTICEMENT, lure, decoy, snare, trap, siren, carrot, attraction, draw, magnet, incentive, temptation, inducement; *informal* come-on.

▸ verb *he was baited at school* TAUNT, tease, goad, pick on, torment, persecute, plague, harry, bother, harass, hound; *informal* needle.

bake verb **1** *bake the fish for 15–20 minutes* COOK, oven-bake, roast, dry-roast.

2 *the earth was baked by the sun* SCORCH, burn, sear, parch, dry (up), desiccate; broil.

balance noun **1** *I tripped and lost my balance* STABILITY, equilibrium, steadiness, footing. ANTONYM instability.

2 *political balance in broadcasting* FAIRNESS, justice, impartiality, evenhandedness, egalitarianism, equal opportunity; parity, equity, equilibrium, equipoise, evenness, symmetry, correspondence, uniformity, equality, equivalence, comparability. ANTONYM imbalance.

3 *this stylistic development provides a balance to the rest of the work* COUNTERBALANCE, counterweight, stabilizer, compensation.

4 *the food was weighed on a balance* SCALE(S), weighing machine.

5 *the balance of the rent* REMAINDER, outstanding amount, rest, residue, difference, remaining part.

▸ verb **1** *she balanced the book on her head* STEADY, stabilize, poise, level.

2 *he balanced his radical remarks with more familiar declarations* COUNTERBALANCE, balance out, offset, even out/up, counteract, compensate for, make up for.

3 *their income and expenditure do not balance* CORRESPOND, agree, tally, match up, concur, coincide, be in agreement, be consistent, equate, be equal.

4 *you need to balance cost against benefit* WEIGH, weigh up, compare, evaluate, consider, assess, appraise, judge.

PHRASES: **in the balance** *thanks to these dismal sales figures, everyone's job is in the balance* UNCERTAIN, undetermined, unsettled, unresolved, unsure, pending, in limbo, up in the air, at a turning point, critical, at a critical stage, at a crisis. **on balance** *on balance, I'd say the scenery for Act II is coming along great* OVERALL, all in all, all things considered, taking everything into consideration/account, by and large, on average.

balanced adjective **1** *a balanced view* FAIR, equitable, just, unbiased, unprejudiced, objective, impartial, evenhanded, dispassionate. ANTONYM partial.

2 *a balanced diet* MIXED, varied; healthy, sensible, well-balanced. ANTONYM unhealthy.

3 *a balanced individual* LEVELHEADED, well-balanced, well-adjusted, mature, stable, sensible, practical, realistic, grounded, with both feet on the ground, pragmatic, reasonable, rational, sane, even-tempered, commonsensical, full of common sense; *informal* together. ANTONYM neurotic.

balcony noun **1** *the balcony of the hotel* veranda, terrace, balustrade, patio.

2 *the applause from the balcony* GALLERY, dress circle, loge, upper tier, upper deck; choir loft; *informal* gods.

bald adjective **1** *a bald head* HAIRLESS, smooth, shaven, depilated; bald-headed; *informal* chrome-domed; *technical* glabrous; *archaic* bald-pated. ANTONYMS hairy, hirsute.

2 *a few bald bushes* LEAFLESS, bare, uncovered. ANTONYMS lush, leafy.

3 *the bald prairie* TREELESS, naked, barren. See note at NAKED. ANTONYM lush.

4 *a bald statement* PLAIN, simple, unadorned, unvarnished, unembellished, undisguised, unveiled, stark, severe, austere, brutal, harsh; blunt, direct, forthright, plain-spoken, straight, straightforward, candid, honest, truthful, realistic, frank, outspoken; *informal* upfront. ANTONYM vague.

balderdash noun See NONSENSE sense 1.

baldness noun *a new treatment for baldness* HAIR LOSS, hairlessness, bald-headedness; *Medicine* alopecia, madarosis; *archaic* bald-patedness, glabreity.

bale noun *a bale of cotton* BUNDLE, bunch, pack, package, parcel.

baleful adjective *she saw her rival's reddened, baleful face* MENACING, threatening, unfriendly, hostile, antagonistic, evil, evil-intentioned, vindictive, wicked, nasty, bitter, acrimonious, malevolent, malicious, malignant, malign, sinister; harmful, injurious, dangerous, destructive, noxious, pernicious, deadly, venomous, poisonous, vitriolic; *literary* malefic, maleficent. ANTONYMS benevolent, friendly.

balk verb **1** *I* ***balk at*** *paying that much* BE UNWILLING TO (BE), draw the line at, be reluctant to (be), hesitate over; eschew, resist, refuse to (be), take exception to; draw back from, flinch from, shrink from, recoil from, demur from, hate to (be). ANTONYM accept.

2 *they were balked by traffic* IMPEDE, obstruct, thwart, hinder, prevent, check, stop, curb, halt, bar, block, forestall, frustrate. See note at THWART. ANTONYM assist.

ball noun **1** *a ball of dough* SPHERE, globe, orb, globule, spherule, spheroid, ovoid.

2 *a musket ball* BULLET, pellet, slug, projectile.

3 *a costume ball* DANCE, dinner dance, masked ball, formal, prom, masquerade; *informal* hop, bop.

4 *everyone had a ball* GOOD TIME, blast, riot.

ballad noun *a ballad sung by Burl Ives* SONG, folk song, chantey, ditty, canzone; poem, tale, saga.

ballast noun *the third balloonist appears to be in need of ballast* STABILIZER, counterbalance, counterweight.

ballet noun. See table on page 65.

BALLET STEPS

arabesque	frappé
arabesque penchée	glissade
à terre	glissé
attitude	grand battement
balancé	grand jeté
ballonné	jeté
ballotté	pas allé
battement	pas de basque
batterie	pas de bourrée
bourreée	pas de chat
brisé	pas de cheval
cabriole	petit battement
cambré	petit jeté
chaîné	piqué
changement de pied	pirouette
chassé	plié
ciseaux	port de bras
couru	promenade
déboîté	relevé
dégagé	retiré
demi-plié	rond de jambe
demi-pointe	sauté
développé	saut de basque
écarté	sissonne
échappé	soubresaut
emboîté	sous-sous
enchaînement	temps levé
entrechat	temps lié
failli	tombé
fondu	tour en l'air
fouetté	tour jeté

balloon noun *sailing by in a balloon* hot-air balloon, barrage balloon; airship, dirigible, Zeppelin, blimp; weather balloon.

▸ verb **1** *her long skirt ballooned in the wind* SWELL (OUT), puff out/up, bulge (out), bag, belly (out), fill (out), billow (out), distend.

2 *the company's debt has ballooned* INCREASE RAPIDLY, soar, rocket, shoot up, escalate, mount, surge, spiral; *informal* go through the ceiling, go through the roof, skyrocket. ANTONYM plummet.

ballot noun *the ballot results will be announced soon* VOTE, poll, election, referendum, plebiscite; show of hands.

ballyhoo noun *informal after all the ballyhoo, the movie was a flop* PUBLICITY, advertising, promotion, marketing, propaganda, push, puffery, buildup, boosting; fuss, excitement; *informal* hype, spiel, hullabaloo, splash.

ballyhooed adjective *a ballyhooed playwright* HYPED, promoted, praised, acclaimed.

balm noun **1** *skin balm* OINTMENT, lotion, cream, salve, liniment, embrocation, rub, gel, emollient, unguent, balsam, moisturizer; *dated* pomade; *archaic* unction. ANTONYMS astringent, irritant.

2 *balm for troubled spirits* RELIEF, comfort, ease, succor, consolation, cheer, solace. ANTONYMS exacerbation, misery.

balmy adjective *the balmy breezes of the West Indies* MILD, gentle, temperate, summery, calm, tranquil, clement, fine, pleasant, benign, soothing, soft. ANTONYMS harsh, wintry.

baloney noun *informal that's a bunch of baloney.* See NONSENSE.

bamboozle verb *informal* See TRICK verb.

ban verb **1** *smoking was banned* PROHIBIT, forbid, veto, proscribe, disallow, outlaw, make illegal, embargo, bar, debar, block, stop, suppress, interdict; *Law* enjoin, restrain. See note at PROHIBIT. ANTONYM permit.

2 *Gary was banned from the playground* EXCLUDE, banish, expel, eject, evict, drive out, force out, oust, remove, get rid of; *informal* boot out, kick out. ANTONYM admit.

▸ noun **1** *a ban on soliciting* PROHIBITION, veto, proscription, embargo, bar, suppression, stoppage, interdict, interdiction, moratorium, injunction.

2 *a ban from international competition* EXCLUSION, banishment, expulsion, ejection, eviction, removal.

banal adjective *banal lyrics* TRITE, hackneyed, clichéd, platitudinous, vapid, commonplace, ordinary, common, stock, conventional, stereotyped, overused, overdone, overworked, stale, worn out, timeworn, tired, threadbare, hoary, hack, unimaginative, humdrum, ho-hum, unoriginal, uninteresting, dull, trivial; *informal* old hat, corny, cornball, played out; *dated* dime-store; *rare* truistic, bromidic. ANTONYM original.

banality noun **1** *the banality of most sitcoms* TRITENESS, vapidity, staleness, unimaginativeness, lack of originality, prosaicness, dullness; *informal* corniness. ANTONYM originality.

2 *they exchanged banalities* PLATITUDE, cliché, truism, old chestnut, stock phrase, bromide, commonplace. ANTONYMS epigram, witticism.

band[1] noun **1** *a band around her waist* BELT, sash, girdle, strap, tape, ring, hoop, loop, circlet, circle, cord, tie, string, thong, ribbon, fillet, strip; *literary* cincture.

2 *the sweater is white with a green band* STRIPE, strip, streak, line, bar, swathe; *technical* stria, striation.

band[2] noun **1** *a band of robbers* GROUP, gang, mob, pack, troop, company, party, crew, body, working party, posse; team, side, lineup; association, society, club, circle, fellowship, partnership, guild, lodge, order, fraternity, confraternity, sodality, brotherhood, sisterhood, sorority, union, alliance, affiliation, institution, league, federation, clique, set, coterie; *informal* bunch.

2 *the band played on* (MUSICAL) GROUP, pop group, ensemble, orchestra; *informal* combo.

▸ verb *local people* ***banded together*** JOIN (UP), team up, join forces, pool resources, get together; amalgamate, unite, form an alliance, form an association, affiliate, federate. ANTONYM split up.

bandage noun *she had a bandage on her foot* DRESSING, covering, gauze, compress, plaster, tourniquet; *trademark* Band-Aid, *trademark* Ace bandage.

▸ verb *she bandaged my knee* BIND, bind up, dress, cover, wrap, swaddle, strap (up).

bandana noun *a red paisley bandana* KERCHIEF, neckerchief; headscarf, babushka.

bandit noun *masked bandits held up the train* ROBBER, thief, outlaw, gunman, crook, mugger, gangster, raider, freebooter, hijacker, looter, marauder; *dated* desperado; *literary* brigand; *historical* rustler, highwayman, reaver.

bandy[1] adjective *bandy legs* BOWED, curved, bent; bowlegged, bandy-legged. ANTONYM straight.

bandy[2] verb **1** *a figure of $40,000 has been* ***bandied about*** | *what's the latest story being* ***bandied about?*** TOSS AROUND/ABOUT, put about, spread (around), discuss, rumor, mention, repeat; *literary* bruit about/abroad.

2 *I'm not going to bandy words with you* EXCHANGE, swap, trade.

bane noun *scurvy was the bane of these seafarers* SCOURGE, plague, curse, blight, pest, nuisance, headache, nightmare, trial, hardship, cross to bear, burden, thorn in one's flesh/side, bitter pill, affliction, trouble, misery, woe, tribulation, misfortune, pain.

bang noun **1** *the door slammed with a bang* THUD, thump, bump, crack, crash, smack, boom, clang, clap, knock, tap, clunk; stamp, stomp, bam, kaboom, kapow, wham, whump, whomp; report, explosion, detonation.

2 *a nasty bang on the head* BLOW, knock, thump, bump, hit, smack, bonk, crack, bash, whack, thwack.

▸ verb **1** *he banged the table with his fist* HIT, strike, beat, thump, hammer, knock, rap, pound, thud, punch, bump, smack, slap, slam, cuff, pummel, buffet, bash, whack, thwack, clobber, clout, clip, wallop, belt, bop, sock, whomp, bust, slug, whale.

2 *fireworks banged in the air* GO BANG, thud, thump, boom, clap, pound, crack, crash, explode, detonate, burst, blow up.

▸ adverb *informal* *the library is bang in the center of town* | *the train arrived bang on time* PRECISELY, exactly, right, directly, immediately, squarely, dead; promptly, prompt, dead on, sharp, on the dot; *informal* smack, slap, smack dab, plumb, on the button, on the nose.

bangle noun *the familiar jingle of Nana's silver bangles* BRACELET, wristlet, anklet, armlet.

banish verb **1** *he was banished for his crime* EXILE, expel, deport, eject, expatriate, ostracize, extradite, repatriate, transport; cast out, oust, evict, throw out, exclude, shut out, ban. ANTONYMS admit, readmit.

2 *he tried to banish his fear* DISPEL, dismiss, disperse, scatter, dissipate, drive away, chase away, shut out, quell, allay. ANTONYM engender.

banister noun *kids always want to slide down the banister* HANDRAIL, railing, rail; baluster; balustrade.

bank[1] noun **1** *the bank of the great river* EDGE, side, shore, coast, embankment, bankside, levee, border, verge, boundary, margin, rim, fringe; *literary* marge, skirt.

2 *a grassy bank* SLOPE, rise, incline, gradient, ramp; mound, ridge, hillock, hummock, knoll; bar, reef, shoal, shelf; accumulation, pile, heap, mass, drift.

3 *a bank of switches* ARRAY, row, line, tier, group, series.

▸ verb **1** *they* ***banked up*** *the earth* PILE (UP), heap (up), stack (up); accumulate, amass, assemble, put together.

2 *the aircraft banked* TILT, LEAN, tip, slant, incline, angle, slope, list, camber, pitch, dip, cant.

bank[2] noun **1** *money in the bank* FINANCIAL INSTITUTION, merchant bank, savings bank, finance company, trust company, credit union.

2 *a blood bank* STORE, reserve, accumulation, stock, stockpile, supply, pool, fund, cache, hoard, deposit; storehouse, reservoir, repository, depository.

▸ verb *I banked the money* DEPOSIT, pay in, invest, lay away.

PHRASE: **bank on** *can the senator bank on your support?* RELY ON, depend on, count on, place reliance on, bargain on, plan on; anticipate, expect; be confident of, be sure of, pin one's hopes/faith on, figure on.

bankroll verb *seven people suspected of helping bankroll resistance to coalition forces were arrested today* FINANCE, pay for, fund, subsidize, invest in.

bankrupt adjective **1** *the company was declared bankrupt* INSOLVENT, failed, ruined, in debt, owing money, in the red, in arrears, in receivership; *informal* bust, belly up, broke, cash-strapped, flat broke. ANTONYMS solvent, in the black.

2 *this government is* ***bankrupt of*** *ideas* BEREFT OF, devoid of, empty of, destitute of; completely lacking in, without, in need of, wanting. ANTONYM teeming with.

▸ verb *the strike nearly bankrupted the union* RUIN, impoverish, reduce to penury/destitution, bring to ruin, bring someone to their knees, wipe out, break; *rare* beggar, pauperize.

bankruptcy noun *many companies were facing bankruptcy* INSOLVENCY, liquidation, failure, ruin, financial ruin, collapse, receivership. ANTONYM solvency.

banner noun **1** *students waved banners* SIGN, placard, poster, notice.

2 *banners fluttered above the troops* FLAG, standard, ensign, color(s), pennant, banderole, guidon; *Nautical* burgee.

banquet noun *the awards banquet* FEAST, dinner; *informal* spread, blowout. ANTONYM snack.

banter noun *a brief exchange of banter* REPARTEE, witty conversation, raillery, wordplay, cut and thrust, kidding, ribbing, badinage, joshing.

▸ verb *sightseers were bantering with the guards* JOKE, jest, quip; *informal* josh, wisecrack.

baptism noun **1** *the baptism ceremony* CHRISTENING, naming.

2 *his baptism as a politician* INITIATION, debut, introduction, inauguration, launch, rite of passage.

baptize verb **1** *he was baptized as a baby* CHRISTEN.

2 *they were baptized into the church* ADMIT, initiate, enroll, recruit, convert.

3 *he was baptized Enoch* NAME, give the name, call, dub; *formal* denominate.

bar noun **1** *an iron bar* ROD, pole, stick, batten, shaft, rail, paling, spar, strut, crosspiece, beam.

2 *a bar of chocolate* BLOCK, slab, cake, tablet, brick, loaf, wedge, ingot.

3 *your drinks are on the bar* COUNTER, table, buffet, stand.

4 *she had a drink in a bar* TAVERN, cocktail lounge, barroom, taproom, pub, after-hours club, lounge, nightclub, speakeasy, roadhouse, beer hall, boîte, club, inn, rathskeller, cantina, bodega; singles bar, sports bar; *informal* watering hole, gin mill, dive, nineteenth hole, *Brit.* public house; *historical* saloon, alehouse.

5 *a bar to promotion* OBSTACLE, impediment, hindrance, obstruction, block, hurdle, barrier, stumbling block. ANTONYM aid.

6 *members of the Bar* LAWYERS, barristers, advocates, counsel, counselors; *chiefly Brit.* solicitors.

7 *the bar across the river mouth* SANDBAR, sandbank, shoal, shallow, reef.

▸ verb **1** *they have barred the door* BOLT, lock, fasten, secure, block, barricade, obstruct. ANTONYMS open, unlock.

2 *I was barred from entering* PROHIBIT, debar, preclude, forbid, ban, interdict, inhibit; exclude, keep out; obstruct, hinder, block; *Law* enjoin. ANTONYMS accept, admit.

▸ preposition *everyone bar me.* See EXCEPT preposition.

barb noun **1** *the hook has a nasty barb* SPIKE, prong, spur, thorn, needle, prickle, spine, quill.

2 *the barbs from his critics* INSULT, sneer, jibe, cutting remark, shaft, slight, brickbat, slur, jeer, taunt; *informal* dig, put-down; (**barbs**) abuse, disparagement, scoffing, scorn, sarcasm, goading.

barbarian noun *the city was besieged by barbarians* SAVAGE, heathen, brute, beast, wild man/woman; ruffian, thug, lout, vandal, boor, hoodlum, hooligan, Neanderthal, troglodyte; philistine; *informal* roughneck, lowlife.

▸ adjective *the barbarian hordes* SAVAGE, uncivilized, barbaric, primitive, heathen, vulgar, wild, brutish, Neanderthal. ANTONYM civilized.

barbaric adjective *barbaric crimes* BRUTAL, barbarous, brutish, bestial, savage, vicious, wicked, cruel, ruthless, merciless, villainous, murderous, heinous, monstrous, vile, inhuman, infernal, dark, fiendish, diabolical. ANTONYM civilized.

barbarity noun *the barbarity of slavery* BRUTALITY, brutalism, cruelty, bestiality, barbarism, barbarousness, savagery, viciousness, wickedness, villainy, baseness, inhumanity; atrocity. ANTONYM benevolence.

barbarous adjective . See BARBARIC.

barbecue noun *a backyard barbecue* COOKOUT, wiener/wienie/weenie roast; BBQ.

▸ verb *they barbecued some steaks* GRILL, spit-roast, broil, charbroil.

barbed adjective *barbed remarks* HURTFUL, wounding, cutting, stinging, mean, spiteful, nasty, cruel, vicious, unkind, snide, scathing, pointed, bitter, acid, caustic, sharp, vitriolic, venomous, poisonous, hostile, malicious, malevolent, vindictive; *informal* bitchy, catty. ANTONYM kindly.

bard noun *literary*. See POET.

bare adjective **1** *a giggling bare infant in her arms* NAKED, unclothed, undressed, uncovered, stripped, having nothing on, nude, in the nude, stark naked; *informal* without a stitch on, buck-naked, butt-naked, mother-naked, in one's birthday suit, in the raw, in the altogether, in the buff. See note at NAKED. ANTONYM clothed.

2 *a bare room* EMPTY, unfurnished, cleared; stark, austere, spartan, unadorned, unembellished, unornamented, plain. ANTONYMS furnished, embellished.

3 *a cupboard **bare of food*** EMPTY OF, devoid of, bereft of; without, lacking, wanting, free from. ANTONYM containing.

4 *a bare landscape* BARREN, bleak, exposed, desolate, stark, arid, desert, lunar; treeless, deforested, bald. ANTONYM lush.

5 *the bare facts* PLAIN, essential, fundamental, basic, straightforward, simple, pure, stark, bald, cold, hard, brutal, harsh.

6 *a bare lead in the race* MERE, no more than, simple; slim, slight, slender, paltry, minimum. ANTONYM comfortable.

▸ verb *he bared his arm* UNCOVER, strip, lay bare, undress, unclothe, denude, expose. ANTONYM cover.

barefaced adjective *a barefaced lie* FLAGRANT, blatant, glaring, obvious, undisguised, unconcealed, naked; shameless, unabashed, unashamed, impudent, audacious, unblushing, brazen.

barely adverb *former hurricane Patricia was barely at tropical storm force* HARDLY, scarcely, just, only just, narrowly, by a very small margin, by the narrowest of margins, by the skin of one's teeth, by a hair's breadth, by a nose; almost not; *informal* by a whisker. ANTONYM easily.

bargain noun **1** *this binder is a bargain at $1.98* GOOD BUY, (good) value for the money, surprisingly cheap; *informal* steal, deal, giveaway, best buy. ANTONYM rip-off.

2 *I'll make a bargain with you* AGREEMENT, arrangement, understanding, deal; contract, pact, compact; pledge, promise.

▸ verb *they bargained over the contract* HAGGLE, negotiate, discuss terms, hold talks, deal, barter, dicker; *formal* treat.

PHRASES: **bargain for/on** *a whole new roof is more than we bargained for* EXPECT, anticipate, be prepared for, allow for, plan for, reckon with, take into account, take into consideration, contemplate, imagine, envisage, foresee, predict; count on, rely on, depend on, bank on, plan on, reckon on, figure on. **in(to) the bargain** *we went to pick out one puppy and came home with two more in the bargain* ALSO, as well, in addition, additionally, besides, on top of that, over and above that, to boot, for good measure.

WORD NOTE enfeoff

My fondness for this word is perverse. It stems in part from the fact that it is so very ancient (it first appears in manuscript texts at the beginning of the fifteenth century); so very English (it connotes the kind of lifestyle associated with knights and realms and demesnes and honor and chivalry); so wonderfully ugly sounding, as though you don't have all your teeth in place when uttering the word, or are suffering an almighty hangover; and so very odd-looking—all those *f's* look as though they should be the old versions of *s's*, the kind of writing you see on ancient charts, as in the cartographic-mystery phrase *Here Be Dragonf.* The literal meaning is quite complicated: to *enfeoff* is literally to give to someone the permanent tenancy of land or estates that are in fact ultimately owned by a lord to whom the enfeoffed person gives loyalty, fealty (an etymologically connected word) and, perhaps, rent (or fee, of course). By association, and in a more up-to-date context, to *enfeoff* someone might be considered as persuading him to make a deal with the devil—to offer him, for example, a position in a loathed political administration to which he must then pay homage. Not a wholly uncommon and unrecognized phenomenon, in other words—and yet le mot juste often escapes one when writing about such a happenstance. *Enfeoff* solves this small problem, at a stroke. **–SW**

barge noun *a barge carrying lumber and dry goods* lighter, canal boat, wherry, scow.

▸ verb *he **barged into** us* PUSH, shove, force, elbow, shoulder, jostle, bulldoze, muscle.

PHRASE: **barge in** *sorry for barging in* BURST IN, break in, butt in, cut in, interrupt, intrude, encroach; *informal* horn in.

bark[1] noun *the bark of a dog* WOOF, yap, yelp, bay.

▸ verb **1** *the collie barked* WOOF, yap, yelp, bay.

2 *"Get out!" he barked* SAY BRUSQUELY, say abruptly, say angrily, snap; shout, bawl, cry, yell, roar, bellow, thunder; *informal* holler. ANTONYM whisper.

bark[2] noun *the bark of a tree* RIND, skin, peel, covering; integument; cork; *technical* cortex.

barn noun *the loft in the barn* OUTBUILDING, shed, cowshed, shelter; stable, stall, outhouse; *archaic* grange, garner.

baron noun **1** *she married a baron* LORD, noble, nobleman, aristocrat, peer.

2 *a steel baron* MAGNATE, tycoon, mogul, captain of industry, nabob, mandarin.

barracks plural noun *confined to the barracks* GARRISON, camp, encampment, depot, billet, quarters, fort, cantonment.

barrage noun **1** *an artillery barrage* BOMBARDMENT, cannonade; gunfire, shelling; salvo, volley, fusillade; *historical* broadside.

2 *a barrage of criticism* DELUGE, stream, storm, torrent, onslaught, flood, shower, spate, tide, avalanche, hail, blaze; abundance, mass, profusion.

barrel noun *oak barrels* CASK, keg, butt, vat, tun, drum, hogshead, kilderkin, barrique, pipe; *historical* firkin.

▸ verb *barreling down the road* CHARGE, plow, stampede, rush, go headlong; zoom.

barren adjective **1** *barren land* UNPRODUCTIVE, infertile, unfruitful, sterile, arid, desert. See note at NAKED. ANTONYM fertile.

2 *archaic a barren woman* INFERTILE, sterile, childless; *technical* infecund. ANTONYM fertile.

3 *a barren exchange of courtesies* POINTLESS, futile, worthless, profitless, valueless, unrewarding, purposeless, useless, vain, aimless, hollow, empty, vacuous, vapid. ANTONYM fruitful.

WORD NOTE **nullipara**

A woman who has never given birth to a child. One of the few nouns referring to the sexual/reproductive/aging status of a woman that is not in any way pejorative, simply because it is almost never used. Should be printed on T-shirts. **—ZS**

barricade noun *a barricade across the street* BARRIER, roadblock, blockade; obstacle, obstruction.

▸ verb *they barricaded the building* SEAL (UP), close up, block off, shut off/up; defend, protect, fortify.

barrier noun **1** *the barrier across the entrance* FENCE, railing, barricade, hurdle, bar, blockade, roadblock.

2 *a barrier to international trade* OBSTACLE, obstruction, hurdle, stumbling block, bar, block, impediment, hindrance, curb.

barring preposition *the Oscars will go on as scheduled, barring any major incidents related to the war* EXCEPT FOR, with the exception of, excepting, in the absence of, if there is/are no, discounting, short of, apart from, but for, other than, aside from, excluding, omitting, leaving out, save for, saving; *informal* outside of.

barter verb **1** *they bartered grain for salt* TRADE, swap, exchange, sell.

2 *you can barter for souvenirs* HAGGLE, bargain, negotiate, discuss terms, deal, dicker; *formal* treat.

base[1] noun **1** *the base of the tower* FOUNDATION, bottom, foot, support, stand, pedestal, plinth. ANTONYM top.

2 *the system uses existing technology as its base* BASIS, foundation, bedrock, starting point, source, origin, root(s), core, key component, heart, backbone.

3 *the troops returned to their base* HEADQUARTERS, camp, site, station, settlement, post, center, starting point.

▸ verb **1** *he based his idea on a movie* FOUND, build, construct, form, ground, root; use as a basis; **(be based on)** derive from, spring from, stem from, originate in, have its origin in, issue from.

2 *the company was based in Quebec* LOCATE, situate, position, install, station, site, establish; garrison.

base[2] adjective *base motives* SORDID, ignoble, low, low-minded, mean, immoral, improper, unseemly, unscrupulous, unprincipled, dishonest, dishonorable, shameful, bad, wrong, evil, wicked, iniquitous, sinful. ANTONYM noble.

baseless adjective *baseless accusations* GROUNDLESS, unfounded, ill-founded, without foundation; unsubstantiated, unproven, unsupported, uncorroborated, unconfirmed, unverified, unattested; unjustified, unwarranted; speculative, conjectural; unsound, unreliable, spurious, specious, trumped up, fabricated, untrue. ANTONYM valid.

bash verb **1** *she bashed him with her stick* STRIKE, hit, beat, thump, slap, smack, bang, knock, batter, pound, pummel; *informal* wallop, clout, belt, whack, thwack, clobber, bop, sock; *archaic* smite.

2 *they* ***bashed into*** *one another* CRASH INTO, run into, bang into, smash into, slam into, knock into, bump into; collide with, hit, meet head-on.

3 *bashing the government* CRITICIZE, censure, assail, attack, condemn, revile, denounce, rail against, cast aspersions on; *informal* pan, slam, hammer, lay into, tear to pieces, trash.

▸ noun **1** *a bash on the head* BLOW, rap, hit, knock, bang, slap, crack, thump, tap; *informal* wallop, clout, belt, whack, bonk, thwack, bop, sock.

2 *Harry's birthday bash.* See PARTY noun sense 1.

bashful adjective *the superhero's alter ego is a sweetly bashful science dork* SHY, reserved, diffident, inhibited, retiring, reticent, reluctant, shrinking; hesitant, timid, apprehensive, nervous, wary, demure, coy, blushing. ANTONYMS bold, confident.

basic adjective **1** *basic human rights* FUNDAMENTAL, essential, primary, principal, cardinal, elementary, elemental, quintessential, intrinsic, central, pivotal, critical, key, focal; vital, necessary, indispensable. ANTONYMS secondary, unimportant.

2 *basic cooking facilities* PLAIN, simple, unsophisticated, straightforward, adequate; unadorned, undecorated, unornamented, without frills; spartan, stark, severe, austere, limited, meager, rudimentary, patchy, sketchy, minimal; unfussy, homely, homespun, meat-and-potatoes, bread-and-butter; rough, rough and ready, crude, makeshift. ANTONYM elaborate.

basically adverb *he's basically a well-behaved dog* FUNDAMENTALLY, essentially, in essence; firstly, first of all, first and foremost, primarily; at heart, at bottom, au fond; principally, chiefly, above all, most of all, mostly, mainly, on the whole, by and large, substantially; intrinsically, inherently; *informal* at the end of the day, when all is said and done.

basics plural noun *this woodworking class is recommended for those who already know the basics* FUNDAMENTALS, essentials, rudiments, (first) principles, foundations, preliminaries, groundwork; essence, basis, core; *informal* nitty-gritty, brass tacks, nuts and bolts, meat and potatoes, bread and butter, ABCs.

basin noun **1** *she poured water into the basin* BOWL, dish, pan; sink, washtub.

2 *a basin among low hills* VALLEY, hollow, dip, depression.

basis noun **1** *the basis of his method* FOUNDATION, support, base; reasoning, rationale, defense; reason, grounds, justification, motivation.

2 *the basis of discussion* STARTING POINT, base, point of departure, beginning, premise, fundamental point/principle, principal constituent, main ingredient, cornerstone, core, heart, thrust, essence, kernel, nub.

3 *on a part-time basis* FOOTING, condition, status, position; arrangement, system, method.

bask verb **1** *I basked in the sun* LAZE, lie, lounge, relax, sprawl, loll, wallow; sunbathe, sun oneself.

2 *she's **basking in** all the glory* REVEL IN, delight in, luxuriate in, wallow in, take pleasure in, rejoice in, glory in, indulge oneself in; enjoy, relish, savor, lap up.

basket noun *baskets decorated with ribbons* hamper, creel, pannier, bushel; wicker basket.

bass adjective *his beautiful bass voice* LOW, deep, low-pitched, resonant, sonorous, rumbling, booming, resounding; baritone. ANTONYM high.

bastard noun **1** *archaic he had fathered a bastard* ILLEGITIMATE CHILD, child born out of wedlock; *dated* love child, by-blow; natural child/son/daughter.

2 *informal he's a real bastard* SCOUNDREL, villain, rogue, rascal, weasel, snake, snake in the grass, miscreant, good-for-nothing, reprobate; *informal* lowlife, creep, nogoodnik, scamp, scalawag, jerk, beast, rat, ratfink, louse, swine, dog, skunk, heel; slimeball, son of a bitch, SOB, scumbag, scumbucket, scuzzball, scuzzbag, dirtbag, sleazeball, sleazebag; *dated* hound, cad; *archaic* blackguard, knave, varlet, whoreson.

▸ adjective **1** *archaic a bastard child* ILLEGITIMATE, born out of wedlock; *dated* natural.

2 *a bastard socialism* ADULTERATED, alloyed, impure, inferior; hybrid, mongrel, patchwork.

bastardize verb *it is unthinkable that I would bastardize my values* ADULTERATE, corrupt, contaminate, weaken, dilute, taint, pollute, debase, distort.

bastion noun **1** *fortified with ditches and bastions* PROJECTION, outwork, breastwork, barbican; *Architecture* bartizan.

2 *a bastion of respectability* STRONGHOLD, bulwark, defender, support, supporter, guard, protection, protector, defense, prop, mainstay.

batch noun *when can we expect the next batch of invoices?* GROUP, quantity, lot, bunch, mass, cluster, raft, set, collection, bundle, pack; consignment, shipment.

bath noun **1** *he lay soaking in the bath* BATHTUB, tub, hot tub, whirlpool, sauna, steam bath, Turkish bath; *trademark* Jacuzzi.

2 *give it a bath* WASH, soak, cleansing, soaking, scrubbing, ablutions; dip; shower.

bathe verb **1** *she bathed and dressed* HAVE/TAKE A BATH, wash; shower.

2 *I bathed in the local swimming pool* SWIM, go swimming, take a dip.

3 *they bathed his wounds* CLEAN, cleanse, wash, rinse, wet, soak, immerse.

4 *the room was bathed in light* SUFFUSE, permeate, pervade, envelop, flood, cover, wash, fill; *literary* mantle.

bathing suit noun *bring a bathing suit and a towel* SWIMSUIT; bikini, monokini, maillot, swimming trunks, swim trunks; swimwear.

bathos noun *the story ends with such a stroke of bathos, you're not sure whether to laugh or scream* ANTICLIMAX, letdown, disappointment, disillusionment; absurdity; *informal* comedown.

WORD NOTE **bathos**

There are a couple of good reasons not to use the word *bathos* without severe provocation. For one thing, it means "an effect of anticlimax created by an unintentional lapse in mood from the sublime to the trivial or ridiculous," so if you're describing a *bathetic* situation, chances are the language you're using to describe the trivial or ridiculous situation won't support the use of an elevated word like *bathos.* When you use an overelevated word in writing that's not so elevated, you're pulling the reader out of your writing, usually with a jerk. Also, many more people know the opposite of *bathos, pathos* (a quality that evokes pity or sadness)—so the risk that your readers will think it's just a typo (and that you mean exactly the opposite of what you actually mean) is a real one. **—EM**

bathroom noun *excuse me, where's the bathroom?* WASHROOM, toilet, ladies'/men's room, restroom, lavatory, powder room, comfort station; urinal; *informal* facilities; little girls'/boys' room, can, john; *Brit.* water closet; *Brit informal* WC, loo, ladies'/gents'; *Military* latrine; *Nautical* head; *dated* commode, privy, outhouse.

baton noun **1** *the conductor's baton* STICK, rod, staff, wand.

2 *police batons* TRUNCHEON, club, billy club, cudgel, bludgeon, stick, nightstick, blackjack, mace; *Irish* shillelagh.

battalion noun **1** *an infantry battalion* regiment, brigade, force, division, squadron, squad, company, section, detachment, contingent, legion, corps, cohort.

2 *a battalion of supporters.* See CROWD noun sense 1.

batten noun *two boards joined with battens* BAR, bolt, rail, shaft; board, strip.

▸ verb *Stephen was **battening down** the shutters* FASTEN, fix, secure, clamp (down), lash, make fast, nail (down), seal.

batter verb *they took turns battering the effigy* PUMMEL, pound, hit repeatedly, buffet, thrash, beat up, clobber, trounce, rain blows on; *informal* knock around/about, beat the living daylights out of, give someone a good hiding, lay into, lace into, do over, rough up.

battered adjective *a battered boat drifted to shore* DAM-

AGED, shabby, run-down, worn out, beat-up, falling to pieces, falling apart, dilapidated, rickety, ramshackle, crumbling, the worse for wear, on its last legs; ABUSED.

battery noun **1** *insert fresh batteries* STORAGE CELL, cell.

2 *a gun battery* EMPLACEMENT, artillery unit; cannonry, ordnance.

3 *a battery of equipment* ARRAY, series, set, bank, group, row, line, lineup, collection.

4 *a battery of tests* SERIES, sequence, cycle, string, succession.

5 *assault and battery* VIOLENCE, assault, mugging.

battle noun **1** *he was killed in the battle* FIGHT, armed conflict, clash, struggle, skirmish, engagement, fray, duel; war, campaign, crusade; fighting, warfare, combat, action, hostilities; *informal* scrap, dogfight, shoot-out; brawl.

2 *a battle at the office* CONFLICT, clash, contest, competition, struggle, turf war; disagreement, argument, altercation, dispute, controversy, tug-of-war.

▸ verb **1** *he has been battling cancer* FIGHT, combat, contend with; resist, withstand, stand up to, confront; war with, feud with; struggle with, strive against.

2 *Mark battled his way to the podium* FORCE, push, elbow, shoulder, fight; struggle, labor.

battle-ax noun **1** *a severe blow from a battle-ax* POLEAX, ax, pike, halberd, tomahawk.

2 *informal she's a real battle-ax.* See HARRIDAN.

battle cry noun **1** *the army's battle cry* WAR CRY, war whoop, rallying call/cry; rebel yell.

2 *the battle cry of the feminist movement* SLOGAN, motto, watchword, catchphrase, mantra.

battlefield noun *what were Vietnam battlefields then are now tourist sites* BATTLEGROUND, field of battle, field of operations, combat zone, theater of war, arena of war, front.

battlement noun *the battlements were abandoned* CASTELLATION, crenellation, parapet, rampart, balustrade, bulwark, wall, bastion, fortification.

batty adjective *informal* See MAD sense 1. See also note at MAD.

bauble noun *gift-shop baubles* TRINKET, knickknack, ornament, frippery, gewgaw, gimcrack, bibelot, kickshaw, tchotchke.

bawdy adjective *bawdy jokes* RIBALD, indecent, risqué, racy, rude, spicy, sexy, suggestive, titillating, naughty, improper, indelicate, indecorous, off-color, earthy, barnyard, broad, locker-room, Rabelaisian; pornographic, obscene, vulgar, crude, coarse, lewd, dirty, filthy, smutty, unseemly, salacious, prurient, lascivious, licentious, X-rated, blue, raunchy; *euphemistic* adult. ANTONYMS clean, innocent.

bawl verb **1** *"Come on!" he bawled* SHOUT, yell, roar, bellow, screech, scream, shriek, howl, whoop, bark, trumpet, thunder; *informal* yammer, holler. ANTONYM whisper.

2 *the children continued to bawl* CRY, sob, weep, shed tears, wail, whine, howl, squall; *rare* ululate. PHRASE: **bawl someone out** *informal* See REPRIMAND.

bay[1] noun *ships were anchored in the bay* COVE, inlet, estuary, indentation, gulf, bight, basin, fjord, arm; natural harbor, anchorage.

bay[2] noun *there was a bay set into the wall* ALCOVE, recess, niche, nook, oriel, opening, hollow, cavity, inglenook; compartment.

bay[3] verb *coyotes baying at the moon* HOWL, bark, yelp, yap, cry, bellow, roar. PHRASE: **at bay** *the smoke did little to keep the mosquitoes at bay* AT A DISTANCE, away, off, at arm's length.

bayonet noun *a man armed with a bayonet* sword, knife, blade, spear, lance, pike, javelin.

bazaar noun **1** *a Turkish bazaar* MARKET, marketplace, mart, exchange, souk.

2 *the church bazaar* RUMMAGE SALE, garage sale, yard sale; fundraiser, charity event; flea market, swap meet; fair, carnival.

be verb **1** *there was once a king* EXIST, have being, have existence; live, be alive, have life, breathe, draw breath, be extant.

2 *the trial is tomorrow at half past one* OCCUR, happen, take place, come about, arise, crop up, transpire, fall, materialize, ensue; *literary* come to pass, befall, betide.

3 *the bed is over there* BE SITUATED, be located, be found, be present, be set, be positioned, be placed, be installed.

4 *it has been like this for hours* REMAIN, stay, last, continue, survive, endure, persist, prevail; wait, linger, hold on, hang on.

beach noun *a sandy beach* SEASIDE, seashore, shore, coast, waterfront, lakeshore, coastline, coastal region, littoral, seaboard, foreshore, water's edge; sands; *literary* strand.

▸ verb *they beached the boat* LAND, ground, strand, run aground, run ashore.

beached adjective *rescuing the beached whale* STRANDED, grounded, aground, ashore, marooned, high and dry, stuck, washed up, washed ashore.

beacon noun *the beacon penetrated the fog* LIGHTHOUSE; signal light, signal fire, danger signal, bonfire, warning light, warning fire; spotlight, searchlight.

bead noun **1** *a string of beads* BALL, pellet, pill, globule, sphere, spheroid, oval, ovoid, orb, round; **(beads)** necklace, rosary, chaplet.

2 *beads of sweat* DROPLET, drop, blob, dot, dewdrop, teardrop. PHRASE: **draw/get a bead on** *I drew a bead on the figure in the attic window* AIM AT, fix on, focus on, zero in on, sight.

beak noun *a bird's beak* BILL, nib, mandible.

beam noun **1** *an oak beam* JOIST, lintel, rafter, purlin; spar, girder, balk, timber, two-by-four, plank; support, strut; scantling, transom, stringer, collar beam, I-beam.

2 *a beam of light coming from the window* RAY, shaft, stream, streak, pencil, finger; flash, gleam, glow, glimmer, glint, flare.

3 *the beam on her face* GRIN, smile, happy expression, bright look. ANTONYM frown.

▸ verb **1** *the signal is* ***beamed out*** BROADCAST, transmit, relay, emit, send/put out, disseminate; direct, aim.

2 *the sun* ***beamed down*** SHINE, radiate, give off light, glare, gleam.

3 *he beamed broadly* GRIN, smile, smirk; *informal* be all smiles. ANTONYM frown.

beaming adjective **1** *his beaming face* GRINNING, smiling, laughing; cheerful, happy, radiant, glowing, sunny, joyful, elated, thrilled, delighted, overjoyed, rapturous, blissful. ANTONYM frowning.

2 *he greeted her with a beaming smile* BRIGHT, CHEERY, sparkling, flashing, brilliant, dazzling, intense, gleaming, radiant.

bean noun See table.

BEANS AND PEAS

adzuki/aduki (bean)	lablab
anasazi bean	lentil
bambara bean	lima bean
black bean	marrowfat pea
black turtle bean	mung (bean)
black-eyed pea	navy bean
broad bean	northern (white) bean
butter bean	peanut
butterfly pea	pigeon pea
cajan pea	pink bean
cannellini bean	pinto bean
carob bean	protein pea
castor bean	pulse
chickpea	purple bean
cluster bean	red bean
congo bean	rice bean
copper bean	runner bean
cowpea	scarlet runner
dhal/dal	snap bean
English pea	snap pea
fava bean	snow pea
field bean	soybean
field pea	split pea
flageolet	string bean
garbanzo bean	sugar pea
garden pea	sugar snap pea
green pea	Swedish brown bean
Great Northern (white) bean	tepary bean
	velvet bean
green bean	wax bean
haricot (bean)	white bean
horsebean	winged bean
hyacinth bean	yam bean
jack bean	yard-long bean
kidney bean	yellow pea

See also table at VEGETABLE.

bear[1] verb **1** *I come bearing gifts* CARRY, bring, transport, move, convey, take, fetch, deliver, tote, lug.

2 *the bag bore my name* DISPLAY, exhibit, be marked with, show, carry, have.

3 *will it bear his weight?* SUPPORT, carry, hold up, prop up.

4 *they can't bear the cost alone* SUSTAIN, carry, support, shoulder, absorb, take on.

5 *she bore no grudge* HARBOR, foster, entertain, nurse, nurture, brood over.

6 *such a solution does not bear close scrutiny* WITHSTAND, stand up to, stand, put up with, take, cope with, handle, sustain, accept.

7 *I can't bear having him around* ENDURE, tolerate, put up with, stand, abide, submit to, experience, undergo, go through, countenance, brave, weather, stomach; *informal* hack, swallow; *formal* brook; *archaic* suffer.

8 *she bore a son* GIVE BIRTH TO, bring forth, deliver, be delivered of, have, produce, spawn, birth; *informal* drop; *literary* beget.

9 *a shrub that bears yellow berries* PRODUCE, yield, give forth, give, grow, provide, supply.

10 *bear left at the junction* VEER, curve, swerve, fork, diverge, deviate, turn, bend.

PHRASES: **bear oneself** *if you bear yourself like a bum, expect to treated as a bum* CONDUCT ONESELF, carry oneself, acquit oneself, act, behave, perform; *formal* comport oneself. **bear down on** *we knew that Sherman's men would be bearing down on us by dawn* ADVANCE ON, close in on, move in on, converge on. **bear fruit** *we're always amazed when one of her crazy ideas actually bears fruit* YIELD RESULTS, get results, succeed, meet with success, be successful, be effective, be profitable, work, go as planned; *informal* pay off, come off, pan out, do the trick. **bear something in mind** *the meals are free, but please bear in mind that you are expected to tip the servers* TAKE INTO ACCOUNT, take into consideration, remember, consider, be mindful, mind, mark, heed. **bear on** *I fail to see how Hugh's personal problem bears on our final decision* BE RELEVANT TO, appertain to, pertain to, relate to, have a bearing on, have relevance to, apply to, be pertinent to. **bear something out** *we're hoping you can bear out his statement* CONFIRM, corroborate, substantiate, endorse, vindicate, give credence to, support, ratify, warrant, uphold, justify, prove, authenticate, verify. **bear with** *if you'll just bear with us, I'm sure the lights will be back on soon* BE PATIENT WITH, show forbearance toward, make allowances for, tolerate, put up with, endure. **bear witness/testimony to** *the majestic windows bear witness to the architect's fascination with natural light* TESTIFY TO, be evidence of, be proof of, attest to, evidence, prove, vouch for; demonstrate, show, establish, indicate, reveal, bespeak.

bear[2] noun *campers are warned that food will attract bears.* See table.

BEARS

Alaskan brown bear	Kodiak bear
American black bear	Malayan sun bear
Asian black bear	panda
black bear	polar bear
blue bear	Siberian brown bear
brown bear	silvertip grizzly (bear)
cave bear (extinct)	sloth bear
cinnamon bear	sun bear
giant panda	white bear
glacier bear	yellow bear
grizzly (bear)	

bearable adjective *volunteer staff can make a hospital stay bearable* TOLERABLE, endurable, supportable, sustainable, sufferable, brookable; acceptable, admissible, manageable. ANTONYM intolerable.

beard noun *a black beard* FACIAL HAIR, whiskers, stubble, five o'clock shadow, bristles; goatee, imperial, Vandyke.

▸ verb *it was up to me to beard the bully* CONFRONT, face, challenge, brave, come face to face with, meet head on; defy, oppose, stand up against, dare, throw down the gauntlet to.

bearded adjective *bearded men* UNSHAVEN, whiskered, whiskery, bewhiskered; stubbly, bristly. ANTONYM clean-shaven.

bearer noun **1** *a lantern-bearer* CARRIER, porter.

2 *the bearer of bad news* MESSENGER, agent, conveyor, carrier, emissary.

3 *the bearer of the documents* HOLDER, possessor, owner.

bearing noun 1 *a man of military bearing* POSTURE, stance, carriage, gait, deportment; *formal* comportment.

2 *a regal bearing* DEMEANOR, manner, air, aspect, attitude, behavior, mien, style.

3 *this has no bearing on the matter* RELEVANCE, pertinence, connection, appositeness, germaneness, importance, significance, application.

4 *a bearing of 15°* DIRECTION, orientation, course, trajectory, heading, tack, path, line, run.

5 *he tormented her beyond bearing* ENDURANCE, tolerance, toleration.

6 (**bearings**) *I lost my bearings* ORIENTATION, sense of direction; whereabouts, location, position.

beast noun 1 *the beasts of the forest* ANIMAL, creature; *informal* critter, varmint.

2 *he is a cruel beast* MONSTER, brute, savage, barbarian, animal, swine, pig, ogre, fiend, demon, devil.

beastly adjective 1 *politics is a beastly profession* AWFUL, horrible, rotten, nasty, foul, objectionable, unpleasant, disagreeable, offensive, vile, abominable, hateful, detestable, terrible, godawful. ANTONYM pleasant.

2 *he was beastly to her* UNKIND, malicious, mean, nasty, unpleasant, unfriendly, spiteful, cruel, vicious, base, foul, malevolent, despicable, contemptible, horrible, horrid, rotten. ANTONYM kind.

beat verb 1 *they were beaten with truncheons* HIT, strike, batter, thump, bang, hammer, punch, knock, thrash, pound, pummel, slap, smack, rain blows on; assault, attack, abuse; cudgel, club, birch; *informal* wallop, belt, bash, whack, thwack, clout, clobber, slug, tan, bop, sock, deck, plug, beat the living daylights out of; *dated* chastise.

2 *the waves **beat upon** the shore* BREAK ON/UPON/AGAINST, dash against; lash against, strike, lap (upon), wash against; splash on/upon/against, roll upon; *literary* plash upon/against, lave against.

3 *the metal is beaten into a die* HAMMER, forge, form, shape, mold, work, stamp, fashion, model.

4 *her heart was still beating* PULSATE, pulse, palpitate, vibrate, throb; pump, pound, thump, thud, hammer, drum; pitter-patter.

5 *the eagle beat its wings* FLAP, flutter, thresh, thrash, wave, vibrate, oscillate.

6 *beat the cream into the mixture* WHISK, mix, blend, whip.

7 *she beat a path through the grass* TREAD, tramp, trample, wear, flatten, press down.

8 *the team they need to beat* DEFEAT, conquer, win against, get the better of, vanquish, trounce, rout, overpower, overcome, subdue; *informal* lick, thrash, whip, wipe the floor with, clobber, cream, shellac, skunk.

9 *he beat the record* SURPASS, exceed, better, improve on, go one better than, eclipse, transcend, top, trump, cap.

▸ noun 1 *the song has a good beat* RHYTHM, pulse, meter, time, measure, cadence; stress, accent.

2 *the beat of hooves* POUNDING, banging, thumping, thudding, booming, hammering, battering, crashing.

3 *the beat of her heart* PULSE, pulsating, vibration, throb, palpitation, reverberation; pounding, thump, thud, hammering, drumming; pitter-patter.

4 *a cop on his beat* CIRCUIT, round, route, way, path.

▸ adjective *informal phew, I'm beat!* See EXHAUSTED sense 1.

PHRASES: **beat a (hasty) retreat.** See RETREAT verb sense 1. **beat it** *informal* . See RUN verb sense 2. **beat someone up** *he just snapped and started beating up his abusive father* ASSAULT, attack, mug, thrash, do over, work over, rough up, lay into, lace into, sail into, beat the living daylights out of, let someone have it, beat up on, knock around/about.

beaten adjective 1 *the beaten team* DEFEATED, losing, unsuccessful, conquered, bettered, vanquished, trounced, routed, overcome, overwhelmed, overpowered, overthrown, bested, subdued, quashed, crushed, broken, foiled, hapless, luckless; *informal* licked, thrashed, losingest, clobbered. ANTONYMS victorious, winning.

2 *a beaten dog* ABUSED, battered, maltreated, ill-treated, mistreated, misused, downtrodden; ASSAULTED, thumped, whacked, hit, thrashed, pummeled, smacked, drubbed; *informal* walloped, belted, bashed, clobbered, knocked around/about, roughed up.

3 *gradually stir in the beaten eggs* WHISKED, whipped, stirred, mixed, blended; frothy, foamy.

4 *a beaten path* TRODDEN, trampled; well-trodden, much trodden, well-used, much traveled, worn, well-worn. ANTONYM untouched.

PHRASE: **off the beaten track/path** *we tried to find a campsite off the beaten track* OUT OF THE WAY, isolated, quiet, private, remote, unfrequented, outlying, secluded, hidden, backwoods, in the back of beyond, in the middle of nowhere, in the hinterlands; *informal* in the sticks. ANTONYMS busy, popular.

beatific adjective 1 *a beatific smile* RAPTUROUS, joyful, ecstatic, seraphic, blissful, serene, happy, beaming.

2 *a beatific vision* BLESSED, exalted, sublime, heavenly, holy, divine, celestial, paradisical, glorious.

beatify verb *he was beatified by Pope Leo XIII* CANONIZE, bless, sanctify, hallow, consecrate, make holy; *rare* macarize.

beatitude noun *the everlasting beatitude* BLESSEDNESS, benediction, grace; bliss, ecstasy, exaltation, supreme happiness, divine joy, divine rapture; saintliness, sainthood.

beau noun *dated* 1 *Sally and her beau* BOYFRIEND, sweetheart, lover, darling, partner, significant other, escort, young man, admirer, suitor; *informal* main squeeze, boy toy.

2 *an eighteenth-century beau* DANDY, fop; *dated* swell, coxcomb, popinjay.

beautiful adjective *beautiful fashion models | a beautiful crystal vase* ATTRACTIVE, pretty, handsome, good-looking, alluring, prepossessing; lovely, charming, delightful, appealing, engaging, winsome; ravishing, gorgeous, stunning, arresting, glamorous, bewitching, beguiling; graceful, elegant, exquisite, aesthetic, artistic, decorative, magnificent; *informal* divine, drop-dead gorgeous, easy on the eye, killer, cute, foxy; *formal* beauteous; *archaic* comely, fair. See word spectrum on page 73. ANTONYM ugly.

beautify verb *efforts to beautify the town center* ADORN, embellish, enhance, decorate, ornament, garnish, gild, smarten up, prettify, enrich, glamorize, spruce up, spiff up, deck (out), trick out, grace; *informal* do up. ANTONYM spoil.

→ ***beautiful***
stunning
ravishing
divine
enchanting
magnificent
exquisite
glamorous
bewitching
beguiling
gorgeous
drop-dead gorgeous
alluring
beauteous
winsome
lovely
charming
comely
delightful
engaging
arresting
elegant
graceful
fetching
seemly
good-looking
prepossessing
foxy
pretty
attractive
cute
appealing
handsome
dapper
natty
bonny
fair
fine
passable
plain
not much to look at
unprepossessing
inelegant
gawky
unappealing
ill-favored
ill-looking
unlovely
unsightly
homely
unpleasant
haggard
lumpish
grim
awful
deformed
disfigured
gross
disgusting
ghastly
frightful
odious
plug-ugly
butt-ugly
reptilian
repellent
repulsive
hideous
misshapen
monstrous
vile
revolting
repugnant
grotesque
ugly ←

beauty noun **1** *the beauty of the scenery* ATTRACTIVENESS, prettiness, good looks, comeliness, allure; loveliness, charm, appeal, eye-appeal, heavenliness; winsomeness, grace, elegance, exquisiteness; splendor, magnificence, grandeur, impressiveness, decorativeness; gorgeousness, glamour; *literary* beauteousness, pulchritude. ANTONYM ugliness.

2 *she is a beauty* BEAUTIFUL WOMAN, belle, vision, Venus, goddess, beauty queen, picture; *informal* babe, hottie, looker, good looker, beaut, siren, doll, arm candy, lovely, stunner, knockout, bombshell, dish, peach, eyeful, fox. ANTONYM hag.

3 *the beauty of this plan* ADVANTAGE, attraction, strength, benefit, boon, blessing, good thing, strong point, virtue, merit, selling point. ANTONYM drawback.

WORD NOTE **pulchritude**

While very useful as a synonym for *sex appeal,* it shouldn't be understood to mean sexy in the manner of the modern desiccated zombie-eyed runway model. Indeed, it stands as a rebuke to that contemporary beauty standard, evoking as it does the plush, statuesque overabundance associated with Broadway chorines of an earlier era. As a bonus you also catch a whiff of the trying-to-be-euphemistic-but-still-vulgar vaudeville patrons ogling them. **—DA**

WORD NOTE **pulchritude**

A paradoxical noun because it means beauty but is itself one of the ugliest words in the language. Same goes for the adjectival form *pulchritudinous.* They're part of a tiny elite cadre of words that possess the very opposite of the qualities they denote. *Diminutive, big, foreign, fancy* (adj), *colloquialism,* and *monosyllabic* are some others; there are at least a dozen more. Inviting your school-age kids to list as many paradoxical words as they can is a neat way to deepen their relationship to English and help them see that words are both symbols for things and very real things themselves. **—DFW**

becalmed adjective *the boats remained becalmed* MOTIONLESS, still, at a standstill, at a halt, unmoving, stuck.

because conjunction *your photos won because they're the best* SINCE, as, in view of the fact that, inasmuch as, owing to the fact that, seeing that/as; *informal* on account of, cuz; *literary* for. ANTONYM despite.

PHRASE: **because of** *because of her exceptionally high scores, she was able to start at Level 3* ON ACCOUNT OF, as a result of, as a consequence of, owing to, due to; thanks to, by/in virtue of; *formal* by reason of.

beckon verb **1** *the guard beckoned to Benny* GESTURE, signal, wave, gesticulate, motion.

2 *the countryside beckons you* ENTICE, invite, tempt, coax, lure, charm, attract, draw, call.

become verb **1** *she became rich* GROW, get, turn, come to be, get to be; *literary* wax.

2 *he became a tyrant* TURN INTO, change into, be transformed into, be converted into.

3 *he became Louisiana's attorney general* BE APPOINTED (AS), be assigned as, be nominated, be elected (as), be made.

4 *the dress becomes her* SUIT, flatter, look good on; set off, show to advantage; *informal* do something for.

5 *it ill becomes him to preach the gospel during a board meeting* BEFIT, suit, behoove. PHRASE: **become of** *whatever became of the guy who designed your terrace?* HAPPEN TO, be the fate of, be the lot of, overtake; *literary* befall, betide.

becoming adjective *that suit's very becoming* FLATTERING, attractive, lovely, pretty, handsome, fetching; stylish, elegant, chic, fashionable, tasteful; *archaic* comely.

bed noun **1** *she got into her bed* cot, cradle, crib, berth; brass bed, bunk bed, camp bed, canopy bed, captain's bed, daybed, featherbed; *trademark* Hide-A-Bed, Murphy bed, sofa bed, spool bed, trundle bed, waterbed, divan, futon, four-poster; *informal* the sack, the hay.

2 *a flower bed* PATCH, plot, border, strip.

3 *built on a bed of stones* BASE, foundation, support, prop, substructure, substratum.

4 *a river bed* BOTTOM, floor, ground. PHRASE: **go to bed** *time to go to bed* RETIRE, call it a day; go to sleep, have/take a nap, get some sleep; *informal* hit the sack, hit the hay, turn in, go (to) beddy-bye, crash, catch forty winks, get some shut-eye, catch some Zs, beat the sheets, meet the sandman, go to slumberland; *literary* slumber.

bedaub verb *literary faces bedaubed with white paint* SMEAR, daub, bespatter, spatter, splatter, cover, coat.

bedding noun *change the bedding* BED LINEN(S), sheets and blankets; bedclothes; bedcovers, bedspread, covers; comforter, duvet.

bedeck verb *a church bedecked with flowers* DECORATE, adorn, ornament, embellish, furnish, garnish, trim, deck, grace, enrich, dress up, trick out; swathe, wreathe, festoon; *informal* do up.

bedevil verb *past mistakes that continue to bedevil her | he accused Congress of allowing "single-interest-group" politics to bedevil U.S. foreign policy* AFFLICT, torment, beset, assail, beleaguer, plague, blight, rack, oppress, harry, curse, dog; harass, distress, trouble, worry, torture; frustrate, vex, annoy, irritate, irk.

bedlam noun *there was bedlam in the stadium* UPROAR, pandemonium, commotion, mayhem, confusion, disorder, chaos, anarchy, lawlessness; furor, upheaval, hubbub, hoopla, turmoil, riot, ruckus, rumpus, tumult, hullabaloo. ANTONYM calm.

bedraggled adjective *the bedraggled search party* DISHEVELED, disordered, untidy, unkempt, tousled, disarranged, in a mess, mussed. ANTONYMS neat, clean.

bedridden adjective *Jake will be bedridden for weeks* CONFINED TO BED, sick in bed, laid up, immobilized, flat on one's back.

bedrock noun **1** *we're digging till we hit bedrock* SUBSTRATUM, substructure, understructure, solid foundation, base, rock base.

2 *the bedrock of our society* CORE, basis, base, foundation, roots, heart, backbone, principle, essence, nitty-gritty; *informal* nuts and bolts.

bedspread noun *a plaid bedspread* COMFORTER, coverlet, quilt, duvet, blanket; spread, bedcover; *dated* counterpane.

beef noun **1** *there's plenty of beef on him* MUSCLE, brawn, bulk; strength, power.

2 *his beef was about the cost* COMPLAINT, criticism, objection, cavil, quibble, grievance, grumble, gripe, grouse.

▸ verb **1** *security was being* ***beefed up*** TOUGHEN UP, strengthen, build up, reinforce, consolidate, augment, improve.

2 *they're constantly beefing about the neighbor's dog* COMPLAIN, grumble, whine, carp, bitch, gripe, bellyache.

beefy adjective *informal the beefy right fielder* MUSCULAR, brawny, hefty, burly, hulking, strapping, well-built, hard-bodied, solid, stalwart, strong, powerful, heavy, robust, sturdy; *informal* hunky, husky. ANTONYM puny.

beer noun *pizza and beer* ALE, brew; *informal* brewski, suds, pint. See table.

BEERS

abbey	Kölsch
ale	Kriek
alt	Kristall
altbier	lager
barley wine	lambic
Berliner Weisse	light
Biere de Garde	malt
bitter	malt liquor
bock	Märzen
brown ale	mild
celery	Muncher
chili	Munich
cream ale	Oktoberfest
diat pils	old ale
doppelbock	oud bruin
Dortmunder	pale ale
draft	pils
dry	pilsner
dunkel	poire
Eisbock	porter
faro	Schwarzbier
franboise	season
ginger	shandy
green	special
Gueuze	Sticke
heavy	stock ale
Hefe	stout
Hell	trappist
honey	Vienna
ice	weiss
India Pale Ale	wheat
Irish ale	Zwickl

See also tables at COCKTAIL, LIQUOR, and WINE.

befall verb *literary* **1** *the same fate befell him* HAPPEN TO, overtake, come upon, be visited on.

2 *tell us what befell* HAPPEN, occur, take place, come about, transpire, materialize; ensue, follow, result; *informal* go down; *literary* come to pass, betide. See note at HAPPEN.

befitting preposition *this is an automobile befitting your fine taste* IN KEEPING WITH, as befits, appropriate to, fit for, suitable for, suited to, proper to, right for, compatible with, consistent with, in character with; *archaic* meet for.

before preposition **1** *he dressed up before going out* PRIOR TO, previous to, earlier than, preparatory to, in preparation for, preliminary to, in anticipation of, in expectation of; in advance of, ahead of, leading up to, on the eve of; *rare* anterior to. ANTONYM after.

2 *he appeared before the judge* IN FRONT OF, in the presence of, in the sight of.

3 *death before dishonor* IN PREFERENCE TO, rather than, sooner than.

▸ adverb *she has ridden before* PREVIOUSLY, before

now/then, until now/then, up to now/then; earlier, formerly, hitherto, in the past, in days gone by; *formal* heretofore.

beforehand adverb *bring any notes you compiled beforehand* IN ADVANCE, ahead of time, in readiness; before, before now/then, earlier (on), previously, already, sooner. ANTONYM afterward.

befriend verb *a charming story in which the toys befriend one another* MAKE FRIENDS WITH, make a friend of; look after, keep an eye on; be of service to, lend a helping hand to, help, protect; side with, stand by, encourage.

befuddled adjective *befuddled from the anesthesia* CONFUSED, muddled, addled, bewildered, disorientated, fazed, perplexed, dazed, dizzy, stupefied, groggy, muzzy, foggy, fuddled, fuzzy, dopey, woozy, befogged, mixed up, discombobulated. ANTONYM clear.

beg verb **1** *he begged on the streets* PANHANDLE, ask for money, seek charity, seek alms; *informal* sponge, cadge, scrounge, bum, mooch.

2 *we* ***begged for*** *mercy* ASK FOR, request, plead for, appeal for, call for, sue for, solicit, seek, press for.

3 *he begged her not to go* IMPLORE, entreat, plead with, appeal to, supplicate, pray to, importune; ask, request, call on, petition; *literary* beseech.

WORD NOTE **beg**

In its main function, *beg* serves as an improved modern synonym for the old *crave,* which now sounds very affected. Both verbs mean "to request earnestly" and imply a sort of subordinate position—I beg a favor, but I demand a right. (*Beseech* and *implore* are close to *beg,* but these bigger words imply a little extra anxiety and/or urgency.) As of 2004, the only really egregious way you can screw up with *beg* is to misuse the phrase *beg the question.* This phrase does not—repeat, not—mean "invite the following obvious question," and sentences like *This begs the question, why are our elected leaders silent on this issue?* are both increasingly common and deeply wrong. The idiom *beg the question* is a compressed Anglicization of the Latin *petitio principii,* which is the name of a particular kind of logical fallacy where one bases a conclusion on a premise that turns out to be just as debatable as the conclusion itself. Genuine examples of begging the question are things like *The death penalty is the just punishment for murder because those who kill forfeit their own right to life* and *True wisdom is speaking and acting judiciously.* Because of its extremely specific origin and meaning, *beg the question* will never mean "invite the question" no matter how widespread the usage becomes. Nor, strictly speaking, will it ever mean "avoid or ignore the real issue," even though a subsidiary def of *beg* is "to dodge or evade." If you want to accuse someone of missing the point, you can say *You're begging the real issue* or something; but it's a boner to use even this sense of *beg* with *question* unless you're talking about a true *petitio principii.* —DFW

THE RIGHT WORD

How badly do you want something? You can **beg** for it, which implies a humble and earnest approach. If you **entreat**, you're trying to get what you want by ingratiating yourself (*she entreated her mother to help her prepare for the exam*). To **plead** involves more urgency (*he pleaded with the judge to spare his life*) and is usually associated with the legal system (*she was advised to plead guilty*). **Beseech** also suggests urgency, as well as an emotional appeal (*he beseeched her to tell the truth*). **Implore** is still stronger, suggesting desperation or great distress (*the look in his mother's eyes implored him to have mercy*). If you really want to get your way, you can **importune**, which means to *beg* not only urgently but persistently and to risk making a pest of yourself (*he importuned her daily to accept his invitation*). **Petition** suggests an appeal to authority (*to petition the government to repeal an unjust law*), while **solicit** suggests petitioning in a courteous, formal way (*soliciting financial support for the school carnival*).

beget verb **1** *literary he begat a son* FATHER, sire, have, bring into the world, give life to, bring into being, spawn.

2 *violence begets violence* CAUSE, give rise to, lead to, result in, bring about, create, produce, generate, engender, spawn, occasion, bring on, precipitate, prompt, provoke, kindle, trigger, spark off, touch off, stir up, whip up, induce, inspire, promote; *literary* enkindle.

beggar noun *he never turned any beggar from his door* PANHANDLER, mendicant, tramp, vagrant, vagabond, hobo; *informal* scrounger, sponger, cadger, freeloader, bum, moocher, mooch.

begin verb **1** *we began work* START, commence, set about, go about, embark on, launch into, get down to, take up; initiate, set in motion, institute, inaugurate, get ahead with; *informal* get cracking on, get going on. ANTONYM cease. See word spectrum on page 16.

2 *he began by saying hello* OPEN, lead off, get underway, get going, get off the ground, start, start off, go ahead, commence; *informal* start the ball rolling, kick off, get the show on the road, fire away, take the plunge. ANTONYMS finish, conclude.

3 *when did the illness begin?* APPEAR, arise, become apparent, make an appearance, spring up, crop up, turn up, come into existence, come into being, originate, start, commence, develop; *literary* come to pass. ANTONYM disappear.

beginner noun *a yoga video for beginners* NOVICE, newcomer, fledgling, neophyte, starter, learner, student, apprentice, trainee; recruit, raw recruit, initiate, freshman; tenderfoot, tyro; postulant, novitiate; *informal* rookie, newbie, cub, greenhorn, new kid (on the block). See note at NOVICE. ANTONYMS expert, veteran.

beginning noun **1** *the beginning of socialism* DAWN, birth, inception, conception, origination, genesis, emergence, rise, start, commencement, starting point, launch, onset, outset; day one; *informal* kickoff. ANTONYM end.

2 *the beginning of the article* OPENING, introduction, start, first part, preamble, opening statement. ANTONYMS end, conclusion.

3 **(beginnings)** *the therapy has its beginnings in China* ORIGIN, source, roots, starting point, birthplace, cradle, spring, fountainhead; genesis, creation; *literary* fount, well spring.

begrudge verb **1** *she begrudged Brian his affluence* ENVY, resent, grudge.

2 *don't begrudge the cost* RESENT, feel aggrieved about, feel bitter about, be annoyed about, be resentful of, grudge, mind, object to, take exception to, regret.

beguile verb **1** *she was beguiled by his beauty* CHARM, attract, enchant, entrancFe, win over, woo, captivate, bewitch, spellbind, dazzle, hypnotize, mesmerize, seduce. See note at TEMPT. ANTONYM repel.

begin
inaugurate
commence
initiate
launch
start
set in motion
set things moving
get under way
kick off
get going
go ahead
take the first step
lay the first stone
start/get/set the ball rolling
put one's shoulder to the wheel
put one's hand to the plow
get down to business
get off the ground
take the plunge
get the show on the road
fire away
get moving
get cracking
get down to it
get to it
get one's finger out
make a start
make a beginning
make the first move
get off one's backside
buckle down
lead up to
build up to
reach the turning point
decelerate
slow down
interrupt
discontinue
cut short
nip in the bud
wind up
put an end to
put a stop to
bring to a stop
bring to an end
bring to a halt
bring to a standstill
bring to a close
draw to a close
come to an end
come to a head
reach a finale
shut down
halt
end
close
stop
cease
finish
deactivate
terminate
conclude
climax
culminate
end

2 *the program has been beguiling children for years* ENTERTAIN, amuse, delight, please, occupy, absorb, engage, distract, divert, fascinate, enthrall, engross. ANTONYM bore.

behalf PHRASE: **on behalf of/on someone's behalf 1** *I am writing on behalf of my client* AS A REPRESENTATIVE OF, as a spokesperson for, for, in the name of, in place of, on the authority of, at the behest of. **2** *a campaign on behalf of recycling* IN THE INTERESTS OF, in support of, for, for the benefit of, for the good of, for the sake of.

behave verb **1** *she behaved badly* CONDUCT ONESELF, act, acquit oneself, bear oneself; *formal* comport oneself; *archaic* deport oneself.

2 *the children behaved themselves* ACT CORRECTLY, act properly, conduct oneself well, be well-behaved, be good; be polite, show good manners, mind one's manners. ANTONYM misbehave.

behavior noun **1** *his behavior was inexcusable* CONDUCT, deportment, bearing, actions, doings; manners, ways; *formal* comportment.

2 *the behavior of these organisms* FUNCTIONING, action, performance, operation, working, reaction, response.

behead verb *dissidents were beheaded* DECAPITATE, cut/chop/lop someone's head off, guillotine.

behest noun *the plan is being pushed through the legislature at the behest of Congressman DeLay* INSTRUCTION, requirement, demand, insistence, bidding, request, wish, desire, will; command, injunction, order, decree, ruling, directive, mandate; *informal* say-so; *rare* rescript.

behind preposition **1** *he hid behind a tree* AT THE BACK/REAR OF, beyond, on the far/other side of, in back of. ANTONYM in front of.

2 *a guard ran behind him* AFTER, following, at the back/rear of, (hard) on the heels of, in the wake of. ANTONYM ahead of.

3 *he was behind the bombings* RESPONSIBLE FOR, at the bottom of, the cause of, the source of, the organizer of; to blame for, culpable of, guilty of.

4 *we're behind you all the way* SUPPORTING, backing, for, on the side of, in agreement with; financing; *informal* rooting for.

▸ adverb **1** *a man followed behind* AFTER, afterward, at the back/end, in the rear. ANTONYMS in front, ahead.

2 *I looked behind* OVER ONE'S SHOULDER, to/toward the back, to/toward the rear, backward. ANTONYM ahead.

3 *we're behind, so don't stop* LATE, running late, behind schedule, behindhand, not on time, behind time.

4 *he was behind with his subscription* IN ARREARS, overdue; late, unpunctual, behindhand.

▸ noun *informal he sat on his behind.* See BUTTOCKS.

PHRASE: **put something behind one** *they put last night's loss to the Orioles behind them* CONSIGN TO THE PAST, put down to experience, regard as water under the bridge, forget about, ignore.

behold verb *literary no eyes beheld them* SEE, observe, view, look at, watch, survey, witness, gaze at/upon, regard, contemplate, inspect, eye; catch sight of, glimpse, spot, spy, notice; *informal* clap eyes on, have/take a gander at, get a load of, eyeball; *literary* espy, descry.

▸ exclamation *archaic* *behold, the prince returns!* LOOK, see; *archaic* lo.

beholden adjective *he is beholden to no one in his determination to defend Malaysia's rights* INDEBTED, in someone's debt, obligated, under an obligation; grateful, owing a debt of gratitude.

behoove verb **1** *it behooves me to go* BE INCUMBENT ON, be obligatory for, be required of, be expected of, be appropriate for.

2 *it ill behooves them to comment* BEFIT, become, suit.

beige adjective *beige curtains* FAWN, pale brown, buff, sand, sandy, oatmeal, khaki, biscuit, coffee, coffee-colored, café au lait, camel, ecru.

being noun **1** *she is warmed by his very being* EXISTENCE, living, life, reality, actuality.

2 *God is alive in the being of man* SOUL, spirit, nature, essence, inner being, inner self, psyche; heart, bosom, breast; *Philosophy* quiddity, pneuma.

3 *an enlightened being* CREATURE, life form, living entity, living thing, soul, living soul, individual, person, human being, human.

belabor verb *don't belabor the point* OVERELABORATE, labor, dwell on, harp on about, hammer away at; overdo, overplay, overdramatize, make too much of, place too much emphasis on; *informal* beat to death, drag out, make a big thing of, blow out of proportion. ANTONYM understate.

belated adjective *a belated anniversary dinner* LATE, overdue, behindhand, behind time, behind schedule, delayed, tardy, unpunctual. ANTONYM early.

belch verb **1** *onions make me belch* BURP.

2 *the furnace belched flames* EMIT, give off, give out, pour out, discharge, disgorge, spew out, spit out, vomit, gush, cough up.

▸ noun *he gave a loud belch* BURP; *formal* eructation.

beleaguered adjective **1** *the beleaguered garrison* BESIEGED, under siege, blockaded, surrounded, encircled, beset, hemmed in, under attack.

2 *a beleaguered government* HARD-PRESSED, troubled, in difficulties, under pressure, under stress, with one's back to the wall, in a tight corner, in a tight spot, up against it; beset, assailed.

belie verb *his eyes belied his words* CONTRADICT, be at odds with, call into question, show/prove to be false, disprove, debunk, discredit, controvert, negate; *formal* confute. ANTONYMS testify to, reveal.

belief noun **1** *it's my belief that age is irrelevant* OPINION, view, conviction, judgment, thinking, way of thinking, idea, impression, theory, conclusion, notion. See note at OPINION.

2 *belief in God* FAITH, trust, reliance, confidence, credence. ANTONYMS disbelief, doubt.

3 *traditional beliefs* IDEOLOGY, principle, ethic, tenet, canon; doctrine, teaching, dogma, article of faith, creed, credo.

believable adjective *contestant number 3 tells the most believable anecdotes | she was completely believable in her role as a federal marshal* CREDIBLE, plausible, likely, tenable, able to hold water, conceivable, imaginable, convincing, creditable, probable, possible, feasible, reasonable, rational, sound, within the bounds of possibility, with a ring of truth. ANTONYM inconceivable.

THE RIGHT WORD

Believable is the most general of these terms, used to describe anything we accept as true, even in the absence of absolute proof (*a believable story about why she was late*). **Credible** also means worthy of belief or confidence and is often used interchangeably with *believable*, but it goes one step further: a *credible* excuse is one that is supported by known facts. **Creditable**, often confused with *credible*, at one time meant worthy of belief but nowadays is used to mean respectable or decent, deserving of honor, reputation, or esteem (*leading a creditable life*). Something that is **convincing** is *believable* because it overcomes doubts or opposition (*a convincing performance*), while something that is **plausible** may appear to be convincing or believable on the surface, but may not be so upon closer examination. **Valid** means legally sound, just, or authoritative; a *valid* criticism seldom provokes opposition. **Cogent**, on the other hand, means having the power to convince; a *cogent* argument is believable because of its clear, forceful, or incisive presentation.

believe verb **1** *I don't believe you* BE CONVINCED BY, trust, have confidence in, consider honest, consider truthful.

2 *do you believe that story?* REGARD AS TRUE, accept, be convinced by, give credence to, credit, trust, put confidence in; *informal* swallow, buy, go for.

3 *I believe he worked for you* THINK, be of the opinion that, have an idea that, imagine, suspect, suppose, assume, presume, take it, conjecture, surmise, conclude, deduce, understand, be given to understand, gather, fancy, guess, dare say; *informal* reckon, figure; *archaic* ween. ANTONYM doubt.

PHRASE: **believe in 1** *she believed in God* BE CONVINCED OF THE EXISTENCE OF, be sure of the existence of. **2** *I believe in lots of exercise* HAVE FAITH IN, pin one's faith on, trust in, have every confidence in, cling to, set (great) store by, value, be convinced by, be persuaded by; subscribe to, approve of; *informal* swear by.

believer noun *a cause with few believers* DEVOTEE, adherent, disciple, follower, supporter. ANTONYMS infidel, skeptic.

belittle verb *Mr. Reese had been warned on two previous occasions to stop belittling his students* DISPARAGE, denigrate, run down, deprecate, depreciate, downgrade, play down, trivialize, minimize, make light of, pooh-pooh, treat lightly, scoff at, sneer at; *formal* derogate; *rare* misprize. ANTONYMS praise, magnify.

bellicose adjective *I cannot endorse the bellicose nature of your organization* BELLIGERENT, aggressive, hostile, warlike, warmongering, hawkish, antagonistic, pugnacious, truculent, confrontational, contentious, militant, combative; *informal* spoiling for a fight, scrappy. See note at HOSTILE. ANTONYM peaceable.

belligerent adjective **1** *a belligerent attitude* HOSTILE, aggressive, threatening, antagonistic, warlike, warmongering, hawkish, pugnacious, bellicose, truculent, confrontational, contentious, militant, combative; *informal* spoiling for a fight, trigger-happy, scrappy. See note at HOSTILE. ANTONYMS peaceable, friendly.

2 *belligerent nations* WARRING, at war, combatant, fighting, battling. ANTONYMS peaceful, neutral.

bellow verb *she bellowed in his ear* ROAR, shout, bawl, thunder, trumpet, boom, bark, yell, shriek, howl, scream; raise one's voice; *informal* holler. ANTONYM whisper.

▸ noun *a bellow of pain* ROAR, shout, bawl, bark, yell, yelp, shriek, howl, scream. ANTONYM whisper.

bellwether noun *a bellwether of change | Disney is a bellwether for the entire entertainment business* HARBINGER, herald, indicator, predictor.

belly noun *he scratched his belly* STOMACH, abdomen, paunch, middle, midriff, girth; *informal* tummy, tum, breadbasket, gut, guts, insides, pot, potbelly, beer belly, spare tire.

▸ verb *her skirt bellied out* BILLOW (OUT), bulge (out), balloon (out), bag (out); distend. ANTONYMS sag, flap.

belong verb **1** *the house belongs to his mother* BE OWNED BY, be the property of, be the possession of, be held by, be in the hands of.

2 *I belong to a book club* BE A MEMBER OF, be in, be affiliated to/with, be allied to, be associated with, be linked to, be an adherent of.

3 *the atlas belongs with the reference books* BE CLASSED, be classified, be categorized, be included, have a place, be located, be situated, be found, lie.

4 *she doesn't belong here* FIT IN, be suited to, have a rightful place, have a home; *informal* go, click.

belonging noun *a sense of belonging* AFFILIATION, acceptance, association, attachment, integration, closeness; rapport, fellow feeling, fellowship. ANTONYM alienation.

belongings plural noun *she could fit all her belongings in one bag* POSSESSIONS, effects, worldly goods, assets, chattels, property; *informal* gear, tackle, kit, things, stuff.

beloved adjective *her beloved brother* DARLING, dear, dearest, precious, adored, much loved, cherished, treasured, prized, highly regarded, admired, esteemed, worshiped, revered, venerated, idolized. ANTONYM hated.

▸ noun *he watched his beloved* SWEETHEART, love, darling, dearest, lover, girlfriend, boyfriend, young lady, young man, beau, lady friend; *informal* steady, main squeeze, swain; *archaic* paramour, doxy.

below preposition **1** *the water rushed below them* BENEATH, under, underneath, further down than, lower than. ANTONYMS above, over.

2 *the result is below average* LESS THAN, lower than, under, not as much as, smaller than. ANTONYMS above, more than.

3 *a captain is below a major* LOWER THAN, under, inferior to, subordinate to, subservient to. ANTONYM above.

▸ adverb **1** *I could see what was happening below* FURTHER DOWN, lower down, in a lower position, underneath, beneath.

2 *read the statements below* UNDERNEATH, following, further on, at a later point.

belt noun **1** *the belt of her coat* SASH, girdle, strap, cummerbund, band; *literary* cincture; *historical* baldric.

2 *farmers in the cotton belt* REGION, area, district, zone, sector, territory; tract, strip, stretch.

▸ verb **1** *she belted them in* FASTEN, tie, bind; *literary* gird.

2 *informal a guy belted him in the face* HIT, strike, smack, slap, bang, beat, punch, thump; *informal* clout, bash, whack, thwack, wallop, sock, clobber, bop, larrup, slug; *archaic* smite.

PHRASE: **below the belt** *bringing up Dana's past to the boss was below the belt* UNFAIR, unjust, unacceptable, inequitable; unethical, unprincipled, immoral, unscrupulous, unsporting, sneaky, dishonorable, dishonest, underhanded; *informal* lowdown, dirty.

bemoan verb *it does no good to bemoan the loss of that job* LAMENT, bewail, mourn, grieve over, sorrow over, regret, cry over; deplore, complain about; *archaic* plain over. See note at MOURN. ANTONYMS rejoice at, applaud.

bemused adjective *bemused expressions on their faces* BEWILDERED, confused, puzzled, perplexed, baffled, mystified, nonplussed, muddled, befuddled, dumbfounded, at sea, at a loss, taken aback, disoriented, disconcerted; *informal* flummoxed, bamboozled, clueless, fazed, discombobulated.

bench noun **1** *he sat on a bench* PEW, stall, settle, seat; bleacher.

2 *a laboratory bench* WORKBENCH, work table, worktop, work surface, counter.

3 *the bench heard the evidence* JUDGES, magistrates, judiciary; court.

▸ verb *the coach benched him for two games* SIDELINE, sit out, cut.

benchmark noun *the settlement became the benchmark for all future negotiations* STANDARD, point of reference, gauge, guide, guideline, guiding principle, norm, touchstone, yardstick, barometer, indicator, measure, model, exemplar, pattern, criterion, specification, convention.

bend verb **1** *the frames can be bent to fit your face* CURVE, angle, hook, bow, arch, flex, crook, hump, warp, contort, distort, deform. ANTONYM straighten.

2 *the highway bends to the left* TURN, curve, incline, swing, veer, deviate, diverge, fork, change course, curl, loop.

3 *he bent down to tie his shoe* STOOP, bow, crouch, hunch, lean down/over. ANTONYM straighten up.

4 *they want to bend me to their will* MOLD, shape, manipulate, direct, force, press, influence, incline, sway.

▸ noun *he came to a bend in the road* CURVE, turn, corner, jog, kink, dogleg, oxbow, zigzag, angle, arc, crescent, twist, crook, deviation, deflection, loop, hairpin turn, hairpin.

PHRASE: **bend over backwards** *informal we've bent over backwards to give you a second chance* TRY ONE'S HARDEST, do one's best, do one's utmost, do all one can, give one's all, make every effort; *informal* do one's damnedest, go all out, pull out all the stops, bust a gut, move heaven and earth.

beneath preposition **1** *we sat beneath the trees* UNDER, underneath, below, at the foot of, at the bottom of; lower than. ANTONYM above.

2 *made to feel beneath them* INFERIOR TO, below, not so important as, lower in status than, subordinate to, subservient to. ANTONYM above.

3 *such an attitude was beneath her* UNWORTHY OF, unbecoming to, degrading to, below. ANTONYM above.

▸ adverb *sand with rock beneath* UNDERNEATH, below, further down, lower down. ANTONYM above.

benediction noun 1 *the priest pronounced the benediction* BLESSING, prayer, invocation; grace, benedicite.

2 *filled with heavenly benediction* BLESSEDNESS, beatitude, bliss, grace.

benefactor, **benefactress** noun *an anonymous benefactor* PATRON, supporter, backer, sponsor; donor, contributor, subscriber; *informal* angel.

beneficent adjective *our wonderful and beneficent Aunt Astrid* BENEVOLENT, charitable, altruistic, humanitarian, neighborly, public-spirited, philanthropic; generous, kind, magnanimous, munificent, unselfish, unstinting, openhanded, liberal, lavish, bountiful; *literary* bounteous. ANTONYMS stingy, mean.

beneficial adjective *ladybugs and other species beneficial to the garden | this information has been highly beneficial* ADVANTAGEOUS, favorable, helpful, useful, of use, of benefit, of assistance, valuable, of value, profitable, rewarding, gainful. ANTONYMS detrimental, disadvantageous.

beneficiary noun *her beneficiaries include several godchildren | about three in five Medicare beneficiaries do not have dependable drug coverage* HEIR, heiress, inheritor, legatee; recipient, receiver, payee, donee, assignee; *Law* devisee, grantee.

benefit noun 1 *for the benefit of others* GOOD, sake, welfare, well-being, advantage, comfort, ease, convenience; help, aid, assistance, service; profit. ANTONYM detriment.

2 *the benefits of working for a large firm* ADVANTAGE, reward, merit, boon, blessing, virtue; bonus; value; *informal* perk; *formal* perquisite. ANTONYMS drawback, disadvantage.

3 *have you applied for this benefit?* SOCIAL SECURITY, welfare, assistance, employment insurance, unemployment, food stamps; charity, donations, gifts, financial assistance.

4 *we have four tickets for tonight's benefit* FUNDRAISER, fundraising event, charity affair, charity event.

▸ verb 1 *the deal benefited them both* BE ADVANTAGEOUS TO, be beneficial to, be of advantage to, be to the advantage of, profit, do good to, be of service to, serve, be useful to, be of use to, be helpful to, be of help to, help, aid, assist, be of assistance to; better, improve, strengthen, boost, advance, further. ANTONYM damage.

2 *they may **benefit from** the scheme* PROFIT FROM, gain from, reap benefits from, reap reward(s) from, make money from; make the most of, exploit, turn to one's advantage, put to good use, do well out of; *informal* cash in on, make a killing from. ANTONYM suffer.

benevolence noun *the benevolence of local businesses* KINDNESS, kindheartedness, bigheartedness, goodness, goodwill, charity, altruism, humanitarianism, compassion, philanthropy; generosity, magnanimity, munificence, unselfishness, openhandedness, beneficence; *literary* bounty, bounteousness. See note at MERCY. ANTONYMS spite, miserliness.

benevolent adjective 1 *a benevolent patriarch* KIND, kindly, kindhearted, bighearted, good-natured, good, benign, compassionate, caring, altruistic, humanitarian, philanthropic; generous, magnanimous, munificent, unselfish, openhanded, beneficent; *literary* bounteous. ANTONYMS unkind, tightfisted.

2 *a benevolent institution* CHARITABLE, nonprofit, not-for-profit; *formal* eleemosynary.

benign adjective 1 *a benign grandfatherly role* KINDLY, kind, warmhearted, good-natured, friendly, warm, affectionate, agreeable, genial, congenial, cordial, approachable, tenderhearted, gentle, sympathetic, compassionate, caring, well-disposed, benevolent. ANTONYMS unfriendly, hostile.

2 *a benign climate* TEMPERATE, mild, gentle, balmy, soft, pleasant, favorable; healthy, wholesome, salubrious. ANTONYMS harsh, unhealthy, unfavorable.

3 *Medicine a benign tumor* HARMLESS, nonmalignant, noncancerous; *Medicine* benignant. ANTONYM malignant.

bent adjective *the bucket had a bent handle* TWISTED, crooked, warped, contorted, deformed, misshapen, out of shape, irregular; bowed, arched, curved, angled, hooked, kinked; *informal* pretzeled.

▸ noun *an artistic bent* INCLINATION, leaning, tendency; talent, gift, flair, aptitude, facility, skill, capability, capacity; predisposition, disposition, instinct, orientation, predilection, proclivity, propensity.

PHRASE: **bent on** *he's bent on going to law school* INTENT ON, determined on, set on, insistent on, resolved on, hell-bent on; committed to, single-minded about, obsessed with, fanatical about, fixated on.

bequeath verb *I **bequeath** the northern campgrounds **to** the Yellow Birch Fishing Club* LEAVE TO, leave in one's will to, hand on/down to, will to, make over to, pass on to, entrust to, grant to, transfer to; donate to, give to; endow on, bestow on, confer on; *Law* demise to, devise to, convey to.

bequest noun *they received a bequest of more than $300,000* LEGACY, inheritance, endowment, settlement; estate, heritage; bestowal; *Law* devise; *Law, dated* hereditament.

berate verb *she berates him so often, he barely hears the words anymore* SCOLD, rebuke, reprimand, reproach, reprove, admonish, chide, criticize, upbraid, take to task, read someone the riot act, haul over the coals; castigate; *informal* tell off, give someone a talking-to, give someone what for, dress down, give someone a dressing-down, give someone a tongue-lashing, rap over the knuckles, bawl out, come down on, tear into, blast; ream out, chew out, zing, take to the woodshed; *dated* call down, rate; *rare* reprehend. See note at SCOLD. ANTONYM praise.

bereavement noun *slowly getting over his bereavement* LOSS, deprivation, dispossession, privation; grief, sorrow, sadness, suffering.

bereft adjective *are you totally **bereft of** common sense?* DEPRIVED OF, robbed of, stripped of, devoid of, bankrupt of; wanting, in need of, lacking, without; *informal* minus, sans, clean out of.

berry noun FRUIT. See table on page 80.

berserk adjective *one of the inmates is berserk* FRENZIED, raving, wild, out of control, amok, on the rampage, frantic, crazy, raging, insane, out of one's mind, hysterical, mad, crazed, maniacal, manic; *informal* bananas, bonkers, nuts, loco, hyper, postal.

berth noun 1 *a four-berth cabin* BUNK, bed, cot, couch, hammock.

BERRIES

akala	jostaberry
aronia berry	juneberry
barberry	juniper berry
bearberry	kiwi
bilberry	lingonberry
black currant	loganberry
black raspberry	maidenhair berry
blackberry	marionberry
blueberry	marlberry
boysenberry	mayhaw
buffalo berry	mulberry
candleberry	nectarberry
cape gooseberry	olallieberry
checkerberry	passionberry
Chinese wolfberry	raspberry
chokeberry	red currant
chokecherry	salmonberry
cloudberry	saskatoon berry
cowberry	serviceberry
cranberry	silvanberry
crowberry	squashberry
darrowberry	strawberry
dewberry	tayberry
elderberry	thimbleberry
fraise des bois	tummelberry
golden raspberry	white currant
gooseberry	whortleberry
grapes	wild blueberry
hackberry	wild strawberry
huckleberry	wineberry
hurtleberry	youngberry

2 *the vessel left its berth* MOORING, dock, slip, anchorage; wharf, pier, jetty, quay.

▸ verb *they berthed at a jetty in Ram's Head Bay* DOCK, moor, land, tie up, make fast.

PHRASE: **give someone/something a wide berth** *they learned to give those gang members a wide berth* AVOID, shun, keep away from, stay away from, steer clear of, keep at arm's length, have nothing to do with; dodge, sidestep, circumvent, skirt around.

beseech verb *literary we beseech your help in permitting us the right to live in a country where human rights are respected* IMPLORE, beg, entreat, importune, plead with, appeal to, exhort, call on, supplicate, importune, pray to, ask, request, petition; *rare* obtest, impetrate, obsecrate. See note at BEG.

beset verb 1 *he is beset by fears* PLAGUE, bedevil, assail, beleaguer, afflict, torment, rack, oppress, trouble, worry, harass, dog, harry.

2 *they were beset by enemy forces* SURROUND, besiege, hem in, shut in, fence in, box in, encircle. See note at ATTACK.

beside preposition 1 *Kate walked beside him* ALONGSIDE, by/at the side of, next to, parallel to, abreast of, at someone's elbow; adjacent to, next door to, cheek by jowl with; bordering, abutting, neighboring.

2 *beside Paula, she felt clumsy* COMPARED WITH/TO, in comparison with/to, by comparison with, next to, against, contrasted with, in contrast to/with. PHRASES: **beside oneself** *she was beside herself with worry* DISTRAUGHT, overcome, out of one's mind, frantic, desperate, distracted, at one's wits' end, frenzied, wound up, worked up; hysterical, unhinged, mad, crazed. **beside the point.** See POINT[1].

besides preposition *who did you ask besides Mary?* IN ADDITION TO, as well as, over and above, above and beyond, on top of; apart from, other than, aside from, but for, save for, not counting, excluding, not including, except, with the exception of, excepting, leaving aside; *informal* outside of.

▸ adverb 1 *there's a lot more besides* IN ADDITION, as well, too, also, in/into the bargain, on top of that, to boot; *archaic* therewithal.

2 *besides, he's always late* FURTHERMORE, moreover, further; anyway, anyhow, in any case, be that as it may; *informal* what's more, anyways.

besiege verb 1 *the Romans besieged Carthage* LAY SIEGE TO, beleaguer, blockade, surround; *archaic* invest.

2 *fans besieged his hotel* SURROUND, mob, crowd around, swarm around, throng around, encircle. See note at ATTACK.

3 *guilt besieged him* OPPRESS, torment, torture, rack, plague, afflict, haunt, harrow, hound, beset, beleaguer, trouble, bedevil, prey on.

4 *he was besieged with requests* OVERWHELM, inundate, deluge, flood, swamp, snow under; bombard.

besmirch verb *literary I'm not trying to besmirch the victim, but the woman had an extensive history of drug-related arrests* SULLY, tarnish, blacken, drag through the mud/mire, stain, taint, smear, disgrace, dishonor, bring discredit to, damage, debase, ruin; slander, malign, defame; *literary* besmear, smirch; *archaic* breathe on. ANTONYMS honor, enhance.

besotted adjective *the poor boy is so obviously besotted with Miss O'Toole* INFATUATED WITH, smitten with, in love with, head over heels in love with, obsessed with; doting on, greatly enamored of; *informal* swept off one's feet by, crazy about, mad about, wild about, carrying a torch for, gaga about/for/over, stuck on, gone on.

bespeak verb *a tree-lined road which bespoke money* INDICATE, be evidence of, be a sign of, denote, point to, testify to, evidence, reflect, demonstrate, show, manifest, display, signify; reveal, betray; *informal* spell; *literary* betoken. ANTONYM belie.

best adjective 1 *the best hotel in Rhode Island* FINEST, greatest, top, foremost, leading, preeminent, premier, prime, first, chief, principal, supreme, of the highest quality, superlative, par excellence, unrivaled, second to none, without equal, nonpareil, unsurpassed, peerless, matchless, unparalleled, unbeaten, unbeatable, optimum, optimal, ultimate, incomparable, ideal, perfect; highest, record-breaking; *informal* star, number-one, a cut above the rest, top-drawer, the Cadillac of, the Rolls-Royce of. ANTONYM worst.

2 *do whatever you think best* MOST ADVANTAGEOUS, most useful, most suitable, most fitting, most appropriate; most prudent, most sensible, most advisable.

▸ adverb 1 *the best-dressed man* TO THE HIGHEST STANDARD, in the best way. ANTONYM worst.

2 *the food he liked best* MOST, to the highest/greatest degree. ANTONYM least.

3 *this is best done at home* MOST ADVANTAGEOUSLY, most usefully, most suitably, most fittingly, most appropriately; most sensibly, most prudently, most wisely; better.

▸ noun 1 *only the best will do* FINEST, choicest, top, cream, choice, prime, elite, crème de la crème, flower, jewel in the crown, nonpareil; *informal* tops, pick of the bunch.

2 *she dressed in her best* BEST CLOTHES, finery, Sunday best; *informal* glad rags.

3 *give her my best* BEST WISHES, regards, kind/kindest regards, greetings, compliments, felicitations, respects; love.

▸ verb *informal she was not to be bested* DEFEAT, beat, get the better of, outdo, outwit, outsmart, worst, be more than a match for, prevail over, vanquish, trounce, triumph over; surpass, outclass, outshine, put someone in the shade, overshadow, eclipse; *informal* lick.

PHRASES: **do one's best** *we'll do our best to make sure you get a good education* DO ONE'S UTMOST, try one's hardest, make every effort, do all one can, give one's all; *informal* bend over backwards, do one's damnedest, go all out, pull out all the stops, bust a gut, break one's neck, move heaven and earth. **had best** *you had best check the pantry for moths* OUGHT TO, should.

bestial adjective *Stanley's bestial behavior* SAVAGE, brutish, brutal, barbarous, barbaric, cruel, vicious, violent, inhuman, subhuman; depraved, degenerate, perverted, debauched, immoral, warped. ANTONYMS civilized, humane.

bestir PHRASE: **bestir oneself** *I doubt he would bestir himself even if the Queen of England showed up* EXERT ONESELF, make an effort, rouse oneself, get going, get moving, get on with it; *informal* shake a leg, look lively, get cracking, get off one's backside.

bestow verb *the honor* ***bestowed upon*** *him* CONFER ON, grant, accord, afford, endow someone with, vest in, present, award, give, donate to, entrust with, vouchsafe. See note at GIVE.

bestride verb 1 *the oil field bestrides the border* EXTEND ACROSS, lie on both sides of, straddle, span, bridge.

2 *he bestrode his horse* STRADDLE, bestraddle, sit/stand astride; mount, get on, get astride.

3 *Italy bestrode Europe in opera* DOMINATE, tower over/above.

best seller noun *another best seller for Michener* BLOCKBUSTER, great success, hit, smash hit, smash, chart-topper, chart-buster, megahit. ANTONYMS failure, flop.

best-selling adjective *the year's best-selling CD* VERY SUCCESSFUL, very popular, boffo; number-one, chart-topping, hit.

bet verb 1 *he bet $10 on the favorite* WAGER, gamble, stake, risk, venture, hazard, chance; put/lay money, speculate.

2 *informal I bet it was your idea* BE CERTAIN, be sure, be convinced, be confident; expect, predict, forecast, guess.

▸ noun 1 *a $20 bet* WAGER, gamble, stake, ante.

2 *informal my bet is that they'll lose* PREDICTION, forecast, guess; opinion, belief, feeling, view, theory.

3 *informal your best bet is to go early* OPTION, choice, alternative, course of action, plan.

bête noire noun *add 'lumpy oatmeal' to his list of bêtes noires* BUGBEAR, PET PEEVE, anathema, thorn in one's side/flesh, bane of one's life, bugaboo, pain, pest. ANTONYM favorite.

betide verb *literary not knowing what would betide* HAPPEN, occur, take place, come about, transpire, arise, chance; result, ensue, follow, develop, supervene; *informal* go down; *formal* eventuate; *literary* come to pass, befall; *archaic* hap.

betoken verb *literary* 1 *a small gift betokening regret* INDICATE, be a sign of, be evidence of, evidence, manifest, mean, signify, denote, represent, show, demonstrate, bespeak.

2 *the blue sky betokened a day of good weather* FORETELL, signal, give notice of, herald, proclaim, prophesy, foreshadow, presage, be a harbinger of, portend, augur, be an omen of, be a sign of, be a warning of, warn of, bode; *literary* foretoken, forebode.

betray verb 1 *he betrayed his own brother* BE DISLOYAL TO, be unfaithful to, double-cross, cross, break faith with, inform on/against, give away, denounce, sell out, stab in the back, break one's promise to; *informal* rat on, fink on, sell down the river, squeal on, rat on/out, finger. ANTONYM be loyal to.

2 *he betrayed a secret* REVEAL, disclose, divulge, tell, give away, leak; unmask, expose, bring out into the open; let slip, let out, let drop, blurt out; *informal* blab, spill, kiss and tell. ANTONYMS conceal, hide.

betrayal noun *betrayal in the workplace | the CIA leak was a serious act of betrayal* DISLOYALTY, treachery, bad faith, faithlessness, falseness, duplicity, deception, double-dealing; breach of faith, breach of trust, stab in the back; double-cross, sellout; *literary* perfidy. ANTONYM loyalty.

betrayer noun *when we find the betrayer, he'll wish he'd never been born* TRAITOR, backstabber, Judas, double-crosser; renegade, quisling, double agent, collaborator, informer, mole, stool pigeon; turncoat, defector; *informal* snake in the grass, stoolie, rat, scab, fink.

betrothal noun *dated the betrothal was announced on St. Swithin's Day* ENGAGEMENT, marriage contract; *archaic* espousal.

betrothed adjective *dated she is betrothed to a man of her parents' choosing* ENGAGED (TO BE MARRIED), promised/pledged in marriage; *literary* affianced; *archaic* plighted, espoused. ANTONYM unattached.

better adjective 1 *better facilities* SUPERIOR, finer, of higher quality; preferable; *informal* a cut above, head and shoulders above, ahead of the pack/field. ANTONYMS worse, inferior.

2 *there couldn't be a better time* MORE ADVANTAGEOUS, more suitable, more fitting, more appropriate, more useful, more valuable, more desirable. ANTONYM worse.

3 *are you better?* HEALTHIER, fitter, stronger; well, cured, healed, recovered; recovering, on the road to recovery, making progress, improving; *informal* on the mend. ANTONYMS worse, sicker.

▸ adverb 1 *I played better today* TO A HIGHER STANDARD, in a superior/finer way.

2 *this may suit you better* MORE, to a greater degree/extent.

3 *the money could be better spent* MORE WISELY, more sensibly, more suitably, more fittingly, more advantageously.

▸ verb 1 *he bettered the record* SURPASS, improve on, beat, exceed, top, cap, trump, eclipse.

2 *refugees who want to better their lot* IMPROVE, ameliorate, raise, advance, further, lift, upgrade, enhance. ANTONYM worsen.

betterment noun *Musharraf spoke of his desire for the betterment of Pakistan and its people* IMPROVEMENT, amelioration, advancement, change for the better, furtherance, upgrading, enhancement; reform, rectification.

between preposition **1** *Philip stood between his parents* IN THE SPACE SEPARATING, in the middle of, with one on either side; amid, amidst; *archaic* betwixt.

2 *the bond between Amy and her mother* CONNECTING, linking, joining; uniting, allying; among.

bevel noun *the bevel that borders the mirror* SLOPE, slant, angle, cant, miter, chamfer, bezel.

beverage noun *soda and other beverages* DRINK, liquid refreshment; *humorous* libation; *archaic* potation. See tables at SOFT DRINK, COCKTAIL, BEER, WINE, and LIQUOR.

bevy noun *a bevy of Vegas headliners* GROUP, crowd, herd, flock, horde, army, galaxy, assemblage, throng, company, gathering, band, body, pack, covey; knot, cluster; *informal* bunch, gaggle, posse.

bewail verb *they bewailed the loss of their cherished freedoms* LAMENT, bemoan, mourn, grieve over, sorrow over, cry over; deplore, complain about, wail about; *archaic* plain over. ANTONYMS rejoice at, applaud.

beware verb *there are loose rocks underfoot, so beware!* BE ON YOUR GUARD, watch out, look out, be alert, be on the lookout, keep your eyes open/peeled, keep an eye out, keep a sharp lookout, be on the qui vive; take care, be careful, be cautious, watch your step; *Golf* fore.

bewilder verb *Sally's words bewildered him* BAFFLE, mystify, bemuse, perplex, puzzle, addle, confuse, confound; *informal* flummox, faze, stump, beat, fox, make someone scratch their head, be all Greek to, floor, discombobulate. ANTONYM enlighten.

bewildered adjective *she looked completely bewildered* BAFFLED, mystified, bemused, perplexed, puzzled, confused, nonplussed, dumbfounded, at sea, at a loss, disorientated, taken aback; *informal* flummoxed, bamboozled; discombobulated.

bewitch verb **1** *the villagers were certain that Ramara had bewitched him* CAST/PUT A SPELL ON, enchant; possess, curse, hex; *archaic* witch.

2 *we were bewitched by the surroundings* CAPTIVATE, enchant, entrance, enrapture, charm, beguile, delight, fascinate, enthrall. ANTONYM repel.

beyond preposition **1** *beyond the trees* ON THE FAR SIDE OF, on the other side of, further away than, behind, past, after, over.

2 *inflation beyond 10 percent* GREATER THAN, more than, exceeding, in excess of, above, over and above, above and beyond, upwards of.

3 *little beyond food was provided* APART FROM, except, other than, besides; *informal* outside of; *formal* save.

▸ adverb *a house with a garden beyond* FURTHER AWAY, further off.

bias noun **1** *he accused the media of bias* PREJUDICE, partiality, partisanship, favoritism, unfairness, one-sidedness; bigotry, intolerance, discrimination, leaning, tendency, inclination, predilection. ANTONYM impartiality.

2 *a dress cut on the bias* DIAGONAL, cross, slant, angle.

▸ verb *this may have biased the result* PREJUDICE, influence, color, sway, weight, predispose; distort, skew, slant.

THE RIGHT WORD

Bias is a predisposition either for or against something; one can have a *bias* against police officers or a *bias* for French food and wines. **Partiality**, on the other hand, is a favorable *bias* (*the partiality of parents for their own children; the partiality of Americans for fast food*), while **prejudice** implies a preconceived and usually negative judgment or opinion (*a decision motivated by racial prejudice*). **Bigotry** is an even stronger term, referring to an intense dislike and often violent hatred for the members of a particular race, religion, or ethnic group. **Narrow-mindedness** also points to rigidly preconceived ideas, but implies that they are the result of lack of education or understanding, rather than outright hostility (*her parents' narrow-mindedness prevented her from meeting any boys her age*). **Parochialism** is another term meaning excessive narrowness of mind (from "parochial," pertaining to a parish or parishes; that is, concerned mainly about local issues), while **provincialism** is narrow-mindedness that results from lack of exposure to cultural or intellectual activity, characteristic of a province or non-urban area. **Intolerance** is a broad term used to describe the inability to put up with almost anything (*parents' intolerance of their children's misbehavior*).

biased adjective *a biased view of the situation* PREJUDICED, partial, partisan, one-sided, blinkered; bigoted, intolerant, discriminatory; distorted, warped, twisted, skewed. See word spectrum at IMPARTIAL. ANTONYM impartial.

Bible noun **1** *he read the Bible* (HOLY) SCRIPTURES, Holy Writ, Good Book, Book of Books. See table.

2 *informal* (**bible**) *the taxi driver's bible* HANDBOOK, manual, ABCs, companion, guide, primer, vade mecum; *rare* enchiridion.

BOOKS OF THE BIBLE

Old Testament	Obadiah
Genesis	Jonah
Exodus	Micah
Leviticus	Nahum
Numbers	Habakkuk
Deuteronomy	Zephaniah
Joshua	Haggai
Judges	Zechariah
Ruth	Malachi
1 Samuel	1 Esdras
2 Samuel	2 Esdras
1 Kings	
2 Kings	**New Testament**
1 Chronicles	Matthew
2 Chronicles	Mark
Ezra	Luke
Nehemiah	John
Tobit	Acts of the Apostles
Judith	Romans
Esther	1 Corinthians
1 Maccabees	2 Corinthians
2 Maccabees	Galatians
3 Maccabees	Ephesians
Job	Philippians
Psalms	Colossians
Proverbs	1 Thessalonians
Ecclesiastes	2 Thessalonians
Song of Solomon/Song of Songs	1 Timothy
	2 Timothy
Wisdom of Solomon	Titus
Ecclesiasticus/Sirach	Philemon
Isaiah	Hebrews
Jeremiah	James
Lamentations	1 Peter
Baruch	2 Peter
Ezekiel	1 John
Daniel	2 John
Hosea	3 John
Joel	Jude
Amos	Revelation

bicker verb *they never bickered before they were married* QUARREL, argue, squabble, wrangle, fight, disagree, dispute, spar, have words, be at each other's throats, lock horns; *informal* scrap, spat. ANTONYM agree.

bicycle noun *her first bicycle was a Schwinn* BIKE, cycle, two-wheeler, mountain bike, ten-speed, racing bike, recumbent; *historical* penny-farthing, ordinary, velocipede.

bid[1] verb **1** *we bid $650 for the antique table* OFFER, make an offer of, put in a bid of, put up, tender, proffer, propose.

2 *she is* ***bidding for*** *a place on the UConn team* TRY TO OBTAIN, try to get, make a pitch for, make a bid for.

▸ noun **1** *a bid of $3,000* OFFER, tender, proposal.

2 *a bid to cut crime* ATTEMPT, effort, endeavor, try; *informal* crack, go, shot, stab; *formal* essay.

bid[2] verb **1** *she bid him farewell* WISH; utter.

2 *literary I did as he bade me* ORDER, command, tell, instruct, direct, enjoin, charge.

3 *literary he bade his companions enter* INVITE TO, ask to, request to.

biddable adjective *her heroines were neither flighty nor biddable* OBEDIENT, acquiescent, compliant, tractable, amenable, complaisant, cooperative, dutiful, submissive; *rare* persuasible. See note at OBEDIENT. ANTONYMS disobedient, uncooperative.

bidding noun *let's make it clear that I am not here at your bidding* COMMAND, order, instruction, decree, injunction, demand, mandate, direction, summons, call; wish, desire; request; *literary* behest; *archaic* hest.

bide PHRASE: **bide one's time** *he was more than willing to bide his time while she was engaged in her lessons* WAIT, sit tight; *informal* stick around, hold on, hang around.

big adjective **1** *a big building* LARGE, sizable, substantial, great, huge, immense, enormous, extensive, colossal, massive, mammoth, vast, tremendous, gigantic, giant, monumental, mighty, gargantuan, elephantine, titanic, mountainous, Brobdingnagian; towering, tall, high, lofty; outsize, oversized; goodly; capacious, voluminous, spacious; king-size(d), man-size, family-size(d), economy-size(d); *informal* jumbo, whopping, mega, humongous, monster, astronomical, ginormous; *formal* commodious. ANTONYMS small, little.

2 *clothing for big people* WELL-BUILT, sturdy, brawny, burly, broad-shouldered, muscular, muscly, rugged, Herculean, bulky, hulking, strapping, thickset, stocky, solid, hefty, large; tall, huge, gigantic; fat, stout, portly, plump, fleshy, paunchy, corpulent, obese; full-figured, big-boned, buxom; roly-poly, rotund, well-fed; *informal* hunky, beefy, husky; *literary* thewy. ANTONYMS small, slight, diminutive.

3 *my big sister* ELDER, older; grown-up, adult, mature, grown.

4 *a big decision* IMPORTANT, significant, major, momentous, weighty, consequential, far-reaching, key, vital, critical, crucial, life-and-death. ANTONYMS unimportant, minor, trivial.

5 *informal a big man in the government* POWERFUL, important, prominent, influential, high-powered, leading, preeminent; major-league. ANTONYMS unimportant, obscure.

6 *informal she has big plans* AMBITIOUS, far-reaching, grandiose, on a grand scale. ANTONYM modest.

7 *he's got a big heart* GENEROUS, kind, kindly, caring, compassionate, loving.

8 *informal East Coast bands are big across the country* POPULAR, successful, in demand, sought-after, all the rage; *informal* hot, in, cool, trendy, now, hip.

PHRASE: **too big for one's britches/boots** *informal sudden popularity has made Scully too big for his britches* CONCEITED, full of oneself, cocky, arrogant, cocksure, above oneself, self-important, puffed-up; vain, self-satisfied, pleased with oneself, smug, complacent; *informal* bigheaded; *literary* vainglorious.

bigheaded adjective *informal their bigheaded drummer is late for every rehearsal* CONCEITED, full of oneself, cocky, arrogant, cocksure, above oneself, self-important; vain, self-satisfied, puffed-up, pleased with oneself, smug, complacent; *informal* too big for one's britches/boots; *literary* vainglorious. ANTONYM modest.

bighearted adjective *Old Fezziwig was Scrooge's bighearted employer* GENEROUS, magnanimous, munificent, openhanded, bountiful, unstinting, unselfish, altruistic, charitable, philanthropic, benevolent; kind, kindly, kindhearted; *literary* bounteous. ANTONYMS mean, stingy.

bigot noun *he was denounced as an anti-Catholic bigot* CHAUVINIST, partisan, sectarian; racist, sexist, homophobe, dogmatist, jingoist. See note at ZEALOT.

bigoted adjective *his bigoted father-in-law* PREJUDICED, biased, partial, one-sided, sectarian, discriminatory; opinionated, dogmatic, intolerant, narrow-minded, blinkered, illiberal; racist, sexist, chauvinistic, jingoistic; warped, twisted, distorted. See note at BIAS. ANTONYM open-minded.

bigwig noun *informal the company bigwigs are flying in for the annual meeting* VIP, (very) important person, notable, dignitary, grandee; celebrity; *informal* somebody, heavyweight, big shot, big gun, big cheese, big fish, big kahuna, big wheel, top gun. ANTONYM nonentity.

bilious adjective **1** *I felt bilious* NAUSEOUS, sick, queasy, nauseated, green around the gills; *rare* qualmish. ANTONYM well.

2 *his bilious disposition.* See IRRITABLE.

3 *a bilious green and pink color scheme* NAUSEATING, sickly, distasteful, dreadful; lurid, garish, loud. ANTONYMS subtle, muted.

bilk verb *informal* See SWINDLE verb.

bill[1] noun **1** *a bill for $60* INVOICE, account, statement, list of charges; check, tab; *archaic* reckoning, score.

2 *a congressional bill* DRAFT LAW, proposed piece of legislation, proposal, measure.

3 *a $20 bill* BANKNOTE, note.

4 *he had been posting bills* POSTER, advertisement, ad, public notice, announcement; flyer, leaflet, handbill.

▸ verb **1** *please bill me for the work* INVOICE, charge, debit, send a statement to.

2 *the concert went ahead as billed* ADVERTISE, announce; schedule, program, timetable; slate.

3 *he was* ***billed as*** *the new Sean Connery* DESCRIBE AS, call, style, label, dub; promote as, publicize as, talk up as, hype as.

bill[2] noun *a bird's bill* BEAK, neb; *technical* mandibles.

billet noun *the troop's billet* QUARTERS, rooms; accommodations, lodging, housing; barracks, cantonment.

▸ verb *two soldiers were billeted here* ACCOMMODATE, quarter, put up, lodge, house; station, garrison.

billow noun 1 *billows of smoke* CLOUD, mass.

2 *archaic* *the billows that break upon the shore* WAVE, roller, breaker.

▸ verb 1 *her dress billowed around her* PUFF UP/OUT, balloon (out), swell, fill (out), belly out.

2 *smoke billowed from the chimney* SWIRL, spiral, roll, undulate, eddy; pour, flow.

billowing adjective ROLLING, swirling, undulating, surging, heaving, billowy, swelling, rippling.

bin noun *the onions go in a bin* CONTAINER, receptacle, holder; drum, canister, box, caddy, can, crate, chest, tin.

bind verb 1 *they bound our hands and feet* TIE (UP), fasten (together), hold together, secure, make fast, attach; rope, strap, lash, fetter, truss, hog-tie, tether. ANTONYMS untie, release.

2 *the experience had* ***bound*** *them* ***together*** UNITE, join, bond, knit together, draw together, yoke together. ANTONYM separate.

3 *we were bound by a rigid timetable* CONSTRAIN, restrict, restrain, trammel, tie hand and foot, tie down, fetter, shackle, hog-tie; hamper, hinder, inhibit.

4 *the edges are bound in a contrasting color* TRIM, hem, edge, border, fringe; finish; *archaic* purfle.

▸ noun *we're in a terrible bind* PREDICAMENT, awkward situation, difficult situation, quandary, dilemma, plight, spot, tight spot; *informal* Catch-22, fix, hole.

binder noun *a new binder for French class* FOLDER, ring binder, three-ring binder; notebook; *trademark* Trapper.

binding adjective *the agreement is binding* IRREVOCABLE, unalterable, inescapable, unbreakable, contractual; compulsory, obligatory, mandatory, incumbent.

binge noun 1 *she was afraid that Howie was on another of his all-night binges* DRINKING BOUT, debauch; *informal* bender, jag, toot, session; *dated* souse; *literary* bacchanal, bacchanalia; *archaic* wassail.

2 *a two-day shopping binge* SPREE; *informal* splurge, spendfest, orgy.

▸ verb *we binged on all the free food* OVERINDULGE, overeat, gorge; *informal* pig out.

biography noun *an unauthorized biography of Pat Nixon* LIFE STORY, life history, life, memoir; *informal* bio.

bird noun *feeding the birds* fowl; chick, fledgling, nestling; *informal* feathered friend, birdie; budgie; *technical* (**birds**) avifauna. See table.

birth noun 1 *Nick arrived just in time for the birth* CHILDBIRTH, delivery, nativity, birthing; blessed/happy event; *formal* parturition; *dated* confinement; *archaic* accouchement, childbed. ANTONYM death.

2 *the birth of science* BEGINNING(S), emergence, genesis, dawn, dawning, rise, start, onset, commencement. ANTONYMS demise, end.

3 *he is of noble birth* ANCESTRY, lineage, blood, descent, parentage, family, extraction, origin, genealogy, heritage, stock, kinship. PHRASE: **give birth to** *she gave birth to twins* HAVE, bear, produce, be delivered of, bring into the world; birth; *informal* drop; *dated* mother; *archaic* bring forth.

birthmark noun *a birthmark shaped like an apple* BEAUTY SPOT/MARK, mole, blemish, nevus.

birthright noun *the presidency of this firm is my birthright* PATRIMONY, inheritance, heritage; right, due, prerogative, privilege; primogeniture.

bisect verb *bisect the exterior angle* CUT IN HALF, halve, divide/cut/split in two, split down the middle; cross, intersect.

bishop noun *a meeting of the bishops* diocesan, metropolitan, suffragan, eparch, exarch; *formal* prelate.

bishopric noun *the local bishopric declared a lengthy statement* DIOCESE, see; episcopate, episcopacy, primacy.

bit noun 1 *a bit of bread* PIECE, portion, segment, section, part; chunk, lump, hunk, slice; fragment, scrap, shred, crumb, grain, speck; spot, drop, pinch, dash, soupçon, modicum; morsel, mouthful, bite, sample; iota, jot, tittle, whit, atom, particle, trace, touch, suggestion, hint, tinge; snippet, snatch, smidgen, tad. ANTONYM lot.

2 *wait a bit* MOMENT, minute, second, (little) while; *informal* sec, jiffy, jiff. PHRASES: **a bit** *he's a bit forgetful* SOMEWHAT, fairly, slightly, rather, quite, a little, moderately; *informal* pretty, sort of, kind of, kinda. **bit by bit** *bit by bit, the truth came out* GRADUALLY, little by little, in stages, step by step, piecemeal, slowly. **in a bit** *I'll see you in a bit* SOON, in a (little) while, in a second, in a minute, in a moment, shortly, in no time, before you know it, before long, directly; *informal* in a jiffy/jiff, in two shakes, in a snap; *literary* ere long, anon.

BIRDS OF NORTH AMERICA

blackbird	nightingale
bluebird	nightjar
blue jay	nuthatch
bobolink	oriole
bobwhite	ovenbird
bunting	phoebe
cardinal	pigeon
catbird	pipit
chat	raven
chickadee	redpoll
chuck-will's-widow	redstart
cowbird	robin
creeper	sapsucker
crossbill	shrike
crow	siskin
cuckoo	skylark
dickcissel	sparrow
dove	starling
finch	swallow
flicker	swift
flycatcher	tanager
gnatcatcher	thrasher
goldfinch	thrush
grackle	titmouse
grosbeak	towhee
hummingbird	veery
junco	vireo
kingbird	warbler
kingfisher	waterthrush
kinglet	waxwing
lark	wheatear
longspur	whippoorwill
magpie	woodpecker
martin	wood thrush
meadowlark	wren
mockingbird	yellowthroat
nighthawk	

See also tables at CHICKEN, PENGUIN, RAPTOR, SEABIRD, SHOREBIRD, and WATERFOWL.

bitch noun *informal* 1 *she's such a bitch* WITCH, shrew, vixen, she-devil, hellcat, harridan, termagant, virago, harpy; *archaic* grimalkin.

2 *a bitch of a job* NIGHTMARE; *informal* bastard, bummer, —— from hell, stinker.

▸ verb *they bitched about the price of oil* COMPLAIN, whine, grumble, grouse; *informal* whinge, moan, grouch, gripe.

bitchy adjective *informal*. See SPITEFUL.

bite verb 1 *the dog bit his arm* SINK ONE'S TEETH INTO, chew, munch, crunch, chomp, tear at, snap at.

2 *the acid* ***bites into*** *the copper* CORRODE, eat into, eat away at, burn (into), etch, dissolve.

3 *a hundred or so retailers should bite* ACCEPT, agree, respond; be lured, be enticed, be tempted; take the bait.

▸ noun 1 *he took a bite of his sandwich* MUNCH, chew, nibble, nip, snap.

2 *he ate it in two bites* MOUTHFUL, piece, bit, morsel.

3 *let's go out for* ***a bite*** A SNACK, a light meal, a quick meal; refreshments; *informal* a little something.

4 *we came back from the picnic covered in insect bites* STING.

5 *the appetizer had a fiery bite* PIQUANCY, pungency, spiciness, strong flavor, tang, zest, sharpness, tartness; *informal* kick, punch, edge, zing.

biting adjective 1 *biting comments* VICIOUS, harsh, cruel, savage, cutting, sharp, bitter, scathing, caustic, acid, acrimonious, acerbic, stinging; vitriolic, hostile, spiteful, venomous, mean, nasty; *informal* bitchy, catty. ANTONYMS mild, gentle.

2 *the biting wind* FREEZING, icy, arctic, glacial; bitter, piercing, penetrating, raw, wintry. ANTONYMS mild, balmy.

bitter adjective 1 *a bitter aftertaste* SHARP, acid, acidic, acrid, tart, sour, biting, unsweetened, vinegary; *technical* acerbic. ANTONYM sweet.

2 *a bitter woman* RESENTFUL, embittered, aggrieved, begrudging, rancorous, spiteful, jaundiced, ill-disposed, sullen, sour, churlish, morose, petulant, peevish, with a chip on one's shoulder. ANTONYMS magnanimous, content.

3 *a bitter blow* PAINFUL, unpleasant, disagreeable, nasty, cruel, awful, distressing, upsetting, harrowing, heartbreaking, heart-rending, agonizing, traumatic, tragic, chilling; *formal* grievous. ANTONYM welcome.

4 *a bitter wind* FREEZING, icy, arctic, glacial; biting, piercing, penetrating, raw, wintry. ANTONYMS warm, balmy.

5 *a bitter dispute* ACRIMONIOUS, virulent, angry, rancorous, spiteful, vicious, vitriolic, savage, ferocious, hate-filled, venomous, poisonous, acrid, nasty, ill-natured. ANTONYM amicable.

bitterness noun 1 *the bitterness of the medicine* SHARPNESS, acidity, acridity, tartness, sourness, harshness; *technical* acerbity. ANTONYM sweetness.

2 *there was no bitterness between them* RESENTMENT, rancor, indignation, grudge, spite, sullenness, sourness, churlishness, moroseness, petulance, pique, peevishness; ACRIMONY, hostility, malice, virulence, antipathy, antagonism, enmity, animus, friction, vitriol, hatred, loathing, venom, poison, nastiness, ill feeling, ill will, bad blood. ANTONYMS magnanimity, contentment, goodwill.

3 *the bitterness of war* TRAUMA, pain, agony, grief; unpleasantness, disagreeableness, nastiness; heartache, heartbreak, distress, desolation, despair, tragedy. ANTONYM delight.

bizarre adjective *bizarre sculptures* STRANGE, peculiar, odd, funny, curious, outlandish, outré, abnormal, eccentric, unconventional, unusual, unorthodox, queer, extraordinary; *informal* weird, wacky, bizarro, oddball, way out, kooky, freaky, off the wall, offbeat. ANTONYMS normal, conventional.

blabber verb *informal*. See BABBLE verb sense 1.

blabbermouth noun *informal* See CHATTERBOX.

black adjective 1 *a black horse* DARK, pitch-black, jet-black, coal-black, ebony, sable, inky. ANTONYM white.

2 *a black night* UNLIT, dark, starless, moonless, wan; *literary* tenebrous, Stygian. ANTONYMS clear, bright.

3 *thirty-seven percent of our advanced-study students are black.* See note below.

4 *the blackest day of the war* TRAGIC, disastrous, calamitous, catastrophic, cataclysmic, fateful, wretched, woeful, awful, terrible; *formal* grievous. ANTONYM joyful.

5 *Mary was in a black mood* MISERABLE, unhappy, sad, wretched, broken-hearted, heartbroken, grief-stricken, grieving, sorrowful, sorrowing, anguished, desolate, despairing, disconsolate, downcast, dejected, sullen, cheerless, melancholy, morose, gloomy, glum, mournful, doleful, funereal, dismal, forlorn, woeful, abject; *informal* blue; *literary* dolorous. ANTONYM cheerful.

6 *black humor* CYNICAL, macabre, weird, unhealthy, ghoulish, morbid, perverted, gruesome; *informal* sick.

7 *a black look* ANGRY, vexed, cross, irritated, incensed. See also ANGRY sense 1. ANTONYM pleased.

8 *archaic a black deed.* WICKED, evil, heinous, villainous, bad. See also WICKED sense 1. ANTONYM virtuous.

PHRASES: **black out** *he blacked out from the pain* FAINT, lose consciousness, pass out, swoon; *informal* go out. **black something out** *we blacked out our homes during the war* DARKEN, shade, turn off the lights in; keep the light out of. **in the black** *our business is finally in the black* SOLVENT, debt-free, out of debt, in credit, financially sound, able to pay one's debts, creditworthy. **black and white** 1 *a black-and-white picture* MONOCHROME, gray-scale. 2 *I wish to see the proposals in black and white* IN PRINT, printed, written down, set down, on paper, recorded, on record, documented. 3 *in black-and-white terms* CATEGORICAL, unequivocal, absolute, uncompromising, unconditional, unqualified, unambiguous, clear, clear-cut.

USAGE NOTE **black**

Black, designating Americans of African heritage, became the most widely used and accepted term in the 1960s and 1970s, replacing **Negro**. It is not usually capitalized: *black Americans*. Through the 1980s, the more formal **African American** replaced **black** in much usage, but both are now generally acceptable. **Afro-American**, an earlier alternative to **black**, is heard mostly in anthropological and cultural contexts. **Colored people**, common earlier in the twentieth century, is now usually regarded as derogatory, although the phrase survives in the full name of the NAACP, the National Association for the Advancement of Colored People. An inversion, **people of color**, has gained some favor, but is also used in reference to other nonwhite ethnic groups: *a gathering spot for African Americans and other people of color interested in reading about their cultures.*

---

blackball verb *Zabel could not support the group's intention to blackball Curtis* REJECT, debar, bar, ban, vote against, blacklist, exclude, shut out; ostracize, expel. ANTONYM admit.

blacken verb **1** *they blackened their faces* BLACK, darken; dirty, make sooty, make smoky, stain, grime, soil. ANTONYMS whiten, clean.

2 *the sky blackened* GROW/BECOME BLACK, darken, dim, grow dim, cloud over. ANTONYMS lighten, brighten.

3 *someone has blackened my name* SULLY, tarnish, besmirch, drag through the mud/mire, stain, taint, smear, disgrace, dishonor, bring discredit to, damage, ruin; slander, defame. ANTONYMS clear, honor.

blacklist verb *the club blacklisted Edwards soon after his arrest* BOYCOTT, ostracize, blackball, spurn, avoid, embargo, steer clear of, ignore; stigmatize; refuse to employ.

black magic noun *the practice of black magic is illegal in this county* SORCERY, witchcraft, wizardry, necromancy, the black arts, devilry; malediction, voodoo, witching, witchery.

blackmail noun *he was accused of blackmail* EXTORTION; *informal* hush money; *formal* exaction.

▸ verb **1** *he was blackmailing the murderer* EXTORT MONEY FROM, threaten; *informal* demand hush money from.

2 *she blackmailed me to work for her* COERCE, pressurize, pressure, force; *informal* lean on, put the screws on, twist someone's arm.

blackout noun **1** *there must have been a blackout—all the clocks are blinking* POWER FAILURE, power outage, brownout.

2 *a news blackout* SUPPRESSION, silence, censorship, gag order, reporting restrictions.

3 *he had a blackout* FAINTING SPELL, faint, loss of consciousness, passing out, swoon, collapse; *Medicine* syncope.

blah noun *informal* **(the blahs)** *looks like he's got a case of the blahs* THE DOLDRUMS, low spirits, a blue funk, depression.

▸ adjective **1** *just feeling kinda blah* LETHARGIC, unenthusiastic, listless, torpid. ANTONYMS energetic, enthusiastic.

2 *there are too many blah subplots* DULL, bland, unexciting, plain-vanilla. ANTONYMS interesting, exciting.

blame verb **1** *he always blames others* HOLD RESPONSIBLE, hold accountable, condemn, accuse, find/consider guilty, assign fault/liability/guilt to, indict, point the finger at, finger, incriminate; *archaic* inculpate. ANTONYM absolve.

2 *they* **blame** *youth crime* **on** *unemployment* ASCRIBE TO, attribute to, impute to, lay at the door of, put down to; *informal* pin.

▸ noun *he was cleared of all blame | Ullman took the blame* RESPONSIBILITY, guilt, accountability, liability, culpability, fault; *informal* rap.

blameless adjective *the company conceded that it was not entirely blameless* INNOCENT, guiltless, above reproach, irreproachable, unimpeachable, in the clear, exemplary, perfect, virtuous, pure, impeccable, faultless; *informal* squeaky clean, *trademark* Teflon. ANTONYM blameworthy.

blameworthy adjective *there is no longer any no doubt that Otis is the blameworthy individual* CULPABLE, reprehensible, indefensible, inexcusable, guilty, criminal, delinquent, wrong, evil, wicked; to blame, at fault, reproachable, responsible, answerable, erring, errant, in the wrong. ANTONYM blameless.

blanch verb **1** *the moonlight blanches her hair* TURN PALE, whiten, lighten, wash out, fade. ANTONYM darken.

2 *his face blanched* PALE, turn pale, turn white, whiten, lose its color, lighten, fade. ANTONYMS color, darken.

3 *blanch the spinach leaves* SCALD, boil briefly.

bland adjective **1** *bland food* TASTELESS, flavorless, insipid, weak, watery, spiceless; *informal* wishy-washy. ANTONYMS tangy, tasty.

2 *a bland film* UNINTERESTING, dull, boring, tedious, monotonous, monochrome, dry, drab, dreary, wearisome; unexciting, unimaginative, uninspiring, uninspired, lackluster, vapid, flat, stale, trite; *informal* blah, plain-vanilla, white-bread, banal, commonplace, humdrum, ho-hum, vacuous, wishy-washy. ANTONYMS interesting, stimulating.

3 *a bland expression* UNEMOTIONAL, emotionless, dispassionate, passionless; inexpressive, cool, impassive; expressionless, blank, wooden, stony, deadpan, hollow, undemonstrative, imperturbable. ANTONYMS emotional, expressive.

WORD NOTE **bland**

Here's an adj that the dictionaries are behind on. *Bland* was originally used of people to mean "suave, smooth, unperturbed, soothingly pleasing" (cf. *blandish, blandishment*), and of things to mean "soft, mild, pleasantly soothing," etc. Only incidentally did it mean "dull, insipid, flavorless." As of 2004, though, *bland* nearly always has a pejorative tinge. Outside of one special semi-medical idiom *(The ulcerous CEO was placed on a bland diet), bland* now tends to imply that whatever's described was trying to be more interesting, piquant, stirring, forceful, magnetic, or engaging than it actually ended up being. **—DFW**

---

blandishments plural noun *the blandishments of advertisers* FLATTERY, cajolery, coaxing, wheedling, persuasion, palaver, honeyed words, smooth talk, blarney; *informal* sweet talk, soft soap, buttering up, smarm.

blank adjective **1** *a blank sheet of paper* EMPTY, unmarked, unused, clear, free, bare, clean, plain. ANTONYM full.

2 *a blank face* EXPRESSIONLESS, deadpan, wooden, stony, impassive, unresponsive, poker-faced, vacuous, empty, glazed, fixed, lifeless, inscrutable. ANTONYM expressive.

3 *"What?" said Maxim, looking blank* BAFFLED, mystified, puzzled, perplexed, stumped, at a loss, stuck, bewildered, dumbfounded, nonplussed, bemused, lost, uncomprehending, at sea, confused; *informal* flummoxed, bamboozled.

4 *a blank refusal* OUTRIGHT, absolute, categorical, unqualified, complete, flat, straight, positive, certain, explicit, unequivocal, clear, clear-cut.

▸ noun *leave a blank where the address will go* SPACE, gap, blank space, empty space; lacuna.

blanket noun *a blanket of cloud* COVERING, layer, coating, carpet, overlay, cloak, mantle, veil, pall, shroud. See table.

▸ adjective *blanket coverage* complete, total, comprehensive, overall, general, mass, umbrella, inclusive, all-inclusive, all-around, wholesale, outright, across-the-board, sweeping, indiscriminate, thorough; universal, international, worldwide, global, nationwide, countrywide, coast-to-coast. ANTONYMS partial, piecemeal.

▸ verb *snow blanketed the mountains* COVER, coat, carpet, overlay; cloak, shroud, swathe, envelop; *literary* mantle.

BLANKETS

acrylic blanket	kambal
afghan	lap robe
baby blanket	Mackinaw blanket
buffalo robe	manta
button blanket	Navajo blanket
comforter	quilt
cotton blanket	receiving blanket
crib blanket	saddle blanket
down comforter	security blanket
duvet	serape
electric blanket	space blanket
fleece blanket	throw
Hudson's Bay blanket™	wool blanket
Indian blanket	

blare verb *sirens blared* BLAST, sound loudly, trumpet, bray, clamor, boom, blat, roar, thunder, bellow, resound. ANTONYM murmur.

▸ noun *the blare of the siren* BLAST, trumpeting, clamor, boom, roar, thunder, bellow, blat. ANTONYM murmur.

blaring adjective *the blaring horns and toxic fumes of city traffic* LOUD, noisy, overloud, deafening, strident; raucous, harsh, dissonant, discordant, cacophonous.

blarney noun *the cop actually fell for her blarney* SMOOTH TALK, honeyed words, flattery, blandishments, cajolery, coaxing, wheedling, persuasion, palaver; *informal* sweet talk, soft soap, smarm, buttering up; baloney, hogwash, bunk, malarkey.

blasé adjective *these children have learned to be blasé about the sound of gunfire* INDIFFERENT, unconcerned, uncaring, casual, nonchalant, offhand, uninterested, apathetic, unimpressed, unmoved, surfeited, jaded, unresponsive, phlegmatic; *informal* laid-back. ANTONYMS concerned, responsive.

blaspheme verb *would you dare to blaspheme in the House of the Lord?* SWEAR, curse, take the Lord's name in vain; *informal* cuss; *archaic* execrate.

blasphemous adjective *a blasphemous mock communion* SACRILEGIOUS, profane, irreligious, irreverent, impious, ungodly, godless. ANTONYM reverent.

blasphemy noun *the nuns would punish me at least three times a week for my blasphemy* PROFANITY, sacrilege, irreligion, irreverence, taking the Lord's name in vain, swearing, curse, cursing, impiety, desecration; *archaic* execration. ANTONYM reverence.

blast noun **1** *the blast from the bomb* SHOCK WAVE, pressure wave.

2 *Friday's blast killed two people* EXPLOSION, detonation, discharge, burst.

3 *a sudden blast of cold air* GUST, rush, gale, squall, wind, draft, waft, puff.

4 *the shrill blast of the trumpets* BLARE, wail, roar, screech, shriek, hoot, honk, beep.

5 *we had a blast* GOOD TIME, ball, riot.

▸ verb **1** *bombers were blasting enemy airfields* BLOW UP, bomb, blow to pieces, dynamite, shell, explode.

2 *guns were* ***blasting away*** FIRE, shoot, blaze, let fly, discharge.

3 *he blasted his horn* HONK, beep, toot, sound.

4 *radios blasting out pop music* BLARE, boom, roar, thunder, bellow, pump, shriek, screech.

5 *informal* *the opposition blasted the government over the deal.* See BERATE.

PHRASE: **blast off** *the rocket blasted off at 8:02* BE LAUNCHED, take off, lift off, leave the ground, become airborne, take to the air.

blasted adjective *informal*. See DAMNED sense 2.

blastoff noun *ten seconds to blastoff* LAUNCH, liftoff, takeoff, ascent, firing. ANTONYM touchdown.

blatant adjective *it was a blatant lie* FLAGRANT, glaring, obvious, undisguised, unconcealed, open; shameless, barefaced, naked, unabashed, unashamed, unblushing, brazen. ANTONYMS inconspicuous, shamefaced.

blather verb *he just blathered about his old girlfriends* PRATTLE, babble, chatter, twitter, prate, go on, run on, rattle on, yap, jabber, maunder, ramble, burble, drivel, blabber, gab; *informal* yak, yatter, yammer, talk a blue streak.

▸ noun *mindless blather* PRATTLE, chatter, twitter, babble, prating, gabble, jabber, rambling; *informal* yatter, twaddle, gobbledygook.

blaze noun **1** *firemen fought the blaze* FIRE, flames, conflagration, inferno, holocaust; forest fire, wildfire, bush fire.

2 *a blaze of light* GLARE, gleam, flash, burst, flare, streak, radiance, brilliance, beam.

▸ verb **1** *the fire blazed for hours* BURN, be alight, be on fire, be in flames, flame.

2 *headlights blazed* SHINE, flash, flare, glare, gleam, glint, dazzle, glitter, glisten.

blazon verb *their name is blazoned across the sails* DISPLAY, exhibit, present, spread, emblazon, plaster; announce, proclaim. See note at ANNOUNCE.

bleach verb *the blinds had been bleached by the sun* TURN WHITE, whiten, turn pale, blanch, lighten, fade, decolorize, peroxide. ANTONYM darken.

▸ noun *a bottle of bleach* chlorine bleach; *trademark* Clorox.

bleak adjective **1** *a bleak landscape* BARE, exposed, desolate, stark, desert, lunar, open, empty, windswept; treeless, without vegetation, denuded. ANTONYM lush.

2 *the future is bleak* UNPROMISING, unfavorable, unpropitious, inauspicious; discouraging, disheartening, depressing, dreary, dim, gloomy, black, dark, grim, hopeless, somber. ANTONYM promising.

3 *a bleak wind* COLD, bitter, biting, raw, freezing, icy.

bleary adjective *his eyes were bleary from exhaustion*

BLURRED, blurry, unfocused; fogged, clouded, dull, misty, watery, rheumy; *archaic* blear. ANTONYM clear.

WORD NOTE **bleary**

There is in the English language no better word for talking about hangovers. **–DA**

bleed verb **1** *his arm was bleeding* LOSE BLOOD, hemorrhage.

2 *the doctor bled him* DRAW BLOOD FROM; *Medicine* exsanguinate; *archaic* phlebotomize.

3 *one color bled into another* FLOW, run, seep, filter, percolate, leach.

4 *sap was bleeding from the trunk* FLOW, run, ooze, seep, exude, weep.

5 *the country was **bled dry** by poachers* DRAIN, sap, deplete, milk, exhaust.

6 *my heart **bleeds for** them* GRIEVE FOR, ache for, sorrow for, mourn for, lament for, feel for, suffer for; sympathize with, pity.

blemish noun **1** *not a blemish marred her skin* IMPERFECTION, flaw, defect, fault, deformity, discoloration, disfigurement; bruise, scar, pit, pock, pimple, blackhead, wart, scratch, cut, gash; mark, streak, spot, smear, speck, blotch, smudge, smut; birthmark, mole; *Medicine* stigma.

2 *the mayor's record is not without blemish* DEFECT, fault, failing, flaw, imperfection, foible, vice; shortcoming, weakness, deficiency, limitation; taint, blot, stain, dishonor, disgrace. ANTONYM virtue.

▸ verb **1** *nothing blemished the coast* MAR, spoil, impair, disfigure, blight, deface, mark, scar; ruin. ANTONYM enhance.

2 *his reign has been blemished by controversy* SULLY, tarnish, besmirch, blacken, blot, taint; spoil, mar, ruin, disgrace, damage, degrade, dishonor; *formal* vitiate.

blend verb **1** *blend the ingredients until smooth* MIX, mingle, combine, merge, fuse, meld, coalesce, integrate, intermix; stir, whisk, fold in; *technical* admix; *literary* commingle.

2 *the new buildings blend with the older ones* HARMONIZE, go (well), fit (in), be in tune, be compatible; coordinate, match, complement.

▸ noun *a blend of bananas, raisins, and ginger* MIXTURE, mix, combination, amalgamation, amalgam, union, marriage, fusion, meld, synthesis, concoction; *technical* admixture.

bless verb **1** *the chaplain blessed the couple* ASK/INVOKE GOD'S FAVOR FOR, give a benediction for; CONSECRATE, sanctify, dedicate (to God), make holy, make sacred; *formal* hallow. ANTONYM curse.

2 *bless the name of the Lord* PRAISE, worship, glorify, honor, exalt, pay homage to, venerate, reverence, hallow; *archaic* magnify.

3 *the gods **blessed** us **with** magical voices* ENDOW WITH, bestow with, furnish with, accord, give, favor with, grace with; confer on; *literary* endue with.

4 *I bless the day you came here* GIVE THANKS FOR, be grateful for, thank; appreciate. ANTONYM rue.

blessed adjective **1** *a blessed place* HOLY, sacred, hallowed, consecrated, sanctified; ordained, canonized, beatified. ANTONYM cursed.

2 *blessed are the meek* FAVORED, fortunate, lucky, privileged, enviable, happy. ANTONYM wretched.

blessing noun **1** *may God give us his blessing* PROTECTION, favor. ANTONYM condemnation.

2 *a special blessing from the priest* BENEDICTION, invocation, prayer, intercession; grace. ANTONYM anathema.

3 *she gave the plan her blessing* SANCTION, endorsement, approval, approbation, favor, consent, assent, agreement; backing, support; *informal* thumbs up, OK, nod.

4 *it was a blessing they didn't have far to go* GODSEND, boon, advantage, benefit, help, bonus, plus; stroke of luck, unmixed blessing, (lucky) break, windfall; *literary* benison. ANTONYM affliction.

blight noun **1** *potato blight* DISEASE, canker, infestation, fungus, mildew, mold.

2 *the blight of aircraft noise* AFFLICTION, scourge, bane, curse, plague, menace, misfortune, woe, trouble, ordeal, trial, nuisance, pest. ANTONYM blessing.

▸ verb **1** *a tree blighted by leaf curl* INFECT, mildew; kill, destroy.

2 *scandal blighted the careers of several politicians* RUIN, wreck, spoil, mar, frustrate, disrupt, undo, end, scotch, destroy, shatter, devastate, demolish; *informal* mess up, foul up, stymie.

blind adjective **1** *he has been blind since birth* SIGHTLESS, unsighted, visually impaired, visionless, unseeing; partially sighted, purblind; *informal* as blind as a bat. ANTONYM sighted.

2 *the government must be blind* IMPERCEPTIVE, unperceptive, insensitive, slow, obtuse, uncomprehending; stupid, unintelligent; *informal* dense, dim, thick, dumb, dopey, dozy. ANTONYM perceptive.

3 *he was **blind to** her shortcomings* UNMINDFUL OF, mindless of, careless of, heedless of, oblivious to, insensible to, unconcerned about, indifferent to. ANTONYM mindful.

4 *blind acceptance of conventional opinion* UNCRITICAL, unreasoned, unthinking, unconsidered, mindless, undiscerning, indiscriminate. ANTONYM discerning.

5 *a blind rage* IMPETUOUS, impulsive, uncontrolled, uncontrollable, wild, unrestrained, immoderate, intemperate, irrational, unbridled.

▸ verb **1** *he was blinded in a car crash* MAKE BLIND, deprive of sight, render sightless; put someone's eyes out.

2 *he was blinded by his faith* DEPRIVE OF JUDGMENT, deprive of perception, deprive of reason, deprive of sense.

3 *they try to blind you with science* OVERAWE, intimidate, daunt, deter, discourage, cow, subdue, dismay; disquiet, discomfit, unsettle, disconcert; disorient, stun, stupefy, confuse, bewilder, bedazzle, confound, perplex, overwhelm; *informal* faze, psych out.

▸ noun **1** *a window blind* SHADE, screen, sunshade, shutter, curtain, awning, canopy; louver, jalousie; Venetian blind, miniblind, vertical blind.

2 *some crook had sent the basketball tickets as a blind* DECEPTION, smokescreen, front, facade, cover, pretext, masquerade, feint, camouflage; trick, ploy, ruse, machination.

blindly adverb *they blindly followed Moscow policy* UNCRITICALLY, unthinkingly, mindlessly, indiscriminately.

blink verb **1** *his eyes did not blink* flutter, flicker, wink, bat.

2 *several red lights began to blink* FLASH, flicker, wink.

3 *no one even blinks at the estimated cost* BE SURPRISED, look twice; *informal* boggle.

4 *after a tense standoff, the union blinked* BACK DOWN, give in, knuckle under, submit, relent.

blinkered adjective *blinkered politicians must be challenged by the voters* NARROW-MINDED, inward-looking, parochial, provincial, insular, small-minded, close-minded, shortsighted; hidebound, illiberal, inflexible, entrenched, prejudiced. ANTONYM broad-minded.

bliss noun **1** *she gave a sigh of bliss* JOY, happiness, pleasure, delight, ecstasy, elation, rapture, euphoria. See note at RAPTURE. ANTONYM misery.

2 *religions promise perfect bliss after death* BLESSEDNESS, benediction, beatitude, glory, heavenly joy, divine happiness; heaven, paradise. ANTONYM hell.

blissful adjective *the blissful honeymooners* ECSTATIC, happy, euphoric, joyful, elated, rapturous, delighted, thrilled, overjoyed, joyous, on cloud nine, in seventh heaven, over the moon, on top of the world.

blister noun **1** *a blister on each heel* vesicle, vesication; pustule, abscess.

2 *check for blisters in the wall covering* BUBBLE, swelling, bulge, protuberance.

blistering adjective **1** *blistering heat* INTENSE, extreme, ferocious, fierce; SCORCHING, searing, blazing, burning, fiery; *informal* boiling, baking, roasting, sweltering. ANTONYMS mild, icy.

2 *a blistering attack on the government* SAVAGE, vicious, fierce, bitter, harsh, scathing, devastating, caustic, searing, vitriolic. ANTONYM mild.

3 *a blistering pace* VERY FAST, breakneck; *informal* blinding. ANTONYM leisurely.

blithe adjective **1** *a blithe disregard for the rules* CASUAL, indifferent, unconcerned, unworried, untroubled, uncaring, careless, heedless, thoughtless; nonchalant, blasé. ANTONYM thoughtful.

2 *literary his blithe, smiling face* HAPPY, cheerful, jolly, merry, joyful, joyous, blissful, ecstatic, euphoric, elated; *dated* gay. ANTONYM sad.

blitz noun **1** *the 1940 blitz on London* BOMBARDMENT, bombing, onslaught, barrage; attack, assault, raid, strike, blitzkrieg.

2 *an expensive new marketing blitz* CAMPAIGN, effort, operation, undertaking.

blizzard noun SNOWSTORM, whiteout, snow squall, snowfall; nor'easter, northeaster.

bloated adjective *bloated bellies* SWOLLEN, distended, tumefied, bulging, inflated, enlarged, expanded, dilated, puffed (up).

blob noun **1** *a blob of cold gravy* DROP, droplet, globule, bead, bubble; *informal* glob.

2 *a blob of ink* SPOT, dab, blotch, blot, dot, smudge; *informal* splotch.

bloc noun *a free-trade bloc* ALLIANCE, coalition, federation, confederation, league, union, partnership, axis, body, association, group.

block noun **1** *a block of cheese* CHUNK, hunk, lump, wedge, cube, brick, slab, bar, piece.

2 *an apartment block* BUILDING, complex, structure, development.

3 *a block of shares* BATCH, group, set, quantity.

4 *a block to Third World development* OBSTACLE, bar, barrier, impediment, hindrance, check, hurdle, stumbling block, handicap, deterrent. ANTONYM aid.

5 *a block in the pipe* BLOCKAGE, obstruction, stoppage, clog, congestion, occlusion, clot.

▸ verb **1** *weeds can block drainage ditches* CLOG (UP), stop up, choke, plug, obstruct, gum up, dam up, congest, jam, close; *informal* gunge up; *technical* occlude. ANTONYM open.

2 *picket lines blocked access to the factory* HINDER, hamper, obstruct, impede, inhibit, restrict, limit; halt, stop, bar, check, prevent. ANTONYM facilitate.

3 *he blocked a shot on the goal line* STOP, deflect, fend off, hold off, repel, parry, repulse.

PHRASES: **block something off** *the bridge was blocked off* CLOSE UP, shut off, seal off, barricade, bar, obstruct. **block something out** *trees blocked out the light* CONCEAL, keep out, blot out, exclude, obliterate, blank out, stop.

blockade noun **1** *a naval blockade of the island* SIEGE; *rare* besiegement.

2 *they erected blockades in the streets* BARRICADE, barrier, roadblock; obstacle, obstruction.

▸ verb *rebels blockaded the capital* BARRICADE, block off, shut off, seal; BESIEGE, surround.

blockage noun *a blockage of leaves in the storm drain* OBSTRUCTION, stoppage, block, occlusion, clog, congestion.

blockhead noun *informal*. See IDIOT.

blond, blonde adjective *blond hair* FAIR, light, yellow, flaxen, golden, platinum, ash blond, strawberry blond, tow-colored; bottle blond, bleached, peroxide. ANTONYM dark.

USAGE NOTE **blond, blonde**

The spellings **blonde** and **blond** correspond to the feminine and masculine forms in French. Although the distinction is usually retained in Britain, American usage since the 1970s has generally preferred the gender-neutral **blond**. The adjective **blonde** may still refer to a woman's (but not a man's) hair color, though use of the noun risks offense (*See that blonde over there?*): the offense arises from the fact that the color of hair is not the person. The adjective applied to inanimate objects (wood, beer) is typically spelled **blond**.

blood noun **1** *he had lost too much blood* PLASMA, vital fluid, gore; *literary* lifeblood, ichor.

2 *a woman of noble blood* ANCESTRY, lineage, bloodline, descent, parentage, family, birth, extraction, origin, genealogy, heritage, stock, kinship.

blood-curdling adjective *a blood-curdling scream* TERRIFYING, frightening, bone-chilling, spine-tingling, chilling, hair-raising, horrifying, alarming; eerie, sinister, horrible; *informal* spooky.

bloodless adjective **1** *a bloodless revolution* NONVIO-

LENT, peaceful, peaceable, pacifist. ANTONYMS bloody, violent.

2 *his face was bloodless* ANEMIC, pale, wan, pallid, ashen, colorless, chalky, waxen, white, gray, pasty, drained, drawn, deathly. ANTONYM ruddy.

3 *a bloodless production* FEEBLE, spiritless, lifeless, listless, halfhearted, unenthusiastic, lukewarm. ANTONYM powerful.

bloodshed noun *another day of bloodshed in Beirut* SLAUGHTER, massacre, killing, wounding; carnage, butchery, bloodletting, bloodbath; violence, fighting, warfare; *literary* slaying.

bloodthirsty adjective *bloodthirsty Vikings* MURDEROUS, homicidal, violent, vicious, barbarous, barbaric, savage, brutal, cutthroat; fierce, ferocious, inhuman.

bloody adjective 1 *his bloody nose* BLEEDING.

2 *bloody medical waste* BLOODSTAINED, blood-soaked, gory; *archaic* sanguinary.

3 *a bloody civil war* VICIOUS, ferocious, savage, fierce, brutal, murderous, barbarous, gory; *archaic* sanguinary.

4 *Brit. informal a bloody nuisance!* See DAMNED sense 2.

bloom noun 1 *orchid blooms* FLOWER, blossom, floweret, floret.

2 *a girl in the bloom of youth* PRIME, perfection, acme, peak, height, heyday; salad days.

3 *the bloom of her skin* RADIANCE, luster, sheen, glow, freshness; BLUSH, rosiness, pinkness, color.

▸ verb 1 *the geraniums bloomed* FLOWER, blossom, open; mature. ANTONYM wither.

2 *their health bloomed in the mountain air* FLOURISH, thrive, prosper, progress, burgeon; *informal* be in the pink. ANTONYM decline.

blossom noun *pink blossoms* FLOWER, bloom, floweret, floret.

▸ verb 1 *the trilliums have blossomed* BLOOM, flower, open, unfold; mature. ANTONYM fade.

2 *the whole region had blossomed* DEVELOP, grow, mature, progress, evolve; flourish, thrive, prosper, bloom, burgeon. ANTONYM decline.

PHRASE: **in blossom** *the cactus is in blossom* IN FLOWER, flowering, blossoming, blooming, in (full) bloom, abloom, open, out; *formal* inflorescent.

blot noun 1 *an ink blot* SPOT, dot, mark, blotch, smudge, patch, dab; *informal* splotch.

2 *the only blot on a clean campaign* BLEMISH, taint, stain, blight, flaw, fault; disgrace, dishonor.

▸ verb 1 *blot the excess water* SOAK UP, absorb, sponge up, mop up; dry up/out; dab, pat.

2 *he had blotted our name forever* TARNISH, taint, stain, blacken, sully, mar; dishonor, disgrace, besmirch. ANTONYM honor.

PHRASE: **blot something out** 1 *Mary blotted out her picture* ERASE, obliterate, delete, efface, rub out, blank out, expunge, eradicate; cross out, strike out, wipe out. 2 *clouds were starting to blot out the stars* CONCEAL, hide, obscure, exclude, obliterate; shadow, eclipse.

blotch noun 1 *pink flowers with dark blotches* PATCH, smudge, dot, spot, blot, dab, daub; *informal* splotch.

2 *his face was covered in blotches* PATCH, mark, freckle, birthmark, discoloration, eruption, nevus.

▸ verb *her face was blotched and swollen* SPOT, mark, smudge, streak, blemish.

blotchy adjective *blotchy skin* MOTTLED, dappled, blotched, patchy, spotty, spotted, smudged, marked; *informal* splotchy.

blow verb 1 *the icy wind blew around us* GUST, bluster, puff, blast, roar, rush, storm.

2 *his ship was blown on to the rocks* SWEEP, carry, toss, drive, push, force.

3 *leaves blew across the road* DRIFT, flutter, waft, float, glide, whirl, move.

4 *he blew a smoke ring* EXHALE, puff, breathe out; emit, expel, discharge, issue.

5 *he blew a trumpet* SOUND, blast, toot, pipe, trumpet; play.

6 *a rear tire had blown* BURST, explode, blow out, split, rupture, puncture.

7 *informal he blew his money on gambling* SQUANDER, waste, misspend, throw away, fritter away, go through, lose, lavish, dissipate, use up; spend recklessly; *informal* splurge.

8 *informal don't blow this opportunity* SPOIL, ruin, bungle, mess up, fudge, muff; WASTE, lose, squander; *informal* botch, screw up, foul up.

9 *his cover was blown* EXPOSE, reveal, uncover, disclose, divulge, unveil, betray, leak.

▸ noun 1 *a blow on the head* KNOCK, BANG, hit, punch, thump, smack, crack, rap, karate chop; *informal* whack, thwack, bonk, bash, clout, sock, wallop.

2 *losing his wife must have been a blow* SHOCK, surprise, bombshell, thunderbolt, jolt; calamity, catastrophe, disaster, upset, setback.

3 *a blow on the guard's whistle* TOOT, blast, blare; whistle.

PHRASES: **blow out** 1 *the matches will not blow out in a strong wind* BE EXTINGUISHED, go out, be put out, stop burning. 2 *the front tire blew out.* See BLOW verb sense 6. 3 *the windows blew out* SHATTER, rupture, crack, smash, splinter, disintegrate; burst, explode, fly apart; *informal* bust. **blow something out** *blow the candles out* EXTINGUISH, put out, snuff, douse, quench, smother. **blow over** *the storm will blow over soon* ABATE, subside, drop off, lessen, ease (off), let up, diminish, fade, dwindle, slacken, recede, tail off, peter out, pass, die down, fizzle out; *dated* remit. **blow up** 1 *a truckload of shells blew up* EXPLODE, detonate, go off, ignite, erupt. 2 *he blows up over every little thing* LOSE ONE'S TEMPER, get angry, rant and rave, go berserk, flare up, erupt; *informal* go mad, go crazy, go wild, hit the roof, fly off the handle. 3 *a crisis blew up* BREAK OUT, erupt, flare up, boil over; emerge, arise. **blow something up** 1 *they blew the plane up* BOMB, blast, destroy; explode, detonate. 2 *blow up the balloons* INFLATE, pump up, fill up, puff up, swell, expand. 3 *I blew the picture up on a photocopier* ENLARGE, magnify, expand, increase. **blow out of proportion** *it was an innocent passing remark that he's blown out of proportion* EXAGGERATE, overstate, overstress, overestimate, magnify, amplify; aggrandize, embellish, elaborate.

blowout noun **1** *the steering is automatic in the event of blowouts* PUNCTURE, flat tire, burst tire; *informal* flat.

2 *informal* *this meal is our last real blowout* FEAST, banquet, celebration, party; *informal* shindig, do, binge.

3 *the game turned into a 17–3 blowout* ROUT, whitewash, walkover, landslide.

blowsy adjective *where does he find these blowsy dames?* UNTIDY, sloppy, scruffy, messy, disheveled, unkempt, frowzy, slovenly; coarse; RED-FACED, ruddy, florid. ANTONYMS tidy, respectable.

blowy adjective *a blowy evening on the houseboat* WINDY, windswept, blustery, gusty, breezy; stormy, squally. ANTONYM still.

blubber[1] noun *whale blubber* FAT, fatty tissue; fatness, plumpness, bulk; beer belly, beer gut, paunch, flab.

blubber[2] verb *informal* *she started to blubber* CRY, sob, weep, snivel; *informal* boo-hoo.

bludgeon noun *hooligans wielding bludgeons* CUDGEL, club, stick, truncheon, baton; nightstick, billy club, blackjack.

▸ verb *he was bludgeoned to death* BATTER, cudgel, club, beat, thrash; clobber, pummel.

blue adjective **1** *bright blue eyes* sky blue, azure, cobalt, sapphire, navy, powder blue, midnight blue, Prussian blue, electric blue, indigo, royal blue, ice-blue, baby blue, air force blue, robin's egg blue, peacock blue, ultramarine, aquamarine, steel blue, slate blue, cyan; *chiefly Brit.* Oxford blue, Cambridge blue; *literary* cerulean.

2 *informal* *Mom was feeling a bit blue* DEPRESSED, down, sad, unhappy, melancholy, miserable, gloomy, dejected, dispirited, downhearted, downcast, despondent, low, glum; *informal* down in the dumps. ANTONYM happy.

blue-collar adjective *blue-collar work* MANUAL, wage, industrial, factory; *informal* lunchpail.

WORD NOTE **blue-collar**

When the literal meaning of a word disappears entirely into its figurative sense, it may become a dead metaphor or a journalistic cliché but may nevertheless be celebrated because it so aptly illustrates the way use ceaselessly modifies language. Such a word is *blue-collar*. It originated as a term for laborers who wore work shirts and no ties. They tended to work with their hands or at a trade; toiled at a factory or a construction site rather than in an office; were underpaid relative to the executive class; and enthusiastically embraced the macho ideal. All that is in *blue-collar*, but the word long ago outlived its literal image. White collars, pink collars, blue collars—you can no longer tell anything from the color of anyone's collar, but the words themselves say a lot about us. As pink is to feminine, blue is to masculine—which may help explain why *blue-collar*, detached from its original meaning, has acquired an extra layer of connotation.

The word (or synonyms thereof) is now used often in the sports pages to describe a basketball or baseball team of millionaires who may make a few million dollars less than the elite teams of the sport. Game six of the 2003 American League Championship Series went in favor of Boston, and a beat writer wondered whether this meant that "the blue-collar Bosox finally stood up to the big, bad Yankees." Another journalist, resisting such a formulation, opined that the "filthy rich" had defeated the "scruffy rich" when the Yankees prevailed. I have heard the Florida Marlins, the team that defeated the Yankees to win the World Series, described as having a "brown bag payroll." That payroll consists of just under fifty million dollars divided, I believe, in twenty-five uneven ways. It's true that the Yankees outspend any other team, but has *blue-collar* become so relative a term that it can modify the status of an infielder with a two million dollar salary or a middle-innings relief pitcher earning what used to be called "a cool million"?

Yes, if only because of the term's connotation. It connotes a tough work ethic, as if to say that, despite any temptation to loaf, these players work hard, practice, prepare, and are, to use another term of the moment, "focused." When *blue-collar* was used regularly to describe the New York Knicks of Patrick Ewing, Charles Oakley, and Anthony Mason, it was a euphemism for "physical," itself a euphemism for playing basketball as if it were hand-to-hand combat under the basket. But it also left the lingering sense that, riches aside, these guys play tough and are unafraid to get hurt, for deep down they remain the kids who played with daring and amazing energy on a neighborhood playground. **—DL**

blueprint noun **1** *blueprints of the aircraft* PLAN, design, diagram, drawing, sketch, map, layout, representation.

2 *a blueprint for similar measures in other countries* MODEL, plan, template, framework, pattern, example, guide, prototype, pilot.

blues plural noun *informal* *a fit of blues* DEPRESSION, sadness, unhappiness, melancholy, misery, sorrow, gloom, dejection, despondency, despair; the doldrums, the dumps, a blue funk.

bluff[1] noun *this threat was dismissed as a bluff* DECEPTION, front, subterfuge, pretense, posturing, sham, fake, deceit, feint, hoax, facade, fraud, charade; trick, ruse, scheme, machination; *informal* put-on.

▸ verb **1** *they are bluffing to hide their guilt* PRETEND, sham, fake, feign, lie, hoax, pose, posture, masquerade, dissemble.

2 *I managed to bluff the board into believing me* DECEIVE, delude, mislead, trick, fool, hoodwink, dupe, hoax, beguile, gull; *informal* con, kid.

bluff[2] adjective *a bluff man* PLAIN-SPOKEN, straightforward, blunt, direct, no-nonsense, frank, open, candid, forthright, unequivocal; hearty, genial, good-natured; *informal* upfront. See note at BRUSQUE.

bluff[3] noun *an impregnable high bluff* CLIFF, promontory, ridge, headland, crag, bank, height, peak, escarpment, scarp, overhang; *rare* eminence.

blunder noun *he shook his head at his blunder* MISTAKE, error, gaffe, slip, oversight, faux pas, misstep, infelicity; *informal* botch, slip-up, boo-boo, blooper, boner, flub. See note at MISTAKE.

▸ verb **1** *the government admitted it had blundered* MAKE A MISTAKE, err, miscalculate, bungle, trip up, be wrong; *informal* slip up, screw up, blow it, goof.

2 *she blundered down the steps* STUMBLE, lurch, stagger, flounder, struggle, fumble, grope.

blunt adjective **1** *a blunt knife* UNSHARPENED, dull, worn, edgeless. ANTONYM sharp.

2 *the leaf is broad with a blunt tip* ROUNDED, flat, obtuse, stubby. ANTONYM pointed.

3 *a blunt message* STRAIGHTFORWARD, frank, plain-spoken, candid, direct, bluff, forthright, unequivocal; BRUSQUE, abrupt, curt, terse, bald, brutal, harsh; stark, unadorned, undisguised, unvarnished; *informal* upfront. See note at BRUSQUE. ANTONYM subtle.

▸ verb **1** *ebony blunts tools very rapidly* DULL, make less sharp. ANTONYM sharpen.

2 *age hasn't blunted my passion for life* DULL, deaden, dampen, numb, weaken, sap, cool, temper, allay, abate; diminish, reduce, decrease, lessen, deplete. ANTONYM intensify.

blur verb **1** *tears blurred her vision* CLOUD, fog, obscure, dim, make hazy, unfocus, soften; *literary* bedim; *archaic* blear. ANTONYMS sharpen, focus.

2 *movies blur the difference between villains and victims* OBSCURE, make vague, confuse, muddle, muddy, obfuscate, cloud, weaken.

▸ noun *a blur on the horizon* INDISTINCT SHAPE, smudge; haze, cloud, mist.

blurred adjective *a blurred photograph* INDISTINCT, blurry, fuzzy, hazy, misty, foggy, shadowy, faint; unclear, vague, indefinite, unfocused, obscure, nebulous.

blurt PHRASE: **blurt something out** *he blurted out his story* BURST OUT WITH, exclaim, call out; DIVULGE, disclose, reveal, betray, let slip, give away; *informal* blab, gush, let on, spill the beans (about), let the cat out of the bag (about).

blush verb *Joan blushed at the compliment* REDDEN, turn/go pink, turn/go red, flush, color, burn up; feel shy, feel embarrassed.

▸ noun *a blush spread across his face* FLUSH, rosiness, pinkness, bloom, (high) color.

bluster verb **1** *he started blustering about the general election* RANT, rave, thunder, bellow, sound off; be overbearing; *informal* throw one's weight around/about.

2 *storms bluster in from the sea* BLAST, gust, storm, roar, rush.

▸ noun *his bluster turned to cooperation* RANTING, thundering, hectoring, bullying; bombast, bravado, bumptiousness, braggadocio.

blustery adjective *a blustery autumn day* STORMY, gusty, blowy, windy, squally, wild, tempestuous, turbulent; howling, roaring. ANTONYM calm.

board noun **1** *a wooden board* PLANK, beam, panel, slat, batten, timber, lath.

2 *the board of directors* COMMITTEE, council, panel, directorate, commission, executive, group.

3 *your room and board will be free* FOOD, meals, provisions, diet, table, bread, rations; keep, maintenance; *informal* grub, nosh, eats, chow.

▸ verb **1** *he boarded the aircraft* GET ON, go aboard, enter, mount, ascend; embark, emplane, entrain; catch; *informal* hop on.

2 *a number of students boarded with them* LODGE, live, reside, be housed, room; *informal* be put up.

3 *they run a facility for boarding dogs* ACCOMMODATE, lodge, take in, put up, house; keep, feed, cater for, billet.

PHRASE: **board something up/over** *shoreline residents are boarding up their windows* COVER UP/OVER, close up, shut up, seal.

board game noun See table at GAME.

boast verb **1** *his mother had been boasting about him* BRAG, crow, swagger, swank, gloat, show off; exaggerate, overstate; *informal* talk big, blow one's own horn, lay it on thick.

2 *the hotel boasts a fine restaurant* POSSESS, have, own, enjoy, pride oneself/itself on.

▸ noun **1** *everyone has tired of listening to your boast* BRAG, self-praise; exaggeration, overstatement, grandiloquence, fanfaronade.

2 *the hall is the boast of the county* PRIDE, joy, wonder, delight, treasure, gem.

boastful adjective *in the first debate he came across as aggressive and boastful* BRAGGING, swaggering, bumptious, puffed up, full of oneself; cocky, conceited, arrogant, egotistical; *informal* swanky, bigheaded, blowhard; *literary* vainglorious. ANTONYM modest.

boat noun *a rowing boat* VESSEL, craft, watercraft, ship; *literary* keel. See table.

▸ verb *they were out boating for hours* SAIL, yacht, paddle, row, cruise.

BOATS

airboat	lifeboat
barge	motorboat
bark/barque	outboard
bateau	outrigger
bidarka	packet (boat)
Boston whaler	paddleboat
bullboat	pedal boat
cabin cruiser	pontoon
canal boat	prahu
canoe	pram
catamaran	punt
catboat	riverboat
cockboat	rowboat
coracle	sailboat
cutter	sampan
dinghy	scow
dory	scull
felucca	shell
ferry	skiff
fishing boat	skipjack
flatboat	steamboat
gig	sternwheeler
gondola	torpedo boat
houseboat	towboat
hydrofoil	trawler
hydroplane	trimaran
iceboat	tugboat
jet boat	umiak
johnboat	water bus
jolly	whaleboat
kayak	whaler
keelboat	wherry
ketch	yacht
launch	yawl

See also tables at SAILING SHIP and SHIP.

bob verb *the bottle bobbed in the water* MOVE UP AND DOWN, bounce, toss, skip, dance, jounce; wobble, jiggle, joggle, jolt, jerk; NOD, incline, dip; wag, waggle.

bode verb *it's that unsettling kind of silence that bodes danger* AUGUR, portend, herald, be a sign of, warn of, foreshadow, be an omen of, presage, indicate, signify, promise, threaten, spell, denote, foretell; prophesy, predict; *literary* betoken, forebode.

bodily adjective *bodily sensations* PHYSICAL, corporeal, corporal, somatic, fleshly; concrete, real, actual, tangible. ANTONYMS spiritual, mental.

body noun **1** *the human body* FIGURE, frame, form, physique, anatomy, skeleton; soma; *informal* bod.

2 *he was hit by shrapnel in the head and body* TORSO, trunk.

3 *the body was exhumed* CORPSE, carcass, skeleton, remains; *informal* stiff; *Medicine* cadaver.

4 *the body of the essay* MAIN PART, central part, core, heart.

5 *a body of water* EXPANSE, mass, area, stretch, tract, sweep, extent.

6 *a growing body of evidence* QUANTITY, amount, volume, collection, mass, corpus.

7 *the representative body of the employers* ASSOCIATION, organization, group, party, company, society, circle, syndicate, guild, corporation, contingent.

8 *add body to your hair* FULLNESS, thickness, substance, bounce, lift, shape. PHRASE: **body and soul** *these young men and women belong to the Corps, body and soul* COMPLETELY, entirely, totally, utterly, fully, thoroughly, wholeheartedly, unconditionally, to the hilt.

THE RIGHT WORD

The problem of what to call the human **body** after it has departed this life is a delicate one. Although a *body* can be either dead or alive, human or animal, a **corpse** is most definitely a dead human body and a **carcass** is the body of a dead animal. The issue has been confused, of course, by the figurative use of *carcass* as a term of contempt (*"Get your carcass out of bed and come down here!"*). While *carcass* is often used humorously, there's nothing funny about *corpse*, a no-nonsense term for a lifeless physical body (*the battlefield was littered with corpses*). A funeral director is likely to prefer the term **remains**, which is a euphemism for the body of the deceased (*he had his wife's remains shipped home for burial*), or **cremains**, if the body has been cremated. A medical student, on the other hand, is much more likely to use the term **cadaver**, which is a corpse that is dissected in a laboratory for scientific study.

bodyguard noun *the singer's former bodyguard* guard, personal guard, protector, guardian, defender; escort, chaperon/chaperone; *informal* heavy, goon, hired gun.

bog noun *the bogs were alive with chirring insects and croaking frogs* MARSH, swamp, muskeg, mire, quagmire, morass, slough, fen, wetland, bogland. PHRASE: **bogged down** *bogged down with endless paperwork* MIRED, stuck, entangled, ensnared, embroiled; hampered, hindered, impeded, delayed, stalled, detained; swamped, overwhelmed.

boggle verb **1** *this data makes the mind boggle* MARVEL, wonder.

2 *it boggles my mind* BAFFLE, astonish, astound, amaze, stagger, overwhelm.

boggy adjective *the boggy expanse behind the ballfields* MARSHY, swampy, miry, fenny, muddy, waterlogged, wet, soggy, sodden; spongy, heavy, sloughy.

bogus adjective *a bogus insurance claim* | *a bogus lottery ticket* FAKE, spurious, false, fraudulent, sham, deceptive; COUNTERFEIT, forged, feigned; make-believe, dummy, pseudo, phony, pretend, fictitious. ANTONYM genuine.

bohemian noun *he is an artist and a Bohemian* NONCONFORMIST, free spirit, dropout; hippie, beatnik; *informal* boho. ANTONYM conservative.

▸ adjective *a Bohemian student life* UNCONVENTIONAL, nonconformist, unorthodox, avant-garde, irregular, offbeat, alternative; artistic; *informal* boho, artsy, artsy-fartsy, way-out. ANTONYM conventional.

boil[1] verb **1** *boil the potatoes* BRING TO A BOIL, simmer, parboil, poach; cook.

2 *the soup is boiling* SIMMER, bubble, stew.

3 *a huge cliff with the sea boiling below* CHURN, seethe, froth, foam; *literary* roil.

▸ noun *bring the stock to a boil* BOILING POINT, rolling boil.

PHRASES: **boil something down** *you have to boil down a lot of tomatoes to make just a few tablespoons of tomato paste* CONDENSE, reduce, concentrate, distill, thicken, compress. ANTONYM dilute.

boil down to *it all boils down to how much money you're willing to spend* COME DOWN TO, amount to, add up to, be in essence.

boil[2] noun *a boil on her neck* SWELLING, spot, pimple, blister, pustule, eruption, carbuncle, wen, abscess, ulcer; *technical* furuncle.

boiling adjective **1** *boiling water* AT BOILING POINT, at 212 degrees Fahrenheit, at 100 degrees Celsius/centigrade; very hot, piping hot; bubbling. ANTONYMS freezing, ice-cold.

2 *informal it was a boiling day* VERY HOT, scorching, blistering, sweltering, sultry, torrid; *informal* broiling, roasting, baking, sizzling. ANTONYMS cold, freezing.

boisterous adjective **1** *a boisterous game of handball* LIVELY, animated, exuberant, spirited, rambunctious; rowdy, unruly, wild, uproarious, unrestrained, undisciplined, uninhibited, uncontrolled, rough, disorderly, riotous, knockabout; noisy, loud, clamorous. See note at VOCIFEROUS. ANTONYMS restrained, quiet.

2 *a boisterous wind* BLUSTERY, gusty, windy, stormy, wild, squally, tempestuous; howling, roaring; *informal* blowy. ANTONYM calm.

bold adjective **1** *bold adventurers* DARING, intrepid, brave, courageous, valiant, valorous, fearless, dauntless, audacious, daredevil; adventurous, heroic, plucky, spirited, confident, assured; *informal* gutsy, spunky, feisty; *literary* temerarious. ANTONYMS timid, unadventurous.

2 *don't be so bold in public* IMPUDENT, insolent, impertinent, brazen, brash, disrespectful, presumptuous, forward; cheeky, fresh.

3 *a bold pattern* STRIKING, vivid, bright, strong, eye-catching, prominent; gaudy, lurid, garish. ANTONYM pale.

4 *departure times are in bold type* HEAVY, thick, pronounced, conspicuous. ANTONYMS light, roman.

THE RIGHT WORD

Is walking up to an attractive stranger and asking him or her to have dinner with you tonight a **bold** move or merely an **aggressive** one? Both words suggest assertive, confident behavior that is a little on the shameless side, but *bold* has a wider range of application. It can suggest self-confidence that borders on impudence (*to be so bold as to call the president by his first name*), but it can also be used to describe a daring temperament that is either courageous or defiant (*a bold investigator who would not give up*). *Aggressive* behavior, on the other hand, usually falls within a narrower range, somewhere between menacing (*aggressive attacks on innocent villagers*) and just plain pushy (*an ag-*

gressive salesperson). **Brazen** implies a defiant lack of modesty (*a brazen stare*), and **presumptuous** goes even further, suggesting over-confidence to the point of causing offense (*a presumptuous request for money*). **Bumptious** behavior can also be offensive, but it is usually associated with the kind of cockiness that can't be helped (*a bumptious young upstart*). An **audacious** individual is bold to the point of recklessness (*an audacious explorer*), which brings it very close in meaning to **intrepid**, suggesting fearlessness in the face of the unknown (*the intrepid settlers of the Great Plains*).

---

bolster verb *an occasional word of thanks would really bolster the staff's morale* STRENGTHEN, reinforce, boost, fortify, renew; support, sustain, buoy up, prop up, shore up, maintain, aid, help; augment, increase. ANTONYM undermine.

bolt noun **1** *the bolt on the shed door* BAR, LOCK, catch, latch, fastener, deadbolt.

2 *nuts and bolts* RIVET, pin, peg, screw.

3 *a bolt whirred over my head* ARROW, quarrel, dart, shaft.

4 *a bolt of lightning* FLASH, thunderbolt, shaft, streak, burst, flare.

5 *Mark made a bolt for the door* DASH, dart, run, sprint, leap, bound.

6 *a bolt of cloth* ROLL, reel, spool; quantity, amount.

▸ verb **1** *he bolted the door* LOCK, bar, latch, fasten, secure.

2 *the lid was bolted down* RIVET, pin, peg, screw; fasten, fix.

3 *Anna bolted from the room* DASH, dart, run, sprint, hurtle, careen, rush, fly, shoot, bound; flee; *informal* tear, scoot, leg it.

4 *he* ***bolted down*** *his breakfast* GOBBLE UP, gulp down, wolf down, guzzle (down), devour; *informal* demolish, polish off, shovel in/down, scarf up.

PHRASES: **a bolt (from) out of the blue** *the department shutdown came as a bolt out of the blue* SHOCK, surprise, bombshell, thunderbolt, revelation. **bolt upright** *in Scene 2, the corpse is supposed to sit suddenly bolt upright* STRAIGHT, rigidly, stiffly. ANTONYM slouching.

bomb noun **1** *they saw bombs bursting on the runway* EXPLOSIVE, incendiary (device); missile, projectile; *dated* blockbuster, bombshell.

2 *countries with the bomb* NUCLEAR WEAPONS, nuclear bombs, atom bombs, A-bombs.

3 *informal their next film was a bomb* FAILURE, flop, megaflop, fiasco, bust, dud, washout, debacle, turkey, dog, clunker.

▸ verb **1** *their headquarters were bombed* BOMBARD, blast, shell, blitz, strafe, pound; attack, assault; blow up, destroy, demolish, flatten, devastate.

2 *informal the show bombed at the box office* FAIL, flop, fall flat, founder.

bombard verb **1** *gun batteries bombarded the islands* SHELL, pound, blitz, strafe, bomb; assail, attack, assault, batter, blast, pelt. See note at ATTACK.

2 *we were bombarded with information* INUNDATE, swamp, flood, deluge, snow under; besiege, overwhelm.

bombastic adjective *these Albanian rivals have alternated violent attacks with bombastic speeches* POMPOUS, blustering, turgid, verbose, orotund, high-flown, high-sounding, overwrought, pretentious, ostentatious, grandiloquent; *informal* highfalutin, puffed up; *rare* fustian.

bona fide adjective *the table is definitely an imitation Chippendale, but the chairs are bona fide | a bona fide endorsement* AUTHENTIC, genuine, real, true, actual; legal, legitimate, lawful, valid, proper; *informal* legit, the real McCoy. See note at GENUINE. ANTONYM bogus.

bonanza noun *those grisly murders of 1872 turned into quite a bonanza for the town, which has thrived as a center of tourism ever since* WINDFALL, godsend, boon, blessing, bonus, stroke of luck, jackpot.

bond noun **1** *the bond between Moira and her son* RELATIONSHIP, tie, link, friendship, fellowship, partnership, association, affiliation, alliance, attachment.

2 *the prisoner struggled with his bonds* CHAINS, fetters, shackles, manacles, irons, restraints.

3 *you've broken your bond* PROMISE, pledge, vow, oath, word (of honor), guarantee, assurance; agreement, contract, pact, bargain, deal.

▸ verb *the extensions are bonded to your hair* JOIN, fasten, fix, affix, attach, secure, bind, stick, fuse.

bondage noun *our own freedom is not so gratifying when we must look upon the bondage of others* SLAVERY, enslavement, servitude, subjugation, subjection, oppression, domination, exploitation, persecution; enthrallment, thraldom; *historical* serfdom, vassalage. ANTONYM liberty.

bonehead noun See IDIOT.

bon mot noun *the dialogue is dry—it's mostly laughless bon mots about relationships* WITTICISM, quip, pun, pleasantry, jest, joke; *informal* wisecrack, one-liner; *rare* apophthegm, equivoque.

bonus noun **1** *the extra space is a real bonus* BENEFIT, advantage, boon, blessing, godsend, stroke of luck, asset, attraction; *informal* plus, pro, perk, gravy; *formal* perquisite. ANTONYM disadvantage.

2 *she's on a good salary and she gets a bonus* GRATUITY, gift, present, reward, prize, lagniappe; incentive, inducement, handout; *informal* sweetener. See note at PRESENT[3]. ANTONYM penalty.

WORD NOTE **lagniappe**

A *lagniappe* is a little something extra given as a bonus or a gift. Without delving too deeply into the murky waters of sound-symbolism, why not use a beautiful word (pronounced lan-**nyap**) for an equally nice thing? **—EM**

---

bon vivant, bon viveur noun *Ben Franklin was admired as a statesman and adored as a bon vivant* HEDONIST, pleasure-seeker, sensualist, sybarite, voluptuary; epicure, gourmet, gastronome. ANTONYM puritan.

bony adjective *his pale, bony face* GAUNT, ANGULAR, skinny, thin, lean, spare, spindly, skin-and-bones, skeletal, emaciated, underweight; *informal* like a bag of bones; *rare* starveling, macilent, gracile. ANTONYM plump.

boo verb *booed by the audience* JEER, heckle, catcall, hiss, hector. ANTONYMS cheer, applaud.

book noun **1** *Nadine and Ian have recommended some good books* VOLUME, tome, publication, title; novel, storybook, anthology, treatise, manual; paperback, hardback, pocket book, e-book.

2 *he scribbled in his book* NOTEBOOK, notepad, pad, memo pad, exercise book, workbook; logbook, ledger, journal, diary.

3 *enter a $400 deposit in the book | the council had to balance its books* LEDGER, account book, record book, balance sheet; **(books)** ACCOUNTS, records.

▸ verb 1 *Dan and Veronica booked a table at the restaurant* RESERVE, make a reservation for, prearrange, order; *formal* bespeak.

2 *we booked a number of events for the festival* ARRANGE, program, schedule, timetable, line up, pencil in, slate.

PHRASE: **by the book** *he's a cop who does everything by the book* ACCORDING TO THE RULES, within the law, lawfully, legally, legitimately; honestly, fairly; *informal* on the level, fair and square.

booking noun *he made a provisional booking for Friday afternoon* RESERVATION, prearrangement; appointment, date; *dated* engagement.

bookish adjective *Swann was always the bookish one in our group* STUDIOUS, scholarly, academic, intellectual, highbrow, erudite, learned, lettered, educated, well-read, knowledgeable; cerebral, serious, earnest; pedantic.

booklet noun *a booklet about Lyme disease* PAMPHLET, brochure, leaflet, handbill, flyer, fact sheet, tract; folder, mailer.

boom noun 1 *the boom of the thunder* REVERBERATION, resonance, thunder, echoing, crashing, drumming, pounding, roar, rumble, explosion.

2 *an unprecedented boom in sales* UPTURN, upsurge, upswing, increase, advance, growth, boost, escalation, improvement, spurt. ANTONYM slump.

▸ verb 1 *thunder boomed overhead* REVERBERATE, resound, resonate; rumble, thunder, blare, echo; crash, roll, clap, explode, bang.

2 *a voice boomed at her* BELLOW, roar, thunder, shout, bawl; *informal* holler. ANTONYM whisper.

3 *the market continued to boom* FLOURISH, burgeon, thrive, prosper, progress, improve, pick up, expand, mushroom, snowball. ANTONYM slump.

boomerang verb *their tax-evading scheme boomeranged, and now they're facing serious legal trouble* BACKFIRE, recoil, reverse, rebound, ricochet; be self-defeating; *informal* blow up in one's face.

booming adjective 1 *a booming voice* RESONANT, sonorous, ringing, resounding, reverberating, carrying, thunderous; strident, stentorian, strong, powerful.

2 *booming business* FLOURISHING, burgeoning, thriving, prospering, prosperous, successful, strong, buoyant; profitable, fruitful, lucrative; *informal* boffo.

boon noun *their help was such a boon* BLESSING, godsend, bonus, plus, benefit, advantage, help, aid, asset; stroke of luck, windfall. ANTONYM curse.

boondocks noun *until I was twelve, we lived in the boondocks* BACKWATER, hinterland, backwoods, backcountry, middle of nowhere; wasteland, bush; *informal* boonies, sticks.

boor noun *a civilized affair guaranteed to separate the boors from the gentlemen* LOUT, oaf, ruffian, thug, yahoo, barbarian, Neanderthal, brute, beast, lubber; *informal* clod, roughneck, troglodyte, pig, peasant.

boorish adjective *we will not tolerate such boorish behavior from our officers* COARSE, uncouth, rude, ill-bred, ill-mannered, uncivilized, unrefined, rough, thuggish, loutish, oafish, lubberly, lumpen; vulgar, unsavory, gross, brutish, Neanderthal; *informal* cloddish. ANTONYM refined.

boost noun 1 *a boost to one's morale | just the boost I needed* UPLIFT, lift, spur, encouragement, help, inspiration, stimulus, pick-me-up; *informal* shot in the arm.

2 *a boost in sales* INCREASE, expansion, upturn, upsurge, upswing, rise, escalation, improvement, advance, growth, boom; hike, jump. ANTONYM decrease.

▸ verb 1 *he phoned to boost her spirits* IMPROVE, raise, uplift, increase, enhance, encourage, heighten, help, promote, foster, stimulate, invigorate, revitalize; *informal* buck up.

2 *they used advertising to boost sales* INCREASE, raise, escalate, improve, strengthen, inflate, push up, promote, advance, foster, stimulate, maximize; facilitate, help, assist, aid; jump-start; *informal* hike, bump up. ANTONYM decrease.

boot[1] noun *muddy boots.*

▸ verb 1 *his shot was booted away by the goalkeeper* KICK, punt; propel, drive.

2 ***boot up** your computer* START UP, fire up, reboot.

PHRASE: **give someone the boot** *informal* See DISMISS sense 1.

boot[2] PHRASE: **to boot** *he's not only intelligent, he's handsome to boot* AS WELL, also, too, besides, in the bargain, in addition, additionally, on top, what's more, moreover, furthermore, likewise; *informal* and all.

booth noun 1 *booths for different vendors* STALL, stand, kiosk.

2 *a phone booth* CUBICLE, kiosk, box, enclosure.

bootleg, bootlegged adjective *bootleg videotapes | bootlegged versions of the software* ILLEGAL, illicit, unlawful, unauthorized, unlicensed, pirated; contraband, smuggled, black-market.

bootlicker noun *informal the little bootlicker brought in cupcakes for Altman's birthday* SYCOPHANT, toady, lickspittle, flatterer, flunky, lackey, yes-man, spaniel, doormat; *informal* brown-noser, brown-nose, suck-up; *vulgar slang* ass-kisser.

booty noun *divvying up the booty* LOOT, plunder, pillage, haul, spoils, stolen goods, ill-gotten gains, pickings; *informal* swag.

booze *informal* noun *fill him up with food and booze* ALCOHOL, alcoholic drink, liquor, drink, spirits, intoxicants; *informal* grog, firewater, rotgut, the hard stuff, the bottle, hooch, moonshine; juice, the sauce. See table at LIQUOR.

▸ verb *he was out boozing with his buddies* DRINK, tipple, imbibe, indulge; *informal* hit the bottle, knock a few back, swill, chug; bend one's elbow.

boozer noun *informal he's a notorious boozer* DRINKER, drunk, drunkard, alcoholic, dipsomaniac, tippler, imbiber, bibber, sot, inebriate; *informal* lush, alky, dipso, soak, boozehound, wino, barfly.

bop verb *informal bopping to the old tunes* DANCE; boogie, jive, groove, disco, rock, stomp; get down, hoof it, cut a/the rug.

bordello noun *she's currently on Broadway, playing the feisty madam of a bordello* BROTHEL, whorehouse; *informal* cathouse; *euphemistic* massage parlor; *dated* bawdy house, house of ill repute; *Law, dated* disorderly house.

border noun **1** *the border of a medieval manuscript* EDGE, MARGIN, perimeter, circumference, periphery; rim, fringe, verge; sides.

2 *the Canadian border* FRONTIER, boundary; borderline, perimeter; marches, bounds.

▸ verb **1** *the fields were bordered by hedges* SURROUND, enclose, encircle, circle, edge, fringe, bound, flank.

2 *the straps are bordered with gold braid* EDGE, fringe, hem; trim, pipe, finish.

3 *the property* ***bordered on*** *the state park* ADJOIN, abut, be next to, be adjacent to, be contiguous with, touch, join, meet, reach.

PHRASE: **border on** *his tone bordered on contempt* VERGE ON, approach, come close to, be comparable to, approximate to, be tantamount to, be similar to, resemble.

THE RIGHT WORD

A **border** is the part of a surface that is nearest to its boundary (*a rug with a flowered border*)—although it may also refer to the boundary line itself (*the border between Vermont and New Hampshire*). A **margin** is a *border* of a definite width that is usually distinct in appearance from what it encloses; but unlike *border*, it usually refers to the blankness or emptiness that surrounds something (*the margin on a printed page*). While *border* and *margin* usually refer to something that is circumscribed, **edge** may refer to only a part of the perimeter (*the edge of the lawn*) or the line where two planes or surfaces converge (*the edge of the table*). *Edge* can also connote sharpness (*the edge of a knife*) and can be used metaphorically to suggest tension, harshness, or keenness (*there was an edge in her voice; take the edge off their nervousness*). **Verge** may also be used metaphorically to describe the extreme limit of something (*on the verge of a nervous breakdown*), but in a more literal sense, it sometimes is used of the line or narrow space that marks the limit or termination of something (*the verge of a desert or forest*). **Brink** denotes the edge of something very steep or an abrupt division between land and water (*the brink of the river*), or metaphorically the very final limit before an abrupt change (*on the brink of disaster*). **Rim** and **brim** apply only to things that are circular or curving. But while *rim* describes the edge or lip of a rounded or cylindrical shape (*the rim of a glass*), *brim* refers to the inner side of the rim when the container is completely full (*a cup filled to the brim with steaming coffee*). However, when one speaks of the *brim* of a hat, it comes closer to the meaning of *margin* or *border*.

borderline noun *the borderline between old and antique* DIVIDING LINE, divide, division, demarcation line, line, cutoff point; threshold, margin, border, boundary.

▸ adjective *borderline cases* MARGINAL, uncertain, indefinite, unsettled, undecided, doubtful, indeterminate, unclassifiable, equivocal; questionable, debatable, controversial, contentious, problematic, ambiguous; *informal* iffy.

bore verb **1** *the movie bored us* STULTIFY, pall on, stupefy, weary, tire, fatigue, send to sleep, leave cold; bore to death, bore to tears; *informal* turn off.

2 *bore a hole in the ceiling* DRILL, pierce, perforate, puncture, punch, cut; tunnel, burrow, mine, dig, gouge, sink.

▸ noun *you can be such a bore* TEDIOUS PERSON/THING, tiresome person/thing, dull person/thing, yawn, bother, nuisance, wet blanket.

boredom noun *his eyes were glassy with boredom* WEARINESS, ennui, apathy, unconcern; frustration, dissatisfaction, restlessness, restiveness, lethargy, lassitude; tedium, dullness, monotony, repetitiveness, flatness, dreariness; *informal* deadliness.

boring adjective *a boring one-man play* TEDIOUS, dull, monotonous, repetitive, unrelieved, unvaried, unimaginative, uneventful; characterless, featureless, colorless, lifeless, insipid, uninteresting, unexciting, uninspiring, unstimulating; unreadable, unwatchable; jejune, flat, bland, dry, stale, tired, banal, lackluster, stodgy, vapid, monochrome, dreary, humdrum, mundane; mind-numbing, wearisome, tiring, tiresome, irksome, trying, frustrating; *informal* deadly, ho-hum, dullsville, dull as dishwater, plain-vanilla. See word spectrum at INTERESTING.

WORD NOTE **boring**

Just as *sexy* (q.v.) is the ultimate compliment, so *boring* is the most dreaded pejorative. Yet in most cases this distressing judgment comes as a surprise. Consider an all too common case. You work hard on a speech, and then realize—within five minutes—that you've misjudged the audience: The tuxedoed salesmen want laughs while they chow down on chicken marsala, not a reconsideration of Plato's theory of epistemology. Your address—were it presented to Oxford dons—might be showered with plaudits and huzzahs, but the overstuffed and half drunk listeners of Amalgmated Business Machines merely shuffle restlessly and glance at their Timex watches and hope that their tormentor—you—will just stop talking as soon as possible. Nonetheless, you doggedly soldier on, while secretly wishing you were dead. Therefore, when your turn comes to describe a performer, book, piece of music, weekly meeting, what have you, be kind and think twice: A man may excuse almost any criticism or insult, but he will never forget and never forgive being called *boring*. **—MD**

borrow verb **1** *we borrowed a lot of money* take as a loan; lease, hire; *informal* scrounge, bum, cadge, mooch. ANTONYM lend.

2 *informal they "borrowed" all of his tools* TAKE, help oneself to, appropriate, commandeer, abscond with, carry off; steal, purloin; *informal* filch, rob, swipe, nab, rip off, lift, "liberate", pinch, heist.

3 *adventurous chefs borrow foreign techniques* ADOPT, take on, acquire, embrace. ANTONYM impart.

bosom noun **1** *the gown was set low over her bosom* BUST, chest; breasts, mammary glands; *informal* boobs, knockers, mammaries, bazooms.

2 *literary the family took Gill into its bosom* PROTECTION, shelter, safety, refuge; heart.

3 *love was kindled within his bosom* HEART, breast, soul, core, spirit.

▸ adjective *bosom friends* CLOSE, intimate, inseparable, faithful, constant, devoted; good, best, favorite.

boss noun *the boss of a large company* HEAD, chief, director, president, principal, chief executive, chair, manager; supervisor, foreman, overseer, controller; employer, owner, proprietor; *informal* number one, kingpin, boss man, boss lady, top dog, bigwig, big cheese, head honcho, big kahuna.

▸ verb *you have no right to* ***boss me around*** ORDER AROUND, dictate to, lord it over, bully, push around, domineer, dominate, pressurize, browbeat; call the shots for, lay down the law on, bulldoze, walk all over, railroad.

bossy adjective *we're hiding from his bossy sister* DOMINEERING, pushy, overbearing, imperious, officious, high-handed, authoritarian, dictatorial, controlling; *informal* high and mighty. ANTONYM submissive.

botch verb *examiners botched the test scores* BUNGLE, mismanage, mishandle, make a mess of, mess up, make a hash of, muff, fluff, foul up, screw up, flub.

bother verb **1** *no one bothered her* DISTURB, trouble, inconvenience, pester, badger, harass, molest, plague, nag, hound, harry, annoy, upset, irritate, hassle, bug, get in someone's hair, get on someone's case, get under a someone's skin, ruffle someone's feathers, rag on, ride.

2 *the incident was too small to bother about* MIND, care, concern oneself, trouble oneself, worry oneself; *informal* give a damn, give a hoot.

3 *there was something bothering him* WORRY, trouble, concern, perturb, disturb, disquiet, disconcert, unnerve; fret, upset, distress, agitate, gnaw at, weigh down; *informal* rattle.

▸ noun **1** *I don't want to put you to any bother* TROUBLE, effort, exertion, inconvenience, fuss, pains.

2 *the food was such a bother to cook* NUISANCE, hassle, pain in the neck, headache, pest, palaver, rigmarole, job, trial, drag, chore, inconvenience, trouble, problem.

bothersome adjective *he's a bothersome man who disrupts every town meeting* ANNOYING, irritating, obnoxious, vexatious, maddening, exasperating; tedious, wearisome, tiresome; troublesome, trying, taxing, awkward, aggravating, pesky, pestilential.

bottle noun **1** *a bottle of whiskey* carafe, flask, decanter, canteen, vessel, pitcher, flagon, magnum, carboy, demijohn.

2 *informal a world blurred by the bottle.* See ALCOHOL.
PHRASE: **bottle something up** *don't bottle up your emotions* SUPPRESS, repress, restrain, withhold, hold in, rein in, inhibit, smother, stifle, contain, conceal, hide, cork, keep a lid on.

bottleneck noun *there's a bottleneck at the intersection of I-91 and I-84* TRAFFIC JAM, jam, congestion, tie-up, holdup, snarl-up, gridlock, logjam, constriction, narrowing, restriction, obstruction, blockage, choke point.

bottom noun **1** *the bottom of the stairs* FOOT, lowest part, lowest point, base; foundation, substructure, underpinning. ANTONYM top.

2 *the bottom of the car* UNDERSIDE, underneath, undersurface, undercarriage, underbelly.

3 *the bottom of Lake Ontario* FLOOR, bed. ANTONYM surface.

4 *the bottom of the standings in the Eastern League* LOWEST POSITION, lowest level. ANTONYM top.

5 *I enjoyed the horseback ride, except for my sore bottom* REAR, rear end, backside, seat, buttocks, rump, derrière; *informal* cheeks, behind, butt, fanny, keister, tush, tail, buns, caboose, duff, heinie, ass, fundament, posterior, gluteus maximus, sit-upon, stern; *Brit. informal* bum, arse; *Anatomy* nates.

6 *police got to the bottom of the mystery* ORIGIN, cause, root, source, basis, foundation; heart, kernel; essence.

▸ adjective *she sat on the bottom step* LOWEST, last, bottommost; *technical* basal. ANTONYMS highest, top.

bottomless adjective **1** *the bottomless pits of hell* FATHOMLESS, unfathomable, endless, infinite, immeasurable.

2 *George's appetite was bottomless* UNLIMITED, limitless, boundless, infinite, inexhaustible, endless, never-ending, everlasting; vast, huge, enormous. ANTONYM limited.

bottom line noun **1** *how will the move affect our bottom line?* PROFIT, net, gain, earnings, return.

2 *the bottom line is passenger safety* CRUX, issue, essential/crucial/main point, heart of the matter, nub.

bough noun *snow-laden pine boughs* BRANCH, limb, arm, offshoot.

boulder noun *a natural formation of boulders* ROCK, stone.

boulevard noun *the third right off of the boulevard* AVENUE, street, road, drive, thoroughfare, way.

bounce verb **1** *the ball bounced* REBOUND, spring back, ricochet, jounce, carom; reflect.

2 *William bounced down the stairs* BOUND, leap, jump, spring, bob, hop, skip, trip, prance.

▸ noun **1** *he reached the door in a single bounce* BOUND, leap, jump, spring, hop, skip.

2 *she had lost her bounce* VITALITY, vigor, energy, vivacity, liveliness, animation, sparkle, verve, spirit, enthusiasm, dynamism; cheerfulness, happiness, buoyancy, optimism; exuberance, ebullience; *informal* get-up-and-go, pep, zing.

PHRASE: **bounce back** *despite our optimistic predictions, sales never bounced back* RECOVER, revive, rally, pick up, be on the mend; perk up, cheer up, brighten up, liven up; *informal* buck up.

bouncing adjective *can we expect a bouncing economy within the next five years?* VIGOROUS, thriving, flourishing, blooming; HEALTHY, strong, robust, fit, in fine fettle; *informal* in the pink.

bouncy adjective **1** *a rather bouncy ride* BUMPY, jolting, jerky, jumpy, jarring, rough.

2 *a bouncy personality* LIVELY, energetic, perky, frisky, jaunty, dynamic, vital, vigorous, vibrant, animated, spirited, buoyant, bubbly, sparkling, vivacious; enthusiastic, ebullient, upbeat; *informal* peppy, zingy, chirpy.

bound[1] adjective **1** *his bound ankles* TIED, chained, fettered, shackled, secured, tied up.

2 *she seemed bound to win* CERTAIN, sure, very likely, destined, fated, doomed.

3 *you're bound by the law to keep quiet* OBLIGATED, obliged, compelled, required, constrained, forced.

4 *the unrest was **bound up** with the region's economic stagnation* CONNECTED, linked, tied, united, allied.

bound[2] verb *hares bound in the fields* LEAP, jump, spring, bounce, hop; skip, bob, dance, prance, gambol, gallop.

▸ noun *he crossed the room with a single bound* LEAP, jump, spring, bounce, hop.

bound[3] verb **1** *corporate freedom is bounded by law* LIMIT, restrict, confine, circumscribe, demarcate, delimit.

2 *the garden is bounded by a hedge* ENCLOSE, surround, encircle, circle, border; close in/off, hem in. PHRASE: **out**

of bounds *this building is out of bounds for all nonmilitary personnel | harassment of our waitresses is strictly out of bounds* OFF LIMITS, restricted, closed off; forbidden, banned, proscribed, illegal, illicit, unlawful, unacceptable, taboo; *informal* no go; *rare* non licet.

boundary noun **1** *the boundary between Alaska and the Yukon Territory* BORDER, frontier, borderline, partition; fenceline.

2 *the boundary between art and advertising* DIVIDING LINE, divide, division, borderline, cutoff point.

3 *the boundary of his estate* BOUNDS, confines, limits, margins, edges, fringes; border, periphery, perimeter.

4 (**boundaries**) *the boundaries of acceptable behavior* LIMITS, parameters, bounds, confines; ambit, compass.

boundless adjective *the pups have boundless energy* LIMITLESS, unlimited, unbounded, untold, immeasurable, abundant; inexhaustible, endless, infinite, interminable, unfailing, ceaseless, everlasting. ANTONYM limited.

bountiful adjective **1** *their bountiful patron* GENEROUS, magnanimous, munificent, openhanded, unselfish, unstinting, lavish; benevolent, beneficent, charitable, philanthropic; *rare* eleemosynary, benignant. ANTONYMS mean, stingy.

2 *a bountiful supply of fresh food* ABUNDANT, plentiful, ample, copious, bumper, superabundant, inexhaustible, prolific, profuse; lavish, generous, handsome, rich; *informal* whopping; *literary* plenteous. ANTONYM meager.

bouquet noun **1** *her bridal bouquet* BUNCH OF FLOWERS, posy, nosegay, spray, corsage, boutonniere.

2 *bouquets go to Ann for a well-planned event* COMPLIMENT, commendation, tribute, accolade; praise, congratulations, applause.

3 *the Chardonnay has a fine bouquet* AROMA, nose, smell, fragrance, perfume, scent, odor. See note at BOUQUET.

bourgeois adjective **1** *a bourgeois family* MIDDLE-CLASS, propertied; CONVENTIONAL, conservative, conformist; provincial, suburban, small-town; *informal* white-bread. ANTONYMS proletarian, unconventional.

2 *bourgeois decadence* CAPITALISTIC, materialistic, money-oriented, commercial. ANTONYM communist.

▸ noun *a proud bourgeois* MEMBER OF THE MIDDLE CLASS, property owner.

WORD NOTE **bourgeois**

When using this word it is essential to remember that it is completely bourgeois to say of something or someone, "How bourgeois." If you do not mind this inference, then the word is at your disposal. **–ZS**

bout noun **1** *a bout of dysentery* ATTACK, fit, spasm, paroxysm, convulsion, eruption, outburst; period, session, spell.

2 *he is fighting his fifth bout* CONTEST, match, fight, prizefight, competition, event, meeting.

bovine adjective **1** *large, bovine eyes* COWLIKE, calflike, taurine.

2 *an expression of bovine amazement* STUPID, slow, ignorant, unintelligent, imperceptive, vacuous, mindless, witless, doltish, dumb, dense, dim, dimwitted, dopey, birdbrained, peabrained, dozy.

▸ noun *a beautiful bovine* COW, heifer, bull, bullock, calf, ox, bison.

WORD NOTE **bovine**

It says something about our assumption that we are a superior species and about our true feelings concerning the animal kingdom that words derived from the names of animals and insects are—when applied to humans—hardly ever flattering. *Waspish. Mousy.* The list goes on. *Foxy,* and perhaps *owlish,* are, I suppose, among the few exceptions. Unfortunately, the temptation to use such words—unfair to humans and animals alike—remains strong because they telegraph so much information, so efficiently. When we hear that someone is *bovine,* or *ferretlike,* we know precisely what is meant. **–FP**

bow[1] verb **1** *the officers bowed* INCLINE THE BODY, incline the head, nod, salaam, kowtow, curtsy, bob, genuflect.

2 *the government* ***bowed to*** *foreign pressure* YIELD TO, submit to, give in to, surrender to, succumb to, capitulate to, defer to, conform to; comply with, accept, heed, observe.

▸ noun *a perfunctory bow* OBEISANCE, salaam, bob, curtsy, nod; *archaic* reverence.

PHRASE: **bow out** *Elwood decided to bow out before the New Hampshire primary* WITHDRAW, resign, retire, step down, pull out, back out; give up, quit, leave, pack it in.

bow[2] noun *the bow of the tanker* PROW, front, stem, nose, head, cutwater.

bow[3] noun **1** *she tied a bow in her hair* LOOP, knot; ribbon.

2 *he bent the rod into a bow* ARC, curve, bend; crescent, half-moon.

3 *an archer's bow* LONGBOW, crossbow; *Archery* recurve.

bowdlerize verb *the English translation was bowdlerized beyond recognition* EXPURGATE, censor, blue-pencil, cut, edit; purge, sanitize, water down; *informal* clean up.

bowel noun **1** (also **bowels**) *a disorder of the bowels* INTESTINE(S), entrails, innards, small intestine, large intestine, colon; *informal* guts, insides, viscera.

2 (**bowels**) *the bowels of the ship* INTERIOR, inside, core, belly; depths, recesses; *informal* innards.

bower noun *a rose-scented bower* ARBOR, pergola, grotto, alcove, sanctuary; gazebo.

bowl noun **1** *she cracked two eggs into a bowl* DISH, basin, pot, crock, mortar; container, vessel, receptacle; *rare* jorum, porringer.

2 *the Hollywood Bowl* STADIUM, arena, amphitheater, colosseum.

▸ verb PHRASE: **bowl someone over 1** *the explosion bowled us over* KNOCK DOWN/OVER, fell, floor, prostrate. **2** *informal I have been bowled over by your generosity* OVERWHELM, astound, astonish, overawe, awe, dumbfound, stagger, stun, amaze, daze, shake, take aback, leave aghast; *informal* floor, flabbergast, blow away.

box[1] noun *a box of cigars* CARTON, pack, packet; case, crate, chest, coffer, casket; container, receptacle.

▸ verb *Muriel* ***boxed up*** *his clothes* PACKAGE, pack, parcel, wrap, bundle, crate, bin.

PHRASE: **box something/someone in** *those two vans have*

boxed in my car HEM IN, fence in, close in, shut in; trap, confine, imprison, intern; surround, enclose, encircle, circle.

box[2] verb **1** *he began boxing professionally* FIGHT, prizefight, spar; brawl; *informal* scrap.

2 *he boxed my ears* STRIKE, smack, cuff, hit, thump, slap, swat, punch, jab, wallop; *informal* belt, bop, sock, clout, clobber, whack, slug; *literary* swinge, smite.

boxer noun *a professional boxer* FIGHTER, pugilist, prizefighter, kick-boxer; *informal* bruiser, scrapper.

boxing noun *the history of boxing* PUGILISM, the sweet science, fighting, sparring, fisticuffs; kick-boxing, prizefighting.

boy noun *the tallest boy in our class* LAD, schoolboy, male child, youth, young man, laddie, stripling. See also CHILD.

boycott verb *they boycotted the elections* SPURN, snub, shun, avoid, abstain from, wash one's hands of, turn one's back on, reject, veto. ANTONYM support.

▸ noun *a boycott of imported lumber* BAN, veto, embargo, prohibition, sanction, restriction; avoidance, rejection, refusal.

boyfriend noun *her old boyfriend was at the reunion* LOVER, sweetheart, beloved, darling, dearest, young man, man friend, man, guy, escort, suitor; PARTNER, significant other, companion; *informal* fella, (main) squeeze, flame, steady, toy boy, boy toy, sugar daddy; *literary* swain; *dated* beau; *archaic* paramour.

boyish adjective *his boyish good looks* YOUTHFUL, young, childlike, adolescent, teenage; immature, juvenile, infantile, childish, babyish, puerile.

bozo noun See FOOL noun sense 1.

brace noun *the aquarium is supported by wooden braces* PROP, beam, joist, batten, rod, post, strut, stay, support, stanchion, bracket.

▸ verb **1** *the plane's wing is braced by a system of rods* SUPPORT, shore up, prop up, hold up, buttress, underpin; strengthen, reinforce.

2 *he braced his hand on the railing* STEADY, secure, stabilize, fix, poise; tense, tighten.

3 *brace yourself for disappointment* PREPARE, get ready, gear up, nerve, steel, galvanize, gird, strengthen, fortify; *informal* psych oneself up.

bracelet noun *gold bracelets* BANGLE, band, circlet, armlet, wristlet, anklet.

bracing adjective *a bracing jog through the snowy field* INVIGORATING, refreshing, stimulating, energizing, exhilarating, reviving, restorative, rejuvenating, revitalizing, rousing, fortifying, strengthening; FRESH, brisk, keen.

bracket noun **1** *each speaker is fixed on a separate bracket* SUPPORT, prop, stay, batten, joist; rest, mounting, rack, frame.

2 *put the words in brackets* PARENTHESIS, square bracket; *Printing* brace.

3 *a higher tax bracket* GROUP, category, grade, classification, set, division, order.

brackish adjective *several species of crab inhabit the brackish water* SLIGHTLY SALTY, saline, salt, briny.

brag verb *he liked to brag about his business connections* BOAST, crow, swagger, swank, bluster, gloat, show off; blow one's own horn, sing one's own praises; *informal* talk big, lay it on thick.

braggart noun *Jeff is a prodigious braggart and a liar* BOASTER, bragger, swaggerer, egotist; *informal* big head, loudmouth, show-off, showboat, blowhard.

braid noun *her hair is in braids* PLAIT, pigtail, twist; cornrows, dreadlocks.

▸ verb **1** *she began to braid her hair* PLAIT, entwine, intertwine, interweave, weave, twist, twine.

2 *the sleeves are braided in scarlet* TRIM, edge, border, pipe, hem, fringe.

brain noun **1** *the disease attacks certain cells in the brain* CEREBRUM, cerebral matter, encephalon; *informal* gray matter.

2 (also **brains**) *success requires brains as well as brawn* INTELLIGENCE, intellect, brainpower, IQ, cleverness, wit(s), reasoning, wisdom, acumen, discernment, judgment, understanding, sense; *informal* gray matter, savvy; smarts.

3 *informal* (**brains**) *Janice is the brains of the family* CLEVER PERSON, intellectual, intellect, thinker, mind, scholar; genius, Einstein; *informal* egghead, brainiac, rocket scientist. ANTONYM dunce.

brainless adjective *is he completely brainless?* STUPID, FOOLISH, witless, unintelligent, ignorant, idiotic, simpleminded, slow-witted, feebleminded, halfwitted, emptyheaded; *informal* dumb, brain-dead, moronic, cretinous, bubbleheaded, thick, dopey, dozy, birdbrained, peabrained, dippy, wooden-headed, chowderheaded. ANTONYM clever.

brainteaser noun *brainteasers for mathematicians* PUZZLE, problem, riddle, conundrum, poser, enigma, stumper.

brainwash verb *the evidence is compelling that these cult members were indeed brainwashed* INDOCTRINATE, condition, reeducate, persuade, influence, propagandize, inculcate.

brainy adjective *informal behind every successful machine is a brainy scientist* CLEVER, intelligent, smart, bright, brilliant, gifted; intellectual, erudite, academic, scholarly, studious, bookish. ANTONYM stupid.

brake noun *a brake on research* CURB, check, restraint, restriction, constraint, control, limitation.

▸ verb *she braked at the traffic lights* SLOW DOWN, slow, decelerate, reduce speed, stop. ANTONYM accelerate.

branch noun **1** *the branches of a tree* BOUGH, limb, arm, offshoot.

2 *a branch of the river* TRIBUTARY, feeder, side stream, fork, side channel, influent.

3 *the judicial branch of government* DIVISION, subdivision, section, subsection, subset, department, sector, part, side, wing.

4 *the corporation's New York branch* OFFICE, bureau, agency; subsidiary, affiliate, offshoot, satellite.

▸ verb **1** *the place where the road branches* FORK, bifurcate, divide, subdivide, split.

2 *narrow paths* ***branched off*** *the road* DIVERGE FROM, deviate from, split off from; fan out from, radiate from.

PHRASE: **branch out** *the company is branching out into the European market* EXPAND, open up, extend; diversify, broaden one's horizons.

brand noun **1** *a new brand of margarine* MAKE, line, label, marque; type, kind, sort, variety; trade name, trademark, proprietary name.

2 *her particular brand of humor* TYPE, kind, sort, variety, class, category, genre, style, ilk, stripe.

3 *the brand on a sheep* IDENTIFICATION, marker, earmark.

▸ verb **1** *the letter M was branded on each animal* MARK, stamp, burn, sear.

2 *the scene was branded on her brain* ENGRAVE, stamp, etch, imprint.

3 *the media branded us as communists* STIGMATIZE, mark out; denounce, discredit, vilify; label.

brandish verb *brandishing a sword* FLOURISH, wave, shake, wield; swing, swish; display, flaunt, show off.

brandy noun applejack, Armagnac, Calvados, cognac, eau-de-vie, grappa, kirsch, marc, mirabelle, slivovitz.

brash adjective *a brash man* SELF-ASSERTIVE, pushy, cocksure, cocky, self-confident, arrogant, bold, audacious, brazen, bumptious, overweening, puffed-up; forward, impudent, insolent, rude. ANTONYM meek.

brassy adjective *we're not at all pleased with your brassy new friends* BRAZEN, forward, bold, self-assertive, pushy, cocksure, cocky, cheeky, saucy, brash; shameless, immodest; loud, vulgar, showy, ostentatious; *informal* flashy. ANTONYMS demure, modest.

brat noun *now that I've met his two little brats, I'm not so sure about this relationship* BADLY BEHAVED CHILD, spoiled child; rascal, wretch, imp, scamp, scapegrace, whippersnapper; minx; *informal* monster, horror, hellion; *archaic* jackanapes.

bravado noun *his bravado seems so phony and overplayed* BOLDNESS, swaggering, bluster; machismo; boasting, bragging, bombast, braggadocio; *informal* showing off.

brave adjective **1** *they put up a brave fight* COURAGEOUS, valiant, valorous, intrepid, heroic, lionhearted, bold, fearless, gallant, daring, plucky, audacious; unflinching, unshrinking, unafraid, dauntless, doughty, mettlesome, stouthearted, spirited; *informal* game, gutsy, spunky. ANTONYM cowardly.

2 *literary* *his medals made a brave show* SPLENDID, magnificent, impressive, fine, handsome.

▸ noun *dated* *an Indian brave* WARRIOR, soldier, fighter.

▸ verb *fans braved freezing temperatures to see them play* ENDURE, put up with, bear, withstand, weather, suffer, go through; face, confront, defy.

WORD NOTE **brave**

Excepting the few who boldly confront oppressive laws or governments (Émile Zola, Anna Akhmatova), or those who join fighting brigades where they risk being killed in battle (Ernst Junger, Andre Malraux), no writer should be referred to as *brave*. Too often modern poets are called brave—or daring or fearless—simply because they write openly about being lonely, sexually frustrated, or drug-dependent. Worse yet, critics sometime present the verbal equivalent of the Silver Star to some assistant professor attempting an unfashionable verse form in his latest contribution to the *Powhatan Review*. That's not quite what placing your life on the line means. Save all those courageous adjectives for coal miners, firefighters and the truly heroic. —MD

bravery noun *the bravery witnessed here today will never be forgotten* COURAGE, valor, intrepidity, nerve, daring, fearlessness, audacity, boldness, dauntlessness, stoutheartedness, heroism; backbone, grit, true grit, pluck, spine, spirit, mettle; *informal* guts, balls, cojones, spunk.

▸ ***bravery***
courage
valor
intrepidity
dauntlessness
doughtiness
pluck
fearlessness
heroism
gallantry
stoutheartedness
manfulness
audacity
daring
determination
resolve
fortitude
mettle
nerve
backbone
spine
balls
guts
cojones
boldness
spirit
grit
spunk
bottle
moxie
sand
gutsiness
gameness
rashness
recklessness
foolishness
lack of sense
lack of gumption
timidity
timorousness
spinelessness
spiritlessness
feebleness
gutlessness
weakness
wimpiness
fearfulness
trepidation
dastardliness
poltroonery
pusillanimity
cravenness
cowardice ◂

bravo exclamation *chants of "Bravo!" went on for several minutes* WELL DONE, splendid, congratulations, brava; encore, take a bow; *informal* attaboy, attagirl.

bravura noun *a display of bravura* SKILL, brilliance, virtuosity, expertise, artistry, talent, ability, flair, éclat, wizardry.

▸ adjective *a bravura performance* VIRTUOSO, masterly, outstanding, excellent, superb, brilliant, dazzling, first-class, expert; *informal* top-notch, mean, ace, A1.

brawl noun *a drunken brawl* FIGHT, skirmish, scuffle, tussle, fray, melee, free-for-all, donnybrook; fisticuffs; *informal* scrap, set-to.

▸ verb *he ended up brawling with photographers* FIGHT, skirmish, scuffle, tussle, exchange blows, grapple, wrestle; *informal* scrap.

brawn noun *he has certainly developed his brawn since high school* PHYSICAL STRENGTH, muscle(s), burliness, huskiness, toughness, power, might; vigor, punch; *informal* beef, beefiness.

brawny adjective *the brawny young hunks at the gym* STRONG, muscular, muscly, well-built, hard-bodied, powerful, mighty, Herculean, strapping, burly, sturdy, husky, rugged; hefty, solid; *informal* beefy, hunky. ANTONYMS puny, weak.

bray verb **1** *a donkey brayed* NEIGH, whinny, hee-haw.

2 *Billy brayed with laughter* ROAR, bellow, trumpet.

brazen adjective *brazen defiance* BOLD, SHAMELESS, unashamed, unabashed, unembarrassed; defiant, impudent, impertinent, cheeky, saucy, insolent, in-your-face; barefaced, blatant, flagrant. See note at BOLD. ANTONYM timid.

PHRASE: **brazen it out** *we were shaking in our boots, but we brazened it out* PUT ON A BOLD FRONT, stand one's ground, be defiant, be unrepentant, be unabashed.

breach noun **1** *a clear breach of the regulations* CONTRAVENTION, violation, infringement, infraction, transgression, neglect; *Law* delict.

2 *a breach between government and Church* RIFT, schism, division, gulf, chasm; disunion, estrangement, discord, dissension, disagreement; split, break, rupture, scission.

3 *a breach in the sea wall* BREAK, rupture, split, crack, fracture; opening, gap, hole, fissure.

▸ verb **1** *the river breached its bank* BREAK (THROUGH), burst (through), rupture; *informal* bust (through).

2 *the changes breached union rules* BREAK, contravene, violate, infringe; defy, disobey, flout, fly in the face of; *Law* infract.

bread noun **1** *a slice of bread.* See table.

2 *his job puts bread on the table.* See FOOD sense 1.

3 *informal I hate doing this, but I need the bread.* See MONEY sense 1.

breadth noun **1** *a breadth of 100 meters* WIDTH, broadness, wideness, thickness; span; diameter.

2 *the breadth of his knowledge* RANGE, extent, scope, depth, reach, compass, scale, degree.

break verb **1** *the mirror broke* SHATTER, smash, crack, snap, fracture, fragment, splinter, fall to bits, fall to pieces; split, burst; *informal* bust.

2 *she had broken her leg* FRACTURE, crack. ANTONYM mend.

3 *the bite had barely broken the skin* PIERCE, puncture, penetrate, perforate; cut.

4 *the coffee machine has broken* STOP WORKING, break down, give out, go wrong, malfunction, crash; *informal* go kaput, conk out, go/be on the blink, go/be on the fritz, give up the ghost.

5 *traders who break the law* CONTRAVENE, violate, fail to observe, fail to comply with, infringe, breach; defy, flout, disobey, fly in the face of. ANTONYMS abide by, keep.

6 *his concentration was broken* INTERRUPT, disturb, interfere with.

7 *they broke for coffee* STOP, pause, have a rest, recess; *informal* take a breather, take five. ANTONYM resume.

8 *a pile of carpets broke his fall* CUSHION, soften the impact of, take the edge off.

9 *the movie broke box-office records* EXCEED, surpass, beat, better, cap, top, outdo, outstrip, eclipse.

10 *habits are difficult to break* GIVE UP, relinquish, drop; *informal* kick, shake, quit.

11 *the strategies used to break the union* DESTROY, crush, quash, defeat, vanquish, overcome, overpower, overwhelm, suppress, cripple; weaken, subdue, cow, undermine.

BREAD AND ROLLS

anadama	johnny cake
bagel	Kaiser roll
baguette	kulick
bannock	landbroed
bara brith	lavash
Barbari	matzo
barmbrack	monkey bread
batter bread	muffin
beaten biscuit	nan
bialy	oatcake
biscuit	oatmeal bread
black bread	onion roll
Boston brown	pain au chocolat
breadstick	pain au levain
brioche	pan de sal
brown bread	pancake
bun	pane francese
challah	panettone
chapati	pappadum
ciabatta	paratha
cinnamon raisin bread	Parker House roll
cinnamon roll	pistolette
cob	pita (bread)
coburg	poori
coffee cake	popover
concha	Portuguese roll
corn dodger	potato bread
corn pone	pretzel
cornbread	Pugliese
Cornish split	pull-apart bread
cottage loaf	Pullman bread
crepe	pumpernickel
crescent roll	raisin bread
crispbread	roll
croissant	roti
crumpet	Russian rye (bread)
dosa	rye (bread)
English muffin	Sally Lunn
farmhouse bread	salt rising bread
ficelle (bread)	salt stick
flapjack	scone
flatbread	seven-grain bread
foccaccia	sourdough bread
French bread	sticky bun
fry bread	stollen
gordita	taralli
grissini	tea bread
hoecake	tea ring
hot cross bun	tortilla
hotcake	vasilopita
houska	waffle
hush puppy	white bread
injera	whole wheat bread
Irish soda bread	wholemeal bread
Italian bread	zephyr bun
Jewish rye (bread)	

12 *her self-control finally broke* GIVE WAY, crack, cave in, yield, go to pieces.

13 *four thousand dollars wouldn't break him* BANKRUPT, ruin, pauperize.

14 *he tried to break the news gently* REVEAL, disclose, divulge, impart, tell; announce, release.

15 *he broke the encryption code* DECIPHER, decode, decrypt, unravel, work out; *informal* figure out.

16 *the day broke fair and cloudless* DAWN, begin, start, emerge, appear.

17 *a political scandal broke* ERUPT, break out.

18 *the weather broke* CHANGE, alter, shift.

19 *waves broke against the rocks* CRASH, dash, beat, pound, lash.

20 *her voice broke as she relived the experience* FALTER, quaver, quiver, tremble, shake.

▸ noun 1 *the magazine has been published without a break since 1950* INTERRUPTION, interval, gap, hiatus; discontinuation, suspension, disruption, cutoff; stop, stoppage, cessation.

2 *a break in the weather* CHANGE, alteration, variation.

3 *let's have a break* REST, respite, recess; stop, pause; interval, intermission; *informal* breather, time out, down time; coffee break.

4 *a weekend break* TIME OFF, vacation, holiday, leave, getaway.

5 *a break in diplomatic relations* RIFT, schism, split, breakup, severance, rupture.

6 *the actress got her first break in 1951* OPPORTUNITY, chance, opening.

PHRASES: **break away** 1 *she attempted to break away* ESCAPE, get away, run away, flee, make off; break free, break loose, get out of someone's clutches; *informal* cut and run. 2 *a group* ***broke away from*** *the main party* LEAVE, secede from, split off from, separate from, part company with, defect from; *Politics* cross the floor from. **break down** 1 *his van broke down.* See BREAK verb sense 4. 2 *pay negotiations broke down* FAIL, collapse, founder, fall through, disintegrate; *informal* fizzle out. 3 *Vicky broke down, sobbing loudly* BURST INTO TEARS; lose control, be overcome, go to pieces, crumble, disintegrate; *informal* crack up, lose it. **break something down** 1 *the police broke the door down* KNOCK DOWN, kick down, smash in, pull down, tear down, demolish. 2 *break big tasks down into smaller parts* DIVIDE, separate. 3 *graphs show how the information can be broken down* ANALYZE, categorize, classify, sort out, itemize, organize; dissect. **break in** 1 *thieves broke in and took her checkbook* COMMIT BURGLARY, break and enter; force one's way in. 2 *"I don't want to interfere," Mrs. Hendry broke in* INTERRUPT, butt in, cut in, interject, interpose, intervene, chime in. **break someone in** *it's Edgar's responsibility to break in the new cooks* TRAIN, initiate; *informal* show someone the ropes. **break into** 1 *thieves broke into a house on Park Street* BURGLE, burglarize, rob; force one's way into. 2 *Phil broke into the discussion* INTERRUPT, butt into, cut in on, intervene in. 3 *he broke into a song* BURST INTO, launch into. **break off** *the cup handle just broke off* SNAP OFF, come off, become detached, become separated. **break something off** 1 *I broke off a branch from the tree* SNAP OFF, pull off, sever, detach. 2 *they threatened to break off diplomatic relations* END, terminate, stop, cease, call a halt to, finish, dissolve; SUSPEND, discontinue; *informal* pull the plug on. **break out** 1 *he* ***broke out of*** *the detention center* ESCAPE FROM, abscond from, flee from; get free of. 2 *fighting broke out* FLARE UP, start suddenly, erupt, burst out. **break up** 1 *the meeting broke up* END, finish, stop, terminate; adjourn; recess. 2 *the crowd began to break up* DISPERSE, scatter, disband, part company. 3 *Danny and I broke up last year* SPLIT UP, separate, part, part company; divorce. 4 *informal the whole cast broke up* BURST OUT LAUGHING, crack up, dissolve into laughter. **break something up** 1 *police tried to break up the crowd* DISPERSE, scatter, disband. 2 *I'm not going to let you break up my marriage* WRECK, ruin, destroy.

breakable adjective *pack the breakable items in bubble wrap* FRAGILE, delicate, flimsy, destructible, brittle, easily broken, easily damaged; *formal* frangible. ANTONYM shatterproof.

breakaway adjective *a breakaway group* SEPARATIST, secessionist, schismatic, splinter; rebel, renegade.

breakdown noun 1 *the breakdown of the negotiations* FAILURE, collapse, disintegration, foundering.

2 *on the death of her father she suffered a breakdown* NERVOUS BREAKDOWN, collapse; *informal* crack-up.

3 *the breakdown of the computer system* MALFUNCTION, failure, crash.

4 *a breakdown of the figures* ANALYSIS, classification, examination, investigation, dissection.

breaker noun *breakers crashed against the cliff* WAVE, roller, comber, whitecap; *informal* (big) kahuna.

break-in noun *the break-in occurred just before midnight* BURGLARY, robbery, theft, raid, breaking and entering, forced entry, break and enter.

breakneck adjective *the breakneck pace of change* EXTREMELY FAST, rapid, speedy, high-speed, lightning, whirlwind.

breakthrough noun *the breakthroughs that will lead us to the cure for this disease cannot happen without adequate funding* ADVANCE, development, step forward, success, improvement; discovery, innovation, revolution; progress, headway. ANTONYM setback.

breakup noun 1 *the breakup of negotiations* END, dissolution; breakdown, failure, collapse, disintegration.

2 *their breakup was very amicable* SEPARATION, split, parting, divorce; estrangement, rift.

breakwater noun *she found a submerged breakwater, constructed of parallel stone walls filled with rubble* SEA WALL, jetty, barrier, mole, bulwark, groin, pier.

breast noun 1 *a baby at her breast* mammary gland, mamma; **(breasts)** BOSOM(S), bust, chest; *informal* boobs, knockers, bazooms, hooters.

2 *feelings of frustration were rising up in his breast* HEART, bosom, soul, core.

breath noun 1 *I took a deep breath* INHALATION, inspiration, gulp of air; exhalation, expiration; *Medicine* respiration.

2 *a breath of wind* PUFF, waft, faint breeze.

3 *a breath of scandal* HINT, suggestion, trace, touch, whisper, murmur, suspicion, whiff, undertone.

4 *there was no breath left in him* LIFE, life force. PHRASE: **take someone's breath away** *his solo on the sax took our*

breath away ASTONISH, astound, amaze, stun, startle, stagger, shock, take aback, dumbfound, jolt, shake up; awe, overawe, thrill, flabbergast, blow away, bowl over, stop someone in their tracks, leave someone speechless.

breathe verb **1** *she breathed deeply* inhale and exhale, respire, draw breath; puff, pant, blow, gasp, wheeze, huff; *Medicine* inspire, expire.

2 *at least I'm still breathing* BE ALIVE, be living, live.

3 *she would breathe new life into the firm* INSTILL, infuse, inject, inspire, impart, imbue.

4 *"Together at last," she breathed* WHISPER, murmur, purr, sigh, say.

breather noun *we could all use a breather* BREAK, REST, respite, breathing space, pause, interval, recess.

breathless adjective **1** *Will arrived flushed and breathless* OUT OF BREATH, panting, puffing, gasping, wheezing, hyperventilating; winded, short of breath.

2 *the crowd was breathless with anticipation* AGOG, open-mouthed, waiting with bated breath, on the edge of one's seat, on tenterhooks, in suspense; excited, impatient.

breathtaking adjective *the breathtaking view from the tower* SPECTACULAR, magnificent, wonderful, awe-inspiring, awesome, astounding, astonishing, amazing, stunning, incredible; thrilling, exciting; *informal* sensational, out of this world, jaw-dropping; *literary* wondrous.

breed verb **1** *elephants breed readily in captivity* REPRODUCE, produce/bear/generate offspring, procreate, multiply, propagate; mate.

2 *she was born and bred in the village* BRING UP, rear, raise, nurture.

3 *the political system bred discontent* CAUSE, bring about, give rise to, lead to, produce, generate, foster, result in; stir up; *literary* beget.

▸ noun **1** *a breed of cow* VARIETY, stock, strain; type, kind, sort.

2 *a new breed of journalist* TYPE, kind, sort, variety, class, brand, genre, generation.

breeding noun **1** *the birds pair for breeding* REPRODUCTION, procreation; mating.

2 *the breeding of laboratory rats* REARING, raising, nurturing.

3 *her aristocratic breeding* UPBRINGING, rearing; parentage, family, pedigree, blood, birth, ancestry.

4 *people of rank and breeding* (GOOD) MANNERS, gentility, refinement, cultivation, polish, urbanity; *informal* class. ANTONYMS bad manners, vulgarity.

breeze noun **1** *a breeze ruffled the leaves* GENTLE WIND, puff of air, gust, cat's paw; *Meteorology* light air; *literary* zephyr.

2 *informal getting your child in and out of the seat is a breeze* EASY TASK, child's play, nothing; *informal* piece of cake, cinch, snap, kids' stuff, cakewalk, five-finger exercise, duck soup.

▸ verb *informal Roger breezed into her office* SAUNTER, stroll, sail, cruise.

breezy adjective **1** *a bright, breezy day* WINDY, fresh, brisk, airy; blowy, blustery, gusty.

2 *his breezy manner* JAUNTY, CHEERFUL, cheery, brisk, carefree, easy, casual, relaxed, informal, lighthearted, lively, buoyant, blithe spirited, sunny, jovial; *informal* upbeat, bright-eyed and bushy-tailed; *dated* gay.

brevity noun **1** *the report is notable for its brevity* CONCISENESS, concision, succinctness, economy of language, pithiness, incisiveness, shortness, compactness. ANTONYM verbosity.

2 *the brevity of human life* SHORTNESS, briefness, transience, ephemerality, impermanence. ANTONYMS lengthiness, permanence.

brew verb **1** *this beer is brewed in Oshkosh* FERMENT, make.

2 *I'll brew some tea* PREPARE, infuse, make, steep, stew.

3 *there's trouble brewing* DEVELOP, loom, threaten, impend, be imminent, be on the horizon, be in the offing.

▸ noun **1** *a home brew* BEER, ale.

2 *a piping hot brew* DRINK, beverage; tea, coffee.

3 *a dangerous brew of political turmoil and violent conflict* MIXTURE, mix, blend, combination, amalgam, mishmash, hodgepodge.

bribe verb *he used his wealth to bribe officials* BUY OFF, pay off, suborn; *informal* grease someone's palm, fix, square.

▸ noun *she accepted bribes* INDUCEMENT, incentive, payola; *informal* payoff, kickback, boodle, sweetener.

bribery noun *the judge dismissed 4 of the 15 bribery counts against two former U.S. Olympic officials* GRAFT, payola, corruption, subornation; *informal* palm-greasing, hush money.

bric-a-brac noun *shelves cluttered with bric-a-brac* ORNAMENTS, knickknacks, trinkets, bibelots, gewgaws, gimcracks, tchotchkes; bits and pieces, odds and ends, things, stuff, junk.

brick noun **1** *bricks and mortar* block, cinder block, firebrick, adobe, clinker.

2 *a brick of ice cream* BLOCK, cube, bar, cake.

bridal adjective *the bridal party* WEDDING, nuptial, marriage, matrimonial, marital, conjugal.

bride noun *Ben's lovely bride* WIFE, marriage partner; newlywed.

bridge noun **1** *a bridge over the river* VIADUCT, overpass, fixed link, aqueduct. See table.

2 *a bridge between rival groups* LINK, connection, bond, tie.

▸ verb **1** *a walkway bridged the highway* SPAN, cross (over), extend across, traverse, arch over.

2 *an attempt to bridge the gap between cultures* JOIN, link, connect, unite; straddle; overcome, reconcile.

TYPES OF BRIDGES

bascule bridge	skew bridge
cantilever bridge	skybridge
catwalk	skywalk
covered bridge	suspension bridge
drawbridge	swing bridge
floating bridge	toll bridge
footbridge	trestle bridge
lift bridge	vertical lift bridge
pontoon bridge	viaduct

bridle noun *a horse's bridle* HARNESS, headgear; hackamore.

▸ verb **1** *military officials bridled at Washington's insistence that they not buy these Russian-made missiles* BRISTLE, take offense, take umbrage, be affronted, be offended, get angry.

2 *he bridled his indignation* CURB, restrain, hold back, control, check, rein in/back; suppress, stifle; *informal* keep a/the lid on.

brief adjective **1** *a brief account* CONCISE, succinct, short, pithy, incisive, abridged, condensed, compressed, abbreviated, compact, thumbnail, capsule, potted; *formal* compendious. ANTONYMS lengthy, long-winded.

2 *a brief visit* SHORT, flying, fleeting, hasty, hurried, quick, cursory, perfunctory; temporary, short-lived, momentary, transient; *informal* quickie. ANTONYMS long, lengthy.

3 *a pair of brief shorts* SKIMPY, scanty, short; revealing.

4 *the boss was rather brief with him* BRUSQUE, abrupt, curt, short, blunt, sharp.

▸ noun **1** *a lawyer's brief* SUMMARY, case, argument, contention; dossier.

2 *a brief of our requirements* OUTLINE, summary, synopsis, précis, sketch, digest.

▸ verb *employees were briefed about the decision* INFORM, tell, update, notify, advise, apprise; prepare, prime, instruct; *informal* fill in, clue in, put in the picture.

briefcase noun ATTACHÉ CASE, attaché, satchel, portfolio, dispatch bag/case, messenger bag.

briefing noun *a press briefing* CONFERENCE, meeting, interview; orientation; *informal* backgrounder, Q & A session.

briefly adverb **1** *Henry paused briefly* MOMENTARILY, temporarily, for a moment, fleetingly.

2 *briefly, the plot is as follows* IN SHORT, in brief, to make/cut a long story short, in a word, in sum, in a nutshell, in essence.

briefs plural noun See UNDERWEAR.

brigade noun **1** *a brigade of soldiers* UNIT, contingent, battalion, regiment, division, squadron, company, platoon, section, corps, troop.

2 *the volunteer ambulance brigade* SQUAD, team, group, band, party, crew, force, outfit.

brigand noun *literary*. See BANDIT.

bright adjective **1** *the bright surface of the metal* SHINING, brilliant, dazzling, beaming, glaring; sparkling, flashing, glittering, scintillating, gleaming, glowing, luminous, radiant; shiny, lustrous, glossy. ANTONYMS dull, dark.

2 *a bright morning* SUNNY, sunshiny, cloudless, clear, fair, fine. ANTONYMS cloudy, overcast.

3 *bright crayons* VIVID, brilliant, intense, strong, bold, glowing, rich; gaudy, lurid, garish; COLORFUL, vibrant; *dated* gay. ANTONYM drab.

4 *a bright guitar sound* CLEAR, vibrant, pellucid; high-pitched.

5 *a bright young graduate* CLEVER, intelligent, quick-witted, smart, canny, astute, intuitive, perceptive; ingenious, resourceful; gifted, brilliant; *informal* brainy. ANTONYMS dimwitted, stupid.

6 *a bright smile* HAPPY, cheerful, cheery, jolly, merry, sunny, beaming; lively, exuberant, buoyant, bubbly, bouncy, perky, chirpy; *dated* gay. ANTONYM cheerless.

7 *a bright future* PROMISING, rosy, optimistic, hopeful, favorable, propitious, auspicious, encouraging, good, golden. ANTONYMS dismal, pessimistic.

▸ adverb *literary the moon shone bright* BRIGHTLY, brilliantly, intensely.

THE RIGHT WORD

Looking for just the right word to capture the quality of the light on a moonlit night or a summer day? All of these adjectives describe an intense, steady light emanating (or appearing to emanate) from a source. **Bright** is the most general term, applied to something that gives forth, reflects, or is filled with light (*a bright and sunny day*; *a bright star*). **Brilliant** light is even more intense or dazzling (*the brilliant diamond on her finger*), and **resplendent** is a slightly more formal, even poetic, way of describing a striking brilliance (*the sky was resplendent with stars*). Poets also prefer adjectives like **effulgent** and **refulgent**, both of which can be applied to an intense, pervading light, sometimes from an unseen source (*her effulgent loveliness*); but *refulgent* specifically refers to reflected light (*a chandelier of refulgent crystal pendants*). **Radiant** is used to describe the power of giving off light, either literally or metaphorically (*a radiant June day*; *the bride's radiant face*); it describes a steady, warm light that is emitted in all directions. Like *radiant*, **luminous** suggests sending forth light, but light of the glow-in-the-dark variety (*the luminous face of the alarm clock*). While diamonds are known for being *brilliant*, fabrics like satin and surfaces like polished wood, which reflect light and take on a gloss or sheen, are often called **lustrous**. If none of these words captures the exact quality of the light you're trying to describe, you can always join the masses and use **shining**, a word that has been overworked to the point of cliché (*my knight in shining armor*).

brighten verb **1** *sunshine brightened the room* ILLUMINATE, light up, lighten, make bright, make brighter, cast/shed light on; *formal* illume.

2 *Sarah* ***brightened up*** *as she thought of her mother's words* CHEER UP, perk up, rally; be enlivened, feel heartened, be uplifted, be encouraged, take heart; *informal* buck up, pep up.

brilliance noun **1** *a philosopher of great brilliance* GENIUS, intelligence, wisdom, sagacity, intellect; talent, ability, prowess, skill, expertise, aptitude; flair, finesse, panache; greatness.

2 *the brilliance and beauty of Paris* SPLENDOR, magnificence, grandeur, resplendence.

3 *the brilliance of the sunshine* BRIGHTNESS, vividness, intensity; sparkle, glitter, glittering, glow, blaze, luminosity, radiance.

brilliant adjective **1** *a brilliant student* BRIGHT, intelligent, clever, smart, astute, intellectual; gifted, talented, able, adept, skillful; elite, superior, first-class, first-rate, excellent; *informal* brainy. ANTONYM stupid.

2 *his brilliant career* SUPERB, glorious, illustrious, impressive, remarkable, exceptional. ANTONYM unremarkable.

3 *a shaft of brilliant light* BRIGHT, shining, blazing, dazzling, vivid, intense, gleaming, glaring, luminous, radiant;

literary irradiant, coruscating. See note at BRIGHT. ANTONYMS obscure, dark.

4 *brilliant green* VIVID, intense, bright, bold, dazzling. ANTONYMS dull, dark.

brim noun 1 *the brim of his hat* peak, visor, shield, shade; fringe.

2 *the cup was filled to its brim* RIM, lip, brink, edge, margin. See note at BORDER.

brimful adjective *a large vessel brimful with water* FULL, filled, brimming, filled/full to the brim, filled to capacity, overfull, running over; *informal* chock-full. ANTONYM empty.

brindle, brindled adjective *a litter of brindle puppies* TAWNY, brownish, brown; DAPPLED, streaked, mottled, speckled, flecked, marbled.

bring verb 1 *he brought a tray* CARRY, fetch, bear, take; convey, transport, tote; move, haul, shift, lug.

2 *Seth brought his bride to the club* ESCORT, conduct, guide, lead, usher, show, shepherd.

3 *the wind changed and brought rain* CAUSE, produce, create, generate, precipitate, lead to, give rise to, result in; stir up, whip up, promote; *literary* beget.

4 *the police contemplated bringing charges* PUT FORWARD, prefer, lay, submit, present, initiate, institute.

5 *this job brings him a regular salary* EARN, make, fetch, bring in, yield, net, gross, return, produce; command, attract. PHRASES: **bring about** *the events that brought about her death* CAUSE, produce, give rise to, result in, lead to, occasion, bring to pass; provoke, generate, engender, precipitate, bring on; *formal* effectuate. **bring around** 1 *she administered CPR and brought him around* WAKE UP, return to consciousness, rouse, bring to. 2 *we would have brought him around, given time* PERSUADE, convince, win over, sway, influence. **bring back** 1 *the smell brought back memories* REMIND ONE OF, put one in mind of, bring/call to mind, conjure up, evoke, summon up. 2 *bring back capital punishment* REINTRODUCE, reinstate, reestablish, revive, resurrect. **bring down** 1 *he was brought down by his own teammate* TRIP, knock over, knock down; foul. 2 *I couldn't bear to bring her down* DEPRESS, sadden, upset, get down, dispirit, dishearten, discourage. 3 *we will bring down the price* DECREASE, reduce, lower, cut, drop; *informal* slash. 4 *the unrest brought down the government* UNSEAT, overturn, topple, overthrow, depose, oust. **bring forward** *why wasn't this brought forward at the last meeting?* PROPOSE, suggest, advance, raise, present, move, submit, lodge. **bring in** *the event brings in a million dollars each year.* See BRING sense 5. **bring on** *what could have brought on this fever?* See BRING ABOUT. **bring out** 1 *they were bringing out a new magazine* LAUNCH, establish, begin, start, found, set up, instigate, inaugurate, market; publish, print, issue, produce. 2 *the shawl brings out the color of your eyes* ACCENTUATE, highlight, emphasize, accent, set off. **bring oneself to** *she could not bring herself to complain* FORCE ONESELF TO, make oneself, bear to. **bring up** 1 *she and Lenny brought up her brother's four children* REAR, raise, care for, look after, nurture, provide for. 2 *I wonder if he'll bring up the matter of the grocery bill* MENTION, allude to, touch on, raise, broach, introduce; voice, air, suggest, propose, submit, put forward, bring forward.

brink noun 1 *the brink of the abyss* EDGE, verge, margin, rim, lip; border, boundary, perimeter, periphery, limit(s).

2 *two countries on the brink of war* VERGE, threshold, point, edge. See note at BORDER.

brio noun *let's give this celebration the brio it deserves!* VIGOR, vivacity, gusto, verve, zest, enthusiasm, vitality, dynamism, animation, spirit, energy; *informal* pep, vim, getup-and-go.

brisk adjective 1 *a brisk pace* QUICK, rapid, fast, swift, speedy, hurried; energetic, lively, vigorous. ANTONYMS slow, sluggish.

2 *business was brisk at the bar* BUSY, bustling, lively, hectic; good. ANTONYM slow.

3 *a brisk breeze* BRACING, fresh, crisp, invigorating, refreshing, stimulating, energizing; biting, keen, chilly, cold; *informal* nippy. ANTONYM sultry.

bristle noun 1 *the bristles on his chin* HAIR, whisker; **(bristles)** stubble, five o'clock shadow; *Zoology* seta/setae.

2 *a hedgehog's bristles* SPINE, prickle, quill, barb.

▸ verb 1 *the hair on the back of his neck bristled* RISE, stand up, stand on end; *literary* horripilate.

2 *she bristled at his tone* TAKE OFFENSE, bridle, take umbrage, be affronted, be offended; get angry, be irritated.

3 *the roof bristled with antennas* ABOUND, overflow, be full, be packed, be crowded, be jammed, be covered; *informal* be thick, be jam-packed, be chock-full.

bristly adjective 1 *bristly little bushes* PRICKLY, spiky, thorny, scratchy, brambly.

2 *the bristly skin of his cheek* STUBBLY, hairy, fuzzy, unshaven, whiskered, whiskery; scratchy, rough, coarse, prickly; *Biology* setaceous, hispid. ANTONYM smooth.

WORD NOTE **setaceous**

From the Latin *saeta* meaning "bristle," we derive this late-eighteenth-century term in its jocular form: "bristly, unshaven." For ambitious novelists only, probably, but acceptance is all in the frequency for these types of slightly pompous Latinate terms. Think of *cornucopia*! **–ZS**

brittle adjective 1 *glass is a brittle material* BREAKABLE, fragile, delicate; splintery; *formal* frangible. ANTONYMS flexible, resilient.

2 *a brittle laugh* HARSH, hard, sharp, grating. ANTONYM soft.

3 *a brittle young woman* EDGY, anxious, unstable, highstrung, tense, excitable, jumpy, skittish, neurotic; *informal* uptight. ANTONYM relaxed.

broach verb 1 *I broached the matter with my parents* BRING UP, raise, introduce, talk about, mention, touch on, air.

2 *he broached a barrel of beer* PIERCE, puncture, tap; OPEN, uncork; *informal* crack open.

broad adjective 1 *a broad flight of steps* WIDE. ANTONYM narrow.

2 *the leaves are two inches broad* WIDE, across, in breadth, in width.

3 *a broad expanse of prairie* EXTENSIVE, vast, immense, great, spacious, expansive, sizable, sweeping, rolling.

4 *a broad range of opportunities* COMPREHENSIVE, inclusive, extensive, wide, all-embracing, eclectic, unlimited. ANTONYM limited.

5 *this report gives a broad outline* GENERAL, nonspecific, unspecific, rough, approximate, basic; loose, vague. ANTONYM detailed.

6 *a broad hint* OBVIOUS, unsubtle, explicit, direct, plain, clear, straightforward, bald, patent, transparent, undisguised, overt. ANTONYM subtle.

7 *a broad Latvian accent* PRONOUNCED, noticeable, strong, thick. ANTONYM slight.

8 *he was attacked in broad daylight* FULL, complete, total; clear, bright.

broadcast verb **1** *the show will be broadcast worldwide* TRANSMIT, relay, air, beam, show, televise, telecast, webcast, simulcast, cablecast, screen.

2 *the result was broadcast far and wide* REPORT, announce, publicize, proclaim; spread, circulate, air, blazon, trumpet. See note at SCATTER.

▸ noun *radio and television broadcasts* PROGRAM, show, production, transmission, telecast, webcast, simulcast, screening.

broaden verb **1** *her smile broadened* WIDEN, expand, stretch (out), draw out, spread; deepen.

2 *the government tried to broaden its political base* EXPAND, enlarge, extend, widen, swell; increase, augment, add to, amplify; develop, enrich, improve, build on.

broadly adverb **1** *the pattern is broadly similar for men and women* IN GENERAL, on the whole, as a rule, in the main, mainly, predominantly; loosely, roughly, approximately.

2 *he was smiling broadly now* WIDELY, openly.

broad-minded adjective *our broad-minded English professor* LIBERAL, tolerant, open-minded, freethinking, progressive, permissive, unprejudiced, unbiased, unbigoted. ANTONYM intolerant.

broadside noun **1** *historical the gunners fired broadsides* SALVO, volley, cannonade, barrage, blast, fusillade.

2 *a broadside against the economic reforms* CRITICISM, censure, polemic, diatribe, tirade; attack, onslaught; *literary* philippic.

brochure noun *college recruitment brochures* BOOKLET, pamphlet, leaflet, flyer, handbill, catalog, handout, prospectus, fact sheet, folder.

broil verb *broil the lamb chops* GRILL, toast, barbecue; cook.

broiling adjective *the sweaty nights and broiling days* HOT, scorching, roasting, baking, boiling (hot), blistering, sweltering, parching, searing, blazing, sizzling, burning (hot), sultry, torrid, tropical, like an oven, like a furnace. ANTONYMS cold, cool.

broke adjective *have you so easily forgotten what it's like to be broke?* PENNILESS, moneyless, bankrupt, insolvent, ruined, down-and-out, without a penny to one's name, without a cent, without one red cent, without two pennies to rub together; poor, poverty-stricken, impoverished, impecunious, penurious, indigent, in penury, needy, destitute, *informal* cleaned out, flat broke, strapped (for cash), bust, busted, hard up, stone broke, as poor as a church mouse.

broken adjective **1** *a broken bottle* SMASHED, shattered, fragmented, splintered, crushed, snapped; in bits, in pieces; destroyed, disintegrated; cracked, split; *informal* in smithereens. ANTONYM whole.

2 *a broken arm* FRACTURED, damaged, injured.

3 *this TV's broken* INOPERATIVE, not working, malfunctioning, faulty, defective, in disrepair, damaged, out of order, broken-down, down; *informal* on the blink, on the fritz, kaput, bust, busted, conked out, acting up, done for. ANTONYMS working, fixed.

4 *broken skin* CUT, ruptured, punctured, perforated.

5 *a broken marriage* FAILED, ended.

6 *broken promises* FLOUTED, violated, infringed, contravened, disregarded, ignored, unkept. ANTONYMS kept, honored.

7 *he was left a broken man* DEFEATED, beaten, subdued; DEMORALIZED, dispirited, discouraged, crushed, humbled; dishonored, ruined.

8 *a night of broken sleep* INTERRUPTED, disturbed, fitful, disrupted, discontinuous, intermittent, unsettled, troubled. ANTONYM uninterrupted.

9 *he pressed on over the broken ground* UNEVEN, rough, irregular, bumpy; rutted, pitted. ANTONYM smooth.

10 *she spoke in broken English* HALTING, hesitating, disjointed, faltering, imperfect. ANTONYM perfect.

broken-down adjective **1** *a broken-down hotel* DILAPIDATED, run-down, ramshackle, tumbledown, in disrepair, beat-up, battered, crumbling, deteriorated, gone to rack and ruin; *informal* fleabag.

2 *a broken-down car* DEFECTIVE, broken, faulty; not working, malfunctioning, inoperative, nonfunctioning; *informal* kaput, conked out, done for.

broken-hearted adjective *his broken-hearted family* HEARTBROKEN, grief-stricken, desolate, devastated, despondent, inconsolable, disconsolate, miserable, depressed, melancholy, wretched, sorrowful, forlorn, heavy-hearted, woeful, doleful, downcast, woebegone, sad, down; *informal* down in/at the mouth; *literary* heartsick. ANTONYM overjoyed.

broker noun *a top Wall Street broker* DEALER, agent; middleman, intermediary, mediator; liaison; stockbroker.

▸ verb *an agreement brokered by the secretariat* ARRANGE, organize, orchestrate, work out, settle, clinch, bring about; negotiate, mediate.

bromide noun See PLATITUDE.

brooch noun *her great aunt's ivory brooch* pin, clip, clasp, badge; *historical* fibula.

brood noun **1** *the bird flew to feed its brood* OFFSPRING, young, progeny; family, hatch, clutch.

2 *informal Gill was the youngest of the brood* FAMILY; children, offspring, youngsters, progeny; *informal* kids.

▸ verb **1** *once the eggs are laid, the male broods them* INCUBATE, hatch.

2 *he slumped in his armchair, brooding* WORRY, fret, agonize, mope, sulk; think, ponder, contemplate, meditate, muse, ruminate.

brook[1] noun *a babbling brook* STREAM, creek, streamlet, rivulet, rill, brooklet, runnel; *Brit.* bourn, burn, beck.

brook[2] verb *formal we brook no violence* TOLERATE, allow, stand, bear, abide, put up with, endure; accept, permit, countenance; *informal* stomach, stand for, hack; *archaic* suffer.

broom noun *mops and brooms* besom, push broom, corn broom, whisk broom.

broth noun *two cups of beef broth* STOCK, bouillon, consommé, soup.

brothel noun *young girls from Nepal are sold to the owners of these brothels* WHOREHOUSE, bordello, massage parlor, cathouse, bagnio; *dated* bawdy house, house of ill repute; *Law, dated* disorderly house.

brother noun **1** *then Steve and his brother Dan showed up* SIBLING; *informal* bro, sib.

2 *they were brothers in crime* COMRADE, colleague, partner, associate, fellow, friend; *informal* pal, chum, mate.

3 *a brother of the order* MONK, cleric, friar, religious, monastic.

brotherhood noun **1** *the ideals of justice and brotherhood* COMRADESHIP, fellowship, brotherliness, fraternalism, kinship; camaraderie, friendship.

2 *a masonic brotherhood* SOCIETY, fraternity, association, alliance, union, league, guild, order, body, community, club, lodge, circle.

brotherly adjective **1** *brotherly rivalry* FRATERNAL, sibling.

2 *brotherly love* FRIENDLY, comradely; affectionate, amicable, kind, devoted, loyal.

brow noun **1** *the doctor wiped his brow* FOREHEAD, temple; *Zoology* frons.

2 *heavy black brows* EYEBROW.

3 *the brow of the hill* SUMMIT, peak, top, crest, crown, head, pinnacle, apex.

browbeat verb *they browbeat the witness into changing her testimony* BULLY, intimidate, force, coerce, compel, hector, dragoon, bludgeon, pressure, pressurize, tyrannize, terrorize, menace; harass, harry, hound; *informal* bulldoze, railroad.

brown adjective *she has brown eyes* hazel, chocolate-colored, coffee-colored, cocoa-colored, nut-brown; brunette; sepia, mahogany, umber, burnt sienna; beige, buff, tan, fawn, camel, café au lait, caramel, chestnut.

browse verb **1** *I visited all the little boutiques, just to browse* LOOK AROUND, window-shop, peruse.

2 *she* ***browsed through*** *the newspaper* SCAN (THROUGH), skim through, glance through, look through, peruse; thumb through, leaf through, flick through; dip into.

3 *three cows were browsing in the meadow* GRAZE, feed, nibble, crop; ruminate.

4 *he spent hours browsing online* SURFING, go from site to site.

bruise noun *a bruise across her forehead* CONTUSION, lesion, mark, black-and-blue mark, discoloration, blackening; injury; swelling, lump, bump, welt; *Medicine* ecchymosis.

▸ verb **1** *her face was badly bruised* injure, mark, discolor.

2 *every one of the apples is bruised* MARK, discolor, blemish; damage, spoil.

3 *Eric's ego was bruised* UPSET, offend, insult, affront, hurt, wound, injure, crush.

brunette adjective *a brunette woman* BROWN-HAIRED, dark, dark-haired.

brunt noun *the brunt of the downsizing was felt most by the warehouse crew* FULL FORCE, force, impact, shock, burden, pressure, weight; effect, repercussions, consequences.

brush noun **1** *a styling brush | camel-hair brushes | a brush and dustpan* hairbrush; toothbrush; paintbrush; scrub brush; whisk broom, sweeper, broom.

2 *he gave the seat a brush with his hand* SWEEP, wipe, dust.

3 *the brush of his lips against her cheek* TOUCH, stroke, skim, graze, nudge, contact; kiss.

4 *a brush with the law* ENCOUNTER, clash, confrontation, conflict, altercation, incident; *informal* run-in.

▸ verb **1** *she brushed her hair* GROOM, comb, neaten, tidy, smooth, arrange, fix, do; curry.

2 *she felt his lips brush her cheek* TOUCH, stroke, caress, skim, sweep, graze, contact; kiss.

3 *she brushed a wisp of hair away* PUSH, move, sweep, clear.

PHRASES: **brush something aside** *she brushed aside his repeated warnings* DISREGARD, ignore, dismiss, shrug off, wave aside; overlook, pay no attention to, take no notice of, neglect, forget about, turn a blind eye to, turn a deaf ear to; reject, spurn; laugh off, make light of, trivialize; *informal* pooh-pooh. **brush someone off** *he tried to help, but she brushed him off* REBUFF, dismiss, spurn, reject; slight, scorn, disdain; ignore, disregard, snub, turn one's back on, give someone the cold shoulder, freeze out; jilt, cast aside, discard. **brush up (on)** *I'm brushing up on my French before our trip to Paris* RELEARN, read up (on), go over, study; improve, sharpen (up), polish up; hone, refine, perfect; *informal* bone up (on).

brush[2] noun *the pheasant scampered into the brush* UNDERGROWTH, bushes, scrub, underwood, underbrush, brushland, brushwood, shrubs, chaparral; thicket, copse; *rare* boscage.

brush-off noun *informal the brush-off was the last thing he expected from her* REJECTION, dismissal, refusal, rebuff, repulse; snub, slight; *informal* kiss-off, gate.

brusque adjective *his brusque manners* CURT, abrupt, blunt, short, sharp, terse, peremptory, gruff; offhand, discourteous, impolite, rude; *informal* snappy. ANTONYM polite.

THE RIGHT WORD

Brusque, which comes from an Italian word meaning rude, describes an abruptness of speech or manner that is not necessarily meant to be rude (*a brusque handshake*; *a brusque reply*). **Curt** is more deliberately unfriendly, suggesting brevity and coldness of manner (*a curt dismissal*). There's nothing wrong with being **blunt**, although it implies an honesty and directness that can border on tactlessness (*a blunt reply to his question about where the money went*). Someone who is **bluff** is usually more likable, possessing a frank, hearty manner that may be a little too outspoken but is seldom offensive (*a bluff man who rarely minced words*). Exhibiting **gruff** or **surly** behavior will not win friends, since both words suggest bad temper if not rudeness. But *gruff* is used to describe a rough or grouchy disposition and, like *bluff*, is applied more often to a man. Anyone who has had to deal with an overworked store clerk while shopping during the holidays knows the meaning of *surly*, which is worse than *gruff*. It describes not only a sour disposition but an outright hostility toward people, and it can apply to someone of either sex (*that surly woman at the customer service desk*).

---

brutal adjective **1** *a brutal attack* SAVAGE, cruel, vicious, ferocious, brutish, barbaric, barbarous, wicked, murderous, bloodthirsty, cold-blooded, callous, heartless, ruthless, merciless, sadistic; heinous, monstrous, abominable, atrocious. See note at CRUELTY. ANTONYMS gentle, humane.

2 *brutal honesty* UNSPARING, unstinting, unembellished, unvarnished, bald, naked, stark, blunt, direct, straightforward, frank, outspoken, forthright, plain-spoken; complete, total.

brute noun *a callous brute* SAVAGE, beast, monster, animal, barbarian, fiend, ogre; sadist; thug, lout, ruffian; *informal* swine, pig.

▸ adjective *brute strength* PHYSICAL, bodily; crude, violent.

bubble noun *the bubbles rose in the glass* globule, bead, blister; air pocket; (**bubbles**) sparkle, fizz, effervescence, froth, head.

▸ verb **1** *the champagne bubbled nicely on the tongue* SPARKLE, fizz, effervesce, foam, froth.

2 *the milk was bubbling above the flame* BOIL, simmer, seethe, gurgle.

3 *she was **bubbling over** with enthusiasm* OVERFLOW, brim over, be filled, gush.

bubbly adjective **1** *a bubbly wine* SPARKLING, bubbling, fizzy, effervescent, gassy, aerated, carbonated; spumante, frothy, foamy. ANTONYM flat.

2 *she was bubbly and full of life* VIVACIOUS, animated, ebullient, exuberant, lively, high-spirited, zestful; sparkling, bouncy, buoyant, carefree; merry, happy, cheerful, perky, sunny, bright; *informal* upbeat, chirpy. ANTONYMS dull, listless.

▸ noun *informal a bottle of bubbly* CHAMPAGNE, sparkling wine, spumante, cava.

buck verb *it takes guts to buck the system* RESIST, oppose, defy, fight, kick against. PHRASES: **buck up** *informal don't worry, I'll buck up soon* CHEER UP, perk up, take heart, pick up, bounce back. **buck someone up** *informal how can we buck you up, pal?* CHEER UP, buoy up, perk up, hearten, uplift, encourage, enliven, give someone a lift; *informal* pep up; *rare* inspirit.

bucket noun **1** *a bucket of cold water* PAIL, scuttle, can, tin, tub; ice bucket, wine cooler.

2 *informal everyone wept buckets* FLOODS, gallons, oceans.

buckle noun *a belt buckle* CLASP, clip, catch, hasp, fastener.

▸ verb **1** *he buckled the belt around his waist* FASTEN, do up, hook, strap, secure, clasp, clip.

2 *the front axle buckled* WARP, bend, twist, curve, distort, contort, deform; bulge, arc, arch; crumple, collapse, give way.

PHRASE: **buckle down** *Isaac finally began to buckle down in his junior year* GET (DOWN) TO WORK, set to work, get down to business; work hard, apply oneself, make an effort, be industrious, be diligent, focus.

bucolic adjective *their farm had been used as the bucolic setting for two major motion pictures* RUSTIC, rural, pastoral, country, countryside; *literary* Arcadian, sylvan, georgic.

bud noun *fresh buds* SPROUT, shoot, blossom; *Botany* plumule.

▸ verb *trees began to bud* SPROUT, shoot, germinate.

budding adjective *a budding artist* PROMISING, up-and-coming, rising, in the making, aspiring, emerging, fledgling, developing, blossoming; *informal* would-be, wannabe.

buddy noun See CHUM.

budge verb **1** *the horses wouldn't budge* MOVE, shift, stir, go.

2 *I couldn't budge the door* DISLODGE, shift, move, reposition.

3 *they refuse to budge on the issue* GIVE IN, give way, yield, change one's mind, acquiesce, compromise, do a U-turn.

budget noun **1** *your budget for the week* FINANCIAL PLAN, forecast; accounts, statement.

2 *a cut in the defense budget* ALLOWANCE, allocation, quota; grant, award, funds, resources, capital.

▸ verb **1** *we have to budget $7,000 for the work* ALLOCATE, allot, allow, earmark, designate, set aside.

2 *budget your finances* SCHEDULE, plan, cost, estimate; ration.

▸ adjective *a budget hotel* CHEAP, inexpensive, economy, affordable, low-cost, low-price, cut-rate, discount, bargain, downmarket. ANTONYM expensive.

buff adjective *a plain buff envelope* BEIGE, yellowish, yellowish-brown, light brown, fawn, sandy, wheaten, biscuit, camel.

▸ verb *he buffed the glass* POLISH, burnish, shine, clean, rub.

▸ noun *informal a film buff* ENTHUSIAST, fan, devotee, lover, admirer; expert, aficionado, authority, pundit; *informal* freak, nut, fanatic, fiend, addict, junkie, bum.

PHRASE: **in the buff** *informal* See NAKED sense 1.

buffer noun *a buffer against market fluctuations* CUSHION, bulwark, shield, barrier, guard, safeguard.

▸ verb *she tried to buffer the children from the troubles* SHIELD, protect, defend, cushion, insulate, screen, guard.

buffet[1] noun **1** *a sumptuous buffet* SMORGASBORD, self-serve meal, serve-yourself meal, spread.

2 *the plates are kept in the buffet* SIDEBOARD, cabinet, cupboard.

buffet[2] verb **1** *rough seas buffeted the coast* BATTER, pound, lash, strike, hit.

2 *he has been buffeted by bad publicity* AFFLICT, trouble, harm, burden, bother, beset, harass, assail, harry, plague, torment, blight, bedevil.

buffoon noun 1 *archaic the king's buffoon* CLOWN, jester, fool, comic, comedian, wag, wit, merry-andrew, harlequin, Punchinello, Pierrot.

2 *they regarded him as a buffoon* FOOL, idiot, dolt, dunce, dunderhead, dullard, ignoramus, dummy, simpleton, jackass; *informal* chump, blockhead, jughead, boob, bozo, doofus, nincompoop, numbskull, numbnuts, dope, twit, nitwit, halfwit, birdbrain. See also ASS sense 2.

bug noun 1 *bugs were crawling everywhere* INSECT, mite; *informal* creepy-crawly, beastie.

2 *informal a stomach bug* ILLNESS, ailment, disorder, infection, disease, sickness, complaint, upset, condition; bacterium, germ, virus.

3 *informal he caught the journalism bug* OBSESSION, enthusiasm, craze, fad, mania, passion, fixation.

4 *the bug planted in his phone* LISTENING DEVICE, hidden microphone, wire, wiretap, tap.

5 *a bug in the software* FAULT, error, defect, flaw; virus; *informal* glitch, gremlin.

▸ verb 1 *her conversations were bugged* RECORD, eavesdrop on, spy on, overhear; wiretap, tap, monitor.

2 *informal she really bugs me.* See ANNOY.

bugbear noun *pseudoscience is a perennial bugbear for legitimate researchers* PET PEEVE, hate, bête noire, anathema, aversion, bugaboo; bane, bane of one's life/existence, irritant, irritation, vexation, thorn in one's flesh/side; nightmare, torment; *informal* pain, pain in the neck, hang-up.

build verb 1 *they were building a tree house* CONSTRUCT, erect, put up, assemble; make, form, create, fashion, model, shape.

2 *they are building a business strategy* ESTABLISH, found, set up, institute, inaugurate, initiate.

3 *the pressure was building* INCREASE, mount, intensify, escalate, grow, rise.

▸ noun *a man of slim build* PHYSIQUE, frame, body, figure, form, shape, stature, proportions; *informal* vital statistics.

PHRASES: **build something in/into** *emergency procedures must be built into every plan* INCORPORATE IN/INTO, include in, absorb into, subsume into, assimilate into. **build on** *we are now in a position to build on all the wonderful legwork that our staff has accomplished* EXPAND ON, enlarge on, develop, elaborate, flesh out, embellish, amplify; refine, improve, perfect. **build up** *the traffic continues to build up* INCREASE, grow, mount (up), intensify, escalate; strengthen. **build something up** 1 *he built up a huge business* ESTABLISH, set up, found, institute, start, create; develop, expand, enlarge. 2 *she built up her stamina* BOOST, strengthen, increase, improve, augment, raise, enhance, swell; *informal* beef up. 3 *I have built up a collection of prints* ACCUMULATE, amass, collect, gather; stockpile, hoard.

builder noun *a house builder | the builders of the transcontinental railroad* CONSTRUCTOR, contractor, creator, maker; planner, architect, deviser, designer; CONSTRUCTION WORKER, bricklayer, laborer.

building noun 1 *a brick building* STRUCTURE, construction, edifice, erection; property, premises, establishment.

2 *the building of power stations* CONSTRUCTION, erection, fabrication, assembly.

buildup noun 1 *the buildup of military strength* INCREASE, growth, expansion, escalation, development, proliferation.

2 *the buildup of carbon dioxide* ACCUMULATION, accretion.

3 *the buildup for the World Cup* PUBLICITY, promotion, advertising, marketing; *informal* hype, ballyhoo, brouhaha, to-do.

built-in adjective 1 *a built-in cupboard* integrated, integral, incorporated.

2 *built-in advantages* INHERENT, intrinsic, inbuilt, innate; essential, implicit, basic, fundamental, deep-rooted.

bulbous adjective *a bulbous growth on the foreleg* BULGING, protuberant, round, fat, rotund; swollen, tumid, distended, bloated.

bulge noun 1 *a bulge in the tire* SWELLING, bump, lump, protuberance, prominence, tumescence.

2 *informal a bulge in the population* SURGE, upsurge, rise, increase, escalation.

▸ verb *his eyes were bulging* SWELL, stick out, puff out, balloon (out), bug out, fill out, belly, distend, tumefy, intumesce; project, protrude, stand out.

THE RIGHT WORD

While all of these verbs mean to extend outward, beyond the normal line or surface of something, it is almost impossible not to associate the word **bulge** with the human body (*a stomach that bulges over a waistband, muscles that bulge beneath a shirt*). *Bulge* suggests a swelling out that is quite noticeable or even abnormal, and that may be the result of internal pressure, although a brick wall can *bulge*, as can a bicep muscle. **Protuberate** is a less common word meaning to swell or stick out, but it does not necessarily imply that anything is abnormal or radically wrong (*he was so thin that his knees protuberated*). To **protrude** is to thrust forth in an unexpected way or to stick out in a way that is abnormal or disfiguring (*her eyes protruded from her skull*). **Project** is the least upsetting of all these words, probably because it is used less often with reference to the human body. Anything that juts out abruptly beyond the rest of a surface is said to *project* (*the balcony projected from the south side of the house*).

bulk noun 1 *the sheer bulk of the bags* SIZE, volume, dimensions, proportions, mass, scale, magnitude, immensity, vastness.

2 *the bulk of entrants were women* MAJORITY, main part, major part, lion's share, preponderance, generality; most, almost all. ANTONYM minority.

bulky adjective *bulky items* LARGE, big, huge, sizable, substantial, massive; king-size, economy-size(d), outsize, oversized, considerable, voluminous; CUMBERSOME, unmanageable, unwieldy, ponderous, heavy, weighty; *informal* jumbo, whopping, hulking, humongous, ginormous. ANTONYMS small, slight.

bulldoze verb 1 *they plan to bulldoze the park* DEMOLISH, knock down, tear down, pull down, flatten, level, raze, clear.

2 *he bulldozed his way through* FORCE, push, shove, barge, elbow, shoulder, jostle, muscle; plunge, crash, sweep, bundle.

3 *informal she tends to bulldoze everyone* BULLY, browbeat, intimidate, dragoon, domineer, hector, pressurize, tyran-

nize, strong-arm, push around, walk all over; railroad, steamroller, lean on, boss.

bullet noun *the bullet was taken to the police lab* ball, shot, cartridge; *informal* slug; (**bullets**) lead, ammunition, ammo.

bulletin noun **1** *a news bulletin* REPORT, dispatch, story, press release, newscast, flash; statement, announcement, message, communication, communiqué.

2 *the society's monthly bulletin* NEWSLETTER, proceedings; newspaper, magazine, digest, gazette, review; tipsheet.

bullish adjective *another bullish candidate has thrown her hat into the ring* CONFIDENT, positive, assertive, self-assertive, assured, self-assured, bold, determined; optimistic, buoyant, sanguine; *informal* feisty, upbeat.

bully noun *the school bully* PERSECUTOR, oppressor, tyrant, tormentor, intimidator; tough guy, thug, ruffian, strong-arm.

▸ verb **1** *the others bully him* PERSECUTE, oppress, tyrannize, browbeat, harass, torment, intimidate, strong-arm, dominate; *informal* push around, bullyrag.

2 *she was bullied into helping* COERCE, pressure, pressurize, press, push; force, compel; badger, goad, prod, browbeat, intimidate, dragoon, strong-arm; *informal* bulldoze, railroad, lean on.

bulwark noun **1** *ancient bulwarks* WALL, rampart, fortification, parapet, stockade, palisade, barricade, embankment, earthwork.

2 *a bulwark of liberty* PROTECTOR, defender, protection, guard, defense, supporter, buttress; mainstay, bastion, stronghold.

bum[1] noun *informal* **1** *the bums sleeping on the sidewalk.* See TRAMP noun sense 1.

2 *you lazy bum* IDLER, loafer, slacker, good-for-nothing, ne'er-do-well, layabout, lounger, shirker; loser.

3 *a ski bum* ENTHUSIAST, fan, aficionado, lover, freak, nut, buff, fanatic, addict.

▸ verb **1** *that summer he bummed around Montreal* LOAF, lounge, idle, wander, drift, meander, dawdle; *informal* mooch, lollygag.

2 *they bummed money off him* BEG, borrow; *informal* scrounge, cadge, sponge, mooch.

▸ adjective *a bum deal* CRUMMY, rotten, pathetic, lousy, pitiful; BAD, poor, second-rate, tinpot, third-rate, second-class, unsatisfactory, inadequate, unacceptable; dreadful, awful, terrible, deplorable, lamentable. ANTONYM excellent.

bum[2] noun *Brit., informal next time I go skating, I'm tying a pillow to my bum!* See BUTTOCKS.

bumbling adjective *the bumbling Inspector Clouseau* BLUNDERING, bungling, inept, clumsy, maladroit, awkward, muddled, klutzy; oafish, clodhopping, lumbering; botched, ham-handed, ham-fisted. ANTONYMS efficient, debonair.

bump noun **1** *I landed with a bump* BANG, crash, smash, smack, crack, jolt, thud, thump; *informal* whack, thwack, bash, bonk, wallop.

2 *a bump in the road | the bump on his head* HUMP, lump, ridge, bulge, knob, protuberance; swelling.

▸ verb **1** *cars **bumped into** each other* HIT, crash into, smash into, smack into, slam into, bang into, knock into, run into, plow into; ram into, collide with, strike.

2 *a cart bumping along the road* BOUNCE, jolt, jerk, rattle, shake.

3 *she got bumped in favor of a rookie* DISPLACE, demote, dislodge, supplant.

PHRASE: **bump into** *informal you'll never guess who we bumped into at the theater* MEET, meet by chance, encounter, run into/across, come across, chance on, happen on.

bumpkin noun *he was very bright, but a bit of a bumpkin* YOKEL, peasant, provincial, rustic, country cousin, hayseed, hillbilly, hick, rube.

bumptious adjective *our bumptious cousin thinks she's God's gift to men* SELF-IMPORTANT, conceited, arrogant, self-assertive, pushy, pompous, overbearing, cocky, swaggering; proud, haughty, overweening, egotistical; *informal* snooty, uppity. See note at BOLD. ANTONYM modest.

bumpy adjective **1** *a bumpy road* UNEVEN, rough, rutted, rutty, pitted, potholed, holey; lumpy, rocky. ANTONYMS smooth, level.

2 *a bumpy ride* BOUNCY, rough, uncomfortable, jolting, lurching, jerky, jarring, bone-shaking. ANTONYMS smooth, comfortable.

bun noun **1** *coffee and a fresh bun* ROLL, sweet bun, hot cross bun, cinnamon bun; hamburger bun, hotdog bun.

2 *informal* (**buns**) *exercises to tighten up those buns* See BUTTOCKS.

bunch noun **1** *a bunch of flowers* BOUQUET, posy, nosegay, spray, corsage; wreath, garland.

2 *a bunch of grapes | a bunch of keys* CLUSTER, clump; knot; group, assemblage.

3 *informal we invited the whole bunch* GROUP, set, circle, company, collection, bevy, band, party; gang, crew, pack; crowd, throng, multitude.

4 *informal I bought **a bunch of** used books* AN ASSORTMENT OF, a bundle of, a collection of; many, lots of, a lot of, loads of, a load of, tons of, a ton of, an abundance of.

▸ verb **1** *he bunched the reins in his hand* BUNDLE, clump, cluster, group, gather; pack.

2 *her skirt bunched at the waist* GATHER, ruffle, pucker, fold, pleat.

3 *the runners **bunched up** behind him* CLUSTER, huddle, gather, congregate, collect, amass, group, crowd.

bundle noun *a bundle of clothes* BUNCH, roll, clump, wad, parcel, sheaf, bale, bolt; package; pile, stack, heap, mass; *informal* load.

▸ verb **1** *she bundled up her things* TIE, pack, parcel, wrap, roll, fold, bind, bale, package.

2 *she was bundled in furs* WRAP, envelop, clothe, cover, muffle, swathe, swaddle, shroud, drape, enfold.

3 *informal he was bundled into a van* shove, push, thrust, manhandle, hurry, rush.

bungle verb *they bungled the robbery* MISHANDLE, mismanage, mess up, spoil, ruin, blunder; *informal* botch, muff, fluff, make a hash of, foul up, screw up, flub, goof up. See word spectrum at ADEPT.

bungling adjective *the work of a bungling amateur* INCOMPETENT, blundering, amateurish, inept, unskillful, maladroit, clumsy, klutzy, awkward, bumbling; *informal* ham-handed, ham-fisted.

bunk noun **1** *there were twelve bunks per dormitory* BERTH, cot, bed. See also note at NONSENSE.

2 *informal the idea was sheer bunk.* See NONSENSE sense 1.

bunkum noun *informal, dated*. See NONSENSE sense 1.

buoy noun *a mooring buoy* FLOAT, marker; bellbuoy, nun buoy, sonobuoy.

▸ verb *the party was buoyed by an election victory* CHEER, cheer up, hearten, rally, invigorate, uplift, lift, encourage, stimulate, inspirit; *informal* pep up, perk up, buck up. ANTONYM depress.

buoyant adjective **1** *a buoyant substance* ABLE TO FLOAT, floating, floatable. ANTONYM leaden.

2 *a buoyant mood* CHEERFUL, cheery, happy, lighthearted, carefree, bright, merry, joyful, bubbly, bouncy, sunny, jolly; lively, jaunty, high-spirited, perky; optimistic, confident, positive; *informal* peppy, upbeat. ANTONYMS depressed, optimistic.

burble verb **1** *two fountains were burbling outside* GURGLE, bubble, murmur, purr, whirr, drone, hum, rumble.

2 *he burbled on* PRATTLE, blather, babble, gabble, prate, drivel, rattle, ramble, maunder, run; *informal* jabber, blabber, yammer, yatter, gab, waffle.

burden noun **1** *a financial burden* ENCUMBRANCE, strain, care, problem, worry, difficulty, trouble, millstone; RESPONSIBILITY, onus, charge, duty, obligation, liability.

2 *they shouldered their burdens* LOAD, weight, cargo, freight.

▸ verb *she thought nothing of burdening us with yet another mouth to feed* LOAD, charge, weigh down, encumber, hamper; overload, overburden; OPPRESS, trouble, worry, harass, upset, distress; haunt, afflict, strain, stress, tax, overwhelm.

burdensome adjective *the care of his parents had become burdensome* ONEROUS, oppressive, troublesome, weighty, worrisome, stressful; vexatious, irksome, trying, difficult; arduous, strenuous, hard, back-breaking, laborious, exhausting, tiring, taxing, demanding, punishing, grueling; *informal* high-maintenance. See note at HEAVY.

bureau noun **1** *an oak bureau* DRESSER, chest of drawers, cabinet, tallboy, highboy.

2 *the tourism bureau* AGENCY, service, office, business, company, firm; DEPARTMENT, division, branch, section.

bureaucracy noun **1** *the ranks of the bureaucracy* CIVIL SERVICE, government, administration; establishment, system, powers that be; ministries, authorities.

2 *unnecessary bureaucracy* RED TAPE, rules and regulations, protocol, officialdom, paperwork.

bureaucrat noun *Washington bureaucrats* OFFICIAL, officeholder, administrator, public servant, civil servant, functionary; mandarin; *derogatory* apparatchik, bean counter, paper shuffler.

burgeon verb *the toy industry is burgeoning* FLOURISH, thrive, prosper, improve, develop; expand, escalate, swell, grow, boom, mushroom, snowball, rocket.

burglar noun *the burglar escaped through the bedroom window* ROBBER, housebreaker, cat burglar, thief, raider, looter, safecracker, intruder, prowler; *informal* second-story man, yegg.

burglary noun **1** *serving time for burglary* HOUSEBREAKING, breaking and entering, theft, stealing, robbery, larceny, thievery, looting, pilferage.

2 *a series of burglaries* BREAK-IN, theft, robbery, raid; *informal* heist.

burgle verb *he confessed to having burgled the senator's office.* ROB, burglarize, loot, steal from, plunder, rifle (through), pillage; break into.

burial noun *a private burial at Vineyard Point Cemetery* BURYING, interment, committal, entombment; funeral, obsequies; *formal* inhumation; *archaic* sepulture. See note at INTERMENT. ANTONYM exhumation.

burial ground noun *a sacred burial ground* CEMETERY, graveyard, churchyard, necropolis; memorial park/garden; *informal* boneyard; *archaic* God's acre; *historical* potter's field.

burlap noun *wall hangings made of burlap and other flammable material* SACKCLOTH, gunny, canvas, hessian.

burlesque noun *a rather risqué burlesque* PARODY, caricature, satire, lampoon, skit, farce; sendup, takeoff, spoof; striptease, strip. See note at CARICATURE.

burly adjective *his burly bodyguards* STRAPPING, well-built, sturdy, brawny, strong, muscular, muscly, thickset, blocky, big, hefty, bulky, stocky, stout, Herculean; *informal* hunky, beefy, husky, hulking; *literary* stalwart, thewy; *technical* mesomorphic. ANTONYM puny.

burn verb **1** *the shed was burning* BE ON FIRE, be alight, be ablaze, blaze, go up, go up in smoke, be in flames, be aflame; smolder, glow.

2 *he burned the letters* SET FIRE TO, set on fire, set alight, light, ignite, touch off; incinerate; *informal* torch.

3 *I burned my dress with the iron* SCORCH, singe, sear, char, blacken, brand, sizzle; scald.

4 *her face burned* BE HOT, be warm, be feverish, be on fire; blush, redden, go red, flush, color.

5 *she* ***is burning with*** *curiosity* BE CONSUMED BY/WITH, be eaten up by/with, be obsessed by/with, be tormented by/with, be beside oneself with.

6 *the energy they* ***burn up*** CONSUME, use up, expend, go/get through, eat up; dissipate. ANTONYM conserve.

THE RIGHT WORD

If you're not an experienced cook, you're likely to **burn** your vegetables, **char** your meat, and, if you put your face too close to the stove, you might even **singe** your eyebrows. All of these verbs mean to injure or bring about a change in something by exposing it to fire or intense heat. *Burn*, which is the most comprehensive term, can mean to change only slightly (*she burned her face by staying out in the sun*) or to destroy completely (*the factory was burned to the ground*). To *char* is to reduce a substance to carbon or charcoal (*the beams in the ceiling were charred by the fire*). Like *char*, **singe** and **scorch** mean to burn only partially or superficially (*scorched the blouse while ironing it*; *singe the chicken before cooking it*). *Singeing* is often done deliberately to remove the hair, bristles, or feathers from the carcass of an animal or bird. **Scald** refers specifically to burning with, or as if with, a hot liquid or steam (*the cook scalded herself when she spilled the boiling water*); it can also mean to parboil or heat to a temperature just below boiling (*scald the milk to make the sauce*). **Sear** is also a term used in cooking, where it means to brown the outside of a piece of meat by subjecting it briefly to intense heat to seal in the juices. When it's human flesh that's being seared in surgery, the correct verb is **cauterize**, which means to burn for healing purposes (*the doctor cauterized the wound to ward off infection*).

---

burning adjective **1** *burning coals* BLAZING, flaming, fiery, ignited, glowing, red-hot, smoldering, igneous; raging, roaring.

2 *burning desert sands* EXTREMELY HOT, red-hot, fiery, blistering, scorching, searing, sweltering, torrid; *informal* baking, boiling (hot), broiling, roasting, sizzling. ANTONYM freezing.

3 *a burning desire* INTENSE, passionate, deep-seated, profound, wholehearted, strong, ardent, fervent, urgent, fierçe, eager, frantic, consuming, uncontrollable.

4 *burning issues* IMPORTANT, crucial, significant, vital, essential, pivotal; urgent, pressing, compelling, critical.

burnish verb *marks can be removed by burnishing the metal* POLISH, shine, buff, rub, gloss.

burp *informal* verb *cucumbers make me burp* BELCH; *formal* eructate; *rare* eruct; *archaic* bolk, rout, ruck.

▸ noun *he let out a loud burp* BELCH; *formal* eructation; *rare* ventosity; *archaic* bolk.

burrow noun *a rabbits' burrow* HOLE, tunnel, warren, dugout; lair, set, den, earth.

▸ verb *the mouse burrows a hole* TUNNEL, dig (out), excavate, grub, mine, bore, channel; hollow out, gouge out.

burst verb **1** *one balloon burst* SPLIT OPEN, rupture, break, tear.

2 *a shell burst in the distance* EXPLODE, blow up, detonate, go off.

3 *water burst through the hole* BREAK, erupt, surge, gush, rush, stream, flow, pour, spill; spout, spurt, jet, spew.

4 *he burst into the room* BARGE, charge, plunge, plow, hurtle, career, careen, rush, dash, tear.

5 *they* ***burst into*** *tears* BREAK OUT IN, launch into, erupt in, have a fit of.

▸ noun **1** *mortar bursts* EXPLOSION, detonation, blast, eruption, bang.

2 *a burst of gunfire* VOLLEY, salvo, fusillade, barrage, discharge; hail, rain.

3 *a burst of activity* OUTBREAK, eruption, flare-up, blaze, attack, fit, rush, gale, storm, surge, upsurge, spurt.

PHRASE: **burst out** *"I don't care!" she burst out* EXCLAIM, blurt, cry, shout, yell; *dated* ejaculate.

bury verb **1** *the dead were buried* INTER, lay to rest, entomb; *informal* put six feet under; *literary* inhume. ANTONYM exhume.

2 *she buried her face in her hands* HIDE, conceal, cover, enfold, engulf, tuck, cup, sink; *literary* enshroud. ANTONYM reveal.

3 *the bullet buried itself in the wood* EMBED, sink, implant, submerge; drive into. ANTONYM extract.

4 *he buried himself in his work* ABSORB, engross, immerse, occupy, engage, busy, involve.

bus noun *take a bus to the airport* MOTORCOACH, coach, school bus, shuttle bus, minibus, double-decker, trolley; *historical* omnibus.

bush noun **1** *a rose bush* SHRUB, brier; **(bushes)** undergrowth, shrubbery.

2 *out in the bush* WILDS, wilderness, forest, woodland, timberland, bush country, bushland; backwoods, hinterland(s), backcountry, backlands; *informal* the sticks, boondocks, boonies.

bush-league adjective *don't get involved with these bush-league investors* SECOND-RATE, mediocre, inferior; provincial, unsophisticated; *informal* small-time, two-bit, rinky-dink.

bushy adjective *Groucho's trademark greasepaint mustache and bushy eyebrows* THICK, shaggy, unruly, fuzzy, bristly, fluffy, woolly; luxuriant. ANTONYMS sleek, wispy.

business noun **1** *Bill's business is electrical engineering* WORK, line of work, occupation, profession, career, employment, job, position; vocation, calling; field, sphere, trade, métier, craft; *informal* biz, racket, game.

2 *whom do you do business with?* TRADE, trading, commerce, dealing, traffic, merchandising; dealings, transactions, negotiations.

3 *her own business* COMPANY, firm, concern, enterprise, venture, organization, operation, corporation, undertaking; office, agency, franchise, practice; *informal* outfit.

4 *none of your business* CONCERN, affair, responsibility, duty, function, obligation; problem, worry; *informal* beeswax, bailiwick.

5 *this thing about the disappearing furniture is a strange business* AFFAIR, matter, thing, case, circumstance, situation, event, incident, happening, occurrence; episode.

businesslike adjective *our meetings are usually conducted in a more businesslike fashion* PROFESSIONAL, efficient, competent, methodical, disciplined, systematic, orderly, organized, structured, practical, pragmatic, routine, slick.

businessman, businesswoman noun *several local businessmen have donated their services* ENTREPRENEUR, business person, industrialist, manufacturer, tycoon, baron, magnate, executive, employer; dealer, trader, broker, merchant, buyer, seller, marketeer, merchandiser, vendor, retailer, supplier.

bust[1] noun **1** *an empire waistline accentuates the bust* CHEST, bosom, breasts.

2 *a bust of Caesar* SCULPTURE, carving, effigy, statue; head and shoulders.

bust[2] *informal* verb **1** *I didn't mean to bust your DVD player* BREAK, smash, fracture, shatter, crack, disintegrate, snap; split, burst.

2 *he promised to bust the counterfeit ring* OVERTHROW, destroy, topple, bring down, ruin, break, overturn, overcome, defeat, get rid of, oust, dislodge.

3 *they were busted for drugs.* See ARREST verb sense 1.

▸ noun *a cache of guns was discovered in the bust* RAID, search; *informal* takedown, shakedown.

PHRASE: **go bust** *their flower shop went bust* FAIL, collapse, fold, go under, founder; go bankrupt, go into receivership, go into liquidation, be wound up; *informal* crash, go broke, go belly up, flop, bomb.

bustle verb *people bustled about* RUSH, dash, hurry, scurry, scuttle, hustle, scamper, scramble; run, tear, charge; *informal* scoot, beetle, buzz, zoom.

▸ noun *the bustle of the market* ACTIVITY, action, liveliness, hustle and bustle, excitement; tumult, hubbub, whirl, commotion; *informal* toing and froing, comings and goings.

bustling adjective *the mall is bustling with holiday shoppers* BUSY, crowded, swarming, teeming, thronged; buzzing, abuzz, buzzy, hectic, lively. ANTONYM deserted.

busy adjective **1** *the campaign volunteers have been busy* OCCUPIED, engaged, involved, employed, working, hard at work; rushed off one's feet, hard-pressed, swamped, up to one's neck; on the job, absorbed, engrossed, immersed, preoccupied; *informal* (as) busy as a bee, on the go, hard at it. ANTONYM idle.

2 *sorry, she's busy at the moment* UNAVAILABLE, engaged, occupied; working, in a meeting, on duty; *informal* tied up. ANTONYM free.

3 *the busy streets of Toronto* HECTIC, active, lively; crowded, bustling, abuzz, swarming, teeming, full, thronged.

4 *a busy design* ORNATE, overelaborate, overblown, overwrought, overdone, fussy, cluttered, overworked. ANTONYMS restrained, quiet.

▸ verb *he busied himself with paperwork* OCCUPY, involve, engage, concern, absorb, engross, immerse, preoccupy; distract, divert.

THE RIGHT WORD

There are varying degrees of busyness. **Busy** implies actively and attentively involved in work or a pastime (*too busy to come to the phone*). It can also be used to describe intensive activity of any kind (*a busy intersection*; *a busy day*). Someone who is **engaged** is also *busy*, but in a more focused way (*engaged in compiling a dictionary*). **Diligent** is used to describe earnest and constant effort, and it often connotes enjoyment of or dedication to what one is doing (*diligent efforts to rescue injured animals*). To be **industrious** is to be more focused still, often with a definite goal in mind (*an industrious employee working for a promotion*). **Sedulous** also applies to goal-oriented activity, but it suggests more close care and perseverance than *industrious* does (*a sedulous investigation of the accident*). The award for concentrated effort goes to the person who is **assiduous**, which suggests painstaking preoccupation with a specific task (*an assiduous student is the one most likely to win his or her teacher's favor*).

busybody noun *I was labeled a snob because I didn't care to belong to her nest of busybodies* MEDDLER, interferer, mischief-maker, troublemaker; gossip, scandalmonger; eavesdropper; *informal* kibitzer, buttinsky, snoop, snooper, Nosy Parker, yenta.

but conjunction **1** *he stumbled but didn't fall* YET, nevertheless, nonetheless, even so, however, still, notwithstanding, despite that, in spite of that, for all that, all the same, just the same; though, although.

2 *this one's expensive, but this one isn't* WHEREAS, conversely, but then, then again, on the other hand, by/in contrast, on the contrary.

▸ preposition *everyone but him* EXCEPT (FOR), apart from, other than, besides, aside from, with the exception of, bar, excepting, excluding, leaving out, save (for), saving.

▸ adverb *he is but a shadow of his former self* ONLY, just, simply, merely, no more than, nothing but; a mere.

PHRASE: **but for** *I would not have survived but for your selfless courage* EXCEPT FOR, if it were not for, were it not for, barring, notwithstanding.

USAGE NOTE **but**

It is a gross canard that beginning a sentence with *but* is stylistically slipshod. In fact, doing so is highly desirable in any number of contexts, as many stylebooks have said (many correctly pointing out that *but* is more effective than *however* at the beginning of a sentence)—e.g.:

• "The group of Adversative conjunctions represented by BUT (called Arrestive) very often fulfil [sic] the office of relating consecutive sentences. . . . An entire paragraph is not unfrequently devoted to arresting or preventing a seeming inference from one preceding, and is therefore appropriately opened by But, Still, Nevertheless, &c." (Alexander Bain, *English Composition and Rhetoric*, 4th ed.; 1877.)

• "*But* (not followed by a comma) always heads its turning sentence; *Nevertheless* usually does (followed by a comma). I am sure, however, that *however* is always better buried in the sentence between commas; *But* is for the quick turn; the inlaid *however* for the more elegant sweep." (Sheridan Baker, *The Practical Stylist*;1962.)

• "Of the many myths concerning 'correct' English, one of the most persistent is the belief that it is somehow improper to begin a sentence with *and*, *but*, *for*, *or*, or *nor*. The construction is, of course, widely used today and has been widely used for generations, for the very good reason that it is an effective means of achieving coherence between sentences and between larger units of discourse, such as paragraphs." (R. W. Pence and D. W. Emery, *A Grammar of Present-Day English*, 2d ed.; 1963.)

• "I can't overstate how much easier it is for readers to process a sentence if you start with *but* when you're shifting direction." (William Zinsser, *On Writing Well*, 6th ed.; 1998.)

• "If you want to begin a sentence by contradicting the last, use *but* instead of *however*." (Christopher Lasch, *Plain Style*; 2002.)

Good writers often begin sentences with *but* and have always done so. Samples from twentieth- and twenty-first-century writers follow:

• "But such simplicity of instinct is scarcely possible for human beings." (Bertrand Russell, *Education and the Good Life*; 1926.)

• "But it must not be assumed that intelligent thinking can play no part in the formation of the goal and of ethical judgments." (Albert Einstein, "Science and Religion" (1939), in *Ideas and Opinions*; 1954.)

• "But he had got used to that and it did not disquiet him." (Ursula K. Le Guin, *The Other Wind*; 2001.)

These are not good writers on bad days. No: they were having good days. In 1963, researcher Francis Christensen found that 8.75% of the sentences in the work of first-rate writers—including H. L. Mencken, Lionel Trilling, and Edmund Wilson—began with coordinating conjunctions (i.e., *and* and *but*). In *The New York Times* (front page during the 1990s) and *U.S. News & World Report* (in 1997), the figure is about the same. To the professional rhetorician, these figures aren't at all surprising.

All this enthusiasm for the construction, though, needs to be tempered to this extent: don't start consecutive sentences with *but*. Also, putting this subordinating conjunction twice in one sentence invariably makes the sentence unwieldy and less easy to read—e.g.: "But this opening misleads because the focus dissipates as the play progresses and the scattershot climax drips with sentiment but is ultimately unsatisfying." (*Pittsburgh Post-Gazette*; Oct. 10, 1997.) (A possible revision: "But this opening misleads because the focus dissipates as the play progresses.

Although the scattershot climax drips with sentiment, it's ultimately unsatisfying.")

The surprisingly common misuse of *but* for *and* often betrays the writer's idiosyncratic prejudice. That is, if you write that someone is "attractive but smart," you're suggesting that this combination of characteristics is atypical—e.g.: "Billy's father . . . is a man of sterling rectitude, poor but honest [read *poor and honest*], determined to pass his upcoming naturalization exams." (*Chicago Tribune*; Oct. 24, 1997.) Is the writer really suggesting that poor people are typically dishonest?

The use of *but* in a negative sense after a pronoun has long caused confusion. Is it "No one but she" or "No one but her"? When *but* is a preposition (meaning "except"), the objective *her* (or *him*) follows. But when *but* is a conjunction, the nominative *she* (or *he*) is proper. The correct form depends on the structure of the sentence. If the verb precedes the *but* phrase, the objective case should be used: "None of the defendants were convicted but him." But if the *but* phrase precedes the verb, the nominative case is proper: "None of the defendants but he were convicted." That sentence is considered equivalent to "None of the defendants were convicted, but he was convicted." (Although that rewording doesn't seem to make literal sense—given that he was one of the defendants—it serves to show the grammar of the sentence excepting him from the absolute word *none*.) *But* thus acts as a conjunction when it precedes the verb in a sentence, as in this one from Thomas Jefferson: "Nobody but we of the craft can understand the diction, and find out what [the statute] means." Here the subject of *can understand* is *nobody*, and the *but* heads the understood clause: "nobody can understand, but we can understand."

The logic here is based on syntax: the native English speaker instinctively rejects as alien-sounding the constructions *me know* in "No one but you and I know what is on these notice boards" and *him knew* in "No one but he knew what this had cost him." **—BG**

---

butch adjective *informal a butch haircut* MASCULINE, manly; mannish, manlike; *informal* macho. ANTONYM effeminate.

butcher noun **1** *a butcher's shop* MEAT SELLER, meat vendor, meat trader.

2 *a Nazi butcher* MURDERER, slaughterer, killer, assassin; *literary* slayer; *dated* cutthroat, homicide.

▸ verb **1** *the goat was butchered* SLAUGHTER, cut up, carve up.

2 *they butchered 150 people* MASSACRE, murder, slaughter, kill, destroy, exterminate, assassinate; *literary* slay.

3 *the studio butchered the film* SPOIL, ruin, mutilate, mangle, mess up, wreck; *informal* make a hash of, screw up, botch.

butler noun *Youngblood has been Mr. Echlin's butler for 40 years* MANSERVANT, servant, chamberlain, man, steward, major-domo, seneschal.

butt noun **1** *the butt of a joke* TARGET, victim, object, subject, dupe; laughingstock.

2 *the butt of a gun* STOCK, end, handle, hilt, haft, helve.

3 *a cigarette butt* STUB, end, tail end, stump, remnant.

4 *informal sitting on his butt.* See BUTTOCKS.

▸ verb **1** *the shop* ***butts up against*** *the house* ADJOIN, abut, be next to, be adjacent to, border (on), be connected to; join, touch.

2 *students butting everyone with their backpacks* RAM, headbutt, bunt; bump, buffet, push, shove. PHRASE: **butt in** *I've asked you not to butt in when your father and I are talking* INTERRUPT, break in, cut in, chime in, interject, intervene, interfere, interpose; *informal* poke one's nose in, put one's oar in.

butter PHRASE: **butter someone up** *informal there she goes, buttering up the boss again* FLATTER, sweet-talk, curry favor with, court, wheedle, cajole, persuade, coax, compliment, get around, prevail on; be obsequious toward, be sycophantic toward, toady to, fawn on, make up to, play up to, ingratiate oneself with, suck up to, be all over, softsoap.

butterfly noun **1** *an unfamiliar species of butterfly* LEPIDOPTERAN. See table.

2 *I had butterflies as I waited* NERVES, anxiety, the jitters.

BUTTERFLIES

admiral	metalmark
aguna	Mexican bluewing
alpine	milkweed butterfly
American lady	mimic
arctic	ministreak
azure	monarch
banner	mourning cloak
beauty	mulberry wing
blue	orange
bolla	orangetip
brushfoot	orion
buckeye	owl butterfly
cabbage white	painted lady
checkered skipper	patch
checkerspot	peacock
clearwing	pearly eye
cloudywing	pixie
comma	powdered skipper
copper	purple
cracker	purplewing
crescent	queen
daggerwing	question mark
Diana	red admiral
dogface	ringlet
dotted blue	roadside skipper
duskywing	satyr
elfin	scallopwing
emperor	scrub hairstreak
flasher	shoemaker
fritillary	silverdrop
giant skipper	silverspot
glassywing	skipper
greenstreak	skipperling
groundstreak	soldier
hairstreak	sootywing
harvester	sulfur/sulphur
heliconian	swallowtail
Julia	tortoiseshell
lady butterfly	viceroy
leaf butterfly	white
leafwing	white admiral
long dash	wood nymph
longtail	yellow
marble	zebra

See also table at MOTH.

buttocks plural noun *stand with your heels and buttocks against the wall* BACKSIDE, rear end, rear, seat, bottom, rump, cheeks, behind, derrière; *informal* butt, fanny, keister, tush, tail, buns, heinie, ass, caboose; fundament, posterior, haunches, gluteus maximus, sit-upon, stern, wazoo; *Brit. informal* bum, arse; *Anatomy* nates.See note at ASS.

button noun **1** *shirt buttons* FASTENER, stud, toggle; hook, catch, clasp, snap fastener, pin.

2 *press the button* SWITCH, knob, control; lever, handle; icon, box.

buttonhole verb *informal*. See ACCOST.

buttress noun **1** *stone buttresses* PROP, support, abutment, brace, shore, pier, reinforcement, stanchion.

2 *a buttress against social collapse* SAFEGUARD, defense, protection, guard; support, prop; bulwark.

▸ verb *authority was buttressed by religion* STRENGTHEN, reinforce, fortify, support, bolster, shore up, underpin, cement, uphold, prop up, defend, sustain, back up.

buxom adjective *a buxom lingerie model* LARGE-BREASTED, big-breasted, bosomy, big-bosomed; shapely, ample, plump, rounded, full-figured, voluptuous, curvaceous, Rubenesque; *informal* busty, built, stacked, chesty, well-endowed, curvy.

buy verb *they bought a new house* PURCHASE, acquire, obtain, get, pick up; take, procure, pay for; invest in; *informal* get hold of, snatch up, snap up, grab, score. ANTONYM sell.

▸ noun *informal a good buy* PURCHASE, investment, acquisition, gain; deal, value, bargain.

▸ ***buy***
procure
purchase
invest in
put money into
make a/the purchase of
acquire
obtain
get
take
secure
pay for
shop for
snap up
score
get hold of
pick up
come by
get one's hands on
lay one's hands on
get one's mitts on
take possession of
handle
traffic in
exchange
barter
trade
vend
auction (off)
dispose of
arrange/negotiate the sale of
put up for sale
offer for sale
put on sale
trade in
deal in
be in the business of
offer for sale
stock
carry
peddle
hawk
retail
sell ◂

buyer noun *a prospective buyer* PURCHASER, customer, consumer, shopper, investor.

buzz noun **1** *the buzz of the bees* HUM, humming, buzzing, murmur, drone.

2 *the buzz of the doorbell* RING, purr, note, tone, beep, bleep, warble, alarm, warning sound.

3 *informal give me a buzz* CALL, ring, phone call, telephone call.

4 *informal the buzz is that he's gone.* See RUMOR.

5 *informal get a buzz out of flying* THRILL, stimulation, glow, tingle; *informal* kick, rush, high, charge.

▸ verb **1** *bees buzzed* HUM, drone, bumble, murmur.

2 *the intercom was buzzing* PURR, warble, sound, ring, beep, bleep.

3 *informal he buzzed around the mall* BUSTLE, scurry, scuttle, hurry, rush, race, dash, tear, chase; *informal* scoot, beetle, whiz, zoom, zip.

4 *the town is buzzing with excitement* HUM, throb, vibrate, pulse, bustle, be abuzz. PHRASE: **buzz off** *I told that little pest to buzz off* SCRAM, go away, be gone/begone, be off; *informal* get lost, take a hike, beat it, bug off, go fly a kite, go suck an egg, vamoose.

by preposition **1** *I broke it by forcing the lid* THROUGH, as a result of, because of, by dint of, by way of, via, by means of; with the help of, with the aid of, by virtue of.

2 *be there by midday* NO LATER THAN, in good time for, at, before.

3 *a house by the lake* NEXT TO, beside, alongside, by/at the side of, adjacent to, side by side with; near, close to, neighboring, adjoining, bordering, overlooking; connected to, contiguous with, attached to.

4 *go by the building* PAST, in front of, beyond.

5 *all right by me* ACCORDING TO, with, as far as —— is concerned.

▸ adverb *people hurried by* PAST, on, along.

PHRASES: **by and by** *by and by, you'll learn the routine* EVENTUALLY, ultimately, finally, in the end, one day, some day, sooner or later, in time, in a while, in the long run, in the fullness of time, in time to come, at length, in the future, in due course, over the long haul. **by oneself** *I built the fireplace by myself* ALONE, on one's own, singly, separately, solitarily, unaccompanied, companionless, unattended, unescorted, solo; unaided, unassisted, without help, by one's own efforts, under one's own steam, independently, single-handed(ly), on one's own initiative; *informal* by one's lonesome.

bye exclamation See GOODBYE.

bygone adjective *it recaptures a bygone era* PAST, former, olden, earlier, previous, one-time, long-ago, of old, ancient, antiquated; departed, dead, extinct, defunct, out of date, outmoded; *literary* of yore. ANTONYMS present, recent.

bylaw noun *the board will be revising its bylaws* RULE, regulation, ordinance.

bypass noun *follow the signs for the bypass* DETOUR, alternate route, alternative route, diversion, shortcut.

▸ verb **1** *bypass the farm* GO AROUND, go past, make a detour around; avoid.

2 *an attempt to bypass the problem* AVOID, evade, dodge, escape, elude, circumvent, get around, shortcut around, skirt, sidestep, steer clear of; *informal* duck.

3 *they bypassed the regulations* IGNORE, pass over, neglect, go over the head of; *informal* short-circuit.

by-product noun *pollution is the by-product of an industrial economy* SIDE EFFECT, consequence, entailment, corollary; ramification, repercussion, spinoff, fallout; fruits.

bystander noun *bystanders witnessed the accident* ONLOOKER, looker-on, passerby, nonparticipant, observer, spectator, eyewitness, witness, watcher, gawker; *informal* rubbernecker.

byword noun **1** *their office was a byword for delay* PERFECT EXAMPLE, classic case, model, exemplar, embodiment, incarnation, personification, epitome.

2 *'vigor' was the byword of the Kennedy years* SLOGAN, motto, maxim, mantra, catchword, watchword, formula; middle name; proverb, adage, saying, dictum.

C

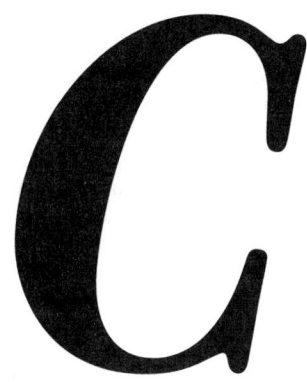

cab noun *she hailed a cab* TAXI, taxicab, hack; rickshaw, trishaw, pedicab.

cabal noun *a cabal of dissidents* CLIQUE, faction, coterie, cell, sect, junta, camarilla; lobby (group), pressure group. See note at PLOT.

cabaret noun **1** *the evening's cabaret* ENTERTAINMENT, show, floor show, performance.

2 *the cabarets of New Orleans* NIGHTCLUB, dinner theater, club, boîte, café; *informal* nightspot, clip joint, honky-tonk.

cabin noun *a cabin by the lake* COTTAGE, log cabin, shack, chantey, hut; chalet; cabana; *historical* camboose.

cabinet noun **1** *a walnut cabinet* CUPBOARD, bureau, bookcase, chest of drawers, sideboard, buffet, dresser, credenza, highboy, tallboy, wardrobe, chiffonier, armoire, wall unit; china cabinet, file cabinet, medicine cabinet.

2 *a meeting of the new cabinet* COUNCIL, administration, ministry, executive, senate.

cable noun **1** *a thick cable moored the ship* ROPE, cord, line, guy, wire; hawser, stay, bridle; choker.

2 *electric cables* WIRE, lead; power line, hydro line, transmission line.

cache noun *a cache of arms* HOARD, store, stockpile, stock, supply, reserve; arsenal; *informal* stash.

cachet noun *for more than fifty years, their winery enjoyed the cachet that others could only envy* PRESTIGE, status, standing, clout, kudos, snob value, stature, preeminence, eminence; street credibility.

cackle verb **1** *the geese cackled at him* SQUAWK, cluck, gabble.

2 *Noel cackled with glee* LAUGH LOUDLY, guffaw, chortle, chuckle.

cacophonous adjective *that cacophonous racket they call music* NOISY, loud, ear-splitting, raucous, discordant, dissonant, jarring, grating, inharmonious, unmelodious, unmusical, tuneless. ANTONYM harmonious.

cacophony noun *despite the cacophony, Rita slept on* DIN, racket, noise, clamor, discord, dissonance, discordance, uproar.

cad noun *dated* See BASTARD noun sense 2.

cadaver noun *Medicine each student is assigned a cadaver* CORPSE, body, dead body, remains, carcass; *informal* stiff; *archaic* corse. See note at BODY.

cadaverous adjective *his cadaverous face* (DEATHLY) PALE, pallid, ashen, gray, whey-faced, sallow, wan, anemic, bloodless, etiolated, corpselike, deathlike; bony, skeletal, emaciated, skin-and-bones, haggard, gaunt, drawn, pinched, hollow-cheeked, hollow-eyed; *informal* like a bag of bones, anorexic. ANTONYMS rosy, plump.

cadence noun *there is a musical cadence in her speech* INTONATION, modulation, lilt, accent, inflection; rhythm, tempo, meter, beat, pulse; *Music* resolution.

cadre noun *a cadre of academic specialists* CORPS, body, team, group, nucleus, core.

café noun *we stopped at a café for a couple of muffins and coffee* COFFEE SHOP, tea room; restaurant, bistro; brasserie, cafeteria; snack bar, diner, eatery.

cafeteria noun LUNCHROOM, luncheonette, lunch counter; snack bar, canteen, café; *informal* caf.

cage noun *animals in cages* ENCLOSURE, pen, pound; coop, hutch; birdcage, aviary; corral.

▸ verb *many animals are caged* CONFINE, shut in/up, pen, coop up, fence in, immure, impound, corral.

cagey adjective *informal he was rather cagey about his plans* SECRETIVE, guarded, cautious, wary, noncommittal, tight-lipped, reticent, evasive; *informal* playing one's cards close to one's chest. ANTONYM open.

cahoots PHRASE: **in cahoots** *informal it turned out that the commissioner was in cahoots with at least two of the managers* IN LEAGUE, colluding, in collusion, conspiring, collaborating, hand in glove, in bed.

cajole verb *I hate it when he cajoles me to go out with his friends* PERSUADE, wheedle, coax, talk into, prevail on, sweet-talk, butter up, soft-soap, seduce, inveigle.

cake noun **1** *chocolate cakes.* See table on page 118.

2 *a cake of soap* BAR, block, brick, slab, tablet, lump.

▸ verb **1** *boots caked with mud* COAT, encrust, plaster, cover.

2 *the blood was beginning to cake* CLOT, congeal, coagulate, solidify, set, inspissate.

PHRASE: **a piece of cake** See CINCH sense 1.

CAKES, PUDDINGS, AND OTHER DESSERTS

ambrosia	Indian pudding
angel food cake	Italian ice
apple crisp	jelly roll
apple pandowdy	kuchen
baba au rhum	Kugelhopf
babka	kulfi
Baked Alaska	lemon chiffon cake
banana pudding	Lord Baltimore cake
banana split	Madeira cake
bananas Foster	madeleine
Banbury tart	marquise
Battenburg cake	Mississippi mud pie
Bavarian cream	mooncake
bavarois	mousse
Black Forest cake	mousseline
blancmange	mud pie
blueberry buckle	nougatine
bombe	panettone
Boston cream pie	panforte
bread pudding	panna cotta
brown Betty	parfait
buche de Noel	pashka
Bundt cake	pavlova
carrot cake	peach Melba
cassata	persimmon pudding
Charlotte Russe	plum pudding
cheesecake	poached pear
cherries in the snow	poires belle-Hélène
cherries jubilee	pot de crème
chocolate pudding	pound cake
chocolate fondue	red velvet cake
clafoutis	rice pudding
cobbler	roulade
coffee cake	sabayon
compote	Sachertorte
coupe	savarin
crème brûlée	semifreddo
crème caramel	sherbet
crepes Suzette	simnel cake
crisp	snow pudding
croquembouche	sorbet
crumb cake	souffle
crumble	spice cake
cupcake	sponge cake
custard	stollen
dacquoise	strawberry shortcake
devil's food cake	streusel
Dobos torte	syllabub
duff	tapioca pudding
dulce de leche	tarte Tatin
Dundee cake	tea cake
financier	timbale
flan	tiramisù
floating island	toffee pudding
flummery	torte
fool	tortoni
fruitcake	tres leches
galette des rois	trifle
gateau	upside-down cake
genoise	vacherin
German chocolate cake	vanilla pudding
gingerbread	wedding cake
granita	whoopie pie
honey cake	zabaglione
hummingbird cake	zuppa inglese
ice cream	

See also tables at CANDY, COOKIE, DOUGHNUT, PASTRY, and PIE.

calamitous adjective *their calamitous adventure became legendary* DISASTROUS, catastrophic, cataclysmic, devastating, dire, tragic; *literary* direful.

calamity noun *she has survived more calamities in the past three months than most people experience in a lifetime* DISASTER, catastrophe, tragedy, cataclysm, adversity, tribulation, affliction, misfortune, misadventure. ANTONYM godsend.

calculate verb **1** *the interest is calculated on a daily basis* COMPUTE, work out, reckon, figure; add up/together, count up, tally, total, tote, tot up.

2 *his words were calculated to wound her* INTEND, mean, aim, design.

3 *we had* ***calculated on*** *a quiet Sunday* EXPECT, count on, anticipate, reckon on, bargain on, figure on.

calculated adjective *a vicious and calculated assault* DELIBERATE, premeditated, planned, preplanned, preconceived, intentional, intended, willful; *Law* prepense. ANTONYM unintentional.

calculating adjective *a crime that only a calculating mind could have planned* CUNNING, crafty, wily, shrewd, sly, scheming, devious, designing, conniving, Machiavellian; *informal* foxy; *archaic* subtle. ANTONYM ingenuous.

calculation noun **1** *the calculation of the overall cost* COMPUTATION, reckoning, adding up, counting up, working out, figuring, totaling up, totting up.

2 *political calculations* ASSESSMENT, judgment; forecast, projection, prediction.

calendar noun *a calendar of events* schedule, agenda, almanac, diary, program, annual, yearbook.

caliber noun **1** *a man of his caliber* QUALITY, merit, distinction, stature, excellence, preeminence; ability, expertise, talent, capability, capacity, proficiency.

2 *questions about the caliber of the officiating* STANDARD, level, quality.

3 *the caliber of a gun* BORE, diameter, gauge.

calibrate verb *calibrate the scale before weighing the packages* ADJUST, measure, set, graduate, correct.

call verb **1** *"Wait for me!" she called* CRY OUT, cry, shout, yell, hail, bellow, roar, bawl, vociferate; *informal* holler.

2 *I'll call you tomorrow* PHONE, telephone, get someone on the phone, give someone a call, give someone a ring, give someone a buzz.

3 *dinner's ready—call the kids* SUMMON, send for, assemble, muster, invite, order.

4 *the vice president called a meeting* CONVENE, summon, assemble; *formal* convoke.

5 *they called their son Liam* NAME, christen, baptize; designate, style, term, dub; *formal* denominate.

6 *yes, I would call him a friend* DESCRIBE AS, regard as, look on as, consider to be.

▸ noun **1** *I heard calls from the auditorium* CRY, shout, yell, roar, scream, exclamation, vociferation; *informal* holler.

2 *the call of the loon* CRY, song, sound.

3 *I'll give you a call tomorrow* PHONE CALL, telephone call, ring; *informal* buzz.

4 *he paid a call on Harold* VISIT, social call.

5 *a call for party unity* APPEAL, request, plea, entreaty.

6 *the last call for passengers on flight 701* SUMMONS, request.

7 *there's no call for expensive wine here* DEMAND, desire, market.

8 *the call of the sea* ATTRACTION, appeal, lure, allure, spell, pull, draw.

9 *it's your call* DECISION, ruling, judgment, verdict.

PHRASES: **call for** *desperate times call for desperate measures* REQUIRE, need, necessitate; justify, warrant. **call off** *we had to call off the trip to Maryland* CANCEL, abandon, scrap, drop, ax, scrub, nix; end, terminate. **call on** **1** *I might call on her later* VISIT, pay a visit to, go and see, drop in on, pop in on, visit with. **2** *he called on the government to hold a plebiscite* APPEAL TO, ask, request, petition, urge, exhort. **3** *we are able to call on qualified staff* HAVE RECOURSE TO, avail oneself of, draw on, make use of. **call the shots** *if she's gonna call the shots from now on, I'm not gonna stick around* BE IN CHARGE, be in control, be the boss, be at the helm/wheel, be in the driver's seat, pull the strings, run the show, rule the roost. **call to mind** *this calls to mind the last constitutional debate* EVOKE, bring to mind, call up, conjure up. **call up** **1** *Roland called me up to ask me out.* See CALL verb sense 2. **2** *they called up the reservists* ENLIST, recruit, conscript; draft. **3** *he was called up from the minors* SELECT, pick, choose. **on call** *Dr. Merton is on call this evening* ON DUTY, on standby, available.

calligraphy noun *the scribe's meticulous calligraphy* HANDWRITING, script, penmanship, hand, pen.

calling noun *when I was four, I knew my calling was photography* PROFESSION, occupation, vocation, call, summons, career, work, employment, job, business, trade, craft, line, line of work; *informal* bag; *archaic* employ.

callous adjective *his callous disregard for other people's feelings* HEARTLESS, unfeeling, uncaring, cold, cold-hearted, hard, as hard as nails, hard-hearted, insensitive, lacking compassion, hard-bitten, hard-nosed, hard-edged, unsympathetic. ANTONYMS kind, compassionate.

callow adjective *she toyed with the emotions of Laughton when he was a callow and insecure young man* IMMATURE, inexperienced, juvenile, adolescent, naive, green, raw, untried, unworldly, unsophisticated; *informal* wet behind the ears. See notes at GULLIBLE, RUDE, YOUTHFUL. ANTONYM mature.

calm adjective **1** *she seemed very calm* SERENE, tranquil, relaxed, unruffled, unperturbed, unflustered, untroubled; equable, even-tempered; placid, unexcitable, unemotional, phlegmatic; composed, 'calm, cool, and collected,' coolheaded, self-possessed; *informal* unflappable, unfazed, nonplussed. ANTONYMS excited, nervous, upset.

2 *the night was calm* WINDLESS, still, tranquil, serene, quiet. ANTONYMS windy, stormy.

3 *the calm waters of the lake* TRANQUIL, still, smooth, glassy, like a millpond; *literary* stilly. ANTONYMS rough, stormy.

▸ noun **1** *calm prevailed* TRANQUILITY, stillness, calmness, quiet, quietness, quietude, peace, peacefulness.

2 *his usual calm deserted him* COMPOSURE, coolness, calmness, self-possession, sangfroid; serenity, tranquility, equanimity, equability, placidness, placidity; *informal* cool, unflappability.

▸ verb **1** *I tried to **calm** him **down*** SOOTHE, pacify, placate, mollify, appease, conciliate, quiet (down), relax. ANTONYMS excite, upset.

2 *she forced herself to **calm down*** COMPOSE ONESELF, recover/regain one's composure, control oneself, pull oneself together, simmer down, cool down/off, take it easy; *informal* get a grip, keep one's shirt on, chill (out), cool one's jets, hang/stay loose, decompress.

THE RIGHT WORD

We usually speak of the weather or the sea as **calm**, meaning free from disturbance or storm. When applied to people and their feelings or moods, *calm* implies an unruffled state, often under disturbing conditions (*to remain calm in the face of disaster*). **Halcyon** is another adjective associated with the weather (*the halcyon days of summer*); it comes from the name of a mythical bird, usually identified with the kingfisher, that builds its nest on the sea and possesses a magical power to calm the winds and waves. **Peaceful** also suggests a lack of turbulence or disorder, although it is usually applied to situations, scenes, and activities rather than to people (*a peaceful gathering of protesters*; *a peaceful resolution to their problems*). **Serene**, **tranquil**, and **placid** are more often used to describe human states of being. *Serene* suggests a lofty and undisturbed calmness (*he died with a serene look on his face*), while *tranquil* implies an intrinsic calmness (*they led a tranquil life in the country*). **Placid** usually refers to a prevailing tendency and is sometimes used disparagingly to suggest a lack of responsiveness or a dull complacency (*with her placid disposition, she seldom got involved in family arguments*).

calumny noun *voters were tired of the candidates' endless barrage of calumny* SLANDER, defamation (of character), character assassination, libel; vilification, traducement, obloquy, verbal abuse; *informal* mudslinging, trash-talk; *rare* contumely. See note at MALIGN.

camaraderie noun *he enjoyed the camaraderie of army life* FRIENDSHIP, comradeship, fellowship, companionship, fraternity, conviviality; mutual support, team spirit, esprit de corps.

cameo noun *they were willing to pay Brando millions just for a cameo* BIT PART, vignette.

camouflage noun **1** *pieces of mossy turf served for camouflage* DISGUISE, concealment, cover, screen.

2 *her indifference was merely camouflage* A FACADE, a front, a false front, a smokescreen, a cover-up, a mask, a blind, a screen, a masquerade, a dissimulation, a pretense.

▸ verb *the van was camouflaged with branches* DISGUISE, hide, conceal, keep hidden, mask, screen, cover (up).

camp[1] noun **1** *a kids' camp* CAMPSITE, campground, encampment, bivouac.

2 *the liberal and conservative camps* FACTION, wing, group, lobby, caucus, bloc, party, coterie, sect, cabal.

▸ verb *they camped in a field* PITCH TENTS, set up camp, encamp, bivouac.

camp[2] *informal* adjective **1** *the camp humor became tiresome after the first twenty minutes* EXAGGERATED, theatrical, affected; *informal* over the top, OTT, camped up, hammy.

2 *a highly camp actor* EFFEMINATE, effete, mincing; *informal* campy. ANTONYM macho.

PHRASE: **camp it up** *he camped it up for the cameras* POSTURE, behave theatrically/affectedly, overact; *informal* ham it up.

campaign noun **1** *Napoleon's Russian campaign* MILITARY OPERATION(S), maneuver(s); crusade, war, battle, offensive, attack.

2 *the campaign to reduce vehicle emissions* CRUSADE, drive, push, struggle; operation, strategy, battle plan.

▸ verb **1** *they are campaigning for political reform* CRUSADE, fight, battle, push, press, strive, struggle, lobby.

2 *she campaigned as a political outsider* RUN FOR OFFICE, stand for office, canvass, barnstorm, electioneer, stump, go on the hustings.

campaigner noun *she was a dedicated campaigner admired even by her opponents for her hard work and sincerity* ACTIVIST, fighter, crusader; champion, advocate, promoter.

camper noun RECREATIONAL VEHICLE, RV, motor home; trailer; *trademark* Winnebago.

can noun *a bag of empty cans for recycling* tin can, aluminum can; canister; spray can; garbage can, trash can.

▸ verb *informal he was canned after being caught stealing office supplies* FIRE, dismiss, ax, let go, lay off, sack.

canal noun **1** *barges chugged up the canal* INLAND WATERWAY, watercourse, channel.

2 *the ear canal* DUCT, tube, passage.

cancel verb **1** *the meeting was canceled* CALL OFF, abandon, scrap, drop, ax, scrub, nix.

2 *his visa has been canceled* ANNUL, invalidate, nullify, declare null and void, void; revoke, rescind, retract, countermand, withdraw; *Law* vacate.

3 *rising unemployment* ***cancelled out*** *earlier economic gains* NEUTRALIZE, counterbalance, counteract, balance (out), countervail, compensate for; negate, nullify, wipe out.

cancer noun **1** *most skin cancers are curable if detected early* MALIGNANT GROWTH, cancerous growth, tumor, malignancy; *technical* carcinoma, sarcoma, melanoma, lymphoma, myeloma.

2 *the cancer of slavery spread across the continent* EVIL, blight, scourge, poison, canker, plague; *archaic* pestilence.

candid adjective **1** *his responses were remarkably candid* FRANK, outspoken, forthright, blunt, open, honest, truthful, sincere, direct, plain-spoken, straightforward, ingenuous, bluff; *informal* upfront, on the level, on the up and up. ANTONYM guarded.

2 *candid shots* UNPOSED, informal, uncontrived, impromptu, natural.

candidate noun *candidates should be computer-literate* APPLICANT, job applicants, job-seeker, interviewee; contender, contestant, nominee.

candle noun *hand-dipped white candles* taper, votive candle; *archaic* glim.

candlestick noun *a pair of brass candlesticks* CANDLE HOLDER, candelabra, menorah, flambeau, sconce.

candor noun *I'm not sure he appreciated my candor* FRANKNESS, openness, honesty, candidness, truthfulness, sincerity, forthrightness, directness, plain-spokenness, bluntness, straightforwardness, outspokenness; *informal* telling it like it is.

candy noun *chocolate candy* bonbon, confectionery, sweet. See table.

CANDY AND OTHER SWEETS

angel's hair	horehound
barfi	jawbreaker
bark	Jordan almond
barley sugar	kiss
boiled sweet	lemon drop
bonbon	licorice
brittle	Life Saver
bubble gum	lollipop
buckeye	lozenge
bullseye	macaroon
burnt peanut	malted milk ball
buttermint	maple sugar
butterscotch	marchpane
candied fruit	marron glacé
candied nut	marshmallow
candied peel	marzipan
candied violet	meringue
candy apple	mint
candy buttons	mostarda di frutta
candy cane	nonpareil
caramel	nougat
caramel apple	nougatine
caramel corn	Nutella
chewing gum	opera cream
chocolate	pastille
chocolate covered	pâte de fruits
cherry	peanut butter cup
comfit	pecan log
cotton candy	penuche
divinity	peppermint patty
dragée	praline
fondant	pulled candy
frangipane	ratafia
friandise	red hot
fruit paste	rock candy
fruit slice	rum ball
fudge	s'more
ganache	saltwater taffy
gianduia	sesame brittle
glyko (spoon sweet)	stroopballetje
gobstopper	Swedish fish
gulab jamun	taffy
gum ball	toffee
gumdrop	torrone
gummy candy	truffle
halvah	Turkish delight
haystack	turtle
heavenly hash	

See also tables at CAKE, COOKIE, DOUGHNUT, PASTRY, and PIE.

cane noun **1** *a silver-topped cane* WALKING STICK, staff; alpenstock; crook, pikestaff.

2 *he was beaten with a cane* STICK, rod, birch; *historical* ferule.

▸ verb *Matthew was caned for bullying* BEAT, strike, hit, flog, thrash, lash, birch, flagellate; *informal* belt, whale.

canine noun *the squad's trained canines* DOG, wolf, fox.

▸ adjective *the shape and build were definitely canine* DOGLIKE, doggish; wolfish, wolflike, lupine; foxlike, vulpine.

canister noun *a canister of Darjeeling tea* CONTAINER, box, tin, can.

canker noun **1** *this plant is susceptible to canker* FUNGAL DISEASE, plant rot; blight.

2 *ear cankers* ULCER, ulceration, infection, sore, abscess, noma.

3 *racism remains a canker.* See CANCER sense 2.

WORD NOTE **noma**

This medical noun signifies an especially icky ulcerous infection of the mouth or genitals. Because the condition most commonly strikes children living in abject poverty/squalor, it's a bit like scrofula. And just as the adj *scrofulous* has gradually extended its sense to mean "corrupt, degenerate, gnarly," so *nomal* seems ripe for similar extension; it could serve as a slightly obscure or erudite synonym for "scrofulous, repulsive, pathetically gross, grossly pathetic" . . . you get the idea. **—DFW**

cannabis noun. See MARIJUANA.

cannibal noun *overblown tales of savage cannibals* MAN-EATER, people-eater; *rare* anthropophagite, anthropophagist.

cannon noun *a Civil War cannon sits near the entrance to the armory* MOUNTED GUN, field gun, piece of artillery; mortar, howitzer; *historical* culverin, falconet.

▸ verb *the couple behind* ***cannoned into*** *us* COLLIDE WITH, hit, run into, crash into, plow into.

cannonade noun *the distant cannonade kept us alert all night* BOMBARDMENT, shelling, gunfire, artillery fire, barrage, pounding.

canny adjective *canny investors* SHREWD, astute, smart, sharp, sharp-witted, discerning, penetrating, discriminating, perceptive, perspicacious, wise, worldly-wise, sagacious; cunning, crafty, wily, as sharp as a tack, savvy; *dated* long-headed. ANTONYM foolish.

canoe noun *a wooden canoe with two seats* dugout, kayak, outrigger, birchbark, pirogue.

▸ verb *we canoed down 200 miles of the Connecticut River* PADDLE.

canon noun **1** *the canons of fair play and equal opportunity* PRINCIPLE, rule, law, tenet, precept; standard, convention, criterion, measure.

2 *a set of ecclesiastical canons* LAW, decree, edict, statute, dictate, decretal.

3 *the Shakespeare canon* LIST OF WORKS, works, writings, oeuvre.

canonical adjective *the canonical method* RECOGNIZED, authoritative, authorized, accepted, sanctioned, approved, established, orthodox. ANTONYM unorthodox.

canonize verb *Bernadette was canonized in 1933* DECLARE TO BE A SAINT; beatify; GLORIFY, deify, idolize.

canopy noun *the canopy gave us some relief from the sun* AWNING, shade, sunshade; marquee; chuppah.

cant[1] noun **1** *religious cant* HYPOCRISY, sanctimoniousness, sanctimony, pietism.

2 *thieves' cant* SLANG, jargon, idiom, argot, patois, speech, terminology, language; *informal* lingo, -speak, -ese. See note at DIALECT.

cant[2] verb *the deck canted some twenty degrees* TILT, lean, slant, slope, incline; tip, list, bank, heel.

▸ noun *the cant of the walls* SLOPE, slant, tilt, angle, inclination.

cantankerous adjective. See GRUMPY.

canteen noun **1** *a canteen of water* CONTAINER, flask, bottle.

2 *the staff canteen* RESTAURANT, cafeteria, refectory, lunchroom, mess hall.

canvass verb **1** *he's canvassing for the Green Party* CAMPAIGN, electioneer, stump, barnstorm.

2 *they promised to canvass all members* POLL, question, ask, survey, interview.

3 *they're canvassing support* SEEK, try to obtain.

canyon noun *burros can be negotiated through the canyon* RAVINE, gorge, gully, defile, couloir; chasm, abyss, gulf, gulch, coulee.

cap noun **1** *his cap blew off in the wind.* See the table at HAT.

2 *a white plastic cap* LID, top; stopper, cork, bung.

3 *the cap on spending* LIMIT, upper limit, ceiling; curb, check.

▸ verb **1** *mountains capped with snow* TOP, crown, cover, coat.

2 *his breakaway goal capped a great game* ROUND OFF, crown, top off, be a fitting climax to.

3 *they tried to cap each other's stories* BEAT, better, improve on, surpass, outdo, outshine, outstrip, top, upstage.

4 *budgets will be capped* SET A LIMIT ON, limit, restrict; curb, control.

capability noun *her professional capabilities | their capability and willingness to tackle tough issues* ABILITY, capacity, power, potential; competence, proficiency, adeptness, aptitude, faculty, wherewithal, experience, skill, skillfulness, talent, flair; *informal* know-how.

capable adjective *a capable young woman* COMPETENT, able, efficient, effective, proficient, accomplished, adept, handy, experienced, skillful, skilled, talented, gifted; *informal* useful. ANTONYM incompetent.

PHRASE: **be capable of** *I'm capable of looking after myself* HAVE THE ABILITY TO, be equal to (the task of), be up to, have what it takes to (be).

capacious adjective *a capacious hotel suite* ROOMY, spacious, ample, big, large, sizable, generous; *formal* commodious. ANTONYMS cramped, small.

capacity noun **1** *the capacity of the freezer* VOLUME, size, magnitude, dimensions, measurements, proportions.

2 *his capacity to inspire trust.* See CAPABILITY.

3 *in his capacity as head librarian* POSITION, post, job, office; role, function.

cape[1] noun *a woolen cape* CLOAK, mantle, cope, wrap, stole, poncho, shawl, tippet, capelet; *historical* pelisse, mantelet.

cape[2] noun *the ship rounded the cape* HEADLAND, promontory, point, spit, head, foreland, horn, hook.

caper verb *children were capering about* SKIP, dance, romp, frisk, gambol, cavort, prance, frolic, leap, hop, jump, rollick.

▸ noun **1** *she did a little caper* DANCE, skip, hop, leap, jump.

2 *informal I'm too old for this kind of caper* STUNT, monkey business, escapade, prank, trick, mischief, foolery, tomfoolery, antics, hijinks, skylarking, lark, shenanigans.

capital noun **1** *Warsaw is the capital of Poland* FIRST CITY, seat of government, metropolis.

2 *she had the capital to pull off the deal* MONEY, finance(s), funds, wherewithal, means, assets, wealth, resources, investment capital; *informal* cash, dough, bread, loot, bucks.

3 *he wrote the name in capitals* CAPITAL LETTERS, uppercase letters, block letters; *informal* caps.

capitalism noun *the capitalism of emerging nations* FREE ENTERPRISE, private enterprise, the free market. ANTONYM communism.

capitalist noun *a capitalist who made his fortune in textiles* FINANCIER, investor, industrialist; magnate, tycoon, entrepreneur, businessman, businesswoman.

capitalize verb *the capacity to capitalize new ventures* FINANCE, fund, underwrite, provide capital for, back; *informal* bankroll, stake, grubstake. PHRASE: **capitalize on** *she tried to capitalize on Sam's misfortune by offering him a high-interest loan* TAKE ADVANTAGE OF, profit from, make the most of, exploit; *informal* cash in on.

capitulate verb *the rebels had been forced to capitulate* SURRENDER, give in/up, yield, concede defeat, give up the struggle, submit, knuckle under; lay down one's arms, raise/show the white flag, throw in the towel. ANTONYMS resist, hold out.

caprice noun 1 *his wife's caprices* WHIM, whimsy, vagary, fancy, fad, quirk, eccentricity, foible.

2 *the staff tired of his caprice* FICKLENESS, changeableness, volatility, capriciousness, unpredictability.

capricious adjective *the capricious workings of fate* FICKLE, inconstant, changeable, variable, mercurial, volatile, unpredictable, temperamental; whimsical, fanciful, flighty, quirky, faddish. ANTONYM consistent.

capsize verb *gale-force winds capsized their small craft* OVERTURN, turn over, turn upside down, upend, flip/tip/keel over, turn turtle; *Nautical* pitchpole; *archaic* overset. ANTONYM right.

capsule noun 1 *he swallowed a capsule* PILL, tablet, lozenge, pastille, drop; *informal* tab.

2 *a space capsule* MODULE, craft, probe.

captain noun 1 *the ship's captain* COMMANDER, master; *informal* skipper.

2 *the team captain* LEADER, head; *informal* boss, skipper.

3 *a captain of industry* MAGNATE, tycoon, industrialist; chief, head, leader, principal; *informal* boss, number one, bigwig, big shot, big gun, big cheese, big kahuna, honcho, top dog, top banana.

▸ verb *a vessel captained by a cutthroat* COMMAND, run, be in charge of, control, manage, govern; *informal* skipper.

caption noun *the captions are written in German* TITLE, heading, wording, head, legend, subtitle; rubric, slogan.

captivate verb *audiences are captivated by his energy* ENTHRALL, charm, enchant, bewitch, fascinate, beguile, entrance, enrapture, delight, attract, allure; engross, mesmerize, spellbind, hypnotize. ANTONYMS repel, bore.

captive noun *release the captives* PRISONER, convict, detainee, inmate, abductee; prisoner of war, POW, internee; *informal* jailbird, con, yardbird, lifer.

▸ adjective *captive wild animals* CONFINED, caged, incarcerated, locked up; jailed, imprisoned, in prison, interned, detained, in captivity, under lock and key, behind bars.

captivity noun *these creatures will languish in captivity* IMPRISONMENT, confinement, internment, incarceration, detention, custody. ANTONYM freedom.

capture verb 1 *the spy was captured in Moscow* CATCH, apprehend, seize, arrest; take prisoner, take captive, imprison, detain, put/throw in jail, put behind bars, put under lock and key, incarcerate; *informal* nab, collar, bag, pick up. ANTONYM free.

2 *guerrillas captured a strategic district* OCCUPY, invade, conquer, seize, take, take over, take possession of.

3 *the music captured the atmosphere of a summer morning* EXPRESS, reproduce, represent, encapsulate.

4 *the tales of pirates captured the children's imaginations* ENGAGE, attract, catch, seize, hold.

▸ noun *he tried to evade capture* ARREST, apprehension, seizure, being taken prisoner, being taken captive, imprisonment.

car noun 1 *he drove up in his car* AUTOMOBILE, motor vehicle, vehicle; *dated* motorcar; *informal* auto, wheels, gas guzzler; jalopy, lemon, junker, clunker, Tin Lizzie, rustbucket. See table.

2 *the dining car* CARRIAGE, coach.

TYPES OF CARS

buggy	minicar
cloth-top	minivan
compact	off-road vehicle/ORV
convertible	patrol car
coupe	race car
cruiser	racing car
dragster	ragtop
electric	roadster
four-by-four/4 × 4	runabout
four-door	sedan
gas-electric	soft-top
GTi	sports car
hardtop	sport-utility vehicle/SUV
hatchback	station wagon
hearse	stretch limo
hot rod	stock car
hybrid	subcompact
jeep	taxi/taxicab
limo/limousine	two-door
low-rider	

carafe noun *a carafe of hot coffee* FLASK, jug, pitcher, decanter, flagon.

caravan noun *a refugee caravan* CONVOY, procession, column, train, cavalcade.

carbuncle noun *treat the carbuncle with hot compresses* BOIL, sore, abscess, pustule, wen; *technical* furuncle.

carcass noun *a mule carcass* CORPSE, dead body, body, remains; *Medicine* cadaver; *informal* stiff, roadkill; *archaic* corse. See note at BODY.

card noun 1 *a piece of stiff card* CARDBOARD, pasteboard, board, Bristol board.

2 *I'll send her a card* GREETING CARD, postcard, notecard.

3 *she produced her card* IDENTIFICATION (CARD), ID, credentials, pass, key card; business card, calling card.

4 *she paid with her card* CREDIT CARD, debit card, bank card, charge card, gold card, platinum card; phone card; *informal* plastic.

5 *the cards were dealt* PLAYING CARD; tarot card; **(cards)** deck/pack of cards. See table on page 123.

6 *informal* *she's such a card!* ECCENTRIC, character; JOKER, wit, wag, jester, clown, comedian; *informal* laugh, scream, hoot, riot, jokester.

CARD GAMES

baccarat	hearts
bezique	monte
blackjack	napoleon
bridge	old maid
canasta	pinochle
cassino/casino	piquet
chemin de fer	poker
contract bridge	rouge-et-noir
cooncan	rummy
crazy eights	setback
cribbage	skat
duplicate bridge	slapjack
écarté	solitaire
euchre	solo
fan-tan	stud poker
faro	three-card monte
five hundred	twenty-one
forty-five	UNO™
gin rummy	war
go fish	whist

cardinal adjective *you've broken one of the cardinal rules* FUNDAMENTAL, basic, main, chief, primary, crucial, pivotal, prime, principal, paramount, preeminent, highest, key, essential. ANTONYM unimportant.

care noun **1** *the care of the child* SAFEKEEPING, SUPERVISION, custody, charge, protection, control, responsibility; guardianship, wardship. ANTONYM neglect.

2 *handle with care* CAUTION, carefulness, heedfulness, heed, attention, attentiveness. ANTONYM carelessness.

3 *she chose her words with care* DISCRETION, judiciousness, forethought, thought, regard, heed, mindfulness; accuracy, precision, discrimination. ANTONYM carelessness.

4 *the cares of the day* WORRY, anxiety, trouble, concern, stress, pressure, strain; sorrow, woe, hardship.

5 *care for the elderly* HELP, aid, assistance, succor, support; concern, consideration, thought, regard, solicitude; *informal* TLC. ANTONYM disregard.

▸ verb *the teachers didn't care about our work* BE CONCERNED, worry (oneself), trouble oneself, concern oneself, bother, mind, be interested; *informal* give a damn, give a hoot.

PHRASE: **care for 1** *he cares for his children* LOVE, be fond of, be devoted to, treasure, adore, dote on, think the world of, worship, idolize. **2** *would you care for a cup of coffee?* LIKE, want, desire, fancy, feel like. **3** *Hospice cares for the terminally ill* LOOK AFTER, take care of, tend (to), attend to, minister to, nurse; be responsible for, keep safe, keep an eye on.

USAGE NOTE **couldn't care less**

Couldn't care less is the correct and logical phrasing, not *could care less*—e.g.: "The American people could care less [read *couldn't care less*] who's White House Chief of Staff." (George Will, on "This Week with David Brinkley"; July 3, 1994.) If you *could care less*, you're saying that you do care some. Invariably, though, writers and speakers who use the phrase mean that they don't care at all. Although some apologists argue that *could care less* is meant to be sarcastic and not to be taken literally, a more plausible explanation is that the *-n't* of *couldn't* has been garbled in sloppy speech and sloppy writing. As American linguist Atcheson L. Hench explains: "A listener has not heard the whole phrase; he has heard a slurred form. *Couldn't care* has two dental stops practically together, *dnt*. This is heard only as *d* and slurring results. The outcome is *I c'd care less*." (*American Speech*, 159; 1973.) **—BG**

careen verb *the car careened down the highway* RUSH, hurtle, career, streak, shoot, race, bolt, dash, speed, run, whiz, zoom, flash, blast, charge, fly, go like the wind, belt, scoot, tear, zip, whip, zap, go like a bat out of hell, bomb, hightail, clip.

career noun **1** *a business career* PROFESSION, occupation, job, vocation, calling, employment, line, line of work, walk of life, métier.

2 *a checkered career* HISTORY, existence, life, course, passage, path.

▸ adjective *a career politician* PROFESSIONAL, permanent, full-time.

▸ verb *they careered down the hill.* See CAREEN.

carefree adjective *she's nothing like her carefree mother* UNWORRIED, untroubled, blithe, airy, nonchalant, insouciant, happy-go-lucky, free and easy, easygoing, relaxed, mellow; *informal* laid-back, loosey-goosey. ANTONYM careworn.

careful adjective **1** *be careful when you go up the stairs* CAUTIOUS, heedful, alert, attentive, watchful, vigilant, wary, on guard, circumspect. See note at VIGILANT. ANTONYM careless.

2 *she'd always been careful with money* PRUDENT, thrifty, frugal, economical, economizing, scrimping, abstemious, sensible; mean, miserly, penny-pinching, parsimonious, niggardly; *informal* stingy. ANTONYM extravagant.

3 *careful consideration of the facts* ATTENTIVE, conscientious, painstaking, meticulous, diligent, deliberate, assiduous, sedulous, scrupulous, punctilious, methodical; *informal* persnickety. ANTONYM inattentive.

careless adjective **1** *careless motorists* INATTENTIVE, incautious, negligent, absentminded, remiss; heedless, irresponsible, impetuous, reckless, foolhardy; cavalier, supercilious, devil-may-care. ANTONYMS careful, attentive.

2 *careless work* SHODDY, slapdash, slipshod, slovenly, negligent, lax, slack, disorganized, hasty, hurried; *informal* sloppy, slaphappy. ANTONYM meticulous.

3 *a careless remark* THOUGHTLESS, insensitive, indiscreet, unguarded, incautious, inadvertent. ANTONYM judicious.

4 *she carried on, **careless of** the time* HEEDLESS OF, unconcerned with, indifferent to, oblivious to.

caress verb *his hands caressed her back* STROKE, touch, fondle, brush, pet; hug, embrace; nuzzle.

caretaker noun JANITOR, custodian, superintendent, maintenance man/woman; curator; concierge, attendant, porter; *informal* super.

▸ adjective *a caretaker government* TEMPORARY, short-term, provisional, substitute, acting, interim, pro tem, stand-in, fill-in, stopgap. ANTONYM permanent.

careworn adjective *Antoine's careworn face told the story of his ordeal* WORRIED, anxious, strained, stressed, dispirited; drained, drawn, gaunt, haggard. ANTONYM carefree.

cargo noun *they work on the docks loading cargo* FREIGHT, load, haul, consignment, delivery, shipment; goods, merchandise, payload, lading.

caricature noun *a caricature of the Baldwin brothers* CARTOON, parody, satire, lampoon, burlesque; *informal* sendup, takeoff.

▸ verb *she has turned to caricaturing her fellow actors* PARODY, satirize, lampoon, make fun of, burlesque, mimic; *informal* send up, take off.

THE RIGHT WORD

Skilled writers and artists who want to poke fun at someone or something have a number of weapons at their disposal. An artist might come up with a **caricature**, which is a drawing or written piece that exaggerates its subject's distinguishing features or peculiarities (*the cartoonist's caricature of the presidential candidate*). A **parody** is similar to a caricature in purpose, but is used of written work, or performances that ridicule an author or performer's work by imitating its language and style for comic effect (*a parody of the scene between Romeo and Juliet*). While a *parody* concentrates on distorting the content of the original work, a **travesty** retains the subject matter but imitates the style in a grotesque or absurd way (*their version of the Greek tragedy was a travesty*). A **lampoon** is a strongly satirical piece of writing that attacks or ridicules an individual or an institution; it is more commonly used as a verb (*to lampoon the government in a local newspaper*). While a *caricature*, a *parody*, and a *travesty* must have an original to imitate, a **burlesque** can be an independent creation or composition; it is a comic or satiric imitation, often a theatrical one, that treats a serious subject lightly or a trivial subject with mock seriousness (*the play was a burlesque of Homer's great epic*). **Mimicry** is something you don't have to be an artist, a writer, or an actor to be good at. Anyone who successfully imitates another person's speech or gestures is a good mimic or impressionist, whether the intent is playful or mocking (*he showed an early talent for mimicry; entertaining his parents with imitations of their friends*).

caring adjective *she spent her final years with a caring granddaughter* KIND, kind-hearted, warmhearted, tender; concerned, attentive, thoughtful, solicitous, altruistic, considerate; affectionate, loving, doting, fond; sympathetic, understanding, compassionate, feeling. ANTONYM cruel.

carnage noun *an unforgettable scene of carnage* SLAUGHTER, massacre, mass murder, butchery, bloodbath, bloodletting, gore; holocaust, pogrom, ethnic cleansing.

carnal adjective *his carnal desires* SEXUAL, sensual, erotic, lustful, lascivious, libidinous, lecherous, licentious; physical, bodily, corporeal, fleshly. ANTONYM spiritual.

carnival noun **1** *the town's carnival* FESTIVAL, fiesta, féte, gala, jamboree, celebration, fest.

2 *he worked at a carnival* FAIR, amusement park, fun fair, ex, amusement show, circus, big top, midway.

carnivorous adjective *the giraffe is not a carnivorous animal* MEAT-EATING, flesh-eating, predatory; raptorial; *rare,* zoophagous, creophagous. ANTONYMS herbivorous, vegetarian.

carol noun *children sang carols* CHRISTMAS SONG, hymn, canticle.

carouse verb *it was pretty stupid to carouse the night before an exam* DRINK AND MAKE MERRY, go on a drinking bout, go on a spree; revel, celebrate, roister; *informal* party, booze, go boozing, binge, go on a binge, go on a bender, paint the town red, rave, whoop it up; *archaic* wassail.

WORD NOTE **mallemaroking**

I rejoice in a language which includes so highly specific a term as this—*the carousing,* it signifies, *of drunken seamen on icebound Greenland whaling ships.* The etymology is unconvincing, and there is some danger that the word may seem a nonce-word, created as a joke to describe a situation so infrequently encountered as not to require a word to denote it. Yet it has enjoyed some publicity in recent years, not least when an editor at *The Guardian* in London noticed that in a later edition of the first dictionary to include it, the definition of *mallemaroking* had been slightly changed to the carousing of drunken seamen in icebound whaling ships—dropping the word *Greenland,* which had hitherto so circumscribed the activity. The same editor wrote a mock-fulmination on a Saturday editorial page: the foul practice of *mallemaroking,* he fumed, previously confined to the Greenland of its birth, seems now to have detached itself from its origins and is fast spreading across the world. It must be stopped immediately, before it is too late. Ever since, the word has enjoyed some small currency, which I would like to see expanded to a subtle degree. The practice being so rare, it is difficult to imagine many writers being able to employ it as a consequence of observation: rather it might be used in sentences such as *I sat in silence on the floe, fancying as I did so that above all the creaking of the bergs and the moaning of the wind, I could hear the faint echo of mallemaroking from the vessels fixed fast out in the Strait.* **—SW**

carp verb *they could always find something to carp about* COMPLAIN, cavil, grumble, grouse, whine, bleat, nag; *informal* gripe, grouch, beef, bellyache, moan, bitch, whinge, kvetch. ANTONYM praise.

carpenter noun *you'll need a carpenter to repair those joists* WOODWORKER, cabinetmaker.

carpet noun **1** *a Turkish carpet* RUG, mat, floor covering. **2** *a carpet of wildflowers* COVERING, blanket, layer, cover, cloak, mantle.

▸ verb *the gravel was carpeted in moss* COVER, coat, overlay, overspread, blanket.

carriage noun **1** *a horse and carriage.* See table.
2 *a railroad carriage* COACH, car, passenger car; flatcar, boxcar.

HORSE-DRAWN CARRIAGES, CARTS, AND WAGONS

barouche	dray
brougham	droshky
buckboard	fiacre
buggy	fly
cab	four-in-hand
cabriolet	gig
calèche	hackney (carriage)
cariole	hansom (cab)
carryall	landau
chaise	phaeton
chariot	post-chaise
chuckwagon	stagecoach
clarence	stanhope
coach	sulky
Conestoga wagon	surrey
coupe	tilbury
covered wagon	trap
curricle	troika
democrat wagon	victoria
dogcart	wagonette

carrier noun *our private carrier delivers more than ten thousand packages a month* BEARER, conveyor, transporter, shipper; courier, hauler, porter.

carry verb **1** *she carried the box into the kitchen* CONVEY, transfer, move, take, bring, bear, lug, tote, fetch, cart.

2 *a cruise line carrying a million passengers a year* TRANSPORT, convey, move, handle.

3 *satellites carry the signal across the country* TRANSMIT, conduct, relay, communicate, convey, dispatch, beam.

4 *the dinghy can carry the weight of the baggage* SUPPORT, sustain, stand; prop up, shore up, bolster.

5 *managers carry most of the responsibility* BEAR, accept, assume, undertake, shoulder, take on (oneself).

6 *she was carrying twins* BE PREGNANT WITH, bear, expect; *technical* be gravid with.

7 *she carried herself with assurance* CONDUCT, bear, hold; act, behave, acquit; *formal* comport.

8 *a resolution was carried* APPROVE, vote for, accept, endorse, ratify, pass; agree to, assent to, rubber-stamp; *informal* OK, give the thumbs up to.

9 *I carried the whole audience* WIN OVER, sway, convince, persuade, influence; motivate, stimulate.

10 *today's paper carried an article on housing policy* PUBLISH, print, communicate, distribute; broadcast, transmit.

11 *we carry a wide range of linens* SELL, stock, keep, keep in stock, offer, have, have for sale, retail, supply.

12 *most toxins carry warnings* DISPLAY, bear, exhibit, show, be marked with.

13 *it carries a penalty of two years' imprisonment* ENTAIL, involve, result in, occasion, have as a consequence.

14 *his voice carried across the field* BE AUDIBLE, travel, reach. PHRASES: **be/get carried away** *I'm afraid I get a bit carried away* LOSE SELF-CONTROL, get overexcited, go too far; *informal* flip, lose it. **carry something off** *she carried off four awards* WIN, secure, gain, achieve, collect; *informal* land, net, bag, scoop. **carry on 1** *they carried on arguing* CONTINUE, keep (on), go on; persist in, persevere in, stick with/at. **2** *informal she was carrying on with other men* HAVE AN AFFAIR, commit adultery, have a fling, play around, mess around, fool around. **3** *informal I was always carrying on* MISBEHAVE, behave badly, get up to mischief, cause trouble, get up to no good, be naughty; clown around, fool around, mess around, act up. **4** *we carried on a conversation* ENGAGE IN, conduct, undertake, be involved in, carry out, perform. **carry out 1** *operations were carried out in secret* CONDUCT, perform, implement, execute. **2** *I carried out my promise to her* FULFILL, carry through, honor, redeem, make good; keep, observe, abide by, comply with, adhere to, stick to, keep faith with.

cart noun **1** *a horse-drawn cart.* See table at CARRIAGE.

2 *carts lined up at the checkout* SHOPPING CART, handcart, pushcart.

▸ verb *informal he had the wreckage carted away* TRANSPORT, convey, haul, move, shift, take; carry, lug.

carte blanche noun *he gave his protégé carte blanche* FREE REIN, a free hand, a blank check.

carton noun *a carton of empty whiskey bottles* BOX, package, cardboard box, container, pack, packet.

cartoon noun **1** *a cartoon of the defense secretary* CARICATURE, parody, lampoon, satire; *informal* takeoff, sendup.

2 *he was reading cartoons* COMIC STRIP, comic, funnies, graphic novel.

3 *they watched cartoons on television* ANIMATED FILM, animation; *informal* toon.

cartridge noun **1** *a toner cartridge* CASSETTE, canister, container, magazine.

2 *a rifle cartridge* BULLET, round, shell, charge, shot.

carve verb **1** *she carved horn handles* SCULPT, sculpture; cut, hew, whittle; form, shape, fashion.

2 *I carved my initials on the tree* ENGRAVE, etch, incise, score.

3 *he carved the roast chicken* SLICE, cut up; chop. PHRASE: **carved in stone** *these are merely suggestions, they're not carved in stone* UNALTERABLE, immutable, unchangeable, irreversible, irrevocable.

carving noun *a carving of Robert E. Lee* SCULPTURE, model, statue, statuette, figure, figurine.

cascade noun *a roaring cascade* WATERFALL, cataract, falls, rapids, white water.

▸ verb *rain cascaded from the roof* POUR, gush, surge, spill, stream, flow, issue, spurt.

case[1] noun **1** *a classic case of overreaction* INSTANCE, occurrence, manifestation, demonstration, exposition, exhibition; example, illustration, specimen, sample, exemplification.

2 *if that is the case, I will have to find somebody else* SITUATION, position, state of affairs, lay of the land; circumstances, conditions, facts; way things stand; *informal* score.

3 *the officers on the case* INVESTIGATION, inquiry, examination, exploration, probe, search, inquest.

4 *only urgent cases were admitted for immediate examination* PATIENT, sick person, invalid, sufferer, victim.

5 *she lost her case* LAWSUIT, (legal) action, legal dispute, suit, trial, legal/judicial proceedings, litigation.

6 *a strong case* ARGUMENT, contention, reasoning, logic, defense, justification, vindication, exposition, thesis.

case[2] noun **1** *a cigarette case* CONTAINER, box, canister, receptacle, holder.

2 *a seed case* CASING, cover, covering, sheath, sheathing, envelope, sleeve, jacket, integument.

3 *a case of wine* CRATE, box, pack.

4 *a glass display case* CABINET, cupboard, buffet.

▸ verb *informal a thief casing the joint* RECONNOITER, inspect, examine, survey, explore, check out.

cash noun **1** *a wallet stuffed with cash* MONEY, currency, hard cash; notes, bank notes, bills; coins, change; *informal* dough, bread, loot, moolah, bucks, dinero, lucre. ANTONYMS check, credit.

2 *a lack of cash* FINANCE(S), money, resources, funds, assets, the means, the wherewithal.

▸ verb *the bank cashed her check* EXCHANGE, change, convert into cash/money; honor, pay, accept.

PHRASE: **cash in on** *the band is cashing in on merchandis-*

ing TAKE ADVANTAGE OF, exploit, milk; make money from, profit from, make a killing from.

cashier noun *the cashier took the check* CHECKOUT GIRL/BOY/PERSON, clerk; bank clerk, teller, banker, treasurer, bursar, purser.

casing noun *a silver-plated casing* COVER, case, shell, envelope, sheath, sheathing, sleeve, jacket, housing.

casino noun *playing the slots in her favorite casino* GAMBLING ESTABLISHMENT, gambling club, gambling den, gaming house.

cask noun *casks of ale for the crew* BARREL, keg, butt, tun, vat, drum, hogshead; *historical* firkin.

casket noun **1** *the casket of a dead soldier* COFFIN, sarcophagus; *informal* box; *humorous* wooden overcoat.

2 *a small casket of jewels* BOX, chest, case, container, receptacle.

casserole noun See table at STEW.

cassette noun *the lecture is available on cassette* TAPE, auidocassette, videocassette, video, cartridge; *dated* eight-track.

cast verb **1** *he cast the stone into the stream* THROW, toss, fling, pitch, hurl, lob; *informal* chuck.

2 *fishermen cast their nets* SPREAD, throw, open out.

3 *she cast a fearful glance over her shoulder* DIRECT, shoot, throw, send.

4 *each citizen cast a vote* REGISTER, record, enter, file, vote.

5 *the fire cast a soft light* EMIT, give off, send out, radiate.

6 *the figures cast shadows* FORM, create, produce; project, throw.

7 *the stags' antlers are cast each year* SHED, lose, discard, slough off.

8 *a figure cast by hand* MOLD, fashion, form, shape, model; sculpt, sculpture, forge.

9 *they were cast as extras* CHOOSE, select, pick, name, nominate.

▸ noun **1** *a cast of the writer's hand* MOLD, die, matrix, shape, casting, model.

2 *a cast of the dice* THROW, toss, fling, pitch, hurl, lob; *informal* chuck.

3 *an inquiring cast of mind* TYPE, sort, kind, character, variety, class, style, stamp, nature.

4 *the cast of our spring musical* ACTORS, performers, players, company, troupe; dramatis personae, characters.

PHRASE: **cast aside** *cast aside the pages marked with an "X"* DISCARD, reject, throw away/out, get rid of, dispose of, abandon.

castaway adjective **1** *castaway sailors* SHIPWRECKED, wrecked, stranded, aground.

2 *castaway clothing* CASTOFF, discarded, used, throwaway.

caste noun *she could not marry outside her caste* CLASS, social class, social order, rank, level, stratum, echelon, status; *dated* estate, station.

castigate verb *Leopold castigated his son for leaving the archbishop's service* REPRIMAND, rebuke, admonish, chastise, chide, censure, upbraid, reprove, reproach, scold, berate, take to task, lambaste, give someone a piece of one's mind; *informal* rake/haul over the coals, tell off, give someone an earful, give someone a tongue-lashing, give someone a roasting, rap someone on the knuckles, slap someone's wrist, dress down, bawl out, give someone hell, blow up at, lay into, blast, zing, have a go at, give someone what for, chew out, ream out; *rare* reprehend. ANTONYMS praise, commend.

castle noun *a drafty old Scottish castle* FORTRESS, fort, stronghold, fortification, keep, citadel.

castrate verb *many of these colts are castrated* NEUTER, geld, cut, desex, unsex, sterilize, fix, alter, doctor; *archaic* emasculate.

casual adjective **1** *a casual attitude to life* INDIFFERENT, apathetic, uncaring, unconcerned; lackadaisical, blasé, nonchalant, insouciant, offhand, flippant; easygoing, free and easy, blithe, carefree, devil-may-care; *informal* laid-back, loosey-goosey, Type-B. ANTONYMS careful, concerned.

2 *a casual remark* OFFHAND, spontaneous, unpremeditated, unthinking, unconsidered, impromptu, throwaway, unguarded; *informal* off-the-cuff. ANTONYM premeditated.

3 *a casual glance* CURSORY, perfunctory, superficial, passing, fleeting; hasty, brief, quick. ANTONYMS careful, thorough.

4 *a casual acquaintance* SLIGHT, superficial. ANTONYMS intimate, close.

5 *casual work* TEMPORARY, part-time, freelance, impermanent, irregular, occasional. ANTONYMS permanent, full-time.

6 *casual sex* PROMISCUOUS, extramarital, free.

7 *a casual meeting changed his life* CHANCE, accidental, unplanned, unintended, unexpected, unforeseen, unanticipated, fortuitous, serendipitous, adventitious. See note at ACCIDENTAL. ANTONYMS intentional, planned.

8 *a casual shirt* INFORMAL, comfortable, leisure, everyday; *informal* sporty. ANTONYMS formal, dressy.

9 *the inn's casual atmosphere* RELAXED, friendly, informal, unceremonious, easygoing, free and easy; *informal* laid-back. ANTONYM formal.

WORD NOTE négligé

So alluring do many of us find words that denote the delicate undergarments of women—of which *negligee* is one, though somewhat old-fashioned and out of favor, lumped these days with the *muumuu,* the *housecoat,* and the *corselette*—that we tend to overlook the noun that was once used to mean a woman's informal attire, and when she was not decked out in what was once called her *complete toilette,* her finery. That word, a single 'e' shorter than the flimsy gown the word suggests nowadays, is *négligé* and it seems a wonderfully appropriate word to reintroduce into more common use today to describe the general informality of clothing that is the style of the moment. It does not denote an appearance so grubbily untidy as to merit *scruffy;* nor is it quite what hotels and cruise ships and restaurants euphemize as *smart casual, resort wear,* or *relaxed.* However, I daresay any restaurant bold enough to suggest *négligé* as the dress code for entry should be prepared for surprise, especially in more risqué neighborhoods. **—SW**

casualty noun *a casualty of war* | *a record of the casualties* VICTIM, fatality, loss, MIA; (**casualties**) dead and injured, missing in action, missing.

casuistry noun *the casuistry about altruism always being ultimately selfish* SOPHISTRY, specious reasoning, speciousness, sophism, equivocation.

cat noun *their pet cats* FELINE, tomcat, tom, kitten, mouser; *informal* pussy (cat), puss, kitty; alley cat; *archaic* grimalkin. See table.

CATS

Domestic	shorthair
Abyssinian	Siamese
American bobtail	Siberian
American curl	Singapura
American shorthair	Somali
American wirehair	Sphynx
angora	tabby
Balinese	Tonkinese
Birman	tortoiseshell
bobtail	Turkish angora
Bombay	Turkish Van
British shorthair	wirehair
Burmese	
calico	**Wild**
chartreux	Bengal tiger
chinchilla (cat)	bobcat
colorpoint shorthair	Canada lynx
Cornish Rex	caracal
curl	catamount
Devon Rex	cheetah
Egyptian mau	clouded leopard
exotic	cougar
ginger	eyra cat
Havana brown	jaguar
Himalayan	jaguarundi
Javanese	kodkod
Japanese bobtail	leopard
Korat	leopard cat
LaPerm	lion
longhair	lynx
Maine coon	margay
Manx	mountain lion
marmalade	ocelot
Norwegian forest cat	oncilla
ocicat	panther
Oriental	puma
Persian	serval
ragdoll	Siberian tiger
Rex	snow leopard
Russian Blue	tiger
Scottish fold	tiger cat
Selkirk Rex	wildcat

cataclysm noun *their homeland was destroyed by a great cataclysm* DISASTER, catastrophe, calamity, tragedy, devastation, holocaust, ruin, ruination, upheaval, convulsion, apocalypse, act of God.

catacombs plural noun *they unearthed the catacombs of an apparently prominent family* UNDERGROUND CEMETERY, crypt, vault, tomb, ossuary.

catalog noun **1** *a library catalog* DIRECTORY, register, index, list, listing, record, archive, inventory.

2 *a mail-order catalog* BROCHURE, mailer, wish book.

▸ verb *the collection is fully cataloged* CLASSIFY, categorize, systematize, index, list, archive, make an inventory of, inventory, record, itemize.

catalyst noun *the governor's speech was a catalyst for debate* STIMULUS, stimulation, spark, sparkplug, spur, incitement, impetus.

catapult verb *the boulder was catapulted into the sea* PROPEL, launch, hurl, fling, send flying, fire, blast, shoot.

cataract noun *the glistening cataract made a spectacular backdrop for our photo shoot* WATERFALL, cascade, falls, rapids, white water.

catastrophe noun *the flood of '82 was the worst catastrophe in the town's history* DISASTER, calamity, cataclysm, holocaust, havoc, ruin, ruination, tragedy; adversity, blight, trouble, trial, tribulation.

catastrophic adjective *the losses were catastrophic* DISASTROUS, calamitous, cataclysmic, apocalyptic, ruinous, tragic, fatal, dire, awful, terrible, dreadful.

catcall noun *the young comics have to learn how to withstand the inevitable catcalls* WHISTLE, boo, hiss, jeer, raspberry, taunt; **(catcalls)** scoffing, abuse, taunting, derision.

WORD NOTE **raspberry**

I am frequently tempted, as an Englishman, to try to induce Americans to introduce Cockney rhyming slang on occasion into their writings, if only to enhance their cosmopolitan air. The general form of this slang is familiar, if a little odd: you take a word, find a two- or three-word phrase that rhymes with it, then cut the final words of the phrase away and employ the first only to denote what you first wanted. An example: *head* rhymes with *loaf of bread.* Cut away *of bread,* and you are left with *loaf*—which term now replaces *head* in all conversation. A stupid person is thus one who *doesn't use his loaf.* Similarly: *tit-for-tat* rhymes with *hat;* slice away *tat,* and the conflated nonce-word *tit-for* is thenceforward used to mean *hat. "Take off your tit-for," the pastor bellowed at the bowler-wearer in church.* The list goes on: *the trouble's on the dog* derives from *the trouble-and-strife,* "the wife," is on the *dog-and-bone,* "the phone"—the wife is on the phone. And while *berk,* which means "a singularly disagreeable fool," comes from *Berkshire Hunt,* and is really very rude indeed, the infinitely more congenial *raspberry* is from *raspberry tart,* it rhymes with *fart,* and is used, says the *Oxford English Dictionary,* to denote the sound of disapproval one makes with one's lips, and which sounds like the *rending of glazed calico.* Sure it does. I suspect it is less than au courant to know how calico sounds—or even what calico is—when noisily showing how you loathe the umpire, or a boring politician. And to be able to describe the sound you make as a raspberry, and to know just why, is to be au courant and cosmopolitan indeed. **—SW**

catch verb **1** *he caught the ball* SEIZE, grab, snatch, take hold of, grasp, grip, trap, clutch, clench; receive, get, intercept. ANTONYM drop.

2 *we've caught the thief* CAPTURE, seize; apprehend, arrest, take prisoner/captive, take into custody; trap, snare, ensnare; net, hook, land; *informal* nab, collar, run in, bust. ANTONYM release.

3 *her heel caught in a hole* BECOME TRAPPED, become entangled, snag.

4 *she caught the last bus* BE IN TIME FOR, make, get; board, get on, step aboard. ANTONYM miss.

5 *they were caught siphoning gas* DISCOVER, find, come upon/across, stumble on, chance on; surprise, catch red-handed, catch in the act.

6 *it caught his imagination* ENGAGE, capture, attract, draw, grab, grip, seize; hold, absorb, engross.

7 *she caught a trace of aftershave* PERCEIVE, notice, observe, discern, detect, note, make out. ANTONYM miss.

8 *I couldn't catch what she was saying* HEAR, perceive, discern, make out; understand, comprehend, grasp, apprehend; *informal* get, get the drift of, figure out.

9 *it caught the flavor of the sixties* EVOKE, conjure up, call to mind, recall, encapsulate, capture.

10 *the blow caught her on the side of her face* HIT, strike, slap, smack, bang. ANTONYM miss.

11 *he caught malaria* BECOME INFECTED WITH, contract, get, fall ill with, be taken ill with, develop, come down with, be struck down with. ANTONYM escape.

12 *the kindling wouldn't catch* IGNITE, start burning, catch fire, kindle.

▸ noun **1** *he inspected the catch* HAUL, net, bag, yield.

2 *he secured the catch* LATCH, lock, fastener, clasp, hasp.

3 *it looks great, but there's a catch* SNAG, disadvantage, drawback, stumbling block, hitch, fly in the ointment, pitfall, complication, problem, hiccup, difficulty; trap, trick, snare; *informal* catch-22.

PHRASES: **catch on 1** *radio soon caught on* BECOME POPULAR, become fashionable, take off, boom, flourish, thrive. **2** *I caught on fast* UNDERSTAND, comprehend, learn, see the light; *informal* latch on, get the picture, get the message, get wise. **catch up to** *police didn't catch up to Swanson until he stopped for gas and food in Great Neck* REACH; be even with; gain on, close in on.

catch-22 noun *he wanted to do the right thing, but either decision would hurt somebody—it was a classic catch-22* DILEMMA, quandary, vicious circle; catch; chicken-and-egg problem.

catching adjective *informal my rash is not catching* INFECTIOUS, contagious; communicable, transmittable, transmissible, infective.

catchphrase noun *I wonder if he regrets having coined the often-mocked catchphrase "read my lips"* SAYING, quotation, quote, slogan, motto, catchword, watchword, byword, buzzword, tag line, mantra.

catchy adjective *I'm not sure what their product is, but they've got a catchy little jingle* MEMORABLE, unforgettable, haunting; appealing, popular; singable, melodious, tuneful, foot-tapping.

categorical adjective *a categorical assurance that annual premiums would not increase* UNQUALIFIED, unconditional, unequivocal, absolute, explicit, express, unambiguous, definite, direct, downright, outright, emphatic, positive, point-blank, conclusive, without reservations, out-and-out. ANTONYMS qualified, equivocal.

categorize verb *we should first categorize them by years of experience* CLASSIFY, class, group, grade, rate, designate; order, arrange, sort, rank; file, catalog, list, index; typecast, pigeonhole, stereotype.

category noun *his music doesn't fit into any conventional category* CLASS, classification, group, grouping, bracket, heading, set; type, sort, kind, variety, species, breed, brand, make, model; grade, order, rank; *informal* pigeonhole.

cater verb **1** *we* ***cater for*** *vegetarians* PROVIDE FOOD FOR, feed, serve, cook for.

2 *a resort* ***catering to*** *older travellers* SERVE, provide for, meet the needs/wants of, accommodate; satisfy, indulge, pander to, gratify.

3 *he seemed to* ***cater to*** *all tastes* TAKE INTO ACCOUNT, take into consideration, allow for, consider, bear in mind, make provision for, have regard for.

caterwaul verb *we could hear those felines caterwauling all night* HOWL, wail, bawl, cry, yell, scream, screech, yowl, ululate.

catharsis noun *the hope was that hypnosis would bring about a catharsis* EMOTIONAL RELEASE, relief, release, venting; purging, purgation, purification, cleansing; *Psychoanalysis* abreaction.

catholic adjective *her musical tastes are quite catholic* UNIVERSAL, diverse, diversified, wide, broad, broad-based, eclectic, liberal, latitudinarian; comprehensive, all-encompassing, all-embracing, all-inclusive. See note at UNIVERSAL. ANTONYM narrow.

cattle plural noun COWS, bovines, oxen, bulls; stock, livestock. See table.

CATTLE

Aberdeen Angus	Highland cattle
African buffalo	Holstein
Alderney	Jersey
Ayrshire	kouprey
banteng	Limousin
beefalo	longhorn
bison	musk ox
Black Angus	ox
Brahman	plains bison
Brown Swiss	Red Angus
buffalo	Red Poll
Charolais	shorthorn
Chianina	Simmental
fighting bull	Texas longhorn
Galloway	water buffalo
gaur	wood bison
gayal	yak
Guernsey	zebu
Hereford	

catty adjective *informal* See SPITEFUL.

caucus noun **1** *the conservative caucus* MEMBERS, party, faction, camp, bloc, group, set, band, ring, cabal, coterie, pressure group.

2 *caucuses will be held in eleven states* MEETING, assembly, gathering, congress, conference, convention, rally, convocation.

cauldron noun *a black cast-iron cauldron* POT, kettle.

cause noun **1** *the cause of the fire* SOURCE, root, origin, beginning(s), starting point; mainspring, base, basis, foundation, fountainhead; originator, author, creator, producer, agent. ANTONYMS effect, result.

2 *there is no cause for alarm* REASON, grounds, justification, call, need, necessity, occasion; excuse, pretext.

3 *the cause of human rights | a good cause* PRINCIPLE, ideal, belief, conviction; object, end, aim, objective, purpose, mission; charity.

4 *he went to plead his cause* CASE, suit, lawsuit, action, dispute.

▸ verb *this disease can cause blindness* BRING ABOUT, give rise to, lead to, result in, create, produce, generate, engender, spawn, bring on, precipitate, prompt, provoke, trigger, make happen, induce, inspire, promote, foster; *literary* beget, enkindle. ANTONYM result from.

caustic adjective **1** *a caustic cleaner* CORROSIVE, corroding, abrasive, mordant, acid.

2 *a caustic comment* SARCASTIC, cutting, biting, mordant, sharp, bitter, scathing, derisive, sardonic, ironic, scornful, trenchant, acerbic, abrasive, vitriolic, acidulous.

caution noun *proceed with caution* CARE, carefulness, heedfulness, heed, attention, attentiveness, alertness, watchfulness, vigilance, circumspection, discretion, prudence.

▸ verb *you were cautioned against taking such rash action* ADVISE, warn, counsel; admonish, exhort.

cautious adjective *a cautious driver* CAREFUL, heedful, attentive, alert, watchful, vigilant, circumspect, prudent; cagey, canny. See note at VIGILANT. ANTONYM reckless.

cavalcade noun *bystanders cheered as the cavalcade passed by* PROCESSION, parade, motorcade, cortège.

cavalier noun *archaic foot soldiers and cavaliers* HORSEMAN, equestrian; cavalryman, trooper, knight.

▸ adjective *a cavalier disregard for danger* OFFHAND, indifferent, casual, dismissive, insouciant, unconcerned; supercilious, patronizing, condescending, disdainful, scornful, contemptuous; *informal* couldn't-care-less, devil-may-care.

cavalry plural noun *he rode with the cavalry during the Mexican War* MOUNTED TROOPS, cavalrymen, troopers, horse; *historical* dragoons, lancers, hussars.

cave noun *the caves at the bottom of the cliff* CAVERN, grotto, underground chamber; cellar, vault, crypt. PHRASE: **cave in 1** *the roof caved in* COLLAPSE, fall in/down, give, give way, crumble, subside. **2** *the manager caved in to their demands* YIELD, surrender, capitulate, submit, give in, back down, make concessions, throw in the towel.

caveat noun *he added the caveat that the results still had to be corroborated* WARNING, caution, admonition; proviso, condition, stipulation, provision, clause, rider, qualification.

caveman, cavewoman noun *were these the drawings of a caveman?* CAVE DWELLER, troglodyte, primitive man/woman, prehistoric man/woman; Neanderthal.

cavern noun *the crude stone steps led down to a dank and cold cavern* LARGE CAVE, grotto, underground chamber/gallery, vault.

cavernous adjective *dinner was served in a cavernous hall* VAST, huge, large, immense, spacious, roomy, airy, capacious, voluminous, extensive, deep; hollow, gaping, yawning; *formal* commodious. ANTONYM small.

cavil verb *he caviled at the cost.* See CARP.

cavity noun *microscopic photos show a surface erose with nodes and cavities* SPACE, chamber, hollow, hole, pocket, pouch; orifice, aperture; socket, gap, crater, pit.

cavort verb *colts cavorted in the pasture* SKIP, dance, romp, jig, caper, frisk, play/horse around, gambol, prance, frolic, lark; bounce, trip, leap, jump, bound, spring, hop; roughhouse, rollick.

cease verb **1** *hostilities had ceased* COME TO AN END, come to a halt, end, halt, stop, conclude, terminate, finish, draw to a close, be over. ANTONYMS start, continue.

2 *they ceased all military activity* BRING TO AN END, bring to a halt, end, halt, stop, conclude, terminate, finish, wind up, discontinue, suspend, break off; *informal* leave off. ANTONYMS start, continue.

PHRASE: **without cease** *they have worked without cease on these prototypes* CONTINUOUSLY, incessantly, unendingly, unremittingly, without a pause, without a break, on and on.

cease-fire noun *a cease-fire was called on Christmas Eve* ARMISTICE, truce, peace, suspension of hostilities.

ceaseless adjective *a ceaseless flow of questions* CONTINUAL, constant, continuous; incessant, unceasing, unending, endless, never-ending, interminable, nonstop, uninterrupted, unremitting, relentless, unrelenting, unrelieved, sustained, persistent, eternal, perpetual. ANTONYM intermittent.

cede verb *the library has ceded ten parking spaces to the hearing clinic* SURRENDER, concede, relinquish, yield, part with, give up; hand over, deliver up, give over, make over, transfer; abandon, forgo, sacrifice; *literary* forsake. See note at RELINQUISH.

ceiling noun *a ceiling was to be set on prices* UPPER LIMIT, maximum, limitation.

celebrate verb **1** *they were celebrating their wedding anniversary* COMMEMORATE, observe, mark, keep, honor, remember, memorialize.

2 *let's all celebrate!* ENJOY ONESELF, have fun, have a good time, have a party, revel, roister, carouse, make merry; *informal* party, go out on the town, paint the town red, whoop it up, make whoopee, live it up, have a ball.

3 *he was celebrated for his achievements* PRAISE, extol, glorify, eulogize, reverence, honor, pay tribute to; *formal* laud.

celebrated adjective *a celebrated hero* ACCLAIMED, admired, highly rated, lionized, revered, honored, esteemed, exalted, vaunted, well-thought-of, ballyhooed; eminent, great, distinguished, prestigious, illustrious, preeminent, estimable, notable, of note, of repute; *formal* lauded. ANTONYM unsung.

celebration noun **1** *the celebration of his 50th birthday* COMMEMORATION, observance, marking, keeping.

2 *a birthday celebration for the twins* PARTY, gathering, festivities, festival, féte, carnival, gala, jamboree, function; *informal* do, bash, shindig, rave.

3 *the celebration of the Eucharist* OBSERVANCE, performance, officiation, solemnization.

celebrity noun **1** *a sports celebrity* FAMOUS PERSON, VIP, very important person, personality, name, big name, famous name, household name, star, superstar; *informal* celeb, somebody, someone, megastar. ANTONYM nonentity.

2 *his celebrity grew* FAME, prominence, renown, eminence, preeminence, stardom, popularity, distinction, note, notability, prestige, stature, repute, reputation. ANTONYM obscurity.

celestial adjective **1** *a celestial body* (IN) SPACE, heavenly, astronomical, extraterrestrial, stellar, astral, planetary. ANTONYMS earthly, terrestrial.

2 *celestial beings* HEAVENLY, holy, saintly, divine, godly, godlike, ethereal, otherworldly; immortal, angelic, seraphic, cherubic. ANTONYMS mundane, hellish.

celibate adjective *an order of celibate brothers* UNMARRIED, single, unwed, spouseless; chaste, virginal, virgin, maidenly, maiden, intact, abstinent, self-denying. See note at CHASTE.

cell noun **1** *a prison cell* ROOM, cubicle, chamber; dungeon, oubliette, lockup.

2 *each cell of the honeycomb* COMPARTMENT, cavity, hole, hollow, section.

3 *terrorist cells* UNIT, faction, arm, section, ring, coterie, group.

cellar noun *the rickety stairs that go down to the cellar* BASEMENT, vault, underground room, lower ground floor, downstairs; cantina; crypt, undercroft. ANTONYM attic.

cement noun *don't step in the wet cement* MORTAR, grout, concrete; ADHESIVE, glue, fixative, gum, paste; superglue; mucilage.

▸ verb *he cemented the sample to a microscope slide* STICK, bond; fasten, fix, affix, attach, secure, bind, glue, gum, paste.

cemetery noun *we gather at the cemetery on Memorial Day* GRAVEYARD, churchyard, burial ground, burying ground, necropolis, memorial park/garden; *informal* boneyard; *historical* potter's field; *archaic* God's acre.

censor noun *the film censors* EXPURGATOR, bowdlerizer; examiner, inspector, editor.

▸ verb *letters home were censored* CUT, delete parts of, make cuts in, blue-pencil; edit, expurgate, bowdlerize, sanitize; *informal* clean up.

EASILY CONFUSED WORDS **censor, censure**

Both **censor** and **censure** are both verbs and nouns, but **censor** means 'to scrutinize, revise, or cut unacceptable parts (from a book, movie, etc.)' or 'a person who does this,' while **censure** means 'to criticize harshly' or 'harsh criticism:' *the DJ won't play the censored tracks*; *some senators considered a resolution of censure to express strong disapproval of the president's behavior.*

censorious adjective *the appointment of censorious watchdogs over the broadcasters* HYPERCRITICAL, overcritical, fault-finding, disapproving, condemnatory, denunciatory, deprecatory, disparaging, reproachful, reproving, censuring, captious, carping, sitting in judgment. ANTONYM complimentary.

censure verb *he was censured for his conduct.* See REPRIMAND verb. See note at REBUKE.

▸ noun *a note of censure* CONDEMNATION, criticism, attack, abuse; reprimand, rebuke, admonishment, reproof, upbraiding, disapproval, reproach, scolding, obloquy; *informal* flak, dressing-down, tongue-lashing; *formal* excoriation, castigation. See note at CENSOR. ANTONYM approval.

center noun *the center of the town* MIDDLE, nucleus, heart, core, hub; middle point, midpoint, halfway point, mean, median. ANTONYM edge.

▸ verb *the story centers on a doctor* FOCUS, concentrate, pivot, hinge, revolve, be based.

USAGE NOTE **center around**

The construction **center around** (as opposed to *center on*, or *revolve around*) has been denounced as incorrect and illogical since it first appeared in the mid-nineteenth century. Although the phrase is common, it defies geometry by confusing the orbit with the fixed point: *the earth revolves around (or its revolution centers on) the sun.* A careful writer will use a precise expression, such as *centers on*, *revolves around*, *concerns*, or *involves*.

centerpiece noun *the tower is the centerpiece of the park* HIGHLIGHT, main feature, high point, best part, climax; focus of attention, focal point, center of attention/interest, magnet, cynosure.

central adjective 1 *occupying a central position* MIDDLE, center, halfway, midway, mid, median, medial, mean; *Anatomy* mesial. ANTONYMS side, extreme.

2 *central Fargo* INNER, innermost, middle, mid; downtown. ANTONYM outer.

3 *their central campaign issue* MAIN, chief, principal, primary, leading, foremost, first, most important, predominant, dominant, key, crucial, vital, essential, basic, fundamental, core, prime, premier, paramount, major, overriding; *informal* number-one. ANTONYMS minor, subordinate.

centralize verb *the state is to centralize its communications network* CONCENTRATE, consolidate, amalgamate, condense, unify, streamline, focus; *Brit.* rationalize. ANTONYM devolve.

ceramics plural noun *an exhibit of Armenian ceramics* POTTERY, pots, china, terra cotta.

cereal noun See table.

CEREAL GRAINS AND PRODUCTS

amaranth	millet
barley	oat bran
bran	oats
buckwheat	polenta
bulgur	quinoa
corn	rice
couscous	rye
farina	semolina
flaxseed	sorghum
grits	spelt
groats	tapioca
hominy	teff
kamut	triticale
kasha	wheat
maize	wheat germ
malt	wild rice
masa	

cerebral adjective *their subversive brand of cerebral comedy* INTELLECTUAL, academic, rational, logical, analytical, scholarly; bookish, brainy. ANTONYM emotional.

ceremonial adjective *a ceremonial occasion* FORMAL, official, state, public; ritual, ritualistic, prescribed, stately, courtly, solemn. See note at FORMAL. ANTONYM informal.

ceremonious adjective *a ceremonious affair at the White House* DIGNIFIED, majestic, imposing, impressive, solemn, ritualistic, stately, formal; courtly, regal, imperial, elegant, grand, glorious, splendid, magnificent, resplendent, portentous; *informal* starchy. See note at FORMAL.

ceremony noun 1 *a wedding ceremony* RITUAL, rite, ceremonial, observance; service, sacrament, liturgy, worship, celebration.

2 *the new queen was proclaimed with due ceremony* POMP, protocol, formalities, niceties, decorum, etiquette, punctilio, politesse.

certain adjective 1 *I'm certain he's guilty* SURE, confident, positive, convinced, in no doubt, satisfied, assured, persuaded. ANTONYM doubtful.

2 *it is certain that more changes are in the offing* UNQUESTIONABLE, sure, definite, beyond question, not in doubt,

indubitable, undeniable, irrefutable, indisputable; obvious, evident, recognized, confirmed, accepted, acknowledged, undisputed, undoubted, unquestioned. ANTONYMS doubtful, possible, unthinkable.

3 *they are certain to win* SURE, very likely, bound, destined. ANTONYM unlikely.

4 *certain defeat* INEVITABLE, assured, destined, predestined; unavoidable, inescapable, inexorable, ineluctable; *informal* in the bag. ANTONYMS possible, unlikely.

5 *there is no certain cure for this* RELIABLE, dependable, trustworthy, foolproof, tried and tested, effective, guaranteed, sure, unfailing, infallible; *informal* sure-fire, idiot-proof, goof-proof. ANTONYM unreliable.

6 *a certain sum of money* DETERMINED, definite, fixed, established, precise. ANTONYMS undefined, undetermined.

7 *a certain lady* PARTICULAR, specific, individual, special.

8 *to a certain extent that is true* MODERATE, modest, medium, middling; limited, small. ANTONYM great.

certainly adverb *this is certainly a forgery* UNQUESTIONABLY, surely, assuredly, definitely, beyond/without question, without doubt, indubitably, undeniably, irrefutably, indisputably; obviously, patently, evidently, plainly, clearly, unmistakably, undisputedly, undoubtedly; *informal* sure as shootin', for sure. ANTONYM possibly.

▸ exclamation *"May I have one?" "Certainly."* YES, definitely, absolutely, sure, by all means, indeed, of course, naturally; affirmative; *informal* OK, okay.

certainty noun 1 *she knew with certainty that he was telling the truth* CONFIDENCE, sureness, positiveness, conviction, certitude, assurance. ANTONYM doubt.

2 *he accepted defeat as a certainty* INEVITABILITY, foregone conclusion; *informal* sure thing, sure bet, no-brainer. ANTONYMS impossibility, possibility.

certificate noun *do you have any type of certificate that proves your ownership?* GUARANTEE, certification, document, authorization, registration, authentication, credentials, accreditation, license, diploma.

certify verb 1 *the aircraft was certified as airworthy* VERIFY, guarantee, attest, validate, confirm, substantiate, endorse, vouch for, testify to; provide evidence, give proof, prove, demonstrate.

2 *a certified hospital* ACCREDIT, recognize, license, authorize, approve, warrant. See note at APPROVE.

certitude noun *the question may never be answered with certitude* CERTAINTY, confidence, sureness, positiveness, conviction, assurance. ANTONYM doubt.

cessation noun *the cessation of hostilities* END, ending, termination, stopping, halting, ceasing, finish, finishing, stoppage, conclusion, winding up, discontinuation, abandonment, suspension, breaking off, cutting short. ANTONYMS start, resumption.

chafe verb 1 *the collar chafed his neck* ABRADE, graze, rub against, gall, scrape, scratch; *Medicine* excoriate.

2 *material chafed by the rock* WEAR AWAY/DOWN, erode, abrade, scour, scrape away.

3 *the bank chafed at the restrictions* BE ANGRY, be annoyed, be irritated, fume, be exasperated, be frustrated.

chaff noun 1 *separating the chaff from the grain* HUSKS, hulls, pods, shells, bran, shucks.

2 *the proposals were so much chaff* GARBAGE, dross, rubbish, trash; *informal* junk, crap, schlock.

3 *good-natured chaff* BANTER, repartee, teasing, ragging, joking, jesting, raillery, badinage, wisecracks, witticism(s); *informal* kidding, ribbing; *formal* persiflage.

▸ verb *the pleasure of chaffing your buddies* TEASE, make fun of, poke fun at, make sport of; *informal* rib, razz, kid, josh, have on, pull someone's leg, pull/jerk/yank someone's chain, goof on.

chagrin noun *Sean showed up at the party, to everyone's chagrin* ANNOYANCE, irritation, vexation, exasperation, displeasure, dissatisfaction, discontent; anger, rage, fury, wrath, indignation, resentment; embarrassment, mortification, humiliation, shame. ANTONYM delight.

chagrined adjective See ANNOYED.

chain noun 1 *he was held in chains* FETTERS, shackles, irons, leg irons, manacles, handcuffs; *informal* cuffs, bracelets; *historical* bilboes.

2 *a chain of events* SERIES, succession, string, sequence, train, course.

▸ verb *she chained her bicycle to the railing* SECURE, fasten, tie, tether, hitch; restrain, shackle, fetter, manacle, handcuff.

chair noun 1 *he sat down on a chair* SEAT. See table.

2 *the chair of the committee.* See CHAIRMAN.

▸ verb *she chairs the economic committee* PRESIDE OVER, take the chair of; lead, direct, run, manage, control, be in charge of.

CHAIRS

Adirondack chair	high chair
armchair	ladder-back (chair)
barber chair	lawn chair
Barcalounger™	lounge chair
barstool	Morris chair
Boston rocker	press-back
butterfly chair	recliner
cane chair	rocker
captain's chair	rocking chair
dentist's chair	sidechair
dining chair	stacking chair
chaise longue	stool
deck chair	straight-backed chair
director's chair	swivel chair
easy chair	task chair
fiddleback (chair)	Windsor chair
fighting chair	wing chair
folding chair	

See also table at SOFA.

chairman, chairwoman noun *the chairman called for a reading of the minutes* CHAIR, chairperson, president, leader, convener; spokesperson, spokesman, spokeswoman.

chalet noun *an A-frame chalet in the Adirondacks* LODGE, cabin, cottage.

chalk PHRASE: **chalk something up** 1 *he has chalked up another success* ACHIEVE, attain, accomplish, gain, earn, win, succeed in making, make, get, obtain, rack up. 2 *I forgot completely—chalk it up to age* ATTRIBUTE, assign, ascribe, put down; blame on, pin on, lay at the door of.

chalky adjective 1 *chalky skin* PALE, bloodless, pallid, colorless, wan, ashen, white, pasty.

2 *chalky bits at the bottom of the glass* POWDERY, gritty, granular.

challenge noun 1 *he accepted the challenge* DARE, provocation; summons.

2 *a challenge to his leadership* TEST, questioning, dispute, stand, opposition, confrontation.

3 *it was proving quite a challenge* PROBLEM, difficult task, test, trial.

▸ verb 1 *we challenged their statistics* QUESTION, disagree with, dispute, take issue with, protest against, call into question, object to.

2 *he challenged one of my men to a duel* DARE, summon, throw down the gauntlet to.

3 *changes that would challenge them* TEST, tax, strain, make demands on; stretch, stimulate, inspire, excite.

USAGE NOTE **challenged**

The use of **challenged** with a preceding adverb, e.g., **physically challenged**, originally intended to give a more positive tone than such terms as **disabled** or **handicapped**, arose in the U.S. in the 1980s. Despite the originally serious intention, the term rapidly became stalled by uses whose intention was to make fun of the attempts at euphemism and whose tone was usually clearly ironic: examples include **cerebrally challenged, follicularly challenged**, etc.

challenging adjective *a challenging crossword puzzle* DEMANDING, testing, taxing, exacting; stretching, exciting, stimulating, inspiring; difficult, tough, hard, formidable, onerous, arduous, strenuous, grueling; *formal* exigent. ANTONYMS easy, uninspiring.

chamber noun 1 *a debating chamber* ROOM, hall, assembly room, auditorium.

2 *archaic we slept safely in our chamber* BEDROOM, room; *literary* bower; *historical* boudoir; *archaic* bedchamber.

3 *the left chamber of the heart* COMPARTMENT, cavity; *Anatomy* auricle, ventricle.

champagne noun *a chilled bottle of our best champagne* SPARKLING WINE; spumante, cava; *informal* bubbly.

champion noun 1 *the world champion* WINNER, titleholder, defending champion, gold medalist, titleist; prizewinner, victor; *informal* champ, number one, king.

2 *a champion of change* ADVOCATE, proponent, promoter, supporter, defender, upholder, backer, exponent; campaigner, lobbyist, crusader, apologist, booster, flag-bearer.

3 *historical the king's champion* KNIGHT, man-at-arms, warrior.

▸ verb *championing the rights of refugees* ADVOCATE, promote, defend, uphold, support, back, stand up for, take someone's part; campaign for, lobby for, fight for, crusade for, stick up for. ANTONYM oppose.

championship noun *Westville won the championship* TITLE, crown, first place, top honors.

chance noun 1 *there was a chance he might be released* POSSIBILITY, prospect, probability, likelihood, likeliness, expectation, anticipation; risk, threat, danger.

2 *I gave her a chance to answer* OPPORTUNITY, opening, occasion, turn, time, window (of opportunity); *informal* shot.

3 *Nichola took an awful chance* RISK, gamble, venture, speculation, long shot, shot in the dark.

4 *pure chance* ACCIDENT, coincidence, serendipity, fate, destiny, fortuity, providence, happenstance; good fortune, luck, good luck, fluke.

▸ adjective *a chance discovery* ACCIDENTAL, fortuitous, adventitious, fluky, coincidental, serendipitous; unintentional, unintended, inadvertent, unplanned. ANTONYM intentional.

▸ verb 1 *I chanced to meet him* HAPPEN. See note at HAPPEN.

2 *she chanced another look* RISK, hazard, venture, try; *formal* essay.

PHRASES: **by chance** *we found a signed first edition completely by chance* FORTUITOUSLY, by accident, accidentally, coincidentally, serendipitously; unintentionally, inadvertently. **chance on/upon** *if you should chance upon a Willie McCovey card, please let me know* COME ACROSS/UPON, run across/into, happen on, light on, stumble on, find by chance, meet (by chance), bump into.

chancy adjective *informal these investments seem too chancy for me* RISKY, unpredictable, uncertain, precarious; unsafe, insecure, tricky, high-risk, hazardous, perilous, parlous; *informal* dicey, hairy. ANTONYM predictable.

change verb 1 *this could change the face of television | things have changed* ALTER, make/become different, adjust, adapt, amend, modify, revise, refine; reshape, refashion, redesign, restyle, revamp, rework, remodel, reorganize, reorder; vary, transform, transfigure, transmute, metamorphose, evolve; *informal* tweak, doctor, rejig; *technical* permute. ANTONYMS preserve, stay the same.

2 *they've changed places* EXCHANGE, substitute, swap, switch, replace, alternate, interchange. ANTONYM keep.

▸ noun 1 *a change of plan* ALTERATION, modification, variation, revision, amendment, adjustment, adaptation; remodeling, reshaping, rearrangement, reordering, restyling, reworking; metamorphosis, transformation, evolution, mutation; *informal* transmogrification.

2 *a change of government* EXCHANGE, substitution, swap, switch, changeover, replacement, alternation, interchange.

3 *I don't have any change* COINS, loose/small change, silver; cash, petty cash; formal specie.

PHRASE: **have a change of heart.** See HEART.

changeable adjective 1 *the weather will be changeable | changeable moods* VARIABLE, inconstant, varying, changing, fluctuating, irregular; erratic, inconsistent, unstable, unsettled, turbulent, protean; fickle, capricious, temperamental, volatile, mercurial, unpredictable, blowing hot and cold; *informal* up and down. ANTONYM constant.

2 *the colors are changeable* ALTERABLE, adjustable, modifiable, variable, mutable, exchangeable, interchangeable, replaceable. ANTONYM invariable.

changeless adjective *the rules around here are changeless* UNCHANGING, unvarying, timeless, static, fixed, permanent, constant, unchanged, consistent, uniform, undeviating; stable, steady, unchangeable, unalterable, invariable, immutable. ANTONYM variable.

channel noun 1 *sailing the North Channel* STRAIT(S), sound, narrows, passage, sea passage.

2 *the water ran down a channel* DUCT, gutter, conduit, trough, culvert, sluice, spillway, race, drain.

3 *a channel for their extraordinary energy* USE, medium, vehicle, way of harnessing; release (mechanism), safety valve, vent.

4 *a channel of communication* MEANS, medium, instrument, mechanism, agency, vehicle, route, avenue.

▸ verb 1 *she* ***channeled out*** *a groove* HOLLOW OUT, gouge (out), cut (out).

2 *many countries channel their aid through charities* CONVEY, transmit, conduct, direct, guide, relay, pass on, transfer.

chant noun 1 *the protesters' chants* SHOUT, cry, call, rallying call, cheer, slogan.

2 *the melodious chant of the monks* INCANTATION, intonation, singing, song, plainsong, recitative.

▸ verb 1 *protesters were chanting slogans* SHOUT, chorus, repeat.

2 *the choir chanted Psalm 118* SING, intone, incant.

chaos noun *police were called in to quell the chaos* DISORDER, disarray, disorganization, confusion, mayhem, bedlam, pandemonium, havoc, turmoil, tumult, commotion, disruption, upheaval, uproar, maelstrom; muddle, mess, shambles, free-for-all; anarchy, lawlessness, entropy; *informal* hullabaloo, hoopla, all hell broken loose. ANTONYM order.

chaotic adjective *the whole town was chaotic* DISORDERLY, disordered, in disorder, in chaos, in disarray, disorganized, topsy-turvy, in pandemonium, in turmoil, in an uproar; in a muddle, in a mess, messy, in a shambles; anarchic, lawless.

chap[1] verb *my skin chapped in the wind* BECOME RAW, become sore, become inflamed, chafe, crack.

chap[2] noun *informal he's a nice chap.* See GUY.

chaperone noun *two teachers attended as chaperones* SUPERVISOR, companion, duenna, escort, minder, den mother.

▸ verb *she was chaperoned by her mother* ACCOMPANY, escort, attend, watch over, keep an eye on, protect, mind.

chapped adjective *chapped hands* DRY, cracked, rough.

chapter noun 1 *the first chapter of the book* SECTION, division, part, portion.

2 *a new chapter in our history* PERIOD, phase, page, stage, epoch, era.

3 *a local chapter of the American Cancer Society* BRANCH, division, subdivision, section, department, lodge, wing, arm.

4 *the cathedral chapter* GOVERNING BODY, council, assembly, convocation, synod, consistory.

char verb *the steaks should be slightly charred* SCORCH, burn, singe, sear, blacken; *informal* toast. See note at BURN.

character noun 1 *a forceful character | the character of a town* PERSONALITY, nature, disposition, temperament, temper, mentality, makeup; features, qualities, properties, traits; spirit, essence, identity, ethos, complexion, tone, feel, feeling.

2 *a woman of character* INTEGRITY, honor, moral strength, moral fiber, rectitude, uprightness; fortitude, strength, backbone, resolve, grit, willpower; *informal* guts, gutsiness.

3 *a stain on his character* REPUTATION, name, good name, standing, stature, position, status.

4 *informal a bit of a character* ECCENTRIC, oddity, madcap, crank, individualist, nonconformist, rare bird, free spirit; *informal* oddball.

5 *a boorish character* PERSON, man, woman, soul, creature, individual, customer.

6 *the characters develop throughout the play* PERSONA, role, part; (**characters**) dramatis personae.

7 *thirty characters per line* LETTER, figure, symbol, sign, mark.

characteristic noun *interesting characteristics* ATTRIBUTE, feature, quality, essential quality, property, trait, aspect, element, facet; mannerism, habit, custom, idiosyncrasy, peculiarity, quirk, oddity, foible.

▸ adjective *his characteristic eloquence* TYPICAL, usual, normal, predictable, habitual; distinctive, particular, special, especial, peculiar, idiosyncratic, defining, singular, unique.

characterize verb 1 *the period was characterized by scientific advancement* DISTINGUISH, make distinctive, mark, typify, set apart.

2 *the women are characterized as prophets of doom* PORTRAY, depict, present, represent, describe; categorize, class, style, brand.

charade noun *our entire relationship is a charade* FARCE, pantomime, travesty, mockery, parody, pretense, act, masquerade.

charge verb 1 *he didn't charge much* ASK IN PAYMENT, ask, levy, demand, want, exact; bill, invoice.

2 *the subscription will be charged to your account* BILL, debit from, take from.

3 *two men were charged with theft* ACCUSE, indict, arraign; prosecute, try, put on trial, inculpate.

4 *they charged him with reforming the system* ENTRUST, burden, encumber, saddle, tax.

5 *the cavalry charged the tanks* ATTACK, storm, assault, assail, fall on, swoop on, descend on; *informal* lay into, tear into. See note at ATTACK.

6 *we charged into the crowd* RUSH, storm, stampede, push, plow, launch oneself, go headlong, steam, barrel, zoom.

7 *his work was charged with energy* SUFFUSE, pervade, permeate, saturate, infuse, imbue, load, fill.

8 *I charge you to stop* ORDER, command, direct, instruct, enjoin; *formal* adjure; *literary* bid.

▸ noun 1 *all customers pay a charge* FEE, payment, price, tariff, amount, sum, fare, levy.

2 *he pleaded guilty to the charge* ACCUSATION, allegation, indictment, arraignment.

3 *an infantry charge* ATTACK, assault, offensive, onslaught, drive, push, thrust.

4 *the child was in her charge* CARE, protection, safekeeping, control; custody, guardianship, wardship; hands.

5 *his charge was to save the business* DUTY, responsibility, task, job, assignment, mission, function; *informal* marching orders.

6 *the safety of my charge* WARD, protégé, dependent.

7 *the judge gave a careful charge to the jury* INSTRUCTION, direction, directive, order, command, dictate, exhortation.

8 *informal I get a real charge out of working hard* THRILL, tingle, glow; excitement, stimulation, enjoyment, pleasure; *informal* kick, buzz, rush.

PHRASE: **in charge of** *I'm in charge of museum security* RESPONSIBLE FOR, in control of, in command of, at the helm/wheel of; MANAGING, running, administering, directing, supervising, overseeing, controlling.

charisma noun *he lacks the charisma we look for in our salespeople* CHARM, presence, personality, force of personality, strength of character; magnetism, attractiveness, appeal, allure.

charismatic adjective *a charismatic leader* CHARMING, fascinating, strong in character; magnetic, captivating, beguiling, attractive, appealing, alluring, winning.

charitable adjective **1** *charitable activities* PHILANTHROPIC, humanitarian, altruistic, benevolent, public-spirited; nonprofit; *formal* eleemosynary.

2 *charitable people* BIGHEARTED, generous, openhanded, free-handed, munificent, bountiful, beneficent; *literary* bounteous.

3 *he was charitable in his judgments* MAGNANIMOUS, generous, liberal, tolerant, easygoing, broad-minded, considerate, sympathetic, lenient, indulgent, forgiving, kind.

charity noun **1** *a children's charity* NONPROFIT ORGANIZATION, voluntary organization, charitable institution; fund, trust, foundation.

2 *we don't need charity* FINANCIAL ASSISTANCE, aid, welfare, relief, financial relief; handouts, gifts, presents, largesse; *historical* alms.

3 *his actions are motivated by charity* PHILANTHROPY, humanitarianism, humanity, altruism, public-spiritedness, social conscience, benevolence, beneficence, munificence.

4 *show a bit of charity* GOODWILL, compassion, consideration, concern, kindness, kindheartedness, tenderness, tenderheartedness, sympathy, indulgence, tolerance, leniency, caritas; *literary* bounteousness. See note at MERCY.

charlatan noun *Doc Brimley didn't go to no fancy halls of ivy, but he was no charlatan* QUACK, sham, fraud, fake, impostor, hoaxer, cheat, deceiver, double-dealer, swindler, fraudster, mountebank; *informal* phony, shark, con man, con artist, scam artist, flimflammer, bunco artist, snake oil salesman; *dated* confidence man/woman. See note at QUACK.

charm noun **1** *people were captivated by her charm* ATTRACTIVENESS, beauty, glamour, loveliness; appeal, allure, desirability, seductiveness, magnetism, charisma.

2 *these traditions retain a lot of charm* APPEAL, drawing power, attraction, allure, fascination.

3 *magical charms* SPELL, incantation, conjuration, magic formula, magic word, mojo, hex.

4 *a lucky charm* TALISMAN, fetish, amulet, mascot, totem, juju.

▸ verb **1** *he charmed them with his singing* DELIGHT, please, win (over), attract, captivate, allure, lure, dazzle, fascinate, enchant, enthrall, enrapture, seduce, spellbind.

2 *he charmed his mother into agreeing* COAX, cajole, wheedle; *informal* sweet-talk, soft-soap; *archaic* blandish.

charming adjective *a charming inn on the cape* | *their charming daughter* DELIGHTFUL, pleasing, pleasant, agreeable, likable, endearing, lovely, lovable, adorable, appealing, attractive, good-looking, prepossessing; alluring, delectable, ravishing, winning, winsome, fetching, captivating, enchanting, entrancing, fascinating, seductive; *informal* heavenly, divine, gorgeous; *literary* beauteous; *archaic* fair, comely. ANTONYM repulsive.

chart noun **1** *check your ideal weight on the chart* GRAPH, table, diagram, histogram; bar chart, pie chart, flow chart; *Computing* graphic.

2 **(charts)** *the song hit the charts at number twelve* top twenty, top ten, list, listing; *dated* hit parade.

▸ verb **1** *the changes were charted accurately* TABULATE, plot, graph, record, register, represent; make a chart/diagram of.

2 *the book charted his progress* FOLLOW, trace, outline, describe, detail, record, document, chronicle, log.

charter noun **1** *a royal charter* AUTHORITY, authorization, sanction, dispensation, consent, permission; permit, license, warrant, franchise.

2 *the UN Charter* CONSTITUTION, code, canon; fundamental principles, rules, laws.

3 *the charter of a yacht* HIRE, hiring, lease, leasing, rent, rental, renting; booking, reservation, reserving.

▸ verb *they chartered a bus* HIRE, lease, rent; book, reserve.

chary adjective *he was chary of broaching the subject* WARY, cautious, circumspect, heedful, careful, on one's guard; distrustful, mistrustful, skeptical, suspicious, dubious, hesitant, reluctant, leery, canny, nervous, apprehensive, uneasy; *informal* cagey, iffy.

chase verb **1** *the cat chased the mouse* PURSUE, run after, give chase to, follow; hunt, track, trail; *informal* tail.

2 *chasing young girls*, PURSUE, run after, make advances to, flirt with; *informal* come on to, hit on; *dated* woo, court, romance, set one's cap for/at, make love to.

3 *she **chased away** the donkeys* DRIVE AWAY, drive off, send away, scare off; *informal* shoo (away), send packing.

4 *she **chased away** all thoughts of him* DISPEL, banish, dismiss, drive away, shut out, put out of one's mind.

▸ noun *they gave up the chase* PURSUIT, hunt, trail.

chasm noun **1** *a deep chasm* GORGE, abyss, canyon, ravine, gully, gulf, defile, couloir, crevasse, fissure, crevice, gulch, coulee.

2 *the chasm between their views* BREACH, gulf, rift; difference, separation, division, dissension, schism, scission.

chassis noun *the chassis of the car is in mint condition* FRAMEWORK, frame, structure, substructure, shell, casing.

chaste adjective **1** *her determination to remain chaste* VIRGINAL, virgin, intact, maidenly, unmarried, unwed; celibate, abstinent, self-restrained, self-denying, continent; innocent, virtuous, pure, pure as the driven snow, sinless, undefiled, unsullied, immaculate; *literary* vestal. ANTONYMS promiscuous, immoral.

2 *a chaste kiss on the cheek* NONSEXUAL, platonic, innocent. ANTONYM passionate.

3 *the dark, chaste interior* PLAIN, simple, bare, unadorned, undecorated, unornamented, unembellished, functional, no-frills, austere. ANTONYM ostentatious.

USAGE NOTE chaste, celibate

Chaste (= untainted by unlawful sexual intercourse; virtuous; sexually continent) is a word that applies to males and females alike—e.g.: "As a young and chaste boy, Yava said, he would often be called on to help construct the sand painting, lending the power of his purity." (*Phoenix Gazette*; June 4, 1993.) Unfortunately, however, a bias pervades the word's usual applications so that it typically refers to women and girls—e.g.: "One view is that a fallen woman who has fully reformed is chaste, while another is that chastity before marriage means physical virginity—a woman can be seduced only once. There is nothing unchaste about marital intercourse and hence, under either view, a widow or divorcee may be an unmarried female of previously chaste character." (Rollin M. Perkins and Ronald N. Boyce, *Criminal Law*, 3d ed.; 1982.)

There is also some confusion about the sense of *chaste*, as opposed to *celibate*. A person who is *chaste* is innocent of unlawful sex—that is, does not engage in sex with anyone other than the person's spouse. So, in both secular law and church law, a person who frequently has sex, but only with his or her spouse, is *chaste*. By contrast, a person who is *celibate* (in the word's original sense and still the only definition in the *Oxford English Dictionary*) abstains from marrying—and sex, too, but only as a consequence of the choice not to marry. The times have passed that meaning by, and today this traditional sense is obsolescent at best. It may remain current with the vow of celibacy that Catholic priests make (i.e., a promise not to marry). But it is almost universally understood, even in that context, to mean "abstaining from sex"—e.g.: "His case underscores the growing debate within the church over whether there is a place in the priesthood for gay men, even celibate ones." (*Boston Globe*; Nov. 25, 2002.) And while many word extensions result in the loss of a useful and unique term, here the shift in meaning of *celibate* has resulted in the creation of a term that has no good substitute—especially since *chaste* sounds archaic, carries outdated connotations about sex, and has drifted toward becoming gender-specific. **—BG**

chasten verb **1** *both men were chastened* SUBDUE, humble, cow, squash, deflate, abase; *informal* flatten, take down a peg or two, put someone in their place, cut down to size, settle someone's hash.

2 *archaic* *the Heaven that chastens us.* See CHASTISE.

chastise verb *the staff were chastised for arriving late* SCOLD, upbraid, berate, reprimand, reprove, rebuke, admonish, chide, censure, lambaste, castigate, lecture, give someone a piece of one's mind, give someone a tongue-lashing, take to task, rake/haul over the coals; *informal* tell off, dress down, bawl out, blow up at, give someone an earful, give someone a roasting, come down on someone like a ton of bricks, slap someone's wrist, rap over the knuckles, give someone hell, give someone what for, chew out, ream out, zing; *archaic* chasten; *rare* reprehend. ANTONYM praise.

chastity noun *a vow of chastity* CELIBACY, chasteness, virginity, abstinence, self-restraint, self-denial, continence; innocence, purity, virtue, morality.

chat noun *I popped in for a chat* TALK, conversation, chitchat, gossip, chatter, heart-to-heart, tête-à-tête; *informal* jaw, confab, chinwag, rap, bull session; *formal* confabulation, colloquy. See note at CONVERSATION.

▸ verb *they chatted with their guests* TALK, gossip, chatter, speak, converse, engage in conversation, tittle-tattle, prattle (on), jabber, babble; *informal* gas, jaw, chew the fat, yap, yak, yatter, yammer, shoot the breeze; *formal* confabulate.

chatter noun *she tired him with her chatter* CHAT, talk, gossip, chitchat, jabbering, jabber, prattling, prattle, babbling, babble, tittle-tattle, blathering, blather; *informal* yammering, yattering, yapping, jawing, chewing the fat; *formal* confabulation, colloquy.

▸ verb *they chattered excitedly.* See BLATHER verb.

chatterbox noun *informal* *he was the office chatterbox* TALKER, chatterer, prattler; *informal* windbag, bigmouth, gasbag, blabbermouth, motormouth.

chatty adjective **1** *he was a chatty person* TALKATIVE, communicative, expansive, unreserved, gossipy, gossiping, garrulous, loquacious, voluble, verbose; *informal* mouthy, talky, gabby, motormouthed. ANTONYM taciturn.

2 *a chatty letter* CONVERSATIONAL, gossipy, informal, casual, familiar, friendly; *informal* newsy. ANTONYM formal.

chauvinism noun *they have a tendency toward small-mindedness and chauvinism* JINGOISM, excessive patriotism, blind patriotism, excessive nationalism, sectarianism, isolationism, flag-waving; xenophobia, racism, ethnocentrism, ethnocentricity; PARTISANSHIP partiality, prejudice, bias, discrimination, bigotry; male chauvinism, antifeminism, misogyny, sexism. See note at JINGOISM.

USAGE NOTE chauvinism, jingoism

Most traditionally, *chauvinism* (/**shoh**-vuh-niz-um/) refers to fanatical patriotism. The word is an eponym from Nicolas Chauvin, a French soldier who was ridiculed for being excessively devoted to Napoleon. By metaphorical extension, the word was broadened to denote excessive pride in people like oneself, especially in reference to males. Today *male chauvinism*, which (as a phrase, not a phenomenon) dates back to the late 1960s, is something of a cliché, being the word's most frequent application. Indeed, some writers have come to use *chauvinism* as if it were synonymous with *male chauvinism*—e.g.: "He betrayed his chauvinism by expressing surprise that I [Diane McFarlin] was an editor." (*Sarasota Herald-Tribune*; Nov. 8, 1998.) To the linguistic traditionalist, these uses (or misuses) are arrant nonsense

The void left by the shift in the meaning of *chauvinism* from national pride to supposed sexual superiority has been filled by *jingoism*. Essentially synonymous with *chauvinism* in its traditional sense, *jingoism* has the added layer of xenophobic and aggressive attitudes toward foreign policy—e.g.: "Gilmour goes overboard in trying to rationalize and justify Kipling's racism and jingoism. He argues, for example, that 'white' in *The White Man's Burden* does not refer to skin color but rather to 'civilization and character' and that Kipling's imperialistic beliefs were essentially humane and benevolent rather than based on greed, paternalism and self-interest." (*Houston Chronicle*; June 23, 2002.). Sometimes the word takes on an even softer sense, suggesting a provincialism or regionalism that is broader than national sovereignty—e.g.: "The prime minister's evident glee that the BA order had gone to a 'European' company is mere jingoism at bottom." (*Wall Street Journal Europe*; Aug. 27, 1998.) **—BG**

chauvinist adjective *chauvinist sentiments* JINGOISTIC, chauvinistic, excessively patriotic, excessively nationalistic, flag-waving, xenophobic, racist, racialist, ethnocentric; bigoted, sexist, male chauvinist, antifeminist, misogynist, woman-hating.

▸ noun *he's a chauvinist* SEXIST, bigot, antifeminist, misogynist, woman-hater; *informal* male chauvinist pig.

cheap adjective **1** *cheap tickets* INEXPENSIVE, low-priced, low-cost, economical, competitive, affordable, reasonable, reasonably priced, budget, economy, bargain, downmarket, cut-rate, reduced, discounted, discount, rock-bottom, giveaway, bargain-basement, low-end, dirt cheap. ANTONYM expensive.

2 *cheap furniture* POOR-QUALITY, second-rate, third-rate, tinpot, substandard, low-grade, inferior, vulgar, shoddy, trashy, tawdry, meretricious, cheapjack, gimcrack, pinchbeck; *informal* rubbishy, chintzy, cheapo, junky, tacky, cheesy, ticky-tacky, kitsch, kitschy, two-bit, dime-store, schlocky. ANTONYM high-class.

3 *she was too cheap to contribute to the fund* MISERLY, stingy, parsimonious, tightfisted, niggardly, chintzy, frugal, penny-pinching, cheeseparing. ANTONYM generous.

4 *the cheap exploitation of suffering* DESPICABLE, contemptible, immoral, unscrupulous, unprincipled, unsavory, distasteful, vulgar, ignoble, shameful. ANTONYM admirable.

5 *he made me feel cheap* ASHAMED, humiliated, mortified, debased, degraded.

cheapen verb 1 *Hetty never cheapened herself* DEMEAN, debase, degrade, lower, humble, devalue, abase, discredit, disgrace, dishonor, shame, humiliate, mortify, prostitute.

2 *cheapening the cost of exports* REDUCE, lower (in price), cut, mark down, discount; *informal* slash.

cheat verb 1 *customers were cheated* SWINDLE, defraud, deceive, trick, scam, dupe, hoodwink, double-cross, gull; *informal* rip off, con, fleece, shaft, hose, sting, bilk, diddle, rook, gyp, finagle, bamboozle, flimflam, put one over on, pull a fast one on, sucker, stiff, hornswoggle; *formal* mulct; *literary* cozen.

2 *the boy cheated death* AVOID, escape, evade, elude; foil, frustrate, thwart.

3 *it's not the first time her husband has cheated* COMMIT ADULTERY, be unfaithful, stray; *informal* two-time, play around; *archaic* cuckold.

▸ noun *a liar and a cheat* SWINDLER, cheater, fraudster, trickster, deceiver, hoaxer, double-dealer, double-crosser, sham, fraud, fake, charlatan, quack, crook, snake oil salesman, mountebank; *informal* con man, con artist, scam artist, shark, sharper, phony, flimflammer, bunco artist; *dated* confidence man/woman.

WORD NOTE **hornswoggle**

A delightfully piratical word for *cheat* or *dupe* or *trick.* If Gilbert and Sullivan never used it, they should have. —**JS**

check verb 1 *troops checked all vehicles* | *I checked her background* EXAMINE, inspect, look at/over, scrutinize, survey; study, investigate, research, probe, look into, inquire into; *informal* check out, give something a once-over.

2 *he checked that the gun was cocked* MAKE SURE, confirm, verify.

3 *two defeats checked their progress* HALT, stop, arrest, cut short; bar, obstruct, hamper, impede, inhibit, frustrate, foil, thwart, curb, block, stall, hold up, retard, delay, slow down; *literary* stay.

4 *her tears could not be checked* SUPPRESS, repress, restrain, control, curb, rein in, stifle, hold back, choke back; *informal* keep a lid on.

▸ noun 1 *a check of the records* EXAMINATION, inspection, scrutiny, perusal, study, investigation, probe, analysis; test, trial, monitoring; checkup; *informal* once-over, look-see.

2 *a check on the abuse of authority* CONTROL, restraint, constraint, curb, limitation.

3 *write a check in the amount of $150* bank draft; traveler's check, certified check, bank check; paycheck.

4 *the waitress arrived with the check* BILL, account, invoice, statement, tab.

PHRASES: **check in** *I checked in at two o'clock sharp* REPORT (ONE'S ARRIVAL), sign in, register. **check out** 1 *we'll be checking out in the morning* LEAVE, vacate, depart; pay the bill, settle up. 2 *the police checked out dozens of leads* INVESTIGATE, look into, inquire into, probe, research, examine, go over; assess, analyze, evaluate; follow up; *informal* give something a once-over, scope out. 3 *she checked herself out in the mirror* LOOK AT, survey, regard, inspect, contemplate; *informal* eyeball. **keep in check** *I try to keep my temper in check* CURB, restrain, hold back, keep a tight rein on, rein in/back; control, govern, master, suppress, stifle; *informal* keep a lid on.

checkered adjective 1 *a checkered tablecloth* CHECKED, plaid, tartan, multicolored, many-colored.

2 *a checkered history* VARIED, mixed, up and down, full of ups and downs, vicissitudinous; unstable, irregular, erratic, inconstant.

checkup noun *I saw the doctor for my annual checkup* EXAMINATION, inspection, evaluation, analysis, survey, probe, test, appraisal; check, health check; *informal* once-over, going-over.

cheek noun *that's enough of your cheek!* See IMPUDENCE.

WORD NOTE **cheek**

An underappreciated term for insolence, sauciness, nerve; also an underappreciated trait in excessively solemn times. *He's got a lot of cheek* is more suggestive and vivid than *He's got a lot of nerve,* or *gall,* or *temerity.* In the same vein, *cheeky bastard* has it all over *impudent bastard.* —**JS**

cheeky adjective. See IMPUDENT.

cheep verb *the summer sounds of bees buzzing and birds cheeping* CHIRP, chirrup, twitter, tweet, peep, chitter, chirr, trill, warble, sing.

cheer noun 1 *the cheers of the crowd* HURRAY, hurrah, whoop, bravo, shout, roar; hosanna, alleluia; **(cheers)** applause, acclamation, clamor, acclaim, ovation. ANTONYM boo.

2 *a time of cheer* HAPPINESS, joy, joyousness, cheerfulness, cheeriness, gladness, merriment, gaiety, jubilation, jollity, jolliness, high spirits, joviality, jocularity, conviviality, lightheartedness; merrymaking, pleasure, rejoicing, revelry. ANTONYM sadness.

3 *Christmas cheer* FARE, food, foodstuffs, eatables, provender; drink, beverages; *informal* eats, nibbles, nosh, grub, chow; *formal* victuals, comestibles.

▸ verb 1 *they cheered their team* APPLAUD, hail, salute, shout for, root for, hurrah, hurray, acclaim, clap for; encourage, support; bring the house down for, holler for, give someone a big hand, put one's hands together for. ANTONYM boo.

2 *the bad weather did little to cheer me* RAISE SOMEONE'S

SPIRITS, make happier, brighten, buoy up, enliven, exhilarate, hearten, gladden, uplift, perk up, boost, encourage, inspirit; *informal* buck up. ANTONYM depress.

PHRASES: **cheer on** *my friends were there to cheer me on* ENCOURAGE, urge on, spur on, drive on, motivate, inspire, fire (up), inspirit, light a fire under. **cheer up** *Leslie cheered up as soon as the grades were posted* PERK UP, brighten (up), become more cheerful, liven up, rally, revive, bounce back, take heart; *informal* buck up.

cheerful adjective **1** *he arrived looking cheerful* HAPPY, jolly, merry, bright, glad, sunny, joyful, joyous, lighthearted, in good/high spirits, sparkling, bubbly, exuberant, buoyant, ebullient, elated, gleeful; breezy, cheery, jaunty, animated, radiant, smiling; jovial, genial, good-humored; carefree, unworried, untroubled, without a care in the world; *informal* upbeat, chipper, chirpy, peppy, bright-eyed and bushy-tailed, full of beans; *dated* gay; *formal* blithe, jocund. ANTONYM sad.

2 *a cheerful room* PLEASANT, attractive, agreeable, cheering, bright, sunny, happy, friendly, welcoming. ANTONYMS drab, dreary.

cheerless adjective *visitors often remarked that the interior of the castle was more cheerless than they had expected* GLOOMY, dreary, dull, dismal, bleak, drab, somber, dark, dim, dingy, funereal; austere, stark, bare, comfortless, unwelcoming, uninviting; miserable, wretched, joyless, depressing, disheartening, dispiriting.

cheers exclamation *informal from Bertie's table we could hear the clinking of glasses and a rousing "Cheers!"* HERE'S TO YOU, good health, your health, skol, prosit, salut, l'chaim; *informal* bottoms up, down the hatch, here's mud in your eye.

cheery adjective See CHEERFUL sense 1.

cheese noun See table.

CHEESES

American	havarti
asadero	Humboldt Fog™
Asiago	jack cheese
Beaufort	Jarlsberg™
Bel Paese™	Laughing Cow™
bleu/blue	Limburger
Bonbel	mascarpone
Boursin	Monterey jack
brick	mozzarella
Brie	Muenster/Munster
Caerphilly	Neufchâtel
Camembert	panir/paneer
cheddar	Parmesan
Cheshire	Parmigiano Reggiano
chèvre	Passendale
colby	pecorino
Cotija	pepper jack
cottage cheese	Port-Salut
cream cheese	pot cheese
Danish blue	provolone
Edam	quark
Emmental	queso fresco
farmer cheese	Red Hawk™
feta	ricotta
fontina	Romano
fresh mozzarella	Roquefort
fromage blanc	Stilton
goat cheese	string cheese
Gorgonzola	Swiss
Gouda	Taleggio
Gruyère	Tilsit

cheesy adjective *informal those cheesy jokes of hers | what a cheesy tie he's wearing* TACKY, cheap, tawdry; trite; *informal* corny, cornball.

chef noun *he was Mitterand's personal chef* COOK, food preparer; chef de cuisine, pastry chef, sous-chef, short-order cook, cordon bleu cook; *informal* cookie.

chemistry noun *there was a chemistry between them* AFFINITY, attraction, rapport, spark.

cherish verb **1** *a woman he could cherish* ADORE, hold dear, love, dote on, be devoted to, revere, esteem, admire; think the world of, set great store by, hold in high esteem; care for, tend to, look after, protect, preserve, keep safe.

2 *I cherish her letters* TREASURE, prize, value highly, hold dear.

3 *they cherished dreams of glory* HARBOR, entertain, possess, hold (on to), cling to, keep in one's mind, foster, nurture.

cherub noun **1** *she was borne up to heaven by cherubs* ANGEL, seraph.

2 *a cherub of 18 months* BABY, infant, toddler, little angel, (tiny) tot; *literary* babe, babe in arms.

cherubic adjective ANGELIC, sweet, cute, adorable, appealing, lovable; innocent, seraphic, saintly.

chest noun **1** *a bullet wound in the chest* BREAST, upper body, torso, trunk; *technical* thorax.

2 *her matronly chest* BUST, bosom; breasts.

3 *an oak chest* BOX, case, casket, crate, trunk, coffer, strongbox. PHRASE: **get off one's chest** *informal I've known what really happened for years, and I'd like to finally get it off my chest* CONFESS, disclose, divulge, reveal, make known, make public, make a clean breast of, bring into the open, tell all about, get a load off one's mind.

chest of drawers noun *each bedroom set comes with two chests of drawers* DRESSER, bureau, cabinet, highboy, tallboy, commode.

chesty adjective *informal* See BUXOM.

chew verb *Carolyn chewed a mouthful of toast* munch, chomp, champ, crunch, nibble, gnaw, eat, consume; *formal* MASTICATE, manducate.

PHRASES: **chew over** *go home and chew it over* MEDITATE ON, ruminate on, think about/over/through, mull over, consider, ponder on, deliberate on, reflect on, muse on, dwell on, give thought to, turn over in one's mind; brood over, puzzle over, rack one's brains about; *informal* kick around, bat around; *formal* cogitate about. **chew the fat** *informal*. See CHAT verb.

chic adjective *a chic yellow belt* STYLISH, elegant, sophisticated, dressy, smart; fashionable, high-fashion, in vogue, up-to-date, up-to-the-minute, contemporary, à la mode, chi-chi, au courant; dapper, dashing, trim; *informal* trendy, with it, happening, snappy, snazzy, modish, du jour, in, funky, natty, swish, fly, spiffy, kicky, tony. ANTONYM unfashionable.

chicanery noun *we didn't catch on to his chicanery until it was too late* TRICKERY, deception, deceit, deceitfulness, duplicity, dishonesty, deviousness, unscrupulousness, underhandedness, subterfuge, fraud, fraudulence, swindling, cheating, duping, hoodwinking; *informal* crookedness, monkey business, hanky-panky, shenanigans, skulduggery, monkeyshines; *archaic* management, knavery.

chicken noun **1** *raising chickens on the farm | buy some boneless chicken* HEN; fowl, poultry. See table.

2 *informal I was afraid of the water, but I was more afraid of being called a chicken.* See COWARD.

▸ adjective *informal Mookie won't come with us, cuz he's chicken.* See COWARDLY.

CHICKENS AND OTHER GROUND BIRDS

Chickens	hazel grouse
bantam	Hungarian partridge
brahma	partridge
Cornish	peafowl/peacock/ peahen
leghorn	pheasant
Plymouth Rock	prairie chicken
Rhode Island Red	ptarmigan
Rock Cornish	quail
Sussex	ringneck
White Rock	ring-necked pheasant
Wyandot	rock ptarmigan
Other Ground Birds	ruffed grouse
black grouse	sage grouse
blue grouse	sharp-tailed grouse
bobwhite	snow partridge
capercaillie	spruce grouse
chukar	tragopan
fool hen	turkey
francolin	willow grouse
grouse	willow ptarmigan
guinea fowl	

chide verb *he wasn't expecting her to chide him right there in front of everyone* SCOLD, chastise, upbraid, berate, reprimand, reprove, rebuke, admonish, censure, lambaste, lecture, give someone a piece of one's mind, take to task, rake/haul over the coals; *informal* tell off, dress down, bawl out, blow up at, give someone an earful, give someone a roasting, give someone a tongue-lashing, come down on someone like a ton of bricks, slap someone's wrist, rap over the knuckles, give someone hell, take to the woodshed, have a go at, give someone what for, chew out, ream out; *formal* castigate; *archaic* chasten; *rare* reprehend. See note at SCOLD. ANTONYM praise.

chief noun **1** *a Wampanoag chief* LEADER, chieftain, grand chief, sachem, sagamore, head, headman, ruler, overlord, master, commander, seigneur, liege lord, liege, potentate, cacique.

2 *the chief of the central bank* HEAD, principal, chief executive, chief executive officer; CEO, president, chair, chairman, chairwoman, chairperson, governor, director, manager; employer, proprietor; *informal* big cheese, big shot, bigwig, skipper, numero uno, honcho, head honcho, boss, padrone.

▸ adjective **1** *the chief rabbi* HEAD, leading, principal, premier, highest, foremost, supreme, arch. ANTONYM subordinate.

2 *their chief aim* MAIN, principal, most important, primary, prime, first, cardinal, central, key, crucial, essential, predominant, preeminent, paramount, overriding, number-one. ANTONYMS secondary, minor.

chiefly adverb *we are interested chiefly in waterfront properties* MAINLY, in the main, primarily, principally, predominantly, mostly, for the most part; usually, habitually, typically, commonly, generally, on the whole, largely, by and large, almost always.

child noun *a well-behaved child | his estate goes directly to his children* YOUNGSTER, little one, boy, girl; baby, newborn, infant, toddler; cherub, angel; schoolboy, schoolgirl; minor, junior, preteen; son, daughter, descendant; *informal* kid, kiddie, tot, tyke, young 'un, lad, rug rat, ankle-biter; *derogatory* brat, guttersnipe, urchin, gamin, gamine; *literary* babe, babe in arms; **(children)** offspring, progeny, issue, brood, descendants.

childbirth noun *complications during childbirth have been drastically reduced* LABOR, delivery, giving birth, birthing, child-bearing; *formal* parturition; *dated* confinement; *literary* travail; *archaic* lying-in, accouchement, childbed.

childhood noun *born into a war-torn environment, they are subject to experiences inappropriate for anyone's childhood* YOUTH, early years, early life, infancy, babyhood, boyhood, girlhood, prepubescence, minority; springtime of life, salad days; *formal* nonage, juvenescence. ANTONYM adulthood.

childish adjective **1** *childish behavior* IMMATURE, babyish, infantile, juvenile, puerile; silly, inane, jejune, foolish, irresponsible. ANTONYM mature.

2 *a round childish face* CHILDLIKE, youthful, young, young-looking, girlish, boyish, baby. ANTONYM adult.

childlike adjective **1** *his grandmother looked almost childlike* YOUTHFUL, young, young-looking, girlish, boyish.

2 *geniuses tend to be rather childlike* INNOCENT, artless, guileless, unworldly, unsophisticated, naive, ingenuous, trusting, unsuspicious, unwary, credulous, gullible; unaffected, without airs, uninhibited, natural, spontaneous; *informal* wet behind the ears.

children plural noun See CHILD.

chill noun **1** *a chill in the air* COLDNESS, chilliness, coolness, iciness, rawness, bitterness, nip. ANTONYM warmth.

2 *he had **a chill*** A COLD, (the) sniffles, (the) shivers, (the) flu/influenza, a fever; *archaic* (the) grippe.

3 *the chill in their relations* UNFRIENDLINESS, lack of warmth, lack of understanding, chilliness, coldness, coolness. ANTONYM friendliness.

▸ verb **1** *the dessert is best chilled* MAKE COLD, make colder, cool (down/off); refrigerate, ice. ANTONYM warm.

2 *his quiet tone chilled Ruth* SCARE, frighten, petrify, terrify, alarm; make someone's blood run cold, chill to the bone, make someone's flesh crawl; *informal* scare the pants off; *archaic* affright. ANTONYMS comfort, reassure.

▸ adjective *a chill wind* COLD, chilly, cool, fresh; wintry, frosty, icy, ice-cold, icy-cold, glacial, polar, arctic, raw, bitter, bitterly cold, biting, freezing, frigid, gelid, hypothermic; *informal* nippy.

PHRASE: **chill out** *informal a place to chill out.* See RELAX sense 1.

chilly adjective **1** *the weather had turned chilly* COOL, cold, crisp, fresh, wintry, frosty, brisk, icy, ice-cold, icy-cold, chill, glacial, polar, arctic, raw, bitter, bitterly cold, freezing, frigid, gelid, hypothermic; *informal* nippy. ANTONYM warm.

2 *a chilly reception* UNFRIENDLY, unwelcoming, cold, cool, frosty, gelid; *informal* standoffish, offish. ANTONYMS warm, friendly.

chime verb **1** *the bells began to chime* RING, peal, toll, sound; ding, dong, clang, boom, bong; *literary* knell.

2 *the clock chimed eight o'clock* STRIKE, sound.

▸ noun *the chimes of the bells* PEAL, pealing, ringing, carillon, toll, tolling; ding-dong, clanging, tintinnabulation; *literary* knell.

PHRASE: **chime in** *"Yes, you do that," Doreen chimed in* INTERJECT, interpose, interrupt, butt in, cut in, join in.

chimera noun *is this great love of hers merely a chimera?* ILLUSION, fantasy, delusion, dream, daydream, pipe dream, figment of the/one's imagination, castle in the air, mirage.

WORD NOTE **chimera**

In Greek mythology, a Chimera is a fire-breathing female monster, usually part lion, goat, and serpent. Because of this derivation, *chimera* and its adjective, *chimerical,* came to mean something illusory, fantastical, hoped-for but impossible. Then scientists learned to make the illusory real, which changed the nature of the word. Gardeners have been grafting twigs from one kind of plant onto stems of another since classical antiquity. Eighteenth-century biologists created chimerical invertebrates using hydras and worms. Medical *chimerism* now refers primarily to organ transplantation, which establishes two genetically different cellular lineages within the transplant recipient. If, after a bone marrow transplant, the new blood-forming system is genetically the donor's, the recipient is a chimera. But so are mermaids and unicorns. **—JS**

chimney noun *a pair of ospreys are nesting on top of the chimney* SMOKESTACK, stack; flue, funnel, vent, stovepipe.

china noun **1** *a cup made of fine china* PORCELAIN.

2 *a table laid with the best china* DISHES, plates, cups and saucers, tableware, chinaware, dinner service; *chiefly Brit.* crockery.

chink noun *a chink in the curtains* OPENING, gap, space, hole, aperture, crack, fissure, crevice, cranny, cleft, split, slit, slot.

▸ verb *the glasses chinked* JINGLE, jangle, clink, tinkle.

chintzy adjective *Marty's family gave us these chintzy end tables* CHEAP, cheesy, shoddy, low-grade, low-end, second-rate, third-rate, kitsch, kitschy, tacky, trashy, gimcrack.

chip noun **1** *wood chips* FRAGMENT, sliver, splinter, shaving, paring, flake.

2 *a chip in the glass* NICK, crack, scratch, notch; flaw, fault.

3 *chiefly Brit. fish and chips* French fries, fries, home fries, frites, pommes frites.

4 *gambling chips* COUNTER, token, check.

▸ verb **1** *a stone chipped my windshield* NICK, crack, scratch; damage.

2 *the plaster had chipped* BREAK (OFF), crack, crumble.

3 *chip the flint to the required shape* WHITTLE, hew, chisel, carve.

PHRASES: **chip away at** *chipping away at their defenses* erode, wear down, wear away, whittle down, corrode, gnaw away at. **chip in** *we can afford the new dishwasher if everybody chips in* CONTRIBUTE, make a contribution, make a donation, pay; *informal* fork out, shell out, cough up, kick in.

chipper adjective *it's nice to see you feeling so chipper* CHEERFUL, lively, perky, high-spirited, cheery, buoyant, sunny, bubbly.

chirp verb *winter is officially over when I hear the robins chirping* TWEET, twitter, cheep, peep, chitter, chirrup, chirr; sing, warble, trill.

chisel verb *how he chiseled this masterpiece out of a chunk of cold rock is beyond me* HEW, engrave, incise, score, chip, carve.

chit-chat noun *informal we ran into each other at the pharmacy and had a little chitchat* SMALL TALK, chatter, gossip, chat, chatting, prattle.

chivalrous adjective **1** *his chivalrous treatment of women* GALLANT, gentlemanly, honorable, respectful, considerate; courteous, polite, gracious, well-mannered, mannerly; *archaic* gentle. ANTONYM rude.

2 *chivalrous pursuits* KNIGHTLY, noble, chivalric; brave, courageous, bold, valiant, valorous, heroic, daring, intrepid. ANTONYM cowardly.

chivalry noun **1** *acts of chivalry* GALLANTRY, gentlemanliness, courtesy, courteousness, politeness, graciousness, mannerliness, good manners. ANTONYM rudeness.

2 *the values of chivalry* KNIGHT ERRANTRY, courtly manners, knightliness, courtliness, nobility; bravery, courage, boldness, valour, heroism, daring, intrepidity; bushido.

choice noun **1** *it's your choice | freedom of choice* SELECTION, election, choosing, picking; decision, say, vote.

2 *you have no other choice* OPTION, alternative, possible course of action.

3 *an extensive choice of wines* RANGE, variety, selection, assortment.

4 *the critics' choice* PREFERENCE, selection, pick, favorite.

▸ adjective *choice plums* SUPERIOR, first-class, first-rate, prime, premier, grade A, best, finest, excellent, select, quality, high-quality, top, top-quality, high-grade, prize, fine, special; hand-picked, carefully chosen; *informal* tip-top, A1, top-notch, blue-ribbon, blue-chip. ANTONYM inferior.

choir noun *the children's choir sang at our wedding* SINGERS, chorus, chorale, choral society, voices, choristers, glee club.

choke verb **1** *Christopher started to choke* GAG, retch, cough, fight for breath.

2 *thick dust choked her* SUFFOCATE, asphyxiate, smother, stifle.

3 *she had been choked to death* STRANGLE, throttle; asphyxiate, suffocate; *informal* strangulate.

4 *the gutters were choked with leaves* CLOG (UP), stop up, block, obstruct, plug, bung up; *technical* occlude.

5 *the Rangers choked in the playoffs* UNDERACHIEVE, underperform, disappoint, lose, collapse, fall apart. PHRASE: **choke back** *we could see that he was choking back tears* SUPPRESS, hold back, fight back, bite back, swallow, check, restrain, control, repress, smother, stifle; *informal* keep a lid on.

choleric adjective *a choleric, self-important little man* BAD-TEMPERED, irascible, irritable, angry, grumpy, grouchy, crotchety, testy, cranky, crusty, cantankerous, curmudgeonly, ill-tempered, peevish, cross, fractious, crabbed, crabby, waspish, prickly, peppery, touchy, short-tempered; snappish, short-fused, ornery. ANTONYMS good-natured, affable.

chomp verb *I could hear her chomping on the celery* MUNCH, crunch, chew, bite; champ.

USAGE NOTE **chomp, champ**

The original and better term for what horses do to their bits is *champ*. *Chomp* is an American variant. (Oddly, American English has transformed *champ* into *chomp*, but *stomp* into *stamp*.) The two spellings have undergone some degree of differentiation. What one *champs* is not actually eaten, but just bitten or gnawed, nervously. But to *chomp* something is to take a bite out of it and usually to consume it. In dialect, *chomp* is colloquially accompanied by the adverb *down* (*chompin' down catfish*). *Chomp* is sometimes mistakenly used in place of *champ* in the idiom—e.g.: "DreamWorks chomps [read *champs*] the bit with 'Whoa, Nelly!' a world-beat rock album by Nelly Furado, on Sept. 26." (*Billboard*; Sept. 16, 2000.) The idiom *champing at the bit* evokes the image of an impatient horse, especially one eager for a race to start. In contemporary print sources, it is slightly more common than the variant form, *chomping at the bit*. **—BG**

choose verb **1** *we chose a quiet country inn* SELECT, pick (out), opt for, settle on, decide on, fix on, take; appoint, name, nominate, vote for, elect.

2 *I'll stay as long as I choose* WISH, want, desire, feel/be inclined, please, like, see fit.

choosy adjective *my cat Kiki was never too choosy when it came to leftovers* FUSSY, finicky, fastidious, overparticular, difficult/hard to please, demanding; *informal* picky, persnickety.

chop verb **1** *chop the potatoes into small pieces* CUT UP, cut into pieces, chop up, cube, dice, hash.

2 *they were out back chopping wood* CHOP UP, cut up, cut into pieces, hew, split.

3 *four fingers were* ***chopped off*** SEVER, cut off, hack off, slice off, lop off, saw off, shear off.

4 *they chopped down large areas of rain forest* CUT DOWN, fell, hack down, clear-cut, harvest.

5 *their training courses were chopped* CUT, ax, abolish, scrap, slash, cancel, terminate, ditch, dump, pull the plug on.

choppy adjective *sailing on choppy waters* ROUGH, turbulent, heavy, heaving, stormy, tempestuous, squally; uneven. ANTONYM calm.

chore noun **1** *he was not accustomed to doing the chores that were now expected of him* TASK, job, duty, errand; **(chores)** work, domestic work, drudgery.

2 *informal spending the afternoon with Millie was a chore* drag, bore, pain.

chortle verb *they were chortling behind their hands, as if we didn't notice* CHUCKLE, laugh, giggle, titter, tee-hee, snigger.

chorus noun **1** *the chorus sang powerfully* CHOIR, ensemble, choral group, choristers, (group of) singers, voices, glee club.

2 *Nancy sang the chorus* REFRAIN. PHRASE: **in chorus** *at least on the library parking issue, we were in chorus* IN UNISON, together, simultaneously, as one, united; in concert, in harmony.

chosen adjective *we will send the tickets for your chosen seating two weeks before the performance* SELECTED, picked, appointed, elected, favored, hand-picked.

chrism noun See note at CREAM.

christen verb **1** *she was christened Sara* BAPTIZE, name, give the name of, call.

2 *a group who were christened "The Magic Circle"* CALL, name, dub, style, term, designate, label, nickname, give the name of; *formal* denominate.

chronic adjective **1** *a chronic illness* PERSISTENT, long-standing, long-term; incurable; *Medicine* immedicable. ANTONYM acute.

2 *chronic economic problems* CONSTANT, continuing, ceaseless, unabating, unending, persistent, long-lasting; severe, serious, acute, grave, dire. ANTONYM temporary.

3 *a chronic liar* INVETERATE, hardened, dyed-in-the-wool, incorrigible; compulsive; *informal* pathological. ANTONYM occasional.

USAGE NOTE **chronic**

Chronic is often used to mean 'habitual, inveterate,' e.g., *a chronic liar*. Some consider this use incorrect. The precise meaning of **chronic** is 'persisting for a long time,' and it is used chiefly of illnesses or other problems: *more than one million people in the United States have chronic bronchitis*.

chronicle noun *a chronicle of the region's past* RECORD, written account, history, annals, archive(s); log, diary, journal.

▸ verb *the events that followed have been chronicled* RECORD, put on record, write down, set down, document, register, report.

chronicler noun *the self-appointed chronicler for the historical society* ANNALIST, historian, archivist, diarist, recorder, reporter.

chronological adjective *put these eight historical events in chronological order, beginning with the earliest* SEQUENTIAL, consecutive, in sequence, in order (of time).

chubby adjective *look how chubby Dad was as a baby!* PLUMP, fat, rotund, portly, dumpy, chunky, well-upholstered, well-rounded; *informal* roly-poly, tubby, pudgy, blubbery, big-boned, full-figured; zaftig, corn-fed. ANTONYM skinny.

chuck verb *informal* **1** *he chucked the letter onto the table* THROW, toss, fling, hurl, pitch, cast, lob.

2 *I chucked the old comics* THROW AWAY/OUT, discard, dispose of, get rid of, dump, scrap, jettison; *informal* ditch, junk, deep-six, trash.

3 *Mary chucked him for another guy* LEAVE, throw over, finish with, break off with, jilt; *informal* dump, ditch.

chuckle verb *Adam chuckled to himself as he drove away* GIGGLE, chortle, titter, tee-hee, snicker, snigger.

chug verb *informal chugging one bottle of Snapple after another* GULP, guzzle, quaff; *informal* swig.

chum noun *informal he's having lunch with a few of his old army chums* FRIEND, buddy, bud, pal; companion, sidekick, intimate; playmate, classmate, schoolmate, workmate; mate; crony; amigo, compadre. ANTONYMS enemy, stranger.

chummy adjective *informal her two ex-husbands have gotten pretty chummy* FRIENDLY, on good terms, close, familiar, intimate; *informal* buddy-buddy, thick, palsy-walsy.

chunk noun *a chunk of cheese* LUMP, hunk, wedge, block, slab, square, nugget, brick, cube, bar, cake.

chunky adjective **1** *a chunky young man* STOCKY, sturdy, thickset, heavily built, well-built, burly, bulky, brawny, solid, heavy. ANTONYM slight.

2 *a chunky sweater* THICK, bulky, heavy-knit. ANTONYMS lightweight, light.

church noun **1** *a village church* PLACE OF WORSHIP, house of God, house of worship; cathedral, abbey, chapel, basilica; synagogue, mosque.

2 *the Methodist Church* DENOMINATION, ecclesial community; creed, faith.

churchyard noun *the old churchyard was overgrown with brambles and goldenrod* CEMETERY, graveyard, burial ground, burying ground, necropolis, memorial park/garden; *informal* boneyard; *historical* potter's field; *archaic* God's acre.

churlish adjective *it seemed churlish to refuse her invitation* RUDE, ill-mannered, ill-bred, discourteous, impolite, unmannerly, uncivil, unchivalrous; inconsiderate, uncharitable, surly, sullen. ANTONYM polite.

churn verb **1** *Mae churned the milk* STIR, agitate, beat, whip, whisk.

2 *the sea churned* HEAVE, boil, swirl, toss, seethe; *literary* roil.

3 *propellers churned up the water* DISTURB, stir up, agitate; *literary* roil. PHRASE: **churn out** *they churn out at least twenty romance novels a year* PRODUCE, make, turn out; *informal* crank out.

chute noun *icy water came rushing down the chute* CHANNEL, slide, shaft, funnel, conduit.

chutzpah noun *informal it took a lot of chutzpah for her to walk in on Owen's bachelor party* AUDACITY, cheek, guts, nerve, boldness, temerity.

cigarette noun *he's outside, having a cigarette informal* smoke, butt, ciggie/ciggy, cancer stick, coffin nail; *Brit. informal* fag.

cinch noun *informal* **1** *it's **a cinch*** AN EASY TASK, child's play, a snap, a walkover, nothing; *informal* a piece of cake, a picnic, a breeze, kids' stuff, a cakewalk, a pushover, duck soup, a walk in the park. ANTONYM challenge.

2 *he was a cinch to take a prize* CERTAINTY, sure thing, sure bet.

cinders plural noun *they sifted through the cinders, looking for her ring* ASHES, ash, embers.

cinema noun **1** *chiefly Brit. the local cinema* MOVIE THEATER, theater, multiplex, movie house; *historical* nickelodeon.

2 *Italian cinema* FILMS, movies, pictures, motion pictures.

cipher noun **1** *information in cipher* CODE, secret writing, cryptograph, cryptogram.

2 *dated a row of ciphers* ZERO, 0, nil, naught/nought.

circa preposition *the year of his birth is circa 1612* APPROXIMATELY, around, about, roughly, something like, on the order of, or so, or thereabouts, more or less, in the region of, give or take; *informal* in the ballpark of. ANTONYM exactly.

circle noun **1** *a circle of gold stars* RING, band, hoop, circlet; halo, disc; *technical* annulus.

2 *her circle of friends* GROUP, set, company, coterie, clique; crowd, band; *informal* gang, bunch, crew.

3 *I don't move in such illustrious circles* SPHERE, world, milieu; society.

▸ verb **1** *seagulls circled above* WHEEL, move around, revolve, rotate, whirl, spiral.

2 *satellites circling the earth* GO AROUND, travel around, circumnavigate; orbit, revolve around.

3 *the abbey was circled by a wall* SURROUND, encircle, ring, enclose, encompass; *literary* gird.

circuit noun **1** *two circuits of the course* LAP, turn, round, circle.

2 *a racing circuit* TRACK, racetrack, raceway, running track, course.

3 *the judge's circuit* TOUR, tour of duty, rounds, regular journey; *informal* beat.

circuitous adjective **1** *a circuitous route* ROUNDABOUT, indirect, winding, meandering, serpentine, tortuous. ANTONYMS direct, straight.

2 *a circuitous discussion* INDIRECT, oblique, roundabout, circumlocutory, periphrastic. ANTONYM to the point.

circular adjective *a circular window* ROUND, disk-shaped, ring-shaped, annular. See note at ROUND.

▸ noun *handing out circulars at the mall* LEAFLET, pamphlet, handbill, flyer, mailer, folder.

circulate verb **1** *the news was widely circulated* SPREAD (AROUND/ABOUT), communicate, disseminate, make known, make public, broadcast, publicize, advertise, propagate, promulgate; distribute, give out, pass around.

2 *fresh air circulates freely* FLOW, course, move around.

3 *they circulated among their guests* SOCIALIZE, mingle.

circulation noun **1** *the circulation of fresh air* FLOW, motion, movement, course, passage.

2 *the circulation of the information* DISSEMINATION, spreading, communication, transmission, making known, putting out/about; broadcasting, publication, propagation, promulgation; distribution, diffusion, issuance.

3 *the magazine had a large circulation* DISTRIBUTION, readership.

circumference noun **1** *the circumference of the pit* PERIMETER, border, boundary; edge, rim, verge, margin, fringe; *literary* marge.

2 *the circumference of his arm* GIRTH, width.

circumlocution noun *when you've finished your circumlocution, maybe you could just get to the point* PERIPHRASIS, discursiveness, long-windedness, verbosity, verbiage, wordiness, prolixity, redundancy, pleonasm, tautology, repetitiveness, repetitiousness.

circumscribe verb *the power of the local agency has been circumscribed by the national organization* RESTRICT, limit, keep within bounds, curb, confine, restrain; regulate, control.

THE RIGHT WORD

Strictly speaking, to **circumscribe** is to draw a line around something to mark its limits or boundary (*a square circumscribed by a circle*). Beyond the realm of geometry, however, it suggests something that is hemmed in on all sides (*a lake circumscribed by mountains*). **Encompass** is used when something is set within a circle or within limits (*a road that encompassed the grounds of the estate; a view that encompassed the harbor*). **Surround** is a less formal word for *circumscribe*, but it can also refer to an undesirable, threatening, or dangerous situation (*surrounded by angry demonstrators; surrounded by skyscrapers*). **Encircle** is similar to *surround* in meaning, but it suggests a tight or quite circular clustering around a central object (*a bowl of fruit encircled by flowers*) or a deliberate attempt to surround someone or something for a definite reason (*to encircle the enemy camp*). **Envelop** is the right word if something is surrounded to the point where it can barely be seen (*a lonely figure enveloped in fog*) or if it is surrounded by layers or folds of an amorphous material (*enveloped in soft cotton to prevent breakage*). **Enclose** is very similar to *envelop*, but it suggests that something has been especially designed to fit around something else for protection or containment (*a ship model enclosed in a glass case*).

---

circumspect adjective *she would have to be circumspect in her dealings with Catherine* CAUTIOUS, wary, careful, chary, guarded, on one's guard; watchful, alert, attentive, heedful, vigilant, leery; *informal* cagey, playing one's cards close to one's chest. See note at VIGILANT. ANTONYM unguarded.

circumstances plural noun **1** *favorable economic circumstances* SITUATION, conditions, state of affairs, position; events, turn of events, incidents, occurrences, happenings; factors, context, background, environment.

2 *Jane explained* ***the circumstances*** *to him* THE FACTS, the details, the particulars, how things stand, the lay of the land; *informal* what's what, the score.

3 *reduced circumstances* FINANCIAL POSITION, lot, lifestyle; resources, means, finances, income.

circumstantial adjective **1** *they have only circumstantial evidence* INDIRECT, inferred, deduced, conjectural; inconclusive, unprovable.

2 *a circumstantial account* DETAILED, particularized, comprehensive, thorough, exhaustive; explicit, specific.

circumvent verb *the checkpoints were easy to circumvent* AVOID, get around, get past, evade, bypass, sidestep, dodge; *informal* duck.

circus noun **1** *the kids enjoyed the circus* CARNIVAL, big top, cirque.

2 *informal the meeting degenerated into* ***a circus*** (A) TURMOIL, chaos, a zoo, bedlam, mayhem, pandemonium.

cistern noun *a cistern of rainwater* TANK, reservoir, container, butt.

citadel noun *they were prisoners within their own citadel* FORTRESS, fort, stronghold, fortification, castle; *archaic* hold.

citation noun **1** *a citation from an eighteenth-century text* QUOTATION, quote, extract, excerpt, passage, line; reference, allusion.

2 *a citation for gallantry* COMMENDATION, mention, honorable mention.

3 *Law a traffic citation* SUMMONS, TICKET, subpoena, writ, court order.

cite verb **1** *cite the passage in full* QUOTE, reproduce.

2 *he cited the case of Roe v. Wade* REFER TO, make reference to, mention, allude to, adduce, instance; specify, name.

3 *he has been cited many times* COMMEND, pay tribute to, praise.

4 *Law the writ cited four of the signatories* SUMMON, summons, serve with a summons, serve with a writ, subpoena.

citizen noun **1** *a Japanese citizen* NATIONAL, subject, passport holder, native.

2 *the citizens of Amsterdam* INHABITANT, resident, native, townsman, townswoman, townsperson, denizen; taxpayer; burgher.

city noun *Phoenix is my favorite city in the Southwest* TOWN, municipality, metropolis, megalopolis, megacity; conurbation, urban area, metropolitan area, urban municipality; borough, township; *informal* burg.

civic adjective *they encourage their children to participate in civic affairs* MUNICIPAL, city, town, urban, metropolitan; public, civil, community, local.

civil adjective **1** *a civil marriage* SECULAR, nonreligious, lay; *formal* laic. ANTONYM religious.

2 *civil aviation* NONMILITARY, civilian. ANTONYM military.

3 *a civil war* INTERNAL, domestic, interior, national. ANTONYMS international, foreign.

4 *he behaved in a civil manner* POLITE, courteous, well-mannered, well-bred, chivalrous, gallant; cordial, genial, pleasant, affable; gentlemanly, ladylike. ANTONYMS discourteous, rude.

civilian noun *family members and other civilians were quickly evacuated from the post* NONCOMBATANT, nonmilitary person, ordinary citizen, private citizen; *informal* civvy.

civility noun **1** *he treated me with civility* COURTESY, courteousness, politeness, good manners, graciousness, consideration, respect, politesse, comity. ANTONYMS disrespect, rudeness.

2 *she didn't waste time on civilities* POLITE REMARK, politeness, courtesy; formality.

civilization noun **1** *a higher stage of civilization* HUMAN DEVELOPMENT, advancement, progress, enlightenment, culture, refinement, sophistication.

2 *ancient civilizations* CULTURE, society, nation, people.

civilize verb *they were trying to civilize people who strongly resented the intrusion* ENLIGHTEN, edify, improve, educate, instruct, refine, cultivate, polish, socialize, humanize.

civilized adjective *his civilized behavior | a civilized society* POLITE, courteous, well-mannered, civil, gentlemanly, ladylike, mannerly; cultured, cultivated, refined, polished, sophisticated; enlightened, educated, advanced, developed. ANTONYMS rude, unsophisticated.

civil servant noun *her first position as a civil servant was in the town hall, issuing dog licenses* PUBLIC SERVANT, government official; bureaucrat, official, administrator, functionary, mandarin; *informal* apparatchik, bean counter, paper shuffler.

clad adjective *he's clad in a hunting outfit* DRESSED, clothed, attired, got up, garbed, rigged out, togged out, costumed; *archaic* appareled; **(clad in)** wearing, sporting.

claim verb **1** *Davies claimed that she was lying* ASSERT, declare, profess, maintain, state, hold, affirm, avow; argue, contend, allege; *formal* aver.

2 *no one claimed the items* LAY CLAIM TO, assert ownership of, formally request.

3 *you can claim compensation* REQUEST, ask for, apply for; demand, exact.

4 *the fire claimed four lives* TAKE, result in the loss of, cause the loss of.

▸ noun **1** *her claim that she was unaware of the problem* ASSERTION, declaration, profession, affirmation, avowal, protestation; contention, allegation.

2 *a claim for damages* REQUEST, application; demand, petition.

3 *we have first* ***claim on*** *their assets* ENTITLEMENT TO, title to, right to.

claimant noun *the claimant was a passenger on the derailed train* APPLICANT, candidate, supplicant; petitioner, plaintiff, litigant, appellant.

clairvoyance noun *I'm not sure how much confidence I have in Miss ZuZu's clairvoyance* ESP, extrasensory perception, sixth sense, psychic powers, second sight; telepathy.

clairvoyant noun *a woman claiming to be a clairvoyant gave a description of the kidnappers* PSYCHIC, fortune teller, crystal-gazer; medium, spiritualist; telepath, mind-reader.

▸ adjective *he didn't tell me about it, and I'm not clairvoyant* PSYCHIC, telepathic, visionary, oracular; *rare* second-sighted.

clam noun See table at MOLLUSK.

clamber verb *Frankie clambered up to the top bunk* SCRAMBLE, climb, scrabble, claw one's way.

clammy adjective **1** *his clammy hands* MOIST, damp, sweaty, sticky; slimy, slippery. ANTONYM dry.

2 *the clammy atmosphere* DAMP, dank, wet; humid, close, muggy, heavy.

clamor noun **1** *her voice rose above the clamor* DIN, racket, rumpus, loud noise, uproar, tumult, shouting, yelling, screaming, roaring; commotion, brouhaha, hue and cry, hubbub, hullabaloo, hoopla.

2 *the clamor for her resignation* DEMAND(S), call(s), urging.

3 *the clamor of the workers* PROTESTS, complaints, outcry.

▸ verb **1** *clamoring crowds* YELL, shout loudly, bay, scream, roar.

2 *scientists are* ***clamoring for*** *a ban* DEMAND, call for, press for, push for, lobby for.

clamorous adjective *a crowd of clamorous children* NOISY, loud, vocal, vociferous, raucous, rowdy; importunate, demanding, insistent, vehement. See note at VOCIFEROUS. ANTONYM quiet.

clamp noun *if the clamp is too loose, its function becomes useless* BRACE, vice, press, clasp; *Music* capo (tasto); *Climbing* jumar.

▸ verb **1** *the sander is clamped on to the workbench* FASTEN, secure, fix, attach; screw, bolt.

2 *a pipe was clamped between his teeth* CLENCH, grip, hold, press, clasp.

PHRASE: **clamp down on** *they promised to clamp down on the drug trafficking in this neighborhood* SUPPRESS, prevent, stop, put a stop/end to, stamp out; crack down on, limit, restrict, control, keep in check.

clampdown noun *informal Barone's clampdown on graft rooted out a lot of unexpected dirt in the department* SUPPRESSION, prevention, stamping out; crackdown, restriction, restraint, curb, check.

clan noun **1** *the Macleod clan* GROUP OF FAMILIES, sept; family, house, dynasty, tribe; *Anthropology* kinship group.

2 *a clan of art collectors* GROUP, set, circle, clique, coterie; crowd, band; *informal* gang, bunch.

clandestine adjective *their clandestine meetings* SECRET, covert, furtive, surreptitious, stealthy, cloak-and-dagger, hole-and-corner, closet, backstairs, backroom; hush-hush. See note at SECRET.

clang noun *the clang of the church bells* REVERBERATION, ringing, ring, ding-dong, bong, peal, chime, toll.

▸ verb *the huge bells clanged* REVERBERATE, resound, ring, bong, peal, chime, toll.

clank noun *the clank of rusty chains* JANGLING, clanging, rattling, clinking, jingling; clang, jangle, rattle, clangor, clink, jingle.

▸ verb *I could hear the chain clanking* JANGLE, rattle, clink, clang, jingle.

clannish adjective *your daughter is part of a very clannish group of girls* CLIQUEY, cliquish, insular, exclusive; unfriendly, unwelcoming.

clap verb **1** *the audience clapped* APPLAUD, clap one's hands, give someone a round of applause, put one's hands together; *informal* give someone a big hand.

2 *he clapped Owen on the back* SLAP, strike, hit, smack, thump; pat; *informal* whack, thwack.

3 *the dove clapped its wings* FLAP, beat, flutter.

▸ noun **1** *everybody gave him a clap* ROUND OF APPLAUSE, handclap; *informal* hand.

2 *a clap on the shoulder* SLAP, blow, smack, thump; pat; *informal* whack, thwack.

3 *a clap of thunder* CRACK, crash, bang, boom; thunderclap.

claptrap noun *sentimental claptrap.* See NONSENSE sense 1.

clarify verb **1** *their report clarified the situation* MAKE CLEAR, shed/throw light on, elucidate, illuminate; EXPLAIN, explicate, define, spell out, clear up. ANTONYM confuse.

2 *clarify the butter* PURIFY, refine; filter, fine.

THE RIGHT WORD

When a biology teacher gets up in front of a class and tries to **explain** how two brown-eyed parents can produce a blue-eyed child, the purpose is to make an entire process or sequence of events understandable. In a less formal sense, to *explain* is to make a verbal attempt to justify certain actions or to make them understood (*she tried to explain why she was so late*). That same teacher might **clarify** a particular exam question that almost everyone in the class got wrong—a word that means to make an earlier event, situation, or statement clear. **Elucidate** is a more formal word meaning to *clarify*, but where the root of the latter refers to clearness, the root of the former refers to light; to *elucidate* is to shed light on something through explanation, illustration, etc. (*the principal's comments were an attempt to elucidate the school's policy on cheating*). A teacher who **explicates** something discusses a complex subject in a point-by-point manner (*to explicate a poem*). If a personal judgment is inserted in making such an explication, the correct word is **interpret** (*to interpret a poem's symbolic meanings*). To **construe** is to make a careful interpretation of something, especially where the meaning is ambiguous. For example, when a class misbehaves in front of a visitor, the teacher is likely to *construe* that behavior as an attempt to cause embarrassment or ridicule.

---

clarity noun **1** *the clarity of his account* LUCIDITY, lucidness, clearness, coherence; *formal* perspicuity. ANTONYMS vagueness, obscurity.

2 *the clarity of the image* SHARPNESS, clearness, crispness, definition. ANTONYM blurriness.

3 *the crystal clarity of the water* LIMPIDITY, limpidness, clearness, transparency, translucence, pellucidity. ANTONYMS murkiness, opacity.

clash noun **1** *clashes between armed gangs* CONFRONTATION, skirmish, fight, battle, engagement, encounter, conflict.

2 *an angry clash* ARGUMENT, altercation, confrontation, shouting match; contretemps, quarrel, disagreement, dispute, run-in.

3 *a clash of tweeds and a striped shirt* MISMATCH, discordance, discord, lack of harmony.

4 *the clash of cymbals* STRIKING, bang, clang, crash.

▸ verb **1** *protesters clashed with police* FIGHT, skirmish, contend, come to blows, come into conflict; do battle.

2 *the mayor clashed with union leaders* DISAGREE, differ, wrangle, dispute, cross swords, lock horns, be at loggerheads.

3 *her red scarf clashed with her coat* BE INCOMPATIBLE, not match, not go, be discordant.

4 *she clashed the cymbals together* BANG, strike, clang, crash.

clasp verb **1** *Ruth clasped his hand* GRASP, grip, clutch, hold tightly; take hold of, seize, grab.

2 *he clasped Joanne in his arms* EMBRACE, hug, enfold, fold, envelop; hold, squeeze.

▸ noun **1** *a gold clasp* FASTENER, fastening, catch, clip, pin; buckle, hasp.

2 *his tight clasp* EMBRACE, hug, cuddle; grip, grasp.

class noun **1** *a hotel of the first class* CATEGORY, grade, rating, classification, group, grouping.

2 *a new class of heart drug* KIND, sort, type, variety, genre, brand; species, genus, breed, strain, stripe.

3 *the middle class* SOCIAL DIVISION, social stratum, rank, level, echelon, group, grouping, income group; social status; *dated* estate; *archaic* condition.

4 *a math class* LESSON, period; seminar, tutorial, workshop, study group.

5 *informal**a woman of class* STYLE, stylishness, elegance, chic, sophistication, taste, refinement, quality, excellence.

▸ verb *the 12-seater is classed as a commercial vehicle* CLASSIFY, categorize, group, grade; order, sort, codify; bracket, designate, label, pigeonhole.

▸ adjective *informal a class player* CLASSY, decent, gracious, respectable, noble.

WORD NOTE class

Class—meaning socioeconomic status—now carries loads of connotation, but often very little meaning. How does one determine a person's "class"? Nowadays, millionaires regard themselves as working stiffs or, at best, as middle class. A salaried employee earning $100,000 a year feels poor if all his neighbors make twice that just from their stock portfolios. In other words, there are no clear markers. Should ghetto drug-lords with shiny BMWs be viewed as members of the "underclass"? Is the owner of a Kwik-E-Mart who pays two college kids to run the register and stock the shelves in the same class as an autoworker at the Ford assembly plant? What if the small-time entrepreneur takes home only $30,000 a year, while the grunt on the line earns $60,000? Nobody, of course, ever admits to being upper class. People with private jets will quietly murmur, after a self-deprecating smile, "Oh, we're just comfortable," or even "We're getting by." In summarizing people's economic status, just say what you think: He's rich, she's poor. Better yet, describe the actual conditions of life: *The Smiths reside in a tract house that cost $40,000, and they can barely afford the mortgage.* —**MD**

---

classic adjective **1** *the classic work on the subject* DEFINITIVE, authoritative; outstanding, first-rate, first-class, best, finest, excellent, superior, masterly.

2 *a classic example of Norman design* TYPICAL, archetypal, quintessential, vintage; model, representative, perfect, prime, textbook. ANTONYM atypical.

3 *a classic style* SIMPLE, elegant, understated; traditional, timeless, ageless.

▸ noun *a classic of the genre* DEFINITIVE EXAMPLE, model, epitome, paradigm, exemplar; great work, masterpiece.

EASILY CONFUSED WORDS classic, classical

Traditionally, **classic** means 'typical, excellent as an example, timeless,' and **classical** means 'of (esp. Greek or Roman) antiquity.' Thus: *John Ford directed many classic Westerns; the museum was built in the classical style.* Great art is considered **classic**, not **classical**, unless it is created in the forms of antiquity. *Classical music* is formal and sophisticated music adhering to certain stylistic principles, especially those of the late eighteenth century, but *a classic folk song* is one that well expresses its culture. A *classical education* exposes a student to *classical* literature, history, and languages (esp. Latin and Greek), but the study of Greek and Latin languages and their literatures is also referred to as *classics*, as in *he majored in classics at college.*

---

classical adjective **1** *classical mythology* ancient Greek, Hellenic, Attic; Latin, ancient Roman.

2 *classical music* TRADITIONAL, long-established; serious, highbrow. ANTONYM modern.

3 *a classical style* SIMPLE, pure, restrained, plain, austere; well-proportioned, harmonious, balanced, symmetrical, elegant. See note at CLASSIC.

classification noun **1** *the classification of diseases* CATEGORIZATION, categorizing, classifying, grouping, grading, ranking, organization, sorting, codification, systematization.

2 *a series of classifications* CATEGORY, class, group, grouping, grade, grading, ranking.

classify verb *we can classify the students into two groups* CATEGORIZE, group, grade, rank, rate, order, organize, range, sort, type, codify, bracket, systematize, systemize; catalog, list, file, index, lump.

classy adjective **1** *a classy hotel* STYLISH, high-class, superior, exclusive, chic, elegant, smart, sophisticated, upscale, upmarket, high-toned; *informal* posh, ritzy, plush, swanky.

2 *a classy organization* DECENT, gracious, respectable, noble.

WORD NOTE **classy**

Classy is a self-defeating word. Think about it: anything described as *classy* generally isn't. *Classy* now means "having superficial trappings of wealth." Fake marble, fake gilt, fake blonde hair, and loud jewelry. Unless you want to imply that something is faux-elegant, use *elegant* or *sophisticated* instead. It's hard even to use *classy* ironically—better to use *swanky*. —EM

clatter verb *the cups clattered on the tray* RATTLE, clank, clink, clunk, clang.

clause noun *a new clause in the treaty* SECTION, paragraph, article, subsection; stipulation, condition, proviso, rider.

claw noun 1 *a bird's claw* TALON, nail; *technical* unguis.

2 *a crab's claw* PINCER, nipper; *technical* chela.

▸ verb *her fingers clawed his shoulders* SCRATCH, lacerate, tear, rip, scrape, graze, dig into.

clay noun 1 *the soil is mainly clay* EARTH, soil, loam.

2 *potter's clay* china clay, kaolin, adobe, ball clay, argil, pug; fireclay.

clean adjective 1 *keep the wound clean* WASHED, scrubbed, cleansed, cleaned; spotless, unsoiled, unstained, unsullied, unblemished, immaculate, pristine, dirt-free; hygienic, sanitary, disinfected, sterilized, sterile, aseptic, decontaminated; laundered; *informal* squeaky clean, as clean as a whistle. ANTONYM dirty.

2 *a clean sheet of paper* BLANK, empty, clear, plain; unused, new, pristine, fresh, unmarked. ANTONYM used.

3 *clean air* PURE, clear, fresh, crisp, refreshing; unpolluted, uncontaminated. ANTONYM polluted.

4 *a clean life* VIRTUOUS, good, upright, upstanding; honorable, respectable, reputable, decent, righteous, moral, exemplary; innocent, pure, chaste; *informal* squeaky clean. ANTONYM guilty.

5 *the firm is clean* INNOCENT, guiltless, blameless, guilt-free, crime-free, above suspicion; *informal* squeaky clean. ANTONYMS dirty, polluted.

6 *a good clean fight* FAIR, honest, sporting, sportsmanlike, honorable, according to the rules; *informal* on the level. ANTONYMS dirty, unfair.

7 *informal they are trying to stay clean* SOBER, teetotal, dry, nondrinking; DRUG-FREE, off drugs; *informal* on the wagon.

8 *a clean cut* NEAT, smooth, crisp, straight, precise. ANTONYM ragged.

9 *a clean break* COMPLETE, thorough, total, absolute, conclusive, decisive, final, irrevocable. ANTONYM partial.

10 *clean lines* SIMPLE, elegant, graceful, streamlined, smooth. ANTONYMS complex, elaborate.

▸ adverb *informal I clean forgot* COMPLETELY, entirely, totally, fully, quite, utterly, absolutely.

▸ verb 1 *Dad cleaned the windows* WASH, cleanse, wipe, sponge, scrub, mop, rinse, scour, swab, hose down, sluice (down), disinfect; shampoo; *literary* lave. ANTONYMS dirty, soil.

2 *I got my clothes cleaned* LAUNDER, dry-clean.

3 *she cleaned the fish* GUT, draw, dress; *formal* eviscerate.

PHRASES: **clean out** *informal those grifters cleaned him out* BANKRUPT, ruin, make insolvent, make penniless, wipe out. **come clean** *informal if you don't come clean, they're going to pin all of this on Kerry* TELL THE TRUTH, tell all, make a clean breast of it; confess, own up, admit guilt, admit to one's crimes/sins; *informal* fess up.

clean-cut adjective *a clean-cut young man from Portland* UPRIGHT, upstanding, respectable, clean-living, wholesome.

cleanse verb 1 *the wound was cleansed* CLEAN (UP), wash, bathe, rinse, disinfect.

2 *cleansing the environment of traces of lead* RID, clear, free, purify, purge.

clear adjective 1 *clear instructions* UNDERSTANDABLE, comprehensible, intelligible, plain, uncomplicated, explicit, lucid, coherent, simple, straightforward, unambiguous, clear-cut, crystal clear; *formal* perspicuous. ANTONYM vague.

2 *a clear case of harassment* OBVIOUS, evident, plain, crystal clear; sure, definite, unmistakable, manifest, indisputable, patent, incontrovertible, irrefutable, beyond doubt, beyond question; palpable, visible, discernible, conspicuous, overt, blatant, glaring; as plain as day, as plain as the nose on one's face. ANTONYMS vague, possible.

3 *clear water* TRANSPARENT, limpid, pellucid, translucent, crystal clear; unclouded. ANTONYMS murky, opaque.

4 *a clear blue sky* BRIGHT, cloudless, unclouded, without a cloud in the sky. ANTONYM cloudy.

5 *her clear complexion* UNBLEMISHED, spot-free. ANTONYMS spotty, pimply.

6 *Rosa's clear voice* DISTINCT, bell-like, as clear as a bell. ANTONYM muffled.

7 *the road was clear* | *a clear view* UNOBSTRUCTED, unblocked, passable, unrestricted, open, unhindered. ANTONYMS limited, obstructed.

8 *a clear conscience* UNTROUBLED, undisturbed, unperturbed, unconcerned, having no qualms; peaceful, at peace, tranquil, serene, calm, easy. ANTONYM guilty.

▸ adverb 1 *stand clear of the doors* AWAY FROM, apart from, at a (safe) distance from, out of contact with.

2 *Tommy's voice came loud and clear* DISTINCTLY, clearly, as clear as a bell, plainly, audibly.

3 *he has time to get clear away* COMPLETELY, entirely, fully, wholly, totally, utterly; *informal* clean.

▸ verb 1 *the sky cleared briefly* BRIGHTEN (UP), lighten, clear up, become bright/brighter, become light/lighter, become sunny.

2 *the drizzle had cleared* DISAPPEAR, go away, end; peter out, fade, wear off, decrease, lessen, diminish.

3 *together they cleared the table* EMPTY, unload, unburden, strip.

4 *clearing drains* UNBLOCK, unstop.

5 *staff cleared the building* EVACUATE, empty; leave.

6 *Karen cleared the dirty dishes* REMOVE, take away, carry away, tidy up.

7 *I cleared the bar on my first attempt* GO OVER, pass over, sail over; jump (over), vault (over), leap (over), hurdle.

8 *he was cleared by an appeals court* ACQUIT, declare innocent, find not guilty; absolve, exonerate; *informal* let off (the hook); *formal* exculpate.

9 *I was cleared to work on the atomic project* AUTHORIZE, give permission, permit, allow, pass, accept, endorse, license, sanction, give approval, give consent; *informal* OK, give the OK, give the thumbs up, give the green light, give the go-ahead.

10 *I cleared $50,000 profit* NET, make/realize a profit of, take home, pocket; gain, earn, make, get, bring in, pull in.

PHRASES: **clear out 1** *informalwe were told to clear out immediately.* See LEAVE[1] sense 1. **2** *we cleared out the junk room* EMPTY (OUT); tidy (up), clean up, clear up. **3** *clear out the old equipment* GET RID OF, throw out/away, discard, dispose of, dump, scrap, jettison; *informal* chuck (out), deep-six, ditch, trash. **clear up 1** *I hope it clears up before the party.* See CLEAR verb sense 1. **2** *we've cleared up the problem* SOLVE, resolve, straighten out, find an/the answer to; get to the bottom of, explain; *informal* crack, figure out.

clearance noun **1** *slum clearance* REMOVAL, clearing, demolition.

2 *you must have clearance to enter* AUTHORIZATION, permission, consent, approval, blessing, leave, sanction, license, dispensation, assent, agreement, endorsement; *informal* the green light, the go-ahead, the thumbs up, the OK, the say-so.

3 *the clearance of a debt* REPAYMENT, payment, paying (off), settling, discharge.

4 *there is plenty of clearance* SPACE, room, room to spare, margin, leeway.

clear-cut adjective *a clear-cut objective* DEFINITE, distinct, clear, well-defined, precise, specific, explicit, unambiguous, unequivocal, black and white, cut and dried. ANTONYM vague.

clearing noun *the trees gave way to a clearing* OPENING, glade, dell.

clearly adverb **1** *write clearly* INTELLIGIBLY, plainly, distinctly, comprehensibly, with clarity; legibly, audibly; *formal* perspicuously.

2 *clearly, substantial changes are needed* OBVIOUSLY, evidently, patently, unquestionably, undoubtedly, without doubt, indubitably, plainly, undeniably, incontrovertibly, irrefutably, doubtless, it goes without saying, needless to say.

USAGE NOTE clearly

Exaggerators like this word, along with its cousins (*obviously*, *undeniably*, *undoubtedly*, and the like). Often a statement prefaced with one of these words is conclusory, and sometimes even exceedingly dubious. As a result—though some readers don't consciously realize it—*clearly* and its ilk are 'weasel words'—that is, unnecessary words that supposedly intensify the meaning of a statement, but actually weaken it. Just how much *clearly* can weaken a statement is evident in the following example, in which the author uses the word to buttress a claim about his own state of mind: "Clearly, I am not to be convinced that this is a small matter." (Stephen White, *The Written Word*; 1984.) **—BG**

cleave[1] verb **1** *cleaving wood for the fire* SPLIT (OPEN), cut (up), hew, hack, chop up; *literary* rive.

2 *cleaving a path through the traffic* PLOW, drive, bulldoze, carve.

cleave[2] PHRASE: **cleave to** *literary* **1** *her tongue clove to the roof of her mouth* STICK (FAST), adhere, be attached. **2** ***cleaving*** *too closely* ***to*** *Moscow's line* ADHERE TO, hold to, abide by, be loyal to, be faithful to.

cleaver noun *the butcher's cleaver* CHOPPER, hatchet, ax, knife; butcher's knife, kitchen knife.

cleft noun **1** *a deep cleft in the rocks* SPLIT, slit, crack, fissure, crevice, rift, break, fracture, rent, breach.

2 *the cleft in his chin* DIMPLE.

▸ adjective *a cleft tail* SPLIT, divided, cloven, bifid.

clemency noun *a fallen dictator who now seeks the clemency he withheld from others* MERCY, mercifulness, leniency, mildness, indulgence, quarter; compassion, humanity, pity, sympathy See note at MERCY. ANTONYM ruthlessness.

clench verb **1** *he stood there clenching his hands* SQUEEZE TOGETHER, clamp together, close/shut tightly; make into a fist.

2 *he clenched the iron bar* GRIP, grasp, grab, clutch, clasp, hold tightly, seize, press, squeeze.

clergy noun *a group of clergy who want to promote religious tolerance* CLERICS, clergymen, clergywomen, churchmen, churchwomen, priests, ecclesiastics, men/women of God; ministry, priesthood, holy orders, the church, the cloth. ANTONYM laity.

clergyman, clergywoman noun *a conference of Massachusetts clergyman* CLERIC, churchman, churchwoman, man/woman of the cloth, man/woman of God, ecclesiastic; priest, minister, pastor, preacher, chaplain, father, bishop, rector, parson, vicar, curate, deacon, deaconess; monk, nun, religious, friar, sister, brother; *informal* reverend, padre, sky pilot, Bible thumper; *dated* divine.

clerical adjective **1** *typing, filing, and other clerical jobs* OFFICE, desk, back-room; administrative, secretarial; white-collar.

2 *her clerical duties as the associate pastor* ECCLESIASTICAL, church, priestly, religious, spiritual, sacerdotal; holy, divine. ANTONYM secular.

clerk noun *give your completed forms to the clerk* OFFICE WORKER, clerical worker, administrator; bookkeeper; cashier, teller; *informal* pencil pusher, paper-shuffler; *historical* scrivener.

clever adjective **1** *a clever young woman* INTELLIGENT, bright, smart, astute, sharp, quick-witted, shrewd; talented, gifted, brilliant, capable, able, competent, apt; educated, learned, knowledgeable, wise; *informal* brainy, clueful, savvy. ANTONYM stupid.

2 *a clever scheme* INGENIOUS, canny, cunning, crafty, artful, slick, neat. ANTONYMS ill-advised, foolish.

3 *she was clever with her hands* SKILLFUL, dexterous, adroit, adept, deft, nimble, handy; skilled, talented, gifted.

4 *a clever remark* WITTY, amusing, droll, humorous, funny. ANTONYM witless.

cliché noun *a good speechwriter will steer clear of clichés* PLATITUDE, hackneyed phrase, commonplace, banality, old saying, maxim, truism, stock phrase, trite phrase; old chestnut.

WORD NOTE **cliché**

One Day at a Time

What goes around comes around.
I made up that phrase this morning.
Do you like it? Would you like to use it?
Be my guest. Help yourself.
You can have your cake and eat it too.
You get the best of both worlds,
six of one and half a dozen of the other.
But don't bite off more than you can chew.
I've been smoke-free now for three years
and there's no such thing as a free lunch.
But say you get your ducks in a row
(your sitting ducks, your lame ducks,
your lucky ducks, your dead ducks),
then, at the last moment of consciousness,
when your whole life flashes before you,
these words will go from your mouth to God's ear
and he (whatever you conceive him to be)
will nod once, with mild eyes,
and say, "Been there. Done that."
—DL

click noun *the click of the timer* CLACK, snap, pop, tick; clink.

▸ verb **1** *cameras clicked* SNAP, clack, tick, pop; clink.

2 *informal* *that night it clicked* BECOME CLEAR, fall into place, come home, make sense, dawn, register, get through, sink in.

3 *informal* *we just clicked* TAKE TO EACH OTHER, get along, be compatible, be like-minded, feel a rapport, see eye to eye; *informal* hit it off, be on the same wavelength.

4 *informal* *this issue hasn't clicked with the voters* GO DOWN WELL, prove popular, be a hit, succeed.

client noun *the waiting room was designed to put the clients at ease* CUSTOMER, buyer, purchaser, shopper, consumer, user; patient; patron, regular; **(clients)** clientele, patronage, public, market; *Law* vendee.

cliff noun *the cliffs of the Southwest are breathtaking* PRECIPICE, rock face, crag, bluff, ridge, escarpment, scar, scarp, ledge, overhang.

climactic adjective *during the climactic scene in Renee's apartment, someone's damn pager started beeping* FINAL, ending, closing, concluding, ultimate; exciting, thrilling, gripping, riveting, dramatic, hair-raising; crucial, decisive, critical.

climate noun **1** *the mild climate* WEATHER CONDITIONS, weather; atmospheric conditions.

2 *they come from a colder climate* REGION, area, zone, country, place; *literary* clime.

3 *the political climate* ATMOSPHERE, mood, feeling, ambience, tenor; tendency, ethos, attitude; milieu; *informal* vibe(s).

climax noun *the climax of his career* PEAK, pinnacle, height, high(est) point, top; acme, zenith; culmination, crowning point, crown, crest; highlight, high spot, high-water mark. ANTONYM nadir.

▸ verb *the event will climax with a concert* CULMINATE, peak, reach a pinnacle, come to a crescendo, come to a head.

climb verb **1** *we climbed the hill* ASCEND, mount, scale, scramble up, clamber up, shinny up; go up, walk up; conquer, gain. ANTONYM descend.

2 *the plane climbed* RISE, ascend, go up, gain altitude. ANTONYMS descend, dive.

3 *the road climbs steeply* SLOPE UPWARD, rise, go uphill, incline upward. ANTONYM drop.

4 *the shares climbed to $10.77* INCREASE, rise, go up; shoot up, soar, rocket. ANTONYMS decrease, fall.

5 *he climbed through the ranks* ADVANCE, rise, move up, progress, work one's way (up).

6 *he climbed out of his car* CLAMBER, scramble; step.

▸ noun *a steep climb* ASCENT, clamber. ANTONYM descent.

PHRASE: **climb down** *Sandy climbed down the ladder* DESCEND, go/come down, move down, shinny down.

clinch verb **1** *he clinched the deal* SECURE, settle, conclude, close, pull off, bring off, complete, confirm, seal, finalize; *informal* sew up, wrap up.

2 *these findings clinched the matter* SETTLE, decide, determine; resolve; *informal* sort out.

3 *Wisconsin State clinched the title* WIN, secure; be victorious, come first, triumph, prevail. ANTONYM lose.

4 *the boxers clinched* GRAPPLE, wrestle, struggle, scuffle.

cling verb *rice grains tend to cling together* STICK, adhere, hold, cohere, bond, bind. PHRASE: **cling (on) to 1** *she clung to him* HOLD ON TO, clutch, grip, grasp, clasp, attach oneself to, hang on to; embrace, hug. **2** *they clung to their beliefs* ADHERE TO, hold to, stick to, stand by, abide by, cherish, remain true to, have faith in; *informal* swear by, stick with.

clinic noun *we took Ralph to the clinic for stitches* MEDICAL CENTER, health center, doctor's office.

clinical adjective **1** *he seemed so clinical* DETACHED, impersonal, dispassionate, objective, uninvolved, distant, remote, aloof, removed, cold, indifferent, neutral, unsympathetic, unfeeling, unemotional. ANTONYM emotional.

2 *the room was clinical* PLAIN, simple, unadorned, unembellished, stark, austere, spartan, bleak, bare; clean; functional, utilitarian, basic, institutional, impersonal, characterless. ANTONYM luxurious.

clink verb *something is clinking near the left rear wheel* DING, ping, jingle, chink, tinkle.

clip[1] noun **1** *a briefcase clip* FASTENER, clasp, hasp, catch, hook, buckle, lock.

2 *a mother-of-pearl clip* BROOCH, pin, badge.

3 *his clip was empty* MAGAZINE, cartridge, cylinder.

▸ verb *he clipped the pages together* FASTEN, attach, fix, join; pin, staple, tack.

clip[2] verb **1** *I clipped the hedge* TRIM, prune, cut, snip, shorten, crop, shear, pare; lop; neaten, shape.

2 *clip the coupon below* REMOVE, cut out, snip out, tear out, detach.

3 *his trailer clipped a parked van* HIT, strike, touch, graze, glance off, run into.

4 *Mom clipped his ear* HIT, cuff, strike, smack, slap, box; *informal* clout, whack, wallop, clobber, sock.

▸ noun **1** *I gave the dog a clip* TRIM, cut, crop, haircut; shear.

2 *a film clip* EXTRACT, excerpt, snippet, cutting, fragment; trailer.

3 *informal* *a clip to the ear* SMACK, cuff, slap; *informal* clout, whack, wallop, sock.

4 *informal* *the truck went at a good clip* SPEED, rate, pace, velocity; *informal* lick.

PHRASE: **clip someone's wings** *if you try to clip her wings, neither one of you will ever be happy* RESTRICT SOMEONE'S FREEDOM, impose limits on, keep under control, stand in the way of; obstruct, impede, frustrate, thwart, fetter, hamstring, handcuff.

clipping noun *a scrapbook filled with pressed flowers and newspaper clippings* CUTTING, snippet, extract, excerpt.

clique noun *almost no one from her clique showed up at the reunion* COTERIE, set, circle, ring, in-crowd, group; club, society, fraternity, sorority; cabal, caucus; *informal* gang.

cloak noun 1 *the cloak over his shoulders* CAPE, poncho, serape, shawl, mantle, wrap, pelisse, burnoose, cope, robe, cowl, djellaba, tippet; cassock, chasuble, pallium; *historical* cardinal.

2 *a cloak of secrecy* COVER, veil, mantle, shroud, screen, mask, shield, blanket.

▸ verb *a peak cloaked in mist* CONCEAL, hide, cover, veil, shroud, mask, obscure, cloud; envelop, swathe, surround.

clobber verb *informal* *I'll clobber him.* See HIT verb sense 1.

clock noun *a grandfather clock* TIMEPIECE, timekeeper, timer; chronometer, chronograph.

▸ verb *informal* *his fastball was clocked at 92 mph* TIME, measure.

clod noun 1 *clods of earth* LUMP, clump, chunk, hunk.

2 *informal* *an insensitive clod.* See IDIOT.

clog noun *dancing in clogs takes a lot of practice* sabot, wooden shoe.

▸ verb *the pipes were clogged* BLOCK, obstruct, congest, jam, choke, bung up, plug, stop up, fill up, gunge up.

cloister noun 1 *the convent's shadowed cloisters* WALKWAY, covered walk, arcade, loggia, gallery.

2 *I was educated in the cloister* ABBEY, monastery, friary, convent, priory, nunnery.

cloistered adjective *the cloistered life of a writer* SECLUDED, sequestered, sheltered, protected, insulated; shut off, isolated, confined, incommunicado; solitary, monastic, reclusive.

close[1] adjective 1 *the town is **close to** Joliette* NEAR, adjacent to; in the vicinity of, in the neighborhood of, within reach of; neighboring, adjoining, abutting, alongside, on the doorstep, a stone's throw (away) from/to, 'a hop, skip, and a jump from'; nearby, at close quarters to; *informal* within spitting distance from/to; *archaic* nigh to. ANTONYMS far, distant.

2 *flying in close formation* DENSE, compact, tight, close-packed, packed, solid; crowded, cramped, congested. ANTONYM sparse.

3 *I was **close to** tears* NEAR, on the verge of, on the brink of, on the point of.

4 *a very close match* EVENLY MATCHED, even, with nothing to choose between them, neck and neck; *informal* even-steven. ANTONYM one-sided.

5 *close relatives* IMMEDIATE, direct, near. ANTONYM distant.

6 *close friends* INTIMATE, dear, bosom; close-knit, tight-knit, inseparable, attached, devoted, faithful; special, good, best, fast, firm; *informal* (as) thick as thieves. ANTONYM casual.

7 *a close resemblance* STRONG, marked, distinct, pronounced. ANTONYM slight.

8 *a close examination* CAREFUL, detailed, thorough, minute, searching, painstaking, meticulous, rigorous, scrupulous, conscientious; attentive, focused. ANTONYM casual.

9 *keep a close eye on them* VIGILANT, watchful, keen, alert.

10 *a close translation* STRICT, faithful, exact, precise, literal; word for word, verbatim. ANTONYM loose.

11 *the weather was hot and close* HUMID, muggy, stuffy, airless, heavy, sticky, sultry, oppressive, stifling. ANTONYM fresh.

close[2] verb 1 *she closed the door* SHUT, pull (shut), push (shut), slam; fasten, secure. ANTONYM open.

2 *close the hole* BLOCK (UP/OFF), stop up, plug, seal (up/off), shut up/off, cork, stopper, bung (up); clog (up), choke, obstruct. ANTONYMS open, unblock.

3 *the enemy was closing fast* CATCH UP, close in, creep up, near, approach, gain on someone.

4 *the gap is closing* NARROW, reduce, shrink, lessen, get smaller, diminish, contract. ANTONYM widen.

5 *his arms closed around her* MEET, join, connect; form a circle.

6 *he closed the meeting* END, conclude, finish, terminate, wind up, break off, halt, discontinue, dissolve; adjourn, suspend. ANTONYMS open, begin.

7 *the factory is to close* SHUT DOWN, close down, cease production, cease trading, go out of business, go bankrupt, go into receivership, go into liquidation; *informal* fold, go bust. See word spectrum at OPEN. ANTONYM open.

8 *he closed a deal* CLINCH, settle, secure, seal, confirm, establish; transact, pull off; complete, conclude, fix, agree, finalize; *informal* wrap up.

▸ noun *the close of the talks* END, finish, conclusion, termination, cessation, completion, resolution, climax, denouement; *informal* outro. ANTONYM beginning.

PHRASE: **close down.** See CLOSE[2] verb sense 7.

closet noun *a clothes closet* CABINET, cupboard, wardrobe, armoire, locker.

▸ adjective *a closet Sherlock Holmes fan* SECRET, covert, private; surreptitious, clandestine, underground, furtive.

▸ verb *David was closeted in his den* SHUT AWAY, sequester, seclude, cloister, confine, isolate.

closure noun *the closure of rural schools* CLOSING DOWN, shutdown; termination, discontinuation, cessation, finish, conclusion; failure; *informal* folding.

clot noun *blood clots* LUMP, clump, mass; thrombus, thrombosis, embolus; *informal* glob, gob.

▸ verb *the blood is likely to clot* COAGULATE, set, congeal, curdle, thicken, solidify.

cloth noun 1 *a maker of cloth* FABRIC, material; textile(s), soft goods.

2 *a cloth to wipe the table* RAG, wipe, duster, sponge; towel; chamois.

clothe verb **1** *they were clothed in silk* DRESS, attire, robe, garb, array, costume, swathe, deck (out), turn out, fit out, rig (out); *informal* get up; *archaic* apparel, habit, invest.

2 *a valley clothed in conifers* COVER, blanket, carpet; envelop, swathe.

clothes plural noun *his clothes are too big for him* CLOTHING, garments, attire, garb, dress, wear, costume; *informal* gear, togs, duds, threads, getup; *formal* apparel; *archaic* raiment, habiliments, vestments.

clothes horse noun See note below.

WORD NOTE **clothes horse**

Clothes horse is in danger of being supplanted by the trendier *fashion victim,* but there's an important distinction. A fashion victim is led astray by the vicissitudes of the prevailing runway looks, without regard to their suitability or attractiveness for the wearer. A clothes horse, while not as concerned with keeping up with the latest fashion, still devotes what some might think to be an unconscionable amount of time and effort to matters of dress. Clothes horses occasionally set the fashion; fashion victims never do. **—EM**

clothing noun See CLOTHES.

cloud noun **1** *dark clouds* storm cloud, cloudbank, cloud cover; mackerel sky. See table.

2 *a cloud of exhaust smoke* MASS, billow; pall, mantle, blanket.

▸ verb **1** *the sky clouded* BECOME CLOUDY, cloud over, become overcast, lower, blacken, darken.

2 *the sand is churned up, clouding the water* MAKE CLOUDY, make murky, dirty, darken, blacken.

3 *anger clouded my judgment* CONFUSE, muddle, obscure, fog, muddy, mar.

PHRASE: **on cloud nine** *Amy was on cloud nine when she passed the bar exam* ECSTATIC, rapturous, joyful, elated, blissful, euphoric, in seventh heaven, walking on air, transported, in raptures, delighted, thrilled, overjoyed, over the moon, on top of the world, tickled pink.

cloudy adjective **1** *a cloudy sky* OVERCAST, clouded; dark, gray, black, leaden, murky; somber, dismal, heavy, gloomy; sunless, starless; hazy, misty, foggy. ANTONYMS clear, bright.

2 *cloudy water* MURKY, muddy, milky, dirty, opaque, turbid. ANTONYM clear.

3 *his eyes grew cloudy* TEARFUL, teary, weepy, lachrymose; moist, watery; misty, blurred. ANTONYMS clear, dry.

clout *informal* noun **1** *a clout on the ear* SMACK, slap, thump, punch, blow, hit, cuff, box, clip; *informal* whack, wallop.

2 *her clout in the business world* INFLUENCE, power, weight, sway, leverage, control, say; dominance, authority; *informal* teeth, muscle.

▸ verb *he clouted me* HIT, strike, punch, smack, slap, cuff, thump, buffet; *informal* wallop, belt, whack, clobber, sock, bop,

cloven adjective *the cloven hoof of an antelope* SPLIT, divided, cleft.

CLOUDS

Cloud Genera
altocumulus
altostratus
cirrocumulus
cirrostratus
cirrus
cumulonimbus
cumulus
nimbostratus
stratocumulus
stratus

Cloud Species
calvus
capillatus
castellanus/castellatus
congestus
fibratus
floccus
fractus
humilis
lenticularis
mediocris
nebulosus
spissatus
stratiformis
stratiformus
uncinus

Cloud Varieties
duplicatus
intortus
lacunosus
mammatus
opacus
perlucidus
radiatus
translucidas
undulatus
vertebratus

Accessory Clouds
scud cloud/pannus
cap cloud/pileus
veil cloud/velum

Stratospheric Clouds
mother-of-pearl/
nacreous
luminous/noctilucent

Other Types and Features
anabatic
anvil/incus
arch/arcus
banner
billow
bow
chinook
cloudlet
contrail
fall streaks
flanking line
Foehn wall
fog
fumulus
funnel cloud
mackerel sky
mamma
mare's tails
mesoscale
nimbus
orographic
praecipitatio
pyrocumulus
rain cloud
storm cloud
streamer
thundercloud
thunderhead
tuba
virga
wall cloud
wave cloud

Types of Anvil Clouds
cumuliform
back-sheared
mushroom

clown noun **1** *a circus clown* COMEDIAN; jester, fool, zany.

2 *the class clown* JOKER, comedian, comic, humorist, wag, wit, prankster, jester, buffoon; *informal* laugh, kidder, wisecracker.

3 *bureaucratic clowns* FOOL, idiot, dolt, ass, simpleton, ignoramus; bungler, blunderer; *informal* moron, meatball, bozo, jackass, chump, numbskull, numbnuts, nincompoop, halfwit, bonehead, knucklehead, fathead, birdbrain, twit, nitwit, twerp.

▸ verb *Harvey* ***clowned around*** FOOL AROUND, play the fool, play around, monkey around; joke (around), jest; *informal* mess around, horse around.

cloying adjective *her romance novels are too cloying for my taste* SICKLY, syrupy, saccharine, oversweet; sickening, nauseating; mawkish, sentimental, twee; *informal* over the top, mushy, slushy, sloppy, gooey, cheesy, corny, cornball, sappy.

club[1] noun **1** *a canoeing club* SOCIETY, association, organization, institution, group, circle, band, body, ring, crew; alliance, league, union.

2 *the city has great clubs* NIGHTCLUB, disco, discotheque, bar.

3 *the top club in the league* TEAM, squad, side, lineup, franchise.

club[2] noun *a wooden club* CUDGEL, truncheon, bludgeon, baton, stick, mace, bat, blackjack, nightstick.

▸ verb *he was clubbed with an iron bar* CUDGEL, bludgeon, bash, beat, hit, strike, batter, belabor; *informal* clout, clobber.

clue noun 1 *give me just one clue | police are searching for clues* HINT, indication, sign, signal, pointer, trace, indicator; lead, tip, tipoff; **(clues)** EVIDENCE, information.

2 *a crossword clue* QUESTION, problem, puzzle, riddle, poser, conundrum. PHRASES: **clue in** *informal if you're missing any of the facts, we can clue you in* INFORM, notify, make aware, prime; keep up to date, keep posted; *informal* tip off, give the lowdown, fill in on, put in the picture, put wise, get/keep up to speed. **not have a clue** *informal you expect me to explain her motives, but I do not have a clue* HAVE NO IDEA, be ignorant, not have an inkling; be baffled, be mystified, be at a loss; *informal* be clueless, not have the faintest/foggiest/slightest idea.

clump noun 1 *a clump of trees* CLUSTER, thicket, group, bunch, assemblage.

2 *a clump of earth* LUMP, clod, mass, wad, glob, gob.

▸ verb 1 *galaxies clump together* CLUSTER, group, collect, gather, assemble, congregate, mass.

2 *they were clumping around upstairs* STAMP, stomp, clomp, tramp, lumber; thump, thud, bang; *informal* galumph.

clumsy adjective 1 *she was terribly clumsy* AWKWARD, uncoordinated, ungainly, graceless, inelegant; inept, maladroit, unskillful, unhandy, accident-prone, like a bull in a china shop, all thumbs; *informal* ham-fisted, butterfingered, having two left feet, klutzy. ANTONYM graceful.

2 *a clumsy contraption* UNWIELDY, cumbersome, bulky, awkward. ANTONYM elegant.

3 *a clumsy remark* GAUCHE, awkward, graceless; unsubtle, uncouth, boorish, crass; tactless, insensitive, thoughtless, undiplomatic, indelicate, ill-judged. ANTONYM tactful.

clunker *informal* noun 1 *his first play was a real clunker* FAILURE, flop, bust, dud, turkey.

2 *he's got loads of money, but he still drives an old clunker* JALOPY, lemon, rustbucket, bucket of bolts, crate.

cluster noun 1 *clusters of berries* BUNCH, clump, mass, knot, group, clutch, bundle, truss.

2 *a cluster of spectators* CROWD, group, knot, huddle, bunch, throng, flock, pack, band; *informal* gang, gaggle.

▸ verb *they clustered around the television* CONGREGATE, gather, collect, group, assemble; huddle, crowd, flock.

clutch[1] verb *she clutched his arm* GRIP, grasp, clasp, cling to, hang on to, clench, hold. PHRASE: **clutch at** *she saved herself by clutching at a branch* REACH FOR, snatch at, make a grab for, catch at, claw at.

clutch[2] noun 1 *a clutch of eggs* GROUP, batch.

2 *a clutch of awards* GROUP, collection; raft, armful; *informal* load, bunch, ton.

clutches plural noun *she's married to a hateful man who has her in his clutches* POWER, control, domination, command, rule, tyranny; hands, hold, grip, grasp, claws, jaws, tentacles; custody.

clutter noun 1 *a clutter of toys* MESS, jumble, litter, heap, tangle, muddle, hodgepodge.

2 *a desk full of clutter* DISORDER, chaos, disarray, untidiness, mess, confusion; litter, rubbish, junk.

▸ verb *the garden was cluttered with tools* LITTER, mess up, disarrange; be strewn, be scattered; *literary* bestrew.

coach[1] noun 1 *an air-conditioned coach shuttled us to the casino* BUS, minibus; *dated* omnibus.

2 *chiefly Brit.* *a railroad coach* CAR, carriage, wagon, compartment, van, Pullman.

3 *a coach and horses* HORSE-DRAWN CARRIAGE, hackney, hansom, gig, landau, brougham.

coach[2] noun *a football coach* INSTRUCTOR, trainer, manager; teacher, tutor, mentor, guru.

▸ verb *she coached Richard in math* INSTRUCT, teach, tutor, school, educate; drill; train.

coagulate verb *a drug that helps the blood to coagulate* CONGEAL, clot, thicken, jell; solidify, harden, set, dry.

coalesce verb *the puddles had coalesced into shallow streams* MERGE, unite, join together, combine, fuse, mingle, blend; amalgamate, consolidate, integrate, homogenize, converge.

coalition noun *the ruling four-party coalition* ALLIANCE, union, partnership, bloc, caucus; federation, league, association, confederation, consortium, syndicate, combine; amalgamation, merger.

coarse adjective 1 *coarse blankets* ROUGH, scratchy, prickly, wiry. ANTONYM soft.

2 *his coarse features* LARGE, rough, rough-hewn, heavy; ugly. ANTONYM delicate.

3 *a coarse boy* OAFISH, loutish, boorish, uncouth, rude, impolite, ill-mannered, uncivil; vulgar, common, rough, uncultured, crass. ANTONYMS sophisticated, refined.

4 *a coarse innuendo* VULGAR, crude, rude, off-color, dirty, filthy, smutty, indelicate, improper, unseemly, crass, tasteless, lewd, prurient, blue, farmyard.

coarsen verb 1 *hands coarsened by work* ROUGHEN, toughen, harden. ANTONYM soften.

2 *I had been coarsened by the army* DESENSITIZE, dehumanize; dull, deaden. ANTONYM refine.

coast noun *the houses along the coast* SEABOARD, coastal region, coastline, seashore, shore, foreshore, shoreline, seaside, waterfront, littoral; *literary* strand.

▸ verb *the car coasted down a hill* FREEWHEEL, cruise, taxi, drift, glide, sail.

coat noun 1 *a winter coat* OVERCOAT, jacket. See table on page 151.

2 *a dog's coat* FUR, hair, wool, fleece; hide, pelt, skin.

3 *a coat of paint* LAYER, covering, coating, skin, film, wash; plating, glaze, varnish, veneer, patina; deposit.

▸ verb *the tube was coated with wax* COVER, paint, glaze, varnish, wash; surface, veneer, laminate, plate, face; daub, smear, cake, plaster.

coating noun See COAT noun sense 3.

coax verb *you have to coax some of the children to speak* PERSUADE, wheedle, cajole, get around; beguile, seduce, inveigle, maneuver; *informal* sweet-talk, soft-soap, butter up, twist someone's arm.

COATS AND JACKETS

anorak	overcoat
bed jacket	parka
blanket coat	peacoat
blazer	pea jacket
bolero	peplum jacket
bomber jacket	puffy jacket/coat
bush jacket	raglan
capote	rain jacket
car coat	raincoat
cardigan	redingote
Chanel jacket	reefer
chesterfield	safari jacket
commuter jacket/coat	shell
cutaway	shirt jacket
dinner jacket	single-breasted
dolman	(jacket/coat)
double-breasted	slicker
jacket/coat	sports coat
doublet	sports jacket
duffle coat	stadium jacket
field coat	storm coat
flight jacket	suit coat
frock coat	surcoat
fur coat	surtout
greatcoat	sweater coat
happi coat	swing coat
jeans jacket	tailcoat
jibba	topcoat
lumberjack jacket	topper
Mackinaw	ulster
mackintosh	whisper jacket
mess jacket	windbreaker
Nehru jacket	trench coat
Norfolk jacket	

cobble PHRASE: **cobble together** *she cobbled together a rough draft* PREPARE ROUGHLY/HASTILY, make roughly/hastily, throw together; improvise, contrive, rig (up), whip up; *informal* rustle up.

cocaine noun *they intercepted a multimillion-dollar shipment of cocaine* informal COKE, crack (cocaine), blow, freebase, nose candy, rock, snow.

cock noun *strutting around like a barnyard cock* ROOSTER, cockerel, capon.

▸ verb **1** *he cocked his head* TILT, tip, angle, incline, dip.

2 *she cocked her little finger* BEND, flex, crook, curve.

3 *the dog cocked its leg* LIFT, raise, hold up.

cockeyed adjective *informal* **1** *that picture is cockeyed* CROOKED, awry, askew, lopsided, tilted, off-center, skewed, skew, misaligned.

2 *a cockeyed scheme* ABSURD, preposterous, ridiculous, ludicrous, farcical, laughable, cockamamie, risible, idiotic, stupid, foolish, silly, inane, imbecilic, half-baked, harebrained; impractical, unfeasible; irrational, illogical, nonsensical, crazy, daft.

cockpit noun *I was invited into the cockpit to meet the pilot* FLIGHT DECK, helm, control room; driver's seat.

cocksure adjective *he won't be so cocksure when he gets in the ring with our boy* ARROGANT, conceited, overweening, overconfident, cocky, proud, vain, self-important, egotistical, presumptuous; smug, patronizing, pompous; *informal* high and mighty, puffed-up. ANTONYM modest.

cocktail noun See table.

cocky adjective *military school has certainly made him less cocky* ARROGANT, conceited, overweening, overconfident, cocksure, self-important, egotistical, presumptuous, boastful, self-assertive; bold, forward, insolent, cheeky, puffed-up. ANTONYM modest.

cocoon verb **1** *he cocooned her in a towel* WRAP, swathe, swaddle, muffle, cloak, enfold, envelop, cover, fold.

2 *he was cocooned in the university* PROTECT, shield, shelter, screen, cushion, insulate, isolate, cloister.

coddle verb *your sons are too old for you to be coddling them* PAMPER, cosset, mollycoddle; spoil, indulge, overindulge, pander to; baby, mother, wait on hand and foot. ANTONYM neglect.

code noun **1** *a secret code* CIPHER, key; hieroglyphics; cryptogram.

2 *a strict social code* MORALITY, convention, etiquette, protocol, value system.

3 *the penal code* LAW(S), rules, regulations; constitution, system.

codify verb *the bill codified these standards for the first time* SYSTEMATIZE, systemize, organize, arrange, order, structure; tabulate, catalog, list, sort, index, classify, categorize, file, log.

coerce verb *he was coerced into giving evidence* PRESSURE, pressurize, press, push, constrain; force, compel, oblige, browbeat, bludgeon, bully, threaten, intimidate, dragoon, twist someone's arm; *informal* railroad, squeeze, lean on. See note at COMPEL.

coercion noun *Johnson claims the police used coercion to extract a confession* FORCE, compulsion, constraint, duress, oppression, enforcement, harassment, intimidation, threats, arm-twisting, pressure.

COCKTAILS AND OTHER MIXED DRINKS

Alabama slammer	merry widow
amaretto sour	mimosa
American Beauty	mint julep
Bellini	mudslide
Black Russian	negroni
Bloody Mary	New York sour
brandy Alexander	old-fashioned
Bronx cocktail	Pimm's cup
Cape Codder	piña colada
champagne cocktail	pink lady
cosmopolitan	pisco sour
Cuba libre	planter's punch
daiquiri	red lion
dirty martini	Rob Roy
fuzzy navel	rum runner
Gibson	rusty nail
gimlet	sangria
gin and tonic	screwdriver
gin rickey	sea breeze
grasshopper	shandy
greyhound	sidecar
Harvey Wallbanger	Singapore sling
highball	sloe gin fizz
hot buttered rum	spritzer
hot toddy	stinger
Irish coffee	tequila sunrise
Jack Rose	toasted almond
kamikaze	Tom and Jerry
Kir royale	Tom Collins
lemon drop	vodka tonic
Long Island iced tea	whiskey sour
mai tai	White Russian
Manhattan	yellow bird
margarita	zombie
martini	

See also tables at BEER, LIQUOR, and WINE.

coffee noun *a cup of coffee and a raspberry danish informal* joe, java. See table.

COFFEES

Altura	Kauai
Amatitlan	Kenya
Angola	Kilimanjaro
Antiqua	Kivu
Arabica	Kona
Baba Budans	Kopi Luwak
Barahona	La Lucie
Blawan	Liberica
Blue Java	Los Volcanos
Blue Mountain	Malabar
Bourbon de Coatepec	Malawi
Bourbon Santos	Malaysia
Brazil	Mandelhing
Bukoba	Maui Kaanapali
Buqisu	Medellin Excelso
Burundi	Mexico
Cameroon	Mocca
Casa Misael	Mocha/Moka
Celebes	Moloka'i
Chamba	Mysore
Chaqqa	Narino
chicory	Nicaragua
China	Oahu
cinnamon roast	Oaxaca
city roast	Panama
Colombia	Papua New Guinea
Costa Rica	Peaberry
Cuba	Puerto Rico
Cucutas	Reunion
Djimmah	Robusta
Ecuador	Rwanda
El Salvador	Santo Domingo
espresso	Santos
Ethiopia	Sulawesi
Ethiopia Harrar	Sumatra
French roast	Tachiras
Greek	Tanzania
Guatemala	Tarrazu
Haiti	Timor
Holualoa	Turkish
Honduras	Uganda
India	Venezuela
Italian roast	Viennese roast
Ituri	Vietnam
Ivory Coast	Yemen
Jamaica	Yirgacheffe
Jampit	Yunnan
Java	Zambia
Kalossi	Zimbabwe

coffer noun **1** *every church had a coffer* STRONGBOX, money box, cashbox, money chest, treasure chest, safe; casket, box.

2 (**coffers**) *the government coffers* FUND(S), reserves, resources, money, finances, wealth, cash, capital, purse; treasury, exchequer; *informal* pork barrel.

coffin noun *a simple pine coffin* casket; sarcophagus; *informal* box; *humorous* wooden overcoat.

cogent adjective *a cogent argument* CONVINCING, compelling, strong, forceful, powerful, potent, weighty, effective; valid, sound, plausible, telling; impressive, persuasive, eloquent, credible, influential; conclusive, authoritative; logical, reasoned, rational, reasonable, lucid, coherent, clear. See note at BELIEVABLE.

cogitate verb *formal I may have to* ***cogitate on*** *that one for a bit* THINK ABOUT/ON/OVER, contemplate, consider, mull over, meditate on, muse on/over, ponder, reflect on, deliberate on/over, ruminate on/over; dwell on, brood on, chew over; *informal* put on one's thinking cap for.

cognate adjective *formal the cognate words in English and German* ASSOCIATED, related, connected, allied, linked; similar, like, alike, akin, kindred, comparable, parallel, corresponding, analogous.

cognition noun *the head injury has impaired his speech and cognition* PERCEPTION, discernment, apprehension, learning, understanding, comprehension, insight; reasoning, thinking, thought.

cognizant adjective *formal* See AWARE sense 1.

cohabit verb *her brother James and this Marilyn Monroe lookalike are cohabiting in Soho* LIVE TOGETHER, live as a couple; *informal* shack up; *dated* live in sin.

cohere verb **1** *the stories cohere into a convincing whole* STICK TOGETHER, hold together, be united, bind, fuse.

2 *this view does not cohere with others* BE CONSISTENT, hang together.

coherent adjective *the patient's speech is more coherent today* LOGICAL, reasoned, reasonable, rational, sound, cogent, consistent, consilient; clear, lucid, articulate; intelligible, comprehensible. ANTONYM muddled.

cohesion noun *the subplots lack cohesion* UNITY, togetherness, solidarity, bond, coherence; connection, linkage.

cohort noun **1** *a Roman army cohort* UNIT, force, corps, division, brigade, battalion, regiment, squadron, company, troop, contingent, legion, phalanx.

2 *the 1940–44 birth cohort of women* GROUP, grouping, category, class, set, division, batch, list; age group, generation.

3 *a party thrown by her departmental cohorts* COLLEAGUE, companion, associate, friend.

coil noun *coils of rope* LOOP, twist, turn, curl, convolution; spiral, helix, corkscrew.

▸ verb *he coiled her hair around his finger* WIND, loop, twist, curl, curve, bend, twine, entwine; spiral, corkscrew.

coin noun **1** *coins in my pocket* penny, nickel, dime, quarter; piece.

2 *large amounts of coin* COINAGE, coins, specie; change, loose change, small change; silver, gold.

▸ verb **1** *dimes were coined* MINT, stamp, strike, cast, punch, die, mold, forge, make.

2 *he coined the term* INVENT, create, make up, conceive, originate, think up, dream up.

coincide verb **1** *the events coincided* OCCUR SIMULTANEOUSLY, happen together, be concurrent, concur, coexist.

2 *their interests do not always coincide* CORRESPOND, tally, agree, accord, concur, match, fit, be consistent, equate, harmonize, be compatible, dovetail, correlate; *informal* square. ANTONYM differ.

coincidence noun **1** *too close to be mere coincidence* ACCIDENT, chance, serendipity, fortuity, providence, happenstance, fate; a fluke.

2 *the coincidence of inflation and unemployment* COOCCURRENCE, coexistence, conjunction, simultaneity, contemporaneity, concomitance.

3 *a coincidence of interests* CORRESPONDENCE, agreement, accord, concurrence, consistency, conformity, harmony, compatibility.

coincidental adjective **1** *a coincidental resemblance* ACCIDENTAL, chance, fluky, random; fortuitous, adventitious, serendipitous; unexpected, unforeseen, unintentional, inadvertent, unplanned.

2 *the coincidental disappearance of the two men* SIMULTANEOUS, concurrent, coincident, contemporaneous, concomitant.

coitus noun *technical* See SEX sense 1.

cold adjective **1** *a cold day* CHILLY, chill, cool, freezing, icy, snowy, wintry, frosty, frigid, gelid; bitter, biting, raw, bone-chilling, nippy, arctic. ANTONYM hot.

2 *I'm very cold* CHILLY, chilled, cool, freezing, frozen, shivery, numb, benumbed; hypothermic. ANTONYM hot.

3 *a cold reception* UNFRIENDLY, inhospitable, unwelcoming, forbidding, cool, frigid, frosty, glacial, lukewarm, indifferent, unfeeling, unemotional, formal, stiff. ANTONYMS friendly, warm.

cold-blooded adjective *a cold-blooded killer* CRUEL, callous, sadistic, inhuman, inhumane, pitiless, merciless, ruthless, unforgiving, unfeeling, uncaring, heartless; savage, brutal, barbaric, barbarous; cold, cold-hearted, unemotional.

cold-hearted adjective *his cold-hearted wife* UNFEELING, unloving, uncaring, unsympathetic, unemotional, unfriendly, uncharitable, unkind, insensitive; hard-hearted, stony-hearted, heartless, hard, cold.

collaborate verb **1** *they collaborated on the project* CO-OPERATE, join forces, team up, band together, work together, participate, combine, ally; pool resources, put —— heads together.

2 *they collaborated with the enemy* COLLUDE, conspire, fraternize, co-operate, consort, sympathize; *informal* be in cahoots.

collaborator noun **1** *his collaborator on the book* CO-WORKER, partner, associate, colleague, confederate; assistant.

2 *a wartime collaborator* QUISLING, fraternizer, collaborationist, colluder, (enemy) sympathizer; traitor, fifth columnist.

collapse verb **1** *the roof collapsed* CAVE IN, fall in, subside, fall down, give (way), crumple, buckle, sag, slump.

2 *he collapsed last night* FAINT, pass out, black out, lose consciousness, keel over, swoon; *informal* conk out.

3 *he collapsed in tears* BREAK DOWN, go to pieces, lose control, be overcome, crumble; *informal* crack up.

4 *peace talks collapsed* BREAK DOWN, fail, fall through, fold, founder, miscarry, come to grief, be unsuccessful; end; *informal* flop, fizzle out.

▸ noun **1** *the collapse of the roof* CAVE-IN, subsidence.

2 *her collapse on stage* FAINTING FIT, faint, blackout, loss of consciousness, swoon; *Medicine* syncope.

3 *the collapse of the talks* BREAKDOWN, failure, disintegration; end.

4 *he suffered a collapse* BREAKDOWN, nervous breakdown, personal crisis, psychological trauma; *informal* crack-up.

collar noun **1** *a shirt collar* NECKBAND, choker; *historical* ruff, gorget, bertha.

2 *a collar around the pipe* RING, band, collet, sleeve, flange.

▸ verb *informal* **1** *he collared a thief* APPREHEND, arrest, catch, capture, seize; take prisoner, take into custody, detain; *informal* nab, pinch, bust, pick up, pull in.

2 *she collared me in the street* ACCOST, waylay, hail, approach, detain, stop, halt, catch, confront, importune; *informal* buttonhole.

collate verb **1** *the system is used to collate information* COLLECT, gather, accumulate, assemble; combine, aggregate, put together; arrange, organize.

2 *we must collate these two sources* COMPARE, contrast, set side by side, juxtapose, weigh against.

collateral noun *she put up her house as collateral for the loan* SECURITY, surety, guarantee, guaranty, insurance, indemnity, indemnification; backing.

colleague noun *Dr. Clinton's colleagues started a scholarship fund in his name* COWORKER, fellow worker, workmate, teammate, associate, partner, collaborator, ally, confederate.

collect verb **1** *he collected the rubbish | she collects Hummel figurines* GATHER, accumulate, assemble; amass, stockpile, pile up, heap up, store (up), hoard, save; mass, accrue. ANTONYMS squander, distribute. See note at GATHER.

2 *a crowd collected in the square* GATHER, assemble, meet, muster, congregate, convene, converge, flock together. ANTONYM disperse.

3 *I must collect the children* FETCH, go/come to get, call for, meet. ANTONYMS take, drop off.

4 *they collect money for charity* RAISE, appeal for, ask for, solicit; obtain, acquire, gather. ANTONYMS give away, distribute.

5 *he paused to* ***collect himself*** RECOVER, regain one's composure, pull oneself together, steady oneself; *informal* get a grip (on oneself). ANTONYMS disperse, distribute.

6 *she collected her thoughts* GATHER, summon (up), muster, get together, marshal. ANTONYMS disperse, distribute.

collected adjective *she is the most collected gymnast on the team* CALM, cool, self-possessed, self-controlled, composed, poised; serene, tranquil, relaxed, unruffled, unperturbed, untroubled; placid, quiet, sedate, phlegmatic; *informal* unfazed, nonplussed, together, laid-back. ANTONYMS excited, hysterical.

collection noun **1** *a collection of stolen items* HOARD, pile, heap, stack, stock, store, stockpile; accumulation, reserve, supply, bank, pool, fund, mine, reservoir.

2 *a collection of shoppers* GROUP, crowd, body, assemblage, gathering, throng; knot, cluster; multitude, bevy, party, band, horde, pack, flock, swarm, mob; *informal* gang, load, gaggle.

3 *a collection of Victorian dolls* SET, series; array, assortment.

4 *a collection of short stories* ANTHOLOGY, selection, compendium, treasury, compilation, miscellany, potpourri.

5 *a collection for the poor* DONATIONS, contributions, gifts, subscription(s); *historical* alms.

6 *a church collection* OFFERING, offertory, tithe.

collective adjective *our collective interests* COMMON, shared, joint, combined, mutual, communal, pooled; united, allied, cooperative, collaborative. ANTONYM individual.

college noun **1** *a college of technology* SCHOOL, academy, university, polytechnic, institute, seminary, conservatoire, conservatory. See table at SCHOOL.

2 *the college of physicians* ASSOCIATION, society, club, institute, body, fellowship, guild, lodge, order, fraternity, league, union, alliance.

collide verb **1** *the trains **collided with** each other* CRASH INTO, hit, strike, impact, run into, bump into, meet head-on, cannon into, plow into, barrel into.

2 *in her work, politics and metaphysics collide* CONFLICT, clash; differ, diverge, disagree, be at odds, be incompatible.

collision noun **1** *a collision in the passing lane* CRASH, accident, impact, smash, bump, hit, fender bender, wreck, pileup.

2 *a collision between two ideas* CONFLICT, clash; disagreement, incompatibility, contradiction.

colloquial adjective *she just loved the colloquial expressions of her Southern in-laws* INFORMAL, conversational, everyday, nonliterary; unofficial, idiomatic, slangy, vernacular, popular, demotic. ANTONYM formal.

collusion noun *there has been collusion between the security forces and paramilitary groups* CONSPIRACY, connivance, complicity, intrigue, plotting, secret understanding, collaboration, scheming.

cologne noun *Ms. Williams wears a cologne that smells like strawberries* SCENT, perfume, fragrance, eau de toilette; aftershave.

colonist noun *the first European colonists of North America* SETTLER, colonizer, colonial, pioneer; immigrant, newcomer, homesteader. ANTONYM native.

colonize verb *the Germans colonized Tanganyika in 1885* SETTLE (IN), people, populate; occupy, take over, seize, capture, subjugate.

colonnade noun *we took a stroll through the colonnade* ROW OF COLUMNS; portico, gallery, stoa, peristyle; arcade.

colony noun **1** *a French colony* SETTLEMENT, dependency, protectorate, satellite, territory, outpost, province.

2 *an artists' colony* COMMUNITY, commune; quarter, district, ghetto.

color noun **1** *the lights changed color* HUE, shade, tint, tone, coloration.

2 *oil color* PAINT, pigment, colorant, dye, stain, tint, wash.

3 *the color in her cheeks* REDNESS, pinkness, rosiness, ruddiness, blush, flush, bloom.

4 *people of every color* SKIN COLORING, skin tone, coloring; race, ethnic group.

5 *anecdotes add color to the text* VIVIDNESS, life, liveliness, vitality, excitement, interest, richness, zest, spice, piquancy, impact, force; *informal* oomph, pizzazz, punch, kick; *literary* salt.

6 *the regimental colors.* See FLAG[1] noun.

▸ verb **1** *the wood was colored blue* TINT, dye, stain, paint, pigment, wash.

2 *she colored* BLUSH, redden, go pink, go red, flush.

3 *the experience colored her outlook* INFLUENCE, affect, taint, warp, skew, distort, bias, prejudice.

4 *they color evidence to make a story sell* EXAGGERATE, overstate, embroider, embellish, dramatize, enhance, varnish; falsify, misreport, manipulate.

colorful adjective **1** *a colorful picture* BRIGHTLY COLORED, vivid, vibrant, brilliant, radiant, rich; gaudy, glaring, garish; multicolored, multicolor, rainbow, varicolored, harlequin, polychromatic, psychedelic, neon, jazzy.

2 *a colorful account* VIVID, graphic, lively, animated, dramatic, fascinating, interesting, stimulating, scintillating, evocative.

colorless adjective **1** *a colorless liquid* UNCOLORED, white, bleached; *literary* achromatic. ANTONYM colored.

2 *her colorless face* PALE, pallid, wan, anemic, bloodless, ashen, white, waxen, pasty, peaked, sickly, drained, drawn, ghostly, deathly. ANTONYM rosy.

3 *a colorless personality* UNINTERESTING, dull, boring, tedious, dry, dreary; unexciting, bland, weak, insipid, vapid, vacuous, feeble, wishy-washy, lame, lifeless, spiritless, anemic, bloodless; nondescript, characterless, plain-vanilla. ANTONYM colorful.

colossal adjective *a colossal building | we made some colossal mistakes* HUGE, massive, enormous, gigantic, giant, mammoth, vast, immense, monumental, prodigious, mountainous, titanic, towering, king-size(d), economy-size(d); *informal* monster, whopping, humongous, jumbo, ginormous. ANTONYM tiny.

column noun **1** *arches supported by massive columns* PILLAR, post, support, upright, baluster, pier, pile, pilaster, stanchion; obelisk, monolith; Doric column, Ionic column, Corinthian column, Tuscan column.

2 *a column in the paper* ARTICLE, piece, item, story, report, account, write-up, feature, review, notice, editorial.

3 *we walked in a column* LINE, file, queue, procession, train, cavalcade, convoy.

columnist noun *a columnist for her school newspaper* WRITER, contributor, journalist, correspondent, newspaperman, newspaperwoman, newsman, newswoman; wordsmith, penman; critic, reviewer, commentator; *informal* scribbler, pencil pusher, hack.

coma noun *doctors do not expect him to come out of the coma* state of unconsciousness; *Medicine* persistent vegetative state.

comatose adjective **1** *he was comatose after the accident* UNCONSCIOUS, in a coma, insensible, insensate.

2 *informal she lay comatose in the sun* INERT, inactive, lethargic, sluggish, torpid, languid; somnolent, sleeping, dormant.

comb verb **1** *she combed her hair* GROOM, brush, untangle, smooth, straighten, neaten, tidy, arrange; curry.

2 *police combed the area* SEARCH, scour, explore, sweep, probe, hunt through, forage through, poke around in, go over, go over with a fine-tooth comb; leave no stone unturned.

combat noun *he was killed in combat* BATTLE, fighting, action, hostilities, conflict, war, warfare.

▸ verb *they tried to combat the disease* FIGHT, battle, tackle, attack, counter, resist, withstand; impede, block, thwart, inhibit; stop, halt, prevent, check, curb.

combatant noun **1** *a combatant in the war* FIGHTER, soldier, serviceman, servicewoman, warrior, trooper.

2 *combatants in the computer market* CONTENDER, adversary, opponent, competitor, challenger, rival.

▸ adjective *combatant armies* WARRING, at war, opposing, belligerent, fighting, battling.

combative adjective *Mosley's combative language* PUGNACIOUS, aggressive, antagonistic, quarrelsome, argumentative, contentious, hostile, truculent, belligerent, bellicose, militant; *informal* spoiling for a fight. ANTONYM conciliatory.

combination noun **1** *a combination of ancient and modern* AMALGAMATION, amalgam, merger, merging, blend, mixture, mix, fusion, marriage, coalition, integration, incorporation, synthesis, composite; *informal* combo.

2 *he acted in combination with his brother* COOPERATION, collaboration, association, union, partnership, league.

combine verb **1** *he combines comedy with tragedy* AMALGAMATE, integrate, incorporate, merge, mix, fuse, blend; bind, join, marry, unify. See note at JOIN.

2 *teachers combined to tackle the problem* CO-OPERATE, collaborate, join forces, get together, unite, team up, throw in one's lot; *informal* gang up.

combustible adjective *piles of combustible material* INFLAMMABLE, flammable, incendiary, ignitable.

combustion noun *the combustion of fossil fuels* BURNING; kindling, ignition.

come verb **1** *come and listen* MOVE NEARER, move closer, approach, advance, draw close/closer, draw near/nearer; proceed; *archaic* draw nigh. ANTONYM go away.

2 *they came last night* ARRIVE, get here/there, make it, appear, come on the scene; approach, enter, turn up, come along, materialize; *informal* show (up), roll in/up, blow in, show one's face. ANTONYM leave.

3 *they* ***came to*** *a stream* REACH, arrive at, get to, make it to; come across, run across, happen on/upon, chance on/upon, come upon, stumble on/upon; end up at, wind up at.

4 *the dress* ***comes to*** *her ankles* EXTEND TO, stretch to, reach, come as far as.

5 *she* ***comes from*** *Italy* BE FROM, be a native of, hail from, originate in; live in, reside in.

6 *attacks came without warning* HAPPEN, occur, take place, come about, transpire, fall, present itself, crop up, materialize, arise, arrive, appear; ensue, follow; *literary* come to pass, befall.

7 *the shoes come in black and brown* BE AVAILABLE, be for sale; be made, be produced.

PHRASES: **come about** *the change came about in 1989* HAPPEN, occur, take place, transpire, fall; crop up, materialize, arise, arrive, appear, surface; ensue, follow; *literary* come to pass, befall. **come across 1** *they came across his friends* MEET/FIND BY CHANCE, meet, run into, run across, come upon, chance on/upon, stumble on/upon, happen on/upon; discover, encounter, find, locate; *informal* bump into. **2** *the emotion comes across* BE COMMUNICATED, be perceived, get across, be clear, be understood, register, sink in, strike home. **3** *she came across as cool* SEEM, appear, look, sound, look to be. **come along 1** *the puppies are coming along nicely* PROGRESS, develop, shape up; come on, turn out; improve, get better, pick up, rally, recover. **2** *come along!* HURRY (UP), be quick, get a move on, come on, look lively, speed up, move faster; *informal* get moving, get cracking, step on it, move it, shake a leg, make it snappy; *dated* make haste. **come apart** *if the straw is too short, the bales will come apart* BREAK APART, break up, fall to bits/pieces, fall apart, disintegrate, come unstuck, separate, split, tear. **come around 1** *the smelling salts helped him come around* REGAIN CONSCIOUSNESS, recover consciousness, come to, come to one's senses, recover, revive, awake, wake up. **2** *I* ***came around to*** *her view* BE CONVERTED TO, be won over by, agree with, change one's mind to, be persuaded by; give way to, yield to, relent to. **3** *Friday the 13th comes around every few months* OCCUR, take place, happen, come up, crop up, arise; recur, reoccur, return, reappear. **4** *come around for a drink* VISIT, stop by, drop by/in/over, come over, pop in/over. **come back** *are you coming back before dinner?* RETURN, get back, arrive home, come home; come again. **come between** *I let my drinking come between me and my family* ALIENATE, estrange, separate, divide, split up, break up, disunite, set at odds. **come by** *where did you ever come by such a magnificent horse?* OBTAIN, acquire, gain, get, find, pick up, procure, secure; buy, purchase; *informal* get one's hands on, get hold of, bag, score, swing. **come down** *the report comes down against a zoning variance in the wetlands* DECIDE, conclude, settle; choose, opt, plump. **come down on** *she came down on him like a ton of bricks.* See REPRIMAND verb. **come down to** *it comes down to two choices: stay in school or find another place to live* AMOUNT TO, add up to, constitute, boil down to, be equivalent to. **come down with** *the whole family has come down with chicken pox* FALL ILL WITH, fall sick with, be taken ill with, show symptoms of, become infected with, get, catch, develop, contract, fall victim to. **come forward** *Vera is always the first to come forward* VOLUNTEER, offer one's services, make oneself available. **come in** *you can't come in without a pass* ENTER, gain admission, cross the threshold. **come into** *Jerry came into a small fortune when his grandfather died* INHERIT, be left, be willed, be bequeathed. **come off** *if you make this meeting come off, you're probably looking at a promotion* SUCCEED, work, turn out well, work out, go as planned, produce the desired result, get results. **come on** *the new bookcases are coming on nicely* PROGRESS, develop, shape up, take shape, come along, turn out; improve. **come out 1** *it came out that he'd been to Rome* BECOME KNOWN, become apparent, come to light, emerge, transpire; get out, be discovered, be uncovered, be revealed, leak out, be disclosed. **2** *my book is coming out* BE PUBLISHED, be issued, be released, be brought out, be printed, go on sale. **3** *the flowers have come out* BLOOM, flower, open. **4** *it will come out all right* END, finish, conclude, work out, turn out; *informal* pan out. **5** *the councilman came out voluntarily* disclose one's homosexuality; *informal* come out of the closet. **come out with** *I didn't really mean to come out with those stupid remarks* UTTER, say, let out, blurt out, burst out with; issue, present. **come through 1** *we came through it OK* SURVIVE, get through, ride out, weather, live through, pull through; withstand, stand up to, endure, surmount, overcome; *informal* stick out. **2** *you* ***came through for*** *us* HELP, be there for. **come to 1** *the bill came to $17.50* AMOUNT TO, add up to, total, run to, equal. **2** *I came to in the ambulance* REGAIN CONSCIOUSNESS, recover consciousness, come around, come to one's senses, recover, revive, awake, wake up. **come up** *whatever comes up, we'll be ready*

ARISE, occur, happen, come about, transpire, emerge, surface, crop up, turn up, pop up. **come up to** **1** *she came up to his shoulder* REACH, come to, be as tall as, extend to. **2** *he never came up to her expectations* MEASURE UP TO, match up to, live up to, fulfill, satisfy, meet, equal, compare with; be good enough for; *informal* hold a candle to. **come up with** *Miranda has come up with a terrific idea* PRODUCE, devise, think up; propose, put forward, submit, suggest, recommend, advocate, introduce, moot.

comeback noun **1** *he made a determined comeback* RESURGENCE, recovery, return, rally, upturn.

2 *informal one of my best comebacks* RETORT, riposte, return, rejoinder; answer, reply, response.

comedian, comedienne noun **1** *a famous comedian* COMIC, comedienne, funny man, funny woman, humorist, gagster, stand-up.

2 *Dad was such a comedian* JOKER, jester, wit, wag, comic, wisecracker, jokester; prankster, clown, fool, buffoon; *informal* laugh, hoot, riot; *informal, dated* card.

comedown noun *informal* **1** *a bit of a comedown for a sergeant* LOSS OF STATUS, loss of face, humiliation, belittlement, demotion, degradation, disgrace.

2 *it's such a comedown after Christmas* ANTICLIMAX, letdown, disappointment, disillusionment, deflation, decline.

comedy noun **1** *he excels in comedy* LIGHT ENTERTAINMENT, comic theater, farce, situation comedy, satire, pantomime, comic opera; burlesque, slapstick; *informal* sitcom. ANTONYMS tragedy, drama.

2 *the comedy in their work* HUMOR, fun, funny side, comical aspect, absurdity, drollness, farce. ANTONYM gravity.

comely adjective *archaic*. See ATTRACTIVE sense 2.

come-on noun *informal the $200 rebate is a come-on for prospective car buyers* INDUCEMENT, incentive, attraction, lure, pull, draw, enticement, bait, carrot, temptation; fascination, charm, appeal, allure.

comeuppance noun *informal the bad guys always get their comeuppance in the final scene* JUST DESERTS, just punishment, due, retribution, requital, what's coming to one.

comfort noun **1** *travel in comfort* EASE, relaxation, repose, serenity, tranquility, contentment, coziness; luxury, opulence, prosperity; bed of roses.

2 *words of comfort* CONSOLATION, solace, condolence, sympathy, commiseration; support, reassurance, cheer.

▸ verb *a friend tried to comfort her* CONSOLE, solace, condole with, commiserate with, sympathize with; support, succor, ease, reassure, soothe, calm; cheer, hearten, uplift. ANTONYMS distress, depress.

comfortable adjective **1** *a comfortable lifestyle* PLEASANT, free from hardship; affluent, well-to-do, luxurious, opulent. ANTONYM harsh.

2 *a comfortable room* COZY, snug, warm, pleasant, agreeable; restful, homelike, homely; *informal* comfy. ANTONYM spartan.

3 *comfortable clothes* LOOSE, loose-fitting, casual; *informal* comfy.

4 *a comfortable pace* LEISURELY, unhurried, relaxed, easy, gentle, sedate, undemanding, slow; *informal* laid-back.

5 *they feel comfortable with each other* AT EASE, relaxed, secure, safe, unworried, contented, happy. ANTONYMS vulnerable, tense.

comforting adjective *Anne gave her a comforting hug* CONSOLING, sympathetic, compassionate, solicitous, tender, warm, caring, loving; supportive, reassuring, soothing, calming; cheering, heartening, encouraging.

comfortless adjective **1** *a comfortless house* GLOOMY, dreary, dismal, bleak, grim, somber; joyless, cheerless, depressing, disheartening, dispiriting, unwelcoming, uninviting; austere, spartan, institutional. ANTONYMS cozy, cheery.

2 *he left her comfortless* MISERABLE, heartbroken, grief-stricken, unhappy, sad, distressed, desolate, devastated, inconsolable, disconsolate, downcast, downhearted, dejected, cheerless, depressed, melancholy, gloomy, glum; *informal* blue, down in the dumps, down in/at the mouth. ANTONYM happy.

comic adjective *a comic play* HUMOROUS, funny, droll, amusing, hilarious, uproarious; comical, farcical, silly, slapstick, zany; witty, jocular; *informal* priceless, side-splitting, rib-tickling; *informal, dated* killing. See word spectrum on page 157. ANTONYM serious.

▸ noun **1** *a professional comic* COMEDIAN, comedienne, funny man/woman, humorist, wit; joker, clown; *informal* kidder, wisecracker.

2 *the paper no longer runs his favorite Sunday comic* comic strip, cartoon, comic book; *informal* funny.

comical adjective **1** *he could be quite comical* FUNNY, comic, humorous, droll, witty, jocular, hilarious, amusing, diverting, entertaining; *informal* jokey, wacky, waggish, side-splitting, rib-tickling, priceless, a scream, a laugh; *informal, dated* killing, a card, a caution. ANTONYM sensible.

2 *they look comical in those suits* SILLY, absurd, ridiculous, laughable, risible, ludicrous, preposterous, foolish; *informal* wacky, crazy. ANTONYM sensible.

coming adjective *the coming election* FORTHCOMING, imminent, impending, approaching; future, expected, anticipated; close, at hand, in store, in the offing, in the pipeline, on the horizon, on the way; *informal* in the cards.

▸ noun *the coming of spring* APPROACH, advance, advent, arrival, appearance, emergence, onset.

command verb **1** *he commanded his men to retreat* ORDER, tell, direct, instruct, call on, require; *literary* bid.

2 *Jones commanded a tank squadron* BE IN CHARGE OF, be in command of, be the leader of; head, lead, control, direct, manage, supervise, oversee; *informal* head up.

3 *they command great respect* RECEIVE, get, gain, secure.

▸ noun **1** *officers shouted commands* ORDER, instruction, directive, direction, commandment, injunction, decree, edict, demand, stipulation, requirement, exhortation, bidding, request.

2 *he had 160 men under his command* AUTHORITY, control, charge, power, direction, dominion, guidance; leadership, rule, government, management, supervision, jurisdiction. See note at JURISDICTION.

comic
uproarious
hysterical
hysterically funny
screamingly funny
hilarious
killing
killingly funny
side-splitting
humorous
comical
absurd
farcical
ridiculous
priceless
funny
zany
silly
slapstick
a barrel of laughs
a scream
a hoot
a laugh
rib-tickling
joking
jocular
amusing
facetious
witty
droll
waggish
diverting
entertaining
boring
bland
depressing
disturbing
distressing
dispiriting
disquieting
moving
upsetting
unhappy
unfortunate
awful
sorry
painful
pitiful
pitiable
piteous
pathetic
cheerless
desolate
dismal
gloomy
disastrous
sorrowful
sad
chilling
miserable
heartbreaking
heart-rending
melancholy
mortifying
wretched
grievous
traumatic
calamitous
doleful
mournful
agonizing
harrowing
tragic

3 *a brilliant command of Italian* KNOWLEDGE, mastery, grasp, comprehension, understanding.

commandeer verb *dozens of private homes were commandeered by the army* SEIZE, take, requisition, appropriate, expropriate, sequestrate, sequester, confiscate, annex, take over, claim, preempt; hijack, arrogate, help oneself to; *informal* walk off with; *Law* distrain.

commander noun *he is commander of an intelligence unit in Bogota* LEADER, head, chief, overseer, controller; commander-in-chief, C in C, commanding officer, CO, officer; *informal* boss, boss man, skipper, numero uno, number one, top dog, kingpin, head honcho, big kahuna.

commanding adjective **1** *a commanding position* DOMINANT, dominating, controlling, superior, powerful, prominent, advantageous, favorable.

2 *a commanding voice* AUTHORITATIVE, masterful, assertive, firm, emphatic, insistent, imperative; peremptory, imperious, dictatorial; *informal* bossy.

commemorate verb *an annual festival to commemorate the liberation of our town* CELEBRATE, pay tribute to, pay homage to, honor, salute, toast; remember, recognize, acknowledge, observe, mark.

commemorative adjective *a commemorative coin that depicts the raising of the flag on Iwo Jima* MEMORIAL, remembrance; celebratory.

commence verb *the meeting will commence at noon* BEGIN, start; get the ball rolling, get going, get underway, get off the ground, set about, embark on, launch into, lead off; open, initiate, inaugurate; *informal* kick off, get the show on the road. ANTONYM conclude.

commencement noun **1** *the commencement of the festivities* BEGINNING, start, opening, outset, onset, launch, initiation, inception, origin; *informal* kickoff.

2 *commencement ceremonies* GRADUATION, convocation.

commend verb **1** *we should commend him* PRAISE, compliment, congratulate, applaud, salute, honor; sing the praises of, pay tribute to, take one's hat off to, pat on the back; *formal* laud. See note at PRAISE. ANTONYM criticize.

2 *I commend her to you without reservation* RECOMMEND, suggest, propose; endorse, advocate, vouch for, speak for, support, back. See note at APPROVE.

3 *formal* *I commend them to your care* ENTRUST, trust, deliver, commit, hand over, give, turn over, consign, assign.

commendable adjective *he tackled the tests with commendable zeal* ADMIRABLE, praiseworthy, creditable, laudable, estimable, meritorious, exemplary, noteworthy, honorable, respectable, fine, excellent. ANTONYM reprehensible.

commendation noun **1** *letters of commendation* PRAISE, congratulation, appreciation; acclaim, credit, recognition, respect, esteem, admiration, homage, tribute.

2 *a commendation for bravery* AWARD, accolade, prize, honor, honorable mention, mention, citation.

commensurate adjective **1** *they had privileges but commensurate duties* EQUIVALENT, equal, corresponding, correspondent, comparable, proportionate, proportional.

2 *a salary **commensurate with** your qualifications* APPROPRIATE TO, in keeping with, in line with, consistent with, corresponding to, according to, relative to; dependent on, based on.

comment noun 1 *their comments on her appearance* REMARK, observation, statement, utterance; pronouncement, judgment, reflection, opinion, view; criticism.

2 *a great deal of comment* DISCUSSION, debate; interest.

3 *a comment in the margin* NOTE, annotation, footnote, gloss, commentary, explanation.

▸ verb 1 *they* ***commented on*** *the food* REMARK ON, speak about, talk about, discuss, mention.

2 *"It will soon be night," he commented* REMARK, observe, reflect, say, state, declare, announce; interpose, interject.

commentary noun 1 *the soccer commentary* NARRATION, description, account, report, review.

2 *textual commentary* EXPLANATION, elucidation, interpretation, exegesis, analysis; assessment, appraisal, criticism; notes, comments.

commentator noun 1 *a television commentator* NARRATOR, announcer, presenter, anchor, anchorman, anchorwoman; reporter, journalist, newscaster, sportscaster; *informal* talking head.

2 *a political commentator* ANALYST, pundit, monitor, observer; writer, speaker.

commerce noun 1 *industry and commerce* TRADE, trading, buying and selling, business, dealing, traffic; (financial) transactions, dealings.

2 *dated human commerce* RELATIONS, dealings, socializing, communication, association, contact, intercourse.

commercial adjective 1 *a vessel built for commercial purposes* TRADE, trading, business, private enterprise, mercantile, sales.

2 *a commercial society* PROFIT-ORIENTED, money-oriented, materialistic, mercenary.

▸ noun *a TV commercial* ADVERTISEMENT, promotion, display; *informal* ad, plug, infomercial.

commercialized adjective *the art world became increasingly commercialized* PROFIT-ORIENTED, money-oriented, commercial, materialistic, mercenary.

commiserate verb *the pastor sat down and* ***commiserated with*** *them after Lester's funeral* OFFER SYMPATHY TO, be sympathetic to, offer condolences to, condole with, sympathize with, empathize with, feel pity for, feel sorry for, feel for; comfort, console.

commiseration noun *a little commiseration may be the most important thing you can offer* CONDOLENCE(S), sympathy, pity, comfort, solace, consolation; compassion, understanding.

commission noun 1 *the dealer's commission* PERCENTAGE, brokerage, share, portion, dividend, premium, fee, consideration, bonus; *informal* cut, take, rake-off, slice.

2 *the commission of building a palace* TASK, employment, job, project, mission, assignment, undertaking; duty, charge, responsibility; *informal* marching orders.

3 *items made under state commission* WARRANT, license, sanction, authority.

4 *an independent commission* COMMITTEE, board, council, panel, directorate, delegation.

5 *the commission of an offense* PERPETRATION, committing, committal, execution.

▸ verb 1 *he was commissioned to paint a portrait* ENGAGE, contract, charge, employ, hire, recruit, retain, appoint, enlist, book, sign up.

2 *they commissioned a sculpture* ORDER; authorize; *formal* bespeak.

PHRASES: **in commission** *the new bathrooms are now in commission* IN SERVICE, in use; working, functional, operative, up and running, in operation, in working order. **out of commission** *more than half of our original computers are out of commission* NOT IN SERVICE, not in use, unserviceable; not working, inoperative, out of order, malfunctioning, broken, down.

commit verb 1 *he committed a murder* CARRY OUT, do, perpetrate, engage in, enact, execute, effect, accomplish; be responsible for; *informal* pull off.

2 *she was committed to their care* ENTRUST, consign, assign, deliver, give, hand over, relinquish; *formal* commend.

3 *they committed themselves to the project* PLEDGE, devote, apply, give, dedicate.

4 *the judge committed him to prison* CONSIGN, send, deliver, confine.

5 *her husband had her committed* HOSPITALIZE, confine, institutionalize, put away; certify.

commitment noun 1 *the pressure of his commitments* RESPONSIBILITY, obligation, duty, tie, liability; task; engagement, arrangement.

2 *her commitment to her students* DEDICATION, devotion, allegiance, loyalty, faithfulness, fidelity.

3 *he made a commitment* VOW, promise, pledge, oath; contract, pact, deal; decision, resolution.

committed adjective *a committed family man* DEVOUT, devoted, dedicated, loyal, faithful, staunch, firm, steadfast, unwavering, wholehearted, keen, passionate, ardent, fervent, sworn, pledged; dutiful, diligent; *informal* card-carrying, hard-core, true blue. ANTONYM apathetic.

committee noun *she appointed a committee to look into the busing issue* BOARD, council, brain trust.

commodious adjective *formal a commodious armchair* ROOMY, capacious, spacious, ample, generous, sizable, large, big, extensive. ANTONYM cramped.

commodity noun *Australian wools are among our most popular foreign commodities* ITEM, material, product, article, object; import, export.

common adjective 1 *the common folk* ORDINARY, normal, average, unexceptional; simple.

2 *a very common art form* USUAL, ordinary, familiar, regular, frequent, recurrent, everyday; standard, typical, conventional, stock, commonplace, run-of-the-mill; *informal* garden variety. See note at PREVALENT. ANTONYM unusual.

3 *a common belief* WIDESPREAD, general, universal, popular, mainstream, prevalent, prevailing, rife, established, conventional, traditional, orthodox, accepted. See note at UNIVERSAL. ANTONYM rare.

4 *the common good* COLLECTIVE, communal, community, public, popular, general; shared, combined. ANTONYMS individual, private.

5 *they are far too common* UNCOUTH, vulgar, coarse, rough, boorish, unladylike, ungentlemanly, ill-bred, uncivilized, unrefined, unsophisticated; lowly, low-born,

low-class, inferior, proletarian, plebeian. ANTONYM refined.

commonly adverb *the hairy woodpecker is commonly mistaken for a downy woodpecker* OFTEN, frequently, regularly, repeatedly, time and (time) again, all the time, routinely, habitually, customarily, oftentimes.

commonplace adjective **1** *a commonplace writing style* ORDINARY, run-of-the-mill, unremarkable, unexceptional, average, mediocre, pedestrian, prosaic, lackluster, dull, bland, uninteresting, mundane; hackneyed, trite, banal, clichéd, predictable, stale, tired, unoriginal; *informal* by-the-numbers, boilerplate, plain-vanilla, dime a dozen, bush-league. ANTONYMS original, outstanding.

2 *a commonplace occurrence* COMMON, normal, usual, ordinary, familiar, routine, standard, everyday, daily, regular, frequent, habitual, typical. ANTONYM unusual.

▸ noun **1** *early death was a commonplace* EVERYDAY EVENT, routine.

2 *a great store of commonplaces* PLATITUDE, cliché, truism, hackneyed phrase, trite phrase, old chestnut, banality; *dated* bromide.

common sense noun *well, at least you had the common sense to call 911* GOOD SENSE, sense, native wit, sensibleness, judgment, levelheadedness, prudence, discernment, canniness, astuteness, shrewdness, wisdom, insight, perception, perspicacity; practicality, capability, resourcefulness, enterprise; *informal* horse sense, gumption, savvy, smarts, street smarts. ANTONYM folly.

commonsensical adjective *the commonsensical thing would have been to check the supply cabinet before ordering more paper* SENSIBLE, reasonable, rational, prudent, smart, practical, realistic, levelheaded.

commotion noun *what's all that commotion in the parking lot?* DISTURBANCE, uproar, tumult, rumpus, ruckus, brouhaha, hoopla, furor, hue and cry, fuss, stir, storm; turmoil, disorder, confusion, chaos, mayhem, havoc, pandemonium; unrest, fracas, riot, breach of the peace, donnybrook; *informal* ruction, ballyhoo, hoo-ha, to-do, hullabaloo.

communal adjective **1** *the kitchen was communal* SHARED, joint, common. ANTONYM private.

2 *they farm on a communal basis* COLLECTIVE, cooperative, community, communalist, combined. ANTONYM individual.

commune noun *she lives in a commune* COLLECTIVE, cooperative, communal settlement, kibbutz.

▸ verb **1** *we pray to commune with God* COMMUNICATE, speak, talk, converse, interface.

2 *she likes to* ***commune with*** *nature* EMPATHIZE WITH, identify with, have a rapport with, feel at one with; relate to, feel close to.

communicable adjective *the spread of communicable diseases* CONTAGIOUS, INFECTIOUS, transmittable, transmissible, transferable, spreadable; *informal* catching.

communicate verb **1** *he communicated the news to his boss* CONVEY, tell, impart, relay, transmit, pass on, announce, report, recount, relate, present; divulge, disclose, mention; spread, disseminate, promulgate, broadcast.

2 *they communicate daily* BE IN TOUCH, be in contact, have dealings, interface, interact, commune, meet, liaise; talk, speak, converse; *informal* have a confab, powwow.

3 *learn how to communicate better* GET ONE'S MESSAGE ACROSS, explain oneself, be understood, get through to someone.

4 *the disease is communicated easily* TRANSMIT, transfer, spread, carry, pass on.

5 *each bedroom communicates with a bathroom* CONNECT WITH, join up with, open on to, lead into.

communication noun **1** *the communication of news* TRANSMISSION, conveyance, divulgence, disclosure; dissemination, promulgation, broadcasting.

2 *there was no communication between them* CONTACT, dealings, relations, connection, association, socializing, intercourse; correspondence, dialogue, talk, conversation, discussion.

3 *an official communication* MESSAGE, statement, announcement, report, dispatch, communiqué, letter, bulletin, correspondence.

communicative adjective *we find that abused children tend to be less communicative than other children* FORTHCOMING, expansive, expressive, unreserved, uninhibited, vocal, outgoing, frank, open, candid; talkative, chatty, loquacious; *informal* gabby.

communion noun **1** *a sense of communion with others* AFFINITY, fellowship, kinship, friendship, fellow feeling, togetherness, closeness, harmony, understanding, rapport, connection, communication, empathy, accord, unity. See note at CONVERSATION.

2 *Christ's presence at Communion* THE EUCHARIST, Holy Communion, the Lord's Supper, Mass.

communiqué noun *a communiqué from the surgeon general is expected this morning* OFFICIAL COMMUNICATION, press release, bulletin, message, missive, dispatch, statement, report, announcement, declaration, proclamation, advisory; *informal* memo.

communist noun & adjective *McCarthy had people suspecting that communists were lurking around every corner* | *communist countries* COLLECTIVIST, leftist, (radical) socialist; Soviet, Bolshevik, Bolshevist, Marxist, Leninist, Trotskyist, Trotskyite, Maoist; *informal, derogatory* commie, red, lefty, Bolshie.

community noun **1** *work done for the community* PUBLIC, general public, populace, people, citizenry, population, collective; residents, inhabitants, citizens.

2 *a suburban community* DISTRICT, region, zone, area, locality, locale, neighborhood; *informal* neck of the woods, hood.

3 *concerns in the immigrant community* GROUP, body, set, circle, clique, faction; *informal* gang, bunch.

4 *a monastic community* BROTHERHOOD, sisterhood, fraternity, sorority, sodality; order, congregation, abbey, convent.

commute verb **1** *they commute by train* TRAVEL TO AND FROM WORK, travel to and fro, travel back and forth.

2 *his sentence was commuted* REDUCE, lessen, lighten, shorten, cut, attenuate, moderate. ANTONYMS increase, uphold.

3 *knight service was commuted for a payment* EXCHANGE, change, substitute, swap, trade, switch.

commuter noun *commuters may see an increase in train fares this spring* DAILY TRAVELER, traveler, passenger; *informal* straphanger.

compact[1] adjective 1 *a compact rug* DENSE, close-packed, tightly packed; thick, tight, firm. ANTONYM loose.

2 *a compact camera* SMALL, little, petite, miniature, mini, small-scale; *informal* teeny, teeny-weeny; little-bitty, itty-bitty; *Scottish* wee. ANTONYM large.

3 *her overview is compact* CONCISE, succinct, condensed, brief, pithy; short and sweet; *informal* snappy; *formal* compendious. ANTONYM rambling.

▸ verb *the snow has been compacted* COMPRESS, condense, pack down, press down, tamp (down), flatten.

compact[2] noun *the warring states signed a compact* TREATY, pact, accord, agreement, contract, bargain, deal, settlement, covenant, concordat; pledge, promise, bond.

companion noun 1 *Harry and his companion* ASSOCIATE, partner, escort, compatriot, confederate; friend, intimate, confidant, confidante, comrade; *informal* pal, chum, crony, sidekick, mate, buddy, amigo, compadre.

2 *a lady's companion* ATTENDANT, aide, helper, assistant, valet, equerry, lady-in-waiting; chaperone; minder.

3 *the tape is a companion to the book* COMPLEMENT, counterpart, twin, match; accompaniment, supplement, addition, adjunct, accessory.

4 *The Gardener's Companion* HANDBOOK, manual, guide, reference book, ABC, primer, vade mecum; *informal* bible.

companionable adjective *the cocker spaniel is a companiable breed* FRIENDLY, affable, cordial, genial, congenial, amiable, easygoing, good-natured, comradely; sociable, convivial, outgoing, gregarious; *informal* chummy, buddy-buddy.

companionship noun *the volunteers do various errands for our elderly clients and provide some much-appreciated companionship* FRIENDSHIP, fellowship, closeness, togetherness, amity, intimacy, rapport, camaraderie, brotherhood, sisterhood; company, society, social contact.

company noun 1 *an oil company* FIRM, business, corporation, establishment, agency, office, bureau, institution, organization, concern, enterprise; conglomerate, consortium, syndicate, multinational; *informal* outfit.

2 *I enjoy his company* COMPANIONSHIP, friendship, fellowship, amity, camaraderie; society, association.

3 *I'm expecting company* GUESTS, house guests, visitors, callers, people; someone.

4 *a company of poets* GROUP, crowd, party, band, assembly, cluster, flock, herd, troupe, throng, congregation; *informal* bunch, gang.

5 *a company of infantry* UNIT, section, detachment, troop, corps, squad, squadron, platoon, battalion, division.

comparable adjective 1 *comparable incomes* SIMILAR, close, near, approximate, akin, equivalent, commensurate, proportional, proportionate; like, matching, homologous.

2 *nobody is* ***comparable with*** *him* EQUAL TO, as good as, in the same league as, able to hold a candle to, on a par with, on a level with; a match for.

comparative adjective *the left the city for the comparative quiet of the country* RELATIVE, in/by comparison.

compare verb 1 *we compared the data sets* CONTRAST, juxtapose, collate, differentiate. See note at CONTRAST.

2 *he was* ***compared to*** *Wagner* LIKEN TO, equate to, analogize to; class with, set side by side with.

3 *the porcelain* ***compares with*** *Dresden's fine china* BE AS GOOD AS, be comparable to, bear comparison with, be the equal of, match up to, be on a par with, be in the same league as, come close to, hold a candle to, be not unlike; match, resemble, emulate, rival, approach. PHRASE: **beyond compare** *their peach cobbler is beyond compare* WITHOUT EQUAL, second to none, in a class of one's own; peerless, matchless, unmatched, incomparable, inimitable, supreme, outstanding, consummate, unique, singular, perfect.

comparison noun 1 *a comparison of the results* JUXTAPOSITION, collation, differentiation.

2 *there's no comparison between them* RESEMBLANCE, likeness, similarity, correspondence, correlation, parallel, parity, comparability.

compartment noun 1 *a secret compartment* SECTION, part, bay, recess, chamber, cavity; pocket.

2 *they put science and religion in separate compartments* DOMAIN, field, sphere, department; category, pigeonhole, bracket, group, set.

compartmentalize verb *we need to compartmentalize the issues we're working on* CATEGORIZE, pigeonhole, group, classify, characterize, stereotype, label, brand; sort, rank, rate.

compass noun *faith cannot be defined within the compass of human thought* SCOPE, range, extent, reach, span, breadth, ambit, limits, parameters, bounds. See note at RANGE.

compassion noun *have you no compassion for a fellow human being?* PITY, sympathy, empathy, fellow feeling, care, concern, solicitude, sensitivity, warmth, love, tenderness, mercy, leniency, tolerance, kindness, humanity, charity. See note at MERCY. ANTONYMS indifference, cruelty.

compassionate adjective *a compassionate concern for the victims* SYMPATHETIC, empathetic, understanding, caring, solicitous, sensitive, warm, loving; merciful, lenient, tolerant, considerate, kind, humane, charitable, bighearted.

compatibility noun *they argue a lot, but they also enjoy a real compatibility* LIKE-MINDEDNESS, similarity, affinity, closeness, fellow feeling, harmony, rapport, empathy, sympathy.

compatible adjective 1 *they were never compatible* WELL SUITED, suited, well matched, like-minded, in tune, in harmony; reconcilable.

2 *her bruising is compatible with a fall* CONSISTENT, congruous, congruent; in keeping.

compatriot noun *Sampras defeated his compatriot Agassi in the final* FELLOW COUNTRYMAN, fellow countrywoman, countryman, countrywoman, fellow citizen.

compel verb 1 *he compelled them to leave their land* FORCE, pressure, press, push, urge; dragoon, browbeat, bully, intimidate, strong-arm; oblige, require, make; *informal* lean on, put the screws on.

2 *they can compel compliance* EXACT, extort, demand, insist on, force, necessitate.

THE RIGHT WORD

A parent faced with a rebellious teenager may try to **compel** him to do his homework by threatening to take away his allowance. *Compel* commonly implies the exercise of authority, the exertion of great effort, or the impossibility of doing anything else (*compelled to graduate from high school by her eagerness to leave home*). It typically requires a personal object, although it is possible to *compel* a reaction or response (*she compels admiration*). **Force** is a little stronger, suggesting the exertion of power, energy, or physical strength to accomplish something or to subdue resistance (*his mother forced him to confess that he'd broken the basement window*). **Coerce** can imply the use of force, but often stops short of using it (*she was coerced into obedience by the threat of losing her telephone privileges*). **Constrain** means *compel*, but by means of restriction, confinement, or limitation (*constrained from dating by his parents' strictness*). **Necessitate** and **oblige** make an action necessary by imposing certain conditions that demand a response (*Her mother's illness obliged her to be more cooperative; it also necessitated giving up her social life*).

compelling adjective **1** *a compelling performance* ENTHRALLING, captivating, gripping, riveting, spellbinding, mesmerizing, absorbing, irresistible. ANTONYM boring.

2 *a compelling argument* CONVINCING, persuasive, cogent, irresistible, powerful, strong, weighty, plausible, credible, sound, valid, telling, conclusive, irrefutable, unanswerable. ANTONYM weak.

compendious adjective *formal a compendious essay on Italian music* SUCCINCT, pithy, short and to the point, concise, compact, condensed, compressed, abridged, summarized, synoptic, capsule; *informal* snappy. ANTONYM expanded.

compendium noun *a compendium of Civil War narratives* COLLECTION, compilation, anthology, treasury, digest; summary, synopsis, précis, outline.

compensate verb **1** *you must compensate for what you did* MAKE AMENDS, make up, make reparation, recompense, atone, requite, pay; expiate, make good, rectify.

2 *we agreed to compensate him for his loss* RECOMPENSE, repay, pay back, reimburse, remunerate, recoup, requite, indemnify.

3 *his flair* ***compensated for*** *his faults* BALANCE (OUT), counterbalance, counteract, offset, make up for, cancel out, neutralize, negative.

compensation noun *my client has not received compensation for the legal fees incurred in 1998* RECOMPENSE, repayment, reimbursement, remuneration, requital, indemnification, indemnity, redress; damages; *informal* comp.

compete verb **1** *they competed in a tennis tournament* TAKE PART, participate, play, be a competitor, be involved; enter.

2 *they had to* ***compete with*** *other firms* CONTEND WITH, vie with, battle (with), wrangle with, jockey with, go head to head with; strive against, pit oneself against; challenge, take on.

3 *no one can* ***compete with*** *Elaine* RIVAL, challenge, keep up with, keep pace with, compare with, match, be in the same league as, come near to, come close to, touch; *informal* hold a candle to.

competence noun **1** *my technical competence* CAPABILITY, ability, competency, proficiency, accomplishment, expertise, adeptness, skill, prowess, mastery, talent; *informal* savvy, know-how.

2 *the competence of the system* ADEQUACY, appropriateness, suitability, fitness; effectiveness; *formal* efficacy.

3 *matters within the competence of the courts* AUTHORITY, power, control, jurisdiction, ambit, scope.

competent adjective **1** *a competent carpenter* CAPABLE, able, proficient, adept, adroit, accomplished, complete, skillful, skilled, credentialed, gifted, talented, expert; good, excellent; *informal* great, mean, wicked, nifty, ace.

2 *she spoke competent French* ADEQUATE, acceptable, satisfactory, reasonable, fair, decent, not bad, all right, average, tolerable, passable, moderate, middling; *informal* OK, okay, so-so, 'comme ci, comme ça'. ANTONYM inadequate.

3 *the court was not competent to hear the case* FIT, suitable, suited, appropriate; qualified, empowered, authorized. ANTONYM unfit.

competition noun **1** *Stephanie won the competition* CONTEST, tournament, match, game, heat, fixture, event.

2 *I'm not interested in competition* RIVALRY, competitiveness, vying; conflict, feuding, fighting; *informal* keeping up with the Joneses.

3 *we must stay ahead of the competition* OPPOSITION, other side, field; enemy; challengers, opponents, rivals, adversaries; *literary* foe.

competitive adjective **1** *a competitive player* AMBITIOUS, zealous, keen, pushy, combative, aggressive. ANTONYM apathetic.

2 *a highly competitive industry* RUTHLESS, aggressive, fierce; Darwinian; *informal* dog-eat-dog, cutthroat.

3 *competitive prices* REASONABLE, moderate; low, inexpensive, cheap, budget, bargain, reduced, discount; rock-bottom, bargain-basement, downmarket. ANTONYM exorbitant.

WORD NOTE **Darwinian**

Given the range of Charles Darwin's accomplishments, the word *Darwinian* could, in theory, mean all sorts of things: *a Darwinian voyage of scientific discovery.* But in fact it's come to signify, more narrowly, the struggle for survival and dominance that furthers evolution and enables a particular species to prevail over its competitors. What I like about the word is how it can also be used to describe certain unattractive sorts of human social behavior, also marked by fierce competition and by the ruthless desire for dominance: *The atmosphere in the classroom—or at the dinner party—was remarkably Darwinian.* **—FP**

competitor noun **1** *the competitors in the race* CONTESTANT, contender, challenger, participant, entrant; runner, player. ANTONYM spectator.

2 *our European competitors* RIVAL, challenger, opponent, adversary; competition, opposition. ANTONYM ally.

compilation noun *a compilation of their greatest hits* COLLECTION, selection, anthology, treasury, compendium, album, corpus; potpourri.

compile verb *he compiled a dossier of patients with tropical diseases* ASSEMBLE, put together, make up, collate, compose, organize, arrange; gather, collect.

complacency noun *the complacency he felt as a math stu-*

dent was abruptly shaken when he took his first calculus exam SMUGNESS, self-satisfaction, self-congratulation, self-regard; gloating, triumph, pride; satisfaction, contentment.

complacent adjective *in this competitive field we can't afford to be complacent* SMUG, self-satisfied, self-congratulatory, self-regarding; gloating, triumphant, proud; pleased, satisfied, content, contented.

complain verb *his dogs were always roaming until someone finally complained* PROTEST, grumble, whine, bleat, carp, cavil, grouse, make a fuss; object, speak out, criticize, find fault; *informal* kick up a fuss, raise a stink, bellyache, moan, snivel, beef, bitch, sound off, gripe, kvetch.

complaint noun **1** *they lodged a complaint* PROTEST, objection, grievance, grouse, cavil, quibble, grumble; charge, accusation, criticism; jeremiad; *informal* beef, gripe, whinge; *Law* plaint.

2 *little cause for complaint* PROTESTATION, objection, exception, grievance, grumbling; criticism, fault-finding, condemnation, disapproval, dissatisfaction; *informal* grousing, bellyaching, nitpicking.

3 *a kidney complaint* DISORDER, disease, infection, affliction, illness, ailment, sickness; condition, problem, upset, trouble.

WORD NOTE **jeremiad**

Deriving from the *Lamentations of Jeremiah* in the Old Testament, the word carries heavy freight, signifying a grievance of biblical proportions, and is grievously overused. **—JS**

complaisant adjective *Willa was too timid to be anything but quiet and complaisant* WILLING, acquiescent, agreeable, amenable, cooperative, accommodating, obliging; biddable, compliant, docile, obedient.

complement noun **1** *the perfect complement to the food* ACCOMPANIMENT, companion, addition, supplement, accessory, trimming.

2 *a full complement of lifeboats* AMOUNT, total, contingent, capacity, allowance, quota.

▸ verb *this sauce complements the dessert* ACCOMPANY, go with, round off, set off, suit, harmonize with; enhance, complete.

EASILY CONFUSED WORDS **complement, compliment; complementary, complimentary**

Complement and **compliment** (and the related words **complementary** and **complimentary**) are frequently confused. Although pronounced alike, they have quite different meanings. As a verb, **complement** means 'to add to something in a way that completes, enhances, or improves it,' as in *The practical work is complemented by tutorials.* **Compliment** means 'admire and praise someone for something,' as in *they complimented Janet on her new necklace.* **Complementary** means 'forming a complement or addition, completing,' as in *I purchased a suit with a complementary shirt and tie.* This can be confused with **complimentary**, for which one sense is 'given freely, as a courtesy': *you must pay for the suit, but the shirt and tie.*

complementary adjective *decorating in complementary colors and patterns* HARMONIOUS, compatible, corresponding, matching, twin; supportive, reciprocal, interdependent. See note at COMPLEMENT. ANTONYM incompatible.

complete adjective **1** *the complete interview* ENTIRE, whole, full, total; uncut, unabridged.

2 *their research was complete* FINISHED, ended, concluded, completed, finalized; accomplished, achieved, discharged, settled, done; *informal* wrapped up, sewn up, polished off. ANTONYM unfinished.

3 *a complete fool* ABSOLUTE, out-and-out, utter, total, real, downright, thoroughgoing, veritable, prize, perfect, unqualified, unmitigated, sheer, arrant, full-out. ANTONYM partial.

▸ verb **1** *he had to complete his training* FINISH, end, conclude, finalize, wind up; *informal* wrap up, sew up, polish off.

2 *the outfit was completed with a veil* FINISH OFF, round off, top off, crown, cap, complement.

3 *complete the application form* FILL IN/OUT, answer.

completely adverb *he'd always been completely honest with her* TOTALLY, entirely, wholly, thoroughly, fully, utterly, absolutely, perfectly, unreservedly, unconditionally, quite, altogether, downright; in every way, in every respect, one hundred percent, every inch, to the hilt; *informal* dead, deadly, to the max.

completion noun *the money ran out before the project's completion* REALIZATION, accomplishment, achievement, fulfillment, consummation, finalization, resolution; finish, end, conclusion, close, cessation.

complex adjective **1** *a complex situation* COMPLICATED, involved, intricate, convoluted, elaborate, impenetrable, Gordian; difficult, knotty, tricky, thorny. ANTONYM simple.

2 *a complex structure* COMPOUND, composite, multiplex.

▸ noun **1** *a complex of roads* NETWORK, system, nexus, web, tissue; combination, aggregation.

2 *informal he had a complex about losing his hair* OBSESSION, fixation, preoccupation; neurosis; *informal* hang-up, thing, bee in one's bonnet.

complexion noun **1** *a pale complexion* SKIN, skin color, skin tone; pigmentation.

2 *this puts an entirely new complexion on things* PERSPECTIVE, angle, slant, interpretation; appearance, light, look.

3 *governments of all complexions* TYPE, kind, sort; nature, character, stamp, ilk, kidney.

complexity noun *an issue of great complexity* COMPLICATION, problem, difficulty; twist, turn, intricacy.

compliance noun **1** ***compliance with** international law* OBEDIENCE TO, observance of, adherence to, conformity to, respect for. ANTONYM violation.

2 *he mistook her silence for compliance* ACQUIESCENCE, agreement, assent, consent, acceptance; complaisance, pliability, docility, meekness, submission. ANTONYM defiance.

compliant adjective *her compliant husband* ACQUIESCENT, amenable, biddable, tractable, complaisant, accommodating, cooperative; obedient, docile, malleable, pliable, submissive, tame, yielding, controllable, unresisting, persuadable, persuasible. See note at OBEDIENT. ANTONYM recalcitrant.

complicate verb *involvement with Adam could only complicate her life* MAKE (MORE) DIFFICULT, make complicated, mix up, confuse, muddle; *informal* mess up, screw up, snarl up. ANTONYM simplify.

complicated adjective *the complicated election process* COMPLEX, intricate, involved, convoluted, tangled, impenetrable, knotty, tricky, thorny, labyrinthine, tortuous, Gordian; confusing, bewildering, perplexing. ANTONYM straightforward.

► ***complicated***
impenetrable
serpentine
involute
involuted
intricate
labyrinthine
Byzantine
Daedalian
Gordian
tortuous
convoluted
cumbersome
involved
elaborate
tangled
complex
perplexing
bewildering
baffling
puzzling
confused
confusing
above one's head
difficult to understand
knotty
tricky
thorny
fiddly
dicey
delicate
requiring special care
feasible
manageable
elementary
undemanding
uninvolved
uncomplicated
unexacting
straightforward
nothing
no sweat
a cinch
a snip
child's play
kids' stuff
plain sailing
as easy as falling off a log
as easy as pie
as easy as ABC
a piece of cake
a five-finger exercise
a doss
a cakewalk
a doddle
a pushover
duck soup
a piece of piss
money for old rope
money for jam
a snap
a breeze
easy-peasy
easy
painless
effortless
simple ◄

complication noun **1** *a complication concerning ownership* DIFFICULTY, problem, obstacle, hurdle, stumbling block; drawback, snag, catch, hitch; *informal* fly in the ointment, headache.

2 *the complication of life in our society* COMPLEXITY, complicatedness, intricacy, convolutedness.

complicity noun *they've been accused of complicity in the destruction of damning evidence* COLLUSION, involvement, collaboration, connivance; conspiracy; *informal* being in cahoots.

compliment noun **1** *an unexpected compliment | he enjoyed the compliments* FLATTERING REMARK, tribute, accolade, commendation, bouquet, pat on the back; **(compliments)** praise, acclaim, admiration, flattery, blandishments, honeyed words. ANTONYM insult.

2 (compliments) *my compliments on your cooking* CONGRATULATIONS, commendations, praise; *informal* props, kudos.

3 (compliments) *Margaret sends her compliments* GREETINGS, regards, respects, good wishes, best wishes, salutations, felicitations.

▸ verb *they complimented his performance* PRAISE, pay tribute to, speak highly/well of, flatter, wax lyrical about, make much of, commend, acclaim, applaud, salute, honor; congratulate someone on. See note at COMPLEMENT. ANTONYM criticize.

complimentary adjective **1** *complimentary remarks* FLATTERING, appreciative, congratulatory, admiring, approving, commendatory, favorable, glowing, adulatory; *informal* rave. ANTONYM derogatory.

2 *complimentary tickets* FREE, free of charge, gratis, for nothing; courtesy; *informal* on the house. See note at COMPLEMENT.

comply verb *Myra **complied with** his wishes* ABIDE BY, observe, obey, adhere to, conform to, hew to, follow, respect; agree to, assent to, go along with, yield to, submit to, defer to; satisfy, fulfill. ANTONYMS ignore, disobey.

component noun *the components of electronic devices* PART, piece, bit, element, constituent, ingredient, building block; unit, module, section.

▸ adjective *the molecule's component elements* CONSTITUENT, integral; basic, essential.

comport PHRASE: **comport oneself** *formal try to comport yourself with a little dignity* BEHAVE, conduct oneself, act, acquit oneself; *archaic* deport oneself.

compose verb **1** *a poem composed by Shelley* WRITE, formulate, devise, make up, think up, produce, invent, concoct; pen, author, draft; score, orchestrate, choreograph.

2 *compose a still life* ORGANIZE, arrange, set out.

3 *the subcommittee is composed of ten senators* MAKE UP, constitute, form. PHRASE: **compose oneself** *you have to compose yourself before you take the stand* CALM DOWN, control oneself, regain one's composure, pull oneself together, collect oneself, steady oneself, keep one's head, relax; *informal* get a grip, keep one's cool, cool one's jets, decompress.

composed adjective *she remained composed throughout the ordeal* CALM, collected, cool, cool as a cucumber, 'cool, calm, and collected', self-controlled, self-possessed; serene, tranquil, relaxed, at ease, unruffled, unperturbed, untroubled; equable, even-tempered, imperturbable; *informal* unflappable, together, laid-back. ANTONYM excited.

composer noun *Berlin was one of the most prolific composers in the history of American music* songwriter, melodist, symphonist, songster, writer; *informal* tunesmith, songsmith.

composite adjective *a composite structure* COMPOUND, complex; combined, blended, mixed.

▸ noun *a composite of plastic and metal* AMALGAMATION, amalgam, combination, compound, fusion, synthesis, mixture, blend; alloy.

composition noun **1** *the composition of the council* MAKEUP, constitution, configuration, structure, formation, form, framework, fabric, anatomy, organization; *informal* setup.

2 *a literary composition* WORK, work of art, creation, opus, oeuvre, piece, arrangement.

3 *we all participated in the composition of the school song* WRITING, creation, formulation, invention, concoction, orchestration.

4 *a school composition* ESSAY, paper, study, piece of writing, theme.

5 *the composition of the painting* ARRANGEMENT, disposition, layout; proportions, balance, symmetry.

6 *an adhesive composition* MIXTURE, compound, amalgam, blend, mix.

compost noun *all of our organic garbage is converted to compost* FERTILIZER, mulch, manure, bone meal, fish meal, blood meal, guano; humus, peat; plant food, top-dressing.

composure noun *most people would have lost their composure after such a disappointing defeat* SELF-CONTROL, self-possession, calm, equanimity, equilibrium, serenity, tranquility; aplomb, poise, presence of mind, sangfroid; imperturbability, placidness, impassivity; *informal* cool.

compound noun **1** *a compound of two elements* AMALGAM, amalgamation, combination, composite, blend, mixture, mix, fusion, synthesis; alloy.

2 *they were contained in the compound* ENCLOSURE, pound, coop; estate, cloister.

▸ adjective *a compound substance* COMPOSITE, complex; blended, fused, combined. ANTONYM simple.

▸ verb **1** *soap compounded with disinfectant* MIX, combine, blend, amalgamate, fuse, synthesize.

2 *his illness compounds their problems* AGGRAVATE, exacerbate, worsen, add to, augment, intensify, heighten, increase, magnify; complicate. ANTONYM alleviate.

PHRASE: **compounded of** *a smell compounded of dust and mold* COMPOSED OF, made up of, formed from.

comprehend verb **1** *Katie couldn't comprehend his message* UNDERSTAND, grasp, take in, see, apprehend, follow, make sense of, fathom, get to the bottom of; unravel, decipher, interpret; *informal* work out, figure out, make head(s) or tail(s) of, get one's head around, get the drift of, catch on to, get.

2 *formal a divine order comprehending all men* COMPRISE, include, encompass, embrace, involve, contain. ANTONYM exclude.

comprehensible adjective *the information must be accurate and comprehensible* INTELLIGIBLE, understandable, accessible; lucid, coherent, clear, plain, explicit, unambiguous, straightforward, fathomable. ANTONYM opaque.

comprehension noun *matters that seemed beyond her comprehension* UNDERSTANDING, grasp, conception, apprehension, cognition, ken, knowledge, awareness, perception; interpretation. ANTONYM ignorance.

comprehensive adjective *a comprehensive review of our defense policy* INCLUSIVE, all-inclusive, complete; thorough, full, extensive, all-embracing, exhaustive, detailed, in-depth, encyclopedic, universal, catholic; far-reaching, radical, sweeping, across the board, wholesale; broad, wide-ranging; *informal* wall-to-wall. ANTONYM limited.

compress verb **1** *the skirt can be compressed into a small bag* SQUEEZE, press, squash, crush, cram, jam, stuff; tamp, pack, compact; constrict; *informal* scrunch.

2 *the text was compressed* ABRIDGE, condense, shorten, cut, abbreviate, truncate; summarize, précis. ANTONYM expand.

comprise verb **1** *the country comprises twenty states* CONSIST OF, be made up of, be composed of, contain, encompass, incorporate; include; *formal* comprehend.

2 *informal this breed comprises half the herd* MAKE UP, constitute, form, compose; account for. See note at INCLUDE.

WORD NOTE **comprise**

It's all very well to criticize others for misusing the language, but this is a word I have misused so many times that I have stopped using it. It means "include, contain" but not "constitute." It has been pointed out to me, more often than I care to admit, that you can say: *The book comprises five sections.* But you should not say: *The book is comprised of five sections.* In the second example, use *compose* instead: *The book is composed of five sections.* I have lost hope of ever getting it straight, so for now I find synonyms, and wait for so many others to make the same mistake that—as so often happens—grammarians simply give up, and decide that both usages are correct. **—FP**

compromise noun **1** *they reached a compromise* AGREEMENT, understanding, settlement, terms, deal, trade-off, bargain; middle ground, happy medium, balance.

2 *a happy marriage needs compromise* GIVE AND TAKE, concession, cooperation. ANTONYM intransigence.

▸ verb **1** *we compromised* MEET EACH OTHER HALFWAY, come to an understanding, make a deal, make concessions, find a happy medium, strike a balance; give and take.

2 *his actions could compromise his reputation* UNDERMINE, weaken, damage, harm; jeopardize, prejudice; discredit, dishonor, shame, embarrass.

compulsion noun **1** *he is under no compulsion to go* OBLIGATION, constraint, coercion, duress, pressure, intimidation.

2 *a compulsion to tell the truth* URGE, impulse, need, desire, drive; obsession, fixation, addiction; temptation.

compulsive adjective **1** *a compulsive desire* IRRESISTIBLE, uncontrollable, compelling, overwhelming, urgent; obsessive.

2 *compulsive eating* OBSESSIVE, obsessional, addictive, uncontrollable.

3 *a compulsive liar* INVETERATE, chronic, incorrigible, incurable, hardened, hopeless, persistent; obsessive, addicted, habitual; *informal* pathological.

4 *it's compulsive viewing* FASCINATING, compelling, gripping, riveting, engrossing, enthralling, captivating.

compulsory adjective *the wearing of seat belts is compulsory* OBLIGATORY, mandatory, required, requisite, necessary, essential; imperative, unavoidable, enforced, demanded, prescribed. ANTONYM optional.

compunction noun *she had no compunction about deceiving them* SCRUPLES, misgivings, qualms, worries, unease, uneasiness, doubts, reluctance, reservations; guilt, regret, contrition, self-reproach. See note at QUALMS.

compute verb *we compute our expenses at the close of each day* CALCULATE, work out, reckon, determine, evaluate, quantify; add up, count up, tally, total, totalize, tot up.

computer noun *your new computers will be able to handle much larger files* PERSONAL COMPUTER, PC, laptop, desktop, terminal; mainframe.

comrade noun *we became comrades back in 1943, working in a field hospital in the Philippines* COMPANION, friend; colleague, associate, partner, coworker, workmate; *informal* pal, crony, mate, chum, buddy.

con *informal* verb *we got conned.* See SWINDLE.

▸ noun **1** *an ex-con.* See CONVICT.

2 *a public relations con.* See SWINDLE.

con artist noun *a shady con artist from Toledo* SWINDLER, fraud, cheater, scam artist, fraudster; *informal* CON MAN, gonif.

concatenation noun *a concatenation of events that had finally led to murder* SERIES, sequence, succession, chain.

concave adjective *a small concave area now filled with rainwater* INCURVATE, curved inward, hollow, depressed, sunken; indented, recessed. ANTONYM convex.

conceal verb **1** *clouds concealed the sun* HIDE, screen, cover, obscure, block out, blot out, mask, shroud, secrete. ANTONYM reveal.

2 *he concealed his true feelings* HIDE, cover up, disguise, mask, veil; keep secret, draw a veil over; suppress, repress, bottle up; *informal* keep a lid on, keep under one's hat. ANTONYMS reveal, confess.

concealed adjective *another piece of concealed evidence was disclosed to Sgt. Kahn* HIDDEN, not visible, out of sight, invisible, covered, disguised, camouflaged, obscured; private, secret.

concealment noun **1** *the concealment of his weapon* HIDING, secretion.

2 *the deliberate concealment of facts* SUPPRESSION, hiding, cover-up, hushing up; whitewash.

concede verb **1** *I had to concede that I'd overreacted* ADMIT, acknowledge, accept, allow, grant, recognize, own, confess; agree. ANTONYM deny.

2 *he conceded the Auvergne to the king* SURRENDER, yield, give up, relinquish, cede, hand over. ANTONYM retain.

PHRASE: **concede defeat** *Colonel Morris vowed never to concede defeat* CAPITULATE, give in, give, surrender, yield, give up, submit, raise the white flag; back down, climb down; *informal* throw in the towel.

conceit noun **1** *his extraordinary conceit* VANITY, narcissism, conceitedness, egotism, self-admiration, self-regard; pride, arrogance, hubris, self-importance; self-satisfaction, smugness; *informal* bigheadedness; *literary* vainglory. See notes at EGOTISM, PRIDE. ANTONYM humility.

2 *the conceits of Shakespeare's verse* IMAGE, imagery, metaphor, simile, trope; PLAY ON WORDS, pun, quip, witticism.

3 *the conceit of time travel* IDEA, notion, fancy.

conceited adjective *she's too conceited to think she might not get the lead role* VAIN, narcissistic, self-centered, egotistic, egotistical, egocentric; proud, arrogant, boastful, full of oneself, self-important, immodest, swaggering; self-satisfied, smug; supercilious, haughty, snobbish; *informal* bigheaded, too big for one's britches, stuck-up, high and mighty, uppity, snotty; *literary* vainglorious.

conceivable adjective *is there any conceivable justification for betraying your family?* IMAGINABLE, possible; plausible, tenable, credible, believable, thinkable, feasible; understandable, comprehensible.

conceive verb **1** *they were unable to conceive* BECOME PREGNANT, become impregnated.

2 *the project was conceived in 1977* THINK UP, think of, dream up, devise, formulate, design, originate, create, develop; *informal* cook up, hatch.

3 *I can hardly conceive what it must be like* IMAGINE, envisage, visualize, picture, think, envision; grasp, appreciate, apprehend; *formal* ideate.

concentrate verb **1** *the government concentrated its efforts* FOCUS, direct, center, centralize. ANTONYM dissipate.

2 *she* **concentrated on** *the movie* FOCUS ON, pay attention to, keep one's mind on, devote oneself to; be absorbed in, be engrossed in, be immersed in.

3 *troops concentrated on the horizon* COLLECT, gather, congregate, converge, mass, cluster, rally. ANTONYM disperse.

4 *the liquid is filtered and concentrated* CONDENSE, boil down, reduce, thicken. ANTONYM dilute.

▸ noun *a fruit concentrate* EXTRACT, decoction, distillation.

concentrated adjective **1** *a concentrated effort* STRENUOUS, concerted, intensive, intense; *informal* all-out. ANTONYM halfhearted.

2 *a concentrated solution* CONDENSED, reduced, evaporated, thickened; undiluted, strong. ANTONYM diluted.

concentration noun **1** *a task requiring concentration* CLOSE ATTENTION, attentiveness, application, single-mindedness, tunnel vision, absorption. ANTONYM inattention.

2 *the concentration of effort* FOCUSING, centralization.

3 *concentrations of seals* GATHERING, cluster, mass, congregation, assemblage.

concept noun *Freud's concept of the superego* IDEA, notion, conception, abstraction; theory, hypothesis; belief, conviction, opinion; image, impression, picture. See note at IDEA.

conception noun **1** *from conception until natural death* INCEPTION OF PREGNANCY, conceiving, fertilization, impregnation, insemination.

2 *the product's conception* INCEPTION, genesis, origination, creation, invention; beginning, origin.

3 *his original conception* PLAN, scheme, project, proposal; intention, aim, idea. See note at IDEA.

4 *my conception of democracy* IDEA, concept, notion, understanding, abstraction; theory, hypothesis; perception, image, impression.

5 *they had no conception of our problems* UNDERSTANDING, comprehension, appreciation, grasp, knowledge; idea, inkling; *informal* clue.

concern verb 1 *the report concerns the war* BE ABOUT, deal with, have to do with, cover; discuss, go into, examine, study, review, analyze; relate to, pertain to.

2 *that doesn't concern you* AFFECT, involve, be relevant to, apply to, have a bearing on, impact on; be important to, interest.

3 *I won't* ***concern myself with*** *your affairs* INVOLVE ONESELF IN, take an interest in, busy oneself with, devote one's time to, bother oneself with.

4 *one thing still concerns me* WORRY, disturb, trouble, bother, perturb, unsettle, make anxious.

▸ noun 1 *a voice full of concern* ANXIETY, worry, disquiet, apprehensiveness, unease, consternation. ANTONYM peace of mind.

2 *his concern for others* SOLICITUDE, consideration, care, sympathy, regard. ANTONYM indifference.

3 *housing is the concern of the council* RESPONSIBILITY, business, affair, charge, duty, job; province, preserve; problem, worry; *informal* bag, bailiwick.

4 *issues that are of concern to women* INTEREST, importance, relevance, significance.

5 *Aboriginal concerns* AFFAIR, issue, matter, question, consideration.

6 *a publishing concern* COMPANY, business, firm, organization, operation, corporation, establishment, house, office, agency; *informal* outfit.

concerned adjective 1 *her mother looked concerned* WORRIED, anxious, upset, perturbed, troubled, distressed, uneasy, apprehensive, agitated.

2 *he is concerned about your welfare* SOLICITOUS, caring; attentive to, considerate of.

3 *all concerned parties* INTERESTED, involved, affected; connected, related, implicated.

concerning preposition *we have new information concerning his disappearance* ABOUT, regarding, relating to, with reference to, referring to, with regard to, as regards, with respect to, respecting, dealing with, on the subject of, in connection with, re, apropos of.

concert noun *a concert at Woolsey Hall featuring a pianist from Estonia* MUSICAL PERFORMANCE, show, production, presentation; recital; *informal* gig. PHRASE: **in concert** *we must take stronger action in concert with our European allies* TOGETHER, jointly, in combination, in collaboration, in cooperation, in league, side by side; in unison.

concerted adjective 1 *make a concerted effort* STRENUOUS, vigorous, intensive, intense, concentrated; *informal* all-out. ANTONYM halfhearted.

2 *concerted action* JOINT, united, collaborative, collective, combined, cooperative. ANTONYM individual.

concession noun 1 *the government made several concessions* COMPROMISE, allowance, exception.

2 *a concession of failure* ADMISSION, acknowledgment, acceptance, recognition, confession. ANTONYM denial.

3 *the concession of territory* SURRENDER, relinquishment, sacrifice, handover. ANTONYMS retention, acquisition.

4 *tax concessions* REDUCTION, cut, discount, deduction, decrease; rebate; *informal* break.

5 *a fast-food concession* STAND, kiosk, stall, counter, vendor.

6 *a logging concession* RIGHT, privilege; license, permit, franchise, warrant, authorization.

concierge noun *the hotel concierge gave us a map of Central Park* DOORKEEPER, doorman, porter, attendant, superintendent.

conciliate verb 1 *he tried to conciliate the peasantry* APPEASE, placate, pacify, mollify, assuage, soothe, humor, reconcile, win over, make peace with. See note at PACIFY. ANTONYM provoke.

2 *he conciliated in the dispute* MEDIATE, act as peacemaker, arbitrate; pour oil on troubled waters.

conciliator noun *even Kaufman, an impartial conciliator, was finding it difficult to trust Henshaw's motives* PEACEMAKER, mediator, go-between, middleman, intermediary, intercessor; dove. ANTONYM troublemaker.

conciliatory adjective *a conciliatory gesture* PROPITIATORY, placatory, appeasing, pacifying, mollifying, peacemaking.

concise adjective *a concise account* SUCCINCT, pithy, incisive, brief, short and to the point, short and sweet; abridged, condensed, compressed, abbreviated, compact; *informal* snappy. See note at TERSE. ANTONYMS lengthy, wordy.

conclave noun *a conclave of American and Japanese business leaders* (PRIVATE) MEETING, gathering, assembly, conference, council, summit; *informal* parley, powwow, get-together.

conclude verb 1 *the meeting concluded at ten* FINISH, end, draw to a close, be over, stop, cease. ANTONYMS commence, start, begin.

2 *she concluded the press conference* BRING TO AN END, close, wind up, terminate, dissolve; *informal* wrap up. ANTONYMS open, start, begin.

3 *an attempt to conclude a cease-fire* NEGOTIATE, broker, agree, come to terms on, settle, clinch, finalize, tie up; bring about, arrange, effect, engineer; *informal* sew up.

4 *I concluded that he was rather unpleasant* DEDUCE, infer, gather, judge, decide, conjecture, surmise, extrapolate, figure, reckon.

conclusion noun 1 *the conclusion of his speech* END, ending, finish, close, termination, windup, cessation; culmination, denouement, peroration, coda; *informal* outro. ANTONYM beginning.

2 *the conclusion of a trade agreement* NEGOTIATION, brokering, settlement, completion, arrangement, resolution.

3 *his conclusions have been verified* DEDUCTION, inference, interpretation, reasoning; opinion, judgment, verdict; assumption, presumption, supposition; *rare* illation. PHRASE: **in conclusion** *in conclusion, I'd like to remind you that Mr. Clark will be signing books in the cafeteria* FINALLY, in closing, to conclude, last but not least; to sum up, in short, to make a long story short.

conclusive adjective 1 *conclusive proof* INCONTROVERTIBLE, undeniable, indisputable, irrefutable, unquestionable, unassailable, convincing, certain, decisive, definitive, definite, positive, categorical, unequivocal; airtight, watertight. ANTONYM unconvincing.

2 *a conclusive win* EMPHATIC, resounding, convincing. ANTONYM narrow.

concoct verb 1 *he planned to concoct a dessert* PREPARE, make, assemble; *informal* fix, rustle up.

2 *this story she has concocted* MAKE UP, dream up, fabricate, invent, trump up; formulate, hatch, brew, cook up.

concoction noun 1 *a concoction containing gin and vodka* MIXTURE, brew, preparation, potion.

2 *a strange concoction of folk pop and Gregorian chant* BLEND, mixture, mix, combination, hybrid.

3 *her story is an improbable concoction* FABRICATION, invention, falsification; *informal* fairy tale.

concomitant adjective *formal the rise of urbanism brought a concomitant risk of crime* ATTENDANT, accompanying, associated, related, connected; resultant, consequent. ANTONYM unrelated.

concord noun *council meetings rarely ended in concord* AGREEMENT, harmony, accord, consensus, concurrence, unity. ANTONYM discord.

concourse noun 1 *the station concourse* ENTRANCE, foyer, lobby, hall.

2 *formal a vast concourse of onlookers* CROWD, group, gathering, assembly, body, company, throng, flock, mass.

concrete adjective 1 *concrete objects* SOLID, material, real, physical, tangible, palpable, substantial, visible, existing. ANTONYMS abstract, imaginary.

2 *concrete proof* DEFINITE, firm, positive, conclusive, definitive; real, genuine, bona fide. ANTONYM vague.

concubine noun *archaic she was the reluctant concubine of Prince Percival* MISTRESS, courtesan, kept woman; lover; *archaic* paramour, doxy; *historical* hetaera.

concupiscence noun See LUST noun sense 1.

concur verb 1 *we concur with this view* AGREE, be in agreement, go along, fall in, be in sympathy; see eye to eye, be of the same mind, be of the same opinion. ANTONYM disagree.

2 *the two events concurred* COINCIDE, be simultaneous, be concurrent, coexist.

concurrent adjective 1 *nine concurrent life sentences* SIMULTANEOUS, coincident, contemporaneous, parallel.

2 *concurrent lines* CONVERGENT, converging, meeting, intersecting.

concussion noun 1 *he suffered a concussion* temporary unconsciousness; brain injury.

2 *the concussion of the blast* FORCE, impact, shock, jolt.

condemn verb 1 *he condemned the suspended players* CENSURE, criticize, denounce, revile, blame, chastise, berate, reprimand, rebuke, reprove, take to task, find fault with; *informal* slam, blast, lay into; *formal* castigate. ANTONYM praise.

2 *he was condemned to death* SENTENCE; convict, find guilty. ANTONYM acquit.

3 *the house has been condemned* DECLARE UNFIT, declare unsafe.

4 *her mistake had condemned her* INCRIMINATE, implicate; *archaic* inculpate.

5 *his illness condemned him to a lonely life* DOOM, destine, damn; consign, assign.

condemnation noun *a comment that provoked widespread condemnation* CENSURE, criticism, strictures, denunciation, vilification; reproof, disapproval; *informal* flak, (a) bad press; *formal* castigation.

condensation noun 1 *windows misty with condensation* MOISTURE, water droplets, steam.

2 *the condensation of the vapor* PRECIPITATION, liquefaction, deliquescence.

3 *a condensation of recent literature* ABRIDGMENT, summary, synopsis, précis, digest.

4 *the condensation of the report* SHORTENING, abridgment, abbreviation, summarization.

condense verb 1 *the water vapor condenses* PRECIPITATE, liquefy, become liquid, deliquesce. ANTONYM vaporize.

2 *he condensed the play* ABRIDGE, shorten, cut, abbreviate, compact; summarize, synopsize, précis; truncate, curtail. ANTONYMS lengthen, expand.

condensed adjective 1 *a condensed text* ABRIDGED, shortened, cut, compressed, abbreviated, reduced, truncated, concise; outline, thumbnail, capsule.

2 *condensed soup* CONCENTRATED, evaporated, reduced; strong, undiluted. ANTONYM diluted.

condescend verb 1 *don't* ***condescend to*** *your reader* PATRONIZE, talk down to, look down one's nose at, look down on, put down.

2 *he condescended to see us* DEIGN, stoop, descend, lower oneself, demean oneself; vouchsafe, see fit, consent.

condescending adjective *she looked us up and down in a condescending manner* PATRONIZING, supercilious, superior, snobbish, snobby, disdainful, lofty, haughty; *informal* snooty, stuck-up.

condition noun 1 *check the condition of your wiring* STATE, shape, order.

2 *they lived in appalling conditions* CIRCUMSTANCES, surroundings, environment, situation, setup, setting, habitat.

3 *she was in top condition* FITNESS, health, form, shape, trim, fettle.

4 *a liver condition* DISORDER, problem, complaint, illness, disease, ailment, sickness, affliction, infection, upset.

5 *a condition of membership* STIPULATION, constraint, prerequisite, precondition, requirement, rule, term, specification, provision, proviso.

▸ verb 1 *their choices are conditioned by the economy* CONSTRAIN, control, govern, determine, decide; affect, touch; form, shape, guide, sway, bias.

2 *our minds are conditioned by habit* TRAIN, teach, educate, guide; accustom, adapt, habituate, mold, inure.

3 *condition the boards with water* TREAT, prepare, prime, temper, process, acclimatize, acclimate, season.

4 *a product to condition your skin* IMPROVE, nourish, tone (up), moisturize.

conditional adjective 1 *their approval is* ***conditional on*** *success* SUBJECT TO, dependent on, contingent on, based on, determined by, controlled by, tied to.

2 *a conditional offer* CONTINGENT, dependent, qualified, with reservations, limited, provisional, provisory.

condolences plural noun *we offer our sincere condolences to his widow* SYMPATHY, commiseration(s), compassion, pity, support, comfort, consolation, understanding.

condom noun *using a condom is only one part of safe sex* CONTRACEPTIVE, prophylactic, sheath; *trademark* Trojan; *informal* rubber; *chiefly Brit. informal* French letter.

condone verb *we cannot condone such dreadful behavior* DISREGARD, accept, allow, let pass, turn a blind eye to, overlook, forget; forgive, pardon, excuse, let go. ANTONYM condemn.

conducive adjective *a environment that is* ***conducive to*** *learning* FAVORABLE TO, beneficial to, advantageous to, opportune to, propitious to, encouraging to, promising to, convenient for, good for, helpful, instrumental in, productive of, useful for. ANTONYM unfavorable.

conduct noun 1 *they complained about her conduct* BEHAVIOR, performance, demeanor; actions, activities, deeds, doings, exploits; habits, manners; *formal* comportment.

2 *the conduct of the elections* MANAGEMENT, running, direction, control, supervision, regulation, administration, organization, coordination, orchestration, handling.

▸ verb 1 *the election was conducted lawfully* MANAGE, direct, run, administer, organize, coordinate, orchestrate, handle, control, oversee, supervise, regulate, carry out/on.

2 *he was conducted through the corridors* ESCORT, guide, lead, usher, show; shepherd, see, bring, take, help.

3 *aluminum conducts heat* TRANSMIT, convey, carry, transfer, impart, channel, relay; disseminate, diffuse, radiate.

PHRASE: **conduct oneself** *I am proud of the way they conducted themselves* BEHAVE, act, acquit oneself, bear oneself; *formal* comport oneself.

conduit noun *spring water enters the brewery through a conduit* CHANNEL, duct, pipe, tube, gutter, trench, culvert, cut, sluice, spillway, flume, chute.

confederacy noun *a confederacy of Indian tribes* FEDERATION, confederation, alliance, league, association, coalition, consortium, syndicate, group, circle; bloc, axis.

confederate adjective *confederate councils* ALLIED, in alliance, in league, cooperating, associated, united, combined, amalgamated.

▸ noun *he was a confederate of the James brothers* ASSOCIATE, partner, accomplice, helper, assistant, ally, collaborator, colleague.

confederation noun *the farmers eventually formed a confederation* ALLIANCE, league, confederacy, federation, association, coalition, consortium, conglomerate, cooperative, syndicate, group, circle; society, union.

confer verb 1 *she went to confer with her colleagues* CONSULT, talk, speak, converse, have a chat, have a tête-à-tête, parley; *informal* have a confab, powwow.

2 *she* ***conferred*** *a knighthood* ***on*** *him* BESTOW ON, present to, grant to, award to, decorate with, honor with, give to, endow with, extend to. See note at GIVE.

conference noun 1 *an international conference* CONGRESS, meeting, convention, seminar, colloquium, symposium, forum, summit.

2 *he gathered them for a conference* DISCUSSION, consultation, debate, talk, conversation, dialogue, chat, tête-à-tête, parley; *informal* confab; *formal* confabulation.

confess verb 1 *he confessed that he had done it* ADMIT, acknowledge, reveal, disclose, divulge, avow, declare, profess; own up, tell all. ANTONYM deny.

2 *they could not make him confess* OWN UP, plead guilty, accept the blame; tell the truth, tell all, make a clean breast of it; *informal* come clean, spill the beans, let the cat out of the bag, get something off one's chest, let on, fess up.

3 *I confess I don't know* ACKNOWLEDGE, admit, concede, grant, allow, own, declare, affirm.

confession noun *they soon got a confession out of him* ADMISSION, acknowledgment, profession; revelation, disclosure, divulgence, avowal; guilty plea.

confidant, fem. confidante noun *he was her business adviser and confidant* CLOSE FRIEND, bosom friend, best friend; intimate; *informal* buddy, chum, pal, crony.

confide verb 1 *he confided his fears to his mother* REVEAL, disclose, divulge, lay bare, betray, impart, declare, intimate, uncover, expose, vouchsafe, tell; confess, admit, give away; *informal* blab, spill.

2 *I need him to* ***confide in*** OPEN ONE'S HEART TO, unburden oneself to, confess to, tell all to.

confidence noun 1 *I have little confidence in these figures* TRUST, belief, faith, credence, conviction. ANTONYMS skepticism, distrust.

2 *she's brimming with confidence* SELF-ASSURANCE, self-confidence, self-possession, assertiveness; poise, aplomb, phlegm; courage, boldness, mettle, nerve. ANTONYMS uncertainty, doubt.

3 *the girls exchanged confidences* SECRET, confidentiality, intimacy.

confident adjective 1 *we are confident that business will improve* OPTIMISTIC, hopeful, sanguine; sure, certain, positive, convinced, in no doubt, satisfied, assured, persuaded.

2 *a confident young man* SELF-ASSURED, assured, self-confident, positive, assertive, self-possessed, self-reliant, poised; coolheaded, phlegmatic, levelheaded, unperturbed, imperturbable, unruffled, at ease; *informal* together, can-do.

confidential adjective 1 *a confidential chat* PRIVATE, personal, intimate, quiet; secret, sensitive, classified, restricted, unofficial, unrevealed, undisclosed, unpublished; *informal* hush-hush, mum; *formal* sub rosa; *archaic* privy.

2 *a confidential friend* TRUSTED, trustworthy, trusty, faithful, reliable, dependable; close, bosom, intimate.

confidentially adverb *I thought we were speaking confidentially* PRIVATELY, in private, in confidence, between ourselves/themselves, off the record, quietly, secretly, in secret, behind closed doors; between you and me and the lamppost; *formal* sub rosa.

configuration noun *proper configuration of the sound system will improve the acoustics* ARRANGEMENT, layout, geography, design, organization, order, grouping, positioning, disposition, alignment; shape, form, appearance, formation, structure, setup, format.

confine verb 1 *they were confined in the house* ENCLOSE, incarcerate, imprison, intern, impound, hold captive, trap; shut in/up, keep, lock in/up, coop (up); fence in, hedge in, wall in/up.

2 *he confined his remarks to the weather* RESTRICT, limit.

confined adjective *she had a fear of confined spaces* CRAMPED, constricted, restricted, limited, small, narrow, compact, tight, uncomfortable, inadequate. ANTONYM roomy.

confinement noun 1 *solitary confinement* IMPRISONMENT, internment, incarceration, custody, captivity, detention, restraint; house arrest.

2 *the confinement of an animal* CAGING, enclosure; quarantine.

3 dated *she went to the hospital for her confinement* LABOR, delivery, birthing; birth, childbirth; *formal* parturition; *archaic* lying-in, childbed.

confines plural noun *these cubs have never ventured beyond the confines of the refuge* LIMITS, margins, extremities, edges, borders, boundaries, fringes, marches; periphery, perimeter.

confirm verb 1 *records confirm the latest evidence* CORROBORATE, verify, prove, validate, authenticate, substantiate, justify, vindicate; support, uphold, back up. ANTONYMS contradict, repudiate.

2 *he confirmed that help was on the way* AFFIRM, reaffirm, assert, assure someone, repeat; promise, guarantee. ANTONYM deny.

3 *his appointment was confirmed by the president* RATIFY, validate, sanction, endorse, formalize, authorize, warrant, accredit, approve, accept. ANTONYM revoke.

confirmation noun 1 *independent confirmation of the deaths* CORROBORATION, verification, proof, testimony, endorsement, authentication, substantiation, evidence.

2 *confirmation of your appointment* RATIFICATION, approval, authorization, validation, sanction, endorsement, formalization, accreditation, acceptance.

confirmed adjective *he's a confirmed gambler* ESTABLISHED, long-standing, committed, dyed-in-the-wool, through and through; staunch, loyal, faithful, devoted, dedicated, steadfast; habitual, compulsive, persistent; unapologetic, unashamed, inveterate, chronic, incurable; *informal* card-carrying.

confiscate verb *the guards confiscated his camera* IMPOUND, seize, commandeer, requisition, appropriate, expropriate, sequester, sequestrate, take (away); *Law* distrain. ANTONYM return.

confiscation noun *the confiscation of illegal weapons* SEIZURE, requisition, appropriation, expropriation, sequestration; *Law* distraint.

conflagration noun *the conflagration spread rapidly through the wooden buildings* FIRE, blaze, flames, inferno, firestorm.

conflate verb *the plot gets weighed down when the writers conflate too many issues into one episode* MIX, blend, fuse, unite, integrate.

conflict noun 1 *industrial conflicts* DISPUTE, quarrel, squabble, disagreement, dissension, clash; discord, friction, strife, antagonism, hostility, disputation, contention; feud, schism. ANTONYM agreement.

2 *the Vietnam conflict* WAR, campaign, battle, fighting, (armed) confrontation, engagement, encounter, struggle, hostilities; warfare, combat. ANTONYM peace.

3 *a conflict between his business and domestic life* CLASH, incompatibility, incongruity, friction; mismatch, variance, difference, divergence, contradiction, inconsistency. ANTONYM harmony.

▸ verb *their interests sometimes conflict* CLASH, be incompatible, vary, be at odds, be in conflict, differ, diverge, disagree, contrast, collide.

conflicting adjective *the two suspects gave conflicting stories* CONTRADICTORY, incompatible, inconsistent, irreconcilable, incongruous, contrary, opposite, opposing, antithetical, clashing, discordant, divergent; at odds.

confluence noun *the confluence of the Rhine and the Mosel* CONVERGENCE, meeting, junction.

conform verb 1 *visitors have to* ***conform to*** *our rules* COMPLY WITH, abide by, obey, observe, follow, keep to, stick to, adhere to, uphold, heed, accept, go along with, fall in with, respect, defer to; satisfy, meet, fulfill. ANTONYM flout.

2 *they refuse to conform* FOLLOW CONVENTION, be conventional, fit in, adapt, adjust, follow the crowd; comply, acquiesce, toe the line, follow the rules; submit, yield; *informal* play it by the book, play by the rules. ANTONYM rebel.

3 *goods must* ***conform to*** *their description* MATCH, fit, suit, answer, agree with, be like, correspond to, be consistent with, measure up to, tally with, square with. ANTONYM differ.

conformist noun *he was too much of a conformist to wear anything but a suit* TRADITIONALIST, conservative, stickler, formalist, diehard, reactionary; *informal* stick-in-the-mud, stuffed shirt. ANTONYMS eccentric, rebel.

confound verb 1 *the figures confounded analysts* AMAZE, astonish, dumbfound, stagger, surprise, startle, stun, throw, shake, discompose, bewilder, bedazzle, baffle, mystify, bemuse, perplex, puzzle, confuse; take aback, shake up, catch off balance; *informal* flabbergast, blow someone's mind, blow away, flummox, faze, stump, beat, fox, discombobulate.

2 *he has always confounded expectations* CONTRADICT, counter, invalidate, negate, go against, quash, explode, demolish, shoot down, destroy, disprove; *informal* poke holes in.

confront verb 1 *Jones confronted the intruder* CHALLENGE, face (up to), come face to face with, meet, accost; stand up to, brave; tackle; *informal* collar. ANTONYM avoid.

2 *the problems that confront us* TROUBLE, bother, burden, distress, worry, oppress, annoy, strain, stress, tax, torment, plague, blight, curse; face, beset.

3 *they must confront their problems* TACKLE, address, face, come to grips with, grapple with, take on, attend to, see to, deal with, take care of, handle, manage. ANTONYM avoid.

4 *she confronted him with the evidence* PRESENT, face.

confrontation noun *I've been trying to avoid a confrontation with his new girlfriend* CONFLICT, clash, fight, battle, encounter, faceoff, engagement, skirmish; hostilities, fighting; *informal* set-to, run-in, dust-up, showdown.

confuse verb 1 *don't confuse students with too much detail* BEWILDER, baffle, mystify, bemuse, perplex, puzzle, confound; *informal* flummox, faze, stump, fox, discombobulate, bedazzle. ANTONYM enlighten.

2 *the authors have confused the issue* COMPLICATE, muddle, jumble, garble, blur, obscure, cloud. ANTONYM simplify.

3 *some people **confuse** strokes **with** heart attacks* MISTAKE FOR, take for, misinterpret as; mix up with, muddle up with, confound with.

confused adjective 1 *they are confused about what is going on* BEWILDERED, bemused, puzzled, perplexed, baffled, mystified, nonplussed, muddled, dumbfounded, at sea, at a loss, taken aback, disoriented, disconcerted; *informal* flummoxed, clueless, fazed, discombobulated.

2 *her confused elderly mother* DEMENTED, bewildered, muddled, addled, befuddled, disoriented, disorientated; unbalanced, unhinged; senile. ANTONYM lucid.

3 *a confused recollection* VAGUE, unclear, indistinct, imprecise, blurred, hazy, woolly, shadowy, dim; imperfect, sketchy. ANTONYMS clear, precise.

4 *a confused mass of bones* DISORDERLY, disordered, disorganized, disarranged, out of order, untidy, muddled, jumbled, mixed up, chaotic, topsy-turvy; *informal* shambolic. ANTONYM neat.

confusing adjective *the instructions are confusing* BEWILDERING, baffling, unclear, perplexing, puzzling, mystifying, disconcerting; ambiguous, misleading, inconsistent, contradictory; unaccountable, inexplicable, impenetrable, unfathomable; complex, complicated.

confusion noun 1 *there is confusion about the new system* UNCERTAINTY, incertitude, unsureness, doubt, ignorance; *formal* dubiety. ANTONYM certainty.

2 *she stared in confusion* BEWILDERMENT, bafflement, perplexity, puzzlement, mystification, befuddlement; shock, daze, wonder, wonderment, astonishment; *informal* head-scratching, discombobulation.

3 *I could not live in this kind of confusion* DISORDER, disarray, disorganization, untidiness, chaos, mayhem; turmoil, tumult, disruption, upheaval, uproar, muddle, mess, shambles; *informal* three-ring circus. ANTONYM order.

4 *a confusion of boxes* JUMBLE, muddle, mess, heap, tangle; *informal* shambles. See note at JUMBLE.

confute verb *formal* *their assertion can certainly be confuted.* See REFUTE. See also note at REFUTE.

congeal verb *the gravy is starting to congeal* COAGULATE, clot, thicken, jell, cake, set, curdle.

congenial adjective 1 *very congenial people* HOSPITABLE, genial, personable, agreeable, friendly, pleasant, likable, amiable, nice; companionable, sociable, sympathetic, comradely, convivial, simpatico; LIKE-MINDED, compatible, kindred, well-suited. See note at PLEASANT. ANTONYM disagreeable.

2 *a congenial environment* PLEASANT, pleasing, agreeable, enjoyable, pleasurable, nice, appealing, satisfying, gratifying, delightful, relaxing, welcoming, hospitable; suitable, well-suited, favorable. ANTONYM unpleasant.

congenital adjective 1 *congenital defects* INBORN, inherited, hereditary, innate, inbred, constitutional, inbuilt, natural, inherent. See note at INHERENT. ANTONYM acquired.

2 *a congenital liar* INVETERATE, compulsive, persistent, chronic, regular, habitual, obsessive, confirmed; incurable, incorrigible, irredeemable, hopeless; unashamed, shameless, pathological.

congested adjective *the tunnels are congested with holiday traffic* CROWDED, overcrowded, full, overflowing, packed, jammed, thronged, teeming, swarming; obstructed, blocked, clogged, choked; *informal* snarled up, gridlocked, jam-packed. ANTONYM clear.

congestion noun *the congestion on I-95 is especially bad near exit 34* CROWDING, overcrowding; obstruction, blockage; traffic jam, bottleneck; *informal* snarl-up, gridlock.

conglomerate noun 1 *the conglomerate was broken up* CORPORATION, company, business, multinational, combine, group, consortium, partnership; firm.

2 *a conglomerate of disparate peoples* MIXTURE, mix, combination, amalgamation, union, marriage, fusion, composite, synthesis; miscellany, hodgepodge. See note at JUMBLE.

▸ adjective *a conglomerate mass* AGGREGATE, agglomerate, amassed, combined.

▸ verb *the debris conglomerated into planets* COALESCE, unite, join, combine, merge, fuse, consolidate, amalgamate, integrate, mingle, intermingle.

congratulate verb 1 *she congratulated him on his marriage* SEND ONE'S BEST WISHES TO, wish someone good luck, wish someone joy; drink to someone's health, toast. ANTONYM curse.

2 *they are to be congratulated* PRAISE, commend, applaud, salute, honor; pay tribute to, regard highly, pat on the back, take one's hat off to. ANTONYM criticize.

PHRASE: **congratulate oneself** *you should **congratulate yourself on** this wonderful accomplishment* TAKE PRIDE IN, feel proud of, flatter oneself on, pat oneself on the back for; take/feel satisfaction in, take pleasure in, glory in, bask in, delight in.

congratulations plural noun 1 *her congratulations on their wedding* GOOD WISHES, best wishes, compliments, felicitations.

2 *you all deserve congratulations* PRAISE, commendation, applause, salutes, honor, acclaim, cheers; approval, admiration, compliments, bouquets, kudos, adulation; a pat on the back.

▸ exclamation *Congratulations! You did it!* BRAVO, brava, mazel tov, kudos; *informal* congrats, attaboy, attagirl, way to go.

congregate verb *war protesters congregated in front of the recruiting office* ASSEMBLE, gather, collect, come together, convene, rally, rendezvous, muster, meet, cluster, group. See note at GATHER. ANTONYM disperse.

congregation noun 1 *the chapel congregation* PARISHIONERS, parish, churchgoers, flock, faithful, followers, believers, fellowship, communicants, laity, brethren, membership; throng, company, assemblage, audience.

2 *congregations of birds* GATHERING, assembly, flock, swarm, bevy, pack, group, body, crowd, mass, multitude, horde, host, mob, throng.

congress noun 1 *a congress of mathematicians* CONFERENCE, convention, seminar, colloquium, symposium, forum, meeting, assembly, gathering, rally, summit.

2 *elections for the new Congress* LEGISLATURE, legislative assembly, senate, house, house of representatives, parliament, convocation, diet, council, chamber.

congruence noun *the congruence of meaning and sound in his music* COMPATIBILITY, consistency, conformity, match, balance, consonance, congruity; agreement, accord, consensus, harmony, unity; *formal* concord. ANTONYM conflict.

conical adjective *a conical roof* CONE-SHAPED, tapered, tapering, pointed, funnel-shaped; *formal* infundibular; *informal* pointy; *Zoology* conoid.

conjectural adjective *your arguments are far too conjectural to be taken seriously* SPECULATIVE, suppositional, theoretical, hypothetical, putative, notional; postulated, inferred, presumed, assumed, presupposed, tentative.

conjecture noun *the information is merely conjecture* SPECULATION, guesswork, surmise, fancy, presumption, assumption, theory, postulation, supposition; inference, (an) extrapolation; an estimate; *informal* a guesstimate, a shot in the dark, a ballpark figure. ANTONYM fact.

▸ verb *I conjectured that the game was over* GUESS, speculate, surmise, infer, fancy, imagine, believe, think, suspect, presume, assume, hypothesize, suppose. ANTONYM know.

conjugal adjective *the conjugal bond must be a two-way relationship* MARITAL, matrimonial, nuptial, marriage, bridal; *Law* spousal; *literary* connubial.

conjunction noun **1** *a theory that the Americas were formed by a conjunction of floating islands* COMING TOGETHER, convergence, union, confluence.

2 *a conjunction of planets* CO-OCCURRENCE, concurrence, coincidence, coexistence, simultaneity, contemporaneity, concomitance, synchronicity, synchrony. PHRASE: **in conjunction with** *in conjunction with our Native American Day, there will be an exhibit of Pequot art in the gymnasium* TOGETHER WITH, along with, accompanying, accompanied by; as well as, in addition to, plus.

conjure verb **1** *he conjured a cigarette out of the air* PRODUCE, make appear, materialize, summon.

2 *the picture that his words* ***conjured up*** BRING TO MIND, call to mind, evoke, summon up, recall, recreate; echo, allude to, suggest, awaken.

conjuring noun *a demonstration of conjuring* MAGIC, illusion, sleight of hand, legerdemain, prestidigitation.

conjuror noun *she was one of the few professional female conjurors of her day* MAGICIAN, illusionist, prestidigitator.

connect verb **1** *electrodes were connected to the device* ATTACH, join, fasten, fix, affix, couple, link, secure, hitch; stick, adhere, fuse, pin, screw, bolt, clamp, clip, hook (up); add, append. See note at JOIN.

2 *rituals* ***connected with*** *Easter* ASSOCIATE WITH, link to/with, couple with; identify with, equate with, relate to.

connection noun **1** *the connection between commerce and art* LINK, relationship, relation, interconnection, interdependence, association; bond, tie, tie-in, correspondence, parallel, analogy.

2 *a poor connection in the plug* ATTACHMENT, joint, fastening, coupling.

3 *he has the right connections* CONTACT, friend, acquaintance, ally, colleague, associate; relation, relative, kin. PHRASE: **in connection with** *a man is being questioned in connection with the murder* REGARDING, concerning, with reference to, with regard to, with respect to, respecting, relating to, in relation to, on, connected with, on the subject of, in the matter of, apropos, re.

conniption noun *informal* See FIT[2] sense 3.

connivance noun *she was wholly unaware of the connivance of her husband and her best friend* COLLUSION, complicity, collaboration, involvement, assistance; tacit consent, conspiracy, intrigue.

connive verb *it is now known that at least two of the directors connived with Officer Cutler in the cover-up* CONSPIRE, collude, collaborate, intrigue, be hand in glove, plot, scheme; *informal* be in cahoots.

conniving adjective *his conniving brother planned the whole dirty affair* SCHEMING, cunning, crafty, calculating, devious, wily, sly, tricky, artful, guileful; manipulative, Machiavellian, disingenuous, deceitful, underhanded, treacherous; *informal* foxy.

connoisseur noun *a connoisseur of fine wines* EXPERT, authority, specialist, pundit, savant; arbiter of taste, aesthete; gourmet, epicure, gastronome; *informal* buff, maven.

connotation noun *there was a connotation of distrust in his voice* OVERTONE, undertone, undercurrent, implication, hidden meaning, nuance, hint, echo, vibrations, association, intimation, suggestion, suspicion, insinuation.

connote verb *he chose a style of dress that would connote toughness* IMPLY, suggest, indicate, signify, hint at, give the impression of, smack of, be associated with, allude to.

EASILY CONFUSED WORDS **connote, denote**

Denote refers to the literal, primary meaning of something; **connote** refers to other characteristics suggested or implied by that thing. Thus, one might say that the word 'mother' **denotes** 'a woman who is a parent' but **connotes** qualities such as 'protection' and 'affection.' **Connotate** is a needless variant of **connote** that, if anything, only adds to the confusion, and therefore should be avoided.

conquer verb **1** *the Franks conquered the Visigoths* DEFEAT, beat, vanquish, trounce, triumph over, be victorious over, get the better of, worst; overcome, overwhelm, overpower, overthrow, subdue, subjugate, quell, quash, crush, rout; *informal* lick, best, hammer, clobber, thrash, paste, demolish, annihilate, wipe the floor with, walk all over, make mincemeat of, massacre, slaughter, cream, shellac, skunk.

2 *Peru was conquered by Spain* SEIZE, take (over), appropriate, subjugate, capture, occupy, invade, annex, overrun.

3 *the first men to conquer Mount Everest* CLIMB, ascend, mount, scale, top, crest.

4 *the way to conquer fear* OVERCOME, get the better of, control, master, get a grip on, deal with, cope with, surmount, rise above, get over; quell, quash, beat, triumph over; *informal* lick.

conqueror noun *they may have uncovered the burial ground of legendary conqueror Genghis Khan* VANQUISHER, conquistador; victor, winner, champion, conquering hero.

conquest noun **1** *the conquest of the Aztecs* DEFEAT, vanquishment, annihilation, overthrow, subjugation, rout, mastery, crushing; victory over, triumph over.

2 *their conquest of the valley* SEIZURE, takeover, capture, occupation, invasion, acquisition, appropriation, subjugation, subjection.

3 *the conquest of K2* ASCENT, climbing, scaling.

4 *she's his latest conquest* CATCH, acquisition, prize, slave; admirer, fan, worshiper; lover, boyfriend, girlfriend.

consanguinity noun See RELATIONSHIP sense 2.

conscience noun *her conscience would not allow her to remain silent* SENSE OF RIGHT AND WRONG, moral sense, inner voice; morals, standards, values, principles, ethics, beliefs; compunction, scruples, qualms.

conscience-stricken adjective *the conscience-stricken teens who set fire to the gazebo* GUILT-RIDDEN, remorseful, ashamed, shamefaced, apologetic, sorry; chastened, contrite, guilty, regretful, rueful, repentant, penitent, abashed, sheepish, compunctious. ANTONYM unrepentant.

conscientious adjective *even Douglas, the most conscientious worker in our department, was laid off* DILIGENT, industrious, punctilious, painstaking, sedulous, assiduous, dedicated, careful, meticulous, thorough, attentive, hard-working, studious, rigorous, particular; religious, strict. ANTONYM casual.

conscious adjective **1** *the patient was conscious* AWARE, awake, alert, responsive, sentient, compos mentis.

2 *he became conscious of people talking* AWARE, mindful, sensible; *formal* cognizant; *rare* regardful. ANTONYM unaware.

3 *a conscious effort* DELIBERATE, intentional, intended, purposeful, purposive, knowing, considered, calculated, willful, premeditated, planned, volitional.

conscript verb *they were conscripted into the army* CALL UP, enlist, recruit, draft; *historical* press, impress.

▸ noun *an army conscript* compulsorily enlisted soldier, recruit, draftee. ANTONYM volunteer.

consecrate verb *the bishop had consecrated two cathedrals in his time* SANCTIFY, bless, make holy, make sacred; dedicate to God, devote, reserve, set apart; anoint, ordain; *formal* hallow. See note at DIVINE.

consecutive adjective *share prices fell for three consecutive days* SUCCESSIVE, succeeding, following, in succession, running, in a row, one after the other, back-to-back, continuous, straight, uninterrupted.

consensus noun **1** *there was consensus among delegates* AGREEMENT, harmony, concurrence, accord, unity, unanimity, solidarity; *formal* concord. ANTONYM disagreement.

2 *the consensus was that they should act* GENERAL OPINION, majority opinion, common view.

consent noun *the consent of all members* AGREEMENT, assent, acceptance, approval, approbation; permission, authorization, sanction, leave; backing, endorsement, support; *informal* go-ahead, thumbs up, green light, OK. ANTONYM dissent.

▸ verb *she* ***consented to*** *surgery* AGREE TO, assent to, yield to, give in to, submit to; allow, give permission for, sanction, accept, approve, go along with. ANTONYM forbid.

consequence noun **1** *a consequence of inflation* RESULT, upshot, outcome, effect, repercussion, ramification, corollary, concomitant, aftermath, aftereffect; fruit(s), product, by-product, end result; *informal* payoff; *Medicine* sequela. ANTONYM cause.

2 *the past is of no consequence* IMPORTANCE, import, significance, account, substance, note, mark, prominence, value, concern, interest; *formal* moment.

consequent adjective *heavy rains and consequent flash flooding are tonight's lead stories* RESULTING, resultant, ensuing, consequential; following, subsequent, successive; attendant, accompanying, concomitant; collateral, associated, related.

consequential adjective **1** *a fire and the consequential smoke damage* RESULTING, resultant, ensuing, consequent; following, subsequent; attendant, accompanying, concomitant; collateral, associated, related. ANTONYMS causal, unrelated.

2 *one of his more consequential initiatives* IMPORTANT, significant, major, momentous, weighty, material, appreciable, memorable, far-reaching, serious. ANTONYM insignificant.

consequently adverb *the doctor has had two emergencies this morning and consequently is running behind schedule* AS A RESULT, as a consequence, so, thus, therefore, ergo, accordingly, hence, for this/that reason, because of this/that, on this/that account; inevitably, necessarily.

conservation noun *the conservation of tropical forests* PRESERVATION, protection, safeguarding, safekeeping; care, guardianship, husbandry, supervision; upkeep, maintenance, repair, restoration; ecology, environmentalism.

conservative adjective **1** *the conservative wing of the party* RIGHT-WING, reactionary, traditionalist; Republican; *Brit.* Tory; *informal* redneck. ANTONYM socialist.

2 *our more conservative neighbors may object to the modern architecture being proposed* TRADITIONALIST, traditional, conventional, orthodox, old-fashioned, dyed-in-the-wool, hidebound, unadventurous, set in one's ways; moderate, middle-of-the-road, buttoned-down; *informal* stick-in-the-mud. ANTONYM radical.

3 *he wore a conservative blue suit* CONVENTIONAL, sober, modest, plain, unobtrusive, restrained, subtle, low-key, demure; *informal* square, straight. ANTONYM ostentatious.

4 *a conservative estimate* LOW, cautious, understated, moderate, reasonable.

▸ noun *liberals and conservatives have found common ground* RIGHT-WINGER, reactionary, rightist, diehard; Republican; *Brit.* Tory.

conservatory noun **1** *a frost-free conservatory* SUMMER HOUSE, belvedere; glasshouse, greenhouse, hothouse.

2 *a teaching job at the conservatory* CONSERVATOIRE, music school, drama school.

conserve verb *fossil fuel should be conserved* PRESERVE, protect, save, safeguard, keep, look after; sustain, prolong, perpetuate; store, reserve, husband. ANTONYM squander.

▸ noun *cherry conserve* JAM, preserve, jelly, marmalade.

consider verb **1** *Isabel considered her choices* THINK ABOUT, contemplate, reflect on, examine, review; mull over, ponder, deliberate on, chew over, meditate on, ruminate on; assess, evaluate, appraise; *informal* size up.

2 *I consider him irresponsible* DEEM, think, believe, judge, adjudge, rate, count, find; regard as, hold to be, reckon to be, view as, see as.

3 *he considered the ceiling* LOOK AT, contemplate, observe, regard, survey, view, scrutinize, scan, examine, inspect; *informal* check out, eyeball.

4 *the inquiry will consider those issues* TAKE INTO CONSIDERATION, take account of, make allowances for, bear in mind, be mindful of, remember, mind, mark, respect, heed, note, make provision for. ANTONYM ignore.

considerable adjective **1** *a considerable amount of money* SIZABLE, substantial, appreciable, significant; goodly, fair, hefty, handsome, decent, worthwhile; ample, plentiful, abundant, great, large, generous; *informal* tidy, not to be sneezed at. ANTONYM paltry.

2 *considerable success* MUCH, great, a lot of, lots of, a great deal of, plenty of, a fair amount of. ANTONYM minor.

3 *a considerable player in the game of politics* DISTINGUISHED, noteworthy, important, significant, prominent, eminent, influential, illustrious; renowned, celebrated, acclaimed. ANTONYM insignificant.

considerably adverb *alcoholic drinks vary considerably in strength* GREATLY, much, very much, a great deal, a lot, lots; significantly, substantially, appreciably, markedly, noticeably; *informal* plenty, seriously.

considerate adjective *the doorman was considerate enough to call her when the mail was delivered* ATTENTIVE, thoughtful, solicitous, mindful, heedful; obliging, accommodating, helpful, cooperative, patient; kind, unselfish, compassionate, sympathetic, caring, charitable, altruistic, generous; polite, sensitive, tactful.

consideration noun **1** *your case needs careful consideration* THOUGHT, deliberation, reflection, contemplation, rumination, meditation; examination, inspection, scrutiny, analysis, discussion; attention, regard; *formal* cogitation.

2 *his health is the prime consideration* FACTOR, issue, matter, concern, detail, aspect, feature.

3 *firms should show more consideration* ATTENTIVENESS, concern, care, thoughtfulness, solicitude; kindness, understanding, respect, sensitivity, tact, discretion; compassion, charity, benevolence. PHRASE: **take into consideration** *the company was willing to take her extended illness into consideration* CONSIDER, give thought to, take into account, allow for, provide for, plan for, make provision for, accommodate, bargain for, reckon with; foresee, anticipate.

considering preposition *considering his size, he was speedy* BEARING IN MIND, taking into consideration, taking into account, keeping in mind, in view of, in light of.

▸ adverb *informal he's been lucky, considering* ALL THINGS CONSIDERED, all in all, on the whole, at the end of the day, when all is said and done.

consign verb **1** *he was **consigned to** Sing Sing* SEND TO, deliver to, hand over to, turn over to, sentence to; confine in, imprison in, incarcerate in, lock up in; (**consign to prison/jail**) *informal* put away, put behind bars, send up the river.

2 *the picture was consigned to the gallery* ASSIGN, allocate, place, put, remit, commit.

3 *the package was consigned by a local company* SEND (OFF), courier, dispatch, transmit, convey, mail, post, ship.

4 *I consigned her picture to the garbage can* DEPOSIT, commit, banish, relegate.

consignment adjective *a consignment clothing shop* SECONDHAND, used, preowned, castoff, hand-me-down.

▸ noun *Dexter has to initial the paperwork for any consignment* DELIVERY, shipment, load, boatload, truckload, cargo; batch; goods.

consist verb **1** *the exhibition **consists of** 180 drawings* BE COMPOSED OF, be made up of, be formed of; comprise, contain, include, incorporate.

2 *style **consists in** the choices that writers make* BE INHERENT IN, lie in, reside in, be present in, be contained in; be expressed by.

consistency noun **1** *the trend shows a degree of consistency* UNIFORMITY, constancy, regularity, evenness, steadiness, stability, equilibrium; dependability, reliability.

2 *mix until the batter is of pouring consistency* THICKNESS, density, viscosity, heaviness, texture; firmness, solidity.

consistent adjective **1** *consistent opinion-poll evidence* CONSTANT, regular, uniform, steady, stable, even, unchanging, undeviating, unfluctuating; dependable, reliable, predictable. ANTONYM irregular.

2 *her injuries were **consistent with** a knife attack* COMPATIBLE WITH, congruous with, consonant with, in tune with, in line with, reconcilable with; corresponding to, conforming to. ANTONYM incompatible.

consolation noun *I realize that mere words are of little consolation* COMFORT, solace, sympathy, compassion, pity, commiseration, empathy; relief, help, support, moral support, encouragement, reassurance.

console[1] verb *she tried to console him* COMFORT, solace, sympathize with, commiserate with, show compassion for, condole with; help, support, cheer (up), hearten, encourage, reassure, soothe. ANTONYM upset.

console[2] noun *a digital console* CONTROL PANEL, instrument panel, dashboard; keyboard, keypad; *informal* dash.

consolidate verb **1** *we consolidated our position in the market* STRENGTHEN, secure, stabilize, reinforce, fortify; enhance, improve.

2 *consolidate the results into an action plan* COMBINE, unite, merge, integrate, amalgamate, fuse, synthesize, bring together, unify. See note at JOIN.

consonance noun *a constitution in consonance with the customs of the people* AGREEMENT, accord, harmony, unison; compatibility, congruity, congruence; *formal* concord.

consonant PHRASE: **consonant with** *these findings are consonant with recent research* IN AGREEMENT WITH, consistent with, in accordance with, in harmony with, compatible with, congruous with, in tune with.

consort noun *the queen and her consort* PARTNER, life partner, companion, mate; spouse, husband, wife, helpmate.

▸ verb *he consorted with other women* ASSOCIATE, keep company, mix, go around, spend time, socialize, fraternize, have dealings; *informal* run around, hang around/out, be thick.

consortium noun *many small business owners felt pressured to join the consortium* ASSOCIATION, alliance, coalition, union, league, guild, syndicate, federation, confederation, confederacy, conglomerate, cooperative, combine, partnership, affiliation, organization; club, society, congress.

conspicuous adjective *a tropical vine with conspicuous blossoms* EASILY SEEN, clear, visible, noticeable, discernible, perceptible, detectable; obvious, manifest, evident, apparent, marked, pronounced, prominent, patent, crystal clear; striking, eye-catching, overt, blatant; distinct, recognizable, unmistakable, inescapable; *informal* as plain as the nose on one's face, standing/sticking out like a sore thumb. See note at NOTICEABLE.

conspiracy noun **1** *a conspiracy to manipulate the results* PLOT, scheme, plan, machination, ploy, trick, ruse, subterfuge; *informal* racket. See note at PLOT.

2 *conspiracy to commit murder* PLOTTING, collusion, intrigue, connivance, machination, collaboration; treason.

conspirator noun *is there any credible evidence of a conspirator working with Oswald?* PLOTTER, schemer, intriguer, colluder, collaborator, conniver.

conspire verb **1** *they admitted conspiring to steal cars* PLOT, scheme, plan, intrigue, machinate, collude, connive, collaborate, work hand in glove; *informal* be in cahoots.

2 *circumstances conspired against them* ACT TOGETHER, work together, combine, unite, join forces; *informal* gang up.

constancy noun **1** *constancy between lovers* FIDELITY, faithfulness, loyalty, commitment, dedication, devotion; dependability, reliability, trustworthiness.

2 *the constancy of Henry's views* STEADFASTNESS, resolution, resolve, firmness, fixedness; determination, perseverance, tenacity, doggedness, staunchness, staying power, obstinacy.

3 *the constancy of their doubt* CONSISTENCY, permanence, persistence, durability, endurance; uniformity, immutability, regularity, stability, steadiness.

constant adjective **1** *the constant background noise* CONTINUAL, continuous, persistent, sustained, around/round-the-clock; ceaseless, unceasing, perpetual, incessant, never-ending, eternal, endless, unabating, nonstop, unrelieved; interminable, unremitting, relentless. See note at RESOLUTE. ANTONYMS fitful, inconstant.

2 *a constant speed* CONSISTENT, regular, steady, uniform, even, invariable, unvarying, unchanging, undeviating, unfluctuating. ANTONYM variable.

3 *a constant friend* FAITHFUL, loyal, devoted, true, fast, firm, unswerving; steadfast, staunch, dependable, trustworthy, trusty, reliable, dedicated, committed. ANTONYM fickle.

4 *constant vigilance* STEADFAST, steady, resolute, determined, tenacious, dogged, unwavering, unflagging.

▸ noun *dread of cancer has been a constant* UNCHANGING FACTOR, given.

constantly adverb *the language is constantly in flux* ALWAYS, all the time, continually, continuously, persistently; around/round the clock, night and day, 'morning, noon, and night'; endlessly, nonstop, incessantly, unceasingly, perpetually, eternally, forever; interminably, unremittingly, relentlessly; *informal* 24-7. ANTONYM occasionally.

constellation noun See table.

THE EIGHTY-EIGHT CONSTELLATIONS

Andromeda: Andromeda	Lacerta: The Lizard
Antlia: The Air Pump	Leo: The Lion
Apus: Bird of Paradise	Leo Minor: The Little Lion
Aquarius: The Water Bearer/Carrier	Lepus: The Hare
Aquila: The Eagle	Libra: The Scales/ Balance
Ara: The Altar	Lupus: The Wolf
Aries: The Ram	Lynx: The Lynx
Auriga: The Charioteer	Lyra: The Harp/Lyre
Boötes: The Herdsman	Mensa: The Table
Caelum: The Chisel	Microscopium: The Microscope
Camelopardalis: The Giraffe	Monoceros: The Unicorn
Cancer: The Crab	Musca: The Fly
Canes: Venatici The Hunting Dogs	Norma: The Rule
Canis Major: The Big Dog	Octans: The Octant
Canis Minor: The Little Dog	Ophiuchus: The Serpent Bearer
Capricornus: The Goat	Orion: The Hunter
Carina: The Ship's Keel	Pavo: The Peacock
Cassiopeia: Cassiopeia	Pegasus: The Flying Horse
Centaurus: The Centaur	Perseus: Perseus
Cepheus: Cepheus	Phoenix: The Firebird
Cetus: The Whale	Pictor: The Easel
Chamaeleon: The Chameleon	Pisces: The Fishes
Circinus: The Compass	Piscis Austrinus: The Southern Fish
Columba: The Dove	Puppis: The Ship's Stern or Poop Deck
Coma Berenices: Berenice's Hair	Pyxis: The Ship's Compass
Corona Australis: The Southern Crown	Reticulum: The Net
Coronas Borealis: The Northern Crown	Sagitta: The Arrow
Corvus: The Crow/Raven	Sagittarius: The Archer
Crater: The Cup	Scorpius: The Scorpion
Crux: The Cross	Sculptor: The Sculptor
Cygnus: The Swan	Scutum: The Shield
Delphinus: The Dolphin	Serpens Caput: The Serpent
Dorado: The Goldfish/Swordfish	Sextans: The Sextant
Draco: The Dragon	Taurus: The Bull
Equuleus: The Little Horse	Telescopium: The Telescope
Eridanus: The River Eridanus	Triangulum: The Triangle
Fornax: The Furnace	Triangulum Australe: The Southern Triangle
Gemini: The Twins	Tucana: The Toucan
Grus: The Crane	Ursa Major: The Great Bear
Hercules: Hercules	Ursa Minor: The Little Bear
Horologium: The Clock	Vela: The Sails
Hydra: The Sea Monster	Virgo: The Virgin
Hydrus: The Sea Serpent	Volans: The Flying Fish
Indus: The Indian	Vulpecula: The Little Fox

consternation noun *much to his colleagues' consternation, Victor was awarded the job in Paris* DISMAY, perturbation, distress, disquiet, discomposure; surprise, amazement, astonishment; alarm, panic, fear, fright, shock. ANTONYM satisfaction.

constituent adjective *constituent parts* COMPONENT, integral; elemental, basic, essential, inherent.

▸ noun **1** *representatives must listen to their constituents* VOTER, elector, member of a constituency.

2 *the constituents of tobacco* COMPONENT, ingredient, element; part, piece, bit, unit; section, portion.

constitute verb **1** *farmers constituted 10 percent of the* *population* AMOUNT TO, add up to, account for, form, make up, compose.

2 *this constitutes a breach of copyright* BE EQUIVALENT TO, be, embody, be tantamount to, be regarded as.

3 *the courts were constituted in 1875* INAUGURATE, establish, initiate, found, create, set up, start, form, organize, develop; commission, charter, invest, appoint, install, empower.

constitution noun 1 *the constitution guarantees our rights* CHARTER, social code, law; bill of rights; rules, regulations, fundamental principles.

2 *the chemical constitution of the dye* COMPOSITION, makeup, structure, construction, arrangement, configuration, formation, anatomy.

3 *she has the constitution of an ox* HEALTH, physical condition, fettle; physique.

constitutional adjective 1 *constitutional powers* LEGAL, lawful, legitimate, authorized, permitted; sanctioned, ratified, warranted, constituted, statutory, chartered, vested, official; by law.

2 *a constitutional weakness* INHERENT, intrinsic, innate, fundamental, essential, organic; congenital, inborn, inbred.

▸ noun *dated she went out for a constitutional.* See WALK noun sense 1.

constrain verb 1 *he felt constrained to explain* COMPEL, force, drive, impel, oblige, coerce, prevail on, require; press, push, pressure. See note at COMPEL.

2 *prices were constrained by government controls* RESTRICT, limit, curb, check, restrain, contain, rein in, hold back, keep down.

constrained adjective *she was uncharacteristically constrained whenever her in-laws were visiting* UNNATURAL, awkward, self-conscious, forced, stilted, strained; restrained, reserved, reticent, guarded. ANTONYM relaxed.

constraint noun 1 *financial constraints* RESTRICTION, limitation, curb, check, restraint, control, damper, rein; hindrance, impediment, obstruction, handicap.

2 *they were able to talk without constraint* INHIBITION, uneasiness, embarrassment; restraint, reticence, guardedness, formality; self-consciousness, awkwardness, stiltedness.

constrict verb 1 *fat constricts the blood vessels* NARROW, make narrower, tighten, compress, contract, squeeze, strangle, strangulate; *archaic* straiten. ANTONYMS expand, dilate.

2 *fear of crime constricts many people's lives* RESTRICT, impede, limit, inhibit, obstruct, interfere with, hinder, hamper.

constriction noun *there was a constriction in her throat* TIGHTNESS, pressure, compression, contraction, cramp; obstruction, blockage, impediment; *Medicine* stricture, stenosis.

construct verb 1 *a new high-rise was being constructed* BUILD, erect, put up, set up, raise, establish, assemble, manufacture, fabricate, create, make. ANTONYM demolish.

2 *he constructed a faultless argument* FORMULATE, form, put together, create, devise, design, compose, work out; fashion, mold, shape, frame.

construction noun 1 *the construction of a new airport* BUILDING, erection, putting up, setting up, establishment; assembly, manufacture, fabrication, creation.

2 *the station was a spectacular construction* STRUCTURE, building, edifice, pile.

3 *you could put an honest construction on their conduct* INTERPRETATION, reading, meaning, explanation, explication, construal; *informal* take, spin.

constructive adjective *constructive criticism* USEFUL, helpful, productive, positive, encouraging; practical, valuable, profitable, worthwhile.

construe verb *I'm not sure you've properly construed what I just said* INTERPRET, understand, read, see, take, take to mean, regard. See note at CLARIFY.

consul noun *he was posing as the French consul* AMBASSADOR, diplomat, chargé d'affaires, attaché, envoy, emissary, plenipotentiary.

consult verb 1 *you need to consult a lawyer* SEEK ADVICE FROM, ask, take counsel from, call on/upon, speak to, turn to, have recourse to; *informal* pick someone's brains.

2 *the government must consult with interested parties* CONFER, have discussions, talk things over, exchange views, communicate, parley, deliberate; *informal* put their heads together.

3 *she consulted her diary* REFER TO, turn to, look at.

consultant noun *she freelanced as a communications consultant* ADVISER, expert, specialist, authority, pundit.

consultation noun 1 *the need for further consultation with industry* DISCUSSION, dialogue, discourse, debate, negotiation, deliberation.

2 *a 30-minute consultation* MEETING, talk, discussion, interview, audience, hearing; appointment, session; *formal* confabulation, colloquy.

consume verb 1 *vast amounts of food and drink were consumed* EAT, devour, ingest, swallow, gobble up, wolf down, guzzle, feast on, snack on; DRINK, gulp down, imbibe; *informal* tuck into, put away, polish off, dispose of, pig out on, down, swill, scarf (down/up).

2 *natural resources are being consumed at an alarming rate* USE (UP), utilize, expend; deplete, exhaust; waste, squander, drain, dissipate, fritter away.

3 *the fire consumed fifty houses* DESTROY, demolish, lay waste, wipe out, annihilate, devastate, gut, ruin, wreck.

4 *Carolyn was consumed with guilt* EAT UP, devour, obsess, grip, overwhelm; absorb, preoccupy.

consumer noun *if you're a satisfied consumer, we've done our job | they provide what consumers ask for* PURCHASER, buyer, customer, shopper; user, end user; client, patron; (**the consumer** or **consumers**) the public, the market.

consuming adjective *his consuming passion for opera* ABSORBING, compelling, compulsive, obsessive, overwhelming; intense, ardent, strong, powerful, burning, raging, fervid, profound, deep-seated.

consummate verb *the deal was finally consummated* COMPLETE, conclude, finish, accomplish, achieve; execute, carry out, perform; *informal* sew up, wrap up; *formal* effectuate.

▸ adjective *his consummate skill | a consummate politician* SUPREME, superb, superlative, superior, accomplished, expert, proficient, skillful, skilled, masterly, master, first-class, talented, gifted, polished, practiced, perfect, ultimate; complete, total, utter, absolute, pure.

consumption noun 1 *food unfit for human consumption* EATING, drinking, ingestion.

2 *the consumption of fossil fuels* USE, using up, utilization, expending, depletion; waste, squandering, dissipation.

contact noun 1 *a disease transmitted through casual contact* TOUCH, touching; proximity, exposure.

2 *foreign diplomats were asked to avoid all contact with him* COMMUNICATION, correspondence, touch; association, connection, intercourse, relations, dealings; *archaic* traffic.

3 *he had many contacts in Germany* CONNECTION, acquaintance, associate, friend.

▸ verb *anyone with information should contact the police* GET IN TOUCH WITH, communicate with, make contact with, approach, notify; telephone, phone, call, speak to, talk to, write to, get hold of.

contagion noun *dated European ships transported contagions to and from the New World* DISEASE, infection, illness, plague, blight; *informal* bug, virus; *archaic* pestilence.

contagious adjective *the disease is highly contagious* INFECTIOUS, communicable, transmittable, transmissible, spreadable; *informal* catching; *dated* infective.

contain verb 1 *the archive contains much unpublished material* INCLUDE, comprise, take in, incorporate, involve, encompass, embrace; consist of, be made up of, be composed of.

2 *the boat contained four people* HOLD, carry, accommodate, seat.

3 *he must contain his anger* RESTRAIN, curb, rein in, suppress, repress, stifle, subdue, quell, swallow, bottle up, hold in, keep in check; control, master.

container noun *a container of leftover beets* RECEPTACLE, vessel, canister, can, box, holder, repository.

contaminate verb *the river was contaminated with photographic chemicals* POLLUTE, adulterate; defile, debase, corrupt, taint, infect, foul, spoil, soil, stain, sully; poison; *literary* befoul. See note at POLLUTE. ANTONYM purify.

contemplate verb 1 *she contemplated her image in the mirror* LOOK AT, view, regard, examine, inspect, observe, survey, study, scrutinize, scan, stare at, gaze at, eye.

2 *he contemplated his fate* THINK ABOUT, ponder, reflect on, consider, mull over, muse on, dwell on, deliberate over, meditate on, ruminate on, chew over, brood on/about, turn over in one's mind; *formal* cogitate.

3 *he was contemplating action for damages* CONSIDER, think about, have in mind, intend, propose; envisage, foresee.

contemplation noun 1 *the contemplation of beautiful objects* VIEWING, examination, inspection, observation, survey, study, scrutiny.

2 *the monks sat in quiet contemplation* THOUGHT, reflection, meditation, consideration, rumination, deliberation, reverie, introspection, brown study; *formal* cogitation, cerebration.

contemplative adjective *a peaceful, contemplative mood* THOUGHTFUL, pensive, reflective, meditative, musing, ruminative, introspective, brooding, deep/lost in thought, in a brown study.

contemporary adjective 1 *contemporary sources* OF THE TIME, of the day, contemporaneous, concurrent, coeval, coexisting, coexistent.

2 *contemporary society* MODERN, present-day, present, current, present-time.

3 *a very contemporary design* MODERN, up-to-date, up-to-the-minute, fashionable; modish, latest, recent; *informal* trendy, with it, du jour. ANTONYMS old-fashioned, out of date.

▸ noun *Chaucer's contemporaries* PEER, fellow; *formal* compeer.

contempt noun 1 *she regarded him with contempt* SCORN, disdain, disrespect, scornfulness, contemptuousness, derision; disgust, loathing, hatred, abhorrence. ANTONYM respect.

2 *he is guilty of contempt of court* DISRESPECT, disregard, slighting. ANTONYM respect.

contemptible adjective *what they said to poor old Mr. Ortiz was contemptible* DESPICABLE, detestable, hateful, reprehensible, deplorable, unspeakable, disgraceful, shameful, ignominious, abject, low, mean, cowardly, unworthy, discreditable, petty, worthless, shabby, cheap, beyond contempt, beyond the pale, sordid; *archaic* scurvy. ANTONYM admirable.

contemptuous adjective *the contemptuous look on your face says it all* SCORNFUL, disdainful, disrespectful, insulting, insolent, derisive, mocking, sneering, scoffing, withering, scathing, snide; condescending, supercilious, haughty, proud, superior, arrogant, dismissive, aloof; *informal* high and mighty, snotty, sniffy. ANTONYM respectful.

contend verb 1 *the pilot had to contend with torrential rain* COPE WITH, face, grapple with, deal with, take on, pit oneself against.

2 *three main groups were contending for power* COMPETE, vie, contest, fight, battle, tussle, go head to head; strive, struggle.

3 *he contends that the judge was wrong* ASSERT, maintain, hold, claim, argue, insist, state, declare, profess, affirm; allege; *formal* aver.

content[1] adjective *she seemed content with life* CONTENTED, satisfied, pleased, gratified, fulfilled, happy, cheerful, glad; unworried, untroubled, at ease, at peace, tranquil, serene. ANTONYMS discontented, dissatisfied.

▸ verb *her reply seemed to content him* SATISFY, please; soothe, pacify, placate, appease, mollify.

▸ noun *a time of content.* See CONTENTMENT.

content[2] noun 1 *foods with a high fiber content* AMOUNT, proportion, quantity.

2 **(contents)** *the contents of a vegetarian sausage* CONSTITUENTS, ingredients, components, elements.

3 **(contents)** *the book's table of contents* CHAPTERS, sections, divisions.

4 *the content of the essay* SUBJECT MATTER, subject, theme, argument, thesis, message, thrust, substance, matter, material, text, ideas.

contented adjective *a contented man.* See CONTENT[1] adjective.

contention noun **1** *a point of contention* DISAGREEMENT, dispute, disputation, argument, discord, conflict, friction, strife, dissension, disharmony. ANTONYM agreement.

2 *we questioned the validity of his contention* ARGUMENT, claim, plea, submission, allegation, assertion, declaration; opinion, stand, position, view, belief, thesis, case. PHRASE: **in contention** *the sisters are in contention for the top ranking* IN COMPETITION, competing, contesting, contending, vying; striving, struggling.

contentious adjective **1** *a contentious issue* CONTROVERSIAL, disputable, debatable, disputed, open to debate, vexed.

2 *a contentious debate* HEATED, vehement, fierce, violent, intense, impassioned.

3 *contentious people.* See QUARRELSOME.

contentment noun *finally being alone brought her a contentment she'd never known* CONTENTEDNESS, content, satisfaction, gratification, fulfillment, happiness, pleasure, cheerfulness; ease, comfort, well-being, peace, equanimity, serenity, tranquility.

contest noun **1** *a boxing contest* COMPETITION, match, tournament, game, meet, event, trial, bout, heat, race.

2 *the contest for the party leadership* FIGHT, battle, tussle, struggle, competition, race.

▸ verb **1** *he intended to contest the seat* COMPETE FOR, contend for, vie for, fight for, try to win, go for.

2 *we contested the decision* OPPOSE, object to, challenge, take a stand against, take issue with, question, call into question.

3 *the issues have been hotly contested* DEBATE, argue about, dispute, quarrel over.

contestant noun *the celebrity contestants play for their favorite charities* COMPETITOR, participant, player, contender, candidate, aspirant, hopeful, entrant.

context noun **1** *the wider historical context* CIRCUMSTANCES, conditions, factors, state of affairs, situation, background, scene, setting.

2 *a quote taken out of context* FRAME OF REFERENCE, contextual relationship; text, subject, theme, topic.

contiguous adjective *the contiguous Gulf states* ADJACENT, neighboring, adjoining, bordering, next-door; abutting, connecting, touching, in contact, proximate.

contingency noun *we've tried to imagine and provide for all possible contingencies* EVENTUALITY, (chance) event, incident, happening, occurrence, juncture, possibility, fortuity, accident, chance, emergency.

contingent adjective **1** *the merger is* ***contingent on*** *government approval* DEPENDENT ON, conditional on, subject to, determined by, hinging on, resting on.

2 *contingent events* CHANCE, accidental, fortuitous, possible, unforeseeable, unpredictable, random, haphazard. See note at ACCIDENTAL.

▸ noun **1** *a contingent of Japanese businessmen* GROUP, party, body, band, company, cohort, deputation, delegation; *informal* bunch, gang.

2 *a contingent of soldiers* DETACHMENT, unit, group.

continual adjective *a service disrupted by continual breakdowns* FREQUENT, repeated, recurrent, recurring, intermittent, regular. ANTONYMS occasional, sporadic.

USAGE NOTE **continual, continuous**

Continual = frequently recurring; intermittent—e.g.: "And [the police are] removing [the homeless]—by police rides to the edge of town, by continual issuing of citations for camping, by mass towing of vehicles and by routine discarding of people's belongings." (*USA Today*; Dec. 3, 1997.) *Continuous* = occurring without interruption; unceasing—e.g.: "Crow Canyon archaeologists want to study the twelfth- and thirteenth-century village to determine exactly when it was inhabited and whether it was occupied continuously or intermittently." (*Santa Fe New Mexican*; Sept. 8, 1996.) A good mnemonic device is to think of the *-ous* ending as being short for "one uninterrupted sequence."

The two words are frequently confused, usually with *continuous* horning in where *continual* belongs—e.g.:

• "Minutes after the arrest, Wayne Forrest, a Deputy Attorney General helping prosecute the case, told the presiding judge, Charles R. DiGisi, that the sheriff's office had been engaged in a 'continuous [read *continual*] course of misconduct' in the Spath case." (*New York Times*; Jan. 18, 1992.)

• "Continuous [read *Continual*] interruptions are frustrating because it often means [read *they often mean*] you have to warm up all over again or don't get a complete workout." (*Montgomery Advertiser*; Jan. 1, 1996.)

The two-word phrase *almost continuous* is correctly replaced by the single-word *continual*—e.g.: "The antidepressant Prozac has been in the news almost continuously [read *continually*] since it was introduced in Belgium in 1986." (*Tampa Tribune*; Nov. 24, 1996.)

A related mistake is to use *continuous* for something that happens at regular (e.g., annual) intervals—e.g.: "The White House tree-lighting ceremony has been held continuously [read *annually*] since 1923." (*Herald-Sun* [Durham, NC]; Dec. 6, 1996.) **—BG**

continually adverb **1** *security measures are continually updated and improved* FREQUENTLY, regularly, repeatedly, recurrently, again and again, time and (time) again; constantly. ANTONYMS occasionally, sporadically.

2 *patients were monitored continually* CONSTANTLY, continuously, around/round the clock, day and night, night and day, 'morning, noon, and night', without a break, nonstop; all the time, the entire time, always, forever, at every turn, incessantly, ceaselessly, endlessly, perpetually, eternally, 24-7. ANTONYMS occasionally, sporadically.

continuance noun **1** *concerned with the continuance of life.* See CONTINUATION.

2 *the prosecution sought a continuance* ADJOURNMENT, postponement, deferment, stay.

continuation noun *the continuation of our relationship seems futile* CARRYING ON, continuance, extension, prolongation, protraction, perpetuation. ANTONYM end.

continue verb **1** *he was unable to continue with his job* CARRY ON, proceed, go on, keep on, persist, press on, persevere; *informal* stick, soldier on. ANTONYM stop.

2 *discussions continued throughout the night* GO ON, carry on, last, extend, be prolonged, run on, drag on. ANTONYMS stop, cease.

3 *we are keen to continue this relationship* MAINTAIN, keep up, sustain, keep going, keep alive, preserve. ANTONYMS suspend, break off.

4 *his willingness to continue in office* REMAIN, stay, carry on, keep going.

5 *we continued our conversation after supper* RESUME,

pick up, take up, carry on with, return to, recommence. ANTONYM end.

continuing adjective *our continuing commitment to customer satisfaction* ONGOING, continuous, sustained, persistent, steady, relentless, rolling, uninterrupted, unabating, unremitting, unrelieved, unceasing. ANTONYM sporadic.

continuity noun *a breakdown in the continutiy of care* CONTINUOUSNESS, uninterruptedness, flow, progression.

continuous adjective *the rain has been continuous since early this morning* UNCEASING, uninterrupted, unbroken, constant, ceaseless, incessant, steady, sustained, solid, continuing, ongoing, without a break, nonstop, around/round-the-clock, persistent, unremitting, relentless, unrelenting, unabating, unrelieved, without respite, endless, unending, never-ending, perpetual, everlasting, eternal, interminable; consecutive, rolling, running; *archaic* without surcease. See note at CONTINUAL. ANTONYMS momentary, temporary.

contort verb *her face was contorted with grief* TWIST, bend out of shape, distort, misshape, warp, buckle, deform.

contour noun *the contour of the moon's surface* OUTLINE, shape, form; lines, curves, figure; silhouette, profile.

contraband noun **1** *contraband was suspected* SMUGGLING, illegal traffic, black marketeering, bootlegging; the black market.

2 *they confiscated the contraband* STOLEN GOODS, swag, bootleg.

▸ adjective *contraband goods* SMUGGLED, black-market, bootleg, under the counter, illegal, illicit, unlawful; prohibited, banned, proscribed, forbidden; *informal* hot.

contraceptive noun *what type of contraceptive did you use?* BIRTH CONTROL; prophylactic, condom, birth control pill, the pill, diaphragm, the sponge, female condom, IUD, cervical cap, morning-after pill, BC/BCP; *trademark* Plan B.

contract noun *a legally binding contract* AGREEMENT, commitment, arrangement, settlement, understanding, compact, covenant, bond; deal, bargain; *Law* indenture.

▸ verb **1** *the market for such goods began to contract* SHRINK, get smaller, decrease, diminish, reduce, dwindle, decline. ANTONYMS expand, increase.

2 *her stomach muscles contracted* TIGHTEN, tense, flex, constrict, draw in, narrow. ANTONYM relax.

3 *she contracted her brow* WRINKLE, knit, crease, purse, pucker.

4 *his name was soon contracted to "Rob"* SHORTEN, abbreviate, cut, reduce; elide. ANTONYMS expand, lengthen.

5 *the company contracted to rebuild the stadium* UNDERTAKE, pledge, promise, covenant, commit oneself, engage, agree, enter an agreement, make a deal.

6 *she contracted rubella* DEVELOP, catch, get, pick up, come down with, be struck down by, be stricken with, succumb to.

7 *he contracted a debt of $3,300* INCUR, run up.

PHRASE: **contract out** *trash collection is contracted out by the town* SUBCONTRACT, outsource, farm out.

contraction noun **1** *the contraction of the industry* SHRINKING, shrinkage, decline, decrease, diminution, dwindling.

2 *the contraction of muscles* TIGHTENING, tensing, flexing.

3 *my contractions started at midnight* LABOR PAINS, labor; cramps.

4 *"goodbye" is a contraction of "God be with you"* ABBREVIATION, short form, shortened form, elision, diminutive.

contradict verb **1** *he contradicted the government's account of the affair* DENY, rebut, dispute, challenge, counter, controvert; *formal* gainsay. ANTONYMS confirm, agree with.

2 *nobody dared to contradict him* ARGUE AGAINST, go against, challenge, oppose; *formal* gainsay.

3 *this research contradicts previous assertions* CONFLICT WITH, be at odds with, be at variance with, be inconsistent with, run counter to, disagree with. ANTONYMS corroborate, support.

contradiction noun **1** *the contradiction between his faith and his lifestyle* CONFLICT, clash, disagreement, opposition, inconsistency, mismatch, variance. ANTONYM agreement.

2 *a contradiction of his statement* DENIAL, refutation, rebuttal, countering. ANTONYMS confirmation, reaffirmation.

contradictory adjective *their contradictory accounts angered the lieutenant* OPPOSED, in opposition, opposite, antithetical, contrary, contrasting, conflicting, at variance, at odds, opposing, clashing, divergent, discrepant, different; inconsistent, incompatible, irreconcilable. See note at OPPOSITE.

contraption noun *he's driving around the yard in another one of his wild contraptions* DEVICE, gadget, apparatus, machine, appliance, mechanism, invention, contrivance; *informal* gizmo, widget, doohickey.

contrary adjective **1** *contrary views* OPPOSITE, opposing, opposed, contradictory, clashing, conflicting, antithetical, incompatible, irreconcilable. See note at OPPOSITE. ANTONYMS compatible, same.

2 *she was sulky and contrary* PERVERSE, awkward, difficult, uncooperative, unhelpful, obstructive, disobliging, recalcitrant, willful, self-willed, stubborn, obstinate, defiant, mulish, pigheaded, intractable; *formal* refractory; *archaic* froward. ANTONYMS cooperative, accommodating.

▸ noun *in fact, the contrary is true* OPPOSITE, reverse, converse, antithesis.

PHRASE: **contrary to** *contrary to what we had predicted, the lemon potatoes were very popular* IN CONFLICT WITH, against, at variance with, at odds with, in opposition to, counter to, incompatible with.

contrast noun **1** *the contrast between rural and urban trends* DIFFERENCE, dissimilarity, disparity, distinction, contradistinction, divergence, variance, variation, differentiation; contradiction, incongruity, opposition, polarity. ANTONYM similarity.

2 *Jane was a complete contrast to Sarah* OPPOSITE, antithesis; foil, complement.

▸ verb **1** *a view that* ***contrasts with*** *his earlier opinion* DIFFER FROM, be at variance with, be contrary to, conflict with, go against, be at odds with, be in opposition to, disagree with, clash with. ANTONYMS resemble, echo.

2 *people* ***contrasted*** *her* ***with*** *her sister* COMPARE WITH/TO, set side by side with, juxtapose with/to; measure against; distinguish from, differentiate from. ANTONYM liken.

EASILY CONFUSED WORDS **contrast, compare**

Contrast means 'note the differences,' whereas **compare** means 'note the similarities' (or, in some cases, inconsistencies).

contravene verb 1 *he contravened several laws* BREAK, breach, violate, infringe; defy, disobey, flout. ANTONYMS comply with, uphold.

2 *the prosecution contravened the rights of the individual* CONFLICT WITH, be in conflict with, be at odds with, be at variance with, run counter to.

contravention noun *a contravention of league rules* BREACH, violation, infringement, neglect, dereliction.

contretemps noun *her little contretemps with Terry* ARGUMENT, quarrel, squabble, disagreement, difference of opinion, dispute; *informal* tiff, set-to, run-in, spat, row.

contribute verb 1 *the government contributed a million dollars* GIVE, donate, put up, subscribe, hand out, grant, bestow, present, provide, supply, furnish; *informal* chip in, pitch in, fork out, shell out, cough up, kick in, ante up, pony up.

2 *an article contributed by Dr. Clouson* SUPPLY, provide, submit.

3 *numerous factors contribute to job satisfaction* PLAY A PART IN, be instrumental in, be a factor in, have a hand in, be conducive to, make for, lead to, cause.

contribution noun 1 *voluntary financial contributions* DONATION, gift, offering, present, handout, grant, subsidy, allowance, endowment, subscription; *formal* benefaction.

2 *contributions from local authors* ARTICLE, piece, story, item, chapter, paper, essay.

contributor noun 1 *the magazine's regular contributors* WRITER, columnist, correspondent.

2 *campaign contributors* DONOR, benefactor, subscriber, supporter, backer, patron, sponsor.

contrite adjective *Joey was so contrite we had to conceal our amusement* REMORSEFUL, repentant, penitent, regretful, sorry, apologetic, rueful, sheepish, hangdog, ashamed, chastened, shamefaced, conscience-stricken, guilt-ridden.

contrition noun *the court-appointed psychiatrist was concerned about her lack of contrition* REMORSE, remorsefulness, repentance, penitence, sorrow, sorrowfulness, regret, ruefulness, pangs of conscience; shame, guilt, compunction; *archaic* rue.

contrivance noun 1 *a mechanical contrivance* DEVICE, gadget, machine, appliance, contraption, apparatus, mechanism, implement, tool, invention; *informal* gizmo, widget, doohickey.

2 *her matchmaking contrivances* SCHEME, stratagem, tactic, maneuver, move, plan, ploy, gambit, wile, trick, ruse, plot, machination.

contrive verb *his opponents contrived a cabinet crisis* BRING ABOUT, engineer, manufacture, orchestrate, stage-manage, create, devise, concoct, construct, plan, fabricate, plot, hatch; *informal* wangle, set up.

contrived adjective *the story's contrived ending is a big letdown* FORCED, strained, studied, artificial, affected, put-on, phony, pretended, false, feigned, fake, manufactured, unnatural; labored, overdone, elaborate. ANTONYM natural.

control noun 1 *China retained control over the region* JURISDICTION, sway, power, authority, command, dominance, government, mastery, leadership, rule, sovereignty, supremacy, ascendancy; charge, management, direction, supervision, superintendence.

2 *strict import controls* RESTRAINT, constraint, limitation, restriction, check, curb, brake, rein; regulation.

3 *her control deserted her* SELF-CONTROL, self-restraint, self-possession, composure, calmness; *informal* cool.

4 *easy-to-use controls* SWITCH, knob, button, dial, handle, lever.

5 *mission control* HEADQUARTERS, HQ, base, center of operations, command post, nerve center.

▸ verb 1 *one family had controlled the company since its formation* BE IN CHARGE OF, run, manage, direct, administer, head, preside over, supervise, superintend, steer; command, rule, govern, lead, dominate, hold sway over, be at the helm; *informal* head up, be in the driver's seat, run the show.

2 *she struggled to control her temper* RESTRAIN, keep in check, curb, check, contain, hold back, bridle, rein in, suppress, repress, master.

3 *public spending was controlled* LIMIT, restrict, curb, cap, constrain; *informal* put the brakes on.

controversial adjective *controversial issues such as abortion* CONTENTIOUS, disputed, at issue, disputable, debatable, arguable, vexed, tendentious; *informal* hot.

controversy noun *being drawn into the political controversy* DISAGREEMENT, dispute, argument, debate, dissension, contention, disputation, altercation, wrangle, wrangling, quarrel, quarreling, war of words, storm; cause célèbre; *informal* hot potato, minefield.

contusion noun *a minor contusion on his elbow* BRUISE, discoloration, injury.

conundrum noun 1 *the conundrums facing policy-makers* PROBLEM, difficult question, difficulty, quandary, dilemma; *informal* poser.

2 *Rod enjoyed conundrums and crosswords* RIDDLE, puzzle, word game; *informal* brainteaser. See note at RIDDLE.

convalesce verb *he went abroad to convalesce* RECUPERATE, get better, recover, get well, get back on one's feet.

convalescence noun *a long period of convalescence* RECUPERATION, recovery, return to health, rehabilitation, improvement.

convalescent adjective *you're still convalescent and you need to rest* RECUPERATING, recovering, getting better, on the road to recovery, improving; *informal* on the mend.

convene verb 1 *he convened a secret meeting* SUMMON, call, call together, order; *formal* convoke.

2 *the committee convened for its final session* ASSEMBLE, gather, meet, come together, congregate. See note at GATHER.

convenience noun **1** *the convenience of the arrangement* EXPEDIENCE, advantage, propitiousness, timeliness; suitability, appropriateness.

2 *for convenience, the handset is wall-mounted* EASE OF USE, usability, usefulness, utility, serviceability, practicality.

3 *the kitchen has all the modern conveniences* APPLIANCE, device, labor-saving device, gadget; amenity; *informal* gizmo.

convenient adjective **1** *a convenient time* SUITABLE, appropriate, fitting, fit, suited, opportune, timely, well-timed, favorable, advantageous, seasonable, expedient.

2 *a hotel that's **convenient for** public transit* NEAR (TO), close to, within easy reach of, well situated for, handy for, not far from, just around the corner from; *informal* a stone's throw from, within spitting distance of.

convent noun *even the hardest work at the convent gave her sense of peace and fulfillment* NUNNERY, MONASTERY, priory, abbey, cloister, religious community.

convention noun **1** *social conventions* CUSTOM, usage, practice, tradition, way, habit, norm; rule, code, canon, punctilio; propriety, etiquette, protocol; *formal* praxis; (**conventions**) mores.

2 *a convention signed by 74 countries* AGREEMENT, accord, protocol, compact, pact, treaty, concordat, entente; contract, bargain, deal.

3 *the party's biennial convention* CONFERENCE, meeting, congress, assembly, gathering, summit, convocation, synod, conclave.

conventional adjective **1** *the conventional wisdom of the day* ORTHODOX, traditional, established, accepted, received, mainstream, prevailing, prevalent, accustomed, customary. ANTONYM unorthodox.

2 *a conventional railroad* NORMAL, standard, regular, ordinary, usual, traditional, typical, common.

3 *a very conventional woman* CONSERVATIVE, traditional, traditionalist, conformist, bourgeois, old-fashioned, of the old school, small-town, suburban; *informal* straight, buttoned-down, square, stick-in-the-mud, fuddy-duddy. ANTONYMS radical, Bohemian.

4 *a conventional piece of work* UNORIGINAL, formulaic, predictable, stock, unadventurous, unremarkable; *informal* humdrum, run-of-the-mill. ANTONYM original.

converge verb **1** *the tracks converge at Union Station* MEET, intersect, cross, connect, link up, coincide, join, unite, merge. ANTONYM diverge.

2 *5,000 protesters **converged on** Capitol Hill* CLOSE IN ON, bear down on, approach, move toward. ANTONYMS diverge, leave.

conversant adjective *the students are **conversant with** a wide range of math skills* FAMILIAR WITH, acquainted with, au fait with, au courant with, at home with, well versed in, well-informed about, knowledgeable about, informed about, abreast of, up-to-date on; *informal* up to speed on, in the loop about; *formal* cognizant of.

conversation noun *he may have overheard our conversation* DISCUSSION, talk, chat, gossip, tête-à-tête, heart-to-heart, exchange, dialogue; *informal* confab, jaw, chitchat, chinwag, gabfest; *formal* confabulation, colloquy.

THE RIGHT WORD

It is nearly impossible for most people to get through a day without having a **conversation** with someone, even if it's only a **chat** with the mailman. Although *conversation* can and does take place in all sorts of contexts, both formal and informal, the word usually implies a relaxed, casual exchange. A *chat* is the least formal of all conversations, whether it's a father talking to his son about girls or two women having a **tête-á-tête** (French for "head to head," meaning a confidential conversation) about their wayward husbands. Men, of course, often complain that women don't understand the meaning of **dialogue**, which is a two-way conversation that may involve opposing points of view. Argument is even more likely to play a role in a **parley**, which formally is a discussion between enemies regarding the terms of a truce. A **colloquy** is the most formal of all conversations (*a colloquy on nuclear disarmament*); it can also be used to jocularly describe a guarded exchange (*a brief colloquy with the arresting officer*). **Communion** is a form of conversation as well—one that may take place on such a profound level that no words are necessary (*communion with nature*).

conversational adjective **1** *conversational English* INFORMAL, chatty, relaxed, friendly; colloquial, idiomatic.

2 *a conversational man* TALKATIVE, chatty, communicative, forthcoming, expansive, loquacious, garrulous.

converse[1] verb *they conversed in low voices* TALK, speak, chat, have a conversation, discourse, communicate; *informal* chew the fat, jaw, visit, shoot the breeze; *formal* confabulate.

converse[2] noun *the converse is also true* OPPOSITE, reverse, obverse, contrary, antithesis, other side of the coin, flip side.

conversion noun **1** *the conversion of waste into energy* CHANGE, changing, transformation, metamorphosis, transfiguration, transmutation, sea change; *humorous* transmogrification.

2 *the conversion of the building* ADAPTATION, alteration, modification, reconstruction, rebuilding, redevelopment, redesign, renovation, rehabilitation.

3 *his religious conversion* REBIRTH, regeneration, reformation.

convert verb **1** *plants convert the sun's energy into chemical energy* CHANGE, turn, transform, metamorphose, transfigure, transmute; *humorous* transmogrify; *technical* permute.

2 *the factory was converted into lofts* ADAPT, turn, change, alter, modify, rebuild, reconstruct, redevelop, refashion, redesign, restyle, revamp, renovate, rehabilitate; *informal* do up, rehab.

3 *they sought to convert sinners* PROSELYTIZE, evangelize, bring to God, redeem, save, reform, re-educate, cause to see the light.

▸ noun *Christian converts* PROSELYTE, neophyte, new believer; *Christianity* catechumen.

convey verb **1** *taxis conveyed guests to the station* TRANSPORT, carry, bring, take, fetch, bear, move, ferry, shuttle, shift, transfer.

2 *he conveyed the information to me* COMMUNICATE, pass on, make known, impart, relay, transmit, send, hand on/off, relate, tell, reveal, disclose.

3 *it's impossible to convey how I felt* EXPRESS, communicate, get across/over, put across/over, indicate, say.

4 *he conveys an air of competence* PROJECT, exude, emit, emanate.

conveyance noun **1** *the conveyance of agricultural produce* TRANSPORTATION, transport, carriage, carrying, transfer, movement, delivery; haulage, portage, cartage, shipment.

2 *formal three-wheeled conveyances* VEHICLE, means/method of transport.

convict verb *he was convicted of sexual assault* FIND GUILTY, sentence. ANTONYM acquit.

▸ noun *two escaped convicts* PRISONER, inmate; criminal, offender, lawbreaker, felon; *informal* jailbird, con, crook, lifer, yardbird.

conviction noun **1** *his conviction for murder* DECLARATION OF GUILT, sentence, judgment. ANTONYM acquittal.

2 *his political convictions* BELIEF, opinion, view, thought, persuasion, idea, position, stance, article of faith. See note at OPINION.

3 *she spoke with conviction* CERTAINTY, certitude, assurance, confidence, sureness, no shadow of a doubt. ANTONYM uncertainty.

convince verb **1** *he convinced me that I was wrong* MAKE CERTAIN, persuade, satisfy, prove to; assure, put/set someone's mind at rest.

2 *I convinced her to marry me* PERSUADE, induce, prevail on/upon, get, talk into, win over, cajole, inveigle.

THE RIGHT WORD

Although it is common to see **convince** and **persuade** used interchangeably, there are distinctions in meaning that careful writers and speakers try to preserve. **Convince** derives from a Latin word meaning 'to conquer, overcome.' **Persuade** derives from a Latin word meaning 'to advise, make appealing, sweeten.' One can **convince** or **persuade** someone with facts or arguments, but, in general, *convincing* is limited to the mind, while *persuasion* results in action (just as *dissuasion* results in nonaction): *the prime minister convinced the council that delay was pointless; the senator persuaded her colleagues to pass the legislation.*

convincing adjective **1** *a convincing argument* COGENT, persuasive, plausible, powerful, potent, strong, forceful, compelling, irresistible, telling, conclusive. See note at BELIEVABLE.

2 *a convincing 5–0 win* RESOUNDING, emphatic, decisive, conclusive.

convivial adjective *our convivial host* FRIENDLY, genial, affable, amiable, congenial, agreeable, good-humored, cordial, warm, sociable, outgoing, gregarious, companionable, clubby, hail-fellow-well-met, cheerful, jolly, jovial, lively; enjoyable, festive.

conviviality noun *the staff at the inn got an excellent rating for their helpfulness and conviviality* FRIENDLINESS, geniality, affability, amiability, bonhomie, congeniality, cordiality, warmth, good nature, sociability, gregariousness, cheerfulness, good cheer, joviality, jollity, gaiety, liveliness.

convocation noun **1** *the students gathered for their convocation* GRADUATION (CEREMONY), commencement.

2 *a convocation of church leaders* ASSEMBLY, gathering, meeting, conference, convention, congress, council, symposium, colloquium, conclave, synod.

convoke verb *formal she claimed to have the power to convoke the spirits of the dead* CONVENE, summon, call together, call.

convoluted adjective *his convoluted answers did nothing to help his credibility* COMPLICATED, complex, involved, elaborate, serpentine, labyrinthine, tortuous, tangled, Byzantine; confused, confusing, bewildering, baffling. ANTONYM straightforward.

convolution noun **1** *crosses adorned with elaborate convolutions* TWIST, turn, coil, spiral, twirl, curl, helix, whorl, loop, curlicue; *Architecture* volute.

2 *the convolutions of the plot* COMPLEXITY, intricacy, complication, twist, turn, entanglement.

convoy noun *a convoy of vehicles* GROUP, fleet, cavalcade, motorcade, cortège, caravan, line, train.

▸ verb *the ship was convoyed by army gunboats* ESCORT, accompany, attend, flank; protect, defend, guard.

convulse verb *his whole body convulsed* SHAKE UNCONTROLLABLY, go into spasms, shudder, jerk, thrash about.

convulsion noun **1** *she had convulsions* FIT, seizure, paroxysm, spasm, attack; *Medicine* ictus.

2 **(convulsions)** *the audience collapsed in convulsions* FITS OF LAUGHTER, paroxysms of laughter, uncontrollable laughter; *informal* hysterics.

3 *the political convulsions of the period* UPHEAVAL, eruption, cataclysm, turmoil, turbulence, tumult, disruption, agitation, disturbance, unrest, disorder.

convulsive adjective *convulsive movements* SPASMODIC, jerky, paroxysmal, violent, uncontrollable; *informal* herky-jerky.

cook verb **1** *Scott cooked dinner* PREPARE, make, put together; *informal* fix, rustle up. See tables on pages 182, 183.

2 *informal he's been cooking the books* FALSIFY, alter, doctor, tamper with, interfere with, massage, manipulate, fiddle.

3 *informal* **(cookin'/cooking)** *we just stopped by to see what's cookin'* HAPPENING, going on, taking place, occurring; *informal* going down.

▸ noun CHEF, food preparer, short-order cook, pastry chef; chef de cuisine, sous-chef, cordon bleu cook; *informal* cookie.

PHRASE: **cook up** *informal he cooked up an alibi so ludicrous that even his own attorney laughed* CONCOCT, devise, contrive, fabricate, trump up, hatch, plot, plan, invent, make up, think up, dream up.

cookie noun See table on page 182.

cooking noun *authentic Italian cooking* CUISINE, cookery, baking; food preparation; food. See tables on pages 182, 183.

▸ adjective *his cooking skills amazing* CULINARY.

cool adjective **1** *a cool breeze* CHILLY, chill, cold, bracing, brisk, crisp, fresh, refreshing, invigorating, nippy. ANTONYMS warm, hot.

2 *a cool response* UNENTHUSIASTIC, lukewarm, tepid, indifferent, uninterested, apathetic, halfhearted; unfriendly, distant, remote, aloof, cold, chilly, frosty, unwelcoming, unresponsive, uncommunicative, undemonstrative, standoffish. ANTONYMS enthusiastic, friendly.

3 *his ability to keep cool in a crisis* CALM, 'calm, cool, and collected', composed, as cool as a cucumber, collected, coolheaded, levelheaded, self-possessed, controlled, self-

COOKING METHODS AND FOOD PREPARATION

bake	grill
barbecue	grind
bard	hard-boil
baste	hash
batter	hull
beat	julienne
blacken	knead
blanch	lard
blend	macerate
boil	marinate
boil down	mash
bone	melt
braise	mince
bread	mix
broil	mold
brown	nap
bruise	pack
butterfly	pan-broil
can	pan-fry
candy	parboil
caramelize	pare
carbonado	pickle
casserole	pipe
char broil	plump
chop	poach
clarify	pot
clean	pound
coat	preserve
coddle	pressure-cook
concentrate	pureé
cream	raise
crisp	reconstitute
crust	reduce
crystallize	refresh
cube	render
curdle	rice
cure	ripen
cut in	roast
deep fry	roll
deglaze	salt
degrease	sauté
dehydrate	scald
desiccate	scallop
devein	score
devil	scramble
dice	sear
draw	shirr
dredge	shock
dress	shred
drizzle	sift
dry	simmer
dry-roast	slice
dunk	smoke
dust	smother
eviscerate	soak
fillet	soft-boil
flake	souse
flambé	steam
float	steep
flute	stew
foam	stir
fold	stir-fry
force	stuff
form	sweat
freeze-dry	temper
frizzle	thread
froth	toast
fry	toss
garnish	whip
glaze	whisk
grate	zest

controlled, poised, serene, tranquil, unruffled, unperturbed, unmoved, untroubled, imperturbable, placid, phlegmatic; *informal* unflappable, together, laid-back. ANTONYMS panic-stricken, agitated.

4 *a cool lack of morality* BOLD, audacious, nerveless; brazen, shameless, unabashed.

5 *informal she thinks she's so cool* FASHIONABLE, stylish, chic, up-to-the-minute, sophisticated; *informal* trendy, funky, with it, hip, big, happening, groovy, phat, kicky, fly.

6 *informal a cool song.* See EXCELLENT.

▸ noun **1** *the cool of the evening* CHILL, chilliness, coldness, coolness. ANTONYM warmth.

2 *Ken lost his cool* SELF-CONTROL, control, composure, self-possession, calmness, equilibrium, calm; aplomb, poise, sangfroid, presence of mind.

verb **1** *cool the sauce in the fridge* CHILL, refrigerate. ANTONYM heat.

2 *her reluctance did nothing to cool his interest* LESSEN, moderate, diminish, reduce, dampen. ANTONYMS inflame, arouse.

3 *Simon's ardor had cooled* SUBSIDE, lessen, diminish, decrease, abate, moderate, die down, fade, dwindle, wane. ANTONYM intensify.

COOKIES

amaretti	macaroon
animal cracker	madeleine
arrowroot cookie	Mallomar™
bar	mandelbrot
biscotti	meltaway
biscuit	meringue
black & white cookie	Mexican wedding
blondie	cookie
brandy snap	molasses cookie
brownie	mostaccioli
butter cookie	oatmeal raisin cookie
chew	Oreo™
chocolate chip cookie	peanut butter cookie
crescent cookie	pecan sandie
crinkle	pepparkakor
crisp	petit beurre
digestive cookie/biscuit	pfeffernüsse
fig bar	pinwheel
Fig Newton™	ratafia (biscuit)
florentine	Rice Krispie Treat™
fortune cookie	rugelach
Garibaldi (biscuit bar)	rusk
ginger cookie	sand tart
gingersnap	sandwich cookie
Girl Scout cookie	shortbread
graham cracker	slice-and-bake cookie
hamantashen	snickerdoodle
haystack cookie	speculoo
hermit	spice cookie
icebox cookie	springerle
jumble cookie	spritz
kiss	sugar cookie
kolacky	sultana (biscuit)
koulourakia	tassie
kringle	tea cake
krumkake	thumbprint cookie
lace cookie	Toll House™ cookie
langue de chat	tuile
lebkuchen	vanilla wafer
lemon bar	wafer
lady finger	whoopie pie
Lorna Doone™	

See also tables at CAKE, CANDY, DOUGHNUT, PASTRY, and PIE.

4 *after a while, she **cooled off*** CALM DOWN, recover/regain one's composure, compose oneself, control oneself, pull oneself together, simmer down.

coop noun *a chicken coop* PEN, run, cage, hutch, enclosure.

▸ verb *he hates being **cooped up** at home* CONFINE, shut in/up, cage (in), pen up/in, keep, detain, trap, incarcerate, immure.

cooperate verb 1 *police and social services cooperated in the operation* COLLABORATE, work together, work side by side, pull together, band together, join forces, team up, unite, combine, pool resources, make common cause, liaise.

2 *he was happy to cooperate* BE OF ASSISTANCE, assist, help, lend a hand, be of service, do one's bit; *informal* play ball.

cooperation noun 1 *cooperation between management and workers* COLLABORATION, joint action, combined effort, teamwork, partnership, coordination, liaison, association, synergy, synergism, give and take, compromise. See note at SYNERGY.

2 *thank you for your cooperation* ASSISTANCE, helpfulness, help, helping hand, aid.

cooperative adjective 1 *a cooperative effort* COLLABORATIVE, collective, combined, common, joint, shared, mutual, united, concerted, coordinated.

2 *pleasant and cooperative staff* HELPFUL, eager to help, glad to be of assistance, obliging, accommodating, willing, amenable, adaptable.

▸ noun *a housing cooperative | a farm cooperative* COMPLEX, commune, collective; joint venture, cooperative enterprise; credit union; pool; *informal* CO-OP.

coordinate verb 1 *exhibitions coordinated by a team of international scholars* ORGANIZE, arrange, order, systematize, harmonize, correlate, synchronize, bring together, fit together, dovetail.

2 *care workers coordinate at a local level* CO-OPERATE, liaise, collaborate, work together, negotiate, communicate, be in contact.

3 *floral designs coordinate with the decor* MATCH, complement, set off; harmonize, blend, fit in, go.

cop *informal* noun *a traffic cop.* See POLICE OFFICER.

▸ verb *he tried to **cop out of** his obligations.* See AVOID sense 2.

cope verb 1 *she couldn't cope on her own* MANAGE, survive, subsist, look after oneself, fend for oneself, carry on, get by/through, bear up, hold one's own, keep one's end up, keep one's head above water; *informal* make it, hack it.

2 *his inability to cope with the situation* DEAL WITH, handle, manage, address, face (up to), confront, tackle, come to grips with, get through, weather, come to terms with.

copious adjective *she took copious notes* ABUNDANT, superabundant, plentiful, ample, profuse, full, extensive, generous, bumper, lavish, fulsome, liberal, overflowing, in abundance, many, numerous; *informal* galore; *literary* plenteous. See note at PREVALENT. ANTONYM sparse.

copse noun *tall firs form a copse at the back of the house* THICKET, grove, wood, coppice, stand, bush, woodlot, brake, brush; *archaic* hurst, holt, boscage.

copulate verb See HAVE SEX at SEX.

TYPES OF COOKING

al dente	gratiné
al forno	grecque
Alfredo	hollandaise
alla taormina	indienne
alla vodka	jardinière
almondine	jerk
amandine	julienne
anglaise	lyonnaise
argenteuil	marinara
au bleu	marinière
au fromage	masala
au gratin	medium
au jus	medium rare
au naturel	meunière
bérnaise	nesselrode
Bolognese	Newburg
bourguignon	niçoise
cacciatore	normande
carbonara	parmigiana
chiffonade	périgord
clamart	parmentier
country fried	piccata
Crécy	pilaf
creole	Pittsburgh style
curried	Provençale
dauphine	puttanesca
en brochette	ranchero
en croûte	rare
en papillote	relleno
espagnole	ripieno
escabeche	roulade
estragon	scallopine
étouffée	stroganoff
farci	subgum
flambé	sunny side up
Florentine	tandoori
forestière	tempura
fra diavolo	tikka
francese	Véronique
Frenched	vindaloo
fricassee	well done
garni	

copulation noun See SEX sense 1.

copy noun 1 *a copy of the report* DUPLICATE, facsimile, photocopy; transcript; reprint; *trademark* Xerox; *dated* carbon (copy), mimeograph, mimeo.

2 *a copy of a sketch by Leonardo da Vinci* REPLICA, reproduction, replication, print, imitation, likeness; counterfeit, forgery, fake; *informal* knockoff.

▸ verb 1 *each form had to be copied* DUPLICATE, photocopy, xerox, run off, reproduce, replicate; *dated* mimeograph.

2 *portraits copied from original paintings by Reynolds* REPRODUCE, replicate; forge, fake, counterfeit.

3 *their sound was copied by a lot of jazz players* IMITATE, reproduce, emulate, follow, echo, mirror, parrot, mimic, ape; plagiarize, steal; *informal* rip off. See note at IMITATE.

coquettish adjective *he easily fell for her coquettish glances* FLIRTATIOUS, flirty, provocative, seductive, inviting, kittenish, coy, arch, teasing, playful; *informal* come-hither, vampish.

cord noun *a two-foot cotton cord* STRING, thread, thong, lace, ribbon, strap, tape, tie, line, rope, cable, wire, ligature; twine, yarn; braid, braiding; elastic, bungee (cord).

cordial adjective *a cordial welcome* FRIENDLY, warm, genial, affable, amiable, pleasant, fond, affectionate, warmhearted, good-natured, gracious, hospitable, welcoming, hearty.

▸ noun *fruit cordial* LIQUEUR, drink.

WORD NOTE cordial

Although the primary meaning of *cordial* is "warm and friendly," in literary writing it is very often used to mean "strongly felt"—so much so that *cordial dislike,* which originally must have been a mostly clever play on the tension between *cordial* as "friendly" and *dislike,* is in danger of becoming a fossilized phrase. If you find yourself writing *cordial dislike* or *cordial loathing,* you may want to consider whether the loathing is really heartfelt, or whether the feeling and the phrase are both halfhearted. **—EM**

cordon noun *a cordon of 500 police* BARRIER, line, row, chain, ring, circle; picket line.

▸ verb *troops* ***cordoned off*** *the area* CLOSE OFF, shut off, seal off, fence off, separate off, isolate, enclose, surround.

core noun **1** *the earth's core* CENTER, interior, middle, nucleus; recesses, bowels, depths; *informal* innards; *literary* midst.

2 *the core of the argument* HEART, heart of the matter, nucleus, nub, kernel, marrow, meat, essence, quintessence, crux, gist, pith, substance, basis, fundamentals; *informal* nitty-gritty, brass tacks, nuts and bolts.

▸ adjective *the core issue* CENTRAL, key, basic, fundamental, principal, primary, main, chief, crucial, vital, essential; *informal* number-one. ANTONYM peripheral.

cork noun *the cork from the wine bottle went flying across the room* STOPPER, stop, plug, peg, spigot, spile.

corner noun **1** *the cart lurched around the corner* BEND, curve, crook, dog-leg; turn, turning, jog, junction, fork, intersection; hairpin turn.

2 *a charming corner of Italy* DISTRICT, region, area, section, quarter, part; *informal* neck of the woods.

3 *he found himself in a tight corner* PREDICAMENT, plight, tight spot, mess, can of worms, muddle, difficulty, problem, dilemma, quandary; *informal* pickle, jam, stew, fix, hole, hot water, bind.

▸ verb **1** *he was eventually cornered by police dogs* DRIVE INTO A CORNER, bring to bay, cut off, block off, trap, hem in, pen in, surround, enclose; capture, catch.

2 *crime syndicates have cornered the stolen car market* GAIN CONTROL OF, take over, control, dominate, monopolize; capture; *informal* sew up.

cornerstone noun *the theory of natural selection is a cornerstone of biological thought* FOUNDATION, basis, keystone, mainspring, mainstay, linchpin, bedrock, base, backbone, key, centerpiece, core, heart, center, crux.

cornucopia noun *these scouts have brought in* ***a cornucopia*** *of young talent* AN ABUNDANCE, a profusion, a plentifulness, a profuseness, a copiousness, an amplitude, a lavishness, a bountifulness, a bounty; a host, a riot; plenty, quantities, scores, a multitude; *informal* millions, a sea, oceans/an ocean, a wealth, lots/a lot, heaps/a heap, masses/a mass, stacks/a stack, piles/a pile, loads/a load, mountains/a mountain, tons/a ton, a slew; *formal* a plenitude.

corny adjective *informal most of our outdoors play was inspired by those corny TV westerns* BANAL, trite, hackneyed, commonplace, clichéd, predictable, hoary, stereotyped, platitudinous, tired, stale, overworked, overused, well-worn; mawkish, sentimental, cloying, syrupy, sugary, saccharine; *informal* cheesy, schmaltzy, mushy, sloppy, cutesy, soppy, cornball, hokey.

corollary noun *job losses are the unfortunate corollary of budget cutting* CONSEQUENCE, result, end result, upshot, effect, repercussion, product, by-product, offshoot.

coronet noun See CROWN noun sense 1.

corporal adjective See CORPOREAL.

corporation noun *the chairman of the corporation* COMPANY, firm, business, concern, operation, house, organization, agency, trust, partnership; conglomerate, group, chain, multinational; *informal* outfit, setup.

corporeal adjective *they tried to bring Satan into corporeal existence* BODILY, fleshly, carnal, corporal, somatic, human, mortal, earthly, physical, material, tangible, concrete, real, actual. See note at TANGIBLE.

corps noun **1** *an army corps* UNIT, division, detachment, section, company, contingent, squad, squadron, regiment, battalion, brigade, platoon.

2 *a corps of trained engineers* GROUP, body, band, cohort, party, gang, pack; team, crew.

corpse noun *the corpse was stolen from the morgue* DEAD BODY, body, carcass, skeleton, remains, mortal remains; *informal* stiff; *Medicine* cadaver. See note at BODY.

corpulent adjective *they provide ample seating for their corpulent clients* FAT, obese, overweight, plump, portly, stout, chubby, paunchy, beer-bellied, heavy, bulky, chunky, well-upholstered, well padded, well covered, meaty, fleshy, rotund, broad in the beam; *informal* tubby, pudgy, beefy, porky, roly-poly, blubbery, corn-fed; *rare* abdominous. ANTONYM thin.

corral noun *she was galloping a pony around the corral* ENCLOSURE, pen, fold, compound, pound, stockade, paddock.

▸ verb **1** *the sheep and goats were corralled at night* ENCLOSE, confine, lock up, shut up, shut in, fence in, pen in, wall in, cage, cage in, coop up.

2 *she corralled some new volunteers* GET, capture, collect, pick up, round up.

correct adjective **1** *the correct answer* RIGHT, accurate, true, exact, precise, unerring, faithful, strict, faultless, flawless, error-free, perfect, letter-perfect, word-perfect; *informal* on the mark, on the nail, bang on, (right) on the money, on the button. ANTONYMS wrong, inaccurate.

2 *correct behavior* PROPER, seemly, decorous, decent, respectable, right, suitable, fit, fitting, befitting, appropriate, apt; approved, accepted, conventional, customary, traditional, orthodox, comme il faut. ANTONYM improper.

▸ verb **1** *proofread your work and correct any mistakes* RECTIFY, put right, set right, right, amend, emend, remedy, repair.

2 *an attempt to correct the trade imbalance* COUNTERACT, offset, counterbalance, compensate for, make up for, neutralize.

3 *the thermostat needs correcting* ADJUST, regulate, fix, set, standardize, normalize, calibrate, fine-tune.

corrective adjective *corrective shoes* REMEDIAL, therapeutic, restorative, curative, reparative, rehabilitative.

correctly adverb **1** *the questions were answered correctly*

ACCURATELY, right, unerringly, precisely, faultlessly, flawlessly, perfectly, without error; *dated* aright.

2 *she behaved correctly at all times* PROPERLY, decorously, with decorum, decently, suitably, fittingly, appropriately, well.

correlate verb **1** *postal codes **correlate with** geographic location* CORRESPOND TO/WITH, match, parallel, agree with, tally with, tie in with, be consistent with, be compatible with, be consonant with, coordinate with, dovetail (with), relate to, conform to; *informal* square with, jibe with. ANTONYM contrast.

2 *we can correlate good health and physical fitness* CONNECT, analogize, associate, relate, compare, set side by side.

correlation noun *the correlation between smoking and lung cancer* CONNECTION, association, link, tie-in, tie-up, relation, relationship, interrelationship, interdependence, interaction, interconnection; correspondence, parallel.

correspond verb **1** *their policies do not **correspond with** their statements* CORRELATE WITH, agree with, be in agreement with, be consistent with, be compatible with, be consonant with, accord with, be in tune with, concur with, coincide with, tally with, tie in with, dovetail (with), fit in with; match, parallel; *informal* square with, jibe with.

2 *a rank corresponding to the American rank of corporal* BE EQUIVALENT, be analogous, be comparable, equate.

3 *Debbie and I corresponded for years* EXCHANGE LETTERS, write, communicate, keep in touch, keep in contact.

correspondence noun **1** *there is some correspondence between the two variables* CORRELATION, agreement, consistency, compatibility, consonance, conformity, similarity, resemblance, parallel, comparability, accord, concurrence, coincidence.

2 *his private correspondence* LETTERS, messages, missives, mail, post; communication.

correspondent noun *the paper's foreign correspondent* REPORTER, journalist, columnist, writer, contributor, newspaperman, newspaperwoman, commentator; *informal* stringer, newshound.

▸ adjective *a correspondent improvement in quality.* See CORRESPONDING.

corresponding adjective *a corresponding revision in the annual budget* COMMENSURATE, parallel, correspondent, matching, correlated, homologous, relative, proportional, proportionate, comparable, equivalent, analogous.

corridor noun *the conference room is at the end of the corridor* PASSAGE, passageway, aisle, gangway, hall, hallway, gallery, arcade.

corroborate verb *the witness can corroborate Brueller's story* CONFIRM, verify, endorse, ratify, authenticate, validate, certify; support, back up, uphold, bear out, bear witness to, attest to, testify to, vouch for, give credence to, substantiate, sustain. ANTONYM contradict.

corrode verb **1** *the iron had corroded* RUST, become rusty, tarnish; wear away, disintegrate, crumble, perish, spoil; oxidize.

2 *acid rain corrodes buildings* WEAR AWAY, eat away (at), gnaw away (at), erode, abrade, consume, destroy.

corrosive adjective *corrosive chemicals* CAUSTIC, corroding, erosive, abrasive, burning, stinging; destructive, damaging, harmful, harsh.

corrugated adjective *panels of corrugated fiberglass* RIDGED, fluted, grooved, furrowed, crinkled, crinkly, puckered, creased, wrinkled, wrinkly, crumpled; *technical* striated.

corrupt adjective **1** *a corrupt official | corrupt practices* DISHONEST, unscrupulous, dishonorable, unprincipled, unethical, amoral, untrustworthy, venal, underhanded, double-dealing, fraudulent, bribable, criminal, illegal, unlawful, nefarious; *informal* crooked, shady, dirty, sleazy. ANTONYMS honest, law-abiding.

2 *the earth was corrupt in God's sight* IMMORAL, depraved, degenerate, reprobate, vice-ridden, perverted, debauched, dissolute, dissipated, bad, wicked, evil, base, sinful, ungodly, unholy, irreligious, profane, impious, impure; *informal* warped. See note at DEPRAVED. ANTONYM moral.

3 *a corrupt text* IMPURE, bastardized, debased, adulterated. ANTONYM pure.

▸ verb **1** *a book that might corrupt its readers* DEPRAVE, pervert, debauch, degrade, warp, lead astray, defile, pollute, sully.

2 *the apostolic writings had been corrupted* ALTER, tamper with, interfere with, bastardize, debase, adulterate.

corruption noun **1** *political corruption* DISHONESTY, unscrupulousness, double-dealing, fraud, fraudulence, misconduct, crime, criminality, wrongdoing; bribery, venality, extortion, profiteering, payola; *informal* graft, grift, crookedness, sleaze. ANTONYM honesty.

2 *his fall into corruption* IMMORALITY, depravity, vice, degeneracy, perversion, debauchery, dissoluteness, decadence, wickedness, evil, sin, sinfulness, ungodliness; *formal* turpitude. ANTONYMS morality, purity.

3 *these figures have been subject to corruption* ALTERATION, bastardization, debasement, adulteration.

corsair noun *archaic* See PIRATE noun sense 1.

corset noun *dated* GIRDLE, panty girdle, foundation garment, foundation, corselette; *historical* stays.

cortège noun **1** *the funeral cortège* PROCESSION, parade, cavalcade, motorcade, convoy, caravan, train, column, file, line.

2 *the prince's cortège* ENTOURAGE, retinue, train, suite; attendants, companions, followers, retainers.

cosmetic adjective *most of the changes were merely cosmetic* SUPERFICIAL, surface, skin-deep, outward, exterior, external.

▸ noun (**cosmetics**) *a new range of cosmetics* MAKEUP, beauty products, beauty aids; *informal* war paint; *rare* maquillage.

cosmic adjective **1** *cosmic bodies* EXTRATERRESTRIAL, in space, from space.

2 *an epic of cosmic dimensions* VAST, huge, immense, enormous, massive, colossal, prodigious, immeasurable, incalculable, unfathomable, fathomless, measureless, infinite, limitless, boundless.

cosmonaut noun See ASTRONAUT.

cosmopolitan adjective **1** *the student body has a cosmopolitan character* MULTICULTURAL, multiracial, international, worldwide, global.

2 *a cosmopolitan audience* WORLDLY, worldly-wise, well

travelled, experienced, unprovincial, cultivated, cultured, sophisticated, suave, urbane, glamorous, fashionable; *informal* jet-setting, cool, hip, stylish. See note at URBANE.

cosset verb *it was hurtful to them to see their father cosseting his stepchildren* PAMPER, indulge, overindulge, mollycoddle, coddle, baby, pet, mother, nanny, nursemaid, pander to, spoil; wait on someone hand and foot.

cost noun **1** *the cost of the equipment* PRICE, asking price, market price, selling price, unit price, fee, tariff, fare, toll, levy, charge, rental; value, valuation, quotation, rate, worth; *informal, humorous* damage.

2 *the human cost of the conflict* SACRIFICE, loss, expense, penalty, toll, price.

3 **(costs)** *we need to make $10,000 to cover our costs* EXPENSES, disbursements, overheads, running costs, operating costs, fixed costs; expenditure, spending, outlay.

▸ verb **1** *the chair costs $186* BE PRICED AT, sell for, be valued at, fetch, come to, amount to; *informal* set someone back, go for.

2 *the proposal has not yet been costed* PUT A PRICE ON, price, value, put a value on, put a figure on.

costly adjective **1** *costly machinery* EXPENSIVE, dear, high-priced, highly priced, overpriced; *informal* steep, pricey, costing an arm and a leg, costing the earth. ANTONYMS cheap, inexpensive.

2 *a costly mistake* CATASTROPHIC, disastrous, calamitous, ruinous; damaging, harmful, injurious, deleterious, woeful, awful, terrible, dreadful; *formal* grievous. ANTONYM beneficial.

costume noun *each contestant wore a costume depicting her state* OUTFIT, garments, (set of) clothes, ensemble; dress, clothing, attire, garb, uniform, livery; *informal* getup, gear, togs, threads; *formal* apparel; *archaic* habit, habiliments, raiment.

coterie noun *a coterie of kindred spirits* CLIQUE, set, circle, inner circle, crowd, in-crowd, band, community, gang.

cottage noun *summers up at Anna and Renzo's cottage* CABIN, lodge; bungalow, country house; shack, chantey.

couch noun *she seated herself on the couch* SOFA, divan, settee, love seat, chesterfield, daybed, davenport, studio couch. See table at SOFA.

▸ verb *his reply was couched in deferential terms* EXPRESS, phrase, word, frame, put, formulate, style, convey, say, state, utter.

cough verb *he coughed loudly* HACK, hawk, bark, clear one's throat, hem.

▸ noun *a loud cough* HACK, bark.

PHRASE: **cough up** *we need to cough up the rent by next Thursday* PAY, pay up, come up with, hand over, dish out, part with; fork out, shell out, lay out, ante up, pony up.

council noun **1** *the town council* LOCAL AUTHORITY, municipal authority, local government, administration, executive, chamber, assembly, corporation.

2 *the Student Council* ADVISORY BODY, board, committee, brain trust, commission, assembly, panel; synod, convocation.

3 *that evening, she held a family council* meeting, gathering, conference, conclave, assembly.

counsel noun **1** *his wise counsel* ADVICE, guidance, counseling, direction, information; hints, recommendations, suggestions, guidelines, tips, pointers, warnings.

2 *the counsel for the defense* LAWYER, advocate, attorney, attorney-at-law, counselor; *chiefly Brit.* solicitor, barrister.

▸ verb *he counseled the team to withdraw from the deal* ADVISE, recommend, direct, advocate, encourage, urge, warn, caution; guide, give guidance.

counselor noun *I discussed college choices with my counselor* ADVISER, consultant, guide, mentor; expert, specialist.

count verb **1** *Vern counted the money again* ADD UP, add together, reckon up, total, tally, calculate, compute, tot up; census; *formal* enumerate; *dated* cast up.

2 *a company with 250 employees, not counting overseas staff* INCLUDE, take into account, take account of, take into consideration, allow for.

3 *I count it a privilege to be asked* CONSIDER, think, feel, regard, look on as, view as, hold to be, judge, deem, account.

4 *it's your mother's feelings that count* MATTER, be of consequence, be of account, be significant, signify, be important, carry weight.

▸ noun **1** *at last count, the committee had 57 members* CALCULATION, computation, reckoning, tally; *formal* enumeration.

2 *her white blood cell count* AMOUNT, number, total.

PHRASES: **count on/upon** **1** *you can count on me* RELY ON, depend on, bank on, trust (in), be sure of, have (every) confidence in, believe in, put one's faith in, take for granted, take as read. **2** *they hadn't counted on his indomitable spirit* EXPECT, reckon on, anticipate, envisage, allow for, be prepared for, bargain for/on, figure on. **down for the count** *informal*. See UNCONSCIOUS adjective sense 1.

countenance noun *his strikingly handsome countenance* FACE, features, physiognomy, profile; (facial) expression, look, appearance, aspect, mien; *informal* mug, puss; *literary* visage, lineaments.

▸ verb *he would not countenance the use of force* TOLERATE, permit, allow, agree to, consent to, give one's blessing to, go along with, hold with, put up with, endure, stomach, swallow, stand for; *formal* brook.

counter[1] noun *the sugar is in a canister on the counter* WORK SURFACE, countertop, work table; bar; checkout (counter).

counter[2] verb **1** *workers countered accusations of dishonesty* RESPOND TO, parry, hit back at, answer, retort to.

2 *the second argument is more difficult to counter* OPPOSE, dispute, argue against/with, contradict, controvert, negate, counteract; challenge, contest; *formal* gainsay, confute. ANTONYM support.

▸ adjective *a counter bid* OPPOSING, opposed, opposite.

PHRASE: **counter to** *nearly all of his proposals are counter to our original agreement* AGAINST, in opposition to, contrary to, at variance with, in defiance of, in contravention of, in conflict with, at odds with.

counteract verb **1** *new measures to counteract drug trafficking* PREVENT, thwart, frustrate, foil, impede, curb, hinder, hamper, check, put a stop to, put/bring a end to, defeat. ANTONYM encourage.

2 *a drug to counteract the side effects* OFFSET, counterbalance, balance (out), cancel out, even out, counterpoise, countervail, compensate for, make up for, remedy; neutralize, nullify, negate, invalidate. ANTONYMS enhance, exacerbate.

counterbalance verb *the risk is counterbalanced by the potential high yields* COMPENSATE FOR, make up for, offset, balance (out), even out, counterpoise, counteract, equalize, neutralize; nullify, negate, undo.

counterfeit adjective *counterfeit $100 bills* FAKE, faked, bogus, forged, imitation, spurious, substitute, ersatz, phony. See note at SPURIOUS. ANTONYM genuine.

▸ noun *the notes were counterfeits* FAKE, forgery, copy, reproduction, imitation; fraud, sham; *informal* phony, knockoff. ANTONYM original.

▸ verb 1 *his signature was hard to counterfeit* FAKE, forge, copy, reproduce, imitate.

2 *he grew tired of counterfeiting interest* FEIGN, simulate, pretend, fake, sham.

countermand verb *orders were being issued and then countermanded* REVOKE, rescind, reverse, undo, repeal, retract, withdraw, quash, overturn, overrule, cancel, annul, invalidate, nullify, negate; *Law* disaffirm, discharge, vacate; *formal* abrogate. ANTONYM uphold.

counterpane noun *dated* See BEDSPREAD.

counterpart noun *the minister held talks with his French counterpart* EQUIVALENT, opposite number, peer, equal, coequal, parallel, complement, analog, match, twin, mate, fellow, brother, sister; *formal* compeer.

countless adjective *bringing relief to countless patients* INNUMERABLE, numerous, untold, a legion of, without number, numberless, unnumbered, limitless, multitudinous, incalculable; *informal* umpteen, no end of, a slew of, loads of, stacks of, heaps of, masses of, oodles of, zillions of, gazillions of; *literary* myriad. ANTONYM few.

countrified adjective *she's traded her uptown apartment for a house in a more countrified setting* RURAL, rustic, pastoral, bucolic, country; idyllic, unspoiled; *literary* Arcadian, sylvan, georgic. ANTONYM urban.

country noun 1 *foreign countries* NATION, (sovereign) state, kingdom, realm, territory, province, principality, palatinate, duchy.

2 *he risked his life for his country* HOMELAND, native land, fatherland, motherland, the land of one's fathers.

3 *every election year, these guys claim to know what **the country** wants* THE PEOPLE, the public, the population, the populace, citizenry, the nation, the body politic; the electors, the voters, the taxpayers, the grass roots; *informal* John Q. Public, Joe Blow, Joe Schmo.

4 *thickly forested country* TERRAIN, land, territory, parts; landscape, scenery, setting, surroundings, environment.

5 *she hated living in the country* COUNTRYSIDE, greenbelt, great outdoors; rural areas, backwoods, back of beyond, hinterland, bush, backcountry; *informal* sticks, middle of nowhere, boondocks, boonies; *Austral.* outback.

▸ adjective *country pursuits* RURAL, countryside, outdoor, rustic, pastoral, bucolic; *literary* sylvan, Arcadian, georgic. ANTONYM urban.

countryman, countrywoman noun 1 *the traditions of his countrymen* COMPATRIOT, fellow citizen.

2 *the countryman takes a great interest in the weather* COUNTRY DWELLER, country cousin, son/daughter of the soil, farmer; rustic, yokel, (country) bumpkin, peasant, provincial; *informal* hayseed, hick, hillbilly, rube; *archaic* swain.

countryside noun 1 *beautiful unspoiled countryside* LANDSCAPE, scenery, surroundings, setting, environment; country, terrain, land.

2 *I was brought up in the countryside.* See COUNTRY noun sense 5.

county noun *families from neighbouring counties* REGION, province, administrative unit, territory, district, area.

coup noun 1 *a violent military coup* SEIZURE OF POWER, coup d'état, putsch, overthrow, takeover, deposition; revolution, palace revolution, rebellion, revolt, insurrection, mutiny, insurgence, uprising.

2 *a major publishing coup* SUCCESS, triumph, feat, accomplishment, achievement, scoop, master stroke, stroke of genius.

coup de grâce noun *the conservative vote in the third district delivered the coup de grâce to Reinhardt's campaign* DEATH BLOW, finishing blow, kiss of death, final blow; *informal* KO, kayo.

couple noun 1 *the next couple is a sister act from Trenton* PAIR, duo, twosome, two; *archaic* twain, brace.

2 *a honeymoon couple* HUSBAND AND WIFE, twosome, partners, lovers; *informal* item.

3 *I have **a couple of** things to do* SOME, a few, a handful of, one or two.

▸ verb 1 *a sense of hope **coupled with** a sense of loss* COMBINE WITH, accompany with, mix with, incorporate with, link with, associate with, connect with/to, ally with; add to, join to; *formal* conjoin with.

2 *a cable is coupled to one of the wheels* CONNECT, attach, join, fasten, fix, link, secure, tie, bind, strap, rope, tether, truss, lash, hitch, yoke, chain, hook (up). ANTONYM detach.

coupon noun 1 *grocery coupons* VOUCHER, token, ticket; *informal* comp, rain check.

2 *fill in the coupon below* FORM, tear-off card.

courage noun *the courage of firefighters is just awesome* BRAVERY, courageousness, pluck, pluckiness, valour, fearlessness, intrepidity, nerve, daring, audacity, boldness, grit, true grit, hardihood, heroism, gallantry; *informal* guts, spunk, moxie, cojones, balls. ANTONYM cowardice.

THE RIGHT WORD

Courage is what makes someone capable of facing extreme danger and difficulty without retreating (*the courage to confront the enemy head-on*). It implies not only bravery and a dauntless spirit but the ability to endure in times of adversity (*a mother's courage in the face of her loss*). Someone who has **guts**, a slang word indicating an admirable display of courage when it really counts (*having the guts to stand up to one's boss*), might also be described as having "intestinal fortitude," a cliché that is more formal and means the same thing. **Fortitude** is the most formal of any of these words; it suggests firmness or strength of mind rather than physical bravery (*the fortitude to stand up for his beliefs*). **Resolution** also implies firmness of mind rather than fearlessness, but the emphasis is on the determination to achieve a goal in spite of opposition or interference (*a woman of strong resolution, not easily held back by her male superiors*). **Tenacity** goes one step beyond *resolution*, adding stubborn persistence and unwillingness to acknowledge defeat (*the tenacity of a bulldog*). **Nerve** and **pluck** are informal words. *Pluck* connotes high spirits, conviction, and eagerness (*the pluck to volunteer her time even after she'd been laid off*), while *nerve* is the cool, unflappable daring with which someone takes a calculated risk (*the nerve to take over the controls and land the plane safely*). *Nerve* can also refer to brashness or even rudeness in social situations (*She had the nerve to go to his house without calling first*).

---

courageous adjective *these Special Olympians are among the most courageous individuals on the planet* BRAVE, plucky, fearless, valiant, valorous, intrepid, heroic, lionhearted, bold, daring, daredevil, audacious, undaunted, unflinching, unshrinking, unafraid, dauntless, indomitable, doughty, mettlesome, venturesome, stouthearted, gallant; *informal* game, gutsy, spunky, ballsy. ANTONYM cowardly.

courier noun *the documents were sent by courier* MESSENGER, runner; letter carrier, mail carrier, delivery man/woman; delivery service.

course noun **1** *the island was not far off our course* ROUTE, way, track, direction, tack, path, line, trail, trajectory, bearing, heading, orbit.

2 *the course of history* PROGRESSION, development, progress, advance, evolution, flow, movement, sequence, order, succession, rise, march, passage, passing.

3 *what is the best course to adopt?* PROCEDURE, plan, plan of action, course of action, line of action, MO, modus operandi, practice, approach, technique, way, means, policy, strategy, program; *formal* praxis.

4 *a waterlogged course* RACECOURSE, raceway, racetrack, track, ground.

5 *I'm taking a French course* CLASS, course of study, program of study, curriculum, syllabus; classes, lectures, studies.

6 *a course of antibiotics* PROGRAM, series, sequence, system, schedule, regimen.

▸ verb *tears coursed down her cheeks* FLOW, pour, stream, run, rush, gush, cascade, flood, roll.

PHRASES: **in due course** *I look forward to hearing from you in due course* AT THE APPROPRIATE TIME, when the time is ripe, in time, in the fullness of time, in the course of time, at a later date, by and by, sooner or later, in the end, eventually. **of course** *there are, of course, exceptions to the rule* NATURALLY, as might be expected, as you/one would expect, needless to say, certainly, to be sure, as a matter of course, obviously, it goes without saying; *informal* natch.

court noun **1** *the court found him guilty* COURT OF LAW, bench, bar, judicature, tribunal; *chiefly Brit.* law court, chancery.

2 *the court of Louis IX* ROYAL HOUSEHOLD, retinue, entourage, train, suite, courtiers, attendants.

3 *she made her way to the queen's court* ROYAL RESIDENCE, palace, castle, château.

▸ verb **1** *a newspaper editor who was courted by senior politicians* CURRY FAVOR WITH, cultivate, try to win over, make up to, ingratiate oneself with; *informal* suck up to, butter up.

2 *he was busily courting public attention* SEEK, pursue, go after, strive for, solicit.

3 *he has often courted controversy* RISK, invite, attract, bring on oneself.

4 *dated* *he's courting her sister* GO OUT WITH, pursue, run after, chase; *informal* date, see, go steady with; *dated* woo, set one's cap for, romance, seek the hand of.

courteous adjective *our courteous staff is available 24 hours a day* POLITE, well-mannered, civil, respectful, well-behaved, well-bred, well-spoken, mannerly; gentlemanly, chivalrous, gallant; gracious, obliging, considerate, pleasant, cordial, urbane, polished, refined, courtly, civilized. ANTONYM rude.

courtesan noun *archaic* See PROSTITUTE noun.

courtesy noun *our customers will be treated with courtesy* POLITENESS, courteousness, good manners, civility, respect, respectfulness; chivalry, gallantry; graciousness, consideration, thought, thoughtfulness, cordiality, urbanity, courtliness.

courtier noun *the princess's courtiers* ATTENDANT, lord, lady, lady-in-waiting, steward, page, squire.

courtly adjective *he gave a courtly bow* REFINED, polished, suave, cultivated, civilized, elegant, urbane, debonair; polite, civil, courteous, gracious, well-mannered, well-bred, chivalrous, gallant, gentlemanly, ladylike, aristocratic, dignified, decorous, formal, stately, ceremonious. ANTONYM uncouth.

courtship noun **1** *a whirlwind courtship* ROMANCE, love affair, affair; engagement.

2 *his courtship of Emma* WOOING, courting, suit, pursuit.

courtyard noun *India and I met in the courtyard for lunch* QUADRANGLE, cloister, square, plaza, piazza, close, enclosure, yard; *informal* quad.

cove noun *a small sandy cove* BAY, inlet, fjord, anchorage.

covenant noun *a breach of the covenant* CONTRACT, agreement, undertaking, commitment, guarantee, warrant, pledge, promise, bond, indenture; pact, deal, settlement, arrangement, understanding.

▸ verb *the landlord covenants to repair the property* UNDERTAKE, contract, guarantee, pledge, promise, agree, engage, warrant, commit oneself, bind oneself.

cover verb **1** *she covered her face with a towel* PROTECT, shield, shelter; hide, conceal, veil. ANTONYMS expose, reveal.

2 *his car was covered in mud* CAKE, coat, encrust, plaster, smother, daub, bedaub.

3 *snow covered the fields* BLANKET, overlay, overspread, carpet, coat; *literary* mantle.

4 *a course covering all aspects of the business* DEAL WITH, consider, take in, include, involve, comprise, incorporate, embrace.

5 *the trial was covered by several newspapers* REPORT ON, write about, describe, commentate on, publish/broadcast details of.

6 *he turned on the radio to cover the noise of the air conditioner* MASK, disguise, hide, camouflage, muffle, block out, stifle, smother.

7 *I'm covering for Jill* STAND IN FOR, fill in for, deputize for, take over from, relieve, take the place of, sit in for, understudy, hold the fort; *informal* sub for, pinch-hit for.

8 *can you make enough to cover your costs?* PAY (FOR), be enough for, fund, finance; pay back, make up for, offset.

9 *your home is covered against damage and loss* INSURE, protect, secure, underwrite, assure, indemnify.

10 *we covered ten miles each day* TRAVEL, journey, go, do, traverse.

▸ noun **1** *a protective cover | a manhole cover.* See COVERING sense 1.

2 *a book cover* BINDING, jacket, dust jacket, dust cover, wrapper.

3 (**covers**) *she pulled the covers over her head* BEDDING, bedclothes, sheets, blankets.

4 *a thick cover of snow* COATING, coat, covering, layer, carpet, blanket, overlay, dusting, film, sheet, veneer, crust, skin, cloak, mantle, veil, pall, shroud.

5 *panicking onlookers ran for cover* SHELTER, protection, refuge, sanctuary, haven, hiding place.

6 *there is considerable game cover around the lake* UNDERGROWTH, vegetation, greenery, woodland, trees, bushes, brush, scrub, plants; covert, thicket, copse.

7 *the company was a cover for an international swindle* FRONT, facade, smokescreen, screen, blind, camouflage, disguise, mask, cloak.

8 *on weekends there's a cover to get in the bar* COVER CHARGE, entry charge, entrance fee, admission charge, price of admission.

PHRASE: **cover up** *the government has tried to cover up the army's role* CONCEAL, hide, keep secret, hush up, draw a veil over, suppress, sweep under the carpet, gloss over, keep dark; *informal* whitewash, keep a/the lid on.

coverage noun **1** *up-to-the-minute coverage of the situation* REPORTAGE, reporting, description, treatment, handling, presentation, investigation, commentary; reports, articles, pieces, stories, ink.

2 *your policy provides coverage against damage by fire* INSURANCE, protection, security, assurance, indemnification, indemnity, compensation.

covering noun **1** *a plastic covering* AWNING, canopy, tarpaulin, cowling, cowl, casing, housing; wrapping, wrapper, cover, envelope, sheath, sleeve, jacket, lid, top, cap.

2 *a covering of snow* LAYER, coating, coat, carpet, blanket, overlay, topping, dusting, film, sheet, veneer, crust, skin, cloak, mantle, veil.

▸ adjective *a covering letter* ACCOMPANYING, explanatory, introductory, prefatory.

coverlet noun *a queen-size flannel coverlet* BEDSPREAD, bedcover, cover, throw, duvet, quilt, eiderdown, comforter; *dated* counterpane.

covert adjective *covert plans to sell arms* SECRET, furtive, clandestine, surreptitious, stealthy, cloak-and-dagger, hole-and-corner, backstairs, backroom, hidden, under-the-table, concealed, private, undercover, underground; *informal* hush-hush. See note at SECRET. ANTONYM overt.

cover-up noun *the aides were implicated in the cover-up* WHITEWASH, concealment, false front, facade, camouflage, disguise, mask, veneer, pretext.

covet verb *even with all they have, they covet the wealth of others* DESIRE, yearn for, crave, have one's heart set on, want, wish for, long for, hanker after/for, hunger after/for, thirst for.

covetous adjective *this covetous man will never be satisfied* GRASPING, greedy, acquisitive, desirous, possessive, envious, green with envy, green-eyed. See notes at GREEDY, JEALOUS.

covey noun *a covey of audition hopefuls were lined up in the lobby* GROUP, gang, troop, troupe, party, company, band, bevy, flock; knot, cluster; *informal* bunch, gaggle, posse, crew.

cow verb *has he cowed you all with his threats?* INTIMIDATE, daunt, browbeat, bully, tyrannize, scare, terrorize, frighten, dishearten, unnerve, subdue; *informal* psych out, bulldoze.

coward noun *the cowards were the first to give up* WEAKLING, milksop, namby-pamby, mouse; *informal* chicken, scaredy-cat, yellow-belly, sissy, baby, candy-ass, milquetoast. ANTONYM hero.

cowardly adjective *he made a cowardly dash for the exit, leaving everyone else behind* FAINT-HEARTED, lily-livered, spineless, chicken-hearted, craven, timid, timorous, fearful, pusillanimous; *informal* yellow, chicken, weak-kneed, gutless, yellow-bellied, wimpish, wimpy. See word spectrum at BRAVERY. ANTONYM brave.

cowboy noun *cowboys on horseback* CATTLEMAN, cowhand, cowman, cowherd, herder, herdsman, drover, stockman, rancher, gaucho, vaquero; *informal* cowpuncher, cowpoke, broncobuster; *dated* buckaroo.

▸ adjective *informal a cowboy pilot* MAVERICK, original, nonconformist, unorthodox, rebel, rebellious.

cower verb *they cowered at the sound of gunfire* CRINGE, shrink, crouch, recoil, flinch, pull back, draw back, tremble, shake, quake, blench, quail, grovel. See note at WINCE.

coy adjective *her coy demeanor is just an act* ARCH, simpering, coquettish, flirtatious, kittenish; demure, shy, modest, bashful, reticent, diffident, self-effacing, shrinking, timid. ANTONYM brazen.

cozen verb *literary* See TRICK verb.

cozy adjective **1** *a cozy country cottage* SNUG, comfortable, warm, homelike, homey, homely, welcoming; safe, sheltered, secure, down-home, homestyle; *informal* comfy, toasty, snug as a bug (in a rug).

2 *a cozy chat* INTIMATE, relaxed, informal, friendly.

crab[1] *the puppies would nose around in the tide pools, intrigued by the darting shiners and scurrying crabs.* See table at CRUSTACEAN.

crab[2] noun *informal we never went to Lacy's house to play because her father was such a crab.* See GROUCH.

crabbed adjective **1** *her crabbed handwriting* CRAMPED, ill-formed, bad, illegible, unreadable, indecipherable, hieroglyphic; shaky, spidery.

2 *a crabbed old man.* See CRABBY.

crabby adjective *sorry, I didn't mean to be so crabby* IRRITABLE, cantankerous, irascible, bad-tempered, grumpy, grouchy, crotchety, tetchy, testy, crusty, curmudgeonly, ill-tempered, ill-humored, peevish, cross, fractious, pettish, crabbed, prickly, waspish; *informal* snappish, snappy, cranky, ornery. ANTONYM affable.

crack noun **1** *a crack in the glass* SPLIT, break, chip, fracture, rupture; crazing.

2 *a crack between two rocks* SPACE, gap, crevice, fissure, cleft, breach, rift, cranny, chink, interstice.

3 *the crack of a rifle* BANG, report, explosion, detonation, pop; clap, crash.

4 *a crack on the head* BLOW, bang, hit, knock, rap, punch, thump, bump, smack, slap; *informal* bash, whack, thwack, clout, wallop, clip, bop.

5 *informal we'll have a crack at it* ATTEMPT, try; *informal* go, shot, stab, whack; *formal* essay.

6 *informal cheap cracks about her clothes* JOKE, witticism, quip; jibe, barb, taunt, sneer, insult; *informal* gag, wisecrack, funny, dig.

▸ verb 1 *the glass cracked in the heat* BREAK, split, fracture, rupture, snap.

2 *she cracked him across the forehead* HIT, strike, smack, slap, beat, thump, knock, rap, punch; *informal* bash, whack, thwack, clobber, clout, clip, wallop, belt, bop, sock, boff, bust, slug.

3 *the witnesses cracked* BREAK DOWN, give way, cave in, go to pieces, crumble, lose control, yield, succumb.

4 *informal the naval code proved harder to crack* DECIPHER, interpret, decode, break, solve, resolve, work out, find the key to; *informal* figure out.

▸ adjective *a crack shot* EXPERT, skilled, skillful, formidable, virtuoso, masterly, consummate, excellent, first-rate, first-class, marvelous, wonderful, magnificent, outstanding, superlative; deadly; *informal* great, superb, fantastic, ace, hotshot, mean, demon, brilliant, crackerjack, bang-up. ANTONYM incompetent.

PHRASES: **crack down on** *a campaign to crack down on crime* SUPPRESS, prevent, stop, put a stop to, put an end to, stamp out, eliminate, eradicate; clamp down on, get tough on, come down hard on, limit, restrain, restrict, check, keep in check, control, keep under control. **crack up** *informal I feel as if I'm about to crack up* BREAK DOWN, have a breakdown, lose control, go to pieces, go out of one's mind, go mad; *informal* lose it, fall/come apart at the seams, go crazy, freak out.

cracked adjective 1 *a cracked cup* CHIPPED, broken, crazed, fractured, splintered, split; damaged, defective, flawed, imperfect.

2 *informal you're cracked!* See MAD sense 1.

crackle verb *bits of dried mosses crackled in the fire* SIZZLE, fizz, hiss, crack, snap, sputter, crepitate.

cradle noun 1 *the baby's cradle* CRIB, bassinet, cot, rocker.

2 *the cradle of democracy* BIRTHPLACE, fount, fountainhead, source, spring, fountain, origin, place of origin, seat; *literary* wellspring.

▸ verb *she cradled his head in her arms* HOLD, support, pillow, cushion, shelter, protect; rest, prop (up).

craft noun 1 *a player with plenty of craft* SKILL, skillfulness, ability, capability, competence, art, talent, flair, artistry, dexterity, craftsmanship, expertise, proficiency, adroitness, adeptness, deftness, virtuosity.

2 *the historian's craft* ACTIVITY, occupation, profession, work, line of work, pursuit.

3 *she used craft to get what she wanted* CUNNING, craftiness, guile, wiliness, artfulness, deviousness, slyness, trickery, duplicity, dishonesty, deceit, deceitfulness, deception, intrigue, subterfuge; wiles, ploys, ruses, schemes, stratagems, tricks.

4 *a sailing craft* VESSEL, ship, boat; *literary* bark/barque.

craftsman, craftswoman noun *the handiwork of East Coast craftsmen* ARTISAN, artist, skilled worker; expert, master; *archaic* artificer.

craftsmanship noun *a fine example of modern craftsmanship* WORKMANSHIP, artistry, craft, art, handiwork, work; skill, skillfulness, expertise, technique.

crafty adjective *a couple of crafty rogues* CUNNING, wily, guileful, artful, devious, sly, tricky, scheming, calculating, designing, sharp, shrewd, astute, canny; duplicitous, dishonest, deceitful; *informal* foxy. ANTONYM honest.

crag noun *the crag is a popular nesting site for eagles* CLIFF, bluff, ridge, precipice, height, peak, tor, escarpment, scarp.

craggy adjective 1 *the craggy cliffs* STEEP, precipitous, sheer, perpendicular; rocky, rugged, ragged.

2 *his craggy face* RUGGED, rough-hewn, strong, manly; weather-beaten, weathered.

cram verb 1 *closets crammed with clothes* FILL, stuff, pack, jam, fill to overflowing, fill to the brim, overload; crowd, overcrowd.

2 *they all crammed into the car* CROWD, pack, pile, squash, squish, squeeze, wedge oneself, force one's way.

3 *he crammed his clothes into a suitcase* THRUST, push, shove, force, ram, jam, stuff, pack, pile, squash, compress, squeeze, wedge.

4 *most of the students are cramming for exams* STUDY, review, bone up.

cramp noun *stomach cramps* MUSCLE/MUSCULAR SPASM, pain, shooting pain, pang, stitch; *Medicine* hyperkinesis.

▸ verb *tighter rules will cramp economic growth* HINDER, impede, inhibit, hamper, constrain, hamstring, interfere with, restrict, limit, shackle; slow down, check, arrest, curb, retard.

cramped adjective 1 *cramped accommodationss* CONFINED, uncomfortable, restricted, constricted, small, tiny, narrow; crowded, packed, congested; *archaic* strait. ANTONYM spacious.

2 *cramped handwriting* SMALL, crabbed, illegible, unreadable, indecipherable, hieroglyphic.

crane noun *the cargo is lifted by a crane* DERRICK, winch, hoist, davit, windlass; block and tackle.

cranium noun *a blow to his cranium* SKULL, head, brain case; *informal* noggin, brainpan.

crank[1] verb *you crank the engine by hand* START, turn (over), get going. PHRASE: **crank up** *informal crank up the volume, Steve* INCREASE, intensify, amplify, heighten, escalate, add to, augment, build up, expand, extend, raise; speed up, accelerate; up, jack up, hike up, step up, bump up, pump up.

crank[2] noun *they're nothing but a bunch of cranks* ECCENTRIC, oddity, madman/madwoman, lunatic; *informal* oddball, freak, weirdo, crackpot, loony, nut, nutcase, head case, maniac, screwball, kook.

cranky adjective *informal the children were tired and cranky.* See CRABBY.

cranny noun *every little cranny was filled with drifted snow* CHINK, crack, crevice, slit, split, fissure, rift, cleft, opening, gap, aperture, cavity, hole, hollow, niche, corner, nook, interstice.

crap noun *informal* 1 *he's talking crap.* See GARBAGE sense 2.

2 *pick up that crap.* See GARBAGE sense 1.

crash verb 1 *the car* ***crashed into*** *a tree* SMASH INTO, collide with, be in collision with, hit, strike, ram, cannon into, plow into, meet head-on, run into, impact.

2 *he crashed his car* SMASH, wreck; *informal* total.

3 *waves* ***crashed against*** *the shore* DASH AGAINST, batter, pound, lash (against), slam (against), be hurled against.

4 *thunder crashed overhead* BOOM, crack, roll, clap, explode, bang, blast, blare, resound, reverberate, rumble, thunder, echo.

5 *informal his clothing company crashed* COLLAPSE, fold, fail, go under, go bankrupt, become insolvent, cease trading, go into receivership, go into liquidation; *informal* go broke, go bust, go belly up.

▸ noun 1 *a crash on the highway* ACCIDENT, collision, road traffic accident, derailment, wreck; *informal* pileup, smash-up, rear-ender.

2 *a loud crash* BANG, smash, smack, crack, bump, thud, clatter, clunk, clang; report, detonation, explosion; noise, racket, clangor, din.

3 *the stock market crash* COLLAPSE, failure, bankruptcy.

▸ adjective *a crash course* INTENSIVE, concentrated, rapid, short; accelerated, immersion.

crass adjective *crass assumptions about women* STUPID, insensitive, mindless, thoughtless, ignorant, witless, oafish, boorish, asinine, coarse, gross, graceless, tasteless, tactless, clumsy, heavy-handed, blundering. ANTONYM intelligent.

crate noun *a crate for their good china* CASE, packing case, chest, box; container, receptacle.

crater noun *the crater has become a lake* HOLLOW, bowl, basin, hole, cavity, depression; *Geology* caldera.

crave verb *he craved professional recognition* LONG FOR, yearn for, desire, want, wish for, hunger for, thirst for, sigh for, pine for, hanker after, covet, lust after, ache for, set one's heart on, dream of, be bent on; *informal* have a yen for, have a jones for, itch for, be dying for.

craven adjective a craven surrender COWARDLY, lily-livered, faint-hearted, chicken-hearted, spineless, timid, timorous, fearful, pusillanimous, weak, feeble; *informal* yellow, chicken, weak-kneed, gutless, yellow-bellied, wimpish; contemptible, abject, ignominious. ANTONYM brave.

craving noun *a craving for chocolate* LONGING, yearning, desire, want, wish, hankering, hunger, thirst, appetite, greed, lust, ache, need, urge; *informal* yen, itch, jones.

crawl verb 1 *they crawled under the table* CREEP, worm one's way, go on all fours, go on hands and knees, wriggle, slither, squirm, scrabble.

2 *informal I'm not going to go* ***crawling to*** *him* GROVEL TO, ingratiate oneself with, be obsequious to, kowtow to, pander to, toady to, truckle to, bow and scrape to, dance attendance on, curry favor with, make up to, fawn on/over; *informal* suck up to, lick someone's boots, butter up.

3 *the place was* ***crawling with*** *soldiers* BE FULL OF, overflow with, teem with, be packed with, be crowded with, be alive with, be overrun with, swarm with, be bristling with, be infested with, be thick with; *informal* be lousy with, be jam-packed with, be chock-full of.

craze noun *the latest fitness craze* FAD, fashion, trend, vogue, enthusiasm, mania, passion, rage, obsession, compulsion, fixation, fetish, fancy, taste, fascination, preoccupation; *informal* thing.

crazed adjective *a crazed murderer* MAD, insane, out of one's mind, deranged, demented, certifiable, psychopathic, lunatic; wild, raving, berserk, manic, maniac, frenzied; *informal* crazy, mental, out of one's head, raving mad, psycho. See also CRAZY sense 1. ANTONYM sane.

crazy adjective *informal* 1 *he was acting like a crazy person* MAD, insane, out of one's mind, deranged, demented, not in one's right mind, crazed, lunatic, non compos mentis, unhinged, mad as a hatter, mad as a March hare; *informal* mental, nutty, nutty as a fruitcake, off one's rocker, not right in the head, round/around the bend, raving mad, batty, bonkers, cuckoo, loopy, ditzy, loony, bananas, loco, with a screw loose, touched, gaga, not all there, out to lunch, crackers, nutso, out of one's tree, wacko, gonzo. ANTONYM sane.

2 *Andrea had a crazy idea* STUPID, foolish, idiotic, silly, absurd, ridiculous, ludicrous, preposterous, farcical, laughable, risible, nonsensical, imbecilic, harebrained, cockamamie, half-baked, impracticable, unworkable, ill-conceived, senseless; *informal* cockeyed, daft, kooky. ANTONYM sensible.

3 *he's* ***crazy about*** *her* PASSIONATE ABOUT, (very) keen on, enamored of, infatuated with, smitten with, devoted to; (very) enthusiastic about, fanatical about; *informal* wild about, mad about, nuts about, hog-wild about, gone on. ANTONYMS indifferent, apathetic.

creak verb *the rusty gate creaked in the wind* SQUEAK, grate, rasp; groan, complain.

cream noun 1 *skin creams* LOTION, ointment, moisturizer, emollient, unguent, cosmetic; salve, rub, embrocation, balm, liniment.

2 *the cream of the crop* BEST, finest, pick, flower, crème de la crème, elite. ANTONYM dregs.

▸ adjective *a cream dress* OFF-WHITE, whitish, cream-colored, creamy, ivory, yellowish-white, ecru.

WORD NOTE **chrism**

Whatever makes up that (usually) white mammalian secretion known as milk is divided into three essential elements—the serous or serum-like liquid, the whey; the casein-like coagulate that can be made into cheese; and that part technically known as the butyraceous or buttery fraction, which floats on the top and is known, of course, as cream. This last word is not simply pleasing and sonorous: it is very ancient, and is freighted with much more than a mere dietary connotation: it enjoys an eleventh-century lexical connection with a word that still survives, if rarely used, and which I think of as one of the prettiest in the tongue: the word for the anointing unguent employed in high church ceremonial, the *chrism.* Chrism both welcomes a child into the world—he is baptized with chrism and wrapped in a chrism-cloth—and it is used to anoint the forehead and lips of one who is departing, and who is given extreme unction. It is tempting merely to use the word oil when writing of such matters: but in fact properly organized churches mix that resinous fragrance known as balm into non-aromatic vegetable oil to make its chrism, and since the ecclesiastical community takes such time and trouble to make the stuff, I advocate using the word, unfamiliar though it may well be. Moreover its connection with cream—before the thirteenth century the words were more or less interchangeable—gives it a certain homely quality that adds to its attraction. **—SW**

creamy adjective **1** *a creamy paste* SMOOTH, thick, velvety, whipped; rich, buttery. ANTONYM lumpy.

2 *creamy flowers* OFF-WHITE, whitish, cream-colored, cream, ivory, yellowish-white.

crease noun **1** *pants with knife-edge creases* FOLD, line, ridge; pleat, tuck; furrow, groove, corrugation.

2 *the creases at the corners of her eyes* WRINKLE, line, crinkle, pucker; **(creases)** crow's feet.

▸ verb *her skirt was creased and stained* CRUMPLE, wrinkle, crinkle, line, scrunch up, rumple, ruck up.

create verb **1** *she has created a work of stunning originality* PRODUCE, generate, bring into being, make, fabricate, fashion, build, construct; design, devise, originate, frame, develop, shape, form, forge.

2 *regular socializing creates good team spirit* BRING ABOUT, give rise to, lead to, result in, cause, breed, generate, engender, produce, make for, promote, foster, sow the seeds of, contribute to. ANTONYM destroy.

3 *the governments planned to create a free-trade zone* ESTABLISH, found, initiate, institute, constitute, inaugurate, launch, set up, form, organize, develop.

creation noun **1** *the creation of a coalition government* ESTABLISHMENT, formation, foundation, initiation, institution, inauguration, constitution; production, generation, fabrication, fashioning, building, construction, origination, development. ANTONYM destruction.

2 *the whole of creation* THE WORLD, the universe, the cosmos; the living world, the natural world, nature, life, living things.

3 *Margaret Atwood's literary creations* WORK, work of art, production, opus, oeuvre; achievement, intellectual property; *informal* brainchild.

creative adjective *our students are encouraged to be creative* INVENTIVE, imaginative, innovative, experimental, original; artistic, expressive, inspired, visionary; enterprising, resourceful.

THE RIGHT WORD

Everyone likes to think that he or she is **creative**, which is used to describe the active, exploratory minds possessed by artists, writers, and inventors (*a creative approach to problem-solving*). Today, however, *creative* has become an advertising buzzword (*creative cooking*, *creative hair-styling*) that simply means new or different. **Original** is more specific and limited in scope. Someone who is *original* comes up with things that no one else has thought of (*an original approach to constructing a doghouse*), or thinks in an independent and creative way (*a highly original filmmaker*). **Imaginative** implies having an active and creative imagination, which often means that the person visualizes things quite differently than the way they appear in the real world (*imaginative illustrations for a children's book*). The practical side of *imaginative* is **inventive**; the *inventive* person figures out how to make things work (*an inventive solution to the problem of getting a wheelchair into a van*). But where an *inventive* mind tends to comes up with solutions to problems it has posed for itself, a **resourceful** mind deals successfully with externally imposed problems or limitations (*A resourceful child can amuse herself with simple wooden blocks*). Someone who is **ingenious** is both *inventive* and *resourceful*, with a dose of cleverness thrown in (*the ingenious idea of using recycled plastic to create a warm, fleecelike fabric*).

creativity noun *her agency is a hotbed of youthful creativity* INVENTIVENESS, imagination, innovation, innovativeness, originality, individuality; artistry, inspiration, vision; enterprise, initiative, resourcefulness.

creator noun **1** *the creator of the series* AUTHOR, writer, designer, deviser, maker, producer; originator, inventor, architect, mastermind, prime mover; *literary* begetter.

2 (the Creator) *the Sabbath is kept to honor the Creator.* See GOD sense 1.

creature noun **1** *the earth and its creatures* ANIMAL, beast, brute; living thing, living being; *informal* critter, varmint. See table at MONSTER.

2 *you're such a lazy creature!* PERSON, individual, human being, character, soul, wretch, customer; *informal* devil, beggar, sort, type.

3 *the boss's truckling creatures* LACKEY, minion, hireling, servant, puppet, tool, cat's paw, pawn; *informal* stooge, yes-man.

credence noun **1** *the government placed little credence in the scheme* BELIEF, faith, trust, confidence, reliance.

2 *later reports lent credence to this view* CREDIBILITY, plausibility, believability; *archaic* credit.

credentials plural noun *checking the driver's credentials* DOCUMENTS, documentation, papers, identity papers, bona fides, ID, ID card, identity card, passport, proof of identity; certificates, diplomas, certification, references.

credibility noun **1** *the whole tale lacks credibility* PLAUSIBILITY, believability, tenability, probability, feasibility, likelihood, credence; authority, cogency.

2 *does he possess the moral credibility the party is looking for?* TRUSTWORTHINESS, reliability, dependability, integrity; reputation, status.

credible adjective *only one of the so-called witnesses could provide a credible story* BELIEVABLE, plausible, tenable, able to hold water, conceivable, likely, probable, possible, feasible, reasonable, with a ring of truth, persuasive. See note at BELIEVABLE.

credit noun **1** *he never got the credit he deserved* PRAISE, commendation, acclaim, acknowledgment, recognition, kudos, glory, esteem, respect, thanks, admiration, tributes, gratitude, appreciation; *informal* bouquets, brownie points, marks.

2 *the speech did his credit no good* REPUTATION, repute, image, name, good name, character, prestige, standing, status, estimation, credibility.

3 *archaic his theory has been given very little credit* CREDENCE, belief, faith, trust, reliance, confidence.

4 *she bought her new car on credit* LOAN, advance, financing; installments; *informal* plastic.

▸ verb **1** *the wise will seldom credit all they hear* BELIEVE, accept, give credence to, trust, have faith in; *informal* buy, swallow, fall for, take something as gospel (truth).

2 *the scheme's success can be credited to the team's frugality* ASCRIBE, attribute, assign, accredit, chalk up, put down.

creditable adjective *her forty years of creditable stage work* COMMENDABLE, praiseworthy, laudable, admirable, honorable, estimable, meritorious, worthy, deserving, respectable. See note at BELIEVABLE. ANTONYM deplorable.

credo noun *he announced his credo in his first editorial* STATEMENT OF BELIEF(S), article of faith, doctrine, creed, axiom, dogma, tenet, canon; theory, thesis, premise, conviction, position; ideology, code of belief.

WORD NOTE **credo**

This credo I hereby affirm. I will never say *marginalize* or use *privilege* as a verb. I will avoid *closure* except perhaps when discussing the endings of poems. I will avoid *gnostic* altogether. I will not say *societal* and *comedic* where *social* and *comic* will serve just as well. I will not say *hegemony* except with irony. I will not put *nestled, cradled,* or *shimmered* in poems, and I will stop reading any poem that has *cupped* in it, or *scrim,* sure signs of *poetical* intent. I will not split infinitives if I can help it. I will use correct grammar, but I will feel free to leave out punctuation marks when it suits my purposes in a poem. I will welcome new oxymorons, as when a friend complains that she has "an ancient computer." I will allow *no-brainer* and *Prozac* and *feng shui* into my poetry, not to mention the *Net,* the *Web,* the *Windows software* that came with the *box,* my *laptop,* my *desktop,* my *ergonomic workstation,* the bad case of *carpal tunnel syndrome* I suffered a few years ago, and other things that would have made no sense to anyone thirty years ago. I will love the language as a living thing that never stops evolving. **—DL**

credulous adjective *he sold 'miracle' cures to desperate and credulous clients* GULLIBLE, naive, too trusting, easily taken in, impressionable, unsuspecting, unsuspicious, unwary, unquestioning; innocent, ingenuous, inexperienced, unsophisticated, unworldly, wide-eyed; *informal* born yesterday, wet behind the ears. See note at GULLIBLE. ANTONYM suspicious.

creed noun **1** *people of many creeds and cultures* FAITH, religion, religious belief, religious persuasion, church, denomination, sect.

2 *his political creed* SYSTEM OF BELIEF, set of beliefs, beliefs, principles, articles of faith, ideology, credo, doctrine, teaching, dogma, tenets, canons.

creek noun *marsh marigolds grow along the creek* STREAM, river, brook, rivulet, freshet, runnel, rill, tributary, watercourse, bourn; *informal* crick. PHRASE: **up a/the creek** *when I saw the condition of the spare tire, I knew we were up a creek* IN TROUBLE, in difficulty/difficulties, in a mess, in a predicament; *informal* in a pickle, in a jam, in a fix.

creep verb *Tim crept out of the house* TIPTOE, steal, sneak, slip, slink, sidle, pad, edge, inch; skulk, prowl.

▸ noun *informal he's such a creep!* See BASTARD noun sense 2.

creeper noun See VINE.

creeps PHRASE: **give someone the creeps** *informal Pam says he's a nice guy, but he still gives me the creeps* REPEL, repulse, revolt, disgust, sicken, nauseate, make someone's flesh creep, make someone's skin crawl; scare, frighten, terrify, horrify; *informal* gross out, freak out, creep out.

creepy adjective *informal the old apple trees look creepy in the dim moonlight* FRIGHTENING, eerie, disturbing, sinister, weird, hair-raising, menacing, threatening, eldritch; *informal* spooky, scary, freaky.

crescent noun *she carved a small crescent into the lid of the box* HALF-MOON, sickle-shape, lunula, lunette; arc, curve, bow.

crest noun **1** *the bird's crest* COMB, plume, tuft of feathers.

2 *the crest of the hill* SUMMIT, peak, top, tip, pinnacle, brow, crown, apex.

3 *our family crest* INSIGNIA, regalia, badge, emblem, heraldic device, coat of arms, arms.

crestfallen adjective *he was crestfallen after his mediocre performance at the tryouts* DOWNHEARTED, downcast, despondent, disappointed, disconsolate, disheartened, discouraged, dispirited, dejected, depressed, desolate, in the doldrums, sad, glum, gloomy, dismayed, doleful, miserable, unhappy, woebegone, forlorn; *informal* blue, bummed, in a blue funk, down in/at the mouth, down in the dumps. ANTONYM cheerful.

crevasse noun *loose rocks fell into the crevasse* CHASM, abyss, fissure, cleft, crack, split, breach, rift, hole, cavity.

crevice noun *the termites crawled into a crevice* CRACK, fissure, cleft, chink, interstice, cranny, nook, slit, split, rift, fracture, breach; opening, gap, hole.

crew noun **1** *the ship's crew* SAILORS, mariners, hands, ship's company, ship's complement.

2 *a crew of cameramen and sound engineers* TEAM, group, company, unit, corps, party, gang.

3 *informal they were a motley crew* CROWD, group, band, gang, mob, pack, troop, swarm, herd, posse; *informal* bunch, tribe.

crib noun **1** *the baby's crib* CRADLE, cot, bassinet.

2 *the oxen's crib* MANGER, stall, feeding trough.

▸ verb *informal she cribbed the plot from a Shakespeare play* COPY, plagiarize, poach, appropriate, steal, "borrow"; *informal* rip off, lift, pinch.

crick noun *a crick in my neck* KINK, pinch, knot, strain, stiffness.

crime noun **1** *kidnapping is a very serious crime* OFFENSE, unlawful act, illegal act, felony, misdemeanor, misdeed, wrong; *informal* no-no.

2 *the increase in crime* LAWBREAKING, delinquency, wrongdoing, criminality, misconduct, illegality, villainy; *informal* crookedness; *Law* malfeasance.

3 *a crime against humanity* SIN, evil, immoral act, wrong, atrocity, abomination, disgrace, outrage. See note at SIN.

criminal noun *a convicted criminal* LAWBREAKER, offender, villain, delinquent, felon, convict, malefactor, wrongdoer, culprit, miscreant; thief, burglar, robber, armed robber, gunman, gangster, terrorist; *informal* crook, con, jailbird, hood, yardbird, perp; *Law* malfeasant.

▸ adjective **1** *criminal conduct* UNLAWFUL, illegal, illicit, lawless, felonious, delinquent, fraudulent, actionable, culpable; villainous, nefarious, corrupt, wrong, bad, evil, wicked, iniquitous; *informal* crooked; *Law* malfeasant. ANTONYM lawful.

2 *informal a criminal waste of taxpayers' money* DEPLORABLE, shameful, reprehensible, disgraceful, inexcusable, unforgivable, unconscionable, unpardonable, outrageous, monstrous, shocking, scandalous, wicked. ANTONYM commendable.

crimp verb *crimp the edges of the pie crust* PLEAT, flute, corrugate, ruffle, fold, crease, crinkle, pucker, gather; pinch, compress, press together, squeeze together.

crimped adjective *crimped blond hair* CURLY, wavy, curled, frizzy.

cringe verb **1** *she cringed as he bellowed in her ear* COWER, shrink, recoil, shy away, flinch, blench, draw back; shake, tremble, quiver, quail, quake.

2 *it makes me cringe when I think of it* WINCE, shudder, squirm, feel embarrassed, feel mortified. See note at WINCE.

crinkle verb *it's impossible to crinkle the paper quietly* WRINKLE, crease, pucker, furrow, corrugate; rumple, crumple, scrunch up, ruck up.

crinkly adjective *a stiff, crinkly fabric* WRINKLED, wrinkly, crinkled, creased, crumpled, rumpled, crimped, corrugated, fluted, puckered, furrowed; wavy.

cripple verb **1** *the accident crippled her* DISABLE, paralyze, immobilize, make lame, incapacitate, handicap, leave someone a paraplegic/quadriplegic.

2 *the company had been crippled by the recession* DEVASTATE, ruin, destroy, wipe out; paralyze, hamstring, bring to a standstill, put out of action, sideline, put out of business, bankrupt, break, bring someone to their knees.

crippled adjective *crippled soldiers* DISABLED, paralyzed, incapacitated, physically handicapped, lame, immobilized, bedridden, in a wheelchair, paraplegic, quadriplegic; *euphemistic* physically challenged.

WORD NOTE **crippled**

To studiously and unerringly substitute *disabled* or *challenged* for *crippled* seems to me to have less to do with the fact that the word itself is demeaning than with a desire to signify our awareness that the disabled have rights, and deserve not only sympathy but respect. Which is entirely laudable and correct. And yet there are instances when *crippled* seems more accurate and less jarring. To say that someone is *hindered* by a *disabled* or *challenged* hand sounds simply peculiar. And to write that a person was *crippled* in an accident sounds worse than saying he was *disabled*—and indeed it is worse. Excising the word from the language signifies a reluctance to face up to the damage that our fragile bodies can sustain, and the harshness of the random fates that befall us every day. **—FP**

crisis noun **1** *the situation had reached a crisis* CRITICAL POINT, turning point, crossroads, watershed, head, moment of truth, zero hour, point of no return, Rubicon, doomsday; *informal* crunch; *Medicine* climacteric.

2 *the current economic crisis* EMERGENCY, disaster, catastrophe, calamity; predicament, plight, mess, trouble, dire straits, difficulty, extremity.

crisp adjective **1** *Sarah ordered scrambled eggs and crisp bacon* CRUNCHY, crispy, brittle, crumbly, friable, breakable; firm, dry. ANTONYM soft.

2 *Grace and Elijah enjoyed the crisp autumn day* INVIGORATING, bracing, brisk, fresh, refreshing, exhilarating, tonic, energizing; cool, chill, chilly, cold, nippy. ANTONYM sultry.

3 *Ms. Stevens's answers were crisp and to the point* BRISK, decisive, businesslike, no-nonsense, incisive, to the point, matter of fact, brusque; terse, succinct, concise, brief, short, short and sweet, laconic, snappy. ANTONYMS soft, sultry, rambling.

4 *crisp white bed linen* SMOOTH, uncreased, ironed; starched. ANTONYM wrinkled.

criterion noun *academic ability is not the sole criterion for allocating funds* STANDARD, specification, measure, gauge, test, scale, benchmark, yardstick, touchstone, barometer; principle, rule, law, canon.

critic noun **1** *a literary critic* REVIEWER, commentator, evaluator, analyst, judge, pundit.

2 *critics of the government* DETRACTOR, attacker, faultfinder, backseat driver, gadfly.

critical adjective **1** *a highly critical report* CENSORIOUS, condemnatory, condemning, denunciatory, disparaging, disapproving, scathing, fault-finding, judgmental, accusatory, negative, unfavorable; *informal* nitpicking, picky. ANTONYM complimentary.

2 *a critical essay* EVALUATIVE, analytical, interpretative, expository, explanatory.

3 *the situation is critical* GRAVE, serious, dangerous, risky, perilous, hazardous, precarious, touch-and-go, in the balance, uncertain, parlous, desperate, dire, acute, life-and-death. ANTONYM safe.

4 *the choice of materials is critical for product safety* CRUCIAL, vital, essential, of the essence, all-important, paramount, fundamental, key, pivotal, decisive, deciding, climacteric. See note at CRUCIAL. ANTONYM unimportant.

criticism noun **1** *she was stung by his criticism* CENSURE, condemnation, denunciation, disapproval, disparagement, opprobrium, fault-finding, attack, broadside, stricture, recrimination; *informal* flak, bad press, panning, put down, knock, slam, brickbats, potshot(s); *formal* excoriation.

2 *literary criticism* EVALUATION, assessment, appraisal, analysis, judgment; commentary, interpretation, explanation, explication, elucidation.

criticize verb *must you criticize everything she does?* FIND FAULT WITH, censure, denounce, condemn, attack, lambaste, pillory, rail against, inveigh against, arraign, cast aspersions on, pour scorn on, disparage, denigrate, give bad press to, run down; *informal* knock, pan, maul, slam, roast, hammer, lay into, lace into, flay, crucify, take apart, pull to pieces, pick holes in, pummel, trash, nitpick; *formal* excoriate. ANTONYM praise.

critique noun *a critique of North American culture* ANALYSIS, evaluation, assessment, appraisal, appreciation, criticism, review, study, commentary, exposition, exegesis.

WORD NOTE **critique**

I went to college in the mid-1980s, and there I got taught that there's no such verb as *to critique.* The professors (both around 50) who hammered this into me explained that *to criticize* meant "to judge the merits and defects of, to analyze, to evaluate" and that *critique* (n.) was simply the noun for "a specific critical commentary or review." Twenty years later, though, dictionaries' primary def of *to criticize* is usually "to find fault with." Even for educated readers, the verb is apt to have negative connotations that it didn't in 1985. This is why some usage authorities now consider *to critique* to be OK; they argue that it can minimize confusion by denoting the neutral, scholarly-type assessment that used to be what *to criticize* meant. Here's the thing, though—it's still only some usage experts who accept *to critique.* Dictionaries' usage panels are usually now split about 50-50 on sentences like *After a run-through, the playwright and director both critiqued the actor's delivery.* And it's not just authorities: a decent percentage of U.S. readers, especially those educated before 1990, still find *to critique* either incorrect or annoying. Why alienate these readers if you don't have to? If you're worried that *criticize* will seem too deprecatory, you can say *evaluate, explicate, analyze, judge . . .* or you can always use the old bury-the-main-verb trick and do *offer a critique of, submit a critique of,* etc. —**DFW**

---

croak verb **1** *"Thank you," I croaked* RASP, squawk, caw, wheeze, gasp.

2 *informal I thought that old mule croaked years ago.* See DIE sense 1.

crock noun **1** *a crock of honey* POT, jar; jug, pitcher, ewer; container, receptacle, vessel.

2 *chiefly Brit.* (**crocks**) *a pile of dirty crocks.* See CROCKERY.

3 *informal his story was a total crock* LIE, falsehood, fib, made-up story, invention, fabrication, deception, (piece of) fiction; (little) white lie, half-truth; *informal* tall tale, whopper.

crockery noun *chiefly Brit. a sink filled with crockery* DISHES, china, tableware; plates, bowls, cups, saucers; *chiefly Brit* crocks.

crony noun *informal he's playing pool with his cronies* FRIEND, companion, bosom friend, intimate, confidant, confidante, familiar, associate, accomplice, comrade; *informal* pal, chum, sidekick, partner in crime, buddy, amigo, compadre, mate; *archaic* compeer.

crook noun **1** *informala small-time crook* CRIMINAL, lawbreaker, offender, villain, delinquent, felon, convict, malefactor, culprit, wrongdoer; rogue, scoundrel, shyster, cheat, scam artist, swindler, racketeer, confidence trickster, snake oil salesman; thief, robber, burglar; *informal* shark, con man, con, jailbird, hood, yardbird; *Law* malfeasant.

2 *the crook of a tree branch* BEND, fork, curve, angle.

▸ verb *he crooked his finger and called the waiter* COCK, flex, bend, curve, curl.

crooked adjective **1** *narrow, crooked streets* WINDING, twisting, zigzag, meandering, tortuous, serpentine. ANTONYM straight.

2 *a crooked spine* BENT, twisted, misshapen, deformed, malformed, contorted, out of shape, wry, warped, bowed, distorted.

3 *the picture over the bed looked crooked* LOPSIDED, askew, awry, off-center, uneven, out of line, asymmetrical, tilted, at an angle, aslant, slanting, cockeyed, wonky.

4 *informal a crooked cop | crooked deals* DISHONEST, unscrupulous, unprincipled, untrustworthy, corrupt, corruptible, venal; criminal, illegal, unlawful, nefarious, fraudulent; *informal* shady, dodgy, hinky. ANTONYMS law-abiding, honest.

croon verb *she'd sit by the old phonograph for hours, listening to Rudy Vallee croon* SING SOFTLY, hum, warble, trill.

crop noun **1** *some farmers lost their entire crop* HARVEST, year's growth, yield; fruits, produce.

2 *a bumper crop of mail* BATCH, lot, assortment, selection, collection, supply, intake.

3 *a rider's crop* WHIP, switch, cane, stick.

▸ verb **1** *she's had her hair cropped* CUT SHORT, cut, clip, shear, shave, lop off, chop off, hack off; dock, bob.

2 *a flock of sheep were cropping the turf* GRAZE ON, browse on, feed on, nibble, eat.

3 *the hay was cropped several times this summer* HARVEST, reap, mow; gather (in), collect, pick, bring home.

PHRASE: **crop up** *things kept cropping up to delay their work* HAPPEN, occur, arise, turn up, spring up, pop up, emerge, materialize, surface, appear, come to light, present itself; *literary* come to pass, befall.

cross noun **1** *a bronze cross* CRUCIFIX, rood.

2 *we all have our crosses to bear* BURDEN, trouble, worry, trial, tribulation, affliction, curse, bane, misfortune, adversity, hardship, vicissitude; millstone, albatross, thorn in one's flesh/side; misery, woe, pain, sorrow, suffering; *informal* hassle, headache.

3 *a cross between a yak and a cow* HYBRID, hybridization, cross-breed, half-breed, mongrel; mixture, amalgam, blend, combination.

▸ verb **1** *they crossed the hills on foot* TRAVEL ACROSS, traverse, range over; negotiate, navigate, cover.

2 *a lake crossed by a fine stone bridge* SPAN, bridge; extend across, stretch across, pass over.

3 *the point where the two roads cross* INTERSECT, meet, join, connect, crisscross.

4 *no one dared cross him* OPPOSE, resist, defy, obstruct, impede, hinder, hamper; contradict, argue with, quarrel with, stand up to, take a stand against, take issue with; *formal* gainsay.

5 *the breed was crossed with the similarly colored Holstein* HYBRIDIZE, cross-breed, interbreed, cross-fertilize, cross-pollinate.

▸ adjective *Jane was getting cross* ANGRY, annoyed, irate, irritated, in a bad mood, vexed, irked, piqued, out of humor, put out, displeased; irritable, short-tempered, bad-tempered, snappish, snappy, crotchety, grouchy, grumpy, fractious, testy, crabby, cranky, mad, hot under the collar, peeved, riled, on the warpath, up in arms, steamed up, sore, bent out of shape, teed off, ticked off, pissed off. ANTONYM pleased.

PHRASE: **cross out** *looking at the manager's starting lineup, it seems that Mitchell's name has been crossed out* DELETE, strike out, ink out, score out, edit out, cancel, obliterate.

cross-examine verb *when McCoy cross-examines a witness, it's not a pretty sight* INTERROGATE, question, cross-question, quiz, catechize, give someone the third degree; *informal* grill, pump, put someone through the wringer.

crossing noun **1** *there should be a traffic light at this crossing* INTERSECTION, crossroads, junction, interchange.

2 *a short ferry crossing* JOURNEY, passage, voyage, trip.

crosswise, crossways adverb *take a ten-inch square of felt and cut it in half crosswise* DIAGONALLY, obliquely, transversely, aslant, at an angle, on the bias; cater-cornered, kitty-corner.

crotch noun *they were taught to knee an assailant in the crotch* GROIN; lap, genitals.

crotchety adjective *it's the dreadful arthritis that has made him so crotchety* BAD-TEMPERED, irascible, irritable, grumpy, grouchy, cantankerous, short-tempered, tetchy, testy, curmudgeonly, ill-tempered, ill-humored, ill-natured, cross-grained, peevish, cross, fractious, pettish, waspish, crabbed, crabby, crusty, prickly, touchy, snappish, snappy, cranky, ornery. ANTONYM good-humored.

crouch verb *the umpire crouches just enough to get a good view of the strike zone* SQUAT, bend (down), hunker down, scrunch down, hunch over, stoop, kneel (down); duck, cower.

crow verb **1** *a cock crowed* CRY, squawk, screech, caw, call.

2 *crowing about your success* BOAST, brag, trumpet, swagger, swank, gloat, show off, preen oneself, sing one's own praises; *informal* talk big, blow one's own horn.

crowd noun **1** *a crowd of people* THRONG, horde, mass, multitude, host, army, battalion, herd, flock, drove, swarm, sea, troupe, pack, press, crush, mob, rabble; collection, company, gathering, assembly, audience, assemblage, congregation; *informal* gaggle, bunch, gang, posse.

2 *she wanted to stand out from the crowd* MAJORITY, multitude, common people, populace, general public, masses, rank and file, hoi polloi; *informal* Joe Public, John Q. Public.

3 *he's been hanging round with a bad crowd* SET, group, circle, clique, coterie; camp; *informal* gang, crew, lot.

4 *the spectacle attracted a capacity crowd* AUDIENCE, spectators, listeners, viewers; house, turnout, attendance, gate; congregation.

▸ verb **1** *reporters crowded around her* CLUSTER, flock, swarm, mill, throng, huddle, gather, assemble, congregate, converge.

2 *the guests all crowded into the dining room* SURGE, push one's way, jostle, elbow one's way; squeeze, pile, cram.

3 *stop crowding me* pressure; harass, hound, pester, harry, badger, nag; *informal* hassle, lean on.

crowded adjective *the pizza place is crowded after every home game | a crowded bus | our villa was crowded with uninvited guests* PACKED, full, mobbed, filled to capacity, full to bursting, congested, overcrowded, overflowing, teeming, swarming, thronged, populous, overpopulated; busy; *informal* jam-packed, stuffed, chockablock, chock-full, bursting at the seams, wall-to-wall, standing room only, SRO; (**crowded with**) full of; *informal* crawling with, lousy with. ANTONYM deserted.

crown noun **1** *a jeweled crown* CORONET, diadem, circlet, tiara; *literary* coronal.

2 *the world heavyweight crown* TITLE, award, accolade, distinction; trophy, cup, medal, plate, shield, belt, prize; laurels, bays, palm(s).

3 *he and his family were loyal servants of the Crown* MONARCH, sovereign, king, queen, emperor, empress; monarchy, royalty; *informal* royals.

4 *the crown of the hill* TOP, crest, summit, peak, pinnacle, tip, head, brow, apex.

▸ verb **1** *David II was crowned in 1331* ENTHRONE, install; invest, induct.

2 *a teaching post at Harvard crowned his career* ROUND OFF, cap, be the climax of, be the culmination of, top off, consummate, perfect, complete, put the finishing touch(es) on/to.

3 *a steeple crowned by a gilded cross* TOP, cap, tip, head, surmount.

4 *informal someone crowned him with a poker.* See HIT verb sense 1.

crucial adjective **1** *negotiations were at a crucial stage* PIVOTAL, critical, key, climacteric, decisive, deciding; life-and-death. ANTONYMS minor, unimportant.

2 *confidentiality is crucial in this case* ALL-IMPORTANT, of the utmost importance, of the essence, critical, preeminent, paramount, essential, vital. ANTONYM unimportant.

THE RIGHT WORD

In any emergency or crisis situation, there is usually a turning point. Such an event is called **critical** if it determines the outcome of a situation (*a critical point in the nuclear disarmament negotiations*; *a critical election for the Democratic Party*). **Crucial** can also refer to a turning point, but it emphasizes the necessity of something happening before a result can be achieved (*the battle was crucial to their victory*), while *critical* suggests more of a balance between positive and negative outcomes (*a critical debate on foreign policy*). **Acute** describes the intensification of a situation that is rapidly approaching a climax (*an acute shortage of O-negative blood*), while **deciding** refers to something that forces a certain outcome (*a deciding factor in his recovery*). **Pressing** and **urgent** are milder words. A situation that is *pressing* may be chronic rather than *acute* (*a pressing need for changes in the political system*), while an *urgent* situation may be approaching a crisis without reference to a specific turning point (*an urgent meeting between the two presidents*). While *urgent* expresses more intensity than *pressing*, neither adjective conveys the same sense of intensity as *crucial*, *critical*, or *acute*.

crucify verb **1** *two thieves were crucified with Jesus* NAIL TO A CROSS; execute, put to death, kill.

2 *she had been crucified by his boastful admission of adultery* DEVASTATE, crush, shatter, cut to the quick, wound, pain, harrow, torture, torment, agonize, persecute.

3 *informal the fans would crucify us if we lost.* See CRITICIZE.

crude adjective **1** *crude oil* UNREFINED, unpurified, unprocessed, untreated; unmilled, unpolished; coarse, raw, natural. ANTONYM refined.

2 *a crude barricade* PRIMITIVE, simple, basic, homespun, rudimentary, rough, rough and ready, rough-hewn, make-do, makeshift, improvised, unfinished, jury-rigged, jerry-built, slapdash; *dated* rude. ANTONYM sophisticated.

3 *crude jokes* VULGAR, rude, naughty, suggestive, bawdy, off-color, indecent, obscene, offensive, lewd, salacious, licentious, ribald, coarse, uncouth, indelicate, tasteless, crass, smutty, dirty, filthy, scatological; *informal* blue. See note at RUDE. ANTONYMS decent, inoffensive.

cruel adjective **1** *a cruel man* BRUTAL, savage, inhuman, barbaric, barbarous, brutish, bloodthirsty, murderous, vicious, sadistic, wicked, evil, fiendish, diabolical, monstrous, abominable; callous, ruthless, merciless, pitiless, remorseless, uncaring, heartless, stony-hearted, hard-hearted, cold-blooded, cold-hearted, unfeeling, unkind, inhumane; *dated* dastardly; *literary* fell. See note at KIND. ANTONYM compassionate.

2 *her death was a cruel blow* HARSH, severe, bitter, harrowing, heartbreaking, heart-rending, painful, agonizing, traumatic; *formal* grievous. ANTONYM mild.

cruelty noun *he treated her with cruelty* BRUTALITY, savagery, inhumanity, barbarity, barbarousness, brutishness, sadism, bloodthirstiness, viciousness, wickedness; lack of compassion, callousness, ruthlessness.

WORD NOTE **The Difference Between Brutality and Cruelty**

In his essay "Notes on the English Character," E. M. Forster casually observes that brutality is considered a German trait and cruelty a Spanish one, just as superficiality is thought to be an American trait and hypocrisy a British one. I understand well enough superficiality and hypocrisy. But I would dearly love to know what Forster thought the difference was between *brutality* and *cruelty.* Let us say that either word implies the inflicting of pain. Is *brutality* akin to ruthlessness, the inflicting of pain as the most effective means to achieve stipulated ends? And is *cruelty* related to sadism, where the viciousness is done for its own sake and not for an imagined advantage? **—DL**

cruise noun *a cruise to the islands* BOAT TRIP, sea trip; voyage, journey.

▸ verb **1** *she cruised across the Atlantic* SAIL, voyage, journey.

2 *a taxi cruised past* DRIVE SLOWLY, drift; *informal* mosey, toodle.

crumb noun *we haven't got a crumb of evidence* FRAGMENT, bit, morsel, particle, speck, scrap, shred, sliver, atom, grain, trace, tinge, mite, iota, jot, whit, ounce, scintilla, soupçon; *informal* smidgen, tad, titch.

crumble verb *the old barn is slowly crumbling* DISINTEGRATE, fall apart, fall to pieces, fall down, break up, collapse, fragment; decay, fall into decay, deteriorate, degenerate, go to rack and ruin, decompose, rot, molder, perish.

crumbly adjective *plant the seedlings in crumbly soil* BRITTLE, breakable, friable, powdery, granular; crisp, crispy.

crumple verb **1** *she crumpled the note in her fist* CRUSH, scrunch up, screw up, squash, squeeze.

2 *his pants were dirty and crumpled* CREASE, wrinkle, crinkle, rumple.

3 *her resistance crumpled* COLLAPSE, give way, cave in, go to pieces, break down, crumble, be overcome.

crunch verb *she hungrily crunched the apple* MUNCH, chomp, bite into.

▸ noun *informal when the crunch comes, she'll be forced to choose* MOMENT OF TRUTH, critical point, crux, crisis, decision time, zero hour, point of no return; showdown.

crusade noun **1** *the medieval crusades* HOLY WAR; jihad.

2 *a crusade against crime* CAMPAIGN, drive, push, movement, effort, struggle; battle, war, offensive.

▸ verb *she likes crusading for the cause of the underdog* CAMPAIGN, fight, do battle, battle, take up arms, work, strive, struggle, agitate, lobby, champion, promote.

crusader noun *she was a crusader against domestic violence* CAMPAIGNER, fighter, champion, advocate; reformer.

crush verb **1** *essential oils are released when the herbs are crushed* SQUASH, squeeze, press, compress; pulp, mash, macerate, mangle; flatten, trample on, tread on; *informal* smush.

2 *your dress will get crushed* CREASE, crumple, rumple, wrinkle, crinkle, scrunch (up).

3 *crush the cookies with a rolling pin* PULVERIZE, pound, grind, break up, smash, crumble; mill; *technical* comminute.

4 *he crushed her in his arms* HUG, squeeze, hold tight, embrace, enfold.

5 *the new regime crushed all popular uprisings* SUPPRESS, put down, quell, quash, stamp out, put an end to, overcome, overpower, defeat, triumph over, break, repress, subdue, extinguish.

6 *Alan was crushed by her words* MORTIFY, humiliate, abash, chagrin, deflate, flatten, demoralize, squash; devastate, shatter; *informal* shoot down in flames, knock the stuffing out of.

▸ noun **1** *the crush of people* CROWD, throng, horde, swarm, sea, mass, pack, press, mob.

2 *informal a teenage crush* INFATUATION, obsession, love, passion; *informal* puppy love.

WORD NOTE **smush**

The informal cousin of *crush* and *smash, smush* is much friendlier than either. There's no evil intent with *smush.* You can smush a cupcake, or a couple more people into a subway car; the cupcake can still be eaten and no one needs to visit the emergency room. *Smash* the cupcake and it goes straight into the garbage. *Crush* the people, and it makes the nightly news. **—EM**

crust noun *a thin crust will form where the twig was snapped off* COVERING, layer, coating, cover, coat, sheet, thickness, film, skin, topping; incrustation, scab.

crustacean See table.

CRUSTACEANS

barnacle	langouste
black tiger shrimp	langoustine
blue crab	lobster
brine shrimp	Norway lobster
copepod	pillbug
crab	prawn
crawdad	roly-poly
crawfish	scampi
crayfish	shrimp
daphnia	snow crab
doodlebug	soft-shell crab
Dungeness crab	spider crab
fiddler crab	spiny lobster
ghost shrimp	squill
hermit crab	stone crab
horseshoe crab	tiger shrimp
king crab	trilobite
krill	wood louse
land crab	

See also table at MOLLUSK.

crusty adjective **1** *crusty French bread* CRISP, crispy, well baked; crumbly, brittle, friable. ANTONYMS soft, soggy.

2 *a crusty old man* IRRITABLE, cantankerous, irascible, bad-tempered, ill-tempered, grumpy, grouchy, crotchety, short-tempered, testy, crabby, curmudgeonly, peevish, cross, fractious, pettish, crabbed, prickly, waspish, peppery, cross-grained; *informal* snappish, cranky, ornery. ANTONYMS affable, good-natured.

crux noun *with whom John will be living is the crux of the situation* NUB, heart, essence, central point, main point, core, center, nucleus, kernel; *informal* bottom line.

cry verb **1** *Mandy started to cry* WEEP, shed tears, sob, wail, cry one's eyes out, bawl, howl, snivel, whimper, squall, mewl, bleat; lament, grieve, mourn, keen; *informal* boo-hoo, blubber, turn on the waterworks; *literary* pule. ANTONYM laugh.

2 *"Wait!" he cried* CALL, shout, exclaim, sing out, yell, shriek, scream, screech, bawl, bellow, roar, vociferate, squeal, yelp, holler; *dated* ejaculate. ANTONYM whisper.

▸ noun **1** *Leonora had a good cry* SOB, weep, crying fit, crying jag; *Technical* vagitus.

2 *a cry of despair* CALL, shout, exclamation, yell, shriek, scream, screech, bawl, bellow, roar, howl, yowl, squeal, yelp, interjection, holler; *dated* ejaculation.

3 *they've issued a cry for help* APPEAL, plea, entreaty, cry from the heart, cri de cœur.

WORD NOTE vagitus

The cry of a newborn baby. Something to add, possibly, to that very short list of questions that must be asked of someone who has just given birth. There is never anything much to say, but you can at least lengthen the period of questions before the awkward silence. Boy or girl? How much did he weigh? What color are his eyes? How loud was his *vagitus?* **–ZS**

crybaby noun *don't be such a crybaby just because you can't watch TV* SISSY, mama's boy; *informal* wimp, wuss, pantywaist.

crypt noun *the fraternity pledges had to spend the night in a crypt* TOMB, vault, mausoleum, burial chamber, sepulcher, catacomb, ossuary, undercroft.

cryptic adjective *she leaves cryptic messages on his answering machine* ENIGMATIC, mysterious, confusing, mystifying, perplexing, puzzling, obscure, abstruse, arcane, oracular, Delphic, ambiguous, elliptical, oblique; *informal* as clear as mud. ANTONYM clear.

crystallize verb **1** *minerals crystallize at different temperatures* FORM CRYSTALS, solidify, harden.

2 *the idea crystallized in her mind* BECOME CLEAR, become definite, take shape, materialize, coalesce; *informal* jell.

cub noun **1** *a lioness and her cubs* **(cubs)** YOUNG, offspring, pups; *archaic* whelps.

2 *don't waste our top writer's time with a routine story—give it to one of the cubs | a cub reporter* TRAINEE, apprentice, probationer, novice, tyro, learner, beginner, tenderfoot; *informal* rookie, newbie, greenhorn. ANTONYM veteran.

cubbyhole noun *the glass-partitioned cubbyhole he called an office* SMALL ROOM, booth, cubicle; den; *informal* cubby.

cube noun **1** *I like my ice to be in conventional cubes* HEXAHEDRON, cuboid, parallelepiped.

2 *a cube of soap* BLOCK, lump, chunk, brick.

cuddle verb **1** *she picked up the baby and cuddled him* HUG, embrace, clasp, hold tight, hold/fold in one's arms, snuggle.

2 *the pair were kissing and cuddling* EMBRACE, hug, caress, pet, fondle; *informal* canoodle, smooch; *informal, dated* spoon, bill and coo.

3 *I cuddled up to him* SNUGGLE, nestle, curl, nuzzle.

cuddly adjective *a cute and cuddly teddy bear* HUGGABLE, soft, warm, cuddlesome, snuggly, cushy; attractive, endearing, lovable.

cudgel noun *a thick wooden cudgel* CLUB, bludgeon, stick, truncheon, baton, mace, blackjack, billy club, nightstick, shillelagh.

▸ verb *the victim was cudgeled to death* BLUDGEON, club, beat, batter, bash.

cue noun *the blinking blue light is my cue to lower the volume* SIGNAL, sign, indication, prompt, reminder; nod, word, gesture.

USAGE NOTE cue, queue

Though pronounced the same, these words have different meanings. *Cue* = (1) a signal to begin; a hint; or (2) a stick used in billiards, pool, or shuffleboard. *Queue* = (1) a line of people or things waiting their turn; or (2) a hanging braid of hair. Not surprisingly, the two are sometimes confused—e.g.:

• "Like most birds, teal don't start their migration based on air temperatures, but take their queue [read *cue*] to head south from the shortening hours of daylight." (*Times-Picayune* [New Orleans]; Sept. 25, 1994.)

• "People were forced to stand in long cues [read *queues*] at five emergency water stations in Amagasaki." (*Daily Yomiuri* [English language/Japan]; Jan. 19, 1995.)

To *cue up* a videotape, an audiotape, or a compact disc is to have it ready for playing at a particular point—e.g.: "His brother cued up the tape, the rousing theme song from 'Rocky.' (*Hartford Courant*; Sept. 17, 1996.)

To *queue up* is to line up—e.g.: "Florida State students queued up for probably the most prized ticket they would ever use." (*Sports Illustrated*; Dec. 2, 1996.)

The braid of hair is spelled *queue*, not *cue*—e.g.: "Instructed by French dancing masters in the stately steps and deep curtsies of the minuet, the young men had indeed to mind their pieds (feet) and queues (pigtails) to keep from losing their balance or their huge wigs." (*Press-Enterprise* [Riverside, CA]; Nov. 15, 1995.) **–BG**

cuff verb *Chris cuffed him on the head* HIT, strike, slap, smack, thump, beat, punch; *informal* clout, wallop, belt, whack, thwack, bash, clobber, bop, sock, boff, slug; *archaic* smite. PHRASE: **off the cuff** *informal* **1** *an off-the-cuff remark* IMPROMPTU, extempore, ad lib; unrehearsed, unscripted, unprepared, improvised, spontaneous, unplanned. **2** *I spoke off the cuff* WITHOUT PREPARATION, without rehearsal, impromptu, ad lib; *informal* off the top of one's head.

cuisine noun *authentic Vietnamese cuisine* COOKING, cookery, food, dishes.

cul-de-sac noun *this is not a through street, it's a cul-de-sac* DEAD END, no exit; blind alley.

cull verb **1** *anecdotes culled from Greek history* SELECT, choose, pick, take, obtain, glean.

2 *he sees culling deer as a necessity* KILL, slaughter, destroy, harvest.

culminate verb *two hours and ten minutes of toe-tapping merriment culminating in the grandest musical finale on Broadway* COME TO A CLIMAX, come to a head, peak, climax, reach a pinnacle; build up to, lead up to; end with, finish with, conclude with.

culmination noun *the gold medal at Nagano was the culmination of her amateur career* CLIMAX, pinnacle, peak, high point, highest point, height, high-water mark, top, summit, crest, apex, zenith, crowning moment, apotheosis, apogee; consummation, completion, finish, conclusion. ANTONYM nadir.

culpability noun *the culpability of Mr. Bidwell's nephew has yet to be determined* GUILT, blame, fault, responsibility, accountability, liability, answerability; guiltiness, blameworthiness.

culpable adjective *I hold you personally culpable* TO BLAME, guilty, at fault, in the wrong, answerable, accountable, responsible, blameworthy, censurable. ANTONYM innocent.

culprit noun *police are doing all they can to catch the culprit* GUILTY PARTY, offender, wrongdoer, perpetrator, miscreant; criminal, malefactor, felon, lawbreaker, delinquent; *informal* baddy, crook, perp.

cult noun **1** *a religious cult* SECT, denomination, group, movement, church, persuasion, body, faction.

2 *the **cult of** eternal youth in Hollywood* OBSESSION WITH, fixation on, mania for, passion for, idolization of, devotion to, worship of, veneration of.

cultivate verb **1** *the peasants cultivated the land* TILL, plow, dig, hoe, farm, work, fertilize, mulch, weed.

2 *they were encouraged to cultivate basic food crops* GROW, raise, rear, plant, sow.

3 *Tessa tried to cultivate her as a friend* win someone's friendship, woo, court, curry favor with, ingratiate oneself with; *informal* get in good with someone, butter up, suck up to.

4 *he wants to cultivate his mind* IMPROVE, better, refine, elevate; educate, train, develop, enrich.

cultivated adjective *believe it or not, Mrs. Cleasby, there are some cultivated young ladies in the Ozarks* CULTURED, educated, well-read, civilized, enlightened, discerning, discriminating, refined, polished; sophisticated, urbane, cosmopolitan.

cultural adjective **1** *cultural differences* ETHNIC, racial, folk; societal, lifestyle.

2 *cultural achievements* AESTHETIC, artistic, intellectual; educational, edifying, civilizing.

culture noun **1** *exposing their children to culture* THE ARTS, the humanities, intellectual achievement; literature, music, painting, philosophy, the performing arts.

2 *a man of culture* INTELLECTUAL/ARTISTIC AWARENESS, education, cultivation, enlightenment, discernment, discrimination, good taste, taste, refinement, polish, sophistication.

3 *Afro-Caribbean culture* CIVILIZATION, society, way of life, lifestyle; customs, traditions, heritage, habits, ways, mores, values.

4 *the culture of crops* CULTIVATION, farming; agriculture, husbandry, agronomy.

cultured adjective *she got her love of art and music from her mother, a vibrant and cultured woman* CULTIVATED, intellectually/artistically aware, artistic, enlightened, civilized, educated, well-educated, well-read, well-informed, learned, knowledgeable, discerning, discriminating, refined, polished, sophisticated; *informal* artsy. ANTONYM ignorant.

culvert noun *they were concerned with the foul smell from the water in the culvert* CHANNEL, conduit, watercourse, trough; drain, gutter, ditch.

cumbersome adjective **1** *a cumbersome diving suit* UNWIELDY, unmanageable, awkward, clumsy, inconvenient, incommodious; bulky, large, heavy, hefty, weighty, burdensome; *informal* hulking, clunky. See note at HEAVY. ANTONYM manageable.

2 *cumbersome procedures* COMPLICATED, complex, involved, inefficient, unwieldy, slow. ANTONYM straightforward.

cumulative adjective *the effects of pollution are cumulative* INCREASING, accumulative, growing, mounting; collective, aggregate, amassed.

cunning adjective *a cunning scheme* CRAFTY, wily, artful, guileful, devious, sly, scheming, designing, calculating, Machiavellian; shrewd, astute, clever, canny; deceitful, deceptive, duplicitous, foxy; *archaic* subtle. ANTONYM honest.

▸ noun *his political cunning* GUILE, craftiness, deviousness, slyness, trickery, duplicity; shrewdness, astuteness.

cup noun **1** *a cup and saucer* teacup, coffee cup, demitasse; mug; *historical* chalice.

2 *the winner was presented with a silver cup* TROPHY, loving cup, award, prize.

cupboard noun *there are clean potholders in the cupboard* CABINET, sideboard, buffet; dresser, armoire, credenza, chiffonier, closet, wardrobe, commode.

Cupid noun *have you been pierced by the arrow of Cupid?* EROS, the god of love; amoretto.

cupidity noun *he did not really see her cupidity until they'd been married for several years* GREED, avarice, avariciousness, acquisitiveness, covetousness, rapacity, materialism, Mammonism; *informal* money-grubbing. ANTONYM generosity.

cupola noun See DOME. See also note below.

USAGE NOTE **copula, cupola**

Copula = (1) a linking verb, such as *be*, *feel*, or *seem*, that expresses a state of being rather than action; or (2) a link or connection in general—e.g.: "This is the age of parsing, a word that once referred to the grammatical analysis of sentences. Now it means playing games with words, as Bill Clinton did with the copula 'is' in worming his way out of charges of illicit copulation." (*San Francisco Chronicle*; Aug. 31, 2001.)

Cupola = an arched or domed roof, as on an astronomical observatory. *Copula* wrongly displaces *cupola* fairly often, probably by writers not versed in architecture—e.g.: "Each has its own copula [read *cupola*], Boston Gables, as well as numerous peaks with windows galore, all topped by a metal roof." (Times-Picayune [New Orleans]; Sept. 30, 2001.) —**BG**

cur noun **1** *a mangy cur* MONGREL, mutt.

2 *informal Neil was beginning to feel like a cur.* See BASTARD noun sense 2.

curable adjective *fortunately, this rash is completely curable* TREATABLE, remediable, medicable, operable.

curative adjective *the natives have used these curative herbs for centuries* HEALING, therapeutic, medicinal, remedial, corrective, restorative, tonic, health-giving.

curb noun *a curb on public spending* RESTRAINT, restriction, check, brake, rein, control, limitation, limit, constraint; *informal* crackdown; *literary* trammel.

▸ verb *he tried to curb his temper* RESTRAIN, hold back/in, keep back, repress, suppress, fight back, bite back, keep in check, check, control, rein in, contain, bridle, subdue; *informal* keep a/the lid on.

curdle verb *the milk was left out so long that it curdled* CLOT, coagulate, congeal, solidify, thicken; turn, sour, ferment.

cure verb **1** *after a long course of treatment, he was cured* HEAL, restore to health, make well/better; *archaic* cleanse.

2 *economic equality cannot cure all social ills* RECTIFY, remedy, put/set right, right, fix, mend, repair, heal, make better; solve, sort out, be the answer/solution to; eliminate, end, put an end to.

3 *the farmers cured their own bacon* PRESERVE, smoke, salt, dry, pickle.

▸ noun **1** *a cure for cancer* REMEDY, medicine, medication, medicament, antidote, antiserum; treatment, therapy; *archaic* physic.

2 *interest rate cuts are not the cure for the problem* SOLUTION, answer, antidote, nostrum, panacea, cure-all; *informal* quick fix, magic bullet, silver bullet.

cure-all noun *aloe has amazing healing properties, but it is not a cure-all* PANACEA, cure for all ills, sovereign remedy, heal-all, nostrum; *informal* magic bullet, silver bullet.

curio noun *a dusty old room full of forgotten curios* TRINKET, knickknack, bibelot, ornament, bauble; objet d'art, collector's item, rarity, curiosity, oddity, kickshaw, tchotchke.

curiosity noun **1** *his evasiveness roused my curiosity* INTEREST, spirit of inquiry, inquisitiveness.

2 *the shop is a treasure trove of curiosities.* See CURIO.

curious adjective **1** *she was curious to know what had happened* INTRIGUED, interested, eager to know, dying to know, agog; inquisitive. ANTONYM uninterested.

2 *her curious behavior* STRANGE, odd, peculiar, funny, unusual, bizarre, weird, eccentric, queer, unexpected, unfamiliar, extraordinary, abnormal, out of the ordinary, anomalous, surprising, incongruous, unconventional, offbeat, unorthodox. ANTONYM ordinary.

curl verb **1** *smoke curled up from his cigarette* SPIRAL, coil, wreathe, twirl, swirl; wind, curve, bend, twist, twist and turn, loop, meander, snake, corkscrew, zigzag.

2 *Ruth curled her arms around his neck* WIND, twine, entwine, wrap.

3 *she washed and curled my hair* CRIMP, perm, wave.

4 *they curled up together on the sofa* NESTLE, snuggle, cuddle.

▸ noun **1** *the tangled curls of her hair* RINGLET, corkscrew, kink, wave.

2 *a curl of smoke* SPIRAL, coil, twirl, swirl, twist, corkscrew, curlicue, helix.

curly adjective *thick, curly hair* WAVY, curling, curled, ringlety, crimped, permed, frizzy, kinky, corkscrew. ANTONYM straight.

curmudgeon noun See GROUCH.

currency noun **1** *foreign currency* MONEY, legal tender, cash, banknotes, bills, notes, coins, coinage, specie.

2 *a term that has gained new currency* PREVALENCE, circulation, exposure; acceptance, popularity.

current adjective **1** *current events* CONTEMPORARY, present-day, modern, present, contemporaneous; topical, in the news, live, burning. ANTONYM past.

2 *the idea is still current* PREVALENT, prevailing, common, accepted, in circulation, circulating, on everyone's lips, popular, widespread. ANTONYM obsolete.

3 *a current driver's license* VALID, usable, up-to-date. ANTONYM expired.

4 *the current prime minister* INCUMBENT, present, in office, in power; reigning. ANTONYMS past, former.

▸ noun **1** *a current of air* FLOW, stream, backdraft, slipstream; airstream, thermal, updraft, draft; undercurrent, undertow, tide.

2 *the current of human life* COURSE, progress, progression, flow, tide, movement.

3 *the current of opinion* TREND, drift, direction, tendency.

curriculum noun *the curriculum choices for history students are extensive* SYLLABUS, course of study, program of study, subjects, modules.

curse noun **1** *she put a curse on him* MALEDICTION, hex, jinx; *formal* imprecation; *literary* anathema; **(a curse)** the evil eye.

2 *the curse of racism* EVIL, blight, scourge, plague, cancer, canker, poison.

3 *the curse of unemployment* AFFLICTION, burden, cross to bear, bane.

4 *muffled curses* OBSCENITY, swear word, expletive, oath, profanity, four-letter word, dirty word, blasphemy; *informal* cuss, cuss word; *formal* imprecation. See table at OATH.

▸ verb **1** *it seemed as if the family had been cursed* PUT A CURSE ON, put the evil eye on, anathematize, damn, hex, jinx; *archaic* imprecate.

2 *she was cursed with feelings of inadequacy* AFFLICT, trouble, plague, bedevil.

3 *drivers cursed and honked their horns* SWEAR, blaspheme, take the Lord's name in vain; *informal* cuss; *archaic* execrate.

cursed adjective **1** *a cursed city* UNDER A CURSE, damned, doomed, ill-fated, ill-starred, jinxed, blighted; *literary* accursed, star-crossed.

2 *informal, dated those cursed children.* See ANNOYING.

cursory adjective *a cursory inspection* PERFUNCTORY, desultory, casual, superficial, token; hasty, quick, hurried, rapid, brief, passing, fleeting. See note at SUPERFICIAL. ANTONYM thorough.

curt adjective *after a curt response to Mary's accusation, he grabbed his coat and headed for the door* TERSE, brusque, abrupt, clipped, blunt, short, monosyllabic, summary; snappish, snappy, sharp, tart; gruff, offhand, unceremonious, ungracious, rude, impolite, discourteous, uncivil. See note at BRUSQUE. ANTONYM expansive.

curtail verb **1** *economic policies designed to curtail spending* REDUCE, cut, cut down, decrease, lessen, pare down, trim, retrench; restrict, limit, curb, rein in; *informal* slash. ANTONYM increase.

2 *his visit was curtailed* SHORTEN, cut short, truncate. ANTONYM lengthen.

curtain noun *he drew the curtains* DRAPE, drapery; window treatment, window hanging, screen, blind(s), shade; valance, café curtain.

▸ verb *the bed was **curtained off** from the rest of the room* CONCEAL, hide, screen, shield; separate, isolate.

curtsy verb *she curtsied to the king* BEND ONE'S KNEE, drop a curtsy, genuflect.

▸ noun *she made a curtsy* BOB, genuflection, obeisance.

curvaceous adjective *a curvaceous young woman* SHAPELY, voluptuous, sexy, full-figured, buxom, full-bosomed, bosomy, Junoesque; *informal* curvy, well-endowed, pneumatic, busty, built, stacked. ANTONYM skinny.

curve noun *the serpentine curves of the river* BEND, turn, loop, curl, twist, hook; arc, arch, bow, undulation, curvature, meander.

▸ verb *the road curved back on itself* BEND, turn, loop, wind, meander, undulate, snake, spiral, twist, coil, curl; arc, arch.

curved adjective *use a large curved needle for the upholstery* BENT, arched, bowed, crescent, curving, wavy, sinuous, serpentine, meandering, undulating, curvilinear, curvy. ANTONYM straight.

cushion noun *a cushion against inflation* PROTECTION, buffer, shield, defense, bulwark.

▸ verb **1** *she cushioned her head on her arms* SUPPORT, cradle, prop (up), rest.

2 *to cushion the blow, wages and pensions were increased* SOFTEN, lessen, diminish, decrease, mitigate, temper, allay, alleviate, take the edge off, dull, deaden.

3 *residents are cushioned from the outside world* PROTECT, shield, shelter, cocoon.

cushy adjective *informal a cushy job* EASY, undemanding; comfortable, secure. ANTONYM difficult.

custodian noun **1** *the school custodian* CARETAKER, janitor, superintendent; *informal* super.

2 *the custodian of the relic* keeper, guardian, steward, protector.

custody noun *the parent who has custody of the child* CARE, guardianship, charge, keeping, safekeeping, wardship, responsibility, protection, tutelage; custodianship, trusteeship. PHRASE: **in custody** *the carjacker is in custody* IN PRISON, in jail, imprisoned, incarcerated, locked up, under lock and key, interned, detained; on remand; *informal* behind bars, doing time, inside.

custom noun **1** *his unfamiliarity with the local customs* TRADITION, practice, usage, observance, way, convention, formality, ceremony, ritual; sacred cow, unwritten rule; mores; *formal* praxis.

2 *it is our custom to visit the Adirondacks in October* HABIT, practice, routine, way, wont; policy, rule.

customarily adverb *we customarily leave at least a fifteen-percent tip* USUALLY, traditionally, normally, as a rule, generally, ordinarily, commonly; habitually, routinely. ANTONYM occasionally.

customary adjective **1** *customary social practices* USUAL, traditional, normal, conventional, familiar, accepted, routine, established, time-honored, regular, prevailing. ANTONYM unusual.

2 *her customary good sense* USUAL, accustomed, habitual, wonted. ANTONYM unusual.

customer noun *Mr. Kanter is one of our best customers* CONSUMER, buyer, purchaser, patron, client, subscriber; shopper.

customs plural noun See TAX noun sense 1.

cut verb **1** *the knife slipped and cut his finger* GASH, slash, lacerate, sever, slit, pierce, penetrate, wound, injure; scratch, graze, nick, incise, score; lance.

2 *cut the pepper into small pieces* CHOP, cut up, slice, dice, cube, mince; carve, hash.

3 *cut back the new growth to about half its length | he should get his hair cut* TRIM, snip, clip, crop, barber, shear, shave; pare; prune, lop, dock; mow.

4 *I went to cut some flowers* PICK, pluck, gather; *literary* cull.

5 *lettering had been cut into the stonework* CARVE, engrave, incise, etch, score; chisel, whittle.

6 *the government cut public spending* REDUCE, cut back/down on, decrease, lessen, retrench, trim, slim down; rationalize, downsize, lower, slash, chop.

7 *the text has been substantially cut* SHORTEN, abridge, condense, abbreviate, truncate; edit; bowdlerize, expurgate.

8 *you need to cut at least ten lines per page* DELETE, remove, take out, excise, blue-pencil, chop.

9 *oil supplies to the area had been cut* DISCONTINUE, break off, suspend, interrupt; stop, end, put an end to.

10 *the point where the line cuts the vertical axis* CROSS, intersect, bisect; meet, join.

11 *she was suspended for cutting classes* SKIP, miss, play truant from; *informal* ditch, play hooky from.

▸ noun **1** *a cut on his jaw* GASH, slash, laceration, incision, wound, injury; scratch, graze, nick.

2 *a cut of beef* piece, section.

3 *informal the directors are demanding their cut* SHARE, portion, bit, quota, percentage; *informal* slice, piece of the pie, piece of the action.

4 *his hair was in need of a cut* HAIRCUT, trim, clip, crop.

5 *a smart cut of the whip* BLOW, slash, stroke.

6 *he followed this with the unkindest cut of all* INSULT, slight, affront, slap in the face, jibe, barb, cutting remark, put-down, dig.

7 *a cut in interest rates* REDUCTION, cutback, decrease, lessening, rollback.

8 *the elegant cut of his jacket* STYLE, design; tailoring, lines, fit.

PHRASES: **cut back** *if profits don't soon improve, we'll have to find ways to cut back | they cut back on medical benefits* ECONOMIZE, downsize, pull/draw in one's horns, tighten one's belt, slim down, scale down; (**cut back on**) cut, cut down, decrease, lessen, retrench, reduce, trim; *informal* slash. **cut down 1** *24 hectares of trees were cut down* FELL, chop down, hack down, saw down, hew. **2** *he was cut down in his prime* KILL, slaughter, shoot down, mow down, gun down; *informal* take out, blow away; *literary* slay. **cut and dried** *the answers to such questions are not always cut and dried* DEFINITE, decided, settled, explicit, specific, precise, unambiguous, clear-cut, unequivocal, black and white, hard and fast. **cut in** *excuse me for cutting in, but Glenda says that dinner's ready* INTERRUPT, butt in, break in, interject, interpose, chime in. **cut off 1** *how did this doll's arm get cut off?* SEVER, chop off, hack off; amputate. **2** *oil and gas supplies were cut off* DISCONTINUE, break off, disconnect, suspend; stop, end, bring to an end. **3** *a community cut off from the mainland by the floodwaters* ISOLATE, separate, keep apart; seclude, closet, cloister, sequester. **cut out 1** *the lifeboat's engines cut out* STOP WORKING, stop, fail, give out, break down; *informal* die, give up the ghost, conk out. **2** *cut out all the diseased wood* REMOVE, take out, excise, extract; snip out, clip out. **3** *it's best to cut out alcohol altogether* GIVE UP, refrain from, abstain from, go without; *informal* quit, lay off, knock off. **cut out of** *his mother cut him out of her will* EXCLUDE FROM, leave out of, omit from, eliminate from. **cut short 1** *they cut short their vacation* BREAK OFF, shorten, truncate, curtail, terminate, end, stop, abort, bring to an untimely end. **2** *several award recipients were cut short during their acceptance speeches* INTERRUPT, cut off, butt in on, break in on.

cutback noun *cutbacks in defense spending* REDUCTION, cut, decrease; economy, saving, rollback. ANTONYM increase.

cute adjective **1** *a cute baby* ENDEARING, adorable, lovable, sweet, lovely, appealing, engaging, delightful, dear, darling, winning, winsome, attractive, pretty; *informal* cutesy, twee.

2 *a cute guy* GOOD-LOOKING, handsome, attractive, gorgeous.

cut-rate adjective *sorry, but I'm not interested in cut-rate tires* CHEAP, marked down, reduced, discount, bargain.

cutthroat noun *dated a band of robbers and cutthroats* MURDERER, killer, assassin; *informal* hit man.

▸ adjective *cutthroat competition between rival firms* RUTHLESS, merciless, fierce, intense, aggressive, dog-eat-dog.

cutting noun **1** *plant cuttings* SCION, slip; graft.

2 *fabric cuttings* PIECE, bit, fragment; trimming.

▸ adjective **1** *a cutting remark* HURTFUL, wounding, barbed, pointed, scathing, acerbic, mordant, caustic, acid, sarcastic, sardonic, snide, spiteful, malicious, mean, nasty, cruel, unkind; *informal* bitchy, catty. ANTONYMS friendly, pleasant.

2 *cutting winter winds* ICY, icy-cold, freezing, arctic, Siberian, glacial, hypothermic, bitter, chilling, chilly, chill; biting, piercing, penetrating, raw, keen, sharp. ANTONYMS balmy, warm.

cyber adjective *our relationship was more cyber than face-to-face.* ELECTRONIC, digital, wired, virtual, web, Internet, Net, online.

cycle noun **1** *the cycle of birth, death, and rebirth* ROUND, rotation; pattern, rhythm.

2 *the painting is one of a cycle of seven* SERIES, sequence, succession, run; set.

▸ verb *Patrick cycled 10 miles each day* RIDE (A BICYCLE), bike, pedal.

cyclical adjective *the cyclical fluctuations in demand* RECURRENT, recurring, regular, repeated; periodic, seasonal, circular.

cyclone noun. See STORM noun sense 1.

cynic noun *he was a cynic who deflated all the hopeful aspirations of his children* SKEPTIC, doubter, doubting Thomas; pessimist, prophet of doom, doomsayer, Cassandra, Chicken Little. ANTONYMS idealist, Pollyanna.

cynical adjective *losing her job after fifteen years of loyal service had left her bitter and cynical* SKEPTICAL, doubtful, distrustful, suspicious, disbelieving; pessimistic, negative, world-weary, disillusioned, disenchanted, jaundiced, sardonic. ANTONYM idealistic.

cynicism noun *theirs was a childhood of absent parents and broken promises, so cynicism was hardly a surprise* SKEPTICISM, doubt, distrust, mistrust, suspicion, disbelief; pessimism, negativity, world-weariness, disenchantment. ANTONYM idealism.

cyst noun *a benign tumor under his left knee* GROWTH, lump; abscess, wen, boil, carbuncle, polyp, humor.

D

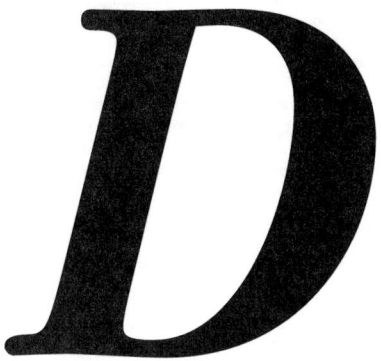

dab verb *she dabbed disinfectant on the cut* PAT, press, touch, blot, mop, swab; daub, apply, wipe, stroke.

▸ noun **1** *a dab of glue* DROP, spot, smear, splash, speck, taste, trace, touch, hint, bit; *informal* smidgen, tad, lick.

2 *apply concealer with light dabs* PAT, touch, blot, wipe.

dabble verb **1** *they dabbled their feet in rock pools* SPLASH, dip; paddle, trail; immerse.

2 *he **dabbled in** politics* TOY WITH, dip into, flirt with, tinker with, trifle with, play with, dally with.

dabbler noun *I'm no expert astronomer, just a dabbler* AMATEUR, dilettante, layman, layperson; trifler, nonprofessional, nonspecialist. ANTONYM professional.

daemon noun *it must have been a magnificent daemon that inhabited the heart and soul of this artist* NUMEN, genius, genius loci, inspiring force, attendant spirit, tutelary spirit, demon.

daft adjective **1** *a daft idea* ABSURD, preposterous, ridiculous, ludicrous, farcical, laughable; idiotic, stupid, foolish, silly, inane, fatuous, harebrained, cockamamie, half-baked, crazy, cockeyed. ANTONYM sensible.

2 *are you daft?* SIMPLEMINDED, stupid, idiotic, slow, witless, feebleminded, empty-headed, vacuous, vapid; unhinged, insane, mad; *informal* thick, dim, dopey, dumb, dimwitted, halfwitted, birdbrained, pea-brained, slow on the uptake, soft in the head, brain-dead, not all there, touched, crazy, mental, nuts, batty, bonkers, crackers, dumb-ass.

daily adjective *a daily event* EVERYDAY, day-to-day, quotidian, diurnal, circadian.

▸ adverb *the museum is open daily* EVERY DAY, once a day, day after day, diurnally.

dainty adjective **1** *a dainty china cup* DELICATE, fine, neat, elegant, exquisite. ANTONYM unwieldy.

2 *a dainty morsel* TASTY, delicious, choice, palatable, luscious, mouthwatering, delectable, toothsome; appetizing, inviting, tempting; *informal* scrumptious, yummy, finger-licking, melt-in-your-mouth. ANTONYMS tasteless, unpalatable.

3 *a dainty eater* FASTIDIOUS, fussy, finicky, particular, discriminating; *informal* choosy, persnickety, picky. ANTONYM undiscriminating.

▸ noun *homemade dainties* DELICACY, tidbit, fancy, luxury, treat; nibble, appetizer; confection, bonbon, goody; *archaic* sweetmeat.

dais noun *each speaker is allowed ten minutes on the dais* PLATFORM, stage, podium, rostrum, stand; soapbox.

dale noun *the green lushness of the dale in springtime* VALLEY, vale; hollow, basin, gully, gorge, ravine, glen; *literary* dell.

dally verb **1** *don't dally on the way to work* DAWDLE, delay, loiter, linger, waste time; lag, trail, straggle, fall behind; amble, meander, drift; *informal* dilly-dally; *archaic* tarry. See note at LOITER. ANTONYM hurry.

2 *he likes dallying with film stars* TRIFLE, toy, amuse oneself, flirt, play fast and loose, philander, carry on, play around.

dam noun *the dam burst* BARRAGE, barrier, wall, embankment, barricade, obstruction.

▸ verb *the river was dammed* BLOCK (UP), obstruct, bung up, close; *technical* occlude.

damage noun **1** *did the thieves do any damage?* HARM, destruction, vandalism; injury, impairment, desecration, vitiation, detriment; ruin, havoc, devastation.

2 *informal what's the damage?* COST, price, expense, charge, total.

3 (damages) *she won $4,300 in damages* COMPENSATION, recompense, restitution, redress, reparation(s); indemnification, indemnity.

▸ verb *the parcel had been damaged* HARM, deface, mutilate, mangle, impair, injure, disfigure, vandalize; tamper with, sabotage; ruin, destroy, wreck, trash; *formal* vitiate. ANTONYM repair.

damaging adjective *the damaging rays of the sun* HARMFUL, detrimental, injurious, hurtful, inimical, dangerous, destructive, ruinous, deleterious; bad, malign, adverse, undesirable, prejudicial, unfavorable; unhealthy, unwholesome. ANTONYM beneficial.

damn verb **1** *they were all damning him* CURSE, put the evil eye on, anathematize, hex, jinx. ANTONYM bless.

2 *we are not going to damn the new product before we try it* CONDEMN, censure, criticize, attack, denounce, revile;

find fault with, deprecate, disparage; *informal* slam, lay into, blast. ANTONYMS acclaim, praise.

▸ noun *informal it's not worth a damn* JOT, whit, iota, rap, scrap, bit; *informal* hoot, two hoots; *dated* a tinker's damn.

▸ exclamation *Damn! I forgot the keys.* DARN, damn it, dammit, drat, shoot, blast, doggone (it), goddammit, hell, rats.

PHRASE: **give a damn** *the only thing she gives a damn about is herself* CARE, mind, concern oneself; *informal* give a hoot.

damnable adjective *a damnable nuisance* UNPLEASANT, disagreeable, objectionable, horrible, horrid, awful, nasty, dreadful, terrible; annoying, irritating, maddening, exasperating; hateful, detestable, loathsome, abominable, beastly.

damned adjective **1** *damned souls* CURSED, doomed, lost, condemned to hell; anathematized; *literary* accursed.

2 *informal this damned car won't start* BLASTED, damn, damnable, confounded, rotten, wretched; *informal* blessed, bloody; *dated* accursed.

damning adjective *Erlich's family was stunned to hear the damning new evidence against her* INCRIMINATING, condemnatory, damnatory; damaging, derogatory; conclusive, strong.

damp adjective *her hair was damp* MOIST, moistened, wettish, dampened, dampish; humid, steamy, muggy, clammy, sweaty, sticky, dank, moisture-laden, wet, wetted; rainy, drizzly, showery, misty, foggy, vaporous, dewy. ANTONYM dry.

▸ noun *the damp in the air* MOISTURE, dampness, humidity, wetness, wet, water, condensation, steam, vapor; clamminess, dankness; rain, dew, drizzle, precipitation, spray; perspiration, sweat. ANTONYM dryness.

▸ verb **1** *sweat damped his hair.* See DAMPEN sense 1.

2 *nothing damped my enthusiasm.* See DAMPEN sense 2.

dampen verb **1** *the rain dampened her face* MOISTEN, damp, wet, dew, water; *literary* bedew. ANTONYM dry.

2 *nothing could dampen her enthusiasm* LESSEN, decrease, diminish, reduce, moderate, damp, put a damper on, throw cold water on, cool, discourage; suppress, extinguish, quench, stifle, curb, limit, check, restrain, inhibit, deter. ANTONYM heighten.

damper noun *the presence of the wretched Inez puts a damper on our fun* CURB, check, restraint, restriction, limit, limitation, constraint, rein, brake, control, impediment; chill, pall, gloom.

dampness noun See DAMP noun.

damsel noun *literary* See GIRL sense 2.

dance verb **1** *he danced with Katherine* sway, trip, twirl, whirl, pirouette, gyrate; *informal* bop, disco, rock, boogie, shake a leg, hoof it, cut a/the rug, trip the light fantastic, get down, mosh, groove.

2 *little girls danced around me* CAPER, cavort, frisk, frolic, skip, prance, gambol, jig; leap, jump, hop, bounce.

3 *flames danced in the fireplace* FLICKER, leap, dart, play, flit, quiver; twinkle, shimmer.

▸ noun **1** *they met at a dance* BALL, masquerade, prom, hoedown, disco; *dated* hop, sock hop. See table.

2 *the last dance had been played* (PIECE OF) DANCE MUSIC.

WORD NOTE **dance**

Dance, the noun, is a piece of music for dancing. Almost all forms of music have at one time been considered suitable for that purpose, but currently *dance music* is limited to: anything unsurprising dominated by an unvarying bass drum pulse between 110 and 130 beats per minute. **—SM**

DANCES

Dance Forms	hornpipe
ballet	hula
ballroom	ländler
belly dancing	lavolta
breakdancing	lion dance
butoh	mazurka
cancan	minuet
Celtic dancing	morris dance
character dancing	musette
contra	pavane
Cossack dancing	polonaise
dancesport	quadrille
disco	roundel
flamenco	saraband
folk dancing	schottische
Highland dancing	sword dance
Irish dancing	syrto
jazz	tarantella
Kathak	zouk
line dancing	
modern dance	**Popular Dances**
round dancing	barn dance
soft shoe	beguine
square dancing	bird dance
step dance	boogaloo
swing	bossa nova
tap dance	break dance
	bunny hop
Aboriginal Dances	bus stop
chicken scratch	butterfly
drum dance	cakewalk
grass dance	carioca
hamatsa	cha-cha
hoop dance	Charleston
rain dance	conga
Red River jig	disco
sun dance	eightsome reel
war dance	foxtrot
	freak
Historical/Folk Dances	frug
allemande	hand jive
bachata	hokey-pokey
bolero	hustle
bourrée	jig
cachucha	jitterbug
capoeira	jive
chaconne	lambada
cinque-pace	Latin hustle
clog dance	limbo
contredanse	lindy (hop)
cotillion	line dance
country dance	locomotion
courante	Macarena
cumbia	mambo
czardas	mashed potato
doppio	merengue
fan dance	monkey
fandango	mosh
farandole	one-step
galliard	paso doble
galop	pogo
gavotte	polka
habanera	quickstep
hasapiko	reel
Highland fling	robot
hopak	rumba
hora	salsa

Popular Dances (*cont'd*)	two-step
samba	Virginia reel
shimmy	waltz
shuffle	watusi
skank	whip
slam dance	
snake dance	**Dancing Events**
stomp	ball
strathspey	barn dance
striptease	cotillion
stroll	hoedown
tango	prom
time warp	rave
turkey trot	Sadie Hawkins dance
tush push	social
twist	sock hop
	tea dance

dancer noun *Miss McCoy was a frustrated dancer who ended up teaching ballet steps to toddlers* danseur, danseuse, ballerina, prima ballerina, premier danseur, danseur noble; *informal* hoofer.

dandle verb *he dandled his little boy on his knee* BOUNCE, jiggle, dance, rock.

dandy noun *he became something of a dandy* FOP, man about town, glamour boy, rake; *informal* sharp dresser, snappy dresser, trendy, dude, pretty boy; *informal, dated* swell; *dated* beau; *archaic* buck, coxcomb, popinjay.

▸ adjective *informal our trip was dandy.* See EXCELLENT.

danger noun **1** *an element of danger* PERIL, hazard, risk, jeopardy; perilousness, riskiness, precariousness, uncertainty, instability, insecurity. ANTONYM safety.

2 *that car is a danger on the roads* MENACE, hazard, threat, risk; *informal* death trap, widow-maker.

3 *a serious danger of fire* POSSIBILITY, chance, risk, probability, likelihood, fear, prospect.

dangerous adjective **1** *a dangerous animal* MENACING, threatening, treacherous; savage, wild, vicious, murderous, desperate. ANTONYM harmless.

2 *dangerous wiring* HAZARDOUS, perilous, risky, high-risk, unsafe, unpredictable, precarious, insecure, touch-and-go, chancy, treacherous; *informal* dicey, hairy. ANTONYM safe.

dangle verb **1** *a chain dangled from his belt* HANG (DOWN), droop, swing, sway, wave, trail, stream.

2 *he dangled the keys* WAVE, swing, jiggle, brandish, flourish.

3 *he dangled money in front of the locals* OFFER, hold out; entice someone with, tempt someone with.

dangling adjective *her dangling earrings* HANGING, drooping, droopy, suspended, pendulous, pendent, trailing, flowing, tumbling.

dank adjective *the dank basement* DAMP, musty, chilly, clammy, moist, wet, unaired, humid. ANTONYM dry.

dapper adjective *doesn't Norm look dapper in his new suit?* SMART, spruce, trim, debonair, neat, well-dressed, well-groomed, well turned out, elegant, chic, dashing; *informal* snazzy, snappy, natty, sharp, spiffy, fly. ANTONYM scruffy.

dapple verb *we dappled the wall by gently flicking the paintbrushes* DOT, spot, fleck, streak, speck, speckle, mottle, marble.

dappled adjective *a dappled horse* SPECKLED, blotched, blotchy, spotted, spotty, dotted, mottled, marbled, flecked, freckled; piebald, pied, brindle, pinto, tabby, calico; patchy, variegated; *informal* splotchy.

dare verb **1** *everyone wanted to say something, but nobody dared* BE BRAVE ENOUGH, have the courage; venture, have the nerve, have the temerity, be so bold as, have the audacity; risk, hazard, take the liberty, stick one's neck out, go out on a limb.

2 *she dared him to go* CHALLENGE, defy, invite, bid, provoke, goad; throw down the gauntlet.

▸ noun *she accepted the dare* CHALLENGE, provocation, goad; gauntlet, invitation.

USAGE NOTE dare

It's been called "one of the subtlest and most variegated verbs in the language" (Robert W. Burchfield, *Points of View*; 1992) and also "one of the trickiest" (William Safire, "Love That Dare," *New York Times*; May 17, 1987). The subtleties arise because *dare* is both an ordinary verb (*he dares you to pick up the snake*) and a modal verb (*he dare not do it himself*). And the form it takes (*dares* vs. *dare* in those examples) changes with that grammatical function.

When *dare* is used as a full verb, it behaves just like most other verbs: it takes an -*s* with a third-person singular subject (*Robert always speaks his mind bluntly and dares anyone to disagree*). The form is identifiable by the presence of an explicit infinitive (with *to*) after *dare* (here, *to disagree*).

Dare was an Old English modal. When it is used as an auxiliary verb (like the modern modals *will*, *must*, and, more closely, *ought*), the infinitive either is missing its *to* (*dare he disagree with Robert?*) or is missing altogether but understood (*he dare not!*). This occurs chiefly, but not only, in interrogative or negative sentences. In those sentences, the form *dares*—although sometimes used mistakenly in striving for correctness—would be unidiomatic, because *dare* in this usage behaves like other uninflected modals (*will he disagree with Robert? | he must not*)

As a modal verb, *dare* raises an interesting question of tense: in reference to past time, should one write (1) "Although challenged to do it, he dare not," or (2) "Although challenged to do it, he dared not"? The *Oxford English Dictionary* endorses the first and calls the second "careless," but that advice was written when that part of the great dictionary was published in 1894 (and the dandy but now archaic *durst* was still available). More recent grammarians are more lenient—e.g.: "As a modal, *dare* exhibits abnormal time reference in that it can be used, without inflection, for past as well as present time: 'The king was so hot-tempered that no one dare tell him the bad news.' The main verb form *dared (to)* might also occur here." (Randolph Quirk et al., *A Comprehensive Grammar of the English Language*; 1985.)

These more modern grammarians' analyses are borne out by actual usage—e.g.: "Mayo said he dared not declare it a little blue heron without confirmation from others." (*Hartford Courant*; Dec. 23, 2001.)

It is odd, however, to see the past-tense form in the set phrase *how dare you*—e.g.: " 'How dared you!' Jon shouted, waving his arms for emphasis. 'That dish was ours, the property of the entire Order! How dared you even think to appropriate it for your own uses!" (Patricia C. Wrede, *Mairelon the Magician*; 1991.)

The form *durst*, which is a past indicative and past subjunctive along with *dared*, is obsolete in American English. In British English, it still occurs rarely, always in a negative sentence or conditional clause in which there is an infinitive either understood or having no *to* (*none durst answer him*).

The exclamatory construction *How dare he do that!* is an idiomatic phrasing of the interrogative *How (does/did he) dare (to) do that?* The subject/actor (*he*) appears after the verb (*dare*) and is always in the nominative case—e.g.:

"How dare she tell taxpayers to take on more responsibility to help neighborhood kids? How dare she be right?" (*Cincinnati Enquirer*; Aug. 18, 2002.) —BG

---

daredevil noun *a young daredevil crashed his car* THRILL-SEEKER, adventurer, madcap, exhibitionist, swashbuckler; stuntman; *informal* show-off.

▸ adjective *a daredevil skydiver* DARING, bold, audacious, intrepid, fearless, madcap, dauntless; heedless, reckless, rash, impulsive, impetuous, foolhardy, incautious, imprudent, harum-scarum. ANTONYMS cowardly, cautious.

daring adjective *a daring attack* BOLD, audacious, intrepid, venturesome, fearless, brave, unafraid, undaunted, dauntless, valiant, valorous, heroic, dashing; madcap, rash, reckless, heedless; *informal* gutsy, spunky, ballsy.

▸ noun *his sheer daring* BOLDNESS, audacity, temerity, fearlessness, intrepidity, bravery, courage, valor, heroism, pluck, spirit, mettle; recklessness, rashness, foolhardiness; *informal* nerve, guts, spunk, grit, moxie, sand, balls.

dark adjective **1** *a dark night* BLACK, pitch-black, jet-black, inky; unlit, unilluminated; starless, moonless; dingy, gloomy, dusky, shadowy, shady; *literary* Stygian. ANTONYM bright.

2 *a dark secret* MYSTERIOUS, secret, hidden, concealed, veiled, covert, clandestine; enigmatic, arcane, esoteric, obscure, abstruse, impenetrable, incomprehensible, cryptic.

3 *dark hair* BRUNETTE, dark brown, chestnut, sable, jet-black, ebony. ANTONYM blond/blonde.

4 *dark skin* SWARTHY, dusky, olive, brown, black, ebony; tanned, bronzed. ANTONYM pale.

5 *dark days* TRAGIC, disastrous, calamitous, catastrophic, cataclysmic; dire, awful, terrible, dreadful, horrible, horrendous, atrocious, nightmarish, harrowing; wretched, woeful. ANTONYM happy.

6 *dark thoughts* GLOOMY, dismal, pessimistic, negative, downbeat, bleak, grim, fatalistic, black, somber; despairing, despondent, hopeless, cheerless, melancholy, glum, grave, morose, mournful, doleful. ANTONYM optimistic.

7 *a dark look* MOODY, brooding, sullen, dour, scowling, glowering, angry, forbidding, threatening, ominous.

8 *dark deeds* EVIL, wicked, sinful, immoral, bad, iniquitous, ungodly, unholy, base; vile, unspeakable, sinister, foul, monstrous, shocking, atrocious, abominable, hateful, despicable, odious, horrible, heinous, execrable, diabolical, fiendish, murderous, barbarous, black; sordid, degenerate, depraved; dishonorable, dishonest, unscrupulous; *informal* lowdown, dirty, crooked, shady. ANTONYMS virtuous, good.

▸ noun **1** *he's afraid of the dark* DARKNESS, blackness, gloom, murkiness, shadow, shade; dusk, twilight, gloaming. ANTONYM light.

2 *she went out after dark* NIGHT, nighttime, darkness; nightfall, evening, twilight, sunset. ANTONYMS dawn, day.

PHRASE: **in the dark** *informal all those months that Luis was running guns for the Contras, his family was completely in the dark* UNAWARE, ignorant, incognizant, oblivious, uninformed, unenlightened, unacquainted, unconversant.

darken verb **1** *the sky darkened* GROW DARK, blacken, dim, cloud over, lower; shade, fog.

2 *his mood darkened* BLACKEN, become angry, become annoyed; sadden, become gloomy, become unhappy, become depressed, become dejected, become dispirited, become troubled.

darkness noun **1** *lights shone in the darkness* DARK, blackness, gloom, dimness, murkiness, shadow, shade; dusk, twilight, gloaming.

2 *darkness fell* NIGHT, nighttime, dark.

3 *the forces of darkness* EVIL, wickedness, sin, iniquity, immorality; devilry, the Devil.

darling noun **1** *good night, my darling* DEAR, dearest, love, lover, sweetheart, sweet, beloved; *informal* honey, hon, angel, pet, sweetie, sugar, babe, baby, treasure.

2 *the darling of the media* FAVORITE, pet, idol, hero, heroine; *informal* blue-eyed boy/girl, fair-haired boy.

▸ adjective **1** *his darling wife* DEAR, dearest, precious, adored, loved, beloved, cherished, treasured, esteemed, worshiped.

2 *a darling little hat* ADORABLE, appealing, charming, cute, sweet, enchanting, bewitching, endearing, dear, delightful, lovely, beautiful, attractive, gorgeous, fetching; *Scottish* bonny.

darn verb *he was darning his socks* MEND, repair, reinforce; sew up, stitch, patch.

▸ exclamation *oh, darn!* See DAMN.

dart noun **1** *a poisoned dart* SMALL ARROW, missile, projectile, flechette.

2 *she made a dart for the door* DASH, rush, run, bolt, break, start, charge, sprint, bound, leap, dive; scurry, scamper, scramble.

▸ verb **1** *Karl darted across the road* DASH, rush, tear, run, bolt, fly, shoot, charge, race, sprint, bound, leap, dive, gallop, scurry, scamper, scramble; *informal* scoot.

2 *he darted a glance at her* DIRECT, cast, throw, shoot, send, flash.

dash verb **1** *he dashed home* RUSH, race, run, sprint, bolt, dart, gallop, career, charge, shoot, hurtle, careen, fly, speed, zoom, scurry, scuttle, scamper; *informal* tear, belt, scoot, zip, whip, hotfoot it, leg it, bomb, barrel. ANTONYM dawdle.

2 *he dashed the glass to the ground* HURL, smash, crash, slam, throw, toss, fling, pitch, cast, project, propel, send; *informal* chuck, heave, sling, peg.

3 *rain dashed against the walls* BE HURLED, crash, smash; batter, strike, beat, pound, lash.

4 *her hopes were dashed* SHATTER, destroy, wreck, ruin, crush, devastate, demolish, blight, overturn, scotch, spoil, frustrate, thwart, check; *informal* blow a hole in, scuttle. ANTONYM raise.

▸ noun **1** *a dash for the door* RUSH, race, run, sprint, bolt, dart, leap, charge, bound, break; scramble.

2 *a dash of salt* PINCH, touch, sprinkle, taste, spot, drop, dab, speck, smattering, sprinkling, splash, bit, modicum, little; *informal* smidgen, tad, lick.

3 *he led off with such dash* VERVE, style, flamboyance, gusto, zest, confidence, self-assurance, élan, flair, vigor, vivacity, sparkle, brio, panache, éclat, vitality, dynamism; *informal* pizzazz, pep, oomph.

dashing adjective **1** *a dashing pilot* DEBONAIR, devil-may-care, raffish, sporty, spirited, lively, dazzling, energetic, animated, exuberant, flamboyant, dynamic, bold, intrepid, daring, adventurous, plucky, swashbuckling; romantic, attractive, gallant.

2 *he looked exceptionally dashing* STYLISH, smart, elegant, chic, dapper, spruce, trim, debonair; fashionable, modish, voguish; *informal* trendy, with it, hip, sharp, snazzy, classy, natty, swish, fly, spiffy.

dastardly adjective *dated their dastardly plan to kidnap Hayes* WICKED, evil, heinous, villainous, diabolical, fiendish, barbarous, cruel, black, dark, rotten, vile, monstrous, abominable, despicable, degenerate, sordid; bad, base, mean, low, dishonorable, dishonest, unscrupulous, unprincipled; *informal* lowdown, dirty, shady, rascally, crooked; beastly. ANTONYM noble.

USAGE NOTE **dastard, dastardly**

Dastard (= coward) is commonly muddled because of the sound association with its harsher rhyme, *bastard*. Although English usage authority H. W. Fowler insisted that *dastard* should be reserved for "one who avoids all personal risk," modern American writers tend to use it as a printable euphemism for the more widely objectionable epithet—e.g.: "Samuel Ramey is the dastard of the piece, the treacherous, lecherous, murderous Assur." (*Los Angeles Times*; May 22, 1994.) British writers, on the other hand, have remained truer to the word's original sense—e.g.: "Last week I moved house from London to Brighton but like a genuine spineless dastard I flatly denied its implications on personal relationships to the last." (*Times* [London]; Feb. 8, 1994.) Recent American dictionaries record one meaning of *dastard* as being "dishonorable, despicable" or "treacherously underhanded." So the new meaning should probably now be considered standard.

Like the noun form, the adjective *dastardly* has been subjected to slipshod extension. Although most dictionaries define it merely as "cowardly," it is now often used as if it meant "sneaky and underhanded; treacherous"—e.g.: "He's b-a-a-a-c-k. Dastardly J. R. Ewing and his oft-manipulated clan rise from TV dustdom to air three times a day on TNN, Cable Channel 37, beginning Monday." (*Tulsa World*; Sept. 27, 1996.) **—BG**

data plural noun (often as singular) *a lack of data on the drug's side effects* FACTS, figures, statistics, details, particulars, specifics; information, intelligence, material, input; *informal* info.

USAGE NOTE **data**

Whether you write "data are" or "data is," you're likely to raise some eyebrows. Technically a plural, *data* has, since the 1940s, been increasingly treated as a mass noun taking a singular verb. But in more or less formal contexts it is preferably treated as a plural—e.g.: "The data are derived from tests performed on expectant mothers." (*Economist*; Mar. 24, 2001.) Many writers use it as a singular, however, risking their credibility with some readers (admittedly a shrinking minority)—e.g.: "No data is offered to suggest that women are being adversely hit by the dearth of articles." (*Globe and Mail* [Canada]; Aug. 24, 1993.)

In the context of computing and related disciplines, the singular use of *data* is common and comfortable—e.g.: "Every time you synchronize your PDA, the data gets backed up to your PC." (PCWorld.com; Feb. 8, 2001.) In one particular use, *data* is rarely treated as a singular: when it begins a clause and is not preceded by the definite article—e.g.: "Data over the last two years suggest that the rate at which gay men get AIDS has finally begun to flatten out." (*New York Times*; Feb. 5, 1989.)

Datum, the "true" singular, is sometimes used when a single piece of information is referred to—e.g.: "We accept the law as a necessary datum, but that is not to say that we are required to accept it in abeyance of our critical faculties." (F. R. Leavis, *The Common Pursuit*; 1952.) Still, in nonscientific contexts, *datum* is likely to sound pretentious.

Because *data* can be either a plural count noun or a singular mass noun, both *many data* and *much data* are correct—e.g.:

• "Numerous expert and representative interests are consulted, and many data assembled, often over a long period." (Carleton K. Allen, *Law in the Making*, 7th ed.; 1964.)

• "But much of the data in present personnel files is highly subjective." (William O. Douglas, *Points of Rebellion*; 1970.)

As Albert C. Baugh, a historian of the English language, put it in 1962, "A student with one year of Latin [knows] that *data* and *phenomena* are plural." Whatever you do, if you use *data* in a context in which its number becomes known, you'll bother some of your readers. Perhaps 50 years from now—maybe sooner, maybe later—everybody will accept it as a collective. But not yet. **—BG**

date noun **1** *the only date he has to remember* DAY, day of the month, occasion, time; year; anniversary.

2 *a later date is suggested for this artifact* AGE, time, period, era, epoch, century, decade, year.

3 *a lunch date* APPOINTMENT, meeting, engagement, rendezvous, assignation; commitment.

4 *informal he's my date for tonight* PARTNER, escort, girlfriend, boyfriend, steady.

▸ verb **1** *the sculpture can be dated accurately* ASSIGN A DATE TO, ascertain the date of, put a date on.

2 *the building* ***dates from*** *the sixteenth century* WAS MADE IN, was built in, originates in, comes from, belongs to, goes back to.

3 *the best films don't date* BECOME OLD-FASHIONED, become outmoded, become dated, show its age.

4 *informal he's dating Jill* GO OUT WITH, take out, go around with, be involved with, see, go steady with; *dated* woo, court.

PHRASE: **to date** *this is all the information we have to date* SO FAR, thus far, yet, as yet, up to now, till now, until now, up to the present (time), hitherto.

WORD NOTE **prochronism**

It is a good thing to know the correct word for your mistakes. Dating an event earlier than it actually happened is a common enough boob made by academics, families, governments, dictators—and it is not always quite accidental. A little *prochronism* goes a long way: to obscure a vital truth, give historical credence to a specious theory, disable the possibilities for change, rewrite an awkward past . . . . With frequent usage and a little tweak of emphasis, it might even be adaptable as a name for a kind of condition for which the sufferer might create a support group. So a husband might say to his wife: "It's not that I forgot our anniversary because I don't care, it's just my prochronism . . . " **—ZS**

dated adjective *the graphics look somewhat dated* OLD-FASHIONED, outdated, outmoded, passé, behind the times, archaic, obsolete, antiquated; unfashionable, unstylish, untrendy; crusty, old world, prehistoric, antediluvian; *informal* old hat, out, uncool. ANTONYM modern.

daub verb *he daubed a rock with paint* SMEAR, bedaub, plaster, splash, spatter, splatter, cake, cover, smother, coat.

▸ noun *daubs of paint* SMEAR, smudge, splash, blot, spot, patch, blotch, splotch.

daughter noun *Nixon's daughter Julie married Eisenhower's grandson* FEMALE CHILD, girl.

daunt verb *wintry conditions did not daunt the runners* DISCOURAGE, deter, demoralize, put off, dishearten, dispirit; intimidate, abash, take aback, throw, cow, overawe, awe, frighten, scare, unman, dismay, disconcert, discompose, perturb, unsettle, unnerve; throw off balance; *informal* rattle, faze, shake up. ANTONYM hearten.

dauntless adjective *only the most dauntless were selected for this dangerous expedition* FEARLESS, determined, resolute, indomitable, intrepid, doughty, plucky, spirited, mettlesome; undaunted, undismayed, unflinching, unshrinking, bold, audacious, valiant, brave, courageous, daring; *informal* gutsy, spunky, feisty.

dawdle verb **1** *they dawdled over breakfast* LINGER, dally, take one's time, be slow, waste time, idle; delay, procrastinate, stall, dilly-dally, lollygag; *archaic* tarry. See note at LOITER. ANTONYM hurry.

2 *Ruth dawdled home* AMBLE, stroll, trail, walk slowly, move at a snail's pace; *informal* mosey, toodle. ANTONYMS hurry, speed.

dawn noun **1** *we got up at dawn* DAYBREAK, sunrise, first light, daylight; first thing in the morning, sun-up. ANTONYM dusk.

2 *the dawn of civilization* BEGINNING, start, birth, inception, origination, genesis, emergence, advent, appearance, arrival, dawning, rise, origin, onset; unfolding, development, infancy; *informal* kickoff. ANTONYM end.

▸ verb **1** *Thursday dawned crisp and sunny* BEGIN, break, arrive, emerge. ANTONYM end.

2 *a bright new future has dawned* BEGIN, start, commence, be born, appear, arrive, emerge; arise, rise, break, unfold, develop. ANTONYM end.

3 *the reality dawned on him* OCCUR TO, come to, strike, hit, enter someone's mind, register with, enter someone's consciousness, cross someone's mind, suggest itself.

WORD NOTE **dawn**

Unless you're Homer, never say *rosy-fingered Dawn.* English is replete with classical tags and hackneyed phrases such as this one, but their use in writing tends to plunge any sentence into bathos. *Rosy-toed Dawn* might work, if you're describing a woman of this name with a dubious penchant for pink nail polish. But, in general, be wary of *the wine-dark sea* or *the melancholy Dane* or *the Bard of Avon* or any other phrase that comes too readily to mind. Or *trippingly to the tongue,* as I originally typed, and then deleted. First thoughts are all too often second-rate clichés. **—MD**

day noun **1** *I stayed for **a day*** A TWENTY-FOUR-HOUR PERIOD, twenty-four hours.

2 *enjoy the beach during the day* DAYTIME, daylight; waking hours. ANTONYM night.

3 *the leading architect of the day* PERIOD, time, age, era, generation.

4 *in his day he had great influence* HEYDAY, prime, time; peak, height, zenith, ascendancy; youth, springtime, salad days. ANTONYM decline.

PHRASES: **day after day** *day after day, we learn of new allegations* REPEATEDLY, again and again, over and over (again), time and (time) again, frequently, often, time after time; 'day in, day out', night and day, all the time; persistently, recurrently, constantly, continuously, continually, relentlessly, regularly, habitually, unfailingly, always, oftentimes; *informal* 24-7; *literary* oft, ofttimes. **day by day 1** *day by day they were forced to retreat* GRADUALLY, slowly, progressively; bit by bit, inch by inch, little by little. **2** *they follow the news day by day* DAILY, every day, day after day; diurnally. **day in, day out.** See DAY AFTER DAY above.

daybreak noun *we'll be packed and ready to go by daybreak* DAWN, crack of dawn, sunrise, first light; daylight, sunup. ANTONYM nightfall.

daydream noun **1** *she was lost in **a daydream*** (A) REVERIE, a trance, (a) fantasy, a vision, fancy, (a) brown study; inattentiveness, woolgathering, preoccupation, absorption, self-absorption, absentmindedness, abstraction.

2 *winning the lottery is just **a daydream*** A DREAM, a pipe dream, a fantasy, a castle in the air, a fond hope; wishful thinking; *informal* pie in the sky.

▸ verb *stop daydreaming!* DREAM, muse, stare into space; fantasize, build castles in the air.

daydreamer noun *it's time you stop being a daydreamer and start focusing on your responsibilities* DREAMER, fantasist, fantasizer, romantic, wishful thinker, idealist; visionary, theorizer, Utopian, Walter Mitty.

daylight noun **1** *do the test in daylight* NATURAL LIGHT, sunlight. ANTONYM darkness.

2 *she went there only in daylight* DAYTIME, day; broad daylight. ANTONYM nighttime.

3 *police moved in at daylight* DAWN, daybreak, (the) break of day, (the) crack of dawn, sunrise, first light, early morning, sunup. ANTONYM nightfall.

day-to-day adjective *my day-to-day routine* REGULAR, everyday, daily, routine, habitual, frequent, normal, standard, usual, typical.

daze verb **1** *he was dazed by his fall* STUN, stupefy; knock unconscious, knock out; *informal* knock the stuffing out of.

2 *she was dazed by the revelations* ASTOUND, amaze, astonish, startle, dumbfound, stupefy, overwhelm, stagger, shock, confound, bewilder, bedazzle, take aback, shake up; *informal* flabbergast, bowl over, blow away.

▸ noun *she is in a daze* STUPOR, trance, haze; spin, whirl, muddle, jumble.

dazzle verb **1** *she was dazzled by the headlights* BLIND TEMPORARILY, deprive of sight.

2 *I was dazzled by the exhibition* OVERWHELM, overcome, impress, move, stir, affect, touch, awe, overawe, leave speechless, take someone's breath away; spellbind, hypnotize; *informal* bowl over, blow away, knock out.

▸ noun **1** *dazzle can be a problem to sensitive eyes* GLARE, brightness, brilliance, shimmer, radiance, shine.

2 *the dazzle of the limelight* SPARKLE, glitter, brilliance, glory, splendor, magnificence, glamour; attraction, lure, allure, draw, appeal; *informal* razzle-dazzle, razzmatazz.

dazzling adjective **1** *the sunlight was dazzling* BRIGHT, blinding, glaring, brilliant.

2 *Jenny's dazzling performance* IMPRESSIVE, remarkable, extraordinary, outstanding, exceptional; incredible, amazing, astonishing, phenomenal, breathtaking, thrilling; excellent, wonderful, magnificent, marvelous, superb, first-rate, superlative, matchless; *informal* mind-blowing, out of this world, fabulous, bang-up, fab, super, sensational, ace, A1, cool, awesome, killer.

deactivate verb *don't forget to deactivate the alarm* DISABLE, defuse, disarm, disconnect, inactivate, make inoperative, immobilize, stop, turn off.

dead adjective 1 *my parents are dead* PASSED ON/AWAY, expired, departed, gone, no more; late, lost, lamented; perished, fallen, slain, slaughtered, killed, murdered; lifeless, extinct; *informal* (as) dead as a doornail, six feet under, pushing up daisies; *formal* deceased; *euphemistic* with God, asleep. ANTONYMS alive, living.

2 *patches of dead ground* BARREN, lifeless, bare, desolate, sterile. ANTONYMS fertile, lush.

3 *a dead language* OBSOLETE, extinct, defunct, disused, abandoned, discarded, superseded, vanished, forgotten; archaic, antiquated, ancient; *literary* of yore. ANTONYMS modern, current.

4 *the phone was dead* NOT WORKING, out of order, inoperative, inactive, in disrepair, broken, malfunctioning, defective; *informal* kaput, conked out, on the blink, on the fritz, bust, busted. ANTONYM in working order.

5 *a dead leg* NUMB, numbed, deadened, desensitized, unfeeling; paralyzed, crippled, incapacitated, immobilized, frozen.

6 *she has dead eyes* EMOTIONLESS, unemotional, unfeeling, impassive, unresponsive, indifferent, dispassionate, inexpressive, wooden, stony, cold; deadpan, flat; blank, vacant. ANTONYM passionate.

7 *his affection for her was dead* EXTINGUISHED, quashed, stifled; finished, over, gone, no more; a thing of the past, ancient history.

8 *a dead town* UNEVENTFUL, uninteresting, unexciting, uninspiring, dull, boring, flat, quiet, sleepy, slow, lackluster, lifeless; *informal* one-horse, dullsville. ANTONYM lively.

9 *dead silence* COMPLETE, absolute, total, utter, out-and-out, thorough, unmitigated. ANTONYM partial.

10 *a dead shot* UNERRING, unfailing, impeccable, sure, true, accurate, precise; deadly, lethal, bang on. ANTONYM poor.

▸ adverb 1 *he was dead serious* COMPLETELY, absolutely, totally, utterly, deadly, perfectly, entirely, quite, thoroughly; definitely, certainly, positively, categorically, unquestionably, undoubtedly, surely; in every way, one hundred percent.

2 *flares were seen dead ahead* DIRECTLY, exactly, precisely, immediately, right, straight, due, squarely; *informal* smack dab.

3 *informal it's dead easy.* See VERY.

deadbeat noun *informal there's no room for deadbeats in the navy* LAYABOUT, loafer, idler, good-for-nothing, bum, sponger; *literary* wastrel.

dead cat bounce See note below.

WORD NOTE **dead cat bounce**

Of Wall Street locutions, my favorite remains *dead cat bounce* to describe the stock market's reflexive if generally small gain on the day after it has fallen steeply like a cat flung out of an upper story window. —DL

deaden verb 1 *surgeons tried to deaden the pain* NUMB, dull, blunt, suppress; alleviate, mitigate, diminish, reduce, lessen, ease, soothe, relieve, assuage, kill. ANTONYM intensify.

2 *the wood paneling deadened any noise* MUFFLE, mute, smother, stifle, dull, dampen; silence, quieten, soften; cushion, buffer, absorb. ANTONYM amplify.

3 *laughing might deaden us to the moral issue* DESENSITIZE, numb, anesthetize; harden (one's heart), toughen, inure. ANTONYM sensitize.

deadline noun *the deadline for manuscript submissions is February 14.* TIME LIMIT, limit, finishing date, target date, cutoff point.

deadlock noun *the negotiations reached a deadlock* STALEMATE, impasse, standoff, logjam; standstill, halt, stop, full stop, dead end.

deadly adjective 1 *these drugs can be deadly* FATAL, lethal, mortal, death-dealing, life-threatening; dangerous, injurious, harmful, detrimental, deleterious, unhealthy; noxious, toxic, poisonous; *literary* deathly. ANTONYMS harmless, beneficial.

2 *deadly enemies* MORTAL, irreconcilable, implacable, unappeasable, unforgiving, remorseless, merciless, pitiless; bitter, hostile, antagonistic.

3 *I noticed their deadly seriousness* INTENSE, great, marked, extreme. ANTONYM mild.

4 *he was deadly pale* DEATHLY, ghostly, ashen, white, pallid, wan, pale; ghastly.

5 *his aim is deadly* UNERRING, unfailing, impeccable, perfect, flawless, faultless; sure, true, precise, accurate, exact, bang on. ANTONYMS inaccurate, poor.

6 *informal life here can be deadly.* See BORING.

▸ adverb *deadly calm* COMPLETELY, absolutely, totally, utterly, perfectly, entirely, wholly, quite, dead, thoroughly; in every way, one hundred percent, to the hilt.

deadpan adjective *his deadpan expression* BLANK, expressionless, inexpressive, impassive, inscrutable, poker-faced, straight-faced; stony, wooden, vacant, fixed, lifeless. ANTONYM expressive.

deaf adjective 1 *she is deaf and blind* HEARING IMPAIRED, hard of hearing; *informal* deaf as a post.

2 *she was **deaf to** their pleading* UNMOVED BY, untouched by, unaffected by, indifferent to, unresponsive to, unconcerned by; unaware of, oblivious to, incognizant of, impervious to.

deafen verb *they were deafened by the explosion* MAKE DEAF, deprive of hearing, impair someone's hearing.

deafening adjective *the deafening noise from the construction site* VERY LOUD, very noisy, overloud, ear-splitting, overwhelming, almighty, mighty, tremendous; booming, thunderous, roaring, resounding, resonant, reverberating. ANTONYM quiet.

deal noun *completion of the deal* AGREEMENT, understanding, pact, bargain, covenant, contract, treaty; arrangement, compromise, settlement; terms; transaction, sale, account; *Law* indenture.

▸ verb 1 *how to **deal with** difficult children* COPE WITH, handle, manage, treat, take care of, take charge of, take in hand, sort out, tackle, take on; control; act toward, behave toward.

2 *the article **deals with** advances in chemistry* CONCERN, be about, have to do with, discuss, consider, cover, per-

tain to; tackle, study, explore, investigate, examine, review, analyze.

3 *the company* ***deals in*** *high-tech goods* TRADE IN, buy and sell; sell, purvey, supply, stock, market, merchandise; traffic, smuggle; *informal* push, flog.

4 *the cards were dealt* DISTRIBUTE, give out, share out, divide out, hand out, pass out, pass around, dole out, dispense, allocate; *informal* divvy up.

5 *the court dealt a blow to government reforms* DELIVER, administer, dispense, inflict, give, impose; aim.

PHRASE: **a great deal/a good deal** *under a great deal of pressure | there's a good deal of unfinished work here* A LOT, a large amount, a fair amount, much, plenty; *informal* lots, loads, heaps, bags, masses, tons, stacks.

dealer noun 1 *an antique dealer* TRADER, merchant, salesman, saleswoman, seller, vendor, purveyor, peddler, hawker; buyer, merchandiser, distributor, supplier, shopkeeper, retailer, wholesaler.

2 *a drug dealer* TRAFFICKER, supplier.

dealing noun 1 *dishonest dealing* BUSINESS METHODS, business practices, business, commerce, trading, transactions; behavior, conduct, actions.

2 **(dealings)** *Canada's dealings with China* RELATIONS, relationship, association, connections, contact, intercourse; negotiations, bargaining, transactions; trade, trading, business, commerce, traffic; *informal* truck, doings.

dean noun 1 *students must have the consent of the dean* FACULTY HEAD, department head, college head, provost, university official; chief, director, principal, president, chancellor, governor.

2 *the dean of Russian literature* DOYEN/DOYENNE, elder statesman, grande dame, grand old man, veteran.

dear adjective 1 *a dear friend* BELOVED, loved, adored, cherished, precious; esteemed, respected, worshiped; close, intimate, bosom, best. ANTONYM hated.

2 *her pictures were too dear to part with* PRECIOUS, treasured, valued, prized, cherished, special.

3 *such a dear man* ENDEARING, adorable, lovable, appealing, engaging, charming, captivating, winsome, lovely, nice, pleasant, delightful, sweet, darling. ANTONYM disagreeable.

4 *the meals are rather dear* EXPENSIVE, costly, high-priced, overpriced, exorbitant, extortionate; *informal* pricey, steep, stiff. ANTONYMS inexpensive, cheap.

▸ noun 1 *don't worry, my dear* DARLING, dearest, love, beloved, sweetheart, sweet, precious, treasure; *informal* sweetie, sugar, honey, hon, baby, pet.

2 *he's such a dear* LOVABLE PERSON; darling, sweetheart, pet, angel, gem, treasure, star.

dearly adverb 1 *I love my son dearly* VERY MUCH, a great deal, greatly, deeply, profoundly, extremely; fondly, devotedly, tenderly.

2 *our freedom has been bought dearly* AT GREAT COST, at a high price, with much suffering, with much sacrifice.

dearth noun *a dearth of trained specialists* LACK, scarcity, shortage, shortfall, want, deficiency, insufficiency, inadequacy, paucity, sparseness, scantiness, rareness; absence. See note at LACK. ANTONYM surfeit.

death noun 1 *her father's death* DEMISE, dying, end, passing, loss of life; eternal rest, quietus; murder, assassination, execution, slaughter, massacre; *informal* curtains; *formal* decease; *archaic* expiry. ANTONYM life.

2 *the death of their dream* END, finish, termination, extinction, extinguishing, collapse, destruction, eradication, obliteration. ANTONYM birth.

3 *Death gestured toward a grave* THE GRIM REAPER, the Dark Angel, the Angel of Death. PHRASE: **put to death** *the czar and his family were put to death* EXECUTE, hang, behead, guillotine, decapitate, electrocute, shoot, gas, crucify, stone; kill, murder, assassinate, eliminate, terminate, exterminate, destroy; *informal* bump off, polish off, do away with, do in, knock off, string up, take out, croak, stiff, blow away, ice, rub out, waste, whack, smoke; *literary* slay.

deathless adjective *our deathless souls* IMMORTAL, undying, imperishable, indestructible; enduring, everlasting, eternal; timeless, ageless. ANTONYMS mortal, ephemeral.

deathly adjective *the wounded soldiers had a deathly pallor* DEATHLIKE, deadly, ghostly, ghastly; ashen, chalky, white, pale, pallid, bloodless, wan, anemic, pasty.

debacle noun *the Watergate break-in became a debacle of the highest order* FIASCO, failure, catastrophe, disaster, mess, ruin; downfall, collapse, defeat; *informal* foul-up, screw-up, hash, botch, washout, snafu.

debar verb 1 *women were debarred from the club* EXCLUDE, ban, bar, disqualify, declare ineligible, preclude, shut out, lock out, keep out, reject, blackball. ANTONYM admit.

2 *the unions were debarred from striking* PREVENT, prohibit, proscribe, disallow, ban, interdict, block, stop; *Law* enjoin, estop. ANTONYM allow.

debase verb 1 *the moral code has been debased* DEGRADE, devalue, demean, cheapen, prostitute, discredit, drag down, tarnish, blacken, blemish; disgrace, dishonor, shame; damage, harm, undermine. See notes at DEPRAVED, HUMBLE. ANTONYM enhance.

2 *the added copper debases the silver* REDUCE IN VALUE, reduce in quality, depreciate; contaminate, adulterate, pollute, taint, sully, corrupt; dilute, alloy.

debatable adjective *the historical accuracy of this account is debatable* ARGUABLE, disputable, questionable, open to question, controversial, contentious; doubtful, dubious, uncertain, unsure, unclear; borderline, inconclusive, moot, unsettled, unresolved, unconfirmed, undetermined, undecided, up in the air, iffy.

debate noun *a debate on the reforms* DISCUSSION, discourse, parley, dialogue; argument, dispute, wrangle, war of words; argumentation, disputation, dissension, disagreement, contention, conflict; negotiations, talks; *informal* confab, powwow.

▸ verb 1 *they will debate the future of rail transport* DISCUSS, talk over/through, talk about, thrash out, hash out, argue, dispute; *informal* kick around, bat around.

2 *he debated whether to call her* CONSIDER, think over/about, chew over, mull over, ponder, revolve, deliberate, contemplate, muse, meditate; *formal* cogitate.

debauch verb 1 *public morals have been debauched* CORRUPT, debase, deprave, warp, pervert, lead astray, ruin.

2 *dated he debauched many women* SEDUCE, deflower, defile, violate; *literary* ravish.

debauched adjective *a fleet commanded by debauched*

young men DISSOLUTE, dissipated, degenerate, corrupt, depraved, sinful, unprincipled, immoral; lascivious, lecherous, lewd, lustful, libidinous, licentious, promiscuous, loose, wanton, abandoned; decadent, profligate, intemperate, sybaritic. ANTONYM wholesome.

debauchery noun *a life of self-absorption and debauchery* DISSIPATION, degeneracy, corruption, vice, depravity; immodesty, indecency, perversion, iniquity, wickedness, sinfulness, impropriety, immorality; lasciviousness, salaciousness, lechery, lewdness, lust, promiscuity, wantonness, profligacy; decadence, intemperance, sybaritism; *formal* turpitude.

debilitate verb *can't you see how these drugs have debilitated you?* WEAKEN, enfeeble, enervate, devitalize, sap, drain, exhaust, weary, fatigue, prostrate; undermine, impair, indispose, incapacitate, cripple, disable, paralyze, immobilize; *informal* knock out, do in. See note at WEAK. ANTONYM invigorate.

debility noun *Sam's obvious debility came as a shock to us* FRAILTY, weakness, enfeeblement, enervation, devitalization, lassitude, exhaustion, weariness, fatigue, prostration; incapacity, indisposition, infirmity, illness, sickness, sickliness; *Medicine* asthenia.

debonair adjective *as debonair as Cary Grant* SUAVE, urbane, sophisticated, cultured, self-possessed, self-assured, confident, charming, gracious, courteous, gallant, chivalrous, gentlemanly, refined, polished, well-bred, genteel, dignified, courtly; well-groomed, elegant, stylish, smart, dashing; *informal* smooth, sharp, cool, slick, fly. ANTONYM unsophisticated.

debrief verb *Soviet scientists were debriefed by the KGB* REVIEW, discuss, examine; cross-examine, interview, interrogate, question, probe, sound out; *informal* grill, pump.

debris noun *the irrigation channels were blocked with debris* DETRITUS, refuse, rubbish, waste, litter, scrap, dross, chaff, flotsam and jetsam; rubble, wreckage; remains, scraps, dregs, trash, garbage, dreck, junk.

debt noun **1** *he couldn't pay his debts* BILL, account, dues, arrears, charges; financial obligation, outstanding payment; check, tab.

2 *his debt to the author* INDEBTEDNESS, obligation; gratitude, appreciation, thanks. PHRASES: **in debt** *the medical bills left them hopelessly in debt* OWING MONEY, in arrears, behind with payments, overdrawn; insolvent, bankrupt, ruined; *informal* in the red. **in someone's debt** *Chris would be forever in his debt* INDEBTED TO, beholden to, obliged to, duty-bound to, honor-bound to, obligated to; grateful (to), thankful (to), appreciative (of).

debtor noun *the debtor was given fourteen days to pay* BORROWER, mortgagor; bankrupt, insolvent, defaulter. ANTONYM creditor.

debunk verb *even the most successful hoax will eventually be debunked* EXPLODE, deflate, quash, discredit, disprove, contradict, controvert, invalidate, negate; challenge, call into question, poke holes in; *formal* confute. ANTONYM confirm.

debut noun *her acting debut was in a forgettable play in Pittsburgh* FIRST APPEARANCE, first performance, launch, coming out, entrance, premiere, introduction, inception, inauguration; *informal* kickoff.

decadence noun **1** *the decadence of modern society* DISSIPATION, degeneracy, debauchery, corruption, depravity, vice, sin, moral decay, immorality; immoderateness, intemperance, licentiousness, self-indulgence, hedonism. ANTONYM morality.

2 *the decadence of nations* DETERIORATION, fall, decay, degeneration, decline, degradation, retrogression. ANTONYM rise.

decadent adjective **1** *decadent city life* DISSOLUTE, dissipated, degenerate, corrupt, depraved, sinful, unprincipled, immoral; licentious, abandoned, profligate, intemperate; sybaritic, hedonistic, pleasure-seeking, self-indulgent.

2 *the decadent empire* DECLINING, decaying, ebbing, degenerating, deteriorating.

decamp verb **1** *he decamped with the profits* ABSCOND, make off, run off/away, flee, bolt, take flight, disappear, vanish, steal away, sneak away, escape, make a run for it, leave, depart; *informal* split, scram, vamoose, cut and run, do a disappearing act, head for the hills, go AWOL, take a powder, go on the lam.

2 *archaic* *the armies decamped* STRIKE ONE'S TENTS, break camp, move on.

decant verb *the wine was decanted into a flask* POUR OFF, draw off, siphon off, drain, tap; transfer.

decapitate verb *traitors were publicly decapitated* BEHEAD, guillotine, put on the block.

decay verb **1** *the corpses had decayed* DECOMPOSE, rot, putrefy, go bad, go off, spoil, fester, perish, deteriorate; degrade, break down, molder, shrivel, wither.

2 *the cities continue to decay* DETERIORATE, degenerate, decline, go downhill, slump, slide, go to rack and ruin, go to seed; disintegrate, fall to pieces, fall into disrepair; fail, collapse; *informal* go to pot, go to the dogs, go into/down the toilet.

▸ noun **1** *signs of decay* DECOMPOSITION, putrefaction, festering; rot, mold, mildew, fungus.

2 *tooth decay* ROT, corrosion, decomposition; caries, cavities, holes.

3 *the decay of American values* DETERIORATION, degeneration, debasement, degradation, decline, weakening, atrophy; crumbling, disintegration, collapse.

decayed adjective *a decayed deer carcass* DECOMPOSED, decomposing, rotten, putrescent, putrid, bad, off, spoiled, far gone, perished; moldy, festering, fetid, rancid, rank; maggoty, wormy.

decaying adjective **1** *decaying fish* DECOMPOSING, decomposed, rotting, rotten, putrescent, putrid, bad, off, perished; moldy, festering, fetid, rancid, rank; maggoty, wormy.

2 *a decaying city* DECLINING, degenerating, dying, crumbling; run-down, tumbledown, ramshackle, shabby, decrepit; in decline, in ruins, on the way out.

decease noun *formal* *her decease was imminent* DEATH, dying, demise, end, passing, loss of life, quietus; *informal* curtains, croaking, snuffing; *archaic* expiry.

deceased adjective *formal* *his deceased relatives* DEAD, expired, departed, gone, no more, passed on/away; late, lost, lamented; perished, fallen, slain, slaughtered, killed, murdered; lifeless, extinct; *informal* (as) dead as a doornail, six feet under, pushing up daisies; *euphemistic* with God, asleep.

deceit noun **1** *her endless deceit* DECEPTION, deceitfulness, duplicity, double-dealing, fraud, cheating, trickery, chicanery, deviousness, slyness, wiliness, guile, bluff, lying, pretense, treachery; *informal* crookedness, monkey business, monkeyshines. ANTONYM honesty.

2 *their life is a deceit* SHAM, fraud, pretense, hoax, fake, blind, artifice; trick, stratagem, device, ruse, scheme, dodge, machination, deception, subterfuge; cheat, swindle; *informal* con, setup, scam, flimflam, bunco.

deceitful adjective **1** *a deceitful woman* DISHONEST, untruthful, mendacious, insincere, false, disingenuous, untrustworthy, unscrupulous, unprincipled, two-faced, duplicitous, double-dealing, underhanded, crafty, cunning, sly, scheming, calculating, treacherous, Machiavellian, sneaky, tricky, foxy, crooked.

2 *a deceitful allegation* FRAUDULENT, counterfeit, fabricated, invented, concocted, made up, trumped up, untrue, false, bogus, fake, spurious, fallacious, deceptive, misleading; *euphemistic* economical with the truth.

deceive verb **1** *she was deceived by a con man* SWINDLE, defraud, cheat, trick, hoodwink, hoax, dupe, take in, mislead, delude, fool, outwit, lead on, inveigle, beguile, double-cross, gull; *informal* con, bamboozle, do, gyp, diddle, rip off, shaft, pull a fast one on, take for a ride, pull the wool over someone's eyes, sucker, snooker, stiff.

2 *he deceived her with another woman* BE UNFAITHFUL TO, cheat on, betray, play someone false; *informal* two-time.

decelerate verb *decelerate when approaching the curve* SLOW DOWN, slow up, ease up, slack up, reduce speed, brake.

decency noun **1** *standards of taste and decency* PROPRIETY, decorum, good taste, respectability, dignity, correctness, good form, etiquette; morality, virtue, modesty, delicacy.

2 *he didn't have the decency to tell me* COURTESY, politeness, good manners, civility, respect; consideration, thoughtfulness, tact, diplomacy.

WORD NOTE **decency**

I recently fell in love with this word when a friend, to whom I had given my novel-in-progress to read, informed me that *decency*—the question of how to lead decent lives and the difficulty of treating others with simple human decency—was the fundamental concern of the characters in my book. To be honest, it hadn't occurred to me. But as soon as I heard it, I realized it was true. Nor had *decency* been, until then, a word that I'd used much. Now I try to use it as often as I can—perhaps in the hope that keeping the word in mind will enable me to practice it more consistently. **—FP**

decent adjective **1** *a decent burial* PROPER, correct, appropriate, apt, fitting, suitable; respectable, dignified, decorous, seemly; nice, tasteful; conventional, accepted, standard, traditional, orthodox; comme il faut.

2 *a very decent fellow* HONORABLE, honest, trustworthy, dependable; respectable, upright, clean-living, virtuous, good; obliging, helpful, accommodating, unselfish, generous, kind, thoughtful, considerate; neighborly, hospitable, pleasant, agreeable, amiable. ANTONYMS dishonest, disobliging.

3 *a job with decent pay* SATISFACTORY, reasonable, fair, acceptable, adequate, sufficient, ample; not bad, all right, tolerable, passable, suitable; *informal* OK, okay, up to snuff. ANTONYM unsatisfactory.

deception noun **1** *they obtained money by deception* DECEIT, deceitfulness, duplicity, double-dealing, fraud, cheating, trickery, chicanery, deviousness, slyness, wiliness, guile, bluff, lying, pretense, treachery; *informal* crookedness, monkey business, monkeyshines.

2 *it was all a deception* TRICK, deceit, sham, fraud, pretense, hoax, fake, blind, artifice; stratagem, device, ruse, scheme, dodge, machination, subterfuge; cheat, swindle; *informal* con, setup, scam, flimflam, bunco. See note at FICTION.

deceptive adjective **1** *distances are very deceptive* MISLEADING, illusory, illusionary, specious; ambiguous; distorted; *literary* illusive.

2 *deceptive practices* DECEITFUL, duplicitous, fraudulent, counterfeit, underhanded, cunning, crafty, sly, guileful, scheming, treacherous, Machiavellian; disingenuous, untrustworthy, unscrupulous, unprincipled, dishonest, insincere, false; *informal* crooked, sharp, shady, sneaky, tricky, foxy.

USAGE NOTE **deceptively**

Deceptively belongs to a very small set of words whose meaning is genuinely ambiguous in that it can be used in similar contexts to mean both one thing and also its complete opposite. A *deceptively smooth surface* is one that appears smooth but in fact is not smooth at all, while a *deceptively spacious room* is one that does not look spacious but is in fact *more* spacious than it appears. But what is a *deceptively steep gradient*? Or a person who is described as *deceptively strong*? To avoid confusion, use with caution (or not at all) unless the context makes clear in what way the thing modified is not what it first appears to be.

decide verb **1** *she decided to become a writer* RESOLVE, determine, make up one's mind, make a decision; elect, choose, opt, plan, aim, have the intention, have in mind.

2 *research to decide a variety of questions* SETTLE, resolve, determine, work out, answer; *informal* sort out, figure out.

3 *the court is to decide the case* ADJUDICATE, arbitrate, adjudge, judge; hear, try, examine; sit in judgment on, pronounce on, give a verdict on, rule on.

decided adjective **1** *they have a decided advantage* DISTINCT, clear, marked, pronounced, obvious, striking, noticeable, unmistakable, patent, manifest; definite, certain, positive, emphatic, undeniable, indisputable, unquestionable; assured, guaranteed.

2 *he was very decided* DETERMINED, resolute, firm, strong-minded, strong-willed, emphatic, dead set, unwavering, unyielding, unbending, inflexible, unshakable, unrelenting, obstinate, stubborn, rock-ribbed.

3 *our future is decided* SETTLED, established, resolved, determined, agreed, designated, chosen, ordained, prescribed; set, fixed; *informal* sewn up, wrapped up.

decidedly adverb *they were decidedly hostile to one another* DISTINCTLY, clearly, markedly, obviously, noticeably, unmistakably, patently, manifestly; definitely, certainly, positively, absolutely, downright, undeniably, unquestionably; extremely, exceedingly, exceptionally, particularly, especially, very; *informal* terrifically, devilishly, ultra, mega, majorly, ever so, dead, real, mighty, awful.

deciding adjective *the deciding factor may be the size of* *your budget* DETERMINING, decisive, conclusive, key, pivotal, crucial, critical, significant, major, chief, principal, prime. See note at CRUCIAL.

decipher verb **1** *he deciphered the code* DECODE, decrypt, break, work out, solve, interpret, unscramble, translate; make sense of, get to the bottom of, unravel; *informal* crack, figure out. ANTONYM encode.

2 *the writing was hard to decipher* MAKE OUT, discern, perceive, read, follow, fathom, make sense of, interpret, understand, comprehend, grasp.

decision noun **1** *they came to a decision* RESOLUTION, conclusion, settlement, commitment, resolve, determination; choice, option, selection.

2 *the judge's decision* VERDICT, finding, ruling, recommendation, judgment, judgment call, pronouncement, adjudication, order, rule, resolve; findings, results; *Law* determination.

3 *his order had a ring of decision* DECISIVENESS, determination, resolution, resolve, firmness; strong-mindedness, purpose, purposefulness.

decisive adjective **1** *a decisive man* RESOLUTE, firm, strong-minded, strong-willed, determined; purposeful, forceful, dead set, unwavering, unyielding, unbending, inflexible, unshakable, obstinate, stubborn, rock-ribbed. See note at RESOLUTE.

2 *the decisive factor* DECIDING, conclusive, determining; key, pivotal, critical, crucial, significant, influential, major, chief, principal, prime.

deck verb **1** *the street was decked with streamers* DECORATE, bedeck, adorn, ornament, trim, trick out, garnish, cover, hang, festoon, garland, swathe, wreathe; embellish, beautify, prettify, enhance, grace, set off; *informal* get up, do up, tart up; *literary* bejewel, bedizen, caparison.

2 *Ingrid was* ***decked out*** *in blue* DRESS (UP), clothe, attire, garb, robe, drape, turn out, fit out, outfit, costume; *informal* doll up, get up, do up, gussy up.

3 *he got up from the table and decked me.* See HIT verb sense 1.

▸ noun *they were lounging on the deck* TERRACE, balcony, veranda, porch, patio.

declaim verb **1** *a preacher declaiming from the pulpit* MAKE A SPEECH, give an address, give a lecture, deliver a sermon; speak, hold forth, orate, preach, lecture, sermonize, moralize; *informal* sound off, spout, speechify, preachify.

2 *they loved to hear Garfield declaim his poetry* RECITE, read aloud, read out loud, read out; deliver; *informal* spout.

3 *he* ***declaimed against*** *the evils of society* SPEAK OUT AGAINST, rail against, inveigh against, fulminate against, rage against, thunder against; rant about, expostulate against; condemn, criticize, attack, decry, disparage.

declamation noun *he delivered a passionate declamation* SPEECH, address, lecture, sermon, homily, discourse, oration, recitation, disquisition, monologue.

declaration noun **1** *they issued a declaration* ANNOUNCEMENT, statement, communication, pronouncement, proclamation, communiqué, edict, advisory.

2 *the declaration of war* PROCLAMATION, notification, announcement, revelation, disclosure, broadcasting.

3 *a declaration of faith* ASSERTION, profession, affirmation, acknowledgment, revelation, disclosure, manifestation, confirmation, testimony, validation, certification, attestation; pledge, avowal, vow, oath, protestation.

declare verb **1** *she declared her political principles* PROCLAIM, announce, state, reveal, air, voice, articulate, express, vent, set forth, publicize, broadcast; *informal* come out with, shout from the rooftops. See note at ANNOUNCE.

2 *he declared that they were guilty* ASSERT, maintain, state, affirm, contend, argue, insist, hold, profess, claim, avow, swear; *formal* aver.

3 *his speech* ***declared*** *him* ***to be*** *a gentleman* SHOW TO BE, reveal as, confirm as, prove to be, attest to someone's being.

decline verb **1** *she declined all invitations* TURN DOWN, reject, brush aside, refuse, rebuff, spurn, repulse, dismiss; forgo, deny oneself, pass up; abstain from, say no to; *informal* give the thumbs down to, give something a miss. ANTONYM accept.

2 *the number of traders has declined* DECREASE, reduce, lessen, diminish, dwindle, contract, shrink, fall off, tail off; drop, fall, go down, slump, plummet; *informal* nosedive, take a header, crash. ANTONYM increase.

3 *standards steadily declined* DETERIORATE, degenerate, decay, crumble, collapse, slump, slip, slide, go downhill, worsen; weaken, wane, ebb; *informal* go to pot, go to the dogs, go into/down the toilet. ANTONYM rise.

▸ noun **1** *a decline in profits* REDUCTION, decrease, downturn, downswing, devaluation, depreciation, diminution, ebb, drop, slump, plunge; *informal* nosedive, crash.

2 *forest decline* DETERIORATION, degeneration, degradation, shrinkage; death, decay.

PHRASE: **in decline** *sadly, our volunteer program is in decline* DECLINING, decaying, crumbling, collapsing, failing; disappearing, dying, moribund; *informal* on its last legs, on the way out.

decode verb *the enemy's battle plans were decoded* DECIPHER, decrypt, work out, solve, interpret, translate; make sense of, get to the bottom of, unravel, unscramble, find the key to; *informal* crack, figure out.

decompose verb **1** *the carcasses will not decompose in these subzero temperatures* DECAY, rot, putrefy, go bad, go off, spoil, fester, perish, deteriorate; degrade, break down, molder, shrivel, wither.

2 *some minerals decompose rapidly* BREAK UP, fragment, disintegrate, crumble, dissolve; break down, decay.

decomposition noun **1** *an advanced state of decomposition* DECAY, putrefaction, putrescence, putridity.

2 *the decomposition of granite* DISINTEGRATION, dissolution; breaking down, decay.

decompress verb **1** *decompress the files before opening them* EXPAND, restore, recover.

2 *you need to take a few minutes to decompress* CALM DOWN, relax, take it easy, wind down; *informal* chill (out), hang loose, stay loose.

deconstruction See note at HAIKU.

decontaminate verb *the space station was decontaminated* SANITIZE, sterilize, disinfect, clean, cleanse, purify; fumigate.

decor noun *the decor in the family room is just awful* DECORATION, furnishing, ornamentation; color scheme.

decorate verb **1** *the door was decorated with a wreath* OR-

NAMENT, adorn, trim, embellish, garnish, furnish, enhance, grace, prettify; festoon, garland, bedeck.

2 *he started to decorate his home* PAINT, WALLPAPER, paper; refurbish, furbish, renovate, redecorate; *informal* do up, spruce up, do over, fix up, give something a facelift.

3 *he was decorated for courage* GIVE A MEDAL TO, honor, cite, reward.

decoration noun 1 *a ceiling with rich decoration* ORNAMENTATION, adornment, trimming, embellishment, garnishing, gilding; beautification, prettification; enhancements, enrichments, frills, accessories, trimmings, finery, frippery.

2 *internal decoration.* See DECOR.

3 *a Christmas tree decoration* ORNAMENT, bauble, trinket, knickknack, spangle; trimming, tinsel.

4 *a decoration won on the battlefield* MEDAL, award, star, ribbon; laurel, trophy, prize.

decorative adjective *mirrors were used as decorative features* ORNAMENTAL, embellishing, garnishing; fancy, ornate, attractive, pretty, showy. ANTONYM functional.

decorous adjective *he behaved toward her in a decorous manner* PROPER, seemly, decent, becoming, befitting, tasteful; correct, appropriate, suitable, fitting; tactful, polite, well-mannered, genteel, respectable; formal, restrained, modest, demure, gentlemanly, ladylike. ANTONYM unseemly.

decorum noun 1 *he had acted with decorum* PROPRIETY, seemliness, decency, good taste, correctness; politeness, courtesy, good manners; dignity, respectability, modesty, demureness. ANTONYM impropriety.

2 *a breach of decorum* ETIQUETTE, protocol, good form, custom, convention; formalities, niceties, punctilios, politeness. ANTONYM impropriety.

decoy noun *a decoy to distract their attention* LURE, bait, red herring; enticement, inducement, temptation, attraction, carrot; snare, trap.

▸ verb *he was decoyed to the mainland* LURE, entice, allure, tempt; entrap, snare, trap.

decrease verb 1 *pollution levels decreased* LESSEN, reduce, drop, diminish, decline, dwindle, fall off; die down, abate, subside, tail off, ebb, wane; plummet, plunge. ANTONYM increase.

2 *decrease the amount of fat in your body* REDUCE, lessen, lower, cut (back/down), curtail; slim down, tone down, deplete, minimize, slash. ANTONYM increase.

▸ noun *a decrease in crime* REDUCTION, drop, decline, downturn, cut, falloff, cutback, diminution, ebb, wane. ANTONYM increase.

decree noun 1 *a presidential decree* ORDER, edict, command, commandment, mandate, proclamation, dictum, fiat; law, bylaw, statute, act; *formal* ordinance.

2 *a court decree* JUDGMENT, verdict, adjudication, ruling, resolution, decision.

▸ verb *he decreed that a stadium should be built* ORDER, command, rule, dictate, pronounce, proclaim, ordain; direct, decide, determine.

decrepit adjective 1 *a decrepit old man* FEEBLE, infirm, weak, weakly, frail; disabled, incapacitated, crippled, doddering, tottering; old, elderly, aged, ancient, senile; *informal* past it, over the hill, no spring chicken. See note at WEAK. ANTONYMS strong, fit.

2 *a decrepit house* DILAPIDATED, rickety, run-down, tumbledown, beat-up, ramshackle, derelict, ruined, in (a state of) disrepair, gone to rack and ruin; battered, decayed, crumbling, deteriorating. ANTONYM sound.

decry verb *she decried the double standards* DENOUNCE, condemn, criticize, censure, attack, rail against, run down, pillory, lambaste, vilify, revile; disparage, deprecate, cast aspersions on; *informal* slam, blast, knock. ANTONYM praise.

dedicate verb 1 *she dedicated her life to the sick* DEVOTE, commit, pledge, give, surrender, sacrifice; set aside, allocate, consign.

2 *a book dedicated to his muse* INSCRIBE, address; assign.

3 *the chapel was dedicated to the Virgin Mary* DEVOTE, assign; bless, consecrate, sanctify; *formal* hallow.

dedicated adjective 1 *a dedicated socialist* COMMITTED, devoted, staunch, firm, steadfast, resolute, unwavering, loyal, faithful, true, dyed-in-the-wool; wholehearted, enthusiastic, single-minded, keen, earnest, zealous, ardent, passionate, fervent; *informal* card-carrying, hardcore. ANTONYM indifferent.

2 *data is accessed by a dedicated machine* EXCLUSIVE, custom built, customized.

dedication noun 1 *athletic excellence requires dedication* COMMITMENT, application, diligence, industry, resolve, enthusiasm, zeal, conscientiousness, perseverance, persistence, tenacity, drive, staying power; hard work, effort. ANTONYMS apathy, laziness.

2 *her dedication to the job* DEVOTION, commitment, loyalty, adherence, allegiance. ANTONYM indifference.

3 *the book has a dedication to her husband* INSCRIPTION, address, message.

4 *the dedication of the church* BLESSING, consecration, sanctification, benediction.

deduce verb *we can deduce from the evidence that Harding was indeed present at the time of the murder* CONCLUDE, reason, work out, infer; glean, divine, intuit, understand, assume, presume, conjecture, surmise, reckon; *informal* figure out.

deduct verb *we'll deduct ten percent from the total* SUBTRACT, take away, take off, debit, dock, discount; abstract, remove, knock off. ANTONYM add.

deduction noun 1 *the deduction of tax* SUBTRACTION, removal, debit, abstraction.

2 *gross pay, before deductions* SUBTRACTION.

3 *she was right in her deduction* CONCLUSION, inference, supposition, hypothesis, assumption, presumption; suspicion, conviction, belief, reasoning; *archaic* illation.

deed noun 1 *kindly deeds* ACT, action; feat, exploit, achievement, accomplishment, endeavor, undertaking, enterprise.

2 *unity must be established in deed and word* FACT, reality, actuality.

3 *a deed to the property* LEGAL DOCUMENT, contract, indenture, instrument.

deem verb *many of these campaigns have been deemed successful* CONSIDER, regard as, judge, adjudge, hold to be, view as, see as, take for, class as, count, find, suppose, reckon; think, believe to be, feel to be; *formal* esteem.

deep adjective **1** *a deep ravine* CAVERNOUS, yawning, gaping, huge, extensive; bottomless, fathomless, unfathomable. ANTONYM shallow.

2 *two inches deep* IN DEPTH, downward, inward, in vertical extent.

3 *deep affection* INTENSE, heartfelt, wholehearted, deep-seated, deep-rooted; sincere, genuine, earnest, enthusiastic, great. ANTONYMS insincere, superficial.

4 *a deep sleep* SOUND, heavy, intense.

5 *a deep thinker* PROFOUND, serious, philosophical, complex, weighty; abstruse, esoteric, recondite, mysterious, obscure; intelligent, intellectual, learned, wise, scholarly; discerning, penetrating, perceptive, insightful.

6 *he was deep in concentration* RAPT, absorbed, engrossed, preoccupied, immersed, lost, gripped, intent, engaged.

7 *a deep mystery* OBSCURE, mysterious, secret, unfathomable, opaque, abstruse, recondite, esoteric, enigmatic, arcane; puzzling, baffling, mystifying, inexplicable.

8 *his deep voice* LOW-PITCHED, low, bass, rich, powerful, resonant, booming, sonorous. ANTONYM high.

9 *a deep red* DARK, intense, rich, strong, bold, warm. ANTONYM light.

▸ noun **1** *literary creatures of deep* SEA, ocean; *informal* drink, briny; *literary* profound.

2 *the deep of night* MIDDLE, midst; depths, dead, thick.

▸ adverb **1** *I dug deep* FAR DOWN, way down, to a great depth.

2 *he brought them deep into woodland* FAR, a long way, a great distance.

deepen verb **1** *his love for her had deepened* GROW, increase, intensify, strengthen, heighten, amplify, augment; *informal* step up.

2 *they deepened the hole* DIG OUT, dig deeper, excavate.

deeply adverb *I am deeply grateful* PROFOUNDLY, greatly, enormously, extremely, very much; strongly, powerfully, intensely, keenly, acutely; thoroughly, completely, entirely; *informal* well, seriously, majorly.

deep-rooted adjective *a deep-rooted distaste for violence* DEEP-SEATED, deep, profound, fundamental, basic; established, ingrained, entrenched, unshakable, inveterate, inbuilt; secure; persistent, abiding, lingering. ANTONYM superficial.

deep-seated adjective See DEEP-ROOTED.

deer noun buck, stag, hart; doe, hind. See table.

DEER

axis	muntjac
barren ground caribou	musk deer
blacktail	Père David's deer
brocket	Peary caribou
caribou	red deer
chital	reindeer
elk	roe
fallow deer	sika
moose	wapiti
mule deer	whitetail
muley	woodland caribou

deface verb *the kids were caught defacing a school building with spray paint* VANDALIZE, disfigure, mar, spoil, ruin, sully, damage, blight, impair, trash.

de facto adverb *the republic is de facto two states* IN PRACTICE, in effect, in fact, in reality, really, actually. ANTONYM de jure.

▸ adjective *de facto control* ACTUAL, real, effective. ANTONYM de jure.

defamation noun *he sued the newspaper for defamation* LIBEL, slander, calumny, character assassination, vilification; scandalmongering, malicious gossip, aspersions, muckraking, abuse; disparagement, denigration; smear, slur; *informal* mudslinging.

defamatory adjective *the candidates abused the debate forum by exchanging defamatory remarks* LIBELOUS, slanderous, calumnious, scandalmongering, malicious, vicious, backbiting, muckraking; abusive, disparaging, denigratory, insulting; *informal* mudslinging, bitchy, catty.

defame verb *she has defamed my character* LIBEL, slander, malign, cast aspersions on, smear, traduce, give someone a bad name, run down, speak ill of, vilify, besmirch, stigmatize, disparage, denigrate, discredit, decry; *informal* do a hatchet job on, drag through the mud, slur; *informal* badmouth, dis; *formal* calumniate. See note at MALIGN. ANTONYM compliment.

default noun **1** *the incidence of defaults on loans* NONPAYMENT, failure to pay, bad debt.

2 *Browne lost the case by default* INACTION, omission, lapse, neglect, negligence, disregard; failure to appear, absence, nonappearance.

▸ verb **1** *the customer defaulted* FAIL TO PAY, not pay, back out, renege; go back on one's word; *informal* welsh, bilk.

2 *the program will default to its own style* REVERT, select automatically.

defeat verb **1** *the army that defeated the rebels* BEAT, conquer, win against, triumph over, get the better of, vanquish; rout, trounce, overcome, overpower, crush, subdue; *informal* lick, thrash, whip, wipe the floor with, make mincemeat of, clobber, slaughter, demolish, cream, skunk, nose out.

2 *these complex plans defeat their purpose* THWART, frustrate, foil, ruin, scotch, debar, derail; obstruct, impede, hinder, hamper; *informal* put the kibosh on, stymie, scuttle.

3 *the motion was defeated* REJECT, overthrow, throw out, dismiss, outvote, turn down; *informal* give the thumbs down.

4 *how to make it work defeats me* BAFFLE, perplex, bewilder, mystify, bemuse, confuse, confound, throw; *informal* beat, flummox, faze, stump.

▸ noun **1** *a crippling defeat* LOSS, conquest, vanquishment; rout, trouncing; downfall; *informal* thrashing, hiding, drubbing, licking, pasting, massacre, slaughter. ANTONYM victory.

2 *the defeat of his plans* FAILURE, downfall, collapse, ruin; rejection, frustration, abortion, miscarriage; undoing, reverse. ANTONYM success.

defeatist adjective *a defeatist attitude* PESSIMISTIC, fatalistic, negative, cynical, despondent, despairing, hopeless, bleak, gloomy. ANTONYM optimistic.

▸ noun PESSIMIST, fatalist, cynic, prophet of doom, doomster; misery, killjoy, worrier; *informal* quitter, wet blanket, worrywart. ANTONYM optimist.

defecate verb *nobody wants to see dogs defecating on the beach* EXCRETE FECES, have a bowel movement, have a BM, evacuate one's bowels, relieve oneself, go to the bathroom; *informal* do/go number two, poop, take a crap, take a dump.

defect[1] noun *he spotted a defect in my work* FAULT, flaw, imperfection, deficiency, weakness, weak spot, inadequacy, shortcoming, limitation, failing; kink, deformity, blemish; mistake, error; *informal* glitch; *Computing* bug.

defect[2] verb *his chief intelligence officer defected* DESERT, change sides, turn traitor, rebel, renege; abscond, quit, jump ship, escape; break faith; secede from, revolt against; *Military* go AWOL; *Politics* cross the floor; *literary* forsake.

defection noun *his defection to the United States* DESERTION, absconding, decamping, flight; apostasy, secession; treason, betrayal, disloyalty; *literary* perfidy.

defective adjective **1** *a defective seat belt* FAULTY, flawed, imperfect, shoddy, inoperative, malfunctioning, out of order, unsound; in disrepair, broken; *informal* on the blink, on the fritz. ANTONYM perfect.

2 *these methods are defective* LACKING, wanting, deficient, inadequate, insufficient.

defector noun *Cuban defectors sought refuge in Miami* DESERTER, turncoat, traitor, renegade, Judas, quisling; *informal* rat.

defend verb **1** *a fort built to defend the border* PROTECT, guard, safeguard, secure, shield; fortify, garrison, barricade; uphold, support, watch over. ANTONYM attack.

2 *he defended his policy* JUSTIFY, vindicate, argue for, support, make a case for, plead for; excuse, explain. ANTONYMS attack, criticize.

3 *the manager defended his players* SUPPORT, back, stand by, stick up for, stand up for, argue for, champion, endorse; *informal* throw one's weight behind. ANTONYM criticize.

defendant noun *does the defendant have counsel?* ACCUSED, prisoner (at the bar); appellant, litigant, respondent; suspect. ANTONYM plaintiff.

defender noun **1** *defenders of the environment* PROTECTOR, guard, guardian, preserver; custodian, watchdog, keeper, overseer.

2 *a defender of colonialism* SUPPORTER, upholder, backer, champion, advocate, apologist, proponent, exponent, promoter; adherent, believer.

defense noun **1** *the defense of the fortress* PROTECTION, guarding, security, fortification; resistance, deterrent.

2 *the enemy's defenses* BARRICADE, fortification; fortress, keep, rampart, bulwark, bastion.

3 *he spoke in defense of his boss* VINDICATION, justification, support, advocacy, endorsement; apology, explanation, exoneration.

4 *more spending on defense* ARMAMENTS, weapons, weaponry, arms; the military, the armed forces.

5 *the prisoner's defense* VINDICATION, explanation, mitigation, justification, rationalization, excuse, alibi, reason; plea, pleading; testimony, declaration, case.

defenseless adjective **1** *defenseless animals* VULNERABLE, helpless, powerless, impotent, weak, susceptible. ANTONYM resilient.

2 *the country is wholly defenseless* UNDEFENDED, unprotected, unguarded, unshielded, unarmed; vulnerable, assailable, exposed, insecure. ANTONYM well-protected.

defensible adjective **1** *a defensible attitude* JUSTIFIABLE, arguable, tenable, defendable, supportable; plausible, sound, sensible, reasonable, rational, logical; acceptable, valid, legitimate; excusable, pardonable, understandable. ANTONYM untenable.

2 *a defensible territory* SECURE, safe, fortified; invulnerable, impregnable, impenetrable, unassailable. ANTONYM vulnerable.

defensive adjective **1** *troops in defensive positions* DEFENDING, protective; wary, watchful.

2 *a defensive response* SELF-JUSTIFYING, oversensitive, prickly, paranoid, neurotic; *informal* uptight.

defer[1] verb *the committee will defer its decision* POSTPONE, put off, delay, hold over, hold off (on), put back; shelve, suspend, stay, put over, table; *informal* put on ice, put on the back burner, back-burner, put in cold storage, mothball. See note at POSTPONE.

defer[2] verb *they* ***deferred to*** *Joseph's judgment* YIELD TO, submit to, give way to, give in to, surrender to, capitulate to, acquiesce to; respect, honor.

deference noun *his writings show excessive deference to the wealthy* RESPECT, respectfulness, dutifulness; submissiveness, submission, obedience, surrender, accession, capitulation, acquiescence, complaisance, obeisance. See note at HONOR. ANTONYM disrespect.

deferential adjective *the hotel's deferential treatment of its elite clientele* RESPECTFUL, humble, obsequious; dutiful, obedient, submissive, subservient, yielding, acquiescent, complaisant, compliant, tractable, biddable, docile.

deferment noun *they sought a temporary deferment of the loan payments* POSTPONEMENT, deferral, suspension, delay, adjournment, interruption, pause; respite, stay, moratorium, reprieve, grace.

defiance noun *he wasn't used to such outspoken defiance* RESISTANCE, opposition, noncompliance, disobedience, insubordination, dissent, recalcitrance, subversion, rebellion; contempt, disregard, scorn, insolence, truculence. ANTONYM obedience.

defiant adjective *he is defiant in the face of critics* INTRANSIGENT, resistant, obstinate, uncooperative, noncompliant, recalcitrant; obstreperous, truculent, dissenting, disobedient, insubordinate, subversive, rebellious, mutinous, feisty. ANTONYM cooperative.

deficiency noun **1** *a vitamin deficiency* INSUFFICIENCY, lack, shortage, want, dearth, inadequacy, deficit, shortfall; scarcity, paucity, absence, deprivation, shortness. ANTONYM surplus.

2 *the team's big deficiency* DEFECT, fault, flaw, imperfection, weakness, weak point, inadequacy, shortcoming, limitation, failing. ANTONYM strength.

deficient adjective **1** *a diet deficient in vitamin A* LACKING, wanting, inadequate, insufficient, limited, poor, scant; low.

2 *deficient leadership* DEFECTIVE, faulty, flawed, inadequate, imperfect, shoddy, weak, inferior, unsound, substandard, second-rate, poor.

deficit noun *a large deficit in the federal budget* SHORTFALL, deficiency, shortage, debt, arrears; negative amount, loss. ANTONYM surplus.

defile verb **1** *her capacity for love had been defiled* SPOIL, sully, mar, impair, debase, degrade; poison, taint, tarnish; destroy, ruin. ANTONYM purify.

2 *the sacred bones were defiled* DESECRATE, profane, violate; contaminate, pollute, debase, degrade, dishonor. See note at POLLUTE. ANTONYM sanctify.

3 *archaic she was defiled by a married man* RAPE, violate; *literary* ravish; *dated* deflower.

definable adjective *she had no definable illness* DETERMINABLE, ascertainable, known, definite, clear-cut, precise, exact, specific.

define verb **1** *the dictionary defines it succinctly* EXPLAIN, expound, interpret, elucidate, describe, clarify; give the meaning of, put into words.

2 *he defined the limits of the law* DETERMINE, establish, fix, specify, designate, decide, stipulate, set out; demarcate, delineate.

3 *the farm buildings defined against the fields* OUTLINE, delineate, silhouette.

definite adjective **1** *a definite answer* EXPLICIT, specific, express, precise, exact, clear-cut, direct, plain, outright; fixed, established, confirmed, concrete. See note at DEFINITIVE. ANTONYM vague.

2 *definite evidence* CERTAIN, sure, positive, conclusive, decisive, firm, concrete, unambiguous, unequivocal, clear, unmistakable, proven; guaranteed, assured, cut and dried. ANTONYMS uncertain, ambiguous.

3 *she had a definite dislike for dogs* UNMISTAKABLE, certain, unequivocal, unambiguous, undisputed, decided, marked, distinct. ANTONYMS vague, slight.

4 *a definite geographical area* FIXED, marked, demarcated, delimited, stipulated, particular. ANTONYM indeterminate.

definitely adverb *it was definitely a case of exploiting child labor* CERTAINLY, surely, for sure, unquestionably, without doubt, without question, undoubtedly, indubitably, positively, absolutely; undeniably, unmistakably, plainly, clearly, obviously, patently, palpably, transparently, unequivocally.

definition noun **1** *the definition of "intelligence"* MEANING, denotation, sense; interpretation, explanation, elucidation, description, clarification, illustration.

2 *the definition of the picture* CLARITY, visibility, sharpness, crispness, acuteness; resolution, focus, contrast.

definitive adjective **1** *a definitive decision* CONCLUSIVE, final, ultimate; unconditional, unqualified, absolute, categorical, positive, definite.

2 *the definitive guide* AUTHORITATIVE, exhaustive, best, finest, consummate; classic, standard, recognized, accepted, official.

EASILY CONFUSED WORDS **definitive, definite**

Definitive in the sense 'decisive, unconditional, final' is sometimes confused with **definite**. **Definite** means 'clearly defined, precise, having fixed limits,' but **definitive** goes further, meaning 'most complete, satisfying all criteria, most authoritative': *although some critics found a few definite weak spots in the author's interpretations, his book was nonetheless widely regarded as the definitive history of the war.* A **definite** decision is simply one that has been made clearly and is without doubt, whereas a **definitive** decision is one that is not only conclusive but also carries the stamp of authority or is a benchmark for the future, as in a Supreme Court ruling. It is a common error to use **definitive** as though it were a more elegant way of saying **definite**.

deflate verb **1** *he deflated the tires* LET DOWN, flatten, void; puncture. ANTONYM inflate.

2 *the balloon deflated* GO DOWN, collapse, shrink, contract. ANTONYMS inflate, expand.

3 *the news had deflated him* SUBDUE, humble, cow, chasten; dispirit, dismay, discourage, dishearten; squash, crush, bring down, take the wind out of someone's sails, knock the stuffing out of. ANTONYM aggrandize.

4 *the budget deflated the economy* REDUCE, slow down, diminish; devalue, depreciate, depress. ANTONYM inflate.

deflect verb **1** *she wanted to deflect attention from herself* TURN ASIDE/AWAY, divert, avert, sidetrack; distract, draw away; block, parry, fend off, stave off.

2 *the ball deflected off the wall* BOUNCE, glance, ricochet, carom; diverge, deviate, veer, swerve, slew.

deform verb *shoes that will not cramp or deform the toes* DISFIGURE, bend out of shape, contort, buckle, warp; damage, impair.

deformed adjective *a deformed skeleton* MISSHAPEN, distorted, dysmorphic, malformed, contorted, out of shape; twisted, crooked, warped, buckled, gnarled; crippled, humpbacked, hunchbacked, disfigured, grotesque; injured, damaged, mutilated, mangled.

deformity noun *a brace used to correct spinal deformities* MALFORMATION, misshapenness, distortion, crookedness; imperfection, abnormality, irregularity; disfigurement; defect, flaw, blemish.

defraud verb *they defrauded thousands of investors* SWINDLE, cheat, rob, embezzle; deceive, dupe, hoodwink, double-cross, trick; *informal* con, do, sting, diddle, rip off, shaft, bilk, rook, gyp, pull a fast one on, put one over on, sucker, snooker, stiff.

defray verb *the reserve funds are not enough to defray the additional costs* PAY (FOR), cover, meet, square, settle, clear, discharge.

deft adjective *a deft piece of footwork | his deft handling of the situation* SKILLFUL, adept, adroit, dexterous, agile, nimble, handy; able, capable, skilled, proficient, accomplished, expert, polished, slick, professional, masterly; clever, shrewd, astute, canny, sharp; *informal* nifty, neat. ANTONYM clumsy.

WORD NOTE **deft**

This neat, adroit word carries an implication of athletic grace even when the subject has nothing to do with sports. *She deftly turned the conversation to another topic,* as well as *She ended the game and match with a deft backhand slice.* **—JS**

defunct adjective *the original contract is defunct* DISUSED, unused, inoperative, nonfunctioning, unusable, obsolete; no longer existing, discontinued; extinct. ANTONYMS working, extant.

defuse verb **1** *he tried to defuse the grenade* DEACTIVATE, disarm, disable, make safe. ANTONYM activate.

2 *an attempt to defuse the tension* REDUCE, lessen, diminish, lighten, relieve, ease, alleviate, moderate, mitigate. ANTONYM intensify.

defy verb 1 *he defied local law* DISOBEY, go against, flout, fly in the face of, disregard, ignore; break, violate, contravene, breach, infringe. ANTONYM obey.

2 *his actions defy belief* ELUDE, escape, defeat; frustrate, thwart, baffle.

3 *he glowered, defying her to mock him* CHALLENGE, dare.

degeneracy noun *the sexual degeneracy and intellectual deterioration of the time* CORRUPTION, decadence, moral decay, dissipation, dissolution, profligacy, vice, immorality, sin, sinfulness, ungodliness; debauchery; *formal* turpitude.

degenerate adjective 1 *a degenerate form of classicism* DEBASED, degraded, corrupt, impure; *formal* vitiated. ANTONYM pure.

2 *her degenerate brother* CORRUPT, decadent, dissolute, dissipated, debauched, reprobate, profligate; sinful, ungodly, immoral, unprincipled, amoral, dishonorable, disreputable, unsavory, sordid, low, ignoble. See note at DEPRAVED. ANTONYM moral.

▸ noun *a group of degenerates* REPROBATE, debauchee, profligate, libertine, roué.

▸ verb 1 *their quality of life had degenerated* DETERIORATE, decline, slip, slide, worsen, lapse, slump, go downhill, regress, retrogress; go to rack and ruin; *informal* go to pot, go to the dogs, hit the skids, go into/down the toilet. ANTONYM improve.

2 *the muscles started to degenerate* WASTE (AWAY), atrophy, weaken.

degradation noun 1 *poverty brings with it degradation* HUMILIATION, shame, loss of self-respect, abasement, indignity, ignominy.

2 *the degradation of women* DEMEANING, debasement, discrediting.

3 *the degradation of the tissues* DETERIORATION, degeneration, atrophy, decay; breakdown.

degrade verb 1 *prisons should not degrade prisoners* DEMEAN, debase, cheapen, devalue; shame, humiliate, humble, mortify, abase, dishonor; dehumanize, brutalize. See note at HUMBLE. ANTONYM dignify.

2 *the polymer will not degrade* BREAK DOWN, deteriorate, degenerate, decay.

degraded adjective 1 *I feel so degraded* HUMILIATED, demeaned, cheapened, cheap, ashamed. ANTONYM proud.

2 *his degraded sensibilities* DEGENERATE, corrupt, depraved, dissolute, dissipated, debauched, immoral, base, sordid. ANTONYMS pure, moral.

degrading adjective *accepting our assistance should not be a degrading experience* HUMILIATING, demeaning, shameful, mortifying, ignominious, undignified, inglorious, wretched.

degree noun 1 *to a high degree* LEVEL, standard, grade, mark; amount, extent, measure; magnitude, intensity, strength; proportion, ratio.

2 *she completed her degree in three years* DIPLOMA, academic program; baccalaureate, bachelor's, master's, doctorate, Ph.D. PHRASES: **by degrees** *rivalries and prejudice were by degrees fading out* GRADUALLY, little by little, bit by bit, inch by inch, step by step, slowly; piecemeal. **to a degree** *without proper instruction, you can operate the machinery only to a degree* TO SOME EXTENT, to a certain extent, up to a point, somewhat.

dehydrate verb 1 *alcohol dehydrates the skin* DRY (OUT), desiccate, dehumidify, effloresce. See note at DRY. ANTONYM hydrate.

2 *frogs can dehydrate quickly* DRY UP/OUT, lose water.

deify verb 1 *she was deified by the early Romans* WORSHIP, revere, venerate, reverence, hold sacred; immortalize.

2 *he was deified by the press* IDOLIZE, lionize, extol, hero-worship; idealize, glorify, aggrandize, put on a pedestal. ANTONYM demonize.

deign verb *he'll never deign to return to his father's house* CONDESCEND, stoop, lower oneself, demean oneself, humble oneself; consent, vouchsafe; *informal* come down from one's high horse.

deity noun *everyone cracked up when Coolidge said she worshiped a deity named Grover* GOD, goddess, divine being, supreme being, divinity, immortal; creator, demiurge; godhead.

dejected adjective *the dejected look on Thomas's face* DOWNCAST, downhearted, despondent, disconsolate, dispirited, crestfallen, disheartened; depressed, crushed, desolate, heartbroken, in the doldrums, sad, unhappy, doleful, melancholy, miserable, woebegone, forlorn, wretched, glum, gloomy; *informal* blue, down in/at the mouth, down in the dumps, in a blue funk. ANTONYM cheerful.

de jure adverb & adjective *Andrew's seat on the board was taken de jure by his brother | he had been de jure king since his father's death* BY RIGHT, rightfully, legally, according to the law; rightful, legal. ANTONYM de facto.

delay verb 1 *we were delayed by the traffic* DETAIN, hold up, make late, slow up/down, bog down; hinder, hamper, impede, obstruct.

2 *they delayed no longer* LINGER, dally, drag one's feet, be slow, hold back, dawdle, waste time; procrastinate, stall, hang fire, mark time, temporize, hesitate, dither, shilly-shally, dilly-dally; *archaic* tarry. ANTONYM hurry.

3 *he may delay the cut in interest rates* POSTPONE, put off, defer, hold over, shelve, suspend, stay; reschedule, put over, push back, table; *informal* put on ice, back-burner, put on the back burner, put in cold storage. See note at POSTPONE. ANTONYM advance.

▸ noun 1 *drivers will face lengthy delays* HOLDUP, wait, detainment; hindrance, impediment, obstruction, setback.

2 *the delay of his trial* POSTPONEMENT, deferral, deferment, stay, respite; adjournment.

3 *I set off without delay* PROCRASTINATION, stalling, hesitation, dithering, dallying, lollygagging, dawdling.

delectable adjective 1 *a delectable meal* DELICIOUS, mouthwatering, appetizing, flavorful, toothsome, palatable; succulent, luscious, tasty; *informal* scrumptious, delish, yummy, finger-licking, lip-smacking, melt-in-your-mouth. ANTONYM unpalatable.

2 *the delectable Ms. Davis* DELIGHTFUL, pleasant, lovely, captivating, charming, enchanting, appealing, beguiling; beautiful, attractive, ravishing, gorgeous, stunning, allur-

ing, sexy, seductive, desirable, luscious; *informal* divine, heavenly, dreamy. ANTONYM unattractive.

delectation noun *chiefly humorous they had all manner of goodies for our delectation* ENJOYMENT, gratification, delight, pleasure, satisfaction, relish; entertainment, amusement, titillation.

delegate noun *union delegates* REPRESENTATIVE, envoy, emissary, commissioner, agent, deputy, commissary; spokesperson, spokesman, spokeswoman; ambassador, plenipotentiary.

▸ verb **1** *she must delegate routine tasks* ASSIGN, entrust, pass on, hand on/over, turn over, devolve, depute, transfer.

2 *they were delegated to negotiate with the Slavs* AUTHORIZE, commission, depute, appoint, nominate, mandate, empower, charge, choose, designate, elect.

delegation noun **1** *the delegation from South Africa* DEPUTATION, legation, mission, diplomatic mission, commission; delegates, representatives, envoys, emissaries, deputies; contingent.

2 *the delegation of tasks to others* ASSIGNMENT, entrusting, giving, devolution, deputation, transference.

delete verb *the offending paragraph was deleted* REMOVE, cut out, take out, edit out, expunge, excise, eradicate, cancel; cross out, strike out, blue-pencil, ink out, scratch out, obliterate, white out; rub out, erase, efface, wipe out, blot out; *Printing* dele. ANTONYM add.

deleterious adjective *the deleterious effects of smoking* HARMFUL, damaging, detrimental, injurious; adverse, disadvantageous, unfavorable, unfortunate, undesirable, bad. ANTONYM beneficial.

deliberate adjective **1** *a deliberate attempt to provoke him* INTENTIONAL, calculated, conscious, intended, planned, studied, knowing, willful, purposeful, purposive, premeditated, preplanned; voluntary, volitional. ANTONYMS accidental, unintentional.

2 *small, deliberate steps* CAREFUL, cautious; measured, regular, even, steady. ANTONYM hasty.

3 *a deliberate worker* METHODICAL, systematic, careful, painstaking, meticulous, thorough. ANTONYM careless.

▸ verb *she* ***deliberated on*** *his words* THINK ABOUT/OVER, ponder, consider, contemplate, reflect on, muse on, meditate on, ruminate on, mull over, give thought to, brood over, dwell on, think on.

deliberately adverb **1** *he deliberately hurt me* INTENTIONALLY, on purpose, purposely, by design, knowingly, wittingly, consciously, purposefully; willfully; *Law* with malice aforethought.

2 *he walked deliberately down the aisle* CAREFULLY, cautiously, slowly, steadily, evenly.

deliberation noun **1** *after much deliberation, I accepted* THOUGHT, consideration, reflection, contemplation, meditation, rumination; *formal* cogitation.

2 *he replaced the glass with deliberation* CARE, carefulness, caution, steadiness.

delicacy noun **1** *the fabric's delicacy* FINENESS, exquisiteness, daintiness, airiness; flimsiness, gauziness, silkiness.

2 *the children's delicacy* SICKLINESS, ill health, frailty, fragility, weakness, debility; infirmity, valetudinarianism.

3 *the delicacy of the situation* DIFFICULTY, trickiness; sensitivity, ticklishness, awkwardness.

4 *treat this matter with delicacy* CARE, sensitivity, tact, discretion, diplomacy, subtlety, sensibility.

5 *an Australian delicacy* CHOICE FOOD, gourmet food, treat, luxury, specialty.

delicate adjective **1** *delicate embroidery* FINE, exquisite, intricate, dainty; flimsy, gauzy, filmy, floaty, diaphanous, wispy, insubstantial. ANTONYMS coarse, crude.

2 *a delicate shade of blue* SUBTLE, soft, muted; pastel, pale, light. ANTONYMS bold, lurid, vibrant.

3 *delicate china cups* FRAGILE, breakable, frail; *formal* frangible. ANTONYMS strong, durable.

4 *his wife is delicate* SICKLY, unhealthy, frail, feeble, weak, debilitated; unwell, infirm; *formal* valetudinarian. ANTONYMS strong, robust, healthy.

5 *a delicate issue* DIFFICULT, tricky, sensitive, ticklish, awkward, problematic, touchy, prickly, thorny; embarrassing; *informal* sticky, dicey.

6 *the matter required delicate handling* CAREFUL, sensitive, tactful, diplomatic, discreet, kid-glove. ANTONYMS inept, clumsy.

7 *his delicate palate* DISCRIMINATING, discerning; FASTIDIOUS, fussy, finicky, dainty; *informal* picky, choosy, persnickety.

8 *a delicate mechanism* SENSITIVE, precision, precise.

delicious adjective **1** *Ezio's delicious sausages* DELECTABLE, mouthwatering, appetizing, tasty, flavorful, toothsome, palatable; succulent, luscious; *informal* scrumptious, delish, yummy, finger-licking, nummy, lip-smacking, melt-in-your-mouth. ANTONYM unpalatable.

2 *a delicious languor stole over her* DELIGHTFUL, exquisite, lovely, pleasurable, pleasant; *informal* heavenly, divine. ANTONYM unpleasant.

delight verb **1** *her manners delighted him* PLEASE GREATLY, charm, enchant, captivate, entrance, thrill; gladden, gratify, appeal to; entertain, amuse, divert; *informal* send, tickle pink, bowl over. ANTONYMS dismay, disgust, displease.

2 *Meg* ***delighted in*** *his touch* TAKE PLEASURE IN, revel in, luxuriate in, wallow in, glory in; adore, love, relish, savor, lap up; *informal* get a kick out of, get a thrill out of, get a charge out of, dig. ANTONYMS loathe, dislike.

▸ noun *she squealed with delight* PLEASURE, happiness, joy, glee, gladness; excitement, amusement; bliss, rapture, elation, euphoria. ANTONYM displeasure.

delighted adjective *a delighted child | the Fitzgeralds were delighted with the kitchen remodeling* PLEASED, glad, happy, thrilled, overjoyed, ecstatic, elated; on cloud nine, walking on air, in seventh heaven, jumping for joy; enchanted, charmed; amused, diverted; gleeful; *informal* over the moon, tickled pink, as pleased as punch, on top of the world, blissed out, on a high.

delightful adjective **1** *a delightful evening* PLEASANT, lovely, pleasurable, enjoyable; amusing, entertaining, diverting; gratifying, satisfying; marvelous, wonderful, splendid, sublime, thrilling; *informal* great, super, fabulous, fab, terrific, heavenly, divine, grand, brilliant, peachy, ducky.

2 *the delightful Sally* CHARMING, enchanting, captivating, bewitching, appealing; sweet, endearing, cute, lovely, adorable, delectable, delicious, gorgeous, ravishing, beautiful, pretty; *informal* dreamy, divine.

delimit verb *their responsibilities will be more strictly delimited* DETERMINE, establish, set, fix, demarcate, define, delineate.

delineate verb **1** *the aims of the study as delineated by the boss* DESCRIBE, set forth/out, present, outline, sketch, depict, represent; map out, define, specify, identify.

2 *a section delineated in red pen* OUTLINE, trace, block in, mark (out/off), delimit.

delinquency noun **1** *teenage delinquency* CRIME, wrongdoing, lawbreaking, lawlessness, misconduct, misbehavior; misdemeanors, offenses, misdeeds.

2 *formal grave delinquency on the host's part* NEGLIGENCE, dereliction of duty, irresponsibility.

delinquent adjective **1** *delinquent teenagers* LAWLESS, lawbreaking, criminal; errant, badly behaved, troublesome, difficult, unruly, disobedient, uncontrollable. ANTONYM well-behaved.

2 *formal delinquent parents face tough penalties* NEGLIGENT, neglectful, remiss, irresponsible, lax, slack, derelict. ANTONYM dutiful.

▸ noun *young delinquents* OFFENDER, wrongdoer, malefactor, lawbreaker, culprit, criminal; hooligan, vandal, mischief-maker, ruffian, hoodlum, lowlife, punk; young offender.

delirious adjective **1** *she was delirious but had lucid intervals* INCOHERENT, raving, babbling, irrational; feverish, frenzied; deranged, demented, unhinged, mad, insane, out of one's mind.

2 *the crowd was delirious during the concert* ECSTATIC, euphoric, elated, thrilled, overjoyed, beside oneself, walking on air, on cloud nine, in seventh heaven, carried away, transported, rapturous; hysterical, wild, frenzied; *informal* blissed out, over the moon, on a high.

delirium noun **1** *she had fits of delirium* DERANGEMENT, dementia, madness, insanity; incoherence, irrationality, hysteria, feverishness, hallucination. ANTONYM lucidity.

2 *the delirium of desire* ECSTASY, rapture, transports, wild emotion, passion, wildness, excitement, frenzy, feverishness, fever; euphoria, elation.

deliver verb **1** *the parcel was delivered to his house* BRING, take, convey, carry, transport, courier; send, dispatch, remit.

2 *the money was* ***delivered up*** *to the official* HAND OVER, turn over, make over, sign over; surrender, give up, yield, cede; consign, commit, entrust, trust.

3 *he was delivered from his enemies* SAVE, rescue, free, liberate, release, extricate, emancipate, redeem.

4 *the court delivered its verdict* UTTER, give, make, read, broadcast; pronounce, announce, declare, proclaim, hand down, return, set forth.

5 *she delivered a deadly blow to his head* ADMINISTER, deal, inflict, give; *informal* land.

6 *he delivered the ball* THROW, pitch, hurl, launch, cast, lob, aim.

7 *the trip delivered everything she wanted* PROVIDE, supply, furnish.

8 *we must* ***deliver on*** *our commitments* FULFILL, live up to, carry out, carry through, make good on.

9 *she returned home to deliver her child* GIVE BIRTH TO, bear, have, bring into the world, birth; *informal* drop; *dated* be delivered of.

deliverance noun **1** *their deliverance from prison* LIBERATION, release, delivery, discharge, rescue, emancipation; salvation; *informal* bailout.

2 *the tone he adopted for such deliverances* UTTERANCE, statement, announcement, pronouncement, declaration, proclamation; lecture, speech.

delivery noun **1** *the delivery of the goods* CONVEYANCE, carriage, transportation, transport, distribution; dispatch, remittance; haulage, shipment.

2 *we get several deliveries a day* CONSIGNMENT, load, shipment.

3 *the midwife had assisted at four deliveries* BIRTH, childbirth; *formal* parturition.

4 *her delivery was stilted* SPEECH, pronunciation, enunciation, articulation, elocution; utterance, recitation, recital, execution.

delude verb *Arthur's children were convinced that his young bride was deluding him* MISLEAD, deceive, fool, take in, trick, dupe, hoodwink, gull, lead on; *informal* con, pull the wool over someone's eyes, lead up the garden path, take for a ride, sucker, snooker.

deluge noun **1** *homes were swept away by the deluge* FLOOD, torrent, spate.

2 *the deluge turned the field into a swamp* DOWNPOUR, torrential rain; thunderstorm, thundershower, rainstorm, cloudburst.

3 *a deluge of complaints* BARRAGE, volley; flood, torrent, avalanche, stream, spate, rush, outpouring, niagara.

▸ verb **1** *homes were deluged by the rains* FLOOD, inundate, submerge, swamp, drown.

2 *we have been deluged with calls* INUNDATE, overwhelm, overrun, flood, swamp, snow under, engulf, bombard.

delusion noun *was her belief in his fidelity just a delusion?* MISAPPREHENSION, misconception, misunderstanding, mistake, error, misinterpretation, misconstruction, misbelief; fallacy, illusion, fantasy.

deluxe adjective *deluxe accommodations* LUXURIOUS, luxury, sumptuous, palatial, opulent, lavish; grand, high-class, quality, exclusive, choice, fancy; expensive, costly, upscale, upmarket; high-end, top-line, top-notch, five-star; *informal* plush, posh, classy, ritzy, swanky, pricey, swank. ANTONYMS basic, cheap.

delve verb **1** *she* ***delved into*** *her pocket* RUMMAGE (AROUND/ABOUT) IN, search, hunt in, scrabble around in, root around/about in, ferret (about/around) in, fish about/around in, dig into/in; go through, rifle through.

2 *we must* ***delve into*** *the matter more deeply* INVESTIGATE, inquire into, probe, explore, research, look into, go into.

demagogue noun *he was drawn into a circle of campus demagogues* RABBLE-ROUSER, agitator, political agitator, soapbox orator, firebrand, fomenter, provocateur.

demand noun **1** *I gave in to her demands* REQUEST, call, command, order, dictate, ultimatum, stipulation.

2 *the demands of a young family* REQUIREMENT, need, desire, wish, want; claim, imposition.

3 *there is a big demand for such toys* MARKET, call, appetite, desire.

▸ verb 1 *workers demanded wage increases* CALL FOR, ask for, request, push for, hold out for; insist on, claim.

2 *Harvey demanded that I tell him the truth* ORDER, command, enjoin, urge; *literary* bid.

3 *"Where is she?" he demanded* ASK, inquire, question, interrogate; challenge.

4 *an activity demanding detailed knowledge* REQUIRE, need, necessitate, call for, involve, entail.

5 *they demanded complete anonymity* INSIST ON, stipulate, make a condition of; expect, look for.

PHRASE: **in demand** *the clerk at Buchanan's said that red kitchen accessories were suddenly in demand* SOUGHT-AFTER, desired, coveted, wanted, requested; marketable, desirable, popular, all the rage, at a premium, big, trendy, hot.

demanding adjective 1 *a demanding task* DIFFICULT, challenging, taxing, exacting, tough, hard, onerous, burdensome, formidable; arduous, uphill, rigorous, grueling, back-breaking, punishing. ANTONYMS easy, effortless.

2 *a demanding child* NAGGING, clamorous, importunate, insistent; trying, tiresome, hard to please; *informal* high-maintenance. ANTONYM easygoing.

demarcate verb *the building lots were demarcated with stakes and orange tape* SEPARATE, divide, mark (out/off), delimit, delineate; bound.

demarcation noun 1 *clear demarcation of function* SEPARATION, distinction, differentiation, division, delimitation, definition.

2 *territorial demarcations* BOUNDARY, border, borderline, frontier; dividing line, divide.

demean verb *such actions demean him in the eyes of the public* DEBASE, lower, degrade, discredit, devalue; cheapen, abase, humble, humiliate, disgrace, dishonor. See note at HUMBLE. ANTONYM dignify.

demeaning adjective *a demeaning experience* DEGRADING, humiliating, shameful, mortifying, abject, ignominious, undignified, inglorious.

demeanor noun *his normally calm demeanor* MANNER, air, attitude, appearance, look; bearing, carriage; behavior, conduct; *formal* comportment.

demented adjective *many of her patients were too demented to benefit from group therapy* MAD, insane, deranged, out of one's mind, crazed, lunatic, unbalanced, unhinged, disturbed, non compos mentis; *informal* crazy, mental, psycho, off one's rocker, nutty, around the bend, raving mad, batty, cuckoo, loopy, loony, bananas, screwy, touched, gaga, not all there, out to lunch, bonkers, crackers, cracked, buggy, nutso, squirrelly, wacko. ANTONYM sane.

dementia noun *her failing memory is not necessarily a symptom of dementia* MENTAL ILLNESS, madness, insanity, derangement, lunacy.

demise noun 1 *her tragic demise* DEATH, dying, passing, loss of life, end, quietus; *formal* decease; *archaic* expiry. ANTONYM birth.

2 *the demise of the Ottoman empire* END, breakup, disintegration, fall, downfall, collapse. ANTONYM start.

demobilize verb *the troops were demobilized* DISBAND, decommission, discharge, demilitarize; *informal* demob.

democracy noun *a democracy in Iraq is quite unlikely for now or any time soon* REPRESENTATIVE GOVERNMENT, elective government; self-government, government by the people; republic, commonwealth. ANTONYM dictatorship.

democratic adjective *a young democratic government* ELECTED, representative, popular, parliamentary; egalitarian, classless; self-governing, autonomous, republican.

demolish verb 1 *they demolished the building* KNOCK DOWN, pull down, tear down, bring down, destroy, flatten, raze (to the ground), level, bulldoze, topple; blow up; dismantle, disassemble. See note at DESTROY. ANTONYM construct.

2 *he demolished her credibility* DESTROY, ruin, wreck; refute, disprove, discredit, overturn, explode; *informal* poke holes in. ANTONYMS confirm, strengthen.

3 *informal our team was demolished.* See TROUNCE.

4 *informal she demolished a bagel.* See DEVOUR sense 1.

demon noun 1 *the demons from hell* DEVIL, fiend, evil spirit; incubus, succubus. ANTONYM angel.

2 *the man was a demon* MONSTER, ogre, fiend, devil, brute, savage, beast, barbarian, animal. ANTONYM saint.

3 *she's a demon on the tennis court* PRO, ace, expert, genius, master, virtuoso, maestro, past master, marvel; star; *informal* hotshot, whiz, buff.

4 *the demon of creativity.* See DAEMON.

demonic, demoniac adjective 1 *demonic powers* DEVILISH, fiendish, diabolical, satanic, Mephistophelean, hellish, infernal; evil, wicked.

2 *the demonic intensity of his playing* FRENZIED, wild, feverish, frenetic, frantic, furious, manic, like one possessed.

demonstrable adjective *the demonstrable links between French and American art* VERIFIABLE, provable, attestable; verified, proven, confirmed; obvious, clear, clear-cut, evident, apparent, manifest, patent, distinct, noticeable; unmistakable, undeniable.

demonstrate verb 1 *his findings demonstrate that boys commit more crimes than girls* SHOW, indicate, determine, establish, prove, confirm, verify, corroborate, substantiate.

2 *she was asked to demonstrate quilting* GIVE A DEMONSTRATION OF, show how something is done; display, show, illustrate, exemplify, demo.

3 *his work demonstrated an analytical ability* REVEAL, bespeak, indicate, signify, signal, denote, show, display, exhibit; bear witness to, testify to; imply, intimate, give away.

4 *they demonstrated against the government* PROTEST, rally, march; stage a sit-in, picket, strike, walk out; mutiny, rebel.

demonstration noun 1 *a dubious demonstration of God's existence* PROOF, substantiation, confirmation, affirmation, corroboration, verification, validation; evidence, indication, witness, testament.

2 *a demonstration of woodcarving* EXHIBITION, presentation, display, exposition, teach-in, demo, expo.

3 *his paintings are a demonstration of his talent* MANIFESTATION, indication, sign, mark, token, embodiment; expression.

4 *an anti-racism demonstration* PROTEST, march, rally, lobby, sit-in; stoppage, strike, walkout, picket (line); *informal* demo.

demonstrative adjective **1** *a very demonstrative family* EXPRESSIVE, open, forthcoming, communicative, unreserved, emotional, effusive, gushing; affectionate, cuddly, loving, warm, friendly, approachable; *informal* touchy-feely, lovey-dovey, huggy. ANTONYM reserved.

2 *the successes are demonstrative of their skill* INDICATIVE, suggestive, illustrative.

3 *demonstrative evidence of his theorem* CONVINCING, definite, positive, telling, conclusive, certain, decisive; incontrovertible, irrefutable, undeniable, indisputable, unassailable. ANTONYM inconclusive.

demoralize verb *the celebratory fuss made about young Browning's promotion has demoralized many of the older employees* DISHEARTEN, dispirit, deject, cast down, depress, dismay, daunt, discourage, unman, unnerve, crush, shake, throw, cow, subdue; break someone's spirit, knock the stuffing out of. ANTONYM hearten.

demoralized adjective *the demoralized army broke and fled* DISPIRITED, disheartened, downhearted, dejected, downcast, low, depressed, despairing; disconsolate, crestfallen, disappointed, dismayed, daunted, discouraged; crushed, humbled, subdued.

demote verb *Calvin was demoted to second lieutenant* DOWNGRADE, relegate, declass, reduce in rank; depose, unseat, displace, oust; *Military* cashier. ANTONYM promote.

demotic adjective *Knox picked up her demotic style of writing when she worked for a newspaper in Madison* POPULAR, vernacular, colloquial, idiomatic, vulgar, common; informal, everyday, slangy. ANTONYM formal.

demur verb *Steve demurred when the suggestion was made* OBJECT, take exception, take issue, protest, cavil, dissent; voice reservations, be unwilling, be reluctant, balk, think twice; drag one's heels, refuse; *informal* boggle, kick up a fuss.

▸ noun *they accepted without demur* OBJECTION, protest, protestation, complaint, dispute, dissent, opposition, resistance; reservation, hesitation, reluctance, disinclination; doubts, qualms, misgivings, second thoughts; a murmur, a word. See note at QUALMS.

demure adjective *a demure Victorian miss* MODEST, unassuming, meek, mild, reserved, retiring, quiet, shy, bashful, diffident, reticent, timid, shrinking, coy; decorous, decent, seemly, ladylike, respectable, proper, virtuous, pure, innocent, chaste; sober, sedate, staid, prim, goody-goody, straitlaced. ANTONYM brazen.

den noun **1** *the mink left its den* LAIR, set, earth, burrow, hole, dugout, covert, shelter, hiding place, hideout.

2 *a notorious drinking den* HAUNT, site, nest, pit, hole; hotbed; *informal* joint, dive.

3 *he scribbled a letter in his den* STUDY, studio, library; family room, living room; sanctum, retreat, sanctuary, hideaway.

denial noun **1** *the reports met with a denial* CONTRADICTION, refutation, rebuttal, repudiation, disclaimer; negation, dissent.

2 *the denial of insurance to certain people* REFUSAL, withholding; rejection, rebuff, repulse, veto, turndown; *formal* declination.

3 *the denial of worldly values* RENUNCIATION, eschewal, repudiation, disavowal, rejection, abandonment, surrender, relinquishment.

denigrate verb *it amused him to denigrate his guests* DISPARAGE, belittle, deprecate, decry, cast aspersions on, criticize, attack; speak ill of, give someone a bad name, defame, slander, libel; run down, abuse, insult, revile, malign, vilify, slur; *informal* badmouth, dis, pull to pieces. ANTONYM extol.

denizen noun *formal the denizens of Grant's Hollow were a quirky lot* INHABITANT, resident, townsman, townswoman, native, local; occupier, occupant, dweller; *archaic* burgher.

denominate verb *formal it's a technique denominated 'threading the needle'* CALL, name, term, designate, style, dub, label, tag, entitle.

denomination noun **1** *a Christian denomination* RELIGIOUS GROUP, sect, cult, movement, body, branch, persuasion, order, school; church.

2 *they demanded bills in small denominations* VALUE, unit, size.

denote verb **1** *the headdresses denoted warriors* DESIGNATE, indicate, be a mark of, signify, signal, symbolize, represent, mean; typify, characterize, distinguish, mark, identify.

2 *his manner denoted an inner strength* SUGGEST, point to, smack of, indicate, show, reveal, intimate, imply, convey, betray, bespeak, spell. See note at CONNOTE.

denouement noun **1** *the film's denouement* FINALE, final scene, epilogue, coda, end, ending, finish, close; culmination, climax, conclusion, resolution, solution. ANTONYM beginning.

2 *the debate had an unexpected denouement* OUTCOME, upshot, consequence, result, end; *informal* payoff. ANTONYM origin.

denounce verb **1** *the Pope denounced abortion* CONDEMN, criticize, attack, censure, decry, revile, vilify, discredit, damn, reject; proscribe; malign, rail against, run down, slur; *informal* knock, slam, hit out at, lay into; *formal* castigate. ANTONYM praise.

2 *he was denounced as a traitor* EXPOSE, betray, inform on; incriminate, implicate, cite, name, accuse.

dense adjective **1** *a dense forest* THICK, close-packed, tightly packed, closely set, close-set, crowded, crammed, compact, solid, tight; overgrown, jungly, impenetrable, impassable. ANTONYM sparse.

2 *dense smoke* THICK, heavy, opaque, soupy, murky, smoggy; concentrated, condensed. ANTONYMS thin, light.

3 *informal they were dense enough to believe me* STUPID, unintelligent, ignorant, brainless, mindless, foolish, slow, witless, simpleminded, empty-headed, vacuous, vapid, idiotic, imbecilic; *informal* thick, dim, moronic, dumb, dopey, dozy, wooden-headed, lamebrained, birdbrained, pea-brained; daft. See note at STUPID. ANTONYM clever.

density noun *a loss of bone density* SOLIDITY, solidness, denseness, thickness, substance, mass; compactness, tightness, hardness.

dent noun **1** *I made a dent in his car* INDENTATION, dimple, dip, depression, hollow, crater, pit, trough.

2 *a nasty dent in their finances* REDUCTION, depletion, deduction, cut. ANTONYM increase.

▸ verb 1 *Jamie dented his bike* INDENT, mark, ding.

2 *the experience dented her confidence* DIMINISH, reduce, lessen, shrink, weaken, erode, undermine, sap, shake, damage, impair.

dentist noun *the dentist recommended extraction of the wisdom teeth* DENTAL SURGEON, orthodontist, periodontist.

denude verb *the autumn winds denude the maples, reminding us of the starkness of winter* STRIP, clear, deprive, bereave, rob; lay bare, uncover, expose; deforest, defoliate; *dated* divest. ANTONYM cover.

deny verb 1 *the report was denied by witnesses* CONTRADICT, controvert, repudiate, challenge, counter, contest, oppose, rebut; *informal* poke holes in; *formal* gainsay. ANTONYM confirm.

2 *he denied the request* REFUSE, turn down, reject, rebuff, repulse, decline, veto, dismiss; *informal* give the thumbs down to, give the red light to, nix. ANTONYM accept.

3 *she had to deny her parents* RENOUNCE, eschew, repudiate, disavow, disown, wash one's hands of, reject, discard, cast aside, abandon, give up; *formal* forswear; *literary* forsake.

deodorant noun *an underarm deodorant* ANTIPERSPIRANT, body spray, perfume, scent; *informal* roll-on.

deodorize verb *sewage waters deodorized without chemicals* FRESHEN, sweeten, purify, disinfect, sanitize, sterilize; fumigate, aerate, air, ventilate.

depart verb 1 *James departed after lunch* LEAVE, go (away), withdraw, absent oneself, abstract oneself, quit, exit, decamp, retreat, retire; make off, run off/away; set off/out, get underway, be on one's way; *informal* make tracks, clear off/out, take off, split. ANTONYM arrive.

2 *the budget departed from the norm* DEVIATE, diverge, digress, drift, stray, veer; differ, vary.

departed adjective *her dear departed father* DEAD, expired, gone, no more, passed on/away; perished, fallen; *informal* six feet under, pushing up daisies; *formal* deceased; with God, asleep.

department noun 1 *the public health department* DIVISION, section, sector, unit, branch, arm, wing; office, bureau, agency, ministry.

2 *the food is Kay's department* DOMAIN, territory, province, area, line; responsibility, duty, function, business, affair, charge, task, concern; *informal* baby, bag, bailiwick.

departure noun 1 *he tried to delay her departure* LEAVING, going, leave-taking, withdrawal, exit, egress, retreat.

2 *a departure from the norm* DEVIATION, divergence, digression, shift; variation, change.

3 *an exciting departure for filmmakers* CHANGE, innovation, novelty, rarity.

depend verb 1 *her career **depends on** a good reference* BE CONTINGENT ON, be conditional on, be dependent on, hinge on, hang on, rest on, rely on; be decided by.

2 *my family **depends on** me* RELY ON, lean on; count on, bank on, trust (in), have faith in, believe in; pin one's hopes on.

dependable adjective *a dependable worker* RELIABLE, trustworthy, trusty, faithful, loyal, unfailing, sure, steadfast, stable; honorable, sensible, responsible.

dependence noun See DEPENDENCY.

dependency noun 1 *her **dependency on** her husband* DEPENDENCE ON, reliance on; need for.

2 *the association of retirement with dependency* HELPLESSNESS, dependence, weakness, defenselessness, vulnerability. ANTONYM independence.

3 *drug dependency* ADDICTION, dependence, reliance; craving, compulsion, fixation, obsession; abuse.

dependent adjective 1 *your placement is **dependent on** her decision* CONDITIONAL ON, contingent on, based on; subject to, determined by, influenced by.

2 *the army is **dependent on** volunteers* RELIANT ON, relying on, counting on; sustained by.

3 *she is **dependent on** drugs* ADDICTED TO, reliant on; *informal* hooked on.

4 *he is ill and dependent* RELIANT, needy; helpless, weak, infirm, invalid, incapable; debilitated, disabled.

▸ noun *providing for his dependents* CHILD, minor; ward, charge, protégé; relative; (**dependents**) offspring, progeny.

depict verb 1 *the painting depicts the Last Supper* PORTRAY, represent, picture, illustrate, delineate, reproduce, render; draw, paint; *literary* limn.

2 *the process depicted by Darwin's theory* DESCRIBE, detail, relate; present, set forth, set out, outline, delineate; represent, portray, characterize.

depiction noun 1 *a depiction of Aphrodite* PICTURE, painting, portrait, drawing, sketch, study, illustration; image, likeness.

2 *the film's depiction of women* PORTRAYAL, representation, presentation, characterization.

deplete verb *the food supply has been depleted* EXHAUST, use up, consume, expend, drain, empty, milk; reduce, decrease, diminish; slim down, cut back. ANTONYM augment.

depletion noun *the depletion of our natural resources* EXHAUSTION, use, consumption, expenditure; reduction, decrease, diminution; impoverishment.

deplorable adjective 1 *your conduct is deplorable* DISGRACEFUL, shameful, dishonorable, unworthy, inexcusable, unpardonable, unforgivable; reprehensible, despicable, abominable, contemptible, execrable, heinous, beyond the pale. ANTONYM admirable.

2 *the garden is in a deplorable state* LAMENTABLE, regrettable, unfortunate, wretched, atrocious, awful, terrible, dreadful, diabolical; sorry, poor, inadequate; *informal* appalling, dire, abysmal, woeful, lousy; *formal* grievous. ANTONYM excellent.

deplore verb 1 *we deplore violence* ABHOR, find unacceptable, frown on, disapprove of, take a dim view of, take exception to; detest, despise; condemn, denounce. ANTONYMS applaud, admire.

2 *he deplored their lack of flair* REGRET, lament, mourn, rue, bemoan, bewail, complain about, grieve over, sigh over. ANTONYM applaud.

deploy verb 1 *forces were deployed at strategic points* POSITION, station, post, place, install, locate, situate, site, establish; base; distribute, dispose.

2 *she deployed all her skills* USE, utilize, employ, take advantage of, exploit; bring into service, call on, turn to, resort to.

deport verb **1** *they were fined and deported* EXPEL, banish, exile, transport, expatriate, extradite, repatriate; evict, oust, throw out; *informal* kick out, boot out, send packing. ANTONYM admit.

2 *archaic* *he deported himself with dignity.* See BEHAVE sense 1.

deportment noun *unprofessional deportment* BEHAVIOR, conduct, performance; manners, practices, actions.

depose verb **1** *the president was deposed* OVERTHROW, unseat, dethrone, topple, remove, supplant, displace; dismiss, oust, drum out, throw out, expel, eject; *informal* chuck out, boot out, get rid of, show someone the door.

2 *Law* *a witness deposed that he had seen me* SWEAR, testify, attest, assert, declare, claim.

deposit noun **1** *a thick deposit of ash* ACCUMULATION, sediment; layer, covering, coating, blanket.

2 *a copper deposit* SEAM, vein, lode, layer, stratum, bed, pipe.

3 *they paid a deposit* DOWN PAYMENT, advance payment, prepayment, installment, retainer, stake.

▸ verb **1** *she deposited her books on the table* PUT (DOWN), place, set (down), unload, rest; drop; *informal* dump, park, plonk, plunk.

2 *the silt deposited by floodwater* LEAVE (BEHIND), precipitate, dump; wash up, cast up.

3 *the gold was deposited at the bank* HOUSE, bank, store, stow, put away; *informal* stash, squirrel away.

deposition noun **1** *Law* *depositions from witnesses* STATEMENT, affidavit, attestation, affirmation, assertion; allegation, declaration; testimony, evidence; *rare* asseveration.

2 *the deposition of calcium* DEPOSITING, accumulation, buildup, precipitation.

depository noun *a book depository* REPOSITORY, cache, store, storeroom, storehouse, warehouse; vault, strongroom, safe, treasury; container, receptacle.

depot noun **1** *the bus depot* TERMINAL, terminus, station, garage; headquarters, base.

2 *an arms depot* STOREHOUSE, warehouse, store, repository, depository, cache; arsenal, magazine, armory, ammunition dump, drop-off.

deprave verb *young minds depraved by pornography* CORRUPT, lead astray, warp, subvert, pervert, debauch, debase, degrade, defile, sully, pollute.

depraved adjective *the depraved patrons of these sex shops* CORRUPT, perverted, deviant, degenerate, debased, immoral, unprincipled; debauched, dissolute, licentious, lecherous, prurient, indecent, sordid; wicked, sinful, vile, iniquitous, nefarious; *informal* warped, twisted, sick.

THE RIGHT WORD

There are many terms to describe the dark side of human nature. Someone who preys on young children would be considered **depraved**, a term that means totally immoral and implies a warped character or a twisted mind (*a depraved man who stole money from his own mother and eventually murdered her*). While *depraved* suggests an absolute condition, **degenerate** is a relative term that implies deterioration from a mental, moral, or physical standard (*her degenerate habits eventually led to her arrest for possession of drugs*). **Corrupt** also suggests a deterioration or loss of soundness, particularly through a destructive or contaminating influence. But unlike *depraved*, which usually applies to the lower end of the human spectrum, people in high positions are often referred to as *corrupt* (*a corrupt politician from a prominent family*). To say that someone or something is **debased** suggests a lowering in quality, value, dignity, or character (*debased by having to spend time in prison*). **Perverted** and **vile** are the strongest of these words describing lack of moral character. *Perverted* suggests a distortion of someone or something from what is right, natural, or true; in a moral sense, it means to use one's appetites or natural desires for other ends than those which are considered normal or natural (*a perverted individual who never should have been left alone with young children*). Most people find criminals who prey on either very old or very young victims to be **vile**, a more general term for whatever is loathsome, repulsive, or utterly despicable (*a vile killer who deserved the maximum sentence*).

depravity noun *the depravity of white slavers* CORRUPTION, vice, perversion, deviance, degeneracy, immorality, debauchery, dissipation, profligacy, licentiousness, lechery, prurience, obscenity, indecency; wickedness, sin, iniquity; *formal* turpitude.

deprecate verb **1** *the school deprecates this behavior* DEPLORE, abhor, disapprove of, frown on, take a dim view of, take exception to, detest, despise; criticize, censure. ANTONYMS praise, overrate.

2 *he deprecates the value of television.* See DEPRECIATE sense 3.

USAGE NOTE **deprecate, depreciate**

The first of these has increasingly encroached on the figurative senses of the second, while the second has retreated into financial contexts. *Deprecate* means "disapprove earnestly"—e.g.: "'Well,' he admitted, deprecatingly, 'one can't suppress one's natural instincts altogether; even if one's reason and self-interest are all the other way.'" (Dorothy L. Sayers, *Gaudy Night*; 1936)

Depreciate, transitively, means "belittle, disparage"; and intransitively, "fall in value" (used in reference to assets or investments).

The familiar phrase *self-deprecating* is, literally speaking, a virtual impossibility, except perhaps for those suffering from extreme neuroses. Thus *self-depreciating*, with *depreciate* in its transitive sense, has historically been viewed as the correct phrase—e.g.: "Sadly, Grizzard did not have the self-depreciating humor of a Jeff Foxworthy, the self-proclaimed redneck comedian." (*St. Louis Post-Dispatch*; July 25, 1996.)

Unfortunately, though, the form *self-deprecating*—despite its mistaken origins—is now 50 times as common in print as *self-depreciating*. Speakers of American English routinely use *self-deprecating*. However grudgingly, we must accord to it the status of standard English—e.g.: "He's smart, articulate, funny, alternately self-deprecating and proud of his success." (*Los Angeles Times*; Sept. 1, 1996.) **—BG**

deprecatory adjective **1** *deprecatory remarks* DISAPPROVING, censorious, critical, scathing, damning, condemnatory, denunciatory, disparaging, denigrating, derogatory, negative, unflattering; disdainful, derisive, snide.

2 *a deprecatory smile* APOLOGETIC, rueful, regretful, sorry, remorseful, contrite, penitent, repentant; shamefaced, sheepish.

depreciate verb **1** *these cars will depreciate quickly* DECREASE IN VALUE, lose value, fall in price.

2 *the decision to depreciate property* DEVALUE, cheapen, reduce, lower in price, mark down, discount.

3 *they depreciate the importance of art* BELITTLE, disparage, denigrate, decry, deprecate, underrate, undervalue, underestimate, diminish, trivialize; disdain, sneer at, scoff at, scorn; *informal* knock, badmouth, sell short, pooh-pooh. See note at DEPRECATE. ANTONYM overrate.

depreciation noun *we are concerned about the depreciation of residential properties* DEVALUATION, devaluing, decrease in value, lowering in value, reduction in value, cheapening, markdown, reduction; decline, downturn, downswing, drop, slump, plunge, tumble, nosedive, crash.

depredation noun *the depredation of the barbarian invasion* PLUNDERING, plunder, looting, pillaging, robbery; devastation, destruction, damage, rape; ravages, raids.

depress verb 1 *the news depressed him* SADDEN, dispirit, cast down, get down, dishearten, demoralize, crush, shake, desolate, weigh down, oppress; upset, distress, grieve, haunt, harrow; *informal* give someone the blues. ANTONYM cheer (up).

2 *new economic policies depressed sales* SLOW DOWN, reduce, lower, weaken, impair; limit, check, inhibit, restrict. ANTONYM encourage.

3 *foreign imports will depress domestic prices* REDUCE, lower, cut, cheapen, keep down, discount, deflate, depreciate, devalue, diminish, ax, slash. ANTONYM raise.

4 *depress each lever in turn* PRESS, push, hold down; thumb, tap; operate, activate. ANTONYM lift.

depressant noun *they were found guilty of drugging Jefferson's horse with depressants* SEDATIVE, tranquilizer, calmative, sleeping pill, soporific, opiate, hypnotic; *informal* downer, trank/tranq; *trademark* Valium; *Medicine* neuroleptic. ANTONYM stimulant.

depressed adjective 1 *he felt lonely and depressed* SAD, unhappy, miserable, gloomy, glum, melancholy, dejected, disconsolate, downhearted, downcast, down, despondent, dispirited, low, heavy-hearted, morose, dismal, desolate; tearful, upset; *informal* blue, down in the dumps, down in/at the mouth. ANTONYM cheerful.

2 *a depressed economy* WEAK, enervated, devitalized, impaired; inactive, flat, slow, slack, sluggish, stagnant. ANTONYM strong.

3 *depressed prices* REDUCED, low, cut, cheap, marked down, discounted, discount; *informal* slashed. ANTONYM inflated.

4 *a depressed part of town* POVERTY-STRICKEN, poor, disadvantaged, underprivileged, deprived, needy, distressed; run-down, slummy. ANTONYM prosperous.

5 *the removal of the tree left a depressed patch of ground* SUNKEN, hollow, concave, indented, recessed. ANTONYM raised.

WORD NOTE **depressed**

Surely this is one of the most overworked words in American English. Who isn't depressed? Maybe those who are *despondent, dispirited, dejected, disconsolate, downhearted,* or *filled with despair.* Not to mention the poor souls who are *under a cloud, down in the dumps,* or even *prostrate with grief.* The scholarly among us frequently suffer from *accidie,* those crossed in love normally feel *heartbroken,* and the spiritually injured know that they have a right to *sing the blues. Melancholy* or *wistful* always sounds rather attractive, and *forlorn* even more so. *Glum* possesses a no-nonsense bluntness, while the poetically *doleful* may easily grow disgustingly *lachrymose. Long-faced* suggests a temporary condition, but *morose* describes a personality type. The *mournful* tend to be a bit histrionic, while those with *sorrows* deserve our sympathy—unless they're *secret sorrows,* which are the purview of Byronic wanderers. The *listless* express their sadness physically, teenagers are *mopey,* and *cheerless* calls to mind a tawdry hotel room with a black rotary phone next to a spongy bed. *Woebegone* has been usurped, with slightly different spelling, by a town in Minnesota, just as haunted houses and February own all the rights to *gloomy.* But don't be *crestfallen:* The synonyms for *depressed* are many and nuanced. We should rouse ourselves from the *doldrums* and use more of them. —**MD**

depressing adjective 1 *depressing thoughts* UPSETTING, distressing, painful, heartbreaking; dismal, bleak, black, somber, gloomy, grave, unhappy, melancholy, sad; wretched, doleful; *informal* morbid, blue.

2 *a depressing room* GLOOMY, bleak, dreary, grim, drab, somber, dark, dingy, funereal, cheerless, joyless, comfortless, uninviting.

depression noun 1 *she seems to be suffering from depression* UNHAPPINESS, sadness, melancholy, melancholia, misery, sorrow, woe, gloom, despondency, low spirits, a heavy heart, despair, desolation, hopelessness; upset, tearfulness; *informal* the dumps, the doldrums, the blues, a funk, a blue funk; *Psychiatry* dysthymia, seasonal affective disorder, SAD.

2 *an economic depression* RECESSION, slump, decline, downturn, standstill; stagnation; the Great Depression; *Economics* stagflation.

3 *a depression in the ground* HOLLOW, indentation, dent, cavity, concavity, dip, pit, hole, sinkhole, trough, crater; basin, bowl.

deprivation noun 1 *unemployment and deprivation* POVERTY, impoverishment, penury, privation, hardship, destitution; need, want, distress, indigence, beggary, ruin; straitened circumstances. ANTONYM wealth.

2 *deprivation of political rights* DISPOSSESSION, withholding, withdrawal, removal, divestment, expropriation, seizure, confiscation; denial, forfeiture, loss; absence, lack. ANTONYM possession.

deprive verb *Adams was **deprived of** her civil rights* DISPOSSESS OF, strip of, divest of, relieve of, deny, rob of; cheat out of; *informal* do out of.

deprived adjective *society's deprived classes* DISADVANTAGED, underprivileged, poverty-stricken, impoverished, poor, destitute, needy, unable to make ends meet.

depth noun 1 *the depth of the caves* DEEPNESS, distance downward, distance inward; drop, vertical extent; *archaic* profundity. ANTONYM shallowness.

2 *the depth of his knowledge* EXTENT, range, scope, breadth, width; magnitude, scale, degree.

3 *her lack of depth* PROFUNDITY, deepness, wisdom, understanding, intelligence, sagacity, discernment, penetration, insight, astuteness, acumen, shrewdness; *formal* perspicuity. ANTONYM shallowness.

4 *a work of great depth* COMPLEXITY, intricacy; profundity, gravity, weight. ANTONYM triviality.

5 *depth of color* INTENSITY, richness, deepness, vividness, strength, brilliance.

6 **(depths)** *the depths of the sea* DEEPEST PART, bottom, floor, bed; abyss. ANTONYM surface.

PHRASE: **in depth** *choose one aspect of the case and investigate it in depth* THOROUGHLY, extensively, comprehensively, rigorously, exhaustively, completely, fully; meticulously, scrupulously, painstakingly.

deputation noun *a deputation on behalf of disabled veterans* DELEGATION, legation, commission, committee, mission, diplomatic mission; contingent, group, party.

depute verb **1** *he was deputed to handle negotiations.* See DESIGNATE sense 1.

2 *the judge deputed smaller cases to others.* See DELEGATE verb sense 1.

deputize verb **1** *he deputized them to keep order in his absence* APPOINT (AS A DEPUTY), designate, delegate, commission, charge, empower, enable.

2 *he* ***deputized for*** *the registrar* STAND IN FOR, sit in for, fill in for, cover for, substitute for, replace, take the place of, understudy for, be a locum for, relieve, take over for; hold down the fort for, act as, act on behalf of; *informal* sub for.

deputy noun *he handed over his duties to his deputy* SECOND, second-in-command, number two; substitute, stand-in, fill-in, relief, understudy, locum tenens; representative, proxy, agent, spokesperson; *informal* sidekick, locum.

▸ adjective *her deputy editor* ASSISTANT, substitute, stand-in, acting, reserve, fill-in, caretaker, temporary, provisional, stopgap, surrogate, interim; *informal* second-string.

deranged adjective *her deranged cousin has finally been locked up* INSANE, mad, disturbed, unbalanced, unhinged, unstable, irrational; crazed, demented, berserk, frenzied, lunatic, certifiable; non compos mentis; *informal* touched, crazy, wacko, mental, psycho. ANTONYM rational.

derelict adjective **1** *a derelict building* DILAPIDATED, ramshackle, run-down, tumbledown, in ruins, falling apart; rickety, creaky, deteriorating, crumbling; neglected, untended, gone to rack and ruin.

2 *a derelict airfield* DISUSED, abandoned, deserted, discarded, rejected, neglected, untended.

3 *he was derelict in his duty* NEGLIGENT, neglectful, remiss, lax, careless, sloppy, slipshod, slack, irresponsible, delinquent.

▸ noun *the derelicts who survive on the streets* TRAMP, vagrant, vagabond, down and out, homeless person, drifter; beggar, mendicant; outcast; *informal* bag lady, hobo, bum.

dereliction noun **1** *buildings were reclaimed from dereliction* DILAPIDATION, disrepair, deterioration, ruin, rack and ruin; abandonment, neglect, disuse.

2 *dereliction of duty* NEGLIGENCE, neglect, delinquency, failure; carelessness, laxity, sloppiness, slackness, irresponsibility; oversight, omission.

deride verb *the kid I used to deride in junior high is now my boss* RIDICULE, mock, scoff at, jibe at, make fun of, poke fun at, laugh at, hold up to ridicule, pillory; disdain, disparage, denigrate, dismiss, slight; sneer at, scorn, insult; *informal* knock, pooh-pooh. ANTONYM praise.

de rigueur adjective **1** *straight hair was de rigueur* FASHIONABLE, in fashion, in vogue, modish, up to date, up-to-the-minute, all the rage, du jour, trendy, with it.

2 *an address is de rigueur for business cards* CUSTOMARY, standard, conventional, normal, orthodox, usual, comme il faut; compulsory, necessary, essential; *informal* done.

derision noun *Quincy's memoirs incited the derision of his siblings* MOCKERY, ridicule, jeers, sneers, taunts; disdain, disparagement, denigration, disrespect, insults; scorn, contempt; lampooning, satire.

derisive adjective *shouting derisive comments* MOCKING, jeering, scoffing, teasing, derisory, snide, sneering; disdainful, scornful, contemptuous, taunting, insulting; scathing, sarcastic.

derisory adjective **1** *a derisory sum* INADEQUATE, insufficient, tiny, small; trifling, paltry, pitiful, miserly, miserable; negligible, token, nominal; ridiculous, laughable, ludicrous, preposterous, insulting; *informal* measly, stingy, lousy, pathetic, piddling, piffling, mingy.

2 *derisory calls from the crowd.* See DERISIVE.

derivation noun **1** *the derivation of theories from empirical observation* DERIVING, induction, deduction, inference; extraction, eliciting.

2 *the derivation of a word* ORIGIN, etymology, root, etymon, provenance, source; origination, beginning, foundation, basis, cause; development, evolution.

derivative adjective *her poetry was derivative* IMITATIVE, unoriginal, uninventive, unimaginative, uninspired; copied, plagiarized, plagiaristic, secondhand; trite, hackneyed, clichéd, stale, stock, banal; *informal* copycat, cribbed, old hat. ANTONYM original.

▸ noun *a derivative of opium* BY-PRODUCT, subsidiary product; spin-off.

derive verb **1** *he derives consolation from his poetry* OBTAIN, get, take, gain, acquire, procure, extract, attain, glean.

2 *"coffee"* ***derives from*** *the Turkish "kahveh"* ORIGINATE IN, stem from, descend from, spring from, be taken from.

3 *his fortune* ***derives from*** *real estate* ORIGINATE IN, be rooted in; stem from, come from, spring from, proceed from, issue from.

derogate verb *formal* **1** *his contribution was derogated by critics* DISPARAGE, denigrate, belittle, deprecate, deflate; decry, discredit, cast aspersions on, run down, criticize; defame, vilify, abuse, insult, attack, pour scorn on; *informal* drag through the mud, knock, slam, bash, badmouth, dis. ANTONYM praise.

2 *the act would* ***derogate from*** *the king's majesty* DETRACT FROM, devalue, diminish, reduce, lessen, depreciate; demean, cheapen. ANTONYMS improve, increase.

3 *behaviors that* ***derogate from*** *the norm* DEVIATE FROM, diverge from, depart from, digress from, stray from; differ from, vary from; conflict with, be incompatible with.

derogatory adjective *a derogatory remark* DISPARAGING, denigratory, deprecatory, disrespectful, demeaning; critical, pejorative, negative, unfavorable, uncomplimentary, unflattering, insulting; offensive, personal, abusive, rude, nasty, mean, hurtful; defamatory, slanderous, libelous; *informal* bitchy, catty. See note at OFFENSE. ANTONYM complimentary.

derring-do noun *dated, or humorous* *what Sir Bluebonnet lacks in physical stature, he hilariously makes up for in charisma and derring-do.* See SPUNK.

USAGE NOTE **derring-do**

Derring-do (= daring action) derives, according to the *Oxford English Dictionary*, from a "chain of misunderstandings and errors." Originally, the term was *dorryng do*, a verb phrase meaning "daring to do." A sixteenth-century misprint in the poetry of John Lydgate (ca. 1370–1450) made it *derrynge do*, which Spenser (1579) misunderstood and used as a noun phrase meaning "manhood, chivalry." Then Sir Walter Scott popularized the phrase in *Ivanhoe* (1820) with the spelling *derring-do*, and this has been settled spelling ever since. But because of its historical and modern associations with *daring*, writers often use the erroneous spelling *daring-do*—e.g.: "Instead, it is also called 'Flower Flange' and has more to do with flowers than fighting and daring-do [read *derring-do*]." (*Knoxville News-Sentinel*; Sept. 25, 1998.) **—BG**

descend verb **1** *the plane started descending* GO DOWN, come down; drop, fall, sink, dive, plummet, plunge, nosedive. ANTONYMS ascend, climb.

2 *she descended the stairs* CLIMB DOWN, go down, come down. ANTONYMS ascend, climb.

3 *the road descends to a village* SLOPE, dip, slant, go down, fall away.

4 *she saw Herb* ***descend from*** *the bus* ALIGHT FROM, disembark, get down from, get off, dismount. ANTONYMS climb aboard, board.

5 *they would not descend to such mean tricks* STOOP, lower oneself, demean oneself, debase oneself; resort, be reduced.

6 *the army descended into chaos* DEGENERATE, deteriorate, decline, sink, slide, fall.

7 *they* ***descended on*** *the fortress* COME IN FORCE ON/UPON, arrive in hordes on; attack, assail, assault, storm, invade, swoop (down) on, charge.

8 *he* ***is descended from*** *a Flemish family* BE A DESCENDANT OF, originate from, issue from, spring from, derive from.

9 *his estates descended to his son* BE HANDED DOWN, be passed down; be inherited by.

descendant noun *Leslie claims to be a descendant of Benjamin Franklin | the legacy left to her descendants* SUCCESSOR, scion; heir; **(descendants)** offspring, progeny, family, lineage; *Law* issue; *archaic* seed, fruit of one's loins. ANTONYM ancestor.

descent noun **1** *the plane began its descent* DIVE, drop; fall, pitch, nosedive.

2 *their descent of the mountain* DOWNWARD CLIMB.

3 *a steep descent* SLOPE, incline, dip, drop, gradient, declivity, slant; hill.

4 *his descent into alcoholism* DECLINE, slide, fall, degeneration, deterioration, regression.

5 *she is of Italian descent* ANCESTRY, parentage, ancestors, family, antecedents; extraction, origin, derivation, birth; lineage, line, genealogy, heredity, stock, pedigree, blood, bloodline; roots, origins.

6 *the descent of property* INHERITANCE, succession.

7 *the sudden descent of the cavalry* ATTACK, assault, raid, onslaught, charge, thrust, push, drive, incursion, foray.

describe verb **1** *he described his experiences* REPORT, recount, relate, tell of, set out, chronicle; detail, catalog, give a rundown of; explain, illustrate, discuss, comment on.

2 *she described him as a pathetic figure* DESIGNATE, pronounce, call, label, style, dub; characterize, class; portray, depict, brand, paint; *literary* limn.

3 *the pen described a circle* DELINEATE, mark out, outline, trace, draw.

WORD NOTE **limn**

This is the phoniest word in the critic's vocabulary, aside from *luminous* to describe a writer's prose (and usually rather gushy prose at that). People are unsure of *limn*'s pronunciation, uncertain of its actual meaning, and generally pretentious when they use it. Most of the time journalists resort to *limn* because they want something fancier than *describe*. Yet while *describe* slips smoothly by without calling much attention to itself, *limn* jumps off the page to strut about and show off. It's one of those words that want to be urbane and debonair, but are somehow really ugly, pushy, nouveau riche. But maybe I'm going out on a limb by saying that. So let's just call *limn* fundamentally, almost viscerally rebarbative. **—MD**

description noun **1** *a description of my travels* ACCOUNT, report, rendition, explanation, illustration; chronicle, narration, narrative, story, commentary; portrayal, portrait; details.

2 *the description of horse racing as "the sport of kings"* DESIGNATION, labeling, naming, dubbing, pronouncement; characterization, classification, branding; portrayal, depiction.

3 *vehicles of every description* SORT, variety, kind, type, category, order, breed, class, designation, specification, genre, genus, brand, make, character, ilk, stripe.

descriptive adjective *descriptive prose* ILLUSTRATIVE, expressive, graphic, detailed, lively, vivid, striking; explanatory, explicative.

descry verb *literary* See NOTICE verb. See also note at DISTINGUISH.

desecrate verb *invaders desecrated the temple* VIOLATE, profane, defile, debase, degrade, dishonor; vandalize, damage, destroy, deface.

desert[1] verb **1** *his wife deserted him* ABANDON, leave, turn one's back on; throw over, jilt, break up with; leave high and dry, leave in the lurch, leave behind, strand; *informal* walk out on, run out on, drop, dump, ditch; *literary* forsake.

2 *his allies were deserting the cause* RENOUNCE, repudiate, relinquish, wash one's hands of, abandon, turn one's back on, betray, disavow; *formal* abjure; *literary* forsake.

3 *soldiers deserted in droves* ABSCOND, defect, run away, make off, decamp, flee, turn tail, take French leave, depart, quit, jump ship; *Military* go AWOL.

desert[2] noun *an expanse of desert* WASTELAND, wastes, wilderness, wilds, barren land; dust bowl.

▸ adjective **1** *desert conditions* ARID, dry, moistureless, parched; scorched, hot; barren, bare, stark, infertile, unfruitful, dehydrated, sterile. ANTONYM fertile.

2 *an uncharted desert island* UNINHABITED, empty, lonely, desolate, bleak; wild, uncultivated.

deserted adjective **1** *a deserted wife* ABANDONED, thrown over, jilted, cast aside; neglected, stranded, marooned, forlorn, bereft; *informal* dumped, ditched, dropped; *literary* forsaken.

2 *a deserted village* EMPTY, uninhabited, unoccupied,

unpeopled, abandoned, evacuated, vacant; untenanted, tenantless, neglected; desolate, lonely, godforsaken. ANTONYM populous.

deserter noun *deserters were shot in full view of their fellow soldiers* ABSCONDER, runaway, fugitive, truant, escapee; renegade, defector, turncoat, traitor.

desertion noun **1** *McKinley's desertion of her family* ABANDONMENT, leaving, jilting.

2 *the desertion of the president's colleagues* DEFECTION; betrayal, renunciation, repudiation, apostasy; *formal* abjuration.

3 *soldiers were prosecuted for desertion* ABSCONDING, running away, truancy, going absent without leave, taking French leave, escape; defection, treason; *Military* going AWOL.

deserve verb *the book deserves our greatest praise* MERIT, earn, warrant, rate, justify, be worthy of, be entitled to, have a right to, be qualified for.

deserved adjective *they clinched a deserved victory* WELL-EARNED, merited, warranted, justified, justifiable; rightful, due, right, just, fair, fitting, appropriate, suitable, proper, apt; *archaic* meet.

deserving adjective **1** *the deserving workers* WORTHY, meritorious, commendable, praiseworthy, admirable, estimable, creditable; respectable, decent, honorable, righteous.

2 *a lapse deserving punishment* MERITING, warranting, justifying, suitable for, worthy of.

desiccated adjective *desiccated coconut* DRIED, dry, dehydrated, powdered. ANTONYM moist.

desideratum noun *integrity was a desideratum* REQUIREMENT, prerequisite, need, indispensable thing, sine qua non, essential, requisite, necessary.

design noun **1** *a design for the offices* PLAN, blueprint, drawing, sketch, outline, map, plot, diagram, draft, representation, scheme, model.

2 *tableware with a gold design* PATTERN, motif, device; style, composition, makeup, layout, construction, shape, form.

3 *his design of reaching the top* INTENTION, aim, purpose, plan, intent, objective, object, goal, end, target; hope, desire, wish, dream, aspiration, ambition.

▸ verb **1** *the church was designed by Hicks* PLAN, outline, map out, draft, draw.

2 *they designed a new engine* INVENT, originate, create, think up, come up with, devise, formulate, conceive; make, produce, develop, fashion; *informal* dream up.

3 *this paper is designed to provoke discussion* INTEND, aim; devise, contrive, purpose, plan; tailor, fashion, adapt, gear; mean, destine. See note at INTEND.

PHRASE: **by design** *things worked out more by accident than by design* DELIBERATELY, intentionally, on purpose, purposefully; knowingly, wittingly, consciously, calculatedly.

designate verb **1** *she designated her successor* APPOINT, nominate, depute, delegate; select, choose, pick, elect, name, identify, assign.

2 *the building was designated a historical site* CLASSIFY, class, label, tag; name, call, entitle, term, dub; *formal* denominate.

designation noun **1** *the designation of a leader* APPOINTMENT, nomination, naming, selection, election.

2 *the designation of wildlife preserves* CLASSIFICATION, specification, definition, earmarking, pinpointing.

3 *the designation "Generalissimo"* TITLE, name, epithet, tag; nickname, byname, sobriquet; *informal* moniker, handle; *formal* denomination, appellation.

designer noun **1** *a designer of office furniture* CREATOR, planner, deviser, inventor, originator; maker; architect, builder.

2 *young designers made the dress* COUTURIER, tailor, dressmaker.

designing adjective *he couldn't compete with the designing young executives he encountered in Washington* SCHEMING, calculating, conniving; cunning, crafty, artful, wily, devious, guileful, manipulative; treacherous, sly, underhanded, deceitful, double-dealing; *informal* crooked, foxy.

desirability noun **1** *the desirability of the property* APPEAL, attractiveness, allure; agreeableness, worth, excellence.

2 *they debated the desirability of gay marriage* ADVISABILITY, advantage, expedience, benefit, merit, value, profit, profitability.

3 *her obvious desirability* ATTRACTIVENESS, sexual attraction, beauty, good looks; charm, seductiveness; *informal* sexiness.

desirable adjective **1** *a desirable location* ATTRACTIVE, sought-after, in demand, popular, desired, covetable, coveted, enviable; appealing, agreeable, pleasant; valuable, good, excellent; *informal* to die for.

2 *it is desirable that they should meet* ADVANTAGEOUS, advisable, wise, sensible, recommendable; helpful, useful, beneficial, worthwhile, profitable, preferable. ANTONYM disadvantageous.

3 *a very desirable woman* SEXUALLY ATTRACTIVE, attractive, beautiful, pretty, appealing; seductive, alluring, enchanting, beguiling, captivating, bewitching, irresistible; *informal* sexy, beddable. ANTONYMS unattractive, ugly.

desire noun **1** *a desire to see the world* WISH, want, aspiration, fancy, inclination, impulse; yearning, longing, craving, hankering, hunger; eagerness, enthusiasm, determination; *informal* yen, itch, jones.

2 *his eyes glittered with desire* LUST, sexual attraction, passion, sensuality, sexuality; lasciviousness, lechery, salaciousness, libidinousness; *informal* the hots, raunchiness, horniness.

▸ verb **1** *they desired peace* WANT, wish for, long for, yearn for, crave, hanker after, be desperate for, be bent on, covet, aspire to; fancy; *informal* have a yen for, have a jones for, yen for, hanker after/for.

2 *she desired him* BE ATTRACTED TO, lust after, burn for, be infatuated by; *informal* fancy, have the hots for, have a crush on, be mad about, be crazy about.

desired adjective **1** *cut the cloth to the desired length* REQUIRED, necessary, proper, right, correct; appropriate, suitable; preferred, chosen, selected.

2 *the desired results* WISHED FOR, wanted, coveted; sought-after, longed for, yearned for; *informal* must-have.

desirous adjective *he was **desirous of** change* EAGER FOR, desiring, anxious for, keen for, craving, yearning for, longing for, hungry for; ambitious for, aspiring to; covetous of, envious of; *informal* dying for, itching for.

desist verb *manufacturers were ordered to* ***desist from*** *dumping chemicals in the river* ABSTAIN FROM, refrain from, forbear from, hold back from, keep from; stop, cease, discontinue, suspend, give up, break off, drop, dispense with, eschew; *informal* lay off, quit. ANTONYM continue.

desk noun *a new PC for each desk* WRITING TABLE, bureau, escritoire, secretaire, rolltop desk, carrel, workstation.

desolate adjective **1** *the desolate prairie* BLEAK, stark, bare, dismal, grim; wild, inhospitable; deserted, uninhabited, godforsaken, abandoned, unpeopled, untenanted, empty, barren; unfrequented, unvisited, isolated, remote. ANTONYM populous.

2 *the news of Rudolph's disappearance left them desolate* MISERABLE, despondent, depressed, disconsolate, devastated, despairing, inconsolable, broken-hearted, grief-stricken, crushed, bereft; sad, unhappy, downcast, down, dejected, forlorn, upset, distressed; *informal* blue, cut up. ANTONYM joyful.

▸ verb **1** *droughts desolated the plains* DEVASTATE, ravage, ruin, lay waste to; level, raze, demolish, wipe out, obliterate.

2 *she was desolated by the loss of her husband* DISHEARTEN, depress, sadden, cast down, make miserable, weigh down, crush, upset, distress, devastate; *informal* shatter.

desolation noun **1** *the desolation of the Gobi Desert* BLEAKNESS, starkness, barrenness, sterility; wildness; isolation, loneliness, remoteness. See note at SOLITUDE.

2 *a feeling of utter desolation* MISERY, sadness, unhappiness, despondency, sorrow, depression, grief, woe; broken-heartedness, wretchedness, dejection, devastation, despair, anguish, distress.

despair noun *let me help you during this time of your despair* HOPELESSNESS, disheartenment, discouragement, desperation, distress, anguish, unhappiness; despondency, depression, disconsolateness, melancholy, misery, wretchedness; defeatism, pessimism. ANTONYMS hope, joy.

▸ verb *don't despair if you can't find a job right away* LOSE HOPE, abandon hope, give up, lose heart, lose faith, be discouraged, be despondent, be demoralized, resign oneself; be pessimistic.

despairing adjective *a despairing look came over his face* HOPELESS, in despair, dejected, depressed, despondent, disconsolate, gloomy, miserable, wretched, desolate, inconsolable; disheartened, discouraged, demoralized, devastated, suicidal; defeatist, pessimistic.

desperado noun *dated a band of armed desperados* BANDIT, criminal, outlaw, lawbreaker, villain, renegade; robber, cutthroat, gangster, pirate.

desperate adjective **1** *a desperate look* DESPAIRING, hopeless; anguished, distressed, wretched, desolate, forlorn, distraught, fraught; out of one's mind, at one's wits' end, beside oneself, at the end of one's rope/tether.

2 *a desperate attempt to escape* LAST-DITCH, last-gasp, eleventh-hour, do-or-die, final; frantic, frenzied, wild; futile, hopeless, doomed.

3 *a desperate shortage of teachers* GRAVE, serious, critical, acute, risky, precarious; dire, awful, terrible, dreadful; urgent, pressing, crucial, vital, drastic, extreme; *informal* chronic.

4 *they were* ***desperate for*** *food* IN GREAT NEED OF, urgently requiring, in want of; eager for, longing for, yearning for, hungry for, crying out for; *informal* dying for.

5 *a desperate act* VIOLENT, dangerous, lawless; reckless, rash, hasty, impetuous, foolhardy, incautious, hazardous, risky; do-or-die.

desperately adverb **1** *he screamed desperately for help* IN DESPERATION, in despair, despairingly, in anguish, in distress; wretchedly, hopelessly, desolately, forlornly.

2 *they are desperately ill* SERIOUSLY, critically, gravely, severely, acutely, dangerously, perilously; very, extremely, dreadfully; hopelessly, irretrievably; *informal* terribly.

3 *he desperately wanted to talk* URGENTLY, pressingly; intensely, eagerly.

desperation noun *her family failed to see her state of desperation* HOPELESSNESS, despair, distress; anguish, agony, torment, misery, wretchedness; discouragement, disheartenment.

despicable adjective *despicable crimes* CONTEMPTIBLE, loathsome, hateful, detestable, reprehensible, abhorrent, abominable, awful, heinous; odious, vile, low, mean, abject, shameful, ignominious, shabby, ignoble, disreputable, discreditable, unworthy; *informal* dirty, rotten, lowdown, lousy; beastly; *archaic* scurvy. ANTONYM admirable.

despise verb *he despised weakness* DETEST, hate, loathe, abhor, execrate, deplore, dislike; scorn, disdain, look down on, deride, sneer at, revile; spurn, shun; *formal* abominate; *archaic or literary* contemn. ANTONYM adore.

THE RIGHT WORD

It's one thing to dislike someone; it's quite another to **despise** or **detest** the person. Both are strong words, used to describe extreme dislike or hatred. *Detest* is probably the purest expression of hatred (*she detested the woman who had raised her, and longed to find her own mother*), while *despise* suggests looking down with great contempt and regarding the person as mean, petty, weak, or worthless (*he despised men whose only concern was their own safety*). **Disdain** carries even stronger connotations of superiority, often combined with self-righteousness (*to disdain anyone lacking a college education*). **Scorn** is a stronger word for *disdain*, and it implies an attitude of not only contempt but of haughty rejection or refusal (*to scorn the woman he'd once loved*). To **loathe** something is to feel utter disgust toward it (*he grew to loathe peanut butter and jelly sandwiches*) and to **abhor** it is to feel a profound, shuddering, repugnance (*she abhorred the very idea of asking her husband for the money*). **Contemn** is a more literary word meaning to treat with disdain, scorn, or contempt.

despite preposition *despite his lack of enthusiasm, Zachary had a pretty good time* IN SPITE OF, notwithstanding, regardless of, in the face of, for all, even with.

despoil verb **1** *a village despoiled by invaders* PLUNDER, pillage, rob, ravage, raid, ransack, rape, loot, sack; devastate, lay waste, ruin. See note at RAVAGE.

2 *the thief despoiled him of all he had* ROB, strip, deprive, dispossess, denude, divest, relieve, clean out.

despoliation noun *the despoliation of the countryside*

PLUNDER, plundering, pillaging, looting, ransacking, ravishing, sacking; ravaging, devastation, ruination, vandalism.

USAGE NOTE **spoliation, despoliation**

A learned word, *spoliation* /spoh-lee-**ay**-shun/ means "the act of ruining, destroying, or spoiling something." In the hands and mouths of the less-than-learned, it's often misspelled and mispronounced *spoilation*. The difference between the form of the verb and of the noun arises from different paths by which the words came into English: in the fourteenth century, *spoil* was borrowed from Old French (*espoille*), whereas in the fifteenth century, *spoliation* was borrowed from Latin (*spoliātio*).

Despoliation (= pillaging, plundering) is often misspelled *despoilation*—a blunder that surprises primarily because it occurs in otherwise highly literate writing—e.g.: "The horrors of gulag and the environmental despoilations [read *despoliations*] of the Soviet era both get their due here." (*Washington Times*; Feb. 27, 1994.)

Oddly, though, the corresponding verb is *despoil*. Why the discrepancy in spelling? The answer again lies in the vagaries of linguistic history. English borrowed the verb in the thirteenth century from Old French (*despoillier*) but the noun in the seventeenth century from Latin (*despoliatio*). And those two forms—for centuries, at any rate—stuck. **—BG**

despondency noun *the despondency of the refugees was captured in this documentary* HOPELESSNESS, despair, discouragement, low spirits, wretchedness; melancholy, gloom, misery, desolation, disappointment, disheartenment, dejection, sadness, unhappiness; *informal* blues, heartache.

despondent adjective *they were tired and despondent* DISHEARTENED, discouraged, dispirited, downhearted, downcast, crestfallen, down, low, disconsolate, despairing, wretched; melancholy, gloomy, morose, dismal, woebegone, miserable, depressed, dejected, sad; *informal* blue, down in/at the mouth, down in the dumps. ANTONYMS hopeful, cheerful.

despot noun *when one despot is deposed for another, the cycle of repression continues* TYRANT, oppressor, dictator, absolute ruler, totalitarian, autocrat; *informal* slave driver.

despotic adjective *a despotic regime* AUTOCRATIC, dictatorial, totalitarian, absolutist, undemocratic, unaccountable; one-party, autarchic, monocratic; tyrannical, tyrannous, oppressive, repressive, draconian, illiberal. ANTONYM democratic.

destabilize verb *the security system has been destabilized* UNDERMINE, weaken, damage, subvert, sabotage, unsettle, upset, disrupt. ANTONYM strengthen.

destination noun *our original destination was Richmond* JOURNEY'S END, end of the line; terminus, stop, stopping place, port of call; goal, purpose, target, end.

destined adjective **1** *he is destined to lead a charmed life* FATED, ordained, predestined, meant; certain, sure, bound, assured, likely; doomed.

2 *computers destined for Pakistan* HEADING, bound, en route, scheduled; intended, meant, designed, designated, allotted, reserved.

destiny noun **1** *master of his own destiny* FUTURE, fate, fortune, doom; lot; *archaic* portion.

2 *she believed their meeting was destiny* FATE, providence; predestination; God's will, kismet, the stars; luck, fortune, chance; karma, serendipity.

destitute adjective **1** *she was left destitute* PENNILESS, poor, impoverished, poverty-stricken, impecunious, without a cent/penny (to one's name); needy, in straitened circumstances, distressed, badly off; *informal* hard up, broke, flat broke, strapped (for cash), without a red cent, dirt poor. ANTONYM rich.

2 *we were* ***destitute of*** *clothing* DEVOID OF, bereft of, deprived of, in need of; lacking, without, deficient in, wanting.

destroy verb **1** *their offices were destroyed by bombing* DEMOLISH, knock down, level, raze (to the ground), fell; wreck, ruin, shatter; blast, blow up, dynamite, explode, bomb. ANTONYMS build, reconstruct.

2 *the new highway would destroy the conservation area* SPOIL, ruin, wreck, disfigure, blight, mar, impair, deface, scar, injure, harm, devastate, damage, wreak havoc on; *informal* total. ANTONYMS restore, preserve.

3 *illness destroyed his career* WRECK, ruin, spoil, disrupt, undo, upset, put an end to, put a stop to, terminate, frustrate, blight, crush, quash, dash, scotch; devastate, demolish, scuttle, sabotage; *informal* mess up, foul up, put the kibosh on, fry, do for, blow a hole in; *archaic* bring to naught. ANTONYMS bolster, help.

4 *the horse had to be destroyed* KILL, put down, put to sleep, slaughter, terminate, exterminate, euthanize.

5 *we will destroy the enemy* ANNIHILATE, wipe out, obliterate, wipe off the face of the earth, eliminate, eradicate, liquidate, finish off, erase; kill, slaughter, massacre, exterminate; *informal* take out, rub out, snuff out, waste, fry, nuke, zap. ANTONYM spare.

THE RIGHT WORD

If you're interested in getting rid of something, you've got a number of options at your disposal. **Destroy** is a general term covering any force that wrecks, ruins, kills, etc. (*to destroy an ant hill by pouring boiling water on it*). If it's a building, you'll want to **demolish** or **raze** it, two words that are generally applied only to very large things. *Raze*is used almost exclusively with structures; it means to bring something down to the level of the ground (*they razed the apartment building to make way for the new hospital*). *Demolish* implies pulling or smashing something to pieces; when used with regard to buildings, it conjures up a vision of complete wreckage and often a heap of rubble (*their new house was demolished by the first hurricane of the season*). But unlike *raze*, *demolish* can also be applied to nonmaterial things (*to demolish the theory with a few simple experiments*). If you **eradicate** something, you eliminate it completely, literally or figuratively, pull it out by the roots (*to eradicate smallpox with a vaccine*) and prevent its reappearance. **Extirpate**, like *eradicate*, implies the utter destruction of something (*the species was extirpated from the park by the flooding*). If you're dealing with cockroaches, you'll probably want to **exterminate** them, which means to wipe out or kill in great numbers. Or better yet, you'll want to **annihilate** them, which is the most extreme word in this group and literally means to reduce to nothingness.

destruction noun **1** *the destruction by allied bombers* DEMOLITION, wrecking, ruination, blasting, bombing; wreckage, ruins.

2 *the destruction of the countryside* DEVASTATION, ruination, blighting, disfigurement, impairment, scarring, harm, desolation.

3 *the destruction of cattle* SLAUGHTER, killing, putting down, extermination, termination.

4 *the destruction of the enemies' forces* ANNIHILATION, obliteration, elimination, eradication, liquidation; killing, slaughter, massacre, extermination.

destructive adjective **1** *the most destructive war* DEVASTATING, ruinous, disastrous, catastrophic, calamitous, cataclysmic; harmful, damaging, detrimental, deleterious, injurious, crippling; violent, savage, fierce, brutal, deadly, lethal.

2 *destructive criticism* NEGATIVE, hostile, vicious, unfriendly; unhelpful, obstructive, discouraging.

desultory adjective *the desultory interest you have in your child's welfare is appalling* CASUAL, cursory, superficial, token, perfunctory, half-hearted, lukewarm; random, aimless, erratic, unmethodical, unsystematic, chaotic, inconsistent, irregular, intermittent, sporadic, fitful. ANTONYM keen.

WORD NOTE **desultory**

One of those not quite onomatopoeic words that nevertheless, syllable by syllable, conjure up a set of images that make their meaning unmistakable and vivid: *De* evoking *depressed, decadent, dead; sul* for *sullen, sulk, sullied; tor* for *torpid;* and *ry* for . . . well, for dragging the thing out needlessly and contributing to the general air of lassitude and half-heartedness that this word beautifully conveys. **—DA**

detach verb *he detached the lamp from its bracket* UNFASTEN, disconnect, disengage, separate, uncouple, remove, loose, unhitch, unhook, free, pull off, cut off, break off. ANTONYM attach.

PHRASE: **detach oneself from 1** *she detached herself from the crowd* FREE ONESELF FROM, separate oneself from, segregate oneself from; move away from, split off from; leave, abandon. **2** *he has detached himself from his family* DISSOCIATE ONESELF FROM, divorce oneself from, alienate oneself from, separate (oneself) from, segregate oneself from, isolate oneself from, cut oneself off from; break away from, disaffiliate oneself from, defect from; leave, quit, withdraw from, break with.

detached adjective **1** *a detached collar* UNFASTENED, disconnected, separated, separate, loosened; untied, unhitched, undone, unhooked, unbuttoned; free, severed, cut off.

2 *a detached observer* DISPASSIONATE, disinterested, objective, uninvolved, outside, neutral, unbiased, unprejudiced, impartial, nonpartisan; indifferent, aloof, remote, distant, impersonal; *informal* cool.

3 *a detached house* STANDING ALONE, separate.

detachment noun **1** *she looked on everything with detachment* OBJECTIVITY, dispassion, disinterest, open-mindedness, neutrality, impartiality; indifference, aloofness.

2 *a detachment of soldiers* UNIT, detail, squad, troop, contingent, outfit, task force, patrol, crew; platoon, company, corps, regiment, brigade, battalion.

3 *retinal detachment* LOOSENING, disconnection, disengagement, separation; removal.

detail noun **1** *the picture is correct in every detail* PARTICULAR, respect, feature, characteristic, attribute, specific, aspect, facet, part, unit, component, constituent; fact, piece of information, point, element, circumstance, consideration.

2 *that's just a detail* UNIMPORTANT POINT, trivial fact, triviality, technicality, nicety, subtlety, trifle, fine point, incidental, inessential, nothing.

3 *records with a considerable degree of detail* PRECISION, exactness, accuracy, thoroughness, carefulness, scrupulousness, particularity.

4 *a guard detail* UNIT, detachment, squad, troop, contingent, outfit, task force, patrol.

5 *I got kitchen detail* DUTY, task, job, chore, charge, responsibility, assignment, function, mission, engagement, occupation, undertaking, errand.

▸ verb **1** *the report details our objections* DESCRIBE, explain, expound, relate, catalog, list, spell out, itemize, particularize, identify, specify; state, declare, present, set out, frame; cite, quote, instance, mention, name.

2 *troops were detailed to prevent their escape* ASSIGN, allocate, appoint, delegate, commission, charge; send, post; nominate, vote, elect, co-opt.

PHRASE: **in detail** *this will be examined in detail in the next chapter* THOROUGHLY, in depth, exhaustively, minutely, closely, meticulously, rigorously, scrupulously, painstakingly, carefully; completely, comprehensively, fully, extensively.

detailed adjective *a detailed description of the assailants* COMPREHENSIVE, full, complete, thorough, exhaustive, all-inclusive; elaborate, minute, intricate; explicit, specific, precise, exact, accurate, meticulous, painstaking; itemized, blow-by-blow. ANTONYM general.

detain verb **1** *they were detained for questioning* HOLD, take into custody, take (in), confine, imprison, lock up, put in jail, intern; arrest, apprehend, seize; *informal* pick up, run in, haul in, nab, collar. ANTONYM release.

2 *don't let me detain you* DELAY, hold up, make late, keep, slow up/down; hinder, hamper, impede, obstruct.

detect verb **1** *no one detected the smell of gas* NOTICE, perceive, discern, be aware of, note, make out, spot, recognize, distinguish, remark, identify, diagnose; catch, sense, see, smell, scent, taste.

2 *they are responsible for detecting fraud* DISCOVER, uncover, find out, turn up, unearth, dig up, root out, expose, reveal.

3 *the hackers were detected* CATCH, hunt down, track down, find, expose, reveal, unmask, smoke out; apprehend, arrest; *informal* nail.

detection noun **1** *the detection of methane* DISCERNMENT, perception, awareness, recognition, identification, diagnosis; sensing, sight, smelling, tasting.

2 *the detection of insider trading* DISCOVERY, uncovering, unearthing, exposure, revelation.

3 *he managed to escape detection* CAPTURE, identification, exposure; apprehension, arrest; notice.

detective noun *they hired a detective to track down Polk's former partner* INVESTIGATOR, private investigator, private detective, police detective, operative; *informal* private eye, PI, sleuth, snoop, shamus, gumshoe, Sherlock; *informal, dated* dick, private dick.

detention noun *he was released after spending a year in detention* CUSTODY, imprisonment, confinement, incarceration, internment, detainment, captivity; arrest, house arrest; quarantine; punishment, discipline.

deter verb **1** *the high cost deterred many* DISCOURAGE, dissuade, put off, scare off; dishearten, demoralize, daunt, intimidate. ANTONYM encourage.

2 *the presence of a guard deters crime* PREVENT, stop, avert, fend off, stave off, ward off, block, halt, check; hinder, impede, hamper, obstruct, foil, forestall, counteract, inhibit, curb. ANTONYM encourage.

detergent noun *laundry detergent* CLEANER, cleanser, cleaning agent; soap, soap powder, dish soap, soap flakes.

deteriorate verb **1** *his health deteriorated* WORSEN, decline, degenerate; fail, slump, slip, go downhill, wane, ebb; *informal* go to pot. ANTONYM improve.

2 *these materials deteriorate if stored wrongly* DECAY, degrade, degenerate, break down, decompose, rot, go off, spoil, perish; break up, disintegrate, crumble, fall apart.

deterioration noun **1** *a deterioration in market conditions* DECLINE, collapse, failure, drop, downturn, slump, *informal* slip, retrogression.

2 *deterioration of the main structure* DECAY, degradation, degeneration, breakdown, decomposition, rot; atrophy, weakening; breakup, disintegration, dilapidation; entropy.

determinate adjective *a determinate hierarchy of authority* FIXED, settled, specified, established, defined, explicit, known, determined, definitive, conclusive, express, precise, categorical, positive, definite.

determination noun **1** *it took great determination to win* RESOLUTION, resolve, willpower, strength of character, single-mindedness, purposefulness, intentness; staunchness, perseverance, persistence, tenacity, staying power; strong-mindedness, backbone; stubbornness, doggedness, obstinacy; spirit, courage, pluck, grit, stout-heartedness; *informal* guts, spunk, balls, moxie; *formal* pertinacity.

2 *the determination of the rent* SETTING, specification, settlement, designation, arrangement, establishment, prescription.

3 *the determination of the speed of light* CALCULATION, discovery, ascertainment, establishment, deduction, divination, diagnosis, discernment, verification, confirmation.

determine verb **1** *chromosomes determine the sex of the embryo* CONTROL, decide, regulate, direct, dictate, govern; affect, influence, mold.

2 *he determined to sell* RESOLVE, decide, make up one's mind, choose, elect, opt; *formal* purpose.

3 *the sum will be determined by an accountant* SPECIFY, set, fix, decide on, settle, assign, designate, arrange, choose, establish, ordain, prescribe, decree.

4 *determine the composition of the fibers* ASCERTAIN, find out, discover, learn, establish, calculate, work out, make out, deduce, diagnose, discern; check, verify, confirm; *informal* figure out.

determined adjective **1** *he was determined to have his way* INTENT ON, bent on, set on, insistent on, resolved to, firm about, committed to; single-minded about, obsessive about.

2 *a very determined man* RESOLUTE, purposeful, purposive, adamant, single-minded, unswerving, unwavering, undaunted, intent, insistent; steadfast, staunch, stalwart; persevering, persistent, indefatigable, tenacious; strong-minded, strong-willed, unshakable, steely, four-square, dedicated, committed; stubborn, dogged, obstinate, inflexible, intransigent, unyielding, immovable, rock-ribbed; *formal* pertinacious. See note at RESOLUTE.

determining adjective *money is the determining factor* DECIDING, decisive, conclusive, final, definitive, key, pivotal, crucial, critical, major, chief, prime.

deterrent noun *the high rate of interest is a deterrent to first-time home buyers* DISINCENTIVE, discouragement, damper, curb, check, restraint; obstacle, hindrance, impediment, obstruction, block, barrier, inhibition. ANTONYM incentive.

detest verb *the only vegetable I truly detest is turnip* ABHOR, hate, loathe, despise, shrink from, be unable to bear, find intolerable, dislike, disdain, have an aversion to; *formal* abominate. See note at DESPISE. ANTONYM love.

detestable adjective *civilized people must not tolerate such detestable inhumanity* ABHORRENT, hateful, loathsome, despicable, abominable, execrable, repellent, repugnant, repulsive, revolting, disgusting, distasteful, horrible, horrid, awful; heinous, reprehensible, obnoxious, odious, offensive, contemptible. See note at OFFENSIVE.

dethrone verb *he devised a plan to dethrone his brother, the king* DEPOSE, unseat, oust, topple, overthrow, bring down, dislodge, displace, supplant, usurp, eject, drum out. ANTONYM crown.

detonate verb **1** *the charge detonated on impact* EXPLODE, go off, blow up, shatter, erupt; ignite; bang, blast, boom.

2 *they detonated the bomb* SET OFF, explode, discharge, let off, touch off, trigger; ignite, kindle.

detonation noun *the detonation of the first atomic bomb* EXPLOSION, discharge, blowing up, ignition; blast, bang, report.

detour noun *the detour will add another twenty minutes to the trip* DIVERSION, circuitous route, indirect route, scenic route; bypass; digression, deviation, shortcut.

detract verb *my reservations should not* ***detract from*** *the book's excellence* BELITTLE, take away from, diminish, reduce, lessen, minimize, play down, trivialize, decry, depreciate, devalue, deprecate.

detractor noun *detractors never deterred me from pursuing my art* CRITIC, disparager, denigrator, deprecator, belittler, attacker, fault-finder, backbiter; slanderer, libeler; *informal* knocker.

detriment noun *local merchants fear the detriment to business that one of these superstores could bring about* HARM, damage, injury, hurt, impairment, loss, disadvantage, disservice, mischief. ANTONYM benefit.

detrimental adjective *erosion can have a detrimental effect on our water* HARMFUL, damaging, injurious, hurtful, inimical, deleterious, destructive, ruinous, disastrous, bad, malign, adverse, undesirable, unfavorable, unfortunate; unhealthy, unwholesome. ANTONYM benign.

detritus noun *areas littered with military detritus* DEBRIS, waste, refuse, rubbish, litter, scrap, flotsam and jetsam, rubble; remains, remnants, fragments, scraps, dregs, leavings, sweepings, dross, scum, trash, garbage; *informal* dreck.

devalue verb *your attempts to devalue Stephen and his*

contributions will not be tolerated BELITTLE, depreciate, disparage, denigrate, decry, deprecate, treat lightly, discredit, underrate, undervalue, underestimate, deflate, diminish, trivialize, run down; *informal* knock, sell short, put down, badmouth, pooh-pooh, pick holes in.

devastate verb **1** *the city was devastated by an earthquake* DESTROY, ruin, wreck, lay waste, ravage, demolish, raze (to the ground), level, flatten; *informal* trash, total. See note at RAVAGE.

2 *he was devastated by the news* SHATTER, shock, stun, daze, dumbfound, traumatize, crush, overwhelm, overcome, distress.

devastating adjective **1** *a devastating cyclone* DESTRUCTIVE, ruinous, disastrous, catastrophic, calamitous, cataclysmic; harmful, damaging, injurious, detrimental; crippling, violent, savage, fierce, dangerous, fatal, deadly, lethal.

2 *devastating news* SHATTERING, shocking, traumatic, overwhelming, crushing, distressing, terrible.

3 *informal he presented devastating arguments* INCISIVE, highly effective, penetrating, cutting; withering, blistering, searing, scathing, fierce, savage, stinging, biting, caustic, harsh, unsparing.

devastation noun **1** *the hurricane left a trail of devastation* DESTRUCTION, ruin, desolation, havoc, wreckage; ruins, ravages.

2 *the devastation of Prussia* DESTRUCTION, wrecking, ruination; demolition, annihilation; despoliation, plunder, pillaging, plundering. See note at DESPOLIATION.

3 *the devastation you have caused the family* SHOCK, trauma, distress, stress, strain, pain, anguish, suffering, upset, agony, misery, heartache.

develop verb **1** *the industry developed rapidly* GROW, expand, spread; advance, progress, evolve, mature; prosper, thrive, flourish, blossom. See note at MATURE.

2 *a plan was developed* INITIATE, instigate, set in motion; originate, invent, form, establish, generate.

3 *children should develop their talents* EXPAND, augment, broaden, supplement, reinforce; enhance, refine, improve, polish, perfect.

4 *a fight developed* START, begin, emerge, erupt, break out, burst out, arise, break, unfold, happen.

5 *he developed the symptoms last week* FALL ILL WITH, be stricken with, succumb to; contract, catch, get, pick up, come down with, become infected with.

development noun **1** *the development of the firm* EVOLUTION, growth, maturation, expansion, enlargement, spread, progress; success.

2 *the development of an idea* FORMING, establishment, initiation, instigation, origination, invention, generation.

3 *keep abreast of developments* EVENT, occurrence, happening, circumstance, incident, situation, issue.

4 *a housing development* COMPLEX, site.

deviant adjective *deviant behavior* ABERRANT, abnormal, atypical, anomalous, irregular, nonstandard; nonconformist, perverse, uncommon, unusual; freakish, strange, odd, peculiar, bizarre, eccentric, idiosyncratic, unorthodox, exceptional; warped, perverted; *informal* kinky, quirky. ANTONYM normal.

▸ noun *we were seen as deviants* NONCONFORMIST, eccentric, maverick, individualist; outsider, misfit; *informal* oddball, weirdo, freak, screwball, kook, odd duck.

deviate verb *do not **deviate from** the original plan* DIVERGE FROM, digress from, drift from, stray from, veer from, swerve from; get sidetracked from, branch off from; differ from, vary from, run counter to, go in opposition to, contrast with.

deviation noun *the slightest deviation could prove disastrous* DIVERGENCE, digression, departure; difference, variation, variance; aberration, abnormality, irregularity, anomaly, inconsistency, discrepancy.

device noun **1** *a device for measuring pressure* IMPLEMENT, gadget, utensil, tool, appliance, apparatus, instrument, machine, mechanism, contrivance, contraption; *informal* gizmo, widget, doohickey.

2 *an ingenious legal device* PLOY, tactic, move, stratagem, scheme, plot, plan, trick, ruse, maneuver, machination, contrivance, expedient, dodge, wile.

3 *their shields bear his device* EMBLEM, symbol, logo, badge, crest, insignia, coat of arms, escutcheon, seal, mark, design, motif; monogram, hallmark, trademark.

devil noun **1** *God and **the Devil*** SATAN, Beelzebub, Lucifer, the Prince of Darkness, the Evil One; *informal* Old Nick.

2 *he drove out the devils from their bodies* EVIL SPIRIT, demon, fiend, bogie; *informal* spook.

3 *look what the cruel devil has done* BRUTE, beast, monster, fiend; villain, sadist, barbarian, ogre.

4 *he's a naughty little devil* RASCAL, rogue, imp, fiend, monkey, wretch; *informal* monster, horror, scamp, tyke, varmint.

5 *informal the poor devils looked ill* WRETCH, unfortunate, creature, soul, person, fellow; *informal* thing, beggar.

devilish adjective **1** *a devilish grin* DIABOLICAL, fiendish, demonic, satanic, demoniac, demoniacal; hellish, infernal; MISCHIEVOUS, wicked, impish, roguish.

2 *a devilish job* DIFFICULT, tricky, ticklish, troublesome, thorny, awkward, problematic.

devil-may-care adjective *devil-may-care stunt pilots* RECKLESS, rash, incautious, heedless, impetuous, impulsive, daredevil, hotheaded, wild, foolhardy, audacious, nonchalant, casual, breezy, flippant, insouciant, happy-go-lucky, easygoing, unworried, untroubled, unconcerned, harum-scarum.

devilment noun See DEVILRY sense 2.

devilry, deviltry noun **1** *some devilry was afoot* WICKEDNESS, evil, sin, iniquity, vileness, badness, wrongdoing, dishonesty, unscrupulousness, villainy, delinquency, devilishness, fiendishness; *informal* crookedness, shadiness.

2 *she had a perverse sense of devilry* MISCHIEF, mischievousness, naughtiness, badness, perversity, impishness; misbehavior, troublemaking, misconduct; pranks, tricks, roguery, devilment; *informal* monkey business, shenanigans.

3 *they dabbled in devilry* BLACK MAGIC, sorcery, witchcraft, wizardry, necromancy, enchantment, incantation; the supernatural, occultism, the occult, the black arts, divination, voodoo, witchery, mojo.

devious adjective **1** *the devious ways in which they bent the rules* UNDERHANDED, deceitful, dishonest, dishonorable, unethical, unprincipled, immoral, unscrupulous, fraudulent, dubious, unfair, treacherous, duplicitous; crafty, cunning, calculating, artful, conniving, scheming, sly, wily; sneaky, furtive, secret, clandestine, surreptitious, covert, snide; *informal* crooked, shady, dirty, lowdown.

2 *a devious route around the coast* CIRCUITOUS, roundabout, indirect, meandering, winding, tortuous.

devise verb *they have devised a way to recycle contaminated oil* CONCEIVE, think up, dream up, work out, formulate, concoct; design, invent, coin, originate; compose, construct, fabricate, create, produce, develop; discover, hit on; hatch, contrive; *informal* cook up.

devitalize verb *the team's enthusiasm was devitalized by the unexpected defeat at Georgetown* WEAKEN, enfeeble, debilitate, enervate, sap, drain, tax, exhaust, weary, tire (out), fatigue, wear out, prostrate; indispose, incapacitate, lay low; *informal* knock out, do in, whack, bush, frazzle, poop. ANTONYM strengthen.

devoid adjective *your argument is **devoid of** logic* FREE OF, empty of, vacant of, bereft of, deprived of, destitute of, bankrupt of; lacking, without, wanting; *informal* minus.

devolution noun *the devolution of power to the regions* DECENTRALIZATION, delegation; redistribution, transfer; surrender, relinquishment.

devolve verb *the move would devolve responsibility to local units* DELEGATE, depute, pass (down/on), download, hand down/over/on, transfer, transmit, assign, consign, convey, entrust, turn over, give, cede, surrender, relinquish, deliver; bestow, grant.

devote verb ALLOCATE, assign, allot, commit, give (over), apportion, consign, pledge; dedicate, consecrate; set aside, earmark, reserve, designate.

devoted adjective LOYAL, faithful, true, staunch, steadfast, constant, committed, dedicated, devout; fond, loving, affectionate, caring, admiring.

devotee noun 1 *a devotee of rock music* ENTHUSIAST, fan, lover, aficionado, admirer; *informal* buff, bum, freak, nut, fiend, fanatic, addict, maniac.

2 *devotees thronged the temple* FOLLOWER, adherent, supporter, advocate, disciple, votary, member, stalwart, fanatic, zealot; believer, worshiper.

devotion noun 1 *her devotion to her husband* LOYALTY, faithfulness, fidelity, constancy, commitment, adherence, allegiance, dedication; fondness, love, admiration, affection, care.

2 *a life of devotion* DEVOUTNESS, piety, religiousness, spirituality, godliness, holiness, sanctity.

3 *morning devotions* RELIGIOUS WORSHIP, worship, religious observance; prayers; prayer meeting, church service.

devotional adjective *the devotional readings for today's service* RELIGIOUS, sacred, spiritual, divine, church, ecclesiastical, faith-based. ANTONYM secular.

devour verb 1 *he devoured his meal* EAT HUNGRILY, eat greedily, gobble (up/down), guzzle, gulp (down), bolt (down), gorge oneself on, wolf (down), feast on, consume, eat up; *informal* demolish, dispose of, make short work of, polish off, shovel down, stuff oneself with, pig out on, put away; *informal* scarf (down/up).

2 *flames devoured the house* CONSUME, engulf, envelop; destroy, demolish, lay waste, devastate; gut, ravage, ruin, wreck.

3 *he was devoured by remorse* AFFLICT, plague, bedevil, trouble, harrow, rack; consume, swallow up, overcome, overwhelm.

devout adjective 1 *a devout Christian* PIOUS, religious, devoted, dedicated, reverent, God-fearing; holy, godly, saintly, faithful, dutiful, righteous, churchgoing, orthodox.

2 *a devout family man* DEDICATED, devoted, committed, loyal, faithful, staunch, genuine, firm, steadfast, unwavering, sincere, wholehearted, keen, enthusiastic, zealous, passionate, ardent, fervent, active, sworn, pledged; *informal* card-carrying, true blue.

dewy adjective 1 *walking on the dewy grass in the morning* MOIST, damp, wet.

2 *dewy innocence.* See DEWY-EYED.

dewy-eyed adjective *dewy-eyed romantics* SENTIMENTAL, nostalgic, wistful, romantic, maudlin, oversweet, misty-eyed; trusting, trustful, naive, dewy, innocent, childlike.

dexterity noun 1 *painting china demanded dexterity* DEFTNESS, adeptness, adroitness, agility, nimbleness, handiness, ability, talent, skill, proficiency, expertise, experience, efficiency, mastery, delicacy, knack, artistry, finesse.

2 *his political dexterity* SHREWDNESS, astuteness, acumen, acuity, intelligence; ingenuity, inventiveness, cleverness, smartness; canniness, sense, discernment, insight, understanding, penetration, perception, perspicacity, discrimination; cunning, artfulness, craftiness; *informal* horse sense, savvy, street smarts.

dexterous adjective 1 *a dexterous flick of the wrist* DEFT, adept, adroit, agile, nimble, neat, handy, able, capable, skillful, skilled, proficient, expert, practiced, polished; efficient, effortless, slick, professional, masterly; *informal* nifty, mean, ace. ANTONYM clumsy.

2 *his dexterous accounting abilities* SHREWD, ingenious, inventive, clever, intelligent, brilliant, smart, sharp, acute, astute, canny, intuitive, discerning, perceptive, insightful, incisive, judicious; cunning, artful, crafty, wily; *informal* on the ball, quick off the mark, quick on the uptake, brainy, savvy. ANTONYM stupid.

diabolical, diabolic adjective *his diabolical plans* DEVILISH, fiendish, satanic, demonic, demoniacal, hellish, infernal, evil, wicked, ungodly, unholy.

diacritic noun See table at ACCENT.

diadem noun *the queen's jeweled diadem* CROWN, coronet, tiara, circlet, chaplet; *literary* coronal.

diagnose verb *perhaps he diagnosed the condition incorrectly* IDENTIFY, determine, distinguish, recognize, detect, pinpoint.

diagnosis noun 1 *the diagnosis of celiac disease* IDENTIFICATION, detection, recognition, determination, discovery, pinpointing.

2 *the results confirmed his diagnosis* OPINION, judgment, verdict, conclusion.

diagonal adjective *the diagonal stripes on the wall make me dizzy* CROSSWISE, crossways, slanting, slanted, aslant, oblique, angled, at an angle; cater-cornered, kitty-cornered.

diagram noun *Jackson's diagrams show the dramatic effects of erosion since 1948* DRAWING, line drawing, sketch, representation, draft, illustration, picture, plan, outline, delineation, figure; *Computing* graphic.

diagrammatic adjective *information presented in a diagrammatic form* GRAPHIC, graphical, representational, representative, schematic, simplified.

dialect noun *the island dialect was influenced by the Spanish in the sixteenth century* REGIONAL LANGUAGE, local language, local speech, vernacular, patois, idiom; regionalisms, localisms; *informal* lingo.

THE RIGHT WORD

When a New York City cab driver calls out the window, "Hey, wassa madda wichoo?" he is using the **vernacular**, which is the authentic, natural pattern of speech among those belonging to a certain community. In some areas of London, on the other hand, one might hear the Cockney **dialect**, which is a form or variety of a language that is confined to a specific group or locality; it has its own pronunciation, usage, and vocabulary, and may persist for generations or even centuries (*he spoke in the dialect of the Appalachian backwoodsman*). A teenager who tells his parents to "Chill out" is using **slang**, which is a very informal language that includes "substitute" vocabulary ("wheels" for *car*, "rug" for *toupee*), grammatical distortions, and other departures from formal or polite usage. **Argot** refers to the slang of a group that feels threatened by the hostility of society as a whole; it traditionally refers to the slang used by criminals and thieves, although it may refer to any peculiar language that a clique or other closely knit group uses to communicate with each other. At one time **cant** was a synonym for *argot*, but now it usually refers to pompous, inflated language or the hackneyed use of words and phrases by members of a particular class or profession (*the cant of the fashion industry*). In contrast to *cant*, which can at least be understood, **jargon** is nearly impossible for the average person to decipher. This term refers to the technical or highly specialized language used by members of an occupational or professional group (*medical jargon, the jargon of the theater*). If you are frustrated because you can't understand the language used by a particular class or group, you're apt to refer to their way of talking as **lingo**, which is a term for any language that is not readily understood (*she tried to reason with the cab driver, but she couldn't understand his lingo*).

dialectic noun *feminism has of course contributed to this dialectic* DISCUSSION, debate, dialogue, logical argument, reasoning, argumentation, polemics; *formal* ratiocination.

dialogue noun **1** *a book consisting of a series of dialogues* CONVERSATION, talk, discussion, interchange, discourse; chat, tête-à-tête, heart-to-heart; *informal* confab, chinwag; *formal* colloquy, confabulation. See note at CONVERSATION.

2 *they called for a serious political dialogue* DISCUSSION, exchange, debate, exchange of views, talk, consultation, conference, parley; talks, negotiations; *informal* powwow, skull session.

WORD NOTE **dialogue**

Noun-wise, the interesting thing about *dialogue* is that it means "a conversation or exchange between two or more people," so it's not wrong to say something like *The council engaged in a long dialogue about the proposal.* Avoid modifying it with certain adjectives, though—*constructive dialogue* and *meaningful dialogue* have, thanks mainly to political cant, become clichés that will glaze readers' eyes. Please also avoid using *dialogue* as a verb—ever. This is despite the facts that (1) Shakespeare occasionally used it as a verb, and (2) there are all sorts of other accepted verbalizations of nouns in English that work the same way; e.g., *to diet* is reduced from "to go on a diet," *to trap* from "to catch in a trap," and so on. Maybe in 30 years, *to dialogue* will be just as standard, but as of now it strikes most literate readers as affected and jargonish. Same with *to transition;* same with *to parent;* same with *to reference;* same with *to gift.* **—DFW**

diameter noun *the diameter of the hole is less than two inches* BREADTH, width, thickness; caliber, bore, gauge.

diametrical, diametric adjective *politically, Taylor was in diametrical opposition to her parents* DIRECT, absolute, complete, exact, extreme, polar, antipodal.

diaphanous adjective *a diaphanous dress* SHEER, fine, delicate, light, thin, insubstantial, floaty, flimsy, filmy, silken, chiffony, gossamer, gossamer-thin, gauzy; translucent, transparent, see-through. ANTONYMS thick, opaque.

diarrhea noun *an outbreak of diarrhea in the camp* loose stools; *informal* the runs, the trots, the squirts, Montezuma's revenge, turista; *Medicine* dysentery; *archaic* the flux. ANTONYM constipation.

diary noun **1** *he put the date in his diary* APPOINTMENT BOOK, engagement book, organizer, personal organizer, daybook, PDA.

2 *her World War II diaries* JOURNAL, memoir, chronicle, log, logbook, history, annal, record.

diatribe noun *he launched into a diatribe against the Catholic Church* TIRADE, harangue, onslaught, attack, polemic, denunciation, broadside, fulmination, condemnation, censure, criticism; *informal* blast; *literary* philippic.

dicey adjective *informal refueling at sea is a bit dicey in bad weather* RISKY, uncertain, unpredictable, touch-and-go, precarious, unsafe, dangerous, fraught with danger, hazardous, perilous, high-risk, difficult; *informal* chancy, hairy, iffy, gnarly. ANTONYM safe.

dichotomy noun *the great dichotomy between theory and practice* CONTRAST, difference, polarity, conflict; gulf, chasm, division, separation, split; *rare* contrariety.

dicker verb *can't you just pay the asking price without dickering?* NEGOTIATE, haggle, bargain, barter.

dictate verb **1** *the president's attempts to dictate policy* PRESCRIBE, lay down, impose, set down, order, command, decree, ordain, direct, determine, decide, control, govern.

2 *you are in no position to* ***dictate to*** *me* GIVE ORDERS TO, order around/about, lord it over; lay down the law to; *informal* boss around/about, push around/about; (**dictate to someone**) throw one's weight around/about.

3 *choice is often dictated by availability* DETERMINE, control, govern, decide, influence, affect.

▸ noun *the dictates of his superior* ORDER, command, commandment, decree, edict, ruling, dictum, diktat, directive, direction, instruction, pronouncement, mandate, requirement, stipulation, injunction, demand; *formal* ordinance; *literary* behest.

dictator noun *a regime that has survived under one dictator for more than forty years* AUTOCRAT, absolute ruler, despot, tyrant, oppressor, autarch.

dictatorial adjective **1** *a dictatorial regime* AUTOCRATIC, undemocratic, totalitarian, authoritarian, autarchic, despotic, tyrannical, tyrannous, absolute, unrestricted, unlimited, unaccountable, arbitrary; *informal* iron-fisted. ANTONYM democratic.

2 *his dictatorial manner* DOMINEERING, autocratic, authoritarian, oppressive, imperious, officious, overweening, overbearing, peremptory, dogmatic, high and mighty; severe, strict; *informal* bossy, high-handed. ANTONYM meek.

dictatorship noun *growing up in the shadow of dictatorship* ABSOLUTE RULE, undemocratic rule, despotism, tyranny, autocracy, autarchy, authoritarianism, totalitarianism, fascism; oppression, repression. ANTONYM democracy.

diction noun 1 *his careful diction* ENUNCIATION, articulation, elocution, locution, pronunciation, speech, intonation, inflection; delivery.

2 *her diction was archaic* PHRASEOLOGY, phrasing, turn of phrase, wording, language, usage, vocabulary, terminology, expressions, idioms.

dictionary noun *dictionaries created by Oxford's American lexicographers* LEXICON, wordbook, word list, glossary; thesaurus.

dictum noun 1 *he received the dictum with evident reluctance* PRONOUNCEMENT, proclamation, direction, injunction, dictate, command, commandment, order, decree, edict, mandate, diktat.

2 *the old dictum "might is right"* SAYING, maxim, axiom, proverb, adage, aphorism, saw, precept, epigram, motto, truism, commonplace, platitude; expression, phrase, tag.

didactic adjective *the didactic photojournalism of Jacob Riis* INSTRUCTIVE, instructional, educational, educative, informative, informational, edifying, improving, preceptive, pedagogic, moralistic.

diddly-squat noun 1 *the contestants who miss the final question go home with diddly-squat* NOTHING, zero; *informal* zilch, zip, nada, diddly, squat.

2 *these guys don't know diddly-squat about roofing* ANYTHING, a thing; *informal* diddly, squat, step one, rule one, word one.

die verb 1 *her father died last year* PASS AWAY, pass on, lose one's life, expire, breathe one's last, meet one's end, meet one's death, lay down one's life, perish, go the way of all flesh, go to one's last resting place, go to meet one's maker, cross the great divide, slip away; *informal* give up the ghost, kick the bucket, croak, buy it, turn up one's toes, cash in one's chips, bite the big one, check out, buy the farm; *archaic* depart this life. ANTONYMS live, survive.

2 *the wind had* ***died down*** ABATE, subside, drop, lessen, ease (off), let up, moderate, fade, dwindle, peter out, wane, ebb, relent, weaken; melt away, dissolve, vanish, disappear; *archaic* remit. ANTONYM intensify.

3 *informal the engine died* FAIL, cut out, give out, stop, break down, stop working; *informal* conk out, go kaput, give up the ghost.

4 *informal she's dying to meet you* LONG, yearn, burn, ache; *informal* itch.

diehard adjective *a diehard hockey fan* HARDLINE, reactionary, ultraconservative, conservative, traditionalist, dyed-in-the-wool, intransigent, inflexible, uncompromising, rigid, entrenched, set in one's ways; staunch, steadfast.

diet[1] noun *health problems related to your diet* SELECTION OF FOOD, food, foodstuffs; *informal* grub, nosh.

▸ verb *she dieted for most of her life* BE ON A DIET, eat sparingly; lose weight, watch one's weight, reduce, slenderize.

diet[2] noun *the diet's lower house* LEGISLATIVE ASSEMBLY, legislature, congress, senate, parliament, council, assembly.

differ verb 1 *the second set of data* ***differed from*** *the first* CONTRAST WITH, be different from, be dissimilar to, be unlike, vary from, diverge from, deviate from, conflict with, run counter to, be incompatible with, be at odds with, go against, contradict. ANTONYM resemble.

2 *the two sides differed over this issue* DISAGREE, conflict, be at variance, be at odds, be in dispute, not see eye to eye. ANTONYM agree.

difference noun 1 *the difference between the two sets of data* DISSIMILARITY, contrast, distinction, differentiation, variance, variation, divergence, disparity, deviation, polarity, gulf, gap, imbalance, contradiction, contradistinction. ANTONYM similarity.

2 *we've had our differences in the past* DISAGREEMENT, difference of opinion, dispute, argument, quarrel, wrangle, contretemps, altercation; *informal* tiff, set-to, run-in, spat, row.

3 *I am willing to pay the difference* BALANCE, remainder, rest, remaining amount, residue.

different adjective 1 *people with different lifestyles* DISSIMILAR, unalike, unlike, contrasting, contrastive, divergent, differing, varying, disparate; poles apart, incompatible, mismatched, conflicting, clashing. ANTONYM similar.

2 *suddenly everything in her life was different* CHANGED, altered, transformed, new, unfamiliar, unknown, strange. ANTONYM the same.

3 *two different occasions* DISTINCT, separate, individual, discrete, independent. ANTONYMS similar, related.

4 *informal he wanted to try something different* UNUSUAL, out of the ordinary, unfamiliar, novel, new, fresh, original, unconventional, exotic, uncommon. ANTONYM ordinary.

differential adjective *technical* 1 *the differential achievements of boys and girls* DIFFERENT, dissimilar, contrasting, unalike, divergent, disparate, contrastive. ANTONYM similar.

2 *the differential features of benign and malignant tumors* DISTINCTIVE, distinguishing. ANTONYM similar.

differentiate verb 1 *he was unable to differentiate between fantasy and reality* DISTINGUISH, discriminate, make/draw a distinction, tell the difference, tell apart. See note at DISTINGUISH.

2 *this differentiates their business from all other booksellers* MAKE DIFFERENT, distinguish, set apart, single out, separate, mark off.

differentiation noun *there is not enough differentiation between the two types of investment* DISTINCTION, distinctness, difference; separation, demarcation, delimitation.

difficult adjective 1 *a very difficult job* HARD, strenuous, arduous, laborious, tough, onerous, burdensome, demanding, punishing, grueling, back-breaking, exhausting, tiring, fatiguing, wearisome; *informal* hellish, killing; *archaic* toilsome. ANTONYM easy.

2 *she found math very difficult* HARD, complicated, complex, involved, impenetrable, unfathomable, over/above one's head, beyond one, puzzling, baffling, perplexing, confusing, mystifying; problematic, intricate, knotty, thorny, ticklish. ANTONYMS simple, straightforward. See note at HARD.

3 *a difficult child* TROUBLESOME, tiresome, trying, exasperating, awkward, demanding, perverse, contrary, recalcitrant, unmanageable, obstreperous, unaccommodating, unhelpful, uncooperative, disobliging; hard to please, fussy, finicky; *formal* refractory. See word spectrum at DOCILE. ANTONYM accommodating.

4 *you've come at a difficult time* INCONVENIENT, awkward, inopportune, unfavorable, unfortunate, inappropriate, unsuitable, untimely, ill-timed. ANTONYM convenient.

5 *the family has been through a difficult year* BAD, tough, grim, dark, black, hard, adverse, distressing; straitened. ANTONYM happy.

difficulty noun **1** *the difficulty of balancing motherhood with a career* STRAIN, trouble, problems, toil, struggle, laboriousness, arduousness; *informal* hassle, stress. ANTONYM ease.

2 *the project has met with one difficulty after another* PROBLEM, complication, snag, hitch, pitfall, handicap, impediment, hindrance, obstacle, hurdle, stumbling block, obstruction, barrier; *informal* fly in the ointment, headache; growing pains.

3 (**difficulties**) *Charles got into difficulties* TROUBLE, predicament, plight, hard times, dire straits; quandary, dilemma; *informal* deep water, a fix, a jam, a spot, a scrape, a stew, a hole, a pickle.

diffidence noun *her diffidence was out of place in this outgoing group* SHYNESS, bashfulness, modesty, self-effacement, meekness, unassertiveness, timidity, humility, hesitancy, reticence, insecurity, self-doubt, uncertainty, self-consciousness.

diffident adjective *underneath his diffident exterior was a passionate temperament* SHY, bashful, modest, self-effacing, unassuming, meek, unconfident, unassertive, timid, timorous, humble, shrinking, reticent, hesitant, insecure, self-doubting, doubtful, uncertain, unsure, self-conscious; *informal* mousy. ANTONYM confident.

diffuse verb *such ideas were diffused widely in the 1970s* SPREAD, spread around, send out, disseminate, scatter, disperse, distribute, put about, circulate, communicate, purvey, propagate, transmit, broadcast, promulgate. See note at SCATTER.

▸ adjective **1** *a diffuse community centered on the church* SPREAD OUT, scattered, dispersed, diasporic.

2 *a diffuse narrative* VERBOSE, wordy, prolix, long-winded, long-drawn-out, discursive, rambling, wandering, meandering, maundering, digressive, circuitous, roundabout, circumlocutory, periphrastic.

diffusion noun *the diffusion of Marxist ideas* SPREAD, dissemination, scattering, dispersal, diaspora, distribution, circulation, propagation, transmission, broadcasting, promulgation.

dig verb **1** *she began to dig the heavy clay soil* TURN OVER, work, break up; till, harrow, plow, shovel.

2 *he took a spade and dug a hole* EXCAVATE, dig out, quarry, hollow out, scoop out, gouge out; cut, bore, tunnel, burrow, mine.

3 *the bodies were hastily* ***dug up*** EXHUME, disinter, unearth.

4 *Winnie dug her elbow into his ribs* POKE, prod, jab, stab, shove, ram, push, thrust, drive.

5 *he'd been* ***digging into*** *my past* DELVE INTO, probe into, search into, inquire into, look into, investigate, research, examine, scrutinize, check up on; *informal* check out.

6 *I* ***dug up*** *some disturbing information* UNCOVER, discover, find (out), unearth, dredge up, root out, ferret out, turn up, reveal, bring to light, expose.

7 *informal, dated* *I dig talking with him.* See ENJOY verb sense 1.

▸ noun **1** *a dig in the ribs* POKE, prod, jab, stab, shove, push.

2 *informal* *they're always making digs at each other* SNIDE REMARK, cutting remark, jibe, jeer, taunt, sneer, insult, barb, insinuation; *informal* wisecrack, crack, put-down.

digest verb *Liz digested this information* ASSIMILATE, absorb, take in, understand, comprehend, grasp; consider, think about, reflect on, ponder, contemplate, mull over.

▸ noun *a digest of their findings* SUMMARY, synopsis, abstract, précis, résumé, summation; compilation; *informal* wrap-up.

digit noun **1** *the door code has ten digits* NUMERAL, number, figure, integer.

2 *we wanted to warm our frozen digits* FINGER, thumb, toe; extremity.

dignified adjective *a dignified and courteous butler* STATELY, noble, courtly, majestic, distinguished, proud, august, lofty, exalted, regal, lordly, imposing, impressive, grand; solemn, serious, grave, formal, proper, ceremonious, decorous, reserved, composed, sedate.

dignify verb *shall we dignify their arrival with some music?* ENNOBLE, enhance, distinguish, add distinction to, honor, grace, exalt, magnify, glorify, elevate.

dignitary noun *the studio is being visited a bunch of foreign dignitaries* WORTHY, personage, VIP, grandee, notable, pillar of society, luminary, leading light, big name; *informal* heavyweight, bigwig, top brass, top dog, big gun, big shot, big cheese, big chief, supremo, big wheel, big kahuna, big enchilada, top banana.

dignity noun **1** *the dignity of the proceedings* STATELINESS, nobility, majesty, regality, courtliness, augustness, loftiness, lordliness, grandeur; solemnity, gravity, gravitas, formality, decorum, propriety, sedateness.

2 *he had lost his dignity* SELF-RESPECT, pride, self-esteem, self-worth.

digress verb *I have digressed from the original plan* DEVIATE, go off on a tangent, get off the subject, get sidetracked, lose the thread, turn aside/away, depart, drift, stray, wander.

digression noun *a book full of long digressions* DEVIATION, detour, diversion, departure, divergence, excursus; aside, incidental remark.

digs plural noun *informal* *his new digs are small, but the location is excellent* HOME, quarters, living quarters, rooms, accommodations; house, apartment; *informal* pad, place; *formal* abode, dwelling, dwelling place, residence, domicile, habitation.

dike noun *the dikes were destroyed in the flood* EMBANKMENT, levee; ditch, trench, gutter.

dilapidated adjective *a row of dilapidated houses* RUNDOWN, tumbledown, ramshackle, broken-down, in disrepair, shabby, battered, beat-up, rickety, shaky, unsound, crumbling, in ruins, ruined, decayed, decaying, decrepit; neglected, uncared-for, untended, the worse for wear, falling to pieces, falling apart, gone to rack and ruin, gone to seed.

dilate verb **1** *her nostrils dilated* ENLARGE, widen, expand, distend. ANTONYM contract.

2 *Diane dilated on the joys of her married life* EXPATIATE, expound, enlarge, elaborate, speak/write at length. ANTONYM contract.

dilatory adjective **1** *he had been dilatory in appointing an executor* SLOW, tardy, unhurried, sluggish, sluggardly, snaillike, lazy. ANTONYMS fast, prompt.

2 *dilatory procedural tactics* DELAYING, stalling, temporizing, procrastinating, time-wasting, filibustering.

dilemma noun *a discussion with a colleague resolved her dilemma* QUANDARY, predicament, Catch-22, vicious circle, plight, mess, muddle; difficulty, problem, trouble, perplexity, confusion, conflict; *informal* no-win situation, fix, tight spot, tight corner, can of worms.

USAGE NOTE **dilemma**

Dilemma should be reserved for reference to a predicament in which a difficult choice must be made between undesirable alternatives: *You see his dilemma? If he moves to London, he may never see his parents again. But if he stays in Seattle, he may be giving up the best job offer of his life.* The weakened use of *dilemma* to mean simply "a difficult situation or problem" (*the dilemma of a teacher shortage*) is recorded as early as the first part of the seventeenth century, but many regard this use as unacceptable and it should be avoided in written English.

dilettante noun *there is no room for the dilettante in this business* DABBLER, amateur, nonprofessional, nonspecialist, layman, layperson. ANTONYM professional.

diligence noun *they set about their tasks with diligence* CONSCIENTIOUSNESS, assiduousness, assiduity, hard work, application, concentration, effort, care, industriousness, rigor, meticulousness, thoroughness; perseverance, persistence, tenacity, dedication, commitment, tirelessness, indefatigability, doggedness.

diligent adjective *diligent workers* INDUSTRIOUS, hardworking, assiduous, conscientious, particular, punctilious, meticulous, painstaking, rigorous, careful, thorough, sedulous, earnest; persevering, persistent, tenacious, zealous, dedicated, committed, unflagging, untiring, tireless, indefatigable, dogged; *archaic* laborious. See note at BUSY. ANTONYM lazy.

dilly noun *a dilly of a traffic jam.* See HUMDINGER.

dilly-dally verb *informal we can't dilly-dally when there are critical decisions to be made* WASTE TIME, dally, dawdle, loiter, linger, take one's time, delay, temporize, stall, procrastinate, pussyfoot around, drag one's feet; dither, hesitate, falter, vacillate, waver, hem and haw; *informal* shilly-shally, lollygag, let the grass grow under one's feet; *archaic* tarry. ANTONYM hurry.

dilute verb **1** *strong bleach can be diluted with water* MAKE WEAKER, weaken, water down; thin out, thin; doctor, adulterate; *informal* cut.

2 *the original plans have been diluted* WEAKEN, moderate, tone down, water down.

▸ adjective *a dilute acid.* See DILUTED.

diluted adjective *a cup of diluted fruit juice* WEAK, dilute, thin, watered down, watery; adulterated. ANTONYM concentrated.

dim adjective **1** *the dim light* FAINT, weak, feeble, soft, pale, dull, subdued, muted. ANTONYM bright.

2 *long dim corridors* DARK, badly lit, ill-lit, dingy, dismal, gloomy, murky; *literary* tenebrous. ANTONYM bright.

3 *a dim figure* INDISTINCT, ill-defined, unclear, vague, shadowy, nebulous, obscured, blurred, blurry, fuzzy. ANTONYM distinct.

4 *dim memories* VAGUE, imprecise, imperfect, unclear, indistinct, sketchy, hazy, blurred, shadowy. ANTONYMS clear, distinct.

5 *informal is she a bit dim?* See STUPID sense 1.

6 *their prospects for the future looked dim* GLOOMY, unpromising, unfavorable, discouraging, disheartening, depressing, dispiriting, hopeless. ANTONYM encouraging.

▸ verb **1** *the lights were dimmed* TURN DOWN, lower, soften, subdue, mute; *literary* bedim. ANTONYM turn up.

2 *my memories have not dimmed with time* FADE, become vague, dwindle, blur. ANTONYM sharpen.

3 *the fighting dimmed hopes of peace* DIMINISH, reduce, lessen, weaken, undermine. ANTONYM intensify.

dimension noun **1** *the dimensions of the room* SIZE, measurements, proportions, extent; length, width, breadth, depth, area, volume, capacity; footage, acreage.

2 *the dimension of the problem* SIZE, scale, extent, scope, magnitude; importance, significance.

3 *the cultural dimensions of the problem* ASPECT, feature, element, facet, side.

diminish verb **1** *the pain will gradually diminish* DECREASE, lessen, decline, reduce, subside, die down, abate, dwindle, fade, slacken off, moderate, let up, ebb, wane, recede, die away/out, peter out; *archaic* remit. ANTONYM increase.

2 *new legislation diminished the courts' authority* REDUCE, decrease, lessen, curtail, cut, cut down/back, constrict, restrict, limit, curb, check; weaken, blunt, erode, undermine, sap. ANTONYM increase.

3 *she lost no opportunity to diminish him* BELITTLE, disparage, denigrate, defame, deprecate, run down; decry, demean, cheapen, devalue; *formal* derogate. ANTONYM boost.

diminution noun *a diminution of freedom reduces the quality of life* REDUCTION, decrease, lessening, decline, dwindling, moderation, fading, fade-out, weakening, ebb.

diminutive adjective *a diminutive breed of parrot* TINY, small, little, petite, elfin, minute, miniature, mini, minuscule, compact, pocket, toy, midget, undersized, short; *informal* teeny, weeny, teeny-weeny, teensy-weensy, itty-bitty, itsy-bitsy, baby, pint-sized, knee-high to a grasshopper, little-bitty; *Scottish* wee. See note at SMALL. ANTONYM enormous.

dimple noun *the dimples on a golf ball* INDENTATION, hollow, cleft.

dimwit noun *informal* See FOOL noun sense 1.

dimwitted adjective *informal* See STUPID senses 1, 2.

din noun *he shouted above the din* NOISE, racket, rumpus, ruckus, cacophony, babel, hubbub, tumult, uproar, commotion, clatter; shouting, yelling, screaming, caterwauling, clamor, clangor, outcry; *informal* hullabaloo. ANTONYM silence.

▸ verb **1** *she had had the evils of drink dinned into her* INSTILL, inculcate, drive, drum, hammer, drill, ingrain; indoctrinate, brainwash.

2 *the sound dinning in my ears* BLARE, blast, clang, clatter, crash, clamor.

dine verb **1** *we dined at a restaurant* HAVE DINNER, have supper, eat; *dated* sup, break bread.

2 *they dined on lobster* EAT, feed on, feast on, banquet on, partake of; *informal* tuck into, chow down on.

diner noun *the diner serves breakfast 24 hours a day* SMALL RESTAURANT, eatery, café, cafeteria, truck stop; *informal* greasy spoon.

dinghy noun BOAT, lifeboat. See also table at BOAT.

dingy adjective *their secret hiding place was a dingy room in the basement* GLOOMY, dark, dull, badly/poorly lit, murky, dim, dismal, dreary, drab, somber, grim, cheerless; dirty, grimy, shabby, faded, worn, dowdy, seedy, rundown; *informal* grungy. ANTONYM bright.

dinky adjective *informal as usual, he made a dinky contribution* TRIFLING, trivial, insignificant, unimportant, negligible, of no account.

dinner noun *dinner will be served on the terrace* EVENING MEAL, supper, main meal; lunch, midday meal; feast, banquet, dinner party; *informal* spread; *humorous* din-din; *formal* repast.

dinosaur noun See table.

DINOSAURS

Acanthopholis	Megaraptor
Albertosaurus	Notoceratops
Allosaurus	Ornithomimus
Amargasaurus	Ouranosaurus
Ankylosaurus	Pachycephalosaurus
Apatosaurus	Parasaurolophus
Baryonyx	Plateosaurus
Brachiosaurus	Protarchaeopteryx
Brontosaurus	Psittacosaurus
Camarasaurus	Pteranodon
Camptosaurus	Quaesitosaurus
Carnotaurus	Riojasaurus
Ceratosaurus	Saichania
Corythosaurus	Saltopus
Deinonychus	Sauropelta
Dilophosaurus	Scelidosaurus
Diplodocus	Scipionyx
Dryosaurus	Sinornithosaurus
Edmontosaurus	Spinosaurus
Euoplocephalus	Stegoceras
Gallimimus	Stegosaurus
Gigantosaurus	Styracosaurus
Homalocephale	Triceratops
Hylaeosaurus	Tröodon
Hypacrosaurus	Tyrannosaurus
Iguanodon	(rex)/T. rex
Janenschia	Ultrasauros
Kentrosaurus	Utahraptor
Lambeosaurus	Velociraptor
Lesothosaurus	Vulcanodon
Maiasaura	Wannanosaurus
Majungatholis	Xiaosaurus
Mamenchisaurus	Yangchuanosuarus
Megalosaurus	Zigongosaurus

diocese noun *Father Lewis comes from a diocese in Maryland* BISHOPRIC, see, eparchy.

dip verb **1** *he dipped a rag in the water* IMMERSE, submerge, plunge, duck, dunk, lower, sink.

2 *the sun dipped below the horizon* SINK, set, drop, go/drop down, fall, descend; disappear, vanish. ANTONYM rise.

3 *the president's popularity has dipped* DECREASE, fall, drop, fall off, decline, diminish, dwindle, slump, plummet, plunge. ANTONYMS rise, increase.

4 *the road dipped* SLOPE DOWN, descend, go down; drop away, fall, sink. ANTONYM rise.

5 *you might have to **dip into** your savings* DRAW ON, use, make use of, have recourse to, spend.

▸ noun **1** *a relaxing dip in the pool* SWIM, bathe; splash, paddle.

2 *give the fish a ten-minute dip in a salt bath* IMMERSION, plunge, ducking, dunking.

3 *chicken satay with peanut dip* SAUCE, dressing.

4 *the hedge at the bottom of the dip* SLOPE, incline, decline, descent; hollow, concavity, depression, basin, indentation.

5 *a dip in sales* DECREASE, fall, drop, downturn, decline, falling-off, slump, reduction, diminution, ebb.

diploma noun *her diploma from Colgate* CERTIFICATE, parchment, sheepskin; degree, accreditation, qualification, license.

diplomacy noun **1** *diplomacy failed to win them independence* STATESMANSHIP, statecraft, negotiation(s), discussion(s), talks, dialogue; international relations, foreign affairs.

2 *Jack's quiet diplomacy* TACT, tactfulness, sensitivity, discretion, subtlety, finesse, delicacy, savoir faire, politeness, thoughtfulness, care, judiciousness, prudence.

diplomat noun *a British diplomat working in Germany* AMBASSADOR, attaché, consul, chargé d'affaires, envoy, nuncio, emissary, plenipotentiary; *archaic* legate.

diplomatic adjective **1** *diplomatic activity* AMBASSADORIAL, consular.

2 *he tried to be diplomatic* TACTFUL, sensitive, subtle, delicate, polite, discreet, thoughtful, careful, judicious, prudent, politic, clever, skillful. ANTONYM tactless.

dire adjective **1** *the dire economic situation* TERRIBLE, dreadful, appalling, frightful, awful, atrocious, grim, alarming; grave, serious, disastrous, calamitous, ruinous, hopeless, irretrievable, wretched, desperate, parlous; *formal* grievous.

2 *he was in dire need of help* URGENT, desperate, pressing, crying, sore, grave, serious, extreme, acute, drastic.

3 *dire warnings of fuel shortages* OMINOUS, gloomy, grim, dismal, unpropitious, inauspicious, unfavorable, pessimistic.

direct adjective **1** *the most direct route* STRAIGHT, undeviating, unswerving; shortest, quickest.

2 *a direct flight* NONSTOP, unbroken, uninterrupted, through.

3 *he is very direct* FRANK, candid, straightforward, honest, open, blunt, plain-spoken, outspoken, forthright, downright, no-nonsense, matter-of-fact, not afraid to call a spade a spade; *informal* upfront.

4 *direct contact with the president* FACE TO FACE, personal, immediate, firsthand.

5 *a direct quotation* VERBATIM, word for word, to the letter, faithful, exact, precise, accurate, correct.

6 *the direct opposite* EXACT, absolute, complete, diametrical.

▸ verb 1 *an economic elite directed the nation's affairs* MANAGE, govern, run, administer, control, conduct, handle, be in charge/control of, preside over, lead, head, rule, be at the helm of; supervise, superintend, oversee, regulate, orchestrate, coordinate; *informal* run the show, call the shots, be in the driver's seat.

2 *was that remark* ***directed at*** *me?* AIM AT, target at, address to, intend for, mean for, design for.

3 *a man in uniform directed them to the hall* GIVE DIRECTIONS, show the way, guide, lead, conduct, accompany, usher, escort.

4 *the judge directed the jury to return a 'not guilty' verdict* INSTRUCT, tell, command, order, charge, require; *literary* bid.

direction noun 1 *a northerly direction* WAY, route, course, line, run, bearing, orientation.

2 *the direction of my research* ORIENTATION, inclination, leaning, tendency, bent, bias, preference; drift, tack, attitude, tone, tenor, mood, current, trend.

3 *his direction of the project* ADMINISTRATION, management, conduct, handling, running, supervision, superintendence, regulation, orchestration; control, command, rule, leadership, guidance.

4 *explicit directions about nursing care* INSTRUCTION, order, command, prescription, rule, regulation, requirement.

directive noun *a directive from the front office* INSTRUCTION, direction, command, order, charge, injunction, prescription, rule, ruling, regulation, law, dictate, decree, dictum, edict, mandate, fiat; *formal* ordinance.

directly adverb 1 *they flew directly to New York* STRAIGHT, right, as the crow flies, by a direct route.

2 *I went directly after breakfast* IMMEDIATELY, at once, instantly, right away, straightaway, posthaste, without delay, without hesitation, forthwith; quickly, speedily, promptly; *informal* pronto.

3 *the houses directly opposite* EXACTLY, right, immediately; diametrically; *informal* bang.

4 *she spoke simply and directly* FRANKLY, candidly, openly, bluntly, forthrightly, without beating around the bush.

director noun *the director of the museum* ADMINISTRATOR, manager, chairman, chairwoman, chairperson, chair, head, chief, principal, leader, governor, president; managing director, chief executive (officer), CEO; supervisor, controller, overseer; *informal* boss, kingpin, top dog, head honcho, numero uno.

directory noun *a directory of past and present members* INDEX, list, listing, register, catalog, record, archive, inventory.

dirge noun *a lone bagpiper played the woeful dirge* ELEGY, lament, burial hymn, threnody, requiem, funeral march; *Irish* keen.

dirt noun 1 *his face was streaked with dirt* GRIME, filth; dust, soot, smut; muck, mud, mire, sludge, slime, ooze, dross; smudges, stains; *informal* crud, yuck, grunge; *Brit.* gunge.

2 *the packed dirt of the road* EARTH, soil, loam, clay, silt; ground.

3 *informal dog dirt.* See EXCREMENT.

4 *informal they tried to dig up dirt on the president* A SCANDAL, gossip, revelations, a rumor, rumors; information.

dirty adjective 1 *a dirty sweatshirt | dirty water* SOILED, grimy, grubby, filthy, mucky, stained, unwashed, greasy, smeared, smeary, spotted, smudged, cloudy, muddy, dusty, sooty; unclean, sullied, impure, tarnished, polluted, contaminated, defiled, foul, unhygienic, unsanitary; *informal* cruddy, yucky, icky, grotty, grungy; *literary* befouled, besmirched, begrimed. ANTONYM clean.

2 *a dirty joke* INDECENT, obscene, rude, naughty, vulgar, smutty, coarse, crude, filthy, bawdy, suggestive, ribald, racy, salacious, risqué, offensive, off-color, lewd, pornographic, explicit, X-rated; *informal* blue, triple-X, XXX; *euphemistic* adult. ANTONYM clean.

3 *dirty tricks* DISHONEST, deceitful, unscrupulous, dishonorable, unsporting, ungentlemanly, below the belt, unfair, unethical, unprincipled; crooked, double-dealing, underhanded, sly, crafty, devious, sneaky. ANTONYMS honest, decent.

4 *informal a dirty cheat* DESPICABLE, contemptible, hateful, vile, low, mean, unworthy, worthless, beyond contempt, sordid; *informal* rotten; *archaic* scurvy. ANTONYMS trustworthy, decent.

5 *a dirty look* MALEVOLENT, resentful, hostile, black, dark; angry, cross, indignant, annoyed, disapproving; *informal* peeved.

▸ verb *he dirtied her nice clean towels* SOIL, stain, muddy, blacken, mess up, mark, spatter, bespatter, smudge, smear, splatter; sully, pollute, foul, defile; *literary* befoul, besmirch, begrime. ANTONYM clean.

disability noun *my disability makes getting into bed a slow process* HANDICAP, disablement, incapacity, impairment, infirmity, defect, abnormality; condition, disorder, affliction.

disable verb 1 *an injury that could disable somebody for life* INCAPACITATE, put out of action, debilitate; handicap, cripple, lame, maim, immobilize, paralyze.

2 *the bomb squad disabled the device* DEACTIVATE, defuse, disarm.

3 *he was disabled from holding public office* DISQUALIFY, prevent, preclude.

disabled adjective 1 *a disabled athlete* HANDICAPPED, incapacitated; debilitated, infirm, out of action; crippled, lame, paralyzed, immobilized, bedridden, paraplegic, quadriplegic, in a wheelchair; *euphemistic* physically challenged, differently abled. See note at HANDICAPPED. ANTONYM able-bodied.

2 *a disabled cargo ship* BROKEN DOWN, out of service, out of commission, wrecked. ANTONYM functioning.

disabuse verb *it isn't easy to* ***disabuse*** *people* ***of*** *something they've been taught to believe in* DISILLUSION ABOUT, undeceive about, set straight on/about, open someone's eyes about, correct on, enlighten on/about, disenchant about, shatter someone's illusions about.

disadvantage noun *the long commute is a big disadvantage of this job* DRAWBACK, snag, downside, stumbling block, fly in the ointment, catch, hindrance, obstacle, impediment; flaw, defect, weakness, fault, handicap, con, trouble, difficulty, problem, complication, nuisance; *informal* minus. ANTONYM benefit.

disadvantaged adjective *disadvantaged families will not be helped by these measures* DEPRIVED, underprivileged, depressed, in need, needy, poor, impoverished, indigent, hard up.

disadvantageous adjective *this puts us in a disadvantageous position* UNFAVORABLE, adverse, unfortunate, unlucky, bad; detrimental, prejudicial, deleterious, harmful, damaging, injurious, hurtful; inconvenient, inopportune, ill-timed, untimely, inexpedient.

disaffected adjective *a plot by disaffected soldiers* DISSATISFIED, disgruntled, discontented, malcontent, frustrated, alienated; disloyal, rebellious, mutinous, seditious, dissident, up in arms; hostile, antagonistic, unfriendly. See note at SOLITUDE. ANTONYM contented.

disagree verb **1** *no one was willing to* ***disagree with*** *him* TAKE ISSUE WITH, challenge, contradict, oppose; be at variance with, be at odds with, not see eye to eye with, differ with, dissent from, be in dispute with, debate with, argue with, quarrel with, wrangle with, clash with, be at loggerheads with, cross swords with, lock horns with; *formal* gainsay.

2 *their accounts disagree on details* DIFFER, be dissimilar, be different, vary, diverge; contradict each other, conflict, clash, contrast.

3 *the spicy food* ***disagreed with*** *her* MAKE ILL, make unwell, nauseate, sicken, upset.

disagreeable adjective **1** *a disagreeable smell* UNPLEASANT, displeasing, nasty, offensive, off-putting, obnoxious, objectionable, horrible, horrid, dreadful, frightful, abominable, odious, repugnant, repulsive, repellent, revolting, disgusting, foul, vile, nauseating, sickening, unpalatable. ANTONYM pleasant.

2 *a disagreeable man* BAD-TEMPERED, ill-tempered, curmudgeonly, cross, crabbed, irritable, grumpy, peevish, sullen, prickly; unfriendly, unpleasant, nasty, mean, mean-spirited, ill-natured, rude, surly, discourteous, impolite, brusque, abrupt, churlish, disobliging. ANTONYM pleasant.

disagreement noun **1** *there was some disagreement over possible solutions* DISSENT, dispute, difference of opinion, variance, controversy, discord, contention, division.

2 *a heated disagreement* ARGUMENT, debate, quarrel, wrangle, squabble, falling-out, altercation, dispute, disputation, war of words, contretemps; *informal* tiff, set-to, blowup, spat, row.

3 *the disagreement between the results of the two assessments* DIFFERENCE, dissimilarity, variation, variance, discrepancy, disparity, divergence, deviation, nonconformity; incompatibility, contradiction, conflict, clash, contrast.

disallow verb *Nguyen's testimony will be disallowed* REJECT, refuse, dismiss, say no to; ban, bar, block, debar, forbid, prohibit; cancel, invalidate, overrule, quash, overturn, countermand, reverse, throw out, set aside; *informal* give the thumbs down to, veto, nix. See note at PROHIBIT.

disappear verb **1** *by 4 o'clock the mist had disappeared* VANISH, pass from sight, be lost to view/sight, recede from view; fade (away), melt away, clear, dissolve, disperse, evaporate, dematerialize; *literary* evanesce. ANTONYM materialize.

2 *this way of life has disappeared* DIE OUT, die, cease to exist, come to an end, end, pass away, pass into oblivion, perish, vanish. ANTONYM survive.

disappoint verb **1** *I'm sorry to have disappointed you* LET DOWN, fail, dissatisfy, dash someone's hopes; upset, dismay, sadden, disenchant, disillusion, shatter someone's illusions, disabuse. ANTONYMS please, satisfy.

2 *his hopes were disappointed* THWART, frustrate, foil, dash, put a damper on; *informal* throw cold water on. ANTONYM fulfill.

disappointed adjective *it was hard to look into those disappointed faces* UPSET, saddened, let down, cast down, disheartened, downhearted, downcast, depressed, dispirited, discouraged, despondent, dismayed, crestfallen, distressed, chagrined; disenchanted, disillusioned; displeased, discontented, dissatisfied, frustrated, disgruntled; *informal* choked, bummed (out), miffed, cut up. ANTONYM pleased.

disappointing adjective *a pretty good movie up until the disappointing ending* REGRETTABLE, unfortunate, sorry, discouraging, disheartening, dispiriting, depressing, dismaying, upsetting, saddening; unsatisfactory; *informal* not all it's cracked up to be.

disappointment noun **1** *his disappointment in the outcome was obvious* SADNESS, regret, dismay, sorrow; dispiritedness, despondency, distress, chagrin; disenchantment, disillusionment; displeasure, dissatisfaction, disgruntlement. ANTONYM satisfaction.

2 *the trip was a bit of a disappointment* LETDOWN, nonevent, anticlimax, washout; *informal* bummer.

disapprobation noun See DISAPPROVAL.

disapproval noun *their strong disapproval of the law* DISAPPROBATION, objection, dislike; dissatisfaction, disfavor, displeasure, distaste; criticism, censure, condemnation, denunciation, deprecation; *informal* thumbs down.

disapprove verb **1** *he* ***disapproved of*** *gamblers* OBJECT TO, have a poor opinion of, look down one's nose at, take exception to, dislike, take a dim view of, look askance at, frown on, be against, not believe in; deplore, criticize, censure, condemn, denounce, decry, deprecate.

2 *the board disapproved the plan* REJECT, veto, refuse, turn down, disallow, throw out, dismiss, rule against; *informal* nix.

disapproving adjective *he cast a disapproving glance* REPROACHFUL, reproving, critical, censorious, condemnatory, condemning, disparaging, denigratory, deprecatory, unfavorable; dissatisfied, displeased, hostile.

disarm verb **1** *the UN must disarm the country* DEMILITARIZE, demobilize.

2 *the militia refused to disarm* LAY DOWN ONE'S ARMS, demilitarize; *literary* beat one's swords into plowshares.

3 *police disarmed the bomb* DEFUSE, disable, deactivate, put out of action, make harmless.

4 *the warmth in his voice disarmed her* WIN OVER, charm, persuade, thaw; mollify, appease, placate, pacify, conciliate, propitiate.

disarmament noun *the public wanted peace and disarmament* DEMILITARIZATION, demobilization, decommissioning; arms reduction, arms limitation, arms control; the zero option.

disarming adjective *a disarming smile* WINNING, charming, irresistible, persuasive, beguiling; conciliatory, mollifying.

disarrange verb *every year the festival gets bigger, and every year the town gets more disarranged* DISORDER, throw into disarray/disorder, put out of place, disorganize, disturb, displace; mess up, make untidy, make a mess of, jumble, mix up, muddle, turn upside-down, scatter; dishevel, tousle, rumple; *informal* turn topsy-turvy, make a shambles of, muss up.

disarray noun *the room was in disarray* DISORDER, confusion, chaos, untidiness, disorganization, dishevelment, mess, muddle, clutter, jumble, tangle, shambles. See note at JUMBLE. ANTONYM tidiness.

disassemble verb *the playground equipment has to be disassembled and moved to another site* DISMANTLE, take apart, take to pieces, take to bits, deconstruct, break up, strip down.

disassociate verb See DISSOCIATE verb.

disaster noun **1** *a subway disaster* CATASTROPHE, calamity, cataclysm, tragedy, act of God, holocaust; accident.

2 *a string of personal disasters* MISFORTUNE, mishap, misadventure, mischance, setback, reversal, stroke of bad luck, blow. ANTONYM blessing.

3 *informal the film was a disaster* FAILURE, fiasco, catastrophe, debacle; *informal* flop, megaflop, dud, bomb, washout, dog, turkey, dead loss. ANTONYM success.

disastrous adjective *a series of disastrous floods* CATASTROPHIC, calamitous, cataclysmic, tragic; devastating, ruinous, harmful, dire, terrible, awful, shocking, appalling, dreadful; black, dark, unfortunate, unlucky, ill-fated, ill-starred, inauspicious; *formal* grievous.

disavow verb *the chairman disavowed the press release* DENY, disclaim, disown, wash one's hands of, repudiate, reject, renounce.

disavowal noun *it's a complete disavowal of responsibility* DENIAL, rejection, repudiation, renunciation, disclaimer.

disband verb *the unit was scheduled to disband* BREAK UP, disperse, demobilize, dissolve, scatter, separate, go separate ways, part company. ANTONYM assemble.

disbelief noun **1** *she stared at him in disbelief* INCREDULITY, astonishment, amazement, surprise, incredulousness; skepticism, doubt, doubtfulness, dubiousness; cynicism, suspicion, distrust, mistrust; *formal* dubiety.

2 *I guess I'll burn in hell for my disbelief* ATHEISM, nonbelief, unbelief, godlessness, irreligion, agnosticism, nihilism.

disbelieve verb *we've learned to disbelieve most of Hubert's explanations* NOT BELIEVE, give no credence to, discredit, discount, doubt, distrust, mistrust, be incredulous, be unconvinced; reject, repudiate, question, challenge; *informal* take with a pinch of salt.

disbeliever noun *they promised to pray for us disbelievers* UNBELIEVER, nonbeliever, atheist, nihilist; skeptic, doubter, agnostic, doubting Thomas, cynic.

disbelieving adjective *he regretted having been so disbelieving* INCREDULOUS, doubtful, dubious, unconvinced; distrustful, mistrustful, suspicious, cynical, skeptical.

disburden verb *how shall I disburden myself of these worries?* RELIEVE, free, liberate, unburden, disencumber, discharge, excuse, absolve.

disburse verb *the proceeds were disbursed weekly* PAY OUT, spend, expend, dole out, dish out, hand out, part with, donate, give; *informal* fork out/over, shell out, lay out, ante up, pony up.

disc, disk noun **1** *the sun was a huge scarlet disc* CIRCLE, round, saucer, discus, ring, round; coin.

2 *computer disks.* See DISK sense 1.

3 *dated an old Stones disc* RECORD, album, LP, vinyl.

discard verb *his old suit has been discarded* DISPOSE OF, throw away/out, get rid of, toss out, jettison, scrap, dispense with, cast aside/off, throw on the scrap heap; reject, repudiate, abandon, drop, have done with, shed; *informal* chuck, dump, ditch, junk, trash, deep-six. ANTONYM keep.

discern verb *they could discern a slender figure, probably a woman, slowly approaching* PERCEIVE, make out, pick out, detect, recognize, notice, observe, see, spot; identify, determine, distinguish; *literary* descry, espy. See note at DISTINGUISH.

discernible adjective *in the fog our flares may be barely discernible* VISIBLE, detectable, noticeable, perceptible, observable, distinguishable, recognizable, identifiable; apparent, evident, distinct, appreciable, clear, obvious, manifest, conspicuous.

discerning adjective *some real treasures for the discerning collector* DISCRIMINATING, judicious, shrewd, clever, astute, intelligent, sharp, selective, sophisticated, tasteful, sensitive, perceptive, percipient, perspicacious, wise, aware, knowing; *informal* clueful.

discharge verb **1** *after his third violation, Vance was discharged* DISMISS, eject, expel, throw out, give someone notice; release, let go, fire, terminate; *Military* cashier; *informal* sack, give someone the sack, boot out, give someone the boot, turf out, give someone their marching orders, show someone the door, send packing, pink-slip, give some the (old) heave-ho. ANTONYMS recruit, engage.

2 *he was discharged from prison* RELEASE, free, set free, let go, liberate, let out. ANTONYM imprison.

3 *oil is routinely discharged from ships* SEND OUT, release, eject, let out, pour out, void, give off.

4 *the swelling will burst and discharge pus* EMIT, exude, ooze, leak. ANTONYM absorb.

5 *he accidentally discharged the gun* FIRE, shoot, let off; set off, trigger, explode, detonate.

6 *the ferry was discharging passengers* UNLOAD, offload, put off; remove. ANTONYM load.

7 *they discharged their duties efficiently* CARRY OUT, perform, execute, conduct, do; fulfill, accomplish, achieve, complete.

8 *the executor must discharge the funeral expenses* PAY, pay off, settle, clear, honor, meet, liquidate, defray, make good; *informal* square.

▸ noun **1** *his discharge from the service* DISMISSAL, release, removal, ejection, expulsion; *Military* cashiering; *informal* the sack, the boot, the ax, a/the pink slip.

2 *her discharge from prison* RELEASE, liberation.

3 *a discharge of diesel oil into the river* LEAK, leakage, emission, release, flow.

4 *a watery discharge from the eyes* EMISSION, secretion, excretion, seepage, suppuration; pus, matter; *Medicine* exudate.

5 *a single discharge of his gun* SHOT, firing, blast; explosion, detonation.

6 *the discharge of their duties* CARRYING OUT, performance, performing, execution, conduct; fulfillment, accomplishment, completion.

7 *the discharge of all debts* PAYMENT, repayment, settlement, clearance, meeting, liquidation.

disciple noun 1 *the disciples of Jesus* APOSTLE, follower.

2 *a disciple of Rousseau* FOLLOWER, adherent, believer, admirer, devotee, acolyte, votary; pupil, student, learner; upholder, supporter, advocate, proponent, apologist.

disciplinarian noun *Mr. Chips was the antithesis of the stern disciplinarian that the boys had come to expect* MARTINET, hard taskmaster, authoritarian, stickler for discipline; tyrant, despot, ramrod; *informal* slave driver.

discipline noun 1 *a lack of proper parental discipline* CONTROL, training, teaching, instruction, regulation, direction, order, authority, rule, strictness, a firm hand; routine, regimen, drill, drilling.

2 *he was able to maintain discipline among his men* GOOD BEHAVIOR, orderliness, control, obedience; self-control, self-discipline, self-government, self-restraint.

3 *sociology is a fairly new discipline* FIELD (OF STUDY), branch of knowledge, subject, area; specialty.

▸ verb 1 *she had disciplined herself to ignore the pain* TRAIN, drill, teach, school, coach; regiment.

2 *she learned to discipline her emotions* CONTROL, restrain, regulate, govern, keep in check, check, curb, keep a tight rein on, rein in, bridle, tame, bring into line.

3 *he was disciplined by management* PUNISH, penalize, bring to book; reprimand, rebuke, reprove, chastise, upbraid; *informal* dress down, give someone a dressing-down, rap on/over the knuckles, give someone a roasting, call (up) on the carpet; *formal* castigate.

disclaimer noun 1 *a disclaimer of responsibility* DENIAL, refusal, rejection. ANTONYMS acceptance, acknowledgment.

2 *Law a deed of disclaimer* RENUNCIATION, relinquishment, resignation, abdication; repudiation, abjuration, disavowal.

disclose verb 1 *the information must not be disclosed to anyone* REVEAL, make known, divulge, tell, impart, communicate, pass on, vouchsafe; release, make public, broadcast, publish, report, unveil; leak, betray, let slip, let drop, give away; *informal* let on, blab, spill the beans, let the cat out of the bag; *archaic* discover, unbosom. ANTONYM conceal.

2 *exploratory surgery disclosed an aneurysm* UNCOVER, reveal, show, expose, bring to light.

disclosure noun 1 *she was embarrassed by this unexpected disclosure* REVELATION, declaration, announcement, news, report; leak.

2 *the disclosure of official information* PUBLISHING, broadcasting; revelation, communication, release, uncovering, unveiling, exposure, exposé; leakage.

discolor verb *smoke will discolor the fabric* STAIN, mark, soil, dirty, streak, smear, spot, tarnish, sully, spoil, mar, blemish; blacken, char; fade, bleach.

discoloration noun *a brown discoloration on the skin* STAIN, mark, streak, spot, blotch, tarnishing; blemish, flaw, defect, bruise, contusion; birthmark, nevus; liver spot, age spot; *informal* splotch.

discolored adjective *he wanted to whiten his discolored teeth* STAINED, marked, spotted, dirty, soiled, tarnished, blackened; bleached, faded, yellowed.

discombobulate verb *informal* See DISCOMFIT.

discomfit verb *her kiss on the cheek discomfited him even more* EMBARRASS, abash, disconcert, discompose, discomfort, take aback, unsettle, unnerve, put someone off their game, ruffle, confuse, fluster, agitate, disorient, upset, disturb, perturb, distress; chagrin, mortify; *informal* faze, rattle, discombobulate.

discomfiture noun *I admit we were somewhat amused by his discomfiture* EMBARRASSMENT, unease, uneasiness, awkwardness, discomfort, discomposure, abashment, confusion, agitation, nervousness, disorientation, perturbation, distress; chagrin, mortification, shame, humiliation; *informal* discombobulation.

discomfort noun 1 *abdominal discomfort* PAIN, aches and pains, soreness, tenderness, irritation, stiffness; ache, twinge, pang, throb, cramp.

2 *the discomforts of life at sea* INCONVENIENCE, difficulty, bother, nuisance, vexation, drawback, disadvantage, trouble, problem, trial, tribulation, hardship; *informal* hassle.

3 *she was unable to hide her discomfort* EMBARRASSMENT, discomfiture, unease, uneasiness, awkwardness, discomposure, confusion, nervousness, perturbation, distress, anxiety; chagrin, mortification, shame, humiliation.

▸ verb *his purpose was to discomfort the president.* See DISCOMFIT.

discomposure noun *she laughed to cover her discomposure* AGITATION, discomfiture, discomfort, uneasiness, unease, confusion, disorientation, perturbation, distress, nervousness; anxiety, worry, consternation, disquiet, disquietude; embarrassment, abashment, chagrin, loss of face; *informal* discombobulation.

disconcert verb *Sheila's unexpected appearance disconcerted him* UNSETTLE, discomfit, throw/catch off balance, take aback, rattle, unnerve, disorient, perturb, disturb, perplex, confuse, bewilder, baffle, fluster, ruffle, shake, upset, agitate, worry, dismay, surprise, take by surprise, startle, put someone off (their game), distract; *informal* throw, faze, discombobulate.

disconcerting adjective *the intense scrutiny was disconcerting* UNSETTLING, unnerving, discomfiting, disturbing, perturbing, troubling, upsetting, worrying, alarming, distracting, off-putting; confusing, bewildering, perplexing.

disconnect verb 1 *the trucks were disconnected from the train* DETACH, disengage, uncouple, decouple, unhook, unhitch, undo, unfasten, unyoke. ANTONYM attach.

2 *she felt as if she were disconnected from the real world* SEPARATE, cut off, divorce, sever, isolate, divide, part, disengage, dissociate, disassociate, remove.

3 *an engineer disconnected the power source* DEACTIVATE, shut off, turn off, switch off, unplug.

disconnected adjective 1 *a world that seemed disconnected from reality* DETACHED, separate, separated, divorced, cut off, isolated, dissociated, disengaged; apart.

2 *a disconnected narrative* DISJOINTED, incoherent, garbled, confused, jumbled, mixed up, rambling, wandering, disorganized, uncoordinated, ill-thought-out.

disconsolate adjective *his partner had to face the disconsolate investors on his own* SAD, unhappy, doleful, woebegone, dejected, downcast, downhearted, despondent, dispirited, crestfallen, cast down, depressed, down, disappointed, disheartened, discouraged, demoralized, low-spirited, forlorn, in the doldrums, melancholy, miserable, long-faced, glum, gloomy; *informal* blue, choked, down in/at the mouth, down in the dumps, in a blue funk; *literary* dolorous. ANTONYM cheerful.

discontent noun *the workers' discontent could no longer be overlooked* DISSATISFACTION, disaffection, discontentment, discontentedness, disgruntlement, grievances, unhappiness, displeasure, bad feelings, resentment, envy; restlessness, unrest, uneasiness, unease, frustration, irritation, annoyance; *informal* a chip on one's shoulder. ANTONYM satisfaction.

discontented adjective *discontented parents attended the meeting in record numbers* DISSATISFIED, disgruntled, fed up, disaffected, discontent, malcontent, unhappy, aggrieved, displeased, resentful; restless, frustrated, irritated, annoyed; *informal* fed up (to the teeth), teed off, ticked off. ANTONYM satisfied.

discontinue verb *ferry service was discontinued* STOP, end, terminate, put an end to, put a stop to, finish, call a halt to, cancel, drop, abandon, dispense with, do away with, get rid of, ax, abolish; suspend, interrupt, break off, withdraw; *informal* cut, pull the plug on, scrap, nix.

discontinuity noun *close examination revealed a discontinuity in the grain pattern* DISCONNECTEDNESS, disconnection, break, lack of unity, disruption, interruption, lack of coherence, disjointedness.

discontinuous adjective *a discontinuous employment record* INTERMITTENT, sporadic, broken, fitful, interrupted, on and off, disrupted, erratic, disconnected.

discord noun 1 *stress resulting from family discord* STRIFE, conflict, friction, hostility, antagonism, antipathy, enmity, bad feeling, ill feeling, bad blood, argument, quarreling, squabbling, bickering, wrangling, feuding, contention, disagreement, dissension, dispute, difference of opinion, disunity, division, opposition; infighting. ANTONYMS accord, harmony.

2 *the music faded in discord* DISSONANCE, discordance, disharmony, cacophony. ANTONYM harmony.

discordant adjective 1 *the messages from Washington and Ottawa were discordant* DIFFERENT, in disagreement, at variance, at odds, divergent, discrepant, contradictory, contrary, in conflict, conflicting, opposite, opposed, opposing, clashing; incompatible, inconsistent, irreconcilable. ANTONYMS harmonious, compatible.

2 *discordant sounds* INHARMONIOUS, tuneless, off-key, dissonant, harsh, jarring, grating, jangling, jangly, strident, shrill, screeching, screechy, cacophonous; sharp, flat. ANTONYMS harmonious, dulcet.

discount noun *students get a 10 percent discount* REDUCTION, deduction, markdown, price cut, cut, rebate.

▸ verb 1 *I'd heard rumors, but I discounted them* DISREGARD, pay no attention to, take no notice of, take no account of, dismiss, ignore, overlook, disbelieve, reject; *informal* take with a pinch of salt, pooh-pooh. ANTONYM believe.

2 *the actual price is discounted in many stores* REDUCE, mark down, cut, lower; *informal* knock down. ANTONYM increase.

3 *show your card and they'll discount 40 percent* DEDUCT, take off, rebate; *informal* knock off, slash off. ANTONYM add.

discourage verb 1 *we want to* ***discourage*** *children* ***from*** *smoking* DETER FROM, dissuade from, disincline from, put off, talk out of; advise against, urge against; *archaic* discountenance from. ANTONYM encourage.

2 *she was discouraged by his hostile tone* DISHEARTEN, dispirit, demoralize, cast down, depress, disappoint; put off, unnerve, daunt, intimidate, cow, crush. ANTONYMS encourage, hearten.

3 *he sought to discourage further conversation* PREVENT, stop, put a stop to, avert, fend off, stave off, ward off; inhibit, hinder, check, curb, put a damper on, throw cold water on. ANTONYM encourage.

discouraged adjective *Doug must be feeling pretty discouraged* DISHEARTENED, dispirited, demoralized, deflated, disappointed, let down, disconsolate, despondent, dejected, cast down, downcast, depressed, crestfallen, dismayed, low-spirited, gloomy, glum, pessimistic, unenthusiastic; put off, daunted, intimidated, cowed, crushed; *informal* down in/at the mouth, down in the dumps, unenthused, bummed.

discouraging adjective *most reports from the area are discouraging* DEPRESSING, demoralizing, disheartening, dispiriting, disappointing, gloomy, off-putting; unfavorable, unpromising, inauspicious. ANTONYM encouraging.

discourse noun 1 *they prolonged their discourse outside the door* DISCUSSION, conversation, talk, dialogue, conference, debate, consultation; parley, powwow, chat, confab; *formal* confabulation, colloquy.

2 *a discourse on critical theory* ESSAY, treatise, dissertation, paper, study, critique, monograph, disquisition, tract; lecture, address, speech, oration; sermon, homily.

▸ verb 1 *he discoursed at length on his favorite topic* HOLD FORTH, expatiate, pontificate; talk, give a talk, give a speech, lecture, sermonize, preach; *informal* spout, sound off; *formal* perorate.

2 *Edward was discoursing with his friends* CONVERSE, talk, speak, debate, confer, consult, parley, chat.

discourteous adjective *it would be discourteous to ignore her* RUDE, impolite, ill-mannered, bad-mannered, disrespectful, uncivil, unmannerly, unchivalrous, ungentlemanly, unladylike, ill-bred, churlish, boorish, crass, ungracious, graceless, uncouth; insolent, impudent, cheeky, audacious, presumptuous; curt, brusque, blunt, offhand, unceremonious, short, sharp; ignorant. ANTONYM polite.

discourtesy noun *these parents seemed unfazed by the discourtesy of their children* RUDENESS, impoliteness, bad manners, incivility, disrespect, ungraciousness, churlishness, boorishness, ill breeding, uncouthness, crassness;

insolence, impudence, impertinence; curtness, brusqueness, abruptness.

discover verb 1 *firemen discovered a body in the debris* FIND, locate, come across/upon, stumble on, chance on, light on, bring to light, uncover, unearth, turn up; track down.

2 *eventually, I discovered the truth* FIND OUT, learn, realize, recognize, fathom, see, ascertain, work out, dig up/out, ferret out, root out; *informal* figure out, dope out.

3 *scientists discovered a new way of dating fossil crustaceans* HIT ON, come up with, invent, originate, devise, design, contrive, conceive of; pioneer, develop.

discoverer noun *the discoverer of penicillin* ORIGINATOR, inventor, creator, deviser, designer; pioneer, explorer.

discovery noun 1 *the discovery of the body* FINDING, location, uncovering, unearthing.

2 *the discovery that she was pregnant* REALIZATION, recognition; revelation, disclosure.

3 *the discovery of new drugs* INVENTION, origination, devising; pioneering.

4 *he failed to take out a patent on his discoveries* FIND, finding; invention, breakthrough, innovation.

discredit verb 1 *an attempt to discredit him and his company* BRING INTO DISREPUTE, disgrace, dishonor, damage the reputation of, blacken the name of, put/show in a bad light, reflect badly on, compromise, stigmatize, smear, tarnish, taint, slur.

2 *that theory has been discredited* DISPROVE, invalidate, explode, refute; *informal* debunk, poke holes in; *formal* confute.

▸ noun 1 *crimes that brought discredit on the administration* DISHONOR, disrepute, disgrace, shame, humiliation, ignominy, infamy, notoriety; censure, blame, reproach, opprobrium; stigma; *dated* disesteem. ANTONYM honor.

2 *the ships were a discredit to the country* DISGRACE, source of shame, reproach. ANTONYM glory.

discreditable adjective *his discreditable conduct* DISHONORABLE, reprehensible, shameful, deplorable, disgraceful, disreputable, blameworthy, ignoble, shabby, objectionable, regrettable, unacceptable, unworthy. ANTONYM praiseworthy.

discreet adjective 1 *discreet inquiries* CAREFUL, circumspect, cautious, wary, chary, guarded; tactful, diplomatic, prudent, judicious, strategic, politic, delicate, sensitive, kid-glove.

2 *discreet lighting* UNOBTRUSIVE, inconspicuous, subtle, low-key, understated, subdued, muted, soft, restrained.

discrepancy noun *the discrepancy between the two sets of figures* DIFFERENCE, disparity, variance, variation, deviation, divergence, disagreement, inconsistency, dissimilarity, mismatch, discordance, incompatibility, conflict. ANTONYM correspondence.

discrete adjective *discrete units of sound* SEPARATE, distinct, individual, detached, unattached, disconnected, discontinuous, disjunct, disjoined. ANTONYM connected.

discretion noun 1 *you can rely on his discretion* CIRCUMSPECTION, carefulness, caution, wariness, chariness, guardedness; TACT, tactfulness, diplomacy, delicacy, sensitivity, prudence, judiciousness.

2 *his sentence would be determined at the discretion of the court* CHOICE, option, preference, disposition, volition; pleasure, liking, wish, will, inclination, desire.

discretionary adjective *a discretionary service charge* OPTIONAL, voluntary, at one's discretion, elective. ANTONYM compulsory.

discriminate verb 1 *he cannot discriminate between fact and fiction* DIFFERENTIATE, distinguish, draw a distinction, tell the difference, tell apart; separate, separate the sheep from the goats, separate the wheat from the chaff. See note at DISTINGUISH.

2 *existing employment policies* ***discriminate against*** *women* BE BIASED AGAINST, be prejudiced against; treat differently, treat unfairly, put at a disadvantage, single out; victimize.

discriminating adjective *she had discriminating tastes* DISCERNING, perceptive, astute, shrewd, judicious, perspicacious, insightful, keen; selective, fastidious, tasteful, refined, sensitive, cultivated, cultured, artistic, aesthetic. ANTONYM indiscriminate.

discrimination noun 1 *racial discrimination* PREJUDICE, bias, bigotry, intolerance, narrow-mindedness, unfairness, inequity, favoritism, one-sidedness, partisanship; sexism, chauvinism, misogyny, racism, racialism, anti-Semitism, heterosexism, ageism, classism; *in South Africa, historical* apartheid. ANTONYM impartiality.

2 *a bland man with no discrimination* DISCERNMENT, judgment, perception, perceptiveness, perspicacity, acumen, astuteness, shrewdness, judiciousness, insight; selectivity, (good) taste, fastidiousness, refinement, sensitivity, cultivation, culture.

discriminatory adjective *the decision against Ms. Rodriquez was discriminatory* PREJUDICIAL, biased, prejudiced, preferential, unfair, unjust, invidious, inequitable, weighted, one-sided, partisan; sexist, chauvinistic, chauvinist, racist, racialist, anti-Semitic, ageist, classist. ANTONYM impartial.

discursive adjective 1 *dull, discursive prose* RAMBLING, digressive, meandering, wandering, maundering, diffuse, long, lengthy, wordy, verbose, long-winded, prolix; circuitous, roundabout, circumlocutory; *informal* waffly. ANTONYM concise.

2 *an elegant discursive style* FLUENT, flowing, fluid, eloquent, expansive. ANTONYM terse.

discuss verb 1 *I discussed the matter with my wife* TALK OVER, talk about, talk through, converse about, debate, confer about, deliberate about, chew over, consider, consider the pros and cons of, thrash out; *informal* kick around, hash out, bat around.

2 *the third chapter discusses this topic in detail* EXAMINE, explore, study, analyze, go into, deal with, treat, consider, concern itself with, tackle.

discussion noun 1 *a long discussion with her husband* CONVERSATION, talk, dialogue, discourse, conference, debate, exchange of views, consultation, deliberation; powwow, chat, tête-à-tête, heart-to-heart, huddle; negotiations, parley; *informal* confab, chitchat, rap (session), skull session, bull session; *formal* confabulation, colloquy.

2 *the book's candid discussion of sexual matters* EXAMINATION, exploration, analysis, study; treatment, consideration.

disdain noun *she looked at him with disdain* CONTEMPT, scorn, scornfulness, contemptuousness, derision, disrespect; disparagement, condescension, superciliousness, hauteur, haughtiness, arrogance, snobbishness, indifference, distaste, dislike, disgust. ANTONYM respect.

▸ verb **1** *she disdained vulgar exhibitionism* SCORN, deride, pour scorn on, regard with contempt, sneer at, sniff at, curl one's lip at, look down one's nose at, look down on; despise; *informal* turn up one's nose at, pooh-pooh. See note at DESPISE.

2 *we disdained his invitation* SPURN, reject, refuse, rebuff, disregard, ignore, snub; decline, turn down, brush aside.

disdainful adjective *Tyler was offended by his disdainful expression* CONTEMPTUOUS, scornful, derisive, sneering, withering, slighting, disparaging, disrespectful, condescending, patronizing, supercilious, haughty, superior, arrogant, proud, snobbish, lordly, aloof, indifferent, dismissive; *informal* high and mighty, hoity-toity, sniffy, snotty; *archaic* contumelious. ANTONYM respectful.

disease noun *herbal preparations to treat tropical diseases* ILLNESS, sickness, ill health; infection, ailment, malady, disorder, complaint, affliction, condition, indisposition, upset, problem, trouble, infirmity, disability, defect, abnormality; pestilence, plague, cancer, canker, blight; *informal* bug, virus. *dated* contagion.

diseased adjective *the diseased trees have been marked with red paint* UNHEALTHY, ill, sick, unwell, ailing, sickly, unsound; infected, septic, contaminated, blighted, rotten, bad, abnormal.

disembark verb *passengers are asked to disembark in single file* GET OFF, step off, leave, pile out; go ashore, debark, detrain, deplane; land, arrive, alight.

disembodied adjective *disembodied faces floated through the smoky mist* BODILESS, incorporeal, discarnate, spiritual; intangible, insubstantial, impalpable; ghostly, spectral, phantom, wraithlike.

USAGE NOTE **disembodied, dismembered**

Disembodied = separated from the physical body, esp. as a spirit. The word is stretched too far when used to describe a body part severed from the torso—e.g.: "Having said all that, did we really need to see the disembodied [read *severed*] heads? In a word: yuck. We got the idea with the hacksaw and the meat cleaver, thanks." (*Arizona Republic*; Nov. 21, 2002.)

Dismembered = (1) (of bodily limbs) cut from the torso; or (2) (of a torso) characterized by having had limbs cut off. This term does not work well with heads—e.g.: "In a flurry of recent TV appearances promoting his new book on families, the former vice president has been seen . . . floating as a dismembered [read *detached*] head in a jar on the Fox cartoon show 'Futurama,' where he's dubbed 'the inventor of the environment.' " (*Christian Science Monitor*; Nov. 19, 2002). **–BG**

disembowel verb *we cleaned and disemboweled the game before returning to the campsite* GUT, draw, remove the guts from; *formal* eviscerate.

disenchanted adjective *disenchanted with politics, he retired from the foreign service* DISILLUSIONED, disappointed, disabused, let down, fed up, dissatisfied, discontented; cynical, soured, jaundiced, sick, indifferent, blasé.

disenchantment noun *the disenchantment of a first love gone sour* DISILLUSIONMENT, disappointment, dissatisfaction, discontent, discontentedness, rude awakening; cynicism.

disengage verb **1** *I disengaged his hand from mine* REMOVE, detach, disentangle, extricate, separate, release, free, loosen, loose, disconnect, unfasten, unclasp, uncouple, undo, unhook, unhitch, untie, unyoke. ANTONYM attach.

2 *UN forces* ***disengaged from*** *the country* WITHDRAW FROM, leave, pull out of, quit, retreat from. ANTONYM enter.

disentangle verb **1** *Allen was disentangling a coil of rope* UNTANGLE, unravel, untwist, unwind, undo, untie, straighten out, smooth out; comb.

2 *he disentangled his fingers from her hair* EXTRICATE, extract, free, remove, disengage, untwine, release, loosen, detach, unfasten, unclasp, disconnect.

disfavor noun *the disfavor of his fellow students* DISAPPROVAL, disapprobation; dislike, displeasure, distaste, dissatisfaction, low opinion; *dated* disesteem.

disfigure verb *junkyards disfigure the landscape* MAR, spoil, deface, scar, blemish, uglify; damage, injure, impair, blight, mutilate, deform, maim, ruin; vandalize. ANTONYM adorn.

disfigurement noun **1** *the disfigurement of Victorian buildings* DEFACEMENT, spoiling, scarring, uglification, mutilation, damage, vandalizing, ruin.

2 *a permanent facial disfigurement* BLEMISH, flaw, defect, imperfection, discoloration, blotch; scar, pockmark; deformity, malformation, abnormality, injury, wound.

disgorge verb **1** *the combine disgorged a stream of grain* POUR OUT, discharge, eject, throw out, emit, expel, spit out, spew out, belch forth, spout; vomit, regurgitate.

2 *they were made to disgorge all the profits* SURRENDER, relinquish, hand over, give up, turn over, yield; *informal* cough up, fork over.

disgrace noun **1** *he brought disgrace on the family* DISHONOR, shame, discredit, ignominy, degradation, disrepute, ill repute, infamy, scandal, stigma, opprobrium, obloquy, condemnation, vilification, contempt, disrespect; humiliation, embarrassment, loss of face; *dated* disesteem. ANTONYM honor.

2 *the unemployment figures are a disgrace* SCANDAL, outrage; discredit, reproach, affront, insult; stain, blemish, blot, black mark; *informal* crime, sin. ANTONYM credit.

▸ verb **1** *you have disgraced the family name* BRING SHAME ON, shame, dishonor, discredit, bring into disrepute, degrade, debase, defame, stigmatize, taint, sully, tarnish, besmirch, stain, blacken, drag through the mud/mire. ANTONYM honor.

2 *he was publicly disgraced* DISCREDIT, dishonor, stigmatize; humiliate, cause to lose face, chasten, humble, demean, put someone in their place, take down a peg or two, cut down to size. ANTONYM honor.

PHRASE: **in disgrace** *Benjamin couldn't bear to return home in disgrace* OUT OF FAVOR, unpopular, under a cloud, disgraced; *informal* in the doghouse.

disgraceful adjective *they caught Warren's disgraceful behavior on videotape* SHAMEFUL, shocking, scandalous, deplorable, despicable, contemptible, beyond contempt, beyond the pale, dishonorable, discreditable, reprehensible, base, mean, low, blameworthy, unworthy, ignoble, shabby, inglorious, outrageous, abominable, atrocious, appalling, dreadful, terrible, disgusting, shameless, vile, odious, monstrous, heinous, iniquitous, unspeakable, loathsome, sordid, nefarious; *archaic* scurvy. ANTONYM admirable.

disgruntled adjective *poor service was the primary complaint of these disgruntled customers* DISSATISFIED, discontented, aggrieved, resentful, fed up, displeased, unhappy, disappointed, disaffected; angry, irate, annoyed, cross, exasperated, indignant, vexed, irritated, piqued, irked, put out, peeved, miffed, bummed, aggravated, hacked off, riled, peed off, PO'd, hot under the collar, in a huff, cheesed off, shirty, sore, teed off, ticked off.

disguise verb *his controlled voice disguised his true feelings* CAMOUFLAGE, conceal, hide, cover up, dissemble, mask, screen, shroud, veil, cloak; gloss over, put up a smokescreen to hide/mask. ANTONYM expose.

PHRASE: **disguise oneself as** *Eleanor disguised herself as a man* DRESS UP AS, pretend to be, pass oneself off as, impersonate, pose as; *formal* personate.

disguised adjective *a disguised investigator* IN DISGUISE, camouflaged; incognito, undercover.

disgust noun *a look of disgust* REVULSION, repugnance, aversion, distaste, nausea, abhorrence, loathing, detestation, odium, horror; contempt, outrage. ANTONYM delight.

▸ verb **1** *the hospital food disgusted me* REVOLT, repel, repulse, sicken, nauseate, turn someone's stomach; *informal* turn off, gross out.

2 *Toby's foul language disgusted her* OUTRAGE, shock, horrify, appall, scandalize, offend.

disgusting adjective **1** *the food was disgusting* REVOLTING, repellent, repulsive, sickening, nauseating, stomach-churning, stomach-turning, off-putting, unpalatable, distasteful, foul, nasty, vomitous; *informal* yucky, icky, gross. ANTONYMS delicious, appealing.

2 *I find racism disgusting* ABHORRENT, loathsome, offensive, appalling, outrageous, objectionable, shocking, horrifying, scandalous, monstrous, unspeakable, shameful, vile, odious, obnoxious, detestable, hateful, sickening, contemptible, despicable, deplorable, abominable, beyond the pale; *informal* gross, ghastly, sick. ANTONYM commendable.

dish noun **1** *a china dish* BOWL, plate, platter, salver, paten; container, receptacle, casserole, tureen; *archaic* trencher, charger; *historical* porringer.

2 *vegetarian dishes* RECIPE, meal, course; **(dishes)** food, fare.

3 *informal she's quite a dish.* See BEAUTY sense 2. PHRASE: **dish out** *they dished out free coffee and bagels to the volunteers* DISTRIBUTE, dispense, issue, hand out/around, give out, pass out/around; deal out, dole out, share out, allocate, allot, apportion.

disharmony noun *there seems to be no desire on either side to end this disharmony* DISCORD, friction, strife, conflict, hostility, acrimony, bad blood, bad feeling, enmity, dissension, disagreement, feuding, quarreling; disunity, division, divisiveness.

dishearten verb *poor reviews disheartened the young author* DISCOURAGE, dispirit, demoralize, cast down, depress, disappoint, dismay, dash someone's hopes; put off, deter, unnerve, daunt, intimidate, cow, crush. ANTONYM encourage.

disheartened adjective *our disheartened soccer team* DISCOURAGED, dispirited, demoralized, deflated, disappointed, let down, disconsolate, despondent, dejected, cast down, downcast, depressed, crestfallen, dismayed, low-spirited, gloomy, glum, pessimistic, unenthusiastic; daunted, intimidated, cowed, crushed; *informal* down in/at the mouth, down in the dumps, unenthused.

disheveled adjective *long and disheveled hair* UNTIDY, unkempt, scruffy, messy, in a mess, disordered, disarranged, rumpled, bedraggled; uncombed, tousled, tangled, tangly, knotted, knotty, shaggy, straggly, windswept, wind-blown, wild; slovenly, slatternly, blowsy, frowzy, mussed (up), mussy. ANTONYM tidy.

dishonest adjective *accused of dishonest business practices* FRAUDULENT, corrupt, swindling, cheating, double-dealing; underhanded, crafty, cunning, devious, treacherous, unfair, unjust, dirty, unethical, immoral, dishonorable, untrustworthy, unscrupulous, unprincipled, amoral; criminal, illegal, unlawful; false, untruthful, deceitful, deceiving, lying, mendacious; *informal* crooked, hinky, shady, tricky, sharp, shifty; *literary* perfidious.

dishonesty noun *Richard was a victim of his business manager's dishonesty* FRAUD, fraudulence, corruption, cheating, chicanery, double-dealing, deceit, deception, duplicity, lying, falseness, falsity, falsehood, untruthfulness; craft, cunning, trickery, artifice, underhandedness, subterfuge, skulduggery, treachery, untrustworthiness, unscrupulousness, criminality, misconduct; *informal* crookedness, dirty tricks, shenanigans; *literary* perfidy. ANTONYM probity.

dishonor noun *the incident brought dishonor upon the police department* DISGRACE, shame, discredit, humiliation, degradation, ignominy, scandal, infamy, disrepute, ill repute, loss of face, disfavor, ill favor, debasement, opprobrium, obloquy; stigma; *dated* disesteem.

▸ verb *his family name has been dishonored* DISGRACE, shame, discredit, bring into disrepute, humiliate, degrade, debase, lower, cheapen, drag down, drag through the mud, blacken the name of, give a bad name to; sully, stain, taint, besmirch, smear, mar, blot, stigmatize.

dishonorable adjective *dishonorable conduct cost Major Pierce her commission* DISGRACEFUL, shameful, disreputable, discreditable, degrading, ignominious, ignoble, blameworthy, contemptible, despicable, reprehensible, shabby, shoddy, sordid, sorry, base, low, improper, unseemly, unworthy; unprincipled, unscrupulous, corrupt, untrustworthy, treacherous, traitorous; *informal* shady, dirty; *literary* perfidious; *archaic* scurvy.

disillusion verb *we pretended to have a happy marriage because we didn't want to disillusion the children* DISABUSE, enlighten, set straight, open someone's eyes; disenchant, shatter someone's illusions, disappoint, make sadder and wiser. ANTONYM deceive.

disillusioned adjective *after Hiram's affair was made public, his wife became disillusioned and withdrawn* DISENCHANTED, disabused, disappointed, let down, discouraged; cynical, sour, negative, world-weary.

disincentive noun *high interest rates are a disincentive to investment* DETERRENT, discouragement, damper, brake, curb, check, restraint, inhibitor; obstacle, impediment, hindrance, obstruction, block, barrier.

disinclination noun *they show a disinclination to face the truth* RELUCTANCE, unwillingness, lack of enthusiasm, indisposition, hesitancy; aversion, dislike, distaste; objection, demur, resistance, opposition. ANTONYM enthusiasm.

disinclined adjective *she was disinclined to abandon the old ways* RELUCTANT, unwilling, unenthusiastic, unprepared, indisposed, ill-disposed, not in the mood, hesitant; loath, averse, antipathetic, resistant, opposed. ANTONYM willing.

disinfect verb *use bleach to disinfect your kitchen surfaces* STERILIZE, sanitize, clean, cleanse, purify, decontaminate; fumigate. ANTONYM contaminate.

disinfectant noun *vinegar is a natural disinfectant* ANTISEPTIC, germicide, sterilizer, cleanser, decontaminant; fumigant.

disingenuous adjective *that innocent, teary-eyed look is just part of a disingenuous act* INSINCERE, dishonest, untruthful, false, deceitful, duplicitous, lying, mendacious; hypocritical.

disinherit verb *Harrison's parents disinherited him when he joined a neo-Nazi cult* CUT SOMEONE OUT OF ONE'S WILL, cut off, dispossess; disown, repudiate, reject, cast off/aside, wash one's hands of, have nothing more to do with, turn one's back on; *informal* cut off without a penny.

disintegrate verb *steam causes the substance to disintegrate* BREAK UP, break apart, fall apart, fall to pieces, fragment, fracture, shatter, splinter; explode, blow up, blow apart, fly apart; crumble, deteriorate, decay, decompose, rot, molder, perish, dissolve, collapse, go to rack and ruin, degenerate; *informal* bust, be smashed to smithereens.

disinter verb *the defense attorney requested that the body be disinterred for further examination* EXHUME, unearth, dig up, disentomb.

disinterest noun **1** *scholarly disinterest* IMPARTIALITY, neutrality, objectivity, detachment, disinterestedness, lack of bias, lack of prejudice; open-mindedness, fairness, fair-mindedness, equity, balance, evenhandedness. ANTONYM bias.

2 *he looked at us with complete disinterest* INDIFFERENCE, lack of interest, unconcern, impassivity; boredom, apathy.

disinterested adjective **1** *disinterested advice* UNBIASED, unprejudiced, impartial, neutral, nonpartisan, detached, uninvolved, objective, dispassionate, impersonal, clinical; open-minded, fair, just, equitable, balanced, evenhanded, with no ax to grind.

2 *he looked at her with disinterested eyes* UNINTERESTED, indifferent, incurious, uncurious, unconcerned, unmoved, unresponsive, impassive, passive, detached, unenthusiastic, lukewarm, bored, apathetic; *informal* couldn't-care-less.

USAGE NOTE **disinterested, uninterested**

Disinterest = (1) impartiality or freedom from bias or from chance of financial benefit; or (2) lack of concern or attention. Leading writers and editors almost unanimously reject sense 2, for which *uninterest* is the better term. Given the overlapping nouns, writers have found it difficult to keep the past-participial adjectives entirely separate, and many have given up the fight to preserve the distinction between them. But the distinction is still best recognized and followed because *disinterested* captures a nuance that no other word quite does. Many influential writers have urged the preservation of its traditional sense. The typically understated A. R. Orage rhapsodized over the word: "No word in the English language is more difficult [than *disinterestedness*] to define or better worth attempting to define. Somewhere or other in its capacious folds it contains all the ideas of ethics and even, I should say, of religion . . . . I venture to say that whoever has understood the meaning of 'disinterestedness' is not far off understanding the goal of human culture." (*Readers and Writers: 1917–1921*; 1922.)

A *disinterested* observer is not merely "impartial" but has nothing to gain from taking a stand on the issue in question. The illustrative quotation that follows deals with journalists' disinterest: "In the film, Wexler's directorial debut, a cameraman portrayed by Robert Forster must wrestle with being a disinterested observer or becoming emotionally involved with what he sees through his lens." (*Los Angeles Times*; Aug. 26, 1996.)

Yet *disinterested* is frequently used (or, in traditionalists' eyes, misused) for *uninterested*—e.g.: "On a day when seeded players fell by the wayside like overripe tomatoes, Agassi looked sickly and almost disinterested [read *uninterested*]." (*Toronto Sun*; June 25, 1996.) **—BG**

WORD NOTE **disinterested**

It is my experience that whenever one is trapped in a bar by a logomaniac, a word-bore, he will sooner or later bring to your notice His View, as though it were worth hearing, of the word *disinterested.* I simply *cannot stand it,* he will say, when young people (who are apparently always to blame for linguistic solecisms) use *disinterested* to mean *not interested,* when of course it properly means *unbiased,* and the word they should be using if they weren't lazy and careless butchers of the tongue, is *uninterested.* Well, I have two pieces of news for you, Mr. Bore. First of all, *disinterested* has been used to mean not interested for a much longer time than it has ever been used to denote "nonpartisan"—nearly 50 seventeenth-century years separate the first use of one meaning from the other. And secondly—a sufficient number of these lazy and (in the logomaniacal view) wrongheaded people, old, young, sensible, and stupid, have lately been employing the word to mean "not interested" that any future editions of a good and nonprescriptive dictionary will be bound to note that this is now a perfectly legitimate way of using the word again, if not the principal one. So forget the argument. Get over it. Though *disinterested* certainly and uniquely does have the sense of "unbiased," it happens that in general use these days—and back in the beginning of the seventeenth century also, it seems—it means "uninterested" too. **—SW**

disjointed adjective *the discussion was too disjointed to follow* UNCONNECTED, disconnected, disunited, discontinuous, fragmented, disorganized, disordered, muddled, mixed up, jumbled, garbled, incoherent, confused; rambling, wandering.

disk, disc noun **1** *a box of blank disks* DISKETTE, floppy disk, floppy; hard disk; zip disk; CD, CD-ROM, DVD.

2 *shape it into the form of a disc.* See DISC sense 1.

dislike verb *a man she had always disliked* FIND DISTASTEFUL, regard with distaste, be averse to, have an aversion to, have no liking/taste for, disapprove of, object to, take exception to; hate, detest, loathe, abhor, despise, be unable to bear/stand, shrink from, shudder at, find repellent; *informal* be unable to stomach; *formal* abominate.

▸ noun *she viewed the other woman with dislike* DISTASTE, aversion, disfavor, disapproval, disapprobation, enmity, animosity, hostility, antipathy, antagonism; hate, hatred, detestation, loathing, disgust, repugnance, abhorrence, disdain, contempt.

dislocate verb **1** *she dislocated her hip* PUT OUT OF JOINT; *informal* put out; *Medicine* luxate.

2 *trade was dislocated by a famine* DISRUPT, disturb, throw into disarray, throw into confusion, play havoc with, interfere with, disorganize, upset, disorder; *informal* mess up.

dislodge verb **1** *replace any stones you dislodge* DISPLACE, knock out of place/position, move, shift; knock over, upset.

2 *economic sanctions failed to dislodge the dictator* REMOVE, force out, drive out, oust, eject, get rid of, evict, unseat, depose, topple, drum out; *informal* kick out, boot out.

disloyal adjective *once judged disloyal, you will never be welcome in this group* UNFAITHFUL, faithless, false, false-hearted, untrue, inconstant, untrustworthy, unreliable, undependable, fickle; treacherous, traitorous, subversive, seditious, unpatriotic, two-faced, double-dealing, double-crossing, deceitful; dissident, renegade; adulterous; *informal* backstabbing, two-timing; *literary* perfidious.

disloyalty noun *the investigation uncovered more cases of disloyalty than anyone had originally suspected* UNFAITHFULNESS, infidelity, inconstancy, faithlessness, fickleness, unreliability, untrustworthiness, betrayal, falseness; duplicity, double-dealing, treachery, treason, subversion, sedition, dissidence; adultery; *informal* backstabbing, two-timing; *literary* perfidy, perfidiousness.

dismal adjective **1** *a dismal look* GLOOMY, glum, melancholy, morose, doleful, woebegone, forlorn, dejected, depressed, dispirited, downcast, despondent, disconsolate, miserable, sad, unhappy, sorrowful, desolate, wretched; *informal* blue, down in the dumps, down in/at the mouth; *literary* dolorous. ANTONYM cheerful.

2 *a dismal hall* DINGY, dim, dark, gloomy, dreary, drab, dull, bleak, cheerless, depressing, uninviting, unwelcoming. ANTONYMS cheerful, bright.

3 *informal a dismal performance.* See POOR sense 2.

dismantle verb *the old opera house was dismantled* TAKE APART, pull apart, pull to pieces, disassemble, break up, break down, strip (down); knock down, pull down, demolish. ANTONYMS assemble, build.

dismay verb *he was dismayed by the change in his friend* APPALL, horrify, shock, shake (up); disconcert, take aback, alarm, unnerve, unsettle, throw off balance, discompose; disturb, upset, distress; *informal* rattle, faze. ANTONYMS encourage, please.

▸ noun *they greeted his decision with dismay* ALARM, shock, surprise, consternation, concern, perturbation, disquiet, discomposure, distress. ANTONYMS pleasure, relief.

dismember verb *coyotes dismembered what was left of the moose* DISJOINT, joint; pull apart, cut up, chop up, butcher. See note at DISEMBODIED.

dismiss verb **1** *the president dismissed five aides* GIVE SOMEONE THEIR NOTICE, get rid of, discharge, terminate; lay off; *informal* sack, give someone the sack, fire, boot out, give someone the boot, give someone their marching orders, show someone the door, can, pink-slip; *Military* cashier. ANTONYM engage.

2 *the guards were dismissed* SEND AWAY, let go; disband, dissolve, discharge. See note at EJECT. ANTONYM assemble.

3 *he dismissed all morbid thoughts* BANISH, set aside, disregard, shrug off, put out of one's mind; reject, deny, repudiate, spurn. ANTONYM entertain.

dismissal noun **1** *the threat of dismissal* TERMINATION, discharge, one's notice; redundancy, laying off; *informal* the sack, sacking, firing, the boot, the ax, one's marching orders, the pink slip; *Military* cashiering. ANTONYM recruitment.

2 *a condescending dismissal* REJECTION, repudiation, repulse, nonacceptance; *informal* kiss-off. ANTONYM acceptance.

dismissive adjective *he was given a dismissive wave and sent on his way* CONTEMPTUOUS, disdainful, scornful, sneering, snide, disparaging, negative. ANTONYM admiring.

dismount verb **1** *the cyclist dismounted* ALIGHT, get off/down.

2 *he was already dismounted* UNSEAT, dislodge, throw, unhorse.

disobedient adjective *he had never been punished for being disobedient* INSUBORDINATE, unruly, wayward, badly behaved, naughty, delinquent, disruptive, troublesome, rebellious, defiant, mutinous, recalcitrant, uncooperative, truculent, willful, intractable, obstreperous; *archaic* contumacious.

disobey verb *she was put on report for willfully disobeying a superior officer* DEFY, go against, flout, contravene, infringe, transgress, violate; disregard, ignore, pay no heed to.

disobliging adjective *our disobliging neighbors* UNHELPFUL, uncooperative, unaccommodating, unreasonable, awkward, difficult; discourteous, uncivil, unfriendly. ANTONYM helpful.

disorder noun **1** *he hates disorder* UNTIDINESS, disorderliness, mess, disarray, chaos, confusion; clutter, jumble; a muddle, a shambles. ANTONYM tidiness.

2 *incidents of public disorder* UNREST, disturbance, disruption, upheaval, turmoil, mayhem, pandemonium; violence, fighting, rioting, lawlessness, anarchy; breach of the peace, fracas, rumpus, ruckus, melee. ANTONYMS order, peace.

3 *a blood disorder* DISEASE, infection, complaint, condition, affliction, malady, sickness, illness, ailment, infirmity, irregularity.

disordered adjective **1** *her gray hair was disordered* UNTIDY, unkempt, messy, in a mess, mussed (up), mussy; disorganized, chaotic, confused, jumbled, muddled, shambolic.

2 *a disordered digestive system* DYSFUNCTIONAL, disturbed, unsettled, unbalanced, upset.

disorderly adjective **1** *a disorderly desk* UNTIDY, disorganized, messy, cluttered; in disarray, in a mess, in a jumble, in a muddle, at sixes and sevens; *informal* shambolic, like a bomb went off. ANTONYM tidy.

2 *disorderly behavior* UNRULY, boisterous, rough, rowdy, wild, riotous; disruptive, troublesome, undisciplined, lawless, unmanageable, uncontrollable, out of hand, out of control. ANTONYM peaceful.

disorganized adjective **1** *a disorganized toolbox* DISORDERLY, disordered, unorganized, jumbled, muddled, untidy, messy, chaotic, topsy-turvy, haphazard, ragtag; in disorder, in disarray, in a mess, in a muddle, in a shambles, shambolic. ANTONYM orderly.

2 *muddled and disorganized* UNMETHODICAL, unsystematic, undisciplined, badly organized, inefficient; haphazard, careless, slapdash; *informal* sloppy, hit-and-miss. ANTONYM organized.

disoriented adjective *the man in the street appears to be disoriented* CONFUSED, bewildered, at sea; lost, adrift, off-course, having lost one's bearings; *informal* not knowing whether one is coming or going.

disown verb *he has been disowned by his parents* REJECT, cast off/aside, abandon, renounce, deny; turn one's back on, wash one's hands of, have nothing more to do with; *literary* forsake.

disparage verb *they disparage Lawrence and his achievements* BELITTLE, denigrate, deprecate, trivialize, make light of, undervalue, underrate, play down; ridicule, deride, mock, scorn, scoff at, sneer at; run down, defame, discredit, speak badly of, cast aspersions on, impugn, vilify, traduce, criticize, slur; *informal* pick holes in, knock, slam, pan, badmouth, dis, pooh-pooh; *formal* calumniate, derogate. See word spectrum at PRAISE. ANTONYMS praise, overrate.

disparaging adjective *disparaging remarks* DEROGATORY, deprecatory, denigratory, belittling; critical, scathing, negative, unfavorable, uncomplimentary, uncharitable; contemptuous, scornful, snide, disdainful; *informal* bitchy, catty; *archaic* contumelious. ANTONYM complimentary.

disparate adjective *our disparate opinions* CONTRASTING, different, differing, dissimilar, unalike, poles apart; varying, various, diverse, diversified, heterogeneous, distinct, separate, divergent; *literary* divers. ANTONYM homogeneous.

disparity noun *a disparity between their stories* DISCREPANCY, inconsistency, imbalance; variance, variation, divergence, gap, gulf; difference, dissimilarity, contrast. ANTONYM similarity.

dispassionate adjective 1 *a calm, dispassionate manner* UNEMOTIONAL, emotionless, impassive, cool, calm, 'calm, cool, and collected', unruffled, unperturbed, composed, self-possessed, self-controlled, unexcitable; *informal* laid-back. ANTONYM emotional.

2 *a dispassionate analysis* OBJECTIVE, detached, neutral, disinterested, impartial, nonpartisan, unbiased, unprejudiced; scientific, analytical. ANTONYM biased.

dispatch verb 1 *all the messages were dispatched* SEND (OFF), post, mail, forward, transmit, e-mail.

2 *the business was dispatched in the morning* DEAL WITH, finish, conclude, settle, discharge, perform; expedite, push through; *informal* make short work of.

3 *the hero dispatched a host of villains* KILL, put to death, take/end the life of; slaughter, butcher, massacre, wipe out, exterminate, eliminate; murder, assassinate, execute; *informal* bump off, do in, do away with, take out, blow away, ice, rub out, waste; *literary* slay. See note at KILL.

▸ noun 1 *files ready for dispatch* SENDING, posting, mailing, e-mailing.

2 *efficiency and dispatch* PROMPTNESS, speed, speediness, swiftness, rapidity, briskness, haste, hastiness; *literary* fleetness, celerity.

3 *the latest dispatch from the front* COMMUNICATION, communiqué, bulletin, report, statement, letter, message; news, intelligence; *informal* memo, info, story, lowdown, scoop; *literary* tidings.

4 *the capture and dispatch of the rogue bull* KILLING, slaughter, massacre, extermination, elimination; murder, assassination, execution; *literary* slaying.

dispel verb *allow me to dispel your fears* BANISH, eliminate, drive away/off, get rid of; relieve, allay, ease, quell. See note at SCATTER.

dispensable adjective *any goods deemed dispensable will not be allowed on board* EXPENDABLE, disposable, replaceable, inessential, nonessential, noncore; unnecessary, redundant, superfluous, surplus to requirements.

dispensation noun 1 *the dispensation of supplies* DISTRIBUTION, supply, supplying, issue, issuing, handing out, doling out, dishing out, sharing out, dividing out; division, allocation, allotment, apportionment.

2 *the dispensation of justice* ADMINISTRATION, administering, delivery, discharge, dealing out, meting out.

3 *a dispensation from the Pope* EXEMPTION, immunity, exception, exoneration, reprieve, remission.

4 *the new constitutional dispensation* SYSTEM, order, arrangement, organization.

dispense verb 1 *servants dispensed the drinks* DISTRIBUTE, pass around, hand out, dole out, dish out, share out; allocate, supply, allot, apportion.

2 *the soldiers dispensed summary justice* ADMINISTER, deliver, issue, discharge, deal out, mete out.

3 *dispensing medicines* PREPARE, make up; supply, provide, sell.

4 *the Pope dispensed him from his impediment* EXEMPT, excuse, except, release, let off, reprieve, absolve. PHRASE: **dispense with** 1 *let's dispense with the formalities* WAIVE, omit, drop, leave out, forgo; do away with, give something a miss. 2 *he dispensed with his crutches* GET RID OF, throw away/out, dispose of, discard; manage without, cope without; *informal* ditch, scrap, dump, deep-six, chuck.

disperse verb 1 *the crowd began to disperse | police dispersed the demonstrators* BREAK UP, split up, disband, scatter, leave, go their separate ways; drive away/off, chase away. ANTONYM assemble.

2 *the fog finally dispersed* DISSIPATE, dissolve, melt away, fade away, clear, lift.

3 *seeds dispersed by birds* SCATTER, disseminate, distribute, spread, broadcast. See note at SCATTER. ANTONYM gather.

dispirited adjective *these overprivileged kids are too easily dispirited* DISHEARTENED, discouraged, demoralized, downcast, low, low-spirited, dejected, downhearted, depressed, disconsolate. ANTONYM heartened.

dispiriting adjective *a dispiriting view of the future* DISHEARTENING, depressing, discouraging, daunting, demoralizing.

displace verb 1 *roof tiles displaced by gales* DISLODGE, dislocate, move, shift, reposition; move out of place, knock out of place/position. ANTONYM replace.

2 *the director was displaced* DEPOSE, dislodge, unseat, remove (from office), dismiss, eject, oust, expel, force out, drive out; overthrow, topple, bring down; *informal* boot out, give someone the boot, show someone the door, bump. ANTONYM reinstate.

3 *English displaced the local language* REPLACE, take the place of, supplant, supersede. See note at REPLACE.

display noun 1 *a display of lights* EXHIBITION, exposition, array, arrangement, presentation, demonstration; spectacle, show, parade, pageant.

2 *they vied to outdo each other in display* OSTENTATION, showiness, extravagance, flamboyance, lavishness, splendor; *informal* swank, flashiness, glitziness.

3 *his display of concern* MANIFESTATION, expression, show.

▸ verb 1 *the paintings are displayed in the art gallery* EXHIBIT, show, put on show/view; arrange, array, present, lay out, set out.

2 *the play displays his many theatrical talents* SHOW OFF, parade, flaunt, reveal; publicize, make known, call/draw attention to. ANTONYM hide.

3 *she displayed a caustic sense of humor* MANIFEST, show evidence of, reveal; demonstrate, show; *formal* evince. ANTONYM conceal.

displease verb *I'd never seen his mom when she wasn't displeased about something* ANNOY, irritate, anger, irk, vex, pique, gall, nettle; put out, upset, aggravate, peeve, needle, bug, rile, miff; *informal* tee off, tick off, piss off.

displeasure noun *the scowl on his face indicated displeasure* ANNOYANCE, irritation, crossness, anger, vexation, pique, rancor; dissatisfaction, discontent, discontentedness, disgruntlement, disapproval; *informal* aggravation. ANTONYM satisfaction.

disposable adjective 1 *disposable plates* THROWAWAY, expendable, single-use.

2 *disposable income* AVAILABLE, usable, spendable.

disposal noun 1 *garbage ready for disposal* THROWING AWAY, discarding, jettisoning, scrapping, recycling; *informal* dumping, ditching, chucking, deep-sixing.

2 *the disposal of the troops in two lines* ARRANGEMENT, arranging, positioning, placement, lining up, disposition, grouping. PHRASE: **at someone's disposal** *the van will be at your disposal all weekend* FOR USE BY, in reserve for, in the hands of, in the possession of.

dispose verb 1 *he disposed the pictures in sequence* ARRANGE, place, put, position, array, set up, form; marshal, gather, group.

2 *the experience disposed him to be kind* INCLINE, encourage, persuade, predispose, make willing, prompt, lead, motivate; sway, influence. PHRASE: **dispose of** 1 *the waste was disposed of* THROW AWAY/OUT, get rid of, discard, jettison, scrap, junk; *informal* dump, ditch, chuck, trash, deep-six. 2 *he had disposed of all his assets* PART WITH, give away, hand over, deliver up, transfer; sell, auction. 3 *informal she disposed of a fourth cupcake.* See CONSUME sense 1.

disposed adjective 1 *they are philanthropically disposed* INCLINED, predisposed, minded.

2 *we are not disposed to argue* WILLING, inclined, prepared, ready, minded, in the mood.

3 *he was disposed to be cruel* LIABLE, apt, inclined, likely, predisposed, prone, tending; capable of.

disposition noun 1 *a nervous disposition* TEMPERAMENT, nature, character, constitution, makeup, mentality.

2 *his disposition to generosity* INCLINATION, tendency, proneness, propensity, proclivity.

3 *the disposition of the armed forces* ARRANGEMENT, positioning, placement, configuration; setup, lineup, layout, array; marshaling, mustering, grouping; *Military* dressing.

4 *Law the disposition of the company's property* DISTRIBUTION, disposal, allocation, transfer; sale, auction.

dispossess verb *the peasants have been dispossessed of their land* DIVEST, strip, rob, cheat (out), deprive; *informal* do out.

disproportionate adjective *the sentence is **disproportionate to** the offense committed* OUT OF PROPORTION TO, not appropriate to, inappropriate to, not commensurate with, incommensurate with, relatively too large/small for; inordinate for, unreasonable for, excessive for, undue for.

disprove verb *Wesley's version of the story should be easy to disprove* REFUTE, prove false, falsify, debunk, negate, invalidate, contradict, confound, controvert, discredit; *informal* poke holes in, blow out of the water, shoot down; *formal* confute.

disputable adjective *some of these figures are disputable* DEBATABLE, open to debate, open to discussion, open to question, arguable, contestable, moot, questionable, doubtful; *informal* iffy.

disputation noun *we'll have no religious disputation in this house* DEBATE, discussion, dispute, argument, arguing, altercation, dissension, disagreement, controversy; polemics.

dispute noun 1 *a subject of dispute* DEBATE, discussion, disputation, argument, controversy, disagreement, quarreling, dissension, conflict, friction, strife, discord. ANTONYM agreement.

2 *they have settled their dispute* QUARREL, argument, altercation, squabble, falling-out, disagreement, difference of opinion, clash, wrangle; *informal* tiff, spat, blowup, scrap, row, rhubarb. See note at QUARREL. ANTONYM agreement.

▸ verb 1 *George disputed with him* DEBATE, discuss, exchange views; quarrel, argue, disagree, clash, fall out, wrangle, bicker, squabble; *informal* have words, have a tiff, have a spat.

2 *they disputed his proposals* CHALLENGE, contest, question, call into question, impugn, quibble over, contradict, controvert, argue about, disagree with, take issue with; *formal* gainsay. ANTONYM accept.

disqualified adjective *the disqualified entrants included a girl who had lied about her age* BANNED, barred, debarred; ineligible. ANTONYM allowed.

disquiet noun *grave public disquiet* UNEASE, uneasiness, worry, anxiety, anxiousness, concern, disquietude; perturbation, consternation, upset, malaise, angst; agitation, restlessness, fretfulness; *informal* jitteriness. ANTONYM calm.

▸ verb *I was disquieted by the news* PERTURB, agitate, upset, disturb, unnerve, unsettle, discompose, disconcert; make uneasy, worry, make anxious; trouble, concern, make fretful, make restless.

disquisition noun *King's eloquent disquisitions on civil rights* ESSAY, dissertation, treatise, paper, tract, article; discussion, lecture, address, presentation, speech, talk.

disregard verb *Annie disregarded the remark* IGNORE, take no notice of, pay no attention/heed to; overlook, turn a blind eye to, turn a deaf ear to, shut one's eyes to, gloss over, brush aside, shrug off; *informal* sneeze at. See note at NEGLECT. ANTONYM heed.

▸ noun *blithe disregard for the rules* INDIFFERENCE, nonobservance, inattention, heedlessness, neglect. ANTONYM attention.

disrepair noun *the outbuildings are in disrepair* DILAPIDATION, decrepitude, shabbiness, collapse, ruin; abandonment, neglect, disuse.

disreputable adjective **1** *he fell into disreputable company* OF BAD REPUTATION, infamous, notorious, louche; dishonorable, dishonest, untrustworthy, unwholesome, villainous, corrupt, immoral; unsavory, slippery, seedy, sleazy; *informal* crooked, shady, shifty, dodgy. ANTONYMS respectable, smart.

2 *filthy and disreputable* SCRUFFY, shabby, down-at-heel, down-at-the-heel(s), seedy, untidy, unkempt, disheveled. ANTONYMS respectable, smart.

disrepute noun *she had brought the family name into disrepute* DISGRACE, shame, dishonor, infamy, notoriety, ignominy, bad reputation; humiliation, discredit, ill repute, low esteem, opprobrium, obloquy. ANTONYM honor.

disrespect noun **1** *disrespect for authority* CONTEMPT, lack of respect, scorn, disregard, disdain. ANTONYM esteem.

2 *he meant no disrespect to anybody* DISCOURTESY, rudeness, impoliteness, incivility, ill/bad manners; insolence, impudence, impertinence. ANTONYM esteem.

disrespectful adjective *no one had ever heard him utter a disrespectful word* DISCOURTEOUS, rude, impolite, uncivil, ill-mannered, bad-mannered; insolent, impudent, impertinent, cheeky, flippant, insubordinate. ANTONYM polite.

disrobe verb *disrobing for the doctor* UNDRESS, strip, take off one's clothes, remove one's clothes.

disrupt verb **1** *the strike disrupted public transit* THROW INTO CONFUSION, throw into disorder, throw into disarray, cause confusion/turmoil in, play havoc with; disturb, interfere with, upset, unsettle; obstruct, impede, hold up, delay, interrupt, suspend; *informal* throw a (monkey) wrench into the works of.

2 *the explosion disrupted the walls of the crater* DISTORT, damage, buckle, warp; shatter; *literary* sunder.

disruptive adjective *he's the most disruptive student in the school* TROUBLESOME, unruly, badly behaved, rowdy, disorderly, undisciplined, wild; unmanageable, uncontrollable, uncooperative, out of control/hand, obstreperous, truculent; *formal* refractory. ANTONYM well-behaved.

dissatisfaction noun *widespread dissatisfaction with the new law* DISCONTENT, discontentment, disaffection, disquiet, unhappiness, malaise, disgruntlement, vexation, annoyance, irritation, anger; disapproval, disapprobation, disfavor, displeasure.

dissatisfied adjective *no one could handle a dissatisfied customer better than Angie* DISCONTENTED, malcontent, unsatisfied, disappointed, disaffected, unhappy, displeased; disgruntled, aggrieved, vexed, annoyed, irritated, angry, exasperated, fed up. ANTONYM contented.

dissect verb **1** *the body was dissected* ANATOMIZE, cut up/open, dismember; vivisect.

2 *the text of the gospels was dissected* ANALYZE, examine, study, scrutinize, pore over, investigate, go over with a fine-tooth comb.

dissection noun **1** *the dissection of corpses* CUTTING UP/OPEN, dismemberment; autopsy, postmortem, necropsy, anatomy, vivisection.

2 *a thorough dissection of their policies* ANALYSIS, examination, study, scrutiny, investigation; evaluation, assessment.

dissemble verb *she's being honest and has no need to dissemble* DISSIMULATE, pretend, feign, act, masquerade, sham, fake, bluff, posture, hide one's feelings, put on a false front.

dissembler noun *he was a born showman and dissembler* LIAR, dissimulator; impostor, humbug, bluffer, fraud, actor, hoaxer, charlatan. See note at QUACK.

disseminate verb *much of our funding is used to disseminate information where it is most needed* SPREAD, circulate, distribute, disperse, promulgate, propagate, publicize, communicate, pass on, put about, make known. See note at SCATTER.

dissension noun *there was dissension within the cabinet* DISAGREEMENT, difference of opinion, dispute, dissent, conflict, friction, strife, discord, antagonism, infighting; argument, debate, controversy, disputation, contention.

dissent verb *two members dissented* DIFFER, disagree, demur, fail to agree, be at variance/odds, take issue; decline/refuse to support, protest, object, dispute, challenge, quibble. ANTONYMS agree, accept.

▸ noun *murmurs of dissent* DISAGREEMENT, difference of opinion, argument, dispute; disapproval, objection, protest, opposition, defiance; conflict, friction, strife, infighting. ANTONYM agreement.

dissenter noun *a chorus of criticism from dissenters* DISSIDENT, objector, protester, disputant; rebel, renegade, maverick, independent; apostate, heretic.

dissertation noun *a fascinating dissertation on the fall of Communism* ESSAY, thesis, treatise, paper, study, discourse, disquisition, tract, monograph.

disservice noun *the posting of inaccurate information does a great disservice to the patrons* UNKINDNESS, bad turn, ill turn, disfavor; injury, harm, hurt, damage, wrong, injustice. ANTONYM favor.

dissidence noun *dissidence within his own party lost him the election* DISAGREEMENT, dissent, discord, discontent; opposition, resistance, protest, sedition.

dissident noun *a jailed dissident* DISSENTER, objector, protester; rebel, revolutionary, recusant, subversive, agitator, insurgent, insurrectionist, refusenik. ANTONYM conformist.

▸ adjective *dissident intellectuals* DISSENTING, disagreeing; opposing, objecting, protesting, rebellious, rebelling, revolutionary, recusant, nonconformist, dissentient. ANTONYM conforming.

dissimilar adjective *families of dissimilar backgrounds* DIFFERENT, differing, unalike, variant, diverse, divergent, heterogeneous, disparate, unrelated, distinct, contrasting; *literary* divers.

dissimilarity noun *the enzymes' structural dissimilarity* DIFFERENCE(S), variance, diversity, heterogeneity, disparateness, disparity, distinctness, contrast, nonuniformity, divergence.

dissimulate verb *she had learned the power of dissimulating to get what she wanted* PRETEND, deceive, feign, act, dissemble, masquerade, pose, posture, sham, fake, bluff, hide one's feelings, be dishonest, put on a false front, lie.

dissimulation noun *he was capable of great dissimulation and hypocrisy* PRETENSE, dissembling, deceit, dishonesty, duplicity, lying, guile, subterfuge, feigning, shamming, faking, bluff, bluffing, posturing, hypocrisy.

dissipate verb **1** *his anger dissipated* DISAPPEAR, vanish, evaporate, dissolve, melt away, melt into thin air, be dispelled; disperse, scatter; *literary* evanesce. See note at SCATTER.

2 *he dissipated his fortune* SQUANDER, fritter (away), misspend, waste, be prodigal with, spend recklessly/freely, spend like water; expend, use up, consume, run through, go through (like water); *informal* blow, splurge.

dissipated adjective *it was in college that he became a dissipated young man* DISSOLUTE, debauched, decadent, intemperate, profligate, self-indulgent, wild, depraved; licentious, promiscuous; drunken. ANTONYM ascetic.

dissipation noun **1** *drunken dissipation* DEBAUCHERY, decadence, dissoluteness, dissolution, intemperance, excess, profligacy, self-indulgence, wildness; depravity, degeneracy; licentiousness, promiscuity; drunkenness. ANTONYM asceticism.

2 *the dissipation of our mineral wealth* SQUANDERING, frittering (away), waste, misspending; expenditure, draining, depletion. ANTONYM preservation.

dissociate verb *the word "spiritual" has become dissociated from religion* SEPARATE, detach, disconnect, sever, cut off, divorce; isolate, alienate, disassociate. ANTONYM relate.

PHRASE: **dissociate oneself from** **1** *he dissociated himself from the Catholic Church* BREAK AWAY FROM, end relations with, sever connections with; withdraw from, quit, leave, disaffiliate from, resign from, pull out of, drop out of, defect from. **2** *he dissociated himself from the statement* DISOWN, reject, disagree with, distance oneself from.

dissociation noun *the dissociation of behavior from consciousness* SEPARATION, disconnection, detachment, severance, divorce, split; segregation, division; *literary* sundering. ANTONYM union.

dissolute adjective *the problems of dissolute teens have become epidemic* DISSIPATED, debauched, decadent, intemperate, profligate, self-indulgent, wild, depraved; licentious, promiscuous; drunken. ANTONYM ascetic.

dissolution noun **1** *the dissolution of the legislative session* CESSATION, conclusion, end, ending, termination, winding up/down, discontinuation, suspension, disbanding; prorogation, recess.

2 *technical* *the dissolution of a polymer in a solvent* DISSOLVING, liquefaction, melting, deliquescence; breaking up, decomposition, disintegration.

3 *the dissolution of the empire* DISINTEGRATION, breaking up; decay, collapse, demise, extinction.

4 *a life of dissolution.* See DISSIPATION sense 1.

dissolve verb **1** *sugar dissolves in water* GO INTO SOLUTION, break down; liquefy, deliquesce, disintegrate.

2 *his hopes dissolved* DISAPPEAR, vanish, melt away, evaporate, disperse, dissipate, disintegrate; dwindle, fade (away), wither; *literary* evanesce.

3 *the crowd dissolved* DISPERSE, disband, break up, scatter, go in different directions.

4 *the assembly was dissolved* DISBAND, disestablish, bring to an end, end, terminate, discontinue, close down, wind up/down, suspend; prorogue, adjourn.

5 *their marriage was dissolved* ANNUL, nullify, void, invalidate, overturn, revoke. PHRASE: **dissolve into/in** *she dissolved into tears* BURST INTO, break (down) into, be overcome with.

dissonant adjective **1** *dissonant sounds* INHARMONIOUS, discordant, unmelodious, atonal, off-key, cacophonous. ANTONYM harmonious.

2 *dissonant colors* INCONGRUOUS, anomalous, clashing, inharmonious; disparate, different, dissimilar. ANTONYMS congruous, complementary.

dissuade verb *his colleagues did nothing to* ***dissuade*** *him* ***from*** *quitting* DISCOURAGE FROM, deter from, prevent from, divert from, stop from; talk out of, persuade against, advise against, argue out of. ANTONYM encourage.

distance noun **1** *they measured the distance* INTERVAL, space, span, gap, extent; length, width, breadth, depth; range, reach.

2 *our perception of distance* REMOTENESS; closeness.

3 *there is a distance between them* ALOOFNESS, remoteness, detachment, unfriendliness; reserve, reticence, restraint, formality; *informal* standoffishness.

▸ verb *he distanced himself from her* WITHDRAW, detach, separate, dissociate, disassociate, isolate, put at a distance.

PHRASE: **in the distance** *there was a cabin in the distance* FAR AWAY/OFF, afar, just in view; on the horizon; *dated* yonder.

distant adjective **1** *distant parts of the world* FARAWAY, far-off, far, far-flung, remote, out of the way, outlying, extrasolar. ANTONYM near.

2 *the distant past* LONG AGO, bygone, olden; ancient, prehistoric; *literary* of yore, olden. ANTONYM recent.

3 *half a mile distant* AWAY, off, apart.

4 *a distant memory* VAGUE, faint, dim, indistinct, unclear, indefinite, sketchy, hazy. ANTONYMS strong, clear.

5 *a distant family connection* REMOTE, indirect, slight. ANTONYM close.

6 *father was always distant* ALOOF, reserved, remote, detached, unapproachable; withdrawn, reticent, taciturn, uncommunicative, undemonstrative, unforthcoming, unresponsive, unfriendly; *informal* standoffish. ANTONYMS friendly, close.

7 *a distant look in his eyes* DISTRACTED, absentminded, faraway, detached, distrait, vague; *informal* spacey. ANTONYM attentive.

distaste noun *they make little secret of their* ***distaste for*** *returning exiles now looking for power* DISLIKE FOR, aversion to/toward, disinclination to/toward, disapproval of, disapprobation of, disdain for, repugnance at/toward, hatred for/of, loathing of. ANTONYM liking.

distasteful adjective **1** *distasteful behavior* UNPLEASANT, disagreeable, displeasing, undesirable; objectionable, offensive, unsavory, unpalatable, obnoxious; disgusting, repellent, repulsive, revolting, repugnant, abhorrent, loathsome, vile. ANTONYMS agreeable, pleasant.

2 *their eggs are distasteful to predators* UNPALATABLE, unsavory, unappetizing, inedible, disgusting. ANTONYM tasty.

distended adjective *a distended abdomen* SWOLLEN, bloated, dilated, engorged, enlarged, inflated, expanded, extended, bulging, protuberant.

distill verb **1** *the water was distilled* PURIFY, refine, filter, treat, process; evaporate and condense.

2 *oil distilled from marjoram* EXTRACT, press out, squeeze out, express.

3 *whiskey is distilled from barley* BREW, ferment.

4 *the solvent is distilled to leave the oil* BOIL DOWN, reduce, concentrate, condense; purify, refine.

distinct adjective **1** *two distinct categories* DISCRETE, separate, different, unconnected; precise, specific, distinctive, individual, contrasting. ANTONYM overlapping.

2 *the tail has distinct black tips* CLEAR, well-defined, unmistakable, easily distinguishable; recognizable, visible, obvious, pronounced, prominent, striking. ANTONYMS indistinct, indefinite.

distinction noun **1** *class distinctions* DIFFERENCE, contrast, dissimilarity, variance, variation; division, differentiation, dividing line, gulf, gap. ANTONYM similarity.

2 *a painter of distinction* IMPORTANCE, significance, note, consequence; renown, fame, celebrity, prominence, eminence, preeminence, repute, reputation; merit, worth, greatness, excellence, quality. ANTONYM mediocrity.

3 *he had served with distinction* HONOR, credit, excellence, merit.

distinctive adjective *the distinctive design in the lace* DISTINGUISHING, characteristic, typical, individual, particular, peculiar, unique, exclusive, special. ANTONYM common.

distinctly adverb **1** *there's something distinctly odd about him* DECIDEDLY, markedly, definitely; clearly, noticeably, obviously, plainly, evidently, unmistakably, manifestly, patently.

2 *Laura spoke quite distinctly* CLEARLY, plainly, intelligibly, audibly, unambiguously.

distinguish verb **1** *distinguishing reality from fantasy* DIFFERENTIATE, tell apart, discriminate between, tell the difference between.

2 *he could distinguish shapes in the dark* DISCERN, see, perceive, make out; detect, recognize, identify; *literary* descry, espy.

3 *this is what distinguishes history from other disciplines* SEPARATE, set apart, make distinctive, make different; single out, mark off, characterize. PHRASE: **distinguish oneself** *she distinguished herself in the air corps* ATTAIN DISTINCTION, be successful, bring fame/honor to oneself, become famous.

THE RIGHT WORD

What we **discern** we see apart from all other objects (*to discern the lighthouse beaming on the far shore*). **Descry** puts even more emphasis on the distant or unclear nature of what we're seeing (*the lookout was barely able to descry a man approaching in the dusk*). To **discriminate** is to perceive the differences between or among things that are very similar; it may suggest that some aesthetic evaluation is involved (*to discriminate between two painters' styles*). **Distinguish** requires making even finer distinctions among things that resemble each other even more closely (*unable to distinguish the shadowy figures moving through the forest*). *Distinguish* can also mean recognizing by some special mark or outward sign (*the sheriff could be distinguished by his silver badge*). **Differentiate**, on the other hand, suggests the ability to perceive differences between things that are easily confused. In contrast to *distinguish*, *differentiate* suggests subtle differences that must be compared in some detail (*the color of her dress was difficult to differentiate from the color of the chair in which she was seated; it took a sharp eye to distinguish where her skirt ended and the upholstery began*) If you have trouble *differentiating* among these closely related verbs, you're not alone.

distinguishable adjective *the differences between the original and the copy were only slightly distinguishable* DISCERNIBLE, recognizable, identifiable, detectable.

distinguished adjective *our distinguished guests* EMINENT, famous, renowned, prominent, well-known; esteemed, respected, illustrious, acclaimed, celebrated, great; notable, important, influential. ANTONYMS unknown, obscure.

distinguishing adjective *does he have any distinguishing features, such as a scar or a birthmark?* DISTINCTIVE, differentiating, characteristic, typical, peculiar, singular, unique.

distorted adjective **1** *a distorted face* TWISTED, warped, contorted, buckled, deformed, malformed, misshapen, disfigured, dysmorphic, crooked, awry, out of shape.

2 *a distorted version* MISREPRESENTED, perverted, twisted, falsified, misreported, misstated, garbled, inaccurate; biased, prejudiced, slanted, colored, loaded, weighted, altered, changed.

distract verb *let's not distract Dionne while she's painting* DIVERT, sidetrack, draw away, disturb, put off.

distracted adjective **1** *she seemed distracted today* PREOCCUPIED, inattentive, vague, abstracted, distrait, absent-minded, faraway, in a world of one's own; bemused, confused, bewildered; troubled, harassed, worried, anxious; *informal* miles away, not with it. ANTONYM attentive.

2 *she was distracted with worry* CRAZED, mad, insane, wild, out of one's head, crazy.

distracting adjective *it's a very distracting noise* DISTURBING, unsettling, intrusive, disconcerting, bothersome, off-putting.

distraction noun **1** *a distraction from the real issues* DIVERSION, interruption, disturbance, interference, hindrance.

2 *frivolous distractions* AMUSEMENT, entertainment, diversion, recreation, leisure pursuit, divertissement.

3 *he was driven to distraction* FRENZY, hysteria, mental distress, madness, insanity, mania; agitation, perturbation.

distrait adjective *he was unusually distrait during breakfast* DISTRACTED, preoccupied, absorbed, abstracted, distant, faraway; absentminded, vague, inattentive, in a brown study, woolgathering, with one's head in the clouds, in a world of one's own; *informal* miles away, not with it, spaced out. ANTONYM alert.

distraught adjective *I first became suspicious when I realized that Frank was not at all distraught over Larry's disappearance* WORRIED, upset, distressed, fraught; overcome, overwrought, beside oneself, out of one's mind, desperate, hysterical, worked up, at one's wits' end; *informal* in a state, unglued.

distress noun **1** *she concealed her distress* ANGUISH, suffering, pain, agony, torment, heartache, heartbreak; misery, wretchedness, sorrow, grief, woe, sadness, unhappiness, desolation, despair. ANTONYM happiness.

2 *a ship in distress* DANGER, peril, difficulty, trouble, jeopardy, risk. ANTONYM safety.

3 *the distress of the refugees* HARDSHIP, adversity, poverty, deprivation, privation, destitution, indigence, impoverishment, penury, need, dire straits. ANTONYM prosperity.

▸ verb *he was distressed by the trial* CAUSE ANGUISH TO, cause suffering to, pain, upset, make miserable; trouble, worry, bother, perturb, disturb, disquiet, agitate, harrow, torment. ANTONYMS calm, please.

distressing adjective *the news was terribly distressing* UPSETTING, worrying, disturbing, disquieting, painful, traumatic, agonizing, harrowing; sad, saddening, heartbreaking, heart-rending; *informal* gut-wrenching. ANTONYM comforting.

distribute verb **1** *the proceeds were distributed among his creditors* GIVE OUT, deal out, dole out, dish out, hand out/around; allocate, allot, apportion, share out, divide out/up, parcel out. ANTONYM collect.

2 *the newsletter is distributed free* CIRCULATE, issue, hand out, deliver.

3 *more than 130 different species are distributed worldwide* DISPERSE, scatter, spread.

distribution noun **1** *the distribution of charity* GIVING OUT, dealing out, doling out, handing out/around, issue, issuing, dispensation; allocation, allotment, apportioning, sharing out, dividing up/out, parceling out.

2 *the geographical distribution of plants* DISPERSAL, dissemination, spread; placement, position, location, disposition.

3 *centers of food distribution* SUPPLY, supplying, delivery, transport, transportation.

4 *the statistical distribution of the problem* FREQUENCY, prevalence, incidence, commonness.

district noun *the most respected contractor in our district* NEIGHBORHOOD, area, region, locality, locale, community, quarter, sector, zone, territory; ward; *informal* neck of the woods.

distrust noun *the general distrust of authority* MISTRUST, suspicion, wariness, chariness, leeriness, lack of trust, lack of confidence; skepticism, doubt, doubtfulness, cynicism; misgivings, qualms, disbelief; *formal* dubiety.

▸ verb *Louise distrusted him* MISTRUST, be suspicious of, be wary/chary of, be leery of, regard with suspicion, suspect; be skeptical of, have doubts about, doubt, be unsure of/about, have misgivings about, wonder about, disbelieve (in).

disturb verb **1** *let's go somewhere where we won't be disturbed* INTERRUPT, intrude on, butt in on, barge in on; distract, disrupt, bother, trouble, pester, harass; *informal* hassle.

2 *don't disturb his papers* DISARRANGE, muddle, rearrange, disorganize, disorder, mix up, interfere with, throw into disorder/confusion, turn upside down.

3 *waters disturbed by winds* AGITATE, churn up, stir up; *literary* roil.

4 *he wasn't disturbed by the allegations* PERTURB, trouble, concern, worry, upset; agitate, fluster, discomfit, disconcert, dismay, distress, discompose, unsettle, ruffle.

disturbance noun **1** *we are concerned about the disturbance to local residents* DISRUPTION, distraction, interference; bother, trouble, inconvenience, upset, annoyance, irritation, intrusion, harassment, hassle.

2 *disturbances among the peasantry* RIOT, fracas, upheaval, brawl, street fight, melee, free-for-all, ruckus, rumpus, rumble, ruction.

3 *emotional disturbance* TROUBLE, perturbation, distress, worry, upset, agitation, discomposure, discomfiture; neurosis, illness, sickness, disorder, complaint.

disturbed adjective **1** *disturbed sleep* DISRUPTED, interrupted, fitful, intermittent, broken.

2 *the children seemed disturbed* TROUBLED, distressed, upset, distraught; unbalanced, unstable, disordered, dysfunctional, maladjusted, neurotic, unhinged; *informal* screwed up, mixed up.

disturbing adjective *he gave us some disturbing information* WORRYING, perturbing, troubling, upsetting; distressing, discomfiting, disconcerting, disquieting, unsettling, dismaying, alarming, frightening.

disunion noun *the disunion of former allies* BREAKING UP, separation, dissolution, partition. ANTONYM federation.

disunite verb *may these states never again be disunited* BREAK UP, separate, divide, split up, partition, dismantle; *literary* sunder. ANTONYM unify.

disunity noun *disunity within the administration* DISAGREEMENT, dissent, dissension, argument, arguing, quarreling, feuding; conflict, strife, friction, discord.

disuse noun *many of the mills fell into disuse* NONUSE, nonemployment, lack of use; neglect, abandonment, desertion, obsolescence; *formal* desuetude.

disused adjective *a disused building* UNUSED, no longer in use, unemployed, idle; abandoned, deserted, vacated, unoccupied, uninhabited.

ditch noun *she rescued a cat from the ditch* TRENCH, trough, channel, dike, drain, gutter, gully, watercourse, conduit; *Archaeology* fosse.

▸ verb **1** *they started ditching the coastal areas* DIG A DITCH IN, trench, excavate, drain.

2 *informal she ditched her old curtains* THROW OUT, throw away, discard, get rid of, dispose of, do away with, deep-six, shed; abandon, drop, shelve, scrap, jettison, throw on the scrap heap; *informal* dump, junk, chuck, pull the plug on, trash.

3 *informal she ditched her husband.* See ABANDON verb sense 3.

dither verb *stop dithering and make a decision* HESITATE, falter, waver, vacillate, change one's mind, be of two minds, be indecisive, be undecided; informal shilly-shally, dilly-dally.

ditzy, ditsy adjective informal *she's almost too convincing in the part of the ditzy secretary* SILLY, foolish, giddy, lightheaded, scatterbrained, featherbrained, harebrained, empty-headed, vacuous, stupid, brainless; skittish, flighty, fickle, capricious, whimsical, inconstant; informal dippy, dizzy, dopey.

diurnal adjective *the patient's moods are determined by diurnal events* DAILY, everyday, quotidian, occurring every/each day.

divan noun *have a rest on the divan* SETTEE, sofa, couch, chesterfield; sofa bed, daybed, studio couch.

dive verb **1** *they dived into the clear water | the plane was diving toward the ground* PLUNGE, nosedive, jump head first, bellyflop; plummet, fall, drop, pitch, dive-bomb.

2 *the islanders dive for oysters* SWIM UNDER WATER; snorkel, scuba dive.

3 *they dove for cover* LEAP, jump, lunge, launch oneself, throw oneself, go headlong, duck.

▸ noun **1** *a dive into the pool* PLUNGE, swan dive, nosedive, jump, bellyflop; plummet, fall, drop, swoop, pitch.

2 *a sideways dive* LUNGE, spring, jump, leap.

3 informal *John got into a fight in some dive* SLEAZY BAR/NIGHTCLUB, seedy bar/nightclub; informal (drinking) joint, hole.

diverge verb **1** *the two roads diverged* SEPARATE, part, fork, divide, split, bifurcate, go in different directions. ANTONYM converge.

2 *areas where our views diverge* DIFFER, be different, be dissimilar; disagree, be at variance, be at odds, conflict, clash. ANTONYM agree.

3 *he diverged from his script* DEVIATE, digress, depart, veer, stray; stray from the point, get off the subject.

divergence noun **1** *the divergence of the human and ape lineages* SEPARATION, dividing, parting, forking, bifurcation.

2 *a marked political divergence* DIFFERENCE, dissimilarity, variance, disparity; disagreement, incompatibility, mismatch.

3 *divergence from standard behavior* DEVIATION, digression, departure, shift, straying; variation, change, alteration.

divergent adjective *divergent points of view* DIFFERING, varying, different, dissimilar, unalike, disparate, contrasting, contrastive; conflicting, incompatible, contradictory, at odds, at variance. ANTONYM similar.

divers adjective literary *Mr. Roosevelt's divers areas of expertise* SEVERAL, many, numerous, multiple, manifold, multifarious, multitudinous; sundry, miscellaneous, assorted, various; literary myriad.

diverse adjective *managing data from diverse databases* VARIOUS, sundry, manifold, multiple; varied, varying, miscellaneous, assorted, mixed, diversified, divergent, heterogeneous, a mixed bag of; different, differing, distinct, unlike, dissimilar; literary divers, myriad.

diversify verb **1** *farmers looking for ways to diversify* BRANCH OUT, expand, extend operations.

2 *a plan aimed at diversifying the economy* VARY, bring variety to; modify, alter, change, transform; expand, enlarge.

diversion noun **1** *the diversion of 19 rivers* REROUTING, redirection, deflection, deviation, divergence.

2 *traffic diversions* DETOUR, bypass, deviation, alternative route.

3 *the noise created a diversion* DISTRACTION, disturbance, smokescreen, feint.

4 *a city full of diversions* ENTERTAINMENT, amusement, pastime, delight, divertissement; fun, recreation, rest and relaxation, pleasure; informal R and R; dated sport.

diversity noun *a diversity of design styles* VARIETY, miscellany, assortment, mixture, mix, mélange, range, array, multiplicity; variation, variance, diversification, heterogeneity, difference, contrast. ANTONYM uniformity.

divert verb **1** *a plan to divert the Fraser River* REROUTE, redirect, change the course of, deflect, channel.

2 *he diverted her from her studies* DISTRACT, sidetrack, disturb, draw away, be a distraction, put off.

3 *the story diverted them* AMUSE, entertain, distract, delight, enchant, interest, fascinate, absorb, engross, rivet, grip, hold the attention of.

diverting adjective *a diverting musical* ENTERTAINING, amusing, enjoyable, pleasing, agreeable, delightful, appealing; interesting, fascinating, intriguing, absorbing, riveting, compelling; humorous, funny, witty, comical. ANTONYM boring.

divest verb *he intends to* ***divest*** *you* ***of*** *your power* DEPRIVE OF, strip of, dispossess of, rob of, cheat out of, trick out of.

divide verb **1** *he divided his estate into separate holdings* SPLIT (UP), cut up, carve up; dissect, bisect, halve, quarter; literary sunder. ANTONYMS unify, join, converge.

2 *a curtain divided her cabin from the galley* SEPARATE, segregate, partition, screen off, section off, split off. ANTONYMS unify, join, converge.

3 *the stairs divide at the mezzanine* DIVERGE, separate, part, branch (off), fork, split (in two), bifurcate. ANTONYMS unify, join, converge.

4 *Jack* ***divided up*** *the cash* SHARE OUT, allocate, allot, apportion, portion out, ration out, parcel out, deal out, dole out, dish out, distribute, dispense; informal divvy up.

5 *he aimed to divide his opponents* DISUNITE, drive apart, break up, split up, set at variance, set at odds; separate, isolate, estrange, alienate; literary tear asunder. ANTONYMS unify, unite.

6 *living things are divided into three categories* CLASSIFY, sort (out), categorize, order, group, grade, rank. ANTONYM combine.

▸ noun *the sectarian divide* BREACH, gulf, gap, split; borderline, boundary, dividing line.

dividend noun **1** *an annual dividend* SHARE, portion, premium, return, gain, profit, commission; informal cut.

2 *the research will produce dividends in the future* BENEFIT, advantage, gain; bonus, extra, plus.

divination noun *he looked to divination for guidance* FORTUNE TELLING, divining, prophecy, prediction, soothsaying, augury; clairvoyance, second sight.

divine adjective **1** *a divine being* GODLY, angelic, seraphic, saintly, beatific; heavenly, celestial, supernal, holy. ANTONYM mortal.

2 *divine worship* RELIGIOUS, holy, sacred, sanctified, consecrated, blessed, devotional.

3 *informal this food is divine.* See EXCELLENT.

▸ noun *dated puritan divines* THEOLOGIAN, clergyman, clergywoman, member of the clergy, churchman, churchwoman, cleric, minister, man/woman of the cloth, preacher, priest; *informal* reverend.

▸ verb 1 *Fergus divined how afraid she was* GUESS, surmise, conjecture, deduce, infer; discern, intuit, perceive, recognize, see, realize, appreciate, understand, grasp, comprehend; *informal* figure (out), savvy.

2 *they divined that this was an auspicious day* FORETELL, predict, prophesy, forecast, foresee, prognosticate. See note at PREDICT.

THE RIGHT WORD

Holy is the only one of these words associated with religion and worship that may be applied directly to the Supreme Being. Something that is *holy* is regarded with the highest reverence because of its connection with God or a god (*Christmas is a holy day in the Christian calendar*). Something that is **sacred**, on the other hand, is set apart as *holy* or is dedicated to some exalted purpose (*sacred music*) but may derive its holiness from a human source rather than from God (*a sacred oath between brothers*). In its strictest sense, **divine** means associated with or derived from God (*the divine right of kings*), but it has also been used to describe anything that is admirable or treasured (*her wedding dress was divine*). **Hallowed** and **consecrated** refer to what has been made sacred or holy, with *hallowed* connotating intrinsic holiness (*they walked on hallowed ground*) and *consecrated* meaning blessed by a formal rite or formally dedicated to some religious use (*the old building had been consecrated as a church*).

diviner noun *she claimed to be a diviner who had received her second sight from an ancient sage* FORTUNE TELLER, clairvoyant, psychic, seer, soothsayer, prognosticator, prophesier, oracle, sibyl, crystal-gazer.

divinity noun 1 *they denied Christ's divinity* DIVINE NATURE, godliness, deity, godhead, holiness.

2 *the study of divinity* THEOLOGY, religious studies, religion, scripture.

3 *a female divinity* DEITY, god, goddess, divine being, supreme being.

division noun 1 *the division of the island | cell division* DIVIDING (UP), breaking up, breakup, carving up, splitting, dissection, bisection; partitioning, separation, segregation.

2 *the division of his assets* SHARING OUT, dividing up, parceling out, dishing out, allocation, allotment, apportionment; splitting up, carving up; *informal* divvying up.

3 *the division between nomadic and urban cultures* DIVIDING LINE, divide, boundary, borderline, border, demarcation line.

4 *each class is divided into nine divisions* SECTION, subsection, subdivision, category, class, group, grouping, set, subset, family.

5 *an independent division of the company* DEPARTMENT, branch, arm, wing, sector, section, subsection, subdivision, subsidiary.

6 *the causes of social division* DISUNITY, disunion, conflict, discord, disagreement, dissension, disaffection, estrangement, alienation, isolation.

divisive adjective *a divisive scheme to set his rivals against each other* ALIENATING, estranging, isolating, schismatic. ANTONYM unifying.

divorce noun 1 *she wants a divorce* DISSOLUTION, annulment, (official) separation. ANTONYM marriage.

2 *a growing divorce between the church and people* SEPARATION, division, split, disunity, estrangement, alienation; schism, gulf, chasm. ANTONYM unity.

▸ verb 1 *her parents have divorced* DISSOLVE ONE'S MARRIAGE, annul one's marriage, end one's marriage, get a divorce.

2 *religion cannot be divorced from morality* SEPARATE, disconnect, divide, dissociate, disassociate, detach, isolate, alienate, set apart, cut off.

divulge verb *he refused to divulge Father O'Neill's whereabouts* DISCLOSE, reveal, tell, communicate, pass on, publish, broadcast, proclaim; expose, uncover, make public, give away, let slip; *informal* spill the beans about, let on about, let the cat out of the bag about. ANTONYM conceal.

divvy verb See DIVIDE verb sense 4.

dizzy adjective 1 *she felt dizzy* GIDDY, lightheaded, faint, unsteady, shaky, muzzy, wobbly; *informal* woozy.

2 *dizzy heights* CAUSING DIZZINESS, causing giddiness, vertiginous.

3 *informal a dizzy blonde.* See DITZY.

do verb 1 *she does most of the manual work* CARRY OUT, undertake, discharge, execute, perform, accomplish, achieve; bring about/off, engineer; *informal* pull off; *formal* effectuate.

2 *they can do as they please* ACT, behave, conduct oneself, acquit oneself; *formal* comport oneself.

3 *regular coffee will do* SUFFICE, be adequate, be satisfactory, fill/fit the bill, serve one's purpose, meet one's needs.

4 *the boys will do the dinner* PREPARE, make, get ready, see to, arrange, organize, be responsible for, be in charge of; *informal* fix.

5 *the company is doing a new range of footwear | a portrait I am doing* MAKE, create, produce, turn out, design, manufacture; paint, draw, sketch; *informal* knock off.

6 *each room was done in a different color* DECORATE, furnish, ornament, deck out, trick out; *informal* do up.

7 *the maid did her hair* STYLE, arrange, adjust; brush, comb, wash, dry, cut; *informal* fix.

8 *I am doing a show to raise money* PUT ON, present, produce; perform in, act in, take part in, participate in.

9 *you've done me a favor* GRANT, pay, render, give.

10 *show me how to do these equations* WORK OUT, figure out, calculate; solve, resolve.

11 *she's doing archaeology* STUDY, learn, take a course in.

12 *what does he do?* HAVE AS A JOB, have as a profession, be employed at, earn a living at.

13 *he is doing well at college* GET ON/ALONG, progress, fare, manage, cope; succeed, prosper.

14 *he was doing 25 mph over the speed limit* DRIVE AT, travel at, move at.

15 *the cyclists do 30 kilometers per day* TRAVEL (OVER), journey, cover, traverse, achieve, notch up, log; *informal* chalk up.

16 *informal we're doing Scotland this summer* VISIT, tour, sightsee in.

▸ noun *informal he invited us to a grand do* PARTY, reception, gathering, celebration, function, social event/occasion, social, soiree; *informal* bash, shindig.

PHRASES: **do away with** 1 *they want to do away with the old customs* ABOLISH, get rid of, discard, remove, eliminate, discontinue, stop, end, terminate, put an end to, put a stop to, dispense with, drop, abandon, give up; *informal* scrap, ditch, dump, deep-six. 2 *informal she tried to do away with her husband.* See KILL verb sense 1. **do in** *informal* 1 *the poor devil's been done in.* See KILL verb sense 1. 2 *the long walk home did me in* WEAR OUT, tire out, exhaust, fatigue, weary, overtire, drain; *informal* take it out of. 3 *I did my back in* INJURE, hurt, damage. **do out of** *informal she nearly succeeded in doing Martin out of his inheritance* SWINDLE OUT OF, cheat out of, trick out of, deprive of; *informal* con out of, diddle out of. **do up** 1 *she did up her bootlace* FASTEN, tie (up), lace, knot; make fast, secure. 2 *informal he's had his house done up* RENOVATE, refurbish, refit, redecorate, decorate, revamp, make over, modernize, improve, spruce up, smarten up; *informal* give something a facelift, rehab. **do without** *we learned to do without many of the luxuries we had become accustomed to* FORGO, dispense with, abstain from, refrain from, eschew, give up, cut out, renounce, manage without; *formal* forswear.

docile adjective *his docile children do everything he asks of them* COMPLIANT, obedient, pliant, dutiful, submissive, deferential, unassertive, cooperative, amenable, accommodating, biddable, malleable. See note at OBEDIENT. ANTONYMS disobedient, willful.

dock[1] noun *his boat was moored at the dock* HARBOR, marina, port, anchorage; wharf, quay, pier, jetty, landing stage.

▸ verb *the ship docked* MOOR, berth, put in, tie up, anchor.

dock[2] verb 1 *they docked the money from his salary* DEDUCT, subtract, remove, debit, take off/away, garnishee; *informal* knock off.

2 *workers had their pay docked* REDUCE, cut, decrease.

3 *the dog's tail was docked* CUT OFF, cut short, shorten, crop, lop; remove, amputate, detach, sever, chop off, take off.

docket noun 1 *he opened a new docket for the account* FILE, dossier, folder.

2 *I looked my name up on the docket* LIST, index; schedule, agenda, program, timetable.

▸ verb *docket the package* DOCUMENT, record, register; label, tag, tab, mark.

doctor noun *Claudio went to see a doctor* PHYSICIAN, MD, medical practitioner, clinician; general practitioner, GP; medic, intern; *informal* doc, medico, quack, sawbones. See table on page 259.

▸ verb 1 *informal he doctored their wounds* TREAT, medicate, cure, heal; tend, attend to, minister to, care for, nurse.

2 *he doctored Stephen's drink* ADULTERATE, contaminate, tamper with, lace; *informal* spike, dope.

3 *the reports have been doctored* FALSIFY, tamper with, interfere with, alter, change; forge, fake; *informal* cook, fiddle with.

▸ ***docile***
compliant
complaisant
submissive
dutiful
tractable
obedient
yielding
deferential
biddable
pliable
easily manipulated
like putty in one's hands
manageable
meek
lamblike
mild
tame
persuadable
passive
unassertive
cooperative
eager to help/please
generous
obliging
accommodating
amenable
considerate
helpful
neighborly
friendly
kindly
agreeable
kind
pleasant
polite
decent
civil
nonconfrontational
disinterested
uninvolved
uninterested
standoffish
unaccommodating
unhelpful
uncooperative
trying
awkward
disobliging
picky
demanding
finicky
fussy
fastidious
particular
critical
cussed
stubborn
pig-headed
unreasonable
tiresome
obstinate
contrary
perverse
exasperating
recalcitrant
obstreperous
refractory
fractious
froward
contrarious
contumacious
difficult ◂

DOCTORS

allergist	neurosurgeon
anesthetist	obstetrician
cardiologist	oncologist
chiropractor	ophthalmologist
clinician	optometrist
consulting physician	orthodontist
dentist	orthopedist
dermatologist	osteopath
endocrinologist	otolaryngologist
family doctor	pathologist
gastroenterologist	pediatrician
general practitioner	plastic surgeon
geriatrician	podiatrist
gynecologist	proctologist
hematologist	psychiatrist
immunologist	radiologist
internist	rheumatologist
naturopath	surgeon
neonatologist	urologist
neurologist	

doctrinaire adjective *doctrinaire Marxists* DOGMATIC, rigid, inflexible, uncompromising; authoritarian, intolerant, fanatical, zealous, extreme.

doctrine noun *the doctrine of the Trinity* CREED, credo, dogma, belief, teaching, ideology; tenet, maxim, canon, principle, precept.

document noun *their lawyer drew up a document* OFFICIAL PAPER, legal paper, certificate, deed, contract, legal agreement; *Law* instrument, indenture.

▸ verb *many aspects of school life have been documented* RECORD, register, report, log, chronicle, archive, put on record, write down; detail, note, describe.

documentary adjective **1** *documentary evidence* RECORDED, documented, registered, written, chronicled, archived, on record, on paper, in writing.

2 *a documentary film* FACTUAL, nonfictional.

▸ noun *a documentary about rural West Virginia* FACTUAL PROGRAM, factual film; program, film, broadcast.

dodder verb *doddering along the sidewalk* TOTTER, teeter, toddle, hobble, shuffle, shamble, falter.

doddering, doddery adjective *a doddering patient who needs constant supervision* TOTTERING, tottery, staggering, shuffling, shambling, faltering, shaky, unsteady, wobbly; feeble, frail, weak.

dodge verb **1** *she dodged into a crowded restaurant* DART, bolt, dive, lunge, leap, spring.

2 *he could easily dodge the two cops* ELUDE, evade, avoid, escape, run away from, lose, shake (off), jink; *informal* give someone the slip, ditch.

3 *the mayor tried to dodge the debate* AVOID, evade, get out of, back out of, sidestep, do an end run; *informal* duck, wriggle out of.

▸ noun **1** *a dodge to the right* DART, bolt, dive, lunge, leap, spring.

2 *a clever dodge | a tax dodge* RUSE, ploy, scheme, tactic, stratagem, subterfuge, trick, hoax, wile, cheat, deception, blind; swindle, fraud; *informal* scam, con, bunco, grift.

doer noun **1** *the doer of unspeakable deeds* PERFORMER, perpetrator, executor, accomplisher, agent.

2 *Daniel is a thinker more than a doer* WORKER, organizer, man/woman of action; *informal* mover and shaker, busy bee.

doff verb *literary he doffed his cap as we walked past* TAKE OFF, remove, strip off, pull off; raise, lift, tip; *dated* divest oneself of. ANTONYM don.

dog noun **1** *she went for a walk with her dog* hound, canine; mongrel, cur; pup, puppy; *informal* doggy/doggie, pooch. See table.

2 *informal you black-hearted dog!* See BASTARD noun sense 2.

3 *informal you're a lucky dog!* See FELLOW sense 1.

▸ verb **1** *they dogged him the length of the country* PURSUE, follow, track, trail, shadow, hound; *informal* tail.

2 *the scheme was dogged by bad weather* PLAGUE, beset, bedevil, beleaguer, blight, trouble.

BREEDS OF DOG

Sporting Dogs
American water spaniel
Brittany (spaniel)
Chesapeake Bay retriever
Clumber spaniel
cocker spaniel
curly-coated retriever
English setter
English springer spaniel
field spaniel
flat-coated retriever
German shorthaired pointer
German wirehaired pointer
golden retriever
Gordon setter
Irish setter
Irish water spaniel
Labrador retriever
pointer
Spinone (Italiano)
Sussex spaniel
vizsla
Weimaraner
Welsh springer spaniel
wirehaired pointing griffon

Hounds
Afghan hound
basenji
basset hound
beagle
black and tan coonhound
bloodhound
bluetick (coonhound)
borzoi
dachshund
foxhound
greyhound
harrier
Ibizan hound
Irish wolfhound
Norwegian elkhound
otterhound
petit basset griffon
Vendéen
pharoah hound
Plott hound
redbone (coonhound)
Rhodesian ridgeback
Saluki
Scottish deerhound
staghound
whippet

Working Dogs
Akita
Alaskan malamute
Anatolian shepherd
Bernese mountain dog
Black Russian terrier
boxer
bullmastiff
Doberman (pinscher)
giant schnauzer
Great Dane
Great Pyrenees
greater Swiss mountain dog
Komondor
kuvasz
mastiff
Neapolitan mastiff
Newfoundland
Portuguese water dog
Rottweiler
St. Bernard
Samoyed
Siberian husky
standard schnauzer

Herding Dogs
Australian cattle dog
Australian shepherd
bearded collie
Belgian Malinois
Belgian sheepdog
Belgian Tervuren
border collie
border terrier
Bouvier des Flandres
Briard
Canaan dog
Cardigan Welsh corgi
collie
German shepherd dog
kelpie
Old English sheepdog
Pembroke Welsh corgi
Polish lowland sheepdog
puli
rough collie
Shetland sheepdog

Terriers
Airedale (terrier)
American Staffordshire terrier
Australian terrier
Bedlington terrier
border terrier
bull terrier
cairn terrier
Dandie Dinmont (terrier)
Glen of Imaal terrier
Irish terrier
Jack Russell terrier
Kerry blue (terrier)
Lakeland terrier
Manchester terrier
miniature bull terrier
miniature schnauzer
Norfolk terrier
Norwich terrier
Scottish terrier
Sealyham terrier
Skye terrier
smooth fox terrier
soft-coated wheaten terrier
Staffordshire bull terrier
Welsh terrier
West Highland (white) terrier
wire fox terrier

Nonsporting Dogs
American Eskimo dog
Bichon Frisé
Boston terrier
bulldog
chow chow
Dalmatian
Finnish spitz
French bulldog
keeshond
Lhasa apso
Löwchen
miniature poodle
schipperke
Shar-Pei
Shiba Inu
standard poodle
Tibetan spaniel
Tibetan terrier

Toy Dogs
affenpinscher
Brussels griffon
Cavalier King Charles spaniel
chihuahua
Chinese crested
English toy spaniel
Havana silk dog/Havanese
Italian greyhound
Japanese chin
Maltese (terrier)
miniature pinscher
papillon
Pekingese/Pekinese
Pomeranian
pug
Shih Tzu
silky terrier
toy Manchester terrier
toy poodle
Yorkshire terrier

Miscellaneous
cockapoo
labradoodle

See also table at WOLF.

dogged adjective *what he lacks in natural talent he makes up for in dogged spirit* TENACIOUS, determined, resolute, resolved, purposeful, persistent, persevering, single-minded, tireless; strong-willed, steadfast, staunch; *formal* pertinacious. See note at STUBBORN. ANTONYM half-hearted.

dogma noun *a dogma of the Sikh religion* TEACHING, belief, tenet, principle, precept, maxim, article of faith, canon; creed, credo, set of beliefs, doctrine, ideology.

dogmatic adjective *your being so dogmatic does not attract me to your religious philosophy* OPINIONATED, peremptory, assertive, insistent, emphatic, adamant, doctrinaire, authoritarian, imperious, dictatorial, uncompromising, unyielding, inflexible, rigid.

doing noun **1** *the doing of the act constitutes the offense* PERFORMANCE, performing, carrying out, execution, implementation, implementing, achievement, accomplishment, realization, completion; *formal* effectuation.

2 *an account of his doings in Boston* EXPLOIT, activity, act, action, deed, feat, achievement, accomplishment; *informal* caper.

3 *that would take some doing* EFFORT, exertion, work, hard work, application, labor, toil, struggle.

doldrums plural noun *winter doldrums* DEPRESSION, melancholy, gloom, gloominess, downheartedness, dejection, despondency, low spirits, despair; inertia, apathy, listlessness, blahs, blue funk, blues. PHRASE: **in the doldrums** *overseas stocks are in the doldrums* INACTIVE, quiet, slow, slack, sluggish, stagnant.

dole verb *we dole out fresh soup and bread every afternoon* DEAL OUT, share out, divide up, allocate, allot, distribute, dispense, hand out, give out, dish out/up, divvy up.

doleful adjective *her doleful eyes* MOURNFUL, woeful, sorrowful, sad, unhappy, depressed, gloomy, morose, melancholy, miserable, forlorn, wretched, woebegone, despondent, dejected, disconsolate, downcast, crestfallen, downhearted; *informal* blue, down in/at the mouth, down in the dumps; *literary* dolorous, heartsick. ANTONYM cheerful.

doll noun **1** *the child was hugging a doll* FIGURE, figurine, action figure, model; toy, plaything; *informal* dolly.

2 *informal* *she was quite a doll.* See BEAUTY sense 2.
PHRASE: **doll oneself up** *informal* *you don't need to doll yourself up for me* DRESS UP; *informal* do oneself up, dress up to the nines, put on one's glad rags.

dollop *informal* noun *a dollop of whipped cream* BLOB, gobbet, lump, ball; *informal* glob.

dolor noun *literary* See MISERY sense 1.

dolorous adjective *literary* See DOLEFUL.

dolphin noun See table at WHALE.

dolt noun See IDIOT.

doltish adjective See STUPID sense 1.

domain noun **1** *they extended their domain* REALM, kingdom, empire, dominion, province, territory, land.

2 *the domain of art* FIELD, area, sphere, discipline, province, world.

dome noun *the distinctive dome of the cathedral* CUPOLA, vault, arched roof, rotunda. See note at CUPOLA.

domestic adjective **1** *domestic commitments* FAMILY, home, household.

2 *she was not at all domestic* stay-at-home, home-loving, homey, housewifely; *humorous* domesticated.

3 *small domestic animals* DOMESTICATED, tame, pet, household.

4 *the domestic car industry* NATIONAL, home, internal.

5 *domestic plants* NATIVE, indigenous.

▸ noun *they worked as domestics* SERVANT, domestic worker, domestic help, maid, housemaid, cleaner, cleaning lady, housekeeper.

domesticated adjective **1** *domesticated animals* TAME, tamed, pet, domestic, trained. ANTONYM wild.

2 *domesticated crops* CULTIVATED, naturalized. ANTONYMS foreign, wild.

3 *humorous* *I'm happily domesticated.* See DOMESTIC sense 2.

domicile *formal* noun *changes of domicile* RESIDENCE, home, house, address, residency, lodging, accommodations; *informal* digs; *formal* dwelling (place), abode, habitation.

▸ verb *he* ***is domiciled*** *in Australia* IS SETTLED, live, make one's home, take up residence.

dominance noun *a position of political dominance* SUPREMACY, superiority, ascendancy, preeminence, predominance, domination, dominion, mastery, power, authority, rule, command, control, sway; *literary* puissance.

dominant adjective 1 *the dominant classes* PRESIDING, ruling, governing, controlling, commanding, ascendant, supreme, authoritative. ANTONYM subservient.

2 *he has a dominant personality* ASSERTIVE, authoritative, forceful, domineering, commanding, controlling, pushy. ANTONYM submissive.

3 *the dominant issues in psychology* MAIN, principal, prime, premier, chief, foremost, primary, predominant, paramount, prominent; central, key, crucial, core; *informal* number-one. ANTONYM secondary.

dominate verb 1 *the Russians dominated Iran in the nineteenth century* CONTROL, influence, exercise control over, command, be in command of, be in charge of, rule, govern, direct, have ascendancy over, have mastery over; *informal* head up, be in the driver's seat, be at the helm of, rule the roost (in), wear the pants (in), have someone in one's hip pocket; *literary* sway.

2 *it dominates the sports scene* PREDOMINATE, prevail, reign, be prevalent, be paramount, be preeminent; *informal* kick butt.

3 *the village is dominated by the viaduct* OVERLOOK, command, tower above/over, loom over.

domination noun *she was put off by the male domination sanctioned by her boyfriend's family* RULE, government, sovereignty, control, command, authority, power, dominion, dominance, mastery, supremacy, superiority, ascendancy, sway.

domineer verb *his mother had always sought out men she could domineer* BROWBEAT, bully, intimidate, push around/about, order about/around, lord it over; dictate to, be overbearing, have under one's thumb, rule with a rod of iron; *informal* boss about/around, walk all over.

domineering adjective *a domineering father and a meek mother had turned her against the idea of marriage* OVERBEARING, authoritarian, imperious, high-handed, autocratic; masterful, dictatorial, despotic, oppressive, iron-fisted, strict, harsh, bossy.

dominion noun 1 *France had dominion over Laos* SUPREMACY, ascendancy, dominance, domination, superiority, predominance, preeminence, hegemony, authority, mastery, control, command, power, sway, rule, government, jurisdiction, sovereignty, suzerainty. See note at JURISDICTION.

2 *a British dominion* DEPENDENCY, colony, protectorate, territory, province, possession; *historical* tributary.

don verb *he donned an overcoat* PUT ON, get dressed in, dress (oneself) in, get into, slip into/on.

donate verb *the proceeds were donated to the American Red Cross* GIVE, give/make a donation of, contribute, make a contribution of, gift, pledge, grant, bestow; *informal* chip in, pitch in, kick in. See note at GIVE.

donation noun *a tax-deductible donation* GIFT, contribution, present, pledge, handout, grant, offering; *formal* benefaction; *historical* alms. See note at PRESENT[3].

done adjective 1 *the job is done* FINISHED, ended, concluded, complete, completed, accomplished, achieved, fulfilled, discharged, executed; *informal* wrapped up, sewn up, polished off. ANTONYM incomplete.

2 *is the meat done?* COOKED (THROUGH), ready. ANTONYMS raw, underdone.

3 *those days are done* OVER, over and done with, at an end, finished, ended, concluded, terminated, no more, dead, gone, in the past. ANTONYMS to come, ongoing.

4 *informal* *that's just not done* PROPER, seemly, decent, respectable, right, correct, in order, fitting, appropriate, acceptable, the done thing. PHRASES: **be/have done with** *she was done with him* BE/HAVE FINISHED WITH, be through with, want no more to do with. **done for** *informal* *if you get caught, you'll be done for* RUINED, finished, destroyed, undone, doomed, lost; *informal* washed up.

Don Juan noun *he was quite the Don Juan in his younger days* WOMANIZER, philanderer, Romeo, Casanova, Lothario, flirt, ladies' man, playboy, seducer, rake, roué, libertine; *informal* skirt-chaser, ladykiller, wolf.

donkey noun 1 *the cart was drawn by a donkey* ASS, jackass, jenny; mule, hinny, burro.

2 *informal* *you silly donkey!* See FOOL noun sense 1.

donnish adjective *the quiet, donnish types* SCHOLARLY, studious, academic, bookish, intellectual, learned, highbrow; *informal* egghead; *dated* lettered.

donor noun *an anonymous donor* GIVER, contributor, benefactor, benefactress; supporter, backer, patron, sponsor, friend, member; *informal* angel.

donut noun See table at DOUGHNUT.

doohickey noun *it's the little red thing next to the blue doohickey* THING, so-and so, whatever it's called; *informal* whatsit, whatnot, doodad, thingy, thingamajig, thingamabob, what's-its-name, whatchamacallit, whatchacallit.

doom noun 1 *his impending doom* DESTRUCTION, downfall, ruin, ruination; extinction, annihilation, death.

2 *archaic* *the day of doom* JUDGMENT DAY, the Last Judgment, doomsday, Armageddon.

▸ verb *we were doomed to fail* DESTINE, fate, predestine, preordain, foredoom, mean; condemn, sentence.

doomed adjective *a doomed voyage* ILL-FATED, ill-starred, cursed, jinxed, foredoomed, damned; *literary* star-crossed.

door noun *many a weary traveler has walked through that door* DOORWAY, portal, opening, entrance, entry, exit. PHRASE: **out of doors** *if the weather's nice, we'll have our dinner out of doors* OUTSIDE, outdoors, in/into the open air, alfresco.

doorman noun *the doorman will call for your car* DOORKEEPER, commissionaire, concierge.

dope noun *informal* 1 *he was caught smuggling dope* (ILLEGAL) DRUGS, narcotics; cannabis, heroin, cocaine.

2 *what a dope!* See FOOL noun sense 1.

3 *give me the dope on Mr. Dixon.* See INTELLIGENCE sense 2.

▸ verb 1 *the horse was doped* DRUG, administer drugs/narcotics to, tamper with, interfere with; sedate.

2 *they doped his drink* ADD DRUGS TO, tamper with, adulterate, contaminate, lace; *informal* spike, doctor.

dopey adjective *informal* *he became dopey and fell into a deep sleep* STUPEFIED, confused, muddled, befuddled, disorientated, groggy, muzzy; *informal* woozy, not with it. ANTONYM alert.

dormant adjective *the tubers lie dormant in the soil until* *spring* ASLEEP, sleeping, resting; INACTIVE, passive, inert, latent, quiescent. See note at LATENT. ANTONYMS awake, active.

dose noun *do not exceed the prescribed dose* MEASURE, measurement, portion, dosage, shot; *informal* hit, fix.

dossier noun *the FBI's dossier on the suspect dates back to 1961* FILE, report, case history; account, notes, document(s), documentation, data, information, evidence.

dot noun *a pattern of tiny dots* SPOT, speck, fleck, speckle; decimal point, period, pixel.

▸ verb **1** *spots of rain dotted his shirt* SPOT, fleck, mark, stipple, freckle, sprinkle; *literary* bestrew, besprinkle.

2 *the streets are dotted with restaurants* SCATTER, pepper, sprinkle, strew.

PHRASE: **on the dot** *informal ring the bell at 1:15 on the dot* PRECISELY, exactly, sharp, prompt, dead on, on the stroke of ——; *informal* on the button, on the nose.

dotage noun *the memoirs she began in her dotage* DECLINING YEARS, winter of one's life, autumn of one's life; advanced years, old age; *literary* eld.

dot-com noun *it's a new dot-com through which they can buy and sell antiques* ONLINE RETAILER, e-business, e-tailer, online business; *informal* clicks and mortar.

dote PHRASE: **dote on** *she doted on the boy* ADORE, love dearly, be devoted to, idolize, treasure, cherish, worship, hold dear; indulge, spoil, pamper.

doting adjective *all her doting admirers* ADORING, loving, besotted, infatuated; affectionate, fond, devoted, caring; uxorious.

dotty adjective *informal* See MAD sense 1.

double adjective **1** *a double garage | double yellow lines* DUAL, duplex, twin, binary, duplicate, in pairs, coupled, twofold. ANTONYM single.

2 *a double helping* DOUBLED, twofold.

3 *a double meaning* AMBIGUOUS, equivocal, dual, two-edged, double-edged, ambivalent, cryptic, enigmatic. ANTONYM unambiguous.

4 *a double life* DECEITFUL, double-dealing, two-faced, dual; hypocritical, false, duplicitous, insincere, deceiving, dissembling, dishonest. ANTONYMS simple, honest.

▸ adverb *we had to pay double* TWICE (OVER), twice the amount, doubly.

▸ noun **1** *if it's not her, it's her double* LOOK-ALIKE, twin, clone, duplicate, exact likeness, replica, copy, facsimile, doppelgänger; *informal* spitting image, dead ringer.

2 *she used a double for the stunts* STAND-IN, substitute.

▸ verb **1** *they doubled his salary* MULTIPLY BY TWO, increase twofold.

2 *the bottom sheet had been doubled up* FOLD (BACK/UP/DOWN/OVER/UNDER), turn back/up/down/over/under, tuck back/up/down/under.

3 *the kitchen can double as a dining room* FUNCTION, do, (also) serve.

PHRASE: **on the double** *hold tight, we'll be there on the double* VERY QUICKLY, as fast as one's legs can carry one, at a run, at a gallop, fast, swiftly, rapidly, speedily, at full speed, at full tilt, as fast as possible; *informal* like (greased) lightning, like the wind, like a bat out of hell, lickety-split, PDQ (pretty damn quick).

double-cross verb *he was double-crossing his family behind their backs* BETRAY, cheat, defraud, trick, hoodwink, mislead, deceive, swindle, be disloyal to, be unfaithful to, play false; *informal* sell down the river.

double-dealing noun *your double-dealing will eventually be your undoing* DUPLICITY, treachery, betrayal, double-crossing, unfaithfulness, untrustworthiness, infidelity, bad faith, disloyalty, breach of trust, fraud, underhandedness, cheating, dishonesty, deceit, deceitfulness, deception, falseness; *informal* crookedness. ANTONYM honesty.

double entendre noun *much of the comedy is derived from racy double entendres* AMBIGUITY, double meaning, innuendo, play on words.

doublespeak noun *they throw in just enough doublespeak to make you forget that they're trying to sell you something you don't really need* EQUIVOCATING, evasion, dodging, beating about the bush, pussyfooting (around); jargon, double-talk, gibberish, gobbledygook; *informal* -speak, -ese, -babble.

doubly adverb *we have to be doubly careful* TWICE AS, in double measure, even more, especially, extra.

doubt noun **1** *there was some doubt as to the caller's identity* UNCERTAINTY, unsureness, indecision, hesitation, dubiousness, suspicion, confusion; queries, questions; *formal* dubiety. See note at UNCERTAINTY. ANTONYM certainty.

2 *a weak leader racked by doubt* INDECISION, hesitation, uncertainty, insecurity, unease, uneasiness, apprehension; hesitancy, vacillation, irresolution. ANTONYMS confidence, conviction.

3 *there is doubt about their motives* SKEPTICISM, distrust, mistrust, doubtfulness, suspicion, cynicism, uneasiness, apprehension, wariness, chariness, leeriness; reservations, misgivings, suspicions; *formal* dubiety. ANTONYM trust.

▸ verb **1** *they doubted my story* DISBELIEVE, distrust, mistrust, suspect, have doubts about, be suspicious of, have misgivings about, have qualms about, feel uneasy about, feel apprehensive about, query, question, challenge. ANTONYM trust.

2 *I doubt whether he will come* THINK SOMETHING UNLIKELY, have (one's) doubts about, question, query, be dubious. ANTONYM be confident.

3 *stop doubting and believe!* BE UNDECIDED, have doubts, be irresolute, be ambivalent, be doubtful, be unsure, be uncertain, be of two minds, hesitate, shilly-shally, waver, vacillate. ANTONYM believe.

PHRASES: **in doubt** **1** *the issue was in doubt* DOUBTFUL, uncertain, open to question, unconfirmed, unknown, undecided, unresolved, in the balance, up in the air; *informal* iffy. **2** *if you are in doubt, ask for advice* IRRESOLUTE, hesitant, vacillating, dithering, wavering, ambivalent; doubtful, unsure, uncertain, of two minds, shilly-shallying, undecided, in a quandary, in a dilemma; *informal* sitting on the fence. **no doubt** *he's no doubt read the note by now* DOUBTLESS, undoubtedly, indubitably, doubtlessly, without (a) doubt; unquestionably, undeniably, incontrovertibly, irrefutably; unequivocally, clearly, plainly, obviously, patently.

doubter noun *this is his chance to confound the doubters* SKEPTIC, doubting Thomas, nonbeliever, unbeliever, disbeliever, cynic, scoffer, questioner, challenger, dissenter. ANTONYM believer.

doubtful adjective **1** *I was doubtful about going* IRRESOLUTE, hesitant, vacillating, dithering, wavering, in doubt, unsure, uncertain, of two minds, shilly-shallying, undecided, in a quandary, in a dilemma, blowing hot and cold. ANTONYMS confident, decisive.

2 *at this point, the verdict is still doubtful* IN DOUBT, uncertain, open to question, unsure, unconfirmed, not definite, unknown, undecided, unresolved, debatable, in the balance, up in the air; *informal* iffy. ANTONYM certain.

3 *the whole trip is looking rather doubtful* UNLIKELY, improbable, dubious, impossible. ANTONYM probable.

4 *they are doubtful of the methods used* DISTRUSTFUL, mistrustful, suspicious, wary, chary, leery, apprehensive; skeptical, unsure, ambivalent, dubious, cynical. ANTONYM trusting.

5 *this decision is of doubtful validity* QUESTIONABLE, arguable, debatable, controversial, contentious; *informal* iffy. ANTONYM sound.

THE RIGHT WORD

If you are **doubtful** about the outcome of a situation, you might be understandably **dubious** about getting involved in it. While all of these adjectives express suspicion, indecision, or a lack of clarity, *doubtful* carries such strong connotations of uncertainty that the thing being described is as good as worthless, unsound, invalid, unlikely, or doomed to fail (*it was doubtful that the plane could land safely*). *Dubious* is not quite as strong, suggesting suspicion, mistrust, or hesitation (*a dubious reputation*). It can also mean inclined to doubt or full of hesitation. If you're *doubtful* about the outcome of a particular situation, it means that you are fairly certain it will not turn out well. If you're *dubious*, on the other hand, it means that you're wavering or hesitating in your opinion. **Questionable** may merely imply the existence of doubt (*a questionable excuse*), but like *dubious*, it also has connotations of dishonesty and immorality (*a place where questionable activities were going on*). **Problematic**, in contrast to both *dubious* and *questionable*, is free from any suggestion of moral judgment or suspicion. It is applied to things that are genuinely uncertain, and to outcomes that are as likely to be positive as negative (*getting everyone in the family to agree could be problematic*). **Ambiguous** and **equivocal** refer to lack of clarity. But while *ambiguous* can refer to either an intentional or unintentional lack of clarity (*her ambiguous replies to our questions*), *equivocal* suggests an intentional wish to remain unclear (*his equivocal responses indicated that he wasn't keen to cooperate*). It can also mean capable of different interpretations (*an equivocal statement that could be taken to mean opposite things*). Something that is **enigmatic** is likely to be intentionally unclear as well (*an enigmatic statement designed to provoke controversy*), although *enigmatic* can also mean perplexing or mysterious.

doubtless adverb *Henry was doubtless glad of the opportunity* UNDOUBTEDLY, indubitably, doubtlessly, no doubt; unquestionably, indisputably, undeniably, incontrovertibly, irrefutably; certainly, surely, of course, indeed.

doughnut noun See table.

doughty adjective *the doughty Sir Lancelot* FEARLESS, dauntless, determined, resolute, indomitable, intrepid, plucky, spirited, bold, valiant, brave, stouthearted, courageous; *informal* gutsy, spunky, feisty, ballsy.

dour adjective *they were barely acknowledged by the dour receptionist* STERN, unsmiling, unfriendly, severe, forbidding, gruff, surly, grim, sullen, solemn, austere, stony. ANTONYMS cheerful, friendly. See note at GLUM.

DOUGHNUTS AND DEEP-FRIED SWEETS

aebleskiver	hojuela
awwamath	jalebi
beignet	jelly doughnut
Berliner	kooksistas
bimuelo	laddu
bismark	longjohn
bitsu-bitsu	loukoumades
buñuelo	malassadas
cala	maple bar
cascaron	nien koh
cenci	oliebollen
chiacchiere	paczki
chrusciki	pampushky
churro	piskota fank
cruller	pizzelle
csoroge	poffertges
dango	puff
farsangi fank	sata andagi
fastnacht	sfenji
fillozes	shisky
French cruller	sopaipilla
fried ice cream	sufganiyot
fritter	viccitelli
funnel cake	zeppole
glazed doughnut	

See also tables at CAKE, CANDY, COOKIE, PASTRY, and PIE.

douse verb **1** *a mob doused the thieves with gas* DRENCH, soak, saturate, wet, splash, slosh.

2 *a guard doused the flames* EXTINGUISH, put out, quench, smother, snuff (out).

dovetail verb **1** *the ends of the logs were dovetailed* JOINT, join, fit together, splice, mortise, tenon.

2 *this will dovetail well with the company's existing activities* FIT IN, go together, be consistent, match, conform, harmonize, be in tune, correspond; *informal* square, jibe.

dowdy adjective *a makeover that took her from dowdy to wow-dy* UNFASHIONABLE, frumpy, old-fashioned, outmoded, out-of-date, inelegant, shabby, frowzy. ANTONYM fashionable.

down[1] adverb **1** *they went down in the elevator* TOWARD A LOWER POSITION, downward, downstairs. ANTONYM up.

2 *she fell down* TO THE GROUND, to the floor, over. ANTONYM up.

▸ preposition **1** *the elevator plunged down the shaft* TO A LOWER POSITION IN, to the bottom of.

2 *I walked down the street* ALONG, to the other end of, from one end of —— to the other.

3 *down the years* THROUGHOUT, through, during.

▸ adjective **1** *I'm feeling a bit down* DEPRESSED, sad, unhappy, melancholy, miserable, wretched, sorrowful, gloomy, dejected, downhearted, despondent, dispirited, low; *informal* blue, down in the dumps, down in/at the mouth. ANTONYM elated.

2 *the computer is down* NOT WORKING, inoperative, malfunctioning, out of order, broken; not in service, out of action, out of commission; *informal* conked out, bust, busted, (gone) kaput, on the fritz, on the blink. ANTONYM working.

▸ verb *informal* **1** *antiaircraft missiles downed the fighter jet* KNOCK DOWN/OVER, knock to the ground, bring down, topple; *informal* deck, floor, flatten.

2 *he downed his beer* DRINK (UP/DOWN), gulp (down), guzzle, quaff, drain, chugalug, slug, finish off; *informal* knock back, put away, scarf (down/up).

▸ noun *the ups and downs of running a business* SETBACKS, upsets, reverses, reversals, mishaps, vicissitudes; *informal* glitches.

PHRASE: **be down on** *informal why do you have to be down on your parents all the time?* DISAPPROVE OF, be against, feel antagonism to, be hostile to, feel ill will toward; *informal* have it in for.

down[2] noun *goose down* SOFT FEATHERS, fine hair; fluff, fuzz, floss, lint.

down-and-out adjective *she had not forgotten what it felt like to be a down-and-out teenager* DESTITUTE, poverty-stricken, impoverished, penniless, insolvent, impecunious; needy, in straitened circumstances, distressed, badly off; homeless, on the streets, vagrant, sleeping rough; *informal* hard up, (flat) broke, strapped (for cash), without a red cent, on skid row. ANTONYM wealthy.

▸ noun *the down-and-outs crowd the subway stations when the weather is bad* POOR PERSON, pauper, indigent; beggar, homeless person, panhandler, vagrant, tramp, drifter, derelict, vagabond, hobo; *informal* have-not, bag lady, bum.

down-at-heel, down-at-the-heel(s) adjective **1** *the resort looks down-at-the-heels* RUN-DOWN, dilapidated, neglected, uncared-for; seedy, insalubrious, squalid, slummy, wretched; *informal* scruffy, scuzzy, flea-bitten.

2 *a down-at-heel laborer* SCRUFFY, shabby, ragged, tattered, mangy, sorry; unkempt, bedraggled, disheveled, ungroomed, seedy, untidy, slovenly; *informal* tatty, scuzzy, grungy; raggedy. ANTONYMS smart, stylish.

downbeat adjective *the mood is decidedly downbeat* PESSIMISTIC, gloomy, negative, defeatist, cynical, bleak, fatalistic, dark, black; despairing, despondent, depressed, dejected, demoralized, hopeless, melancholy, glum.

downcast adjective *it's too nice a day to be looking so downcast* DESPONDENT, disheartened, discouraged, dispirited, downhearted, crestfallen, down, low, disconsolate, despairing; sad, melancholy, gloomy, glum, morose, doleful, dismal, woebegone, miserable, depressed, dejected; *informal* blue, down in/at the mouth, down in the dumps. ANTONYM elated.

downfall noun *the shah's downfall* UNDOING, ruin, ruination; defeat, conquest, deposition, overthrow; nemesis, destruction, annihilation, elimination; end, collapse, fall, crash, failure; debasement, degradation, disgrace; Waterloo. ANTONYM rise.

downgrade verb **1** *plans to downgrade three workers* DEMOTE, lower, reduce/lower in rank; relegate. ANTONYM promote.

2 *I won't downgrade their achievement* DISPARAGE, denigrate, detract from, run down, belittle; *informal* badmouth, dis. ANTONYM praise.

downhearted adjective *of the children, little Robbie was the most downhearted* DESPONDENT, disheartened, discouraged, dispirited, downcast, crestfallen, down, low, disconsolate, wretched; melancholy, gloomy, glum, morose, doleful, dismal, woebegone, miserable, depressed, dejected, sorrowful, sad; *informal* blue, down in/at the mouth, down in the dumps. ANTONYM elated.

download verb *I downloaded a new version of my browser* LOAD, copy, transfer, upload.

downpour noun *they met when huddled under an awning during a sudden downpour* RAINSTORM, cloudburst, deluge, shower; thunderstorm, thundershower; torrential/pouring rain.

downright adjective **1** *downright lies* COMPLETE, total, absolute, utter, thorough, out-and-out, outright, sheer, arrant, pure, real, veritable, categorical, unmitigated, unadulterated, unalloyed, unequivocal.

2 *her downright attitude.* See FORTHRIGHT.

▸ adverb *that's downright dangerous* THOROUGHLY, utterly, positively, profoundly, really, completely, totally, entirely; unquestionably, undeniably, in every respect, through and through; *informal* plain.

downside noun *the downside is all the travel, which keeps me from my family* DRAWBACK, disadvantage, snag, stumbling block, catch, pitfall, fly in the ointment; handicap, limitation, trouble, difficulty, problem, complication, nuisance; hindrance; weak spot/point; *informal* minus. ANTONYM advantage.

down-to-earth adjective *I guess we weren't expecting the son of those weirdos to be so charming and down-to-earth* PRACTICAL, sensible, realistic, matter-of-fact, responsible, reasonable, rational, logical, balanced, sober, pragmatic, levelheaded, commonsensical, sane. ANTONYM idealistic.

downtown noun *the tax incentives are designed to bring business back to downtown* CITY CENTER, (central) business district, urban core; inner city; *informal* concrete jungle.

▸ adjective *downtown shoppers want better parking facilities* CENTRAL, metropolitan, metro, urban; uptown, midtown.

downtrodden adjective *thousands of downtrodden families arrived at the border, only to be turned away* OPPRESSED, subjugated, persecuted, repressed, tyrannized, crushed, enslaved, exploited, victimized, bullied; disadvantaged, underprivileged, powerless, helpless; abused, maltreated.

downward adjective *profits are in a downward trend* DESCENDING, downhill, falling, sinking, dipping; earthbound, earthward.

downy adjective *the downy white fibers of autumn's milkweed* SOFT, velvety, smooth, fleecy, fluffy, fuzzy, feathery, furry, woolly, silky.

dowry noun *Belinda's dowry included an acre of fertile pasture and two young mules* MARRIAGE SETTLEMENT, (marriage) portion; *archaic* dot.

doze verb *she was dozing at her desk when the supervisor walked by* CATNAP, nap, drowse, sleep lightly, rest; *informal* snooze, catch forty winks, get some shut-eye, catch some Zs; *literary* slumber.

▸ noun *a little doze before dinner might be just what you need* CATNAP, nap, siesta, light sleep, drowse, rest; *informal* snooze, forty winks; *literary* slumber.

PHRASE: **doze off** *the guy in front of us would doze off between all the musical numbers* FALL ASLEEP, go to sleep, drop off; *informal* nod off, drift off, sack out, conk out.

dozy adjective *she did look a bit dozy, but I never suspected drugs* DROWSY, sleepy, half asleep, somnolent; lethargic, listless, enervated, inactive, languid, weary, tired, fatigued, logy, heavy-eyed; *informal* dopey, yawny.

drab adjective **1** *a drab interior* COLORLESS, gray, dull, washed out, muted, lackluster; dingy, dreary, dismal, cheerless, gloomy, somber. ANTONYMS bright, cheerful.

2 *a drab existence* UNINTERESTING, dull, boring, tedious, monotonous, dry, dreary; unexciting, unimaginative, uninspiring, insipid, lackluster, flat, stale, wishy-washy, colorless; lame, tired, sterile, anemic, barren, tame; middle-of-the-road, run-of-the-mill, mediocre, nondescript, characterless, mundane, unremarkable, humdrum, plain-vanilla. ANTONYM interesting.

draconian adjective *collaborators suffered draconian reprisals* HARSH, severe, strict, extreme, drastic, stringent, tough; cruel, oppressive, ruthless, relentless, punitive; authoritarian, despotic, tyrannical, repressive. ANTONYM lenient.

draft[1] noun **1** *the draft of his speech* PRELIMINARY VERSION, rough outline, plan, skeleton, abstract; main points, bare bones.

2 *a draft of the building* PLAN, blueprint, design, diagram, drawing, sketch, map, layout, representation.

3 *a bank draft* CHECK, order, money order, bill of exchange.

draft[2] noun **1** *the draft made Robyn shiver* CURRENT OF AIR, rush of air; waft, wind, breeze, gust, puff, blast; *informal* blow.

2 *a deep draft of beer* GULP, drink, swallow, mouthful, slug; *informal* swig, swill.

drag verb **1** *she dragged the chair backward* HAUL, pull, tug, heave, lug, draw; trail, trawl, tow; *informal* yank.

2 *the day dragged* BECOME TEDIOUS, pass slowly, creep along, hang heavy, wear on, go on too long, go on and on.

▸ noun **1** *the drag of the air brakes* PULL, resistance, tug.

2 *informal* *work can be a drag* BORE, nuisance, bother, trouble, pest, annoyance, trial, chore, vexation; *informal* pain, pain in the neck, headache, hassle.

PHRASES: **drag on** *their feud has dragged on for years* PERSIST, continue, go on, carry on, extend, run on, be protracted, endure, prevail. **drag out** *let's not drag out the Q&A session with issues that can't be addressed at this point* PROLONG, protract, draw out, spin out, string out, extend, lengthen, carry on, keep going, continue.

dragoon noun *historical* *the dragoons charged* CAVALRYMAN, mounted soldier; *historical* knight, chevalier, hussar; *archaic* cavalier.

▸ verb *he dragooned his friends into participating* COERCE, pressure, press, push; force, compel, impel; hound, harass, nag, harry, badger, goad, pester; browbeat, bludgeon, bully, twist someone's arm, strong-arm; *informal* railroad.

drag queen noun. See TRANSVESTITE.

drain verb **1** *a valve for draining the tank* EMPTY (OUT), void, clear (out), evacuate, unload. ANTONYM fill.

2 *drain off any surplus liquid* DRAW OFF, extract, withdraw, remove, siphon off, pour out, pour off; milk, bleed, tap, void, filter, discharge.

3 *the water drained away to the sea* FLOW, pour, trickle, stream, run, rush, gush, flood, surge; leak, ooze, seep, dribble, issue, filter, bleed, leach.

4 *more people would just drain our resources* USE UP, exhaust, deplete, consume, expend, get through, sap, strain, tax; milk, bleed. ANTONYM replenish.

▸ noun **1** *the drain filled with water* SEWER, channel, conduit, ditch, culvert, duct, pipe, gutter, trough; sluice, spillway, race, flume, chute.

2 *a drain on the battery* STRAIN, pressure, burden, load, tax, demand.

dram noun *a dram of peach brandy* DRINK, nip, sip, drop, finger, splash, little, spot, taste.

drama noun **1** *a television drama* PLAY, show, piece, theatrical work, dramatization.

2 *he is studying drama* ACTING, the theater, the stage, the performing arts, dramatic art(s), stagecraft.

3 *she liked to create a drama* INCIDENT, scene, spectacle, crisis; excitement, thrill, sensation; disturbance, commotion, turmoil; dramatics, theatrics.

dramatic adjective **1** *dramatic art* THEATRICAL, theatric, thespian, stage, dramaturgical; *formal* histrionic.

2 *a dramatic increase* CONSIDERABLE, substantial, sizable, goodly, fair, marked, noticeable, measurable, perceptible, obvious, appreciable; significant, notable, noteworthy, remarkable, extraordinary, exceptional, phenomenal; *informal* tidy. ANTONYM insignificant.

3 *dramatic scenes set in the city* EXCITING, stirring, action-packed, sensational, spectacular; startling, unexpected, tense, gripping, riveting, fascinating, thrilling, hair-raising; rousing, lively, electrifying, impassioned, moving. ANTONYM boring.

4 *dramatic headlands* STRIKING, impressive, imposing, spectacular, breathtaking, dazzling, sensational, awesome, awe-inspiring, remarkable, outstanding, incredible, phenomenal. ANTONYM unimpressive.

5 *a dramatic gesture* EXAGGERATED, theatrical, ostentatious, actressy, stagy, showy, splashy, melodramatic, overdone, histrionic, affected, mannered, artificial; *informal* hammy, ham, campy. ANTONYMS natural, unaffected.

dramatist noun *Fonda plays the part of dramatist Lillian Hellman* PLAYWRIGHT, writer, scriptwriter, screenwriter, scenarist, dramaturge.

dramatize verb **1** *the novel was dramatized* TURN INTO A PLAY/MOVIE/MOTION PICTURE/FILM, adapt for the stage/screen.

2 *the tabloids dramatized the event* EXAGGERATE, overdo, overstate, hyperbolize, magnify, amplify, inflate; sensationalize, embroider, color, aggrandize, embellish, elaborate; *informal* blow up (out of all proportion).

drape verb **1** *she draped a shawl around her* WRAP, wind, swathe, sling, hang.

2 *the chair was draped with dirty laundry* COVER, envelop, swathe, shroud, deck, festoon, overlay, cloak, wind, enfold, sheathe.

3 *he draped one leg over the arm of his chair* DANGLE, hang, suspend, droop, drop.

drastic adjective *drastic measures were necessary* EXTREME, serious, desperate, radical, far-reaching, momentous, substantial; heavy, severe, harsh, rigorous; oppressive, draconian. ANTONYM moderate.

draw verb **1** *he drew the house* SKETCH, make a drawing (of), delineate, outline, draft, rough out, illustrate, render, represent, trace; portray, depict.

2 *she drew her chair closer to the fire* PULL, haul, drag, tug, heave, lug, trail, tow; *informal* yank.

3 *the train drew into the station* MOVE, go, come, proceed, progress, travel, advance, pass, drive; inch, roll, glide, cruise; forge, sweep; back.

4 *she drew the curtains* CLOSE, shut, lower; open, part, pull back, pull open, fling open, raise.

5 *the doctor drew some fluid off the knee* DRAIN, extract, withdraw, remove, suck, pump, siphon, milk, bleed, tap.

6 *he drew his gun* PULL OUT, take out, produce, fish out, extract, withdraw; unsheathe.

7 *I drew on my line of credit* WITHDRAW, take out.

8 *while I draw breath* BREATHE IN, inhale, inspire, respire.

9 *she was drawing huge audiences* ATTRACT, interest, win, capture, catch, engage, lure, entice; absorb, occupy, rivet, engross, fascinate, mesmerize, spellbind, captivate, enthrall, grip.

10 *what conclusion can we draw?* DEDUCE, infer, conclude, derive, gather, glean.

▸ noun **1** *the match ended in a draw* TIE, dead heat, stalemate.

2 *the draw of the city* ATTRACTION, lure, allure, pull, appeal, glamour, enticement, temptation, charm, seduction, fascination, magnetism.

PHRASES: **draw on** *you can always draw on your carpentry skills* CALL ON, have recourse to, avail oneself of, turn to, look to, fall back on, rely on, exploit, use, employ, utilize, bring into play. **draw out 1** *he drew out a gun.* See DRAW verb sense 6. **2** *they always drew out their goodbyes* PROLONG, protract, drag out, spin out, string out, extend, lengthen. **3** *you'll have to carefully draw him out with specific questions* ENCOURAGE TO TALK, put at ease. **draw up 1** *a car drew up beside us* STOP, pull up, halt, come to a standstill, brake, park; arrive. **2** *we drew up a list* COMPOSE, formulate, frame, write down, draft, prepare, think up, devise, work out; create, invent, design. **3** *he drew up his forces in battle array* ARRANGE, marshal, muster, assemble, group, order, range, rank, line up, dispose, position, array.

drawback noun *one of the drawbacks of the bigger screen is a slight loss in resolution* DISADVANTAGE, snag, downside, stumbling block, catch, hitch, pitfall, fly in the ointment; weak spot/point, weakness, imperfection; handicap, limitation, trouble, difficulty, problem, complication; hindrance, obstacle, impediment, obstruction, inconvenience, discouragement, deterrent; *informal* minus, hiccup, (monkey) wrench in the works. ANTONYM benefit.

drawing noun **1** *a drawing of our poodles, Skibby and Popo* SKETCH, picture, illustration, representation, portrayal, delineation, depiction, composition, study; diagram, outline, design, plan.

2 *she won the Christmas drawing* RAFFLE, lottery, sweepstake, sweep, ballot, lotto.

drawl verb *by the time he drawls a complete sentence, I'll be old and gray* SAY SLOWLY, speak slowly; drone.

drawn adjective *she looked pale and drawn* PINCHED, haggard, drained, wan, hollow-cheeked; fatigued, tired, exhausted; tense, stressed, strained, worried, anxious, harassed, fraught; *informal* hassled.

dread verb *I used to dread going to school* FEAR, be afraid of, worry about, be anxious about, have forebodings about; be terrified by, tremble/shudder at, shrink from, quail from, flinch from; *informal* get cold feet about.

▸ noun *she was filled with dread* FEAR, apprehension, trepidation, anxiety, worry, concern, foreboding, disquiet, unease, angst; fright, panic, alarm; terror, horror; *informal* the jitters, the creeps, the shivers, the heebie-jeebies. ANTONYM confidence.

▸ adjective *the dread disease* AWFUL, frightful, terrible, horrible, dreadful; feared, frightening, alarming, terrifying, dire, dreaded.

dreadful adjective **1** *a dreadful accident* TERRIBLE, frightful, horrible, grim, awful, dire; horrifying, alarming, shocking, distressing, appalling, harrowing; ghastly, fearful, horrendous; tragic, calamitous; *formal* grievous. ANTONYM mild.

2 *a dreadful meal* UNPLEASANT, disagreeable, nasty; frightful, shocking, awful, abysmal, atrocious, disgraceful, deplorable, very bad, repugnant; poor, inadequate, inferior, unsatisfactory, distasteful; *informal* pathetic, woeful, crummy, rotten, sorry, third-rate, lousy, godawful. ANTONYMS pleasant, agreeable.

3 *you're a dreadful flirt* OUTRAGEOUS, shocking; inordinate, immoderate, unrestrained.

dreadfully adverb **1** *I'm dreadfully hungry* EXTREMELY, very, really, exceedingly, tremendously, exceptionally, extraordinarily; decidedly, most, particularly; *informal* terrifically, terribly, desperately, awfully, devilishly, mega, seriously, majorly, ever so, real, mighty, awful; *informal, dated* frightfully.

2 *she missed James dreadfully* VERY MUCH, much, lots, a lot, a great deal, intensely, desperately.

3 *the company performed dreadfully* TERRIBLY, awfully, very badly, atrociously, appallingly, abominably, poorly; *informal* abysmally, pitifully.

dream noun **1** *I awoke from my dreams* REM sleep; nightmare; vision, fantasy, hallucination.

2 *she went around in a dream* DAYDREAM, reverie, trance, daze, stupor, haze.

3 *he realized his childhood dream* AMBITION, aspiration, hope; goal, aim, objective, grail, intention, intent, target; desire, wish, yearning; daydream, fantasy, pipe dream.

4 *he's an absolute dream* DELIGHT, joy, marvel, wonder, gem, treasure; beauty, vision.

▸ verb **1** *she dreamed about her own funeral* HAVE A DREAM, have a nightmare.

2 *I* ***dreamt of*** *making the Olympic team* FANTASIZE ABOUT, daydream about; WISH FOR, hope for, long for, yearn for, hanker after, set one's heart on; aspire to, aim for, set one's sights on.

3 *she's always dreaming* DAYDREAM, be in a trance, be lost in thought, be preoccupied, be abstracted, stare into space, muse, be in la-la land.

4 *I wouldn't dream of being late* THINK, consider, contemplate, conceive.

▸ adjective *his dream home* IDEAL, perfect, fantasy.

PHRASE: **dream up** *I dreamed up some new excuse* THINK UP, invent, concoct, devise, hatch, contrive, create, work out, come up with; *informal* cook up.

dreamer noun *part of me will always be a dreamer* FANTASIST, daydreamer; romantic, sentimentalist, idealist, wishful thinker, Don Quixote; Utopian, visionary. ANTONYM realist.

dreamland noun **1** *I drift off to dreamland* SLEEP; *humorous* the land of Nod.

2 *they must be living in dreamland* THE LAND OF MAKE-BELIEVE, fairyland, cloudland, la-la land, never-never land, paradise, Utopia, heaven, Shangri-La.

dreamlike adjective *they use lighting and smoke to give the scene a dreamlike effect* UNREAL, illusory, imaginary, unsubstantial, chimerical, ethereal, phantasmagorical, trancelike; surreal; nightmarish, Kafkaesque; hazy, shadowy, faint, indistinct, unclear; *literary* illusive.

dreamy adjective **1** *a dreamy expression* DAYDREAMING, dreaming; pensive, thoughtful, reflective, meditative, ruminative; lost in thought, preoccupied, distracted, rapt, inattentive, woolgathering, vague, absorbed, absent-minded, with one's head in the clouds, in a world of one's own; *informal* miles away. ANTONYMS alert, attentive.

2 *you and your ideas are a bit too dreamy for me* IDEALISTIC, romantic, starry-eyed, impractical, unrealistic, Utopian, quixotic; *chiefly Brit. informal* airy-fairy. ANTONYMS realistic, practical.

3 *a dreamy recollection* DREAMLIKE, vague, dim, hazy, shadowy, faint, indistinct, unclear. ANTONYMS clear, sharp.

4 *informal Tasha's friend Rick is really dreamy* ATTRACTIVE, handsome, good-looking; appealing, lovely, delightful; *informal* heavenly, divine, gorgeous, hot, cute. ANTONYMS unattractive, ugly.

dreary adjective **1** *the dreary hours spent in a jail cell* DULL, drab, uninteresting, flat, tedious, wearisome, boring, unexciting, unstimulating, uninspiring, soul-destroying; humdrum, monotonous, uneventful, unremarkable, featureless, ho-hum. ANTONYM exciting.

2 *she thought of dreary things* SAD, miserable, depressing, gloomy, somber, grave, mournful, melancholic, joyless, cheerless. ANTONYM cheerful.

3 *a dreary day* GLOOMY, dismal, dull, dark, dingy, murky, overcast; depressing, somber. ANTONYM bright.

dregs plural noun **1** *the dregs from a bottle of wine* SEDIMENT, deposit, residue, accumulation, sludge, lees, grounds, remains; *technical* residuum.

2 *the dregs of humanity* SCUM, refuse, riffraff, outcasts, deadbeats; underclass, untouchables, lowest of the low, great unwashed, hoi polloi; *informal* trash.

drench verb *the rain has drenched us to the bone* SOAK, saturate, wet through, permeate, douse, souse; drown, swamp, inundate, flood; steep, bathe.

dress verb **1** *he dressed quickly* PUT ON CLOTHES, clothe oneself, get dressed.

2 *she was dressed in a suit* CLOTHE, attire, garb, deck out, trick out, costume, array, robe; *informal* get up, doll up.

3 *they dress for dinner every day* WEAR FORMAL CLOTHES, wear evening dress, dress up.

4 *dressing the house for the holidays* DECORATE, trim, deck, adorn, ornament, embellish, beautify, prettify; festoon, garland, garnish.

5 *they dressed his wounds* BANDAGE, cover, bind, wrap, swathe; doctor, care for.

6 *dress the chicken* PREPARE, get ready; clean.

7 *the field was dressed with manure* FERTILIZE, enrich, manure, mulch, compost, top-dress.

8 *he dressed Michelle's hair* STYLE, groom, arrange, do; comb, brush; preen, primp; *informal* fix.

9 *Military the battalion dressed its ranks* LINE UP, align, straighten, arrange, order, dispose; fall in.

▸ noun **1** *a long blue dress* gown, robe, shift, frock. See table.

2 *fancy dress* CLOTHES, clothing, garments, attire; costume, outfit, ensemble, garb; *informal* gear, getup, togs, duds, glad rags, threads, Sunday best; *formal* apparel; *archaic* raiment.

PHRASES: **dress down 1** *even the execs dress down on Fridays* DRESS INFORMALLY, dress casually. **2** *never dress down an employee in front of his colleagues.* See REPRIMAND verb. **dress up 1** *Angela loved dressing up* DRESS SMARTLY, dress formally, wear evening dress; *informal* doll oneself up, put on one's glad rags, gussy oneself up. **2** *Hugh dressed up as Santa Claus* DISGUISE ONESELF, dress; put on fancy dress, put on a costume.

DRESSES

A-line dress	muumuu
baby doll	off-the-shoulder dress
ballgown	pinafore
caftan	princess dress
chemise	sack dress
cheongsam	sari
coat dress	sarong
cocktail dress	sheath
dirndl	shift
empire dress	shirtdress
evening dress/gown	shirtwaist
gown	skimmer
granny dress	slip dress
halter dress	strapless dress
housedress	sundress
jumper	tank dress
kimono	tea gown
little black dress	tube dress
maternity dress	tunic
Mother Hubbard	wedding gown

dressing noun **1** *salad dressing* SAUCE, condiment, dip. See table at SAUCE.

2 *they put fresh dressings on her burns* BANDAGE, covering, plaster, gauze, lint, compress; *trademark* Band-Aid.

3 *an organic dressing for the vegetable garden* FERTILIZER, manure, compost, dung, guano; bone meal, blood meal, fish meal; mulch; top-dressing.

dressmaker noun *her dressmaker was the young widow of Colonel Wilcox* TAILOR, seamstress, needlewoman; clothier; couturier, designer.

dressy adjective *we weren't quite as dressy as some of the other guests* SMART, formal; elaborate, ornate; stylish, elegant, chic, fashionable, fancy, black-tie; *informal* snappy, snazzy, natty, trendy, gussied up. ANTONYM casual.

dribble verb **1** *the baby started to dribble* DROOL, slaver, slobber, salivate, drivel.

2 *rainwater dribbled down her face* TRICKLE, drip, fall, drizzle; ooze, seep.

3 *dribble the ball* BOUNCE.

▸ noun 1 *there was dribble on his chin* SALIVA, spittle, spit, slaver, slobber, drool.

2 *a dribble of sweat* TRICKLE, drip, driblet, stream, drizzle; drop, splash.

dried adjective *the dried corn can be used in a variety of recipes* DEHYDRATED, desiccated, dry, dried up, moistureless.

drift verb 1 *his raft drifted down the river* BE CARRIED, be borne; float, bob, waft, meander.

2 *the guests drifted away* WANDER, meander, stray, putter, dawdle.

3 *don't allow your attention to drift* STRAY, digress, deviate, diverge, veer, get sidetracked.

4 *snow drifted over the path* PILE UP, bank up, heap up, accumulate, gather, amass.

▸ noun 1 *a drift from the country to urban areas* MOVEMENT, shift, flow, transfer, relocation, gravitation.

2 *the pilot had not noticed any drift* DEVIATION, digression.

3 *he caught her drift* GIST, essence, meaning, sense, substance, significance; thrust, import, tenor; implication, intention; direction, course.

4 *a drift of deep snow* PILE, heap, bank, mound, mass, accumulation.

drifter noun *a lonesome drifter who had come from parts unknown* WANDERER, traveler, transient, roamer, itinerant, tramp, vagabond, vagrant, hobo, bum.

drill noun 1 *a hydraulic drill* DRILLING TOOL, boring tool, auger, (brace and) bit, gimlet, awl, bradawl.

2 *they learned military drills* TRAINING, instruction, coaching, teaching; (physical) exercises, workout.

3 *Estelle knew the drill* PROCEDURE, routine, practice, regimen, program, schedule; method, system.

▸ verb 1 *drill the piece of wood* BORE A HOLE IN, make a hole in; bore, pierce, puncture, perforate.

2 *a sergeant drilling new recruits* TRAIN, instruct, coach, teach, discipline; exercise, put someone through their paces.

3 *his mother had drilled politeness into him* INSTILL, hammer, drive, drum, din, implant, ingrain; teach, indoctrinate, brainwash.

drink verb 1 *she drank her coffee* SWALLOW, gulp down, quaff, guzzle, imbibe, sip, consume; *informal* swig, down, knock back, put away, swill, chug.

2 *he never drank* DRINK ALCOHOL, tipple, indulge; carouse; *informal* hit the bottle, booze, booze it up, knock a few back, get tanked up, go on a bender, bend one's elbow.

3 *let's **drink to** success* TOAST, salute.

▸ noun 1 *he took a sip of his drink* BEVERAGE, liquid refreshment; bracer, nightcap, nip; *humorous* libation; *archaic* potation. See tables at COCKTAIL, SOFT DRINK.

2 *she turned to drink* ALCOHOL, liquor, alcoholic drink; *informal* booze, hooch, the hard stuff, firewater, rotgut, moonshine, the bottle, the sauce. See table at LIQUOR.

3 *she took a drink of her wine* SWALLOW, gulp, sip, draft, slug; *informal* swig, swill.

4 *informal he fell into **the drink*** THE SEA, the ocean, the water; *informal* the briny, Davy Jones's locker; *literary* the deep.

PHRASE: **drink something in** *I'll just sit here and drink in the scenery* ABSORB, assimilate, digest, ingest, take in; be rapt in, be lost in, be fascinated by, pay close attention to.

drinkable adjective *running low on drinkable water* POTABLE, fit to drink, palatable; pure, clean, safe, unpolluted, untainted, uncontaminated.

drinker noun *I had no idea he was such a drinker.* See DRUNK noun.

drip verb 1 *there was a faucet dripping* DRIBBLE, leak.

2 *sweat dripped from his chin* DROP, dribble, trickle, drizzle, run, splash, plop; leak, emanate, issue.

▸ noun 1 *a bucket to catch the drips* DROP, dribble, spot, trickle, splash.

2 *informal that drip who fancies you* bore; ninny, milksop, namby-pamby; *informal* creep; wimp, sissy, wuss, candy-ass, pantywaist.

drive verb 1 *I can't drive a car* OPERATE, handle, manage; pilot, steer.

2 *he drove to the police station* TRAVEL BY CAR, motor.

3 *I'll drive you to the airport* CHAUFFEUR, run, give someone a lift/ride, take, ferry, transport, convey, carry.

4 *the engine drives the front wheels* POWER, propel, move, push.

5 *he drove a nail into the board* HAMMER, screw, ram, sink, plunge, thrust, propel, knock.

6 *she drove her cattle to market* IMPEL, urge; herd, round up, shepherd.

7 *a desperate mother driven to crime* FORCE, compel, prompt, precipitate; oblige, coerce, pressure, goad, spur, prod.

8 *he drove his staff extremely hard* WORK, push, tax, exert.

▸ noun 1 *an afternoon drive* EXCURSION, outing, trip, jaunt, tour; ride, run, journey; *informal* spin.

2 *the house has a long drive* DRIVEWAY, approach, access road.

3 *sexual drive* URGE, appetite, desire, need; impulse, instinct.

4 *she lacked the drive to succeed* MOTIVATION, ambition, single-mindedness, willpower, dedication, doggedness, tenacity; enthusiasm, zeal, commitment, aggression, spirit; energy, vigor, verve, vitality, pep; *informal* getup-and-go.

5 *an anticorruption drive* CAMPAIGN, crusade, movement, effort, push, appeal.

PHRASE: **drive at** *I can see what you're driving at, but you're wrong* SUGGEST, imply, hint at, allude to, intimate, insinuate, indicate; refer to, mean, intend; *informal* get at.

drivel noun *he was talking complete drivel* NONSENSE, twaddle, claptrap, balderdash, gibberish, rubbish, mumbo-jumbo, garbage; *informal* poppycock, piffle, tripe, bull, hogwash, baloney, codswallop, flapdoodle, jive, guff, bushwa; *informal, dated* tommyrot, bunkum. See note at NONSENSE.

▸ verb *you always **drivel on*** TALK NONSENSE, talk rubbish, babble, ramble, gibber, blather, prattle, gabble, waffle.

driver verb *the driver failed to signal* MOTORIST, chauffeur; pilot, operator.

driving adjective *the party's driving force* MOVING, motivating, dynamic, stimulating, energetic, inspirational.

drizzle noun **1** *they shivered in the drizzle* FINE RAIN, light shower, spray, mist.

2 *a drizzle of syrup* TRICKLE, dribble, drip, stream, rivulet; sprinkle, sprinkling.

▸ verb **1** *it's beginning to drizzle* RAIN LIGHTLY, shower, spot, spit, sprinkle.

2 *drizzle the cream over the fruit* TRICKLE, drip, dribble, pour, splash, sprinkle.

droll adjective *a droll remark that started everyone laughing* FUNNY, humorous, amusing, comic, comical, mirthful, hilarious; clownish, farcical, zany, quirky; jocular, lighthearted, facetious, witty, whimsical, wry, tongue-in-cheek; *informal* waggish, wacky, side-splitting, rib-tickling. ANTONYM serious.

drone verb **1** *a plane droned overhead* HUM, buzz, whirr, vibrate, murmur, rumble, purr.

2 *he* ***droned on*** *about right and wrong* SPEAK BORINGLY, go on and on, talk at length; intone, pontificate; *informal* spout, sound off, jaw, spiel, speechify.

▸ noun **1** *the drone of aircraft taking off* HUM, buzz, whirr, vibration, murmur, purr.

2 *drones supported by taxpayers' money* HANGER-ON, parasite, leech, passenger, bottom feeder; idler, loafer, layabout, good-for-nothing, do-nothing; *informal* lazybones, scrounger, sponger, freeloader, slacker.

drool verb *after the stroke he was continually drooling* SALIVATE, dribble, slaver, slobber.

▸ noun *a trickle of drool* SALIVA, spit, spittle, dribble, slaver, slobber.

droop verb **1** *the dog's tail is drooping* HANG (DOWN), dangle, sag, flop; wilt, sink, slump, drop.

2 *his eyelids were drooping* CLOSE, shut, fall.

3 *the news made her droop* BE DESPONDENT, lose heart, give up hope, become dispirited, become dejected; flag, languish, wilt.

droopy adjective **1** *the plant was looking droopy* HANGING (DOWN), hanging limply, dangling, falling, dropping, draped; bent, bowed, stooping; drooping, sagging, flopping, wilting; *Botany* cernuous.

2 *after he left she felt droopy* DESPONDENT, dejected, depressed, down, sad, unhappy, melancholy, miserable, gloomy, dispirited, downhearted, downcast, low, glum; *informal* down in the dumps.

WORD NOTE **cernuous**

Quite often writers find themselves in need of an adjective to describe the eloquent curve of such varied items as bent-over old men (and their beards), bowed trees and bowing servants, an attack of impotence, wilting flowers, and so on. Too often *drooping* is resorted to here. Why not use instead this sonorous mid-17th-century word, chiefly botanical, but perfectly serviceable in all the cases listed above and more. Avoids the insistent comic overtones of *droop,* adding a touch of dignity to the scene. **—ZS**

drop verb **1** *Eric dropped the box* LET FALL, let go of, lose one's grip on; release, unhand, relinquish. ANTONYMS lift, hold on to.

2 *water drops from the cave roof* DRIP, fall, dribble, trickle, run, plop, leak.

3 *a plane dropped out of the sky* FALL, descend, plunge, plummet, dive, nosedive, tumble, pitch. ANTONYM rise.

4 *she dropped to her knees* FALL, sink, collapse, slump, tumble. ANTONYM rise.

5 *informal I was so tired I thought I would drop* COLLAPSE, faint, pass out, black out, swoon, keel over; *informal* conk out.

6 *the track drops from the ridge* SLOPE DOWNWARD, slant downward, descend, go down, fall away, sink, dip. ANTONYM lift.

7 *the exchange rate dropped* DECREASE, lessen, reduce, diminish, depreciate; fall, decline, dwindle, sink, slump, plunge, plummet, drop off. ANTONYM increase.

8 *you can drop algebra if you wish* GIVE UP, drop out of, finish with, withdraw from; discontinue, end, stop, cease, halt; abandon, forgo, relinquish, dispense with, have done with; *informal* pack in, quit. ANTONYMS take up, continue.

9 *he was dropped from the team* EXCLUDE, discard, expel, oust, throw out, leave out; dismiss, discharge, let go; *informal* boot out, kick out. ANTONYMS pick, keep.

10 *he dropped his unsuitable friends* ABANDON, desert, throw over; renounce, disown, turn one's back on, wash one's hands of; reject, give up, cast off; neglect, shun; *literary* forsake. ANTONYM keep.

11 *he dropped all reference to compensation* OMIT, leave out, eliminate, take out, delete, cut, erase. ANTONYMS insert, include.

12 *the taxi* ***dropped*** *her* ***off*** DELIVER, bring, take, convey, carry, transport; leave, unload. ANTONYM pick up.

13 *drop the gun on the ground* PUT, place, deposit, set, lay, leave; *informal* pop, plonk. ANTONYM pick up.

14 *she dropped names* MENTION, refer to, hint at; bring up, raise, broach, introduce; show off.

15 *the team has yet to drop a point* LOSE, concede, give away. ANTONYMS gain, win.

▸ noun **1** *a drop of water* DROPLET, blob, globule, bead, bubble, tear, dot; *informal* glob; **(drops of water/rain)** *rare* stillicide.

2 *it needs a drop of oil* SMALL AMOUNT, little, bit, dash, spot; dribble, driblet, sprinkle, trickle, splash; dab, speck, smattering, sprinkling, modicum; *informal* smidgen, tad. ANTONYM great deal.

3 *a lemon drop* CANDY, lozenge, pastille.

4 *a small drop in profits* DECREASE, reduction, decline, falloff, downturn, slump; cut, cutback, curtailment; depreciation. ANTONYM increase.

5 *I walked to the edge of the drop* CLIFF, abyss, chasm, gorge, gully, precipice; slope, descent, incline.

PHRASES: **drop back/behind** *he dropped back and was soon lost in the crowd* FALL BACK/BEHIND, get left behind, lag behind; straggle, linger, dawdle, dally, hang back, loiter, bring/take up the rear, dilly-dally. **drop off 1** *trade dropped off sharply.* See DROP verb sense 7. **2** *she kept dropping off* FALL ASLEEP, doze (off), nap, catnap, drowse; *informal* nod off, drift off, snooze, take forty winks.

drop out of *he dropped out of his studies.* See DROP verb sense 8.

WORD NOTE **stillicide**

Of incredible value to the crime writer or anybody else wishing to build suspense into a landscape, *stillicide* is the falling of water, especially in drops, or a succession of drops. Inexplicably underused—every day brings a new way to employ it. **—ZS**

dropout noun **1** *a high school dropout* QUITTER; idler, layabout, loafer, deadbeat, delinquent, burnout.

2 *a sixties dropout* NONCONFORMIST, hippie, beatnik, Bohemian, free spirit, rebel; *informal* oddball, eccentric.

droppings plural noun *pigeon droppings* EXCREMENT, excreta, feces, stools, dung, ordure, manure; *informal* poo.

dross noun *trying to find something decent among the discount-house dross* RUBBISH, junk; debris, chaff, detritus, flotsam and jetsam, garbage, trash, dreck.

drought noun *this year's drought was devastating to cotton growers* DRY SPELL, lack of rain, shortage of water.

drove noun **1** *a drove of cattle* HERD, flock, pack.

2 *they came in droves* CROWD, swarm, horde, multitude, mob, throng, host, mass, army, herd.

drown verb **1** *he nearly drowned* SUFFOCATE IN WATER, inhale water; go to a watery grave.

2 *the valleys were drowned* FLOOD, submerge, immerse, inundate, deluge, swamp, engulf.

3 *his voice was* ***drowned out*** *by the music* MAKE INAUDIBLE, overpower, overwhelm, override; muffle, deaden, stifle, extinguish.

drowse verb *they like to drowse in the sun* DOZE, nap, catnap, rest; *informal* snooze, get forty winks, get some shut-eye, catch some Zs.

▸ noun *she had been woken from her drowse* DOZE, light sleep, nap, catnap, rest, siesta; *informal* snooze, forty winks, shut-eye.

drowsy adjective **1** *the pills made her drowsy* SLEEPY, dozy, groggy, somnolent; tired, weary, fatigued, exhausted, yawning, nodding; lethargic, sluggish, torpid, listless, languid; *informal* snoozy, dopey, yawny, dead beat, all in, dog-tired, bone-weary. ANTONYM alert.

2 *a drowsy afternoon* SOPORIFIC, sleep-inducing, sleepy, somniferous; narcotic, sedative, tranquilizing; lulling, soothing. ANTONYM invigorating.

drubbing noun **1** *I gave him a good drubbing* BEATING, thrashing, walloping, thumping, battering, pounding, pummeling, slapping, punching, pelting; *informal* hammering, licking, clobbering, belting, bashing, pasting, tanning, kicking.

2 *informal* *New York's 8–1 drubbing by Anaheim.* See DEFEAT noun sense 1.

drudge noun *a household drudge* MENIAL WORKER, slave, lackey, servant, laborer, worker, cog; *informal* gofer, runner, bottle-washer, serf.

▸ verb *archaic* *he drudged in the fields.* See TOIL verb sense 1.

drudgery noun *she swore her daughters would never be condemned to a life of drudgery* HARD WORK, menial work, donkey work, toil, labor; chores. See note at LABOR.

drug noun **1** *drugs prescribed by doctors* MEDICINE, medication, medicament, pharmaceutical; remedy, cure, antidote.

2 *she was under the influence of drugs* NARCOTIC, stimulant, hallucinogen; *informal* dope.

▸ verb **1** *he was drugged* ANESTHETIZE, narcotize; poison; knock out, stupefy; *informal* dope.

2 *she drugged his coffee* ADD DRUGS TO, tamper with, adulterate, contaminate, lace, poison; *informal* dope, spike, doctor.

drug addict noun See ADDICT sense 1.

drugged adjective *they found Tom and his drugged friends camped out in the living room* STUPEFIED, insensible, befuddled; delirious, hallucinating, narcotized; anesthetized, knocked out; *informal* stoned, coked, high (as a kite), doped, tripping, spaced out, wasted, wrecked. ANTONYM sober.

drum noun **1** *the beat of a drum* percussion instrument; bongo, tom-tom, snare drum, kettledrum, bodhrán; *historical* tambour.

2 *the steady drum of raindrops* BEAT, rhythm, patter, tap, pounding, thump, thud, rattle, pitter-patter, pit-a-pat, rat-a-tat, thrum.

3 *a drum of radioactive waste* CANISTER, barrel, cylinder, tank, bin, can; container.

▸ verb **1** *she drummed her fingers on the desk* TAP, beat, rap, thud, thump; tattoo, thrum.

2 *the rules were drummed into us at school* INSTILL, drive, din, hammer, drill, implant, ingrain, inculcate.

PHRASES: **drum out of** *Kazwell was running the organization into the ground, until the other members drummed him out* EXPEL, dismiss, throw out, oust; drive out, get rid of; exclude, banish; *informal* give someone the boot, boot out, kick out, give someone their marching orders, show someone the door, send packing. **drum up** *leaflets were distributed in hopes of drumming up support for the campaign* ROUND UP, gather, collect; summon, attract; canvass, solicit, petition.

WORD NOTE **drum**

A *drum* is anything that makes a pleasing sound when struck repeatedly, typically involving a stretched membrane and a resonator. This can include a dried squash, a body of water, or even your stomach (but not your head). More kinds of drums: *kick* (or *bass*) drum, *timpani, conga, taiko, tongue drum, thunder drum, ocean drum, hand drum, tabla, talking drum, water drum.* **—SM**

drunk adjective *he was so drunk he couldn't stand up* INTOXICATED, inebriated, inebriate, impaired, drunken, tipsy, under the influence; *informal* plastered, smashed, bombed, sloshed, sozzled, sauced, lubricated, well-oiled, wrecked, juiced, blasted, stinko, blitzed, half-cut, fried, wasted, hopped up, gassed, polluted, pissed, tanked (up), soaked, out of one's head/skull, loaded, trashed, hammered, soused, buzzed, befuddled, besotted, pickled, pixilated, canned, cockeyed, blotto, blind drunk, roaring drunk, dead drunk, punch-drunk, ripped, stewed, tight, merry, the worse for wear, far gone, pie-eyed, in one's cups, three sheets to the wind; *Brit. informal* bladdered, lashed; *literary* crapulous. ANTONYM sober.

▸ noun *a brilliant artist, he was also a tortured drunk* DRUNKARD, inebriate, drinker, tippler, imbiber, sot; heavy drinker, problem drinker, alcoholic, dipsomaniac; *informal* boozer, soak, lush, wino, alky, rummy, barfly; *archaic* toper. ANTONYM teetotaler.

WORD NOTE **crapulous**

Like *factitious, costive,* and *jejune,* this is one of those words that people hesitate to use because they know it doesn't quite mean what they think. Moreover, it looks and sounds vulgar, though being a forceful adjective for drunkenness and other forms of intemperance. *Factitious* suggests a portmanteau coupling of *factual* and *fictitious*—which is almost right since it means "contrived" or "sham." *Costive*—that is, "slow, sluggish, constipated"—has nothing to do with cost, while *jejune* properly means "insubstantial and insipid" rather than "callow and childish." Most prose should aspire to clarity, but not at the price of an impoverished diction. Writers ought to use these tricky words sometimes, not only to keep such useful terms current but also to lend a little panache to their prose. **—MD**

THE RIGHT WORD

Anyone who is obviously or legally under the influence of alcohol is said to be **drunk**. **Drunken** means the same thing, but only *drunk* should be used predicatively, that is, after a linking verb (*she was drunk*) while *drunken* is more often used to modify a noun (*a drunken sailor*) and, in some cases, to imply habitual drinking to excess. *Drunken* is also used to modify nouns that do not refer to a person (*a drunken celebration*). To say **intoxicated** or **inebriated** is a more formal and less offensive way of calling someone *drunk*, with *intoxicated* implying that the individual is only slightly drunk, and *inebriated* implying drunkenness to the point of excitement or exhilaration (*the streets were filled with inebriated revelers*). **Tight** and **tipsy** are two of the more common slang expressions (there are literally hundreds more) meaning *drunk*. Like *intoxicated, tipsy* implies that someone is only slightly drunk, while *tight* implies obvious drunkenness but without any loss of muscular coordination. An elderly woman who has had one sherry too many might be described as *tipsy*, but someone who has been drinking all evening and is still able to stand up and give a speech might be described as *tight*. Either condition is preferable to being **blotto**, a word that means drunk to the point of incomprehensibility or unconsciousness.

drunken adjective **1** *drunken revelers.* See DRUNK adjective. See also note at DRUNK.

2 *a drunken all-night party* DEBAUCHED, dissipated, carousing, roistering, intemperate, unrestrained, uninhibited, abandoned; bacchanalian, Bacchic; *informal* boozy.

drunkenness noun *his bouts of drunkenness* INTOXICATION, inebriation, insobriety, tipsiness, impairment; intemperance, overindulgence, debauchery; heavy drinking, alcoholism, dipsomania.

dry adjective **1** *the dry desert* ARID, parched, droughty, scorched, baked; waterless, moistureless, rainless; dehydrated, desiccated, thirsty, bone dry. ANTONYM wet.

2 *dry leaves* PARCHED, dried, withered, shriveled, wilted, wizened; crisp, crispy, brittle; dehydrated, desiccated. ANTONYM fresh.

3 *the rolls were dry* HARD, stale, old, past its best. ANTONYMS moist, fresh.

4 *a dry well* WATERLESS, empty.

5 *I'm really dry* THIRSTY, dehydrated; *informal* parched, gasping.

6 *it was dry work* THIRSTY, thirst-making; hot; strenuous, arduous.

7 *dry toast* UNBUTTERED, butterless, plain.

8 *the dry facts* BARE, simple, basic, fundamental, stark, bald, hard, straightforward. ANTONYM embellished.

9 *a dry debate* DULL, uninteresting, boring, unexciting, tedious, tiresome, wearisome, dreary, monotonous; unimaginative, sterile, flat, bland, lackluster, stodgy, prosaic, humdrum, mundane; *informal* deadly. ANTONYMS lively, interesting.

10 *a dry sense of humor* WRY, subtle, laconic, sharp; ironic, sardonic, sarcastic, cynical; satirical, mocking, droll; *informal* waggish.

11 *a dry response to his cordial advance* UNEMOTIONAL, indifferent, impassive, cool, cold, emotionless; reserved, restrained, impersonal, formal, stiff, wooden. ANTONYMS emotional, expressive.

12 *this is a dry state* TEETOTAL, prohibitionist, alcohol-free, nondrinking, abstinent, sober; *informal* on the wagon.

13 *dry white wine* CRISP, sharp, piquant, tart, bitter. ANTONYM sweet.

▸ verb **1** *the sun dried the ground* PARCH, scorch, bake; dehydrate, desiccate, dehumidify. ANTONYM moisten.

2 *dry the leaves completely* DEHYDRATE, desiccate; wither, shrivel. ANTONYM moisten.

3 *he dried the spills with a paper towel* TOWEL, rub; mop up, blot up, soak up, absorb.

4 *she dried her eyes* WIPE, rub, dab.

5 *methods of drying meat* DESICCATE, dehydrate; preserve, cure, smoke.

PHRASES: **dry out** *she dried out on her thirtieth birthday and has been sober ever since* GIVE UP DRINKING, give up alcohol, become a teetotaler, go on the wagon. **dry up** *foreign investment may dry up* DWINDLE, subside, peter out, wane, taper off, ebb, come to a halt/end, run out, give out, disappear, vanish.

THE RIGHT WORD

Almost anything lacking in moisture (in relative terms)—whether it's a piece of bread, the basement of a house, or the state of Arizona—may be described as **dry**, a word that also connotes a lack of life or spirit (*a dry lecture on cell division*). **Arid**, on the other hand, applies to places or things that have been deprived of moisture and are therefore extremely or abnormally *dry* (*one side of the island was arid*); it is most commonly used to describe a desertlike region or climate that is lifeless or barren. **Desiccated** is used as a technical term for something from which moisture has been removed, and in general use it suggests lifelessness, although it is applied very often to people who have lost their vitality (*a desiccated old woman who never left her house*) or to animal and vegetable products that have been completely deprived of their vital juices (*desiccated oranges hanging limply from the tree*). **Dehydrated** is very close in meaning to *desiccated* and is often the preferred adjective when describing foods from which the moisture has been extracted (*they lived on dehydrated fruit*). *Dehydrated* may also refer to an unwanted loss of moisture (*the virus had left him seriously dehydrated*), as may the less formal term **parched**, which refers to an undesirable or uncomfortable lack of water in either a human being or a place (*parched with thirst; the parched landscape*). **Sere** is associated primarily with places and means *dry* or *arid* (*a harsh, sere land where few inhabitants could survive*).

dual adjective *a futuristic car with dual engines* DOUBLE, twofold, binary; duplicate, twin, matching, paired, coupled. ANTONYM single.

dub verb **1** *he was dubbed "the world's sexiest man"* NICKNAME, call, name, label, christen, term, tag, entitle, style; designate, characterize, nominate; *formal* denominate.

2 *she dubbed him "Sir Elton John"* KNIGHT, invest.

dubiety noun *formal the dubiety of Henry's fate* DOUBTFULNESS, uncertainty, unsureness, incertitude; ambiguity, ambivalence, confusion; hesitancy, doubt. See note at UNCERTAINTY.

dubious adjective **1** *I was rather dubious about the idea* DOUBTFUL, uncertain, unsure, hesitant; undecided, indefinite, unresolved, up in the air; vacillating, irresolute; skeptical, suspicious; *informal* iffy. See note at DOUBTFUL. ANTONYMS certain, definite.

2 *dubious business practices* SUSPICIOUS, suspect, untrustworthy, unreliable, questionable; *informal* shady, fishy. ANTONYM trustworthy.

duck[1] noun *a pair of ducks were nesting on the edge of our pond male* : drake; *female* : duck; *young* : duckling. See table at WATERFOWL.

duck[2] verb **1** *he ducked behind the wall* BOB DOWN, bend (down), stoop (down), crouch (down), squat (down), hunch down, hunker down; cower, cringe.

2 *she was ducked in the river* DIP, dunk, plunge, immerse, submerge, lower, sink.

3 *informal they cannot duck the issue forever* SHIRK, dodge, evade, avoid, elude, escape, back out of, shun, eschew, sidestep, bypass, circumvent; *informal* cop out of, get out of, wriggle out of, dipsy-doodle around.

duct noun *a ventilation duct* TUBE, channel, canal, vessel; conduit, culvert; pipe, pipeline, outlet, inlet, flue, shaft, vent; *Anatomy* ductus.

ductile adjective **1** *ductile metals* PLIABLE, pliant, flexible, supple, plastic, tensile; soft, malleable, workable, bendable; *informal* bendy. ANTONYM brittle.

2 *efforts to keep the oppressed people ductile* DOCILE, obedient, submissive, meek, mild, lamblike; willing, accommodating, amenable, cooperative, compliant, malleable, tractable, biddable, persuadable. ANTONYM intransigent.

dud noun *their new product is a dud* FAILURE, flop, letdown, disappointment; *informal* washout, lemon, nohoper, nonstarter, dead loss, clunker. ANTONYM success.

▸ adjective **1** *a dud typewriter* DEFECTIVE, faulty, unsound, inoperative, broken, malfunctioning; *informal* bust, busted, kaput, conked out. ANTONYM sound.

2 *a dud $50 bill* COUNTERFEIT, fraudulent, forged, fake, faked, false, bogus; invalid, worthless; *informal* phony. ANTONYM genuine.

dude noun *informal* See FELLOW sense 1.

dudgeon PHRASE: **in high dudgeon** *the sponsors from Cleveland stormed out in high dudgeon* INDIGNANTLY, resentfully, angrily, furiously; in a temper, in anger, with displeasure; *informal* in a huff, seeing red.

due adjective **1** *their fees were due* OWING, owed, payable; outstanding, overdue, unpaid, unsettled, undischarged, delinquent.

2 *the chancellor's statement is due today* EXPECTED, anticipated, scheduled for, awaited; required.

3 *the respect due to a great artist* DESERVED BY, merited by, warranted by; appropriate to, fit for, fitting for, right for, proper to.

4 *he drove without due care* PROPER, correct, rightful, suitable, appropriate, apt; adequate, sufficient, enough, satisfactory, requisite.

▸ noun **1** *he attracts more criticism than is his due* RIGHTFUL TREATMENT, fair treatment, just punishment; right, entitlement; just deserts; *informal* comeuppance.

2 *members have paid their dues* FEE, subscription, charge; payment, contribution.

▸ adverb *he hiked due north* DIRECTLY, straight, exactly, precisely, dead.

PHRASE: **due to 1** *her death was due to an infection* ATTRIBUTABLE TO, caused by, ascribed to, because of, put down to. **2** *the train was canceled due to staff shortages* BECAUSE OF, owing to, on account of, as a consequence of, as a result of, thanks to, in view of; *formal* by reason of.

USAGE NOTE **due to**

The use of **due to** as a prepositional phrase meaning 'because of,' as in *he had to retire due to an injury* first appeared in print in 1897, and traditional grammarians have opposed this prepositional usage for a century on the grounds that it is a misuse of the adjectival phrase **due to** in the sense of 'attributable to, likely or expected to' (*the train is due to arrive at 11:15*), or 'payable to' (*render unto Caesar what is due to Caesar*). Nevertheless, this prepositional usage is now widespread and common in all types of literature and must be regarded as standard English.

Avoid the wordy phrase **due to the fact that** and use *because* instead, especially in writing.

duel noun **1** *he was killed in a duel* AFFAIR OF HONOR; single combat; (sword) fight, confrontation, face-off, shoot-out.

2 *a chess duel* CONTEST, match, game, meet, encounter.

▸ verb *they dueled with swords* FIGHT A DUEL, fight, battle, combat, contend.

dulcet adjective *the dulcet sounds of the zither* SWEET, soothing, mellow, honeyed, mellifluous, euphonious, pleasant, agreeable; melodious, melodic, lilting, lyrical, silvery, golden. ANTONYM harsh.

dull adjective **1** *a dull novel* UNINTERESTING, boring, tedious, monotonous, unrelieved, unvaried, unimaginative, uneventful; characterless, featureless, colorless, lifeless, insipid, unexciting, uninspiring, unstimulating, jejune, flat, bland, dry, stale, tired, banal, lackluster, ho-hum, stodgy, dreary, humdrum, mundane; mind-numbing, wearisome, tiring, tiresome, irksome, dullsville. ANTONYM interesting.

2 *a dull morning* OVERCAST, cloudy, gloomy, dark, dismal, dreary, somber, gray, murky, sunless. ANTONYMS sunny, bright.

3 *dull colors* DRAB, dreary, somber, dark, subdued, muted, lackluster, faded, washed out, muddy, dingy. ANTONYM bright.

4 *a dull sound* MUFFLED, muted, quiet, soft, faint, indistinct; stifled, suppressed. ANTONYMS loud, resonant.

5 *the chisel became dull* BLUNT, unsharpened, edgeless, worn down. ANTONYM sharp.

6 *a rather dull child* UNINTELLIGENT, stupid, slow, witless, vacuous, empty-headed, stunned, brainless, mindless, foolish, idiotic; *informal* dense, dim, moronic, halfwitted, thick, dumb, dopey, dozy, bovine, slow on the uptake, wooden-headed, fat-headed. See note at STUPID. ANTONYM clever.

7 *her cold made her feel dull* SLUGGISH, lethargic, enervated, listless, languid, torpid, slow, sleepy, drowsy, weary, tired, fatigued; apathetic; *informal* dozy, dopey, yawny, logy. ANTONYM lively.

▸ verb 1 *the pain was dulled by drugs* LESSEN, decrease, diminish, reduce, dampen, blunt, deaden, allay, ease, soothe, assuage, alleviate. ANTONYM intensify.

2 *sleep dulled her mind* NUMB, benumb, deaden, desensitize, stupefy, daze. ANTONYM enliven.

3 *rain dulled the sky* DARKEN, blacken, dim, veil, obscure, shadow, fog. ANTONYM brighten.

4 *the somber atmosphere dulled her spirit* DAMPEN, lower, depress, crush, sap, extinguish, smother, stifle. ANTONYMS raise, brighten.

dullard noun *the guy at the video store turned out to be a real dullard* IDIOT, fool, stupid person, simpleton, ignoramus, oaf, dunce, dolt; *informal* moron, cretin, imbecile, nincompoop, dope, chump, nitwit, dimwit, birdbrain, peabrain, numbskull, numbnuts, fathead, dumbo, dumdum, donkey, doofus, goof, bozo, dummy, zombie.

duly adverb 1 *the document was duly signed* PROPERLY, correctly, appropriately, suitably, fittingly.

2 *he duly arrived to collect Alice* AT THE RIGHT TIME, on time, punctually.

dumb adjective 1 *she stood dumb while he shouted* MUTE, speechless, tongue-tied, silent, at a loss for words; taciturn, uncommunicative, untalkative, tight-lipped, close-mouthed; *informal* mum.

2 *informal he is not as dumb as you'd think* STUPID, unintelligent, ignorant, dense, brainless, mindless, foolish, slow, dull, simple, empty-headed, stunned, vacuous, vapid, idiotic, half-baked, imbecilic, bovine; *informal* thick, dim, moronic, dopey, dozy, thickheaded, fat-headed, bird-brained, pea-brained; daft. See note at STUPID. ANTONYM clever.

dumbfound verb *she was dumbfounded by Bruce's actions* ASTONISH, astound, amaze, stagger, surprise, startle, stun, confound, stupefy, daze, take aback, stop someone in their tracks, strike dumb, leave open-mouthed, leave aghast; *informal* flabbergast, floor, bowl over.

dumbfounded adjective *a dumbfounded audience* ASTONISHED, astounded, amazed, staggered, surprised, startled, stunned, confounded, nonplussed, stupefied, dazed, dumbstruck, open-mouthed, speechless, thunderstruck; taken aback, disconcerted; *informal* flabbergasted, flummoxed, bowled over, blown away, floored.

dummy noun 1 *a store-window dummy* MANNEQUIN, model, figure.

2 *the book is just a dummy* MOCK-UP, imitation, likeness, look-alike, representation, substitute, sample; replica, reproduction; counterfeit, sham, fake, forgery; *informal* dupe.

3 *informal you're a dummy.* See IDIOT.

▸ adjective *a dummy attack on the airfield* SIMULATED, feigned, pretended, practice, trial, mock, make-believe; *informal* pretend, phony, virtual. ANTONYM real.

dump noun 1 *take the garbage to the dump* TRANSFER STATION, garbage dump, landfill (site), rubbish heap, dumping ground; dustheap, slag heap.

2 *informal the house is a dump* HOVEL, shack, slum; mess; hole, pigsty.

▸ verb 1 *he dumped his bag on the table* PUT DOWN, set down, deposit, place, unload; drop, throw down; *informal* park, plonk (down), plunk (down).

2 *they will dump asbestos at the site* DISPOSE OF, get rid of, throw away/out, discard, jettison; *informal* ditch, junk, deep-six.

3 *informal he dumped her* ABANDON, desert, leave, jilt, break up with, finish with, throw over; *informal* walk out on, rat on, drop, ditch.

dumpling noun *chicken and dumplings* pirogi, wonton, knish, matzo ball, doughboy, potsticker, gnocchi, kreplach.

dumps PHRASE: **down in the dumps** *informal why so down in dumps, Mrs. Herbert?* UNHAPPY, sad, depressed, gloomy, glum, melancholy, miserable, dejected, despondent, dispirited, downhearted, downcast, down, low, heavy-hearted, dismal, desolate; tearful, upset, blue, down in/at the mouth.

dumpy adjective *the boots make him look dumpy* SHORT, squat, stubby; PLUMP, stout, chubby, chunky, portly, fat, bulky, tubby, roly-poly, pudgy, porky. ANTONYMS tall, slender.

dun[1] adjective *a dun cow* GRAYISH-BROWN, brownish, mousy, muddy, khaki, umber.

dun[2] verb *you can't dun me for her debts* IMPORTUNE, press, plague, pester, nag, harass, hound, badger, hassle, bug.

dunce noun *Uncle Abraham was a bit of a dunce, but most people got along with him* FOOL, idiot, stupid person, simpleton, ignoramus, dullard; *informal* dummy, dumbo, thickhead, nitwit, dimwit, halfwit, moron, cretin, imbecile, dope, boob, chump, numbskull, numbnuts, nincompoop, fathead, airhead, birdbrain, peabrain, ninny, ass, doofus, goof, meatball, schmuck, bozo, lummox. ANTONYM genius.

dune noun *no vehicles allowed within 20 yards of the dunes* BANK, mound, hillock, hummock, knoll, ridge, heap, drift.

dung noun *flies swarm around the fresh dung* MANURE, muck; excrement, feces, droppings, scat, ordure, cowpats; *informal* cow pies, cow patties, cow flops, cow chips, horse apples, turds.

dungeon noun *the castle dungeon is now a tourist attraction* UNDERGROUND PRISON, oubliette; cell, jail, lockup.

duo noun *a talented duo* TWOSOME, pair, couple.

dupe verb *they were duped by a con man* DECEIVE, trick, hoodwink, hoax, swindle, defraud, cheat, double-cross; gull, mislead, take in, fool, inveigle; *informal* con, do, rip off, diddle, shaft, bilk, rook, pull the wool over someone's eyes, pull a fast one on, sucker, snooker.

▸ noun *an innocent dupe in her game* VICTIM, gull, pawn, puppet, instrument; fool, innocent; *informal* sucker, chump, stooge, sitting duck, fall guy, pigeon, patsy, sap.

duplicate noun *a duplicate of the invoice* COPY, photocopy, facsimile, reprint; replica, reproduction, clone; *dated* carbon copy; *informal* dupe; *trademark* Xerox.

▸ adjective *duplicate keys* MATCHING, identical, twin, corresponding, equivalent.

▸ verb 1 *she will duplicate the newsletter* COPY, photocopy, xerox, reproduce, replicate, reprint, run off; *dated* mimeograph.

2 *a feat difficult to duplicate* REPEAT, do again, redo, replicate.

duplicity noun *he got caught up in the duplicity of his crooked partners* DECEITFULNESS, deceit, deception, double-dealing, underhandedness, dishonesty, fraud, fraudulence, sharp practice, chicanery, trickery, subterfuge, skulduggery, treachery; *informal* crookedness, shadiness, dirty tricks, shenanigans, monkey business; *literary* perfidy. ANTONYM honesty.

durability noun *they demonstrated the durability of the plastic* IMPERISHABILITY, durableness, longevity; resilience, strength, sturdiness, toughness, robustness. ANTONYM fragility.

durable adjective 1 *durable carpets* HARDWEARING, long-lasting, heavy-duty, industrial-strength, tough, resistant, imperishable, indestructible, strong, sturdy. ANTONYM delicate.

2 *a durable peace* LASTING, long-lasting, long-term, enduring, persistent, abiding; stable, secure, firm, deep-rooted, permanent, undying, everlasting. ANTONYM short-lived.

duration noun *the duration of recovery varies from patient to patient* FULL LENGTH, time, time span, time scale, period, term, span, fullness, length, extent, continuation.

duress noun *their confessions were extracted under duress* COERCION, compulsion, force, pressure, intimidation, constraint; threats; *informal* arm-twisting.

during conjunction *the museum is closed during December* THROUGHOUT, through, in, in the course of, for the time of.

dusk noun *we launch the patrol boats at dusk* TWILIGHT, nightfall, sunset, sundown, evening, close of day; semi-darkness, gloom, murkiness; *literary* gloaming, eventide. ANTONYM dawn.

dusky adjective 1 *the dusky countryside* SHADOWY, dark, dim, gloomy, murky, shady; unlit, unilluminated; sunless, moonless. ANTONYM bright.

2 *dated* *a dusky complexion* DARK-SKINNED, dark, olive-skinned, swarthy, ebony, black; tanned, bronzed, coppery, brown. ANTONYM fair.

dust noun 1 *the desk was covered in dust* DIRT, grime, filth, smut, soot; fine powder.

2 *they fought in the dust* EARTH, soil, dirt; ground.

▸ verb 1 *she dusted her mantelpiece* WIPE, clean, brush, sweep, mop.

2 *dust the cake with powdered sugar* SPRINKLE, scatter, powder, dredge, sift, cover, strew.

dusty adjective 1 *the floor was dusty* DIRTY, grimy, grubby, unclean, soiled, mucky, sooty; undusted; *informal* grungy, cruddy. ANTONYM clean.

2 *dusty sandstone* POWDERY, crumbly, chalky, friable; granular, gritty, sandy.

3 *a dusty pink* MUTED, dull, faded, pale, pastel, subtle; grayish, darkish, dirty. ANTONYM bright.

dutiful adjective *Clarence's dutiful niece* CONSCIENTIOUS, responsible, dedicated, devoted, attentive; obedient, compliant, submissive, biddable; deferential, reverent, reverential, respectful, good. See note at OBEDIENT. ANTONYM remiss.

duty noun 1 *she was free of any duty* RESPONSIBILITY, obligation, commitment; allegiance, loyalty, faithfulness, fidelity, homage.

2 *it was his duty to attend the king* JOB, task, assignment, mission, function, charge, place, role, responsibility, obligation; *dated* office.

3 *the duty was raised on alcohol* TAX, levy, tariff, excise, toll, fee, payment, rate, countervail; dues. PHRASES: **off duty** *I'll be off duty at midnight* NOT WORKING, at leisure, on leave, off (work), free. **on duty** *there is always a supervisor on duty* WORKING, at work, busy, occupied, engaged; *informal* on the job.

dwarf noun 1 *she married a dwarf who worked in her father's circus* SMALL PERSON, short person; midget, pygmy, manikin, homunculus.

2 *the wizard captured the dwarf* GNOME, goblin, hobgoblin, troll, imp, elf, brownie, leprechaun.

▸ adjective *dwarf conifers* MINIATURE, small, little, tiny, toy, pocket, diminutive, baby, pygmy, stunted, undersized, undersize; *informal* mini, teeny, teeny-weeny, itsy-bitsy, pint-sized, little-bitty, vertically challenged; *Scottish* wee. ANTONYM giant.

▸ verb 1 *the buildings dwarf the trees* DOMINATE, tower over, loom over, overshadow, overtop.

2 *her progress was dwarfed by her sister's success* OVERSHADOW, outshine, surpass, exceed, outclass, outstrip, outdo, top, trump, transcend; diminish, minimize.

dwell verb *formal* *gypsies dwell in these caves* RESIDE, live, be settled, be housed, lodge, stay; *informal* put up; *formal* abide, be domiciled. PHRASE: **dwell on** *I'm not one to dwell on the past* LINGER OVER, mull over, muse on, brood about/over, think about; be preoccupied by, be obsessed by, eat one's heart out over; harp on about, discuss at length.

dwelling noun *formal* *their dwellings were simple but pristine, both inside and out* RESIDENCE, home, house, accommodationss; quarters, rooms, lodgings; *informal* place, pad, digs; *formal* abode, domicile, habitation.

dwindle verb 1 *the population dwindled* DIMINISH, decrease, reduce, lessen, shrink; fall off, tail off, drop, fall, slump, plummet; disappear, vanish, die out; *informal* nosedive. ANTONYM increase.

2 *her career dwindled* DECLINE, deteriorate, fail, slip, slide, fade, go downhill, go to rack and ruin; *informal* go to pot, go to the dogs, hit the skids, go down the tubes, go down the drain, go down the toilet. ANTONYM flourish.

dye noun *a blue dye* COLORANT, coloring, color, dyestuff, pigment, tint, stain, wash.

▸ verb *the gloves were dyed* COLOR, tint, pigment, stain, wash.

dyed-in-the-wool adjective *a dyed-in-the-wool socialist* INVETERATE, confirmed, entrenched, established, long-standing, deep-rooted, diehard; complete, absolute, thorough, thoroughgoing, out-and-out, true blue; firm, unshakable, staunch, steadfast, committed, devoted, dedicated, loyal, unswerving, full bore; *informal* card-carrying.

dying adjective 1 *his dying aunt* TERMINALLY ILL, at

death's door, on one's deathbed, near death, fading fast, expiring, moribund, not long for this world, in extremis; *informal* on one's last legs, having one foot in the grave.

2 *a dying art form* DECLINING, vanishing, fading, ebbing, waning; *informal* on the way out. ANTONYM thriving.

3 *her dying words* FINAL, last; deathbed. ANTONYM first.

▸ noun *he took her dying very hard* DEATH, demise, passing, loss of life, quietus; *formal* decease.

dynamic adjective *he was eclipsed by his more dynamic colleagues* ENERGETIC, spirited, active, lively, zestful, vital, vigorous, forceful, powerful, positive; high-powered, aggressive, bold, enterprising; magnetic, passionate, fiery, high-octane; *informal* go-getting, peppy, full of get-up-and-go, full of vim and vigor, gutsy, spunky, feisty, go-ahead. ANTONYM halfhearted.

dynamism noun *the dynamism in his performance* ENERGY, spirit, liveliness, zestfulness, vitality, vigor, forcefulness, power, potency, positivity; aggression, drive, ambition, enterprise; magnetism, passion, fire; *informal* pep, get-up-and-go, vim and vigor, guts, feistiness, gumption.

dynasty noun *the fourth king of the Shang dynasty* BLOODLINE, line, ancestral line, lineage, house, family, ancestry, descent, succession, genealogy, family tree; regime, rule, reign, empire, sovereignty.

dyspeptic adjective *he never became the dyspeptic old man his father had been* BAD-TEMPERED, short-tempered, irritable, snappish, testy, tetchy, touchy, crabby, crotchety, grouchy, cantankerous, peevish, cross, disagreeable, waspish, prickly; *informal* on a short fuse, cranky, ornery.

dysphesia noun See note below.

WORD NOTE **dysphesia**

This is a medical noun with some timely nonmedical applications. Educated writers already use *aphasia* to refer to a brain-centered inability to use language, which is close but not identical to the medical meaning. *Dysphesia* can be similarly extended from its technical def to mean really severe difficulties with forming coherent sentences. As anyone who's listened to our current president knows, there are speakers whose lack of facility goes way beyond the range of *clumsy* or *inarticulate.* Our president's public English, like that of his father before him, is *dysphesiac.* —**DFW**

E

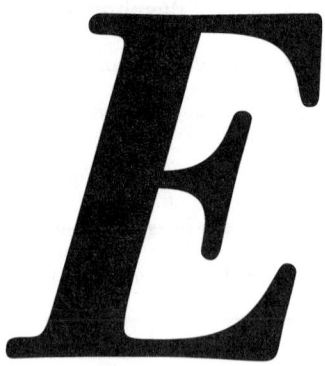

each pronoun *there are 47 books and each must be read* EVERY ONE, each one, each and every one, all, the whole lot.

▸ adjective *he visited each month* EVERY, each and every, every single.

▸ adverb *they gave $10 each* APIECE, per person, per capita, from each, individually, respectively, severally.

eager adjective **1** *small eager faces* KEEN, enthusiastic, avid, fervent, ardent, motivated, wholehearted, dedicated, committed, earnest; *informal* gung-ho. ANTONYM apathetic.

2 *we were eager for news* ANXIOUS, impatient, longing, yearning, wishing, hoping, hopeful; on the edge of one's seat, on tenterhooks, on pins and needles; *informal* itching, gagging, dying. ANTONYM uninterested.

THE RIGHT WORD

You've heard of the "eager beaver"? Anyone who has a strong interest or an impatient desire to pursue or become involved in something is called **eager** (*eager to get started; an eager learner*). Someone who is especially *eager* might be called **avid**, a word that implies greed or insatiable desire (*an avid golfer, he was never at home on weekends*). **Ardent** combines eagerness with intense feelings of passion or devotion (*an ardent lover; an ardent theatergoer*), while **fervent** suggests an eagerness that is ready, at least figuratively, to boil over (*their fervent pleas could not be ignored*). Anyone who is deeply interested in something or who shows a spirited readiness to act is called **keen** (*he was keen on bicycling*), while **zealous** implies the kind of eagerness that pushes all other considerations aside (*a zealous environmentalist*). **Enthusiastic** may connote participation rather than expectation: One can be *eager* to take a trip to Switzerland, an *ardent* student of Swiss history, and an *avid* outdoorsperson who is *keen* on hiking, but one is usually called *enthusiastic* about a trip to Switzerland when it is under way or is over; *enthusiastic* also very often applies to someone who outwardly and forcefully expresses eagerness.

eagerness noun *the eagerness of potential buyers* KEENNESS, enthusiasm, avidity, fervor, zeal, wholeheartedness, earnestness, commitment, dedication; impatience, desire, longing, yearning, hunger, appetite, ambition, yen.

eagle noun. See table at RAPTOR.

ear noun **1** *an infection of the ear* inner ear, middle ear, outer ear.

2 *he had the ear of the president* ATTENTION, notice, heed, regard, consideration.

3 *he has an ear for a good song* APPRECIATION, discrimination, perception. PHRASE: **play it by ear** *until we know all the facts, we'll have to play it by ear* IMPROVISE, extemporize, ad lib; make it up as one goes along, think on one's feet, wing it, fly by the seat of one's pants.

WORD NOTE **auricular**

Originally a multitasking late medieval word meaning "of confession: spoken only to the ear, private," now flattened out into the more general (and probably more functional) "of or pertaining to the ear." In the seventeenth century it became a beautiful synecdoche for one's little finger—the finger most easily fit into an ear. Not recommended for most of us, but surely still of use (in both in its confessional and anatomical form) to poet-types and lovers. **—ZS**

early adjective **1** *early copies of the book* ADVANCE, forward; initial, preliminary, first; pilot, trial. ANTONYM late.

2 *an early death* UNTIMELY, premature, unseasonable, before time.

3 *early man* PRIMITIVE, ancient, prehistoric, primeval; *literary* of yore. ANTONYM modern.

4 *an early official statement* PROMPT, timely, quick, speedy, rapid, fast. ANTONYM overdue.

▸ adverb **1** *Rachel has to get up early* IN THE EARLY MORNING; at dawn, at daybreak, at first light. ANTONYM late.

2 *they hoped to leave school early* BEFORE THE USUAL TIME; prematurely, too soon, ahead of time, ahead of schedule; *literary* betimes.

earmark verb *the cash had been earmarked for the firm* SET ASIDE, keep (back), reserve; designate, assign, mark; allocate, allot, devote, pledge, give over.

▸ noun *he has all the earmarks of a leader* CHARACTERISTICS, attribute, feature, hallmark, quality.

earn verb **1** *they earned $20,000* BE PAID, take home, gross, net; receive, get, make, obtain, collect, bring in; *informal* pocket, bank, rake in.

2 *he has earned their trust* DESERVE, merit, warrant, justify, be worthy of; gain, win, secure, establish, obtain, procure, get, acquire; *informal* clinch. ANTONYM lose.

earnest adjective **1** *he is dreadfully earnest* SERIOUS, solemn, grave, sober, humorless, staid, intense; committed, dedicated, keen, diligent, zealous; thoughtful, cerebral, deep, profound. ANTONYMS frivolous, apathetic.

2 *earnest prayer* DEVOUT, heartfelt, wholehearted, sincere, impassioned, fervent, ardent, intense, urgent. ANTONYM halfhearted.

PHRASE: **in earnest 1** *we are in earnest about stopping crime* SERIOUS, sincere, wholehearted, genuine; committed, firm, resolute, determined. **2** *he started writing in earnest* ZEALOUSLY, purposefully, determinedly, resolutely; passionately, wholeheartedly.

earnestly adverb *we earnestly prayed for his recovery* SERIOUSLY, solemnly, gravely, intently; sincerely, resolutely, firmly, ardently, fervently, eagerly.

earnings plural noun *their combined earnings paid for this house* INCOME, wages, salary, stipend, pay, payment, fees; revenue, yield, profit, takings, proceeds, avails, dividends, return, remuneration.

earth noun **1** *the moon orbits the earth* WORLD, globe, planet.

2 *a trembling of the earth* LAND, ground, terra firma; floor.

3 *he plowed the earth* SOIL, clay, loam; dirt, sod, turf; ground.

4 *the earth rejoiced* HUMANITY, humankind, mankind, (all) people; *humorous* earthlings.

5 *the fox's earth* DEN, lair, set, burrow, warren, hole; retreat, shelter, hideout, hideaway.

earthenware noun *her original line of earthenware* POTTERY, stoneware; china, porcelain; pots, crockery.

earthly adjective **1** *the earthly environment* TERRESTRIAL, telluric. ANTONYM extraterrestrial.

2 *the promise of earthly delights* WORLDLY, temporal, mortal, human; material; carnal, fleshly, bodily, physical, corporeal, sensual. ANTONYMS spiritual, heavenly.

3 *informal there is no earthly explanation for this* FEASIBLE, possible, likely, conceivable, imaginable.

earthquake noun *assessing the damage from the earthquake* EARTH TREMOR, tremor, shock, foreshock, aftershock, convulsion, seismic activity; *informal* quake.

earthy adjective **1** *an earthy smell* SOIL-LIKE, dirtlike.

2 *she was a simple, earthy girl* DOWN-TO-EARTH, unsophisticated, unrefined, simple, plain, unpretentious, natural.

3 *Emma's earthy language* BAWDY, ribald, off-color, racy, rude, vulgar, lewd, crude, foul, coarse, uncouth, unseemly, indelicate, indecent, obscene; *informal* blue, locker-room, barnyard.

ease noun **1** *he defeated them all with ease* EFFORTLESSNESS, no trouble, simplicity; deftness, adroitness, proficiency, mastery. ANTONYM difficulty.

2 *his ease of manner* NATURALNESS, casualness, informality, amiability, affability; unconcern, composure, nonchalance, insouciance. ANTONYMS stiffness, formality.

3 *he couldn't find any ease* PEACE, calm, tranquility, serenity; repose, restfulness, quiet, security, comfort. ANTONYMS trouble, disturbance.

4 *a life of ease* AFFLUENCE, wealth, prosperity, luxury, plenty; comfort, contentment, enjoyment, well-being. ANTONYMS poverty, hardship.

▸ verb **1** *the alcohol eased his pain* RELIEVE, alleviate, mitigate, soothe, palliate, moderate, dull, deaden, numb; reduce, lighten, diminish. ANTONYM aggravate.

2 *the rain **eased off*** ABATE, subside, die down, let up, slack off, diminish, lessen, peter out, relent, come to an end. ANTONYM worsen.

3 *work helped to ease her mind* CALM, pacify, soothe, comfort, console, quieten; hearten, gladden, uplift, encourage.

4 *we want to ease their adjustment* FACILITATE, expedite, assist, help, aid, advance, further, forward, simplify. ANTONYM hinder.

5 *he eased out the cork* GUIDE, maneuver, inch, edge; slide, slip, squeeze.

PHRASE: **at ease/at one's ease** *she felt completely at ease in their mountain retreat* RELAXED, calm, serene, tranquil, unworried, contented, content, happy; comfortable.

easily adverb **1** *she won the race easily* EFFORTLESSLY, comfortably, simply; with ease, without difficulty, without a hitch, smoothly; skillfully, deftly, smartly; *informal* no sweat, hands down.

2 *he's easily the best* UNDOUBTEDLY, without doubt, without question, indisputably, undeniably, definitely, certainly, clearly, obviously, patently; by far, far and away, by a mile.

east adjective *an east wind* EASTERN, easterly, eastward, oriental.

easy adjective **1** *the task was very easy* UNCOMPLICATED, undemanding, unchallenging, effortless, painless, trouble-free, facile, simple, straightforward, elementary; *informal* easy as pie, a piece of cake, child's play, kids' stuff, a cinch, no sweat, a breeze, smooth sailing, duck soup, a snap. ANTONYMS difficult, challenging.

2 *easy babies* DOCILE, manageable, amenable, tractable, compliant, pliant, acquiescent, obliging, cooperative, easygoing. ANTONYMS difficult, demanding.

3 *an easy target* VULNERABLE, susceptible, defenseless; naive, gullible, trusting. ANTONYMS streetwise, savvy.

4 *Dave's easy manner* NATURAL, casual, informal, unceremonious, unreserved, uninhibited, unaffected, easygoing, amiable, affable, genial, good-humored; carefree, nonchalant, unconcerned, laid-back. ANTONYM formal.

5 *an easy life* CALM, tranquil, serene, quiet, peaceful, untroubled, contented, relaxed, comfortable, secure, safe; *informal* cushy. ANTONYMS stressful, chaotic.

6 *an easy pace* LEISURELY, unhurried, comfortable, undemanding, easygoing, gentle, sedate, moderate, steady. ANTONYM demanding.

7 *informal people think she's easy* PROMISCUOUS, unchaste, loose, wanton, abandoned, licentious, debauched; *informal* sluttish, slutty, whorish. ANTONYM chaste.

easygoing adjective *Fred was easygoing and a pleasure to work with* RELAXED, even-tempered, placid, mellow, mild, happy-go-lucky, carefree, free and easy, nonchalant, insouciant, imperturbable; amiable, considerate, undemanding, patient, tolerant, lenient, broad-minded, understanding; good-natured, pleasant, agreeable; *informal* laid-back, unflappable, Type-B, low-maintenance. ANTONYMS tense; intolerant.

eat verb 1 *we ate a hearty breakfast* CONSUME, devour, ingest, partake of; gobble (up/down), bolt (down), wolf (down); swallow, chew, munch, chomp; *informal* guzzle, nosh, put away, chow down on, tuck into, demolish, dispose of, polish off, pig out on, scarf (down).

2 *we ate at a local restaurant* HAVE A MEAL, consume food, feed, snack; breakfast, lunch, dine; feast, banquet; *informal* graze, nosh; *dated* sup.

3 *acidic water can **eat away at** pipes* ERODE, corrode, wear away/down/through, burn through, consume, dissolve, disintegrate, crumble, decay; damage, destroy.

eatable adjective *the casserole was barely eatable* EDIBLE, palatable, digestible; fit to eat, fit for consumption.

eatery noun See table at RESTAURANT.

eats plural noun *informal come on in for some eats* FOOD, sustenance, nourishment, fare; eatables, snacks, tidbits; *informal* nosh, grub, chow, vittles, chuck.

eavesdrop verb *sorry, I refuse to **eavesdrop on** Kenny for you* LISTEN IN ON, spy on; monitor, tap, wiretap, record, overhear; *informal* snoop on, bug.

ebb verb 1 *the tide ebbed* RECEDE, go out, retreat, flow back, fall back/away, subside. ANTONYM come in.

2 *his courage began to ebb* DIMINISH, dwindle, wane, fade away, peter out, decline, flag, let up, decrease, weaken, disappear. ANTONYMS increase, intensify.

▸ noun 1 *the ebb of the tide* RECEDING, retreat, subsiding.

2 *the ebb of the fighting* ABATEMENT, subsiding, easing, dying down, de-escalation, decrease, decline, diminution.

ebony adjective *his ebony eyes* BLACK, jet-black, pitch-black, coal-black, sable, inky, sooty, raven, dark.

ebullience noun *the director's ebullience inspires the cast* EXUBERANCE, buoyancy, cheerfulness, cheeriness, merriment, jollity, sunniness, jauntiness, lightheartedness, high spirits, elation, euphoria, jubilation; animation, sparkle, vivacity, enthusiasm, perkiness; *informal* chirpiness, bounciness, pep.

ebullient adjective *in an ebullient mood* EXUBERANT, buoyant, cheerful, joyful, cheery, merry, jolly, sunny, jaunty, lighthearted, elated; animated, sparkling, vivacious, irrepressible; *informal* bubbly, bouncy, peppy, upbeat, chirpy, smiley, full of beans; *dated* gay. ANTONYM depressed.

eccentric adjective *eccentric behavior* UNCONVENTIONAL, uncommon, abnormal, irregular, aberrant, anomalous, odd, queer, strange, peculiar, weird, bizarre, outlandish, freakish, extraordinary; idiosyncratic, quirky, nonconformist, outré; *informal* way out, offbeat, freaky, oddball, wacky, kooky. ANTONYM conventional.

▸ noun *he was something of an eccentric* ODDITY, odd fellow, character, individualist, individual, free spirit; misfit; *informal* oddball, odd duck, weirdo, freak, nut, head case, crank, wacko, kook, screwball, crackpot.

eccentricity noun *Sidney's eccentricity was more charming than alarming* UNCONVENTIONALITY, singularity, oddness, strangeness, weirdness, quirkiness, freakishness; peculiarity, foible, idiosyncrasy, caprice, whimsy, quirk; *informal* nuttiness, screwiness, freakiness, kookiness.

ecclesiastic noun *a high ecclesiastic.* See CLERGYMAN.

▸ adjective *ecclesiastic embroidery.* See ECCLESIASTICAL.

ecclesiastical adjective *his ecclesiastical duties* PRIESTLY, ministerial, clerical, ecclesiastic, canonical, sacerdotal; church, churchly, religious, spiritual, holy, divine; *informal* churchy.

echelon noun *he reached the upper echelons of government* LEVEL, rank, grade, step, rung, tier, position, order.

echo noun 1 *a faint echo of my shout* REVERBERATION, reflection, ringing, repetition, repeat.

2 *the scene she described was an echo of the photograph* DUPLICATE, copy, replica, imitation, mirror image, double, match, parallel; *informal* look-alike, spitting image, dead ringer.

3 *a faint echo of their love* TRACE, vestige, remnant, ghost, shadow, memory, recollection, remembrance; reminder, sign, mark, token, souvenir, indication, suggestion, hint; evidence.

▸ verb 1 *his laughter echoed around the room* REVERBERATE, resonate, resound, reflect, ring, vibrate.

2 *Bill echoed Rex's words* REPEAT, restate, reiterate; copy, imitate, parrot, mimic; reproduce, recite, quote, regurgitate; *informal* recap.

WORD NOTE **echo**

An artificial echo can be called a *delay, slapback, doubling, chorus, flange, phasing, ambience, room tone,* or *reverb.* A *delay* is one or more distinct repetitions. A *slapback* is one distinct echo. *Doubling* is one echo too immediate to be heard distinctly. *Chorus, flange,* and *phasing* are one quick echo (doubling) at varying speeds, producing a whooshing or wobbling sound. *Ambience,* or *room tone,* is many quick echoes blended into an illusion of small space. *Reverb* is many echoes blended into an illusion of cavernous space. —**SM**

éclat noun *the woodwinds were quite spirited, but the strings lacked éclat* STYLE, flamboyance, confidence, élan, dash, flair, vigor, gusto, verve, zest, sparkle, brio, panache, dynamism, spirit; *informal* pizzazz, pep, oomph.

eclectic adjective *an eclectic mix of party music* WIDE-RANGING, broad-based, extensive, comprehensive, encyclopedic; varied, diverse, catholic, all-embracing, multifaceted, multifarious, heterogeneous, miscellaneous, assorted.

eclipse noun 1 *the eclipse of the sun* BLOTTING OUT, blocking, covering, obscuring, concealing, darkening; *Astronomy* occultation.

2 *the eclipse of the empire* DECLINE, fall, failure, decay, deterioration, degeneration, weakening, collapse.

▸ verb 1 *the sun was eclipsed by the moon* BLOT OUT, block, cover, obscure, hide, conceal, obliterate, darken; shade; *Astronomy* occult.

2 *the system was eclipsed by new methods* OUTSHINE, overshadow, surpass, exceed, outclass, outstrip, outdo, top, trump, transcend, upstage.

economic adjective 1 *economic reform* FINANCIAL, monetary, budgetary, fiscal; commercial.

2 *an economic alternative to carpeting* CHEAP, inexpensive, low-cost, economical, cut-rate, discount, bargain. ANTONYM expensive.

economical adjective 1 *an economical car* CHEAP, inexpensive, low-cost, budget, economy, economic; cut-rate, discount, bargain. ANTONYM expensive.

2 *a very economical shopper* THRIFTY, provident, prudent, sensible, frugal, sparing, abstemious; mean, parsimonious, penny-pinching, miserly, stingy. ANTONYM spendthrift.

THE RIGHT WORD

If you don't like to spend money unnecessarily, you may simply be **economical**, which means that you manage your finances wisely and avoid any unnecessary expenses. If you're **thrifty**, you're both industrious and clever in managing your resources (*a thrifty shopper who never leaves home without her coupons*). **Frugal**, on the other hand, means that you tend to be sparing with money—sometimes getting a little carried away in your efforts—by avoiding any form of luxury or lavishness (*too frugal to take a taxi, even at night*). If you're **sparing**, you exercise such restraint in your spending that you sometimes deprive yourself (*sparing to the point where she allowed herself only one new item of clothing a season*). If you're **provident**, however, you're focused on providing for the future (*never one to be provident, she spent her allowance the day she received it*). **Miserly** and **parsimonious** are both used to describe frugality in its most extreme form. But while being *frugal* might be considered a virtue, being *parsimonious* is usually considered to be a fault or even a vice (*they could have been generous with their wealth, but they chose to lead a parsimonious life*). And no one wants to be called *miserly*, which implies being stingy out of greed rather than need (*so miserly that he reveled in his riches while those around him were starving*).

economize verb *they economized by growing their own vegetables* SAVE (MONEY), cut costs; cut back, make cutbacks, retrench, budget, make economies, be thrifty, be frugal, scrimp, cut corners, tighten one's belt, watch the/one's pennies.

economy noun **1** *the nation's economy* WEALTH, (financial) resources; financial system, financial management.

2 *one can combine good living with economy* THRIFT, thriftiness, providence, prudence, careful budgeting, economizing, saving, scrimping, restraint, frugality, abstemiousness. ANTONYM extravagance.

ecstasy noun *the ecstasy of loving him* RAPTURE, bliss, elation, euphoria, transports, rhapsodies; joy, jubilation, exultation. See note at RAPTURE. ANTONYM misery.

ecstatic adjective *the news of Sophie's safe return made them ecstatic* ENRAPTURED, elated, in raptures, euphoric, rapturous, joyful, overjoyed, blissful; on cloud nine, in seventh heaven, beside oneself with joy, jumping for joy, delighted, thrilled, exultant; *informal* over the moon, on top of the world, blissed out.

ecumenical adjective *the local churches are sponsoring an ecumenical service on the green* NONDENOMINATIONAL, universal, catholic, latitudinarian, all-embracing, all-inclusive. See note at UNIVERSAL. ANTONYM denominational.

eddy noun *small eddies at the river's edge* SWIRL, whirlpool, vortex, maelstrom.

▸ verb *cold air eddied around her* SWIRL, whirl, spiral, wind, circulate, twist; flow, ripple, stream, surge, billow.

edge noun **1** *the edge of the lake* BORDER, boundary, extremity, fringe, margin, side; lip, rim, brim, brink, verge; perimeter, circumference, periphery, limits, bounds. See note at BORDER. ANTONYM middle.

2 *she had an edge in her voice* SHARPNESS, severity, bite, sting, asperity, acerbity, acidity, trenchancy; sarcasm, acrimony, malice, spite, venom. ANTONYM kindness.

3 *they have an edge over their rivals* ADVANTAGE, lead, head start, the whip hand, the upper hand; superiority, dominance, ascendancy, supremacy, primacy; *informal* inside track. ANTONYM disadvantage.

▸ verb **1** *poplars edged the orchard* BORDER, fringe, verge, skirt; surround, enclose, encircle, circle, encompass, bound.

2 *a nightie edged with lace* TRIM, pipe, band, decorate, finish; border, fringe; bind, hem.

3 *he edged closer to the fire* CREEP, inch, work one's way, pick one's way, ease oneself; sidle, steal, slink.

PHRASE: **on edge** *they were always on edge when Uncle Herman visited.* See EDGY sense 1.

edgy adjective **1** *everyone was edgy as the deadline approached* TENSE, nervous, on edge, anxious, apprehensive, uneasy, unsettled; twitchy, jumpy, keyed up, restive, skittish, neurotic, insecure; irritable, touchy, tetchy, testy, crotchety, prickly; *informal* uptight, wired, snappy, strung out. ANTONYM calm.

2 *an edgy new novel* CUTTING-EDGE, on-the-edge, fringe, avant-garde, innovative, original, offbeat; gritty. ANTONYM conventional.

WORD NOTE **edgy, hip**

There are fake words. One of them is *edgy,* as *New York Times* columnist David Brooks notes in today's paper (October 25, 2003). "Edginess," he writes, "is the garment that mainstream institutions wear when they want to look slightly but safely rebellious." Possibly so, but maybe the more salient point is that it remains a cultural imperative to rebel, or to be perceived as rebellious, as if James Dean in *Rebel Without a Cause* or Marlon Brando in *The Wild One* were better examples to follow than such models of rectitude as, say, Gregory Peck as a journalist fighting prejudice in *Gentleman's Agreement* or Gary Cooper enforcing the law in *High Noon.*

I remember the year everyone began using the word *edgy.* It was 1996. An Anne Klein chemise had an *edgy* look. A few years later you heard the word used routinely by film critics and book reviewers. An *edgy* movie was deliberately off-center and had a dark side. David Lynch made *edgy* movies and TV shows. *Mulholland Drive* featured a fractured, dreamy narrative that took radical, unexplained turns. It was weird but in a hip way.

Hip would be the ultimate word in this category, a word in such universal use that it may be destined toward the oblivion that follows overexposure. But *hip* had a kernel of meaning at one time, and a core of mystery, that continues to beguile. To Norman Mailer the distinction between *hip* and *square* seemed all-important. I remember, from an essay of his that I read in high school, that in various categories of taste and judgment, from music to philosophy, there was a square paragon and a hip one. One of Mailer's examples sticks all these years later: D. H. Lawrence was hip, Aldous Huxley square. I have given up trying to figure out why. Maybe it was that Lawrence represented seduction by touch and Huxley seduction by talking the girl into it. The widespread use of *hip* as a term of praise today may mean nothing less than the defeat of the *straight.* No one wants to be *straight* if the alternative is hip. Straight implies narrow-mindedness and a lack of curiosity. Hip are jeans, hip-hugging or not. Straight is a suit—a word increasingly used to denote not clothes but the person wearing them: a faceless, characterless fellow, perhaps an accountant or lawyer, in the company's employ. Better to be hip and in the know, on the cusp, ahead of the curve, especially if you can project an edgy appearance.

There's a moment in his 1956 rendition of "You Brought a New Kind of Love To Me" when Frank Sinatra substitutes the words "I'm hip" for "I know." That's a smart use of the word. The greatest parodic use I have ever seen was in the headline of a little story about the late Sammy Davis, Jr., original member of the Rat Pack. The story was about his having hip reconstruction surgery. The headline: "Sammy Davis to Get Hip." —**DL**

---

edible adjective *these berries may not be edible* SAFE TO EAT, fit for human consumption, wholesome, good to eat; consumable, digestible, palatable; *formal* comestible.

edict noun *rules established by government edict* DECREE, order, command, commandment, mandate, proclamation, pronouncement, dictate, fiat, promulgation; law, statute, act, bill, ruling, injunction; *formal* ordinance.

edification noun *formal I read Latin for my own personal edification* EDUCATION, instruction, tuition, teaching, training, tutelage, guidance; enlightenment, cultivation, information; improvement, development.

USAGE NOTE **edification**

In the phrase *for your edification* (= for your moral or intellectual instruction), the word *edification* is sometimes misused to mean "for your enjoyment" or the like—e.g.:

- "Dennis has come to the Tishomingo Lodge and Casino to perform daredevil dives for the edification [read *thrill*] of the casino guests." (*Rocky Mountain News* [Denver]; Feb. 15, 2002.)
- "Everyone says vaguely snotty things about each other and hidden cameras record, for our edification [read *titillation*], sundry couples' first kisses." (*Daily News of Los Angeles*; June 2, 2002.)
- "Quinn and his best friend Creedy (Gerard Butler) reenact the climactic light-saber battle between Luke Skywalker and Darth Vader for the edification [read *enjoyment*] of the local children." (*Austin American-Statesman*; July 12, 2002.) —**BG**

---

edifice noun *the imposing new edifice on Whitfield Street* BUILDING, structure, construction, erection, pile, complex; property, development, premises.

edify verb *formal students who have no desire to be edified should leave my classroom and take up thumb-twiddling* EDUCATE, instruct, teach, school, tutor, train, guide; enlighten, inform, cultivate, develop, improve, better.

WORD NOTE **edifying**

Though, strictly speaking, it still means instructive, one hardly hears this word (or, for that matter, *edify* and *edification*) used anymore without a slightly ironic edge. *The listeners were subjected to an edifying speech about the lecturer's accomplishments. Her discourse on table manners was intended for our edification.* Perhaps it's because the slightly old-fashioned diction evokes an era in which writers and speakers commonly felt the urge or obligation to raise the moral, spiritual, and intellectual level of their audiences, and because we have grown impatient with, or cynical about, the wish to improve us in that way. *Improving,* a word of which I'm also fond, has a similar connotation, possibly more ironic. *The novel contained many improving moral lessons.* —**FP**

---

edit verb **1** *she edited the text* CORRECT, check, copyedit, improve, emend, polish; modify, adapt, revise, rewrite, reword, rework, redraft; shorten, condense, cut, abridge; *informal* clean up, blue-pencil.

2 *this volume was edited by a consultant* SELECT, choose, assemble, organize, put together.

3 *he edited the school newspaper* BE THE EDITOR OF, direct, run, manage, head, lead, supervise, oversee, preside over; *informal* be the boss of.

edition noun *the latest edition includes candid photos from the peace rally* ISSUE, number, volume, impression, publication; version, revision.

educate verb *it's nearly impossible to educate children who hate being in school* TEACH, school, tutor, instruct, coach, train, drill; guide, inform, enlighten; inculcate, indoctrinate; *formal* edify.

educated adjective *her assistant was an educated and creative young man* INFORMED, literate, schooled, tutored, well-read, learned, knowledgeable, enlightened; intellectual, academic, erudite, scholarly, cultivated, cultured; *dated* lettered.

education noun **1** *the education of young children* TEACHING, schooling, tuition, tutoring, instruction, coaching, training, tutelage, guidance; indoctrination, inculcation, enlightenment; *formal* edification.

2 *a woman of some education* LEARNING, knowledge, literacy, scholarship, enlightenment.

educational adjective **1** *a stuffy educational establishment* ACADEMIC, scholastic, school, learning, teaching, pedagogic, instructional.

2 *an educational experience* INSTRUCTIVE, instructional, educative, informative, illuminating, pedagogic, enlightening, didactic, heuristic; *formal* edifying.

educative adjective. See EDUCATIONAL sense 2.

educator noun *Mr. Chips is one of the most beloved educators in fiction* TEACHER, tutor, instructor, schoolteacher; educationalist, educationist; lecturer, professor; guide, mentor, guru; *formal* pedagogue; *dated* schoolmaster, schoolmistress, schoolmarm; *archaic* schoolman.

eerie adjective *eerie sounds from the swamp* UNCANNY, sinister, ghostly, unnatural, unearthly, supernatural, otherworldly; strange, abnormal, odd, weird, freakish; creepy, scary, spooky, freaky, frightening; bone-chilling, spine-chilling, hair-raising, blood-curdling, terrifying.

efface verb **1** *the chalk drawings were effaced by the rain* ERASE, eradicate, expunge, blot out, rub out, wipe out, remove, eliminate; delete, cancel, obliterate.

2 *he attempted to **efface himself*** MAKE ONESELF INCONSPICUOUS, keep out of sight, keep out of the limelight, lie low, keep a low profile, withdraw (oneself).

effect noun **1** *the effect of these changes* RESULT, consequence, upshot, outcome, repercussions, ramifications; end result, conclusion, culmination, corollary, concomitant, aftermath; fruit(s), product, by-product, payoff; *Medicine* sequela. ANTONYM cause.

2 *the effect of the drug* IMPACT, action, effectiveness, influence; power, potency, strength; success; *formal* efficacy.

3 *the new rules come into effect tomorrow* FORCE, operation, enforcement, implementation, effectiveness; validity, lawfulness, legality, legitimacy.

4 *some words to that effect* SENSE, meaning, theme, drift, import, intent, intention, tenor, significance, message; gist, essence, spirit.

5 (**effects**) *the dead man's effects* BELONGINGS, possessions, goods, worldly goods, chattels, goods and chattels; property, paraphernalia; *informal* gear, tackle, things, stuff.

▸ verb *they effected many changes* ACHIEVE, accomplish, carry out, realize, manage, bring off, execute, conduct, engineer, perform, do, perpetrate, discharge, complete, consummate; cause, bring about, create, produce, make; provoke, occasion, generate, engender, actuate, initiate; *formal* effectuate. See note at AFFECT.

PHRASES: **in effect** *the battle had, in effect, already been won* REALLY, in reality, in truth, in fact, in actual fact, effectively, essentially, in essence, practically, to all intents and purposes, all but, as good as, more or less, almost, nearly, just about; *informal* pretty much; *literary* well-nigh, nigh on. **take effect** **1** *these measures will take effect in May* COME INTO FORCE, come into operation, become operative, begin, become valid, become law, apply, be applied. **2** *the drug started to take effect* WORK, act, be effective, produce results. See note at EFFECT.

effective adjective **1** *an effective treatment* SUCCESSFUL, effectual, potent, powerful; helpful, beneficial, advantageous, valuable, useful; *formal* efficacious. ANTONYMS ineffective, weak.

2 *a more effective argument* CONVINCING, compelling, strong, forceful, potent, weighty, sound, valid; impressive, persuasive, plausible, credible, authoritative; logical, reasonable, lucid, coherent, cogent, eloquent; *formal* efficacious. ANTONYM weak.

3 *the new law will become effective next week* OPERATIVE, in force, in effect; valid, official, lawful, legal, binding; *Law* effectual. ANTONYM invalid.

4 *Korea was under effective Japanese control* VIRTUAL, practical, essential, actual, implicit, tacit. ANTONYM theoretical.

THE RIGHT WORD

All of these adjectives mean producing or capable of producing a result, but they are not interchangeable. Use **effective** when you want to describe something that produces a definite effect or result (*an effective speaker who was able to rally the crowd's support*) and **efficacious** when it produces the desired effect or result (*an efficacious remedy that cured her almost immediately*). If something produces the desired effect or result in a decisive manner, use **effectual** (*an effectual recommendation that got him the job*), an adjective that is often employed when looking back after an event is over (*an effectual strategy that finally turned the tide in their favor*). Reserve the use of **efficient** for when you want to imply skill and economy of energy in producing the desired result (*so efficient in her management of the company that layoffs were not necessary*). When applied to people, *efficient* means capable or competent (*an efficient homemaker*) and places less emphasis on the achievement of results and more on the skills involved.

effectiveness noun *we were impressed by the effectiveness of the nontoxic pesticide* SUCCESS, productiveness, potency, power; benefit, advantage, value, virtue, usefulness; *formal* efficacy.

effectual adjective **1** *effectual political action* EFFECTIVE, successful, productive, constructive; worthwhile, helpful, beneficial, advantageous, valuable, useful; *formal* efficacious. See note at EFFECTIVE.

2 *Law an effectual document* VALID, authentic, bona fide, genuine, official; lawful, legal, legitimate, binding, legally binding, contractual.

effeminate adjective *an effeminate bartender* WOMANISH, effete, foppish, unmanly, feminine; *informal* camp, campy, flaming. ANTONYM manly.

effervescence noun **1** *wines of uniform effervescence* FIZZ, fizziness, sparkle, gassiness, carbonation, aeration, bubbliness.

2 *his cheeky effervescence* VIVACITY, liveliness, animation, high spirits, ebullience, exuberance, buoyancy, sparkle, gaiety, jollity, cheerfulness, perkiness, breeziness, enthusiasm, irrepressibility, vitality, zest, energy, dynamism, pep, bounce, spunk.

effervescent adjective **1** *an effervescent drink* FIZZY, sparkling, carbonated, aerated, gassy, bubbly. ANTONYMS flat, still.

2 *effervescent young people* VIVACIOUS, lively, animated, high-spirited, bubbly, ebullient, buoyant, sparkling, scintillating, lighthearted, jaunty, happy, jolly, cheery, cheerful, perky, sunny, enthusiastic, irrepressible, vital, zestful, energetic, dynamic; *informal* bright-eyed and bushy-tailed, peppy, bouncy, upbeat, chirpy, full of beans. ANTONYM depressed.

effete adjective **1** *effete trendies* AFFECTED, pretentious, precious, mannered, overrefined; ineffectual; *informal* la-di-da. ANTONYM unpretentious.

2 *an effete young man* EFFEMINATE, unmanly, girlish, feminine; soft, timid, cowardly, lily-livered, spineless, pusillanimous; *informal* sissy, wimpish, wimpy. ANTONYM manly.

3 *the fabric of society is effete* WEAK, enfeebled, enervated, worn out, exhausted, finished, drained, spent, powerless, ineffectual. ANTONYM powerful.

WORD NOTE **effete**

Here's a word on which some dictionaries and usage authorities haven't caught up with the realities of literate usage. Yes, the traditional meaning of *effete* is "depleted of vitality, washed out, exhausted"—and in a college paper for an older prof you'd probably want to use it in only that way. But a great many educated people accept *effete* now also as a pejorative synonym for *elite* or *elitist,* one with an added suggestion of effeminacy, over-refinement, pretension, and/or decadence; and in this writer's opinion it is not a boner to use *effete* this way, since no other word has quite its connotative flavor. Traditionalists who see this evolved def as an error often blame Spiro Agnew's characterization of some liberal group or other as an "effete corps of impudent snobs," but there are deeper reasons for this evolution, such as that *effete* derives from the Latin *effētus,* which meant "worn out from bearing children" and thus had an obvious feminine connotation. Or that, historically, *effete* was often used to describe artistic movements that had exhausted their vitality, and one of the main characteristics of a kind of art's exhaustion was its descent into excessive refinement/foppery/decadence. **—DFW & EM**

efficacious adjective *formal a change in diet may be quite efficacious* EFFECTIVE, effectual, successful, productive, constructive, potent; helpful, beneficial, advantageous, valuable, useful. See note at EFFECTIVE.

efficacy noun *formal the efficacy of prescription drugs*

EFFECTIVENESS, success, productiveness, potency, power; benefit, advantage, value, virtue, usefulness.

efficiency noun **1** *we need to make changes to improve efficiency* ORGANIZATION, order, orderliness, regulation, coherence; productivity, effectiveness.

2 *I compliment you on your efficiency* COMPETENCE, capability, ability, proficiency, adeptness, expertise, professionalism, skill, effectiveness.

efficient adjective **1** *efficient techniques* ORGANIZED, methodical, systematic, logical, orderly, businesslike, streamlined, productive, effective, cost-effective, labor-saving. See note at EFFECTIVE. ANTONYM disorganized.

2 *an efficient secretary* COMPETENT, capable, able, proficient, adept, skillful, skilled, effective, productive, organized, businesslike. ANTONYM incompetent.

effigy noun *protestors threw water-balloon "bombs" at an effigy of the president* STATUE, statuette, sculpture, model, dummy, figurine; likeness, image; bust.

effluent noun *the effluent from papermaking contains may contaminants* (LIQUID) WASTE, sewage, waste water, effluvium, outflow, discharge, emission.

effort noun **1** *they made an effort to work together* ATTEMPT, try, endeavor; *informal* crack, shot, stab; *formal* essay.

2 *his score was a fine effort* ACHIEVEMENT, accomplishment, attainment, result, feat; undertaking, enterprise, work; triumph, success, coup.

3 *the job requires little effort* EXERTION, energy, work, endeavor, application, labor, power, muscle, toil, strain; *informal* sweat, elbow grease.

effortless adjective *he makes the most complex dance moves look effortless* EASY, undemanding, unchallenging, painless, simple, uncomplicated, straightforward, elementary; fluent, natural; *informal* as easy as pie, child's play, kids' stuff, a cinch, no sweat, a breeze, duck soup, a snap. ANTONYM difficult.

effrontery noun *Stearns had the effrontery to counter the admiral's directive* IMPUDENCE, impertinence, cheek, insolence, cockiness, audacity, temerity, presumption, nerve, gall, shamelessness, impoliteness, disrespect, bad manners; *informal* brass, face, chutzpah, sauce, sass. See note at TEMERITY.

effusion noun **1** *an effusion of poisonous gas* OUTFLOW, outpouring, rush, current, flood, deluge, emission, discharge, emanation; spurt, surge, jet, stream, torrent, gush, flow.

2 *reporters' flamboyant effusions* OUTBURST, outpouring, gushing, rhapsody; wordiness, verbiage.

effusive adjective *effusive compliments* GUSHING, gushy, unrestrained, extravagant, fulsome, demonstrative, lavish, enthusiastic, lyrical; expansive, wordy, verbose, over the top. See note at SENTIMENTAL. ANTONYM restrained.

egg noun *the eggs are suspended in a gelatinous mass* OVUM; gamete, germ cell; (**eggs**) roe, spawn, seed. PHRASE: **egg someone on** *Earl didn't really want to enter the talent contest, but his friends egged him on* URGE, goad, incite, provoke, push, drive, prod, prompt, induce, impel, spur on; encourage, exhort, motivate, galvanize.

egghead noun *informal Frances fits right in with all the chess-club eggheads* INTELLECTUAL, thinker, academic, scholar, sage; bookworm, highbrow; expert, genius, mastermind; *informal* brain, whiz, brainiac, rocket scientist. ANTONYM dunce.

ego noun *the defeat was a bruise to his ego* SELF-ESTEEM, self-importance, self-worth, self-respect, self-image, self-confidence.

egocentric adjective *Ivy has finally outgrown her egocentric friends* SELF-CENTERED, egomaniacal, egoistic, egotistic, self-interested, selfish, self-seeking, self-absorbed, narcissistic, vain, self-important. ANTONYM altruistic.

egotism, egoism noun *Darla's egotism will always thwart her chances for a lasting relationship* SELF-CENTEREDNESS, egomania, egocentricity, self-interest, selfishness, self-seeking, self-serving, self-regard, self-love, narcissism, self-admiration, vanity, conceit, self-importance; boastfulness. See also note at PRIDE.

THE RIGHT WORD

Is the handsome, arrogant, successful politician who thinks the world revolves around him an egoist or an egotist? **Egotism** is a negative term that combines extreme self-preoccupation with a tendency to show off or attract attention, while **egoism** is a more neutral term for those who are preoccupied with their own needs and interests but do not necessarily consider themselves superior (*the egoism of teenagers is well-documented*). There is nothing neutral about **conceit**, which carries strong connotations of superiority and a failure to see oneself realistically (*he was so rich and powerful that conceit came easily*). **Vanity**, on the other hand, is not based so much on feelings of superiority as it is on a love for oneself and a craving for the admiration of others (*his vanity drove him to cosmetic surgery*). **Narcissism** and **solipsism** were once considered technical terms drawn from psychology and philosophy, respectively, but nowadays they are also in the general language. *Narcissism* means self-love and preoccupation with one's physical or mental attributes (*the beautiful young actress had a reputation for narcissism*), while *solipsism* refers to someone who is completely wrapped up in his or her own concerns (*the solipsism of the theoretical mathematician*).

egotist, egoist noun *boxing is a sport that breeds egotists* SELF-SEEKER, egocentric, egomaniac, narcissist; boaster, braggart; *informal* show-off, big head, showboat.

egotistic, egoistic adjective *Archie's egotistic lifestyle has alienated many people over the years* SELF-CENTERED, selfish, egocentric, egomaniacal, self-interested, self-seeking, self-absorbed, narcissistic, vain, conceited, self-important; boastful.

egregious adjective *an egregious error of judgment* SHOCKING, appalling, terrible, awful, horrendous, frightful, atrocious, abominable, abhorrent, outrageous; monstrous, heinous, dire, unspeakable, shameful, unforgivable, intolerable, dreadful; *formal* grievous. ANTONYM marvelous.

egress noun **1** *the egress from the gallery was blocked* EXIT, way out, escape route. ANTONYM entrance.

2 *a means of egress* DEPARTURE, exit, withdrawal, retreat, exodus; escape. ANTONYM entry.

eight cardinal number *we certainly heard a talented eight this evening* OCTET, eightsome, octuplets; *Poetry* octrain, octameter; *Music* octuplet, octave; *technical* octad; *rare* ogdoad, octarchy.

ejaculate verb **1** *the male ejaculates* EMIT SEMEN, climax, have an orgasm, orgasm; *informal* come.

2 *dated "What?" he ejaculated* EXCLAIM, cry out, call out, yell, blurt out, come out with.

ejaculation noun 1 *the ejaculation of fluid* EMISSION, ejection, discharge, release, expulsion.

2 *premature ejaculation* EMISSION OF SEMEN, climax, orgasm.

3 *dated the conversation consisted of ejaculations* EXCLAMATION, interjection; call, shout, yell.

eject verb 1 *the volcano ejected ash* EMIT, spew out, discharge, give off, send out, belch, vent; expel, release, disgorge, spout, vomit, throw up.

2 *the pilot had time to eject* BAIL OUT, escape, get out.

3 *they were ejected from the hall* EXPEL, throw out, turn out, cast out, remove, oust; evict, banish; *informal* kick out, boot out, chuck out, give someone the bum's rush. ANTONYM admit.

4 *he was ejected from his post* DISMISS, remove, discharge, oust, expel, ax, throw out, force out, drive out; *informal* sack, fire, send packing, boot out, kick out, chuck out, give someone their marching orders, show someone the door. ANTONYM appoint.

THE RIGHT WORD

Want to get rid of someone? You can **eject** him or her, which means to throw or cast out (*he was ejected from the meeting room*). If you hope the person never comes back, use **expel**, a verb that suggests driving someone out of a country, an organization, etc., for all time (*to be expelled from school*); it can also imply the use of voluntary force (*to expel air from the lungs*). If you exercise force or the power of law to get rid of someone or something, **oust** is the correct verb (*ousted after less than two years in office*). If as a property owner you are turning someone out of a house or a place of business, you'll want to **evict** the person (*she was evicted for not paying the rent*). **Dismiss** is by far the mildest of these terms, suggesting that you are rejecting or refusing to consider someone or something (*to dismiss a legal case*). It is also commonly used of loss of employment (*dismissed from his job for excessive tardiness*).

ejection noun 1 *the ejection of electrons* EMISSION, discharge, expulsion, release; elimination.

2 *their ejection from the grounds* EXPULSION, removal; eviction, banishment, exile.

3 *his ejection from office* DISMISSAL, removal, discharge, expulsion.

eke verb *I had to* **eke out** *my remaining funds* HUSBAND, use sparingly, be thrifty with, be frugal with, be sparing with, use economically; *informal* go easy on. ANTONYM squander.

PHRASE: **eke out a living** *they barely eked out a living* SUBSIST, survive, get by, scrape by, make ends meet, keep body and soul together, keep the wolf from the door, keep one's head above water.

ekphrastic adjective See note below.

WORD NOTE **ekphrastic**

My candidate for the ugliest word in the language is *ekphrastic*. An *ekphrastic* poem is one that has a painting or other work of art as its subject, and that's a legitimate category, God knows. But I'd go to lengths to avoid using *ekphrastic*, which, in addition to sounding academic and pompous, sounds plain ugly—with the *ek* succeeded so soon by the *ic*. I believe the second-ugliest word is *carbuncular*, as in the "young man carbuncular" who beds the typist in T. S. Eliot's "The Waste Land"; Eliot wants us to see this fellow as a sort of human pimple. There's a three-way tie for third place, courtesy of the medical profession: *colonoscopy, catheter, oncology.* **—DL**

elaborate adjective 1 *an elaborate plan* COMPLICATED, complex, intricate, involved; detailed, painstaking, careful; tortuous, convoluted, serpentine, Byzantine. ANTONYMS simple, plain.

2 *an elaborate plasterwork ceiling* ORNATE, decorated, embellished, adorned, ornamented, fancy, fussy, busy, ostentatious, extravagant, showy, baroque, rococo, florid; *informal* fancy-schmancy. ANTONYMS simple, plain.

▸ verb *both sides refused to* **elaborate on** *their reasons* EXPAND ON, enlarge on, add to, flesh out, put flesh on the bones of, add detail to, expatiate on; develop, fill out, embellish, embroider, enhance, amplify.

élan noun *they performed with uncommon élan* FLAIR, style, panache, confidence, dash, éclat; energy, vigor, vitality, liveliness, brio, esprit, animation, vivacity, zest, verve, spirit, pep, sparkle, enthusiasm, gusto, eagerness, feeling, fire; *informal* pizzazz, zing, zip, vim, oomph.

elapse verb *how much time has elapsed?* PASS, go by/past, wear on, slip by/away/past, roll by/past, slide by/past, steal by/past, tick by/past.

elastic adjective 1 *elastic material* STRETCHY, elasticized, stretchable, springy, flexible, pliant, pliable, supple, yielding, plastic, resilient. See note at FLEXIBLE. ANTONYM rigid.

2 *an elastic concept of nationality* ADAPTABLE, flexible, adjustable, accommodating, variable, fluid, versatile. ANTONYM inflexible.

▸ noun *buying elastics for her hair* RUBBER BAND, elastic band, scrunchie.

elasticity noun 1 *the skin's natural elasticity* STRETCHINESS, flexibility, pliancy, suppleness, plasticity, resilience, springiness, give.

2 *the elasticity of the term* ADAPTABILITY, flexibility, adjustability, fluidity, versatility.

elated adjective *Sally and Marv were elated at the idea of becoming grandparents* THRILLED, delighted, overjoyed, ecstatic, euphoric, very happy, joyous, gleeful, jubilant, beside oneself, exultant, rapturous, in raptures, walking on air, on cloud nine, in seventh heaven, jumping for joy, in transports of delight; *informal* on top of the world, over the moon, on a high, tickled pink. ANTONYM miserable.

elation noun *the declaration of peace is indeed cause for our greatest elation* EUPHORIA, ecstasy, happiness, delight, transports of delight, joy, joyousness, glee, jubilation, exultation, bliss, rapture.

elbow verb *he elbowed his way through the crowd* PUSH, shove, force, shoulder, jostle, barge, muscle, bulldoze.

elbow room noun *the committee desires more elbow room within the confines of the organization* ROOM TO MANEUVER, room, space, breathing space, personal space, scope, opportunity, freedom, play, free rein, license, latitude, leeway.

elder adjective *his elder brother* OLDER, senior, big.

▸ noun *the native elders* LEADER, senior figure, patriarch, father.

elderly adjective *her elderly mother* AGED, old, advanced in years, aging, long in the tooth, past one's prime; gray-haired, grizzled, hoary; in one's dotage, decrepit, doddering, doddery, senescent; *informal* getting on, past it, over the hill, no spring chicken. ANTONYM youthful.

▸ noun **(the elderly)** *health care for the elderly* OLD PEOPLE, the aged, senior citizens; geriatrics, seniors; retired people, retirees, golden agers; *informal* oldsters, geezers.

elect verb **1** *a new president was elected* VOTE FOR, VOTE IN, return, cast one's vote for; choose, pick, select.

2 *she elected to stay behind* CHOOSE, decide, opt, vote.

▸ adjective *the president-elect* FUTURE, -to-be, designate, chosen, elected, coming, next, appointed.

▸ noun **(the elect)** *it is not the elect who need better health care and safer schools* THE CHOSEN, the elite, the favored; the crème de la crème.

election noun *announcing the results of the election* BALLOT, vote, popular vote, ballot box; poll(s); acclamation; primary.

electioneer verb *we electioneered for Stevenson in the fifties* CAMPAIGN, canvass, go on the hustings.

elector noun *my thanks to the faithful electors who brought me to this place* VOTER, member of the electorate, constituent.

electric adjective **1** *an electric kettle* ELECTRIC-POWERED, electrically operated, battery-operated.

2 *the atmosphere was electric* EXCITING, charged, electrifying, thrilling, heady, dramatic, intoxicating, dynamic, stimulating, galvanizing, rousing, stirring, moving; tense, knife-edge, explosive, volatile.

electricity noun *cabins with no electricity* POWER, electric power, energy, current, static.

electrify verb *lecturers who electrify their students* EXCITE, thrill, stimulate, arouse, rouse, inspire, stir (up), exhilarate, intoxicate, galvanize, move, fire (with enthusiasm), fire someone's imagination, invigorate, animate; startle, jolt, shock, light a fire under; *informal* give someone a thrill, give someone a charge.

elegance noun **1** *he was attracted by her elegance* STYLE, stylishness, grace, gracefulness, taste, tastefulness, sophistication; refinement, dignity, beauty, poise, charm, culture; suaveness, urbanity, panache.

2 *the elegance of the idea* NEATNESS, simplicity; ingenuity, cleverness, inventiveness.

elegant adjective **1** *an elegant black outfit* STYLISH, graceful, tasteful, sophisticated, classic, chic, smart, fashionable, modish; refined, dignified, poised, beautiful, lovely, charming, artistic, aesthetic; cultivated, polished, cultured; dashing, debonair, suave, urbane. ANTONYM gauche.

2 *an elegant solution* NEAT, simple, effective; ingenious, clever, deft, intelligent, inventive. ANTONYMS messy, unwieldy.

WORD NOTE **elegant**

I like the subtle sense of economy that *elegant* imparts to what otherwise might be just a synonym for *graceful.* When you say that a fastball or a legal brief or a dance move is elegant, you're saying that you admire not just its beauty but also its efficiency—that it gets the job done with surprisingly few wasted components or motions, and even with an ingenious shortcut or two. This is one of those words I like so much that I have to stop myself from overusing it. **—DA**

elegiac adjective *an elegiac piece for small orchestra* MOURNFUL, melancholic, melancholy, plaintive, sorrowful, sad, lamenting, doleful; funereal, dirgelike; nostalgic, valedictory, poignant; *literary* dolorous. ANTONYM cheerful.

elegy noun *an elegy for his father* LAMENT, requiem, threnody, dirge; *literary* plaint; *Irish* keen.

element noun **1** *an essential element of the game* COMPONENT, constituent, part, section, portion, piece, segment, bit; aspect, factor, feature, facet, ingredient, strand, detail, point; member, unit, module, item.

2 *there is an element of truth in this stereotype* TRACE, touch, hint, smattering, soupçon.

3 (elements) *the elements of political science* BASICS, essentials, principles, first principles; foundations, fundamentals, rudiments; *informal* nuts and bolts, ABCs.

4 (elements) *I braved the elements* WEATHER, climate, meteorological conditions, atmospheric conditions; wind, rain, snow.

elemental adjective **1** *the elemental principles of accounting* BASIC, primary, fundamental, essential, root, underlying; rudimentary.

2 *elemental forces* NATURAL, atmospheric, meteorological, environmental, climatic.

elementary adjective **1** *an elementary astronomy course* BASIC, rudimentary, fundamental; preparatory, introductory, initiatory, entry-level; *informal* 101. ANTONYM advanced.

2 *a lot of the work is elementary* EASY, simple, straightforward, uncomplicated, undemanding, painless, child's play, plain sailing; *informal* as easy as pie, as easy as ABC, a piece of cake, no sweat, kids' stuff. ANTONYMS complicated, difficult.

elephantine adjective *a tropical plant with elephantine leaves* ENORMOUS, huge, gigantic, very big, massive, giant, immense, tremendous, colossal, mammoth, gargantuan, vast, prodigious, monumental, titanic; hulking, bulky, heavy, weighty, ponderous, lumbering; *informal* jumbo, whopping, humongous, monster, ginormous. ANTONYM tiny.

elevate verb **1** *we need a breeze to elevate the kite* RAISE, lift (up), raise up/aloft, upraise; hoist, hike up, haul up. ANTONYM lower.

2 *he was elevated to senior writer* PROMOTE, upgrade, advance, move up, raise, prefer; ennoble, exalt, aggrandize; *informal* move up the ladder. ANTONYM demote.

elevated adjective **1** *an elevated highway* RAISED, upraised, high up, aloft; overhead.

2 *elevated language* LOFTY, grand, exalted, fine, sublime; inflated, pompous, bombastic, orotund. ANTONYMS lowly, base.

3 *the gentry's elevated status* HIGH, higher, high-ranking, of high standing, lofty, superior, exalted, eminent; grand, noble. ANTONYMS lowly, humble.

elevation noun **1** *his elevation to the directorship* PROMOTION, upgrading, advancement, advance, preferment, aggrandizement; ennoblement; *informal* step up the ladder.

2 *15,000–30,000 feet in elevation* ALTITUDE, height.

3 *elevations in excess of 8,000 feet* HEIGHT, hill, mountain, mount; *formal* eminence.

4 *elevation of thought* GRANDEUR, greatness, nobility, loftiness, majesty, sublimity.

elf noun *elves inhabit the great hollow trees* PIXIE, fairy, sprite, imp, brownie; dwarf, gnome, goblin, hobgoblin; leprechaun, puck, troll.

elfin adjective *her elfin little brother charmed all the aunts and uncles* ELFLIKE, elfish, elvish, pixielike; puckish, impish, playful, mischievous; dainty, delicate, small, petite, slight, little, tiny, diminutive.

elicit verb *your sarcastic remarks will no doubt elicit a negative response* OBTAIN, draw out, extract, bring out, evoke, call forth, bring forth, induce, prompt, generate, engender, trigger, provoke; *formal* educe.

eligible adjective 1 *those people eligible to vote* ENTITLED, permitted, allowed, qualified, able.

2 *an eligible bachelor* DESIRABLE, suitable; available, single, unmarried, unattached, unwed.

eliminate verb 1 *a policy that would eliminate inflation* REMOVE, get rid of, put an end to, do away with, end, stop, terminate, eradicate, destroy, annihilate, stamp out, wipe out, extinguish.

2 *he was eliminated in the first round of competition* KNOCK OUT, beat; exclude, rule out, disqualify.

elite noun *hobnobbing with Southport's elite* BEST, pick, cream, crème de la crème, flower, nonpareil, elect; high society, jet set, beautiful people, beau monde, haut monde, glitterati; aristocracy, nobility, upper class. ANTONYM dregs.

elixir noun *a homemade elixir purported to enhance virility* POTION, concoction, brew, philter, decoction, mixture; medicine, tincture; extract, essence, concentrate, distillate, distillation; *literary* draft.

elliptical adjective 1 *an elliptical shape* OVAL, egg-shaped, elliptic, ovate, ovoid, oviform, ellipsoidal.

2 *elliptical phraseology* CRYPTIC, abstruse, ambiguous, obscure, oblique, Delphic; terse, concise, succinct, compact, economic, laconic, sparing, abridged.

elocution noun *the producers brought in a teacher to help with her elocution* PRONUNCIATION, enunciation, articulation, diction, speech, intonation, vocalization, modulation; phrasing, delivery, public speaking.

elongate verb 1 *an exercise that elongates the muscles* LENGTHEN, extend, stretch (out). ANTONYM shorten.

2 *the high notes were elongated* PROLONG, protract, draw out, sustain. ANTONYM shorten.

eloquence noun *the eloquence of his sermons* FLUENCY, articulateness, expressiveness, silver tongue, persuasiveness, forcefulness, power, potency, effectiveness; oratory, rhetoric, grandiloquence, magniloquence; *informal* gift of the gab, way with words.

eloquent adjective 1 *an eloquent speaker* FLUENT, articulate, expressive, silver-tongued; persuasive, strong, forceful, powerful, potent, well-expressed, effective, lucid, vivid, graphic; smooth-tongued, glib. ANTONYM inarticulate.

2 *her glance was more eloquent than words* EXPRESSIVE, meaningful, suggestive, revealing, telling, significant, indicative.

elsewhere adverb *the negatives are stored in one place, and the prints are stored elsewhere* SOMEWHERE ELSE, in/at/to another place, in/at/to a different place, hence; not here, not present, absent, away, abroad, out. ANTONYM here.

elucidate verb *Sherwood's diaries may help elucidate his motives* EXPLAIN, make clear, illuminate, throw/shed light on, clarify, clear up, sort out, unravel, spell out; interpret, explicate; gloss. See note at CLARIFY. ANTONYM confuse.

elucidation noun *the manual provides elucidation useful to the beginner* EXPLANATION, clarification, illumination; interpretation, explication; gloss.

elude verb *Holbrook eluded the police for several weeks* EVADE, avoid, get away from, dodge, escape from, run from, run away from; lose, shake off, give the slip to, slip away from, throw off the scent; *informal* slip through someone's fingers, slip through the net.

elusive adjective 1 *her elusive husband* DIFFICULT TO FIND; evasive, slippery; *informal* always on the move.

2 *an elusive quality* INDEFINABLE, intangible, impalpable, ambiguous.

Elysian adjective *an Elysian vision* HEAVENLY, paradisal, paradisiacal, celestial, divine; *literary* empyrean.

Elysium noun *Greek Mythology* *human souls conveyed to Elysium* HEAVEN, paradise, the Elysian fields; eternity, the afterlife, the next world, the hereafter; *Scandinavian Mythology* Valhalla; *Classical Mythology* the Islands of the Blessed; *Arthurian Legend* Avalon.

emaciated adjective *emaciated bodies* THIN, skeletal, bony, gaunt, wasted; scrawny, skinny, scraggy, skin and bones, rawboned, sticklike, waiflike; starved, underfed, undernourished, underweight, half-starved; cadaverous, shriveled, shrunken, withered; *informal* anorexic, like a bag of bones. ANTONYM fat.

e-mail, email noun *I haven't read my e-mail today* ELECTRONIC MAIL, text messaging; correspondence, communication, message(s), mail, memo(s), letter(s).

▸ verb *e-mail your résumé before noon Friday* SEND ELECTRONICALLY, transmit, forward, mail.

emanate verb 1 *warmth emanated from the fireplace* ISSUE, spread, radiate, be sent forth/out.

2 *the proposals emanated from a committee* ORIGINATE, stem, derive, proceed, spring, issue, emerge, flow, come.

3 *he emanated an air of power* EXUDE, emit, radiate, give off/out, send out/forth.

emanation noun 1 *an emanation of his tortured personality* PRODUCT, consequence, result, fruit.

2 *radon gas emanation* DISCHARGE, emission, radiation, effusion, outflow, outpouring, flow, leak; *technical* efflux.

emancipate verb *the young Cowles emancipated his father's serfs* FREE, liberate, set free, release, deliver, discharge; unchain, unfetter, unshackle, untie, unyoke; *rare* disenthrall. ANTONYM enslave.

emancipated adjective *emancipated women* LIBERATED, independent, unconstrained, uninhibited; free.

emasculate verb 1 *the opposition emasculated the committee's proposal* WEAKEN, enfeeble, debilitate, erode, undermine, cripple; remove the sting from, pull the teeth out of; *informal* water down.

2 *archaic the ganders should be emasculated at three months.* See CASTRATE.

embalm verb 1 *his body had been embalmed* PRESERVE, mummify, lay out.

2 *the poem ought to embalm his memory* PRESERVE, conserve, enshrine, immortalize.

embankment noun *a steep grassy embankment* BANK, mound, ridge, earthwork, causeway, barrier, levee, dam, dike.

embargo noun *an embargo on oil sales* BAN, bar, prohibition, stoppage, interdict, proscription, veto, moratorium; restriction, restraint, block, barrier, impediment, obstruction; boycott.

▸ verb *arms sales were embargoed* BAN, bar, prohibit, stop, interdict, debar, proscribe, outlaw; restrict, restrain, block, obstruct; boycott. ANTONYM allow.

embark verb 1 *the passengers were not allowed to embark until 4:30* BOARD SHIP, go on board, go aboard; *informal* hop on, jump on.

2 *he* ***embarked on*** *a new career* BEGIN, start, commence, undertake, set about, take up, turn one's hand to, get down to; enter into, venture into, launch into, plunge into, engage in, settle down to; *informal* get cracking on, get going on, have a go/crack/shot at.

embarrass verb *his parents would show up drunk and embarrass him* MORTIFY, shame, put someone to shame, humiliate, abash, chagrin, make uncomfortable, make self-conscious; discomfit, disconcert, discompose, upset, distress; *informal* show up, discombobulate.

embarrassed adjective *the officer's flashlight caught a pair of embarrassed teens in the back seat* MORTIFIED, red-faced, blushing, abashed, shamed, ashamed, shamefaced, humiliated, chagrined, awkward, self-conscious, uncomfortable, sheepish; discomfited, disconcerted, upset, discomposed, flustered, agitated, distressed; shy, bashful, tongue-tied; *informal* with egg on one's face, wishing the earth would swallow one up.

embarrassing adjective *many embarrassing moments have been preserved on videotape* HUMILIATING, shaming, shameful, mortifying, ignominious; awkward, uncomfortable, cringeworthy, compromising; disconcerting, discomfiting, upsetting, distressing.

embarrassment noun 1 *he was scarlet with embarrassment* MORTIFICATION, humiliation, shame, shamefacedness, chagrin, awkwardness, self-consciousness, sheepishness, discomfort, discomfiture, discomposure, agitation, distress; shyness, bashfulness.

2 *his current financial embarrassment* DIFFICULTY, predicament, plight, problem, mess, imbroglio; *informal* bind, jam, pickle, fix, scrape.

3 *an embarrassment of riches* SURPLUS, excess, overabundance, superabundance, glut, surfeit, superfluity; abundance, profusion, plethora.

embassy noun 1 *the Italian embassy* CONSULATE, legation.

2 *historical the king sent an embassy to the rebels* ENVOY, representative, delegate, emissary; delegation, deputation, legation, mission, diplomatic mission.

embed, imbed verb *rhinestones are then embedded in the leather trim* IMPLANT, plant, set, fix, lodge, root, insert, place; sink, drive, hammer, ram.

embellish verb 1 *weapons embellished with precious metal* DECORATE, adorn, ornament; beautify, enhance, grace; trim, garnish, gild; deck, bedeck, festoon, emblazon; *literary* bejewel, bedizen.

2 *the legend was embellished in later retellings* ELABORATE, embroider, expand on, exaggerate.

embellishment noun 1 *architectural embellishments* DECORATION, ornamentation, adornment; beautification, enhancement, trimming, trim, garnishing, gilding.

2 *we wanted the truth, not romantic embellishments* ELABORATION, addition, exaggeration.

ember noun *a hot ember | shoveling out the embers* GLOWING COAL, live coal; cinder; **(embers)** ashes, residue.

embezzle verb *he's accused of embezzling donated funds* MISAPPROPRIATE, steal, thieve, pilfer, purloin, appropriate, defraud someone of, siphon off, pocket, help oneself to; abstract; *informal* rob, rip off, skim, line one's pockets with, pinch.

embezzlement noun *four corporate managers were indicted for embezzlement* MISAPPROPRIATION, theft, stealing, robbery, thieving, pilfering, purloining, pilferage, appropriation, swindling; fraud, larceny.

embittered adjective *after twenty years of Neil's infidelity, can you blame her for being embittered?* BITTER, resentful, rancorous, jaundiced, aggrieved, sour, frustrated, dissatisfied, alienated, disaffected.

emblazon verb 1 *shirts emblazoned with the company name* ADORN, decorate, ornament, embellish; inscribe.

2 *a flag with a hammer and sickle emblazoned on it* DISPLAY, depict, show.

emblem noun *their emblem is an eagle perched atop a cannon* SYMBOL, representation, token, image, figure, mark, sign; crest, badge, device, insignia, stamp, seal, heraldic device, coat of arms, shield; logo, trademark, brand.

THE RIGHT WORD

When it comes to representing or embodying the invisible or intangible, you can't beat a **symbol**. It applies to anything that serves as an outward sign of something immaterial or spiritual (*the cross as a symbol of salvation; the crown as a symbol of monarchy*), although the association between the symbol and what it represents does not have to be based on tradition or convention and may, in fact, be quite arbitrary (*the annual gathering at the cemetery became a symbol of the family's long and tragic history*). An **emblem** is a visual symbol or pictorial device that represents the character or history of a family, a nation, or an office (*the eagle is an emblem of the United States*). It is very close in meaning to **attribute**, which is an object that is conventionally associated with either an individual, a group, or an abstraction (*the spiked wheel as an attribute of St. Catherine; the scales as an attribute of Justice*). An **image** is also a visual representation or embodiment, but in a much broader sense (*veins popping, he was the image of the angry father*). **Sign** is often used in place of *symbol* to refer to a simple representation of an agreed-upon meaning (*the upraised fist as a sign of victory; the white flag as a sign of surrender*), but a *symbol* usually embodies a wider range of meanings, while a *sign* can be any object, event, or gesture from which information can be deduced (*her faltering voice was a sign of her nervousness*). A **token**, on the other hand, is something offered as a symbol or reminder (*he *gave her his class ring as a token of his devotion*) and a **type**, particularly in a religious context, is a symbol or representation of something not present (*Jerusalem as the type of heaven; the paschal lamb as the type of Christ*).

---

emblematic, emblematical adjective 1 *a situation emblematic of the industrialized twentieth century* SYMBOLIC, representative, demonstrative, suggestive, indicative.

2 *emblematic works of art* ALLEGORICAL, symbolic, metaphorical, parabolic, figurative.

embodiment noun *the embodiment of the hippie culture* PERSONIFICATION, incarnation, realization, manifestation, avatar, expression, representation, actualization, symbol, symbolization, materialization; paradigm, epitome, paragon, soul, model; type, essence, quintessence, exemplification, example, exemplar, ideal; *formal* reification.

embody verb 1 *he embodies the spirit of industrial capitalism* PERSONIFY, realize, manifest, symbolize, represent, express, concretize, incarnate, epitomize, stand for, typify, exemplify; *formal* reify, hypostatize.

2 *the changes embodied in the gun control legislation* INCORPORATE, include, contain, encompass; assimilate, consolidate, integrate, organize, systematize; combine.

embolden verb *emboldened by the brandy, he walked over to her table* FORTIFY, make brave/braver, encourage, hearten, strengthen, brace, stiffen the resolve of, lift the morale of; rouse, stir, stimulate, cheer, rally, fire, animate, inspirit, invigorate; *informal* buck up. See note at ENCOURAGE. ANTONYM dishearten.

embrace verb 1 *he embraced her warmly* HUG, take/hold in one's arms, hold, cuddle, clasp to one's bosom, clasp, squeeze, clutch; caress; enfold, enclasp, encircle, envelop, entwine oneself around; *informal* canoodle, clinch.

2 *most states have embraced the concept* WELCOME, welcome with open arms, accept, take up, take to one's heart, adopt; espouse, support, back, champion.

3 *the faculty embraces a wide range of departments* INCLUDE, take in, comprise, contain, incorporate, encompass, cover, involve, embody, subsume, comprehend.

▸ noun *a fond embrace* HUG, cuddle, squeeze, clinch, caress, clasp; bear hug.

embrocation noun *an embrocation of comfrey and aloe* OINTMENT, lotion, cream, rub, salve, emollient, liniment, balm, unguent.

embroider verb 1 *a cushion embroidered with a pattern of golden keys* SEW, stitch; decorate, adorn, ornament, embellish.

2 *she embroidered her stories with colorful detail* ELABORATE, embellish, enlarge on, exaggerate, touch up, dress up, gild, color; *informal* jazz up.

embroidery noun 1 *the girls were taught embroidery* NEEDLEWORK, needlepoint, needlecraft, sewing, tatting, crewel work, tapestry.

2 *fanciful embroidery of the facts* ELABORATION, embellishment, adornment, ornamentation, coloring, enhancement; exaggeration, overstatement, hyperbole.

embroil verb *I don't want to get embroiled in your crazy schemes* INVOLVE, entangle, ensnare, enmesh, catch up, mix up, bog down, mire.

embryo noun 1 *a human embryo* FETUS, fertilized egg, unborn child/baby, zygote.

2 *the embryo of a capitalist economy* GERM, nucleus, seed; rudimentary version, rudiments, basics, beginning, start.

embryonic adjective 1 *an embryonic chick* FETAL, unborn, unhatched; in utero.

2 *an embryonic prodemocracy movement* RUDIMENTARY, undeveloped, unformed, immature, incomplete, incipient, inchoate; fledgling, budding, nascent, emerging, developing, early, germinal. ANTONYM mature.

emcee noun *Billy Crystal will repeat his role as emcee* MASTER OF CEREMONIES, MC, host, hostess, ringmaster, chairman.

emend verb *the editors select letters for publication and may emend content at their own discretion* CORRECT, rectify, repair, fix; improve, enhance, polish, refine, amend; edit, rewrite, revise, copyedit, redraft, recast, rephrase, reword, rework, alter, change, modify; *rare* redact.

emerge verb 1 *a policeman emerged from the alley* COME OUT, appear, come into view, become visible, surface, materialize, manifest oneself, issue, come forth.

2 *several unexpected facts emerged* BECOME KNOWN, become apparent, be revealed, come to light, come out, turn up, transpire, unfold, prove to be the case.

emergence noun *the emergence of a new generation* APPEARANCE, arrival, coming, materialization; advent, inception, dawn, birth, origination, start, development, rise.

emergency noun 1 *a military emergency* CRISIS, urgent situation, extremity, exigency; accident, disaster, catastrophe, calamity; difficulty, plight, predicament, danger.

2 *get her down to emergency right away* emergency room, ER.

▸ adjective 1 *an emergency meeting* URGENT, crisis; impromptu, extraordinary.

2 *emergency supplies* RESERVE, standby, backup, fallback, in reserve.

emergent adjective *an emergent democracy* EMERGING, developing, rising, dawning, budding, embryonic, infant, fledgling, nascent, incipient, inchoate.

emigrate verb *her Swedish ancestors emigrated in 1901* MOVE ABROAD, move overseas, leave one's country, migrate; relocate, resettle; defect. ANTONYM immigrate.

emigration noun *the main incentive for emigration was the promise of higher wages* MOVING ABROAD, moving overseas, expatriation, migration; exodus, diaspora; relocation, resettling; defection.

eminence noun 1 *his eminence as a scientist* FAME, celebrity, illustriousness, distinction, renown, preeminence, notability, greatness, prestige, importance, reputation, repute, note; prominence, superiority, stature, standing.

2 *various legal eminences* IMPORTANT PERSON, dignitary, luminary, worthy, grandee, notable, notability, personage, leading light, VIP; *informal* somebody, someone, big shot, big gun, heavyweight.

3 *formal* *the hotel's eminence above the sea* ELEVATION, height, rise.

eminent adjective 1 *an eminent man of letters* ILLUSTRIOUS, distinguished, renowned, esteemed, preeminent, notable, noteworthy, great, prestigious, important, influential, affluential, outstanding, noted, of note; famous, celebrated, prominent, well-known, lionized, acclaimed, exalted, revered, august, venerable. ANTONYM unknown.

2 *the eminent reasonableness of their claims* OBVIOUS, clear, conspicuous, marked, singular, signal; total, complete, utter, absolute, thorough, perfect, downright, sheer.

EASILY CONFUSED WORDS **eminent, imminent, immanent**

Eminent, **imminent**, and **immanent** are frequently confused. **Eminent** means 'outstanding, famous': *the book was written by an eminent authority on folk art.* **Imminent** means 'about to happen': *people brushed aside the possibility that war was imminent.* **Immanent**, often used in religious or philosophical contexts, means 'inherent': *we can philosophize that death is immanent in life, but this doesn't make it easier.*

eminently adverb *this vehicle is eminently suitable for rough terrain* VERY, greatly, highly, exceedingly, extremely, particularly, exceptionally, supremely, uniquely; obviously, clearly, conspicuously, markedly, singularly, signally, outstandingly, strikingly, notably, surpassingly; totally, completely, utterly, absolutely, thoroughly, perfectly, downright.

emissary noun *Clinton praised King Hussein as a bold emissary for peace* ENVOY, ambassador, delegate, attaché, consul, plenipotentiary; agent, representative, deputy; messenger, courier; nuncio.

emission noun *controlling the emission of carbon dioxide* DISCHARGE, release, outpouring, outflow, leak, excretion, secretion, ejection; emanation, radiation, effusion, ejaculation, disgorgement, issuance.

emit verb 1 *the hydrocarbons emitted from vehicle exhausts* DISCHARGE, release, give out/off, pour out, send forth, throw out, void, vent, issue; leak, ooze, excrete, disgorge, secrete, eject, ejaculate; spout, belch, spew out; emanate, radiate, exude. ANTONYM absorb.

2 *he emitted a loud cry* UTTER, voice, let out, produce, give vent to, come out with, vocalize.

emollient adjective *a rich emollient shampoo* MOISTURIZING, soothing, softening.

▸ noun *she applied an emollient* MOISTURIZER, cream, lotion, oil, rub, salve, unguent, balm; *technical* humectant.

emolument noun *formal his name alone is worth the emolument they're willing to offer* SALARY, pay, payment, wage(s), earnings, allowance, stipend, honorarium, reward, premium; fee, charge, consideration; income, profit, gain, return.

emotion noun 1 *she was good at hiding her emotions* FEELING, sentiment; reaction, response.

2 *overcome by emotion, she turned away* PASSION, strength of feeling, warmth of feeling.

3 *responses based purely on emotion* INSTINCT, intuition, gut feeling; sentiment, the heart.

THE RIGHT WORD

A **feeling** can be almost any subjective reaction or state—pleasant or unpleasant, strong or mild, positive or negative—that is characterized by an emotional response (*a feeling of insecurity; a feeling of pleasure*). An **emotion** is a very intense feeling, which often involves a physical as well as a mental response and implies outward expression or agitation (*to be overcome with emotion*) **Passion** suggests a powerful or overwhelming emotion, with connotations of sexual love (*their passion remained undiminished after 30 years of marriage*) or intense anger (*a passion for revenge*). There is more intellect and less feeling in **sentiment**, which is often applied to an emotion inspired by an idea (*political sentiments; antiwar sentiments*). *Sentiment* also suggests a refined or slightly artificial feeling (*a speech marked by sentiment rather than passion*). **Affect** is a formal psychological term that refers to an observed emotional state (*heavily sedated, he spoke without affect*).

emotional adjective 1 *an emotional young man* PASSIONATE, hot-blooded, ardent, fervent, excitable, temperamental, melodramatic, tempestuous; demonstrative, responsive, tender, loving, feeling, sentimental, sensitive. ANTONYMS cold, apathetic.

2 *he paid an emotional tribute to his wife* POIGNANT, moving, touching, affecting, powerful, stirring, emotive, heartrending, heartwarming, impassioned, dramatic; haunting, pathetic, sentimental; *informal* tear-jerking. ANTONYM unfeeling.

3 *during the speech we all became a little emotional* TEARFUL, teary-eyed, sad, choked up, weepy; *formal, literary* lachrymose. ANTONYM dry-eyed.

4 *their emotional needs are often ignored* SPIRITUAL, inner, psychological, psychic, of the heart. ANTONYM material.

emotionless adjective *emotionless faces* UNEMOTIONAL, unfeeling, dispassionate, passionless, unexpressive, inexpressive, cool, cold, cold-blooded, impassive, indifferent, detached, remote, aloof; toneless, flat, dead, expressionless, blank, wooden, stony, deadpan, vacant, poker-faced.

emotive adjective 1 *a highly emotive book.* See EMOTIONAL sense 2.

2 *an emotive issue* CONTROVERSIAL, contentious, inflammatory; sensitive, delicate, difficult, problematic, touchy, awkward, prickly, ticklish.

empathize verb *John could* ***empathize with*** *the survivors* IDENTIFY WITH, sympathize with, be in sympathy with, understand, share the feelings of, be in tune with; be on the same wavelength as, talk the same language as; relate to, feel for, have insight into; *informal* put oneself in someone else's shoes.

emperor noun *the emperor of Japan* RULER, sovereign, king, monarch, potentate; *historical* czar, kaiser, mikado, khan.

emphasis noun 1 *the curriculum gave more emphasis to reading and writing* PROMINENCE, importance, significance, value; stress, weight, accent, attention, priority, preeminence, urgency, force.

2 *the emphasis is on the word "little"* STRESS, accent, accentuation, weight, prominence; beat; *Prosody* ictus.

emphasize verb *the profile emphasizes Orgento's dedication to feeding the hungry* STRESS, underline, highlight, focus attention on, point up, lay stress on, draw attention to, spotlight, foreground, play up, make a point of; bring to the fore, insist on, belabor; accent, accentuate, underscore; *informal* press home, rub it in. ANTONYM understate.

emphatic adjective 1 *an emphatic denial* VEHEMENT, firm, wholehearted, forceful, forcible, energetic, vigorous, direct, assertive, insistent; certain, definite, out-and-out, one hundred percent; decided, determined, categorical, unqualified, unconditional, unequivocal, unambiguous, absolute, explicit, downright, outright, clear. ANTONYMS hesitant, tentative.

2 *an emphatic victory* CONCLUSIVE, decisive, decided, unmistakable; resounding, telling; *informal* thundering. ANTONYM narrow.

empire noun 1 *the Ottoman Empire* KINGDOM, realm, domain, territory, imperium; commonwealth; power, world power, superpower.

2 *a worldwide shipping empire* ORGANIZATION, corporation, multinational, conglomerate, consortium, company, business, firm, operation.

3 *his dream of empire* POWER, rule, ascendancy, supremacy, command, control, authority, sway, dominance, domination, dominion.

empirical adjective *many of these predictions have received empirical confirmation* EXPERIENTIAL, practical, heuristic, firsthand, hands-on; observed, evidence-based, seen, demonstrable. ANTONYM theoretical.

employ verb 1 *she employed a chauffeur* HIRE, engage, recruit, take on, secure the services of, sign up, sign, put on the payroll, enroll, appoint; retain, contract; indenture, apprentice. ANTONYM dismiss.

2 *Julio was employed in carving a stone figure* OCCUPY, engage, involve, keep busy, tie up; absorb, engross, immerse.

3 *the team employed subtle psychological tactics* USE, utilize, make use of, avail oneself of; apply, exercise, practice, put into practice, exert, bring into play, bring to bear; draw on, resort to, turn to, have recourse to.

employed adjective *it is a myth that most employed people have adequate health insurance for their families* WORKING, in work, in employment, holding down a job; earning, wage-earning, waged, breadwinning.

employee noun *each employee receives a Thanksgiving turkey | the slowdown has been a hard blow to our employees* WORKER, member of staff, staffer; blue-collar worker, white-collar worker, laborer, hand, hired hand; wage earner; *informal* desk jockey; **(employees)** personnel, staff, workforce, human resources.

employer noun 1 *his employer gave him a glowing reference* MANAGER, boss, proprietor, director, chief executive, chief, president, head man, head woman; *informal* boss man, skipper; padrone.

2 *the largest private-sector employer in Ohio* COMPANY, firm, business, organization, manufacturer.

employment noun 1 *she found employment as a clerk* WORK, service, labor; a job, a post, a position, a situation, an occupation, a profession, a trade, a line of work, a calling, a vocation, a craft, a pursuit; *archaic* employ.

2 *the employment of children* HIRING, hire, engagement, taking on; apprenticing.

3 *the employment of nuclear weapons* USE, utilization, application, exercise.

emporium noun *a furniture emporium* STORE, shop, outlet, retail outlet, superstore, megastore, department store, chain store, supermarket; establishment.

empower verb 1 *the act empowered police to arrest dissenters* AUTHORIZE, entitle, permit, allow, license, sanction, warrant, commission, delegate, qualify, enable, equip. ANTONYM forbid.

2 *movements to empower the poor* EMANCIPATE, unshackle, set free, liberate. ANTONYM enslave.

empress noun *an exhibit of gowns worn by the empress* RULER, sovereign, queen, monarch, potentate; *historical* czarina.

emptiness noun *she had filled an emptiness in his life* VOID, vacuum, empty space, vacuity, gap, vacancy, hole, lack.

empty adjective 1 *an empty house* VACANT, unoccupied, uninhabited, untenanted, bare, desolate, deserted, abandoned; clear, free. ANTONYM full.

2 *an empty threat* MEANINGLESS, hollow, idle, vain, futile, worthless, useless, nugatory, insubstantial, ineffective, ineffectual. ANTONYMS meaningful, serious.

3 *without her, my life is empty* FUTILE, pointless, purposeless, worthless, meaningless, valueless, of no value, useless, of no use, aimless, senseless, hollow, barren, insignificant, inconsequential, trivial. ANTONYM worthwhile.

4 *his eyes were empty* BLANK, expressionless, vacant, deadpan, wooden, stony, impassive, absent, glazed, fixed, lifeless, emotionless, unresponsive. ANTONYM expressive.

▸ verb 1 *I emptied the dishwasher* UNLOAD, unpack, void; clear, evacuate. ANTONYMS fill, load.

2 *he emptied out the contents of the case* REMOVE, take out, extract, tip out, pour out, dump out, drain.

empty-headed adjective *they treat her like some empty-headed bimbo* STUPID, foolish, silly, unintelligent, idiotic, brainless, witless, vacuous, stunned, vapid, featherbrained, birdbrained, harebrained, scatterbrained, thoughtless, imbecilic; *informal* halfwitted, dumb, dim, airheaded, brain-dead, dippy, dizzy, dopey, flaky, soft in the head, slow on the uptake, ditzy, dumb-ass. ANTONYM intelligent.

empyrean *literary* adjective *the empyrean regions* HEAVENLY, celestial, ethereal; upper.

▸ noun **(the empyrean)** *sing it to the empyrean!* HEAVEN, the heavens, the sky, the skies, the upper regions, the stratosphere; *literary* the ether, the wide blue yonder, the firmament, the welkin.

emulate verb *they tried to emulate Lucy's performance* IMITATE, copy, mirror, echo, follow, model oneself on; match, equal, parallel, be on a par with, be in the same league as, come close to; compete with, contend with, rival, surpass; take a leaf out of someone's book.

enable verb *the brace will enable you to walk more steadily* ALLOW, permit, let, give the means, equip, empower, make able, fit; make possible, facilitate; authorize, entitle, qualify; *formal* capacitate. ANTONYM prevent.

enact verb 1 *the charter was enacted in 1982* PASS, make law, legislate; approve, ratify, sanction, authorize; impose, lay down, bring down. ANTONYM repeal.

2 *members of the church enacted the Nativity* ACT OUT, act, perform, appear in, stage, mount, put on, present.

enactment noun 1 *the enactment of a Bill of Rights* PASSING; ratification, sanction, approval, authorization; imposition.

2 *congressional enactments* ACT, law, bylaw, ruling, rule, regulation, statute, measure; *formal* ordinance; **(enactments)** legislation.

enamel noun *shiny red enamel* COATING, lacquer, varnish, glaze, finish.

enamored adjective *she was secretly* ***enamored of*** *the prince* IN LOVE WITH, infatuated with, besotted with, smitten with, captivated by, enchanted by, fascinated by, bewitched by, beguiled by; keen on, taken with; *informal* mad about, crazy about, wild about, bowled over by, stuck on, hot for, sweet on, carrying a torch for, moonstruck by; *literary* ensorcelled by.

encampment noun *Dolan and Martini reached the encampment only minutes before daybreak* CAMP, military camp, bivouac, cantonment; campsite, camping ground; tents.

encapsulate verb **1** *their conclusions are encapsulated in one sentence* SUMMARIZE, sum up, give the gist of, put in a nutshell; capture, express.

2 *seeds encapsulated in resin* ENCLOSE, encase, contain, envelop, enfold, sheath, cocoon, surround.

enchant verb *these tales are sure to enchant your little ones* | *mermaids enchanted the sailors* CAPTIVATE, charm, delight, enrapture, entrance, enthrall, beguile, bewitch, spellbind, fascinate, hypnotize, mesmerize, rivet, grip, transfix; *rare* ensorcell; *informal* bowl someone over. ANTONYM bore.

WORD NOTE **ensorcell**

An Elizabethan term that might be of use to modern cultural commentators. Meaning "enchant, bewitch, fascinate," it is an elegant addition to the clutch of terms we usually use to describe the effect our televisions have on us. **—ZS**

enchanter noun *an evil enchanter named Norg* WIZARD, witch, sorcerer, warlock, magician, necromancer, magus; witch doctor, medicine man, shaman; *archaic* mage; *rare* thaumaturge.

enchanting adjective *an enchanting ballerina* CAPTIVATING, charming, delightful, bewitching, beguiling, adorable, lovely, attractive, appealing, engaging, winning, fetching, winsome, alluring, disarming, seductive, irresistible, fascinating; *dated* taking.

enchantment noun **1** *a race of giants skilled in enchantment* MAGIC, witchcraft, sorcery, wizardry, necromancy; charms, spells, incantations, mojo; *rare* thaumaturgy.

2 *the enchantment of the garden by moonlight* ALLURE, delight, charm, beauty, attractiveness, appeal, fascination, irresistibility, magnetism, pull, draw, lure.

3 *being with him was sheer enchantment* BLISS, ecstasy, heaven, rapture, joy.

enchantress noun *the enchantress put a curse on all the young men of Underwood Village* WITCH, sorceress, magician, fairy; Circe, siren.

encircle verb *". . . and the smoke, it encircled his head like a wreath"* SURROUND, enclose, circle, girdle, ring, encompass; close in, shut in, fence in, wall in, hem in, confine; *literary* gird, engirdle. See note at CIRCUMSCRIBE.

enclose verb **1** *tall trees enclosed the campsite* SURROUND, circle, ring, girdle, encompass, encircle; confine, close in, shut in, corral, fence in, wall in, hedge in, hem in; *literary* gird, engirdle. See note at CIRCUMSCRIBE.

2 *please enclose a stamped addressed envelope* INCLUDE, insert, put in; send.

enclosure noun *they drove the donkeys into the enclosure* PADDOCK, fold, pen, compound, stockade, ring, yard; sty, coop, corral.

encomium noun *formal the poet's encomium to the king* EULOGY, panegyric, paean, accolade, tribute, testimonial; praise, acclaim, acclamation, homage.

encompass verb **1** *the apartment buildings encompass common recreational grounds, complete with swimming pool and tennis court* SURROUND, enclose, encircle, circumscribe, bound, border; *literary* gird, engird; *rare* compass. See note at CIRCUMSCRIBE.

2 *the debates encompassed a vast range of subjects* COVER, embrace, include, incorporate, take in, contain, comprise, involve, deal with, range across; *formal* comprehend.

encounter verb **1** *I encountered a teacher I used to know* MEET, meet by chance, run into, come across/upon, stumble across/on/upon, chance on/upon, happen on/upon; *informal* bump into.

2 *we encountered a slight problem* EXPERIENCE, hit, run into, come up against, face, be faced with, confront.

▸ noun **1** *an unexpected encounter* MEETING, chance meeting.

2 *a violent encounter between police and demonstrators* BATTLE, fight, clash, confrontation, struggle, skirmish, engagement; *informal* run-in, set-to, scrap.

encourage verb **1** *the players were encouraged by the crowd's response* HEARTEN, cheer, buoy up, uplift, inspire, motivate, spur on, stir, stir up, fire up, stimulate, invigorate, vitalize, revitalize, embolden, fortify, rally; *informal* buck up, pep up, give a shot in the arm to. ANTONYM discourage.

2 *she had encouraged him to go* PERSUADE, coax, urge, press, push, pressure, pressurize, prod, goad, egg on, prompt, influence, sway; *informal* put ideas into one's head. ANTONYM dissuade.

3 *the municipal government must encourage local businesses* SUPPORT, back, champion, promote, further, foster, nurture, cultivate, strengthen, stimulate; help, assist, aid, boost, fuel. ANTONYM hinder.

THE RIGHT WORD

To **encourage** is to give active help or to raise confidence to the point where one dares to do what is difficult (*encouraged by her teacher, she set her sights on attending Harvard*). **Embolden** also entails giving confidence or boldness, but it implies overcoming reluctance or shyness (*success as a public speaker emboldened her to enter politics*). To **hearten** is to put one's heart into or to renew someone's spirit (*heartened by the news of his recovery*), and to **inspire** is to infuse with confidence, resolution, or enthusiasm (*inspired by her mother's example, she started exercising regularly*). To **foster** is to encourage by nurturing or extending aid (*to foster the growth of small businesses by offering low-interest loans*); in some contexts, *foster* suggests an unwise or controversial kind of help (*to foster rebellion among local farmers*). **Instigate** also implies that what is being encouraged is not necessarily desirable (*to instigate a fight*), while **stimulate** is a more neutral term meaning to rouse to action or effort (*to stimulate the growth of crops; to stimulate an interest in literature*).

encouragement noun **1** *she needed a bit of encouragement* HEARTENING, cheering up, inspiration, motivation, stimulation, fortification; support, morale-boosting, a boost, a shot in the arm.

2 *they required no encouragement to get back to work* PERSUASION, coaxing, urging, pep talk, pressure, prodding, prompting; spur, goad, inducement, incentive, bait, motive; *informal* carrot.

3 *the encouragement of foreign investment* SUPPORT, backing, championship, championing, sponsoring, promotion, furtherance, furthering, fostering, nurture, cultivation; help, assistance, boosterism.

encouraging adjective **1** *an encouraging start* PROMISING, hopeful, auspicious, propitious, favorable, bright, rosy; heartening, reassuring, cheering, comforting, welcome, pleasing, gratifying.

2 *my parents were very encouraging* SUPPORTIVE, understanding, helpful; positive, responsive, enthusiastic, boosterish.

encroach verb *she didn't want to **encroach on** his privacy* INTRUDE ON, trespass on, impinge on, obtrude on, impose oneself on, invade, infiltrate, interrupt, infringe on, violate, interfere with, disturb; *informal* horn in on, muscle in on; *archaic* entrench on.

encroachment noun *the **encroachment on** their territory* INTRUSION ON, trespass on, invasion of, infiltration of, incursion into, appropriation of; infringement of, impingement on.

encumber verb **1** *her movements were encumbered by her heavy skirts* HAMPER, hinder, obstruct, impede, cramp, inhibit, restrict, limit, constrain, restrain, bog down, retard, slow (down); inconvenience, disadvantage, handicap. See note at HINDER.

2 *they are encumbered with debt* BURDEN, load, weigh down, saddle; overwhelm, tax, stress, strain, overload, overburden.

encumbrance noun **1** *he soon found the old equipment a great encumbrance* HINDRANCE, obstruction, obstacle, impediment, constraint, handicap, inconvenience, nuisance, disadvantage, drawback; *literary* trammel; *archaic* cumber.

2 *she knew she was an encumbrance to him* BURDEN, responsibility, obligation, liability, weight, load, stress, strain, pressure, trouble, worry; millstone, albatross, cross to bear; *informal* ball and chain.

encyclopedic adjective *his encyclopedic knowledge of food* COMPREHENSIVE, complete, thorough, thoroughgoing, full, exhaustive, in-depth, wide-ranging, all-inclusive, all-embracing, all-encompassing, universal, vast; *formal* compendious.

end noun **1** *the end of the road* EXTREMITY, furthermost part, limit; margin, edge, border, boundary, periphery; point, tip, tail end, tag end, terminus. ANTONYMS beginning, middle.

2 *the end of the novel* CONCLUSION, termination, ending, finish, close, resolution, climax, finale, culmination, denouement; epilogue, coda, peroration. ANTONYM beginning.

3 *wealth is a means and not an end in itself* AIM, goal, purpose, objective, object, holy grail, target; intention, intent, design, motive; aspiration, wish, desire, ambition.

4 *the commercial end of the business* ASPECT, side, section, area, field, part, share, portion, segment, province.

5 *his end might come at any time* DEATH, dying, demise, passing, expiry, quietus; doom, extinction, annihilation, extermination, destruction; downfall, ruin, ruination, Waterloo; *informal* curtains; *formal* decease. ANTONYM birth.

▸ verb **1** *the show **ended with** a wedding scene* FINISH WITH, conclude with, terminate with, come to an end with, draw to a close with, close with, stop with, cease with; culminate in, climax with, build up to, lead up to, come to a head with. ANTONYMS begin, start.

2 *she ended their relationship* BREAK OFF, call off, bring to an end, put an end to, stop, finish, terminate, discontinue, curtail; dissolve, cancel, annul; *informal* can, ax. ANTONYM begin. See word spectrum at BEGIN.

endanger verb *the pollutants endanger the fish* IMPERIL, jeopardize, risk, put at risk, put in danger, expose to danger; threaten, pose a threat to, be a danger to, be detrimental to, damage, injure, harm; *archaic* peril.

endearing adjective *the baby ducklings are endearing* LOVABLE, adorable, cute, sweet, dear, delightful, lovely, charming, appealing, attractive, engaging, winning, captivating, enchanting, beguiling, winsome.

endearment noun **1** *his murmured endearments* TERM OF AFFECTION, term of endearment, pet name; (**endearments**) sweet nothings, sweet talk.

2 *he spoke to her without endearment* AFFECTION, fondness, tenderness, feeling, sentiment, warmth, love, liking, care.

endeavor verb *the company endeavored to expand its activities* TRY, attempt, seek, undertake, aspire, aim, set out; strive, struggle, labor, toil, work, exert oneself, apply oneself, do one's best, do one's utmost, give one's all, be at pains; *informal* have a go, have a shot, have a stab, give something one's best shot, do one's damnedest, go all out, bend over backwards; *formal* essay.

▸ noun **1** *an endeavor to build a more buoyant economy* ATTEMPT, try, bid, effort, venture; *informal* go, crack, shot, stab; *formal* essay.

2 *several days of endeavor* EFFORT, exertion, striving, struggling, laboring, toil, struggle, labor, hard work, application, industry; pains; *informal* sweat, 'blood, sweat, and tears', elbow grease; *literary* travail.

3 *an extremely unwise endeavor* UNDERTAKING, enterprise, venture, exercise, activity, exploit, deed, act, action, move; scheme, plan, project; *informal* caper.

ending noun *a happy ending* END, finish, close, closing, conclusion, resolution, summing-up, windup, denouement, finale; cessation, stopping, termination, discontinuation. ANTONYM beginning.

endless adjective **1** *a woman with endless energy* UNLIMITED, limitless, infinite, inexhaustible, boundless, unbounded, untold, immeasurable, measureless, incalculable; abundant, abounding, great; bottomless, ceaseless, unceasing, unending, without end, everlasting, constant, continuous, continual, interminable, unfading, unfailing, perpetual, eternal, enduring, lasting. See note at ETERNAL. ANTONYMS limited, transient.

2 *as children we played endless games* COUNTLESS, innumerable, untold, legion, numberless, unnumbered, numerous, very many, manifold, multitudinous, multifarious; a great number of, infinite numbers of, a multitude of; *informal* umpteen, no end of, loads of, stacks of, heaps of, masses of, oodles of, scads of, zillions of, gazillions of; *literary* myriad, divers. ANTONYM few.

endorse verb **1** *endorse a product* SUPPORT, back, agree with, approve (of), favor, subscribe to, recommend, champion, stick up for, uphold, affirm, sanction; *informal* throw one's weight behind, okay. See note at APROVE. ANTONYM oppose.

2 *endorse a check* COUNTERSIGN, sign, autograph, authenticate; *rare* chirographate.

endorsement noun *the proposal won their overwhelming endorsement* SUPPORT, backing, approval, seal of approval, agreement, recommendation, championship, patronage, affirmation, sanction; *informal* buy-in.

endow verb 1 *the CEO endowed a hospital for sick kids* FINANCE, fund, pay for, provide for, subsidize, support financially, put up the money for; establish, found, set up, institute.

2 *nature endowed fish with gills* PROVIDE, supply, furnish, equip, invest, favor, bless, grace, gift; give, bestow; *literary* endue.

endowment noun 1 *the endowment of a Chair of Botany* FUNDING, financing, subsidizing; establishment, foundation, institution.

2 *her will contained a generous endowment* BEQUEST, legacy, inheritance; gift, present, grant, award, donation, contribution, subsidy, settlement; *formal* benefaction.

3 *his natural endowments* QUALITY, characteristic, feature, attribute, facility, faculty, ability, talent, gift, strength, aptitude, capability, capacity.

endurable adjective *it was cold but endurable* BEARABLE, tolerable, supportable, manageable, sustainable. ANTONYM unbearable.

endurance noun 1 *she pushed him beyond the limit of his endurance* TOLERATION, tolerance, sufferance, forbearance, patience, acceptance, resignation, stoicism.

2 *the race is a test of endurance* STAMINA, staying power, fortitude, perseverance, persistence, tenacity, doggedness, grit, indefatigability, resolution, determination; *formal* pertinacity.

endure verb 1 *he endured years of pain* UNDERGO, go through, live through, experience, meet, encounter; cope with, deal with, face, suffer, tolerate, put up with, brave, bear, withstand, sustain, weather; *Brit.* thole.

2 *I cannot endure such behavior* TOLERATE, bear, put up with, suffer, take, abide; *informal* hack, stand for, stomach, swallow, hold with; *formal* brook.

3 *our love will endure forever* LAST, live, live on, go on, survive, abide, continue, persist, persevere, remain, stay. ANTONYM fade.

WORD NOTE **thole**

In the northern parts of Britain, particularly Northern Ireland, you can still hear this heartbreaking synonym for *allow* or *permit.* It comes into its own in times of trouble, for its strongest meaning is "to endure something without complaint or resistance"; to be afflicted and to suffer. When someone dies in Northern Ireland, it is not uncommon to say to the bereaved "You'll have to thole," both as a fact and a consolation. **—ZS**

enduring adjective *our enduring faith* LASTING, long-lasting, abiding, durable, continuing, persisting, eternal, perennial, permanent, unending, everlasting; constant, stable, steady, steadfast, fixed, firm, unwavering, unfaltering, unchanging; *literary* amaranthine. ANTONYM short-lived.

enemy noun *he and his brother have been enemies for years* | *the enemy would strike at dawn* OPPONENT, adversary, foe, rival, antagonist, combatant, challenger, competitor, opposer; (**the enemy**) the opposition, the competition, the other side, the opposing side. ANTONYMS ally, friend.

energetic adjective 1 *an energetic teacher* ACTIVE, lively, dynamic, zestful, spirited, animated, vital, vibrant, bouncy, bubbly, exuberant, ebullient, perky, frisky, sprightly, tireless, indefatigable, enthusiastic; *informal* peppy, feisty, full of beans, bright-eyed and bushy-tailed. See word spectrum on page 293. ANTONYMS lethargic, inactive.

2 *energetic exercises* VIGOROUS, strenuous, brisk; hard, arduous, demanding, taxing, tough, rigorous. ANTONYM gentle.

3 *an energetic advertising campaign* FORCEFUL, vigorous, high-powered, all-out, determined, bold, powerful, potent; intensive, hard-hitting, pulling no punches, aggressive, high-octane; *informal* punchy, in-your-face. ANTONYM halfhearted.

energize verb 1 *people are energized by his ideas* ENLIVEN, liven up, animate, vitalize, invigorate, perk up, excite, electrify, stimulate, stir up, fire up, rouse, motivate, move, drive, spur on, encourage, galvanize; *informal* pep up, buck up, jump-start, kick-start, give a shot in the arm to, turbocharge.

2 *floor sensors energized by standing passengers* ACTIVATE, trigger, trip, operate, actuate, switch on, turn on, start, start up, power.

energy noun *a good night's sleep will restore their energy* VITALITY, vigor, life, liveliness, animation, vivacity, spirit, spiritedness, verve, enthusiasm, zest, vibrancy, spark, sparkle, effervescence, ebullience, exuberance, buoyancy, sprightliness; strength, stamina, forcefulness, power, dynamism, drive; fire, passion, ardor, zeal; *informal* zip, zing, pep, pizzazz, punch, bounce, oomph, moxie, mojo, go, get-up-and-go, vim and vigor, feistiness.

enervate verb *the hot weather enervated her* EXHAUST, tire, fatigue, weary, wear out, devitalize, drain, sap, weaken, enfeeble, debilitate, incapacitate, prostrate; *informal* knock out, do in, shatter. ANTONYM invigorate.

enervation noun *his enervation is due to a lingering illness* FATIGUE, exhaustion, tiredness, weariness, lassitude, weakness, feebleness, debilitation, indisposition, prostration.

enfeeble verb *enfeebled from malnutrition* WEAKEN, debilitate, incapacitate, indispose, lay low; drain, sap, exhaust, tire, fatigue, devitalize. ANTONYM strengthen.

enfold verb 1 *the summit was enfolded in white cloud* ENVELOP, engulf, sheathe, swathe, swaddle, cocoon, shroud, veil, cloak, drape, cover; surround, enclose, encase, encircle; *literary* enshroud, mantle.

2 *he enfolded her in his arms* CLASP, hold, fold, wrap, squeeze, clutch, gather; embrace, hug, cuddle; *literary* embosom.

enforce verb 1 *the sheriff enforced the law* IMPOSE, apply, administer, implement, bring to bear, discharge, execute, prosecute.

2 *they cannot enforce cooperation between the parties* FORCE, compel, coerce, exact, extort; *archaic* constrain.

enforced adjective *an enforced break from work* COMPULSORY, obligatory, mandatory, involuntary, forced, im-

energetic
dynamic
vigorous
vital
zestful
spirited
sprightly
lively
animated
bouncy
bubbly
perky
frisky
go-go
sparky
zippy
peppy
bright-eyed and bushy-tailed
full of get-up-and-go
full of vim and vigor
full of beans
on the go
on the move
bustling
sporty
spry
agile
nimble
mobile
busy
involved
occupied
absorbed
unmovable
immobile
stationary
inert
lacking energy
uninterested
unenergetic
indifferent
impassive
lukewarm
lackadaisical
half-hearted
inactive
vigorless
spiritless
lifeless
sluggish
passive
limp
heavy
dull
effete
shiftless
torpid
supine
idle
apathetic
slothful
enervated
indolent
languid
languishing
languorous
listless

posed, required, requisite, stipulated, prescribed, contractual, binding, necessary, unavoidable, inescapable. ANTONYM voluntary.

enfranchise verb **1** *women were enfranchised in Manitoba in 1916* GIVE THE VOTE TO, give suffrage to, grant suffrage to.

2 *historical he enfranchised his slaves* EMANCIPATE, liberate, free, set free, release; unchain, unyoke, unfetter, unshackle.

engage verb **1** *tasks that engage children's interest* CAPTURE, catch, arrest, grab, snag, draw, attract, gain, win, hold, grip, captivate, engross, absorb, occupy. ANTONYM lose.

2 *he engaged a landscaper to do the job* EMPLOY, hire, recruit, take on, secure the services of, put on the payroll, enroll, appoint. ANTONYM dismiss.

3 *he engaged to pay them $10,000* CONTRACT, promise, agree, pledge, vow, covenant, commit oneself, bind oneself, undertake, enter into an agreement.

4 *the chance to* ***engage in*** *many social activities* PARTICIPATE IN, take part in, join in, become involved in, go in for, partake in/of, share in, play a part/role in; have a hand in, be a party to, enter into.

5 *infantry units engaged the enemy* FIGHT, do battle with, wage war on/against, attack, take on, set upon, clash with, skirmish with; encounter, meet.

6 *he engaged the gears* INTERLOCK, interconnect, mesh, intermesh, fit together, join, join together, unite, connect, couple. ANTONYM disengage.

engaged adjective **1** *he's otherwise engaged* BUSY, occupied, unavailable; *informal* tied up. See note at BUSY. ANTONYMS free, unoccupied.

2 *she's engaged to an American guy* BETROTHED, promised in marriage, pledged in marriage; attached; *informal* spoken for; *literary* affianced; *archaic* plighted, espoused. ANTONYM unattached.

engagement noun **1** *they broke off their engagement* MARRIAGE CONTRACT; *dated* betrothal; *archaic* espousal.

2 *a social engagement* APPOINTMENT, meeting, arrangement, commitment; date, assignation, rendezvous; *literary* tryst.

3 *the first engagement of the war* BATTLE, fight, clash, confrontation, encounter, conflict, skirmish; warfare, action, combat, hostilities; *informal* dogfight.

engaging adjective **1** *an engaging young person* CHARMING, appealing, attractive, pretty, delightful, lovely, pleasing, pleasant, agreeable, likable, winsome, enchanting, captivating. ANTONYM unappealing.

2 *an engaging story* INTERESTING, engrossing, gripping, involving, absorbing, fascinating. ANTONYM boring.

engender verb **1** *his works engendered considerable controversy* CAUSE, be the cause of, give rise to, bring about, occasion, lead to, result in, produce, create, generate, arouse, rouse, inspire, provoke, prompt, kindle, trigger, spark, stir up, whip up, induce, incite, instigate, foment; *literary* beget, enkindle.

2 *archaic he engendered six children* FATHER, sire, bring into the world, spawn, breed; *literary* beget.

engine noun **1** *a power-generating engine* MOTOR, machine, mechanism; jet, turbojet, turboprop, turbofan, turbine, generator.

2 *the main engine of change* CAUSE, agent, instrument, originator, initiator, generator.

3 *historical engines of war* DEVICE, contraption, apparatus, machine, appliance, mechanism, implement, instrument, tool.

engineer noun **1** *a structural engineer* designer, planner, builder. See table.

2 *the ship's engineer* OPERATOR, driver, controller.

3 *the prime engineer of the approach* ORIGINATOR, deviser, designer, architect, inventor, developer, creator; mastermind.

▸ verb *he engineered a takeover deal* BRING ABOUT, arrange, pull off, bring off, contrive, maneuver, manipulate, negotiate, organize, orchestrate, choreograph, mount, stage, mastermind, originate, manage, stage-manage, coordinate, control, superintend, direct, conduct; *informal* wangle.

BRANCHES OF ENGINEERING

aerospace	geotechnical
aeronautical	human
agricultural	industrial
architectural	knowledge
bioengineering	mechanical
biomedical	mechatronic
chemical	metallurgical
civil	mineral
computer	petroleum
electrical	nuclear
electromechanical	software
electronic	structural
environmental	systems
genetic	textile
geoenvironmental	transportation
geophysical	

engrained adjective. See INGRAINED.

engrave verb **1** *my name was engraved on the ring* CARVE, inscribe, cut (in), incise, chisel, chase, score, notch, etch, imprint, impress.

2 *the image was engraved in his memory* FIX, set, imprint, stamp, brand, impress, embed, etch.

engraving noun *an engraving of a clipper ship* ETCHING, print, impression, lithograph; plate, dry point, woodcut, linocut.

engross verb *Poppa's stories will engross them* ABSORB, engage, rivet, grip, hold, interest, involve, occupy, preoccupy; fascinate, captivate, enthrall, intrigue.

engrossed adjective *Leopold is* ***engrossed in*** *his stamp collection* ABSORBED IN, involved in, interested in, engaged in, occupied by/with, preoccupied by/with, immersed in, caught up in, riveted by, gripped by, rapt in, fascinated by/with, intent on, captivated by, enthralled by/with, intrigued by/with.

engrossing adjective *an engrossing murder mystery* ABSORBING, interesting, riveting, gripping, captivating, compelling, fascinating, intriguing, enthralling, engaging; *informal* unputdownable.

engulf verb *waves engulfed the sand castles* INUNDATE, flood, deluge, immerse, swamp, swallow up, submerge; bury, envelop, overwhelm.

enhance verb *background music will enhance the mood* INCREASE, add to, intensify, heighten, magnify, amplify, inflate, strengthen, build up, supplement, augment, boost, raise, lift, elevate, exalt; improve, enrich, complement. ANTONYM diminish.

enigma noun *how it works is an enigma to me* MYSTERY, puzzle, riddle, conundrum, paradox, problem, quandary; a closed book; *informal* poser. See note at RIDDLE.

enigmatic adjective *photos of his wife, the enigmatic artist Georgia O'Keeffe* MYSTERIOUS, inscrutable, puzzling, mystifying, baffling, perplexing, impenetrable, unfathomable, sphinxlike, Delphic, oracular; cryptic, elliptical, ambiguous, equivocal, paradoxical, obscure, oblique, secret. See note at DOUBTFUL.

enjoin verb *I enjoin you to admit your mistake* URGE, encourage, admonish, press; instruct, direct, require, order, command, tell, call on, demand, charge; *formal* adjure; *literary* bid. See note at PROHIBIT.

enjoy verb **1** *he enjoys playing the piano* LIKE, love, be fond of, be entertained by, take pleasure in, be keen on, delight in, appreciate, relish, revel in, adore, lap up, savor, luxuriate in, bask in; *informal* get a kick out of, get a thrill out of, dig. ANTONYMS dislike, hate.

2 *she had always enjoyed good health* BENEFIT FROM, have the benefit of; be blessed with, be favored with, be endowed with, be possessed of, possess, own, boast. ANTONYMS dislike, lack.

PHRASE: **enjoy oneself** *she travels just to enjoy herself* HAVE FUN, have a good time, have the time of one's life; make merry, celebrate, revel, disport; *informal* party, love life, have a ball, have a whale of a time, whoop it up, let one's hair down.

enjoyable adjective *a most enjoyable movie* ENTERTAINING, amusing, agreeable, pleasurable, diverting, engaging, delightful, to one's liking, pleasant, congenial, convivial, lovely, fine, good, great, delicious, delectable, satisfying, gratifying; marvelous, wonderful, magnificent, splendid; *informal* super, fantastic, fabulous, fab, terrific, magic, killer. See note at PLEASANT.

enjoyment noun *he has brought enjoyment to millions* PLEASURE, fun, entertainment, amusement, diversion, recreation, relaxation; delight, happiness, merriment, joy, gaiety, jollity; satisfaction, gratification, liking, relish, gusto; *humorous* delectation.

enlarge verb **1** *they enlarged the scope of their research* EXTEND, expand, grow, add to, amplify, augment, magnify, build up, supplement; widen, broaden, stretch, lengthen; elongate, deepen, thicken. ANTONYM reduce.

2 *the lymph glands had enlarged* SWELL, distend, bloat, bulge, dilate, tumefy, blow up, puff up, balloon. ANTONYM shrink.

3 *he* ***enlarged on*** *this subject* ELABORATE ON, expand on, add to, build on, flesh out, add detail to, expatiate on; develop, fill out, embellish, embroider.

enlargement noun *the enlargement of the park* EXPANSION, extension, growth, amplification, augmentation, addition, magnification, widening, broadening, lengthening; elongation, deepening, thickening; swelling, distension, dilation.

enlighten verb *please enlighten us about the latest developments* INFORM, tell, make aware, open someone's eyes, notify, illuminate, apprise, brief, update, bring up to date; disabuse, set straight; *informal* put in the picture, clue in, fill in, put wise, bring up to speed.

enlightened adjective *without a free press there cannot be an enlightened people* INFORMED, well-informed, aware, sophisticated, advanced, developed, liberal, open-minded, broad-minded, educated, knowledgeable, wise; civilized, refined, cultured, cultivated. ANTONYM benighted.

enlightenment noun *sharing her musical enlightenment*

with her children INSIGHT, understanding, awareness, wisdom, education, learning, knowledge; illumination, awakening, instruction, teaching; sophistication, advancement, development, open-mindedness, broad-mindedness; culture, refinement, cultivation, civilization.

enlist verb **1** *he **enlisted in** the scouts* JOIN UP WITH, join, enroll in, sign up for, volunteer for.

2 *he was enlisted in the army* RECRUIT, call up, enroll, sign up; conscript; draft, induct; *archaic* levy.

3 *he enlisted the help of a friend* OBTAIN, engage, secure, win, get, procure.

enliven verb **1** *a meeting enlivened by her wit and vivacity* LIVEN UP, spice up, add spice to, ginger up, vitalize, leaven; *informal* perk up, pep up. See note at QUICKEN.

2 *the visit had enlivened my mother* CHEER UP, brighten up, liven up, raise someone's spirits, uplift, gladden, buoy up, animate, vivify, vitalize, invigorate, restore, revive, refresh, rejuvenate, stimulate, rouse, boost, exhilarate, light a fire under; *informal* perk up, buck up, pep up.

en masse adverb *the angry audience walked out en masse* (ALL) TOGETHER, as a group, as one, en bloc, as a whole, wholesale; unanimously, with one voice.

enmesh verb *before he knew it, Reid was enmeshed in the gang mentality* EMBROIL, entangle, ensnare, snare, trap, entrap, ensnarl, involve, catch up, mix up, bog down, mire.

enmity noun *a world free from enmity between nations and races* HOSTILITY, animosity, antagonism, friction, antipathy, animus, acrimony, bitterness, rancor, resentment, aversion, ill feeling, bad feeling, ill will, bad blood, hatred, hate, loathing, odium; malice, spite, spitefulness, venom, malevolence. See word spectrum at AMITY. ANTONYM friendship.

ennoble verb *the original vision of the modern Olympic Games was to ennoble and strengthen sports* DIGNIFY, honor, exalt, elevate, raise, enhance, add dignity to, distinguish; magnify, glorify, aggrandize. ANTONYM demean.

ennui noun *an ennui bred of long familiarity* BOREDOM, tedium, listlessness, lethargy, lassitude, languor, weariness, enervation; malaise, dissatisfaction, melancholy, depression, world-weariness, Weltschmerz.

enormity noun **1** *the enormity of the task* IMMENSITY, hugeness; size, extent, magnitude, greatness.

2 *the enormity of his crimes* WICKEDNESS, evil, vileness, baseness, depravity; outrageousness, monstrousness, hideousness, heinousness, horror, atrocity; villainy, cruelty, inhumanity, mercilessness, brutality, savagery, viciousness.

3 *the enormities of the regime* OUTRAGE, horror, evil, atrocity, barbarity, abomination, monstrosity, obscenity, iniquity; crime, sin, violation, wrong, offense, disgrace, injustice, abuse.

USAGE NOTE **enormity**

This word is imprecisely used to mean 'great size,' as in *it is difficult to comprehend the enormity of the continent,* but the original and preferred meaning is 'extreme wickedness,' as in *the enormity of the mass murders.* To indicate enormous size, the words *enormousness, immensity, vastness, hugeness,* etc., are preferable.

enormous adjective *enormous waves battered the shore* HUGE, vast, immense, gigantic, very big, great, giant, massive, colossal, mammoth, tremendous, mighty, monumental, epic, prodigious, mountainous, king-size(d), economy-size(d), titanic, towering, elephantine, gargantuan, Brobdingnagian; *informal* mega, monster, whopping, humongous, jumbo, astronomical, ginormous. ANTONYM tiny.

enormously adverb **1** *an enormously important factor* VERY, extremely, really, exceedingly, exceptionally, tremendously, immensely, hugely; singularly, particularly, eminently; *informal* terrifically, awfully, seriously, desperately, ultra, damn, damned, darn, darned; real, mighty. ANTONYMS slightly, moderately.

2 *prices vary enormously* CONSIDERABLY, greatly, widely, very much, a great deal, a lot. ANTONYMS slightly, not at all.

enough adjective *they had enough food* SUFFICIENT, adequate, ample, the necessary; *informal* plenty of. ANTONYM insufficient.

▸ pronoun *there's enough for everyone* SUFFICIENT, plenty, a sufficient amount, an adequate amount, as much as necessary; a sufficiency, an ample supply; one's fill.

en passant adverb *the report mentions, en passant, certain features of the Danish system* IN PASSING, incidentally, by the way, parenthetically, while on the subject, apropos.

enrage verb *the scheme is bound to enrage union members* ANGER, infuriate, incense, madden, inflame; antagonize, provoke, exasperate; *informal* drive mad/crazy, drive up the wall, make someone see red, make someone's blood boil, make someone's hackles rise, get someone's back up, get someone's dander up; *informal* tick off, piss off, burn up. ANTONYM placate.

enraged adjective *an enraged mob* FURIOUS, infuriated, very angry, irate, incensed, raging, incandescent, fuming, ranting, raving, seething, beside oneself; *informal* mad, hopping mad, wild, livid, boiling, apoplectic, hot under the collar, on the warpath, foaming at the mouth, steamed up, fit to be tied, pissed off, PO'd; *literary* wrathful. ANTONYM calm.

enrapture verb *enraptured by the music* DELIGHT, enchant, captivate, charm, enthrall, entrance, bewitch, beguile, transport, thrill, excite, exhilarate, intoxicate, take someone's breath away; *informal* bowl over, blow someone's mind; *literary* ravish.

enrich verb *enrich the soil with nitrogen* ENHANCE, improve, better, add to, augment; supplement, complement; boost, elevate, raise, lift, refine. ANTONYM spoil.

enroll verb **1** *they both **enrolled for** the course* REGISTER FOR, sign up/on for, put one's name down for, apply for, volunteer for; enter, join.

2 *280 new members were enrolled* ACCEPT, admit, take on, register, sign on/up, recruit, engage; empanel.

en route adverb *he was en route from Delaware to Illinois* ON THE WAY, in transit, during the journey, along/on the road, on the move; coming, going, proceeding, traveling.

ensconce verb *Agnes ensconced herself in their bedroom* SETTLE, install, plant, position, seat, sit; establish, nestle; hide away, tuck away; *informal* park, plonk.

ensemble noun **1** *a Bulgarian folk ensemble* GROUP, band; company, troupe, cast, chorus, corps; *informal* combo.

2 *the buildings present a charming provincial ensemble*

WHOLE, entity, unit, body, set, combination, composite, package; sum, total, totality, entirety, aggregate.

3 *a pink and black ensemble* OUTFIT, costume, suit; separates, coordinates; *informal* getup.

enshrine verb *the following rights should be enshrined in the treaty* PRESERVE, entrench, set down, lay down, set in stone, embody, incorporate, contain, include, treasure, immortalize, cherish.

enshroud verb *literary gray clouds enshrouded the city* ENVELOP, veil, shroud, swathe, cloak, cloud, enfold, surround, bury; cover, conceal, obscure, blot out, hide, mask; *literary* mantle.

ensign noun *the ship flew a Greek ensign* FLAG, standard, color(s), banner, pennant, pennon, streamer, banderole.

enslave verb *there were few natives left to enslave* SUBJUGATE, suppress, tyrannize, oppress, dominate, exploit, persecute; *rare* enthrall, bind, yoke; disenfranchise. ANTONYMS liberate, emancipate.

enslavement noun *the enslavement of the captured soldiers* SLAVERY, servitude, bondage, forced labor; exploitation, oppression, bonds, chains, fetters, shackles, yoke; *historical* thralldom. ANTONYM liberation.

ensnare verb *the larvae construct pits to ensnare their prey* CAPTURE, catch, trap, entrap, snare, net; entangle, embroil, enmesh.

ensue verb *Evelyn showed up unexpectedly and a fierce argument ensued* RESULT, follow, develop, proceed, succeed, emerge, stem, arise, derive, issue; occur, happen, take place, come next/after, transpire, supervene; *formal* eventuate; *literary* come to pass, befall.

ensure verb **1** *ensure that the surface is completely clean* MAKE SURE, make certain, see to it; check, confirm, establish, verify.

2 *legislation to ensure equal opportunities for all* SECURE, guarantee, assure, certify, safeguard, set the seal on, clinch, entrench.

entail verb *first, we'll need to know exactly what the job entails* INVOLVE, necessitate, require, need, demand, call for; mean, imply; cause, produce, result in, lead to, give rise to, occasion.

entangle verb **1** *their parachutes became entangled* TWIST, intertwine, entwine, tangle, ravel, snarl, knot, coil, mat.

2 *the fish are easily entangled in fine nets* CATCH, capture, trap, snare, ensnare, entrap, enmesh.

3 *he was entangled in a lawsuit* INVOLVE, implicate, embroil, mix up, catch up, bog down, mire.

entanglement noun **1** *their entanglement in the war* INVOLVEMENT, embroilment.

2 *romantic entanglements* AFFAIR, relationship, love affair, romance, amour, fling, dalliance, liaison, involvement, intrigue; complication.

entente noun *they didn't want to jeopardize the entente with the Netherlands* UNDERSTANDING, agreement, arrangement, entente cordiale, settlement, deal; alliance, treaty, pact, accord, convention, concordat.

enter verb **1** *police entered the house from the side* GO IN/INTO, come in/into, get in/into, set foot in, cross the threshold of, gain access to, infiltrate, access. ANTONYM leave.

2 *a bullet entered his chest* PENETRATE, pierce, puncture, perforate; *literary* transpierce. ANTONYM leave.

3 *he entered politics in 1979* GET INVOLVED IN, join, throw oneself into, engage in, embark on, take up; participate in, take part in, play a part/role in, contribute to. ANTONYM leave.

4 *the planning entered a new phase* REACH, move into, get to, begin, start, commence. ANTONYM finish.

5 *they entered the military at eighteen* JOIN, become a member of, enroll in/for, enlist in, volunteer for, sign up for; take up. ANTONYM leave.

6 *she entered a cooking competition* SIGN ON/UP FOR, put one's name down for, register for, enroll in/for, go in for; compete in, take part in, participate in.

7 *the cashier entered the details in a ledger* RECORD, write, set down, put down, take down, note, jot down; put on record, minute, register, log. ANTONYM erase.

8 *please enter your password* KEY (IN), type (in).

9 *Law he entered a plea of guilty* SUBMIT, register, lodge, record, file, put forward, present. ANTONYM withdraw.

enterprise noun **1** *a joint enterprise* UNDERTAKING, endeavor, venture, exercise, activity, operation, task, business, proceeding; project, scheme, plan, program, campaign.

2 *we want candidates with enterprise* INITIATIVE, resourcefulness, imagination, entrepreneurialism, ingenuity, inventiveness, originality, creativity; quick-wittedness, cleverness; enthusiasm, dynamism, drive, ambition, energy; boldness, daring, courage, leadership; *informal* gumption, get-up-and-go, oomph.

3 *a profit-making enterprise* BUSINESS, company, firm, venture, organization, operation, concern, corporation, establishment, partnership; *informal* outfit, setup.

enterprising adjective *an enterprising farmer is now charging visitors* RESOURCEFUL, entrepreneurial, imaginative, ingenious, inventive, creative; quick-witted, clever, bright, sharp, sharp-witted; enthusiastic, dynamic, proactive, ambitious, energetic; bold, daring, courageous, adventurous; *informal* go-ahead, take-charge, self-motivated. ANTONYM unimaginative.

entertain verb **1** *she wrote plays to entertain them* AMUSE, divert, delight, please, charm, cheer, interest; *informal* bring the house down; engage, occupy, absorb, engross. ANTONYM bore.

2 *he entertains foreign visitors* RECEIVE, host, play host/hostess to, invite (around/round/over), throw a party for; wine and dine, feast, cater for, feed, treat, welcome, féte.

3 *we don't entertain much* RECEIVE GUESTS, have people around/round/over, have company, throw/have a party.

4 *I would never entertain such an idea* CONSIDER, give consideration to, contemplate, think about, give thought to; countenance, tolerate, support; *formal* brook. ANTONYM reject.

entertainer noun *a family of entertainers* PERFORMER, artiste, artist.

entertaining adjective *Ben is an entertaining companion* DELIGHTFUL, enjoyable, diverting, amusing, pleasing, agreeable, appealing, engaging, interesting, fascinating, absorbing, compelling; humorous, funny, comical; *informal* fun.

entertainment noun **1** *he reads for entertainment* AMUSEMENT, pleasure, leisure, recreation, relaxation, fun, enjoyment, interest, diversion.

2 *an entertainment for the emperor* SHOW, performance, presentation, production, extravaganza, spectacle, pageant.

enthrall verb *the exhibit of Calder's early mobiles enthralled us* CAPTIVATE, charm, enchant, bewitch, fascinate, beguile, entrance, delight; win, ensnare, absorb, engross, rivet, grip, transfix, hypnotize, mesmerize, spellbind. ANTONYM bore.

enthralling adjective *her travel journals are enthralling* FASCINATING, entrancing, enchanting, bewitching, captivating, charming, beguiling, delightful; absorbing, engrossing, compelling, riveting, gripping, exciting, spellbinding; *informal* unputdownable.

enthuse verb **1** *I* ***enthused about*** *the idea* RAVE ABOUT, be enthusiastic about, gush over, wax lyrical about, be effusive about, get all worked up about, rhapsodize about; praise to the skies, extol; *informal* go wild/mad/crazy about/over/for, ballyhoo.

2 *he enthuses people* MOTIVATE, inspire, stimulate, encourage, spur (on), galvanize, rouse, excite, stir (up), fire; *rare* inspirit.

USAGE NOTE **enthuse**

The verb **enthuse** is a back-formation from the noun **enthusiasm** and, like many verbs formed from nouns in this way, it is regarded by traditionalists as unacceptable. **Enthuse** has been in the language for more than 150 years, but, before using the word in formal writing, be aware that readers familiar with its Greek meaning may find casual usage misguided or irritating. **Enthusiasm** derives from a word originally meaning 'to become inspired or possessed by a god' (*en* 'in' + *theos* 'god'). From the traditionalist point of view, *inspired* or *excited* is preferable to *enthused*.

enthusiasm noun **1** *she worked with enthusiasm* EAGERNESS, keenness, ardor, fervor, passion, zeal, zest, gusto, energy, verve, vigor, vehemence, fire, spirit, avidity; wholeheartedness, commitment, willingness, devotion, earnestness; *informal* get-up-and-go. ANTONYMS apathy, half-heartedness.

2 *he responded to the proposal with enthusiasm* INTEREST, admiration, approval, support, encouragement. ANTONYMS apathy, disinterest.

3 *they put their enthusiasms to good use* INTEREST, passion, obsession, mania; inclination, preference, penchant, predilection, fancy; pastime, hobby, recreation, pursuit.

enthusiast noun *a railroad enthusiast* FAN, devotee, aficionado, lover, admirer, follower; expert, connoisseur, authority, pundit; *informal* buff, bum, freak, fanatic, nut, fiend, addict, maniac; geek, eager beaver. See note at ZEALOT.

enthusiastic adjective *an enthusiastic supporter of Latin American baseball* EAGER, keen, avid, ardent, fervent, passionate, ebullient, zealous, vehement; excited, wholehearted, committed, devoted, fanatical, earnest; *informal* hog-wild, can-do, gung-ho, rah-rah, psyched. See note at EAGER.

entice verb *he tried to entice us by promising a screen test at his studio* TEMPT, lure, allure, attract, appeal to; invite, persuade, convince, beguile, coax, woo, court; seduce, lead on; *informal* sweet-talk. See note at TEMPT.

enticement noun *on my budget, I have to resist the enticement of colorful packaging and clever advertising* LURE, temptation, allure, attraction, appeal, draw, pull, bait; charm, seduction, fascination; *informal* come-on.

enticing adjective *the Thanksgiving table was an enticing sight* TEMPTING, alluring, attractive, appealing, inviting, seductive, beguiling, charming; magnetic, irresistible.

entire adjective **1** *I devoted my entire life to him* WHOLE, complete, total, full; undivided. ANTONYM partial.

2 *only one of the vases is entire* INTACT, unbroken, undamaged, unimpaired, unscathed, unspoiled, perfect, in one piece. ANTONYMS partial, broken.

3 *they are in entire agreement* ABSOLUTE, total, utter, out-and-out, thorough, wholehearted; unqualified, unreserved, outright. ANTONYMS partial, qualified.

entirely adverb **1** *that's entirely out of the question* ABSOLUTELY, completely, totally, wholly, utterly, quite; altogether, in every respect, thoroughly, downright, one hundred percent.

2 *a gift entirely for charitable purposes* SOLELY, only, exclusively, purely, merely, just, alone.

entirety noun *I'll give you ten bucks for the entirety* WHOLE, total, aggregate, totality, sum total. ANTONYM part.

PHRASE: **in its entirety** *we heard his miserable life story, in its entirety* COMPLETELY, entirely, totally, fully, wholly; in every respect, in every way, one hundred percent, all the way, every inch, to the hilt, to the core.

entitle verb **1** *this pass entitles you to visit the museum* QUALIFY, make eligible, authorize, allow, permit; enable, empower.

2 *a chapter entitled "Comedy and Tragedy"* TITLE, name, call, label, head, designate, dub; *formal* denominate.

entitlement noun *their entitlement to benefits* RIGHT, prerogative, claim; permission, dispensation, privilege.

entity noun **1** *a single entity* BEING, creature, individual, organism, life form; person; body, object, article, thing.

2 *the distinction between entity and nonentity* EXISTENCE, being; life, living, animation; substance, essence, reality, actuality.

entomb verb *mummified bodies entombed in the pyramids* INTER, lay to rest, bury; *informal* plant; *literary* inhume, sepulcher.

entourage noun *Elvis's entourage* RETINUE, escort, cortège, train, suite; court, staff, bodyguard(s); attendants, companions, retainers; *informal* posse.

entrails plural noun *the entrails are removed by the butcher* INTESTINES, bowels, guts, viscera, internal organs, vital organs; offal; *informal* insides, innards.

entrance[1] noun **1** *the main entrance* ENTRY, way in, entryway, entranceway, access, approach; door, portal, gate; opening, mouth; entrance hall, foyer, lobby, porch. ANTONYM exit.

2 *the entrance of Mrs. Salter* APPEARANCE, arrival, entry, ingress, coming. ANTONYMS exit, departure.

3 *he was refused entrance* ADMISSION, admittance, entry, right of entry, access, ingress.

entrance[2] verb **1** *I was entranced by her beauty* ENCHANT, bewitch, beguile, captivate, mesmerize, hypnotize, spellbind; enthrall, engross, absorb, fascinate; stun, stupefy, overpower, electrify; charm, dazzle, delight; *informal* bowl over, knock out.

2 *Orpheus entranced the wild beasts* CAST A SPELL ON, bewitch, hex, spellbind, hypnotize, mesmerize.

entrance fee noun *the club charges an entrance fee* ADMISSION, cover charge, cover, entry charge, ticket.

entrant noun 1 *university entrants* NEW MEMBER, new arrival, beginner, newcomer, freshman, recruit; novice, neophyte, tenderfoot; *informal* rookie, newbie, greenhorn.

2 *a prize will be awarded to the best entrant* COMPETITOR, contestant, contender, participant; candidate, applicant.

entrap verb 1 *fishing lines can entrap wildlife* TRAP, snare, snag, ensnare, entangle, enmesh; catch, capture.

2 *he was entrapped by an undercover policeman* ENTICE, lure, inveigle; bait, decoy, trap; lead on, trick, deceive, dupe, hoodwink, sting; *informal* set up, frame.

entreat verb *my lord, I entreat you to believe me* IMPLORE, beg, plead with, pray, ask, request; bid, enjoin, appeal to, call on, petition, solicit, importune; *literary* beseech. See note at BEG.

entreaty noun *he ignored Gert's entreaties* PLEA, appeal, request, petition; suit, application, claim; solicitation, supplication; prayer.

entrée noun 1 *there are a dozen entrées on the menu* MAIN COURSE, main dish.

2 *an excellent entrée into the profession* MEANS OF ENTRY, entry, entrance, ingress; route, path, avenue, way, key, passport; *informal* in.

entrench verb *post-Communist countries strive to entrench their new press freedoms* ESTABLISH, settle, lodge, set, root, install, plant, embed, seat; enshrine; *informal* dig (oneself) in.

entrenched adjective *they tend to cling to entrenched attitudes* INGRAINED, established, confirmed, fixed, firm, deep-seated, deep-rooted; unshakable, indelible, ineradicable, inexorable.

entrepreneur noun *a newsletter for young entrepreneurs* BUSINESSMAN/BUSINESSWOMAN, enterpriser, speculator, tycoon, magnate, mogul; dealer, trader; promoter, impresario; *informal* wheeler-dealer, whiz kid, mover and shaker, go-getter, high flyer, hustler, idea man/person.

entropy noun *if a new, conscientious government is not poised to step in, liberation may engender only entropy* DETERIORATION, degeneration, crumbling, decline, degradation, decomposition, breaking down, collapse; disorder, chaos.

entrust verb 1 *he was entrusted with the task* CHARGE, invest, endow; burden, encumber, saddle.

2 *the powers* ***entrusted to*** *the treasury department* ASSIGN TO, confer on, bestow on, vest in, consign to; delegate to, depute to, devolve to; give to, grant to, vouchsafe to.

3 *she entrusted them to the hospital* HAND OVER, give custody of, turn over, commit, consign, deliver; *formal* commend.

entry noun 1 *my moment of entry* APPEARANCE, arrival, entrance, ingress, coming. ANTONYMS departure, exit.

2 *the entry to the building.* See ENTRANCE[1] sense 1.

3 *he was refused entry* ADMISSION, admittance, entrance, access, ingress.

4 *entries in the cash book* ITEM, record, note, listing; memo, memorandum; account.

5 *data entry* RECORDING, archiving, logging, documentation, capture, keying.

6 *we must pick a winner from the entries* CONTESTANT, competitor, contender, entrant, participant; candidate, applicant; submission, entry form, application.

entry-level adjective *entry-level management* INTRODUCTORY, elementary, basic, first, starter, junior.

entwine verb *her hair was entwined with ropes of pearls* WIND AROUND, twist around, coil around; weave, intertwine, interlace, interweave; entangle, tangle; twine, braid, plait, wreathe, knit.

enumerate verb 1 *he enumerated four objectives* LIST, itemize, set out, give; cite, name, specify, identify, spell out, detail, particularize.

2 *they enumerated voters* CALCULATE, compute, count, add up, tally, total, number, quantify; reckon, work out, tot up.

enunciate verb 1 *she enunciated each word slowly* PRONOUNCE, articulate; say, speak, utter, voice, vocalize, sound.

2 *a document enunciating the policy* EXPRESS, state, put into words, declare, profess, set forth, assert, affirm; put forward, air, proclaim.

envelop verb *enveloped in a blanket, safe in his mother's arms* SURROUND, cover, enfold, engulf, encircle, encompass, cocoon, sheathe, swathe, enclose; cloak, screen, shield, veil, shroud. See note at CIRCUMSCRIBE.

envelope noun *she tore open the envelope* WRAPPER, wrapping, sleeve, cover, covering, casing, package.

enviable adjective *of the three candidates, St. Clair has the enviable advantage of experience* DESIRABLE, desired, favored, sought-after, admirable, covetable, attractive; fortunate, lucky; *informal* to die for.

envious adjective *she felt envious of her friend's beauty* JEALOUS, covetous, desirous; grudging, begrudging, resentful; bitter. See note at JEALOUS.

environment noun 1 *birds from many environments* HABITAT, territory, domain; surroundings, environs, conditions.

2 *the hospital environment* SITUATION, SETTING, milieu, background, backdrop, scene, location; context, framework; sphere, world, realm; ambience, atmosphere.

3 (**the environment**) *the impact of pesticides on the environment* THE NATURAL WORLD, nature, the earth, the planet, the ecosystem, the biosphere, Mother Nature; wildlife, flora and fauna, the countryside.

environmentalist noun *environmentalists and industrialists must unite to save the world's forests* CONSERVATIONIST, preservationist, ecologist, nature lover; *informal* tree hugger, green, greenie.

environs plural noun *the environs of Milwaukee* SURROUNDINGS, surrounding area, vicinity, purlieu; locality, neighborhood, district, region; precincts.

envisage verb *can you envisage the factories of the future?* IMAGINE, contemplate, visualize, envision, picture; conceive of, think of; foresee.

envision verb 1 *it was envisioned that the hospital would* *open soon* PLAN, envisage, predict, forecast, foresee, anticipate, expect; intend, mean.

2 *he envisioned a big shiny condominium* VISUALIZE, imagine, envisage, picture; conceive of, dream of, think of, see.

envoy noun *a UN envoy has visited the home of Myanmar's opposition leader* AMBASSADOR, emissary, diplomat, consul, attaché, chargé d'affaires, plenipotentiary; nuncio; representative, delegate, proxy, surrogate, liaison, spokesperson; agent, intermediary, mediator; *informal* go-between; *historical* legate.

envy noun 1 *a pang of envy* JEALOUSY, covetousness; resentment, bitterness, discontent; the green-eyed monster.

2 *the firm is the envy of Europe* FINEST, best, pride, top, cream, jewel, flower, leading light, the crème de la crème.

▸ verb 1 *I admired and envied her* BE ENVIOUS OF, be jealous of; begrudge, be resentful of.

2 *we envied her lifestyle* COVET, desire, aspire to, wish for, want, long for, yearn for, hanker after, crave.

ephemeral adjective *last year's ephemeral fashions* TRANSITORY, transient, fleeting, passing, short-lived, momentary, brief, short; temporary, impermanent, short-term; fly-by-night. See note at TEMPORARY. ANTONYM permanent.

epic noun 1 *the epics of Homer* HEROIC POEM; story, saga, legend, romance, chronicle, myth, fable, tale.

2 *a big Hollywood epic* LONG FILM; *informal* blockbuster.

▸ adjective 1 *a traditional epic poem* HEROIC, long, grand, monumental, Homeric, Miltonian.

2 *their epic journey* AMBITIOUS, heroic, grand, great, Herculean; very long, monumental; adventurous.

epicure noun *this Caribbean island will help you meet your own inner epicure* GOURMET, gastronome, gourmand, connoisseur; *informal* foodie.

epicurean noun *a generous, life-loving epicurean* HEDONIST, sensualist, pleasure-seeker, sybarite, voluptuary, bon vivant, bon viveur; epicure, gourmet, gastronome, connoisseur, gourmand.

▸ adjective *epicurean excesses* HEDONISTIC, sensualist, pleasure-seeking, self-indulgent, good-time, sybaritic, voluptuary, lotus-eating; decadent, unrestrained, extravagant, intemperate, immoderate; gluttonous, gourmandizing. See note at SENSUOUS.

epidemic noun 1 *an epidemic of typhoid* OUTBREAK, plague, pandemic, epizootic.

2 *a joyriding epidemic* SPATE, rash, wave, eruption, outbreak, craze; flood, torrent; upsurge, upturn, increase, growth, rise.

▸ adjective *the craze is now epidemic* RIFE, rampant, widespread, wide-ranging, extensive, pervasive; global, universal, ubiquitous; endemic, pandemic, epizootic.

THE RIGHT WORD

A disease that quickly and severely affects a large number of people and then subsides is an **epidemic**: *throughout the Middle Ages, successive epidemics of the plague killed millions.* **Epidemic** is also used as an adjective: *she studied the causes of epidemic cholera.* A disease that is continually present in an area and affects a relatively small number of people is **endemic**: *malaria is endemic in* (or *to*) *hot, moist climates.* A **pandemic** is a widespread epidemic that may affect entire continents or even the world: *the pandemic of 1918 ushered in a period of frequent epidemics of gradually diminishing severity.* Thus, from an epidemiologist's point of view, the Black Death in Europe and AIDS in sub-Saharan Africa are pandemics rather than epidemics.

epigram noun *a collection of humorous epigrams from old gravestones* WITTICISM, quip, jest, pun, bon mot; saying, maxim, adage, aphorism, apophthegm, epigraph; *informal* one-liner, wisecrack, (old) chestnut. See note at SAYING.

epigrammatic adjective *her epigrammatic verses* CONCISE, succinct, pithy, aphoristic; incisive, short and sweet; witty, clever, quick-witted, piquant, sharp, gnomic, laconic; *informal* snappy. ANTONYM expansive.

epilogue noun *the book is summarized in the epilogue* AFTERWORD, postscript, PS, coda, codicil, appendix, tailpiece, supplement, addendum, postlude, rider, back matter; conclusion. ANTONYM prologue.

episode noun 1 *the best episode of his career* INCIDENT, event, occurrence, happening; occasion, experience, adventure, exploit; matter, affair, thing; interlude, chapter.

2 *the final episode of the series* INSTALLMENT, chapter, passage; part, portion, section, component; program, show.

3 *an episode of illness* PERIOD, spell, bout, attack, phase; *informal* patch.

episodic adjective 1 *episodic wheezing* INTERMITTENT, sporadic, periodic, fitful, irregular, spasmodic, occasional. ANTONYM continuous.

2 *an episodic account of the war* IN EPISODES, in installments, in sections, in parts.

epistle noun *formal* *the historical backdrop of St. Paul's epistles* LETTER, missive, communication, dispatch, note, line; news, correspondence.

epitaph noun *the epitaphs on their tombstones* ELEGY, commemoration, obituary; inscription, legend.

epithet noun *Marion is better known by his epithet, the 'Swamp Fox'* SOBRIQUET, nickname, byname, title, name, label, tag; description, designation; *informal* moniker, handle; *formal* appellation, denomination.

epitome noun *Cary Grant will always be the epitome of the debonair man* PERSONIFICATION, embodiment, incarnation, paragon; essence, quintessence, archetype, paradigm; exemplar, model, soul, example; height.

epitomize verb *a nation that has come to epitomize socialism* EMBODY, encapsulate, typify, exemplify, represent, manifest, symbolize, illustrate, sum up; personify; *formal* reify.

epoch noun *England's Tudor epoch* ERA, age, period, time, span, stage; eon.

equable adjective 1 *an equable man* EVEN-TEMPERED, calm, composed, collected, self-possessed, relaxed, easygoing; nonchalant, insouciant, mellow, mild, tranquil, placid, stable, levelheaded; imperturbable, unexcitable, untroubled, well-balanced, serene; *informal* unflappable, together, laid-back. ANTONYMS temperamental, excitable.

2 *an equable climate* STABLE, constant, uniform, unvarying, consistent, unchanging, changeless; moderate, temperate. ANTONYMS uneven, extreme.

equal adjective 1 *lines of equal length* IDENTICAL, uniform, alike, like, the same, equivalent; matching, even, comparable, similar, corresponding. See note at SAME. ANTONYM different.

2 *fares* ***equal to*** *a month's wages* EQUIVALENT TO, identical to, amounting to; proportionate to; commensurate with, on a par with. ANTONYMS more than, less than.

3 *equal treatment before the law* UNBIASED, impartial, nonpartisan, fair, just, equitable; unprejudiced, nondiscriminatory, egalitarian; neutral, objective, disinterested. ANTONYM discriminatory.

4 *an equal contest* EVENLY MATCHED, even, balanced, level; on a par, on an equal footing; *informal* fifty-fifty, neck and neck. ANTONYM uneven.

▸ noun *they did not treat him as their equal* EQUIVALENT, peer, fellow, coequal, like; counterpart, match, parallel.

▸ verb **1** *two plus two equals four* BE EQUAL TO, be equivalent to, be the same as; come to, amount to, make, total, add up to.

2 *he equaled the world record* MATCH, reach, parallel, be level with, measure up to.

3 *the fable equals that of any other poet* BE AS GOOD AS, be a match for, measure up to, equate with; be in the same league as, rival, compete with.

PHRASE: **equal to** *trust me, I am equal to the task* CAPABLE OF, fit for, up to, good enough for, strong enough for; suitable for, suited to, appropriate for.

equality noun **1** *we promote equality for women* FAIRNESS, equal rights, equal opportunities, equity, egalitarianism; impartiality, evenhandedness; justice.

2 *equality between supply and demand* PARITY, similarity, comparability, correspondence; likeness, resemblance; uniformity, evenness, balance, equilibrium, consistency, homogeneity, agreement, congruence, symmetry.

equalize verb *attempts to equalize their earnings* MAKE EQUAL, make even, even out/up, level, regularize, standardize, balance, square, match; bring into line.

equanimity noun *she confronted the daily crises with equanimity* COMPOSURE, calm, level-headedness, self-possession, coolheadedness, presence of mind; serenity, tranquility, phlegm, imperturbability, equilibrium; poise, assurance, self-confidence, aplomb, sangfroid, nerve; *informal* cool. ANTONYM anxiety.

equate verb **1** *he equates criticism with treachery* IDENTIFY, compare, liken, associate, connect, link, relate, class, bracket.

2 *the rent equates to $24 per square foot* CORRESPOND, be equivalent, amount; equal.

3 *moves to equate supply and demand* EQUALIZE, balance, even out/up, level, square, tally, match; make equal, make even, make equivalent.

equation noun **1** *a quadratic equation* MATHEMATICAL PROBLEM, sum, calculation, question.

2 *the equation of success with riches* IDENTIFICATION, association, connection, matching; equivalence, correspondence, agreement, comparison.

3 *other factors came into the equation* SITUATION, problem, case, question; quandary, predicament.

equatorial adjective *equatorial regions* TROPICAL, hot, humid, sultry. ANTONYM polar.

equestrian adjective *an equestrian statue* ON HORSEBACK, mounted, riding.

▸ noun *tracks for equestrians* RIDER, horseback rider, horseman, horsewoman, jockey.

equilibrium noun **1** *the equilibrium of the economy* BALANCE, symmetry, equipoise, parity, equality; stability. ANTONYM imbalance.

2 *his equilibrium was never shaken* COMPOSURE, calm, equanimity, sangfroid; level-headedness, coolheadedness, imperturbability, poise, presence of mind; self-possession, self-command; impassivity, placidity, tranquility, serenity; *informal* cool. ANTONYMS nervousness, agitation.

equip verb **1** *the boat was equipped with a flare gun* PROVIDE, furnish, supply, issue, stock, provision, arm, endow, rig.

2 *the course will equip them for the workplace* PREPARE, qualify, suit, train, ready.

equipment noun *taking inventory of our equipment* APPARATUS, paraphernalia, articles, appliances, impedimenta; tools, utensils, implements, instruments, hardware, gadgets, gadgetry; stuff, things; kit, tackle, rig; resources, supplies; trappings, appurtenances, accoutrements; *informal* gear; *dated* equipage; *Military* matériel, baggage.

equitable adjective *a plan to distribute the burden of taxes in an equitable way* FAIR, just, impartial, evenhanded, unbiased, unprejudiced, egalitarian; disinterested, objective, neutral, nonpartisan, open-minded; *informal* fair and square. ANTONYM unfair.

equity noun **1** *the equity of Finnish society* FAIRNESS, justness, impartiality, egalitarianism; objectivity, balance, open-mindedness.

2 *he owns 25% of the equity in the property* VALUE, worth; ownership, rights, proprietorship.

equivalence noun *equivalence of birth and death rates in human populations is rare* EQUALITY, sameness, interchangeability, comparability, correspondence; uniformity, similarity, likeness, nearness.

equivalent adjective *a degree or equivalent qualification* EQUAL, identical; similar, comparable, corresponding, analogous, homologous, commensurate, parallel, synonymous; approximate, near. See note at SAME.

▸ noun *the Australian press is touting her as the equivalent of Dolly Parton* COUNTERPART, parallel, alternative, match, analog, twin, clone, opposite number; equal, peer; version; *rare* coequal.

equivocal adjective *an equivocal statement* AMBIGUOUS, indefinite, noncommittal, vague, imprecise, inexact, inexplicit, hazy; unclear, cryptic, enigmatic, pettifogging; ambivalent, uncertain, unsure, indecisive. See note at DOUBTFUL. ANTONYM definite.

equivocate verb *you have equivocated too often in the past* PREVARICATE, be evasive, be noncommittal, be vague, be ambiguous, dodge the question, beat around the bush, hedge; vacillate, shilly-shally, waver; temporize, hesitate, stall, hem and haw; *informal* pussyfoot around, sit on the fence; *rare* tergiversate. See note at LIE[1].

era noun *the Roosevelt era* EPOCH, age, period, phase, time, span, eon; generation.

eradicate verb *a total of three monthly applications will eradicate the termites* ELIMINATE, get rid of, remove, obliterate; exterminate, destroy, annihilate, kill, wipe out; abolish, stamp out, extinguish, quash; erase, efface, excise, expunge, expel; *informal* zap, nuke, wave goodbye to. See note at DESTROY.

erase verb 1 *they erased his name from all lists* DELETE, rub out, wipe off, blot out, cancel; efface, expunge, excise, remove, obliterate, eliminate, cut.

2 *the old differences in style were erased* DESTROY, wipe out, obliterate, eradicate, abolish, stamp out, quash.

erect adjective 1 *she held her body erect* UPRIGHT, straight, vertical, perpendicular; standing. ANTONYMS bent, flaccid.

2 *an erect penis* ENGORGED, enlarged, swollen, tumescent; hard, stiff, rigid. ANTONYM limp.

3 *the dog's fur was erect* BRISTLING, standing on end, upright. ANTONYM flat.

▸ verb *erecting a new barn* BUILD, construct, put up; assemble, put together, fabricate. ANTONYMS demolish, dismantle.

erection noun 1 *the erection of a house* CONSTRUCTION, building, assembly, fabrication, elevation.

2 *a bleak concrete erection* BUILDING, structure, edifice, construction, pile.

3 *a normal erection* ERECT PENIS, phallus; tumescence; *informal, vulgar* boner, hard-on.

ergo adverb *I'm a writer, ergo I write* THEREFORE, consequently, so, as a result, hence, thus, accordingly, for that reason, that being the case, on that account; *formal* whence; *archaic* wherefore.

ergonomic adjective *an ergonomic keyboard* WELL-DESIGNED, usable, user-friendly; comfortable, safe.

erode verb *waves and weather are seriously eroding the north side of the island* WEAR AWAY/DOWN, abrade, grind down, crumble; weather; eat away at, dissolve, corrode, rot, decay; undermine, weaken, deteriorate, destroy.

erosion noun *erosion has dramatically affected the topography here over the past two hundred years* WEARING AWAY, abrasion, attrition; weathering; dissolution, corrosion, decay; deterioration, disintegration, destruction.

erotic adjective *erotic literature* SEXY, sexually arousing, sexually stimulating, titillating, suggestive; pornographic, sexually explicit, lewd, smutty, hard-core, soft-core, dirty, racy, risqué, ribald, naughty; sexual, sensual, amatory; seductive, alluring, tantalizing; *informal* blue, X-rated, steamy, raunchy, bootylicious; *euphemistic* adult.

err verb *the judge had erred in not allowing new evidence* MAKE A MISTAKE, be wrong, be in error, be mistaken, blunder, fumble, be incorrect, miscalculate, get it wrong; sin, lapse; *informal* slip up, screw up, foul up, goof, make a boo-boo, drop the ball, bark up the wrong tree.

errand noun *one of my errands is to stop at the pharmacy for batteries* TASK, job, chore, assignment; collection, delivery; mission, undertaking.

errant adjective 1 *the errant officers were suspended* OFFENDING, guilty, culpable, misbehaving, delinquent, lawbreaking; troublesome, unruly, wayward, disobedient. ANTONYMS innocent, law-abiding.

2 *archaic a knight errant* TRAVELING, wandering, itinerant, roaming, roving, voyaging. ANTONYM sedentary.

erratic adjective *the test results were too erratic for useful analysis* UNPREDICTABLE, inconsistent, changeable, variable, inconstant, irregular, fitful, unstable, turbulent, unsettled, changing, varying, fluctuating, mutable; unreliable, undependable, volatile, spasmodic, mercurial, capricious, fickle, temperamental, moody. ANTONYM consistent.

erring adjective *the jury agreed that the erring party should pay full restitution* OFFENDING, guilty, culpable, misbehaving, errant, delinquent, lawbreaking, aberrant, deviant.

erroneous adjective *an erroneous accusation* WRONG, incorrect, mistaken, in error, inaccurate, untrue, false, fallacious; unsound, specious, faulty, flawed; *informal* way out, full of holes. ANTONYM correct.

error noun *leaving the door unlocked was my error* MISTAKE, inaccuracy, miscalculation, blunder, oversight; fallacy, misconception, delusion; misprint, erratum; *informal* slip-up, boo-boo, goof. See note at MISTAKE. PHRASE: **in error** *millions of tax dollars were collected in error* WRONGLY, by mistake, mistakenly, incorrectly; accidentally, by accident, inadvertently, unintentionally, by chance.

ersatz adjective *ersatz coffee* ARTIFICIAL, substitute, imitation, synthetic, fake, false, faux, mock, simulated; pseudo, sham, bogus, spurious, counterfeit; manufactured, man-made; *informal* phony, wannabe. See note at SPURIOUS. ANTONYM genuine.

erstwhile adjective *Candi's erstwhile tennis instructor* FORMER, old, past, one-time, sometime, ex-, late, then; previous; *formal* quondam. ANTONYM present.

erudite adjective *our erudite cousin, Norma* LEARNED, scholarly, educated, knowledgeable, well-read, well-informed, intellectual; intelligent, clever, academic, literary; bookish, highbrow, sophisticated, cerebral; *informal* brainy; *dated* lettered. See note at KNOWLEDGE. ANTONYM ignorant.

erupt verb 1 *the volcano erupted* EMIT LAVA, become active, flare up; explode.

2 *fighting erupted* BREAK OUT, flare up, start suddenly; ensue, arise, happen.

3 *a boil erupted on her temple* APPEAR, break out, flare up, come to a head, suppurate, emerge.

eruption noun 1 *a volcanic eruption* DISCHARGE, ejection, emission; explosion.

2 *an eruption of violence* OUTBREAK, flare-up, upsurge, outburst, explosion; wave, spate.

3 *a skin eruption* RASH, outbreak, breakout, inflammation.

escalate verb 1 *prices have escalated* INCREASE RAPIDLY, soar, rocket, shoot up, mount, spiral, climb, go up, inflate; *informal* go through the ceiling, go through the roof, skyrocket. ANTONYM plunge.

2 *the dispute escalated* GROW, develop, mushroom, increase, heighten, intensify, accelerate. ANTONYM shrink.

escalation noun 1 *an escalation in oil prices* INCREASE, rise, hike, growth, leap, upsurge, upturn, climb.

2 *an escalation of the conflict* INTENSIFICATION, aggravation, exacerbation, magnification, amplification, augmentation; expansion, buildup.

escapade noun *famous for his flying escapades* EXPLOIT, stunt, caper, antic(s), spree, shenanigan, hijinks; adventure, venture, mission; deed, feat, trial, experience; incident, occurrence, event.

escape verb 1 *he escaped from prison* RUN AWAY/OFF, get out, break out, break free, make a break for it, bolt, flee, take flight, make off, take off, abscond, take to one's heels, make one's getaway, make a run for it; disappear, vanish, slip away, sneak away; *informal* cut and run, skedaddle, vamoose, fly the coop, take French leave, go on the lam.

2 *he escaped his pursuers* GET AWAY FROM, escape from, elude, avoid, dodge, shake off; *informal* give someone the slip.

3 *they escaped injury* AVOID, evade, dodge, elude, miss, cheat, sidestep, circumvent, steer clear of; *informal* duck.

4 *lethal gas escaped* LEAK (OUT), seep (out), discharge, emanate, issue, flow (out), pour (out), gush (out), spurt (out), spew (out).

▸ noun 1 *his escape from prison* GETAWAY, breakout, jailbreak, bolt, flight; disappearance, vanishing act.

2 *a narrow* ***escape from*** *death* AVOIDANCE OF, evasion of, circumvention of.

3 *a gas escape* LEAK, leakage, spill, seepage, discharge, effusion, emanation, outflow, outpouring; gush, stream, spurt.

4 *an escape from boredom* DISTRACTION, diversion.

escapee noun *two of the escapees are thought to be wounded* RUNAWAY, escaper, absconder; jailbreaker, fugitive; truant; deserter, defector.

escapism noun *romance novels offer a form of escapism that many people thoroughly enjoy* FANTASY, fantasizing, daydreaming, daydreams, reverie; imagination, flight(s) of fancy, pipe dreams, wishful thinking, woolgathering; *informal* pie in the sky. ANTONYM realism.

eschew verb *he firmly eschewed political involvement* ABSTAIN FROM, refrain from, give up, forgo, shun, renounce, steer clear of, have nothing to do with, fight shy of; relinquish, reject, disavow, abandon, spurn, wash one's hands of, drop; *informal* kick, pack in; *formal* forswear, abjure.

escort noun 1 *a police escort* GUARD, bodyguard, protector, minder, attendant, chaperone; entourage, retinue, cortège; protection, defense, convoy.

2 *her escort for the evening* COMPANION, partner; *informal* date; *formal* attendant.

3 *an agency dealing with escorts* PAID COMPANION, hostess; geisha; gigolo.

▸ verb *he escorted her down the aisle* CONDUCT, accompany, guide, lead, usher, shepherd, bring, take; drive, walk.

esoteric adjective *in attendance were more than 50 antiques dealers brimming with esoteric knowledge* ABSTRUSE, obscure, arcane, recherché, rarefied, recondite, abstract; enigmatic, inscrutable, cryptic, Delphic; complex, complicated, incomprehensible, opaque, impenetrable, mysterious.

especial adjective 1 *especial care is required* PARTICULAR, special, extra special, superior, exceptional, extraordinary; unusual, out of the ordinary, uncommon, remarkable, singular.

2 *her especial brand of charm* DISTINCTIVE, individual, special, particular, distinct, peculiar, personal, own, unique, specific.

especially adverb 1 *complaints poured in, especially from Toronto* MAINLY, mostly, chiefly, principally, largely; substantially, particularly, primarily, generally, usually, typically.

2 *a committee especially for the purpose* EXPRESSLY, specially, specifically, exclusively, just, particularly, explicitly.

3 *he is especially talented* EXCEPTIONALLY, particularly, specially, very, extremely, singularly, strikingly, distinctly, unusually, extraordinarily, uncommonly, uniquely, remarkably, outstandingly, really; *informal* seriously, majorly.

espionage noun *an American pilot suspected of espionage* SPYING, infiltration; eavesdropping, surveillance, reconnaissance, intelligence, undercover work.

espousal noun *Will's recent espousal of neo-Nazism has distressed his family and perplexed his friends* ADOPTION, embracing, acceptance; support, championship, encouragement, defense; sponsorship, promotion, endorsement, advocacy, approval.

espouse verb *do you espouse the political beliefs of your parents?* ADOPT, embrace, take up, accept, welcome; support, back, champion, favor, prefer, encourage; promote, endorse, advocate. ANTONYM reject.

espy verb *literary he espied a niche up in the rocks* CATCH SIGHT OF, glimpse, see, spot, spy, notice, observe, discern, pick out, detect; *literary* behold.

essay noun 1 *he wrote an essay* ARTICLE, composition, study, paper, dissertation, thesis, discourse, treatise, disquisition, monograph; commentary, critique, theme.

2 *formal his first essay in telecommunications* ATTEMPT, effort, endeavor, try, venture, trial, experiment, undertaking.

essence noun 1 *the very essence of economics* QUINTESSENCE, soul, spirit, nature; core, heart, crux, nucleus, substance; principle, fundamental quality, sum and substance, warp and woof, reality, actuality; *informal* nitty-gritty.

2 *essence of ginger* EXTRACT, concentrate, distillate, elixir, decoction, juice, tincture; scent, perfume, oil. PHRASES: **in essence** *in essence, his essays are the products of an indoctrinated young mind* ESSENTIALLY, basically, fundamentally, primarily, principally, chiefly, predominantly, substantially; above all, first and foremost; effectively, virtually, to all intents and purposes; intrinsically, inherently. **of the essence** *absolute secrecy is of the essence.* See ESSENTIAL adjective sense 1.

essential adjective 1 *it is essential to remove the paint* CRUCIAL, necessary, key, vital, indispensable, important, all-important, of the essence, critical, imperative, mandatory, compulsory, obligatory; urgent, pressing, paramount, preeminent, high-priority, nonnegotiable; *informal* must-have. See note at NECESSARY. ANTONYMS unimportant, optional.

2 *the essential simplicity of his style* BASIC, inherent, fundamental, quintessential, intrinsic, underlying, characteristic, innate, primary, elementary, elemental; central, pivotal, vital. See note at INHERENT. ANTONYM secondary.

▸ noun 1 *an essential for broadcasters* NECESSITY, prerequisite, requisite, requirement, need; condition, precondition, stipulation; sine qua non; *informal* must, must-have.

2 *the essentials of the job* FUNDAMENTALS, basics, rudiments, first principles, foundations, bedrock; essence, basis, core, kernel, crux, sine qua non; *informal* nitty-gritty, brass tacks, nuts and bolts, meat and potatoes.

establish verb 1 *they established an office in Moscow* SET

UP, start, initiate, institute, form, found, create, inaugurate; build, construct, install.

2 *evidence to establish his guilt* PROVE, demonstrate, show, indicate, signal, exhibit, manifest, attest to, evidence, determine, confirm, verify, certify, substantiate.

established adjective 1 *established practice* ACCEPTED, traditional, orthodox, habitual, set, fixed, official; usual, customary, common, normal, general, prevailing, accustomed, familiar, expected, routine, typical, conventional, standard.

2 *an established composer* WELL-KNOWN, recognized, esteemed, respected, famous, prominent, noted, renowned.

establishment noun 1 *the establishment of a democracy* FOUNDATION, institution, formation, inception, creation, installation; inauguration, start, initiation.

2 *a dressmaking establishment* BUSINESS, firm, company, concern, enterprise, venture, organization, operation; factory, plant, store, shop, office, practice; *informal* outfit, setup.

3 *educational establishments* INSTITUTION, place, premises, foundation, institute.

4 **(the Establishment)** *they dare to poke fun at the Establishment* THE AUTHORITIES, the powers that be, the system, the ruling class; the hierarchy, the oligarchy; *informal* Big Brother.

estate noun 1 *the Knowltons' estate* PROPERTY, grounds, garden(s), park, parkland, land(s), landholding, manor, territory; *historical* seigneury.

2 *a coffee estate* PLANTATION, farm, holding; forest, vineyard; ranch.

3 *he left an estate worth $610,000* ASSETS, capital, wealth, riches, holdings, fortune; property, effects, possessions, belongings; *Law* goods and chattels.

esteem noun *she was held in high esteem* RESPECT, admiration, acclaim, approbation, appreciation, favor, recognition, honor, reverence; estimation, regard, opinion.

▸ verb 1 *such ceramics are highly esteemed* RESPECT, ADMIRE, value, regard, acclaim, appreciate, like, prize, treasure, favor, revere.

2 *formal I would esteem it a favor if you could speak to him.* See DEEM.

THE RIGHT WORD

If you're a classical music aficionado, you might **appreciate** a good symphony orchestra, **admire** someone who plays the oboe, and **esteem** the works of Beethoven above all other classical composers. All three of these verbs are concerned with recognizing the worth of something, but in order to *appreciate* it, you have to understand it well enough to judge it critically. If you *admire* something, you appreciate its superiority (*to admire a pianist's performance*), while *esteem* goes one step further, implying that your admiration is of the highest degree (*a musician esteemed throughout the music world*). You **prize** what you value highly or cherish, especially if it is a possession (*she prized her Stradivarius violin*), while **regard** is a more neutral term meaning to look at or to have a certain mental view of something, either favorable or unfavorable (*to regard him as a great musician; to regard her as a ruthless competitor*). To **respect** is to have a deferential regard for someone or something because of its worth or value (*to respect the conductor's interpretation of the music*).

estimate verb 1 *estimate the cost* CALCULATE ROUGHLY, approximate, guess; evaluate, judge, gauge, reckon, rate, determine; *informal* guesstimate, ballpark.

2 *we estimate it to be worth $50,000* CONSIDER, believe, reckon, deem, judge, rate, gauge.

▸ noun 1 *an estimate of the cost* ROUGH CALCULATION, approximation, estimation, rough guess; costing, quotation, valuation, evaluation; *informal* guesstimate.

2 *his estimate of Paul's integrity* EVALUATION, estimation, judgment, rating, appraisal, opinion, view.

estimation noun 1 *an estimation of economic growth* ESTIMATE, approximation, rough calculation, rough guess, evaluation; *informal* guesstimate, ballpark figure.

2 *she rated highly in Janice's estimation* ASSESSMENT, evaluation, judgment, perception; esteem, opinion, view.

estrange verb *Arafat was urged not to estrange the Bush White House* ALIENATE, antagonize, turn away, drive away, distance; sever, set at odds with; drive a wedge between (oneself and).

estrangement noun *the estrangement between Vita and her family* ALIENATION, antagonism, antipathy, disaffection, hostility, unfriendliness; variance, difference; parting, separation, divorce, breakup, split, breach, schism. See note at SOLITUDE.

estuary noun *we paddled down the estuary, observing herons and ospreys* (RIVER) MOUTH, delta; *archaic* embouchure, debouchure, debouchment, discharge, disemboguement.

et cetera adverb *they make their own linguini, fettuccini, ziti, lasagna, et cetera* AND SO ON, and so forth, and the rest, and/or the like, and suchlike, among others, et al., etc.; *informal* and what have you, and whatnot, and on and on, yadda yadda yadda.

etch verb *the metal is etched with a dilute acid* ENGRAVE, carve, inscribe, incise, chase, score, print, mark.

etching noun *Picasso's etchings were often relatively large and bold* ENGRAVING, print, impression, block, plate; woodcut, linocut.

eternal adjective 1 *eternal happiness* EVERLASTING, never-ending, endless, perpetual, undying, immortal, abiding, permanent, enduring, infinite, boundless, timeless; amaranthine. ANTONYM transient.

2 *eternal vigilance* CONSTANT, continual, continuous, perpetual, persistent, sustained, unremitting, relentless, unrelieved, uninterrupted, unbroken, never-ending, nonstop, around/round-the-clock, endless, ceaseless. ANTONYM intermittent.

THE RIGHT WORD

There are some things in life that seem to exist beyond the boundaries of time. **Endless** is the most informal and has the broadest scope of all these adjectives. It can mean without end in time (*an endless argument*) or space (*the endless universe*), and it implies never stopping, or going on continuously as if in a circle (*to consult an endless succession of doctors*). **Unending** is a less formal word used to describe something that endures or has no end, and it can be used either in an approving sense (*unending devotion*) or a disapproving one (*unending conflict*). **Never-ending** is a more emphatic term than *unending*; it, too, can be used in either a positive or a negative sense (*a never-ending delight; a never-ending source of embarrassment*). In contrast, **interminable** is almost always used in a disapproving or negative sense for something that lasts a long time (*interminable delays in construction*). **Everlasting** refers to something that will continue to exist once it is created, while **eternal** implies that it has always existed and will continue to exist in the future. In Christian theology, for example, believers in the *eternal* God look forward to *everlasting* life.

---

eternally adverb 1 *I shall be eternally grateful* FOREVER, permanently, perpetually, (for) evermore, for ever and ever, for eternity, in perpetuity, enduringly; forevermore; *informal* until the cows come home; *archaic* for aye.

2 *the drummer is eternally complaining* CONSTANTLY, continually, continuously, always, all the time, persistently, repeatedly, regularly; day and night, night and day, nonstop; endlessly, incessantly, perpetually; interminably, relentlessly; *informal* 24-7.

eternity noun 1 *the memory will remain for eternity* EVER, all time, perpetuity.

2 *Theology souls destined for eternity* THE AFTERLIFE, everlasting life, life after death, the hereafter, the afterworld, the next world; heaven, paradise, immortality.

3 *informal I waited an eternity for you* A LONG TIME, an age, ages, a lifetime; hours, years, eons; forever; *informal* donkey's years, a month of Sundays, a coon's age.

ethereal adjective *melodic phrases of ethereal beauty* DELICATE, exquisite, dainty, elegant, graceful; fragile, airy, fine, subtle; unearthly. ANTONYMS substantial, earthly.

ethical adjective 1 *an ethical dilemma* MORAL, social, behavioral. See note at MORAL.

2 *an ethical investment policy* MORAL, right-minded, principled, irreproachable; righteous, high-minded, virtuous, good, morally correct; clean, lawful, just, honorable, reputable, respectable, noble, worthy; praiseworthy, commendable, admirable, laudable; whiter than white, saintly, impeccable, politically correct; *informal* squeaky clean, PC.

ethics plural noun *your so-called newspaper is clearly not burdened by a sense of ethics* MORAL CODE, morals, morality, values, rights and wrongs, principles, ideals, standards (of behavior), value system, virtues, dictates of conscience.

ethnic adjective *a wide spectrum of ethnic groups* RACIAL, race-related, ethnological; cultural, national, tribal, ancestral, traditional.

ethos noun *responsibility for the ethos of the school* SPIRIT, character, atmosphere, climate, mood, feeling, tenor, essence; disposition, rationale, morality, moral code, value system, principles, standards, ethics.

etiquette noun *the article includes tips on etiquette* PROTOCOL, manners, accepted behavior, rules of conduct, decorum, good form; courtesy, propriety, formalities, niceties, punctilios; custom, convention; *Computing* netiquette; *informal* the done thing; *formal* politesse.

etymology noun *the etymology of a word may be unknown* DERIVATION, word history, development, origin, source.

eulogize verb *the police eulogized the positive effect of speed cameras* EXTOL, acclaim, sing the praises of, praise to the skies, wax lyrical about, rhapsodize about, rave about, enthuse about, ballyhoo, hype. See note at PRAISE. ANTONYM criticize.

eulogy noun *a graveside eulogy* ACCOLADE, panegyric, paean, tribute, compliment, commendation; praise, acclaim; plaudits, bouquets; *formal* encomium. ANTONYM attack.

euphemism noun *'influential person' is the local euphemism for underworld don* POLITE TERM, indirect term, circumlocution, substitute, alternative, understatement, genteelism.

euphemistic adjective *the textbooks reportedly use the euphemistic term 'advance' instead of 'invade' to describe Japan's takeover of the Korean Peninsula* POLITE, substitute, mild, understated, indirect, neutral, evasive; diplomatic, inoffensive, genteel; periphrastic, circumlocutory, mealy-mouthed.

euphonious adjective *the euphonious chorus of songbirds* PLEASANT-SOUNDING, sweet-sounding, mellow, mellifluous, dulcet, sweet, honeyed, lyrical, silvery, golden, lilting, soothing; harmonious, melodious; *informal* easy on the ear. ANTONYM cacophonous.

euphoria noun *the euphoria of victory* ELATION, happiness, joy, delight, glee; excitement, exhilaration, jubilation, exultation; ecstasy, bliss, rapture. See note at RAPTURE. ANTONYM misery.

euphoric adjective *they received a euphoric welcome* ELATED, happy, joyful, delighted, gleeful; excited, exhilarated, jubilant, exultant; ecstatic, blissful, rapturous, transported, on cloud nine, in seventh heaven; *informal* on top of the world, over the moon, on a high.

eureka exclamation *Eureka! The word 'borage' completes the crossword puzzle!* BINGO, I've got it, that's it.

euthanasia noun *both veterinarians recommended euthanasia as the most merciful procedure* MERCY KILLING, assisted suicide; *rare* quietus.

evacuate verb 1 *local residents were evacuated* REMOVE, clear, move out, take away, shift.

2 *they evacuated the bombed town* LEAVE, vacate, abandon, desert, move out of, quit, withdraw from, retreat from, decamp from, flee, depart from, escape from.

3 *police evacuated the area* CLEAR, empty.

4 *patients couldn't evacuate their bowels* EMPTY (OUT), void, open, move, purge; defecate.

5 *he evacuated the contents of his stomach* EXPEL, eject, discharge, excrete, void, empty (out), vomit up.

evade verb 1 *they evaded the guards* ELUDE, avoid, dodge, escape (from), steer clear of, keep at arm's length, sidestep; lose, leave behind, shake off; *informal* give someone the slip. ANTONYMS confront, run into.

2 *he evaded the question* AVOID, dodge, sidestep, bypass, shirk, hedge, skirt around, fudge, be evasive about; *informal* duck. ANTONYM face.

evaluate verb *the house was most recently evaluated in 2002* ASSESS, judge, gauge, rate, estimate, appraise, analyze, examine, get the measure of; *informal* size up, check out.

evaluation noun *proper evaluation of the results is critical* ASSESSMENT, appraisal, judgment, gauging, rating, estimation, consideration; analysis, examination, test, review.

evanescent adjective *literary operating on an evanescent budget* VANISHING, fading, evaporating, melting away, disappearing; ephemeral, fleeting, short-lived, short-term, transitory, transient, fugitive, temporary. See note at TEMPORARY. ANTONYM permanent.

evangelical adjective 1 *evangelical Christianity* SCRIPTURAL, biblical; fundamentalist.

2 *an evangelical preacher* EVANGELISTIC, evangelizing, missionary, crusading, proselytizing; *informal* Bible-thumping.

evangelist noun *the first evangelist I ever heard of was Billy Graham* PREACHER, missionary, gospeler, proselytizer, crusader; *informal* Bible-thumper.

evangelistic adjective. See EVANGELICAL sense 2.

evangelize verb *his calling is to evangelize the downtrodden in these poor neighborhoods | evangelizing in the West Indies* CONVERT, proselytize, redeem, save, preach to, recruit; act as a missionary, missionize, crusade, campaign.

evaporate verb 1 *the water evaporated* VAPORIZE, become vapor, volatilize; dry up. ANTONYM condense.

2 *the rock salt is washed and evaporated* DRY OUT, dehydrate, desiccate, dehumidify. ANTONYM wet.

3 *the feeling has evaporated* END, pass, pass away, fizzle out, peter out, wear off, vanish, fade, disappear, dissolve, melt away. ANTONYM materialize.

evasion noun 1 *the evasion of immigration control* AVOIDANCE, elusion, circumvention, dodging, sidestepping.

2 *she grew tired of all the evasion* PREVARICATION, evasiveness, beating around the bush, hedging, pussyfooting, hemming and hawing, equivocation, vagueness, temporization; *rare* tergiversation.

evasive adjective *the judge was infuriated by the defendant's evasive answers* EQUIVOCAL, prevaricating, elusive, ambiguous, noncommittal, vague, inexplicit, unclear; roundabout, indirect; *informal* cagey, shifty, slippery. See word spectrum at FRANK.

eve noun 1 *the **eve of** the election* DAY BEFORE, evening before, night before; period (just) before.

2 *literary a winter's eve* EVENING, night; end of day, close of day; twilight, dusk, sunset, sundown, nightfall; *literary* eventide, evenfall, gloaming. ANTONYM morning.

even adjective 1 *an even surface* FLAT, smooth, uniform, featureless; unbroken, undamaged; level, plane. ANTONYM bumpy.

2 *an even temperature* UNIFORM, constant, steady, stable, consistent, unvarying, unchanging, regular. ANTONYMS variable, irregular.

3 *they all have an even chance* EQUAL, the same, identical, like, alike, similar, comparable, parallel. ANTONYM unequal.

4 *the score was even* TIED, drawn, level, all square, balanced; neck and neck; *informal* even-steven. ANTONYM unequal.

5 *an even disposition* EVEN-TEMPERED, balanced, stable, equable, placid, calm, composed, poised, cool, relaxed, easy, imperturbable, unexcitable, unruffled, untroubled; *informal* together, laid-back, unflappable. ANTONYMS excitable, moody.

▸ verb 1 *the canal bottom was **evened out*** FLATTEN, level (off/out), smooth (off/out), plane; make uniform, make regular.

2 ***even up** the portions* EQUALIZE, make equal, balance, square; standardize, regularize, homogenize.

▸ adverb 1 *it got even colder* STILL, yet, more, all the more.

2 *even the best hitters missed the ball* SURPRISINGLY, unexpectedly, paradoxically.

3 *she is afraid, even ashamed, to ask for help* INDEED, you could say, veritably, in truth, actually, or rather; *dated* nay.

4 *she could **not even** afford food* NOT SO MUCH AS, hardly, barely, scarcely.

PHRASES: **even as** *we laugh even as we empathize with his discomfort* WHILE, whilst, as, just as, at the very time that, during the time that. **even so** *I feel better, but the doubts persist even so* NEVERTHELESS, nonetheless, all the same, just the same, anyway, anyhow, still, yet, however, notwithstanding, despite that, in spite of that, for all that, be that as it may, in any event, at any rate; *informal* anyhoo, anyways. **get even** *Waite thinks he's struck the final blow, but I'll get even* HAVE ONE'S REVENGE, avenge oneself, take vengeance, even the score, settle the score, hit back, give as good as one gets, pay someone back, repay someone, reciprocate, retaliate, take reprisals, exact retribution; give someone their just deserts; *informal* give someone a taste of their own medicine, settle someone's hash; *literary* be revenged.

evenhanded adjective *for reasons we have yet to analyze, our older teachers are far more evenhanded than the younger ones* FAIR, just, equitable, impartial, unbiased, unprejudiced, nonpartisan, nondiscriminatory; disinterested, detached, objective, neutral. ANTONYM biased.

evening noun *they met in town nearly every evening* NIGHT, late afternoon, end of day, close of day; twilight, dusk, nightfall, sunset, sundown; *literary* eve, eventide, evenfall, gloaming.

event noun 1 *an annual event* OCCURRENCE, happening, proceeding, incident, affair, circumstance, occasion, phenomenon; function, gathering; *informal* bash.

2 *the team lost the event* COMPETITION, contest, tournament, round, heat, match, fixture; race, game, bout. PHRASES: **in any event** *we may not join you for dinner, but in any event we'll see you at the theater* REGARDLESS, whatever happens, come what may, no matter what, at any rate, in any case, anyhow, anyway, even so, still, nevertheless, nonetheless; *informal* anyways, anyhoo. **in the event** *in the event, they squabbled and the plan fell through* AS IT TURNED OUT, as it happened, in the end; as a result, as a consequence.

even-tempered adjective *Zaslawski was secretly and deeply envious of anyone with a loving and even-tempered father* SERENE, calm, composed, tranquil, relaxed, easygoing, mellow, unworried, untroubled, unruffled, imperturbable, placid, equable, stable, levelheaded; *informal* unflappable, together, laid-back. ANTONYM excitable.

eventful adjective *a long and eventful day* BUSY, action-packed, full, lively, active, hectic, strenuous; momentous, significant, important, historic, consequential, fateful. ANTONYM dull.

eventual adjective *the eventual outcome of the competition* FINAL, ultimate, concluding, closing, end; resulting, ensuing, consequent, subsequent.

eventuality noun *it is impossible to anticipate every eventuality* EVENT, incident, occurrence, happening, development, phenomenon, situation, circumstance, case, contingency, chance, likelihood, possibility, probability; outcome, result.

eventually adverb *the culprit will be caught eventually* IN

THE END, in due course, by and by, in time, after some time, after a bit, finally, at last, over the long haul; ultimately, in the long run, at the end of the day, one day, some day, sometime, at some point, sooner or later.

eventuate verb *formal* **1** *you never know what might eventuate.* See HAPPEN sense 1.

2 *the fight* ***eventuated in*** *his death* RESULT IN, end in, lead to, give rise to, bring about, cause.

ever adverb **1** *the best I've ever done* AT ANY TIME, at any point, on any occasion, under any circumstances, on any account; up till now, until now.

2 *he was ever the optimist* ALWAYS, forever, eternally, until hell freezes over, until the cows come home.

3 *an ever increasing rate of crime* CONTINUALLY, constantly, always, endlessly, perpetually, incessantly, unremittingly.

4 *will she ever learn?* AT ALL, in any way.

everlasting adjective **1** *everlasting love* ETERNAL, endless, never-ending, perpetual, undying, abiding, enduring, infinite, boundless, timeless. See note at ETERNAL. ANTONYM transient.

2 *his everlasting complaints* CONSTANT, continual, continuous, persistent, relentless, unrelieved, uninterrupted, unabating, endless, interminable, never-ending, nonstop, incessant. ANTONYM occasional.

every adjective **1** *he exercised every day* EACH, each and every, every single.

2 *we make every effort to satisfy our clients* ALL POSSIBLE, the utmost.

everybody pronoun *everybody complains about taxes* EVERYONE, every person, each person, all, one and all, all and sundry, the whole world, the public; *informal* 'every Tom, Dick, and Harry'; *dated* every man jack.

everyday adjective **1** *the everyday demands of a baby* DAILY, day-to-day, quotidian.

2 *everyday drugs like acetaminophen* COMMONPLACE, ordinary, common, usual, regular, familiar, conventional, run-of-the-mill, standard, stock; household, domestic; *informal* garden variety. ANTONYM unusual.

everyone pronoun See EVERYBODY.

everything pronoun *everything is half price* EACH ITEM, each thing, every single thing, the lot, the whole lot; all; *informal* the whole kit and caboodle, the whole shebang, the whole schmear, the whole ball of wax, the whole nine yards. ANTONYM nothing.

everywhere adverb *McDonald's restaurants are found everywhere* ALL OVER, all around, ubiquitously, in every nook and cranny, far and wide, near and far, high and low, 'here, there, and everywhere'; throughout the land, the world over, worldwide, globally; *informal* all over the place, everyplace, all over the map. ANTONYM nowhere.

evict verb *Leonard took no pleasure in evicting tenants* EXPEL, eject, oust, remove, dislodge, turn out, throw out, drive out; dispossess, expropriate; *informal* chuck out, kick out, boot out, bounce, give someone the (old) heave-ho, throw someone out on their ear, give someone the bum's rush, give someone their walking papers. See note at EJECT.

eviction noun *a notice of eviction was left in the mailbox* EXPULSION, ejection, ousting, removal, dislodgment, displacement, banishment; dispossession, expropriation; *Law* ouster.

evidence noun **1** *they found evidence of his plotting* PROOF, confirmation, verification, substantiation, corroboration, affirmation, attestation.

2 *the court accepted her evidence* TESTIMONY, statement, attestation, declaration, avowal, submission, claim, contention, allegation; *Law* deposition, representation, affidavit.

3 *evidence of a struggle* SIGNS, indications, pointers, marks, traces, suggestions, hints; manifestation.

▸ verb *the rise of racism is evidenced here* INDICATE, show, reveal, display, exhibit, manifest; testify to, confirm, prove, substantiate, endorse, bear out; *formal* evince. ANTONYM disprove.

PHRASE: **in evidence** *team spirit was in evidence* NOTICEABLE, conspicuous, obvious, perceptible, visible, on view, on display, plain to see; palpable, tangible, unmistakable, undisguised, prominent, striking, glaring; *informal* as plain as the nose on your face, sticking out like a sore thumb, staring someone in the face.

evident adjective *the fact that he loves his family is evident* OBVIOUS, apparent, noticeable, conspicuous, perceptible, visible, discernible, clear, clear-cut, plain, manifest, patent; palpable, tangible, distinct, pronounced, marked, striking, glaring, blatant; unmistakable, indisputable; *informal* as plain as the nose on your face, sticking out like a sore thumb, as clear as day.

evidently adverb **1** *he was evidently dismayed* OBVIOUSLY, clearly, plainly, visibly, manifestly, patently, distinctly, markedly; unmistakably, undeniably, undoubtedly.

2 *evidently, she believed herself superior* SEEMINGLY, apparently, as far as one can tell, from all appearances, on the face of it; it seems (that), it appears (that).

evil adjective **1** *an evil deed* WICKED, bad, wrong, immoral, sinful, foul, vile, dishonorable, corrupt, iniquitous, depraved, reprobate, villainous, nefarious, vicious, malicious; malevolent, sinister, demonic, devilish, diabolical, fiendish, dark; monstrous, shocking, despicable, atrocious, heinous, odious, contemptible, horrible, execrable; *informal* lowdown, dirty. ANTONYMS good, virtuous.

2 *an evil spirit* CRUEL, mischievous, pernicious, malignant, malign, baleful, vicious; destructive, harmful, hurtful, injurious, detrimental, deleterious, inimical, bad, ruinous. ANTONYMS good, beneficial.

3 *an evil smell* UNPLEASANT, disagreeable, nasty, horrible, foul, disgusting, filthy, vile, noxious. ANTONYM pleasant.

▸ noun **1** *the evil in our midst* WICKEDNESS, bad, badness, wrongdoing, sin, ill, immorality, vice, iniquity, degeneracy, corruption, depravity, villainy, nefariousness, malevolence; devil; *formal* turpitude.

2 *nothing but evil would ensue* HARM, pain, misery, sorrow, suffering, trouble, disaster, misfortune, catastrophe, affliction, woe, hardship.

3 *the evils of war* ABOMINATION, atrocity, obscenity, outrage, enormity, crime, monstrosity, barbarity.

evince verb *formal his letters evince the excitement he felt* REVEAL, show, make plain, manifest, indicate, display, exhibit, demonstrate, evidence, attest to; convey, communicate, proclaim, bespeak; *informal* ooze. ANTONYM conceal.

eviscerate verb *formal the goat had been skinned and eviscerated* DISEMBOWEL, gut, draw, dress.

evocative adjective *evocative photos from our childhood* REMINISCENT, suggestive, redolent; expressive, vivid, graphic, powerful, haunting, moving, poignant.

evoke verb *the music evoked some forgotten memories* BRING TO MIND, put one in mind of, conjure up, summon (up), invoke, elicit, induce, kindle, stimulate, stir up, awaken, arouse, call forth; recall, echo, capture.

evolution noun **1** *the evolution of Bolshevism* DEVELOPMENT, advancement, growth, rise, progress, expansion, unfolding; transformation, adaptation, modification, revision.

2 *his interest in evolution* DARWINISM, natural selection.

evolve verb *our little tea party evolved into an all-night bash* DEVELOP, progress, advance; mature, grow, expand, spread; alter, change, transform, adapt, metamorphose; *humorous* transmogrify.

exacerbate verb *each party blames the other for exacerbating the problem* AGGRAVATE, worsen, inflame, compound; intensify, increase, heighten, magnify, add to, amplify, augment; *informal* add fuel to the fire/flames. See note at EXASPERATE. ANTONYM reduce.

exact adjective **1** *an exact description* PRECISE, accurate, correct, faithful, close, true; literal, strict, faultless, perfect, impeccable; explicit, detailed, minute, meticulous, thorough; *informal* on the nail, on the mark, bang on, on the money, on the button. ANTONYM inaccurate.

2 *an exact manager* CAREFUL, meticulous, painstaking, punctilious, conscientious, scrupulous, exacting; methodical, organized, orderly. ANTONYM careless.

▸ verb **1** *she exacted high standards from them* DEMAND, require, insist on, request, impose, expect; extract, compel, force, squeeze.

2 *they exacted a terrible vengeance on him* INFLICT, impose, administer, apply.

exacting adjective **1** *an exacting training routine* DEMANDING, stringent, testing, challenging, onerous, arduous, laborious, taxing, grueling, punishing, hard, tough. ANTONYM easy.

2 *an exacting boss* STRICT, stern, severe, firm, demanding, tough, harsh; inflexible, uncompromising, unyielding, unsparing; *informal* persnickety. ANTONYM easygoing.

exactly adverb **1** *it's exactly as I expected it to be* PRECISELY, entirely, absolutely, completely, totally, just, quite, in every way, in every respect, one hundred percent, every inch; *informal* to a T, on the money.

2 *write the quotation out exactly* ACCURATELY, precisely, correctly, unerringly, faultlessly, perfectly; verbatim, word for word, letter for letter, to the letter, faithfully.

▸ exclamation *"She escaped?" "Exactly."* PRECISELY, yes, that's right, just so, quite so, quite, indeed, absolutely; *informal* you got it.

PHRASE: **not exactly** *I'm not exactly a spring chicken* BY NO MEANS, not at all, in no way, certainly not; not really.

exaggerate verb *the conflict was exaggerated by the media* OVERSTATE, overemphasize, overestimate, magnify, amplify, aggrandize, inflate; embellish, embroider, elaborate, overplay, dramatize; hyperbolize, stretch the truth; *informal* lay it on thick, make a mountain out of a molehill, blow out of all proportion, blow up, make a big thing of. ANTONYM understate.

exaggerated adjective *an exaggerated account of my exploits* OVERSTATED, inflated, magnified, amplified, aggrandized, excessive; hyperbolic, elaborate, overdone, overplayed, overblown, over-dramatized, melodramatic, sensational; *informal* over the top.

exaggeration noun *his testimony was a laughable mix of contradiction and exaggeration* OVERSTATEMENT, overemphasis, magnification, amplification, aggrandizement; dramatization, elaboration, embellishment, embroidery, hyperbole, overkill, gilding the lily.

exalt verb **1** *they exalted their hero* EXTOL, praise, acclaim, esteem; pay homage to, revere, venerate, worship, lionize, idolize, look up to; *informal* put on a pedestal, laud. ANTONYMS disparage, despise.

2 *this power exalts the peasant* ELEVATE, promote, raise, advance, upgrade, ennoble, dignify, aggrandize. ANTONYM lower.

3 *his works exalt the emotions* UPLIFT, elevate, inspire, excite, stimulate, enliven, exhilarate. ANTONYM depress.

exaltation noun **1** *a heart full of exaltation* ELATION, joy, rapture, ecstasy, bliss, happiness, delight, gladness.

2 *their exaltation of Shakespeare* PRAISE, acclamation, reverence, veneration, worship, adoration, idolization, lionization.

exalted adjective **1** *his exalted office* HIGH, high-ranking, elevated, superior, lofty, eminent, prestigious, illustrious, distinguished, esteemed.

2 *his exalted aims* NOBLE, lofty, high-minded, elevated; inflated, pretentious.

3 *she felt spiritually exalted* ELATED, exultant, jubilant, joyful, rapturous, ecstatic, blissful, transported, happy, exuberant, exhilarated; *informal* high.

exam noun. See EXAMINATION sense 3.

examination noun **1** *artifacts spread out for examination* SCRUTINY, inspection, perusal, study, investigation, consideration, analysis, appraisal, evaluation.

2 *a medical examination* INSPECTION, checkup, assessment, appraisal; probe, test, scan; *informal* once-over, overhaul.

3 *a school examination* TEST, exam, quiz, assessment; oral, midterm, final; paper, term paper.

4 Law *the examination of witnesses* INTERROGATION, questioning, cross-examination, inquisition.

examine verb **1** *they examined the bank records* INSPECT, scrutinize, investigate, look at, study, scan, sift (through), probe, appraise, analyze, review, survey; *informal* check out.

2 *students were examined after a year* TEST, quiz, question; assess, appraise.

3 Law *name the witnesses to be examined* INTERROGATE, question, quiz, cross-examine; catechize, give the third degree to, probe, sound out; *informal* grill, pump.

examiner noun *the accounts are checked by an independent examiner* ASSESSOR, questioner, interviewer, tester, appraiser, marker, inspector; auditor, analyst; adjudicator, judge, scrutineer.

example noun **1** *a fine example of Chinese porcelain* SPECIMEN, sample, exemplar, exemplification, instance, case, illustration, case in point.

2 *we must follow their example* PRECEDENT, lead, model, pattern, exemplar, ideal, standard, template, paradigm; role model, object lesson. See note at MODEL.

3 *he was hanged as an example to others* WARNING, caution, lesson, deterrent, admonition; moral. PHRASE: **for example** *she's met several Hall of Famers—for example, Brooks Robinson and Johnny Mize* FOR INSTANCE, e.g., by way of illustration, such as, as, like; in particular, case in point, namely, viz., to wit.

exasperate verb *her bratty children exasperate their teachers* INFURIATE, incense, anger, annoy, irritate, madden, enrage, antagonize, provoke, irk, vex, get on someone's nerves, ruffle someone's feathers, rub the wrong way; *informal* aggravate, rile, bug, needle, get someone's back up, get someone's goat, tee off, tick off. ANTONYM please.

EASILY CONFUSED WORDS **exasperate, exacerbate**

The verbs **exasperate** and **exacerbate** are sometimes confused. **Exasperate**, the more common of the two, means 'to irritate or annoy to an extreme degree' (*He e-mails me stupid jokes all day long. It's exasperating!*). **Exacerbate** means 'to increase the bitterness or severity' of something (*why does she insist on saying 'helpful' things that only exacerbate matters?*).

exasperating adjective *twirling his mustache is just one of his exasperating habits* INFURIATING, annoying, irritating, maddening, provoking, irksome, vexatious, trying, displeasing; *informal* aggravating.

exasperation noun *she provoked exasperation among her colleagues* IRRITATION, annoyance, vexation, anger, fury, rage, ill humor, crossness, testiness, tetchiness; disgruntlement, discontent, displeasure, chagrin; *informal* aggravation.

excavate verb **1** *she excavated a narrow tunnel* DIG, dig out, bore, hollow out, scoop out; burrow, tunnel, sink, gouge.

2 *numerous artifacts have been excavated* UNEARTH, dig up, uncover, reveal; disinter, exhume.

excavation noun **1** *the excavation of a grave* UNEARTHING, digging up; disinterment, exhumation.

2 *the excavation of a moat* DIGGING, hollowing out, boring, channeling.

3 *implements found in the excavations* HOLE, pit, trench, trough; archaeological site.

exceed verb **1** *the cost will exceed $400* BE MORE THAN, be greater than, be over, go beyond, overreach, top.

2 *Brazil exceeds the U.S. in fertile land* SURPASS, outdo, outstrip, outshine, outclass, transcend, top, cap, beat, excel, better, eclipse, overshadow; *informal* best, leave standing, be head and shoulders above.

exceedingly adverb *an exceedingly comfortable home* EXTREMELY, exceptionally, especially, tremendously, very, really, truly, awfully, seriously, totally, completely; *formal* most; *informal* mega, ultra, real, mighty; *archaic* exceeding.

excel verb **1** *he excelled at football* SHINE, be excellent, be outstanding, be skillful, be talented, be preeminent, reign supreme; stand out, be the best, be unparalleled, be unequaled, be second to none, be unsurpassed.

2 *she excelled him in her work* SURPASS, outdo, outshine, outclass, outstrip, beat, top, transcend, exceed, better, pass, eclipse, overshadow; *informal* best, be head and shoulders above, be a cut above.

excellence noun *a center of medical excellence* DISTINCTION, quality, superiority, brilliance, greatness, merit, caliber, eminence, preeminence, supremacy; skill, talent, virtuosity, accomplishment, mastery.

excellent adjective *a cruise ship with excellent accommodations* VERY GOOD, superb, outstanding, exceptional, marvelous, wonderful, magnificent; preeminent, perfect, matchless, unbeatable, peerless, supreme, prime, first-rate, first-class, superlative, splendid, fine, beautiful, exemplary; *informal* A1, ace, great, terrific, tremendous, fantastic, fabulous, splendiferous, fab, top-notch, dandy, divine, blue-ribbon, blue-chip, bang-up, skookum, class, awesome, magic, wicked, mean, cool, out of this world, hunky-dory, A-OK, brilliant, killer. ANTONYMS inferior, poor.

except preposition *every day except Monday* EXCLUDING, not including, excepting, omitting, not counting, but, besides, apart from, aside from, barring, bar, other than, saving; with the exception of, save for; *informal* outside of. ANTONYM including.

▸ verb *lawyers are all crooks, present company excepted* EXCLUDE, omit, leave out, count out, disregard; exempt. ANTONYM include.

exception noun *this case is an exception* ANOMALY, irregularity, deviation, special case, isolated example, peculiarity, abnormality, oddity; misfit, aberration; *informal* freak; bad apple. PHRASES: **take exception to** *Lydia took exception to their criticism of her husband* OBJECT TO, take offense at, take umbrage at, demur at, disagree with; resent, argue against, protest against, oppose, complain about, shudder at; *informal* kick up a fuss about, raise a stink about. **with the exception of** *all of the sopranos, with the exception of Dia, will wear black dresses with red sashes.* See EXCEPT preposition.

exceptionable adjective *formal*. See OBJECTIONABLE.

exceptional adjective **1** *the drought was exceptional* UNUSUAL, uncommon, abnormal, atypical, extraordinary, out of the ordinary, rare, unprecedented, unexpected, surprising; strange, odd, freakish, anomalous, peculiar, weird; *informal* freaky, something else. ANTONYMS normal, usual.

2 *her exceptional ability* OUTSTANDING, extraordinary, remarkable, special, excellent, phenomenal, prodigious; unequaled, unparalleled, unsurpassed, peerless, matchless, nonpareil, first-rate, first-class; *informal* A1, top-notch. ANTONYM average.

exceptionally adverb **1** *it was exceptionally cold* UNUSUALLY, uncommonly, abnormally, atypically, extraordinarily, unexpectedly, surprisingly; strangely, oddly; *informal* weirdly, freakily.

2 *an exceptionally acute mind* EXCEEDINGLY, outstandingly, extraordinarily, remarkably, especially, phenomenally, prodigiously.

excerpt noun *an excerpt from the poem* EXTRACT, part, section, piece, portion, snippet, clip, bit, sample; reading, citation, quotation, quote, line, passage.

▸ verb QUOTE, extract, cite.

excess noun **1** *an excess of calcium* SURPLUS, surfeit, overabundance, superabundance, superfluity, glut. ANTONYMS lack, dearth.

2 *the excess is turned into fat* REMAINDER, rest, residue; leftovers, remnants; surplus, extra, difference.

3 *a life of excess* OVERINDULGENCE, intemperance, immoderation, profligacy, lavishness, extravagance, decadence, self-indulgence. ANTONYMS moderation, restraint.

▸ adjective *excess skin oils* SURPLUS, superfluous, redundant, unwanted, unneeded, excessive; extra.

PHRASE: **in excess of** *the book sold in excess of 10,000 copies* MORE THAN, over, above, upwards of, beyond.

excessive adjective **1** *excessive alcohol consumption* IMMODERATE, intemperate, imprudent, overindulgent, unrestrained, uncontrolled, lavish, extravagant; superfluous.

2 *the cost is excessive* EXORBITANT, extortionate, unreasonable, outrageous, undue, uncalled for, extreme, inordinate, unwarranted, disproportionate, too much, de trop; *informal* over the top.

excessively adverb *her father had excessively high standards* INORDINATELY, unduly, unnecessarily, unreasonably, ridiculously, overly; very, extremely, exceedingly, exceptionally, impossibly; immoderately, intemperately; ad nauseam.

exchange noun **1** *the exchange of ideas* INTERCHANGE, trade, trading, swapping, traffic, trafficking.

2 *a broker on the exchange* STOCK EXCHANGE, money market; bourse.

3 *an acrimonious exchange* CONVERSATION, dialogue, talk, discussion, chat; debate, argument, altercation, row; *formal* confabulation, colloquy.

▸ verb *we exchanged shirts* TRADE, swap, switch, change, interchange.

PHRASES: **exchange blows** *they exchanged blows out in the parking lot* FIGHT, brawl, scuffle, tussle; *informal* scrap, have a set-to. **exchange words** *the children would tearfully listen from upstairs when their parents exchanged words* ARGUE, quarrel, squabble, have an argument, have a disagreement.

excise[1] noun *the excise on liquor* DUTY, tax, levy, tariff.

excise[2] verb **1** *the tumors were excised* CUT OUT/OFF/AWAY, take out, extract, remove; *technical* resect.

2 *all unnecessary detail should be excised* DELETE, cross out/through, strike out, score out, cancel, put a line through; erase, scratch; *informal* ditch, nix, kill; *Printing* dele.

excitable adjective *the horses are very excitable* TEMPERAMENTAL, mercurial, volatile, emotional, sensitive, high-strung, unstable, nervous, tense, edgy, jumpy, twitchy, uneasy, neurotic; *informal* uptight, wired. ANTONYM placid.

excite verb **1** *the prospect of a vacation excited me* THRILL, exhilarate, animate, enliven, rouse, stir, stimulate, galvanize, electrify, inspirit; *informal* buck up, pep up, give someone a buzz, give someone a kick, give someone a charge. ANTONYMS bore, depress.

2 *she wore a chiffon nightgown to excite him* AROUSE, arouse sexually, stimulate, titillate, inflame; *informal* turn someone on, get someone going. ANTONYM turn off.

3 *his clothes excited envy* PROVOKE, stir up, rouse, arouse, kindle, trigger (off), spark (off), incite, cause; *literary* enkindle.

excited adjective **1** *they were excited about the prospect* THRILLED, exhilarated, animated, enlivened, electrified; enraptured, intoxicated, feverish, adrenalized, enthusiastic; *informal* high, high as a kite, fired up, psyched.

2 *excited lovers* AROUSED, sexually aroused, stimulated, titillated, inflamed; *informal* turned on, hot, horny, sexed up.

excitement noun **1** *the excitement of seeing a leopard in the wild* THRILL, pleasure, delight, joy; *informal* kick, buzz, charge, high.

2 *excitement in her eyes* EXHILARATION, elation, animation, enthusiasm, eagerness, anticipation, feverishness; *informal* pep, vim, zing.

3 *their excitement was mutual* AROUSAL, sexual arousal, passion, stimulation, titillation.

exciting adjective **1** *an exciting story* THRILLING, exhilarating, action-packed, stirring, rousing, stimulating, intoxicating, electrifying, invigorating; gripping, compelling, powerful, dramatic.

2 *an exciting encounter with her lover* AROUSING, sexually arousing, stimulating, sexually stimulating, titillating, erotic, sexual, sexy; *informal* raunchy, steamy.

exclaim verb *"Well, I never!" she exclaimed* CRY OUT, cry, declare, blurt out; call, call out, shout, yell; *dated* ejaculate.

exclamation noun *an exclamation of amazement* CRY, call, shout, yell, interjection.

exclude verb **1** *women were excluded from many scientific societies* KEEP OUT, deny access to, shut out, debar, disbar, bar, ban, prohibit, ostracized. ANTONYMS admit, accept.

2 *the clause excluded any judicial review* ELIMINATE, rule out, preclude, foreclose; *formal* except. ANTONYM allow for.

3 *the price excludes postage* BE EXCLUSIVE OF, not include. ANTONYM include.

4 *he excluded his own name from the list* LEAVE OUT/OFF, omit, miss out. ANTONYM include.

exclusive adjective **1** *an exclusive club* SELECT, chic, high-class, elite, fashionable, stylish, elegant, premier, grade A; expensive, upscale, upmarket, high-toned; *informal* posh, ritzy, classy, tony.

2 *a room for your exclusive use* SOLE, unshared, unique, only, individual, personal, private. ANTONYM partial.

3 *prices **exclusive of** sales tax* NOT INCLUDING, excluding, leaving out, omitting, excepting. ANTONYM inclusive.

4 *mutually exclusive alternatives* INCOMPATIBLE, irreconcilable.

▸ noun *a six-page exclusive* SCOOP, exposé, special.

excoriate verb **1** *Medicine the skin had been excoriated* ABRADE, rub away, rub raw, scrape, scratch, chafe; strip away, skin.

2 *formal he was excoriated in the press.* See CRITICIZE.

excrement noun *cleaning up the ferrets' excrement* FECES, excreta, stools, droppings; waste matter, ordure, dung; *informal* poop, poo, dirt, turds, caca.

excrescence noun **1** *an excrescence on his leg* GROWTH, lump, swelling, nodule, outgrowth.

2 *the new buildings were an excrescence* EYESORE, blot on the landscape, monstrosity.

excrete verb *waste products are excreted from the body* EXPEL, pass, void, discharge, eject, evacuate; defecate, urinate. ANTONYM ingest.

excruciating adjective *excruciating pain* AGONIZING, severe, acute, intense, violent, racking, searing, piercing, stabbing, raging; unbearable, unendurable; *informal* splitting, killing.

excursion noun *a lovely excursion to Nassau* TRIP, outing, jaunt, expedition, journey, tour; day trip, day out, side trip, drive, run, ride; *informal* junket, spin, sortie. See note at JOURNEY.

excusable adjective *it's an excusable mistake* FORGIVABLE, pardonable, defensible, justifiable; venial. ANTONYM unforgivable.

excuse verb **1** *eventually she excused him* FORGIVE, pardon, absolve, exonerate, acquit; *informal* let someone off (the hook); *formal* exculpate. ANTONYMS punish, blame.

2 *such conduct can never be excused* JUSTIFY, defend, condone, vindicate; forgive, overlook, disregard, ignore, tolerate, sanction. ANTONYM condemn.

3 *she has been excused from her duties* LET OFF, release, relieve, exempt, absolve, free.

▸ noun **1** *that's no excuse for stealing* JUSTIFICATION, defense, reason, explanation, mitigating circumstances, mitigation, vindication.

2 *an excuse to get away* PRETEXT, ostensible reason, pretense; *informal* story, alibi.

3 *informal that pathetic* ***excuse for*** *a man!* TRAVESTY OF, poor specimen of; *informal* apology for.

execrable adjective *an execrable piece of work* APPALLING, atrocious, lamentable, egregious, awful, dreadful, terrible; disgusting, deplorable, disgraceful, frightful, reprehensible, abhorrent, loathsome, odious, hateful, vile, abysmal, lousy, godawful. ANTONYM admirable.

execute verb **1** *he was convicted and executed* PUT TO DEATH, kill; hang, behead, guillotine, electrocute, send to the (electric) chair, shoot, put before a firing squad; *informal* string up, fry. See note at KILL.

2 *the corporation executed a series of financial deals* CARRY OUT, accomplish, bring off/about, achieve, complete, engineer, conduct; *informal* pull off; *formal* effectuate.

3 *a well-executed act* PERFORM, present, render; stage.

execution noun **1** *the execution of the plan* IMPLEMENTATION, carrying out, accomplishment, bringing off/about, engineering, attainment, realization.

2 *the execution of the play* PERFORMANCE, presentation, rendition, rendering, staging.

3 *thousands were sentenced to execution* CAPITAL PUNISHMENT, the death penalty; the gibbet, the gallows, the noose, the rope, the scaffold, the guillotine, the firing squad, the electric chair, the chair.

executioner noun *today he meets his executioner* HANGMAN; *historical* headsman.

executive adjective *executive powers* ADMINISTRATIVE, decision-making, managerial; lawmaking.

▸ noun **1** *top-level bank executives* CHIEF, head, director, senior official, senior manager, CEO, chief executive officer; *informal* boss, exec, suit, big cheese.

2 *the executive has increased in number* ADMINISTRATION, management, directorate; government, legislative body.

exegesis noun *the exegesis of ancient texts* INTERPRETATION, explanation, exposition, explication.

exemplar noun *Luciano is an exemplar of decorum* EPITOME, perfect example, paragon, ideal, exemplification, textbook example, embodiment, essence, quintessence; paradigm, model, role model, template.

exemplary adjective **1** *her exemplary behavior* PERFECT, ideal, model, faultless, flawless, impeccable, irreproachable; excellent, outstanding, admirable, commendable, laudable, above/beyond reproach; textbook. ANTONYM deplorable.

2 *exemplary jail sentences* DETERRENT, cautionary, warning, admonitory; *rare* monitory.

3 *her works are exemplary of cutting-edge feminism* REPRESENTATIVE, illustrative, characteristic, typical.

exemplify verb **1** *this story exemplifies current trends* TYPIFY, epitomize, be a typical example of, represent, be representative of, symbolize.

2 *he exemplified his point with an anecdote* ILLUSTRATE, give an example of, demonstrate.

exempt adjective *they are* ***exempt from*** *all charges* FREE FROM, not liable to, not subject to, exempted from, excepted from, excused of/from, absolved of. ANTONYM subject to.

▸ verb *he had been exempted from military service* EXCUSE, free, release, exclude from, give/grant immunity, spare, absolve from; *informal* let off (the hook), grandfather. See note at ABSOLVE.

exemption noun *exemption from the road tax* IMMUNITY, exception, dispensation, indemnity, exclusion, freedom, release, relief, absolution.

exercise noun **1** *exercise improves your heart* PHYSICAL ACTIVITY, a workout, working out; gymnastics, sports, games, physical education, physical training, aerobics, body conditioning, calisthenics; *informal* phys ed.

2 *Mr. Nixon's translation exercises* TASK, piece of work, problem, assignment, activity; *Music* étude.

3 *the exercise of professional skill* USE, utilization, employment; practice, application.

4 (exercises) *military exercises* MANEUVERS, operations; war games.

▸ verb **1** *she exercised every day* WORK OUT, do exercises, train; *informal* pump iron.

2 *he must learn to exercise patience* USE, employ, make use of, utilize; practice, apply.

WORD NOTE sexercise

There is a case for this word replacing *exercise* altogether. The *Oxford English Dictionary* gives the secondary meaning of an "exercise designed to enhance sexual attractiveness or improve sexual performance," but it is hard to think of a form of "personal exercise" which aims at anything else. It has a more specific definition, however; that of sexual activity "perceived as exercise." Of all the pointless mid-twentieth-century additions to our workout vocabularies, this is the most worthy of continuation in the language. **—ZS**

exert verb **1** *he exerted considerable pressure on me* BRING TO BEAR, apply, exercise, employ, use, utilize, deploy.

2 *Geoff had been* ***exerting himself*** STRIVE, try hard, make an/every effort, endeavor, do one's best, do one's utmost, give one's all, push oneself, drive oneself, work hard; *infor-*

mal go all out, pull out all the stops, bend/lean over backwards, do one's damnedest, do one's darnedest, move heaven and earth, bust one's chops.

exertion noun **1** *she was panting with exertion* EFFORT, strain, struggle, toil, endeavor, hard work, labor; *literary* travail.

2 *the exertion of pressure* USE, application, exercise, employment, utilization.

exhale verb **1** *she exhaled her cigarette smoke* BREATHE OUT, blow out, puff out. ANTONYM inhale.

2 *the jungle exhaled mists of early morning* GIVE OFF, emanate, send forth, emit.

exhaust verb **1** *the effort had exhausted him* TIRE OUT, wear out, overtire, fatigue, weary, tire, drain, run someone into the ground; *informal* do in, take it out of one, wipe out, knock out, burn out, poop, tucker out. ANTONYMS invigorate, refresh.

2 *the country has exhausted its reserves* USE UP, run through, go through, consume, finish, deplete, spend, empty, drain, run out of; *informal* blow. ANTONYM replenish.

3 *we've exhausted the subject* TREAT THOROUGHLY, say all there is to say about, do to death, overwork.

exhausted adjective **1** *I worked until I was exhausted* TIRED OUT, worn out, weary, dead-tired, dog-tired, bone-tired, ready to drop, drained, fatigued, enervated; *informal* beat, done in, all in, bushed, zonked, bagged, knocked out, wiped out, burned out, pooped, tuckered out, tapped out, fried, whipped. See note at TIRED.

2 *exhausted reserves* USED UP, consumed, finished, spent, depleted; empty, drained.

exhausting adjective *an exhausting day of moving furniture* TIRING, wearying, taxing, fatiguing, wearing, enervating, draining; arduous, strenuous, onerous, demanding, grueling; *informal* killing, murderous.

exhaustion noun **1** *sheer exhaustion forced Mona to give up* EXTREME TIREDNESS, overtiredness, fatigue, weariness, burnout.

2 *the exhaustion of fuel reserves* CONSUMPTION, depletion, using up, expenditure; draining, emptying.

exhaustive adjective *an exhaustive study of Icelandic history* COMPREHENSIVE, all-inclusive, complete, full, full-scale, encyclopedic, sweeping, thorough, in-depth; detailed, meticulous, painstaking. ANTONYM perfunctory.

exhibit verb **1** *the paintings were exhibited at the Wadsworth* PUT ON DISPLAY/SHOW, display, show, put on public view, showcase; set out, lay out, array, arrange.

2 *Luke exhibited signs of jealousy* SHOW, reveal, display, manifest; express, indicate, demonstrate, present; *formal* evince.

▸ noun **1** *exhibit A is a handwritten letter* OBJECT, item, piece, showpiece; display; evidence.

2 *people flocked to the exhibit.* See EXHIBITION sense 1.

exhibition noun **1** *an exhibition of Inuit sculpture* (PUBLIC) DISPLAY, show, showing, presentation, demonstration, exposition, showcase, exhibit.

2 *a convincing exhibition of concern* DISPLAY, show, demonstration, manifestation, expression.

exhibitionist noun *I'm not enough of an exhibitionist to dress up as Frank-N-Furter* POSTURER, poser, self-publicist; extrovert; *informal* show-off, showboat.

exhilarate verb *the fireworks display exhilarated us* THRILL, excite, intoxicate, elate, delight, enliven, animate, invigorate, energize, vitalize, stimulate; *informal* give someone a thrill, give someone a buzz, give someone a charge.

exhilaration noun *a feeling of exhilaration* ELATION, euphoria, exultation, exaltation, joy, happiness, delight, joyousness, jubilation, rapture, ecstasy, bliss.

exhort verb *Clinton exhorted state legislatures to beef up educational standards and help put welfare recipients to work* URGE, encourage, call on, enjoin, charge, press; bid, appeal to, entreat, implore, beg; *formal* adjure; *literary* beseech. See note at INCITE.

exhortation noun **1** *no amount of exhortation had any effect* URGING, encouragement, persuasion, pressure; warning.

2 *the government's exhortations to voters* ENTREATY, appeal, call, charge, injunction; admonition, warning.

exhume verb *the district attorney is requesting that Baker's body be exhumed* DISINTER, dig up, unearth. ANTONYM bury.

exigency noun **1** *the exigencies of the continuing war* NEED, demand, requirement, necessity.

2 *financial exigency* URGENCY, crisis, difficulty, pressure.

exiguous adjective *formal Bob Cratchit's exiguous wages* MEAGER, inadequate, insufficient, small, scanty, paltry, negligible, modest, deficient, miserly, niggardly, beggarly; *informal* measly, stingy, piddling. ANTONYMS ample, generous.

exile noun **1** *his exile from the land of his birth* BANISHMENT, expulsion, expatriation, deportation.

2 *political exiles* ÉMIGRÉ, expatriate; displaced person, refugee, deportee; *informal* expat; *historical* DP.

▸ verb *he was exiled from his country* EXPEL, banish, expatriate, deport, drive out, throw out, outlaw.

exist verb **1** *animals existing in the distant past* LIVE, be alive, be living; be; happen.

2 *the liberal climate that existed during his presidency* PREVAIL, occur, be found, be in existence; be the case.

3 *she had to exist on a low income* SURVIVE, subsist, live, support oneself; manage, make do, get by, scrape by, make ends meet.

existence noun **1** *the industry's continued existence* ACTUALITY, being, existing, reality; survival, continuation.

2 *her suburban existence* WAY OF LIFE, way of living, life, lifestyle. PHRASE: **in existence** *there are millions of unidentified species in existence.* See EXISTENT.

existent adjective *species that are no longer existent* IN EXISTENCE, alive, existing, living, extant; surviving, remaining, undestroyed.

existentialism noun See note below.

WORD NOTE **existentialism**

In post–World War II New York, *existentialism* seemed sexy, bohemian, and antiacademic. It was an "action philosophy," a survivor's answer to nihilistic despair, and it went well with berets and saxophones, Abstract Expressionists in cold water lofts, and heroes of novels searching for authenticity in a universe of chance. For a certain extraordinary period of time, everyone wanted to be existential. Not everyone knew what this meant exactly, but everyone wanted the distinction. Misused and overused, the very word *existential* began to function as a sort of highbrow condiment of choice, the squiggle of French mustard that spiced up the hot dog of a banal observation. It was irresistible. To Norman Mailer, *existential* signified the cool of John F. Kennedy at the Democratic National Convention in Los Angeles in 1960—or maybe it meant a mutual climax achieved by anal intercourse. If you wore sunglasses in the subway and listened to Miles Davis, you were probably existential.

Such perhaps is the fate of certàin avant-garde movements in art or thought. They arrive with the intent to move heaven and earth, and after they've gone, what they leave is their faded stylishness, and it's the same old hard earth, and heaven's as remote as ever. **—DL**

---

exit noun **1** *the fire exit* WAY OUT, door, egress, escape route; doorway, gate, gateway, portal. ANTONYM entrance.

2 *take the second exit* TURNING, turnoff, turn, junction.

3 *his sudden exit* DEPARTURE, leaving, withdrawal, going, decamping, retreat; flight, exodus, escape. ANTONYM arrival.

▸ verb *the doctor had just exited* LEAVE, go (out), depart, withdraw, retreat. ANTONYM enter.

exodus noun *the exodus of refugees from Albania* MASS DEPARTURE, withdrawal, evacuation, leaving; migration, emigration; flight, escape, fleeing.

exonerate verb **1** *the inquiry exonerated them* ABSOLVE, clear, acquit, find innocent, discharge; *formal* exculpate. See note at ABSOLVE. ANTONYMS charge, convict.

2 *Pope Clement V exonerated the king from his oath* RELEASE, discharge, free, liberate; excuse, exempt, except, dispense; *informal* let off. ANTONYM hold to.

exorbitant adjective *exorbitant interest rates* EXTORTIONATE, excessively high, excessive, prohibitive, outrageous, unreasonable, inflated, unconscionable, huge, enormous; *informal* steep, stiff, sky-high, over the top, rip-off. ANTONYM reasonable.

exorcise verb **1** *exorcising an evil spirit* DRIVE OUT, cast out, expel.

2 *they exorcised the house* PURIFY, cleanse, purge.

exotic adjective **1** *exotic birds* FOREIGN, nonnative, tropical; introduced, imported. ANTONYM native.

2 *exotic places* FOREIGN, faraway, far-off, far-flung, distant. ANTONYMS familiar, nearby.

3 *Carlotta's exotic appearance* STRIKING, colorful, eye-catching, flamboyant; unusual, unconventional, out of the ordinary, foreign-looking, extravagant, outlandish, orchidaceous; *informal* offbeat, off the wall. ANTONYM conventional.

WORD NOTE **orchidaceous**

With its botanical derivation, *orchidaceous* applied to people means exceedingly showy (not that there's anything wrong with that), flamboyant, even flaming, in the gay sense of the word. **—JS**

---

expand verb **1** *metals expand when heated* INCREASE IN SIZE, become larger, enlarge; swell, dilate, inflate; lengthen, stretch, thicken, fill out. ANTONYMS shrink, contract.

2 *the company is expanding* GROW, become/make larger, become/make bigger, increase in size, increase in scope, upsize; extend, augment, broaden, widen, develop, diversify, build up; branch out, spread, proliferate. ANTONYMS shrink, scale down.

3 *the senator* ***expanded on*** *the proposals* ELABORATE ON, enlarge on, go into detail about, flesh out, develop, expatiate on.

4 *she learned to expand and flourish among new acquaintances* RELAX, unbend, become relaxed, grow friendlier, loosen up. ANTONYMS tense up, clam up.

expanse noun *an expanse of wheat and barley* AREA, stretch, sweep, tract, swathe, belt, region; sea, carpet, blanket, sheet.

expansion noun **1** *expansion and contraction of blood vessels* ENLARGEMENT, increase in size, swelling, dilation; lengthening, elongation, stretching, thickening. ANTONYM contraction.

2 *the expansion of the company* GROWTH, increase in size, enlargement, extension, development; spread, proliferation, multiplication. ANTONYM reduction in size.

3 *an expansion of a lecture given last year* ELABORATION, enlargement, amplification, development. ANTONYMS abridgment, summary.

expansive adjective **1** *expansive grassland* EXTENSIVE, sweeping, rolling.

2 *expansive coverage* WIDE-RANGING, extensive, broad, wide, comprehensive, thorough, full-scale.

3 *Bethany became engagingly expansive* COMMUNICATIVE, forthcoming, sociable, friendly, outgoing, affable, chatty, talkative, garrulous, effusive, loquacious, voluble.

expatiate verb *he expatiated on the topic of volunteerism* SPEAK/WRITE AT LENGTH, go into detail, expound, dwell, dilate, expand, enlarge, elaborate; *formal* perorate.

expatriate noun *expatriates working overseas* EMIGRANT, nonnative, émigré, migrant; *informal* expat. ANTONYM national.

▸ adjective *expatriate workers* EMIGRANT, living abroad, nonnative, foreign, émigré; *informal* expat. ANTONYMS indigenous, native.

▸ verb *he was expatriated* EXILE, deport, banish, expel. ANTONYM repatriate.

expect verb **1** *I expect she'll be late* SUPPOSE, presume, think, believe, imagine, assume, surmise; *informal* guess, reckon, figure.

2 *a 10 percent rise was expected* ANTICIPATE, await, look for, hope for, look forward to; contemplate, bargain for/on, bank on; predict, forecast, envisage, envision.

3 *we expect total loyalty* REQUIRE, ask for, call for, want, insist on, demand.

expectancy noun **1** *feverish expectancy* ANTICIPATION, expectation, eagerness, excitement.

2 *life expectancy* LIKELIHOOD, probability, outlook, prospect.

expectant adjective **1** *expectant fans* EAGER, excited, psyched, agog, waiting with bated breath, hopeful; in suspense, on tenterhooks.

2 *an expectant mother* PREGNANT; *informal* expecting, with a bun in the oven; *chiefly Brit. informal* preggers; *technical* gravid; *dated* in the family way; *archaic* with child.

expectation noun **1** *her expectations were unrealistic* SUPPOSITION, assumption, presumption, conjecture, surmise, calculation, prediction, hope.

2 *tense with expectation* ANTICIPATION, expectancy, eagerness, excitement, suspense.

expecting adjective *informal*. See EXPECTANT sense 2.

expedient adjective *a politically expedient strategy* CONVENIENT, advantageous, in one's own interests, useful, of use, beneficial, of benefit, helpful; practical, pragmatic, politic, prudent, wise, judicious, sensible.

▸ noun *a temporary expedient* MEASURE, means, method, stratagem, scheme, plan, move, tactic, maneuver, device, contrivance, ploy, machination, dodge.

expedite verb *our legal assistants can help expedite the paperwork* SPEED UP, accelerate, hurry, hasten, step up, quicken, precipitate, dispatch; advance, facilitate, ease, make easier, further, promote, aid, push through, urge on, boost, stimulate, spur on, help along, catalyze, fast-track. ANTONYM delay.

expedition noun **1** *an expedition to the South Pole* JOURNEY, voyage, tour, odyssey; exploration, safari, trek, hike. See note at JOURNEY.

2 *informal a shopping expedition* TRIP, excursion, outing, jaunt.

3 *all members of the expedition* GROUP, team, party, crew, band, squad.

expeditious adjective *an expeditious review* SPEEDY, swift, quick, rapid, fast, brisk, efficient; prompt, punctual, immediate, instant; *literary* fleet. ANTONYM slow.

expel verb **1** *the opposition leader was expelled from her party* THROW OUT, eject, bar, ban, debar, drum out, oust, remove, get rid of, dismiss; *Military* cashier; *informal* chuck out, sling out, kick out, boot out, give someone the bum's rush. See note at EJECT. ANTONYM admit.

2 *he was expelled from the country* BANISH, exile, deport, evict, expatriate, drive out, throw out.

3 *Dolly expelled a hiss* LET OUT, discharge, eject, issue, send forth.

expend verb **1** *they had already expended $75,000* SPEND, pay out, disburse, dole out, get through, waste, fritter (away), dissipate; *informal* fork out, dish out, shell out, lay out, cough up, blow, splurge, ante up. ANTONYMS save, conserve.

2 *children expend a lot of energy* USE UP, use, utilize, consume, eat up, deplete, get through, burn through. ANTONYM conserve.

expendable adjective **1** *an accountant decided Mathers was expendable* DISPENSABLE, replaceable, nonessential, inessential, unnecessary, noncore, unneeded, not required, superfluous, disposable. ANTONYMS indispensable, essential.

2 *an expendable satellite launcher* DISPOSABLE, throwaway, single-use.

expenditure noun **1** *the expenditure of funds* SPENDING, paying out, outlay, use, disbursement, doling out, waste, wasting, frittering (away), dissipation. ANTONYMS saving, conservation.

2 *reducing public expenditure* COSTS, spending, payments, expenses, overheads. ANTONYM income.

expense noun **1** *the expense of entertaining* COST, price, charge, outlay, fee, tariff, levy, payment; *informal, humorous* damage.

2 **(expenses)** *regular expenses* OVERHEAD, costs, outlay, expenditure(s), charges, bills, payment(s); incidentals.

3 *tax cuts come at the expense of social programs* SACRIFICE, cost, loss.

expensive adjective *an expensive meal* COSTLY, high-priced, dear; overpriced, exorbitant, extortionate; *informal* steep, pricey, costing an arm and a leg, big-ticket, costing the earth. ANTONYMS cheap, economical.

experience noun **1** *qualifications and experience* SKILL, knowledge, practical knowledge, understanding; background, record, history; maturity, worldliness, sophistication; *informal* know-how.

2 *an enjoyable experience* INCIDENT, occurrence, event, happening, episode; adventure, exploit, escapade.

3 *his first* ***experience of*** *business* INVOLVEMENT IN, participation in, contact with, acquaintance with, exposure to, observation of, awareness of, insight into.

▸ verb *some policemen experience harassment* UNDERGO, encounter, meet, come into contact with, come across, come up against, face, be faced with.

experienced adjective **1** *an experienced pilot* KNOWLEDGEABLE, skillful, skilled, expert, accomplished, adept, adroit, master, consummate; proficient, trained, competent, capable, well trained, well versed; seasoned, practiced, mature, veteran. ANTONYM novice.

2 *she deluded herself that she was experienced* WORLDLY WISE, worldly, sophisticated, suave, urbane, mature, knowing; *informal* streetwise, street smart. ANTONYM naive.

experiment noun **1** *carrying out experiments* TEST, investigation, trial, examination, observation; assessment, evaluation, appraisal, analysis, study.

2 *these results have been established by experiment* RESEARCH, experimentation, observation, analysis, testing.

▸ verb *they experimented with new ideas* CONDUCT EXPERIMENTS, carry out trials/tests, conduct research; test, trial, do tests on, try out, assess, appraise, evaluate.

experimental adjective **1** *the experimental stage* EXPLORATORY, investigational, trial, test, pilot; speculative, conjectural, hypothetical, tentative, preliminary, untested, untried.

2 *experimental music* INNOVATIVE, innovatory, new, original, radical, avant-garde, cutting-edge, alternative, unorthodox, unconventional; *informal* way-out.

WORD NOTE **experimental**

Strictly, *experimental* music is a style of composition in which the actual sound produced is beside the point. Historically, it was a genre lasting from August 29, 1952, the day of the premiere of John Cage's 4'33" (the 'silent' piece), until the 1974 publication of Michael Nyman's book *Experimental Music: Cage and Beyond,* which negated the genre by defining its limits. **—SM**

expert noun *she is an art expert* SPECIALIST, authority, pundit; adept, maestro, virtuoso, master, past master, wizard; connoisseur, aficionado; *informal* ace, buff, pro, techie, whiz, hotshot, maven, crackerjack.

▸ adjective *an expert chess player* SKILLFUL, skilled, adept, accomplished, talented, fine; master, masterly, brilliant, virtuoso, magnificent, outstanding, great, exceptional, excellent, first-class, first-rate, superb; proficient, good, able, capable, experienced, practiced, knowledgeable; *informal* ace, crack, mean. ANTONYM incompetent.

expertise noun *a high level of expertise in psychiatry is required* SKILL, skillfulness, expertness, prowess, proficiency, competence; knowledge, mastery, ability, aptitude, facility, capability; *informal* know-how.

expiate verb *the desire to expiate his sins* ATONE FOR, make amends for, make up for, do penance for, pay for, redress, redeem, offset, make good.

expire verb **1** *my contract has expired* RUN OUT, become invalid, become void, lapse; END, finish, stop, come to an end, terminate.

2 *the spot where he expired* DIE, pass away/on, breathe one's last; *informal* kick the bucket, bite the dust, croak, buy it, buy the farm; *dated* depart this life.

3 *technical the breath is then expired* BREATHE OUT, exhale, blow out, expel.

expiry noun **1** *the expiry of the lease* LAPSE, expiration.

2 *the expiry of her term of office* END, finish, termination, conclusion.

3 *archaic the sad expiry of their friend* DEATH, demise, passing (away/on), dying; *formal* decease.

explain verb **1** *a technician explained the procedure* DESCRIBE, give an explanation of, make clear, make intelligible, spell out, put into words; elucidate, expound, explicate, clarify, throw/shed light on; gloss, interpret. See note at CLARIFY.

2 *nothing could explain his newfound wealth* ACCOUNT FOR, give an explanation for, give a reason for; justify, give a justification for, give an excuse for, vindicate, legitimize.

explanation noun **1** *an explanation of the ideas contained in the essay* CLARIFICATION, simplification; description, report, statement; elucidation, exposition, expounding, explication; gloss, interpretation, commentary, exegesis.

2 *I owe you an explanation* ACCOUNT, reason; justification, excuse, alibi, defense, vindication, story, answers.

explanatory adjective *write two or three explanatory paragraphs* EXPLAINING, descriptive, describing, illustrative, interpretive, instructive, expository.

expletive noun *she let out an expletive and slammed the phone down* SWEAR WORD, obscenity, profanity, oath, curse, four-letter word, dirty word; *informal* cuss word, cuss; *formal* imprecation; (**expletives**) bad language, foul language, strong language, swearing.

explicable adjective *it is our understanding of history that makes the present more explicable* EXPLAINABLE, understandable, comprehensible, accountable, intelligible, interpretable.

explicate verb *I'm not sure anyone could fully explicate the works of Joyce* EXPLAIN, make explicit, clarify, make plain/clear, spell out, untangle; interpret, translate, elucidate, expound, illuminate, throw light on. See note at CLARIFY.

explicit adjective **1** *explicit instructions* CLEAR, plain, straightforward, crystal clear, easily understandable; precise, exact, specific, unequivocal, unambiguous; detailed, comprehensive, exhaustive. ANTONYM vague.

2 *sexually explicit material* GRAPHIC, uncensored, candid, full-frontal, hard-core.

explode verb **1** *a bomb has exploded* BLOW UP, detonate, go off, burst (apart), fly apart, erupt.

2 *exploding the first atomic device* DETONATE, set off, let off, discharge. ANTONYMS disarm, defuse.

3 *he exploded in anger* LOSE ONE'S TEMPER, blow up, get angry, become enraged, get mad; *informal* fly off the handle, hit the roof, blow one's cool/top/stack, go wild, go bananas, go ballistic, see red, go off the deep end, go crackers, go postal.

4 *the city's population is exploding* INCREASE SUDDENLY/RAPIDLY, mushroom, snowball, escalate, multiply, burgeon, rocket, skyrocket.

5 *exploding the myths about men* DISPROVE, refute, invalidate, negate, discredit, debunk, dispel, belie, give the lie to; *informal* poke holes in, blow out of the water; *formal* confute. ANTONYM confirm.

exploit verb **1** *we should exploit this new technology* UTILIZE, harness, use, make use of, turn/put to good use, make the most of, capitalize on, benefit from; *informal* cash in on.

2 *exploiting the workers* TAKE ADVANTAGE OF, abuse, impose on, treat unfairly, misuse, ill-treat; *informal* walk (all) over, take for a ride, rip off.

▸ noun *his exploits brought him notoriety* FEAT, deed, act, adventure, stunt, escapade; achievement, accomplishment, attainment; *informal* lark, caper.

exploitation noun **1** *the exploitation of mineral resources* UTILIZATION, use, making use of, making the most of, capitalization on; *informal* cashing in on.

2 *the exploitation of the poor* TAKING ADVANTAGE, abuse, misuse, ill-treatment, unfair treatment, oppression.

exploration noun **1** *the exploration of space* INVESTIGATION, study, survey, research, inspection, examination, scrutiny, observation; consideration, analysis, review.

2 *explorations into the mountains* EXPEDITION, trip, journey, voyage; *archaic* peregrination; (**explorations**) travels.

exploratory adjective *exploratory surgery* INVESTIGATIVE, investigational, explorative, probing, fact-finding; experimental, trial, tentative, test, preliminary, provisional.

explore verb **1** *they explored all the possibilities* INVESTIGATE, look into, consider; examine, research, survey, scrutinize, study, review, go over with a fine-tooth comb; *informal* check out.

2 *a rare chance to explore the Galapagos Islands* TRAVEL OVER/IN/THROUGH, tour, range over; survey, take a look at, inspect, investigate, reconnoiter, wander through.

explorer noun *the street is named after Peary, the Arctic explorer* TRAVELER, discoverer, voyager, adventurer; surveyor, scout, prospector.

explosion noun **1** *Edward heard the explosion* DETONATION, eruption, blowing up; bang, blast, boom, kaboom.

2 *an explosion of anger* OUTBURST, flare-up, outbreak, eruption, storm, rush, surge; fit, paroxysm, attack.

3 *the explosion of human populations* SUDDEN/RAPID INCREASE, mushrooming, snowballing, escalation, multiplication, burgeoning, rocketing, skyrocketing.

explosive adjective **1** *explosive gases* VOLATILE, inflammable, flammable, combustible, incendiary.

2 *Biff's explosive temper* FIERY, stormy, violent, volatile, angry, passionate, tempestuous, turbulent, touchy, irascible, hotheaded, short-tempered.

3 *an explosive situation* TENSE, charged, highly charged, overwrought; dangerous, perilous, hazardous, sensitive, delicate, unstable, volatile.

4 *explosive population growth* SUDDEN, dramatic, rapid; mushrooming, snowballing, escalating, rocketing, skyrocketing, accelerating.

▸ noun *stocks of explosives* BOMB, incendiary (device).

exponent noun *the new premier is an exponent of free trade* ADVOCATE, supporter, proponent, upholder, backer, defender, champion; promoter, propagandist, campaigner, fighter, crusader, enthusiast, apologist; *informal* cheerleader, booster. ANTONYMS critic, opponent.

export verb **1** *exporting raw materials* SELL OVERSEAS/ABROAD, send overseas/abroad, ship overseas/abroad, market overseas/abroad, trade internationally. ANTONYM import.

2 *she is trying to export her ideas to Japan* TRANSMIT, spread, disseminate, circulate, communicate, pass on; *literary* bruit about/abroad.

expose verb **1** *at low tide, the sands are exposed* REVEAL, uncover, lay bare. ANTONYM cover.

2 *he was* ***exposed to*** *asbestos* MAKE VULNERABLE TO, subject to, lay open to, put at risk of/from, put in jeopardy of/from. ANTONYM protect.

3 *they were* ***exposed to*** *liberal ideas* INTRODUCE TO, bring into contact with, make aware of, familiarize with, acquaint with. ANTONYM keep away.

4 *he was exposed as a liar* UNCOVER, reveal, unveil, unmask, detect, find out; discover, bring to light, bring into the open, make known; denounce, condemn; *informal* spill the beans on, blow the whistle on.

exposé noun *a poorly written exposé on the Hollywood drug scene* REVELATION, disclosure, exposure; report, feature, piece, column; *informal* tell-all, scoop. ANTONYM cover-up.

exposed adjective *an exposed hillside* UNPROTECTED, unsheltered, open to the elements/weather; vulnerable, defenseless, undefended. ANTONYM sheltered.

exposition noun **1** *a lucid exposition* EXPLANATION, description, elucidation, explication, interpretation; account, commentary, appraisal, assessment, discussion, exegesis.

2 *the exposition will feature 200 exhibits* EXHIBITION, fair, trade fair, trade show, show, expo, display, presentation, demonstration, exhibit.

expository adjective *expository dialogue* EXPLANATORY, descriptive, describing, explicatory, explicative, interpretative, exegetical.

expostulate verb *Jim* ***expostulated with*** *the teacher's opinion to no avail* REMONSTRATE WITH, disagree with, argue with, take issue with, protest against, reason against, express disagreement with, raise objections to, rail against.

exposure noun **1** *the exposure of the lizard's vivid blue tongue* REVEALING, revelation, uncovering, baring, laying bare.

2 *exposure to harmful chemicals* SUBJECTION, vulnerability, laying open.

3 *suffering from exposure* HYPOTHERMIA, cold, frostbite.

4 ***exposure to*** *great literature* INTRODUCTION TO, experience of/with, contact with, familiarity with, acquaintance with, awareness of.

5 *the exposure of a banking scandal* UNCOVERING, revelation, disclosure, unveiling, unmasking, discovery, detection; denunciation, condemnation.

6 *we're getting a lot of exposure* PUBLICITY, coverage, publicizing, advertising, public interest/attention, media interest/attention, ink; *informal* hype, face time.

7 *a southern exposure* OUTLOOK, aspect, view; position, setting, location.

expound verb **1** *he expounded his theories* PRESENT, put forward, set forth, propose, propound; explain, give an explanation of, detail, spell out, describe.

2 *a treatise expounding Chomsky's theories* EXPLAIN, interpret, explicate, elucidate; comment on, give a commentary on. PHRASE: **expound on** *he expounded on the virtues of books* ELABORATE ON, expand on, expatiate on, discuss at length.

express[1] verb **1** *community leaders expressed their anger* COMMUNICATE, convey, indicate, show, demonstrate, reveal, make manifest, put across/over, get across/over; articulate, put into words, utter, voice, give voice to; state, assert, proclaim, profess, air, make public, give vent to; *formal* evince.

2 *all the juice is expressed* SQUEEZE OUT, press out, extract. PHRASE: **express oneself** *he had difficulty expressing himself* COMMUNICATE ONE'S THOUGHTS/OPINIONS/VIEWS, put thoughts into words, speak one's mind, say what's on one's mind.

express[2] adjective *an express bus* RAPID, swift, fast, quick, speedy, high-speed; nonstop, direct. ANTONYMS slow, local.

express[3] adjective **1** *an express reference to confidential matters* EXPLICIT, clear, direct, obvious, plain, distinct, unambiguous, unequivocal; specific, precise, crystal clear, certain, categorical. ANTONYM implied.

2 *one express purpose* SOLE, specific, particular, exclusive, specified, fixed.

expression noun **1** *the free expression of opposition views* UTTERANCE, uttering, voicing, pronouncement, declaration, articulation, assertion, setting forth; dissemination, circulation, communication, spreading, promulgation.

2 *an expression of sympathy* INDICATION, demonstration, show, exhibition, token; communication, illustration, revelation.

3 *an expression of harassed fatigue* LOOK, appearance, air, manner, countenance, mien.

4 *a timeworn expression* IDIOM, phrase, idiomatic expression; proverb, saying, adage, maxim, axiom, aphorism, saw, motto, platitude, cliché.

5 *these pieces are very different in expression* EMOTION, feeling, spirit, passion, intensity; style, intonation, tone.

6 *essential oils obtained by expression* SQUEEZING, pressing, extraction, extracting.

expressionless adjective **1** *his face was expressionless* INSCRUTABLE, deadpan, poker-faced; blank, vacant, emotionless, unemotional, inexpressive; glazed, stony, wooden, impassive. ANTONYM expressive.

2 *a flat, expressionless tone* DULL, dry, toneless, monotonous, boring, tedious, flat, wooden, unmodulated, unvarying, devoid of feeling/emotion. ANTONYMS interesting, lively.

expressive adjective 1 *an expressive shrug* ELOQUENT, meaningful, demonstrative, suggestive. ANTONYM expressionless.

2 *an expressive song* EMOTIONAL, full of emotion/feeling, passionate, poignant, moving, stirring, evocative, powerful, emotionally charged. ANTONYM unemotional.

3 *his diction is very expressive of his upbringing* INDICATIVE, demonstrative, revealing.

expressly adverb 1 *he was expressly forbidden to discuss the matter* EXPLICITLY, clearly, directly, plainly, distinctly, unambiguously, unequivocally; absolutely; specifically, categorically, pointedly, emphatically.

2 *a machine expressly built for spraying paint* SOLELY, specifically, particularly, specially, exclusively, just, only, explicitly.

expropriate verb *legislation to expropriate land from absentee landlords* SEIZE, take away, take over, take, appropriate, take possession of, requisition, commandeer, claim, acquire, sequestrate, confiscate; *Law* distrain.

expulsion noun 1 *expulsion from the party* REMOVAL, debarment, dismissal, exclusion, discharge, ejection, drumming out. ANTONYM admission.

2 *the expulsion of bodily wastes* DISCHARGE, ejection, excretion, voiding, evacuation, elimination, passing.

expunge verb *a moment that cannot be expunged from his memory* ERASE, remove, delete, rub out, wipe out, efface; cross out, strike out, blot out, destroy, obliterate, scratch, eradicate, eliminate, deep-six.

expurgate verb *a book that had been expurgated for use in schools* CENSOR, bowdlerize, blue-pencil, cut, edit; clean up, sanitize, make acceptable, make palatable, water down, tame.

exquisite adjective 1 *exquisite antique glass* BEAUTIFUL, lovely, elegant, fine; magnificent, superb, excellent, wonderful, ornate, well-crafted, well-made, perfect; delicate, fragile, dainty, subtle.

2 *exquisite taste* DISCRIMINATING, discerning, sensitive, selective, fastidious; refined, cultivated, cultured, educated.

3 *exquisite agony* INTENSE, acute, keen, piercing, sharp, severe, racking, excruciating, agonizing, harrowing, searing; unbearable, unendurable.

extant adjective *extant manuscripts* STILL EXISTING, in existence, existent, surviving, remaining, undestroyed.

extemporary, extemporaneous adjective See EXTEMPORE.

extempore adjective *an extempore speech* IMPROMPTU, spontaneous, unscripted, ad lib, extemporary, extemporaneous; improvised, unrehearsed, unplanned, unprepared, off the top of one's head; *informal* off-the-cuff; *formal* ad libitum. ANTONYM rehearsed.

▸ adverb *he was speaking extempore* SPONTANEOUSLY, extemporaneously, ad lib, without preparation, without rehearsal, off the top of one's head; *informal* off the cuff; *formal* ad libitum.

extemporize verb *jazz musicians extemporize freely* IMPROVISE, ad lib, play it by ear, think on one's feet; *informal* wing it, fly by the seat of one's pants.

extend verb 1 *he attempted to extend his dominions* EXPAND, enlarge, increase, make larger, make bigger; lengthen, widen, broaden. ANTONYMS reduce, shrink.

2 *the garden extends down to the road* CONTINUE, carry on, run on, stretch (out), reach, lead.

3 *we have extended our range of services* WIDEN, expand, broaden; augment, supplement, increase, add to, enhance, develop. ANTONYM narrow.

4 *extending the life of the charter* PROLONG, lengthen, increase; stretch out, protract, spin out, string out. ANTONYM shorten.

5 *extend your arms and legs* STRETCH OUT, spread out, reach out, straighten out.

6 *he extended a hand in greeting* HOLD OUT, reach out, hold forth; offer, give, outstretch, proffer.

7 *we wish to extend our thanks to Mr. Bayes* OFFER, proffer, give, grant, bestow, accord. PHRASE: **extend to** *her tolerance did not always extend to her staff* INCLUDE, take in, incorporate, encompass.

extended adjective *an extended legal battle* PROLONGED, protracted, long-lasting, long-drawn-out, spun out, long, dragged out, strung out, lengthy; *informal* marathon.

extension noun 1 *they are planning a new extension* ADDITION, adjunct, annex, wing, supplementary building, ell, add-on.

2 *an extension of knowledge* EXPANSION, increase, enlargement, widening, broadening, deepening; augmentation, enhancement, development, growth, continuation.

3 *an extension of opening hours* PROLONGATION, lengthening, increase.

4 *I need an extension on my essay* POSTPONEMENT, more/extra time, deferral, delay.

extensive adjective 1 *a mansion with extensive grounds* LARGE, large-scale, sizable, substantial, considerable, ample, expansive, great, vast.

2 *extensive knowledge* COMPREHENSIVE, thorough, exhaustive; broad, wide, wide-ranging, catholic, eclectic.

extent noun 1 *two acres in extent* AREA, size, expanse, length; proportions, dimensions.

2 *the full extent of her father's illness* DEGREE, scale, level, magnitude, scope; size, breadth, width, reach, range.

extenuate verb *rare I've no wish to extenuate his transgressions* EXCUSE, mitigate, palliate, make allowances for, make excuses for, defend, vindicate, justify; diminish, lessen, moderate, qualify, play down.

extenuating adjective *a just decision must allow for extenuating circumstances* MITIGATING, excusing, exonerative, palliative, justifying, justificatory, vindicating; *formal* exculpatory.

exterior adjective *the exterior walls* OUTER, outside, outermost, outward, external. ANTONYM interior.

▸ noun *the exterior of the building* OUTSIDE, outer surface, external surface, outward appearance, facade.

exterminate verb *they were hired to exterminate the car-*

penter ants KILL, put to death, take/end the life of, dispatch; slaughter, butcher, massacre, wipe out, eliminate, eradicate, annihilate; murder, assassinate, execute, slay; *informal* do away with, bump off, do in, take out, blow away, ice, rub out, waste. See note at DESTROY.

extermination noun *the extermination of mob rivals* KILLING, murder, assassination, putting to death, execution, dispatch, slaughter, massacre, liquidation, elimination, eradication, annihilation, slaying.

external adjective **1** *an external wall* OUTER, outside, outermost, outward, exterior. ANTONYM internal.

2 *an external examiner* OUTSIDE, independent, nonresident, from elsewhere. ANTONYM in-house.

extinct adjective **1** *an extinct species* VANISHED, lost, died out, no longer existing, no longer extant, wiped out, destroyed, gone. ANTONYM extant.

2 *an extinct volcano* INACTIVE. ANTONYM dormant.

extinction noun *efforts to save the California condor from extinction* DYING OUT, disappearance, vanishing; extermination, destruction, elimination, eradication, annihilation.

extinguish verb **1** *the fire was extinguished* DOUSE, put out, stamp out, smother, beat out. ANTONYM light.

2 *all hope was extinguished* DESTROY, end, finish off, put an end to, bring to an end, terminate, remove, annihilate, wipe out, erase, eliminate, eradicate, obliterate; *informal* take out, rub out. ANTONYM start up.

extirpate verb *those who tried to extirpate Christianity* WEED OUT, destroy, eradicate, stamp out, root out, wipe out, eliminate, suppress, crush, put down, put an end to, get rid of. See note at DESTROY.

extol verb *nutritionists extol the virtues of fiber* PRAISE ENTHUSIASTICALLY, go into raptures about/over, wax lyrical about, sing the praises of, praise to the skies, acclaim, exalt, eulogize, adulate, rhapsodize over, rave about, enthuse about/over; *informal* go wild about, go on about, ballyhoo; *formal* laud; *archaic* panegyrize. See note at PRAISE. ANTONYM criticize.

extort verb *he was convicted of extorting money from local residents* FORCE, extract, exact, wring, wrest, screw, squeeze, obtain by threat(s), blackmail someone for; *informal* put the bite on someone for; soak, rook.

extortion noun *arrested on a charge of extortion* BLACKMAIL, shakedown; *formal* exaction.

extortionate adjective *extortionate prices* EXORBITANT, excessively high, excessive, outrageous, unreasonable, inordinate, inflated, exacting, harsh, severe, oppressive; *informal* over the top; grasping, bloodsucking, avaricious, greedy, money-grubbing.

extortionist noun *a politician who numbered bootleggers and extortionists among his friends* RACKETEER, extortioner, extorter, blackmailer; *informal* bloodsucker, vampire.

extra adjective *extra income* ADDITIONAL, more, added, supplementary, further, auxiliary, ancillary, subsidiary, secondary, bonus.

▸ adverb **1** *working extra hard* EXCEPTIONALLY, particularly, specially, especially, very, extremely; unusually, extraordinarily, uncommonly, remarkably, outstandingly, amazingly, incredibly, really, awfully, terribly; *informal* seriously, mucho, majorly.

2 *we charge extra for cheese* IN ADDITION, additionally, as well, also, too, besides, on top (of that); *archaic* withal.

▸ noun **1** *an optional extra* ADDITION, supplement, adjunct, addendum, add-on, bonus.

2 *a group of tourists were hired as extras for the scene on the bus* WALK-ON, supernumerary, spear carrier.

extract verb **1** *he extracted the videocassette* TAKE OUT, draw out, pull out, remove, withdraw; free, release, extricate. ANTONYM insert.

2 *extracting money* WREST, exact, wring, screw, squeeze, obtain by force, obtain by threat(s), extort, blackmail someone for; *informal* put the bite on someone for.

3 *the roots are crushed to extract the juice* SQUEEZE OUT, express, press out, obtain. ANTONYMS add, infuse.

4 *the figures are extracted from the report* EXCERPT, select, reproduce, copy, take. ANTONYM insert.

5 *ideas extracted from a variety of theories* DERIVE, develop, evolve, deduce, infer, obtain; *formal* educe.

▸ noun **1** *an extract from his article* EXCERPT, passage, citation, quotation; (**excerpts**) analects.

2 *an extract of the ginseng root* DECOCTION, distillation, distillate, abstraction, concentrate, essence, juice.

extraction noun **1** *the extraction of gallstones* REMOVAL, taking out, drawing out, pulling out, withdrawal; freeing, release, extrication. ANTONYM insertion.

2 *the extraction of grape juice* SQUEEZING, expressing, pressing, obtaining.

3 *a man of Irish extraction* DESCENT, ancestry, parentage, ancestors, family, antecedents; lineage, line, origin, derivation, birth; genealogy, heredity, stock, pedigree, blood, bloodline; roots, origins; *rare* filiation, stirps.

extradite verb *the Russians extradited him to Germany* DEPORT, send, ship, deliver, hand over; repatriate.

extradition noun *detainees awaiting extradition* DEPORTATION, repatriation, expulsion.

extraneous adjective **1** *extraneous considerations* IRRELEVANT, immaterial, beside the point, unrelated, unconnected, inapposite, inapplicable, superfluous.

2 *extraneous noise* EXTERNAL, outside, exterior.

extraordinary adjective **1** *an extraordinary coincidence* REMARKABLE, exceptional, amazing, astonishing, astounding, sensational, stunning, incredible, unbelievable, phenomenal; striking, outstanding, momentous, impressive, singular, memorable, unforgettable, unique, noteworthy; out of the ordinary, unusual, uncommon, rare, surprising; *informal* fantastic, terrific, tremendous, stupendous, awesome; *literary* wondrous.

2 *extraordinary speed* VERY GREAT, tremendous, enormous, immense, prodigious, stupendous, monumental.

extraterrestrial adjective & noun See ALIEN adjective sense 3, noun sense 2.

extravagance noun **1** *a fit of extravagance* PROFLIGACY, improvidence, wastefulness, prodigality, lavishness.

2 *the costliest brand is an extravagance* LUXURY, indulgence, self-indulgence, treat, extra, nonessential.

3 *the extravagance of the decor* ORNATENESS, elaborateness, embellishment, ornamentation; ostentation, overelaborateness, excessiveness, exaggeration, outrageousness, immoderation, excess.

extravagant adjective **1** *an extravagant lifestyle* SPENDTHRIFT, profligate, improvident, wasteful, prodigal, lavish. ANTONYM thrifty.

2 *extravagant gifts* EXPENSIVE, costly, lavish, high-priced, high-cost; valuable, precious; *informal* pricey, costing the earth. ANTONYM cheap.

3 *extravagant prices* EXORBITANT, extortionate, excessive, high, unreasonable. ANTONYMS reasonable, low.

4 *extravagant praise* EXCESSIVE, immoderate, exaggerated, gushing, unrestrained, effusive, fulsome. See note at PROFUSE. ANTONYM moderate.

5 *decorated in an extravagant style* ORNATE, elaborate, decorated, ornamented, fancy; overelaborate, gaudy, garish, ostentatious, exaggerated, baroque, rococo; *informal* lavish, flashy, glitzy. ANTONYM plain.

extravaganza noun *a star-studded extravaganza to raise funds for AIDS research* SPECTACULAR, display, spectacle, show, pageant, gala; blowout, barn burner.

extreme adjective **1** *extreme danger* UTMOST, very great, greatest, greatest possible, maximum, maximal, highest, supreme, great, acute, enormous, severe, high, exceptional, extraordinary. ANTONYM slight.

2 *extreme measures* DRASTIC, serious, desperate, dire, radical, far-reaching, momentous, consequential; heavy, sharp, severe, austere, harsh, tough, strict, rigorous, oppressive, draconian. ANTONYM mild.

3 *extreme views* RADICAL, extremist, immoderate, fanatical, revolutionary, rebel, subversive, militant, far-right, far-left. ANTONYM moderate.

4 *extreme sports* DANGEROUS, hazardous, risky, high-risk, adventurous. ANTONYMS tame, safe.

5 *the extreme north* FURTHEST, farthest, furthermost, far, very, utmost; *archaic* outmost. ANTONYM near.

▸ noun **1** *the two extremes* OPPOSITE, antithesis, side of the coin, (opposite) pole, antipode.

2 *this attitude is taken to its extreme in the following quote* LIMIT, extremity, highest/greatest degree, maximum, height, top, zenith, peak, ne plus ultra.

PHRASE: **in the extreme** *David was generous in the extreme.* See EXTREMELY.

extremely adverb *even on the hottest days, the caverns are extremely cold* VERY, exceedingly, exceptionally, especially, extraordinarily, in the extreme, tremendously, immensely, vastly, hugely, intensely, acutely, singularly, uncommonly, unusually, decidedly, particularly, supremely, highly, remarkably, really, truly, mightily; *informal* terrifically, awfully, terribly, devilishly, majorly, seriously, mega, ultra, damn, damned, ever so, real, mighty, awful, way, darned, gosh-darn; *archaic* exceeding. ANTONYMS slightly, barely.

extremist noun *the attack was carried out by a group of right-wing extremists* FANATIC, radical, zealot, fundamentalist, hard-liner, militant, activist; *informal* ultra. See note at ZEALOT. ANTONYM moderate.

extremity noun **1** *the eastern extremity* LIMIT, end, edge, side, farthest point, boundary, border, frontier; perimeter, periphery, margin; *literary* bourn, marge.

2 *she lost feeling in her extremities* FINGERS AND TOES, hands and feet, limbs.

3 *the extremity of the violence* INTENSITY, magnitude, acuteness, ferocity, vehemence, fierceness, violence, severity, seriousness, strength, power, powerfulness, vigor, force, forcefulness.

4 *in extremity he will send for her* DIRE STRAITS, trouble, difficulty, hard times, hardship, adversity, misfortune, distress; (a) crisis, an emergency, (a) disaster, (a) catastrophe, calamity; a predicament, a plight, mess, a dilemma; *informal* a fix, a pickle, a jam, a spot, a bind, a hole, a sticky situation, hot water, deep water.

extricate verb *there's always someone who can extricate these wealthy little brats from their run-ins with the law* EXTRACT, free, release, disentangle, get out, remove, withdraw, disengage; *informal* get someone/oneself off the hook.

extrinsic adjective *climate, geography, and other extrinsic factors* EXTERNAL, extraneous, exterior, outside, outward. ANTONYM intrinsic.

extrovert noun *like many extroverts, he was unhappy inside* OUTGOING PERSON, sociable person, socializer, life of the party. ANTONYM introvert.

▸ adjective *Raj's extrovert personality* OUTGOING, extroverted, sociable, gregarious, genial, affable, friendly, unreserved. ANTONYM introverted.

extrude verb *machines extrude the plastics that become jars and bottles* FORCE OUT, thrust out, express, eject, expel, release, emit.

exuberant adjective **1** *exuberant guests dancing on the terrace* EBULLIENT, buoyant, cheerful, jaunty, lighthearted, high-spirited, exhilarated, excited, elated, exultant, euphoric, joyful, cheery, merry, jubilant, vivacious, enthusiastic, irrepressible, energetic, animated, full of life, lively, vigorous, adrenalized; *informal* bubbly, bouncy, chipper, chirpy, full of beans; *literary* blithe. ANTONYM gloomy.

2 *an exuberant welcome* EFFUSIVE, extravagant, fulsome, expansive, gushing, gushy, demonstrative. ANTONYM restrained.

3 *an exuberant coating of mosses* LUXURIANT, lush, rich, dense, thick, abundant, profuse, plentiful, prolific. ANTONYM meager.

exude verb **1** *milkweed exudes a milky sap* GIVE OFF/OUT, discharge, release, emit, issue; ooze, weep, secrete, excrete.

2 *slime exudes from the fungus* OOZE, seep, issue, escape, discharge, flow, leak.

3 *he exuded self-confidence* EMANATE, radiate, ooze, emit; display, show, evince, exhibit, manifest, transmit, embody.

exult verb **1** *her opponents exulted when she left* REJOICE, be joyful, be happy, be delighted, be elated, be ecstatic, be overjoyed, be jubilant, be rapturous, be in raptures, be thrilled, jump for joy, be on cloud nine, be in seventh heaven; celebrate, cheer; *informal* be over the moon, be on top of the world; *literary* joy; *archaic* jubilate. ANTONYM sorrow.

2 *he **exulted in** his triumph* REJOICE AT/IN, take delight in, find/take pleasure in, find joy in, enjoy, revel in, glory in, delight in, relish, savor; be/feel proud of, congratulate oneself on. ANTONYM sorrow.

exultant adjective *the exultant winners waved to the crowd* JUBILANT, thrilled, triumphant, delighted, exhilarated, happy, overjoyed, joyous, joyful, gleeful, excited, rejoicing, ecstatic, euphoric, elated, rapturous, in raptures, enraptured, on cloud nine, in seventh heaven; *rare* exilient; *informal* over the moon, jumping for joy.

WORD NOTE **exilient**

With this word we could rid the world forever of the phrase *jumping for joy,* for it means exactly that; a useful synonym for *exultant; rapturous. Exilience* makes a change from *ebullience,* and is more specifically concerned with delight, which *ebullience* (though often used in this way) is not. **–ZS**

exultation noun *a gold medalist filled with exultation* JUBILATION, rejoicing, happiness, pleasure, joy, gladness, delight, glee, elation, cheer, euphoria, exhilaration, delirium, ecstasy, rapture, exuberance.

eye noun **1** *he rubbed his eyes* EYEBALL; *informal* peeper, baby blues; *literary* or *humorous* orb.

2 *sharp eyes* EYESIGHT, vision, sight, powers of observation, perception, visual perception.

3 *an eye for a bargain* APPRECIATION, awareness, alertness, perception, consciousness, feeling, instinct, intuition, nose.

4 *his thoughtful eye* WATCH, observance, gaze, stare, regard; observation, surveillance, vigilance, contemplation, scrutiny.

5 **(eyes)** *to desert was despicable in their eyes* OPINION, thinking, way of thinking, mind, view, viewpoint, point of view, attitude, standpoint, perspective, belief, judgment, assessment, analysis, estimation.

6 *the eye of a needle* HOLE, opening, aperture, eyelet, slit, slot.

7 *the eye of the storm* CENTER, middle, heart, core, hub, thick.

▸ verb *I saw him intently eyeing that antique car* LOOK AT, observe, view, gaze at, stare at, regard, contemplate, survey, scrutinize, consider, glance at; watch, keep an eye on, keep under observation; ogle, leer at, make eyes at; *informal* have/take a gander at, check out, size up, eyeball; *literary* behold.

PHRASES: **lay/set/clap eyes on** *informal have you ever laid your eyes on a more beautiful sailboat?* SEE, observe, notice, spot, spy, catch sight of, glimpse, catch/get a glimpse of; *literary* behold, espy, descry. **see eye to eye** *even best friends can't expect to see eye to eye on everything* AGREE, concur, be in agreement, be of the same mind/opinion, be in accord, think as one; be on the same wavelength, get on/along.

eye candy noun *most critics panned the film as being little more than 96 minutes of eye candy* VISUAL FEAST, eyeful; gloss, tinsel, veneer, decoration, glitter, flamboyance, gaudiness; ritz, glitz, garishness, razzle-dazzle, razzmatazz; sight for sore eyes.

eye-catching adjective *eye-catching designs adorn each door* STRIKING, arresting, conspicuous, dramatic, impressive, spectacular, breathtaking, dazzling, amazing, stunning, sensational, remarkable, distinctive, unusual, out of the ordinary.

eyelash noun *long brown eyelashes* LASH; *Anatomy* cilium.

eyesight noun *my eyesight is perfect* SIGHT, vision, faculty of sight, ability to see, visual perception, perception.

eyesore noun *what's left of the old factory is a danger and an eyesore* MONSTROSITY, blot (on the landscape), mess, scar, blight, disfigurement, blemish, ugly sight.

eyewitness noun *several eyewitnesses were questioned by the police* OBSERVER, onlooker, witness, bystander, spectator, watcher, viewer, passerby, gawker; *literary* beholder.

F

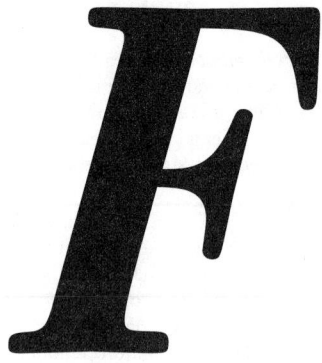

fable noun **1** *the fable of the wary fox* MORAL TALE, tale, parable, allegory.

2 *the fables of ancient Greece* MYTH, legend, saga, epic, folk tale, folk story, fairy tale, mythos, folklore, mythology. See note at FICTION.

fabled adjective **1** *a fabled god-giant of Finnish myth* LEGENDARY, mythical, mythic, mythological, fabulous, folkloric, fairy-tale; fictitious, fantastic, imaginary, imagined, made-up.

2 *the fabled quality of French wine* CELEBRATED, renowned, famed, famous, well-known, legendary, prized, noted, notable, acclaimed, esteemed, prestigious, of repute, of high standing.

fabric noun **1** *the finest silk fabric* CLOTH, material, textile, tissue. See table.

2 *the fabric of society* STRUCTURE, infrastructure, framework, frame, form, composition, construction, foundations, warp and woof.

FABRICS

acetate
acid-washed
acrylic
alpaca
angora
astrakhan
baize
barathea
batik
batiste
bengaline
bombazine
bouclé
broadcloth
brocade
buckram
buckskin
bunting
burlap
calico
cambric
camel hair
canvas
cashmere
cavalry twill
challis
chambray
charmeuse
chenille
chiffon
chino
chintz
ciré
cloqué
corduroy
cotton
crash
crepe
cretonne
crinoline
crushed velvet
Dacron
damask
denim
dimity
drill
drugget
duck
duffel
dupioni
faille
felt
fishnet
flannel
flannelette
fleece
foulard
gabardine
gauze
gingham
Gore-Tex™
grasscloth
grenadine
grosgrain
gunny
Harris tweed
herringbone
hopsack
horsehair
huckaback
ikat
jaconet
jacquard
jean
jersey
kente
kersey
khaddar
khaki
knit
lace
lamé
lawn
leatherette
leno
linen
loden
Lurex™
Lycra™
mackintosh
madras
melton
merino
mohair
moiré
muslin
nainsook
nankeen
Naugahyde™
nylon
oilcloth
organdy
organza
Orlon™
ottoman
oxford cloth
paisley
panne
pashmina
peachskin
peau de soie
percale
piqué
plaid
plissé
plush
polar fleece
polycotton
polyester
pongee
poplin
ramie
rayon
sateen
satin
saxony
seersucker
serge
shantung
sharkskin
silk
spandex
suede
swansdown
taffeta
tartan
tattersall
terrycloth
ticking
toile
toweling
tricot
tulle
tweed
twill
Ultrasuede™
veiling
velour
velvet
velveteen
vicuña
Viyella™
voile
webbing
whipcord
wool
worsted

fabricate verb **1** *he fabricated research data* FALSIFY, fake, counterfeit, cook; invent, make up. See note at LIE[1].

2 *fabricating a pack of lies* CONCOCT, make up, dream up, invent, trump up; *informal* cook up.

3 *you will have to fabricate an exhaust system* MAKE, create, manufacture, produce; construct, build, assemble, put together, form, fashion.

fabrication noun **1** *the story was a complete fabrication* INVENTION, concoction, (piece of) fiction, falsification, lie, untruth, falsehood, fib, myth, made-up story, fairy story/tale, cock-and-bull story; white lie, half-truth, exaggeration; *informal* tall tale, whopper. See note at FICTION.

2 *the lintels are galvanized after fabrication* MANUFACTURE, creation, production; construction, building, assembly, forming, fashioning.

fabulous adjective **1** *fabulous wealth* TREMENDOUS, stupendous, prodigious, phenomenal, remarkable, exceptional; astounding, amazing, fantastic, breathtaking, staggering, unthinkable, unimaginable, incredible, unbelievable, unheard of, untold, undreamed of, beyond one's wildest dreams; *informal* mind-boggling, mind-blowing, jaw-dropping.

2 *informal we had a fabulous time.* See EXCELLENT.

3 *a fabulous horselike beast* MYTHICAL, legendary, mythic, mythological, fabled, folkloric, fairy-tale; fictitious, imaginary, imagined, made up.

facade noun **1** *a vinyl-sided facade* FRONT, frontage, face, elevation, exterior, outside.

2 *a facade of bonhomie* SHOW, front, appearance, pretense, simulation, affectation, semblance, illusion, act, masquerade, charade, mask, cloak, veil, veneer.

face noun **1** *a beautiful face* COUNTENANCE, physiognomy, features; *informal* mug; puss; *literary* visage; *archaic* front.

2 *her face grew sad* (FACIAL) EXPRESSION, look, appearance, air, manner, bearing, countenance, mien.

3 *he made a face at the sourness of the drink* GRIMACE, scowl, wry face, wince, frown, glower, pout, moue.

4 *a cube has six faces* SIDE, aspect, flank, surface, plane, facet, wall, elevation.

5 *a watch face* DIAL, display.

6 *changing the face of the industry* APPEARANCE, outward appearance, aspect, nature, image.

7 *he put on a brave face* FRONT, show, display, act, appearance, facade, exterior, mask, masquerade, pretense, pose, veneer.

8 *criticism should never cause the recipient to lose face* RESPECT, honor, esteem, regard, admiration, approbation, acclaim, approval, favor, appreciation, popularity, prestige, standing, status, dignity; self-respect, self-esteem.

▸ verb **1** *the hotel faces the sea* LOOK OUT ON, front on to, look toward, be facing, look over/across, overlook, give on to, be opposite (to).

2 *you'll just have to face the facts* ACCEPT, become reconciled to, get used to, become accustomed to, adjust to, acclimatize oneself to; learn to live with, cope with, deal with, come to terms with, become resigned to.

3 *he faces a humiliating rejection* BE CONFRONTED BY, be faced with, encounter, experience, come into contact with, come up against.

4 *the problems facing our police force* BESET, worry, distress, trouble, bother, confront; harass, oppress, vex, irritate, exasperate, strain, stress, tax; torment, plague, blight, bedevil, curse; *formal* discommode.

5 *he faced the challenge boldly* BRAVE, face up to, encounter, meet, meet head-on, confront; oppose, resist, withstand.

6 *a wall faced with stucco* COVER, clad, veneer, overlay, surface, dress, put a facing on, laminate, coat, line.

PHRASES: **face to face** *the two men stood face to face* FACING (EACH OTHER), opposite (each other), across from each other. **on the face of it** *on the face on it, the peace talks are going quite well* OSTENSIBLY, to all appearances, to all intents and purposes, at first glance, on the surface, superficially; apparently, seemingly, outwardly, it seems (that), it would seem (that), it appears (that), it would appear (that), as far as one can see/tell, by all accounts.

faceless adjective *they are just faceless people to him, individuals whose needs he can simply ignore* ANONYMOUS, unknown, nameless; characterless, nondescript, undistinguished, featureless.

facelift noun **1** *she's planning to have a facelift* COSMETIC SURGERY, plastic surgery, nip and tuck.

2 *informal the theater is reopening after a facelift* RENOVATION, redecoration, refurbishment, revamp, revamping, makeover, reconditioning, overhauling, modernization, restoration, repair, redevelopment, rebuilding, reconstruction, refit.

facet noun **1** *the many facets of the gem* SURFACE, face, side, plane.

2 *other facets of his character* ASPECT, feature, side, dimension, characteristic, detail, point, ingredient, strand; component, constituent, element.

facetious adjective *unfortunately, they took my facetious remarks seriously* FLIPPANT, flip, glib, frivolous, tongue-in-cheek, ironic, sardonic, joking, jokey, jocular, playful, sportive, teasing, mischievous; witty, amusing, funny, droll, comic, comical, lighthearted, jocose. ANTONYM serious.

facile adjective **1** *a facile explanation* SIMPLISTIC, superficial, oversimplified; shallow, glib, jejune, naive; dime-store.

2 *he achieved a facile victory* EFFORTLESS, easy, undemanding, unexacting, painless, trouble-free.

USAGE NOTE facile

Always meaning "easy" in one sense or another, *facile* may connote either proficiency or shallowness. The writer must achieve clarity through context. Sometimes the word connotes the ease that comes with artistic mastery—e.g.: "Nicolai Dobrev played the jester, a noble baritone with a facile instrument." (*Boston Herald*; Mar. 30, 2002.) More often, it connotes triteness or oversimplification—e.g.: "But most mental health experts say closure is no holy grail, only rendered so by people seeking facile solutions to complex problems." (*Christian Science Monitor*; Mar. 28, 2002.) **—BG**

facilitate verb *private funding has facilitated our research* MAKE EASY/EASIER, ease, make possible, make smooth/smoother, smooth the way for; enable, assist, help (along), aid, oil the wheels of, expedite, speed up, accelerate, forward, advance, promote, further, encourage, catalyze, be a catalyst for. ANTONYM impede.

facility noun **1** *parking facilities* PROVISION, space, means, potential, equipment.

2 *the facilities consisted of an old wooden outhouse* WASHROOM, toilet, restroom, bathroom.

3 *a wealth of local facilities* AMENITY, resource, service, advantage, convenience, benefit.

4 *a medical facility* ESTABLISHMENT, center, place, station, location, premises, site, post, base; *informal* joint, outfit, setup.

5 *his facility for drawing* APTITUDE, talent, gift, flair, bent, skill, knack, genius; ability, proficiency, competence, capability, capacity, faculty; expertness, adeptness, prowess, mastery, artistry.

facing[1] noun **1** *green velvet facings* COVERING, trimming, lining, interfacing.

2 *brick facing on a concrete core* SIDING, facade, cladding, veneer, skin, surface, front, coating, covering, dressing, overlay, lamination, plating.

facing[2] preposition *the two stone jackals sit facing each other* OPPOSITE (TO), face to face with, across from; *informal* eyeball to eyeball with; *archaic* fronting.

WORD NOTE **fornent, fornenst**

This is an excellent synonym for *opposite to, facing,* and also *alongside.* It has a secondary discursive usage: "with regard to, concerning." Before dismissing this word as an arch and archaic poeticism, it should be remembered that it is common in Northern Ireland, used in an everyday way by everyday people. It is one of the many prepositions the English took to Ireland and then forgot to bring home with them when they left. This should be their loss and not the rest of the world's. Worth attempting in a novel if only to see what happens. **—ZS**

facsimile noun *a facsimile of the manuscript* COPY, reproduction, duplicate, photocopy, replica, likeness, print, reprint, printout, offprint, fax; *trademark* Xerox; *dated* carbon copy, photostat, mimeograph. ANTONYM original.

fact noun **1** *it is a fact that the water is polluted* REALITY, actuality, certainty; truth, verity, gospel. ANTONYMS lie, fiction.

2 *every fact was double-checked* DETAIL, piece of information, particular, item, specific, element, point, factor, feature, characteristic, ingredient, circumstance, aspect, facet; **(facts)** information.

3 *an accessory after the fact* EVENT, happening, occurrence, incident, act, deed. PHRASE: **in fact** *Mr. Hartmann was in fact present at the time of the shooting* ACTUALLY, in actuality, in actual fact, really, in reality, in point of fact, as a matter of fact, as it happens, in truth, to tell the truth; *archaic* in sooth, verily.

faction noun **1** *a faction of the party* CLIQUE, coterie, caucus, cabal, bloc, camp, group, grouping, sector, section, wing, arm, branch, set; ginger group, pressure group.

2 *the council was split by faction* INFIGHTING, dissension, dissent, dispute, discord, strife, conflict, friction, argument, disagreement, controversy, quarreling, wrangling, bickering, squabbling, disharmony, disunity, schism.

factious adjective *factious parties have weakened the movement* DIVIDED, split, schismatic, discordant, conflicting, argumentative, disagreeing, disputatious, quarreling, quarrelsome, clashing, warring, at loggerheads, at odds, rebellious, mutinous. ANTONYM harmonious.

factitious adjective *the papers are shamelessly printing these factitious accounts* BOGUS, fake, specious, false, counterfeit, fraudulent, spurious, sham, mock, feigned, affected, pretended, contrived, engineered, inauthentic, ersatz; *informal* phony, pseudo, pretend. ANTONYM genuine.

factor noun *this had been a key factor in his decision to withdraw* ELEMENT, part, component, ingredient, strand, constituent, point, detail, item, feature, facet, aspect, characteristic, consideration, influence, circumstance.

factory noun *jobs in the factories were getting harder to find* PLANT, works, yard, mill, workshop, shop; *informal* sweatshop.

factotum noun *back then, these wealthy college boys made sure their personal factotums were just a whistle away* HANDYMAN, jack of all trades; assistant, man Friday, gal/girl Friday; gofer; *informal* Mr./Ms. Fix-It.

factual adjective *a factual report from the chairman* TRUTHFUL, true, accurate, authentic, historical, genuine, fact-based; true-to-life, correct, exact, honest, faithful, literal, verbatim, word for word, well-documented, unbiased, objective, unvarnished; *formal* veridical. ANTONYM fictitious.

faculty noun **1** *the faculty of speech* POWER, capability, capacity, facility, wherewithal, means; **(faculties)** senses, wits, reason, intelligence.

2 *an unusual faculty for unearthing contributors* ABILITY, proficiency, competence, capability, potential, capacity, facility; aptitude, talent, gift, flair, bent, skill, knack, genius; expertise, expertness, adeptness, adroitness, dexterity, prowess, mastery, artistry.

3 *conflict between students and faculty* STAFF, teachers, professors, instructors.

4 *the arts faculty* DEPARTMENT, school, division, section.

fad noun *when I was a kid, no fad was more apparent than the coonskin cap* CRAZE, vogue, trend, fashion, mode, enthusiasm, passion, obsession, mania, rage, compulsion, fixation, fetish, fancy, whim, fascination; *informal* thing.

fade verb **1** *the paintwork has faded* BECOME PALE, become bleached, become washed out, lose color, discolor; grow dull, grow dim, lose luster. ANTONYM brighten.

2 *sunlight had faded the picture* BLEACH, wash out, make pale, blanch, whiten. ANTONYMS brighten, enhance.

3 *remove the flower heads as they fade* WITHER, wilt, droop, shrivel, die.

4 *the afternoon light began to fade* DIM, grow dim, grow faint, fail, dwindle, die away, wane, disappear, vanish, decline, melt away; *literary* evanesce. ANTONYM increase.

5 *the Communist movement was* ***fading away*** DECLINE, die out, diminish, deteriorate, decay, crumble, collapse, fail, fall, sink, slump, go downhill; *informal* go to pot, go to the dogs; *archaic* retrograde. ANTONYM thrive.

fail verb **1** *the enterprise had failed* BE UNSUCCESSFUL, not succeed, fall through, fall flat, collapse, founder, backfire, meet with disaster, come to nothing, come to naught; *informal* flop, bomb. ANTONYM succeed.

2 *he has failed the final French examination* BE UNSUCCESSFUL IN, not pass; not make the grade on; *informal* FLUNK, botch, blow, screw up, bungle. ANTONYM pass.

3 *at his lowest point, his friends failed him* LET DOWN, disappoint; desert, abandon, betray, be disloyal to; *literary* forsake. ANTONYM support.

4 *the crops failed* DIE, wither; be deficient, be insufficient, be inadequate. ANTONYM thrive.

5 *daylight failed* FADE, dim, die away, wane, disappear, vanish.

6 *the ventilation system failed* BREAK DOWN, break, stop working, cut out, crash; malfunction, go wrong, develop a fault; *informal* conk out, go on the blink, go on the fritz. ANTONYM work.

7 *Joe's health was failing* DETERIORATE, degenerate, decline, fade, wane, ebb. ANTONYM improving.

8 *900 businesses are failing a week* COLLAPSE, crash, go under, go bankrupt, go into receivership, go into liquidation, cease trading; *informal* fold, flop, go bust, go broke, go belly-up. ANTONYM thrive.

PHRASE: **without fail** *without fail, Carlos leaves for lunch at 12:05 every day* WITHOUT EXCEPTION, unfailingly, regularly, invariably, predictably, conscientiously, religiously, whatever happened.

failing noun *Deborah accepted him despite his failings* FAULT, shortcoming, weakness, imperfection, defect, flaw, frailty, foible, idiosyncrasy, vice. ANTONYM strength.

▸ preposition *failing financial assistance, you will be bankrupt* IN THE ABSENCE OF, lacking, barring, absent, without.

failure noun 1 *the failure of the assassination attempt* LACK OF SUCCESS, nonfulfillment, defeat, collapse, foundering. ANTONYM success.

2 *all his schemes had been a failure* FIASCO, debacle, catastrophe, disaster; *informal* flop, megaflop, washout, dead loss, snafu, clinker, dud, no-go. ANTONYM success.

3 *she was regarded as a failure* LOSER, underachiever, ne'er-do-well, disappointment; *informal* no-hoper, dead loss, dud, write-off. ANTONYM success.

4 *his failure in duty* NEGLIGENCE, dereliction; omission, oversight.

5 *a crop failure* INADEQUACY, insufficiency, deficiency, dearth, scarcity, shortfall.

6 *the failure of the camera* BREAKING DOWN, breakdown, malfunction; crash.

7 *company failures* COLLAPSE, crash, bankruptcy, insolvency, liquidation, closure. ANTONYM success.

faint adjective 1 *a faint mark* INDISTINCT, vague, unclear, indefinite, ill-defined, imperceptible, unobtrusive; pale, light, faded. ANTONYM clear.

2 *a faint cry* QUIET, muted, muffled, stifled; feeble, weak, whispered, murmured, indistinct; low, soft, gentle. ANTONYM loud.

3 *a faint possibility* SLIGHT, slender, slim, small, tiny, negligible, remote, vague, unlikely, improbable; *informal* minuscule. ANTONYM great.

4 *faint praise* UNENTHUSIASTIC, halfhearted, weak, feeble. ANTONYM strong.

5 *I suddenly felt faint* DIZZY, giddy, lightheaded, unsteady; *informal* woozy.

▸ verb *she thought he would faint* PASS OUT, lose consciousness, black out, keel over, swoon; *informal* flake out, conk out, zonk out, go out like a light.

▸ noun *a dead faint* BLACKOUT, fainting fit, loss of consciousness, swoon; *Medicine* syncope.

faint-hearted adjective *come now, my faint-hearted friend, I'll get you to safety* TIMID, timorous, nervous, easily scared, fearful, afraid; cowardly, craven, spineless, pusillanimous, lily-livered; *informal* chicken, chicken-hearted, yellow-bellied, gutless, sissy, wimpy, wimpish. ANTONYM brave.

faintly adverb 1 *Maria called his name faintly* INDISTINCTLY, softly, gently, weakly; in a whisper, in a murmur, in a low voice. ANTONYM loudly.

2 *he looked faintly bewildered* SLIGHTLY, vaguely, somewhat, quite, fairly, rather, a little, a bit, a touch, a shade; *informal* sort of, kind of, kinda. ANTONYM extremely.

fair[1] adjective 1 *the courts were generally fair* JUST, equitable, honest, upright, honorable, trustworthy; impartial, unbiased, unprejudiced, nonpartisan, neutral, evenhanded; lawful, legal, legitimate; *informal* legit, on the level; on the up and up. ANTONYMS unjust, biased.

2 *fair weather* FINE, dry, bright, clear, sunny, cloudless; warm, balmy, clement, benign, pleasant. ANTONYM inclement.

3 *fair winds* FAVORABLE, advantageous, benign; on one's side, in one's favor. ANTONYM unfavorable.

4 *fair hair* BLOND/BLONDE, yellowish, golden, flaxen, light, light brown, ash blond. ANTONYM dark.

5 *Hermione's fair skin* PALE, light, light-colored, white, creamy. ANTONYM dark.

6 *archaic the fair maiden's heart.* See BEAUTIFUL.

7 *the restaurant was fair* REASONABLE, passable, tolerable, satisfactory, acceptable, respectable, decent, all right, good enough, pretty good, not bad, average, middling; *informal* OK, so-so, [comme ci, comme ça]. PHRASE: **fair and square** *face it, I beat you fair and square* HONESTLY, fairly, without cheating, without foul play, by the book; lawfully, legally, legitimately; *informal* on the level, on the up and up.

fair[2] noun 1 *a country fair* CARNIVAL, festival, exhibition; midway.

2 *an antiques fair* MARKET, bazaar, flea market, exchange, sale; *dated* emporium.

3 *a new art fair* EXHIBITION, exhibit, display, show, presentation, exposition.

fairly adverb 1 *all students were treated fairly* JUSTLY, equitably, impartially, without bias, without prejudice, evenhandedly; lawfully, legally, legitimately, by the book; equally, the same.

2 *the pipes are in fairly good condition* REASONABLY, passably, tolerably, adequately, moderately, quite, relatively, comparatively; *informal* pretty, kind of, kinda, sort of.

fair-minded adjective *all you can do now is pray for a fair-minded jury* FAIR, just, evenhanded, equitable, impartial, nonpartisan, unbiased, unprejudiced; honest, honorable, trustworthy, upright, decent; *informal* on the level; on the up and up.

fairy noun *we were gleefully certain that little fairies inhabited our woods* SPRITE, pixie, elf, imp, brownie, puck, leprechaun; *literary* faerie, fay.

fairy tale, fairy story noun **1** *the movie was inspired by a fairy tale* FOLK TALE, folk story, traditional story, myth, legend, fantasy, fable.

2 *informal she accused him of telling fairy tales* LIE, white lie, fib, half-truth, untruth, falsehood, tall tale, story, fabrication, invention, fiction; *informal* whopper, cock-and-bull story.

faith noun **1** *he justified his boss's faith in him* TRUST, belief, confidence, conviction; optimism, hopefulness, hope. ANTONYM mistrust.

2 *she gave her life for her faith* RELIGION, church, sect, denomination, (religious) persuasion, (religious) belief, ideology, creed, teaching, doctrine. PHRASES: **break faith with** *our own chairman has broken faith with this organization* BE DISLOYAL TO, be unfaithful to, be untrue to, betray, play someone false, break one's promise to, fail, let down; double-cross, deceive, cheat, stab in the back. **keep faith with** *Mrs. Grimes has always kept faith with everyone in my department* BE LOYAL TO, be faithful to, be true to, stand by, stick by, keep one's promise to.

faithful adjective **1** *his faithful assistant* LOYAL, constant, true, devoted, true-blue, unswerving, staunch, steadfast, dedicated, committed; trusty, trustworthy, dependable, reliable. See note at RESOLUTE. ANTONYMS traitorous, unreliable.

2 *a faithful copy* ACCURATE, precise, exact, errorless, unerring, faultless, true, close, strict; realistic, authentic; *informal* on the mark, bang on, on the money. ANTONYM inaccurate.

faithless adjective **1** *her faithless lover* UNFAITHFUL, disloyal, inconstant, false, untrue, adulterous, traitorous; fickle, flighty, untrustworthy, unreliable, undependable; deceitful, two-faced, double-crossing; *informal* cheating, two-timing, backstabbing; *literary* perfidious.

2 *a faithless society* UNBELIEVING, nonbelieving, irreligious, disbelieving, agnostic, atheistic; pagan, heathen.

fake noun **1** *the sculpture was a fake* FORGERY, counterfeit, copy, pirate(d) copy, sham, fraud, hoax, imitation, mock-up, dummy, reproduction; *informal* phony, rip-off, knockoff, dupe.

2 *that doctor is a fake* CHARLATAN, fraud, fraudster, mountebank, sham, quack, humbug, impostor, hoaxer, cheat, trickster; *informal* phony, con man, con artist, scam artist. See note at QUACK.

▸ adjective **1** *fake $50 bills* COUNTERFEIT, forged, fraudulent, sham, imitation, pirate(d), false, bogus; invalid, inauthentic; *informal* phony, dud. ANTONYM genuine.

2 *fake diamonds* IMITATION, artificial, synthetic, simulated, reproduction, replica, ersatz, faux, man-made, dummy, false, mock, bogus; *informal* pretend, phony, pseudo. ANTONYM genuine.

3 *a fake accent* FEIGNED, faked, put-on, assumed, invented, affected, pseudo; unconvincing, artificial, mock; *informal* phony. ANTONYM authentic.

▸ verb **1** *the certificate was faked* FORGE, counterfeit, falsify, mock up, copy, pirate, reproduce, replicate; doctor, alter, tamper with.

2 *she faked a yawn* FEIGN, pretend, simulate, put on, affect.

fall verb **1** *bombs began to fall* DROP, descend, come down, go down; plummet, plunge, sink, dive, tumble; cascade. ANTONYM rise.

2 *he tripped and fell* TOPPLE OVER, tumble over, keel over, fall down/over, go head over heels, go headlong, collapse, take a spill, pitch forward; trip, stumble, slip; *informal* come a cropper. ANTONYM get up.

3 *the river began to fall* SUBSIDE, recede, ebb, flow back, fall away, go down, sink. ANTONYMS rise, flood.

4 *inflation will fall* DECREASE, decline, diminish, fall off, drop off, lessen, dwindle; plummet, plunge, slump, sink; depreciate, cheapen, devalue; *informal* go through the floor, nosedive, take a header, crash. ANTONYMS rise, increase.

5 *the Mogul empire fell* DECLINE, deteriorate, degenerate, go downhill, go to rack and ruin; decay, wither, fade, fail; *informal* go to the dogs, go to pot, go down the toilet. ANTONYMS rise, flood, increase, flourish.

6 *those who fell in the war* DIE, perish, lose one's life, be killed, be slain, be lost, meet one's death; *informal* bite the dust, croak, buy it, buy the farm. ANTONYM flourish.

7 *the town **fell to** the barbarians* SURRENDER TO, yield to, submit to, give in to, capitulate to, succumb to; be taken by, be defeated by, be conquered by, be overwhelmed by. ANTONYM resist.

8 *Easter falls on April 11th* OCCUR, take place, happen, come about; arise; *literary* come to pass.

9 *night fell* COME, arrive, appear, arise, materialize.

10 *she fell ill* BECOME, grow, get, turn.

11 *more tasks may **fall to** him* BE THE RESPONSIBILITY OF, be the duty of, be borne by, be one's job; come someone's way.

▸ noun **1** *an accidental fall* TUMBLE, trip, spill, topple, slip; collapse; *informal* nosedive, header, cropper.

2 *a fall in sales* DECLINE, falloff, drop, decrease, cut, dip, reduction, downswing; plummet, plunge, slump; *informal* nosedive, crash. ANTONYM increase.

3 *the fall of the Roman Empire* DOWNFALL, collapse, ruin, ruination, failure, decline, deterioration, degeneration; destruction, overthrow, demise. ANTONYMS increase, rise, ascent.

4 *the fall of the city* SURRENDER, capitulation, yielding, submission; defeat. ANTONYM rise.

5 *a steep fall down to the ocean* DESCENT, declivity, slope, slant, incline, downgrade. ANTONYM ascent.

6 *the fall of man* SIN, wrongdoing, transgression, error, offense, lapse, fall from grace, original sin.

7 (**falls**) *rafting trips below the falls* WATERFALL, cascade, cataract; rapids, white water.

PHRASES: **fall apart** *the old teacup fell apart in my hands* FALL TO PIECES, fall to bits, come apart (at the seams); disintegrate, fragment, break up, break apart, crumble, decay, perish; *informal* bust. **fall asleep** *I almost fell asleep at work* DOZE OFF, drop off, go to sleep; *informal* nod off, go off, drift off, crash, conk out, go out like a light, sack out. **fall away** *the ground here falls away abruptly* SLOPE DOWN, slope, slant down, go down, drop, drop away, descend, dip, sink, plunge. **fall back** *the troops were ordered to fall back* RETREAT, withdraw, back off, draw back, pull back, pull away, move away. **fall back on** *I can always fall back on my career in landscaping* RESORT TO, turn to, look to, call on, have recourse to; rely on, depend on, lean on. **fall behind** 1 *the other walkers fell behind* LAG, lag behind, trail, trail behind, be left behind, drop back, bring up the rear; straggle, dally, dawdle, hang back. 2 *they fell behind on their payments* GET INTO DEBT, get into arrears, default, be in the red. **fall for** 1 *she fell for John* FALL IN LOVE WITH, become infatuated with, lose one's heart to, take a fancy to, be smitten with/by, be attracted to; *informal* have the hots for. 2 *she won't fall for that trick* BE DECEIVED BY, be duped by, be fooled by, be taken in by, believe, trust, be convinced by; *informal* go for, buy, swallow (hook, line, and sinker). **fall in** 1 *the roof fell in* COLLAPSE, cave in, crash in, fall down; give way, crumble, disintegrate. 2 *the soldiers fell in* GET IN FORMATION, get in line, line up, take one's position. 3 *he fell in with a bad crowd* GET INVOLVED, take up, join up, go around, make friends; *informal* hang, hang out. **fall off.** See FALL verb sense 4. **fall on** *the army fell on the rebels* ATTACK, assail, assault, fly at, set about, set upon; pounce upon, ambush, surprise, rush, storm, charge; *informal* jump, lay into, have a go at. **fall out** *let's not fall out over something so silly* QUARREL, argue, row, fight, squabble, bicker, have words, disagree, be at odds, clash, wrangle, cross swords, lock horns, be at loggerheads, be at each other's throats; *informal* scrap. **fall short** *we sincerely hope that our fund-raising efforts will not fall short* BE DEFICIENT, be inadequate, be insufficient, be wanting, be lacking, disappoint; *informal* not come up to scratch, not come up to snuff. **fall short of** *the results fell short of what was expected* FAIL TO MEET, fail to reach, fail to live up to. **fall through** *the deal fell through* FAIL, be unsuccessful, come to nothing, miscarry, abort, go awry, collapse, founder, come to grief; *informal* fizzle out, flop, fold, come a cropper, go over like a lead balloon.

fallacious adjective *we almost printed his fallacious information* ERRONEOUS, false, untrue, wrong, incorrect, flawed, inaccurate, mistaken, misinformed, misguided; specious, spurious, bogus, fictitious, fabricated, made up; groundless, unfounded, ill-founded, unproven, unsupported, uncorroborated; *informal* phony, full of holes. ANTONYM correct.

fallacy noun *the fallacy that Abner Doubleday invented the game of baseball* MISCONCEPTION, misbelief, delusion, mistaken impression, error, misapprehension, misinterpretation, misconstruction, mistake; untruth, inconsistency, myth.

fallback noun & adjective *the teaching degree is my fallback | we periodically review the fallback procedures* BACKUP, reserve, contingency, auxiliary, spare, alternative.

fallen adjective 1 *fallen heroes* DEAD, perished, killed, slain, slaughtered, murdered; lost, late, lamented, departed, gone; *formal* deceased.

2 *dated fallen women* IMMORAL, loose, promiscuous, unchaste, sinful, impure, sullied, tainted, dishonored, ruined.

fallible adjective *what good is a fallible security system?* ERROR-PRONE, errant, liable to err, open to error; imperfect, flawed, weak.

fallout noun *the fallout from the scandal led to her resignation* REPERCUSSION(S), reverberation(s), aftermath, effect(s), consequence(s).

fallow adjective 1 *fallow farmland* UNCULTIVATED, unplowed, untilled, unplanted, unsown; unused, dormant, resting, empty, bare. ANTONYM cultivated.

2 *a fallow trading period* INACTIVE, dormant, quiet, slack, slow, stagnant; barren, unproductive. ANTONYM busy.

false adjective 1 *a false report* INCORRECT, untrue, wrong, erroneous, fallacious, flawed, distorted, inaccurate, imprecise; untruthful, fictitious, concocted, fabricated, invented, made up, trumped up, unfounded, spurious; counterfeit, forged, fraudulent. ANTONYMS correct, truthful.

2 *a false friend* FAITHLESS, unfaithful, disloyal, untrue, inconstant, treacherous, traitorous, two-faced, double-crossing, deceitful, dishonest, duplicitous, untrustworthy, unreliable; untruthful; *informal* cheating, two-timing, backstabbing; *literary* perfidious. ANTONYM faithful.

3 *false pearls.* See FAKE adjective, sense 2.

falsehood noun 1 *a downright falsehood* LIE, untruth, fib, falsification, fabrication, invention, fiction, story, cock-and-bull story, flight of fancy; half truth; *informal* tall story, tall tale, fairy tale, whopper. See note at FICTION. ANTONYM truth.

2 *he accused me of falsehood* LYING, mendacity, untruthfulness, fibbing, fabrication, invention, perjury, telling stories; deceit, deception, pretense, artifice,double-crossing, treachery; *literary* perfidy. ANTONYM honesty.

falsify verb 1 *she falsified the accounts* FORGE, fake, counterfeit, fabricate; alter, change, doctor, tamper with, fudge, manipulate, adulterate, corrupt, misrepresent, misreport, distort, warp, embellish, embroider; *informal* cook.

2 *the theory is falsified by the evidence* DISPROVE, refute, debunk, negate, negative, invalidate, contradict, controvert, confound, demolish, discredit; *informal* poke holes in, blow out of the water; *formal* confute.

falsity noun *the falsity of his assertions* UNTRUTHFULNESS, untruth, fallaciousness, falseness, falsehood, fictitiousness, inaccuracy; mendacity, fabrication, dishonesty, deceit.

falter verb 1 *the government faltered* HESITATE, delay, drag one's feet, stall; waver, vacillate, waffle, be indecisive, be irresolute, blow hot and cold, hem and haw; *informal* sit on the fence, dilly-dally, shilly-shally.

2 *she faltered over his name* STAMMER, stutter, stumble; hesitate, flounder.

3 *the economy was faltering* STRUGGLE, stumble, flounder, founder, be in difficulty.

fame noun *a designer of international fame* RENOWN, celebrity, stardom, popularity, prominence; note, distinction, esteem, importance, account, consequence, greatness, eminence, prestige, stature, repute; notoriety, infamy. ANTONYM obscurity.

famed adjective *famed for his grace and artistry* FAMOUS, celebrated, well-known, prominent, noted, notable, renowned, respected, esteemed, acclaimed; notorious, infamous. ANTONYM unknown.

familiar adjective 1 *a familiar task* WELL-KNOWN, recognized, accustomed; common, commonplace, everyday, day-to-day, ordinary, habitual, usual, customary, routine, standard, stock, mundane, run-of-the-mill; *literary* wonted.

2 *are you **familiar with** the subject?* ACQUAINTED WITH, conversant with, versed in, knowledgeable of, well-

informed in/of; skilled in, proficient in; at home with, no stranger to, au fait with, au courant with; *informal* up on, in the know about.

3 *a familiar atmosphere* INFORMAL, casual, relaxed, easy, comfortable; friendly, unceremonious, unreserved, open, natural, unpretentious. ANTONYM formal.

4 *he is too familiar with the teachers* PRESUMPTUOUS, overfamiliar, disrespectful, forward, bold, impudent, impertinent. ANTONYM formal.

familiarity noun **1** *her* ***familiarity with*** *Asian politics* ACQUAINTANCE WITH, awareness of, experience with/of, insight into, knowledge of, understanding of, comprehension of, grasp of, skill in, proficiency in.

2 *she was affronted by his familiarity* PRESUMPTION, overfamiliarity, presumptuousness, forwardness, boldness, audacity, cheek, impudence, impertinence, disrespect; liberties.

3 *our familiarity allows us to tease one another* CLOSENESS, intimacy, attachment, affinity, friendliness, friendship, amity; *informal* chumminess.

familiarize verb *let me* ***familiarize*** *you* ***with*** *our new phone setup* MAKE CONVERSANT WITH, make familiar with, acquaint with; accustom to, habituate to, instruct in, teach in, educate in, school in, prime in, introduce to; brief in/about; *informal* put in the picture about/with, give the lowdown on, fill in on, get up to speed on/with.

family noun **1** *I met his family* RELATIVES, relations, kin, next of kin, kinsfolk, kindred, one's (own) flesh and blood, nearest and dearest, people, connections; extended family, in-laws; clan, tribe; *informal* folks.

2 *he had the right kind of family* ANCESTRY, parentage, pedigree, genealogy, background, family tree, descent, lineage, bloodline, blood, extraction, stock; forebears, forefathers, antecedents, roots, origins.

3 *she is married with* ***a family*** CHILDREN, little ones, youngsters; offspring, progeny, descendants, scions, heirs; a brood; *Law* issue; *informal* kids, kiddies, tots.

4 *the warbler family* TAXONOMIC GROUP, order, class, genus, species; stock, strain, line; *Zoology* phylum.

family tree noun *the Internet has helped me trace my family tree* ANCESTRY, genealogy, descent, lineage, line, bloodline, pedigree, background, extraction, derivation; family, dynasty, house; forebears, forefathers, antecedents, roots, origins.

famine noun *a nation threatened by famine* FOOD SHORTAGES, scarcity of food; starvation, malnutrition. ANTONYM plenty.

famished adjective *the hikers were famished by the time they reached camp* RAVENOUS, hungry, starving, starved, empty, unfed; *informal* peckish. ANTONYM full.

famous adjective *an exhibit featuring the artwork of famous actors* WELL KNOWN, prominent, famed, popular; renowned, noted, eminent, distinguished, esteemed, celebrated, respected; of distinction, of repute; illustrious, acclaimed, great, legendary, lionized; having one's name in lights; notorious, infamous. ANTONYM unknown.

fan[1] noun *a ceiling fan* VENTILATOR, blower, air conditioner.

▸ verb **1** *she fanned her face* COOL, aerate, ventilate; freshen, refresh.

2 *they fanned public fears* INTENSIFY, increase, agitate, inflame, exacerbate; stimulate, stir up, whip up, fuel, kindle, spark, arouse.

3 *the police squad* ***fanned out*** SPREAD (OUT), branch (out); outspread.

fan[2] noun *a basketball fan* ENTHUSIAST, devotee, admirer, lover; supporter, follower, disciple, adherent, zealot; expert, connoisseur, aficionado; *informal* buff, bum, fiend, freak, nut, addict, junkie, fanatic, groupie.

fanatic noun **1** *a religious fanatic* ZEALOT, extremist, militant, dogmatist, devotee, adherent; sectarian, bigot, partisan, radical, diehard; *informal* maniac. See note at ZEALOT.

2 *informal a hockey fanatic.* See FAN[2] .

fanatical adjective **1** *they are fanatical about their faith* ZEALOUS, extremist, extreme, militant, dogmatic, radical, diehard; intolerant, single-minded, blinkered, inflexible, uncompromising, hardcore.

2 *he was fanatical about tidiness* ENTHUSIASTIC, eager, keen, overkeen, fervent, ardent, passionate; obsessive, obsessed, fixated, compulsive; *informal* wild, gung-ho, nuts, crazy, hog-wild.

fancier noun *a pigeon fancier* ENTHUSIAST, lover, hobbyist; expert, connoisseur, aficionado; *informal* buff.

fanciful adjective **1** *a fanciful story* FANTASTIC, far-fetched, unbelievable, extravagant; ridiculous, absurd, preposterous; imaginary, made-up, make-believe, mythical, fabulous; *informal* tall, hard to swallow. ANTONYM literal.

2 *a fanciful girl* IMAGINATIVE, inventive; whimsical, impractical, dreamy, quixotic; out of touch with reality, in a world of one's own. ANTONYM down-to-earth.

3 *a fanciful building* ORNATE, exotic, fancy, imaginative, extravagant, fantastic; curious, bizarre, eccentric, unusual. ANTONYM practical.

fancy verb **1** *she fancied him.* See LIKE sense 1.

2 *I fancied I could see lights* THINK, imagine, believe, be of the opinion, be under the impression; reckon.

▸ adjective *fancy clothes* ELABORATE, ornate, ornamental, decorative, adorned, embellished, intricate; ostentatious, showy, flamboyant; luxurious, lavish, extravagant, expensive; *informal* flashy, jazzy, ritzy, snazzy, posh, classy; fancy-schmancy. See word spectrum at PLAIN. ANTONYM plain.

▸ noun *she took a fancy to you* LIKING, taste, inclination; urge, wish, whim, impulse, notion, whimsy, hankering, craving; *informal* yen, itch.

fanfare noun **1** *a fanfare announced her arrival* TRUMPET CALL, flourish, fanfaronade; *archaic* trump.

2 *the project was greeted with great fanfare* FUSS, commotion, show, display, ostentation, flashiness, pageantry, splendor; *informal* ballyhoo, hype, pizzazz, razzle-dazzle, glitz.

fantasize verb *they both wanted a film career, but while Dionne was out scrambling for parts, Heidi stayed home and fantasized* DAYDREAM, dream, muse, make-believe, pretend, imagine; build castles in the air, build castles in Spain, live in a dream world.

fantastic adjective **1** *a fantastic car* MARVELOUS, wonderful, sensational, outstanding, superb, super, excellent, first-rate, first-class, dazzling, out of this world, breathtaking; *informal* great, terrific, fabulous, ace, magic, cool, wicked, awesome, brilliant, killer. ANTONYM ordinary.

2 *a fantastic notion* FANCIFUL, extravagant, extraordinary, irrational, wild, absurd, far-fetched, nonsensical, incredible, unbelievable, unthinkable, implausible, improbable, unlikely, doubtful, dubious; strange, peculiar, odd, queer, weird, eccentric, whimsical, capricious; visionary, romantic; *informal* crazy, cockeyed, off the wall. ANTONYM rational.

3 *fantastic shapes* STRANGE, weird, bizarre, outlandish, queer, peculiar, grotesque, freakish, surreal, exotic; elaborate, ornate, intricate. ANTONYM ordinary.

4 *his fantastic accuracy* TREMENDOUS, remarkable, great, terrific, impressive, outstanding, phenomenal.

fantasy noun **1** *a mix of fantasy and realism* IMAGINATION, fancy, invention, make-believe; creativity, vision; daydreaming, reverie. ANTONYMS realism, truth.

2 *his fantasy about being famous* DREAM, daydream, pipe dream, fanciful notion, wish; fond hope, chimera, delusion, illusion; *informal* pie in the sky.

far adverb **1** *we walked far that afternoon* A LONG WAY, a great distance, a good way; afar.

2 *her charm far outweighs any flaws* MUCH, considerably, markedly, immeasurably, greatly, significantly, substantially, appreciably, noticeably; to a great extent, by a long way, by far, by a mile, easily. ANTONYM slightly.

▸ adjective **1** *far places* DISTANT, faraway, far-off, remote, out of the way, far-flung, outlying. ANTONYMS near, neighboring.

2 *the far side of the campus* FURTHER, more distant; opposite. ANTONYM near.

PHRASES: **by far** *this is by far the best essay we've read today* BY A GREAT AMOUNT, by a good deal, by a long way, by a mile, far and away; undoubtedly, without doubt, without question, positively, absolutely, easily; significantly, substantially, appreciably, much. **far and away.** See BY FAR (above). **far and near** *people came from far and near in hopes of witnessing a miracle* EVERYWHERE, [here, there, and everywhere], far and wide, all over (the world), throughout the land, worldwide; *informal* all over the place; all over the map. **far and wide.** See FAR AND NEAR (above). **far from** *staff were far from happy* NOT, not at all, nowhere near; the opposite of, the antithesis of, anything but. **go far** *we always knew that Rudy would go far* BE SUCCESSFUL, succeed, prosper, flourish, thrive, get on, get on in the world, make good, set the world on fire; *informal* make a name for oneself, make one's mark, go places, do all right for oneself, find a place in the sun. **go too far** *one of these days, you're going to go too far and they're going to haul you away* GO TO EXTREMES, go overboard, overdo it, go over the top, not know when to stop. **so far 1** *nobody has noticed so far* UP TO THIS POINT, up to now, as yet, thus far, hitherto, up to the present, to date. **2** *his liberalism only extends so far* TO A CERTAIN EXTENT, up to a point, to a degree, within reason, within limits.

faraway adjective **1** *faraway places* DISTANT, far off, far, remote, far-flung, outlying, extrasolar; obscure, out of the way, off the beaten track/path. ANTONYM nearby.

2 *a faraway look in her eyes* DREAMY, daydreaming, abstracted, absentminded, distracted, preoccupied, vague; lost in thought, somewhere else, not with us, in a world of one's own; *informal* miles away. ANTONYM alert.

farce noun **1** *the stories approach farce* SLAPSTICK COMEDY, slapstick, burlesque, vaudeville, buffoonery. ANTONYM tragedy.

2 *the trial was a farce* MOCKERY, travesty, absurdity, sham, pretense, masquerade, charade, joke, waste of time; *informal* shambles.

farcical adjective **1** *the idea is farcical* RIDICULOUS, preposterous, ludicrous, absurd, laughable, risible, nonsensical; senseless, pointless, useless; silly, foolish, idiotic, stupid, harebrained, cockamamie; *informal* crazy, daft.

2 *farcical goings-on* MADCAP, zany, slapstick, comic, comical, clownish, amusing; hilarious, uproarious; *informal* wacky.

fare noun **1** *we paid the fare* TICKET PRICE; price, cost, charge, fee, toll, tariff; transport cost.

2 *the taxi picked up a fare* PASSENGER, traveler, customer.

3 *they eat simple fare* FOOD, meals, sustenance, nourishment, nutriment, foodstuffs, provender, eatables, provisions; cooking, cuisine; diet; *informal* grub, nosh, eats, chow; *formal* comestibles, victuals.

4 *typical Hollywood fare* OFFERING(S), wares; menu.

▸ verb *how are you faring?* GET ON, get along, cope, manage, do, muddle through/along, survive; *informal* make out.

farewell exclamation *farewell, New York* GOODBYE, so long, bye, bye-bye, see you (later), cheers; adieu, au revoir, ciao, adios, sayonara; bon voyage; *informal, dated* toodle-oo.

▸ noun *an emotional farewell* GOODBYE, valediction, adieu; leave-taking, parting, departure; send-off.

far-fetched adjective *a far-fetched story about alien abduction* IMPROBABLE, unlikely, implausible, unconvincing, dubious, doubtful, incredible, unbelievable, unthinkable; contrived, fanciful, unrealistic, ridiculous, absurd, preposterous; *informal* hard to swallow, fishy.

farm noun *a farm of 100 acres* RANCH, farmstead, plantation, estate, family farm, dairy farm, hobby farm; farmland, market garden.

▸ verb **1** *he farmed locally* WORK THE LAND, be a farmer, cultivate the land; rear livestock.

2 *they farm the land* CULTIVATE, till, work, plow, dig, plant.

3 *the family farms sheep* BREED, rear, keep, raise, tend.

PHRASE: **farm something out** *we farmed out the warehouse construction to another firm* CONTRACT OUT, outsource, subcontract, delegate.

farmer noun *the independent Tennessee farmers have been hurt by this careless legislation* AGRICULTURIST, agronomist, rancher, smallholder, peasant; farmhand, *historical* habitant, grazier.

farming noun *her family's been in farming since the 1700s* AGRICULTURE, cultivation, ranching, land management, farm management; husbandry; agronomy, agribusiness.

far out adjective *informal* See UNCONVENTIONAL.

farrago noun *the decor was an appalling farrago of random items and mismatched colors* HODGEPODGE, mishmash, ragbag, potpourri, jumble, mess, confusion, mélange, gallimaufry, hash, assortment, miscellany, mixture, conglomeration, medley. See note at JUMBLE.

far-reaching adjective *a reduction in funding will have far-reaching implications* EXTENSIVE, wide-ranging, comprehensive, widespread, all-embracing, overarching, across the board, sweeping, blanket, wholesale; important, significant, radical, major, consequential.

farsighted adjective *reaping the benefits of her farsighted investments* PRESCIENT, visionary, percipient, shrewd, discerning, judicious, canny, prudent.

farther adverb *he'd like to live even farther from the city* MORE FAR, farther away, further, further away, more remote, more distant, more removed.

▸ adjective *the farther side of the field* MORE DISTANT, more remote, remoter, farther away/off, further, further (away/off); far, other, opposite.

EASILY CONFUSED WORDS **farther, farthest; further, furthest**

Traditionally, **farther** and **farthest** were used in referring to physical distance: *the falls were still two or three miles farther up the path.* **Further** and **furthest** were restricted to figurative or abstract senses: *we decided to consider the matter further.* Although **farther** and **farthest** are still restricted to measurable distances, **further** and **furthest** are now common in both senses: *those plants should be furthest from the window.*

farthest adjective *the farthest island in the chain is uninhabited* MOST DISTANT, most remote, remotest, farthest away, furthest, furthest away, farthermost, furthermost; (most) outlying, (most) outer, outermost, extreme, uttermost, ultimate; *archaic* outmost. ANTONYM nearest.

▸ adverb *Charlie threw his discus the farthest* MOST DISTANT, farthest away, furthest, furthest away, at/for the greatest distance. See note at FARTHER.

fascinate verb *the space program fascinates me* INTEREST, captivate, engross, absorb, enchant, enthrall, entrance, transfix, rivet, mesmerize, engage, compel; lure, tempt, entice, draw; charm, attract, intrigue, divert, entertain. ANTONYM bore.

fascinating adjective *the book is a fascination study of Southern schools during the Civil War* INTERESTING, captivating, engrossing, absorbing, enchanting, enthralling, spellbinding, riveting, engaging, compelling, compulsive, gripping, thrilling; alluring, tempting, irresistible; charming, attractive, intriguing, diverting, entertaining.

fascination noun *crime and criminals are topics of endless fascination* INTEREST, preoccupation, passion, obsession, compulsion; allure, lure, charm, attraction, intrigue, appeal, pull, draw.

fascism noun *his brand of so-called patriotism sure seems like fascism to me* AUTHORITARIANISM, totalitarianism, dictatorship, despotism, autocracy; Nazism, rightism; nationalism, xenophobia, racism, anti-Semitism; jingoism, isolationism; neofascism, neo-Nazism.

fascist noun *he was branded a fascist* AUTHORITARIAN, totalitarian, autocrat, extreme right-winger, rightist; Nazi, blackshirt; nationalist, xenophobe, racist, anti-Semite, jingoist; neofascist, neo-Nazi. ANTONYM liberal.

▸ adjective *a fascist regime* AUTHORITARIAN, totalitarian, dictatorial, despotic, autocratic, undemocratic, illiberal; Nazi, extreme right-wing, rightist, militarist; nationalist(ic), xenophobic, racist, jingoistic. ANTONYM democratic.

fashion noun **1** *the fashion for tight clothes* VOGUE, trend, craze, rage, mania, fad; style, look; tendency, convention, custom, practice; *informal* thing.

2 *the world of fashion* CLOTHES, clothing design, couture; the garment industry; *informal* the rag trade.

3 *it needs to be run in a sensible fashion* MANNER, way, method, mode, style; system, approach.

▸ verb *the model was fashioned from lead* CONSTRUCT, build, make, manufacture, fabricate, tailor, contrive; cast, shape, form, mold, sculpt; forge, hew.

PHRASES: **after a fashion** *the arrangement worked after a fashion* TO A CERTAIN EXTENT, in a way, somehow, somehow or other, in a manner of speaking, in its way. **in fashion** *are these hideous shoes really in fashion?* FASHIONABLE, in vogue, up-to-date, up-to-the-minute, all the rage, chic, à la mode; *informal* trendy, with it, cool, in, the in thing, hot, big, hip, happening, now, sharp, groovy, tony, fly. **out of fashion** *sorry, Dad, that necktie is completely out of fashion* UNFASHIONABLE, dated, old-fashioned, out of date, outdated, outmoded, behind the times; unstylish, untrendy, unpopular, passé, démodé; *informal* old hat, out, square, uncool.

fashionable adjective *a fashionable spa in Newport* IN VOGUE, voguish, in fashion, popular, up-to-date, up-to-the-minute, modern, all the rage, du jour, modish, à la mode, trendsetting; stylish, chic; *informal* trendy, classy, with it, cool, in, hot, big, hip, happening, now, snazzy, spiffy, tony, fly.

fast[1] adjective **1** *a fast pace* SPEEDY, quick, swift, rapid; fast-moving, fast-paced, high-speed, turbo, sporty; accelerated, express, blistering, breakneck, pell-mell; hasty, hurried; *informal* nippy, zippy, blinding, supersonic; *literary* fleet. ANTONYM slow.

2 *he held the door fast* SECURE, fastened, tight, firm, closed, shut; immovable, unbudgeable. ANTONYM loose.

3 *a fast color* INDELIBLE, lasting, permanent, stable. ANTONYM temporary.

4 *fast friends* LOYAL, devoted, faithful, firm, steadfast, staunch, true, bosom, inseparable; constant, enduring, unswerving.

5 *a fast woman* PROMISCUOUS, licentious, dissolute, debauched, impure, unchaste, wanton, abandoned, of easy virtue; sluttish, whorish; intemperate, immoderate, shameless, sinful, immoral; *informal* easy; *dated* loose. ANTONYM chaste.

▸ adverb **1** *she drove fast* QUICKLY, rapidly, swiftly, speedily, briskly, at speed, at full tilt; hastily, hurriedly, in a hurry, posthaste, pell-mell; like a shot, like a flash, on the double, at the speed of light; *informal* lickety-split, PDQ (pretty damn quick), nippily, like (greased) lightning, hell-bent for leather, like mad, like the wind, like a bat out of hell; *literary* apace. ANTONYM slowly.

2 *his wheels were stuck fast* SECURELY, firmly, immovably, fixedly.

3 *he's fast asleep* DEEPLY, sound, completely.

4 *she lived fast and dangerously* WILDLY, dissolutely, intemperately, immoderately, recklessly, self-indulgently, extravagantly.

fast[2] verb *we must fast and pray* EAT NOTHING, abstain from food, refrain from eating, go without food, go hungry, starve oneself; go on a hunger strike. ANTONYM eat.

▸ noun *a five-day fast* PERIOD OF FASTING, period of abstinence; hunger strike; diet. ANTONYM feast.

fasten verb **1** *he fastened the door* BOLT, lock, secure, make fast, chain, seal. ANTONYM unlock.

2 *they fastened splints to his leg* ATTACH, fix, affix, clip, pin, tack; stick, bond, join. ANTONYM remove.

3 *he fastened his horse to a tree* TIE, tie up, bind, tether, truss, fetter, lash, hitch, anchor, strap, rope. ANTONYM untie.

4 *the dress fastens at the front* BUTTON (UP), zip (up), do up, close. ANTONYM undo.

5 *his gaze fastened on me* FOCUS, fix, be riveted, concentrate, zero in, zoom in, direct at.

6 *blame had been* ***fastened on*** *the underling* ASCRIBE TO, attribute to, assign to, chalk up to; pin on, lay at the door of.

7 *critics* ***fastened on*** *the end of the report* SINGLE OUT, concentrate on, focus on, pick out, fix on, seize on.

fastener noun *we'll replace any missing or broken fastener* BUTTON, clasp, strap, tie, buckle, zipper, catch, snap, hook and eye; *trademark* Velcro.

fastidious adjective *he was fastidious about personal hygiene* SCRUPULOUS, punctilious, painstaking, meticulous; perfectionist, fussy, finicky, overparticular; critical, overcritical, hypercritical, hard to please, exacting, demanding; *informal* persnickety, nitpicking, choosy, picky, anal. ANTONYM lax.

fat adjective **1** *a fat man* PLUMP, stout, overweight, large, chubby, portly, flabby, paunchy, potbellied, beer-bellied, meaty, of ample proportions, heavyset; obese, corpulent, fleshy, gross; *informal* plus-sized, big-boned, tubby, roly-poly, well-upholstered, beefy, porky, blubbery, chunky, pudgy. ANTONYMS thin, skinny.

2 *fat bacon* FATTY, greasy, oily, oleaginous; *formal* pinguid. ANTONYM lean.

3 *a fat book* THICK, big, chunky, bulky, substantial, voluminous; long. ANTONYM thin.

4 *informal a fat salary* LARGE, substantial, sizable, considerable; generous, lucrative. ANTONYM small.

▸ noun **1** *exercises to burn away the fat* FATTY TISSUE, adipose tissue, cellulite; blubber; flab; *informal* spare tire, love handles.

2 *eggs fried in sizzling fat* COOKING OIL, grease; lard, suet, butter, margarine.

fatal adjective **1** *a fatal disease* DEADLY, lethal, mortal, death-dealing; terminal, incurable, untreatable, inoperable, malignant; *literary* deathly. ANTONYMS harmless, superficial.

2 *a fatal mistake* DISASTROUS, devastating, ruinous, catastrophic, calamitous, dire; costly; *formal* grievous. ANTONYMS harmless, beneficial.

fatalism noun *Paulette's fatalism made her come across as pretty morose* PASSIVE ACCEPTANCE, resignation, stoicism, acceptance of the inevitable; pessimism, defeatism, negativism, negative thinking, doom and gloom; predeterminism.

fatality noun *news of this fatality has spread quickly* DEATH, casualty, mortality, victim; fatal accident.

▸ ***fat***
obese
corpulent
Falstaffian
rotund
endomorphic
roly-poly
stout
stocky
porky
portly
paunchy
dumpy
chunky
fleshy
tubby
overweight
well-upholstered
well-padded
well-rounded
corn-fed
ample
pudgy
fattish
chubby
plump
zaftig
buxom
full-figured
curvy
shapely
well-proportioned
mesomorphic
muscular
athletic
sleek
rangy
lean
lanky
spare
slender
slim
ectomorphic
svelte
willowy
sylphlike
slight
skinny
spindly
gangly
reedy
weedy
scrawny
scraggy
underfed
underweight
bony
angular
spindle-shanked
raw-boned
pinched
hollow-cheeked
gaunt
as thin as a reed
stick-like
emaciated
skeletal
anorexic
cadaverous
gracile
macilent
thin ◂

fate noun **1** *what has fate in store for me?* DESTINY, providence, the stars, chance, luck, serendipity, fortune, kismet, karma.

2 *my fate was in their hands* FUTURE, destiny, outcome, end, lot.

3 *a similar fate would befall other killers* DEATH, demise, end; retribution, sentence.

4 *Mythology* **(the Fates)** *the Fates will decide* the weird sisters; the Parcae, the Moirai, the Norns; 'Clotho, Lachesis, and Atropos'.

▸ verb **(be fated)** *his daughter was fated to face the same problem* BE PREDESTINED, be preordained, be destined, be meant, be doomed; be sure, be certain, be bound, be guaranteed.

fateful adjective **1** *that fateful day* DECISIVE, critical, crucial, pivotal; momentous, important, key, significant, historic, portentous; *informal* earth-shattering, earth-shaking. See note at OMINOUS. ANTONYMS unimportant, trivial.

2 *their fateful defeat in 1812* DISASTROUS, ruinous, calamitous, devastating, tragic, terrible.

father noun **1** *his mother and father* DAD; daddy, pop, pa, dada, papa; old man, patriarch, paterfamilias.

2 *literary the religion of my fathers* ANCESTOR, forefather, forebear, predecessor, antecedent, progenitor, primogenitor. ANTONYM descendant.

3 *the father of democracy* ORIGINATOR, initiator, founder, inventor, creator, maker, author, architect.

4 *the city fathers* LEADER, elder, patriarch, official.

5 **(Father)** *our heavenly Father* GOD, Lord, Lord God.

6 (often **Father**) *ask the father to pray for you* PRIEST, pastor, parson, clergyman, cleric, minister, preacher; *informal* reverend, padre.

▸ verb PARENT, be the father of, bring into the world, spawn, sire, breed; *literary* beget; *archaic* engender.

fatherland noun *returning to his fatherland after forty years* NATIVE LAND, native country, homeland, mother country, motherland, land of one's birth.

fatherly adjective *she appreciated his fatherly advice* PATERNAL, fatherlike; protective, supportive, encouraging, affectionate, caring, sympathetic, indulgent.

fathom verb **1** *Charlotte tried to fathom her cat's expression* UNDERSTAND, comprehend, work out, make sense of, grasp, divine, puzzle out, get to the bottom of; interpret, decipher, decode; *informal* make head(s) or tail(s) of, crack.

2 *fathoming the ocean* MEASURE THE DEPTH OF, sound, plumb.

fatigue noun TIREDNESS, weariness, sleepiness, drowsiness, exhaustion, enervation, languor, lethargy, torpor, prostration. ANTONYM energy.

▸ verb *the troops were fatigued* TIRE (OUT), exhaust, wear out, drain, weary, wash out, overtire, prostrate, enervate; *informal* knock out, take it out of, do in, poop, bush, wear to a frazzle. See note at TIRED. ANTONYM invigorate.

WORD NOTE **fatigue**

Tiredness and *sleepiness* are synonyms representing the need for sleep, while *drowsiness* conveys mental impairment; *languor* is a pleasant sleepiness. *Lethargy* and *torpor* are extreme sleepiness. *Exhaustion* is extreme fatigue, or extreme weariness or lack of energy. **—SM**

fatness noun *persons with varying degrees of fatness were chosen for the stress tests* PLUMPNESS, stoutness, heaviness, chubbiness, portliness, rotundity, flabbiness, paunchiness; obesity, corpulence; *informal* tubbiness, pudginess. ANTONYM thinness.

fatten verb **1** *fattening livestock* MAKE FAT/FATTER, feed (up), build up.

2 *we're sending her home to **fatten up*** PUT ON WEIGHT, gain weight, get heavier, grow fatter, fill out. ANTONYMS lose weight, slim down.

fatty adjective *avoid fatty foods* GREASY, oily, fat, oleaginous; high-fat. ANTONYM lean.

fatuous adjective *the irritation of fatuous questions* SILLY, foolish, stupid, inane, idiotic, vacuous, asinine; pointless, senseless, ridiculous, ludicrous, absurd; *informal* dumb, daft. ANTONYM sensible.

Faulknerian adjective See note below.

WORD NOTE **Faulknerian**

Sometimes scholars, book publicists, or English majors will refer to a new Southern novel as *Faulknerian.* Or they might dub an evocative passage in a short story *Proustian.* Or describe a hellish scene as *Dantesque.* They might even resort to *Shakespearean, Sophoclean,* or *Joycean.* All perfectly good words, and all with the same drawback: they don't really mean much. Even those who know *Sanctuary* and *Absalom! Absalom!* won't be sure what *Faulknerian* signifies. Does it refer to intricately structured novels, long, convoluted sentences, grotesque characters, multigenerational sagas, doomed Southern aristocrats, crude melodrama, soaring authorial ambition, or what? Great writers aren't reducible to adjectives; they contain multitudes and their works are as rich and varied as the world around us. Rather than adopt this convenient, if vague shorthand, just describe the book or poem as it is and then, if need be, compare it to some precisely noted aspect of Balzac, Faulkner, or whomever. **—MD**

fault noun **1** *he has his faults* DEFECT, failing, imperfection, flaw, blemish, shortcoming, weakness, frailty, foible, vice. ANTONYMS merit, strength.

2 *engineers have located the fault* DEFECT, flaw, imperfection, bug; error, mistake, inaccuracy; *informal* glitch, gremlin.

3 *it was not my fault* RESPONSIBILITY, liability, culpability, blameworthiness, guilt.

4 *don't blame one child for another's faults* MISDEED, wrongdoing, offense, misdemeanor, misconduct, indiscretion, peccadillo, transgression; *informal* no-no. See note at SIN.

▸ verb *you couldn't fault any of the players* FIND FAULT WITH, criticize, attack, censure, condemn, reproach; complain about, quibble about, moan about; *informal* knock, slam, gripe about, beef about, pick holes in.

PHRASES: **at fault** *no one is at fault* TO BLAME, blameworthy, culpable; responsible, guilty, in the wrong. **to a fault** *Katherine is very giving, sometimes to a fault* EXCESSIVELY, unduly, immoderately, overly, needlessly.

THE RIGHT WORD

No one is perfect. But when it comes to cataloguing your own imperfections, it's best to start with your **foibles**—the slight weaknesses or eccentricities for which you will be most quickly forgiven. You also have a good chance of being forgiven for your **shortcomings**, which are not necessarily damaging to others (*his ardent devotion to his dog was a shortcoming that was readily overlooked*). **Failing** suggests a more severe shortcoming, usually with more serious consequences (*chronic tardiness was one of her failings*), but a *failing* can also be a weakness of character that you're not responsible for and perhaps not even aware of (*pride is a common failing among those who have met with great success early in life*). **Fault** also implies failure—but not necessarily a serious failure—to reach moral perfection (*his major fault was his outspokenness*). While *fault* usually indicates something inherent in your nature rather than external to it, a **flaw** can be either superficial (*a flaw in his otherwise immaculate appearance*) or profound (*a personality flaw that made her impossible to work with*), and it can refer to things as well as people (*a flaw in the table's finish*). A **blemish** is usually a physical flaw (*a facial blemish*), although it can be anything that disfigures or mars the perfection or someone or something (*a blemish on her otherwise spotless academic record*). You can get rid of a blemish and even overcome your shortcomings, but a **defect** is a flaw so serious that you may never be able to get rid of it (*a defect in his hearing*).

---

fault-finding noun *he came to expect nothing but fault-finding from his wife* CRITICISM, captiousness, caviling, quibbling; complaining, grumbling, carping, moaning; *informal* nitpicking, griping, grousing, bellyaching. ANTONYM praise.

faultless adjective *speaking faultless English* PERFECT, flawless, without fault, error-free, impeccable, accurate, precise, exact, correct, exemplary. ANTONYM flawed.

faulty adjective **1** *a faulty electric blanket* MALFUNCTIONING, broken, damaged, defective, not working, out of order; *informal* on the blink, acting up, kaput, bust, busted, on the fritz. ANTONYM working.

2 *her logic is faulty* DEFECTIVE, flawed, unsound, inaccurate, incorrect, erroneous, fallacious, wrong. ANTONYM sound.

fauna noun *studying the fauna of Guatemala* WILDLIFE, animals, living creatures.

faux pas noun *excuse my faux pas* MISTAKE, blunder, gaffe, indiscretion, impropriety, solecism, barbarism; *informal* boo-boo, blooper. See note at MISTAKE.

favor noun **1** *will you do me a favor?* SERVICE, good turn, good deed, kindness, act of kindness, courtesy. ANTONYM disservice.

2 *she looked on him with favor* APPROVAL, approbation, goodwill, kindness, benevolence. ANTONYM disapproval.

3 *they showed favor to one of the players* FAVORITISM, bias, partiality, partisanship.

4 *you shall receive the king's favor* PATRONAGE, backing, support, assistance.

▸ verb **1** *she favors the modest option* PREFER, lean toward, opt for, tend toward, be in favor of; approve (of), advocate, support, ANTONYM oppose.

2 *he favors his son over his daughter* TREAT PARTIALLY, be biased toward, prefer.

3 *the conditions favored the other team* BENEFIT, advantage, help, assist, aid, be of service to, do a favor for. ANTONYM hinder.

4 *he favored Lucy with a smile* OBLIGE, honor, gratify, humor, indulge.

PHRASE: **in favor of** *we're in favor of a strike* ON THE SIDE OF, pro, (all) for, giving support to, approving of, sympathetic to.

favorable adjective **1** *a favorable assessment of his ability* APPROVING, commendatory, complimentary, flattering, glowing, enthusiastic; good, pleasing, positive; *informal* rave. ANTONYM critical.

2 *conditions are favorable* ADVANTAGEOUS, beneficial, in one's favor, good, right, suitable, fitting, appropriate; propitious, auspicious, promising, encouraging. ANTONYM disadvantageous.

3 *a favorable reply* POSITIVE, affirmative, assenting, agreeing, approving; encouraging, reassuring. ANTONYM negative.

favorably adverb *judged favorably by their superiors* POSITIVELY, approvingly, sympathetically, enthusiastically, appreciatively.

favored adjective *the president's favored candidate for chief of staff* PREFERRED, favorite, recommended, chosen, choice.

favorite adjective *his favorite aunt* BEST-LOVED, most-liked, favored, dearest; preferred, chosen, choice.

▸ noun **1** *Brutus was Caesar's favorite* (FIRST) CHOICE, pick, preference, pet, darling, the apple of one's eye; *informal* blue-eyed boy/girl, golden boy/girl, fair-haired boy/girl.

2 *the favorite in the first race* EXPECTED WINNER, probable winner, odds-on favorite, top seed, top pick, front runner.

favoritism noun *we want one rule for everyone and no favoritism* PARTIALITY, partisanship, preferential treatment, favor, prejudice, bias, inequality, unfairness, discrimination.

fawn verb *they were **fawning over** the president* BE OBSEQUIOUS TO, be sycophantic to, curry favor with, flatter, play up to, crawl to, ingratiate oneself with, dance attendance on; *informal* suck up to, be all over, brown-nose, toady.

fawning adjective *her fawning personal staff* OBSEQUIOUS, servile, sycophantic, flattering, ingratiating, unctuous, oleaginous, groveling, crawling; *informal* bootlicking, smarmy, sucky, brown-nosing, toadying.

fay *literary* *Father would tell us that the dandelion down was spun by a little fay who lived in our apple tree.* See FAIRY. See also note at FEY.

faze verb *the storm doesn't seem to faze your dog* DISCONCERT, perturb, disturb, unnerve, unsettle, daunt, disorientate, put off, throw (off), rattle.

USAGE NOTE **faze, phase**

Faze = disconcert; daunt. *Phase* (verb) = carry out (a plan, program, etc.) in stages. *Phase* for *faze* is an increasingly common blunder—e.g.: "Others said they had weathered so many rumors that nothing phased [read *fazed*] them anymore." (*Boston Globe*; June 6, 1995.) The opposite error (*faze* for *phase*) also occurs, but more rarely—e.g.: "All that while shooting guard Art Mlotkowski, shadowed all over the court by Northport senior Rob Sanicola, was fazed [read *phased*] out of the offense." (*Newsday* [New York]; Feb. 26, 1995.) —**BG**

---

fear noun **1** *he felt fear at entering the house* TERROR, fright, fearfulness, horror, alarm, panic, agitation, trepidation, dread, consternation, dismay, distress; anxiety, worry, angst, unease, uneasiness, apprehension, apprehensiveness, nervousness, nerves, perturbation, foreboding; *informal* the creeps, the shivers, the willies, the heebie-jeebies, jitteriness, twitchiness, butterflies (in the stomach).

2 *she overcame her fears* PHOBIA, aversion, antipathy, dread, bugbear, nightmare, horror, terror; anxiety, neurosis; *informal* hang-up.

3 *there's no fear of my leaving you alone* LIKELIHOOD, likeliness, prospect, possibility, chance, probability; risk, danger.

▸ verb **1** *she feared her husband* BE AFRAID OF, be fearful of, be scared of, be apprehensive of, dread, live in fear of, be terrified of; be anxious about, worry about, feel apprehensive about.

2 *he fears heights* HAVE A PHOBIA ABOUT, have a horror of, take fright at.

3 *he feared to tell them* BE TOO AFRAID, be too scared, hesitate, dare not.

4 *they* ***feared for*** *his health* WORRY ABOUT, feel anxious about, feel concerned about, have anxieties about.

5 *all who fear the Lord* STAND IN AWE OF, revere, reverence, venerate, respect.

6 *I fear that you may be right* SUSPECT, have a (sneaking) suspicion, be inclined to think, be afraid, have a hunch, think it likely.

fearful adjective **1** *they are fearful of being overheard* AFRAID, frightened, scared (stiff), scared to death, terrified, petrified; alarmed, panicky, nervous, tense, apprehensive, uneasy, worried (sick), anxious; *informal* jittery, jumpy.

2 *the guards were fearful* NERVOUS, trembling, quaking, cowed, daunted; timid, timorous, faint-hearted; *informal* jittery, jumpy, twitchy, keyed up, in a cold sweat, a bundle of nerves; *informal* spooked.

3 *a fearful accident* HORRIFIC, terrible, dreadful, awful, appalling, frightful, ghastly, horrible, horrifying, horrendous, terribly bad, shocking, atrocious, abominable, hideous, monstrous, gruesome.

fearfully adverb *she opened the door fearfully* APPREHENSIVELY, uneasily, nervously, timidly, timorously, hesitantly, with one's heart in one's mouth.

fearless adjective *fearless warriors* BOLD, brave, courageous, intrepid, valiant, valorous, gallant, plucky, lionhearted, heroic, daring, audacious, indomitable, doughty; unafraid, undaunted, unflinching; *informal* gutsy, spunky, ballsy, feisty. ANTONYMS timid, cowardly.

fearsome adjective *the crocodile's teeth were a fearsome sight* FRIGHTENING, scary, horrifying, terrifying, menacing, chilling, spine-chilling, hair-raising, alarming, unnerving, daunting, formidable, forbidding, dismaying, disquieting, disturbing.

feasible adjective *a feasible solution* PRACTICABLE, practical, workable, achievable, attainable, realizable, viable, realistic, sensible, reasonable, within reason; suitable, possible, expedient; *informal* doable. ANTONYM impractical.

feast noun **1** *a wedding feast* BANQUET, celebration meal, lavish dinner; entertainment; revels, festivities; *informal* blowout, spread.

2 *the feast of St. Stephen* (RELIGIOUS) FESTIVAL, feast day, saint's day, holy day, holiday.

3 *a feast for the eyes* TREAT, delight, joy, pleasure.

▸ verb **1** *they* ***feasted on*** *lobster* GORGE ON, dine on, eat one's fill of, overindulge in, binge on; eat, devour, consume, partake of; *informal* stuff one's face with, stuff oneself with, pig out on, chow down on.

2 *they feasted the returning heroes* HOLD A BANQUET FOR, throw a party for, wine and dine, entertain lavishly, regale, treat, féte.

feat noun *his gaining access to the imperial palace was no small feat* ACHIEVEMENT, accomplishment, attainment, coup, triumph; undertaking, enterprise, venture, operation, exercise, endeavor, effort, performance, exploit.

feather noun *the size and markings of this feather would indicate a barred owl* PLUME, quill, flight feather, tail feather; *Ornithology* covert, plumule; (**feathers**) plumage, feathering, down.

feature noun **1** *a typical feature of French music* CHARACTERISTIC, attribute, quality, property, trait, hallmark, trademark; aspect, facet, factor, ingredient, component, element, theme; peculiarity, idiosyncrasy, quirk.

2 *her delicate features* FACE, countenance, physiognomy; *informal* mug, kisser; puss, pan; *literary* visage, lineaments.

3 *she made a feature of her garden sculptures* CENTERPIECE, (special) attraction, highlight, focal point, focus (of attention).

4 *she writes features at the newspaper* ARTICLE, piece, item, report, story, column, review, commentary, write-up.

5 *tonight's feature stars Clint Eastwood* MOVIE, film; main show, main event; *informal* flick, pic.

▸ verb **1** *PBS is featuring a week of live concerts* PRESENT, promote, make a feature of, give prominence to, focus attention on, spotlight, highlight.

2 *she is to feature in a major advertising campaign* STAR, appear, participate, play a part.

febrile adjective *the febrile patients were given intravenous fluids* FEVERISH, hot, burning, flushed, sweating; *informal* having a temperature.

feces plural noun *the feces were examined for parasites* EXCREMENT, bodily waste, waste matter, ordure, dung, manure; excreta, stools, droppings; dirt, filth, muck, mess, night soil; *informal* poop, pooh, doo-doo, turds, poo, caca.

feckless adjective *the feckless bum hasn't gotten off our sofa for ten days* USELESS, worthless, incompetent, inept, good-for-nothing, ne'er-do-well; lazy, idle, slothful, indolent, irresponsible, shiftless; *informal* no-good, no-account.

WORD NOTE **feckless**

The obscene-sounding first syllable gives punch and an air of harsh condemnation to this synonym for *irresponsible,* conveying "not merely irresponsible, but also unforgivably blithe, and, in one's blitheness, causing great harm." Highly useful in the George W. era. —**DA**

WORD NOTE **feckless**

A totally great adjective. One reason that the slippage in the meaning of *effete* is OK (see note at EFFETE) is that we can use *feckless* to express what *effete* used to mean. *Feckless* primarily means "deficient in efficacy, lacking vigor or determination, feeble"; but it can also mean "careless, profligate, irresponsible." The word appears most often now in connection with wastoid youths, bloated bureaucracies—anyone who's culpable for his own haplessness. The great thing about using *feckless* is that it lets you be extremely dismissive and mean without sounding mean; you just sound witty and classy. The word's also fun to use because of the soft-*e* assonance and the *k* sound—and the triply assonant noun form is even more fun. **—DFW**

fecund adjective *the fecund wheat fields* FERTILE, fruitful, productive, high-yielding; rich, lush, flourishing, thriving. See note at FERTILE. ANTONYM barren.

federate verb *several tribes federated in an attempt to stem the tide of white colonial expansionism* CONFEDERATE, combine, unite, unify, merge, amalgamate, integrate, join (up), band together, team up.

federation noun *a federation of Protestant denominations* CONFEDERATION, confederacy, league; combination, alliance, coalition, union, syndicate, guild, consortium, partnership, cooperative, association, amalgamation; *informal* federacy.

fed up adjective *I'm **fed up with** the game playing in politics* SICK AND TIRED OF, weary of, tired of, sick of; **(be fed up with)** have had it up to here with, have had enough of.

fee noun *for the quality of work, I think the fee was reasonable* PAYMENT, wage, salary, allowance; price, cost, charge, tariff, rate, amount, sum, figure; **(fees)** remuneration, dues, earnings, pay; *formal* emolument.

feeble adjective **1** *he was very old and feeble* WEAK, weakly, weakened, frail, infirm, delicate, sickly, ailing, unwell, poorly, enfeebled, enervated, debilitated, incapacitated, decrepit, etiolated. See note at WEAK. ANTONYM strong.

2 *a feeble argument* INEFFECTIVE, ineffectual, inadequate, unconvincing, implausible, unsatisfactory, poor, weak, flimsy. ANTONYM effective.

3 *he's too feeble to stand up to his boss* COWARDLY, craven, faint-hearted, spineless, spiritless, lily-livered, chinless; timid, timorous, fearful, unassertive, weak, ineffectual, wishy-washy; *informal* wimpy, sissy, sissified, gutless, chicken. ANTONYMS forceful, brave.

4 *a feeble light* FAINT, dim, weak, pale, soft, subdued, muted. ANTONYM strong.

feeble-minded adjective *he's not as feebleminded as he pretends to be* STUPID, idiotic, imbecilic, foolish, witless, doltish, empty-headed, vacuous; *informal* halfwitted, moronic, dumb, dim, dopey, dippy; daft. ANTONYM clever.

feed verb **1** *feed the kids* GIVE FOOD TO, provide (food) for, cater for, cook for.

2 *feed the baby* NURSE, breast-feed, suckle; bottle-feed.

3 *too many cows feeding in a small area* GRAZE, browse, crop, pasture; eat, consume food, chow down.

4 *the birds **feed on** a varied diet* LIVE ON/OFF, exist on, subsist on, eat, consume.

5 *feeding one's self-esteem* STRENGTHEN, fortify, support, bolster, reinforce, boost, fuel, encourage.

6 *she fed secrets to the Russians* SUPPLY, provide, give, deliver, furnish, issue, pass on.

▸ noun *feed for goats and sheep* FODDER, food, forage, pasturage, herbage, provender; *formal* comestibles.

feedback noun *we welcome feedback from the viewers* RESPONSE, reaction, comments, criticism; reception, reviews.

feel verb **1** *she felt the fabric* TOUCH, stroke, caress, fondle, finger, thumb, handle.

2 *she felt a breeze on her back* PERCEIVE, sense, detect, discern, notice, be aware of, be conscious of.

3 *you will not feel any pain* EXPERIENCE, undergo, go through, bear, endure, suffer.

4 *he felt his way toward the door* GROPE, fumble, scrabble, pick.

5 *feel the temperature of the water* TEST, try (out), check, assess.

6 *he feels that he should go to the meeting* BELIEVE, think, consider (it right), be of the opinion, hold, maintain, judge; *informal* reckon, figure.

7 *I feel that he is only biding his time* SENSE, have a (funny) feeling, get the impression, have a hunch, intuit.

8 *the air feels damp* SEEM, appear, strike one as.

▸ noun **1** *the divers worked by feel* (SENSE OF) TOUCH, tactile sense, feeling (one's way).

2 *the feel of the paper* TEXTURE, surface, finish; weight, thickness, consistency, quality.

3 *the feel of a room* ATMOSPHERE, ambience, aura, mood, feeling, air, impression, character, tenor, spirit, flavor; *informal* vibrations, vibes.

4 *a feel for languages* APTITUDE, knack, flair, bent, talent, gift, faculty, ability.

PHRASES: **feel for** *tell your mother we certainly feel for her* SYMPATHIZE WITH, be sorry for, pity, feel pity for, feel sympathy for, feel compassion for, be moved by; commiserate with, condole with. **feel like** *I feel like some lemon meringue pie* WANT, would like, wish for, desire, fancy, feel in need of, long for; *informal* yen for, be dying for.

feeler noun **1** *the fish has two feelers on its head* ANTENNA, tentacle, tactile/sensory organ; *Zoology* antennule.

2 *the committee put out feelers* TENTATIVE INQUIRY/PROPOSAL, advance, approach, overture, probe.

feel-good adjective *it's a feel-good movie that everyone in the family will enjoy* HEARTWARMING, uplifting, positive, warm and fuzzy, sentimental, softhearted, mawkish, touchy-feely.

feeling noun **1** *assess the fabric by feeling* (SENSE OF) TOUCH, feel, tactile sense, using one's hands.

2 *a feeling of nausea* SENSATION, sense, consciousness.

3 *I had a feeling that I would win* SUSPICION, sneaking suspicion, notion, inkling, hunch, funny feeling, feeling in one's bones, fancy, idea; presentiment, premonition; *informal* gut feeling.

4 *the strength of her feeling* LOVE, affection, fondness, tenderness, warmth, warmness, emotion, sentiment; passion, ardor, desire. See note at EMOTION.

5 *a rush of feeling* COMPASSION, sympathy, empathy, fellow feeling, concern, solicitude, solicitousness, tenderness, love; pity, sorrow, commiseration.

6 *he had hurt her feelings* SENSIBILITIES, sensitivities, self-esteem, pride.

7 *my feeling is that it is true* OPINION, belief, view, impression, intuition, instinct, hunch, estimation, guess.

8 *a feeling of peace* ATMOSPHERE, ambience, aura, air, feel, mood, impression, spirit, quality, flavor; *informal* vibrations, vibes.

▸ adjective *a feeling man* SENSITIVE, warm, warmhearted, tender, tenderhearted, caring, sympathetic, kind, compassionate, understanding, thoughtful.

feign verb **1** *she lay still and feigned sleep* SIMULATE, fake, sham, affect, give the appearance of, make a pretense of.

2 *he's not really ill, he's only feigning* PRETEND, put it on, fake, sham, bluff, masquerade, play-act; *informal* kid.

feigned adjective *he accepted the invitation with feigned enthusiasm* PRETENDED, simulated, affected, artificial, insincere, put-on, fake, false, sham; *informal* pretend, phony. ANTONYM sincere.

feint noun *the attack on the main gate was a feint* BLUFF, blind, ruse, deception, subterfuge, hoax, trick, ploy, device, dodge, sham, pretense, cover, smokescreen, distraction, contrivance; deke; *informal* red herring.

feisty adjective *the part of Annie called for a just-so balance of adorable and feisty* SPIRITED, spunky, plucky, gutsy, ballsy.

WORD NOTE **feisty**

Be sure you know how to pronounce this word (and any others you might use). *Feisty, idyll,* and their tricky ilk may easily trap the innocent into sounding ignorant or ill-educated. People who know the correct pronunciations are likely to wince at your first mistake, then grow acutely embarrassed each time you repeat it. **—MD**

felicitations plural noun *on the occasion of your marriage, felicitations from us all* CONGRATULATIONS, good wishes, best wishes, regards, kind regards, blessings, compliments, respects.

felicitous adjective **1** *his nickname was particularly felicitous* APT, well-chosen, fitting, suitable, appropriate, apposite, pertinent, germane, relevant. ANTONYM inappropriate.

2 *the room's only felicitous feature* FAVORABLE, advantageous, good, pleasing. ANTONYM unfortunate.

felicity noun **1** *domestic felicity* HAPPINESS, joy, joyfulness, joyousness, bliss, delight, cheerfulness; contentedness, satisfaction, pleasure. ANTONYM unhappiness.

2 *David expressed his feelings with his customary felicity* ELOQUENCE, aptness, appropriateness, suitability, suitableness, applicability, fitness, relevance, pertinence. ANTONYM inappropriateness.

feline adjective *she moved with feline grace* CATLIKE, graceful, sleek, sinuous.

▸ noun *her pet feline* CAT, kitten; *informal* puss, pussy (cat), kitty (cat); *archaic* grimalkin.

fell[1] verb **1** *all the dead sycamores had to be felled* CUT DOWN, chop down, hack down, saw down, clear.

2 *she felled him with one punch* KNOCK DOWN/OVER, knock to the ground, strike down, bring down, bring to the ground, prostrate; knock out, knock unconscious; *informal* deck, floor, flatten, down, lay out, KO.

fell[2] adjective *literary a fell intent* MURDEROUS, savage, violent, vicious, fierce, ferocious, barbarous, barbaric, monstrous, cruel, ruthless; *archaic* sanguinary. PHRASE: **in one fell swoop** *this may resolve two crises in one fell swoop* ALL AT ONCE, together, at the same time, in one go.

fellow noun **1** *informal he's a decent sort of fellow* MAN, boy; person, individual, soul; *informal* guy, character, customer, joe, devil, bastard, chap, dude, hombre; *dated* dog.

2 *he exchanged glances with his fellows* COMPANION, friend, comrade, partner, associate, coworker, colleague; peer, equal, contemporary, confrere; *informal* chum, pal, buddy. PHRASE: **fellow feeling** *the fellow feeling he had for his jilted brother came from recent experience* SYMPATHY, empathy, feeling, compassion, care, concern, solicitude, solicitousness, warmth, tenderness, (brotherly) love; pity, sorrow, commiseration.

fellowship noun **1** *a community bound together in fellowship* COMPANIONSHIP, companionability, sociability, comradeship, camaraderie, friendship, mutual support; togetherness, solidarity; *informal* chumminess.

2 *the church fellowship* ASSOCIATION, society, club, league, union, guild, affiliation, alliance, fraternity, confraternity, brotherhood, sorority, sodality, benevolent society.

felon noun *does stealing a pair of socks make me a felon?* CONVICT, crook, criminal, outlaw; malefactor, wrongdoer; *informal* con.

felony noun See CRIME sense 1.

female adjective *female attributes* FEMININE, womanly, ladylike. ANTONYM male.

▸ noun *the author was a female.* See WOMAN sense 1.

feminine adjective **1** *a very feminine young woman* WOMANLY, ladylike; girlish; soft, delicate, gentle, graceful; *informal* girly. ANTONYM masculine.

2 *he seemed slightly feminine* EFFEMINATE, womanish, unmanly, effete, epicene; *informal* sissy, sissified, wimpy. ANTONYM manly.

femininity noun *she was a woman truly comfortable with her femininity* WOMANLINESS, feminineness, womanly qualities, feminine qualities.

feminism noun *a longtime advocate of feminism* THE WOMEN'S MOVEMENT, the feminist movement, women's liberation, female emancipation, women's rights; *informal* women's lib.

femme fatale noun *she was a femme fatale who had a particular appetite for wealthy older men* SEDUCTRESS, temptress, siren, enchantress; Delilah, Lorelei; *informal* vamp, man-eater, home wrecker.

fen noun *in spring, the fen smelled of fresh skunk cabbage* MARSH, marshland, salt marsh, fenland, wetland, bog, peat bog, swamp, swampland.

fence noun **1** *a gap in the fence* BARRIER, fencing, enclosure, barricade, stockade, palisade, fenceline; railing.

2 *informal a fence dealing mainly in jewelry* RECEIVER (OF STOLEN GOODS), dealer.

▸ verb **1** *they fenced off many acres* ENCLOSE, surround, circumscribe, encircle, circle, encompass; *archaic* compass.

2 *he* ***fenced in*** *his chickens* CONFINE, pen in, coop up, shut in/up, separate off; enclose, surround, corral.

3 *she fences as a hobby* SWORD-FIGHT; duel.

PHRASE: **(sitting) on the fence** *informal voters tend to shy away from candidates who are on the fence* UNDECIDED, uncommitted, uncertain, unsure, vacillating, wavering, dithering, hesitant, doubtful, ambivalent, of two minds, in a quandary, hemming and hawing, wishy-washy; neutral, impartial, nonpartisan.

fend verb *they were unable to **fend off** the invasion* WARD OFF, head off, stave off, hold off, repel, repulse, resist, fight off, defend oneself against, prevent, stop, block, intercept, hold back. PHRASE: **fend for oneself** *the children were forced to fend for themselves* TAKE CARE OF ONESELF, look after oneself, provide for oneself, manage (by oneself), cope alone, stand on one's own two feet.

feral adjective **1** *feral dogs* WILD, untamed, untamable, undomesticated, untrained. ANTONYMS tame, pet.

2 *a feral snarl* FIERCE, ferocious, vicious, savage, predatory, menacing, bloodthirsty.

ferment verb **1** *the beer continues to ferment* UNDERGO FERMENTATION, brew; effervesce, fizz, foam, froth.

2 *an environment that ferments disorder* CAUSE, bring about, give rise to, generate, engender, spawn, instigate, provoke, incite, excite, stir up, whip up, foment; *literary* beget, enkindle.

▸ noun *a ferment of revolutionary upheaval* FEVER, furor, frenzy, tumult, storm, rumpus; turmoil, upheaval, unrest, disquiet, uproar, agitation, turbulence, disruption, confusion, disorder, chaos, mayhem; *informal* hoo-ha, to-do.

ferocious adjective **1** *ferocious animals* FIERCE, savage, wild, predatory, aggressive, dangerous. ANTONYMS gentle, tame.

2 *a ferocious attack* BRUTAL, vicious, violent, bloody, barbaric, savage, sadistic, ruthless, cruel, merciless, heartless, bloodthirsty, murderous; *literary* fell. ANTONYM gentle.

3 *informal a ferocious headache* INTENSE, strong, powerful, fierce, severe, extreme, acute, unbearable, raging; *informal* hellish. ANTONYM mild.

ferocity noun *the ferocity of his speech was startling* SAVAGERY, brutality, barbarity, fierceness, violence, bloodthirstiness, murderousness; ruthlessness, cruelty, pitilessness, mercilessness, heartlessness.

ferret verb **1** *she ferreted in her handbag* RUMMAGE, feel around, grope around, forage around, fish around/about, poke around/about; search through, hunt through, rifle through.

2 ***ferreting out** misdemeanors* UNEARTH, uncover, discover, detect, search out, bring to light, track down, dig up, root out, nose out, snoop around for.

ferry noun *the Block Island ferry from New London* PASSENGER BOAT, passenger ship, ferry boat, car ferry; ship, boat, vessel; *historical* packet, packet boat.

▸ verb *the new cars were ferried to the island* TRANSPORT, convey, carry, ship, run, take, bring, shuttle.

fertile adjective **1** *the soil is fertile* FECUND, fruitful, productive, high-yielding, rich, lush.

2 *fertile couples* ABLE TO CONCEIVE, able to have children; *technical* fecund. ANTONYM barren.

3 *a fertile brain* IMAGINATIVE, inventive, innovative, creative, visionary, original, ingenious; productive, prolific. ANTONYM unimaginative.

THE RIGHT WORD

A **fertile** woman is one who has the power to produce offspring, just as *fertile* soil produces crops and a *fertile* imagination produces ideas. This adjective pertains to anything in which seeds (or thoughts) can take root and grow. A woman with ten children might be described as **fecund**, which means that she is not only capable of producing many offspring but has actually done it. A woman can be *fertile*, in other words, without necessarily being *fecund*. **Fruitful**, whose meaning is very close to that of *fecund* when used to describe plants and may replace *fertile* in reference to soil or land, pertains specifically to something that promotes fertility or fecundity (*a fruitful downpour*). It can also apply in a broader sense to anything that bears or promotes results (*a fruitful idea; a fruitful discussion*). While it's one thing to call a woman with a large family *fecund*, **prolific** is more usually applied to animals or plants in the literal sense of fertility, and suggests reproducing in great quantity or with rapidity. Figuratively, prolific is often used of highly productive creative efforts (*a prolific author with 40 titles published*).

fertilization noun *the sex of the embryo is determined at fertilization* CONCEPTION, impregnation, insemination; pollination, propagation.

fertilize verb **1** *the field was fertilized* FEED, mulch, compost, green manure, manure, dress, top-dress, add fertilizer to.

2 *these orchids are fertilized by insects* POLLINATE, cross-pollinate, cross-fertilize, fecundate.

fertilizer noun *we use only organic fertilizer* MANURE, plant food, compost, dressing, top dressing, dung.

fervent adjective *a fervent prayer* IMPASSIONED, passionate, intense, vehement, ardent, sincere, fervid, heartfelt; enthusiastic, zealous, fanatical, hardcore, wholehearted, avid, eager, keen, committed, dedicated, devout; *literary* perfervid. See note at EAGER. ANTONYM apathetic.

WORD NOTE **fervent**

Too often restricted to descriptions of religious and political fanatics, *fervent* is more versatile. It adds an atmosphere of feverish intensity to the description of almost any human endeavor or interest. I like its positive connotations: its use can be a sweet way of paying tribute to the depth of someone's passion for whatever brings them ongoing, everyday pleasure—a friendship, a hobby, a favorite movie. **—DA**

WORD NOTE **fervent**

A beautiful and expressive word that combines the phonological charms of *verve* and *fever.* Lots of writers, though, seem to think that *fervent* is synonymous with *fervid,* and most dictionaries don't do much to disabuse them. The truth is that there's a hierarchical trio of zeal-type adjectives, all with roots in the Latin verb *fervēre* (= to boil). Even though *fervent* can also mean "glowingly hot" (as in *Fingering his ascot, Aubrey gazed abstractedly at the brazier's fervent coals*), it's actually just the baseline term, more or less synonymous with *ardent. Fervid* is the next level up; it connotes even more passion/devotion/eagerness than *fervent.* At the top is *perfervid,* which means "extravagantly, rabidly, uncontrollably zealous or impassioned." *Perfervid* deserves to be used more, not only for its internal alliteration and metrical pizzazz but because its deployment shows that the writer knows the differences between the three *fervēre*-words. **—DFW**

fervid adjective *fervid protestations of love* FERVENT, ardent, passionate, impassioned, intense, vehement, wholehearted, heartfelt, sincere, earnest; *literary* perfervid.

fervor noun *even the smallest of tasks he tackled with fervor* PASSION, ardor, intensity, zeal, vehemence, emotion, warmth, earnestness, avidity, eagerness, keenness, enthusiasm, excitement, animation, vigor, energy, fire, spirit, zest, fervency. ANTONYM apathy.

fester verb **1** *his deep wound festered* SUPPURATE, become septic, become infected, form pus, weep; *Medicine* be purulent; *archaic* rankle.

2 *the garbage festered* ROT, molder, decay, decompose, putrefy, go bad, spoil, deteriorate.

3 *their resentment festered* RANKLE, eat away, gnaw away, brew, smolder.

festival noun **1** *the town's fall festival* FAIR, carnival, fiesta, jamboree, celebrations, festivities, fest.

2 *fasting precedes the festival* HOLY DAY, feast day, saint's day, commemoration, day of observance.

festive adjective *a festive mood* JOLLY, merry, joyous, joyful, happy, jovial, lighthearted, cheerful, jubilant, convivial, high-spirited, mirthful, uproarious; celebratory, holiday, carnival; Christmassy; *archaic* festal.

festivity noun **1** **(festivities)** *food plays an important part in the festivities* CELEBRATION, festival, entertainment, party, jamboree; merrymaking, feasting, revelry, jollification; revels, fun and games; *informal* bash.

2 *the festivity of Opening Day* JUBILATION, merriment, gaiety, cheerfulness, cheer, joyfulness, jollity, conviviality, high spirits, revelry.

festoon noun *festoons of paper flowers* GARLAND, chain, lei, swathe, swag, loop.

▸ verb *the room was festooned with streamers* DECORATE, adorn, ornament, trim, deck (out), hang, loop, drape, swathe, garland, wreathe, bedeck; *informal* do up/out, get up, trick out; *literary* bedizen.

fetch verb **1** *he went to fetch a doctor* (GO AND) GET, go for, call for, summon, pick up, collect, bring, carry, convey, transport.

2 *the land could fetch a million dollars* SELL FOR, bring in, raise, realize, yield, make, command, cost, be priced at; *informal* go for, set one back, pull in.

fetching adjective *give this note to the fetching young lady in the blue dress* ATTRACTIVE, appealing, sweet, pretty, good-looking, lovely, delightful, charming, prepossessing, captivating, enchanting, irresistible; *Scottish* bonny; *informal* divine, heavenly; killer; *archaic* comely, fair.

fete noun *join us for a fun-filled fête on the grounds of the Adams House* GALA, bazaar, fair, festival, fiesta, jubilee, carnival; fundraiser, charity event.

fetid adjective *a fetid pile of garbage* STINKING, smelly, foul-smelling, malodorous, reeking, pungent, acrid, high, rank, foul, noxious, humming; *informal* funky; *literary* noisome, miasmic, miasmal; *Brit. informal* minging, pongy. ANTONYM fragrant.

fetish noun **1** *he developed a bodybuilding fetish* FIXATION, obsession, compulsion, mania; weakness, fancy, fascination, fad; *informal* thing, hang-up.

2 *an African fetish* JUJU, talisman, charm, amulet; totem, idol, image, effigy.

fetter verb **1** *the captive was fettered* SHACKLE, manacle, handcuff, clap in irons, put in chains, chain (up); *informal* cuff; *literary* enfetter.

2 *these obligations fetter the company's powers* RESTRICT, restrain, constrain, limit; hinder, hamper, impede, obstruct, hamstring, inhibit, check, curb, trammel; *informal* hog-tie.

fetters plural noun *bound by fetters of iron* SHACKLES, manacles, handcuffs, irons, leg irons, chains, restraints; *informal* cuffs, bracelets; *historical* bilboes.

fettle noun *my, you certainly are in fine fettle* SHAPE, trim, fitness, physical fitness, health, state of health; condition, form, repair, state of repair, order, working order.

fetus noun *an ultrasonic photo of the fetus* EMBRYO, unborn baby/child.

feud noun *tribal feuds* VENDETTA, conflict; rivalry, hostility, enmity, strife, discord; quarrel, argument, falling out. See note at QUARREL.

▸ verb *he feuded with his teammates* QUARREL, fight, argue, bicker, squabble, fall out, dispute, clash, differ, be at odds; *informal* scrap.

fever noun **1** *he developed a fever* FEVERISHNESS, high temperature, febrility; *Medicine* pyrexia; *informal* TEMPERATURE.

2 *a fever of excitement* FERMENT, frenzy, furor; ecstasy, rapture.

3 *Stanley Cup fever* EXCITEMENT, frenzy, agitation, passion.

fevered adjective **1** *her fevered brow* FEVERISH, febrile, hot, burning.

2 *a fevered imagination* EXCITED, agitated, frenzied, overwrought, fervid.

feverish adjective **1** *she's really feverish* FEBRILE, fevered, hot, burning; *informal* having a temperature.

2 *feverish excitement* FRENZIED, frenetic, hectic, agitated, excited, restless, nervous, worked up, overwrought, frantic, furious, hysterical, wild, uncontrolled, unrestrained.

few adjective **1** *police are revealing few details* NOT MANY, hardly any, scarcely any; a small number of, a small amount of, one or two, a handful of; little. See note at LESS. ANTONYM many.

2 *comforts here are few* SCARCE, scant, meager, insufficient, in short supply; thin on the ground, few and far between, infrequent, uncommon, rare; negligible. ANTONYM plentiful.

▸ pronoun **(a few)** *there weren't many biscuits, but we saved you a few* A SMALL NUMBER, a handful, one or two, a couple, two or three; not many, hardly any.

fey adjective *it will be difficult for critics to pigeonhole Dean as the fey favorite of Volvo-driving, Chardonnay-sipping elitists.* See WHIMSICAL sense 1.

USAGE NOTE fey, fay

Fey derives from the Old English *fæge* ("doomed to die") and carries the related sense "in an unusually excited state (like one about to die)." By an extension, the word came to mean "whimsical, otherworldly, eccentric," perhaps from confusion with *fay* (= a fairy or elf). This shift in meaning was noticed as early as 1950. Today the word's original meaning is all but forgotten—e.g.: "An upsurge of book sales in cyberspace could have dramatic effects on the fortunes of the already fey and contradictory world of book publishing." (*Washington Post*, Aug. 4, 1997.) —**BG**

fiancée, masc. **fiancé** noun *he presented his fiancée with a pair of emerald earrings* BETROTHED, wife-to-be, husband-to-be, bride-to-be, future wife/husband, prospective spouse; *informal, dated* intended.

fiasco noun *the picnic was a fiasco* FAILURE, disaster, catastrophe, debacle, shambles, farce, mess, wreck; *informal* flop, washout, snafu. ANTONYM success.

fiat noun *a political union imposed through imperial fiat* DECREE, edict, order, command, commandment, injunction, proclamation, mandate, dictum, diktat.

fib noun *you're telling a fib* LIE, untruth, falsehood, made-up story, invention, fabrication, deception, (piece of) fiction; (little) white lie, half-truth; *informal* tall story/tale, whopper. See note at LIE[1]. ANTONYM truth.

fiber noun **1** *fibers from the murderer's sweater* THREAD, strand, filament; *technical* fibril.

2 *natural fibers* MATERIAL, cloth, fabric.

3 *fiber in the diet* ROUGHAGE, bulk.

fickle adjective *the fickle Loretta has a different boyfriend every month* CAPRICIOUS, changeable, variable, volatile, mercurial; inconstant, undependable, unsteady, unfaithful, faithless, flighty, giddy, skittish; fair-weather; *technical* labile; *literary* mutable. ANTONYM constant.

fiction noun **1** *the popularity of South American fiction* NOVELS, stories, (creative) writing, (prose) literature; *informal* lit.

2 *the president dismissed the allegation as absolute fiction* FABRICATION, invention, lies, fibs, untruth, falsehood, fantasy, nonsense. ANTONYM fact.

THE RIGHT WORD

If a young child tells you there is a dinosaur under his bed, you might assume that his story is a **fiction**, but it is probably a **figment**. A *fiction* is a story that is invented either to entertain or to deceive (*her excuse was ingenious, but it was pure fiction*), while *figment* suggests the operation of fancy or imagination (*a figment of his imagination*). If a child hides his sandwich under the sofa cushions and tells you that a dinosaur ate it, this would be a **fabrication**, which is a story that is intended to deceive. Unlike a *figment*, which is mostly imagined, a *fabrication* is a false but thoughtfully constructed story in which some truth is often interwoven (*the city's safety record was a fabrication designed to lure tourists downtown*). A **falsehood** is basically a lie—a statement or story that one knows to be false but tells with intent to deceive (*a deliberate falsehood about where the money had come from*). A **deception**, on the other hand, is an act that deceives but not always intentionally (*a foolish deception designed to prevent her parents from worrying*). A **fable** is a fictitious story that deals with events or situations that are clearly fantastic, impossible, or incredible. It often gives animals or inanimate objects the power to speak and conveys a lesson of practical wisdom, as in *Aesop's Fables*.

fictional adjective *fictional characters* FICTITIOUS, fictive, invented, imaginary, made up, make-believe, unreal, fabricated, mythical. ANTONYM real.

fictitious adjective **1** *a fictitious name* FALSE, fake, fabricated, sham; bogus, spurious, assumed, affected, adopted, feigned, invented, made up; *informal* pretend, phony. ANTONYM genuine.

2 *a fictitious character*. See FICTIONAL.

fiddle *informal* noun *she played the fiddle* VIOLIN, viola.

▸ verb **1** *he fiddled with a coaster* FIDGET, play, toy, twiddle, fuss, fool about/around; finger, thumb, handle; *informal* mess around/about.

2 *he fiddled with the dials* ADJUST, tinker, play around, meddle, interfere.

3 *fiddling the figures* FALSIFY, manipulate, massage, rig, distort, misrepresent, doctor, alter, tamper with, interfere with; *informal* fix, flimflam, cook (the books).

fidelity noun **1** *fidelity to her husband* FAITHFULNESS, loyalty, constancy; trueheartedness, trustworthiness, dependability, reliability; *formal* troth. ANTONYMS infidelity, disloyalty.

2 *fidelity to your king* LOYALTY, allegiance, obedience; *historical* homage, fealty. ANTONYM disloyalty.

3 *the fidelity of the reproduction* ACCURACY, exactness, precision, preciseness, correctness; strictness, closeness, faithfulness, authenticity. ANTONYM inaccuracy.

fidget verb **1** *the audience began to fidget* MOVE RESTLESSLY, wriggle, squirm, twitch, jiggle, shuffle, be agitated; *informal* be jittery.

2 *she fidgeted with her scarf* PLAY, fuss, toy, twiddle, fool around; *informal* fiddle, mess around.

▸ noun **1** *his convulsive fidgets* TWITCH, wriggle, squirm, jiggle, shuffle, tic, spasm.

2 *what a fidget you are!* FLIBBERTIGIBBET, restless person, bundle of nerves.

fidgety adjective *why is the dog so fidgety?* RESTLESS, restive, on edge, uneasy, antsy, nervous, keyed up, anxious, agitated; *informal* jittery, twitchy.

field noun **1** *a large plowed field* MEADOW, pasture, paddock, grassland, pastureland; *literary* lea, sward; *archaic* glebe.

2 *a soccer field* PLAYING FIELD, ground, sports field; *Brit.* pitch. See table at TRACK AND FIELD.

3 *the field of biotechnology* AREA, sphere, discipline, province, department, domain, sector, branch, subject; *informal* bailiwick.

4 *your field of vision* SCOPE, range, sweep, reach, extent.

5 *she is well ahead of the field* COMPETITORS, entrants, competition; applicants, candidates, possibles.

▸ verb **1** *she fielded the ball* CATCH, stop, retrieve; return, throw back.

2 *they can field an army of about one million* DEPLOY, position, range, dispose.

3 *he fielded some awkward questions* DEAL WITH, handle, cope with, answer, reply to, respond to.

▸ adjective **1** *field experience* PRACTICAL, hands-on, applied, experiential, empirical. ANTONYM theoretical.

2 *field artillery* MOBILE, portable, transportable, movable, maneuverable, light.

fiend noun **1** *a fiend had taken possession of him* DEMON, devil, evil spirit; *informal* spook.

2 *a fiend bent on global evildoing* VILLAIN, beast, brute, barbarian, monster, ogre, sadist, evildoer, swine.

3 *informal* *a drug fiend* ADDICT, abuser, user; *informal* junkie, ——head, ——freak.

4 *informal* *a fitness fiend* ENTHUSIAST, maniac; devotee, fan, lover, fanatic, addict, buff, freak, nut.

fiendish adjective 1 *a fiendish torturer* WICKED, cruel, vicious, evil, malevolent, villainous; brutal, savage, barbaric, barbarous, inhuman, murderous, ruthless, merciless; *dated* dastardly.

2 *a fiendish plot* CUNNING, clever, ingenious, crafty, canny, wily, devious, shrewd; *informal* sneaky.

3 *a fiendish puzzle* DIFFICULT, complex, challenging, complicated, intricate, involved, knotty, thorny, tricky.

fierce adjective 1 *a fierce black mastiff* FEROCIOUS, savage, vicious, aggressive. ANTONYM gentle.

2 *fierce competition* AGGRESSIVE, cutthroat, competitive; keen, intense, strong, relentless. ANTONYM mild.

3 *fierce, murderous jealousy* INTENSE, powerful, vehement, passionate, impassioned, fervent, fervid, ardent. ANTONYM mild.

4 *a fierce wind* POWERFUL, strong, violent, forceful; stormy, blustery, gusty, tempestuous. ANTONYMS gentle, mild.

5 *a fierce pain* SEVERE, extreme, intense, acute, awful, dreadful; excruciating, agonizing, piercing. ANTONYM mild.

fiery adjective 1 *the fiery breath of dragons* BURNING, blazing, flaming; on fire, ablaze, igneous; *literary* afire.

2 *a fiery red* BRIGHT, brilliant, vivid, intense, deep, rich.

3 *her fiery spirit* PASSIONATE, impassioned, ardent, fervent, fervid, spirited; quick-tempered, volatile, explosive, aggressive, determined, resolute.

fiesta noun *a five-day fiesta* FESTIVAL, carnival, holiday, celebration, party.

fight verb 1 *two men were fighting* BRAWL, exchange blows, attack each other, assault each other, hit each other, punch each other; struggle, grapple, wrestle; *informal* scrap, have a set-to, roughhouse, engage in fisticuffs.

2 *they fought in the First World War* (DO) BATTLE, go to war, take up arms, be a soldier; engage, meet, clash, skirmish.

3 *a war fought for freedom* ENGAGE IN, wage, conduct, prosecute, undertake.

4 *they are always fighting* QUARREL, argue, bicker, squabble, fall out, have a fight, have a row, wrangle, be at odds, disagree, differ, have words, bandy words, be at each other's throats, be at loggerheads; *informal* scrap.

5 *fighting against wage reductions* CAMPAIGN, strive, battle, struggle, contend, crusade, agitate, lobby, push, press.

6 *they will fight the decision* OPPOSE, contest, contend with, confront, challenge, combat, dispute, quarrel with, argue against/with, strive against, struggle against.

7 *Tyler fought the urge to stick his tongue out* REPRESS, restrain, suppress, stifle, smother, hold back, fight back, keep in check, curb, control, rein in, choke back; *informal* keep the lid on.

▸ noun 1 *a fight outside a club* BRAWL, fracas, melee, rumpus, skirmish, sparring match, struggle, scuffle, altercation, clash, disturbance; fisticuffs; *informal* scrap, set-to, donnybrook.

2 *a heavyweight fight* BOXING MATCH, bout, match.

3 *Japan's fight against Russia* BATTLE, engagement, clash, conflict, struggle; war, campaign, crusade, action, hostilities.

4 *a fight with my girlfriend* ARGUMENT, quarrel, squabble, row, wrangle, disagreement, falling-out, contretemps, altercation, dispute; *informal* tiff, spat, scrap, cat fight, blowup.

5 *their fight for control of the company* STRUGGLE, battle, campaign, push, effort.

6 *she had no fight left in her* WILL TO RESIST, resistance, spirit, courage, pluck, pluckiness, grit, strength, backbone, determination, resolution, resolve, resoluteness, aggression, aggressiveness; *informal* guts, spunk, moxie.

PHRASES: **fight back** 1 *if the enemy attacks, we will fight back* RETALIATE, counterattack, strike back, hit back, respond, reciprocate, return fire, give tit for tat. 2 *Russ fought back tears.* See FIGHT verb sense 7. **fight off** *they tried in vain to fight off the swarming locusts* REPEL, repulse, beat off/back, ward off, fend off, keep/hold at bay, drive away/back, force back.

fighter noun 1 *a guerrilla fighter* SOLDIER, fighting man/woman, warrior, combatant, serviceman, servicewoman, trooper, mercenary; *archaic* man-at-arms.

2 *the fighter was knocked to the ground* BOXER, pugilist, prizefighter; wrestler.

3 *enemy fighters* WARPLANE, armed aircraft.

fighting adjective *a fighting man* VIOLENT, combative, aggressive, pugnacious, truculent, belligerent, bellicose, scrappy. ANTONYM peaceful.

▸ noun *200 were injured in the fighting* VIOLENCE, hostilities, conflict, action, combat; warfare, war, battles, skirmishing, rioting. ANTONYM peace.

figment noun *a figment of his very creative imagination* INVENTION, creation, fabrication; hallucination, illusion, delusion, fancy, vision. See note at FICTION.

figurative adjective *the example given was meant to be figurative* METAPHORICAL, nonliteral, symbolic, allegorical, representative, emblematic. ANTONYM literal.

figure noun 1 *the production figure* STATISTIC, number, quantity, amount, level, total, sum; (**figures**) data, information.

2 *the second figure was 9* DIGIT, numeral, numerical symbol.

3 *he can't put a figure on it* PRICE, cost, amount, value, valuation.

4 (**figures**) *I'm good with figures* ARITHMETIC, mathematics, math, calculations, computation, numbers.

5 *her petite figure* PHYSIQUE, build, frame, body, proportions, shape, form.

6 *a dark figure emerged* SILHOUETTE, outline, shape, form.

7 *a figure of authority* PERSON, personage, individual, man, woman, character, personality; representative, embodiment, personification, epitome.

8 *life-size figures* HUMAN REPRESENTATION, effigy, model, statue.

9 *geometrical figures* SHAPE, pattern, design, motif.

10 *see figure 4* DIAGRAM, illustration, drawing, picture, plate.

▸ verb **1** *a beast figuring in Egyptian legend* FEATURE, appear, be featured, be mentioned, be referred to, have prominence, crop up.

2 *a way to figure the values* CALCULATE, work out, total, reckon, compute, determine, assess, put a figure on, crunch the numbers, tot up.

3 *informal I figured that I didn't have a chance* SUPPOSE, think, believe, consider, expect, take it, suspect, sense; assume, dare say, conclude, take it as read, presume, deduce, infer, extrapolate, gather, guess.

4 *"Charlotte's late." "That figures."* MAKE SENSE, seem reasonable, stand to reason, be to be expected, be logical, follow, ring true.

PHRASES: **figure on** *they figured on paying about $100* PLAN ON, count on, rely on, bank on, bargain on, depend on, pin one's hopes on; anticipate, expect to (be). **figure out** *he tried to figure out how to switch on the lamp* WORK OUT, fathom, puzzle out, decipher, ascertain, make sense of, think through, get to the bottom of; understand, comprehend, see, grasp, get the hang of, get the drift of; *informal* crack; *Brit. informal* twig.

figurehead noun **1** *the president was just a figurehead* TITULAR HEAD, nominal leader, leader in name only, front man, cipher, token, mouthpiece, puppet, instrument.

2 *the figurehead on the ship* CARVING, bust, sculpture, image, statue.

figure skating noun. See table.

FIGURE SKATING TERMS

axel	over-rotation
camel spin	pairs skating
compulsory figures	toe pick
death spiral	precision skating
flip	quad
flying	salchow
free skate	serpentine
ice dancing	sit spin
lift	spin
loop	spread-eagle
Lutz	toe loop

filament noun *the fragile filament inside the bulb* FIBER, thread, strand; *technical* fibril.

file[1] noun **1** *he opened the file* FOLDER, portfolio, binder, document case.

2 *we have files on all the major companies* DOSSIER, document, record, report; data, information, documentation, annals, archives.

3 *the computer file was searched* DATA, document, text.

4 *the director needed updating on the Uecker file* DOSSIER, department, front.

▸ verb **1** *file the documents correctly* CATEGORIZE, classify, organize, put in place/order, order, arrange, catalog, record, store, archive.

2 *Debbie has filed for divorce* APPLY, register, ask.

3 *two women have filed a civil suit against him* BRING, press, lodge, place; *formal* prefer.

file[2] noun *a file of boys* LINE, column, row, string, chain, procession, queue.

▸ verb *we filed out into the parking lot* WALK IN A LINE, march, parade, troop.

file[3] verb *she filed her nails* SMOOTH, buff, rub (down), polish, shape; scrape, abrade, rasp, sandpaper.

filial adjective *a display of filial affection* DUTIFUL, devoted, compliant, respectful, affectionate, loving.

filibuster noun *many hours in committee are characterized by filibuster* STONEWALLING, delaying tactics, procrastination, obstruction, temporizing.

▸ verb *the opposition are filibustering* WASTE TIME, stall, play for time, stonewall, sandbag, procrastinate, buy time, employ delaying tactics.

filigree noun *decorated with gold filigree* TRACERY, fretwork, latticework, scrollwork, lacework, quilling.

fill verb **1** *he filled a bowl with cereal* MAKE FULL, fill up, fill to the brim, top up, charge. ANTONYM empty.

2 *guests filled the parlor* CROWD INTO, throng, pack (into), occupy, squeeze into, cram (into); overcrowd, overfill.

3 *he was filling his shelves* STOCK, pack, load, supply, replenish, restock, refill.

4 *fill all the holes with a spackling compound* BLOCK UP, stop (up), plug, seal, caulk. ANTONYM unblock.

5 *the perfume filled the room* PERVADE, permeate, suffuse, be diffused through, penetrate, infuse, perfuse.

6 *he was going to fill a government post* OCCUPY, hold, take up; *informal* hold down.

7 *we had just filled a big order* CARRY OUT, complete, fulfill, execute, discharge. PHRASES: **fill in** *while Mr. Grant is on vacation, Luis will be filling in* SUBSTITUTE, deputize, stand in, cover, take over, act as stand-in, take the place of; *informal* sub, step into someone's shoes/boots, pinch-hit. **fill in on** *when we get home, you can fill us in on the details* INFORM OF, advise of, tell about, acquaint with, apprise of, brief on, update with; *informal* put in the picture about, bring up to speed on. **fill something in/out** *fill in these forms he filled out the questionnaire* COMPLETE, answer. **fill out** *the puppies will begin to fill out once they start getting proper nutrition* GROW FATTER, become plumper, flesh out, put on weight, gain weight, get heavier.

filling noun *filling for cushions* STUFFING, padding, wadding, filler.

▸ adjective *a filling meal* SUBSTANTIAL, hearty, ample, satisfying, square; heavy.

fillip noun *their support provided a fillip to her campaign* STIMULUS, stimulation, boost, incentive, impetus; tonic, spur, push, aid, help; *informal* shot in the arm.

film noun **1** *a film of sweat* LAYER, coat, coating, covering, cover, sheet, patina, overlay.

2 *Emma was watching a film* MOVIE, picture, feature film, motion picture; *informal* flick, pic; *dated* moving picture, talkie.

3 *she would like to work in film* MOVIES, cinema, pictures, the motion picture industry.

▸ verb **1** *he immediately filmed the next scene* RECORD (ON FILM), shoot, capture on film, video.

2 *his eyes had* ***filmed over*** CLOUD (OVER), mist (over), haze (over); become blurred, blur; *archaic* blear.

film star noun. See MOVIE STAR.

filmy adjective *a filmy black blouse* DIAPHANOUS, transparent, see-through, translucent, sheer, gossamer; delicate, fine, light, thin, silky. ANTONYMS thick, opaque.

filter noun *a carbon filter* STRAINER, sifter; riddle; gauze, netting.

▸ verb 1 *the farmers filter the water* SIEVE, strain, sift, filtrate, clarify, purify, refine, treat.

2 *the rain had filtered through her jacket* SEEP, percolate, leak, trickle, ooze.

filth noun 1 *stagnant pools of filth* DIRT, muck, grime, mud, mire, sludge, slime, ooze; excrement, excreta, dung, manure, ordure, sewage; rubbish, refuse, dross; pollution, contamination, filthiness, uncleanness, foulness, nastiness, garbage, crud, grunge, gunge, trash.

2 *I felt sick after reading that filth* PORNOGRAPHY, pornographic literature/films, dirty books, smut, obscenity, indecency; *informal* porn, porno.

filthy adjective 1 *the room was filthy* DIRTY, grimy, muddy, slimy, unclean, mucky; foul, squalid, sordid, nasty, soiled, sullied; polluted, contaminated, unhygienic, unsanitary; *informal* cruddy, grungy; *literary* besmirched; *formal* feculent. ANTONYM clean.

2 *his face was filthy* UNWASHED, unclean, dirty, grimy, smeared, grubby, muddy, mucky, black, blackened, stained; *literary* begrimed. ANTONYM clean.

3 *filthy jokes* OBSCENE, indecent, dirty, smutty, rude, improper, coarse, bawdy, vulgar, lewd, racy, raw, off-color, earthy, barnyard, locker-room, ribald, risqué, "adult", pornographic, explicit; *informal* blue, porn, porno, X-rated. ANTONYMS clean, polite.

4 *you filthy brute!* DESPICABLE, contemptible, nasty, low, base, mean, vile, obnoxious; *informal* dirty (rotten), low-down, no-good.

5 *he was in a filthy mood* BAD, foul, bad-tempered, ill-tempered, irritable, grumpy, grouchy, cross, fractious, peevish; *informal* cranky, ornery. ANTONYM good.

▸ adverb *filthy rich* VERY, extremely, tremendously, immensely, remarkably, excessively, exceedingly; *informal* stinking, awfully, terribly, seriously, mega, majorly, ultra, damn.

final adjective 1 *the final year of study* LAST, closing, concluding, finishing, end, terminating, ultimate, eventual. ANTONYM first.

2 *their decisions are final* IRREVOCABLE, unalterable, absolute, conclusive, irrefutable, incontrovertible, indisputable, unchallengeable, binding. ANTONYM provisional.

▸ noun *the Stanley Cup final* DECIDER, clincher, final game/match. ANTONYM qualifier.

finale noun *the show's spectacular finale* CLIMAX, culmination; end, ending, finish, close, conclusion, termination; denouement, last act, final scene. ANTONYM beginning.

finality noun *an answer delivered with finality* CONCLUSIVENESS, decisiveness, decision, definiteness, definitiveness, certainty, certitude; irrevocability, irrefutability.

finalize verb *they had yet to finalize a peace treaty* CONCLUDE, complete, clinch, settle, work out, secure, wrap up, wind up, put the finishing touches to; reach an agreement on, agree on, come to terms on; *informal* sew up.

finally adverb 1 *she finally got her man to the altar* EVENTUALLY, ultimately, in the end, after a long time, at (long) last; in the long run, in the fullness of time.

2 *finally, wrap the ribbon around the edge* LASTLY, last, in conclusion, to conclude, to end.

3 *this should finally dispel that common misconception* CONCLUSIVELY, irrevocably, decisively, definitively, for ever, for good, once and for all.

finance noun 1 *he knows about finance* FINANCIAL AFFAIRS, money matters, fiscal matters, economics, money management, commerce, business, investment.

2 *short-term finance* FUNDS, assets, money, capital, resources, cash, reserves, revenue, income; funding, backing, sponsorship.

▸ verb *the project was financed by grants* FUND, pay for, back, capitalize, endow, subsidize, invest in; underwrite, guarantee, sponsor, support, bankroll.

financial adjective *our financial picture has improved* MONETARY, money, economic, pecuniary, fiscal, banking, commercial, business, investment.

THE RIGHT WORD

What's the difference between a **financial** crisis and a **fiscal** one? It all depends on who's having trouble with money and the scale of the difficulties. *Financial* usually applies to money matters involving large sums or transactions of considerable importance (*the auction was a financial success*). *Fiscal* refers specifically to the financial affairs of a government, organization, or corporation (*the end of the company's fiscal year*), while **pecuniary** refers to money matters of a more personal or practical nature and is preferred to *financial* when money is being discussed on a smaller scale (*pecuniary motives, pecuniary assistance, pecuniary difficulties*). Of all these words, **monetary** refers most directly to money as such and is often used when discussing the coinage, distribution, and circulation of money (*the European monetary system; the monetary unit of a country*).

financier noun *a corporate financier* INVESTOR, speculator, banker, capitalist, industrialist, businessman, businesswoman, stockbroker; *informal* money man, backer.

find verb 1 *I found the book I wanted* LOCATE, spot, pinpoint, unearth, obtain; search out, nose out, track down, root out; come across/upon, run across/into, chance on, light on, happen on, stumble on, encounter; *informal* bump into; *literary* espy.

2 *they say they've found a cure for rabies* DISCOVER, invent, come up with, hit on.

3 *the police found her purse* RETRIEVE, recover, get back, regain, repossess. ANTONYM lose.

4 *I hope you find peace* OBTAIN, acquire, get, procure, come by, secure, gain, earn, achieve, attain.

5 *I found the courage to speak* SUMMON (UP), gather, muster (up), screw up, call up.

6 *caffeine **is found** in coffee and tea* BE (PRESENT), occur, exist, be existent, appear.

7 *you'll find that it's a lively area* DISCOVER, become aware, realize, observe, notice, note, perceive, learn.

8 *I find their decision strange* CONSIDER, think, believe to be, feel to be, look on as, view as, see as, judge, deem, regard as.

9 *he was found guilty* JUDGE, adjudge, adjudicate, deem, rule, declare, pronounce.

10 *her barb found its mark* ARRIVE AT, reach, attain, achieve; hit, strike.

▸ noun **1** *an archaeological find* DISCOVERY, acquisition, asset.

2 *this table is a real find* GOOD BUY, bargain; godsend, boon.

PHRASE: **find out** *let us know what you find out about the theft* DISCOVER, become aware, learn, detect, discern, perceive, observe, notice, note, get/come to know, realize; bring to light, reveal, expose, unearth, disclose; *informal* figure out, cotton on, catch on, get wise (to), savvy; *Brit. informal* twig.

finding noun **1** *the finding of the leak* DISCOVERY, location, locating, detection, detecting, uncovering.

2 *the tribunal's findings* CONCLUSION, decision, verdict, pronouncement, judgment, ruling, rule, decree, order, recommendation, resolve; *Law* determination.

fine[1] adjective **1** *fine wines* EXCELLENT, first-class, first-rate, great, exceptional, outstanding, quality, superior, splendid, magnificent, exquisite, choice, select, prime, supreme, superb, wonderful, superlative, of high quality, second to none; *informal* A1, top-notch, blue-ribbon, blue-chip, splendiferous. ANTONYM poor.

2 *a fine citizen* WORTHY, admirable, praiseworthy, laudable, estimable, upright, upstanding, respectable.

3 *the initiative is fine, but it's not enough on its own* ALL RIGHT, acceptable, suitable, good (enough), passable, satisfactory, adequate, reasonable, tolerable; *informal* OK. ANTONYM unsatisfactory.

4 *I feel fine* IN GOOD HEALTH, well, healthy, all right, (fighting) fit, as fit as a fiddle, blooming, thriving, in good shape, in good condition, in fine fettle; *informal* OK, in the pink. ANTONYM ill.

5 *a fine day* FAIR, dry, bright, clear, sunny, without a cloud in the sky, warm, balmy, summery. ANTONYM inclement.

6 *a fine old house* IMPRESSIVE, imposing, striking, splendid, grand, majestic, magnificent, stately.

7 *fine clothes* ELEGANT, stylish, expensive, smart, chic, fashionable; fancy, sumptuous, lavish, opulent; *informal* flashy, swanky, ritzy, plush.

8 *a fine mind* KEEN, quick, alert, sharp, bright, brilliant, astute, clever, intelligent, perspicacious. ANTONYM slow.

9 *fine china* DELICATE, fragile, dainty. ANTONYM coarse.

10 *fine hair* THIN, light, delicate, wispy, flyaway. ANTONYM thick.

11 *a fine point* SHARP, keen, acute, sharpened, razor-sharp. ANTONYMS thick, blunt.

12 *fine material* SHEER, light, lightweight, thin, flimsy; diaphanous, filmy, gossamer, silky, transparent, translucent, see-through. ANTONYMS thick, coarse.

13 *fine sand* FINE-GRAINED, powdery, powdered, dusty, ground, crushed; *technical* comminuted. ANTONYM coarse.

14 *fine detailed work* INTRICATE, delicate, detailed, elaborate, dainty, meticulous.

15 *a fine distinction* SUBTLE, ultra-fine, nice, hair-splitting, nitpicking.

16 *people's finer feelings* ELEVATED, lofty, exalted, noble; refined, sensitive, cultivated, cultured, civilized, sophisticated. ANTONYM coarse.

17 *fine taste* DISCERNING, discriminating, refined, cultivated, cultured, critical. ANTONYM vulgar.

▸ adverb *informal you're doing fine* WELL, all right, not badly, satisfactorily, adequately, nicely, tolerably; *informal* OK, good. ANTONYM badly.

fine[2] noun *heavy fines* (FINANCIAL) PENALTY, sanction, fee, charge.

▸ verb *they were fined for breaking environmental laws* PENALIZE, impose a fine on, charge.

finery noun *all dressed up in her finery* REGALIA, best clothes, best, Sunday best; *informal* glad rags.

finesse noun **1** *masterly finesse* SKILL, skillfulness, expertise, subtlety, flair, panache, élan, polish, artistry, virtuosity, mastery.

2 *a modicum of finesse* TACT, tactfulness, discretion, diplomacy, delicacy, sensitivity, perceptiveness, savoir faire.

3 *a clever finesse* WINNING MOVE, trick, stratagem, ruse, maneuver, artifice, machination.

finger noun *he wagged his finger at the cat* DIGIT, thumb, index finger, forefinger; *informal* pinkie.

▸ verb **1** *she fingered her brooch uneasily* TOUCH, feel, handle, stroke, rub, caress, fondle, toy with, play (around) with, fiddle with.

2 *no one fingered the culprit* IDENTIFY, recognize, pick out, spot; inform on, point the finger at; *informal* rat on, squeal on, tell on, blow the whistle on, snitch on.

finicky adjective *their fancy words and finicky manners* FUSSY, fastidious, punctilious, over-particular, difficult, exacting, demanding; *informal* picky, choosy, persnickety; *archaic* nice.

finish verb **1** *Mrs. Porter had just finished the task* COMPLETE, end, conclude, stop, cease, terminate, bring to a conclusion/end/close, wind up; crown, cap, round off, put the finishing touches to; accomplish, discharge, carry out, do, get done, fulfill; *informal* wrap up, sew up, polish off. ANTONYM start.

2 *Sarah has finished school* LEAVE, give up, drop; stop, discontinue, have done with, complete; *informal* pack in, quit. ANTONYMS begin, continue.

3 *Hitch finished his dinner* CONSUME, eat, devour, drink, finish off, polish off, gulp (down); use (up), exhaust, empty, drain, get through, run through; *informal* down. ANTONYM start.

4 *the program has finished* END, come to an end, stop, conclude, come to a conclusion/end/close, cease. ANTONYMS start, begin.

5 *some items were finished in a black lacquer* VARNISH, lacquer, veneer, coat, stain, wax, shellac, enamel, glaze.

▸ noun **1** *the finish of filming* END, ending, completion, conclusion, close, closing, cessation, termination; final part/stage, finale, denouement; *informal* sewing up, polishing off. ANTONYMS start, beginning.

2 *a gallop to the finish* FINISHING LINE, finishing post, tape.

3 *an antiquated paint finish* VENEER, lacquer, lamination, glaze, coating, covering; surface, texture.

PHRASE: **finish off 1** *the executioners finished them off* KILL, take/end the life of, execute, terminate, exterminate, liquidate, get rid of; *informal* wipe out, do in, bump off, take out, dispose of, do away with, ice, rub out, waste. **2** *financial difficulties finished off the business* OVERWHELM, overcome, defeat, get the better of, worst, bring down; *informal* drive to the wall, best.

finished adjective **1** *the finished job* COMPLETED, concluded, terminated, over (and done with), at an end; accomplished, executed, discharged, fulfilled, done; *informal* wrapped up, sewn up, polished off; *formal* effectuated. ANTONYM incomplete.

2 *a finished performance* ACCOMPLISHED, polished, flawless, faultless, perfect; expert, proficient, masterly, impeccable, virtuoso, skillful, skilled, professional. ANTONYMS crude, unpolished.

3 *he was finished* RUINED, defeated, beaten, wrecked, doomed, bankrupt, broken; *informal* washed up, through.

finite adjective *there is a finite amount of water in the system* LIMITED, restricted, determinate, fixed.

fire noun **1** *a fire broke out* BLAZE, conflagration, inferno; flames, burning, combustion; forest fire, wildfire, brush fire.

2 *he lacked fire* DYNAMISM, energy, vigor, animation, vitality, vibrancy, exuberance, zest, élan; passion, ardor, zeal, spirit, verve, vivacity, vivaciousness; enthusiasm, eagerness, gusto, fervor, fervency; *informal* pep, vim, go, getup-and-go, oomph.

3 *rapid machine-gun fire* GUNFIRE, firing, flak, bombardment.

4 *they directed their fire at the state legislature* CRITICISM, censure, condemnation, denunciation, opprobrium, admonishments, brickbats; hostility, antagonism, animosity; *informal* flak.

▸ verb **1** *howitzers firing shells* LAUNCH, shoot, discharge, let fly with.

2 *someone fired a gun* SHOOT, discharge, let off, set off.

3 *informal he was fired* DISMISS, discharge, give someone their notice, lay off, let go, get rid of, ax, cashier; *informal* sack, give someone the sack, boot out, give someone the boot, give someone their marching orders, pink-slip; *Brit.* make redundant.

4 *the engine fired* START, get started, get going.

5 *the stories fired my imagination* STIMULATE, stir up, excite, awaken, arouse, rouse, inflame, animate, inspire, motivate.

PHRASES: **catch fire** *it was amazing that neither of the adjoining buildings caught fire* IGNITE, catch light, burst into flames, go up in flames. **on fire 1** *the restaurant was on fire* BURNING, alight, ablaze, blazing, aflame, in flames; *literary* afire. **2** *she was on fire with passion* ARDENT, passionate, fervent, excited, eager, enthusiastic.

firearm noun *an unregistered firearm* GUN, weapon, rifle, pistol, handgun, revolver; *informal* shooter, piece, heat.

firebrand noun *a group of political firebrands* RADICAL, revolutionary, agitator, rabble-rouser, incendiary, subversive, troublemaker.

fireproof adjective *fireproof coveralls* NONFLAMMABLE, incombustible, fire resistant, flame resistant, flame retardant, heatproof. ANTONYM inflammable.

fireworks plural noun **1** *there are fireworks after every Friday night game* PYROTECHNICS, firecrackers.

2 *his stubbornness has produced some fireworks* UPROAR, trouble, mayhem, fuss; tantrums, hysterics.

firm[1] adjective **1** *the ground is fairly firm* HARD, solid, unyielding, resistant; solidified, hardened, compacted, compressed, dense, stiff, rigid, frozen, set. ANTONYMS soft, yielding.

2 *firm foundations* SECURE, secured, stable, steady, strong, fixed, fast, set, taut, tight; immovable, irremovable, stationary, motionless. ANTONYM unstable.

3 *a firm handshake* STRONG, vigorous, sturdy, forceful. ANTONYM limp.

4 *I was very firm about what I wanted | a firm supporter* RESOLUTE, determined, decided, resolved, steadfast; adamant, emphatic, insistent, single-minded, in earnest, wholehearted; unfaltering, unwavering, unflinching, unswerving, unbending; hardline, committed, dyed-in-the-wool. ANTONYM irresolute.

5 *firm friends* CLOSE, good, intimate, inseparable, dear, special, fast; constant, devoted, loving, faithful, longstanding, steady, steadfast, rock-steady. ANTONYM distant.

6 *firm plans* DEFINITE, fixed, settled, decided, established, confirmed, agreed; unalterable, unchangeable, irreversible. ANTONYM indefinite.

firm[2] noun *an accounting firm* COMPANY, business, concern, enterprise, organization, corporation, conglomerate, office, bureau, agency, consortium; *informal* outfit, setup.

firmament noun *literary gazing up to* ***the firmament*** THE SKY, heaven; the heavens, the skies; *literary* the empyrean, the welkin.

first adjective **1** *the first chapter* EARLIEST, initial, opening, introductory. ANTONYMS last, closing.

2 *first principles* FUNDAMENTAL, basic, rudimentary, primary; key, cardinal, central, chief, vital, essential.

3 *our first priority* FOREMOST, principal, highest, greatest, paramount, top, uppermost, prime, chief, leading, main, major; overriding, predominant, prevailing, central, core, dominant; *informal* number-one. ANTONYM last.

4 *first prize* TOP, best, prime, premier, winner's, winning.

▸ adverb **1** *the room they had first entered* AT FIRST, to begin with, first of all, at the outset, initially.

2 *she would eat first* BEFORE ANYTHING ELSE, first and foremost, now.

3 *she wouldn't go—she'd die first!* IN PREFERENCE, sooner, rather.

▸ noun *it was a first for both of us* NOVELTY, new experience; unknown territory.

first aid noun *everyone should learn the fundamentals of first aid* CARE, treatment, help, medical attention, assistance, ministrations.

first-class adjective *a first-class hotel* SUPERIOR, first-rate, high-quality, top-quality, high-grade, five-star; prime, premier, premium, grade A, best, finest, select, exclusive, excellent, superb; *informal* A1, top-notch, blue-ribbon, blue-chip. ANTONYM poor.

first-hand adjective *her firsthand experience in grant writing* DIRECT, immediate, personal, hands-on, experiential, empirical, evidence-based, eye-witness. ANTONYMS vicarious, indirect.

first name noun *her first name is Gretchen* FORENAME, given name, Christian name. ANTONYM surname.

first-rate adjective *they have done a first-rate job* TOP-QUALITY, high-quality, top-grade, first-class, second to none, fine; superlative, excellent, superb, outstanding, exceptional, exemplary, marvelous, magnificent, splendid; *informal* top-notch, blue-ribbon, blue-chip, ace, A1, super, great, terrific, tremendous, bang-up, skookum, fantastic, killer.

fiscal adjective *figures for the past fiscal year show a trend of improvement* budgetary; financial, economic, monetary, money. See note at FINANCIAL.

fish noun *we caught enough fish to live on for a week.* See table.

▸ verb **1** *we can fish in Putnam's Pond* GO FISHING, angle, cast, trawl, troll, seine.

2 *she fished for her purse* SEARCH, delve, look, hunt; grope, fumble, ferret (about/around), root around/about, rummage (around/about).

3 *I'm not* ***fishing for*** *compliments* TRY TO GET, seek to obtain, solicit, angle for, aim for, hope for, cast around/about for, be after.

PHRASE: **fish out** *I fished my earring out of the cake batter* PULL OUT, haul out, remove, extricate, extract, retrieve; rescue from, save from.

fisherman noun *a favorite vacation spot for fishermen* ANGLER, fisher, fisheries worker.

fishing noun *their family activities include tennis and fishing* ANGLING, trawling, trolling, seining, ice fishing, catching fish.

fishy adjective **1** *a fishy smell* FISHLIKE, piscine.

2 *round fishy eyes* EXPRESSIONLESS, inexpressive, vacant, lackluster, glassy.

3 *informal there was something fishy going on* SUSPICIOUS, questionable, dubious, doubtful, suspect; odd, queer, peculiar, strange; *informal* funny, shady, crooked, sketchy.

fission noun *the radioactive materials absorb neutrons and undergo fission* SPLITTING, division, dividing, rupture, breaking, severance. ANTONYM fusion.

fissure noun *the flood was blamed on an unreported fissure in the dam* OPENING, crevice, crack, cleft, breach, crevasse, chasm; break, fracture, fault, rift, rupture, split.

fist noun *he tried to look tough by waving his fists at us* CLENCHED HAND; *informal* duke, mitt.

fit[1] adjective **1** *fit for human habitation | he is a fit subject for such a book* SUITABLE, good enough; relevant, pertinent, apt, appropriate, suited, apposite, fitting; *archaic* meet. ANTONYM unsuitable.

2 *is he fit to look after a child?* COMPETENT, able, capable; ready, prepared, qualified, trained, equipped. ANTONYM incapable.

3 *informal you look fit to commit murder!* READY, prepared, all set, in a fit state, likely, about; *informal* psyched up.

4 *he looked tanned and fit* HEALTHY, well, in good health, in (good) shape, in (good) trim, in good condition, fighting fit, as fit as a fiddle; athletic, muscular, well-built, strong, robust, hale and hearty, in the pink. ANTONYM unwell.

FISH

albacore (tuna)	limpet
amberjack	lox
anchovy	lutefisk
angelfish	mackerel
anglerfish	mahimahi
bacalao	mako (shark)
barbel	monkfish
barracuda	moray eel
bass	orange roughy
blackfish	parrotfish
blenny	perch
blowfish	pilchard
bluefish	pollack
bonito	pompano
bream	rainbow trout
brill	ray
brisling	red mullet
buffalo fish	red snapper
burbot	rockfish
butterfish	rouget
carp	sablefish
catfish	salmon
char	sand dab
cod/codfish	sardine
conger eel	scrod
crappie	sea bass
cusk	sea bream
dogfish	sea trout
dolphinfish	shad
dorado	shark
dory	skate
Dover sole	smelt
eel	snapper
finnan (haddie)	sole
flounder	sprat
fluke	striped bass
flying fish	sturgeon
fugu	sunfish
goby	swordfish
grouper	tarpon
grunion	tilapia
grunt	tilefish
haddock	torsk
hake	trout
halibut	tuna
herring	turbot
John Dory	wahoo
kingfish	whitefish
kipper	wrasse
lamprey	yellowtail
lemon sole	

▸ verb **1** *have your carpets fitted professionally* LAY, position, place, put in place/position, fix.

2 *cameras fitted with a backlight button* EQUIP, provide, supply, fit out, furnish.

3 *concrete slabs were* ***fitted together*** JOIN, connect, put together, piece together, attach, unite, link (together), slot together.

4 *a sentence that fits her crimes* MATCH, suit, be appropriate to, correspond to, tally with, go with, accord with, correlate to, be congruous with, be congruent with, be consonant with.

5 *an MA fits you for a professional career* QUALIFY, prepare, make ready, train, groom.

▸ noun *the degree of fit between a school's philosophy and practice* CORRELATION, correspondence, agreement, consistency, equivalence, match, similarity, compatibility, concurrence.

PHRASE: **fit in** *he never fit in with the academic crowd*

CONFORM, be in harmony, blend in, be in line, be assimilated into.

fit[2] noun 1 *an epileptic fit* CONVULSION, spasm, paroxysm, seizure, attack; *Medicine* ictus.

2 *a fit of the giggles* OUTBREAK, outburst, attack, bout, spell.

3 *my mother would have a fit if she knew* TANTRUM, fit of temper, outburst of anger/rage, frenzy; *informal* blowout, hissy fit, conniption (fit). PHRASE: **in/by fits and starts** *she writes in fits and starts yet manages to complete a new book almost every year.* SPASMODICALLY, intermittently, sporadically, erratically, irregularly, fitfully, haphazardly.

fitful adjective *a fitful night's sleep* INTERMITTENT, sporadic, spasmodic, broken, disturbed, disrupted, patchy, irregular, uneven, unsettled; *informal* herky-jerky.

fitness noun 1 *marathon running requires tremendous fitness* GOOD HEALTH, strength, robustness, vigor, athleticism, toughness, physical fitness, muscularity; good condition, good shape, well-being.

2 *his fitness for active service* SUITABILITY, capability, competence, ability, aptitude; readiness, preparedness, eligibility.

fitted adjective *a fitted sheet* SHAPED, contoured, fitting tightly, fitting well.

fitting noun 1 *bathroom fittings* FURNISHINGS, furniture, fixtures, equipment, appointments, appurtenances.

2 *the fitting of catalytic converters* INSTALLATION, installing, putting in, fixing.

▸ adjective *a fitting conclusion* APT, appropriate, suitable, apposite; fit, proper, right, seemly, correct; *archaic* meet. ANTONYM unsuitable.

five cardinal number *a talented five from Tucson* QUINTET, fivesome; quintuplets; *technical* pentad.

fix verb 1 *he fixed my washing machine* REPAIR, mend, put right, put to rights, get working, restore (to working order); overhaul, service, renovate, recondition.

2 *signs were fixed to utility poles* FASTEN, attach, affix, secure; join, connect, couple, link; install, implant, embed; stick, glue, pin, nail, screw, bolt, clamp, clip.

3 *his words are fixed in my memory* STICK, lodge, embed, burned, branded.

4 *his eyes were fixed on the ground* FOCUS, direct, level, point, train.

5 *informal* *Laura was fixing her hair* ARRANGE, put in order, adjust; style, groom, comb, brush; *informal* do.

6 *informal* *Chris will fix supper* PREPARE, cook, make, get; *informal* rustle up, whip up.

7 *let's fix a date for the meeting* DECIDE ON, select, choose, resolve on; determine, settle, set, arrange, establish, allot; designate, name, appoint, specify.

8 *chemicals are used to fix the dye* MAKE PERMANENT, make fast, set.

9 *informal* *the fight was fixed* RIG, arrange fraudulently; tamper with, influence; *informal* fiddle.

10 *informal* *don't tell anybody, or I'll fix you!* GET ONE'S REVENGE ON, avenge oneself on, get even with, get back at, take reprisals against, punish, deal with; sort someone out.

11 *the cat has been fixed* CASTRATE, neuter, geld, spay, desex, sterilize; *informal* doctor, alter.

▸ noun *informal* 1 *they are in a bit of a fix* PREDICAMENT, plight, difficulty, awkward situation, corner, tight spot; mess, mare's nest, dire straits; *informal* pickle, jam, hole, scrape, bind, sticky situation.

2 *he needed his fix* DOSE; *informal* hit.

3 *a quick fix for the coal industry* SOLUTION, answer, resolution, way out, remedy, cure, placebo; *informal* magic bullet, band-aid solution.

4 *the result was a complete fix* FRAUD, swindle, trick, charade, sham; *informal* setup, fiddle.

PHRASE: **fix up** *informal* *we need to get Dolly fixed up with a job* PROVIDE, supply, furnish.

fixated adjective *she's been **fixated on** photography* OBSESSED WITH, preoccupied with, obsessive about; focused on, keen on, gripped by, engrossed in, immersed in, wrapped up in, enthusiastic about, fanatical about; *informal* hooked on, wild for/about, nuts for/about, crazy for/about.

fixation noun *his sports fixation has gotten intolerable* OBSESSION, preoccupation, mania, addiction, compulsion; *informal* thing, bug, craze, fad.

fixed adjective 1 *there are fixed ropes on the rock face* FASTENED, secure, fast, firm; riveted, moored, anchored.

2 *a fixed period of time* PREDETERMINED, set, established, arranged, specified, decided, agreed, determined, confirmed, prescribed, allotted, definite, defined, explicit, precise.

fixture noun 1 *fixtures and fittings* FIXED APPLIANCE, installation, unit.

2 *she's a fixture at the bar* RESIDENT, lifer, permanent feature; *informal* part of the furniture.

fizz verb *the soda really fizzes when you first open the bottle* EFFERVESCE, sparkle, bubble, froth; *literary* spume.

▸ noun 1 *the fizz in champagne* EFFERVESCENCE, sparkle, fizziness, bubbles, bubbliness, gassiness, carbonation, froth.

2 *informal* *their set is a little lacking in fizz* EBULLIENCE, exuberance, liveliness, life, vivacity, animation, vigor, energy, verve, dash, spirit, sparkle, zest, fire; *informal* pizzazz, pep, zip, oomph.

3 *the fizz of the static* CRACKLE, crackling, buzz, buzzing, hiss, hissing, white noise; *literary* susurration.

fizzle verb *the loudspeaker fizzled* CRACKLE, buzz, hiss, fizz, crepitate.

▸ noun 1 *electric fizzle.* See FIZZ noun sense 3.

2 *the whole thing turned out to be a fizzle* FAILURE, fiasco, debacle, disaster; *informal* flop, washout, letdown, dead loss, snafu.

PHRASE: **fizzle out** *the viewers' enthusiasm pretty much fizzled out after the first season* PETER OUT, die off, ease off, cool off, flatline; tail off, wither away, wind down.

fizzy adjective *fizzy root beer* EFFERVESCENT, sparkling, carbonated, gassy, bubbly, frothy; spumante, frizzante. ANTONYMS still, flat.

flab noun *informal* *daily walking has trimmed off my abdominal flab* FAT, excessive weight, fatness, plumpness, lard; paunch, potbelly, beer belly.

flabbergast verb *informal* See ASTONISH.

flabby adjective 1 *his flabby stomach* SOFT, loose, flaccid, slack, untoned, drooping, sagging. ANTONYM firm.

2 *a flabby child* FAT, fleshy, overweight, plump, chubby, portly, rotund, broad in the beam, of ample proportions, obese, corpulent; *informal* tubby, roly-poly, well-upholstered. ANTONYM thin.

flaccid adjective 1 *a flaccid muscle* SOFT, loose, flabby, slack, lax; drooping, sagging. ANTONYM firm.

2 *his play seemed flaccid* LACKLUSTER, lifeless, listless, uninspiring, unanimated, tame, dull, vapid. ANTONYM spirited.

flag[1] noun *he raised the flag* BANNER, standard, ensign, pennant, banderole, streamer, jack, gonfalon; colors; Stars and Stripes, Old Glory, Union Jack; Jolly Roger; *Canadian* Red Ensign, Maple Leaf.

▸ verb *flag the misspelled words* INDICATE, identify, point out, mark, label, tag, highlight.

PHRASE: **flag down** *we had no luck flagging down a cab* HAIL, wave down, signal to stop, stop, halt.

flag[2] verb 1 *they were flagging toward the finish* TIRE, grow tired/weary, weaken, grow weak, wilt, droop, fade, run out of steam. ANTONYM revive.

2 *my energy flags in the afternoon* FADE, decline, wane, ebb, diminish, decrease, lessen, dwindle; wither, melt away, peter out, die away/down. ANTONYM increase.

flagellate verb *my pa is gonna flagellate me if I don't get home before dark* FLOG, whip, beat, scourge, lash, birch, strap, belt, cane, thrash, horsewhip, tan/whip someone's hide.

flagrant adjective *it was a flagrant distortion of the facts* BLATANT, glaring, obvious, overt, conspicuous, barefaced, shameless, brazen, undisguised, unconcealed; outrageous, scandalous, shocking, disgraceful, dreadful, terrible, gross.

flagship adjective *our flagship product is an environment-friendly electric lawn mower* TOP-OF-THE-LINE, topline, premium, prime, leading, champion, best, top.

flagstone noun *the landscapers unearthed a beautiful flagstone walkway, perhaps laid a hundred years ago* PAVING SLAB, paving stone, slab, flag.

flail verb 1 *he fell headlong, his arms flailing* WAVE, swing, thrash about, flap about.

2 *I was flailing about in the water* FLOUNDER, struggle, thrash, writhe, splash.

3 *he flailed their shoulders with his cane* THRASH, beat, strike, flog, whip, lash, scourge, cane; *informal* wallop, whack.

flair noun 1 *a flair for publicity* APTITUDE, talent, gift, instinct, (natural) ability, facility, skill, bent, feel, knack.

2 *she dressed with flair* STYLE, stylishness, panache, dash, élan, poise, elegance; taste, good taste, discernment, discrimination; *informal* class, pizzazz.

flak noun 1 *my aircraft had been damaged by flak* ANTI-AIRCRAFT FIRE, shelling, gunfire; bombardment, barrage, salvo, volley.

2 *informal he has come in for a lot of flak* CRITICISM, censure, disapproval, disapprobation, hostility, complaints; opprobrium, obloquy, calumny, vilification, abuse, brickbats; *formal* castigation, excoriation.

flake[1] noun 1 *flakes of pastry* SLIVER, wafer, shaving, paring; chip, scale; fragment, scrap, shred; *technical* lamina.

2 *informal Geoff can be such a flake* DITZ, space cadet, airhead, fool, scatterbrain.

▸ verb *the paint was flaking* PEEL (OFF), chip, blister, come off (in layers).

flake[2] PHRASE: **flake out** *informal she flaked out in her chair* FALL ASLEEP, go to sleep, drop off; collapse, faint, pass out, lose consciousness, black out, swoon; *informal* conk out, nod off, sack out.

flaky adjective 1 *flaky skin* FLAKING, peeling, scaly, blistering, scabrous.

2 *a flaky person* FOOLISH, silly, frivolous, flighty, spacey, new-agey.

flamboyant adjective 1 *her flamboyant personality* EXUBERANT, confident, lively, animated, vibrant, vivacious. ANTONYMS modest, restrained.

2 *a flamboyant cravat* COLORFUL, brightly colored, bright, vibrant, vivid; dazzling, eye-catching, bold; showy, ostentatious, gaudy, garish, lurid, loud; *informal* jazzy, flashy. ANTONYMS dull, restrained.

3 *a flamboyant architectural style* ELABORATE, ornate, fancy; baroque, rococo. ANTONYM simple.

flame noun 1 **(flames)** *a sheet of flames* FIRE, blaze, conflagration, inferno.

2 **(flames)** *the flames of her anger* PASSION, warmth, ardor, fervor, fervency, fire, intensity.

3 *informal an old flame* SWEETHEART, boyfriend, girlfriend, lover, partner; *informal* beau; *dated* steady.

▸ verb 1 *logs crackled and flamed* BURN, blaze, be ablaze, be alight, be on fire, be in flames, be aflame.

2 *Erica's cheeks flamed* BECOME RED, go red, blush, flush, redden, grow pink/crimson/scarlet, color, glow.

PHRASE: **in flames** *the cabin was in flames* ON FIRE, burning, alight, flaming, blazing, ignited; *literary* afire.

flame-proof adjective *flame-proof gloves* NONFLAMMABLE, noninflammable, flame-resistant, fire-resistant, flame-retardant. ANTONYM flammable.

flaming adjective 1 *a flaming bonfire* BLAZING, ablaze, burning, on fire, in flames, aflame; *literary* afire.

2 *flaming hair* BRIGHT, brilliant, vivid; red, reddish-orange, ginger, titian.

3 *a flaming altercation* FURIOUS, violent, vehement, frenzied, angry, passionate.

4 *in a flaming temper* FURIOUS, enraged, fuming, seething, incensed, infuriated, angry, raging, livid; *literary* wrathful.

flammable adjective *the proper storage of flammable solvents* INFLAMMABLE, burnable, combustible.

flank noun 1 *the horse's flanks* SIDE, haunch, quarter, thigh.

2 *the southern flank of the army* SIDE, wing.

▸ verb *the garden is flanked by two rivers* EDGE, bound, line, border, fringe.

flap verb 1 *the mallards flapped their wings* BEAT, flutter, agitate, wave, wag, swing.

2 *the flag flapped in the breeze* FLUTTER, fly, blow, swing, sway, ripple, stir.

▸ noun 1 *pockets with buttoned flaps* FOLD, overlap, covering.

2 *a few flaps of the wing* FLUTTER, fluttering, beat, beating, waving.

3 *informal I'm in a desperate flap* PANIC, fluster, state, dither, twitter, stew, tizzy.

4 *informal she created a flap with her controversial statement* FUSS, commotion, stir, hubbub, storm, uproar; controversy, brouhaha, furor; *informal* to-do, ballyhoo, hoo-ha.

flare noun 1 *the flare of the match* BLAZE, flash, dazzle, burst, flicker.

2 *a flare set off by the crew* DISTRESS SIGNAL, rocket, beacon, light, signal.

3 *a flare of anger* BURST, rush, eruption, explosion, spasm, access.

▸ verb 1 *the wick flared* BLAZE, flash, flare up, flame, burn; glow, flicker.

2 *her nostrils flared* SPREAD, broaden, widen; dilate.

PHRASE: **flare up** 1 *the wooden houses flared up like matchsticks* BURN, blaze, go up in flames. 2 *his injury has flared up again* RECUR, reoccur, reappear; break out, start suddenly, erupt. 3 *I flared up at him* LOSE ONE'S TEMPER, become enraged, fly into a temper, go berserk; *informal* blow one's top, fly off the handle, go mad, go bananas, hit the roof, go off the deep end, flip out, explode, have a fit, go crackers, flip one's wig, blow one's stack, go ballistic, go postal, have a conniption fit.

flash verb 1 *a torch flashed* LIGHT UP, shine, flare, blaze, gleam, glint, sparkle, burn; blink, wink, flicker, shimmer, twinkle, glimmer, glisten, scintillate; *literary* glister, coruscate.

2 *informal he was flashing his money around* SHOW OFF, flaunt, flourish, display, parade.

3 *informal he flashed at me* EXPOSE ONESELF.

4 *racing cars flashed past* ZOOM, streak, tear, shoot, dash, dart, fly, whistle, hurtle, careen, rush, bolt, race, speed, career, whiz, whoosh, buzz; *informal* belt, zap, bomb; barrel.

▸ noun 1 *a flash of light* FLARE, blaze, burst; gleam, glint, sparkle, flicker, shimmer, twinkle, glimmer.

2 *a basic uniform with no flashes* EMBLEM, insignia, badge; stripe, bar, chevron, brevet, wings.

3 *a sudden flash of inspiration* BURST, outburst, wave, rush, surge, flush.

▸ adjective *informal a flash sports car.* See FLASHY.

PHRASE: **in/like a flash** *the police were there in a flash* INSTANTLY, suddenly, abruptly, immediately, all of a sudden; quickly, rapidly, swiftly, speedily; in an instant/moment, in a (split) second, in a trice, in the blink of an eye; *informal* in a jiff, in a jiffy.

flashy adjective *informal a flashy outfit for the dance number* OSTENTATIOUS, flamboyant, showy, conspicuous, extravagant, expensive; vulgar, tasteless, brash, lurid, garish, loud, gaudy; *informal* snazzy, fancy, swanky, flash, jazzy, glitzy. ANTONYM understated.

flask noun *a flask of warm brandy* BOTTLE, container; hip flask, vacuum flask; *trademark* Thermos.

flat adjective 1 *a flat surface* LEVEL, horizontal; smooth, even, uniform, regular, plane. ANTONYMS vertical, uneven.

2 *the sea was flat* CALM, still, pacific, tranquil, glassy, undisturbed, without waves, like a millpond. ANTONYM choppy.

3 *a flat wooden box* SHALLOW, low-sided. ANTONYM deep.

4 *flat sandals* LOW, low-heeled, without heels.

5 *the teacher's flat voice* MONOTONOUS, toneless, droning, boring, dull, tedious, uninteresting, unexciting, soporific; bland, dreary, colorless, featureless, emotionless, expressionless, lifeless, spiritless, lackluster, plain-vanilla. ANTONYMS exciting, emotional.

6 *he felt too flat to get out of bed* DEPRESSED, dejected, dispirited, despondent, downhearted, disheartened, low, low-spirited, down, unhappy, blue; without energy, enervated, sapped, weary, tired out, worn out, exhausted, drained; *informal* down in the dumps. ANTONYMS cheerful, energized.

7 *the market was flat* SLOW, inactive, sluggish, slack, quiet, depressed. ANTONYM busy.

8 *a flat tire* DEFLATED, punctured, burst. ANTONYM inflated.

9 *a flat fee* FIXED, set, regular, unchanging, unvarying, invariable.

10 *a flat denial* OUTRIGHT, direct, absolute, definite, positive, straight, plain, explicit; firm, resolute, adamant, assertive, emphatic, categorical, unconditional, unqualified, unequivocal.

▸ adverb 1 *she lay down flat on the floor* STRETCHED OUT, outstretched, spread-eagle, sprawling, prone, supine, prostrate, recumbent.

2 *informal she turned me down flat* OUTRIGHT, absolutely, firmly, resolutely, adamantly, emphatically, insistently, categorically, unconditionally, unequivocally.

▸ noun (**flats**) *they race their bikes across the flats* TIDAL FLATS, mud flats, tideland, intertidal area.

PHRASE: **flat out** *I'd been working flat out* HARD, as hard as possible, for all one's worth, to the limit, all out; at full speed, as fast as possible, at full tilt, full bore, full throttle, in high gear; *informal* like crazy, like mad, like the wind, firing on all cylinders, like a bat out of hell.

flatten verb 1 *Flynn flattened the crumpled paper* MAKE FLAT, make even, smooth (out/off), level (out/off).

2 *the cows flattened the grass* COMPRESS, press down, crush, squash, compact, trample.

3 *tornadoes can flatten buildings in seconds* DEMOLISH, raze (to the ground), tear down, knock down, destroy, wreck, devastate, obliterate; *informal* total.

4 *informal Griff flattened him with a single punch* KNOCK DOWN/OVER, knock to the ground, fell, prostrate; *informal* floor, deck.

flatter verb 1 *it amused him to flatter her* COMPLIMENT, praise, express admiration for, say nice things about, fawn over; cajole, humor, flannel, blarney; *informal* sweet-talk, soft-soap, brown-nose, butter up, play up to, slobber over; *formal* laud. ANTONYM insult.

2 *I was flattered to be asked* HONOR, gratify, please, delight; *informal* tickle pink. ANTONYM offend.

3 *a hairstyle that flattered her* SUIT, become, look good on, go well with; *informal* do something for. ANTONYM clash with.

flatterer noun *he's got all the flatterers that money can buy* SYCOPHANT, bootlicker, brown-noser, toady, lickspittle, flunky, lackey, yes-man, doormat, stooge, cringer, suck, suck-up.

flattering adjective **1** *flattering remarks* COMPLIMENTARY, praising, favorable, commending, admiring, applauding, appreciative, good; fulsome, honeyed, sugary, cajoling, silver-tongued, honey-tongued; fawning, oily, obsequious, ingratiating, servile, sycophantic; *informal* sweet-talking, soft-soaping, crawling, bootlicking; *formal* encomiastic.

2 *it was very flattering to be nominated* PLEASING, gratifying, honoring, gladdening.

3 *her most flattering dress* BECOMING, enhancing.

flattery noun *she's simply not vain enough to fall for your flattery* PRAISE, adulation, compliments, blandishments, honeyed words; fawning, blarney, cajolery; *formal* encomium; *informal* sweet talk, soft soap, snow job, buttering up, toadying.

flatulence noun **1** *medications that help with flatulence* (INTESTINAL) GAS, wind; *informal* farting, tooting; *formal* flatus.

2 *the flatulence of his latest recordings* POMPOSITY, pompousness, pretension, pretentiousness, grandiloquence, bombast, turgidity.

flaunt verb *he flaunts his young wife as if she were the prize heifer at the county fair* SHOW OFF, display ostentatiously, make a (great) show of, put on show/display, parade; brag about, crow about, vaunt; *informal* flash.

USAGE NOTE **flaunt, flout**

Confusion about these terms is so distressingly common that some dictionaries have thrown in the towel and now treat *flaunt* as a synonym of *flout*. *Flout* means "contravene or disregard; treat with contempt." *Flaunt* means "show off or parade something in an ostentatious manner," but is often incorrectly used for *flout*, perhaps because it is misunderstood as a telescoped version of *flout* and *taunt*—e.g.: "In Washington, the White House issued a statement that deplored the Nigerian Government's 'flaunting [read *flouting*] of even the most basic international norms and universal standards of human rights.' " (*New York Times*; Nov. 11, 1995.)

Of course, *flaunt* is more often used correctly—e.g.: "He donates millions to religious and charitable groups, yet flaunts his own wealth." (*Fortune*; Aug. 18, 1997.) *Flout*, meanwhile, almost never causes a problem. Here it's correctly used: "A record rider turnout, fueled by the mayor's earlier pledge to end the escort and crack down on cyclists flouting traffic laws, poured into the streets on an improvised route." (*San Francisco Examiner*; Aug. 3, 1997.) But the rare mistake of misusing *flout* for *flaunt* does sometimes occur—e.g.: "Mr. Talton was soon joined by almost two dozen other conservative Republicans who filed en masse into the clerk's office to flout [read *flaunt*] their disapproval for their colleague and fellow party member." (*Dallas Morning News*; May 25, 2000.)

One federal appellate judge who misused *flaunt* for *flout* in a published opinion—only to be corrected by judges who later quoted him—appealed to *Webster's Third New International Dictionary of the English Language*, which accepts as standard any usage that can be documented with any frequency. The judge then attempted to justify his error and pledged to persist in it. Seeking refuge in a nonprescriptive dictionary, however, merely ignores the all-important distinction between formal contexts, in which strict standards of usage must apply, and informal contexts, in which venial faults of grammar or usage may, if we are lucky, go unnoticed (or unmentioned). **—BG**

flavor noun **1** *the flavor of prosciutto* TASTE, savor, tang.

2 *cilantro gives a distinctive flavor to the sauce* FLAVORING, seasoning, tastiness, tang, relish, bite, piquancy, pungency, spice, spiciness, zest; *informal* zing, zip.

3 *a strong international flavor* CHARACTER, quality, feel, feeling, ambience, atmosphere, aura, air, mood, tone; spirit, essence, nature.

4 *this excerpt will give a flavor of the report* IMPRESSION, suggestion, hint, taste.

▸ verb *spices for flavoring food* ADD FLAVOR TO, add flavoring to, season, spice (up), add piquancy to, ginger up, enrich; *informal* pep up.

PHRASE: **flavor of the month** *informal sure, it's great to be flavor of the month, but where will you be a year from now?* ALL THE RAGE, the latest thing, the fashion, in vogue; a one-hit wonder; *informal* hot, in.

flavoring noun **1** *this cheese is often combined with other flavorings* SEASONING, spice, herb, additive; condiment, dressing.

2 *vanilla flavoring* EXTRACT, flavor, essence, concentrate, distillate.

flaw noun *the reactor's design flaw | a flaw in his character* DEFECT, blemish, fault, imperfection, deficiency, weakness, weak spot/point/link, inadequacy, shortcoming, limitation, failing, foible; *literary* hamartia; *Computing* bug; *informal* glitch. See note at FAULT. ANTONYM strength.

flawed adjective **1** *a flawed mirror* FAULTY, defective, unsound, imperfect; broken, cracked, torn, scratched, deformed, distorted, warped, buckled. ANTONYM flawless.

2 *the findings were flawed* UNSOUND, defective, faulty, distorted, inaccurate, incorrect, erroneous, imprecise, fallacious, misleading. ANTONYM sound.

flawless adjective *a flawless performance* PERFECT, unblemished, unmarked, unimpaired; whole, intact, sound, unbroken, undamaged, mint, pristine; impeccable, immaculate, consummate, accurate, correct, faultless, error-free, unerring; exemplary, model, ideal, copybook; *Theology* inerrant. ANTONYM flawed.

flay verb **1** *the martyrs were killed and flayed* SKIN, strip the skin off; *Medicine* excoriate.

2 *informal he flayed his critics.* See CRITICIZE.

fleck noun *flecks of pale blue* SPOT, mark, dot, speck, speckle, freckle, patch, smudge, streak, blotch, dab; *informal* splotch; *rare* macula.

▸ verb *the deer's flanks were flecked with white* SPOT, mark, dot, speckle, bespeckle, freckle, stipple, stud, bestud, blotch, mottle, streak, splash, spatter, bespatter, scatter, sprinkle; *informal* splotch.

fledgling noun *a woodpecker fledgling* CHICK, baby bird, nestling.

▸ adjective *fledgling industries* EMERGING, emergent, sunrise, dawning, embryonic, infant, nascent; developing, in the making, budding, up-and-coming, rising. ANTONYMS declining, mature.

flee verb **1** *she fled to her room* RUN (AWAY/OFF), run for it, make a run for it, dash, take flight, be gone, make off, take off, take to one's heels, make a break for it, bolt, beat a (hasty) retreat, make a quick exit, make one's getaway, escape; *informal* beat it, clear off/out, vamoose, skedaddle, split, leg it, turn tail, scram, light out, cut out, peel out; *archaic* fly.

2 *they fled the country* RUN AWAY FROM, leave hastily, escape from; *informal* skip; *archaic* fly.

fleece noun *a sheep's fleece* WOOL, coat.

▸ verb *informal we were fleeced by a scalper.* See SWINDLE verb.

fleecy adjective *a fleecy robe* FLUFFY, woolly, downy, soft, fuzzy, furry, velvety, shaggy; *technical* floccose, pilose. ANTONYM coarse.

fleet[1] noun *the fleet set sail* NAVY, naval force, (naval) task force, armada, flotilla, squadron, convoy.

fleet[2] adjective *literary as fleet as a greyhound* NIMBLE, agile, lithe, lissome, acrobatic, supple, light-footed, light on one's feet, spry, sprightly; quick, fast, swift, rapid, speedy, brisk, smart; *informal* zippy, twinkle-toed.

fleeting adjective *ours was a fleeting romance* BRIEF, short, short-lived, quick, momentary, cursory, transient, ephemeral, fugitive, passing, transitory; *literary* evanescent. See note at TEMPORARY. ANTONYM lasting.

flesh noun **1** *you need more flesh on your bones* MUSCLE, meat, tissue, brawn; *informal* beef.

2 *she carries too much flesh* FAT, weight; *Anatomy* adipose tissue; *informal* blubber, flab.

3 *a fruit with juicy flesh* PULP, soft part, marrow, meat.

4 *the pleasures of the flesh* THE BODY, human nature, physicality, carnality, animality; sensuality, sexuality. PHRASES: **one's (own) flesh and blood** *how can you deny your own flesh and blood?* FAMILY, relative(s), relation(s), blood relation(s), kin, kinsfolk, kinsman, kinsmen, kinswoman, kinswomen, kindred, nearest and dearest, people; *informal* folks. **flesh out 1** *he really fleshed out for his latest movie role* PUT ON WEIGHT, gain weight, get heavier, grow fat/fatter, fatten up, get fat, fill out. **2** *the story line should be fleshed out a bit* EXPAND (ON), elaborate on, add to, build on, add flesh to, put flesh on (the bones of), add detail to, expatiate on, supplement, reinforce, augment, fill out, enlarge on. **in the flesh** *look, it's Sean Penn, in the flesh* IN PERSON, before one's (very) eyes, in front of one; in real life, live; physically, bodily, in bodily/human form, incarnate.

fleshly adjective *resisting fleshly temptations* CARNAL, physical, animal, bestial; sexual, sensual, erotic, lustful. ANTONYMS spiritual, noble.

fleshy adjective *the trim athlete has become a fleshy couch potato* PLUMP, chubby, portly, fat, obese, overweight, stout, corpulent, full-figured, heavyset, paunchy, well padded, well covered, well-upholstered, rotund; *informal* tubby, pudgy, beefy, porky, roly-poly, blubbery, corn-fed. ANTONYM thin.

flex verb **1** *you must flex your elbow* BEND, crook, hook, cock, angle, double up. ANTONYM straighten.

2 *Rachel flexed her cramped muscles* TIGHTEN, tauten, tense (up), tension, contract. ANTONYM relax.

flexibility noun **1** *the flexibility of wood* PLIABILITY, suppleness, pliancy, plasticity; elasticity, stretchiness, springiness, spring, resilience, bounce; *informal* give. ANTONYM rigidity.

2 *the flexibility of a mixed portfolio* ADAPTABILITY, adjustability, variability, versatility, open-endedness, freedom, latitude. ANTONYM inflexibility.

3 *the flexibility shown by the local authority* COOPERATION, amenability, accommodations, tolerance, willingness to compromise. ANTONYM intransigence.

flexible adjective **1** *flexible tubing* PLIABLE, supple, bendable, pliant, plastic; elastic, stretchy, whippy, springy, resilient, bouncy; *informal* bendy. ANTONYM rigid.

2 *a flexible arrangement* ADAPTABLE, adjustable, variable, versatile, open-ended, open, free. ANTONYM inflexible.

3 *the need to be flexible toward tenants* ACCOMMODATING, amenable, willing to compromise, cooperative, tolerant, easygoing. ANTONYM intransigent.

THE RIGHT WORD

If you can bend over and touch your toes, you are **flexible**. But a dancer or gymnast is **limber**, an adjective that specifically applies to a body that has been brought into condition through training (*to stay limber, she did yoga every day*). *Flexible* applies to whatever can be bent without breaking, whether or not it returns to its original shape (*a flexible plastic hose; a flexible electrical conduit*); it does not necessarily refer, as *limber* does, to the human body. Unlike *flexible*, **resilient** implies the ability to spring back into shape after being bent or compressed, or to recover one's health or spirits quickly (*so young and resilient that she was back at work in a week*). **Elastic** is usually applied to substances or materials that are easy to stretch or expand and that quickly recover their shape or size (*pants with an elastic waist*), while **supple** is applied to whatever is easily bent, twisted, or folded without breaking or cracking (*a soft, supple leather*). When applied to the human body, *supple* suggests the ability to move effortlessly. **Pliant** and **pliable** may used to describe either people or things that are easily bent or manipulated. *Pliant* suggests a tendency to bend without force or pressure from the outside, while *pliable* suggests the use of force or submission to another's will. A *pliant* person is merely adaptable, but a *pliable* person is easy to influence and eager to please.

flick noun *a flick of the wrist* JERK, snap, flip, whisk.

▸ verb **1** *he flicked the switch* CLICK, snap, flip, jerk.

2 *the horse flicked its tail* SWISH, twitch, wave, wag, waggle, shake.

PHRASE: **flick through** *flick through the pages and try to find a hairstyle you like* THUMB (THROUGH), leaf through, flip through, skim through, scan, look through, browse through, dip into, glance at/through, peruse, run one's eye over.

flicker verb **1** *the lights flickered* GLIMMER, glint, flare, dance, gutter; twinkle, sparkle, blink, wink, flash, scintillate; *literary* glister, coruscate.

2 *his eyelids flickered* FLUTTER, quiver, tremble, shiver, shudder, spasm, jerk, twitch.

flight noun **1** *the history of flight* AVIATION, flying, air transport, aerial navigation, aeronautics.

2 *a flight to Rome* AIRPLANE/PLANE TRIP, air trip, trip/journey by air.

3 *the flight of a baseball* TRAJECTORY, path through the air, track, orbit.

4 *a flight of birds* FLOCK, skein, covey, swarm, cloud.

5 *his headlong flight from home* ESCAPE, getaway, hasty departure, exit, exodus, decamping, breakout, bolt, disappearance.

6 ***a flight of stairs*** STAIRCASE, set of steps, set of stairs. PHRASES: **put someone to flight** *the king's infantry put our demoralized militia to flight* CHASE AWAY/OFF, drive back/away/off/out, scatter (to the four winds), disperse, repel, repulse, rout, stampede, scare off; *informal* send packing. **take flight** *the cowards took flight as the enemy approached* FLEE, run (away/off), run for it, make a run for it, be gone, make off, take off, take to one's heels, make a break for it, bolt, beat a (hasty) retreat, make a quick exit, make one's getaway, escape; *informal* beat it, clear off/out, vamoose, skedaddle, split, leg it, turn tail, scram, light out, bug out, cut out, peel out; *archaic* fly.

flighty adjective *his flighty sister has changed her college major four times* FICKLE, inconstant, mercurial, whimsical, capricious, skittish, volatile, impulsive; irresponsible, giddy, reckless, wild, careless, thoughtless. ANTONYMS steady, responsible.

flimsy adjective **1** *a flimsy building* INSUBSTANTIAL, fragile, breakable, frail, shaky, unstable, wobbly, tottery, rickety, ramshackle, makeshift; jerry-built, badly built, shoddy, chintzy, gimcrack. ANTONYM sturdy.

2 *a flimsy garment* THIN, light, fine, filmy, floaty, diaphanous, sheer, delicate, insubstantial, wispy, gossamer, gauzy. ANTONYM thick.

3 *flimsy evidence* WEAK, feeble, poor, inadequate, insufficient, thin, unsubstantial, unconvincing, implausible, unsatisfactory. ANTONYM sound.

flinch verb **1** *he flinched at the noise* WINCE, start, shudder, quiver, jerk, shy. See note at WINCE.

2 *she never* ***flinched from*** *her duty* SHRINK FROM, recoil from, shy away from, swerve from, demur from; dodge, evade, avoid, duck, balk at, jib at, quail at, fight shy of.

fling verb *he flung the ax into the river* THROW, toss, sling, hurl, cast, pitch, lob; *informal* chuck, heave.

▸ noun **1** *a birthday fling* GOOD TIME, spree, bit of fun, night on the town; fun and games, revels, larks; *informal* binge.

2 *she had a brief fling with him* AFFAIR, love affair, relationship, romance, affaire (de cœur), amour, flirtation, dalliance, liaison, entanglement, involvement, attachment.

flip verb **1** *the wave* ***flipped*** *the dinghy* ***over*** | *the plane flipped on to its back* OVERTURN, turn over, tip over, roll (over), upturn, capsize; upend, invert, knock over; keel over, topple over, turn turtle; *archaic* overset.

2 *he flipped the key through the air* THROW, flick, toss, fling, sling, pitch, cast, spin, lob; *informal* chuck; *dated* shy.

3 *I flipped the transmitter switch* FLICK, click, snap. PHRASE: **flip through** *mindlessly flipping through the magazine* THUMB (THROUGH), leaf through, flick through, skim through, scan, look through, browse through, glance at/through, peruse, run one's eye over.

flip-flop noun *the senator did a sudden flip-flop on gun control* ABOUT-FACE, U-turn, volte-face, reversal, turnaround, one-eighty, change of heart; *informal* U-ey.

flippancy noun *your flippancy was inappropriate during an obviously serious moment* FRIVOLITY, levity, facetiousness; disrespect, irreverence, cheek, impudence, impertinence; sauce, sassiness. ANTONYMS seriousness, respect.

flippant adjective *a flippant remark* FRIVOLOUS, facetious, tongue-in-cheek; disrespectful, irreverent, cheeky, impudent, impertinent; *informal* flip, waggish. ANTONYMS serious, respectful.

flirt verb **1** *it amused him to* ***flirt with*** *her* TRIFLE WITH, toy with, tease, lead on.

2 *those conservatives who* ***flirted with*** *fascism* DABBLE IN, toy with, trifle with, amuse oneself with, play with, tinker with, dip into, scratch the surface of.

3 *he is* ***flirting with*** *danger* COURT, risk, not fear, invite.

▸ noun *Anna was quite a flirt* TEASE, trifler, philanderer, coquette, heartbreaker.

flirtation noun *a bit of mild flirtation* COQUETRY, teasing, trifling.

flirtatious adjective *her blatantly flirtatious manner* COQUETTISH, flirty, kittenish, teasing.

flit verb *dragonflies flitted across the pond* DART, dance, skip, play, dash, trip, flutter, bob, bounce.

float verb **1** *oil floats on water* STAY AFLOAT, stay on the surface, be buoyant, be buoyed up. ANTONYM sink.

2 *the balloon floated in the air* HOVER, levitate, be suspended, hang, defy gravity.

3 *a cloud floated across the moon* DRIFT, glide, sail, slip, slide, waft. ANTONYM rush.

4 *they have just floated that idea* SUGGEST, put forward, come up with, submit, moot, propose, advance, test the popularity of; *informal* run something up the flagpole (to see who salutes). ANTONYM withdraw.

floating adjective **1** *floating seaweed* BUOYANT, on the surface, afloat, drifting. ANTONYM sunken.

2 *floating helium balloons* HOVERING, levitating, suspended, hanging, defying gravity. ANTONYM grounded.

3 *floating voters* UNCOMMITTED, undecided, of two minds, torn, split, uncertain, unsure, wavering, vacillating, indecisive, blowing hot and cold, undeclared; *informal* sitting on the fence. ANTONYM committed.

4 *a floating population* UNSETTLED, transient, temporary, variable, fluctuating; migrant, wandering, nomadic, on the move, migratory, traveling, drifting, roving, roaming, itinerant, vagabond. ANTONYM settled.

5 *a floating exchange rate* VARIABLE, changeable, changing, fluid, fluctuating. ANTONYM fixed.

flock noun **1** *a flock of sheep* HERD, drove.

2 *a flock of birds* FLIGHT, congregation, covey, clutch.

3 *flocks of people* CROWD, throng, horde, mob, rabble, mass, multitude, host, army, pack, swarm, sea; *informal* gaggle.

▸ verb **1** *people flocked around McCartney* GATHER, collect, congregate, assemble, converge, mass, crowd, throng, cluster, swarm.

2 *tourists flock to the place* STREAM, go in large numbers, swarm, crowd, troop.

flog verb *the thief was flogged* WHIP, scourge, flagellate, lash, birch, switch, cane, thrash, beat; tan someone's hide.

flood noun **1** *a flood warning* INUNDATION, swamping, deluge, high water; torrent, overflow, flash flood, freshet, spate.

2 *a flood of tears* OUTPOURING, torrent, rush, stream, gush, surge, cascade.

3 *a flood of complaints* SUCCESSION, series, string, chain; barrage, volley, battery; avalanche, torrent, stream, tide, spate, storm, shower, cascade. ANTONYM trickle.

▸ verb 1 *the whole town was flooded* INUNDATE, swamp, deluge, immerse, submerge, drown, engulf.

2 *the river could flood* OVERFLOW, burst its banks, brim over, run over.

3 *imports are flooding the domestic market* GLUT, swamp, saturate, oversupply.

4 *refugees flooded in* POUR, stream, flow, surge, swarm, pile, crowd. ANTONYM trickle.

floodgate noun *heavy rains may prove too much for the East Creek floodgate* SLUICE, watergate; lock, dam, weir.

floor noun 1 *he sat on the floor* GROUND, flooring.

2 *the second floor* STORY, level, deck, tier.

▸ verb 1 *he floored his attacker* KNOCK DOWN, knock over, bring down, fell, prostrate; *informal* lay out.

2 *informal the question floored him* BAFFLE, defeat, confound, perplex, puzzle, mystify; *informal* beat, flummox, stump, fox.

flop verb 1 *he flopped into a chair* COLLAPSE, slump, crumple, subside, sink, drop.

2 *his hair flopped over his eyes* HANG (DOWN), dangle, droop, sag, loll.

3 *informal the play flopped* BE UNSUCCESSFUL, fail, not work, fall flat, founder, misfire, backfire, be a disappointment, do badly, lose money, be a disaster; *informal* bomb, tank, flame out, come a cropper, bite the dust, blow up in someone's face. ANTONYM succeed.

▸ noun *informal the play was a flop* FAILURE, disaster, debacle, catastrophe, loser; *informal* washout, also-ran, dog, lemon, nonstarter, clinker, turkey. ANTONYM success.

floppy adjective *the rabbit's floppy ears* LIMP, flaccid, slack, flabby, relaxed; drooping, droopy; loose, flowing. ANTONYMS erect, stiff.

florid adjective 1 *a florid complexion* RUDDY, red, red-faced, rosy, rosy-cheeked, pink; flushed, blushing, high-colored; *archaic* sanguine. ANTONYM pale.

2 *florid plasterwork* ORNATE, fancy, elaborate, embellished, curlicued, extravagant, flamboyant, baroque, rococo, fussy, busy. ANTONYM plain.

3 *florid prose* FLOWERY, flamboyant, high-flown, high-sounding, grandiloquent, ornate, fancy, bombastic, elaborate, turgid, pleonastic; *informal* highfalutin; *rare* fustian. ANTONYM plain.

flotsam noun *search and salvage crews are gathering flotsam by the boatfuls* WRECKAGE, cargo, remains; debris, detritus, waste, dross, refuse, scrap, trash, garbage, rubbish; *informal* dreck, junk.

flounce[1] verb *she flounced off to her room* STORM, stride angrily, sweep, stomp, stamp, march, strut.

flounce[2] noun *a lace flounce* FRILL, ruffle, ruff, peplum, jabot, furbelow, ruche.

flounder verb 1 *people were floundering in the water* STRUGGLE, thrash, flail, twist and turn, splash, stagger, stumble, reel, lurch, blunder, squirm, writhe.

2 *she floundered, not knowing quite what to say* STRUGGLE, be out of one's depth, have difficulty, be confounded, be confused; *informal* scratch one's head, be flummoxed, be clueless, be foxed, be fazed, be floored, be beaten.

3 *more firms are floundering* STRUGGLE FINANCIALLY, be in dire straits, face financial ruin, be in difficulties, face bankruptcy/insolvency, founder. See note at FOUNDER[2]. ANTONYM prosper.

flourish verb 1 *ferns flourish in the shade* GROW, thrive, prosper, do well, burgeon, increase, multiply, proliferate; spring up, shoot up, bloom, blossom, bear fruit, burst forth, run riot. ANTONYMS die, wither.

2 *the arts flourished* THRIVE, prosper, bloom, be in good health, be vigorous, be in its heyday; progress, make progress, advance, make headway, develop, improve; evolve, make strides, move forward (in leaps and bounds), expand; *informal* be in the pink, go places, go great guns, get somewhere. ANTONYM decline.

3 *he flourished the sword at them* BRANDISH, wave, shake, wield; swing, twirl, swish; display, exhibit, flaunt, show off.

flout verb *countless retailers flout the law by selling cigarettes to children* DEFY, refuse to obey, disobey, break, violate, fail to comply with, fail to observe, contravene, infringe, breach, commit a breach of, transgress against; ignore, disregard. See note at FLAUNT. ANTONYM observe.

flow verb 1 *the water flowed down the channel* RUN, course, glide, drift, circulate; trickle, seep, ooze, dribble, drip, drizzle, spill; stream, swirl, surge, sweep, gush, cascade, pour, roll, rush.

2 *many questions flow from today's announcement* RESULT, proceed, arise, follow, ensue, derive, stem, accrue; originate, emanate, spring, emerge; be caused by, be brought about by, be produced by, be consequent on.

▸ noun *a good flow of water* MOVEMENT, motion, current, flux, circulation; trickle, ooze, percolation, drip; stream, swirl, surge, gush, rush, spate, tide.

flower noun 1 *blue flowers* BLOOM, blossom, floweret, floret. See table.

2 *the flower of the nation's youth* BEST, finest, pick, choice, cream, crème de la crème, elite. ANTONYM dregs.

PARTS OF FLOWERS

androecium	peduncle
anther	perianth
bract	petal
calyx	placenta
capitulum	pollen
carpel	rachis
catkin	receptacle
corolla	sepal
corymb	spadix
cyme	spathe
filament	spike
floret	spikelet
glume	spur
gynoecium	stamen
involucre	stigma
nectary	style
ovary	tassel
ovule	tepal
palea	torus
panicle	umbel
pedicel	whorl

flowery adjective 1 *flowery fabrics* FLORAL, flower-patterned.

2 *flowery language* FLORID, flamboyant, ornate, fancy, convoluted; high-flown, high-sounding, magniloquent, grandiloquent, baroque, orotund, overblown, pleonastic;

informal highfalutin, purple, fancy-dancy, fancy-schmancy; *rare* fustian. ANTONYM plain.

flowing adjective **1** *long flowing hair* LOOSE, free, unconfined, draping. ANTONYMS stiff, curly.

2 *the new model will have soft, flowing lines* SLEEK, streamlined, aerodynamic, smooth, clean; elegant, graceful; *technical* faired. ANTONYM jagged.

3 *he writes in an easy, flowing style* FLUENT, fluid, free-flowing, effortless, easy, natural, smooth. ANTONYMS stilted, halting.

fluctuate verb *profits fluctuate from month to month* VARY, change, differ, shift, alter, waver, swing, oscillate, alternate, rise and fall, go up and down, seesaw, yo-yo, be unstable.

fluctuation noun *a natural fluctuation in temperature* VARIATION, change, shift, alteration, swing, movement, oscillation, alternation, rise and fall, seesawing, yo-yoing, instability, unsteadiness. ANTONYM stability.

flue noun *periodically check the flue for obstructions* DUCT, tube, shaft, vent, pipe, passage, channel, conduit; funnel, chimney, smokestack.

fluent adjective **1** *a fluent campaign speech* ARTICULATE, eloquent, expressive, communicative, coherent, cogent, illuminating, vivid, well-written/spoken. ANTONYM inarticulate.

2 *fluent in French* ARTICULATE; **(be fluent in)** have a (good) command of.

3 *a very fluent running style* FREE-FLOWING, smooth, effortless, easy, natural, fluid; graceful, elegant; regular, rhythmic. ANTONYM jerky.

fluff noun **1** *fluff on her sleeve* FUZZ, lint, dust, dustballs, dust bunnies.

2 *informal he only made a few fluffs* MISTAKE, error, slip, misstep, flub, slip of the tongue; wrong note, slip-up; *formal* lapsus linguae.

▸ verb *informal Penney fluffed the shot | he fluffed his only line* FUMBLE, make a mess of, bungle, miss, deliver badly, muddle up, forget; *informal* mess up, make a hash of, botch, foul up, screw up, flub, goof up. ANTONYM succeed in.

fluffy adjective *the gloves have a fluffy lining* FLEECY, woolly, fuzzy, hairy, feathery, downy, furry; soft. ANTONYM rough.

fluid noun *the fluid seeps up the tube* LIQUID, watery substance, solution. ANTONYM solid.

▸ adjective **1** *a fluid substance* FREE-FLOWING; liquid, liquefied, melted, molten, runny, running. ANTONYM solid.

2 *his plans were still fluid* ADAPTABLE, flexible, adjustable, open-ended, open, open to change, changeable, variable. ANTONYM firm.

3 *the fluid state of affairs* FLUCTUATING, changeable, subject/likely to change, shifting, ever-shifting, inconstant; unstable, unsettled, turbulent, volatile, mercurial, protean. ANTONYM static.

4 *he stood up in one fluid movement* SMOOTH, fluent, flowing, effortless, easy, continuous, seamless; graceful, elegant. ANTONYM jerky.

fluke noun *what a nice fluke, finding you here* CHANCE, coincidence, accident, twist of fate; piece of luck, stroke of good luck/fortune, serendipity.

fluky adjective *a fluky encounter with her ex-husband led to a reconciliation* LUCKY, fortunate, providential, timely, opportune, serendipitous, expedient, heaven-sent, auspicious, propitious, felicitous; chance, fortuitous, accidental, unintended. ANTONYM planned.

flummox verb *informal at age ten, he created intricate math problems that flummoxed his teachers* BAFFLE, perplex, puzzle, bewilder, mystify, bemuse, confuse, confound; *informal* faze, stump, beat, fox, be all Greek to, floor, discombobulate.

WORD NOTE **flummox**

There is greater intensity and more imagination in *flummox* than in its near relatives, *baffle, perplex, confuse;* the comical sound of the word adds to its strength—though the same can be said for *discombobulate. Flummoxed* conjures up a figure in momentary speechless paralysis, whereas *discombobulated* suggests a human contraption coming all to pieces. **—JS**

flunky noun **1** *a flunky brought us drinks* SERVANT, lackey, steward, butler, footman, valet, attendant, page.

2 *government flunkies searched his offices* MINION, lackey, hireling, subordinate, underling, servant; creature, instrument, cat's paw; *informal* stooge, gofer.

flurried adjective *I was so flurried that I broke the cork* AGITATED, flustered, ruffled, in a panic, worked up, beside oneself, overwrought, perturbed, frantic; *informal* in a flap, in a state, in a twitter, in a fluster, in a dither, in a tizzy. ANTONYM calm.

flurry noun **1** *snow flurries* SWIRL, whirl, eddy, billow, shower, gust.

2 *a flurry of activity* BURST, outbreak, spurt, fit, spell, bout, rash, eruption; fuss, stir, bustle, hubbub, commotion, disturbance, furor; *informal* to-do, flap.

3 *a flurry of imports* SPATE, wave, flood, deluge, torrent, stream, tide, avalanche; series, succession, string, outbreak, rash, explosion, run, rush. ANTONYMS dearth, trickle.

flush[1] verb **1** *Shane flushed in embarrassment* BLUSH, redden, go pink, go red, go crimson, go scarlet, color (up). ANTONYM pale.

2 *fruit helps to flush toxins from the body* RINSE, wash, sluice, swill, cleanse, clean.

3 *they flushed out the snipers* DRIVE, chase, force, dislodge, expel, frighten, scare.

▸ noun **1** *a flush crept over her face* BLUSH, reddening, high color, color, rosiness, pinkness, ruddiness, bloom. ANTONYM paleness.

2 *the flush of youth* BLOOM, glow, freshness, radiance, vigor, rush.

flush[2] adjective *informal* **1** *the company was **flush with** cash* WELL SUPPLIED WITH, well provided with, well stocked with, replete with, overflowing with, bursting with, brimming with, loaded with, overloaded with, teeming with, stuffed with, swarming with, thick with, solid with; full of, abounding in, rich in, abundant in; *informal* awash with, jam-packed with, chock-full of. ANTONYM bereft.

2 *the years when cash was flush* PLENTIFUL, abundant, in abundance, copious, ample, profuse, superabundant; *in-*

formal galore; *literary* plenteous, bounteous. See note at WEALTHY. ANTONYMS lacking, low.

flushed adjective **1** *flushed faces* RED, pink, ruddy, glowing, reddish, pinkish, rosy, florid, high-colored, healthy-looking, aglow, burning, feverish; blushing, red-faced, embarrassed, shamefaced. ANTONYM pale.

2 *flushed with success* ELATED, excited, thrilled, exhilarated, happy, delighted, overjoyed, joyous, gleeful, jubilant, exultant, ecstatic, euphoric, rapturous; *informal* blissed out, over the moon, high, on a high. ANTONYM dismayed.

fluster verb *she was flustered by his presence* UNSETTLE, make nervous, unnerve, agitate, ruffle, upset, bother, put on edge, disquiet, disturb, worry, perturb, disconcert, confuse, throw off balance, confound; *informal* rattle, faze, put into a flap, throw into a tizzy, discombobulate. ANTONYM calm.

▸ noun *I was in a terrible fluster* STATE OF AGITATION, state of anxiety, nervous state, panic, frenzy, fret; *informal* dither, flap, tizz, tizzy, twitter, state, sweat. ANTONYM state of calm.

fluted adjective *a roof supported by fluted columns* GROOVED, channeled, furrowed, ribbed, corrugated, ridged. ANTONYMS smooth, plain.

flutter verb **1** *butterflies fluttered around* FLIT, hover, flitter, dance.

2 *a tern was fluttering its wings* FLAP, move up and down, beat, quiver, agitate, vibrate, whiffle.

3 *she fluttered her eyelashes* FLICKER, bat.

4 *flags fluttered* FLAP, wave, ripple, undulate, quiver; fly.

5 *her heart fluttered* BEAT WEAKLY, beat irregularly, palpitate, miss/skip a beat, quiver, go pit-a-pat; *Medicine* exhibit arrhythmia.

▸ noun **1** *the flutter of wings* BEATING, flapping, quivering, agitation, vibrating.

2 *a flutter of dark eyelashes* FLICKER, bat.

3 *the flutter of the flags* FLAPPING, waving, rippling.

4 *a flutter of nervousness* TREMOR, wave, rush, surge, flash, stab, flush, tremble, quiver, shiver, frisson, chill, thrill, tingle, shudder, ripple, flicker.

flux noun *the flux of vapor in the tube* CONTINUOUS CHANGE, changeability, variability, inconstancy, fluidity, instability, unsteadiness, fluctuation, variation, shift, movement, oscillation, alternation, rise and fall, seesawing, yo-yoing. ANTONYM stability.

fly verb **1** *a bird flew overhead* TRAVEL THROUGH THE AIR, wing its way, wing, glide, soar, wheel; hover, hang; take wing, take to the air, mount.

2 *they flew to Paris* TRAVEL BY AIRPLANE/PLANE, travel by air, jet.

3 *military planes flew in food supplies* TRANSPORT BY AIRPLANE/PLANE, transport by air, airlift, lift, jet.

4 *he could fly a plane* PILOT, operate, control, maneuver, steer.

5 *the ship was flying a red flag* DISPLAY, show, exhibit, bear; have hoisted, have run up.

6 *flags flew in the town* FLUTTER, flap, wave.

7 *doesn't time fly?* GO QUICKLY, fly by/past, pass swiftly, slip past, rush past.

8 *the runners flew by.* See SPEED verb sense 1.

9 *archaic the beaten army had to fly.* See FLEE sense 1.

PHRASES: **fly at** *he flew at Rodriguez with fire in his eyes* ATTACK, assault, pounce on, set upon, set about, let fly at, turn on, round on, lash out at, hit out at, fall on; *informal* lay into, tear into, lace into, sail into, pitch into, let someone have it, jump, have a go at, light into. **let fly.** See LET.

fly-by-night adjective **1** *a fly-by-night character* UNRELIABLE, undependable, untrustworthy, disreputable; DISHONEST, deceitful, dubious, unscrupulous; *informal* iffy, shady, sketchy, shifty, slippery, crooked, hinky; bent. ANTONYMS reputable,, reliable.

2 *fly-by-night business enterprises* SHORT-LIVED, ephemeral, superficial, fleeting. ANTONYMS long-standing, reliable.

flyer, flier noun **1** *frequent flyers* AIR TRAVELER, airline/air passenger, airline customer, jet-setter.

2 *flyers killed in the war* PILOT, airman, airwoman; *dated* aviator, aviatrix, aeronaut.

3 *we distributed flyers promoting our cleaning business* LEAFLET, handout, bill, handbill, brochure, circular, advertisement, junk mail.

flying adjective **1** *a flying beetle* WINGED; AIRBORNE, in the air, in flight.

2 *a flying visit* BRIEF, short, lightning, fleeting, hasty, rushed, hurried, quick, whistle-stop, cursory, perfunctory; *informal* quickie. ANTONYM long.

foam noun *the foam on the waves* FROTH, spume, surf; fizz, effervescence, bubbles, head; lather, suds.

▸ verb *the water foamed* FROTH, spume; fizz, effervesce, bubble; lather; ferment, rise; boil, seethe, simmer.

foamy adjective *beat the egg whites until foamy* FROTHY, foaming, spumy, bubbly, aerated, bubbling; sudsy; whipped, whisked.

focus noun **1** *schools are a focus of community life* CENTER, focal point, central point, center of attention, hub, pivot, nucleus, heart, cornerstone, linchpin, cynosure.

2 *the focus is on helping people* EMPHASIS, accent, priority, attention, concentration.

3 *the main focus of this chapter* SUBJECT, theme, concern, subject matter, topic, issue, thesis, point, thread; substance, essence, gist, matter.

4 *the resulting light beams are brought to a focus at the eyepiece* FOCAL POINT, point of convergence.

▸ verb **1** *she focused her binoculars on the tower* BRING INTO FOCUS; aim, point, turn.

2 *the investigation will* ***focus on*** *areas of social need* CONCENTRATE ON, center on, zero in on, zoom in on; address itself to, pay attention to, pinpoint, revolve around, have as its starting point.

PHRASES: **in focus** *submit only those snapshots that are in focus* SHARP, crisp, distinct, clear, well-defined, well focused. **out of focus** *the shots are slightly out of focus, which gives them an eerie quality* BLURRED, unfocused, indistinct, blurry, fuzzy, hazy, misty, cloudy, lacking definition, nebulous.

WORD NOTE focus

Focus is now the noun of choice for expressing what people used to mean by *concentration* (*Sampras's on-court focus was phenomenal*) and *emphasis* (*Our focus is on sat-*

isfying the needs of our customers). Adjectivized, it seems often to serve as an approving synonym for *driven* or *monomaniacal*: *He's the most focused warehouse manager we've ever had.* As a verb, it seems isomorphic with the older *to concentrate*: *Focus, people!*; *The Democrats hope that the campaign will focus on the economy; We need to focus on finding solutions instead of blaming each other*; etc. Notice, with respect to those last two sample sentences, how the verb phrase *to focus on* can take as its object either a thing-noun ("economy") or an *ing*-word ("finding"), and how its grammar is slightly different in these two cases. With a noun, *to focus on* means "to concentrate attention or effort on," i.e., the direct object is built right into the verb phrase; but with *ing*-words, it means "to direct toward a particular goal"—there's always a direct object like "attention/efforts/energies" that's suppressed but understood, and the *ing*-word functions as an indirect object. Given the speed with which *to focus* has supplanted *to concentrate,* it's a little surprising that nobody objects to its somewhat jargony New Age feel—but nobody seems to. Maybe this is because the word is only one of many film and drama terms that have lately entered mainstream usage, e.g., *to foreground* (= to feature, to give top priority to); *to background* (= to downplay, to relegate to the back burner); *scenario* (= an outline of some hypothetical sequence of events), *dialogue* (see note at DIALOGUE), and so on. —**DFW**

---

foe noun *a well-armed foe* ENEMY, adversary, opponent, rival, antagonist, combatant, challenger, competitor, opposer, opposition, competition, other side. See word spectrum at FRIEND. ANTONYM friend.

fog noun *we can't set sail in this fog* MIST, smog, murk, haze, ice fog; *archaic* sea smoke; *literary* brume, fume.

▸ verb **1** *the windshield* ***fogged up*** | *his breath fogged the glass* STEAM UP, mist over, cloud over, film over, make/become misty. ANTONYM clear.

2 *his brain was fogged with sleep* MUDDLE, daze, stupefy, fuddle, befuddle, bewilder, confuse, befog; *literary* bedim, becloud.

foggy adjective **1** *the weather was foggy* MISTY, smoggy, hazy, murky. ANTONYM clear.

2 *she was foggy with sleep* | *a foggy memory* MUDDLED, fuddled, befuddled, confused, at sea, bewildered, dazed, stupefied, numb, groggy, fuzzy, bleary; dark, dim, hazy, shadowy, cloudy, blurred, obscure, vague, indistinct, unclear; *informal* dopey, woolly, woozy, out of it. ANTONYM lucid.

foible noun *tolerating each other's foibles* WEAKNESS, failing, shortcoming, flaw, imperfection, blemish, fault, defect, limitation; quirk, kink, idiosyncrasy, eccentricity, peculiarity. See note at FAULT. ANTONYM strength.

foil[1] verb *their escape attempt was foiled* THWART, frustrate, counter, balk, impede, obstruct, hamper, euchre, hinder, snooker, cripple, scotch, derail, scupper, scuttle, smash; stop, block, prevent, defeat; *informal* do for, put paid to, stymie, cook someone's goose. See note at THWART. ANTONYM assist.

foil[2] noun *Abbott was the perfect foil to Costello* CONTRAST, complement, antithesis, relief.

foist verb *why are you trying to* ***foist*** *your crummy old furniture* ***on*** *me?* IMPOSE ON, force on, thrust on, offload on, unload on, dump on, palm off on; pass off on; saddle someone with, land someone with.

fold[1] verb **1** *I folded the cloth* DOUBLE (OVER/UP), crease, turn under/up/over, bend; tuck, gather, pleat.

2 *fold the cream into the chocolate mixture* MIX, blend, stir gently, incorporate.

3 *he folded her in his arms* ENFOLD, wrap, envelop; take, gather, clasp, squeeze, clutch; embrace, hug, cuddle, cradle.

4 *the firm folded last year* FAIL, collapse, founder; go bankrupt, become insolvent, cease trading, go into receivership, go into liquidation, be closed (down), be shut (down); *informal* crash, go bust, go broke, go under, go belly up.

▸ noun *there was a fold in the paper* CREASE, wrinkle, crinkle, pucker, furrow; pleat, gather.

fold[2] noun **1** *the sheep were in their fold* ENCLOSURE, pen, paddock, pound, compound, ring, corral; sheepfold.

2 *they welcomed Joe back into the fold* COMMUNITY, group, body, company, mass, flock, congregation, assembly.

folder noun *it's the blue folder labeled "Taxes"* FILE, binder, portfolio, envelope, sleeve, wallet.

foliage noun *the plant is grown for its striking foliage* LEAVES, leafage; greenery, vegetation, verdure.

folk noun *informal* **1** *the local folk* PEOPLE, individuals, 'men, women, and children', (living) souls, mortals; citizenry, inhabitants, residents, populace, population; *formal* denizens.

2 *my folks came from the north* PARENTS, RELATIVES, relations, blood relations, family, nearest and dearest, people, kinsfolk, kinsmen, kinswomen, kin, kith and kin, kindred, flesh and blood.

folklore noun *Adrian is fascinated by the local folklore* MYTHOLOGY, lore, oral history, tradition, folk tradition; legends, fables, myths, folk tales, folk stories, old wives' tales; mythos.

follow verb **1** *we'll let the others follow* COME BEHIND, come after, go behind, go after, walk behind. ANTONYM lead.

2 *he was expected to follow his father in the business* SUCCEED, replace, take the place of, take over from; *informal* step into someone's shoes, fill someone's shoes/boots.

3 *people used to* follow *the band* ***around*** ACCOMPANY, go along with, go around with, travel with, escort, attend, trail around with, string along with; *informal* tag along with. ANTONYM lead.

4 *the KGB followed her everywhere* SHADOW, trail, stalk, track, dog, hound; *informal* tail.

5 *follow the instructions* OBEY, comply with, conform to, adhere to, stick to, keep to, hew to, act in accordance with, abide by, observe, heed, pay attention to. ANTONYM flout.

6 *penalties may* ***follow from*** *such behavior* RESULT FROM, arise from, be a consequence of, be caused by, be brought about by, be a result of, come after, develop from, ensue from, emanate from, issue from, proceed from, spring from, flow from, originate from, stem from. ANTONYM lead to.

7 *I couldn't follow what he said* UNDERSTAND, comprehend, apprehend, take in, grasp, fathom, appreciate, see; *informal* make head(s) or tail(s) of, get, figure out, savvy, wrap/get one's head around, wrap/get one's mind around, get the drift of. ANTONYM misunderstand.

8 *she followed her mentor in her poetic style* IMITATE, copy, mimic, ape, reproduce, mirror, echo; emulate, take as a pattern, take as an example, take as a model, adopt the style of, model oneself on, take a leaf out of someone's book.

9 *he follows the Pacers* BE A FAN OF, be a supporter of, support, be a follower of, be an admirer of, be a devotee of, be devoted to. ANTONYM dislike.

PHRASES: **follow through** *they lack the resources to follow the project through* COMPLETE, bring to completion, see something through; continue with, carry on with, keep on with, keep going with, stay with; *informal* stick something out. **follow up** *I've got a hunch and I'm going to follow it up* INVESTIGATE, research, look into, dig into, delve into, make inquiries into, inquire about, ask questions about, pursue, chase up; *informal* check out, scope out.

follower noun **1** *the president's closest followers* ACOLYTE, assistant, attendant, companion; henchman, minion, lackey, servant; *informal* hanger-on, sidekick. ANTONYM leader.

2 *a follower of Christ* DISCIPLE, apostle, supporter, defender, champion; believer, true believer, worshiper. ANTONYM opponent.

3 *followers of winter sports* FAN, enthusiast, admirer, devotee, lover, supporter, adherent.

following noun *his devoted following* ADMIRERS, supporters, backers, fans, adherents, devotees, advocates, patrons, public, audience, circle, retinue, train. ANTONYM opposition.

▸ adjective **1** *the following day* NEXT, ensuing, succeeding, subsequent. ANTONYM preceding.

2 *the following questions* below, further on; these; *formal* hereunder, hereinafter. ANTONYMS preceding, aforementioned.

folly noun *the folly of youth* FOOLISHNESS, foolhardiness, stupidity, idiocy, lunacy, madness, rashness, recklessness, imprudence, injudiciousness, irresponsibility, thoughtlessness, indiscretion; *informal* craziness. ANTONYM wisdom.

foment verb *accused of fomenting civil unrest* INSTIGATE, incite, provoke, agitate, excite, stir up, whip up, encourage, urge, fan the flames of. See note at INCITE.

fond adjective **1** *she was* ***fond of*** *dancing* KEEN ON, partial to, addicted to, enthusiastic about, passionate about; attached to, attracted to, enamored of, in love with, having a soft spot for; *informal* into, hooked on, gone on, sweet on, struck on. ANTONYM indifferent.

2 *her fond husband* ADORING, devoted, doting, loving, caring, affectionate, warm, tender, kind, attentive, uxorious. ANTONYM unfeeling.

3 *a fond hope* UNREALISTIC, naive, foolish, overoptimistic, deluded, delusory, absurd, vain, Panglossian. ANTONYM realistic.

fondle verb *gently fondling the puppies | a priest who had inappropriately fondled several children* CARESS, stroke, pat, pet, finger, tickle, play with; maul, molest; *informal* paw, grope, feel up, touch up, cop a feel of.

fondness noun **1** *they look at each other with such fondness* AFFECTION, love, liking, warmth, tenderness, kindness, devotion, endearment, attachment, friendliness. ANTONYM hatred.

2 *a fondness for spicy food* LIKING, love, taste, partiality, keenness, inclination, penchant, predilection, relish, passion, appetite; weakness, soft spot; *informal* thing, yen, jones. ANTONYM dislike.

food noun **1** *French food* NOURISHMENT, sustenance, nutriment, fare; bread, daily bread; cooking, cuisine; foodstuffs, edibles, provender, refreshments, meals, provisions, rations; solids; *informal* eats, eatables, nosh, grub, chow, vittles; *formal* comestibles; *literary* viands; *dated* victuals; *archaic* commons, meat, aliment.

2 *food for the cattle* FODDER, feed, provender, forage.

foodie noun *informal his father was a foodie who worked for an international magazine* GOURMET, epicure, gastronome, gourmand.

fool noun **1** *you've acted like a complete fool* IDIOT, ass, blockhead, dunce, dolt, ignoramus, imbecile, cretin, dullard, simpleton, moron, clod; *informal* nitwit, halfwit, dope, ninny, nincompoop, chump, dimwit, dingbat, dipstick, goober, coot, goon, dumbo, dummy, ditz, dumdum, fathead, numbskull, numbnuts, dunderhead, thickhead, airhead, flake, lamebrain, zombie, nerd, peabrain, birdbrain, jughead, jerk, donkey, twit, goat, dork, twerp, schmuck, bozo, boob, turkey, schlep, chowderhead, dumbhead, goofball, goof, goofus, galoot, lummox, klutz, putz, schlemiel, sap, meatball, dumb cluck.

2 *she made a fool of me* LAUGHINGSTOCK, dupe, butt, gull, cat's paw; *informal* stooge, sucker, fall guy, sap.

3 *historical the fool in King James's court* JESTER, court jester, clown, buffoon, joker, zany.

▸ verb **1** *he'd been fooled by a mere child* DECEIVE, trick, hoax, dupe, take in, mislead, delude, hoodwink, sucker, bluff, gull; swindle, defraud, cheat, double-cross; *informal* con, bamboozle, pull a fast one on, take for a ride, pull the wool over someone's eyes, put one over on, have on, diddle, fiddle, sting, shaft, snooker, stiff, euchre, hornswoggle; *literary* cozen.

2 *I'm not fooling, I promise* PRETEND, make believe, feign, put on an act, act, sham, fake; joke, jest; *informal* kid; have someone on.

PHRASE: **fool around 1** *someone's been fooling around with the controls* FIDDLE, play (around), toy, trifle, meddle, tamper, interfere, monkey (around); *informal* mess (around). **2** *informal my husband's been fooling around* PHILANDER, womanize, flirt, have an affair, commit adultery, cheat; *informal* play around, mess around, carry on, play the field, sleep around.

foolery noun *the foolery in this dormitory has gotten out of hand* CLOWNING, fooling, tomfoolery, buffoonery, silliness, foolishness, stupidity, idiocy; antics, capers; *informal* larks, shenanigans, didoes; *archaic* harlequinade.

foolhardy adjective *their foolhardy plans* RECKLESS, rash, irresponsible, impulsive, hotheaded, impetuous, bullheaded, daredevil, devil-may-care, madcap, harebrained, precipitate, hasty, overhasty; *literary* temerarious. See note at TEMERITY. ANTONYM prudent.

foolish adjective *don't let your foolish impulses get you into trouble* STUPID, silly, idiotic, witless, brainless, mindless, unintelligent, thoughtless, half-baked, imprudent, incautious, injudicious, unwise; ill-advised, ill-considered, impolitic, rash, reckless, foolhardy, daft; *informal* dumb, dim, dimwitted, halfwitted, thick, harebrained, crack-brained, crackpot, pea-brained, wooden-headed, dumb-ass, chowderheaded. See note at ABSURD. ANTONYMS sensible, wise.

foolishness noun *I regretted my foolishness* FOLLY, stupidity, idiocy, imbecility, silliness, inanity, thoughtlessness, imprudence, injudiciousness, lack of foresight, lack of sense, irresponsibility, indiscretion, foolhardiness, rashness, recklessness. ANTONYMS sense, wisdom.

foolproof adjective *a foolproof security system* INFALLIBLE, dependable, reliable, trustworthy, certain, sure, guaranteed, safe, sound, tried and tested; watertight, airtight, flawless, perfect; *informal* sure-fire, idiot-proof, goof-proof; *formal* efficacious. ANTONYM flawed.

foot noun 1 **(feet)** *my feet hurt informal* tootsies, dogs, boats; *Brit. informal* trotters.

2 *the animal's foot* paw, hoof, pad; *Brit.* trotter.

3 *the foot of the hill* BOTTOM, base, lowest part; end; foundation. PHRASE: **foot the bill** *informal as usual, the taxpayers will have to foot the bill* PAY (THE BILL), settle up; *informal* pick up the tab, pick up the check, cough up (the money/dough), fork out (the money/dough), shell out (the money/dough).

footing noun 1 *Natalie lost her footing* FOOTHOLD, toehold, grip, purchase.

2 *a solid financial footing* BASIS, base, foundation.

3 *on an equal footing* STANDING, status, position; condition, arrangement, basis; relationship, terms.

footling adjective *don't bother me with your footling problems* TRIVIAL, trifling, petty, insignificant, inconsequential, picayune, unimportant, minor, small, time-wasting; *informal* piddling, fiddling. ANTONYMS important, large.

footnote noun *informative footnotes* NOTE, marginal note, annotation, comment, gloss; aside, incidental remark, digression.

footprint noun *the footprints led us to the cave* FOOTMARK, footstep, mark, impression; **(footprints)** track(s), spoor.

footstep noun 1 *he heard a footstep* FOOTFALL, step, tread, stomp, stamp.

2 *footsteps in the sand* FOOTPRINT, footmark, mark, impression; **(footsteps)** track(s), spoor.

fop noun *he was known as quite a fop in the old neighborhood, always dressed to the nines and whistling a cheery tune* DANDY, man about town, poseur; *informal* snappy dresser, trendoid, hipster; *archaic* coxcomb, popinjay.

foppish adjective *you don't want to be prancing around a joint like this in those foppish threads* DANDYISH, dandified, dapper, dressy; affected, preening, vain; effeminate, girly, mincing; *informal* natty, sissy, camp, campy.

forage verb *Colonel Kendricks sent out a small party to forage for provisions* HUNT, search, look, rummage around, ferret, root about/around, nose around/about, scavenge.

▸ noun 1 *forage for the horses* FODDER, feed, food, provender.

2 *a nightly forage for food* HUNT, search, look, quest, rummage, scavenge.

foray noun *the foray was met with little resistance* RAID, attack, assault, incursion, swoop, strike, onslaught, sortie, sally, push, thrust; *archaic* onset.

forbear verb *can you **forbear from** drinking?* REFRAIN FROM, abstain from, desist from, keep from, restrain oneself from, stop oneself from, hold back from, withhold from; resist the temptation to (be); eschew, avoid, decline to (be). ANTONYM persist.

forbearance noun *we are proud of the forbearance you have demonstrated during these difficult weeks* TOLERANCE, patience, resignation, endurance, fortitude, stoicism; leniency, clemency, indulgence; restraint, self-restraint, self-control. See note at ABSTINENCE.

forbearing adjective *she taught me to be forbearing at the moments when I least wanted to be* PATIENT, tolerant, easygoing, lenient, clement, forgiving, understanding, accommodating, indulgent; long-suffering, resigned, stoic; restrained, self-controlled. See note at LENIENT. ANTONYMS impatient, intolerant.

forbid verb *the law forbids gender discrimination* PROHIBIT, ban, outlaw, make illegal, veto, proscribe, disallow, embargo, bar, debar, interdict; *Law* enjoin, restrain. See word spectrum on page 356. See also note at PROHIBIT. ANTONYM permit.

forbidding adjective 1 *a forbidding manner* HOSTILE, unwelcoming, unfriendly, off-putting, unsympathetic, unapproachable, grim, stern, hard, tough, frosty. ANTONYM friendly.

2 *the dark castle looked forbidding* THREATENING, ominous, menacing, sinister, brooding, daunting, formidable, fearsome, frightening, chilling, disturbing, disquieting. See note at OMINOUS. ANTONYM inviting.

force noun 1 *he pushed with all his force* STRENGTH, power, energy, might, effort, exertion; impact, pressure, weight, impetus. ANTONYM weakness.

2 *they used force to achieve their aims* COERCION, compulsion, constraint, duress, oppression, harassment, intimidation, threats; *informal* arm-twisting, bullying tactics.

3 *the force of the argument* COGENCY, potency, weight, effectiveness, soundness, validity, strength, power, significance, influence, authority; *informal* punch; *formal* efficacy. ANTONYM weakness.

4 *a force for good* AGENCY, power, influence, instrument, vehicle, means.

5 *a peace-keeping force* BODY, body of people, group, outfit, party, team; detachment, unit, squad; *informal* bunch.

▸ verb 1 *he was forced to pay* COMPEL, coerce, make, constrain, oblige, impel, drive, pressurize, pressure, press, push, press-gang, bully, dragoon, bludgeon; *informal* put the screws on, lean on, twist someone's arm. See note at COMPEL.

2 *the door had to be forced* BREAK OPEN, burst open, knock down, smash down, kick in.

3 *water was forced through a hole* PROPEL, push, thrust, shove, drive, press, pump.

4 *they forced a confession out of the kids* EXTRACT, elicit, exact, extort, wrest, wring, drag, screw, squeeze.

PHRASE: **in force** 1 *the law is now in force* EFFECTIVE, in operation, operative, operational, in action, valid. 2 *her fans were out in force* IN GREAT NUMBERS, in hordes, in full strength.

forced adjective 1 *forced entry* VIOLENT, forcible.

2 *forced repatriation* ENFORCED, forcible, compulsory, obligatory, mandatory, involuntary, imposed, required,

forbid
proscribe
interdict
enjoin
ban
bar
debar
outlaw
make illegal
prohibit
block
veto
rule out
stop
declare taboo
preclude
exclude
give the red light to
give the thumbs down to
put the kibosh on
disallow
restrain
put a stop to
put an end to
tolerate
turn a blind eye to
turn a deaf ear to
overlook
countenance
admit of
brook
let
suffer
acquiesce in
accede to
enable
give someone/something the nod
OK
give the OK to
give the green light to
say the word
allow
authorize
qualify
grant
grant someone the right
agree to
approve of
license
give the go-ahead to
give the thumbs up to
give someone permission/authorization/leave
consent to
assent to
give one's consent/assent to
give one's blessing to
legalize
legitimatize
legitimate
entitle
empower
sanction
permit

stipulated, dictated, ordained, prescribed. ANTONYM voluntary.

3 *a forced smile* STRAINED, unnatural, artificial, false, feigned, simulated, contrived, labored, stilted, studied, mannered, affected, unconvincing, insincere, hollow; *informal* phony, pretend, put on. ANTONYM natural.

forceful adjective **1** *a forceful personality* DYNAMIC, energetic, assertive, authoritative, vigorous, powerful, strong, pushy, driving, determined, insistent, commanding, dominant, domineering; *informal* bossy, in-your-face, go-ahead, feisty. ANTONYMS weak, submissive.

2 *a forceful argument* COGENT, convincing, compelling, strong, powerful, potent, weighty, effective, well-founded, telling, persuasive, irresistible, eloquent, coherent. ANTONYMS weak, unconvincing.

forcible adjective **1** *forcible entry* FORCED, violent.

2 *forcible repatriation.* See FORCED sense 2.

ford noun *a ford across the Khutzeymateen* CROSSING PLACE, crossing; shallow place.

▸ verb *we tried to ford the river* CROSS, traverse; wade across, walk across, drive across, travel across, make it across, make one's way across.

forebear noun ANCESTOR, forefather, antecedent, progenitor, primogenitor. ANTONYM descendant.

forebode verb *literary the scarlet sky forebodes the visitation of mischief* PRESAGE, augur, portend, herald, warn of, forewarn of, foreshadow, be an omen of, indicate, signify, signal, promise, threaten, spell, denote; *literary* betoken, foretoken. See note at OMINOUS.

foreboding noun **1** *a feeling of foreboding* APPREHENSION, anxiety, trepidation, disquiet, unease, uneasiness, misgiving, suspicion, worry, fear, fearfulness, dread, alarm; *informal* the willies, the heebie-jeebies, the jitters, the creeps. ANTONYM calm.

2 *their forebodings proved justified* PREMONITION, presentiment, bad feeling, sneaking suspicion, funny feeling, intuition; *archaic* presage.

forecast verb *they forecast record profits* PREDICT, prophesy, prognosticate, foretell, foresee, forewarn of. See note at PREDICT.

▸ noun *a gloomy forecast* PREDICTION, prophecy, forewarning, prognostication, augury, divination, prognosis.

forefather noun See FOREBEAR.

forefront noun *her first CD propelled her to the forefront of the music scene* VANGUARD, van, spearhead, head, lead, front, fore, front line, cutting edge, avant-garde. ANTONYMS rear, background.

forego verb See FORGO.

foregoing adjective *the foregoing circumstances are no longer applicable to this argument* PRECEDING, aforesaid, aforementioned, previously mentioned, earlier, above; previous, prior, antecedent. ANTONYM following.

foregone PHRASE: **a foregone conclusion** *a rental increase is a foregone conclusion* CERTAINTY, inevitability, matter of course, predictable result; *informal* sure thing, no-brainer.

foreground noun **1** *the foreground of the picture* FRONT, fore.

2 *in the foreground of the political drama* FOREFRONT, vanguard, van, spearhead, head, lead, front, fore, front line, cutting edge.

forehead noun *she brushed the hair from her forehead* BROW, temple.

foreign adjective **1** *foreign branches of American banks* OVERSEAS, exotic, distant, external, alien, nonnative. ANTONYMS domestic, native.

2 *the concept is very foreign to us* UNFAMILIAR, unknown, unheard of, strange, alien; novel, new. ANTONYM familiar.

foreigner noun *her unease with foreigners* ALIEN, nonnative, stranger, outsider; immigrant, landed immigrant, refugee, settler, newcomer. ANTONYM native.

foreman, forewoman noun *report any injury to the foreman* SUPERVISOR, overseer, superintendent, team leader; foreperson; captain; ramrod, straw boss.

foremost adjective *the foremost impressionist of his age* LEADING, principal, premier, prime, top, top-level, greatest, best, supreme, preeminent, outstanding, most important, most prominent, most influential, most illustrious, most notable; ranking, number-one, star. ANTONYM minor.

forerunner noun **1** *archosaurs were the forerunners of dinosaurs* PREDECESSOR, precursor, antecedent, ancestor, forebear; prototype. ANTONYM descendant.

2 *a headache may be the forerunner of other complaints* PRELUDE, herald, harbinger, precursor, sign, signal, indication, warning.

foresee verb *I foresee much good fortune in your future* ANTICIPATE, predict, forecast, expect, envisage, envision, see; foretell, prophesy, prognosticate; *literary* foreknow.

foreshadow verb *those things that foreshadow war are sadly upon us* SIGNAL, indicate, signify, mean, be a sign of, suggest, herald, be a harbinger of, warn of, portend, prefigure, presage, promise, point to, anticipate; *informal* spell; *literary* forebode, foretoken, betoken, adumbrate; *archaic* foreshow. See note at PREDICT.

WORD NOTE **adumbrate**

Ever since I found in my childhood paintbox a small square of reddish-brown watercolor pigment labeled *burnt umber,* I have been enchanted with the wonderfully euphonious catalog of words that revolve around the letters *umb,* and which generally have something to do with the Latin for *shadow.* To be sure, *cucumber* (like its ancestor *cowcumber,* a form which we are haughtily informed no well-taught person still uses) has no connection, and the verb *cumber,* meaning "to hinder," has only the most tenuous link, via an Old French term connected to *cumulus,* which defines a cloud that, among other attributes, spreads an unusually large and dark shadow below it. In my shadowland of fine-sounding words we find *umbrella, penumbra, sombrero, somber,* the Italian province of *Umbria*—the land of shadows—and here, *adumbrate,* which sounds more euphonious than all the rest, and in my view should be used as often as possible whenever you want to sketch or outline or otherwise prefigure or, of course, foreshadow something. When the edge of a thundercloud passes across the sun and you look up and draw your sweater around your shoulder and shudder—the chill you feel at that moment nicely adumbrates the storm to come. **—SW**

foresight noun *my lack of foresight has cost me dearly* FORETHOUGHT, planning, farsightedness, vision, anticipation, prudence, care, caution, precaution, readiness, preparedness. ANTONYM hindsight.

forest noun *the cooling shade of the forest* WOOD(S), woodland, timberland, trees, bush, plantation; jungle, rain forest, pinewood; *archaic* greenwood; taiga, boreal forest, Carolinian forest, Acadian forest.

forestall verb *they were unable to forestall Roosevelt's reelection* PREEMPT, get in before; anticipate, second-guess; nip in the bud, thwart, frustrate, foil, stave off, ward off, fend off, avert, preclude, obviate, prevent; *informal* beat someone to it.

forestry noun *a college degree in forestry* FOREST MANAGEMENT, tree growing, agroforestry; *technical* arboriculture, silviculture, dendrology.

foretaste noun *the parade is a foretaste of the spectacle to come* SAMPLE, taster, taste, preview, specimen, example, teaser; indication, suggestion, hint, whiff; warning, forewarning, omen.

foretell verb **1** *the locals can foretell a storm* PREDICT, forecast, prophesy, prognosticate; foresee, anticipate, envisage, envision, see. See note at PREDICT.

2 *dreams can foretell the future* INDICATE, foreshadow, prefigure, anticipate, warn of, point to, signal, portend, augur, presage, be an omen of; *literary* forebode, foretoken, betoken; *archaic* foreshow.

forethought noun *without forethought, you'll just keep stumbling through life* ANTICIPATION, planning, forward planning, provision, precaution, prudence, care, caution; foresight, farsightedness, vision. ANTONYMS impulse, recklessness.

forever adverb **1** *their love would last forever* FOR ALWAYS, evermore, for ever and ever, for good, for all time, until the end of time, until hell freezes over, eternally, forevermore, perpetually, in perpetuity; *informal* until the cows come home, until kingdom come; *archaic* for aye.

2 *he was forever banging into things* ALWAYS, continually, constantly, perpetually, incessantly, endlessly, persistently, repeatedly, regularly; nonstop, day and night, 'morning, noon, and night'; all the time, the entire time; *informal* 24-7. ANTONYMS never, occasionally.

forewarn verb *the building would have been torched if the authorities had not been forewarned* WARN, warn in advance, give advance warning, give fair warning, give notice, apprise, inform; alert, caution, put someone on their guard; *informal* tip off.

forewarning noun *the dogs howled a forewarning of death* OMEN, sign, indication, portent, presage, warning, harbinger, foreshadowing, augury, signal, promise, threat, hint, straw in the wind, writing on the wall, canary in the coal mine; *literary* foretoken.

foreword noun *he wrote the foreword to one of her books* PREFACE, introduction, prologue, preamble; *informal* intro, lead-in; *formal* exordium, prolegomenon, proem. ANTONYM conclusion.

forfeit verb *latecomers will forfeit their places* LOSE, be deprived of, surrender, relinquish, sacrifice, give up, yield, renounce, forgo; *informal* pass up, lose out on. ANTONYM retain.

▸ noun *they are liable to a forfeit* PENALTY, sanction, punishment, penance; fine; confiscation, loss, relinquishment, forfeiture, surrender; *Law* sequestration.

forge[1] verb **1** *smiths forged swords* HAMMER OUT, beat into shape, fashion.

2 *they forged a partnership* BUILD, construct, form, create, establish, set up.

3 *he forged her signature* FAKE, falsify, counterfeit, copy, imitate, reproduce, replicate, simulate.

forge[2] verb *they forged through swamps* ADVANCE STEADILY, advance gradually, press on, push on, soldier on, march on, push forward, make progress, make headway. PHRASE: **forge ahead** *Jack's horse forged ahead and took the lead* ADVANCE RAPIDLY, progress quickly, make rapid progress, increase speed.

forged adjective *forged oil paintings* FAKE, faked, false, counterfeit, imitation, copied, pirated; sham, bogus; *informal* phony, dud. ANTONYM genuine.

forgery noun **1** *guilty of forgery* COUNTERFEITING, falsification, faking, copying, pirating.

2 *the painting was a forgery* FAKE, counterfeit, fraud, sham, imitation, replica, copy, pirate copy; *informal* phony.

forget verb **1** *he forgot where he was* FAIL TO REMEMBER, fail to recall, fail to think of; *informal* disremember. ANTONYM remember.

2 *I never forget my briefcase* LEAVE BEHIND, fail to take/bring.

3 *I forgot to close the door* NEGLECT, fail, omit.

4 *you can forget that idea* STOP THINKING ABOUT, put out of one's mind, shut out, blank out, pay no heed to, not worry about, ignore, overlook, take no notice of; abandon, say goodbye to, deep-six.

forgetful adjective **1** *I'm so forgetful these days* ABSENTMINDED, amnesic, amnesiac, vague, disorganized, dreamy, abstracted; *informal* scatterbrained, having a mind/memory like a sieve. ANTONYM reliable.

2 ***forgetful of*** *the time* HEEDLESS OF, careless of, unmindful of; inattentive to, negligent about, oblivious to, unconcerned about, indifferent to, not bothered about. ANTONYM heedful.

forgetfulness noun **1** *his excuse was forgetfulness* ABSENTMINDEDNESS, amnesia, poor memory, a lapse of memory, vagueness, abstraction; *informal* scattiness. ANTONYM reliability.

2 *a forgetfulness of duty* NEGLECT, heedlessness, carelessness, disregard; inattention, obliviousness, lack of concern, indifference. ANTONYM heed.

forgivable adjective *an occasional oversight is forgivable* PARDONABLE, excusable, condonable, understandable, tolerable, permissible, allowable, justifiable.

forgive verb **1** *she would not forgive him* PARDON, excuse, exonerate, absolve; make allowances for, feel no resentment toward, feel no malice toward, harbor no grudge against, bury the hatchet with; let bygones be bygones; *informal* let off (the hook); *formal* exculpate. ANTONYMS blame, resent. See note at ABSOLVE.

2 *you must forgive his rude conduct* EXCUSE, overlook, disregard, ignore, pass over, make allowances for, allow; turn a blind eye to, turn a deaf ear to, wink at, indulge, tolerate. ANTONYM punish.

forgiveness noun *we beg your forgiveness* PARDON, absolution, exoneration, remission, dispensation, indulgence, clemency, mercy; reprieve, amnesty; *archaic* shrift. ANTONYMS mercilessness, punishment.

forgiving adjective *Cromwell was not renowned for his forgiving nature* MERCIFUL, lenient, compassionate, magnanimous, humane, softhearted, forbearing, tolerant, indulgent, understanding. ANTONYMS merciless, vindictive.

forgo, forego verb *not willing to forgo our dental insurance* DO WITHOUT, go without, give up, waive, renounce, surrender, relinquish, part with, drop, sacrifice, abstain from, refrain from, eschew, cut out; *informal* swear off; *formal* forswear, abjure. ANTONYM keep.

forgotten adjective *Vivaldi's operas are largely forgotten* UNREMEMBERED, out of mind, past recollection, beyond/past recall, consigned to oblivion; left behind; neglected, overlooked, ignored, disregarded, unrecognized. ANTONYM remembered.

fork verb *the road forks at the south end of the lake* SPLIT, branch (off), divide, subdivide, separate, part, diverge, go in different directions, bifurcate; *technical* divaricate, ramify.

forked adjective *the hawk's distinctive forked tail* SPLIT, branching, branched, bifurcate(d), Y-shaped, V-shaped, pronged, divided; *technical* divaricate. ANTONYM straight.

forlorn adjective **1** *he sounded forlorn* UNHAPPY, sad, miserable, sorrowful, dejected, despondent, disconsolate, wretched, abject, down, downcast, dispirited, downhearted, crestfallen, depressed, melancholy, gloomy, glum, mournful, despairing, doleful, woebegone; *informal* blue, down in/at the mouth, down in the dumps; *rare* lachrymose. ANTONYM happy.

2 *a forlorn garden* DESOLATE, deserted, abandoned, forsaken, forgotten, neglected. ANTONYM cared for.

3 *a forlorn attempt* HOPELESS, vain, with no chance of success; useless, futile, pointless, purposeless, unavailing, nugatory; *archaic* bootless. ANTONYMS hopeful, sure-fire.

form noun **1** *the general form of the landscape | form is less important than content* SHAPE, configuration, formation, structure, construction, arrangement, appearance, exterior, outline, format, layout, design.

2 *the human form* BODY, shape, figure, stature, build, frame, physique, anatomy; *informal* vital statistics.

3 *the infection takes different forms* MANIFESTATION, appearance, embodiment, incarnation, semblance, shape, guise.

4 *sponsorship is a form of advertising* KIND, sort, type, class, classification, category, variety, genre, brand, style; species, genus, family.

5 *put the mixture into a form* MOLD, cast, shape, matrix, die.

6 *what is the form here?* ETIQUETTE, social practice, custom, usage, use, modus operandi, habit, wont, protocol, procedure, rules, convention, tradition, fashion, style; *formal* praxis.

7 *you have to fill in a form* QUESTIONNAIRE, document, coupon, paper, sheet.

8 *in top form* FITNESS, condition, fettle, shape, trim, health.

▸ verb **1** *the pads are formed from mild steel* MAKE, construct, build, manufacture, fabricate, assemble, put together; create, produce, concoct, devise, contrive, frame, fashion, shape.

2 *he formed a plan* FORMULATE, devise, conceive, work out, think up, lay, draw up, put together, produce, fashion, concoct, forge, hatch, incubate, develop; *informal* dream up.

3 *they plan to form a company* SET UP, establish, found, launch, float, create, bring into being, institute, start (up), get going, initiate, bring about, inaugurate. ANTONYM dissolve.

4 *a mist was forming* MATERIALIZE, come into being/existence, crystallize, emerge, spring up, develop; take shape, appear, loom, show up, become visible. ANTONYM disappear.

5 *the horse may form bad habits* ACQUIRE, develop, get, pick up, contract, slip into, get into. ANTONYMS avoid, break.

6 *the warriors formed themselves into a diamond pattern* ARRANGE, draw up, line up, assemble, organize, sort, order, range, array, dispose, marshal, deploy.

7 *the parts of society form an integrated whole* CONSTITUTE, make, make up, compose, add up to.

8 *the city formed a natural meeting point* CONSTITUTE, serve as, act as, function as, perform the function of, do duty for, make.

9 *teachers form the minds of children* DEVELOP, mold, shape, train, teach, instruct, educate, school, drill, discipline, prime, prepare, guide, direct, inform, enlighten, inculcate, indoctrinate, edify.

PHRASE: **good form** *it is not good form to leave visitors on their own* GOOD MANNERS, manners, polite behavior, correct behavior, convention, etiquette, protocol; *informal* the done thing.

formal adjective **1** *a formal dinner* CEREMONIAL, ceremonious, ritualistic, ritual, conventional, traditional; stately, courtly, solemn, dignified; elaborate, ornate, dressy; black-tie. ANTONYM informal.

2 *a very formal manner* ALOOF, reserved, remote, detached, unapproachable; stiff, prim, stuffy, staid, ceremonious, correct, proper, decorous, conventional, precise, exact, punctilious, unbending, inflexible, straitlaced; *informal* buttoned-down, standoffish. ANTONYMS informal, casual.

3 *a formal garden* SYMMETRICAL, regular, orderly, arranged, methodical, systematic. ANTONYM informal.

4 *formal permission* OFFICIAL, legal, authorized, approved, validated, certified, endorsed, documented, sanctioned, licensed, recognized, authoritative. ANTONYMS informal, unofficial.

5 *formal education* CONVENTIONAL, mainstream; school, institutional. ANTONYM informal.

THE RIGHT WORD

Formal suggests a suit-and-tie approach to certain situations—reserved, conventional, obeying all the rules (*an engraved invitation to a formal dinner requiring black tie or evening gown*). **Proper**, in this regard, implies scrupulously correct behavior that observes rules of etiquette (*the proper way to serve a guest; the proper spoon for dessert*). **Punctilious** behavior observes all the proper formalities (a *"punctilio"* is a detail or fine point), but may verge on the annoying (*her punctilious attention to the correct placement of silverware made setting the table an ordeal*). Someone (usually a man) who likes to show off just how *formal* and *proper* he can be runs the risk of becoming the most dreaded dinner guest of all: the **pompous** ass. *Pompous* individuals may derive more than the normal amount of pleasure from participating in **ceremonial** acts or events, which are those performed according to set rules, but **ceremonious** suggests a less negative and more ritualized approach to formality (*the Japanese woman could not have been more ceremonious than when she was carrying out the ceremonial serving of tea*).

formality noun **1** *the formality of the occasion* CEREMONY, ceremoniousness, ritual, conventionality, red tape, protocol, decorum; stateliness, courtliness, solemnity. ANTONYM informality.

2 *his formality was off-putting* ALOOFNESS, reserve, remoteness, detachment, unapproachability; stiffness, primness, stuffiness, staidness, correctness, decorum, punctiliousness, inflexibility; *informal* standoffishness. ANTONYM informality.

3 (**formalities**) *we keep the formalities to a minimum* OFFICIAL PROCEDURE, bureaucracy, red tape, paperwork.

4 *the medical examination is just a formality* ROUTINE, routine practice, normal procedure.

format noun *the journal's new format* DESIGN, style, presentation, appearance, look; form, shape, size; arrangement, plan, structure, scheme, composition, configuration.

formation noun **1** *the formation of the island's sand ridges* EMERGENCE, coming into being, genesis, development, evolution, shaping, origination. ANTONYMS destruction, disappearance.

2 *the formation of a new government* ESTABLISHMENT, setting up, start, initiation, institution, foundation, inception, creation, inauguration, launch, flotation. ANTONYM dissolution.

3 *the aircraft were flying in tight formation* CONFIGURATION, arrangement, pattern, array, alignment, positioning, disposition, order.

formative adjective **1** *at a formative stage* DEVELOPMENTAL, developing, growing, malleable, impressionable, susceptible.

2 *a formative influence* DETERMINING, controlling, influential, guiding, decisive, forming, shaping, determinative.

former adjective **1** *the former bishop* ONE-TIME, erstwhile, sometime, ex-, late; PREVIOUS, foregoing, preceding, earlier, prior, past, last. ANTONYMS future, next.

2 *in former times* EARLIER, old, past, bygone, olden, longago, gone by, long past, of old; *literary* of yore. ANTONYMS future, present.

3 *the former of the two* FIRST-MENTIONED, first. ANTONYM latter.

formerly adverb *this is Mr. Kane, formerly of Kane Industries* PREVIOUSLY, earlier, before, until now/then, hitherto, née, once, once upon a time, at one time, in the past; *formal* heretofore.

formidable adjective **1** *a formidable curved dagger* INTIMIDATING, forbidding, daunting, disturbing, alarming, frightening, disquieting, brooding, awesome, fearsome, ominous, foreboding, sinister, menacing, threatening, dangerous. ANTONYMS pleasant-looking, comforting.

2 *a formidable task* ONEROUS, arduous, taxing, difficult, hard, heavy, laborious, burdensome, strenuous, backbreaking, uphill, Herculean, monumental, colossal; demanding, tough, challenging, exacting; *formal* exigent; *archaic* toilsome. ANTONYM easy.

3 *a formidable pianist* CAPABLE, able, proficient, adept, adroit, accomplished, seasoned, skillful, skilled, gifted, talented, masterly, virtuoso, expert, knowledgeable, qualified; impressive, powerful, mighty, terrific, tremendous, great, complete, redoubtable; *informal* mean, wicked, deadly, nifty, crack, ace, magic, crackerjack. ANTONYM weak.

formless adjective *a formless heap* SHAPELESS, amorphous, unshaped, indeterminate; structureless, unstructured. ANTONYMS shaped, definite.

formula noun **1** *a legal formula* FORM OF WORDS, set expression, phrase, saying, aphorism.

2 *a peace formula* RECIPE, prescription, blueprint, plan, method, procedure, technique, system; template.

3 *a formula for removing grease* PREPARATION, concoction, mixture, compound, creation, substance.

formulaic adjective *the homes here are not the products of a formulaic design* CONVENTIONAL, stock, unoriginal, stereotypical, uninspired, clichéd, paint-by-number.

formulate verb **1** *the miners formulated a plan* DEVISE, conceive, work out, think up, lay, draw up, put together, form, produce, fashion, concoct, contrive, forge, hatch, prepare, develop; *informal* dream up.

2 *this is how Marx formulated his question* EXPRESS, phrase, word, put into words, frame, couch, put, articulate, convey, say, state, utter.

fornication noun *formal the nuns warned us about the spiritual price one pays for fornication* EXTRAMARITAL SEX, extramarital relations, adultery, infidelity, unfaithfulness, cuckoldry; premarital sex; *informal* hanky-panky.

forsake verb *literary* **1** *he forsook his wife* ABANDON, desert, leave, leave high and dry, turn one's back on, cast aside, break (up) with; jilt, strand, leave stranded, leave in the lurch, throw over; *informal* walk out on, run out on, dump, ditch, can. ANTONYMS return to, stay with.

2 *I won't forsake my vegetarian principles* RENOUNCE, abandon, relinquish, dispense with, disclaim, disown, disavow, discard, wash one's hands of; give up, drop, jettison, do away with, ax; *informal* ditch, scrap, scrub, junk; *formal* forswear. ANTONYM keep (to).

forswear verb *formal we are formally forswearing the use of chemical weapons* RENOUNCE, relinquish, reject, forgo, disavow, abandon, deny, repudiate, give up, wash one's hands of; eschew, abstain from, refrain from; *informal* kick, pack in, quit, swear off; *Law* disaffirm; *literary* forsake; *formal* abjure, abnegate. ANTONYMS adhere to, persist with, take up.

fort noun *dozens of settlers in the area sought refuge within the confines of the fort* FORTRESS, castle, citadel, blockhouse, stronghold, redoubt, fortification, bastion; fastness.

forte noun *acting had always been her forte* STRENGTH, strong point, specialty, strong suit, talent, special ability, skill, bent, gift, métier; *informal* thing. ANTONYM weakness.

forth adverb **1** *smoke billowed forth* OUT, outside, away, off, ahead, forward, into view; into existence.

2 *from that day forth* ONWARD, onwards, on, forward; for ever, into eternity; until now.

forthcoming adjective **1** *forthcoming events* IMMINENT, impending, coming, upcoming, approaching, future; close, (close) at hand, in store, in the wind, in the air, in the offing, in the pipeline, on the horizon, on the way, on us, about to happen. ANTONYMS past, current.

2 *no reply was forthcoming* AVAILABLE, ready, at hand, accessible, obtainable, at someone's disposal, obtained, given, vouchsafed to someone; *informal* up for grabs, on tap. ANTONYM unavailable.

3 *he was not very forthcoming about himself* COMMUNICATIVE, talkative, chatty, loquacious, vocal; expansive, expressive, unreserved, uninhibited, outgoing, frank, open, candid; *informal* gabby. ANTONYM uncommunicative.

forthright adjective *a forthright statement to the press about her involvement in the cover-up* FRANK, direct, straightforward, honest, candid, open, sincere, outspoken, straight, blunt, plain-spoken, no-nonsense, downright, bluff, matter-of-fact, to the point; *informal* upfront. ANTONYMS secretive, evasive.

forthwith adverb *all hostages are to be released forthwith* IMMEDIATELY, at once, instantly, directly, right away, straightaway, posthaste, without delay, without hesitation; quickly, speedily, promptly; *informal* pronto. ANTONYM sometime.

fortification noun *fortifications loomed ominously along the high banks of the river* RAMPART, wall, defense, bulwark, palisade, stockade, redoubt, earthwork, bastion, parapet, barricade.

fortify verb **1** *the knights fortified their citadel* BUILD DEFENSES AROUND, strengthen, secure, protect. ANTONYMS weaken, expose.

2 *the wall had been fortified* STRENGTHEN, reinforce, toughen, consolidate, bolster, shore up, brace, buttress. ANTONYM weaken.

3 *I'll have a drink to fortify me* INVIGORATE, strengthen, energize, enliven, liven up, animate, vitalize, rejuvenate, restore, revive, refresh; *informal* pep up, buck up, give a shot in the arm to. ANTONYMS sedate, subdue.

fortitude noun COURAGE, bravery, endurance, resilience, mettle, moral fiber, strength of mind, strength of character, strong-mindedness, backbone, spirit, grit, true grit, doughtiness, steadfastness; *informal* guts. See note at COURAGE. ANTONYM faint-heartedness.

fortnight noun *they took enough supplies to last **a fortnight*** TWO WEEKS. See note below.

WORD NOTE **fortnight**

Unless you are carrying a UK passport, using the word *fortnight* is an embarrassing affectation. Argue all you want that it's inefficient to use "two weeks" when there's a perfectly good single word with the same meaning, but if you are that set on efficiency as the highest goal for a language, English is already the wrong choice for you. If you are going to use *fortnight* as a speaker of American English, be prepared for "huh?" at best and outright ridicule at worst. **—EM**

fortress noun *the fortress fell into the hands of the French* FORT, castle, citadel, blockhouse, stronghold, redoubt, fortification, bastion; fastness.

fortuitous adjective **1** *a fortuitous resemblance* CHANCE, adventitious, unexpected, unanticipated, unpredictable, unforeseen, unlooked-for, serendipitous, casual, incidental, coincidental, random, accidental, inadvertent, unintentional, unintended, unplanned, unpremeditated. ANTONYM predictable. See note at ACCIDENTAL.

2 *the Red Wings were saved by a fortuitous rebound* LUCKY, fluky, fortunate, providential, advantageous, timely, opportune, serendipitous, heaven-sent. ANTONYM unlucky.

USAGE NOTE fortuitous

The traditional, etymological meaning of **fortuitous** is 'happening by chance': a *fortuitous meeting* is a chance meeting, which might turn out to be either a good thing or a bad thing. In modern uses, however, **fortuitous** tends more often to be used to refer to fortunate outcomes, and the word has become more or less a synonym for 'lucky' or 'fortunate.' This use is frowned upon as being not etymologically correct and is best avoided except in informal contexts.

fortunate adjective **1** *he was fortunate that the punishment was so slight* LUCKY, favored, blessed, blessed with good luck, in luck, having a charmed life, charmed; *informal* sitting pretty. ANTONYM unfortunate.

2 *in a fortunate position* FAVORABLE, advantageous, providential, auspicious, welcome, heaven-sent, beneficial, propitious, fortuitous, opportune, happy, felicitous. ANTONYM unfavorable.

3 *the society gives generously to less fortunate people* WEALTHY, rich, affluent, prosperous, well off, moneyed, well-to-do, well-heeled, opulent, comfortable; favored, privileged. ANTONYM underprivileged.

fortunately adverb *fortunately no one was injured in the collision* LUCKILY, by good luck, by good fortune, as luck would have it, propitiously; mercifully, thankfully; thank goodness, thank God, thank heavens, thank the stars.

fortune noun **1** *fortune favored him* CHANCE, accident, coincidence, serendipity, destiny, fortuity, providence, happenstance.

2 *a change of fortune* LUCK, fate, destiny, predestination, the stars, serendipity, karma, kismet, lot.

3 **(fortunes)** *an upswing in the team's fortunes* CIRCUMSTANCES, state of affairs, condition, position, situation; plight, predicament.

4 *he made his fortune in steel* WEALTH, riches, substance, property, assets, resources, means, possessions, treasure, estate.

5 *informal this dress cost* ***a fortune*** A HUGE AMOUNT, a vast sum, a king's ransom, millions, billions; *informal* a small fortune, a mint, a bundle, a pile, a wad, an arm and a leg, a pretty penny, a tidy sum, big money, big bucks, gazillions, megabucks, top dollar. ANTONYM pittance.

fortune teller noun *for two bucks you could get a reading from a gypsy fortune teller* CLAIRVOYANT, crystal-gazer, psychic, prophet, seer, oracle, soothsayer, augur, diviner, sibyl; palmist, palm-reader.

forum noun **1** *forums were held for staff to air grievances* MEETING, assembly, gathering, rally, conference, seminar, convention, symposium, colloquium, caucus; *informal* get-together; *formal* colloquy.

2 *a forum for discussion* SETTING, place, scene, context, stage, framework, backdrop; medium, means, apparatus, auspices.

3 *the Roman forum* PUBLIC MEETING PLACE, marketplace, agora.

forward adverb **1** *the traffic moved forward* AHEAD, forward, onward, onwards, on, further.

2 *the winner stepped forward* TOWARD THE FRONT, out, forth, into view.

3 *from that day forward* ONWARD, onwards, on, forth; for ever, into eternity; until now.

▸ adjective **1** *in a forward direction* MOVING FORWARD, moving forward, moving ahead, onward, advancing, progressing, progressive. ANTONYM backward.

2 *the fortress served as the Austrian army's forward base against the Russians* FRONT, advance, foremost, head, leading, frontal. ANTONYM rear.

3 *forward planning* FUTURE, forward-looking, for the future, prospective.

4 *the girls seemed very forward* BOLD, BRAZEN, brazen-faced, barefaced, brash, shameless, immodest, audacious, daring, presumptuous, familiar, overfamiliar, pert; *informal* fresh. ANTONYM shy.

▸ verb **1** *my mother forwarded me your e-mail* SEND ON, mail on, redirect, re-address, pass on.

2 *the goods were forwarded by sea* SEND, dispatch, transmit, carry, convey, deliver, ship.

forward-looking adjective *the forward-looking countries of Europe forged ahead* PROGRESSIVE, enlightened, dynamic, pushing, bold, enterprising, ambitious, pioneering, innovative, modern, avant-garde, positive, reforming, radical; *informal* go-ahead, go-getting. ANTONYM backward-looking.

forwards adverb See FORWARD adverb.

fossil noun *we could detect fossils in the cornerstone of the building* PETRIFIED REMAINS, petrified impression, remnant, relic.

fossilized adjective **1** *fossilized remains* petrified, ossified.

2 *a fossilized idea* ARCHAIC, antiquated, antediluvian, old-fashioned, quaint, outdated, outmoded, behind the times, anachronistic, stuck in time; *informal* prehistoric.

foster verb **1** *he fostered the arts* ENCOURAGE, promote, further, stimulate, advance, forward, cultivate, nurture, strengthen, enrich; help, aid, abet, assist, contribute to, support, back, be a patron of. See note at ENCOURAGE. ANTONYMS neglect, suppress.

2 *they started fostering children* BRING UP, rear, raise, care for, take care of, look after, nurture, provide for; mother, parent.

foul adjective **1** *a foul stench* DISGUSTING, revolting, repulsive, repugnant, abhorrent, loathsome, offensive, sickening, nauseating, nauseous, stomach-churning, stomach-turning, distasteful, obnoxious, objectionable, odious, noxious, vomitous; *informal* ghastly, gruesome, gross, putrid, yucky, skanky, beastly; *literary* miasmic, noisome, mephitic. ANTONYM fragrant.

2 *a pile of foul laundry* DIRTY, filthy, mucky, grimy, grubby, muddy, muddied, unclean, unwashed; squalid, sordid, soiled, sullied, scummy; rotten, defiled, decaying, putrid, putrefied, smelly, fetid; *informal* cruddy, yucky, icky; *rare* feculent. ANTONYM clean.

3 *he had been foul to her* UNKIND, malicious, mean, nasty, unpleasant, unfriendly, spiteful, cruel, vicious, base, malevolent, despicable, contemptible; *informal* horrible, horrid, rotten; beastly. ANTONYMS pleasant, kind.

4 *foul weather* INCLEMENT, unpleasant, disagreeable, bad; rough, stormy, squally, gusty, windy, blustery, wild, blowy, rainy, wet. ANTONYM fair.

5 *foul drinking water* CONTAMINATED, polluted, infected, tainted, impure, filthy, dirty, unclean; *rare* feculent. ANTONYM clean.

6 *a foul deed* EVIL, wicked, bad, wrong, immoral, sinful, vile, dishonorable, corrupt, iniquitous, depraved, villainous, nefarious, vicious, malicious; malevolent, sinister, demonic, devilish, diabolical, fiendish, dark; monstrous, shocking, despicable, atrocious, heinous, odious, contemptible, horrible, execrable; *informal* lowdown, dirty. ANTONYM righteous.

7 *foul language* VULGAR, crude, coarse, filthy, dirty, obscene, indecent, indelicate, naughty, lewd, smutty, ribald, salacious, scatological, offensive, abusive. ANTONYM mild.

8 *a foul tackle* ILLEGAL; unfair, unsporting, unsportsmanlike, below the belt, dirty. ANTONYM fair.

▸ verb **1** *the river had been fouled with waste* DIRTY, infect, pollute, contaminate, poison, taint, sully, soil, stain, blacken, muddy, splash, spatter, smear, blight, defile, make filthy. ANTONYM clean up.

2 *the vessel had fouled her nets* TANGLE UP, entangle, snarl, catch, entwine, enmesh, twist. ANTONYM disentangle.

foul-mouthed adjective *your foul-mouthed friends are not welcome in this house* VULGAR, crude, coarse; obscene, rude, smutty, dirty, filthy, indecent, indelicate, offensive, lewd, X-rated, scatological, foul, abusive.

found verb **1** *she founded her company in 2002* ESTABLISH, set up, start (up), begin, get going, institute, inaugurate, launch, float, form, create, bring into being, originate, develop. ANTONYMS dissolve, liquidate.

2 *they founded a new city* BUILD, construct, erect, put up; plan, lay plans for. ANTONYMS abandon, demolish.

PHRASE: **be founded on** *our relationship must be founded on trust* BE BASED ON, be built on, be constructed on; be grounded in, be rooted in; rest, hinge, depend.

foundation noun **1** *the foundations of a building* FOOTING, foot, base, substructure, infrastructure, underpinning; bottom, bedrock, substratum.

2 *the report has a scientific foundation* BASIS, starting point, base, point of departure, beginning, premise; principles, fundamentals, rudiments; cornerstone, core, heart, thrust, essence, kernel.

3 *there was no foundation for the claim* JUSTIFICATION, grounds, defense, reason, rationale, cause, basis, motive, excuse, call, pretext, provocation.

4 *an educational foundation* ENDOWED INSTITUTION, charitable body, funding agency, source of funds, endowment.

WORD NOTE **foundation garments**

Some writers love assignments and exercises, and one I like involves taking familiar two-word phrases, misconstruing at least one of the terms in each case, and using the results to trigger a narrative. *Foundation garments* can be construed correctly to refer to a woman's underclothes—or creatively to indicate a suit worn by officials of the Guggenheim, Ford, MacArthur, or Rockefeller foundations. *Lemon peel* suggests a variety of striptease done beneath hot yellow lights. *Body shop* is a place that provides corpses—for a stiff price. The idea of a hospital used for military purposes popped into my head when my friend Bill Wadsworth told me that as a boy he thought *General Anesthesia* was related to Princess Anastasia and that both came out of Tolstoy. I used to think *trial and error* was a comment on the judiciary. Now I think it designates a court where the verdict is always wrong, so to be tried there is itself a punishment.

In sum: a famous executive at a philanthropic foundation goes to a strip club. Later, the stripper's corpse turns up in a back alley where the stuffed shirt lies unconscious. He is charged with a crime he does not remember having committed. His restored memory is his punishment, which cures him as he lies in the hospital ward where strange ideological debates and disputes keep going on around him.

All this is proof, perhaps, that metaphoric invention is a species of deliberate error. **—DL**

founder[1] noun *the founder of modern physics* ORIGINATOR, creator, (founding) father, prime mover, architect, engineer, designer, developer, pioneer, author, planner, inventor, mastermind; *literary* begetter.

founder[2] verb **1** *the ship foundered* SINK, go to the bottom, go down, be lost at sea.

2 *the scheme foundered* FAIL, be unsuccessful, not succeed, fall flat, fall through, collapse, backfire, meet with disaster, come to nothing, come to naught; *informal* flatline, flop, bomb. ANTONYM succeed.

3 *their horses foundered in the river* STUMBLE, trip, trip up, lose one's balance, lose/miss one's footing, slip, stagger, lurch, totter, fall, tumble, topple, sprawl, collapse.

EASILY CONFUSED WORDS **founder, flounder**

It is easy to confuse the words **founder** and **flounder**, not only because they sound similar but also because the contexts in which they are used overlap. **Founder** means, in its general and extended use, 'fail or come to nothing, sink out of sight' (*the scheme foundered because of lack of organizational backing*). **Flounder**, on the other hand, means 'struggle, move clumsily, be in a state of confusion' (*new recruits floundering about in their first week*).

foundling noun *it was during the Depression that Mrs. Aronson took in eight little foundlings and raised them as her own* ABANDONED INFANT, waif, stray, orphan, outcast.

fountain noun **1** *a fountain of water* JET, spray, spout, spurt, well, fount, cascade.

2 *a fountain of knowledge* SOURCE, fount, font, well; reservoir, fund, mass, mine.

four cardinal number *their infield is indeed a fabulous four, leading the league in every defensive category* QUARTET, foursome, tetralogy, quadruplets; *technical* tetrad; *rare* quadrumvirate.

foxy adjective *informal* **1** *a foxy character* CRAFTY, wily, artful, guileful, devious, sly, scheming, designing, calculating, Machiavellian; shrewd, astute, clever, canny; deceitful, deceptive, duplicitous; *archaic* subtle.

2 *a foxy lady* SEXY, sexually attractive, hot, cute, seductive, luscious, toothsome; *informal* bootylicious.

foyer noun *you may hang your coats in the foyer* ENTRANCE HALL, hall, hallway, entrance, entry, entranceway, entryway, porch, reception area, atrium, concourse, lobby, narthex.

fracas noun *the fracas in the alley drew the attention of a passing patrol car* DISTURBANCE, brawl, melee, rumpus, skirmish, struggle, scuffle, scrum, clash, fisticuffs, altercation; *informal* scrap, dust-up, set-to, donnybrook.

fraction noun **1** *a fraction of the population* PART, subdivision, division, portion, segment, slice, section, sector; proportion, percentage, ratio, measure. ANTONYM whole.

2 *only a fraction of the collection* TINY PART, fragment, snippet, snatch, smattering, selection. See note at FRAGMENT.

3 *he moved a fraction closer* TINY AMOUNT, little, bit, touch, soupçon, trifle, mite, shade, jot; *informal* smidgen, smidge, tad.

fractious adjective **1** *fractious children* GRUMPY, bad-tempered, irascible, irritable, crotchety, grouchy, cantankerous, short-tempered, tetchy, testy, curmudgeonly, ill-tempered, ill-humored, peevish, cross, waspish, crabby, crusty, prickly, touchy; *informal* snappish, cranky, ornery. ANTONYMS contented, affable.

2 *the fractious opposition party* WAYWARD, unruly, uncontrollable, unmanageable, out of hand, obstreperous, difficult, headstrong, recalcitrant, intractable; disobedient, insubordinate, disruptive, disorderly, undisciplined; contrary, willful; *formal* refractory; *archaic* contumacious. ANTONYM dutiful.

fracture noun **1** *the risk of vertebral fracture* BREAKING, breakage, cracking, fragmentation, splintering, rupture.

2 *tiny fractures in the rock* CRACK, split, fissure, crevice, break, rupture, breach, rift, cleft, chink, interstice; crazing.

▸ verb *the glass fractured* BREAK, crack, shatter, splinter, split, rupture; *informal* bust.

fragile adjective **1** *fragile porcelain* BREAKABLE, easily broken; delicate, dainty, fine, flimsy; eggshell; *formal* frangible. ANTONYMS durable, robust.

2 *the fragile cease-fire* TENUOUS, shaky, insecure, unreliable, vulnerable, flimsy. ANTONYM durable.

3 *she is still very fragile* WEAK, delicate, frail, debilitated; ill, unwell, ailing, poorly, sickly, infirm, enfeebled. ANTONYM strong.

fragment noun **1** *meteorite fragments* PIECE, bit, particle, speck; chip, shard, sliver, splinter; shaving, paring, snippet, scrap, flake, shred, wisp, morsel.

2 *a fragment of conversation* SNATCH, snippet, scrap, bit.

▸ verb *explosions caused the granite to fragment* BREAK UP, break, break into pieces, crack open/apart, shatter, splinter, fracture; disintegrate, fall to pieces, fall apart.

THE RIGHT WORD

The whole is equal to the sum of its **parts**—*part* being a general term for any of the components of a whole. But how did the whole come apart? **Fragment** suggests that breakage has occurred (*fragments of pottery*) and often refers to a brittle substance such as glass or pottery. **Segment** suggests that the whole has been separated along natural or pre-existing lines of division (*a segment of an orange*), and **section** suggests a substantial and clearly separate *part* that fits closely with other parts to form the whole (*a section of a bookcase*). **Fraction** usually suggests a less substantial but still clearly delineated *part*(*a fraction of her income*), and a **portion** is a *part* that has been allotted or assigned to someone (*her portion of the program*). Finally, the very frequently used **piece** is any *part* that is separate from the whole.

fragmentary adjective *fragmentary evidence* INCOMPLETE, fragmented, disconnected, disjointed, broken, discontinuous, piecemeal, sketchy, uneven, patchy.

fragrance noun **1** *the fragrance of spring flowers* SWEET SMELL, scent, perfume, bouquet; aroma, redolence, nose. See note at SMELL.

2 *a bottle of fragrance* PERFUME, scent, eau de toilette, toilet water; eau de cologne, cologne; aftershave.

fragrant adjective *an infusion of fragrant herbs* SWEET-SCENTED, sweet-smelling, scented, perfumed, aromatic, odoriferous, odiferous, perfumy; *literary* redolent. ANTONYM smelly.

frail adjective **1** *a frail old lady* WEAK, delicate, feeble, enfeebled, debilitated; infirm, ill, ailing, unwell, sickly, poorly, in poor health. See note at WEAK. ANTONYMS strong, fit.

2 *a frail structure* FRAGILE, breakable, easily damaged, delicate, flimsy, insubstantial, unsteady, unstable, rickety; *formal* frangible. ANTONYMS sturdy, robust.

frailty noun **1** *the frailty of old age* INFIRMITY, weakness, enfeeblement, debility; fragility, delicacy; ill health, sickliness. ANTONYM strength.

2 *his many frailties* WEAKNESS, fallibility; weak point, flaw, imperfection, defect, failing, fault, shortcoming, deficiency, inadequacy, limitation. ANTONYM strength.

frame noun **1** *a tubular metal frame* FRAMEWORK, structure, substructure, skeleton, chassis, shell, casing, body, bodywork; support, scaffolding, foundation, infrastructure.

2 *his tall, slender frame* BODY, figure, form, shape, physique, build, size, proportions.

3 *a picture frame* SETTING, mount, mounting.

▸ verb **1** *he had the picture framed* MOUNT, set in a frame.

2 *the legislators who frame the regulations* FORMULATE, draw up, draft, plan, shape, compose, put together, form, devise, create, establish, conceive, think up, originate; *informal* dream up.

PHRASE: **frame of mind** *what was your frame of mind at the time just preceding the accident?* MOOD, state of mind, humor, temper, disposition.

frame-up noun *informal he spent six years behind bars, the victim of a clever frame-up* CONSPIRACY, plot; trick, trap, entrapment; *informal* put-up job, setup.

framework noun **1** *a metal framework* FRAME, substructure, infrastructure, structure, skeleton, chassis, shell, body, bodywork; support, scaffolding, foundation.

2 *the framework of society* STRUCTURE, shape, fabric, order, scheme, system, organization, construction, configuration, composition, warp and woof; *informal* makeup.

franchise noun **1** *the extension of the franchise to women* SUFFRAGE, the vote, the right to vote, voting rights, enfranchisement.

2 *the company lost its TV franchise* WARRANT, charter, license, permit, authorization, permission, sanction, privilege.

frank adjective **1** *he was quite frank with me* CANDID, direct, forthright, plain, plain-spoken, straight, straightforward, explicit, to the point, matter-of-fact; open, honest, truthful, sincere; outspoken, bluff, blunt, unsparing, not afraid to call a spade a spade; *informal* upfront. ANTONYM evasive.

2 *she looked at the child with frank admiration* OPEN, undisguised, unconcealed, naked, unmistakable, clear, obvious, transparent, patent, manifest, evident, perceptible, palpable; blatant, barefaced, flagrant. ANTONYM concealed. *See word spectrum on page 364.*

frankly adverb **1** *frankly, I couldn't care less* TO BE FRANK, to be honest, to tell you the truth, to be truthful, in all honesty, as it happens.

frank
honest
candid
sincere
truthful
forthright
straightforward
bluff
blunt
not afraid to call a spade a spade
outspoken
uninhibited
plain-spoken
downright
open
forthcoming
direct
upfront
unvarnished
bald
straightforward
guileless
on the level
genuine
ingenuous
innocent
artless
transparent
simple
natural
talkative

choosing one's words

discreet
reticent
unforthcoming
uncommunicative
quiet
reserved
self-contained
close
close-mouthed
tight-lipped
introverted
taciturn
silent
playing one's cards close to one's chest
artful
tricky
crafty
cunning
sneaky
calculating
designing
conniving
scheming
wily
sly
guileful
furtive
veiled
shrouded
under the table
hole-and-corner
back-alley
cloak-and-dagger
hugger-mugger
secretive
dishonest
conspiratorial
evasive

2 *he stated the case quite frankly* CANDIDLY, directly, plainly, straightforwardly, forthrightly, openly, honestly, without beating about the bush, without mincing one's words, without prevarication, point-blank; bluntly, outspokenly, with no holds barred.

frantic adjective *the families of the missing passengers were frantic* PANIC-STRICKEN, panicky, beside oneself, at one's wits' end, distraught, overwrought, worked up, agitated, distressed; frenzied, wild, frenetic, fraught, feverish, hysterical, desperate; *informal* in a state, in a tizzy, wound up, het up, in a flap, tearing one's hair out. ANTONYM calm.

fraternity noun 1 *a spirit of fraternity* BROTHERHOOD, fellowship, kinship, friendship, (mutual) support, solidarity, community, union, togetherness; sisterhood.

2 *the teaching fraternity* PROFESSION, body of workers; band, group, set, circle.

3 *a college fraternity* SOCIETY, club, association; group, set.

fraternize verb *the musicians were told not to fraternize with the dancers* ASSOCIATE, mix, consort, socialize, keep company, rub elbows; *informal* hang around, hang out, run around, hobnob, be thick with.

fraud noun 1 *he was arrested for fraud* FRAUDULENCE, cheating, swindling, embezzlement, deceit, deception, double-dealing, chicanery, sharp practice.

2 *social insurance frauds* SWINDLE, racket, deception, trick, cheat, hoax; *informal* scam, con, rip-off, sting, gyp, fiddle, bunco, hustle, grift.

3 *they exposed him as a fraud* IMPOSTOR, fake, sham, charlatan, quack, mountebank; swindler, gonif, snake oil salesman, fraudster, racketeer, cheat, confidence trickster; *informal* phony, con man, con artist, scam artist.

fraudulent adjective *a fraudulent stock transaction* DISHONEST, cheating, swindling, corrupt, criminal, illegal, unlawful, illicit; deceitful, double-dealing, duplicitous, dishonorable, unscrupulous, unprincipled; *informal* crooked, shady, dirty. ANTONYM honest.

fraught adjective 1 *their world is **fraught with** danger* FULL OF, filled with, rife with; attended by, accompanied by.

2 *she sounded a bit fraught* ANXIOUS, worried, stressed, upset, distraught, overwrought, worked up, antsy, agitated, distressed, distracted, desperate, frantic, panic-stricken, panic-struck, panicky; beside oneself, at one's wits' end, at the end of one's tether/rope; *informal* wound up, in a state, in a flap, in a cold sweat, tearing one's hair out, having kittens.

fray[1] verb 1 *cheap fabric soon frays* UNRAVEL, wear, wear thin, wear out/through, become worn.

2 *her nerves were frayed* STRAIN, tax, overtax, put on edge.

fray[2] noun *two men started the fray* BATTLE, fight, engagement, conflict, clash, skirmish, altercation, tussle, struggle, scuffle, melee, brawl, fracas; *informal* scrap, set-to.

frayed adjective 1 *a frayed shirt collar* WORN, well-worn, threadbare, tattered, ragged, holey, moth-eaten, in holes, the worse for wear; *informal* tatty, raggedy, dog-eared.

2 *his frayed nerves* STRAINED, fraught, tense, edgy, stressed.

freak noun 1 *a genetically engineered freak* ABERRATION, abnormality, irregularity, oddity; monster, monstrosity, mutant; freak of nature.

2 *the accident was a complete freak* ANOMALY, aberration, rarity, oddity, unusual occurrence; fluke, twist of fate.

3 *informal they were dismissed as a bunch of freaks* ODDITY, eccentric, misfit; crank, lunatic; *informal* oddball, weirdo, nutcase, nut, wacko, kook.

4 *informal a fitness freak* ENTHUSIAST, fan, devotee, lover, aficionado; *informal* fiend, nut, fanatic, addict, maniac.

▸ adjective *a freak storm | a freak result* UNUSUAL, anomalous, aberrant, atypical, unrepresentative, irregular, fluky, exceptional, unaccountable, bizarre, queer, peculiar, odd, freakish; unpredictable, unforeseeable, unexpected, unanticipated, surprising; rare, singular, isolated. ANTONYM normal.

▸ verb *informal he **freaked out*** GO CRAZY, go mad, go out of one's mind, go to pieces, crack, snap, lose control; panic, become hysterical; *informal* lose it, lose one's cool, crack up, go ape, go postal.

freakish adjective *freakish weather.* See FREAK adjective.

freaky adjective *informal* See ODD senses 1, 2.

WORD NOTE **freaky**

John Donne began some of his poems with a robust imperative. "The Canonization," for example, opens: "For God's sake hold your tongue, and let me love." Donne wrote seduction poems in the tone of one used to giving orders and getting his way. Now that "getting freaky" has become a synonym for "getting naked," an imitation of the great poet's manner wedded to the American collegiate vernacular might produce this opening line: "Hey, ugly, let's get freaky." **—DL**

freckle noun *the sun brings out the freckles on his face* SPECKLE, fleck, dot, spot, mole, blotch, macula.

free adjective **1** *admission is free* WITHOUT CHARGE, free of charge, for nothing; complimentary, gratis; *informal* for free, on the house.

2 *she was **free of** any pressures* UNENCUMBERED BY, unaffected by, clear of, without, rid of; exempt from, not liable to, safe from, immune to, excused from; *informal* sans, minus.

3 *I'm free this afternoon* UNOCCUPIED, not busy, available, between appointments; off duty, off work, off; on vacation, on leave; at leisure, with time on one's hands, with time to spare. ANTONYMS busy, occupied, unavailable.

4 *the bathroom's free now* VACANT, empty, available, unoccupied, not taken, not in use. ANTONYM occupied.

5 *a citizen of a free nation* INDEPENDENT, self-governing, self-governed, self-ruling, self-determining, nonaligned, sovereign, autonomous; democratic. ANTONYM dependent.

6 *the killer is still free* ON THE LOOSE, at liberty, at large; loose, unconfined, unbound, untied, unchained, untethered, unshackled, unfettered, unrestrained. ANTONYM captive.

7 *you are free to leave* ALLOWED, permitted; ABLE, in a position to. ANTONYM unable.

8 *the free flow of water* UNIMPEDED, unobstructed, unrestricted, unhampered, clear, open, unblocked. ANTONYM obstructed.

9 *she was free with her money* GENEROUS, liberal, openhanded, unstinting, bountiful; lavish, extravagant, prodigal. ANTONYM mean.

10 *his free and hearty manner* FRANK, open, candid, direct, plain-spoken; unrestrained, unconstrained, free and easy, uninhibited.

▸ verb **1** *three of the hostages were freed* RELEASE, set free, let go, liberate, discharge, deliver; set loose, let loose, turn loose, untie, unchain, unfetter, unshackle, unleash; *literary* disenthrall. See word spectrum at IMPRISON. ANTONYMS confine, lock up.

2 *the victims were freed by firefighters* EXTRICATE, release, get out, pull out, pull free; rescue, set free. ANTONYM trap.

3 *they wish to be freed from all legal ties* EXEMPT, except, excuse, relieve, unburden, disburden.

PHRASES: **free and easy** *the restaurant's free and easy atmosphere* EASYGOING, relaxed, casual, informal, unceremonious, unforced, natural, open, spontaneous, uninhibited, friendly; tolerant, liberal; *informal* laid-back.
a free hand *he was allowed a free hand in appointing new staff* FREE REIN, carte blanche, freedom, liberty, license, latitude, leeway, a blank check.

freebooter noun *the islands offered sanctuary to freebooters* PIRATE, marauder, raider; bandit, robber; adventurer, swashbuckler; *historical* privateer; *archaic* buccaneer, corsair.

freedom noun **1** *a desperate bid for freedom* LIBERTY, liberation, release, deliverance, delivery, discharge; *literary* disenthrallment; *historical* manumission. See note at LIBERTY. ANTONYM captivity.

2 *revolution was the only path to freedom* INDEPENDENCE, self-government, self-determination, self-rule, home rule, sovereignty, nonalignment, autonomy; democracy. ANTONYM dependence.

3 *freedom from local political accountability* EXEMPTION, immunity, dispensation; impunity. ANTONYM liability.

4 *freedom to choose your course of treatment* RIGHT, entitlement, privilege, prerogative; scope, latitude, leeway, flexibility, space, breathing space, room, elbow room; license, leave, free rein, a free hand, carte blanche, a blank check. ANTONYM restriction.

free-for-all noun *we got out just before the argument turned into a free-for-all* BRAWL, fight, scuffle, tussle, struggle, confrontation, clash, altercation, fray, fracas, melee, rumpus, disturbance; breach of the peace; *informal* scrap, set-to.

freelance adjective *freelance writers are invited to submit articles* SELF-EMPLOYED, independent, contract.

freethinker noun *the freethinkers in her household were so unlike the strict Roman Catholics in his family* NONCONFORMIST, individualist, independent, maverick; agnostic, atheist, nonbeliever, unbeliever. ANTONYM conformist.

free will noun *Americans take for granted their blessed right to free will* SELF-DETERMINATION, freedom of choice, autonomy, liberty, independence. PHRASE: **of one's own free will** *I pursued a modeling career of my own free will* VOLUNTARILY, willingly, readily, freely, without reluctance, without compulsion, of one's own accord, of one's own volition, of one's own choosing.

freeze verb **1** *the stream had frozen* ICE OVER, ice up, solidify. ANTONYMS thaw, melt.

2 *my fingers froze* become frozen, become frostbitten. ANTONYMS thaw, warm up.

3 *the campers stifled in summer and froze in winter* BE VERY COLD, be numb with cold, turn blue with cold, shiver, be chilled to the bone/marrow. ANTONYM overheat.

4 *she froze in horror* STOP DEAD, stop in one's tracks, stop, stand (stock) still, go rigid, become motionless, become paralyzed. ANTONYM run away.

5 *the price of gasoline was frozen* FIX, hold, peg, set; limit, restrict, cap, confine, regulate; hold/keep down. ANTONYM change.

PHRASE: **freeze out** *informal she was frozen out by her husband's relatives* EXCLUDE, leave out, shut out, cut out, ignore, ostracize, spurn, snub, shun, turn one's back on, cold-shoulder, give someone the cold shoulder, leave out in the cold.

freezing adjective **1** *a freezing wind* BITTER, bitterly cold, icy, chill, frosty, glacial, wintry, subzero, hypothermic; raw, biting, piercing, bone-chilling, penetrating, cutting, numbing; arctic, polar, Siberian. ANTONYM balmy.

2 *you must be freezing* FROZEN, extremely cold, numb with cold, chilled to the bone/marrow, frozen stiff, shivery, shivering; *informal* frozen to death. ANTONYM hot.

freight noun **1** *freight carried by rail* GOODS, cargo, load, consignment, delivery, shipment; merchandise.

2 *our reliance on air freight* TRANSPORTATION, transport, conveyance, carriage, portage, haulage.

French fries noun FRIES, French-fried potatoes, pommes frites, frites, home fries, shoestring potatoes, curly fries; *chiefly Brit.* chips.

frenetic adjective *the frenetic bustle of the city* FRANTIC, wild, frenzied, hectic, fraught, feverish, fevered, mad, manic, hyperactive, energetic, intense, amped-up, fast and furious, turbulent, tumultuous. ANTONYM calm.

frenzied adjective *frenzied holiday shoppers* FRANTIC, wild, frenetic, hectic, fraught, feverish, fevered, mad, crazed, manic, intense, furious, uncontrolled, out of control. ANTONYM calm.

frenzy noun **1** *the crowd whipped itself into a state of frenzy* HYSTERIA, madness, mania, delirium, feverishness, fever, wildness, agitation, turmoil, tumult; wild excitement, euphoria, elation, ecstasy.

2 *a frenzy of anger* FIT, paroxysm, spasm, bout.

frequency noun *the frequency of errors* RATE OF OCCURRENCE, incidence, amount, commonness, prevalence; *Statistics* distribution.

frequent adjective **1** *frequent bouts of chest infection* RECURRENT, recurring, repeated, periodic, continual, one after another, successive; many, numerous, lots of, several. ANTONYM few.

2 *a frequent business traveler* HABITUAL, regular. ANTONYM occasional.

▸ verb *he frequented chic nightclubs* VISIT, patronize, spend time in, visit regularly, be a regular visitor to, haunt; *informal* hang out at.

frequenter noun *a **frequenter** of Ed's Bar & Grill* HABITUÉ OF, patron of, regular at, regular visitor to, regular customer at/of, regular client of, familiar face at.

frequently adverb *he frequently attends church* REGULARLY, often, very often, all the time, habitually, customarily, routinely; many times, a lot, many a time, lots of times, again and again, time and again, over and over again, repeatedly, recurrently, continually, oftentimes; *literary* oft, ofttimes.

fresh adjective **1** *fresh fruit* NEWLY PICKED, garden-fresh, crisp, unwilted; raw, natural, unprocessed. ANTONYMS stale, processed.

2 *a fresh sheet of paper* CLEAN, blank, empty, clear, white; unused, new, pristine, unmarked, untouched. ANTONYM used.

3 *a fresh approach* NEW, recent, latest, up-to-date, modern, modernistic, ultra-modern, newfangled; original, novel, different, innovative, unusual, unconventional, unorthodox; radical, revolutionary; *informal* offbeat. ANTONYM old.

4 *fresh recruits* YOUNG, youthful; new, inexperienced, naive, untrained, unqualified, untried, raw; *informal* wet behind the ears. ANTONYM experienced.

5 *he felt fresh and happy to be alive* REFRESHED, rested, restored, revived; (as) fresh as a daisy, energetic, vigorous, invigorated, full of vim and vigor, lively, vibrant, spry, sprightly, bright, alert, perky; *informal* full of beans, raring to go, bright-eyed and bushy-tailed, chirpy, chipper. ANTONYM tired.

6 *her fresh complexion* HEALTHY, healthy-looking, clear, bright, youthful, blooming, glowing, unblemished; fair, rosy, rosy-cheeked, pink, ruddy. ANTONYM healthy.

7 *the night air was fresh* COOL, crisp, refreshing, invigorating, tonic; pure, clean, clear, uncontaminated, untainted. ANTONYMS stale, stifling.

8 *a fresh wind* CHILLY, chill, cool, cold, brisk, bracing, invigorating; strong; *informal* nippy. ANTONYMS sultry, warm.

9 *informal don't get fresh with me* IMPUDENT, sassy, saucy, brazen, shameless, forward, bold, cheeky, impertinent, insolent, presumptuous, disrespectful, rude, pert, (as) bold as brass; *informal* lippy, mouthy. ANTONYM polite.

freshen verb **1** *this will freshen your breath* REFRESH, deodorize, cleanse; revitalize, restore.

2 *she went to **freshen up** before dinner* WASH, wash up, bathe, shower; tidy oneself (up), spruce oneself up, smarten oneself up, groom oneself, primp oneself; *informal* titivate oneself, doll oneself up; *formal, humorous* perform one's ablutions.

3 *the waitress freshened their coffee* REFILL, top up, fill up, replenish.

freshman noun *a freshman at Bennington* NEW STUDENT, first-year student, undergraduate; newcomer, new recruit, probationer; beginner, learner, novice, tenderfoot; *informal* frosh, undergrad, rookie, greenhorn.

fret verb **1** *she was fretting about Jonathan* WORRY, be anxious, feel uneasy, be distressed, be upset, upset oneself, concern oneself; agonize, sigh, pine, brood, eat one's heart out.

2 *his absence began to fret her* TROUBLE, bother, concern, perturb, disturb, disquiet, disconcert, distress, upset, alarm, panic, agitate; *informal* eat away at.

fretful adjective *the long wait in traffic was making us fretful* DISTRESSED, upset, miserable, unsettled, uneasy, ill at ease, uncomfortable, edgy, agitated, worked up, tense, stressed, restive, fidgety, antsy; querulous, irritable, cross, fractious, peevish, petulant, out of sorts, bad-tempered, irascible, grumpy, crotchety, captious, testy, tetchy, cranky, het up, uptight, twitchy, crabby.

friable adjective *plant the bulbs in friable soil* CRUMBLY, easily crumbled; powdery, dusty, chalky, soft; dry, crisp, brittle.

friar noun *a young friar led us the meditation gardens* MONK, brother, religious, cenobite, contemplative; prior, abbot.

friction noun 1 *a lubrication system that reduces friction* ABRASION, rubbing, chafing, grating, rasping, scraping; resistance, drag.

2 *there was considerable friction between father and son* DISCORD, strife, conflict, disagreement, dissension, dissent, infighting, opposition, contention, dispute, disputation, arguing, argument, quarreling, bickering, squabbling, wrangling, fighting, feuding, rivalry; hostility, animosity, antipathy, enmity, antagonism, resentment, acrimony, bitterness, bad feeling, ill feeling, ill will, bad blood. ANTONYM harmony.

friend noun 1 *a close friend* COMPANION, soul mate, intimate, confidante, confidant, familiar, alter ego, second self, playmate, playfellow, classmate, schoolmate, workmate; ally, associate; sister, brother; best friend, kindred spirit, bosom buddy, bosom friend; *informal* pal, chum, sidekick, crony, main man, mate, buddy, bud, amigo, compadre, homeboy, homegirl, homie; *archaic* compeer. ANTONYM enemy.

2 *the friends of the National Ballet* PATRON, backer, supporter, benefactor, benefactress, sponsor; well-wisher, defender, champion; *informal* angel.

friendless adjective *caring for those who are poor and friendless* ALONE, all alone, by oneself, solitary, lonely, with no one to turn to, lone, without friends, companionless, unbefriended, unpopular, unwanted, unloved, abandoned, rejected, forsaken, shunned, spurned, forlorn, lonesome. ANTONYM popular.

friendliness noun *her host's friendliness* AFFABILITY, amiability, geniality, congeniality, bonhomie, cordiality, good nature, good humor, warmth, affection, demonstrativeness, conviviality, joviality, companionability, sociability, gregariousness, camaraderie, neighborliness, hospitableness, approachability, accessibility, openness, kindness, kindliness, sympathy, amenability, benevolence.

friendly adjective 1 *a friendly woman* AFFABLE, amiable, genial, congenial, cordial, warm, affectionate, demonstrative, convivial, companionable, sociable, gregarious, outgoing, comradely, neighborly, hospitable, approachable, easy to get on with, accessible, communicative, open, unreserved, easygoing, good-natured, kindly, benign, amenable, agreeable, obliging, sympathetic, well-disposed, benevolent; *informal* chummy, buddy-buddy.

2 *friendly conversation* AMICABLE, congenial, cordial, pleasant, easy, relaxed, casual, informal, unceremonious; close, intimate, familiar. ANTONYM hostile.

3 *a friendly wind swept the boat to the shore* FAVORABLE, advantageous, helpful; lucky, providential. ANTONYM unfavorable.

4 *a kid-friendly hotel* COMPATIBLE, suited, adapted, appropriate.

friendship noun 1 *lasting friendships* RELATIONSHIP, close relationship, attachment, mutual attachment, association, bond, tie, link, union.

2 *old ties of love and friendship* AMITY, camaraderie, friendliness, comradeship, companionship, fellowship, fellow feeling, closeness, affinity, rapport, understanding, harmony, unity; intimacy, mutual affection. ANTONYM enmity.

friend
friend
intimate
compeer
confidant/confidante
soul mate
second self
alter ego
best friend
bosom friend
fidus Achates
boon companion
sister/brother
close friend
ally
comrade
confrère
companion
pal
sidekick
crony
main man
mate
amigo/amiga
compadre
paisan
homeboy/homegirl
homie/homey
buddy
bosom buddy
chum
playmate
playfellow
classmate
schoolmate
colleague
workmate
associate
contact
connection
acquaintance
competitor
opponent
opposer
challenger
combatant
adversary
antagonist
rival
hostile party
hostile
foe
enemy
foe

fright noun 1 *she was paralyzed with fright* FEAR, fearfulness, terror, horror, alarm, panic, dread, trepidation, dismay, nervousness, apprehension, apprehensiveness, perturbation, disquiet; *informal* jitteriness, twitchiness.

2 *the experience gave everyone* ***a fright*** A SCARE, a shock, a surprise, a turn, a jolt, a start; the shivers, the shakes; *informal* the jitters, the heebie-jeebies, the willies, the creeps, a cold sweat, butterflies (in one's stomach).

3 *informal* *she looked an absolute fright* UGLY SIGHT, eye-

sore, monstrosity; *informal* mess, sight, state, blot on the landscape.

frighten verb *the fighting in the streets frightened us* SCARE, startle, alarm, terrify, petrify, shock, chill, panic, shake, disturb, dismay, unnerve, unman, intimidate, terrorize, cow, daunt; strike terror into, put the fear of God into, chill someone to the bone/marrow, make someone's blood run cold; *informal* scare the living daylights out of, scare stiff, scare someone out of their wits, scare witless, scare to death, scare the pants off, spook, make someone's hair stand on end, make someone jump out of their skin, give someone the heebie-jeebies, make someone's hair curl, scare the bejesus out of; *archaic* affright.

frightening adjective *a frightening story about bloodthirsty aliens* TERRIFYING, horrifying, alarming, startling, white-knuckle, chilling, spine-chilling, hair-raising, blood-curdling, bone-chilling, disturbing, unnerving, intimidating, daunting, dismaying, upsetting, harrowing, traumatic; eerie, sinister, fearsome, nightmarish, macabre, menacing; eldritch; *informal* scary, spooky, creepy, hairy.

frightful adjective *the house was in a frightful mess* HORRIBLE, horrific, ghastly, horrendous, serious, awful, dreadful, terrible, nasty, grim, dire, unspeakable; alarming, shocking, terrifying, harrowing, appalling, fearful; hideous, gruesome, grisly; *informal* horrid; *formal* grievous.

frigid adjective **1** *a frigid January night* VERY COLD, bitterly cold, bitter, freezing, frozen, frosty, icy, gelid, chilly, chill, wintry, bleak, subzero, arctic, Siberian, bone-chilling, polar, glacial, hypothermic; *informal* nippy. ANTONYMS hot, tropical.

2 *frigid politeness* STIFF, formal, stony, wooden, unemotional, passionless, unfeeling, indifferent, unresponsive, unenthusiastic, austere, distant, aloof, remote, reserved, unapproachable; frosty, cold, icy, cool, unsmiling, forbidding, unfriendly, unwelcoming, hostile; *informal* offish, standoffish. ANTONYM friendly.

frill noun **1** *a full skirt with a wide frill* RUFFLE, flounce, ruff, furbelow, jabot, peplum, ruche, ruching, fringe; *archaic* purfle.

2 *a comfortable apartment with no-frills* OSTENTATION, ornamentation, decoration, embellishment, fanciness, fuss, chi-chi, gilding, excess; trimmings, extras, additions, nonessentials, luxuries, extravagances, superfluities.

frilly adjective *a frilly white apron* RUFFLED, flounced, frilled, crimped, ruched, trimmed, lacy, frothy; fancy, ornate; *informal* fancy-dancy, fancy-schmancy.

fringe noun **1** *the city's northern fringe* PERIMETER, periphery, border, borderline, margin, rim, outer edge, edge, extremity, limit; outer limits, limits, borders, bounds, outskirts; *literary* marge. ANTONYM middle.

2 *the curtains with the yellow fringe* EDGING, edge, border, trimming, frill, flounce, ruffle; tassels; *archaic* purfle.

▸ adjective *fringe theater* UNCONVENTIONAL, unorthodox, alternative, avant-garde, experimental, innovative, left-field, innovatory, radical, extreme; peripheral; off-off Broadway; *informal* offbeat, way out. ANTONYM mainstream.

▸ verb **1** *a robe of gold, fringed with black velvet* TRIM, edge, hem, border, bind, braid; decorate, adorn, ornament, embellish, finish; *archaic* purfle.

2 *the lake is fringed by a belt of trees* BORDER, edge, bound, skirt, line, surround, enclose, encircle, circle, girdle, encompass, ring; *literary* gird.

fringe benefit noun *our fringe benefits include free eye exams and discounted theater tickets* EXTRA, added extra, additional benefit, privilege, bonus; *informal* perk; *formal* perquisite.

frippery noun **1** *a functional building with not a hint of frippery* OSTENTATION, showiness, embellishment, adornment, ornamentation, ornament, decoration, trimming, gilding, prettification, gingerbread; finery, frou-frou; *informal* bells and whistles.

2 *roadside shops full of fripperies* TRINKET, bauble, knickknack, gewgaw, gimcrack, bibelot, ornament, novelty, trifle, kickshaw, tchotchke; *archaic* gaud.

frisk verb **1** *the spaniels frisked around my ankles* FROLIC, gambol, cavort, caper, scamper, skip, dance, romp, trip, prance, leap, spring, hop, jump, bounce.

2 *the officer frisked him* SEARCH, check, inspect.

frisky adjective *frisky squirrels* LIVELY, bouncy, bubbly, perky, active, energetic, animated, zestful, full of vim and vigor; playful, coltish, skittish, spirited, high-spirited, in high spirits, exuberant; *informal* full of beans, zippy, peppy, bright-eyed and bushy-tailed; *literary* frolicsome.

fritter verb *he **frittered away** his inheritance* SQUANDER, waste, misuse, misspend, dissipate; overspend, spend like water, be prodigal with, run through, get through; *informal* blow, splurge, pour/throw down the drain. ANTONYM save.

frivolity noun *everyone needs a little frivolity now and again* LIGHTHEARTEDNESS, levity, joking, jocularity, gaiety, fun, frivolousness, silliness, foolishness, flightiness, skittishness; superficiality, shallowness, flippancy, vacuity, empty-headedness.

frivolous adjective **1** *a frivolous girl* SKITTISH, flighty, giddy, silly, foolish, superficial, shallow, irresponsible, thoughtless, featherbrained, empty-headed, peabrained, birdbrained, vacuous, vapid; *informal* dizzy, dippy, ditzy, flaky. ANTONYMS sensible, serious.

2 *frivolous remarks* FLIPPANT, glib, facetious, joking, jokey, lighthearted; fatuous, inane, senseless, thoughtless; *informal* flip. ANTONYM serious.

3 *new rules to stop frivolous lawsuits* TIME-WASTING, pointless, trivial, trifling, minor, petty, insignificant, unimportant. ANTONYM important.

frizzle verb *their hair was frizzled* CURL, coil, crimp, crinkle, kink, wave, frizz. ANTONYM straighten.

frizzy adjective *the doll's frizzy hair* CURLY, curled, corkscrew, ringlety, crimped, crinkly, kinky, frizzed; permed. ANTONYM straight.

frog legs plural noun See note below.

USAGE NOTE **frog legs, frogs legs, frog's legs, frogs legs**

Some cookbook authors write *frog legs*—e.g., Irma S. Rombauer and Marion Rombauer Becker (*Joy of Cooking*; 1975), Jacqueline Killeen (*The Whole World Cookbook*; 1979), and Emeril Lagasse (*Louisiana Real & Rustic*; 1996). Others, perhaps a majority of writers on culinary matters, write *frogs' legs*—e.g., Ruth R. Tyndall (*Eat Yourself Full*; 1967), Helen Corbitt (*Helen Corbitt Cooks for Company*; 1974), and Pierre Franey (*More 60-Minute Gourmet*; 1981).

This form appears to be a direct translation of the French *cuisses de grenouilles* (= legs of frogs, or frogs' legs).

The other forms are less defensible. At least one writer—Jacques Pepin (*La Methode*; 1979)—uses *frog's legs*, as if they were served always in pairs (and carefully matched up). Some writers indecisively mix two or more forms—e.g., Alan Davidson, in *The Oxford Companion to Food* (1999), uses both *frog legs* and *frogs' legs*.

Those citations don't quite reflect general usage in newspapers and journals. Of 1,600 examples checked in Westlaw's ALLNEWS database in January 2002, the breakdown was as follows: *frog legs*—880 (55%); *frogs' legs*—450 (28%); *frog's legs*—194 (12%); and *frogs legs*—76 (5%). Likewise, informal surveys suggest that most cultivated speakers who would order this item say *frog legs*. The cookbook writers' preference for *frogs' legs* seems a mite pedantic. In any event, the two forms to be avoided are *frog's legs* (unless you're talking about a particular frog) and *frogs legs* (unless you eat them without utensils or napkins). **—BG**

---

frolic verb *children frolicked on the sand* PLAY, amuse oneself, romp, disport oneself, frisk, gambol, cavort, caper, cut capers, scamper, skip, dance, prance, leap about, jump about; *dated* sport.

▸ noun *the youngsters enjoyed their frolic* ANTIC, caper, game, romp, escapade; **(frolics)** fun, fun and games, hijinks, merrymaking, amusement, skylarking.

frolicsome adjective *literary* *the dogs love to be free and frolicsome* PLAYFUL, frisky, fun-loving, jolly, merry, gleeful, lighthearted, exuberant, high-spirited, spirited, lively, perky, coltish, kittenish; mischievous, impish, roguish; *informal* peppy, zippy, full of beans.

front noun **1** *the front of the boat* FORE, foremost part, forepart, anterior, forefront, nose, head; bow, prow; foreground. ANTONYMS rear, back.

2 *the store's front* FRONTAGE, face, facing, facade; window.

3 *the battlefield surgeons who work at the front* FRONT LINE, firing line, vanguard, van; trenches.

4 *the front of the line* HEAD, beginning, start, top, lead. ANTONYM back.

5 *she kept up a brave front* APPEARANCE, air, face, manner, demeanor, bearing, pose, exterior, veneer, (outward) show, act, pretense, affectation.

6 *the shop was a front for his real business* COVER, cover-up, false front, blind, disguise, facade, mask, cloak, screen, smokescreen, camouflage.

▸ adjective *the front runners* LEADING, lead, first, foremost; in first place. ANTONYM last.

▸ verb *the houses **fronted on** a reservoir* OVERLOOK, look out on/over, face (toward), lie opposite (to); have a view of, command a view of.

PHRASE: **in front** *it looks as if Carson is now in front* AHEAD, to/at the fore, at the head, up ahead, in the vanguard, in the van, in the lead, leading, coming first; *informal* up front.

frontier noun *the lakes sit astride the U.S.-Canadian frontier* BORDER, boundary, borderline, dividing line, demarcation line; perimeter, limit, edge, rim, bounds.

frost noun **1** *bushes covered with frost* ICE CRYSTALS, ice, rime, verglas; hoarfrost, ground frost, black frost; *informal* Jack Frost; *archaic* hoar.

2 *there was frost in his tone* COLDNESS, coolness, frostiness, ice, iciness, frigidity; hostility, unfriendliness, stiffness, aloofness; *informal* standoffishness.

frosty adjective **1** *a frosty morning* FREEZING, cold, icy-cold, bitter, bitterly cold, chill, wintry, frigid, glacial, hypothermic, arctic; frozen, icy, gelid; *informal* nippy; *literary* rimy.

2 *her frosty gaze* COLD, frigid, icy, glacial, unfriendly, inhospitable, unwelcoming, forbidding, hostile, stony, stern, steely, hard.

froth noun *the froth on top of his beer* FOAM, head; bubbles, frothiness, fizz, effervescence; lather, suds; scum; *literary* spume.

▸ verb *the liquid frothed up* BUBBLE, fizz, effervesce, foam, lather; churn, seethe; *literary* spume.

frothy adjective **1** *a frothy liquid* FOAMING, foamy, bubbling, bubbly, fizzy, sparkling, effervescent, gassy, carbonated; sudsy; *literary* spumy.

2 *a frothy daytime show* LIGHTWEIGHT, light, superficial, shallow, slight, insubstantial; trivial, trifling, frivolous.

frown verb **1** *she frowned at him* SCOWL, glower, glare, lower, make a face, look daggers, give someone a black look; knit/furrow one's brows; *informal* give someone a dirty look. ANTONYM smile.

2 *public displays of affection were **frowned on*** DISAPPROVE OF, view with disfavor, dislike, look askance at, not take kindly to, take a dim view of, take exception to, object to, have a low opinion of.

frowzy adjective **1** *a frowzy old biddy* SCRUFFY, unkempt, untidy, messy, disheveled, slovenly, slatternly, bedraggled, down-at-the-heels, badly dressed, dowdy, raggedy.

2 *a frowzy room* DINGY, gloomy, dull, drab, dark, dim; stuffy, close, musty, stale, stifling; shabby, seedy, rundown.

frozen adjective **1** *the frozen ground* ICY, ice-covered, icebound, frosty, frosted, gelid; frozen solid, hard, (as) hard as iron; *literary* rimy. ANTONYM thawed.

2 *his hands were frozen* FREEZING, icy, very cold, chilled to the bone/marrow, numb, numbed, frozen stiff, frostbitten; *informal* frozen to death. ANTONYMS hot, boiling.

frugal adjective **1** *a hard-working, frugal woman* THRIFTY, economical, careful, cautious, prudent, provident, unwasteful, sparing, scrimping; abstemious, abstinent, austere, self-denying, ascetic, monkish, spartan; parsimonious, miserly, niggardly, cheeseparing, penny-pinching, close-fisted; *informal* tightfisted, tight, stingy. See note at ECONOMICAL. ANTONYM extravagant.

2 *their frugal breakfast* MEAGER, scanty, scant, paltry, skimpy; plain, simple, spartan, inexpensive, cheap, economical. ANTONYM lavish.

fruit noun **1** *fruit for dessert.* See table on page 370.

2 *the fruits of their labors* REWARD, benefit, profit, product, return, yield, legacy, issue; result, outcome, upshot, consequence, effect.

fruitful adjective **1** *a fruitful tree* FERTILE, fecund, prolific, high-yielding; fruit-bearing, fruiting. See note at FERTILE. ANTONYM barren.

2 *fruitful discussions* PRODUCTIVE, constructive, useful, of use, worthwhile, helpful, beneficial, valuable, rewarding, profitable, advantageous, gainful, successful, effective, effectual, well-spent. ANTONYM futile.

FRUITS

abiu	jujube
achocha	kiwi fruit
akebia	kumquat
akee/ackee	langsat
ambarella	lemon
ananas	lime
apple	longan
apricot	loquat
atemoya	lychee
avocado	mamey
azarole	mameyito
bael	mandarin
banana	mango
banana flower	mangosteen
baobab	medlar
Barbados cherry	melon
barberry	monstera
beach plum	mountain apple
bearberry	moya
bergamot	mulberry
berry	muskmelon
bignay	mysore raspberry
bilberry	naranjilla
bilimbi	nectarine
biriba	noni
blackberry	orange
blackberry jam fruit	papaya
blood orange	passion fruit
blueberry	pawpaw
Brazilian cherry	peach
breadfruit	peanut butter fruit
buffaloberry	pear
cabelluda	pepino
calamansi	persimmon
cantaloupe	pineapple
carambola	pitahaya
casaba	plantain
chayote	plum
cherimoya	pomegranate
cherry	pomelo
Chinese wolfberry	prickly pear
chokecherry	prune
cherry plum	pummelo
citron	quince
clementine	rambutan
cloudberry	raspberry
coconut	rhubarb
corossolier	rollinia
cranberry	rose apple
Crenshaw melon	salak
crowberry	salmonberry
currant	santol
damson	sapodilla
date	sapote
dewberry	satsuma
durian	serviceberry
eggfruit	soursop
elderberry	spanspek
feijoa	squashberry
fig	star fruit
gamboge	starapple
gooseberry	strawberry
grape	Surinam cherry
grapefruit	tamarillo
greengage	tamarind
ground cherry	ugli fruit
guava	wampee
hackberry	water apple
honeydew (melon)	watermelon
huckleberry	wax jambu
ilama	whortleberry
jaboticaba	winter melon
jackfruit	yuzu

See also tables at APPLE and BERRY.

fruition noun *when the project comes to its fruition, you will be favorably impressed* FULFILLMENT, realization, actualization, materialization, achievement, attainment, accomplishment, resolution; success, completion, consummation, conclusion, close, finish, perfection, maturity, maturation, ripening, ripeness; implementation, execution, performance.

fruitless adjective *fruitless negotiations* FUTILE, vain, in vain, to no avail, to no effect, idle; pointless, useless, worthless, wasted, hollow; ineffectual, ineffective, inefficacious; unproductive, unrewarding, frustrating, profitless, unsuccessful, unavailing, barren, for naught; abortive; *archaic* bootless. ANTONYM productive.

frumpy adjective *the clothes made her look frumpy* DOWDY, frumpish, unfashionable, old-fashioned; drab, dull, homely, shabby, scruffy. ANTONYM fashionable.

frustrate verb **1** *his plans were frustrated* THWART, defeat, foil, block, stop, put a stop to, counter, spoil, check, balk, disappoint, forestall, dash, scotch, quash, crush, derail, snooker; obstruct, impede, hamper, hinder, hamstring, stand in the way of; *informal* stymie, foul up, screw up, put the kibosh on, do for; *informal* scuttle. See note at THWART. ANTONYMS help, facilitate.

2 *the delays frustrated her* EXASPERATE, infuriate, annoy, anger, vex, irritate, irk, try someone's patience; disappoint, discontent, dissatisfy, discourage, dishearten, dispirit; *informal* aggravate, bug, miff. ANTONYM please.

frustration noun **1** *he clenched his fists in frustration* EXASPERATION, annoyance, anger, vexation, irritation; disappointment, dissatisfaction, discontentment, discontent; *informal* aggravation.

2 *the frustration of her attempts to introduce changes* THWARTING, defeat, prevention, foiling, blocking, spoiling, circumvention, forestalling, disappointment, derailment; obstruction, hampering, hindering; failure, collapse.

fry verb *fry the onions in the skillet* COOK, sauté, sear, brown, sizzle, frizzle, pan-fry, deep-fry.

fuddled adjective *the fumes are making me dizzy and fuddled* STUPEFIED, addled, befuddled, confused, muddled, bewildered, dazed, stunned, muzzy, groggy, foggy, fuzzy, vague, disorientated, disoriented, at sea; *informal* dopey, woozy, fazed, not with it, discombobulated.

fuddy-duddy noun *informal stop being such a fuddy-duddy and listen to the kids' music* (OLD) FOGEY, conservative, traditionalist, conformist; fossil, dinosaur, troglodyte, mossback, museum piece, stick-in-the-mud, square, stuffed shirt, dodo.

fudge verb **1** *the mayor tried to fudge the issue* EVADE, avoid, dodge, skirt, duck, gloss over; hedge on, prevaricate about, vacillate on, be noncommittal on, stall on, beat around the bush about, equivocate on, hem and haw on; *informal* cop out on, sit on the fence about; *rare* tergiversate about.

2 *the government has been fudging figures* ADJUST, manipulate, massage, put a spin on, juggle, misrepresent, misreport, bend; tamper with, tinker with, interfere with, doctor, falsify, distort; *informal* cook, fiddle with.

fuel noun **1** *the car ran out of fuel* GAS, gasoline, diesel, petroleum, propane; power source; *Brit.* petrol.

2 *she added more fuel to the fire* FIREWOOD, wood, kindling, logs; coal, coke, anthracite; oil, kerosene, propane, lighter fluid; heat source.

3 *we all need fuel to keep our bodies going* NOURISHMENT, food, sustenance, nutriment, nutrition.

4 *his antics added fuel to the opposition's cause* ENCOURAGEMENT, ammunition, stimulus, incentive; provocation, goading.

▸ verb 1 *power stations fueled by low-grade coal* POWER, fire, charge.

2 *the rumors fueled anxiety among opposition* FAN, feed, stoke up, inflame, intensify, stimulate, encourage, provoke, incite, whip up; sustain, keep alive.

fugitive noun *a hunted fugitive* ESCAPEE, runaway, deserter, absconder; refugee.

▸ adjective 1 *a fugitive criminal* ESCAPED, runaway, on the run, on the loose, at large; wanted; *informal* AWOL, on the lam.

2 *the fugitive nature of life* FLEETING, transient, transitory, ephemeral, fading, momentary, short-lived, short, brief, passing, impermanent, here today and gone tomorrow; *literary* evanescent.

fulfill verb 1 *she fulfilled a lifelong ambition to visit Israel* ACHIEVE, attain, realize, actualize, make happen, succeed in, bring to completion, bring to fruition, satisfy.

2 *she failed to fulfill her duties* CARRY OUT, perform, accomplish, execute, do, discharge, conduct; complete, finish, conclude, perfect.

3 *they fulfilled the criteria* MEET, satisfy, comply with, conform to, fill, answer.

fulfilled adjective *the new job has me feeling fulfilled* SATISFIED, content, contented, happy, pleased; serene, placid, untroubled, at ease, at peace. ANTONYM discontented.

full adjective 1 *her glass was full* FILLED, filled up, filled to capacity, filled to the brim, brimming, brimful. ANTONYM empty.

2 *streets **full of** people* CROWDED WITH, packed with, crammed with, congested with; teeming with, swarming with, thick with, thronged with, overcrowded with, overrun with; abounding with, bursting with, overflowing with; *informal* jam-packed with, wall-to-wall with, stuffed with, chockablock with, chock-full of, bursting at the seams with, packed to the gunwales with, awash with. ANTONYM empty.

3 *all the seats were full* OCCUPIED, taken, in use, unavailable. ANTONYMS empty, unoccupied.

4 *I'm full* REPLETE, full up, satisfied, well-fed, sated, satiated, surfeited; gorged, glutted; *informal* stuffed. ANTONYM hungry.

5 *she'd had a full life* EVENTFUL, interesting, exciting, lively, action-packed, busy, energetic, active. ANTONYM uneventful.

6 *a full list of available facilities* COMPREHENSIVE, thorough, exhaustive, all-inclusive, all-encompassing, all-embracing, in depth; complete, entire, whole, unabridged, uncut. ANTONYMS selective, incomplete.

7 *a fire engine driven at full speed* MAXIMUM, top, greatest, highest. ANTONYM low.

8 *she had a full figure* PLUMP, well-rounded, rounded, buxom, shapely, ample, curvaceous, voluptuous, womanly, Junoesque; *informal* busty, curvy, well-upholstered, well-endowed, zaftig. ANTONYM thin.

9 *a full skirt* LOOSE-FITTING, loose, baggy, voluminous, roomy, capacious, billowing. ANTONYMS tight, tight-fitting.

10 *his full baritone voice* RESONANT, rich, sonorous, deep, vibrant, full-bodied, strong, fruity, clear. ANTONYM thin.

11 *the full flavor of a Bordeaux* RICH, intense, full-bodied, strong, deep. ANTONYMS watery, thin.

▸ adverb 1 *she looked full into his face* DIRECTLY, right, straight, squarely, square, dead, point-blank; *informal* bang, plumb.

2 *you knew full well I was leaving* VERY, perfectly, quite; *informal* darn, damn, damned, darned; *chiefly Brit.* bloody.

PHRASES: **in full** *my letter was published in full* IN ITS ENTIRETY, in toto, in total, unabridged, uncut. **to the full** *live your life to the full* FULLY, thoroughly, completely, to the utmost, to the limit, to the maximum, for all one's worth.

full-blooded adjective *a full-blooded price war* UNCOMPROMISING, all-out, out and out, committed, vigorous, strenuous, intense; full-blown, unrestrained, uncontrolled, unbridled, hard-hitting, pulling no punches. ANTONYM halfhearted.

full-blown adjective *a full-blown crisis* FULLY DEVELOPED, full-scale, full-blooded, fully fledged, complete, total, thorough, entire; advanced.

full-bodied adjective *a full-bodied claret* FULL-FLAVORED, flavorful, full of flavor, rich, mellow, fruity, robust, strong, well-matured. ANTONYM tasteless.

full-grown adjective *how full-grown men can act so childishly is beyond me* ADULT, mature, grown-up, of age; fully grown, fully developed, fully fledged, in one's prime, in full bloom, ripe. ANTONYM infant.

fullness noun 1 *the fullness of the information they provide* COMPREHENSIVENESS, completeness, thoroughness, exhaustiveness, all-inclusiveness.

2 *the fullness of her body* PLUMPNESS, roundedness, roundness, shapeliness, curvaceousness, voluptuousness, womanliness; *informal* curviness.

3 *the recording has a fullness and warmth* RESONANCE, richness, intensity, depth, vibrancy, strength, clarity, three-dimensionality. PHRASE: **in the fullness of time** *in the fullness of time, Ricardo would realize they were right* IN DUE COURSE, when the time is ripe, eventually, in time, in time to come, one day, some day, sooner or later; ultimately, finally, in the end.

full-scale adjective 1 *a full-scale model* FULL-SIZE, life-size. ANTONYM small-scale.

2 *a full-scale public inquiry* THOROUGH, comprehensive, extensive, exhaustive, complete, all-out, all-encompassing, all-inclusive, all-embracing, thoroughgoing, wide-ranging, sweeping, in-depth, far-reaching. ANTONYM partial.

fully adverb 1 *I fully agree with him* COMPLETELY, entirely, wholly, totally, quite, utterly, perfectly, altogether, thoroughly, in all respects, in every respect, without reservation, without exception, to the hilt. ANTONYMS partly, nearly.

2 *fully two minutes must have passed* AT LEAST, no less

than, no fewer than, easily, without exaggeration. ANTONYM nearly.

fully fledged adjective *only fully fledged technicians should be working on the main transformers* TRAINED, qualified, proficient, experienced; mature, fully developed, full-grown. ANTONYM novice.

fulminate verb *homeowners fulminated against the tax hikes* PROTEST, rail against, rage about, rant about, thunder about, storm about, vociferate against, declaim, inveigh against, speak out against, make/take a stand against; denounce, decry, condemn, criticize, censure, disparage, attack, execrate; *informal* mouth off about; *formal* excoriate.

fulmination noun *the fulminations of media moralists* PROTEST, objection, complaint, rant, tirade, diatribe, harangue, invective, railing, obloquy; denunciation, condemnation, criticism, censure, attack, broadside, brickbats; *formal* excoriation; *literary* philippic.

fulsome adjective *he paid fulsome tribute to his secretary* EXCESSIVE, extravagant, overdone, immoderate, inordinate, over-appreciative, flattering, adulatory, fawning, unctuous, ingratiating, cloying, saccharine; enthusiastic, effusive, rapturous, glowing, gushing, profuse, generous, lavish; *informal* over the top, smarmy.

WORD NOTE **fulsome**

Revenge is a dish best savored when taken cold. At last, some years after writing *The Professor and the Madman,* I can now have my say in reply to those who accused me of misusing the word *fulsome.* I imagine I must have had 60 letters from readers, all professing outrage that in the book I had employed the phrase *The most fulsome remarks made about the volunteers . . .* and had in doing so misapplied and misunderstood the word grotesquely. *Fulsome,* they thundered, means "physically loathsome, foul, disgusting." How dare I to misuse it so—and in, of all places, *a book about words?* Does this not place the credibility of the entire book at stake? Well, I can reply at last: no it does not, because *fulsome* does mean exactly what I wanted it to mean: "abundant, plentiful, tending to cloying overabundance" usually used in reference to gross or excessive flattery, over-demonstrative affection, or the like. The readers who fulminated so were using out-of-date dictionaries, or prescriptive texts that demanded rather than described how words should, in the opinions of a small band of editors, be used. *Fulsome,* admittedly once laden with pejorative senses, has lately come to mean "abundant and excessive." Words evolve (as the *Oxford English Dictionary* constantly reminds us) and they do so evidently rather more rapidly than does the thinking and lexical understanding (this being the revenge, here supped on cold) of some of my correspondents. **—SW**

fumble verb **1** *she fumbled for her keys* GROPE, fish, search blindly, scrabble around.

2 *he fumbled about in the dark* STUMBLE, blunder, flounder, lumber, stagger, totter, lurch; **(fumble about/around)** feel one's way, grope one's way.

3 *the quarterback fumbled the ball* MISS, drop, mishandle, bobble.

4 *she fumbled her lines* MESS UP, make a mess of, bungle, mismanage, mishandle, spoil; *informal* make a hash of, fluff, botch, muff, flub.

▸ noun *a fumble from the goaltender* SLIP, mistake, error, gaffe; *informal* slip-up, boo-boo.

fume noun **(fumes) 1** *a fire giving off toxic fumes* SMOKE, vapor, gas, effluvium; exhaust; pollution.

2 *stale wine fumes* SMELL, odor, stink, reek, stench, fetor, funk; *literary* miasma.

▸ verb **1** *fragments of lava were fuming and sizzling* EMIT SMOKE, emit gas, smoke; *archaic* reek.

2 *Elsa was still fuming at his arrogance* BE FURIOUS, be enraged, be very angry, seethe, be livid, be incensed, boil, be beside oneself, spit; rage, rant and rave; *informal* be hot under the collar, foam at the mouth, see red.

fumigate verb *the prisoners' quarters are fumigated once a month* DISINFECT, purify, sterilize, sanitize, decontaminate, cleanse, clean out. ANTONYM soil.

fun noun **1** *I joined in with the fun did you have fun?* ENJOYMENT, entertainment, amusement, pleasure; jollification, merrymaking; recreation, diversion, leisure, relaxation; a good time, a great time; *informal* R and R (rest and recreation), a ball. ANTONYM boredom.

2 *she's full of fun* MERRIMENT, cheerfulness, cheeriness, jollity, joviality, jocularity, high spirits, gaiety, mirth, laughter, hilarity, glee, gladness, lightheartedness, levity. ANTONYM misery.

3 *he became a figure of fun* RIDICULE, derision, mockery, laughter, scorn, contempt, jeering, sneering, jibing, teasing, taunting. ANTONYM respect.

▸ adjective *informal a fun evening* ENJOYABLE, entertaining, amusing, diverting, pleasurable, pleasing, agreeable, interesting.

PHRASES: **in fun** *the teasing was all in fun* PLAYFUL, in jest, as a joke, tongue in cheek, lighthearted, for a laugh. **make fun of** *the kids who made fun of Marty were total jerks* TEASE, poke fun at, ridicule, mock, laugh at, taunt, jeer at, scoff at, deride; parody, lampoon, caricature, satirize; *informal* rib, kid, have on, pull someone's leg, send up, rag on, razz.

USAGE NOTE **fun**

The use of **fun** as an adjective meaning 'enjoyable,' as in *we had a fun evening*, is not fully accepted in standard English and should only be used in informal contexts. There are signs, however, that this situation is changing, given the recent appearance in American English of comparative and superlative forms **funner** and **funnest**, formed as if **fun** were a normal adjective. The adjectival forms **funner** and **funnest** have not 'arrived' in all the dictionaries, however, and if employed at all, they should be used sparingly and not in formal written English.

function noun **1** *the main function of the machine* PURPOSE, task, use, role.

2 *my function was to select and train the recruits* RESPONSIBILITY, duty, role, concern, province, activity, assignment, obligation, charge; task, job, mission, undertaking, commission; capacity, post, situation, office, occupation, employment, business.

3 *a function attended by local dignitaries* SOCIAL EVENT, party, social occasion, affair, gathering, reception, soiree, jamboree, gala, meet-and-greet; *informal* do, bash, shindig.

▸ verb **1** *the electrical system had ceased to function* WORK, go, run, be in working/running order, operate, be operative.

2 *the museum **functions as** an educational center* ACT AS, serve as, operate as; perform as, work as, play the role of, do duty as.

functional adjective **1** *a small functional kitchen* PRACTICAL, useful, utilitarian, utility, workaday, serviceable; minimalist, plain, simple, basic, modest, unadorned, unostentatious, no-frills, without frills; impersonal, characterless, soulless, institutional, clinical.

2 *the machine is now fully functional* WORKING, in working order, functioning, in service, in use; going, running, operative, operating, in operation, in commission, in action; *informal* up and running.

functionary noun *a Capitol Hill functionary* OFFICIAL, officeholder, public servant, civil servant, bureaucrat, administrator, apparatchik; *informal* bean counter.

fund noun **1** *an emergency fund for refugees* COLLECTION, kitty, reserve, pool, purse; endowment, foundation, trust, grant, investment; savings, nest egg; *informal* stash.

2 **(funds)** *I was very short of funds* MONEY, cash, ready money; wealth, means, assets, resources, savings, capital, reserves, the wherewithal; *informal* dough, bread, loot.

3 *his fund of stories* STOCK, store, supply, accumulation, collection, bank, pool; mine, reservoir, storehouse, treasury, treasure house, hoard, repository; *informal* pork barrel.

▸ verb *the agency was funded by a federal grant* FINANCE, pay for, back, capitalize, sponsor, put up the money for, subsidize, underwrite, endow, support, maintain; *informal* foot the bill for, pick up the tab for, bankroll, stake.

fundamental adjective *fundamental principles* BASIC, underlying, core, foundational, rudimentary, elemental, elementary, basal, root; primary, prime, cardinal, first, principal, chief, key, central, vital, essential, important, indispensable, necessary, crucial, pivotal, critical; structural, organic, constitutional, inherent, intrinsic. ANTONYMS secondary, unimportant.

fundamentally adverb *she was, fundamentally, a good person* ESSENTIALLY, in essence, basically, at heart, at bottom, deep down, au fond; primarily, above all, first and foremost, first of all; *informal* at the end of the day, when all is said and done, when you get right down to it.

fundamentals plural noun *the fundamentals of the job* BASICS, essentials, rudiments, foundations, basic principles, first principles, preliminaries; crux, crux of the matter, heart of the matter, essence, core, heart, base, bedrock; *informal* nuts and bolts, nitty-gritty, brass tacks, ABC, meat and potatoes.

funeral noun **1** *he'd attended a funeral* BURIAL, interment, entombment, committal, inhumation, laying to rest; cremation; obsequies, last offices, memorial service; *archaic* sepulture.

2 *informal ignore my advice if you like—it's your funeral* RESPONSIBILITY, problem, worry, concern, business, affair; *informal* headache.

funereal adjective **1** *the funereal atmosphere* SOMBER, gloomy, mournful, melancholy, lugubrious, sepulchral, miserable, doleful, woeful, sad, sorrowful, cheerless, joyless, bleak, dismal, depressing, dreary; grave, solemn, serious; *literary* dolorous. ANTONYM cheerful.

2 *funereal colors* DARK, black, drab.

fungus noun *the fungus will flourish in a dark, moist environment* MUSHROOM, toadstool; mold, mildew, rust; *Biology* saprophyte.

funk noun *he was in **a funk** because his wife ran out on him* A (STATE OF) DEPRESSION, a bad mood, a low, the dumps, the doldrums, a blue funk.

funky adjective **1** *Shannah liked funky music* GROOVY, bluesy, jazzy, syncopated.

2 *funky clothing* COOL, trendy, fashionable, hip, supercool.

3 *funky smell* UNPLEASANT, smelly; weird.

funnel noun **1** *fluid was poured through the funnel* TUBE, pipe, channel, conduit.

2 *smoke poured from the ship's funnels* CHIMNEY, flue, vent.

▸ verb *the money was funneled back into the forestry industry* CHANNEL, feed, direct, pump, convey, move, pass; pour, filter, trickle down.

funny adjective **1** *a funny movie these guys are really funny* AMUSING, humorous, witty, comic, comical, droll, facetious, jocular, jokey; hilarious, hysterical, riotous, uproarious; entertaining, diverting, sparkling, scintillating; silly, farcical, slapstick; *informal* side-splitting, rib-tickling, laugh-a-minute, wacky, zany, off the wall, a scream, rich, priceless; *informal, dated* killing. ANTONYMS serious, unamusing.

2 *a funny coincidence* STRANGE, peculiar, odd, queer, weird, bizarre, curious, freakish, freak, quirky; mysterious, mystifying, puzzling, perplexing; unusual, uncommon, anomalous, irregular, abnormal, exceptional, singular, out of the ordinary, extraordinary.

3 *there's something funny about him* SUSPICIOUS, suspect, dubious, untrustworthy, questionable; *informal* shady, sketchy, fishy. ANTONYM trustworthy.

fur noun *coarse brown hair* HAIR, wool; coat, fleece, pelt; *Zoology* pelage.

furious adjective **1** *she was furious when she learned about it* ENRAGED, infuriated, very angry, irate, incensed, raging, incandescent, fuming, ranting, raving, seething, beside oneself, outraged; *informal* mad, hopping mad, wild, livid, boiling, apoplectic, hot under the collar, on the warpath, foaming at the mouth, steamed up, fit to be tied; *literary* wrathful. ANTONYM calm.

2 *a furious debate* HEATED, hot, passionate, fiery, "lively"; fierce, vehement, violent, wild, unrestrained, tumultuous, turbulent, tempestuous, stormy. ANTONYM calm.

furnish verb **1** *the bedrooms are elegantly furnished* FIT OUT, provide with furniture, appoint, outfit.

2 *grooms furnished us with horses for our journey* SUPPLY, provide, equip, provision, issue, kit out, present, give, offer, afford, purvey, bestow; *informal* fix up.

furniture noun *most of the bedroom furniture is mahogany* FURNISHINGS, fittings, movables, appointments, effects; *Law* chattels; *informal* stuff, things.

furor noun *her memoirs caused a furor* COMMOTION, uproar, outcry, fuss, upset, brouhaha, foofaraw, palaver, pother, tempest, agitation, pandemonium, disturbance, hubbub, rumpus, tumult, turmoil; stir, excitement; *informal* song and dance, to-do, hoo-ha, hullabaloo, ballyhoo, flap, stink.

furrow noun **1** *furrows in a plowed field* GROOVE, trench, rut, trough, channel, hollow.

2 *the furrows on either side of her mouth* WRINKLE, line, crease, crinkle, crow's foot, corrugation.

▸ verb *his brow furrowed* WRINKLE, crease, line, crinkle, pucker, screw up, scrunch up, corrugate.

furry adjective *a furry little mouse* COVERED WITH FUR, hairy, downy, fleecy, soft, fluffy, fuzzy, woolly.

further adverb **1** *further information* ADDITIONAL, more, extra, supplementary, supplemental, other; new, fresh.

2 *further, it gave him an excellent excuse not to attend.* See FURTHERMORE.

3 *she's transferring to a school further from home.* See FARTHER.

▸ adjective *the further end of the hall.* See FARTHER.

▸ verb *an attempt to further his career* PROMOTE, advance, forward, develop, facilitate, aid, assist, help, help along, lend a hand to, abet; expedite, hasten, speed up, catalyze, accelerate, step up, spur on, oil the wheels of, give a push to, boost, encourage, cultivate, nurture, foster. See note at FARTHER. ANTONYM impede.

furtherance noun *the furtherance of his business interests* PROMOTION, furthering, advancement, forwarding, development, facilitation, aiding, assisting, helping, abetting; hastening, acceleration, boosting, encouragement, cultivation, nurturing, fostering. ANTONYM hindrance.

furthermore adverb *furthermore, you'll have access to a better library* MOREOVER, further, what's more, also, additionally, in addition, besides, as well, too, to boot, on top of that, over and above that, into the bargain, by the same token; *archaic* withal.

furthest adjective *the furthest car on the left is mine.* See FARTHEST.

▸ adverb *Lynda had to walk the furthest.* See FARTHEST. See note at FARTHER.

furtive adjective *they met in seedy dives to craft their furtive plans* SECRETIVE, secret, surreptitious, clandestine, hidden, covert, conspiratorial, cloak-and-dagger, backroom, backstairs, sly, sneaky, under-the-table; sidelong, sideways, oblique, indirect; *informal* hush-hush, shifty. See note at SECRET. ANTONYM open.

fury noun **1** *she exploded with fury* RAGE, anger, wrath, outrage, spleen, temper; crossness, indignation, umbrage, annoyance, exasperation; *literary* ire, choler. ANTONYM good humor.

2 *the fury of the storm* FIERCENESS, ferocity, violence, turbulence, tempestuousness, savagery; severity, intensity, vehemence, force, forcefulness, power, strength. ANTONYM mildness.

3 *she turned on her mother like a fury* VIRAGO, hellcat, termagant, spitfire, vixen, shrew, harridan, dragon, gorgon; **(Furies)** *Greek Mythology* Eumenides.

fuse verb **1** *a band that fuses rap with rock* COMBINE, amalgamate, put together, join, unite, marry, blend, merge, meld, mingle, integrate, intermix, intermingle, synthesize; coalesce, compound, alloy; *technical* admix; *literary* commingle. ANTONYM separate.

2 *metal fused to a base of colored glass* BOND, stick, bind, weld, solder; melt, smelt. ANTONYM disconnect.

fusillade noun *a fusillade of missiles* SALVO, volley, barrage, bombardment, cannonade, battery, burst, blast, hail, shower, rain, stream; *historical* broadside.

fusion noun *the fusion of cells* BLEND, blending, combination, amalgamation, joining, union, marrying, bonding, merging, melding, mingling, integration, intermixture, intermingling, synthesis; coalescence.

fuss noun **1** *what's all the fuss about?* ADO, excitement, agitation, pother, stir, commotion, confusion, disturbance, brouhaha, uproar, furor, palaver, foofaraw, tempest in a teapot, much ado about nothing; bother, fluster, flurry, bustle; *informal* hoo-ha, to-do, ballyhoo, song and dance, performance, pantomime.

2 *they settled in with very little fuss* BOTHER, trouble, inconvenience, effort, exertion, labor; *informal* hassle.

3 *he didn't put up a fuss* PROTEST, complaint, objection, grumble, grouse; *informal* gripe.

▸ verb *he was still* ***fussing over*** *his clothes* WORRY ABOUT, fret about, be anxious about, be agitated about, make a big thing out of; *informal* flap about, be in a tizzy over/about, be in a stew over/about.

fussbudget noun *informal* *he's such a fussfudget, he gets upset if one hair is out of place* FUSSY PERSON, worrier, perfectionist, stickler, grumbler; *informal* nitpicker, old woman, fuss, fusspot.

fussy adjective **1** *he's very fussy about what he eats* FINICKY, particular, overparticular, fastidious, discriminating, selective, dainty; hard to please, difficult, exacting, demanding; faddish; *informal* persnickety, choosy, picky.

2 *a fussy, frilly bridal gown* OVERELABORATE, overdecorated, ornate, fancy, overdone; busy, cluttered.

fusty adjective **1** *the room smelt fusty* STALE, musty, dusty; stuffy, airless, unventilated; damp, mildewed, mildewy. ANTONYMS fresh, airy.

2 *a fusty conservative* OLD-FASHIONED, out of date, outdated, behind the times, antediluvian, backward-looking; fogeyish; *informal* square, uncool. ANTONYMS modern, up-to-date.

futile adjective *they piled on thousands of sandbags in a futile attempt to hold back the river* FRUITLESS, vain, pointless, useless, ineffectual, ineffective, inefficacious, to no effect, of no use, in vain, to no avail, unavailing; unsuccessful, failed, thwarted; unproductive, barren, unprofitable, abortive; impotent, hollow, empty, forlorn, idle, hopeless; *archaic* bootless. ANTONYM useful.

futility noun *the futility of his actions* FRUITLESSNESS, pointlessness, uselessness, vanity, ineffectiveness, inefficacy; failure, barrenness, unprofitability; impotence, hollowness, emptiness, forlornness, hopelessness.

future noun **1** *his plans for* ***the future*** THE TIME TO COME, the time ahead; what lies ahead, (the) coming times. ANTONYM past.

2 *she knew her future lay in acting* DESTINY, fate, fortune; prospects, expectations, chances.

▸ adjective **1** *a future date* LATER, to come, following, ensuing, succeeding, subsequent, coming.

2 *his future wife* TO BE, destined; intended, planned, prospective.

PHRASE: **in future** *in future, let's bring plenty of extra batteries* FROM NOW ON, after this, in the future, from this day forward, hence, henceforward, subsequently, in time to come, down the road; *formal* hereafter.

fuzz noun *the soft fuzz on his cheeks* HAIR, down; fur, fluff, fleeciness; *informal* peach fuzz.

fuzzy adjective **1** *her fuzzy hair* FRIZZY, fluffy, woolly; downy, soft.

2 *a fuzzy picture* BLURRY, blurred, indistinct, unclear, bleary, misty, distorted, out of focus, unfocused, lacking definition, nebulous; ill-defined, indefinite, vague, hazy, imprecise, inexact, loose, woolly.

3 *my mind was fuzzy* CONFUSED, muddled, addled, fuddled, befuddled, groggy, disoriented, disorientated, mixed up, fazed, foggy, dizzy, stupefied, benumbed.

G

gab *informal* verb *they were all gabbing away like crazy* CHATTER, chitter-chatter, chat, talk, gossip, gabble, babble, prattle, jabber, blather, blab; *informal* yak, yackety-yak, yabber, yatter, yammer, blabber, blah-blah, jaw, gas, mouth off, natter, run off at the mouth. PHRASE: **the gift of (the) gab** *Reverend Lilly was a charming young man blessed with the gift of gab* ELOQUENCE, fluency, expressiveness, a silver tongue; persuasiveness; *informal* a way with words, blarney.

gabble verb *he gabbled on in a panicky way* JABBER, babble, prattle, rattle, blabber, gibber, blab, drivel, twitter, sputter.

▸ noun *the boozy gabble of the crowd* JABBERING, babbling, chattering, gibbering, babble, chatter, rambling.

gabby adjective *informal* See TALKATIVE.

gad verb *informal she's been **gadding about** in Europe* GALLIVANT ABOUT, traipse around, flit around, run around, travel around, roam (about/around).

gadabout noun *informal Marc and Patty linked up with some other gadabouts in Paris* PLEASURE-SEEKER; traveler, globetrotter, wanderer, drifter.

gadget noun *Everett had to buy every new gadget on the market* APPLIANCE, apparatus, instrument, implement, tool, utensil, contrivance, contraption, machine, mechanism, device, labor-saving device, convenience, invention; *informal* gizmo, widget. See table at APPLIANCE.

gaffe noun *I made some real gaffes at work* BLUNDER, mistake, error, slip, faux pas, indiscretion, impropriety, miscalculation, gaucherie, solecism; *informal* slip-up, howler, boo-boo, fluff, flub, blooper, goof.

gag[1] verb **1** *a dirty rag was used to gag her mouth* SMOTHER, block, plug, stifle, stop up, muffle.

2 *the government tried to gag its critics* SILENCE, muzzle, mute, muffle, suppress, stifle; censor, curb, check, restrain, fetter, shackle, restrict.

3 *the stench made her gag* RETCH, heave, dry-heave.

▸ noun *his scream was muffled by the gag* MUZZLE, tie, restraint.

gag[2] noun *informal a film full of lame gags* JOKE, jest, witticism, quip, pun, play on words, double entendre; practical joke, stunt, lark; *informal* crack, wisecrack, one-liner.

gaiety noun **1** *the gaiety of Susannah's youth had been supplanted by the cares of widowhood* CHEERFULNESS, lightheartedness, happiness, merriment, glee, gladness, joy, joie de vivre, joyfulness, joyousness, delight, high spirits, good spirits, good humor, cheeriness, jollity, mirth, joviality, exuberance, elation; liveliness, vivacity, animation, effervescence, sprightliness, zest, zestfulness; *informal* chirpiness, bounce, pep; *literary* blitheness. ANTONYM misery.

2 *the hotel restaurant was a scene of gaiety* MERRYMAKING, festivity, fun, fun and games, frolics, revelry, jollification, celebration, pleasure; *informal* partying; *dated* sport.

gaily adverb **1** *she skipped gaily along the path* MERRILY, cheerfully, cheerily, happily, joyfully, joyously, blithely, jauntily, gleefully.

2 *gaily painted boats* BRIGHTLY, colorfully, brilliantly.

gain verb **1** *he gained a scholarship to the college* OBTAIN, get, secure, acquire, come by, procure, attain, achieve, earn, win, garner, capture, clinch, pick up, carry off, reap; *informal* land, net, bag, scoop, wangle, swing, walk away/off with. See note at GET. ANTONYM lose.

2 *they stood to gain from the deal* PROFIT, make money, reap benefits, benefit, do well; *informal* make a killing. ANTONYM lose.

3 *the dog gained weight* PUT ON, increase in. ANTONYM lose.

4 *the others were **gaining on** us* CATCH UP WITH/ON, catch someone up, catch, close (in) on, near.

5 *we finally gained the ridge* REACH, arrive at, get to, come to, make, attain, set foot on; *informal* hit, wind up at.

▸ noun **1** *his gain from the deal* PROFIT, advantage, benefit, reward; percentage, takings, yield, return, winnings, receipts, proceeds, dividend, interest; *informal* pickings, cut, take, divvy, slice, piece of the pie. ANTONYM loss.

2 *a price gain of 7.5 percent* INCREASE, rise, increment, augmentation, addition. ANTONYM decrease.

PHRASE: **gain time** *the district attorney had run out of plausible ways to gain time* PLAY FOR TIME, stall, procrastinate, delay, temporize, hold back, hang back, hang fire, dally, drag one's feet.

gainful adjective *a gainful investment* PROFITABLE, paid, well-paid, remunerative, lucrative, moneymaking; rewarding, fruitful, worthwhile, useful, productive, constructive, beneficial, advantageous, valuable.

gainsay verb *formal* *it was difficult to gainsay his claim* DENY, dispute, disagree with, argue with, dissent from, contradict, repudiate, challenge, oppose, contest, counter, controvert, rebut. ANTONYM confirm.

gait noun *there was a new liveliness to her gait* WALK, step, stride, pace, tread, bearing, carriage; *formal* comportment.

gala noun *the annual summer gala* FÊTE, fair, festival, carnival, pageant, jubilee, jamboree, party, garden party, celebration; festivities.

▸ adjective *a gala occasion* FESTIVE, celebratory, merry, joyous, joyful; diverting, entertaining, enjoyable, spectacular.

galaxy noun *the search for life in other galaxies* STAR SYSTEM, solar system, constellation; stars, heavens.

gale noun **1** *a howling gale.* See STORM noun sense 1.

2 *gales of laughter* PEAL, howl, hoot, shriek, scream, roar; outburst, burst, fit, paroxysm, explosion.

gall[1] noun **1** *she had the gall to ask for money* EFFRONTERY, impudence, impertinence, cheek, cheekiness, insolence, audacity, temerity, presumption, cockiness, nerve, shamelessness, disrespect, bad manners; *informal* face, chutzpah; sauce, sass. See note at TEMERITY.

2 *scholarly gall was poured on this work* BITTERNESS, resentment, rancor, bile, spleen, malice, spite, spitefulness, malignity, venom, vitriol, poison.

gall[2] noun **1** *this was a gall that she frequently had to endure* IRRITATION, irritant, annoyance, vexation, nuisance, provocation, bother, torment, plague, thorn in one's side/flesh; *informal* aggravation, bore, headache, hassle, pain, pain in the neck, pain in the butt.

2 *a bay horse with a gall on its side* SORE, ulcer, ulceration; abrasion, scrape, scratch, graze, chafe.

▸ verb *it galled him that he had to wake early* IRRITATE, annoy, vex, anger, infuriate, exasperate, irk, pique, nettle, put out, displease, antagonize, get on someone's nerves, make someone's hackles rise, rub the wrong way; *informal* aggravate, peeve, miff, rile, needle, get (to), bug, get someone's goat, get/put someone's back up, get someone's dander up, drive mad/crazy, drive round/around the bend, drive up the wall, tee off, tick off, rankle.

gallant adjective **1** *his gallant countrymen* BRAVE, courageous, valiant, valorous, bold, plucky, daring, fearless, intrepid, heroic, lionhearted, stouthearted, doughty, mettlesome, dauntless, undaunted, unflinching, unafraid; *informal* gutsy, spunky. ANTONYM cowardly.

2 *her gallant companion* CHIVALROUS, princely, gentlemanly, honorable, courteous, polite, mannerly, attentive, respectful, gracious, considerate, thoughtful. ANTONYM discourteous.

gallantry noun **1** *he received medals for gallantry* BRAVERY, courage, courageousness, valor, pluck, pluckiness, nerve, daring, boldness, fearlessness, dauntlessness, intrepidity, heroism, mettle, grit, stoutheartedness; *informal* guts, spunk, moxie.

2 *she acknowledged his selfless gallantry* CHIVALRY, chivalrousness, gentlemanliness, courtesy, courteousness, politeness, good manners, attentiveness, graciousness, respectfulness, respect.

gallery noun **1** *the art gallery* MUSEUM; exhibition room, display room.

2 *they sat up in the gallery* BALCONY, circle, dress circle, loges; *informal* gods.

3 *a long gallery with doors along each side* PASSAGE, passageway, corridor, walkway, arcade.

galling adjective *his hypocrisy was galling* ANNOYING, irritating, vexing, vexatious, infuriating, maddening, irksome, provoking, exasperating, trying, tiresome, troublesome, bothersome, displeasing, disagreeable; *informal* aggravating.

gallivant verb *my days of gallivanting are long past* FLIT, jaunt, run; roam, wander, travel, rove; *informal* gad.

gallop verb *Paul galloped across the clearing* RUSH, race, run, sprint, bolt, dart, dash, career, charge, shoot, hurtle, careen, hare, fly, speed, zoom, streak; *informal* tear, belt, pelt, scoot, zip, whip, hotfoot it, hightail it, bomb, barrel. ANTONYM amble.

gallows plural noun **1** *the wooden gallows* GIBBET, scaffold, gallows tree.

2 *they were condemned to* ***the gallows*** HANGING, being hanged, the noose, the rope, the gibbet, the scaffold, execution.

galore adjective *up in the attic were old trunks and hatboxes galore* APLENTY, in abundance, in profusion, in great quantities, in large numbers, by the dozen; to spare; everywhere, all over (the place); *informal* by the truckload.

galvanize verb *the reverend's words galvanized our group into action* JOLT, shock, startle, impel, stir, spur, prod, urge, motivate, stimulate, electrify, excite, rouse, arouse, awaken; invigorate, fire, animate, vitalize, energize, exhilarate, thrill, catalyze, inspire, light a fire under; *informal* give someone a shot in the arm.

gambit noun *the most ambitious financial gambit in history* STRATAGEM, scheme, plan, tactic, maneuver, move, course/line of action, device; machination, ruse, trick, ploy, wangle.

gamble verb **1** *he started to gamble more often* BET, place/lay a bet on something, stake money on something, back the horses, game; *informal* play the ponies.

2 *investors are gambling that the British pound will fall* TAKE A CHANCE, take a risk; *informal* stick one's neck out, go out on a limb.

▸ noun **1** *his grandfather enjoyed a gamble* BET, wager, speculation; game of chance.

2 *I took a gamble and it paid off* RISK, chance, hazard, shot in the dark, leap of faith; pig in a poke, pot luck; *rare* salto.

WORD NOTE salto

Throw the moldy journalistic "leap of faith" out of your phrase closet, and replace it with this, its exact synonym. If you want to speak not figuratively but practically, it has a couple of real-life applications. It will also do for any daring or flying leaps you make in the world, and if you are a gymnast, it sounds more vigorous than the usual somersault. **–ZS**

gambol verb *lambs gamboled in the pasture* FROLIC, frisk, cavort, caper, skip, dance, romp, prance, leap, hop, jump, spring, bound, bounce; play; *dated* sport.

game noun **1** *Andrew and his friends invented a new*

game PASTIME, diversion, entertainment, amusement, distraction, divertissement, recreation, sport, activity. See table. See also table at CARD.

2 *the team hasn't lost a game all season* MATCH, contest, tournament, meet; final, playoff.

3 *I spoiled his little game* SCHEME, plot, ploy, stratagem, strategy, gambit, tactics; trick, device, maneuver, wile, dodge, ruse, machination, contrivance, subterfuge; prank, practical joke; *informal* scam; *archaic* shift.

4 *she lived off fish and game* WILD ANIMALS, wild fowl, big game.

▸ adjective **1** *they weren't game enough to join in* BRAVE, courageous, plucky, bold, daring, intrepid, valiant, stouthearted, mettlesome; fearless, dauntless, undaunted, unflinching; *informal* gutsy, spunky.

2 *I need a bit of help—are you game?* WILLING, prepared, ready, disposed, of a mind; eager, keen, enthusiastic, up for it.

▸ verb *they were drinking and gaming all evening* GAMBLE, bet, place/lay bets.

GAMES

Children's Games	Table Games and Board Games
blindman's bluff/buff	air hockey
catch	backgammon
cat's cradle	bagatelle
charades	Battleship™
cops and robbers	billiards
cowboys and Indians	bingo
dodge ball	Boggle™
double dutch	Candyland™
duck, duck, goose	checkers
follow-the-leader	chess
four square	Chinese checkers
freeze tag	Chutes and Ladders™
hangman	Clue™
hide-and-seek	dominoes
hopscotch	foosball
jacks	go
kickball	jigsaw puzzle
kick the can	kriegspiel
leapfrog	Life™
marbles	Monopoly™
monkey in the middle	Operation™
musical chairs	pachisi/Parcheesi™
pin the tail on the donkey	pickup sticks
red light, green light	pinball
Red Rover	pool
ring-around-the-rosie	Risk™
Simon Says	Rummy Kub™
spud	Scrabble™
tag	Sorry!™
telephone	table-top hockey
tetherball	Trivial Pursuit™
tic-tac-toe	Yahtzee™
tiddlywinks	
tug of war	
twenty questions	
Twister™	

gamin, fem. gamine noun *dated the gamins that inhabit the alley* URCHIN, ragamuffin, waif, stray; *derogatory* guttersnipe.

gamut noun *the complete gamut of human emotion* RANGE, spectrum, span, scope, sweep, compass, area, breadth, reach, extent, catalog, scale; variety. See note at RANGE.

gang noun **1** *a gang of tough-looking boys* BAND, group, crowd, pack, horde, throng, mob, herd, swarm, troop, cluster; company, gathering; *informal* posse, bunch, gaggle, load.

2 *informal Shania was one of our gang* CIRCLE, social circle, social set, group, clique, in-crowd, coterie, cabal, lot, ring; *informal* crew, rat pack.

3 *a gang of workmen* CREW, team, group, squad, shift, detachment, unit.

▸ verb *they all* ***ganged up*** *to put me down* CONSPIRE, cooperate, collude, work together, act together, combine, join forces, team up, get together, unite, ally.

gangling, gangly adjective *she's no longer a gangling teenager with braces* LANKY, rangy, tall, thin, skinny, spindly, stringy, bony, angular, scrawny, spare; awkward, uncoordinated, ungainly, gawky, inelegant, graceless, ungraceful; *dated* spindle-shanked. ANTONYM squat.

gangster noun *Prohibition was a boon era for gangsters* HOODLUM, gang member, racketeer, robber, ruffian, thug, tough, villain, lawbreaker, criminal; gunman; Mafioso; *informal* mobster, crook, lowlife, hit man, hood; *dated* desperado.

gap noun **1** *a gap in the shutters* OPENING, aperture, space, breach, chink, slit, slot, vent, crack, crevice, cranny, cavity, hole, orifice, interstice, perforation, break, fracture, rift, rent, fissure, cleft, divide.

2 *a gap between meetings* PAUSE, intermission, interval, interlude, break, breathing space, breather, respite, hiatus, recess.

3 *a gap in our records* OMISSION, blank, lacuna, void, vacuity.

4 *the gap between rich and poor* CHASM, gulf, rift, split, separation, breach; contrast, difference, disparity, divergence, imbalance.

gape verb **1** *she gaped at him in astonishment* STARE, stare open-mouthed, stare in wonder, goggle, gaze, ogle; *informal* rubberneck, gawk.

2 *a padded coat that gaped at every seam* OPEN WIDE, open up, yawn; part, split.

gaping adjective *a gaping hole* CAVERNOUS, yawning, wide, broad; vast, huge, enormous, immense, extensive.

garage noun **1** *he let them park in his garage* CARPORT.

2 *she took her car to the garage* SERVICE STATION, gas station.

3 *a new bus garage was to be built* DEPOT, station, terminus, terminal, base, headquarters.

garage sale noun *we spent all morning going to garage sales* YARD SALE, tag sale, lawn sale; rummage sale, white elephant sale.

garb noun *men and women in riding garb* CLOTHES, clothing, garments, attire, dress, costume, outfit, wear, uniform, livery, regalia; *informal* gear, getup, togs, duds; *formal* apparel; *archaic* raiment, habiliment, vestments.

▸ verb *both men were garbed in black* DRESS, clothe, attire, fit out, turn out, deck (out), costume, robe; *informal* get up; *archaic* apparel.

garbage noun **1** *the garbage is taken to landfill sites* TRASH, rubbish, refuse, waste, detritus, litter, junk, scrap; scraps, leftovers, remains, slops; *informal* crap.

2 *most of what he says is garbage* NONSENSE, balderdash, claptrap, twaddle, blather; dross, rubbish; *informal* hogwash, baloney, tripe, jive, bilge, bull, crap, bunk, poppycock, piffle, bunkum.

garble verb *the message was garbled in transmission* MIX UP, muddle, jumble, confuse, obscure, distort, scramble; misstate, misquote, misreport, misrepresent, mistranslate, misinterpret, misconstrue, twist.

garden noun PLOT, bed, patch; flower bed, flower garden, vegetable garden, herb garden; victory garden; *chiefly Brit.* yard, lawn. PHRASE: **lead someone up the garden path** *informal he led her up the garden path and then disappeared with her savings* DECEIVE, mislead, delude, hoodwink, dupe, trick, entrap, beguile, take in, fool, pull the wool over someone's eyes, gull; *informal* con, pull a fast one on, string along, take for a ride, put one over on.

gardening noun *gardening is their favorite weekend pursuit* HORTICULTURE, yardwork, landscaping.

gargantuan adjective *a gargantuan wedding cake* HUGE, enormous, vast, gigantic, very big, giant, massive, colossal, mammoth, immense, mighty, monumental, mountainous, titanic, towering, tremendous, elephantine, king-size(d), economy-size(d), prodigious; *informal* mega, monster, whopping, humongous, jumbo, ginormous. ANTONYM tiny.

garish adjective *garish party decorations* GAUDY, lurid, loud, harsh, glaring, violent, showy, glittering, brassy, brash; tasteless, in bad taste, tawdry, vulgar, unattractive, bilious; *informal* flash, flashy, tacky, tinselly, neon. ANTONYM drab.

garland noun *a garland of flowers* FESTOON, lei, wreath, ring, circle, swag; coronet, crown, coronal, chaplet, fillet.

▸ verb *gardens garlanded with colored lights* FESTOON, wreathe, swathe, hang; adorn, ornament, embellish, decorate, deck, trim, dress, bedeck, array; *literary* bedizen.

garment noun *the brown tweed is a lovely garment* | *all of her garments seem to be red* ITEM OF CLOTHING, article of clothing; *informal* getup; (**garments**) clothes, clothing, dress, garb, outfit, costume, attire; *informal* gear, togs, duds, threads; *formal* apparel.

garner verb *Edward garnered ideas from his travels* GATHER, collect, accumulate, amass, assemble, reap.

garnish verb *garnish the dish with chopped parsley* DECORATE, adorn, ornament, trim, dress, embellish; enhance, grace, beautify, prettify, add the finishing touch to.

▸ noun *keep a few sprigs for a garnish* DECORATION, adornment, trim, trimming, ornament, ornamentation, embellishment, enhancement, finishing touch; *Cooking* chiffonade.

garret noun *there were two straw beds in the garret* LOFT, attic, mansard.

garrison noun **1** *the enemy garrison had been burned alive* TROOPS, militia, soldiers, forces; armed force, military detachment, unit, platoon, brigade, squadron, battalion, corps.

2 *forces from three garrisons* FORTRESS, fort, fortification, stronghold, citadel, camp, encampment, cantonment, command post, base, station; barracks.

▸ verb **1** *French infantry garrisoned the town* DEFEND, guard, protect, barricade, shield, secure; man, occupy.

2 *troops were garrisoned in various regions* STATION, post, put on duty, deploy, assign, install; base, site, place, position; billet.

garrulous adjective **1** *a garrulous old man* TALKATIVE, loquacious, voluble, verbose, chatty, chattering, gossipy; effusive, expansive, forthcoming, conversational, communicative; *informal* mouthy, gabby, gassy, windy, having the gift of the gab, motormouthed. See note at TALKATIVE. ANTONYMS taciturn, reticent.

2 *his garrulous reminiscences* LONG-WINDED, wordy, verbose, prolix, long, lengthy, rambling, wandering, maundering, meandering, digressive, diffuse, discursive; gossipy, chatty; *informal* windy, gassy. ANTONYM concise.

gas noun *the car uses only unleaded gas* FUEL, gasoline; *Brit.* petrol; *informal* juice.

gash noun *a gash on his forehead* LACERATION, cut, wound, injury, slash, tear, incision; slit, split, rip, rent; scratch, scrape, graze, abrasion; *Medicine* lesion.

▸ verb *he gashed his hand on some broken glass* LACERATE, cut (open), wound, injure, hurt, slash, tear, gouge, puncture, slit, split, rend; scratch, scrape, graze, abrade.

gasoline noun. See GAS.

gasp verb **1** *I gasped in surprise* CATCH ONE'S BREATH, draw in one's breath, gulp; exclaim, cry (out).

2 *she collapsed on the ground, gasping* PANT, puff, wheeze, breathe hard, choke, fight for breath.

▸ noun *a gasp of dismay* GULP; exclamation, cry; sharp inhalation.

gas station noun *stop at the gas station and check the oil* service station, filling station.

gastric adjective *gastric pain* STOMACH, intestinal, enteric, duodenal, celiac, abdominal, ventral.

gate noun *they barged threw the gate without stopping* GATEWAY, doorway, entrance, entryway; exit, egress, opening; door, portal; barrier, turnstile.

gather verb **1** *we gathered in the hotel lobby* CONGREGATE, assemble, meet, collect, come/get together, convene, muster, rally, converge; cluster together, crowd, mass, flock together. ANTONYM scatter.

2 *she* ***gathered*** *her family* ***together*** SUMMON, call together, bring together, assemble, convene, rally, round up, muster, marshal. ANTONYM disperse.

3 *knickknacks he had gathered over the years* COLLECT, accumulate, amass, garner, accrue; store, stockpile, hoard, put away/by, lay by/in; *informal* stash away, squirrel away.

4 *they gathered corn from the fields* HARVEST, reap, crop; pick, pluck; collect.

5 *the show soon gathered a fanatical following* ATTRACT, draw, pull, pull in, collect, pick up.

6 *I gather that environmentalism is the hot issue* UNDERSTAND, be given to understand, believe, be led to believe, think, conclude, deduce, infer, assume, take it, surmise, fancy; hear, hear tell, learn, discover.

7 *he gathered her to his chest* CLASP, clutch, pull, embrace, enfold, hold, hug, cuddle, squeeze; *literary* embosom.

8 *his tunic was gathered at the waist* PLEAT, shirr, pucker, tuck, fold, ruffle.

THE RIGHT WORD

Gather is the most general of these terms meaning to come or bring together. It implies bringing widely scattered things or people to one place but with no particular arrangement (*to gather shells at the beach; to gather the fam-*

ily in the living room). **Collect**, on the other hand, implies both selectivity (*to collect evidence for the trial*) and organization (*to collect butterflies as a hobby*). To *gather* one's thoughts means to bring them together because they have been previously scattered; to *collect* one's thoughts is to organize them. **Assemble** pertains to objects or people who are brought together for a purpose (*to assemble data for a report; to assemble Congress so that legislation will be passed*), while **congregate** may be more spontaneous, done as a free choice (*people congregated in front of the palace, hoping to catch a glimpse of the queen*). **Convene** is a formal word meaning to *assemble* or meet in a body (*to convene an international conference on the subject of global warming*) **Marshal** and **muster** are usually thought of as military terms. *Muster* implies bringing together the parts or units of a force (*troops mustered for inspection*), and *marshal* suggests a very orderly and purposeful arrangement (*to marshal the allied forces along the battle front*).

---

gathering noun **1** *she rose to address the gathering* ASSEMBLY, meeting, convention, rally, turnout, congress, convocation, conclave, council, synod, forum; congregation, audience, crowd, group, throng, mass, multitude; *informal* get-together; *formal* concourse.

2 *the gathering of data for a future book* COLLECTING, collection, garnering, amassing, compilation, accumulation, accrual, cumulation, building up.

gauche adjective *Rose was embarrassed by her gauche relatives* AWKWARD, gawky, inelegant, graceless, ungraceful, ungainly, maladroit, klutzy, inept; lacking in social grace(s), unsophisticated, uncultured, uncultivated, unrefined, raw, inexperienced, unworldly. ANTONYMS elegant, sophisticated.

gaudy adjective *the motel rooms were clean but howlingly gaudy* GARISH, lurid, loud, overbright, glaring, harsh, violent, showy, glittering, brassy, ostentatious; tasteless, in bad taste, tawdry, vulgar, unattractive, bilious; *informal* flash, flashy, tacky, kitsch, kitschy. ANTONYMS drab, tasteful.

gauge noun **1** *the temperature gauge* MEASURING DEVICE, measuring instrument, meter, measure; indicator, dial, scale, display.

2 *exports are an important gauge of economic activity* MEASURE, indicator, barometer, point of reference, guide, guideline, touchstone, yardstick, benchmark, criterion, test, litmus test.

3 *guitar strings of a different gauge* SIZE, diameter, thickness, width, breadth; measure, capacity, magnitude; bore, caliber.

▸ verb **1** *astronomers can gauge the star's intrinsic brightness* MEASURE, calculate, compute, work out, determine, ascertain; count, weigh, quantify, put a figure on, pin down.

2 *it is difficult to gauge how effective the ban was* ASSESS, evaluate, determine, estimate, form an opinion of, appraise, get the measure of, judge, guess; *informal* guesstimate, size up.

gaunt adjective **1** *a gaunt, graying man* HAGGARD, drawn, thin, lean, skinny, spindly, spare, bony, angular, rawboned, pinched, hollow-cheeked, scrawny, scraggy, as thin as a rail, cadaverous, skeletal, emaciated, skin-and-bones; wasted, withered, etiolated; *informal* like a bag of bones; *dated* spindle-shanked. See note at THIN. ANTONYM plump.

2 *the gaunt ruin of the dark tower* BLEAK, stark, desolate, bare, gloomy, dismal, somber, grim, stern, harsh, forbidding, uninviting, cheerless. ANTONYM cheerful.

gauzy adjective *a gauzy summer fabric* TRANSLUCENT, transparent, sheer, see-through, fine, delicate, flimsy, filmy, gossamer, diaphanous, chiffony, wispy, thin, light, insubstantial, floaty. ANTONYMS opaque, thick.

gawk verb *informal I somehow managed not to gawk at his gorgeous roommate* GAPE, goggle, gaze, ogle, stare, stare open-mouthed; *informal* rubberneck.

gawky adjective *how can you convince a fourteen-year-old boy that he will not always be so gawky?* AWKWARD, ungainly, gangling, maladroit, clumsy, klutzy, inelegant, uncoordinated, graceless, ungraceful; unconfident, unsophisticated. ANTONYM graceful.

gay adjective **1** *gay men and women* HOMOSEXUAL, lesbian; *informal* queer.

2 *dated her children were all chubby and gay.* See CHEERFUL sense 1.

▸ noun See HOMOSEXUAL.

USAGE NOTE gay

Gay meaning 'homosexual,' dating back to the 1930s (if not earlier), became established in the 1960s as the term preferred by homosexual men to describe themselves. It is now the standard accepted term throughout the English-speaking world. As a result, the centuries-old other senses of **gay** meaning either 'carefree' or 'bright and showy,' once common in speech and literature, are much less frequent. The word **gay** cannot be readily used unselfconsciously today in these older senses without sounding old-fashioned or arousing a sense of double entendre, despite concerted attempts by some to keep them alive.

Gay in its modern sense typically refers to men (**lesbian** being the standard term for homosexual women), but in some contexts it can be used of both men and women.

---

gaze verb *he **gazed at** her* STARE AT, look fixedly at, gape at, goggle at, eye, look at, study, scrutinize, take a good look at; ogle, leer at; *informal* gawk at, rubberneck, eyeball.

▸ noun *her piercing gaze* STARE, fixed look, gape; regard, inspection, scrutiny.

gazebo noun *the gazebo in the park is being painted white* SUMMERHOUSE, pavilion, belvedere; arbor, bower.

gazette noun *it's in this week's gazette* NEWSPAPER, paper, journal, periodical, organ, newsletter, bulletin; *informal* rag.

gear noun *informal* **1** *his fishing gear* EQUIPMENT, apparatus, paraphernalia, articles, appliances, impedimenta; tools, utensils, implements, instruments, gadgets; stuff, things; kit, rig, tackle, odds and ends, bits and pieces, trappings, appurtenances, accoutrements, regalia; *archaic* equipage.

2 *I'll go back to the hotel and pick up my gear* BELONGINGS, possessions, effects, personal effects, property, paraphernalia, odds and ends, bits and pieces, bags, baggage, luggage; *Law* chattels; *informal* things, stuff.

3 *police in riot gear* CLOTHES, clothing, garments, outfits, attire, garb; dress, wear; *informal* togs, duds, getup, threads; *formal* apparel.

gel verb See JELL.

gelatinous adjective *stir over low heat until the mixture becomes gelatinous* JELLYLIKE, glutinous, viscous, viscid, mucilaginous, sticky, gluey, gummy, slimy; *informal* gooey, gunky.

geld verb *Mitch selects the horses that are to be gelded* CASTRATE, neuter, fix, alter, desex, doctor.

gem noun **1** *rubies and other gems* JEWEL, gemstone, stone, precious stone, semiprecious stone; solitaire, cabochon; *archaic* bijou. See table.

2 *the gem of the collection* BEST, finest, pride, prize, treasure, flower, pearl, jewel in the crown; pick, choice, cream, the crème de la crème, elite, acme; *informal* one in a million, bee's knees.

GEMSTONES

agate	jade
alexandrite	jasper
almandine	jet
amber	lapis lazuli
amethyst	malachite
aquamarine	marcasite
beryl	moss agate
bloodstone	olivine
carbuncle	onyx
carnelian	opal
cat's-eye	pearl
chalcedony	peridot
chrysoberyl	pyrope
chrysoprase	rose quartz
citrine	ruby
corundum	sapphire
demantoid	sardonyx
diamond	smoky quartz
emerald	sunstone
fire opal	tiger's eye
garnet	topaz
girasol	tourmaline
hyacinth	turquoise
jacinth	zircon

gender noun See SEX sense 3.

USAGE NOTE **gender, sex**

The word **gender** has been used since the fourteenth century primarily as a grammatical term, referring to the classes of noun in Latin, Greek, German, and other languages designated as *masculine*, *feminine*, or *neuter*. It has also been used since the fourteenth century in the sense 'the state of being male or female,' but this did not become a common standard use until the mid twentieth century. Although the words **gender** and **sex** both have the sense 'the state of being male or female,' they are typically used in slightly different ways: **sex** tends to refer to biological differences, while **gender** tends to refer to cultural or social ones.

genealogy noun *our genealogy has been difficult to determine* LINEAGE, line, line of descent, family tree, bloodline; pedigree, ancestry, extraction, heritage, parentage, birth, family, dynasty, house, stock, blood, roots.

general adjective **1** *this is suitable for general use* WIDESPREAD, common, extensive, universal, wide, popular, public, mainstream; established, conventional, traditional, orthodox, accepted. See note at UNIVERSAL. ANTONYM restricted.

2 *a general pay increase* COMPREHENSIVE, overall, across the board, blanket, umbrella, mass, wholesale, sweeping, broad-ranging, inclusive, companywide; universal, global, worldwide, nationwide. ANTONYM localized.

3 *general knowledge* MISCELLANEOUS, mixed, assorted, diversified, composite, heterogeneous, eclectic. ANTONYM specialist.

4 *the general practice* USUAL, customary, habitual, traditional, normal, conventional, typical, standard, regular; familiar, accepted, prevailing, routine, run-of-the-mill, established, everyday, ordinary, common. ANTONYM exceptional.

5 *a general description* BROAD, imprecise, inexact, rough, loose, approximate, unspecific, vague, woolly, indefinite; *informal* ballpark. ANTONYM detailed.

generality noun **1** *the debate has moved on from generalities* GENERALIZATION, general statement, general principle, sweeping statement; abstraction, extrapolation. ANTONYM specific.

2 *the generality of this principle* UNIVERSALITY, comprehensiveness, all-inclusiveness, broadness.

generally adverb **1** *summers were generally hot* NORMALLY, in general, as a rule, by and large, more often than not, almost always, mainly, mostly, for the most part, predominantly, on the whole; usually, habitually, customarily, typically, ordinarily, commonly.

2 *popular opinion veers generally to the left* OVERALL, in general terms, generally speaking, all in all, broadly, on average, basically, effectively.

3 *the method was generally accepted* WIDELY, commonly, extensively, universally, popularly.

generate verb **1** *moves to generate extra business* CAUSE, give rise to, lead to, result in, bring about, create, make, produce, engender, spawn, precipitate, prompt, provoke, trigger, spark off, stir up, induce, promote, foster.

2 *captive animals may not* ***generate offspring*** PROCREATE, breed, reproduce, father offspring, sire offspring, mother offspring, spawn offspring, create offspring, produce offspring, have offspring; *literary* beget offspring; *archaic* engender offspring.

generation noun **1** *people of the same generation* AGE, age group, peer group.

2 **(generations)** *generations ago* AGES, years, eons, a long time, an eternity; *informal* donkey's years.

3 *the next generation of computers* CROP, batch, wave, range.

4 *the generation of novel ideas* CREATION, production, initiation, origination, inception, inspiration.

5 *human generation* PROCREATION, reproduction, breeding; creation.

generator noun *crank up the generator* ENGINE, dynamo, alternator, magneto, cell, turbine, turbocharger, pump, windmill.

generic adjective **1** *a generic classification for similar offenses* GENERAL, common, collective, nonspecific, inclusive, all-encompassing, broad, comprehensive, blanket, umbrella. See note at UNIVERSAL. ANTONYM specific.

2 *generic drugs are cheaper than brand-name ones* UNBRANDED, nonproprietary, no-name. ANTONYM specific.

generosity noun **1** *the generosity of our host* LIBERALITY, lavishness, magnanimity, munificence, openhandedness, free-handedness, unselfishness; kindness, benevolence, altruism, charity, big-heartedness, goodness; *literary* bounteousness.

2 *the generosity of the food portions* ABUNDANCE, plentifulness, copiousness, lavishness, liberality, largeness.

generous adjective **1** *she is generous with money* LIBERAL, lavish, magnanimous, munificent, giving, openhanded, free-handed, bountiful, unselfish, ungrudging, free, indulgent, prodigal; *literary* bounteous. ANTONYMS mean, stingy.

2 *it was generous of them to offer* MAGNANIMOUS, kind, benevolent, altruistic, charitable, noble, big-hearted, honorable, good; unselfish, self-sacrificing. ANTONYMS mean, selfish.

3 *a generous amount of fabric* LAVISH, plentiful, copious, ample, liberal, large, great, abundant, profuse, bumper, opulent, prolific; *informal* galore; *literary* bounteous, plenteous. ANTONYM meager.

genesis noun **1** *the hatred had its genesis in something dark* ORIGIN, source, root, beginning, start.

2 *the genesis of his neurosis* FORMATION, development, evolution, emergence, inception, origination, creation, formulation, propagation.

genial adjective *my genial colleagues* FRIENDLY, affable, cordial, amiable, warm, easygoing, approachable, sympathetic; good-natured, good-humored, cheerful; neighborly, hospitable, companionable, comradely, sociable, convivial, outgoing, gregarious; *informal* chummy. ANTONYM unfriendly.

genitals plural noun *male genitals* PRIVATE PARTS, genitalia, sexual organs, reproductive organs, pudenda; crotch, groin, nether regions; *informal* privates.

genius noun **1** *the world knew of his genius* BRILLIANCE, intelligence, intellect, ability, cleverness, brains, erudition, wisdom, fine mind; artistry, flair. ANTONYM stupidity.

2 *she has a genius for organization* TALENT, gift, flair, aptitude, facility, knack, bent, ability, expertise, capacity, faculty; strength, forte, brilliance, skill, artistry.

3 *he is a genius* BRILLIANT PERSON, gifted person, mastermind, Einstein, intellectual, great intellect, brain, mind; prodigy; *informal* egghead, bright spark, brainiac, rocket scientist. ANTONYM dunce.

genocide noun *a tyrant guilty of genocide* MASS MURDER, mass homicide, massacre; annihilation, extermination, elimination, liquidation, eradication, decimation, butchery, bloodletting; pogrom, ethnic cleansing, holocaust.

genre noun *historical fiction is my favorite genre of literature* CATEGORY, class, classification, group, set, list; type, sort, kind, breed, variety, style, model, school, stamp, cast, ilk.

WORD NOTE **genre**

Genre in pop music is mostly racism: *soul, rhythm-and-blues, urban,* etc., are euphemisms for any music made by African-Americans; *singer-songwriter, new wave, electropop, soft rock,* etc., are categories exclusive of them. *Billboard* magazine, the music industry's paper of record, used to have three charts: *Race, Folk,* and *Pop. Race* meant African-Americans; *Folk* meant European-Americans from the South; *Pop* was everything else. Nowadays there are many more charts, but the organizing principle—social exclusion—is identical. We would not call all music by Jews *klezmer,* nor would we file Alice Walker under "soul" writers. Please use musical labels advisedly. **—SM**

genteel adjective *she never quite fit in with Harold's genteel family* REFINED, respectable, decorous, mannerly, well-mannered, courteous, polite, proper, correct, seemly; well-bred, cultured, sophisticated, ladylike, gentlemanly, dignified, gracious; affected. See note at URBANE. ANTONYM uncouth.

gentility noun *an air of old-fashioned gentility* REFINEMENT, distinction, breeding, sophistication; respectability, punctiliousness, decorum, good manners, politeness, civility, courtesy, graciousness, correctness; affectation, ostentation.

gentle adjective **1** *his manner was gentle* KIND, tender, sympathetic, considerate, understanding, compassionate, benevolent, good-natured; humane, lenient, merciful, clement; mild, placid, serene, sweet-tempered. ANTONYM brutal.

2 *a gentle breeze* LIGHT, soft. ANTONYM strong.

3 *a gentle slope* GRADUAL, slight, easy. ANTONYM steep.

4 *archaic a woman of gentle birth.* See NOBLE adjective sense 1.

gentleman noun *a fine steed suitable for a gentleman such as yourself* MAN; nobleman; *informal* gent; *archaic* cavalier.

gentlemanly adjective *gentlemanly manners came naturally to him* CHIVALROUS, gallant, honorable, noble, courteous, civil, mannerly, polite, gracious, considerate, thoughtful; well-bred, cultivated, cultured, refined, suave, urbane. ANTONYM rude.

gentry noun *posing as a member of the gentry* UPPER CLASSES, privileged classes, elite, high society, haut monde, smart set; establishment, aristocracy; *informal* upper crust, top drawer.

genuine adjective **1** *a genuine Picasso* AUTHENTIC, real, actual, original, bona fide, true, veritable; attested, undisputed; *informal* the real McCoy, honest-to-goodness, honest-to-God, the real thing, kosher. ANTONYM bogus.

2 *a genuine person* SINCERE, honest, truthful, straightforward, direct, frank, candid, open; artless, natural, unaffected; *informal* straight, upfront, on the level, on the up and up. ANTONYM insincere.

THE RIGHT WORD

A car salesperson might claim that the seats of that pricey sedan you're considering are made from **genuine** leather, a word that applies to anything that is really what it is claimed or represented to be. If you're in the market for a Model T Ford, however, you'll want to make sure that the car is **authentic**, which emphasizes formal proof or documentation that an object is what it is claimed to be. Use **bona fide** when sincerity is involved (*a bona fide offer*), and **legitimate** when you mean lawful or in accordance with established rules, principles, and standards (*a legitimate business*). **Veritable** implies correspondence with the truth but not necessarily a literal or strict correspondence with reality (*a veritable supermarket for car-buyers*). How will it feel to drive that Mercedes out of the showroom? You won't know until you're the **actual** owner of the car—a word that means existing in fact rather than in the imagination.

genus noun **1** *Biology a large genus of plants* subdivision, division, group, subfamily.

2 *a new genus of music* TYPE, sort, kind, genre, style, variety, category, class; breed, brand, family, stamp, cast, ilk.

geography noun. See table on page 383.

BRANCHES OF GEOGRAPHY

biogeography	hypsography
cartography	meteorology
climatology	oceanography
demography	orography
geology	physical geography
geomorphology	political geography
geopolitics	seismology
glaciology	topography
human geography	volcanology
hydrology	

germ noun **1** *this detergent kills germs* MICROBE, microorganism, bacillus, bacterium, virus; *informal* bug.

2 *a fertilized germ* EMBRYO, bud; seed, spore, ovule; egg, ovum.

3 *the germ of an idea* START, beginning(s), seed, embryo, bud, root, rudiment; origin, source, potential; core, nucleus, kernel, essence.

germane adjective *your question is not germane to the topic at hand* RELEVANT, pertinent, applicable, apposite, material; apropos, appropriate, apt, fitting, suitable; connected, related, akin. ANTONYM irrelevant.

germinate verb **1** *the grain is allowed to germinate* SPROUT, shoot (up), bud; develop, grow, spring up; *dated* vegetate.

2 *the idea began to germinate* DEVELOP, take root, grow, incubate, emerge, evolve, mature, expand, advance, progress.

gestation noun **1** *a gestation of thirty days* PREGNANCY, incubation; development, maturation.

2 *the law underwent a period of gestation* DEVELOPMENT, evolution, formation, emergence, origination.

gesticulate verb *they frantically gesticulated to get someone's attention* GESTURE, signal, motion, wave, sign.

gesticulation noun *she didn't know his wild gesticulation was a warning of danger* GESTURING, gesture, hand movement, signals, signs; wave, indication; body language.

gesture noun **1** *a gesture of surrender* SIGNAL, sign, motion, indication, gesticulation; show.

2 *a symbolic gesture* ACTION, act, deed, move.

▸ verb *he gestured to her* SIGNAL, motion, gesticulate, wave, indicate, give a sign.

get verb **1** *where did you get that hat?* ACQUIRE, obtain, come by, receive, gain, earn, win, come into, take possession of, be given; buy, purchase, procure, secure; gather, collect, pick up, hook, net, land; achieve, attain; *informal* get one's hands on, get one's mitts on, get hold of, grab, bag, score. ANTONYM give.

2 *I got your letter* RECEIVE, be sent, be in receipt of, be given. ANTONYM send.

3 *your tea's getting cold* BECOME, grow, turn, go.

4 *get the children from school* FETCH, collect, go for, call for, pick up, bring, deliver, convey, ferry, transport. ANTONYM leave.

5 *the chairman gets $650,000 a year* EARN, be paid, take home, bring in, make, receive, collect, gross; *informal* pocket, bank, rake in, net, bag.

6 *have the police got their man?* APPREHEND, catch, arrest, capture, seize; take prisoner, take into custody, detain, put in jail, put behind bars, imprison, incarcerate; *informal* collar, grab, nab, nail, run in, pinch, bust, pick up, pull in.

7 *I got a taxi* TRAVEL BY/ON/IN; take, catch, use.

8 *she got the flu* SUCCUMB TO, develop, come/go down with, get sick with, fall victim to, be struck down with, be afflicted by/with; become infected with, catch, contract, fall ill with, be taken ill with.

9 *I got a pain in my arm* EXPERIENCE, suffer, be afflicted with, sustain, feel, have.

10 *I got him on the radio* CONTACT, get in touch with, communicate with, make contact with, reach; phone, call, radio; speak to, talk to; *informal* get hold of.

11 *I didn't get what he said* HEAR, discern, distinguish, make out, perceive, follow, take in.

12 *I don't get the joke* UNDERSTAND, comprehend, grasp, see, fathom, follow, perceive, apprehend, unravel, decipher; *informal* get the drift of, catch on to, latch on to, figure out.

13 *we got there early* ARRIVE, reach, come, make it, turn up, appear, come on the scene, approach, enter, present oneself, come along, materialize, show one's face; *informal* show (up), roll in/up, blow in.

14 *we got her to go* PERSUADE, induce, prevail on/upon, influence.

15 *I'd like to get to meet him* CONTRIVE, arrange, find a way, manage; *informal* work it, fix it.

16 *I'll get supper* PREPARE, get ready, cook, make, assemble, muster, concoct; *informal* fix, rustle up.

17 *informal* *I'll get him for that* TAKE REVENGE ON, exact/wreak revenge on, get one's revenge on, avenge oneself on, take vengeance on, get even with, pay back, get back at, exact retribution on, give someone their just deserts.

18 *you really got me with that third question* BAFFLE, perplex, puzzle, bewilder, mystify, bemuse, confuse, confound; *informal* flummox, faze, stump, beat, fox, discombobulate.

19 *what gets me is how neurotic she is* ANNOY, irritate, exasperate, anger, irk, vex, provoke, incense, infuriate, madden, try someone's patience, ruffle someone's feathers; *informal* aggravate, peeve, miff, rile, get to, needle, get someone's back up, get on someone's nerves, get someone's goat, drive mad, make someone see red, tee off, tick off. PHRASES: **get about** *he uses a wheelchair to get about* MOVE ABOUT, move around, travel. **get across** *a photo will help you get the message across* COMMUNICATE, impart, convey, transmit, make clear, express. **get ahead** *the desire to get ahead* PROSPER, flourish, thrive, do well; succeed, make it, advance, get on in the world, go up in the world, make good, become rich; *informal* go places, get somewhere, make the big time. **get along 1** *can't you try to get along with his family?* BE FRIENDLY, be compatible, get on; agree, see eye to eye, concur, be in accord; *informal* hit it off, be on the same wavelength. **2** *she was getting along well at school* FARE, manage, progress, advance, get on, get by, do, cope; succeed. **get around** *Toby really gets around* TRAVEL, circulate, socialize, do the rounds. **get at 1** *it's difficult to get at the pipes* ACCESS, get to, reach, touch. **2** *she had been got at by enemy agents* CORRUPT, suborn, influence, bribe, buy off, pay off; *informal* fix, square. **3** *informal* *what are you getting at?* IMPLY, suggest, intimate, insinuate, hint, mean, drive at, allude to. **get**

away *the prisoners got away* ESCAPE, run away/off, break out, break free, break loose, bolt, flee, take flight, make off, take off, decamp, abscond, make a run for it; slip away, sneak away; *informal* cut and run, skedaddle, do a disappearing act. **get away with** *he's been getting away with every kind of wrongdoing since he was three* ESCAPE BLAME FOR, escape punishment for. **get back** **1** *they should get back before dawn* RETURN, come home, come back. **2** *she got her gloves back from the lost and found* RETRIEVE, regain, win back, recover, recoup, reclaim, repossess, recapture, redeem; find (again), trace. **get back at** *she wasted years of her life thinking about getting back at her ex-husband* TAKE REVENGE ON, exact/wreak revenge on, avenge oneself on, take vengeance on, get even with, pay back, retaliate on/against, exact retribution on, give someone their just deserts. **get by** *he had just enough money to get by* MANAGE, cope, survive, exist, subsist, muddle through/along, scrape by, make ends meet, make do, keep the wolf from the door; *informal* make out. **get down** *her poetry always gets me down* DEPRESS, sadden, make unhappy, make gloomy, dispirit, dishearten, demoralize, discourage, crush, weigh down, oppress; upset, distress; *informal* give someone the blues, make someone fed up. **get lost** *do us a favor and get lost!* See SCRAM. **get off** **1** *Sally got off the bus* STEP OFF, alight (from), dismount (from), descend (from), disembark (from), leave, exit. **2** *informal he was arrested but got off* ESCAPE PUNISHMENT, be acquitted, be absolved, be cleared, be exonerated. **get on** **1** *we got on the train* BOARD, enter, step aboard, climb on, mount, ascend, catch; *informal* hop on, jump on. **2** *how are you getting on?* FARE, manage, progress, get along, do, cope, get by, survive, muddle through/along; succeed, prosper; *informal* make out. **3** *we don't get on too well.* See GET ALONG sense 1. **get on with** **1** *she got on with her job* CONTINUE (WITH), proceed with, go ahead with, carry on with, go on with, press on with, persist with/in, persevere with; keep at; *informal* stick with/at. **2** **get out** **1** *the prisoners got out.* See GET AWAY. **2** *the news got out* BECOME KNOWN, become common knowledge, come to light, emerge, transpire; come out, be uncovered, be revealed, be divulged, be disseminated, be disclosed, be reported, be released, leak out. **get out of** *how do you plan to get out of this mess?* EVADE, dodge, shirk, avoid, escape, sidestep; *informal* duck (out of), wriggle out of, cop out of. **get over** **1** *I just got over the flu* RECOVER FROM, recuperate from, get better after, shrug off, survive. **2** *we tried to get over this problem* OVERCOME, surmount, get the better of, master, find an/the answer to, get a grip on, deal with, cope with, sort out, take care of, crack, rise above; *informal* lick. **get together** **1** *get together the best writers* COLLECT, gather, assemble, bring together, rally, muster, marshal, congregate, convene, amass; *formal* convoke. **2** *we must get together soon* MEET, meet up, rendezvous, see each other, socialize. **get up** *he seldom gets up before noon* GET OUT OF BED, rise, stir, rouse oneself; *informal* surface; *formal* arise.

THE RIGHT WORD

Get is a very broad term meaning to come into possession of. You can *get* something by fetching it (*get some groceries*), by receiving it (*get a birthday gift*), by earning it (*get interest on a bank loan*), or by any of a dozen other familiar means. It is such a common, over-used word that many writers try to substitute **obtain** for it whenever possible, perhaps because it sounds less colloquial. But it can also sound pretentious (*all employees were required to obtain an annual physical exam*) and should be reserved for contexts where the emphasis is on seeking something out (*to obtain blood samples*). **Acquire** often suggests a continued, sustained, or cumulative acquisition (*to acquire poise as one matures*), but it can also hint at deviousness (*to acquire the keys to the safe*). Use **procure** if you want to emphasize the effort involved in bringing something to pass (*procure a mediated divorce settlement*) or if you want to imply maneuvering to possess something (*procure a reserved parking space*). But beware: *Procure* is so often used to describe the act of obtaining partners to gratify the lust of others (*to procure a prostitute*) that it has acquired somewhat unsavory overtones. **Gain** also implies effort, usually in *getting* something advantageous or profitable (*gain entry, gain victory*). In a similar vein, **secure** underscores the difficulty involved in bringing something to pass and the desire to place it beyond danger (*secure a permanent peace; secure a lifeline*). **Attain** should be reserved for achieving a high goal or desirable result (*If she attains the summit of Mt. Everest, she will secure for herself a place in mountaineering history*).

getaway noun *he made his getaway in broad daylight* ESCAPE, breakout, bolt for freedom, flight; disappearance, vanishing act.

get-together noun *a friendly get-together at Pete's house* PARTY, meeting, gathering, social event, social; *informal* do, bash.

getup noun *informal check out Stacey's wild getup* OUTFIT, clothes, costume, ensemble, suit, clothing, dress, attire, garments, garb; *informal* gear, togs, duds, threads; *formal* apparel.

get-up-and-go noun *informal your grandfather has more getup-and-go than you do* DRIVE, initiative, enterprise, enthusiasm, eagerness, ambition, motivation, dynamism, energy, gusto, vim, vigor, vitality, verve, fire, fervor, zeal, commitment, spirit; *informal* gumption, oomph, pep. ANTONYM apathy.

ghastly adjective **1** *a ghastly stabbing* TERRIBLE, horrible, grim, awful, dire; frightening, terrifying, horrifying, alarming; distressing, shocking, appalling, harrowing; dreadful, frightful, horrendous, monstrous, gruesome, grisly; *informal* gut-wrenching. ANTONYM pleasant.

2 *informal a ghastly building* UNPLEASANT, objectionable, disagreeable, distasteful, awful, terrible, dreadful, detestable, insufferable, vile; *informal* horrible, horrid. ANTONYM charming.

3 *a ghastly pallor* PALE, white, pallid, pasty, wan, bloodless, peaked, ashen, gray, waxy, blanched, drained, pinched, green, sickly, ghostly, ghostlike; *informal* like death warmed over. ANTONYMS ruddy, healthy.

ghost noun **1** *his ghost haunts the crypt* SPECTER, phantom, wraith, spirit, presence; apparition; *informal* spook. See also the table at SPIRIT.

2 *the ghost of a smile* TRACE, hint, suggestion, impression, suspicion, tinge; glimmer, semblance, shadow, whisper.

ghostly adjective *a ghostly vision at the end of the hallway* SPECTRAL, ghostlike, phantom, wraithlike, phantasmal, phantasmic; unearthly, unnatural, supernatural; insubstantial, shadowy; eerie, weird, uncanny; frightening, spine-chilling, hair-raising, blood-curdling, bone-chilling, terrifying, chilling, sinister; *informal* creepy, scary, spooky.

ghoulish adjective *most of his stories feature at least one* *terribly ghoulish character* MACABRE, grisly, gruesome, grotesque, ghastly; unhealthy, horrible, unwholesome.

giant noun *the mythical giant of the forest* COLOSSUS, behemoth, Brobdingnagian, mammoth, monster, leviathan, titan; giantess; *informal* jumbo, whopper. ANTONYM dwarf.

▸ adjective *a giant balloon* HUGE, colossal, massive, enormous, gigantic, very big, mammoth, vast, immense, monumental, mountainous, titanic, towering, elephantine, king-size(d), economy-size(d), gargantuan, Brobdingnagian; substantial, hefty; *informal* mega, monster, whopping, humongous, jumbo, hulking, bumper, ginormous. ANTONYM miniature.

gibber verb *he rocks in his chair, gibbering to himself* PRATTLE, babble, ramble, drivel, jabber, gabble, burble, twitter, mutter, mumble; *informal* yammer, blabber, jibber-jabber, blather, yak.

gibberish noun *am I going deaf, or is she speaking gibberish?* NONSENSE, garbage, balderdash, blather, rubbish; *informal* drivel, gobbledygook, mumbo-jumbo, tripe, hogwash, baloney, bilge, bull, bunk, guff, eyewash, piffle, twaddle, poppycock.

gibe, jibe noun *vicious gibes* SNIDE REMARK, cutting remark, taunt, sneer, jeer, insult, barb; *informal* dig, put-down.

▸ verb *even when her family gibed, Angela pursued her dream of becoming an astronaut* JEER, taunt, mock, scoff, sneer.

giddy adjective **1** *just one beer would make him feel giddy* DIZZY, lightheaded, faint, weak, vertiginous; unsteady, shaky, wobbly; *informal* woozy. ANTONYM steady.

2 *she was young and giddy* FLIGHTY, silly, frivolous, skittish, irresponsible, flippant, whimsical, capricious; featherbrained, scatty, thoughtless, heedless, carefree; *informal* dippy, ditzy, flaky. ANTONYM sensible.

gift noun **1** *he gave the staff a gift* PRESENT, handout, donation, offering, bestowal, bonus, award, endowment; tip, gratuity; largesse; *informal* freebie, perk; *formal* benefaction. See note at PRESENT[3].

2 *Marlin possessed a gift for interior design* TALENT, flair, aptitude, facility, knack, bent, ability, expertise, capacity, capability, faculty; endowment, strength, genius, brilliance, skill, artistry.

▸ verb *he gifted a composition to the orchestra* PRESENT, give, bestow, confer, donate, endow, award, accord, grant; hand over, make over.

gifted adjective *a gifted young percussionist* TALENTED, skillful, skilled, accomplished, expert, consummate, master(ly), virtuoso, first-rate, able, apt, adept, proficient; intelligent, clever, bright, brilliant; precocious; *informal* crack, top-notch, ace. ANTONYM inept.

gigantic adjective *the new houses on Long Hill Road are gigantic* HUGE, enormous, vast, extensive, very big, very large, giant, massive, colossal, mammoth, immense, monumental, mountainous, titanic, towering, elephantine, king-size(d), economy-size(d), gargantuan; *informal* mega, monster, whopping, humongous, jumbo, hulking, bumper, ginormous. ANTONYM tiny.

giggle noun & verb *she suppressed a giggle | he giggled at the picture* TITTER, snigger, snicker, tee-hee, chuckle, chortle, laugh.

gigolo noun *she was mortified to learn her husband had been a gigolo in LA when he was twenty-something* PLAYBOY, escort, male escort, paid escort; lover; *informal* toy boy.

gild verb **1** *she gilded the picture frame* GOLD-PLATE; cover with gold, paint gold.

2 *he tends to gild the truth* ELABORATE, embellish, embroider; camouflage, disguise, dress up, color, exaggerate, expand on; *informal* jazz up.

gimcrack adjective *they lived in gimcrack villas you'd be afraid to sneeze in* SHODDY, jerry-built, flimsy, insubstantial, thrown together, makeshift; inferior, poor-quality, second-rate, cheap, cheapjack; tawdry, kitsch, kitschy, chintzy, trashy, dime-store; *informal* tacky, junky, cheapo, schlocky.

gimmick noun *the trivia contest was a gimmick to sell more newspapers* PUBLICITY STUNT, contrivance, scheme, stratagem, ploy; *informal* shtick.

gingerly adverb *he stepped gingerly on to the ice* CAUTIOUSLY, carefully, with care, warily, charily, circumspectly, delicately; heedfully, watchfully, vigilantly, attentively; hesitantly, timidly. ANTONYM recklessly.

gird verb **1** *the island was girded by rocks* SURROUND, enclose, encircle, circle, encompass, border, bound, edge, skirt, fringe; close in, confine.

2 *they girded themselves for war* PREPARE, get ready, gear up; nerve, steel, galvanize, brace, fortify; *informal* psych oneself up.

girdle noun **1** *her stockings were held up by her girdle* CORSET, panty girdle, corselet, foundation garment; truss.

2 *a diamond-studded girdle* BELT, sash, cummerbund, waistband, strap, band, girth, cord.

▸ verb *a garden girdled the house* SURROUND, enclose, encircle, circle, encompass, circumscribe, border, bound, skirt, edge; *literary* gird.

girl noun **1** *a five-year-old girl* FEMALE CHILD, daughter; schoolgirl; *Scottish* lass, lassie. See also CHILD.

2 *he settled down with a nice girl* YOUNG WOMAN, young lady, miss, mademoiselle; *Scottish* lass, lassie; *informal* chick, gal, grrrl, babe; *literary* maid, damsel, ingenue.

3 *his girl left him.* See GIRLFRIEND.

girlfriend noun *Danny's new girlfriend is from Massachusetts* SWEETHEART, lover, partner, significant other, main squeeze, girl, woman; fiancée; *informal* steady; *dated* lady friend, lady friend, lady love, betrothed; *archaic* leman.

girlish adjective *her girlish giggles* GIRLY, youthful, childlike, childish, immature; feminine.

girth noun **1** *a tree ten feet in girth* CIRCUMFERENCE, perimeter; width, breadth.

2 *he tied the towel around his girth* STOMACH, midriff, middle, abdomen, belly, gut; *informal* tummy, tum.

3 *a horse's girth* cinch.

gist noun *the gist of her essay is an indictment of the religious right* ESSENCE, substance, central theme, heart of the matter, nub, kernel, marrow, meat, burden, crux;

thrust, drift, sense, meaning, significance, import; *informal* nitty-gritty.

give verb **1** *she gave them $2000* PRESENT WITH, provide with, supply with, furnish with, let someone have; hand (over to), offer, proffer; award, grant (to), bestow on/upon, accord, confer on, make over to; donate to, contribute to. ANTONYMS receive, take.

2 *can I give him a message?* CONVEY TO, pass on to, impart to, communicate to, transmit to; send, deliver (to), relay to; tell (to).

3 *a baby given into their care* ENTRUST, commit, consign, assign; *formal* commend.

4 *she gave her life for them* SACRIFICE, give up, relinquish; devote, dedicate.

5 *he gave her time to think* ALLOW, permit, grant, accord; offer.

6 *this leaflet gives our opening times* SHOW, display, set out, indicate, detail, list.

7 *they gave no further trouble* CAUSE, make, create, occasion.

8 *garlic gives flavor* PRODUCE, yield, afford, impart, lend.

9 *she gave a party* ORGANIZE, arrange, throw, host, hold, have, provide.

10 *Dominic gave a bow* PERFORM, execute, make, do.

11 *she gave a shout* UTTER, let out, emit, produce, make.

12 *he gave Larry a beating* ADMINISTER, deliver, deal, inflict, impose.

13 *the door gave* GIVE WAY, cave in, collapse, break, fall apart; bend, buckle.

▸ noun *informal there isn't enough give in the jacket* ELASTICITY, flexibility, stretch, stretchiness; slack, play.

PHRASES: **give away 1** *he refused to believe that his own sister had given him away* BETRAY, inform on; *informal* rat on, blow the whistle on, sell down the river, rat out, finger. **2** *his face gave little away* REVEAL, disclose, divulge, let slip, leak, let out. **3** *Kellie gave away all of her possessions* DONATE, make a gift of, confer, contribute, will, bequeath; distribute; sacrifice; get rid of, dispose of, relent, throw in the towel/sponge. **give in** *in the end, Dolan was forced to give in* CAPITULATE, concede defeat, admit defeat, give up, surrender, yield, submit, back down, give way, defer, relent, throw in the towel. **give off** *the lantern gives off a powerful glow* EMIT, produce, send out, throw out; discharge, release, exude, vent. **give out 1** *the gas reserves have finally given out* RUN OUT, be used up, be consumed, be exhausted, be depleted; fail, flag; dry up. **2** *thousands of leaflets were given out* DISTRIBUTE, issue, hand out, pass around, dispense; dole out, dish out, mete out; allocate, allot. **give up. 1** See GIVE IN (above). **2** *when did you give up drinking?* STOP, cease, discontinue, desist from, abstain from, cut out, renounce, forgo; resign from, stand down from; *informal* quit, kick, swear off, leave off, pack in, lay off.

THE RIGHT WORD

You **give** a birthday present, **grant** a favor, **bestow** charity, and **confer** an honor. While all of these verbs mean to convey something or transfer it from one's own possession to that of another, the circumstances surrounding that transfer dictate which word is the best one. *Give* is the most general, meaning to pass over, deliver, or transmit something (*give him encouragement*). *Grant* implies that a request or desire has been expressed, and that the receiver is dependent on the giver's discretion (*grant permission for the trip*). **Award** suggests that the giver is in some sense a judge, and that the thing given is deserved (*award a scholarship*), while *bestow* implies that something is given as a gift and may imply condescension on the part of the giver (*bestow a large sum of money on a needy charity*). To *confer* is to give an honor, a privilege, or a favor; it implies that the giver is a superior (*confer a knighthood; confer a college degree*). **Donate** implies that the giving is to a public cause or charity (*donate a painting to the local art museum*), and to **afford** is to give or bestow as a natural consequence (the window afforded a fine view of the mountains).

give and take noun *there has to be some give and take on both sides* COMPROMISE, concession; cooperation, reciprocity, teamwork, interplay.

given adjective **1** *a given number of years* SPECIFIED, stated, designated, set, particular, specific; prescribed, agreed, appointed, prearranged, predetermined. ANTONYM unspecified.

2 *she was given to fits of temper* PRONE, liable, inclined, disposed, predisposed, apt, likely.

▸ preposition *given the issue's complexity, a brief summary is difficult* CONSIDERING, in view of, bearing in mind, in the light of; assuming.

▸ noun *his aggression is taken as a given* ESTABLISHED FACT, reality, certainty.

giver noun *Lynette threw her indolent nephews out of the house, vowing that her days as the "family giver" were over* DONOR, contributor, donator, benefactor, benefactress, provider; supporter, backer, patron, sponsor, subscriber.

glacial adjective **1** *glacial conditions* FREEZING, cold, icy, ice-cold, subzero, frozen, gelid, wintry; arctic, polar, Siberian, hypothermic; bitter, biting, raw; *literary* chill. ANTONYMS tropical, hot.

2 *Beverly's tone was glacial* UNFRIENDLY, hostile, unwelcoming; frosty, icy, cold, chilly. ANTONYMS warm, friendly.

3 *they proceeded at a glacial pace* SLOW, lugubrious, unhurried, leisurely, steady, sedate, slow-moving, plodding, dawdling, sluggish, sluggardly, lead-footed. ANTONYMS fast, brisk.

glad adjective **1** *I'm really glad you're coming* PLEASED, happy, delighted, thrilled, overjoyed, elated, gleeful; gratified, grateful, thankful; *informal* tickled pink, over the moon. ANTONYMS dismayed, annoyed.

2 *I'd be glad to help* WILLING, eager, happy, pleased, delighted; ready, prepared. ANTONYMS unwilling, reluctant.

3 *glad tidings* PLEASING, welcome, happy, joyful, cheering, heartening, gratifying. ANTONYMS unwelcome, distressing.

gladden verb *it gladdens us to see you so happy* DELIGHT, please, make happy, elate; cheer, cheer up, hearten, buoy up, give someone a lift, uplift; gratify; *informal* tickle someone pink, buck up. ANTONYM sadden.

gladly adverb *we gladly accepted the senator's invitation* WITH PLEASURE, happily, cheerfully; willingly, readily, eagerly, freely, ungrudgingly; *archaic* fain, lief.

glamorous adjective **1** *a glamorous woman* BEAUTIFUL, attractive, lovely, bewitching, enchanting, beguiling; elegant, chic, stylish, fashionable; charming, charismatic, appealing, alluring, seductive; *informal* classy, glam. ANTONYMS dowdy, drab.

2 *a glamorous lifestyle* EXCITING, thrilling, stimulating; dazzling, glittering, glossy, colorful, exotic; *informal* ritzy, glitzy, jet-setting. ANTONYMS boring, dull.

glamour noun 1 *she had undeniable glamour* BEAUTY, allure, attractiveness; elegance, chic, style; charisma, charm, magnetism, desirability.

2 *the glamour of show business* ALLURE, attraction, fascination, charm, magic, romance, mystique, exoticism, spell; excitement, thrill; glitter, bright lights; *informal* glitz, glam, tinsel.

glance verb 1 *Rachel glanced at him* LOOK BRIEFLY, look quickly, peek, peep; glimpse; *informal* have a gander.

2 *I **glanced through** the report* READ QUICKLY, scan, skim through, leaf through, flip through, thumb through, browse (through); dip into.

3 *a bullet **glanced off** the ice* RICOCHET OFF, rebound off, be deflected off, bounce off; graze, clip.

4 *sunlight glanced off her hair* REFLECT, flash, gleam, glint, glitter, glisten, glimmer, shimmer.

▸ noun *a glance at his watch* PEEK, peep, brief look, quick look, glimpse; *informal* gander.

PHRASE: **at first glance** *at first glance, the plastic stemware could have been mistaken for crystal* ON THE FACE OF IT, on the surface, at first sight, to the casual eye, to all appearances; apparently, seemingly, outwardly, superficially, it would seem, it appears, as far as one can see/tell, by all accounts.

glare verb 1 *she glared at him* SCOWL, glower, stare angrily, look daggers, frown, lower, give someone a black look, look threateningly; *informal* give someone a dirty look.

2 *the sun glared out of the sky* BLAZE, beam, shine brightly, be dazzling, be blinding.

▸ noun 1 *a cold glare* SCOWL, glower, angry stare, frown, black look, threatening look; *informal* dirty look.

2 *the harsh glare of the lights* BLAZE, dazzle, shine, beam; radiance, brilliance, luminescence.

glaring adjective 1 *glaring lights* DAZZLING, blinding, blazing, strong, bright, harsh. ANTONYMS soft, dim.

2 *a glaring omission* OBVIOUS, conspicuous, unmistakable, inescapable, unmissable, striking; flagrant, blatant, outrageous, gross; overt, patent, transparent, manifest; *informal* standing/sticking out like a sore thumb. ANTONYMS inconspicuous, minor.

glass noun 1 *a glass of water* TUMBLER, drinking vessel; goblet, flute, schooner, chalice.

2 *we sell china and glass* GLASSWARE, stemware, crystal, crystalware.

glasses plural noun *Hale looks older in his glasses* EYEGLASSES, eyewear, spectacles; *informal* specs; bifocals.

glassy adjective 1 *the glassy surface of the lake* SMOOTH, mirrorlike, gleaming, shiny, glossy, polished, vitreous; slippery, icy; clear, transparent, translucent; calm, still, flat. ANTONYM rough.

2 *a glassy stare* EXPRESSIONLESS, glazed, blank, vacant, fixed, motionless; emotionless, impassive, lifeless, wooden, vacuous. ANTONYM expressive.

glaze verb 1 *the pots are glazed when dry* VARNISH, enamel, lacquer, japan, shellac, paint; gloss.

2 *pastry glazed with caramel* COVER, coat; ice, frost.

3 *his eyes glazed over* BECOME GLASSY, go blank; mist over, film over.

▸ noun 1 *pottery with a blue glaze* VARNISH, enamel, lacquer, finish, coating; luster, shine, gloss.

2 *a cake with an apricot glaze* COATING, topping; icing, frosting.

gleam verb *the new silver tea service positively gleams* SHINE, glimmer, glint, glitter, shimmer, sparkle, twinkle, flicker, wink, glisten, flash; *literary* glister.

▸ noun 1 *a gleam of light* GLIMMER, glint, shimmer, twinkle, sparkle, flicker, flash; beam, ray, shaft.

2 *the gleam of brass* SHINE, luster, gloss, sheen; glint, glitter, glimmer, sparkle; brilliance, radiance, glow; *literary* glister.

3 *a gleam of hope* GLIMMER, flicker, ray, spark, trace, suggestion, hint, sign.

glean verb *what were you able to glean from questioning the witness?* OBTAIN, get, take, draw, derive, extract, cull, garner, gather; learn, find out.

glee noun *Agnes clapped her hands together with glee* DELIGHT, pleasure, happiness, joy, gladness, elation, euphoria; amusement, mirth, merriment; excitement, gaiety, exuberance; relish, triumph, jubilation, satisfaction, gratification. ANTONYM disappointment.

gleeful adjective *the gleeful bunch over there must have been rooting for the Patriots* DELIGHTED, pleased, joyful, happy, glad, overjoyed, elated, euphoric; amused, mirthful, merry, exuberant; jubilant; *informal* over the moon.

glib adjective *glib phrases rolled off his tongue* SLICK, pat, fast-talking, smooth-talking; disingenuous, insincere, facile, shallow, superficial, flippant; smooth, silver-tongued, urbane; *informal* flip, sweet-talking. See note at TALKATIVE. ANTONYM sincere.

glide verb 1 *a gondola glided past* SLIDE, slip, sail, float, drift, flow; coast, freewheel, roll; skim, skate.

2 *seagulls gliding over the waves* SOAR, wheel, plane; fly.

3 *he glided out of the door* SLIP, steal, slink.

glimmer verb *moonlight glimmered on the lawn* GLEAM, shine, glint, flicker, shimmer, glisten, glow, twinkle, sparkle, glitter, wink, flash; *literary* glister.

▸ noun 1 *a glimmer of light* GLEAM, glint, flicker, shimmer, glow, twinkle, sparkle, flash, ray.

2 *a glimmer of hope* GLEAM, flicker, ray, trace, sign, suggestion, hint.

glimpse noun *a glimpse of her face* BRIEF LOOK, quick look; glance, peek, peep; sight, sighting.

▸ verb *he glimpsed a figure* CATCH SIGHT OF, notice, discern, spot, spy, sight, pick out, make out; *literary* espy, descry.

glint verb *the diamond glinted* SHINE, gleam, catch the light, glitter, sparkle, twinkle, wink, glimmer, shimmer, glisten, flash; *literary* glister.

▸ noun *the glint of the silver* GLITTER, gleam, sparkle, twinkle, glimmer, flash.

glisten verb *the sea glistened in the morning light* SHINE, sparkle, twinkle, glint, glitter, glimmer, shimmer, wink, flash; *literary* glister.

glitter verb *crystal glittered in the candlelight* SHINE, sparkle, twinkle, glint, gleam, shimmer, glimmer, wink, flash, catch the light; *literary* glister.

▸ noun **1** *the glitter of light on the water* SPARKLE, twinkle, glint, gleam, shimmer, glimmer, flicker, flash; brilliance, luminescence.

2 *the glitter of show business* GLAMOUR, excitement, thrills, attraction, appeal; dazzle; *informal* razzle-dazzle, razzmatazz, glitz, ritziness.

gloat verb *Richard's been gloating ever since he won the lottery* DELIGHT, relish, take great pleasure, revel, rejoice, glory, exult, triumph, crow; boast, brag, be smug, congratulate oneself, preen oneself, pat oneself on the back; rub one's hands together; *informal* rub it in.

global adjective **1** *the global economy* WORLDWIDE, international, world, intercontinental.

2 *a global view of the problem* COMPREHENSIVE, overall, general, all-inclusive, all-encompassing, encyclopedic, universal, blanket; broad, far-reaching, extensive, sweeping.

globalize verb *plans to globalize the company* INTERNATIONALIZE, go global, expand worldwide.

globe noun **1** *every corner of the globe* WORLD, earth, planet.

2 *the sun is a globe* SPHERE, orb, ball, spheroid, round.

globular adjective *the large globular blossoms are usually pink or red* SPHERICAL, spheric, spheroidal, round, globe-shaped, ball-shaped, orb-shaped, rounded, bulbous. See note at ROUND.

globule noun *a globule of gravy on the tablecloth* DROPLET, drop, bead, tear, ball, bubble, pearl; *informal* blob, glob.

gloom noun **1** *she peered into the gloom* DARKNESS, dark, dimness, blackness, murkiness, shadows, shade; dusk, twilight, gloaming. ANTONYM light.

2 *his gloom deepened* DESPONDENCY, depression, dejection, melancholy, melancholia, downheartedness, unhappiness, sadness, glumness, gloominess, misery, sorrow, woe, wretchedness; despair, pessimism, hopelessness; *informal* the blues, the dumps. ANTONYM happiness.

gloomy adjective **1** *a gloomy room* DARK, shadowy, sunless, dim, somber, dingy, dismal, dreary, murky, unwelcoming, cheerless, comfortless, funereal; *literary* Stygian. ANTONYMS bright, sunny.

2 *Joanna looked gloomy* DESPONDENT, downcast, downhearted, dejected, dispirited, disheartened, discouraged, demoralized, crestfallen; depressed, desolate, low, sad, unhappy, glum, melancholy, miserable, woebegone, mournful, forlorn, morose; *informal* blue, down in/at the mouth, down in the dumps; *literary* dolorous. ANTONYMS happy, cheerful.

3 *gloomy forecasts about the economy* PESSIMISTIC, depressing, downbeat, disheartening, disappointing; unfavorable, bleak, bad, black, somber, grim, cheerless, hopeless. ANTONYMS upbeat, optimistic.

glorify verb **1** *they gather to glorify God* PRAISE, extol, exalt, worship, revere, reverence, venerate, pay homage to, honor, adore, thank, give thanks to; *formal* laud; *archaic* magnify.

2 *a poem to glorify the memory of the dead* ENNOBLE, exalt, elevate, dignify, enhance, augment, promote; praise, celebrate, honor, extol, lionize, acclaim, applaud, hail; glamorize, idealize, romanticize, enshrine, immortalize; *formal* laud. ANTONYM dishonor.

glorious adjective **1** *a glorious victory* ILLUSTRIOUS, celebrated, famous, acclaimed, distinguished, honored; outstanding, great, magnificent, noble, triumphant. ANTONYM undistinguished.

2 *glorious views* WONDERFUL, marvelous, magnificent, superb, sublime, spectacular, lovely, fine, delightful; *informal* super, great, stunning, fantastic, terrific, tremendous, sensational, heavenly, divine, gorgeous, fabulous, fab, awesome, ace, killer; *literary* wondrous, beauteous. ANTONYMS miserable, horrid.

glory noun **1** *a sport that won him glory* RENOWN, fame, prestige, honor, distinction, kudos, eminence, acclaim, praise; celebrity, recognition, reputation; *informal* bouquets. ANTONYMS shame, obscurity.

2 *glory to the Lord* PRAISE, worship, adoration, veneration, honor, reverence, exaltation, homage, thanksgiving, thanks.

3 *a house restored to its former glory* MAGNIFICENCE, splendor, resplendence, grandeur, majesty, greatness, nobility; opulence, beauty, elegance. ANTONYMS lowliness, modesty.

4 *the glories of Vermont* WONDER, beauty, delight, marvel, phenomenon; sight, spectacle.

▸ verb *we* ***gloried in*** *our independence* TAKE PLEASURE IN, revel in, rejoice in, delight in; relish, savor; congratulate oneself on, be proud of, boast about, bask in; *informal* get a kick out of, get a thrill out of.

gloss[1] noun **1** *the gloss of her hair* SHINE, sheen, luster, gleam, patina, brilliance, shimmer. See note at POLISH.

2 *beneath the gloss of success* FACADE, veneer, surface, show, camouflage, disguise, mask, smokescreen; window dressing.

▸ verb **1** *she glossed her lips* MAKE GLOSSY, shine; glaze, polish, burnish.

2 *he tried to* ***gloss over*** *his problems* CONCEAL, cover up, hide, disguise, mask, veil; shrug off, brush aside, play down, minimize, understate, make light of; *informal* brush under the carpet.

gloss[2] noun *glosses in the margin* EXPLANATION, interpretation, exegesis, explication, elucidation; annotation, note, footnote, commentary, comment, rubric; translation, definition; *historical* scholium.

▸ verb *difficult words are glossed in a footnote* EXPLAIN, interpret, explicate, define, elucidate; annotate; translate, paraphrase.

glossy adjective **1** *a glossy wooden floor* SHINY, gleaming, lustrous, brilliant, shimmering, glistening, satiny, sheeny, smooth, glassy; polished, lacquered, glazed. ANTONYMS dull, lusterless.

2 *a glossy magazine* EXPENSIVE, high-quality; stylish, fashionable, glamorous; attractive, artistic, upmarket; *informal* classy, ritzy, glitzy. ANTONYMS downmarket, cheap.

glove noun MITTEN, mitt, gauntlet. See table.

GLOVES AND MITTS

baseball glove	gauntlets
boxing gloves	hockey gloves
buckskin gloves	kid gloves
capeskin gloves	leather gloves
catcher's mitt	mittens
deerskin gloves	opera gloves
doeskins	oven mitt
dress gloves	rubber gloves
driving gloves	suede gloves
gardening gloves	surgical gloves

glow verb **1** *lights glowed from the windows* SHINE, radiate, gleam, glimmer, flicker, flare; luminesce.

2 *a fire glowed in the hearth* RADIATE HEAT, smolder, burn.

3 *she glowed with embarrassment* FLUSH, blush, redden, color (up), go pink, go scarlet; burn.

4 *she glowed with pride* TINGLE, thrill; beam.

▸ noun **1** *the glow of the fire* RADIANCE, light, shine, gleam, glimmer, incandescence, luminescence; warmth, heat.

2 *a glow spread over her face* FLUSH, blush, rosiness, pinkness, redness, high color; bloom, radiance. ANTONYM pallor.

3 *a warm glow deep inside her* HAPPINESS, contentment, pleasure, satisfaction.

glower verb *she glowered at him* SCOWL, glare, look daggers, frown, lower, give someone a black look; *informal* give someone a dirty look.

▸ noun *the glower on his face* SCOWL, glare, frown, black look; *informal* dirty look.

glowing adjective **1** *glowing coals* BRIGHT, shining, radiant, glimmering, flickering, twinkling, incandescent, luminous, luminescent; lit (up), lighted, illuminated, ablaze; aglow, smoldering.

2 *his glowing cheeks* ROSY, pink, red, flushed, blushing; radiant, blooming, ruddy, florid; hot, burning.

3 *glowing colors* VIVID, vibrant, bright, brilliant, rich, intense, strong, radiant, warm.

4 *a glowing report* COMPLIMENTARY, favorable, enthusiastic, positive, commendatory, admiring, lionizing, rapturous, rhapsodic, adulatory; fulsome; *informal* rave.

glue noun *a tube of glue* ADHESIVE, fixative, gum, paste, cement; epoxy, epoxy resin, size, sizing, mucilage, stickum.

▸ verb **1** *the planks were glued together* STICK, gum, paste; affix, fix, cement, bond.

2 *informal she **is glued to** the television* BE RIVETED TO, be gripped by, be hypnotized by, be mesmerized by.

glum adjective *Gary sure looks glum today* GLOOMY, downcast, downhearted, dejected, despondent, crestfallen, disheartened; depressed, desolate, unhappy, doleful, melancholy, miserable, woebegone, mournful, forlorn, in the doldrums, morose; *informal* blue, down in/at the mouth, in a blue funk, down in the dumps. ANTONYM cheerful.

THE RIGHT WORD

All happy people are alike, to paraphrase Tolstoy, but each unhappy person is unhappy in his or her own way. A **sullen** person is gloomy, untalkative, and ill-humored by nature; a **glum** person is usually silent because of low spirits or depressing circumstances (*to be glum in the face of a plummeting stock market*). **Melancholy** suggests a more or less chronic sadness (*her melancholy was the result of an unhappy childhood*), while a person who is **saturnine** has a forbiddingly gloomy and taciturn nature (*his request was met with a saturnine and scornful silence*). **Dour** refers to a grim and bitter outlook or disposition (*a dour old woman who never smiled*), and **doleful** implies a mournful sadness (*the child's doleful expression as his parents left*). Someone or something described as **lugubrious** is mournful or gloomy in an affected or exaggerated way (*lugubrious songs about lost love*).

glut noun *a glut of cars* SURPLUS, excess, surfeit, superfluity, overabundance, superabundance, oversupply, plethora. ANTONYM dearth.

▸ verb *the factories are glutted* OVERLOAD, cram, cram full, overfill, oversupply, saturate, flood, inundate, deluge, swamp, congest; *informal* stuff.

glutinous adjective *a glutinous white liquid* STICKY, viscous, viscid, tacky, gluey, gummy, treacly; adhesive; *informal* gooey, cloggy, gloppy.

glutton noun *I can barely stomach being at the same table with that glutton* GOURMAND, overeater, big eater, gorger, gobbler; *informal* pig, greedy pig, guzzler.

gluttonous adjective *doesn't anyone ever feed those gluttonous children?* GREEDY, gourmandizing, voracious, insatiable, wolfish; *informal* piggish, piggy. See note at GREEDY.

gluttony noun *the gluttony you displayed last evening was reprehensible* GREED, greediness, overeating, gourmandism, gourmandizing, voracity, insatiability; *informal* piggishness.

gnarled adjective **1** *a gnarled tree trunk* KNOBBLY, knotty, knotted, gnarly, lumpy, bumpy, nodular; twisted, bent, crooked, distorted, contorted.

2 *gnarled hands* TWISTED, bent, misshapen; arthritic; rough, wrinkled, wizened.

gnash verb *she wailed and gnashed her teeth* GRIND, grate, rasp, grit; *archaic* gristbite.

gnaw verb **1** *the dog gnawed at a bone* CHEW, chomp, champ, bite, munch, crunch; nibble.

2 *the pressures are **gnawing away at** their independence* ERODE, wear away, wear down, eat away (at); consume, devour.

3 *the doubts **gnawed at** her* NAG, plague, torment, torture, trouble, distress, worry, haunt, oppress, burden, hang over, bother, fret; niggle at.

go verb **1** *he's gone into town* MOVE, proceed, make one's way, advance, progress, pass; walk, travel, journey; *literary* betake oneself.

2 *the road goes to Michigan Avenue* EXTEND, stretch, reach; lead.

3 *the money will go to charity* BE GIVEN, be donated, be granted, be presented, be awarded; be devoted; be handed (over).

4 *it's time to go* LEAVE, depart, go away, withdraw, absent oneself, make an exit, exit; set off, start out, get underway, be on one's way; decamp, retreat, retire, make off, clear out, run off, run away, flee, make a move; *informal* make tracks, push off, beat it, take off, skedaddle, scram, split, scoot. ANTONYMS arrive, come.

5 *how quickly the years* ***go by*** PASS, elapse, slip by/past, roll by/past, tick away; fly by/past.

6 *a golden age that has gone for good* DISAPPEAR, vanish, be no more, cease to exist, come to an end, be over, run its course, fade away; finish, end, cease. ANTONYM return.

7 *when your money* ***is gone****, you'll come crawling back* BE USED UP, be spent, be exhausted, be consumed, be drained, be depleted.

8 *I'd like to see my grandchildren before I go* DIE, pass away, pass on, lose one's life, expire, breathe one's last, perish, go to meet one's maker; *informal* give up the ghost, kick the bucket, croak, buy it, bite the big one, buy the farm, check out; *archaic* decease, depart this life.

9 *the bridge went suddenly* COLLAPSE, give way, fall down, cave in, crumble, disintegrate.

10 *his hair had gone gray* BECOME, get, turn, grow.

11 *he heard the bell go* MAKE A SOUND, sound, reverberate, resound; ring, chime, peal, toll, clang.

12 *everything went well* TURN OUT, work out, develop, come out; result, end (up); *informal* pan out.

13 *those colors don't go* MATCH, be harmonious, harmonize, blend, be suited, be complementary, coordinate, be compatible. ANTONYM clash.

14 *my car won't go* FUNCTION, work, run, operate.

15 *where does the cutlery go?* BELONG, be kept.

16 *this all goes to prove my point* CONTRIBUTE, help, serve; incline, tend.

▸ noun 1 *her second go* ATTEMPT, try, effort, bid, endeavor; *informal* shot, stab, crack, bash, whirl, whack; *formal* essay.

2 *he has plenty of go in him* ENERGY, vigor, vitality, life, liveliness, spirit, verve, enthusiasm, zest, vibrancy, sparkle; stamina, dynamism, drive, push, determination; *informal* pep, punch, oomph, get-up-and-go.

PHRASES: **go about** *Ruth went about with her housework* SET ABOUT, begin, embark on, start, commence, address oneself to, get down to, get to work on, get going on, undertake; approach, tackle, attack; *informal* get cracking on/with. **go along with** *I'm willing to go along with that idea* AGREE TO/WITH, fall in with, comply with, cooperate with, acquiesce in, assent to, follow; submit to, yield to, defer to. **go around** 1 *the wheels were going around* SPIN, revolve, turn, rotate, whirl. 2 *a nasty rumor is going around* BE SPREAD, be circulated, be put about, circulate, be broadcast. **go away.** See GO verb sense 4. **go back on** *she went back on her promise* RENEGE ON, break, fail to honor, default on, repudiate, retract; do an about-face; *informal* cop out (of). **go by** *we have to go by his decision* OBEY, abide by, comply with, keep to, conform to, follow, heed, defer to, respect. **go down** 1 *the ship went down* SINK, founder, go under. 2 *interest rates are going down* DECREASE, get lower, fall, drop, decline; plummet, plunge, slump. 3 *informal they went down in the first round* LOSE, be beaten, be defeated. 4 *his name will go down in history* BE REMEMBERED, be recorded, be commemorated, be immortalized. **go far** *stick with your aunts' company and you'll go far* BE SUCCESSFUL, succeed, be a success, do well, get on, get somewhere, get ahead, make good; *informal* make a name for oneself, make one's mark. **go for** 1 *I went for the tuna* CHOOSE, pick, opt for, select, decide on, settle on. 2 *the dog went for her* ATTACK, assault, hit, strike, beat up, assail, set upon, rush at, lash out at; *informal* lay into, rough up, have a go at, beat up on. 3 *she goes for younger men* BE ATTRACTED TO, like, fancy; prefer, favor, choose; *informal* have a thing about. **go in for** *until I got to San Juan, I'd never gone in for water sports* TAKE PART IN, participate in, engage in, get involved in, join in, enter into, undertake; practice, pursue; espouse, adopt, embrace. **go into** *you should have gone into the subject more thoroughly* INVESTIGATE, examine, inquire into, look into, research, probe, explore, delve into; consider, review, analyze. **go off** *the bomb went off* EXPLODE, detonate, blow up. **go on** 1 *the lecture went on for hours* LAST, continue, carry on, run on, proceed; endure, persist; take. 2 *she went on about her cruise* TALK AT LENGTH, ramble, rattle on, chatter, prattle, blather, twitter; *informal* gab, yak, yabber, yatter, run off at the mouth, mouth off. 3 *I'm not sure what went on* HAPPEN, take place, occur, transpire; *informal* go down; *literary* come to pass, betide. **go out** 1 *the lights went out* BE TURNED OFF, be extinguished; stop burning. 2 *he's* ***going out with*** *Kate* SEE, date, take out, be someone's boyfriend/girlfriend, be involved with; *informal* go steady with, go with; *dated* court, woo, step out with. **go over** 1 *go over the figures* EXAMINE, study, scrutinize, inspect, look at/over, scan, check; analyze, appraise, review. 2 *we are going over our lines* REHEARSE, practice, read through, run through. **go through** 1 *the terrible things she has gone through* UNDERGO, experience, face, suffer, be subjected to, live through, endure, brave, bear, tolerate, withstand, put up with, cope with, weather. 2 *she went through hundreds of dollars* SPEND, use up, run through, get through, expend, deplete, burn up; waste, squander, fritter away. 3 *she went through Sue's bag* SEARCH, look through, hunt through, rummage in/through, rifle through. 4 *I have to go through the report* EXAMINE, study, scrutinize, inspect, look over, scan, check; analyze, appraise, review. 5 *the deal has gone through* BE COMPLETED, be concluded, be brought off; be approved, be signed, be rubber-stamped, be given the green light. **go under** *another local restaurant has gone under* GO BANKRUPT, be shut (down), go into receivership, go into liquidation, become insolvent, be liquidated, cease trading; fail; *informal* go broke, go belly up, fold. **go without** 1 *I went without breakfast* ABSTAIN FROM, refrain from, forgo, do without, deny oneself. 2 *the children did not go without* BE DEPRIVED, be in want, go short, go hungry, be in need.

goad noun 1 *he applied his goad to the cows* PROD, spike, staff, crook, rod.

2 *a goad to political change* STIMULUS, incentive, encouragement, inducement, fillip, spur, prod, prompt, catalyst; motive, motivation.

▸ verb *we were goaded into action* PROVOKE, spur, prod, egg on, hound, badger, incite, rouse, stir, move, stimulate, motivate, prompt, induce, encourage, urge, inspire; impel, pressure, dragoon.

go-ahead *informal* noun *they gave the go-ahead for the scheme* PERMISSION, consent, leave, license, dispensation, warrant, clearance; authorization, assent, agreement, approval, endorsement, sanction, blessing, nod; *informal* thumbs up, OK, green light.

▸ adjective *go-ahead companies* ENTERPRISING, resourceful, innovative, ingenious, original, creative; progressive, pioneering, modern, forward-looking, enlightened; enthusiastic, ambitious, entrepreneurial, high-powered; bold, daring, audacious, adventurous, dynamic; *informal* go-getting.

goal noun *I never numbered wealth as one of my goals* OBJECTIVE, aim, end, target, design, intention, intent, plan, purpose; (holy) grail; ambition, aspiration, wish, dream, brass ring, desire, hope.

goat noun **1** *a herd of goats* billy goat, nanny goat, kid.

2 *be careful of that old goat* LECHER, libertine, womanizer, seducer, Don Juan, Casanova, Lothario, Romeo; pervert, debauchee, rake; *informal* lech, dirty old man, ladykiller, wolf.

gobble verb *must you gobble your food so? | he* ***gobbled down*** *every last crumb | the dogs* ***gobbled up*** *their kibble* EAT GREEDILY, EAT HUNGRILY, guzzle, bolt, gulp (down), devour, wolf (down), gorge (oneself) on; *informal* tuck into, put away, pack away, demolish, polish off, shovel in/down, stuff one's face with, pig out on; *informal* scoff (down/up), scarf (down/up), inhale; *rare* gluttonize, gourmandize, ingurgitate.

gobbledygook, gobbledegook noun *informal a letter full of legal gobbledygook* GIBBERISH, claptrap, nonsense, rubbish, balderdash, blather, garbage; *informal* mumbo-jumbo, drivel, tripe, hogwash, baloney, bilge, bull, bunk, guff, eyewash, piffle, twaddle, poppycock, phooey, hooey.

go-between noun *history will recognize Carter's skills as a go-between* INTERMEDIARY, middleman, agent, broker, liaison, contact; negotiator, interceder, intercessor, mediator.

goblet noun *the goblets go on the right* WINE GLASS, water glass, chalice; glass, tumbler, cup, beaker.

goblin noun *the goblins of Yekov would make their surreptitious jaunts into town every third moon* HOBGOBLIN, gnome, dwarf, troll, imp, elf, brownie, fairy, pixie, leprechaun.

god noun **1 (God)** *a gift from God* THE LORD, the Almighty, the Creator, the Maker, the Godhead; Allah, Jehovah, Yahweh; (God) the Father, (God) the Son, the Holy Ghost/Spirit, the Holy Trinity; the Great Spirit, Gitchi Manitou; *humorous* the Man Upstairs.

2 *sacrifices to appease the gods* DEITY, goddess, divine being, celestial being, divinity, immortal, avatar. See table.

3 *wooden gods* IDOL, graven image, icon, totem, talisman, fetish, juju.

godforsaken adjective *this godforsaken town holds no future for you* WRETCHED, miserable, dreary, dismal, depressing, grim, cheerless, bleak, desolate, gloomy; deserted, neglected, isolated, remote, backward. ANTONYM charming.

godless adjective **1** *a godless society* ATHEISTIC, unbelieving, agnostic, skeptical, heretical, faithless, irreligious, ungodly, unholy, impious, profane; infidel, heathen, idolatrous, pagan; satanic, devilish. ANTONYM religious.

2 *godless pleasures* IMMORAL, wicked, sinful, wrong, evil, bad, iniquitous, corrupt; irreligious, sacrilegious, profane, blasphemous, impious; depraved, degenerate, de-

GODS AND GODDESSES

Greek
Aeolus
Amphitrite
Aphrodite
Apollo (Phoebus)
Ares
Artemis
Asclepius
Athena
Cronus
Demeter
Dionysus
Eos
Eros
Gaia
Hebe
Hecate
Helios
Hephaestus
Hera
Hermes
Hestia
Hygeia
Hymen
Hypnos
Iris
Momus
Nemesis
Nereus
Oceanus
Orpheus
Pan
Paris
Persephone
Phaethon
Philemon
Pluto
Poseidon
Priapus
Proteus
Selene
Serapis
Tartarus
Tethys
Themis
Tyche
Uranus
Victory
Zeus

Roman
Aesculapius
Aurora
Bellona
Ceres
Cupid
Diana
Faunus
Flora
Fortuna
Juno
Jupiter
Luna
Maia
Mars
Mercury
Minerva
Mithras
Morpheus
Neptune
Orcus
Saturn
Venus
Vesta
Vulcan

Scandinavian
Aegir
the Aesir
Asgard
Aurvandil
Balder
Bil
Bragi
Eastre/Ostara
Forseti
Frey
Freya
Frigga
Fulla
Gefjon
Heimdall
Hel
Hermod
Hodur
Idun
Loki
Nanna
Niord
the Norns
Odin
Ran
Sif
Skadi
Thor
Tyr
Ull
Vali
the Valkyries
the Vanir
Vidar
the Waves
Ymir

Middle Eastern
Anshar
Anu
Apsu
Aruru
Assur
Astarte
Baal
Dagan
Ea
Ellil
Ishtar
Ishum
Lahmu
Marduk
Moloch
Mummu
Nanaja
Nergal
Ningal
Ninmah
Ninurta
Nissaba
Qingu
Shamash
Sin
Tammuz
Tiamat

Indian/Hindu/Vedic
Agni
Brahma
Ganesha
Ganga
Hanuman
Indra

continued next page

Kali	Khonsu
Krishna	Maat
Kubera	Mut
Lakshmi	Nut
Parvati	Osiris
Ram	Ptah
Saraswati	Ra
Shiva	Sekhmet
Soma	Seth
Surya	Thoth
Varuna	
Vayu	**Mesoamerican**
Vishnu	Chalchiuhtlicue
Yama	Coatlicue
	Huitzilopochtli
Egyptian	Hunab Ku
Amun/Ammon	Huracán
Anubis	Itzamna
Apis	Kukulkán
Bastet	Mictlantecuhtli
Bes	Quetzalcóatl
Hathor	Teotihuacan
Horus	Tezcatlipoca
Isis	

bauched, perverted, decadent; impure. ANTONYM virtuous.

godlike adjective *the godlike giants of Roman mythology* DIVINE, godly, superhuman; angelic, seraphic; spiritual, heavenly, celestial; sacred, holy, saintly.

godly adjective *their claims of a godly agenda do not jibe with their hateful activities* RELIGIOUS, devout, pious, reverent, believing, God-fearing, saintly, holy, prayerful, spiritual, churchgoing.

godsend noun *the state subsidies have been a godsend to our preschool center* BOON, blessing, bonus, plus, benefit, advantage, help, aid, asset; stroke of luck, windfall, manna (from heaven). ANTONYM curse.

go-getter noun *he wasn't enough of a go-getter to make it as a salesman* ACHIEVER, high flyer, success story, high achiever, man/woman of action; bigwig, mover and shaker, wheeler-dealer, hustler.

goings-on plural noun *the goings-on at his Hollywood parties have become legendary* EVENTS, happenings, affairs, business; mischief, misbehavior, misconduct, funny business; *informal* monkey business, hanky-panky, shenanigans.

gold noun **1** *she won the gold* GOLD MEDAL, first prize.
2 *he struck gold* PAY DIRT, the jackpot, the bull's-eye.

golden adjective **1** *her golden hair* BLOND/BLONDE, yellow, fair, flaxen, tow-colored. ANTONYMS dark, raven.

2 *a golden time* SUCCESSFUL, prosperous, flourishing, thriving; favorable, providential, lucky, fortunate; happy, joyful, glorious. ANTONYMS unsuccessful, unhappy.

3 *a golden opportunity* EXCELLENT, fine, superb, splendid; special, unique; favorable, opportune, promising, bright, full of promise; advantageous, profitable, valuable, providential.

4 *the golden girl of tennis* FAVORITE, favored, popular, admired, beloved, pet; acclaimed, applauded, praised; brilliant, consummate, gifted; *informal* blue-eyed; *formal* lauded.

golf noun See note and table.

USAGE NOTE **golf**

One may either *play golf* (the phrase dates from ca. 1575) or simply *golf* (ca. 1800)—that is, *golf* can be a verb as well as a noun. Most golfers use the older phrasing and say that they *play golf* (*I'll be playing golf on Saturday*), whereas nowadays nongolfers tend to be the ones who use *golf* as a verb (*she'll be golfing on Saturday*). In modern print sources, *played golf* is 20 times as common as *golfed.* Writers on golf often disparage the verb *golf* as symptomatic of linguistic dufferdom—e.g.: One writer states: "If you call yourself a golfer, you never use *golf* as a verb. You never say 'We went golfing.' *Golf* to a golfer is a noun. A guy tells you he 'golfs,' and you know he's clueless." (*San Francisco Examiner*, June 14, 1998.) If you're serious about golf and writing, stick to the noun uses of *golf*. That will never get anyone teed off. —BG

GOLF TERMS

Scoring	**On a Golf Course**
ace	apron
albatross	back nine
birdie	bunker
bogey	caddy
bye	card
dormie	collar
double bogey	cup
double eagle	divot
eagle	dogleg
halve	fairway
handicap	flag
hole-in-one	flagstick
match play	foursome
par	fringe
penalty	front nine
stroke play	gallery
	golf bag
Shots	golf ball
address	golf cart
approach	green
backswing	greens fee
bisque	greenskeeper
carry	hazard
chip shot	hole
cut	leader board
draw	links
drive	lip
duck hook	nineteenth hole
duff	pin
fade	rough
fat	sand trap
flier	stick
fore!	tee
gimme	trap
honor	turn
hook	water hazard
lag	
loft	**Types of Club**
mulligan	brassie
pitch shot	driver
pull	iron
putt	jigger
recovery	long iron
run-up	putter
shank	sand wedge
short game	short iron
slice	wedge
stroke	wood
waggle	
	Related Activities
Ball Position	driving range
lie	miniature golf
pin-high	mini-golf
stymie	snow golf

gone adjective 1 *I wasn't gone long* AWAY, absent, off, out; missing, unavailable. ANTONYM present.

2 *those days are gone* PAST, over, over and done with, no more, done, finished, ended; forgotten, dead and buried. ANTONYMS here, extant.

3 *the milk's all gone* USED UP, consumed, finished, spent, depleted; at an end. ANTONYM replenished.

4 *an aunt of mine, long since gone* DEAD, deceased, expired, departed, no more, passed on/away; late, lost, lamented; perished, fallen; defunct, extinct; *informal* six feet under, pushing up daisies; *euphemistic* with God, asleep, at peace; *rare* demised, exanimate. ANTONYM alive.

goo noun *informal what's that goo on the seat?* STICKY SUBSTANCE, ooze, sludge, muck; *informal* gunk, crud, gloop, glop.

good adjective 1 *a good product* FINE, superior, quality; excellent, superb, outstanding, magnificent, exceptional, marvelous, wonderful, first-rate, first-class, sterling; satisfactory, acceptable, not bad, all right; *informal* great, OK, A1, jake, hunky-dory, ace, terrific, fantastic, fabulous, fab, top-notch, blue-chip, blue-ribbon, bang-up, killer, class, awesome, wicked; smashing, brilliant. ANTONYM bad.

2 *a good person* VIRTUOUS, righteous, upright, upstanding, moral, ethical, high-minded, principled; exemplary, law-abiding, irreproachable, blameless, guiltless, unimpeachable, honorable, scrupulous, reputable, decent, respectable, noble, trustworthy; meritorious, praiseworthy, admirable; whiter than white, saintly, saintlike, angelic; *informal* squeaky clean. ANTONYM wicked.

3 *the children are good at school* WELL-BEHAVED, obedient, dutiful, polite, courteous, respectful, deferential, compliant. ANTONYM naughty.

4 *a good thing to do* RIGHT, correct, proper, decorous, seemly; appropriate, fitting, apt, suitable; convenient, expedient, favorable, opportune, felicitous, timely; *archaic* meet.

5 *a good driver* CAPABLE, able, proficient, adept, adroit, accomplished, skillful, skilled, talented, masterly, virtuoso, expert; *informal* great, mean, wicked, nifty, ace, crackerjack. ANTONYM inept.

6 *a good friend* CLOSE, intimate, dear, bosom, special, best, firm, valued, treasured; loving, devoted, loyal, faithful, constant, reliable, dependable, trustworthy, trusty, true, unfailing, staunch.

7 *the dogs are in good condition* HEALTHY, fine, sound, tiptop, hale and hearty, fit, robust, sturdy, strong, vigorous. ANTONYMS poor, ill.

8 *a good time was had by all* ENJOYABLE, pleasant, agreeable, pleasurable, delightful, great, nice, lovely; amusing, diverting, jolly, merry, lively; *informal* super, fantastic, fabulous, fab, terrific, grand, brilliant, killer, peachy, ducky. ANTONYMS unpleasant, terrible.

9 *it was good of you to come* KIND, kindhearted, goodhearted, thoughtful, generous, charitable, magnanimous, gracious; altruistic, unselfish, selfless. ANTONYMS unkind, thoughtless.

10 *a good time to call* CONVENIENT, suitable, appropriate, fitting, fit; opportune, timely, favorable, advantageous, expedient, felicitous, happy, providential. ANTONYM inconvenient.

11 *bananas are good for you* WHOLESOME, healthy, healthful, nourishing, nutritious, nutritional, beneficial, salubrious. ANTONYMS bad, unhealthy.

12 *are these eggs good?* EDIBLE, safe to eat, fit for human consumption; fresh, wholesome, consumable; *formal* comestible. ANTONYMS bad, inedible.

13 *good food* DELICIOUS, tasty, mouthwatering, appetizing, flavorful, delectable, toothsome, palatable; succulent, luscious; *informal* scrumptious, delish, yummy, lip-smacking, finger-licking, nummy, melt-in-your-mouth.

14 *a good reason* VALID, genuine, authentic, legitimate, sound, bona fide; convincing, persuasive, telling, potent, cogent, compelling. ANTONYM unconvincing.

15 *we waited a good hour* WHOLE, full, entire, complete, solid.

16 *a good number of them* CONSIDERABLE, sizable, substantial, appreciable, significant; goodly, fair, reasonable; plentiful, abundant, great, large, generous; *informal* tidy. ANTONYM small.

17 *wear your good clothes* BEST, finest, nicest; special, party, Sunday, formal, dressy, smart, smartest. ANTONYMS casual, everyday.

18 *good weather* FINE, fair, dry; bright, clear, sunny, cloudless; calm, windless; warm, mild, balmy, clement, pleasant, nice. ANTONYMS bad, inclement.

▸ noun 1 *issues of good and evil* VIRTUE, righteousness, goodness, morality, integrity, rectitude; honesty, truth, honor, probity; propriety, worthiness, merit; blamelessness, purity. ANTONYM wickedness.

2 *it's all for your good* BENEFIT, advantage, profit, gain, interest, welfare, well-being; enjoyment, comfort, ease, convenience; help, aid, assistance, service; behalf. ANTONYM disadvantage.

▸ exclamation *good, that's settled* FINE, very well, all right, right, all right then, yes, agreed; *informal* okay, OK, okey-dokey.

PHRASES: **for good** *those days are gone for good* FOREVER, permanently, for always, evermore, forevermore, for ever and ever, for eternity, never to return, forevermore; *informal* for keeps, until the cows come home, until hell freezes over; *archaic* for aye. **make good 1** *if I don't get away from my family, I'll never make good* SUCCEED, be successful, be a success, do well, get ahead, reach the top; prosper, flourish, thrive; *informal* make it, make the grade, make a name for oneself, make one's mark, get somewhere, arrive. **2** *he promised to make good any damage* REPAIR, mend, fix, put right, see to; restore, remedy, rectify. **3** *they made good their escape* EFFECT, conduct, perform, implement, execute, carry out; achieve, accomplish, succeed in, realize, attain, engineer, bring about, bring off. **4** *he will make good his promise* FULFILL, carry out, implement, discharge, honor, redeem; keep, observe, abide by, comply with, stick to, heed, follow, be bound by, live up to, stand by, adhere to.

goodbye exclamation *Goodbye! See you all next year!* FAREWELL, adieu, au revoir, ciao, adios; bye, bye-bye, so long, see you later, see you, sayonara; bon voyage; cheers; *informal* toodle-oo. ANTONYM hello.

▸ noun (often **goodbyes**) *we said our goodbyes at the door* PARTING, leave-taking, send-off.

good-for-nothing adjective *a good-for-nothing bum* USELESS, worthless, incompetent, inefficient, inept, ne'er-do-well; lazy, idle, slothful, indolent, shiftless; *informal* no-good, lousy. ANTONYM worthy.

▸ noun *lazy good-for-nothings* NE'ER-DO-WELL, layabout, do-nothing, idler, loafer, lounger, sluggard, shirker, underachiever; *informal* slacker, lazybones, couch potato.

good-humored adjective *Disney insisted on hiring only the most good-humored of personnel* GENIAL, affable, cordial, friendly, amiable, easygoing, approachable, good-natured, cheerful, cheery; companionable, comradely, sociable, convivial; *informal* chummy. ANTONYM grumpy.

good-looking adjective *a good-looking couple* ATTRACTIVE, beautiful, pretty, handsome, lovely, stunning, striking, arresting, gorgeous, prepossessing, fetching, captivating, bewitching, beguiling, engaging, charming, enchanting, appealing, delightful; sexy, seductive, alluring, tantalizing, irresistible, ravishing, desirable; *Scottish* bonny; *informal* hot, easy on the eye, drop-dead gorgeous, cute, foxy, bodacious; *literary* beauteous; *archaic* comely, fair. ANTONYM ugly.

goodly adjective *I'll bet he paid a goodly sum for that car* LARGE, largish, sizable, substantial, considerable, respectable, significant, decent, generous, handsome; *informal* tidy, serious. ANTONYM paltry.

good-natured adjective *the crowd was rowdy but good-natured* WARMHEARTED, friendly, amiable; neighborly, benevolent, kind, kindhearted, generous, unselfish, considerate, thoughtful, obliging, helpful, supportive, charitable; understanding, sympathetic, easygoing, accommodating. ANTONYM malicious.

goodness noun **1** *she must have seen some goodness in him* VIRTUE, good, righteousness, morality, integrity, rectitude; honesty, truth, truthfulness, honor, probity; propriety, decency, respectability, nobility, worthiness, worth, merit, trustworthiness; blamelessness, purity.

2 *the neighbor's goodness toward us* KINDNESS, kindliness, tenderheartedness, humanity, mildness, benevolence, graciousness; tenderness, warmth, affection, love, goodwill; sympathy, compassion, care, concern, understanding, tolerance, generosity, charity, leniency, clemency, magnanimity.

3 *slow cooking retains the food's goodness* NUTRITIONAL VALUE, nutrients, wholesomeness, nourishment.

THE RIGHT WORD

Of all these words denoting moral excellence, **goodness** is the broadest in meaning. It describes an excellence so well established that it is thought of as inherent or innate and is associated with kindness, generosity, helpfulness, and sincerity (*she has more goodness in her little finger than most people have in their whole body*). **Morality**, on the other hand, is moral excellence based on a code of ethical conduct or religious teaching (*his behavior was kept in line by fear of punishment rather than morality*). Although it is often used as a synonym for *goodness*, **virtue** suggests moral excellence that is acquired rather than innate and that is consciously or steadfastly maintained, often in spite of temptations or evil influences (*her virtue was as unassailable as her noble character*). **Rectitude** is used to describe strict adherence to the rules of just or right behavior and carries strong connotations of sternness and self-discipline (*he had a reputation for rectitude and insisted on absolute truthfulness*). **Probity** describes an honesty or integrity that has been tried and proved (*as mayor, she displayed a probity that was rare in a politician*).

goods plural noun **1** *he dispatched the goods* MERCHANDISE, wares, stock, commodities, produce, products, articles; imports, exports.

2 *the dead woman's goods* PROPERTY, possessions, worldly possessions, effects, chattels, valuables; *informal* things, stuff, junk, gear, bits and pieces.

good-tempered adjective *she was never as good-tempered as her twin brother* EQUABLE, even-tempered, imperturbable; unruffled, unflustered, untroubled, well-balanced; easygoing, mellow, mild, calm, relaxed, cool, at ease; placid, stable, levelheaded; cheerful, upbeat; *informal* unflappable, laid-back. ANTONYM moody.

goodwill noun *your acts of goodwill have not gone unnoticed* BENEVOLENCE, compassion, goodness, kindness, consideration, charity; cooperation, collaboration; friendliness, amity, thoughtfulness, decency, sympathy, understanding, neighborliness. ANTONYM hostility.

goody-goody adjective *informal her goody-goody sister gave us a lecture on how to behave in public* SELF-RIGHTEOUS, sanctimonious, pious; prim and proper, straitlaced, prudish, priggish, puritanical, moralistic; *informal* square.

gooey adjective *informal* **1** *a gooey mess* STICKY, viscous, viscid; gluey, tacky, gummy, treacly, syrupy; *informal* icky, gloppy.

2 *a gooey movie* SENTIMENTAL, mawkish, cloying, sickly, saccharine, sugary, syrupy; romantic, twee; *informal* slushy, sloppy, mushy, schmaltzy, lovey-dovey, cheesy, corny, soppy; cornball, sappy.

goof verb *I think I goofed on the question about the gold standard* BLUNDER, err, mess up, fluff, flub, slip up, make a mistake. See note at MISTAKE.

▸ noun *he acts like such a goof.* See FOOL sense 1.

PHRASE: **goof off** *I didn't want Mr. Lester to think I was just goofing off* MESS AROUND/ABOUT, fool around, clown, act up, play the fool.

goose noun gander, gosling. See table at WATERFOWL.

gore[1] noun *the book's gratuitous gore* BLOOD, bloodiness; bloodshed, slaughter, carnage, butchery.

gore[2] verb *he was gored by a bull* PIERCE, stab, stick, impale, spear, horn.

gorge noun *the river runs through a gorge* RAVINE, canyon, gully, defile, couloir; chasm, gulf; gulch, coulee.

▸ verb **1** *they gorged themselves on cake* STUFF, cram, fill; glut, satiate, overindulge, overfill; *informal* pig out.

2 *vultures **gorged on** the flesh* DEVOUR, guzzle, gobble, gulp (down), wolf (down); *informal* demolish, polish off, scoff (down), down, stuff one's face with; scarf (down/up).

gorgeous adjective **1** *a gorgeous woman.* See GOOD-LOOKING.

2 *a gorgeous view* SPECTACULAR, splendid, superb, wonderful, grand, impressive, awe-inspiring, awesome, amazing, stunning, breathtaking, incredible; *informal* sensational, fabulous, fantastic.

3 *gorgeous uniforms* RESPLENDENT, magnificent, sumptuous, luxurious, elegant, opulent; dazzling, brilliant. ANTONYM drab.

gory adjective **1** *a gory ritual slaughter* GRISLY, gruesome, violent, bloody, brutal, savage; ghastly, frightful, horrid, fearful, hideous, macabre, horrible, horrific; shocking, appalling, monstrous, unspeakable; *informal* blood-and-guts.

2 *gory pieces of flesh* BLOODY, bloodstained, bloodsoaked.

gospel noun 1 **(the Gospel)** *the Gospel according to John* CHRISTIAN TEACHING, Christian doctrine, Christ's teaching; the word of God, the good news, the New Testament.

2 *don't treat this as gospel* THE TRUTH; fact, actual fact, reality, actuality, factuality, the case, a certainty.

3 *her gospel of nonviolence* DOCTRINE, dogma, teaching, principle, ethic, creed, credo, ideology, ideal; belief, tenet, canon.

gossamer noun *her dress swirled like gossamer* COBWEBS; silk, gauze, chiffon.

▸ adjective *a gossamer veil* GAUZY, gossamery, fine, diaphanous, delicate, filmy, floaty, chiffony, cobwebby, wispy, thin, light, insubstantial, flimsy; translucent, transparent, see-through, sheer.

gossip noun 1 *tell me all the gossip* RUMOR(S), tittle-tattle, whispers, canards, tidbits; scandal, hearsay; *informal* dirt, buzz, scuttlebutt.

2 *she's such a gossip* SCANDALMONGER, gossipmonger, tattler, busybody, muckraker, flibbertigibbet.

▸ verb *she gossiped about Dean's wife* SPREAD RUMORS, spread gossip, talk, whisper, tell tales, tittle-tattle, tattle; *informal* dish the dirt.

gouge verb *a tunnel had been gouged out of the mountain* SCOOP, hollow, excavate; cut, dig, scrape, scratch.

gourmand noun *his brother is a shameless gourmand who is eating us out of house and home* GLUTTON, overeater, big eater, gobbler, gorger; *informal* pig, greedy pig, guzzler.

gourmet noun *a restaurant lauded by the most discriminating gourmets* GASTRONOME, epicure, epicurean; connoisseur; *informal* foodie.

govern verb 1 *he governs the province* RULE, preside over, reign over, control, be in charge of, command, lead, dominate; run, head, administer, manage, regulate, oversee, supervise; *informal* be in the driver's seat of.

2 *the rules governing social behavior* DETERMINE, decide, control, regulate, direct, rule, dictate, shape; affect, influence, sway, act on, mold, modify, impact on.

government noun 1 *the government announced further cuts* ADMINISTRATION, executive, regime, authority, powers that be, directorate, council, leadership; cabinet, ministry; *informal* feds; **(the government)** Washington.

2 *her job was the government of the district* RULE, governing, running, leadership, control, administration, regulation, management, supervision.

governor noun *the governor of the island has issued a weather alert* LEADER, ruler, chief, head; *historical* intendant; premier, president, viceroy, chancellor; administrator, principal, director, chairperson, chair, superintendent, commissioner, controller; *informal* boss.

gown noun *a blue gown with seed pearls on the bodice* DRESS, evening gown, prom dress, prom gown, wedding gown; frock, shift; robe, dressing gown.

grab verb 1 *Jessica grabbed his arm* SEIZE, grasp, snatch, take hold of, grip, clasp, clutch; take; *informal* glom on to.

2 *informal I'll grab another drink* GET, acquire, obtain; buy, purchase, procure; secure, snap up; gather, collect, garner; achieve, attain; *informal* get one's hands on, get one's mitts on, get hold of, bag, score, nab.

▸ noun *she made a grab for his gun* LUNGE, snatch.

PHRASE: **up for grabs** *informal dozens of prizes are up for grabs* AVAILABLE, obtainable, to be had, for the taking; for sale, on the market; *informal* for the asking, on tap, gettable.

grace noun 1 *the grace of a ballerina* ELEGANCE, poise, gracefulness, finesse; suppleness, agility, nimbleness, light-footedness. ANTONYMS inelegance, stiffness.

2 *he at least had the grace to look sheepish* COURTESY, decency, (good) manners, politeness, decorum, respect, tact. ANTONYM effrontery.

3 *she fell from grace* FAVOR, approval, approbation, acceptance, esteem, regard, respect; goodwill. ANTONYM disfavor.

4 *he lived there by grace of the king* FAVOR, goodwill, generosity, kindness, indulgence; *formal* benefaction.

5 *they have five days' grace to decide* DEFERMENT, deferral, postponement, suspension, adjournment, delay, pause; respite, stay, moratorium, reprieve.

6 *who would like to say this evening's grace?* BLESSING, prayer of thanks, thanksgiving, benediction.

▸ verb 1 *the occasion was graced by the president* DIGNIFY, distinguish, honor, favor; enhance, ennoble, glorify, elevate, aggrandize, upgrade.

2 *a mosaic graced the floor* ADORN, embellish, decorate, ornament, enhance; beautify, prettify, enrich, bedeck.

graceful adjective *our dancers must be both muscular and graceful* ELEGANT, fluid, fluent, natural, neat; agile, supple, nimble, light-footed.

graceless adjective *Ms. Oakes has turned two dozen graceless eighth graders into a well-choreographed chorus line* GAUCHE, maladroit, inept, awkward, unsure, unpolished, unsophisticated, uncultured, unrefined; clumsy, ungainly, ungraceful, inelegant, uncoordinated, gawky, gangling, bumbling; tactless, thoughtless, inconsiderate; *informal* ham-handed, ham-fisted, klutzy.

gracious adjective 1 *a gracious hostess* COURTEOUS, polite, civil, chivalrous, well-mannered, mannerly, decorous; tactful, diplomatic; kind, benevolent, considerate, thoughtful, obliging, accommodating, indulgent, magnanimous; friendly, amiable, cordial, hospitable. ANTONYM rude.

2 *gracious colonial buildings* ELEGANT, stylish, tasteful, graceful; comfortable, luxurious, sumptuous, opulent, grand, high-class; *informal* swanky, plush. ANTONYMS shabby, crude.

3 *God's gracious intervention* MERCIFUL, compassionate, kind; forgiving, lenient, clement, forbearing, humane, tenderhearted, sympathetic; indulgent, generous, magnanimous, benign, benevolent. ANTONYM cruel.

gradation noun 1 *a gradation of ability* RANGE, scale, spectrum, span; progression, hierarchy, ladder, pecking order.

2 *each of the bands has a number of color gradations within it* LEVEL, grade, rank, position, status, stage, standard, echelon, rung, step, notch; class, stratum, group, grouping, set.

grade noun 1 *a higher grade of steel* CATEGORY, set, class, classification, grouping, group, bracket.

2 *his job is of the lowest grade* RANK, level, echelon, standing, position, class, status, order; step, rung, stratum, tier.

3 *she got the best grades in the class* MARK, score; assessment, evaluation, appraisal.

4 *he's in grade 5* YEAR; class.

5 *a steep grade.* See GRADIENT.

▸ verb 1 *eggs are graded by size* CLASSIFY, class, categorize, bracket, sort, group, arrange, pigeonhole; rank, evaluate, rate, value.

2 *the essays have been graded* SCORE, mark, assess, judge, evaluate, appraise.

3 *the colors grade into one another* BLEND, shade, merge, pass.

PHRASE: **make the grade** *informal he lacked the experience to make the grade* QUALIFY, be up to scratch, come up to standard, pass, pass muster, measure up; succeed, win through; *informal* be up to snuff, cut it, cut the mustard.

gradient noun 1 *the gradient of Miller's Hill Road is less steep than it was fifty years ago* SLOPE, incline, hill, rise, ramp, bank; declivity, grade.

2 *the gradient of the line* STEEPNESS, angle, slant, slope, inclination.

gradual adjective 1 *a gradual transition* SLOW, measured, unhurried, cautious; piecemeal, step-by-step, progressive, continuous, systematic, steady. ANTONYMS abrupt, sudden.

2 *a gradual slope* GENTLE, moderate, slight, easy. ANTONYM steep.

gradually adverb *the icicles gradually got longer throughout the day | gradually add the flour mixture* SLOWLY, slowly but surely, cautiously, gently, gingerly; piecemeal, little by little, bit by bit, inch by inch, by degrees; progressively, systematically; regularly, steadily.

graduate verb 1 *he wants to teach when he graduates* GET ONE'S DIPLOMA, get one's degree, pass one's exams, complete/finish one's studies.

2 *she wants to graduate to serious drama* PROGRESS, advance, move up.

3 *a thermometer graduated in Fahrenheit* CALIBRATE, mark off, measure out, grade.

graduation noun *President Carter spoke at our graduation* GRADUATION CEREMONY, graduation exercises, commencement, convocation.

graffiti noun *the graffiti on the underpass* STREET ART, spray-painting, inscriptions, drawings; defacement, vandalism.

graft[1] noun 1 *grafts may die from lack of water* SCION, cutting, shoot, offshoot, bud, sprout, sprig.

2 *a skin graft* TRANSPLANT, implant.

▸ verb 1 *graft a bud onto the stem* AFFIX, join, insert, splice.

2 *tissue is grafted on to the cornea* TRANSPLANT, implant.

3 *a mansion grafted on to a farmhouse* ATTACH, add, join.

graft[2] noun *sweeping measures to curb official graft* CORRUPTION, bribery, dishonesty, deceit, fraud, unlawful practices, illegal means, payola; *informal* palm-greasing, hush money, kickbacks, crookedness. ANTONYM honesty.

grain noun 1 *the local farmers grow grain* CEREAL, cereal crops. See table at CEREAL.

2 *a grain of wheat* KERNEL, seed, grist.

3 *grains of sand* GRANULE, particle, speck, mote, mite; bit, piece; scrap, crumb, fragment, morsel.

4 *a grain of truth* TRACE, hint, tinge, suggestion, shadow; bit, soupçon; scintilla, ounce, iota, jot, whit, scrap, shred; *informal* smidgen, smidge, tad.

5 *the grain of the lumber* TEXTURE, surface, finish; weave, pattern.

grammar noun *the editors of this newspaper need a refresher course in grammar* SYNTAX, sentence structure, rules of language, morphology; linguistics.

grammatical adjective 1 *the grammatical structure of a sentence* SYNTACTIC, morphological; linguistic.

2 *a grammatical sentence* WELL-FORMED, correct, proper; acceptable, allowable.

grand adjective 1 *a grand hotel* MAGNIFICENT, imposing, impressive, awe-inspiring, splendid, resplendent, majestic, monumental; palatial, stately, large; luxurious, sumptuous, lavish, opulent, upmarket, upscale; *informal* fancy, posh, plush, classy, swanky, five-star. ANTONYMS inferior, unimpressive.

2 *a grand scheme* AMBITIOUS, bold, epic, big, extravagant.

3 *a grand old lady* AUGUST, distinguished, illustrious, eminent, esteemed, honored, venerable, dignified, respectable; preeminent, prominent, notable, renowned, celebrated, famous; aristocratic, noble, regal, blue-blooded, high-born, patrician; *informal* upper-crust. ANTONYMS ordinary, humble.

4 *a grand total of $2,000* COMPLETE, comprehensive, all-inclusive, inclusive; final. ANTONYM partial.

5 *the grand staircase* MAIN, principal, central, prime; biggest, largest. ANTONYMS minor, secondary.

6 *informal you're doing a grand job* EXCELLENT, very good, marvelous, first-class, first-rate, wonderful, outstanding, sterling, fine, splendid, superb, terrific, fabulous, great; *informal* super, ace, killer; smashing, brilliant. ANTONYM poor.

▸ noun *informal a check for ten grand* THOUSAND DOLLARS; *informal* thou, K/Ks; G/Gs, gee/gees.

grandeur noun *the grandeur of the Rockies | the grandeur of a royal wedding* SPLENDOR, magnificence, impressiveness, glory, resplendence, majesty, greatness; stateliness, pomp, ceremony.

grandfather noun 1 *his grandfather lives here informal* granddad, grandad, grandpa, gramps, grampy, granddaddy, grandaddy, poppa.

2 *the grandfather of modern liberalism* FOUNDER, inventor, originator, creator, initiator; father, founding father, pioneer.

3 *our pioneering grandfathers* FOREFATHER, forebear, ancestor, progenitor, antecedent.

▸ verb *federal funding was eliminated for these air-polluting road projects, but a loophole has grandfathered the previously funded projects* EXEMPT, excuse, free, exclude, grant immunity to, spare, absolve; *informal* let off (the hook).

grandiloquent adjective *grandiloquent speeches* POMPOUS, bombastic, magniloquent, pretentious, ostentatious, high-flown, orotund, florid, flowery; overwrought, overblown, overdone; *informal* highfalutin, purple. ANTONYM understated.

grandiose adjective **1** *the court's grandiose facade* MAGNIFICENT, impressive, grand, imposing, awe-inspiring, splendid, resplendent, majestic, glorious, elaborate; palatial, stately, luxurious, opulent; *informal* plush, swanky, flash. ANTONYMS humble, unimpressive.

2 *a grandiose plan* AMBITIOUS, bold, overambitious, extravagant, high-flown, flamboyant; *informal* over the top. ANTONYMS humble, modest.

WORD NOTE **grandiose**

Only a few of the synonyms shown here make it clear that while to be *grand* is one thing, to be *grandiose* is quite another. Something *grandiose* is pretentiously grand; grand with a self-satisfied smirk. There's a terrible tendency, when deciding between similar-sounding synonyms, such as *grand* and *grandiose,* to always choose the longer. If you have this bad habit, make sure the extra syllables aren't also carrying an extra weight of meaning that you don't intend. **—EM**

grandmother noun *informal* grandma, gramma, granny, grannie, gran, nana.

grant verb **1** *he granted them leave of absence* ALLOW, accord, permit, afford, vouchsafe. ANTONYM refuse.

2 *he granted them $20,000* GIVE, award, bestow on, confer on, present with, provide with, endow with, supply with. See note at GIVE.

3 *I grant that the difference is not absolute* ADMIT, accept, concede, yield, allow, appreciate, recognize, acknowledge, confess; agree. ANTONYM deny.

▸ noun *a grant from the council* ENDOWMENT, subvention, award, donation, bursary, allowance, subsidy, contribution, handout, allocation, gift; scholarship.

granular adjective *two new inches of granular snow* POWDER, powdered, powdery, grainy, granulated, gritty.

granulated adjective *granulated tea leaves* POWDERED, crushed, crumbled, ground, minced, grated, pulverized; particulate.

granule noun *minute granules of gold* GRAIN, particle, fragment, bit, crumb, morsel, mote, speck.

graph noun *use graphs to analyze your data* CHART, diagram; bar chart, pie chart, histogram, scatter diagram.

▸ verb *we graphed the new prices* PLOT, trace, draw up, delineate.

graphic adjective **1** *a graphic representation of language* VISUAL, symbolic, pictorial, illustrative, diagrammatic; drawn, written.

2 *a graphic account of the war* VIVID, explicit, expressive, detailed; uninhibited, powerful, colorful, rich, lurid, shocking; realistic, descriptive, illustrative; telling, effective. ANTONYM vague.

▸ noun *Computing* *this printer's good enough for graphics* PICTURE, illustration, image; diagram, graph, chart; (**graphics**) art, visual art.

THE RIGHT WORD

A photograph of a car accident on the front page of a newspaper might be described as **graphic**, while a photograph of a mountain village would be called **picturesque**. Both adjectives are used to describe things that have visual impact or that produce a strong, clear impression, but *graphic* means having the power to evoke a strikingly lifelike representation, whether it is in pictures or in words (*the driving instructor gave them a graphic description of what happens in a 50-mph head-on collision*). **Vivid** is a more general term suggesting something that is felt, seen, heard, or apprehended with a sense of intense reality (*the vivid colors of the landscape; a vivid memory of the horrors of war*). Something that is **pictorial** aims to present a vivid picture (*a pictorial writing style*), while **picturesque** usually applies to scenes, pictures, etc. that are visually striking because they are panoramic, quaint, or unusual (*from a distance the village looked picturesque, but up close it was seen to be rundown*).

grapple verb **1** *the policemen grappled with him* WRESTLE, struggle, tussle; brawl, fight, scuffle, battle.

2 *he grappled his prey* SEIZE, grab, catch, catch hold of, take hold of, grasp.

3 *she is* ***grappling with*** *her problems* TACKLE, confront, face, deal with, cope with, come to grips with; apply oneself to, devote oneself to.

grasp verb **1** *she grasped his hands* GRIP, clutch, clasp, hold, clench; catch, seize, grab, snatch, latch on to. ANTONYM release.

2 *everybody grasped the important points* UNDERSTAND, comprehend, follow, take in, perceive, see, apprehend, assimilate, absorb; *informal* get, catch on to, figure out, get one's head around, take on board.

3 *he grasped the opportunity* TAKE ADVANTAGE OF, act on; seize, leap at, snatch, jump at, pounce on. ANTONYMS miss, overlook.

▸ noun **1** *his grasp on her hand* GRIP, hold; clutch, clasp, clench.

2 *his domineering mother's grasp* CONTROL, power, clutches, command, domination, rule, tyranny.

3 *a prize lay within their grasp* REACH, scope, power, limits, range; sights.

4 *your grasp of history* UNDERSTANDING, comprehension, perception, apprehension, awareness, grip, knowledge; mastery, command.

grasping adjective *a grasping corporate executive* AVARICIOUS, acquisitive, greedy, rapacious, mercenary, materialistic; mean, miserly, parsimonious, niggardly, hoarding, selfish, possessive, close; *informal* tightfisted, tight, stingy, money-grubbing, cheap, grabby.

grass noun *fertilize the grass* TURF, sod; lawn, green.

grassroots adjective *a grassroots movement* POPULAR, of-the-people, bottom-up, nonhierarchical, rank-and-file.

grate verb **1** *she grated the cheese* SHRED, pulverize, mince, grind, granulate, crush, crumble.

2 *her bones grated together* GRIND, rub, rasp, scrape, jar, grit, creak.

3 *the tune is beginning to grate* IRRITATE, set someone's teeth on edge, jar; annoy, nettle, chafe, fret; *informal* aggravate, get on someone's nerves, get under someone's skin, get someone's goat.

grateful adjective *we were all grateful to Rita* THANKFUL, appreciative; indebted, obliged, obligated, in someone's debt, beholden.

gratification noun *a generation that has come to demand* *instant gratification* SATISFACTION, fulfillment, indulgence, relief, appeasement; pleasure, enjoyment, relish.

gratify verb **1** *it gratified him to be seen with her* PLEASE, gladden, make happy, delight, make someone feel good, satisfy; *informal* tickle pink, buck up. See note at PLEASANT. ANTONYM displease.

2 *he gratified her desires* SATISFY, fulfill, indulge, comply with, pander to, cater to, give in to, satiate, feed, accommodate. ANTONYM frustrate.

grating[1] adjective **1** *the chair made a grating noise* SCRAPING, scratching, grinding, rasping, jarring.

2 *a grating voice* HARSH, raucous, strident, piercing, shrill, screechy; discordant, cacophonous; hoarse, rough, gravelly. ANTONYMS harmonious, pleasing.

3 *it's written in grating language* IRRITATING, annoying, infuriating, irksome, maddening, displeasing, tiresome; jarring, unsuitable, inappropriate; *informal* aggravating. ANTONYMS pleasing, appropriate.

grating[2] noun *a strong iron grating* GRID, grate, grille, lattice, trellis, mesh.

gratis adverb *the room was provided gratis, courtesy of the casino* FREE, free of charge, without charge, for nothing, at no cost, gratuitously; *informal* on the house, for free.

gratitude noun *Chip was miffed by his nephew's lack of gratitude* GRATEFULNESS, thankfulness, thanks, appreciation, indebtedness; recognition, acknowledgment, credit.

gratuitous adjective *there was one moment of nudity in the movie, and it was ridiculously gratuitous* UNJUSTIFIED, uncalled for, unwarranted, unprovoked, undue; indefensible, unjustifiable; needless, unnecessary, inessential, unmerited, groundless, senseless, wanton, indiscriminate; excessive, immoderate, inordinate, inappropriate. ANTONYM necessary.

gratuity noun *I'm not allowed to accept this gratuity* TIP, gift, present, donation, reward, handout; bonus, extra; baksheesh. See note at PRESENT[3].

grave[1] noun *she left flowers at his grave* BURIAL SITE, gravesite, cemetery plot, tomb, sepulcher, vault, burial chamber, mausoleum, crypt; last resting place.

grave[2] adjective **1** *a grave matter* SERIOUS, important, weighty, profound, significant, momentous; critical, acute, urgent, pressing; dire, terrible, awful, dreadful; *formal* exigent. ANTONYM trivial.

2 *Jackie looked grave* SOLEMN, serious, sober, unsmiling, grim, somber; severe, stern, dour. ANTONYM cheerful.

gravel noun *two truckloads of gravel* PEBBLES, stones, grit, aggregate, shingle.

gravelly adjective **1** *a gravelly beach* PEBBLY, stony, gritty, shingly.

2 *his gravelly voice* HUSKY, gruff, throaty, deep, croaky, rasping, grating, harsh, rough.

gravestone noun *the inscription on his gravestone* HEADSTONE, tombstone, stone, monument, memorial.

graveyard noun CEMETERY, burial ground, burying ground, necropolis, columbarium, memorial park/garden; *informal* boneyard; *historical* potter's field.

gravitas noun *a man of gravitas* DIGNITY, seriousness, solemnity, gravity, sobriety; authority, weightiness. ANTONYM frivolity.

gravitate verb *take her to a bar, and she automatically gravitates to the lowlifes* MOVE, head, drift, be drawn, be attracted; tend, lean, incline.

gravity noun **1** *the gravity of the situation* SERIOUSNESS, importance, significance, weight, consequence, magnitude; acuteness, urgency, exigence; awfulness, dreadfulness; *formal* moment.

2 *the gravity of his demeanor* SOLEMNITY, seriousness, somberness, sobriety, soberness, severity, grimness, humorlessness, dourness; gloominess.

gray adjective **1** *a gray suit* silvery, silver-gray, gunmetal, slate, charcoal, smoky.

2 *his gray hair* WHITE, silver, hoary.

3 *a gray day* CLOUDY, overcast, dull, sunless, gloomy, dreary, dismal, somber, bleak, murky. ANTONYMS sunny, bright.

4 *her face looked gray* ASHEN, wan, pale, pasty, pallid, colorless, bloodless, white, waxen; sickly, peaked, drained, drawn, deathly. ANTONYM ruddy.

5 *the gray daily routine* CHARACTERLESS, colorless, nondescript, insipid, jejune, unremarkable, flat, bland, dry, stale; dull, uninteresting, boring, tedious, monotonous, monochrome. ANTONYM lively.

6 *their policy regarding unmarried couples is a gray area* AMBIGUOUS, unclear, uncertain, doubtful, indefinite, indistinct, indeterminate, debatable, open to question. ANTONYMS black and white, certain.

▸ verb *the population grayed* AGE, grow old, mature.

graze[1] verb *the deer grazed* FEED, eat, nibble, browse.

graze[2] verb **1** *she grazed her knuckles on the box* SCRAPE, abrade, skin, scratch, chafe, bark, scuff, rasp; cut, nick.

2 *his shot grazed the far post* TOUCH, brush, shave, skim, kiss, scrape, clip, glance off.

▸ noun *grazes on the skin* SCRATCH, scrape, abrasion, cut; *Medicine* trauma.

grease noun **1** *engines covered in grease* OIL, lubricant, lubricator, lubrication.

2 *the kitchen was filmed with grease* FAT, oil, cooking oil, animal fat; lard, suet.

3 *his hair was smothered with grease* GEL, lotion, cream; *dated* brilliantine; *trademark* Brylcreem.

▸ verb *grease the old hinges | grease a baking dish* LUBRICATE, oil, smear/coat/spray with oil, butter.

greasy adjective **1** *a plate of greasy food* FATTY, oily, buttery, oleaginous; *formal* pinguid. ANTONYM lean.

2 *greasy hair* OILY. ANTONYM dry.

3 *the pole was very greasy* SLIPPERY, slick, slimy, slithery, oily; *informal* slippy. ANTONYM dry.

4 *a greasy little man* INGRATIATING, obsequious, sycophantic, fawning, toadying, groveling; effusive, gushing, gushy; unctuous, oily; *informal* smarmy, slimy, bootlicking.

great adjective **1** *they showed great interest* CONSIDERABLE, substantial, significant, appreciable, special, serious; exceptional, extraordinary. ANTONYM little.

2 *a great expanse of water* LARGE, big, extensive, expansive, broad, wide, sizable, ample; vast, immense, huge, enormous, massive; *informal* humongous, whopping, ginormous. ANTONYM small.

3 *you great fool!* ABSOLUTE, total, utter, out-and-out, downright, thoroughgoing, complete; perfect, positive, prize, sheer, arrant, unqualified, consummate, veritable.

4 *great writers* PROMINENT, eminent, important, distinguished, illustrious, celebrated, honored, acclaimed, admired, esteemed, revered, renowned, notable, famous, famed, well-known; leading, top, major, principal, first-rate, matchless, peerless, star. ANTONYM minor.

5 *the great navies in world history* POWERFUL, dominant, influential, strong, potent, formidable, redoubtable; leading, important, foremost, major, chief, principal. ANTONYM minor.

6 *a great castle* MAGNIFICENT, imposing, impressive, awe-inspiring, grand, splendid, majestic, sumptuous, resplendent. ANTONYM modest.

7 *a great sportsman* EXPERT, skillful, skilled, adept, accomplished, talented, fine, masterly, master, brilliant, virtuoso, marvelous, outstanding, first-class, superb; *informal* crack, ace, A1, class. ANTONYM poor.

8 *a great fan of rugby* ENTHUSIASTIC, eager, keen, zealous, devoted, ardent, fanatical, passionate, dedicated, committed. ANTONYM unenthusiastic.

9 *we had a great time* ENJOYABLE, delightful, lovely, pleasant, congenial; exciting, thrilling; excellent, marvelous, wonderful, fine, splendid, very good; *informal* terrific, fantastic, fabulous, splendiferous, fab, super, grand, cool, hunky-dory, killer, swell. ANTONYM bad.

greatly adverb *your donations are greatly appreciated* VERY MUCH, considerably, substantially, appreciably, significantly, markedly, sizably, seriously, materially, profoundly; enormously, vastly, immensely, tremendously, mightily, abundantly, extremely, exceedingly; *informal* plenty, majorly. ANTONYM slightly.

greatness noun **1** *a child destined for greatness* EMINENCE, distinction, illustriousness, repute, high standing; importance, significance; celebrity, fame, prominence, renown.

2 *her greatness as a writer* GENIUS, prowess, talent, expertise, mastery, artistry, virtuosity, skill, proficiency; flair, finesse; caliber, distinction.

grebe See table at WATERFOWL.

greed, greediness noun **1** *human greed* AVARICE, cupidity, acquisitiveness, covetousness, rapacity; materialism, mercenariness; *rare* pleonexia, *informal* money-grubbing, affluenza. ANTONYM generosity.

2 *her mouth watered with greed* GLUTTONY, hunger, voracity, insatiability; gourmandism, intemperance, overeating, self-indulgence; *informal* piggishness. ANTONYM temperance.

3 *their greed for power* DESIRE, appetite, hunger, thirst, craving, longing, lust, yearning, hankering; avidity, eagerness; *informal* yen, itch. ANTONYM indifference.

WORD NOTE **pleonexia**

An ancient word for a contemporary condition. Where *pleonexia* does the linguistic work that simple *greed* or *avarice* does not, is in its diagnosis of a covetousness that is not healthy, that is abnormal. It is a word that needs to be added to the more harmless terms with which we describe the modern consumer. *Pleonexia* is a heightened and unhealthy condition, as *anorexia* is the pathological extremity of a brand of asceticism. There is need, then there is desire, then there is greed, and then there is *pleonexia*. **—ZS**

greedy adjective **1** *a greedy eater* GLUTTONOUS, ravenous, voracious, intemperate, self-indulgent, insatiable, wolfish; *informal* piggish, piggy.

2 *a greedy capitalist* AVARICIOUS, acquisitive, covetous, grasping, materialistic, mercenary, possessive; *informal* money-grubbing, money-grabbing, grabby.

3 *she is greedy for an award* EAGER, avid, hungry, craving, longing, yearning, hankering; impatient, anxious; *informal* dying, itching.

THE RIGHT WORD

The desire for money and the things it can buy is often associated with Americans. But not all Americans are **greedy**, which implies an insatiable desire to possess or acquire something, beyond what one needs or deserves (*greedy for profits*). Someone who is *greedy* for food might be called **gluttonous**, which emphasizes consumption as well as desire (*a gluttonous appetite for sweets*), but *greedy* is a derogatory term only when the object of longing is itself evil or when it cannot be possessed without harm to oneself or others (*a reporter greedy for information*). A *greedy* child may grow up to be an **avaricious** adult, which implies a fanatical greediness for money or other valuables. **Rapacious** is an even stronger term, with an emphasis on taking things by force (*so rapacious in his desire for land that he forced dozens of families from their homes*). **Acquisitive**, on the other hand, is a more neutral word suggesting a willingness to exert effort in acquiring things (*an acquisitive woman who filled her house with antiques and artwork*), and not necessarily material things (*a probing, acquisitive mind*). **Covetous**, in contrast to *acquisitive*, implies an intense desire for something as opposed to the act of acquiring or possessing it. It is often associated with the Ten Commandments (*Thou shalt not covet thy neighbor's wife*) and suggests a longing for something that rightfully belongs to another.

green adjective **1** *a green scarf* viridescent; olive, jade, pea green, emerald (green), lime (green), sea green; *literary* virescent, glaucous.

2 *a green island* VERDANT, grassy, leafy, verdurous. ANTONYM barren.

3 **(Green)** *he promotes Green issues* ENVIRONMENTAL, ecological, conservation, ecocentric, eco-.

4 *a green alternative to diesel* ENVIRONMENTALLY FRIENDLY, nonpolluting, ecological; ozone-friendly. ANTONYM polluting.

5 *green bananas* UNRIPE, immature. ANTONYM ripe.

6 *green firewood* UNSEASONED, not aged; pliable, supple. ANTONYMS seasoned, dry.

7 *the new lieutenant was green* INEXPERIENCED, unversed, callow, immature; new, raw, unseasoned, untried; inexpert, untrained, unqualified, ignorant; simple, unsophisticated, unpolished; naive, innocent, ingenuous, credulous, gullible, unworldly; *informal* wet behind the ears, born yesterday. ANTONYM experienced.

8 *he went green* PALE, wan, pallid, ashen, ashen-faced, pasty, pasty-faced, gray, whitish, washed out, blanched, drained, pinched, sallow; sickly, nauseous, ill, sick, unhealthy. ANTONYM ruddy.

▸ noun **1** *a canopy of green over the road* FOLIAGE, greenery, plants, leaves, leafage, vegetation.

2 *a village green* PARK, common, grassy area, lawn, sward.

3 *eat your* ***greens*** VEGETABLES, leafy vegetables, salad; *informal* veggies.

4 *Greens are against multinationals* ENVIRONMENTALIST, conservationist, preservationist, nature lover, eco-activist; *informal, derogatory* tree hugger, greenie.

greenery noun *the greenery of the summer landscape* FOLIAGE, vegetation, plants, green, leaves, leafage, undergrowth, underbrush, plant life, flora, herbage, verdure.

greenhorn noun *informal* See NOVICE sense 1.

green light noun *he was given the green light to implement his proposals* AUTHORIZATION, permission, approval, assent, consent, sanction; leave, clearance, warranty, agreement, imprimatur, one's blessing, the seal/stamp of approval, the rubber stamp, the nod; authority, license, dispensation, empowerment, freedom, liberty; *informal* the OK, the go-ahead, the thumbs up, the say-so. ANTONYM the red light, refusal.

greet verb **1** *she greeted Hank cheerily* SAY HELLO TO, address, salute, hail; welcome, meet, receive.

2 *the decision was greeted with outrage* RECEIVE, acknowledge, respond to, react to, take.

greeting noun **1** *he shouted a greeting* HELLO, salute, salutation, address; welcome; acknowledgment. ANTONYM farewell.

2 (**greetings**) *birthday greetings* BEST WISHES, good wishes, congratulations, felicitations; compliments, regards, respects.

gregarious adjective **1** *he was fun-loving and gregarious* SOCIABLE, company-loving, convivial, companionable, outgoing, friendly, affable, amiable, genial, warm, comradely; *informal* chummy. ANTONYM unsociable.

2 *gregarious fish* SOCIAL, living in groups.

grid noun **1** *a metal grid* GRATING, mesh, grille, gauze, lattice.

2 *the grid of streets* NETWORK, matrix, reticulation.

grief noun **1** *he was overcome with grief* SORROW, misery, sadness, anguish, pain, distress, heartache, heartbreak, agony, torment, affliction, suffering, woe, desolation, dejection, despair; mourning, mournfulness, bereavement, lamentation; *literary* dolor, dole. ANTONYM joy.

2 *informal the police gave me a lot of grief* TROUBLE, annoyance, bother, irritation, vexation, harassment; *informal* aggravation, hassle.

grief-stricken adjective *grief-stricken families gathered at the church* SORROWFUL, sorrowing, miserable, sad, heartbroken, broken-hearted, anguished, pained, distressed, tormented, suffering, woeful, doleful, desolate, despairing, devastated, upset, inconsolable, wretched; mourning, grieving, mournful, bereaved, lamenting; *literary* dolorous, heartsick. ANTONYM joyful.

grievance noun **1** *social and economic grievances* INJUSTICE, wrong, injury, ill, unfairness; affront, insult, indignity.

2 *students voiced their grievances* COMPLAINT, criticism, objection, grumble, grouse; ill feeling, bad feeling, resentment, bitterness, pique; *informal* gripe; *Brit.* whinge, moan, grouch, niggle, beef, bone to pick.

grieve verb **1** *she grieved for her father* MOURN, lament, sorrow, be sorrowful; cry, sob, weep, shed tears, weep and wail, beat one's breast. See note at MOURN. ANTONYM rejoice.

2 *it grieved me to leave her* SADDEN, upset, distress, pain, hurt, wound, break someone's heart, make someone's heart bleed. ANTONYM please.

grievous *formal* adjective **1** *his death was a grievous blow* SERIOUS, severe, grave, bad, critical, dreadful, terrible, awful, crushing, calamitous; painful, agonizing, traumatic, wounding, damaging, injurious; sharp, acute. ANTONYMS slight, trivial.

2 *a grievous sin* HEINOUS, grave, deplorable, shocking, appalling, atrocious, gross, dreadful, egregious, iniquitous. ANTONYMS venial, trivial.

grim adjective **1** *his grim expression* STERN, forbidding, uninviting, unsmiling, dour, formidable, harsh, steely, flinty, stony; cross, churlish, surly, sour, ill-tempered; fierce, ferocious, threatening, menacing, implacable, ruthless, merciless. ANTONYMS amiable, pleasant.

2 *grim humor* BLACK, dark, mirthless, bleak, cynical. ANTONYM lighthearted.

3 *the asylum holds some grim secrets* DREADFUL, dire, ghastly, horrible, horrendous, horrid, terrible, awful, appalling, frightful, shocking, unspeakable, grisly, gruesome, hideous, macabre; depressing, distressing, upsetting, worrying, unpleasant.

4 *a grim little hovel* BLEAK, dreary, dismal, dingy, wretched, miserable, depressing, cheerless, comfortless, joyless, gloomy, uninviting; *informal* godawful. ANTONYM cheery.

5 *grim determination* RESOLUTE, determined, firm, decided, steadfast, dead set; obstinate, stubborn, obdurate, unyielding, intractable, uncompromising, unshakable, unrelenting, relentless, dogged, tenacious. ANTONYM irresolute.

grimace noun *his mouth twisted into a grimace* SCOWL, frown, sneer; face.

▸ verb *Nina grimaced at Joe* SCOWL, frown, sneer, glower, lower; make a face, make faces. ANTONYM smile.

grime noun *her skirt was smeared with grime* DIRT, filth, grunge, mud, mire, smut, soot, dust; *informal* muck, crud, gunge.

▸ verb *concrete grimed by diesel exhaust* BLACKEN, dirty, stain, soil; *literary* begrime, besmirch.

grimy adjective *grimy old rags* DIRTY, grubby, grungy, mucky, soiled, stained, smeared, filthy, smutty, sooty, dusty, muddy; *informal* yucky, cruddy; *literary* besmirched, begrimed. ANTONYM clean.

grin verb *Liam grinned at us* SMILE, smile broadly, beam, smile from ear to ear, grin like a Cheshire cat; smirk; *informal* be all smiles.

▸ noun *a silly grin* SMILE, broad smile; smirk. See note at SMILE. ANTONYMS frown, scowl.

grind verb **1** *the sandstone is ground into powder* CRUSH, pound, pulverize, mill, granulate, crumble, smash, press; *technical* triturate, comminute.

2 *a knife being ground on a wheel* SHARPEN, whet, hone, file, strop; smooth, polish, sand, sandpaper.

3 *one tectonic plate grinds against another* RUB, grate, scrape, rasp.

▸ noun *the daily grind* DRUDGERY, toil, hard work, labor, exertion, chores, slog; *informal* sweat; *literary* travail. See note at LABOR.

PHRASE: **grind out** *the composing department grinds out*

hundreds of pages a day PRODUCE, generate, crank out, turn out; *informal* churn out.

grip verb 1 *she gripped the edge of the table* GRASP, clutch, hold, clasp, take hold of, clench, grab, seize, cling to; squeeze, press; *informal* glom on to. ANTONYMS release, hold lightly.

2 *Harry was gripped by a sneezing fit* AFFLICT, affect, take over, beset, rack, convulse.

3 *we were gripped by the drama* ENGROSS, enthrall, absorb, rivet, spellbind, hold spellbound, bewitch, fascinate, hold, mesmerize, enrapture; interest. ANTONYMS bore, repel.

▸ noun 1 *a tight grip* GRASP, hold.

2 *the wheels lost their grip on the road* TRACTION, purchase, friction, adhesion, resistance.

3 *he was in the grip of an obsession* CONTROL, power, hold, stranglehold, chokehold, clutches, command, mastery, influence.

4 *I had a pretty good* ***grip on*** *the situation* UNDERSTANDING OF, comprehension of, grasp of, command of, perception of, awareness of, apprehension of, conception of; *formal* cognizance of.

5 *a leather grip* TRAVEL BAG, traveling bag, suitcase, bag, overnight bag, flight bag.

PHRASE: **come to grips with** *you need to come to grips with the divorce* DEAL WITH, cope with, handle, grasp, tackle, undertake, take on, grapple with, face, face up to, confront.

gripe *informal* verb *he's always griping about something* COMPLAIN, grumble, grouse, protest, whine, bleat; *informal* moan, bellyache, beef, bitch, kvetch; *Brit.* whinge.

▸ noun *employees' gripes* COMPLAINT, grumble, grouse, grievance, objection; cavil, quibble, niggle; *informal* moan, beef, kvetch; *Brit.* whinge.

gripping adjective *a gripping spy novel* ENGROSSING, enthralling, absorbing, riveting, captivating, spellbinding, bewitching, fascinating, compulsive, compelling, mesmerizing; thrilling, exciting, action-packed, dramatic, stimulating; *informal* unputdownable, page-turning. ANTONYM boring.

grisly adjective *the grisly details of the crime* GRUESOME, ghastly, frightful, horrid, horrifying, fearful, hideous, macabre, spine-chilling, horrible, horrendous, grim, awful, dire, dreadful, terrible, horrific, shocking, appalling, abominable, loathsome, abhorrent, odious, monstrous, unspeakable, disgusting, repulsive, repugnant, revolting, repellent, sickening; *informal* gross.

gristly adjective *a gristly pot roast* STRINGY, sinewy, fibrous; tough, leathery, chewy.

grit noun 1 *the grit from the paths* SAND, dust, dirt; gravel, pebbles, stones.

2 *just the grit we're looking for in a candidate* COURAGE, bravery, pluck, mettle, backbone, spirit, strength of character, strength of will, moral fiber, steel, nerve, fortitude, toughness, hardiness, resolve, resolution, determination, tenacity, perseverance, endurance; *informal* guts, spunk.

▸ verb *Gina gritted her teeth* CLENCH, clamp together, shut tightly; grind, gnash.

gritty adjective 1 *a gritty floor* SANDY, gravelly, pebbly, stony; powdery, dusty.

2 *a gritty performance* COURAGEOUS, brave, plucky, mettlesome, stouthearted, valiant, bold, spirited, intrepid, tough, determined, resolute, purposeful, dogged, tenacious; *informal* gutsy, spunky, feisty.

3 *a gritty look at urban life* REALISTIC, uncompromising, tough, true-to-life, unidealized, graphic, sordid.

grizzled adjective *Grampa tugged at his grizzled beard* GRAY, graying, silver, silvery, snowy, white, salt-and-pepper; gray-haired, hoary.

groan verb 1 *she groaned and rubbed her stomach* MOAN, whimper, cry, call out.

2 *they were groaning about the management* COMPLAIN, grumble, grouse; *informal* moan, niggle, beef, bellyache, bitch, gripe.

3 *the old wooden door groaned* CREAK, squeak; grate, rasp.

▸ noun 1 *a groan of anguish* MOAN, cry, whimper.

2 *their moans and groans* COMPLAINT, grumble, grouse, objection, protest, grievance; *informal* grouch, moan, beef, gripe.

3 *the groan of the elevator* CREAKING, creak, squeak, grating, grinding.

groggy adjective *the sedative made him groggy* DAZED, stupefied, in a stupor, befuddled, fuddled, dizzy, disoriented, disorientated, punch-drunk, shaky, unsteady, wobbly, weak, faint, muzzy; *informal* dopey, woozy, not with it.

groom verb 1 *she groomed her pony* CURRY, brush, comb, clean, rub down.

2 *his dark hair was carefully groomed* BRUSH, comb, arrange, do; tidy, spruce up, smarten up, preen, primp; *informal* fix.

3 *they were groomed for stardom* PREPARE, prime, ready, condition, tailor; coach, train, instruct, drill, teach, school.

▸ noun 1 *a groom took his horse* STABLE HAND, stableman, stable boy, stable girl; *historical* equerry.

2 *the bride and groom* BRIDEGROOM; newly married man, newlywed.

groove noun *water trickled down the grooves* FURROW, channel, trench, trough, canal, gouge, hollow, indentation, rut, gutter, cutting, cut, fissure; *Carpentry* rabbet.

grooved adjective *panels of grooved plastic* FURROWED, fluted, corrugated, ribbed, ridged.

grope verb 1 *she groped for her glasses* FUMBLE, scrabble, fish, ferret, rummage, feel, search, hunt.

2 *informal one of the men started groping her* FONDLE, touch; *informal* paw, maul, feel up, touch up.

gross adjective 1 *the child was pale and gross* OBESE, corpulent, overweight, fat, big, large, fleshy, flabby, portly, bloated; *informal* porky, pudgy, tubby, blubbery, roly-poly. ANTONYM slender.

2 *men of gross natures* BOORISH, coarse, vulgar, loutish, oafish, thuggish, brutish, philistine, uncouth, crass, common, unrefined, unsophisticated, uncultured, uncultivated; *informal* cloddish. ANTONYM refined.

3 *informal the place smelled gross* DISGUSTING, repellent, repulsive, abhorrent, loathsome, foul, nasty, obnoxious, sickening, nauseating, stomach-churning, unpalatable; vomitous; *informal* yucky, icky, gut-churning. ANTONYMS pleasant, lovely.

4 *a gross distortion of the truth* FLAGRANT, blatant, glaring, obvious, overt, naked, barefaced, shameless, brazen, audacious, undisguised, unconcealed, patent, transparent, manifest, palpable; out and out, utter, complete. ANTONYM minor.

5 *their gross income* TOTAL, whole, entire, complete, full, overall, combined, aggregate; before deductions, before tax, pretax. ANTONYM net.

▸ verb *she grosses over a million dollars a year* EARN, make, bring in, take, get, receive, collect; *informal* rake in.

grotesque adjective **1** *a grotesque creature* MALFORMED, deformed, misshapen, misproportioned, distorted, twisted, gnarled, mangled, mutilated; ugly, unsightly, monstrous, hideous, freakish, unnatural, abnormal, strange, odd, peculiar; *informal* weird, freaky. ANTONYM normal.

2 *grotesque mismanagement of funds* OUTRAGEOUS, monstrous, shocking, appalling, preposterous; ridiculous, ludicrous, farcical, unbelievable, incredible.

grotto noun *seven pounds of cocaine was found stashed in a remote grotto* CAVE, cavern, hollow; pothole, underground chamber.

grouch noun *informal an ill-mannered grouch* GRUMBLER, complainer, moaner, curmudgeon; *informal* grump, sourpuss, whiner, sorehead, crab.

▸ verb *informal there's not a lot to grouch about* GRUMBLE, complain, grouse, whine, bleat, carp, cavil; *informal* moan; *Brit.* whinge, gripe, beef, bellyache, bitch, sound off, kvetch.

grouchy adjective *there's no need to be so grouchy* GRUMPY, cross, irritable, bad-tempered, crotchety, crabby, cantankerous, curmudgeonly, testy, tetchy, huffy, snappish, waspish, prickly; *informal* snappy, cranky.

ground noun **1** *she collapsed on the ground* FLOOR, earth, terra firma; flooring; *informal* deck.

2 *the soggy ground* EARTH, soil, dirt, clay, loam, turf, clod, sod; land, terrain.

3 **(grounds)** *the mansion's grounds* ESTATE, lawn(s), yard(s), gardens, park, parkland, land, acres, property, surroundings, holding, territory; *archaic* demesne.

4 **(grounds)** *grounds for dismissal* REASON, cause, basis, base, foundation, justification, rationale, argument, premise, occasion, excuse, pretext, motive, motivation.

5 **(grounds)** *coffee grounds* SEDIMENT, precipitate, settlings, dregs, lees, deposit, residue.

▸ verb **1** *the boat grounded on a sandbar* RUN AGROUND, run ashore, beach, land.

2 *an assertion grounded on results of several studies* BASE, found, establish, root, build, construct, form.

3 *they were grounded in classics and history* INSTRUCT, coach, teach, tutor, educate, school, train, drill, prime, prepare; familiarize with, acquaint with.

PHRASES: **hold one's ground** *he tried to dissuade me with his negative remarks, but I held my ground* STAND FIRM, stand fast, make a stand, stick to one's guns, dig in one's heels. **gain ground** *we failed to gain ground in that last campaign* ADVANCE, progress, make headway; catch up, close in.

groundbreaking adjective See INNOVATIVE.

groundless adjective *groundless accusations* BASELESS, without basis, without foundation, ill-founded, unfounded, unsupported, uncorroborated, unproven, empty, idle, unsubstantiated, unwarranted, unjustified, unjustifiable, without cause, without reason, without justification, unreasonable, irrational, illogical, misguided.

groundswell noun *a groundswell of activity* UPSURGE, surge, rise, increase, escalation, outbreak, outburst, wave, upwelling.

groundwork noun *their predecessors did all the groundwork and got none of the credit* PRELIMINARY WORK, preliminaries, preparations, spadework, legwork, donkey work; planning, arrangements, organization, homework; basics, essentials, fundamentals, underpinning, foundation.

group noun **1** *the exhibits were divided into three distinct groups* CATEGORY, class, classification, grouping, set, lot, batch, bracket, type, sort, kind, variety, family, species, genus, breed; grade, grading, rank, status.

2 *a group of tourists* CROWD, party, body, band, company, gathering, congregation, assembly, collection, cluster, flock, pack, troop, gang; *informal* bunch, pile.

3 *a coup attempt by a group within the legislature* FACTION, division, section, clique, coterie, circle, set, ring, camp, bloc, caucus, cabal, fringe movement, splinter group.

4 *the women's group* ASSOCIATION, club, society, league, guild, circle, union, sorority, fraternity.

5 *a small group of trees* CLUSTER, knot, collection, mass, clump.

6 *a local singing group* BAND, ensemble, act; *informal* combo, outfit.

▸ verb **1** *patients were grouped according to their symptoms* CATEGORIZE, classify, class, catalog, sort, bracket, pigeonhole, grade, rate, rank; prioritize, triage.

2 *extra chairs were grouped around the table* PLACE, arrange, assemble, organize, range, line up, dispose.

3 *the two parties* ***grouped together*** UNITE, join together/up, team up, gang up, join forces, get together, ally, form an alliance, affiliate, combine, marry, merge, pool resources; collaborate, work together, pull together, cooperate.

grouse verb *she groused about the food* GRUMBLE, complain, protest, whine, bleat, carp, cavil, make a fuss; *informal* moan, bellyache, gripe, beef, bitch, grouch, sound off, kvetch.

▸ noun *our biggest grouse was about the noise* GRUMBLE, complaint, grievance, objection, cavil, quibble; *informal* moan, beef, gripe, grouch.

grove noun *dozens of rabbits inhabit this grove* COPSE, woods, wood, thicket, bush, stand, woodlot, coppice; orchard, plantation; *archaic* hurst, holt.

grovel verb **1** *George groveled at his feet, begging for mercy* PROSTRATE ONESELF, lie, kneel, cringe.

2 *she was not going to* ***grovel to*** *him* BE OBSEQUIOUS TO, fawn on, kowtow to, bow and scrape to, toady to, truckle to, abase oneself to, humble oneself to; curry favor with, flatter, dance attendance on, make up to, play up to, ingratiate oneself with; *informal* crawl to, suck up to, lick someone's boots.

grow verb **1** *the boys had grown* GET BIGGER, get taller, get larger, increase in size. ANTONYM shrink.

2 *sales and profits continue to grow* INCREASE, swell, multiply, snowball, mushroom, balloon, build up, mount up, pile up; *informal* skyrocket. ANTONYM decline.

3 *flowers grew among the rocks* SPROUT, germinate, shoot up, spring up, develop, bud, burst forth, bloom, flourish, thrive, burgeon.

4 *he grew vegetables* CULTIVATE, produce, propagate, raise, rear, nurture, tend; farm.

5 *the family business grew* EXPAND, extend, develop, progress, make progress; flourish, thrive, burgeon, prosper, succeed, boom. ANTONYMS fail, decline.

6 *the modern fable grew from an ancient myth* ORIGINATE, stem, spring, arise, emerge, issue; develop, evolve.

7 *Leonora grew bored* BECOME, get, turn, begin to feel.

growl verb *why is your dog growling at us?* SNARL, bark, yap, bay.

grown-up noun *she wanted to be treated like a grown-up* ADULT, (grown) woman, (grown) man, mature woman, mature man. ANTONYM child.

▸ adjective *she has two grown-up daughters* ADULT, mature, of age; fully grown, full-grown, fully developed.

growth noun **1** *population growth* INCREASE, expansion, augmentation, proliferation, multiplication, enlargement, mushrooming, snowballing, rise, escalation, buildup. ANTONYM decrease.

2 *the growth of plants* DEVELOPMENT, maturation, growing, germination, sprouting; blooming. ANTONYM withering.

3 *the marked growth of local enterprises* EXPANSION, extension, development, progress, advance, advancement, headway, spread; rise, success, boom, upturn, upswing. ANTONYMS failure, decline.

4 *a growth on his jaw* TUMOR, malignancy, cancer; lump, excrescence, outgrowth, swelling, nodule; cyst, polyp.

grub noun **1** *a small black grub* LARVA; maggot; caterpillar.

2 *informal we'll grab some grub on the way.* See FOOD sense 1.

▸ verb **1** *they* ***grubbed up*** *the weeds* DIG UP, unearth, uproot, root up/out, pull up/out, tear out.

2 *he began grubbing around in the trash* RUMMAGE, search, hunt, delve, dig, scrabble, ferret, root, rifle, fish, poke.

grubby adjective *his grubby work clothes* DIRTY, grimy, filthy, mucky, unwashed, stained, soiled, smeared, spotted, muddy, dusty, sooty; unhygienic, unsanitary; *informal* cruddy, yucky; *literary* befouled, begrimed. ANTONYM clean.

grudge noun *a former employee with a grudge* GRIEVANCE, resentment, bitterness, rancor, pique, umbrage, dissatisfaction, disgruntlement, bad feelings, hard feelings, ill feelings, ill will, animosity, antipathy, antagonism, enmity, animus; *informal* a chip on one's shoulder.

▸ verb *he grudges the time the meetings use up* BEGRUDGE, resent, feel aggrieved about, be resentful of, mind, object to, take exception to, take umbrage at.

grudging adjective *her grudging apology* RELUCTANT, unwilling, forced, halfhearted, unenthusiastic, hesitant; begrudging, resentful. ANTONYM eager.

grueling adjective *a grueling hike through the snow* EXHAUSTING, tiring, fatiguing, wearying, taxing, draining, debilitating; demanding, exacting, difficult, hard, arduous, strenuous, laborious, back-breaking, harsh, severe, stiff, stressful, punishing, crippling; *informal* killing, murderous, hellish.

gruesome adjective *Arnie's gruesome Halloween mask frightened the little kids* GRISLY, ghastly, frightful, horrid, horrifying, hideous, horrible, horrendous, grim, awful, dire, dreadful, terrible, horrific, shocking, appalling, disgusting, repulsive, repugnant, revolting, repellent, sickening; loathsome, abhorrent, odious, monstrous, unspeakable; *informal* sick, gross. ANTONYM pleasant.

gruff adjective **1** *a gruff reply | his gruff exterior* ABRUPT, brusque, curt, short, blunt, bluff, no-nonsense; laconic, taciturn; surly, churlish, grumpy, crotchety, curmudgeonly, crabby, cross, bad-tempered, short-tempered, ill-natured, crusty, tetchy, bearish, ungracious, unceremonious; *informal* grouchy. See note at BRUSQUE. ANTONYMS friendly, courteous.

2 *a gruff voice* ROUGH, guttural, throaty, gravelly, husky, croaking, rasping, raspy, growly, hoarse, harsh; low, thick. ANTONYMS mellow, soft.

grumble verb *they grumbled about the disruption* COMPLAIN, grouse, whine, mutter, bleat, carp, cavil, protest, make a fuss; *informal* moan, bellyache, beef, bitch, grouch, sound off, gripe, kvetch; *Brit.* whinge.

▸ noun *his customers' grumbles* COMPLAINT, grievance, protest, cavil, quibble, criticism, grouse; *informal* grouch, moan, beef, bitch, gripe.

grumpy adjective *Matthau's grumpy old man was a tour de force* BAD-TEMPERED, crabby, ill-tempered, short-tempered, crotchety, tetchy, testy, waspish, prickly, touchy, irritable, irascible, crusty, cantankerous, curmudgeonly, bearish, surly, ill-natured, churlish, ill-humored, peevish, pettish, cross, fractious, disagreeable, snappish; *informal* grouchy, snappy, cranky, shirty, ornery. ANTONYM good-humored.

WORD NOTE **grumpy**

This word is overused, especially when there are so many other, more evocative synonyms. Try *tetchy* for the kind of grumpy that's quick to take offense; *churlish* for the grumpiness born of entitlement (think of the overpaid cellphone yapper cutting you off), *peevish* for the complaining, fault-finding grumpiness of the vague and wavering old man; *fractious* for the grumpiness of the unpleasable overtired child; *pettish* for the grumpiness of the spoiled beauty; *waspish* for the snappish, tightlipped grumpiness of the thin and elderly spinster; and *shirty* for the insolent grumpiness of the person who knows he's being thwarted and doesn't much like it. **—EM**

guarantee noun **1** *all repairs have a one-year guarantee* WARRANTY.

2 *a guarantee that the hospital will stay open* PROMISE, assurance, word (of honor), pledge, vow, oath, bond, commitment, covenant.

3 *banks usually demand* ***a guarantee*** *for loans* COLLATERAL, security, surety, a guaranty, earnest.

▸ verb **1** *he agreed to guarantee the loan* UNDERWRITE, put up collateral for.

2 *can you guarantee that he wasn't involved?* PROMISE, swear, swear to the fact, pledge, vow, undertake, give one's word, give an assurance, give an undertaking, take an oath.

guard verb **1** *infantry guarded the barricaded bridge* PROTECT, stand guard over, watch over, keep an eye on; cover, patrol, police, defend, shield, safeguard, keep safe, secure.

2 *the prisoners were guarded by armed men* KEEP UNDER SURVEILLANCE, keep under guard, keep watch over, mind.

3 *forest wardens must* ***guard against*** *poachers* BEWARE OF, keep watch for, be alert to, keep an eye out for, be on the lookout for, be on the alert for.

▸ noun **1** *border guards* SENTRY, sentinel, security guard, watchman, night watchman; protector, defender, guardian; lookout, watch; garrison.

2 *her prison guard* WARDEN, warder, keeper; jailer; *informal* screw; *archaic* turnkey.

3 *he let his guard slip and they escaped* VIGILANCE, vigil, watch, surveillance, watchfulness, caution, heed, attention, care, wariness.

4 *a metal guard* SAFETY GUARD, safety device, protective device, shield, screen, fender; bumper, buffer.

PHRASES: **off (one's) guard** *the explosion from the furnace room caught everyone off guard* UNPREPARED, unready, inattentive, unwary, with one's defenses down, cold, unsuspecting; *informal* napping, asleep at the wheel. **on one's guard** *homeowners should be on their guard* VIGILANT, alert, on the alert, wary, watchful, cautious, careful, heedful, chary, circumspect, on the lookout, on the qui vive, on one's toes, prepared, ready, wide awake, attentive, observant, keeping one's eyes peeled.

guarded adjective *they showed guarded enthusiasm for the proposal* CAUTIOUS, careful, circumspect, wary, chary, on one's guard, reluctant, reticent, noncommittal, restrained, reserved; *informal* buttoned-up, cagey.

guardian noun *Linwood has been my guardian since I was three* PROTECTOR, defender, preserver, custodian, warden, guard, keeper; conservator, curator, caretaker, steward, trustee.

guerrilla noun *the communications canter was raided by leftist guerrillas from the north* FREEDOM FIGHTER, irregular, member of the resistance, partisan; rebel, radical, revolutionary, revolutionist; terrorist.

guess verb **1** *he guessed she was about 40* ESTIMATE, hazard a guess, reckon, gauge, judge, calculate; hypothesize, postulate, predict, speculate, conjecture, surmise; *informal* guesstimate.

2 *informal I guess I owe you an apology* SUPPOSE, think, imagine, expect, suspect, dare say; *informal* reckon, figure.

▸ noun *my guess was right* HYPOTHESIS, theory, prediction, postulation, conjecture, surmise, estimate, belief, opinion, reckoning, judgment, supposition, speculation, suspicion, impression, feeling; *informal* guesstimate, shot in the dark.

guesswork noun *the educated guesswork we rely on in our research* GUESSING, conjecture, surmise, supposition, assumptions, presumptions, speculation, hypothesizing, theorizing, prediction; approximations, rough calculations; hunches; *informal* guesstimates, ballpark figures.

guest noun **1** *I have two guests coming to dinner* VISITOR, house guest, caller; company; *archaic* visitant. ANTONYM host.

2 *hotel guests* PATRON, client, visitor, boarder, lodger, roomer. ANTONYMS host, landlord, landlady.

▸ adjective *a guest speaker* INVITED, featured, special.

guest house noun *we stayed at a little guest house on Block Island* INN, bed and breakfast, B&B, hotel, motel; boarding house.

guff noun *informal* See NONSENSE sense 1.

guffaw verb *he guffawed at his own punch line* LAUGH HEARTILY, laugh loudly, roar with laughter, roar, bellow, cackle.

guidance noun **1** *she looked to her father for guidance* ADVICE, counsel, direction, instruction, enlightenment, information; recommendations, suggestions, tips, hints, pointers, guidelines.

2 *work continued under the guidance of a project supervisor* DIRECTION, control, leadership, management, supervision, superintendence, charge; handling, conduct, running, overseeing.

guide noun **1** *our guide took us back to the hotel* ESCORT, attendant, tour guide, docent, cicerone; usher, chaperone; *historical* dragoman.

2 *she is an inspiration and a guide* ADVISER/ADVISOR, mentor, counselor; guru.

3 *the light acted as a guide for shipping* POINTER, marker, indicator, signpost, mark, landmark; guiding light, sign, signal, beacon.

4 *the techniques outlined are meant as a guide* MODEL, pattern, blueprint, template, example, exemplar; standard, touchstone, measure, benchmark, yardstick, gauge.

5 *a pocket guide to the Aleutians.* See GUIDEBOOK.

▸ verb **1** *he guided her to her seat* LEAD, conduct, show, show the way, usher, shepherd, direct, steer, pilot, escort, accompany, attend; see, take, help, assist.

2 *the chairperson must guide the meeting* DIRECT, steer, control, manage, command, lead, conduct, run, be in charge of, have control of, pilot, govern, preside over, superintend, supervise, oversee; handle, regulate.

3 *he was always there to guide me* ADVISE, counsel, give advice to, direct, give direction to.

guidebook noun *he's written a guidebook that rates all the places to dine and lodge in the area* GUIDE, travel guide, travelogue, vade mecum; field guide; companion, handbook, directory; *informal* bible.

guideline noun *the zoning commission's strict guidelines* RECOMMENDATION, instruction, direction, suggestion, advice; regulation, rule, principle, guiding principle; standard, criterion, measure, gauge, yardstick, benchmark, touchstone; procedure, parameter.

guild noun *the copper craftsmen have formed a guild* ASSOCIATION, society, union, league, organization, company, cooperative, fellowship, club, order, lodge, brotherhood, fraternity, sisterhood, sorority.

guile noun *Georgia was the only one among us not taken in by Owen's guile* CUNNING, craftiness, craft, artfulness, art, artifice, wiliness, slyness, deviousness; wiles, ploys, schemes, stratagems, maneuvers, tricks, subterfuges, ruses; deception, deceit, duplicity, underhandedness, double-dealing, trickery. ANTONYM honesty.

guileless adjective *how can you take advantage of someone so sweet and guileless?* ARTLESS, ingenuous, naive, open, genuine, natural, simple, childlike, innocent, unsophisticated, unworldly, unsuspicious, trustful, trusting; honest, truthful, sincere, straightforward. ANTONYM scheming.

guilt noun **1** *the proof of his guilt* CULPABILITY, guiltiness, blameworthiness; wrongdoing, wrong, criminality, misconduct, sin. ANTONYM innocence.

2 *a terrible feeling of guilt* SELF-REPROACH, self-condemnation, shame, a guilty conscience, pangs of conscience; remorse, remorsefulness, regret, contrition, contriteness, compunction. ANTONYM innocence.

guiltless adjective *the victims here are these guiltless children* INNOCENT, blameless, not to blame, without fault, above reproach, above suspicion, in the clear, unimpeachable, irreproachable, faultless, sinless, spotless, immaculate, unsullied, uncorrupted, undefiled, untainted, unblemished, untarnished, impeccable; *informal* squeaky clean, whiter than white, as pure as the driven snow. ANTONYM guilty.

guilty adjective **1** *the guilty party* CULPABLE, to blame, at fault, in the wrong, blameworthy, responsible; erring, errant, delinquent, offending, sinful, criminal; *archaic* peccant. ANTONYM innocent.

2 *I still feel guilty about it* ASHAMED, guilt-ridden, conscience-stricken, remorseful, sorry, contrite, repentant, penitent, regretful, rueful, abashed, shamefaced, sheepish, hangdog; in sackcloth and ashes. ANTONYM unrepentant.

guise noun **1** *the god appeared in the guise of a swan* LIKENESS, outward appearance, appearance, semblance, form, shape, image; disguise.

2 *additional payments were made under the guise of consulting fees* PRETENSE, disguise, front, facade, cover, blind, screen, smokescreen.

gulf noun **1** *our ship sailed into the gulf* INLET, bay, bight, cove, fjord, estuary, sound.

2 *the ice gave way and a gulf widened slowly* HOLE, crevasse, fissure, cleft, split, rift, pit, cavity, chasm, abyss, void; ravine, gorge, canyon, gully.

3 *a growing gulf between rich and poor* DIVIDE, division, separation, gap, breach, rift, split, chasm, abyss; difference, contrast, polarity.

gull[1] noun *the gulls went into a comical frenzy when we dumped the old bait overboard.* See table at SEABIRD.

gull[2] verb *he gulled Lisa's entire family before he skipped town* HOODWINK, fool, dupe, deceive, delude, hoax, trick, mislead, lead on, take in, swindle, cheat, double-cross; *informal* pull the wool over someone's eyes, pull a fast one on, put one over on, bamboozle, con, sucker, snooker; *literary* cozen.

gullet noun *the bird's gullet* ESOPHAGUS, throat, maw, pharynx; crop, craw; *archaic* throttle, gorge.

gullible adjective *he was a swindler who preyed on gullible elderly widows* CREDULOUS, naive, overtrusting, overtrustful, easily deceived, easily taken in, exploitable, dupable, impressionable, unsuspecting, unsuspicious, unwary, ingenuous, innocent, inexperienced, unworldly, green; *informal* wet behind the ears, born yesterday. ANTONYM suspicious.

THE RIGHT WORD

Some people will believe anything. Those who are truly **gullible** are the easiest to deceive, which is why they so often make fools of themselves. Those who are merely **credulous** might be a little too quick to believe something, but they usually aren't stupid enough to act on it. **Trusting** suggests the same willingness to believe (*a trusting child*), but it isn't necessarily a bad way to be (*a person so trusting he completely disarmed his enemies*). No one likes to be called **naïve** because it implies a lack of street smarts (*she's so naïve she'd accept a ride from a stranger*), but when applied to things other than people, it can describe a simplicity and absence of artificiality that is quite charming (*the naïve style in which nineteenth-century American portraits were often painted*). Most people would rather be thought of as **ingenuous**, meaning straightforward and sincere (*an ingenuous confession of the truth*), because it implies the simplicity of a child without the negative overtones. **Callow**, however, comes down a little more heavily on the side of immaturity and almost always goes hand-in-hand with youth. Whether young or old, someone who is **unsophisticated** suffers because of lack of experience.

gully noun **1** *a steep icy gully* RAVINE, canyon, gorge, pass, defile, couloir, gulch, coulee, draw.

2 *water runs from the drainpipe into a gully* CHANNEL, conduit, trench, ditch, drain, culvert, cut, gutter.

gulp verb **1** *she gulped her juice* SWALLOW, guzzle (down), quaff, swill down, down; *informal* swig, knock back, chug, chugalug. ANTONYM sip.

2 *he **gulped down** the rest of his meal* GOBBLE (DOWN), guzzle (down), devour, bolt down, wolf down; *informal* put away, demolish, polish off, shovel in/down, scoff (down). ANTONYM nibble.

3 *Lisa **gulped back** her tears* CHOKE BACK, fight back, hold back/in, suppress, stifle, smother.

▸ noun *a gulp of cold beer* MOUTHFUL, swallow, draft; *informal* swig.

gum noun *photographs stuck down with gum* GLUE, adhesive, fixative, paste, epoxy, epoxy resin, mucilage.

▸ verb *the receipts were gummed into a book* STICK, glue, paste; fix, affix, attach, fasten.

PHRASE: **gum up** *check to see if the valves are gummed up* CLOG (UP), choke (up), stop up, plug; obstruct; *informal* bung up, gunge up; *technical* occlude.

gummy adjective *the price tag left a gummy residue* STICKY, tacky, gluey, adhesive, resinous, viscous, viscid, glutinous, mucilaginous; *informal* gooey.

gumption noun *informal we never thought Clarence would have the gumption to stand up to the committee—and actually get what he wanted* INITIATIVE, resourcefulness, enterprise, ingenuity, imagination; astuteness, shrewdness, acumen, sense, common sense, wit, mother wit, practicality; spirit, backbone, pluck, mettle, nerve, courage, wherewithal; *informal* get-up-and-go, spunk, oomph, moxie, savvy, horse sense, (street) smarts.

gun noun *the illegal trafficking of drugs and guns* FIREARM, pistol, revolver, rifle, shotgun, carbine, automatic, handgun, semiautomatic, machine gun, Uzi; weapon; *informal* piece, gat, heater.

gunfire noun *the sound of distant gunfire* GUNSHOTS, shots, shooting, firing, sniping; artillery fire, strafing, shelling; tracer fire.

gunman noun *a lone gunman apparently hid in the stairwell for several hours* ARMED ROBBER, gangster, terrorist; sniper, gunfighter; assassin, murderer, killer; *informal* hit man, hired gun, gunslinger, mobster, shootist, hood.

gurgle verb *the water swirled and gurgled* BABBLE, burble, tinkle, bubble, ripple, murmur, purl, splash; *literary* plash.

▸ noun *the gurgle of a small brook* BABBLING, tinkling, bubbling, rippling, trickling, murmur, murmuring, purling, splashing; *literary* plashing.

guru noun **1** *a Hindu guru and mystic* SPIRITUAL TEACHER, teacher, tutor, sage, mentor, spiritual leader, leader, master; *Hinduism* swami, maharishi. ANTONYM disciple.

2 *a management guru* EXPERT, authority, pundit, leading light, master, specialist; *informal* whiz. ANTONYM amateur.

gush verb **1** *water gushed through the weir* SURGE, burst, spout, spurt, jet, stream, rush, pour, spill, well out, cascade, flood; flow, run, issue.

2 *everyone gushed about the script* ENTHUSE, rave, be enthusiastic, be effusive, rhapsodize, go into raptures, wax lyrical, praise to the skies; *informal* go mad, go wild, go crazy.

▸ noun *a gush of water* SURGE, stream, spurt, jet, spout, outpouring, outflow, burst, rush, cascade, flood, torrent; *technical* efflux.

gushing, gushy adjective *Randall was embarrassed by the gushing praise* EFFUSIVE, enthusiastic, overenthusiastic, unrestrained, extravagant, lavish, fulsome, rhapsodic, lyrical; *informal* over the top. ANTONYM restrained.

gust noun **1** *a sudden gust of wind* FLURRY, blast, puff, blow, rush; squall.

2 *gusts of laughter* OUTBURST, burst, eruption, fit, paroxysm; gale, peal, howl, hoot, shriek, roar.

▸ verb *wind gusted around the chimneys* BLOW, bluster, flurry, roar.

gusto noun *neighbors remembered the slain soldier as a friendly kid who played sports with gusto* ENTHUSIASM, relish, appetite, enjoyment, delight, glee, pleasure, satisfaction, appreciation, liking; zest, zeal, fervor, verve, keenness, avidity. ANTONYMS apathy, distaste.

gusty adjective *it's too gusty for a picnic* BLUSTERY, windy, breezy; squally, stormy, tempestuous, wild, turbulent; *informal* blowy. ANTONYM calm.

gut noun **1** *he had an ache in his gut* STOMACH, belly, abdomen, solar plexus; intestines, bowels; *informal* tummy, tum, insides, innards.

2 *fish heads and guts* ENTRAILS; intestines, viscera; offal; gurry; *informal* insides, innards.

3 *informal* (**guts**) *Nicola had the guts to say what she felt* COURAGE, bravery, backbone, nerve, pluck, spirit, boldness, audacity, daring, grit, fearlessness, feistiness, toughness, determination; *informal* spunk, moxie. See note at COURAGE.

▸ adjective *informal a gut feeling* INSTINCTIVE, instinctual, intuitive, deep-seated; knee-jerk, automatic, involuntary, spontaneous, unthinking, visceral.

▸ verb **1** *clean, scale, and gut the trout* REMOVE THE GUTS FROM, disembowel, draw; *formal* eviscerate.

2 *the church was gutted by fire* DEVASTATE, destroy, demolish, wipe out, lay waste, ravage, consume, ruin, wreck.

gutless adjective *informal* See COWARDLY.

gutsy adjective *informal Lacey made a gutsy move by hiring an ex-con* BRAVE, courageous, plucky, bold, daring, fearless, adventurous, audacious, valiant, intrepid, heroic, lionhearted, undaunted, unflinching, unshrinking, unafraid, dauntless, indomitable, doughty, stouthearted; spirited, determined, resolute; *informal* spunky, gutty, feisty, ballsy.

gutter noun *gutters clogged with leaves* DRAIN, sluice, sluiceway, culvert, spillway, sewer; channel, conduit, pipe; rain gutter; trough, trench, ditch, furrow, cut.

guttural adjective *the man who called had a guttural voice* THROATY, husky, gruff, gravelly, growly, growling, croaky, croaking, harsh, rough, rasping, raspy; deep, low, thick.

guy noun *informal he's a handsome guy* MAN, fellow, gentleman; youth, boy; *informal* lad, fella, gent, chap, dude, joe, Joe Blow, Joe Schmo, hombre.

guzzle verb *she **guzzled down** the orange juice* GULP DOWN, swallow, quaff, down, swill; *informal* knock back, swig, slug.

gym noun **1** *she exercised at the local gym* GYMNASIUM, health club, fitness center, recreation center, spa; *informal* rec center.

2 *gym was his least favorite class* PHYSICAL EDUCATION; gymnastics; *informal* phys ed., PE.

GYMNASTIC EVENTS

asymmetric bars	rhythmic (gymnastics)
balance beam	ribbons
balls	rings
clubs	ropes
floor exercise	sports aerobics
high bar	teamgym
hoops	trampoline
horizontal bar	tumbling
parallel bars	uneven bars
pommel horse	vault
power tumbling	

gypsy noun *a caravan of gypsies* ROMANY, Rom, traveler, nomad, rover, roamer, wanderer.

gyrate verb *the disk gyrates atop an aluminum pole* ROTATE, revolve, wheel, turn around, whirl, circle, pirouette, twirl, swirl, spin, swivel.

H

habit noun **1** *it was his habit to go for a run every morning* CUSTOM, practice, routine, wont, pattern, convention, way, norm, tradition, matter of course, rule, usage.

2 *her many irritating habits* MANNERISM, way, quirk, foible, trick, trait, idiosyncrasy, peculiarity, singularity, oddity, eccentricity, feature; tendency, propensity, inclination, bent, proclivity, disposition, predisposition.

3 *his cocaine habit* ADDICTION, dependence, dependency, craving, fixation, compulsion, obsession, weakness; *informal* monkey on one's back.

4 *a monk's habit* GARMENT(S), dress, garb, clothes, clothing, attire, outfit, costume; *informal* gear; *formal* apparel. PHRASES: **habit of mind** *a scientific habit of mind* DISPOSITION, temperament, character, nature, makeup, constitution, frame of mind, bent. **in the habit of** *they were in the habit of phoning each other daily* ACCUSTOMED TO, used to, given to, wont to, inclined to.

habitable adjective *it's not the Ritz, but it's habitable* FIT TO LIVE IN, inhabitable, fit to occupy, in good repair, livable; *formal* tenantable.

habitat noun *the habitat of the spotted turtle has been greatly diminished* NATURAL ENVIRONMENT, natural surroundings, home, domain, haunt; *formal* habitation.

habitation noun **1** *a house fit for human habitation* OCCUPANCY, occupation, residence, residency, living in, tenancy.

2 *formal his main habitation* RESIDENCE, place of residence, house, home, seat, lodging place, billet, quarters, living quarters, rooms, accommodations; *informal* pad, digs; *formal* dwelling, dwelling place, abode, domicile.

habitual adjective **1** *her father's habitual complaints* CONSTANT, persistent, continual, continuous, perpetual, nonstop, recurrent, repeated, frequent; interminable, incessant, ceaseless, endless, never-ending; *informal* eternal. ANTONYMS occasional, infrequent.

2 *habitual drinkers* INVETERATE, confirmed, compulsive, obsessive, incorrigible, hardened, ingrained, dyed-in-the-wool, chronic, regular; addicted; *informal* pathological. ANTONYM occasional.

3 *his habitual secretiveness* CUSTOMARY, accustomed, regular, usual, normal, set, fixed, established, routine, common, ordinary, familiar, traditional, typical, general, characteristic, standard, time-honored; *literary* wonted. ANTONYM unaccustomed.

habituate verb *poverty had habituated their children to a life of hopelessness* ACCUSTOM, make used, familiarize, adapt, adjust, attune, acclimatize, acculturate, condition; inure, harden; acclimate.

habitué noun *the habitués of Scully's Bar* FREQUENT VISITOR, regular visitor, regular customer, regular client, regular patron, familiar face, regular, patron, frequenter, haunter.

hack[1] verb *Stuart hacked the padlock off* CUT, chop, hew, lop, saw; slash. PHRASE: **hack it** *informal he tried to run his own commercial fishing outfit, but he couldn't hack it* COPE, manage, get on/by, carry on, come through, muddle along/through; stand it, tolerate it, bear it, endure it, put up with it; *informal* handle it, abide it, stick it out.

hack[2] noun **1** *a tabloid hack* JOURNALIST, reporter, newspaperman, newspaperwoman, writer; *informal* journo, scribbler; *archaic* penny-a-liner.

2 *office hacks* DRUDGE, menial, menial worker, factotum; *informal* gofer.

hacker noun *informal viruses that are the brainchildren of these malicious hackers informal* CYBERPUNK, pirate, computer criminal, hacktivist.

WORD NOTE **hacker**

This word shouldn't be totally abandoned to its contemporary cyber-connotation, since it's great for describing amateur athletes. When you are flailing away with your club or racket or bat, getting nowhere but persisting out of sheer obstinacy and love of the game, you're a hacker . . . there is no other word for it. **—DA**

hackle PHRASE: **make someone's hackles rise** *Julie's compulsive criticizing made her sister's hackles rise* ANNOY, irritate, exasperate, anger, incense, infuriate, irk, nettle, vex, put out, provoke, gall, antagonize, get on someone's nerves, ruffle someone's feathers, rankle with; rub the wrong way; *informal* aggravate, peeve, needle, rile, make someone see red, make someone's blood boil, get someone's back up, get someone's goat, get someone's dander up, bug, tee off, tick off, burn up.

hackneyed adjective *your hackneyed arguments fail to*

persuade anyone OVERUSED, overdone, overworked, worn out, timeworn, platitudinous, vapid, stale, tired, threadbare; trite, banal, hack, clichéd, hoary, commonplace, common, ordinary, stock, conventional, stereotyped, predictable; unimaginative, unoriginal, uninspired, prosaic, dull, boring, pedestrian, run-of-the-mill, boilerplate, routine; *informal* old hat, cheesy, corny, played out. ANTONYM original.

Hades noun See HELL sense 1.

haft noun *gripping the haft of the knife* HANDLE, shaft, hilt, butt, stock, grip, handgrip, helve, shank.

hag noun *we'd all heard tales of a wizened hag who lived alone on the far side of the mountain* CRONE, old woman, gorgon; *informal* witch, crow, cow, old bag.

haggard adjective *he looked terrible, all pale and haggard* DRAWN, tired, exhausted, drained, careworn, unwell, unhealthy, spent, washed out, run-down; gaunt, pinched, peaked, hollow-cheeked, hollow-eyed, thin, emaciated, wasted, cadaverous; pale, wan, gray, ashen. ANTONYM healthy.

haggle verb *John spent nearly every Saturday morning haggling at flea markets and garage sales* BARTER, bargain, negotiate, dicker, quibble, wrangle; beat someone down, drive a hard bargain.

haiku noun See note below.

WORD NOTE **haiku**

Haikus have three lines
consisting of five, seven
and five syllables.

Japanese poets
once owned the market with their
seasonal blossoms.

By the placid pond
sat a frog, poised to leap, and
then you heard a splash.

A bird in the pines,
black, and nothing else but snow,
in branches of sky.

For a poet less
wedded to nature, haikus
have other uses.

The economy
of the haiku makes it apt
for aphorisms.

Here's an example
about a term that people
use to show they're smart:

Deconstruction

Deconstruction is
one of those words that means what
you want it to mean.
—DL

hail[1] verb **1** *a friend hailed him from the upper deck* CALL OUT TO, shout to, address; greet, say hello to, salute.

2 *he hailed a cab* FLAG DOWN, wave down, signal to.

3 *critics hailed the film as a masterpiece* ACCLAIM, praise, applaud, rave about, extol, eulogize, hymn, lionize, sing the praises of, make much of, glorify, cheer, salute, toast, ballyhoo; *formal* laud.

4 *Rick **hails from** Australia* COME FROM, be from, be a native of, have one's roots in.

hail[2] noun *a hail of bullets* BARRAGE, volley, shower, rain, torrent, burst, stream, storm, avalanche, onslaught; bombardment, cannonade, battery, blast, salvo; *historical* broadside.

▸ verb *tons of dust hailed down on us* BEAT, shower, rain, fall, pour; pelt, pepper, batter, bombard, assail.

hair noun **1** *her thick black hair* LOCKS, curls, ringlets, mane, mop; shock of hair, head of hair; tresses.

2 *I like your hair* HAIRSTYLE, haircut, cut, coiffure; *informal* hairdo, do, coif.

3 *a dog with short, blue-gray hair* FUR, wool; coat, fleece, pelt; mane. PHRASES: **a hair's breadth** *she won by a hair's breadth* THE NARROWEST OF MARGINS, a narrow margin, the skin of one's teeth, a split second, a nose, a whisker. **let one's hair down** *informal even the chairman of the board has to let his hair down once in a while* ENJOY ONESELF, have a good time, have fun, make merry, let oneself go; *informal* have a ball, whoop it up, paint the town red, live it up, have a whale of a time, let it all hang out. **make someone's hair stand on end** *the truth about Corrine would make your hair stand on end* HORRIFY, shock, appall, scandalize, stun; make someone's blood run cold; *informal* make someone's hair curl, turn someone's hair white. **split hairs** *you missed the point because you were so busy splitting hairs* QUIBBLE, cavil, carp, niggle; *informal* nitpick; *archaic* pettifog.

hairdo noun *informal* See HAIRSTYLE.

hairdresser noun *the hairdresser suggested adding highlights* HAIRSTYLIST, stylist, coiffeur, coiffeuse; barber.

hairless adjective *all the guys on our swim team have gone hairless* BALD, bald-headed; shaven, shaved, shorn, clean-shaven, beardless, smooth, smooth-faced, depilated; tonsured; *technical* glabrous; *archaic* bald-pated. ANTONYM hairy.

hairpiece noun *they claim the hairpiece was worn by an aide of George Washington* WIG, toupee, periwig; *informal* rug.

hair-raising adjective *the hair-raising stories we would tell around the campfire* TERRIFYING, frightening, petrifying, alarming, chilling, horrifying, shocking, spine-chilling, blood-curdling, bone-chilling, white-knuckle, fearsome, nightmarish; eerie, sinister, weird, ghostly, unearthly; eldritch; *informal* hairy, spooky, scary, creepy.

hair-splitting adjective *his hair-splitting aunt had gotten even more critical with age* PEDANTIC, pettifogging; quibbling, niggling, caviling, carping, critical, overcritical, hypercritical; *informal* nitpicking, persnickety, picky.

hairstyle noun *a new hairstyle for the prom* HAIRCUT, cut, style, hair, coiffure; *informal* hairdo, do, coif. See table on page 409.

hairy adjective **1** *animals with hairy coats* SHAGGY, bushy, long-haired; woolly, furry, fleecy, fuzzy; *Botany & Zoology* pilose.

2 *his hairy face* BEARDED, bewhiskered, mustachioed; unshaven, stubbly, bristly; *formal* hirsute.

3 *informal a hairy situation* RISKY, dangerous, perilous, hazardous, touch-and-go; tricky, ticklish, difficult, awkward; *informal* dicey, sticky.

WORD NOTE **hairy**

There are maybe more descriptors for various kinds of hair and hairiness than any other word-set in English, and some of them are extremely strange and fun. The more pedestrian terms like *shaggy, unshorn, bushy, coiffed,* and so on we'll figure you already know. The adj *barbigerous* is an extremely uptown synonym for *bearded. Cirrose* and *cirrous,* from the Latin *cirrus* meaning "curl" or "fringe" (as in *cirrus clouds*), can both be used to refer to somebody's curly or tufty or wispy/feathery hair—Nicolas Cage's hair in *Adaptation* is cirrose. *Crinite* means "hairy or possessed of a hair-like appendage," though it's mainly a botanical term and would be a bit eccentric applied to a person. *Crinose,* however, is a people-adj that means "having a lot of hair," especially in the sense of one's hair being really long. The related noun *crinosity* is antiquated but not obsolete and can be used to refer to somebody's hair in an amusingly donnish way, as in *Madonna's normally platinum crinosity is now a maternal brown. Glabrous,* which is the loveliest of all hair-related adjectives, means having no hair (on a given part) at all. Please note that *glabrous* means more baby's-bottom-hairless than bald or shaved, though if you wanted to describe a bald person in an ironically fancy way you could talk about his *glabrous dome* or something. *Hirsute* is probably the most familiar upmarket synonym for *hairy,* totally at home in any kind of formal writing. Like that of many hair-related adjectives, *hirsute*'s original use was in botany (where it means "covered with coarse or bristly hairs"), but in regular usage its definition is much more general. Not so with the noun *hirsutism,* though, which is still semi-medical and means having a truly pathological amount of hair and/or hair that's unusually or unevenly distributed—the point is that the noun's not really a synonym for *hairiness. Hispid* means "covered with stiff or rough little hairs" and could apply to a military pate or unshaved jaw. *Hispidulous* is mainly just a puffed-up form of *hispid* and should be avoided. *Lanate* and *lanated* mean "having or being composed of woolly hairs." A prettier and slightly more familiar way to describe woolly hair is with the adjective *flocculent.* (There's also *floccose,* but this is used mainly of odd little hairy fruits like kiwi and quince.) Then there are the *pil*-based words, all derived from the Latin *pilus* (= hair). *Pilose,* another fairly common adj, means "covered with fine soft hair." Deceptively similar-looking is *pilous,* which is a more hardcore-science adj that the *OED** defines as "characterized by or abounding in hair, hairy," citing as an example the following (unexplained, thus kind of troubling) sentence: *It is covered with a rough pilous epidermis. Pilous*'s own similarity to *pileous* is not deceptive, since the latter, a medical adjective, means "consisting of or pertaining to hair"; e.g., certain hair-intensive cancerous growths are classified as *pileous tumors.* On the other hand, pileous tumors are sometimes also called *piliferous tumors,* wherein the latter adj means "having or producing hair" (in botany, *piliferous* means "tipped with a hair," as in certain weird leaves). There's also *piligerous,* which means "covered or clothed in hair" and is used primarily of animals, and *piliated,* which comes from the plural of *pilus* and is used to describe certain kinds of hairy or fringe-intensive bacteria. Last but not least is the noun *pilimiction,* which names a hopefully very rare medical disorder "in which piliform or hair-like bodies are passed in the urine." Outside of maybe describing some kind of terribly excruciated facial expression as *pilimictive,* however, it's hard to imagine a mainstream use for *pilimiction.* (One *pil*-word N.B.: It so happens that the adjective *pubescent* literally means "covered with soft downy hairs," so technically it qualifies as a synonym for *pilose*; but as of 2004 almost no reader will take *pubescent* this way, so I'd stick with *pilose.*) *Tomentose* means "covered with dense little matted hairs"—baby chimps, hobbits' feet, and Robin Williams are all tomentose. *Ulotrichous,* which is properly classed with *lannate* and *flocculent,* is an old and extremely fancy term for "crisply woolly hair." Be advised that it is also, if not exactly a racist adj, certainly a racial one—A.C. Haddon's *Races of Man,* from the early 1900s, famously classified races according to three basic hair types: *leiotrichous* (straight), *cymotrichous* (wavy), and *ulotrichous.*

Now go do the right thing.

*N.B. If you're thinking of using any of the more esoteric adjectives here, you'd be well advised to keep an *OED* close at hand. This is not simply a gratuitous plug of another Oxford U. Press product. The fact is that some of these hair-related terms aren't in other dictionaries; plus, the terms are often specialized enough that you're going to want not just an abstract definition but a couple sample sentences so that you can see how the words are actually used. Only the *OED* has both defs and in-context samples for just about every significant word in the language. Actually, why not screw appearances and just state the obvious: No really serious writer should be without an *OED,* whether it's bought or stolen or hacked into the online version of or whatever you need to do. Nothing else comes close. **—DFW**

halcyon adjective *the halcyon days of our youth* HAPPY, golden, idyllic, carefree, blissful, joyful, joyous, contented; flourishing, thriving, prosperous, successful; serene, calm, tranquil, peaceful. See note at CALM.

hale adjective *fair weather and a hale crew* HEALTHY, fit, fighting fit, well, in good health, bursting with health, in fine fettle, strong, robust, vigorous, hardy, sturdy, hearty, lusty, able-bodied; *informal* in the pink, as right as rain. ANTONYM unwell.

half adjective *a half grapefruit* HALVED, bisected, divided in two. ANTONYM whole.

▸ adverb **1** *the chicken is half cooked* PARTIALLY, partly, incompletely, inadequately, insufficiently; in part, part, slightly. ANTONYMS fully, completely.

2 *I'm half inclined to believe you* TO A CERTAIN EXTENT/DEGREE, to some extent/degree, (up) to a point, in part, partly, in some measure. ANTONYM fully.

▸ noun *the first half of the show* PORTION, section, part, period; 50 percent.

half-baked adjective **1** *half-baked theories* ILL-CONCEIVED, harebrained, cockamamie, ill-judged, impractical, unrealistic, unworkable, ridiculous, absurd; *informal* crazy, crackpot, cockeyed. ANTONYM sensible.

2 *her half-baked nephew* FOOLISH, stupid, silly, idiotic, simpleminded, feebleminded, empty-headed, featherbrained, featherheaded, brainless, witless, unintelligent, ignorant; *informal* dim, dopey, dumb, thick, halfwitted, dimwitted, birdbrained, dozy. ANTONYM sensible.

HAIRSTYLES

Afro	French braid
beehive	French twist
blunt cut	marcel (wave)
bob	Mohawk
body wave	mullet
bouffant	pageboy
bowl cut	perm
braids	permanent wave
brush cut	pigtails
bun	pixie cut
buzz/buzz cut	pompadour
chignon	ponytail
cornrows	razor cut
crewcut	ringlets
DA/duck's ass	shag
dreadlocks	shingle
ducktail	spike
feathercut	updo
flat-top	

half-hearted adjective *the halfhearted applause was not exactly encouraging* UNENTHUSIASTIC, cool, lukewarm, tepid, apathetic, indifferent, uninterested, unconcerned, languid, listless; perfunctory, cursory, superficial, desultory, feeble, lackluster. ANTONYM enthusiastic.

halfway adjective *the halfway point* MIDWAY, middle, mid, central, center, intermediate; *Anatomy* medial, mesial.

▸ adverb **1** *he started running down the passage and then stopped halfway* MIDWAY, in the middle, in the center; partway, part of the way.

2 *she seemed halfway friendly* TO SOME EXTENT/DEGREE, in some measure, relatively, comparatively, moderately, somewhat, (up) to a point; just about, almost, nearly.

PHRASE: **meet someone halfway** *I was willing to meet him halfway* COMPROMISE, come to terms, reach an agreement, make a deal, make concessions, find the middle ground, strike a balance; give and take.

halfwit noun *informal* See FOOL noun sense 1.

halfwitted adjective *informal* See STUPID sense 1.

hall noun **1** *hang your coat in the hall* ENTRANCE HALL, hallway, entry, entrance, lobby, foyer, vestibule; atrium, concourse; passageway, passage, corridor, entryway.

2 *we booked a hall for the wedding* BANQUET HALL, community center, assembly room, meeting room, chamber; auditorium, concert hall, theater.

hallmark noun **1** *the hallmark on silver* ASSAY MARK, official mark, stamp of authenticity.

2 *tiny bubbles are the hallmark of fine champagnes* MARK, distinctive feature, characteristic, sign, sure sign, telltale sign, badge, stamp, trademark, indication, indicator, calling card.

hallowed adjective *trespassing on hallowed ground* HOLY, sacred, consecrated, sanctified, blessed; revered, venerated, honored, sacrosanct, worshiped, divine, inviolable. See note at DIVINE.

hallucinate verb *the fever made her hallucinate* HAVE HALLUCINATIONS, see things, be delirious, fantasize; *informal* trip, see pink elephants.

hallucination noun *are you sure that what you saw wasn't a hallucination?* DELUSION, illusion, figment of the imagination, vision, apparition, mirage, chimera, fantasy; **(hallucinations)** delirium, phantasmagoria; *informal* trip, pink elephants.

halo noun *a stunning depiction of the angel's halo* RING OF LIGHT, nimbus, aureole, glory, crown of light, corona; *technical* halation; *rare* gloriole.

halt verb **1** *Jen halted and turned around* STOP, come to a halt, come to a stop, come to a standstill; pull up, draw up. ANTONYMS start, go.

2 *a further strike has halted production* STOP, bring to a stop, put a stop to, bring to an end, put an end to, terminate, end, wind up; suspend, break off, arrest; impede, check, curb, stem, block, stall, hold back; *informal* pull the plug on, put the kibosh on. ANTONYMS start, continue.

▸ noun **1** *the car drew to a halt* STOP, standstill.

2 *a halt in production* STOPPAGE, stopping, discontinuation, break, suspension, pause, interval, interruption, hiatus; cessation, termination, close, end.

halting adjective **1** *a halting conversation* | *halting English* HESITANT, faltering, hesitating, stumbling, stammering, stuttering; broken, imperfect. ANTONYM fluent.

2 *his halting gait* UNSTEADY, awkward, faltering, stumbling, limping, hobbling. ANTONYMS steady, nimble.

ham-handed adjective *his ham-handed treatment of the situation* CLUMSY, bungling, incompetent, amateurish, inept, unskillful, inexpert, maladroit, gauche, awkward, inefficient, bumbling, useless; *informal* ham-fisted, klutzy; all thumbs. ANTONYM expert.

WORD NOTE **ham-fisted**

I prefer *ham-fisted* to *ham-handed.* If pressed to explain, I would probably mutter something nonsensical about how *ham-fisted* emphasizes the lack of dexterous fingers: not only are your hands like unto hams, your clumsy hammy fingers are balled into useless fists. *Cack-handed* is another great word, when you need that extra helping of derision that only a Briticism can dish out. **—EM**

hammer noun *a hammer and chisel* mallet, beetle, gavel, sledgehammer, jackhammer.

▸ verb **1** *the alloy is hammered into a circular shape* BEAT, forge, shape, form, mold, fashion, make.

2 *Sally **hammered at** the door* BATTER, pummel, beat, bang, pound; strike, hit, knock on, thump on; cudgel, bludgeon, club; *informal* bash, wallop, clobber, whack, thwack.

3 *they **hammered away at** their nonsmoking campaign* WORK HARD AT, labor at, slog away at, plod away at, grind away at, slave away at, work like a dog on, put one's nose to the grindstone for; persist with, persevere with, press on with; *informal* stick at, plug away at, work one's tail off on/for, soldier on with.

4 *antiracism had been **hammered into** her* DRUM INTO, instill in, inculcate into, knock into, drive into; drive home to, impress upon; ingrain into.

5 *informal we've hammered them twice this season.* See TROUNCE.

PHRASE: **hammer out** *the committee sat for three hours hammering out a new budget* THRASH OUT, work out, agree on, sort out, decide on, bring about, effect, produce, broker, negotiate, reach an agreement on.

hamper[1] noun *a picnic hamper* BASKET, pannier, wickerwork basket; box, container.

hamper[2] verb *the search was hampered by fog* HINDER, obstruct, impede, inhibit, retard, balk, thwart, foil, curb, delay, set back, slow down, hobble, hold up, interfere with; restrict, constrain, trammel, block, check, curtail, frustrate, cramp, bridle, handicap, cripple, hamstring, shackle, fetter; *informal* stymie, hog-tie, throw a (monkey) wrench in the works of. See note at HINDER. ANTONYM help.

hamstring verb **1** *cattle were killed or hamstrung* CRIPPLE, lame, disable, incapacitate.

2 *he felt hamstrung by the regulations.* See HAMPER[2].

hand noun **1** *big, strong hands* palm, fist; *informal* paw, mitt, duke, hook, meathook.

2 *the clock's second hand* POINTER, indicator, needle, arrow, marker.

3 **(hands)** *the frontier posts remained in government hands* CONTROL, power, charge, authority; command, responsibility, guardianship, management, care, supervision, jurisdiction; possession, keeping, custody; clutches, grasp, thrall; disposal; *informal* say-so.

4 *let me give you **a hand*** HELP, a helping hand, assistance, aid, support, succor, relief; a good turn, a favor.

5 *a document written in his own hand* HANDWRITING, writing, script, calligraphy.

6 *a ranch hand* WORKER, workman, laborer, operative, hired hand, roustabout, peon; cowboy.

▸ verb *she handed each of us an envelope* PASS, give, let someone have; throw, toss; present to.

PHRASES: **at hand** *the time for courage is at hand* IMMINENT, approaching, coming, about to happen, on the horizon; impending. **big hand** *informal her fans gave her a big hand* ROUND OF APPLAUSE, clap, handclap, ovation, standing ovation; applause, handclapping. **close at hand** *keep the manual close at hand* READILY AVAILABLE, available, handy, to hand, within reach, accessible, close, close by, near, nearby, at the ready, at one's fingertips, at one's disposal, convenient; *informal* get-at-able. **hand down** *this bracelet has been handed down from four generations* PASS ON, pass down; bequeath, will, leave, make over, give, gift, transfer; *Law* demise, devise. **hand in glove** *working hand in glove with their former adversaries* IN CLOSE COLLABORATION, in close association, in close cooperation, very closely, in partnership, in league, in collusion; *informal* in cahoots, in bed. **hand out** *volunteers were asked to hand out pamphlets* DISTRIBUTE, give out, pass out/around, dole out, dish out, deal out, mete out, issue, dispense; allocate, allot, apportion, disburse; circulate, disseminate. **hand over** *they handed over the stolen goods to the authorities* YIELD, give, give up, pass, grant, entrust, surrender, relinquish, cede, turn over, deliver up, forfeit, sacrifice. **hands down** *we won hands down* EASILY, effortlessly, with ease, with no trouble, without effort; *informal* by a mile, no sweat. **try one's hand at** *I regret that I never tried my hand at waterskiing* HAVE A GO AT, make an attempt at, have a shot at; attempt, try, try out, give something a try; *informal* have a stab at, give something a whirl; *formal* essay.

handbag noun *a leather handbag* PURSE, bag, shoulder bag, clutch purse, evening bag; pocketbook; *historical* reticule.

handbill noun *annoyed by the handbills on our windshield* NOTICE, advertisement, flyer, leaflet, circular, handout, pamphlet, brochure, fact sheet; *informal* ad.

handbook noun *the handbook explains our late-fee policy* MANUAL, instructions, instruction manual, how-to guide; almanac, companion, directory, compendium; guide, guidebook, vade mecum.

handcuff verb *Martini was handcuffed to the radiator* MANACLE, shackle, fetter; restrain, clap/put someone in irons; *informal* cuff.

handcuffs plural noun *when her lawyer came, Paula was still in handcuffs* MANACLES, shackles, irons, fetters, bonds, restraints; *informal* cuffs, bracelets.

handful noun 1 ***a handful of** bad apples* A FEW, a small number of, a small amount of, a small quantity of, one or two, some, not many, a scattering of, a trickle of.

2 *informal* *the child is a real handful* NUISANCE, problem, bother, irritant, thorn in someone's flesh/side; *informal* pest, headache, pain, pain in the neck, pain in the butt.

handgun noun *British lawmakers will vote on a proposal to ban all handguns* PISTOL, revolver, gun, sidearm, six-shooter, .38, derringer; *informal* piece, Saturday night special, rod, roscoe; *trademark* Colt, Luger.

handicap noun 1 *a visual handicap* DISABILITY, physical abnormality, mental abnormality, defect, impairment, affliction, deficiency, dysfunction.

2 *a handicap to the competitiveness of the industry* IMPEDIMENT, hindrance, obstacle, barrier, bar, obstruction, encumbrance, constraint, restriction, check, block, curb; disadvantage, drawback, stumbling block, difficulty, shortcoming, limitation; ball and chain, albatross, millstone (around someone's neck), burden, liability; *literary* trammel. ANTONYMS benefit, advantage.

▸ verb *lack of funding handicapped the research* HAMPER, impede, hinder, impair, hamstring; restrict, check, obstruct, block, curb, bridle, hold back, constrain, trammel, limit, encumber; *informal* stymie. ANTONYMS help, advance.

handicapped adjective *accommodations for handicapped customers* DISABLED, incapacitated, disadvantaged, crippled; infirm, invalid; *euphemistic* physically challenged, differently abled.

USAGE NOTE **handicapped**

Handicapped in the sense referring to a person's mental or physical disabilities is first recorded in the early twentieth century. For a brief period in the second half of the twentieth century, it looked as if **handicapped** would be replaced by **disabled**, but both words are now acceptable and interchangeable in standard American English, and neither word has been overtaken by newer coinages such as *differently abled* or *physically challenged*.

handicraft noun *a prime example of early American handicraft* CRAFT, handiwork, craftwork; craftsmanship, workmanship, artisanship, art, skill.

handiwork noun *the jewelry is the handiwork of Chinese smiths* CREATION, product, work, achievement; handicraft, craft, craftwork.

handkerchief noun *a monogrammed handkerchief* HANKY; kerchief, bandanna; tissue.

handle verb 1 *the equipment must be handled with care* HOLD, pick up, grasp, grip, lift; feel, touch, finger; *informal* paw.

2 *a car that is easy to handle* CONTROL, drive, steer, operate, maneuver, manipulate.

3 *she handled the problems well* DEAL WITH, manage, tackle, take care of, take charge of, attend to, see to, sort out, apply oneself to, take in hand; respond to, field.

4 *the advertising company that is handling the account* ADMINISTER, manage, control, conduct, direct, guide, supervise, oversee, be in charge of, take care of, look after.

5 *the traders handled goods manufactured in the Rhineland* TRADE IN, deal in, buy, sell, supply, peddle, traffic in, purvey, hawk, tout, market.

▸ noun *the knife's handle* HAFT, shank, stock, shaft, grip, handgrip, hilt, helve, butt; knob.

hand-me-down adjective *hand-me-down clothes* SECONDHAND, used, handed-down, passed-on, castoff, worn, old, pre-owned, thrift-store/thrift-shop; *informal* preloved. ANTONYM new.

handout noun 1 **(handouts)** *she existed on handouts*

CHARITY, aid, benefit, financial support, donations, subsidies, welfare; *historical* alms.

2 *a photocopied handout* LEAFLET, pamphlet, brochure, fact sheet; handbill, flyer, notice, circular.

hand-picked adjective *six hand-picked contestants will be flown to Ireland for the finals* SPECIALLY CHOSEN, selected, invited; select, elite; choice.

handsome adjective 1 *a handsome man* GOOD-LOOKING, attractive, striking, gorgeous; *informal* hunky, drop-dead gorgeous, hot, cute. ANTONYM ugly.

2 *a handsome woman of 30* STRIKING, imposing, prepossessing, elegant, stately, dignified, statuesque, good-looking, attractive, personable. ANTONYM plain.

3 *a handsome profit* SUBSTANTIAL, considerable, sizable, princely, large, big, ample, bumper; *informal* tidy, whopping, not to be sneezed at, ginormous. ANTONYM meager.

handwriting noun *barely legible handwriting* WRITING, script, hand, pen; penmanship, calligraphy, chirography; *informal* scrawl, scribble, chicken scratch.

handy adjective 1 *a handy reference tool* USEFUL, convenient, practical, easy-to-use, well-designed, user-friendly, user-oriented, helpful, functional, serviceable. ANTONYM inconvenient.

2 *keep your credit card handy* READILY AVAILABLE, available, at hand, near at hand, within reach, accessible, ready, close, close by, near, nearby, at the ready, at one's fingertips; *informal* get-at-able.

3 *he's handy with a needle and thread* SKILLFUL, skilled, dexterous, deft, nimble-fingered, adroit, able, adept, proficient, capable; good with one's hands; *informal* nifty. ANTONYM inept.

handyman noun *Mrs. Odetts looked in the classifieds for a handyman* REPAIRMAN, odd-job man, factotum, jack of all trades; *informal* do-it-yourselfer, Mr. Fixit, fixit man.

hang verb 1 *lights hung from the trees* BE SUSPENDED, dangle, hang down, be pendent, swing, sway.

2 *hang the pictures at eye level* PUT UP, fix, attach, affix, fasten, post, display, suspend, pin up, nail up.

3 *the room was hung with streamers* DECORATE, adorn, drape, festoon, deck out, trick out, bedeck, array, garland, swathe, cover, ornament; *literary* bedizen.

4 *he was hanged for murder* STRING UP, send to the gallows.

5 *a pall of smoke hung over the city* HOVER, float, drift, be suspended. PHRASES: **hang around** *informal* 1 *they spent their time hanging around in bars* LOITER, linger, wait around, waste time, kill time, mark time, while away the/one's time, cool one's heels, twiddle one's thumbs; frequent, be a regular visitor to, haunt; *informal* hang out in. 2 *she's hanging around with a gang of marketing types* ASSOCIATE, mix, keep company, socialize, fraternize, consort, rub elbows; *informal* hang out, run around, be thick, hobnob. **hang on** 1 *he **hung on to** her coat* HOLD ON TO, hold fast to, grip, clutch, grasp, hold tightly to, cling to. 2 *her future hung on their decision* DEPEND ON, be dependent on, turn on, hinge on, rest on, be contingent on, be determined by, be decided by.

3 *I'll hang on as long as I can* PERSEVERE, hold out, hold on, go on, carry on, keep on, keep going, keep at it, continue, persist, stay with it, struggle on, plod on; *informal* soldier on, stick to/at it, stick it out, hang in there.

4 *informal hang on, let me think* WAIT, wait a minute, wait a second, hold on, stop; hold the line/phone; *informal* hold your horses, sit tight, wait a sec. **hang over someone** *the threat of budget cuts is hanging over us* BE IMMINENT, threaten, be close, be impending, impend, loom, be on the horizon.

hangdog adjective *his hangdog expression betrayed his alleged confidence* SHAMEFACED, sheepish, abashed, ashamed, guilty-looking, abject, cowed, dejected, downcast, crestfallen, woebegone, disconsolate. ANTONYM unabashed.

hanger-on noun *here comes Mr. Bigshot and his creepy hangers-on* FOLLOWER, flunky, toady, camp follower, sycophant, parasite, leech, bottom feeder; henchman, minion, lackey, vassal; acolyte; cohort; *informal* groupie, sponger, freeloader, passenger, sidekick.

hanging noun *silk wall hangings* DRAPE, curtain; drapery; tapestry, textile art.

▸ adjective *hanging fronds of honeysuckle* PENDENT, dangling, trailing, tumbling; suspended.

hangout noun *McMurphy's is one of our hangouts* HAUNT, favorite spot, meeting place, territory; den, refuge, retreat, stomping ground, stamping ground, home away from home.

hang-up noun *Louie has a hang-up about dirty windows* NEUROSIS, phobia, preoccupation, fixation, obsession, idée fixe; inhibition, mental block, psychological block, block, difficulty; *informal* complex, thing, bee in one's bonnet.

hank noun *a hank of yarn* COIL, skein, length, roll, loop, twist, piece; lock, ringlet, curl.

hanker verb *I hanker to go home* YEARN, long, crave, desire, wish, want, hunger, thirst, lust, ache, pant, be eager, be desperate, be eating one's heart out; fancy, pine; *informal* be dying, have a yen, itch.

hankering noun *I had a sudden hankering for a BLT* LONGING, yearning, craving, desire, wish, hunger, thirst, urge, ache, lust, appetite, fancy; *informal* yen, itch; *archaic* appetency. ANTONYM aversion.

hanky-panky noun *informal hanky-panky among public officials is always newsworthy* MISBEHAVIOR, naughtiness, infidelity, unfaithfulness, adultery, philandering, fooling around; funny business, mischief, goings-on, misconduct, chicanery, dishonesty, deception, deceit, trickery, intrigue, skulduggery, subterfuge, machinations; *informal* monkey business, shenanigans, carryings-on.

haphazard adjective *Shelley's haphazard piles of laundry* RANDOM, unplanned, unsystematic, unmethodical, disorganized, disorderly, irregular, indiscriminate, chaotic, hit-and-miss, arbitrary, aimless, careless, casual, slapdash, slipshod; chance, accidental; *informal* higgledy-piggledy.

hapless adjective *the hapless victims of exploitation* UNFORTUNATE, unlucky, luckless, out of luck, ill-starred, ill-fated, jinxed, cursed, doomed; unhappy, forlorn, wretched, miserable, woebegone; *informal* down on one's luck; *literary* star-crossed. ANTONYM lucky.

WORD NOTE **hapless, unfortunate**

I have a great affection for words with a vaguely nineteenth-century (in this case, somewhat Dickensian) tone, and I find myself using them whenever it is remotely appropriate. *She was the hapless victim of the thoughtlessness of her elders. Unfortunate,* which is, in my view, nearly synonymous with *hapless,* is another such word. *The unfortunate young fellow failed to notice the oncoming train.* How interesting that using one ever-so-slightly dated word or expression inspires us to use others, such as *elders,* or *young fellow.* And how telling that both words—quaint relics of another era—are adjectives meant to convey sympathy for those who are suffering or who have suffered, often through no fault of their own. **—FP**

happen verb **1** *remember what happened last time he was here* OCCUR, take place, come about; ensue, result, transpire, materialize, arise, crop up, come up, present itself, supervene; *informal* go down; *formal* eventuate; *literary* come to pass, betide.

2 *I wonder what* ***happened to*** *Joe?* BECOME OF; *literary* befall, betide.

3 *they happened to be in* CHANCE, have the good/bad luck.

4 *she* ***happened on*** *a blue jay's nest* DISCOVER, find, find by chance, come across, chance on, stumble on, hit on.

THE RIGHT WORD

When things **happen**, they come to pass either for a reason or by chance (*it happened the day after school started; she happened upon the scene of the accident*), but the verb is more frequently associated with chance (*it happened to be raining when we got there*). **Occur** can also refer either to something that comes to pass either accidentally or as planned, but it should only be used interchangeably with *happen* when the subject is a definite or actual event (*the tragedy occurred last winter*). Unlike *happen, occur* also carries the implication of something that presents itself to sight or mind (*it never occurred to me that he was lying*). **Transpire** is a more formal (and some would say undesirable) word meaning to *happen* or *occur,* and it conveys the sense that something has leaked out or become known (*he told her exactly what had transpired while she was away*). While things that *happen, occur,* or *transpire* can be either positive or negative, when something **befalls** it is usually unpleasant (*he had no inkling of the disaster that would befall him when he got home*).

happening noun *bizarre happenings* OCCURRENCE, event, incident, proceeding, affair, doing, circumstance, phenomenon, episode, experience, occasion, development, eventuality.

▸ adjective *informal a happening nightspot* FASHIONABLE, modern, popular, new, latest, up-to-date, up-to-the-minute, in fashion, in vogue, le dernier cri; *informal* trendy, funky, hot, cool, with it, hip, in, big, now, groovy. ANTONYM old-fashioned.

happily adverb **1** *he smiled happily* CONTENTEDLY, cheerfully, cheerily, merrily, delightedly, joyfully, joyously, gaily, gleefully.

2 *I will happily do as you ask* GLADLY, willingly, readily, freely, cheerfully, ungrudgingly, with pleasure; *archaic* fain.

3 *happily, we are living in enlightened times* FORTUNATELY, luckily, thankfully, mercifully, by good luck, by good fortune, as luck would have it; thank goodness, thank God, thank heavens, thank the Lord.

happiness noun *trying to rediscover the happiness we once knew* PLEASURE, contentment, satisfaction, cheerfulness, merriment, gaiety, joy, joyfulness, joviality, jollity, glee, delight, good spirits, lightheartedness, well-being, enjoyment; exuberance, exhilaration, elation, ecstasy, jubilation, rapture, bliss, blissfulness, euphoria, transports of delight.

happy adjective **1** *Melissa looked happy and excited* CHEERFUL, cheery, merry, joyful, jovial, jolly, jocular, gleeful, carefree, untroubled, delighted, smiling, beaming, grinning, in good spirits, in a good mood, lighthearted, pleased, contented, content, satisfied, gratified, buoyant, radiant, sunny, blithe, joyous, beatific; thrilled, elated, exhilarated, ecstatic, blissful, euphoric, overjoyed, exultant, rapturous, in seventh heaven, on cloud nine, walking on air, jumping for joy, jubilant; *informal* chirpy, over the moon, on top of the world, tickled pink, on a high, as happy as a clam; *formal* jocund. See word spectrum on page 414. ANTONYM sad.

2 *we will be happy to advise you* GLAD, pleased, delighted; willing, ready, disposed. ANTONYM unwilling.

3 *a happy coincidence* FORTUNATE, lucky, favorable, advantageous, opportune, timely, well-timed, convenient. ANTONYM unfortunate.

happy-go-lucky adjective *what's wrong with letting your children be happy-go-lucky?* EASYGOING, carefree, casual, free and easy, devil-may-care, blithe, nonchalant, insouciant, blasé, unconcerned, untroubled, unworried, lighthearted, laid-back. ANTONYM anxious.

harangue noun *a ten-minute harangue* TIRADE, diatribe, lecture, polemic, rant, fulmination, broadside, attack, onslaught; criticism, condemnation, censure, admonition, sermon; declamation, speech; *informal* blast; *literary* philippic.

▸ verb *he harangued his erstwhile colleagues* RANT AT, hold forth to, lecture, shout at; berate, criticize, attack; *informal* sound off at, mouth off to.

harass verb **1** *tenants who harass their neighbors* PERSECUTE, intimidate, hound, harry, plague, torment, bully, bedevil; pester, bother, worry, disturb, trouble, provoke, stress; *informal* hassle, bug, ride, give someone a hard time, get on someone's case.

2 *they were sent to harass the enemy flanks* HARRY, attack, beleaguer, set upon, assail.

harassed adjective *the job left her totally harassed* STRESSED, stressed out, strained, worn out, hard-pressed, careworn, worried, troubled, beleaguered, under pressure, at the end of one's tether, at the end of one's rope; *informal* hassled. ANTONYM carefree.

harassment noun *the report cites three separate accusations of harassment* PERSECUTION, intimidation, pressure, force, coercion; *informal* hassle.

harbinger noun *I long to see the robins, crocuses, and other harbingers of spring* HERALD, sign, indication, signal, portent, omen, augury, forewarning, presage; forerunner, precursor, messenger; *literary* foretoken.

harbor noun **1** *a picturesque harbor* PORT, dock, haven, marina; mooring, moorage, anchorage; waterfront.

2 *a safe harbor for me* REFUGE, haven, safe haven, shelter, sanctuary, retreat, place of safety, port in a storm.

▸ verb **1** *he is harboring a dangerous criminal* SHELTER, conceal, hide, shield, protect, give sanctuary to; take in, put up, accommodate, house.

happy
exuberant
elated
exhilarated
ecstatic
euphoric
thrilled
exultant
joyful
overjoyed
jumping for joy
delighted
in seventh heaven
on cloud nine
over the moon
walking on air
blissed out
beaming
on top of the world
buoyant
blithe
gay
blissful
gleeful
jovial
tickled pink
merry
as pleased as Punch
as happy as a clam
jolly
smiling
cheerful
sunny
tickled to death
light-hearted
in a good mood
carefree
happy-go-lucky
untroubled
cheery
content
out of sorts
low-spirited
down
depressed
crestfallen
down in the mouth
down in the dumps
blue
dejected
downcast
bowed down
downhearted
unhappy
glum
dismal
gloomy
doleful
melancholy
broken-hearted
despondent
woebegone
miserable
mournful
forlorn
despairing
disconsolate
sorrowful
woeful
wretched
heartbroken
grief-stricken
inconsolable
sad

2 *Rose had harbored a grudge against him* BEAR, nurse, nurture, cherish, entertain, foster, hold on to, cling to.

hard adjective **1** *hard ground* FIRM, solid, rigid, stiff, resistant, unbreakable, inflexible, impenetrable, unyielding, solidified, hardened, compact, compacted, dense, close-packed, compressed; steely, tough, strong, stony, rocklike, flinty, as hard as stone; frozen; *literary* adamantine. ANTONYM soft.

2 *hard physical work* ARDUOUS, strenuous, tiring, fatiguing, exhausting, wearying, back-breaking, grueling, heavy, laborious; difficult, taxing, exacting, testing, challenging, demanding, punishing, tough, formidable, onerous, rigorous, uphill, Herculean; *informal* murderous, killing, hellish; *formal* exigent; *archaic* toilsome. ANTONYM easy.

3 *hard workers* DILIGENT, hard-working, industrious, sedulous, assiduous, conscientious, energetic, keen, enthusiastic, zealous, earnest, persevering, persistent, unflagging, untiring, indefatigable; studious. ANTONYM lazy.

4 *a hard problem* DIFFICULT, puzzling, perplexing, baffling, bewildering, mystifying, knotty, thorny, problematic, complicated, complex, intricate, involved; insoluble, unfathomable, impenetrable, incomprehensible, unanswerable. ANTONYM simple.

5 *times are hard* HARSH, grim, difficult, bad, bleak, dire, tough, austere, unpleasant, uncomfortable, straitened, spartan; dark, distressing, painful, awful. ANTONYM comfortable.

6 *a hard taskmaster* STRICT, harsh, firm, severe, stern, tough, rigorous, demanding, exacting; callous, unkind, unsympathetic, cold, heartless, hard-hearted, unfeeling; intransigent, unbending, uncompromising, inflexible, implacable, stubborn, obdurate, unyielding, unrelenting, unsparing, grim, ruthless, merciless, pitiless, cruel; standing no nonsense, ruling with a rod of iron. ANTONYMS kind, easygoing.

7 *a hard winter* BITTERLY COLD, cold, bitter, harsh, severe, bleak, freezing, icy, icy-cold, arctic. ANTONYM mild.

8 *a hard blow* FORCEFUL, heavy, strong, sharp, smart, violent, powerful, vigorous, mighty, hefty, tremendous. ANTONYMS light, gentle.

9 *hard facts* RELIABLE, definite, true, confirmed, substantiated, undeniable, indisputable, unquestionable, verifiable. ANTONYMS unverified, questionable.

10 *hard cider* ALCOHOLIC, strong, intoxicating, potent; *formal* spirituous. ANTONYM nonalcoholic.

11 *hard drugs* ADDICTIVE, habit-forming; strong, harmful.

▸ adverb **1** *George pushed the door hard* FORCEFULLY, forcibly, roughly, powerfully, strongly, heavily, sharply, vigorously, energetically, with all one's might, with might and main. ANTONYM gently.

2 *they worked hard* DILIGENTLY, industriously, assiduously, conscientiously, sedulously, busily, enthusiastically, energetically, doggedly, steadily; *informal* like mad, like crazy.

3 *this prosperity has been hard won* WITH DIFFICULTY, with effort, after a struggle, painfully, laboriously. ANTONYM easily.

4 *her death hit him hard* SEVERELY, badly, acutely, deeply, keenly, seriously, profoundly, gravely; *formal* grievously. ANTONYM slightly.

5 *it was raining hard* HEAVILY, strongly, in torrents, in sheets; steadily; *informal* cats and dogs, buckets. ANTONYM lightly.

6 *my mother looked hard at me* CLOSELY, attentively, intently, critically, carefully, keenly, searchingly, earnestly, sharply. ANTONYM casually.

PHRASES: **hard and fast** *get used to it—the curfew here is hard and fast* DEFINITE, fixed, set, strict, rigid, binding, clear-cut, cast-iron, ironclad; inflexible, immutable, unchangeable, incontestable. **hard by** CLOSE TO, right by, beside, near (to), nearby, not far from, a stone's throw from, on the doorstep of; *informal* within spitting distance of, [a hop, skip, and jump away from]. **hard feelings** *I had no idea that our separation had left him with such hard feelings* RESENTMENT, animosity, ill feeling, ill will, bitterness, bad blood, resentfulness, rancor, malice, acrimony, antagonism, antipathy, animus, friction, anger, hostility, hate, hatred. **hard up** *informal* *this administration ignores the families that are hard up* POOR, short of money, badly off, impoverished, impecunious, in reduced circumstances, unable to make ends meet; penniless, destitute, poverty-stricken; *informal* broke, strapped for cash, strapped.

THE RIGHT WORD

For the student who doesn't read well, homework is **hard** work, which means that it demands great physical or mental effort. An English assignment to write an essay might be particularly **difficult**, meaning that it not only requires effort but skill. Where *hard* suggests toil, *difficult* emphasizes complexity (*a difficult math problem*). Memorizing long lists of vocabulary words would be **laborious**, which is even more restrictive than *hard* and suggests prolonged, wearisome toil with no suggestion of the skill required and no reference to the complexity of the task. Reading *War and Peace*, however, would be an **arduous** task, because it would require a persistent effort over a long period of time. A school assignment may be *difficult*, but is usually not *arduous*; that is, it may require skill rather than perseverance. It may also be *arduous* without being particularly *difficult*, as when a student is asked to write "I will not throw spitballs" five hundred times. A student who is new to a school may find it especially **trying**, which implies that it taxes the individual's patience, skill, or capabilities.

hard-bitten adjective *a hard-bitten FBI agent* HARDENED, tough, cynical, unsentimental, hardheaded, case-hardened, as tough as nails; *informal* hard-nosed, hard-edged, hard-boiled. ANTONYM sentimental.

hard-boiled adjective *informal* See HARD-BITTEN.

hard-core adjective *hard-core socialists* DIEHARD, staunch, dedicated, committed, steadfast, dyed-in-the-wool, long-standing; hardline, extreme, entrenched, radical, intransigent, uncompromising, rigid.

harden verb **1** *this glue will harden in four hours* SOLIDIFY, set, congeal, clot, coagulate, stiffen, thicken, cake, cure, inspissate; freeze, crystallize; ossify, calcify, petrify. ANTONYM liquefy.

2 *their suffering had hardened them* TOUGHEN, desensitize, inure, case-harden, harden someone's heart; deaden, numb, benumb, anesthetize; brutalize. ANTONYM soften.

hardened adjective **1** *he was hardened to the violence he had seen* INURED, desensitized, deadened; accustomed, habituated, acclimatized, used.

2 *a hardened criminal* INVETERATE, seasoned, habitual, chronic, compulsive, confirmed, dyed-in-the-wool; incorrigible, incurable, irredeemable, unregenerate.

hardheaded adjective *a hardheaded jurist* UNSENTIMENTAL, practical, pragmatic, businesslike, realistic, sensible, rational, clear-thinking, coolheaded, down-to-earth, matter-of-fact, no-nonsense, with both feet on the ground; tough, hard-bitten; shrewd, astute, sharp, sharp-witted; *informal* hard-nosed, hard-edged, hard-boiled. ANTONYMS idealistic, sentimental.

hard-hearted adjective *he's not nearly as hard-hearted as he pretends to be* UNFEELING, heartless, cold, hard, callous, unsympathetic, uncaring, unloving, unconcerned, indifferent, unmoved, unkind, uncharitable, unemotional, cold-hearted, cold-blooded, mean-spirited, stony-hearted, having a heart of stone, as hard as nails, cruel. ANTONYM compassionate.

hard-hitting adjective *a hard-hitting ad campaign* UNCOMPROMISING, blunt, forthright, frank, honest, direct, tough; critical, unsparing, strongly worded, straight-talking, pulling no punches, not mincing one's words, not beating around/about the bush.

hardiness noun *in New England, you should select plants for their hardiness* ROBUSTNESS, strength, toughness, ruggedness, sturdiness, resilience, stamina, vigor; healthiness, good health. ANTONYM frailty.

hardline adjective *one of President Mugabe's key hardline allies* UNCOMPROMISING, strict, extreme, tough, diehard, immoderate, inflexible, intransigent, firm, intractable, unyielding, undeviating, unwavering, single-minded, not giving an inch; *rare* indurate. ANTONYMS moderate, flexible.

hardly adverb *we hardly know each other* SCARCELY, barely, only just, slightly.

hard-nosed adjective *informal* *hard-nosed reporters* TOUGH-MINDED, unsentimental, no-nonsense, hardheaded, hard-bitten, pragmatic, realistic, down-to-earth, practical, rational, shrewd, astute, businesslike; *informal* hard-boiled, hard-edged. ANTONYM sentimental.

hard-pressed adjective **1** *the hard-pressed infantry* UNDER ATTACK, hotly pursued, harried.

2 *the hard-pressed construction industry* IN DIFFICULTIES, under pressure, troubled, beleaguered, harassed, with one's back to/against the wall, in a tight corner, in a tight spot, between a rock and a hard place; overburdened, overworked, overloaded, stressed-out; *informal* up against it.

hardship noun *by age six, she was a refugee and no stranger to hardship* PRIVATION, deprivation, destitution, poverty, austerity, penury, want, need, neediness, impecuniousness; misfortune, distress, suffering, affliction, trouble, pain, misery, wretchedness, tribulation, adversity, trials, trials and tribulations, dire straits; *literary* travails. ANTONYMS prosperity, ease.

hardware noun *our garage became the receptacle for all his father's hardware* EQUIPMENT, apparatus, gear, paraphernalia, tackle, kit, machinery; tools, articles, implements, instruments, appliances.

hard-working adjective *even the hard-working employees got stiffed at bonus time* DILIGENT, industrious, conscientious, assiduous, sedulous, painstaking, persevering, unflagging, untiring, tireless, indefatigable, studious;

keen, enthusiastic, zealous, busy, with one's shoulder to the wheel, with one's nose to the grindstone. ANTONYM lazy.

hardy adjective *our tiny frail baby has grown into a strapping hardy man* ROBUST, healthy, fit, strong, sturdy, tough, rugged, hearty, lusty, vigorous, hale and hearty, fit as a fiddle, fighting fit, in fine fettle, in good health, in good condition; *dated* stalwart. ANTONYM delicate.

hare-brained adjective **1** *a hare-brained scheme* ILL-JUDGED, rash, foolish, foolhardy, reckless, madcap, wild, silly, stupid, ridiculous, absurd, idiotic, asinine, imprudent, impracticable, unworkable, unrealistic, unconsidered, half-baked, ill-thought-out, ill-advised, ill-conceived; *informal* crackpot, cockeyed, crazy, daft. ANTONYM sensible.

2 *a hare-brained kid* FOOLISH, silly, idiotic, unintelligent, empty-headed, scatterbrained, featherbrained, birdbrained, pea-brained, brainless, giddy; *informal* dippy, dizzy, flaky, dopey, dotty, airheaded. ANTONYM intelligent.

harem noun *the inner rooms of the harem* SERAGLIO; zenana; women's quarters.

hark verb *literary hark, I hear a warning note* LISTEN, lend an ear, pay attention, attend, mark; *archaic* hearken, give ear. PHRASE: **hark back to** *why hark back to such unpleasant memories?* RECALL, call to mind, bring to mind, look back on, evoke, put one in mind of.

harlequin noun *historical the gaily garbed harlequins of his court* JESTER, joker, merry-andrew.

▸ adjective *a harlequin pattern* MULTICOLORED, many-colored, colorful, parti-colored, varicolored, many-hued, rainbow, variegated, jazzy, kaleidoscopic, psychedelic, polychromatic, checkered; *archaic* motley.

harlot noun *archaic stay off that street, unless you want to be mistaken for a harlot* PROSTITUTE, whore, fille de joie, call girl; promiscuous woman; *informal* hooker, hustler, tramp; *dated* streetwalker, hussy, lady of the evening, tart, pro, member of the oldest profession, scarlet woman, loose woman, fallen woman, cocotte, wanton; *archaic* strumpet, courtesan, trollop, doxy, trull.

harm noun **1** *the voltage is not sufficient to cause harm* INJURY, hurt, pain, trauma; damage, impairment, mischief. ANTONYM benefit.

2 *I can't see any harm in it* EVIL, wrong, ill, wickedness, iniquity, sin. ANTONYM good.

▸ verb **1** *he's never harmed anybody in his life* INJURE, hurt, wound, lay a finger on, maltreat, mistreat, misuse, ill-treat, ill-use, abuse, molest.

2 *this could harm her Olympic prospects* DAMAGE, hurt, spoil, mar, do mischief to, impair.

harmful adjective *the harmful rays of the sun* DAMAGING, injurious, detrimental, dangerous, deleterious, unfavorable, negative, disadvantageous, unhealthy, unwholesome, hurtful, baleful, destructive; noxious, hazardous, poisonous, toxic, deadly, lethal; bad, evil, malign, malignant, malevolent, corrupting, subversive, pernicious. ANTONYM beneficial.

harmless adjective **1** *a harmless substance* SAFE, innocuous, benign, gentle, mild, wholesome, nontoxic, nonpoisonous, nonirritant, nonirritating, hypoallergenic; nonaddictive. ANTONYMS dangerous, toxic.

2 *he seems harmless enough* INOFFENSIVE, innocuous, unobjectionable, unexceptionable. ANTONYM objectionable.

harmonious adjective **1** *harmonious music* TUNEFUL, melodious, melodic, sweet-sounding, mellifluous, dulcet, lyrical; euphonious, euphonic, harmonic, polyphonic; *informal* easy on the ear. ANTONYM discordant.

2 *their harmonious relationship* FRIENDLY, amicable, cordial, amiable, congenial, easy, peaceful, peaceable, cooperative; compatible, sympathetic, united, attuned, in harmony, in rapport, in tune, in accord, of one mind, seeing eye to eye. ANTONYM hostile.

3 *a harmonious blend of traditional and modern* CONGRUOUS, coordinated, balanced, in proportion, compatible, well-matched, well-balanced; *literary* consilient. ANTONYM incongruous.

harmonize verb **1** *colors that harmonize in a pleasing way* COORDINATE, go together, match, blend, mix, balance; be compatible, be harmonious, suit each other. ANTONYM clash.

2 *a plan to harmonize tax laws across the country* COORDINATE, systematize, correlate, integrate, synchronize, make consistent, homogenize, bring in line, bring in tune.

harmony noun **1** *musical harmony* EUPHONY, polyphony; tunefulness, melodiousness, mellifluousness. ANTONYM dissonance.

2 *the harmony of the whole structure* BALANCE, symmetry, congruity, consonance, coordination, compatibility. ANTONYM incongruity.

3 *the villagers live together in harmony* ACCORD, agreement, peace, peacefulness, amity, amicability, friendship, fellowship, cooperation, understanding, consensus, unity, sympathy, rapport, like-mindedness; unison, union, concert, oneness, synthesis; *formal* concord. ANTONYM disagreement.

harness noun *a horse's harness* TACK, tackle, equipment; trappings; yoke; *archaic* equipage.

▸ verb **1** *he harnessed his horse* HITCH UP, put in harness, yoke, couple.

2 *attempts to harness solar energy* CONTROL, exploit, utilize, use, employ, make use of, put to use; channel, mobilize, apply, capitalize on.

harp PHRASE: **harp on about** *the way she harps on about his shortcomings, it's a wonder he can stand to be with her* KEEP ON ABOUT, go on about, keep talking about, dwell on, make an issue of; labor the point of.

harpoon noun *the whalers were equipped with harpoons* SPEAR, trident, dart, barb, gaff, leister.

harridan noun *Steve tried to scare us with stories of the evil harridan Miss Duffy, who in reality was the sweetest teacher in Coolidge Elementary* SHREW, termagant, virago, harpy, vixen, nag, hag, crone, dragon, ogress; fishwife, hellcat, she-devil, gorgon; martinet, tartar; *informal* old bag, old bat, battle-ax, witch; *archaic* scold.

harried adjective *harried mothers with their crying children* HARASSED, beleaguered, flustered, agitated, bothered, vexed, stressed, beset, plagued; *informal* hassled, up against it.

harrow verb *his words harrowed her very soul* DISTRESS, trouble, bother, afflict, grieve, torment, disturb, pain, hurt, mortify. ANTONYM comfort.

harrowing adjective *a harrowing experience for the hostages* DISTRESSING, distressful, traumatic, upsetting; shocking, disturbing, painful, haunting, appalling, horrifying.

harry verb **1** *they harried the retreating enemy* ATTACK, assail, assault; charge, rush, strike, set upon; bombard, shell, strafe.

2 *the government was harried by a new lobby* HARASS, hound, bedevil, torment, pester, bother, worry, badger, nag, plague; *informal* hassle, bug, lean on, give someone a hard time.

harsh adjective **1** *a harsh voice* GRATING, jarring, rasping, strident, raucous, brassy, discordant, unharmonious, unmelodious; screeching, shrill; rough, coarse, hoarse, gruff, croaky. ANTONYMS soft, dulcet.

2 *harsh colors* GLARING, bright, dazzling; loud, garish, gaudy, lurid, bold. ANTONYM subdued.

3 *his harsh rule over them* CRUEL, savage, barbarous, despotic, dictatorial, tyrannical, tyrannous; ruthless, merciless, pitiless, relentless, unmerciful; severe, strict, intolerant, illiberal, iron-fisted; hard-hearted, heartless, unkind, inhuman, inhumane. ANTONYMS kind, enlightened.

4 *they took harsh measures to end the crisis* SEVERE, stringent, draconian, firm, stiff, hard, stern, rigorous, grim, uncompromising; punitive, cruel, brutal. ANTONYM lenient.

5 *harsh words* RUDE, discourteous, uncivil, impolite; unfriendly, sharp, bitter, abusive, unkind, disparaging; abrupt, brusque, curt, gruff, short, surly, offhand. ANTONYM friendly.

6 *harsh conditions* AUSTERE, grim, spartan, hard, comfortless, inhospitable, stark, bleak, desolate. ANTONYM comfortable.

7 *a harsh winter* HARD, severe, cold, bitter, bleak, freezing, icy; arctic, polar, Siberian. ANTONYMS balmy, mild.

8 *harsh detergents* ABRASIVE, strong, caustic; coarse, rough. ANTONYMS gentle, mild.

harum-scarum adjective *the rules were too restrictive for a couple of harum-scarum teens like Bella and Maud* RECKLESS, impetuous, impulsive, imprudent, rash, wild; daredevil, madcap, hotheaded, harebrained, foolhardy, incautious, careless, heedless; *informal* devil-may-care; *literary* temerarious. ANTONYM cautious.

harvest noun **1** *we all helped with the harvest* HARVESTING, reaping, picking, collecting.

2 *a poor harvest* YIELD, crop, vintage; fruits, produce.

3 *the experiment yielded a meager harvest* RETURN, result, fruits; product, output, effect; consequence.

▸ verb **1** *he harvested the wheat* GATHER (IN), bring in, reap, pick, collect.

2 *she harvested many honors* ACQUIRE, obtain, gain, get, earn; accumulate, amass, gather, collect; *informal* land, net, bag, rake in, scoop up.

hash noun *a whole hash of excuses* MIXTURE, assortment, variety, array, mix, miscellany, selection, medley, mishmash, ragbag, gallimaufry, potpourri, hodgepodge. PHRASE: **make a hash of** *informal he was sorry to have made such a hash of the travel arrangements* BUNGLE, fluff, flub, mess up, make a mess of; mismanage, mishandle, ruin, wreck; botch, muff, muck up, foul up, screw up, blow.

hassle *informal* noun **1** *parking is such a hassle* INCONVENIENCE, bother, nuisance, problem, trouble, struggle, difficulty, annoyance, irritation, thorn in one's side/flesh, fuss; *informal* aggravation, stress, headache, pain, pain in the neck.

2 *she got into a hassle with that guy.* See QUARREL noun.

▸ verb *they were hassling him to pay up* HARASS, pester, nag, keep on at, badger, hound, harry, bother, torment, plague; *informal* bug, give someone a hard time, get on someone's case, breathe down someone's neck.

hassled adjective *informal we were feeling pretty hassled and asked if we could be seated away from that annoying couple* HARASSED, agitated, stressed (out), harried, frayed, flustered; beleaguered, hounded, plagued, bothered, beset, tormented; under pressure; *informal* up against it, hot and bothered. ANTONYM calm.

haste noun *working with feverish haste* SPEED, hastiness, hurriedness, swiftness, rapidity, quickness, briskness; *formal* expedition. ANTONYM delay.

PHRASE: **in haste** *the curtains look as if they were hung in haste* QUICKLY, rapidly, fast, speedily, with urgency, in a rush, in a hurry.

hasten verb **1** *we hastened back home* HURRY, rush, dash, race, fly, shoot; scurry, scramble, dart, bolt, sprint, run, gallop; go fast, go quickly, go like lightning, go hell-bent for leather; *informal* tear, scoot, zip, zoom, belt, hotfoot it, bomb, hightail, barrel; *dated* make haste. ANTONYMS dawdle, crawl.

2 *chemicals can hasten aging* SPEED UP, accelerate, quicken, precipitate, advance, hurry on, step up, spur on, catalyze; facilitate, aid, assist, boost. ANTONYMS slow down, delay.

hastily adverb **1** *Meg retreated hastily* QUICKLY, hurriedly, fast, swiftly, rapidly, speedily, briskly, without delay, posthaste; with all speed, as fast as possible, at breakneck speed, at a run, on the double; *informal* PDQ (pretty damn quick), like lightning, like greased lightning, like the wind, like a bat out of hell, lickety-split.

2 *an agreement was hastily drawn up* HURRIEDLY, speedily, quickly; on the spur of the moment, prematurely.

hasty adjective **1** *hasty steps* QUICK, hurried, fast, swift, rapid, speedy, brisk; *literary* fleet. ANTONYM slow.

2 *hasty decisions* RASH, impetuous, impulsive, reckless, precipitate, spur-of-the-moment, premature, unconsidered, unthinking; *literary* temerarious. See note at SUPERFICIAL. ANTONYM considered.

hat noun *please remove your hat* CAP, beret, bonnet. See table on page 418.

hatch verb **1** *the duck hatched her eggs* INCUBATE, brood.

2 *the plot that you* ***hatched up*** *last night* DEVISE, conceive, concoct, brew, invent, plan, design, formulate; think up, dream up; *informal* cook up.

hatchet noun *a small hatchet with an oak handle* AX, tomahawk, cleaver, mattock.

hate verb **1** *they hate each other* LOATHE, detest, despise, dislike, abhor, execrate; be repelled by, be unable to bear/stand, find intolerable, recoil from, shrink from; *formal* abominate. ANTONYM love.

2 *I hate to bother you* BE SORRY, be reluctant, be loath, be unwilling, be disinclined; regret, dislike.

▸ noun **1** *feelings of hate* HATRED, loathing, detestation, dislike, distaste, abhorrence, abomination, execration, aversion; hostility, enmity, animosity, antipathy, revulsion, disgust, contempt, odium. ANTONYM love.

2 *a hate of mine is filling in forms* PEEVE, pet peeve, bugbear, bane, bête noire, bogey, aversion, thorn in one's flesh/side, bugaboo. ANTONYM love.

hateful adjective *his hateful letters were presented as evidence* DETESTABLE, horrible, horrid, unpleasant, awful, nasty, disagreeable, despicable, objectionable, insufferable, revolting, loathsome, abhorrent, abominable, execrable, odious, disgusting, distasteful, obnoxious, offensive, vile, heinous, ghastly, beastly, godawful. ANTONYM delightful.

hatred noun *he finally overcame the hatred he felt for his unfaithful wife* LOATHING, hate, detestation, dislike, distaste, abhorrence, abomination, execration; aversion, hostility, ill will, ill feeling, enmity, animosity, antipathy; revulsion, disgust, contempt, odium.

haughtiness noun *people were quickly put off by her haughtiness* ARROGANCE, conceit, pride, hubris, hauteur, vanity, self-importance, pomposity, condescension, disdain, contempt; snobbishness, snobbery, superciliousness; *informal* snootiness. ANTONYM modesty.

HATS AND HEADCOVERINGS

alpine hat	knit cap
balaclava	leghorn
balmoral	mantilla
baseball cap	matador's hat
beanie	miter
bearskin	mobcap
beaver	mortarboard
beret	nightcap
bicorne	opera hat
bird's nest hat	panama hat
biretta	petasus
boater	picture hat
bonnet	pillbox
bowler	pith helmet
busby	porkpie
cap	sailor hat
chapeau	sallet
chauffeur's cap	shako
chef's hat	shovel hat
cloche	silk hat
cocked hat	ski cap
coif	skimmer
coolie hat	skullcap
coonskin (cap)	snap-brim
cowboy hat	sombrero
crown	sou'wester
deerstalker	Stetson™
derby	stocking cap
Dolly Varden	stovepipe hat
dunce cap	straw hat
engineer's cap	sunbonnet
fedora	tam
fez	tam-o'-shanter
forage cap	tarboosh
gangster hat	tarpaulin
gaucho hat	ten-gallon hat
glengarry	topi
graduation cap	toque
hard hat	toreador hat
headdress	tricorne
helmet	trilby
high hat	turban
homburg	Viking hat/helmet
hunting cap	watch cap
Juliet cap	wide-awake
kaffiyeh	yarmulke
kepi	zucchetto

haughty adjective *he is both haughty and disdainful* PROUD, arrogant, vain, conceited, snobbish, superior, self-important, pompous, supercilious, condescending, patronizing; scornful, contemptuous, disdainful; full of oneself, above oneself; *informal* stuck-up, snooty, hoity-toity, uppity, uppish, big-headed, high and mighty, la-di-da. ANTONYM humble.

haul verb **1** *she hauled the basket along* DRAG, pull, tug, heave, lug, hump, draw, tow; *informal* yank.

2 *a contract to haul coal* TRANSPORT, convey, carry, ship, ferry, move.

▸ noun *the thieves abandoned their haul* BOOTY, loot, plunder; spoils, stolen goods, ill-gotten gains; *informal* swag, boodle.

haunches plural noun *the dog just sat there on its haunches, staring at me* RUMP, hindquarters, rear, rear end, seat; buttocks, thighs, derrière, bottom; behind, backside; *Anatomy* nates; *informal* butt, fanny, tush, bum, heinie; *humorous* fundament, posterior, gluteus maximus.

haunt verb **1** *a ghost haunts this house* APPEAR IN, materialize in; visit.

2 *he haunts street markets* FREQUENT, patronize, visit regularly; loiter in, linger in; *informal* hang out in.

3 *the sight haunted me for years* TORMENT, disturb, trouble, worry, plague, burden, beset, beleaguer; prey on, weigh on, gnaw at, nag at, weigh heavily on, obsess; *informal* bug.

▸ noun *a favorite haunt of artists* HANGOUT, stomping ground, stamping ground, meeting place; territory, domain, resort, retreat, spot.

haunted adjective **1** *a haunted house* POSSESSED, cursed; ghostly, eerie; *informal* spooky, scary.

2 *her haunted eyes* TORMENTED, anguished, troubled, tortured, worried, disturbed.

haunting adjective *the haunting background music* EVOCATIVE, emotive, affecting, moving, touching, stirring, powerful; poignant, nostalgic, wistful, elegiac; memorable, indelible, unforgettable.

hauteur noun *two years in the army seems to have taken the edge off his hauteur* HAUGHTINESS, superciliousness, arrogance, pride, conceit, snobbery, snobbishness, superiority, self-importance; disdain, condescension; airs and graces; *informal* snootiness, uppishness.

have verb **1** *he had a new car* POSSESS, own, be in possession of, be the owner of; be blessed with, boast, enjoy; keep, retain, hold, occupy.

2 *the apartment has five rooms* COMPRISE, consist of, contain, include, incorporate, be composed of, be made up of; encompass; *formal* comprehend.

3 *they had dinner together* EAT, consume, devour, partake of; drink, imbibe, quaff; *informal* demolish, dispose of, put away, scoff (down), scarf (down/up).

4 *she had a letter from Mark* RECEIVE, get, be given, be sent, obtain, acquire, come by, take receipt of. ANTONYMS send, give.

5 *we've decided to have a party* ORGANIZE, arrange, hold, give, host, throw, put on, lay on, set up, fix up.

6 *she's going to have a baby* GIVE BIRTH TO, bear, be delivered of, bring into the world, produce; *informal* drop; *archaic* beget.

7 *we are having guests for dinner* ENTERTAIN, be host to, cater for, receive; invite over, ask over/around, wine and dine; accommodate, put up.

8 *he had trouble finding the restaurant* EXPERIENCE, encounter, face, meet, find, run into, go through, undergo.

9 *I have a headache* BE SUFFERING FROM, be afflicted by, be affected by, be troubled with.

10 *I had a good time* EXPERIENCE; enjoy.

11 *many of them have doubts* HARBOR, entertain, feel, nurse, nurture, sustain, maintain.

12 *he had little patience* MANIFEST, show, display, exhibit, demonstrate.

13 *she had them line up according to height* MAKE, ask to, request to, get to, tell to, require to, induce to, prevail upon to; order to, command to, direct to, force to.

14 *I can't have you insulting me* TOLERATE, endure, bear, support, accept, put up with, go along with, take, countenance; permit to, allow to; *informal* stand, abide, stomach; *formal* brook.

15 *I **have to** get up at six* MUST, be obliged to, be required to, be compelled to, be forced to, be bound to.

16 *informal I'd been had* TRICK, fool, deceive, cheat, dupe, take in, hoodwink, swindle; *informal* con, diddle, rip off, shaft, hose, sucker, snooker. PHRASES: **have had it** *informal* 1 *they admit that they've had it* HAVE NO CHANCE, have no hope, have failed, be finished, be defeated, have lost; *informal* have flopped, have come a cropper, have bought the farm. 2 *if you tell anyone, you've had it* BE IN TROUBLE, be in for a scolding; *informal* be in hot water, be in deep doodoo, be toast, be dead meat. **have on** *she had a blue dress on* BE WEARING, be dressed in, be clothed in, be attired in, be decked out in, be robed in.

haven noun 1 *a safe haven* REFUGE, retreat, shelter, sanctuary, asylum; port in a storm, oasis, sanctum.

2 *they stopped in a small haven* ANCHORAGE, harbor, harborage, port, moorage, mooring; cove, inlet, bay.

haversack noun *they looked like little soldiers with their khaki haversacks* KNAPSACK, backpack, rucksack, pack.

havoc noun 1 *the hurricane caused havoc* DEVASTATION, destruction, damage, desolation, ruination, ruin; disaster, catastrophe.

2 *hyperactive children create havoc* DISORDER, chaos, disruption, mayhem, bedlam, pandemonium, turmoil, tumult, uproar; commotion, furor, a three-ring circus; *informal* hullabaloo.

hawk[1] noun *every October we meet at Dobbs' Hill to watch the red-tailed hawks.* See table at RAPTOR.

hawk[2] verb *hawking his wares on the street* PEDDLE, sell, tout, vend, trade in, traffic in, push.

hawk-eyed adjective *a hawk-eyed security guard intercepted the would-be bomber* VIGILANT, observant, alert, eagle-eyed, sharp-eyed; on the alert, on the lookout, with one's eyes peeled; *informal* not missing a trick, on the ball. ANTONYM inattentive.

hay noun *soon the barns will be filled with hay* FORAGE, dried grass, silage, fodder, straw, herbage. PHRASE: **make hay while the sun shines** *Jack was a firm believer in making hay while the sun shines* make the most of an opportunity, take advantage of something, strike while the iron is hot, seize the day, carpe diem.

haywire adjective *informal the binding machine has gone haywire | by midnight, the negotiations were completely haywire* OUT OF CONTROL, erratic, faulty, malfunctioning, out of order; chaotic, confused, disorganized, disordered, topsy-turvy; *informal* on the blink, on the fritz.

hazard noun 1 *the hazards of radiation* DANGER, risk, peril, threat, menace; problem, pitfall.

2 *literary the laws of hazard* CHANCE, probability, fortuity, luck, fate, destiny, fortune, providence.

▸ verb 1 *he hazarded a guess* VENTURE, advance, put forward, volunteer, float; conjecture, speculate, surmise; *formal* opine.

2 *it's too risky to hazard money on* RISK, jeopardize, gamble, stake, bet, chance; endanger, imperil.

hazardous adjective *a hazardous construction site* RISKY, dangerous, unsafe, perilous, precarious, fraught with danger; unpredictable, uncertain, chancy, high-risk, insecure, touch-and-go; *informal* dicey, hairy. ANTONYMS safe, certain.

haze noun 1 *a thick haze on the sea* MIST, fog, cloud; smoke, vapor, steam.

2 *a haze of euphoria* BLUR, daze, confusion, muddle, befuddlement.

hazy adjective 1 *a hazy day* MISTY, foggy, cloudy, overcast; smoggy, murky.

2 *hazy memories* VAGUE, indistinct, unclear, faint, dim, nebulous, shadowy, blurred, fuzzy, confused.

head noun 1 *she scratched her head thoughtfully* skull, cranium, crown; *informal* nut, noodle, noggin, dome.

2 *he had to use his head* BRAIN(S), brainpower, intellect, intelligence; wit(s), wisdom, mind, sense, reasoning, common sense; *informal* savvy, gray matter, smarts.

3 *she had a good head for business* APTITUDE, faculty, talent, gift, capacity, ability; mind, brain.

4 *the head of the church* LEADER, chief, controller, governor, superintendent, commander, captain; director, manager; principal, president, premier; chieftain, headman, sachem; CEO; *informal* boss, boss man, kingpin, top dog, Mr. Big, skipper, ringleader, numero uno, head honcho, big kahuna.

5 *the head of the line* FRONT, beginning, start, fore, forefront; top.

6 *the head of the river* SOURCE, origin, headspring, headwater; *literary* wellspring.

7 *beer with **a head*** FROTH, foam, bubbles, spume, fizz, effervescence; suds.

▸ adjective *the head waiter* CHIEF, principal, leading, main, first, foremost, prime, premier, senior, top, highest, supreme, superior, top-ranking, ranking. ANTONYM subordinate.

▸ verb 1 *the procession was headed by the mayor* LEAD, be at the front of; be first, lead the way.

2 *Dr. Jones heads a research team* COMMAND, control, lead, run, manage, direct, supervise, superintend, oversee, preside over, rule, govern, captain; *informal* be the boss of.

3 *she was **heading for** the exit* MOVE TOWARD, make for,

aim for, go in the direction of, be bound for, make a beeline for; set out for, start out for.

PHRASES: **at the head of** *Stasha will now be at the head of the department* IN CHARGE OF, controlling, commanding, leading, managing, running, directing, supervising, overseeing; at the wheel of, at the helm of. **come to a head** *the violence came to a head after two civilians were killed* REACH A CRISIS, come to a climax, reach a critical point, reach a crossroads. **go to someone's head 1** *the wine has gone to my head* INTOXICATE SOMEONE, befuddle someone, make someone drunk; *informal* make someone woozy; *formal* inebriate someone. **2** *her victory went to her head* MAKE SOMEONE CONCEITED, make someone full of themselves, turn someone's head, puff someone up. **head off 1** *he went to head off the cars* INTERCEPT, divert, deflect, redirect, reroute, draw away, turn away. **2** *they headed off a confrontation* FORESTALL, avert, ward off, fend off, stave off, hold off, nip in the bud, keep at bay; prevent, avoid, stop. **keep one's head** *Richie kept his head throughout the confrontation* KEEP/STAY CALM, keep one's self-control, maintain one's composure; *informal* keep one's cool, keep one's shirt on, keep it together, cool one's jets. **lose one's head** *you cannot lose your head in the courtroom* LOSE CONTROL, lose one's composure, lose one's equilibrium, go to pieces; panic, get flustered, get confused, get hysterical; *informal* lose one's cool, freak out, crack up.

headache noun **1** *I've got a headache* PAIN IN THE HEAD, migraine; neuralgia; *informal* head.

2 *informal* *their behavior was a headache for the teacher* NUISANCE, trouble, problem, bother, bugbear, pest, worry, inconvenience, vexation, irritant, thorn in one's side; *informal* aggravation, hassle, pain (in the neck).

head case noun *informal* *it seems that every family has at least one head case* MANIAC, lunatic, madman, madwoman; *informal* loony, nut, nutcase, fruitcake, crank, crackpot, screwball, crazy, kook, wacko, dingbat, loon.

head first adjective & adverb See HEADLONG.

heading noun **1** *chapter headings* TITLE, caption, legend, subtitle, subheading, rubric, headline.

2 *this topic falls under four main headings* CATEGORY, division, classification, class, section, group, grouping, subject, topic.

headland noun *his family owns all of the houses on the headland* CAPE, promontory, point, head, foreland, peninsula, bluff.

headlong adverb **1** *he fell headlong into the tent* HEAD FIRST, on one's head. ANTONYM feet first.

2 *she rushed headlong to join the craze* WITHOUT THINKING, without forethought, precipitously, impetuously, rashly, recklessly, carelessly, heedlessly, hastily, head first. ANTONYM cautiously.

▸ adjective *a headlong dash* BREAKNECK, whirlwind; reckless, precipitate, precipitous, hasty, careless, heedless, head-first. ANTONYM cautious.

head-on adjective **1** *a head-on collision* DIRECT, full on.

2 *a head-on confrontation* DIRECT, face to face, personal; *informal* eyeball to eyeball.

headquarters plural noun *the report was immediately dispatched to headquarters* THE HEAD OFFICE, the main office, HQ, the base, the nerve center, the war room, mission control, the command post.

headstone noun *the heavy salt air up here is erosive to these old headstones* GRAVESTONE, tombstone, stone, grave marker, monument, memorial.

headstrong adjective *our middle child is the most headstrong* WILLFUL, strong-willed, stubborn, obstinate, unyielding, obdurate; contrary, perverse, wayward, unruly; *formal* refractory. ANTONYM tractable.

heads-up noun *if we see Mr. Klein's car pull in, we'll give you **a heads-up*** WARNING, forewarning, notice, advance notice, a/the tip-off, a/the red flag.

headway PHRASE: **make headway** *critics charge that the ground troops are making no headway in their purported mission* MAKE PROGRESS, progress, make strides, gain ground, advance, proceed, move, get ahead, come along, take shape.

heady adjective **1** *heady wine* POTENT, intoxicating, strong; alcoholic, vinous; *formal* spirituous. ANTONYM nonalcoholic.

2 *the heady days of my youth* EXHILARATING, exciting, thrilling, stimulating, invigorating, electrifying, rousing; *informal* mind-blowing. ANTONYM boring.

heal verb **1** *he heals sick people* MAKE BETTER, make well, cure, treat, restore to health. ANTONYM make worse.

2 *his knee had healed* GET BETTER, get well, be cured, recover, mend, improve. ANTONYM get worse.

3 *time will heal the pain of grief* ALLEVIATE, ease, assuage, palliate, relieve, help, lessen, mitigate, attenuate, allay. ANTONYM aggravate.

4 *we tried to heal the rift* PUT RIGHT, set right, repair, remedy, resolve, correct, settle; conciliate, reconcile, harmonize; *informal* patch up. ANTONYM worsen.

healing adjective *the healing properties of aloe* CURATIVE, therapeutic, medicinal, remedial, corrective, reparative; tonic, restorative, health-giving, healthful, beneficial. ANTONYM harmful.

health noun **1** *he was restored to health* WELL-BEING, healthiness, fitness, good condition, good shape, fine fettle; strength, vigor, wellness. ANTONYM illness.

2 *bad health forced him to retire* PHYSICAL STATE, physical shape, condition, constitution.

healthful adjective *a healthful environment* HEALTHY, health-giving, beneficial, good for one, salubrious; wholesome, nourishing, nutritious. See note at SANITARY. ANTONYM unhealthy.

healthy adjective **1** *a healthy baby* WELL, in good health, fine, fit, in good trim, in good shape, in fine fettle, in tip-top shape; blooming, thriving, hardy, robust, strong, vigorous, fighting fit, fit as a fiddle, the picture of health; *informal* OK, in the pink, right as rain. ANTONYM ill.

2 *a healthy diet* HEALTH-GIVING, healthful, good for one; wholesome, nutritious, nourishing; beneficial, salubrious. ANTONYM unwholesome.

heap noun **1** *a heap of boxes* PILE, stack, mound, mountain, mass, quantity, load, lot, jumble; collection, accumulation, assemblage, store, hoard.

2 *informal* *we have **heaps of** room | **a heap of** troubles* A LOT OF, a fair amount of, much, plenty of, a good deal of, a great deal of, an abundance of, a wealth of, a profusion of;

(a great) many, a large number of, numerous, scores of; *informal* hundreds of, thousands of, millions of, a load of, loads of, a pile of, piles of, oodles of, stacks of, lots of, masses of, scads of, reams of, oceans of, miles of, tons of, zillions of.

▸ verb *she heaped logs on the fire* PILE UP, pile, stack up, stack, make a mound of; assemble, collect.

PHRASE: **heap on/upon** *they heaped praise on her* SHOWER ON, lavish on, load on; bestow on, confer on, give, grant, vouchsafe, favor with.

hear verb **1** *she can't hear* PERCEIVE SOUND; have hearing.

2 *she could hear men's voices* PERCEIVE, make out, discern, catch, get, apprehend; overhear.

3 *I heard that radio show* LISTEN TO, catch.

4 *they heard that I had moved* BE INFORMED, be told, find out, discover, learn, gather, glean, ascertain, get word, get wind.

5 *a jury heard the case* TRY, judge; adjudicate (on), adjudge, pass judgment on.

6 *I totally hear what you're saying* ACKNOWLEDGE, understand, sympathize with, recognize, get, perceive.

hearing noun **1** *the wolf's acute hearing* ABILITY TO HEAR, auditory perception, sense of hearing, aural faculty.

2 *she moved out of hearing* EARSHOT, hearing distance, hearing range, auditory range.

3 *I had a fair hearing* CHANCE TO SPEAK, opportunity to be heard; interview, audience.

4 *he gave evidence at the hearing* TRIAL, court case, inquiry, inquest, tribunal; investigation, inquisition.

hearsay noun *that's all hearsay, and I don't care to listen to such tripe* RUMOR, gossip, tittle-tattle, idle talk; stories, tales; *informal* the grapevine, scuttlebutt, loose lips.

heart noun **1** *my heart stopped beating informal* ticker.

2 *he poured out his heart* EMOTIONS, feelings, sentiments; soul; love, affection, passion.

3 *she has no heart* COMPASSION, sympathy, humanity, feeling(s), fellow feeling, tenderness, softness, empathy, understanding; kindness, goodwill.

4 *they may lose heart* ENTHUSIASM, keenness, eagerness, spirit, determination, resolve, purpose, courage, nerve, willpower, fortitude; *informal* guts, spunk.

5 *the heart of the city* CENTER, middle, hub, core, nucleus, eye, bosom. ANTONYM edge.

6 *the heart of the matter* ESSENCE, crux, core, nub, root, gist, meat, marrow, pith, substance, kernel; *informal* nitty-gritty. ANTONYM peripherals.

PHRASES: **after one's own heart** *Lucie was always a girl after my own heart* LIKE-MINDED, of the same mind, kindred, compatible, congenial, sharing one's tastes; *informal* on the same wavelength. **at heart** *he's a good kid at heart* DEEP DOWN, basically, fundamentally, essentially, in essence, intrinsically; really, actually, truly, in fact; *informal* when you get right down to it. **by heart** *I know the lyrics by heart* FROM MEMORY, down pat, by rote, word for word, verbatim, word-perfect. **do one's heart good** *it does my heart good to see the children getting along* CHEER ONE (UP), please one, gladden one, make one happy, delight one, hearten one, gratify one, make one feel good, give one a lift; *informal* tickle someone pink. **eat one's heart out** *Adam will eat his heart out when he hears about Julia's engagement* PINE, long, ache, brood, mope, fret, sigh, sorrow, yearn, agonize; grieve, mourn, lament. **from the bottom of one's heart** *everything in that poem I meant from the bottom of my heart* SINCERELY, earnestly, fervently, passionately, truly, genuinely, heartily, with all sincerity. **give/lose one's heart to** *so, which young lady have you given your heart to this week?* FALL IN LOVE WITH, fall for, be smitten by; *informal* fall head over heels for, be swept off one's feet by, develop a crush on. **have a change of heart** *it seems that the Smiths have had a change of heart about selling their house* CHANGE ONE'S MIND, flip-flop, change one's tune, have second thoughts, have a rethink, think again, think twice; *informal* get cold feet, do a U-turn, pull a U-ey. **have a heart** *come on, have a heart and let Sandy keep the puppy* BE COMPASSIONATE, be kind, be merciful, be lenient, be sympathetic, be considerate, have mercy. **heart and soul** *the volunteers were into the campaign heart and soul* WHOLEHEARTEDLY, enthusiastically, eagerly, zealously; absolutely, completely, entirely, fully, utterly, to the hilt, one hundred percent. **take heart** *your cards and letters helped us to take heart* BE ENCOURAGED, be heartened, be comforted; cheer up, brighten up, perk up, liven up, revive. **with one's heart in one's mouth** *she slowly made her way down the dark cellar stairs with her heart in her mouth* IN ALARM, in fear, fearfully, apprehensively, on edge, with trepidation, in suspense, in a cold sweat, with bated breath, on tenterhooks; *informal* with butterflies in one's stomach, in a state, in a stew, in a sweat.

heartache noun *a life of heartache* ANGUISH, grief, suffering, distress, unhappiness, misery, sorrow, sadness, heartbreak, via dolorosa, pain, hurt, agony, angst, despondency, despair, woe, desolation. ANTONYM happiness.

heartbreak noun. See HEARTACHE.

heartbreaking adjective *heartbreaking news from the doctor* DISTRESSING, upsetting, disturbing, heart-rending, sad, tragic, painful, traumatic, agonizing, harrowing; pitiful, poignant, plaintive, moving, tearjerker, tearjerking, gut-wrenching. ANTONYM comforting.

heartbroken adjective *the disqualified gymnasts were heartbroken* ANGUISHED, devastated, broken-hearted, heavy-hearted, grieving, grief-stricken, inconsolable, crushed, shattered, desolate, despairing; upset, distressed, miserable, sorrowful, sad, downcast, disconsolate, crestfallen, despondent; *informal* down in the dumps.

heartburn noun *the chest pains may indicate something more serious than heartburn* INDIGESTION, dyspepsia, acid reflux, pyrosis.

hearten verb *the letter from Daphne will hearten him* CHEER (UP), encourage, raise someone's spirits, boost, buoy up, perk up, inspirit, uplift, elate; comfort, reassure; *informal* buck up, pep up. See note at ENCOURAGE.

heartfelt adjective *her heartfelt confession* SINCERE, genuine, from the heart; earnest, profound, deep, wholehearted, ardent, fervent, passionate, enthusiastic, eager; honest, bona fide. ANTONYM insincere.

heartily adverb **1** *we heartily welcome the changes* WHOLEHEARTEDLY, sincerely, genuinely, warmly, profoundly, with all one's heart; eagerly, enthusiastically, earnestly, ardently.

2 *they were heartily sick of her* VERY, extremely, thoroughly, completely, absolutely, really, exceedingly, immensely, most, downright, quite, seriously; *informal* real, mighty.

heartless adjective *Amelia had known more than her share of heartless men* UNFEELING, unsympathetic, unkind, uncaring, unconcerned, insensitive, inconsiderate, hard-hearted, stony-hearted, cold-hearted, mean-spirited; cold, callous, cruel, merciless, pitiless, inhuman. ANTONYM compassionate.

heart-rending adjective *their heart-rending testimonies had the audience in tears* DISTRESSING, upsetting, disturbing, heartbreaking, sad, tragic, painful, traumatic, harrowing; pitiful, poignant, plaintive, moving, tearjerker, tearjerking, gut-wrenching.

heartsick adjective *literary we were heartsick when we read the story of his misfortune* DESPONDENT, dejected, depressed, desolate, downcast, forlorn, unhappy, sad, upset, miserable, wretched, woebegone, inconsolable, grieving, grief-stricken, heavy-hearted, broken-hearted.

heartthrob noun *informal the heartthrob of her day was Tyrone Power* IDOL, pinup, star, superstar; *informal* dreamboat, Adonis.

heart-to-heart adjective *a heart-to-heart chat* INTIMATE, personal, man-to-man, woman-to-woman; candid, honest, truthful, sincere.

▸ noun *they had a long heart-to-heart* PRIVATE CONVERSATION, tête-à-tête, one-to-one, chat, talk, word; *informal* confab.

heartwarming adjective *tonight's heartwarming episode reunites Dan's family for a memorable Thanksgiving* TOUCHING, moving, heartening, stirring, uplifting, pleasing, cheering, gladdening, encouraging, gratifying. ANTONYM distressing.

hearty adjective **1** *a hearty character* EXUBERANT, jovial, ebullient, cheerful, uninhibited, effusive, lively, loud, animated, vivacious, energetic, spirited, dynamic, enthusiastic, eager; warm, cordial, friendly, affable, amiable, good natured. ANTONYM introverted.

2 *hearty congratulations* WHOLEHEARTED, heartfelt, sincere, genuine, real, true; earnest, fervent, ardent, enthusiastic. ANTONYM halfhearted.

3 *a hearty woman of sixty-five* ROBUST, healthy, hardy, fit, flourishing, blooming, fighting fit, fit as a fiddle; vigorous, sturdy, strong; *informal* full of vim. ANTONYM frail.

4 *a hearty meal* SUBSTANTIAL, large, ample, sizable, filling, generous, square, solid; healthy. ANTONYM light.

heat noun **1** *a plant sensitive to heat* WARMTH, hotness, warmness, high temperature; hot weather, warm weather, sultriness, mugginess, humidity; heat wave, hot spell. ANTONYM cold.

2 *he took the heat out of the dispute* PASSION, intensity, vehemence, warmth, fervor, fervency; enthusiasm, excitement, agitation; anger, fury. ANTONYM apathy.

3 *a female bear in heat* ESTRUS, season, sexual receptivity.

▸ verb **1** *the food was heated* WARM, warm up, heat up, make hot, make warm; reheat, cook, microwave; *informal* nuke, zap. ANTONYMS cool, chill.

2 *the pipes expand as they **heat up*** BECOME HOT, become warm, get hotter, get warmer, increase in temperature. ANTONYM cool (down).

3 *he calmed down as quickly as he had **heated up*** BECOME IMPASSIONED, become excited, become animated; get angry, become enraged.

heated adjective **1** *a heated swimming pool* WARM, hot; thermal.

2 *a heated argument* VEHEMENT, passionate, impassioned, animated, spirited, lively, intense, fiery; angry, bitter, furious, fierce, stormy, tempestuous.

3 *Robert grew heated as he spoke of the risks* EXCITED, animated, inflamed, worked up, wound up, keyed up; *informal* het up, in a state.

heathen noun **1** *the evangelist preached to the heathens* PAGAN, infidel, idolater, heretic, unbeliever, disbeliever, nonbeliever, atheist, agnostic, skeptic; *archaic* paynim. ANTONYM believer.

2 *heathens who spoil good whiskey with ice* PHILISTINE, boor, oaf, ignoramus, lout, yahoo, vulgarian, plebeian; *informal* pleb, peasant.

▸ adjective *a heathen practice* PAGAN, infidel, idolatrous, heathenish; unbelieving, nonbelieving, atheistic, agnostic, heretical, faithless, godless, irreligious, ungodly, unholy; barbarian, barbarous, uncivilized, uncultured, primitive, ignorant, philistine.

heave verb **1** *she heaved the sofa backward* HAUL, pull, lug, drag, draw, tug, heft; *informal* hump, yank.

2 *informal she heaved a brick at him* THROW, fling, cast, toss, hurl, lob, pitch; *informal* chuck, sling.

3 *he heaved a sigh of relief* LET OUT, breathe, give, sigh; emit, utter.

4 *the sea heaved* RISE AND FALL, roll, swell, surge, churn, seethe, swirl.

5 *she heaved into the sink* RETCH, gag; vomit, be sick, get sick; *informal* throw up, puke, hurl, spew, barf, upchuck, ralph.

heaven noun **1** *the good will have a place in heaven* PARADISE, nirvana, Zion; the hereafter, the next world, the next life, Elysium, the Elysian Fields, Valhalla; *literary* the empyrean. ANTONYMS hell, purgatory.

2 *a good book is my idea of heaven* BLISS, ecstasy, rapture, contentment, happiness, delight, joy, seventh heaven; paradise, Utopia, nirvana. ANTONYM misery.

3 **(the heavens)** *he observed the heavens* THE SKY, the skies, the upper atmosphere, the stratosphere, space; *literary* the firmament, the vault of heaven, the blue, the (wild/wide) blue yonder, the welkin, the empyrean, the azure, the upper regions, the sphere, the celestial sphere. PHRASES: **in seventh heaven** *we're all in seventh heaven with this new swimming pool* ECSTATIC, euphoric, thrilled, elated, delighted, overjoyed, on cloud nine, walking on air, jubilant, rapturous, jumping for joy, transported, delirious, blissful; *informal* over the moon, on top of the world, on a high, tickled pink, as happy as a clam. **move heaven and earth** *I'm going to get this promotion, even if I have to move heaven and earth to do it* TRY ONE'S HARDEST, do one's best, do one's utmost, do all one can, give one's all, spare no effort, put oneself out; strive, exert oneself, work hard; *informal* bend over backwards, do one's damnedest, pull out all the stops, go all out, bust a gut.

heavenly adjective **1** *heavenly choirs* DIVINE, holy, celestial, supernal; angelic, seraphic, cherubic; *literary* empyrean. ANTONYMS mortal, infernal.

2 *heavenly constellations* CELESTIAL, cosmic, stellar, astral; planetary; extraterrestrial, superterrestrial. ANTONYMS terrestrial, earthly.

3 *informal* *a heavenly morning* DELIGHTFUL, wonderful, glorious, perfect, excellent, sublime, idyllic, first-class, first-rate; blissful, pleasurable, enjoyable; exquisite, beautiful, lovely, gorgeous, enchanting; *informal* divine, super, great, fantastic, fabulous, terrific. ANTONYM dreadful.

heaven-sent adjective *the audition was a heaven-sent opportunity* AUSPICIOUS, providential, propitious, felicitous, opportune, golden, favorable, advantageous, serendipitous, lucky, happy, good, fortunate. ANTONYM inopportune.

heavily adverb **1** *Dad walked heavily* LABORIOUSLY, slowly, ponderously, woodenly, stiffly; with difficulty, painfully, awkwardly, clumsily. ANTONYMS easily, quickly.

2 *we were heavily defeated* DECISIVELY, conclusively, roundly, soundly; utterly, completely, thoroughly. ANTONYM narrowly.

3 *he drank heavily* EXCESSIVELY, to excess, immoderately, copiously, inordinately, intemperately, a great deal, too much, overmuch. ANTONYM moderately.

4 *the area is heavily planted with trees* DENSELY, closely, thickly. ANTONYMS lightly, sparsely.

5 *I became heavily involved in politics* DEEPLY, very, extremely, greatly, exceedingly, tremendously, profoundly; *informal* seriously, ever so.

heavy adjective **1** *a heavy box* WEIGHTY, hefty, substantial, ponderous; solid, dense, leaden; burdensome; *informal* hulking, weighing a ton. ANTONYM light.

2 *a heavy man* OVERWEIGHT, fat, obese, corpulent, large, bulky, stout, stocky, portly, plump, paunchy, fleshy; *informal* hulking, tubby, beefy, porky, pudgy. ANTONYM thin.

3 *a heavy blow to the head* FORCEFUL, hard, strong, violent, powerful, vigorous, mighty, hefty, sharp, smart, severe. ANTONYM gentle.

4 *a gardener did the heavy work for me* ARDUOUS, hard, physical, laborious, difficult, strenuous, demanding, tough, onerous, back-breaking, grueling; *archaic* toilsome. ANTONYM easy.

5 *a heavy burden of responsibility* ONEROUS, burdensome, demanding, challenging, difficult, formidable, weighty; worrisome, stressful, trying, crushing, oppressive. ANTONYMS undemanding, moderate.

6 *heavy fog* DENSE, thick, soupy, murky, impenetrable. ANTONYMS light, wispy.

7 *a heavy sky* OVERCAST, cloudy, clouded, gray, dull, gloomy, murky, dark, black, stormy, leaden, lowering. ANTONYMS sunny, bright.

8 *heavy rain* TORRENTIAL, relentless, copious, teeming, severe. ANTONYMS light, intermittent.

9 *heavy soil* CLAYEY, muddy, sticky, wet. ANTONYMS friable, dry.

10 *a heavy fine* SIZABLE, hefty, substantial, colossal, big, considerable; stiff; *informal* tidy, whopping, steep, astronomical. ANTONYM small.

11 *heavy seas* TEMPESTUOUS, turbulent, rough, wild, stormy, choppy, squally. ANTONYM calm.

12 *heavy fighting* INTENSE, fierce, vigorous, relentless, all-out, severe, serious. ANTONYM halfhearted.

13 *a heavy drinker* IMMODERATE, excessive, intemperate, overindulgent, unrestrained, uncontrolled. ANTONYM moderate.

14 *a heavy meal* SUBSTANTIAL, filling, hearty, large, big, ample, sizable, generous, square, solid. ANTONYM light.

15 *their diet is* ***heavy on*** *vegetables* ABOUNDING IN, abundant in, lavish with, profuse with, unstinting with, using a lot of. ANTONYM light on.

16 *he felt heavy and very tired* LETHARGIC, listless, sluggish, torpid, languid, apathetic, logy. ANTONYMS energetic, animated.

17 *a heavy heart* SAD, sorrowful, melancholy, gloomy, downcast, downhearted, heartbroken, dejected, disconsolate, demoralized, despondent, depressed, crestfallen, desolate, down; *informal* blue; *literary* dolorous. ANTONYM cheerful.

18 *these poems are rather heavy* TEDIOUS, difficult, dull, dry, serious, heavy going, dreary, boring, turgid, uninteresting.

19 *branches heavy with blossoms* LADEN, loaded, covered, filled, groaning, bursting, teeming, abounding.

20 *a heavy crop* BOUNTIFUL, plentiful, abundant, large, bumper, rich, copious, considerable, sizable, profuse; *informal* whopping; *literary* plenteous. ANTONYM meager.

21 *he has heavy features* COARSE, rough, rough-hewn, unrefined; rugged, craggy. ANTONYM delicate.

THE RIGHT WORD

Trying to move a refrigerator out of a third-floor apartment is difficult because it is **cumbersome**, which means that it is so heavy and bulky that it becomes unwieldy or awkward to handle. Cartons filled with books, on the other hand, are merely **heavy**, which implies greater density and compactness than the average load. A huge oak dining table might be described as **massive**, which stresses largeness and solidity rather than weight, while something that is **ponderous** is too large or too *massive* to move, or to be moved quickly (*a ponderous printing press*). Most of these terms can be used figuratively as well. *Heavy*, for example, connotes a pressing down on the mind, spirits, or senses (*heavy with fatigue; a heavy heart*) and *ponderous* implies a dull and labored quality (*a novel too ponderous to read*). **Burdensome**, which refers to something that is not only *heavy* but must be carried or supported, is even more likely to be used in an abstract way to describe something that is difficult but can, with effort, be managed (*a burdensome task*). Both a package and a problem may be described as **weighty**, meaning actually (as opposed to relatively) heavy; but it is more commonly used to mean very important or momentous (*weighty matters to discuss*).

heavy-handed adjective **1** *they are heavy-handed with the equipment* CLUMSY, awkward, maladroit, unhandy, inept, unskillful; *informal* ham-handed, ham-fisted, all thumbs. ANTONYM dexterous.

2 *heavy-handed policing* INSENSITIVE, oppressive, overbearing, high-handed, harsh, stern, severe, tyrannical, despotic, ruthless, merciless; tactless, undiplomatic, inept. ANTONYM sensitive.

heavy-hearted adjective *dozens of heavy-hearted supporters gathered to hear his concession speech* MELANCHOLY, sad, sorrowful, mournful, gloomy, depressed, desolate, despondent, dejected, downhearted, downcast, crestfallen, disconsolate, glum, miserable, wretched, dismal, morose, woeful, woebegone, doleful, unhappy; *informal* down in the dumps, down in/at the mouth, blue; *literary* dolorous. ANTONYM cheerful.

heckle verb *he was heckled by the drunk in the back of the room* JEER, taunt, jibe at, shout down, boo, hiss, harass; *informal* give someone a hard time. ANTONYM cheer.

hectic adjective *the trip to the airport was hectic* FRANTIC, frenetic, frenzied, feverish, manic, busy, active, fast and furious, fast-paced; lively, brisk, bustling, buzzing, abuzz. ANTONYM leisurely.

hector verb *we remembered being hectored by Sue's big brother on the playground* BULLY, intimidate, browbeat, harass, torment, plague; coerce, strong-arm; threaten, menace; *informal* bulldoze.

hedge noun **1** *high hedges* HEDGEROW, bushes; windbreak.

2 *an excellent hedge against a fall in the dollar* SAFEGUARD, protection, shield, screen, guard, buffer, cushion; insurance, security.

3 *his analysis is full of hedges* EQUIVOCATION, evasion, fudge, quibble, qualification; temporizing, uncertainty, prevarication, vagueness.

▸ verb **1** *fields hedged with forsythia* SURROUND, enclose, encircle, ring, border, edge, bound.

2 *she was* ***hedged in*** *by her limited education* CONFINE, restrict, limit, hinder, obstruct, impede, constrain, trap; hem in.

3 *he hedged at every new question* PREVARICATE, equivocate, vacillate, quibble, hesitate, stall, dodge the issue, be noncommittal, be evasive, be vague, beat around the bush, pussyfoot around, mince one's words; hem and haw; *informal* sit on the fence, duck the question.

4 *the company hedged its position on the market* SAFEGUARD, protect, shield, guard, cushion; cover, insure.

hedonism noun *they feel that television promotes hedonism among all its viewers, especially children* SELF-INDULGENCE, pleasure-seeking, self-gratification, lotus-eating, sybaritism; intemperance, immoderation, extravagance, luxury, high living. ANTONYM self-restraint.

hedonist noun *they were a couple of shameless hedonists who planned to live a fun-filled, childless life* SYBARITE, sensualist, voluptuary, pleasure-seeker, bon viveur, bon vivant; epicure, gastronome. ANTONYM ascetic.

hedonistic adjective *he's become less hedonistic since getting married* SELF-INDULGENT, pleasure-seeking, sybaritic, lotus-eating, epicurean, good-time; unrestrained, intemperate, immoderate, extravagant, decadent.

heed verb *heed the warnings* PAY ATTENTION TO, take notice of, take note of, pay heed to, attend to, listen to; bear in mind, be mindful of, mind, mark, consider, take into account, follow, obey, adhere to, abide by, observe, take to heart, be alert to. ANTONYM disregard.

▸ noun *he paid no heed* ATTENTION, notice, note, regard; consideration, thought, care.

heedful adjective *the governor is about to deliver a statement regarding the hurricane, and it is imperative that everyone is heedful* ATTENTIVE, careful, mindful, cautious, prudent, circumspect; alert, aware, wary, chary, watchful, vigilant, on guard, on the alert.

heedless adjective *the evacuation warnings were clear, but he was heedless and didn't get out in time* UNMINDFUL, taking no notice, paying no heed, unheeding, disregardful, neglectful, oblivious, inattentive, blind, deaf; incautious, imprudent, rash, reckless, foolhardy, improvident, unwary.

heel[1] noun **1** *shoes with low heels* wedge, stiletto.

2 *the heel of a loaf* TAIL END, end, crust, remnant, remainder, remains.

3 *informal you're such a heel to have left Liz at the altar* SCOUNDREL, rogue, rascal, reprobate, miscreant; *informal* beast, rat, louse, swine, snake, scumbag, scumbucket, scuzzball, sleazeball, sleazebag, stinker.

heel[2] verb *the ship heeled to starboard* LEAN OVER, list, careen, tilt, tip, incline, keel over.

heft verb *Doug helped us heft the kegs up into the truck.* LIFT, lift up, raise, raise up, heave, hoist, haul; carry, lug, tote; *informal* cart, hump, schlep.

▸ noun *the heft of the urn surprised us* WEIGHT, heaviness, bulk.

hefty adjective **1** *a hefty young man* BURLY, heavy, sturdy, strapping, bulky, brawny, husky, strong, muscular, large, big, solid, well-built; portly, stout; *informal* hulking, hunky, beefy. ANTONYMS slight, gaunt.

2 *a hefty kick* POWERFUL, violent, hard, forceful, heavy, mighty. ANTONYM feeble.

3 *hefty loads of lumber* HEAVY, weighty, bulky, big, large, substantial, massive, ponderous; unwieldy, cumbersome, burdensome, hulking. ANTONYM light.

4 *a hefty fine* SUBSTANTIAL, sizable, considerable, stiff, extortionate, large, excessive; *informal* steep, astronomical, whopping. ANTONYMS paltry, small.

hegemony noun *the Prussian hegemony of the nineteenth century* LEADERSHIP, dominance, dominion, supremacy, authority, mastery, control, power, sway, rule, sovereignty.

height noun **1** *the height of the wall* SIZE, tallness, extent upward, vertical measurement, elevation, stature, altitude. ANTONYM width.

2 *the mountain heights* SUMMIT, top, peak, crest, crown, tip, cap, pinnacle, apex, brow, ridge. ANTONYM base.

3 *the height of their fame* HIGHEST POINT, crowning moment, peak, acme, zenith, apogee, pinnacle, climax, high-water mark. ANTONYM nadir.

4 *the height of bad manners* EPITOME, acme, zenith, quintessence, very limit; ultimate, utmost; ne plus ultra.

5 (heights) *he is terrified of heights* HIGH PLACES, high ground; precipices, cliffs.

heighten verb **1** *the roof had to be heightened* RAISE, make higher, lift (up), elevate. ANTONYM lower.

2 *her pleasure was heightened by guilt* INTENSIFY, increase, enhance, add to, augment, boost, strengthen, deepen, magnify, amplify, aggravate, reinforce. ANTONYM reduce.

heinous adjective *heinous crimes* ODIOUS, wicked, evil, atrocious, monstrous, abominable, detestable, contemptible, reprehensible, despicable, egregious, horrific, terrible, awful, abhorrent, loathsome, hideous, unspeakable, execrable; iniquitous, villainous, beyond the pale. ANTONYM admirable.

heir, heiress noun *Mr. Richfield's heirs would squander the old tycoon's fortune in less than twelve years* SUCCES-

SOR, next in line, inheritor, beneficiary, legatee; descendant, scion; *Law* devisee.

heist noun *informal* See ROBBERY.

helicopter noun *informal* CHOPPER, copter, eggbeater, whirlybird.

helix noun *the teacher's crude drawing of a DNA double helix* SPIRAL, coil, corkscrew, curl, curlicue, twist, gyre, whorl, convolution; *technical* volute, volution.

hell noun **1** *they feared hell* THE NETHERWORLD, the Inferno, the infernal regions, the abyss; eternal damnation, perdition; hellfire, fire and brimstone; Hades, Sheol, Acheron, Gehenna, Tophet; *literary* the pit. ANTONYM heaven.

2 *he made her life hell* A MISERY, torture, agony, a torment, a nightmare, an ordeal; anguish, wretchedness, woe. ANTONYM paradise.

PHRASES: **give hell** *informal* **1** *when I found out, I gave him hell* REPRIMAND SEVERELY, rebuke, admonish, chastise, castigate, chide, upbraid, reprove, scold, berate, remonstrate with, reprehend, take to task, lambaste; read the riot act, give a piece of one's mind, rake/haul over the coals; *informal* tell off, dress down, give an earful, give a roasting, rap over the knuckles, let have it, bawl out, come down hard on, lay into, blast, chew out. **2** *she gave me hell when I was her assistant* HARASS, hound, plague, harry, bother, trouble, bully, intimidate, pick on, victimize, terrorize; *informal* hassle, give a hard time. **raise hell** *informal* **1** *they were hollering and raising hell* CAUSE A DISTURBANCE, cause a commotion, be noisy, run riot, run wild, go on the rampage, be out of control; *informal* raise the roof. **2** *he raised hell with the planners* REMONSTRATE, expostulate, be angry, be furious; argue; *informal* kick up a fuss, raise a stink.

hell-bent adjective *once he's hell-bent on something, there's no stopping him* INTENT, bent, determined, set, dead set, insistent, fixed, resolved; single-minded, fixated. ANTONYM halfhearted.

hellish adjective **1** *the hellish face of Death* INFERNAL, Hadean, chthonic; diabolical, fiendish, satanic, demonic; evil, wicked. ANTONYM angelic.

2 *informal a hellish week* HORRIBLE, rotten, awful, terrible, dreadful, ghastly, horrid, vile, foul, appalling, atrocious, horrendous, frightful; difficult, unpleasant, nasty, disagreeable; stressful, taxing, tough, hard, frustrating, fraught, traumatic, grueling; *informal* murderous, lousy; beastly, hellacious. ANTONYM wonderful.

hello exclamation *hello, Maxie, how've you been?* HI, howdy, hey, hiya, ciao, aloha.

helm noun *he took the helm* TILLER, wheel; steering gear, rudder. PHRASE: **at the helm** *Judith will be at the helm while I am in New Jersey* IN CHARGE, in command, in control, responsible, in authority, at the wheel, in the driver's seat, in the saddle, holding the reins, running the show, calling the shots.

help verb **1** *can you help me please?* ASSIST, aid, lend a (helping) hand to, give assistance to, come to the aid of; be of service to, be of use to; do someone a favor, do someone a service, do someone a good turn, bail someone out, come to someone's/the rescue, give someone a leg up; *informal* get someone out of a tight spot, save someone's bacon, save someone's skin. ANTONYM hinder.

2 *this credit card helps cancer research* SUPPORT, contribute to, give money to, donate to; promote, boost, back; further the interests of, bankroll. ANTONYM impede.

3 *sore throats are helped by lozenges* RELIEVE, soothe, ease, alleviate, make better, improve, assuage, lessen; remedy, cure, heal. ANTONYM worsen.

▸ noun **1** *I'll take help wherever I can find it | this may be of help to you* ASSISTANCE, aid, a helping hand, support, succor, advice, guidance; benefit, use, advantage, service, comfort; *informal* a shot in the arm.

2 *he sought help for his eczema* RELIEF, alleviation, improvement, assuagement, healing; a remedy, a cure, a restorative.

3 *they treated the help badly* DOMESTIC WORKER, domestic servant, cleaner, cleaning lady, housekeeper, maid, hired help, helper.

▸ exclamation *we heard the faint cries of "Help!" in the distance* SOS, mayday.

PHRASES: **cannot help** *he could not help laughing* BE UNABLE TO STOP, be unable to refrain from, be unable to keep from. **help oneself to** *Tara helped herself to one of the photo albums that we left on the table* STEAL, take, appropriate, borrow, liberate, pocket, lift, purloin, commandeer; *informal* swipe, nab, filch, walk off with, run off with, pinch.

helper noun *the teachers' helpers are treated to a picnic lunch at the end of each school year* ASSISTANT, aide, helpmate, helpmeet, deputy, auxiliary, second, right-hand man/woman, attendant, acolyte; coworker, workmate, teammate, associate, colleague, partner; *informal* sidekick.

helpful adjective **1** *the staff are helpful* OBLIGING, eager to please, kind, accommodating, supportive, cooperative; sympathetic, boosterish, neighborly, charitable. ANTONYMS unsympathetic, unobliging.

2 *we found your comments helpful* USEFUL, of use, beneficial, valuable, profitable, advantageous, fruitful, worthwhile, constructive; informative, instructive. ANTONYM useless.

3 *a helpful new tool* HANDY, useful, convenient, practical, easy-to-use, functional, serviceable; *informal* neat, nifty. ANTONYM inconvenient.

helping noun *the helpings are very generous* PORTION, serving, piece, slice, share, ration, allocation; *informal* dollop.

helpless adjective *the cubs are born blind and helpless* DEPENDENT, incapable, powerless, impotent, weak; defenseless, vulnerable, exposed, unprotected, open to attack; paralyzed, disabled. ANTONYM independent.

helpmate, helpmeet noun *he thanked his wife of twenty years for being his helpmate and best friend* HELPER, assistant, attendant; supporter, friend, companion; spouse, partner, life partner, mate, husband, wife.

helter-skelter adverb *they ran helter-skelter down the hill* HEADLONG, pell-mell, hotfoot, posthaste, hastily, hurriedly, at full tilt, hell-bent for leather; recklessly, precipitately, heedlessly, wildly; *informal* like a bat out of hell, like the wind, like greased lightning, lickety-split.

▸ adjective *a helter-skelter collection of houses* DISORDERED, disorderly, chaotic, muddled, jumbled, untidy, haphazard, disorganized, topsy-turvy; *informal* higgledy-piggledy. ANTONYM orderly.

hem noun *the hem of her dress* EDGE, edging, border, trim, trimming. PHRASES: **hem in 1** *a bay hemmed in by pine trees* SURROUND, border, edge, encircle, circle, ring, enclose, skirt, fringe, encompass, corral. **2** *we were hemmed in by the rules* RESTRICT, confine, trap, hedge in, fence in; constrain, restrain, limit, curb, check. **hem and haw** *they hem and haw every time we ask for an explanation* HESITATE, dither, vacillate, be indecisive, equivocate, waver; *informal* blow hot and cold, shilly-shally.

he-man noun *informal he was very masculine without being an arrogant he-man* MUSCLEMAN, strongman, macho man, iron man; Hercules, Samson, Tarzan; *informal* hunk, tough guy, alpha male, beefcake, studmuffin, bruiser. ANTONYM wimp.

hence adverb *the amount of traffic—and hence the amount of pollution—will be reduced* CONSEQUENTLY, as a consequence, for this reason, therefore, ergo, thus, so, accordingly, as a result, because of that, that being so.

henceforth, henceforward adverb *henceforth, we will accept only photo IDs* FROM NOW ON, as of now, in (the) future, hence, subsequently, from this day on, from this day forth; *formal* hereafter.

henchman noun *he leaves all the dirty work to his henchmen* RIGHT-HAND MAN, assistant, aide, helper; underling, minion, man Friday, lackey, flunky, stooge; bodyguard; *informal* sidekick, crony, heavy, goon.

henpecked adjective *the prosecution characterized him as a henpecked husband who finally snapped* BROWBEATEN, downtrodden, bullied, dominated, subjugated, oppressed, intimidated; meek, timid, cringing, long-suffering; *informal* under someone's thumb. ANTONYM domineering.

herald noun **1** *historical a herald announced the armistice* MESSENGER, courier; proclaimer, announcer, crier.

2 *the first herald of spring* HARBINGER, sign, indicator, indication, signal, prelude, portent, omen; forerunner, precursor; *literary* foretoken.

▸ verb **1** *shouts heralded their approach* PROCLAIM, announce, broadcast, publicize, declare, trumpet, blazon, advertise.

2 *the speech heralded a policy change* SIGNAL, indicate, announce, spell, presage, augur, portend, promise, foretell; usher in, pave the way for, be a harbinger of; *literary* foretoken, betoken.

herb noun. See table. See also table at SPICE.

Herculean adjective **1** *a Herculean task* ARDUOUS, grueling, laborious, back-breaking, onerous, strenuous, difficult, formidable, hard, tough, huge, massive, uphill; demanding, exhausting, taxing; *archaic* toilsome. ANTONYM easy.

2 *his Herculean build* STRONG, muscular, muscly, powerful, robust, solid, strapping, brawny, burly; *informal* hunky, beefy, hulking. ANTONYM puny.

herd noun **1** *a herd of cows* drove, flock, pack, fold; group, collection.

2 *a herd of actors* CROWD, group, bunch, horde, mob, host, pack, multitude, throng, swarm, company.

3 *they consider themselves above the herd* COMMON PEOPLE, masses, rank and file, crowd, commonality, plebeians; hoi polloi, mob, proletariat, rabble, riffraff, great unwashed; *informal* proles, plebs.

▸ verb **1** *we herded the sheep into the pen* DRIVE, shepherd, guide; round up, gather, collect, corral.

2 *we all herded into the room* CROWD, pack, flock; cluster, huddle.

3 *they herd reindeer* TEND, look after, keep, watch (over), mind, guard.

herdsman noun CATTLEMAN, cowherd, cowhand, cowman, cowboy, rancher, shepherd, ranchero, stockman, herder, drover; *informal* cowpuncher, cowpoke; *archaic* herd.

here adverb **1** *they lived here* AT/IN THIS PLACE, at/in this spot, at/in this location.

2 *I am here now* PRESENT, in attendance, attending, at hand; available. ANTONYM absent.

3 *come here tomorrow* TO THIS PLACE, to this spot, to this location, over here, nearer, closer; *literary* hither.

4 *here is your opportunity* NOW, at this moment, at this point, at this point in time, at this juncture, at this stage. PHRASE: **here and there 1** *clumps of crabgrass here and there* IN VARIOUS PLACES, in different places; at random. **2** *they darted here and there* BACK AND FORTH, around, about, to and fro, hither and thither, in all directions.

hereafter adverb *formal nothing I say hereafter is intended to offend* FROM NOW ON, after this, as of now, from this moment forth, from this day forth, from this day forward, subsequently, in (the) future, hence, henceforth, henceforward; *formal* hereinafter.

▸ noun **(the hereafter)** *our preparation for the hereafter* LIFE AFTER DEATH, the afterlife, the afterworld, the next world; eternity, heaven, paradise.

HERBS

basil	lemon basil
bay leaf	lemon verbena
bee balm	lemongrass
black cohosh	lovage
boldo leaf	marjoram
borage	Mexican pepperleaf
bouquet garni	mint
burdock	mugwort
burnet	myrtle
calamint	oregano
calendula	pandanus
capers	parsley
catnip	pennyroyal
chervil	peppermint
Chinese parsley	perilla
chives	ramson
cicely	rice paddy herb
cilantro	rocket
coriander	rosemary
costmary	rue
cress	sage
curry leaf	savory
dandelion	saw leaf
dill	shiso
feverfew	sorrel
fines herbes	sweet basil
horehound	tarragon
hyssop	Thai basil
Kaffir lime leaf	thyme
laurel leaf	wormwood
lavender	yarrow
lemon balm	

hereditary adjective **1** *a hereditary right* INHERITED; bequeathed, willed, handed-down, passed-down, passed-on, transferred; ancestral, family, familial.

2 *a hereditary disease* GENETIC, congenital, inborn, inherited, inbred, innate; in the family, in the blood, in the genes.

heredity noun *heredity is a major factor in the diagnosis of many conditions* CONGENITAL TRAITS, genetic makeup, genes; ancestry, descent, extraction, parentage.

heresy noun *an age in which scientists were often accused of heresy* DISSENSION, dissent, nonconformity, heterodoxy, unorthodoxy, apostasy, blasphemy, freethinking; agnosticism, atheism, nonbelief; idolatry, paganism.

heretic noun *heretics were banished or put to death* DISSENTER, nonconformist, apostate, freethinker, iconoclast; agnostic, atheist, nonbeliever, unbeliever, idolater, idolatress, pagan, heathen; *archaic* paynim. ANTONYMS conformist, believer.

heritage noun **1** *they stole his heritage* INHERITANCE, birthright, patrimony; legacy, bequest.

2 *Hawaii's cultural heritage* TRADITION, history, past, background; culture, customs.

3 *his Greek heritage* ANCESTRY, lineage, descent, extraction, parentage, roots, background, heredity.

hermaphrodite noun *we had to name two species that occur naturally as hermaphrodites* ANDROGYNE, intersex, epicene; *Biology* bisexual, gynandromorph.

▸ adjective *hermaphrodite creatures* ANDROGYNOUS, intersex, hermaphroditic, hermaphroditical, epicene; *Biology* bisexual.

hermetic adjective *the documents are stored in a hermetic box* AIRTIGHT, tight, sealed, zip-locked, vacuum-packed; watertight, waterproof.

hermit noun *just because I prefer to live alone doesn't make me a hermit* RECLUSE, solitary, loner, ascetic, marabout, troglodyte; *historical* anchorite, anchoress; *archaic* eremite.

hero noun **1** *the heroes of Guadalcanal* BRAVE PERSON, brave man/woman, man/woman of courage, man/woman of the hour, lionheart, warrior, knight; champion, victor, conqueror. ANTONYMS coward, loser.

2 *a football hero* STAR, superstar, megastar, idol, celebrity, luminary; ideal, paragon, shining example, demigod; favorite, darling; *informal* celeb. ANTONYMS unknown, nobody.

3 *the hero of the film* (MALE) PROTAGONIST, principal (male) character, principal (male) role, main character, title character, starring role, star part; (male) lead, lead actor, leading man. ANTONYMS villain, supporting character, supporting role.

heroic adjective *firefighters perform heroic acts every single day* BRAVE, courageous, valiant, valorous, lionhearted, superhuman, intrepid, bold, fearless, daring, audacious; unafraid, undaunted, dauntless, doughty, plucky, manly, stouthearted, mettlesome; gallant, chivalrous, noble; *informal* gutsy, spunky, ballsy.

heroin noun *addicted to heroin* OPIATE; *informal* H, horse, skag, junk, sugar, China White, smack.

heroine noun **1** *she's a heroine—she saved my baby | the heroines of the air corps* BRAVE WOMAN, hero, woman of courage, woman of the hour; victor, winner, conqueror. ANTONYMS coward, loser.

2 *the literary heroine of Moscow* STAR, superstar, megastar, idol, celebrity, luminary; ideal, paragon, shining example; favorite, darling, queen; *informal* celeb. ANTONYMS unknown, nobody.

3 *the film's heroine* (FEMALE) PROTAGONIST, principal (female) character, principal (female) role, main character, title character; (female) lead, lead actress, leading lady; prima donna, diva. ANTONYMS villain, supporting character, supporting role.

heroism noun *an award for his heroism* BRAVERY, courage, valor, intrepidity, boldness, daring, audacity, fearlessness, dauntlessness, pluck, stout-heartedness, lionheartedness; backbone, spine, grit, spirit, mettle; gallantry, chivalry; *informal* guts, spunk, balls, cojones, moxie.

hero-worship noun *the hero-worship of his fans soon became unsettling to him* IDOLIZATION, adulation, admiration, lionization, idealization, worship, adoration, veneration.

hesitancy noun. See HESITATION.

hesitant adjective **1** *she is hesitant about buying* UNCERTAIN, undecided, unsure, doubtful, dubious, skeptical; tentative, nervous, reluctant, gun-shy; indecisive, irresolute, hesitating, dithering, vacillating, wavering, waffling, blowing hot and cold; ambivalent, of two minds, hemming and hawing; *informal* iffy. ANTONYMS certain, decisive.

2 *a hesitant child* LACKING CONFIDENCE, diffident, timid, shy, bashful, insecure, tentative. ANTONYM confident.

hesitate verb **1** *she hesitated, unsure of what to say* PAUSE, delay, wait, shilly-shally, dither, stall, temporize; be of two minds, be uncertain, be unsure, be doubtful, be indecisive, hedge, equivocate, fluctuate, vacillate, waver, waffle, have second thoughts, think twice; *informal* dilly-dally, blow hot and cold, get cold feet, hem and haw.

2 *don't hesitate to contact me* BE RELUCTANT, be unwilling, be disinclined, scruple; have misgivings about, have qualms about, shrink from, demur from, think twice about, balk at; *informal* miss a beat.

hesitation noun *she answered without hesitation* HESITANCY, uncertainty, unsureness, doubt, doubtfulness, dubiousness; irresolution, irresoluteness, indecision, indecisiveness, hesitance; equivocation, vacillation, waffling, wavering, second thoughts; dithering, stalling, dawdling, temporization, delay; reluctance, disinclination, unease, ambivalence; *informal* cold feet; *formal* dubiety.

heterodox adjective *their heterodox sister was home from college, spouting her liberal views* UNORTHODOX, nonconformist, dissenting, dissident, rebellious, renegade; heretical, blasphemous, recusant, apostate, skeptical; freethinking, unconventional. ANTONYM orthodox.

heterogeneous adjective *a heterogeneous collection of art* DIVERSE, varied, varying, variegated, miscellaneous, assorted, mixed, sundry, disparate, multifarious, different, differing, motley; *informal* hodgepodge, mixed-bag; *literary* divers. ANTONYM homogeneous.

heterosexual adjective *most of my heterosexual friends are single* STRAIGHT; *informal* hetero, het.

hew verb **1** *the logs are freshly hewn* CHOP, hack, cut, lop, ax, cleave, split; fell.

2 *steps had been hewn into the rock wall* CUT, carve, chisel, shape, fashion, sculpt.

heyday noun *during his heyday, he was quite the matinee idol* PRIME, peak, height, pinnacle, summit, apex, acme, zenith, climax, high point; day, time, bloom, flowering; prime of life, salad days, halcyon days, glory days.

hiatus noun *the spring hiatus gave us time to rethink our next project* PAUSE, break, gap, lacuna, interval, intermission, interlude, interruption, suspension, lull, respite, time out, time off, recess; *informal* breather, letup.

hibernate verb **1** *bears hibernate in winter* LIE DORMANT, lie torpid, sleep; overwinter.

2 *he wanted to hibernate in front of a fire for the night* HOLE UP, escape, withdraw, retreat, cocoon.

hick noun *informal a hick from the sticks* BUMPKIN, country bumpkin, yokel, rustic, country dweller, peasant, provincial, country cousin; *informal* hillbilly, hayseed, rube.

▸ adjective **1** *a hick town* RURAL, rustic, backwater, backwoods, outlying; jerkwater.

2 *hick attitudes* SMALL-TOWN, unsophisticated, rural, narrow-minded, small-minded, parochial; *informal* bush-league.

hidden adjective **1** *a hidden camera* CONCEALED, secret, undercover, invisible, unseen, out of sight, closeted, covert; secluded, tucked away; camouflaged, disguised, masked, cloaked. ANTONYM visible.

2 *a hidden meaning* OBSCURE, unclear, veiled, clouded, shrouded, concealed; cryptic, mysterious, secret, abstruse, arcane; ulterior, deep, subliminal, coded. ANTONYMS clear, obvious.

hide[1] verb **1** *he hid the money* CONCEAL, secrete, put out of sight; camouflage; lock up, stow away, tuck away, squirrel away, cache; *informal* stash. ANTONYMS flaunt, expose.

2 *they hid in an air vent* CONCEAL ONESELF, sequester oneself, hide out, take cover, keep out of sight; lie low, go underground; *informal* hole up.

3 *clouds hid the moon* OBSCURE, block out, blot out, obstruct, cloud, shroud, veil, blanket, envelop, eclipse. ANTONYM reveal.

4 *he could not hide his dislike* CONCEAL, keep secret, cover up, keep quiet about, hush up, bottle up, suppress, curtain, bury; disguise, dissemble, mask, camouflage; *informal* keep under one's hat, keep a/the lid on. ANTONYM disclose.

hide[2] noun *the hide should be tanned quickly* SKIN, pelt, coat; leather.

hideaway noun *the cabin in Maine is our hideaway* RETREAT, refuge, hiding place, hideout, den, bolt-hole, shelter, sanctuary, sanctum; hermitage, secret place.

hidebound adjective *hidebound traditionalists* CONSERVATIVE, reactionary, conventional, orthodox; fundamentalist, diehard, hardline, dyed-in-the-wool, set in one's ways, unyielding, inflexible; narrow-minded, small-minded, intolerant, uncompromising, rigid; prejudiced, bigoted. ANTONYM liberal.

hideous adjective *the scenes were too hideous to watch* UGLY, repulsive, repellent, unsightly, revolting, gruesome, grotesque, monstrous, ghastly; *informal* as ugly as sin; awful, terrible, appalling, dreadful, frightful, horrible, horrendous, horrific, horrifying, shocking, sickening, unspeakable, abhorrent, heinous, abominable, foul, vile, odious, execrable. ANTONYMS beautiful, pleasant.

hideout noun *the gang had a hideout up in the mountains* HIDING PLACE, hideaway, retreat, refuge, shelter, safe house, sanctuary, sanctum.

hiding PHRASE: **in hiding** *the fugitive is in hiding* HIDDEN, concealed, lying low, underground, in a safe house.

hiding place noun See HIDEOUT.

hierarchy noun *in the corporate hierarchy, Curt is about six levels below the CEO* PECKING ORDER, order, ranking, chain of command, grading, gradation, ladder, scale, range.

higgledy-piggledy *informal* adjective *a big higgledy-piggledy pile of papers* DISORDERED, disorderly, disorganized, untidy, messy, chaotic, jumbled, muddled, confused, unsystematic, irregular; out of order, in disarray, in a mess, in a muddle, haphazard; *informal* all over the place, upside-down, topsy-turvy. ANTONYM tidy.

▸ adverb *the cars were parked higgledy-piggledy* IN DISORDER, in a muddle, in a jumble, in disarray, untidily, haphazardly, anyhow; *informal* all over the place, helter-skelter, topsy-turvy, every which way, pell-mell, any old how.

high adjective **1** *a high mountain* TALL, lofty, towering, soaring, elevated, giant, big; multistory, high-rise. ANTONYMS short, low.

2 *a high position in the government* HIGH-RANKING, high-level, leading, top, top-level, prominent, preeminent, foremost, senior; influential, powerful, important, elevated, prime, premier, exalted, ranking; *informal* top-notch, chief. ANTONYMS low-ranking, lowly.

3 *high principles* HIGH-MINDED, noble, lofty, moral, ethical, honorable, exalted, admirable, upright, honest, virtuous, righteous. ANTONYM amoral.

4 *high prices* INFLATED, excessive, unreasonable, expensive, costly, exorbitant, extortionate, prohibitive, dear; *informal* steep, stiff, pricey. ANTONYMS reasonable, low.

5 *high winds* STRONG, powerful, violent, intense, extreme, forceful; BLUSTERY, gusty, stiff, squally, tempestuous, turbulent, howling, roaring. ANTONYMS light, calm.

6 *the high life* LUXURIOUS, lavish, extravagant, grand, opulent; sybaritic, hedonistic, epicurean, decadent; upmarket, upscale; *informal* fancy, classy, swanky. ANTONYM abstemious.

7 *I have a high opinion of you* FAVORABLE, good, positive, approving, admiring, complimentary, commendatory, flattering, glowing, adulatory, rapturous. ANTONYM unfavorable.

8 *a high note* | *his high voice* HIGH-PITCHED, high-frequency; soprano, treble, falsetto, shrill, sharp, piercing, penetrating. ANTONYMS low, low-pitched, deep.

9 *informal they were high before they even got to the party* INTOXICATED, inebriated, drugged, on drugs, stupefied, befuddled, delirious, hallucinating; *informal* STONED, wired, hopped up, high as a kite, tripping, hyped up, doped up, coked, spaced out, wasted, wrecked. ANTONYMS sober, straight.

10 ***high in** fiber* ELEVATED IN, rich in, ample in, loaded with, plentiful in, full of; *informal* chock-full of, jam-packed with. ANTONYM deficient.

▸ noun *prices were at a rare high* HIGH LEVEL, high point, peak, high-water mark; pinnacle, zenith, acme, height. ANTONYM low.

▸ adverb *a jet flew high overhead* AT GREAT HEIGHT, high up, far up, way up, at altitude; in the air, in the sky, on high, aloft, overhead. ANTONYM low.

PHRASES: **high and dry** *we track down these guys who have left their wives and children high and dry* DESTITUTE, helpless, in the lurch, in difficulties; abandoned, stranded, marooned. **high and low** *I searched high and low for my keys* EVERYWHERE, all over, all around, far and wide, 'here, there, and everywhere,' extensively, thoroughly, widely, in every nook and cranny; *informal* all over the place, all over the map. **high and mighty** *informal he feels high and mighty just because he was lucky enough to keep his job* SELF-IMPORTANT, condescending, patronizing, pompous, disdainful, supercilious, superior, snobbish, snobby, haughty, conceited, above oneself; *informal* stuck-up, puffed up, snooty, hoity-toity, la-di-da, uppity, full of oneself, too big for one's britches/boots. **on a high** *informal she was obviously on a high after Joey proposed* ECSTATIC, euphoric, exhilarated, delirious, elated, ebullient, thrilled, overjoyed, beside oneself, walking on air, on cloud nine, in seventh heaven, jumping for joy, in raptures, in high spirits, exultant, jubilant; excited, overexcited; *informal* blissed out, over the moon, on top of the world.

high achiever noun See GO-GETTER.

high-born adjective *her high-born father had given up his inheritance to marry a lowly seamstress* NOBLE, aristocratic, well-born, titled, patrician, blue-blooded, upper-class, genteel; *informal* upper-crust, top-drawer; *archaic* gentle. ANTONYM lowly.

highbrow adjective *his work has a highbrow following* INTELLECTUAL, scholarly, bookish, well-read, literary, cultured, academic, educated, lettered, sophisticated, erudite, learned, cerebral; *informal* brainy, egghead, inkhorn. ANTONYM lowbrow.

▸ noun *highbrows who hate rap music* INTELLECTUAL, scholar, academic, bluestocking, bookish person, thinker; *informal* egghead, brain, bookworm, brainiac.

high-class adjective *the casino's high-class hotel* SUPERIOR, upper-class, first-rate; excellent, select, elite, choice, premier, top, top-flight; luxurious, deluxe, upscale, high-quality, top-quality, upmarket; *informal* top-notch, blue-ribbon, five-star, top-drawer, A1, ritzy, tony, classy, posh.

high-end adjective *high-end dining* TOP-LINE, deluxe, best, top of the line, superior, top-notch, high-grade, upscale, upmarket, choice, first-class, first-rate, fancy; expensive, high-priced, pricey, costly.

highfalutin adjective *informal* See PRETENTIOUS.

high-flown adjective *one of his high-flown ideas finally panned out* GRAND, extravagant, elaborate, flowery, lofty, ornate, overblown, overdone, overwrought, grandiloquent, magniloquent, grandiose, orotund, inflated, high-sounding; affected, pretentious, bombastic, pompous, turgid; *informal* windy, purple, highfalutin, la-di-da. ANTONYM plain.

high-handed adjective *I'll not be subordinate to any high-handed individual, male or female* IMPERIOUS, arbitrary, peremptory, arrogant, haughty, domineering, supercilious, pushy, overbearing, heavy-handed, lordly, magisterial; inflexible, rigid; autocratic, authoritarian, dictatorial, tyrannical; *informal* bossy, high and mighty. ANTONYM modest.

high-impact adjective *a high-impact sales pitch* IMPRESSIVE, bold, compelling, effective; punchy; forceful, powerful, high-powered, potent, hard-hitting; intensive, energetic, dynamic; *informal* high-octane.

highland noun *Peru's Andean highland* UPLANDS, highlands, mountains, hills, heights, moors; upland, tableland, plateau.

highlight noun *the highlight of his career* HIGH POINT, best part, climax, peak, pinnacle, height, acme, zenith, summit, crowning moment, high-water mark, centerpiece. ANTONYM nadir.

▸ verb *he has highlighted shortcomings in the plan* SPOTLIGHT, call attention to, point out, single out, focus on, underline, feature, play up, show up, bring out, accentuate, accent, give prominence to, zero in on, stress, emphasize.

highly adverb **1** *a highly dangerous substance* VERY, extremely, exceedingly, particularly, most, really, thoroughly, decidedly, distinctly, exceptionally, immensely, greatly, inordinately, singularly, extraordinarily; *informal* awfully, terribly, majorly, seriously, supremely, desperately, hugely, ultra, oh-so, damn, damned; real, mighty, awful; *dated* frightfully. ANTONYM slightly.

2 *he was highly regarded* FAVORABLY, well, appreciatively, admiringly, approvingly, positively, glowingly, enthusiastically. ANTONYM unfavorably.

high-maintenance adjective *Ernie's high-maintenance girlfriend* DEMANDING, challenging, exacting, difficult, hard to please, needy.

high-minded adjective *high-minded civil libertarians* HIGH-PRINCIPLED, principled, honorable, moral, upright, upstanding, right-minded, noble, good, honest, decent, ethical, righteous, virtuous, worthy, idealistic. ANTONYM unprincipled.

high-pitched adjective *a high-pitched scream* HIGH, high-frequency, shrill, sharp, piercing; soprano, treble, falsetto. ANTONYMS low-pitched, deep.

high-powered adjective *high-powered career women* DYNAMIC, ambitious, energetic, assertive, enterprising, vigorous; forceful, powerful, potent, aggressive; *informal* go-getting, high-octane.

high-pressure adjective **1** *high-pressure sales tactics* FORCEFUL, insistent, persistent, pushy; intensive, high-powered, aggressive, coercive, compelling, not taking no for an answer.

2 *a high-pressure job* DEMANDING, stressful, nerve-racking, tense, pressured.

high-priced adjective *high-priced luxury cars* EXPENSIVE, costly, dear, big-ticket, high-end; overpriced, exorbitant, extortionate; *informal* pricey, steep, stiff.

high-profile adjective *he gladly stays behind the scenes, managing the business affairs of his high-profile wife* PROMINENT, well-known, famous, renowned, celebrated, legendary, notable, noteworthy, distinguished, eminent; visible, conspicuous; notorious, infamous.

high-ranking adjective See HIGH adjective sense 2.

high-risk adjective See RISKY.

high-sounding adjective See HIGH-FLOWN.

high-speed adjective *a high-speed chase on the highway* FAST, quick, rapid, speedy, swift, breakneck, lightning, brisk, express; *informal* zippy, supersonic; *literary* fleet. ANTONYM slow.

high-spirited adjective *a high-spirited horse* LIVELY, spirited, full of fun, fun-loving, animated, zestful, bouncy, bubbly, sparkling, vivacious, buoyant, cheerful, joyful, exuberant, ebullient, jaunty, irrepressible; *informal* chirpy, peppy, full of beans; *literary* frolicsome.

high spirits plural noun *the high spirits of these young competitors is indeed infectious* LIVELINESS, vitality, spirit, zest, energy, bounce, sparkle, vivacity, buoyancy, cheerfulness, good humor, joy, joyfulness, exuberance, ebullience, joie de vivre; *informal* pep, zing.

high-strung adjective *a high-strung woman answered the phone and started accusing me of harassing her* NERVOUS, excitable, agitated, temperamental, sensitive, unstable; brittle, on edge, edgy, jumpy, jittery, restless, anxious, tense, stressed, overwrought, neurotic; *informal* worked up, uptight, twitchy, wired, wound up, het up, strung out. ANTONYM easygoing.

highway noun *we got off the highway in Litchfield* MAIN ROAD, main route; parkway, throughway, freeway, expressway, turnpike.

hijack verb *two flight attendants thwarted Girard's attempt to hijack the plane* COMMANDEER, seize, take over, take control; skyjack, carjack; appropriate, expropriate, confiscate, co-opt.

hijinks plural noun *our college hijinks* ANTICS, pranks, escapades, stunts, practical jokes, tricks; fun, fun and games, skylarking, mischief, silliness, horseplay, tomfoolery, clowning; *informal* shenanigans, capers, monkey business.

hike noun *a five-mile hike* WALK, trek, tramp, trudge, slog, footslog, march; ramble.

▸ verb *they hiked across the island* WALK, trek, tramp, tromp, trudge, slog, footslog, march; ramble, rove, traipse; *informal* hoof it, leg it.

PHRASE: **hike up** 1 *Roy hiked up his trousers* HITCH UP, pull up, hoist, lift, raise; *informal* yank up. 2 *they hiked up the price* INCREASE, raise, up, put up, boost up, mark up, push up, inflate; *informal* jack up, bump up.

hilarious adjective *the final scene is hilarious* VERY FUNNY, hysterically funny, hysterical, uproarious, riotous, rollicking, farcical, rib-tickling; humorous, comic, amusing, entertaining jocular, jovial, laughable; *informal* side-splitting, gut-busting, knee-slapping, thigh-slapping, priceless, a scream, a hoot.

hilarity noun *we always enjoy a great deal of hilarity when we get together* AMUSEMENT, mirth, laughter, merriment, lightheartedness, levity, fun, humor, jocularity, jollity, gaiety, delight, glee, exuberance, high spirits; comedy.

hill noun 1 *the top of the hill* HIGH GROUND, prominence, hillock, foothill, hillside, rise, mound, mount, knoll, butte, hummock, mesa; bank, bluff, ridge, slope, incline, gradient; (**hills**) heights, highland(s), downs, elevation; *Geology* drumlin; *formal* eminence.

2 *a hill of garbage* HEAP, pile, stack, mound, mountain, mass.

hillbilly noun *informal* See HICK.

hillock noun *the lovely green hillocks in the distance* MOUND, small hill, prominence, elevation, rise, knoll, hummock, hump, dune; bank, ridge, knob; *formal* eminence.

hilt noun *the hilt of his sword* HANDLE, haft, handgrip, grip, shaft, shank, helve. PHRASE: **to the hilt** *we will support our leaders to the hilt* COMPLETELY, fully, wholly, totally, absolutely, entirely, utterly, unreservedly, unconditionally, in every respect, in all respects, one hundred percent, every inch, to the full, to the maximum extent, all the way, body and soul, heart and soul.

hind adjective *the left hind leg* BACK, rear, hinder, hindmost, posterior; dorsal. ANTONYMS fore, front.

hinder verb *budget cuts have hindered our progress* HAMPER, obstruct, impede, inhibit, retard, balk, prevent, thwart, foil, curb, delay, arrest, interfere with, set back, slow down, hobble, hold back, hold up, stop, halt; restrict, restrain, constrain, block, check, curtail, frustrate, cramp, handicap, cripple, hamstring; *informal* stymie, throw a wrench in the works. See note at PROHIBIT. ANTONYM facilitate.

THE RIGHT WORD

If you're about to set off on a cross-country trip by car and wake up to find that a foot of snow has fallen overnight, it would be correct to say that the weather has **hindered** you. But if you're trying to drive through a snowstorm and are forced to creep along at a snail's pace behind a snowplow, it would be correct to say you were **impeded**. To *hinder* is to delay or hold something back, especially something that is under way or is about to start (*she entered college but was hindered by poor study habits*); it connotes a thwarting of progress, either deliberate or accidental. *Impede*, on the other hand, means to slow the progress of someone or something by a deliberate act; it implies that the obstacles are more serious and suggests that movement or progress is so slow that it is painful or frustrating (*the shoes were so tight they impeded his circulation*). Both **hamper** and **encumber** involve hindering by outside forces. To *hamper* is to impede by placing restraints on someone or something so as to make action difficult (*hampered by family responsibilities*), while **encumber** means to hinder by the placing of a burden (*encumbered with several heavy suitcases*). To **obstruct** is to place obstacles in the way, often bringing progress or movement to a complete halt (*obstruct traffic; obstruct justice*). **Prevent** suggests precautionary or restraining measures (*the police prevented him from entering the burning building*) and is also used to describe a nonhuman agency or cause that hinders something (*the snow prevented us from leaving that day*).

hindrance noun *bad weather was the primary hindrance to our rescue efforts* IMPEDIMENT, obstacle, barrier, bar, obstruction, handicap, block, hurdle, restraint, restriction, limitation, encumbrance, interference; complication, delay, drawback, setback, difficulty, inconvenience, snag, catch, hitch, check, stumbling block; *informal* fly in the ointment, hiccup, wrench in the works. ANTONYM help.

hinge verb *our future* ***hinges on*** *the election* DEPEND ON, hang on, rest on, turn on, center on, pivot on, be contingent on, be dependent on, be conditional on; be determined by, be decided by, revolve around.

hint noun 1 *a hint that he would leave* CLUE, inkling, suggestion, indication, indicator, sign, signal, pointer, intimation, insinuation, innuendo, mention, whisper.

2 *handy hints about painting* TIP, suggestion, pointer, clue, guideline, recommendation; advice, help; *informal* how-to.

3 *a hint of mint* TRACE, touch, suspicion, suggestion, dash, soupçon, tinge, modicum, whiff, taste, undertone; *informal* smidgen, tad, speck.

▸ verb *what are you **hinting at**?* IMPLY, insinuate, intimate, suggest, indicate, signal; allude to, refer to, drive at, mean; *informal* get at.

hinterland noun *Jody always worried that his father would take them back to the hinterland* BACKWOODS, backwater, wilds, wilderness, bush, back of beyond, backcountry; *informal* sticks, middle of nowhere, boondocks, boonies; *Austral.* outback.

hip adjective *informal* 1 *a hip pair of rhinestone-studded sunglasses* FASHIONABLE, stylish, popular, all the rage, in fashion, in vogue, up-to-the-minute; *informal* trendy, cool, styling/stylin', with it, in, hot, big, happening, now, groovy, funky, sharp, the in thing, phat, kicky, tony, fly. See note at EDGY.

2 *I'm **hip to** what you're saying* WISE TO, clued in to, tuned in to, in the know about, in touch with, up to speed with.

hippie noun *yesterday's hippies are today's ad execs* FLOWER CHILD, Bohemian, beatnik, long-hair, free spirit, nonconformist, dropout.

hips plural noun *just swing your hips to the music* PELVIS, hindquarters, haunches, thighs.

hire verb 1 *they hire labor in line with demand* EMPLOY, engage, recruit, appoint, take on, sign up, enroll, commission, enlist, contract. ANTONYMS dismiss, lay off.

2 *we hired a car* RENT, lease, charter, let, sublet.

hired gun noun *Heccabe was a hired gun, working secretly for the state* MERCENARY, hit man, assassin, gunman, soldier of fortune, thug, hired thug; EXPERT, specialist; *informal* hotshot; *historical* condottiere.

hired hand noun *Rick worked as our hired hand during summer vacations* LABORER, worker, employee, help, assistant; peon, menial, drudge.

hirsute adjective *formal they described him as unusually large and hirsute* HAIRY, shaggy, bushy, hair-covered; woolly, furry, fleecy, fuzzy; bearded, unshaven, bristly.

hiss verb 1 *the escaping gas hissed* FIZZ, fizzle, whistle, wheeze; *rare* sibilate.

2 *the audience hissed* JEER, catcall, boo, heckle, whistle, hoot; scoff, jibe.

▸ noun 1 *the hiss of the steam* FIZZ, fizzing, whistle, hissing, sibilance, wheeze, pfft; *rare* sibilation.

2 *the speaker received hisses* JEER, catcall, boo, whistle; abuse, scoffing, taunting, derision.

hissy fit noun *just try to ignore her if she has one of her hissy fits* TEMPER TANTRUM, tantrum, angry outburst, fit of temper, paroxysm, paroxysm of rage, histrionics; fit of pique, snit, huff.

historic adjective *the historic first flight at Kitty Hawk* SIGNIFICANT, notable, important, momentous, consequential, memorable, newsworthy, unforgettable, remarkable; famous, famed, celebrated, renowned, legendary; landmark, sensational, groundbreaking, epoch-making, red-letter, earth-shattering. ANTONYM insignificant.

USAGE NOTE **historic, historical**

Historical, meaning "of or relating to or occurring in history," is called upon for use far more frequently than historic. **Historic** means "historically significant" *the Alamo is a historic building*. An event that makes history is historic; momentous happenings or developments are historic—e.g.: "The Supreme Court's historic decision about whether mentally competent, dying patients and their doctors have the right to hasten death won't be known for months." (*USA Today*, Jan. 10, 1997). A documented fact, event, or development—perhaps having no great importance—is *historical*. E.g.: "Despite the historical data, some people just don't feel comfortable knowing their loan's rate can drift up 5 or 6 points." (Chicago Sun-Times, Jan. 24, 1997). Examples of *historic* used incorrectly for *historical* could easily run for several pages—e.g.: "The Sunday Trading Act, which formally became law yesterday, removes historic [read *historical*] anomalies of the kind that allowed shopkeepers to sell pornographic magazines but not Bibles on the Sabbath, and instant but not ground coffee." (*Times* (London), Aug. 27, 1994). "The odds are now on a further easing of monetary policy and there is a good historic [read *historical*] correlation between falling interest rates and a rising stock market." (*Financial Times*, June 13, 1996). "Rape is also an historic [read a *historical*] soldiers' sport." (*Harper's Magazine*, Jan. 2003). The far less common mistake is misusing *historical* for *historic*—e.g.: "Gary Pinkel didn't know what to expect after Toledo and Nevada found themselves going into a historical [read *historic*] overtime in the Las Vegas Bowl." (*Austin Am.-Statesman*, Dec. 16, 1995). —BG

historical adjective 1 *historical evidence* DOCUMENTED, recorded, chronicled, archival; authentic, factual, actual, true. ANTONYMS mythical, legendary.

2 *historical figures* PAST, bygone, ancient, old, former; *literary* of yore.See note at HISTORIC. ANTONYM contemporary.

history noun 1 *my interest in history* THE PAST, former times, historical events, the olden days, the old days, bygone days, long ago, yesterday, antiquity; *literary* days of yore, yesteryear.

2 *a history of the Boxer Rebellion* CHRONICLE, archive, record, diary, report, narrative, account, study, tale, story, saga; memoir.

3 *she gave details of her history* BACKGROUND, past, life story, biography, experiences, backstory; antecedents.

histrionic adjective *a histrionic account of her divorce* MELODRAMATIC, theatrical, dramatic, exaggerated, stagy, showy, affected, artificial, overacted, overdone; *informal* hammy, ham, campy.

histrionics plural noun *how about a little more plain-talking sincerity and a little less histrionics?* DRAMATICS, theatrics, tantrums; affectation, staginess, artificiality.

hit verb 1 *she hit her child* STRIKE, slap, smack, spank, cuff, punch, thump, swat; beat, thrash, batter, pound, pummel, box someone's ears; whip, flog, cane; *informal* whack, wallop, bash, bop, clout, clip, clobber, sock, swipe, crown, beat the living daylights out of, knock someone around, belt, tan, lay into, let someone have it, deck, floor, slug; *literary* smite.

2 *a car hit the barrier* CRASH INTO, run into, smash into,

smack into, knock into, bump into, plow into, collide with, meet head-on, impact.

3 *informal spending will hit $180 million* REACH, touch, arrive at, rise to, climb to.

4 *it hit me that I had forgotten* OCCUR TO, strike, dawn on, come to; enter one's head, cross one's mind, come to mind, spring to one's mind.

▸ noun 1 *he received a hit from behind* BLOW, thump, punch, knock, bang, cuff, slap, smack, spank, tap, crack, stroke, welt, karate chop; impact, collision, bump, crash; *informal* whack, thwack, wallop, bash, belt, clout, sock, swipe, clip, slug.

2 *he directed many big hits* SUCCESS, box-office success, sellout, winner, triumph, sensation; best seller; *informal* smash, smash hit, megahit, knockout, crowd-pleaser, chart-topper, chart-buster, wow, biggie, number one. ANTONYM failure.

PHRASES: **hit back** *if you're gonna come after me with lies and innuendo, I'm gonna hit back* RETALIATE, respond, reply, react, counter, defend oneself. **hit hard** *the tragedy hit her hard* DEVASTATE, affect badly, hurt, harm, leave a mark on; upset, shatter, crush, shock, overwhelm, traumatize. **hit home** *the documentary on teen suicide painfully hit home* HAVE THE INTENDED EFFECT, strike home, hit the mark, register, be understood, get through, sink in. **hit it off** *informal Mark and Mika hit it off almost immediately* GET ON WELL, get along, get on, be friends, be friendly, be compatible, be well matched, feel a rapport, see eye to eye, take to each other, warm to each other; *informal* click, get on like a house on fire, be on the same wavelength. **hit on/upon** 1 *he hit on the truth | Cagney hit upon a great idea for the finale* DISCOVER, come up with, think of, conceive of, dream up, work out, invent, create, devise, design, pioneer; uncover, stumble on, happen upon, chance on, light on, come upon. 2 *he tried to hit on me* FLIRT WITH, show interest in, make eyes at, come on to, make advances to/toward.

hitch verb 1 *Tom hitched the pony to his cart* HARNESS, yoke, couple, fasten, connect, attach, tether, tie.

2 *she hitched the blanket around her* PULL, jerk, tug, hike, lift, raise, yank, shift.

3 *informal they hitched a ride informal* THUMB. See also HITCHHIKE.

▸ noun *it went without a hitch* PROBLEM, difficulty, snag, catch, setback, hindrance, obstacle, obstruction, complication, impediment, stumbling block, barrier; holdup, interruption, delay; *informal* headache, glitch, hiccup.

hitchhike verb *they hitchhiked across the Texas Panhandle informal* HITCH, thumb a ride/lift, thumb rides/lifts.

hither adverb *literary* See HERE sense 3.

hitherto adverb *hitherto a part of French West Africa, Benin achieved independence in 1960* PREVIOUSLY, formerly, earlier, before, beforehand; so far, thus far, to date, as yet, until now, until then, till now, till then, up to now, up to then; *formal* heretofore.

hit man noun *Bennie had been a hit man for the Guiletti family* ASSASSIN, killer, murderer, gunman, hired gun.

hit-or-miss, hit-and-miss adjective *even his approach to finding a job is hit-or-miss* ERRATIC, haphazard, disorganized, undisciplined, unmethodical, uneven; careless, slapdash, slipshod, casual, cursory, lackadaisical, random, aimless, undirected, indiscriminate; *informal* sloppy. ANTONYM meticulous.

hoard noun *a secret hoard of gold* CACHE, stockpile, stock, store, collection, supply, reserve, reservoir, fund, accumulation; treasury, treasure house, treasure trove; *informal* stash.

▸ verb *they hoarded rations* STOCKPILE, store, store up, stock up on, put aside, put by, lay by, lay up, set aside, stow away, buy up; cache, amass, collect, save, gather, garner, accumulate, squirrel away, put aside for a rainy day; *informal* stash away, salt away. ANTONYM squander.

hoarse adjective *voices hoarse from shouting* ROUGH, harsh, throaty, gruff, husky, growly, gravelly, grating, scratchy, raspy, rasping, raucous, croaky, croaking, with a frog in one's throat. ANTONYMS mellow, clear.

hoary adjective 1 *hoary cobwebs* GRAYISH-WHITE, gray, white, snowy, silver, silvery; frosty; *literary* rimy.

2 *a hoary old man* GRAY-HAIRED, white-haired, silver-haired, grizzled; elderly, aged, old, ancient, venerable *informal* over the hill. ANTONYM young.

hoax noun *the Piltdown man was perhaps the most successful hoax of the twentieth century* PRACTICAL JOKE, joke, jest, prank, trick; ruse, deception, fraud, bluff, confidence trick; *informal* con, spoof, scam, setup.

hobble verb *Luke hobbled into the post office* LIMP, walk with difficulty, walk lamely, move unsteadily, walk haltingly; shamble, totter, dodder, stagger, falter, stumble, lurch.

hobby noun *writing poetry is just one of my hobbies* PASTIME, leisure activity, leisure pursuit; sideline, side interest, diversion, avocation; recreation, entertainment, amusement.

hobgoblin noun *he believed there were hobgoblins under his bed* GOBLIN, imp, sprite, elf, brownie, pixie, puck, leprechaun, gnome; bogey, bugbear, bogeyman.

hobnob verb *informal she sought out every opportunity to hobnob with the rich and famous* ASSOCIATE, mix, fraternize, socialize, keep company, spend time, go around, mingle, consort, network, rub shoulders, rub elbows; *informal* hang around/out, be thick, schmooze.

hobo noun *Charlie, a well-known hobo among the locals, was in fact an eccentric millionaire who drifted in and out of town for more than twenty years* TRAMP, vagrant, vagabond, derelict; *informal* bum, down-and-out; drifter, transient, itinerant.

hock verb *informal* See PAWN verb.

hocus-pocus noun 1 *a little hocus-pocus and—presto!—the tiger disappears* MAGIC, sleight of hand, conjuring, witchcraft, wizardry, sorcery; deception, sham, devilry, trickery; *informal* scam.

2 *she dismissed it as so much hocus-pocus* NONSENSE, rubbish, garbage, balderdash, malarkey, baloney, bunk, hogwash, bull, hokum.

hodgepodge noun *a rambling hodgepodge of Chinese modern and art deco* MIXTURE, mix, mixed bag, assortment, random collection, conglomeration, jumble, ragbag, grab bag, miscellany, medley, salmagundi, potpourri, patchwork, pastiche; mélange, mishmash, hash, confusion, farrago, gallimaufry. See note at JUMBLE.

hoedown noun *Sportsmen's Hall was all decked out for*

the hoedown PARTY, shindig, hootenanny, bash, jamboree, dance, barn dance, fête, celebration.

hog noun *a prize-winning hog* PIG, sow, swine, porker, piglet, boar; *informal* piggy.

▸ verb *informal he hogged the limelight* MONOPOLIZE, dominate, take over, corner, control. ANTONYM share.

hogwash noun *informal* See NONSENSE sense 1.

hoi polloi noun *in days long past, the royal family would not have deigned to commune with the hoi polloi* MASSES, common people, populace, public, multitude, rank and file, lower order(s), plebeians, proletariat; mob, herd, rabble, riffraff, great unwashed; *informal* plebs, proles; *historical* third estate.

hoist verb *we hoisted the mainsail* RAISE, raise up, lift, lift, haul up, heave up, jack up, hike up, winch up, pull up, heft up, upraise, uplift, elevate, erect. ANTONYM lower.

▸ noun *a mechanical hoist* LIFTING GEAR, crane, winch, block and tackle, pulley, windlass, derrick; *Nautical* sheerlegs.

hoity-toity adjective *informal oh, just look at Miss Prissface and her hoity-toity friends* SNOBBISH, snobby, haughty, disdainful, conceited, proud, pretentious, arrogant, supercilious, superior, imperious, above oneself, self-important; *informal* high and mighty, snooty, stuck-up, puffed-up, uppity, uppish, la-di-da.

hokey adjective *informal* See CORNY.

hokum noun *informal* See NONSENSE sense 1.

hold verb **1** *she held a suitcase* CLASP, clutch, grasp, grip, clench, cling to, hold on to; carry, bear. ANTONYMS release, let go of.

2 *I wanted to hold her* EMBRACE, hug, clasp, cradle, enfold, squeeze, fold in one's arms, cling to.

3 *do you hold a degree?* POSSESS, have, own, bear, carry, have to one's name.

4 *the branch held my weight* SUPPORT, bear, carry, take, keep up, sustain, prop up, shore up.

5 *the police were holding him* DETAIN, hold in custody, imprison, lock up, put behind bars, put in prison, put in jail, incarcerate, keep under lock and key, confine, constrain, intern, impound; *informal* put away. ANTONYMS release, let go.

6 *try to hold the audience's attention* MAINTAIN, keep, occupy, engross, absorb, interest, captivate, fascinate, enthrall, rivet, mesmerize, transfix; engage, catch, capture, arrest. ANTONYM lose.

7 *he held a senior post* OCCUPY, have, fill; *informal* hold down.

8 *the tank holds 250 gallons* TAKE, contain, accommodate, fit; have a capacity of, have room for.

9 *the court held that there was no evidence* MAINTAIN, consider, take the view, believe, think, feel, deem, be of the opinion; judge, rule, decide; *informal* reckon; *formal* opine, esteem.

10 *let's hope the good weather holds* PERSIST, continue, carry on, go on, hold out, keep up, last, endure, stay, remain. ANTONYM end.

11 *the offer still holds* BE AVAILABLE, be valid, hold good, stand, apply, remain, exist, be the case, be in force, be in effect.

12 *they held a meeting* CONVENE, call, summon; conduct, have, organize, run; *formal* convoke. ANTONYM disband.

13 *hold your fire* STOP, halt, restrain, check, cease, discontinue; *informal* break off, give up; hold back, suppress, repress, refrain from using, stifle, withhold. ANTONYM resume.

▸ noun **1** *she kept a hold on my hand* GRIP, grasp, clasp, clutch.

2 *Tom had a hold over his father* INFLUENCE, power, control, dominance, authority, command, leverage, sway, mastery, dominion.

3 *the military tightened their hold on the capital* CONTROL, grip, power, stranglehold, chokehold, dominion, authority.

PHRASES: **get hold of** *informal I'll try to get hold of Stevenson this evening* CONTACT, get in touch with, communicate with, make contact with, reach, notify; phone, call, speak to, talk to. **hold back 1** *if you feel like singing, don't hold back* HESITATE, pause, stop oneself, restrain oneself, desist, forbear. **2** *Jane held back her tears* SUPPRESS, fight back, choke back, stifle, smother, subdue, rein in, repress, curb, control, keep a tight rein on; *informal* keep a lid on. **3** *don't hold anything back from me* WITHHOLD, hide, conceal, keep secret, keep hidden, keep quiet about, keep to oneself, hush up; *informal* sit on, keep under one's hat. **4** *you'll never make it in music if you keep letting your parents hold you back* HINDER, hamper, impede, obstruct, inhibit, hobble, check, curb, block, thwart, balk, hamstring, restrain, frustrate, stand in someone's way. **hold dear** *she holds this house dear* CHERISH, treasure, prize, appreciate, adore, value highly, care for/about; *informal* put on a pedestal. **hold down 1** *they will hold down inflation* KEEP DOWN, keep low, freeze, fix. **2** *informal she held down two jobs* OCCUPY, have, do, fill. **3** *the people can be held down only so long* OPPRESS, repress, suppress, subdue, subjugate, keep down, keep under, tyrannize, dominate. **hold forth** *he was holding forth on the qualities of good wine* SPEAK AT LENGTH, talk at length, go on, sound off; declaim, spout, pontificate, orate, preach, sermonize; *informal* speechify, drone on. **hold off 1** *the rain held off* STAY AWAY, keep off, not come, delay. **2** *we held off the swarms of ants as long as we could* RESIST, repel, repulse, rebuff, parry, deflect, fend off, stave off, ward off, keep at bay. **hold on 1** *hold on, I'll be right there* WAIT, wait a minute, just a moment, just a second; stay here, stay put; hold the line; *informal* just a sec, hang on, sit tight, hold your horses. **2** *if only they could hold on just a little longer* KEEP GOING, persevere, survive, last, continue, struggle on, carry on, go on, hold out, see it through, stay the course; *informal* soldier on, stick it out, hang in there. **hold on to 1** *he held on to the chair* CLUTCH, hang on to, clasp, grasp, grip, cling to. **2** *they can't hold on to their staff* RETAIN, keep, hang on to. **hold one's own.** See OWN. **hold out 1** *the small band of weary soldiers held out until reinforcements arrived* PERSIST, last, remain; persevere, continue. **2** *Celia held out her hands* EXTEND, proffer, offer, present; outstretch, reach out, stretch out, put out. **hold over** *the family gathering was held over until late January* POSTPONE, put off, put back, delay, defer, suspend, shelve, put over, table, take a rain check on; *informal* put on ice, put on the back burner, put in cold storage, mothball. **hold up 1** *the argument doesn't hold up* BE CONVINCING, be logical, hold water, bear examination, be sound. **2** *they held up the trophy* DISPLAY, hold aloft, exhibit, show (off), flourish, brandish; *informal* flash. **3** *concrete pillars hold up the bridge* SUPPORT, bear, carry, take, keep up, prop up, shore up, buttress. **4** *our flight was held up for hours* DELAY, detain, make late, set back, keep back, retard, slow up. **5** *a lack of cash has held up progress* OBSTRUCT, impede, hinder, hamper, inhibit, arrest, balk, thwart, curb, hamstring, frustrate, foil, interfere with, stop; *informal* stymie, hog-tie. **6** *two gunmen held up the bank* ROB; *informal* stick up. **hold water.** See WATER. **with no holds barred** *you can tell us everything that happened, with no holds barred* CANDIDLY, honestly, frankly, directly, openly, bluntly; *informal* point-blank, without mincing one's words.

holder noun **1** *a knife holder* CONTAINER, receptacle, case, casing, cover, covering, housing, sheath; stand, rest, rack.

2 *are you the holder of a major credit card?* BEARER, owner, possessor, keeper; custodian.

holding pattern PHRASE: **in a holding pattern** *the project is in a holding pattern until the board reviews our most recent progress* IN LIMBO, up in the air, on hold, undecided, undetermined, unresolved; *informal* on the back burner, treading water.

holdings plural noun *her holdings are distressingly meager* ASSETS, funds, capital, resources, savings, investments, securities, equities, bonds, stocks and shares, reserves; property, possessions.

holdup noun **1** *I ran into a series of holdups* DELAY, setback, hitch, snag, obstruction, difficulty, problem, trouble, stumbling block; *informal* tie-up, logjam; traffic jam, gridlock, bottleneck, roadblock; snarl-up, glitch, hiccup.

2 *a bank holdup* ROBBERY, raid, armed robbery, armed raid; theft, burglary, mugging; *informal* stickup, heist.

hole noun **1** *a hole in the roof* OPENING, aperture, gap, space, orifice, vent, chink, breach, break; crack, leak, rift, rupture; puncture, perforation, cut, split, gash, slit, rent, tear, crevice, fissure.

2 *a hole in the ground* PIT, ditch, trench, cavity, crater, depression, indentation, hollow; well, borehole, excavation, dugout; cave, cavern, pothole.

3 *the gopher's hole* BURROW, lair, den, earth, set; retreat, shelter.

4 *there are holes in their argument* FLAW, fault, defect, weakness, shortcoming, inconsistency, discrepancy, loophole; error, mistake.

5 *informal* *I was living in a real hole* HOVEL, slum, shack; *informal* dump, dive, pigsty, hole in the wall, rathole, sty.

6 *informal* *she has dug herself into a hole* PREDICAMENT, difficult situation, awkward situation, corner, tight corner, quandary, dilemma; crisis, emergency, difficulty, trouble, plight, dire straits, imbroglio; *informal* fix, jam, mess, bind, scrape, spot, tight spot, pickle, sticky situation, can of worms, hot water. PHRASES: **hole up 1** *the bears hole up in winter* HIBERNATE, lie dormant. **2** *informal* *the snipers holed up in a farmhouse* HIDE (OUT), conceal oneself, secrete oneself, shelter, take cover, lie low. **poke holes in** *informal* *it was pretty easy to poke holes in Dr. Delvecchio's theories* FIND FAULT WITH, pick apart, deconstruct, query, quibble with; deflate, puncture. **in the hole** *the diner was in the hole within six months after Abdul's sons took over* IN DEBT, in arrears, in deficit, overdrawn, behind; *informal* in the red.

holiday noun **1** *Presidents' Day is a federal holiday* DAY OF OBSERVANCE, festival, feast day, féte, fiesta, celebration, anniversary, jubilee; saint's day, holy day.

2 chiefly *Brit.* *Sara and Lou's ten-day holiday* VACATION, break, rest, respite, recess; time off, time out, leave, furlough, sabbatical; trip, tour, journey, voyage; *informal* getaway; *formal* sojourn.

holier-than-thou adjective *you will never sell your opinions to me with that holier-than-thou attitude* SANCTIMONIOUS, self-righteous, smug, self-satisfied; priggish, pious, pietistic, Pharisaic. ANTONYM humble.

holler *informal* verb *he hollers when he's hungry* SHOUT, yell, cry, cry out, vociferate, call, call out, roar, bellow, bawl, bark, howl; boom, thunder, shriek, screech. ANTONYM whisper.

▸ noun *a euphoric holler* SHOUT, cry, yell, cheer, roar, bellow, bawl, howl, outcry; *informal* whoop. ANTONYM whisper.

hollow adjective **1** *each fiber has a hollow core* EMPTY, void, unfilled, vacant. ANTONYM solid.

2 *hollow cheeks* SUNKEN, gaunt, deep-set, concave, depressed, indented; *rare* incurvate.

3 *a hollow sound* DULL, low, flat, toneless, expressionless; muffled, muted.

4 *a hollow victory* MEANINGLESS, empty, valueless, worthless, useless, pyrrhic, nugatory, futile, fruitless, profitless, pointless. ANTONYM worthwhile.

5 *a hollow promise* INSINCERE, hypocritical, feigned, false, sham, deceitful, cynical, spurious, untrue, two-faced; *informal* phony, pretend. ANTONYM sincere.

▸ noun **1** *a hollow under the tree* HOLE, pit, cavity, crater, trough, bowl, cave, cavern; depression, indentation, dip, dent; niche, nook, cranny, recess.

2 *the village lay in a hollow* VALLEY, vale, dale, basin, glen. *literary* dell.

▸ verb *a tunnel hollowed out of a mountain* GOUGE, scoop, dig, shovel, cut; excavate, channel.

holocaust noun *fears of a nuclear holocaust* CATACLYSM, disaster, catastrophe; destruction, devastation, annihilation; massacre, slaughter, mass murder, extermination, extirpation, carnage, butchery; genocide, ethnic cleansing, pogrom.

holy adjective **1** *holy men* SAINTLY, godly, saintlike, pious, pietistic, religious, devout, God-fearing, spiritual; righteous, good, virtuous, angelic, sinless, pure, numinous, beatific; canonized, beatified, ordained. See note at DIVINE. ANTONYMS sinful, irreligious.

2 *a Jewish holy place* SACRED, consecrated, hallowed, sanctified, sacrosanct, venerated, revered, divine, religious, blessed, dedicated. ANTONYM cursed.

homage noun *the memorial concert for Mrs. Quinn was a most appropriate display of homage* RESPECT, honor, reverence, worship, obeisance, admiration, esteem, adulation, acclaim; tribute, acknowledgment, recognition; accolade, panegyric, paean, encomium, salute, eulogy. See note at HONOR. PHRASE: **pay homage to** *they paid* *homage to the local boy who became president* HONOR, acclaim, applaud, salute, praise, commend, pay tribute to, take one's hat off to; *formal* laud.

home noun **1** *they fled their homes* RESIDENCE, place of residence, house, apartment, flat, bungalow, cottage; accommodations, property, quarters, rooms, lodgings; a roof over one's head; address, place; *informal* pad, digs; hearth, nest; *formal* domicile, abode, dwelling, dwelling place, habitation.

2 *an Italian stonemason far from his home.* See HOMELAND.

3 *a home for the elderly* INSTITUTION, nursing home, retirement home, rest home; children's home; hospice, shelter, refuge, retreat, asylum, hostel, halfway house.

4 *the home of fine wines* ORIGIN, source, cradle, fount, fountainhead.

▸ adjective **1** *the home market* DOMESTIC, internal, local, national, interior. ANTONYMS foreign, international.

2 *home movies | the sale of home produce* HOMEMADE, homegrown, family.

PHRASES: **at home** **1** *I was at home all day* IN, in one's house, present, available, indoors, inside, here. **2** *she felt very much at home* AT EASE, comfortable, relaxed, content; in one's element, on one's own turf. **3** *he is* ***at home with*** *mathematics* CONFIDENT WITH, conversant with, proficient in; used to, familiar with, au fait with, au courant with, skilled in, experienced in, well versed in. **bring home to someone** *Sylvia's overdose brought home to them the fragility of their own lives* MAKE SOMEONE REALIZE, make someone understand, make someone aware, make clear to someone; drive home to someone, impress upon someone, draw attention to, focus attention on, underline, highlight, spotlight, emphasize, stress; *informal* clue someone in to. **hit home.** See HIT HOME at HIT. **home free** *when the inspector at the third checkpoint nodded at Mitchell, I knew we were home free | I passed the final flag with so much stamina that I knew I was home free* SAFE, secure, out of danger, off the hook; assured of success, the winner, victorious; *informal* golden. **home in on** *the reporters immediately wanted to home in on his broken engagement* FOCUS ON, concentrate on, zero in on, center on, fix on; highlight, spotlight, target, underline, pinpoint, track, zoom in on. **nothing to write home about** *informal the amusement park was enjoyable enough, but nothing to write home about* UNEXCEPTIONAL, mediocre, ordinary, commonplace, indifferent, average, middle-of-the-road, run-of-the-mill, garden variety; boring, mundane, humdrum, ho-hum; tolerable, passable, adequate, fair; *informal* OK, so-so, 'comme ci, comme ça,' plain-vanilla, no great shakes, not so hot.

homegrown adjective *our homegrown fruits and vegetables* LOCAL, native, indigenous, domestic.

homeland noun *she left her homeland to settle in Japan with her husband's family* NATIVE LAND, country of origin, home, birthplace, hometown; roots, fatherland, motherland, mother country, land of one's fathers; the old country.

homeless adjective *homeless people* OF NO FIXED ADDRESS, without a roof over one's head, on the streets, vagrant, displaced, dispossessed, destitute, down-and-out.

▸ noun *charities for the homeless* PEOPLE OF NO FIXED ADDRESS, vagrants, down-and-outs, street people, tramps, vagabonds, itinerants, transients, migrants, derelicts, drifters, hoboes; *informal* bag ladies, bums.

homely adjective **1** *she's rather homely* UNATTRACTIVE, plain, unprepossessing, unlovely, ill-favored, ugly; *informal* not much to look at. ANTONYM attractive.

2 *a homely atmosphere.* See HOMEY sense 1.

3 *homely pursuits.* See HOMEY sense 2.

homemade adjective **1** *homemade bread and jam* HOMESTYLE, homespun, simple, basic, plain; rustic, folksy; *informal* like Mom used to make.

2 *a homemade bomb* HANDMADE, makeshift, jerry-built, rudimentary; crude, rough, unsophisticated.

homeowner noun *homeowners in the Scotch Hill section have drafted a petition against the proposed landfill on Fuller Drive* OWNER, householder, resident, occupant, proprietor.

homespun adjective *homespun rural philosophy* UNSOPHISTICATED, plain, simple, basic, unpolished, unrefined, rustic, folksy; coarse, rough, crude, rudimentary, bush-league. ANTONYM sophisticated.

homey adjective **1** *the house is homey yet elegant* COZY, homelike, homely, comfortable, snug, welcoming, informal, relaxed, intimate, warm, pleasant, cheerful, friendly, congenial, hospitable; *informal* comfy. ANTONYMS uncomfortable, formal.

2 *life on the mountain was simple and homey* UNSOPHISTICATED, homely, unrefined, unpretentious, plain, simple, modest, domestic; everyday, ordinary. ANTONYM sophisticated.

homicidal adjective *his homicidal tendencies went undetected for years* MURDEROUS, violent, brutal, savage, ferocious, vicious, bloody, bloodthirsty, barbarous, barbaric; deadly, lethal, mortal; *literary* fell; *archaic* sanguinary.

homicide noun *we're investigating a homicide that took place in this building* MURDER, killing, slaughter, butchery, massacre; assassination, execution, extermination; patricide, matricide, infanticide; *literary* slaying.

homily noun *a guest preacher delivered today's homily* SERMON, lecture, discourse, address, lesson, talk, speech, oration.

homogeneous adjective *should the members of a society become so homogeneous that any trace of cultural diversity vanishes?* UNIFORM, identical, unvaried, consistent, indistinguishable, homologous, homogenized; alike, similar, the same, much the same, all of a piece, melting-pot. ANTONYM different.

homogenize verb *my job is to homogenize all you precious little 'individuals' into one fighting machine* MAKE UNIFORM, make similar, standardize, unite, integrate, fuse, merge, blend, meld, coalesce, amalgamate, combine. ANTONYM diversify.

homosexual adjective *we decided to march with our homosexual friends* GAY, lesbian, homoerotic, same-sex; *informal* queer, camp, pink, lavender, homo; *literary* Uranian. ANTONYM heterosexual. See note at GAY.

▸ noun *she has a serious crush on William, who, unfortunately for her, is a homosexual* GAY, lesbian; *informal* queer, queen, dyke, butch, femme; *literary* Uranian. ANTONYM heterosexual.

hone verb *she honed the machete with a large strop | Brian's skills on the tuba were honed over the summer* SHARPEN, whet, strop, grind, file; polish, refine, improve, enhance, fine-tune. ANTONYMS blunt, dull, atrophy.

honest adjective **1** *an honest man* UPRIGHT, honorable, moral, ethical, principled, righteous, right-minded, respectable; virtuous, good, decent, fair, law-abiding, high-minded, upstanding, incorruptible, truthful, trustworthy, reliable, conscientious, scrupulous, reputable; *informal* on the level, trusty. ANTONYMS unscrupulous, dishonest.

2 *I haven't been honest with you* TRUTHFUL, sincere, candid, frank, open, forthright, ingenuous, straight; straightforward, plain-speaking, matter-of-fact; *informal* upfront, aboveboard, on the level. ANTONYM insincere.

3 *an honest mistake* GENUINE, true, bona fide, legitimate; *informal* legit, honest-to-goodness.

honestly adverb **1** *he earned the money honestly* FAIRLY, lawfully, legally, legitimately, honorably, decently, ethically, in good faith, by the book; openly, on the level, aboveboard.

2 *we honestly believe this is for the best* SINCERELY, genuinely, truthfully, truly, wholeheartedly; really, frankly, actually, seriously, to be honest, to tell you the truth, to be frank, in all honesty, in all sincerity; *informal* Scout's honor.

▸ exclamation *Honestly! I don't know what to do with you!* FOR HEAVEN'S SAKE, for goodness' sake, for Pete's sake, really, sheesh, jeepers.

honesty noun **1** *I can attest to his honesty* INTEGRITY, uprightness, honorableness, honor, morality, morals, ethics, principles, high principles, righteousness, right-mindedness; virtue, goodness, probity, high-mindedness, fairness, incorruptibility, truthfulness, trustworthiness, reliability, dependability, rectitude.

2 *they spoke with honesty about their fears* SINCERITY, candor, frankness, directness, bluntness, truthfulness, truth, openness, straightforwardness.

honey noun *informal here, honey, wear my jacket* SWEETHEART, darling, dear, dearest, love; *informal* angel, sweetie, sugar, pet.

honeyed adjective *honeyed words* SWEET, sugary, pleasant, flattering, adulatory; dulcet, soothing, soft, mellow, mellifluous; saccharine, syrupy, unctuous. ANTONYM harsh.

honk verb *what good will honking your horn do?* BEEP, blow, blare, blast, sound, hoot.

honor noun **1** *a man of honor* INTEGRITY, honesty, uprightness, ethics, morals, morality, principles, high principles, righteousness, high-mindedness; virtue, goodness, decency, probity, character, good character, scrupulousness, worth, fairness, justness, trustworthiness, reliability, dependability. ANTONYMS unscrupulousness, dishonor.

2 *a mark of honor* DISTINCTION, recognition, privilege, glory, kudos, cachet, prestige, merit, credit; importance, illustriousness, notability; respect, esteem, approbation. ANTONYM disgrace.

3 *our honor is at stake* REPUTATION, name, good name, good credit, character, esteem, repute, image, standing, stature, status, popularity.

4 *he was welcomed with honor* ACCLAIM, acclamation, applause, accolades, adoration, tributes, compliments, salutes, bouquets; homage, praise, veneration, glory, reverence, adulation, exaltation; *dated* laud. ANTONYM contempt.

5 *she had the honor of meeting the first lady* PRIVILEGE, pleasure, pride, joy; compliment, favor, distinction. ANTONYM shame.

6 *military honors* ACCOLADE, award, reward, prize, decoration, distinction, medal, ribbon, star, laurel.

7 *dated she died defending her honor* CHASTITY, virginity, maidenhead, purity, innocence, modesty; *archaic* virtue, maidenhood.

▸ verb **1** *we should honor our parents* ESTEEM, respect, admire, defer to, look up to; appreciate, value, cherish, adore; reverence, revere, venerate, worship; *informal* put on a pedestal. ANTONYM disrespect.

2 *they were honored at a special ceremony* APPLAUD, acclaim, praise, salute, recognize, celebrate, commemorate, commend, hail, lionize, exalt, eulogize, pay homage to, pay tribute to, sing the praises of; *formal* laud. ANTONYMS disgrace, criticize.

3 *he honored the contract* FULFILL, observe, keep, obey, heed, follow, carry out, discharge, implement, execute, effect; keep to, abide by, adhere to, comply with, conform to, be true to, live up to. ANTONYM disobey.

THE RIGHT WORD

The Ten Commandments instruct us to "**Honor** thy father and mother." But what does *honor* entail? While all of these nouns describe the respect or esteem that one shows to another, *honor* implies acknowledgment of a person's right to such respect (*honor one's ancestors; honor the dead*). **Homage** is honor with praise or tributes added, and it connotes a more worshipful attitude (*pay homage to the king*). **Reverence** combines profound respect with love or devotion (*he treated his wife with reverence*), while **deference** suggests courteous regard for a superior, often by yielding to the person's status or wishes (*show deference to one's elders*). **Obeisance** is a show of honor or reverence by an act or gesture of submission or humility, such as a bow or a curtsy (*the schoolchildren were instructed to pay obeisance when the Queen arrived*).

honorable adjective **1** *an honorable man* HONEST, moral, ethical, principled, righteous, right-minded; decent, respectable, estimable, virtuous, good, upstanding, upright, worthy, noble, fair, just, truthful, trustworthy, law-abiding, reliable, reputable, creditable, dependable. See note at MORAL. ANTONYM crooked.

2 *an honorable career* ILLUSTRIOUS, distinguished, eminent, great, glorious, renowned, acclaimed, prestigious, noble, creditable, admirable. ANTONYM deplorable.

honorarium noun *each technical adviser receives an annual honorarium of $500* FEE, payment, consideration, allowance, stipend; remuneration, pay, expenses, compensation, recompense, reward; *formal* emolument.

honorary adjective *she has received honorary diplomas from eleven colleges and universities worldwide* TITULAR, symbolic, in name only, ceremonial, nominal, unofficial, token.

hood noun *they wore sunglasses and hoods to disguise*

themselves HEAD COVERING, cowl, snood, headscarf, amice.

hoodlum noun *he was roughed up by a bunch of hoodlums* THUG, lout, delinquent, vandal, ruffian, hooligan, lowlife; gangster, crook, mobster, criminal; *informal* tough, bruiser, goon, hood, punk, rowdy.

hoodwink verb *Jimmy was hoodwinked by his own brother* DECEIVE, trick, dupe, outwit, fool, delude, inveigle, cheat, take in, hoax, mislead, lead on, defraud, double-cross, swindle, gull, scam; *informal* con, bamboozle, hornswoggle, fleece, do, have, sting, gyp, shaft, rip off, lead up the garden path, pull a fast one on, put one over on, take for a ride, pull the wool over someone's eyes, sucker, snooker; *literary* cozen.

hook noun **1** *she hung her jacket on the hook* PEG, coat rack.

2 *the dress has six hooks* FASTENER, fastening, catch, clasp, hasp, clip, pin.

3 *I had a fish on the end of my hook* FISHHOOK, barb, gaff, snare, snag.

4 *a right hook to the chin* PUNCH, blow, hit, cuff, thump, smack; *informal* belt, bop, sock, clout, whack, wallop, slug; *informal* boff.

▸ verb **1** *they hooked baskets onto the ladder* ATTACH, hitch, fasten, fix, secure, clasp. See note at PAIR.

2 *he hooked his thumbs in his belt* CURL, bend, crook, loop, curve.

3 *he hooked a 24-pound pike* CATCH, land, net, take; bag, snare, trap.

PHRASES: **by hook or by crook** *I'll get to Hollywood by hook or by crook* BY ANY MEANS, somehow (or other), no matter how, in one way or another, by fair means or foul. **hook, line, and sinker** *they believed her phony alibi hook, line, and sinker* COMPLETELY, totally, utterly, entirely, wholly, absolutely, through and through, one hundred percent, 'lock, stock, and barrel.' **off the hook** *informal Mr. Lee paid the fine, so now Tammy is off the hook* OUT OF TROUBLE, in the clear, free, home free; acquitted, cleared, reprieved, exonerated, absolved; *informal* let off.

hooked adjective **1** *a hooked nose* CURVED, hook-shaped, hooklike, aquiline, angular, bent, crooked. ANTONYM straight.

2 *informal he is* ***hooked on*** *reality TV* KEEN ON, enthusiastic about, addicted to, obsessed with, infatuated with, fixated on, fanatical about; *informal* mad about, crazy about, wild about, nuts about.

3 *she had the audience hooked* CAPTIVATED, enthralled, entranced, bewitched, charmed. ANTONYM indifferent.

hooker noun *informal* See PROSTITUTE noun.

hooligan noun *I want you to stop hanging around with those hooligans* TROUBLEMAKER, delinquent, juvenile delinquent, mischief-maker, vandal; rowdy, ruffian, yahoo.

hoop noun *a simple gold hoop* RING, band, circle, circlet, bracelet, (hoop) earring, loop; *technical* annulus.

hooray exclamation *Hooray! We won!* HURRAH, hallelujah, bravo, hot dog, wahoo, yahoo, whoopee, yay, yippee.

hoot noun **1** *the hoot of an owl* SCREECH, shriek, call, cry.

2 *hoots of derision* SHOUT, yell, cry, snort, howl, shriek, whoop, whistle; boo, hiss, jeer, catcall.

3 *informal the party was a hoot* GOOD TIME, scream, laugh, blast, riot, giggle, barrel of laughs; *dated* caution.

▸ verb **1** *an owl hooted* SCREECH, shriek, cry, call.

2 *they hooted in disgust* SHOUT, yell, cry, howl, shriek, whistle; boo, hiss, jeer, heckle, catcall.

PHRASE: **give a hoot** *informal obviously you don't give a hoot about clean air* CARE, be concerned, mind, be interested, be bothered, trouble oneself about; *informal* give a damn.

hop verb **1** *he hopped over the fence* JUMP, bound, spring, bounce, leap, vault.

2 *informal she hopped over the Atlantic* GO, dash; travel, journey; jet, fly; *informal* pop, whip, nip.

▸ noun **1** *the rabbit had a hop around* JUMP, bound, bounce, leap, spring.

2 *informal a short hop by taxi* JOURNEY, distance, ride, drive, run, trip, jaunt; flight; *informal* hop, skip, and a jump.

hope noun **1** *I had high hopes* ASPIRATION, desire, wish, expectation, ambition, aim, goal, plan, design; dream, daydream, pipe dream.

2 *a life filled with hope* HOPEFULNESS, optimism, expectation, expectancy; confidence, faith, trust, belief, conviction, assurance; promise, possibility. ANTONYM pessimism.

3 *have we any hope of winning?* CHANCE, prospect, likelihood, probability, possibility; *informal* shot.

▸ verb **1** *he's* ***hoping for*** *a medal* EXPECT, anticipate, look for, be hopeful of, pin one's hopes on, want; wish for, long for, dream of.

2 *we're hoping to address the issue* AIM, intend, be looking, have the intention, have in mind, plan, aspire.

hopeful adjective **1** *he remained hopeful* OPTIMISTIC, full of hope, confident, positive, buoyant, sanguine, expectant, bullish, cheerful, lighthearted; *informal* upbeat.

2 *hopeful signs* PROMISING, encouraging, heartening, inspiring, reassuring, auspicious, favorable, optimistic, propitious, bright, rosy.

▸ noun *the Democratic hopeful for 2004* CANDIDATE, aspirant, prospect, possibility; nominee, competitor, contender; *informal* up-and-comer.

hopefully adverb **1** *he rode on hopefully* OPTIMISTICALLY, full of hope, confidently, buoyantly, sanguinely; expectantly.

2 *hopefully it will finish soon* IF ALL GOES WELL, God willing, with luck, with any luck; most likely, probably; conceivably, feasibly; *informal* knock on wood, fingers crossed.

USAGE NOTE hopefully

Four points about this word: First, it was widely condemned from the 1960s to the 1980s. Briefly, the objections are that (1) *hopefully* properly means "in a hopeful manner" and shouldn't be used in the radically different sense "I hope" or "it is to be hoped"; (2) if the extended sense is accepted, the original sense will be forever lost; and (3) in constructions such as "Hopefully, it won't rain this afternoon," the writer illogically ascribes an emotion (*hopefulness*) to a nonperson. *Hopefully* isn't analogous to *curiously* (= it is a curious fact that), *fortunately* (= it is a fortunate thing that), and *sadly* (= it is a sad fact that). How so? Unlike all those other sentence adverbs, *hopefully* can't be resolved into any longer expression involving the word *hopeful*—but only *hope* (e.g., *it is to be hoped that* or *I hope that*).

Second, whatever the merits of those arguments, the battle is now over. *Hopefully* is now a part of American English, and it has all but lost its traditional meaning—e.g.: "Hopefully, one day we will all grow older." (*San Diego Union-Tribune*; Nov. 26, 1997.) Sometimes, the word is genuinely ambiguous (if the original meaning is considered still alive)—e.g.: "Dave Krieg will take the snaps and, hopefully, hand off to RB Garrison Hearst." (*USA Today*; Sept. 1, 1995.) (Is Krieg hoping for the best when Hearst runs? Or is the writer hoping that Krieg won't pass the football or hand off to another running back?) Indeed, the original meaning of *hopefully* is alive, even if moribund—e.g.: "Officials recently have pointed hopefully to signs of increased usage of the garage." (*Boston Globe*; Oct. 9, 1994.)

Third, some stalwarts continue to condemn the word, so that anyone using it in the new sense is likely to have a credibility problem with some readers—e.g.

• "Professor Michael Dummett, an Oxford logician, condemns the new usage of *hopefully* because only a person can be hopeful, and in many such cases there is nobody around in the sentence to be hopeful." (*Daily Telegraph* [UK]; Dec. 11, 1996.)

• "Although various adverbs may be used to modify entire clauses, *hopefully* isn't among them—yet. I only hope I won't have to concede that it is until I'm an old, old woman." (Barbara Wallraff, *Word Court*; 2000.)

Fourth, though the controversy swirling around this word has subsided, any use of it is likely to distract some readers. Avoid it in all senses if you're concerned with your credibility: if you use it in the traditional way, many readers will think it odd; if you use it in the newish way, a few readers will tacitly tut-tut you.

Throughout the late twentieth century, the common wisdom was that the use of *hopefully* as a sentence adverb had begun sometime around the early 1930s. Then, in 1999, a lexicographic scholar named Fred Shapiro, using computer-assisted research, traced it back to Cotton Mather's 1702 book, *Magnalia Christi Americana*, in this sentence: "Chronical diseases, which evidently threaten his Life, might hopefully be relieved by his removal." The evidence then skips to 1851, then to the 1930s. **—BG**

---

hopeless adjective **1** *she felt weary and hopeless* DESPAIRING, desperate, wretched, forlorn, pessimistic, defeatist, resigned; dejected, downhearted, despondent, demoralized; *archaic* woebegone.

2 *a hopeless case* IRREMEDIABLE, beyond hope, lost, beyond repair, irreparable, irreversible; helpless, incurable; impossible, no-win, unwinnable, futile, unworkable, impracticable, useless; *archaic* bootless.

3 *Joseph was hopeless at tennis* BAD, awful, terrible, dreadful, horrible, atrocious; inferior, incompetent, inadequate, unskilled; *informal* pathetic, useless, lousy, rotten.

4 *a hopeless romantic* INCURABLE, incorrigible, chronic, compulsive; complete, utter, absolute, total, out-and-out; inveterate, confirmed, established, dyed-in-the-wool.

horde noun *a horde of fans stormed the playing field* CROWD, mob, pack, gang, group, troop, army, legion, swarm, mass, herd, rabble; throng, multitude, host, band, flock, drove, press, crush; *informal* crew, tribe, pile.

horizon noun **1** *the sun rose above the horizon* SKYLINE.

2 *she wanted to broaden her horizons* OUTLOOK, perspective, perception; range of experience, range of interests, scope, prospect, ambit, compass, orbit. PHRASE: **on the horizon** *a better life for us is on the horizon* IMMINENT, impending, due, close, near, approaching, coming, forthcoming, at hand, on the way, about to happen, upon us, in the offing, in the pipeline, in the air, in the wings, in the cards, just around the corner, coming down the pike; brewing, looming, threatening, menacing.

horizontal adjective **1** *a horizontal surface* level, flat, plane, smooth, even; straight, parallel. ANTONYM vertical.

2 *she was horizontal on the bed* FLAT, supine, prone, prostrate, recumbent. ANTONYM upright.

3 *a horizontal move* LATERAL, sideways.

horny adjective *informal she admitted to being a bit horny during dinner* AROUSED, sexually aroused, oversexed, excited, stimulated, titillated, inflamed, passionate; lecherous, lascivious, lustful, salacious, lewd; *informal* turned on, hot, hot to trot, hot and bothered; *formal* concupiscent.

horrendous adjective See HORRIBLE.

horrible adjective **1** *a horrible murder* DREADFUL, awful, terrible, shocking, appalling, horrifying, horrific, horrendous, horrid, hideous, grisly, ghastly, gruesome, gory, harrowing, heinous, vile, unspeakable; nightmarish, macabre, spine-chilling, blood-curdling; loathsome, monstrous, abhorrent, hateful, hellish, execrable, abominable, atrocious, sickening, foul. ANTONYMS pleasant, agreeable.

2 *informal a horrible little man* NASTY, horrid, disagreeable, unpleasant, detestable, awful, dreadful, terrible, appalling, horrendous, foul, repulsive, repugnant, repellent, ghastly; obnoxious, hateful, odious, hideous, objectionable, insufferable, vile, loathsome, abhorrent; *informal* frightful, godawful. ANTONYMS pleasant, agreeable.

horrid adjective See HORRIBLE.

horrific adjective *a horrific accident* DREADFUL, horrendous, horrible, frightful, fearful, awful, terrible, atrocious, heinous; horrifying, shocking, appalling, harrowing, gruesome; hideous, grisly, gory, ghastly, unspeakable, monstrous, nightmarish, sickening.

horrify verb **1** *she horrified us with ghastly tales* FRIGHTEN, scare, terrify, petrify, paralyze, alarm, panic, terrorize, fill with fear, scare someone out of their wits, frighten the living daylights out of, make someone's hair stand on end, make someone's blood run cold, give someone the creeps; *informal* scare the pants off, spook; *archaic* affright.

2 *he was horrified by her remarks* SHOCK, appall, outrage, scandalize, offend; disgust, revolt, nauseate, sicken.

horror noun **1** *children screamed in horror* TERROR, fear, fright, alarm, panic; dread, trepidation. ANTONYM delight.

2 *to her horror she found herself alone* DISMAY, consternation, perturbation, alarm, distress; disgust, outrage, shock. ANTONYM satisfaction.

3 *the horror of the tragedy* AWFULNESS, frightfulness, savagery, barbarity, hideousness; atrocity, outrage.

4 *informal**he's a little horror* RASCAL, devil, imp, monkey; *informal* terror, scamp, scalawag, tyke, varmint.

5 *informal her new dress is a horror* EYESORE, monstrosity, abomination, blot, disgrace, mess, sight. ANTONYM beauty.

horror-struck, horror-stricken adjective *the witnesses to the collision were horror-struck* HORRIFIED, terrified, petrified, frightened, afraid, fearful, scared, panic-stricken, scared/frightened to death, scared witless; shocked, appalled, aghast; *informal* scared stiff, freaked out.

hors d'oeuvre noun See APPETIZER.

horse noun *Nadine boards and grooms horses* EQUINE, mount, charger, cob, nag; pony; foal, yearling, colt, stallion, gelding, mare, filly; bronco; *dated* stepper; *archaic* steed. See table. PHRASE: **horse around** *informal they knew better than to horse around when their father came home* FOOL AROUND, play, have fun, clown around, monkey around.

HORSES

American saddle horse	mustang
Andalusian	Newfoundland pony
Appaloosa	palomino
Arabian	Percheron
Belgian	polo pony
Canadian	Quarter Horse
cayuse	racehorse
Chincoteague pony	Shetland pony
Clydesdale	shire horse
Dartmoor pony	Standardbred
Falabella	Tennessee Walking Horse
Hanoverian	thoroughbred
Lippizzaner	Waler
Morgan	

horseman, horsewoman noun *a stately parade of horsemen* RIDER, equestrian, jockey; cavalryman, trooper; *historical* hussar, dragoon; *archaic* cavalier.

horseplay noun *the brothers' horseplay was not looked on too kindly by Aunt Smitty* TOMFOOLERY, fooling around, roughhousing, clowning, buffoonery, fun; pranks, antics, hijinks; *informal* shenanigans, monkey business.

horse sense noun *informal* See COMMON SENSE.

horticulture noun *your gardener apparently knows very little about horticulture* GARDENING, landscaping, cultivation; floriculture, arboriculture, agriculture.

hosanna noun *the people's hosannas greeted him as he rode into the city* SHOUT OF PRAISE, alleluia, hurrah, hurray, hooray, cheer, paean.

hose noun **1** *a flexible green hose.* See PIPE noun sense 1.
2 *some new black dress hose.* See HOSIERY.

hoser noun *informal* See IDIOT.

hosiery noun *rinsing out some hosiery* STOCKINGS, tights, nylons, hose, pantyhose, leotards; socks.

hospice noun See HOME noun sense 3.

hospitable adjective *my hospitable in-laws* WELCOMING, friendly, congenial, genial, sociable, convivial, cordial, courteous; gracious, well-disposed, amenable, helpful, obliging, accommodating, neighborly, warm, kind, generous, bountiful.

hospital noun *the hospitals were overwhelmed with cases of influenza* INFIRMARY, medical center, health center, clinic, sanatorium, hospice; *Military* field hospital; *dated* asylum.

hospitality noun *we found nothing but hospitality among the Ukrainians* FRIENDLINESS, hospitableness, warm reception, welcome, helpfulness, neighborliness, warmth, kindness, congeniality, geniality, cordiality, courtesy, amenability, generosity, entertainment, catering, food.

host[1] noun **1** *the host greeted the guests* PARTY-GIVER, hostess, entertainer. ANTONYM guest.

2 *the host of a TV series* PRESENTER, anchor, anchorman, anchorwoman, announcer, master of ceremonies, ringmaster; *informal* emcee.

▸ verb **1** *Diane hosted a dinner party* GIVE, have, hold, throw, put on, provide, arrange, organize.

2 *Jack hosted the show* PRESENT, introduce, front, anchor, announce; *informal* emcee .

3 *she hosted her colleagues from overseas* ENTERTAIN, play host/hostess to; receive, welcome; take in, house, provide accommodations for, put up.

host[2] noun **1** *a host of memories* MULTITUDE, lot, abundance, wealth, profusion; *informal* load, heap, mass, pile, ton, number; *literary* myriad.

2 *a host of movie stars* CROWD, throng, group, flock, herd, swarm, horde, mob, army, legion, pack, tribe, troop; assemblage, congregation, gathering.

hostage noun *all of the hostages were released unharmed* CAPTIVE, prisoner, inmate, detainee, internee; victim, abductee, prey; human shield, pawn, instrument.

hostel noun *we save a little money by staying in no-frills hostels whenever we can* CHEAP HOTEL, bed and breakfast, B&B, inn, boarding house, guest house, dormitory, residence, lodging, accommodations; YMCA, YWCA; shelter, refuge, asylum.

hostile adjective **1** *a hostile attack* UNFRIENDLY, unkind, bitter, unsympathetic, malicious, vicious, rancorous, venomous, poisonous, virulent; antagonistic, aggressive, confrontational, belligerent, truculent, vitriolic; bellicose, pugnacious, warlike. ANTONYMS friendly, mild.

2 *hostile conditions* UNFAVORABLE, adverse, bad, harsh, grim, hard, tough, brutal, fierce, inhospitable, forbidding, menacing, threatening. ANTONYM favorable.

3 *they are* ***hostile to*** *the idea* OPPOSED TO, averse to, antagonistic to, ill-disposed to, disapproving of, unsympathetic to, antipathetic to; opposing, against, inimical to; *informal* anti, down on.

THE RIGHT WORD

Few people have trouble recognizing hostility when confronted with it. Someone who is **hostile** displays an attitude of intense ill will and acts like an enemy (*the audience grew hostile after waiting an hour for the show to start*). Both **bellicose** and **belligerent** imply a readiness or eagerness to fight, but the former is used to describe a state of mind or temper (*after drinking all night, he was in a bellicose mood*), while the latter is normally used to describe someone who is actively engaged in hostilities (*the belligerent brothers were at it again*). While *hostile* and *belligerent* usually apply to people, **adverse** and **inimical** are used describe tendencies or influences. *Inimical* means having an antagonistic tendency (*remarks that were inimical to everything she believed in*), and *adverse* means turned toward something in opposition (*an adverse wind; under adverse circumstances*). Unlike *hostile*, *adverse* and *inimical* need not connote the involvement of human feeling.

hostility noun **1** *he glared at her with hostility* ANTAGONISM, unfriendliness, enmity, malevolence, malice, unkindness, rancor, venom, hatred, loathing; resentment, animosity, antipathy, acrimony, ill will, ill feeling; aggression, belligerence.

2 *their hostility to the present regime* OPPOSITION, antagonism, aversion, resistance, dissidence.

3 **(hostilities)** *a cessation of hostilities* FIGHTING, conflict, armed conflict, combat, aggression, warfare, war, bloodshed, violence.

hot adjective **1** *hot food* HEATED, piping hot, sizzling, steaming, roasting, boiling (hot), searing, scorching, scalding, burning, red-hot. ANTONYMS cold, chilled.

2 *a hot day* VERY WARM, balmy, summery, tropical, scorching, broiling, searing, blistering; sweltering, torrid, sultry, humid, muggy, close, boiling, baking, roasting. ANTONYMS cold, chilly.

3 *she felt very hot* FEVERISH, fevered, febrile; burning, flushed, sweaty; *rare* pyretic.

4 *a hot chili* SPICY, spiced, highly seasoned, peppery, fiery, strong; piquant, pungent, aromatic, zesty. ANTONYM mild.

5 *hot competition* FIERCE, intense, keen, competitive, cutthroat, dog-eat-dog, ruthless, aggressive, strong. ANTONYM weak.

6 *informal hot gossip* NEW, fresh, recent, late, up to date, up-to-the-minute; just out, hot off the press(es), real-time. ANTONYMS old, stale.

7 *informal this band is hot* POPULAR, in demand, sought-after, in favor; fashionable, in vogue, all the rage; *informal* big, in, now, hip, trendy, cool. ANTONYMS out of fashion, unpopular.

8 *she thought Mark was hot* GOOD-LOOKING, sexy, attractive, gorgeous, handsome, beautiful; *archaic* comely, fair. ANTONYM unappealing.

9 *hot goods* STOLEN, illegally obtained, purloined, pilfered, illegal, illicit, unlawful; smuggled, fenced, bootleg, contraband. ANTONYM lawful.

10 *her dancing made him hot* AROUSED, sexually aroused, excited, stimulated, titillated, inflamed; *informal* turned on, hot to trot. ANTONYM frigid.

PHRASES: **blow hot and cold** *when it comes to her romantic interest in him, she blows hot and cold* VACILLATE, dither, shilly-shally, waver, be indecisive, change one's mind, be undecided, be uncertain, be unsure, hem and haw. **hot and heavy** *isn't it a bit too soon for them to be so hot and heavy with each other?* intense, ardent, passionate, fervid. **have the hots for** *Liza admits that she has the hots for Ryan* be (sexually) attracted to, desire, lust after; *informal* have a crush on, have a thing for, be crazy about. **hot on the heels/trail of** *the marketing mavens are hot on the heels of this latest craze* CLOSE BEHIND, directly after, right after, straight after, hard on the heels of, following closely. **hot under the collar** *informal* See ANGRY sense 1.

hot air noun *informal* See NONSENSE sense 1.

hotbed noun *a hotbed of crime* BREEDING GROUND, den, nest, stronghold, flash point, cradle, seedbed.

hot-blooded adjective *he's not exactly the hot-blooded Latin lover I thought he'd be* PASSIONATE, amorous, amatory, ardent, fervid, lustful, libidinous, lecherous, sexy, virile; *informal* horny. ANTONYM cold.

hot-button adjective *hot-button issues* SENSITIVE, thorny, ticklish, touchy, delicate, controversial, difficult, tough, troublesome; complicated, complex, involved, intricate; current, contemporary, topical, in the news.

hot dog noun See table at SAUSAGE.

hotel noun *we booked separate rooms at the hotel* INN, motel, boarding house, guest house, bed and breakfast, B&B, hostel, lodge, accommodations, lodging.

hot
searing
sweltering
scorching
stifling
roasting
parching
blistering
oven-like
oppressive
tropical
boiling
boiling hot
blazing hot
baking
torrid
sultry
close
airless
muggy
humid
summery
balmy
clement
pleasant
fair
temperate
fresh
cool
crisp
brisk
nippy
chill
sharp
raw
bleak
snowy
frosty
icy
ice-cold
icy-cold
wintry
bitter
bitterly cold
penetrating
biting
piercing
freezing
glacial
polar
arctic
Siberian
frigid
gelid
brumal
cold

hotfoot PHRASE: **hotfoot it** *informal we'd better hotfoot it to the airport* HURRY, dash, run, rush, race, sprint, bolt, dart, career, careen, charge, shoot, hurtle, fly, speed, zoom, streak; *informal* tear, belt, scoot, clip, leg it, go like a bat out of hell, bomb, hightail it; *archaic* hie.

hotheaded adjective *Desi could camp it up as the hotheaded Cuban bandleader* IMPETUOUS, impulsive, headstrong, reckless, rash, irresponsible, foolhardy, madcap, devil-may-care; excitable, volatile, explosive, fiery, hot-tempered, quick-tempered, unruly.

hothouse noun **1** *tomatoes grew in the hothouse* GREENHOUSE, conservatory.

2 *society was becoming a hothouse of narcissism* BREEDING GROUND, hotbed, seedbed.

▸ adjective *the school has a hothouse atmosphere* INTENSE, oppressive, stifling; overprotected, sheltered, insular, isolated, shielded; sensitive.

hotly adverb 1 *a hotly contested issue* VEHEMENTLY, vigorously, strenuously, fiercely, passionately, heatedly; angrily, indignantly. ANTONYM calmly.

2 *a hotly anticipated new movie* EAGERLY, enthusiastically, extremely, highly, hugely, heartily.

hotshot noun *informal a young broadcasting hotshot* EXPERT, master, genius, virtuoso, maestro, adept, past master, champion, star; *informal* demon, ace, wizard, pro, whiz; maven, crackerjack. ANTONYM amateur.

▸ adjective *a hotshot lawyer* EXCELLENT, first-rate, first-class, marvelous, wonderful, magnificent, outstanding, superlative, formidable, virtuoso, masterly, expert, champion, consummate, skillful, adept; prominent, celebrated, renowned, eminent, famous, high-profile, important, prestigious, notable, well-known; superb, brilliant; *informal* great, terrific, super, tremendous, top-notch, crack, ace, A1, mean, awesome, fantastic, sensational, fabulous, fab, fancy-pants; blue-ribbon, blue-chip, top-drawer *slang* wicked. ANTONYM mediocre.

hot spot noun 1 *a local hot spot* POPULAR DESTINATION, fashionable destination, trendy place, happenin'/happening place; restaurant, eatery, eating place, bar, club.

2 *the Middle East has become the latest hot spot* DANGEROUS PLACE, trouble spot, problem area.

hot-tempered adjective *he is hot-tempered and capable of violence* IRASCIBLE, quick-tempered, short-tempered, irritable, fiery, bad-tempered; touchy, volatile, testy, tetchy, fractious, prickly, peppery, hotheaded, pugnacious; *informal* snappish, snappy, on a short fuse. ANTONYM easygoing.

hot tub noun *soaking in the hot tub* WHIRLPOOL, spa; *trademark* Jacuzzi.

hound noun *take the hounds out for a run* DOG, hunting dog, canine, mongrel, cur; *informal* doggy, pooch, mutt, pup. See table at DOG.

▸ verb 1 *she was hounded by the press* PURSUE, chase, follow, shadow, be hot on someone's heels, hunt (down), stalk, track, trail, tail, dog; harass, hassle, persecute, harry, pester, bother, badger, torment, bedevil; *informal* bug, give someone a hard time, devil.

2 *they hounded him out of office* FORCE, drive, pressure, pressurize, push, urge, coerce, impel, dragoon, strong-arm; nag, bully, browbeat; *informal* bulldoze, railroad, hustle.

house noun 1 *a new development with 200 houses* RESIDENCE, home, place of residence; homestead; a roof over one's head; *formal* habitation, dwelling (place), abode, domicile. See table.

2 *you'll wake the whole house!* HOUSEHOLD, family, occupants; clan, tribe; *informal* brood.

3 *the house of Windsor* FAMILY, clan, tribe; dynasty, line, bloodline, lineage, ancestry, family tree.

4 *a printing house* FIRM, business, company, corporation, enterprise, establishment, institution, organization, operation; *informal* outfit, setup.

5 *the country's upper house* LEGISLATIVE ASSEMBLY, legislative body, legislature, chamber, council, congress, senate, parliament, diet.

6 *the house applauded* AUDIENCE, crowd, spectators, viewers, listeners; assembly, congregation.

7 *they filled the house* theater, auditorium, amphitheater, hall, gallery, stalls.

▸ verb 1 *they can house twelve employees* ACCOMMODATE, provide accommodations for, give someone a roof over their head, lodge, quarter, board, billet, take in, sleep, put up; harbor, shelter.

2 *this panel houses the main switch* CONTAIN, hold, store; cover, protect, enclose.

PHRASE: **on the house** *informal drinks are on the house* FREE, free of charge, without charge, at no cost, for nothing, gratis; complimentary; *informal* for free, comp.

HOUSES

adobe house	house trailer
A-frame	igloo
apartment	in-law apartment
apartment house	log cabin
attached house	longhouse
beach house	maisonette
bi-level	manor
brownstone	mansion
bungalow	mobile home
bunkhouse	octagon house
cabin	penthouse
Cape Cod	prefabricated house/prefab
carriage house	quadruplex
chalet	raised ranch
clapboard house	ranch house
coach house	row house
colonial	semidetached
cottage	solar house
country house	split-level
detached	tepee
dormitory	townhouse
double-wide (trailer)	tract house
duplex	trailer
Dutch colonial	triplex
farmhouse	Tudor
frame house	two-family house
galerie house	Victorian
garrison house	wickiup
Georgian	wigwam
hacienda	
half-timbered house	

household noun *the household was asleep* FAMILY, house, occupants, residents, ménage; clan, tribe; *informal* brood.

▸ adjective *household goods* DOMESTIC, family; everyday, ordinary, common, commonplace, regular, practical, workaday.

householder noun *the householder has not responded to the served notice* HOMEOWNER, owner, occupant, resident; tenant, leaseholder; proprietor, landlady, landlord, freeholder.

housekeeper noun See MAID sense 1.

housework noun *we all do our share of the housework* DOMESTIC WORK, housecleaning, housekeeping, homemaking; chores, cleaning; home economics.

housing noun 1 *they invested in housing* HOUSES, homes, residences, apartment buildings, condominiums; accommodations, lodging, living quarters, shelter; *formal* dwellings, dwelling places, habitations.

2 *the housing for the antenna* CASING, covering, case, cover, holder, sheath, jacket, shell, carapace, capsule.

hovel noun *living in the most dismal hovels* SHACK, slum, chantey, hut; *informal* dump, hole, dive, pigsty.

hover verb **1** *helicopters hovered overhead* BE SUSPENDED, be poised, hang, levitate, float; fly.

2 *she hovered anxiously nearby* LINGER, loiter, wait (around); *informal* hang around/about, stick around.

however adverb **1** *however, gaining weight is not inevitable* NEVERTHELESS, nonetheless, but, still, yet, though, although, even so, for all that, despite that, in spite of that; anyway, anyhow, be that as it may, all the same, having said that, notwithstanding; *informal* still and all.

2 *however you look at it* IN WHATEVER WAY, regardless of how, no matter how.

howl noun **1** *the howl of a wolf* BAYING, howling, bay, cry, yowl, bark, yelp.

2 *a howl of anguish* WAIL, cry, yell, yelp, yowl; bellow, roar, shout, shriek, scream, screech.

▸ verb **1** *dogs howled in the distance* BAY, cry, yowl, bark, yelp.

2 *a baby started to howl* WAIL, cry, yell, yowl, bawl, bellow, shriek, scream, screech, caterwaul; *informal* holler.

3 *the movie was so funny, we just howled* LAUGH, guffaw, roar; be doubled up, split one's sides; *informal* crack up, be in stitches, be rolling in the aisles, be on the floor.

howler noun *informal laying that center tile in upside down was a real howler* MISTAKE, error, blunder, faux pas, fault, gaffe, slip; *formal* solecism; *informal* slip-up, goof-up, boo-boo, botch, blooper, pratfall.

hub noun **1** *the hub of the wheel* PIVOT, axis, fulcrum, center, middle.

2 *the hub of family life* CENTER, core, heart, middle, focus, focal point, central point, nucleus, kernel, nerve center, polestar. ANTONYM periphery.

hubbub noun **1** *her voice was lost in the hubbub* NOISE, din, racket, commotion, clamor, cacophony, babel, ruckus; *informal* rumpus, hullabaloo.

2 *she fought through the hubbub* CONFUSION, chaos, pandemonium, bedlam, mayhem, disorder, disturbance, turmoil, tumult, uproar, fracas, havoc, brouhaha, hustle and bustle.

hubris noun *the hubris among economists was shaken* ARROGANCE, conceit, haughtiness, hauteur, pride, self-importance, egotism, pomposity, superciliousness, superiority; *informal* big-headedness, cockiness. ANTONYM humility.

huckster noun *the hucksters along the boardwalk* TRADER, dealer, seller, purveyor, vendor, salesman, salesperson, peddler, hawker; *informal* pusher.

huddle verb **1** *they huddled together* CROWD, cluster, gather, bunch, throng, flock, herd, collect, group, congregate, mass; press, pack, squeeze. ANTONYM disperse.

2 *he huddled beneath the sheets* CURL UP, snuggle, nestle, hunch up.

▸ noun **1** *a huddle of passengers* CROWD, cluster, bunch, knot, group, throng, flock, press, pack; collection, assemblage; *informal* gaggle.

2 *the team went into a huddle* CONSULTATION, discussion, debate, talk, parley, meeting, conference; *informal* confab, powwow.

hue noun *a lovely hue of lilac* COLOR, shade, tone, tint, tinge.

hue and cry noun See HULLABALOO.

huff noun *he ran out in a huff* BAD MOOD, fit of pique, temper, tantrum, rage; *informal* snit, state, grump, hissy fit.

huffy adjective *don't get all huffy about it* IRRITABLE, irritated, annoyed, cross, grumpy, grouchy, bad-tempered, crotchety, crabby, cantankerous, moody, petulant, sullen, sulky, surly; touchy, testy, tetchy; *informal* snappy, cranky, miffed.

hug verb **1** *they hugged each other* EMBRACE, cuddle, squeeze, clasp, clutch, cradle, cling to, hold close, hold tight, take/fold someone in one's arms, clasp someone to one's bosom.

2 *our route hugged the coastline* FOLLOW CLOSELY, keep close to, stay near to, follow the course of.

3 *we hugged the comforting thought* CLING TO, hold on to, cherish, hold dear; harbor, nurse, foster, retain, keep in mind.

▸ noun *there were hugs as we left* EMBRACE, cuddle, squeeze, bear hug, clasp, hold, clinch.

huge adjective *a huge battleship* ENORMOUS, vast, immense, large, big, great, massive, colossal, prodigious, gigantic, gargantuan, mammoth, monumental; giant, towering, elephantine, mountainous, monstrous, titanic; epic, Herculean, Brobdingnagian; *informal* jumbo, mega, monster, king-size(d), economy-size(d), oversized, super-size(d), whopping, humongous, honking, hulking, astronomical, cosmic, ginormous. ANTONYM tiny.

hugely adverb *a hugely expensive legal battle* VERY, extremely, exceedingly, enormously, most, really, particularly, tremendously, greatly, highly, decidedly, exceptionally, immensely, inordinately, extraordinarily, vastly; very much, to a great extent; *informal* terrifically, awfully, terribly, majorly, seriously, mega, ultra, oh-so, ever so, damn, damned, real, mighty, awful; frightfully; *archaic* exceeding.

hulk noun **1** *the rusting hulks of ships* WRECK, shipwreck, wreckage, ruin, derelict; shell, skeleton, hull.

2 *a great hulk of a man* GIANT, lump, blob, clod; oaf; *informal* clodhopper, ape, gorilla, lummox, lubber.

hulking adjective *informal a hulking black dog lumbered down the stairs* LARGE, big, heavy, sturdy, burly, brawny, hefty, strapping; bulky, weighty, massive, ponderous; clumsy, awkward, ungainly, lumbering, lumpish, oafish; *informal* beefy, clunky, clodhopping. ANTONYM small.

hull noun **1** *the ship's hull* FRAMEWORK, body, shell, frame, skeleton, structure; fuselage.

2 *seed hulls* SHELL, husk, pod, case, covering, integument, calyx, shuck; *Botany* pericarp, legume.

hullabaloo noun *informal the hullabaloo outside the police station attracted reporters by the dozen* FUSS, commotion, hue and cry, uproar, outcry, clamor, storm, furor, hubbub, ruckus, brouhaha; pandemonium, mayhem, tumult, turmoil, hurly-burly, rumpus, palaver; *informal* hoo-ha, to-do, song and dance, stink.

hum verb **1** *the engine was humming* PURR, drone, murmur, buzz, thrum, whine, whir, throb, vibrate, rumble.

2 *she hummed a tune* sing, croon, murmur, drone.

3 *the workshops are humming* BE BUSY, be active, be lively, buzz, bustle, be a hive of activity, throb, pulsate; *informal* be happening.

▸ noun *a low hum of conversation* MURMUR, drone, purr, buzz, mumble.

human adjective **1** *they're only human* MORTAL, flesh and blood; fallible, weak, frail, imperfect, vulnerable, susceptible, erring, error-prone; physical, bodily, fleshly.

2 *the human side of politics* COMPASSIONATE, humane, kind, considerate, understanding, sympathetic, tolerant; approachable, accessible.

3 *in human form* ANTHROPOMORPHIC, anthropoid, humanoid, hominid.

▸ noun *the link between humans and animals* PERSON, human being, personage, mortal, member of the human race; man, woman; individual, soul, living soul, being; Homo sapiens; earthling.

humane adjective *the humane treatment of animals* COMPASSIONATE, kind, considerate, understanding, sympathetic, tolerant; lenient, forbearing, forgiving, merciful, mild, gentle, tender, clement, benign, humanitarian, benevolent, charitable; warmhearted, tenderhearted, softhearted. ANTONYM cruel.

humanitarian adjective **1** *a humanitarian act* COMPASSIONATE, humane; unselfish, altruistic, generous, magnanimous, benevolent, merciful, kind, sympathetic. ANTONYM selfish.

2 *a humanitarian organization* CHARITABLE, philanthropic, public-spirited, socially concerned, welfare; *rare* eleemosynary.

▸ noun *Mrs. Roosevelt would be most gratified to be remembered as a humanitarian* PHILANTHROPIST, altruist, benefactor, patron, social reformer, good Samaritan; do-gooder; *archaic* philanthrope.

humanities plural noun *if higher education becomes any more driven by corporate objectives, the humanities will be grappling for survival* ARTS, liberal arts, literature, philosophy; classics, classical studies, classical literature.

humanity noun **1** *humanity evolved from the apes* HUMANKIND, mankind, man, people, human beings, humans, the human race, mortals; Homo sapiens.

2 *the humanity of Christ* HUMAN NATURE, humanness, mortality.

3 *he praised them for their humanity* COMPASSION, brotherly love, fraternity, fellow feeling, philanthropy, humaneness, kindness, consideration, understanding, sympathy, tolerance; leniency, mercy, mercifulness, clemency, pity, tenderness; benevolence, charity, goodness, magnanimity, generosity.

humanize verb *we attempt to humanize these young men before we send them out to find jobs* CIVILIZE, improve, better; educate, enlighten, instruct; socialize, refine, polish; *formal* edify.

humankind noun See HUMANITY sense 1.

humble adjective **1** *her bearing was humble* MEEK, deferential, respectful, submissive, diffident, self-effacing, unassertive; unpresuming, modest, unassuming, self-deprecating; subdued, chastened. ANTONYMS proud, overbearing.

2 *a humble background* LOWLY, working-class, lower-class, poor, undistinguished, mean, modest, ignoble, lowborn, plebeian, underprivileged; common, ordinary, simple, inferior, unremarkable, insignificant, inconsequential. ANTONYM noble.

3 *my humble abode* MODEST, plain, simple, ordinary, unostentatious, unpretentious. ANTONYM grand.

▸ verb *he had to humble himself to ask for my help* HUMILIATE, abase, demean, lower, degrade, debase; mortify, shame, abash; *informal* cut down to size, deflate, make eat humble pie, take down a peg or two, settle someone's hash, make eat crow.

THE RIGHT WORD

While all of these verbs mean to lower in one's own estimation or in the eyes of others, there are subtle distinctions among them. **Humble** and **humiliate** sound similar, but *humiliate* emphasizes shame and the loss of self-respect and usually takes place in public (*humiliated by her tearful outburst*), while *humble* is a milder term implying a lowering of one's pride or rank (*to humble the arrogant professor by pointing out his mistake*). **Abase** suggests groveling or a sense of inferiority and is usually used reflexively (*got down on his knees and abased himself before the king*), while **demean** is more likely to imply a loss of dignity or social standing (*refused to demean herself by marrying a common laborer*). When used to describe things, **debase** means a deterioration in the quality or value of something (*a currency debased by the country's political turmoil*), but in reference to people it connotes a weakening of moral standards or character (*debased himself by accepting bribes*). **Degrade** is even stronger, suggesting the destruction of a person's character through degenerate or shameful behavior (*degraded by long association with criminals*).

humdinger noun *informal Some of Hedda's hats were real humdingers* AMAZING THING; *informal* jim-dandy, dandy, dilly, beaut, lollapalooza, ripsnorter, peach, doozy, lulu, whopper.

humdrum adjective *they were quite wrong in assuming that the lighthouse keeper led a lonely and humdrum life* MUNDANE, dull, dreary, boring, tedious, monotonous, prosaic; unexciting, uninteresting, uneventful, unvaried, repetitive, unremarkable; routine, ordinary, everyday, day-to-day, workaday, quotidian, run-of-the-mill, commonplace, garden variety, pedestrian; *informal* plain-vanilla, ho-hum. ANTONYMS remarkable, exciting.

humidity noun *a climate of warm temperatures and high humidity* MUGGINESS, humidness, closeness, sultriness, stickiness, steaminess, airlessness, stuffiness, clamminess; dampness, damp, dankness, moisture, moistness, wetness, dewiness. ANTONYMS freshness, aridity.

humiliate verb *he was humiliated in front of the whole school* EMBARRASS, mortify, humble, shame, put to shame, disgrace, chagrin; discomfit, chasten, abash, deflate, crush, squash; abase, debase, demean, degrade, lower; belittle, cause to feel small, cause to lose face; *informal* show up, put down, cut down to size, take down (a peg or two), put someone in their place, make someone eat crow. See note at HUMBLE.

humiliation noun *the humiliation of having been left at the altar* EMBARRASSMENT, mortification, shame, indignity, ignominy, disgrace, discomfiture, dishonor, degradation, discredit, belittlement, opprobrium; loss of face; *informal* blow to one's pride/ego, slap in the face, kick in the teeth, comedown. ANTONYM honor.

humility noun *he accepted the award with sincere humil-*

ity MODESTY, humbleness, meekness, diffidence, unassertiveness; lack of pride, lack of vanity; servility, submissiveness. ANTONYM pride.

hummock noun See HILL sense 1.

humor noun **1** *the humor of the film* COMEDY, comical aspect, funny side, fun, amusement, funniness, hilarity, jocularity; absurdity, ludicrousness, drollness; satire, irony, farce.

2 *the stories are spiced up with humor* JOKES, joking, jests, jesting, quips, witticisms, bon mots, funny remarks, puns, sallies, badinage; wit, wittiness, funniness, comedy, drollery; *informal* gags, wisecracks, cracks, kidding, waggishness, one-liners. See note at WIT.

3 *his good humor was infectious* MOOD, temper, disposition, temperament, nature, state of mind, frame of mind; spirits.

▸ verb *she was always humoring him* INDULGE, accommodate, pander to, cater to, yield to, give way to, give in to, go along with; pamper, spoil, baby, overindulge, mollify, placate, gratify, satisfy.

humorist noun *the sports editor was looking for a humorist to write a brief daily column during the course of the Olympic Games* COMIC WRITER, wit, wag; comic, funny man/woman, comedian, comedienne, stand-up comic, joker, jester, clown, wisecracker; *informal* cutup.

humorless adjective *her humorless father had scared off a whole string of suitors before Ted came along* SERIOUS, solemn, sober, somber, grave, grim, dour, unsmiling, stony-faced, saturnine; gloomy, glum, sad, melancholy, dismal, joyless, cheerless, lugubrious; boring, tedious, dull, dry. ANTONYM jovial.

humorous adjective *a humorous account of our expedition* AMUSING, funny, comic, comical, entertaining, diverting, witty, jocular, jocose, lighthearted, tongue-in-cheek, wry, facetious, laughable, risible; hilarious, uproarious, riotous, zany, farcical, droll; *informal* priceless, side-splitting, gut-busting, rib-tickling, knee-slapping, thigh-slapping. ANTONYM serious.

hump noun *the hump made her look old and slouchy* PROTUBERANCE, prominence, lump, bump, knob, protrusion, projection, bulge, swelling, hunch; growth, outgrowth.

hunch verb **1** *he hunched his shoulders* ARCH, curve, hump, bend, bow. ANTONYM straighten.

2 ***I hunched up** as small as I could* CROUCH, huddle, curl; hunker down, bend, stoop, slouch, squat, duck. ANTONYM stretch (out).

▸ noun **1** *the hunch on his back* PROTUBERANCE, hump, lump, bump, knob, protrusion, prominence, bulge, swelling; growth, outgrowth.

2 *my hunch is that he'll be back* FEELING, feeling in one's bones, guess, suspicion, impression, conjecture, inkling, idea, sense, notion, fancy, intuition, premonition, presentiment; *informal* gut feeling, gut instinct.

hunger noun **1** *she was faint with hunger* LACK OF FOOD, hungriness, ravenousness, emptiness; starvation, malnutrition, famine, malnourishment, undernourishment.

2 *a hunger for news* DESIRE, craving, longing, yearning, hankering, appetite, thirst; want, need; *informal* itch, yen.
PHRASE: **hunger after/for** *all actors hunger after such a role* DESIRE, crave, covet; long for, yearn for, pine for, ache for, hanker after, thirst for, lust for; want, need; *informal* have a yen for, itch for, be dying for.

hungry adjective **1** *I was really hungry* RAVENOUS, empty, in need of food, hollow, faint from/with hunger; starving, starved, famished; malnourished, undernourished, underfed; *informal* peckish, able to eat a horse; *archaic* esurient. ANTONYM full.

2 *they are hungry for success* EAGER, keen, avid, longing, yearning, aching, pining, greedy, covetous; craving, hankering; *informal* itching, dying, hot. ANTONYM indifferent.

hunk noun **1** *a hunk of bread* CHUNK, piece, wedge, block, slab, lump, square; gobbet.

2 *informal he's such a hunk* GOOD-LOOKING MAN, heartthrob, macho man; *informal* babe, stud, studmuffin, dreamboat, (male) specimen, looker, beefcake, chick magnet, babe magnet, he-man, hottie.

hunt verb **1** *they hunted deer* CHASE, stalk, pursue, course, run down; track, trail, follow, hound, shadow; *informal* tail.

2 *police are **hunting for** her* SEARCH FOR, look for, look high and low for, scour the area for, sweep the area for, comb the area for; seek, try to find; scout around, rummage around/about, root around/about, fish around/about.

▸ noun **1** *the thrill of the hunt* CHASE, pursuit.

2 *police have stepped up their hunt* SEARCH, look, quest, manhunt.

hunter noun *many local hunters support stricter gun laws* HUNTSMAN, huntswoman, trapper, stalker, woodsman; nimrod; predator; Orion. See note at NIMROD.

hurdle noun **1** *his leg hit a hurdle* FENCE, jump, barrier, barricade, bar, railing, rail.

2 *the final hurdle to overcome* OBSTACLE, difficulty, problem, barrier, bar, snag, stumbling block, impediment, obstruction, complication, hindrance, hitch; *informal* headache, hiccup, glitch, fly in the ointment, wrench in the works.

hurl verb **1** *he hurled an eraser at her head* THROW, toss, fling, pitch, cast, lob, bowl, launch, catapult; project, propel, let fly, fire; *informal* chuck, heave, sling, peg. *dated* shy.

2 *informal she felt like she was going to hurl.* See VOMIT.

hurricane noun See STORM noun sense 1.

hurried adjective **1** *a hurried greeting* QUICK, fast, swift, rapid, speedy, brisk, hasty, abrupt; cursory, perfunctory, brief, short, fleeting, flying, passing, superficial, slapdash. ANTONYMS slow, leisurely.

2 *a hurried decision* HASTY, rushed, speedy, quick, expeditious; impetuous, impulsive, precipitate, precipitous, rash, incautious, imprudent, spur-of-the-moment. ANTONYM considered.

hurriedly adverb *she got up and dressed hurriedly* HASTILY, speedily, quickly, fast, rapidly, swiftly, briskly; without delay, at top speed, at full tilt, full bore, full out, on the double; headlong, posthaste; *informal* like the wind, like greased lightning, double-quick, lickety-split.

hurry verb **1** *hurry or you'll be late* BE QUICK, hurry up, hurry it up, hasten, speed up, speed it up, press on, push on; run, dash, rush, race, fly; scurry, scramble, scuttle, sprint; *informal* get a move on, move it, step on it, get cracking, get moving, shake a leg, hightail it, chop-chop, tear, zip, zoom, hotfoot it, leg it, get the lead out; *dated* make haste; *archaic* hie. ANTONYMS dawdle, move slowly.

2 *she hurried him out* HUSTLE, hasten, push, urge, drive, spur, goad, prod.

▸ noun *in all the hurry, we forgot* RUSH, haste, flurry, hustle and bustle, confusion, commotion, hubbub, turmoil; race, scramble, scurry.

hurt verb **1** *my back hurts* BE PAINFUL, be sore, be tender, cause pain, cause discomfort; ache, smart, sting, burn, throb; *informal* be killing (one).

2 *Dad hurt his leg* INJURE, wound, damage, abuse, disable, incapacitate, maim, mutilate, wrench; bruise, cut, gash, graze, scrape, scratch, lacerate. ANTONYM heal.

3 *his words hurt her* DISTRESS, pain, wound, sting, upset, sadden, devastate, grieve, mortify; cut to the quick. ANTONYMS please, comfort.

4 *high interest rates are hurting the economy* HARM, damage, be detrimental to, weaken, blight, impede, jeopardize, undermine, ruin, wreck, sabotage, cripple. ANTONYMS improve, benefit.

▸ noun *she apologized for the hurt she had caused* DISTRESS, pain, suffering, injury, grief, misery, anguish, agony, trauma, woe, upset, sadness, sorrow; harm, damage, trouble. ANTONYM joy.

▸ adjective **1** *my hurt hand* INJURED, wounded, bruised, grazed, cut, gashed, battered, sore, painful, aching, smarting, throbbing. ANTONYM healed.

2 *Anne's hurt expression* PAINED, injured, distressed, anguished, upset, sad, mortified, offended; *informal* miffed, peeved, sore. ANTONYM pleased.

hurtful adjective *the effects of hurtful remarks may last a lifetime* UPSETTING, distressing, wounding, painful, injurious; unkind, cruel, nasty, mean, malicious, spiteful, vindictive; cutting, barbed, poisonous; *informal* catty, bitchy.

hurtle verb *they hurtled out of the classroom and into the gymnasium* SPEED, rush, run, race, sprint, bolt, dash, career, charge, careen, shoot, streak, flash, gallop, fly, scurry, go like the wind; *informal* belt, tear, scoot, whiz, zoom, go like a bat out of hell, hightail it, barrel.

husband noun *Chris's husband is a South American businessman* SPOUSE, partner, life partner, mate, consort, man, helpmate, helpmeet; groom, bridegroom; *informal* hubby, old man, one's better half, other half, significant other.

husbandry noun **1** *farmers have new methods of husbandry* FARM MANAGEMENT, land management, farming, agriculture, agronomy; cultivation; animal husbandry, ranching.

2 *the careful husbandry of their resources* CONSERVATION, management; economy, thrift, thriftiness, frugality.

hush verb *will somebody please hush those kids in the back row?* SILENCE, quiet, quiet down, shush; soothe, calm, pacify; gag, muzzle, muffle, mute; *informal* shut up.

▸ exclamation *someone's coming, everybody hush!* BE QUIET, keep quiet, quiet, quiet down, be silent, stop talking, hold your tongue; *informal* shut up, shh, hush up, shut your mouth, shut your face, shut your trap, button your lip, pipe down, put a sock in it, give it a rest, save it, not another word.

▸ noun *a hush descended* SILENCE, quiet, quietness; stillness, peace, peacefulness, calm, lull, tranquility. ANTONYM noise.

PHRASE: **hush up** *management took steps to hush up the dangers* KEEP SECRET, conceal, hide, suppress, cover up, keep quiet about; obscure, veil, sweep under the carpet; *informal* sit on, keep under one's hat.

hush-hush adjective *informal* See SECRET adjective sense 1.

husk noun *the husk of the coconut* SHELL, hull, pod, case, covering, integument, shuck; *Botany* pericarp, legume.

husky adjective **1** *a husky voice* THROATY, gruff, gravelly, hoarse, croaky, rough, guttural, harsh, rasping, raspy; deep. ANTONYMS shrill, soft.

2 *Paddy was a husky guy* STRONG, muscular, muscly, muscle-bound, big, brawny, hefty, burly, hulking, strapping, thickset, solid, powerful, heavy, robust, sturdy, stalwart, blocky, Herculean, well-built; *informal* beefy, hunky; *literary* thewy. ANTONYM puny.

hussy noun *in this farcical version, Juliet is portrayed as a shameless hussy* MINX, coquette, tease, seductress, Lolita, Jezebel; slut, harlot, loose woman; *informal* floozy, tart, vamp, tramp; *dated* trollop; *archaic* jade, strumpet.

hustle verb **1** *I was hustled away* MANHANDLE, push, shove, thrust, frogmarch, whisk, bundle.

2 *we'll have to hustle to catch the bus* rush, hurry, be quick, hasten; speed up, press on; *informal* get a move on, step on it, get moving, get cracking, shake a leg.

3 *if you want it, you'll have to hustle for it* WORK, work hard, strive, endeavor, apply oneself, exert oneself; *informal* pull out all the stops.

4 *informal* *don't be hustled into joining some cause you don't believe in* COERCE, force, compel, pressure, pressurize, badger, pester, hound, harass, nag, harry, urge, goad, prod, spur; browbeat, bulldoze, bludgeon, steamroller, strong-arm; *informal* railroad, fast-talk. PHRASE: **hustle and bustle** *I need the hustle and bustle of the city* ACTIVITY, bustle, tumult, hubbub, action, liveliness, animation, excitement, agitation, commotion, flurry, whirl; *informal* ballyhoo, hoo-ha, hullabaloo.

hut noun *we spent two nights in a rustic little hut near the village* SHACK, chantey, cabin, log cabin, shelter, shed, lean-to, hovel; hovel; cabana.

hybrid noun *a hybrid between a brown and an albino mouse* CROSS, cross-breed, mixed breed, half-breed, half-blood; mixture, blend, amalgamation, combination, composite, compound, fusion.

▸ adjective *a hybrid organization* COMPOSITE, cross-bred, interbred, mongrel; heterogeneous, mixed, blended, compound, amalgamated, hyphenated.

hygiene noun *they teach preschoolers the fundamentals of personal hygiene* CLEANLINESS, sanitation, sterility, purity, disinfection; public health, environmental health.

hygienic adjective *keeping the kitchen hygienic* SANITARY, clean, germ-free, disinfected, sterilized, sterile, antiseptic, aseptic, unpolluted, uncontaminated, salubrious, healthy, wholesome, purified; *informal* squeaky clean. See note at SANITARY. ANTONYM unsanitary.

hymn noun *singing the old familiar hymns* RELIGIOUS SONG, song of praise, anthem, canticle, chorale, psalm, paean, carol; spiritual.

hype *informal* noun *her work relies on hype and headlines* PUBLICITY, advertising, promotion, marketing, exposure; *informal* ballyhoo, promo.

▸ verb *a stunt to hype a new product* PUBLICIZE, advertise, promote, push, boost, merchandise, build up; *informal* plug.

hyper adjective *this new medication seems to make him even more hyper* HYPERACTIVE, overactive, active, energetic; busy, fidgety; excited, frantic, frenetic, frenzied, adrenalized, feverish; *informal* keyed-up, fired-up, amped-up, psyched, high-energy, caffeinated, pumped, pumped up, turbocharged.

hyperbole noun *the media hyperbole that accompanied their championship series* EXAGGERATION, overstatement, magnification, embroidery, embellishment, excess, overkill, rhetoric; *informal* purple prose, puffery. ANTONYM understatement.

hypnotic adjective *hypnotic music* MESMERIZING, mesmeric, spellbinding, entrancing, bewitching, irresistible, magnetic, compelling, enthralling, captivating, charming; soporific, sleep-inducing, sedative, numbing; *Medicine* stupefacient.

hypnotize verb **1** *he had been hypnotized as a stunt* MESMERIZE, put into a trance.

2 *they were hypnotized by the dancers* ENTRANCE, mesmerize, spellbind, enthrall, transfix, captivate, bewitch, charm, enrapture, grip, rivet, absorb, fascinate, magnetize.

hypochondriac noun *a hypochondriac who depends on her pills* VALETUDINARIAN, neurotic.

▸ adjective *her hypochondriac husband* VALETUDINARIAN, hypochondriacal, malingering, health-obsessed; neurotic, paranoid, phobic.

hypocrisy noun *must politics be the perennial benchmark of hypocrisy?* DISSIMULATION, false virtue, cant, posturing, affectation, speciousness, empty talk, insincerity, falseness, deceit, dishonesty, mendacity, pretense, duplicity; sanctimoniousness, sanctimony, pietism, piousness; *informal* phoniness, fraud. ANTONYM sincerity.

hypocrite noun *I've been made to feel inadequate my whole life by someone who turns out to be a total hypocrite* PRETENDER, dissembler, deceiver, liar, pietist, sanctimonious person, plaster saint; *informal* phony, fraud, sham, fake.

hypothesis noun *his 'steady state' hypothesis of the origin of the universe* THEORY, theorem, thesis, conjecture, supposition, postulation, postulate, proposition, premise, assumption; notion, concept, idea, possibility.

hypothetical adjective *the scenario I suggested was strictly hypothetical* THEORETICAL, speculative, conjectured, conjectural, notional, suppositional, supposed, putative, assumed; academic. ANTONYM actual.

hysteria noun *his fictional account of an alien invasion caused not-so-fictional hysteria among the radio audience* FRENZY, feverishness, hysterics, fit of madness, derangement, mania, delirium; panic, alarm, distress. ANTONYM calm.

hysterical adjective **1** *Janet became hysterical* OVERWROUGHT, overemotional, out of control, frenzied, frantic, wild, feverish, crazed; beside oneself, driven to distraction, distraught, agitated, berserk, manic, delirious, unhinged, deranged, out of one's mind, raving; *informal* in a state.

2 *informal her attempts to dance were hysterical* HILARIOUS, uproarious, very funny, very amusing, comical, farcical; *informal* hysterically funny, priceless, side-splitting, rib-tickling, gut-busting, knee-slapping, thigh-slapping, a scream, a hoot, a barrel of laughs; *dated* killing.

hysterics plural noun *informal* **1** *a fit of hysterics* HYSTERIA, wildness, feverishness, irrationality, frenzy, loss of control, delirium, derangement, mania.

2 *the girls collapsed in hysterics* FITS OF LAUGHTER, gales of laughter, peals of laughter, paroxysms of laughter, uncontrollable laughter, convulsions, fits; *informal* stitches.

I

I pronoun See note below.

WORD NOTE **I**

Certainly the graceful use of *I* takes practice, and should be among the principal goals of any writer. Few of us wish to sound egotistical or self-centered (whether in prose or person), but attempts to avoid saying *I* usually lead to various off-putting alternatives. *This writer, this reviewer,* and their like seem both weaselly and slightly offensive, marking out the user as somehow superior to the unwashed masses, among whom the reader must usually count himself. *One* also carries a whiff of snooty, aristocratic disdain. Either use *I* or recast your expressions to avoid the first person altogether. **—MD**

ice noun **1** *a roof covered with ice* FROZEN WATER, icicles; black ice, frost, rime, glaze.

2 *the ice in her voice* COLDNESS, coolness, frost, frostiness, iciness; hostility, unfriendliness; stiffness, aloofness. ANTONYMS warmth, friendliness.

▸ verb **1** *the lake has **iced over*** FREEZE, FREEZE OVER, turn into ice, harden, solidify; *archaic* glaciate. ANTONYM thaw.

2 *she had iced the cake* FROST, cover with icing, glaze.

PHRASES: **on ice** *informal.* See PENDING adjective sense 1. **on thin ice** *we're standing on thin ice by testing Russia's patience* IN A RISKY SITUATION, at risk, in peril, imperiled, living dangerously, living on the edge.

ice-cold adjective *an ice-cold beer | the night winds were ice-cold* ICY, freezing, glacial, gelid, subzero, frozen, wintry, frigid; arctic, polar, Siberian, hypothermic; bitter, biting, cutting, bone-chilling, raw, chilly, frosty, nippy; *literary* rimy. ANTONYM hot.

iced adjective *add sprigs of fresh mint to your iced drinks* ICE-COLD, cold, chilled, refrigerated; frosty, icy, frozen.

icing noun *a cake with pink icing* GLAZE, frosting, topping, fondant, piping.

icon noun **1** *an icon of the Blessed Virgin* IMAGE, idol, portrait, picture, representation, likeness, symbol, sign; figure, statue.

2 *he became a teen icon* IDOL, paragon, hero, heroine; celebrity, superstar, star; favorite, darling.

iconoclast noun *in terms of the money culture in Washington, Rep. Linda Smith is an iconoclast* CRITIC, skeptic; heretic, unbeliever, dissident, dissenter, infidel; rebel, renegade, mutineer.

icy adjective **1** *icy roads* FROZEN, frozen over, iced over, frosty, frosted, ice-bound, ice-covered, iced up; slippery; *literary* rimy.

2 *an icy wind* FREEZING, cold, chill, chilly, chilling, nippy, frigid, frosty, biting, cutting, bitter, raw, arctic, wintry, glacial, Siberian, hypothermic, polar, gelid. ANTONYMS hot, warm.

3 *an icy voice* UNFRIENDLY, hostile, forbidding, unwelcoming, inhospitable; cold, cool, chilly, frigid, frosty, glacial, gelid; haughty, stern, hard. ANTONYM friendly.

ID noun *show your ID to the guy at the front entrance* IDENTIFICATION, (identification/identity) papers, bona fides, documents, credentials.

idée fixe noun See OBSESSION.

idea noun **1** *the idea of death scares her* CONCEPT, notion, conception, thought; image, visualization; hypothesis, postulation.

2 *our idea is to open a new shop* PLAN, scheme, design, proposal, proposition, suggestion, brainchild, vision; aim, intention, purpose, objective, object, goal, target.

3 *Liz had other ideas on the subject* THOUGHT, theory, view, opinion, feeling, belief, attitude, conclusion; *informal* take.

4 *I had an idea that it might happen* SENSE, feeling, suspicion, inkling, hunch, clue, theory, notion, impression; *dated* fancy.

5 *I get the idea* MEANING, significance, sense, import, essence, gist, drift; point, aim, intention, purport, implication; design, motive.

6 *an idea of the cost* ESTIMATE, estimation, approximation, guess, conjecture, rough calculation; *informal* guesstimate.

THE RIGHT WORD

If you have an **idea** it might refer to something perceived through the senses (*I had no idea it was so cold out*), to something visualized (*the idea of a joyous family outing*), or to something that is the product of the imagination (*a great idea for raising money*). *Idea* is a comprehensive word that applies to almost any aspect of mental activity. A **thought**, on the other hand, is an idea that is the result of meditation, reasoning, or some other intellectual activity (*she hadn't given much thought to the possibility of losing*). A **notion** is a vague or capricious idea, often without any sound basis (*he had a notion that he could get there by hitchhiking*). A widely held idea of what something is or should be is a **concept** (*the concept of loyalty was beyond him*), while a **conception** is a concept that is held by an individual or small group and that is often colored by imagination and feeling (*her conception of marriage as a romantic ideal*). An idea that is triggered by something external is an **impression**, a word that suggests a half-formed mental picture or superficial view (*he made a good impression; she had the impression that everything would be taken care of*).

---

ideal adjective **1** *ideal flying weather* PERFECT, best possible, consummate, supreme, excellent, flawless, faultless, exemplary, classic, model, ultimate, quintessential. ANTONYM bad.

2 *an ideal concept* ABSTRACT, theoretical, conceptual, notional; hypothetical, speculative, conjectural, suppositional. ANTONYM concrete.

3 *an ideal world* UNATTAINABLE, unachievable, impracticable, chimerical; unreal, fictitious, hypothetical, theoretical, ivory-towered, imaginary, illusory, idealized, idyllic, visionary, Utopian, fairy-tale. ANTONYMS attainable, real.

▸ noun **1** *no woman could be the ideal he imagined for himself* PERFECTION, paragon, epitome, shining example, ne plus ultra, nonpareil, dream.

2 *an ideal to aim at* MODEL, pattern, exemplar, standard, example, paradigm, archetype, prototype; yardstick, lodestar. See note at MODEL.

3 *a liberal ideal* PRINCIPLE, standard, value, belief, conviction, persuasion; **(ideals)** morals, morality, ethics, ideology, creed.

idealist noun *the title character is a liberal idealist set up to lose a senatorial election* UTOPIAN, visionary, wishful thinker, pipe-dreamer, fantasist, romantic, dreamer, daydreamer, stargazer; Walter Mitty, Don Quixote; *rare* fantast.

idealistic adjective *some say I'm drawing a wildly idealistic portrait of what the Church can become* UTOPIAN, visionary, romantic, quixotic, dreamy, unrealistic, impractical, starry-eyed; fanciful; *informal* with one's head in the clouds; *chiefly Brit. informal* airy-fairy.

idealize verb *they tend to idealize the postwar years* ROMANTICIZE, glorify, be unrealistic about, look at through rose-colored glasses, paint a rosy picture of, glamorize; deify, put on a pedestal.

ideally adverb *ideally, it would be a good thing to provide rehabilitation* IN A PERFECT WORLD; preferably, if possible, by choice, by preference, as a matter of choice, rather; all things being equal, theoretically, hypothetically, in theory, in principle, on paper.

identical adjective **1** *wearing identical badges* INDISTINGUISHABLE, (exactly) the same, uniform, twin, duplicate, interchangeable, synonymous, undifferentiated, homogeneous, of a piece, cut from the same cloth; alike, like, matching, like (two) peas in a pod; similar. ANTONYMS different, unlike.

2 *I used the identical technique* SAME, very same, selfsame, very, one and the same; aforementioned, aforesaid, aforenamed, above, above-stated; foregoing, preceding. See note at SAME. ANTONYM different.

identifiable adjective *what identifiable features should we be looking for?* DISTINGUISHABLE, recognizable, known; noticeable, perceptible, discernible, appreciable, detectable, observable, perceivable, ascertainable, visible; distinct, marked, conspicuous, unmistakable, clear. ANTONYM unrecognizable.

identification noun **1** *the identification of the suspect* RECOGNITION, singling out, pinpointing, naming; discerning, distinguishing; *informal* fingering.

2 *early identification of problems* DETERMINATION, establishment, ascertainment, discovery, diagnosis, divination; verification, confirmation.

3 *may I see your identification?* ID, (identity/identification) papers, bona fides, documents, credentials; ID card, identity card, pass, badge, warrant, license, permit, passport.

4 *the identification of Nonconformity with Victorian values* ASSOCIATION, link, linkage, connection, tie, interconnection, interrelation, interdependence.

5 *his identification with the music is evident* EMPATHY, rapport, relationship, fellow feeling, sympathetic cord.

identify verb **1** *the driver was identified by two witnesses* RECOGNIZE, single out, pick out, spot, point out, pinpoint, put one's finger on, put a name to, name, know; discern, distinguish; remember, recall, recollect; *informal* finger; *formal* espy.

2 *I identified four problem areas* DETERMINE, establish, ascertain, make out, diagnose, discern, distinguish; verify, confirm; *informal* figure out, get a fix on, peg.

3 *they identify professional sports with wealth and glamour* ASSOCIATE, link, connect, relate, bracket, couple; mention in the same breath as, put side by side with.

4 *Peter* ***identifies with*** *the hero* EMPATHIZE WITH, be in tune with, have a rapport with, feel at one with, sympathize with; be on the same wavelength as, speak the same language as; understand, relate to, feel for.

identity noun **1** *the identity of the owner* NAME, ID; specification.

2 *she was afraid of losing her identity* INDIVIDUALITY, self, selfhood; personality, character, originality, distinctiveness, differentness, singularity, uniqueness.

3 *a case of mistaken identity* IDENTIFICATION, recognition, naming, singling out.

ideology noun *the party has to jettison outdated ideology and give up its stranglehold on power* BELIEFS, ideas, ideals, principles, ethics, morals; doctrine, creed, credo, faith, teaching, theory, philosophy; tenets, canon(s); conviction(s), persuasion; *informal* ism.

idiocy noun *a seventeenth-century antidote to idiocy was to rub the forehead with beaver testicles* STUPIDITY, folly, foolishness, foolhardiness, ignorance; madness, insanity, lunacy, nonsense; silliness, brainlessness, thoughtlessness, senselessness, irresponsibility, imprudence, ineptitude, inanity, absurdity, ludicrousness, fatuousness; *informal* craziness. ANTONYM sense.

idiom noun *these musicians all work in the gospel idiom* LANGUAGE, mode of expression, turn of phrase, style, speech, locution, diction, usage, phraseology, phrasing, phrase, vocabulary, terminology, parlance, jargon, argot, cant, patter, tongue, vernacular; *informal* lingo.

idiomatic adjective *the president lacks an ear for idiomatic English* VERNACULAR, colloquial, everyday, conversational; natural, grammatical, correct.

idiosyncrasy noun *traveling with her own fruitcake is one of the queen's idiosyncrasies | Fenway's Green Monster is perhaps the most recognizable ballpark idiosyncrasy* PECULIARITY, oddity, eccentricity, mannerism, trait, singularity, quirk, tic, whim, vagary, caprice, kink; fetish, foible, crotchet, habit, characteristic; individuality; unorthodoxy, unconventionality.

idiosyncratic adjective *of the great idiosyncratic detectives of fiction, Nero Wolfe is my favorite* DISTINCTIVE, individual, individualistic, characteristic, peculiar, typical, special, specific, unique, one-of-a-kind, personal; eccentric, unconventional, irregular, anomalous, odd, quirky, offbeat, queer, strange, weird, wacky, wingy, bizarre, freakish, abnormal; *informal* freaky, far out, off the wall.

idiot noun *informal that idiot was driving way too fast* FOOL, ass, halfwit, dunce, dolt, ignoramus, cretin, moron, imbecile, simpleton; *informal* dope, ninny, nincompoop, chump, dimwit, dumbo, dummy, dum-dum, loon, dork, sap, jackass, blockhead, jughead, bonehead, knucklehead, fathead, numbskull, numbnuts, dumb-ass, doofus, clod, dunderhead, ditz, lummox, dipstick, thickhead, meathead, meatball, woodenhead, airhead, pinhead, lamebrain, peabrain, birdbrain, jerk, nerd, donkey, nitwit, twit, boob, twerp, schmuck, bozo, turkey, chowderhead, dingbat. ANTONYM genius.

idiotic adjective *her latest comedy is fanciful without being idiotic* STUPID, silly, foolish, witless, brainless, mindless, thoughtless, unintelligent; imprudent, unwise, ill-advised, ill-considered, half-baked, foolhardy; absurd, senseless, pointless, nonsensical, inane, fatuous, ridiculous; *informal* dumb, dim, dimwitted, halfwitted, dopey, harebrained, pea-brained, wooden-headed, thickheaded, dumb-ass.

idle adjective **1** *an idle person* LAZY, indolent, slothful, work-shy, shiftless, inactive, sluggish, lethargic, listless; slack, lax, lackadaisical, good-for-nothing; *rare* otiose. ANTONYM industrious.

2 *being idle won't pay the bills* UNEMPLOYED, jobless, out-of-work, redundant, between jobs, workless, unwaged, unoccupied. ANTONYM employed.

3 *they left the machine idle* INACTIVE, unused, unoccupied, unemployed, disused; not in use, out of use, out of action, inoperative, nonfunctioning, out of service. ANTONYM working.

4 *their idle hours* UNOCCUPIED, spare, empty, vacant, unfilled, available. ANTONYMS busy, full.

5 *idle remarks* FRIVOLOUS, trivial, trifling, vain, minor, petty, lightweight, shallow, superficial, insignificant, unimportant, worthless, paltry, niggling, peripheral, inane, fatuous; unnecessary, time-wasting. ANTONYMS meaningful, serious.

6 *idle threats* EMPTY, meaningless, pointless, worthless, vain, hollow, insubstantial, futile, ineffective, ineffectual; groundless, baseless. ANTONYM serious.

▸ verb **1** *Lily idled on the window seat* DO NOTHING, be inactive, vegetate, take it easy, mark time, twiddle one's thumbs, kill time, languish, laze, lounge, loll, loaf, loiter; *informal* hang around, veg out, bum around, lollygag. See note at LOITER.

2 *he let the engine idle* RUN IN NEUTRAL, run.

idler noun *Orwell immersed himself in the world of tramps and idlers* LOAFER, layabout, good-for-nothing, ne'er-do-well, lounger, shirker, sluggard; *informal* slacker, slob, lazybones, slowpoke; *literary* wastrel. ANTONYM workaholic.

idol noun **1** *idols deemed un-Islamic were summarily destroyed* ICON, representation of a god, image, effigy, statue, figure, figurine, fetish, totem; graven image, false god, golden calf.

2 *a teen idol* HERO, HEROINE, star, superstar, icon, celebrity; favorite, darling, pet, beloved; *informal* pinup, heartthrob, dreamboat, golden boy/girl.

idolatry noun *the prophets railed against idolatry* IDOLIZATION, fetishization, fetishism, idol worship, adulation, adoration, reverence, veneration, glorification, lionization, hero-worshiping.

idolize verb *the kids idolize their fighter-pilot father* HERO-WORSHIP, worship, revere, venerate, deify, lionize; stand in awe of, reverence, look up to, admire, adore, exalt; *informal* put on a pedestal. See note at REVERE.

idyll noun See UTOPIA.

idyllic adjective *the once idyllic islands are now subjected to martial law* PERFECT, wonderful, blissful, halcyon, happy; ideal, idealized; heavenly, paradisal, Utopian, Elysian; peaceful, picturesque, bucolic, unspoiled; *literary* Arcadian.

if conjunction **1** *if the rain holds out, we can walk* ON THE CONDITION THAT, provided (that), providing (that), presuming (that), supposing (that), assuming (that), as long as, given that, in the event that.

2 *if I miss curfew, she lays down the law* WHENEVER, every time.

3 *a useful, if unintended innovation* ALTHOUGH, albeit, but, yet, while; even though, despite being; *chiefly Brit.* whilst.

▸ noun *there is one if in all this* UNCERTAINTY, doubt; condition, stipulation, provision, proviso, constraint, precondition, requirement, specification, restriction.

WORD NOTE if

Most dictionaries' usage notes for *if* are long and involved; it might be English's hardest conjunction. From experience born of repeated personal humiliation, I can tell you that there are two main ways to mess up with *if* and make your writing look weak. The first is to use *if* for *whether.* They are not synonyms—*if* is used to express a conditional, *whether* to introduce alternative possibilities. True, abstract grammatical distinctions are hard to remember in the heat of composition, but in this case there's a great simple test: If you can coherently insert an "or not" after either the conjunction or the clause it introduces, you need *whether.* Examples: *He didn't know whether [or not] it would rain*; *She asked me straight out whether I was a fetishist [or not]*; *We told him to call if [or not?* no*] he needed a ride [or not?* no*].* The second kind of snafu involves a basic rule for using commas with subordinating conjunctions (which are what *if* is one of). A subordinating conjunction signals the reader that the clause it's part of is dependent; common subordinating conjunctions include *before, after, while, unless, if, as,* and *because.* For most kinds of sentences, the relevant rule is easy and worth remembering: Use a comma after the subordinating conjunction's clause only if that clause comes before the independent clause that completes the thought; if the subordinating conjunction's clause comes after the independent clause, there's no comma. Example: *If I were you, I'd put down that hatchet* vs. *I'd put down that hatchet if I were you.* —**DFW**

---

iffy adjective *informal* **1** *an iffy neighborhood* DUBIOUS, doubtful, questionable, shaky; substandard, second-rate, inferior; sketchy.

2 *the date was a bit iffy* UNCERTAIN, undecided, unsettled, unsure, unresolved, in doubt, dubious, ambivalent; *informal* up in the air, borderline.

ignite verb **1** *he escaped moments before the gas ignited* CATCH FIRE, burst into flames, combust; be set off, explode. ANTONYM go out.

2 *his cigarette ignited the blanket* LIGHT, set fire to, set on fire, set alight, kindle, spark, touch off; *informal* set/put a match to. ANTONYM extinguish.

3 *the campaign failed to ignite voter interest* AROUSE, kindle, trigger, spark, instigate, excite, provoke, stimulate, animate, stir up, whip up, rally, jump-start, incite, fuel. ANTONYM dampen.

ignoble adjective *the ignoble tradition of mudslinging* DISHONORABLE, unworthy, base, shameful, contemptible, despicable, dastardly, vile, degenerate, shabby, sordid, mean; improper, unprincipled, discreditable; humble, low, lowly, common, plebeian.

ignominious adjective *Wahid made an ignominious exit after 21 months in power* HUMILIATING, undignified, embarrassing, mortifying; ignoble, inglorious; disgraceful, shameful, dishonorable, discreditable. ANTONYM glorious.

ignominy noun *the Braves face the ignominy of losing three straight games to the league's worst team* SHAME, humiliation, embarrassment, mortification; disgrace, dishonor, discredit, degradation, scandal, infamy, indignity, ignobility, loss of face. ANTONYM honor.

ignoramus noun See FOOL noun sense 1.

USAGE NOTE **ignoramus**

Until 1934 in England, if a grand jury considered the evidence of an alleged crime insufficient to prosecute, it would endorse the bill *ignoramus*, meaning literally "we do not know" or "we know nothing of this." Long before, though, the word *ignoramus* had come to mean, by extension, "an ignorant person." In 1615, George Ruggle wrote a play called *Ignoramus*, about a lawyer who knew nothing about the law; this fictional lawyer soon gave his name to all manner of know-nothings, whether lawyers or nonlawyers. The modern nonlegal meaning appears most frequently—e.g.: "There's no surprise—or challenge—in watching a sycophantic, misogynistic ignoramus like Burdette win out over the self-effacing, truth-loving Hutchinson." (*Chicago Tribune*; Aug. 5, 1997.)

The plural is *ignoramuses*. The form *ignorami* is a pseudo-learned blunder, since in Latin *ignoramus* is a verb and not one of the Latin nouns ending in *-us*. —**BG**

---

ignorance noun **1** *our* ***ignorance of*** *Islam* INCOMPREHENSION OF, unawareness of, unconsciousness of, unfamiliarity with, inexperience with, lack of knowledge about, lack of information about; *informal* cluelessness about. ANTONYMS understanding, familiarity.

2 *both ignorance and poverty contribute to the growing problem of forced child labor* LACK OF KNOWLEDGE, lack of education, unenlightenment, illiteracy; lack of intelligence, stupidity, foolishness, idiocy. ANTONYMS knowledge, education.

ignorant adjective **1** *the plight of these ignorant children should be an international concern* UNEDUCATED, unknowledgeable, untaught, unschooled, untutored, untrained, illiterate, unlettered, unlearned, unread, uninformed, unenlightened, benighted; inexperienced, unworldly, unsophisticated. ANTONYM educated.

2 *they were* ***ignorant of*** *working-class life* WITHOUT KNOWLEDGE OF, unaware of, unconscious of, oblivious to, incognizant of, unfamiliar with, unacquainted with, uninformed about, ill-informed about, unenlightened about, unconversant with, inexperienced in/with, naive about, green about; *informal* in the dark about, clueless about. ANTONYM knowledgeable.

THE RIGHT WORD

Someone who knows nothing about growing things might be called **ignorant** by a farmer who never went to high school but has spent his life in the fields. Although all of these adjectives refer to a lack of knowledge, *ignorant* refers to a lack of knowledge in general (*a foolish, ignorant person*) or to a lack of knowledge of some particular subject (*ignorant of the fine points of financial management*). A professor of art history might refer to someone who doesn't know how to look at a painting as **uneducated** or **untutored**, both of which refer to a lack of formal education in schools (*she was very bright but basically uneducated, and completely untutored in the fine arts*). Someone who cannot read or write is **illiterate**, a term that may also denote a failure to display civility or cultivated behavior (*the professor routinely referred to his students as illiterate louts*). Someone who is **unlettered** lacks a knowledge of fine literature (*a scientist who was highly trained but unlettered*); it also implies being able to read and write, but with no skill in either of these areas. **Unlearned** is similar to *ignorant* in that it refers to a lack of learning in general or in a specific subject (*an unlearned man who managed to become a millionaire*), but it does not carry the same negative connotations. **Uninformed** refers to a lack of definite information or data. For example, one can be highly intelligent and well educated but still *uninformed* about the latest developments in earthquake prediction.

---

ignore verb **1** *he ignored the customers* DISREGARD, take no notice of, pay no attention to, pay no heed to; turn a blind eye to, turn a deaf ear to, tune out. ANTONYM pay attention to. See note at NEGLECT.

2 *he was ignored by the journalists* SNUB, slight, spurn, shun, disdain, look right through, pass over, look past; *informal* give someone the brush-off, give someone the cold shoulder. ANTONYM acknowledge.

3 *doctors ignored her husband's instructions* SET ASIDE, pay no attention to, take no account of; break, contravene, fail to comply with, fail to observe, disregard, disobey, breach, defy, flout; *informal* pooh-pooh. ANTONYM obey.

ilk noun *the rap metal of Kid Rock and his ilk* TYPE, sort, class, category, group, set, breed, strain, bracket, genre, make, model, kind, brand, vintage, stamp, style, family, variety.

ill adjective **1** *she was feeling rather ill* UNWELL, sick, not (very) well, ailing, poorly, sickly, peaked, indisposed, infirm; out of sorts, not oneself, bad, off, in a bad way, far gone; bedridden, valetudinarian; queasy, nauseous, nauseated; *informal* under the weather, laid up, rotten, crummy, lousy, pukey, dizzy, woozy, green around the gills, like death warmed over. ANTONYMS well, healthy.

2 *the ill effects of smoking* HARMFUL, damaging, detrimental, deleterious, adverse, injurious, hurtful, destructive, pernicious, dangerous; unhealthy, unwholesome, poisonous, noxious; *literary* malefic, maleficent. ANTONYMS good, beneficial.

3 *ill feelings had divided them for years* HOSTILE, antagonistic, acrimonious, inimical, antipathetic; unfriendly, unsympathetic, unkind; resentful, spiteful, malicious, vindictive, malevolent, bitter. ANTONYMS friendly, warm.

4 *an ill omen* UNLUCKY, adverse, unfavorable, unfortunate, unpropitious, inauspicious, unpromising, infelicitous, ominous, sinister; *literary* direful. ANTONYM auspicious.

5 *ill manners* RUDE, discourteous, impolite, improper; impertinent, insolent, impudent, uncivil, disrespectful; *informal* ignorant. ANTONYMS good, polite.

6 *the ill management of the front office* BAD, poor, incompetent, unsatisfactory, inadequate, inexpert, deficient. ANTONYMS good, competent.

▸ noun 1 **(ills)** *the ills of society* PROBLEMS, troubles, evils, difficulties, misfortunes, trials, tribulations; worries, anxieties, concerns; *informal* headaches, hassles; *archaic* travails.

2 *he wished them no ill* HARM, hurt, injury, damage, pain, trouble, misfortune, suffering, distress.

3 **(ills)** *the body's ills* ILLNESSES, ailments, disorders, complaints, afflictions, sicknesses, diseases, maladies, infirmities.

▸ adverb 1 *such behavior ill becomes a chief executive* POORLY, badly, imperfectly. ANTONYM well.

2 *the look on her face boded ill for her opponents* UNFAVORABLY, adversely, badly, inauspiciously. ANTONYMS well, auspiciously.

3 *he can ill afford the loss of income* BARELY, scarcely, hardly, only just, (only) with difficulty, just possibly. ANTONYM easily.

4 *we are ill prepared for another flood* INADEQUATELY, unsatisfactorily, insufficiently, imperfectly, poorly, badly. ANTONYMS well, satisfactorily.

PHRASES: **ill at ease** *Ritchie was cautioned not to appear ill at ease in the courtroom* AWKWARD, uneasy, uncomfortable, embarrassed, self-conscious, out of place, inhibited, gauche; restless, restive, fidgety, discomfited, worried, anxious, on edge, edgy, nervous, tense, high-strung; *informal* twitchy, jittery, discombobulated, antsy. **speak ill of** *we never heard him once speak ill of his ex-wife* DENIGRATE, disparage, criticize, be critical of, speak badly of, be malicious about, blacken the name of, run down, insult, abuse, attack, revile, malign, vilify, slur; *informal* badmouth, dis, bitch about, slag; *formal* derogate; *rare* asperse.

ill-advised adjective *an ill-advised business venture* UNWISE, injudicious, misguided, imprudent, ill-considered, ill-judged, impolitic; foolhardy, foolish, harebrained, rash, reckless, irresponsible; *informal* crazy, idiotic, crackpot, madcap. ANTONYMS wise, judicious.

ill-bred adjective See ILL-MANNERED.

ill-conceived adjective *the atrium's ill-conceived design has received much criticism* BADLY PLANNED, badly thought out, harebrained, ill-advised, ill-considered, ill-judged, misjudged, injudicious, imprudent, unwise, hasty, rash.

ill-considered adjective See ILL-ADVISED.

ill-defined adjective *an ill-defined property line | the ill-defined messages in his art* VAGUE, indistinct, unclear, imprecise, nebulous, shadowy, obscure; blurred, fuzzy, hazy, woolly.

ill-disposed adjective *the court may be* ***ill-disposed to*** *foreign companies* HOSTILE TO, antagonistic to, unfriendly to, unsympathetic to, antipathetic to, inimical to, unfavorable to, adverse to, averse to, at odds with; *informal* anti, down on. ANTONYM friendly.

illegal adjective *illegal campaign contributions* UNLAWFUL, illicit, illegitimate, criminal, felonious; unlicensed, unauthorized, unsanctioned; outlawed, banned, forbidden, prohibited, proscribed, taboo; contraband, black-market, bootleg; *Law* malfeasant; *informal* crooked, shady, sketchy. ANTONYMS lawful, legitimate.

illegible adjective *nearly a billion prescriptions are rechecked each year because of physicians' illegible handwriting* UNREADABLE, indecipherable, unintelligible, incomprehensible, hieroglyphic; scrawled, scribbled, crabbed, cramped.

illegitimate adjective 1 *illegitimate share trading* ILLEGAL, unlawful, illicit, criminal, felonious; unlicensed, unauthorized, unsanctioned; prohibited, outlawed, banned, forbidden, proscribed; fraudulent, corrupt, dishonest; *Law* malfeasant; *informal* crooked, shady. ANTONYMS legal, lawful.

2 *dated her illegitimate children* BORN OUT OF WEDLOCK, bastard, unfathered; *archaic* natural, misbegotten; **(illegitimate child)** love child. ANTONYM legitimate.

ill-fated adjective *an ill-fated rebellion* DOOMED, blighted, damned, cursed, accursed, ill-starred, unlucky, hapless, jinxed; disastrous, unfortunate; *literary* star-crossed.

ill-favored adjective *he was particularly ill-favored after a night of drunken debauchery* UNATTRACTIVE, plain, ugly, homely, unprepossessing, displeasing; *informal* not much to look at. ANTONYM attractive.

ill humor noun See IRRITABILITY.

ill-humored adjective *oddly enough, the ill-humored Dr. Lowe was one of the most popular instructors* BAD-TEMPERED, ill-tempered, short-tempered, in a (bad) mood, cross; irritable, irascible, sullen, tetchy, testy, crotchety, touchy, cantankerous, curmudgeonly, peevish, fractious, waspish, prickly, pettish; grumpy, grouchy, crabbed, crabby, splenetic, dyspeptic, choleric; *informal* snappish, on a short fuse, soreheaded, cranky, ornery. ANTONYM amiable.

illiberal adjective *we're hoping they will withdraw the most illiberal and intrusive of these measures* INTOLERANT, narrow-minded, unenlightened, conservative, reactionary; fundamentalist, puritanical; undemocratic, authoritarian, repressive, totalitarian, despotic, tyrannical, oppressive, draconian, fascist. ANTONYMS tolerant, progressive.

illicit adjective 1 *illicit drugs* ILLEGAL, unlawful, illegitimate, criminal, felonious; outlawed, banned, forbidden, prohibited, proscribed; unlicensed, unauthorized, unsanctioned; contraband, black-market, bootleg; *Law* malfeasant. ANTONYMS lawful, legal.

2 *an illicit love affair* TABOO, forbidden, impermissible, unacceptable, adulterous; secret, clandestine, furtive. ANTONYM aboveboard.

illimitable adjective See LIMITLESS.

illiteracy noun **1** *for these villagers, poverty and illiteracy go hand in hand* INABILITY TO READ OR WRITE.

2 *technological illiteracy* IGNORANCE, unawareness, inexperience, unenlightenment, lack of knowledge, lack of education; *informal* cluelessness; *literary* nescience.

illiterate adjective **1** *an illiterate peasant* UNABLE TO READ OR WRITE, unlettered.

2 *too many voters are politically illiterate* IGNORANT, unknowledgeable, unenlightened, uneducated, unschooled, untaught, untutored, untrained, uninstructed, uninformed, unread, unlearned; *informal* clueless; *literary* nescient. See note at IGNORANT.

ill-judged adjective See ILL-ADVISED.

ill-mannered adjective *we never encountered the ill-mannered locals you had warned us about* BAD-MANNERED, discourteous, rude, impolite, uncivil, abusive, disagreeable; insolent, impertinent, impudent, cheeky, presumptuous, audacious, disrespectful; badly behaved, ill-behaved, boorish, loutish, oafish, uncouth, uncivilized, unmannered, ill-bred, vulgar, crass; *informal* ignorant. See note at RUDE. ANTONYM polite.

ill-natured adjective *Cinderella's ill-natured stepsisters* MEAN, nasty, spiteful, malicious, disagreeable; poisonous, venomous, bitter; ill-tempered, bad-tempered, moody, irritable, irascible, surly, sullen, peevish, petulant, fractious, cross, crabbed, crabby, tetchy, testy, grouchy, waspish; *informal* bitchy. ANTONYMS good-natured, sweet.

illness noun *more than fifty students have been diagnosed with the same illness* SICKNESS, disease, ailment, complaint, disorder, malady, affliction, indisposition; ill health, poor health, infirmity; infection, virus; *informal* bug; *dated* contagion. ANTONYM good health.

illogical adjective *it is illogical to assume that there will never be a cure for Parkinson's disease* IRRATIONAL, unreasonable, unsound, unreasoned, unjustifiable, groundless, unfounded; incorrect, erroneous, invalid, spurious, faulty, flawed, fallacious, unscientific; specious, sophistic, casuistic; absurd, preposterous, untenable; *informal* full of holes, off the wall. ANTONYM logical.

ill-starred adjective See ILL-FATED.

ill-tempered adjective *retirement didn't suit Uncle Luke, who soon became sullen and ill-tempered* BAD-TEMPERED, short-tempered, quick-tempered, ill-humored, moody; in a (bad) mood, cross, irritable, irascible, tetchy, testy, crotchety, touchy, cantankerous, curmudgeonly, peevish, fractious, waspish, prickly, pettish; grumpy, grouchy, crabbed, crabby, disagreeable, splenetic, dyspeptic, choleric; *informal* snappish, snippy, short-fused, on a short fuse, soreheaded, cranky, ornery, bitchy.

ill-timed adjective *our ill-timed vacation landed us in the worst-hit area during the hurricane* UNTIMELY, mistimed, badly timed; premature, hasty; inconvenient, inopportune; inappropriate, unsuitable, malapropos; unfavorable, unfortunate. ANTONYMS timely, opportune.

ill-treated adjective *there is no telling how long these animals have been ill-treated* ABUSED, mistreated, beaten, molested, misused, oppressed; harmed, injured, damaged, manhandled; *informal* knocked around/about, roughed up.

illuminate verb **1** *the bundle was illuminated by the torch* LIGHT (UP), lighten, throw light on, brighten, shine on, irradiate; *literary* illumine, illume, enlighten. ANTONYM darken.

2 *the manuscripts were illuminated* DECORATE, illustrate, embellish, adorn, ornament.

3 *documents often illuminate people's thought processes* CLARIFY, elucidate, explain, reveal, shed light on, give insight into, demystify; exemplify, illustrate; *informal* spell out. ANTONYMS confuse, conceal.

illuminating adjective *the lectures have been interesting as well as illuminating* INFORMATIVE, enlightening, explanatory, instructive, instructional, edifying, helpful, educational, revealing; *informal* tell-all.

illumination noun **1** *a floodlight provided illumination* LIGHT, lighting, radiance, gleam, glow, glare; shining, gleaming, glowing; brilliance, luminescence; *literary* illumining, irradiance, lucency, lambency, effulgence, refulgence. ANTONYM darkness.

2 *the illumination of a manuscript* DECORATION, illustration, embellishment, adornment, ornamentation.

3 *these books give illumination on the subject* CLARIFICATION, elucidation, explanation, revelation, explication.

4 *it was an era of great illumination* ENLIGHTENMENT, insight, understanding, awareness; learning, education, edification. ANTONYM ignorance.

illusion noun **1** *he had destroyed her illusions* DELUSION, misapprehension, misconception, false impression; fantasy, fancy, dream, chimera; fool's paradise, self-deception.

2 *the lighting increases the illusion of depth* APPEARANCE, impression, semblance; misperception, false appearance; *rare* simulacrum.

3 *it's just an illusion* MIRAGE, hallucination, apparition, figment of the imagination, trick of the light, trompe l'oeil; deception, trick, smoke and mirrors.

4 *Copperfield's amazing illusions* (MAGIC) TRICK, conjuring trick; **(illusions)** magic, conjuring, sleight of hand, legerdemain.

illusory adjective *the comfort these theories give is illusory* DELUSORY, delusive; illusionary, imagined, imaginary, fanciful, fancied, unreal, chimerical; sham, false, fallacious, fake, bogus, mistaken, erroneous, misguided, untrue; *informal* all in one's mind. See note at OSTENSIBLE. ANTONYM genuine.

illustrate verb **1** *the photographs that illustrate the book* DECORATE, adorn, ornament, accompany, embellish; add pictures/drawings to, provide artwork for.

2 *this can be illustrated through a brief example* EXPLAIN, explicate, elucidate, clarify, make plain, demonstrate, show, emphasize; *informal* get across.

3 *his sense of humor was illustrated by his screen saver* EXEMPLIFY, typify, epitomize, show, demonstrate, display, represent, encapsulate.

illustrated adjective *an illustrated collection of poems* WITH ILLUSTRATIONS, with pictures, with drawings, pictorial.

illustration noun **1** *the illustrations in children's books*

PICTURE, drawing, sketch, figure, image, plate, print, artwork; visual aid.

2 *by way of illustration* EXEMPLIFICATION, demonstration, showing; example, typical case, case in point, object lesson, analogy.

illustrative adjective *the parables are wonderfully illustrative* EXEMPLIFYING, explanatory, elucidative, explicative, expository, exegetical; demonstrative, descriptive, representative, indicative, emblematic, symbolic, typical; *rare* evincive.

illustrious adjective *the book falls short of its illustrious cinematic predecessor* EMINENT, distinguished, acclaimed, notable, noteworthy, prominent, preeminent, foremost, leading, important, influential; renowned, famous, famed, well-known, celebrated, legendary; esteemed, honored, respected, venerable, august, highly regarded, well-thought-of, of distinction; brilliant, glorious, stellar. ANTONYMS lackluster, unknown.

ill will noun *the ill will between the two families predates anyone's memory* ANIMOSITY, hostility, enmity, acrimony, animus, hatred, hate, loathing, antipathy; ill feeling, bad feeling, bad blood, antagonism, unfriendliness, dislike; spite, spitefulness, resentment, hard feelings, bitterness, malice, rancor; *informal* grudge, friction. ANTONYM goodwill.

image noun **1** *an image of St. Bartholomew* LIKENESS, resemblance; depiction, portrayal, representation; statue, statuette, sculpture, bust, effigy; painting, picture, portrait, drawing, sketch.

2 *images of the planet Neptune* PICTURE, photograph, snapshot, photo.

3 *he contemplated his image in the mirror* REFLECTION, mirror image, likeness.

4 *the image of this country as democratic* CONCEPTION, impression, idea, perception, notion; mental picture, vision; character, reputation; appearance, semblance. See note at EMBLEM.

5 *biblical images* SIMILE, metaphor, metonymy; figure of speech, trope, turn of phrase; imagery.

6 *his heartthrob image* PUBLIC PERCEPTION, persona, profile, reputation, stature, standing; face, front, facade, mask, guise.

7 *I'm the image of my grandfather* DOUBLE, living image, look-alike, clone, copy, twin, duplicate, exact likeness, mirror image, doppelgänger; *informal* spitting image, dead ringer, carbon copy; *archaic* similitude.

8 *a graven image* IDOL, icon, fetish, totem.

▸ verb *she imaged imposing castles* ENVISAGE, envision, imagine, picture, see in one's mind's eye.

imagery noun See IMAGE sense 5.

imaginable adjective *they did everything imaginable to save the farm* THINKABLE, conceivable, supposable, believable, credible, creditable; possible, plausible, feasible, tenable, within reason, under the sun.

imaginary adjective *his imaginary friends* UNREAL, nonexistent, fictional, fictitious, pretend, make-believe, mythical, mythological, fabulous, fanciful, storybook, fantastic; made-up, dreamed-up, invented, concocted, fancied; illusory, illusive, a figment of one's imagination, *archaic* visionary. ANTONYMS real, actual.

imagination noun **1** *a vivid imagination* CREATIVE POWER, fancy, vision; *informal* mind's eye.

2 *you need imagination in dealing with these problems* CREATIVITY, imaginativeness, creativeness; vision, inspiration, inventiveness, invention, resourcefulness, ingenuity; originality, innovation, innovativeness.

3 *the album captured the public's imagination* INTEREST, fascination, attention, passion, curiosity.

imaginative adjective *imaginative writers | an imaginative solution* CREATIVE, visionary, inspired, inventive, resourceful, ingenious; original, innovative, innovatory, unorthodox, unconventional; fanciful, whimsical, fantastic; *informal* offbeat, off the wall, zany. See note at CREATIVE.

imagine verb **1** *imagine sitting through five hours of steady air turbulence* VISUALIZE, envisage, envision, picture, see in the mind's eye; dream up, think up/of, conjure up, conceive, conceptualize; *formal* ideate.

2 *I imagine he was at home* ASSUME, presume, expect, take it, presuppose; suppose, think (it likely), dare say, surmise, believe, be of the view, figure; *informal* guess, reckon; *formal* opine.

imbalance noun *China now has the greatest gender imbalance in the world* DISPARITY, variance, variation, lack of harmony; disproportion, lopsidedness, unevenness, inequality; gulf, breach, gap.

imbecile noun See FOOL noun sense 1.

imbed verb See EMBED.

imbibe verb *formal* **1** *they'd imbibed too much whiskey* DRINK, consume, quaff, guzzle, gulp (down); *informal* knock back, down, swill, chug.

2 *he had imbibed liberally* DRINK (ALCOHOL), take strong drink, tipple; *informal* booze, knock a few back, hit the bottle, bend one's elbow.

3 *imbibing local history* ASSIMILATE, absorb, soak up, take in, drink in, digest, learn, acquire, grasp, pick up, familiarize oneself with.

imbroglio noun *the company may not survive another legal imbroglio* COMPLICATED SITUATION, complication, problem, difficulty, predicament, trouble, confusion, quandary, entanglement, muddle, mess, quagmire, morass, sticky situation; *informal* bind, jam, pickle, fix, corner, hole, scrape.

imbue verb *the painting has become deeply imbued with the idea of Basque separatism* PERMEATE, saturate, diffuse, suffuse, pervade, bathe, drench, steep; impregnate, inject, inculcate, ingrain, instill, invest, inspire, breathe; fill.

imitate verb **1** *other artists have imitated her style* EMULATE, copy, model oneself on, follow, echo, parrot; *informal* rip off, knock off, pirate.

2 *he imitated Richard Nixon* MIMIC, do an impression of, impersonate, ape; parody, caricature, burlesque, travesty; *informal* take off, send up, make like, mock; *formal* personate.

THE RIGHT WORD

A young girl might **imitate** her mother by answering the phone in exactly the same tone of voice, while a teenager who deliberately *imitates* the way her mother talks for the purpose of irritating her would more accurately be said to **mimic** her. *Imitate* implies following something as an example or model (*he imitated the playing style of his music teacher*), while *mimic* suggests imitating someone's mannerisms for fun or ridicule (*they liked to mimic the teacher's southern drawl*). To **copy** is to imitate or reproduce something as closely as possible (*he copied the style of dress and speech used by the other gang members*). When someone assumes another person's appearance or mannerisms, sometimes for the purpose of perpetrating a fraud, he or she is said to **impersonate** (*arrested for impersonating a police officer; a comedian well known for impersonating political figures*). **Ape** and **mock** both imply an unflattering imitation. Someone who mimics in a contemptuous way is said to *ape* (*he entertained everyone in the office by aping the boss's phone conversations with his wife*), while someone who imitates with the intention of belittling or irritating is said to *mock* (*the students openly mocked their teacher's attempt to have a serious discussion about sex*).

---

imitation noun **1** *an imitation of a sailor's hat* COPY, simulation, reproduction, replica; counterfeit, forgery, rip off.

2 *learning by imitation* EMULATION, copying, echoing, parroting.

3 *a perfect imitation of Elvis* IMPERSONATION, impression, parody, mockery, caricature, burlesque, travesty, lampoon, pastiche; mimicry, mimicking, imitating, aping; *informal* send-up, takeoff, spoof.

▸ adjective *imitation ivory* ARTIFICIAL, synthetic, simulated, man-made, manufactured, ersatz, substitute; mock, sham, fake, faux, bogus, knockoff, pseudo, phony. ANTONYMS real, genuine.

imitative adjective **1** *imitative crime* SIMILAR, like, mimicking; *informal* copycat.

2 *I found the film empty and imitative* DERIVATIVE, unoriginal, unimaginative, uninspired, uninventive, plagiarized, plagiaristic, slavish; clichéd, hackneyed, stale, trite, banal, rehashed; *informal* cribbed, old hat. ANTONYM original.

imitator noun **1** *she has many imitators* COPIER, emulator, follower, mimic, plagiarist, ape, parrot; *informal* copycat.

2 *an imitator of famous torch singers.* See IMPERSONATOR.

immaculate adjective **1** *an immaculate white shirt* CLEAN, spotless, ultraclean, pristine, unsoiled, unstained, unsullied; shining, shiny, gleaming; neat, tidy, spick-and-span; *informal* squeaky clean, as clean as a whistle. ANTONYM dirty.

2 *a guitar in immaculate condition* PERFECT, pristine, mint, as good as new; flawless, faultless, unblemished, unspoiled, undamaged; excellent, impeccable; *informal* tip-top, A1. ANTONYMS worn, damaged.

3 *his immaculate service record* UNBLEMISHED, spotless, impeccable, unsullied, undefiled, untarnished, stainless; pure, virtuous, incorrupt, above reproach; *informal* squeaky clean, as pure as the driven snow. ANTONYMS defiled, reproachable.

immanent adjective See INHERENT. See also note at EMINENT.

immaterial adjective **1** *the difference in our ages was immaterial* IRRELEVANT, unimportant, inconsequential, insignificant, of no matter/consequence, of little account, beside the point, neither here nor there. ANTONYMS significant, important.

2 *the immaterial soul* INTANGIBLE, incorporeal, bodiless, disembodied, impalpable, ethereal, insubstantial, metaphysical; spiritual, unearthly, supernatural. ANTONYMS tangible, physical.

immature adjective **1** *an immature Stilton cheese* UNRIPE, not mature, premature, unmellowed; undeveloped, unformed, unfinished, raw, embryonic. ANTONYM ripe.

2 *an extremely immature girl* CHILDISH, babyish, infantile, juvenile, adolescent, puerile, sophomoric, jejune, callow, green, tender, young, inexperienced, unsophisticated, unworldly, naive; *informal* wet behind the ears. See note at YOUTHFUL. ANTONYMS mature, worldly.

immeasurable adjective *the immeasurable riches provided to us by nature* INCALCULABLE, inestimable, innumerable, untold; limitless, boundless, unbounded, unlimited, illimitable, infinite, countless, never-ending, interminable, endless, inexhaustible; vast, immense, extensive, great, abundant; *informal* no end of; *literary* myriad.

immediate adjective **1** *the UN called for immediate action* INSTANT, instantaneous, swift, prompt, fast, speedy, rapid, brisk, quick, expeditious; sudden, hurried, hasty, precipitate; *informal* snappy. ANTONYMS delayed, gradual.

2 *their immediate concerns* CURRENT, present, existing, actual; urgent, pressing, exigent. ANTONYMS past, future.

3 *the immediate past* RECENT, not long past, just gone, latest. ANTONYM remote.

4 *our immediate neighbors* NEAREST, near, close, closest, next-door; adjacent, adjoining, contiguous. ANTONYM distant.

5 *the immediate cause of death* DIRECT, primary. ANTONYM indirect.

immediately adverb **1** *it was necessary to make a decision immediately* STRAIGHTAWAY, at once, right away, instantly, now, directly, promptly, forthwith, this/that (very) minute, this/that instant, there and then, then and there, on the spot, here and now, without delay, without further ado, posthaste; quickly, as fast as possible, speedily, as soon as possible; *informal* ASAP, pronto, double-quick, on the double, PDQ, in/like a flash, like a shot, tout de suite; *humorous* toot sweet; *archaic* forthright.

2 *I sat immediately behind him* DIRECTLY, right, exactly, precisely, squarely, just, dead; *informal* smack dab.

immemorial adjective *immemorial customs* ANCIENT, (very) old, age-old, antediluvian, timeless, archaic, venerable, long-standing, timeworn, time-honored, tried and true; traditional; *literary* of yore.

immense adjective *an immense brick church | immense jars of mayonnaise* HUGE, vast, massive, enormous, gigantic, colossal, great, very large/big, monumental, towering, tremendous; giant, elephantine, monstrous, mammoth, titanic, king-size(d), economy-size(d); *informal* mega, monster, whopping, humongous, jumbo, astronomical, cosmic, ginormous, Brobdingnagian. ANTONYM tiny.

immensely adverb *it was an immensely difficult decision* EXTREMELY, very, exceedingly, exceptionally, extraordinarily, tremendously, hugely, singularly, distinctly, outstandingly, uncommonly, unusually, decidedly, particularly, eminently, supremely, highly, remarkably, really, truly, mightily, thoroughly, in the extreme; *informal* terrifically, awfully, fearfully, terribly, devilishly, frightfully, seriously, mega, damn, damned, ever so, real, mighty, powerful, awful, darned; *informal, dated* devilish; *archaic* exceeding. ANTONYM slightly.

immerse verb **1** *litmus paper turns red on being immersed in acid* SUBMERGE, dip, dunk, duck, sink, plunge; soak, drench, saturate, marinate, wet, douse, souse, steep.

2 *Elliot was* ***immersed in*** *his work* ABSORB IN, engross in, occupy by/with, engage in, involve in/with, bury in, swamp with, lose (oneself) in; busy with, preoccupy with, fixate on/upon.

immigrant noun *they will convene to discuss the civil liberties of immigrants* NEWCOMER, settler, migrant, emigrant; nonnative, foreigner, alien, outsider; expatriate; *informal* expat. ANTONYM native.

imminent adjective *a cease-fire was imminent* IMPENDING, close (at hand), near, (fast) approaching, coming, forthcoming, on the way, in the offing, in the pipeline, on the horizon, in the air, just around the corner, coming down the pike, expected, anticipated, brewing, looming, threatening, menacing; *informal* in the cards. See note at EMINENT.

immobile adjective **1** *she sat immobile for a long time* MOTIONLESS, without moving, still, stock-still, static, stationary; rooted to the spot, rigid, frozen, transfixed, like a statue, not moving a muscle. ANTONYM moving.

2 *I dreaded being immobile* UNABLE TO MOVE, immobilized; paralyzed, crippled. ANTONYM mobile.

immobilize verb *the virus has immobilized the House's internal communication system | it is important to immobilize the injured part of the body* PUT OUT OF ACTION, disable, make inoperative, inactivate, deactivate, paralyze, freeze, cripple; bring to a standstill, halt, stop; restrain, stabilize.

immoderate adjective *immoderate spending* EXCESSIVE, heavy, intemperate, unrestrained, unrestricted, uncontrolled, unlimited, unbridled, uncurbed, overindulgent, imprudent, reckless; undue, inordinate, unreasonable, unjustified, unwarranted, uncalled for, outrageous; extravagant, lavish, exorbitant, prodigal, profligate, wanton, dissipated.

immodest adjective *the deputy minister complained that the dance was too immodest for the memorial ceremony* INDECOROUS, improper, indecent, indelicate, immoral; forward, bold, brazen, impudent, shameless, loose, wanton; *informal* fresh, cheeky, saucy, brassy.

immoral adjective *the legality of the fugitive slave laws does not alter the fact that they were deeply immoral* UNETHICAL, bad, morally wrong, wrongful, wicked, evil, foul, unprincipled, unscrupulous, dishonorable, dishonest, unconscionable, iniquitous, disreputable, corrupt, depraved, vile, villainous, nefarious, base, miscreant; sinful, godless, impure, unchaste, unvirtuous, shameless, degenerate, debased, debauched, dissolute, reprobate, lewd, obscene, perverse, perverted; licentious, wanton, promiscuous, loose; *informal* shady, lowdown, crooked, sleazy. ANTONYMS ethical, chaste.

EASILY CONFUSED WORDS **immoral, amoral**

Immoral means 'failing to adhere to moral standards.' **Amoral** means 'without, or not concerned with, moral standards.' An **immoral** person commits acts that violate society's moral norms. An **amoral** person has no understanding of these norms, or no sense of right and wrong. Whereas **amoral** may be simply descriptive, **immoral** is always judgmental.

immorality noun *he charged that the overseas press was prone to lies and immorality* WICKEDNESS, immoral behavior, badness, evil, vileness, corruption, dishonesty, dishonorableness; sinfulness, ungodliness, unchastity, sin, depravity, villainy, vice, degeneracy, debauchery, dissolution, perversion, lewdness, obscenity, wantonness, promiscuity; *informal* shadiness, crookedness; *formal* turpitude.

immortal adjective **1** *our souls are immortal* UNDYING, deathless, eternal, everlasting, never-ending, endless, lasting, enduring, ceaseless; imperishable, indestructible, inextinguishable, immutable, perpetual, permanent, unfading.

2 *an immortal children's classic* TIMELESS, perennial, classic, time-honored, enduring; famous, famed, renowned, legendary, great, eminent, outstanding, acclaimed, celebrated.

▸ noun **1** *Greek temples of the immortals* GOD, GODDESS, deity, divine being, supreme being, divinity.

2 *one of the immortals of literature* GREAT, hero, legend, god, celebrity, star, Olympian.

immortality noun **1** *the immortality of the gods* ETERNAL LIFE, everlasting life, deathlessness; indestructibility, imperishability.

2 *the book has achieved immortality* TIMELESSNESS, legendary status, lasting fame/renown.

immortalize verb *the battle was immortalized by Pushkin* COMMEMORATE, memorialize, eternalize; celebrate, deify, exalt, glorify; eulogize, pay tribute to, honor, salute.

immovable adjective **1** *lock your bike to something immovable* FIXED, secure, stable, moored, anchored, rooted, braced, set firm, set fast; stuck, jammed, stiff, unbudgeable, four-square. ANTONYM mobile.

2 *there he was, silent and immovable* MOTIONLESS, unmoving, immobile, stationary, still, stock-still, not moving a muscle, rooted to the spot; transfixed, paralyzed, frozen. ANTONYMS moving, in motion.

3 *she was immovable in her loyalties* STEADFAST, unwavering, unswerving, resolute, determined, firm, unshakable, adamant, unfailing, dogged, tenacious, inflexible, unyielding, unbending, uncompromising, obdurate, obstinate, iron-willed; *informal* rock-steady, diehard. ANTONYMS fickle, unsure.

immune adjective *they are* ***immune to*** *hepatitis B | this company seems to be* ***immune to*** *fluctuations in the economy* RESISTANT TO, not subject to, not liable to, unsusceptible to, not vulnerable to; protected from, safe from, secure against, not in danger of; impervious to, invulnerable to, unaffected by. ANTONYM susceptible.

immunity noun **1** *an* ***immunity to*** *malaria* RESISTANCE TO, nonsusceptibility to; ability to fight off, protection against, defenses against; immunization against, inoculation against.

2 *immunity from prosecution* EXEMPTION, exception, freedom, release, dispensation, amnesty.

3 *diplomatic immunity* INDEMNITY, privilege, prerogative, right, liberty, license; legal exemption, impunity, protection.

immunize verb *have these children been* ***immunized against*** *rubella?* VACCINATE AGAINST, inoculate against; protect from, safeguard against.

immure verb *those immured in the Gulag had horrific stories to tell* CONFINE, intern, shut up, lock up, incarcerate, imprison, jail, cage, put behind bars, put under lock and key, hold captive, hold prisoner; detain, hold.

immutable adjective *the subtext of the liturgy had always been God's immutable power* FIXED, set, rigid, inflexible, permanent, established, carved in stone; unchanging, unchanged, unvarying, unvaried, static, constant, lasting, enduring, steadfast. ANTONYM variable.

imp noun **1** *our neighborhood imps are, for the most part, harmless* RASCAL, monkey, devil, troublemaker, urchin; *informal* scamp, brat, monster, horror, terror, tyke, whippersnapper, hellion, varmint, rapscallion; *archaic* scapegrace.

2 *this trickster of Indian myth is an inscrutable imp possessed of satanic charisma* HOBGOBLIN, goblin, elf, sprite, pixie, brownie, fairy, puck; demon, little devil; *archaic* bugbear.

impact noun **1** *the force of the impact* COLLISION, crash, smash, bump, bang, knock.

2 *the job losses will have a major impact* EFFECT, influence, significance, meaning; consequences, repercussions, ramifications, reverberations.

▸ verb **1** *a comet impacted the earth sixty million years ago* CRASH INTO, smash into, collide with, hit, strike, ram, smack into, bang into, slam into.

2 *high interest rates have impacted retail spending* AFFECT, influence, have an effect on, make an impression on; hit, touch, change, alter, modify, transform, shape.

USAGE NOTE **impact**

Impact has traditionally been only a noun. In recent years, however, it has undergone a semantic shift that has allowed it to act as a verb. Such use has become widespread (and also widely condemned by stylists)—e.g.: "The researchers concluded that this low level of intensity may have impacted [read *affected*] the results." (*Tampa Tribune*; July 17, 1997.) This use of the word would be perfectly acceptable if *impact* were performing any function not as ably performed by *affect* or *influence*. If *affect* as a verb is not sufficiently straightforward in context, then the careful writer might use *have an impact on*, which, though longer, is probably better than the jarring impact of *impacted*. Reserve *impact* for noun uses and *impacted* for wisdom teeth.

Interestingly, *impact* as a verb might have arisen partly in response to widespread diffidence about the spelling of *affect* (often confused with *effect*). **—BG**

impair verb *sagging eyelid skin can impair eyesight* HAVE A NEGATIVE EFFECT ON, damage, harm, diminish, reduce, weaken, lessen, decrease, impede, hinder, hobble; undermine, compromise; *formal* vitiate. ANTONYMS improve, enhance.

impaired adjective **1** *visually impaired* DISABLED, handicapped, incapacitated; *euphemistic* challenged, differently abled.

2 *driving while impaired* DRUNK, intoxicated, under the influence, inebriated; *informal* bombed, high, stoned, wasted, smashed, plastered, soused.

impairment noun See HANDICAP noun sense 1.

impale verb *her knife impaled the counter like a javelin* STICK, skewer, spear, spike, transfix, harpoon; pierce, stab, run through; *literary* transpierce.

impalpable adjective *his skin was sallow and his pulse impalpable | impalpable clouds* INTANGIBLE, insubstantial, incorporeal, immaterial; indefinable, elusive, imperceptible, undescribable.

impart verb **1** *she had news to impart* COMMUNICATE, pass on, convey, transmit, relay, relate, recount, tell, make known, make public, report, announce, proclaim, herald, spread, disseminate, circulate, promulgate, broadcast; disclose, reveal, divulge; *informal* let on about, blab, blurt.

2 *the picture imparts some color to the drab office* GIVE, bestow, confer, grant, lend, afford, provide, supply.

impartial adjective *can the United Nations be trusted as an impartial arbiter of world affairs?* UNBIASED, unprejudiced, neutral, nonpartisan, nondiscriminatory, disinterested, detached, dispassionate, objective, open-minded, equitable, evenhanded, fair, fair-minded, just; without favoritism, without fear or favor. ANTONYMS biased, partisan.

impassable adjective *the farm-to-market roads were impassable* UNPASSABLE, unnavigable, untraversable, im-

▸ ***impartial***
disinterested
objective
unbiased
unprejudiced
nonpartisan
nondiscriminatory
dispassionate
detached
uncommitted
tolerant
broad-minded
nonaligned
neutral
fair-minded
even-handed
indifferent
unemotional
stiff
unbending
narrow-minded
one-sided
subjective
unfair
inequitable
partial
partisan
blinkered
distorted
loaded
weighted
warped
twisted
skewed
intolerant
sectarian
chauvinistic
chauvinist
discriminatory
prejudiced
parti pris
bigoted
anti-Semitic
heterosexist
homophobic
sexist
racist
biased ◂

penetrable; closed, blocked, barricaded; dense, thick, blind.

impasse noun *an impasse in the peace talks poses new challenges* DEADLOCK, dead end, stalemate, standoff; standstill, halt, stoppage, stop; *informal* Catch-22.

impassioned adjective *an impassioned commentary about the state of American politics* EMOTIONAL, heartfelt, wholehearted, earnest, sincere, fervent, ardent, passionate, fervid, intense, burning; vehement, zealous, heated; *literary* perfervid.

impassive adjective *Woodgate sat with his arms folded and remained impassive* EXPRESSIONLESS, unexpressive, inexpressive, inscrutable, unreadable, blank, deadpan, poker-faced, straight-faced; stony, wooden, unresponsive, cold, unmoved, indifferent; serene, calm, peaceful, unruffled, dispassionate, cool, unemotional. ANTONYM expressive.

impatience noun **1** *he was shifting in his seat with impatience* RESTLESSNESS, restiveness, agitation, nervousness, anxiety; eagerness, keenness; *informal* jitteriness.

2 *a burst of impatience* IRRITABILITY, testiness, tetchiness, irascibility, querulousness, peevishness, petulance, frustration, exasperation, annoyance, pique.

impatient adjective **1** *Elaine grew impatient* RESTLESS, restive, agitated, nervous, anxious, tense, ill at ease, edgy, jumpy, keyed up; *informal* twitchy, jittery, uptight, high-strung. ANTONYMS calm, indifferent.

2 *they are impatient to get back home* ANXIOUS, eager, keen, yearning, longing, aching, agog; *informal* itching, dying, raring, gung-ho, straining at the leash. ANTONYM reluctant.

3 *why must you be so impatient with the children?* IRRITATED, annoyed, angry, testy, tetchy, snappy, cross, querulous, peevish, piqued, short-tempered; abrupt, curt, brusque, terse, short; *informal* peeved. ANTONYMS even-tempered, pleased.

impeach verb **1** *congressional moves to impeach the president* INDICT, charge, accuse, lay charges against, arraign, take to court, put on trial, prosecute.

2 *the headlines impeached their clean image* CHALLENGE, question, disparage, criticize, call into question, raise doubts about, cast aspersions on. ANTONYM confirm.

impeccable adjective *the lieutenant's record is impeccable* FLAWLESS, faultless, unblemished, spotless, immaculate, stainless, perfect, exemplary; sinless, irreproachable, blameless, guiltless; *informal* squeaky clean. ANTONYMS imperfect, sinful.

impecunious adjective *she left Evansville to escape the solicitations of her impecunious relatives* PENNILESS, poor, impoverished, indigent, insolvent, hard up, poverty-stricken, needy, destitute; in straitened circumstances, unable to make ends meet; *informal* (flat) broke, strapped (for cash); *formal* penurious. ANTONYM wealthy.

impede verb *your efforts to impede our progress will be unsuccessful* HINDER, obstruct, hamper, hold back/up, delay, interfere with, disrupt, retard, slow (down), hobble, cripple; block, check, stop, scupper, scuttle, thwart, frustrate, balk, foil, derail; *informal* stymie, throw a (monkey) wrench in the works of; *dated* cumber. See note at HINDER. ANTONYM facilitate.

impediment noun **1** *an impediment to economic improvement* HINDRANCE, obstruction, obstacle, barrier, bar, block, handicap, check, curb, restriction, limitation; setback, difficulty, snag, hitch, hurdle, stumbling block; *informal* fly in the ointment, hiccup, (monkey) wrench in the works, glitch; *archaic* cumber.

2 *a speech impediment* DEFECT; stammer, stutter, lisp.

impel verb **1** *financial difficulties impelled her to seek work* FORCE, compel, constrain, oblige, require, make, urge, exhort, press, pressurize, drive, push, spur, prod, goad, incite, prompt, persuade.

2 *vital energies impel him in unforeseen directions* PROPEL, drive, move, get going, get moving.

impending adjective *a smarter grid could warn of impending blackouts* IMMINENT, close (at hand), near, nearing, approaching, coming, forthcoming, upcoming, to come, on the way, about to happen, in store, in the offing, on the horizon, in the air/wind, brewing, looming, threatening, menacing; *informal* coming down the pike, in the cards.

impenetrable adjective **1** *impenetrable armor* IMPERVIOUS, impermeable, indestructible, solid, thick, unyielding; impregnable, inviolable, invulnerable, unassailable, unpierceable; *informal* bulletproof. ANTONYMS permeable, vulnerable.

2 *a dark, impenetrable forest* IMPASSABLE, unpassable, inaccessible, unnavigable, untraversable; dense, thick, overgrown; *archaic* thickset. ANTONYMS sparse, accessible.

3 *an impenetrable clique* EXCLUSIVE, closed, secretive, secret, private; restrictive, restricted, limited. ANTONYM open.

4 *impenetrable statistics* INCOMPREHENSIBLE, unfathomable, inexplicable, unintelligible, inscrutable, unclear, baffling, bewildering, puzzling, perplexing, enigmatic, cryptic, confusing, abstruse, opaque; complex, complicated, difficult. ANTONYM clear.

impenitent adjective *the hardness of their impenitent hearts* UNREPENTANT, unrepenting, uncontrite, remorseless, unashamed, unapologetic, unabashed.

imperative adjective **1** *it is imperative that you find him* VITALLY IMPORTANT, of vital importance, all-important, vital, crucial, critical, essential, necessary, indispensable, urgent; compulsory, obligatory, mandatory. ANTONYMS unimportant, optional.

2 *the imperative note in her voice* PEREMPTORY, commanding, imperious, authoritative, masterful, dictatorial, magisterial, assertive, firm, insistent. ANTONYM submissive.

imperceptible adjective *the imperceptible shift of constellations | an imperceptible rustle of cellophane* UNNOTICEABLE, undetectable, indistinguishable, indiscernible, invisible, inaudible, inappreciable, impalpable, unobtrusive, inconspicuous, unseen; slight, small, tiny, minute, microscopic, infinitesimal, subtle, faint, fine, negligible, inconsequential; indistinct, unclear, obscure, vague, indefinite, hard to make out. ANTONYMS noticeable, obvious.

imperfect adjective **1** *the goods were returned as imperfect* FAULTY, flawed, defective, shoddy, unsound, inferior, second-rate, below standard, substandard; damaged, blemished, torn, broken, cracked, scratched; *informal* not up to snuff, not up to scratch, crummy, lousy. ANTONYM flawless.

2 *an imperfect form of the manuscript* INCOMPLETE, unfinished, half-done; unpolished, unrefined, rough. ANTONYM complete

3 *she spoke imperfect Arabic* BROKEN, faltering, halting, hesitant, rudimentary, limited. ANTONYMS flawless, fluent.

imperfection noun **1** *the glass is free from imperfections* DEFECT, fault, flaw, deformity, discoloration, disfigurement; crack, scratch, chip, nick, pit, dent; blemish, stain, spot, mark, streak. ANTONYM strength.

2 *he was aware of his imperfections* FLAW, fault, failing, deficiency, weakness, vice, weak point, fallibility, shortcoming, foible, inadequacy, frailty, limitation, chink in one's armor. ANTONYM perfection.

3 *the imperfection of the fossil record* INCOMPLETENESS, patchiness, deficiency; roughness, crudeness. ANTONYM completeness.

imperial adjective **1** *imperial banners* ROYAL, regal, monarchical, sovereign, kingly, queenly, princely.

2 *her imperial bearing* MAJESTIC, grand, august, dignified, proud, stately, noble, aristocratic, regal; magnificent, imposing, impressive.

3 *our customers thought we were imperial.* See IMPERIOUS.

imperil verb *allowing access to the detainee would imperil national security* ENDANGER, jeopardize, risk, put in danger, put in jeopardy, expose to danger, hazard; threaten, pose a threat to; *archaic* peril.

imperious adjective *Black tells stories of imperious judges and duplicitous witnesses* PEREMPTORY, high-handed, commanding, imperial, overbearing, overweening, domineering, authoritarian, dictatorial, autocratic, authoritative, lordly, assertive, bossy, arrogant, haughty, presumptuous; *informal* pushy, high and mighty.

imperishable adjective *it was the movie version that gave the novelist imperishable fame* ENDURING, everlasting, undying, deathless, immortal, perennial, long-lasting; indestructible, inextinguishable, ineradicable, unfading, permanent, never-ending, never dying, durable; *literary* sempiternal, perdurable.

impermanent adjective *the methods they're proposing for reforestation are risky and impermanent* TEMPORARY, transient, transitory, passing, fleeting, momentary, ephemeral, fugitive; short-lived, brief, here today and gone tomorrow; *literary* evanescent.

impermeable adjective *an impermeable vault* WATERTIGHT, waterproof, damp-proof, airtight, (hermetically) sealed, vacuum-packed, zip-locked.

impersonal adjective **1** *an impersonal judgment* NEUTRAL, unbiased, nonpartisan, unprejudiced, objective, detached, disinterested, dispassionate, without favoritism. ANTONYM biased.

2 *their impersonal relationships extended even to their own wives and children* ALOOF, distant, remote, reserved, withdrawn, unemotional, unsentimental, dispassionate, cold, cool, indifferent, unconcerned; formal, stiff, businesslike; *informal* starchy, standoffish, wooden. ANTONYMS emotional, warm.

impersonate verb *impersonating the boss during a meeting was not your smartest move* IMITATE, mimic, do an impression of, ape, copy, parrot; parody, caricature, burlesque, travesty, satirize, lampoon; masquerade as, pose as, pass oneself off as; *informal* take off, send up, make like; *formal* personate. See note at IMITATE.

impersonation noun *the president seemed genuinely amused by the impersonations of the first family* IMPRESSION, imitation; parody, caricature, burlesque, travesty, lampoon, pastiche; *informal* takeoff, send-up; *formal* personation.

impersonator noun *a dozen skydiving Elvis impersonators* IMITATOR, impressionist, mimic; parodist, lampooner.

impertinence noun *I'll refrain from answering with the impertinence your question deserves* RUDENESS, insolence, impoliteness, bad manners, discourtesy, disrespect, incivility; impudence, cheek, cheekiness, audacity, presumption, temerity, effrontery, nerve, gall, boldness, cockiness, brazenness; *informal* brass, sauce, sass, sassiness, chutzpah, lip, back talk, guff; *archaic* assumption.

impertinent adjective *impertinent remarks* RUDE, insolent, impolite, ill-mannered, bad-mannered, uncivil, discourteous, disrespectful; impudent, cheeky, audacious, bold, brazen, brash, presumptuous, forward; tactless, undiplomatic; *informal* saucy, pert, sassy, smart-alecky. ANTONYM polite.

THE RIGHT WORD

All of these adjectives mean exceeding the bounds of propriety; the easiest way to distinguish **impertinent** from the others is to think of its root: *impertinent* behavior is not pertinent—in other words, it is inappropriate or out of place. The *impertinent* individual has a tendency to be rude or presumptuous toward those who are entitled to deference or respect (*it was an impertinent question to ask a woman who had just lost her husband*). The **intrusive** person is unduly curious about other people's affairs (*her constant questions about the state of their marriage were intrusive and unwelcome*), while **obtrusive** implies objectionable actions rather than an objectionable disposition. The *obtrusive* person has a tendency to thrust himself or herself into a position where he or she is conspicuous and apt to do more harm than good (*they tried to keep him out of the meeting because his presence would be obtrusive*). To be **meddlesome** is to have a prying or inquisitive nature and a tendency to interfere in an annoying way in other people's affairs (*a meddlesome neighbor*). **Impudent** and **insolent** are much stronger words for inappropriate behavior. Young people are often accused of being *impudent*, which means to be *impertinent* in a bold and shameless way (*an impudent young man who had a lot to learn about tact*). Anyone who is guilty of insulting and contemptuously arrogant behavior might be called *insolent* (*he was so insolent to the arresting officer that he was handcuffed*).

imperturbable adjective *the guide dogs are trained to be imperturbable* SELF-POSSESSED, composed, calm, cool, and collected, coolheaded, self-controlled, serene, relaxed, unexcitable, even-tempered, placid, phlegmatic; unperturbed, unflustered, unruffled; *informal* unflappable, unfazed, nonplussed, laid-back; *rare* equanimous. ANTONYMS excitable, edgy.

impervious adjective **1** *he seemed* ***impervious to*** *the chill wind* UNAFFECTED BY, untouched by, immune to, invulnerable to, insusceptible to, resistant to, indifferent to, heedless of, insensible to, unconscious of, oblivious to; proof against.

2 *an impervious rain jacket* IMPERMEABLE, impenetrable, impregnable, waterproof, watertight, water-resistant, repellent; (hermetically) sealed, zip-locked. ANTONYM permeable.

impetuous adjective **1** *an impetuous decision* IMPULSIVE, rash, hasty, overhasty, reckless, heedless, careless, foolhardy, bullheaded, headstrong, incautious, imprudent, injudicious, ill-considered, unthought-out; spontaneous, impromptu, spur-of-the-moment, precipitate, precipitous, hurried, rushed; *informal* devil-may-care, harum-scarum, hotheaded. See note at TEMERITY. ANTONYMS considered, cautious.

2 *an impetuous flow of water* TORRENTIAL, powerful, forceful, vigorous, violent, raging, relentless, uncontrolled; rapid, fast, fast-flowing, swift. ANTONYM sluggish.

impetus noun **1** *the flywheel lost all its impetus* MOMENTUM, propulsion, impulsion, motive force, driving force, drive, thrust; energy, force, power, push, strength.

2 *the sales force were given fresh impetus* MOTIVATION, stimulus, incitement, incentive, inducement, inspiration, encouragement, boost, fillip, springboard; *informal* a shot in the arm.

impiety noun **1** *a world of impiety and immorality* GODLESSNESS, ungodliness, unholiness, irreligion, irreverence, sinfulness, sin, vice, transgression, wrongdoing, immorality, unrighteousness, blasphemy, sacrilege; apostasy, atheism, agnosticism, paganism, heathenism, nonbelief, unbelief. ANTONYM holiness.

2 *not even motherhood was immune to impiety* IRREVERENCE, disrespect, impertinence, insolence, mockery, derision. ANTONYM reverence.

impinge verb **1** *these issues* ***impinge on*** *all of us* AFFECT, have an effect on, touch, have a bearing on, influence, have/make an impact on, leave a mark on.

2 *the proposed highway would* ***impinge on*** *parkland* ENCROACH ON, intrude on, infringe (on), invade, trespass on, obtrude, cut through, interfere with; violate; *informal* horn in on.

impious adjective *the impious magistrate of the Sung dynasty* GODLESS, ungodly, unholy, irreligious, sinful, wicked, immoral, unrighteous, sacrilegious, heretical, profane, blasphemous, irreverent; apostate, atheistic, agnostic, pagan, heathen, faithless, nonbelieving, unbelieving, *rare* nullifidian.

impish adjective **1** *he takes an impish delight in shocking the press* MISCHIEVOUS, naughty, wicked, devilish, rascally, roguish, playful, sportive; mischief-making, full of mischief.

2 *an impish grin* ELFIN, elflike, pixieish, puckish; mischievous, roguish, sly.

implacable adjective *the computer hacker has become the new implacable foe* UNAPPEASABLE, unforgiving, unsparing; inexorable, intransigent, inflexible, unyielding, unbending, uncompromising, unrelenting, relentless, ruthless, remorseless, merciless, heartless, pitiless, cruel, hard, harsh, stern, tough, iron-fisted.

implant verb **1** *the microchip is implanted under the skin* INSERT, embed, bury, lodge, place; graft.

2 *he implanted the idea in my mind* INSTILL, inculcate, insinuate, introduce, inject, plant, sow, root, lodge.

▸ noun *a silicone implant* TRANSPLANT, graft, implantation, insert.

implausible adjective *a swift conclusion to the negotiations is implausible* | *another one of his implausible excuses* UNLIKELY, improbable, questionable, doubtful, debatable; unrealistic, unconvincing, far-fetched, incredible, unbelievable, unimaginable, inconceivable, fantastic, fanciful, ridiculous, absurd, preposterous, outrageous; *informal* hard to swallow, cock and bull. ANTONYM convincing.

implement noun *garden implements* TOOL, utensil, instrument, device, apparatus, gadget, contraption, appliance, machine, contrivance; *informal* gizmo; (**implements**) equipment, kit, tackle, accoutrements, paraphernalia. See note at TOOL.

▸ verb *the cost of implementing the new law* EXECUTE, apply, put into effect, put into action, put into practice, carry out/through, perform, enact; fulfill, discharge, accomplish, bring about, achieve, realize, actualize, phase in; *formal* effectuate.

implicate verb **1** *he had been implicated in a financial scandal* INCRIMINATE, compromise; involve, connect, link, embroil, enmesh, ensnare, entangle; *archaic* inculpate; *informal* finger.

2 *viruses are* ***implicated in*** *the development of cancer* INVOLVE IN, concern with, associate with, connect to/with.

implication noun **1** *he was smarting at their implication* SUGGESTION, insinuation, innuendo, hint, intimation, imputation.

2 *important political implications* CONSEQUENCE, result, ramification, repercussion, reverberation, effect, significance.

3 *his implication in the murder case* INCRIMINATION, involvement, connection, entanglement, association; *dated* inculpation.

implicit adjective **1** *implicit assumptions* IMPLIED, hinted at, suggested, insinuated; unspoken, unexpressed, undeclared, unstated, tacit, unacknowledged, taken for granted; inherent, latent, underlying, inbuilt, incorporated; understood, inferred, deducible. ANTONYM explicit.

2 *an implicit trust in human nature* ABSOLUTE, complete, total, wholehearted, perfect, utter; unqualified, unconditional, categorical; unshakable, unquestioning, firm, steadfast. ANTONYM limited.

implicitly adverb *a man in whom they implicitly believed* COMPLETELY, absolutely, totally, wholeheartedly, utterly, unconditionally, unreservedly, without reservation.

implied adjective See IMPLICIT.

implore verb *his mother implored him to continue studying* PLEAD WITH, beg, entreat, beseech, appeal to, ask, request, call on; exhort, urge, enjoin, press, push, petition, bid, importune; supplicate. See note at BEG.

imply verb **1** *are you implying he is mad?* INSINUATE, suggest, hint (at), intimate, say indirectly, indicate, give someone to understand, convey the impression, signal. See note at INFER.

2 *the forecasted traffic increase implies more roads* INVOLVE, entail; mean, point to, signify, indicate, signal, connote, denote; necessitate, require, presuppose.

impolite adjective *Devon was consistently impolite, always interrupting and making the most doltish remarks* RUDE, bad-mannered, ill-mannered, discourteous, uncivil, disrespectful, inconsiderate, boorish, churlish, ill-bred, ungentlemanly, unladylike, ungracious; insolent, impudent, impertinent, cheeky; loutish, rough, crude, vulgar, indelicate, indecorous, tactless, gauche, uncouth; *informal* ignorant, lippy, saucy; *archaic* contumelious. ANTONYMS polite, well-mannered.

impolitic adjective *it was impolitic of you to alienate the very people who could finance our program* IMPRUDENT, unwise, injudicious, incautious, irresponsible; ill-judged, ill-advised, misguided, rash, reckless, foolhardy, foolish, shortsighted; undiplomatic, tactless, thoughtless. ANTONYMS prudent, wise.

import verb **1** *Greenland imports just about everything that is consumed* BUY FROM ABROAD, bring in, ship in. ANTONYM export.

2 *practices imported from the business world* DERIVE, obtain, take, extract, glean; *informal* steal, crib, filch.

▸ noun **1** *a tax on **imports*** IMPORTED GOODS, foreign goods, imported merchandise, foreign merchandise, imported commodities, foreign commodities.

2 *the import of foreign books* IMPORTATION, importing, introduction, bringing in, bringing from abroad, shipping in.

3 *a matter of great import* IMPORTANCE, significance, consequence, momentousness, magnitude, substance, weight, note, gravity, seriousness; *formal* moment. ANTONYM insignificance.

4 *the full import of her words* MEANING, sense, essence, gist, drift, purport, connotation, message, thrust, point, substance, implication.

importance noun **1** *the signing of the treaty was an event of immense importance* SIGNIFICANCE, momentousness, import, consequence, note, noteworthiness, substance; seriousness, gravity, weightiness, urgency.

2 *she had a fine sense of her own importance* POWER, influence, authority, sway, weight, dominance; prominence, eminence, preeminence, prestige, notability, worth, stature; *informal* clout, pull.

important adjective **1** *an important meeting* SIGNIFICANT, consequential, momentous, of great import, major; critical, crucial, vital, pivotal, decisive, urgent, historic; serious, grave, weighty, material; *formal* of great moment. ANTONYM trivial.

2 *the important thing is that you do well in your exams* MAIN, chief, principal, key, major, salient, prime, foremost, paramount, overriding, crucial, vital, critical, essential, significant; central, fundamental; *informal* number-one. ANTONYM inessential.

3 *the school was important to the community* OF VALUE, valuable, (highly) prized, beneficial, necessary, essential, indispensable, vital; of concern, of interest, relevant, pertinent. ANTONYMS irrelevant, of no concern.

4 *he was an important man* POWERFUL, influential, of influence, well-connected, high-ranking, high-powered; prominent, eminent, preeminent, notable, noteworthy, of note; distinguished, esteemed, respected, prestigious, celebrated, famous, great; *informal* affluential, major league. ANTONYM insignificant.

importune verb *he importuned her for some spare change* BEG, beseech, entreat, implore, plead with, appeal to, call on, lobby; harass, pester, press, badger, bother, nag, harry; *informal* hassle, bug. See note at BEG.

impose verb **1** *he imposed his ideas on the art director* FOIST, force, inflict, press, urge; *informal* saddle someone with, land someone with.

2 *new taxes will be imposed* LEVY, charge, apply, enforce; set, establish, institute, introduce, bring into effect.

3 *it was never my intention to **impose on** you* TAKE ADVANTAGE OF, exploit, take liberties with, treat unfairly; bother, trouble, disturb, inconvenience, put out, put to trouble, be a burden on; *informal* walk all over.

imposing adjective *an imposing mansion* IMPRESSIVE, striking, arresting, eye-catching, dramatic, spectacular, stunning, awesome, awe-inspiring, formidable, splendid, grand, grandiose, majestic, stately, august. ANTONYM modest.

imposition noun **1** *the imposition of an alien culture* IMPOSING, foisting, forcing, inflicting.

2 *the imposition of tax on consumables* LEVYING, charging, application, applying, enforcement, enforcing, enjoining; setting, establishment, introduction, institution.

3 *it would be no imposition* BURDEN, encumbrance, strain, bother, worry; *informal* hassle, drag.

impossible adjective **1** *gale-force winds made fishing impossible* NOT POSSIBLE, out of the question, unfeasible, impractical, impracticable, nonviable, unworkable; unthinkable, unimaginable, inconceivable, absurd. ANTONYM easy.

2 *an impossible dream* UNATTAINABLE, unachievable, unobtainable, unwinnable, hopeless, impractical, implausible, far-fetched, outrageous, preposterous, ridiculous, absurd, impracticable, unworkable, futile. ANTONYM attainable.

3 *informal* *an impossible customer* UNREASONABLE, objectionable, difficult, awkward; intolerable, unbearable, unendurable; exasperating, maddening, infuriating, irritating; *informal* high maintenance. ANTONYM bearable.

impossibly adverb *their entrance exam is impossibly difficult* UNREASONABLY, extremely, exceedingly, exceptionally, unduly, unnecessarily, ridiculously, overly. See note at EXCESSIVELY.

WORD NOTE **impossibly**

This is one of those adverbs that's formed from an adjective and can modify only modifiers, never verbs. Using these sorts of adverbs—*impossibly fast, extraordinarily yummy, irreducibly complex*—is an upscale educated speech tic that translates well to writing. Not only can the adverbs be as colorful/funny/snarky as you like, but the device is a neat way to up the formality of your prose without sacrificing personality; it makes the writer sound like an actual person, albeit a classy one. The big caveat is that you can't use these special-adverb-plus-adjective constructions more than once every few sentences or your prose starts to look like it's trying too hard. **—DFW**

impostor noun *it turned out the meter reader was an impostor | the biometrics cannot be duplicated by impostors* IMPERSONATOR, masquerader, pretender, imitator, deceiver, hoaxer, trickster, fraudster, swindler; fake, fraud, sham, phony, scammer. See note at QUACK.

imposture noun *Barton's imposture was recognized as such only after he had fled town* MISREPRESENTATION, pretense, deceit, deception, trickery, artifice, subterfuge, feint; hoax, trick, ruse, dodge; *informal* con, scam, flim-flam.

impotent adjective **1** *the legal sanctions are impotent* POWERLESS, ineffective, ineffectual, inadequate, weak, feeble, useless, worthless, futile; *literary* impuissant. ANTONYMS powerful, effective.

2 *natural forces that humans are impotent to control* UNABLE, incapable, powerless, helpless. ANTONYM able.

impound verb 1 *officials began impounding documents* CONFISCATE, appropriate, take possession of, seize, commandeer, expropriate, requisition, sequester, sequestrate; *Law* distrain.

2 *the cattle were impounded* PEN IN, shut up/in, fence in, enclose, cage, confine, corral.

3 *criminals impounded in prison* LOCK UP, incarcerate, imprison, confine, intern, immure, hold captive, hold prisoner.

impoverish verb 1 *his widow had been impoverished* MAKE POOR, make penniless, reduce to penury, bankrupt, beggar, ruin, bring to ruin, make insolvent; *rare* pauperize.

2 *the trees were impoverishing the soil* WEAKEN, sap, exhaust, deplete, enervate; *informal* bleed. ANTONYM enrich.

impoverished adjective 1 *an impoverished peasant farmer* POOR, poverty-stricken, penniless, destitute, indigent, impecunious, needy, beggared, beggarly, pauperized, down-and-out, bankrupt, ruined, insolvent; *informal* (flat) broke, hard up, dirt poor, on skid row; *formal* penurious. ANTONYMS rich, wealthy.

2 *the soil is impoverished* WEAKENED, exhausted, drained, sapped, depleted, spent; barren, unproductive, unfertile, unfruitful. ANTONYMS rich, fertile.

impracticable adjective *a repeat autopsy would be impracticable* UNWORKABLE, unfeasible, nonviable, unachievable, unattainable, unrealizable; impractical, impossible. ANTONYMS workable, feasible.

impractical adjective 1 *an impractical suggestion* UNREALISTIC, unworkable, unfeasible, nonviable, impracticable; ill-thought-out, impossible, absurd, wild; *informal* cockeyed, crackpot, crazy. ANTONYMS practical, sensible.

2 *impractical white ankle boots* UNSUITABLE, not sensible, inappropriate, unserviceable. ANTONYMS practical, sensible.

3 *an impractical scholar* IDEALISTIC, unrealistic, romantic, dreamy, fanciful, quixotic; *informal* ivory-tower, blue-sky, starry-eyed; *chiefly Brit. informal* airy-fairy. ANTONYMS practical, down-to-earth.

imprecation noun See CURSE noun senses 1, 4.

imprecise adjective 1 *a rather imprecise definition* VAGUE, loose, indefinite, inexplicit, indistinct, nonspecific, unspecific, sweeping, broad, general; hazy, fuzzy; *informal* loosey-goosey, woolly, sketchy, nebulous, ambiguous, equivocal, uncertain. ANTONYM narrow.

2 *an imprecise estimate* INEXACT, approximate, estimated, rough, ballpark. ANTONYM exact.

impregnable adjective 1 *the fortress is impregnable* INVULNERABLE, impenetrable, unassailable, inviolable, secure, strong, well fortified, well defended; invincible, unconquerable, unbeatable, indestructible. ANTONYM vulnerable.

2 *he displayed a calm, impregnable certainty* UNASSAILABLE, unbeatable, undefeatable, unshakable, invincible, unconquerable, invulnerable. ANTONYMS shaky, vulnerable.

impregnate verb 1 *a pad impregnated with natural oils* INFUSE, soak, steep, saturate, drench; permeate, pervade, suffuse, imbue.

2 *the woman he had impregnated* MAKE/GET PREGNANT, inseminate, fertilize; *informal* get/put in the family way; *informal, vulgar* knock up; *informal, dated* get into trouble; *archaic* fecundate, get with child.

impresario noun *a theatrical impresario* ORGANIZER, (stage) manager, producer; promoter, publicist, showman; director, conductor, maestro.

impress verb 1 *Hazel had impressed him* MAKE AN IMPRESSION ON, have an impact on, influence, affect, move, stir, rouse, excite, inspire; dazzle, awe, overawe, take someone's breath away, amaze, astonish; *informal* grab, blow someone away, stick in someone's mind. ANTONYM disappoint.

2 *goldsmiths impressed his likeness on medallions* IMPRINT, print, stamp, mark, emboss, punch.

3 *you must* ***impress upon*** *her the need to save* EMPHASIZE TO, stress to, bring home to, instill in, inculcate into, drum into.

impression noun 1 *he got the impression that she was hiding something* FEELING, feeling in one's bones, sense, fancy, (sneaking) suspicion, inkling, premonition, intuition, presentiment, hunch; notion, idea, funny feeling, gut feeling.

2 *a favorable impression* OPINION, view, image, picture, perception, judgment, verdict, estimation. See note at IDEA.

3 *school made a profound impression on me* IMPACT, effect, influence.

4 *the cap had left a circular impression* INDENTATION, dent, mark, outline, imprint.

5 *he did a good impression of their science teacher* IMPERSONATION, imitation; parody, caricature, burlesque, travesty, lampoon; *informal* takeoff, send-up, spoof; *formal* personation.

6 *an artist's impression of the gardens* REPRESENTATION, portrayal, depiction, rendition, interpretation, picture, drawing.

impressionable adjective *his music has anxious parents concerned about what impressionable children may hear and think* EASILY INFLUENCED, suggestible, susceptible, persuadable, pliable, malleable, pliant, trusting, naive, innocent, wide-eyed, credulous, gullible.

impressive adjective 1 *an impressive building* MAGNIFICENT, majestic, imposing, splendid, spectacular, grand, awe-inspiring, striking, stunning, breathtaking; *informal* mind-blowing, jaw-dropping. ANTONYM ordinary.

2 *it was an impressive performance* ADMIRABLE, masterly, accomplished, expert, skilled, skillful, consummate; excellent, outstanding, first-class, first-rate, fine, superb; *informal* awesome, great, mean, nifty, ace, crackerjack, bang-up. ANTONYM mediocre.

imprint verb 1 *patterns can be imprinted in the clay* STAMP, print, impress, mark, emboss, brand, inscribe, etch.

2 *the image was imprinted into his mind* FIX, establish, stick, lodge, implant, plant, embed, instill, impress, inculcate.

▸ noun 1 *her feet left imprints on the floor* IMPRESSION, print, mark, indentation.

2 *colonialism has left its imprint* IMPACT, lasting effect, influence, impression, mark, trace.

imprison verb *we expect to imprison another two dozen individuals by the end of this month alone* INCARCERATE, send to prison, jail, lock up, put away, intern, detain, hold prisoner, hold captive; confine, shut up, cage; *informal* put behind bars. ANTONYMS free, release.

imprisoned adjective *imprisoned dissidents* INCARCERATED, in prison, in jail, jailed, locked up, interned, detained, held prisoner, held captive; *informal* behind bars, doing time, under lock and key, inside.

► ***imprison***
immure
confine
hold captive
intern
incarcerate
shut up
impound
cage
trap
corral
pen (in/up)
fence in
hedge in
hurdle
rail in
coop (up)
mew up
box up/in
wall in/up
lock up/in
hem in
close in
gird
compass
encompass
surround
ring
encircle
enclose
set limits around
impose limitations on/upon
authorize someone's comings and goings
grant a leave of absence
let go
set free
release
set loose
let loose
turn loose
unleash
untie
uncage
unchain
unfetter
unshackle
unmanacle
discharge
let off
let off the hook
clear
spare
set at liberty
pardon
reprieve
deliver
liberate
emancipate
disenthrall
manumit
free ◄

improbability noun *many chose to believe in the improbability of a second world war* UNLIKELIHOOD, implausibility; doubtfulness, uncertainty, dubiousness; *informal* fat chance, long shot.

improbable adjective **1** *it seemed improbable that the hot weather would continue* UNLIKELY, doubtful, dubious, debatable, questionable, uncertain; unthinkable, inconceivable, unimaginable, incredible; *informal* iffy. ANTONYM certain.

2 *an improbable explanation* UNCONVINCING, unbelievable, incredible, ridiculous, absurd, preposterous, outrageous; far-fetched, fantastic, fanciful. ANTONYM believable.

impromptu adjective *an impromptu lecture* UNREHEARSED, unprepared, unscripted, extempore, extemporized, extemporaneous, improvised, spontaneous, unplanned; *informal* off-the-cuff, offhand, spur-of-the-moment, ad-lib. See note at SPONTANEOUS. ANTONYMS prepared, rehearsed.

► adverb *they played the song impromptu* EXTEMPORE, spontaneously, extemporaneously, without preparation, without rehearsal; *informal* off the cuff, off the top of one's head, on the spur of the moment, ad lib.

improper adjective **1** *it is improper for policemen to accept gifts* INAPPROPRIATE, unacceptable, unsuitable, unprofessional, irregular; unethical, corrupt, immoral, dishonest, dishonorable. ANTONYMS appropriate, acceptable.

2 *it was improper for young ladies to drive a young man home* UNSEEMLY, indecorous, unfitting, unbecoming, undignified, unladylike, ungentlemanly; indecent, immodest, immoral; scandalous, shocking, offensive. ANTONYMS proper, fitting.

3 *improper limericks* INDECENT, risqué, off color, indelicate, naughty, suggestive, smutty, vulgar, crude, obscene; *informal* raunchy, steamy, blue, X-rated. ANTONYM decent.

4 *improper installation will affect performance* INCORRECT, wrong, inaccurate, erroneous, mistaken. ANTONYM correct.

impropriety noun **1** *a suggestion of impropriety* WRONGDOING, misconduct, dishonesty, corruption, unscrupulousness, unprofessionalism, irregularity; unseemliness, indecorousness, indelicacy, indecency, immorality.

2 *fiscal improprieties* TRANSGRESSION, misdemeanor, offense, misdeed, misconduct, crime; indiscretion, mistake, peccadillo, solecism; *archaic* trespass.

improve verb **1** *ways to improve the service* MAKE BETTER, better, ameliorate, upgrade, update, refine, enhance, boost, build on, raise, polish, fix (up), amend; *informal* tweak; *formal* meliorate. ANTONYM worsen.

2 *communications improved during the eighteenth century* GET BETTER, advance, progress, develop; make headway, make progress, pick up, look up. ANTONYM deteriorate.

3 *the dose is not repeated if patient improves* RECOVER, get better, recuperate, gain strength, rally, revive, get back on one's feet, get over something; be on the road to recovery, be on the mend; *informal* turn the corner, take a turn for the better, bounce back. ANTONYM deteriorate.

4 *resources are needed to improve the offer* INCREASE, make larger, raise, augment, enhance, boost, supplement, top up; *informal* up, hike up, bump up, soup up, beef up. ANTONYMS decrease, diminish.

PHRASE: **improve on** *how could anyone improve on his*

brilliant analysis? SURPASS, better, do better than, outdo, exceed, beat, top, cap.

improvement noun *identifying the areas most in need of improvement | passengers will notice many new improvements* ADVANCE, development, upgrade, refinement, renovation, enhancement, advancement, upgrading, amelioration, betterment; boost, lift, rise, augmentation, raising, step up; rally, recovery, upswing, upturn.

improvident adjective *one consequence of a healthy economy may be a generation of improvident youth* SPENDTHRIFT, thriftless, wasteful, prodigal, profligate, extravagant, lavish, free-spending, immoderate, excessive; imprudent, irresponsible, careless, reckless, heedless. ANTONYMS thrifty, conservative.

improvise verb **1** *she was improvising in front of the cameras* EXTEMPORIZE, ad lib, speak impromptu; *informal* speak off the cuff, speak off the top of one's head, wing it; jam, scat.

2 *she improvised a playhouse for the kids* CONTRIVE, devise, throw together, cobble together, rig up; *informal* whip up, rustle up.

improvised adjective **1** *an improvised speech* IMPROMPTU, unrehearsed, unprepared, unscripted, extempore, extemporized, spontaneous, unplanned; *informal* off-the-cuff, ad-libbed, spur-of-the-moment. See note at SPONTANEOUS. ANTONYMS prepared, rehearsed.

2 *an improvised shelter* MAKESHIFT, thrown together, cobbled together, rough and ready, crude, make-do, temporary, jerry-built, jury-rigged, slapdash.

imprudent adjective *a series of imprudent marriages* UNWISE, injudicious, incautious, indiscreet, misguided, ill-advised, ill-judged; thoughtless, unthinking, improvident, irresponsible, shortsighted, foolish; rash, reckless, heedless. ANTONYM sensible.

impudence noun *her irrepressible impudence landed her in the principal's office about a million times* IMPERTINENCE, insolence, effrontery, audacity, cheek, cheekiness, cockiness, brazenness, brass, boldness; presumption, presumptuousness, disrespect, flippancy, bumptiousness, brashness; rudeness, impoliteness, ill manners, gall; *informal* chutzpah, nerve, sauce, sass, sassiness.

impudent adjective *the oblivious couple and their impudent children were asked to leave* IMPERTINENT, insolent, cheeky, cocky, brazen, bold, audacious; presumptuous, forward, disrespectful, insubordinate, bumptious, brash; rude, impolite, ill-mannered, discourteous, ill-bred; *informal* saucy, lippy, sassy, brassy, smart-alecky; *archaic* contumelious. See note at IMPERTINENT. ANTONYM polite.

impugn verb *are you impugning my judgment?* CALL INTO QUESTION, challenge, question, dispute, query, take issue with.

impulse noun **1** *she had an impulse to run and hide* URGE, instinct, drive, compulsion, itch; whim, desire, fancy, notion, inclination, temptation.

2 *passions provide the main impulse of poetry* INSPIRATION, stimulation, stimulus, incitement, motivation, encouragement, incentive, spur, catalyst, impetus, thrust.

3 *impulses from the spinal cord to the muscles* PULSE, current, wave, signal. PHRASE: **on (an) impulse** *I agreed to bungee-jump on an impulse | they claimed the robbery was not planned, that they did it on impulse* IMPULSIVELY, spontaneously, on the spur of the moment, without forethought, without premeditation.

impulsive adjective **1** *he had an impulsive nature* IMPETUOUS, spontaneous, hasty, passionate, emotional, uninhibited; rash, reckless, careless, imprudent, foolhardy, unwise, madcap, devil-may-care, daredevil. ANTONYM cautious.

2 *an impulsive decision* IMPROMPTU, snap, spontaneous, unpremeditated, spur-of-the-moment, extemporaneous; impetuous, precipitate, hasty, rash; sudden, ill-considered, ill-thought-out, whimsical. See note at SPONTANEOUS. ANTONYM premeditated.

impunity noun *the lawsuit attempts to fight the impunity that these military officials have enjoyed for too long* IMMUNITY, indemnity, exemption (from punishment), freedom from liability, nonliability, license; amnesty, dispensation, reprieve, pardon, exoneration; stay of execution; privilege, favoritism, special treatment, carte blanche. ANTONYM liability.

PHRASE: **with impunity** *they boldly break laws at will, and do so with impunity* WITHOUT PUNISHMENT, with no ill consequences, scot-free, unpunished.

impure adjective **1** *impure gold* ADULTERATED, mixed, combined, blended, alloyed; *technical* admixed. ANTONYM pure.

2 *the water was impure* CONTAMINATED, polluted, tainted, unwholesome, poisoned; dirty, filthy, foul, unclean, defiled; unhygienic, unsanitary; *literary* befouled. ANTONYM clean.

3 *impure thoughts* IMMORAL, sinful, wrongful, wicked; unchaste, lustful, lecherous, lewd, lascivious, prurient, obscene, indecent, ribald, risqué, improper, crude, coarse, debased, degenerate; *formal* concupiscent. ANTONYM chaste.

impurity noun **1** *the impurity of the cast iron* ADULTERATION, debasement, degradation, corruption; contamination, pollution.

2 *the impurities in beer* CONTAMINANT, pollutant, foreign body, foreign matter; dross, dirt, filth.

3 *sin and impurity* IMMORALITY, sin, sinfulness, wickedness; unchastity, lustfulness, lechery, lecherousness, lewdness, lasciviousness, prurience, obscenity, dirtiness, crudeness, indecency, ribaldry, impropriety, vulgarity, depravity, coarseness; *formal* concupiscence.

impute verb *the worst of these mistakes have been unfairly **imputed to** Dr. Irvine* ATTRIBUTE TO, ascribe to, assign to, credit to; connect with, associate with.

in preposition **1** *she was hiding in the closet* INSIDE, within, in the middle of; surrounded by, enclosed by.

2 *he was covered in mud* WITH, by.

3 *he put a candy in his mouth* INTO, inside.

4 *they met in 1921* DURING, in the course of, over.

5 *I'll see you in half an hour* AFTER, at the end of, following; within, in less than, in under.

▸ adverb **1** *his mom walked in* INSIDE, indoors, into the room, into the house/building.

2 *the tide's in* HIGH, at its highest level, rising.

▸ adjective **1** *no one is in* PRESENT, (at) home; inside, indoors, in the house/room.

2 *informal* *sculpted beards are in* FASHIONABLE, in fashion, in vogue, popular, stylish, modern, modish, chic, à la mode, de rigueur, trendy, cool, all the rage, du jour, with it, the in thing, hip, hot. ANTONYMS unfashionable, unpopular.

PHRASES: **in for** *we're probably in for some rain* DUE FOR, in line for; expecting, about to undergo/receive. **in for it** *when Dad gets home, you're gonna be in for it* IN TROUBLE, about to be punished; *informal* in hot/deep water. **in on** *we were never in on the whole story* PRIVY TO, aware of, acquainted with, informed about/of, apprised of; *informal* wise to, in the know about, hip to. **ins and outs** *informal no one expects you to learn all the ins and outs on your first day of work* DETAILS, particulars, facts, features, characteristics, nuts and bolts; *informal* nitty gritty. **in with** *her principal mission was to get in with as many senior executives as possible* IN FAVOR WITH, popular with, friendly with, friends with, on good terms with; liked by, admired by, accepted by.

inability noun *the state's inability to build a credible case against him* LACK OF ABILITY, incapability, incapacity, powerlessness, impotence, helplessness; incompetence, ineptitude, unfitness, inefficacy.

inaccessible adjective **1** *inaccessible woodlands* UNREACHABLE, out of reach, unapproachable; cutoff, isolated, remote, insular, in the back of beyond, out of the way, lonely, solitary, godforsaken.

2 *the book was elitist and inaccessible* INCOMPREHENSIBLE, impenetrable, inscrutable, baffling; obscure, esoteric, abstruse, recondite, arcane; elitist, exclusive, pretentious.

3 *the lecturer was inaccessible to students* UNAPPROACHABLE, aloof, distant, unfriendly, standoffish.

inaccuracy noun **1** *the inaccuracy of recent opinion polls* INCORRECTNESS, inexactness, imprecision, erroneousness, mistakenness, fallaciousness, faultiness. ANTONYM correctness.

2 *the article contained a number of inaccuracies* ERROR, mistake, fallacy, slip, slip-up, oversight, fault, blunder, gaffe; erratum, solecism; *informal* howler, typo, blooper, goof.

inaccurate adjective *inaccurate reports* INEXACT, imprecise, incorrect, wrong, erroneous, careless, faulty, imperfect, flawed, defective, unsound, unreliable; fallacious, false, mistaken, untrue; *informal* wide of the mark.

inaction noun *the mayor was criticized for his inaction* INACTIVITY, nonintervention; neglect, negligence, apathy, inertia, indolence, sluggishness, lethargy, idleness.

inactive adjective **1** *I was terribly inactive over the holidays* IDLE, indolent, lazy, lifeless, slothful, lethargic, inert, sluggish, unenergetic, listless, torpid, sedentary.

2 *the computer is currently inactive* INOPERATIVE, nonfunctioning, idle; not working, out of service, unused, not in use; dormant.

inactivity noun **1** *long periods of inactivity* IDLENESS, indolence, laziness, lifelessness, slothfulness, lethargy, inertia, sluggishness, listlessness, inaction, torpor. ANTONYM action.

2 *government inactivity* INACTION, nonintervention; neglect, negligence, apathy, passivity. ANTONYM action.

inadequacy noun **1** *the inadequacy of available resources* INSUFFICIENCY, deficiency, deficit, scarcity, sparseness, dearth, paucity, shortage, want, lack, undersupply; paltriness, meagerness. ANTONYMS abundance, surplus.

2 *her feelings of personal inadequacy* INCOMPETENCE, incapability, unfitness, ineffectiveness, inefficiency, inefficacy, inexpertness, ineptness, uselessness, impotence, powerlessness; inferiority, mediocrity. ANTONYM competence.

3 *the inadequacies of the present system* SHORTCOMING, defect, fault, failing, weakness, weak point, limitation, flaw, imperfection. ANTONYM strength.

inadequate adjective **1** *inadequate water supplies* INSUFFICIENT, deficient, poor, scant, scanty, scarce, sparse, in short supply; paltry, meager, niggardly, beggarly, limited; *informal* measly, pathetic; *formal* exiguous. ANTONYM sufficient.

2 *an inadequate typist* INCOMPETENT, incapable, unsatisfactory, unfit, unacceptable, ineffective, ineffectual, inefficient, unskillful, inexpert, inept, amateurish, substandard, poor, useless, inferior; *informal* not up to scratch, not up to snuff, no great shakes, lame, shabby. ANTONYM competent.

inadmissible adjective *inadmissible evidence* UNALLOWABLE, not allowed, invalid, unacceptable, impermissible, disallowed, forbidden, prohibited, precluded.

inadvertent adjective *an inadvertent omission* UNINTENTIONAL, unintended, accidental, unpremeditated, unplanned, innocent, uncalculated, unconscious, unthinking, unwitting, involuntary; careless, negligent. ANTONYM deliberate.

inadvisable adjective *traveling to the village is inadvisable for the president at this time* UNWISE, ill-advised, imprudent, ill-judged, ill-considered, injudicious, impolitic, foolish, misguided; *Medicine* contraindicated. ANTONYMS wise, shrewd.

inalienable adjective *China of course contends that Taiwan is an inalienable part of China* INVIOLABLE, absolute, sacrosanct; untransferable, nontransferable, nonnegotiable; *Law* indefeasible.

inane adjective *another one of Craig's inane schemes* SILLY, foolish, stupid, fatuous, idiotic, ridiculous, ludicrous, absurd, senseless, asinine, frivolous, vapid; childish, puerile; *informal* dumb, moronic, ditzy, daft. ANTONYM sensible.

inanimate adjective *in the dream sequence, several of the inanimate objects in his bedroom come to life* LIFELESS, insentient, without life, inorganic; dead, defunct. ANTONYM living.

inapplicable adjective *they argued that executive privilege was simply inapplicable in the face of the grand jury subpoena* IRRELEVANT, immaterial, not germane, not pertinent, unrelated, unconnected, extraneous, beside the point; unsuitable, inapposite; *formal* impertinent. ANTONYM relevant.

inappropriate adjective *children's access to the Internet may expose them to inappropriate material* UNSUITABLE, unfitting, unseemly, unbecoming, unbefitting, improper, impolite; incongruous, out of place/keeping, inapposite, inapt, infelicitous, ill-suited; ill-judged, ill-advised; *informal* out of order/line; *formal* malapropos. ANTONYM suitable.

inapt adjective . See INAPPROPRIATE.

inarticulate adjective **1** *an inarticulate young man* TONGUE-TIED, lost for words, unable to express oneself. ANTONYM silver-tongued.

2 *an inarticulate reply* UNINTELLIGIBLE, incomprehensible, incoherent, unclear, indistinct, mumbled, muffled. ANTONYM fluent.

3 *inarticulate rage* UNSPOKEN, silent, unexpressed, wordless, speechless, unvoiced. ANTONYM vocal.

inattentive adjective **1** *an inattentive student* DISTRACTED, lacking concentration, preoccupied, absent-minded, daydreaming, dreamy, abstracted, distrait; *informal* miles away, spaced out. ANTONYM alert.

2 *inattentive service.* See NEGLIGENT.

inaudible adjective *inaudible voices* UNHEARD, out of earshot; indistinct, imperceptible, faint, muted, soft, low, muffled, whispered, muttered, murmured, mumbled; silent, soundless, noiseless, hushed; ultrasonic.

inaugural adjective *the inaugural meeting of the Geographic Society* OPENING, FIRST, launching, initial, introductory, initiatory, maiden. ANTONYM final.

inaugurate verb **1** *he inaugurated a new trade policy* INITIATE, begin, start, commence, institute, launch, start off, get going, get underway, set in motion, get off the ground, establish, found, lay the foundations of; bring in, usher in, introduce; *informal* kick off.

2 *the new president will be inaugurated in January* ADMIT TO OFFICE, install, instate, swear in; invest, ordain; crown, enthrone.

3 *the library was inaugurated on Jefferson's birthday* OPEN, declare open, unveil; dedicate, consecrate.

inauspicious adjective *after an inauspicious start, the Giants ended the season in first place* UNPROMISING, unpropitious, unfavorable, unfortunate, infelicitous, unlucky, ill-omened, ominous; discouraging, disheartening, bleak. ANTONYM promising.

inborn adjective *inborn allergic reactions* INNATE, congenital, connate, instinctive, inherent, natural, inbred, inherited, hereditary, in one's genes. See note at INHERENT.

incalculable adjective *artifacts of incalculable value | incalculable losses* INESTIMABLE, untold, indeterminable, immeasurable, incomputable; infinite, endless, limitless, boundless, measureless; enormous, immense, huge, vast, innumerable, countless.

incandescent adjective **1** *incandescent fragments of lava* WHITE-HOT, red-hot, burning, fiery, blazing, ablaze, aflame; glowing, aglow, radiant, bright, brilliant, luminous, sparkling; *literary* fervid, lucent; *rare* igneous.

2 *an incandescent speech* PASSIONATE, ardent, fervent, fervid, intense, impassioned, spirited, fiery.

incantation noun *I was more amused than entranced by the flickering candles and spooky incantations* CHANT, invocation, conjuration, magic spell/formula, charm, hex, enchantment, mojo; intonation, recitation.

incapable adjective **1** *the job should never have been assigned to an incapable crew* INCOMPETENT, inept, inadequate, lacking ability, not good enough, leaving much to be desired, inexpert, unskillful, ineffective, ineffectual, inefficacious, feeble, unfit, unqualified, unequal to the task; *informal* not up to it, not up to snuff, useless, hopeless. ANTONYM competent.

2 *he was judged to be mentally incapable* INCAPACITATED, incompetent, helpless, powerless, impotent. ANTONYM competent.

3 *they are incapable of supporting themselves* UNABLE TO (BE), not capable of, lacking the ability to (be), not equipped to (be), lacking the experience to (be). ANTONYM able.

incapacitated adjective *Ivan did not expect to be incapacitated for more than a few days* DISABLED, debilitated, indisposed, unfit, impaired; immobilized, paralyzed, out of action, out of commission, hors de combat; *informal* laid up. ANTONYM fit.

incapacity noun *the doctors were baffled by the severity of her physical incapacity* DISABILITY, incapability, inability, debility, impairment, indisposition; impotence, powerlessness, helplessness; incompetence, inadequacy, ineffectiveness. ANTONYM capability.

incarcerate verb *Luckins returned to the site where she had been incarcerated nearly fifty years earlier* IMPRISON, put in prison, send to prison, jail, lock up, put under lock and key, put away, intern, confine, detain, hold, immure, put in chains, hold prisoner, hold captive; *informal* put behind bars. ANTONYMS release, set free.

incarceration noun *eight years of incarceration* IMPRISONMENT, internment, confinement, detention, custody, captivity, restraint; *informal* time; *archaic* durance, duress.

incarnate adjective *the chairman has been labeled "evil incarnate" by various conservationists* IN HUMAN FORM, in the flesh, in physical form, in bodily form, made flesh; corporeal, physical, fleshly, embodied, personified.

incarnation noun **1** *the incarnation of artistic genius* EMBODIMENT, personification, exemplification, type, epitome; manifestation, bodily form, avatar.

2 *a previous incarnation* LIFETIME, life, existence.

incautious adjective *my uncle's history of incautious behavior is hardly a secret* RASH, unwise, careless, heedless, thoughtless, reckless, unthinking, imprudent, misguided, ill-advised, ill-judged, injudicious, impolitic, unguarded, foolhardy, foolish. ANTONYM circumspect.

incendiary adjective **1** *an incendiary bomb* COMBUSTIBLE, flammable, inflammable.

2 *an incendiary speech* INFLAMMATORY, rabble-rousing, provocative, seditious, subversive; contentious, controversial.

▸ noun *a political incendiary* AGITATOR, demagogue, rabble-rouser, firebrand, troublemaker, agent provocateur, revolutionary, insurgent, subversive.

incense verb See ENRAGE.

incensed adjective See ENRAGED.

incentive noun *only financial incentives will curb the polluting activities of major industries* INDUCEMENT, motivation, motive, reason, stimulus, stimulant, spur, impetus, encouragement, impulse; incitement, goad, provocation; attraction, lure, bait; *informal* carrot, sweetener, come-on. ANTONYM deterrent.

inception noun *the airline plans to file for bankruptcy, seven years after its inception* BEGINNING, commencement, start, birth, dawn, genesis, origin, outset; establishment, institution, foundation, founding, formation, initiation, setting up, origination, constitution, inauguration, opening, debut, day one; *informal* kickoff. See note at ORIGIN. ANTONYM end.

incessant adjective *their dog's incessant barking* CEASELESS, unceasing, constant, continual, unabating, interminable, endless, unending, never-ending, everlasting, eternal, perpetual, continuous, nonstop, around/round-the-clock, uninterrupted, unbroken, unremitting, persistent, relentless, unrelenting, unrelieved, sustained. ANTONYMS intermittent, occasional.

incessantly adverb *Hong Kongers worry incessantly about preserving their political autonomy* CONSTANTLY, continually, all the time, nonstop, without stopping, without a break, around/round the clock, interminably, unremittingly, ceaselessly, endlessly; *informal* 24-7. ANTONYM occasionally.

inchoate adjective *their government should not interfere in the inchoate market forces* RUDIMENTARY, undeveloped, unformed, immature, incipient, embryonic; beginning, fledgling, developing.

incidence noun *an increased incidence of heart disease* OCCURRENCE, prevalence; rate, frequency; amount, degree, extent.

incident noun **1** *incidents in his youth* EVENT, occurrence, episode, experience, happening, occasion, proceeding, eventuality, affair, business; adventure, exploit, escapade; matter, circumstance, fact, development.

2 *police were investigating the incident* DISTURBANCE, fracas, melee, commotion, rumpus, scene; fight, skirmish, clash, brawl, free-for-all, encounter, conflict, ruckus, confrontation, altercation, contretemps; *informal* ruction.

3 *the journey was not without incident* EXCITEMENT, adventure, drama; danger, peril.

incidental adjective **1** *incidental details* LESS IMPORTANT, secondary, subsidiary; minor, peripheral, background, nonessential, inessential, unimportant, insignificant, inconsequential, tangential, extrinsic, extraneous, superfluous. ANTONYMS essential, crucial.

2 *an incidental discovery* CHANCE, accidental, by chance, by accident, random; fortuitous, serendipitous, adventitious, coincidental, unlooked-for, unexpected, fluky. See note at ACCIDENTAL. ANTONYM deliberate.

3 *the risks* ***incidental to*** *the job* CONNECTED WITH, related to, associated with, accompanying, attending, attendant on, concomitant to/with. ANTONYM unrelated.

incidentally adverb **1** *incidentally, I haven't had a reply yet* BY THE WAY, by the by, by the bye, in passing, en passant, speaking of which; parenthetically; *informal* BTW, as it happens.

2 *the infection was discovered incidentally* BY CHANCE, by accident, accidentally, fortuitously, by a fluke, by happenstance; coincidentally, by coincidence.

incinerate verb *we would incinerate our household trash in a barrel in the backyard.* BURN, reduce to ashes, consume by fire, carbonize; cremate.

incipient adjective *the system detects incipient problems early* DEVELOPING, growing, emerging, emergent, dawning, just beginning, inceptive, initial, inchoate; nascent, embryonic, fledgling, in its infancy, germinal. ANTONYM full-blown.

incision noun **1** *a surgical incision* CUT, opening, slit.

2 *incisions on the marble* NOTCH, carving, etching, engraving, inscription, score; nick, scratch, scarification.

incisive adjective *an incisive commentator* PENETRATING, acute, sharp, sharp-witted, razor-sharp, keen, astute, trenchant, shrewd, piercing, cutting, perceptive, insightful, percipient, perspicacious, discerning, analytical, clever, smart, quick; concise, succinct, pithy, to the point, brief, crisp, clear, effective; *informal* punchy, heads-up, on the ball; *rare* sapient. ANTONYMS rambling, vague.

incite verb **1** *we're hoping that last night's incident will not incite altercations in the stadium today* STIR UP, whip up, encourage, fan the flames of, stoke up, fuel, kindle, ignite, inflame, stimulate, instigate, provoke, excite, arouse, awaken, inspire, engender, trigger, spark off, ferment, foment; *literary* enkindle. ANTONYM suppress.

2 *she incited him to commit murder* EGG ON, encourage, urge, goad, provoke, spur on, drive, stimulate, push, prod, prompt, induce, impel; arouse, rouse, excite, inflame, sting, prick; *informal* put up to. ANTONYMS discourage, deter.

THE RIGHT WORD

The best way to start a riot is to **incite** one, which means to urge or stimulate to action, either in a favorable or an unfavorable sense. If you **instigate** an action, however, it implies that you are responsible for initiating it and that the purpose is probably a negative or evil one (*the man who instigated the assassination plot*). **Foment** suggests agitation or incitement over an extended period of time (*foment a discussion; foment the rebellion that leads to war*). An instigator, in other words, is someone who initiates the idea, while a fomenter is someone who keeps it alive. You can **provoke** a riot in the same way that you instigate one, but the emphasis here is on spontaneity rather than on conscious design (*her statement provoked an outcry from animal rights activists*). To **arouse** is to awaken a feeling or elicit a response (*my presence in the junkyard aroused suspicion*), or to open people's eyes to a situation (*we attempted to arouse public awareness*). But once you've aroused people, you may have to **exhort** them, meaning to urge or persuade them, by appealing to their sympathy or conscience, to take constructive action.

incivility noun *Cadet Anderson was reprimanded for incivility* RUDENESS, discourtesy, impoliteness, bad manners, disrespect, boorishness, ungraciousness; insolence, impertinence, impudence. ANTONYM politeness.

inclement adjective *inclement weather* COLD, chilly, bleak, wintry, freezing, snowy, icy; wet, rainy, drizzly, damp; stormy, blustery, wild, rough, squally, windy; unpleasant, bad, foul, nasty, brutal, severe, extreme, harsh. ANTONYMS fine, sunny.

inclination noun **1** *his political inclination* TENDENCY, propensity, proclivity, leaning, predisposition, disposition, predilection, desire, wish, impulse, bent, bias; liking, affection, penchant, partiality, preference, appetite, fancy, interest, affinity; stomach, taste; *informal* yen. ANTONYM aversion.

2 *an inclination of his head* BOWING, bow, bending, nod, nodding, lowering.

incline verb **1** *his prejudice inclines him to overlook obvious facts* PREDISPOSE, lead, make, make of a mind, dispose, prejudice, bias; prompt, induce, influence, sway; persuade, convince.

2 *I* ***incline to*** *the opposite view* PREFER, favor, go for; tend to, lean to, swing to, veer to, gravitate to, be drawn to.

3 *he inclined his head* BEND, bow, nod, bob, lower, dip.

▸ noun *a steep incline* SLOPE, gradient, pitch, ramp, bank, ascent, rise, upslope, dip, descent, declivity, downslope; hill, grade, downgrade.

inclined adjective **1** *if you feel so inclined* DISPOSED, of a mind, willing, ready, prepared; predisposed.

2 *she's inclined to gossip* PRONE, given, liable, likely, apt, wont.

3 *an inclined floor* SLOPING, sloped, slanted, leaning, angled, oblique, at/on a slant, at an angle.

include verb **1** *activities include sports and drama* INCORPORATE, comprise, encompass, cover, embrace, involve, take in, number, contain; consist of, be made up of, be composed of; *formal* comprehend. ANTONYM exclude.

2 *don't forget to include the cost of repairs* ALLOW FOR, count, take into account, take into consideration. ANTONYMS omit, leave out.

THE RIGHT WORD

Include has a broader meaning than **comprise**. In the sentence *the accommodations comprise two bedrooms, bathroom, kitchen, and living room*, the word **comprise** implies that there are no accommodations other than those listed. **Include** can be used in this way too, but it is also used in a nonrestrictive way, implying that there may be other things not specifically mentioned that are part of the same category, as in *the price includes a special welcome pack*. Careful writers will avoid superfluous uses of "including . . . and more," commonly found in advertising. The 'and more' is superfluous because **including** or **includes** implies that there is more than what is listed.

inclusive adjective *an inclusive travel package* ALL-INCLUSIVE, with everything included, comprehensive, in toto; overall, full, all-around, umbrella, blanket, across-the-board, catch-all, all-encompassing.

incognito adverb & adjective *you'll be traveling incognito* UNDER AN ASSUMED NAME, under a false name, in disguise, disguised, under cover, in plain clothes, camouflaged, unidentified; secretly, anonymously.

incoherent adjective **1** *a long, incoherent speech* UNCLEAR, confused, unintelligible, incomprehensible, hard to follow, disjointed, disconnected, disordered, mixed up, garbled, jumbled, scrambled, muddled; rambling, wandering, disorganized, illogical; inarticulate, mumbling, slurred. ANTONYM intelligible.

2 *she was incoherent and shivering* DELIRIOUS, raving, babbling, hysterical, irrational. ANTONYM lucid.

income noun *annual income* EARNINGS, salary, pay, remuneration, wages, stipend; revenue, receipts, takings, profits, gains, proceeds, turnover, yield, dividend, means, take; *formal* emolument. ANTONYM expenditure.

incoming adjective **1** *the incoming train* ARRIVING, entering; approaching, coming (in), inbound. ANTONYM outgoing.

2 *the incoming president* NEWLY ELECTED, newly appointed, succeeding, new, next, future; elect, to-be, designate. ANTONYM outgoing.

incommensurate adjective See DISPROPORTIONATE.

incommodious adjective *the rooms were clean but quite incommodious* UNCOMFORTABLE, small, cramped, tiny. ANTONYM spacious.

incommunicable adjective See INDESCRIBABLE.

incommunicado adjective *Padilla has been held incommunicado in a South Carolina navy brig* ISOLATED, out of reach/touch, sequestered, unreachable, secluded.

incomparable adjective *the incomparable Maggie Smith is once again the deputy headmistress of Hogwarts* WITHOUT EQUAL, beyond compare, unparalleled, matchless, peerless, unmatched, without parallel, beyond comparison, second to none, in a class of its/one's own, unequaled, unrivaled, inimitable, nonpareil, par excellence; transcendent, superlative, surpassing, unsurpassed, unsurpassable, supreme, top, best, outstanding, consummate, singular, unique, rare, perfect; *informal* one-in-a-million; *formal* unexampled. ANTONYMS ordinary, commonplace.

incompatible adjective **1** *she and McBride are totally incompatible* UNSUITED, mismatched, ill-matched; worlds apart, poles apart, like night and day. ANTONYMS well-matched, suited.

2 *incompatible economic objectives* IRRECONCILABLE, conflicting, opposed, opposing, opposite, contradictory, antagonistic, antipathetic; clashing, inharmonious, discordant; mutually exclusive; poles apart, worlds apart, night and day. ANTONYMS compatible, complementary.

3 *his theory was* ***incompatible with*** *that of his predecessor* INCONSISTENT WITH, at odds with, out of keeping with, at variance with, inconsonant with, different to, divergent from, contrary to, in conflict with, in opposition to, antithetical to, (diametrically) opposed to, counter to, irreconcilable with. ANTONYM consistent.

incompetence noun *Ms. Russell's dismissal was based only on her incompetence* INEPTITUDE, ineptness, inability, lack of ability, lack of skill, lack of proficiency; inadequacy, ineffectiveness, inefficiency, deficiency, insufficiency; amateurishness, clumsiness; *informal* uselessness. ANTONYM prowess.

incompetent adjective *not only is the staff overpaid, they're incompetent* INEPT, unskillful, unskilled, inexpert, amateurish, unprofessional, bungling, blundering, clumsy, inadequate, substandard, inferior, ineffective, deficient, inefficient, ineffectual, wanting, lacking, leaving much to be desired; incapable, unfit, unqualified; *informal* useless, pathetic, ham-fisted, not up to it, not up to scratch, bush league.

incomplete adjective **1** *the project is still incomplete* UNFINISHED, uncompleted, partial, half-finished, half-done, half-completed.

2 *inaccurate or incomplete information* DEFICIENT, insufficient, imperfect, defective, partial, patchy, sketchy, fragmentary, fragmented.

incomprehensible adjective *the patient's muttering was incomprehensible | the judge ruled that the original contract was too incomprehensible to be binding* UNINTELLIGIBLE, impossible to understand, impenetrable, unclear, indecipherable, inscrutable, beyond one's comprehension, beyond one, beyond one's grasp, complicated, complex, involved, baffling, bewildering, mystifying, unfathomable, puzzling, cryptic, confusing, perplexing; abstruse, esoteric, recondite, arcane, mysterious, Delphic; *informal* over one's head, all Greek. ANTONYMS intelligible, clear.

inconceivable adjective *even his oldest rivals thought the charges of treason against him were inconceivable* UNBELIEVABLE, beyond belief, incredible, unthinkable, unimaginable, extremely unlikely; impossible, beyond the bounds of possibility, out of the question, preposterous, ridiculous, ludicrous, absurd, incomprehensible; *informal* hard to swallow. ANTONYM likely.

inconclusive adjective *the defendant was confident that the evidence would be inconclusive* INDECISIVE, proving nothing; indefinite, indeterminate, unresolved, unproved, unsettled, still open to question/doubt, debatable, unconfirmed; moot; vague, ambiguous; *informal* up in the air, left hanging.

incongruous adjective **1** *the women visiting the mission looked incongruous in their smart hats and fur coats* OUT OF PLACE, out of keeping, inappropriate, unsuitable, unsuited; wrong, strange, odd, curious, queer, absurd, bizarre. ANTONYM appropriate.

2 *an incongruous collection of objects* ILL-MATCHED, ill-assorted, mismatched, unharmonious, discordant, dissonant, conflicting, clashing, jarring, incompatible, different, dissimilar, contrasting, disparate. ANTONYM harmonious.

inconsequential adjective *their efforts to save the Bixner Building were ultimately inconsequential* INSIGNIFICANT, unimportant, of little/no consequence, neither here nor there, incidental, inessential, nonessential, immaterial, irrelevant; negligible, inappreciable, inconsiderable, slight, minor, trivial, trifling, petty, paltry, measly; *informal* piddling, piffling. ANTONYMS significant, important, of great consequence.

inconsiderate adjective *she reproached her son for being routinely inconsiderate to his wife* THOUGHTLESS, unthinking, insensitive, selfish, self-centered, unsympathetic, uncaring, heedless, unmindful, unkind, uncharitable, ungracious, impolite, discourteous, rude, disrespectful; tactless, undiplomatic, indiscreet, indelicate. ANTONYM thoughtful.

inconsistent adjective **1** *his inconsistent behavior* ERRATIC, changeable, unpredictable, variable, varying, changing, inconstant, unstable, irregular, fluctuating, unsteady, unsettled, uneven; self-contradictory, contradictory, paradoxical; capricious, fickle, flighty, whimsical, unreliable, mercurial, volatile, blowing hot and cold, ever-changing, chameleonlike; *technical* labile.

2 *he had done nothing* ***inconsistent with*** *his morality* INCOMPATIBLE WITH, conflicting with, in conflict with, at odds with, at variance with, differing from, contrary to, in opposition to, (diametrically) opposed to, irreconcilable with, out of keeping with, out of step with; antithetical to.

inconsolable adjective *those left homeless by the fire were inconsolable* HEARTBROKEN, broken-hearted, grief-stricken, beside oneself with grief, devastated, wretched, sick at heart, desolate, despairing, distraught, comfortless; miserable, unhappy, sad; *literary* heartsick.

inconspicuous adjective *the flaw in the carpeting is inconspicuous | wearing inconspicuous street clothes, Swann escaped through the crowd* UNOBTRUSIVE, unnoticeable, unremarkable, unspectacular, unostentatious, undistinguished, unexceptional, modest, unassuming, discreet, hidden, concealed; unseen, in the background, low-profile. ANTONYM noticeable.

inconstant adjective *an inconstant friend* FICKLE, faithless, unfaithful, false, wayward, unreliable, untrustworthy, capricious, volatile, flighty, unpredictable, erratic, blowing hot and cold; changeable, mutable, mercurial, variable, irregular; *informal* cheating, two-timing. ANTONYM faithful.

incontestable adjective See INCONTROVERTIBLE.

incontinent adjective *incontinent hysteria* UNRESTRAINED, lacking self-restraint, uncontrolled, unbridled, unchecked, unfettered; uncontrollable, ungovernable. ANTONYM restrained.

incontrovertible adjective *he realizes that his forensic findings are not incontrovertible* INDISPUTABLE, incontestable, undeniable, irrefutable, unassailable, beyond dispute, unquestionable, beyond question, indubitable, beyond doubt, unarguable, undebatable; certain, sure, definite, definitive, proven, decisive, conclusive, demonstrable, emphatic, categorical, airtight, watertight. ANTONYM questionable.

inconvenience noun **1** *we apologize for any inconvenience caused by the delay* TROUBLE, bother, problems, disruption, difficulty, disturbance; vexation, irritation, annoyance; *informal* aggravation, hassle.

2 *his early arrival was clearly an inconvenience* NUISANCE, trouble, bother, problem, vexation, worry, trial, bind, bane, irritant, thorn in someone's side; *informal* headache, pain, pain in the neck, pain in the butt, drag, aggravation, hassle.

▸ verb *I don't want to inconvenience you* TROUBLE, bother, put out, put to any trouble, disturb, impose on, burden, incommode; *informal* hassle, plague; *formal* discommode.

inconvenient adjective *symptoms can range from merely inconvenient to downright life-changing* AWKWARD, difficult, inopportune, untimely, ill-timed, unsuitable, inappropriate, unfortunate; tiresome, troublesome, irritating, annoying, vexing, bothersome; *informal* aggravating.

incorporate verb **1** *the region was incorporated into Moldavian territory* ABSORB, include, subsume, assimilate, integrate, take in, swallow up.

2 *the model incorporates some advanced features* INCLUDE, contain, comprise, embody, embrace, build in, encompass.

3 *literary references were incorporated with photographs* BLEND, mix, mingle, meld; combine, unite, join.

incorporeal adjective *in the past, the incorporeal and invisible God was never represented* INTANGIBLE, impalpable, nonphysical; bodiless, disembodied, discarnate, immaterial; spiritual, ethereal, unsubstantial, insubstantial, transcendental; ghostly, spectral, supernatural. ANTONYM tangible.

incorrect adjective **1** *an incorrect answer* WRONG, erroneous, in error, mistaken, inaccurate, imprecise, wide of the mark, off target; untrue, false, fallacious; *informal* out, way out.

2 *incorrect behavior* INAPPROPRIATE, wrong, unsuitable, inapt, inapposite; ill-advised, ill-considered, ill-judged, injudicious, unacceptable, unfitting, out of keeping, improper, unseemly, unbecoming, indecorous; *informal* out of line, out of order.

incorrigible adjective *an incorrigible flirt* INVETERATE, habitual, confirmed, hardened, dyed-in-the-wool, incurable, chronic, irredeemable, hopeless, beyond hope; impenitent, unrepentant, unapologetic, unashamed; bad, naughty, terrible. ANTONYM repentant.

incorruptible adjective **1** *an incorruptible man* HONEST, honorable, trustworthy, principled, high-principled, unbribable, moral, ethical, good, virtuous. ANTONYM venal.

2 *an incorruptible substance* IMPERISHABLE, indestructible, indissoluble, enduring, everlasting. ANTONYM perishable.

increase verb **1** *demand is likely to increase* GROW, get bigger, get larger, enlarge, expand, swell; rise, climb, escalate, soar, surge, rocket, shoot up, spiral; intensify, strengthen, extend, heighten, stretch, spread, widen; multiply, snowball, mushroom, proliferate, balloon, build up, mount up, pile up, accrue, accumulate; *literary* wax. ANTONYM decrease.

2 *higher expectations will increase user demand* ADD TO, make larger, make bigger, augment, supplement, top up, build up, extend, raise, swell, inflate; magnify, maximize, intensify, strengthen, heighten, amplify; *informal* up, jack up, hike up, bump up, torque up, crank up. ANTONYM reduce.

▸ noun *the increase in size | an increase in demand* GROWTH, rise, enlargement, expansion, extension, multiplication, elevation, inflation; increment, addition, augmentation; magnification, intensification, amplification, climb, escalation, surge, upsurge, upswing, spiral, spurt; *informal* hike. ANTONYMS decrease, reduction.

increasingly adverb *the regime became increasingly draconian* MORE AND MORE, progressively, to an increasing extent, ever more.

incredible adjective **1** *I find his story incredible* UNBELIEVABLE, beyond belief, hard to believe, unconvincing, far-fetched, implausible, improbable, highly unlikely, dubious, doubtful; inconceivable, unthinkable, unimaginable, impossible; *informal* hard to swallow, cock-and-bull.

2 *an incredible feat of engineering* MAGNIFICENT, wonderful, marvelous, spectacular, remarkable, phenomenal, prodigious, breathtaking, extraordinary, unbelievable, amazing, stunning, astounding, astonishing, awe-inspiring, staggering, formidable, impressive, supreme, great, awesome, superhuman; *informal* fantastic, terrific, tremendous, stupendous, mind-boggling, mind-blowing, jaw-dropping, out of this world, far-out; *literary* wondrous.

EASILY CONFUSED WORDS **incredible, incredulous**

Believability is at the heart of both **incredible** and **incredulous**, but there is an important distinction in the respective uses of these two adjectives. **Incredible** means 'unbelievable' or 'not convincing' and can be applied to a situation, statement, policy, or threat to a person: *I find this testimony incredible.* **Incredulous** means 'disinclined to believe, skeptical'—the opposite of *credulous, gullible*—and is usually applied to a person's attitude: *he managed to look simultaneously incredulous and bored by her story.*

incredulous adjective *Chung was incredulous when the congressman was not more forthcoming in his first broadcast interview about the case* DISBELIEVING, skeptical, unbelieving, distrustful, mistrustful, suspicious, doubtful, dubious, unconvinced; cynical. See note at INCREDIBLE.

increment noun *the three-percent increment is unlikely to make much difference to the price* INCREASE, addition, supplement, gain, augmentation, accretion, addendum; enlargement, enhancement, boost; *informal* hike. ANTONYM reduction.

incremental adjective *the incremental increases in wages have been slow this year* GRADUAL, progressive, steady, step-by-step; increasing, growing.

incriminate verb *no witnesses to last night's shooting have incriminated Mr. Jackson* IMPLICATE, involve, enmesh; blame, accuse, denounce, inform against, point the finger at; entrap; *informal* frame, set up, stick/pin the blame on, rat on; *archaic* inculpate.

inculcate verb *the beliefs* ***inculcated in*** *him by his father* INSTILL IN, implant in, fix in, impress in, imprint in; hammer into, drum into, drive into, drill into.

incumbent adjective **1** *it is* ***incumbent on*** *you* ***to*** *tell them* NECESSARY FOR ONE TO, essential that, required that, imperative that; compulsory for one to, binding on one to, mandatory that.

2 *the incumbent president* CURRENT, present, in office, in power; reigning.

▸ noun *the first incumbent of the post* HOLDER, bearer, occupant.

incur verb *it is astonishing how many expenses they incurred in just one evening | these actions are likely to incur the coach's wrath* BRING UPON ONESELF, expose oneself to, lay oneself open to; run up; attract, invite, earn, arouse, cause, give rise to, be liable/subject to, meet with, sustain, experience, contract.

incurable adjective **1** *an incurable illness* UNTREATABLE, inoperable, irremediable; terminal, fatal, mortal; chronic.

2 *an incurable romantic* INVETERATE, dyed-in-the-wool, confirmed, established, long-established, long-standing, absolute, complete, utter, thorough, out-and-out, through and through; unashamed, unapologetic, unrepentant, incorrigible, hopeless.

incursion noun *an Israeli* ***incursion into*** *the Palestinian camp left nine dead* ATTACK ON, assault on, raid on, invasion of, storming of, overrunning of, foray into, blitz on, sortie into, sally into/against, advance on/into, push into, thrust into, infiltration of. ANTONYM retreat.

indebted adjective *nations we assumed would be indebted to us have turned a blind eye* BEHOLDEN, under an obligation, obliged, obligated, grateful, thankful, in debt, owing a debt of gratitude.

indecent adjective **1** *indecent photographs* OBSCENE, dirty, filthy, rude, coarse, naughty, vulgar, gross, crude, lewd, salacious, improper, smutty, off-color; pornographic, offensive, prurient, sordid, scatological; ribald, risqué, racy; *informal* porn, porno, X-rated, XXX, raunchy, blue; *euphemistic* adult.

2 *they left the dinner table with indecent haste* UNSEEMLY, improper, indecorous, unceremonious, indelicate, unbecoming, ungentlemanly, unladylike, unfitting, unbefitting; untoward, unsuitable, inappropriate; in bad taste, tasteless, unacceptable, offensive, crass.

indecipherable adjective *indecipherable handwriting* ILLEGIBLE, unreadable, hard to read, unintelligible, unclear; scribbled, scrawled, hieroglyphic, cramped, crabbed.

indecision noun *many an opportunity has been lost to indecision* INDECISIVENESS, irresolution, hesitancy, hesitation, tentativeness; ambivalence, doubt, doubtfulness, uncertainty, incertitude; vacillation, wavering, equivocation, second thoughts; shilly-shallying, dithering, temporizing, hemming and hawing, dilly-dallying, sitting on the fence; *formal* dubiety.

indecisive adjective **1** *an indecisive result* INCONCLUSIVE, proving nothing, settling nothing, open, indeterminate, undecided, unsettled, borderline, indefinite, unclear, ambiguous, vague; *informal* up in the air.

2 *an indecisive leader* IRRESOLUTE, hesitant, tentative, weak; vacillating, equivocating, dithering, wavering, faltering; ambivalent, divided, blowing hot and cold, of two minds, in a dilemma, in a quandary, torn; doubtful, unsure, uncertain; undecided, uncommitted; *informal* iffy, sitting on the fence, wishy-washy, shilly-shallying, waffling, waffly.

indecorous adjective *they swaggered in sporting wild hair and the most indecorous attire* IMPROPER, unseemly, unbecoming, undignified, immodest, indelicate, indecent, unladylike, ungentlemanly; inappropriate, incorrect, unsuitable, undesirable, unfitting, in bad taste, ill-bred, vulgar.

indeed adverb **1** *there was, indeed, quite a furor* AS EXPECTED, to be sure; in fact, in point of fact, as a matter of fact, in truth, actually, as it happens/happened, if truth be told, admittedly; *archaic* in sooth.

2 *"May I join you?" "Yes, indeed."* CERTAINLY, assuredly, of course, naturally, without (a) doubt, without question, by all means, yes; *informal* you bet, I'll say; *informal* indeedy.

3 *you are indeed clever* VERY, extremely, exceedingly, tremendously, immensely, singularly, decidedly, particularly, remarkably, really.

indefatigable adjective *the indefatigable Cosby spoke at eight different colleges* TIRELESS, untiring, unflagging, unwearied; determined, tenacious, dogged, single-minded, assiduous, industrious, hard-working, unswerving, unfaltering, unwavering, unshakable, resolute, indomitable; persistent, relentless, unremitting.

indefensible adjective *Smith admitted that her remarks about Collins were indefensible* INEXCUSABLE, unjustifiable, unjustified, unpardonable, unforgivable; uncalled for, unprovoked, gratuitous, unreasonable, unnecessary; insupportable, unacceptable, unwarranted, unwarrantable; flawed, wrong, untenable, unsustainable.

indefinable adjective *the flavor is indefinable* HARD TO DEFINE, hard to describe, indescribable, inexpressible, nameless; vague, obscure, nebulous, impalpable, intangible, elusive.

indefinite adjective **1** *an indefinite period* INDETERMINATE, unspecified, unlimited, unrestricted, undecided, undetermined, undefined, unfixed, unsettled, unknown, uncertain; limitless, infinite, endless, immeasurable. ANTONYMS fixed, limited.

2 *an indefinite idea* VAGUE, ill-defined, unclear, imprecise, inexact, loose, general, nebulous, fuzzy, hazy, obscure, ambiguous, equivocal. ANTONYM clear.

indelible adjective *indelible memories* INERADICABLE, permanent, lasting, ingrained, persisting, enduring, unfading, unforgettable, haunting, never to be forgotten.

indelicate adjective **1** *an indelicate question* INSENSITIVE, tactless, inconsiderate, undiplomatic, impolitic. ANTONYM tactful.

2 *an indelicate sense of humor* VULGAR, rude, crude, tasteless, bawdy, racy, risqué, ribald, earthy, indecent, improper, naughty, indecorous, off-color, dirty, smutty, raunchy. ANTONYMS polite, clean.

indemnity noun **1** *indemnity against loss* INSURANCE, assurance, protection, security, indemnification, surety, guarantee, warranty, safeguard.

2 *the company was paid $100,000 in indemnity* COMPENSATION, reimbursement, recompense, repayment, restitution, payment, redress, reparation(s), damages.

3 *legislative indemnity* SALARY, wages, pay, remuneration, earnings.

indent verb *the shoreline is indented by marshes, harbors, and tidal inlets* NOTCH, make an indentation in, nick; depress, impress, mark, imprint; scallop, groove, furrow.

▸ noun See INDENTATION.

indentation noun *the indentation in the side of the refrigerator is barely visible* HOLLOW, depression, dip, dent, indent, cavity, concavity, pit, trough; dimple, cleft; nick, notch, groove; impression, imprint, mark; recess, bay, inlet, cove.

indenture noun *the validity of the indenture was in question* CONTRACT, agreement, compact, deal, covenant, bond.

▸ verb *Taylor was indentured by the age of twelve* BIND, contract, employ, apprentice; *Law* article.

independence noun **1** *the struggle for Quebec independence* SELF-GOVERNMENT, self-rule, home rule, separation, self-determination, sovereignty, autonomy, freedom, liberty.

2 *he valued his independence* SELF-SUFFICIENCY, self-reliance, autonomy, freedom, liberty. See note at LIBERTY.

3 *financial independence* FREEDOM, comfort, ease.

independent adjective **1** *an independent country* SELF-GOVERNING, self-ruling, self-determining, sovereign, autonomous, free, nonaligned. ANTONYMS subservient, dependent.

2 *two independent groups of biologists verified the results* SEPARATE, different, unconnected, unrelated, dissociated, discrete. ANTONYM connected.

3 *independent schools* PRIVATE, private-sector, non-state-run, fee-paying; privatized, denationalized. ANTONYMS public, state-run.

4 *her grown-up, independent children* SELF-SUFFICIENT, self-supporting, self-reliant, standing on one's own two feet. ANTONYM dependent.

5 *independent advice* IMPARTIAL, unbiased, unprejudiced, neutral, disinterested, uninvolved, uncommitted, detached, dispassionate, objective, nonpartisan, nondiscriminatory. ANTONYM biased.

6 *an independent spirit* FREETHINKING, free, individualistic; unconventional, maverick, bold, unconstrained, unfettered, untrammeled. ANTONYMS orthodox, constrained.

independently adverb *I prefer to work independently* ALONE, on one's own, separately, unaccompanied, solo, autonomously; unaided, unassisted, without help, by one's own efforts, under one's own steam, single-handed, single-handedly, on one's own initiative. ANTONYMS jointly, assisted.

indescribable adjective *indescribable joy* INEXPRESSI-

BLE, indefinable, beyond words/description, ineffable, incommunicable; unutterable, unspeakable.

indestructible adjective *indestructible plastics* UNBREAKABLE, shatterproof, durable; lasting, enduring, everlasting, perennial, deathless, undying, immortal, inextinguishable, imperishable; *informal* heavy-duty, industrial-strength; *literary* adamantine. ANTONYMS fragile, breakable.

indeterminate adjective **1** *an indeterminate period of time* UNDETERMINED, uncertain, unknown, unspecified, unstipulated, indefinite, unfixed. ANTONYM known.

2 *some indeterminate figures* VAGUE, indefinite, unspecific, unclear, nebulous, indistinct; amorphous, shapeless, formless; hazy, faint, fuzzy, shadowy, dim. ANTONYMS definite, clear.

index noun **1** *the library's subject index* LIST, listing, inventory, catalog, register, directory.

2 *literature is an index to its time* GUIDE, sign, indication, indicator, gauge, measure, signal, mark, evidence, symptom, token; clue, hint.

▸ verb *he indexed his sources* LIST, catalog, make an inventory of, itemize, inventory, record.

indicate verb **1** *sales indicate a growing market* POINT TO, be a sign of, be evidence of, evidence, demonstrate, show, testify to, bespeak, be a symptom of, be symptomatic of, denote, connote, mark, signal, signify, suggest, imply; manifest, reveal, betray, display, reflect, represent; *formal* evince; *literary* betoken.

2 *the president indicated his willingness to use force* STATE, declare, make known, communicate, announce, mention, express, reveal, divulge, disclose; put it on record; admit.

3 *please indicate your preferences on the form* SPECIFY, designate, mark, stipulate; show.

4 *he indicated the direction we needed to go* POINT TO, point out, gesture toward.

indicated adjective *in such cases surgery is indicated* ADVISABLE, recommended, suggested, desirable, preferable, best, sensible, wise, prudent, in someone's best interests; necessary, needed, required, called for.

indication noun *there was no indication of injury* SIGN, signal, indicator, symptom, mark, manifestation, demonstration, show, evidence, attestation, proof; pointer, guide, hint, clue, intimation, omen, augury, portent, warning, forewarning. See note at SIGN.

indicative adjective *the results are indicative of a possible warming trend* SYMPTOMATIC, expressive, suggestive, representative, emblematic, symbolic; typical, characteristic.

indicator noun *the test is used as an indicator of performance* MEASURE, gauge, barometer, guide, index, mark, sign, signal, symptom; bellwether, herald, hint; standard, touchstone, yardstick, benchmark, criterion, point of reference, guideline, test, litmus test.

indict verb *the teenager was* ***indicted for*** *second-degree robbery* CHARGE WITH, accuse of, arraign for, take to court for, put on trial for, bring to trial for, prosecute for; cite for, impeach for. ANTONYM acquit.

indifference noun **1** *his apparent indifference infuriated her* LACK OF CONCERN, unconcern, disinterest, lack of interest, lack of enthusiasm, apathy, nonchalance, insouciance; boredom, unresponsiveness, impassivity, dispassion, detachment, coolness.

2 *a matter of indifference* UNIMPORTANCE, insignificance, irrelevance, inconsequentiality.

indifferent adjective **1** *an indifferent shrug* UNCONCERNED, uninterested, uncaring, casual, nonchalant, offhand, uninvolved, unenthusiastic, apathetic, lukewarm, phlegmatic, blasé, insouciant; unimpressed, bored, unmoved, unresponsive, impassive, dispassionate, detached, cool. ANTONYMS heedful, caring.

2 *an indifferent performance* MEDIOCRE, ordinary, average, middling, middle-of-the-road, uninspired, undistinguished, unexceptional, unexciting, unremarkable, run-of-the-mill, pedestrian, prosaic, lackluster, forgettable, amateur, amateurish; *informal* OK, so-so, 'comme ci, comme ça,' fair-to-middling, no great shakes, bush-league. ANTONYM brilliant.

indigenous adjective *indigenous species* NATIVE, original, aboriginal, autochthonous; local, domestic, homegrown; earliest, first. See note at NATIVE.

indigent adjective *indigent families* POOR, impecunious, destitute, penniless, impoverished, insolvent, poverty-stricken; needy, in need, hard up, disadvantaged, badly off; *informal* (flat) broke, strapped (for cash), on skid row, down-and-out; *formal* penurious. ANTONYM rich.

▸ noun *a shelter for the city's indigents* VAGRANT, homeless person, down-and-out, beggar, pauper, derelict, have-not; *informal* bum.

indigestion noun *my indigestion was probably caused by the fried shrimp* DYSPEPSIA, heartburn, hyperacidity, stomachache; upset stomach; *informal* bellyache, tummy ache, collywobbles; *technical* pyrosis.

indignant adjective *after the shabby way you've treated me, why shouldn't I be indignant?* AGGRIEVED, resentful, affronted, disgruntled, displeased, cross, angry, mad, annoyed, offended, exasperated, irritated, piqued, nettled, in high dudgeon, chagrined; *informal* peeved, vexed, irked, put out, miffed, aggravated, riled, in a huff, huffy, ticked off, sore.

indignation noun *she was filled with indignation at having been blamed unjustly* RESENTMENT, umbrage, affront, disgruntlement, displeasure, anger, outrage, annoyance, irritation, exasperation, vexation, offense, pique; *informal* aggravation; *literary* ire.

indignity noun *the indignity of being dumped by one's wife* SHAME, humiliation, loss of self-respect, loss of pride, loss of face, embarrassment, mortification, ignominy; disgrace, dishonor, stigma, discredit; affront, insult, abuse, mistreatment, injury, offense, injustice, slight, snub, discourtesy, disrespect; *informal* slap in the face, kick in the teeth.

indirect adjective **1** *an indirect effect* INCIDENTAL, accidental, unintended, unintentional, secondary, subordinate, ancillary, concomitant.

2 *the indirect route* ROUNDABOUT, circuitous, wandering, meandering, serpentine, winding, tortuous, zigzag.

3 *an indirect answer* OBLIQUE, inexplicit, implicit, implied, allusive, mealy-mouthed; backhanded.

indirectly adverb **1** *we're all affected, if only indirectly* INCIDENTALLY, secondarily, concomitantly, consequentially, contingently, accidentally.

2 *I heard about it indirectly* SECONDHAND, at second

hand, from others, in a roundabout way; *informal* through the grapevine.

3 *he referred to the subject indirectly* OBLIQUELY, by implication, allusively, by hinting.

indiscernible adjective See IMPERCEPTIBLE.

indiscreet adjective *indiscreet office romances* IMPRUDENT, unwise, impolitic, injudicious, incautious, irresponsible, ill-judged, ill-advised, misguided, ill-considered, careless, thoughtless, rash, unwary, hasty, reckless, precipitate, impulsive, foolhardy, foolish, shortsighted; undiplomatic, indelicate, tactless, insensitive; untimely, infelicitous; immodest, indecorous, unseemly, improper.

indiscretion noun 1 *he was prone to indiscretion* IMPRUDENCE, injudiciousness, incaution, irresponsibility; carelessness, rashness, recklessness, impulsiveness, foolhardiness, foolishness, folly; tactlessness, thoughtlessness, insensitivity; *humorous* foot-in-mouth disease.

2 *his past indiscretions* BLUNDER, lapse, gaffe, mistake, faux pas, error, slip, impropriety; misdemeanor, transgression, peccadillo, solecism, misdeed; *informal* slip-up. See note at SIN.

indiscriminate adjective *their choice of furnishings is appallingly indiscriminate* NONSELECTIVE, unselective, undiscriminating, uncritical, aimless, hit-or-miss, haphazard, random, arbitrary, unsystematic, undirected; wholesale, general, sweeping, blanket; thoughtless, unthinking, inconsiderate, casual, careless. ANTONYM selective.

indispensable adjective *the volunteers' help has been indispensable* ESSENTIAL, necessary, all-important, of the utmost importance, of the essence, vital, must-have, crucial, key, needed, required, requisite, imperative; invaluable. See note at NECESSARY. ANTONYM superfluous.

indisposed adjective 1 *my wife is indisposed* ILL, unwell, sick, on the sick list, poorly, ailing, not (very) well, out of sorts, out of action, hors de combat; *informal* under the weather, laid up. ANTONYM well.

2 *she was indisposed to help him* RELUCTANT, unwilling, disinclined, loath, unprepared, not disposed, not keen. ANTONYM willing.

indisposition noun See ILLNESS.

indisputable adjective *the photographs are what really made the facts indisputable* INCONTROVERTIBLE, incontestable, undeniable, irrefutable, beyond dispute, unassailable, unquestionable, beyond question, indubitable, not in doubt, beyond doubt, beyond a shadow of a doubt, unarguable, airtight, watertight; unequivocal, unmistakable, certain, sure, definite, definitive, proven, decisive, conclusive, demonstrable, self-evident, clear, clear-cut, plain, obvious, manifest, patent, palpable. ANTONYM questionable.

indistinct adjective 1 *the distant shoreline was indistinct* BLURRED, out of focus, fuzzy, hazy, misty, foggy, cloudy, shadowy, dim, nebulous; unclear, obscure, vague, faint, indistinguishable, indiscernible, barely perceptible, hard to see, hard to make out. ANTONYM clear.

2 *the last two digits are indistinct* INDECIPHERABLE, illegible, unreadable, hard to read. ANTONYM legible.

3 *indistinct sounds* MUFFLED, muted, low, quiet, soft, faint, inaudible, hard to hear; muttered, mumbled. ANTONYMS audible, clear.

indistinguishable adjective 1 *the two girls were indistinguishable* IDENTICAL, difficult to tell apart, like (two) peas in a pod, like Tweedledum and Tweedledee, very similar, two of a kind. ANTONYM dissimilar.

2 *the image had become indistinguishable | the voices are indistinguishable* UNINTELLIGIBLE, incomprehensible, hard to make out, indistinct, unclear; inaudible. ANTONYM clear.

individual adjective 1 *exhibitions devoted to individual artists* SINGLE, separate, discrete, independent, solo; sole, lone, solitary, isolated.

2 *the fashion world was eager to be rocked by her individual style* CHARACTERISTIC, distinctive, distinct, typical, particular, peculiar, personal, personalized, special; original, unique, exclusive, singular, idiosyncratic, different, unusual, novel, unorthodox, atypical, out of the ordinary, one of a kind.

▸ noun 1 *Ed was never a particularly happy individual* PERSON, human being, mortal, soul, creature; man, boy, woman, girl; character, personage; *informal* type, sort, customer, guy.

2 *the anthology is dedicated to the math professor who most encouraged her to be an individual* INDIVIDUALIST, free spirit, nonconformist, original, eccentric, character, maverick, rare bird, something else.

WORD NOTE individual

As a noun, this word has one legitimate use, which is to distinguish a single person from some larger group: *One of the enduring oppositions of British literature is that between the individual and society*; *Boy, she's a real individual.* It is not a synonym for *person* despite the fact that much legal, bureaucratic, and public-statement prose uses it that way—which is to say that it looms large in turgid crap like *Law-enforcement personnel apprehended the individual as he was attempting to exit the premises. Individual* for *person* and *an individual* for *someone* are pretentious, deadening puff-words; eschew them. (For more on puff-words, please see note at UTILIZE.) **—DFW**

individualistic adjective *an individualistic approach to symphonic composition* UNCONVENTIONAL, unorthodox, atypical, singular, unique, original, nonconformist, independent, individual, freethinking; eccentric, maverick, strange, odd, peculiar, quirky, queer, idiosyncratic; *informal* off-the-wall.

individuality noun *the need to assert our individuality* DISTINCTIVENESS, distinction, uniqueness, originality, singularity, particularity, peculiarity, differentness, separateness; personality, character, identity, self, ego.

individually adverb *the applications will be reviewed individually* ONE AT A TIME, one by one, singly, separately, severally, independently, apart. ANTONYM together.

indoctrinate verb *armed with an evil political agenda, they set out to indoctrinate the nation's idealistic youth* BRAINWASH, propagandize, proselytize, inculcate, instill, reeducate, persuade, convince, condition, program, mold, discipline; instruct, teach, train, school, drill.

indolence noun *his musical gifts dissolved in the indolence of his nature* LAZINESS, idleness, slothfulness, sloth, shiftlessness, inactivity, inaction, inertia, sluggishness, lifelessness, lethargy, languor, languidness, torpor, torpidity; *rare* otiosity; *literary* hebetude.

indolent adjective *those who choose to remain aimless and* *indolent will never benefit from our self-help programs* LAZY, idle, slothful, loafing, do-nothing, sluggardly, shiftless, lackadaisical, languid, inactive, inert, sluggish, lethargic, torpid; slack, good-for-nothing, feckless. ANTONYMS industrious, energetic.

indomitable adjective *the indomitable spirit of this team* INVINCIBLE, unconquerable, unbeatable, unassailable, invulnerable, unshakable, unsinkable; indefatigable, unyielding, unbending, stalwart, stouthearted, lionhearted, strong-willed, strong-minded, steadfast, staunch, resolute, firm, determined, intransigent, inflexible, adamant; unflinching, courageous, brave, valiant, heroic, intrepid, fearless, plucky, gritty. ANTONYM submissive.

indoors adverb *the ceremony was held indoors | I spent the day indoors* INSIDE, in, within; in one's home, at home, under the roof.

indubitable adjective *indubitable testimony* UNQUESTIONABLE, undoubtable, indisputable, unarguable, undebatable, incontestable, undeniable, irrefutable, incontrovertible, unmistakable, unequivocal, certain, sure, positive, definite, absolute, conclusive, watertight, ironclad; beyond doubt, beyond the shadow of a doubt, beyond dispute, beyond question, not in question, not in doubt; *informal* sure as shootin'. ANTONYM doubtful.

induce verb **1** *the pickets induced many workers to stay away* PERSUADE, convince, prevail upon, get, make, prompt, move, inspire, influence, encourage, motivate; coax into, wheedle into, cajole into, talk into, prod into; *informal* twist someone's arm. ANTONYM dissuade.

2 *how to induce hypnosis* BRING ABOUT, cause, produce, effect, create, give rise to, generate, instigate, engender, occasion, set in motion, lead to, result in, trigger, whip up, stir up, kindle, arouse, rouse, foster, promote, encourage; *literary* beget, enkindle; *rare* effectuate. ANTONYM prevent.

inducement noun *customers responded best to such inducements as rebates and low interest rates* INCENTIVE, encouragement, attraction, temptation, stimulus, bait, lure, pull, draw, spur, goad, impetus, motive, motivation, provocation; bribe, reward; *informal* carrot, come-on, sweetener. ANTONYM deterrent.

induct verb **1** *the new ministers were* ***inducted into*** *the cabinet* ADMIT TO, allow into, introduce to, initiate into, install in, instate in, swear into; appoint to.

2 *he* ***inducted*** *me* ***into*** *the skills of magic* INTRODUCE TO, acquaint with, familiarize with, make conversant with; ground in, instruct in, teach in, educate in, school in.

indulge verb **1** *Seth indulged his passion for vintage stemware* SATISFY, gratify, fulfill, feed, accommodate; yield to, give in to, give way to.

2 *she seldom* ***indulged in*** *sentimentality* WALLOW IN, give oneself up to, give way to, yield to, abandon oneself to, give free rein to; luxuriate in, revel in, lose oneself in.

3 *she did not indulge her children* PAMPER, spoil, overindulge, coddle, mollycoddle, cosset, baby, spoon-feed, pander to, wait on hand and foot, cater to someone's every whim, kill with kindness. PHRASE: **indulge oneself** *it's healthy to indulge yourself once in a while* TREAT ONESELF, give oneself a treat; go on a spree. *informal* go to town, splurge.

indulgence noun **1** *the indulgence of all his desires* SATISFACTION, gratification, fulfillment, satiation, appeasement; accommodation; slaking, quenching. ANTONYMS denial, withholding.

2 *excessive indulgence contributed to his ill health* SELF-GRATIFICATION, self-indulgence, overindulgence, intemperance, immoderation, excess, excessiveness, lack of restraint, extravagance, decadence; *rare* sybaritism. ANTONYMS moderation, restraint.

3 *they viewed vacations as an indulgence* EXTRAVAGANCE, luxury, treat, nonessential, extra, frill. ANTONYM necessity.

4 *his mother's indulgence made him ungovernable* PAMPERING, coddling, mollycoddling, spoiling, cosseting, babying. ANTONYM strictness.

5 *I ask for your indulgence* TOLERANCE, forbearance, understanding, kindness, compassion, sympathy, forgiveness, leniency, mercy, clemency, liberality. ANTONYMS severity, harshness.

indulgent adjective *the children took advantage of their indulgent sitter* PERMISSIVE, easygoing, liberal, tolerant, forgiving, forbearing, lenient, kind, kindly, generous, softhearted, compassionate, understanding, sympathetic; fond, doting, soft; compliant, obliging, accommodating. See note at LENIENT. ANTONYM strict.

industrial adjective **1** *industrial areas of the city* MANUFACTURING, factory; commercial, business, trade.

2 *industrial plastic* HEAVY-DUTY, durable, strong, tough, rugged.

industrialist noun *nineteenth-century industrialists* MANUFACTURER, factory owner; captain of industry, big businessman, magnate, tycoon, capitalist, financier.

industrious adjective *the industrious immigrants who founded our town in 1826* HARD-WORKING, diligent, assiduous, conscientious, steady, painstaking, sedulous, persevering, unflagging, untiring, tireless, indefatigable, studious; busy, as busy as a bee, active, bustling, energetic, on the go, vigorous, determined, dynamic, zealous, productive; with one's shoulder to the wheel, with one's nose to the grindstone. See note at BUSY. ANTONYM indolent.

industry noun **1** *Canadian industry* MANUFACTURING, production; construction.

2 *the publishing industry* BUSINESS, trade, field, line (of business); *informal* racket.

3 *the kitchen was a hive of industry* ACTIVITY, busyness, energy, vigor, productiveness; hard work, industriousness, diligence, application, dedication. ANTONYM inactivity.

inebriated adjective *an apparently inebriated boater stunned diners at a waterfront restaurant when he docked his craft in the buff* DRUNK, intoxicated, inebriate, impaired, drunken, tipsy, under the influence; *informal* plastered, smashed, bombed, sloshed, sozzled, sauced, lubricated, well-oiled, wrecked, juiced, blasted, stinko, blitzed, half-cut, fried, gassed, polluted, tanked (up), soaked, out of one's head/skull, loaded, trashed, buzzed, befuddled, besotted, pickled, pixilated, canned, cockeyed, blotto, blind drunk, roaring drunk, dead drunk, punch-drunk, ripped, stewed, tight, the worse for wear, far gone, pie-eyed, three sheets to the wind; *vulgar slang* shit-faced; *Brit. informal* bladdered, lashed; *informal, dated* in one's cups, merry; *literary* crapulous. See note at DRUNK. ANTONYM sober.

inedible adjective *the stew looked fabulous but it was inedible* UNEATABLE, indigestible, unsavory, unpalatable, unappetizing, unwholesome; stale, rotten, off, bad, unfit to eat.

ineffable adjective **1** *the ineffable, surging joy of the Beatles* INDESCRIBABLE, inexpressible, beyond words, beyond description, begging description; indefinable, unutterable, untold, unimaginable; overwhelming, breathtaking, awesome, marvelous, wonderful, staggering, amazing.

2 *the ineffable name of God* UNUTTERABLE, not to be uttered, not to be spoken, unmentionable, forbidden, taboo.

ineffective adjective **1** *an ineffective scheme* UNSUCCESSFUL, unproductive, fruitless, unprofitable, abortive, futile, purposeless, useless, worthless, ineffectual, inefficient, inefficacious, inadequate; feeble, inept, lame; *archaic* bootless.

2 *an ineffective president* INEFFECTUAL, inefficient, inefficacious, unsuccessful, powerless, impotent, lame-duck; inadequate, incompetent, incapable, unfit, inept, bungling, weak, poor; *informal* useless, hopeless.

ineffectual adjective . See INEFFECTIVE senses 1, 2.

inefficient adjective **1** *an inefficient worker* INEFFECTIVE, ineffectual, unproductive, incompetent, inept, incapable, unfit, unskillful, inexpert, amateurish, unprofessional; disorganized, unprepared; negligent, lax, sloppy, slack, careless; *informal* lousy, useless, good-for-nothing.

2 *inefficient processes* UNECONOMICAL, wasteful, unproductive, time-wasting, slow; deficient, disorganized, unsystematic.

inelegant adjective **1** *an inelegant laugh* UNREFINED, uncouth, unsophisticated, unpolished, uncultivated; ill-bred, coarse, vulgar, rude, impolite, unmannerly, tasteless. ANTONYM refined.

2 *an inelegant maneuver* GRACELESS, ungraceful, ungainly, uncoordinated, awkward, clumsy, lumbering; inept, unskillful, inexpert; *informal* having two left feet, clunky. ANTONYM graceful.

ineligible adjective *the aforementioned agencies will be ineligible to participate in any federally funded assistance program* UNQUALIFIED, unsuitable, unacceptable, undesirable, inappropriate, unworthy; ruled out, disqualified, disentitled; *Law* incompetent. ANTONYM qualified.

inept adjective *his mother could pitch a wicked fastball, but she was completely inept in the kitchen* INCOMPETENT, unskillful, unskilled, inexpert, amateurish; clumsy, awkward, maladroit, bungling, blundering; unproductive, unsuccessful, ineffectual, not up to scratch; *informal* ham-handed, ham-fisted, butterfingered, klutzy, all thumbs. ANTONYM competent.

inequality noun *Dominicans spoke out against the social inequality in their country* IMBALANCE, inequity, inconsistency, variation, variability; divergence, polarity, disparity, discrepancy, dissimilarity, difference; bias, prejudice, discrimination, unfairness.

inequitable adjective *inequitable salaries for similar positions* UNFAIR, unjust, unequal, uneven, unbalanced, one-sided, discriminatory, preferential, biased, partisan, partial, prejudiced. ANTONYM fair.

inequity noun *the inequity of the law* UNFAIRNESS, injustice, unjustness, discrimination, partisanship, partiality, favoritism, bias, prejudice.

inert adjective *forces that once drove the economy have become inert* UNMOVING, motionless, immobile, inanimate, still, stationary, static; dormant, sleeping; unconscious, comatose, lifeless, insensible, insensate, insentient; idle, inactive, sluggish, lethargic, indolent, stagnant, listless, torpid. ANTONYM active.

inertia noun *by the nature of its own inertia, the coal industry has remained an unshakable constant* INACTIVITY, inaction, inertness; unchanged state, stationary condition, stasis.

inescapable adjective *meeting the future in-laws is inescapable* UNAVOIDABLE, inevitable, ineluctable, inexorable; assured, sure, certain, guaranteed; necessary, required, compulsory, mandatory; *rare* ineludible. ANTONYM avoidable.

inessential adjective See NONESSENTIAL.

inestimable adjective *inestimable damage* IMMEASURABLE, incalculable, innumerable, unfathomable, indeterminable, measureless, countless, untold; limitless, boundless, unlimited, infinite, endless, inexhaustible; *informal* no end of; *literary* myriad. ANTONYM few.

inevitable adjective *at this point, war is inevitable* UNAVOIDABLE, inescapable, inexorable, ineluctable; assured, certain, sure, fixed; fated, destined, predestined, predetermined; *rare* ineludible. ANTONYM uncertain.

inevitably adverb *the epidemic of tobacco-related disease that will inevitably come* NATURALLY, necessarily, automatically, as a matter of course, of necessity, inescapably, unavoidably, certainly, surely, definitely, undoubtedly, incontrovertibly; *informal* like it or not; *formal* perforce.

inexact adjective *inexact diagnostic practices* IMPRECISE, inaccurate, approximate, rough, crude, general, vague, fuzzy, ill-defined; *informal* off-base, ballpark.

inexcusable adjective *our report found inexcusable national security weaknesses* INDEFENSIBLE, unjustifiable, unwarranted, unpardonable, unforgivable; blameworthy, censurable, reprehensible, deplorable, unconscionable, disgraceful, unacceptable, unreasonable.

inexhaustible adjective **1** *her patience is inexhaustible* UNLIMITED, limitless, illimitable, infinite, boundless, endless, never-ending, unfailing, everlasting; immeasurable, incalculable, inestimable, untold; copious, abundant, plentiful, bottomless. ANTONYM limited.

2 *the dancers were inexhaustible* TIRELESS, indefatigable, untiring, unwearied, unwearying, unfaltering, unflagging, unremitting, persevering, persistent, dogged. ANTONYMS weary, lacking stamina.

inexorable adjective **1** *the inexorable advance of science* RELENTLESS, unstoppable, inescapable, inevitable, unavoidable, irrevocable, unalterable; persistent, continuous, nonstop, steady, interminable, incessant, unceasing, unremitting, unrelenting.

2 *inexorable creditors* INTRANSIGENT, unbending, unyielding, inflexible, adamant, obdurate, immovable, unshakable; implacable, unappeasable, severe, hard, unforgiving, unsparing, uncompromising, ruthless, relentless, pitiless, merciless.

inexpensive adjective *inexpensive wine* CHEAP, low-priced, low-cost, modest, economical, competitive, affordable, reasonable, budget, bargain, cut-rate, reduced, discounted, discount, rock-bottom, giveaway, downmarket, low-end; *informal* bargain-basement, dirt cheap.

inexperienced adjective *she's inexperienced, but we expect her to become an excellent teacher* UNSEASONED, unpracticed, untrained, unschooled, unqualified, unskilled, amateur; ignorant, unversed, inexpert; ill-equipped, ill-prepared; naive, unsophisticated, callow, immature, green, unworldly; *informal* wet behind the ears.

inexpert adjective *inexpert installation spoils the windows irreparably* UNSKILLED, unskillful, amateur, amateurish, unprofessional, inexperienced; inept, incompetent, maladroit, uncoordinated, clumsy, bungling, blundering; *informal* ham-handed, ham-fisted, butterfingered.

inexplicable adjective *these inexplicable acts of vandalism have left the community stunned* UNACCOUNTABLE, unexplainable, incomprehensible, unfathomable, impenetrable, insoluble; baffling, puzzling, perplexing, mystifying, bewildering, confusing; mysterious, strange. ANTONYM understandable.

inexpressible adjective *my grief is inexpressible* INDESCRIBABLE, indefinable, unutterable, unspeakable, ineffable, beyond words, nameless; unimaginable, inconceivable, unthinkable, untold.

inexpressive adjective *a room of inexpressive faces* EXPRESSIONLESS, impassive, emotionless; inscrutable, unreadable, blank, vacant, glazed, glassy, lifeless, deadpan, wooden, stony; poker-faced, straight-faced.

inextinguishable adjective *his inextinguishable passion for literature* IRREPRESSIBLE, unquenchable, indestructible, undying, immortal, imperishable, unfailing, unceasing, ceaseless, enduring, everlasting, eternal, persistent.

inextricable adjective **1** *our lives are inextricable* INSEPARABLE, indivisible, entangled, tangled, mixed up.

2 *an inextricable situation* INESCAPABLE, unavoidable, ineluctable.

infallible adjective **1** *an infallible sense of timing* UNERRING, unfailing, faultless, flawless, impeccable, perfect, precise, accurate, meticulous, scrupulous.

2 *an infallible remedy* UNFAILING, unerring, guaranteed, dependable, trustworthy, reliable, sure, certain, safe, foolproof, effective; *informal* sure-fire; *formal* efficacious.

infamous adjective **1** *an infamous train robber* NOTORIOUS, disreputable; legendary, fabled, famed. ANTONYM reputable.

2 *infamous misconduct* ABOMINABLE, outrageous, shocking, shameful, disgraceful, dishonorable, discreditable, contemptible, unworthy; monstrous, atrocious, nefarious, appalling, dreadful, terrible, heinous, egregious, detestable, despicable, loathsome, hateful, vile, unspeakable, unforgivable, iniquitous, scandalous; *informal* dirty, filthy, lowdown. ANTONYM honorable.

infamy noun **1** *public infamy* NOTORIETY, disrepute, ill fame, disgrace, discredit, shame, dishonor, ignominy, scandal, censure, blame, disapprobation, condemnation.

2 *she was punished for her alleged infamy* WICKEDNESS, evil, vileness, iniquity, depravity, degeneracy, immorality; sin, wrongdoing, offense, abuse; *formal* turpitude.

infancy noun **1** *his twin died in infancy* BABYHOOD, early childhood.

2 *music video was in its infancy* BEGINNINGS, early days, early stages; seeds, roots; start, commencement, rise, emergence, genesis, dawn, birth, inception. ANTONYM end.

infant noun *a fretful infant* BABY, newborn, young child, (tiny) tot, little one, papoose; *Medicine* neonate; *informal* tiny; *literary* babe, babe in arms, suckling.

▸ adjective *an infant stage* DEVELOPING, emergent, emerging, embryonic, nascent, incipient, new, fledgling, budding, up-and-coming.

infantile adjective *it's time you outgrew your infantile behavior* CHILDISH, babyish, immature, puerile, juvenile, adolescent, jejune; silly, inane, fatuous.

infantry noun *the infantry, as usual, took the worst of the battle* INFANTRYMEN, foot soldiers, foot guards; the ranks; *informal* GIs; cannon fodder; *Military slang* grunts; *historical* footmen.

infatuated adjective *Kyle was hopelessly **infatuated with** his cousin's girlfriend* BESOTTED WITH, in love with, head over heels about, obsessed with, taken with, lovesick for, moonstruck over; enamored of, attracted to, devoted to, captivated by, enthralled by, enchanted by, bewitched by, under the spell of; *informal* smitten with, sweet on, keen on, hot for, gone on, hung up on, mad about, crazy about, nuts about, stuck on, carrying a torch for.

infect verb **1** *he didn't want to infect others with his chicken pox* PASS INFECTION TO, spread disease to, contaminate.

2 *nitrates were infecting rivers* CONTAMINATE, pollute, taint, foul, dirty, blight, damage, ruin; poison.

3 *his high spirits infected everyone* AFFECT, influence, have an impact on, touch; excite, inspire, stimulate, animate.

infection noun *a treatable skin infection* DISEASE, virus; disorder, condition, affliction, complaint, illness, ailment, sickness, infirmity; contamination, poison, septicemia, suppuration; *informal* bug; *dated* contagion; *Medicine* sepsis.

infectious adjective **1** *infectious disease* CONTAGIOUS, communicable, transmittable, transferable, spreadable; epidemic; *informal* catching; *dated* infective.

2 *her laughter is infectious* IRRESISTIBLE, compelling, persuasive, contagious, catching.

infer verb *is it really possible to infer that a crime was committed, given this flimsy evidence?* DEDUCE, conclude, conjecture, surmise, reason, interpret; gather, understand, presume, assume, take it, extrapolate; read between the lines, figure (out); *informal* reckon.

USAGE NOTE infer

Properly used, *infer* means "deduce; reason from premises to a conclusion"—e.g.: "We get no sense of the man himself from this book except what we can infer from the biographical facts that Mr. Magida presents." (*New York Times*; Aug. 18, 1996.)

Writers frequently misuse *infer* when *imply* (= hint at; suggest) would be the correct word—e.g.: "And no team is, of course, inferring [read *implying*] that Dallas isn't talented." (*New York Times*; Jan. 12, 1996.) Remember: a speaker or writer *implies* something without putting it expressly. A listener or reader *infers* beyond what has been literally expressed. Or, as Theodore Bernstein put it, "The *implier* is the pitcher; the *inferrer* is the catcher." (*The Careful Writer*; 1965.) Stylists agree that the important distinction between these words deserves to be maintained. **—BG**

inference noun *there should be no inference drawn from the fact that he chooses not to be a witness* DEDUCTION, conclusion, reasoning, conjecture, speculation, guess, presumption, assumption, supposition, reckoning, extrapolation.

inferior adjective **1** *poorer people were thought to be innately inferior* SECOND-CLASS, lesser, lower in status, lower-ranking, subordinate, second-fiddle, junior, minor; subservient, lowly, humble, menial, beneath one. ANTONYM superior.

2 *inferior accommodations* SECOND-RATE, substandard, low-quality, low-grade, downmarket, bush-league, unsatisfactory, shoddy, deficient; poor, bad, awful, dreadful, wretched; *informal* crummy, scuzzy, rotten, lousy, third-rate, tinpot, rinky-dink. ANTONYM luxury.

▸ noun *how dare she treat him as an inferior?* SUBORDINATE, junior, underling, minion, menial, peon. ANTONYM superior.

infernal adjective **1** *the infernal regions* HELLISH, nether, subterranean, underworld, chthonic, Tartarean; satanic, devilish, diabolical, fiendish, demonic.

2 *informal an infernal nuisance* DAMNABLE, wretched, confounded; annoying, irritating, infuriating, irksome, detestable, exasperating; *informal* damned, damn, blasted, blessed, pesky, aggravating; *informal, dated* cursed.

infertile adjective **1** *infertile soil* BARREN, unfruitful, unproductive; sterile, impoverished, arid.

2 *she was infertile* STERILE, barren; childless, unable to procreate/reproduce, impotent; *Medicine* infecund.

infest verb *without follow-up treatment, a new horde of ants will infest the building* OVERRUN, spread through, invade, infiltrate, pervade, permeate, inundate, overwhelm; beset, plague, swarm.

infested adjective *the bedding was infested with fleas* OVERRUN, swarming, teeming, crawling, alive, ridden, lousy; plagued, beset.

infidel noun *a holy war against the infidels* UNBELIEVER, disbeliever, nonbeliever, agnostic, atheist; heathen, pagan, idolater, heretic, freethinker, dissenter, nonconformist; *archaic* paynim; *rare* nullifidian.

infidelity noun *even after reconciliation, she could not forgive his infidelity* UNFAITHFULNESS, adultery, cuckoldry, disloyalty, extramarital sex; deceit, falseness; affair, liaison, fling, amour; *informal* fooling/playing around, cheating, two-timing, hanky-panky; *formal* fornication. ANTONYM faithfulness.

infiltrate verb *spies were prepared to infiltrate the enemy camp* INSINUATE ONESELF INTO, worm one's way into, sneak into, slip into, get into, invade, penetrate, enter; permeate, pervade, seep into/through, soak into.

infiltrator noun *once identified, the infiltrators were subjected to grueling questioning* SPY, secret agent, undercover agent, operative, informant, informer, mole, plant, spook; intruder, interloper, subversive.

infinite adjective **1** *the universe is infinite* BOUNDLESS, unbounded, unlimited, limitless, never-ending, interminable; immeasurable, fathomless, imponderable; extensive, vast; immense, great, huge, enormous. ANTONYMS limited, small.

2 *infinite resources* COUNTLESS, uncountable, inestimable, innumerable, numberless, immeasurable, incalculable, untold, myriad. ANTONYM limited.

infinitesimal adjective *these infinitesimal organisms can cause monstrously huge problems* MINUTE, tiny, minuscule, very small; microscopic, imperceptible, indiscernible; *informal* teeny, wee, teeny-weeny, itsy-bitsy, little-bitty. ANTONYM enormous.

infinity noun **1** *the infinity of space* ENDLESSNESS, infinitude, infiniteness, boundlessness, limitlessness; vastness, immensity.

2 *an infinity of accessories* INFINITE NUMBER, great number; abundance, profusion, host, multitude, mass, wealth; *informal* heap, stack.

infirm adjective *how long has he been so infirm?* FRAIL, weak, feeble, debilitated, decrepit, disabled; ill, unwell, sick, sickly, indisposed, ailing. See note at WEAK. ANTONYM healthy.

infirmity noun *the family would never openly discuss Aunt Erma's infirmity* ILLNESS, malady, ailment, disease, disorder, sickness, affliction, complaint, indisposition, frailty, weakness; disability, impairment.

inflame verb **1** *his opinions inflamed his rival* ENRAGE, incense, anger, madden, infuriate, exasperate, provoke, antagonize, rile; *informal* make someone see red, make someone's blood boil. ANTONYM placate.

2 *the case inflamed passions against the pit bull* INCITE, arouse, rouse, provoke, stir up, whip up, kindle, ignite, touch off, foment, inspire, stimulate, agitate. ANTONYMS calm, dampen.

3 *he inflamed an already tense situation* AGGRAVATE, exacerbate, intensify, worsen, compound. ANTONYM soothe.

inflamed adjective **1** *the cut became inflamed* SWOLLEN, puffed up; red; raw, sore, painful, tender; infected, septic.

2 *inflamed feelings* ANGRY, infuriated, furious, enraged; excited, aroused, stimulated, titillated.

inflammable adjective *inflammable fabrics* FLAMMABLE, combustible, incendiary, ignitable; volatile, unstable. ANTONYM fireproof.

inflammation noun *apply ice to the inflammation* SWELLING, puffiness; redness; rawness, soreness, tenderness; infection, festering, suppuration, septicity.

inflammatory adjective *neither senator condemned the inflammatory language used by Sharpton* PROVOCATIVE, incendiary, inflaming, inciting, agitating, stirring, rousing, provoking, fomenting, rabble-rousing, seditious, subversive, mutinous; fiery, passionate; controversial, contentious.

inflate verb **1** *she inflated the mattress* BLOW UP, fill up, fill with air, aerate, pump up; dilate, distend, swell. ANTONYM deflate.

2 *the demand inflated prices* INCREASE, raise, boost, escalate, put up; *informal* hike up, jack up, bump up, boost (up). ANTONYMS decrease, depress.

3 *the figures were inflated by the press* EXAGGERATE, magnify, overplay, overstate, enhance, embellish, increase, amplify, augment. ANTONYMS play down, understate, soft-pedal.

inflated adjective **1** *an inflated balloon* BLOWN UP, aerated, filled, puffed up/out, pumped up; distended, expanded, engorged, swollen.

2 *inflated prices* HIGH, sky-high, excessive, unreasonable, prohibitive, outrageous, exorbitant, extortionate; *informal* steep, stiff, pricey.

3 *an inflated opinion of himself* EXAGGERATED, magnified, aggrandized, immoderate, overblown, overstated.

4 *inflated language* HIGH-FLOWN, extravagant, exaggerated, elaborate, flowery, ornate, overblown, overwrought, grandiloquent, magniloquent, lofty, grandiose; affected, pretentious, bombastic, tumid; *informal* windy, highfalutin.

inflection noun *when I read my lines, he'd gently correct my pronunciation and inflection.* STRESS, cadence, rhythm, accent, intonation, pitch, emphasis, modulation, lilt, tone.

inflexible adjective **1** *his inflexible attitude* STUBBORN, obstinate, obdurate, intractable, intransigent, unbending, immovable, unaccommodating; hidebound, single-minded, pigheaded, mulish, uncompromising, adamant, firm, resolute, diehard, dyed-in-the-wool; *formal* refractory. ANTONYMS accommodating, flexible.

2 *inflexible rules* UNALTERABLE, unchangeable, immutable, unvarying; firm, fixed, set, established, entrenched, hard and fast, carved in stone; stringent, strict, hardline, ironclad. ANTONYM flexible.

3 *inflexible plastic* RIGID, stiff, unyielding, unbending, unbendable; hard, firm, inelastic. ANTONYMS pliable, flexible.

inflict verb **1** *he* ***inflicted*** *an injury* ***on*** *James* ADMINISTER TO, deliver to, deal out to, dispense to, mete out to; impose on, exact on, wreak on; cause to, give to; *informal* dish out to.

2 *I won't inflict myself on you any longer* IMPOSE, force, thrust, foist; saddle someone with, burden someone with.

influence noun **1** *the influence of parents on their children* EFFECT, impact; control, sway, hold, power, authority, mastery, domination, supremacy; guidance, direction; pressure.

2 *a bad* ***influence on*** *young girls* EXAMPLE TO, (role) model for, guide for, inspiration to.

3 *political influence* POWER, authority, sway, leverage, weight, pull, standing, prestige, stature, rank; *informal* clout, muscle, teeth.

▸ verb **1** *bosses can influence our careers* AFFECT, have an impact on, impact, determine, guide, control, shape, govern, decide; change, alter, transform.

2 *an attempt to influence the jury* SWAY, bias, prejudice, suborn; pressure, coerce; dragoon, intimidate, browbeat, brainwash; *informal* twist someone's arm, lean on, put ideas into one's head.

influential adjective **1** *an influential leader* POWERFUL, dominant, controlling, strong, authoritative, persuasive; important, affluential, prominent, distinguished, eminent. ANTONYMS unimportant, impotent.

2 *she was influential in shaping his career* INSTRUMENTAL, significant, important, crucial, pivotal. ANTONYM insignificant.

influx noun **1** *an influx of tourists* INUNDATION, rush, stream, flood, incursion; invasion, intrusion.

2 *influxes of river water* INFLOW, inrush, flood, inundation.

inform verb **1** *she informed him that she was ill* TELL, notify, apprise, advise, impart to, communicate to, let someone know; brief, prime, enlighten, send word to, give/supply information to; *informal* fill someone in, clue someone in.

2 *he* ***informed on*** *two of the suspects* DENOUNCE, give away, betray, incriminate, inculpate, report, finger; sell out, stab in the back; *informal* rat on/out, squeal on, tell on, blab on, tattle on, blow the whistle on, sell down the river, snitch on.

3 *the articles were informed by feminism* SUFFUSE, pervade, permeate, infuse, imbue, inspire; characterize.

informal adjective **1** *an informal chat* UNOFFICIAL, casual, relaxed, easygoing, unceremonious; open, friendly, intimate; simple, unpretentious, easy; *informal* unstuffy, laid-back, chummy. ANTONYMS official, formal.

2 *informal language* COLLOQUIAL, vernacular, idiomatic, demotic, popular; familiar, everyday, unofficial; simple, natural, unpretentious; *informal* slangy, chatty, folksy. ANTONYMS literary, formal.

3 *informal clothes* CASUAL, relaxed, comfortable, everyday, sloppy, leisure; *informal* comfy, cazh. ANTONYM formal.

informant noun See INFORMER.

information noun *we'll give you the latest information* DETAILS, particulars, facts, figures, statistics, data; knowledge, intelligence; instruction, advice, guidance, direction, counsel, enlightenment; news, word; *informal* info, lowdown, dope, dirt, inside story, scoop, poop. See note at KNOWLEDGE.

informative adjective *he hosts TV's most informative game show* INSTRUCTIVE, instructional, illuminating, enlightening, revealing, explanatory; factual, educational, educative, edifying, didactic; *informal* newsy.

informed adjective *our informed listeners tell us we've reported the wrong concert dates* KNOWLEDGEABLE, enlightened, literate, educated; sophisticated, cultured; briefed, versed, up to date, up to speed, in the know, au courant, au fait; *informal* hip, in the loop. ANTONYM ignorant.

informer noun *a Libyan informer for the CIA* INFORMANT, betrayer, traitor, Judas, double-crosser, collaborator, spy, double agent, fifth columnist, infiltrator, plant, tattletale; *informal* rat, squealer, whistle-blower, snake in the grass, snitch, fink, stool pigeon, stoolie, canary.

infraction noun *leaving the grounds before noon is an infraction of the rules | Hurley has been cited for another infraction* VIOLATION, contravention, breach, transgression, infringement, offense; neglect, dereliction, noncompliance; *Law* contumacy.

infrequent adjective *her infrequent visits* RARE, uncommon, unusual, exceptional, few (and far between), as rare/scarce as hen's teeth; unaccustomed, unwonted; isolated, scarce, scattered; sporadic, irregular, intermittent, seldom; *informal* once in a blue moon. ANTONYM common.

infringe verb **1** *the statute infringed constitutionally guaranteed rights* CONTRAVENE, violate, transgress, break, breach; disobey, defy, flout, fly in the face of; disregard, ignore, neglect; go beyond, overstep, exceed; *Law* infract. ANTONYMS obey, comply with.

2 *the surveillance* ***infringed on*** *his rights* RESTRICT, limit, curb, check, encroach on; undermine, erode, diminish, weaken, impair, damage, compromise. ANTONYM preserve.

infuriate verb *the governor's veto is likely to infuriate child-care providers statewide* ENRAGE, incense, anger, inflame; exasperate, antagonize, provoke, rile, annoy, irritate, aggravate, madden, nettle, gall, irk, vex, get on someone's nerves, try someone's patience, rankle; *informal* make someone see red, get someone's back up, make someone's blood boil, needle, ride, tick off, tee off, piss off, PO, wind up, get to, bug. ANTONYMS please, humor.

infuriating adjective *it's infuriating that they leave that dog outside to bark all day* EXASPERATING, maddening, annoying, irritating, irksome, vexatious, trying, tiresome; *informal* aggravating, pesky, infernal.

infuse verb **1** *she was infused with pride* FILL, suffuse, imbue, inspire, charge, pervade, permeate.

2 *he infused new life into the group* INSTILL, breathe, inject, impart, inculcate, introduce, add.

3 *infuse the dried herbs in hot oil* STEEP, brew, stew, soak, immerse, marinate.

ingenious adjective *an ingenious economist | the kids in her science class have devised an ingenious machine for sorting recyclables* INVENTIVE, creative, imaginative, original, innovative, pioneering, resourceful, enterprising, inspired; clever, intelligent, smart, brilliant, masterly, talented, gifted, skillful; astute, sharp-witted, quick-witted, shrewd; elaborate, sophisticated. See note at CREATIVE.

ingenuity *the boundless ingenuity of da Vinci* INVENTIVENESS, creativity, imagination, innovation, enterprise, insight, perception, perceptiveness, intuition, inspiration; finesse, flair, artistry; genius, intelligence, cleverness, brilliance; talent, skill, mastery; acumen, astuteness, sharpness, shrewdness; *informal* thinking outside the box.

ingenuous adjective *she had never before met a grown man so ingenuous* NAIVE, innocent, simple, childlike, trusting, unwary; unsuspicious, unworldly, wide-eyed, inexperienced, green; open, sincere, honest, frank, candid, forthright, artless, guileless, genuine, upfront. See note at GULLIBLE. ANTONYM artful.

ingest verb *you may gargle with the solution but do not ingest it* CONSUME, swallow, take in, eat, devour, imbibe, drink; *informal* gobble up, wolf down, put away, down, inhale, scarf (down).

inglorious adjective *her association with the blackmailers brought an inglorious end to an otherwise brilliant career* SHAMEFUL, dishonorable, ignominious, discreditable, disgraceful, scandalous; humiliating, mortifying, demeaning, ignoble, undignified, wretched, shabby.

ingrained, engrained adjective **1** *ingrained attitudes* ENTRENCHED, established, deep-rooted, deep-seated, fixed, firm, unshakable, ineradicable; inveterate, dyed-in-the-wool, abiding, enduring, stubborn. See note at INHERENT. ANTONYM transient.

2 *ingrained dirt* GROUND-IN, fixed, implanted, embedded; permanent, indelible, ineradicable. ANTONYM superficial.

ingratiate PHRASE: **ingratiate oneself** *he has **ingratiated himself with** President Jiang by running ideological education campaigns* CURRY FAVOR WITH, cultivate, win over, get in good with; toady to, grovel to, fawn over, kowtow to, play up to, pander to, flatter, court, wheedle, schmooze; *informal* suck up to, lick someone's boots, butter up, brown-nose.

ingratiating adjective *a forced and ingratiating smile* SYCOPHANTIC, toadying, fawning, unctuous, obsequious; flattering, insincere; smooth-tongued, slick; greasy, oily, saccharine; *informal* smarmy, slimy.

ingratitude noun *these sanctions have sent a message of ingratitude to the many honest and hard-working officers* UNGRATEFULNESS, thanklessness, lack of appreciation, nonrecognition.

ingredient adjective *crystallized iodine is a legal ingredient of an illegal drug* CONSTITUENT, component, element; part, piece, bit, strand, portion, unit, feature, aspect, attribute; (**ingredients**) contents, makings.

ingress noun *two doors offer ingress to the station* ENTRY, entrance, entryway, entrée, access, admittance, admission; way in, approach, passage. ANTONYM exit.

in-group noun INNER CIRCLE, in-crowd, popular crowd, clique, set, circle, coterie; *informal* gang, bunch, crew.

inhabit verb *outside of the research team, humans do not inhabit this island* LIVE IN/ON, occupy; settle (in/on), people, populate, colonize; dwell in/on, reside in/on, tenant, lodge in/on, have one's home in/on; *formal* be domiciled in/on, abide in/on.

inhabitant noun *the inhabitants have organized a protest* RESIDENT, occupant, occupier, dweller, squatter, settler; local, native; *formal* denizen; (**inhabitants**) population, populace, people, public, community, citizenry, townsfolk, townspeople.

inhale verb *inhale deeply | we'd rather not inhale your cigar smoke* BREATHE IN, inspire, draw in, suck in, take in, sniff in, drink in.

inharmonious adjective **1** *inharmonious sounds* UNMELODIOUS, discordant, unharmonious, unmusical, dissonant, off-key; grating, harsh, cacophonous; *rare* absonant. ANTONYM musical.

2 *once you've endured a dinner with her family you will never again think that your relatives are inharmonious* ANTAGONISTIC, argumentative, quarrelsome, captious, disputatious, belligerent, confrontational, combative. ANTONYM congenial.

inherent adjective *inherent traits* INTRINSIC, innate, immanent, built-in, indwelling, inborn, ingrained, deep-rooted; essential, fundamental, basic, structural, organic; natural, instinctive, instinctual, congenital, native. ANTONYM acquired.

THE RIGHT WORD

A quality that is **inherent** is a permanent part of a person's nature or essence (*an inherent tendency to fight back*). If it is **ingrained**, it is deeply wrought into his or her substance or character (*ingrained prejudice against women*). **Inborn** and **innate** are nearly synonymous, sharing the basic sense of existing at the time of birth, but *innate* is usually preferred in an abstract or philosophical context (*innate defects; innate ideas*), while *inborn* is reserved for human characteristics that are so deep-seated they seem to have been there from birth (*an inborn aptitude for the piano*). **Congenital** also means from the time of one's birth, but it is primarily used in medical contexts and refers to problems or defects (*congenital color-blindness; a congenital tendency toward schizophrenia*). **Intrinsic** and **essential** are broader terms that can apply to things as well as people. Something that is *essential* is part of the essence or constitution of something (*an essential ingredient; essential revisions in the text*), while an *intrinsic* quality is one that belongs naturally to a person or thing (*her intrinsic fairness; an intrinsic weakness in the design*).

---

inherit verb **1** *she inherited his farm* BECOME HEIR TO, come into/by, be bequeathed, be left, be willed, receive; *Law* be devised.

2 *Richard inherited the title* SUCCEED TO, assume, take over, come into; *formal* accede to.

inheritance noun **1** *a comfortable inheritance* LEGACY, bequest, endowment, bestowal, provision; birthright, heritage, patrimony; *Law* devise.

2 *his* ***inheritance of*** *the title* SUCCESSION TO, accession to, assumption of, elevation to.

inhibit verb **1** *the obstacles that inhibit change* IMPEDE, hinder, hamper, hold back, discourage, interfere with, obstruct, slow down, retard; curb, check, suppress, restrict, fetter, cramp, frustrate, stifle, prevent, block, thwart, foil, stop, halt. See note at THWART. ANTONYMS encourage, allow.

2 *she feels inhibited from taking part* PREVENT, disallow, exclude, forbid, prohibit, preclude, ban, bar, interdict. ANTONYM encourage.

inhibited adjective *witnesses should not be inhibited to reveal what they know | she was so inhibited that most people thought she was cold and unfeeling* SHY, reticent, reserved, self-conscious, diffident, bashful, coy; wary, reluctant, hesitant, insecure, unconfident, unassertive, timid; withdrawn, repressed, constrained, undemonstrative; *informal* uptight, anal-retentive.

inhibition noun **1** *they overcame their inhibitions* SHYNESS, reticence, self-consciousness, reserve, diffidence; wariness, hesitancy, hesitation, insecurity; timidity; repression, reservation; psychological block; *informal* hang-up.

2 *writing without inhibition* HINDRANCE, hampering, discouragement, obstruction, impediment, suppression, repression, restriction, restraint, constraint, cramping, stifling, prevention; curb, check, bar, barrier.

inhospitable adjective **1** *the inhospitable landscape* UNINVITING, unwelcoming; bleak, forbidding, cheerless, hostile, savage, wild, harsh, inimical; uninhabitable, barren, bare, austere, desolate, stark, spartan. ANTONYMS welcoming, cheery.

2 *forgive me if I seem inhospitable* UNWELCOMING, unfriendly, unsociable, antisocial, unneighborly, uncongenial; aloof, cool, cold, frosty, distant, remote, indifferent, uncivil, discourteous, ungracious; ungenerous, unkind, unsympathetic; *informal* standoffish. ANTONYMS welcomng, warm, friendly.

inhuman adjective **1** *inhuman treatment* CRUEL, harsh, inhumane, brutal, callous, sadistic, severe, savage, vicious, barbaric; monstrous, heinous, egregious; merciless, ruthless, pitiless, remorseless, cold-blooded, heartless, hard-hearted, dastardly; unkind, inconsiderate, unfeeling, uncaring; *informal* beastly. ANTONYM humane.

2 *he ran at an inhuman pace* SUPERHUMAN, unearthly, extraordinary, phenomenal, exceptional, incredible, unbelievable.

inhumane adjective See INHUMAN sense 1.

inimical adjective *an inimical gaze | policies inimical to democracy* HARMFUL, injurious, detrimental, deleterious, prejudicial, damaging, hurtful, destructive, ruinous, pernicious; antagonistic, contrary, antipathetic, unfavorable, adverse, opposed; hostile, unkind, unsympathetic, unfriendly, ill-disposed, malevolent; unwelcoming, cold, frosty; *literary* malefic. See note at HOSTILE. ANTONYMS friendly, favorable.

inimitable adjective *after years of trying to imitate Hitchcock, I finally accepted the fact that the master is inimitable* INCOMPARABLE, unparalleled, unrivaled, peerless, matchless, unequaled, unsurpassable, superlative, supreme, perfect, beyond compare, second to none, in a class of one's own; unique, distinctive, individual, sui generis; *formal* unexampled.

iniquity noun **1** *many runaways become the pawns of these merchants of iniquity* WICKEDNESS, sinfulness, immorality, impropriety; vice, evil, sin; villainy, criminality; odiousness, atrocity, egregiousness; outrage, monstrosity, obscenity, reprehensibility; *formal* turpitude. ANTONYMS morality, virtue.

2 *I will forgive their iniquity* SIN, crime, transgression, wrongdoing, wrong, violation, offense, vice. ANTONYMS goodness, virtue.

initial adjective *the initial stages* BEGINNING, opening, commencing, starting, inceptive, embryonic, fledgling; first, early, primary, preliminary, elementary, foundational, preparatory; introductory, inaugural. ANTONYM final.

▸ verb *he initialed the warrant* PUT ONE'S INITIALS ON, initialize, sign, ink, countersign, autograph, endorse, inscribe, witness, verify.

initially adverb *initially, we thought it might be pilot error* AT FIRST, at the start, at the outset, in/at the beginning, to begin with, to start with, originally.

initiate verb **1** *the government initiated the scheme* BEGIN, start (off), commence; institute, inaugurate, launch, instigate, establish, set up, start the ball rolling on; originate, pioneer; *informal* kick off, spark. ANTONYM finish.

2 *he was initiated into a cult* ADMIT, induct, install, incorporate, enlist, enroll, recruit, sign up, swear in; ordain, invest. ANTONYM expel.

3 *she was* ***initiated into*** *the business of publishing* TEACH ABOUT, instruct in, tutor in, school in, prime in, ground in; familiarize with, acquaint with; indoctrinate; *informal* show someone the ropes in/within.

▸ noun *the initiates were put through the customary opening-day paces* NOVICE, starter, beginner, newcomer; student, pupil, learner, trainee, apprentice; recruit, new recruit, raw recruit, tyro, neophyte; postulant, novitiate; *informal* rookie, newbie, new kid (on the block), greenhorn.

initiation noun **1** *the initiation of the program* BEGINNING, starting, commencement; institution, inauguration, launch, opening, instigation, actuation, origination, devising, inception; establishment, setting up; *informal* kickoff. ANTONYM finish.

2 *a rite of initiation into the tribe* INDUCTION, introduction, admission, admittance, installation, incorporation, ordination, investiture, enlistment, enrollment, recruitment; baptism. ANTONYM expulsion.

initiative noun **1** *employers are looking for people with initiative* SELF-MOTIVATION, resourcefulness, inventiveness, imagination, ingenuity, originality, creativity, enterprise; drive, dynamism, ambition, motivation, spirit, energy, vision; *informal* get-up-and-go, pep, moxie, spunk, gumption.

2 *a recent initiative on recycling* PLAN, scheme, strategy, stratagem, measure, proposal, step, action, approach.

inject verb 1 *he injected a painkiller* ADMINISTER, introduce; *informal* shoot (up), mainline.

2 *a pump injects air into the valve* INSERT, introduce, feed, push, force, shoot. See note at INSERT.

3 *he injected new life into the team* INTRODUCE, instill, infuse, imbue, breathe.

4 *she injected a note of realism into the debate* INTERJECT, interpose, throw in, add, contribute.

injection noun 1 *every time I go to the doctor's, I seem to be due for another injection* INOCULATION, vaccination, immunization, booster (shot); *informal* jab, shot, needle, hypo, fix.

2 *her injection of humor into the discussion was a godsend* INTRODUCTION, infusion, instilling, imbuing, inculcation.

injudicious adjective *he now regrets his injudicious comments* IMPRUDENT, unwise, inadvisable, ill-advised, misguided; ill-considered, ill-judged, incautious, hasty, rash; inappropriate, impolitic, inexpedient; foolish, foolhardy, harebrained. ANTONYM prudent.

injunction noun *the injunction prevents Sunday trading* ORDER, ruling, directive, command, instruction; decree, edict, dictum, dictate, fiat, mandate, writ; warning, caution, admonition.

injure verb 1 *he injured his foot* HURT, wound, damage, harm; cripple, lame, disable; maim, mutilate, deform, mangle, break.

2 *his comments injured her reputation* DAMAGE, mar, impair, spoil, ruin, blight, blemish, tarnish, blacken.

3 *dated my actions have injured no one* WRONG, abuse, do an injustice to, offend against, maltreat, mistreat, ill-use.

injured adjective 1 *his injured arm* HURT, wounded, damaged, sore, bruised; crippled, lame, disabled; maimed, mutilated, deformed, mangled, broken, fractured. ANTONYM healthy.

2 *the injured party* WRONGED, offended, maltreated, mistreated, ill-used, harmed; defamed, maligned, insulted, dishonored. ANTONYM offending.

3 *an injured tone* UPSET, hurt, wounded, offended, reproachful, pained, aggrieved; displeased, unhappy, put out, disgruntled, cut to the quick. ANTONYMS healthy, offending.

injurious adjective *the searing summer sun could prove injurious | an injurious story* HARMFUL, damaging, deleterious, detrimental, hurtful, baleful; disadvantageous, unfavorable, undesirable, adverse, inimical, unhealthy, pernicious; insulting, libelous, wrongful; *literary* malefic.

injury noun 1 *minor injuries* WOUND, bruise, cut, gash, laceration, scratch, graze, abrasion, contusion, lesion; *Medicine* trauma.

2 *they escaped without injury* HARM, hurt, damage, pain, suffering, impairment, affliction; disfigurement.

3 *the injury to her feelings* OFFENSE, abuse; affront, insult, slight, snub, indignity, slap in the face; wrong, wrongdoing, injustice.

injustice noun 1 *the injustice of the world* UNFAIRNESS, unjustness, inequity, corruption; cruelty, tyranny, repression, exploitation; bias, prejudice, discrimination, intolerance.

2 *his sacking was an injustice* WRONG, offense, crime, sin, misdeed, outrage, atrocity, scandal, disgrace, affront; *informal* raw deal.

inkling noun *I had no inkling of their intentions* IDEA, notion, sense, impression, conception, suggestion, indication, whisper, glimmer; (sneaking) suspicion, fancy, hunch, feeling; hint, clue, intimation, sign; *informal* the foggiest (idea), the faintest (idea).

inky adjective 1 *the inky darkness* BLACK, jet-black, pitch-black; sable, ebony, dark, raven; *literary* Stygian.

2 *inky fingers* INK-STAINED, stained, blotchy, smudged.

inlaid adjective *an inlaid design of glass beads in the tile | an inlaid floor* INSET, set, studded, lined, paneled, laid; ornamented, decorated; mosaic, intarsia, marquetry.

inland adjective 1 *inland areas* INTERIOR, inshore, central, internal, upcountry, upriver; landlocked. ANTONYM coastal.

2 *inland trade* DOMESTIC, internal, home, local; national, provincial. ANTONYM international.

▸ adverb *the goods were carried inland* UPCOUNTRY, upriver, inshore, to the interior.

inlet noun 1 *we drifted toward a marshy inlet* COVE, bay, bight, estuary, fjord, sound, armlet, salt chuck.

2 *a fresh-air inlet* VENT, flue, shaft, duct, channel, passage, pipe, pipeline, opening.

inmate noun 1 *at least two dozen inmates were treated for minor injuries following the prison fire* PRISONER, convict, captive, detainee, internee; *informal* jailbird, con, yardbird, lifer.

2 *from our treehouse we would watch the inmates of Twin Oaks Hospital tending to their pretty little gardens* PATIENT, in-patient; convalescent; resident, inhabitant, occupant.

inn noun *the inn where Longfellow stayed* HOTEL, guest house, lodge, bed and breakfast, B&B, hostel; tavern, bar, hostelry, taproom, pub, public house, watering hole; *French* auberge; *dated* alehouse.

innards plural noun 1 *the pig's innards* ENTRAILS, internal organs, viscera, intestines, bowels, guts; *informal* insides.

2 *the innards of the engine* (INNER) WORKINGS, mechanism, machinery, components, parts.

innate adjective *an innate talent for woodworking* INBORN, inbred, inherent, indwelling, natural, intrinsic, instinctive, intuitive, unlearned; hereditary, inherited, in the blood, in the family; inbuilt, deep-rooted, deep-seated, hard-wired, connate. See note at INHERENT. ANTONYM acquired.

inner adjective 1 *the inner gates* INTERNAL, interior, inside, inmost, innermost. ANTONYM external.

2 *the premier's inner circle* PRIVILEGED, restricted, exclusive, private, confidential, intimate.

3 *inner feelings* HIDDEN, secret, deep, underlying, unapparent; veiled, unrevealed. ANTONYM apparent.

4 *one's inner life* MENTAL, intellectual, psychological, spiritual, emotional.

innermost adjective 1 *the innermost shrine* CENTRAL, middle, internal, interior.

2 *her innermost feelings* DEEPEST, deep-seated, inward,

underlying, intimate, private, personal, secret, hidden, concealed, unexpressed, unrevealed, unapparent; true, real, honest.

innkeeper noun *relatively few innkeepers maintain a constant Internet connection* LANDLORD, landlady, hotelier, hotel owner, proprietor, manager, host, hostess; licensee, barkeeper, barkeep; publican, restaurateur.

innocence noun **1** *he protested his innocence* GUILTLESSNESS, blamelessness, irreproachability.

2 *the innocence of Sleeping Beauty is beyond the comprehension of these young girls* VIRGINITY, chastity, chasteness, purity; integrity, morality, decency; *dated* honor; *archaic* virtue.

3 *she took advantage of his innocence* NAIVETÉ, ingenuousness, credulity, inexperience, gullibility, simplicity, unworldliness, guilelessness, greenness.

innocent adjective **1** *he was entirely innocent* GUILTLESS, blameless, in the clear, unimpeachable, irreproachable, above suspicion, faultless; honorable, honest, upright, law-abiding; *informal* squeaky clean. ANTONYM guilty.

2 *innocent fun* HARMLESS, benign, innocuous, safe, inoffensive. ANTONYM harmful.

3 *Alcott's depiction of innocent girls* VIRTUOUS, pure, moral, decent, righteous, upright, wholesome; demure, modest, chaste, virginal; impeccable, spotless, sinless, unsullied, incorrupt, undefiled; *informal* squeaky clean, lily-white, pure as the driven snow. ANTONYM sinful.

4 *she is* ***innocent of*** *guile* FREE FROM, without, lacking (in), clear of, ignorant of, unaware of, untouched by.

5 *at the innocent age of twelve* NAIVE, ingenuous, trusting, credulous, unsuspicious, unwary, unguarded; impressionable, gullible, easily led; inexperienced, unworldly, unsophisticated, green; simple, artless, guileless, wide-eyed; *informal* wet behind the ears, born yesterday. ANTONYMS worldly, seasoned.

▸ noun *an innocent in a strange land* INGÉNUE, unworldly person; child, baby, babe; novice; *informal* greenhorn; *literary* babe in arms.

USAGE NOTE **innocent**

Innocent properly means 'harmless,' but it has long been extended in general language to mean 'not guilty.' The jury (or judge) in a criminal trial does not, strictly speaking, find a defendant 'innocent.' Rather, a defendant may be *guilty* or *not guilty* of the charges brought. In common use, however, owing perhaps to the concept of the *presumption of innocence*, which instructs a jury to consider a defendant free of wrongdoing until proven guilty on the basis of evidence, *not guilty* and *innocent* have come to be thought of as synonymous.

innocuous adjective **1** *an innocuous fungus* HARMLESS, safe, nontoxic, innocent; edible, eatable. ANTONYMS harmful, toxic.

2 *an innocuous comment* INOFFENSIVE, unobjectionable, unexceptionable, harmless, mild, tame, anodyne, soft-focus. ANTONYM offensive.

innovation noun *no appliance manufacturer can survive without an ongoing commitment to innovation* CHANGE, alteration, revolution, upheaval, transformation, metamorphosis, breakthrough; new measures, new methods, modernization, novelty, newness; creativity, originality, ingenuity, inspiration, inventiveness; *informal* a shake up.

innovative adjective *Philco's design was considered the most innovative of the season* ORIGINAL, new, novel, fresh, unusual, unprecedented, avant-garde, experimental, inventive, ingenious, creative; advanced, modern, state-of-the-art, pioneering, groundbreaking, revolutionary, radical, newfangled.

innuendo noun *his innuendoes were usually just thinly veiled sexual remarks* INSINUATION, suggestion, intimation, implication, hint, overtone, undertone, allusion, reference; aspersion, slur.

innumerable adjective *innumerable letters and telegrams flooded the courtroom during the trial* COUNTLESS, untold, legion, without number, numberless, unnumbered, multitudinous, incalculable, limitless; *informal* umpteen, a slew of, no end of, loads of, stacks of, heaps of, masses of, oodles of, zillions of, gazillions of; *literary* myriad. ANTONYM few.

inoculation noun *the school nurse has no record of your child's most recent inoculation* IMMUNIZATION, vaccination, vaccine; injection, booster; *informal* jab, shot, hypo, needle.

inoffensive adjective *many people are challenging your contention that these were inoffensive remarks* HARMLESS, innocuous, unobjectionable, unexceptionable; nonviolent, nonaggressive, mild, peaceful, peaceable, gentle; tame, innocent.

inoperable adjective **1** *an inoperable tumor* UNTREATABLE, incurable, irremediable; malignant; terminal, fatal, deadly, lethal; *archaic* immedicable. ANTONYM curable.

2 *the machine was left inoperable.* See INOPERATIVE sense 1.

3 *the agreement is now inoperable* IMPRACTICAL, unworkable, unfeasible, unrealistic, nonviable, impracticable, unsuitable. ANTONYM feasible.

inoperative adjective **1** *the fan is inoperative* DEFECTIVE, out of order, out of service, down, unserviceable, unusable, inoperable, bust/busted, out of action, shot, broken, faulty, on the blink, on the fritz, out of commission, acting up, kaput. ANTONYM working.

2 *the contract is inoperative* VOID, null and void, invalid, ineffective, nonviable; canceled, revoked, terminated; worthless, valueless, unproductive, abortive. ANTONYM valid.

inopportune adjective *the embassy's decision to release that statement was unfortunate and inopportune* INAPPROPRIATE, unsuitable, malapropos, unfavorable, unfortunate, infelicitous, inexpedient; untimely, ill-timed, ill-chosen, unseasonable; awkward, difficult, inconvenient, disruptive. ANTONYM appropriate.

inordinate adjective *don't you think this is an inordinate amount of luggage for one weekend?* EXCESSIVE, undue, unreasonable, unjustifiable, unwarrantable, disproportionate, unwarranted, unnecessary, needless, uncalled for, gratuitous, exorbitant, extreme; outrageous, immoderate, extravagant, intemperate; *informal* over the top. ANTONYMS moderate, conservative.

WORD NOTE **inordinate**

As an adjective to express over-the-top-ness, especially the over-the-top-ness of something intangible, I'm inordinately fond of *inordinate.* It doesn't pass as much judgment as *unreasonable,* or flaunt as much as *outrageous.* It's inordinately susceptible to overuse. A little inordinateness is more than enough. **—EM**

---

input noun **1** *an error resulted from invalid input* DATA, details, information, material; facts, figures, statistics, particulars, specifics; *informal* info.

2 *I value your input* CONTRIBUTION, offering, idea, opinion.

▸ verb *she was hired to input the data from an old system* FEED IN, put in, load, insert; key in, type in, enter; code, store.

inquest noun See INQUIRY sense 2.

inquire verb **1** *I inquired about part-time training courses* ASK, make inquiries, question someone, request/solicit information.

2 *the commission will* ***inquire into*** *the state of health care* INVESTIGATE, conduct an inquiry into/about/regarding, probe, look into; research, examine, explore, delve into, study; *informal* check out.

inquiring See INQUISITIVE.

inquiry noun **1** *an inquiry about our location* QUESTION, query.

2 *an inquiry into alleged security leaks* INVESTIGATION, probe, examination, review, analysis, exploration; inquest, hearing.

inquisition noun *what started as a few friendly questions soon turned into a not-so-friendly inquisition* INTERROGATION, questioning, quizzing, cross-examination; investigation, inquiry, inquest, hearing; *informal* grilling; *Law* examination.

inquisitive adjective *we laughed when Brian said his sister was studying journalism—she was always such an inquisitive little pest* CURIOUS, interested, intrigued, prying, spying, eavesdropping, intrusive, busybody, meddlesome, snooping; inquiring, questioning, probing, searching; *informal* nosy, Nosy Parker, snoopy. ANTONYM uninterested.

inroads plural noun *our department has made appreciable and positive inroads since receiving an unfavorable report last spring* ADVANCE, progress, forward movement, headway.

insane adjective **1** *she was declared insane* MENTALLY ILL, mentally disordered, of unsound mind, certifiable; psychotic, schizophrenic; mad, deranged, demented, out of one's mind, non compos mentis, unhinged, unbalanced, unstable, disturbed, crazed; *informal* crazy, (stark) raving mad, not all there, bushed, bonkers, cracked, psycho, batty, cuckoo, loony, loopy, loco, nuts, screwy, bananas, crackers, wacko, off one's rocker, out of one's tree, around the bend, mad as a hatter, buggy. ANTONYM sane.

2 *insane laughter* MANIACAL, psychotic, crazed, hysterical. ANTONYM normal.

3 *an insane suggestion* FOOLISH, idiotic, stupid, silly, senseless, nonsensical, absurd, ridiculous, ludicrous, lunatic, preposterous, fatuous, inane, asinine, harebrained, half-baked; impracticable, implausible, irrational, illogical; *informal* crazy, mad, cockeyed, daft. ANTONYM sensible.

4 *I just looked at next week's schedule, and now I'm completely insane* MAD, crazy; angry, furious, annoyed; *informal* aggravated, foaming at the mouth, hot under the collar ANTONYMS calm, contented.

insanity noun **1** *insanity runs in her family* MENTAL ILLNESS, madness, dementia; lunacy, instability; mania, psychosis; *informal* craziness.

2 *it would be insanity to take this loan* FOLLY, foolishness, madness, idiocy, stupidity, lunacy, silliness; *informal* craziness.

insatiable adjective *an insatiable appetite for expensive jewelry* UNQUENCHABLE, unappeasable, uncontrollable; voracious, gluttonous, greedy, hungry, ravenous, wolfish; avid, eager, keen; *informal* piggy; *literary* insatiate.

inscribe verb **1** *his name was inscribed above the door* CARVE, write, engrave, etch, cut, incise; imprint, stamp, impress, mark.

2 *a book inscribed to him by the author* DEDICATE, address, name, sign.

inscription noun **1** *the inscription on the sarcophagus* ENGRAVING, etching; wording, writing, lettering, legend, epitaph, epigraph.

2 *the book had an inscription* DEDICATION, message; signature, autograph.

inscrutable adjective *John Law was a financial genius with inscrutable motives* ENIGMATIC, mysterious, unreadable, inexplicable, unexplainable, incomprehensible, impenetrable, unfathomable, unknowable; opaque, abstruse, arcane, obscure, cryptic. ANTONYM transparent.

insect noun See table on page 483.

insecure adjective **1** *an insecure young man* UNCONFIDENT, uncertain, unsure, doubtful, hesitant, self-conscious, unassertive, diffident, unforthcoming, shy, timid, retiring, timorous, inhibited, introverted; anxious, fearful, worried; *informal* mousy. ANTONYM confident.

2 *an insecure railing* UNSTABLE, rickety, rocky, wobbly, shaky, unsteady, precarious; weak, flimsy, unsound, unsafe; *informal* jerry-built. ANTONYM stable.

insecurity noun **1** *he hid his insecurity* LACK OF CONFIDENCE, self-doubt, diffidence, unassertiveness, timidity, uncertainty, nervousness, inhibition; anxiety, worry, unease.

2 *the insecurity of our situation* VULNERABILITY, defenselessness, peril, danger; instability, fragility, frailty, shakiness, unreliability.

insensible adjective **1** *she was insensible on the floor* UNCONSCIOUS, insensate, senseless, insentient, inert, comatose, knocked out, passed out, blacked out; stunned, numb, numbed; *informal* out (cold), down for the count, out of it, zonked out, dead to the world. ANTONYM conscious.

2 *he was* ***insensible to*** *the risks* UNAWARE OF, ignorant of, unconscious of, unmindful of, oblivious to, incognizant of; indifferent to, impervious to, deaf to, blind to, unaffected by; *informal* in the dark about. ANTONYM aware.

3 *he showed insensible disregard* INSENSITIVE, dispassionate, cool, emotionless, unfeeling, unconcerned, detached, indifferent, hardened, tough, callous; *informal* hard-boiled. ANTONYM sensitive.

insensitive adjective **1** *an insensitive bully* HEARTLESS, unfeeling, inconsiderate, thoughtless, thick-skinned; hard-hearted, cold-blooded, uncaring, unconcerned, unsympathetic, unkind, callous, cruel, merciless, pitiless. ANTONYM compassionate.

2 *he was* ***insensitive to*** *her feelings* IMPERVIOUS TO, oblivious to, unaware of, unresponsive to, indifferent to, unaffected by, unmoved by, untouched by; *informal* in the dark about.

inseparable adjective **1** *inseparable friends* DEVOTED, bosom, close, fast, firm, good, best, intimate, faithful; *informal* as thick as thieves, joined at the hip.

2 *the laws are inseparable* INDIVISIBLE, indissoluble, inextricable, entangled; (one and) the same.

INSECTS

ant	gnat
alderfly	Goliath beetle
amberwing	grasshopper
ant lion	greenbottle
aphid	harvester ant
army ant	Hercules beetle
assassin bug	honeybee
backswimmer	hornet
bee	horsefly
bedbug	housefly
beetle	ichneumon
blackfly	Japanese beetle
blowfly	June bug
bluebottle	katydid
boatman	ladybug
boll weevil	leafcutter
booklouse	leafhopper
borer	lightning bug
botfly	locust
bristletail	louse
bumblebee	mayfly
butterfly	mealy bug
caddisfly	Mexican bean beetle
carpenter ant	mosquito
carpenter bee	moth
carpet beetle	mud dauber
carrion beetle	no-see-um
chafer	paper wasp
chinch bug	pismire
cicada	potato beetle
click beetle	praying mantis
cluster fly	rhinoceros beetle
coccid	roach
cockroach	robber fly
Colorado beetle	rose chafer
corn borer	rove beetle
crane fly	sandfly
cricket	sawfly
cuckoo bee	sawyer
cucumber beetle	scarab beetle
damselfly	scorpion fly
darner	shadfly
deathwatch beetle	snout beetle
deerfly	snowflea
diving beetle	spittlebug
dobsonfly	springtail
doodlebug	squash bug
dragonfly	stag beetle
dung beetle	stink bug
earwig	stonefly
elater	termite
emmet	tiger beetle
engraver beetle	tsetse fly
fire ant	walking stick
firefly	water beetle
flea	wasp
froghopper	weevil
fruit fly	white ant
furniture beetle	whitefly
gall wasp	yellow jacket
glowworm	

insert verb **1** *he inserted a tape in the machine* PUT, place, push, thrust, slide, slip, load, fit, slot, lodge, install; *informal* pop, stick. ANTONYMS extract, take out.

2 *she inserted a clause* ENTER, introduce, add, incorporate, interpolate, interpose, interject. ANTONYM remove.

▸ noun *the newspaper carried an insert* ENCLOSURE, insertion, supplement; circular, advertisement, pamphlet, leaflet; *informal* ad.

THE RIGHT WORD

If you want to put something in a fixed place between or among other things, you can **insert** it (*insert a new paragraph in an essay; insert photographs in the text of a book*). If it's a liquid, you'll probably want to **inject** it (*inject the flu vaccine*), although to inject can also mean to add something new or different (*inject some humor into an otherwise dreary speech*). If it's a person, you should **introduce** him or her, which suggests placing the individual in the midst of a group so as to become part of it. You can also introduce things (*introduce a new subject into the curriculum*), but if the thing you're introducing is extraneous or lacks authorization, you may have to **interpolate** it (*interpolate editorial comments*). If you have remarks, statements, or questions to introduce in an abrupt or forced manner, you'll have to **interject** them (*in the midst of his speech, she interjected what she felt were important details*). If you interject too often, however, you risk offending the speaker and may have to ask someone to **mediate**, which means to settle a dispute or bring about a compromise by taking a stand midway between extremes.

inside noun **1** *the inside of a volcano* INTERIOR, inner part; center, core, middle, heart. ANTONYM exterior.

2 *informal my insides are aching* STOMACH, gut, internal organs, bowels, intestines; *informal* belly, tummy, guts, innards, viscera.

▸ adjective **1** *his inside pocket* INNER, interior, internal, innermost. ANTONYM outer.

2 *inside information* CONFIDENTIAL, classified, restricted, privileged, private, secret, exclusive; *informal* hush-hush. ANTONYM public.

▸ adverb **1** *she ushered me inside* INDOORS, within, in.

2 *how do you feel inside?* INWARDLY, within, secretly, privately, deep down, at heart, emotionally, intuitively, instinctively.

3 *informal if I get caught again I'll be back inside* IN PRISON, in jail, in custody; locked up, imprisoned, incarcerated; *informal* behind bars, doing time.

insidious adjective *the insidious bond between big money and political decisions* STEALTHY, subtle, surreptitious, cunning, crafty, treacherous, artful, sly, wily, shifty, underhanded, indirect; *informal* sneaky.

insight noun **1** *your insight has been invaluable* INTUITION, discernment, perception, awareness, understanding, comprehension, apprehension, appreciation, penetration, acumen, perspicacity, judgment, acuity; vision, wisdom, prescience; *informal* savvy.

2 *an* ***insight into*** *the government* UNDERSTANDING OF, appreciation of, revelation about; introduction to; *informal* eye-opener about.

insightful adjective *he gives an insightful analysis of the text* INTUITIVE, perceptive, discerning, penetrating, penetrative, astute, percipient, perspicacious, sagacious, wise, judicious, shrewd, sharp, sharp-witted, razor-sharp, keen, incisive, acute, imaginative, appreciative, intelligent, thoughtful, sensitive, deep, profound; visionary, farsighted, prescient; *informal* savvy, right-brained.

insignia noun *I thought from the insignia that he was at least a colonel* BADGE, crest, emblem, symbol, sign, device, mark, seal, logo, colors.

insignificant adjective *the raises the kitchen staff received were insignificant* UNIMPORTANT, trivial, trifling, negligible, inconsequential, of no account, inconsiderable; nugatory, paltry, petty, insubstantial, frivolous, pointless, worthless, meaningless, irrelevant, immaterial, peripheral; *informal* piddling.

insincere adjective *voters respond favorably to even the most insincere campaign promises, as long as they hear just what they want* FALSE, fake, hollow, artificial, feigned, pretended, put-on, inauthentic; disingenuous, hypocritical, cynical, deceitful, deceptive, duplicitous, double-dealing, two-faced, lying, untruthful, mendacious; *informal* phony, pretend.

insinuate verb *he insinuated that she lied* IMPLY, suggest, hint, intimate, indicate, let it be known, give someone to understand; *informal* make out. PHRASE: **insinuate oneself into** *he is trying to insinuate himself into their family* WORM ONE'S WAY INTO, ingratiate oneself with, curry favor with; foist oneself on, introduce oneself into, edge one's way into, insert oneself into; infiltrate, invade, sneak into, maneuver oneself into, intrude on, impinge on; *informal* muscle in on.

insinuation noun *she made many unkind insinuations regarding Lewis's parental ability* IMPLICATION, inference, suggestion, hint, intimation, connotation, innuendo, reference, allusion, indication, undertone, overtone; aspersion, slur, allegation.

insipid adjective **1** *insipid coffee* TASTELESS, flavorless, bland, weak, wishy-washy; unappetizing, unpalatable. ANTONYM tasty.

2 *insipid pictures* UNIMAGINATIVE, uninspired, uninspiring, characterless, flat, uninteresting, lackluster, dull, drab, boring, dry, humdrum, ho-hum, monochrome, tedious, run-of-the-mill, commonplace, pedestrian, trite, tired, hackneyed, stale, lame, wishy-washy, colorless, anemic, lifeless. ANTONYMS interesting, imaginative.

insist verb **1** *she insisted that they pay up* DEMAND, command, require, dictate; urge, exhort.

2 *he insisted that he knew nothing* MAINTAIN, assert, hold, contend, argue, protest, claim, vow, swear, declare, stress, repeat, reiterate; *formal* aver. PHRASE: **insist on** *she insisted on her children's going to college* BE SET ON, be intent on, persist in, stand firm about, stand one's ground about, be resolute about, be emphatic about, be adamant about, not take no for an answer about; *informal* stick to one's guns about.

insistent adjective **1** *Tony's insistent questioning* PERSISTENT, determined, adamant, importunate, tenacious, unyielding, dogged, unrelenting, tireless, inexorable; demanding, pushy, forceful, urgent; clamorous, vociferous; emphatic, firm, assertive.

2 *the insistent rattle of the fan* INCESSANT, constant, unremitting, repetitive; obtrusive, intrusive, loud.

insolent adjective *Dan is an inveterate wise guy who can't help making insolent cracks as he narrates the tale* IMPERTINENT, impudent, cheeky, ill-mannered, bad mannered, unmannerly, rude, impolite, uncivil, discourteous, disrespectful, insubordinate, contemptuous; audacious, bold, cocky, brazen; insulting, abusive; *informal* fresh, lippy, saucy, pert, sassy, smart-alecky; *archaic* contumelious. See note at IMPERTINENT. ANTONYM polite.

insoluble adjective **1** *some problems are insoluble* UNSOLVABLE, unanswerable, unresolvable; unfathomable, impenetrable, unexplainable, inscrutable, inexplicable.

2 *these minerals are insoluble in water* INDISSOLUBLE, incapable of dissolving.

insolvency noun See BANKRUPTCY.

insolvent adjective *even his family never suspected that Chet was insolvent* BANKRUPT, ruined, wiped out, in receivership; penniless, poor, impoverished, impecunious, destitute, without a penny (to one's name), in debt, in arrears; *informal* bust, (flat) broke, belly up, in the red, hard up, strapped (for cash), cleaned out; *formal* penurious.

insomnia noun *I've tried every wild remedy for insomnia, including cinnamon baths and standing on my head* SLEEPLESSNESS, wakefulness, restlessness, inability to sleep.

insouciance noun *through his own profligacy and insouciance in raising money, he brought about the very thing he had hoped to avoid* NONCHALANCE, unconcern, indifference, heedlessness, calm, equanimity, composure, ease, airiness; *informal* cool. ANTONYM anxiety.

insouciant adjective *only outwardly did he possess an insouciant attitude about the disease* NONCHALANT, untroubled, unworried, unruffled, unconcerned, indifferent, blasé, heedless, careless; relaxed, calm, equable, serene, composed, easy, easygoing, carefree, free and easy, happy-go-lucky, lighthearted, airy, blithe, mellow; *informal* cool, laid-back, slaphappy.

inspect verb *by all means, inspect any part of the house you wish* EXAMINE, check, scrutinize, investigate, vet, test, monitor, survey, study, look over, peruse, scan, explore, probe; assess, appraise, review, audit; *informal* check out, give something a/the once-over.

inspection noun *on further inspection, we detected a slight crack in the pipe* EXAMINATION, checkup, survey, scrutiny, probe, exploration, observation, investigation; assessment, appraisal, review, evaluation; *informal* once-over, going-over, look-see.

inspector noun *the inspector's report is due here by noon* EXAMINER, scrutineer, investigator, surveyor, assessor, appraiser, reviewer, analyst; observer, overseer, supervisor, monitor, watchdog, ombudsman; auditor.

inspiration noun **1** *her work is a real inspiration to others* GUIDING LIGHT, example, model, muse, motivation, encouragement, influence, spur, stimulus, lift, boost, incentive, impulse, catalyst.

2 *his work lacks inspiration* CREATIVITY, inventiveness, innovation, ingenuity, genius, imagination, originality; artistry, insight, vision; finesse, flair.

3 *she had a sudden inspiration* BRIGHT IDEA, revelation, flash; *informal* brainwave, brainstorm, eureka moment.

inspire verb **1** *the landscape inspired him to write* STIMULATE, motivate, encourage, influence, rouse, move, stir, energize, galvanize, incite; animate, fire, excite, spark, inspirit, incentivize, affect. See note at ENCOURAGE.

2 *the film inspired a musical* GIVE RISE TO, lead to, bring about, cause, prompt, spawn, engender; *literary* beget.

3 *Charles inspired awe in her* AROUSE, awaken, prompt, induce, ignite, trigger, kindle, produce, bring out; *literary* enkindle.

inspired adjective *toe-tapping melodies and inspired lyrics* OUTSTANDING, wonderful, marvelous, excellent, magnificent, fine, exceptional, first-class, first-rate, virtuoso, supreme, superlative, brilliant; innovative, ingenious, imaginative, original; *informal* tremendous, superb, super, ace, wicked, awesome, out of this world. ANTONYMS dull, poor.

inspiring adjective *inspiring essays* INSPIRATIONAL, encouraging, heartening, uplifting, stirring, rousing, stimulating, electrifying; moving, affecting, impassioned, influential.

instability noun **1** *the instability of political life* UNRELIABILITY, uncertainty, unpredictability, insecurity, riskiness; impermanence, inconstancy, changeability, variability, fluctuation, mutability, transience. ANTONYMS certainty, steadiness.

2 *emotional instability* VOLATILITY, unpredictability, variability, capriciousness, flightiness, fickleness, changeability, vacillation. ANTONYM steadiness.

3 *the instability of the foundations* UNSTEADINESS, unsoundness, shakiness, frailty, fragility, weakness. ANTONYM soundness.

install verb **1** *a photocopier was installed in the office* PUT, position, place, locate, situate, station, site, lodge; insert. ANTONYM remove.

2 *the college installs its new president this afternoon* SWEAR IN, induct, instate, inaugurate, invest; appoint; ordain, consecrate, anoint; enthrone, crown. ANTONYM remove.

3 *she installed herself behind the table* ENSCONCE, establish, position, settle, seat, lodge, plant; sit (down); *informal* plonk, park.

4 *you'll need to install new software* LOAD, store.

installment noun **1** *I pay monthly installments* PART PAYMENT; deferred payment, premium.

2 *a story published in installments* PART, portion, section, segment, bit; chapter, episode, volume, issue.

instance noun *an instance of racism* EXAMPLE, exemplar, occasion, occurrence, case; illustration.

▸ verb *they instanced the previous case as an example* CITE, quote, refer to, mention, allude to, give; specify, name, identify, draw attention to, put forward, offer, advance.

PHRASE: **in the first instance** See IN THE FIRST PLACE at PLACE.

instant adjective **1** *instant access to your money* IMMEDIATE, instantaneous, on-the-spot, prompt, swift, speedy, rapid, quick, express, lightning; sudden, precipitate, abrupt; *informal* snappy, PDQ (pretty damn/darn quick). ANTONYM delayed.

2 *instant meals* PREPREPARED, precooked, ready-made, ready-mixed, heat-and-serve, fast; microwaveable.

▸ noun **1** *come here this instant!* MOMENT, minute, second; juncture, point.

2 *it all happened in an instant* MOMENT, minute, trice, (split) second, wink/blink/twinkling of an eye, flash, no time (at all), heartbeat; *informal* sec, jiffy, jiff, snap.

instantaneous adjective *it doesn't have the instantaneous delivery aspect of the Internet but you'll get much higher resolution* IMMEDIATE, instant, on-the-spot, prompt, swift, speedy, rapid, quick, express, expedutious, lightning; sudden, hurried, precipitate; *informal* snappy, PDQ (pretty damn/darn quick); *literary* fleet. ANTONYM delayed.

instantly adverb *she fell asleep almost instantly* IMMEDIATELY, at once, straightaway, right away, instantaneously; suddenly, abruptly, all of a sudden; forthwith, then and there, here and now, this/that minute, this/that instant; quickly, rapidly, speedily, promptly; in an instant, in a moment, in a (split) second, in a trice, in/like a flash, like a shot, in the twinkling of an eye, in no time (at all), before you know it; *informal* in a jiffy, in a jiff, pronto, like (greased) lightning, stat, on the double, tout de suite.

instead adverb *instead, let's take the train* AS AN ALTERNATIVE, alternatively, alternately; on second thoughts, all things being equal. PHRASE: **instead of** *I'll have the blue instead of the yellow, please* AS AN ALTERNATIVE TO, as a substitute for, as a replacement for, in place of, in lieu of, in preference to; rather than, as opposed to, as against, as contrasted with, before.

instigate verb **1** *the committee instigated formal proceedings* SET IN MOTION, get underway, get off the ground, start, commence, begin, initiate, launch, institute, set up, inaugurate, establish, organize; actuate, generate, bring about; start the ball rolling on, kick off. See note at ENCOURAGE. ANTONYM halt.

2 *the liberal clergy is instigating a movement of political reform* INCITE, encourage, urge, provoke, goad, spur (on), initiate, stimulate, push (for), prompt, induce; arouse, rouse, inflame, excite, stir up; *informal* root on. See note at INCITE. ANTONYMS dissuade, quell.

instigation noun **1** *it was primarily Aaron's instigation that brought the festival into being* PROMPTING, suggestion, recommendation; request, entreaty, demand, insistence; wish, desire, persuasion; *formal* instance.

2 *foreign instigation is suspected to be at the root of this disturbance* INCITEMENT, initiation, provocation, stirring up, fomentation, inducement, encouragement.

instigator noun *the instigators behind the crime wave* INITIATOR, prime mover, motivator, architect, designer, planner, inventor, mastermind, originator, author, creator, agent; founder, pioneer, founding father; agitator, fomenter, troublemaker, ringleader, rabble-rouser.

instill verb **1** *we instill vigilance in our children* INCULCATE, implant, ingrain, impress, imprint, introduce; engender, produce, generate, induce, inspire, promote, foster; drum (into), drill (into).

2 *he instilled Monet with a love of nature* IMBUE, inspire, infuse, inculcate, inject; indoctrinate; teach.

instinct noun **1** *some instinct told me to be careful* NATURAL TENDENCY, inherent tendency, inclination, urge, drive, compulsion, need; intuition, feeling, hunch, sixth sense, insight; nose.

2 *his instinct for music* TALENT, gift, ability, aptitude, faculty, skill, flair, feel, genius, knack, bent.

instinctive adjective *an instinctive understanding of machinery | an instinctive urge to scream* INTUITIVE, natural, instinctual, innate, inborn, inherent; unconscious, subconscious, intuitional; automatic, reflex, knee-jerk, mechanical, spontaneous, involuntary, impulsive; *informal* gut, second nature. ANTONYMS learned, voluntary.

institute noun See INSTITUTION sense 1.

▸ verb *Ingersoll has asked us to institute the new hiring policies before December 31* INITIATE, set in motion, get underway, get off the ground, get going, start, commence, begin, launch; set up, inaugurate, found, establish, organize, generate, bring about; start the ball rolling on; *informal* kick off. ANTONYM end.

institution noun **1** *an academic institution* ESTABLISHMENT, organization, institute, foundation, center; academy, school, college, university; society, association, body, guild, federation, consortium.

2 *how much do we know about the quality of medical care in these institutions?* HOSPITAL, NURSING HOME, retirement home, old-age home, old folks' home, (residential) home; asylum, mental institution; sanatorium.

3 *the institution of marriage* PRACTICE, custom, convention, tradition, habit; phenomenon, fact; system, policy; idea, notion, concept, principle.

4 *the institution of legal proceedings* INITIATION, instigation, launch, start, commencement, beginning, inauguration, generation, origination.

institutional adjective **1** *an institutional framework for discussions* ORGANIZED, established, bureaucratic, conventional, procedural, prescribed, set, routine, formal, systematic, systematized, methodical, businesslike, orderly, coherent, structured, regulated.

2 *the rooms are rather institutional* IMPERSONAL, formal, regimented, uniform, unvaried, monotonous; insipid, bland, uninteresting, dull; unappealing, uninviting, unattractive, unwelcoming, dreary, drab, colorless; stark, spartan, bare, clinical, sterile, austere.

instruct verb **1** *the union instructed them to strike* ORDER, direct, command, tell, enjoin, require, call on, mandate, charge; *literary* bid.

2 *do not attempt to operate the binder until you've been thoroughly instructed* TEACH, school, coach, train, enlighten, inform, educate, tutor, guide, prepare, prime.

3 *the judge instructed the jury to consider all of the facts* INFORM, tell, notify, apprise, advise, brief, prime; *informal* fill someone in, clue someone in.

instruction noun **1** *my instructions are to be obeyed at all times* ORDER, command, directive, direction, decree, edict, injunction, mandate, dictate, commandment, bidding; requirement, stipulation; *informal* marching orders; *literary* behest.

2 (**instructions**) *read the instructions* DIRECTIONS, key, rubric, specification, how-tos; handbook, manual, guide, tutorial.

3 *most of the instruction we received was combat-related* TEACHING, coaching, schooling, education, tutelage, tuition; lessons, classes, lectures; training, preparation, grounding, guidance.

instructive adjective *the manual is not sufficiently instructive* INFORMATIVE, instructional, informational, illuminating, enlightening, explanatory; educational, educative, edifying, didactic, pedagogic, heuristic; improving, moralistic, homiletic; useful, helpful.

instructor noun *Heilbrun was briefly an instructor at Brooklyn College* TEACHER, schoolteacher, educator, professor; mentor, tutor; coach, trainer; adviser, counselor, guide; *formal* pedagogue.

instrument noun **1** *a wound made with a sharp instrument* IMPLEMENT, tool, utensil; device, apparatus, contrivance, gadget. See note at TOOL.

2 *check all the cockpit instruments* MEASURING DEVICE, gauge, meter; indicator, dial, display; avionics.

3 *Tony tuned his instruments* MUSICAL INSTRUMENT. See table on page 487.

4 *drama can be an instrument of learning* AGENT, agency, cause, channel, medium, means, mechanism, vehicle, organ.

5 *he is a mere instrument* PAWN, puppet, creature, dupe, cog; tool, cat's paw; *informal* stooge.

instrumental adjective *the space program has always been instrumental in our efforts to make medical advances* INVOLVED, active, influential, contributory; helpful, useful, of service; significant, important, crucial, critical, essential, pivotal, key; (**be instrumental in**) play a part in, contribute to, be a factor in, have a hand in; add to, help, promote, advance, further; be conducive to, lead to, cause.

insubordinate adjective *she defended her insubordinate behavior by exposing corruption in high places* DISOBEDIENT, unruly, wayward, errant, badly behaved, disorderly, undisciplined, delinquent, troublesome, rebellious, defiant, recalcitrant, uncooperative, willful, intractable, unmanageable, uncontrollable; awkward, difficult, perverse, contrary; disrespectful, cheeky. ANTONYM obedient.

insubordination noun *one quickly learns at West Point that insubordination is a serious matter* DISOBEDIENCE, unruliness, indiscipline, bad behavior, misbehavior, misconduct, delinquency, insolence; rebellion, defiance, mutiny, revolt; recalcitrance, willfulness, awkwardness, perversity; *informal* acting-up; *Law* contumacy.

insubstantial adjective **1** *an insubstantial structure* FLIMSY, fragile, breakable, weak, frail, slight, unstable, shaky, wobbly, rickety, ramshackle, jerry-built. ANTONYM sturdy.

2 *insubstantial evidence* WEAK, flimsy, feeble, poor, inadequate, insufficient, tenuous, insignificant, unconvincing, implausible, unsatisfactory, paltry. ANTONYM sound.

3 *insubstantial visions* INTANGIBLE, impalpable, untouchable, discarnate, unsubstantial, incorporeal; imaginary, unreal, illusory, spectral, ghostlike, vaporous, immaterial. ANTONYM tangible.

4 *an insubstantial amount* SMALL, negligible, inconsequential, inconsiderable, trifling, measly; *informal* piddling. ANTONYMS ample, generous.

insufferable adjective **1** *the heat was insufferable* INTOLERABLE, unbearable, unendurable, insupportable, unacceptable, oppressive, overwhelming, overpowering; *informal* too much. ANTONYM bearable.

2 *his win made him insufferable* CONCEITED, arrogant, boastful, cocky, cocksure, full of oneself, self-important, swaggering; vain, puffed up, self-satisfied, self-congratulatory, smug; *informal* bigheaded, too big for one's britches, too big for one's boots; *literary* vainglorious. ANTONYM modest.

MUSICAL INSTRUMENTS

Stringed	
acoustic guitar	recorder
aeolian harp	soprano saxophone
balalaika	tenor saxophone
bandura	tin whistle
banjo	**Keyboard**
bass guitar	baby grand
bass viol	calliope
bouzouki	carillon
cello	celesta/celeste
Celtic harp	clavichord
cimbalom	clavier
cittern	grand piano
classical guitar	harmonium
contrabass	harpsichord
double bass	melodeon
dulcimer	organ
fiddle	piano
gittern	pianola
guitar	pipe organ
harp	player piano
hurdy-gurdy	spinet
kora	synthesizer
koto	virginals
electric guitar	**Brass**
lute	althorn
lyre	baritone
mandolin	bugle
rebec	cornet
samisen	euphonium
sarangi	flugelhorn
sarod	French horn
sitar	helicon
string bass	horn
tamboura	mellophone
theorbo	sackbut
trigon	saxhorn
twelve-string guitar	slide trombone
ukulele	sousaphone
veena	trombone
viol	trumpet
viola	tuba
viola d'amore	**Percussion**
viola da braccio	anvil
viola da gamba	bass drum
violin	bells
violoncello	bongo drum
Welsh harp	chimes
zither	conga drum
Wind	crescent
alto saxophone	cymbals
bass clarinet	drums
basset horn	glockenspeil
bassoon	gong
clarinet	kettledrum
cor anglais	maracas
didgeridoo	marimba
English horn	snare drum
lute	steel drum
harmonica	tambourine
kazoo	timpani
oboe	traps
ocarina	triangle
panpipes	vibraharp
pennywhistle	vibraphone
piccolo	xylophone

insufficient adjective *the emergency lighting is insufficient | insufficient funds* INADEQUATE, deficient, poor, scant, scanty; not enough, too little, too few, too small; scarce, sparse, in short supply, lacking, wanting; paltry, meager, niggardly; incomplete, restricted, limited; *informal* measly, pathetic, piddling.

insular adjective **1** *insular attitudes* NARROW-MINDED, small-minded, inward-looking, parochial, provincial, small-town, shortsighted, hidebound, blinkered; set in one's ways, inflexible, rigid, entrenched; illiberal, intolerant, prejudiced, bigoted, biased, partisan, xenophobic; *informal* redneck. ANTONYMS broad-minded, tolerant.

2 *an insular existence* ISOLATED, inaccessible, cutoff, segregated, detached, solitary, lonely, hermitic. ANTONYM cosmopolitan.

insulate verb **1** *pipes must be insulated* WRAP, sheathe, cover, coat, encase, enclose, envelop; heatproof, soundproof; pad, cushion.

2 *they were insulated from the impact of the war* PROTECT, save, shield, shelter, screen, cushion, buffer, cocoon; isolate, segregate, sequester, detach, cut off.

insult verb *he insulted my wife* ABUSE, be rude to, slight, disparage, discredit, libel, slander, malign, defame, denigrate, cast aspersions on, call someone names, put someone down; offend, affront, hurt, humiliate, wound; *informal* badmouth, dis; *formal* derogate, calumniate; *rare* asperse. ANTONYM compliment.

▸ noun *he hurled insults at us* ABUSIVE REMARK, jibe, affront, slight, barb, slur, indignity; injury, libel, slander, defamation; abuse, disparagement, aspersions; *informal* dig, crack, put-down, slap in the face, kick in the teeth, cheap shot, low blow.

insulting adjective *once you send that insulting message, there's no taking it back* ABUSIVE, rude, offensive, disparaging, belittling, derogatory, deprecatory, disrespectful, uncomplimentary, pejorative; disdainful, derisive, scornful, contemptuous; defamatory, slanderous, libelous, scurrilous, blasphemous; *informal* bitchy, catty, snide. See note at OFFENSIVE.

insupportable adjective **1** *his arrogance was insupportable* INTOLERABLE, insufferable, unbearable, unendurable; oppressive, overwhelming, overpowering; *informal* too much. ANTONYM bearable.

2 *this view is insupportable* UNJUSTIFIABLE, indefensible, inexcusable, unwarrantable, unreasonable, untenable; unjustified, baseless, groundless, unfounded, unsupported, unsubstantiated, unconfirmed, uncorroborated, invalid; implausible, weak, flawed, specious, defective. ANTONYMS defensible, justified.

insurance noun **1** *insurance for his new car* INDEMNITY, indemnification, assurance, (financial) protection, security, coverage.

2 *insurance against a third world war* PROTECTION, defense, safeguard, security, hedge, precaution, provision, surety; immunity; guarantee, warranty; *informal* backstop.

insure verb *the high cost of insuring a teenage driver* PROVIDE INSURANCE FOR, indemnify, cover, assure, protect, underwrite; guarantee, warrant.

insurgent adjective *insurgent forces* REBELLIOUS, rebel, revolutionary, mutinous, insurrectionist; renegade, seditious, subversive. ANTONYM loyal.

▸ noun *the insurgents are gaining popularity* REBEL, revolutionary, revolutionist, mutineer, insurrectionist, agitator, subversive, renegade, incendiary; guerrilla, freedom fighter, anarchist, terrorist. ANTONYM loyalist.

insurmountable adjective *I refuse to believe that any of the problems mentioned here today are insurmountable* INSUPERABLE, unconquerable, invincible, unassailable; overwhelming, hopeless, impossible.

insurrection noun *Spann later died in a prison insurrection by Taliban and al Qaeda prisoners* REBELLION, revolt, uprising, mutiny, revolution, insurgence, riot, sedition, subversion; civil disorder, unrest, anarchy; coup (d'état).

intact adjective *we expect to find the house intact when we get back* WHOLE, entire, complete, unbroken, undamaged, unimpaired, faultless, flawless, unscathed, untouched, unspoiled, unblemished, unmarked, perfect, pristine, inviolate, undefiled, unsullied, virgin, in one piece; sound, solid. ANTONYM damaged.

intangible adjective **1** *the shadows were more intangible than usual as they shifted with each quavering bough and passing cloud* IMPALPABLE, untouchable, incorporeal, discarnate, abstract; ethereal, insubstantial, immaterial, airy; ghostly, spectral, unearthly, supernatural.

2 *team spirit may be intangible, but we wouldn't have gotten to the finals without it* INDEFINABLE, indescribable, inexpressible, nameless; vague, obscure, abstract, unclear, indefinite, undefined, subtle, elusive.

integral adjective **1** *an integral part of human behavior* ESSENTIAL, fundamental, basic, intrinsic, inherent, constitutive, innate, structural; vital, necessary, requisite. ANTONYMS peripheral, incidental.

2 *the dryer has integral cord storage* BUILT-IN, integrated, incorporated, included. ANTONYM peripheral.

3 *an integral approach to learning* UNIFIED, integrated, comprehensive, composite, combined, aggregate; complete, whole. ANTONYMS partial, fragmented.

integrate verb *reserve forces will be more closely integrated with the regular forces* COMBINE, amalgamate, merge, unite, fuse, blend, mingle, coalesce, consolidate, meld, intermingle, mix; incorporate, unify, assimilate, homogenize; desegregate. ANTONYM separate.

integrated adjective **1** *an integrated package of services* UNIFIED, united, consolidated, amalgamated, combined, merged, fused, homogeneous, assimilated, cohesive, complete; *Brit.* joined-up.

2 *an integrated school* DESEGREGATED, nonsegregated, unsegregated, mixed, multicultural.

integrity noun **1** *I never doubted his integrity* HONESTY, probity, rectitude, honor, good character, principle(s), ethics, morals, righteousness, morality, virtue, decency, fairness, scrupulousness, sincerity, truthfulness, trustworthiness. ANTONYM dishonesty.

2 *the integrity of the federation* UNITY, unification, coherence, cohesion, togetherness, solidarity. ANTONYM division.

3 *the structural integrity of the aircraft* SOUNDNESS, strength, sturdiness, solidity, durability, stability, stoutness, toughness. ANTONYM fragility.

intellect noun **1** *a film that appeals to one's intellect* MIND, brain(s), intelligence, reason, understanding, thought, brainpower, sense, judgment, wisdom, wits; *informal* gray matter, IQ, brain cells, smarts.

2 *one of the finest intellects* THINKER, intellectual, sage; mind, brain.

intellectual adjective **1** *her intellectual capacity* MENTAL, cerebral, cognitive, psychological; rational, abstract, conceptual, theoretical, analytical, logical; academic. ANTONYM physical.

2 *an intellectual man* INTELLIGENT, clever, academic, educated, well-read, lettered, erudite, cerebral, learned, knowledgeable, literary, bookish, highbrow, scholarly, studious, enlightened, sophisticated, cultured, donnish; *informal* brainy. ANTONYM stupid.

▸ noun *"The Simpsons" is among the most revered TV shows among intellectuals* HIGHBROW, learned person, academic, bookworm, man/woman of letters, bluestocking; thinker, brain, scholar, genius, Einstein, polymath, mastermind; *informal* egghead, brains, brainiac, rocket scientist. ANTONYM dunce.

intelligence noun **1** *a man of great intelligence* INTELLECTUAL CAPACITY, mental capacity, intellect, mind, brain(s), IQ, brainpower, judgment, reasoning, understanding, comprehension; acumen, wit, sense, insight, perception, penetration, discernment, smartness, canniness, astuteness, intuition, acuity, cleverness, brilliance, ability; *informal* braininess.

2 *we're awaiting the latest intelligence from our operatives* INFORMATION, facts, details, particulars, data, knowledge, reports, inside story; *informal* info, dope, skinny, lowdown.

3 *intelligence operation* INFORMATION GATHERING, surveillance, observation, reconnaissance, spying, espionage, infiltration, ELINT, humint; *informal* recon.

intelligent adjective **1** *an intelligent writer* CLEVER, bright, brilliant, quick-witted, quick on the uptake, smart, canny, astute, intuitive, insightful, perceptive, perspicacious, discerning; knowledgeable; able, gifted, talented; *informal* brainy.

2 *an intelligent being* RATIONAL, higher-order, capable of thought.

intelligentsia plural noun *this antidemocratic system is supported by the political intelligentsia who call themselves democratic, even progressive* INTELLECTUALS, intelligent people, academics, scholars, literati, cognoscenti, illuminati, highbrows, thinkers, brains; intelligent; *informal* eggheads. ANTONYM masses.

intelligible adjective *finally, an owner's manual that's actually intelligible* COMPREHENSIBLE, understandable; accessible, digestible, user-friendly, penetrable, fathomable; lucid, clear, coherent, plain, simple, explicit, precise, unambiguous, self-explanatory; *formal* exoteric.

intemperate adjective *a man of intemperate taste may soon find himself with little left to taste* IMMODERATE, excessive, undue, inordinate, extreme, unrestrained, uncontrolled; self-indulgent, overindulgent, extravagant, lavish, prodigal, profligate; imprudent, reckless, wild; dissolute, debauched, wanton, dissipated. ANTONYM moderate.

intend verb *I intend to lease a car | what does Mark intend to do about the broken gate?* PLAN, mean, have in mind, have the intention, aim, propose; aspire, hope, expect, be resolved, be determined; want, wish; contemplate, think of, envisage, envision; design, earmark, designate, set aside; *formal* purpose.

THE RIGHT WORD

If you **intend** to do something, you may or may not be serious about getting it done (*I intend to clean out the garage some day*) but at least you have a goal in mind. Although **mean** can also imply either a firm resolve (*I mean to go, with or without her permission*) or a vague intention (*I've been meaning to write her for weeks*), it is a less formal word that usually connotes a certain lack of determination or a weak resolve. **Plan**, like *mean* and *intend*, may imply a vague goal (*I plan to tour China some day*), but it is often used to suggest that you're taking active steps (*I plan to leave as soon as I finish packing*). **Aim** indicates that you have an actual goal or purpose in mind and that you're putting some effort behind it (*I aim to be the first woman president*), without the hint of failure conveyed by *mean*. If you **propose** to do something, you declare your intention ahead of time (*I propose that we set up a meeting next week*), and if you **purpose** to do it, you are even more determined to achieve your goal (*I purpose to write a three-volume history of baseball in America*). **Design** suggests forethought in devising a plan (*design a strategy that will keep everyone happy*).

---

intended adjective *the hit was not intended* DELIBERATE, intentional, calculated, conscious, planned, studied, knowing, willful, purposeful, done on purpose, premeditated, preplanned, preconceived. ANTONYM accidental.

▸ noun *informal* *when will we meet your intended?* FIANCÉE, FIANCÉ, bride-to-be, wife-to-be, husband-to-be, future wife, future husband, prospective spouse; *formal* betrothed.

intense adjective **1** *intense heat* EXTREME, great, acute, fierce, severe, high; exceptional, extraordinary; harsh, strong, powerful, potent, overpowering, vigorous; *informal* serious. ANTONYM mild.

2 *a very intense young man* PASSIONATE, impassioned, ardent, fervent, zealous, vehement, fiery, emotional; earnest, eager, animated, spirited, vigorous, energetic, fanatical, committed. ANTONYM apathetic.

THE RIGHT WORD

Intense and **intensive** are similar in meaning, but they differ in emphasis. **Intense** tends to relate to subjective responses—emotions and how we feel—while **intensive** tends to relate to objective descriptions. Thus *an intensive course* simply describes the type of course: one that is designed to cover a lot of ground in a short time. On the other hand, in *the course was intense*, the word **intense** describes how someone felt about the course.

---

intensify verb *leaders here are fearful that yesterday's bombing will intensify the fighting north of the city* ESCALATE, increase, step up, boost, raise, strengthen, augment, reinforce; pick up, build up, heighten, deepen, extend, expand, amplify, magnify; aggravate, exacerbate, worsen, inflame, compound. ANTONYMS abate, lessen.

intensity noun **1** *the intensity of the sun* STRENGTH, power, potency, force; severity, ferocity, vehemence, fierceness, harshness; magnitude, greatness, acuteness, extremity.

2 *many here today remember the intensity in Dr. King's voice* PASSION, ardor, fervor, fervency, zeal, vehemence, fire, heat, emotion; eagerness, animation, spirit, vigor, strength, energy; fanaticism. ANTONYMS apathy, indifference.

intensive adjective *an intensive search of the area* | *an intensive course in Russian* THOROUGH, thoroughgoing, in-depth, rigorous, exhaustive; all-inclusive, comprehensive, all-embracing, all-encompassing, complete, full; vigorous, strenuous; concentrated, condensed, accelerated; detailed, minute, close, meticulous, scrupulous, painstaking, methodical, careful. See note at INTENSE. ANTONYMS cursory, superficial.

intent noun *he tried to figure out his father's intent* AIM, intention, purpose, objective, object, goal, target; design, plan, scheme; wish, desire, ambition, idea, aspiration.

▸ adjective **1** *he was **intent on** proving his point* BENT ON, set on, insistent on, hell-bent on; committed to, obsessive about, obsessed with fanatical about, fixated on; determined to; anxious to, resolved to, impatient to.

2 *an intent expression* ATTENTIVE, absorbed, engrossed, fascinated, enthralled, rapt, riveted; focused, earnest, concentrating, intense, studious, preoccupied; alert, watchful.

PHRASE: **for/to all intents and purposes** *if you sublet your apartment, realize that you are—for all intents and purposes—a landlord* IN EFFECT, effectively, in essence, essentially, virtually, practically; more or less, just about, all but, as good as, in all but name, almost, nearly; *informal* pretty much, pretty well; *literary* nigh on. ANTONYMS by no means, in no way.

intention noun **1** *it is his intention to be leader.* See INTENT noun.

2 *he managed, without intention, to upset me* INTENT, intentionality, deliberateness, design, calculation, meaning; premeditation, forethought, preplanning; *Law* malice aforethought.

intentional adjective *intentional contamination of our food supply is a real threat* DELIBERATE, calculated, conscious, intended, planned, meant, studied, knowing, willful, purposeful, purposive, done on purpose, premeditated, preplanned, preconceived; *rare* witting.

intentionally adverb *she would never intentionally hurt anyone* DELIBERATELY, on purpose, purposely, purposefully, by design, knowingly, wittingly, consciously; premeditatedly, calculatedly, in cold blood, willfully, wantonly; *Law* with malice aforethought. ANTONYM accidentally.

intently adverb *the bobcat was crouched, motionless, intently fixed on its quarry* ATTENTIVELY, closely, keenly, earnestly, hard, carefully, fixedly, raptly, sharply, steadily.

inter verb See BURY sense 1.

interact verb *how the children interact is a primary focus of our observations* COMMUNICATE, interface, connect, cooperate; meet, socialize, mix, be in contact, have dealings, work together.

interactive adjective *for an interactive version of this game, visit our website* TWO-WAY, responsive, able to react/respond; hands-on, direct.

intercede verb *a third party was called in to intercede* MEDIATE, intermediate, arbitrate, conciliate, negotiate, moderate; intervene, interpose, step in, act; plead, petition, advocate.

intercept verb *the ball was intercepted* | *a nearby Coast Guard cutter was able to intercept the gunrunners before they reached the harbor* STOP, head off, cut off; catch, seize, grab, snatch; obstruct, impede, interrupt, block, check, detain; ambush, challenge, waylay.

intercession noun *four Serbs were released after intercession by NATO-led peacekeepers in Kosovo* MEDIATION, intermediation, arbitration, conciliation, negotiation; intervention, involvement; pleading, petition, entreaty, agency; diplomacy.

interchange verb *the watch comes with five different straps, which can be interchanged to match your outfit* SUBSTITUTE, transpose, switch, alternate; exchange, swap, trade; reverse, invert, replace.

▸ noun 1 *the interchange of ideas* EXCHANGE, trade, swap, barter, give and take, traffic, reciprocation, reciprocity; *archaic* truck.

2 *a highway interchange* JUNCTION, intersection, crossing; overpass, exit (ramp), cloverleaf.

interchangeable adjective *the attachments for these two vacuum cleaners are interchangeable* SIMILAR, identical, indistinguishable, alike, the same, uniform, twin, undifferentiated; corresponding, commensurate, equivalent, synonymous, comparable, equal; transposable.

intercom noun *a familiar voice on the intercom entreated us to hurry to the loading dock* public address system, PA system, paging system; loudspeaker, squawk box; baby monitor.

interconnected adjective *our lives have always been interconnected | interconnected office phones* CONNECTING, connected, interconnecting; joined, linked, fused, intertwined.

intercourse noun 1 *social intercourse* DEALINGS, relations, relationships, association, connections, contact; interchange, communication, communion, correspondence; negotiations, bargaining, transactions; trade, traffic, commerce; *informal* doings, truck.

2 *she did not consent to intercourse* SEXUAL INTERCOURSE, sex, lovemaking, sexual relations, intimacy, coupling, mating, copulation, penetration; *informal* nookie, whoopee; *technical* coitus, coition; *formal* fornication; *dated* carnal knowledge.

interdict noun *they breached an interdict* PROHIBITION, ban, bar, veto, proscription, interdiction, embargo, moratorium, injunction. ANTONYM permission.

▸ verb 1 *they interdicted foreign commerce* PROHIBIT, forbid, ban, bar, veto, proscribe, embargo, disallow, debar, outlaw; stop, suppress; *Law* enjoin. See note at PROHIBIT. ANTONYM permit.

2 *efforts to interdict the flow of heroin* INTERCEPT, stop, head off, cut off; obstruct, impede, block; detain. ANTONYM facilitate.

interest noun 1 *we listened with interest* ATTENTIVENESS, attention, absorption; heed, regard, notice; curiosity, inquisitiveness; enjoyment, delight, enthusiasm. ANTONYM boredom.

2 *places of interest* ATTRACTION, appeal, fascination, charm, beauty, allure. ANTONYM repulsion.

3 *this will be of interest to those involved* CONCERN, consequence, importance, import, significance, note, relevance, value, weight; *formal* moment. ANTONYM irrelevance.

4 *her interests include reading* HOBBY, pastime, leisure pursuit, recreation, diversion, amusement; passion, enthusiasm; *informal* thing, bag, cup of tea.

5 *a financial interest in the firm* STAKE, share, claim, investment, stock, equity; involvement, concern.

6 *what is your interest in the case?* INVOLVEMENT, partiality, partisanship, preference, loyalty; bias, prejudice.

7 *his attorney guarded his interests* CONCERN, business, affair.

8 *her savings earned interest* DIVIDENDS, profits, returns; a percentage.

▸ verb 1 *a topic that interests you* APPEAL TO, be of interest to, attract, intrigue, fascinate; absorb, engross, rivet, grip, captivate; amuse, divert, entertain; arouse one's curiosity, whet one's appetite; *informal* float someone's boat, tickle someone's fancy. ANTONYM bore.

2 *can I* ***interest*** *you* ***in*** *a drink?* persuade to have, tempt to have; sell.

PHRASE: **in someone's best interests** *there was bitter disagreement over which treatment would be in their father's best interest* OF (THE MOST) BENEFIT TO, to the advantage of; for the sake of, for the benefit of.

interested adjective 1 *an interested crowd* ATTENTIVE, intent, absorbed, engrossed, fascinated, riveted, gripped, captivated, rapt, agog; intrigued, inquisitive, curious; keen, eager; *informal* all ears, nosy, snoopy. ANTONYMS uninterested, bored.

2 *the government consulted with interested groups* CONCERNED, involved, affected, connected, related. ANTONYM uninvolved.

3 *no interested party can judge the contest* PARTISAN, partial, biased, prejudiced, preferential. ANTONYMS disinterested, nonpartisan.

interesting adjective *a dramatic look inside the classroom that makes for some interesting television* ABSORBING, engrossing, fascinating, riveting, gripping, compelling, compulsive, captivating, engaging, enthralling; appealing, attractive; amusing, entertaining, stimulating, thought-provoking, diverting, intriguing. ANTONYM boring.

interfere verb 1 *we don't let emotion* ***interfere with*** *our duty* IMPEDE, obstruct, stand in the way of, hinder, inhibit, restrict, constrain, hamper, handicap, cramp, check, block; disturb, disrupt, influence, impinge on, affect, confuse.

2 *she tried not to* ***interfere in*** *his life* BUTT INTO, barge into, pry into, intrude into, intervene in, get involved in, encroach on, impinge on; meddle in, tamper with; *informal* poke one's nose into, horn in on, muscle in on, stick one's oar in.

interference noun 1 *they resent state interference* INTRUSION, intervention, intercession, involvement, trespass, meddling, prying; *informal* butting in.

2 *radio interference* DISRUPTION, disturbance, distortion, static.

interim noun *in the interim they did more research* MEANTIME, meanwhile, intervening time; interlude, interval.

▸ adjective *an interim advisory body* PROVISIONAL, temporary, pro tem, stopgap, short-term, fill-in, caretaker, acting, transitional, makeshift, improvised, impromptu. ANTONYM permanent.

interior adjective 1 *the house has interior paneling* INSIDE, inner, internal, intramural. ANTONYM exterior.

2 *the interior waterways of British Columbia* INLAND, inshore, noncoastal, inner, innermost, central, upcountry, upland. ANTONYM outer.

3 *an interior monologue* INNER, mental, spiritual, psychological; private, personal, intimate, secret.

▸ noun 1 *the yacht's interior* INSIDE, inner part, inner area, depths, recesses, bowels, belly; center, core, heart, nucleus; *informal* innards. ANTONYMS exterior, outside.

2 *the interior of the province* CENTER, heartland, hinterland, backcountry, bush. ANTONYM borderland.

→ ***interesting***
absorbing
riveting
transfixing
captivating
engrossing
spellbinding
enthralling
entrancing
beguiling
fascinating
gripping
compulsive
engaging
stimulating
exciting
action-packed
intriguing
appealing
attractive
thought-provoking
compelling
unputdownable
entertaining
diverting
amusing
facetious
(plain) vanilla
a dime a dozen
routine
run-of-the-mill
nothing to write home about
ordinary
conventional
unoriginal
unremarkable
unimaginative
monotonous
repetitive
colorless
flat
lifeless
bland
tired
banal
lame
uninspiring
plodding
pedestrian
lackluster
humdrum
mundane
dreary
stale
grey
dull
tedious
stiff
leaden
wooden
mechanical
sterile
insipid
jejune
deadly
tiresome
mind-numbing
soul-destroying
boring ←

interject verb **1** *may I interject a comment?* INTERPOSE, introduce, throw in, interpolate, add, insert. See note at INSERT.

2 *please refrain from interjecting during each speaker's two-minute introductory remarks* INTERRUPT, intervene, cut in, break in, butt in, chime in; have one's say *informal* put one's oar in, put one's two cents in.

interlace verb *Albright was careful to interlace her tough remarks with compliments for the prime minister* INTERWEAVE, mingle, mesh, entwine, intertwine, twine; intersperse, sprinkle, punctuate.

interlock verb *the puzzle pieces are designed to interlock* INTERCONNECT, interlink, engage, mesh, intermesh, join, unite, connect, couple.

interloper noun *we were made to feel more like interlopers than vacationers* INTRUDER, encroacher, trespasser, invader, infiltrator; uninvited guest; outsider, stranger, alien; *informal* gatecrasher, buttinsky.

interlude noun *the scene in the hospital room was a welcome interlude in this relentlessly high-paced adventure* INTERVAL, intermission, break, recess, pause, respite, rest, breathing space, halt, gap, stop, stoppage, hiatus, lull; *informal* breather, time out.

intermediary noun *the deal was concluded through an intermediary* MEDIATOR, go-between, negotiator, intervenor, intercessor, arbitrator, arbiter, conciliator, peacemaker; middleman, broker.

intermediate adjective *an intermediate stage in the cell's development* IN-BETWEEN, middle, mid, midway, halfway, median, medial, intermediary, intervening, transitional.

interment noun See BURIAL.

USAGE NOTE **interment, internment**

Interment = burial (*interment will take place just after the funeral service*). *Internment* = detention, esp. of aliens in wartime (*the internment of Japanese Americans during World War II*). *Interment* is sometimes, especially in obituaries, confounded with *internment*—e.g.: "Graveside ceremony and internment [read *interment*] will be at Hillside Cemetery in Peekskill immediately following." (*Times Union* [Albany]; Aug. 22, 2000.)

interminable adjective *the interminable silence was finally broken by the plaints of her crying infant* (SEEMINGLY) ENDLESS, never-ending, unending, nonstop, everlasting, ceaseless, unceasing, incessant, constant, continual, uninterrupted, sustained; monotonous, tedious, long-winded, overlong, rambling. See note at ETERNAL.

intermingle verb *marinating overnight allows the flavors to intermingle* MIX, intermix, mingle, blend, fuse, merge, combine, amalgamate, integrate, unite; *rare* commix, admix; *literary* commingle.

intermission noun *refreshments are available during the intermission* INTERVAL, interlude, halftime, entr'acte, break, recess, pause, rest, respite, breathing space, lull, gap, stop, stoppage, halt, hiatus; cessation, suspension; *informal* breather, time out.

intermittent adjective *intermittent bursts of gunfire* SPORADIC, irregular, fitful, spasmodic, broken, fragmentary, discontinuous, isolated, random, patchy, scattered; occasional, infrequent, periodic, episodic, on and off; *informal* herky-jerky. ANTONYM continuous.

intern verb 1 *the refugees were interned in camps* CONFINE, detain, hold (captive), lock up, imprison, incarcerate, impound, jail; *informal* put away.

2 *she's interning with an accounting firm* APPRENTICE, train; *Law* article.

▸ noun *an intern at a local firm* TRAINEE, apprentice, probationer, (summer) student, novice, beginner.

internal adjective 1 *the internal structure of the building* INNER, interior, inside, intramural; central. ANTONYM external.

2 *Canada's internal affairs* DOMESTIC, home, interior, civil, local; national, federal, provincial, state. ANTONYM foreign.

3 *an internal battle with herself* MENTAL, psychological, emotional; personal, private, secret, hidden.

international adjective *international business concerns* GLOBAL, worldwide, intercontinental, universal; multinational. ANTONYMS national, local.

Internet noun *available on the Internet* WORLD WIDE WEB, Web, WWW, cyberspace, Net, information superhighway, Infobahn.

▸ adjective *Internet cafés* CYBER, wired, online, virtual, digital, Web, Web-based, e-, Net.

internment noun *camps were established for the internment of suspected terrorist sympathizers* DETENTION, confinement, custody, captivity, imprisonment, incarceration. See note at INTERMENT.

interplay noun *the interplay between fighter and trainer* INTERACTION, interchange, exchange; teamwork, cooperation, reciprocation, reciprocity, give and take.

interpolate verb *language models can be interpolated online* INSERT, interpose, interject, enter, add, incorporate, inset, put, introduce. See note at INSERT.

interpose verb 1 *he interposed himself between the girls* INSINUATE, insert, place, put.

2 *I must interpose a note of caution* INTRODUCE, insert, interject, add, put in; *informal* slip in.

3 *they interposed to uphold the truce* INTERVENE, intercede, step in, involve oneself; interfere, intrude, butt in, cut in, meddle; *informal* barge in, horn in, muscle in.

interpret verb 1 *the rabbis interpret the Jewish laws* EXPLAIN, elucidate, expound, explicate, clarify, illuminate, shed light on. See note at CLARIFY.

2 *the remark was interpreted as an invitation* UNDERSTAND, construe, take (to mean), see, regard.

3 *the symbols are difficult to interpret* DECIPHER, decode, unscramble, make intelligible; understand, comprehend, make sense of, figure out; *informal* crack.

4 *he interpreted the role of Hamlet* PERFORM, act, play, render, depict, portray.

interpretation noun 1 *the interpretation of the Bible's teachings* EXPLANATION, elucidation, expounding, exposition, explication, exegesis, clarification.

2 *they argued over interpretation* MEANING, understanding, construal, connotation, explanation, inference.

3 *the interpretation of experimental findings* ANALYSIS, evaluation, review, study, examination.

4 *his interpretation of the sonata* RENDITION, rendering, execution, presentation, performance, portrayal.

interpreter noun 1 *he spoke through an interpreter | interpreters were brought in to read the German messages* TRANSLATOR, transcriber, transliterator.

2 *a fine interpreter of this role* PERFORMER, presenter, exponent; singer, player, actor, dancer.

3 *interpreters of Soviet history* ANALYST, evaluator, reviewer, critic.

interrogate verb *the suspects were interrogated in separate rooms* QUESTION, cross-question, cross-examine, quiz, catechize; interview, examine, debrief, give someone the third degree; *informal* pump, grill.

interrogation noun *he was taken to the police station for interrogation* QUESTIONING, cross-questioning, cross-examination, quizzing; interview, debriefing, inquiry, the third degree; *informal* grilling; *Law* examination.

interrupt verb 1 *she opened her mouth to interrupt* CUT IN (ON), break in (on), barge in (on), intervene (in), put one's oar in, put one's two cents in, interject; *informal* butt in (on), chime in (with).

2 *the band had to interrupt their tour* SUSPEND, adjourn, discontinue, break off, put on hold; stop, halt, cease, end, bring to an end/close; *informal* put on ice, put on the back burner.

3 *the coastal plain is **interrupted by** large lagoons* BREAK (UP) BY, punctuate by/with; pepper with, strew with, dot with, scatter with, sprinkle with.

4 *their view was interrupted by houses* OBSTRUCT, impede, block, restrict, hamper.

interruption noun 1 *he was not pleased at her interruption* CUTTING IN, barging in, intervention, intrusion; *informal* butting in.

2 *an interruption of the power supply* DISCONTINUATION, breaking off, suspension, disruption, stopping, stoppage, halting, cessation.

3 *an interruption in her career* INTERVAL, interlude, break, pause, gap, hiatus.

intersect verb 1 *the lines intersect at right angles* CROSS, crisscross; *technical* decussate.

2 *the cornfield is intersected by a track* BISECT, divide, cut in two/half, cut across/through, crosscut; cross, traverse.

intersection noun 1 *the intersection of two lines* CROSSING, crisscrossing; meeting.

2 *the driver stopped at an intersection* JUNCTION, interchange, crossroads, corner, cloverleaf.

intersperse verb 1 *giant poppies were interspersed among the rocks* SCATTER, disperse, spread, strew, dot, sprinkle, pepper.

2 *the beech trees are interspersed with pines* INTERMIX, mix, mingle, diversified, punctuate.

intertwine verb *a wreath of laurel, intertwined with daffodils* ENTWINE, interweave, interlace, twist, braid, plait, splice, knit, weave, mesh.

interval noun 1 *Baldwin made two speeches in the interval* INTERIM, interlude, intervening time, intervening period, meantime, meanwhile.

2 *short intervals between contractions* STRETCH, period, time, spell; break, pause, gap.

3 *intervals of still water* OPENING, distance, span, space, area.

intervene verb **1** *had the war not intervened, they might have married* OCCUR, happen, take place, arise, crop up, come about; *literary* come to pass, befall, betide.

2 *she intervened in the dispute* INTERCEDE, involve oneself, get involved, interpose oneself, step in; mediate, referee; interfere, intrude, meddle, interrupt.

interview noun *all applicants will be called for an interview* MEETING, discussion, conference, examination, interrogation; audience, talk, dialogue, exchange, conversation.

▸ verb *we interviewed seventy subjects for the survey* TALK TO, have a discussion with, have a dialogue with; question, interrogate, cross-examine, meet with; poll, canvass, survey, sound out; *informal* grill, pump; *Law* examine.

interviewer noun *her first stint as an interviewer was for her fifth-grade newsletter* QUESTIONER, interrogator, examiner, assessor, appraiser; journalist, reporter.

interweave verb **1** *the threads are interwoven* INTERTWINE, entwine, interlace, splice, braid, plait; twist together, weave together, wind together; *Nautical* marry.

2 *their fates were interwoven* INTERLINK, link, connect; intermix, mix, merge, blend, interlock, bind together, knit together, fuse.

intestinal adjective *he was treated for an intestinal complaint* ENTERIC, gastro-enteric, duodenal, celiac, gastric, ventral, stomach, abdominal.

intestines plural noun *the intestines are used in pet foods* GUT, guts, entrails, viscera; *informal* insides, innards.

intimacy noun **1** *the sisters reestablished their old intimacy* CLOSENESS, togetherness, affinity, rapport, attachment, familiarity, friendliness, friendship, amity, affection, warmth, confidence; *informal* chumminess.

2 *the memory of their intimacy* SEXUAL RELATIONS, (sexual) intercourse, sex, lovemaking; *dated* carnal knowledge; *formal* copulation, (sexual) congress; *technical* coitus.

intimate[1] adjective **1** *an intimate friend of Picasso's* CLOSE, bosom, dear, cherished, faithful, devoted, fast, firm, familiar; *informal* chummy. ANTONYM distant.

2 *an intimate atmosphere* FRIENDLY, warm, welcoming, hospitable, relaxed, informal; cozy, comfortable, snug; *informal* comfy. ANTONYMS formal, cold.

3 *intimate thoughts* PERSONAL, private, confidential, secret; innermost, inner, inward, deep, deepest; unspoken, undisclosed.

4 *an intimate knowledge of the music industry* DETAILED, thorough, exhaustive, deep, in-depth, profound; direct, personal, immediate, firsthand; *informal* up-close-and-personal. ANTONYMS sketchy, superficial.

5 *intimate relations* SEXUAL, carnal, romantic, amorous, amatory. ANTONYMS nonsexual, platonic.

▸ noun *his circle of intimates* CLOSE FRIEND, best friend, bosom friend, confidant, confidante; *informal* chum, pal, crony, buddy, bosom buddy, bud; *chiefly Brit. informal* mate.

intimate[2] verb **1** *he intimated to the committee his decision to retire* ANNOUNCE, state, proclaim, declare, make known, make public, publicize, disclose, reveal, divulge, set forth.

2 *her feelings were subtly intimated* IMPLY, suggest, hint at, insinuate, indicate, signal, allude to, refer to, convey; *informal* get at, drive at.

intimation noun *the first intimation of trouble came when the police began going door to door* SUGGESTION, hint, indication, sign, signal, inkling, suspicion, impression; clue, undertone, whisper, wind; communication, notification, notice, warning.

intimidate verb *Rico sent his goons to intimidate the local merchants* FRIGHTEN, menace, terrify, scare, terrorize, cow, dragoon, subdue; THREATEN, browbeat, bully, pressure, harass, harry, hassle, hound, torment, tyrannize, persecute; *informal* lean on, push around, bulldoze, railroad, twist someone's arm, strong-arm.

intolerable adjective *the drilling noise had become intolerable* UNBEARABLE, insufferable, unsupportable, insupportable, unendurable, beyond endurance, too much to bear; unacceptable; *informal* too much. ANTONYM bearable.

intolerance **1** *clearly she had not inherited her parents' racial intolerance* BIGOTRY, narrow-mindedness, small-mindedness, illiberality, parochialism, provincialism; prejudice, bias, partisanship, partiality, discrimination; injustice, inequality. See note at BIAS.

2 *lactose intolerance* SENSITIVITY, hypersensitivity; allergy.

intolerant adjective **1** *intolerant in religious matters* BIGOTED, narrow-minded, small-minded, parochial, provincial, illiberal; prejudiced, biased, partial, partisan, discriminatory.

2 *foods to which you are intolerant* ALLERGIC, sensitive, hypersensitive.

intonation noun **1** *she read with the wrong intonation* INFLECTION, pitch, tone, timbre, cadence, lilt, rise and fall, modulation, speech pattern; accentuation, accent, emphasis, stress.

2 *the intonation of hymns* CHANTING, intoning, incantation, recitation, singing.

intoxicate verb **1** *one glass of wine intoxicated him* INEBRIATE, make drunk, make someone's head spin, befuddle, go to someone's head; *informal* make someone woozy.

2 *she became intoxicated by sci-fi literature at age ten* EXHILARATE, thrill, elate, delight, captivate, enthrall, entrance, enrapture, excite, stir, rouse, invigorate, inspire, fire with enthusiasm, electrify, transport; *informal* give someone a buzz, give someone a kick, give someone a thrill, bowl over.

intoxicated adjective *several passengers later said they suspected the driver of being intoxicated* DRUNK, inebriated, inebriate, impaired, drunken, tipsy, under the influence; *informal* plastered, smashed, bombed, sloshed, sozzled, hammered, sauced, lubricated, well-oiled, wrecked, juiced, blasted, stinko, blitzed, half-cut, fried, gassed, polluted, pissed, tanked (up), soaked, out of one's head, out of one's skull, loaded, trashed, buzzed, befuddled, hopped up, besotted, pickled, pixilated, canned, cockeyed, wasted, blotto, blind drunk, roaring drunk, dead drunk, punch-drunk, ripped, stewed, tight, high, merry, the worse for wear, far gone, pie-eyed, in one's cups, three sheets to the wind; *Brit. informal* bladdered, lashed; *literary* crapulous. See note at DRUNK. ANTONYM sober.

intoxicating adjective **1** *intoxicating drink* ALCOHOLIC, strong, hard, fortified, potent, stiff, intoxicant; *formal* spirituous.

2 *an intoxicating sense of freedom* HEADY, exhilarating, thrilling, exciting, rousing, stirring, stimulating, invigorating, electrifying; strong, powerful, potent; *informal* mind-blowing. ANTONYM nonalcoholic.

intractable adjective **1** *intractable problems* UNMANAGEABLE, uncontrollable, difficult, awkward, troublesome, demanding, burdensome. ANTONYM manageable.

2 *an intractable man* STUBBORN, obstinate, obdurate, inflexible, headstrong, willful, unbending, unyielding, uncompromising, unaccommodating, uncooperative, difficult, awkward, perverse, contrary, pigheaded, stiff-necked. See note at STUBBORN. ANTONYM compliant.

intransigent adjective *both Palestinian and Israeli leaders have grown increasingly intransigent* UNCOMPROMISING, inflexible, unbending, unyielding, diehard, unshakable, unwavering, resolute, rigid, unaccommodating, uncooperative, stubborn, obstinate, obdurate, pigheaded, single-minded, iron-willed, stiff-necked. ANTONYM compliant.

intrepid adjective *our intrepid leader inspired us to forge ahead* FEARLESS, unafraid, undaunted, unflinching, unshrinking, bold, daring, gallant, audacious, adventurous, heroic, dynamic, spirited, indomitable; brave, courageous, valiant, valorous, stouthearted, stalwart, plucky, doughty; *informal* gutsy, spunky, ballsy. See note at BOLD. ANTONYM timid.

intricate adjective *intricate designs etched into the glass* | *an intricate plot* COMPLEX, complicated, convoluted, tangled, entangled, twisted; elaborate, ornate, detailed, baroque, delicate; involuted; bewildering, confusing, perplexing, labyrinthine, Byzantine; *informal* fiddly.

intrigue verb *her answer intrigued him* INTEREST, be of interest to, fascinate, arouse someone's curiosity, arouse someone's interest, pique someone's curiosity, pique someone's interest, attract.

▸ noun **1** *political intrigue* SECRET PLAN, plotting, plot, conspiracy, collusion, conniving, scheme, scheming, stratagem, machination, trickery, double-dealing, underhandedness, subterfuge; *informal* dirty tricks. See note at PLOT.

2 *Rick's intrigue with his brother's wife caused the family immeasurable grief* (LOVE) AFFAIR, affair of the heart, liaison, amour, fling, flirtation, dalliance, tryst; adultery, infidelity, unfaithfulness, indiscretion; *informal* fooling around, playing around, hanky-panky.

intriguing adjective *intriguing stories* INTERESTING, fascinating, absorbing, compelling, gripping, riveting, captivating, engaging, enthralling, enchanting, attractive, appealing.

intrinsic adjective *an intrinsic eye for fashion* INHERENT, innate, inborn, inbred, congenital, connate, natural; deep-rooted, deep-seated, indelible, ineradicable, ingrained; integral, basic, fundamental, essential; built-in. See note at INHERENT.

introduce verb **1** *she has introduced a new system* INSTITUTE, initiate, launch, inaugurate, establish, found; bring in, usher in, set in motion, start, begin, commence, get going, get underway, originate, pioneer, kick off.

2 *she introduced new legislation* PROPOSE, put forward, suggest, bring to the table, submit; set forth, raise, broach, bring up, mention, air, float; *informal* run something up the flagpole.

3 *she introduced Lindsey to the young man* PRESENT (FORMALLY), make known, acquaint with.

4 *introducing nitrogen into canned beer* INSERT, inject, put, force, shoot, feed. See note at INSERT.

5 *she introduced a note of severity into her voice* INSTILL, infuse, inject, add, insert.

6 *Clayton introduces the program each week* ANNOUNCE, present, give an introduction to; start off, begin, open.

introduction noun **1** *the introduction of democratic reforms* INSTITUTION, establishment, initiation, launch, inauguration, foundation; start, commencement, debut, inception, origination. ANTONYM abolition.

2 *an* ***introduction to*** *the king* (FORMAL) PRESENTATION TO; meeting with, audience with.

3 *the book's introduction* FOREWORD, preface, preamble, prologue, prelude; opening (statement), beginning; *informal* intro, lead-in, prelims; *formal* proem, prolegomenon. ANTONYM afterword.

4 ***an introduction to*** *hothouse gardening* A PRIMER OF, a basic explanation of, a brief account of; the basics of, the rudiments of, the fundamentals of.

5 *freshmen would soon experience the traditional* ***introduction to*** *school life* INITIATION INTO, induction into, inauguration into, baptism into.

introductory adjective **1** *the introductory chapter* OPENING, initial, starting, initiatory, first; prefatory, preliminary, leadoff. ANTONYM final.

2 *an introductory course* ELEMENTARY, basic, rudimentary, primary; initiatory, preparatory, entry-level, survey; *informal* 101. ANTONYM advanced.

introspection noun *the first lady's book is heavy on photos and light on introspection* SELF-ANALYSIS, self-examination, soul-searching, introversion, self-observation; contemplation, meditation, thoughtfulness, thought, pensiveness, reflection, rumination; *informal* navel-gazing; *formal* cogitation.

introspective adjective *an introspective poet* INWARD-LOOKING, self-analyzing, introverted, introvert, brooding; contemplative, thoughtful, pensive, meditative, reflective; *informal* navel-gazing.

introverted adjective *his introverted parents were uncomfortable with the rowdy friends he brought home from college* SHY, reserved, withdrawn, reticent, diffident, retiring, quiet; introspective, introvert, inward-looking, self-absorbed; pensive, contemplative, thoughtful, meditative, reflective. ANTONYM extroverted.

intrude verb *there will never be a consensus on just how entitled the press is to* ***intrude on*** *the lives of celebs* ENCROACH ON, impinge on, interfere in, trespass on/upon, infringe on, obtrude on/into, invade, violate, disturb, disrupt, interrupt; meddle in, barge in on; *informal* horn in on, muscle in on, poke one's nose into.

intruder noun *the intruder turned out to be a raccoon in the garage* TRESPASSER, interloper, invader, infiltrator; burglar, housebreaker, thief, prowler.

intrusion noun *victims of illegal computer intrusion* ENCROACHMENT, invasion, incursion, intervention, infringement, impingement; disturbance, disruption, interruption.

intrusive adjective *an intrusive journalist* INTRUDING, invasive, obtrusive, unwelcome, pushy; meddlesome, prying, impertinent, interfering; *informal* nosy, snoopy. See note at IMPERTINENT.

intuition noun **1** *he works according to intuition* INSTINCT, intuitiveness; sixth sense, clairvoyance, second sight.

2 *this confirms an intuition I had* HUNCH, feeling (in one's bones), inkling, (sneaking) suspicion, idea, sense, notion; premonition, presentiment; *informal* gut feeling, gut instinct.

intuitive adjective *an intuitive grasp of the truth* INSTINCTIVE, instinctual; innate, inborn, inherent, natural, congenital; unconscious, subconscious, right-brained, involuntary, visceral; *informal* gut.

inundate verb **1** *a flood inundated the temple* FLOOD, deluge, overrun, swamp, drown, submerge, engulf.

2 *we have been inundated with complaints* OVERWHELM, overrun, overload, bog down, swamp, besiege, snow under, bombard, glut.

inure verb *they had become inured to poverty* HARDEN, toughen, season, temper, condition; accustom, habituate, familiarize, acclimatize, adjust, adapt, desensitize. ANTONYM sensitize.

invade verb **1** *the army invaded the town* OCCUPY, conquer, capture, seize, take (over), annex, win, gain, secure; march into, storm. ANTONYM withdraw from.

2 *someone had invaded our privacy* INTRUDE ON, violate, encroach on, infringe on, trespass on, obtrude on, disturb, disrupt; *informal* horn in on, muscle in on, barge in on. ANTONYM respect.

3 *every summer, tourists invaded the beach* OVERRUN, swarm, overwhelm, inundate.

invader noun *invaders surprised them at dawn* ATTACKER, aggressor, raider, marauder; occupier, conqueror; intruder, interloper.

invalid[1] noun *a home for invalids* ILL PERSON, sick person, valetudinarian; patient, convalescent, shut-in.

▸ adjective *her invalid husband* ILL, sick, sickly, ailing, unwell, infirm, in poor health, indisposed; incapacitated, bedridden, housebound, frail, feeble, weak, debilitated. ANTONYM healthy.

invalid[2] adjective **1** *the law was invalid* (LEGALLY) VOID, null and void, unenforceable, not binding, illegitimate, inapplicable. ANTONYM binding.

2 *the theory is invalid* FALSE, untrue, inaccurate, faulty, fallacious, spurious, unconvincing, unsound, weak, wrong, wide of the mark, off target; untenable, baseless, ill-founded, groundless; *informal* full of holes. ANTONYM true.

invalidate verb **1** *the court invalidated the statute* RENDER INVALID, void, nullify, annul, negate, cancel, disallow, overturn, overrule; *informal* nix. See note at VOID.

2 *this case invalidates the general argument* DISPROVE, refute, contradict, negate, belie, discredit, debunk; weaken, undermine, explode; *informal* poke holes in; *formal* confute.

invaluable adjective *an invaluable member of the organization* INDISPENSABLE, crucial, critical, key, vital, necessary, irreplaceable, all-important; immeasurable, incalculable, inestimable, priceless. ANTONYM dispensable.

invariably adverb *we say we'll order light, but we invariably end up with platters of fried food* ALWAYS, on every occasion, at all times, without fail, without exception; everywhere, in all places, in all cases, in all instances; regularly, consistently, repeatedly, habitually, unfailingly, religiously; constantly, steadily. ANTONYMS sometimes, never.

invasion noun **1** *the invasion of the island* OCCUPATION, capture, seizure, annexation, annexing, takeover; storming, incursion, attack, assault. ANTONYM withdrawal.

2 *an invasion of tourists* INFLUX, inundation, flood, rush, torrent, deluge, avalanche, juggernaut.

3 *an invasion of my privacy* VIOLATION, infringement, interruption, intrusion, encroachment, disturbance, disruption, breach. ANTONYM respect.

invective noun *the invective that spewed from Claude's lips left everyone speechless* ABUSE, insults, expletives, swear words, swearing, curses, foul language, foul language, vituperation; denunciation, censure, vilification, revilement, reproach, castigation, recrimination; *informal* tongue-lashing, trash talk; *formal* obloquy, contumely. ANTONYM praise.

inveigh verb *he was one of the few Wall Streeters willing to **inveigh against** corporate greed* FULMINATE AGAINST, declaim against, protest (against), rail against/at, rage at, remonstrate against; denounce, censure, condemn, decry, criticize; disparage, denigrate, run down, abuse, vituperate, vilify, impugn; *informal* sound off about, blast, dis, slam. ANTONYM support.

inveigle verb *planted in colleges throughout the country are brainwashed members whose only mission is to inveigle unsuspecting students into the cult* ENTICE, tempt, lure, seduce, beguile; wheedle, cajole, coax, persuade; *informal* sweet-talk, soft-soap, con, sucker, snow. See note at TEMPT.

invent verb **1** *Louis Braille invented an alphabet for the blind* ORIGINATE, create, design, devise, contrive, develop, innovate; conceive, think up, dream up, come up with, pioneer; coin.

2 *they invented the story for a laugh* MAKE UP, fabricate, concoct, hatch, dream up, conjure up; *informal* cook up.

invention noun **1** *the invention of the telescope* ORIGINATION, creation, innovation, devising, development, design.

2 *medieval inventions* INNOVATION, creation, design, contraption, contrivance, construction, device, gadget; *informal* brainchild.

3 *she played with taste and invention* INVENTIVENESS, originality, creativity, imagination, inspiration.

4 *the story was a total invention* FABRICATION, concoction, (piece of) fiction, story, tale; lie, untruth, falsehood, fib, myth, fantasy, make-believe; *informal* tall tale, cock-and-bull story.

inventive adjective *a well-intentioned and fairly inventive kids' movie* CREATIVE, original, innovative, imaginative, ingenious, resourceful; unusual, fresh, novel, new, newfangled; experimental, avant-garde, groundbreaking, revolutionary, unorthodox, unconventional. See note at CREATIVE. ANTONYMS unimaginative, hackneyed.

inventor noun *the inventor of the separating zipper* ORIG-

INATOR, creator, innovator; designer, deviser, developer, maker, producer; author, architect; pioneer, mastermind, father, progenitor.

inventory noun *an inventory of all their belongings | our inventory of leaf rakes is low* LIST, listing, catalog, record, register, checklist, log, archive; stock, supply, store.

▸ verb *I inventoried his collection of music boxes* LIST, catalog, record, register, log, document.

inverse adjective *inverse snobbery.* See REVERSE adjective sense 2.

▸ noun *alkalinity is the inverse of acidity.* See OPPOSITE noun.

invert verb *the crew inverted the mast* TURN UPSIDE DOWN, upend, upturn, turn around/about, turn inside out, turn back to front, transpose, reverse, flip (over).

invest verb **1** *he **invested in** a soap company* PUT MONEY INTO, provide capital for, fund, back, finance, subsidize, bankroll, underwrite; buy into, buy shares in; *informal* grubstake.

2 *they invested $18 million* SPEND, expend, put in, venture, speculate, risk; *informal* lay out.

3 *they **invested in** a new car* PURCHASE, buy, procure.

4 *the scene was invested with magic* IMBUE, infuse, charge, steep, suffuse, permeate, pervade.

5 *the powers **invested in** the bishop* VEST IN, confer on, bestow on, grant to, entrust to, put in the hands of.

investigate verb *police are still investigating this apparent murder* INQUIRE INTO, look into, go into, probe, explore, scrutinize, conduct an investigation into, make inquiries about; inspect, analyze, study, examine, consider, research; *informal* check out, suss out, scope out, dig, get to the bottom of.

investigation noun *we cannot determine the cause of the fire without further investigation* EXAMINATION, inquiry, study, inspection, exploration, consideration, analysis, appraisal; research, scrutiny, perusal; probe, review, (background) check, survey.

investigator noun *investigators searching the ship on Monday found a cache of weapons* INSPECTOR, examiner, inquirer, inquisitor, explorer, analyzer; researcher, fact-finder, scrutineer, prober, searcher, auditor; detective.

investiture noun *the investiture of archbishops* INAUGURATION, appointment, installation, initiation, swearing in; ordination, consecration, crowning, enthronement.

investment noun **1** *some tips for responsible investment* INVESTING, speculation; funding, backing, financing, underwriting; buying shares.

2 *it's a good investment* VENTURE, speculation, risk, gamble; asset, acquisition, holding, possession; *informal* grubstake.

3 *an investment of $305,000* STAKE, share, money/capital invested.

4 *a substantial investment of time* CONTRIBUTION, surrender, loss, forfeiture, sacrifice.

investor noun *Chinese investors have moved billions of dollars into Hong Kong* SHAREHOLDER, buyer; backer, financier, venture capitalist.

inveterate adjective **1** *an inveterate gambler* CONFIRMED, hardened, incorrigible, addicted, habitual, compulsive, obsessive; *informal* pathological, chronic.

2 *an inveterate liberal* STAUNCH, steadfast, committed, devoted, dedicated, dyed-in-the-wool, out and out, diehard, hard-core.

3 *inveterate corruption* INGRAINED, deep-seated, deep-rooted, entrenched, congenital, ineradicable, incurable.

invidious adjective **1** *that put her in an invidious position* UNPLEASANT, awkward, difficult; undesirable, unenviable; odious, hateful, detestable. ANTONYM pleasant.

2 *an invidious comparison* UNFAIR, unjust, iniquitous, unwarranted; deleterious, detrimental, discriminatory. ANTONYM fair.

invigorate verb *invigorated by the chilly autumn air | the need to invigorate the peace process in the Middle East* REVITALIZE, energize, refresh, revive, vivify, brace, rejuvenate, enliven, liven up, perk up, wake up, animate, galvanize, fortify, stimulate, rouse, exhilarate; *informal* buck up, pep up, breathe new life into. See note at QUICKEN. ANTONYM tire.

invincible adjective *invincible superheroes* INVULNERABLE, indestructible, unconquerable, unbeatable, indomitable, unassailable; impregnable, inviolable; *informal* bulletproof. ANTONYM vulnerable.

inviolable adjective See INALIENABLE.

inviolate adjective *the insignia of the Red Cross was regarded as virtually inviolate* UNTOUCHABLE, inviolable, safe from harm; UNTOUCHED, undamaged, unhurt, unharmed, unscathed; unspoiled, unflawed, unsullied, unstained, undefiled, unprofaned, perfect, pristine, pure; intact, unbroken, whole, entire, complete.

invisible adjective *when the glue dries, it is invisible* UNABLE TO BE SEEN, not visible; undetectable, indiscernible, inconspicuous, imperceptible; unseen, unnoticed, unobserved, hidden, veiled, obscured, out of sight.

invitation noun **1** *an invitation to dinner* REQUEST TO ATTEND, call, summons; offer; card, note; *informal* invite.

2 *an open door is an invitation to a thief* ENCOURAGEMENT, provocation, temptation, lure, magnet, bait, enticement, attraction, allure; *informal* come-on.

invite verb **1** *they invited us to Sunday brunch* ASK, summon, have someone over, request someone's company, request the pleasure of someone's company.

2 *we invite your comments* ASK FOR, request, call for, appeal for, solicit, seek, summon.

3 *airing such views invites trouble* PROVOKE, induce, cause, create, generate, engender, foster, encourage, lead to; incite, elicit, bring on oneself, arouse, call forth.

inviting adjective *the inviting aromas wafting from her kitchen* TEMPTING, enticing, alluring, beguiling; attractive, appealing, pleasant, agreeable, delightful; appetizing, mouthwatering; fascinating, enchanting, entrancing, captivating, intriguing, irresistible, seductive. ANTONYM repellent.

invoice noun *an invoice for the goods* BILL, account, statement (of charges), check; *informal* tab; *archaic* reckoning.

▸ verb *we'll invoice you for the damage* BILL, charge, send an invoice/bill to.

invoke verb **1** *he invoked his statutory rights* CITE, refer to, adduce, instance; resort to, have recourse to, turn to.

2 *I invoked the Madonna* APPEAL TO, pray to, call on, supplicate, entreat, solicit, beg, implore; *literary* beseech.

3 *invoking spirits* SUMMON, call (up), conjure (up).

involuntary adjective *an involuntary urge* SPONTANEOUS, instinctive, unconscious, unintentional, uncontrollable; reflex, automatic; *informal* knee-jerk. ANTONYM deliberate.

involve verb **1** *the inspection involved a lot of work* REQUIRE, necessitate, demand, call for; entail, mean, imply, presuppose. ANTONYM preclude.

2 *I try to involve everyone in key decisions* INCLUDE, count in, bring in, take into account, take note of; incorporate, encompass, touch on, embrace, comprehend, cover. ANTONYM exclude.

involved adjective **1** *social workers* ***involved in*** *the case* ASSOCIATED WITH, connected with, concerned in/with. ANTONYM unconnected.

2 *he had been involved in drug dealing* IMPLICATED, incriminated, inculpated, embroiled, entangled, caught up; *informal* mixed up.

3 *a long and involved story* COMPLICATED, intricate, complex, elaborate; convoluted, impenetrable, unfathomable. ANTONYM straightforward.

4 *very* ***involved with*** *the organization* ENGROSSED IN, absorbed in, immersed in, caught up in, preoccupied by, busy with, engaged in/with, intent on. ANTONYM uninterested.

involvement noun **1** *his involvement in a plot to overthrow the government* PARTICIPATION, action, hand; collaboration, collusion, complicity, implication, incrimination, inculpation; association, connection, attachment, entanglement.

2 *emotional involvement* ATTACHMENT, friendship, intimacy; relationship, relations, bond.

invulnerable adjective *acts of terrorism have reminded us that no nations are invulnerable* IMPERVIOUS, insusceptible, immune; indestructible, impenetrable, impregnable, unassailable, inviolable, invincible, secure; proof (against); *informal* bulletproof.

inward adjective **1** *an inward curve* TOWARD THE INSIDE, going in; concave. ANTONYM outward.

2 *an inward smile* INTERNAL, inner, interior, innermost; private, personal, hidden, secret, veiled, masked, concealed, unexpressed. ANTONYM external.

▸ adverb *the door opened inward.* INSIDE, into the interior, inwards, within.

inwardly adverb *inwardly, George blamed himself* INSIDE, internally, within, deep down (inside), in one's heart (of hearts); privately, secretly, confidentially; *literary* inly.

inwards adverb See INWARD.

iota noun *nothing she said made an iota of difference* BIT, speck, mite, scrap, shred, ounce, scintilla, atom, jot, grain, whit, trace; *informal* smidgen, smidge, tad; *archaic* scruple.

irascible adjective *this hot weather has put everyone in an irascible mood* IRRITABLE, quick-tempered, short-tempered, hot-tempered, testy, touchy, tetchy, edgy, crabby, petulant, waspish, dyspeptic, snappish; cross, surly, crusty, grouchy, grumpy, cranky, cantankerous, curmudgeonly, ill-natured, peevish, querulous, fractious; *informal* prickly, snippy. ANTONYMS even-tempered, good-natured.

irate adjective *several irate customers demanded a full refund* ANGRY, furious, infuriated, incensed, enraged, fuming, seething, cross, mad, livid; raging, ranting, raving, in a frenzy, beside oneself, outraged, up in arms; indignant, exasperated, annoyed, irritated, irked, vexed, piqued, choleric; *informal* foaming at the mouth, hot under the collar, seeing red, cheesed off, hopping mad, PO'd, fit to be tied; *literary* wrathful; *archaic* wroth. ANTONYMS calm, contented.

ire noun *literary the plans provoked the ire of conservationists* ANGER, rage, fury, wrath, outrage, temper, crossness, spleen; annoyance, exasperation, irritation, displeasure, indignation, vexation, chagrin, pique; *literary* choler.

iridescent adjective *an iridescent film of oil on the puddle* OPALESCENT, nacreous; shimmering, luminous, glittering, sparkling, dazzling, shining, gleaming, glowing, lustrous, scintillating; kaleidoscopic, rainbow-colored, multicolored; *literary* glistering, coruscating, effulgent, scintillant.

irk verb *clearly, the prosecutor's opening questions irked him* IRRITATE, annoy, gall, pique, nettle, exasperate, try someone's patience; anger, infuriate, madden, incense, get on someone's nerves; antagonize, provoke; *informal* get someone's dander up, ruffle someone's feathers, make someone's hackles rise; rub the wrong way, get (someone's goat), get/put someone's back up, make someone's blood boil, peeve, miff, frost, rile, aggravate, needle, get to, bug, drive mad/crazy, tee off, tick off, piss off, PO, rankle, ride, drive up the wall, make someone see red. ANTONYM please.

irksome adjective *the irksome babbling of the couple upstairs* IRRITATING, annoying, vexing, vexatious, galling, exasperating, disagreeable; tiresome, wearisome, tedious, trying, troublesome, bothersome, nettlesome, obnoxious, awkward, difficult, boring, uninteresting; infuriating, maddening; *informal* infernal.

iron noun **1** *a ship built of iron* metal, pig iron, cast iron, wrought iron.

2 **(irons)** *they were clapped in irons* MANACLES, shackles, fetters, chains, handcuffs; *informal* bracelets, cuffs.

▸ adjective **1** *an iron law of politics* INFLEXIBLE, unbreakable, absolute, unconditional, categorical, incontrovertible, infallible. ANTONYM flexible.

2 *an iron will* UNCOMPROMISING, unrelenting, unyielding, unbending, resolute, resolved, determined, firm, rigid, steadfast, unwavering, steely; *literary* adamantine. ANTONYM flexible.

PHRASE: **iron out** *it's time we iron out our differences* RESOLVE, straighten out, sort out, smooth out, clear up, settle, put right, solve, remedy, rectify, fix, mend, eliminate, eradicate, erase, get rid of; harmonize, reconcile.

ironic adjective **1** *Edward's tone was ironic* SARCASTIC, sardonic, cynical, mocking, satirical, caustic, wry. ANTONYM sincere.

2 *it's ironic that a former illiterate is now a successful writer* PARADOXICAL, incongruous. ANTONYM logical.

irony noun **1** *that note of irony in her voice* SARCASM, causticity, cynicism, mockery, satire, sardonicism. See note at WIT. ANTONYM sincerity.

2 *the irony of the situation* PARADOX, incongruity, incongruousness. ANTONYM logic.

irradiate verb **1** *her smile irradiated the room* ILLUMINATE, light (up), cast light upon, brighten, shine on; *literary* illumine, illume.

2 *irradiated with gamma rays* RADIATE, charge, blast,

shoot; infuse, permeate, saturate, flood; *informal* zap, nuke.

irrational adjective *an irrational fear of insects* UNREASONABLE, illogical, groundless, baseless, unfounded, unjustifiable; absurd, ridiculous, ludicrous, preposterous, silly, foolish, senseless. ANTONYMS reasonable, logical.

irreconcilable adjective **1** *irreconcilable views about religion* INCOMPATIBLE, at odds, at variance, conflicting, clashing, antagonistic, mutually exclusive, diametrically opposed; disparate, poles apart. ANTONYMS compatible, similar.

2 *irreconcilable enemies* IMPLACABLE, unappeasable, uncompromising, inflexible; mortal, bitter, deadly, sworn, out-and-out.

irrefutable adjective *irrefutable evidence* INDISPUTABLE, undeniable, unquestionable, incontrovertible, incontestable, beyond question, beyond doubt, conclusive, definite, definitive, decisive, certain, positive, sure; *informal* sure as shootin'.

irregular adjective **1** *irregular features | an irregular coastline* ASYMMETRICAL, nonuniform, uneven, crooked, misshapen, lopsided, twisted; unusual, peculiar, strange, bizarre; jagged, ragged, serrated, indented. ANTONYM straight.

2 *irregular surfaces* ROUGH, bumpy, uneven, pitted, rutted; lumpy, knobbly, gnarled. ANTONYM smooth.

3 *an irregular heartbeat* INCONSISTENT, unsteady, uneven, fitful, patchy, variable, varying, changeable, changing, inconstant, erratic, unstable, unsettled, spasmodic, intermittent, fluctuating; *informal* herky-jerky. ANTONYM steady.

4 *irregular financial dealings* AGAINST THE RULES, out of order, improper, illegitimate, unscrupulous, unethical, unprofessional, unacceptable; *informal* shady. ANTONYM aboveboard.

5 *irregular clothing* FLAWED, damaged, imperfect, discarded, rejected, throwaway.

irregularity noun **1** *the irregularity of the coastline* ASYMMETRY, nonuniformity, unevenness, crookedness, lopsidedness; jaggedness, raggedness, indentation.

2 *the irregularity of the surface* ROUGHNESS, bumpiness, unevenness; lumpiness.

3 *irregularity in the fabric* FLAW, damage, imperfection; blemish, mark, spot, stain.

4 *the irregularity of the bus service* INCONSISTENCY, unsteadiness, unevenness, fitfulness, patchiness, instability, variability, changeableness, fluctuation, unpredictability, unreliability.

5 *financial irregularities* IMPROPRIETY, wrongdoing, misconduct, dishonesty, corruption, immorality; *informal* shadiness, crookedness, dodginess.

6 *the staff noted any irregularity in operation* ABNORMALITY, unusualness, strangeness, oddness, singularity, anomaly, deviation, aberration, peculiarity, idiosyncrasy.

irrelevant adjective *the judge ruled that the victim's use of drugs was irrelevant* BESIDE THE POINT, immaterial, not pertinent, not germane, off the subject, unconnected, unrelated, peripheral, extraneous, inapposite, inapplicable; unimportant, inconsequential, insignificant, trivial; *formal* impertinent.

irreligious adjective *it was a great miscalculation to assess America as an irreligious society* ATHEISTIC, unbelieving, nonbelieving, agnostic, heretical, faithless, godless, ungodly, impious, profane, infidel, barbarian, heathen, pagan; secular, humanist. ANTONYMS pious, God-fearing.

irreparable adjective *irreparable damage to the landing module* IRREVERSIBLE, irrevocable, irrecoverable, unrepairable, beyond repair, unrectifiable; hopeless. ANTONYM repairable.

irreplaceable adjective *an irreplaceable set of engraved wine glasses* UNIQUE, invaluable, priceless, unrepeatable, one-of-a-kind, incomparable, unparalleled; treasured, prized, cherished.

irrepressible adjective **1** *the desire for freedom is irrepressible* INEXTINGUISHABLE, unquenchable, uncontainable, uncontrollable, indestructible, undying, everlasting.

2 *his irrepressible personality* EBULLIENT, exuberant, buoyant, sunny, breezy, jaunty, lighthearted, high-spirited, vivacious, animated, full of life, lively; *informal* bubbly, bouncy, peppy, chipper.

irreproachable adjective *her irreproachable character* IMPECCABLE, above/beyond reproach, blameless, faultless, flawless, unblemished, untarnished, spotless, immaculate, exemplary, model, outstanding, exceptional, admirable, perfect; *informal* squeaky clean; *trademark* Teflon. ANTONYM reprehensible.

irresistible adjective **1** *irresistible snakeskin stilettos | his irresistible smile* ENTICING, tempting, alluring, inviting, seductive; attractive, desirable, fetching, glamorous, appealing, delightful; ravishing, captivating, beguiling, tantalizing, enchanting, charming, fascinating, magnetic. ANTONYMS undesirable, off-putting.

2 *an irresistible impulse to scream* UNCONTROLLABLE, overwhelming, overpowering, compelling, compulsive, irrepressible, ungovernable, besetting; unavoidable, inexorable, unpreventable, inescapable, driving, potent, forceful, urgent, imperative; obsessive. ANTONYM controllable.

irresolute adjective *once again, faced with an important issue, this legislative body sits irresolute and utterly useless* INDECISIVE, hesitant, vacillating, equivocating, dithering, wavering, shilly-shallying; ambivalent, blowing hot and cold, of two minds, hemming and hawing, in a dilemma, in a quandary, torn; doubtful, in doubt, unsure, uncertain, undecided, wishy-washy; *informal* sitting on the fence. ANTONYM decisive.

irrespective adjective *each member has one vote,* ***irrespective of*** *the number of shares held* REGARDLESS OF, without regard to/for, notwithstanding, whatever, no matter what, without consideration of.

irresponsible adjective *such irresponsible behavior is unthinkable for a man your age* RECKLESS, rash, careless, thoughtless, foolhardy, foolish, impetuous, impulsive, devil-may-care, delinquent, derelict, negligent, harebrained; unreliable, undependable, untrustworthy, flighty, immature. ANTONYM sensible.

irreverent adjective *no one was amused by his irreverent joke-telling* DISRESPECTFUL, disdainful, scornful, contemptuous, derisive, disparaging; impertinent, impudent, cheeky, saucy, flippant, rude, discourteous. ANTONYM respectful.

irreversible adjective *irreversible damage* IRREPARABLE, beyond repair, irremediable, irrevocable, permanent; unalterable, unchangeable, immutable, carved in stone; *Law* peremptory. ANTONYM temporary.

irrevocable adjective *an irrevocable commitment* IRREVERSIBLE, unalterable, unchangeable, immutable, final, binding, permanent, carved in stone; *Law* peremptory. ANTONYM temporary.

irrigate verb **1** *the river can be used to irrigate thousands of adjacent acres* WATER, bring water to, soak, flood, inundate.

2 *have you irrigated the wound?* FLUSH, wash (out), cleanse; flood.

irritability noun *she walked in with the irritability of a wounded bear* IRASCIBILITY, testiness, touchiness, grumpiness, moodiness, grouchiness, (bad) mood, cantankerousness, curmudgeonliness, bad temper, short temper, ill humor, peevishness, crossness, fractiousness, pettishness, crabbiness, tetchiness, waspishness, prickliness, crankiness, orneriness; *literary* choler. ANTONYM good humor.

irritable adjective *being out of work made him irritable* BAD-TEMPERED, short-tempered, irascible, tetchy, testy, touchy, grumpy, grouchy, moody, crotchety, in a (bad) mood, cantankerous, bilious, curmudgeonly, ill-tempered, annoyed, cross, ill-humored, peevish, fractious, pettish, crabby, bitchy, waspish, prickly, splenetic, dyspeptic, choleric; *informal* cranky, ornery, shirty, on a short fuse, soreheaded. ANTONYM easygoing.

WORD NOTE **shirty**

An apt, infrequently used term for irritable or easily annoyed, as in, *Well, you don't have to get all shirty about it,* which virtually guarantees an increase in shirtiness. **—JS**

irritant noun See IRRITATION sense 2.

irritate verb **1** *they seem to enjoy irritating me* ANNOY, vex, make angry, make cross, anger, exasperate, irk, gall, pique, nettle, put out, antagonize, get on someone's nerves, try someone's patience, ruffle someone's feathers, make someone's hackles rise; infuriate, madden, provoke, pester, rub the wrong way; *informal* aggravate, hassle, miff, rile, needle, get to, bug, get in someone's hair, get under someone's skin, get someone's dander up, rattle someone's cage, get/put someone's back up, drive mad/crazy, drive someone around the bend, drive up the wall, drive bananas, tee off, tick off, burn up, rankle, ride. See note at AGGRAVATE. ANTONYM pacify.

2 *paint fumes irritate my throat* INFLAME, aggravate; pain, hurt; chafe, abrade, scratch, rasp; *rare* excoriate. ANTONYM soothe.

irritated adjective *we had never before seen the commissioner so irritated* ANNOYED, cross, angry, vexed, exasperated, irked, piqued, nettled, put out, fed up, disgruntled, in a bad mood, in a temper, testy, in a huff, huffy, aggrieved; irate, infuriated, incensed; *informal* aggravated, peeved, miffed, mad, riled, hot under the collar, teed off, ticked off, PO'd, sore; *archaic* wroth. ANTONYM good-humored.

irritating adjective *a slow Web site is irritating to your customers* ANNOYING, infuriating, exasperating, maddening, trying, tiresome, vexing, vexatious, obnoxious, irksome, nagging, niggling, galling, grating, aggravating, pestilential.

irritation noun **1** *she tried not to show her irritation* ANNOYANCE, exasperation, vexation, indignation, impatience, crossness, displeasure, chagrin, pique; anger, rage, fury, wrath, aggravation; *literary* ire. ANTONYM delight.

2 *I realize my presence is an irritation for you* IRRITANT, annoyance, thorn in someone's side/flesh, bother, trial, torment, plague, inconvenience, nuisance, aggravation, pain (in the neck), headache, burr under someone's saddle. ANTONYM pleasure.

island noun *she lived on an island* ISLE, islet; atoll; **(islands)** archipelago.

▸ verb *he was islanded from the problems of real life* ISOLATE, cloister, seclude; separate, detach, cut off.

isolate verb **1** *the police isolated the area* CORDON OFF, seal off, close off, fence off.

2 *doctors isolated the patients* separate, set/keep apart, segregate, detach, cut off, shut away, keep in solitude, quarantine, cloister, seclude, sequester. ANTONYM integrate.

3 *I have isolated the problem* IDENTIFY, single out, pick out, point out, spot, recognize, distinguish, pinpoint, locate.

isolated adjective **1** *isolated communities* REMOTE, out of the way, outlying, off the beaten track/path, secluded, lonely, godforsaken, far-flung, inaccessible, cutoff, incommunicado, in the backwoods, in the back of beyond, in the back concessions, in the boonies/boondocks, in the middle of nowhere, in the sticks, in the tall timbershinterland. ANTONYM accessible.

2 *he lived an isolated existence* SOLITARY, lonely, companionless, friendless; secluded, cloistered, segregated, unsociable, reclusive, hermitic, lonesome. ANTONYM sociable.

3 *an isolated incident* UNIQUE, lone, solitary; unusual, uncommon, exceptional, anomalous, abnormal, untypical, atypical, freak. ANTONYMS common, everyday.

issue noun **1** *the committee discussed the issue* MATTER, matter in question, question, point, point at issue, affair, case, subject, topic; problem, bone of contention.

2 *the issue of a special stamp* ISSUING, publication, publishing, printing; circulation, distribution.

3 *the latest issue of our magazine* EDITION, number, copy, installment, volume, publication.

4 *Law she died without issue* OFFSPRING, descendants, heirs, successors, children, progeny, family; *archaic* seed, fruit (of one's loins).

5 *an issue of water* DISCHARGE, emission, release, outflow, outflowing, secretion, emanation, exudation, effluence; *technical* efflux.

▸ verb **1** *the mayor issued a statement* SEND OUT, put out, release, deliver, publish, announce, pronounce, broadcast, communicate, circulate, distribute, disseminate, transmit.

2 *the students were issued with new uniforms* SUPPLY, provide, furnish, arm, equip, fit out, rig out; *Brit.* kit out; *informal* fix up.

3 *the smell of onion issued from the kitchen* EMANATE, emerge, exude, flow (out/forth), pour (out/forth); be emitted.

4 *large profits might* **issue from** *the deal* RESULT FROM, follow, ensue from, stem from, spring (forth) from, arise from, proceed from, come (forth) from; be the result of, be brought on/about by, be produced by.

PHRASES: **at issue** *at issue here is what constitutes 'art'* IN QUESTION, in dispute, under discussion, under consideration, for debate. **take issue with** *we'll get nowhere if you have to take issue with everything that anybody says* DISAGREE WITH, be in dispute with, be in contention with, be at variance with, be at odds with, argue with, quarrel with; challenge, dispute, (call into) question. ANTONYM agree with.

WORD NOTE **issues**

In a therapy-saturated culture, *issues* has come to mean "problems." It started out referring to neurotic problems, as in *He's got father issues,* or, not even requiring an adjective, *she has issues,* then devolved into the general: *I'm late because I had parking issues.* A *New York Times* article in January 2004 described a brown-headed cowbird that apparently can't sing and engage in visual courtship display at the same time as having *multitasking issues.* In the software industry, *issues* is a euphemism for "bugs": rather than acknowledge a bug in one of its products, a company might say, *This is a known issue.* **—JS**

it pronoun See notes below.

USAGE NOTE **it is I, it is me**

Generally, the nominative pronoun (here *I*) is the complement of a linking verb (*this is she* | *it was he*). But *it is me* and *it's me* are fully acceptable, especially in informal contexts.

In 1937, editor Walter Barnes wrote, "The facts surrounding the case of 'It is me' are: 1. This expression is in accepted use in informal situations. 2. It is preferable to 'It is I' whenever the speaker wishes to emphasize his own personal identity. It is so used and has been so used by dozens of reputable writers from Shakespeare to the present, including . . . Emerson, Meredith, and Stevenson. 3. So far as anyone knows, it has been in good colloquial use for three or four centuries, though for most of that time, the grammarians have been grumbling about it. 4. Many careful, sensitive speakers and writers employ both 'It is me' and 'It is I,' depending on the desired shade of meaning." ("Stepchildren of the Mother Tongue," *Review of Reviews*; Mar. 1937.)

Of course, those with even a smattering of French know that *it's me* answers nicely to *c'est moi*. Good writers have long found the English equivalent serviceable—e.g.: "But Silver . . . called out to know if that were me." (Robert Louis Stevenson, *Treasure Island*; 1883.)

In *The Second Tree from the Corner* (1954), E. B. White told an amusing story about the fear that so many writers have of making a mistake: "One time a newspaper sent us to a morgue to get a story on a woman whose body was being held for identification. A man believed to be her husband was brought in. Somebody pulled the sheet back; the man took one agonizing look, and cried, 'My God, it's her!' When we reported this grim incident, the editor diligently changed it to 'My God, it's she!' "

Similar problems arise in the third person, as in *it is him*. The editors of *Newsweek* approve the phrase *it's him*—e.g.: "Rostenkowski simply signed an expense-account voucher for stamps that Smith converted into cash. The first time he says he witnessed the alleged scheme, in 1989, 'I was no doubt taken aback when I saw his [Rostenkowski's] name on the [$2,000] voucher. I couldn't believe it was him.' Most Democrats on Capitol Hill still can't believe it's him." (*Newsweek*; Aug. 2, 1993.) **—BG**

USAGE NOTE **its, it's**

The possessive form of *it* is *its*; the contraction for *it is* is *it's*. But the two words are often confounded—e.g.: "Potter County was ordered by the state to do something about overcrowding in it's [read *its*] system." (*Canyon News* [TX]; Jan. 13, 1994.)

Confusion is just as much a problem in British English as it is in American English—e.g.: "But fear not because fashion does award it's [read *its*] very own New Year's Honour's list of modern classics." (*Independent* [UK]; Jan. 16, 2000.)

Also, the possessive *its* should never be used—as it sometimes is—as a personal pronoun in place of *his, her,* or *his or her*. **—BG**

itch noun **1** *I have an itch on my back* tingling, irritation, prickle, prickling, tickle, tickling, itchiness.

2 *informal* *the itch to travel* LONGING, yearning, craving, ache, hunger, thirst, keenness, urge, hankering; wish, fancy, desire; *informal* yen.

▸ verb **1** *my scar really itches* tingle, prickle, tickle, be irritated, be itchy.

2 *informal* *he itched to help her* LONG, yearn, ache, burn, crave, hunger, thirst, be eager, be desperate; want, wish, desire, pine, fancy; *informal* have a yen, be dying.

item noun **1** *an item of farm equipment* | *the main item in a moose's diet* THING, article, object, artifact, piece, product; element, constituent, component, ingredient.

2 *a news item* REPORT, story, account, article, piece, write-up, bulletin, feature.

3 *I hear they are an item* COUPLE, twosome, partners, lovers; *informal* thing.

itemize verb *they itemized thirty-two design flaws in the reactor type* LIST, catalog, inventory, record, document, register, detail, specify, identify; enumerate, number.

itinerant adjective *itinerant traders* TRAVELING, peripatetic, wandering, roving, roaming, touring, saddlebag, nomadic, gypsy, migrant, vagrant, vagabond, of no fixed address.

▸ noun *an encampment of itinerants* TRAVELER, wanderer, roamer, rover, nomad, gypsy, migrant, transient, drifter, vagabond, hobo, vagrant, tramp.

itinerary noun *the old stone chapel should be on every visitor's itinerary* TRAVEL PLAN, schedule, timetable, agenda, program, tour; (planned) route.

J

jab verb *he jabbed the officer with his finger* POKE, prod, dig, nudge, butt, ram; thrust, stab, push.

▸ noun **1** *a jab in the ribs* POKE, prod, dig, nudge, butt; thrust, stab, push.

2 *felled by a left jab* PUNCH, blow, hit, whack, smack, cuff.

3 *exchanging verbal jabs* INSULT, cutting remark, barb; *informal* dig, put-down.

jabber verb *they jabbered nonstop* PRATTLE, babble, chatter, twitter, prate, yap, gabble, rattle on, blather; *informal* yak, yammer, yabber, yatter, blab, blabber.

▸ noun *stop your jabber!* PRATTLE, babble, chatter, chattering, twitter, twittering, gabble, blather; *informal* yabbering, yatter, blabber.

jack noun *a phone jack* SOCKET, outlet, plug, connection. PHRASE: **jack something up** **1** *they jacked up the car* RAISE, hoist, lift (up), winch up, lever up, hitch up, elevate. **2** *informal they may need to jack up interest rates* INCREASE, raise, up, mark up; *informal* hike (up), bump up, boost.

jacket noun See table at COAT.

jackpot noun *this week's lottery jackpot* TOP PRIZE, first prize; pool, kitty, pot, gold mine, bonanza. PHRASE: **hit the jackpot** *informal Ingalls may have hit the jackpot with this latest novel* STRIKE IT RICH, strike gold, succeed; *informal* clean up, hit the big time, score.

jaded adjective *a taste exotic enough for the most jaded palate | the uninspired writing of a jaded journalist* SURFEITED, sated, satiated, glutted; dulled, blunted, deadened, inured; TIRED, weary, wearied; unmoved, blasé, apathetic. ANTONYM fresh.

jag noun **1** *Joe caught his pants on a jag in the rock* SHARP PROJECTION, point, protrusion, barb, thorn, spur, snag, tooth.

2 *a crying jag* BINGE, spree, bout, indulgence, overindulgence.

jagged adjective *don't give your dog a jagged bone* SPIKY, barbed, ragged, rough, uneven, irregular, broken; jaggy, snaggy; serrated, sawtooth, sawtoothed, indented. ANTONYM smooth.

jail noun *he was thrown into the local jail* PRISON, penitentiary, penal institution, lockup, detention center, jailhouse, stockade, correctional facility, reformatory, reform school; *informal* clink, slammer, big house, jug, brig, can, pen, hoosegow, cooler, cage, slam, pokey.

▸ verb *she was jailed for killing her husband* IMPRISON, put in prison, send to prison, incarcerate, lock up, put away, intern, detain, hold (prisoner/captive), put into detention, put behind bars, put inside. ANTONYMS acquit, release.

jailer noun WARDEN, prison officer, guard; captor; *informal* screw.

jalopy noun *informal she just loves to drive that old jalopy around town* DILAPIDATED CAR; *informal* clunker, lemon, bucket of bolts, wreck, Tin Lizzie, rustbucket, heap, junker, beater.

jam[1] verb **1** *he jammed a finger in each ear* STUFF, shove, force, ram, thrust, press, push, stick, squeeze, cram.

2 *hundreds of people jammed into the hall* CROWD, pack, pile, press, squeeze, squish, cram, wedge; throng, mob, occupy, fill, overcrowd, obstruct, block, congest.

3 *the rudder had jammed* STICK, become stuck, catch, seize (up), become trapped.

4 *dust can jam the mechanism* IMMOBILIZE, paralyze, disable, cripple, put out of action, bring to a standstill; clog.

5 *we were just jamming and his amp blew* IMPROVISE, play (music), extemporize, ad lib.

▸ noun **1** *a traffic jam* CONGESTION, holdup, bottleneck, gridlock, backup, tie-up, snarl-up.

2 *informal we are in a real jam* PREDICAMENT, plight, tricky situation, difficulty, problem, quandary, dilemma, muddle, mess, imbroglio, mare's nest, dire straits; *informal* pickle, stew, fix, hole, scrape, bind, tangle, spot, tight spot, corner, tight corner, hot/deep water, can of worms.

jam[2] noun *raspberry jam* PRESERVE, conserve, jelly, marmalade, fruit spread, compote, (fruit) butter.

jamboree noun RALLY, gathering, convention, conference; festival, fête, fiesta, gala, carnival, celebration; *informal* bash, shindig, hoedown.

jangle verb *keys jangled at his waist* CLANK, clink, jingle, tinkle.

▸ noun *the jangle of his chains* CLANK, clanking, clink, clinking, jangling, jingle, jingling, tintinnabulation.

janitor noun *the janitor's supply closet* CUSTODIAN, caretaker, cleaner, maintenance man/worker, superintendent.

jar[1] noun *a jar of honey* (GLASS) CONTAINER, pot, crock, receptacle, cookie jar, mason jar, ginger jar.

jar[2] verb **1** *each step jarred my whole body* JOLT, jerk, shake, shock, concuss, rattle, vibrate.
2 *the play's symbolism jarred with the realism of its setting* CLASH, conflict, contrast, be incompatible, be at variance, be at odds, be inconsistent, be discordant.

jargon noun *the brochure is written in legal jargon* SPECIALIZED LANGUAGE, slang, cant, idiom, argot, patter; *informal* -speak, -ese, -babble, newspeak, journalese, bureaucratese, technobabble, psychobabble; double-talk, doublespeak; gibberish, gobbledygook, blather. See note at DIALECT.

jarring adjective *the striped wallpaper and plaid curtains make a jarring combination | the portrait of his dead children was a jarring reminder of his drunken driving* CLASHING, conflicting, contrasting, incompatible, incongruous; discordant, dissonant, inharmonious, harsh, grating, strident, shrill, cacophonous; irritating, disturbing. ANTONYM harmonious.

jaundiced adjective *a jaundiced view of the world* BITTER, resentful, cynical, soured, disenchanted, disillusioned, disappointed, pessimistic, skeptical, distrustful, suspicious, misanthropic; envious, jealous.

jaunt noun *a jaunt around Manhattan* TRIP, pleasure trip, outing, excursion, day trip, day out; tour, drive, ride, run; *informal* spin. See note at JOURNEY.

jaunty adjective *Kevin looked pretty jaunty for the awards show | a jaunty musical score* CHEERFUL, cheery, happy, merry, jolly, joyful; lively, perky, bright, buoyant, bubbly, bouncy, breezy, in good spirits, exuberant, ebullient; carefree, blithe, airy, lighthearted, nonchalant, insouciant, happy-go-lucky; *informal* bright-eyed and bushy-tailed, chirpy. ANTONYMS depressed, serious.

jaw noun **1** *a broken jaw* JAWBONE, lower/upper jaw, jowl; *Anatomy* mandible, maxilla.
2 **(jaws)** *the wolf held the rat in its jaws* MOUTH, maw, muzzle; teeth, fangs; *informal* chops.

jazz noun *their band plays mostly jazz.* See table. PHRASE: **jazz up** *informal let's jazz up this boring decor* ENLIVEN, liven up, brighten up, make more interesting/exciting, add (some) color to, ginger up, spice up; *informal* perk up, pep up.

TYPES OF JAZZ

acid	hard bop
Afro-Cuban	harmolodics
avant-garde	hot
barrelhouse	jive
bebop	Latin
big band	mainstream
boogie-woogie	manouche
bop	modal
cool	modern
Dixieland	New Orleans
electronic	nu
free	progressive
fusion	ragtime
gutbucket	stomp
gypsy	swing

jazzy adjective *that's one jazzy bedspread* FUNKY, hip, vibrant, lively, spirited, bold, exciting, flamboyant, showy, gaudy, flashy; bright, colorful, brightly colored, striking, eye-catching, vivid. ANTONYM dull.

jealous adjective **1** *he was jealous of his sister's popularity* ENVIOUS, covetous, desirous; resentful, grudging, begrudging, green (with envy). ANTONYMS proud, admiring.
2 *a jealous lover* SUSPICIOUS, distrustful, mistrustful, doubting, insecure, anxious; possessive, overprotective. ANTONYM trusting.
3 *they are very jealous of their rights* PROTECTIVE, vigilant, watchful, heedful, mindful, careful, solicitous. ANTONYM careless.

THE RIGHT WORD

Envious implies wanting something that belongs to another and to which one has no particular right or claim (*envious of her good fortune*). **Jealous** may refer to a strong feeling of envy (*it is hard not to be jealous of a man with a job like his*), or it may imply an intense effort to hold on to what one possesses (*jealous of what little time she has to herself*); it is often associated with distrust, suspicion, anger, and other negative emotions (*a jealous wife*). Someone who is **covetous** has fallen prey to an inordinate or wrongful desire, usually for a person or thing that rightfully belongs to another. In other words, a young man might be *jealous* of the other men who flirt with his girlfriend, while they might be *envious* of her obvious preference for him. But the young man had better not be *covetous* of his neighbor's wife.

jealousy noun **1** *he was consumed with jealousy* ENVY, covetousness; resentment, resentfulness, bitterness, spite; *informal* the green-eyed monster.
2 *the jealousy of his long-suffering wife* SUSPICION, suspiciousness, distrust, mistrust, insecurity, anxiety; possessiveness, overprotectiveness.

WORD NOTE **jealousy**

I remember being taught in school that *jealousy* was not the same as *envy. Jealousy,* or so I was given to understand, had a specifically romantic or sexual connotation, whereas *envy* had a broader meaning. It is possible to be envious of another's success, but one is jealous of a successful rival for the affections of one's boyfriend. Othello was jealous, but not envious. Now, it seems, the meanings have been conflated and blurred, and one routinely hears that someone is jealous of someone else's fame. This seems to me regrettable. I think that the two emotions—material envy and romantic jealousy—are not at all the same, and a clear linguistic distinction between them should be established and maintained. **—FP**

jeans plural noun See note below.

WORD NOTE **jeans**

Why do some words last while others fade into oblivion? There was a time when *dungarees* and *jeans* vied on an equal footing for the linguistic market in blue denim pants. *Jeans* won that competition handily, in a rout, rather in the way that a company achieves dominance in an industry.

The linguistic process is a little like capitalism, then, but purer, with no antitrust legislation or zealous attorneys general to limit the monopoly. **—DL**

jeer verb *the demonstrators* ***jeered at*** *the police* TAUNT, mock, scoff at, ridicule, sneer at, deride, insult, abuse, heckle, catcall at, boo, whistle at, jibe at, hiss at. ANTONYM cheer.

▸ noun *the jeers of the crowd* TAUNT, sneer, insult, shout, jibe, boo, hiss, catcall; derision, teasing, scoffing, abuse, scorn, heckling, catcalling; *informal* raspberry, Bronx cheer. ANTONYM applause.

jell, gel verb **1** *leave the mixture to jell* SET, stiffen, solidify, thicken, harden; cake, congeal, jellify, coagulate, clot.

2 *things started to jell very quickly* TAKE SHAPE, fall into place, come together, take form, work out; crystallize.

jelly noun *grape jelly* PRESERVE, marmalade, jam; aspic, gelatin.

jeopardize verb *accused of jeopardizing the health of their children* THREATEN, endanger, imperil, risk, put at risk, put in danger/jeopardy; hazard, stake; leave vulnerable; compromise, be a danger to, pose a threat to. ANTONYM safeguard.

jeopardy noun *the peace talks are* ***in jeopardy*** IN DANGER, in peril; at risk. ANTONYMS safety, security.

jerk noun **1** *she gave the reins a jerk* YANK, tug, pull, wrench, tweak, twitch.

2 *the elevator stopped with a jerk* JOLT, lurch, bump, start, jar, bang, bounce, shake, shock.

3 *informal I showed up for the party on the wrong night and felt like a complete jerk.* See FOOL noun sense 1.

4 *informal Tim is such a jerk for screaming at her in public.* See BASTARD noun sense 2.

▸ verb **1** *she jerked her arm free* YANK, tug, pull, wrench, wrest, drag, pluck, snatch, seize, rip, tear.

2 *the car jerked along* JOLT, lurch, bump, rattle, bounce, shake, jounce.

jerky adjective *it was a very jerky ride* CONVULSIVE, spasmodic, fitful, twitchy, shaky; JOLTING, lurching, bumpy, bouncy, jarring. ANTONYM smooth.

jerry-built adjective *we entered our jerry-built monstrosity in the raft race and won second prize* SHODDY, makeshift, badly built, gimcrack, flimsy, insubstantial, rickety, ramshackle, crude, chintzy; inferior, poor-quality, second-rate, third-rate, tinpot, low-grade. ANTONYM sturdy.

jest verb *I think he's jesting* fool around, play a practical joke, tease, kid, pull someone's leg, pull/jerk/yank someone's chain, have someone on; fun; joke, quip, gag, tell jokes, crack jokes; *informal* wisecrack.

▸ noun *jests were bandied about freely* JOKE, witticism, funny remark, gag, quip, sally, pun; crack, wisecrack, one-liner.

PHRASE: **in jest** *those sarcastic remarks were made in jest* IN FUN, as a joke, tongue in cheek, playfully, jokingly, facetiously, frivolously, for a laugh.

jester noun **1** *historical a court jester* FOOL, court fool, court jester, clown, harlequin, pantaloon; *archaic* buffoon, merry-andrew.

2 *the class jester* JOKER, clown, comedian, comic, humorist, wag, wit, prankster, jokester, trickster, buffoon; *informal* card, hoot, scream, laugh, wisecracker, barrel of laughs, smart-ass, smart aleck.

jet[1] noun **1** *a jet of water* STREAM, spurt, squirt, spray, spout; gush, rush, surge, burst.

2 *an executive jet* JET PLANE, jetliner; aircraft, plane, jumbo jet.

jet[2] adjective *her glossy jet hair* BLACK, jet-black, pitch-black, ink-black, ebony, raven, sable, sooty.

jettison verb **1** *six aircraft jettisoned their loads* DUMP, drop, ditch, discharge, throw out, unload, throw overboard.

2 *he jettisoned his unwanted papers | the scheme was jettisoned* DISCARD, dispose of, throw away/out, get rid of; reject, scrap, abandon, drop; *informal* chuck (out), dump, ditch, ax, trash, junk, deep-six. ANTONYMS keep, retain.

jetty noun *we'd walk out on the jetty at low tide to look for starfish* PIER, landing stage, landing, quay, wharf, dock; breakwater, mole, groin, dike, dockominium, levee.

Jew See note below.

WORD NOTE **Jew**

A student of mine—a Jewish man—took me to task once for writing that an essay he had submitted, and which in my view was trying too hard (and failing) to be amusing, had about it *an unfortunate Jackie Mason-ish tone.* This, he said, was an example of the insidious, all-pervading nature of anti-Semitism, which infects almost all who are not of Jewish faith or forebears. I replied that I was merely comparing his style with that of a comedian I have long found singularly unfunny—but the damage was done. I am tarred with a brush, at least in this young man's mind, from which it is impossible to ever be cleansed. Hence my particular need to tiptoe through the lexical and social minefield of whether, and when, it is currently acceptable to use the word *Jew,* instead of the adjectival form, *Jewish.* There is an answer: *Jewish* and *Jew* are essentially interchangeable—*he is a Jew, he is Jewish* —in a purely technical sense, describing one as being of Hebrew descent (from the Semitic tribe, descendants of Abraham, Isaac, and Jacob), a follower of the religion of Judaism. But there is one sense in which *Jew* and *Jewish* are not the same: in medieval times in England the monarchs forbade Christians from setting up as moneylenders, but gave Jews the monopoly to do so, making Jews their protégés. So to be a Jew was to be a lender of money, a usurer and, by association, one who strikes hard bargains. This specific use, though perhaps of historical interest, is today highly offensive. Indeed, it is so unpleasant to many that it suggests the word should never be used, since one risks, even if using it in an innocent way, conferring the opprobrious inference that was intended in crueler times. Rarely would I suggest ever abandoning a word, or at least being extremely circumspect about its use: but in this case, I do. And it goes without saying that when used attributively—*Jew boy*—or as a verb to denote miserly behavior—*to Jew down*—it is highly offensive too. **—SW**

jewel noun **1** *priceless jewels* GEM, gemstone, (precious) stone, brilliant; baguette; *informal* sparkler, rock; *archaic* bijou. See table at GEM.

2 *the jewel of his collection* FINEST EXAMPLE/SPECIMEN, showpiece, pride (and joy), cream, crème de la crème, jewel in the crown, masterpiece, nonpareil, glory, prize, boast, pick, ne plus ultra.

jewelry noun *a locked box for her jewelry* JEWELS, gems, gemstones, precious stones; costume jewelry, trinkets; *informal* bling; *archaic* bijoux. See table on page 504.

jibe[1] noun *cruel jibes.* See GIBE.

▸ verb *Simon jibed in a sarcastic way.* See GIBE.

JEWELRY

ankle bracelet	French-hook earrings
anklet	freshwater pearls
armlet	girandole
bangle	hoop earrings
beads	ID bracelet
bracelet	lavalier
brooch	lever-back earrings
cameo	locket
carcanet	mood ring
chain	necklace
chandelier earrings	nose ring
charm	pendant
charm bracelet	pin
choker	powerbeads
circlet	ring
clip	scarfpin
clip-on earrings	signet ring
collar	solitaire
coronet	stickpin
cuff	stud earrings
cufflinks	studs
cultured pearls	teardrop earrings
dangle earrings	tiara
eardrops	tie pin
earrings	toe ring
engagement ring	torc/torque
estate jewelry	torsade
eternity ring	wedding band/ring
fibula	wristlet
fob	wristwatch

jibe[2] verb *their story doesn't quite jibe with the evidence* AGREE, be in accord, be consistent, square, fit.

jiffy, jiff PHRASE: **in a jiffy/jiff** *informal I'll be there in a jiffy* (VERY) SOON, in a second, in a minute, in a moment, momentarily, in a trice, in a flash, shortly, any second, any minute (now), in no time (at all), directly; *informal* in a sec, in a snap, in two shakes (of a lamb's tail), in a wink, in a twinkle; *archaic* anon.

jig noun *Georgia did a cheerful little jig down the hall* DANCE, lively dance, skip, hop, prance.

jiggle verb *Ron nervously jiggled his foot* SHAKE, joggle, waggle, wiggle; fidget, wriggle, squirm, quiver, tremble.

jilt verb *do you think she's jilted him?* LEAVE, walk out on, throw over, finish with, break up with, spurn, chuck, ditch, dump, drop, run out on, give someone the old heave-ho; *literary* forsake.

jingle noun **1** *the jingle of money* CLINK, chink, tinkle, jangle, ding-a-ling, ring, ding, ping, chime, tintinnabulation.

2 *advertising jingles* SLOGAN, catchphrase; ditty, song, rhyme, tune.

▸ verb *the keys jingled* CLINK, chink, tinkle, jangle, ring, ding, ping, chime.

jingoism noun *a newspaper known for its jingoism* EXTREME PATRIOTISM, chauvinism, extreme nationalism, xenophobia, flag-waving; hawkishness, militarism, belligerence, bellicosity. See note at CHAUVINISM.

WORD NOTE **jingoism**

I don't know why this word has always seemed to me to be onomatopoeic. Somehow the sound of it evokes, for me, the attitude and political stance it describes—an aggressive, bullying, rowdy, and mindless nationalism: *The voters worried that the candidate's jingoism might involve the country in a senseless war.* In fact, the origin of *jingo* is thought to be a corruption of *Jesus,* and *by jingo* can be traced to a nineteenth-century English music-hall ditty about the foreign policy of the day. I much prefer it to its near relative, *chauvinism*—named for one of Napoleon's soldiers—with its more refined, deceptively polite, and less boisterous associations. **–FP**

jinx noun *after years of bad luck they finally broke the jinx* CURSE, spell, malediction; evil eye, black magic, voodoo, bad luck, hex.

▸ verb *the family is jinxed* CURSE, cast a spell on, put the evil eye on, hex.

jitters plural noun *informal stories like that give me* ***the jitters*** NERVOUSNESS, nerves, edginess, uneasiness, anxiety, anxiousness, tension, agitation, restlessness; stage fright; *informal* butterflies (in one's stomach), the willies, the creeps, collywobbles, the heebie-jeebies, jitteriness, the jim-jams.

jittery adjective *informal the company's accounting troubles left stock investors jittery* NERVOUS, on edge, edgy, tense, anxious, agitated, ill at ease, uneasy, keyed up, overwrought, jumpy, on tenterhooks, worried, apprehensive; *informal* with butterflies in one's stomach, twitchy, uptight, het up, in a tizzy, spooky, squirrelly, antsy. ANTONYM calm.

job noun **1** *my job involves a lot of traveling* OCCUPATION, profession, trade, position, career, work, line of work, livelihood, post, situation, appointment, métier, craft; vocation, calling; vacancy, opening; *humorous* McJob.

2 *this job will take three months* TASK, piece of work, assignment, project; chore, errand; undertaking, venture, operation, enterprise, business.

3 *it's your job to protect her* RESPONSIBILITY, duty, charge, task; role, function, mission; *informal* department.

4 *informal a bank job* ROBBERY, theft, holdup, burglary, break-in; *informal* stickup, heist.

jobless adjective *as of today, Young is among the jobless* UNEMPLOYED, out-of-work, out of a job, between jobs, laid off, unwaged, on the dole; *Brit.* redundant. ANTONYM employed.

jockey noun *legendary jockey Willie Shoemaker won his first horse race when he was 17* RIDER, horseman, horsewoman, equestrian.

▸ verb *on the eve of the primary, with McCain running even with Bush in New Hampshire polls, both men jockeyed for position* MANEUVER, ease, edge, work, steer; compete, contend, vie; struggle, fight, scramble, jostle.

jocular adjective *my jocular uncle* HUMOROUS, funny, witty, comic, comical, amusing, droll, waggish, jokey, hilarious, facetious, tongue-in-cheek, teasing, playful; lighthearted, jovial, cheerful, cheery, merry; *formal* jocose, ludic. ANTONYM solemn.

jocund adjective *formal* See CHEERFUL sense 1.

jodhpur noun See note below.

USAGE NOTE **jodhpur**

jodhpur /**jod**-per/ derives from the city of Jodhpur, India. The word (almost invariably used in the plural) refers to a type of flared-at-the-thigh pants used in English horse-riding. Through a kind of visual metathesis, the word is often mispronounced /jod-fər/. And believe it or not, this error pervades the horse-riding industry. The mispronunciation sometimes results in the obvious misspelling—e.g.: "Wealthy suburbanites clad in fancy jodphurs [read jodhpurs] and riding boots will replace overall-clad cowboys like Mizer." (*Palm Beach Post,* 14 July 2002.) By inevitable extension, the misspelling also goes back to the source of the word—e.g.: "His name is Ali Akbar Khan, above, whose family traces its musical roots to the sixteenth century, when an ancestor was court musician to the Emperor Akbar, as Ali Akbar Khan was to the Maharajah of Jodphur [read Jodhpur] in his 20's." (*N.Y. Times,* 7 Nov. 2002.) How did Jodhpur, a town in northwestern India, come to be famously associated with riding pants? It seems that Rao Raja Hanut Singh, who represented Jodhpur at Queen Victoria's 60th jubilee in 1897, had designed some comfortable riding trousers that ballooned at the thigh and narrowed at the knee so that they could be tucked into boots. While in London, he had the pants copied by a London tailor, who then began making and selling them. By 1899, the pants were well on their way to international popularity. **—BG**

---

jog verb **1** *he jogged along the road* RUN SLOWLY, trot, lope, dog-trot; *dated* jog-trot.

2 *something jogged her memory* STIMULATE, prompt, stir, activate, refresh; prod, jar, nudge.

▸ noun **1** *he set off at a jog* RUN, trot, lope, dog-trot; *dated* jog trot.

2 *a jog in the road* BEND, turn, curve, corner, zigzag, kink, dogleg.

joie de vivre noun *if there is one symbol that represents French society and its joie de vivre, it is the Paris café* JOYFULNESS, cheerfulness, cheeriness, lightheartedness, happiness, joy, gaiety, high spirits, élan, jollity, joviality, exuberance, ebullience, liveliness, vivacity, verve, effervescence, buoyancy, zest, zestfulness; *informal* pep, zing; *literary* blitheness. ANTONYMS sobriety, depression.

join verb **1** *we joined a bunch of sticks together* FASTEN, attach, tie, bind, couple, connect, unite, link, yoke, weld, fuse, glue.

2 *the two clubs have joined together* COMBINE, amalgamate, merge, join forces, unify, unite.

3 *we joined them in their venture* TEAM UP WITH, band together with, cooperate with, collaborate with.

4 *she joined the volleyball team* SIGN UP WITH, enlist in, enroll in, enter, become a member of, be part of.

5 *where the Ottawa River joins the St. Lawrence* MEET, reach, abut, touch, adjoin, border on, connect with.

THE RIGHT WORD

It is possible for an individual to **join** an investment club, to **consolidate** his or her financial resources, and to **combine** a background in economics with a strong interest in retirement planning. All of these words mean to bring together or to attach two or more things. *Join* is the general term for bringing into contact or conjunction two discrete things (*join two pieces of wood; join one's friends in celebration*), while **conjoin** emphasizes both the separateness of the things that are joined and the unity that results (*her innate brilliance, conjoined with a genuine eagerness to learn, made her the ideal candidate for the job*). In contrast, to *combine* is to mix or mingle things together, often to the point where they merge with one another (*combine the ingredients for a cake*). *Consolidate* also implies a merger of distinct and separate elements, but the emphasis here is on achieving greater compactness, strength, or efficiency (*consolidate their furnishings and buy a new house together*). **Connect** implies a loose or obvious attachment of things to each other, but with each thing's identity or physical separateness preserved (*the two families were connected by blood; she connected the computer to the printer*). In a physical context, it differs from *join* in that it implies an intervening element that permits movement; in other words, the bones are *connected* by ligaments, but bricks are *joined* by mortar. When things are joined or combined so closely that they form a single thing, they are said to **unite** (*the parties were united in their support of the new law*).

---

joint noun **1** *cracks in the joint* JUNCTURE, junction, join, intersection, confluence, nexus, link, linkage, connection; weld, seam; *Anatomy* commissure.

2 *the hip joint* ball-and-socket joint, hinge joint, articulation.

3 *informal a classy joint* ESTABLISHMENT, restaurant, bar, club, nightclub, place; hole, dump, dive. See also BAR sense 4.

4 *informal he rolled a joint* marijuana cigarette, cannabis cigarette; *informal* reefer, doobie, roach, jay, blunt, spliff.

▸ adjective *matters of joint interest | a joint effort* COMMON, shared, communal, collective; mutual, cooperative, collaborative, concerted, combined, united, bilateral, multilateral. ANTONYM separate.

jointly adverb *Hitachi and NEC will jointly develop business software* TOGETHER, in partnership, in cooperation, cooperatively, in conjunction, in collaboration, in concert, as one, in combination, mutually; in league, in alliance; in collusion.

joke noun **1** *they were telling jokes* FUNNY STORY, jest, witticism, quip; pun, play on words; *informal* gag, wisecrack, crack, one-liner, rib-tickler, knee-slapper, thigh-slapper, punch line, groaner.

2 *playing stupid jokes* TRICK, practical joke, prank, lark, stunt, hoax, jape; *informal* spoof.

3 *informal he soon became a joke to us* LAUGHINGSTOCK, object of ridicule, stooge, butt; *Brit. informal* Aunt Sally.

4 *informal the present system is a joke* FARCE, travesty, waste of time.

▸ verb **1** *she laughed and joked with the guests* TELL JOKES, crack jokes; jest, banter, quip; *informal* wisecrack, josh.

2 *they didn't realize you were only joking* FOOL, fool around, play a trick, play a practical joke, tease; *informal* kid, fun, pull (someone's leg), pull/jerk/yank someone's chain, make a monkey out of someone, put someone on.

joker noun HUMORIST, comedian, comedienne, comic, wit, clown, card, jokester, jester, wisecracker, wag; prankster, practical joker, hoaxer, trickster.

jolly adjective *he returned in a jolly mood* CHEERFUL, happy, cheery, good-humored, jovial, merry, sunny, joyful, joyous, lighthearted, in high spirits, bubbly, exuberant, ebullient, gleeful, mirthful, genial, affable, fun-loving; *informal* chipper, chirpy, perky, bright-eyed and bushy-tailed, hail-fellow-well-met; *formal* jocund, jocose; *dated* gay; *literary* blithe. ANTONYM miserable.

▸ noun (**jollies**) *people who get their jollies reading the tabloids* PLEASURE, thrill, enjoyment, excitement, titillation; *informal* kicks.

jolt verb **1** *the train jolted the passengers to one side* PUSH, thrust, jar, bump, knock, bang; shake, joggle, jog.

2 *the car jolted along* BUMP, bounce, jerk, rattle, lurch, shudder, jounce; *Brit.* judder.

3 *she was jolted out of her reverie* STARTLE, surprise, shock, stun, shake, take aback; astonish, astound, amaze, stagger, stop someone in their tracks; *informal* rock, floor.

▸ noun **1** *a series of sickening jolts* BUMP, bounce, shake, jerk, lurch.

2 *he woke up with a jolt* START, jerk, jump.

3 *the sight of the dagger gave him a jolt* FRIGHT, the fright of one's life, shock, scare, surprise; wake-up call.

jostle verb **1** *jostled by the crowd* BUMP INTO/AGAINST, knock into/against, bang into, collide with, plow into, jolt; PUSH, shove, elbow, mob, shoulder; *informal* barrel into, bulldoze.

2 *media empires jostle to catch the eye of Asian readers and viewers* STRUGGLE, vie, jockey, scramble, crowd one another.

jot verb *I've* ***jotted down*** *a few details* WRITE DOWN, note down, make a note of, take down, put on paper; scribble, scrawl.

▸ noun *not a jot of evidence* IOTA, scrap, shred, whit, grain, crumb, ounce, (little) bit, jot or tittle, speck, atom, particle, scintilla, trace, hint; *informal* smidgen, tad.

journal noun **1** *a medical journal* PERIODICAL, magazine, gazette, digest, review, newsletter, bulletin; newspaper, paper, tabloid, broadsheet; daily, weekly, monthly, quarterly.

2 *he keeps a journal* DIARY, daily record, daybook, log, logbook, chronicle.

journalism noun *a career in journalism* THE PRESS, the fourth estate, REPORTING, news writing, news broadcasting, news coverage, reportage, feature writing, photojournalism, sensationalism, the newspaper business; articles, reports, features, pieces, stories.

journalist noun *another journalist has been wounded in Bosnia* REPORTER, correspondent, columnist, writer, commentator, reviewer; investigative journalist, photojournalist, newspaperman, newspaperwoman, newsman, newswoman, newshound, newshawk, hack, stringer.

journey noun *their journey around the world* TRIP, expedition, excursion, tour, trek, voyage, junket, cruise, ride, drive, jaunt; crossing, passage, flight; travels, wandering, globe-trotting; odyssey, pilgrimage; peregrination.

▸ verb *they journeyed south* TRAVEL, go, voyage, sail, cruise, fly, hike, trek, ride, drive, make one's way; take/go on a trip, go on an expedition, tour, rove, roam.

THE RIGHT WORD

While all of these nouns refer to a course of travel to a particular place, usually for a specific purpose, there is a big difference between a **jaunt** to the nearest beach and an **expedition** to the rainforest. While a **trip** may be either long or short, for business or pleasure, and taken at either a rushed or a leisurely pace (*a ski trip; a trip to Europe*), a **journey** suggests that a considerable amount of time and distance will be covered and that the travel will take place over land (*a journey into the Australian outback*). A long trip by water or through air or space is a **voyage** (*a voyage to the Galapagos Islands; a voyage to Mars*), while a short, casual trip for pleasure or recreation is a *jaunt* (*a jaunt to the local shopping mall*). **Excursion** also applies to a brief pleasure trip, usually no more than a day in length, that returns to the place where it began (*an afternoon excursion to the zoo*). Unlike the rest of these nouns, *expedition* and **pilgrimage** apply to *journeys* that are undertaken for a specific purpose. An *expedition* is usually made by an organized group or company (*a scientific expedition; an expedition to locate new sources of oil*), while a *pilgrimage* is a journey to a place that has religious or emotional significance (*the Muslims' annual pilgrimage to Mecca; a pilgrimage to the place where her father died*).

---

joust verb *knights jousted with lances* TOURNEY; fight, spar, clash; *historical* tilt.

▸ noun *a medieval joust* TOURNAMENT, tourney; combat, contest, fight, battle, clash; *historical* tilt.

jovial adjective *his jovial manner* CHEERFUL, jolly, happy, cheery, good-humored, convivial, genial, good-natured, friendly, amiable, affable, sociable, outgoing; smiling, merry, sunny, joyful, joyous, high-spirited, exuberant; chipper, chirpy, perky, bright-eyed and bushy-tailed, hail-fellow-well-met; *formal* jocund, jocose; *dated* gay; *literary* blithe. ANTONYM miserable.

joy noun **1** *whoops of joy* DELIGHT, great pleasure, joyfulness, jubilation, triumph, exultation, rejoicing, happiness, gladness, glee, exhilaration, exuberance, elation, euphoria, bliss, ecstasy, rapture; enjoyment, felicity, joie de vivre, jouissance; *literary* jocundity. ANTONYM misery.

2 *it was a joy to be with her* PLEASURE, source of pleasure, delight, treat, thrill. ANTONYM trial.

joyful adjective **1** *his joyful mood* CHEERFUL, happy, jolly, merry, sunny, joyous, lighthearted, in good spirits, bubbly, exuberant, ebullient, cheery, smiling, mirthful, radiant; jubilant, overjoyed, thrilled, ecstatic, euphoric, blissful, on cloud nine, elated, delighted, gleeful; jovial, genial, good-humored; *informal* chipper, chirpy, peppy, over the moon, on top of the world, upbeat; *dated* gay; *formal* jocund; *literary* blithe. ANTONYMS sad, miserable.

2 *joyful news* PLEASING, happy, good, cheering, gladdening, welcome, heartwarming. ANTONYM distressing.

3 *a joyful occasion* HAPPY, cheerful, merry, jolly, festive, joyous. ANTONYMS sad, depressing.

joyless adjective **1** *a joyless man* GLOOMY, melancholy, morose, lugubrious, glum, somber, saturnine, sullen, dour, humorless. ANTONYM cheerful.

2 *a joyless room* DEPRESSING, cheerless, gloomy, dreary, bleak, dispiriting, drab, dismal, desolate, austere, somber; unwelcoming, uninviting, inhospitable; *literary* drear. ANTONYMS cheerful, welcoming.

joyous adjective . See JOYFUL senses 1, 3.

jubilant adjective *a jubilant crowd* OVERJOYED, exultant, triumphant, joyful, rejoicing, exuberant, elated, thrilled, gleeful, euphoric, ecstatic, enraptured, in raptures, walking on air, in seventh heaven, on cloud nine; *informal* over the moon, on top of the world, tickled pink, on a high. ANTONYM despondent.

jubilation noun *we couldn't conceal our jubilation* EXULTATION, joy, joyousness, elation, euphoria, rejoicing, ecstasy, rapture, glee, gleefulness, exuberance.

jubilee noun *Queen Elizabeth II's golden jubilee* ANNIVERSARY, commemoration; celebration, festival, jamboree; festivities, revelry.

judge noun **1** *the judge sentenced him to five years* JUSTICE, magistrate, sheriff, jurist.

2 *a panel of judges will select the winner* ADJUDICATOR, arbiter, arbitrator, assessor, evaluator, referee, ombudsman, ombudsperson, appraiser, examiner, moderator, mediator.

▸ verb **1** *we judged that it was too late to proceed* FORM THE OPINION, conclude, decide; consider, believe, think, deem, view; deduce, gather, infer, gauge, estimate, guess, surmise, conjecture; regard as, look on as, take to be, rate as, class as; *informal* reckon, figure.

2 *the case was judged by a tribunal* TRY, hear; adjudicate, decide, give a ruling on, give a verdict on.

3 *she was judged innocent of murder* ADJUDGE, pronounce, decree, rule, find.

4 *the competition will be judged by last year's winner* ADJUDICATE, arbitrate, mediate, moderate.

5 *entries were judged by a panel of experts* ASSESS, appraise, evaluate; examine, review.

judgment noun **1** *his temper could affect his judgment* DISCERNMENT, acumen, shrewdness, astuteness, sense, common sense, perception, perspicacity, percipience, acuity, discrimination, reckoning, wisdom, wit, judiciousness, prudence, canniness, sharpness, sharp-wittedness, powers of reasoning, reason, logic; savvy, horse sense, street smarts, gumption.

2 *a court judgment* VERDICT, decision, adjudication, ruling, pronouncement, decree, finding; sentence.

3 *critical judgment* ASSESSMENT, evaluation, appraisal; review, analysis, criticism, critique. PHRASE: **against one's better judgment** *I paid the asking price, against my better judgment* RELUCTANTLY, unwillingly, grudgingly.

judgmental adjective *he's compulsively judgmental* CRITICAL, censorious, condemnatory, disapproving, disparaging, deprecating, negative, overcritical, hypercritical.

judicial adjective *a judicial inquiry* LEGAL, juridical, judicatory; official.

EASILY CONFUSED WORDS **judicial, judicious, judiciary**

Judicial means 'relating to judgment and the administration of justice': *the judicial system*; *judicial robes*. Do not confuse it with **judicious**, which means 'prudent, reasonable': *his new album requires judicious use of the skip button*. **Judiciary**, usually a noun and sometimes an adjective, refers to the judicial branch of government, the court system, or judges collectively.

judicious adjective *following a judicious course of action* WISE, sensible, prudent, politic, shrewd, astute, canny, sagacious, commonsensical, sound, well-advised, discerning, percipient, intelligent, smart; *informal* heads-up. See note at JUDICIAL. ANTONYM ill-advised.

jug noun *a jug of cider* PITCHER, carafe, flask, flagon, bottle, decanter, ewer, crock, jar, urn; *historical* amphora.

juggle verb **1** *juggling three part-time jobs* HANDLE, manage, deal with, multitask.

2 *the auditors suspect that the books had been juggled* TAMPER WITH, manipulate, falsify, alter, rig; *informal* fudge, fix, doctor, cook.

juice noun **1** *the juice from two lemons* LIQUID, fluid, sap; extract; nectar.

2 *informal he ran out of juice on the last lap* ENERGY, power, stamina, steam.

juicy adjective **1** *a juicy peach* SUCCULENT, tender, moist; ripe; *archaic* mellow. ANTONYM dry.

2 *informal juicy gossip* SENSATIONAL, very interesting, fascinating, lurid; scandalous, racy, risqué, spicy; *informal* hot. ANTONYM dull.

3 *informal juicy profits* | *a juicy role* SUBSTANTIAL, large, sizable, generous; profitable, lucrative, remunerative; DESIRABLE, appealing, attractive; *informal* tidy, whopping, to die for. ANTONYMS insignificant, undesirable.

jumble noun *a jumble of books and toys* UNTIDY HEAP, clutter, muddle, mess, confusion, disarray, tangle, imbroglio; HODGEPODGE, mishmash, miscellany, motley collection, mixed bag, medley, jambalaya, farrago, gallimaufry.

▸ verb *the photographs are all* ***jumbled up*** MIX UP, muddle up, disarrange, disorganize, disorder, put in disarray.

THE RIGHT WORD

Confusion is a very broad term, applying to any indiscriminate mixing or mingling that makes it difficult to distinguish individual elements or parts (*a confusion of languages*). The typical teenager's bedroom is usually a **jumble** of books, papers, clothing, CDs, and soda cans—the word suggests physical disorder and a mixture of dissimilar things. If the disorder exists on a figurative level, it is usually called a **hodgepodge** (*a hodgepodge of ideas, opinions, and quotations, with a few facts thrown in for good measure*). **Conglomeration** refers to a collection of dissimilar things, but with a suggestion that the collection is random or inappropriate (*a conglomeration of decorating styles*). A **mélange** can be a mixture of foods (*add peppers or zucchini to the mélange*), but it can also be used in a derogatory way (*an error-filled mélange of pseudoscience, religion, and fanciful ideas*). A **farrago** is an irrational or confused mixture of elements and is usually worse than a *conglomeration* (*a farrago of doubts, fears, hopes, and desires*), while a **muddle** is less serious and suggests confused thinking and lack of organization (*their bank records were in a complete muddle*). **Disarray** implies disarrangement and is most appropriately used when order or discipline has been lost (*his unexpected appearance threw the meeting into disarray*).

jumbo adjective *informal* See HUGE.

jump verb **1** *the cat jumped off his lap* | *Flora began to jump around* LEAP, spring, bound, hop; skip, caper, dance, prance, frolic, cavort.

2 *he jumped the fence* VAULT (OVER), leap over, clear, sail over, hop over, hurdle.

3 *pretax profits jumped* RISE, go up, shoot up, soar, surge, climb, increase; *informal* skyrocket.

4 *the noise made her jump* START, jerk, jolt, flinch, recoil; *informal* jump out of one's skin.

5 *Polly* ***jumped at*** *the chance* ACCEPT EAGERLY, leap at, welcome with open arms, seize on, snap up, grab, pounce on.

6 *the place was jumping* ROCK, hop, buzz, be lively, be wild.

7 *two guys jumped him in the alley* ASSAULT, assail, set upon, mug, attack, pounce on.

▸ noun **1** *a short jump across the ditch* LEAP, spring, vault, bound, hop.

2 *a jump in profits* RISE, leap, increase, upsurge, upswing, upturn; *informal* hike.

3 *I woke up with a jump* START, jerk, involuntary movement, spasm.

PHRASES: **jump the gun** *informal several radio stations*

have jumped the gun by announcing winners long before the polls have closed in certain districts ACT PREMATURELY, act too soon, be too/overly hasty, be precipitate, be rash; *informal* be ahead of oneself. **jump to it** *informal* *this year, students will really have to jump to it if they hope to get a hot meal before the kitchen closes* HURRY UP, get a move on, be quick; *informal* get cracking, shake a leg, look lively, look sharp, get the lead out; *dated* make haste.

jump-start verb *efforts to jump-start the stalled economy* REVITALIZE, stimulate, energize, boost, spark, ignite, fire up.

jumpy adjective **1** *informal he was tired and jumpy* NERVOUS, on edge, edgy, tense, anxious, ill at ease, uneasy, restless, fidgety, keyed up, overwrought, on tenterhooks; *informal* a bundle of nerves, jittery, uptight, het up, in a tizzy; strung out; squirrelly, antsy. ANTONYMS calm, relaxed.

2 *jumpy black-and-white footage* JERKY, jolting, lurching, bumpy, jarring; fitful, convulsive.

junction noun **1** *the junction between the roof and the wall* JOINT, intersection, join, bond, seam, connection, juncture; *Anatomy* commissure.

2 *the junction of the two rivers* CONFLUENCE, convergence, meeting point, juncture.

3 *turn right at the next junction* INTERSECTION, crossroads, crossing, interchange; turn, turnoff, exit; traffic circle, cloverleaf.

juncture noun **1** *at this juncture, I am unable to tell you* POINT, point in time, time, moment, moment in time; period, occasion, phase.

2 *the juncture of the pipes.* See JUNCTION sense 1.

3 *the juncture of the rivers.* See JUNCTION sense 2.

jungle noun **1** *the Amazon jungle* TROPICAL FOREST, (tropical) rain forest, wilderness.

2 *the jungle of bureaucracy* COMPLEXITY, confusion, complication, chaos, mess; labyrinth, maze, tangle, web.

junior adjective **1** *the junior members of the family* YOUNGER, youngest. ANTONYMS senior, older.

2 *a junior position in the firm* LOW-RANKING, lower-ranking, entry-level, subordinate, lesser, lower, minor, secondary. ANTONYMS senior, higher-ranking.

junk *informal* noun *an attic full of junk* RUBBISH, clutter, odds and ends, bric-a-brac, bits and pieces; garbage, trash, refuse, litter, scrap, waste, debris, detritus, dross; *informal* crap.

▸ verb *time to junk the old pickup* THROW AWAY/OUT, discard, get rid of, dispose of, scrap, toss out, jettison; *informal* chuck, dump, ditch, deep-six, trash.

junket noun *informal the company sponsored a New Year's Eve gambling junket* excursion, outing, spree, trip, jaunt; celebration, party, jamboree, feast, festivity; *informal* bash, shindig.

junkie noun **1** *a heroin junkie* ADDICT, abuser; *informal* druggie, stoner, -freak, -head.

2 *a sci-fi junkie* FAN, enthusiast, devotee, lover, fanatic, aficionado; freak, nut, buff, bum.

junta noun *Myanmar's military junta has freed five more opposition lawmakers* FACTION, cabal, clique, camarilla, party, set, ring, gang, league, confederacy.

jurisdiction noun **1** *an area under French jurisdiction* AUTHORITY, control, power, dominion, rule, administration, command, sway, leadership, sovereignty, hegemony.

2 *foreign jurisdictions* TERRITORY, region, province, district, area, domain, realm.

THE RIGHT WORD

The **authority** of our elected officials refers to their *power* (often conferred by rank or office) to give orders, require obedience, or make decisions. Their authority is normally limited by their **jurisdiction**, which is a legally predetermined division of a larger whole, within which someone has a right to rule or decide (*the matter was beyond his jurisdiction*). The president of the United States has more **power** than any other American official, which means that he has the ability to exert force or control over something. He does not, however, have the *authority* to make laws on his own. As commander in chief, he does have **command** over the nation's armed forces, implying that he has the kind of authority that can enforce obedience. Back in the days when Great Britain had **dominion**, or supreme authority, over the American colonies, it was the king of England who held **sway** over this country's economic and political life—an old-fashioned word that stresses the sweeping scope of one's power. But his **sovereignty**, which emphasizes absolute or autonomous rule over something considered as a whole, was eventually challenged. The rest, as they say, is history.

just adjective **1** *a just and democratic society* FAIR, fair-minded, equitable, evenhanded, impartial, unbiased, objective, neutral, disinterested, unprejudiced, open-minded, nonpartisan; honorable, upright, decent, honest, righteous, moral, virtuous, principled. ANTONYM unfair.

2 *a just reward* DESERVED, well deserved, well earned, earned, merited; rightful, due, fitting, appropriate, suitable; *formal* condign; *archaic* meet. ANTONYM undeserved.

3 *just criticism* VALID, sound, well-founded, justified, justifiable, warranted, legitimate. ANTONYMS unfair, wrongful.

▸ adverb **1** *I just saw him* A MOMENT AGO, a second ago, a short time ago, very recently, not long ago.

2 *she's just right for him* EXACTLY, precisely, absolutely, completely, totally, entirely, perfectly, utterly, wholly, thoroughly, in all respects; *informal* to a T, dead.

3 *we just made it* NARROWLY, only just, by a hair's breadth; barely, scarcely, hardly; *informal* by the skin of one's teeth, by a whisker.

4 *she's just a child* ONLY, merely, simply, but, nothing but, no more than.

5 *the color's just fantastic* REALLY, absolutely, completely, positively, entirely, totally, quite; indeed, truly.

PHRASE: **just about** *informal that's just about all I can eat at one meal* NEARLY, almost, practically, all but, virtually, as good as, more or less, to all intents and purposes; *informal* pretty much; *literary* well-nigh, nigh on.

justice noun **1** *I appealed to his sense of justice* FAIRNESS, justness, fair play, fair-mindedness, equity, evenhandedness, impartiality, objectivity, neutrality, disinterestedness, honesty, righteousness, morals, morality.

2 *they were determined to exact justice* PUNISHMENT, judgment, retribution, compensation, just deserts.

3 *an order made by the justices* JUDGE, magistrate, jurist.
PHRASE: **do justice to** *the movie didn't do justice to the book* consider fairly, be worthy of.

justifiable adjective *justifiable criticism* VALID, legitimate, warranted, well-founded, justified, just, reasonable; defensible, tenable, supportable, acceptable. ANTONYM indefensible.

justification noun *there's no justification for their rudeness* GROUNDS, reason, basis, rationale, premise, rationalization, vindication, explanation; defense, argument, apologia, apology, case.

justify verb **1** *directors must justify the expenditure* GIVE GROUNDS FOR, give reasons for, give a justification for, explain, give an explanation for, account for; defend, answer for, vindicate.

2 *the situation justified further investigation* WARRANT, be good reason for, be a justification for.

justly adverb **1** *he is justly proud of his achievement* JUSTIFIABLY, with (good) reason, legitimately, rightly, rightfully, deservedly. ANTONYM unjustifiably.

2 *they were treated justly* FAIRLY, with fairness, equitably, evenhandedly, impartially, without bias, objectively, without prejudice, fairly and squarely. ANTONYM unfairly.

jut verb *the face of the cliff is sheer, except for one shelf of rock that* ***juts out*** STICK OUT, project, protrude, bulge out, overhang.

juvenile adjective **1** *juvenile offenders* YOUNG, teenage, adolescent, boyish, girlish, junior, pubescent, prepubescent, youthful. See note at YOUTHFUL. ANTONYM adult.

2 *juvenile behavior* CHILDISH, immature, puerile, infantile, babyish; jejune, inexperienced, callow, green, unsophisticated, sophomoric, naive, foolish, silly. ANTONYM mature.

▸ noun *two juveniles fled the scene* YOUNG PERSON, youngster, child, teenager, adolescent, youth, boy/girl, minor, junior; *informal* kid, punk. ANTONYM adult.

juxtapose verb *the exhibit juxtaposes works by Van Gogh and Gauguin* PLACE SIDE BY SIDE, set side by side, collocate, mix; compare, contrast.

K

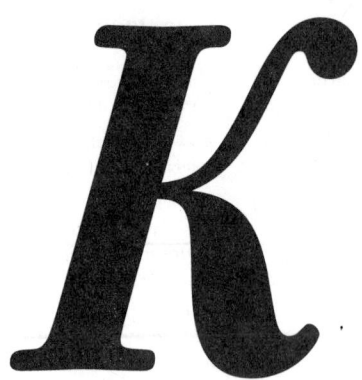

kaleidoscopic adjective **1** *kaleidoscopic swirls in the puddles* MULTICOLORED, many-colored, multicolor, many-hued, variegated, parti-colored, varicolored, psychedelic, rainbow, polychromatic. ANTONYM monochrome.

2 *the kaleidoscopic political landscape* EVER-CHANGING, changeable, shifting, fluid, protean, variable, inconstant, fluctuating, unpredictable, impermanent. ANTONYMS fixed, constant.

kaput *informal* adjective *the TV's kaput* BROKEN, malfunctioning, broken-down, inoperative; defunct, dead; *informal* conked out, on the fritz, done for. PHRASE: **go kaput** *it's anybody's guess which will go kaput first, the washer or the dryer* BREAK DOWN, go wrong, stop working, give out, go haywire; *informal* conk out, go belly up.

keel PHRASES: **on an even keel** *finally, the relationship seems to be on an even keel* steady, on track, on course, untroubled. **keel over 1** *the boat keeled over* CAPSIZE, turn turtle, turn upside down, founder; overturn, turn over, flip (over), tip over. **2** *the slightest activity made him keel over* COLLAPSE, faint, pass out, black out, lose consciousness, swoon.

keen adjective **1** *his publishers were keen to capitalize on his success* EAGER, anxious, intent, impatient, determined, ambitious, champing at the bit; *informal* raring, itching, dying. See note at EAGER. ANTONYM reluctant.

2 *a keen birdwatcher* ENTHUSIASTIC, avid, eager, ardent, passionate, fervent, impassioned; conscientious, committed, dedicated, zealous. ANTONYMS apathetic, halfhearted.

3 *they are **keen on** horses | a girl he was **keen on*** ENTHUSIASTIC ABOUT, interested in, passionate about; attracted to, fond of, taken with, smitten with, enamored of, infatuated with; *informal* struck on, hot on/for, mad about, crazy about, nuts about. ANTONYMS indifferent, unenthusiastic.

4 *a keen cutting edge* SHARP, sharpened, honed, razor-sharp. ANTONYM blunt.

5 *keen eyesight* ACUTE, sharp, discerning, sensitive, perceptive, clear. ANTONYM weak.

6 *a keen mind* ACUTE, penetrating, astute, incisive, sharp, perceptive, piercing, razor-sharp, perspicacious, shrewd, discerning, clever, intelligent, brilliant, bright, smart, wise, canny, percipient, insightful. ANTONYMS dull, stupid.

7 *a keen wind* COLD, icy, freezing, harsh, raw, bitter; penetrating, piercing, biting. ANTONYM gentle.

8 *a keen sense of duty* INTENSE, acute, fierce, passionate, burning, fervent, ardent, strong, powerful.

THE RIGHT WORD

A knife can be **sharp**, even **keen**, but it can't be **astute**. While *keen* and *sharp* mean having a fine point or edge, they also pertain to mental agility and perceptiveness. You might describe someone as having a *keen* mind, which suggests the ability to grapple with complex problems, or to observe details and see them as part of a larger pattern (*a keen appreciation of what victory would mean for the Democratic party*) or a *keen* wit, which suggests an incisive or stimulating sense of humor. Someone who is *sharp* has an alert and rational mind, but is not necessarily well grounded in a particular field and may in some cases be cunning or devious (*sharp enough to see how the situation might be turned to her advantage*). An **astute** mind, in contrast, is one that has a thorough and profound understanding of a given subject or field (*an astute understanding of the legal principles involved*). Like *sharp*, **shrewd** implies both practicality and cleverness, but with an undercurrent of self-interest (*a shrewd salesperson*). **Acute** is close in meaning to *keen*, but with more emphasis on sensitivity and the ability to make subtle distinctions (*an acute sense of smell*). While a keen mind might see only superficial details, a **penetrating** mind would focus on underlying causes (*a penetrating analysis of the plan's feasibility*). **Perspicacious** is the most formal of these terms, meaning both perceptive and discerning (*a perspicacious remark; perspicacious judgment*).

keep verb **1** *you should keep all the old forms* RETAIN, hold on to, keep hold of, retain possession of, keep possession of, not part with; save, store, conserve, put aside, set aside; *informal* hang on to, stash away. ANTONYMS throw away, lose.

2 *I tried to keep calm* REMAIN, continue to be, stay, carry on being, persist in being.

3 *he keeps talking about the Super Bowl* PERSIST IN, keep on, carry on, continue, do something constantly. ANTONYMS stop, give up.

4 *I won't keep you long* DETAIN, keep waiting, delay, hold up, retard, slow down.

5 *most people kept the rules | he had to keep his promise*

COMPLY WITH, obey, observe, conform to, abide by, adhere to, stick to, heed, follow; fulfill, carry out, act on, make good, honor, keep to, stand by. ANTONYMS disobey, break.

6 *keeping the old traditions* PRESERVE, keep alive/up, keep going, carry on, perpetuate, maintain, uphold, sustain. ANTONYMS discard, abandon.

7 *that's where we keep the linen* STORE, house, stow, put (away), place, deposit.

8 *she keeps rabbits* BREED, rear, raise, farm; own, have as a pet.

9 *God keep you | keep them from harm* LOOK AFTER, care for, take care of, mind, watch over; PRESERVE, protect, keep safe, shield, shelter, safeguard, defend, guard. ANTONYMS neglect, endanger.

10 *she kept their whereabouts from us* KEEP SECRET, keep hidden, hide, conceal, withhold.

11 *worry kept her from sleeping* PREVENT, stop, restrain, hold back. ANTONYMS enable, allow.

▸ noun *money to pay for his keep* MAINTENANCE, upkeep, sustenance, board, room and board, lodging, food, livelihood.

PHRASES: **keep at** *she's determined to keep at her studies until she passes the bar exam* PERSEVERE WITH/IN/AT, persist in/with, keep going with, carry on with, press on with, work away at, continue with; *informal* stick at, plug away at, hammer away at. **keep something back** 1 *she kept back some of the money* RESERVE, keep in reserve, put aside/by, set aside; retain, hold back, hold on to, not part with; *informal* stash away. 2 *she kept back the details* WITHHOLD, keep secret, keep hidden, conceal, suppress, keep quiet about. 3 *she could hardly keep back her tears* SUPPRESS, stifle, choke back, fight back, hold back/in, repress, keep in check, contain, smother, swallow, bite back. **keep from** *it's hard to keep from smoking* REFRAIN FROM, stop oneself, restrain oneself from, prevent oneself from, forbear from, avoid. **keep off** 1 *we ask that you please keep off the playing field* STAY OFF, not enter, keep away from, stay away from, not trespass on. 2 *Maud tried to keep off political subjects* AVOID, steer clear of, stay away from, evade, dodge, sidestep, bypass, skirt around; *informal* duck. 3 *you should keep off alcohol* ABSTAIN FROM, do without, refrain from, give up, forgo, not touch; *informal* swear off; *formal* forswear. **keep on** *they kept on working | despite our exhaustion, we agreed to keep on* CONTINUE, go on, carry on, persist in, persevere in; soldier on, struggle on, keep going. **keep something up** *keep up the good work* CONTINUE (WITH), keep on with, keep going with, carry on with, persist with, persevere with. **keep up with** *she walked fast to keep up with them* KEEP PACE WITH, keep abreast of; match, equal.

keeper noun *Gregor is the keeper of the tennis courts and adjacent grounds* GUARDIAN, custodian, curator, administrator, overseer, steward, caretaker.

keeping PHRASE: **in keeping with** *in keeping with the patriotic theme, we've asked the band to conclude with a Sousa medley* CONSISTENT WITH, in harmony with, in accord with, in agreement with, in line with, in character with, compatible with; appropriate to, befitting, suitable for.

keepsake noun *a box with concert programs, pressed corsages, and other keepsakes* MEMENTO, souvenir, reminder, remembrance, token; party favor, bomboniere.

keg noun *the beer is delivered in kegs* BARREL, cask, vat, butt, tun, hogshead; *historical* firkin.

ken noun *their conversation was beyond my ken* KNOWLEDGE, awareness, perception, vision, understanding, grasp, comprehension, realization, appreciation, consciousness.

kerchief noun *we wore red kerchiefs for the cowgirl number* BANDANA, headscarf, babushka.

kernel noun 1 *the kernel of a nut* seed, grain, core; nut.

2 *the kernel of the argument* ESSENCE, core, heart, essentials, quintessence, fundamentals, basics, nub, gist, substance; *informal* nitty-gritty.

3 *a kernel of truth* NUCLEUS, germ, grain, nugget.

key noun 1 *I put my key in the lock* door key, latchkey, pass key, master key.

2 *the key to the mystery | the key to success* ANSWER, clue, solution, explanation; basis, foundation, requisite, precondition, means, way, route, path, passport, secret, formula.

▸ adjective *a key figure* CRUCIAL, central, essential, indispensable, pivotal, critical, dominant, vital, principal, prime, primary, chief, major, leading, main, important, significant. ANTONYM peripheral.

keyboard noun. See table at INSTRUMENT.

keynote noun *the keynote of this year's conference is 'Adequate and Affordable Health Care'* THEME, salient point, gist, substance, burden, tenor, pith, marrow, essence, heart, core, basis, essential feature/element, crux.

keystone noun *the keystone of the government's policy* FOUNDATION, basis, linchpin, cornerstone, base, principle, guiding principle, core, heart, center, crux, fundament.

kibosh PHRASE: **put the kibosh on** *informal* *inclement weather can put the kibosh on a promising vintage* PUT A STOP TO, stop, halt, put an end to, quash, block, cancel, scotch, thwart, prevent, suppress; *informal* stymie; scuttle.

kick verb 1 *she kicked the ball over the fence* BOOT, punt, drop-kick; *informal* hoof.

2 *informal* *he was struggling to kick his drug habit* GIVE UP, break, abandon, end, stop, cease, desist from, renounce; *informal* shake, pack in, leave off, quit.

▸ noun 1 *that kick landed the ball across the street* BLOW WITH THE FOOT, punt; *informal* boot. See table at SWIMMING.

2 *informal* *I get a kick out of driving a race car* THRILL, excitement, stimulation, tingle; fun, enjoyment, amusement, pleasure, gratification; *informal* buzz, high, rush, charge.

3 *informal* *a drink with a powerful kick* POTENCY, stimulant effect, strength, power; tang, zest, bite, piquancy, edge, pungency; *informal* punch.

4 *informal* *a health kick* CRAZE, enthusiasm, obsession, mania, passion; fashion, vogue, trend; *informal* fad.

PHRASES: **kick someone/something around** *informal* 1 *I'm tired of getting kicked around* ABUSE, mistreat, maltreat, push around, trample on, take for granted; *informal* boss around, walk all over. 2 *they began to kick around some ideas* DISCUSS, talk over, debate, thrash out, consider, toy with, play with. **kick back** *informal* *I just wanna* *kick back and watch some TV* RELAX, unwind, take it easy, rest, slow down, let up, ease up/off, sit back, chill (out), hang loose. **kick off** *informal we'll kick off with a brief description of how a timeshare works | they kicked off the ceremony with a parade of cadets* START, commence, begin, get going, get off the ground, get underway; open, start off, set in motion, launch, initiate, introduce, inaugurate, usher in. **kick someone out** *informal most of us were given one-week suspensions from school, but Andy and Olivia were actually kicked out* EXPEL, eject, banish, exile, throw out, oust, evict, get rid of, ax; dismiss, discharge; *informal* chuck (out), send packing, boot out, give someone their marching orders, give someone their walking papers, give someone the gate, give someone the (old) heave-ho, sack, bounce, fire, give someone the bum's rush.

kickback noun **1** *the kickback from the gun* RECOIL, kick, rebound.

2 *informal they paid kickbacks to politicians* BRIBE, payment, inducement; *informal* payola, payoff, boodle.

kickoff noun *informal breakfast on the boat was a great kickoff to the weekend* BEGINNING, start, commencement, launch, outset, opening.

kick-start verb *if the project isn't kick-started soon, it's going to be dropped altogether* START UP, fire up, jump-start, turn on, get something moving, get something off the ground, energize.

kid[1] noun *informal they have three kids* CHILD, youngster, little one, baby, toddler, tot, infant, boy/girl, young person, minor, juvenile, adolescent, teenager, youth, stripling; offspring, son/daughter; *informal* kiddie, shaver, young 'un, rug rat, ankle-biter, munchkin, whippersnapper; *derogatory* brat; *literary* babe.

kid[2] verb *informal* **1** *I'm not kidding | stop kidding me* JOKE, tease, jest, chaff, be facetious, fool around, pull (someone's) leg, pull/jerk/yank someone's (chain), have (someone) on, rib.

2 *don't kid yourself* DELUDE, deceive, fool, trick, hoodwink, hoax, beguile, dupe, gull; *informal* con, pull the wool over (someone's) eyes.

kidnap verb *they attempted to kidnap the president's child* ABDUCT, carry off, capture, seize, snatch, take hostage.

kill verb **1** *gangs killed twenty-seven people* MURDER, take/end the life of, assassinate, eliminate, terminate, dispatch, finish off, put to death, execute; slaughter, butcher, massacre, wipe out, annihilate, exterminate, mow down, shoot down, cut down, cut to pieces; *informal* bump off, polish off, do away with, do in, knock off, take out, croak, stiff, blow away, liquidate, dispose of, ice, snuff, rub out, waste, whack, smoke; *euphemistic* neutralize; *literary* slay.

2 *this would kill all hopes of progress* DESTROY, put an end to, end, extinguish, dash, quash, ruin, wreck, shatter, smash, crush, scotch, thwart; *informal* put the kibosh on, stymie, scuttle.

3 *we had to kill several hours at the airport* WHILE AWAY, fill (up), occupy, pass, spend, waste.

4 *informal you must rest or you'll kill yourself* EXHAUST, wear out, tire out, overtax, overtire, fatigue, weary, sap, drain, enervate, knock out.

5 *informal my feet were killing me* HURT, cause pain to, torture, torment, cause discomfort to; be painful, be sore, be uncomfortable.

6 *a shot to kill the pain* ALLEVIATE, assuage, soothe, allay, dull, blunt, deaden, stifle, suppress, subdue.

7 *informal an opposition attempt to kill the bill* VETO, defeat, vote down, rule against, reject, throw out, overrule, overturn, put a stop to, quash, squash.

8 *informal Noel killed the engine* TURN OFF, switch off, stop, shut off/down, cut.

▸ noun **1** *the hunter's kill* PREY, quarry, victim, bag.

2 *the wolf was moving in for the kill* DEATH BLOW, killing, dispatch, finish, end, coup de grâce.

THE RIGHT WORD

When it comes to depriving someone or something of life, the options are seemingly endless. To **kill** is the most general term, meaning to cause the death of a person, animal, or plant, with no reference to the manner of killing, the agent, or the cause (*killed in a car accident*). Even inanimate things may be killed (*Congress killed the project when they vetoed the bill*). To **slay** is to kill deliberately and violently; it is used more often in written than in spoken English (*a novel about a presidential candidate who is slain by his opponent*). **Murder** implies a malicious and premeditated killing of one person by another (*a gruesome murder carried out by the son-in-law*), while **assassinate** implies that a politically important person has been murdered, often by someone hired to do the job (*assassinate the head of the guerilla forces*). Someone who is put to death by a legal or military process is said to be **executed** (*execute by lethal injection*), but if someone is killed primarily to get rid or him or her, the appropriate verb is **dispatch**, which also suggests speed or promptness (*after delivering the secret documents, the informer was dispatched*). While **slaughter** is usually associated with the killing of animals for food, it can also apply to a mass killing of humans (*the slaughter of innocent civilians provoked a worldwide outcry*). **Massacre** also refers to the brutal murder of large numbers of people, but it is used more specifically to indicate the wholesale destruction of a relatively defenseless group of people (*the massacre of Bethlehem's male children by King Herod*).

killer noun **1** *police are searching for the killer* MURDERER, assassin, slaughterer, butcher, serial killer, gunman; executioner, hit man, cutthroat; *literary* slayer; *dated* homicide.

2 *a major killer* CAUSE OF DEATH, fatal illness, deadly illness, threat to life, scourge.

killing noun *a brutal killing* MURDER, assassination, homicide, manslaughter, elimination, putting to death, execution; slaughter, massacre, butchery, carnage, bloodshed, extermination, annihilation; *literary* slaying.

▸ adjective **1** *a killing blow* DEADLY, lethal, fatal, mortal, death-dealing; murderous, homicidal; *literary* deathly.

2 *informal a killing schedule* EXHAUSTING, grueling, punishing, taxing, draining, wearing, prostrating, crushing, tiring, fatiguing, debilitating, enervating, arduous, tough, demanding, onerous, strenuous, rigorous; *informal* murderous.

PHRASE: **make a killing** *informal Tess made a killing in real estate* MAKE A LARGE PROFIT, make a/one's fortune, make money, rake it in, clean up, cash in, make a pretty penny, make big bucks.

killjoy noun *uh-oh, here comes that killjoy Walter* SPOILSPORT, wet blanket, damper, party pooper; prophet of doom.

kilter PHRASE: **out of kilter** *jet lag has left me completely* *out of kilter* AWRY, off balance, unbalanced, out of order, disordered, confused, muddled, disoriented, out of tune, out of whack, out of step; *humorous* discombobulated. See also OFF-KILTER.

kin noun *their own kin* RELATIVES, relations, family (members), kindred, kith and kin; flesh and blood, nearest and dearest; kinsfolk, kinsmen, kinswomen, people; *informal* folks.

kind adjective *she is such a kind and caring person* KINDLY, good-natured, kindhearted, warmhearted, caring, affectionate, loving, warm; considerate, helpful, thoughtful, obliging, unselfish, selfless, altruistic, good, attentive; compassionate, sympathetic, understanding, big-hearted, benevolent, benign, friendly, neighborly, hospitable, well-meaning, public-spirited. ANTONYMS inconsiderate, mean.

▸ noun **1** *all kinds of gifts* | *the kinds of bird that could be seen* SORT, type, variety, style, form, class, category, genre; genus, species, race, breed; flavor.

2 *they were different in kind* | *the first of its kind* CHARACTER, nature, essence, quality, disposition, makeup; type, style, stamp, manner, description, mold, cast, temperament, ilk, stripe.

PHRASE: **kind of** *informal it was kind of spicy* RATHER, quite, fairly; somewhat, a little, slightly, a shade; *informal* pretty, sort of; a bit, kinda, a touch, a tad.

kindle verb **1** *he kindled a fire* LIGHT, ignite, set alight, set light to, set fire to, put a match to. ANTONYMS extinguish, douse.

2 *the Beatles kindled my interest in music* ROUSE, arouse, wake, awake, awaken; stimulate, inspire, stir (up), excite, evoke, provoke, fire, inflame, trigger, activate, spark off; *literary* waken, enkindle.

kindliness noun *grateful for his kindliness* KINDNESS, benevolence, warmth, gentleness, tenderness, care, humanity, sympathy, compassion, understanding; generosity, charity, kindheartedness, warm-heartedness, solicitousness, thoughtfulness.

kindly adjective *a kindly old lady* BENEVOLENT, kind, kindhearted, warmhearted, generous, gentle, warm, good-natured, compassionate, caring, loving, benign, well meaning; helpful, thoughtful, considerate, good-hearted, nice, friendly, neighborly. ANTONYMS unkind, cruel.

▸ adverb **1** *she spoke kindly* BENEVOLENTLY, good-naturedly, warmly, affectionately, tenderly, lovingly, compassionately; considerately, thoughtfully, helpfully, obligingly, generously, selflessly, unselfishly, sympathetically. ANTONYMS unkindly, harshly.

2 *kindly explain what you mean* PLEASE, if you please, if you wouldn't mind; *archaic* prithee, pray.

kindness noun *he thanked her for her kindness* KINDLINESS, kindheartedness, warm-heartedness, affection, warmth, gentleness, concern, care; consideration, helpfulness, thoughtfulness, unselfishness, selflessness, altruism, compassion, sympathy, understanding, big-heartedness, benevolence, benignity, friendliness, hospitality, neighborliness; generosity, magnanimity, charitableness.

kindred noun *his mother's kindred* FAMILY, relatives, relations, kin, kith and kin, one's own flesh and blood; kinsfolk, kinsmen/kinswomen, people; *informal* folks.

▸ adjective **1** *industrial relations and kindred subjects* RE-

▸ ***kind***
compassionate
caring
feeling
charitable
altruistic
generous
gracious
lenient
humane
merciful
clement
philanthropic
public-spirited
sympathetic
understanding
good-natured
kind-hearted
big-hearted
amiable
soft-hearted
warm-hearted
good-hearted
warm
obliging
cooperative
accommodating
considerate
helpful
thoughtful
friendly
neighborly
courteous
nice
well-intentioned
well-meaning
inoffensive
cool
unfriendly
unsympathetic
uncharitable
uncaring
unfeeling
mean
catty
beastly
shitty
bitchy
spiteful
malicious
heartless
cold-blooded
bloodless
hard
harsh
callous
merciless
pitiless
savage
barbaric
inhumane
sadistic
cut-throat
bloodthirsty
vicious
murderous
sanguinary
cruel ◂

LATED, allied, connected, comparable, similar, like, parallel, associated, analogous. ANTONYM unrelated.

2 *a kindred spirit* LIKE-MINDED, in sympathy, in harmony, in tune, of one mind, akin, similar, like, compatible; *informal* on the same wavelength. ANTONYMS unsympathetic, alien.

king noun 1 *the king of France* RULER, sovereign, monarch, crowned head, Crown, emperor, prince, potentate, lord. See also the table at RULER.

2 *informal* *the king of country music* STAR, leading light, luminary, superstar, giant, master; *informal* supremo, megastar.

kingdom noun 1 *his kingdom stretched to the sea* REALM, domain, dominion, country, empire, principality, duchy, land, nation, state, sovereign state, province, territory.

2 *the third floor was Henderson's little kingdom* DOMAIN, province, realm, sphere, dominion, territory, arena, zone.

3 *the plant kingdom* DIVISION, category, classification, grouping, group.

kingly adjective 1 *kingly power* ROYAL, regal, monarchical, sovereign, imperial, princely.

2 *kingly robes* REGAL, majestic, stately, noble, lordly, dignified, distinguished, courtly; splendid, magnificent, grand, glorious, rich, gorgeous, resplendent, princely, superb, sumptuous; *informal* splendiferous.

kingpin noun *Washington's list of suspected drug kingpins* BOSS, head, number one, big cheese, bigwig, top dog. ANTONYM lackey.

kink noun 1 *your fishing line should have no kinks in it* CURL, twist, twirl, loop, crinkle; knot, tangle, entanglement.

2 *there are still some kinks to iron out* FLAW, defect, imperfection, problem, complication, hitch, snag, shortcoming, weakness; *informal* hiccup, glitch.

3 *a kink in my neck* CRICK, stiffness, pinch, knot.

kinky adjective 1 *informal* *kinky underwear* PROVOCATIVE, sexy, erotic, titillating, naughty, indecent, immodest.

2 *informal* *a kinky relationship* PERVERSE, abnormal, deviant, unconventional, unnatural, degenerate, depraved, perverted; *informal* pervy.

3 *Catriona's long kinky hair* CURLY, crimped, curled, curling, frizzy, frizzed, wavy.

kinship noun 1 *the value of kinship in society* family ties, blood ties, common ancestry, consanguinity.

2 *she felt kinship with the others* AFFINITY, sympathy, rapport, harmony, understanding, empathy, closeness, fellow feeling, bond, compatibility; similarity, likeness, correspondence, concordance.

kinsman, kinswoman noun *his namesake and distant kinsman* RELATIVE, relation, family member; cousin, aunt, uncle, nephew, niece.

kiosk noun *the kiosks along the boardwalk* BOOTH, stand, stall, concession, counter, newsstand; information booth.

kiss verb 1 *he kissed her on the lips* | *they kissed* give a kiss to, brush one's lips against, blow a kiss to; *informal* peck, smooch, canoodle, neck, buss, make out, lock lips; *formal/humorous* osculate.

2 *allow your foot just to kiss the floor* BRUSH (AGAINST), caress, touch (gently), stroke, skim over.

▸ noun 1 *a kiss on the cheek* | *a passionate kiss* peck, smack, smooch, buss, French kiss; X; *formal/humorous* osculation.

2 *the kiss of the flowers against her cheeks* GENTLE TOUCH, caress, brush, stroke.

kit noun 1 *the sculptor's kit* EQUIPMENT, tools, implements, instruments, gadgets, utensils, appliances, tools of the trade, gear, tackle, hardware, paraphernalia; *informal* things, stuff, (the) necessaries; *Military* accoutrements.

2 *a model airplane kit* SET (OF PARTS), do-it-yourself kit.

kitschy, kitsch adjective *the kitschy accessories are hilarious* TACKY, tawdry, showy, gimcrack, gaudy, cheap, tasteless, vulgar.

klutz noun *informal* *in senior year he transcended the moniker "Klass Klutz" and won the role of Petruchio* STUMBLEBUM, butterfingers; oaf, schlub, galoot, lug, lummox, boor, ape.

WORD NOTE **galoot**

Words that combine derision and affection are rare and ought to be taken advantage of. This word lets you make fun of a tall, gangly, clumsy guy for being tall, gangly, and clumsy, but conveys as well the linguistic equivalent of a chuck under the chin. *Galoot* is also less familiar (and funnier sounding) than the equivalent *lug,* and unlike *lug,* has only one meaning. **—DA**

knack noun 1 *a knack for making money* GIFT, talent, flair, genius, instinct, faculty, ability, capability, capacity, aptitude, aptness, bent, forte, facility; TECHNIQUE, method, trick, skill, adroitness, art, expertise; **(a knack for)** *informal* the hang of.

2 *his **knack of** getting injured at the wrong time* TENDENCY TO, propensity for, habit of, proneness to, aptness to, bent for, liability to, predisposition to, inclination to.

knapsack noun *with knapsacks on their backs* BACKPACK, rucksack, haversack, pack, kit bag.

knave noun *archaic* See JERK noun sense 3.

knead verb *kneading the dough* PUMMEL, work, pound, squeeze, shape, mold.

knee-jerk adjective *is it a well-thought-out plan or a knee-jerk reaction to FBI and CIA infighting?* IMPULSIVE, automatic, spontaneous, instinctive, mechanical, unthinking, hasty, rash, reckless, impetuous, precipitate.

kneel verb *they knelt to pray* FALL TO ONE'S KNEES, get down on one's knees, genuflect; *historical* kowtow.

knell noun *literary* 1 *the knell of the ship's bell* TOLL, tolling, dong, resounding, reverberation; death knell; *archaic* tocsin.

2 *this sounded the knell for the project* END, beginning of the end, death knell, death warrant.

knickknack noun *it's no fun dusting all her knickknacks* TRINKET, novelty, gewgaw, bibelot, ornament, trifle, bauble, gimcrack, curio, tchotchke; memento, souvenir, kickshaw; *archaic* gaud.

knife noun *a sharp knife* CUTTING TOOL, blade, cutter. See table.

▸ verb *the victims had been knifed* STAB, hack, gash, run

through, slash, lacerate, cut, pierce, jab, stick, spike, impale, transfix, bayonet, spear.

KNIVES AND DAGGERS

bolo	palette knife
bowie knife	parang
bread knife	paring knife
butcher knife	penknife
butter knife	pocket knife
carving knife	poniard
chef's knife	putty knife
clasp knife	scalpel
cleaver	sheath knife
dagger	shiv
dirk	skean
fish knife	skean-dhu
hunting knife	steak knife
jackknife	stiletto
kirpan	Swiss Army knife
kris	switchblade
kukri	table knife
lancet	ulu
machete	utility knife

knight noun *knights in armor* CAVALIER, cavalryman, horseman; lord, noble, nobleman; *historical* chevalier, paladin, banneret. PHRASE: **knight in shining armor** *she clung to the fantasy of her knight in shining armor* SIR GALAHAD, knight on a white charger/horse/steed, rescuer, savior, champion, hero, liberator, defender, protector, guardian, guardian angel.

knightly adjective *tales of knightly deeds* GALLANT, noble, valiant, heroic, courageous, brave, bold, valorous; chivalrous, courteous, honorable. ANTONYM ignoble.

knit verb **1** *Bertram learned to knit in medical school, to keep his fingers nimble.* See table.

2 *disparate regions began to knit as one* UNITE, unify, come together, draw together, become closer, bond, fuse, coalesce, merge, meld, blend.

3 *Marcus knitted his brows* FURROW, tighten, contract, gather, wrinkle.

▸ noun *silky knits in pretty shades* KNITTED GARMENT, knitwear, woolen; sweater, pullover, jersey, cardigan.

KNITTING AND CROCHETING TERMS

afghan stitch	garter stitch
Aran	gauge
argyle	intarsia
back loop	knit stitch
bind off	knitwise
block	moss stitch
bobble	pick up
bobbin	picot
casting on	purl stitch
casting off	purlwise
cable needle	ribbing
cable stitch	seed stitch
chain	selvage stitch
circular needle	shaker knit
crochet hook	single crochet
cross	slip stitch
double crochet	stockinette
double-knit	triple crochet
drop a stitch	twist
eyelet	wrap yarn
Fair Isle	yarn
fisherman's knit	yarn over
front loop	

knob noun **1** *the drake has a black bill with a knob at the base* LUMP, bump, protuberance, protrusion, bulge, swelling, knot, node, nodule, ball, boss.

2 *the knobs on the radio* DIAL, button.

3 *she turned the knob on the door* DOORKNOB, handle, door handle.

knock verb **1** *he knocked on the door* BANG, tap, rap, thump, pound, hammer; strike, hit, beat.

2 *she knocked her knee on the table* BUMP, bang, hit, strike, crack; injure, hurt, bruise; *informal* bash, thwack.

3 *he* ***knocked into*** *an elderly man* COLLIDE WITH, bump into, bang into, be in collision with, run into, crash into, smash into, plow into, bash into.

4 *informal I'm not knocking the company.* See CRITICIZE.

▸ noun **1** *a sharp knock at the door* TAP, rap, rat-tat-tat, knocking, bang, banging, pounding, hammering, drumming, thump, thud.

2 *the casing is tough enough to withstand knocks* BUMP, blow, bang, jolt, jar, shock; collision, crash, smash, impact.

3 *informal this isn't a knock on Dave.* See CRITICISM sense 1.

4 *life's hard knocks* SETBACK, reversal, defeat, failure, difficulty, misfortune, bad luck, mishap, blow, disaster, calamity, disappointment, sorrow, trouble, hardship; *informal* kick in the teeth.

PHRASES: **knock something back** *informal we can watch the game and knock back a few beers* SWALLOW, gulp down, drink (up), quaff, guzzle, slug, down, swig, drain, swill (down), toss off, scarf (down). **knock someone/something down** *he deliberately knocked down the display of toilet paper in aisle 3* FELL, floor, flatten, bring down, knock to the ground; knock over, run over/down; DEMOLISH, pull down, tear down, destroy; raze (to the ground), level, bulldoze. **knock it off!** *informal it's not funny anymore, so just knock it off!* STOP IT; *informal* cut it out, give it a rest, pack it in, that's enough, lay off. **knock someone out 1** *I hit him and knocked him out* KNOCK UNCONSCIOUS, knock senseless; floor, prostrate, put out cold, KO, kayo. **2** *in the second match, Canada was knocked out* ELIMINATE, beat, defeat, vanquish, overwhelm, trounce. **3** *informal walking that far knocked her out* EXHAUST, wear out, tire (out), overtire, fatigue, weary, drain; *informal* do in, take it out of. **4** *informal the view knocked me out* OVERWHELM, stun, stupefy, amaze, astound, astonish, stagger, take someone's breath away; impress, dazzle, enchant, awe, entrance; *informal* bowl over, flabbergast, blow away. **knock someone up** *informal, vulgar she's not the first girl he's knocked up* GET/MAKE PREGNANT, impregnate; *informal* put in the family way.

knockout noun **1** *the match was won by a knockout* KO, finishing blow, coup de grâce, stunning blow, kayo, TKO (technical knockout).

2 *informal she's a knockout!* BEAUTY, babe, bombshell, vision, dream, hottie, dish, looker, eye-catcher, peach, heartthrob, fox, arm candy.

3 *informal the performance was a knockout* MASTERPIECE, sensation, marvel, wonder, triumph, success, feat, coup, master stroke, tour de force; *informal* humdinger, doozy, stunner.

knoll noun *she walked up the grassy knoll* MOUND, hillock, rise, hummock, hill, drumlin, hump, bank, ridge, elevation.

knot noun **1** *make a small knot* TIE, twist, loop, bow, hitch, half hitch, clove hitch, join, fastening; square knot, reef knot, slip knot, overhand knot, granny knot; tangle, entanglement.

2 *a knot in the wood* NODULE, gnarl, node; lump, knob, swelling, gall, protuberance, bump, burl.

▸ verb *a long blue scarf was knotted around her waist* TIE (UP), fasten, secure, bind, do up.

knotted adjective *knotted hair* TANGLED, tangly, knotty, entangled, matted, snarled, unkempt, uncombed, tousled; *informal* mussed up.

knotty adjective **1** *a knotty legal problem* COMPLEX, complicated, involved, intricate, convoluted, involuted; difficult, hard, thorny, taxing, awkward, tricky, problematic, troublesome. ANTONYMS straightforward, simple.

2 *knotty roots* GNARLED, knotted, knurled, nodular, knobbly, lumpy, bumpy.

3 *a knotty piece of thread* KNOTTED, tangled, tangly, twisted, entangled, snarled, matted.

know verb **1** *who knows I'm here?* BE AWARE, realize, be conscious, be informed; notice, perceive, see, sense, recognize; *informal* be clued in, savvy.

2 *I think Mary knows his address* HAVE KNOWLEDGE OF, be informed of, be apprised of; *formal* be cognizant of.

3 *you should know the rules beforehand* BE FAMILIAR WITH, be conversant with, be acquainted with, have knowledge of, be versed in, have mastered, have a grasp of, understand, comprehend; have learned, have memorized, be up to speed on.

4 *I know only a few people here* BE ACQUAINTED WITH, have met, be familiar with; be friends with, be friendly with, be on good terms with, be close to, be intimate with.

5 *he had known better times* EXPERIENCE, go through, live through, undergo, taste.

6 *my brothers don't know a saucepan from a frying pan* DISTINGUISH, tell (apart), differentiate, discriminate; recognize, pick out, identify.

know-how noun *informal good old American know-how* KNOWLEDGE, expertise, skill, skillfulness, expertness, proficiency, understanding, mastery, technique; ability, capability, competence, capacity, adeptness, dexterity, deftness, aptitude, adroitness, ingenuity, faculty; *informal* savvy.

knowing adjective **1** *a knowing smile* SIGNIFICANT, meaningful, eloquent, expressive, suggestive; ARCH, sly, mischievous, impish, teasing, playful.

2 *she's a very knowing child* SOPHISTICATED, worldly, worldly-wise, urbane, experienced; knowledgeable, well-informed, enlightened; shrewd, astute, canny, sharp, wily, perceptive.

3 *a knowing infringement of the rules* DELIBERATE, intentional, conscious, calculated, willful, done on purpose, premeditated, planned, preconceived.

knowingly adverb *a civil court jury agreed that the auto maker did not knowingly design a faulty vehicle* DELIBERATELY, intentionally, consciously, wittingly, on purpose, by design, premeditatedly, willfully.

know-it-all noun *informal when did you become such a know-it-all?* SMARTY-PANTS, smart aleck, wise guy, wise apple, smarty, wiseacre, smart-ass, wiseass.

knowledge noun **1** *his knowledge of history | technical knowledge* UNDERSTANDING, comprehension, grasp, command, mastery; expertise, skill, proficiency, expertness, accomplishment, adeptness, capacity, capability; *informal* know-how. ANTONYM ignorance.

2 *people anxious to display their knowledge* LEARNING, erudition, education, scholarship, schooling, wisdom. ANTONYMS ignorance, illiteracy.

3 *he slipped away without my knowledge* AWARENESS, consciousness, realization, cognition, apprehension, perception, appreciation; *formal* cognizance. ANTONYM unawareness.

4 *an intimate* ***knowledge of*** *the countryside* FAMILIARITY WITH, acquaintance with, intimacy with.

5 *inform the police of your knowledge* INFORMATION, facts, intelligence, news, reports; *informal* info, (the) lowdown.

THE RIGHT WORD

How much do you know? **Knowledge** applies to any body of facts gathered by study, observation, or experience, and to the ideas inferred from these facts (*an in-depth knowledge of particle physics; firsthand knowledge about the company*). **Information** may be no more than a collection of data or facts (*information about vacation resorts*) gathered through observation, reading, or hearsay, with no guarantee of their validity (*false information that led to the arrest*). **Scholarship** emphasizes academic knowledge or accomplishment (*a special award for scholarship*), while **learning** is knowledge gained not only by study in schools and universities but by individual research and investigation (*a man of education and learning*), which puts it on a somewhat higher plane. **Erudition** is on a higher plane still, implying bookish knowledge that is beyond the average person's comprehension (*exhibit extraordinary erudition in a doctoral dissertation*). **Pedantry**, on the other hand, is a negative term for a slavish attention to obscure facts or details or an undue display of learning (*the pedantry of modern literary criticism*). You can have extensive *knowledge* of a subject and even exhibit *erudition*, however, without attaining **wisdom**, the superior judgment and understanding that is based on both knowledge and experience.

knowledgeable adjective **1** *Beryl was a knowledgeable woman* WELL-INFORMED, learned, well-read, educated, well-educated, erudite, scholarly, cultured, cultivated, enlightened. ANTONYM ignorant.

2 *he is* ***knowledgeable about*** *modern art* ACQUAINTED WITH, familiar with, (well) versed in, conversant with, au courant with, au fait with; having a knowledge of, up on, up to date with, up to speed on, abreast of, plugged in to, (well) grounded in. ANTONYM ill-informed.

known adjective **1** *a known criminal* RECOGNIZED, well-known, widely known, noted, celebrated, notable, notorious; acknowledged, self-confessed, declared, overt.

2 *the known world* FAMILIAR, known about, well-known; studied, investigated.

knuckle PHRASE: **knuckle under** *the hostages agreed that they would not knuckle under* SURRENDER, submit, capitulate, give in/up, yield, give way, succumb, back down, admit defeat, lay down one's arms, throw in the towel, climb down, quit, raise the white flag.

kosher *informal* adjective *buying pearls in the subway didn't seem quite kosher* PROPER, aboveboard, genuine, correct, legitimate, legit, fine, admissible, acceptable, orthodox.

kowtow verb **1** *they **kowtowed to** the emperor* PROSTRATE ONESELF BEFORE, bow (down) to/ before, genuflect to/before, do/make obeisance to/before, fall on one's knees before, kneel before.

2 *she didn't have to **kowtow to** a boss* GROVEL TO, be obsequious to, be servile to, be sycophantic to, fawn over/on, cringe to, bow and scrape to, toady to, truckle to, abase oneself before, humble oneself to; curry favor with, dance attendance on, ingratiate oneself with, suck up to, kiss up to, brown-nose, lick someone's boots.

kudos noun *kudos to you, Mrs. DeHaven, for a lifetime of quiet courage and unwavering generosity | much kudos comes with the job* PRAISE, glory, honor, status, standing, distinction, fame, celebrity; admiration, respect, esteem, acclaim, prestige, cachet, credit, full marks, props.

L

label noun **1** *the price is clearly stated on the label* TAG, ticket, sticker, marker, tab.

2 *a designer label* BRAND, brand name, trade name, trademark, make, logo.

3 *the label the media came up with for me* DESIGNATION, description, tag; name, epithet, nickname, title, sobriquet, pet name, cognomen; *formal* denomination, appellation.

▸ verb **1** *label each jar with the date* TAG, put labels on, ticket, mark.

2 *tests labeled him an underachiever* CATEGORIZE, classify, class, describe, designate, identify; mark, stamp, brand, condemn, pigeonhole, stereotype, typecast; call, name, term, dub, nickname.

labor noun **1** *manual labor* WORK, hard work, toil, exertion, industry, drudgery, effort, menial work; *informal* slog, grind, sweat, scut work; *literary* travail, moil. ANTONYMS rest, leisure.

2 *management and labor need to cooperate* WORKERS, employees, workmen, workforce, staff, working people, blue-collar workers, laborers, labor force, proletariat. ANTONYM management.

3 *the labors of Hercules* TASK, job, chore, mission, assignment.

4 *a difficult labor* CHILDBIRTH, birth, delivery, nativity; contractions, labor pains; *formal* parturition; *literary* travail; *dated* confinement; *archaic* lying-in, accouchement, childbed.

▸ verb **1** *a project on which he had labored for many years* WORK, work hard, toil, slave (away), grind away, struggle, strive, exert oneself, work one's fingers to the bone, work like a dog, work like a Trojan; *informal* slog away, plug away; *literary* travail, moil.

2 *she labored to unite the party* STRIVE, struggle, endeavor, work, try, work hard, try hard, make every effort, do one's best, do one's utmost, do all one can, give one's all, go all out, fight, put oneself out, apply oneself, exert oneself; *informal* bend/lean/fall over backwards, pull out all the stops, bust a gut, bust one's chops.

3 *there is no need to labor the point* OVEREMPHASIZE, belabor, overstress, overdo, strain, overplay, make too much of, exaggerate, dwell on, harp on.

4 *Rex was **laboring under** a misapprehension* SUFFER FROM, be a victim of, be deceived by, be misled by.

THE RIGHT WORD

Most people have to **work** for a living, meaning that they have to exert themselves mentally or physically in return for a paycheck. But *work* is not always performed by humans (*a machine that works like a charm*). **Labor** is not only human but usually physical work (*the labor required to build a stone wall*), although it can also apply to intellectual work of unusual difficulty (*the labor involved in writing a symphony*). Anyone who has been forced to perform **drudgery** knows that it is the most unpleasant, uninspiring, and monotonous kind of labor (*a forklift that eliminates the drudgery of stacking boxes; the drudgery of compiling a phone book*). A **grind** is even more intense and unrelenting than drudgery, emphasizing work that is performed under pressure in a dehumanizing way (*the daily grind of classroom teaching*). **Toil** suggests labor that is prolonged and very tiring (*farmers who toil endlessly in the fields*), but not necessarily physical (*mothers who toil to teach their children manners*). Those who **travail** endure pain, anguish, or suffering (*his hours of travail ended in heartbreak*).

labored adjective **1** *labored breathing* STRAINED, difficult, forced, laborious.

2 *Wang's labored alibi only hurt his defense* CONTRIVED, strained, stilted, forced, stiff, unnatural, artificial, overdone, ponderous, overelaborate, laborious, unconvincing, overwrought.

laborer noun *auto-industry laborers* WORKMAN, worker, working man/woman, manual worker, unskilled worker, day laborer, blue-collar worker, hired hand, hand, peon, roustabout, drudge, menial; *informal* grunt; *archaic* mechanic, cottier.

laborious adjective **1** *a laborious job* ARDUOUS, hard, heavy, difficult, strenuous, grueling, punishing, exacting, tough, onerous, burdensome, back-breaking, labor-intensive, trying, challenging; tiring, fatiguing, exhausting, wearying, wearing, taxing, demanding, wearisome, tedious, boring, time-consuming; *archaic* toilsome. See note at HARD. ANTONYM easy.

2 *Doug's laborious writing style* LABORED, strained, forced, contrived, affected, stiff, stilted, unnatural, artificial, overwrought, heavy, ponderous, convoluted. ANTONYMS natural, effortless.

labyrinth noun **1** *a labyrinth of little streets* MAZE, warren, network, complex, web, entanglement.

2 *the labyrinth of conflicting regulations* TANGLE, web, morass, jungle, confusion, entanglement, convolution; jumble, mishmash.

labyrinthine adjective **1** *labyrinthine corridors* MAZELIKE, winding, twisting, serpentine, meandering, wandering, rambling.

2 *a labyrinthine system* COMPLICATED, intricate, complex, involved, tortuous, convoluted, involuted, tangled, elaborate; confusing, puzzling, mystifying, bewildering, baffling.

lace noun **1** *a dress trimmed with white lace* openwork, lacework, tatting; passementerie, needlepoint (lace), filet, bobbin lace, pillow lace, torchon lace, needle lace, point lace, Battenberg lace, Chantilly lace, Mechlin lace, Valenciennes.

2 *brown shoes with laces* SHOELACE, bootlace, shoestring, lacing, tie.

▸ verb **1** *he **laced up** his running shoes* FASTEN, do up, tie up, secure, knot. ANTONYM untie.

2 *he laced his fingers into mine* ENTWINE, intertwine, twine, entangle, interweave, link; braid, plait.

3 *tea laced with rum* FLAVOR, mix (in), blend, fortify, strengthen, stiffen, season, spice (up), enrich, liven up; doctor, adulterate; *informal* spike.

4 *her brown hair was laced with gray* STREAK, stripe, striate, line.

PHRASE: **lace into** *informal* **1** *Danny laced into him.* See BEAT SOMEONE UP at BEAT. **2** *the newspaper laced into the prime minister.* See CRITICIZE.

lacerate verb *the nail has lacerated his left arm* CUT (OPEN), gash, slash, tear, rip, rend, shred; score, scratch, scrape, graze; wound, injure, hurt.

laceration noun *a bleeding laceration* GASH, cut, wound, injury, tear, slash; scratch, scrape, abrasion, graze.

lachrymose adjective See TEARFUL sense 1. ANTONYMS cheerful, comic.

lack noun *a lack of cash* ABSENCE, want, need, deficiency, dearth, insufficiency, shortage, shortfall, scarcity, paucity, unavailability, deficit. ANTONYM abundance.

▸ verb *they lack sufficient resources* BE WITHOUT, be in need of, need, be lacking, require, want, be short of, be deficient in, be bereft of, be low on, be pressed for, have insufficient; *informal* be strapped for. ANTONYMS have, possess.

THE RIGHT WORD

To suffer from a **lack** of food means to be partially or totally without it; to be in **want** of food also implies a lack, but with an emphasis on the essential or desirable nature of what is lacking; for example, you may experience a complete *lack* of pain following surgery, but you would be in *want* of medication if pain were suddenly to occur. **Absence**, on the other hand, refers to the complete nonexistence of something or someone. A *lack* of dairy products in your diet implies that you're not getting enough; an *absence* of dairy products implies that you're not getting any at all. If the scarcity or lack of something makes it costly, or if something is in distressingly low supply, the correct word is **dearth** (*a dearth of water in the desert; a dearth of nylon stockings during World War II*). A **shortage** of something is a partial insufficiency of an established, required, or accustomed amount (*a shortage of fresh oranges after the late-season frost*), while **privation** is the negative state or absence of a corresponding positive (*they suffered from hunger, cold, and other privations*).

lackadaisical adjective *I was lackadaisical about my training* LETHARGIC, apathetic, listless, sluggish, spiritless, passionless; careless, lazy, lax, unenthusiastic, half-hearted, lukewarm, indifferent, unconcerned, casual, offhand, blasé, insouciant, relaxed; *informal* laid-back, easygoing, couldn't-care-less. ANTONYM enthusiastic.

WORD NOTE **lackadaisical**

Lackadaisical is such a deliberate word that its use is nearly oxymoronic. No one ever uses *lackadaisical* carelessly or without thinking; it's always put in calculatedly and consciously. *Insouciant* is the same way—troubled to be untroubled. **—EM**

lackey noun **1** *lackeys helped them from their carriage* SERVANT, flunky, footman, manservant, valet, steward, butler, attendant, houseboy, domestic; *archaic* scullion.

2 *one of the manager's lackeys* TOADY, flunky, sycophant, flatterer, minion, hanger-on, lickspittle, brown-noser, spaniel, pawn, underling, stooge; *informal* yes-man, trained seal, bootlicker, doormat, drudge, peon.

lacking adjective **1** *proof was lacking* ABSENT, missing, nonexistent, unavailable. ANTONYMS present, plentiful.

2 *they found the department lacking on two counts* DEFICIENT, defective, inadequate, wanting, flawed, faulty, insufficient, unacceptable, impaired, imperfect, inferior. ANTONYM perfect.

3 *he seemed to be **lacking in** common sense* WITHOUT, devoid of, bereft of; DEFICIENT IN, low on, short on, in need of; *informal* minus. ANTONYM full of.

lackluster adjective *a lackluster performance* UNINSPIRED, uninspiring, unimaginative, dull, humdrum, colorless, characterless, bland, dead, insipid, vapid, flat, dry, lifeless, tame, prosaic, spiritless, lusterless; boring, monotonous, dreary, tedious; *informal* blah. ANTONYM inspired.

laconic adjective **1** *his laconic comment* BRIEF, concise, terse, succinct, short, pithy. See note at TERSE. ANTONYM verbose.

2 *their laconic press agent* TACITURN, uncommunicative, reticent, quiet, reserved, silent, unforthcoming, brief. ANTONYM loquacious.

lacquer noun *a shiny black lacquer* VARNISH, shellac, gloss, glaze, enamel, finish, polish.

lad noun *informal a lad of eight* BOY, schoolboy, youth, youngster, juvenile, stripling; *informal* kid, whippersnapper; *derogatory* brat. See also CHILD.

ladder noun **1** *she climbed down the ladder* steps, set of steps; rope ladder, stepladder, extension ladder.

2 *the academic ladder* HIERARCHY, scale, grading, ranking, pecking order.

laden adjective *a tray laden with plates* LOADED, burdened, weighed down, encumbered, overloaded, piled high, fully charged; full, filled, packed, stuffed, crammed; *informal* chock-full, chockablock.

la-di-da adjective *informal Bernice and her la-di-da friends* SNOBBISH, pretentious, affected, mannered, pompous, conceited, haughty; *informal* snooty, stuck-up, high and mighty, hoity-toity, uppity, snotty. ANTONYMS unpretentious, down-to-earth.

ladle verb *he was **ladling out** the contents of the pot* SPOON OUT, scoop out, dish up/out, serve.

▸ noun *a soup ladle* SPOON, scoop, dipper.

lady noun **1** *several ladies were present* WOMAN, female; *informal* dame; *derogatory* broad; *literary* maid, damsel; *archaic* wench.

2 *lords and ladies* NOBLEWOMAN, duchess, countess, peeress, viscountess, baroness; *archaic* gentlewoman.

ladylike adjective *as ladylike as Audrey Hepburn* GENTEEL, polite, refined, well-bred, cultivated, polished, decorous, proper, respectable, seemly, well-mannered, cultured, sophisticated, elegant, modest; feminine, womanly. ANTONYM coarse.

lag verb *I'm sorry to be **lagging behind*** FALL BEHIND, straggle, fall back, trail (behind), hang back, not keep pace, bring up the rear; dawdle, dilly-dally. See note at LOITER. ANTONYM keep up.

laggard noun *there'll be no laggards on my watch, Mr. Tyler* STRAGGLER, loiterer, lingerer, dawdler, sluggard, snail, idler, loafer; *informal* lazybones, slacker, slowpoke, foot-dragger.

lagoon noun *swimming in the moonlit lagoon* BAY, inland sea, lake, bight, pool.

laid-back adjective *informal you must try to be more laid-back* RELAXED, easygoing, free and easy, casual, nonchalant, unexcitable, imperturbable, unruffled, blasé, cool, equable, even-tempered, low-maintenance, insouciant, calm, unperturbed, unflustered, unflappable, unworried, unconcerned, unbothered; leisurely, unhurried, Type-B; stoical, phlegmatic, tolerant. ANTONYM uptight.

lair noun **1** *the lair of a large python* DEN, burrow, hole, tunnel, cave.

2 *a villain's lair* HIDEOUT, hiding place, hideaway, refuge, sanctuary, haven, shelter, retreat.

laissez-faire noun *an agenda that embraces the concept of laissez-faire* FREE ENTERPRISE, free trade, nonintervention, free-market capitalism, market forces.

▸ adjective *he has argued for a laissez-faire policy regarding the Internet | Elliott's laissez-faire approach to parenting* NONINTERVENTIONIST, noninterventional, noninterfering; uninvolved, indifferent; lax, loose, permissive, nonrestrictive, liberal, libertarian; *informal* hands-off.

lake noun *the frozen lake* POND, pool, tarn, reservoir, slough, lagoon, water, waterhole, watering hole, inland sea; oxbow (lake), pothole (lake), glacial lake; *Scottish* loch; *literary* mere.

lam PHRASE: **on the lam** *Butch and his gang are on the lam* ON THE LOOSE, at large, on the run, escaped, fugitive, in flight.

lambaste verb *the coach was lambasted in the media* CRITICIZE, chastise, censure, take to task, harangue, rail at, rant at, fulminate against; upbraid, scold, reprimand, rebuke, castigate, chide, reprove, admonish, berate; *informal* lay into, tear into, give someone a dressing-down, dress down, give someone what for, give someone a tongue-lashing, tell off, bawl out, chew out; *formal* excoriate.

lambent adjective *the lambent light from a distant campfire* FLICKERING, fluttering, incandescent, twinkling, dancing, radiant, brilliant.

lame adjective **1** *the mare was lame* LIMPING, hobbling; crippled, disabled, incapacitated; *dated* game. ANTONYM able-bodied.

2 *a lame excuse* FEEBLE, weak, thin, flimsy, poor, sorry; unconvincing, implausible, unlikely. ANTONYM convincing.

lamebrain noun See IDIOT.

lament noun **1** *the widow's laments* WAIL, wailing, lamentation, moan, moaning, weeping, crying, sob, sobbing, keening; jeremiad; complaint.

2 *a lament for the dead* DIRGE, requiem, elegy, threnody, monody; keen.

▸ verb **1** *the mourners lamented* MOURN, grieve, sorrow, wail, weep, cry, sob, keen, beat one's breast. See note at MOURN. ANTONYMS celebrate, rejoice.

2 *he lamented the modernization of the buildings* BEMOAN, bewail, complain about, deplore, rue; protest against, object to, oppose, fulminate against, inveigh against, denounce.

lamentable adjective *lamentable living conditions* DEPLORABLE, regrettable, sad, terrible, awful, wretched, woeful, dire, disastrous, grave, appalling, dreadful, pitiful, shameful, sorrowful, unfortunate. ANTONYM wonderful.

lamentation noun *the survivors' lamentation* WEEPING, wailing, crying, sobbing, moaning, lament, keening, grieving, mourning.

laminate verb *the machine laminates cards and documents in clear plastic* COVER, overlay, coat, surface, face; veneer, glaze, plasticize.

lamp noun *we had plenty of illumination from our lamps* LIGHT, lantern; floor lamp, table lamp, bedside lamp, banker's lamp, gooseneck lamp; chandelier; candelabra; *trademark* Tiffany lamp; floodlight, spotlight, strobe light, arc lamp; fluorescent lamp, track lights; lava lamp; sunlamp; flashlight; streetlight, streetlamp; Chinese lantern, Japanese lantern; storm lantern, hurricane lamp, oil lamp, kerosene lamp; *trademark* Coleman lamp.

lampoon verb *he was mercilessly lampooned* SATIRIZE, mock, ridicule, make fun of, caricature, burlesque, parody, tease; *informal* roast, send up.

▸ noun *a lampoon of student life* SATIRE, burlesque, parody, skit, caricature, impersonation, travesty, mockery; *informal* send-up, takeoff, spoof. See note at CARICATURE.

lance noun *a knight with a lance* SPEAR, pike, javelin; harpoon.

land noun **1** *publicly owned land* GROUNDS, fields, terrain, territory, open space; property, landholding, acres, acreage, lands, real estate, realty, estate; *historical* demesne.

2 *fertile land* SOIL, earth, loam, topsoil, humus; tillage.

3 *many people are leaving **the land*** THE COUNTRYSIDE, the country, rural areas, farmland, agricultural land.

4 *Tunisia is a land of variety* COUNTRY, nation, nation state, state, realm, kingdom, province; region, area, domain.

5 *the lookout sighted land to the east* TERRA FIRMA, dry land; coast, coastline, shore. ANTONYM sea.

▸ verb **1** *Canadian troops landed at Juno Beach* DISEMBARK, go ashore, debark, alight, get off. ANTONYM embark.

2 *our ship landed at New London* DOCK, moor, berth, put in, anchor, drop anchor. ANTONYM set sail.

3 *their plane landed in Chicago* TOUCH DOWN, make a landing, come in to land, come down. ANTONYM take off.

4 *a bird landed on the branch* PERCH, settle, come to rest, alight. ANTONYM fly off.

5 *informal Nick landed the job of editor* OBTAIN, get, acquire, secure, be appointed to, gain, net, win, achieve, attain, carry off; *informal* bag.

6 *informal Joanne's drug habit* ***landed*** *her* ***in*** *big trouble* BRING, lead to, drive to, cause to be in.

7 *informal he landed a left hook that staggered Curry* INFLICT, deal, deliver, administer, dispense, score, mete out.

landing noun **1** *a forced landing* ALIGHTING, landfall; arrival; touchdown, splashdown, reentry; docking. ANTONYMS takeoff, departure.

2 *the ferry landing* HARBOR, berth, dock, jetty, landing stage, pier, quay, slip, wharf, slipway.

landlord, landlady noun *the landlady had objected to the noise* PROPERTY OWNER, proprietor, proprietress, lessor, householder, landowner; slumlord. ANTONYM tenant.

landmark noun **1** *the cliff is a landmark for hikers* MARKER, mark, indicator, beacon, cairn.

2 *one of Arizona's most famous landmarks* MONUMENT, distinctive feature, prominent feature.

3 *the ruling was hailed as a landmark* TURNING POINT, milestone, watershed, critical point, benchmark.

▸ adjective *a landmark decision* PRECEDENT-SETTING, normative, consequential, historic.

landscape noun *the landscape of Tahiti* SCENERY, countryside, topography, country, terrain; outlook, view, vista, prospect, aspect, panorama, perspective, sweep.

landslide noun **1** *floods and landslides* rockslide, mudslide; avalanche.

2 *the Democrats enjoyed a landslide* DECISIVE VICTORY, overwhelming majority, triumph, sweep.

lane noun **1** *country lanes* road, street, byroad, byway, alley, alleyway, back alley, back lane, track.

2 *bicycle lanes* | *a three-lane highway* TRACK, way, course; road division; express lane.

language noun **1** *the structure of language* SPEECH, writing, communication, conversation, speaking, talking, talk, discourse; words, vocabulary.

2 *the English language* TONGUE, mother tongue, native tongue; dialect, patois, slang, idiom, jargon, argot, cant; *informal* lingo.

3 *the booklet is written in simple, everyday language* WORDING, phrasing, phraseology, style, vocabulary, terminology, expressions, turns of phrase, parlance, form/mode of expression, usages, locutions, choice of words, idiolect; *informal* lingo.

languid adjective **1** *a languid wave of the hand* RELAXED, unhurried, languorous, slow; listless, lethargic, sluggish, lazy, idle, indolent, apathetic; *informal* laid-back. ANTONYM energetic.

2 *languid days in the sun* LEISURELY, languorous, relaxed, restful, lazy. ANTONYM action-packed.

3 *she was pale and languid* SICKLY, weak, faint, feeble, frail, delicate; tired, weary, fatigued. ANTONYM vigorous.

languish verb **1** *the plants languished and died* WEAKEN, deteriorate, decline; wither, droop, wilt, fade, waste away; *informal* go downhill. ANTONYMS thrive, flourish.

2 *the general is now languishing in prison* WASTE AWAY, rot, be abandoned, be neglected, be forgotten, suffer, experience hardship.

languor noun **1** *the sultry languor that was stealing over her* LASSITUDE, lethargy, listlessness, torpor, fatigue, weariness, sleepiness, drowsiness; laziness, idleness, indolence, inertia, sluggishness, apathy. ANTONYM vigor.

2 *the languor of a hot day* STILLNESS, tranquility, calm, calmness; oppressiveness, heaviness.

lanky adjective *a lanky cowboy* TALL AND THIN, THIN, slender, slim, lean, lank, skinny, spindly, scrawny, spare, bony, gangling, gangly, gawky, rangy. ANTONYM short and stocky.

lantern noun See LAMP.

lap[1] noun *Liam sat on Santa's lap* KNEE, knees, thighs.

lap[2] noun *a race of eight laps* CIRCUIT, leg, circle, revolution, round; length.

▸ verb **1** *she lapped the other runners* OVERTAKE, outstrip, leave behind, pass, go past; catch up with; *informal* leapfrog.

2 *literary he was lapped in blankets* WRAP, swathe, envelop, enfold, swaddle.

lap[3] verb **1** *waves lapped against the sea wall* SPLASH, wash, swish, slosh, break, beat, strike, dash, roll; *literary* plash.

2 *the dog lapped water out of a puddle* DRINK, lick up, swallow, slurp, gulp. PHRASE: **lap something up** *he was lapping up the accolades* RELISH, revel in, savor, delight in, glory in, enjoy.

lapse noun **1** *a lapse of concentration* FAILURE, failing, slip, error, mistake, blunder, fault, omission, hiccup; *informal* slip-up.

2 *his lapse into petty crime* DECLINE, fall, falling, slipping, drop, deterioration, degeneration, backsliding, regression, retrogression, descent, sinking, slide.

3 *a lapse of time* INTERVAL, gap, pause, interlude, lull, hiatus, break.

▸ verb **1** *our membership has lapsed* EXPIRE, become void, become invalid, run out.

2 *she lapsed into self-pity* REVERT, relapse; drift, slide, slip, sink; deteriorate, decline, fall, degenerate, backslide, regress, retrogress.

lapsed adjective **1** *a lapsed Catholic* NONPRACTICING, backsliding, apostate; former. ANTONYM practicing.

2 *a lapsed membership* EXPIRED, void, invalid, out of date. ANTONYM valid.

larceny noun *his police record included two counts of larceny* THEFT, stealing, robbery, pilfering, thieving; burglary, housebreaking, breaking and entering; *informal* filching, swiping, pinching; *formal* peculation.

large adjective 1 *a large house | large numbers of people* BIG, great, huge, sizable, substantial, immense, enormous, colossal, massive, mammoth, vast, prodigious, tremendous, gigantic, giant, monumental, stupendous, gargantuan, elephantine, titanic, mountainous, monstrous; towering, tall, high; mighty, voluminous; king-size(d), economy-size(d), family-size(d), man-size(d), giant-size(d); *informal* jumbo, whopping, mega, humongous, monster, astronomical, ginormous. ANTONYM small.

2 *a large man* BIG, burly, heavy, tall, bulky, thickset, chunky, strapping, hulking, hefty, muscular, brawny, solid, powerful, sturdy, strong, rugged; full-figured, buxom; fat, plump, overweight, chubby, stout, meaty, fleshy, portly, rotund, flabby, paunchy, obese, corpulent; *informal* hunky, roly-poly, beefy, tubby, well-upholstered, pudgy, well-fed, big-boned, corn-fed. ANTONYMS small, thin.

3 *a large supply of wool* ABUNDANT, copious, plentiful, ample, liberal, generous, lavish, bountiful, bumper, boundless, good, considerable, superabundant; *literary* plenteous. ANTONYM meager.

4 *the measure has large economic implications* WIDE-REACHING, far-reaching, wide, sweeping, large-scale, broad, extensive, comprehensive, exhaustive. ANTONYM trivial.

PHRASES: **at large** 1 *fourteen criminals are still at large* AT LIBERTY, free, loose, on the loose, on the run, fugitive, on the lam. 2 *society at large* AS A WHOLE, generally, in general. **by and large** *the children, by and large, treated him well* ON THE WHOLE, generally, in general, all things considered, all in all, for the most part, in the main, as a rule, overall, almost always, mainly, mostly; on average, on balance.

largely adverb *the population in this district is largely of retirement age* MOSTLY, mainly, to a large/great extent, chiefly, predominantly, primarily, principally, for the most part, in the main; usually, typically, commonly.

large-scale adjective *a large-scale program* EXTENSIVE, wide-ranging, far-reaching, exhaustive, comprehensive; mass, nationwide, global.

largesse noun 1 *Bob took advantage of his friend's largesse* GENEROSITY, liberality, munificence, bounty, bountifulness, beneficence, altruism, charity, philanthropy, magnanimity, benevolence, charitableness, openhandedness, kindness, big-heartedness; *formal* benefaction. ANTONYM stinginess.

2 *distributing largesse to the locals* GIFTS, presents, handouts, grants, aid; patronage, sponsorship, backing, help; alms. See note at PRESENT[3].

lark *informal* noun *we were just having a bit of* ***a lark*** FUN, good fun, amusement, a laugh, a joke; an escapade, a prank, a trick, a jape, a practical joke.

lascivious adjective *his lascivious jokes are not funny* LECHEROUS, lewd, lustful, licentious, libidinous, salacious, lubricious, prurient, dirty, smutty, naughty, indecent, ribald; *informal* blue; *formal* concupiscent.

lash verb 1 *he lashed the beast repeatedly* WHIP, flog, flagellate, beat, thrash, horsewhip, scourge, birch, belt, strap, cane, switch; strike, hit; *informal* wallop, whack, tan (someone's hide), larrup, whale.

2 *rain lashed the windowpanes* BEAT AGAINST, dash against, pound, batter, strike, hit, knock.

3 *the tiger began to lash its tail* SWISH, flick, twitch, whip.

4 *two boats were lashed together* FASTEN, bind, tie (up), tether, hitch, knot, rope, make fast.

▸ noun 1 *he brought the lash down upon the prisoner's back* WHIP, horsewhip, scourge, thong, flail, strap, birch, cane, switch; *historical* cat-o'-nine-tails, cat, knout.

2 *twenty lashes* STROKE, blow, hit, strike, welt, thwack; *archaic* stripe.

PHRASE: **lash out at** *the president lashed out at the opposition* CRITICIZE, chastise, censure, attack, condemn, denounce, lambaste, rail at/against, harangue, pillory; berate, upbraid, rebuke, reproach; *informal* lay into, tear into, blast; *formal* castigate.

lassitude noun *prolonged periods of lassitude* LETHARGY, listlessness, weariness, languor, sluggishness, tiredness, fatigue, torpor, lifelessness, apathy. ANTONYM vigor.

lasso noun *the cowhand's lasso* LARIAT, rope.

last adjective 1 *the last woman in line* REARMOST, hindmost, endmost, at the end, at the back, furthest (back), final, ultimate. ANTONYMS first, leading.

2 *Rembrandt spent his last years in Amsterdam* CLOSING, concluding, final, ending, end, terminal; later, latter. ANTONYMS initial, early.

3 *I'd be the last person to say anything against him* LEAST LIKELY, most unlikely, most improbable; least suitable, most unsuitable, most inappropriate, least appropriate. ANTONYMS first, most likely.

4 *we met last year* THE PREVIOUS, the preceding; the prior, the former. ANTONYM next.

5 *this was his last chance* FINAL, only remaining.

▸ adverb *the entrant arriving last is eliminated* AT THE END, at/in the rear.

▸ noun *the most important business was left to the last* END, ending, finish, close, conclusion, finale, termination. ANTONYM beginning.

PHRASES: **at last** *at last, the rain stopped* FINALLY, at long last, after a long time, in the end, eventually, ultimately, in (the fullness of) time. **last word** 1 *that's my last word* FINAL DECISION, definitive statement, conclusive comment. 2 *she was determined to have the last word* CONCLUDING REMARK, final say, closing statement. 3 *the last word in luxury and efficiency* BEST, peak, acme, epitome, latest; pinnacle, apex, apogee, ultimate, height, zenith, nonpareil, crème de la crème; *archaic* nonsuch. **last hurrah** *Sunday's performance was Shelley's last hurrah* SWAN SONG, grand finale, finale, curtain call.

EASILY CONFUSED WORDS **last, latest**

In precise usage, **latest** means 'most recent' (*my latest project is wallpapering my dining room*), and **last** means 'final' (*the last day of the school year will be June 18*). But *last* is often used in place of *latest*, especially in informal contexts: *I read his last novel.*

last[2] verb 1 *the hearing lasted for six days* CONTINUE, go on, carry on, keep on, keep going, proceed; stay, remain, persist.

2 *how long will he last as manager?* SURVIVE, endure, hold on, hold out, keep going, persevere; *informal* stick it out, hang on.

3 *the car is built to last* ENDURE, wear well, stand up, bear up; *informal* go the distance.

last-ditch adjective *a last-ditch effort to save the old church* LAST-MINUTE, last-chance, eleventh-hour, last-resort, desperate, do-or-die, last-gasp, final.

lasting adjective *a lasting friendship* ENDURING, long-lasting, long-lived, abiding, continuing, long-term, surviving, persisting, permanent; durable, constant, stable, established, secure, long-standing; unchanging, irreversible, immutable, eternal, undying, everlasting, unending, never-ending, unfading, changeless, indestructible, unceasing, unwavering, unfaltering. ANTONYM ephemeral.

lastly adverb *lastly, I would like to thank my parents* FINALLY, in conclusion, to conclude, to sum up, to end, last, ultimately. ANTONYM firstly.

latch noun *he lifted the latch* FASTENING, catch, fastener, clasp, lock.

▸ verb *Jess latched the back door* FASTEN, secure, make fast, lock.

late adjective **1** *the train was late* BEHIND SCHEDULE, behind time, behindhand; tardy, running late, overdue, belated, delayed. ANTONYMS punctual, early.

2 *her late husband* DEAD, departed, lamented, passed on/away, deceased. ANTONYMS alive, existing.

▸ adverb **1** *she had arrived late* BEHIND SCHEDULE, behind time, behindhand, belatedly, tardily, at the last minute, at the buzzer. ANTONYM early.

2 *I was working late* AFTER HOURS, after office hours, overtime.

3 *don't stay out late* LATE AT NIGHT; *informal* till all hours.

PHRASE: **of late** *he's not felt well of late.* See LATELY.

lately adverb *we haven't seen much of you lately* RECENTLY, of late, latterly, in recent times, in the past few days, in the last couple of weeks.

lateness noun *Dinny is known for her lateness* UNPUNCTUALITY, tardiness, delay, dilatoriness.

latent adjective *his latent skills* DORMANT, untapped, unused, undiscovered, hidden, concealed, underlying, invisible, unseen, undeveloped, unrealized, unfulfilled, potential.

THE RIGHT WORD

All of these words refer to what is not currently observable or showing signs of activity. A **latent** talent is one that has not yet manifested itself, while **potential** suggests a talent that exists in an undeveloped state (*a potential concert violinist*). A child may have certain *latent* qualities of which his or her parents are unaware; but teachers are usually quick to spot a *potential* artist or poet in the classroom. **Dormant** and **quiescent** are less frequently associated with people and more often associated with things. A volcano might be described as *dormant*, which applies to anything that is currently inactive but has been active in the past and is capable of becoming active again in the future. *Dormant* carries the connotation of sleeping (*plants that are dormant in the winter*), while *quiescent* means motionless (*a quiescent sea*), emphasizing inactivity without referring to past or future activity. **Abeyant**, like *dormant*, means suspended or temporarily inactive, but it is most commonly used as a noun (*personal rights and privileges kept in abeyance until the danger had passed*).

later adjective *a later chapter* SUBSEQUENT, following, succeeding, future, upcoming, to come, ensuing, next; *formal* posterior; *archaic* after. ANTONYM earlier.

▸ adverb **1** *later, the film rights were sold* SUBSEQUENTLY, eventually, then, next, later on, after this/that, afterward, at a later date, in the future, in due course, by and by, in a while, in time. See note at SOONER.

2 *two days later a letter arrived* AFTERWARD, later on, after, after that, subsequently, following; *formal* thereafter. See word spectrum at NOW.

lateral adjective **1** *lateral movements* SIDEWAYS, sidewise, sideward, edgewise, edgeways, oblique, horizontal.

2 *lateral thinking* UNORTHODOX, inventive, creative, imaginative, original, innovative, nonlinear.

latest adjective **1** *the latest reports from Iraq* MOST RECENT, newest, just released, up-to-the-minute.

2 *the latest Paris designs* NEWEST, just out, fresh, freshest, up-to-date, state-of-the-art, au courant, dernier cri, current, modern, contemporary, fashionable, in fashion, in vogue; newfangled; *informal* in, with it, trendy, hip, hot, big, funky, happening, cool. See note at LAST. ANTONYMS old, unfashionable.

lather noun *rich, soapy lather* FOAM, froth, suds, soapsuds; bubbles; *literary* spume. PHRASE: **in a lather** *Hannah is in a lather over the chemistry exam* AGITATED, flustered, distressed, worked up, strung out, keyed up, in a state, in a tizzy, in a dither, in a twitter, upset.

latitude noun **1** *Toronto and Nice are on the same latitude* parallel. ANTONYM longitude.

2 *he gave them a lot of latitude* FREEDOM, scope, leeway, space, breathing space, flexibility, liberty, independence, free rein, license, room to maneuver, elbow room, wiggle room, freedom of action. See note at RANGE. ANTONYM restriction.

latter adjective **1** *the latter stages of development* LATER, closing, end, concluding, final; latest, most recent. ANTONYM initial.

2 *Russia chose the latter option* LAST-MENTIONED, second, last, later. ANTONYM former.

latter-day adjective *a latter-day puritan* MODERN, present-day, current, contemporary.

lattice noun *the ivy-covered lattice* GRID, latticework, fretwork, open framework, openwork, trellis, trelliswork, espalier, grille, network, mesh.

laud verb *a single lauded by the music press* PRAISE, extol, hail, applaud, acclaim, commend, sing the praises of, speak highly of, pay tribute to, lionize, eulogize, rhapsodize over/about; *informal* rave about; *archaic* magnify, panegyrize. See note at PRAISE. ANTONYM criticize.

laudable adjective *thanked for their laudable contributions of time and talent* PRAISEWORTHY, commendable, admirable, meritorious, worthy, deserving, creditable, estimable. ANTONYM shameful.

laudatory adjective *a laudatory front-page endorsement* COMPLIMENTARY, praising, congratulatory, extolling, adulatory, commendatory, approbatory, flattering, celebratory, eulogizing, panegyrical; *informal* glowing; *formal* encomiastic. ANTONYM disparaging.

laugh verb **1** *Norma started to laugh excitedly* CHUCKLE, chortle, guffaw, cackle, giggle, titter, twitter, snigger, snicker, yuk, tee-hee, burst out laughing, roar/hoot/howl with laughter, crack up, dissolve into laughter, split one's sides, be (rolling) on the floor, be doubled up, be killing oneself (laughing); *informal* be in stitches, be rolling in the aisles.

2 *people **laughed at** his theories* RIDICULE, mock, deride, scoff at, jeer at, sneer at, jibe at, make fun of, poke fun at, scorn; lampoon, satirize, parody; dismiss; *informal* send up, pooh-pooh.

▸ noun 1 *he gave a short laugh* CHUCKLE, chortle, guffaw, giggle, titter, twitter, tee-hee, snigger, snicker, yuk, roar/hoot/howl of laughter, belly laugh, horse laugh.

2 *informal he was a laugh* JOKER, jokester, wag, wit, clown, jester, prankster, character; *informal* card, hoot, scream, riot, gas, barrel of laughs.

3 *informal I entered the contest for a laugh* JOKE, prank, jest, escapade, caper, practical joke; *informal* hoot, lark.

PHRASE: **laugh something off** *you have to just laugh off their stupid remarks* DISMISS, make a joke of, make light of, shrug off, brush aside, scoff at; *informal* pooh-pooh.

laughable adjective 1 *the government's new education policy is laughable* RIDICULOUS, ludicrous, absurd, risible, preposterous; foolish, silly, idiotic, stupid, asinine, nonsensical, crazy, insane, outrageous, harebrained, cockamamie; *informal* cockeyed, daffy.

2 *if it weren't so tragic, it'd be laughable* AMUSING, funny, humorous, hilarious, uproarious, comical, comic, farcical.

laughingstock noun *their new airport has been called the laughingstock of world air travel* BUTT, dupe, spectacle, figure of fun, stooge, fall guy.

laughter noun *the sound of laughter* LAUGHING, chuckling, chortling, guffawing, giggling, tittering, twittering, cackling, sniggering; *informal* hysterics.

launch verb 1 *they've launched the shuttle | the rocket has launched* SEND INTO ORBIT, blast off, take off, lift off.

2 *he launched the boat* SET AFLOAT, put to sea, put into the water.

3 *a chair was launched at him* THROW, hurl, fling, pitch, lob, let fly; fire, shoot; *informal* chuck, heave, sling.

4 *the government launched a new campaign* SET IN MOTION, get going, get underway, start, commence, begin, embark on, initiate, inaugurate, set up, organize, introduce, bring into being; *informal* kick off, roll out.

5 *he **launched into** a tirade* START, commence, burst into.

launder verb *the linens are laundered each Thursday* WASH, wash and iron, clean; dry-clean.

laundry noun 1 *a big pile of laundry* WASHING, wash, dirty clothes.

2 *the facilities include a laundry* LAUNDRY ROOM, launderette; trademark Laundromat; cleaners, dry cleaners.

laurels plural noun *enjoying all the laurels befitting such an accomplished young woman* HONORS, tributes, praise, plaudits, accolades, kudos, acclaim, acclamation, credit, glory, honor, distinction, fame, renown, prestige, recognition.

lavatory noun See BATHROOM.

lavish adjective 1 *lavish parties* SUMPTUOUS, luxurious, costly, expensive, opulent, grand, splendid, rich, fancy, posh; *informal* fancy-schmancy. ANTONYM meager.

2 *lavish hospitality* GENEROUS, liberal, bountiful, open-handed, unstinting, unsparing, free, munificent, extravagant, prodigal. ANTONYM frugal.

3 *lavish amounts of champagne* ABUNDANT, copious, plentiful, liberal, prolific, generous; *literary* plenteous. See note at PROFUSE. ANTONYM scant.

▸ verb *she **lavished** money **on** her children* GIVE FREELY TO, spend generously on, bestow on, heap on, shower with.

law noun 1 *a new law was passed* REGULATION, statute, enactment, act, bill, decree, edict, bylaw, rule, ruling, ordinance, dictum, command, order, directive, pronouncement, proclamation, dictate, fiat.

2 *a career in law* THE LEGAL PROFESSION, the bar.

3 *informal on the run from the law.* See POLICE noun.

4 *the laws of the game* RULE, regulation, principle, convention, instruction, guideline.

5 *a moral law* PRINCIPLE, rule, precept, directive, injunction, commandment, belief, creed, credo, maxim, tenet, doctrine, canon.

law-abiding adjective *law-abiding citizens* HONEST, righteous, honorable, upright, upstanding, good, decent, virtuous, moral, dutiful, obedient, compliant. ANTONYM criminal.

lawbreaker noun *to her dying day, Bobbie never believed that her son was a lawbreaker* CRIMINAL, offender, wrongdoer, malefactor, evildoer, transgressor, miscreant; villain, rogue, ruffian, felon; *Law* malfeasant; *informal* crook, con, jailbird, hood; *archaic* miscreant.

lawful adjective *the lawful seizure of weapons* LEGITIMATE, legal, licit, just, permissible, permitted, allowable, allowed, rightful, sanctioned, authorized, warranted, within the law; *informal* legit. ANTONYMS illegal, criminal.

lawless adjective *a lawless country* UNGOVERNABLE, unruly, disruptive, anarchic, disorderly, rebellious, insubordinate, riotous, mutinous; uncivilized, wild. ANTONYM orderly.

lawlessness noun *he was the first sheriff to bring the town's lawlessness under control* ANARCHY, disorder, chaos, unruliness, criminality, crime.

lawn noun *mowing the lawn* GRASS, yard, front yard, backyard, dooryard.

lawsuit noun *the actor is now involved in a lawsuit against his former business manager* LEGAL ACTION, suit, case, action, legal proceedings, judicial proceedings, proceedings, litigation, trial, legal dispute, legal contest.

lawyer noun *O'Donnell's lawyers are confident that the case will be dismissed* ATTORNEY, counsel, counselor, legal practitioner, legal professional, legal adviser, member of the bar, litigator, advocate; *chiefly Brit.* barrister, solicitor; *informal* ambulance chaser, mouthpiece, legal eagle, legal beagle.

lax adjective *lax discipline in schools* SLACK, slipshod, negligent, remiss, careless, heedless, unmindful, slapdash, offhand, casual; easygoing, lenient, permissive, liberal, indulgent, overindulgent; *informal* sloppy. See note at LENIENT. ANTONYM strict.

lay[1] verb 1 *Curtis laid the newspaper on the table* PUT, place, set, put down, set down, deposit, rest, situate, locate, position; *informal* stick, dump, park, plunk.

2 *the act laid the foundation for the new system* SET IN PLACE, put in place, set out; set up, establish.

3 *I'll lay money that Michelle will be there* BET, wager, gamble, stake, risk, hazard, venture; **(lay money)** give odds, speculate.

4 *they are going to lay charges* BRING, press, bring forward, lodge, register, place, file.

5 *she* ***laid*** *the blame* ***on*** *Maxwell* ASSIGN TO, attribute to, ascribe to, allot to, attach to; **(lay the blame on)** hold someone accountable, hold someone responsible, find guilty.

6 *we* ***laid out*** *plans for the next voyage* DEVISE, arrange, make, make ready, prepare, work out, hatch, design, plan, scheme, plot, conceive, put together, draw up, produce, develop, concoct, formulate, cook up.

7 *this will lay responsibility on the court* IMPOSE, apply, entrust, vest, place, put; inflict, encumber, saddle, charge, burden.

8 *we laid the trap and waited* SET, prepare, devise, bait. See note at LIE². PHRASES: **lay something aside 1** *farmers laying aside areas for conservation* PUT ASIDE, put to one side, keep, save. **2** *developers must lay aside their conservatism* ABANDON, cast aside, set aside, reject, renounce, repudiate, disregard, forget, discard; *literary* forsake. **lay something bare** *his private life has been laid bare* REVEAL, disclose, divulge, show, expose, exhibit, uncover, unveil, unmask, make known, make public. **lay something down 1** *he laid down his glass* PUT DOWN, set down, place down, deposit, rest; *informal* plunk down. **2** *they were forced to lay down their weapons* RELINQUISH, surrender, give up, yield, cede. **3** *the ground rules have been laid down* FORMULATE, stipulate, set down, draw up, frame; prescribe, ordain, dictate, decree; enact, pass, decide, determine, impose, codify. **lay down the law** *too many parents have relinquished their right to lay down the law* BE DOGMATIC, be in charge (of the rules), set the rules, be domineering, be the boss, call the shots. **lay eyes on** *informal something clicked the first time they laid eyes on each other* SEE, spot, observe, regard, view, catch sight of, set eyes on; *literary* behold, espy, descry. **lay hands on** *wait till I lay my hands on you!* CATCH, lay/get hold of, get one's hands on, seize, grab, grasp, capture. **lay into** *informal* **1** *the general's henchmen were encouraged to publicly lay into dissenters.* See ASSAULT verb sense 1. **2** *he laid into her with a string of insults.* See CRITICIZE. **lay it on thick** *informal oh, brother, can he lay it on thick when he wants to impress a girl* EXAGGERATE, overdo it, embellish the truth; flatter, praise, soft-soap, pile it on, sweet-talk. **lay off** *informal* **1** *I have to lay off beer* GIVE UP, abstain from, desist from, cut out. **2** *I lay off work at 5* QUIT, pack in, leave off, stop. **3** *lay off, you big jerk!* BACK OFF, give it a rest, enough already, shut up, stop it. **4** *three more couriers were laid off today* DISMISS, let go, discharge, give notice to, release; *informal* sack, fire, ax, give someone their marching orders, pink-slip, give someone the boot, give someone the (old) heave-ho. **lay out 1** *Robyn laid the plans out on the desk* SPREAD OUT, set out, display, exhibit. **2** *a paper laying out our priorities* OUTLINE, sketch out, rough out, detail, draw up, formulate, work out, frame, draft. **3** *informal he had to lay out $70.* See PAY verb sense 2. **lay waste to** *any further testing at this site will lay waste to an irreplaceable ecosystem* DEVASTATE, wipe out, destroy, demolish, annihilate, raze, ruin, wreck, level, flatten, ravage, pillage, sack, despoil.

USAGE NOTE

The verb **lay** means, broadly, 'put something down': *they are going to lay the carpet*. The past tense and the past participle of **lay** is **laid**: *they laid the groundwork*; *she had laid careful plans*.

The verb **lie**, on the other hand, means 'assume a horizontal or resting position': *why don't you lie on the floor?*

In practice, many speakers inadvertently get the **lay** forms and the **lie** forms into a tangle of right and wrong usage. Here are some examples of typical incorrect usage: *have you been laying on the sofa all day?* (should be **lying**); *he lay the books on the table* (should be **laid**); *I had laid in this position so long, my arm was stiff* (should be **lain**).

---

lay² adjective **1** *a lay preacher* NONCLERICAL, nonordained, secular, temporal.

2 *a lay audience* NONPROFESSIONAL, amateur, nonspecialist, nontechnical, untrained, unqualified.

layabout noun *I want Carmen and the rest of these layabouts out of here by noon* IDLER, loafer, slacker, lazybones, lounger, flâneur, shirker, sluggard, laggard, slugabed, malingerer, good-for-nothing; *informal* lazybones, couch potato; *literary* wastrel.

layer noun *a layer of fresh snow* COATING, sheet, coat, film, covering, blanket, skin, thickness; stratum, band.

layman noun. See LAYPERSON.

layoff noun *a companywide layoff* DISMISSAL, discharge; *informal* sacking, firing; downsizing; the sack, the boot, the ax. ANTONYM recruitment.

layout noun **1** *the layout of the house* ARRANGEMENT, geography, design, organization; plan, map; blueprint.

2 *the magazine's layout* DESIGN, arrangement, presentation, style, format; structure, organization, composition, configuration.

layperson noun **1** *a prayer book for laypeople* UNORDAINED PERSON, member of the congregation, layman, laywoman, member of the laity.

2 *engineering sounds highly specialized to the layperson* LAYMAN, nonexpert, nonprofessional, amateur, nonspecialist, dilettante.

laze verb *lazing by the river* RELAX, unwind, idle, do nothing, loaf (around/about), lounge (around/about), loll (around/about), lie (around/about), take it easy; *informal* hang around, veg (out), bum (around).

lazy adjective *the lazy volunteers were sent home* IDLE, indolent, slothful, work-shy, shiftless, inactive, sluggish, lethargic; remiss, negligent, slack, lax, lackadaisical. ANTONYM industrious.

lazybones noun *informal everyone in that family is a lazybones* IDLER, loafer, layabout, lounger, good-for-nothing, do-nothing, shirker, sluggard, laggard, slugabed, flâneur; *informal* slacker, couch potato; *literary* wastrel. ANTONYM go-getter.

leach verb *the chemicals leach into our drinking water* DRAIN, filter, percolate, seep, filtrate, strain.

lead¹ verb **1** *Michelle led them into the house* GUIDE, conduct, show, show the way, lead the way, usher, escort, steer, pilot, shepherd; accompany, see, take. ANTONYM follow.

2 *he led us to believe they were lying* CAUSE, induce, prompt, move, persuade, influence, drive, condition, make; incline, dispose, predispose.

3 *this might* ***lead to*** *job losses* RESULT IN, cause, bring on/about, give rise to, be the cause of, make happen, create, produce, occasion, effect, generate, contribute to, promote; provoke, stir up, spark off, arouse, foment, instigate; involve, necessitate, entail; *formal* effectuate. ANTONYM prevent.

4 *he led a march to the city center* BE AT THE HEAD OF, be at the front of, head, spearhead; precede. ANTONYM follow.

5 *she led a coalition of radicals* BE THE LEADER OF, be the head of, preside over, head, command, govern, rule, be in charge of, be in command of, be in control of, run, control, direct, be at the helm of; administer, organize, manage; reign over, be in power over; *informal* head up. ANTONYM serve in.

6 *the Bengals were leading at halftime* BE AHEAD, be winning, be (out) in front, be in the lead, be first, be on top. ANTONYM trail.

7 *the champion was leading the field* BE AT THE FRONT OF, be first in, be ahead of, head; outrun, outstrip, outpace, leave behind, draw away from; outdo, outclass, beat; *informal* leave standing. ANTONYM trail.

8 *I just want to lead a normal life* EXPERIENCE, have, live, spend.

▸ noun 1 *I was in* ***the lead*** *early on* THE LEADING POSITION, first place, the van, the vanguard; ahead, in front, winning.

2 *they took the lead in the personal computer market* FIRST POSITION, forefront, primacy, dominance, superiority, ascendancy; preeminence, supremacy, advantage, upper hand, whip hand.

3 *playing the lead* LEADING ROLE, star/starring role, title role, principal part; principal character, male lead, female lead, leading man, leading lady.

4 *a Labrador on a lead* LEASH, tether, rope, chain, cord.

5 *detectives were following up a new lead* CLUE, hint, tip, tip-off, suggestion, indication, sign, pointer.

▸ adjective *the lead position* LEADING, first, top, foremost, front, head; chief, principal, main, premier.

PHRASES: **lead something off** *let's lead off the meeting with a few words from Mr. Diaz* BEGIN, start (off), commence, open; *informal* kick off. **lead someone on** *were you leading her on with that talk about marriage?* DECEIVE, mislead, delude, hoodwink, dupe, trick, fool, pull the wool over someone's eyes; *informal* string along, lead up the garden path, take for a ride, fleece, inveigle, hornswoggle, scam. **lead the way** 1 *he led the way to the kitchen* GUIDE SOMEONE, conduct someone, show someone the way. 2 *our corporation is leading the way in new technologies* TAKE THE INITIATIVE, break (new) ground, blaze a trail, prepare the way, be at the forefront. **lead up to** *perhaps these informal meetings will lead up to a more formal relationship* PREPARE THE WAY FOR, pave the way for, lay the groundwork for, set the scene for, work up/around to.

lead[2] noun *informal get that lead down to forensics immediately* BULLET, slug, pellet; shot, buckshot, ammunition

PHRASE: **get the lead out** *come on you guys—get the lead out!* HURRY UP, get a move on, be quick; *informal* get cracking, shake a leg, look lively, look sharp; *dated* make haste.

leaden adjective 1 *he moved on leaden feet* SLUGGISH, heavy, lumbering, slow, burdensome, cumbersome.

2 *leaden prose* BORING, dull, unimaginative, uninspired, monotonous, heavy, labored, wooden, lifeless, plodding; depressing.

3 *a leaden sky* GRAY, grayish, black, dark; cloudy, gloomy, overcast, dull, sunless, oppressive, threatening; *literary* tenebrous.

leader noun 1 *the leader of the Democratic Party | world leaders have agreed to meet in Geneva* CHIEF, head, principal; commander, captain; superior, headman; chairman, chairwoman, chairperson, chair; (managing) director, CEO, manager, superintendent, supervisor, overseer, administrator, employer, master, mistress; president, premier, governor; ruler, monarch, king, queen, sovereign, emperor; *informal* boss, skipper, number one, numero uno, honcho, sachem, padrone. ANTONYMS follower, supporter.

2 *the uncontested leader in genetic engineering* PIONEER, front runner, world leader, world-beater, innovator, trailblazer, groundbreaker, trendsetter, torchbearer, pathfinder.

leadership noun 1 *firm leadership* GUIDANCE, direction, control, management, superintendence, supervision; organization, government.

2 *the leadership of the Rainbow Coalition* DIRECTORSHIP, governorship, governance, administration, captaincy, control, ascendancy, supremacy, rule, command, power, dominion, influence.

leading adjective 1 *he played the leading role* MAIN, chief, major, prime, most significant, most important, principal, foremost, key, central, focal, preeminent, paramount, dominant, essential. ANTONYMS subordinate, secondary.

2 *the nation's leading steel companies* MOST IMPORTANT, most powerful, affluential, foremost, chief, preeminent, outstanding, dominant, most influential. ANTONYMS minor, secondary.

3 *last season's leading scorer* TOP, highest, best, first; front, lead; unparalleled, matchless, star. ANTONYMS worst, last.

leaf noun 1 *sycamore leaves* LEAFLET, frond, blade, needle; *Botany* cotyledon, blade, bract.

2 *a leaf in a book* PAGE, sheet, folio.

▸ verb *he* ***leafed through*** *the documents* FLIP THROUGH, thumb through, flick through, skim through/over, browse through, glance through/over, riffle through, rifle through; scan, run one's eye over, peruse.

PHRASE: **turn over a new leaf** *how many released prisoners actually turn over a new leaf?* REFORM, improve, mend one's ways, make a fresh start, change for the better; *informal* go straight.

leaflet noun *leaflets about fire prevention* PAMPHLET, booklet, brochure, handbill, circular, flyer, fact sheet, handout, bulletin.

league noun 1 *a league of nations* ALLIANCE, confederation, confederacy, federation, union, association, coalition, consortium, affiliation, guild, cooperative, partnership, fellowship, syndicate.

2 *the best team in the league* big league(s), major league(s), minor league(s), American League, National League, intramural league, Little League, bush league.

3 *the store is not in the same league* CLASS, group, circle, category, level.

▸ verb *they* ***leagued together*** *with other companies* ALLY, join forces, join together, unite, band together, affiliate, combine, amalgamate, confederate, team up, join up.

PHRASE: **in league with** *in league with the drug cartel* COLLABORATING WITH, cooperating with, in alliance with, allied with, conspiring with, hand in glove with; *informal* in cahoots with, in bed with.

leak verb 1 *oil leaking from the tanker* SEEP (OUT), escape, ooze (out), secrete, bleed, emanate, issue, drip, dribble, drain; discharge, exude.

2 *civil servants leaked information to the press* DISCLOSE, divulge, reveal, make public, tell, impart, pass on, relate, communicate, expose, broadcast, publish, release, let slip, bring into the open; *informal* blab; **(leak news/information)** let the cat out of the bag, spill the beans.

▸ noun 1 *check that there are no leaks in the pipe* HOLE, opening, aperture, puncture, perforation, gash, slit, nick, rent, break, crack, fissure, rupture.

2 *a gas leak* DISCHARGE, leakage, seepage, drip, escape.

3 *leaks to the media* DISCLOSURE, revelation, exposé, leakage, tip-off.

lean[1] verb 1 *Polly* ***leaned against*** *the door* REST ON/AGAINST, recline on/against, be supported by.

2 *trees leaning in the wind* SLANT, incline, bend, tilt, be at an angle, slope, tip, list.

3 *he* ***leans toward*** *existentialist philosophy* TEND TOWARD, incline toward, gravitate toward; have a preference for, have a penchant for, be partial to, have a liking for, have an affinity with.

4 *a strong shoulder to* ***lean on*** DEPEND ON, be dependent on, rely on, count on, bank on, have faith in, trust (in).

5 *informal he* ***leaned on*** *me to change my mind* INTIMIDATE, coerce, browbeat, bully, threaten, put pressure on, harass, hassle; *informal* twist someone's arm, put the screws on, hold a gun to someone's head.

lean[2] adjective 1 *a tall, lean man* SLIM, thin, slender, spare, wiry, lanky, skinny. See note at THIN. ANTONYM fat.

2 *a lean harvest* MEAGER, sparse, poor, mean, inadequate, insufficient, paltry, scanty, deficient, insubstantial. ANTONYMS plentiful, abundant.

3 *lean times* HARD, bad, difficult, tough, impoverished, poverty-stricken. ANTONYM prosperous.

leaning noun *my leaning is definitely toward a more liberal agenda* INCLINATION, tendency, bent, proclivity, propensity, penchant, predisposition, predilection, partiality, preference, bias, attraction, liking, fondness, taste; *informal* yen.

leap verb 1 *he* ***leaped over*** *the gate* JUMP OVER, jump, vault over, vault, spring over, bound over, hop (over), hurdle, leapfrog, clear.

2 *Claudia leapt to her feet* SPRING, jump, jump up, hop, bound.

3 *we leapt into the car* RUSH, hurry, hasten.

4 *she* ***leaped at*** *the chance* ACCEPT EAGERLY, grasp (with both hands), grab, take advantage of, seize (on), jump at.

5 *don't* ***leap to*** *conclusions* FORM HASTILY, reach hurriedly; hurry to, hasten to, jump to, rush to.

6 *profits leapt in January* INCREASE RAPIDLY, soar, rocket, skyrocket, shoot up, escalate.

▸ noun 1 *an easy leap* JUMP, vault, spring, bound, hop, skip.

2 *a leap of 33%* SUDDEN RISE, surge, upsurge, upswing, upturn.

PHRASE: **by/in leaps and bounds** *his health has improved by leaps and bounds* RAPIDLY, swiftly, quickly, speedily.

learn verb 1 *learning a foreign language* ACQUIRE A KNOWLEDGE OF, acquire skill in, become competent in, become proficient in, grasp, master, take in, absorb, assimilate, digest, familiarize oneself with; study, read up on, be taught, have lessons in; *informal* get the hang of, bone up on.

2 *she learned the poem in just a few minutes* MEMORIZE, learn by heart, commit to memory, get down pat; *archaic* con.

3 *he learned that the school would shortly be closing* DISCOVER, find out, become aware, be informed, hear, hear tell; gather, understand, ascertain, establish; *informal* get wind of the fact, get wise to the fact; *Brit. informal* suss out.

learned adjective *the most learned man in their community* SCHOLARLY, erudite, well-educated, knowledgeable, well-read, well-informed, lettered, cultured, intellectual, academic, literary, bookish, highbrow, studious; *informal* brainy. ANTONYM ignorant.

learner noun See NOVICE sense 1.

learning noun 1 *a center of learning* STUDY, studying, education, schooling, tuition, teaching, academic work; research.

2 *the astonishing range of his learning* SCHOLARSHIP, knowledge, education, erudition, intellect, enlightenment, illumination, edification, book learning, information, understanding, wisdom. See note at KNOWLEDGE. ANTONYM ignorance.

lease noun *a 15-year lease* RENTAL AGREEMENT, leasehold, charter; rental, tenancy, tenure, period of occupancy.

▸ verb 1 *the film crew leased a large hangar* RENT, charter.

2 *they leased the mill to a reputable family* RENT, rent out, let, let out; sublet, sublease.

leash noun *keep your dog on a leash* LEAD, tether, rope, chain, restraint.

▸ verb 1 *she leashed the dog* PUT A/THE LEASH ON, put a/the lead on, tether, tie up, secure, restrain.

2 *the fury in her face was barely leashed* CURB, control, keep under control, check, restrain, hold back, suppress, rein in.

PHRASE: **straining at the leash** *thousands of young actors are straining at the leash just for the chance to audition* EAGER, impatient, anxious, enthusiastic; *informal* itching, dying.

least adjective *I have not the least idea what this means* SLIGHTEST, smallest, minutest, tiniest, littlest. PHRASE: **at**

least *check in at least one hour before takeoff* AT THE MINIMUM, no/not less than; more than; anyway, at all events, leastways/leastwise.

leather noun See table.

TYPES OF LEATHER

alligator	Nubuck™
buckskin	oxhide
buff	patent leather
calfskin	pigskin
capeskin	rawhide
chamois	Russia leather
chrome leather	sealskin
cordovan	shagreen
cowhide	shammy
crocodile	sheepskin
deerskin	snakeskin
doeskin	suede
full-grain leather	whitleather
goatskin	
grain leather	**Imitation Leather**
kid	Broncohide™
kidskin	DuraSuede™
lambskin	leatherette
Levant morocco	leatherlike vinyl
mocha	Naugahyde™
morocco	pleather
nappa/napa	

leathery adjective **1** *leathery skin* ROUGH, rugged, leathered, hard, hardened, wrinkled, furrowed, lined, weather-beaten, callous, gnarled.

2 *a leathery cut of beef* TOUGH, hard, gristly, chewy, stringy, rubbery.

leave[1] verb **1** *I left the hotel* DEPART FROM, go away from, go from, withdraw from, retire from, take oneself off from, exit from, take one's leave of, pull out of, be gone from, decamp from, disappear from, vacate, absent oneself from; say one's farewells/goodbyes to, quit; *informal* push off from, shove off from, clear out/off of, cut and run from, split, vamoose from, scoot from. ANTONYMS arrive, stay.

2 *the next morning we left for Taipei* SET OFF, head, make; set sail.

3 *he's left his wife* ABANDON, desert, cast aside, jilt, throw over; *informal* dump, ditch, drop, walk/run out on; *literary* forsake. ANTONYM stay with.

4 *he left his job in November* QUIT, resign from, retire from, step down from, withdraw from, pull out of, give up; pack it in, call it quits.

5 *she left her purse on a bus* LEAVE BEHIND, forget, lose, mislay.

6 *I thought I'd leave it to the experts* ENTRUST, hand over, pass on, refer; delegate.

7 *he left her $100,000* BEQUEATH, will, endow, hand down to, make over to.

8 *the speech left some feelings of disappointment* CAUSE, produce, generate, give rise to. PHRASE: **leave someone/something out 1** *Adam left out the address* OMIT, fail to include, overlook, forget; skip, miss. **2** *when the roster for Game 2 was drawn up, Harvey was left out* EXCLUDE, omit, pass over; eliminate, cut, drop.

leave[2] noun **1** *the judge granted leave to appeal* PERMISSION, consent, authorization, sanction, warrant, dispensation, approval, clearance, blessing, assent, license; *informal* the go-ahead, the green light, the OK, the rubber stamp, the nod.

2 *he was on leave* VACATION, break, time off, holiday, furlough, sabbatical, leave of absence. PHRASE: **take one's leave of** *he took his leave of us* BID FAREWELL TO, say goodbye to.

leaven verb **1** *yeast leavens the bread* RAISE, make rise, puff up, expand.

2 *formal proceedings leavened by humor* PERMEATE, infuse, pervade, imbue, suffuse, transform; enliven, liven up, invigorate, energize, electrify, ginger up, season, spice (up), perk up, brighten up, lighten, lift; *informal* buck up, pep up.

lecher noun *her blind date turned out to be a lecher* LECHEROUS MAN, libertine, womanizer, debauchee, rake, roué, profligate, wanton; Don Juan, Casanova, Lothario, Romeo; *informal* lech, dirty old man, (old) goat, wolf, skirt-chaser; *archaic* fornicator.

lecherous adjective *the lecherous creep who lives in our building* LUSTFUL, licentious, lascivious, libidinous, prurient, lewd, salacious, lubricious, debauched, dissolute, wanton, dissipated, degenerate, depraved, dirty, filthy; *formal* concupiscent. ANTONYM chaste.

lecture noun **1** *a lecture on children's literature* SPEECH, talk, address, discourse, disquisition, presentation, oration, lesson.

2 *Dave got a lecture about his daydreaming* SCOLDING, chiding, reprimand, rebuke, reproof, reproach, upbraiding, berating, admonishment, sermon; *informal* dressing-down, talking-to, tongue-lashing, roasting; *formal* castigation.

▸ verb **1** *lecturing on the dangers of drugs* GIVE A LECTURE, give a talk, talk, make a speech, speak, give an address, discourse, hold forth, declaim, expatiate; *informal* spout, sound off.

2 *she lectures at Colgate University* TEACH, give instruction, give lessons.

3 *she was lectured for her gossiping* SCOLD, chide, reprimand, rebuke, reprove, reproach, upbraid, berate, chastise, admonish, lambaste, rake/haul over the coals, take to task; *informal* give someone a dressing-down, give someone a talking-to, tell off, bawl out; *formal* castigate.

lecturer noun *a guest lecturer from Yale* UNIVERSITY TEACHER, college teacher, professor, tutor, educator; academic, academician, preceptor; *formal* pedagogue.

ledge noun *a collection of teapots on the ledge | a rock ledge* SHELF, sill, mantel, mantelpiece, shelving; projection, protrusion, overhang, ridge, prominence.

ledger noun *a sales ledger* BOOK, account book, record book, register, log, accounts; records, books; balance sheet, financial statement.

lee noun *the lee of the wall* SHELTER, protection, cover, refuge, safety, security.

leech noun *the welfare system is supposed to help the needy, not to feed the leeches* PARASITE, bloodsucker; *informal* scrounger, sponger, bottom feeder, freeloader.

leer verb *Henry* **leered at** *her* OGLE, look lasciviously at, look suggestively at, eye, check out; *informal* give someone a/the once-over, lust after/over.

▸ noun *a sly leer* LECHEROUS LOOK, lascivious look, ogle; *informal* the once-over, the eye.

leery adjective *be leery of these slick salesmen* WARY, cautious, careful, guarded, chary, suspicious, distrustful; worried, anxious, apprehensive, hesitant, uncertain.

leeway noun *enforcement officials now have more leeway in prosecuting offenders* FREEDOM, scope, latitude, space, room, liberty, flexibility, license, free hand, free rein.

left adjective *it's in my left pocket | move to the left side* LEFT-HAND, sinistral; *Nautical* port, larboard; *Heraldry* sinister. ANTONYMS right, starboard.

left-handed adjective 1 *a left-handed golfer* sinistral; *informal* southpaw. ANTONYM right-handed.

2 *a left-handed compliment* BACKHANDED, ambiguous, equivocal, double-edged; dubious, ironic, sardonic, insincere, hypocritical. ANTONYM forthright.

leftover noun 1 *a leftover from the 60s* RESIDUE, SURVIVOR, vestige, legacy, throwback.

2 **(leftovers)** *put the leftovers in the fridge* UNEATEN FOOD, leavings, remainder, scraps, remnants, remains; excess, surplus.

▸ adjective *leftover food* REMAINING, left, uneaten, unconsumed; excess, surplus, superfluous, unused, unwanted, spare.

left-wing adjective *the committee's left-wing policies* LIBERAL, leftist, left-of-center, left-leaning; socialist, communist; Labor/Labour, Marxist, Bolshevik; *informal* commie, lefty, red, pinko. ANTONYMS right-wing, conservative.

leg noun 1 *Lee broke his leg* LOWER LIMB, limb, shank; *informal* pin.

2 *the first leg of a European tour* PART, stage, portion, segment, section, phase, stretch, lap. PHRASES: **give someone a leg up** *we all want to give our kids a leg up in the world* HELP/ASSIST SOMEONE, give someone assistance, lend someone a helping hand, give someone a boost. **leg it** *informal* See RUN verb sense 1. **on its/one's last legs** *the barn is on its last legs* DILAPIDATED, worn out, rickety, about to fall apart, about to become obsolete; failing, dying, terminal, on one's deathbed. **pull someone's leg** *is Julie really sick or is she just pulling my leg?* TEASE SOMEONE, make fun of someone, tease, joke, make fun, fool, jest, joke with someone, play a (practical) joke on someone, play a trick on someone, make a monkey out of someone; hoax someone, fool someone, deceive someone, lead someone on, hoodwink someone, dupe someone, beguile someone, gull someone; *informal* kid someone, have someone on, rib someone, take someone for a ride, put someone on. **stretch one's legs** *we always like to stretch our legs after dinner* GO FOR A WALK, take a stroll, walk, stroll, move about, get some exercise.

legacy noun 1 *a legacy from a great aunt* BEQUEST, inheritance, heritage, endowment, gift, patrimony, settlement, birthright; *formal* benefaction.

2 *a legacy of the residential schools* CONSEQUENCE, effect, upshot, spin-off, repercussion, aftermath, by-product, result.

legal adjective *the legal sale of alcoholic beverages* LAWFUL, legitimate, licit, within the law, legalized, valid; permissible, permitted, allowable, allowed, aboveboard, admissible, acceptable; authorized, sanctioned, licensed, constitutional; *informal* legit. ANTONYM criminal.

legalize verb *where do you stand on legalizing marijuana?* MAKE LEGAL, decriminalize, legitimize, legitimate, permit, allow, authorize, sanction, license, validate; regularize, normalize; *informal* OK. ANTONYM prohibit.

legatee noun See BENEFICIARY.

legend noun 1 *Arthurian legends* MYTH, saga, epic, tale, story, folk tale, folk story, fairy tale, fable, mythos, folklore, lore, mythology, fantasy, oral history, folk tradition; urban myth.

2 *film legends* CELEBRITY, star, superstar, icon, phenomenon, luminary, leading light, giant; *informal* celeb, megastar.

legendary adjective 1 *legendary knights* FABLED, heroic, traditional, fairy-tale, storybook, mythical, mythological. ANTONYMS factual, historical.

2 *a legendary figure in sports* FAMOUS, celebrated, famed, renowned, acclaimed, illustrious, esteemed, honored, exalted, venerable, well-known, popular, prominent, distinguished, great, eminent, preeminent, high-profile; *formal* lauded.

legerdemain noun 1 *stage magicians practicing legerdemain* SLEIGHT OF HAND, conjuring, magic, wizardry; *formal* prestidigitation; *rare* thaumaturgy.

2 *a piece of management legerdemain* TRICKERY, cunning, artfulness, craftiness, chicanery, skulduggery, deceit, deception, artifice.

legible adjective *large, legible handwriting* READABLE, easy to read, easily deciphered, clear, plain, neat, decipherable, intelligible.

legion noun 1 *a military legion* BRIGADE, regiment, battalion, company, troop, division, squadron, squad, platoon, phalanx, unit, force.

2 *the legions of TV cameras* HORDE, throng, multitude, host, crowd, mass, mob, gang, swarm, flock, herd, score, army, pack.

▸ adjective *her fans are legion* NUMEROUS, countless, innumerable, incalculable, many, abundant, plentiful; *literary* myriad.

legislate verb *we urge Congress to legislate against human cloning* MAKE LAWS, pass laws, enact laws, formulate laws; authorize, decree, order, sanction.

legislation noun *pushing for stronger gun legislation* LAW(S), body of laws, rules, rulings, regulations, acts, bills, statutes, enactments, ordinances.

legislative adjective *a legislative assembly* LAWMAKING, judicial, juridical, parliamentary, governmental, policymaking.

legislator noun *let your legislators know how you feel about the state income tax* LAWMAKER, lawgiver; representative, congressman, congresswoman, senator; parliamentarian.

legislature noun *the new Hong Kong legislature* LEGISLATIVE BODY, congress, legislative assembly, parliament, senate, house of representatives, council, diet.

legitimate adjective 1 *the only form of legitimate gambling* LEGAL, lawful, licit, legalized, authorized, permitted, permissible, allowable, allowed, admissible, sanctioned, approved, licensed, statutory, constitutional; *informal* legit, street legal. ANTONYM illegal.

2 *the legitimate heir* RIGHTFUL, lawful, genuine, authentic, real, true, proper, authorized, sanctioned, acknowledged, recognized. See note at GENUINE. ANTONYMS false, fraudulent.

3 *legitimate grounds for doubt* VALID, sound, well-founded, justifiable, reasonable, sensible, just, fair, bona fide. ANTONYM illegal.

legitimize verb *China's revised constitution will legitimize citizens' rights to hold private property* VALIDATE, legitimate, permit, authorize, sanction, license, condone, justify, endorse, support; legalize. ANTONYM outlaw.

leisure noun *the balance between leisure and work* FREE TIME, spare time, time off; recreation, relaxation, inactivity, pleasure; *informal* R and R, downtime. ANTONYM work.

PHRASE: **at your leisure** *Form A may be completed at your leisure* AT YOUR CONVENIENCE, when it suits you, in your own (good/sweet) time, without haste, unhurriedly.

leisurely adjective *a leisurely stroll through town* UNHURRIED, relaxed, easy, gentle, sedate, comfortable, restful, undemanding, slow, lazy. ANTONYM hurried.

lemon noun *informal her Yugo was a real lemon* DEFECTIVE CAR; disappointment, letdown; *informal* clunker, junker, jalopy, Tin Lizzie, bucket of bolts, rustbucket, beater.

lend verb **1** *I'll lend you my towel* LOAN, let someone use; advance. See note at LOAN. ANTONYM borrow.

2 *these examples lend weight to his assertions* ADD, impart, give, bestow, confer, provide, supply, furnish, contribute. ANTONYM detract.

PHRASES: **lend an ear** *when Travers gets up to speak, I hope you'll lend an ear* LISTEN, pay attention, take notice, be attentive, concentrate, heed, pay heed; *informal* be all ears; *archaic* hearken. **lend a hand** *I'm here to lend a hand with the harvest* HELP, help out, give a helping hand, assist, give assistance, make a contribution, do one's bit; *informal* pitch in. **lend itself to** *the terrain lends itself to downhill skiing* BE SUITABLE FOR, be suited to, be appropriate for, be applicable for.

length noun **1** *a length of three or four yards | the whole length of the valley* EXTENT, distance, linear measure, span, reach; area, expanse, stretch, range, scope.

2 *a considerable length of time* PERIOD, duration, stretch, span.

3 *a length of blue silk* PIECE, swatch, measure.

4 *the press criticized the length of her speech* LENGTHINESS, extent, prolixity, wordiness, verbosity, long-windedness. PHRASE: **at length 1** *the preacher spoke at length* FOR A LONG TIME, for ages, for hours, interminably, endlessly, ceaselessly, unendingly. **2** *Everett was questioned at length* THOROUGHLY, fully, in detail, in depth, comprehensively, exhaustively, extensively. **3** *his search led him, at length, to Seattle* AFTER A LONG TIME, eventually, in time, finally, at last, at long last, in the end, ultimately.

lengthen verb *he lengthened his stride to keep up | as the spring days lengthen* ELONGATE, make longer, extend, prolong, protract, stretch out, drag out; expand, widen, broaden, enlarge; grow/get longer, draw out. ANTONYM shorten.

lengthy adjective **1** *a lengthy civil war* LONG, very long, long-lasting, prolonged, extended; *informal* marathon. ANTONYM short.

2 *lengthy discussions* PROTRACTED, overlong, long-drawn-out; verbose, wordy, prolix, long-winded; tedious, boring, interminable. ANTONYM brief.

lenient adjective *Brother Andrew was a lenient teacher* MERCIFUL, clement, forgiving, forbearing, tolerant, charitable, humane, indulgent, easygoing, magnanimous, sympathetic, compassionate, mild. See note at MERCY. ANTONYM severe.

THE RIGHT WORD

Not all parents approach discipline in the same way. Someone who is **lenient** is willing to lower his or her standards of strictness when it comes to imposing discipline (*the principal was lenient with the students who had been caught playing hooky*). A parent who is **forbearing** struggles against giving in to negative feelings and is therefore able to abstain from hasty or ill-tempered actions, no matter what the provocation (*her father's forbearing attitude meant that she escaped with only a lecture*). **Indulgent** goes beyond forbearing and suggests catering to someone's whims (*an indulgent parent who seldom denied her child anything*). **Lax** is a negative kind of leniency involving laziness or indifference (*a lax mother who never imposed a curfew*), while **merciful** suggests a relaxing of standards on the basis of compassion (*a merciful mother who understood her daughter's anger*). To be **permissive** is also to be extremely lenient—an approach that connotes tolerance to the point of passivity (*the children's utter disregard for the rules was the result of their permissive upbringing*).

lesbian noun *the title character is a nineteen-year-old lesbian* HOMOSEXUAL WOMAN, gay woman; *informal* butch, femme; *offensive* dyke, bulldyke, queer. ANTONYMS heterosexual, straight woman.

▸ adjective *a long-term lesbian partnership* HOMOSEXUAL, gay, same-sex; Sapphic, homoerotic; *informal* butch; *offensive* dykey, queer. ANTONYM straight.

lesion noun *symptoms include clusters of red lesions* WOUND, injury, bruise, abrasion, contusion; ulcer, ulceration, sore, running sore, abscess; *Medicine* trauma.

less pronoun *the fare is* ***less than*** *$1* A SMALLER AMOUNT THAN, not so/as much as, under, below. ANTONYM more.

▸ adjective *there was less noise now* NOT SO MUCH, smaller, slighter, shorter, reduced; fewer.

▸ adverb *we must use the car less* TO A LESSER DEGREE, to a smaller extent, not so/as much.

▸ preposition *figure the list price less 10 percent* MINUS, subtracting, excepting, without. ANTONYM plus.

USAGE NOTE less, fewer

Strictly, *less* applies to singular nouns (*less tonic water, please*) or units of measure (*less than six ounces of epoxy*). *Fewer* applies to plural nouns (*fewer guests arrived than expected*) or numbers of things (*we have three fewer members this year*). The exception in using *fewer* occurs when count nouns essentially function as mass nouns because the units are so very numerous or they aren't considered discrete items (the idea of individual units becomes meaningless). Hence *less* is used correctly with time and money: one isn't, ordinarily, talking about the number of years or the number of dollars but rather the amount of time or the amount of money—e.g.:

• "On that mantra, Larry Clark has built a $45 million-a-year company in less than five years." (*Arizona Business Gazette*; Nov. 30, 1995.)

• "Okay, how about $50 a month for such an apartment—less than two dollars a day?" (*Village Voice*; Apr. 29, 1997.)

Fewer, in fact, is incorrect when intended to refer to a period of time—e.g.: "You can run from sea level to the sky and back to earth in as fast as 45 minutes (so far), but even today, going round-trip in fewer [read *less*] than 60 minutes carries a special cachet." (*Anchorage Daily News*; June 29, 1997.) But if the units of time are thought of as wholes, and not by fractions, then *fewer* is called for (*fewer days abroad | fewer weeks spent apart*). Hence we say *less documentation* but *fewer documents*; *less whispering* but *fewer remarks*; *less of a burden* but *fewer burdens*; *less fattening* but *fewer calories*.

Fastidious writers and editors preserve the old distinction. But the loose usage crops up often—e.g.: "You will have less [read *fewer*] people to call and haunt about paying for their outfits and buying their accessories." (*Boston Herald* [magazine]; Oct. 19, 1997.) The linguistic hegemony by which *less* has encroached on *fewer*'s territory is probably now irreversible. What has clinched this development is something as mundane as the express checkout lines in supermarkets. They're typically bedecked with signs cautioning, "15 items or less." These signs are all but ubiquitous in the United States. But the occasional more literate supermarket owner uses a different sign: "15 or fewer items."

Finally, even with the strict usage, it's sometimes a close call whether a thing is a mass noun or a count noun, and hence whether *less* or *fewer* is proper. Take, for example, a percentage: should it be "less than 10% of the homeowners were there" or "fewer than 10% of the homeowners were there"? One could argue that a percentage is something counted (i.e., 10 out of 100), and thus requires *fewer*. One could also argue that a percentage is a collective mass noun (akin, e.g., to money), and thus requires *less*. The latter is the better argument because most percentages aren't whole numbers anyway. And even if it were a toss-up between the two theories, it's sound to choose *less*, which is less formal in tone than *fewer*.

If, in strict usage, *less* applies to singular nouns and *fewer* to plural nouns, the choice is clear: "one less golfer on the course," not "one fewer golfer." This is tricky only because *less* is being applied to a singular count noun, whereas it usually applies to a mass noun. Lyricist Hal David got it right in "One Less Bell to Answer" (1970). Nearly a quarter of the time, however, writers use *one fewer*, an awkward and unidiomatic phrase. One can't help thinking that this is a kind of hypercorrection induced by underanalysis of the *less*-vs.-*fewer* question.

Lesser, like *less*, refers to quantity, but is confined to use as an adjective before a singular noun and following an article (*the lesser crime*) or alone before a plural noun (*lesser athletes*), thus performing a function no longer idiomatically possible with less. Dating from the thirteenth century, this formal usage allows *lesser* to act as an antonym of *greater*. **—BG**

---

lessen verb **1** *the new law did little to lessen the stigma* REDUCE, make less/smaller, minimize, decrease; allay, assuage, alleviate, attenuate, palliate, ease, dull, deaden, blunt, moderate, mitigate, dampen, soften, tone down, dilute, weaken. ANTONYM increase.

2 *the pain began to lessen* GROW LESS, grow smaller, decrease, diminish, decline, subside, abate; fade, die down/off, let up, ease off, tail off, drop (off/away), fall, dwindle, ebb, wane, recede. ANTONYM increase.

3 *his behavior lessened him in their eyes* DIMINISH, degrade, discredit, devalue, belittle. ANTONYM aggrandize.

lesser adjective **1** *a lesser offense* LESS IMPORTANT, minor, secondary, subsidiary, marginal, ancillary, auxiliary, supplementary, peripheral; inferior, insignificant, unimportant, petty. ANTONYMS greater, primary.

2 *you look down at us lesser mortals* SUBORDINATE, minor, inferior, second-class, subservient, lowly, humble. ANTONYM superior.

lesson noun **1** *a math lesson* CLASS, session, seminar, tutorial, lecture, period, period of instruction/teaching.

2 (lessons) *they should be industrious at their lessons* EXERCISES, assignments, schoolwork, homework, study.

3 *reading the lesson in church* BIBLE READING, scripture, text, reading, passage.

4 *Stuart's accident should be a lesson to all parents* WARNING, deterrent, caution; example, exemplar, message, moral.

let verb **1** *let him sleep for now* ALLOW TO, permit to, give permission to, give leave to, authorize to, sanction to, grant the right to, license to, empower to, enable to, entitle to; *archaic* suffer to. ANTONYMS prevent, prohibit.

2 *Wilcox opened the door to let her through* ALLOW TO GO, permit to pass; make way for.

PHRASES: **let someone down** *I'm afraid I've let the team down* FAIL, fail to support, disappoint, disillusion; abandon, desert, leave stranded, leave in the lurch. **let something down** *Maryann let down the hem on her mother's old prom dress* LENGTHEN, make longer. **let fly 1** *he **let fly** with a brick* HURL, fling, throw, propel, pitch, lob, toss, launch; shoot, fire, blast; *informal* chuck, sling, heave. **2** *she **let fly** at Geoffrey* LOSE ONE'S TEMPER WITH, lash out at, scold, chastise, chide, rant at, inveigh against, rail against; explode at, burst out at, let someone have it; *formal* excoriate. **let go** *don't let go of the steering wheel* RELEASE, release one's hold on, loose/loosen one's hold on, relinquish; *archaic* unhand. **let someone go** *they let half of the warehouse crew go* DISMISS, discharge, lay off, give notice to; *informal* sack, fire, ax, give someone their marching orders, send packing, give someone the boot, give someone the (old) heave-ho, can, pink-slip. **let someone in** *they seemed reluctant to let me in* ALLOW TO ENTER, allow in, admit, open the door to; receive, welcome, greet. **let someone in on something** *we can't let you in on the details just yet* INCLUDE IN, count in on, admit in on, allow to share in, let participate in, inform about, tell about. **let someone off 1** *informal I'll let you off this time* PARDON, forgive, grant an amnesty to; deal leniently with, be merciful to, have mercy on; acquit, absolve, exonerate, clear, vindicate; *informal* let someone off the hook; *formal* exculpate. **2** *he let me off work* EXCUSE FROM, exempt from, spare from. **let on** *informal* **1** *I never let on that I felt anxious* REVEAL, make known, tell, disclose, mention, divulge, let slip, give away, make public; blab; *informal* let the cat out of the bag, give the game away. **2** *he let on that he'd won* PRETEND, feign, affect, make out, make believe, simulate. **let something out 1** *I let out a cry of triumph* UTTER, emit, give, give vent to, produce, issue, express, voice, release. **2** *she let out that he'd given her a lift home* REVEAL, make known, tell, disclose, mention, divulge, let slip, give away, let it be known, blurt out. **let someone out** *they let me out of the hospital on Monday* RELEASE, liberate, (set) free, let go, discharge; set/turn loose, allow to leave. **let up** *informal* **1** *the rain has let up* ABATE, lessen, decrease, diminish, subside, relent, slacken, die down/off, ease (off), tail off; ebb, wane, dwindle, fade; stop, cease, finish. **2** *you never let up, do you?* RELAX, ease up/off, slow down; pause, break (off), take a break, rest, stop; *informal* take a breather. **3** *I promise I'll let up on him* TREAT LESS SE-

VERELY, be more lenient with, be kinder to; *informal* go easy on.

letdown noun *the movie was a big letdown after reading the book* DISAPPOINTMENT, anticlimax, comedown, nonevent, fiasco, setback, blow, disadvantage; *informal* washout.

lethal adjective *a lethal dose of arsenic* FATAL, deadly, mortal, death-dealing, life-threatening, murderous, killing; poisonous, toxic, noxious, venomous; dangerous, destructive, harmful, pernicious; *literary* deathly, nocuous. ANTONYMS harmless, safe.

lethargic adjective *feeling depressed and lethargic* SLUGGISH, inert, inactive, slow, torpid, lifeless; languid, listless, lazy, idle, indolent, shiftless, slothful, apathetic, weary, tired, fatigued.

lethargy noun *the lethargy may be related to his latest medication* SLUGGISHNESS, inertia, inactivity, inaction, slowness, torpor, torpidity, lifelessness, listlessness, languor, laziness, idleness, indolence, shiftlessness, sloth, apathy, passivity, weariness, tiredness, lassitude, fatigue, inanition; *literary* hebetude. ANTONYMS vigor, energy.

letter noun **1** *capital letters* ALPHABETICAL CHARACTER, character, sign, symbol, mark, figure, rune; *Linguistics* grapheme.

2 *he wrote Len a letter* WRITTEN MESSAGE, message, written communication, communication, note, line, missive, dispatch; correspondence, news, information, intelligence, word; post, mail; *formal* epistle. See table.

3 **(letters)** *a man of letters* LEARNING, scholarship, erudition, education, knowledge; intellect, intelligence, enlightenment, wisdom, sagacity, culture. PHRASE: **to the letter** *he followed her instructions to the letter* STRICTLY, precisely, exactly, accurately, closely, faithfully, religiously, punctiliously, literally, verbatim, in every detail.

TYPES OF LETTERS

acknowledgment letter	letter of credit
acceptance letter	letter of intent
air letter	letter of introduction
billet-doux	letter of recommendation
bread-and-butter letter	letter of thanks
business letter	love letter
chain letter	mash letter
circular	memo
cover letter	memorandum
dead letter	newsletter
Dear John letter	open letter
dunning letter	poison-pen letter
e-mail/email	rejection letter
fan letter	thank-you note
form letter	

lettered adjective *in colonial Brattleboro, this household of lettered young women was quite a curiosity* LEARNED, erudite, academic, educated, well-educated, well-read, widely read, knowledgeable, intellectual, well-schooled, enlightened, cultured, cultivated, scholarly, bookish, highbrow, studious, cerebral. ANTONYM ill-educated.

letup noun *informal there can be no letup in the war against drugs* ABATEMENT, lessening, decrease, diminishing, diminution, decline, relenting, remission, slackening, weakening, relaxation, dying down, easing off, tailing off, dropping away/off; respite, break, breather, interval, hiatus, suspension, cessation, stop, pause.

Levant See note below.

WORD NOTE **Levant**

To restore a pleasing word that, for one of any number of reasons, has been dropped from the popular lexicon, to something approaching its former status and glory, is a duty that a writer is, in my view, obliged to undertake from time to time. Back in the 1930s Georgette Heyer rescued *delope*—"to fire one's dueling pistol harmlessly into the air"—from oblivion, and deserves much gratitude for keeping it in currency. These days I am keen to see that the word *Levant,* an at-risk lexeme, remains in circulation. It is a word with a charming etymology, in that it comes from the French verb "to rise," and denotes the place from which the sun seems to rise each morning—the East. Specifically it means the countries on the eastern shore of the Mediterranean—Turkey to Egypt, via Palestine and Israel—all of which, in a decidedly nonpolitical, but agnostically geographical description, were for centuries lumped together as *the Levant.* (Of course, the world being spheroidal, someone's east is another person's west, so to an inhabitant of India, the Levantine countries would be those where the sun sets, in the West, and there may well be a Hindi term suggesting so) . There is a raw Mediterranean east wind still called a *levanter,* known to yachtsmen who also know the *simoom* and the *sirocco;* but people of *Levantine* stock, and the Levant from which they come, are half-vanished terms, due for a prompt and enthusiastic revival and a swift and lasting rescue. **—SW**

level adjective **1** *a smooth and level surface* FLAT, smooth, even, uniform, plane, flush, plumb. ANTONYMS uneven, bumpy.

2 *he kept his voice level* UNCHANGING, steady, unvarying, even, uniform, regular, constant, invariable, unaltering; calm, unemotional, composed, equable, unruffled, serene, tranquil. ANTONYMS shaky, unsteady.

3 *his eyes were **level with** hers* ALIGNED WITH, on the same level as, on a level with, at the same height as, in line with. ANTONYMS uneven, above, below.

▸ noun **1** *she is at a managerial level* RANK, standing, status, position; echelon, degree, grade, gradation, stage, standard, rung; class, stratum, group, grouping, set, classification.

2 *a high level of unemployment* QUANTITY, AMOUNT, extent, measure, degree, volume, size, magnitude, intensity, proportion.

3 *the level of water is rising* HEIGHT, altitude, elevation.

4 *the sixth level* FLOOR, story, deck.

▸ verb **1** *tilt the pan to level the mixture* MAKE LEVEL, level out/off, make even, even out, make flat, flatten, smooth, smooth out, make uniform.

2 *bulldozers leveled the building* RAZE, demolish, flatten, topple, destroy; tear down, knock down, pull down, bulldoze.

3 *he leveled his opponent with a single blow* KNOCK DOWN, lay out, flatten, floor, fell; knock out; *informal* KO, kayo.

4 *Carl leveled the playing field* EQUALIZE, make equal, equal, even, even up, make level.

5 *he leveled his pistol at me* AIM, point, direct, train, focus, turn, sight.

6 *informal I knew you'd **level with** me* BE FRANK WITH, be open with, be honest with, be aboveboard with, tell the truth to, tell all to, hide nothing from, be straightforward with, be upfront with; *informal* come clean with, set the record straight with.

PHRASE: **on the level** *informal Urbana is such a smooth talker, we never know for sure if she's on the level* GENUINE, straight, honest, aboveboard, fair, true, sincere, straightforward, trustworthy; *informal* upfront, on the up and up.

levelheaded adjective *how did those nitwits end up with such levelheaded children?* SENSIBLE, practical, realistic, prudent, pragmatic, wise, reasonable, rational, mature, judicious, sound, sober, businesslike, no-nonsense, composed, calm, 'calm, cool, and collected', confident, well-balanced, equable, coolheaded, self-possessed, having one's feet on the ground; *informal* unflappable, together, grounded. ANTONYMS excitable, foolish.

lever noun **1** *you can insert a lever and pry the rail off* CROWBAR, bar, jimmy.

2 *he pulled the lever* HANDLE, grip, pull, switch.

▸ verb *he levered the door open* PRY, prize, force, wrench, pull, wrest, heave; *informal* jimmy.

leverage noun **1** *the long handles provide increased leverage* GRIP, purchase, hold; support, anchorage, force, strength.

2 *the union's leverage at the bargaining table* INFLUENCE, power, authority, weight, sway, pull, control, say, dominance, advantage, pressure; *informal* clout, muscle, teeth, bargaining chip.

levitate noun *the spaceship slowly levitated over the cornfield* FLOAT, rise, rise into the air, hover, be suspended, glide, hang, fly, soar up.

levity noun *without some occasional levity, the working environment is no better than a sweatshop* LIGHTHEARTEDNESS, high spirits, vivacity, liveliness, cheerfulness, cheeriness, humor, gaiety, fun, jocularity, hilarity, frivolity, amusement, mirth, laughter, merriment, glee, comedy, wit, wittiness, jollity, joviality. ANTONYM seriousness.

levy verb *the government's right to levy taxes* IMPOSE, charge, exact, raise, collect; *rare* mulct.

▸ noun **1** *the levy of taxes* IMPOSITION, raising, collection; *formal* exaction.

2 *the levy on alcohol* TAX, tariff, toll, excise, duty, imposition, impost; *rare* mulct.

lewd adjective **1** *a lewd old man* LECHEROUS, lustful, licentious, lascivious, dirty, prurient, salacious, lubricious, libidinous; debauched, depraved, degenerate, decadent, dissipated, dissolute, perverted, wanton; *formal* concupiscent; *archaic* lickerish. ANTONYM chaste.

2 *a lewd song* VULGAR, crude, smutty, dirty, filthy, obscene, pornographic, coarse, off-color, unseemly, indecent, salacious; rude, racy, risqué, naughty, bawdy, ribald; *informal* blue, raunchy, X-rated, XXX, porno; *euphemistic* adult. ANTONYM clean.

lexicon noun *an illustrated lexicon* DICTIONARY, wordbook, vocabulary list, glossary, thesaurus.

liability noun **1** *journalists' liability for defamation* ACCOUNTABILITY, responsibility, legal responsibility, answerability; blame, culpability, guilt, fault. ANTONYM immunity.

2 *they have big liabilities* FINANCIAL OBLIGATIONS, debts, arrears, dues. ANTONYM asset.

3 *she was proving to be a liability* HINDRANCE, encumbrance, burden, handicap, nuisance, inconvenience; obstacle, impediment, disadvantage, weakness, weak link, shortcoming; millstone around one's neck, albatross, Achilles heel. ANTONYMS advantage, asset.

liable adjective **1** *they are liable for negligence* RESPONSIBLE, legally responsible, accountable, answerable, chargeable, blameworthy, at fault, culpable, guilty. See note at RESPONSIBLE.

2 *my income is liable to fluctuate wildly* LIKELY, inclined, tending, disposed, apt, predisposed, prone, given.

3 *areas* ***liable to*** *flooding* EXPOSED TO, prone to, subject to, susceptible to, vulnerable to, in danger of, at risk of.

liaise verb *social services liaised with the police* COOPERATE, work together, collaborate; communicate, network, interface, interact, link up.

liaison noun **1** *Dave was my liaison with the district manager* INTERMEDIARY, mediator, middleman, contact, link, connection, go-between, representative, agent.

2 *a secret liaison* LOVE AFFAIR, affair, relationship, romance, attachment, fling, amour, romantic entanglement, entanglement, tryst; *informal* hanky-panky.

liar noun *even in a court of law, Jeff was a shameless liar* DECEIVER, fibber, perjurer, false witness, fabricator, equivocator; fabulist; *informal* storyteller.

libation noun **1** *they pour libations into the holy well* LIQUID OFFERING, offering, tribute, oblation.

2 *humorous would you like a libation?* (ALCOHOLIC) DRINK, beverage, liquid refreshment; dram, draft, nip, shot; *informal* tipple, nightcap, pick-me-up; *archaic* potation.

libel noun *she sued two newspapers for libel* DEFAMATION, defamation of character, character assassination, calumny, misrepresentation, scandalmongering; aspersions, denigration, vilification, disparagement, derogation, insult, slander, malicious gossip; lie, slur, smear, untruth, false report; *informal* mudslinging, bad-mouthing.

▸ verb *she alleged the magazine had libeled her* DEFAME, malign, slander, blacken someone's name, sully someone's reputation, speak ill/evil of, traduce, smear, cast aspersions on, drag someone's name through the mud, besmirch, tarnish, taint, tell lies about, stain, impugn someone's character/integrity, vilify, denigrate, disparage, run down, stigmatize, discredit, slur; *informal* dis, bad-mouth; *formal* derogate, calumniate. See note at MALIGN.

liberal adjective **1** *the values of a liberal society* TOLERANT, unprejudiced, unbigoted, broad-minded, open-minded, enlightened; permissive, free, free and easy, easygoing, libertarian, indulgent, lenient. ANTONYMS narrow-minded, bigoted.

2 *a liberal social agenda* PROGRESSIVE, advanced, modern, forward-looking, forward-thinking, progressivist, enlightened, reformist, radical. ANTONYMS reactionary, conservative.

3 *a liberal education* WIDE-RANGING, broad-based, general.

4 *a liberal interpretation of divorce laws* FLEXIBLE, broad, loose, rough, free, general, nonliteral, nonspecific, imprecise, vague, indefinite. ANTONYMS strict, to the letter.

5 *a liberal coating of paint* ABUNDANT, copious, ample, plentiful, generous, lavish, luxuriant, profuse, considerable, prolific, rich; *literary* plenteous. ANTONYM scant.

6 *they were liberal with their cash* GENEROUS, openhanded, unsparing, unstinting, ungrudging, lavish, free, munificent, bountiful, beneficent, benevolent, bighearted, philanthropic, charitable, altruistic, unselfish; *literary* bounteous. ANTONYMS careful, miserly.

liberate verb **1** *they liberated the prisoners* SET FREE, free, release, let out, let go, set/let loose, save, rescue; emancipate, enfranchise. ANTONYMS imprison, enslave.

2 *he liberated a trinket from her jewelry box* STEAL, take; *informal* swipe, nab, pinch, borrow.

libertine noun *an unrepentant libertine* PHILANDERER, playboy, rake, roué, Don Juan, Lothario, Casanova, Romeo; lecher, seducer, womanizer, adulterer, debauchee, profligate, wanton; *informal* skirt-chaser, ladykiller, lech, wolf; *formal* fornicator.

liberty noun **1** *personal liberty* FREEDOM, independence, free rein, license, self-determination, free will, latitude. ANTONYMS constraint, slavery.

2 *the fight for liberty* INDEPENDENCE, freedom, autonomy, sovereignty, self-government, self-rule, self-determination; civil liberties, human rights. ANTONYM tyranny.

3 *the liberty to go where you please* RIGHT, birthright, prerogative, entitlement, privilege, permission, sanction, authorization, authority, license, power. ANTONYM constraint.

PHRASES: **at liberty 1** *he was at liberty for three months* FREE, on the loose, loose, at large, unconfined; escaped, out, on the lam. **2** *you are at liberty to leave* FREE, permitted, allowed, authorized, able, entitled, eligible. **take liberties with** *I'd appreciate it if you would refrain from taking liberties with me* ACT WITH FAMILIARITY TOWARD, show disrespect to/toward, act with impropriety with/toward, act indecorously with, be impudent with, act with impertinence to/toward; take advantage of, exploit.

PHRASE: **take the liberty** *may I take the liberty to order champagne?* PRESUME, venture, be so bold as.

THE RIGHT WORD

The Fourth of July is the day on which Americans commemorate their nation's **independence**, a word that implies the ability to stand alone, without being sustained by anything else. While *independence* is usually associated with countries or nations, **freedom** and **liberty** more often apply to individuals. But unlike *freedom*, which implies an absence of restraint or compulsion (*the freedom to speak openly*), *liberty* implies the power to choose among alternatives rather than merely being unrestrained (*the liberty to select their own form of government*). *Freedom* can also apply to many different types of oppressive influences (*freedom from interruption; freedom to leave the room at any time*), while *liberty* often connotes deliverance or release (*he gave the slaves their liberty*). **License** may imply the *liberty* to disobey rules or regulations imposed on others, especially when there is an advantage to be gained in doing so (*poetic license*). But more often it refers to an abuse of *liberty* or the power to do whatever one pleases (*a license to sell drugs*). **Permission** is an even broader term than *license*, suggesting the capacity to act without interference or censure, usually with some degree of approval or authority (*permission to be absent from his post*).

libidinous adjective *libidinous impulses* LUSTFUL, lecherous, lascivious, lewd, carnal, salacious, prurient, licentious, libertine, lubricious, dissolute, debauched, depraved, degenerate, decadent, dissipated, wanton, promiscuous; *informal* wolfish; *formal* concupiscent.

libido noun *alcohol may impair your libido* SEX DRIVE, sexual appetite; sexual desire, desire, passion, sensuality, sexuality, lust, lustfulness; *informal* horniness; *formal* concupiscence.

license noun **1** *a driver's license* PERMIT, certificate, document, documentation, authorization, warrant; certification, credentials; pass, papers.

2 *you have license to make changes* PERMISSION, authority, right, a free hand, leave, authorization, entitlement, privilege, prerogative; liberty, freedom, power, latitude, scope, free rein, carte blanche, a blank check, the go-ahead. See note at LIBERTY.

3 *poetic license* DISREGARD FOR THE FACTS, inventiveness, invention, creativity, imagination, fancy, freedom, looseness.

▸ verb *we're licensed to sell beer* PERMIT, allow, authorize, grant/give authority, grant/give permission, grant/give a license; certify, empower, entitle, enable, give approval, let, qualify, sanction; *informal* rubber stamp. ANTONYM ban.

licentious adjective *a book that exaggerates the licentious behavior of the rich and famous* DISSOLUTE, dissipated, debauched, degenerate, immoral, naughty, wanton, decadent, depraved, sinful, corrupt; lustful, lecherous, lascivious, libidinous, prurient, lubricious, lewd, promiscuous, lickerish; *formal* concupiscent. ANTONYM moral.

licit adjective See LEGITIMATE sense 1.

lick verb **1** *the spaniel licked his face* PASS ONE'S TONGUE OVER, touch with one's tongue, tongue; lap.

2 *informal they licked the home team 3–0.* See DEFEAT verb sense 1.

3 *informal we've got that problem licked* OVERCOME, get the better of, find an answer/solution to, conquer, beat, control, master, curb, check.

▸ noun *informal* **1** *a lick of paint* DAB, bit, drop, dash, spot, touch, splash; *informal* smidgen.

2 *a guitar lick* SHORT SOLO, riff, line, theme.

PHRASE: **lick someone's boots/shoes** *nobody licks the boss's boots with more finesse than Little Miss* SUCK UP TO, toady to, be servile to, be obsequious to, fawn over, flatter, butter up, ingratiate oneself with, brown-nose with/to.

lickety-split adverb *they ran out of here lickety-split* AT FULL SPEED, very quickly, on the double, as fast as one's legs can carry one, at a gallop, headlong, pell-mell, hell-bent for leather, like the wind, like a bat out of hell, at full tilt.

licking noun *informal* **1** *the Mariners took a licking* DEFEAT, beating, trouncing, thrashing; *informal* hiding, pasting, hammering, drubbing, shellacking.

2 *Ray got the worst licking of his life* THRASHING, beating, flogging, whipping; *informal* walloping, hiding, pasting, whaling.

lid noun *the lid of a saucepan* COVER, top, cap, covering.
PHRASES: **put a lid on it** *hey, chatterbox, put a lid on it* STOP TALKING, BE QUIET, hold your tongue; *informal* shut up, hush up, shut your mouth, shut your face, shut your trap, button your lip, pipe down, put a sock in it, give it a rest, save it, not another word. **blow the lid off** *informal intelligence officials have blown the lid off the so-called crusade against corruption* EXPOSE, reveal, make known,

make public, bring into the open, disclose, divulge; *informal* spill the beans, blab.

lie[1] noun *loyalty had made him tell lies* UNTRUTH, falsehood, fib, fabrication, deception, invention, fiction, piece of fiction, falsification; (little) white lie, half-truth, exaggeration; *informal* tall tale, whopper, taradiddle. ANTONYM truth.

▸ verb *he lied to the police* TELL AN UNTRUTH, TELL A LIE, fib, dissemble, dissimulate, misinform, mislead, tell a white lie, perjure oneself, commit perjury, prevaricate; *informal* lie through one's teeth, stretch the truth; *formal* forswear oneself.

THE RIGHT WORD

If your spouse asks you whether you remembered to mail the tax forms and you say "Yes," even though you know they're still sitting on the passenger seat of your car, you're telling a **lie**, which is a deliberately false statement. If you launch into a lengthy explanation of the day's frustrations and setbacks, the correct word would be **prevaricate**, which is to quibble, dodge the point, or confuse the issue so as to avoid telling the truth. If you tell your spouse that you would have mailed the taxes, but then you started thinking about an important deduction you might be entitled to take and decided it would be unwise to mail them without looking into it, you're **rationalizing**, which is to come up with reasons that put your own behavior in the most favorable possible light. If you say that there was an accident in front of the post office that prevented you from finding a parking space and there really wasn't, **fabricate** is the correct verb, meaning that you've invented a false story or excuse without the harsh connotations of *lie* (*she fabricated an elaborate story about how they got lost on their way home*). **Equivocate** implies saying one thing and meaning another; it usually suggests the use of words that have more than one meaning, or whose ambiguity may be misleading. For example, if your spouse says, "Did you take care of the taxes today?" you might equivocate by saying "Yes," you took care of them—meaning that you finished completing the forms and sealing them in the envelope, but that you didn't actually get them to the post office. To **fib** is to tell a falsehood about something unimportant; it is often used as a euphemism for *lie* (*a child who fibs about eating his vegetables*).

lie[2] verb **1** *he was lying on a bed* RECLINE, lie down, lie back, be recumbent, be prostrate, be supine, be prone, be stretched out, sprawl, rest, repose, lounge, loll. ANTONYM stand.

2 *her handbag lay on a chair* BE PLACED, be situated, be positioned, rest.

3 *lying on the border of Switzerland and Austria* BE SITUATED, be located, be placed, be found, be sited.

4 *the difficulty lies in building real quality into the products* CONSIST, be inherent, be present, be contained, exist, reside. PHRASES: **lie heavy on** *keeping these secrets from her family lies heavy on her* TROUBLE, worry, bother, torment, oppress, nag, prey on one's mind, plague, niggle at, gnaw at, haunt; *informal* bug. **lie low** *Nate and Rizzo will have to lie low until the trial is over* HIDE, go into hiding, conceal oneself, keep out of sight, go underground, hide out; *informal* hole up. See note at LAY.

USAGE NOTE **lie**

In the sense of telling an untruth, the verb is inflected *lie, lied, lied.*

The more troublesome inflections belong to the senses of reclining, being placed, and being situated: *lie, lay, lain.* A murderer may *lie in wait.* Yesterday he *lay in wait.* And for several days he *has lain in wait*—e.g.: "The Ramseys say an intruder may have lay [read *lain*] in wait for hours before killing the 6-year-old beauty queen." (*Austin American-Statesman*; Mar. 18, 2000.) **—BG**

life noun **1** *the joy of giving life to a child* EXISTENCE, being, living, animation; sentience, creation, viability. ANTONYMS death, nonexistence.

2 *threats to life on the planet* LIVING THINGS, living beings, living creatures, the living; human/animal/plant life, fauna, flora, ecosystems; human beings, humanity, humankind, mankind, man.

3 *an easy life* WAY OF LIFE, lifestyle, situation, fate, lot.

4 *the last nine months of his life* LIFETIME, life span, days, time on earth, existence.

5 *he is full of life* VIVACITY, animation, liveliness, vitality, verve, high spirits, exuberance, zest, buoyancy, enthusiasm, energy, vigor, dynamism, élan, gusto, brio, bounce, spirit, fire; movement; *informal* oomph, pizzazz, pep, zing, zip, vim.

6 *the life of the party* MOVING SPIRIT, vital spirit, spirit, life force, lifeblood, heart, soul.

7 *more than 1,500 lives were lost in the accident* PERSON, human being, individual, soul.

8 *I really wanted a new car, but that's life* THE WAY OF THE WORLD, the way things go, the human condition; fate, destiny, providence, kismet, karma, fortune, luck, chance; *informal* the way the cookie crumbles, the breaks. PHRASES: **come to life 1** *the kids are finally coming to life* BECOME ACTIVE, come alive, wake up, awaken, arouse, rouse, stir; *literary* waken. **2** *the carved angel suddenly came to life* BECOME ANIMATE, come alive. **for dear life** *we held on to the rope for dear life* DESPERATELY, with all one's might, for all one is worth, as fast/hard as possible, like the devil. **give one's life 1** *he would give his life for her* DIE FOR, lay down one's life for, sacrifice oneself for, offer one's life for, die to save. **2** *he gave his life to the company* DEDICATE ONESELF, devote oneself, give oneself, surrender oneself.

life-and-death adjective *a life-and-death decision* VITAL, of vital importance, crucial, critical, urgent, pressing, pivotal, momentous, important, all-important, key, serious, grave, significant; *informal* earth-shattering; *formal* of great moment. ANTONYM trivial.

lifeblood noun *the lifeblood of Hong Kong is trade, especially with China* LIFE FORCE, life, essential constituent, driving force, vital spark, inspiration, stimulus, essence, crux, heart, soul, core.

lifeless adjective **1** *a lifeless body* DEAD, departed, perished, gone, no more, passed on/away, stiff, cold, (as) dead as a doornail; *formal* deceased; *rare* demised. ANTONYM alive.

2 *a lifeless rag doll* INANIMATE, without life, inert, insentient. ANTONYM animate.

3 *a lifeless landscape* BARREN, sterile, bare, desolate, stark, arid, infertile, uncultivated, uninhabited; bleak, colorless, characterless, soulless.

4 *a lifeless performance* LACKLUSTER, spiritless, apathetic, torpid, lethargic; dull, monotonous, boring, tedious, dreary, unexciting, expressionless, emotionless, colorless, characterless. ANTONYMS vibrant, lively.

lifelike adjective *the doll is so lifelike* REALISTIC, true to life, representational, faithful, exact, precise, detailed, vivid, graphic, natural, naturalistic; *Art* kitchen-sink. ANTONYM unrealistic.

lifelong adjective *a lifelong commitment* LASTING, long-lasting, long-term, constant, stable, established, steady, enduring, permanent. ANTONYM ephemeral.

lifestyle noun *their privileged lifestyle* WAY OF LIFE, way of living, life, situation, fate, lot; conduct, behavior, customs, culture, habits, ways, mores; *Anthropology* lifeway.

lifetime noun **1** *he did a lot in his lifetime* LIFE SPAN, life, days, duration of life, one's time (on earth), existence, one's career.

2 *it would take **a lifetime*** ALL ONE'S LIFE, a very long time, an eternity, years (on end), eons; *informal* ages (and ages), an age.

lift verb **1** *lift the pack onto your back* RAISE, hoist, heave, haul up, heft, raise up/aloft, elevate, hold high; pick up, grab, take up, scoop up, snatch up; winch up, jack up, lever up; *informal* hump; *literary* upheave. ANTONYMS drop, put down.

2 *the news lifted his spirits* BOOST, raise, buoy up, elevate, cheer up, perk up, uplift, brighten up, gladden, encourage, stimulate, revive; *informal* buck up. ANTONYM subdue.

3 *the fog had lifted* CLEAR, rise, disperse, dissipate, disappear, vanish, dissolve. ANTONYM appear.

4 *the ban has been lifted* CANCEL, remove, withdraw, revoke, rescind, annul, void, discontinue, end, stop, terminate. ANTONYMS establish, impose.

5 *he lifted his voice* AMPLIFY, raise, make louder, increase. ANTONYMS soften, quieten.

6 *informal he lifted sections from a 1986 article* PLAGIARIZE, pirate, copy, reproduce, poach, steal; *informal* crib, rip off, pinch.

7 *informal she lifted a wallet.* See STEAL verb sense 1.

▸ noun **1** *give me a lift up* PUSH, boost, hoist, heave, thrust, shove.

2 *he gave me **a lift** to the airport* A RIDE, a drive, transportation.

3 *that goal will give his confidence a real lift* BOOST, fillip, stimulus, impetus, encouragement, spur, push; improvement, enhancement; *informal* shot in the arm, pick-me-up.

PHRASE: **lift off** *the helicopters lifted off at 1030 hours* TAKE OFF, become airborne, take to the air, take wing; be launched, blast off, rise.

light[1] noun **1** *the light of candles* ILLUMINATION, brightness, luminescence, luminosity, shining, gleaming, gleam, brilliance, radiance, luster, glowing, glow, blaze, glare, dazzle; sunlight, moonlight, starlight, lamplight, firelight; ray of light, beam of light; *literary* effulgence, refulgence, lambency. ANTONYM darkness.

2 *there was a light on in the hall* LAMP, wall light; headlight, headlamp, sidelight; streetlight, floodlight; lantern; flashlight.

3 *have you got a light?* MATCH, (cigarette) lighter.

4 *we'll wait for the light* DAYLIGHT, daylight hours, daytime, day; dawn, morning, daybreak, sunrise; natural light, sunlight. ANTONYMS darkness, nighttime.

5 *he saw the problem in a different light* ASPECT, angle, slant, approach, interpretation, viewpoint, standpoint, context, hue, complexion.

6 *light dawned on Loretta* UNDERSTANDING, enlightenment, illumination, comprehension, insight, awareness, knowledge. ANTONYM ignorance.

7 *an eminent legal light* EXPERT, authority, master, leader, guru, leading light, luminary.

▸ verb *Alan lit the kindling* SET ALIGHT, set light to, set burning, set on fire, set fire to, put/set a match to, ignite, kindle, spark (off). ANTONYM extinguish.

▸ adjective **1** *a light, cheerful room* BRIGHT, full of light, well-lit, well-illuminated, sunny. ANTONYMS dark, gloomy. See word spectrum on page 537.

2 *light shades of blue and rose* LIGHT-COLORED, light-toned, pale, pale-colored, pastel. ANTONYMS dark, deep.

3 *light hair* FAIR, light-colored, blond/blonde, golden, flaxen. ANTONYMS dark, brunette.

PHRASES: **bring something to light** *the surprise inspection brought some incriminating evidence to light* REVEAL, disclose, expose, uncover, unearth, dig up/out, bring to notice, identify. **come to light** *a fact important to this case has just come to light* BE DISCOVERED, be uncovered, be unearthed, come out, become known, become apparent, appear, materialize, emerge. **in (the) light of** *in light of this new information, there is no reason to continue our questioning* TAKING INTO CONSIDERATION, taking into account, considering, bearing in mind, taking note of, in view of. **light into** *informal* **1** *we started lighting into our attackers.* See SET ON/UPON at SET[1] . **2** *my father lit into me for being late.* See SCOLD verb. **light on/upon** *we'd almost given up when we lit upon this article about Mathew's murder trial* COME ACROSS, chance on/upon, hit on/upon, happen on/upon, stumble on/upon/across, find, discover, uncover, come up with. **light up** **1** *the dashboard lit up* BECOME BRIGHT, brighten, lighten, shine, gleam, flare, blaze, glint, sparkle, shimmer, glisten, scintillate. **2** *he lit up outside the bar* START SMOKING, light a cigarette. **light something up** **1** *a flare lit up the night sky* MAKE BRIGHT, brighten, illuminate, lighten, throw/cast light on, shine on, irradiate; *literary* illumine, illume. **2** *her enthusiasm lit up her face* ANIMATE, irradiate, brighten, cheer up, enliven. **throw/cast/shed (some) light on** *perhaps I can shed some light on this problem* EXPLAIN, elucidate, clarify, clear up, interpret. **out like a light** *after a day at the beach, these kids will be out like a light by eight o'clock* ASLEEP, unconscious, comatose; *informal* out cold, dead to the world.

light[2] adjective **1** *it's light enough to carry* EASY TO LIFT, not heavy, lightweight; easy to carry, portable. See word spectrum on page 537. ANTONYM heavy.

2 *a light cotton robe* FLIMSY, lightweight, insubstantial, thin; delicate, floaty, gauzy, gossamer, diaphanous. ANTONYMS heavy, thick.

3 *she is light on her feet* NIMBLE, agile, lithe, limber, lissome, graceful; light-footed, fleet-footed, quick, quick-moving, spry, sprightly; *informal* twinkle-toed; *literary* fleet, lightsome. ANTONYM clumsy.

4 *a light soil* FRIABLE, sandy, easily dug, workable, crumbly, loose. ANTONYMS dense, heavy.

5 *a light dinner* SMALL, modest, simple, easily digested; *informal* low-cal. ANTONYMS heavy, rich.

light
effulgence
refulgence
lambency
fulguration
luminescence
luminosity
shine
blaze
glare
dazzle
incandescence
brightness
radiance
luster
gleam
ray of light
shaft of light
beam of light
sunlight
electric light
gaslight
lamplight
firelight
illumination
phosphorescence
glow
glimmer
half-light
dusk
gloaming
twilight
crepuscule
sunset
sundown
evening
evenfall
eventide
nightfall
owl light
moonlight
starlight
dimness
shadow
gloom
dullness
shade
murk
tenebrosity
dark

6 *light duties* EASY, simple, undemanding, untaxing; *informal* cushy. ANTONYMS hard, burdensome.

7 *his eyes gleamed with light mockery* GENTLE, mild, moderate, slight; playful, lighthearted. ANTONYM serious.

8 *light reading* ENTERTAINING, lightweight, diverting, undemanding, frivolous, superficial, trivial. ANTONYMS serious, deep.

9 *a light heart* CAREFREE, lighthearted, cheerful, cheery, happy, merry, jolly, blithe, bright, sunny; buoyant, bubbly, jaunty, bouncy, breezy, optimistic, positive, upbeat, ebullient; *dated* gay.

10 *this is no light matter* UNIMPORTANT, insignificant, trivial, trifling, petty, inconsequential, superficial. ANTONYMS serious, important.

11 *light footsteps* GENTLE, delicate, soft, dainty; faint, indistinct. ANTONYM heavy.

12 *her head felt light* DIZZY, giddy, lightheaded, faint, vertiginous; *informal* woozy.

lighten[1] verb **1** *the first touch of dawn lightened the sky* MAKE LIGHTER, make brighter, brighten, light up, illuminate, throw/cast light on, shine on, irradiate; *literary* illumine, illume. ANTONYM darken.

2 *he used lemon juice to lighten his hair* WHITEN, make whiter, bleach, blanch, make paler. ANTONYM darken.

lighten[2] verb **1** *lightening the burden of taxation* MAKE LIGHTER, lessen, reduce, decrease, diminish, ease; alleviate, mitigate, allay, relieve, palliate, assuage. ANTONYMS increase, intensify.

2 *his smile lightened her spirits* CHEER (UP), brighten, gladden, hearten, perk up, lift, enliven, boost, buoy (up), uplift, revive, restore, revitalize. ANTONYM depress.

light-fingered adjective *our light-fingered cashier* THIEVING, stealing, pilfering, shoplifting, dishonest; *informal* sticky-fingered, crooked. ANTONYM honest.

lightheaded adjective *sit down if you're feeling lightheaded* DIZZY, giddy, faint, light in the head, vertiginous, reeling; *informal* woozy.

lighthearted adjective *a lighthearted musical* CAREFREE, cheerful, cheery, happy, merry, glad, playful, jolly, jovial, joyful, gleeful, ebullient, high-spirited, lively, blithe, bright, sunny, buoyant, vivacious, bubbly, jaunty, bouncy, breezy; entertaining, amusing, diverting; *informal* chirpy, upbeat; *dated* gay. ANTONYM miserable.

lightly adverb **1** *Hermione kissed him lightly on the cheek* SOFTLY, gently, faintly, delicately. ANTONYMS hard, heavily.

2 *season very lightly with paprika* SPARINGLY, slightly, sparsely, moderately, delicately. ANTONYMS intensely, abundantly.

3 *he has gotten off lightly* WITHOUT SEVERE PUNISHMENT, easily, leniently, mildly. ANTONYM severely.

4 *her views are not to be dismissed lightly* CARELESSLY, airily, heedlessly, without consideration, indifferently, unthinkingly, thoughtlessly, uncaringly, flippantly, breezily, frivolously. ANTONYM seriously.

light
airy
feathery
floaty
weightless
slight
flimsy
insubstantial
lightweight
manageable
transportable
portable
compact
close-packed
firm
thick
solid
hefty
large
big
hulking
substantial
weighing a ton
weighty
burdensome
dense
ponderous
massive
leaden
heavy

lightweight adjective **1** *a lightweight jacket* THIN, light, flimsy, insubstantial; summery. ANTONYMS heavy, thick.

2 *lightweight entertainment* TRIVIAL, insubstantial, superficial, shallow, unintellectual, undemanding, frivolous; of little merit/value; *informal* Mickey Mouse. ANTONYM profound.

▸ noun *he's no lightweight* AMATEUR, second-rater, unimportant person, insignificant person, nobody, nonentity, no-name, small fry.

likable, likeable adjective *a likable guy* PLEASANT, nice, friendly, agreeable, affable, amiable, genial, personable, charming, popular, good-natured, engaging, appealing, endearing, convivial, congenial, simpatico, winning, delightful, enchanting, lovable, adorable, sweet; *informal* darling, lovely. ANTONYM unpleasant.

like[1] verb **1** *I like Tony* BE FOND OF, be attached to, have a soft spot for, have a liking for, have regard for, think well of, admire, respect, esteem; be attracted to, fancy, find attractive, be keen on, be taken with; be infatuated with, carry a torch for; *informal* be crazy about, have a crush on, have a thing for, have the hots for, dig, take a shine to. ANTONYM hate.

2 *she likes gardening* ENJOY, have a taste for, have a preference for, have a liking for, be partial to, find/take pleasure in, be keen on, find agreeable, have a penchant for, have a passion for, find enjoyable; appreciate, love, adore, relish; *informal* have a thing about, be into, be mad about, be hooked on, get a kick out of. ANTONYM hate.

3 *feel free to say what you like* CHOOSE, please, wish, want, see fit, think fit, care to, will.

4 *how would she like it if someone did that to her?* FEEL ABOUT, regard, think about, consider.

like[2] preposition **1** *you're just like a teacher* SIMILAR TO, the same as, identical to.

2 *the figure landed like a cat* IN THE SAME WAY AS, in the same manner as, in the manner of, in a similar way to.

3 *cities like Joplin* SUCH AS, for example, for instance; in particular, namely.

4 *he sounded mean, which isn't like him* CHARACTERISTIC OF, typical of, in character with.

▸ noun *we'll never see his like again* EQUAL, match, equivalent, counterpart, twin, parallel; *rare* compeer.

▸ adjective *a like situation* SIMILAR, much the same, comparable, corresponding, resembling, alike, analogous, parallel, equivalent, cognate, related, kindred; identical, same, matching. ANTONYM dissimilar.

WORD NOTE **like**

Setting aside the adolescent propensity for *like* as a syntactical oral hiccup, there is no more grating solecism than this word's use as a conjunction. Such a practice transforms good writers into country bumpkins. By comparison, the widely abused *hopefully* and the inexcusable *irregardless* sound positively learned. Admittedly, this is a prejudice, since *like* has been employed as a conjunction (at least in speech) for centuries. Still, it's hard not to wince when reading *like I said* or *He was running like he was a man on fire.* Nearly always *as* or *as if* is called for. A useful hint: Avoid *like* when it would connect two independent clauses. Drop the words *he was* from the second example and *like* would be acceptable: *He was running like a man on fire.* If confused, stick with using *like* for comparisons: *He was, like Job, a man on fire.* **—MD**

likelihood noun *the likelihood of getting a fair trial in this court is slim | smoking greatly increases the likelihood of lung disease* PROBABILITY, chance, prospect, possibility, likeliness, odds, feasibility; risk, threat, danger; hope, promise.

likely adjective **1** *it seemed likely that a scandal would break* PROBABLE, distinctly possible, to be expected, odds-on, possible, plausible, imaginable; expected, anticipated, predictable, predicted, foreseeable; *informal* in the cards. ANTONYMS improbable, impossible.

2 *a likely explanation* PLAUSIBLE, reasonable, feasible, acceptable, believable, credible, tenable, conceivable. ANTONYMS incredible, unbelievable.

3 *a likely story!* UNLIKELY, implausible, unbelievable, incredible, untenable, unacceptable, inconceivable. ANTONYM believable.

4 *a likely place for a picnic* SUITABLE, appropriate, apposite, fit, fitting, acceptable, right; promising, hopeful.

▸ adverb *he was likely dead* PROBABLY, in all probability, presumably, no doubt, doubtlessly; *informal* (as) like as not, chances are.

likeness noun **1** *her likeness to Anne is quite uncanny* RESEMBLANCE, similarity, similitude, correspondence. ANTONYM dissimilarity.

2 *she appeared in the likeness of a ghost* SEMBLANCE, guise, appearance, outward form, form, shape, image.

3 *a likeness of the president* REPRESENTATION, image, depiction, portrayal; picture, drawing, sketch, painting, portrait, photograph, study; statue, sculpture.

THE RIGHT WORD

Two sisters who are only a year apart in age and who are very similar to each other in terms of appearance and personality would be said to bear a **likeness** to one another. **Similarity** applies to people or things that are merely somewhat alike (*there was a similarity between the two women, both of whom were raised in the Midwest*), while **resemblance** suggests a similarity only in appearance or in superficial or external ways (*with their short hair and blue eyes, they bore a strong resemblance to each other*). **Affinity** adds to *resemblance* a natural kinship, temperamental sympathy, common experience, or some other relationship (*she has an affinity for young children*). **Similitude** is a more literary word meaning *likeness* or *similarity* in reference to abstract things (*a similitude of the truth*). An **analogy** is a comparison of things that are basically unlike but share certain attributes or circumstances (*he drew an analogy between the human heart and a bicycle pump*).

likewise adverb **1** *an ambush was out of the question, likewise poison* ALSO, in addition, too, as well, to boot; besides, moreover, furthermore.

2 *encourage your family and friends to do likewise* THE SAME, similarly, correspondingly, in the same way, in similar fashion.

liking noun *his **liking for** fine wine* FONDNESS FOR, love of, affection for, penchant for, attachment to; enjoyment of, appreciation of, taste for, passion for; preference for, partiality to, predilection to; desire for, fancy for.

lilt noun *the lilt of her Scottish accent* CADENCE, rise and fall, inflection, intonation, rhythm, swing, beat, pulse, tempo.

limb noun **1** *his sore limbs* ARM, LEG, appendage; *archaic* member.

2 *the limbs of the tree* BRANCH, bough, offshoot, shoot.
PHRASE: **go out on a limb** *the government would not go out on a limb* BE PUT IN A PRECARIOUS POSITION, become vulnerable, be put in a risky situation; *informal* be sticking one's neck out.

limber adjective *I have to practice to keep myself limber* LITHE, supple, nimble, lissome, flexible, fit, agile, acrobatic, loose-jointed, loose-limbed. See note at FLEXIBLE. ANTONYM stiff.

PHRASE: **limber up** *limbering up for the marathon* WARM UP, loosen up, get into condition, get into shape, practice, train, stretch.

limbo PHRASE: **in limbo** *our mortgage approval is in limbo* IN ABEYANCE, unattended to, unfinished; suspended, deferred, postponed, put off, pending, on ice, in cold storage; unresolved, undetermined, up in the air, uncertain; *informal* on the back burner, on hold, treading water, in the balance.

limelight noun *she was once again enjoying the limelight* FOCUS OF ATTENTION, public attention, public interest, media attention, public eye, glare of publicity, prominence, spotlight; center stage. ANTONYM obscurity.

limit noun 1 *the city limits* BOUNDARY, border, bound, frontier, edge, demarcation line; perimeter, outside, confine, periphery, margin, rim.

2 *a limit of 4,500 people* MAXIMUM, ceiling, limitation, upper limit; restriction, check, control, restraint.

3 *resources are stretched to the limit* UTMOST, breaking point, greatest extent.

4 *informal* *I've reached **my limit**!* ONE'S/THE BREAKING POINT, the last straw; *informal* the end, it, one's wits' end, one's/the max.

▸ verb *the pressure to limit costs* RESTRICT, curb, cap, check, hold in check, restrain, put a brake on, freeze, regulate, control, govern, delimit.

PHRASE: **off limits** *access to their mother's workshop was strictly off limits* OUT OF BOUNDS, forbidden, banned, restricted, unacceptable, taboo.

limitation noun 1 *a limitation on the number of guests* RESTRICTION, curb, restraint, control, check; bar, barrier, block, deterrent. ANTONYM increase.

2 *he is aware of his own limitations* IMPERFECTION, flaw, defect, failing, shortcoming, weak point, deficiency, failure, frailty, weakness, foible. ANTONYM strength.

limited adjective 1 *limited resources* RESTRICTED, finite, little, tight, slight, in short supply, short; meager, scanty, sparse, few, insubstantial, deficient, inadequate, insufficient, paltry, poor, minimal. ANTONYMS ample, boundless.

2 *the limited powers of the council* RESTRICTED, curbed, checked, controlled, restrained, delimited, rangebound, qualified. ANTONYM absolute.

limitless adjective *a seemingly limitless supply of free software* BOUNDLESS, unbounded, unlimited, illimitable; infinite, endless, never-ending, unending, everlasting, untold, immeasurable, bottomless, fathomless; unceasing, interminable, inexhaustible, constant, perpetual.

limp[1] verb *she limped out of the house* HOBBLE, walk with a limp, walk lamely, walk unevenly, walk haltingly, hitch, falter, stumble, lurch.

▸ noun *walking with **a limp*** LAMENESS, a hobble, an uneven gait; *Medicine* claudication.

limp[2] adjective 1 *a limp handshake* SOFT, flaccid, loose, slack, lax; floppy, drooping, droopy, sagging. ANTONYM firm.

2 *we were all limp with exhaustion* TIRED, fatigued, weary, exhausted, worn out; lethargic, listless, spiritless, weak. ANTONYM energetic.

limpid adjective 1 *a limpid pool* CLEAR, transparent, glassy, crystal clear, crystalline, translucent, pellucid, unclouded. ANTONYM opaque.

2 *his limpid prose* LUCID, clear, plain, understandable, intelligible, comprehensible, coherent, explicit, unambiguous, simple, vivid, sharp, crystal clear; *formal* perspicuous. ANTONYM unintelligible.

line[1] noun 1 *he drew a line through the name* dash, rule, bar, score; underline, underscore, stroke, slash; *technical* stria, striation.

2 *there were lines around her eyes* WRINKLE, furrow, crease, groove, crinkle, crow's foot, laugh line.

3 (usu. **lines**) *the classic lines of the exterior* CONTOUR, outline, configuration, shape, figure, delineation, profile.

4 *the line between Canada and the United States* BOUNDARY, boundary line, limit, border, borderline, demarcation line, dividing line, edge, margin, perimeter, frontier.

5 (usu. **lines**) *behind enemy lines* POSITION, formation, defense, fieldwork, front (line); trenches.

6 *he put the wash on the line* CLOTHESLINE; cord rope, string, cable, wire, thread, twine, strand.

7 *they waited in a line* ROW, file, lineup, queue.

8 *a line of figures* COLUMN, row.

9 *a long line of bad decisions* SERIES, sequence, succession, chain, string, set, cycle.

10 *a line of flight* COURSE, route, track, path, way, run.

11 *they took a very tough line with the industry | the party line* COURSE OF ACTION, course, procedure, technique, tactic, tack; policy, practice, approach, plan, program, position, stance, philosophy.

12 *her own line of thought* COURSE, direction, drift, tack, tendency, trend.

13 *informal* *he fed me a line* STORY, piece of fiction, fabrication; *informal* spiel.

14 (**lines**) *he couldn't remember his lines* WORDS, part, script, speech.

15 *my line is engineering* LINE OF WORK, work, line of business, business, field, trade, occupation, employment, profession, job, career, specialty, forte, province, department, sphere, area, area of expertise.

16 *a new line of cologne* BRAND, kind, sort, type, variety, make.

17 *a noble line* ANCESTRY, family, parentage, birth, descent, lineage, extraction, genealogy, roots, origin, background; stock, bloodline, pedigree.

18 *the opening line of the poem* SENTENCE, phrase, clause, utterance; passage, extract, quotation, quote, citation.

19 *I should drop Ralph a line* NOTE, letter, card, postcard, e-mail, message, communication, missive, memorandum; correspondence, word; *informal* memo; *formal* epistle.

▸ verb 1 *her face was lined with age* FURROW, wrinkle, crease, pucker, mark with lines.

2 *the driveway was lined by poplars* BORDER, edge, fringe, bound, rim.

PHRASES: **draw the line at** *we draw the line at keg parties* STOP SHORT OF/AT, refuse to accept, balk at; object to, take issue with, take exception to. **in line** 1 *they stood in line for food* IN A ROW, in a file, in a lineup; *chiefly Brit.* in a queue. 2 *the advertisements are in line with the editorial style* IN AGREEMENT, in accord, in accordance, in harmony, in step, in compliance. 3 *he stood in line with the target* IN ALIGNMENT, aligned, level, at the same height; side by side. 4 *the referee kept him in line* UNDER CONTROL, in order, in check. **in line for** *Laine is in line for a senior position* A CANDIDATE FOR, in the running for, on the short list for, being considered for. **get a line on** *were you able to get a line on their upcoming projects?* learn something about, find out about, be informed about, hear about, hear tell about. **lay it on the line** *go ahead, lay it on the line, I can take it* SPEAK FRANKLY, speak honestly, be direct, pull no punches, be blunt, not mince one's words, call a spade a spade; *informal* give it to someone straight. **line up** 1 *line up for inspection* FORM A LINE, get into rows/columns, fall in; *chiefly Brit.* queue up; *Military* dress.

2 *they lined them up against the wall* ARRANGE IN LINES, put in rows, arrange in columns, align, range; *Military* dress. 3 *we've lined up an all-star cast* ASSEMBLE, put together, organize, prepare, arrange, prearrange, fix up; book, schedule. **on the line** *a firefighter's life is on the line every day* AT RISK, in danger, in jeopardy, endangered, imperiled. **toe the line** *the choice is yours: toe the line or pack your bags* CONFORM, obey the rules, observe the rules, comply with the rules, abide by the rules, follow the rules; *informal* play by the rules.

line[2] verb *they lined the handbags with a quilted rayon* PUT A LINING IN, interline, face, back, pad. PHRASE: **line one's pockets** *informal he had lined his pockets with campaign funds* MAKE MONEY, accept bribes, embezzle money; *informal* feather one's nest, graft, grift, be on the make.

lineage noun *tracing his paternal lineage* ANCESTRY, family, parentage, birth, descent, line, extraction, derivation, genealogy, roots, origin, background; stock, bloodline, breeding, pedigree.

linear adjective *linear motion* STRAIGHT, direct, undeviating, as straight as an arrow; sequential.

lineup noun 1 *a star-studded lineup* LIST OF PERFORMERS, cast, company, bill, program, schedule.

2 *the Oilers' lineup* LIST OF PLAYERS, roster, team, squad, side.

linger verb 1 *the crowd lingered for a long time* WAIT AROUND, stay, remain, wait, stay put; loiter, dawdle, dally, take one's time; *informal* stick around, hang around, hang on; *archaic* tarry. ANTONYM leave.

2 *the infection can linger for many years* PERSIST, continue, remain, stay, endure, carry on, last, keep on/up. ANTONYMS vanish, disappear.

lingerie noun *fine silk lingerie* WOMEN'S UNDERWEAR, underclothes, underclothing, undergarments, foundation garments; nightwear, nightclothes; *informal* undies, underthings. See also the table at UNDERWEAR.

lingering adjective 1 *lingering doubts* REMAINING, surviving, persisting, abiding, nagging, niggling.

2 *a slow, lingering death* PROTRACTED, prolonged, long-drawn-out, long-lasting.

lingo noun *informal he quickly picked up the musicians' lingo* LANGUAGE, tongue, dialect; jargon, terminology, slang, argot, cant, patter; *informal* -ese, -speak, mumbo-jumbo. See note at DIALECT.

link noun 1 *a chain of steel links* LOOP, ring, connection, connector, coupling, joint.

2 *the links between transport and the environment* CONNECTION, relationship, association, linkage, tie-up.

3 *their links with the labor movement* BOND, tie, attachment, connection, relationship, association, affiliation.

4 *he was an important link in our operation* COMPONENT, constituent, element, part, piece.

▸ verb 1 *four boxes were linked together* JOIN, connect, fasten, attach, bind, unite, combine, amalgamate; clamp, secure, fix, tie, couple, yoke, hitch.

2 *the evidence linking him with the murder* ASSOCIATE, connect, relate, join, bracket.

lionhearted adjective *the lionhearted champion of freedom* BRAVE, courageous, valiant, gallant, intrepid, valorous, fearless, bold, daring; stouthearted, stalwart, heroic, doughty, plucky, manly; *informal* gutsy, spunky, ballsy. ANTONYM cowardly.

lionize verb *popular myths have lionized a man who was in fact little more than a petty thief* CELEBRATE, fête, glorify, honor, exalt, acclaim, admire, praise, extol, applaud, hail, venerate, eulogize; *formal* laud. ANTONYM vilify.

lip noun 1 *the lip of the crater* EDGE, rim, brim, border, verge, brink.

2 *informal don't give me any lip!* INSOLENCE, impertinence, impudence, cheek, cheekiness, rudeness, audacity, effrontery, disrespect; *informal* mouth, back-talk, guff, sauce. PHRASES: **bite one's lip** *I wanted to say something about that hideous dress, but I bit my lip* KEEP QUIET, keep one's mouth shut, say nothing, bite one's tongue. **keep a stiff upper lip** *in my neighborhood, you learned early to keep a stiff upper lip when life ain't all sweetness and roses* KEEP CONTROL OF ONESELF, not show emotion, appear unaffected; *informal* keep one's cool.

liquefy verb *it was so warm in the kitchen that the brie started to liquefy* MAKE/BECOME LIQUID, condense; *Brit.* liquidize, melt; deliquesce. ANTONYM solidify.

liqueur noun. See table at LIQUOR.

liquid adjective 1 *liquid fuels* FLUID, liquefied; melted, molten, thawed, dissolved; *Chemistry* hydrous. ANTONYMS solid, gaseous.

2 *her liquid eyes* CLEAR, limpid, crystal clear, crystalline, pellucid, unclouded, bright. ANTONYMS cloudy, opaque.

3 *liquid sounds* PURE, clear, mellifluous, dulcet, mellow, sweet, sweet-sounding, soft, melodious, harmonious. ANTONYMS disharmonious, cacophonous.

4 *liquid assets* CONVERTIBLE, disposable, usable, spendable. ANTONYMS tied up, unavailable.

▸ noun *a vat of liquid* FLUID, moisture; liquor, solution, juice.

liquidate verb 1 *the company was liquidated* CLOSE DOWN, wind up, put into liquidation, dissolve, disband.

2 *he liquidated his share portfolio* CONVERT TO CASH, convert, cash in, sell off, sell up.

3 *liquidating the public debt* PAY OFF, pay, pay in full, settle, clear, discharge, square, honor.

4 *informal* *they were liquidated in bloody purges.* See KILL verb sense 1.

liquor noun **1** *he liked his liquor* ALCOHOL, spirits, drink, alcoholic drink, intoxicating liquor, intoxicant; *informal* grog, firewater, rotgut, the hard stuff, the bottle, hooch, moonshine; juice, the sauce. See table.

2 *strain the liquor into the sauce* STOCK, broth, bouillon, juice, liquid.

LIQUORS AND LIQUEURS

Whiskey	raki
bourbon	sake
Canadian	schnapps
whisky/whiskey	tequila
grain whiskey	vodka
Irish whiskey	
malt whiskey	**Liqueurs**
rye	absinthe
Scotch whisky/whiskey	advocaat
single malt	amaretto
sour mash	anisette
usquebaugh	Baileys™
	Benedictine™
Brandy	cassis
applejack	Campari™
Armagnac™	Chambord™
Calvados™	Chartreuse™
cherry brandy	Cointreau™
cognac	crème de cacao
Courvoisier™	crème de cassis
eau-de-vie	crème de menthe
grappa	curaçao
kirsch	Drambuie™
marc	Frangelico™
mirabelle	Galliano™
	Grand Marnier™
Gin	Irish Cream
Hollands	Kahlúa™
London gin	kümmel
sloe gin	Lillet™
	maraschino
Rum	Midori™
Bacardi™	ratafia
cachaca	pastis
demerara (rum)	Pernod™
tafia	Pimm's™
	Rémy Martin™
Other Spirits	sambuca
aquavit	Slivovitz™
arrack	Southern Comfort™
cachaça	Tia Maria™
ouzo	triple sec

See also tables at BEER, COCKTAIL, and WINE.

lissome adjective See LITHE.

list[1] noun *a list of the world's wealthiest people* CATALOG, inventory, record, register, roll, file, index, directory, listing, checklist, enumeration.

▸ verb *the accounts are listed alphabetically* RECORD, register, make a list of, enter; itemize, enumerate, catalog, file, log, categorize, inventory; classify, group, sort, rank, alphabetize, index.

list[2] verb *the boat listed to one side* LEAN, lean over, tilt, tip, heel, heel over, keel over, careen, cant, pitch, incline, slant, slope, bank.

listen verb **1** *are you listening?* HEAR, pay attention, be attentive, attend, concentrate; keep one's ears open, prick up one's ears; *informal* be all ears, lend an ear; *literary* hark; *archaic* hearken.

2 *policy-makers should* ***listen to*** *popular opinion* PAY ATTENTION TO, take heed of, heed, take notice of, take note of, mind, mark, bear in mind, take into consideration, take into account, tune in to. PHRASE: **listen in** *she handed him a note that said that the police were listening in* EAVESDROP, spy, overhear, tap, wiretap, bug, monitor.

listless adjective *this heat makes me listless | a listless performance* LETHARGIC, enervated, spiritless, lifeless, languid, languorous, inactive, inert, sluggish, torpid. ANTONYM energetic. See word spectrum at ENERGETIC.

litany noun **1** *reciting the litany* PRAYER, invocation, supplication, devotion; *archaic* orison.

2 *a litany of complaints* RECITAL, recitation, enumeration; list, listing, catalog, inventory.

literacy noun *testing for literacy* ABILITY TO READ AND WRITE, reading/writing proficiency; learning, book learning, education, scholarship, schooling.

literal adjective **1** *the literal sense of the word "dreadful"* STRICT, factual, plain, simple, exact, straightforward; unembellished, undistorted; objective, correct, true, accurate, genuine, authentic. ANTONYM figurative.

2 *a literal translation* WORD-FOR-WORD, verbatim, letter-for-letter; exact, precise, faithful, close, strict, accurate. ANTONYM loose.

literary adjective **1** *literary works* WRITTEN, poetic, artistic, dramatic.

2 *her literary friends* SCHOLARLY, learned, intellectual, cultured, erudite, bookish, highbrow, bluestocking, lettered, academic, cultivated; well-read, widely read, educated, well-educated.

3 *literary language* FORMAL, written, poetic, dramatic; elaborate, ornate, flowery; inkhorn.

literary device noun See table at RHETORICAL.

literate adjective **1** *many of the workers were not literate* ABLE TO READ/WRITE, educated, schooled. ANTONYM illiterate.

2 *her literate friends* EDUCATED, well-educated, well-read, widely read, scholarly, learned, knowledgeable, lettered, cultured, cultivated, sophisticated, well-informed. ANTONYM ignorant.

3 *he was computer literate* KNOWLEDGEABLE, well-versed, savvy, smart, conversant, competent; *informal* up on, up to speed on. ANTONYM ignorant.

WORD NOTE **literate**

"Not least, the prose is brisk, charming, and *literate.*" How often a writer intends this last adjective as a compliment, an accolade on the order of calling the style elegant and witty. But to praise an author's prose as *literate* is to offer faint praise at best. Sentences should always be literate—isn't that the rock-bottom desideratum of any writing? Moreover, the term is vague. Does it mean readable? That all the words in the sentences are properly spelled? Or is it a synonym for educated? Rather than resorting to this wan assertion of mere competence, as if the jowly novelist under review was still learning his letters from a hornbook, try to describe the actual style: *This is prose that works hard to be amiable, almost good-neighborly, one working stiff jawing with another under the backyard shade trees.* Better too much color and precision than the wearily ho-hum and lukewarm. —MD

---

literature noun 1 *English literature* WRITTEN WORKS, writings, writing, creative writing, literary texts, compositions.

2 *the literature on prototype theory* PUBLICATIONS, published writings, texts, reports, studies.

3 *election literature* PRINTED MATTER, brochures, leaflets, pamphlets, circulars, flyers, handouts, handbills, bulletins, fact sheets, publicity, propaganda, notices.

lithe adjective *lithe dancers* AGILE, graceful, supple, limber, lithesome, loose-limbed, nimble, deft, flexible, lissome, slender, slim, willowy. ANTONYM clumsy.

litigation noun *his attorneys advised him to avoid the litigation that Comstock was suggesting* LEGAL PROCEEDINGS, legal action, lawsuit, legal dispute, legal case, case, suit, prosecution, indictment.

litter noun 1 *never drop litter* GARBAGE, refuse, junk, waste, debris, scraps, leavings, fragments, detritus, trash, rubbish.

2 *the litter of papers around her* CLUTTER, jumble, muddle, mess, heap, disorder, untidiness, confusion, disarray; *informal* shambles.

3 *a litter of kittens* BROOD, family.

4 *she was carried on a litter* SEDAN CHAIR, palanquin; stretcher.

▸ verb 1 *clothes littered the floor* MAKE UNTIDY, mess up, make a mess of, clutter up, be strewn about, be scattered about; *informal* make a shambles of.

2 *a paper littered with quotes* FILL, pack, load, clutter.

little adjective 1 *a little writing desk* SMALL, small-scale, compact; mini, miniature, tiny, minute, minuscule; toy, baby, pocket, undersized, dwarf, midget, wee; *informal* teeny-weeny, teensy-weensy, itsy-bitsy, itty-bitty, little-bitty, half-pint, vest-pocket, li'l, micro. See note at SMALL. ANTONYMS big, large.

2 *a little man* SHORT, small, slight, petite, diminutive, tiny; elfin, dwarfish, midget, pygmy, Lilliputian; *informal* teeny-weeny, pint-sized, peewee. ANTONYMS big, large.

3 *my little sister* YOUNG, younger, junior, small, baby, infant. ANTONYMS big, elder.

4 *I was a bodyguard for a little while* BRIEF, short, short-lived; fleeting, momentary, transitory, transient; fast, quick, hasty, cursory. ANTONYM long.

5 *a few little problems* MINOR, unimportant, insignificant, trivial, trifling, petty, paltry, inconsequential, nugatory; *informal* dinky, piddling. ANTONYMS important, significant.

6 *they have little political influence* HARDLY ANY, not much, slight, scant, limited, restricted, modest, little or/to no, minimal, negligible. ANTONYM considerable.

7 *you little sneak* CONTEMPTIBLE, mean, spiteful, petty, small-minded.

▸ adverb 1 *he is little known as a singer | they little thought* HARDLY, barely, scarcely, not much, not at all, slightly, only slightly. ANTONYM well.

2 *his art has been little seen in Canada* RARELY, seldom, infrequently, hardly, hardly ever, scarcely, scarcely ever, not much. ANTONYM often.

PHRASES: **a little** 1 *add a little vinegar* SOME, a small amount of, a bit of, a touch of, a soupçon of, a dash of, a taste of, a spot of; a shade of, a suggestion of, a trace of, a hint of, a suspicion of; a dribble of, a splash of, a pinch of, a sprinkling of, a speck of; *informal* a smidgen of, a tad of. 2 *after a little, Oliver came in* A SHORT TIME, a little while, a bit, an interval, a short period; a minute, a moment, a second, an instant; *informal* a sec, a mo, a jiffy. 3 *this reminds me a little of the Adriatic* SLIGHTLY, faintly, remotely, vaguely; somewhat, a little bit, to some degree. **little by little** *little by little, the house fell into disrepair* GRADUALLY, slowly, by degrees, by stages, step by step, bit by bit, progressively; subtly, imperceptibly.

liturgy noun *the Anglican liturgy* RITUAL, worship, service, ceremony, rite, observance, celebration, sacrament; tradition, custom, practice, rubric; *formal* ordinance.

livable adjective 1 *renovations made the house livable* HABITABLE, inhabitable, fit to live in, in good repair; suitable, acceptable, passable; comfortable, cozy.

2 *life has become livable again* BEARABLE, endurable, tolerable, supportable, sufferable.

live[1] verb 1 *the greatest mathematician who ever lived* EXIST, be alive, be, have life; breathe, draw breath, walk the earth. ANTONYMS die, be dead.

2 *I **live in** Arkansas* RESIDE IN, have one's home in, have one's residence in, be settled in; be housed in, lodge in; inhabit, occupy, populate; *formal* dwell in, be domiciled in.

3 *they lived quietly* PASS/SPEND ONE'S LIFE, have a lifestyle; behave, conduct oneself; *formal* comport oneself.

4 *she had lived a difficult life* EXPERIENCE, spend, pass, lead, have, go through, undergo.

5 *Fred lived by his wits* SURVIVE, make a living, earn one's living, eke out a living; subsist, support oneself, sustain oneself, make ends meet, keep body and soul together.

6 *you should get out there and live* ENJOY ONESELF, enjoy life, have fun, live life to the full/fullest. PHRASES: **live it up** *informal they're living it up in Hawaii* LIVE EXTRAVAGANTLY, live in the lap of luxury, live in clover; carouse, revel, enjoy oneself, have a good time, go on a spree; *informal* party, paint the town red, have a ball, live high on/off the hog; *archaic* wassail. **live off/on** *the gulls live off discarded fish* SUBSIST ON, feed on/off, eat, consume.

live[2] adjective 1 *live bait* LIVING, alive, having life, breathing, animate, sentient. ANTONYMS dead, inanimate.

2 *a live performance* IN THE FLESH, personal, in person, not recorded. ANTONYM recorded.

3 *a live wire* ELECTRIFIED, charged, powered, active; *informal* hot. ANTONYM inactive.

4 *live coals* HOT, glowing, red hot, aglow; burning, alight, flaming, aflame, blazing, ignited, on fire; *literary* afire.

5 *a live grenade* UNEXPLODED, explosive, active; unstable, volatile. ANTONYM inactive.

PHRASE: **live wire** *informal that Goldie is a real live wire* ENERGETIC PERSON; *informal* fireball, human dynamo, powerhouse, life of the party.

livelihood noun *thousands of people relied on that one factory for their livelihood* INCOME, source of income, means of support, living, subsistence, keep, maintenance, sustenance, nourishment, daily bread; job, work, employment, occupation, vocation; *informal* bread and butter.

lively adjective 1 *a lively young woman* ENERGETIC, active, animated, dynamic, full of life, outgoing, spirited, high-spirited, vivacious, enthusiastic, vibrant, buoyant, exuberant, effervescent, cheerful; bouncy, bubbly, perky, sparkling, zestful; *informal* full of beans, chirpy, chipper, peppy. ANTONYMS listless, lifeless.

2 *a lively bar* BUSY, crowded, bustling, buzzing; vibrant, boisterous, jolly, festive; *informal* buzzy, hopping. ANTONYMS quiet, dead.

3 *a lively debate* HEATED, vigorous, animated, spirited, enthusiastic, forceful; exciting, interesting, memorable. ANTONYMS lifeless, dull.

4 *a lively portrait of the local community* VIVID, colorful, striking, graphic, bold, strong. ANTONYMS lifeless, dull.

liven PHRASES: **liven up** *we livened up when Edie arrived* BRIGHTEN UP, cheer up, perk up, revive, rally, pick up, bounce back; *informal* buck up. **liven someone/something up** *the new sofa livens up the whole room* BRIGHTEN UP, cheer up, enliven, animate, raise someone's spirits, perk up, spice up, make lively, wake up, invigorate, revive, refresh, vivify, galvanize, stimulate, stir up, get going; *informal* buck up, pep up.

livid adjective **1** *informal Mom was absolutely livid.* See FURIOUS sense 1.

2 *a livid bruise* PURPLISH, bluish, dark, discolored, purple, grayish-blue; bruised; angry, black and blue. See note at PALE[2].

living noun **1** *she cleaned floors for a living* LIVELIHOOD, (source of) income, means of support, subsistence, keep, maintenance, sustenance, nourishment, daily bread; job, work, employment, occupation, vocation; *informal* bread and butter.

2 *healthy living* WAY OF LIFE, lifestyle, way of living, life; conduct, behavior, activities, habits.

▸ adjective **1** *living organisms* ALIVE, live, having life, animate, sentient; breathing, existing, existent; *informal* alive and kicking. See note at ALIVE. ANTONYMS dead, extinct.

2 *a living language* CURRENT, contemporary, present; in use, active, surviving, extant, persisting, remaining, existing, in existence. ANTONYMS dead, extinct.

3 *a living hell* COMPLETE, total, utter, absolute, real, veritable, perfect, out-and-out, downright.

living room noun *there is no phone in the living room* SITTING ROOM, front room, family room, living area, great room, den, lounge.

lizard noun. See table at REPTILE.

load noun **1** *he has **a load** to deliver* CARGO, freight, a consignment, a delivery, a shipment, goods, merchandise; a pack, a bundle, a parcel; a truckload, a shipload, a boatload, a vanload.

2 *informal I bought **a load of** clothes* A LOT OF, a great deal of, a large amount/quantity of, an abundance of, a wealth of, a mountain of; many, plenty of; *informal* a heap of, a mass of, a pile of, a stack of, a ton of, lots of, heaps of, masses of, piles of, stacks of, tons of.

3 *a heavy teaching load* COMMITMENT, responsibility, duty, obligation, charge, burden; trouble, worry, strain, pressure.

▸ verb **1** *we quickly loaded the van* FILL, fill up, pack, charge, stock, stack, lade.

2 *Larry loaded boxes into the jeep* PACK, stow, store, stack, bundle; place, deposit, put away.

3 *loading the committee with responsibilities* BURDEN, weigh down, saddle, charge; overburden, overwhelm, encumber, tax, strain, trouble, worry.

4 *Richard loaded Marshal with honors* REWARD, ply, regale, shower.

5 *he loaded a gun* PRIME, charge, prepare to fire/use.

6 *load the cassette into the camcorder* INSERT, put, place, slot.

7 *the dice are loaded against him* BIAS, rig, fix; weight.

loaded adjective **1** *a loaded freight train* FULL, filled, laden, packed, stuffed, crammed, brimming, stacked; *informal* chock-full, chockablock.

2 *a loaded gun* PRIMED, charged, armed, ready to fire.

3 *informal they have no money worries; they're loaded.* See RICH sense 1.

4 *informal he came home from the party loaded.* See INTOXICATED.

5 *loaded dice* BIASED, rigged, fixed; juiced; weighted.

6 *a loaded question* CHARGED, sensitive, delicate.

loaf verb *he was just loafing all day at the beach* LAZE, lounge, loll, idle, waste time; *informal* hang around, bum around, futz around.

loafer noun *Sandler plays a loafer with six months to pass grades 1 through 12* IDLER, layabout, good-for-nothing, lounger, shirker, sluggard, laggard, slugabed; *informal* slacker, slob, lazybones, bum.

loan noun *a loan of $7,000* CREDIT, advance; mortgage, overdraft; lending, moneylending.

▸ verb **1** *he loaned me his car* LEND, advance, give credit; give on loan, lease, charter.

2 *the majority of exhibits have been loaned* BORROW, receive/take on loan.

WORD NOTE **loan**

If you use *loan* as a verb in anything other than ultra-informal speech, you're marking yourself as ignorant or careless. As of 2004, the verb *to lend* never comes off as fussy or pretentious, merely as correct. —**DFW**

loath adjective *they were loath to take risks* RELUCTANT, unwilling, disinclined, ill-disposed; averse, opposed, resistant. ANTONYM willing.

loathe verb *I loathe their so-called music* HATE, detest, abhor, execrate, have a strong aversion to, feel repugnance toward, not be able to bear/stand, be repelled by. See note at DESPISE. ANTONYM love.

loathing noun *the loathing she feels for Karyn is understandable* HATRED, hate, detestation, abhorrence, abomination, execration, odium; antipathy, dislike, hostility, animosity, ill feeling, bad feeling, malice, animus, enmity, aversion; repugnance.

loathsome adjective *his first wife was a loathsome creature* HATEFUL, detestable, abhorrent, repulsive, odious, repugnant, repellent, disgusting, revolting, sickening, abominable, despicable, contemptible, reprehensible, execrable, damnable; vile, horrible, hideous, nasty, obnoxious, gross, foul, horrid; *informal* yucky.

lob verb *they lobbed grenades onto the gun platform* THROW, toss, fling, pitch, hurl, pelt, sling, launch, propel; *informal* chuck, heave.

lobby noun **1** *the hotel lobby* ENTRANCE HALL, hallway, entrance, hall, vestibule, foyer, reception area.

2 *the antigun lobby* SPECIAL INTEREST GROUP, interest group, pressure group; movement, campaign, crusade; lobbyists, supporters; faction, camp.

▸ verb **1** *readers are urged to lobby their legislators* SEEK TO INFLUENCE, try to persuade, bring pressure to bear on, importune, sway; petition, solicit, appeal to, pressurize.

2 *a group **lobbying for** better rail services* CAMPAIGN FOR, crusade for, press for, push for, ask for, call for, demand; promote, advocate, champion.

local adjective **1** *local government* COMMUNITY, district, neighborhood, regional, city, town, municipal, county. ANTONYMS national, global.

2 *a local restaurant* NEIGHBORHOOD, nearby, near, at hand, close by; accessible, handy, convenient.

3 *a local infection* CONFINED, restricted, contained, localized. ANTONYMS general, widespread.

▸ noun *complaints from the locals* LOCAL PERSON, native, inhabitant, resident. ANTONYM outsider.

locale noun *the advantages of living in a rural locale* PLACE, site, spot, area; position, location, setting, scene, venue, background, backdrop, environment; neighborhood, district, region, locality.

localize verb *our efforts to localize the conflict* LIMIT, restrict, confine, contain, circumscribe, concentrate, delimit. ANTONYM generalize.

locate verb **1** *help me locate this photograph* FIND, discover, pinpoint, detect, track down, unearth, sniff out, smoke out, search out, ferret out, uncover.

2 *a company located near Pittsburgh* SITUATE, site, position, place, base; put, build, establish, found, station, install, settle.

location noun *we've found the perfect location for our family reunion* POSITION, place, situation, site, locality, locale, spot, whereabouts, point; scene, setting, area, environment; bearings, orientation; venue, address; *technical* locus.

lock noun *the lock on the door* BOLT, catch, fastener, clasp, bar, hasp, latch.

▸ verb **1** *he locked the door* BOLT, fasten, bar, secure, seal; padlock, latch, chain. ANTONYMS unlock, open.

2 *they locked arms* JOIN, interlock, intertwine, link, mesh, engage, unite, connect, yoke, mate; couple. ANTONYMS separate, divide.

3 *the wheels locked* BECOME STUCK, stick, jam, become/make immovable, become/make rigid.

4 *he locked her in an embrace* CLASP, grasp, embrace, hug, squeeze, clench.

PHRASES: **lock horns** *he's locked horns with every boss he's ever had* ARGUE, quarrel, fight, disagree, squabble, bicker. **lock lips** *informal I saw you locking lips with Quinn* KISS; *informal* smooch, peck, neck, canoodle, make out. **lock someone out of** *we were locked out of the conference* KEEP OUT OF, shut out of/from, refuse entrance to, deny admittance to; exclude from, bar from, debar from, ban from. **lock someone up** *take him away and lock him up* IMPRISON, jail, incarcerate, send to prison, put behind bars, put under lock and key, put in chains, clap in irons, cage, pen, coop up; *informal* put away, put inside.

lockup noun *Eileen spent the night in lockup | the lockup in this town is a historical landmark* JAIL, prison, cell, detention center, jailhouse, penitentiary; *informal* slammer, jug, can, brig, clink, big house, cooler, hoosegow, cage, pen, pokey.

locomotion noun *the lemur's amusingly agile locomotion* MOVEMENT, motion, moving; travel, traveling; mobility, motility; walking, running; progress, progression, passage; *formal* perambulation.

lodge noun **1** *a hunting lodge* HOUSE, cottage, cabin, chalet.

2 *we'll eat up at the lodge* MAIN HALL, main building, dining hall.

3 *a beaver's lodge* DEN, lair, hole, set; retreat, haunt, shelter.

4 *a Masonic lodge* HALL, clubhouse, meeting room.

5 *the porter's lodge* GATEHOUSE, cottage.

▸ verb **1** *William lodged at our house* RESIDE, board, stay, live, rent rooms, be put up, be quartered, room; *formal* dwell, be domiciled, sojourn; *archaic* abide.

2 *they were lodged at an inn* ACCOMMODATE, put up, take in, house, board, billet, quarter, shelter.

3 *we lodged a complaint* SUBMIT, register, enter, put forward, advance, lay, present, tender, proffer, put on record, record, file.

4 *the bullet lodged in his back* BECOME FIXED, embed itself, become embedded, become implanted, get/become stuck, stick, catch, become caught, wedge.

lodging noun *the lodging provided at the farm was charming* ACCOMMODATIONS, rooms, chambers, living quarters, place to stay, a roof over one's head, housing, shelter; *informal* digs, pad, nest; *formal* abode, residence, dwelling, dwelling place, habitation.

lofty adjective **1** *a lofty tower* TALL, high, giant, towering, soaring, skyscraping. ANTONYMS low, short.

2 *lofty ideals* NOBLE, exalted, high, high-minded, worthy, grand, fine, elevated, sublime. ANTONYMS base, lowly.

3 *lofty disdain* HAUGHTY, arrogant, disdainful, supercilious, condescending, scornful, patronizing, contemptuous, self-important, conceited, snobbish; aloof, standoffish; *informal* stuck-up, snooty, snotty, hoity-toity. ANTONYM modest.

log noun **1** *a fallen log* BRANCH, trunk; piece of wood; (**logs**) timber, firewood.

2 *a log of phone calls* RECORD, register, logbook, journal, diary, minutes, chronicle, daybook, record book, ledger, account, tally.

▸ verb **1** *all complaints are logged* REGISTER, record, make a note of, note down, write down, jot down, put in writing, enter, file.

2 *the pilot had logged 95 hours* ATTAIN, achieve, chalk up, make, do, go.

3 *he was injured while logging* CUT DOWN TREES, chop down trees, fell trees, clear cut, harvest trees.

PHRASE: **log in** *just go to our Web site and log in* SIGN IN, register, enter, log on.

logger noun *the logger takes a percentage of the proceeds from the mill* LUMBERJACK, lumberman, woodcutter, woodsman; *informal* jack, pulp cutter, chaser, faller, high rigger, skidder, handlogger, hooktender, bull of the woods; *historical* woodman.

loggerheads plural noun PHRASE: **at loggerheads** *the European Union and United States are at loggerheads over how to reduce greenhouse gases* IN DISAGREEMENT, at odds, at variance, wrangling, quarreling, disagreeing, disputing, locking horns, at daggers drawn, in conflict, fighting, at war; *informal* at each other's throats.

logic noun **1** *this case appears to defy all logic* REASON, judgment, logical thought, rationality, wisdom, sense, good sense, common sense, sanity; *informal* horse sense.

2 *the logic of their argument* REASONING, line of reasoning, rationale, argument, argumentation.

logical adjective **1** *information displayed in a logical fashion* REASONED, well-reasoned, reasonable, rational, left-brained, sound, cogent, well-thought-out, valid; coherent, clear, well-organized, systematic, orderly, methodical, analytical, consistent, objective. ANTONYMS illogical, irrational.

2 *the logical outcome* NATURAL, reasonable, sensible, understandable; predictable, unsurprising, only to be expected, most likely, likeliest, obvious. ANTONYMS unlikely, surprising.

logistics plural noun *the logistics of deploying forces in Afghanistan* ORGANIZATION, planning, plans, management, arrangement, administration, orchestration, coordination, execution, handling, running.

logjam noun *health-care reform is trapped in a merciless political logjam* DEADLOCK, stalemate, tie; impasse, bottleneck, barrier, block.

logo noun *a sweatshirt with the company logo* EMBLEM, trademark, brand, device, figure, symbol, design, sign, mark; insignia, crest, seal.

loiter verb **1** *he loitered at bus stops* LINGER, wait, skulk; loaf, lounge, idle, laze, waste time, lollygag; *informal* hang around; *archaic* tarry.

2 *they loitered along the river bank* DAWDLE, dally, stroll, amble, saunter, meander, drift, putter, take one's time; *informal* dilly-dally, mosey.

THE RIGHT WORD

Someone who hangs around downtown after the stores are closed and appears to be deliberately wasting time is said to **loiter**, a verb that connotes improper or sinister motives (*the police warned the boys not to loiter*). To **dawdle** is to pass time leisurely or to pursue something halfheartedly (*dawdle in a stationery shop; dawdle over a sinkful of dishes*). Someone who **dallies** dawdles in a particularly pleasurable and relaxed way, with connotations of amorous activity (*he dallied with his girlfriend when he should have been delivering papers*). **Idle** suggests that the person makes a habit of avoiding work or activity (*idle away the hours of a hot summer day*), while **lag** suggests falling behind or failing to maintain a desirable rate of progress (*she lagged several yards behind her classmates as they walked to the museum*).

loll verb **1** *he lolled in an armchair* LOUNGE, sprawl, drape oneself, stretch oneself; slouch, slump; laze, luxuriate, put one's feet up, lean back, sit back, recline, relax, take it easy, take a load off.

2 *her head lolled to one side* HANG DOWN, hang loosely, hang, droop, dangle, sag, drop, flop.

lollygag verb See LOITER sense 1.

lone adjective *a lone police officer* SOLITARY, single, solo, unaccompanied, unescorted, alone, by oneself/itself, sole, companionless; detached, isolated.

WORD NOTE **lone**

If you want to use *lone* in the poetic sense of "lonely, unfrequented, uninhabited," realize that this use will recall for many readers the last line of Shelley's "Ozymandias": "The lone and level sands stretch far away." If you don't want to evoke this poem, you might want to use another word, such as *desolate* or *unpeopled.* **—EM**

lonely adjective **1** *I felt very lonely* ISOLATED, alone, lonesome, friendless, with no one to turn to, forsaken, abandoned, rejected, unloved, unwanted, outcast; gloomy, sad, depressed, desolate, forlorn, cheerless, down, blue. ANTONYM popular.

2 *the lonely life of a writer* SOLITARY, unaccompanied, lone, by oneself/itself, companionless. ANTONYM sociable.

3 *a lonely road* DESERTED, uninhabited, unfrequented, unpopulated, desolate, isolated, remote, out of the way, secluded, off the beaten track/path, in the back of beyond, godforsaken; *informal* in the middle of nowhere. ANTONYMS populous, crowded.

loner noun *a loner from parts unknown* RECLUSE, introvert, lone wolf, hermit, solitary, misanthrope, outsider; *historical* anchorite.

long[1] adjective *a long silence* LENGTHY, extended, prolonged, extensive, protracted, long-lasting, long-drawn-out, drawn-out, spun out, dragged out, seemingly endless, lingering, interminable. ANTONYMS short, brief.

PHRASE: **before long** *we'll be in Kentucky before long* SOON, shortly, presently, in the near future, in a little while, by and by, in a minute, in a moment, in a second; *informal* anon, in a jiffy; *dated* directly; *literary* ere long.

long[2] verb *I **longed for** a vacation* YEARN FOR, pine for, ache for, hanker for/after, hunger for, thirst for, itch for, be eager for, be desperate for; crave, dream of, set one's heart on; *informal* have a yen for, be dying for.

longevity noun *the longevity of this potted rubber tree is phenomenal* LENGTH OF LIFE, life span, lifetime, shelf life; durability, endurance, resilience, strength, robustness.

longing noun *a longing for the countryside* YEARNING, pining, craving, ache, burning, hunger, thirst, hankering; *informal* yen, itch.

▸ adjective *a longing look* YEARNING, pining, craving, hungry, thirsty, hankering, wistful, covetous.

long-lasting adjective *our long-lasting friendship* ENDURING, lasting, abiding, long-lived, long-running, long-established, long-standing, lifelong, deep-rooted, time-honored, traditional, permanent. ANTONYMS short-lived, ephemeral.

long shot noun **1** *it's a long shot, but you could win big* GAMBLE, venture, speculation, risk, chance, outside chance.

2 *he was the long shot in the sprint* UNDERDOG, dark horse, weaker one, little guy, David. PHRASE: **not by a long shot** See NOT BY A LONG SHOT at SHOT[1] .

long-standing adjective *a long-standing business partnership* WELL-ESTABLISHED, long-established; time-honored, traditional, age-old; abiding, enduring, long-lived, surviving, persistent, prevailing, perennial, deep-rooted, long-term, confirmed. ANTONYMS new, recent.

long-suffering adjective *her long-suffering parents* PATIENT, forbearing, tolerant, uncomplaining, stoic, stoical, resigned; easygoing, indulgent, charitable, accommodating, forgiving, understanding. ANTONYMS impatient, complaining.

long-winded adjective *long-winded speeches* VERBOSE, wordy, lengthy, long, overlong, prolix, prolonged, protracted, long-drawn-out, interminable; discursive, diffuse, rambling, tortuous, meandering, repetitious, maundering; *informal* windy. ANTONYMS concise, succinct, laconic.

look verb **1** *Mrs. Wright* ***looked at*** *him* GLANCE AT, gaze at, stare at, gape at, peer at; peep at, peek, take a look at; watch, observe, view, regard, examine, inspect, eye, scan, scrutinize, survey, study, contemplate, consider, take in, ogle; *informal* take a gander at, rubberneck, goggle, give someone/something a/the once-over, get a load of, eyeball; *literary* behold. ANTONYM ignore.

2 *her room* ***looked out on*** *Broadway* COMMAND A VIEW OF, face, overlook, front.

3 *they looked shocked* SEEM, seem to be, appear, appear to be, have the appearance/air of being, give the impression of being, give every appearance/indication of being, strike someone as being.

▸ noun **1** *here's the latest analysis—let's give it a look* GLANCE, view, examination, study, inspection, observation, scan, survey, peep, peek, glimpse, gaze, stare; *informal* eyeful, gander, look-see, once-over, squint.

2 *the look on her face* EXPRESSION, mien.

3 *that rustic look* APPEARANCE, air, aspect, bearing, cast, manner, mien, demeanor, facade, impression, effect.

4 *this year's look* FASHION, style, vogue, mode.

PHRASES: **look after** *Janie looks after our goats and llamas* TAKE CARE OF, care for, attend to, minister to, tend, mind, keep an eye on, keep safe, be responsible for, protect; nurse, babysit, house-sit. **look back on** *those songs really make me look back on my college days* REFLECT ON, think back to, remember, recall, reminisce about, harken back to. **look down on** *we never understood why Papa looked down on the Italian families in our building* DISDAIN, scorn, regard with contempt, look down one's nose at, sneer at, despise. **look for** *he's looking for a book about begonias* SEARCH FOR, hunt for, try to find, seek, try to track down, forage for, scout out, quest for/after. **look forward to** *I look forward to Rebecca's call* AWAIT WITH PLEASURE, eagerly anticipate, lick one's lips over, be unable to wait for, count the days until. **look into** *they promised to look into our complaints* INVESTIGATE, inquire into, ask questions about, go into, probe, explore, follow up, research, study, examine; *informal* check out, give something a/the once-over, scope out. **look like** *in his overcoat he looks like an undertaker* RESEMBLE, bear a resemblance to, look similar to, take after, have the look of, have the appearance of, remind one of, make one think of; *informal* be the spitting image of, be a dead ringer for. **look on/upon** *people he looked on as friends took advantage of him* REGARD, consider, think of, deem, judge, see, view, count, reckon. **look out** *you'll get burned if you don't look out* BEWARE, watch out, be on (one's) guard, be alert, be wary, be vigilant, be careful, take care, be cautious, pay attention, take heed, keep one's eyes open/peeled, keep an eye out; watch your step. **look something over** *he looked over the engineer's reports* INSPECT, examine, scan, cast an eye over, take stock of, vet, view, look through, peruse, read through, check out; *informal* give something a/the once-over, eyeball. **look to 1** *we must look to the future* CONSIDER, think about, turn one's thoughts to, focus on, take heed of, pay attention to, attend to, address, mind, heed. **2** *they look to the government for help* TURN TO, resort to, have recourse to, fall back on, rely on. **look up 1** *things are looking up* IMPROVE, get better, pick up, come along/on, progress, make progress, make headway, perk up, rally, take a turn for the better. **2** *she looked up his number* SEARCH FOR, look for, try to find. **look someone up** *informal I'll look you up next time I'm in Tacoma* GO TO VISIT, pay a visit to, call on, go to see, look in on, visit with, go see; *informal* drop in on, drop by, pop by. **look up to** *some of the more self-centered ballplayers resent the responsibility of having thousands of kids look up to them* ADMIRE, have a high opinion of, think highly of, hold in high regard, regard highly, rate highly, respect, esteem, value, venerate.

look-alike noun *a contest to see who is the most convincing Alfred E. Neuman look-alike* DOUBLE, twin, clone, duplicate, exact likeness, replica, copy, facsimile, doppelgänger; *informal* spitting image, dead ringer.

lookout noun **1** *he saw the smoke from the lookout* OBSERVATION POST, lookout point, lookout station, lookout tower, watchtower.

2 *a scenic lookout* VIEW, vista, prospect, panorama, scene, aspect, outlook.

3 *he agreed to act as lookout* WATCHMAN, watch, guard, sentry, sentinel. PHRASE: **be on the lookout/keep a lookout** *be on the lookout for enemy aircraft* KEEP WATCH, keep an eye out, keep one's eyes peeled, keep a vigil, be alert, be vigilant, be on the qui vive.

loom verb **1** *ghostly shapes loomed out of the fog* EMERGE, appear, come into view, take shape, materialize, reveal itself.

2 *the church loomed above him* SOAR, tower, rise, rear up; overhang, overshadow, dominate.

3 *without reforms, disaster looms* BE IMMINENT, be on the horizon, impend, threaten, brew, be just around the corner, be in the air/wind. PHRASE: **loom large** *the impending cutbacks loom large* DOMINATE, be important, be significant, be of consequence; count, matter.

loon[1] noun *informal are you some kind of a loon, mowing your lawn at two o'clock in the morning?* FOOL, idiot, ass, halfwit, dunce, dolt, ignoramus, moron, imbecile, simpleton; lunatic; *informal* dope, ninny, nincompoop, dimwit, jackass, blockhead, jughead, bonehead, knucklehead, fathead, numbskull, dumb-ass, dunderhead, ditz, dipstick, thickhead, meathead, meatball, woodenhead, airhead, pinhead, lamebrain, peabrain, birdbrain, jerk, nitwit, twit, boob, loony, nut, nutcase, fruitcake, crank, crackpot, screwball, crazy, kook, wacko, dingbat.

loon[2] noun *the first time I heard the bizarre wail of a loon, I just about jumped out of my skin.* See table at WATERFOWL.

loony adjective *informal at first we thought Hoskins was a bit amusing, but now we think he's plum loony.* See CRAZY sense 1.

loop noun *a loop of rope* COIL, hoop, ring, circle, noose, oval, spiral, curl, bend, curve, arc, twirl, whorl, twist, hook, helix, convolution.

▸ verb 1 *Dave looped rope around their hands* COIL, wind, twist, snake, wreathe, spiral, curve, bend, turn.

2 *he looped the cables together* FASTEN, tie, join, connect, knot, bind.

loophole noun *a loophole in the regulations* MEANS OF EVASION, means of avoidance; window, gap, opening.

loose adjective 1 *a loose floorboard* NOT FIXED IN PLACE, not secure, unsecured, unattached; detached, unfastened, untied; wobbly, unsteady, movable. ANTONYMS secure, tight.

2 *she wore her hair loose* UNTIED, unpinned, unbound, hanging free, down, flowing.

3 *there's a wolf loose* FREE, at large, at liberty, on the loose, escaped; unconfined, untied, unchained, untethered, stray. ANTONYM secure.

4 *a loose interpretation* VAGUE, indefinite, inexact, imprecise, approximate; broad, general, rough; liberal; *informal* ballpark. ANTONYMS literal, narrow.

5 *a loose jacket* BAGGY, generously cut, slack, roomy; oversized, shapeless, sagging, saggy, sloppy. ANTONYMS tight, form-fitting.

6 *dated a loose woman* PROMISCUOUS, of easy virtue, fast, wanton, unchaste, immoral; licentious, dissolute; *dated* fallen. ANTONYM chaste.

7 *loose talk* INDISCREET, unguarded, free, gossipy, gossiping. ANTONYMS discreet, guarded.

▸ verb 1 *loose the dogs* FREE, set free, unloose, turn loose, set loose, let loose, let go, release; untie, unchain, unfasten, unleash. ANTONYM confine.

2 *the fingers loosed their hold* RELAX, slacken, loosen; weaken, lessen, reduce, diminish, moderate. ANTONYM tighten.

PHRASES: **at loose ends** *ever since the factory closed, Don has been at loose ends* WITH NOTHING TO DO, unoccupied, unemployed, at leisure, idle, adrift, with time to kill; bored, twiddling one's thumbs, hanging/kicking around. **on the loose** *an inmate from Wickham Hall is on the loose* FREE, at liberty, at large, escaped; on the run, fugitive, wanted; *informal* on the lam.

loose-limbed adjective *loose-limbed gymnasts* SUPPLE, limber, lithe, lissome, willowy; agile, nimble, flexible.

loosen verb 1 *loosen the clothesline | you simply loosen two screws* MAKE SLACK, slacken, unstick; UNFASTEN, detach, release, disconnect, undo, unclasp, unlatch, unbolt. ANTONYM tighten.

2 *her fingers loosened* BECOME SLACK, slacken, become loose, let go, ease; work loose, work free. ANTONYM tighten.

3 *Philip loosened his grip* WEAKEN, relax, slacken, loose, lessen, reduce, moderate, diminish. ANTONYM tighten.

PHRASE: **loosen up** *you need to loosen up* RELAX, unwind, ease up, calm down; *informal* lighten up, go easy, chill out, kick back.

loot noun *a bag full of loot* BOOTY, spoils, plunder, stolen goods, contraband, pillage; *informal* swag, hot goods, ill-gotten gains, take.

▸ verb *troops looted the cathedral* PLUNDER, pillage, despoil, ransack, sack, raid, rifle, rob, burgle, burglarize.

lop verb *they've* ***lopped off*** *the dead branches* CUT (OFF), chop off, hack off, saw off, hew (off), ax; prune, sever, clip, trim, snip (off), dock, crop.

lopsided adjective *my gingerbread house is lopsided* CROOKED, askew, awry, off-center, uneven, out of line, asymmetrical, tilted, at an angle, aslant, slanting; off-balance, off-kilter; *informal* cockeyed. ANTONYMS even, level, balanced.

loquacious adjective *a loquacious little boy* TALKATIVE, voluble, communicative, expansive, garrulous, unreserved, chatty, gossipy, gossiping; *informal* having the gift of gab, gabby, gassy, motormouthed, talky, windy. See note at TALKATIVE. ANTONYMS reticent, taciturn.

lord noun 1 *the lord of the manor* MASTER, ruler, leader, chief, superior, monarch, sovereign, king, emperor, prince, governor, commander, suzerain, liege, liege lord. ANTONYMS servant, inferior.

2 *let us pray to* ***the Lord*** GOD, the Father, the Almighty, the Creator; Jehovah, Adonai, Yahweh, Elohim, Allah; Jesus Christ, the Messiah, the Savior, the Son of God, the Redeemer, the Lamb of God, the Prince of Peace, the King of Kings; *informal* the Man Upstairs.

3 *a press lord* MAGNATE, tycoon, mogul, captain, baron, king; industrialist, proprietor; *informal* big shot, (head) honcho; *derogatory* fat cat. PHRASE: **lord it over someone** *in our schooldays, you used to lord it over us* ORDER ABOUT/AROUND, dictate to, domineer, ride roughshod over, pull rank on, tyrannize, have under one's thumb; *informal* boss around, walk all over, push around; throw one's weight around.

lore noun 1 *Arthurian lore* MYTHOLOGY, myths, legends, stories, traditions, folklore, fables, oral tradition, mythos.

2 *baseball lore* KNOWLEDGE, learning, wisdom; *informal* know-how.

lose verb 1 *I've lost my watch* MISLAY, misplace, be unable to find, lose track of, leave (behind), fail to keep/retain, fail to keep sight of. ANTONYM find.

2 *he's lost a lot of blood* BE DEPRIVED OF, suffer the loss of; no longer have. ANTONYMS keep, regain.

3 *he lost his pursuers* ESCAPE FROM, evade, elude, dodge, avoid, give someone the slip, shake off, throw off, throw off the scent; leave behind, outdistance, outstrip, outrun.

4 *they lost their way* STRAY FROM, wander from, depart from, go astray from, fail to keep to.

5 *you've lost your chance* MISS, waste, squander, fail to grasp, fail to take advantage of, let pass, neglect, forfeit; *informal* pass up, lose out on. ANTONYM seize.

6 *they always lose at lacrosse* BE DEFEATED, be beaten, suffer defeat, be the loser, be conquered, be vanquished, be trounced; *informal* go down, take a licking, be bested. ANTONYM win.

7 *you can lose the phony accent* DISCARD, get rid of, dispose of, dump, jettison, throw out, drop. PHRASES: **lose out** *if we don't act soon, we'll lose out* BE DEPRIVED OF AN OPPORTUNITY, fail to benefit, be disadvantaged, be the loser. **lose out on** *the town has lost out on a tourist opportunity* BE UNABLE TO TAKE ADVANTAGE OF, fail to benefit from; *informal* miss out on.

loser noun **1** *the loser still gets the silver medal* DEFEATED PERSON, also-ran, runner-up. ANTONYM winner.

2 *informal he's a complete loser* FAILURE, underachiever, ne'er-do-well, write-off, has-been; MISFIT, freak, unpopular person; *informal* geek, dweeb, nerd, hoser; flop, no-hoper, washout, lemon. ANTONYM success.

loss noun **1** *the loss of the documents* MISLAYING, misplacement, forgetting. ANTONYMS recovery, finding.

2 *loss of earnings* DEPRIVATION, disappearance, privation, forfeiture, diminution, erosion, reduction, depletion.

3 *the loss of her husband* DEATH, dying, demise, passing (away/on), end; *formal* decease; *archaic* expiry.

4 **(losses)** *Canadian losses in the war* CASUALTIES, fatalities, victims; dead; missing; death toll, number killed/dead.

5 *a loss of $15,000* DEFICIT, debit, debt, indebtedness, deficiency. ANTONYMS gain, profit.

PHRASE: **at a loss** *I'm at a loss about what just happened* BAFFLED, nonplussed, mystified, puzzled, perplexed, bewildered, bemused, at sixes and sevens, confused, dumbfounded, stumped, stuck, blank; *informal* clueless, flummoxed, bamboozled, fazed, floored, beaten, discombobulated.

lost adjective **1** *her lost keys* MISSING, mislaid, misplaced, vanished, disappeared, gone missing, gone astray, forgotten, nowhere to be found; absent, not present, strayed; irretrievable, unrecoverable.

2 *I think we're lost* OFF COURSE, off track, disorientated, having lost one's bearings, going around in circles, adrift, at sea, astray.

3 *a lost opportunity* MISSED, forfeited, neglected, wasted, squandered, gone by the boards; *informal* down the drain.

4 *lost traditions* BYGONE, past, former, one-time, previous, old, olden, departed, vanished, forgotten, consigned to oblivion, extinct, dead, gone.

5 *lost species and habitats* EXTINCT, died out, defunct, vanished, gone; DESTROYED, wiped out, ruined, wrecked, exterminated, eradicated.

6 *a lost cause* HOPELESS, beyond hope, futile, forlorn, failed, beyond remedy, beyond recovery.

7 *lost souls* DAMNED, fallen, irredeemable, irreclaimable, irretrievable, past hope, past praying for, condemned, cursed, doomed; *literary* accursed. ANTONYM saved.

8 *lost in thought* ENGROSSED, absorbed, rapt, immersed, deep, intent, engaged, wrapped up.

lot pronoun ***lots** of friends* | ***a lot** of money* A LARGE AMOUNT, a fair amount, a good/great deal, a great quantity, quantities, an abundance, a wealth, a profusion, plenty, a mass; a large number, a considerable number, scores; *informal* hundreds, thousands, millions, billions, gazillions, loads, masses, heaps, a pile, a stack, piles, oodles, stacks, scads, reams, wads, pots, oceans, a mountain, mountains, miles, tons, zillions, gobs, a bunch; **(lots of/a lot of)** many, a great many, numerous, more —— than one can shake a stick at. ANTONYMS a little, not much, a few, not many.

▸ noun **1** *the books were auctioned in lots* ITEM, article; batch, set, collection, group, bundle, quantity, assortment, parcel.

2 *his lot in life* FATE, destiny, fortune, doom; situation, circumstances, state, condition, position, plight, predicament.

3 *playing ball in a vacant lot* PATCH OF GROUND, piece of ground, plot, area, tract, parcel, plat.

▸ adverb *I work in pastels **a lot*** A GREAT DEAL, a good deal, to a great extent, much; often, frequently, regularly. ANTONYM a little.

PHRASES: **draw/cast lots** *we drew lots to see who gets to drive* toss/flip a coin, draw straws, throw/roll (the) dice. **throw in one's lot with** *he threw in his lot with the conspirators* JOIN FORCES WITH, join up with, form an alliance with, ally with, align oneself with, link up with, make common cause with.

lotion noun *scented hand lotion* OINTMENT, cream, salve, balm, rub, emollient, moisturizer, lubricant, gel, unguent, liniment, embrocation.

lottery noun **1** *play the lottery* RAFFLE, drawing, prize drawing, sweepstake(s), lotto.

2 *life is a lottery* GAMBLE, speculation, venture, risk, game of chance, matter of luck; *informal* crapshoot.

loud adjective **1** *loud music* NOISY, blaring, booming, deafening, roaring, thunderous, thundering, ear-splitting, ear-piercing, piercing; carrying, clearly audible; lusty, powerful, forceful, stentorian; *Music* forte, fortissimo. ANTONYMS quiet, soft.

2 *loud complaints* VOCIFEROUS, clamorous, insistent, vehement, emphatic, urgent. ANTONYM gentle.

3 *a loud T-shirt* GARISH, gaudy, flamboyant, lurid, glaring, showy, ostentatious; vulgar, tasteless; *informal* flash, flashy, kitsch, kitschy, tacky. ANTONYMS sober, tasteful.

loudmouth noun *informal coworkers characterize him as an egocentric loudmouth* BRAGGART, boaster, bragger, blusterer, swaggerer; *informal* blabbermouth, big mouth, blowhard, show-off.

loudspeaker noun *a message came over the loudspeaker* PUBLIC ADDRESS SYSTEM, PA (system), intercom; SPEAKER, monitor, woofer, tweeter; megaphone; *informal* squawk box.

lounge verb *he just lounges in his room* LAZE, lie, loll, lie back, lean back, recline, stretch oneself, drape oneself, relax, rest, repose, take it easy, put one's feet up, unwind, luxuriate; sprawl, slump, slouch, flop; loaf, idle, do nothing; *informal* take a load off, kick back.

▸ noun **1** *a hotel lounge* BAR, pub, club, barroom, taproom.

2 *an airport lounge* WAITING AREA, reception room.

3 *she sat in the lounge* LIVING ROOM, sitting room, front room, salon, family room; *dated* parlor, drawing room.

lousy *informal* adjective **1** *a lousy film.* See AWFUL sense 2.

2 *the lousy, double-crossing snake!* See DESPICABLE.

3 *I felt lousy.* See ILL adjective sense 1. PHRASE: **be lousy with** *the restaurant was lousy with screaming little brats.* See CRAWL sense 3.

lout noun *drunken louts* RUFFIAN, hooligan, thug, boor, barbarian, oaf, hoodlum, rowdy, lubber; *informal* tough, roughneck, bruiser, yahoo, lug. ANTONYM gentleman.

lovable adjective *lovable baby gorillas* ADORABLE, dear, sweet, cute, charming, darling, lovely, likable, delightful, captivating, enchanting, engaging, bewitching, pleasing, appealing, winsome, winning, fetching, endearing. ANTONYMS hateful, loathsome.

love noun 1 *his friendship with Helen grew into love* DEEP AFFECTION, fondness, tenderness, warmth, intimacy, attachment, endearment; devotion, adoration, doting, idolization, worship; passion, ardor, desire, lust, yearning, infatuation, besottedness. ANTONYM hatred.

2 *her **love for** fashion | a **love of** good food* LIKING OF/FOR, enjoyment of, appreciation of/for, taste for, delight for/in, relish of, passion for, zeal for, appetite for, zest for, enthusiasm for, keenness for, fondness for, soft spot for, weakness for, bent for, proclivity for, inclination for, disposition for, partiality for, predilection for, penchant for.

3 *their love for their fellow human beings* COMPASSION, care, caring, regard, solicitude, concern, friendliness, friendship, kindness, charity, goodwill, sympathy, kindliness, altruism, unselfishness, philanthropy, benevolence, fellow feeling, humanity.

4 *he was her one true love* BELOVED, loved one, love of one's life, dear, dearest, dear one, darling, sweetheart, sweet, angel, honey; lover, inamorato, inamorata, amour; *archaic* paramour.

5 *their love will survive* RELATIONSHIP, love affair, romance, liaison, affair of the heart, amour.

6 *my mother sends her love* BEST WISHES, regards, good wishes, greetings, kind/kindest regards.

▸ verb 1 *she loves him* CARE VERY MUCH FOR, feel deep affection for, hold very dear, adore, think the world of, be devoted to, dote on, idolize, worship; be in love with, be infatuated with, be smitten with, be besotted with; *informal* be mad/crazy/nuts/wild about, have a crush on, carry a torch for. ANTONYM hate.

2 *Laura loved painting* LIKE VERY MUCH, delight in, enjoy greatly, have a passion for, take great pleasure in, derive great pleasure from, relish, savor; have a weakness for, be partial to, have a soft spot for, have a taste for, be taken with; *informal* get a kick out of, have a thing about, be mad/crazy/nuts/wild about, be hooked on, get off on. ANTONYM hate.

PHRASES: **fall in love with** *she didn't mean to fall in love with him* BECOME INFATUATED WITH, give/lose one's heart to; *informal* fall for, be bowled over by, be swept off one's feet by, develop a crush on. **in love with** *he's in love with Gillian* INFATUATED WITH, besotted with, enamored of, smitten with, consumed with desire for; captivated by, bewitched by, enthralled by, entranced by, moonstruck by; devoted to, doting on; *informal* mad/crazy/nuts/wild about.

WORD NOTE **love**

The rhymes with *love* are limited to *above, dove, glove, of,* and *shove. Romance* is much better; at least it rhymes with *dance.*

The skies above
Contain a dove
Wearing the glove I'm dreaming of;
To rhyme with *love,*
Words you must shove.

So don't burden us with any more strained rhymes; either use the word in the middle of a line *(I love you)* or use a different word. This is why we have a thesaurus. See also note at ROMANCE. **—SM**

love affair noun 1 *he had a love affair with a teacher* RELATIONSHIP, affair, romance, liaison, affair of the heart, affaire de cœur, intrigue, fling, amour, involvement, romantic entanglement; flirtation, dalliance.

2 *informal a **love affair with** sports* ENTHUSIASM FOR, mania for, devotion for, passion for.

loveless adjective *a loveless marriage* PASSIONLESS, unloving, unfeeling, heartless, cold, icy, frigid, undersexed. ANTONYMS loving, passionate.

lovelorn adjective *my lovelorn son thinks the world has come to an end* LOVESICK; pining, languishing; spurned, jilted, rejected, forsaken.

lovely adjective 1 *a lovely young woman* BEAUTIFUL, pretty, attractive, good-looking, appealing, handsome, adorable, exquisite, sweet, personable, charming; enchanting, engaging, winsome, seductive, sexy, gorgeous, alluring, ravishing, glamorous; *informal* tasty, knockout, stunning, drop-dead gorgeous; killer, cute, foxy, hot; *formal* beauteous; *archaic* comely, fair. ANTONYMS ugly, hideous.

2 *a lovely view* SCENIC, picturesque, pleasing, easy on the eye; magnificent, stunning, splendid.

3 *informal we had a lovely day* DELIGHTFUL, very pleasant, very nice, very agreeable, marvelous, wonderful, sublime, superb, magical; *informal* terrific, fabulous, heavenly, divine, amazing, glorious. ANTONYM horrible.

lover noun 1 *she had a secret lover* BOYFRIEND, GIRLFRIEND, beloved, love, darling, sweetheart, inamorata, inamorato; mistress; partner, significant other, main squeeze; *informal* bit on the side, toy boy, boy toy; *dated* ladylove, beau; *archaic* swain, concubine, paramour.

2 *a dog lover* DEVOTEE, admirer, fan, enthusiast, aficionado; *informal* buff, freak, nut, junkie.

WORD NOTE **lover**

Despite centuries of precedent, *lover* does not rhyme with *another.* In our stupid language the only rhymable word for *lover* that you can really use much is *beau,* so let's all use it in speech every day till it sounds less dated. Remember: *beau.* **—SM**

lovesick adjective *mooning around like a lovesick teenager* LOVELORN, pining, languishing, longing, yearning, infatuated; frustrated.

loving adjective *her loving husband* AFFECTIONATE, fond, devoted, adoring, doting, solicitous, demonstrative; caring, tender, warm, warmhearted, close; amorous, ardent, passionate, amatory. ANTONYMS cold, cruel.

low adjective 1 *a low fence* SHORT, small, little; squat, stubby, stunted, dwarf; shallow. ANTONYM high.

2 *low prices* CHEAP, economical, moderate, reasonable, modest, bargain, budget, bargain-basement, rock-bottom, cut-rate. ANTONYMS high, expensive.

3 *supplies were low* SCARCE, scanty, scant, skimpy, meager, sparse, few, little, paltry; reduced, depleted, diminished. ANTONYMS plentiful, abundant.

4 *low quality* INFERIOR, substandard, poor, bad, low-grade, low-end, below par, second-rate, unsatisfactory, deficient, defective, shoddy. ANTONYMS high, superior.

5 *of low birth* HUMBLE, lowly, low-ranking, plebeian, proletarian, peasant, poor; common, ordinary. ANTONYMS superior, noble.

6 *low expectations* UNAMBITIOUS, unaspiring, modest. ANTONYMS high, ambitious.

7 *a low opinion* UNFAVORABLE, poor, bad, adverse, negative. ANTONYMS high, favorable, good.

8 *a low blow.* See LOWDOWN adjective.

9 *low humor* UNCOUTH, uncultured, unsophisticated, rough, rough-hewn, unrefined, tasteless, crass, common, vulgar, coarse, crude. ANTONYMS high, exalted.

10 *a low voice* QUIET, soft, faint, gentle, muted, subdued, muffled, hushed, quieted, whispered, stifled. ANTONYM loud.

11 *a low note* BASS, baritone, low-pitched, deep, rumbling, booming, sonorous.

12 *she was feeling low* DEPRESSED, dejected, despondent, downhearted, downcast, low-spirited, down, morose, miserable, dismal, heavy-hearted, mournful, forlorn, woebegone, gloomy, glum, crestfallen, dispirited; without energy, enervated, flat, sapped, weary; *informal* down in/at the mouth, down in the dumps, blue. ANTONYM cheerful.

▸ noun *the dollar fell to an all-time low* NADIR, low point, lowest point, lowest level, minimum, depth, rock bottom. ANTONYMS high, zenith.

lowbrow adjective *a lowbrow action movie* MASS-MARKET, tabloid, popular, intellectually undemanding, lightweight, accessible, unpretentious; uncultured, unsophisticated, trashy, philistine, simplistic, downmarket; *informal* dumbed-down. ANTONYMS highbrow, intellectual.

lowdown *informal* adjective *a lowdown trick* UNFAIR, mean, despicable, reprehensible, contemptible, lamentable, disgusting, shameful, low, cheap, underhanded, foul, unworthy, shabby, base, dishonorable, unprincipled, sordid; *informal* rotten, dirty; beastly; *dated* dastardly. ANTONYMS kind, honorable.

▸ noun *he gave us the lowdown* FACTS, information, story, intelligence, news, inside story; *informal* info, rundown, score, scoop, word, dope, dirt, poop, skinny.

lower adjective 1 *the lower house of Parliament* SUBORDINATE, inferior, lesser, junior, minor, secondary, lower-level, subsidiary, subservient. ANTONYMS upper, senior.

2 *her lower lip* BOTTOM, bottommost, nether, under; underneath, further down, beneath. ANTONYMS upper, higher, top.

3 *a lower price* CHEAPER, reduced, cut, slashed. ANTONYMS higher, increased.

▸ verb 1 *she lowered the mask* MOVE DOWN, let down, take down, haul down, drop, let fall. ANTONYMS raise, lift up.

2 *lower your voice* SOFTEN, modulate, quiet, hush, tone down, muffle, turn down, mute. ANTONYMS raise, intensify.

3 *they are lowering their prices* REDUCE, decrease, lessen, bring down, mark down, cut, slash, ax, diminish, curtail, prune, pare (down). ANTONYM increase.

4 *the water level lowered* SUBSIDE, fall (off), recede, ebb, wane; abate, die down, let up, moderate, diminish, lessen.

5 *don't lower yourself to their level* DEGRADE, debase, demean, abase, humiliate, downgrade, discredit, shame, dishonor, disgrace; belittle, cheapen, devalue; **(lower oneself)** stoop, sink, descend. ANTONYM boost.

lowering adjective *the lowering western sky* OVERCAST, dark, leaden, gray, cloudy, clouded, gloomy, threatening, menacing, promising rain.

low-grade adjective *low-grade building materials* POOR-QUALITY, inferior, substandard, second-rate; shoddy, cheap, reject, trashy, gimcrack, chintzy, rubbishy; *informal* two-bit, schlocky, bum, cheapjack. ANTONYMS top-quality, first-class.

low-key adjective *she conducted a low-key campaign* RESTRAINED, modest, understated, muted, subtle, quiet, low-profile, inconspicuous, unostentatious, unobtrusive, discreet, toned-down; casual, informal, mellow, laid-back. ANTONYMS ostentatious, obtrusive.

lowly adjective *that's right Mrs. Tynesdale, I used to be your lowly stable boy* HUMBLE, low, low-born, low-ranking, plebeian, proletarian; common, ordinary, plain, average, modest, simple; inferior, ignoble, subordinate, obscure. ANTONYMS aristocratic, exalted.

loyal adjective *she was loyal to her country* FAITHFUL, true, devoted; constant, steadfast, staunch, dependable, reliable, trusted, trustworthy, trusty, dutiful, dedicated, unchanging, unwavering, unswerving; patriotic. ANTONYM treacherous.

loyalty noun *my grandparents never doubted each other's loyalty* ALLEGIANCE, faithfulness, obedience, adherence, homage, devotion; steadfastness, staunchness, trueheartedness, dependability, reliability, trustworthiness, duty, dedication, commitment; patriotism; *historical* fealty. ANTONYM treachery.

lubricant noun *tubes of lubricant* GREASE, oil, lubrication, emollient, lotion, unguent; *informal* lube.

lubricate verb *lubricating the hinges* OIL, GREASE; wax, polish; facilitate, smooth, ease; *informal* lube.

lucid adjective 1 *a lucid description* INTELLIGIBLE, comprehensible, understandable, cogent, coherent, articulate; clear, transparent; plain, simple, vivid, sharp, straightforward, unambiguous; *formal* perspicuous. ANTONYMS confusing, ambiguous.

2 *he was not lucid enough to explain* RATIONAL, sane, in one's right mind, in possession of one's faculties, compos mentis, able to think clearly, balanced, clearheaded, sober, sensible; *informal* all there. See note at SENSIBLE. ANTONYMS muddled, confused.

luck noun 1 *with luck you'll make it* GOOD FORTUNE, good luck; a fluke, a stroke of luck; *informal* a lucky break. ANTONYMS bad luck, misfortune.

2 *I wish you luck* SUCCESS, prosperity, good fortune, good luck. ANTONYMS failure, misfortune.

3 *it is a matter of luck whether it hits or misses* FORTUNE, fate, destiny, Lady Luck, lot, the stars, karma, kismet; fortuity, serendipity; chance, accident, a twist of fate. PHRASES: **in luck** *you're in luck, there's one blue sweater left in your size* FORTUNATE, lucky, blessed with good luck, born under a lucky star; successful, having a charmed life. **out of luck** *sorry, you're out of luck—the bus left just five minutes ago* UNFORTUNATE, unlucky, luckless, hapless, unsuccessful, cursed, jinxed, ill-fated; *informal* down on one's luck; *literary* star-crossed.

luckily adverb *luckily, we took the Great Elms Bridge, which was not flooded over* FORTUNATELY, happily, providentially, opportunely, by good fortune, as luck would have it, propitiously; mercifully, thankfully. ANTONYM unfortunately.

luckless adjective *his luckless father died penniless and alone* UNLUCKY, unfortunate, unsuccessful, hapless, out of luck, cursed, jinxed, doomed, ill-fated; *informal* down on one's luck, losingest; *literary* star-crossed. ANTONYM lucky.

lucky adjective **1** *the lucky winner* FORTUNATE, in luck, blessed, favored, born under a lucky star, charmed; successful, prosperous. ANTONYM unfortunate.

2 *a lucky escape* PROVIDENTIAL, fortunate, advantageous, timely, opportune, serendipitous, expedient, heaven-sent, auspicious; chance, fortuitous, fluky, accidental. ANTONYM untimely.

► ***lucky***
blessed
heaven-sent
charmed
providential
auspicious
felicitous
fortuitous
propitious
advantageous
serendipitous
fortunate
born under a lucky star
born with a silver spoon in one's mouth
in luck
jammy
favorable
encouraging
hopeful
optimistic
making the best of a bad situation
down on one's luck
out of luck
accident-prone
ill-omened
ill-fated
ill-starred
star-crossed
inauspicious
unpropitious
hapless
ill-fated
ill-omened
luckless
doomed
jinxed
wretched
miserable
blighted
damned
cursed
unlucky ◄

lucrative adjective *a lucrative business* PROFITABLE, profit-making, gainful, remunerative, moneymaking, paying, high-income, well-paid, bankable; rewarding, worthwhile; thriving, flourishing, successful, booming. ANTONYM unprofitable.

ludicrous adjective *a ludicrous idea* ABSURD, ridiculous, farcical, laughable, risible, preposterous, foolish, mad, insane, idiotic, stupid, inane, silly, asinine, nonsensical; *informal* crazy. See note at ABSURD. ANTONYM sensible.

lug verb *she lugged her groceries to the door* CARRY, lift, bear, tote, heave, hoist, shoulder; haul, drag, tug, tow, transport, move, convey, shift; *informal* hump, schlep.

► noun *informal you big lug!* See OAF.

luggage noun *a rack for the luggage* BAGGAGE; bags, suitcases, cases, trunks. See also BAG noun sense 2.

lugubrious adjective *lugubrious hymns | their lugubrious aunt* MOURNFUL, gloomy, sad, unhappy, doleful, glum, melancholy, woeful, miserable, woebegone, forlorn, somber, solemn, serious, sorrowful, morose, dour, cheerless, joyless, dismal; funereal, sepulchral; *informal* down in/at the mouth; *literary* dolorous. See note at GLUM. ANTONYM cheerful.

WORD NOTE **lugubrious**

Loaded with baggy, pendulous vowels, *lugubrious* sounds as sad and dismal as its meaning. The mournful face of Peter Lorre comes to mind, as do performances by Lon Chaney and (perhaps it's just the cognate) Bela Lugosi. **–JS**

lukewarm adjective **1** *lukewarm coffee* TEPID, slightly warm, warmish, at room temperature, chambré. ANTONYMS hot, cold.

2 *a lukewarm response* INDIFFERENT, cool, halfhearted, apathetic, unenthusiastic, tepid, perfunctory, noncommittal, lackadaisical; *informal* laid-back, unenthused, couldn't-care-less. ANTONYM enthusiastic.

lull verb **1** *the sound of the bells lulled us to sleep* SOOTHE, calm, hush; rock. ANTONYMS waken, agitate.

2 *his honeyed words lulled their suspicions* ASSUAGE, allay, ease, alleviate, soothe, quiet, quieted; reduce, diminish; quell, banish, dispel. ANTONYM aggravate.

3 *they lulled us into a false sense of security* DECEIVE, dupe, trick, fool, hoodwink.

► noun **1** *a lull in the fighting* PAUSE, respite, interval, break, hiatus, suspension, interlude, intermission, breathing space; *informal* letup, breather.

2 *the lull before the storm* CALM, stillness, quiet, tranquility, peace, silence, hush. ANTONYM activity.

lullaby noun CRADLE SONG, berceuse.

lumber verb *elephants lumbered past* LURCH, stumble, trundle, shamble, shuffle, waddle; trudge, clump, stump, plod, tramp, tromp; *informal* galumph.

► noun *a truckload of quality lumber* TIMBER, wood, boards, planks.

lumbering adjective *he was a lumbering bear of a man* CLUMSY, awkward, heavy-footed, slow, blundering, bumbling, inept, maladroit, uncoordinated, ungainly, ungraceful, gauche, lumpish, hulking, ponderous; *informal* clodhopping. ANTONYMS nimble, agile.

lumberjack noun. See LOGGER.

luminary noun *the luminaries of the art world* LEADING LIGHT, guiding light, inspiration, role model, hero, heroine, leader, expert, master; lion, legend, celebrity, personality, great, giant; *informal* bigwig, rainmaker, VIP. ANTONYM nobody.

luminous adjective *the luminous face of the alarm clock* SHINING, bright, brilliant, radiant, dazzling, glowing, gleaming, scintillating, lustrous; luminescent, phosphorescent, fluorescent, incandescent. See note at BRIGHT. ANTONYM dark.

lummox noun See OAF.

lump[1] noun **1** *a lump of coal* CHUNK, hunk, piece, mass, block, wedge, slab, cake, nugget, ball, brick, cube, pat, knob, clod, gobbet, dollop, wad; *informal* glob, gob.

2 *a lump on his head* SWELLING, bump, bulge, protuberance, protrusion, growth, outgrowth, nodule, hump; goose egg.

3 **(lumps)** *take your lumps* HARD KNOCKS, defeats, losses.

▸ verb *it is out of ignorance that they* ***lump together*** *all modern artists* COMBINE, put together, group, bunch, aggregate, unite, pool, merge, collect, throw together, consider together.

lump[2] verb *informal like it or lump it* PUT UP WITH, bear, endure, suffer, take, tolerate, accept.

lunacy noun **1** *originality demands a degree of lunacy* INSANITY, madness, mental illness, dementia, mania, psychosis; *informal* craziness. ANTONYM sanity.

2 *the lunacy of gambling* FOLLY, foolishness, stupidity, silliness, idiocy, madness, recklessness, foolhardiness, imprudence, irresponsibility; *informal* craziness. ANTONYMS sense, prudence.

lunatic noun *he drives like a lunatic* MANIAC, madman, madwoman, imbecile, psychopath, psychotic; fool, idiot; eccentric; *informal* loony, nut, nutcase, head case, psycho, moron, screwball, crackpot, fruitcake, loon.

▸ adjective **1** *a lunatic prisoner.* See MAD sense 1.

2 *a lunatic idea.* See MAD sense 3.

lunch noun *my usual lunch includes soup and a sandwich* MIDDAY MEAL, luncheon, brunch, light meal, snack. PHRASE: **out to lunch** *some of these therapists are more out to lunch than their patients* CRAZY, out of one's mind, mad; out of touch, out of it, unaware, absentminded; cuckoo, batty, flaky, spacey, nutty, wingy, off one's rocker.

lunchbox noun *her lunchbox is the one with Miss Piggy on the front* LUNCH PAIL, lunch bucket.

lunge noun *Darren made a lunge at his attacker* THRUST, jab, stab, dive, rush, charge.

▸ verb *he lunged at Finn with a knife* THRUST, dive, spring, launch oneself, rush, make a grab.

lurch verb **1** *he lurched into the kitchen* STAGGER, stumble, wobble, sway, reel, roll, weave, pitch, totter, blunder.

2 *the ship lurched* SWAY, reel, list, heel, rock, roll, pitch, toss, jerk, shake, flounder, swerve, teeter. PHRASE: **leave someone in the lurch** *Wally talked us into taking part in the protest, and then he just left us in the lurch* LEAVE IN TROUBLE, let down, leave stranded, leave high and dry, abandon, desert.

lure verb *consumers are frequently lured into debt* TEMPT, entice, attract, induce, coax, persuade, inveigle, allure, seduce, win over, cajole, beguile, bewitch, ensnare. See note at TEMPT. ANTONYMS deter, put off.

▸ noun *the lure of the stage* TEMPTATION, enticement, attraction, pull, draw, appeal; inducement, allurement, fascination, interest, magnet; *informal* come-on.

lurid adjective **1** *lurid colors* BRIGHT, brilliant, vivid, glaring, shocking, fluorescent, flaming, dazzling, intense; gaudy, loud, showy, bold, garish, tacky. ANTONYMS muted, subtle.

2 *the lurid details* SENSATIONAL, sensationalist, exaggerated, overdramatized, colorful; salacious, graphic, explicit, unrestrained, prurient, shocking; gruesome, gory, grisly; *informal* juicy, full-frontal. ANTONYMS discreet, restrained.

WORD NOTE **lurid**

Lurid and *garish* are both vivid words with similar meanings. What *lurid* gives you that *garish* doesn't is a hint of sleaze. And complexity, too: it is one of those words that usefully take you in two divergent emotional directions at once, suggesting that the object described is both sordid and appealing. (*Louche* does this too.) —**DA**

lurk verb *is someone lurking in the bushes?* SKULK, loiter, lie in wait, lie low, hide, conceal oneself, take cover, keep out of sight.

luscious adjective **1** *luscious fruit* DELICIOUS, succulent, lush, juicy, mouthwatering, lip-smacking, sweet, tasty, appetizing; *informal* scrumptious, yummy, nummy; *literary* ambrosial. ANTONYM unappetizing.

2 *a luscious well-tanned beauty* SEXY, sexually attractive, nubile, ravishing, gorgeous, seductive, alluring, sultry, beautiful, stunning; *informal* drop-dead gorgeous, hot, curvy, foxy, cute. ANTONYMS plain, scrawny.

lush adjective **1** *lush vegetation* LUXURIANT, rich, abundant, profuse, exuberant, riotous, prolific, vigorous; dense, thick, rank, rampant; *informal* jungly. See note at PROFUSE. ANTONYMS barren, meager.

2 *a lush, ripe peach* SUCCULENT, luscious, juicy, soft, tender, ripe. ANTONYM shriveled.

3 *a lush apartment* LUXURIOUS, deluxe, sumptuous, palatial, opulent, lavish, elaborate, extravagant, fancy; *informal* plush, ritzy, posh, swanky, swank. ANTONYM austere.

lust noun **1** *his lust for her* SEXUAL DESIRE, sexual appetite, sexual longing, ardor, desire, passion; libido, sex drive, sexuality, biological urge; lechery, lasciviousness, concupiscence; *informal* horniness, the hots, randiness.

2 *a lust for power* GREED, desire, craving, covetousness, eagerness, avidity, cupidity, longing, yearning, hunger, thirst, appetite, hankering. ANTONYM aversion.

▸ verb **1** *he* ***lusted after*** *his employer's wife* DESIRE, be consumed with desire for, find sexually attractive, crave, covet, ache for, burn for; *informal* have the hots for, fancy, have a thing about/for, drool over.

2 *she* ***lusted after*** *adventure* CRAVE, desire, covet, want, wish for, long for, yearn for, dream of, hanker for, hanker after, hunger for, thirst for, ache for. ANTONYMS dread, avoid.

luster noun **1** *her hair lost its luster* SHEEN, gloss, shine, glow, gleam, shimmer, burnish, polish, patina. See note at POLISH. ANTONYM dullness.

2 *the luster of the Milky Way* BRILLIANCE, brightness, radiance, sparkle, dazzle, flash, glitter, glint, gleam, luminosity, luminescence.

lustful adjective *a lustful look* LECHEROUS, lascivious, libidinous, licentious, salacious, goatish; wanton, unchaste, impure, naughty, immodest, indecent, dirty, prurient; passionate, sensual, sexy, erotic; *informal* horny, randy, raunchy, lusty; *formal* concupiscent. ANTONYMS chaste, pure.

lustrous adjective *lustrous black hair* SHINY, shining, satiny, glossy, gleaming, shimmering, burnished, polished; radiant, bright, brilliant, luminous; dazzling, sparkling, glistening, twinkling. See note at BRIGHT. ANTONYM dull.

lusty adjective **1** *a lusty baby* HEALTHY, strong, fit, vigorous, robust, hale and hearty, energetic; rugged, sturdy, muscular, muscly, strapping, hefty, husky, burly, powerful; *informal* beefy; *dated* stalwart. ANTONYMS feeble, weak.

2 *lusty singing* LOUD, vigorous, hearty, strong, powerful, forceful. ANTONYMS feeble, weak.

3 *informal lusty young men.* See LUSTFUL.

luxuriant adjective *luxuriant vegetation* LUSH, rich, abundant, profuse, exuberant, riotous, prolific, vigorous; dense, thick, rank, rampant; *informal* jungly. See note at PROFUSE. ANTONYMS barren, sparse.

EASILY CONFUSED WORDS **luxuriant, luxurious**

Luxuriant and **luxurious** are sometimes confused. **Luxuriant** means 'lush, profuse, prolific': *forests of dark luxuriant foliage; luxuriant black eyelashes*). **Luxurious**, a much more common word, means 'supplied with luxuries, extremely comfortable': *a luxurious mansion.*

luxuriate verb *luxuriating in a bubble bath* REVEL, bask, delight, take pleasure, wallow; (**luxuriate in**) enjoy, relish, savor, appreciate; *informal* get a kick out of, get a thrill out of. ANTONYM dislike.

luxurious adjective **1** *a luxurious hotel* OPULENT, sumptuous, deluxe, rich, grand, palatial, splendid, magnificent, well appointed, extravagant, fancy, upscale, upmarket, five-star; *informal* plush, posh, classy, ritzy, swanky, swank. ANTONYMS poor, austere, spartan.

2 *a luxurious lifestyle* SELF-INDULGENT, sensual, pleasure-loving, pleasure-seeking, epicurean, hedonistic, sybaritic. See notes at LUXURIANT, SENSUOUS. ANTONYM abstemious.

luxury noun **1** *we'll live in luxury* OPULENCE, luxuriousness, sumptuousness, grandeur, magnificence, splendor, lavishness, the lap of luxury, a bed of roses, (the land of) milk and honey; *informal* the life of Riley. ANTONYMS austerity, poverty.

2 *a TV is his only luxury* INDULGENCE, extravagance, self-indulgence, nonessential, treat, extra, frill. ANTONYM necessity.

lying noun *she was no good at lying* UNTRUTHFULNESS, fabrication, fibbing, perjury, white lies; falseness, falsity, dishonesty, mendacity, telling stories, invention, misrepresentation, deceit, duplicity; *literary* perfidy. ANTONYM honesty.

▸ adjective *he was a lying womanizer* UNTRUTHFUL, false, dishonest, mendacious, deceitful, deceiving, duplicitous, double-dealing, two-faced; *literary* perfidious. ANTONYM truthful.

lynch verb *DeLuca was lynched by Yardley's mob* EXECUTE ILLEGALLY, hang, kill; *informal* string up.

lyrical adjective **1** *lyrical love poetry* EXPRESSIVE, emotional, deeply felt, personal, subjective, passionate, lyric.

2 *she was lyrical about her success* ENTHUSIASTIC, rhapsodic, effusive, rapturous, ecstatic, euphoric, carried away. ANTONYM unenthusiastic.

lyrics plural noun *Cole Porter wrote the music and lyrics* WORDS, libretto, book, text, lines.

M

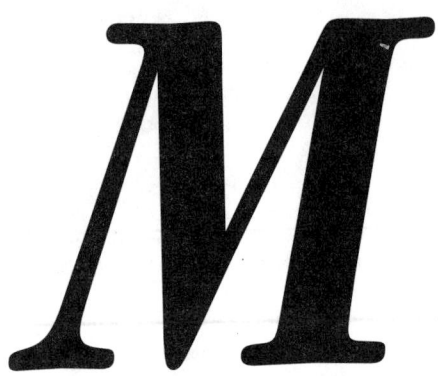

macabre adjective **1** *a macabre ritual* GRUESOME, grisly, grim, gory, morbid, ghastly, unearthly, grotesque, hideous, horrific, shocking, dreadful, loathsome, repugnant, repulsive, sickening.

2 *a macabre joke* BLACK, weird, unhealthy; *informal* sick.

mace noun *the thug wielded a mace* CLUB, cudgel, stick, staff, shillelagh, bludgeon, truncheon, nightstick, billy club, blackjack.

Machiavellian adjective *their Machiavellian plot to inherit Aunt Lorinda's estate* DEVIOUS, cunning, crafty, artful, wily, sly, scheming, treacherous, two-faced, tricky, double-dealing, unscrupulous, deceitful, dishonest; *literary* perfidious; *informal* foxy. ANTONYMS straightforward, ingenuous.

machinations plural noun *they were always wary of the machinations of rival gangs* SCHEMING, schemes, plotting, plots, intrigues, conspiracies, ruses, tricks, wiles, stratagems, tactics, maneuvering. See note at PLOT.

machine noun **1** *a threshing machine* APPARATUS, appliance, device, contraption, contrivance, mechanism, engine, gadget, tool.

2 *an efficient publicity machine* ORGANIZATION, system, structure, arrangement, machinery; *informal* setup.

3 *he's an eating machine* POWERHOUSE, human dynamo; wonder, phenomenon, sensation; automaton.

machinery noun **1** *printing machinery* EQUIPMENT, apparatus, hardware, gear, tackle, plant; mechanism; instruments, tools; gadgetry, technology.

2 *the machinery of government* WORKINGS, organization, system, structure, administration, institution; *informal* setup.

machismo noun *don't be struttin' your machismo around here, buster* (AGGRESSIVE) MASCULINITY, toughness, male chauvinism, sexism, virility, manliness; bravado; *informal* testosterone, macho.

macho adjective *a macho man* (AGGRESSIVELY) MALE, (unpleasantly) masculine; manly, virile, red-blooded; *informal* butch. ANTONYM wimpish.

▸ noun *macho is out.* See MACHISMO.

mad adjective **1** *he felt he was going mad* INSANE, mentally ill, certifiable, deranged, demented, of unsound mind, out of one's mind, not in one's right mind, sick in the head, crazy, crazed, lunatic, non compos mentis, unhinged, disturbed, raving, psychotic, psychopathic, mad as a hatter, mad as a March hare; *informal* CRAZY, mental, off one's nut, nuts, nutty, nutty as a fruitcake, nutso, off one's rocker, not right in the head, round/around the bend, (stark) raving mad, bats, batty, buggy, bonkers, dotty, cuckoo, cracked, loopy, loony, bananas, loco, screwy, schizoid, psycho, touched, gaga, not all there, not right upstairs, crackers, out of one's tree, meshuga, wacko, gonzo; **(be mad)** have a screw loose, have bats in the/one's belfry; **(go mad)** lose one's reason, lose one's mind, take leave of one's senses, lose one's marbles, crack up. ANTONYM sane.

2 *I'm still mad at him | don't get mad* ANGRY, furious, infuriated, irate, raging, enraged, fuming, incensed, seeing red, beside oneself; *informal* livid, sore; *literary* wrathful; **(get mad)** lose one's temper, get in a rage, rant and rave; *informal* explode, go off the deep end, go ape, flip, flip out, flip one's wig. ANTONYMS unruffled, calm.

3 *some mad scheme* FOOLISH, insane, stupid, lunatic, foolhardy, idiotic, senseless, absurd, impractical, silly, inane, asinine, wild, unwise, imprudent; *informal* crazy, crackpot, crack-brained, daft. ANTONYM sensible.

4 *informal he's* ***mad about*** *jazz* ENTHUSIASTIC ABOUT, passionate about; ardent about, fervent about, avid about, fanatical about; devoted to, infatuated with, in love with, hot for; *informal* crazy about, nuts about, wild about, hooked on, gone on, nutso about. ANTONYM indifferent.

5 *it was a mad dash to get ready* FRENZIED, frantic, frenetic, feverish, wild, hectic, manic. PHRASE: **like mad** *informal* **1** *I ran like mad* FAST, quickly, rapidly, speedily, hastily, hurriedly. **2** *he had to fight like mad* ENERGETICALLY, enthusiastically, madly, furiously, with a will, for all one is worth, passionately, intensely, ardently, fervently; *informal* like crazy, hammer and tongs.

WORD NOTE batty

There's a gentle sweetness to this term for *crazy:* it conjures up an elderly woman pottering harmlessly about the garden, hair coming undone every which way, talking to herself (or the plants or the birds), oblivious to creatures of the human persuasion. It is closer to *eccentric,* or *deeply peculiar,* than to the harsher *nuts, wacko, bonkers,* or *bats.* It is not clear why *bats* (or *nuts*) are synonyms for *crazy*—considering that bats have radar, their flight is anything but.

Still, before people knew about the radar, bat flight must have looked, well, nuts. *Batty* may derive from the phrase *bats in the belfry,* or from the name of the prominent English physician, William Battie (sometimes Batty), who wrote a *Treatise on Madness* in 1758, and advocated therapeutic asylums rather than prisons for the insane. **–JS**

---

madcap adjective **1** *a madcap scheme* RECKLESS, rash, foolhardy, foolish, harebrained, wild, hasty, imprudent, ill-advised; *informal* crazy, crackpot, crack-brained.

2 *a madcap comedy* ZANY, eccentric, unconventional.

▸ noun *she was a boisterous madcap* ECCENTRIC, crank, madman/madwoman, maniac, lunatic; oddity, character; *informal* crackpot, oddball, weirdo, loony, nut, screwball, loon.

madden verb **1** *what maddens people most is his vagueness* INFURIATE, exasperate, irritate; incense, anger, enrage, provoke, upset, agitate, vex, irk, make someone's hackles rise, make someone see red; *informal* aggravate, make someone's blood boil, make livid, get someone's goat, get someone's back up, tee off, tick off, steam someone up.

2 *they were maddened with pain* DRIVE MAD, drive insane, derange, unhinge, unbalance; *informal* drive round/around the bend.

made-up adjective **1** *a made-up story* INVENTED, fabricated, trumped up, concocted, fictitious, fictional, false, untrue, specious, spurious, bogus, apocryphal, imaginary, mythical.

2 *she was made up for the evening* WEARING MAKEUP; *informal* dolled up, decked out.

madhouse noun *informal* **1** *his father is shut up in a madhouse* MENTAL HOSPITAL, mental institution, psychiatric hospital, asylum; *informal* nuthouse, funny farm, loony bin; *dated* lunatic asylum.

2 *when we arrived, it was **a madhouse*** BEDLAM, mayhem, chaos, pandemonium, an uproar, turmoil, disorder, madness, all hell broken loose, a (three-ring) circus, a zoo.

madly adverb **1** *she was smiling madly* INSANELY, deliriously, wildly, like a lunatic; *informal* crazily. ANTONYM sanely.

2 *madly snapping pictures* FAST, furiously, hurriedly, quickly, speedily, hastily, energetically; *informal* like mad, like crazy. ANTONYM slowly.

3 *informal she was madly in love with him* INTENSELY, fervently, wildly, unrestrainedly, to distraction. ANTONYM slightly.

4 *informal a madly eccentric pair* VERY, extremely, really, exceedingly, exceptionally, remarkably, extraordinarily, immensely, tremendously, wildly, hugely; *informal* awfully, terribly, terrifically, fantastically. ANTONYM slightly.

madman, madwoman noun *there was a madman on the loose* LUNATIC, maniac, psychotic, psychopath, sociopath; *informal* loony, nut, nutcase, head case, psycho, screwball, loon.

madness noun **1** *today madness is called mental illness* INSANITY, mental illness, dementia, derangement; lunacy, instability; mania, psychosis; *informal* craziness. ANTONYM sanity.

2 *it would be madness to do otherwise* FOLLY, foolishness, idiocy, stupidity, insanity, lunacy, silliness; *informal* craziness. ANTONYMS common sense, good sense.

3 *it's absolute madness in here* BEDLAM, mayhem, chaos, pandemonium, craziness, uproar, turmoil, disorder, all hell broken loose, (three-ring) circus. ANTONYM calm.

maelstrom noun **1** *a maelstrom in the sea* WHIRLPOOL, vortex, eddy, swirl; *literary* Charybdis.

2 *the maelstrom of war* TURBULENCE, tumult, turmoil, disorder, disarray, chaos, confusion, upheaval, pandemonium, bedlam, whirlwind.

maestro noun **1** *blues maestro Eric Clapton* VIRTUOSO, master, expert, genius, wizard, prodigy; *informal* ace, whiz, pro, hotshot. ANTONYMS novice, beginner.

2 *the maestro took the podium* CONDUCTOR, (music) director.

magazine noun *a monthly fashion magazine* JOURNAL, periodical, serial, supplement, quarterly, monthly, weekly, newsmagazine; *informal* glossy, mag, zine, fanzine.

magenta adjective *the blouse is white with magenta pinstripes* REDDISH-PURPLE, purplish-red, crimson, plum, carmine red, fuchsia; *literary* incarnadine.

magic noun **1** *do you believe in magic?* SORCERY, witchcraft, wizardry, necromancy, enchantment, the supernatural, occultism, the occult, black magic, the black arts, voodoo, hoodoo, mojo, shamanism; charm, hex, spell, jinx.

2 *he does magic at children's parties* CONJURING TRICKS, sleight of hand, legerdemain, illusion, prestidigitation.

3 *the magic of the stage* ALLURE, attraction, excitement, fascination, charm, glamour.

4 *her dancing is pure magic* SKILL, brilliance, ability, accomplishment, adeptness, adroitness, deftness, dexterity, aptitude, expertise, art, finesse, talent.

▸ adjective **1** *a magic spell* SUPERNATURAL, enchanted, occult.

2 *a magic place* FASCINATING, captivating, charming, glamorous, magical, enchanting, entrancing, spellbinding, magnetic, irresistible, hypnotic.

3 *informal we were magic together* MARVELOUS, wonderful, excellent, admirable; *informal* terrific, fabulous, brilliant.

magical adjective **1** *magical incantations* SUPERNATURAL, magic, occult, shamanistic, mystical, paranormal, preternatural, otherworldly.

2 *the news had a magical effect* EXTRAORDINARY, remarkable, exceptional, outstanding, incredible, phenomenal, unbelievable, amazing, astonishing, astounding, stunning, staggering, marvelous, magnificent, wonderful, sensational, breathtaking, miraculous; *informal* fantastic, fabulous, stupendous, out of this world, terrific, tremendous, brilliant, mind-boggling, mind-blowing, awesome; *literary* wondrous.

3 *this magical place* ENCHANTING, entrancing, spellbinding, bewitching, beguiling, fascinating, captivating, alluring, enthralling, charming, attractive, lovely, delightful, beautiful; *informal* dreamy, heavenly, divine, gorgeous. ANTONYMS dull, boring.

magician noun **1** *she imagined she was a magician* SORCERER, sorceress, witch, wizard, warlock, enchanter, enchantress, necromancer, shaman.

2 *Houdini was a great magician* CONJUROR, illusionist, prestidigitator.

3 *he is a magician on the ice* GENIUS, marvel, wizard.

magisterial adjective 1 *a magisterial pronouncement* AUTHORITATIVE, masterful, assured, lordly, commanding, assertive. ANTONYM humble.

2 *his magisterial style of questioning* DOMINEERING, dictatorial, autocratic, imperious, overbearing, peremptory, high-handed, arrogant, supercilious, patronizing; *informal* bossy. ANTONYMS hesitant, tentative.

magnanimous adjective *her magnanimous contributions to the art world* GENEROUS, charitable, benevolent, beneficent, big-hearted, handsome, princely, altruistic, philanthropic, unselfish, chivalrous, noble; forgiving, merciful, lenient, indulgent, clement. ANTONYMS mean-spirited, selfish.

magnate noun *the industrial magnates of the nineteenth century* TYCOON, mogul, captain of industry, baron, lord, king, magnifico; industrialist, proprietor; *informal* big shot, big cheese, (head) honcho; *derogatory* fat cat.

magnet noun 1 *you can test if it's steel by using a magnet* LODESTONE; electromagnet, solenoid.

2 *a magnet for tourists* ATTRACTION, focus, draw, lure, mecca.

magnetic adjective *a magnetic personality* ALLURING, attractive, fascinating, captivating, enchanting, enthralling, appealing, charming, prepossessing, engaging, entrancing, seductive, inviting, irresistible, charismatic.

magnetism noun *the sheer magnetism of his physical presence* ALLURE, attraction, fascination, appeal, draw, drawing power, pull, charm, enchantment, seductiveness, magic, spell, charisma.

magnification noun *the fine lines are visible only under magnification* ENLARGEMENT, enhancement, increase, augmentation, extension, expansion, amplification, intensification, inflation. ANTONYM reduction.

magnificence noun *the magnificence of Broadway* SPLENDOR, grandeur, impressiveness, glory, majesty, nobility, pomp, stateliness, elegance, sumptuousness, opulence, luxury, lavishness, richness, brilliance, dazzle, skill, virtuosity. ANTONYMS modesty, tawdriness, weakness.

magnificent adjective 1 *a magnificent view of the mountains* SPLENDID, spectacular, impressive, striking, glorious, superb, majestic, awesome, awe-inspiring, breathtaking. ANTONYM uninspiring.

2 *a magnificent apartment overlooking the lake* SUMPTUOUS, resplendent, grand, impressive, imposing, monumental, palatial, stately, opulent, luxurious, lavish, rich, dazzling, beautiful, elegant; *informal* splendiferous, ritzy, posh, swanky. ANTONYMS modest, tawdry, cheap.

3 *a magnificent performance* MASTERLY, skillful, virtuoso, brilliant. ANTONYMS poor, weak.

magnify verb 1 *the lens magnifies the image* ENLARGE, boost, enhance, maximize, increase, augment, extend, expand, amplify, intensify; *informal* blow up. ANTONYM reduce.

2 *they magnified the problem* EXAGGERATE, overstate, overemphasize, overplay, dramatize, color, embroider, embellish, inflate, make a mountain out of (a molehill); *informal* blow up (out of all proportion), make a big thing out of. ANTONYMS minimize, understate.

magnitude noun 1 *the magnitude of the task* IMMENSITY, vastness, hugeness, enormity; size, extent, expanse, greatness, largeness, bigness. ANTONYM smallness.

2 *events of tragic magnitude* IMPORTANCE, import, significance, weight, consequence, mark, notability, note; *formal* moment. ANTONYM triviality.

PHRASE: **of the first magnitude** *we are witnessing a historic event of the first magnitude* OF THE UTMOST IMPORTANCE, of the greatest significance, very important, of great consequence; *formal* of great moment.

maid noun 1 *the maid cleared the table* FEMALE SERVANT, maidservant, housemaid, domestic, housekeeper; help, cleaner, cleaning woman/lady; *dated* parlormaid, lady's maid, chambermaid.

2 *literary a village maid and her swain* GIRL, young woman, young lady, lass, miss, ingenue; *literary* maiden, damsel, nymph; *archaic* wench.

maiden noun *literary a pretty young maiden.* See MAID sense 2.

▸ adjective 1 *a maiden aunt* UNMARRIED, spinster, unwed, unwedded, single, husbandless, celibate.

2 *a maiden voyage* FIRST, initial, inaugural, introductory, initiatory, virgin.

WORD NOTE **spinster**

An apparently innocent word that would seem to mean "an unmarried woman," until we compare the *spinster* to her male counterpart—the *bachelor*—at which point the word reveals its true colors. A bachelor, we might assume, has chosen to remain unmarried, a state which does not reflect on his attractiveness, and indeed may make him even more appealing. Whereas a spinster has had the misfortune of having been unable to find a man. That must be why one sees—especially on TV—the growing use of the term *bachelorette,* while, so far, we have yet to use the term *spinsterette.* There are many apparently gender-neutral words which in fact have gender-specific associations. For example, one rarely sees the verb *to scold* used in reference to men who harangue us. **—FP**

mail noun *the mail arrived* letters, correspondence; postal system, postal service, post office; delivery, collection; e-mail; *chiefly Brit.* post; *informal* snail mail.

▸ verb *we mailed the card* SEND, dispatch, post, direct, forward, redirect, ship, express, courier; e-mail.

mailman noun *the mailman usually gets here before noon* POSTAL WORKER; postman, mail carrier, letter carrier.

maim verb *a dog maimed by a coyote* INJURE, wound, cripple, disable, incapacitate, impair, mar, mutilate, lacerate, disfigure, deform, mangle.

main adjective *the main item* PRINCIPAL, chief, head, leading, foremost, most important, major, ruling, dominant, central, focal, key, prime, master, premier, primary, first, first-line, fundamental, supreme, predominant, (most) prominent, preeminent, paramount, overriding, cardinal, crucial, critical, pivotal, salient, elemental, essential, staple. ANTONYMS subsidiary, minor.

▸ noun *a burst water main* PIPE, channel, duct, conduit.

PHRASE: **in the main** *in the main, we want the menu to offer a nice selection of kosher alternatives.* See MAINLY.

mainly adverb *the people on the island are mainly tourists* MOSTLY, for the most part, in the main, on the whole, largely, by and large, to a large extent, predominantly, chiefly, principally, primarily; generally, usually, typically, commonly, on average, as a rule, almost always.

mainspring noun *the mainspring of anticommunism* MOTIVE, motivation, impetus, driving force, incentive, impulse, prime mover, reason, fountain, fount, wellspring, root, generator.

mainstay noun *agriculture is the mainstay of their economy* CENTRAL COMPONENT, central figure, centerpiece, prop, linchpin, cornerstone, pillar, bulwark, buttress, chief support, backbone, anchor, foundation, base, staple.

mainstream adjective *the mainstream audience may not be ready for these graphic sculptures* NORMAL, conventional, ordinary, orthodox, conformist, accepted, established, recognized, common, usual, prevailing, popular. ANTONYM fringe.

maintain verb **1** *they wanted to maintain peace* PRESERVE, conserve, keep, retain, keep going, keep alive, keep up, prolong, perpetuate, sustain, carry on, continue. ANTONYMS break (off), discontinue.

2 *the association maintains its private roads* KEEP IN GOOD CONDITION, keep in (good) repair, keep up, service, care for, take good care of, look after. ANTONYM neglect.

3 *the cost of maintaining a dog* SUPPORT, provide for, keep, sustain; nurture, feed, nourish. ANTONYM neglect.

4 *he always maintained his innocence | he maintains that he is innocent* INSIST (ON), declare, assert, protest, affirm, avow, profess, claim, allege, contend, argue, swear (to), hold to; *formal* aver. ANTONYM deny.

maintenance noun **1** *the maintenance of peace* PRESERVATION, conservation, keeping, prolongation, perpetuation, carrying on, continuation, continuance. ANTONYMS breakdown, discontinuation.

2 *car maintenance* UPKEEP, service, servicing, repair(s), care. ANTONYM neglect.

3 *the maintenance of his children* SUPPORT, keeping, upkeep, sustenance; nurture, feeding, nourishment. ANTONYM neglect.

4 *absent fathers are forced to pay maintenance* FINANCIAL SUPPORT, child support, alimony, provision; keep, subsistence, living expenses.

majestic adjective *the majestic Rocky Mountains | his father's majestic presence* STATELY, dignified, distinguished, solemn, magnificent, grand, splendid, resplendent, glorious, sumptuous, impressive, august, noble, awe-inspiring, monumental, palatial; statuesque, Olympian, imposing, marvelous, sonorous, resounding, heroic. ANTONYMS modest, wretched.

major adjective **1** *the major North American writers* GREATEST, best, finest, most important, chief, main, prime, principal, capital, cardinal, leading, star, foremost, outstanding, first-rate, preeminent, arch-; *informal* major league, big league. ANTONYM minor.

2 *an issue of major importance* CRUCIAL, vital, great, considerable, paramount, utmost, prime; *informal* serious. ANTONYM little.

3 *a major factor* IMPORTANT, big, significant, weighty, crucial, key, sweeping, substantial. ANTONYM trivial.

4 *major surgery* SERIOUS, radical, complicated, difficult. ANTONYM minor.

majority noun **1** *the majority of cases* LARGER PART/NUMBER, greater part/number, best/better part, most, more than half; plurality, bulk, mass, weight, (main) body, preponderance, predominance, generality, lion's share. ANTONYM minority.

2 *a majority in the election* (WINNING) MARGIN, superiority of numbers/votes; landslide.

3 *my youngest child has reached majority* LEGAL AGE, adulthood, manhood/womanhood, maturity; age of consent, coming of age.

USAGE NOTE **majority**

Strictly speaking, **majority** should be used with countable nouns to mean 'the greater number': *the majority of cases*. The use of **majority** with uncountable nouns to mean 'the greatest part' (*I spent the majority of the day reading*), although common in informal contexts, is not considered good standard English.

make verb **1** *he makes models* CONSTRUCT, build, assemble, put together, manufacture, produce, fabricate, create, form, fashion, model. ANTONYM destroy.

2 *I didn't want to go but she made me* FORCE, compel, coerce, press, drive, pressure, oblige, require; have someone do something, prevail on, dragoon, bludgeon, strongarm, impel, constrain; *informal* railroad.

3 *don't make such a noise* CAUSE, create, give rise to, produce, bring about, generate, engender, occasion, effect, set up, establish, institute, found, develop, originate; *literary* beget.

4 *she made a little bow* PERFORM, execute, give, do, accomplish, achieve, bring off, carry out, effect.

5 *they made him chairman* APPOINT, designate, name, nominate, select, elect, vote in, install; induct, institute, invest, ordain.

6 *he had made a will* FORMULATE, frame, draw up, devise, make out, prepare, compile, compose, put together; draft, write, pen.

7 *I've made a mistake* PERPETRATE, commit, be responsible for, be guilty of, be to blame for.

8 *he's made a lot of money* ACQUIRE, obtain, gain, get, realize, secure, win, earn; gross, net, clear; bring in, take (in), rake in. ANTONYM lose.

9 *he made dinner* PREPARE, get ready, put together, concoct, cook, dish up, throw together, whip up, brew; *informal* fix.

10 *we've got to make a decision* REACH, come to, settle on, determine on, conclude.

11 *she made a short announcement* UTTER, give, deliver, give voice to, enunciate, recite, pronounce.

12 *the sofa makes a good bed* BE, act as, serve as, function as, constitute, do duty for.

13 *he'll make the team* GAIN A PLACE IN, get into, gain access to, enter; achieve, attain.

14 *he just made his train* CATCH, get, arrive/be in time for, arrive at, reach; get to. ANTONYM miss.

▸ noun **1** *what make is the car?* BRAND, marque, label.

2 *a man of a different make from his brother* CHARACTER, nature, temperament, temper, disposition, kidney, mold, stamp.

PHRASES: **make as if/though** *he made as if to run away* FEIGN, pretend, make a show/pretense of, affect, feint, make out. **make believe** *we encourage the children to make believe* PRETEND, fantasize, daydream, build castles in the air, dream, imagine, play-act, play. **make do** *we have precious little but we make do | we'll have to make do with just one income* SCRAPE BY, get by, manage, cope, survive, muddle through, improvise, make ends meet, keep the wolf from the door, keep one's head above water; *informal* make out; (**make do with**) make the best of, get by on, put up with. **make for** 1 *she made for the door* GO FOR/TOWARD, head for/toward, aim for, make one's way toward, move toward, direct one's steps toward, steer a course toward, be bound for, make a beeline for. 2 *constant arguing doesn't make for a happy marriage* CONTRIBUTE TO, be conducive to, produce, promote, facilitate, foster. **make it** 1 *he'll never make it as a singer* SUCCEED, be a success, distinguish oneself, get ahead, make good; *informal* make the grade, arrive. 2 *she's very ill—is she going to make it?* SURVIVE, come through, pull through, get better, recover. **make love.** See HAVE SEX at SEX. **make off with** *they made off with all the wedding gifts* TAKE, steal, purloin, pilfer, abscond with, run away/off with, carry off, snatch; kidnap, abduct; *informal* walk away/off with, swipe, filch, nab, lift, "liberate", "borrow", snitch, pinch; heist. **make out** *informal* 1 *how did you make out?* GET ON/ALONG, fare, do, proceed, go, progress, manage, survive, cope, get by. 2 *I could just make out a figure in the distance* SEE, discern, distinguish, perceive, pick out, detect, observe, recognize; *literary* descry, espy. 3 *he couldn't make out what she was saying* UNDERSTAND, comprehend, follow, grasp, fathom, work out, make sense of, interpret, decipher, make head(s) or tail(s) of, get, get the drift of, catch. 4 *she made out that he was violent* ALLEGE, claim, assert, declare, maintain, affirm, suggest, imply, hint, insinuate, indicate, intimate, impute; *formal* aver. 5 *he made out a receipt for $20* WRITE OUT, fill out, fill in, complete, draw up. 6 *they made out in the back seat* KISS, neck, caress, pet; *informal* smooch, canoodle, fool around. **make over** *Grandpa made over the deed to Uncle Marc* TRANSFER, sign over, turn over, hand over/on/down, give, leave, bequeath, bestow, pass on, assign, consign, entrust; *Law* devolve. **make up** 1 *let's kiss and make up* BE FRIENDS AGAIN, bury the hatchet, declare a truce, make peace, forgive and forget, shake hands, become reconciled, settle one's differences, mend fences, call it quits. 2 *exports make up 42% of earnings* CONSTITUTE, form, compose, account for. 3 *Gina brought a friend to make up a foursome* COMPLETE, round off/out, finish. 4 *the pharmacist made up the prescription* PREPARE, mix, concoct, put together. 5 *he made up an excuse* INVENT, fabricate, concoct, dream up, think up, hatch, trump up; devise, manufacture, formulate, coin; *informal* cook up. 6 *she made up her face* APPLY MAKEUP/COSMETICS TO, powder; (**make oneself up**) *informal* put on one's face, do/paint one's face, apply one's war paint, doll oneself up. **make up for** 1 *she tried to make up for what she'd said* ATONE FOR, make amends for, compensate for, make recompense for, make reparation for, make redress for, make restitution for, expiate. 2 *job satisfaction can make up for low pay* OFFSET, counterbalance, counteract, compensate for; balance, neutralize, cancel out, even up, redeem. **make up one's mind** *you need to make up your mind about the job offer* DECIDE, come to a decision, make/reach a decision; settle on a plan of action, come to a conclusion, reach a conclusion; determine, resolve. **make way** *make way for the paramedics* MOVE ASIDE, clear the way, make a space, make room, stand back.

make-believe noun *that was sheer make-believe* FANTASY, pretense, daydreaming, imagination, invention, fancy, dream, fabrication, play-acting, dreaming in technicolor, charade, masquerade, dress-up. ANTONYM reality.

▸ adjective *make-believe adventures* IMAGINARY, imagined, made-up, fantasy, dreamed-up, fanciful, fictitious, fictive, feigned, fake, mock, sham, simulated; *informal* pretend, phony. ANTONYMS real, actual.

makeover noun *the kitchen is long overdue for a makeover* TRANSFORMATION, renovation, overhaul, new look, remodeling, refurbishment, reconditioning, improvement; *informal* facelift.

maker noun *the makers of fine furniture* CREATOR, manufacturer, constructor, builder, producer, fabricator, inventor, architect, designer.

makeshift adjective *we stayed dry under some makeshift shelter* TEMPORARY, provisional, interim, stopgap, make-do, standby, rough and ready, improvised, ad hoc, extempore, jury-rigged, jerry-built, thrown together, cobbled together. ANTONYM permanent.

makeup noun 1 *she used excessive makeup* COSMETICS, maquillage; greasepaint, face paint; *informal* war paint.

2 *the cellular makeup of plants* COMPOSITION, constitution, structure, configuration, arrangement, organization, formation.

3 *jealousy isn't part of his makeup* CHARACTER, nature, temperament, personality, disposition, mentality, persona, psyche; *informal* what makes someone tick.

making noun 1 *the making of cars* MANUFACTURE, mass-production, building, construction, assembly, production, creation, putting together, fabrication, forming, molding, forging. ANTONYM destruction.

2 (**makings**) *she has the makings of a champion* QUALITIES, characteristics, ingredients; potential, promise, capacity, capability; essentials, essence, beginnings, rudiments, basics, stuff. PHRASE: **in the making** *a hero in the making* BUDDING, up and coming, emergent, developing, nascent, potential, promising, incipient.

maladjusted adjective *a home for maladjusted kids* DISTURBED, unstable, neurotic, unbalanced, unhinged, dysfunctional; *informal* mixed up, screwed up, messed up. ANTONYMS normal, stable.

maladroit adjective *the judge reprimanded Palermo for his maladroit handling of the case* BUNGLING, awkward, inept, clumsy, bumbling, incompetent, unskillful, heavy-handed, gauche, tactless, inconsiderate, undiplomatic, impolitic; *informal* ham-fisted, all thumbs, klutzy. ANTONYMS adroit, skillful.

malady noun *every time we visit Jerry, he has a new malady* ILLNESS, sickness, disease, infection, ailment, disorder, complaint, indisposition, affliction, infirmity, syndrome; *informal* bug, virus.

malaise noun *he showed no sign of emerging from his grief and malaise* UNHAPPINESS, uneasiness, unease, discomfort, melancholy, depression, despondency, dejection, angst, ennui; lassitude, listlessness, languor, weariness;

indisposition, ailment, infirmity, illness, sickness, disease. ANTONYMS comfort, well-being.

malapropism noun *she's famous for her hilarious malapropisms* WRONG WORD, solecism, misuse, misapplication, infelicity, slip of the tongue, Freudian slip, blunder.

malcontent noun *a group of malcontents* TROUBLEMAKER, mischief-maker, agitator, dissident, rebel, rabble-rouser; discontent, complainer, grumbler, moaner, whiner; *informal* grouch, grump, bellyacher, kvetch, squeaky wheel.

▸ adjective *a malcontent employee.* See DISCONTENTED.

male adjective *it's his male jealousy, which is nearly always unfounded* MASCULINE, virile, manly, macho; red-blooded. ANTONYM female.

▸ noun *two males walked past.* See MAN noun sense 1.

THE RIGHT WORD

We speak of a **male** ancestor, a **masculine** scent, and a **manly** activity, but only of women as **mannish**. While all of these adjectives apply to what is characteristic of the male of the species (particularly the human species), *male* can refer to plants or animals as well as human beings and is used to describe whatever is biologically distinguished from the female sex (*an all-male choir; a male cat; a male holly bush*). *Masculine* refers to the qualities, characteristics, and behaviors associated with or thought to be appropriate to men and boys (*a masculine handshake*). *Manly* emphasizes the desirable qualities that a culture associates with a mature man, such as courage and independence (*the manly virtues; the manly sport of football*). **Manful** differs from *manly* primarily in its emphasis on sturdiness and resoluteness (*a manful effort to hold back tears*). **Virile** is a stronger word than *masculine* or *manly* and is applied only to mature men; it suggests the vigor, muscularity, and forcefulness—and especially the sexual potency—associated with mature manhood (*a virile man who looked like Charlton Heston in his youth*).

malediction noun *the maledictions of the evil Dr. Krepling* CURSE, damnation, oath; spell, hex, jinx; *formal* imprecation; *literary* anathema; *archaic* execration. ANTONYM blessing.

malefactor noun *she is studying the psychological profiles of three teenage malefactors* WRONGDOER, miscreant, offender, criminal, culprit, villain, lawbreaker, felon, evildoer, delinquent, hooligan, hoodlum; sinner, transgressor; *informal* crook, thug; *archaic* trespasser.

malevolent adjective *a malevolent glare* MALICIOUS, hostile, evil-minded, baleful, evil-intentioned, venomous, evil, malign, malignant, rancorous, vicious, vindictive, vengeful; *literary* malefic, maleficent. ANTONYM benevolent.

malformed adjective *a mythical island of malformed creatures* DEFORMED, misshapen, misproportioned, ill-proportioned, disfigured, distorted, crooked, contorted, twisted, warped; abnormal, grotesque, dysmorphic, monstrous. ANTONYMS perfect, normal, healthy.

malfunction verb *the computer has malfunctioned* CRASH, go wrong, break down, fail, stop working, go down; *informal* conk out, go kaput, blow up, act up.

▸ noun *a computer malfunction* CRASH, breakdown, fault, failure, bug; *informal* glitch.

malice noun *she had intended no malice toward him* SPITE, malevolence, ill will, vindictiveness, vengefulness, revenge, malignity, evil intentions, animus, enmity, rancor; *informal* bitchiness, cattiness; *literary* maleficence. ANTONYM benevolence.

malicious adjective *their malicious cousin Charles would mysteriously disappear at sea* SPITEFUL, malevolent, evil-intentioned, vindictive, vengeful, malign, mean, nasty, hurtful, mischievous, wounding, cruel, unkind; *informal* bitchy, catty; *literary* malefic, maleficent. ANTONYM benevolent.

malign adjective *a malign influence* HARMFUL, evil, bad, baleful, hostile, inimical, destructive, malignant, injurious; *literary* malefic, maleficent. ANTONYM beneficial.

▸ verb *he maligned an innocent man* DEFAME, slander, libel, blacken someone's name/character, smear, vilify, speak ill of, cast aspersions on, run down, traduce, denigrate, disparage, slur, abuse, revile; *informal* badmouth, dis, knock; *formal* derogate, calumniate. ANTONYM praise.

THE RIGHT WORD

Do you want to ruin someone's life? You can **malign** someone, which is to say or write something evil without necessarily lying (*she was maligned for her past association with radical causes*). To **calumniate** is to make false and malicious statements about someone; the word often implies that you have seriously damaged that person's good name (*after leaving his job, he spent most of his time calumniating and ridiculing his former boss*). To **defame** is to cause actual injury to someone's good name or reputation (*he defamed her by accusing her of being a spy*). If you don't mind risking a lawsuit, you can **libel** the person, which is to write or print something that defames him or her (*the tabloid libeled the celebrity and ended up paying the price*). **Slander**, which is to defame someone orally, is seldom a basis for court action but can nevertheless cause injury to someone's reputation (*after a loud and very public argument, she accused him of slandering her*). If all else fails, you can **vilify** the person, which is to engage in abusive name-calling (*even though he was found innocent by the jury, he was vilified by his neighbors*).

malignant noun **1** *a malignant disease* VIRULENT, very infectious, invasive, uncontrollable, dangerous, deadly, fatal, incurable, life-threatening. ANTONYM curable.

2 *a malignant growth* CANCEROUS; *technical* metastatic. ANTONYM benign.

3 *a malignant thought* SPITEFUL, malicious, malevolent, evil-intentioned, vindictive, vengeful, malign, mean, nasty, hurtful, mischievous, wounding, cruel, unkind; *informal* bitchy, catty; *literary* malefic, maleficent. ANTONYM benevolent.

malinger verb *he was put on report for malingering* PRETEND TO BE ILL, feign (an) illness, fake (an) illness; shirk; *informal* goof off.

malingerer noun *you won't find any whiners or malingerers in this outfit* SHIRKER, idler, layabout, loafer; *informal* slacker, goof-off, goldbrick.

mall noun *we met at the mall to get our ears pierced* SHOPPING CENTER, (shopping) plaza, shopping complex, strip mall, mini-mall, galleria, megamall, marketplace.

malleable adjective **1** *a malleable substance* PLIABLE, ductile, plastic, pliant, soft, workable. ANTONYM hard.

2 *a malleable young woman* EASILY INFLUENCED, suggestible, susceptible, impressionable, pliable, amenable, compliant, tractable; biddable, complaisant, manipulable, persuadable, like putty in someone's hands. ANTONYM intractable.

malnutrition noun *the malnutrition of millions around the world is shameful* UNDERNOURISHMENT, malnourishment, poor diet, inadequate diet, unhealthy diet, lack of food; hunger, starvation.

malodorous adjective *several tenants in the building had complained about the malodorous apartment on the second floor* FOUL-SMELLING, evil-smelling, fetid, smelly, stinking (to high heaven), reeking, rank, high, putrid, noxious; *informal* stinky, funky; *literary* noisome, mephitic. See note at ODOROUS. ANTONYM fragrant.

malpractice noun *her foot surgeon was found guilty of malpractice* WRONGDOING, (professional) misconduct, breach of ethics, unprofessionalism, unethical behavior; negligence, carelessness, incompetence.

maltreat verb See MISTREAT.

mama's boy noun *he overcame his reputation as a mama's boy by becoming a champion bodybuilder* MILKSOP, namby-pamby, coward, weakling, mollycoddle; *informal* sissy, baby, wuss, wimp, milquetoast, drip, pantywaist; *archaic* poltroon.

mammoth adjective *a crisis of mammoth proportions* HUGE, enormous, gigantic, giant, colossal, massive, vast, immense, mighty, stupendous, monumental, Herculean, epic, prodigious, mountainous, monstrous, titanic, towering, elephantine, king-size(d), economy-size(d), gargantuan, Brobdingnagian; *informal* mega, monster, whopping, honking, humongous, bumper, jumbo, astronomical, ginormous. ANTONYM tiny.

man noun **1** *a handsome man* MALE, adult male, gentleman; *informal* guy, fellow, fella, joe, geezer, gent, bloke, chap, dude, hombre; (**men**) menfolk.

2 *all men are mortal* HUMAN BEING, human, person, mortal, individual, personage, soul.

3 *the evolution of man* THE HUMAN RACE, the human species, *Homo sapiens*, humankind, humanity, human beings, humans, people, mankind.

4 *the men voted to go on strike* WORKER, workman, laborer, hand, blue-collar worker; staff.

5 *have you met her new man?* BOYFRIEND, partner, husband, spouse, lover, admirer, fiancé; common-law husband, live-in lover, significant other, main squeeze; *informal* toy boy, sugar daddy, intended; *dated* beau, steady, young man.

6 *his man brought him a cocktail.* See MANSERVANT.

▸ verb **1** *the office is manned from 9 to 5* STAFF, crew, occupy, people.

2 *firefighters manned the pumps* OPERATE, work, use, utilize.

PHRASES: **man to man** *can we speak man to man?* FRANKLY, openly, honestly, directly, candidly, plainly, forthrightly, without beating about the bush; woman to woman. **to a man** *the squad volunteered, to a man, to work another full shift in the rescue mission* WITHOUT EXCEPTION, with no exceptions, bar none, one and all, everyone, each and every one, unanimously, as one.

USAGE NOTE **man**

Traditionally, the word **man** has been used to refer not only to adult males but also to human beings in general, regardless of sex. There is a historical explanation for this: in Old English, the principal sense of **man** was 'a human being,' and the words *wer* and *wif* were used to refer specifically to 'a male person' and 'a female person,' respectively. Subsequently, **man** replaced *wer* as the normal term for 'a male person,' but the older sense 'a human being' remained in use.

In the second half of the twentieth century, the generic use of **man** to refer to 'human beings in general' (*reptiles were here long before man appeared on the earth*) became problematic; the use is now often regarded as sexist or old-fashioned. In some contexts, terms such as **the human race** or **humankind** may be used instead of **man** or **mankind**.

manacle verb *the unruly inmates were manacled to the bars in the cell* SHACKLE, fetter, chain, put/clap in irons, handcuff, restrain; secure; *informal* cuff.

manacles plural noun *he claimed there were no manacles that could hold him* HANDCUFFS, shackles, chains, irons, fetters, restraints, bonds; *informal* cuffs, bracelets.

manage verb **1** *she manages a staff of 80 people* BE IN CHARGE OF, run, be head of, head, direct, control, preside over, lead, govern, rule, command, superintend, supervise, oversee, administer, organize, conduct, handle, guide, be at the helm of; *informal* head up.

2 *he managed a smile* ACCOMPLISH, achieve, do, carry out, perform, undertake, bring about/off, effect, finish; succeed in, contrive, engineer.

3 *will you be able to manage without him?* COPE, get along/on, make do, be/fare/do all right, carry on, survive, get by, muddle through/along, fend for oneself, shift for oneself, make ends meet, weather the storm; *informal* make out, hack it.

4 *she can't manage that horse* CONTROL, handle, master; cope with, deal with.

manageable adjective **1** *a manageable amount of work* ACHIEVABLE, doable, practicable, possible, feasible, reasonable, attainable, viable. ANTONYMS impractical, impossible.

2 *a manageable child* COMPLIANT, tractable, pliant, pliable, malleable, biddable, docile, amenable, governable, controllable, accommodating, acquiescent, complaisant, yielding. ANTONYM unmanageable.

3 *a manageable program* USER-FRIENDLY, easy to use, handy. ANTONYM unwieldy.

management noun **1** *he's responsible for the management of the firm* ADMINISTRATION, running, managing, organization; charge, care, direction, leadership, control, governing, governance, ruling, command, superintendence, supervision, overseeing, conduct, handling, guidance, operation.

2 *workers are disputing with management* MANAGERS, employers, directors, board of directors, board, directorate, executives, administrators, administration; owners, proprietors; *informal* bosses, top brass.

manager noun **1** *the plant manager* EXECUTIVE, head of department, supervisor, principal, administrator, head, director, managing director, CEO, employer, superintendent, foreman, forewoman, overseer; proprietor; *informal* boss, chief, head honcho.

2 *the band's manager* ORGANIZER, controller, comptroller; impresario.

mandate noun 1 *they won a mandate to form the government* AUTHORITY, approval, acceptance, ratification, endorsement, sanction, authorization.

2 *a mandate from the UN* INSTRUCTION, directive, decree, command, order, injunction, edict, charge, commission, bidding, ruling, fiat; *formal* ordinance.

▸ verb 1 *catalytic converters were mandated in 1975* MAKE MANDATORY, legislate, authorize, require by law; designate.

2 *they were mandated to strike* INSTRUCT, order, direct, command, tell, require, charge, call on.

mandatory adjective *a high school diploma is mandatory* OBLIGATORY, compulsory, binding, required, requisite, necessary, essential, imperative. ANTONYM optional.

maneuver verb 1 *I maneuvered the car into the space* STEER, guide, drive, negotiate, navigate, pilot, direct, manipulate, move, work, jockey.

2 *he maneuvered things to suit himself* MANIPULATE, contrive, manage, engineer, devise, plan, fix, organize, arrange, set up, orchestrate, choreograph, stage-manage; *informal* wangle.

3 *he began maneuvering for the party leadership* INTRIGUE, plot, scheme, plan, lay plans, conspire, pull strings.

▸ noun 1 *a tricky parking maneuver* OPERATION, exercise, activity, move, movement, action.

2 *diplomatic maneuvers* STRATAGEM, tactic, gambit, ploy, trick, dodge, ruse, plan, scheme, operation, device, plot, machination, artifice, subterfuge, intrigue.

3 **(maneuvers)** *military maneuvers* TRAINING EXERCISES, exercises, war games, operations.

manfully adverb *they manfully righted the toppled van* BRAVELY, courageously, boldly, gallantly, pluckily, heroically, intrepidly, fearlessly, valiantly, dauntlessly; resolutely, determinedly, hard, strongly, vigorously, with might and main, like a Trojan; with all one's strength, to the best of one's abilities, as best one can, desperately. See note at MALE.

manger noun *they laid fresh hay in the manger* TROUGH, feeding trough, feeder, crib.

mangle verb 1 *the bodies were mangled beyond recognition* MUTILATE, maim, disfigure, damage, injure, crush; hack, cut up, lacerate, tear apart, butcher, maul.

2 *he's mangling the English language* SPOIL, ruin, mar, mutilate, make a mess of, wreck; *informal* murder, make a hash of, butcher.

mangy adjective 1 *a mangy cat* SCABBY, scaly, scabrous, diseased.

2 *a mangy old armchair* SCRUFFY, moth-eaten, shabby, worn; dirty, squalid, sleazy, seedy, flea-bitten; *informal* tatty, raggedy-ass, the worse for wear, scuzzy.

manhandle verb 1 *tourists were manhandled by the protestors* PUSH, shove, jostle, hustle; maltreat, ill-treat, mistreat, maul, molest; *informal* paw, rough up, roust.

2 *we manhandled the piano down the stairs* HEAVE, haul, push, shove; pull, tug, drag, lug, carry, lift, maneuver; *informal* hump.

manhood noun 1 *the transition from boyhood to manhood* MATURITY, sexual maturity, adulthood.

2 *an insult to his manhood* VIRILITY, manliness, machismo, masculinity, maleness; mettle, spirit, strength, fortitude, determination, bravery, courage, intrepidity, valor, heroism, boldness.

mania noun 1 *fits of mania* MADNESS, derangement, dementia, insanity, lunacy, psychosis, mental illness; delirium, frenzy, hysteria, raving, wildness.

2 *his mania for gadgets* OBSESSION, compulsion, fixation, fetish, fascination, preoccupation, infatuation, passion, enthusiasm, desire, urge, craving; craze, fad, rage; *informal* thing, yen.

maniac noun 1 *a homicidal maniac* LUNATIC, madman, madwoman, psychopath; *informal* loony, fruitcake, nutcase, nut, psycho, mental case, head case, sicko, screwball, crazy, loon.

2 *informal a techno maniac* ENTHUSIAST, fan, devotee, aficionado; *informal* freak, fiend, fanatic, nut, buff, bum, addict.

WORD NOTE **mentalist**

Before this word vanishes into pure comedy (where in England in particular it now resides), its original meaning should be restated. It is not a synonym for a *nutcase* or a *maniac.* It refers to a person whose tastes are for mental rather than material pleasures, or whose artistic aim is the expression of thought. Of course, such a person in the current climate might as well be a *mentalist* (in the contemporary sense) and is best advised to take note of the original, rare-seventeenth-century definition, of a *mentalist:* "a person who conceals his or her real thoughts." **—ZS**

manic adjective 1 *a manic grin* MAD, insane, deranged, demented, maniacal, lunatic, wild, crazed, demonic, hysterical, raving, unhinged, unbalanced; *informal* crazy. ANTONYM sane.

2 *manic activity* FRENZIED, feverish, frenetic, hectic, intense; *informal* hyper, mad. ANTONYM calm.

manifest verb 1 *she manifested signs of depression* DISPLAY, show, exhibit, demonstrate, betray, present, reveal; *formal* evince. ANTONYM hide.

2 *his positive potential* ***is manifested by*** *his art* BE EVIDENCE OF, be a sign of, indicate, show, attest to, reflect, bespeak, prove, establish, evidence, substantiate, corroborate, confirm; *literary* betoken. ANTONYM mask.

▸ adjective *his manifest lack of interest* OBVIOUS, clear, plain, apparent, evident, patent, palpable, distinct, definite, blatant, overt, glaring, barefaced, explicit, transparent, conspicuous, undisguised, unmistakable, noticeable, perceptible, visible, recognizable. ANTONYM secret.

manifestation noun 1 *the manifestation of anxiety* DISPLAY, demonstration, show, exhibition, presentation.

2 *manifestations of global warming* SIGN, indication, evidence, token, symptom, testimony, proof, substantiation, mark, reflection, example, instance. See note at SIGN.

3 *a supernatural manifestation* APPARITION, appearance, materialization, visitation.

manifesto noun *a party manifesto that would change the course of world politics* POLICY STATEMENT, mission statement, platform, (little) red book, program, declaration, proclamation, pronouncement, announcement.

manifold adjective *the problems are manifold* MANY, numerous, multiple, multifarious, legion, diverse, various, several, varied, different, miscellaneous, assorted, sundry; *literary* myriad, divers.

manipulate verb **1** *he manipulated some knobs and levers* OPERATE, work; turn, pull.

2 *she manipulated the muscles of his back* MASSAGE, rub, knead, feel, palpate.

3 *the government tried to manipulate the situation* CONTROL, influence, use/turn to one's advantage, exploit, maneuver, engineer, steer, direct, gerrymander; twist someone around one's little finger.

4 *they accused him of manipulating the data* FALSIFY, rig, distort, alter, change, doctor, massage, juggle, tamper with, tinker with, interfere with, misrepresent; *informal* cook, fiddle with.

manipulative adjective *his manipulative partner eventually stole the business out from under him* SCHEMING, calculating, cunning, crafty, wily, shrewd, devious, designing, conniving, Machiavellian, artful, guileful, slippery, slick, sly, unscrupulous, disingenuous; *informal* foxy.

manipulator noun *a ruthless political manipulator* EXPLOITER, user, maneuverer, conniver, puppet master, wheeler-dealer; *informal* operator.

mankind noun *for the good of all mankind* THE HUMAN RACE, man, humanity, human beings, humans, *Homo sapiens*, humankind, people, men and women.

manly adjective **1** *his manly physique* VIRILE, masculine, strong, muscular, muscly, strapping, well-built, sturdy, robust, rugged, tough, powerful, brawny, red-blooded, vigorous; *informal* hunky. See note at MALE. ANTONYM effeminate.

2 *their manly deeds* BRAVE, courageous, bold, valiant, valorous, fearless, plucky, macho, manful, intrepid, daring, heroic, lionhearted, gallant, chivalrous, swashbuckling, adventurous, stouthearted, dauntless, doughty, resolute, determined, stalwart; *informal* gutsy, spunky, ballsy. ANTONYM cowardly.

man-made adjective *man-made fabrics* ARTIFICIAL, synthetic, manufactured, fabricated; imitation, ersatz, simulated, mock, fake, phony, counterfeit, plastic. ANTONYMS natural, real.

mannequin noun **1** *mannequins in a department store window* DUMMY, model, figure.

2 *mannequins on the catwalk* MODEL, fashion model, supermodel.

manner noun **1** *it was dealt with in a very efficient manner* WAY, fashion, mode, means, method, system, style, approach, technique, procedure, process, methodology, modus operandi, form.

2 *what manner of creature is it?* KIND, sort, type, variety, nature, breed, brand, stamp, class, category, genre, order.

3 *her rather unfriendly manner* DEMEANOR, air, aspect, attitude, bearing, cast, behavior, conduct; mien; *formal* comportment.

4 **(manners)** *aristocratic manners* CUSTOMS, habits, ways, practices, conventions, usages.

5 **(manners)** *it's bad manners to stare* BEHAVIOR, conduct, way of behaving; form.

6 **(manners)** *you ought to teach him some manners* CORRECT BEHAVIOR, etiquette, social graces, good form, protocol, politeness, decorum, propriety, gentility, civility, Ps and Qs.

mannered adjective *his highly mannered style of prose* AFFECTED, pretentious, unnatural, artificial, contrived, stilted, stiff, forced, put-on, theatrical, precious, stagy, camp; *informal* pseudo. ANTONYM natural.

mannerism noun *she built an act around the mannerisms she'd picked up from her Jewish mother and Italian aunts* IDIOSYNCRASY, quirk, oddity, foible, trait, peculiarity, habit, characteristic, tic.

mannish adjective *she adopted a mannish appearance for the stage* UNFEMININE, unwomanly, masculine, unladylike, Amazonian; *informal* butch. See note at MALE. ANTONYMS feminine, girlish.

manservant noun *my manservant Roderick will be at your disposal* VALET, attendant, retainer, equerry, man, steward, butler, houseman, footman, flunky, page, houseboy, lackey.

mansion noun *a tour of Beverly Hills mansions* STATELY HOME, hall, manor, manor house, country house; *informal* palace; *formal* residence. ANTONYM hovel.

manslaughter noun *the jury will decide if she is guilty of manslaughter* KILLING, murder, homicide, assassination; *literary* slaying.

mantle noun **1** *a dark green velvet mantle* CLOAK, cape, shawl, wrap, stole; *historical* pelisse.

2 *a thick mantle of snow* COVERING, layer, blanket, sheet, veil, curtain, canopy, cover, cloak, pall, shroud.

3 *the mantle of leadership* ROLE, burden, onus, duty, responsibility.

▸ verb *heavy mists mantled the forest* COVER, envelop, veil, cloak, curtain, shroud, swathe, wrap, blanket, conceal, hide, disguise, mask, obscure, surround, clothe; *literary* enshroud.

mantra noun *their newest mantra is "stay connected"* SLOGAN, motto, maxim, catchphrase, catchword, watchword, byword, buzzword, tag (line).

manual adjective **1** *manual work* DONE WITH ONE'S HANDS, by hand, laboring, physical, blue-collar.

2 *a manual drill* HAND-OPERATED, hand, nonelectric, nonautomatic.

▸ noun *a training manual* HANDBOOK, instruction book, instructions, guide, how-to book, companion, ABC, primer, guidebook, A to Z; *informal* bible.

manufacture verb **1** *the company manufactures laser printers* MAKE, produce, mass-produce, build, construct, assemble, put together, create, fabricate, turn out, process, engineer.

2 *a story manufactured by the press* MAKE UP, invent, fabricate, concoct, hatch, dream up, think up, trump up, devise, formulate, frame, contrive; *informal* cook up.

▸ noun *the manufacture of aircraft engines* PRODUCTION, making, manufacturing, mass-production, construction, building, assembly, creation, fabrication, prefabrication, processing.

manufacturer noun *local manufacturers are important*

sources of tax revenue MAKER, producer, builder, constructor, creator; factory owner, industrialist, captain of industry.

manure noun *spread composted manure over the strawberry plants* DUNG, muck, excrement, droppings, ordure, guano, cow pats; fertilizer; *informal* cow chips, road apples, horse apples, buffalo chips, cow-pies, cow patties, cow flops; turds, scat.

manuscript noun *the preservation of ancient manuscripts* DOCUMENT, text, script, paper, typescript, draft; codex, palimpsest, scroll; autograph, holograph.

many adjective **1** *many animals were killed* NUMEROUS, a great/good deal of, a lot of, plenty of, countless, innumerable, scores of, crowds of, droves of, an army of, a horde of, a multitude of, a multiplicity of, multitudinous, multiple, untold; several, various, sundry, diverse, assorted, multifarious; copious, abundant, profuse, an abundance of, a profusion of; *informal* lots of, umpteen, loads of, masses of, stacks of, scads of, heaps of, piles of, bags of, tons of, oodles of, dozens of, hundreds of, thousands of, millions of, billions of, zillions of, gazillions of, a slew of, a boatload of, more —— than one can shake a stick at; *literary* myriad, divers. ANTONYM few.

2 *sacrificing the individual for the sake of the many* PEOPLE, common people, masses, multitude, populace, public, rank and file; *informal* hoi polloi, common herd, mob, proletariat, riffraff, great unwashed, proles. ANTONYM few.

map noun *we'll never find their house without a map* PLAN, chart, cartogram, survey, plat, plot; road map, street map, guide; atlas, globe; relief map, contour map; Mercator projection, Peters projection.

▸ verb *the region was mapped from the air* CHART, plot, delineate, draw, depict, portray.

PHRASE: **map out** *he mapped out the plan for our campaign* OUTLINE, set out, lay out, sketch out, trace out, rough out, block out, delineate, detail, draw up, formulate, work out, frame, draft, plan, plot out, arrange, design, program.

mar verb **1** *an ugly scar marred his features* SPOIL, impair, disfigure, detract from, blemish, scar; mutilate, deface, deform. ANTONYM enhance.

2 *the celebrations were marred by violence* SPOIL, ruin, impair, damage, wreck; harm, hurt, blight, taint, tarnish, sully, stain, pollute; *informal* foul up; *formal* vitiate.

marauder noun *the placed chains across the river to keep out marauders* RAIDER, plunderer, pillager, looter, robber, pirate, freebooter, bandit, highwayman, rustler; *literary* brigand; *archaic* buccaneer, corsair, reaver.

marauding adjective *marauding Mongols destroyed their village* PREDATORY, rapacious, thieving, plundering, pillaging, looting, freebooting, piratical.

march verb **1** *the men marched past* STRIDE, walk, troop, step, pace, tread; footslog, slog, tramp, tromp, hike, trudge; parade, file, process.

2 *she marched in without even knocking* STRIDE, strut, stalk, flounce, storm, stomp, sweep.

3 *time **marches on*** ADVANCE, progress, move on, roll on.

▸ noun **1** *a long march* HIKE, trek, tramp, slog, footslog, walk; route march, forced march.

2 *police in riot gear charged the march* PARADE, procession, cortège; demonstration, protest.

3 *the march of technology* PROGRESS, advance, progression, development, evolution; passage.

margin noun **1** *the margin of the lake* EDGE, side, verge, border, perimeter, brink, brim, rim, fringe, boundary, limits, periphery, bound, extremity; *literary* bourn, skirt. See note at BORDER.

2 *there's no margin for error* LEEWAY, latitude, scope, room, room to maneuver, space, allowance, extra, surplus.

3 *they won by a narrow margin* GAP, majority, amount, difference.

marginal adjective **1** *the difference is marginal* SLIGHT, small, tiny, minute, insignificant, minimal, negligible.

2 *a marginal case* BORDERLINE, disputable, questionable, doubtful.

marginalize verb *the new management seems to be trying to marginalize our department* SIDELINE, trivialize; isolate, cut off, shut out; disenfranchise, alienate, estrange, discriminate against.

marijuana noun *the illegal cultivation of marijuana* CANNABIS, hashish, hemp, sinsemilla; informal POT, dope, grass, weed, Mary Jane, bud, hash, bhang, kef, ganja, locoweed; reefer, doob, spliff, toke, roach.

marinate verb *marinate the ribs in a mixture of beer, honey, and orange rind* STEEP, soak, souse, immerse, marinade, bathe.

marine adjective **1** *marine plants* SEAWATER, sea, saltwater, oceanic; aquatic; *technical* pelagic.

2 *a marine vessel* MARITIME, nautical, naval; seafaring, seagoing, oceangoing.

mariner noun *an old mariner from Gloucester* SAILOR, seaman, seafarer; *informal* sea dog, salt, bluejacket; *Brit.* matelot, shellback.

marital adjective *Fred was unable to cope with Leah's desire to dissolve their marital bond* MATRIMONIAL, married, wedded, conjugal, nuptial, marriage, wedding; spousal; *literary* connubial.

maritime adjective **1** *maritime law* NAVAL, marine, nautical; seafaring, seagoing, sea, oceangoing.

2 *maritime regions* COASTAL, seaside, littoral.

mark noun **1** *a dirty mark* BLEMISH, streak, spot, fleck, dot, blot, stain, smear, speck, speckle, blotch, smudge, smut, fingermark, fingerprint; bruise, discoloration; birthmark; *informal* splotch; *technical* stigma.

2 *a punctuation mark* SYMBOL, sign, character; diacritic.

3 *books bearing the mark of a well-known bookseller* LOGO, seal, stamp, imprint, symbol, emblem, device, insignia, badge, brand, trademark, monogram, hallmark, logotype, watermark.

4 *unemployment passed the three million mark* POINT, level, stage, degree.

5 *a mark of respect* SIGN, token, symbol, indication, badge, emblem; symptom, evidence, proof.

6 *the war left its mark on him* IMPRESSION, imprint, traces; effect, impact, influence.

7 *the mark of a civilized society* CHARACTERISTIC, feature, trait, attribute, quality, hallmark, calling card, badge, stamp, property, indicator.

8 *he got good marks for math* GRADE, grading, rating, score, percentage.

9 *the bullet missed its mark* TARGET, goal, aim, bull's-eye; objective, object, end.

▸ verb **1** *be careful not to mark the paintwork* DISCOLOR, stain, smear, smudge, streak, blotch, blemish; dirty, pockmark, bruise; *informal* splotch; *literary* smirch.

2 *her possessions were clearly marked* PUT ONE'S NAME ON, name, initial, label, identify; hallmark, watermark, brand.

3 *I've marked the relevant passages* INDICATE, label, flag, tick, check off, highlight; show, identify, designate, delineate, denote, specify.

4 *a festival to mark the town's 200th anniversary* CELEBRATE, observe, recognize, acknowledge, keep, honor, solemnize, pay tribute to, salute, commemorate, remember, memorialize.

5 *the incidents marked a new phase in their campaign* REPRESENT, signify, be a sign of, indicate, herald.

6 *his style is marked by simplicity and concision* CHARACTERIZE, distinguish, identify, typify, brand, signalize, stamp.

7 *I have a pile of essays to mark* ASSESS, evaluate, grade, appraise, correct.

8 *it'll cause trouble, you mark my words!* TAKE HEED OF, heed, listen to, take note of, pay attention to, attend to, note, mind, bear in mind, take into consideration.

PHRASES: **make one's mark** *she intends to make her mark in Hollywood* BE SUCCESSFUL, distinguish oneself, succeed, be a success, prosper, get ahead, make good; *informal* make it, make the grade. **mark down** *the prices will be marked down after Christmas* REDUCE, decrease, lower, cut, put down, discount; *informal* slash. **mark up** *they were accused of marking up the cost before offering a discount* INCREASE, raise, up, put up, hike (up), escalate; *informal* jack up. **quick off the mark** *an elite force that was more quick off the mark than any fighting element in the sector* ALERT, quick, quick-witted, bright, clever, perceptive, sharp, sharp-witted, observant, wide awake, on one's toes; *informal* on the ball, quick on the uptake. **wide of the mark** *his answer was wide of the mark* INACCURATE, incorrect, wrong, erroneous, off target, out, mistaken, misguided, misinformed.

marked adjective *we see a marked improvement in Sally's grades* NOTICEABLE, pronounced, decided, distinct, striking, clear, glaring, blatant, unmistakable, obvious, plain, manifest, patent, palpable, prominent, signal, significant, conspicuous, notable, recognizable, identifiable, distinguishable, discernible, apparent, evident; written all over one. ANTONYM imperceptible.

market noun **1** *I'll get some sugar when I'm at the market* GROCERY STORE, supermarket, store, convenience store; farmers' market.

2 *browsing through old postcards at the antiques market* MARKETPLACE, mart, flea market, bazaar, fair; *archaic* emporium.

3 *there's no market for such goods* DEMAND, call, want, desire, need, requirement.

4 *the market is sluggish* STOCK MARKET, trading, trade, business, commerce, buying and selling, dealing.

▸ verb *the product was marketed worldwide* SELL, retail, vend, merchandise, trade, peddle, hawk; advertise, promote.

PHRASE: **on the market** *these are the finest pearls on the market today* ON SALE, (up) for sale, available, obtainable, on the block.

marksman, markswoman noun *a self-taught marksman* SNIPER, sharpshooter, good shot; *informal* crack shot, deadeye, shootist.

maroon verb *schoolboys marooned on a desert island* STRAND, cast away, cast ashore, shipwreck; abandon, leave behind, leave, leave in the lurch, desert, forsake; *informal* leave high and dry.

marriage noun **1** *a proposal of marriage* (HOLY) MATRIMONY, wedlock.

2 *the marriage took place at St. Margaret's* WEDDING, wedding ceremony, marriage ceremony, nuptials, union. ANTONYMS divorce, separation.

3 *a marriage of jazz, pop, and gospel* UNION, alliance, fusion, mixture, mix, blend, amalgamation, combination, merger. ANTONYM separation.

married adjective **1** *a married couple* WEDDED, wed; *informal* spliced, hitched, coupled. ANTONYM single.

2 *married bliss* MARITAL, matrimonial, conjugal, nuptial; *Law* spousal; *literary* connubial.

marry verb **1** *the couple married last year* GET/BE MARRIED, wed, be wed, become man and wife; *informal* tie the knot, walk down the aisle, take the plunge, get spliced, get hitched, say "I do"; *dated* plight/pledge one's troth.

2 *John wanted to marry her* WED; *informal* make an honest woman of; *archaic* espouse. ANTONYM divorce.

3 *the show marries poetry with art* JOIN, unite, combine, fuse, mix, blend, merge, amalgamate, link, connect, couple, knit, yoke. ANTONYM separate.

marsh noun *a pair of great blue herons made regular visits to the marsh* SWAMP, marshland, bog, peat bog, muskeg, swampland, morass, mire, moor, quagmire, slough, fen, fenland, wetland, bayou.

marshal verb **1** *they marshaled an army* ASSEMBLE, gather (together), collect, muster, call together, draw up, line up, align, array, organize, group, arrange, deploy, position, order, dispose; mobilize, rally, round up. See note at GATHER.

2 *guests were marshaled to their seats* USHER, guide, escort, conduct, lead, shepherd, steer, take.

marsupial noun See table.

MARSUPIALS

antechinus	pademelon
bandicoot	phalanger
cuscus	pygmy possum
dasyure	quoll
flying phalanger	rat kangaroo
honey possum	ringtail
kangaroo	Tasmanian devil
koala	wallaby
numbat	wombat
opossum/possum	

martial adjective *their martial exploits* MILITARY, soldierly, soldier-like, army, naval; warlike, fighting, combative, bellicose, hawkish, pugnacious, militaristic.

martial art noun *trained in several martial arts* aikido, jiu-jitsu, judo, karate, kung fu, tae kwon do, Tai chi, kendo, krav maga, capoeira.

martyrdom noun *the martyrdom of Peter* DEATH, suffering, torture, torment, persecution, agony, ordeal; killing, sacrifice, self-sacrifice, crucifixion, immolation, burning, auto-da-fé; *Christianity* Passion.

marvel verb *she marveled at their courage* BE AMAZED, be astonished, be surprised, be awed, stand in awe, wonder; stare, gape, goggle, not believe one's eyes/ears, be dumbfounded; *informal* be flabbergasted.

▸ noun *he's a marvel* WONDER, miracle, sensation, spectacle, phenomenon; *informal* something else, something to shout about.

marvelous adjective **1** *his solo climb was marvelous* AMAZING, astounding, astonishing, awesome, breathtaking, sensational, remarkable, spectacular, stupendous, staggering, stunning; phenomenal, prodigious, miraculous, extraordinary, incredible, unbelievable; *literary* wondrous. ANTONYM commonplace.

2 *marvelous weather* EXCELLENT, splendid, wonderful, magnificent, superb, glorious, sublime, lovely, delightful, too good to be true; *informal* super, great, amazing, fantastic, terrific, tremendous, sensational, heavenly, divine, gorgeous, grand, fabulous, fab, marvy, awesome, to die for, magic, ace, killer, wicked, mind-blowing, jaw-dropping, far out, out of this world; smashing, brilliant, boss; *informal, dated* swell, dreamy. ANTONYM awful.

masculine adjective **1** *a masculine trait* MALE, man's, men's; male-oriented. See note at MALE. ANTONYM feminine.

2 *a powerfully masculine man* VIRILE, macho, manly, muscular, muscly, strong, strapping, well built, rugged, robust, brawny, powerful, red-blooded, vigorous; *informal* hunky. ANTONYMS weak, effeminate.

3 *a rather masculine woman* MANNISH, boyish, unfeminine, unwomanly, Amazonian; *informal* butch.

masculinity noun *he's the picture of masculinity* VIRILITY, manliness, maleness, machismo, vigor, strength, muscularity, ruggedness, robustness; *informal* testosterone.

mash verb *mash the potatoes* SMASH, crush, purée, cream, pulp, squash, pound, beat, rice.

▸ noun *first pound the garlic to a mash* PULP, purée, mush, paste.

mask noun **1** *she wore a mask to conceal her face* DISGUISE, false face; *historical* domino, visor.

2 *he dropped his mask of good humor* PRETENSE, semblance, veil, screen, front, false front, facade, veneer, blind, disguise, guise, concealment, cover, cover-up, cloak, camouflage.

▸ verb *poplar trees masked the factory* HIDE, conceal, disguise, cover up, obscure, screen, cloak, camouflage, veil.

masquerade noun **1** *a grand masquerade* MASKED BALL, masque, fancy-dress party, costume party.

2 *he couldn't keep up the masquerade much longer* PRETENSE, deception, pose, act, front, facade, disguise, dissimulation, bluff, play-acting, make-believe; *informal* put-on.

▸ verb *a woman* ***masquerading as*** *a man* PRETEND TO BE, pose as, pass oneself off as, impersonate, disguise oneself as.

Mass noun *we attended the six o'clock Mass* EUCHARIST, Holy Communion, Communion, service, liturgy.

mass noun **1** *a soggy mass of fallen leaves* PILE, heap; accumulation, aggregation, accretion, concretion, buildup; *informal* batch, wad.

2 *a mass of cyclists* CROWD, horde, large group, throng, host, troop, army, herd, flock, drove, swarm, mob, pack, press, crush, flood, multitude.

3 *the mass of our students are licensed drivers* MAJORITY, greater part/number, best/better part, major part, bulk, main body, lion's share; **(the mass)** most.

4 **(masses)** *bringing the news to the masses* COMMON PEOPLE, populace, public, people, rank and file, crowd, third estate; *derogatory* hoi polloi, mob, proletariat, common herd, great unwashed.

5 *informal a mass of food.* See LOT noun sense 1.

▸ adjective *mass hysteria* WIDESPREAD, general, wholesale, universal, large-scale, extensive, pandemic.

▸ verb *they began massing troops in the region* ASSEMBLE, marshal, gather together, muster, round up, mobilize, rally.

massacre noun **1** *a cold-blooded massacre of innocent civilians* SLAUGHTER, wholesale/mass slaughter, indiscriminate killing, mass murder, mass execution, annihilation, liquidation, decimation, extermination; carnage, butchery, bloodbath, bloodletting, pogrom, genocide, ethnic cleansing, holocaust, night of the long knives; *literary* slaying.

2 *informal the game was an 8–0 massacre.* See ROUT noun sense 2.

▸ verb **1** *thousands were brutally massacred* SLAUGHTER, butcher, murder, kill, annihilate, exterminate, execute, liquidate, eliminate, decimate, wipe out, mow down, cut down, put to the sword, put to death; *literary* slay. See note at KILL.

2 *informal they were massacred in the final round.* See TROUNCE.

massage noun *her physical therapy includes massage* RUB, rubdown, rubbing, kneading, palpation, manipulation, pummeling; body rub, back rub; shiatsu, reflexology, acupressure, hydromassage, Swedish massage, osteopathy; effleurage, tapotement.

▸ verb **1** *he massaged her tired muscles* RUB, knead, palpate, manipulate, pummel, work.

2 *the statistics have been massaged* ALTER, tamper with, manipulate, doctor, falsify, juggle, fiddle with, tinker with, distort, change, rig, interfere with, misrepresent; *informal* fix, cook, fiddle.

massive adjective *a massive iceberg* HUGE, enormous, vast, immense, large, big, mighty, great, colossal, tremendous, prodigious, gigantic, gargantuan, mammoth, monstrous, monumental, giant, towering, elephantine, mountainous, titanic; epic, Herculean, Brobdingnagian; *informal* monster, jumbo, mega, whopping, humongous, hulking, honking, bumper, astronomical, ginormous. See note at HEAVY. ANTONYM tiny.

mast noun **1** *a ship's mast* spar, boom, yard, gaff, foremast, mainmast, topmast, mizzen-mast, mizzen, royal mast.

2 *the mast on top of the building* FLAGPOLE, flagstaff, pole, post, rod, upright; aerial, transmitter, pylon.

master noun **1** *historical he acceded to his master's wishes* LORD, overlord, lord and master, ruler, sovereign, monarch, liege (lord), suzerain. ANTONYMS servant, underling.

2 *the dog's master* OWNER, keeper.

3 *a chess master* EXPERT, adept, genius, past master, maestro, virtuoso, professional, doyen, authority, champion; *informal* ace, pro, wizard, whiz, hotshot, maven, crackerjack. ANTONYMS novice, amateur.

4 *the master of the ship* CAPTAIN, commander; *informal* skipper.

5 *their spiritual master* GURU, teacher, leader, guide, mentor; rabbi, swami, Maharishi. ANTONYMS acolyte, disciple.

▸ verb 1 *I managed to master my fears* OVERCOME, conquer, beat, quell, quash, suppress, control, overpower, triumph over, subdue, vanquish, subjugate, prevail over, govern, curb, check, bridle, tame, defeat, get the better of, get a grip on, get over; *informal* lick.

2 *it took ages to master the technique* LEARN, become proficient in, know inside out, know (frontward and) backwards; pick up, grasp, understand; *informal* get the hang of.

▸ adjective 1 *a master craftsman* EXPERT, adept, proficient, skilled, skillful, deft, dexterous, adroit, practiced, experienced, masterly, accomplished, complete, demon, brilliant; *informal* crack, ace, mean, crackerjack.

2 *the master bedroom* PRINCIPAL, main, chief; biggest.

masterful adjective 1 *a masterful man* COMMANDING, powerful, imposing, magisterial, lordly, authoritative; dominating, domineering, overbearing, overweening, imperious. ANTONYM weak.

2 *their masterful handling of the situation* EXPERT, adept, clever, masterly, skillful, skilled, adroit, proficient, deft, dexterous, accomplished, polished, consummate; *informal* crack, ace. ANTONYM inept.

THE RIGHT WORD

Masterful and **masterly** overlap in meaning and are sometimes confused. **Masterful** can mean 'domineering,' but it also means 'very skillful, masterly.' Note, however, that **masterful** used in this 'masterly' sense generally describes a person (*he has limited talent, but he's masterful at exploiting it*), while **masterly** usually describes an achievement or action (*that was a masterly response to our opponents' arguments*).

masterly adjective See note at MASTERFUL.

mastermind verb *he masterminded the whole campaign* PLAN, control, direct, be in charge of, run, conduct, organize, arrange, preside over, orchestrate, stage-manage, engineer, manage, coordinate; conceive, devise, originate, initiate, think up, frame, hatch, come up with; *informal* be the brains behind.

▸ noun *the mastermind behind the project* GENIUS, mind, intellect, author, architect, organizer, originator, prime mover, initiator, inventor; *informal* brain, brains, idea man.

masterpiece noun *Vivaldi's masterpiece* PIÈCE DE RÉSISTANCE, chef-d'œuvre, masterwork, magnum opus, finest/best work, tour de force.

mastery noun 1 *her mastery of the language* PROFICIENCY, ability, capability; knowledge, understanding, comprehension, familiarity, command, grasp, grip.

2 *they played with tactical mastery* SKILL, skillfulness, expertise, dexterity, finesse, adroitness, virtuosity, prowess, deftness, proficiency; *informal* know-how.

3 *man's mastery over nature* CONTROL, domination, command, ascendancy, supremacy, preeminence, superiority; triumph, victory, the upper hand, the whip hand, rule, government, power, sway, authority, jurisdiction, dominion, sovereignty.

masticate verb *strong jaws enable them to masticate the bones of their prey* CHEW, munch, champ, chomp, crunch, eat; *formal* manducate.

mat noun 1 *the fat cat sat on the mat* RUG, runner, carpet, doormat, welcome mat, bath mat, hearth rug, floor cloth; dhurrie, numdah; kilim, flokati, tatami.

2 *he placed his glass on the mat* COASTER, placemat, table mat.

3 *a thick mat of hair* MASS, tangle, knot, mop, thatch, shock, mane.

▸ verb *his hair was matted with blood* TANGLE, entangle, knot, snarl up.

match noun 1 *we won the match* CONTEST, competition, game, tournament, event, trial, test, meet, matchup; bout, fight; derby; playoff, replay, rematch, engagement; *Scottish & Canadian* bonspiel.

2 *he was no match for the champion* EQUAL, rival, equivalent, peer, counterpart; *formal* compeer.

3 *the vase was an exact match of the one she already owned* LOOK-ALIKE, double, twin, duplicate, mate, fellow, companion, counterpart; replica, copy; *informal* spitting image, dead ringer.

4 *a love match* MARRIAGE, betrothal, relationship, partnership, union.

▸ verb 1 *the curtains matched the duvet cover* GO WITH, coordinate with, complement, suit; be the same as, be similar to.

2 *did their statements match?* CORRESPOND, be in agreement, tally, agree, match up, coincide, accord, conform, square.

3 *no one can match him at chess* EQUAL, be a match for, measure up to, compare with, parallel, be in the same league as, be on a par with, touch, keep pace with, keep up with, emulate, rival, vie with, compete with, contend with; *informal* hold a candle to.

matching adjective *red suede boots with a matching handbag | pick the two matching blocks from the pile* CORRESPONDING, equivalent, parallel, analogous; coordinating, complementary; paired, twin, identical, like, like (two) peas in a pod, alike. ANTONYMS different, clashing.

matchless adjective *her sister's matchless beauty* INCOMPARABLE, unrivaled, inimitable, beyond compare/comparison, unparalleled, unequaled, without equal, peerless, second to none, unsurpassed, unsurpassable, nonpareil, unique, consummate, perfect, rare, transcendent, surpassing; *formal* unexampled.

mate noun 1 *she's finally found her ideal mate* PARTNER, life partner, husband, wife, spouse, lover, live-in lover, significant other, companion, helpmate, helpmeet, consort; *informal* better half, other half, main squeeze, hubby, missus, missis, old lady, old man.

2 *this sock has lost its mate* MATCH, fellow, twin, companion, other half, equivalent.

3 *informal he's gone out with his mates.* See CHUM.

▸ verb *pandas rarely mate in captivity* BREED, couple, copulate.

material noun 1 *the decomposition of organic material* MATTER, substance, stuff, medium.

2 *the materials for a new building* CONSTITUENT, raw material, element, component.

3 **(materials)** *cleaning materials* THINGS, items, articles, stuff, necessaries.

4 *curtain material* FABRIC, cloth, textiles.

5 *material for a magazine article* INFORMATION, data, facts, facts and figures, statistics, evidence, details, particulars, background, notes; *informal* info, dope, lowdown.

▸ adjective 1 *the material world* PHYSICAL, corporeal, tangible, nonspiritual, mundane, worldly, earthly, secular, temporal, concrete, real, solid, substantial. ANTONYMS spiritual, abstract.

2 *she was too fond of material comforts* SENSUAL, physical, carnal, corporal, fleshly, bodily, creature. ANTONYMS intellectual, aesthetic.

3 *information that could be material to the inquiry* RELEVANT, pertinent, important, applicable, germane; apropos, to the point; vital, essential, key. ANTONYMS immaterial, irrelevant.

4 *the storms caused material damage* SIGNIFICANT, major, important. ANTONYM insignificant.

materialistic adjective *nonessential products that appeal to our materialistic society* CONSUMERIST, acquisitive, greedy; worldly, capitalistic, bourgeois.

materialize verb 1 *the forecasted rain did not materialize* HAPPEN, occur, come about, take place, come into being, transpire; *informal* come off; *formal* eventuate; *literary* come to pass.

2 *Harry materialized at the door* APPEAR, turn up, arrive, make/put in an appearance, present oneself/itself, emerge, surface, reveal oneself/itself, show one's face, pop up; *informal* show up.

maternal adjective 1 *her maternal instincts* MOTHERLY, protective, caring, nurturing, loving, devoted, affectionate, fond, warm, tender, gentle, kind, kindly, comforting.

2 *his maternal grandparents* ON ONE'S MOTHER'S SIDE; *dated* on the distaff side.

mathematical adjective 1 *mathematical symbols* ARITHMETICAL, numerical; statistical, algebraic, geometric, trigonometric.

2 *mathematical precision* RIGOROUS, meticulous, scrupulous, punctilious, scientific, strict, precise, exact, accurate, pinpoint, correct, careful, unerring.

BRANCHES OF MATHEMATICS

algebra	geometry
analysis	integral calculus
applied mathematics	mechanics
arithmetic	number theory
calculus	plane geometry
combinatorics	probability theory
computational mathematics	quadratics
conics	set theory
differential calculus	solid geometry
foundations	statistics
game theory	topology
geodesy	trigonometry

matrimonial adjective See MARITAL.

matrimony noun *the sacrament of holy matrimony* MARRIAGE, wedlock, union; nuptials. ANTONYM divorce.

matted adjective *the cat's matted fur* TANGLED, tangly, knotted, knotty, tousled, disheveled, uncombed, unkempt; *informal* ratty, mussy.

matter noun 1 *decaying vegetable matter* MATERIAL, substance, stuff.

2 *the heart of the matter* AFFAIR, business, proceeding, situation, circumstance, event, happening, occurrence, incident, episode, experience; subject, topic, issue, question, point, point at issue, case, concern.

3 *it is of little matter now* IMPORTANCE, consequence, significance, note, import, weight; *formal* moment.

4 *what's the matter?* PROBLEM, trouble, difficulty, complication; upset, worry.

5 *the matter of the book* CONTENT, subject matter, text, argument, substance.

▸ verb *it doesn't matter what you wear* BE IMPORTANT, make any/a difference, be of importance, be of consequence, be relevant, count; *informal* cut any ice.

PHRASES: **as a matter of fact** *as a matter of fact, I was the one who sent the flowers* ACTUALLY, in (actual) fact, in point of fact, as it happens, really, believe it or not, in reality, in truth, to tell the truth. **no matter** *I ordered a blue tablecloth, but no matter, the green one looks just fine* IT DOESN'T MATTER, it makes no difference, it's not important, never mind, don't worry about it.

matter-of-fact adjective *Desmond is too creative and fanciful to fit in with such matter-of-fact people* UNEMOTIONAL, practical, down-to-earth, sensible, realistic, rational, sober, unsentimental, pragmatic, businesslike, commonsensical, levelheaded, hardheaded, no-nonsense, factual, literal, straightforward, straight-out, plain, unembellished, unvarnished, unadorned; unimaginative, prosaic.

mature adjective 1 *a mature woman* ADULT, grown-up, grown, fully grown, full-grown, of age, fully developed, in one's prime, middle-aged. ANTONYM adolescent.

2 *he's very mature for his age* SENSIBLE, responsible, adult, levelheaded, reliable, dependable; wise, discriminating, shrewd, sophisticated. ANTONYM childish.

3 *mature cheese* RIPE, ripened, mellow; ready to eat/drink. ANTONYMS fresh, unripe.

4 *on mature reflection, he decided not to go* CAREFUL, thorough, deep, considered. ANTONYMS impulsive, unthinking.

▸ verb 1 *kittens mature when they are about a year old* BE FULLY GROWN, be full-grown; come of age, reach adulthood, reach maturity.

2 *he's matured since he left home* GROW UP, become more sensible, become more adult; blossom.

3 *leave the cheese to mature* RIPEN, mellow; age.

4 *their friendship didn't have time to mature* DEVELOP, grow, evolve, bloom, blossom, flourish, thrive.

THE RIGHT WORD

Most of us would prefer to **mature** rather than simply **age**. *Mature* implies gaining wisdom, experience, or sophistication as well as adulthood; when applied to other living things, it indicates fullness of growth and readiness for normal functioning (*a mature crop of strawberries*). To *age*, on the other hand, is to undergo the changes that result from the passage of time, often with an emphasis on the negative or destructive changes that accompany growing old (*the tragedy aged him five years*). **Develop** is like *mature* in that it means to undergo a series of positive changes to attain perfection or effectiveness, but it can refer to a part as well as a whole organism (*the kitten's eyesight had begun to develop at three weeks*). **Ripen** is a less formal word meaning to *mature*, but it usually applies to fruit (*the apples ripened in the sun*). **Mellow** suggests the tempering or moderation of harshness that comes with time or experience. With its connotations of warmth, mildness, and sweetness, it is a more positive word than *mature* or *age* (*to mellow as one gets older*).

---

maturity noun **1** *her progress from childhood to maturity* ADULTHOOD, majority, coming-of-age, manhood, womanhood.

2 *he displayed a maturity beyond his years* RESPONSIBILITY, sense, levelheadedness; wisdom, discrimination, shrewdness, sophistication.

maudlin adjective **1** *maudlin self-pity* SENTIMENTAL, oversentimental, emotional, overemotional, tearful, lachrymose; *informal* weepy, misty-eyed. See note at SENTIMENTAL.

2 *a maudlin ballad* MAWKISH, sentimental, oversweet, oversentimental; *informal* tearjerker, tearjerking, mushy, slushy, sloppy, schmaltzy, cheesy, corny, soppy, cornball, three-hankie.

maul verb **1** *he had been mauled by a lion* SAVAGE, attack, tear to pieces, lacerate, claw, scratch.

2 *the customers are not allowed to maul our dancers* MOLEST, feel, fondle, manhandle; *informal* grope, paw.

3 *informal his book was mauled by the critics.* See CRITICIZE.

maunder verb **1** *he maundered on about his problems* RAMBLE, prattle, blather, rattle, chatter, jabber, babble; *informal* yak, yatter.

2 *she maundered across the road* WANDER, drift, meander, amble, putter.

mausoleum noun *the Dirkson family mausoleum dates back to 1878* TOMB, sepulcher, crypt, vault, charnel house, burial chamber, catacomb.

maverick noun *Torrey was the maverick in the family, the only one who valued freedom over an inheritance* INDIVIDUALIST, nonconformist, free spirit, unorthodox person, original, eccentric; rebel, dissenter, dissident, enfant terrible; *informal* cowboy, loose cannon. ANTONYM conformist.

maw noun **1** *a cat scrub its maw with its forelegs* MOUTH, jaws, muzzle; throat, gullet; *informal* trap, chops, kisser.

2 *he walked forward into the gaping maw of the tunnel* ENTRANCE, opening, gap, hole, chasm, black hole, abyss.

mawkish adjective *he keeps sending her these mawkish greeting cards* SENTIMENTAL, oversentimental, maudlin, cloying, sickly, saccharine, sugary, oversweet, syrupy, nauseating; *informal* mushy, slushy, sloppy, schmaltzy, weepy, cutesy, lovey-dovey, cheesy, corny, soppy, cornball, hokey, tearjerker, tearjerking, three-hankie. See note at SENTIMENTAL.

maxim noun *the maxim "you can't cheat an honest man" is posted on the wall above his desk* SAYING, adage, aphorism, proverb, motto, saw, axiom, dictum, precept, epigram; truism, cliché. See note at SAYING.

maximum adjective *the maximum amount* GREATEST, highest, biggest, largest, top, topmost, most, utmost, maximal. ANTONYM minimum.

▸ noun *production levels are near their maximum* UPPER LIMIT, limit, utmost, uttermost, greatest, most, extremity, peak, height, ceiling, top, apex; *informal* max. ANTONYM minimum.

maybe adverb *maybe the bus will be on time today* PERHAPS, possibly, conceivably, it could be (that), it is possible (that), for all one knows; *literary* peradventure, perchance.

mayhem noun *no one would confess to how the mayhem started* CHAOS, disorder, havoc, bedlam, pandemonium, tumult, uproar, turmoil, commotion, all hell broken loose, maelstrom, trouble, disturbance, confusion, riot, anarchy, violence, insanity, madness; *informal* madhouse.

maze noun *the mainland's city streets were a baffling maze to the islanders* LABYRINTH, complex network, warren; web, tangle, jungle, snarl; puzzle.

meadow noun *Holsteins and Guernseys grazed lazily in the meadows along Route 24* FIELD, paddock; pasture, pastureland, prairie; *literary* lea, mead.

meager adjective **1** *their meager earnings* INADEQUATE, scanty, scant, paltry, limited, restricted, modest, insufficient, sparse, deficient, negligible, skimpy, slender, poor, miserable, pitiful, puny, miserly, niggardly, beggarly; *informal* measly, stingy, pathetic, piddling; *formal* exiguous. ANTONYM abundant.

2 *a tall, meager man* THIN, lean, skinny, spare, scrawny, gangling, gangly, spindly, stringy, bony, rawboned, gaunt, underweight, underfed, undernourished, emaciated, skeletal. ANTONYM fat.

meal noun *each meal on the cruise ship was spectacular* snack; *informal* bite (to eat), spread, blowout, feed; *formal* repast, collation; *literary* refection. See table.

TYPES OF MEALS

bag lunch	lunch
banquet	luncheon
barbecue	picnic
blue plate special	potluck (supper/dinner)
box lunch	power lunch
breakfast	prix fixe
brunch	rijsttafel
buffet	salad bar
clambake	smorgasbord
continental breakfast	supper
cookout	table d'hôte
dinner	takeout
feast	tea
high tea	wienie/wiener roast

mean[1] verb **1** *flashing lights mean the road is blocked* SIGNIFY, convey, denote, designate, indicate, connote, show, express, spell out; stand for, represent, symbolize; imply, suggest, intimate, hint at, insinuate, drive at, refer to, allude to, point to; *literary* betoken.

2 *she didn't mean to break it* INTEND, aim, plan, design, have in mind, contemplate, purpose, propose, set out, aspire, desire, want, wish, expect. See note at INTEND.

3 *he was hit by a bullet meant for a soldier* INTEND, design; destine, predestine.

4 *the closures will mean a rise in unemployment* ENTAIL, involve, necessitate, lead to, result in, give rise to, bring about, cause, engender, produce.

5 *this means a lot to me* MATTER, be important, be significant.

6 *a red sky in the morning usually means rain* PRESAGE, portend, foretell, augur, promise, foreshadow, herald, signal, bode; *literary* betoken.

mean[2] adjective **1** *a mean trick* UNKIND, nasty, unpleasant, spiteful, malicious, unfair, cruel, shabby, foul, despicable, contemptible, obnoxious, vile, odious, loathsome, base, low; *informal* horrible, horrid, hateful, rotten, low-down; beastly. ANTONYM kind.

2 *he's too mean to leave a tip* MISERLY, niggardly, close-fisted, parsimonious, penny-pinching, cheeseparing, Scroogelike; *informal* tightfisted, stingy, tight, mingy, money-grubbing, cheap; *formal* penurious. ANTONYMS generous, munificent.

3 *the truth was obvious to even the meanest intelligence* INFERIOR, poor, limited, restricted.

4 *their mean origins* LOWLY, humble, ordinary, low, low-born, modest, common, base, proletarian, plebeian, obscure, ignoble, undistinguished; *archaic* baseborn. ANTONYM noble.

5 *informal he's a mean cook.* See EXCELLENT.

mean[3] noun *a mean between frugality and miserliness* MIDDLE COURSE, middle way, midpoint, happy medium, golden mean, compromise, balance; median, norm, average.

▸ adjective *the mean temperature* AVERAGE, median, middle, medial, medium, normal, standard.

meander verb **1** *the river meandered gently* ZIGZAG, wind, twist, turn, curve, curl, bend, snake.

2 *we meandered along the path* STROLL, saunter, amble, wander, ramble, drift, maunder; *informal* mosey, tootle, toodle.

meandering adjective **1** *a meandering stream* WINDING, windy, zigzag, zigzagging, twisting, turning, curving, serpentine, sinuous, twisty. ANTONYM straight.

2 *meandering reminiscences* RAMBLING, maundering, circuitous, roundabout, digressive, discursive, indirect, tortuous, convoluted. ANTONYM succinct.

meaning noun **1** *the meaning of his remark* SIGNIFICANCE, sense, signification, import, gist, thrust, drift, implication, tenor, message, essence, substance, purport, intention.

2 *the word has several different meanings* DEFINITION, sense, explanation, denotation, connotation, interpretation, nuance.

3 *my life has no meaning* VALUE, validity, worth, consequence, account, use, usefulness, significance, point.

4 *his smile was full of meaning* EXPRESSIVENESS, significance, eloquence, implications, insinuations.

▸ adjective *a meaning look.* See MEANINGFUL sense 3.

meaningful adjective **1** *a meaningful remark* SIGNIFICANT, relevant, important, consequential, telling, material, valid, worthwhile. ANTONYM inconsequential.

2 *a meaningful relationship* SINCERE, deep, serious, in earnest, significant, important.

3 *a meaningful glance* EXPRESSIVE, eloquent, pointed, significant, meaning; pregnant, speaking, telltale, revealing, suggestive, charged, loaded.

meaningless adjective **1** *a jumble of meaningless words* UNINTELLIGIBLE, incomprehensible, incoherent.

2 *she felt her life was meaningless* FUTILE, pointless, aimless, empty, hollow, blank, vain, purposeless, valueless, useless, of no use, worthless, senseless, trivial, trifling, unimportant, insignificant, inconsequential. ANTONYM worthwhile.

means plural noun **1** *the best means to achieve your goal* METHOD, way, manner, mode, measure, technique, expedient, agency, medium, instrument, channel, vehicle, avenue, course, process, procedure.

2 *she doesn't have the means to support herself* MONEY, resources, capital, income, finance, funds, cash, wherewithal, assets; *informal* dough, bread, moola.

3 *a man of means* WEALTH, riches, affluence, substance, fortune, property, money, capital. PHRASES: **by all means** *by all means you must have dinner with us* OF COURSE, certainly, definitely, surely, absolutely, with pleasure; *informal* sure thing. **by means of** *the load was raised by means of a crane* USING, utilizing, employing, through, with the help of; as a result of, by dint of, by way of, by virtue of. **by no means** *the result is by no means certain* NOT AT ALL, in no way, not in the least, not in the slightest, not the least bit, not by a long shot, certainly not, absolutely not, definitely not, on no account, under no circumstances; *informal* no way.

meantime PHRASE: **in the meantime** See MEANWHILE sense 1.

meanwhile adverb **1** *meanwhile, I'll stay here* FOR NOW, for the moment, for the present, for the time being, meantime, in the meantime, in the interim, in the interval.

2 *cook for a further half hour; meanwhile, make the stuffing* AT THE SAME TIME, simultaneously, concurrently.

measly adjective **1** *her measly salary* PALTRY, meager, scanty, niggardly, miserable, inadequate, insufficient; *informal* pathetic, stingy.

2 *you measly little twerp* CONTEMPTIBLE, worthless, wretched, inconsequential, inferior.

measurable adjective **1** *a measurable amount* QUANTIFIABLE, computable.

2 *a measurable improvement* APPRECIABLE, noticeable, significant, visible, perceptible, definite, obvious.

measure verb **1** *they measured the length of the room* CALCULATE, compute, count, meter, quantify, weigh, size, evaluate, assess, gauge, plumb, determine.

2 *she did not need to* ***measure*** *herself* ***against*** *some ideal* COMPARE WITH, pit against, set against, test against, judge by.

▸ noun **1** *cost-cutting measures* ACTION, act, course (of action), deed, proceeding, procedure, step, means, expedient; maneuver, initiative, program, operation.

2 *the House passed the measure* STATUTE, act, bill, law, legislation.

3 *the original dimensions were in metric measure* SYSTEM, standard, units, scale.

4 *a measure of egg white* QUANTITY, amount, portion.

5 *the students retain* ***a measure*** *of independence* A CERTAIN AMOUNT, an amount, a certain degree, a degree; some.

6 *sales are the measure of the company's success* YARD-

STICK, test, standard, barometer, touchstone, litmus test, criterion, benchmark.

PHRASES: **beyond measure** *it irritates him beyond measure that she is always right* IMMENSELY, extremely, vastly, greatly, excessively, immeasurably, incalculably, infinitely. **for good measure** *she added a couple of chili peppers for good measure* AS A BONUS, as an extra, into the bargain, to boot, in addition, besides, as well. **get/have the measure of** *she wants to get the measure of Kate before they meet at the Olympics* EVALUATE, assess, gauge, judge, understand, fathom, read, be wise to, see through; *informal* have someone's number. **measure up** *he was cut from the Corps because he just couldn't measure up* PASS MUSTER, match up, come up to standard, fit/fill the bill, be acceptable; *informal* come up to scratch, make the grade, cut the mustard, be up to snuff. **measure up to** *we didn't measure up to their standards* MEET, come up to, equal, match, bear comparison with, be on a level with; achieve, satisfy, fulfill.

measured adjective **1** *his measured steps* REGULAR, steady, even, rhythmic, rhythmical, unfaltering; slow, dignified, stately, sedate, leisurely, unhurried.

2 *his measured tones* THOUGHTFUL, careful, carefully chosen, studied, calculated, planned, considered, deliberate, restrained.

measureless adjective *Otto's measureless charm* BOUNDLESS, limitless, unlimited, unbounded, untold, immense, vast, endless, inexhaustible, infinite, illimitable, immeasurable, incalculable. ANTONYM limited.

measurement noun **1** *measurement of the effect is difficult* QUANTIFICATION, computation, calculation, mensuration; evaluation, assessment, gauging.

2 *all measurements are given in metric units* SIZE, dimension, proportions, magnitude, amplitude; mass, bulk, volume, capacity, extent; value, amount, quantity, area, length, height, depth, weight, width, range.

meat noun **1** *you need to cut down on your consumption of meat.* FLESH, animal flesh. See table.

2 *archaic meat and drink* FOOD, nourishment, sustenance, provisions, rations, fare, foodstuff(s), provender, daily bread; *informal* grub, eats, chow, nosh, vittles; *formal* comestibles; *dated* victuals; *literary* viands.

3 *the meat of the matter* SUBSTANCE, pith, marrow, heart, kernel, core, nucleus, nub, essence, essentials, gist, fundamentals, basics; *informal* nitty-gritty.

meaty adjective **1** *a tall, meaty man* BEEFY, brawny, burly, muscular, muscly, powerful, sturdy, strapping, well-built, solidly built, thickset; fleshy, stout.

2 *a good, meaty story* INTERESTING, thought-provoking, three-dimensional, stimulating; substantial, satisfying, meaningful, deep, profound.

mechanic noun *ask the mechanic for an estimate on the repairs* TECHNICIAN, ENGINEER, repairman, serviceman; *informal* grease monkey.

mechanical adjective **1** *a mechanical device* MECHANIZED, machine-driven, automated, automatic, power-driven, robotic. ANTONYM manual.

2 *a mechanical response* AUTOMATIC, unthinking, unconscious, robotic, involuntary, reflex, knee-jerk, gut, habitual, routine, unemotional, unfeeling, lifeless; perfunctory, cursory, careless, casual. ANTONYM conscious.

MEAT

Types of Meat
alligator
antelope
armadillo
bear
beaver
beefalo
bison
boar
buffalo
caiman
capon
caribou
cervena
chicken
Cornish hen
duck
elk
emu
fowl
frog legs
game
goat
goose
grouse
guinea fowl
hare
kangaroo
kid
lamb
llama
moose
muscovy duck
musk ox
muskrat
mutton
ostrich
partridge
pheasant
pigeon
pork
poultry
poussin
pullet
rabbit
raccoon
rattlesnake
snail
squab
squirrel
turkey
turtle
veal
venison
wild boar
wild turkey
wood pigeon
yak

Cuts of Meat
American leg
arm roast
arm steak
baby back rib
back fat
back rib
bacon
baron
belly
blade
blade Boston
blade chop
blade loin
Boston shoulder
braciola
brains
breast
brisket
burger
butt
butterfly
butterfly chop
Canadian bacon
cap steak
caul
center loin
center rib
charcuterie
charqui
chateaubriand
chitterlings
chop
chuck
chuck blade roast
club steak
cold cut
corned beef
country style rib
cross rib roast
crosscut shank
crown roast
cubed steak
culotte steak
cushion shoulder
cutlet
Delmonico
drumstick
eye of round
fatback
filet
filet mignon
fillet
flank
flanken
flitch
foie gras
fore shank
frenched leg
gammon
gizzards
ground chuck
ground round
ground sirloin
ham
hamburger
heart
heel of round
hindshank
hock
jowl
Kansas City strip
kidney
knuckles
lard
leg of lamb
liver
loin
lung
marrow
medallion
mountain oyster
neck
neck slice
New York sirloin
noisette
numbles
offal
oxtail
paillard
pastrami

picnic	sirloin chop
pig tail	sirloin tip
pig's foot	skirt steak
pin bone sirloin	slab bacon
plate	sparerib
porterhouse	Spencer steak
pot roast	spleen
prairie oyster	square shoulder
prosciutto	St. Louis style rib
rack	standing rib roast
rib	steak
rib chop	steamboat round
rib eye	stew meat
rib roast	stomach
rib tip	strip steak
riblet	suet
roast	sweetbread
rolled leg	Swiss steak
rolled roast	T-bone
round bone sirloin	tenderloin
rump	testicle
saddle	thigh
Salisbury steak	tongue
salt pork	top loin
sandwich steak	top sirloin
shank	tournedo
shell steak	triangle steak
shin	tripe
short loin	tri-tip
short rib	umbles
shortplate	veal
shoulder	wedge bone sirloin
sirloin	wing

mechanism noun **1** *an electrical mechanism* MACHINE, piece of machinery, appliance, apparatus, device, instrument, contraption, gadget; *informal* gizmo.

2 *the train's safety mechanism* MACHINERY, workings, works, movement, action, gears, components.

3 *a formal mechanism for citizens to lodge complaints* PROCEDURE, process, system, operation, method, technique, means, medium, agency, channel.

medal noun *they gathered once every five years to display their medals and share war stories* DECORATION, ribbon, star, badge, laurel, palm, award; honor.

meddle verb **1** *don't* ***meddle in*** *my affairs* INTERFERE IN/WITH, butt in/into, intrude on/into, intervene in, pry into; *informal* poke one's nose in, horn in on, muscle in on, snoop into, stick one's oar in, kibitz in.

2 *someone had been meddling with her things* FIDDLE, interfere, tamper, tinker, fool around.

meddlesome adjective *my meddlesome neighbor is peering out the window at us* INTERFERING, meddling, intrusive, prying, busybody; *informal* nosy. See note at IMPERTINENT.

media noun ***the media*** *went wild with the story of Jackson's arrest* THE PRESS, the fourth estate, the news, the papers; broadcasting, publishing.

USAGE NOTE **media, medium**

Strictly speaking, the first is the plural of the second (*the media were overreacting*). But *media*—as a shortened form of communications *media*—is increasingly used as a mass noun (*the media was overreacting*). While that usage still makes some squeamish, it must be accepted as standard. But it's still possible (and preferable) to draw the line at *medias*, which has recently raised its ugly head—e.g.: "The staff will use several medias [read *media*] and visuals to help get their points across." (*Virginian-Pilot & Ledger Star* [Norfolk]; Jan. 17, 1996.)

Mediums is the correct plural when the sense of *medium* is "a clairvoyant or spiritualist"—e.g.: "Contact is initiated by the deceased, and no psychics, mediums or devices are involved." (*St. Petersburg Times*; Oct. 14, 1996.) Otherwise, the form should be avoided—e.g.: "Reporters for printed mediums [read *media*] also focus criticism on television for using all-purpose experts to express an opinion on a wide variety of subjects." (*New York Times*; May 4, 1990.) **—BG**

median adjective the median score for this test is 73 medial, mean, middle, average, mid, central, intermediate.

mediate verb **1** *the UN tried to mediate between the two countries* ARBITRATE, conciliate, moderate, act as peacemaker, make peace; intervene, step in, intercede, act as an intermediary, liaise.

2 *a tribunal was set up to mediate disputes* RESOLVE, settle, arbitrate in, umpire, reconcile, referee; mend, clear up; *informal* patch up. See note at INSERT.

3 *he attempted to mediate a solution to the conflict* NEGOTIATE, bring about, effect; *formal* effectuate.

mediation noun *mediation between victims and offenders* ARBITRATION, conciliation, reconciliation, intervention, intercession, good offices; negotiation, shuttle diplomacy.

mediator noun *the mediator in their salary dispute* ARBITRATOR, arbiter, negotiator, conciliator, peacemaker, go-between, middleman, intermediary, moderator, intervenor, intercessor, broker, honest broker, liaison officer; umpire, referee, adjudicator, judge.

medicinal adjective *an infusion of medicinal herbs* CURATIVE, healing, remedial, therapeutic, restorative, corrective, health-giving; medical.

FORMS OF MEDICATION

balsam	lotion
cachet	lozenge
caplet	nasal spray
capsule	nebulizer
cream	ointment
drip	pastille
drops	pill
enema	poultice
gargle	powder
hypodermic	rub
inhalant	salve
injectable	suppository
intravenous	tablet

medicine noun **1** *the practice of medicine.* See table on page 572.

2 *take your medicine* MEDICATION, medicament, drug, prescription, pharmaceutical, dose, treatment, remedy, cure; nostrum, panacea, cure-all; *informal* meds; *archaic* physic. See table on this page.

medicine man noun *she wouldn't let the mission clinic treat her without approval from the local medicine man* SHAMAN, healer; witch doctor.

medieval adjective **1** *medieval times* OF THE MIDDLE AGES, of the Dark Ages, Dark-Age; Gothic. ANTONYM modern.

2 *informal his attitudes are positively medieval* PRIMITIVE, antiquated, archaic, antique, antediluvian, old-fashioned, out of date, outdated, outmoded, anachronistic, passé, obsolete; *informal* horse-and-buggy. ANTONYM modern.

BRANCHES OF MEDICINE

anesthesiology (anesthesia)	obstetrics (pregnancy, childbirth)
allopathy (conventional drugs)	odontology (teeth)
audiology (hearing)	oncology (cancer)
cardiology (heart)	ophthalmology (eyes)
chiropody (feet)	orthodontics (teeth alignment)
cytology (cells)	orthopedics (bones)
dentistry (teeth)	otology (ear)
dermatology (skin)	otorhinolaryngology (ear, nose, throat)
embryology (embryos)	pediatrics (children)
endocrinology (glands, hormones)	pathology (diseases)
epidemiology (disease control)	periodontics (gums)
etiology (disease causes)	pharmacology (drugs)
family practice (general medicine)	physiotherapy (manipulation, exercise)
gastroenterology (stomach, intestines)	podiatry (feet)
general practice (general medicine)	proctology (rectum)
geriatrics (the elderly)	prosthetics (artificial body parts)
gerontology (old age)	prosthodontics (artificial teeth)
gynecology (women)	psychiatry (mental illness)
hematology (blood)	radiology (radiation)
histology (tissues)	serology (blood sera)
immunology (immune system)	surgery (incisions)
internal medicine (internal organs)	symptomatology (symptoms)
myology (muscles)	therapeutics (disease treatment)
neurology (nervous system)	toxicology (poisons)
nosology (disease classification)	urology (kidneys, urinary tract)
nuclear medicine (radioactivity)	veterinary medicine (animals)

mediocre adjective a mediocre performance ORDINARY, average, middling, middle-of-the-road, uninspired, undistinguished, indifferent, unexceptional, unexciting, unremarkable, run-of-the-mill, pedestrian, prosaic, lackluster, forgettable, amateur, amateurish; *informal* OK, so-so, 'comme ci, comme ça', plain-vanilla, fair-to-middling, no great shakes, not up to much, bush-league. ANTONYM excellent.

meditate verb *please allow me more time to meditate* CONTEMPLATE, think, consider, ponder, muse, reflect, deliberate, ruminate, chew the cud, brood, mull something over; be in a brown study, be deep/lost in thought, debate with oneself; pray; *informal* put on one's thinking cap; *formal* cogitate.

meditation noun *cultivating the presence of God through meditation* CONTEMPLATION, thought, thinking, musing, pondering, consideration, reflection, deliberation, rumination, brooding, reverie, brown study, concentration; prayer; *formal* cogitation.

medium noun **1** *using technology as a medium for job creation* radio was the first great medium of mass communication MEANS, method, way, form, agency, avenue, channel, vehicle, organ, instrument, mechanism. See note at MEDIA. See also table at ART.

2 *organisms growing in their natural medium* HABITAT, element, environment, surroundings, milieu, setting, conditions.

3 *she consulted a medium* SPIRITUALIST, spiritist, necromancer, channeler; fortune teller, clairvoyant, psychic.

4 *a happy medium* MIDDLE WAY, middle course, middle ground, middle, mean, median, midpoint; compromise, golden mean.

▸ adjective *medium height* AVERAGE, middling, medium-sized, middle-sized, moderate, normal, standard.

medley noun *a medley of Beatles songs | a vegetable medley* ASSORTMENT, miscellany, mixture, mélange, variety, mixed bag, grab bag, mix, collection, selection, potpourri, patchwork, bricolage; motley collection, ragbag, gallimaufry, mishmash, jumble, hodgepodge, salmagundi.

meek adjective *they called her Miss Mouse because she was so meek* SUBMISSIVE, yielding, obedient, compliant, tame, biddable, tractable, acquiescent, deferential, timid, unprotesting, unresisting, like a lamb to the slaughter; quiet, mild, gentle, docile, lamblike, shy, diffident, unassuming, self-effacing. ANTONYM assertive.

meet verb **1** *I met an old friend on the train* ENCOUNTER, meet up with, come face to face with, run into, run across, come across/upon, chance on, happen on, stumble across/on; *informal* bump into.

2 *she first met Paul at a party* GET TO KNOW, be introduced to, make the acquaintance of.

3 *the committee met on Saturday* ASSEMBLE, gather, come together, get together, congregate, convene.

4 *the place where three roads meet* CONVERGE, connect, touch, link up, intersect, cross, join.

5 *she met death bravely* FACE, encounter, undergo, experience, go through, suffer, endure, bear; cope with, handle.

6 *the announcement was met with widespread hostility* GREET, receive, answer, treat.

7 *he does not meet the job's requirements* FULFILL, satisfy, fill, measure up to, match (up to), conform to, come up to, comply with, answer.

8 *shipowners would meet the cost of oil spills* PAY, settle, clear, honor, discharge, pay off, square.

▸ noun *a track meet* EVENT, tournament, game, match, contest, competition.

PHRASE: **meet someone halfway** See HALFWAY.

meeting noun **1** *he stood up to address the meeting* GATHERING, assembly, conference, congregation, convention, summit, forum, convocation, conclave, council, rally, caucus; *informal* get-together.

2 *she demanded a meeting with the councilman* CONSULTATION, audience, interview.

3 *he intrigued her on their first meeting* ENCOUNTER, contact; appointment, assignation, rendezvous; *literary* tryst.

4 *the meeting of land and sea* CONVERGENCE, coming together, confluence, conjunction, union, junction, abutment; intersection, T-junction, crossing.

mega adjective *informal she signed a mega contract.* See HUGE.

megalomania noun *the megalomania during the "up" phases of his bipolar disorder has gotten worse* DELUSIONS OF GRANDEUR, folie de grandeur, thirst/lust for power; self-importance, egotism, conceit, conceitedness.

melancholy adjective *a melancholy expression* SAD, sorrowful, unhappy, desolate, mournful, lugubrious, gloomy, despondent, dejected, depressed, downhearted, downcast, disconsolate, glum, miserable, wretched, dismal, morose, woeful, woebegone, doleful, joyless, heavy-hearted; *informal* down in the dumps, down in/at the mouth, blue; *literary* atrabilious. See note at GLUM. ANTONYM cheerful.

▸ noun *a feeling of melancholy* SADNESS, sorrow, unhappiness, woe, desolation, melancholia, dejection, depression, despondency, cafard, gloom, gloominess, misery; *informal* the dumps, the blues.

mélange noun *a mélange of different cultures* MIXTURE, medley, assortment, blend, variety, mixed bag, grab bag, mix, miscellany, selection, potpourri, patchwork, bricolage; motley collection, ragbag, gallimaufry, hash, mishmash, jumble, hodgepodge. See note at JUMBLE.

meld verb *the molten metals are melded into a durable alloy* BLEND, merge, combine, fuse, mesh, alloy.

melee noun *people were trampled in the melee* FRACAS, disturbance, rumpus, tumult, commotion, ruckus, disorder, fray; brawl, fight, scuffle, struggle, skirmish, scrimmage, free-for-all, tussle; *informal* scrap, set-to, ruction, slugfest.

mellifluous adjective *mellifluous dinner music* SWEET-SOUNDING, dulcet, honeyed, mellow, soft, liquid, silvery, soothing, rich, smooth, euphonious, harmonious, tuneful, musical. ANTONYM cacophonous.

mellow adjective **1** *a mellow mood* GENIAL, affable, amiable, good-humored, good-natured, amicable, pleasant, relaxed, easygoing, low-maintenance, placid; jovial, jolly, cheerful, happy, merry.

2 *the mellow tone of his voice* DULCET, sweet-sounding, tuneful, melodious, mellifluous; soft, smooth, warm, full, rich.

3 *a mellow wine* FULL-BODIED, mature, well matured, full-flavored, rich, smooth. See note at MATURE. PHRASE: **mellow out** *you need to mellow out* RELAX, unwind, loosen up, de-stress, slow down, take it easy; *informal* chill (out), take a (chill) pill, decompress.

melodious adjective *the pleasure of hearing her melodious singing voice* TUNEFUL, melodic, musical, mellifluous, dulcet, sweet-sounding, silvery, harmonious, euphonious, lyrical; *informal* easy on the ear. ANTONYM discordant.

melodramatic adjective *the early soap operas of radio days were exceedingly melodramatic* EXAGGERATED, histrionic, overdramatic, overdone, operatic, sensationalized, overemotional, overwrought, sentimental, extravagant; theatrical, stagy, actressy; *informal* hammy.

melody noun *familiar melodies* TUNE, air, strain, theme, song, refrain, piece of music; *informal* ditty.

melt verb **1** *the snow was beginning to melt* THAW, liquefy, defrost, soften, dissolve, deliquesce.

2 *his smile melted her heart* SOFTEN, disarm, touch, affect, move.

3 *his anger* ***melted away*** VANISH, disappear, fade away, dissolve, evaporate; *literary* evanesce.

meltdown noun *informal she was heading for a meltdown and we chose to ignore the signs* BREAKDOWN, nervous breakdown, mental collapse; *informal* freak-out, crack-up, fit, tantrum; disintegration, collapse.

member noun **1** *a member of the club* SUBSCRIBER, associate, affiliate, life member, card-carrying member.

2 *a member of a mathematical set* CONSTITUENT, element, component, part, portion, piece, unit.

3 *archaic many victims had injured members* LIMB, organ; arm, leg, appendage.

membrane noun *the sensitive membranes in the mouth* LAYER, sheet, skin, film, tissue, integument, overlay; *technical* pellicle.

memento noun *she kept the painted clamshell as a memento from our trip to Cape Cod* SOUVENIR, keepsake, reminder, remembrance, token, memorial bomboniere; trophy, relic.

memo noun *informal* See MEMORANDUM.

memoir noun **1** *a touching memoir of her childhood* ACCOUNT, history, record, chronicle, narrative, story, portrayal, depiction, sketch, portrait, profile, biography, monograph.

2 **(memoirs)** *he published his memoirs in 1955* AUTOBIOGRAPHY, life story, memories, recollections, reminiscences; journal, diary.

memorable adjective *thank you for making our visit so memorable | a memorable theme song* UNFORGETTABLE, indelible, catchy, haunting; momentous, significant, historic, notable, noteworthy, important, consequential, remarkable, special, signal, outstanding, extraordinary, striking, vivid, arresting, impressive, distinctive, distinguished, famous, celebrated, renowned, illustrious, glorious.

memorandum noun *a memorandum from the general* MESSAGE, communication, note, e-mail, letter, missive, directive; reminder, aide-mémoire; *informal* memo.

memorial noun **1** *the war memorial* MONUMENT, cenotaph, mausoleum; statue, plaque, cairn; shrine; tombstone, gravestone, headstone.

2 *the festival is a memorial to his life's work* TRIBUTE, testimonial; remembrance, memento.

▸ adjective *a memorial service* COMMEMORATIVE, remembrance, commemorating.

memorize verb *we have to memorize a poem in French* COMMIT TO MEMORY, remember, learn by heart, get off by heart, learn, learn by rote, become word-perfect in, get something down pat; *archaic* con.

memory noun **1** *she is losing her memory* ABILITY TO REMEMBER, powers of recall.

2 *happy memories of her young days* RECOLLECTION, remembrance, reminiscence; impression.

3 *the town built a statue in memory of him* COMMEMORATION, remembrance; honor, tribute, recognition, respect.

4 *a computer's memory* MEMORY BANK, store, cache, disk, RAM, ROM, hard drive.

menace noun **1** *an atmosphere full of menace* THREAT, ominousness, intimidation, warning, ill omen.

2 *a menace to urban society* DANGER, peril, risk, hazard, threat; jeopardy.

3 *that dog is a menace* NUISANCE, pest, annoyance, plague, torment, terror, troublemaker, mischief-maker, thorn in someone's side/flesh.

▸ verb **1** *gorillas are still menaced by poaching* THREATEN, be a danger to, put at risk, jeopardize, imperil.

2 *a gang of skinheads menaced local residents* INTIMIDATE, threaten, terrorize, frighten, scare, terrify.

menacing adjective THREATENING, ominous, intimidating, frightening, terrifying, alarming, forbidding, black, thunderous, glowering, unfriendly, hostile, sinister, baleful, warning; *formal* minatory. ANTONYM friendly.

mend verb **1** *workmen were mending faulty cabling* REPAIR, fix, put back together, piece together, restore; sew (up), stitch, darn, patch, cobble; rehabilitate, renew, renovate; *informal* patch up. ANTONYMS break, worsen.

2 *they mended their quarrel* PUT/SET RIGHT, set straight, straighten out, sort out, rectify, remedy, cure, right, resolve, square, settle, put to rights, correct, retrieve, improve, make better. ANTONYMS break, worsen.

mendacious adjective LYING, untruthful, dishonest, deceitful, false, dissembling, insincere, disingenuous, hypocritical, fraudulent, double-dealing, two-faced, two-timing, duplicitous, perjured; untrue, fictitious, falsified, fabricated, fallacious, invented, made up; *informal* full of crap; *literary* perfidious. ANTONYM truthful.

mendicant noun See BEGGAR noun sense 1.

menial adjective *a menial job* UNSKILLED, lowly, humble, low-status, inferior, degrading; routine, humdrum, boring, dull.

▸ noun *they were treated like menials* SERVANT, drudge, minion, joe-boy, factotum, lackey, hired hand; *informal* wage slave, gofer, peon, grunt; *archaic* scullion.

menstruation noun *tribal ceremonies regarding menstruation* PERIOD, menses, menorrhea, menstrual cycle; menarche; *informal* one's/that time of the month; *informal, dated* the curse.

mental adjective **1** *mental faculties* INTELLECTUAL, cerebral, brain, rational, cognitive. ANTONYM physical.

2 *a mental disorder* PSYCHIATRIC, psychological, psychogenic.

3 *informal he's completely mental.* See MAD sense 1.

mentality noun **1** *I can't understand the mentality of these people* WAY OF THINKING, mind set, cast of mind, frame of mind, turn of mind, mind, psychology, mental attitude, outlook, disposition, makeup.

2 *a person of limited mentality* INTELLECT, intellectual capabilities, intelligence, IQ, (powers of) reasoning, rationality; *informal* brains, smarts.

mentally adverb *mentally, I was prepared to deal with the situation* IN ONE'S MIND, in one's head, inwardly, intellectually, cognitively.

mention verb **1** *don't mention the war* ALLUDE TO, refer to, touch on/upon; bring up, raise, broach, introduce, moot.

2 *Jim mentioned that he'd met them before* STATE, say, indicate, let someone know, disclose, divulge, reveal.

3 *I'll gladly mention your work to my friends* RECOMMEND, commend, put in a good word for, speak well of.

▸ noun **1** *he made no* ***mention of*** *your request* REFERENCE TO, allusion to, remark of/about/regarding, statement about/regarding, announcement of, indication of.

2 *my book got a mention on the show* RECOMMENDATION, commendation, a good word.

PHRASES: **don't mention it** *"Sorry for being late." "Oh, don't mention it."* DON'T APOLOGIZE, it doesn't matter, it makes no difference, it's not important, never mind, don't worry. **not to mention** *if the party's canceled, we'll have to notify the guests, not to mention the caterers* IN ADDITION TO, as well as; not counting, not including, to say nothing of, aside from, besides.

mentor noun **1** *his political mentors* ADVISER, guide, guru, counselor, consultant; confidant(e).

2 *regular meetings between mentor and trainee* TRAINER, teacher, tutor, instructor.

menu noun **1** *she studied the menu before ordering* BILL OF FARE, carte du jour, table d'hôte; wine list.

2 *a drop-down menu* LIST OF COMMANDS, options, toolbar.

meow verb *a stray cat meowed at the back door* MEW, mewl, cry.

mephitic adjective *literary* See MALODOROUS.

mercantile adjective *her grandfather had invested in several mercantile interests at the turn of the century* COMMERCIAL, trade, trading, business, merchant, sales.

mercenary adjective **1** *mercenary self-interest* MONEY-ORIENTED, grasping, greedy, acquisitive, avaricious, covetous, bribable, venal, materialistic; *informal* money-grubbing.

2 *mercenary soldiers* HIRED, paid, bought, professional.

▸ noun *a group of mercenaries* SOLDIER OF FORTUNE, professional soldier, hired soldier, gunman; *informal* hired gun; *historical* condottiere.

merchandise noun *a wide range of merchandise* GOODS, wares, stock, commodities, lines, produce, products.

▸ verb *a new product that can be easily merchandised* PROMOTE, market, sell, retail; advertise, publicize, push; *informal* plug.

merchant noun *a tea merchant from Bombay* TRADER, dealer, wholesaler, broker, agent, seller, buyer, buyer and seller, vendor, distributor, peddler, retailer, shopkeeper, storekeeper.

merciful adjective **1** *God is merciful* FORGIVING, compassionate, clement, pitying, forbearing, lenient, humane, mild, kind, softhearted, tenderhearted, gracious, sympathetic, humanitarian, liberal, tolerant, indulgent, generous, magnanimous, benign, benevolent. See note at LENIENT. ANTONYM cruel.

2 *a merciful silence fell* WELCOME, blessed. PHRASE: **be merciful to** *the judge was inclined to be merciful to first offenders* HAVE MERCY ON, have pity on, show mercy to, spare, pardon, forgive, be lenient to; *informal* go/be easy on, let off.

mercifully adverb *mercifully, everyone escaped unharmed* LUCKILY, fortunately, happily, thank goodness, thank God, thank heavens.

merciless adjective *the merciless Cossacks who invaded Siberia* RUTHLESS, remorseless, pitiless, unforgiving, unsparing, implacable, inexorable, relentless, unremitting, inflexible, inhumane, inhuman, unsympathetic, unfeeling, intolerant, rigid, severe, cold-blooded, hard-hearted, stony-hearted, heartless, harsh, callous, cruel, brutal, barbarous, cutthroat. ANTONYM compassionate.

mercurial adjective *a mercurial temperament* VOLATILE, capricious, temperamental, excitable, fickle, changeable, unpredictable, variable, protean, mutable, erratic, quicksilver, inconstant, inconsistent, unstable, unsteady, fluctuating, ever-changing, moody, flighty, wayward, whimsical, impulsive; *technical* labile. ANTONYM stable.

mercy noun **1** *he showed no mercy to the others* LENIENCY, clemency, compassion, grace, pity, charity, forgiveness, forbearance, quarter, humanity; soft-heartedness, tenderheartedness, kindness, sympathy, liberality, indulgence, tolerance, generosity, magnanimity, beneficence. ANTONYMS ruthlessness, cruelty.

2 *we must be thankful for small mercies* BLESSING, godsend, boon, favor, piece/stroke of luck, windfall. PHRASE: **at the mercy of 1** *they found themselves at the mercy of the tyrant* IN THE POWER OF, under/in the control of, in the clutches of, subject to. **2** *he was at the mercy of the elements* DEFENSELESS AGAINST, vulnerable to, exposed to, susceptible to, prey to, (wide) open to.

THE RIGHT WORD

If you want to win friends and influence people, it's best to start with **benevolence**, a general term for goodwill and kindness (*a grandfather's benevolence*). **Charity** is even better, suggesting generous giving (*the baker gave him bread out of charity*) but also meaning tolerance and understanding of others (*she viewed his selfish behavior with charity*). **Compassion** is a feeling of sympathy or sorrow for someone else's misfortune (*he has shown compassion for the homeless*), and often includes showing **mercy**. Aside from its religious overtones, *mercy* means compassion or kindness in our treatment of others, especially those who have offended us or who deserve punishment (*mercy toward the pickpocket*). **Clemency** is mercy shown by someone whose duty or function it is to administer justice or punish offenses (*the judge granted clemency*), while **leniency** emphasizes gentleness, softness, or lack of severity, even if it isn't quite deserved (*a father's leniency in punishing his young son*).

mere adjective *it costs **a mere** $11.00* NO MORE THAN, just, only, merely; no better than; a paltry, a measly, an insignificant, an ordinary, a minor, a little, a piddling, a piffling.

merely adverb *the buttons are merely decorative* ONLY, purely, solely, simply, just, but.

meretricious adjective *the meretricious glitter of the whole charade* WORTHLESS, valueless, cheap, tawdry, trashy, Brummagem, tasteless, kitsch, kitschy; false, artificial, fake, imitation; *informal* tacky, chintzy.

merge verb **1** *the company merged with a firm based in Peoria* JOIN (TOGETHER), join forces, amalgamate, unite, affiliate, team up, link (up). ANTONYM separate.

2 *the two organizations were merged* AMALGAMATE, bring together, join, consolidate, conflate, unite, unify, combine, incorporate, integrate, link (up), knit, yoke. ANTONYM separate.

3 *the two colors merged* MINGLE, blend, fuse, mix, intermix, intermingle, coalesce; *literary* commingle.

merger noun *a pending merger between two Russian oil companies* AMALGAMATION, combination, union, fusion, coalition, affiliation, unification, incorporation, consolidation, link-up, alliance. ANTONYM split.

merit noun **1** *composers of outstanding merit* EXCELLENCE, quality, caliber, worth, worthiness, credit, value, distinction, eminence. ANTONYM inferiority.

2 *the merits of the scheme* GOOD POINT, strong point, advantage, benefit, value, asset, plus. ANTONYMS fault, disadvantage.

▸ verb *the accusation did not merit a response* DESERVE, earn, be deserving of, warrant, rate, justify, be worthy of, be worth, be entitled to, have a right to, have a claim to/on.

Meritage *trademark* See note below.

USAGE NOTE **Meritage**

"Some people find the word 'Meritage' meritorious. Others find it meretricious. But most people have no idea what it means." (*Denver Post*; June 8, 1994.) And the dictionaries provide no help: as of early 2003, no major dictionary had an entry on the term—which has an interesting history.

In 1988, California winemakers sponsored an international contest to create an upscale term for a table wine blended from two or more Bordeaux varietals grown in the United States. A California grocery-store wine buyer won the contest with "Meritage," a portmanteau word formed by combining *merit* with *heritage*. The word rhymes with *heritage*; it's pronounced /**mer**-it-ij/. Yet many wine enthusiasts mistakenly give it a Frenchified pronunciation (/mar-i-**tahzh**/), which has become lamentably widespread.

To help keep prices reasonable, insist on the unpretentious pronunciation rhyming with *heritage*. With the faux-French affectation, prices will surely get out of hand. **—BG**

meritorious adjective *an award for meritorious conduct* PRAISEWORTHY, laudable, commendable, admirable, estimable, creditable, worthy, deserving, excellent, exemplary, good. ANTONYM discreditable.

merriment noun *we got caught up in the merriment of the occasion* HIGH SPIRITS, high-spiritedness, exuberance, cheerfulness, gaiety, fun, effervescence, verve, buoyancy, levity, zest, liveliness, cheer, joy, joyfulness, joyousness, jolliness, jollity, happiness, gladness, jocularity, conviviality, festivity, merrymaking, revelry, mirth, glee, gleefulness, laughter, hilarity, lightheartedness, amusement, pleasure. ANTONYM misery.

merry adjective *merry throngs of students* CHEERFUL, cheery, in high spirits, high-spirited, bright, sunny, smiling, lighthearted, buoyant, lively, carefree, without a care in the world, joyful, joyous, jolly, convivial, festive, mirthful, gleeful, happy, glad, laughing; *informal* chirpy; *formal* jocund; *dated* gay; *literary* blithe. ANTONYM miserable.

PHRASE: **make merry** *I'm afraid we may have made merry a bit too long last night.* HAVE FUN, have a good time, enjoy oneself, have a party, celebrate, carouse, feast, 'eat, drink, and be merry', revel, roister; *informal* party, have a ball.

mesh noun *wire mesh* NETTING, net, network; web, webbing, lattice, latticework.

▸ verb **1** *one gear meshes with the other* ENGAGE, connect, lock, interlock.

2 *our ideas just do not mesh* HARMONIZE, fit together, match, dovetail.

mesmerize verb *the dancers mesmerized us* ENTHRALL, hold spellbound, entrance, dazzle, bedazzle, bewitch, charm, captivate, enchant, fascinate, transfix, grip, hypnotize.

mess noun **1** *please clear up the mess* UNTIDINESS, disorder, disarray, clutter, shambles, jumble, muddle, chaos.

2 *don't step in the dog mess* EXCREMENT, muck, feces, excreta.

3 *I've got to get out of this mess* PLIGHT, predicament, tight spot/corner, difficulty, trouble, quandary, dilemma, problem, muddle, mix-up, imbroglio; *informal* jam, fix, pickle, stew, scrape. PHRASES: **make a mess of** *he made a mess of the project* MISMANAGE, mishandle, bungle, fluff, spoil, ruin, wreck; *informal* mess up, botch, make a hash of, foul up. **mess around** *don't mess around with any of the equipment* FOOL AROUND, fiddle about/around, play around; fidget, toy, trifle, tamper, tinker, interfere, meddle, monkey (around/about). **mess up** 1 *he messed up my kitchen* DIRTY; clutter up, disarrange, jumble, dishevel, rumple; *informal* muss up; *literary* befoul. 2 *informal Eddie really messed things up.* See MAKE A MESS OF above.

message noun 1 *are there any messages for me?* COMMUNICATION, piece of information, news, note, memorandum, memo, e-mail, letter, missive, report, bulletin, communiqué, dispatch.

2 *the message of his teaching* MEANING, sense, import, idea; point, thrust, gist, essence, content, subject (matter), substance, implication, drift, lesson. PHRASE: **get the message** *informal what do I have to say to make you get the message?* UNDERSTAND, get the point, comprehend; *informal* catch on, get the picture.

messenger noun *the messenger arrived by motorcycle* COURIER, runner, envoy, emissary, agent, go-between, message-bearer; postman, letter carrier, mailman; *historical* herald; *archaic* legate.

messy adjective 1 *messy oil spills | messy hair* DIRTY, filthy, grubby, soiled, grimy; mucky, muddy, slimy, sticky, sullied, spotted, stained, smeared, smudged; disheveled, scruffy, unkempt, rumpled, matted, tousled, bedraggled, tangled; *informal* yucky, grungy. ANTONYM clean.

2 *a messy kitchen* DISORDERLY, disordered, in a muddle, chaotic, confused, disorganized, in disarray, disarranged; untidy, cluttered, in a jumble; *informal* like a bomb's hit it, shambolic. ANTONYMS orderly, tidy.

3 *a messy legal battle* COMPLEX, intricate, tangled, confused, convoluted; unpleasant, nasty, bitter, acrimonious. ANTONYMS straightforward, amicable.

metal noun See table.

METALS AND ALLOYS

aluminum	mercury
antimony	nickel
brass	pewter
bronze	platinum
cast iron	silver
chrome steel	solder
chromium	stainless steel
copper	steel
cupronickel	tin
gold	titanium
gunmetal	tungsten
iron	uranium
iridium	white gold
lead	zinc
magnesium	

metallic adjective 1 *a metallic sound* TINNY, jangling, jingling; grating, harsh, jarring, dissonant.

2 *metallic paint* METALIZED, burnished; shiny, glossy, lustrous.

metamorphosis noun *his amazing metamorphosis from gawky hayseed to sexy pop star* TRANSFORMATION, mutation, transmutation, change, alteration, conversion, modification, remodeling, reconstruction; *humorous* transmogrification; *formal* transubstantiation.

metaphor noun *the profusion of metaphors in her everyday speech has gotten pretty tiresome* FIGURE OF SPEECH, image, trope, analogy, comparison, symbol, word painting/picture.

metaphoric, metaphorical adjective *the writer meant it in a metaphoric sense* FIGURATIVE, allegorical, symbolic; imaginative, extended. ANTONYM literal.

metaphysical adjective 1 *metaphysical questions* ABSTRACT, theoretical, conceptual, notional, philosophical, speculative, intellectual, academic.

2 *Good and Evil are inextricably linked in a metaphysical battle* TRANSCENDENTAL, spiritual, supernatural, paranormal.

mete PHRASE: **mete out** *they were instructed to mete out harsh punishment* DISPENSE, hand out, allocate, allot, apportion, issue, deal out, dole out, dish out, assign, administer.

meteor noun *legend has it that he traveled to Earth on the tail of a meteor* falling star, shooting star, meteorite, meteoroid, bolide.

METEOR SHOWERS

Meteor Shower and Approx. peak date	Perseids (August 12)
Quadrantids (January 4)	Draconids (October 8)
April Lyrids (April 22)	Orionids (October 22)
Eta Aquarids (May 5)	Taurids (November 4)
June Lyrids (June 16)	Leonids (November 17)
June Boötids (June 27)	Geminids (December 14)
South Delta Aquarids (July 27)	Ursids (December 23)

meteoric adjective *her meteoric rise to fame* RAPID, lightning, swift, fast, quick, speedy, accelerated, instant, sudden, spectacular, dazzling, brilliant. ANTONYM gradual.

meteorologist noun *meteorologists are predicting an early winter* WEATHER FORECASTER, weatherman, weatherwoman.

method noun 1 *they use very old-fashioned methods* PROCEDURE, technique, system, practice, routine, modus operandi, process; strategy, tactic, plan.

2 *there's a method to his madness* ORDER, orderliness, organization, structure, form, system, logic, planning, design, sense. ANTONYM disorder.

methodical adjective *a methodical approach to the evaluation* ORDERLY, well-ordered, well-organized, (well) planned, efficient, businesslike, systematic, structured, logical, analytic, disciplined; meticulous, punctilious.

meticulous adjective *the etchers give meticulous attention to each piece* CAREFUL, conscientious, diligent, scrupulous, punctilious, painstaking, accurate; thorough, studious, rigorous, detailed, perfectionist, fastidious, methodical, particular. ANTONYM careless.

métier noun 1 *he had another métier besides teaching* OCCUPATION, job, work, profession, business, employment, career, vocation, trade, craft, line (of work), specialty.

2 *improvisation is more my métier* FORTE, strong point, strength, specialty, talent, bent; *informal* thing, cup of tea.

metropolis noun *their trip to the booming metropolis made them eager to return to their little house in the sticks*

CAPITAL (CITY), chief town, county town; big city, conurbation, megalopolis, megacity.

mettle noun **1** *a man of mettle* SPIRIT, fortitude, strength of character, moral fiber, steel, determination, resolve, resolution, backbone, grit, true grit, courage, courageousness, bravery, valor, fearlessness, daring; *informal* guts, spunk, balls.

2 *Frazer was of a very different mettle* CALIBER, character, disposition, nature, temperament, personality, makeup, stamp.

mew verb *the cat mewed plaintively* MEOW, mewl, cry.

mewl verb *the baby fretted and mewled* WHIMPER, cry, whine; *literary* pule.

miasma noun *literary* *the miasma from the stagnant swamp made us choke and gag* STINK, reek, stench, fetor, smell, fume, odor, whiff; gas, cloud, smog, vapor.

miasmic, miasmal adjective *literary* *we were horrified to learn that they would bathe in this miasmic water* FOUL-SMELLING, fetid, smelly, stinking (to high heaven), reeking, rank, putrid, noxious, malodorous; *literary* noisome, mephitic.

microbe noun *a culture of isolated microbes* MICROORGANISM, bacillus, bacterium, virus, germ; *informal* bug.

microscopic adjective *microscopic fibers found in the suspect's car* TINY, very small, minute, infinitesimal, minuscule; little, micro, diminutive; *informal* teeny, weeny, teeny-weeny, teensy-weensy, itsy-bitsy, little-bitty; *Scottish* wee. ANTONYM huge.

midday noun *the bells chime at midday* NOON, twelve noon, high noon, noontide, noonday. ANTONYM midnight.

middle noun **1** *a shallow dish with a spike in the middle* CENTER, midpoint, halfway point, dead center, focus, hub; eye, heart, core, kernel. ANTONYM outside.

2 *he had a towel around his middle* MIDRIFF, waist, belly, stomach, abdomen; *informal* tummy, tum, gut.

▸ adjective **1** *the middle point* CENTRAL, mid, mean, medium, medial, median, midway, halfway.

2 *the middle level* INTERMEDIATE, intermediary.

middle-class adjective *she rails against her parents' middle-class values, and yet she lives rent-free in their middle-class home* BOURGEOIS, conventional, mainstream, plain-vanilla; suburban, white-picket-fence, Waspish, WASP, yuppie.

middleman noun *I'd rather avoid the middleman and buy direct from the manufacturer* INTERMEDIARY, intercessor, go-between, liaison, mediator; dealer, broker, agent, factor, wholesaler, distributor.

middling adjective *a town of the middling kind, neither rich nor poor* AVERAGE, standard, normal, middle-of-the-road; moderate, ordinary, commonplace, everyday, workaday, tolerable, passable; run-of-the-mill, fair, mediocre, undistinguished, unexceptional, unremarkable; *informal* OK, so-so, 'comme ci, comme ça', fair-to-middling, plain-vanilla.

midget noun *the inhabitants must have been midgets* SMALL PERSON, dwarf, homunculus, Lilliputian, gnome, pygmy; *informal* shrimp.

▸ adjective **1** *a story about midget matadors* DIMINUTIVE, dwarfish, petite, very small, pygmy; *informal* pint-sized, peewee. ANTONYM giant.

2 *a midget camera* MINIATURE, pocket, dwarf, baby, mini. ANTONYM giant.

midnight noun *we'll meet under the clock tower at midnight* TWELVE MIDNIGHT, the middle of the night, the witching hour. ANTONYM midday.

midpoint noun *the Franklin Lane exit is considered the midpoint between the north and south ends of town* CENTER (POINT), middle, halfway point, midway point.

midriff noun *exercises designed to tighten your flabby midriff* STOMACH, belly, midsection, waist, middle, abdomen, tummy.

midst *literary* noun *in the midst of the confusion, one strong and sturdy voice broke through and was heard* MIDDLE, center, heart, core, midpoint, kernel, nub; depth(s), thick; (**in the midst of**) in the course of, halfway through, at the heart/core of. PHRASE: **in our midst** *there is a hero in our midst* AMONG US, in our group, with us.

midway adverb *he was explaining what happened and then just stopped midway* HALFWAY, in the middle, at the midpoint, in the center; part-way, at some point.

mien noun *a scowling mien that did nothing to boost our confidence* APPEARANCE, look, expression, countenance, aura, demeanor, attitude, air, manner, bearing; *formal* comportment.

miffed adjective *informal* See ANNOYED.

might noun *she hit him with all her might* STRENGTH, force, power, vigor, energy, brawn, powerfulness, forcefulness.

mightily adverb **1** *she is mightily pleased with herself* EXTREMELY, exceedingly, enormously, immensely, tremendously, hugely, very (much); *informal* awfully, majorly, mega, mighty, plumb.

2 *Ann and I labored mightily* STRENUOUSLY, energetically, powerfully, hard, with all one's might, with might and main, all out, heartily, vigorously, diligently, assiduously, persistently, indefatigably; *informal* like mad, like crazy.

mighty adjective **1** *a mighty blow* POWERFUL, forceful, violent, vigorous, hefty, thunderous. ANTONYM feeble.

2 *a mighty warrior* FEARSOME, ferocious; big, tough, robust, muscular, strapping. ANTONYMS puny, tiny.

3 *mighty industrial countries* DOMINANT, influential, strong, powerful, important, predominant. ANTONYM insignificant.

4 *mighty oak trees* HUGE, enormous, massive, gigantic, big, large, giant, colossal, mammoth, immense; *informal* monster, whopping, humongous, jumbo(-sized), ginormous. ANTONYM tiny.

▸ adverb *informal* *I'm mighty pleased to see you* EXTREMELY, exceedingly, enormously, immensely, tremendously, hugely, mightily, very (much); *informal* awfully, majorly, mega, plumb, right; *informal, dated* frightfully.

migrant noun *they exploited the Puerto Rican migrants who toiled in their orchards for dismal wages* IMMIGRANT, EMIGRANT; nomad, itinerant, traveler, vagrant, transient, rover, wanderer, drifter.

▸ adjective *migrant workers* TRAVELING, wandering, drifting, nomadic, roving, roaming, itinerant, vagrant, transient.

migrate verb **1** *cities grew rapidly as rural populations migrated in search of jobs* RELOCATE, resettle, move (house); immigrate; emigrate, go abroad, go overseas, pull up stakes; *dated* remove.

2 *wildebeest migrate across the Serengeti* ROAM, wander, drift, rove, travel (around).

migratory adjective *a winter haven for migratory species* MIGRANT, migrating, moving, traveling.

mild adjective **1** *a mild tone of voice* GENTLE, tender, softhearted, tenderhearted, sensitive, sympathetic, warm, placid, calm, tranquil, serene, peaceable, good-natured, mild-mannered, amiable, affable, genial, easygoing. ANTONYM harsh.

2 *a mild punishment* LENIENT, light; compassionate, merciful, humane. ANTONYMS harsh, cruel.

3 *he was eyeing her with mild interest* SLIGHT, faint, vague, minimal, nominal, moderate, token, feeble. ANTONYM strong.

4 *mild weather* WARM, balmy, temperate, clement. ANTONYMS cold, severe.

5 *a mild curry* BLAND, insipid, tame. ANTONYMS spicy, piquant.

mildew noun See MOLD[2].

milestone noun *the invention of the electron microscope was a milestone in diagnostic medicine* LANDMARK, significant event, achievement, highlight, watershed, benchmark, touchstone.

milieu noun *the political milieu in New England* ENVIRONMENT, sphere, background, backdrop, setting, context, atmosphere; location, conditions, surroundings, environs; *informal* stomping grounds, stamping grounds, turf.

militant adjective *militant supporters* AGGRESSIVE, violent, belligerent, bellicose, vigorous, forceful, active, fierce, combative, pugnacious; radical, extremist, extreme, zealous, fanatical.

▸ noun *the demands of the militants* ACTIVIST, extremist, radical, young turk, zealot.

militaristic adjective *their militaristic leaders* WARMONGERING, warlike, martial, hawkish, pugnacious, combative, aggressive, belligerent, bellicose. ANTONYM peaceable.

military adjective *military activity* FIGHTING, service, army, armed, defense, martial. ANTONYM civilian.

▸ noun *the military took power* (ARMED) FORCES, services, militia; army, navy, air force, marines, coast guard.

militate verb *his resentment of others in the company* ***militates against*** *his own chances for advancement* TEND TO PREVENT, work against, hinder, discourage, prejudice, be detrimental to.

milk verb **1** *Pam was milking the cows* DRAW MILK FROM, express milk from.

2 *milk a little of the liquid* DRAW OFF, siphon (off), pump off, tap, drain, extract.

3 *milking rich clients* EXPLOIT, take advantage of, cash in on, suck dry; *informal* bleed, squeeze, fleece.

milksop noun See MAMA'S BOY.

milky adjective *a milky complexion* PALE, white, milk-white, whitish, off-white, cream, creamy, chalky, pearly, nacreous, ivory, alabaster; cloudy, frosted, opaque. ANTONYM swarthy.

mill noun **1** *a steel mill* FACTORY, (processing) plant, works, workshop, shop, foundry.

2 *a pepper mill* GRINDER, crusher, quern.

▸ verb *the wheat is milled into flour* GRIND, pulverize, powder, granulate, pound, crush, press; *technical* comminute, triturate.

PHRASE: **mill around/about** *people were milling about in the streets* THRONG, swarm, crowd.

millstone noun *a lifetime of lying and stealing had become the very millstone that would crush him* BURDEN, encumbrance, dead weight, cross to bear, albatross, load; duty, responsibility, obligation, liability, misfortune.

mime noun *a mime of someone fencing* PANTOMIME, charade, dumb show.

▸ verb *she mimed picking up a phone* ACT OUT, pantomime, gesture, simulate, represent.

mimic verb **1** *she mimicked his accent* IMITATE, copy, impersonate, do an impression of, ape, caricature, parody, lampoon, burlesque, parrot; *informal* send up, take off, spoof. See note at IMITATE.

2 *most hoverflies mimic wasps* RESEMBLE, look like, have the appearance of, simulate; *informal* make like.

▸ noun *he was a superb mimic* IMPERSONATOR, impressionist, imitator, parodist, caricaturist, lampooner, lampoonist; *informal* copycat; *archaic* ape.

mimicry noun *the bird's mimicry amazed us* IMITATION, imitating, impersonation, copying, aping. See note at CARICATURE.

mince verb **1** *mince the meat and onions* GRIND, chop up, cut up, dice, hash, chop fine.

2 *she minced out of the room* WALK AFFECTEDLY; *informal* sashay, flounce, strut. PHRASE: **not mince (one's) words** I'll not mince words: you need to stick to this exercise program or you're looking at serious health problems TALK STRAIGHT, not beat around the bush, call a spade a spade, speak straight from the heart, pull no punches, not put too fine a point on it, tell it like it is, talk turkey.

mincing adjective *no one dared to laugh at the young master's mincing walk* AFFECTED, dainty, effeminate, pretentious, dandified, foppish; *informal* camp.

mind noun **1** *expand your mind* BRAIN, intelligence, intellect, intellectual capabilities, brains, brainpower, wits, understanding, reasoning, judgment, sense, head; *informal* gray matter, brain cells, smarts.

2 *he kept his mind on the job* ATTENTION, thoughts, concentration, attentiveness.

3 *the tragedy affected her mind* SANITY, mental faculties, senses, wits, reason, reasoning, judgment; *informal* marbles.

4 *Justin's words stuck in her mind* MEMORY, recollection.

5 *the country's great minds* INTELLECT, thinker, brain, scholar, academic.

6 *I've a mind to complain* INCLINATION, desire, wish, urge, notion, fancy, intention, will.

7 *we're of the same mind* OPINION, way of thinking, outlook, attitude, view, viewpoint, point of view.

▸ verb **1** *do you mind if I smoke?* CARE, object, be bothered, be annoyed, be upset, take offense, disapprove, dislike it, look askance; *informal* give a damn, give a hoot.

2 *mind the step!* BE CAREFUL OF, watch out for, look out for, beware of, be on one's guard for, be wary of.

3 ***mind you*** *wipe your feet* BE/MAKE SURE (THAT) YOU, see (that) you; remember to, don't forget to.

4 *her husband was minding the baby* LOOK AFTER, take care of, keep an eye on, attend to, care for, tend, babysit.

5 *mind what your mother says* PAY ATTENTION TO, heed, pay heed to, attend to, take note/notice of, note, mark, listen to, be mindful of; obey, follow, comply with.

PHRASES: **be of two minds** *I am of two minds about going to law school* BE UNDECIDED, be uncertain, be unsure, hesitate, waver, vacillate, hem and haw; *informal* dilly-dally, shilly-shally. **bear/keep in mind** *just bear in mind that I've never used a Mac* REMEMBER, note, be mindful of, take note of; *formal* take cognizance of. **cross one's mind** *did it ever cross your mind that he just doesn't want to go?* OCCUR TO ONE, enter one's mind/head, strike one, hit one, dawn on one. **give someone a piece of one's mind.** *I'd really like to give that lying Patterson a piece of my mind.* See REPRIMAND verb. **have in mind** *now, for the curtains, do you have a specific pattern in mind?* THINK OF, contemplate; intend, plan, propose, desire, want, wish. **never mind** **1** *never mind the cost* DON'T BOTHER ABOUT, don't worry about, disregard, forget. **2** *never mind, it's all right now* DON'T APOLOGIZE, forget it, don't worry about it, it doesn't matter. **out of one's mind** **1** *you must be out of your mind!* See MAD sense 1. **2** *I've been out of my mind with worry* FRANTIC, beside oneself, distraught, in a frenzy. **put someone in mind of** *the view here puts me in mind of Amsterdam* REMIND OF, recall, conjure up, suggest; RESEMBLE, look like. **to my mind** *to my mind, this is a clear case of blackmail* IN MY OPINION, in my view, as I see it, in my estimation, in my book, if you ask me.

mindful adjective *with mindful steps we slowly made our way down the gorge* AWARE, conscious, sensible, alive, alert, acquainted, heedful, wary, chary; *informal* wise, hip; *formal* cognizant, regardful. ANTONYM heedless.

mindless adjective **1** *a mindless idiot* STUPID, idiotic, brainless, imbecilic, imbecile, asinine, witless, foolish, empty-headed, slow-witted, obtuse, featherbrained, doltish; *informal* dumb, pig-ignorant, brain-dead, cretinous, moronic, thick, birdbrained, pea-brained, dopey, dim, halfwitted, dippy, fat-headed, boneheaded, chowderheaded.

2 *mindless acts of vandalism* UNTHINKING, thoughtless, senseless, gratuitous, wanton, indiscriminate, unreasoning.

3 *a mindless task* MECHANICAL, automatic, routine; tedious, boring, monotonous, brainless, mind-numbing. PHRASE: **mindless of** *the birds flock to the feeders, mindless of the humans nearby* INDIFFERENT TO, heedless of, unaware of, unmindful of, careless of, blind to.

mine noun **1** *a coal mine* PIT, excavation, quarry, workings, diggings; strip mine, open-pit mine, placer (mine), hardrock mine.

2 *a mine of information* RICH SOURCE, repository, store, storehouse, reservoir, gold mine, treasure house, treasury, reserve, fund, wealth, stock.

3 *he was killed by a mine* EXPLOSIVE, land mine, limpet mine, magnetic mine, depth charge.

▸ verb **1** *the iron ore was mined from shallow pits* QUARRY, excavate, dig (up), extract, remove; strip-mine, pan.

2 *medical data was mined for relevant statistics* SEARCH, delve into, scour, scan, read through, survey.

3 *the entrance to the harbor had been mined* DEFEND WITH MINES, lay with mines.

miner noun *the trapped miners were rescued* DIGGER, collier, gold panner; *dated* sourdough.

mingle verb **1** *fact and fiction are skillfully mingled in his novels* MIX, blend, intermingle, intermix, interweave, interlace, combine, merge, fuse, unite, join, amalgamate, meld, mesh; *literary* commingle. ANTONYMS separate, be separated.

2 *wedding guests mingled in the lobby* SOCIALIZE, circulate, fraternize, get together, associate with others; *informal* hobnob, rub elbows. ANTONYMS separate, part.

miniature adjective *a miniature railroad* SMALL-SCALE, mini; tiny, little, small, minute, baby, toy, pocket, dwarf, pygmy, minuscule, diminutive, vest-pocket; *informal* teeny, teeny-weeny, teensy, teensy-weensy, itsy-bitsy, eensy, eensy-weensy; *Scottish* wee. See note at SMALL. ANTONYM giant.

minimal adjective *with minimal care, you can have a beautiful terrarium* VERY LITTLE, minimum, the least (possible); nominal, token, negligible. ANTONYM maximum.

minimize verb **1** *the aim is to minimize costs* KEEP DOWN, keep at/to a minimum, reduce, decrease, cut down, lessen, curtail, diminish, prune; *informal* slash. ANTONYMS maximize, increase.

2 *we should not minimize his contribution* BELITTLE, make light of, play down, underestimate, underrate, downplay, undervalue, understate; *informal* pooh-pooh; *archaic* hold cheap. ANTONYM exaggerate.

minimum noun *costs will be kept to the minimum* LOWEST LEVEL, lower limit, bottom level, rock bottom, nadir; least, lowest, slightest. ANTONYM maximum.

▸ adjective *the minimum amount of effort* MINIMAL, least, smallest, least possible, slightest, lowest, minutest.

minion noun *if working for you means being your minion, I'm not the person you're looking for* UNDERLING, henchman, flunky, lackey, hanger-on, follower, servant, hireling, vassal, stooge, toady, sycophant; *informal* yes-man, trained seal, bootlicker, brown-noser, suck-up.

minister noun **1** *our minister visited me in the hospital* CLERGYMAN, clergywoman, cleric, ecclesiastic, pastor, vicar, rector, priest, parson, deacon, father, man/woman of the cloth, man/woman of God, churchman, churchwoman; curate, chaplain; *informal* reverend, padre, Holy Joe, sky pilot.

2 *a government minister* MEMBER OF THE GOVERNMENT, cabinet minister, secretary of state, undersecretary.

3 *the Canadian minister in Egypt* AMBASSADOR, chargé d'affaires, plenipotentiary, envoy, emissary, diplomat, consul, representative; *archaic* legate.

▸ verb *doctors were* ***ministering to*** *the injured* TEND TO, care for, take care of, look after, nurse, treat, attend to, see to, administer to, help, assist.

ministrations plural noun *her mother's anxious ministra-*

tions ATTENTION, treatment, help, assistance, aid, care, services; *informal* TLC.

ministry noun **1** *he's training for the ministry* HOLY ORDERS, the priesthood, the cloth, the church.

2 *the ministry of Jesus* TEACHING, preaching, evangelism.

3 *the ministry for foreign affairs* (GOVERNMENT) DEPARTMENT, bureau, agency, office.

minor adjective **1** *a minor problem* SLIGHT, small; unimportant, insignificant, inconsequential, inconsiderable, subsidiary, negligible, trivial, trifling, paltry, petty, nickel-and-dime; *informal* piffling, piddling. ANTONYM major.

2 *a minor poet* LITTLE KNOWN, unknown, lesser, unimportant, insignificant, obscure, minor-league; *informal* small-time, two-bit. ANTONYM important.

▸ noun *the heir to the throne was a minor* CHILD, infant, youth, adolescent, teenager, boy, girl; *informal* kid, kiddie. ANTONYM adult.

minstrel noun *historical a band of gay minstrels* MUSICIAN, singer, balladeer, poet; *historical* troubadour, jongleur; *literary* bard.

mint noun *informal the bank made* ***a mint*** *out of the deal* A VAST SUM OF MONEY, a king's ransom, millions, billions; *informal* a (small) fortune, a tidy sum, a bundle, a pile, big money, big bucks, megabucks.

▸ adjective *in mint condition* BRAND NEW, pristine, perfect, immaculate, unblemished, undamaged, unmarked, unused, first-class, excellent.

▸ verb **1** *the shilling was minted in 1742* COIN, stamp, strike, cast, forge, manufacture.

2 *the slogan had been freshly minted* CREATE, invent, make up, think up, dream up, coin.

minuscule adjective *she notices even the minuscule defects* TINY, minute, microscopic, nanoscale, very small, little, micro, diminutive, miniature, baby, dwarf, Lilliputian; *informal* teeny, teeny-weeny, teensy, teensy-weensy, itsy-bitsy, eensy, eensy-weensy; *Scottish* wee. ANTONYM huge.

minute[1] noun **1** *it'll only take a minute* MOMENT, short time, little while, second, instant; *informal* sec, jiff, jiffy, flash.

2 *at that minute, Tony walked in* POINT, point in time, moment, instant, juncture.

3 (**minutes**) *their objection was noted in the minutes* RECORD(S), proceedings, log, notes; transcript, summary, résumé. PHRASES: **in a minute** *the biscuits will be done in a minute* VERY SOON, in a moment, in a second, in an instant, in a trice, shortly, any minute (now), in a short time, in (less than) no time, before long, momentarily; *informal* anon, in two shakes, in a snap; *literary* ere long. **this minute** *you get in here this minute!* AT ONCE, immediately, directly, this second, instantly, straightaway, right now, right away, forthwith; *informal* pronto, straight off, right off, tout de suite. **up-to-the-minute** *stay tuned for up-to-the-minute fashion tips* LATEST, newest, up-to-date, modern, fashionable, smart, chic, stylish, all the rage, in vogue, hip; *informal* trendy, with it, in, styling, phat. **wait a minute** *if you'll just wait a minute, I'm sure we can get to the bottom of this* BE PATIENT, wait a moment/second, hold on; *informal* hang on, hold your horses.

minute[2] adjective **1** *minute particles.* See MINUSCULE.

2 *a minute chance of success* NEGLIGIBLE, slight, infinitesimal, minimal, insignificant, inappreciable. ANTONYM significant. See note at SMALL.

3 *minute detail* EXHAUSTIVE, painstaking, meticulous, rigorous, scrupulous, punctilious, detailed, precise, accurate. ANTONYM cursory.

minutiae plural noun *the captain cannot be concerned with the minutiae of shipboard life* DETAILS, niceties, finer points, particulars, trivia, trivialities.

miracle noun *his recovery was a blessed miracle* WONDER, marvel, sensation, phenomenon, supernatural phenomenon, mystery.

miraculous adjective **1** *the miraculous help of St. Blaise* SUPERNATURAL, preternatural, inexplicable, unaccountable, magical.

2 *a miraculous escape* AMAZING, astounding, remarkable, extraordinary, incredible, unbelievable, sensational, marvelous, phenomenal; *informal* mind-boggling, mind-blowing, out of this world.

mirage noun *could it be that her face was just a mirage?* OPTICAL ILLUSION, hallucination, phantasmagoria, apparition, fantasy, chimera, vision, figment of the/one's imagination; *literary* phantasm.

mire noun **1** *it's a mire out there* SWAMP, bog, morass, quagmire, slough; swampland, wetland, marshland.

2 *they were stuck in the mire* MUD, slime, dirt, filth, muck.

3 *struggling to pull Russia out of the mire* MESS, difficulty, plight, predicament, tight spot, trouble, quandary, muddle; *informal* jam, fix, pickle, hot water.

▸ verb **1** *Frank's horse got mired in a bog* BOG DOWN, sink (down).

2 *he has become mired in lawsuits* ENTANGLE, tangle up, embroil, catch up, mix up, involve.

mirror noun **1** *a quick look in the mirror* reflecting surface; full-length mirror, hand mirror, side mirror, rearview mirror; *chiefly Brit.* looking glass, glass.

2 *his life was a mirror of her own* REFLECTION, twin, replica, copy, match, parallel.

▸ verb *her music mirrored the mood of desperation* REFLECT, match, reproduce, imitate, simulate, copy, mimic, echo, parallel, correspond to.

mirth noun *we could not hold back our mirth* MERRIMENT, high spirits, cheerfulness, cheeriness, hilarity, glee, laughter, gaiety, buoyancy, blitheness, euphoria, exhilaration, lightheartedness, joviality, joy, joyfulness, joyousness. ANTONYM misery.

misadventure noun *their journey to the Olympics began as one misadventure after another* ACCIDENT, problem, difficulty, misfortune, mishap; setback, reversal (of fortune), stroke of bad luck, blow, contretemps; failure, disaster, tragedy, calamity, woe, trial, tribulation, catastrophe.

misanthrope noun *he was going to join a group of misanthropes but he disliked all the members* HATER OF MANKIND, cynic; recluse, hermit; *informal* grouch, grump.

misanthropic adjective *she became more and more misanthropic in high school, to the consternation of her parents and teachers* ANTISOCIAL, unsociable, unfriendly, reclusive, uncongenial, cynical, jaundiced.

misapprehend verb *I fear you have misapprehended my intentions* MISUNDERSTAND, misinterpret, misconstrue, misconceive, mistake, misread, get the wrong idea about, take something the wrong way.

misappropriate verb *he confessed to having misappropriated millions from his clients* EMBEZZLE, expropriate, steal, thieve, pilfer, pocket, help oneself to, make off with; *informal* swipe, filch, rip off, snitch, pinch.

misbegotten adjective **1** *a misbegotten scheme* ILL-CONCEIVED, ill-advised, badly planned, badly thought-out, harebrained.

2 *you misbegotten scoundrel!* CONTEMPTIBLE, despicable, wretched, miserable, confounded; *informal* infernal, damned; *dated* cursed, accursed.

3 *archaic misbegotten children.* See ILLEGITIMATE sense 2.

misbehave verb *our parents would never let us misbehave in public* BEHAVE BADLY, be misbehaved, be naughty, be disobedient, disobey, get up to mischief, get up to no good; be bad-mannered, be rude; *informal* carry on, act up.

miscalculate verb *please recheck the bill, as I believe you've miscalculated* MISJUDGE, make a mistake (about), calculate wrongly, estimate wrongly, overestimate, underestimate, overvalue, undervalue; misconstrue, misinterpret, misunderstand; go wrong, err, be wide of the mark.

miscalculation noun *auditors detected a significant miscalculation in the budget* ERROR OF JUDGMENT, misjudgment, mistake, overestimate, underestimate.

miscarriage noun **1** *she's had a miscarriage* STILLBIRTH, spontaneous abortion.

2 *the miscarriage of the project* FAILURE, foundering, ruin, ruination, collapse, breakdown, thwarting, frustration, undoing, nonfulfillment, mismanagement.

miscarry verb **1** *the shock caused her to miscarry* LOSE ONE'S BABY, have a miscarriage, abort, have a spontaneous abortion.

2 *our plan miscarried* GO WRONG, go awry, go amiss, be unsuccessful, be ruined, fail, misfire, abort, founder, come to nothing, fall through, fall flat; *informal* flop, go up in smoke. ANTONYM succeed.

miscellaneous adjective *he does miscellaneous jobs around the studio* VARIOUS, varied, different, assorted, mixed, sundry, diverse, disparate; diversified, motley, multifarious, ragtag, heterogeneous, eclectic, odd; *literary* divers.

miscellany noun *amid the miscellany on these shelves are some rare treasures* ASSORTMENT, mixture, mélange, blend, variety, mixed bag, grab bag, mix, medley, diversity, assemblage, potpourri, pastiche, mishmash, ragbag, salmagundi, gallimaufry, hodgepodge, hash; selection, collection, anthology, treasury.

mischief noun **1** *the boys are always getting into mischief* NAUGHTINESS, bad behavior, misbehavior, mischievousness, misconduct, disobedience; pranks, tricks, capers, nonsense, devilry, funny business; *informal* monkey business, shenanigans, carryings-on.

2 *the mischief in her eyes* IMPISHNESS, roguishness, devilment.

mischievous adjective **1** *a mischievous child* NAUGHTY, badly behaved, misbehaving, disobedient, troublesome, full of mischief; rascally, roguish. ANTONYM well-behaved.

2 *a mischievous smile* PLAYFUL, teasing, wicked, impish, roguish, arch.

misconception noun *a popular misconception about science* MISAPPREHENSION, misunderstanding, mistake, error, misinterpretation, misconstruction, misreading, misjudgment, misbelief, miscalculation, false impression, illusion, fallacy, delusion. See note at MISNOMER.

misconduct noun **1** *allegations of misconduct* WRONGDOING, unlawfulness, lawlessness, crime, felony, criminality, sin, sinfulness; unethical behavior, unprofessionalism, malpractice, negligence, impropriety.

2 *he was reprimanded for his misconduct* MISBEHAVIOR, bad behavior, misdeeds, misdemeanors, disorderly conduct, mischief, naughtiness, rudeness.

misconstrue verb *Pete's shyness is misconstrued as unfriendliness* MISUNDERSTAND, misinterpret, misconceive, misapprehend, mistake, misread; be mistaken about, get the wrong idea about, get it/someone wrong.

miscreant noun *the South Street playground has been taken over by a pack of drug-dealing miscreants* CRIMINAL, culprit, wrongdoer, malefactor, offender, villain, lawbreaker, evildoer, delinquent, hoodlum, reprobate; *Law* malfeasant.

misdeed noun See MISDEMEANOR.

misdemeanor noun *he turned a blind eye to his son's misdemeanors* WRONGDOING, evil deed, crime, felony; misdeed, misconduct, offense, error, peccadillo, transgression, sin; *informal* no-no; *archaic* trespass, misdoing.

miser noun *one wonders how happy a miser could ever be* PENNY-PINCHER, Scrooge, pinchpenny; *informal* skinflint, money-grubber, cheapskate, tightwad, piker. ANTONYM spendthrift.

miserable adjective **1** *I'm too miserable to eat* UNHAPPY, sad, sorrowful, dejected, depressed, downcast, downhearted, down, despondent, disconsolate, wretched, glum, gloomy, dismal, melancholy, woebegone, doleful, forlorn, heartbroken; *informal* blue, down in/at the mouth, down in the dumps. ANTONYMS happy, contented.

2 *their miserable surroundings* DREARY, dismal, gloomy, drab, wretched, depressing, grim, cheerless, bleak, desolate; poor, shabby, squalid, seedy, dilapidated; *informal* flea-bitten. ANTONYM luxurious.

3 *miserable weather* UNPLEASANT, disagreeable, depressing; wet, rainy, stormy; *informal* rotten. ANTONYMS glorious, lovely.

4 *a miserable old grouch* GRUMPY, sullen, gloomy, bad-tempered, ill-tempered, ill-natured, dour, surly, sour, glum, moody, unsociable, saturnine, lugubrious, irritable, churlish, cantankerous, crotchety, cross, crabby, cranky, grouchy, testy, peevish, crusty, waspish. ANTONYMS cheerful, good-natured.

5 *miserable wages* INADEQUATE, meager, scanty, paltry, small, poor, pitiful, niggardly; *informal* measly, stingy, pathetic; *formal* exiguous. ANTONYMS generous, adequate.

6 *all that fuss about a few miserable dollars* WRETCHED, confounded; *informal* blithering, blessed, damned, blasted; *dated* accursed.

miserly adjective **1** *his miserly uncle* MEAN, niggardly, close-fisted, parsimonious, penny-pinching, cheeseparing, Scroogelike; *informal* tightfisted, stingy, tight, mingy, money-grubbing, cheap; *formal* penurious. See note at ECONOMICAL. ANTONYM generous.

2 *the prize is a miserly $300.* See MEAGER sense 1.

misery noun 1 *periods of intense misery* UNHAPPINESS, distress, wretchedness, suffering, anguish, anxiety, angst, torment, pain, grief, heartache, heartbreak, despair, despondency, dejection, depression, desolation, gloom, melancholy, melancholia, woe, sadness, sorrow; *informal* the dumps, the blues; *literary* dolor. ANTONYMS contentment, pleasure.

2 *the miseries of war* AFFLICTION, misfortune, difficulty, problem, ordeal, trouble, hardship, deprivation; pain, sorrow, trial, tribulation, woe.

misfire verb *the plan had misfired* GO WRONG, go awry, be unsuccessful, fail, founder, fall through, fall flat; backfire; *informal* flop, go up in smoke.

misfit noun they prided themselves on being the class misfits NONCONFORMIST, eccentric, maverick, individualist, square peg in a round hole; *informal* oddball, odd duck, weirdo, freak, screwball.

misfortune noun *the loss of their home in the flood was only the first of several misfortunes* PROBLEM, difficulty, setback, trouble, adversity, stroke of bad luck, reversal (of fortune), misadventure, mishap, blow, failure, accident, disaster, catastrophe; sorrow, misery, woe, trial, tribulation, tragedy.

misgiving noun *we finally gave our consent to the marriage, but we still had misgivings* QUALM, doubt, reservation; suspicion; **(misgivings)** distrust, mistrust, lack of confidence, second thoughts; trepidation, skepticism, unease, uneasiness, anxiety, apprehension, disquiet. See note at QUALMS.

misguided adjective 1 *the policy is misguided* ERRONEOUS, fallacious, unsound, misplaced, misconceived, ill-advised, ill-considered, ill-judged, ill-founded, inappropriate, unwise, injudicious, imprudent.

2 *you are quite misguided* MISINFORMED, misled, wrong, mistaken, deluded, confused; *informal* off base.

mishandle verb 1 *the officer mishandled the situation* BUNGLE, fumble, make a mess of, mismanage, spoil, ruin, wreck; *informal* botch, make a hash of, mess up, screw up, fluff.

2 *he mishandled his dog* BULLY, persecute, ill-treat, mistreat, maltreat, manhandle, abuse, knock around, hit, beat; *informal* beat up.

3 *the equipment could be dangerous if mishandled* MISUSE, abuse, handle/treat roughly.

mishap noun *even a minor mishap can have serious consequences* ACCIDENT, trouble, problem, difficulty, setback, adversity, misfortune, blow; failure, disaster, tragedy, catastrophe, calamity, mischance, misadventure.

mishmash noun *a mishmash of colors and patterns* JUMBLE, confusion, ragbag, patchwork, farrago, assortment, medley, miscellany, mixture, mélange, blend, mix, potpourri, conglomeration, bricolage, gallimaufry, salmagundi, hodgepodge, hash.

misinform verb *we're sorry to tell you that you've been deliberately misinformed* MISLEAD, misguide, give wrong information, delude, take in, deceive, lie to, hoodwink; *informal* lead up the garden path, take for a ride, give someone a bum steer.

misinterpret verb *his proposal was misinterpreted* MISUNDERSTAND, misconceive, misconstrue, misapprehend, mistake, misread; confuse, be mistaken, get the wrong idea, take amiss.

misjudge verb *she misjudged her opponent's stamina* GET THE WRONG IDEA ABOUT, get wrong, judge incorrectly, estimate wrongly, be wrong about, miscalculate, misread; overestimate, underestimate, overvalue, undervalue, underrate.

mislay verb *I've mislaid my keys* LOSE, misplace, put in the wrong place, be unable to find, forget the whereabouts of. ANTONYM find.

mislead verb *Caroline deliberately misled her* DECEIVE, delude, take in, lie to, fool, hoodwink, throw off the scent, pull the wool over someone's eyes, misguide, misinform, give wrong information to; *informal* lead up the garden path, take for a ride, give someone a bum steer.

misleading adjective *a leaflet full of misleading statements* DECEPTIVE, confusing, deceiving, equivocal, ambiguous, fallacious, specious, spurious, false.

mismanage verb *the accountant had mismanaged their personal finances* BUNGLE, make a mess of, mishandle, spoil, ruin, wreck; *informal* botch, make a hash of, mess up, screw up, fluff.

mismatched adjective *mismatched socks | a mismatched couple* ILL-ASSORTED, ill-matched, incongruous, unsuited, incompatible, inconsistent, at odds; out of keeping, clashing, dissimilar, unalike, different, at variance, disparate, unrelated, divergent, contrasting. ANTONYM matching.

misnomer noun *scientists say "killer whale" is a misnomer for what is one of the gentlest marine creatures known to man* INACCURATE NAME/LABEL/DESIGNATION, wrong name/label/designation, inappropriate name/label/designation.

USAGE NOTE misnomer, misconception

Speakers and writers frequently misuse this word, meaning "an inappropriate name," to mean "a popular misconception"—e.g.: " 'The last I remember, only 7 percent of Division I programs operate in the black. The common misnomer [read *misconception*] is that people see this as a multi-million-dollar business.' " (*Times Union* [Albany]; Dec. 24, 2000.) Oddly enough, this mistake is itself a kind of misnomer based on a misconception. Although the error is less common in edited text, it does surface—e.g.: "The old theory that was heard at UW for years is that the school needs a big-name coach. That's really a misnomer [read *misconception*] because UW usually has succeeded in developing its own big-name coach." (*Wyoming Tribune-Eagle*; Nov. 21, 2002.)

Typically, when the term is used correctly it will accompany a misleading word or title, often in quotation marks—e.g.: "Old countries are sometimes world-weary and cynical, urging a 'realism' that is sometimes a misnomer for the moral corruption they know so very well." (*Washington Post*; Oct. 15, 2002.) —**BG**

misogynist noun *he apparently deserved his reputation as a misogynist* WOMAN-HATER; antifeminist, (male) chauvinist, sexist; *informal* male chauvinist pig.

misplace verb *he had misplaced the tickets* LOSE, mislay, put in the wrong place, be unable to find, forget the whereabouts of. ANTONYM find.

misplaced adjective 1 *his affections were misplaced* MIS-

GUIDED, unwise, ill-advised, ill-considered, ill-judged, inappropriate.

2 *misplaced keys* LOST, mislaid, missing.

misprint noun *the book is full of misprints* MISTAKE, error, typographical error, erratum; *informal* typo.

misquote verb *my original statement has been misquoted* MISREPORT, misrepresent, misstate, take/quote out of context, distort, twist, slant, bias, put a spin on, falsify.

misrepresent verb *you are misrepresenting the views of the government* GIVE A FALSE ACCOUNT, misreport, misquote, quote/take out of context, misinterpret, put a spin on, skew, warp, falsify, distort, misstate, exaggerate.

miss[1] verb 1 *the shot missed her by inches* FAIL TO HIT, be/go wide of, fall short of. ANTONYM hit.

2 *Mandy missed the ball* FAIL TO CATCH, drop, fumble, bobble, fluff, flub, mishandle, screw up. ANTONYM catch.

3 *I've missed my bus* BE TOO LATE FOR, fail to catch/get. ANTONYM catch.

4 *I missed what you said* FAIL TO HEAR, mishear.

5 *you can't miss the station* FAIL TO SEE/NOTICE, overlook. ANTONYMS see, notice.

6 *she never missed a class* FAIL TO ATTEND, be absent from, play truant from, cut, skip. ANTONYM attend.

7 *don't miss this exciting opportunity!* LET SLIP, fail to take advantage of, let go, let pass, pass up.

8 *I left early to miss rush hour* AVOID, beat, evade, escape, dodge, sidestep, elude, circumvent, steer clear of, find a way around, bypass.

9 *she missed him when he was away* PINE FOR, yearn for, ache for, long for, long to see.

▸ noun *one hit and three misses* FAILURE, omission, slip, blunder, error, mistake.

miss[2] noun *a lovely miss* YOUNG WOMAN, young lady, girl, schoolgirl, missy; *Scottish* lass, lassie; *French* mademoiselle; *informal* girlie, chick, doll, gal; *literary* maiden, maid, damsel; *archaic* wench.

misshapen adjective *his misshapen feet* DEFORMED, malformed, distorted, crooked, twisted, warped, out of shape, bent, asymmetrical, irregular, misproportioned, ill-proportioned, disfigured, dysmorphic, grotesque.

missing adjective 1 *his wallet is missing* LOST, mislaid, misplaced, absent, gone (astray), gone AWOL, unaccounted for; disappeared, vanished. ANTONYM at hand.

2 *passion was missing from her life* ABSENT, not present, lacking, wanting. ANTONYM present.

mission noun 1 *a mercy mission to Africa* ASSIGNMENT, commission, expedition, journey, trip, undertaking, operation; task, job, labor, work, duty, charge, trust.

2 *her mission in life* VOCATION, calling, goal, aim, quest, purpose, function, life's work.

3 *a trade mission* DELEGATION, deputation, commission, legation.

4 *a teacher in a mission* missionary post, missionary station, missionary school.

5 *a bombing mission* SORTIE, operation, raid.

missionary noun *Liddell died in occupied China, where he had been a missionary* EVANGELIST, apostle, proselytizer, preacher, minister, priest; *historical* black robe.

missive noun *take this missive to Lieutenant Baxter* MESSAGE, communication, letter, word, note, e-mail, memorandum, line, communiqué, dispatch, news; *informal* memo; *formal* epistle; *literary* tidings.

misspent adjective *our misspent youth* WASTED, dissipated, squandered, thrown away, frittered away, misused, misapplied.

misstep noun *the number of missteps in this department is inexcusable* MISTAKE, error, blunder, slip, faux pas, infelicity; *informal* blooper, boner, flub, slip-up.

mist noun *the mist was clearing* HAZE, fog, smog, murk, cloud, drizzle.

mistake noun *I assumed it had been a mistake* ERROR, fault, inaccuracy, omission, slip, blunder, miscalculation, misunderstanding, oversight, misinterpretation, gaffe, faux pas, solecism; *informal* slip-up, boo-boo, blooper, boner, goof, flub.

▸ verb 1 *did I mistake your meaning?* MISUNDERSTAND, misinterpret, get wrong, misconstrue, misread.

2 *children often* ***mistake*** *vitamin pills* ***for*** *candies* CONFUSE WITH, mix up with, take for, misinterpret as.

PHRASES: **be mistaken** *I'm afraid you are mistaken—I've never been here before* BE WRONG, be in error, be under a misapprehension, be misinformed, be misguided; *informal* be barking up the wrong tree. **make a mistake** *he admits he's made a mistake* GO WRONG, err, make an error, blunder, miscalculate; *informal* slip up, make a boo-boo, drop the ball, goof (up).

THE RIGHT WORD

It would be a **mistake** to argue with your boss the day before he or she evaluates your performance, but to forget an important step in an assigned task would be an **error**. Although these nouns are used interchangeably in many contexts, a *mistake* is usually caused by poor judgment or a disregard of rules or principles (*it was a mistake not to tell the truth at the outset*), while an *error* implies an unintentional deviation from standards of accuracy or right conduct (*a mathematical error*). A **blunder** is a careless, stupid, or blatant mistake involving behavior or judgment; it suggests awkwardness or ignorance on the part of the person who makes it (*his blunder that ruined the evening*). A **slip** is a minor and usually accidental mistake that is the result of haste or carelessness (*her slip of the tongue spoiled the surprise*), while a **faux pas** (which means "false step" in French) is an embarrassing breach of etiquette (*it was a faux pas to have meat at the table when so many of the guests were vegetarians*). **Goofs** and **bloopers** are humorous mistakes. A *blooper* is usually a mix-up in speech, while to *goof* is to make a careless error that is honestly admitted (*she shrugged her shoulders and said, "I goofed!"*)

mistaken adjective *they were acting on mistaken information* WRONG, erroneous, inaccurate, incorrect, false, fallacious, unfounded, misguided, misinformed. ANTONYM correct.

mistakenly adverb 1 *she mistakenly assumed that she knew him* WRONGLY, in error, erroneously, incorrectly, falsely, fallaciously, inaccurately. ANTONYM correctly.

2 *Matt mistakenly opened the letter* BY ACCIDENT, accidentally, inadvertently, unintentionally, unwittingly, unconsciously, by mistake. ANTONYM intentionally.

mistimed adjective *his interruption was terribly mistimed* ILL-TIMED, badly timed, inopportune, inappropriate, inconvenient, malapropos, untimely, unseasonable. ANTONYM opportune.

mistreat verb *he's in prison for mistreating his children* ILL-TREAT, maltreat, abuse, knock about/around, hit, beat, strike, molest, injure, harm, hurt; misuse, mishandle; *informal* beat up, rough up, mess up, kick around.

mistress noun *her husband's mistress turned out to be one of her friends* LOVER, girlfriend, kept woman; courtesan, concubine, hetaera; *informal* the other woman; *archaic* paramour.

mistrust verb **1** *I mistrust his motives* BE SUSPICIOUS OF, be mistrustful of, be distrustful of, be skeptical of, be wary of, be chary of, distrust, have doubts about, have misgivings about, have reservations about, suspect.

2 *don't mistrust your impulses* QUESTION, challenge, doubt, have no confidence in, have no faith in.

▸ noun **1** *mistrust of Russia was widespread* SUSPICION, distrust, doubt, misgivings, wariness.

2 *their mistrust of David's competence* QUESTIONING, lack of confidence in, lack of faith in, doubt about.

mistrustful adjective *Sheila's unlikely stories made him even more mistrustful* SUSPICIOUS, chary, wary, distrustful, doubtful, dubious, uneasy, skeptical, leery.

misty adjective **1** *misty weather* HAZY, foggy, cloudy; smoggy. ANTONYM clear.

2 *a misty outline* BLURRY, fuzzy, blurred, clouded, dim, indistinct, unclear, vague. ANTONYMS sharp, distinct.

3 *misty memories* VAGUE, unclear, indefinite, hazy, nebulous. ANTONYM clear.

misunderstand verb *she misunderstood his motives* MISAPPREHEND, misinterpret, misconstrue, misconceive, mistake, misread; be mistaken, get the wrong idea, receive a false impression; *informal* be barking up the wrong tree, miss the boat.

misunderstanding noun **1** *a fundamental misunderstanding of juvenile crime* MISINTERPRETATION, misconstruction, misreading, misapprehension, misconception, the wrong idea, false impression.

2 *we have had some misunderstandings* DISAGREEMENT, difference (of opinion), dispute, falling-out, quarrel, argument, altercation, squabble, wrangle, row, clash; *informal* spat, scrap, tiff, rhubarb.

misuse verb **1** *misusing public funds* PUT TO WRONG USE, misemploy, embezzle, use fraudulently; abuse, squander, waste.

2 *she had been misused by her husband.* See MISTREAT.

▸ noun **1** *a misuse of company assets* WRONG USE, embezzlement, fraud; squandering, waste.

2 *the misuse of drugs* ILLEGAL USE, abuse.

mitigate verb *the worst symptoms have been mitigated* ALLEVIATE, reduce, diminish, lessen, weaken, lighten, attenuate, take the edge off, allay, ease, assuage, palliate, relieve, tone down. See note at ALLEVIATE. ANTONYM aggravate.

mitigating adjective *if not for mitigating circumstances, he would have been convicted* EXTENUATING, justificatory, justifying, vindicating, qualifying; face-saving; *formal* exculpatory.

mix verb **1** *mix all the ingredients together* BLEND, mix up, mingle, combine, put together, jumble; fuse, unite, unify, join, amalgamate, incorporate, meld, marry, coalesce, homogenize, intermingle, intermix; *technical* admix; *literary* commingle. ANTONYM separate.

2 *she mixes with all sorts* ASSOCIATE, socialize, fraternize, keep company, consort; mingle, circulate, rub elbows; *informal* hang out/around, hobnob, network.

3 *we just don't mix* BE COMPATIBLE, get along/on, be in harmony, see eye to eye, agree; *informal* hit it off, click, be on the same wavelength.

▸ noun *a mix of ancient and modern* MIXTURE, blend, mingling, combination, compound, fusion, alloy, union, amalgamation; medley, mélange, collection, selection, assortment, variety, mixed bag, grab bag, miscellany, potpourri, jumble, ragbag, patchwork, bricolage, farrago, gallimaufry, salmagundi, hodgepodge.

PHRASES: **mix up 1** *mix up the ingredients.* See MIX verb sense 1. **2** *I mixed up the dates* CONFUSE, get confused, muddle (up), get muddled up, mistake. **mixed up in** *how did she get mixed up in a car-theft ring?* INVOLVED IN, embroiled in, caught up in.

mixed adjective **1** *a mixed collection* ASSORTED, varied, variegated, miscellaneous, disparate, diverse, diversified, motley, sundry, jumbled, heterogeneous. ANTONYM homogeneous.

2 *mixed breeds* HYBRID, cross-bred, interbred, mongrel, half-caste. ANTONYM pure.

3 *mixed reactions* AMBIVALENT, equivocal, contradictory, conflicting, confused, muddled. ANTONYM unequivocal.

mixed up adjective *informal sorry, I'm still a little mixed up* CONFUSED, befuddled, bemused, bewildered, muddled; disturbed, neurotic, unbalanced; *informal* hung up, messed up, at sea.

mixer noun **1** *a kitchen mixer* BLENDER, food processor, beater; churn.

2 *he attended a mixer* GATHERING, social, function, get-together, meet-and-greet.

mixture noun **1** *the pudding mixture* BLEND, mix, brew, combination, concoction; composition, compound, alloy, amalgam.

2 *a strange mixture of people* ASSORTMENT, miscellany, medley, mélange, blend, variety, mixed bag, grab bag, mix, diversity, collection, selection, potpourri, mishmash, ragbag, patchwork, bricolage, farrago, gallimaufry, salmagundi, hodgepodge, hash.

3 *genetically, the animal is a mixture* CROSS, cross-breed, mongrel, hybrid, half-breed, half-caste.

mix-up noun *there was some sort of mix-up in the birth records* CONFUSION, muddle, misunderstanding, mistake, error; *informal* screw-up.

moan noun **1** *moans of pain* GROAN, wail, whimper, sob, cry.

2 *the moan of the wind* SIGH, murmur, sough.

3 *informal there were moans about the delay* COMPLAINT, complaining, grouse, grousing, grumble, grumbling, whine, whining, carping; *informal* gripe, griping, grouching, bellyaching, bitching, beef, beefing.

▸ verb **1** *he moaned in agony* GROAN, wail, whimper, sob, cry.

2 *the wind moaned in the trees* SIGH, murmur, sough.

3 *informal you're always moaning about the weather* COMPLAIN, grouse, grumble, whine, carp; *informal* gripe, grouch, bellyache, bitch, beef, kvetch.

mob noun 1 *troops dispersed the mob* CROWD, horde, multitude, rabble, mass, throng, group, gang, gathering, assemblage.

2 (**Mob**) *he was hiding from the Mob* MAFIA, Cosa Nostra, Camorra.

3 *the mob was excluded from political life* COMMON PEOPLE, masses, rank and file, commonality, third estate, plebeians, proletariat; hoi polloi, lower classes, rabble, riffraff, great unwashed; *informal* proles, plebs.

▸ verb 1 *the band's lead singer was mobbed when he visited Vancouver* SURROUND, swarm, besiege, jostle.

2 *reporters mobbed her hotel* CROWD (INTO), fill, pack, throng, press into, squeeze into.

mobile adjective 1 *both patients are mobile* ABLE TO MOVE (AROUND), moving, walking; *Zoology* motile; *Medicine* ambulant. ANTONYM motionless.

2 *a mobile library* TRAVELING, transportable, portable, movable; itinerant, peripatetic. ANTONYM stationary.

3 *highly mobile young people* ADAPTABLE, flexible, versatile, adjustable. ANTONYM static.

mobility noun 1 *restricted mobility* ABILITY TO MOVE, movability.

2 *the mobility of Billy's face* EXPRESSIVENESS, eloquence, animation.

3 *mobility in the workforce* ADAPTABILITY, flexibility, versatility, adjustability.

mobilize verb 1 *the government mobilized the troops* MARSHAL, deploy, muster, rally, call up, assemble, mass, organize, prepare.

2 *mobilizing support for the party* GENERATE, arouse, awaken, excite, incite, provoke, foment, prompt, stimulate, stir up, galvanize, encourage, inspire, whip up; *literary* enkindle.

mobster noun *their mother always pretended she didn't know they were mobsters* GANGSTER, hoodlum, criminal, crook, gang member; Mafioso, capo, godfather, don; *informal* goon, hood, goodfella.

mock verb 1 *they mocked her accent* RIDICULE, jeer at, sneer at, deride, scorn, make fun of, laugh at, scoff at, tease, taunt; *informal* josh, rag on, pull/jerk/yank someone's chain.

2 *they mocked the way he speaks* PARODY, ape, take off, satirize, lampoon, imitate, impersonate, mimic; *informal* send up. See note at IMITATE.

▸ adjective *mock leather* IMITATION, artificial, man-made, simulated, synthetic, ersatz, fake, reproduction, dummy, sham, false, faux, spurious, bogus, counterfeit, inauthentic, pseudo; *informal* pretend, phony. ANTONYM genuine.

mockery noun 1 *the mockery in his voice* RIDICULE, derision, jeering, sneering, contempt, scorn, scoffing, teasing, taunting, sarcasm.

2 *the trial was a mockery* TRAVESTY, charade, farce, parody.

mode noun 1 *an informal mode of policing* MANNER, way, fashion, means, method, system, style, approach, technique, procedure, process, practice.

2 *the camera is in manual mode* FUNCTION, position, operation.

3 *the mode for activewear* FASHION, vogue, style, look, trend; craze, rage, fad.

model noun 1 *a working model* REPLICA, copy, representation, mock-up, dummy, imitation, duplicate, reproduction, facsimile.

2 *the Canadian model of health care* PROTOTYPE, stereotype, archetype, type, version; mold, template, framework, pattern, design, blueprint.

3 *she was a model of patience* IDEAL, paragon, perfect example/specimen; perfection, acme, epitome, nonpareil, crème de la crème.

4 *a runway model* FASHION MODEL, supermodel, mannequin.

5 *an artist's model* SUBJECT, poser, sitter.

6 *the latest model of car* VERSION, type, design, variety, kind, sort.

▸ adjective 1 *model trains* REPLICA, TOY, miniature, dummy, imitation, duplicate, reproduction, facsimile.

2 *model farms* PROTOTYPICAL, prototypal, archetypal.

3 *a model teacher* IDEAL, perfect, exemplary, classic, flawless, faultless.

THE RIGHT WORD

Most parents try to set a good **example** for their children, although they may end up setting a bad one. An *example*, in other words, is a precedent for imitation, either good or bad. Most parents would do better to provide a **model** for their children, which refers to a person or thing that is to be followed or imitated because of its excellence in conduct or character. *Model* also connotes a physical shape to be copied closely (*a ship's model, a model airplane*). Not all children regard their parents as an **ideal** to which they aspire, a word that suggests an imagined perfection or a standard based upon a set of desirable qualities (*the ideal gentleman; the ideal of what an artist should be*); but young people's lives often end up following the **pattern** established by their parents, meaning that their lives follow the same basic configuration or design. While **prototype** and **archetype** are often used interchangeably, they really mean quite different things. An *archetype* is a perfect and unchanging form that existing things or people can approach but never duplicate (*the archetype of a mother*), while a *prototype* is an early, usually unrefined version of something that later versions reflect but may depart from (*a prototype for a hydrogen-fueled car*). **Paradigm** can refer to an example that serves as a model, but today its use is primarily confined to a grammatical context, where it means a set giving all the various forms of a word, such as the conjugation of a verb.

moderate adjective 1 *moderate success* AVERAGE, modest, medium, middling, ordinary, common, commonplace, everyday, workaday; tolerable, passable, adequate, fair; mediocre, indifferent, unexceptional, unremarkable, run-of-the-mill; *informal* OK, so-so, 'comme ci, comme ça', fair-to-middling, plain-vanilla, no great shakes, not up to much. ANTONYMS great, massive.

2 *moderate prices* REASONABLE, acceptable; inexpensive, low, fair, modest. ANTONYMS outrageous, unreasonable.

3 *moderate views* MIDDLE-OF-THE-ROAD, nonextreme, nonradical, centrist. ANTONYM extreme.

4 *moderate behavior* RESTRAINED, controlled, sober; tolerant, lenient. ANTONYM unreasonable.

▸ verb 1 *the wind has moderated somewhat* DIE DOWN, abate, let up, calm down, lessen, decrease, diminish; recede, weaken, subside. ANTONYM increase.

2 *you can help to moderate her anger* CURB, control, check, temper, restrain, subdue; repress, tame, lessen, decrease,

lower, reduce, diminish, alleviate, allay, appease, assuage, ease, soothe, calm, tone down. ANTONYMS exacerbate, aggravate.

3 *the panel was moderated by one of the writers* CHAIR, take the chair of, preside over.

moderately adverb *a moderately successful farmer* SOMEWHAT, quite, rather, fairly, reasonably, comparatively, relatively, to some extent; tolerably, passably, adequately; *informal* pretty.

moderation noun 1 *he urged them to show moderation* SELF-RESTRAINT, restraint, self-control, self-discipline; temperance, leniency, fairness. See note at ABSTINENCE.

2 *a moderation of their confrontational style* RELAXATION, easing (off), reduction, abatement, weakening, slackening, tempering, softening, diminution, diminishing, lessening; decline, modulation, modification, mitigation, allaying; *informal* letup. PHRASE: **in moderation** *I quit drinking because I wasn't able to drink in moderation* IN MODERATE QUANTITIES/AMOUNTS, within (sensible) limits; moderately.

modern adjective 1 *modern times* PRESENT-DAY, contemporary, present, current, twenty-first-century, latter-day, modern-day, recent. ANTONYM past.

2 *her clothes are very modern* FASHIONABLE, in fashion, in style, in vogue, up to date, all the rage, trend-setting, stylish, styling/stylin', voguish, modish, chic, à la mode; the latest, new, newest, newfangled, modernistic, advanced; *informal* trendy, cool, in, with it, now, hip, phat, happening, kicky, tony, fly. ANTONYMS out of date, old-fashioned.

modernize verb 1 *they are modernizing their manufacturing facilities* UPDATE, bring up to date, streamline, overhaul; renovate, remodel, refashion, revamp.

2 *we must modernize to survive* GET UP TO DATE, move with the times, innovate; *informal* get in the swim, get with it, go with the flow.

modest adjective 1 *she was modest about her poetry* SELF-EFFACING, self-deprecating, humble, unpretentious, unassuming, unostentatious; shy, bashful, self-conscious, diffident, reserved, reticent, coy. ANTONYMS conceited, boastful.

2 *modest success* MODERATE, fair, limited, tolerable, passable, adequate, satisfactory, acceptable, unexceptional. ANTONYMS great, runaway.

3 *a modest house* SMALL, ordinary, simple, plain, humble, inexpensive, unostentatious, unpretentious. ANTONYMS grandiose, grand.

4 *her modest dress* DECOROUS, decent, seemly, demure, proper. ANTONYM flamboyant.

modesty noun 1 *Hannah's modesty cloaks many talents* SELF-EFFACEMENT, humility, unpretentiousness; shyness, bashfulness, self-consciousness, reserve, reticence, timidity.

2 *the modesty of his aspirations* LIMITED SCOPE, moderation.

3 *the modesty of his home* UNPRETENTIOUSNESS, simplicity, plainness.

modicum noun *I'd like to leave while I still have a modicum of my self-respect* SMALL AMOUNT, particle, speck, fragment, scrap, crumb, grain, morsel, shred, dash, drop, pinch, soupçon, jot, iota, whit, atom, smattering, scintilla, hint, suggestion, tinge; *informal* smidgen, tad.

modification noun 1 *the design is undergoing modification* ALTERATION, adjustment, change, adaptation, refinement, revision.

2 *some minor modifications were made* REVISION, refinement, improvement, amendment, adaptation, adjustment, change, alteration.

3 *the modification of his views* SOFTENING, moderation, tempering, qualification.

modify verb 1 *their economic policy has been modified* ALTER, change, adjust, adapt, amend, revise, reshape, refashion, restyle, revamp, rework, remodel, refine; *informal* tweak, doctor.

2 *he modified his more extreme views* MODERATE, revise, temper, soften, tone down, qualify.

modish adjective *modish outfits for spring* FASHIONABLE, stylish, chic, modern, contemporary, all the rage, in vogue, voguish, up-to-the-minute, à la mode, du jour; *informal* trendy, cool, with it, in, now, hip, styling/stylin', happening, phat, funky, kicky, tony, fly.

modulate verb 1 *the cells modulate the body's response* REGULATE, adjust, set, modify, moderate.

2 *she modulated her voice* ADJUST, change the tone of, temper, soften.

modus operandi noun *leaving an open Bible on the floor is part of the burglar's modus operandi* METHOD (OF WORKING), way, MO, manner, technique, style, procedure, approach, methodology, strategy, plan, formula; *formal* praxis.

mogul noun *Hollywood movie moguls* MAGNATE, tycoon, VIP, notable, personage, baron, captain, king, lord, grandee, nabob; *informal* bigwig, big shot, big cheese, top dog, top banana, big kahuna, big enchilada.

moist adjective 1 *the air was moist* DAMP, dampish, steamy, humid, muggy, clammy, dank, wet, wettish, soggy, sweaty, sticky. ANTONYM dry.

2 *a moist fruitcake* SUCCULENT, juicy, soft. ANTONYM dry.

3 *her eyes grew moist* TEARFUL, watery, misty, dewy.

moisten verb *they moisten the towels with almond-scented hot water* DAMPEN, wet, damp, water, humidify; *literary* bedew.

moisture noun *too much moisture is bad for the tiny seedlings* WETNESS, wet, water, liquid, condensation, dew, steam, vapor, dampness, damp, humidity, clamminess, mugginess, dankness, wateriness.

moisturizer noun *a face moisturizer with aloe and shea butter* LOTION, cream, balm, emollient, salve, unguent, lubricant; *technical* humectant.

mojo noun *informal* 1 *get your mojo working* MAGIC, voodoo, hoodoo, wizardry, sorcery; charm, lucky charm, amulet, talisman, churinga.

2 *he's lost his mojo* ENERGY, vitality, spirit, zest, verve; power, dynamism, drive; fire, passion, ardor, zeal; *informal* zip, zing, pep, pizzazz, punch, bounce, oomph, moxie, go, get-up-and-go, vim and vigor, feistiness.

mold[1] noun 1 *the molten metal is poured into a mold* CAST, die, form, matrix, shape, template, pattern, frame.

2 *an actress in the traditional Hollywood mold* PATTERN, form, shape, format, model, kind, type, style; archetype, prototype.

3 *he is a figure of heroic mold* CHARACTER, nature, temper-

ament, disposition; caliber, kind, sort, variety, stamp, type.

▸ verb **1** *a figure molded from clay* SHAPE, form, fashion, model, work, construct, make, create, manufacture, sculpt, sculpture; forge, cast.

2 *molding foreign policy* DETERMINE, direct, control, guide, lead, influence, shape, form, fashion, make.

mold[2] noun *walls stained with mold* MILDEW, fungus, dry rot, must, moldiness, mustiness.

molder verb *bags of garbage are moldering on the hot sidewalks* DECAY, decompose, rot (away), go moldy, go off, go bad, spoil, putrefy.

moldy adjective *everything in the cellar was moldy* MILDEWED, mildewy, musty, moldering, fusty; decaying, decayed, rotting, rotten, bad, spoiled, far gone, decomposing.

mole noun **1** *the mole on his left cheek* MARK, birthmark, freckle, blotch, spot, blemish, beauty spot, beauty mark.

2 *an undercover mole* SPY, agent, secret agent, undercover agent, operative, plant, infiltrator, sleeper, informant, informer; *informal* spook; *archaic* intelligencer.

molest verb **1** *the crowd molested the police* HARASS, harry, hassle, pester, bother, annoy, beset, persecute, torment; *informal* roust.

2 *he molested a ten-year-old boy* (SEXUALLY) ABUSE, (sexually) assault, interfere with, rape, violate; *informal* grope, paw, fondle; *literary* ravish. See note at ATTACK.

mollify verb **1** *they tried to mollify the protesters* APPEASE, placate, pacify, conciliate, soothe, calm (down). See note at PACIFY. ANTONYM enrage.

2 *mollifying the fears of the public* ALLAY, assuage, alleviate, mitigate, ease, reduce, moderate, temper, tone down, soften; *informal* blunt. ANTONYM inflame.

mollusk noun See table.

MOLLUSKS

Bivalves	**Gastropods**
bar clam	abalone
bay scallop	conch
cherrystone clam	cowrie
clam	haliotis
cockle	limpet
gaper	murex
geoduck	nudibranch
littleneck	periwinkle
mussel	ram's-horn-snail
oyster	sea slug
pearl oyster	sea snail
pecten	slug
piddock	snail
quahog	volute
razor clam	whelk
scallop	winkle
sea scallop	
steamer	**Cephalopods**
teredo	cuttlefish
zebra mussel	nautilus
	octopus
	squid

See also table at CRUSTACEAN.

mollycoddle verb *his parents mollycoddle him* PAMPER, cosset, coddle, spoil, indulge, overindulge, pet, baby, nanny, wait on hand and foot.

▸ noun *the boy's a mollycoddle!* See MAMA'S BOY.

WORD NOTE **mollycoddle**

Use this word at every opportunity. If you have to change your hero from a strapping lumberjack to an effete interior decorator just to use this word, do it. Don't hesitate. **—EM**

molten adjective *vats of molten iron* LIQUEFIED, liquid, fluid, melted, flowing.

moment noun **1** *he thought for a moment* LITTLE WHILE, short time, bit, minute, instant, second, split second; *informal* sec.

2 *the moment they met* POINT (IN TIME), time, hour.

3 *formal issues of little moment* IMPORTANCE, import, significance, consequence, note, weight, concern, interest. PHRASE: **in a moment** *the show will start in a moment* VERY SOON, in a minute, in a second, in a trice, shortly, any minute (now), in the twinkling of an eye, in (less than) no time, in no time at all, momentarily; *informal* in a jiff, in a jiffy, in two shakes (of a lamb's tail), in the blink of an eye, in a snap, in a heartbeat, in a flash; *literary* ere long.

momentarily adverb **1** *he paused momentarily* BRIEFLY, fleetingly, for a moment, for a second, for an instant.

2 *my husband will be here momentarily.* See IN A MOMENT at MOMENT.

momentary adjective *a momentary lapse in power* BRIEF, short, short-lived, fleeting, passing, transient, transitory, ephemeral; *literary* evanescent. ANTONYM lengthy.

momentous adjective *a momentous decision* IMPORTANT, significant, historic, portentous, critical, crucial, life-and-death, decisive, pivotal, consequential, of consequence, far-reaching, earth-shattering, earth-shaking; *formal* of moment. ANTONYM insignificant.

momentum noun *we gained momentum going down the Killingworth hill* IMPETUS, energy, force, power, strength, thrust, speed, velocity.

monarch noun *Elizabeth II has been Britain's reigning monarch since 1953* SOVEREIGN, ruler, the Crown, crowned head, potentate; king, queen, emperor, empress, prince, princess.

monastery noun *the monastery was temporarily occupied by Nazis* RELIGIOUS COMMUNITY; friary, abbey, priory, nunnery, cloister, convent.

monastic adjective **1** *a monastic community* CLOISTERED, cloistral, claustral.

2 *a monastic existence* AUSTERE, ascetic, simple, solitary, monkish, celibate, quiet, cloistered, sequestered, secluded, reclusive, hermitlike, hermitic, incommunicado.

monetary adjective *her sharp monetary instincts got us through the recession in very good sharp* FINANCIAL, fiscal, pecuniary, money, cash, economic, budgetary. See note at FINANCIAL.

money noun **1** *have you got money for train fare?* CASH, hard cash, ready money; the means, the wherewithal, funds, capital, finances, (filthy) lucre; coins, change, specie, silver, currency, bills, (bank) notes; *informal* dough, bread, bucks, loot, greenbacks, moola, dinero, shekels, mazuma; *archaic* pelf.

2 *she married him for his money* WEALTH, riches, fortune, affluence, assets, liquid assets, resources, means.

3 *the money here is better* PAY, salary, wages, remuneration; *formal* emolument. PHRASES: **for my money** *for my money,* *they are the better team* IN MY OPINION, to my mind, in my view, as I see it, personally, in my estimation, in my judgment, if you ask me. **in the money** *informal we're finally in the money*. See MONEYED.

moneyed adjective *she's got two brothers—one is broke and the other is moneyed* RICH, wealthy, affluent, well-to-do, well off, prosperous, in clover, opulent, of means, of substance; *informal* in the money, rolling in it, loaded, stinking/filthy rich, well-heeled, made of money. ANTONYM poor.

money-grubbing adjective *informal his money-grubbing ex-wife will be collecting alimony until he drops dead* ACQUISITIVE, avaricious, grasping, money-grabbing, gold-digging, rapacious, mercenary, materialistic.

money-making adjective *it wasn't the moneymaking enterprise we had hoped it would be* PROFITABLE, profit-making, remunerative, lucrative, successful, financially rewarding. ANTONYM loss-making.

mongrel noun *a curly-tailed mongrel* CROSS-BREED, cross, mixed breed, half-breed; cur, mutt; *informal* Heinz 57.

▸ adjective *a mongrel bitch* CROSS-BRED, of mixed breed, half-breed, interbred, mixed. ANTONYM pedigree.

monitor noun **1** *a fetal monitor* DETECTOR, scanner, recorder; listening device; security camera.

2 *UN monitors* OBSERVER, watchdog, overseer, supervisor.

3 *a computer monitor* SCREEN, video display terminal, VDT.

▸ verb *his movements were closely monitored* OBSERVE, watch, track, keep an eye on, keep under observation, keep watch on, keep under surveillance, record, note, oversee; *informal* keep tabs on.

monk noun *the monks teach a class in organic gardening* brother, religious, cenobite, contemplative, mendicant; friar; abbot, prior; novice, oblate, postulant; lama, marabout.

monkey noun **1** SIMIAN, primate, ape. See table at PRIMATE.

2 *you little monkey!* See RASCAL. PHRASES: **make a monkey (out) of** *she made a monkey out of Clark in front of his friends* MAKE SOMEONE LOOK FOOLISH, make a fool of, make a laughingstock of, ridicule, make fun of, poke fun at. **monkey with** *don't monkey with those switches* TAMPER WITH, fiddle with, interfere with, meddle with, tinker with, play with; *informal* mess with.

monkey business noun *informal they better not try any monkey business when Ms. Bergdahl is around* MISCHIEF, misbehavior, mischievousness, devilry, devilment, tomfoolery; dishonesty, trickery, chicanery, skulduggery; *informal* shenanigans, funny business, hanky-panky, monkeyshines.

monolith noun *no one knows for sure who erected these monoliths and why* STANDING STONE, menhir, megalith, sarsen (stone).

monolithic adjective **1** *a monolithic building* MASSIVE, huge, vast, colossal, gigantic, immense, giant, enormous; featureless, characterless.

2 *the old monolithic Communist party* INFLEXIBLE, rigid, unbending, unchanging, fossilized.

monologue noun *Letterman's nightly monologue* SOLILOQUY, speech, address, lecture, sermon, homily; *formal* oration.

monomania noun *his interest in the subject verges on monomania* OBSESSION, fixation, consuming passion, mania, compulsion.

monopolize verb **1** *the company has monopolized the market* CORNER, control, take over, gain control/dominance over; *archaic* engross.

2 *he monopolized the conversation* DOMINATE, take over; *informal* hog.

3 *she monopolized the guest of honor* TAKE UP ALL THE ATTENTION OF, keep to oneself; *informal* tie up.

monotonous adjective **1** *a monotonous job* TEDIOUS, boring, dull, uninteresting, unexciting, wearisome, tiresome, repetitive, repetitious, unvarying, unchanging, unvaried, humdrum, ho-hum, routine, mechanical, mind-numbing, soul-destroying; colorless, featureless, dreary; *informal* deadly, samey, dullsville. ANTONYM interesting.

2 *a monotonous voice* TONELESS, flat, uninflected, soporific.

monotony noun **1** *the monotony of everyday life* TEDIUM, tediousness, lack of variety, dullness, boredom, repetitiveness, uniformity, routineness, wearisomeness, tiresomeness; lack of excitement, uneventfulness, dreariness, colorlessness, featurelessness; *informal* deadliness.

2 *the monotony of her voice* TONELESSNESS, flatness.

monster noun **1** *legendary sea monsters* FABULOUS CREATURE, mythical creature. See table on page 589.

2 *her husband is a monster* BRUTE, fiend, beast, devil, demon, barbarian, savage, animal; *informal* swine, pig.

3 *the boy's a little monster* RASCAL, imp, monkey, wretch, devil; *informal* horror, scamp, scalawag, tyke, varmint, hellion; *archaic* scapegrace, rapscallion.

4 *he's a monster of a man* GIANT, mammoth, colossus, leviathan, titan; *informal* jumbo.

▸ adjective *informal a monster truck*. See HUGE.

monstrosity noun **1** *a concrete monstrosity* EYESORE, blot on the landscape, excrescence, horror.

2 *a biological monstrosity* MUTANT, mutation, freak (of nature), monster, abortion.

monstrous adjective **1** *a monstrous creature* GROTESQUE, hideous, ugly, ghastly, gruesome, horrible, horrific, horrifying, grisly, disgusting, repulsive, repellent, dreadful, frightening, terrifying, malformed, misshapen. ANTONYM lovely.

2 *a monstrous tidal wave*. See HUGE.

3 *monstrous acts of violence* APPALLING, heinous, egregious, evil, wicked, abominable, terrible, horrible, dreadful, vile, outrageous, shocking, disgraceful; unspeakable, despicable, vicious, savage, barbaric, barbarous, inhuman, beastly. ANTONYMS admirable, good.

month noun See table on page 589.

monument noun **1** *a stone monument* MEMORIAL, statue, pillar, column, obelisk, cross; cenotaph, tomb, mausoleum, shrine.

2 *a monument was placed over the grave* GRAVESTONE, headstone, tombstone, grave marker, plaque.

3 *a monument to a past era of aviation* TESTAMENT, record, reminder, remembrance, memorial, commemoration.

MONSTERS AND CREATURES

abominable snowman	kraken
Argus	leviathan
basilisk	Lilith
banshee	Loch Ness Monster
behemoth	loup-garou
Bigfoot	lycanthrope
bogie	manticore
brownie	mermaid
Cadborosaurus (Caddy)	merman
Cerberus	Minotaur
centaur	Nessie
Chimera	Ogopogo
chupacabra	orc
cockatrice	Pegasus
Cthulhu	phoenix
Cyclops	Sasquatch
demon	satyr
devil	Scylla
dragon	sea serpent
elf	sea snake
erl-king	shape-shifter
fairy	siren
faun	Sphinx
Frankenstein	thunderbird
gnome	Tiamat
goblin	troll
Gorgon	Typhon
Grendel	unicorn
griffin	urchin
harpy	vampire
hippogriff	werewolf
hobbit	windigo
Hydra	witch
jinn	yeti

See also table at SPIRIT.

monumental adjective **1** *a monumental task* HUGE, great, enormous, gigantic, massive, colossal, mammoth, immense, tremendous, mighty, stupendous.

2 *a monumental error in judgment* TERRIBLE, dreadful, awful, colossal, staggering, huge, enormous, unforgivable, egregious.

3 *her monumental achievement* IMPRESSIVE, striking, outstanding, remarkable, magnificent, majestic, stupendous, ambitious, large-scale, grand, awe-inspiring, important, significant, distinguished, memorable, immortal.

mooch verb *he was always mooching money from us* BEG, ask for money, borrow; *informal* scrounge, bum, sponge, cadge.

▸ noun *she is such a mooch* BEGGAR *informal* bum, scrounger, sponger, cadger, freeloader, moocher.

mood noun **1** *she's in a good mood* FRAME/STATE OF MIND, humor, temper; disposition, spirit, tenor.

2 *he's obviously in* ***a mood*** A BAD MOOD, a (bad) temper, a sulk, a fit of pique; low spirits, the doldrums, the blues, a blue funk; *informal* the dumps.

3 *the mood of the film* ATMOSPHERE, feeling, spirit, ambience, aura, character, tenor, flavor, feel, tone. PHRASE: **in the mood** *I don't like to go to the casino unless I'm in the mood* IN THE RIGHT FRAME OF MIND, wanting to, inclined to, disposed to, minded to, eager to, willing to.

moody adjective *how can she live with that moody man?* TEMPERAMENTAL, emotional, volatile, capricious, changeable, mercurial; sullen, sulky, morose, glum, depressed, dejected, despondent, doleful, dour, sour, saturnine, manic-depressive; *informal* blue, down in the dumps, down in/at the mouth. ANTONYMS even-tempered, cheerful.

moon noun *viewing the eclipse of the moon* SATELLITE.

▸ verb **1** *stop* ***mooning about*** WASTE TIME, loaf, idle, mope; *informal* lollygag.

2 *he's mooning over her photograph* MOPE, pine, brood, daydream, fantasize, be in a reverie.

PHRASES: **many moons ago** *informal we stayed at that hotel many moons ago* A LONG TIME AGO, ages ago, years ago. **once in a blue moon** *informal Donnie brings me flowers once in a blue moon* HARDLY EVER, scarcely ever, rarely, very seldom. **over the moon** *informal I'm over the moon just thinking about our upcoming cruise.* See ECSTATIC.

moonshine noun *informal* **1** *they brewed up a batch of moonshine* ALCOHOL, bootleg liquor, drink; *informal* booze, shine, hooch, white lightning, homebrew; rotgut, firewater.

2 *that story's a lot of moonshine, and you know it.* See NONSENSE sense 1.

moor[1] verb *a boat was moored to the quay* TIE UP, secure, make fast, fix firmly, anchor, berth, dock.

moor[2] noun *a walk on the moor* UPLAND, moorland; heath.

MONTHS OF THE YEAR

Gregorian Calendar	**Hindu Calendar**
January	Chaitra
February	Vaisakha
March	Jyaistha
April	Asadha
May	Sravana
June	Bhadra
July	Asvina
August	Kartika
September	Agrahayana/Margasirsa
October	Pausa
November	Magha
December	Phalguna

Jewish Calendar	**Chinese Agricultural Calendar**
Nisan	Li Chun
Iyyar	Yu Shui
Sivan	Jing Zhe
Thammuz	Chun Fen
Ab	Qing Ming
Elul	Gu Yu
Tishri	Li Xia
Hesvan	Xiao Man
Kislev	Mang Zhong
Tebet	Xia Zhi
Sebat	Xiao Shu
Adar	Da Shu
	Li Qui
Islamic Calendar	Chu Shu
Muharram	Bai Lu
Safar	Qui Fen
Rabi I	Han Lu
Rabi II	Shuang Jiang
Jumada I	Li Dong
Jumada II	Xiao Xue
Rajab	Da Xue
Shaban	Dong Zhi
Ramadan	Xiao Han
Shawwal	Da Han
Dhu al-Qadah	
Dhu al-Hijjah	

moot adjective *a moot point* DEBATABLE, open to discussion/question, arguable, questionable, at issue, open to doubt, disputable, controversial, contentious, disputed, unresolved, unsettled, up in the air.

▸ verb *the idea was first mooted in the 1930s* RAISE, bring up, broach, mention, put forward, introduce, advance, propose, suggest.

mop noun *her tousled mop of hair* SHOCK, mane, tangle, mass.

▸ verb *a man was mopping the floor* WASH, clean, wipe, swab.

PHRASE: **mop up** 1 *I mopped up the spilled coffee* WIPE UP, clean up, sponge up. 2 *troops mopped up the last pockets of resistance* FINISH OFF, deal with, dispose of, take care of, clear up, eliminate.

mope verb 1 *it's no use moping* BROOD, sulk, be miserable, be despondent, pine, eat one's heart out, fret, grieve; *informal* be down in the dumps, be down in/at the mouth; *literary* repine.

2 *she was moping about the house* LANGUISH, moon, idle, loaf; *informal* lollygag.

moral adjective 1 *moral issues* ETHICAL, social, having to do with right and wrong.

2 *a moral man* VIRTUOUS, good, righteous, upright, upstanding, high-minded, principled, honorable, honest, just, noble, incorruptible, scrupulous, respectable, decent, clean-living, law-abiding. ANTONYM dishonorable.

3 *moral support* PSYCHOLOGICAL, emotional, mental.

▸ noun 1 *the moral of the story* LESSON, message, meaning, significance, signification, import, point, teaching.

2 *he has no morals* MORAL CODE, code of ethics, (moral) values, principles, standards, (sense of) morality, scruples.

THE RIGHT WORD

You can be an **ethical** person without necessarily being a **moral** one, since *ethical* implies conformity with a code of fair and honest behavior, particularly in business or in a profession (*an ethical legislator who didn't believe in cutting deals*), while *moral* refers to generally accepted standards of goodness and rightness in character and conduct—especially sexual conduct (*the moral values she'd learned from her mother*). In the same way, you can be **honorable** without necessarily being **virtuous**, since *honorable* suggests dealing with others in a decent and ethical manner, while *virtuous* implies the possession of moral excellence in character (*many honorable businesspeople fail to live a virtuous private life*). **Righteous** is similar in meaning to **virtuous** but also implies freedom from guilt or blame (*righteous anger*); when the righteous person is also somewhat intolerant and narrow-minded, *self-righteous* might be a better adjective. Someone who makes a hypocritical show of being righteous is often described as **sanctimonious**—in other words, acting like a saint without having a saintly character.

morale noun *Bob Hope was the champion of troop morale* CONFIDENCE, self-confidence, self-esteem, spirit(s), team spirit, enthusiasm.

morality noun 1 *the morality of nuclear weapons* ETHICS, rights and wrongs, ethicality.

2 *a sharp decline in morality* VIRTUE, goodness, good behavior, righteousness, rectitude, uprightness; morals, principles, honesty, integrity, propriety, honor, justice, decency; ethics, standards/principles of behavior, mores, standards. See note at GOODNESS.

moralize verb *it isn't your job to moralize to me* PONTIFICATE, sermonize, lecture, preach.

morass noun 1 *the muddy morass* QUAGMIRE, swamp, bog, marsh, muskeg, mire, marshland, wetland, slough, moor.

2 *a morass of paperwork* CONFUSION, chaos, muddle, tangle, entanglement, imbroglio, jumble, clutter; *informal* logjam.

moratorium noun *a moratorium on nuclear testing* EMBARGO, ban, prohibition, suspension, postponement, stay, stoppage, halt, freeze, standstill, respite.

morbid adjective 1 *a morbid fascination with contemporary warfare* GHOULISH, macabre, unhealthy, gruesome, unwholesome; abnormal, aberrant, disturbing, worrisome; *informal* sick, weird. ANTONYM wholesome.

2 *I felt decidedly morbid* GLOOMY, glum, melancholy, morose, dismal, somber, doleful, despondent, dejected, sad, depressed, downcast, down, disconsolate, miserable, unhappy, downhearted, dispirited, low; *informal* blue, down in the dumps, down in/at the mouth. ANTONYM cheerful.

mordant adjective *a mordant sense of humor* CAUSTIC, trenchant, biting, cutting, acerbic, sardonic, sarcastic, scathing, acid, sharp, keen; critical, bitter, virulent, vitriolic.

more adjective *I could do with some more clothes* ADDITIONAL, further, added, extra, increased, new, other, supplementary. ANTONYMS less, fewer.

▸ adverb 1 *he was able to concentrate more on his writing* TO A GREATER EXTENT, further, some more, better.

2 *he was rich, and more, he was handsome.* See MOREOVER.

▸ pronoun *we're going to need more* EXTRA, an additional amount, an additional amount, an addition, an increase. ANTONYMS less, fewer.

PHRASE: **more or less** *the jar holds more or less 18 pickles* APPROXIMATELY, roughly, nearly, almost, close to, about, of/on the order of, in the region of.

moreover adverb *Lindsey is going to the wedding, and moreover, she'll be singing at the reception* BESIDES, furthermore, what's more, in addition, also, as well, too, to boot, additionally, on top of that, into the bargain, more, likewise; *archaic* withal.

mores plural noun *the mores of the day would have prevented her from voicing political opinions* CUSTOMS, conventions, ways, way of life, traditions, practices, habits; *Anthropology* lifeways; *formal* praxis.

moribund adjective 1 *the patient was moribund* DYING, expiring, terminal, on one's deathbed, near death, at death's door, not long for this world. ANTONYMS thriving, recovering.

2 *the moribund shipbuilding industry* DECLINING, in decline, waning, dying, stagnating, stagnant, crumbling, on its last legs. ANTONYM flourishing.

morning noun 1 *I've got a meeting **this morning*** BEFORE NOON, before lunch/lunchtime, this a.m.; *literary* this morn, this forenoon.

2 *morning is on its way* DAWN, daybreak, sunrise, first

light, sunup; *literary* dayspring, dawning, aurora, cock crow. PHRASE: **morning, noon, and night** *she stayed at his bedside morning, noon, and night* ALL THE TIME, without a break, constantly, continually, incessantly, ceaselessly, perpetually, unceasingly; *informal* 24-7.

moron noun *what moron left ice cream on the stove?* FOOL, idiot, ass, blockhead, dunce, dolt, ignoramus, imbecile, cretin, dullard, simpleton, clod; *informal* nitwit, halfwit, dope, ninny, nincompoop, chump, dimwit, dingbat, dipstick, goober, coot, goon, dumbo, dummy, ditz, dumdum, fathead, numbskull, numbnuts, dunderhead, thickhead, airhead, flake, lamebrain, zombie, nerd, peabrain, birdbrain, jughead, jerk, donkey, twit, goat, dork, twerp, schmuck, bozo, boob, turkey, schlep, chowderhead, dumbhead, goofball, goof, goofus, galoot, lummox, klutz, putz, schlemiel, sap, meatball, dumb cluck. ANTONYM genius.

moronic adjective *a succession of moronic game shows* STUPID, FOOLISH, senseless, brainless, mindless, idiotic, imbecile, insane, lunatic, asinine, ridiculous, ludicrous, absurd, preposterous, silly, inane, witless, half-baked, empty-headed, unintelligent, slow-witted, weak-minded; *informal* crazy, dumb, brain-dead, cretinous, imbecilic, doltish, thick, thickheaded, birdbrained, pea-brained, pinheaded, dopey, dim, dimwitted, halfwitted, dippy, fatheaded, blockheaded, boneheaded, lamebrained, chuckleheaded, dunderheaded, muttonheaded; daft, dumb-ass, chowderheaded.

morose adjective *Louis sat alone, looking morose* SULLEN, sulky, gloomy, bad-tempered, ill-tempered, dour, surly, sour, glum, moody, ill-humored, melancholy, melancholic, brooding, broody, doleful, miserable, depressed, dejected, despondent, downcast, unhappy, low, down, grumpy, irritable, churlish, cantankerous, crotchety, cross, crabby, cranky, grouchy, testy, snappish, peevish, crusty; *informal* blue, down in the dumps, down in/at the mouth. ANTONYM cheerful.

morsel noun *we sampled morsels of their splendid desserts* MOUTHFUL, bite, nibble, bit, soupçon, taste, spoonful, forkful, sliver, drop, dollop, spot, gobbet, tidbit.

mortal adjective **1** *mortal remains | all men are mortal* PERISHABLE, physical, bodily, corporeal, fleshly, earthly; human, impermanent, transient, ephemeral.

2 *a mortal blow* DEADLY, fatal, lethal, death-dealing, murderous, terminal.

3 *mortal enemies* IRRECONCILABLE, deadly, sworn, bitter, out-and-out, implacable.

4 *a mortal sin* UNPARDONABLE, unforgivable. ANTONYM venial.

5 *living in mortal fear* EXTREME, (very) great, terrible, awful, dreadful, intense, severe, grave, dire, unbearable.

▸ noun *we are mere mortals* HUMAN BEING, human, person, man/woman; earthling.

mortality noun **1** *a sense of his own mortality* IMPERMANENCE, transience, ephemerality, perishability; humanity; corporeality.

2 *the causes of mortality* DEATH, loss of life, dying.

mortify verb **1** *I'd be mortified if my friends found out* EMBARRASS, humiliate, chagrin, discomfit, shame, abash, horrify, appall.

2 *he was mortified at being excluded* HURT, wound, affront, offend, put out, pique, irk, annoy, vex; *informal* rile.

3 *mortifying the flesh* SUBDUE, suppress, subjugate, control; discipline, chasten, punish.

mortuary noun *flowers were sent to the mortuary* funeral parlor, funeral home; morgue.

mosaic noun *the mosaic in the front hallway was commissioned by Colonel Reed in 1842* PATTERN, design, arrangement, collection, collage, picture, pastiche.

most pronoun *most of the guests brought gifts* NEARLY ALL, almost all, the greatest part/number, the majority, the bulk, the preponderance. ANTONYMS little, few.

PHRASE: **for the most part** See MOSTLY senses 1, 2.

mostly adverb **1** *the other passengers were mostly businessmen* MAINLY, for the most part, on the whole, in the main, largely, chiefly, predominantly, principally, primarily.

2 *I mostly wear jeans* USUALLY, generally, in general, for the most part, as a rule, ordinarily, normally, customarily, typically, most of the time, almost always, on average, on balance.

mote noun *do you know how it feels to have not even a mote of hope?* SPECK, particle, grain, spot, fleck, atom, scintilla.

motel noun *all the motels in the region were booked for the season* HOTEL, inn, motor inn, motor court, lodge; accommodations, lodging, rooms.

moth noun *in summer, we'd sit on the steps and watch the moths flit about the porch light.* See table.

MOTHS

acrea moth	Io moth
armyworm moth	Isabella moth
bagworm moth	leopard moth
black witch	luna moth
buck moth	lunate moth
bumblebee moth	meal moth
burnet	Mediterranean flour moth
carpenter moth	noctuid
carpet moth	oakworm moth
cecropia	Pandora moth
clearwing	pantry moth
clothes moth	pitch twigmoth
codling moth	plume moth
cotton leafworm moth	polyphemus moth
ctenuchid	Promethea moth
cutworm moth	prominent
Cynthia	regal/royal moth
dagger moth	rosy maple moth
day moth	salt marsh moth
diamondback moth	satin moth
dried leaf moth	saturnid
emperor moth	silkworm/silk moth
flannel moth	snout moth
forester	sphinx
geometer	tentmaker
grain moth	three-spotted fillip
green cloverworm moth	tiger moth
gypsy moth	tortrix
handmaid	tussock
hawk moth	underwing
honey-locust moth	wax moth
hummingbird moth	yucca moth
imperial moth	Zimmerman pine moth
Indian meal moth	

See also table at BUTTERFLY.

moth-eaten adjective *a moth-eaten tweed jacket* THREADBARE, worn (out), well-worn, old, shabby, scruffy, tattered, ragged; *informal* tatty, the worse for wear, raggedy.

mother noun **1** *I will ask my mother* FEMALE PARENT, materfamilias, matriarch; *informal* mom, mommy, ma, mama; old lady, old woman; *chiefly Brit. informal* mum, mummy.

2 *the foal's mother* DAM.

3 *necessity is the mother of invention* SOURCE, origin, genesis, fountainhead, inspiration, stimulus; *literary* wellspring.

4 *informal a mother of a storm informal* HUMDINGER, dilly, doozy, lulu, whopper.

▸ verb **1** *she mothered her husband* LOOK AFTER, care for, take care of, nurse, protect, tend, raise, rear; pamper, coddle, cosset, fuss over. ANTONYM neglect.

2 *she mothered two sets of twins* GIVE BIRTH TO, have, bear, produce, birth; *archaic* be brought to bed of.

▸ adjective *my mother tongue* NATIVE, first, original; ancestral.

motherly adjective *thanks for your motherly advice* MATERNAL, maternalistic, protective, caring, loving, devoted, affectionate, fond, warm, tender, gentle, kind, kindly, understanding, compassionate.

motif noun **1** *a colorful tulip motif* DESIGN, pattern, decoration, figure, shape, device, emblem, ornament.

2 *a recurring motif in her work* THEME, idea, concept, subject, topic, leitmotif, element.

motion noun **1** *the rocking motion of the boat | a planet's motion around the sun* MOVEMENT, moving, locomotion, rise and fall, shifting; progress, passage, passing, transit, course, travel, traveling.

2 *a motion of the hand* GESTURE, movement, signal, sign, indication; wave, nod, gesticulation.

3 *the motion failed to obtain a majority* PROPOSAL, proposition, recommendation, suggestion.

▸ verb *he motioned her to sit down* GESTURE, signal, direct, indicate; wave, beckon, nod, gesticulate.

PHRASES: **in motion** *remain seated while the bus is in motion* MOVING, on the move, going, traveling, running, functioning, operational. **set/put in motion** *they have set in motion a formal review of the law* START, commence, begin, activate, initiate, launch, get underway, get going, get off the ground; trigger off, set off, spark off, generate, cause.

motionless adjective *the leaves were motionless in the still night air* UNMOVING, still, stationary, stock-still, immobile, static, not moving a muscle, rooted to the spot, transfixed, paralyzed, frozen. ANTONYM moving.

motivate verb **1** *she was primarily motivated by the desire for profit* PROMPT, drive, move, inspire, stimulate, influence, activate, impel, push, propel, spur (on).

2 *it's the teacher's job to motivate the child* INSPIRE, stimulate, encourage, spur (on), excite, inspirit, incentivize, fire with enthusiasm.

motivation noun **1** *his motivation was financial* MOTIVE, motivating force, incentive, stimulus, stimulation, inspiration, inducement, incitement, spur, reason; *informal* carrot.

2 *keep up the staff's motivation* ENTHUSIASM, drive, ambition, initiative, determination, enterprise; *informal* get-up-and-go.

motive noun **1** *the motive for the attack* REASON, motivation, motivating force, rationale, grounds, cause, basis, object, purpose, intention; incentive, inducement, incitement, lure, inspiration, stimulus, stimulation, spur.

2 *religious motives in art* MOTIF, theme, idea, concept, subject, topic, leitmotif.

▸ adjective *motive power* KINETIC, driving, impelling, propelling, propulsive, motor.

motley adjective *a motley collection of vintage fabrics* MISCELLANEOUS, disparate, diverse, assorted, varied, diversified, heterogeneous; *informal* ragtag, raggle-taggle. ANTONYM homogeneous.

WORD NOTE **motley**

The word *motley* is on an unfortunate downward slide. For reasons to do with police officers and a rock band it has become irrevocably attached to the word *crew* and now conjures up visions of something shabby—varied in its shabbiness—but definitely shabby, unlikely-looking. When we hear in *As You Like It,* "O that I were a fool! I am ambitious for a motley coat," we only wonder why. How exactly *motley* got its down-at-heel associations is unclear. It means simply "diversified in color, multicolored, variegated" and should be, by rights, as value-free as its synonyms. True, the noun has the secondary meaning "incongruous mixture" and true, *motley* is itself a synecdoche for a jester's incongruously colored coat—but shabby? Untrustworthy? Suspicious? Even dangerous? *Motley* needs rehabilitation. **—ZS**

motor home noun See CAMPER.

mottled adjective *mottled horses* BLOTCHY, blotched, spotted, spotty, speckled, streaked, streaky, marbled, flecked, freckled, dappled, stippled; piebald, skewbald, brindled, brindle, pinto, calico; *informal* splotchy.

motto noun *the town's motto is "Tolerance and Prosperity"* MAXIM, saying, proverb, aphorism, adage, saw, axiom, apophthegm, formula, expression, phrase, dictum, precept; slogan, catchphrase, mantra; truism, cliché, platitude.

mound noun **1** *a mound of leaves* HEAP, pile, stack, mountain; mass, accumulation, assemblage.

2 *high on the mound* HILLOCK, hill, knoll, rise, hummock, hump, embankment, bank, ridge, elevation; *Geology* drumlin.

▸ verb *mound up the rice on a serving plate* PILE (UP), heap (up).

mount verb **1** *he mounted the stairs* GO UP, ascend, climb (up), scale. ANTONYM descend.

2 *the committee mounted the platform* CLIMB ON TO, jump on to, clamber on to, get on to.

3 *they mounted their horses* GET ASTRIDE, bestride, get on to, hop on to.

4 *the museum is mounting an exhibition* (PUT ON) DISPLAY, exhibit, present, install; organize, put on, stage.

5 *the company mounted a takeover bid* ORGANIZE, stage, prepare, arrange, set up; launch, set in motion, initiate.

6 *their losses mounted rapidly* INCREASE, grow, rise, escalate, soar, spiral, shoot up, rocket, climb, accumulate, build up, multiply. ANTONYMS decrease, diminish.

7 *cameras were mounted above the door* INSTALL, place, fix, set, put up, put in position.

mountain noun **1** *a range of mountains* PEAK, height, mount, prominence, summit, pinnacle, alp; (**mountains**) range, sierra, cordillera, massif.

2 ***a mountain*** *of work* A GREAT DEAL, a lot; a profusion, an abundance, a quantity, a backlog; *informal* a heap, a pile, a stack, a slew, lots, loads, heaps, piles, tons, masses; gobs. PHRASE: **move mountains** 1 *faith can move mountains* PERFORM MIRACLES, work/do wonders. 2 *his fans move mountains to attend his performances* MAKE EVERY EFFORT, pull out all the stops, do one's utmost/best; *informal* bend/lean over backwards.

mountainous adjective 1 *a mountainous region* HILLY, craggy, rocky, alpine; upland, highland. ANTONYM flat.

2 *mountainous waves* HUGE, enormous, gigantic, massive, giant, colossal, immense, tremendous, mighty; *informal* whopping, humongous, ginormous. ANTONYM tiny.

mountebank noun *that mountebank is going to rue the day he ever set foot in our fair town* SWINDLER, charlatan, confidence trickster, fraud, fraudster, impostor, trickster, hoaxer; *informal* con man, flimflammer, snake oil salesman, sharp, grifter, bunco artist. See note at QUACK.

mourn verb 1 *Isobel mourned her husband* GRIEVE FOR, sorrow over, lament for, weep for.

2 *he mourned the loss of the beautiful buildings* DEPLORE, bewail, bemoan, rue, regret.

THE RIGHT WORD

Not everyone exhibits unhappiness in the same way. **Grieve** is the strongest of these verbs, implying deep mental anguish or suffering, often endured alone and in silence (*she grieved for years over the loss of her baby*). **Mourn** is more formal and often more public; although it implies deep emotion felt over a period of time, that emotion may be more ceremonial than sincere (*the people mourned the loss of their leader*). **Lament** comes from a Latin word meaning to wail or weep, and it therefore suggests a vocal or verbal expression of loss (*The shrieking women lamented their husbands' deaths*). **Bemoan** also suggests suppressed or inarticulate sounds of *grief*, often expressing regret or disapproval (*to bemoan one's fate*). **Sorrow** combines deep sadness with regret and often pertains to a less tragic loss than *grieve* or *mourn* (*sorrow over a lost love*), while **rue** has even stronger connotations of regret and repentance (*she rued the day she was born*).

mournful adjective *mournful music* SAD, sorrowful, doleful, melancholy, melancholic, woeful, grief-stricken, miserable, unhappy, heartbroken, broken-hearted, gloomy, dismal, desolate, dejected, despondent, depressed, downcast, disconsolate, woebegone, forlorn, rueful, lugubrious, joyless, cheerless; *literary* dolorous. ANTONYM cheerful.

mourning noun 1 *a period of mourning* GRIEF, grieving, sorrowing, lamentation, lament, keening, wailing, weeping.

2 *she was dressed in mourning* BLACK (CLOTHES), (widow's) weeds; *archaic* sables.

mouse noun. See table at RODENT.

mousy adjective 1 *mousy hair* LIGHTISH BROWN, brownish, brownish-gray, dun-colored; dull, lackluster.

2 *a small, mousy woman* TIMID, quiet, fearful, timorous, shy, self-effacing, diffident, unassertive, unforthcoming, withdrawn, introverted, introvert.

mouth noun 1 *open your mouth* lips, jaws; maw, muzzle; *informal* trap, chops, kisser, puss.

2 *the mouth of the cave* ENTRANCE, opening, entry, way in, access, ingress.

3 *the mouth of the bottle* OPENING, rim, lip.

4 *the mouth of the river* OUTFALL, outlet, debouchment; estuary.

5 *informal don't give me any mouth* IMPUDENCE, insolence, impertinence, effrontery, presumption, presumptuousness, rudeness, disrespect, cheek, cheekiness; *informal* lip, sauce, sass, sassiness, back talk.

▸ verb 1 *he mouthed platitudes* UTTER, speak, say; pronounce, enunciate, articulate, voice, express; say insincerely, say for form's sake, pay lip service to.

2 *he mouthed the words to the song* LIP-SYNCH.

PHRASES: **down in/at the mouth** *informal* . See UNHAPPY sense 1. **keep one's mouth shut** *informal just keep your mouth shut and no one will get hurt* SAY NOTHING, keep quiet, not breathe a word, not tell a soul; *informal* keep mum, not let the cat out of the bag. **mouth off** *informal* 1 *he was mouthing off about politics again* RANT, spout, declaim, sound off. 2 *the students mouthed off to their teacher* TALK INSOLENTLY, be disrespectful.

mouthful noun 1 *a mouthful of pizza* BITE, nibble, taste, bit, piece; spoonful, forkful.

2 *a mouthful of beer* SIP, swallow, drop, gulp, slug; *informal* swig.

3 *"sesquipedalian" is a bit of a mouthful* TONGUE-TWISTER, long word, difficult word.

mouthpiece noun 1 *the flute's mouthpiece* EMBOUCHURE.

2 *a mouthpiece for the government* SPOKESPERSON, spokesman, spokeswoman, speaker, agent, representative, propagandist, voice; organ, channel, vehicle, instrument.

movable adjective 1 *movable objects* PORTABLE, transportable, transferable; mobile.

2 *movable dates* VARIABLE, changeable, alterable. ANTONYM fixed.

move verb 1 *she moved to the door* | *don't move!* GO, walk, proceed, progress, advance; budge, stir, shift, change position.

2 *he moved the chair closer to the fire* CARRY, transport, transfer, shift.

3 *things were moving too fast* (MAKE) PROGRESS, make headway, advance, develop.

4 *he urged the council to move quickly* TAKE ACTION, act, take steps, do something, take measures; *informal* get moving.

5 *she's moved to Rotterdam* RELOCATE, move away, change one's address, leave, go away, go down the road, decamp, pull up stakes.

6 *I was deeply moved by the story* AFFECT, touch, impress, shake, upset, disturb, make an impression on.

7 *she was moved to act* INSPIRE, prompt, stimulate, motivate, provoke, influence, rouse, induce, incite.

8 *they are not prepared to move on this issue* CHANGE, budge, shift one's ground, change one's tune, change

one's mind, have second thoughts; make a U-turn, do an about-face.

9 *she moves in the art world* CIRCULATE, mix, socialize, keep company, associate; *informal* hang out/around.

10 *I move that we adjourn* PROPOSE, submit, suggest, advocate, recommend, urge.

▸ noun **1** *his eyes followed her every move* MOVEMENT, motion, action; gesture, gesticulation.

2 *his recent move to Sarasota* RELOCATION, change of address, transfer, posting.

3 *the latest move in the war against drugs* INITIATIVE, step, action, act, measure, maneuver, tactic, stratagem.

4 *it's your move* TURN, go; opportunity, chance.

PHRASES: **get a move on** *informal c'mon guys, let's get a move on* HURRY UP, speed (it) up, move faster; *informal* get cracking, get moving, step on it, shake a leg, hop to it; *dated* make haste. **make a move** *waiting for the other side to make a move* DO SOMETHING, take action, act, take the initiative; *informal* get moving. **on the move 1** *she's always on the move* TRAVELING, in transit, moving, journeying, on the road; *informal* on the go. **2** *the economy is on the move* PROGRESSING, making progress, advancing, developing.

movement noun **1** *Rachel made a sudden movement | there was almost no movement* MOTION, move; gesture, gesticulation, sign, signal; action, activity.

2 *the movement of supplies* TRANSPORTATION, shift, shifting, conveyance, moving, transfer.

3 *the labor movement* POLITICAL GROUP, party, faction, wing, lobby, camp.

4 *a movement to declare war on poverty* CAMPAIGN, crusade, drive, push.

5 *there have been movements in the financial markets* DEVELOPMENT, change, fluctuation, variation.

6 *the movement toward equality* TREND, tendency, drift, swing.

7 *some movement will be made by the end of the month* PROGRESS, progression, advance.

8 *a symphony in three movements* PART, section, division.

movie noun **1** *a horror movie | they rented a movie* FILM, motion picture, picture, feature (film); video, DVD; *informal* flick, pic; *dated* moving picture.

2 *we're going to the movies* MOVIE THEATER, cinema, multiplex, silver screen, cinematheque; *informal* big screen; *dated* movie house.

movie star noun *the glamorous life of a movie star* (MOVIE/FILM) ACTOR/ACTRESS, film star, leading man, leading lady, lead; celebrity, star, starlet, matinee idol, superstar; *informal* celeb.

moving adjective **1** *moving parts | a moving train* IN MOTION, operating, operational, working, going, on the move, active; movable, mobile. ANTONYMS fixed, stationary.

2 *a moving book* AFFECTING, touching, poignant, heartwarming, heart-rending, emotional, disturbing; inspiring, inspirational, stimulating, stirring.

THE RIGHT WORD

A movie about the Holocaust might be described as **moving**, since it arouses emotions or strong feelings, particularly feelings of pathos. A movie about a young girl's devotion to her dog might more accurately be described as **touching**, which means arousing tenderness or compassion, while a movie dealing with a young girl's first experience with love would be **poignant**, since it pierces one's heart or keenly affects one's sensibilities. While *poignant* implies a bittersweet response that combines pity and longing or other contradictory emotions, **pathetic** means simply moving one to pity (*a pathetic scene in which the dog struggled to save his drowning mistress*). Almost any well-made film can be **affecting**, a more general term that suggests moving one to tears or some other display of feeling (*the affecting story of a daughter's search for her birth mother*).

mow verb *she had mown the lawn* CUT (DOWN), trim; crop, clip, prune, manicure. PHRASE: **mow down** *they were ordered to mow down the student protestors* KILL, run down, gun down, shoot down, cut down, cut to pieces, butcher, slaughter, massacre, annihilate, wipe out; *informal* blow away.

much adjective *did you get much help?* A LOT OF, a great/good deal of, a great/large amount of, plenty of, ample, copious, abundant, plentiful, considerable; *informal* lots of, loads of, heaps of, masses of, tons of, piles of, mucho. ANTONYM little.

▸ adverb **1** *it didn't hurt much* GREATLY, to a great extent/degree, a great deal, a lot, considerably, appreciably.

2 *does he come here much?* OFTEN, frequently, many times, repeatedly, regularly, habitually, routinely, usually, normally, commonly; *informal* a lot.

▸ pronoun *he did much for our team* A LOT, a great/good deal, plenty; *informal* lots, loads, heaps, masses.

muck noun **1** *I'll just clean off the muck* DIRT, grime, filth, mud, slime, mess; *informal* crud, gunk, grunge, gunge, guck, glop.

2 *spreading muck on the fields* DUNG, manure, ordure, excrement, excreta, droppings, feces, sewage, sludge, biosolids; *informal* cow chips, horse apples.

mucky adjective *get your mucky boots out of here* DIRTY, filthy, grimy, muddy, grubby, messy, soiled, stained, smeared, slimy, sticky, bespattered; *informal* cruddy, grungy, grotty, yucky; *literary* besmirched, begrimed, befouled. ANTONYM clean.

mucous adjective *the bug leaves a mucous trail behind it* GLUTINOUS, gelatinous, mucilaginous, mucoid, viscous, viscid.

WORD NOTE **mucous**

Mucous, an adj, is not synonymous with the noun *mucus*. It's worth noting this not only because the two words are fun but because so many people don't know the difference. *Mucus* means the unmentionable stuff itself. *Mucous* refers to (1) something that makes or secretes mucus, as in *The next morning, his mucous membranes were in rocky shape indeed*, or (2) something that consists of or resembles mucus, as in *The mucous consistency of its eggs kept the diner's breakfast trade minimal.* —**DFW**

mud noun *we trekked through the mud* MIRE, sludge, ooze, silt, clay, dirt, soil. PHRASE: **as clear as mud** *Dr. Elena's lectures are as clear as mud* UNCLEAR, unintelligible, opaque, unfathomable, incomprehensible, baffling, perplexing, inscrutable.

muddle verb **1** *you've **muddled** things **up*** CONFUSE, mix up, jumble (up), disarrange, disorganize, disorder, disturb, mess up.

2 *she became muddled* BEWILDER, confuse, bemuse, perplex, puzzle, baffle, mystify.

▸ noun 1 *the files are in a muddle* MESS, confusion, jumble, tangle, mishmash, chaos, disorder, disarray, disorganization, imbroglio, hodgepodge. See note at JUMBLE.

2 *a bureaucratic muddle* BUNGLE, mix-up, misunderstanding; *informal* foul-up, snafu.

PHRASE: **muddle along/through** *don't worry, we'll muddle through* COPE, manage, get by/along, scrape by/along, make do.

muddy adjective 1 *muddy ground* WATERLOGGED, boggy, marshy, swampy, squishy, mucky, slimy, spongy, wet, soft, heavy; *archaic* quaggy.

2 *muddy shoes* MUD-CAKED, muddied, dirty, filthy, mucky, grimy, soiled; *literary* begrimed. ANTONYM clean.

3 *muddy water* MURKY, cloudy, muddied, turbid, riled. ANTONYM clear.

4 *a muddy pink* DINGY, dirty, drab, dull, sludgy.

▸ verb 1 *don't muddy your boots* MAKE MUDDY, dirty, soil, spatter, bespatter; *literary* besmirch, begrime.

2 *these results muddy the situation* MAKE UNCLEAR, obscure, confuse, obfuscate, blur, cloud, befog. ANTONYM clarify.

muffle verb 1 *everyone was muffled up in coats* WRAP (UP), swathe, enfold, envelop, cloak.

2 *the sound of their footsteps was muffled* DEADEN, dull, dampen, mute, soften, quiet, tone down, mask, stifle, smother.

muffled adjective *we thought we heard muffled voices* INDISTINCT, faint, muted, dull, soft, stifled, smothered. ANTONYM loud.

mug noun 1 *a china mug* CUP, glass; stein, flagon, tankard; *archaic* stoup.

2 *informal her ugly mug.* See FACE noun sense 1.

▸ verb *informal he was mugged by three youths* ASSAULT, attack, set upon, beat up, rob; *informal* jump, rough up, lay into, do over.

mugger noun *attacked by a mugger in the park.* See ROBBER.

muggy adjective *a muggy August afternoon* HUMID, close, sultry, sticky, oppressive, airless, stifling, suffocating, stuffy, clammy, damp, heavy. ANTONYM fresh.

mulish adjective *they're both too mulish to ever resolve anything* OBSTINATE, stubborn, pigheaded, recalcitrant, intransigent, unyielding, inflexible, bullheaded, stiff-necked.

mull PHRASE: **mull over** *I'll have to mull it over before making a final decision* PONDER, consider, think over/about, reflect on, contemplate, turn over in one's mind, chew over, cogitate on, give some thought to.

multicolored adjective *these crazy kids and their multicolored hair* KALEIDOSCOPIC, psychedelic, colorful, multicolor, many-colored, many-hued, rainbow, variegated, polychromatic. ANTONYM monochrome.

multifarious adjective *our multifarious ethnic traditions* DIVERSE, many, numerous, various, varied, diversified, multiple, multitudinous, multiplex, manifold, multifaceted, different, heterogeneous, miscellaneous, assorted; *literary* myriad, divers. ANTONYM homogeneous.

multiple adjective *words with multiple meanings* NUMEROUS, many, various, different, diverse, several, manifold, multifarious, multitudinous; *literary* myriad, divers. ANTONYM single.

multiplicity noun *the multiplicity of species* ABUNDANCE, scores, mass, host, array, variety; range, diversity, heterogeneity, plurality, profusion; *informal* loads, stacks, heaps, masses, tons; *literary* myriad.

multiply verb 1 *their difficulties seem to be multiplying* INCREASE, grow, become more numerous, accumulate, proliferate, mount up, mushroom, snowball. ANTONYM decrease.

2 *the rabbits have multiplied* BREED, reproduce, procreate.

multitude noun 1 ***a multitude*** *of birds* A LOT, a great/large number, a great/large quantity, a host, a horde, a mass, a swarm, an abundance, a profusion; scores, quantities, droves; *informal* a slew, lots, loads, masses, stacks, heaps, piles, tons, dozens, hundreds, thousands, millions, gazillions.

2 *Father Philip addressed the multitude* CROWD, gathering, assembly, congregation, flock, throng, horde, mob; *formal* concourse.

3 *political power in the hands of the multitude* COMMON PEOPLE, people, populace, masses, rank and file, commonality, plebeians; hoi polloi, mob, proletariat, common herd; *informal* great unwashed, rabble, proles, plebs.

multitudinous adjective *the multitudinous stars* NUMEROUS, many, abundant, profuse, prolific, copious, multifarious, innumerable, countless, numberless, infinite; *literary* divers, myriad.

mum[1] *informal* adjective *he was keeping mum* SILENT, quiet, mute, dumb, tight-lipped, unforthcoming, reticent.
PHRASE: **mum's the word** *informal remember, when we get back to the house, mum's the word* SAY NOTHING, keep quiet, don't breathe a word, don't tell a soul, keep it secret, keep it to yourself, keep it under your hat; *informal* don't let on, don't let the cat out of the bag.

mum[2] noun *chiefly Brit. informal my mum looks after me.* See MOTHER noun sense 1.

mumble verb *he mumbles on purpose just to annoy me* MUTTER, murmur, speak indistinctly, talk under one's breath.

mumbo-jumbo noun *their ad campaign is just a lot of mumbo-jumbo* NONSENSE, gibberish, claptrap, rubbish, balderdash, blather, hocus-pocus; *informal* gobbledygook, bafflegab.

munch verb *the rustle we heard turned out to be giraffes munching leaves* CHEW, champ, chomp, masticate, crunch, eat, gnaw, nibble, snack, chow down on.

mundane adjective 1 *her mundane life* HUMDRUM, dull, boring, tedious, monotonous, tiresome, wearisome, unexciting, uninteresting, uneventful, unvarying, unremarkable, repetitive, repetitious, routine, ordinary, everyday, day-to-day, run-of-the-mill, commonplace, workaday; *informal* plain-vanilla, ho-hum. ANTONYMS extraordinary, imaginative.

2 *the mundane world* EARTHLY, worldly, terrestrial, mate-

rial, temporal, secular, areligious; *literary* sublunary. ANTONYM spiritual.

municipal adjective *land use is controlled by the municipal authorities* CIVIC, civil, metropolitan, urban, city, town, borough. ANTONYM rural.

municipality noun *the municipality of Springfield* BOROUGH, town, city, district, precinct, township.

munificent adjective *a munificent bequest* GENEROUS, bountiful, openhanded, magnanimous, philanthropic, princely, handsome, lavish, liberal, charitable, bighearted, beneficent; *literary* bounteous. ANTONYM mean.

mural noun *a mural by Diego Rivera.* See PICTURE noun sense 1.

murder noun **1** *a brutal murder* KILLING, homicide, assassination, liquidation, extermination, execution, slaughter, butchery, massacre; manslaughter; *literary* slaying.

2 *informal driving there was murder* HELL, hell on earth, a nightmare, an ordeal, a trial, misery, torture, agony.

▸ verb **1** *someone tried to murder him* KILL, put to death, assassinate, execute, liquidate, eliminate, dispatch, butcher, slaughter, massacre, wipe out; *informal* bump off, do in, do away with, knock off, blow away, blow someone's brains out, take out, dispose of, ice, rub out, smoke, waste; *literary* slay. See note at KILL.

2 *informal Anna was murdering a Mozart sonata.* See MANGLE sense 2.

3 *informal he murdered his opponent.* See TROUNCE.

murderer, murderess noun *the murderer was finally brought to justice* KILLER, assassin, serial killer, butcher, slaughterer; *informal* hit man, gunman, hired gun; *literary* slayer.

murderous adjective **1** *a murderous attack* HOMICIDAL, brutal, violent, savage, ferocious, fierce, vicious, bloodthirsty, barbarous, barbaric; fatal, lethal, deadly, mortal, death-dealing; *archaic* sanguinary.

2 *informal a murderous schedule* ARDUOUS, grueling, strenuous, punishing, onerous, exhausting, taxing, difficult, rigorous; *informal* killing, hellish.

WORD NOTE **murderous**

I like to use this word as a synonym for *threatening,* especially when referring to weather—gathering storm clouds, vicious lightning, etc. It's fun to anthropomorphize natural phenomena. —**DA**

murky adjective **1** *a murky winter afternoon* DARK, gloomy, gray, leaden, dull, dim, overcast, cloudy, clouded, sunless, dismal, dreary, bleak; *literary* tenebrous. ANTONYMS bright, sunny.

2 *murky water* DIRTY, muddy, cloudy, turbid, riled, roily. ANTONYM clear.

3 *her murky past* QUESTIONABLE, suspicious, suspect, dubious, dark, mysterious, secret; *informal* shady, sketchy. ANTONYMS spotless, innocent.

murmur noun **1** *his voice was a murmur* WHISPER, undertone, mutter, mumble.

2 *they left without a murmur* COMPLAINT, grumble, grouse; *informal* gripe, moan.

3 *the murmur of bees* HUM, humming, buzz, buzzing, thrum, thrumming, drone; sigh, rustle; *literary* susurration, murmuration.

▸ verb **1** *he heard them murmuring in the hall* MUTTER, mumble, whisper, talk under one's breath, speak softly.

2 *no one murmured at the delay* COMPLAIN, mutter, grumble, grouse; *informal* gripe, moan.

3 *the wind was murmuring through the trees* RUSTLE, sigh; burble, purl; *literary* whisper.

muscle noun **1** *he had muscle but no brains* STRENGTH, power, muscularity, brawn, burliness; *informal* beef, beefiness; *literary* thew.

2 *financial muscle* INFLUENCE, power, strength, might, force, forcefulness, weight; *informal* clout. PHRASE: **muscle in on** *informal we don't like people muscling in on our private affairs* INTERFERE WITH, force one's way into, impose oneself on, encroach on; *informal* horn in on, barge in on.

muscular adjective **1** *muscular tissue* FIBROUS, sinewy.

2 *he's very muscular* STRONG, brawny, muscly, sinewy, powerfully built, well muscled, hard-bodied, burly, strapping, sturdy, powerful, athletic; *Physiology* mesomorphic; *informal* hunky, beefy, muscle-bound; *literary* thewy.

3 *a muscular economy* VIGOROUS, robust, strong, powerful, dynamic, potent, active.

muse[1] noun *the poet's muse* INSPIRATION, creative influence, stimulus; *formal* afflatus. See table.

THE NINE MUSES

Calliope (epic poetry)	Polyhymnia (sacred song and oratory)
Clio (history)	Terpsichore (dance and choral song)
Erato (lyric and love poetry)	Thalia (comedy)
Euterpe (music)	Urania (astronomy)
Melpomene (tragedy)	

muse[2] verb *I **mused on** Toby's story* PONDER, consider, think over/about, mull over, reflect on, contemplate, turn over in one's mind, chew over, give some thought to, cogitate on; think about, be lost in contemplation/thought over, daydream about.

mush noun **1** *some sort of grayish mush* PAP, pulp, slop, paste, purée, mash, porridge; *informal* gloop, goo, gook, glop, sludge, guck.

2 *romantic mush* SENTIMENTALITY, mawkishness; *informal* schmaltz, corn, slush, slop.

mushroom noun *the mushrooms thrive in this warm wet weather* FUNGUS, button mushroom, cep, chanterelle, cremini, enoki, field mushroom, honey mushroom, horse mushroom, matsutake, morel, oyster mushroom, pine mushroom, porcini, portobello, shiitake, death cap, bolete.

▸ verb *ecotourism mushroomed in the 1980s* PROLIFERATE, grow/develop rapidly, burgeon, spread, increase, expand, boom, explode, snowball, rocket, skyrocket; thrive, flourish, prosper. ANTONYM contract.

mushy adjective **1** *cook until the fruit is mushy* SOFT, semiliquid, pulpy, sloppy, spongy, squashy, squishy; *informal* gooey. ANTONYM firm.

2 *informal a mushy movie* SENTIMENTAL, mawkish, emotional, saccharine, oversweet; *informal* slushy, schmaltzy, weepy, tearjerker, tearjerking, corny, soppy, cornball, sappy, hokey, three-hankie, cheesy. See note at SENTIMENTAL.

music noun See table.

WORD NOTE **music**

After the musical revolutions of the twentieth century, the synonyms for *music* have increased to include *art* and *theater* at least, and maybe *listening,* or even *activity;* but older synonyms such as *melody* and *tune* seem like special cases. **—SM**

MUSIC

Types of Music
a cappella
acid house
acid rock
alternative
barbershop
barrelhouse
bebop
bluegrass
blues
boogie-woogie
calypso
chant
choral
country
country and western
dancehall
death metal
disco
Dixieland
easy listening
electronica
emo
flamenco
folk
funk
gangsta
gospel
Goth
grunge
hard rock
heavy metal
hip hop
industrial
jazz
jungle
klezmer
Latin
mariachi
Motown
New Age
new country
new wave
opera
pop
progressive rock
punk
rap
reggae
rhythm and blues
rock
rockabilly
rock and roll
salsa
ska
soul
swing
technofunk
thrash metal
trance
trip hop
world music
zydeco

Musical Directions
a cappella (unaccompanied)
accelerando/accel (accelerating)
adagio (slowly)
ad libitum/ad lib (at will)
al fine (to the end)
allargando (broadening)
allegretto (fairly lively)
allegro (lively)
al segno (as far as the sign)
andante (moderately slow)
andantino (slightly faster than andante)
arco (with the bow)
assai (very)
a tempo (in the original tempo)
bis (repeat)
con brio (with vigor)
con moto (with movement)
crescendo/cresc (becoming louder)
da capo/DC (from the beginning)
dal segno/DS (from the sign)
decrescendo/decresc (becoming quieter)
diminuendo/dim (becoming quieter)
dolce (sweetly)
fine (end)
forte/f (loudly)
forte piano (loudly then immediately softly)
fortissimo/ff (very loudly)
glissando (sliding)
larghetto (fairly slowly)
largo (very slowly)
legato (tied/smoothly)
lento (slowly)
maestoso (majestically)
marcato (accented)
meno (less)
meno mosso (less quickly)
mezzo (half)
mezzo forte/mf (fairly loudly)
mezzo piano/mp (fairly softly)
moderato (at a moderate pace)
molto (very)
mosso (fast and with animation)
moto (motion)
non troppo (not too much)
obbligato (not to be omitted)
ped. (pedal)
pianissimo/pp (very softly)
piano/p (softly)
più (more)
pizzicato/pizz (plucked)
poco (a little)
rallentando/rall (slowing down)
ritardando/rit (slowing down)
ritenuto (suddenly more slowly)
scherzando (playfully)
segno (sign)
sempre (always/throughout)
sforzando/sf/sfz (strongly accented)
smorzando (dying away)
sordino (with a mute)
sostenuto/sost (sustained)
sotto voce (in an undertone)
staccato/stacc (detached)
tacet (voice/instrument remains silent)
tenuto/ten (held)
troppo (too much)
tutti (all players/singers)
vivace (lively)

musical adjective *musical poetry* TUNEFUL, melodic, melodious, harmonious, sweet-sounding, sweet, mellifluous, euphonious, euphonic. ANTONYM discordant.

musician noun *the club is looking for musicians* PLAYER, performer, instrumentalist, accompanist, soloist, virtuoso, maestro; *historical* minstrel.

musing noun *in my musing of late, I have decided that I need more purpose in my life* MEDITATION, thinking, contemplation, deliberation, pondering, reflection, rumination, introspection, daydreaming, reverie, dreaming, preoccupation, brooding; *formal* cogitation.

muss verb *informal don't be mussing your hair before the photo shoot* RUFFLE, tousle, dishevel, rumple, mess up, make a mess of, disarrange, make untidy.

must[1] verb *I must go* OUGHT TO, should, have (got) to, need to, be obliged to, be required to, be compelled to.

▸ noun *informal this video is **a must*** NOT TO BE MISSED, very good; a necessity, essential, a requirement, a requisite.

must[2] noun *a smell of must* MOLD, mustiness, moldiness, mildew, fustiness, decay, rot.

muster verb **1** *they mustered 50,000 troops* ASSEMBLE, mobilize, rally, raise, summon, gather (together), mass, collect, convene, call up, call to arms, recruit, conscript, draft; *archaic* levy. See note at GATHER.

2 *reporters mustered outside her house* CONGREGATE, assemble, gather together, come together, collect together, convene, mass, rally.

3 *she mustered her courage* SUMMON (UP), screw up, call up, rally.

▸ noun *the colonel called a muster* ROLL CALL, assembly, rally, meeting, gathering, assemblage, congregation, convention; parade, review.

PHRASE: **pass muster** *as far as Dean's parents are concerned, I'll never pass muster* BE GOOD ENOUGH, come up to standard, come up to scratch, measure up, be acceptable/adequate, fill/fit the bill; *informal* make the grade, come/be up to snuff.

musty adjective **1** *the room smelled musty* MOLDY, stale, fusty, damp, dank, mildewy, smelly, stuffy, airless, unventilated; *informal* funky. ANTONYMS fresh, fragrant.

2 *the play seemed musty* UNORIGINAL, uninspired, unimaginative, hackneyed, stale, flat, tired, banal, trite, clichéd, old-fashioned, outdated; *informal* old hat. ANTONYM fresh.

mutable adjective *the mutable nature of fashion* CHANGEABLE, variable, varying, fluctuating, shifting, inconsistent, unpredictable, inconstant, fickle, uneven, unstable, protean; *literary* fluctuant. ANTONYM invariable.

mutant noun *is this insect some sort of mutant?* FREAK (OF NATURE), deviant, monstrosity, monster, mutation.

mutate verb *rhythm and blues mutated into rock and roll* CHANGE, metamorphose, evolve; transmute, transform, convert; *humorous* transmogrify.

mutation noun 1 *cells that have undergone mutation* ALTERATION, change, variation, modification, transformation, metamorphosis, transmutation; *humorous* transmogrification.

2 *a genetic mutation* MUTANT, freak (of nature), deviant, monstrosity, monster, anomaly.

mute adjective 1 *she remained mute* SILENT, speechless, dumb, unspeaking, tight-lipped, taciturn; *informal* mum, tongue-tied. ANTONYMS voluble, talkative.

2 *a mute appeal* WORDLESS, silent, dumb, unspoken, unvoiced, unexpressed. ANTONYM spoken.

3 *the forest was mute* QUIET, silent, hushed. ANTONYM noisy.

4 *he was deaf and mute* DUMB, unable to speak; *Medicine* aphasic.

▸ verb 1 *the noise was muted by the heavy curtains* DEADEN, muffle, dampen, soften, quieten, hush; stifle, smother, suppress. ANTONYM amplify.

2 *Bruce muted his criticisms* RESTRAIN, soften, tone down, moderate, temper. ANTONYM intensify.

muted adjective 1 *the muted hum of traffic* MUFFLED, faint, indistinct, quiet, soft, low.

2 *muted colors* SUBDUED, pastel, delicate, subtle, understated, restrained.

mutilate verb 1 *the bodies had been mutilated* MANGLE, maim, disfigure, butcher, dismember; cripple.

2 *the painting was mutilated* VANDALIZE, damage, deface, ruin, spoil, destroy, wreck, violate, desecrate; *informal* trash.

mutinous adjective *your mutinous scheme has failed* REBELLIOUS, insubordinate, subversive, seditious, insurgent, insurrectionary, rebel, riotous.

mutiny noun *there was a mutiny over wages* INSURRECTION, rebellion, revolt, riot, uprising, insurgence, insubordination. See note at UPRISING.

▸ verb *thousands of soldiers mutinied* RISE UP, rebel, revolt, riot, disobey/defy authority, be insubordinate.

mutt noun *informal* See MONGREL noun.

mutter verb 1 *a group of men stood muttering* TALK UNDER ONE'S BREATH, murmur, mumble, whisper, speak in an undertone.

2 *the players muttered about the salary freezes* GRUMBLE, complain, grouse, carp, whine; *informal* moan, gripe, beef, whinge, kvetch.

mutual adjective *our interest in boating is mutual* RECIPROCAL, reciprocated, returned; common, joint, shared.

USAGE NOTE **mutual**

Traditionalists consider using **mutual** to mean 'common to two or more people' (*a mutual friend*; *a mutual interest*) to be incorrect, holding that the sense of reciprocity is necessary (*mutual respect*; *mutual need*). However, both senses are well established and acceptable in standard English.

muzzle noun 1 *the dog's velvety muzzle* SNOUT, nose, mouth, maw.

2 *the muzzle of a gun* BARREL, end.

▸ verb *attempts to muzzle the media* GAG, silence, censor, stifle, restrain, check, curb, fetter.

muzzy adjective 1 *she felt muzzy* GROGGY, lightheaded, faint, dizzy, befuddled, befogged, dazed, fuddled; *informal* dopey, woozy. ANTONYM clear.

2 *a muzzy image* BLURRED, blurry, fuzzy, unfocused, unclear, ill-defined, foggy, hazy. ANTONYM clear.

myopic adjective 1 *a myopic patient* NEARSIGHTED; *chiefly Brit.* shortsighted. ANTONYM farsighted.

2 *the government's myopic attitude* UNIMAGINATIVE, uncreative, unadventurous, narrow-minded, small-minded, short-term, shortsighted. ANTONYM farsighted.

myriad *literary* noun ***a myriad*** *of insects* A MULTITUDE, a large/great number, a large/great quantity, scores, quantities, a mass, a host, droves, a horde; *informal* lots, loads, masses, stacks, scads, tons, hundreds, thousands, millions, gazillions.

▸ adjective *the myriad lights of the city* INNUMERABLE, countless, infinite, numberless, untold, unnumbered, immeasurable, multitudinous, numerous; *literary* divers.

WORD NOTE **myriad**

As an adj, *myriad* means "an indefinitely large number [of something]" (*The Local Group comprises myriad galaxies*) or "made up of a great many diverse elements" (*the myriad plant life of Amazonia*). As a noun, it's used with an article and *of* to mean "a large number" (*The new CFO faced a myriad of cash-flow problems*). What's odd is that some authorities consider only the adjectival *myriad* correct—there's about a 50-50 chance that a given copyeditor will query *a myriad of*—even though the noun usage has a much longer and more distinguished history. It's really only in nineteenth-century poetry that *myriad* starts showing up as an adj. So *myriad*'s situation right now is confusing. It's tempting simply to recommend avoiding the noun usage so that there's no chance a reader will be bugged. The truth, though, is that any reader who's bugged by *a myriad of* is both persnickety and wrong—and you can usually rebut sniffy teachers, copyeditors, et. al. by directing them to Coleridge's "Myriad myriads of lives teemed forth . . . ."
—DFW

myself pronoun See note below.

USAGE NOTE **myself**

Myself is best used either reflexively (*I have decided to exclude myself from consideration*) or intensively (*I myself have seen that*; *I've done that myself*). The word shouldn't appear as a substitute for *I* or *me* (*my wife and myself were delighted to see you*). Using it that way, as an "untriggered reflexive," is thought somehow to be modest, as if the reference were less direct. Yet it's no less direct, and the user may unconsciously cause the reader or listener to assume an intended jocularity, or that the user is somewhat doltish—e.g.:

• "Those ins and outs are largely a self-learning process, though knowing the experience of someone like myself [read *me*] might make the learning shorter, easier, and a lot less painful." (Mark H. McCormack, *What They Don't Teach You at Harvard Business School*; 1984.)

• "The exclusion of women and women's concerns is self-defeating. For instance, myself and other women in Hollywood [read *many women in Hollywood, including me*,] would deliver millions of dollars of profit to the film industry if we could make films and television shows about the lives of real women." (*Los Angeles Times*; Oct. 22, 1989.)

• "My wife and myself [read *I*] were in a religious cult for over 15 years before the leader fell over dead." (*Pantagraph* [Bloomington, IL]; Apr. 6, 1997. **—BG**

---

mysterious adjective **1** *he vanished in mysterious circumstances* PUZZLING, strange, peculiar, curious, funny, queer, odd, weird, bizarre, mystifying, inexplicable, baffling, perplexing, incomprehensible, unexplainable, unfathomable. ANTONYM straightforward.

2 *he was being very mysterious* ENIGMATIC, inscrutable, secretive, reticent, evasive, furtive, surreptitious. ANTONYMS straightforward, open.

mystery noun **1** *his death remains a mystery* PUZZLE, enigma, conundrum, riddle, secret, problem, unsolved problem. See note at RIDDLE.

2 *her past is shrouded in mystery* SECRECY, obscurity, uncertainty, mystique.

3 *reading a classic mystery* THRILLER, murder mystery, detective story/novel, murder story, crime novel; *informal* whodunit.

mystic, mystical adjective **1** *a mystic experience* SPIRITUAL, religious, transcendental, paranormal, otherworldly, supernatural, occult, metaphysical.

2 *mystic rites* SYMBOLIC, symbolical, allegorical, representational, metaphorical.

3 *a figure of mystical significance* CRYPTIC, concealed, hidden, abstruse, arcane, esoteric, inscrutable, inexplicable, unfathomable, mysterious, secret, enigmatic.

mystify verb *Houdini mystified his audiences* BEWILDER, puzzle, perplex, baffle, confuse, confound, bemuse, bedazzle, throw; *informal* flummox, stump, bamboozle, fox.

mystique noun *a certain mystique still surrounds the family* CHARISMA, glamour, romance, mystery, magic, charm, appeal, allure.

myth noun **1** *ancient Greek myths* FOLK TALE, folk story, legend, tale, story, fable, saga, mythos, lore, folklore, mythology.

2 *the myths surrounding childbirth* MISCONCEPTION, fallacy, false notion, old wives' tale, fairy tale/story, fiction; *informal* tall tale, cock-and-bull story, urban myth/legend.

mythical adjective **1** *mythical beasts* LEGENDARY, mythological, fabled, fabulous, folkloric, fairy-tale, storybook; fantastical, imaginary, imagined, fictitious, storied.

2 *her mythical child* IMAGINARY, fictitious, make-believe, fantasy, invented, made-up, nonexistent; *informal* pretend.

WORD NOTE **storied**

The first time I saw this word in a major newspaper—used, as I recall, to describe a street which had a particularly colorful history, one on which many notable events had transpired—I thought it was a typo. I have since seen it used more often to refer to a place or thing to which all sorts of stories and legends are attached. So I have learned that it is indeed a word, but I still don't happen to like it. Perhaps that's because it somehow seems like a participle, which would make *story* a verb along the lines of *journal*, as in *to journal*, which is, in my opinion, one of the most repellent current usages. **—FP**

---

mythological adjective *great mythological beasts* FABLED, fabulous, folkloric, fairy-tale, legendary, mythical, mythic, traditional; fictitious, imaginary.

mythology noun *no ancient culture is without its mythology* MYTH(S), legend(s), folklore, folk tales, folk stories, lore, tradition.

N

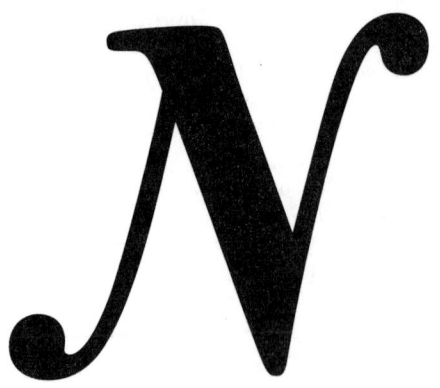

nab verb *informal* *they nabbed the suspect outside of his trailer* CATCH, capture, apprehend, arrest, seize, grab; *informal* nail, pull in, pick up.

nabob noun *the nabobs of Wall Street* VERY RICH PERSON, tycoon, magnate, millionaire, billionaire, multimillionaire; *informal* fat cat.

nadir noun *the nadir of his career* LOWEST POINT, lowest level, all-time low, bottom, rock-bottom; *informal* pits. ANTONYM zenith.

nag[1] verb **1** *she's constantly nagging me* HARASS, badger, give someone a hard time, hound, harry, criticize, carp, find fault with, keep on at, grumble at, go on at; henpeck; *informal* hassle, get on someone's case, ride.

2 *this has been nagging me for weeks* TROUBLE, worry, bother, plague, torment, niggle, prey on one's mind; annoy, irritate; *informal* bug, aggravate.

▸ noun *don't be such a nag* SHREW, harpy, termagant, harridan; *archaic* scold.

nag[2] noun *she rode the nag into town* WORN-OUT HORSE, old horse, hack; *informal* plug; *archaic* jade.

nagging adjective **1** *his nagging wife* SHREWISH, complaining, grumbling, fault-finding, scolding, carping, criticizing.

2 *a nagging pain* PERSISTENT, continuous, niggling, unrelenting, unremitting, unabating.

nail noun **1** *fastened with nails* TACK, spike, pin, rivet; finishing nail, roofing nail, hobnail, brad.

2 *polishing her nails* FINGERNAIL, thumbnail, toenail.

▸ verb **1** *a board was nailed to the wall* FASTEN, attach, fix, affix, secure, tack, hammer, pin.

2 *informal* *he nailed the suspect* CATCH, capture, apprehend, arrest, seize; *informal* collar, nab, pull in, pick up.

3 *she nailed that somersault* PERFORM WELL, succeed in, execute, complete, bring about/off; *informal* land, pull off, score.

PHRASES: **hard as nails** *he regretted having been a father who always acted as if he were hard as nails* CALLOUS, hard-hearted, heartless, unfeeling, unsympathetic, uncaring, insensitive, unsentimental, hard-bitten, tough, lacking compassion. **hit the nail on the head** *when Arthur said that Donna couldn't be trusted, he really hit the nail on the head* GET IT RIGHT, get it, guess correctly, speak (the) truth.

naive adjective *don't be fooled by his naive manner of speaking* INNOCENT, unsophisticated, artless, ingenuous, inexperienced, guileless, unworldly, trusting; gullible, credulous, immature, callow, raw, green, wide-eyed; *informal* wet behind the ears, born yesterday. See note at GULLIBLE. ANTONYM worldly.

naiveté noun *we were not expecting such naiveté in a thirty-year-old woman from Queens* INNOCENCE, ingenuousness, guilelessness, artlessness, unworldliness, trustfulness; gullibility, credulity, immaturity, callowness.

naked adjective **1** *naked sunbathers* NUDE, bare, in the nude, stark naked, having nothing on, stripped, unclothed, undressed; *informal* without a stitch on, in one's birthday suit, in the buff, in the raw, in the altogether, buck-naked, butt-naked, mother-naked. ANTONYMS clothed, dressed.

2 *a naked flame* UNPROTECTED, uncovered, exposed, unguarded. ANTONYM covered.

3 *the naked branches of the trees* BARE, barren, denuded, stripped, uncovered.

4 *I felt naked and exposed* VULNERABLE, helpless, weak, powerless, defenseless, exposed, open to attack.

5 *the naked truth* | *naked hostility* UNDISGUISED, plain, unadorned, unvarnished, unqualified, stark, bald; overt, obvious, open, patent, evident, apparent, manifest, unmistakable, blatant.

THE RIGHT WORD

Someone who isn't wearing any clothes is **naked**; this adjective is usually associated with revealing a part or all of the body (*her naked shoulder; a naked man ran from the burning building*). A *naked* person who appears in a painting or photograph is called a **nude**, a euphemistic but more socially acceptable term referring to the unclothed human body. **Bare** can describe the branches of a tree as well as human limbs; it implies the absence of the conventional or appropriate covering (*a bare wooden floor; bare legs; four bare walls*). **Bald** also suggests a lack of covering, but it refers particularly to a lack of natural covering, especially hair (*a bald head*). **Barren** implies a lack of vegetation, and it also connotes destitution and fruitlessness (*a barren wasteland devoid of life*). A *bald* artist might paint a *nude* woman whose *bare* arms are extended against a *barren* winter landscape.

---

namby-pamby adjective *her new boyfriend is the essence of virility—nothing like that namby-pamby guy she used to date* WEAK, feeble, spineless, effeminate, effete; ineffectual; *informal* wimpy, sissy.

name noun **1** *her name's Emma* designation, honorific, title, tag, epithet, label; *informal* moniker, handle; *formal* denomination, appellation.

2 *the top names in the fashion industry* CELEBRITY, star, superstar, VIP, leading light, big name, luminary; expert, authority; *informal* celeb, somebody, megastar, big shot, bigwig, big gun, great, giant.

3 *the good name of the firm* REPUTATION, character, repute, standing, stature, esteem, prestige, cachet, kudos; renown, popularity, notability, distinction.

▸ verb **1** *they named the baby Phoebe* CALL, give a name to, dub; label, style, term, title, entitle; baptize, christen; *formal* denominate.

2 *he named the woman in the photograph* IDENTIFY, specify.

3 *he has named his successor* CHOOSE, select, pick, decide on, nominate, designate.

nameless adjective **1** *a nameless photographer* UNNAMED, unidentified, anonymous, incognito, unspecified, unacknowledged, uncredited; unknown, unsung, uncelebrated.

2 *nameless fears* UNSPEAKABLE, unutterable, inexpressible, indescribable; indefinable, vague, unspecified.

namely adverb *I want to go someplace warm, namely Aruba* THAT IS, that is to say, in other words, to be specific, specifically, viz., to wit.

nanny noun *the children's nanny* CAREGIVER, caretaker, babysitter, au pair, governess; *dated* nursemaid, nurse.

nap[1] verb *they were napping on the sofa* DOZE, sleep, sleep lightly, take a nap, catnap, rest, take a siesta; *informal* snooze, catch forty winks, get some shut-eye, catch some Zs, catch a few Zs.

▸ noun ***a nap** will make you feel better* (SOME) SLEEP, a little sleep, a catnap, a siesta, a doze, a lie-down, (a/some) rest, a little rest; *informal* a snooze, forty winks, (some) shut-eye, a little shut-eye, (some) beauty sleep/rest, a little beauty sleep/rest, a power nap.

PHRASE: **catch someone napping** *the teacher had warned us to be ever prepared, but the unannounced test caught most of us napping* CATCH OFF GUARD, catch unawares, surprise, take by surprise, catch out, find unprepared; *informal* catch someone with their pants down.

nap[2] noun *the nap of the velvet* PILE, fibers, threads, weave, surface, grain.

napkin noun *the napkin goes to the left of the plate* table napkin, dinner napkin, cocktail napkin, serviette; paper towel; linen.

narcissism noun *his emotional development was hindered by his mother's narcissism* VANITY, self-love, self-admiration, self-absorption, self-obsession, conceit, self-centeredness, self-regard, egotism, egoism. See note at EGOTISM. ANTONYM modesty.

narcissistic adjective *she was never happy in the narcissistic life that her press agent and manager had crafted for her* VAIN, self-loving, self-admiring, self-absorbed, self-obsessed, conceited, self-centered, self-regarding, egotistic, egotistical, egoistic; *informal* full of oneself.

narcotic noun *addicted to narcotics* SOPORIFIC (DRUG), opiate, sleeping pill; painkiller, pain reliever, analgesic, anodyne, palliative, anesthetic; tranquilizer, sedative; *informal* downer, dope; *Medicine* stupefacient.

▸ adjective *a narcotic sleeping pill* SOPORIFIC, sleep-inducing, opiate; painkilling, pain-relieving, analgesic, anodyne, anesthetic, tranquilizing, sedative; *Medicine* stupefacient.

narrate verb *the story is narrated by an English butler* TELL, relate, recount, describe, chronicle, give a report of, report; voice-over.

narrative noun *an interesting narrative about her year in Bolivia* ACCOUNT, chronicle, history, description, record, report, story.

narrator noun **1** *the narrator of "The Arabian Nights"* STORYTELLER, teller of tales, relater, chronicler, raconteur, anecdotalist. ANTONYMS listener, audience.

2 *the film's narrator* VOICE-OVER, commentator, speaker.

narrow adjective **1** *the path became narrow* SMALL, tapered, tapering, narrowing; *archaic* strait. ANTONYMS wide, broad.

2 *her narrow waist* SLENDER, slim, slight, spare, attenuated, thin. ANTONYM broad.

3 *a narrow space* CONFINED, cramped, tight, restricted, limited, constricted. ANTONYM spacious.

4 *a narrow range of products* LIMITED, restricted, circumscribed, small, inadequate, insufficient, deficient. ANTONYMS wide, broad.

5 *a narrow view of the world.* See NARROW-MINDED.

6 *nationalism in the narrowest sense of the word* STRICT, literal, exact, precise. ANTONYM broad.

7 *a narrow escape* BY A VERY SMALL MARGIN, close, near, by a hair's breadth; *informal* by a whisker.

▸ verb *the path narrowed | narrowing the gap between rich and poor* GET/BECOME/MAKE NARROWER, get/become/make smaller, taper, diminish, decrease, reduce, contract, shrink, constrict; *archaic* straiten.

narrowly adverb **1** *one bullet narrowly missed him* ONLY JUST, just, barely, scarcely, hardly, by a hair's breadth; *informal* by a whisker.

2 *she looked at me narrowly* CLOSELY, carefully, searchingly, attentively.

narrow-minded adjective *our school has no place for such narrow-minded teaching* INTOLERANT, illiberal, reactionary, conservative, parochial, provincial, insular, small-minded, petty, blinkered, inward-looking, narrow, hidebound, prejudiced, bigoted; *informal* redneck. See note at BIAS. ANTONYM tolerant.

narrows plural noun *these narrows were first navigated in the sixteenth century* STRAIT(S), sound, channel, waterway, passage, sea passage, neck.

nascent adjective *the nascent economic recovery* JUST BEGINNING, budding, developing, growing, embryonic, incipient, young, fledgling, evolving, emergent, dawning, burgeoning.

nastiness noun **1** *my mother tried to shut herself off from* *all the nastiness of life* UNPLEASANTNESS, disagreeableness, offensiveness, vileness, foulness.

2 *her uncharacteristic nastiness* UNKINDNESS, unpleasantness, unfriendliness, disagreeableness, rudeness, churlishness, spitefulness, maliciousness, meanness, ill temper, ill nature, viciousness, malevolence; *informal* bitchiness, cattiness.

nasty adjective **1** *a nasty smell* UNPLEASANT, disagreeable, disgusting, distasteful, awful, dreadful, horrible, terrible, vile, foul, abominable, frightful, loathsome, revolting, repulsive, odious, sickening, nauseating, repellent, repugnant, horrendous, appalling, atrocious, offensive, objectionable, obnoxious, unsavory, unappetizing, off-putting; noxious, foul-smelling, smelly, stinking, rank, fetid, malodorous, mephitic; *informal* ghastly, horrid, gruesome, diabolical, yucky, skanky, godawful, gross, beastly, lousy, funky; *literary* miasmal, noisome. ANTONYMS pleasant, delightful.

2 *the weather turned nasty* UNPLEASANT, disagreeable, foul, filthy, inclement; wet, stormy, cold, blustery, blizzardy. ANTONYMS sunny, pleasant.

3 *she can be really nasty* UNKIND, unpleasant, unfriendly, disagreeable, rude, churlish, spiteful, malicious, mean, ill-tempered, ill-natured, vicious, malevolent, obnoxious, hateful, hurtful; *informal* bitchy, catty. ANTONYMS nice, charming.

4 *a nasty accident | a nasty cut* SERIOUS, dangerous, bad, awful, dreadful, terrible, severe; painful, ugly. ANTONYMS minor, slight.

5 *she had the nasty habit of appearing unannounced* ANNOYING, irritating, infuriating, disagreeable, unpleasant, maddening, exasperating.

6 *they wrote nasty things on the wall* OBSCENE, indecent, offensive, crude, rude, dirty, filthy, vulgar, foul, gross, disgusting, pornographic, smutty, lewd; *informal* sick, X-rated. ANTONYMS polite, decent.

nation noun *an independent nation* COUNTRY, sovereign state, state, land, realm, kingdom, republic; fatherland, motherland; people, race.

national adjective **1** *national politics* STATE, public, federal, governmental; civic, civil, domestic, internal. ANTONYMS local, international.

2 *a national strike.* See NATIONWIDE.

▸ noun *a Canadian national* CITIZEN, subject, native; voter.

nationalism noun *their extreme nationalism was frightening* PATRIOTISM, patriotic sentiment, flag-waving, xenophobia, chauvinism, jingoism. See notes at CHAUVINISM, JINGOISM.

nationality noun **1** *what is your nationality?* CITIZENSHIP.

2 *all the main nationalities of Ethiopia* ETHNIC GROUP, ethnic minority, tribe, clan, race, nation.

nationwide adjective *a nationwide talent search* NATIONAL, countrywide, general, widespread, extensive. ANTONYM local.

native noun *a native of Rome, New York* INHABITANT, resident, local; citizen, national; aborigine, autochthon; *formal* dweller. ANTONYM foreigner.

▸ adjective **1** *the native peoples* INDIGENOUS, original, first, earliest, aboriginal, autochthonous. ANTONYM immigrant.

2 *native produce | native plants* DOMESTIC, homegrown, homemade, local; indigenous. ANTONYM imported.

3 *a native instinct for politics* INNATE, inherent, inborn, instinctive, intuitive, natural; hereditary, inherited, congenital, inbred, connate. ANTONYM acquired.

4 *her native tongue* MOTHER, vernacular, first.

THE RIGHT WORD

A **native** New Yorker is probably not **indigenous**, although both words apply to persons or things that belong to or are associated with a particular place by birth or origin. *Native* means born or produced in a specific region or country (*native plants; native dances*), but it can also apply to persons or things that were introduced from elsewhere some time ago—which is the case with most New Yorkers who consider themselves natives. *Indigenous*, on the other hand, is more restricted in meaning; it applies only to someone or something that is not only native but was not introduced from elsewhere (*the pumpkin is indigenous to America*). Generally speaking, *native* applies to individual organisms, while *indigenous* applies to races or species. Something that is **endemic** is prevalent in a particular region because of special conditions there that favor its growth or existence (*heather is endemic in the Scottish Highlands; malaria is endemic in Central America*). There are no longer any **aboriginal** New Yorkers, a word that refers to the earliest known inhabitants of a place or to ancient peoples who have no known ancestors and have inhabited a region since its earliest historical time. Australia is known for its *aboriginal* culture, which was preserved for centuries through geographical isolation.

Native American See note below.

USAGE NOTE Native American

The term *Native American* proliferated in the 1970s to denote groups served by the federal Bureau of Indian Affairs: American Indians as well as the Eskimos and Aleuts of Alaska. Later, the term was interpreted as including Native Hawaiians and Pacific Islanders, and it fell into disfavor among some Indian and Alaskan groups, who came to prefer *American Indian* and *Alaska Native*. Yet views are unpredictable: some consider *Native American* more respectful than *American Indian*.

As an equivalent to *American Indian*, the phrase *Native American* was long thought to be a twentieth-century innovation. In fact, the phrase *Native American*—though it came into vogue in the early and mid-1970s—dates back to at least 1737 in this sense. And it made literal sense (for the most part) in 1737, since at that time most people who had been born in the New World were indigenous—not of European descent. By the nineteenth century, when the phrase *native American* (lowercase *n-*) was fairly common, it had become ambiguous, since it often referred to any person born in the United States, whether of indigenous or of European descent. Here, in a mid-twentieth-century passage, it refers to place of birth: "Dr. Flesch . . . was born in Vienna, but writes more like a native American than do most native Americans; in fact, he teaches the natives how to write like natives; it is always amazing to recall that he came to America as lately as the 1930's." (Gorham Munson, *The Written Word*, rev. ed.; 1949.)

The phrase *indigenous American*, which is a more logical and etymologically correct way of referring to an American Indian, does have some support—e.g.: "Hundreds of high schools and colleges have dropped their Indian symbols over the past 30 years as many indigenous American groups and their members have called for sports teams to drop the names." (*J. News* [Westchester Co., NY]; June 3,

2002.) Meanwhile, the synonymous phrase *autochthonous American* hasn't ever caught on. No surprise there. **–BG**

---

natty adjective *informal he's looking pretty darn natty in that new suit* SMART, stylish, fashionable, dapper, debonair, dashing, spruced up, well-dressed, chic, elegant, trim; *informal* snazzy, trendy, snappy, nifty, sassy, spiffy, fly, kicky, styling/stylin', sharp. ANTONYM scruffy.

natural adjective **1** *a natural occurrence* NORMAL, ordinary, everyday, usual, regular, common, commonplace, typical, routine, standard, established, customary, accustomed, habitual. ANTONYMS abnormal, exceptional. See note at NORMAL.

2 *natural produce* UNPROCESSED, organic, pure, wholesome, unrefined, pesticide-free, additive-free. ANTONYMS artificial, refined.

3 *Alex is a natural leader* BORN, naturally gifted, untaught.

4 *his natural instincts* INNATE, inborn, inherent, native, instinctive, intuitive; hereditary, inherited, inbred, congenital, connate. ANTONYM acquired.

5 *she seemed very natural* UNAFFECTED, spontaneous, uninhibited, relaxed, unselfconscious, genuine, open, artless, guileless, ingenuous, unpretentious, without airs. ANTONYMS self-conscious, false, affected.

6 *it was quite natural to think that* REASONABLE, logical, understandable, (only) to be expected, predictable. ANTONYM unreasonable.

naturalist noun *the wildlife preserve employs a team of naturalists from around the world* NATURAL HISTORIAN, life scientist, wildlife expert; biologist, botanist, zoologist, ornithologist, entomologist, ecologist.

naturalistic adjective *her sculptures are so naturalistic they seem to breathe* REALISTIC, real-life, true-to-life, lifelike, graphic, representational, faithful, photographic. ANTONYM abstract.

naturalize verb **1** *he was naturalized in 1950* GRANT CITIZENSHIP TO, make a citizen, enfranchise, give a passport to.

2 *they naturalized new species of grass and wildflowers* ESTABLISH, introduce, acclimatize, domesticate; acclimate.

naturally adverb **1** *he's naturally shy* BY NATURE, by character, inherently, innately, congenitally.

2 *try to act naturally* NORMALLY, in a natural manner/way, unaffectedly, spontaneously, genuinely, unpretentiously; *informal* natural. ANTONYM self-consciously.

3 *naturally, they wanted everything kept quiet* OF COURSE, as might be expected, needless to say; obviously, clearly, it goes without saying. ANTONYM surprisingly.

WORD NOTE naturally

Writers generally hope that their sentences smoothly interlock, and that any reader's eyes pass swiftly down the page without effort. To assist in creating this frictionless continuity, we sometimes turn to words like *naturally* or phrases like *of course, in fact,* and *that said.* These usually appear at the start of a sentence, simultaneously announcing new material while subtly or overtly hearkening back to earlier content. The occasional use of these locutions to promote continuity is fine, but all too often they merely signal slack writing. In themselves such words don't actually carry any meaning; they are simply syntactic grace notes—and employed too often they grow into verbal tics. As much as possible, cast out these fawning connectives and make your thinking the dynamic that sweeps the reader along. Prefer concision to clutter, the meaningful to the vacuous. **–MD**

---

nature noun **1** *the beauty of nature* THE NATURAL WORLD, Mother Nature, Mother Earth, the environment; wildlife, flora and fauna, the countryside; the universe, the cosmos.

2 *such crimes are, by their very nature, difficult to hide* ESSENCE, inherent/basic/essential qualities, inherent/basic/essential features, character, complexion.

3 *it was not in her nature to argue* CHARACTER, personality, disposition, temperament, makeup, psyche, constitution.

4 *experiments of a similar nature* KIND, sort, type, variety, category, ilk, class, species, genre, style, cast, order, kidney, mold, stamp, stripe.

naught, nought noun *all his efforts will have been for naught* NOTHING, nothing at all, no point, no purpose, no effect; nil, zero; *informal* zilch, zip, nada, diddly-squat.

naughty adjective **1** *a naughty boy* BADLY BEHAVED, disobedient, bad, misbehaved, misbehaving, wayward, defiant, unruly, insubordinate, willful, delinquent, undisciplined, uncontrollable, ill-mannered, ungovernable, unbiddable, disorderly, disruptive, fractious, recalcitrant, wild, wicked, obstreperous, difficult, troublesome, awkward, contrary, perverse, incorrigible; mischievous, playful, impish, roguish, rascally; *informal* bratty; *formal* refractory. ANTONYM well-behaved.

2 *naughty jokes* INDECENT, risqué, rude, racy, ribald, bawdy, suggestive, improper, indelicate, indecorous; vulgar, dirty, filthy, smutty, crude, coarse, obscene, lewd, pornographic; *informal* raunchy, saucy; *euphemistic* adult. ANTONYM decent.

nausea noun **1** *symptoms include nausea and headaches* SICKNESS, biliousness, queasiness; vomiting, retching, gagging; upset stomach; travel-sickness, seasickness, carsickness, airsickness.

2 *it induces a feeling of nausea* DISGUST, revulsion, repugnance, repulsion, distaste, aversion, loathing, abhorrence.

nauseating adjective *the smell was nauseating* SICKENING, nauseous, stomach-churning, emetic, sickly; disgusting, revolting, offensive, loathsome, obnoxious, foul, vomitous; *informal* gross, gut-churning, gut-wrenching.

nauseous adjective **1** *the food made her feel nauseous* SICK, nauseated, queasy, bilious, green around the gills, ill, unwell; seasick, carsick, airsick, travel-sick; *informal* barfy; *rare* qualmish.

2 *a nauseous stench.* See NAUSEATING.

nautical adjective *a library of nautical history and literature* MARITIME, marine, naval, seafaring; boating, sailing.

navel noun **1** *so, does that mean Adam and Eve had no navels? informal* belly button; *Anatomy* umbilicus.

2 *the navel of Byzantine culture* CENTER, central point, hub, focal point, focus, nucleus, heart, core; *literary* omphalos.

navigable adjective *after October, these waters are not navigable by ordinary craft* PASSABLE, negotiable, traversable; clear, open, unobstructed, unblocked.

navigate verb **1** *he navigated the yacht across the Atlantic* STEER, pilot, guide, direct, helm, captain; *Nautical* con; *informal* skipper.

2 *the upper reaches are dangerous to navigate* SAIL ACROSS/OVER, sail, travel/journey/voyage across/over, cross, traverse, negotiate, pass.

3 *I'll drive—you can navigate* MAP-READ, give directions, plan the route.

navigator noun *he had learned to be an able navigator by the time he was twelve* HELMSMAN, steersman, pilot, guide, wheelman.

navy noun **1** *a 600-ship navy* FLEET, flotilla, armada, naval force.

2 *a navy blazer* NAVY BLUE, dark blue, midnight blue, indigo.

near adverb **1** *her children live near.* See NEARBY adverb.

2 *near perfect conditions* ALMOST, just about, nearly, practically, virtually; *literary* well-nigh.

▸ preposition *a hotel near the seafront* CLOSE TO, close by, a short distance from, in the vicinity of, in the neighborhood of, within reach of, a stone's throw away from; *informal* within spitting distance of.

▸ adjective **1** *the nearest house* CLOSE, nearby, close/near at hand, at hand, a stone's throw away, within reach, accessible, handy, convenient; *informal* within spitting distance. ANTONYM far.

2 *the final judgment is near* IMMINENT, in the offing, close/near at hand, at hand, (just) around the corner, impending, looming. ANTONYMS remote, distant.

3 *a near relation* CLOSELY RELATED, close, related. ANTONYM distant.

4 *a near escape* NARROW, close, by a hair's breadth; *informal* by a whisker.

▸ verb **1** *by dawn we were nearing Moscow* APPROACH, draw near/nearer to, get close/closer to, advance toward, close in on.

2 *the death toll is nearing 3,000* VERGE ON, border on, approach.

nearby adjective *one of the nearby villages* NOT FAR AWAY/OFF, close/near at hand, close by, close, near, within reach, at hand, neighboring; accessible, handy, convenient. ANTONYM faraway.

▸ adverb *her mother lives nearby* CLOSE BY, close/near at hand, near, close, a short distance away, in the neighborhood, in the vicinity, at hand, within reach, on the doorstep, (just) around the corner.

nearly adverb *it was nearly midnight* ALMOST, just about, about, more or less, practically, virtually, all but, as good as, not far off, to all intents and purposes; not quite; *informal* pretty much, pretty well; *literary* well-nigh.

near miss noun *two airliners were involved in a near miss yesterday* CLOSE THING, near thing, narrow escape, close call; *informal* close shave.

nearsighted adjective *I'm too nearsighted to go without my glasses* MYOPIC; *informal* as blind as a bat; *archaic* purblind. ANTONYM farsighted.

neat adjective **1** *the bedroom was neat and clean* TIDY, orderly, well-ordered, in (good) order, shipshape, in apple-pie order, spick-and-span, uncluttered, straight, trim. ANTONYM untidy.

2 *he's very neat* SMART, dapper, trim, well-groomed, well-turned-out, spruce; *informal* natty. ANTONYM shabby.

3 *her neat script* WELL-FORMED, regular, precise, elegant, well-proportioned.

4 *this neat little gadget* COMPACT, well designed, handy.

5 *his neat footwork* SKILLFUL, deft, dexterous, adroit, adept, expert; *informal* nifty. ANTONYM clumsy.

6 *a neat solution* CLEVER, ingenious, inventive.

7 *neat gin* UNDILUTED, straight, unmixed; *informal* straight up.

8 *informal we had a really neat time.* See WONDERFUL.

neatly adverb **1** *neatly arranged papers* TIDILY, methodically, systematically; smartly, sprucely.

2 *the point was neatly put* CLEVERLY, aptly, elegantly.

3 *a neatly executed turn* SKILLFULLY, deftly, adroitly, adeptly, expertly.

nebulous adjective **1** *the figure was nebulous* INDISTINCT, indefinite, unclear, vague, hazy, cloudy, fuzzy, misty, blurred, blurry, foggy; faint, shadowy, obscure, formless, amorphous. ANTONYM clear.

2 *nebulous ideas* VAGUE, ill-defined, unclear, hazy, uncertain, indefinite, indeterminate, imprecise, unformed, muddled, confused, ambiguous. ANTONYM well-defined.

necessarily adverb *an increase in fees does not necessarily guarantee a balanced budget* AS A CONSEQUENCE, as a result, automatically, as a matter of course, certainly, surely, definitely, incontrovertibly, undoubtedly, inevitably, unavoidably, inescapably, ineluctably, of necessity; *formal* perforce.

necessary adjective **1** *parental permission is necessary* OBLIGATORY, requisite, required, compulsory, mandatory, imperative, needed, de rigueur; essential, indispensable, vital.

2 *a necessary consequence* INEVITABLE, unavoidable, inescapable, inexorable, ineluctable; predetermined, preordained.

THE RIGHT WORD

Food is **essential** to human life, which means that we must have it to survive. *Essential* can also apply to something that makes up the *essence*, or necessary qualities or attributes, of a thing (*a good safecracker is essential to our plan*). Clothing is **indispensable** in Northern climates, which means that it cannot be done without if the specified or implied purpose—in this case, survival—is to be achieved. **Necessary** applies to something without which a condition cannot be fulfilled (*cooperation was necessary to gather the harvest*), although it generally implies a pressing need rather than absolute indispensability. **Requisite** refers to that which is required by the circumstances (*the requisite skills for a botanist*) and generally describes a requirement that is imposed from the outside rather than an inherent need.

necessitate verb *the additional enrollment necessitates an additional staff person* MAKE NECESSARY, entail, involve, mean, require, demand, call for, be grounds for, warrant, constrain, force. See note at COMPEL.

necessitous adjective *distributing milk to necessitous mothers* NEEDY, poor, short of money, disadvantaged, underprivileged, in straitened circumstances, impoverished, poverty-stricken, penniless, impecunious, destitute, pauperized, indigent, without a cent to one's name; *informal* hard up; *formal* penurious. ANTONYM wealthy.

necessity noun **1** *the microwave is now regarded as a necessity* ESSENTIAL, indispensable item, requisite, prerequisite, necessary, basic, sine qua non, desideratum; *informal* must-have.

2 *political necessity forced him to resign* FORCE OF CIRCUMSTANCE, obligation, need, call, exigency; force majeure.

3 *the necessity of growing old* INEVITABILITY, certainty, inescapability, inexorability, ineluctability.

4 *necessity made them steal* POVERTY, need, neediness, want, deprivation, privation, penury, destitution, indigence. PHRASE: **of necessity** *the renovations will, of necessity, require a more aggressive fund-raising campaign* NECESSARILY, inevitably, unavoidably, inescapably, ineluctably; as a matter of course, naturally, automatically, certainly, surely, definitely, incontrovertibly, undoubtedly; *formal* perforce.

neck noun *the cop grabbed Malloy by the neck* nape, scruff; *technical* cervix; *archaic* scrag.

▸ verb *informal they were necking in the parking lot* KISS, caress, pet; *informal* smooch, make out, canoodle; *informal, dated* spoon.

PHRASE: **neck and neck** *going into the third lap, Christian and Perry are neck and neck* LEVEL, equal, tied, side by side, close; *informal* even-steven.

necklace noun *a simple gold necklace* CHAIN, choker, necklet; beads, pearls; pendant, locket; *historical* torc.

necromancer noun *a convention of spiritualists and necromancers* SORCERER, sorceress, (black) magician, wizard, warlock, witch, enchantress, occultist, diviner; spiritualist, medium; *rare* thaumaturge, thaumaturgist.

necromancy noun *Juma had been a practitioner of necromancy in some small village in Central America* SORCERY, (black) magic, witchcraft, witchery, wizardry, the occult, occultism, voodoo, hoodoo; divination; spiritualism.

necropolis noun *overlooking the woeful sea is the home to many a lost soldier, a rolling green necropolis* CEMETERY, graveyard, churchyard, burial ground; *informal* boneyard; *historical* potter's field, God's acre.

need verb **1** *do you need money?* REQUIRE, be in need of, have need of, want; be crying out for, be desperate for; demand, call for, necessitate, entail, involve; lack, be without, be short of.

2 *you needn't come* HAVE TO, be obliged to, be compelled to.

3 *she needed him so much* YEARN FOR, pine for, long for, desire, miss.

▸ noun **1** *there's no need to apologize* NECESSITY, obligation, requirement, call, demand.

2 *basic human needs* REQUIREMENT, essential, necessity, want, requisite, prerequisite, demand, desideratum.

3 *their need was particularly pressing* NEEDINESS, want, poverty, deprivation, privation, hardship, destitution, indigence.

4 *my hour of need* DIFFICULTY, trouble, distress; crisis, emergency, urgency, extremity.

PHRASE: **in need** *these children are in need* NEEDY, necessitous, deprived, disadvantaged, underprivileged, poor, impoverished, poverty-stricken, destitute, impecunious, indigent; *formal* penurious.

needful adjective *formal we'll do whatever is needful* NECESSARY, needed, required, requisite; essential, imperative, vital, indispensable.

needle noun **1** *a needle and thread* bodkin.

2 *the virus is transmitted via needles* hypodermic needle, syringe; *informal* hypo.

3 *the needle on the meter* INDICATOR, pointer, marker, arrow, hand.

4 *put the needle on the record* STYLUS.

▸ verb *informal he needled her too much* GOAD, provoke, bait, taunt, pester, harass, prick, prod, sting, tease; IRRITATE, annoy, anger, vex, irk, nettle, pique, exasperate, infuriate, get on someone's nerves, rub the wrong way, ruffle someone's feathers, try someone's patience; *informal* aggravate, rile, niggle, get in someone's hair, hassle, get to, bug, miff, peeve, get/put someone's back up, get under someone's skin, get at, ride.

needless adjective *needless details* UNNECESSARY, inessential, nonessential, unneeded, undesired, unwanted, uncalled for; gratuitous, pointless; dispensable, expendable, superfluous, redundant, excessive, supererogatory. ANTONYM necessary.

PHRASE: **needless to say** *needless to say, we are grateful for any and all donations* OF COURSE, as one would expect, not unexpectedly, it goes without saying, obviously, naturally; *informal* natch.

needlework noun *some of the surgeons keep their fingers nimble with needlework* SEWING, stitching, embroidery, needlepoint, needlecraft, tapestry, crewel (work). See table at SEWING.

needy adjective *collecting food and blankets for needy families* POOR, deprived, disadvantaged, underprivileged, necessitous, in need, needful, hard up, in straitened circumstances, poverty-stricken, indigent, impoverished, pauperized, destitute, impecunious, penniless, moneyless; *informal* broke, strapped (for cash), busted; *formal* penurious. ANTONYM wealthy.

ne'er-do-well noun *I don't want to end up a ne'er-do-well like my old man* GOOD-FOR-NOTHING, layabout, loafer, idler, shirker, sluggard, slugabed, drone; *informal* lazybones, bum; *archaic* wastrel.

nefarious adjective *the nefarious long-lost brother returns to steal Iris's inheritance* WICKED, evil, sinful, iniquitous, egregious, heinous, atrocious, vile, foul, abominable, odious, depraved, monstrous, fiendish, diabolical, unspeakable, despicable; villainous, criminal, corrupt, illegal, unlawful; *dated* dastardly. ANTONYM good.

negate verb **1** *they negated the court's ruling* INVALIDATE, nullify, neutralize, cancel; undo, reverse, annul, void, revoke, rescind, repeal, retract, countermand, overrule, overturn; *informal* nix; *formal* abrogate. See note at VOID. ANTONYMS validate, confirm.

2 *he has never successfully negated Henderson's central theory* DISPROVE, prove wrong, prove false, refute, debunk, discredit, invalidate; *informal* poke holes in; *formal* confute. ANTONYM confirm.

negation noun **1** *negation of the findings* DENIAL, contradiction, repudiation, refutation, rebuttal; nullification, cancellation, revocation, repeal, retraction; *formal* abrogation.

2 *evil is not just the negation of goodness* OPPOSITE, reverse, antithesis, contrary, inverse, converse; absence, want.

negative adjective 1 *a negative reply* OPPOSING, opposed, contrary, anti-, dissenting, saying "no", in the negative. ANTONYMS positive, affirmative.

2 *stop being so negative* PESSIMISTIC, defeatist, gloomy, cynical, fatalistic, dismissive, antipathetic, critical; unenthusiastic, uninterested, unresponsive. ANTONYMS positive, optimistic.

3 *a negative effect on the economy* HARMFUL, bad, adverse, damaging, detrimental, unfavorable, disadvantageous. ANTONYMS good, favorable.

▸ noun *he murmured a negative* "NO", refusal, rejection, veto; dissension, contradiction; denial; *informal* thumbs-down.

neglect verb 1 *she neglected the children* FAIL TO LOOK AFTER, leave alone, abandon, desert; *literary* forsake. ANTONYMS cherish, look after.

2 *he's neglecting his work* PAY NO ATTENTION TO, let slide, not attend to, be remiss about, be lax about, leave undone, shirk. ANTONYM concentrate on.

3 *don't neglect our advice* DISREGARD, ignore, pay no attention to, take no notice of, pay no heed to, overlook; disdain, scorn, spurn. ANTONYM heed.

4 *I neglected to inform her* FAIL, omit, forget. ANTONYM remember.

▸ noun 1 *the place had an air of neglect* DISREPAIR, dilapidation, deterioration, shabbiness, disuse, abandonment; *rare* desuetude.

2 *her doctor was guilty of neglect* NEGLIGENCE, dereliction of duty, carelessness, heedlessness, unconcern, laxity, slackness, irresponsibility; *formal* delinquency. ANTONYM care.

3 *the* ***neglect of*** *women's concerns* DISREGARD OF/FOR, ignoring of, overlooking of; inattention to, indifference to, heedlessness to. ANTONYM attention.

THE RIGHT WORD

One of the most common reasons why people fail to arrive at work on time is that they **neglect** to set their alarm clocks, a verb that implies a failure to carry out some expected or required action, either intentionally or through carelessness. Some people, of course, choose to **disregard** their employer's rules pertaining to tardiness, which implies a voluntary, and sometimes deliberate, inattention. Others hear the alarm go off and simply **ignore** it, which suggests not only a deliberate decision to **disregard** something but a stubborn refusal to face the facts. No doubt they hope their employers will **overlook** their frequent late arrivals, which implies a failure to see or to take action, which can be either intentional or due to haste or lack of care (*to overlook minor errors*). But they also hope no one will **slight** them for their conduct when it comes to handing out raises and promotions, which means to **disregard** or **neglect** in a disdainful way.

neglected adjective 1 *neglected animals* UNCARED FOR, abandoned; mistreated, maltreated; *literary* forsaken.

2 *a neglected cottage* DERELICT, dilapidated, tumbledown, ramshackle, untended.

3 *a neglected masterpiece of prose* DISREGARDED, forgotten, overlooked, ignored, unrecognized, unnoticed, unsung, underestimated, undervalued, unappreciated.

neglectful adjective See NEGLIGENT.

negligent adjective *a negligent safety inspector* NEGLECTFUL, remiss, careless, lax, irresponsible, inattentive, heedless, thoughtless, unmindful, forgetful; slack, sloppy, derelict; *formal* delinquent. ANTONYM dutiful.

negligible adjective *the defects are negligible* TRIVIAL, trifling, insignificant, unimportant, minor, inconsequential; minimal, small, slight, inappreciable, infinitesimal, nugatory, petty; paltry, inadequate, insufficient, meager, pitiful; *informal* minuscule, piddling, measly; *formal* exiguous. ANTONYM significant.

negotiable adjective 1 *salary is negotiable* OPEN TO DISCUSSION, discussable, flexible, open to modification; unsettled, undecided.

2 *the pathway was negotiable* PASSABLE, navigable, crossable, traversable; clear, unblocked, unobstructed.

3 *negotiable checks* transferable; valid.

negotiate verb 1 *she refused to negotiate* DISCUSS TERMS, talk, consult, parley, confer, debate; compromise; mediate, intercede, arbitrate, moderate, conciliate; bargain, haggle.

2 *he negotiated a new contract* ARRANGE, broker, work out, thrash out, agree on; settle, clinch, conclude, pull off, bring off, transact; *informal* sort out, swing.

3 *I negotiated the obstacles* GET AROUND, get past, get over, clear, cross; surmount, overcome, deal with, cope with.

negotiation noun 1 (**negotiations**) *the negotiations resume next week* DISCUSSION(S), talks, deliberations; conference, debate, dialogue, consultation; mediation, arbitration, conciliation.

2 *the negotiation of the deal* ARRANGEMENT, brokering; settlement, conclusion, completion, transaction.

negotiator noun *they brought in an impartial negotiator to help settle the dispute* MEDIATOR, arbitrator, arbiter, moderator, go-between, middleman, intermediary, intercessor, intervener, conciliator; representative, spokesperson, broker, bargainer.

neigh verb *the sight of smoke made the horses neigh* WHINNY, bray.

neighborhood noun 1 *a quiet neighborhood* DISTRICT, area, locality, locale, quarter, community; part, region, zone; *informal* neck of the woods, hood, nabe, stomping ground, stamping ground.

2 *in the neighborhood of Greensboro* VICINITY, environs, purlieus, precincts, vicinage. PHRASE: **in the neighborhood of** *a new roof will be in the neighborhood of $4,000* APPROXIMATELY, about, around, roughly, in the region of, of/on the order of, nearly, almost, close to, just about, practically, there or thereabouts, circa.

neighboring adjective *the owner of the neighboring property* ADJACENT, adjoining, bordering, connecting, abutting; proximate, near, close, close/near at hand, next-door, nearby, in the vicinity. ANTONYM remote.

neighborly adjective *most of the tenants here are pretty neighborly* OBLIGING, helpful, friendly, kind, amiable, amicable, affable, genial, agreeable, hospitable, companionable, well disposed, civil, cordial, good-natured, nice, pleasant, generous; considerate, thoughtful, unselfish, decent. ANTONYM unfriendly.

nemesis noun **1** *they were beaten in the final by their nemesis* ARCHRIVAL, adversary, foe, opponent, arch enemy.

2 *this could be the bank's nemesis* DOWNFALL, undoing, ruin, ruination, destruction, Waterloo.

3 *the nemesis that his crime deserved* RETRIBUTION, vengeance, punishment, just deserts; fate, destiny.

neologism noun *the delightful neologisms of Lewis Carroll* NEW WORD, new expression, new term, new phrase, coinage; made-up word, nonce word.

neophyte noun **1** *a neophyte of the monastery* NOVICE, novitiate; postulant, catechumen.

2 *cooking classes are offered to neophytes* BEGINNER, learner, novice, newcomer; initiate, tyro, fledgling; trainee, apprentice, probationer, tenderfoot; *informal* rookie, newbie, greenhorn. See note at NOVICE.

ne plus ultra noun *the ne plus ultra of jazz pianists* LAST WORD, ultimate, perfect example, height, acme, zenith, epitome, quintessence.

nepotism noun *hiring my daughter was not nepotism—it was just good business* FAVORITISM, preferential treatment, the old boy network, looking after one's own, bias, partiality, partisanship. ANTONYM impartiality.

nerd noun *informal the nerds running the world's technology are certainly getting the last laugh* BORE; *informal* dork, dweeb, nimrod, geek, drip, loser; techie.

nerve noun **1** *the nerves that transmit pain* nerve fiber, neuron, axon, dendrite.

2 *the match will be a test of nerve* CONFIDENCE, assurance, coolheadedness, self-possession; courage, bravery, pluck, boldness, intrepidity, fearlessness, daring; determination, willpower, spirit, backbone, fortitude, intestinal fortitude, mettle, grit, true grit, stout-heartedness; *informal* guts, spunk, moxie. See note at COURAGE.

3 *he had the nerve to ask her out again* AUDACITY, cheek, effrontery, gall, temerity, presumption, boldness, brazenness, impudence, impertinence, arrogance, cockiness; *informal* face, front, chutzpah.

4 *pre-wedding nerves* ANXIETY, tension, nervousness, stress, worry, cold feet, apprehension; *informal* butterflies (in one's stomach), the jitters, the shakes, the heebie-jeebies. PHRASE: **get on someone's nerves** *her squeaky voice gets on my nerves* IRRITATE, annoy, irk, anger, bother, vex, provoke, displease, exasperate, infuriate, gall, pique, needle, ruffle someone's feathers, try someone's patience; jar on, grate on, rankle; rub the wrong way; *informal* aggravate, get to, bug, miff, peeve, rile, nettle, get someone's goat, tick off.

nerve-racking adjective *it's the waiting that's the most nerve-racking* STRESSFUL, anxious, worrying, fraught, nail-biting, tense, difficult, trying, worrisome, daunting, frightening; *informal* scary, hairy.

nervous adjective **1** *a nervous woman* HIGH-STRUNG, anxious, edgy, tense, excitable, jumpy, skittish, brittle, neurotic; timid, mousy, shy, fearful. ANTONYMS relaxed, calm.

2 *he was so nervous he couldn't eat* ANXIOUS, worried, apprehensive, on edge, edgy, tense, stressed, agitated, uneasy, restless, worked up, keyed up, overwrought, jumpy; fearful, frightened, scared, shaky, in a cold sweat, gun-shy; *informal* with butterflies in one's stomach, jittery, twitchy, in a state, uptight, wired, in a flap, het up, strung out, having kittens. ANTONYMS relaxed, calm.

3 *a nervous disorder* NEUROLOGICAL, neural.

nervous breakdown noun *the boss's nervous breakdown almost destroyed the company* MENTAL COLLAPSE, breakdown, collapse, crisis, trauma; nervous exhaustion, mental illness; *informal* crack-up.

nervousness noun *she began chattering out of nervousness* ANXIETY, edginess, tension, agitation, stress, worry, apprehension, uneasiness, disquiet, fear, trepidation, perturbation, alarm; *informal* butterflies (in one's stomach), the jitters, the willies, the heebie-jeebies, the shakes.

nervy adjective *it was a nervy move* AUDACIOUS, impudent, brazen, cheeky, bold, plucky; *informal* gutsy, spunky, ballsy.

nest noun **1** *the birds built a nest* ROOST, aerie.

2 *the animals disperse rapidly from the nest* LAIR, den, burrow.

3 *a cozy love nest* HIDEAWAY, hideout, retreat, shelter, refuge, den.

4 *a nest of intrigue* HOTBED, den, breeding ground, cradle.

nest egg noun *her nest egg wasn't much, but it was enough to keep the wolves from the door* SAVINGS, life savings, cache, funds, reserve.

nestle verb *the little ones nestled under the cozy quilt with their mother* SNUGGLE, cuddle, huddle, nuzzle, settle, burrow.

Net noun *their first communication was through **the Net*** THE INTERNET, the World Wide Web, the Web; *dated* cyberspace, the information superhighway, the infobahn.

net[1] noun **1** *fishermen mending their nets* FISHING NET, dragnet, drift net, trawl (net), landing net, gill net, cast net, seine.

2 *a dress of green net* NETTING, meshwork, webbing, tulle, fishnet, openwork, lace, latticework.

3 *he managed to escape the net* TRAP, snare.

▸ verb *they netted big criminals* CATCH, capture, trap, entrap, snare, ensnare, bag, hook, land; *informal* nab, collar.

net[2] adjective **1** *net earnings* AFTER TAX, after deductions, take-home, final; *informal* bottom line. ANTONYM gross.

2 *the net result* FINAL, end, ultimate, closing; overall, actual, effective.

▸ verb *she netted $50,000* EARN, make, get, gain, obtain, acquire, accumulate, clear, take home, bring in, pocket, realize, be paid; *informal* rake in.

nether adjective *the nether regions* LOWER, low, bottom, bottommost, under, basal; underground. ANTONYM upper.

netherworld noun *their souls were doomed to wander **the netherworld*** HELL, the underworld, the infernal regions, the abyss; eternal damnation, perdition; Hades, Acheron, Gehenna, Tophet, Sheol; *literary* the pit. ANTONYM heaven.

nettle verb *I try not to be nettled by her, but it isn't easy* IRRITATE, annoy, irk, gall, vex, anger, exasperate, infuriate, provoke; upset, displease, offend, affront, pique, get on someone's nerves, try someone's patience, ruffle someone's feathers; rub the wrong way, rankle; *informal* peeve, aggravate, miff, rile, needle, get to, bug, get someone's goat, tick off.

network noun **1** *a network of arteries* WEB, lattice, net, matrix, mesh, crisscross, grid, reticulum, reticulation; *Anatomy* plexus.

2 *a network of lanes* MAZE, labyrinth, warren, tangle.

3 *a network of friends* SYSTEM, complex, nexus, web, webwork.

neurosis noun *has he been diagnosed with an actual neurosis?* MENTAL ILLNESS, mental disorder, psychological disorder; psychoneurosis, psychopathy; obsession, phobia, fixation; *Medicine* neuroticism.

neurotic adjective **1** *Medicine neurotic patients* MENTALLY ILL, mentally disturbed, unstable, unbalanced, maladjusted; psychopathic, phobic, obsessive-compulsive. ANTONYMS stable, well balanced.

2 *a neurotic, self-obsessed woman* OVERANXIOUS, oversensitive, nervous, tense, high-strung, strung-out, paranoid; obsessive, fixated, hysterical, overwrought, worked-up, irrational, twitchy. ANTONYMS laid-back, calm.

neuter adjective *the traumatic abuses of his childhood left him feeling more neuter than masculine* ASEXUAL, sexless, unsexed; androgynous, epicene.

▸ verb *have your pets neutered* STERILIZE, castrate, spay, geld, fix, desex, alter, doctor; *archaic* emasculate.

neutral adjective **1** *a neutral judge* IMPARTIAL, unbiased, unprejudiced, objective, open-minded, nonpartisan, disinterested, dispassionate, detached, impersonal, unemotional, indifferent, uncommitted. ANTONYMS biased, partisan.

2 *Switzerland remained neutral* UNALIGNED, nonaligned, unaffiliated, unallied, uninvolved; noncombatant. ANTONYMS partisan, combatant.

3 *a neutral topic of conversation* INOFFENSIVE, bland, unobjectionable, unexceptionable, anodyne, unremarkable, ordinary, commonplace; safe, harmless, innocuous. ANTONYMS provocative, offensive.

4 *a neutral background* PALE, light; beige, cream, taupe, oatmeal, ecru, buff, fawn, gray; colorless, uncolored, achromatic; indeterminate, insipid, nondescript, dull, drab. ANTONYMS bright, colorful.

neutralize verb *if the internal dissension is not neutralized, we have no hope of moving forward* COUNTERACT, offset, counterbalance, balance, counterpoise, countervail, compensate for, make up for; cancel out, nullify, negate; equalize.

never adverb **1** *his room is never tidy* NOT EVER, at no time, not at any time, not once; *literary* ne'er. ANTONYM always.

2 *she will never agree to it* NOT AT ALL, certainly not, not for a moment, under no circumstances, on no account, nevermore; *informal* no way, not on your life, not in a million years, when pigs fly, when hell freezes over. ANTONYMS certainly, definitely.

never-ending adjective *never-ending noise* INCESSANT, continuous, unceasing, ceaseless, constant, continual, perpetual, uninterrupted, unbroken, steady, unremitting, relentless, persistent, interminable, nonstop, endless, unending, everlasting, eternal. See note at ETERNAL.

nevertheless adverb *nevertheless, it makes sense to take a few precautions* NONETHELESS, even so, however, but, still, yet, though; in spite of that, despite that, be that as it may, for all that, that said, just the same, all the same; notwithstanding, regardless, anyway, anyhow, still and all.

new adjective **1** *new technology* RECENTLY DEVELOPED, up to date, latest, current, state-of-the-art, contemporary, advanced, recent, modern, cutting-edge, leading-edge. ANTONYMS old, existing.

2 *new ideas* NOVEL, original, fresh, imaginative, creative, experimental; contemporary, modernist, up to date; newfangled, ultramodern, avant-garde, futuristic; *informal* way out, far out. ANTONYMS old-fashioned, hackneyed.

3 *is your boat new?* UNUSED, brand new, pristine, fresh, in mint condition. ANTONYMS old, secondhand.

4 *we have to find a new approach* DIFFERENT, another, alternative; unfamiliar, unknown, strange; unaccustomed, untried. ANTONYM present.

5 *they had a new classroom built* ADDITIONAL, extra, supplementary, further, another, fresh. ANTONYM existing.

6 *I came back a new woman* REINVIGORATED, restored, revived, improved, refreshed, regenerated, reborn.

newbie noun *informal* See NEWCOMER sense 2.

newborn adjective *newborn babies* JUST BORN, recently born.

▸ noun *the bacteria are dangerous to newborns* YOUNG BABY, tiny baby, infant; *Medicine* neonate.

newcomer noun **1** *a newcomer to the village* (NEW) ARRIVAL, immigrant, settler; stranger, outsider, foreigner, alien; *informal* johnny-come-lately, new kid on the block.

2 *photography tips for the newcomer* BEGINNER, novice, learner; trainee, apprentice, tyro, initiate, neophyte, tenderfoot; *informal* rookie, newbie, greenhorn.

newfangled adjective *newfangled digital technology* NEW, the latest, modern, ultramodern, up-to-the-minute, state-of-the-art, advanced, contemporary, new-generation; *informal* trendy, flash. ANTONYM dated.

newly adverb *a newly discovered species of moth* RECENTLY, just, only just, lately, freshly; not long ago, a short time ago, only now, of late; new-.

news noun *they were stunned by the news of his death* REPORT, announcement, story, account; article, news flash, newscast, headlines, press release, communication, communiqué, bulletin; message, dispatch, statement, intelligence; disclosure, revelation, word, talk, gossip; *informal* scoop; *literary* tidings.

newspaper noun *the front-page story in today's newspaper* PAPER, journal, gazette, tabloid, broadsheet, local (paper), daily (paper), weekly (paper); scandal sheet; *informal* rag, tab.

newsworthy adjective *our annual pig festival is the most newsworthy event in the county* INTERESTING, topical, notable, noteworthy, important, significant, momentous, historic, remarkable, sensational. ANTONYM unremarkable.

next adjective **1** *the next chapter* FOLLOWING, succeeding, upcoming, to come. ANTONYMS previous, preceding.

2 *the next house in the street* NEIGHBORING, adjacent, adjoining, next-door, bordering, connected, attached; closest, nearest.

▸ adverb *where shall we go next?* THEN, after, afterward/afterward, after this/that, following that/this, later, subsequently; *formal* thereafter, thereupon. ANTONYM before.

PHRASE: **next to** *she sat down next to a window* BESIDE, by, alongside, by the side of, next door to, adjacent to, side by side with; close to, near, neighboring, adjoining.

nibble verb **1** *they* ***nibbled at*** *mangoes* TAKE SMALL BITES FROM, pick at, gnaw at, peck at, snack on; toy with; taste, sample; *informal* graze on.

2 *the mouse nibbled his finger* PECK, nip, bite.

▸ noun **1** *the fish enjoyed a nibble on the lettuce* BITE, gnaw, chew; taste.

2 *a few nibbles before dinner* MORSEL, mouthful, bite; snack, tidbit, canapé, hors d'oeuvre.

nice adjective **1** *have a nice time* ENJOYABLE, pleasant, agreeable, good, satisfying, gratifying, delightful, marvelous; entertaining, amusing, diverting, lovely, great. ANTONYM unpleasant.

2 *a nice landlord* PLEASANT, likable, agreeable, personable, congenial, amiable, affable, genial, friendly, charming, delightful, engaging; sympathetic, simpatico, compassionate, good. ANTONYM nasty.

3 *nice manners* POLITE, courteous, civil, refined, polished, genteel, elegant. ANTONYMS unrefined, rough.

4 *that's a rather nice distinction* SUBTLE, fine, delicate, minute, precise, strict, close; careful, meticulous, scrupulous. ANTONYMS approximate, rough.

5 *it's a nice day* FINE, pleasant, agreeable; dry, sunny, warm, mild. ANTONYMS stormy, nasty.

USAGE NOTE **nice**

Nice originally had a number of meanings, including 'fine, subtle, discriminating' (*they are not very nice in regard to the company they keep*); 'refined in taste, hard to please, fastidious' (*for company so nice, the finest caterers would be engaged*); and 'precise, strict' (*she has a nice sense of decorum*). The popular overuse of **nice** to mean 'pleasant, agreeable, satisfactory' has rendered the word trite: *we had a very nice time*; *this is a nice room*; *he's a nice boy.*

nicety noun **1** *legal niceties* SUBTLETY, fine point, nuance, refinement, detail.

2 *great nicety of control* PRECISION, accuracy, exactness, meticulousness.

niche noun **1** *a niche in the wall* RECESS, alcove, nook, cranny, hollow, bay, cavity, cubbyhole, pigeonhole.

2 *he found his niche in life* IDEAL POSITION, place, function, vocation, calling, métier, job.

nick verb **1** *I nicked my toe* CUT, scratch, incise, gouge, gash, score.

2 *Brit. informal* *she nicked his wallet.* See STEAL verb sense 1, 2.

▸ noun *a slight nick in the surface* CUT, scratch, incision, notch, chip, gouge, gash; dent, indentation.

PHRASE: **in the nick of time** *as usual, the Lone Ranger arrived in the nick of time* JUST IN TIME, not a moment too soon, at the critical moment, at the last second; *informal* at the buzzer, just under the wire.

nickname noun *'Bambi' is the nickname my sister gave me when I was a baby* SOBRIQUET, byname, tag, label, epithet, cognomen; pet name, diminutive, endearment; *informal* moniker; *formal* appellation.

nifty adjective *informal* **1** *nifty camerawork* SKILLFUL, deft, agile, capable. ANTONYM clumsy.

2 *a nifty little gadget* USEFUL, handy, practical.

3 *a nifty suit* FASHIONABLE, stylish, smart.

niggardly adjective **1** *a niggardly person* CHEAP, mean, miserly, parsimonious, close-fisted, penny-pinching, cheeseparing, grasping, ungenerous, illiberal; *informal* stingy, tight, tightfisted. ANTONYM generous.

2 *niggardly rations* MEAGER, inadequate, scanty, scant, skimpy, paltry, sparse, insufficient, deficient, short, lean, small, slender, poor, miserable, pitiful, puny; *informal* measly, stingy, pathetic, piddling. ANTONYMS lavish, abundant.

WORD NOTE **niggardly**

I was once giving a speech to a group of students in South Carolina, and happened to make reference to the *niggardly* pay raise that was then being offered to a group of local strikers—whereupon three members of the audience, two of them white and one black, walked out in evident protest. Much the same had happened in Washington, DC, a month or so before: a local civil servant was excoriated for having used the same word, one which, to some ill-educated members of his audience, was deemed to be—since it had a similarity of sound—racist and offensive. Of course, most users of this book will, ipso facto, be educated and liberally rounded people, and even if unaware of the precise etymology will know that this synonym for "parsimonious" has no connection whatsoever with the presently offensive and generally unusable word *nigger* (my caveat here refers only to the accepted and acceptable use of *nigger* within some racially and socially circumscribed communities). *Niggardly* almost certainly comes from a Scandinavian term for "a stingy person," and it is, so far as is known, ethnically and chromatically untainted. So even if only to annoy the ignorant and pedantic watchdogs of correctness, this word should, I think, be used frequently. There is a much nobler reason to do so also, of course: it is a quite splendid-sounding and -looking word, easy on both the eye and the ear. **—SW**

niggle verb **1** *his behavior does niggle me* IRRITATE, annoy, bother, provoke, exasperate, upset, gall, irk, rankle with; *informal* rile, get to, bug.

2 *he niggles about the prices* COMPLAIN, quibble, nitpick, fuss, carp, cavil, grumble, gripe, grouse, moan.

▸ noun *niggles about the lack of equipment* QUIBBLE, trivial complaint, criticism, grumble, grouse, cavil; *informal* gripe, moan, beef.

night noun *they did all their dirty dealing during the night* nighttime; hours of darkness, darkness, dark; nightfall, sunset. ANTONYM day.

PHRASE: **night and day** *wartime factories ran night and day* ALL THE TIME, around/round the clock, [morning, noon, and night], [day in, day out], ceaselessly, endlessly, incessantly, unceasingly, interminably, constantly, perpetually, continually, relentlessly; *informal* 24-7.

nightclub noun *we hit all the hot nightclubs* CLUB, nightspot, disco, discotheque, bar, lounge. See also BAR noun sense 4.

nightfall noun *we lock the doors at nightfall* SUNSET, sundown, dusk, twilight, evening, close of day, dark; *literary* eventide. ANTONYM dawn.

nightly adjective **1** *nightly raids* EVERY NIGHT, each night, night after night.

2 *his nightly wanderings* NOCTURNAL, nighttime.

▸ adverb *a band plays there nightly* EVERY NIGHT, each night, night after night.

nightmare noun **1** *she woke from a nightmare* BAD DREAM, night terrors; *archaic* incubus.

2 *the journey was a nightmare* ORDEAL, trial, torment, horror, hell, misery, agony, torture, murder; curse, bane.

nightmarish adjective *a nightmarish creature clawed at the door* UNEARTHLY, spine-chilling, hair-raising, horrific, macabre, hideous, unspeakable, gruesome, grisly, ghastly, harrowing, disturbing, Kafkaesque; *informal* scary, creepy.

nightstick noun *the patrol officer's nightstick* BLUDGEON, truncheon, club, billy club, stick.

nihilism noun *she could not accept Bacon's nihilism, his insistence that man is a futile being* SKEPTICISM, negativity, cynicism, pessimism; disbelief, unbelief, agnosticism, atheism.

nihilist noun *he contends that his being a nihilist should not discount his ability to teach biblical history* SKEPTIC, negativist, cynic, pessimist; disbeliever, unbeliever, agnostic, atheist.

nil noun *our chances of getting there on time were nil* NOTHING, none; zero, 0, naught/nought; *Tennis* love; *informal* zilch, zip, nada, a goose egg, nix; *dated* cipher.

nimble adjective **1** *he was nimble on his feet* AGILE, sprightly, light, spry, lively, quick, graceful, lithe, limber; skillful, deft, dexterous, adroit; *informal* nippy, twinkle-toed; *literary* lightsome. ANTONYM clumsy.

2 *a nimble mind* QUICK-WITTED, quick, alert, lively, wide awake, observant, astute, adroit, perceptive, penetrating, discerning, shrewd, sharp; intelligent, bright, smart, clever, brilliant; *informal* brainy, quick on the uptake. ANTONYM dull.

nimrod noun **1** *a secluded paradise for anglers and nimrods.* See HUNTER.

2 *informal the kids we used to think of as nimrods are now the leaders of our local industry.* See NERD.

USAGE NOTE **nimrod**

According to all the standard dictionaries, this word means "a skillful hunter." The term derives from the name of a king of Shinar (Southern Babylonia)—that is, King Nimrod, who is described in Genesis as a mighty hunter. And the word is often used in this traditional sense—e.g.: "Some sportsmen, of course, would say Mealey has a fatal flaw . . . . Nimrods and anglers believe he's too cozy with groups as varied as ranchers, miners, loggers and even environmentalists." (*Spokesman-Review* [Spokane]; Aug. 5, 1997.) In late-twentieth-century slang, though, the word has come to mean "a simpleton; dunderhead; blockhead"—e.g.:

• "Hey all you mack daddies (cool guys) out there: if you don't want to sound like a nimrod (geek) on your next trip to kili cali (Southern California), don't get all petro (worried)." (*Washington Post*; July 20, 1997.)

• "V.P. Marketing: 'You'd call Messier that to his face?' Quinn: 'No, I'm calling it to yours, ya nimrod.' " (*Financial Post* [Canada]; July 31, 1997.)

Though this sense isn't recorded in most standard dictionaries, it certainly exists and is well known among the younger generations. For now, it remains slang. But it surely threatens to kill off the hunter sense. **—BG**

nincompoop noun *informal* See IDIOT.

nip verb *the child nipped her* BITE, nibble, peck; pinch, tweak, squeeze, grip.

▸ noun *a nip in the air* CHILL, biting cold, iciness.

PHRASE: **nip something in the bud** *before your children start spending most of their free time in front of the television or computer, nip it in the bud* CUT SHORT, curtail, check, curb, thwart, frustrate, stop, halt, arrest, stifle, obstruct, block, squash, quash, subdue, crack down on, stamp out; *informal* put the kibosh on.

nipple noun *the mother dog's nipples* TEAT; *informal* tit; *Anatomy* mammilla.

nippy adjective *it's a bit nippy in here* COLD, chilly, icy, bitter, raw. ANTONYM warm.

nirvana noun *there are no shortcuts to nirvana* PARADISE, heaven; bliss, ecstasy, joy, peace, serenity, tranquility; enlightenment. ANTONYM hell.

nitpicking adjective *informal* See PEDANTIC.

nitty-gritty noun *informal now let's get to the nitty-gritty of managing your own business* BASICS, essentials, fundamentals, substance, quintessence, heart of the matter; nub, crux, gist, meat, kernel, marrow; *informal* brass tacks, bottom line; nuts and bolts.

nitwit noun *informal* See IDIOT.

nix verb *Eileen's parents nixed the idea of a camping trip* REJECT, veto, turn down, scrap, scrub, ditch, scuttle, stymie, call off, put the kibosh on.

no exclamation *no, I will not go on a date with your cousin Ralph* absolutely not, most certainly not, of course not, under no circumstances, by no means, not at all, negative, never, not really; *informal* nope, uh-uh, nah, not on your life, no way, no way José, ixnay; *archaic* nay. ANTONYM yes.

nobility noun **1** *a member of the nobility* ARISTOCRACY, aristocrats, peerage, peers (of the realm), lords, nobles, noblemen, noblewomen, patricians; *informal* aristos.

2 *the nobility of his deed* VIRTUE, goodness, honor, decency, integrity; magnanimity, generosity, selflessness.

noble adjective **1** *a noble family* ARISTOCRATIC, patrician, blue-blooded, high-born, titled; *archaic* gentle. ANTONYM humble.

2 *a noble cause* RIGHTEOUS, virtuous, good, honorable, upright, decent, worthy, moral, ethical, reputable; magnanimous, unselfish, generous. ANTONYM dishonorable.

3 *a noble pine forest* MAGNIFICENT, splendid, grand, stately, imposing, dignified, proud, striking, impressive, majestic, glorious, awesome, monumental, statuesque, regal, imperial. ANTONYM unimpressive.

▸ noun *Scottish nobles* ARISTOCRAT, nobleman, noblewoman, lord, lady, peer, peeress, peer of the realm, patrician; *informal* aristo.

nobody pronoun *nobody was home* NO ONE, none, not a soul, nary a soul.

▸ noun *stop thinking of yourself as a nobody* NONENTITY, no-name, zero, nonperson, no-hoper, nothing; loser, lightweight. See word spectrum at STAR.

no-brainer noun *accepting their job offer was a no-*

brainer EASY DECISION, easy task; foregone conclusion, sure thing, certainty, given.

nod verb **1** *she nodded her head* INCLINE, bob, bow, dip.

2 *he nodded to me to start* SIGNAL, gesture, gesticulate, motion, sign, indicate.

▸ noun **1** *she gave a nod to the manager* SIGNAL, indication, sign, cue; gesture.

2 *a quick nod of his head* INCLINATION, bob, bow, dip.

3 *Halifax will get the nod as host city* APPROVAL, selection, sanction, endorsement; *informal* OK, A-OK, green light, thumbs up.

PHRASE: **nod off** *give me a pillow and I'll nod off right this second* FALL ASLEEP, go to sleep, doze off, drop off; *informal* drift off, go out like a light, sack out, drift into the arms of Morpheus.

node noun *the node of the branches* JUNCTION, intersection, interchange, fork, confluence, convergence, crossing.

noise noun *I have a headache from all the noise* SOUND, din, hubbub, clamor, racket, uproar, tumult, commotion, pandemonium, babel; *informal* hullabaloo. ANTONYM silence.

noiseless adjective *a noiseless air purifier* SILENT, quiet, hushed, soundless.

noisome adjective See ODIOUS.

noisy adjective **1** *a noisy crowd* ROWDY, clamorous, boisterous, turbulent, uproarious, riotous, rambunctious, rackety; chattering, talkative, vociferous, shouting, screaming. ANTONYM quiet.

2 *noisy music* LOUD, fortissimo, blaring, booming, overloud, deafening, thunderous, tumultuous, clamorous, ear-splitting, piercing, strident, cacophonous, raucous. ANTONYM soft.

nomad noun *a photojournalist who lived with a clan of nomads for six months* ITINERANT, traveler, migrant, wanderer, roamer, rover; gypsy, Bedouin; transient, drifter, vagabond, vagrant, tramp.

nominal adjective **1** *the nominal head of the campaign* IN NAME ONLY, titular, formal, official; theoretical, supposed, ostensible, so-called. ANTONYM real.

2 *a nominal rent* TOKEN, symbolic; tiny, minute, minimal, small, insignificant, trifling; *informal* minuscule, piddling, piffling. ANTONYM considerable.

nominate verb **1** *you may nominate a candidate* PROPOSE, recommend, suggest, name, put forward, present, submit.

2 *he nominated his assistant* APPOINT, select, choose, elect, commission, designate, name, delegate.

nominee noun *we'll hold a Q & A session with the nominees on Monday evening* CANDIDATE, contender, contestant, prospect, runner, choice, possibility.

no-name noun *on that team I was just a no-name* NOBODY, nonentity, zero, nonperson, insignificant person.

▸ adjective *a no-name product* UNBRANDED, generic, nonproprietary.

nonbeliever noun *her family condemned her for marrying a nonbeliever* UNBELIEVER, disbeliever, skeptic, doubter, doubting Thomas, cynic, nihilist; atheist, agnostic, freethinker; infidel, pagan, heathen.

nonce PHRASE: **for the nonce** *for the nonce, I'll be the acting chairman* FOR THE TIME BEING, temporarily, pro tem, for now, for the moment, for the interim, for a while, for the present, in the meantime; provisionally.

nonchalant adjective *she acts nonchalant, but I think she's quite nervous* CALM, composed, unconcerned, cool, [calm, cool, and collected], cool as a cucumber; indifferent, blasé, dispassionate, apathetic, casual, insouciant; *informal* laid-back. ANTONYM anxious.

noncommittal adjective *please advise your client that this court expects something more substantial than a string of noncommittal responses* EVASIVE, equivocal, guarded, circumspect, reserved; discreet, uncommunicative, tactful, diplomatic, vague; *informal* cagey. PHRASE: **be noncommittal** *he was noncommittal about their chances of success* EQUIVOCATE, give nothing away, dodge the issue, sidestep the issue, hedge, pussyfoot around, beat around the bush, temporize, shilly-shally, vacillate, waver; hem and haw; *informal* duck the question, sit on the fence.

non compos mentis adjective See INSANE sense 1.

nonconformist noun *our college has the reputation of being a haven for nonconformists* DISSENTER, dissentient, protester, rebel, renegade, schismatic; freethinker, apostate, heretic; individualist, free spirit, maverick, eccentric, original, deviant, misfit, dropout, outsider, Bohemian.

nondescript adjective *he was of average height and build, and even his clothes were nondescript* UNDISTINGUISHED, unremarkable, unexceptional, featureless, characterless, faceless, unmemorable, lackluster; ordinary, commonplace, average, run-of-the-mill, mundane, garden-variety; uninteresting, uninspiring, colorless, bland, dull. ANTONYM distinctive.

nondrinker noun *Irene's been a nondrinker ever since the drunk-driving incident* TEETOTALER, abstainer; recovering alcoholic; dry, prohibitionist.

none pronoun **1** *none of the fish are unusual* NOT ONE, not a (single) one. ANTONYM all.

2 *none of this concerns me* NO PART, not a bit, not any. ANTONYM all.

3 *none can know better than you* NOT ONE, no one, nobody, not a soul, not a single person, no man. ANTONYM all.

PHRASE: **none the ——** *we were left none the wiser* NOT AT ALL, not a bit, not the slightest bit, in no way, by no means any.

nonentity noun *the tragedy is that, even after all the therapy we can provide, many of these kids will continue to be the nonentities that they've been taught to be* NOBODY, unimportant person, zero, nonperson, no-name, nothing, small fry, mediocrity; *informal* no-hoper, loser. ANTONYM celebrity.

nonessential adjective *nonessential items such as colognes and cosmetics are not permitted* UNNECESSARY, inessential, unessential, noncore, needless, unneeded, superfluous, uncalled for, redundant, dispensable, expendable, unimportant, extraneous.

nonetheless adverb *I doubt you have much to add—nonetheless, we want to hear your side of the story* NEVERTHELESS, even so, however, but, still, yet, though; in spite of that, despite that, be that as it may, for all that, that said, just the same, all the same; notwithstanding, regardless, anyway, anyhow, still and all.

nonexistent adjective *studio honchos would feed the press stories of the nonexistent guy-girl romances of their homosexual stars* IMAGINARY, imagined, unreal, fictional, fictitious, made up, invented, fanciful; fantastic, mythical; illusory, hallucinatory, chimerical, notional, shadowy, insubstantial; missing, absent; *literary* illusive. ANTONYM real.

nonintervention noun *a policy of nonintervention is not appropriate when the fundamental freedoms of others are in jeopardy and their very lives at risk* LAISSEZ-FAIRE, nonparticipation, noninterference, inaction, passivity, neutrality; live and let live.

nonobservance noun *we take the nonobservance of curfew very seriously* INFRINGEMENT, breach, violation, contravention, transgression, noncompliance, infraction; dereliction, neglect.

no-nonsense adjective *we like your no-nonsense approach* STRAIGHTFORWARD, forthright, upfront, pragmatic, down-to-earth, down-to-business, matter-of-fact.

nonpareil adjective *a nonpareil storyteller* INCOMPARABLE, matchless, unrivaled, unparalleled, unequaled, peerless, beyond compare, second to none, unsurpassed, unbeatable, inimitable; unique, consummate, superlative, supreme; *formal* unexampled. ANTONYM mediocre.

▸ noun *without a doubt, theirs is the nonpareil* BEST, finest, crème de la crème, peak of perfection, elite, jewel in the crown, ne plus ultra, paragon; *archaic* nonesuch.

nonpartisan adjective *the moderator must remain nonpartisan throughout the debates* UNBIASED, impartial, neutral, objective.

nonplussed verb **1** *Nick was nonplussed by the suggestion that he'd acted unkindly* SURPRISED, stunned, dumbfounded, confounded, taken aback, disconcerted, thrown, thrown off balance; puzzled, perplexed, mystified, baffled, bemused, bewildered; *informal* fazed, flummoxed, stumped, bamboozled, discombobulated.

2 *Tex remained nonplussed throughout the scandal* UNPERTURBED, unruffled, unfazed, composed.

USAGE NOTE **nonplussed**

In standard use, **nonplussed** means 'surprised and confused': *the hostility of the new neighbor's refusal left Mrs. Walker nonplussed.* In American English, a new use has developed in recent years, meaning 'unperturbed'—more or less the opposite of its traditional meaning: *hoping to disguise his confusion, he tried to appear nonplussed.* This new use probably arose on the assumption that **non-** was the normal negative prefix and must therefore have a negative meaning. Although the use is common, it is not yet considered standard. Note that the correct spelling is *nonplussed*, not *nonplused.*

nonsense noun **1** *that's a lot of damn nonsense* RUBBISH, gibberish, claptrap, balderdash, blarney; *informal* hogwash, baloney, rot, moonshine, garbage, jive, tripe, drivel, bilge, bull, guff, bunk, bosh, BS, eyewash, piffle, poppycock, phooey, hooey, malarkey, hokum, twaddle, gobbledygook, codswallop, flapdoodle, hot air; *dated* bunkum, tommyrot; *vulgar slang* bullshit, crap. ANTONYM (good) sense.

2 *she stands no nonsense* MISCHIEF, naughtiness, bad behavior, misbehavior, misconduct, misdemeanor; pranks, tricks, clowning, buffoonery, funny business; *informal* tomfoolery, monkey business, shenanigans, hanky-panky. ANTONYM good behavior.

3 *they dismissed the concept as nonsense* ABSURDITY, folly, stupidity, ludicrousness, inanity, foolishness, idiocy, insanity, madness. ANTONYMS (good) sense, wisdom.

▸ exclamation *"Nonsense!" she retorted* RUBBISH, balderdash; *informal* no way, get out of here, get real, phooey, puh-leeze, hooey, poppycock, come off it, like hell; *dated* pshaw.

THE RIGHT WORD

If you write or speak in an obscure, senseless, or unintelligible manner, you'll probably be accused of producing **nonsense**. It is the most general of these nouns and may refer to behavior as well as to what is said (*the demonstrators were told in no uncertain terms to stop this nonsense or leave the room*). **Twaddle** refers to silly, empty utterances from people who know nothing about a subject but who write or talk about it anyway (*I was sick of her twaddle about the dangers of electromagnetic fields*). **Bunk** (short for bunkum) applies to an utterance that strikes the popular fancy even though it is lacking in worth or substance (*the speech, which received enthusiastic applause, was pure bunk*). **Poppycock** applies to nonsense that is full of complex, confused, or clichéd ideas (*the report was a strange combination of logical thinking and outright poppycock*). **Bull** is a slang term for deceitful and often boastful writing or speech (*he gave them a line of bull*). Perhaps the most insulting of these terms is **drivel**, which implies a steady flow of inane, idle, or nonsensical speech or writing similar to what might be expected from a very young child or an idiot (*his first novel was full of romantic drivel*).

nonsensical adjective **1** *her nonsensical way of talking* MEANINGLESS, senseless, illogical. ANTONYMS logical, rational.

2 *a nonsensical generalization* FOOLISH, insane, stupid, idiotic, illogical, irrational, senseless, absurd, silly, inane, harebrained, ridiculous, ludicrous, preposterous; *informal* crazy, crackpot, nutty; daft. ANTONYMS sane, sensible.

nonstop adjective *nonstop entertainment* CONTINUOUS, constant, continual, perpetual, incessant, unceasing, ceaseless, endless, uninterrupted, round-the-clock; unremitting, relentless, persistent, never-ending. ANTONYM occasional.

▸ adverb *we worked nonstop* CONTINUOUSLY, continually, incessantly, unceasingly, ceaselessly, all the time, constantly, perpetually, around/round the clock, day and night, steadily, relentlessly, persistently; *informal* 24-7. ANTONYM occasionally.

nonviolent adjective *a nonviolent demonstration* PEACEFUL, peaceable, orderly, well-behaved.

noodle noun *overcooked noodles.* See table on page 613.

nook noun *the children's library has cozy nooks for quiet reading* RECESS, corner, alcove, niche, cranny, bay, inglenook, cavity, cubbyhole, pigeonhole; opening, gap, aperture; hideaway, hiding place, hideout, shelter.

noon noun *the bank closes at noon* MIDDAY, twelve o'clock, twelve hundred hours, twelve noon, high noon, noon hour, noonday; *literary* noontime, noontide.

no one pronoun *no one shed a tear when he was fired* NOBODY, not a soul, not anyone, not a single person, never a one, none.

norm noun **1** *norms of diplomatic behavior* CONVEN-

TION, standard; criterion, yardstick, benchmark, touchstone, rule, formula, pattern, guide, guideline, model, exemplar.

2 *such teams are now **the norm*** STANDARD, usual, the rule; normal, typical, average, unexceptional, par for the course, expected.

normal adjective **1** *they issue books in the normal way* USUAL, standard, ordinary, customary, conventional, habitual, accustomed, expected, wonted; typical, stock, common, everyday, regular, routine, established, set, fixed, traditional, time-honored. ANTONYM unusual.

2 *a normal couple* ORDINARY, average, typical, run-of-the-mill, middle-of-the-road, common, conventional, mainstream, unremarkable, unexceptional, garden-variety, a dime a dozen.

THE RIGHT WORD

Most of us want to be regarded as **normal**, an adjective that implies conformity with established norms or standards and is the opposite of abnormal (*a normal body temperature; normal intelligence*). **Regular**, like *normal*, is usually preferred to its opposite (irregular) and implies conformity to prescribed standards or established patterns (*their regular monthly meeting; a regular guy*), but *normal* carries stronger connotations of conformity within prescribed limits and sometimes allows for a wider range of differences. Few of us think of ourselves as **ordinary**, a term used to describe what is commonplace or unexceptional (*an ordinary person wearing ordinary clothes*), although many people are ordinary in some ways and extraordinary in others. **Average** also implies conformity with what is regarded as normal or ordinary (*a woman of average height*), although it tends to emphasize the middle ground and to exclude both positive and negative extremes. **Typical** applies to persons or things possessing the representative characteristics of a type or class (*a typical teenager*). Someone or something described as **natural** behaves or operates in accordance with an inherent nature or character (*his fears were natural for one so young*), while **usual** applies to that which conforms to common or ordinary use or occurrence (*we paid the usual price*).

normality noun *after a season of elections, it takes some time to return to normality* NORMALCY, business as usual, the daily round; routine, order, regularity.

normally adverb **1** *she wanted to walk normally* NATURALLY, conventionally, ordinarily; as usual, as normal.

2 *normally we'd keep quiet about this* USUALLY, ordinarily, as a rule, generally, in general, mostly, for the most part, by and large, mainly, most of the time, on the whole; typically, customarily, traditionally.

north adjective *the north winds can be brutal* NORTHERN, northerly, polar, Arctic, boreal.

nose noun **1** *a punch on the nose* snout, muzzle, proboscis, trunk; *informal* beak, snoot, schnoz, schnozzola, sniffer, honker.

2 *a nose for scandal* INSTINCT, feeling, sixth sense, intuition, insight, perception.

3 *wine with a fruity nose* SMELL, bouquet, aroma, fragrance, perfume, scent, odor.

4 *the plane's nose dipped* nose cone, bow, prow, front end.

▸ verb **1** *the dog nosed the ball* NUZZLE, nudge, push.

2 *she's **nosing into** my business* PRY INTO, inquire about/into, poke around/about, interfere in/with, meddle in/with; be a busybody about, stick/poke one's nose in/into; *informal* be nosy about, snoop around/into.

3 *he nosed the car into the traffic* EASE, inch, edge, move, maneuver, steer, guide.

PHRASES: **by a nose** *Harris won the third race by a nose* JUST, only just, barely, narrowly, by a hair's breadth, by the skin of one's teeth, by a whisker. **nose around/about** *you check the bedrooms and we'll nose around the kitchen* INVESTIGATE, explore, ferret around/through, rummage around/through, search; delve into, peer into; prowl around; *informal* snoop around/about. **nose out** *a team of trained dogs help us to nose out the armed passengers* DETECT, find, discover, bring to light, track down, dig up, ferret out, root out, uncover, unearth, sniff out. **on the nose** *informal the plane landed at 7:15 on the nose* EXACTLY, precisely, sharp, on the dot, on the button, promptly, prompt, dead on, bang on.

nosedive noun **1** *the plane went into a nosedive* DIVE, descent, drop, plunge, plummet, fall. ANTONYM climb.

2 *informal the dollar took a nosedive* FALL, drop, plunge, plummet, tumble, decline, slump; *informal* crash.

▸ verb **1** *the device nosedived to earth* DIVE, plunge, pitch, drop, plummet.

2 *informal costs have nosedived* FALL, take a header, drop, sink, plunge, plummet, tumble, slump, go down, decline; *informal* crash. ANTONYMS soar, rise.

nosh *informal* noun *all kinds of nosh.* See FOOD sense 1.

▸ verb *they noshed on smoked salmon.* See EAT sense 1.

nostalgia noun *a nostalgia for traditional values* REMINISCENCE, remembrance, recollection; wistfulness, regret, sentimentality; homesickness.

nostalgic adjective *music that evokes nostalgic memories of our youth* WISTFUL, evocative, romantic, sentimental; dewy-eyed, misty-eyed, maudlin; homesick.

nostrum noun **1** *they have to prove their nostrums work* MEDICINE, patent medicine, potion, elixir, panacea, cure-all, wonder drug, quack remedy; *informal* magic bullet.

2 *right-wing nostrums* MAGIC FORMULA, recipe for success, remedy, cure, prescription, answer.

nosy adjective *informal the nosy guy next door is always peeking out through the curtains* PRYING, inquisitive, curious, spying, eavesdropping, intrusive; *informal* snooping, snoopy.

NOODLES

bean curd	mung bean
bean thread	naeng myun
cellophane	pirogi
chasoba	quenelle
chow fun	ramen
dang myun	rice
dumpling	rice sheet
e-fu	rice stick
egg	rice vermicelli
farfel	Sevian
glass	shirataki
gooksu	soba
harusame	somen
Hokkien	spaetzle
knodel	udon
kreplach	wheat
lo mein	won ton
mei fun	

See also table at PASTA.

notable adjective 1 *notable examples of workmanship* NOTEWORTHY, remarkable, outstanding, important, significant, momentous, memorable; marked, striking, impressive; uncommon, unusual, special, exceptional, signal. ANTONYMS unremarkable, insignificant.

2 *a notable author* PROMINENT, important, well-known, famous, affluential, famed, noted, distinguished, great, eminent, illustrious, respected, esteemed, renowned, celebrated, acclaimed, influential, prestigious, of note. ANTONYMS obscure, unknown.

▸ noun *movie stars and other notables* CELEBRITY, public figure, VIP, personage, notability, dignitary, worthy, luminary; star, superstar, icon, name, big name; *informal* celeb, somebody, bigwig, big shot, big cheese, big fish, megastar, big kahuna, high muckamuck. ANTONYMS nonentity, no-name.

notably adverb *these are notably short-lived birds* REMARKABLY, especially, specially, very, extremely, exceptionally, singularly, particularly, peculiarly, distinctly, significantly, unusually, extraordinarily, strikingly, uncommonly, incredibly, really, decidedly, surprisingly, conspicuously; in particular, primarily, principally.

notation noun 1 *algebraic notation* SYMBOLS, alphabet, syllabary, script; code, cipher, hieroglyphics.

2 *notations in the margin* ANNOTATION, jotting, comment, footnote, entry, memo, gloss, explanation.

notch noun 1 *a notch in the end of the arrow* NICK, cut, incision, score, scratch, slit, slot, groove, cleft, indentation.

2 *her opinion of Nick dropped a notch* DEGREE, level, rung, point, mark, measure, grade.

▸ verb *notch the plank* NICK, cut, score, incise, carve, scratch, slit, gouge, groove, furrow.

note noun 1 *a note in her diary* RECORD, entry, item, notation, jotting, memorandum, reminder, aide-mémoire; *informal* memo.

2 **(notes)** *his notes were read at the next meeting* MINUTES, records, details; report, account, commentary, transcript, proceedings, transactions; synopsis, summary, outline.

3 *notes in the margins* ANNOTATION, footnote, commentary, comment; marginalia, exegesis.

4 *he dropped me a note* MESSAGE, communication, letter, line; *formal* epistle, missive.

5 *this note is legal tender* BILL; banknote; **(notes)** paper money.

6 *this is worthy of note* ATTENTION, consideration, notice, heed, observation, regard.

7 *a composer of note* DISTINCTION, importance, eminence, prestige, fame, celebrity, acclaim, renown, repute, stature, standing, consequence, account.

8 *a note of hopelessness in her voice* TONE, intonation, inflection, sound; hint, indication, sign, element, suggestion.

▸ verb 1 *we will note your suggestion* BEAR IN MIND, be mindful of, consider, observe, heed, take notice of, pay attention to, take in.

2 *the letter noted the ministers' concern* MENTION, refer to, touch on, indicate, point out, make known, state.

3 *note the date in your diary* WRITE DOWN, put down, jot down, take down, inscribe, enter, mark, record, register, pencil (in).

notebook noun *a new notebook for French class* NOTEPAD, scratch pad, exercise book, workbook, memo pad, tablet, writing tablet; register, logbook, log, diary, daybook, journal, record.

noted adjective *a noted authority on the boll weevil* RENOWNED, well-known, famous, famed, prominent, celebrated; notable, of note, important, eminent, distinguished, illustrious, acclaimed, esteemed; of distinction, of repute. ANTONYM unknown.

noteworthy adjective *her work in the field of anthropology is noteworthy* NOTABLE, interesting, significant, important; remarkable, impressive, striking, outstanding, memorable, unique, special; unusual, extraordinary, singular, rare. ANTONYM unexceptional.

nothing noun 1 *all my efforts add up to nothing* NOT A THING, not anything, nil, zero, naught/nought; *informal* zilch, zip, nada, diddly-squat, squat. ANTONYM something.

2 *forget it—it's nothing* A TRIFLING MATTER, a trifle; neither here nor there; *informal* no big deal.

3 *he treats her as a nothing* NOBODY, unimportant person, nonentity, no-name, nonperson. ANTONYM celebrity.

4 *the share value fell to nothing* ZERO, naught/nought, 0; *Tennis* love. PHRASES: **be/have nothing to do with** 1 *it has nothing to do with you* BE UNCONNECTED WITH, be unrelated to, not concern; be irrelevant to, be inapplicable to, be inapposite to. 2 *I'll have nothing to do with him* AVOID, shun, ignore, have no contact with, steer clear of, give a wide berth to. **for nothing** 1 *she hosted the show for nothing* FREE, free of charge, gratis, without charge, at no cost; *informal* for free, on the house. 2 *all this trouble for nothing* IN VAIN, to no avail, to no purpose, with no result, needlessly, pointlessly. **nothing but** *he's nothing but a nuisance* MERELY, only, just, solely, simply, purely, no more than.

nothingness noun 1 *the nothingness of death* OBLIVION, nullity, blankness; void, vacuum; *rare* nihility.

2 *the nothingness of it all overwhelmed him* UNIMPORTANCE, insignificance, triviality, pointlessness, uselessness, worthlessness.

notice noun 1 *nothing escaped his notice* ATTENTION, observation, awareness, consciousness, perception; regard, consideration, scrutiny; watchfulness, vigilance, attentiveness.

2 *a notice on the wall* POSTER, bill, handbill, advertisement, announcement, bulletin; flyer, leaflet, pamphlet; sign, card; *informal* ad.

3 *show times may change without notice* NOTIFICATION, warning, advance warning, announcement; information, news, communication, word.

4 *I handed in my notice* RESIGNATION.

5 *the play got bad notices* REVIEW, write-up, critique, criticism.

▸ verb *I noticed that the door was open* OBSERVE, perceive, note, see, discern, detect, spot, distinguish, mark, remark, descry; *literary* behold. ANTONYM overlook.

PHRASE: **take no notice of** *he took no notice of anything I said* IGNORE, pay no attention to, disregard, pay no heed to, take no account of, brush aside, shrug off, turn a blind eye to, pass over, let go, overlook; look the other way (from).

noticeable adjective *a fresh coat of paint will make a noticeable difference* DISTINCT, evident, obvious, apparent, manifest, patent, plain, clear, marked, conspicuous, front-and-center, unmistakable, undeniable, pronounced, prominent, striking, arresting; perceptible, discernible, detectable, observable, visible, appreciable.

THE RIGHT WORD

A scratch on someone's face might be **noticeable**, while a scar that runs from cheekbone to chin would be **conspicuous**. When it comes to describing the things that attract our attention, *noticeable* means readily noticed or unlikely to escape observation (*a noticeable facial tic; a noticeable aversion to cocktail parties*), while *conspicuous* implies that the eye (or mind) cannot miss it (*her absence was conspicuous*). Use **prominent** when you want to describe something that literally or figuratively stands out from its background (*a prominent nose; a prominent position on the committee*). It can also apply to persons or things that stand out so clearly they are generally known or recognized (*a prominent citizen*). Someone or something that is **outstanding** rises above or beyond others and is usually superior to them (*an outstanding student*). **Remarkable** applies to anything that is noticeable because it is extraordinary or exceptional (*remarkable blue eyes*). **Striking** is an even stronger word, used to describe something so out of the ordinary that it makes a deep and powerful impression on the observer's mind or vision (*a striking young woman over six feet tall*).

notification noun **1** *the notification of the victim's wife* INFORMING, telling, alerting, filling in.

2 *she received notification that he was on the way* INFORMATION, word, advice, news, intelligence; communication, message; *literary* tidings.

notify verb *we will notify you as soon as possible* INFORM, tell, advise, brief, apprise, let someone know, put in the picture, fill in; alert, warn.

notion noun **1** *he had a notion that something was wrong* IDEA, belief, conviction, opinion, view, thought, impression, perception; hypothesis, theory; feeling, funny feeling, suspicion, sneaking suspicion, hunch. See note at IDEA.

2 *Claire had no notion of what he meant* UNDERSTANDING, idea, awareness, knowledge, clue, inkling.

3 *he got a notion to return* IMPULSE, inclination, whim, desire, wish; *dated* fancy.

notional adjective *the notional line between East and West* HYPOTHETICAL, theoretical, speculative, conjectural, suppositional, putative, conceptual; imaginary, fanciful, unreal, illusory. ANTONYM actual.

notoriety noun *his undeserved notoriety* INFAMY, disrepute, ill repute, bad name, dishonor, discredit; *dated* ill fame.

notorious adjective *a notorious gunman of the Old West* INFAMOUS, scandalous; well known, famous, famed, legendary.

notwithstanding preposition *notwithstanding his workload, he is a dedicated father* DESPITE, in spite of, regardless of, for all.

▸ adverb *she is bright and ambitious—notwithstanding, she is now jobless* NEVERTHELESS, nonetheless, even so, all the same, in spite of this, despite this, however, still, yet, that said, just the same, anyway, in any event, at any rate.

▸ conjunction ***notwithstanding that*** *the rain was torrential, they played on* ALTHOUGH, even though, though, in spite of the fact that, despite the fact that.

nought noun. See NAUGHT.

nourish verb **1** *patients must be well nourished* FEED, provide for, sustain, maintain.

2 *we nourish the talents of children* ENCOURAGE, promote, foster, nurture, cultivate, stimulate, boost, advance, assist, help, aid, strengthen, enrich.

3 *the hopes Emma nourished* CHERISH, nurture, foster, harbor, nurse, entertain, maintain, hold, have.

nourishing adjective *a nourishing snack* NUTRITIOUS, nutritive, wholesome, good for one, healthy, health-giving, healthful, beneficial, sustaining. ANTONYM unhealthy.

nourishment noun FOOD, sustenance, nutriment, nutrition, subsistence, provisions, provender, fare; *informal* grub, nosh, chow, eats, vittles, scoff, chuck; *formal* comestibles; *dated* victuals.

nouveau riche plural noun *we appeal to the nouveau riche for much of our funding* new rich, parvenus, arrivistes, upstarts, social climbers, vulgarians.

novel[1] noun *curl up with a good novel* BOOK, paperback, hardcover; STORY, tale, narrative, romance, roman à clef; piece of fiction; best seller, blockbuster; potboiler, pulp (fiction).

novel[2] adjective *a novel way of making money* NEW, original, unusual, unfamiliar, unconventional, unorthodox; different, fresh, imaginative, innovative, innovatory, inventive, modern, neoteric, avant-garde, pioneering, groundbreaking, revolutionary; rare, unique, singular, unprecedented; experimental, untested, untried; strange, exotic, newfangled. ANTONYM traditional.

WORD NOTE **novel**

Novel manages to pack into five positive letters what *unusual, unprecedented, unfamiliar, unconventional, untested, untried, unknown,* and *unorthodox* have to signal with unwieldy and negative *un-* prefixes. Why use a negative-looking word for a positive thing when *novel* is so tidily neat and comes without a whiff of disapproval? **—EM**

novelist noun *Kafka was a Czech novelist who wrote in German* WRITER, author, fictionist, man/woman of letters, scribe; *informal* penman, scribbler.

novelty noun **1** *the novelty of our approach* ORIGINALITY, newness, freshness, unconventionality, unfamiliarity; difference, imaginativeness, creativity, innovation, modernity.

2 *we sell seasonal novelties* KNICKKNACK, trinket, bauble, toy, trifle, gewgaw, gimcrack, ornament, kickshaw.

novice noun **1** *a five-day course for novices* BEGINNER, learner, neophyte, newcomer, initiate, tyro, fledgling; apprentice, trainee, probationer, student, pupil, tenderfoot; *informal* rookie, newbie, greenhorn. ANTONYMS expert, veteran.

2 *a novice who was never ordained* NEOPHYTE, novitiate; postulant, proselyte, catechumen.

THE RIGHT WORD

All of these nouns are used to describe someone who has not yet acquired the skills and experience needed to qualify for a trade, a career, a profession, or a sphere of life.

Beginner is the most general and informal term, used to describe someone who has begun to acquire the necessary skills but has not yet mastered them (*violin lessons for beginners*). An **apprentice** is also a beginner, usually a young person, who is serving under a more experienced master or teacher to learn the skills of a trade or profession (*an apprentice to one of the great Renaissance painters*); in a broad sense, *apprentice* refers to any beginner whose efforts are unpolished. **Novice** implies that the person lacks training and experience (*a novice when it came to writing fiction*), while **neophyte** is a less negative term, suggesting that the person is eagerly learning the ways, methods, or principles of something (*he was a neophyte at this type of sailing*). A **probationer** is a beginner who is undergoing a trial period, during which he or she must prove an aptitude for a certain type of work or life (*she was a lowly probationer, with no privileges or status*).

---

novitiate noun **1** *his novitiate lasts a year* PROBATIONARY PERIOD, probation, trial period, test period, apprenticeship, training period, traineeship, training, initiation.

2 *two young novitiates* NOVICE, neophyte; postulant, proselyte, catechumen.

now adverb **1** *I'm extremely busy now* AT THE MOMENT, at present, at the present (time/moment), at this moment in time, currently, presently.

2 *television is now the main source of news* NOWADAYS, today, these days, in this day and age; in the present climate.

3 *you must leave now* AT ONCE, straightaway, right away, right now, this minute, this instant, immediately, instantly, directly, without further ado, promptly, without delay, as soon as possible; *informal* pronto, straight off, ASAP.

PHRASES: **as of now** *as of now, cigarettes are banned in this house* FROM THIS TIME ON, from now on, henceforth, from this day forward, in (the) future; *formal* hereafter. **for now** *for now, we'll just have salad* FOR THE TIME BEING, for the moment, for the present, for the meantime, for the nonce. **not now** *I promise I will, but not now* LATER, later on, sometime, one day, some day, one of these days, sooner or later, in due course, by and by, eventually, ultimately. **now and again** *now and again, we like to visit the gallery* OCCASIONALLY, now and then, from time to time, sometimes, every so often, (every) now and again, at times, on occasion(s), (every) once in a while; periodically, once in a blue moon.

nowadays adverb *nowadays, it seems as if everyone is obsessed with staying young* THESE DAYS, today, at the present time, in these times, in this day and age, now, currently, at the moment, at present, at this moment in time; in the present climate, presently.

nowhere PHRASE: **in the middle of nowhere** *I wasn't born in the middle of nowhere, you know* BACK OF BEYOND, rural areas, backwoods, hinterland, bush, backcountry; *informal* sticks, boondocks, boonies; *Austral.* outback.

noxious adjective *noxious fumes* POISONOUS, toxic, deadly, harmful, dangerous, pernicious, damaging, destructive; unpleasant, nasty, disgusting, awful, dreadful, horrible, terrible; vile, revolting, foul, nauseating, appalling, offensive; malodorous, fetid, putrid; *informal* ghastly, horrid; *literary* noisome. ANTONYM innocuous.

nuance noun *the nuances of light are very effective* FINE DISTINCTION, subtle difference; shade, shading, gradation, variation, degree; subtlety, nicety, overtone.

nub noun *the nub of the argument* CRUX, central point,

now
forthwith
instanter
without delay
quickly
with all speed
then and there
there and then
here and now
without further/more ado
in/like a flash
before you can say Jack Robinson
on the spot
double quick
in double quick time
pronto
tout de suite
straight off
toot sweet
lickety-split
this (very) minute
this instant
asap
as soon as possible
pdq
pretty damn quick
as quickly as possible
promptly
at once
straight away
right away
right now
directly
sooner rather than later
in short order

next

by and by
in a while
after a bit
sooner or later
in time
in due course
following this/that
at a later time
at a later date
in the future
in time to come
at a future time/date
at some point in the future
later on
after this/that
some day
one day
one of these days
one of these fine days
eventually
at some time in the future
at some point in the future
at a future time/date
in the fullness of time
in the long run
in the end
at the end of the day
when all is said and done
subsequently
afterwards
eventually
finally
ultimately
later

main point, core, heart, heart of the matter, nucleus, essence, quintessence, kernel, marrow, meat, pith; gist, substance; *informal* nitty-gritty.

nubile adjective *tempted by Frankie's nubile girlfriend* SEXUALLY MATURE; sexually attractive, desirable, sexy, luscious; marriageable; *informal* beddable.

nucleus noun *the nucleus of the international banking world* CORE, center, central part, heart, nub, hub, middle, eye, focus, focal point, pivot, crux.

nude adjective NAKED, stark naked, bare, unclothed, undressed, disrobed, stripped, unclad, au naturel, without a stitch on, in one's birthday suit, in the raw, in the altogether, in the buff; *informal* buck-naked, butt-naked, mother-naked. See note at NAKED. ANTONYM clothed.

nudge verb **1** *he nudged Ben* POKE, elbow, dig, prod, jog, jab.

2 *the canoe nudged a bank* TOUCH, bump (against), push (against), run into.

3 *we nudged them into action* PROMPT, encourage, stimulate, prod, galvanize.

4 *unemployment was nudging 3,000,000* APPROACH, near, come close to, be verging on, border on.

▸ noun **1** *Maggie gave him a nudge* POKE, prod, jog, jab, push, dig (in the ribs).

2 *after a nudge, she remembered Lillian* REMINDER, prompt, prompting, prod, encouragement.

nudity noun *there was one brief moment of nudity* NAKEDNESS, bareness, state of undress, undress; *informal* one's birthday suit.

nugatory adjective **1** *a nugatory observation* WORTHLESS, unimportant, inconsequential, valueless, trifling, trivial, insignificant, meaningless.

2 *the shortages will render our hopes nugatory* FUTILE, useless, vain, unavailing, null, invalid.

nugget noun *a nugget of gold | doughy nuggets in the stew* LUMP, nub, chunk, piece, hunk, wad, gobbet; *informal* gob.

nuisance noun *I find these long journeys a nuisance* ANNOYANCE, inconvenience, bore, bother, irritation, problem, trouble, trial, burden; pest, plague, thorn in one's side/flesh; *informal* pain, pain in the neck, hassle, bind, drag, chore, aggravation, headache, nudnik. ANTONYM blessing.

nuke verb *informal* **1** *they nuked the enemy* BOMB, bombard, attack, destroy, demolish, flatten; shell, torpedo, blow up.

2 *she nuked the leftovers for five minutes* MICROWAVE, reheat, warm, cook; irradiate; zap.

null adjective *their marriage was declared null* INVALID, null and void, void; annulled, nullified, canceled, revoked. ANTONYM valid.

nullify verb **1** *they nullified the legislation* ANNUL, render null and void, void, invalidate; repeal, reverse, rescind, revoke, disallow, cancel, abolish; countermand, do away with, terminate, quash; *Law* vacate; *formal* abrogate. See note at VOID. ANTONYM ratify.

2 *the costs would nullify any tax relief* CANCEL OUT, neutralize, negate, negative.

numb adjective *his fingers were numb* WITHOUT SENSATION, without feeling, numbed, benumbed, desensitized, insensible, senseless, unfeeling; anesthetized; dazed, stunned, stupefied, paralyzed, immobilized, frozen. ANTONYM sensitive.

▸ verb *the cold numbed her senses* DEADEN, benumb, desensitize, dull; anesthetize; daze, stupefy, paralyze, immobilize, freeze. ANTONYM sensitize.

number noun **1** *a whole number* NUMERAL, integer, figure, digit; character, symbol; decimal, unit; cardinal number, ordinal number.

2 *a large number of complaints* AMOUNT, quantity; total, aggregate, tally; quota.

3 *the wedding of one of their number* GROUP, company, crowd, circle, party, band, crew, set, gang.

4 *the band performed another number* SONG, piece (of music), tune, track; routine, sketch, dance, act.

▸ verb **1** *visitors numbered more than two million* ADD UP TO, amount to, total, come to.

2 *he numbers the fleet at a thousand* CALCULATE, count, total, compute, reckon, tally; assess, tot up; *formal* enumerate.

3 *each paragraph is numbered* assign a number to, mark with a number; itemize, enumerate.

4 *he numbers her among his friends* INCLUDE, count, reckon, deem.

5 *his days are numbered* LIMIT, restrict, fix.

PHRASES: **a number of** *she's collected a number of ashtrays* SEVERAL, various, quite a few, sundry. **without number** *the nights I've worried about those kids is without number* COUNTLESS, innumerable, unlimited, endless, limitless, untold, numberless, uncountable, uncounted; numerous, many, multiple, manifold, legion.

numberless adjective *there are numberless questions to be answered* INNUMERABLE, countless, unlimited, endless, limitless, untold, uncountable, uncounted; numerous, many, multiple, manifold, legion; *informal* more —— than one can shake a stick at; *literary* myriad.

numbing adjective **1** *menthol has a numbing effect* DESENSITIZING, deadening, benumbing, anesthetic, anesthetizing; paralyzing.

2 *numbing cold* FREEZING, raw, bitter, biting, arctic, icy.

3 *numbing boredom* STUPEFYING, mind-numbing, boring, stultifying, soul-destroying; soporific.

numbskull noun *informal* See IDIOT.

numeral noun *your password should have at least one numeral* NUMBER, integer, figure, digit; character, symbol, unit.

numerous adjective *numerous studies have been published on the subject* MANY, very many, a lot of, scores of, countless, numberless, innumerable; several, quite a few, various; plenty of, copious, a quantity of, an abundance of, a profusion of, a multitude of; frequent; *informal* umpteen, lots of, loads of, masses of, stacks of, heaps of, bags of, tons of, oodles of, hundreds of, thousands of, millions of, gazillions of, more —— than one can shake a stick at; *literary* myriad. ANTONYM few.

numinous adjective *the numinous beauty of these ancient relics* SPIRITUAL, religious, divine, holy, sacred; mysterious, otherworldly, unearthly, transcendent.

nun noun *my favorite English teacher was a nun named Sister George* SISTER, abbess, prioress, Mother Superior,

Reverend Mother; novice; bride of Christ, religious, conventual, contemplative, canoness; *literary* vestal; *historical* anchoress.

nuncio noun *Father Mike was in a dither over the nuncio's visit* (PAPAL) AMBASSADOR, legate, envoy, messenger.

nunnery noun *the younger children stayed at a nunnery until the end of the war* CONVENT, priory, abbey, cloister, religious community.

nuptial adjective *our nuptial vows* MATRIMONIAL, marital, marriage, wedding, conjugal, bridal; married, wedded; *literary* connubial; *Law* spousal.

nuptials plural noun *we attended the young duke's nuptials* WEDDING, wedding ceremony, marriage, union; *archaic* espousal.

nurse noun **1** *skilled nurses* CAREGIVER, RN, LPN, nurse practitioner, physician's assistant, health care worker; *informal* Florence Nightingale.

2 *she had been his nurse in childhood* NANNY, nursemaid, governess, au pair, babysitter; wet nurse.

▸ verb **1** *they nursed smallpox patients* CARE FOR, take care of, look after, tend, minister to.

2 *I nursed my sore finger* TREAT, medicate, tend; dress, bandage, soothe, doctor.

3 *Rosa was nursing her baby* BREAST-FEED, suckle, feed; wet-nurse.

4 *they nursed old grievances* HARBOR, foster, entertain, bear, have, hold (on to), cherish, cling to, retain.

nursemaid noun See NURSE noun sense 2.

nurture verb **1** *she nurtured her children into adulthood* BRING UP, care for, take care of, look after, tend, rear, raise, support, foster; parent, mother. ANTONYM neglect.

2 *we nurtured these plants* CULTIVATE, grow, keep, tend.

3 *he nurtured my love of art* ENCOURAGE, promote, stimulate, develop, foster, cultivate, boost, contribute to, assist, help, abet, strengthen, fuel. ANTONYM hinder.

▸ noun **1** *we are what nature and nurture have made us* UPBRINGING, rearing, raising, child care; training, education. ANTONYM nature.

2 *the nurture of ideas* ENCOURAGEMENT, promotion, fostering, development, cultivation.

nut noun **1** *nuts in their shells* kernel, nutmeat. See table.

2 *informal some nut arrived at the office* MANIAC, lunatic, madman, madwoman; eccentric; *informal* loony, nutcase, fruitcake, head case, crank, crackpot, weirdo, screwball, crazy, dingbat, loon.

3 *informal a health nut* ENTHUSIAST, fan, devotee, aficionado; *informal* freak, fiend, fanatic, addict, buff, bum. PHRASE: **off one's nut** *informal*. See MAD sense 1.

nutrition noun *the child was not receiving adequate nutrition* NOURISHMENT, nutriment, nutrients, sustenance, food; *informal* grub, chow, nosh, vittles; *literary* viands; *dated* victuals.

nutritious adjective *a nutritious fruit drink* NOURISHING, good for one, full of nutrients, nutritive, nutritional, wholesome, healthy, healthful, beneficial, sustaining.

nuts adjective *informal* **1** *they thought we were nuts.* See MAD sense 1.

2 *he's **nuts about** her* INFATUATED WITH, devoted to, in love with, smitten with, enamored of, hot for, keen on; *informal* mad about, crazy about, nutty about, wild about, hooked on, gone on.

nuts and bolts plural noun *the nuts and bolts of running an airline* PRACTICAL DETAILS, fundamentals, basics, practicalities, essentials, mechanics, rudiments, ABCs; *informal* nitty-gritty, ins and outs, brass tacks, meat and potatoes.

nutty adjective *informal* **1** *they're all nutty.* See MAD sense 1.

2 *she's **nutty about** Elvis.* See NUTS sense 2.

nuzzle verb **1** *the horse nuzzled at her pocket* NUDGE, nose, prod, push, root.

2 *she **nuzzled up to** her boyfriend* SNUGGLE UP TO, cuddle up to, nestle close to, embrace, hug.

nymph noun **1** *a nymph with winged sandals* SPRITE, sylph, spirit. See note at SPIRIT.

2 *literary a slender nymph with brown eyes* GIRL, belle, nymphet, sylph, ingenue; young woman, young lady; *Scottish* lass; *literary* maid, maiden, damsel.

EDIBLE NUTS AND SEEDS

acorn	filbert
almond	gingko nut
areca nut	hazelnut
beechnut	hickory nut
betel nut	horse chestnut
black walnut	litchi (nut)
Brazil (nut)	macadamia (nut)
breadnut	nutmeg
bunya nut	peanut
butternut	pecan
candlenut	pignoli
cashew (nut)	pignut
chestnut	pine nut
chinquapin/chinkapin	piñon/pinyon (nut)
cobnut	pistachio (nut)
coco de mer	pumpkin seed
coconut	sesame seed
cohune/cahoun (nut)	souari nut
cola/kola nut	Spanish peanut
corozo	sunflower seed
English walnut	walnut

O

oaf noun *the oaf upstairs with his television on full blast* LOUT, boor, barbarian, Neanderthal, churl, bumpkin, yokel; FOOL, dolt, dullard; *informal* idiot, imbecile, moron, halfwit, cretin, ass, jackass, goon, yahoo, ape, baboon, clod, blockhead, meathead, meatball, bonehead, knucklehead, chucklehead, lamebrain, palooka, lug, bozo, boob, chowderhead, lummox, klutz, goofus, doofus, dork, turkey, dingbat; *Brit. informal* twit, nerk, git, yob; *archaic* lubber.

oafish adjective *his oafish brother* STUPID, foolish, idiotic, cretinous; UNGAINLY, loutish, awkward, clumsy, lumbering, apelike, cloddish, Neanderthal, uncouth, uncultured, boorish, rough, coarse, brutish, ill-mannered, unrefined, rough-hewn; *informal* blockheaded, moronic, boneheaded, halfwitted, lamebrained, thickheaded; *archaic* lubberly.

oar noun PADDLE, scull, blade. PHRASE: **put one's oar in/put in one's oar** *sometimes I like to put my oar in and my advice can be a little tactless* MEDDLE, interfere, butt in, intrude, intervene, pry; *informal* poke one's nose in, horn in on, muscle in on, snoop, kibitz.

oasis noun **1** *an oasis near Cairo* WATERING HOLE, watering place, waterhole, spring.

2 *the park is an oasis filled with half a million flowers and thousands of lights* REFUGE, haven, retreat, sanctuary, sanctum, shelter, harbor, asylum.

oath noun **1** *an oath of allegiance* VOW, pledge, sworn statement, promise, avowal, affirmation, word, word of honor, bond, guarantee; *formal* troth.

2 *he uttered a stream of oaths* SWEAR WORD, profanity, expletive, four-letter word, dirty word, obscenity, vulgarity, curse, malediction, blasphemy; *informal* cuss, cuss word; *formal* imprecation. See table.

obdurate adjective *the brass were also obdurate in their opposition to having women in any combat positions* STUBBORN, obstinate, intransigent, inflexible, unyielding, unbending, pigheaded, bullheaded, mulish, stiff-necked; headstrong, unshakable, intractable, unpersuadable, immovable, inexorable, uncompromising, iron-willed, adamant, firm, determined. See note at STUBBORN. ANTONYMS malleable, tractable.

WORD NOTE **obdurate**

Obdurate is a member of that select company of left-handed words that sound better than what they actually mean—highly useful. It fits nicely into the classic tripartite sentence of comparison: "I'm *uncompromising;* you're *obdurate;* he's *pigheaded.*" **—EM**

obedience noun *the party leadership wants blind obedience to their policies* COMPLIANCE, acquiescence, tractability, amenability; DUTIFULNESS, duty, deference, observance of the law/rules; SUBMISSIVENESS, submission, conformity, docility, tameness, subservience, obsequiousness, servility. ANTONYMS disobedience, rebellion

OATHS AND CURSES

arse	fuck it
(*British*) ass	God Almighty
bastard	goddammit
bejesus	gol darn it
bleep	good God
blimey	good Lord
(*British*) bloody hell	heck
(*British*) bosh	hell
brother	hell's bell's
bull	holy crap
bullshit	holy Moses
by Jove	holy shit
Christ	jeez
confound it	jeez Louise
crap	Jesus
crapola	Jesus Christ
crikey	Jesus H. Christ
(*British*) criminy	merde
dadburn it	mother of God
dammit	my ass
damn	phooey
damnation	pish
damn it	piss off
dang	poop
darn	sacre bleu
doggone it	sheesh
drat	shit
durn	shoot
durn it	son of a bitch
fie	son of a gun
for Christ's sake	tarnation
for the love of God	what the hell
fuck	what the Sam Hill

obedient adjective *obviously, you want an obedient dog for security work* COMPLIANT, acquiescent, tractable, amenable; DUTIFUL, good, law-abiding, deferential, respectful, duteous, well trained, well disciplined, manageable, governable; DOCILE, tame, biddable, meek, passive, submissive, unresisting, yielding; malleable, pliable, pliant, subservient, obsequious, servile. ANTONYMS disobedient, rebellious.

THE RIGHT WORD

Children and animals may be expected to obey, but nowadays **obedient** is seldom used to describe adult human beings without a suggestion that they are allowing someone else to assume too great a degree of authority (*are we to believe that Cinderella became the prince's demure, obedient wife?*). The critical note is stronger in **biddable**. A biddable person is excessively meek and ready to obey any instruction, without questioning either its wisdom or the authority of the person giving it (*he could barely think for herself, having been so biddable to his domineering parents*). **Docile** (from Latin *docilis* 'teachable') has similar implications, but in addition to unquestioning obedience it suggests a general reluctance to complain or rebel, even where such behavior would be justified (*employers depended on the regime for a cheap and docile workforce*). **Dutiful** may evoke a sneer, suggesting the virtuous, yet dull (*his dutiful niece spent most of her life caring for him*) or the perfunctory fulfillment of an obligation (*a dutiful postcard to his mother*). One of the oldest (and still living) meanings of **compliant** is 'reshaping under pressure' (*conversion of the gel to a much less compliant glass*). This helps to explain the principal modern sense of the adjective, '(excessively) disposed to agree with others or obey rules' (*compliant legislators loyally followed party policy*). In the computer age a further sense, 'technically compatible,' has developed (*the system is Windows compliant*).

obeisance noun **1** *he made a very formal, elaborate gesture of obeisance* RESPECT, homage, worship, adoration, reverence, veneration, honor, submission, deference. See note at HONOR.

2 *he made a half-bow, half-curtsy, a sort of unisex obeisance* BOW, curtsy, bob, genuflection, salaam; *historical* kowtow.

obelisk noun *an obelisk marks the mass grave where Custer was buried* PILLAR, column, needle, shaft, monolith, monument.

obese adjective *a physician would describe her as a young obese white female* FAT, overweight, corpulent, gross, stout, fleshy, heavy, portly, plump, paunchy, potbellied, beer-bellied, broad in the beam, bulky, bloated, flabby, Falstaffian; *informal* porky, roly-poly, blubbery, pudgy, well-upholstered. ANTONYMS thin, skinny, emaciated.

obesity noun *businesses are developing programs to fight workers' obesity* FATNESS, corpulence, stoutness, portliness, plumpness, chubbiness, rotundity, flabbiness, grossness. ANTONYMS thinness, emaciation.

obey verb **1** *I was honor-bound to obey* DO WHAT SOMEONE SAYS, carry out someone's orders; SUBMIT TO, defer to, bow to, yield to, give in to.

2 *he refused to obey the order* CARRY OUT, perform, act on, execute, discharge, implement, fulfill.

3 *NRA activists point out that criminals don't obey gun laws* COMPLY WITH, adhere to, observe, abide by, act in accordance with, conform to, respect, follow, keep to, stick to.

4 *she wants me to just obey and shut up* FOLLOW ORDERS, do as one's told, play it by the book, toe the line. ANTONYMS disobey, defy, ignore.

obfuscate verb **1** *mere rationalizations to obfuscate rather than clarify the real issue* OBSCURE, confuse, make unclear, blur, muddle, complicate, muddy, cloud, befog. ANTONYM clarify.

2 *her work became more and more obfuscated by mathematics and jargon* BEWILDER, mystify, puzzle, perplex, confuse, baffle, confound, bemuse, befuddle, nonplus; *informal* flummox.

obituary noun *the local paper ran a full-page obituary* DEATH NOTICE, eulogy; *informal* obit; *rare* necrology.

object noun **1** *wooden objects* THING, article, item, device, gadget, entity; *informal* doodad, thingamajig, thingamabob, whatsit, whatchamacallit, thingy, doohickey, dingus.

2 *he spent five years as the object of a frenzied manhunt* TARGET, butt, focus, recipient, victim.

3 *the object was to let everyone have a voice in the decision* OBJECTIVE, aim, goal, target, purpose, end, plan; ambition, design, intent, intention, point, idea.

▸ verb *people attending the meeting* ***objected to*** *nearly every element of the new ordinance* PROTEST (AGAINST), lodge a protest against oppose, raise objections to, express disapproval of, take exception to, take issue with, take a stand against, argue against, quarrel with, condemn, draw the line at, demur at, disapprove of, mind, complain about, cavil at, quibble about; beg to differ with; *informal* kick up a fuss/stink about, kvetch about. ANTONYMS approve, accept.

objection noun *he lodged an official objection with the town council* PROTEST, protestation, demur, demurral, demurrer, complaint, expostulation, grievance, cavil, quibble; OPPOSITION, argument, counterargument, disagreement, disapproval, dissent; *informal* gripe, beef.

objectionable adjective *there is restricted access to objectionable material* UNPLEASANT, offensive, disagreeable, distasteful, displeasing, off-putting, undesirable, obnoxious, unacceptable; NASTY, disgusting, awful, terrible, dreadful, frightful, horrid, appalling, insufferable, intolerable, odious, vile, foul, unsavory, repulsive, repellent, repugnant, revolting, abhorrent, loathsome, hateful, detestable, reprehensible, deplorable; *informal* ghastly, horrible, beastly; *formal* exceptionable, rebarbative. ANTONYMS pleasant, agreeable.

objective adjective **1** *I was hoping to get an objective and pragmatic report* IMPARTIAL, unbiased, unprejudiced, nonpartisan, disinterested, neutral, uninvolved, evenhanded, equitable, fair, fair-minded, just, open-minded, dispassionate, detached, neutral. ANTONYMS biased, partial, prejudiced.

2 *eight objective measurements to track student performance* FACTUAL, actual, real, empirical, evidence-based, verifiable. ANTONYM subjective.

▸ noun *you can't achieve your objectives unless people understand them* AIM, intention, purpose, target, goal, intent, object, end; idea, point, design, plan, ambition, aspiration, desire, hope.

objectively adverb *encourage people to look at the information objectively and see how it will affect them* IMPARTIALLY, without bias, without prejudice, evenhandedly, dispassionately, detachedly, equitably, fairly, justly, open-mindedly, with an open mind. ANTONYMS one-sidedly, with prejudice.

objectivity noun *the quest for total objectivity is unrealistic* IMPARTIALITY, absence/lack of bias, absence/lack of prejudice, fairness, fair-mindedness, neutrality, even-handedness, justice, open-mindedness, disinterest, detachment, dispassion, neutrality.

oblation noun *he poured the first oblation to the household gods* RELIGIOUS OFFERING, offering, sacrifice, peace offering, burnt offering, gift of thanks, first fruits, libation.

obligate verb *signing the agreement does not obligate you to stay through the end of the program* OBLIGE, compel, commit, bind, require, constrain, force, impel.

obligation noun **1** *no obligation may be placed upon you without your consent* DUTY, commitment, responsibility moral imperative; FUNCTION, task, job, assignment, commission, burden, charge, onus, liability, accountability, requirement, debt; *literary* trust.

2 *he felt an obligation to tip well* DUTY, compulsion, indebtedness; duress, necessity, pressure, constraint. PHRASE: **under (an) obligation** *the district attorney is under obligation to investigate | they don't understand that they are under obligation to intervene* BEHOLDEN, obliged, in someone's debt, indebted, obligated, compelled, duty-bound, honor-bound.

obligatory adjective *top hat and tails are obligatory for men* COMPULSORY, mandatory, prescribed, required, demanded, statutory, enforced, binding, incumbent; requisite, necessary, imperative, unavoidable, inescapable, essential. ANTONYMS optional, voluntary.

oblige verb **1** *it was impractical to oblige taxis to carry infant seats* REQUIRE, compel, bind, constrain, obligate, leave with no option but, force. See note at COMPEL.

2 *she was kind enough to oblige* DO SOMEONE A FAVOR, accommodate, help, assist, serve; indulge, humor, gratify someone's wishes.

obliged adjective *if anyone could tell me what's wrong with this file, I'd be obliged* THANKFUL, (most) grateful, (most) appreciative; beholden, indebted, in someone's debt. PHRASE: **much obliged** *I really appreciate the ride—much obliged!* THANK YOU, thanks, many thanks, thanks a lot, thanks (so) very much, thanks so much, thank you kindly; *informal* thanks a million.

obliging adjective *he was obliging enough to carry all the bags* HELPFUL, accommodating, willing, cooperative, considerate, complaisant, agreeable, amenable, generous, kind, neighborly, hospitable, friendly, pleasant, good-natured, amiable, gracious, unselfish, civil, courteous, polite, decent. ANTONYMS inconsiderate, uncooperative.

oblique adjective **1** *an oblique line* SLANTING, slanted, sloping, at an angle, angled, diagonal, aslant, slant, slantwise, skew, askew, cater-cornered, kitty-corner. ANTONYM straight.

2 *an oblique reference to an inside joke* INDIRECT, inexplicit, roundabout, circuitous, circumlocutory, implicit, implied, elliptical, evasive, backhanded. ANTONYMS direct, explicit.

3 *an oblique glance* SIDELONG, sideways, furtive, covert, sly, surreptitious.

obliquely adverb **1** *was the rope, strung across this road obliquely, a real weapon or just a simpleminded booby trap?* DIAGONALLY, at an angle, slantwise, sideways, sidelong, aslant.

2 *she was an embarrassment, someone who could only be spoken of obliquely* INDIRECTLY, in a roundabout way, not in so many words, circuitously, evasively.

obliterate verb **1** *I briefly contemplated trying to obliterate the logo with nail polish remover* ERASE, eradicate, expunge, efface, wipe out, blot out, rub out, block out, remove all traces of.

2 *I want to see the super-turtle obliterate an entire Japanese district in under a minute* DESTROY, wipe out, annihilate, demolish, eliminate, decimate, liquidate, wipe off the face of the earth, wipe off the map; *informal* zap, nuke. ANTONYM create.

3 *she slapped her puff over her face, trying to obliterate it with powder* OBSCURE, hide, conceal, blot out, block (out), cover, screen.

oblivion noun **1** *they drank themselves into oblivion* UNCONSCIOUSNESS, insensibility, a stupor, stupefaction, senselessness; a coma, a blackout; *literary* the waters of Lethe. ANTONYM consciousness.

2 *luckily, he was able to rescue that design from oblivion* OBSCURITY, limbo, anonymity, nonexistence, nothingness, neglect, disregard. ANTONYM fame.

oblivious adjective ***oblivious to*** *the conversation around the table | utterly and happily* ***oblivious of*** *the effect he was having upon his audience* UNAWARE OF, unconscious of, heedless of, unmindful of, insensible of/to, unheeding of, ignorant of, incognizant of, blind to, deaf to, unsuspecting of, unobservant of; INSENSITIVE TO, unconcerned with, impervious to, unaffected by, indifferent to, *informal* clueless. ANTONYMS aware, conscious; sensitive.

WORD NOTE **clueless**

Well before Amy Heckerling used it in transplanting Jane Austen's *Emma* to Beverly Hills, *clueless* was an ingenious upgrade of "doesn't get it." Other weak alternatives include *out of it* and possibly *spacey*, but *clueless* is in a league of its own. From San Francisco: "Favorite variant: after someone says something particularly clueless, you say, 'Cluephone—it's for you!'" **—JS**

obloquy noun **1** *he was able to control the press of New York City, so as to hold me up to obloquy* VILIFICATION, opprobrium, vituperation, condemnation, denunciation, abuse, criticism, censure, defamation, denigration, calumny, insults; *informal* flak; *formal* castigation, excoriation; *archaic* contumely. ANTONYM praise.

2 *there is no moral obloquy connected with getting drunk in Japan* DISGRACE, dishonor, shame, discredit, stigma, humiliation, loss of face, ignominy, odium, opprobrium, disfavor, disrepute, ill repute, infamy, stain, notoriety, scandal. ANTONYM honor.

obnoxious adjective **1** *the gasoline-powered pump made an obnoxious racket* UNPLEASANT, disagreeable, nasty, distasteful, offensive, objectionable, unsavory, unpalatable, off-putting, awful, terrible, dreadful, frightful, revolting, repulsive, repellent, repugnant, disgusting, odious, vile, foul, abhorrent, loathsome, nauseating, sickening, hateful, insufferable, intolerable, detestable, abominable, despicable, contemptible; *informal* horrible, horrid, ghastly, gross, putrid, yucky, godawful, beastly, skanky; *literary* noisome. ANTONYMS delightful, fragrant.

2 *I prayed I could express myself without being obnoxious* ANNOYING, tiresome, irritating; overbearing, bumptious; unpleasant, nasty; *informal* bratty, pesky. ANTONYMS pleasant, charming.

obscene adjective 1 *a vengeful lover sent obscene photos of his former girlfriend to her new partner* PORNOGRAPHIC, INDECENT, smutty, salacious, dirty, filthy, X-rated, explicit, lewd, rude, vulgar, coarse, crude, offensive, immoral, improper, impure, off-color, degenerate, depraved, debauched; lubricious, risqué, erotic, carnal, lascivious, licentious, bawdy; scatological, profane; *informal* blue, porn, porno, skin; *euphemistic* adult. ANTONYMS pure, clean, decent.

2 *I was watching obscene amounts of daytime TV* SHOCKING, scandalous, vile, foul, atrocious, outrageous, heinous, odious, abhorrent, abominable, disgusting, hideous, repugnant, offensive, objectionable, repulsive, revolting, repellent, loathsome, nauseating, sickening, awful, dreadful, terrible, frightful.

obscenity noun 1 *the over-the-top obscenity of the musical interludes* INDECENCY, immorality, impropriety, salaciousness, smuttiness, smut, lewdness, impurity, crudeness, vulgarity, dirtiness, dirt, filth, coarseness, crudity; profanity; eroticism, carnality, lasciviousness, licentiousness.

2 *he attacked, first with obscenities, and then with fists* EXPLETIVE, swear word, oath, profanity, curse, four-letter word, dirty word, blasphemy; *informal* cuss, cuss word; *formal* imprecation.

3 *they claimed that nearly a third of UN member states practiced human rights obscenities* ATROCITY, (act of) brutality, (act of) cruelty, (act of) savagery, (act of) inhumanity, crime, evil.

obscure adjective 1 *the truth is that many aspects of a war's outcome remain obscure for years* UNCLEAR, uncertain, unknown, in doubt, doubtful, dubious, mysterious, hazy, vague, indeterminate, concealed, hidden. ANTONYMS clear, obvious.

2 *obscure references to Proust* ABSTRUSE, recondite, arcane, esoteric; mystifying, puzzling, perplexing, baffling, ambiguous, cryptic, enigmatic, Delphic, oracular, oblique, opaque, elliptical, unintelligible, incomprehensible, impenetrable, unfathomable; *informal* as clear as mud. ANTONYMS clear, plain.

3 *rumors from open-mouth radio shows and obscure web sites* LITTLE KNOWN, unknown, unheard of, unnoticed, undistinguished, unimportant, insignificant, inconsequential, minor, lowly; nameless, anonymous; unsung, unrecognized, forgotten. ANTONYMS famous, renowned.

4 *an obscure shape* INDISTINCT, faint, vague, nebulous, ill-defined, unclear, blurred, blurry, misty, hazy; dark, dim, shadowy; *literary* tenebrous; *archaic* caliginous. ANTONYM distinct.

▸ verb 1 *a shy and abject manner obscured her prettiness* HIDE, conceal, cover, veil, shroud, screen, mask, cloak, cast a shadow over, shadow, block (out), obliterate, eclipse, darken; *literary* bedim, enshroud. ANTONYM reveal.

2 *human rights are often obscured by the shadow of politics* CONFUSE, complicate, obfuscate, cloud, blur, muddy; muddy the waters of; *literary* befog, becloud. ANTONYMS illuminate, clarify.

THE RIGHT WORD

Obscure is the general term for something that is unclear or not easy to understand; **abstruse** and **recondite** are more formal terms. **Obscure** often expresses dissatisfaction at one's inability to identify something (*the causation of his mental disorder is obscure*), or, more critically, refers to something that's not sufficiently clearly expressed (*the law is too obscure to interpret correctly | we find it difficult to address your obscure complaints*). A reference to, say, "an obscure congressman" is a dismissive comment, suggesting that this is someone not only little known but perhaps deservedly so. **Abstruse** is more precise in its meaning—'difficult to understand'—and usually implies that the subject would be puzzling to most anyone (*reading her essays, one wonders if even she can understand her abstruse philosophy*). **Recondite** denotes topics that are known and understood by only a few experts: *recondite though their theme may be, they demonstrate that it is not without relevance*. There is often a critical suggestion that difficulty or obscurity has been deliberately sought out or magnified.

obscurity noun 1 *the novel plots Carlotta's rise from obscurity to stardom* INSIGNIFICANCE, inconspicuousness, unimportance, anonymity; limbo, twilight, oblivion. ANTONYM fame.

2 *small-minded intellectuals who had accused him of obscurity* INCOMPREHENSIBILITY, impenetrability, unintelligibility, opacity; abstruseness, arcaneness, esotericism. ANTONYM clarity.

3 *there may be obscurities but no answerless riddles* ENIGMA, puzzle, mystery, ambiguity.

obsequies plural noun *they left the sad obsequies to my men* FUNERAL RITES, funeral service, funeral, burial, interment, entombment, inhumation, last offices; *formal* exequies; *archaic* sepulture.

obsequious adjective *an elderly gentlemen surrounded by obsequious heirs* SERVILE, ingratiating, sycophantic, fawning, unctuous, oily, oleaginous, groveling, cringing, subservient, submissive, slavish; *informal* brown-nosing, bootlicking, smarmy; *vulgar slang* ass-kissing. ANTONYM domineering.

THE RIGHT WORD

If you want to get ahead with your boss, you might trying being **obsequious**, which suggests an attitude of inferiority that may or may not be genuine, but that is assumed in order to placate a superior in hopes of getting what one wants (*a "goody two shoes" whose obsequious behavior made everyone in the class cringe*). While **subservient** may connote similar behavior, it is more often applied to those who are genuinely subordinate or dependent and act accordingly (*a timid, subservient child who was terrified of making a mistake*). **Servile** is a stronger and more negative term, suggesting a cringing submissiveness (*the dog's servile obedience to her master*). **Slavish**, suggesting the status or attitude of a slave, is often used to describe strict adherence to a set of rules or a code of conduct (*a slavish adherence to the rules of etiquette*).

observable adjective *that will certainly cause an observable change in the instrument reading* NOTICEABLE, visible, perceptible, perceivable, detectable, conspicuous, distinguishable, discernible, recognizable, evident, apparent, manifest, obvious, patent, palpable, overt, clear, distinct, plain, unmistakable. ANTONYM hidden.

observance noun 1 *elders responsible for the correct observance of sacred rites* COMPLIANCE WITH, adherence to, accordance with, respect for, observation of, obedience to; keeping of, obeying of, fulfillment of, following of, honoring of; *archaic* abidance by. ANTONYM disregard.

2 *a Catholic calendar of saints' days and religious observances* RITE, ritual, ceremony, ceremonial, celebration, practice, service, office, festival, tradition, custom, convention, formality, form; *formal* praxis.

observant adjective 1 *the farmer whose weather eye has been usurped by the radio has become less observant* ALERT, sharp-eyed, sharp, eagle-eyed, hawk-eyed, having eyes like a hawk, watchful, heedful, aware; on the lookout, on the qui vive, on guard, attentive, vigilant, having one's eyes open/peeled; *informal* beady-eyed, not missing a trick, on the ball. ANTONYM inattentive.

2 *observant Jews* PRACTICING, obedient, conforming, conformist; law-abiding, orthodox, devout.

observation noun 1 *the patient has been brought in for observation | whatever the reason, many people are irrationally afraid of snakes, and this makes for poor observation* MONITORING, watching, scrutiny, examination, inspection, survey, surveillance, consideration, study, review.

2 *who was the recipient of that flattering observation?* REMARK, comment, statement, utterance, pronouncement, declaration; OPINION, impression, thought, reflection; *Law* obiter dictum.

3 *the **observation of** the law* OBSERVANCE OF, compliance with, adherence to, respect for, obedience to, keeping of, obeying of, heeding of.

observe verb 1 *I observed this wheelchair dude in the vestibule waiting for me | other behavioral problems have been observed in our patient population* NOTICE, see, note, perceive, discern, detect, spot; *literary* espy, descry, behold. ANTONYM overlook.

2 *I may not even observe them unawares* WATCH, look at, eye, contemplate, view, witness, survey, regard, keep an eye on, scrutinize, keep under observation, keep (a) watch on, keep under surveillance, monitor, check out, keep a weather eye on, keep tabs on, spy on; *informal* eyeball.

3 *She'd observed that the Christmas tree looked underdecorated* REMARK, comment, say, mention, note, declare, announce, state, pronounce; *formal* opine.

4 *both countries agreed to observe the cease-fire* COMPLY WITH, abide by, keep, obey, adhere to, heed, honor, be heedful of, respect, follow, consent to, acquiesce in, accept, fulfill. ANTONYMS disregard, ignore.

5 *this year he observed the anniversary at a ceremony on the South Lawn* COMMEMORATE, mark, keep, memorialize, solemnize, remember, recognize, celebrate.

observer noun 1 *a casual observer might not have noticed* SPECTATOR, onlooker, watcher, looker-on, fly on the wall, viewer, witness, eyewitness, bystander; *informal* rubberneck; *literary* beholder.

2 *industry observers expect the deal to be finalized today* COMMENTATOR, reporter; monitor.

obsess verb *being thin is obsessing her* PREOCCUPY, be uppermost in someone's mind, prey on someone's mind, prey on, possess, haunt, consume, plague, torment, hound, bedevil, beset, take control of, control, take over, have a hold on, rule, eat up, have a grip on, grip.PHRASE: **be obsessed** *he **was obsessed with** his roommate's sister | I **am obsessed by** a desire to win* BE FIXATED ON/UPON, be preoccupied with, be possessed by, be consumed with/by (thoughts of), have an obsession with; be infatuated with, be besotted with, be smitten with; *informal* have a thing about/for, be hung up about/on, have it bad for.

obsession noun *that new car has become his obsession* FIXATION, ruling/consuming passion, passion, mania, idée fixe, compulsion, preoccupation, infatuation, addiction, fetish, craze, hobbyhorse; phobia, complex, neurosis; *informal* a bee in one's bonnet, hang-up, thing.

obsessive adjective *her obsessive behavior includes relentless tidying* ALL-CONSUMING, consuming, compulsive, controlling, obsessional, fanatic, fanatical, neurotic, excessive, overkeen, besetting, tormenting, inescapable, pathological.

obsolescent adjective *much of the business etiquette our parents knew is obsolescent* DYING OUT, on the decline, declining, waning, on the wane, disappearing, past its prime, aging, moribund, on its last legs, old-fashioned, outmoded, downlevel, on the way out; obsolete, outdated, out of date, behind the times.

obsolete adjective *most of the machinery in their Somerville plant is obsolete | obsolete hairstyles* OUTDATED, out of date, outmoded, old-fashioned, démodé, passé, out of fashion; no longer in use, disused, fallen into disuse, behind the times, superannuated, outworn, antiquated, antediluvian, anachronistic, discontinued, old, dated, archaic, ancient, fossilized, extinct, defunct, dead, bygone, out; *informal* prehistoric. See note at OLD. ANTONYMS cutting-edge, the latest, modern.

obstacle noun *blindness is not the worst obstacle I've had to overcome* BARRIER, hurdle, stumbling block, obstruction, bar, block, impediment, hindrance, snag, catch, drawback, hitch, handicap, deterrent, complication, difficulty, problem, disadvantage, curb, check; *informal* fly in the ointment, monkey wrench (in the works). ANTONYMS advantage, aid.

obstinacy noun *Zach's obstinacy contributed to his unfavorable performance evaluation* STUBBORNNESS, inflexibility, intransigence, intractability, obduracy, mulishness, pigheadedness, willfulness, contrariness, perversity, recalcitrance, refractoriness, implacability, rigidity, uncooperativeness; persistence, tenacity, tenaciousness, pertinacity, doggedness, single-mindedness. ANTONYM flexibility.

obstinate adjective *it's unusual for two such obstinate people to have a happy marriage* STUBBORN, unyielding, inflexible, unbending, intransigent, intractable, obdurate, mulish, bullheaded, stubborn as a mule, pigheaded, self-willed, strong-willed, headstrong, willful, contrary, perverse, recalcitrant, refractory, uncooperative, unmanageable, stiff-necked, rigid, uncompromising, implacable, unrelenting, immovable, unshakable; persistent, tenacious, pertinacious, dogged, single-minded. See note at STUBBORN. ANTONYM compliant.

obstreperous adjective *the hotel manager was accustomed to dealing with obstreperous guests* UNRULY, unmanageable, disorderly, undisciplined, uncontrollable, rowdy, disruptive, truculent, difficult, refractory, rebellious, mutinous, riotous, out of control, wild, turbulent, uproarious, boisterous; noisy, loud, clamorous, raucous, vociferous; *informal* rambunctious. See note at VOCIFEROUS. ANTONYMS quiet, restrained.

obstruct verb 1 *ensure that the air vents are not obstructed* BLOCK (UP), clog (up), get in the way of, jam (up), cut off, shut off, bung up, choke, dam up; barricade, bar; *technical* occlude. ANTONYM clear.

2 *he was charged with obstructing traffic* HOLD UP, bring to a standstill, stop, halt, block.

3 *fears that the regime would obstruct the distribution of food* IMPEDE, hinder, interfere with, hamper, hobble, block, interrupt, hold up, stand in the way of, frustrate, thwart, balk, inhibit, hamstring, sabotage; slow down, retard, delay, stonewall, stall, stop, halt, stay, restrict, limit, curb, put a brake on, bridle; *informal* stymie. See note at HINDER. ANTONYMS facilitate, further.

obstruction noun *wealthy property owners have created one obstruction after another to undermine the low-income housing project* OBSTACLE, barrier, stumbling block, hurdle, bar, block, impediment, hindrance, snag, difficulty, catch, drawback, hitch, handicap, deterrent, curb, check, restriction; blockage, stoppage, congestion, bottleneck, holdup, jam; *Medicine* occlusion; *informal* fly in the ointment, monkey wrench (in the works).

obstructive adjective *he pursued his dreams of being a musician despite the efforts of his obstructive parents* UNHELPFUL, uncooperative, unsupportive, awkward, difficult, unaccommodating, disobliging, perverse, contrary; *archaic* froward, contrarious. ANTONYMS helpful, supportive.

obtain verb 1 *the newspaper obtained a copy of the letter* GET, acquire, come by, secure, procure, come into the possession of, pick up, be given; gain, earn, achieve, attain; *informal* get hold of, get/lay one's hands on, get one's mitts on, land, net. See note at GET. ANTONYMS relinquish, lose.

2 *formal rules obtaining in other jurisdictions* PREVAIL, be in force, apply, exist, be in use, be in effect, stand, hold, be the case.

obtainable adjective *use dried herbs only when fresh ones are not obtainable* AVAILABLE, to be had, in circulation, on the market, in season, at one's disposal, at hand, attainable, procurable, accessible, realizable, gettable; *informal* up for grabs, on tap, get-at-able.

obtrusive adjective *a car dealership on this stretch of road would be too obtrusive | she wears the most obtrusive outfits* CONSPICUOUS, prominent, noticeable, obvious, unmistakable; intrusive, out of place; bold, loud, showy, gaudy, garish, flashy; *informal* sticking/standing out like a sore thumb. See note at IMPERTINENT. ANTONYMS unobtrusive, inconspicuous.

obtuse adjective *he frustrated his teachers by pretending to be obtuse* STUPID, slow-witted, slow, dull-witted, unintelligent, ignorant, simpleminded, witless; insensitive, imperceptive, uncomprehending; *informal* dim, dimwitted, dense, dumb, slow on the uptake, halfwitted, brain-dead, moronic, cretinous, thick, dopey, lamebrained, dumb-ass, dead from the neck up, boneheaded, chowderheaded. See note at STUPID. ANTONYMS clever, astute.

obviate verb *our latest agreement obviates any further discussion of the matter* PRECLUDE, prevent, remove, get rid of, do away with, get around, rule out, eliminate, make/render unnecessary.

obvious adjective *it's obvious that they don't get along | her intentions are obvious* CLEAR, crystal clear, plain, plain to see, evident, apparent, manifest, patent, conspicuous, pronounced, transparent, palpable, prominent, marked, decided, distinct, noticeable, unmissable, perceptible, visible, discernible; unmistakable, indisputable, self-evident, incontrovertible, incontestable, undeniable, beyond doubt, beyond question, as clear as day, staring someone in the face; overt, open, undisguised, unconcealed, frank, glaring, blatant, written all over someone; *informal* as plain as the nose on one's face, sticking/standing out like a sore thumb, right under one's nose. ANTONYMS imperceptible, obscure.

obviously adverb *they were obviously thrilled to hear your good news | obviously, I had forgotten her name* CLEARLY, evidently, plainly, patently, visibly, discernibly, manifestly, noticeably; unmistakably, undeniably, incontrovertibly, demonstrably, unquestionably, indubitably, undoubtedly, without doubt, doubtless; of course, naturally, needless to say, it goes without saying. See note at CLEARLY. ANTONYM perhaps.

occasion noun 1 *a previous occasion* TIME, instance, moment, juncture, point; event, occurrence, affair, incident, episode, experience; situation, case, circumstance.

2 *a family occasion* SOCIAL EVENT, event, affair, function, celebration, party, get-together, gathering; *informal* do, bash.

3 *I doubt if the occasion will arise* OPPORTUNITY, right moment, opportune time, chance, opening, window.

4 *it's the first time I've had occasion to complain* REASON, cause, call, grounds, justification, need, motive, inducement.

▸ verb *her situation occasioned a good deal of sympathy* CAUSE, give rise to, bring about, result in, lead to, prompt, elicit, call forth, evoke, make for, produce, create, arouse, generate, engender, precipitate, provoke, stir up, inspire, spark (off), trigger; *literary* beget.

PHRASE: **on occasion.** See OCCASIONALLY.

occasional adjective *the admiral made occasional appearances on board our ship* INFREQUENT, intermittent, irregular, sporadic, odd, random; periodic; uncommon, rare, isolated, few and far between, sometime. ANTONYMS regular, frequent.

occasionally adverb *I occasionally have wine with dinner* SOMETIMES, from time to time, (every) now and then, (every) now and again, at times, every so often, (every) once in a while, on occasion; periodically, at intervals; irregularly, sporadically, infrequently, intermittently, on and off, off and on. ANTONYMS often, frequently.

occlude verb *a blood clot has occluded the coronary artery* BLOCK (UP), stop (up), obstruct, clog (up), close, shut, plug (up), choke.

occult noun *his interest in* ***the occult*** THE SUPERNATURAL, the paranormal, supernaturalism, magic, black magic, witchcraft, sorcery, necromancy, wizardry, the black arts, occultism, diabolism, devil worship, devilry, voodoo, hoodoo, white magic, witchery, mysticism; *rare* theurgy.

▸ adjective 1 *occult powers* SUPERNATURAL, magic, magical, mystical, mystic, psychic, preternatural, paranormal transcendental; Kabbalistic, hermetic.

2 *the typically occult language of the time* ESOTERIC, arcane, recondite, abstruse, secret; obscure, incomprehensible, impenetrable, puzzling, perplexing, mystifying, mysterious, enigmatic.

occupancy noun *our occupancy is temporary* OCCUPATION, tenancy, tenure, residence, residency, inhabitation,

habitation, living, lease, holding, possession; *formal* dwelling.

occupant noun 1 *the occupants of the houses* RESIDENT, inhabitant, owner, householder, tenant, renter, leaseholder, lessee; addressee, occupier; *formal* dweller.

2 *the first occupant of the post* INCUMBENT, holder.

occupation noun 1 *his father's occupation* JOB, profession, work, line of work, trade, employment, position, post, situation, business, career, field, métier, vocation, calling, craft.

2 *her leisure occupations* PASTIME, activity, hobby, pursuit, interest, entertainment, recreation, amusement, diversion, divertissement.

3 *a property suitable for occupation by seniors* RESIDENCE, residency, habitation, inhabitation, occupancy, tenancy, tenure, lease, living in, possession; *formal* dwelling.

4 *the Roman occupation of Britain* CONQUEST, capture, invasion, seizure, takeover, annexation, overrunning, subjugation, subjection, appropriation; COLONIZATION, rule, control, possession, suzerainty.

occupational adjective *occupational hazards | occupational choices* JOB-RELATED, work, professional, vocational, employment, business, career.

occupied adjective 1 *tasks that kept her occupied all day* BUSY, engaged, working, at work, active; immersed, preoccupied, absorbed, engrossed; *informal* tied up, wrapped up, hard at it. ANTONYM idle.

2 *all the tables were occupied* IN USE, full, engaged, taken, unavailable. ANTONYMS available, empty, free.

3 *only two of the apartments are occupied* INHABITED, lived-in, tenanted, settled. ANTONYMS vacant, empty.

occupy verb 1 *Carol occupied the basement apartment* LIVE IN, inhabit, be the tenant of, lodge in; move into, take up residence in, make one's home in; people, populate, settle; *formal* reside in, dwell in.

2 *two windows occupied almost the whole of the end wall* TAKE UP, fill, fill up, cover, use up.

3 *he occupies a senior post at the firm* HOLD, fill, be in, have, hold down.

4 *I need something to occupy my mind* ENGAGE, busy, employ, distract, absorb, engross, preoccupy, hold, interest, involve, entertain, amuse, divert.

5 *the region was occupied by Soviet troops* CAPTURE, seize, take possession of, conquer; invade, overrun; take over, garrison, hold, annex, subjugate, colonize.

occur verb 1 *the accident occurred at about 3:30* HAPPEN, take place, come about, transpire, materialize, arise, crop up; *informal* go down; *literary* come to pass, befall, betide; *formal* eventuate. See note at HAPPEN.

2 *the disease occurs chiefly in tropical climates* BE FOUND, be present, exist, appear, prevail, present itself, manifest itself, turn up.

3 *an idea occurred to her* ENTER ONE'S HEAD/MIND, cross one's mind, come to mind, spring to mind, strike one, hit one, dawn on one, suggest itself, present itself.

occurrence noun 1 *vandalism used to be a rare occurrence* EVENT, incident, happening, phenomenon, affair, matter, circumstance.

2 *the occurrence of cancer increases with age* EXISTENCE, instance, appearance, manifestation, materialization, development; frequency, incidence, rate, prevalence; *Statistics* distribution.

ocean noun 1 *the ocean was calm* SEA; *informal* drink, briny, chuck, salt chuck; *literary* deep, waves, main.

2 *informal* ***oceans*** *of energy* A LOT, a great/good deal, plenty, an abundance, a great/large amount; *informal* lots, tons, loads, heaps, scads, oodles, gobs; *vulgar slang* shitload. ANTONYMS dearth, lack.

octopus noun See note below.

USAGE NOTE octopus

Because this word is actually of Greek origin—not Latin—the classical plural is *octopodes* (ok-**top**-uh-deez), not *octopi*. But the standard plural is *octopuses*. Still, some writers mistakenly use the supposed Latin plural—e.g.: "The nearby mangrove swamps have become nurseries and breeding grounds for a whole new ecosystem, including sponges, octopi [read *octopuses*], shrimp, oysters, sharks, fiddler crabs, and man." (*Christian Science Monitor*; Mar. 14, 1984.)

Occasionally the pedantic *octopodes* appears, but it is relatively rare—e.g.: "The baby octopus salad, made with finger-sized octopodes, whole and purplish, were marinated in a tasty, sesame oil dressing and lightly sprinkled with sesame seeds." (*Newsday* [New York]; Oct. 19, 2001.) **—BG**

odd adjective 1 *an odd man* STRANGE, peculiar, weird, queer, funny, bizarre, abnormal, eccentric, unusual, unconventional, outlandish, quirky, zany; *informal* wacky, kooky, screwy, freaky, oddball, offbeat, off the wall, out there. ANTONYMS normal, conventional.

2 *quite a few odd things had happened* STRANGE, unusual, peculiar, funny, curious, bizarre, weird, uncanny, queer, outré, unexpected, unfamiliar, abnormal, atypical, anomalous, different, out of the ordinary, out of the way, exceptional, rare, extraordinary, remarkable, puzzling, mystifying, mysterious, perplexing, baffling, unaccountable, uncommon, irregular, singular, deviant, aberrant, freak, freakish; *informal* fishy, freaky. ANTONYMS ordinary, usual. See word spectrum on page 626.

3 *we have the odd drink together | he does odd jobs for friends* OCCASIONAL, casual, irregular, isolated, random, sporadic, periodic; miscellaneous, various, varied, sundry. ANTONYMS regular, scheduled.

4 *odd socks* MISMATCHED, unmatched, unpaired; single, lone, solitary, extra, surplus, leftover, remaining.

5 *when you've got an odd ten minutes, stop by my office* SPARE, free, available, unoccupied; between appointments, between engagements. PHRASE: **odd man out** *no matter what our group planned to do over school vacations, Cassidy was always odd man out* OUTSIDER, exception, oddity, nonconformist, maverick, individualist, misfit, fish out of water, square peg in a round hole.

oddity noun 1 *she was regarded as a bit of an oddity* ECCENTRIC, misfit, square peg in a round hole, maverick, nonconformist, odd one, rare bird, crank; *informal* character, oddball, weirdo, crackpot, nut, freak, screwball, kook, queer/odd fish, queer/odd duck. ANTONYMS conformist, average Joe.

2 *his work remains an oddity in some respects* ANOMALY, aberration, curiosity, rarity.

3 *there was a real oddity about their artwork* STRANGE-

odd
peculiar
strange
queer
bizarre
outré
unconventional
unorthodox
unfamiliar
curious
uncanny
unusual
weird
freakish
freaky
aberrant
deviant
outlandish
offbeat
out of the ordinary
exceptional
remarkable
unexpected
irregular
uncommon
unique
singular
atypical
abnormal
anomalous
different
special
noteworthy
extraordinary
rare
memorable
worth mentioning
not worth mentioning
adequate
satisfactory
passable
not bad
average
typical
standard
normal
usual
customary
expected
uneventful
everyday
run-of-the-mill
garden-variety
commonplace
unexceptional
nothing to write home about
conventional
middle-of-the-road
suburban
pedestrian
prosaic
quotidian
hackneyed
workaday
mundane
humdrum
bland
plain-vanilla
nondescript
colorless
undistinguished
unremarkable
quotidian
ordinary

NESS, peculiarity, oddness, weirdness, bizarreness, eccentricity, queerness, unconventionality, outlandishness, *informal* wackiness, kookiness.

4 *the oddities of human nature* PECULIARITY, idiosyncrasy, eccentricity, quirk, irregularity, twist.

oddments plural noun **1** *oddments of fabric* SCRAPS, remnants, odds and ends, bits, pieces, bits and pieces, leftovers, fragments, snippets, ends, shreds, tail ends.

2 *a cellar full of oddments.* See ODDS AND ENDS at ODDS.

odds plural noun **1** ***odds are*** *that he is no longer alive* THE LIKELIHOOD IS, the probability is, chances are, there's a good chance.

2 *the odds are in our favor against all odds* ADVANTAGE, edge; superiority, supremacy, ascendancy. PHRASES: **at odds 1** *Duncan and Eliza have been at odds all week* IN CONFLICT, in disagreement, on bad terms, at cross purposes, at loggerheads, quarreling, arguing, on the outs, at daggers drawn, at each other's throats. **2** *your behavior is* ***at odds with*** *the interests of the company* AT VARIANCE WITH, not in keeping with, out of keeping with, out of line with, in opposition to, conflicting with, contrary to, incompatible with, inconsistent with, irreconcilable with. **odds and ends** BITS AND PIECES, bits, pieces, stuff, paraphernalia, things, sundries, miscellanea, bric-a-brac, knickknacks, oddments, junk.

odious adjective *the odious procedures of the military government | the dumpsite was especially odious in summer* REVOLTING, repulsive, repellent, repugnant, disgusting, offensive, objectionable, vile, foul, abhorrent, loathsome, nauseating, sickening, hateful, detestable, execrable, abominable, monstrous, appalling, reprehensible, deplorable, insufferable, intolerable, despicable, contemptible, unspeakable, atrocious, awful, terrible, dreadful, frightful, obnoxious, unsavory, unpalatable, unpleasant, disagreeable, nasty, noisome, distasteful; *informal* ghastly, horrible, horrid, gross, godawful; beastly. ANTONYMS delightful, pleasant.

odium noun *during the trial, he sensed his family's distrust and odium* DISGUST, abhorrence, repugnance, revulsion, loathing, detestation, hatred, hate, obloquy, dislike, distaste, disfavor, antipathy, animosity, animus, enmity, hostility, contempt; disgrace, shame, opprobrium, discredit, dishonor. ANTONYM approval.

odor noun **1** *an odor of sweat* SMELL, stench, stink, reek, whiff, fetor; *informal* funk; *literary* miasma.

2 *the pleasing odor of fresh-roasted coffee* AROMA, smell, scent, fragrance, bouquet, perfume. See note at SMELL.

3 *an odor of suspicion* ATMOSPHERE, air, aura, quality, flavor, savor, hint, suggestion, impression, whiff.

odoriferous, odiferous adjective *it was an especially odoriferous patch of the garden, where the hyacinths, lilacs, and red ramblers take turns blooming from one end of the season to the other.* See FRAGRANT. See also note at ODOROUS.

odorless adjective *an odorless lotion* UNSCENTED, fragrance-free; inodorous, deodorized.

odorous adjective *the dogs have been rolling in something quite odorous* SMELLY, foul-smelling, malodorous, pungent, acrid, evil-smelling, stinking, reeking, fetid, rank; *informal* stinky; *Brit. informal* minging, pongy; *literary* miasmic, miasmal, noisome, mephitic; *rare* olid.

USAGE NOTE **odorous, odoriferous, malodorous**

In practice, *odorous* (= having a pronounced odor) is neutral in connotation (*an odorous bouquet* ¦ *an odorous locker room*). Although, in *A Dictionary of Contemporary American Usage* (1957), the Evanses insisted that *odorous* be "strictly confined to pleasant fragrances", today it is used with a negative sense about twice as often as a positive one. *Malodorous* carries even stronger negative connotations (*a malodorous bathroom*). *Odoriferous*, a frequently misused term, has historically had positive connotations in the sense "fragrant" (*odoriferous rose gardens*). It shouldn't be used in reference to foul odors—e.g.: "The only thing that gave him trouble was finding a toad; the rest of the stuff, though mostly nasty and odoriferous [read *odorous* or *malodorous*], was obtained with little difficulty." (Theodore R. Cogswell, "The Wall Around the World" (1953), in *The Mammoth Book of Fantasy*, Mike Ashley ed.; 2001.)

Odiferous is an erroneous shortening of *odoriferous*, and it's often misused for *odorous* or *malodorous*. Only someone familiar with garlic plants knows whether the odor in the following example is nice or foul (probably the latter): "They are underplanted with useful plants ranging from fragrant peppermint to odiferous [read *malodorous*, *odorous*, or, if pleasant-smelling, *odoriferous*] garlic chives." (*Boston Herald*; Aug. 3, 1997.)

Just as *odious* (= offensive) is sometimes misused to describe a foul smell, so *odoriferous* is sometimes misused to mean "corrupt" or at least "suspicious"—e.g.: "There does seem to be something odoriferous underfoot." (*Orlando Sentinel Tribune*; Dec. 29, 2002.) Unfortunately, the use is common enough that at least one dictionary (*Merriam-Webster's Collegiate Dictionary*, 11th ed.; 2003) lists "morally offensive" as an alternative definition of *odoriferous*. In one sense that's understandable, because corruption and bad smells have always been associated (the usage passes the sniff test). But in a larger sense it's unfortunate, since we can't clearly distinguish all the odor words we already have—and it just continues the degeneration of the word's connotations. **—BG**

odyssey noun *Magellan's great odyssey* | *the book details her odyssey from housewife to world leader* JOURNEY, voyage, trek, travels, quest, crusade, pilgrimage, wandering, journeying; *archaic* peregrination.

off adverb **1** *Kate's off today* AWAY, absent, out, unavailable, not at work, off duty, on leave, on vacation; free, at leisure; *Brit.* on holiday. ANTONYMS in, at work, working.

2 *the game's off* CANCELED, postponed, called off, shelved. ANTONYM on.

▸ adjective **1** *the fish was a bit off* ROTTEN, bad, stale, moldy, sour, rancid, turned, spoiled, putrid, putrescent; (of beer) skunky. ANTONYM fresh.

2 *informal I felt decidedly off* UNWELL, ill, out of sorts, not oneself, sick, indisposed, bad; *informal* under the weather, not up to par, lousy, crummy; *vulgar slang* crappy. ANTONYM well.

PHRASE: **off and on** *I still play tennis, but only off and on* PERIODICALLY, at intervals, on and off, (every) once in a while, every so often, (every) now and then/again, from time to time, occasionally, sometimes, intermittently, irregularly. ANTONYM regularly.

offbeat adjective *informal an offbeat suggestion* | *offbeat clothes* UNCONVENTIONAL, unorthodox, unusual, eccentric, idiosyncratic, outré, strange, bizarre, weird, peculiar, odd, freakish, outlandish, out of the ordinary, Bohemian, alternative, zany, quirky; *informal* wacky, freaky, way-out, off the wall, kooky, oddball. ANTONYMS conventional, ordinary.

off-color adjective *off-color jokes* SMUTTY, dirty, rude, crude, filthy, suggestive, indecent, indelicate, risqué, racy, bawdy, naughty, blue, vulgar, ribald, broad, salacious, coarse, obscene; *informal* raunchy; *euphemistic* adult.

offend verb **1** *I'm sorry if I offended him* HURT SOMEONE'S FEELINGS, give offense to, affront, displease, upset, distress, hurt, wound; annoy, anger, exasperate, irritate, vex, pique, gall, irk, nettle, ruffle someone's feathers, tread on someone's toes; rub the wrong way; *informal* rile, rattle, peeve, needle, miff, put someone's nose out of joint, put someone's back up; *vulgar slang* piss off.

2 *the smell of cigarette smoke offended him* DISPLEASE, be distasteful to, be disagreeable to, be offensive to, disgust, repel, revolt, sicken, nauseate, be repugnant to; *informal* turn off, gross out. ANTONYMS please, delight.

3 *criminals who offend again and again* BREAK THE LAW, commit a crime, do wrong, sin, go astray, transgress; *archaic* trespass.

offended adjective *he was offended because she had forgotten their anniversary* UPSET, INSULTED, affronted, aggrieved, displeased, hurt, wounded, disgruntled, put out, annoyed, angry, cross, exasperated, indignant, irritated, piqued, vexed, irked, stung, galled, nettled, resentful, in a huff, huffy, in high dudgeon; *informal* riled, miffed, peeved, aggravated, sore, teed off, ticked off; *vulgar slang* pissed off. ANTONYM pleased.

offender noun *my client is not the offender in this case* WRONGDOER, CRIMINAL, lawbreaker, miscreant, malefactor, felon, delinquent, culprit, guilty party, outlaw, sinner, transgressor; *Law* malfeasant.

offense noun **1** *he denied having committed any offense* CRIME, illegal/unlawful act, misdemeanor, breach of the law, felony, wrongdoing, wrong, misdeed, peccadillo, sin, transgression, infringement; *Law* malfeasance; *informal* no-no; *archaic* trespass; *rare* malefaction. See note at SIN.

2 *an offense to basic justice* AFFRONT, slap in the face, insult, outrage, violation, slight.

3 *I do not want to cause offense* ANNOYANCE, anger, resentment, indignation, irritation, exasperation, wrath, displeasure, hard/bad/ill feelings, disgruntlement, pique, vexation, animosity, antipathy.

4 *planning our next offense* ATTACK, offensive, assault, onslaught, invasion, incursion, foray, sortie. PHRASE: **take offense** *his jokes were very insulting, and many of us took offense* BE/FEEL OFFENDED, take exception, take something personally, feel affronted, be/feel resentful, take something amiss, take umbrage, be/get/feel upset, be/get/feel annoyed, be/get/feel angry, get into a huff.

offensive adjective **1** *offensive remarks* INSULTING, insolent, derogatory, disrespectful, hurtful, wounding, abusive; annoying, exasperating, irritating, galling, provocative, outrageous; rude, impertinent, discourteous, uncivil, impolite; crude, vulgar, coarse, improper, indecent; *formal* exceptionable. ANTONYMS complimentary, polite, courteous.

2 *an offensive smell* UNPLEASANT, disagreeable, nasty, distasteful, displeasing, objectionable, off-putting, awful, terrible, dreadful, frightful, obnoxious, abominable, disgusting, repulsive, repellent, repugnant, revolting, abhorrent, loathsome, detestable, odious, vile, foul, sickening, nauseating; *informal* ghastly, horrible, horrid, gross, putrid, godawful, beastly; *literary* noisome, mephitic. ANTONYMS pleasant, delightful.

3 *an offensive air strike* HOSTILE, attacking, aggressive, invading, incursive, combative, belligerent, on the attack. ANTONYM defensive.

▸ noun *a military offensive* ATTACK, assault, onslaught, drive, invasion, push, thrust, charge, sortie, sally, foray, raid, incursion, offense, blitz, campaign. PHRASE: **take the offensive** *our fleet will take the offensive within the next 48 hours* LAUNCH AN ATTACK, begin to attack, attack first, strike the first blow.

THE RIGHT WORD

Looking for just the right word to express your dislike, distaste, disgust, or aversion to something? **Offensive** is a relatively mild adjective, used to describe anyone or anything that is unpleasant or disagreeable (*she found his remarks offensive; the offensive sight of garbage piled in the alley*). If you want to express strong dislike for someone or something that deserves to be disliked, use **detestable** (*a detestable man who never had a kind word for anyone*). If something is so offensive that it provokes a physical as well as a moral or intellectual response, use **odious** (*the odious treatment of women during the war in Bosnia*), and if you instinctively draw back from it, use **repugnant** (*the very thought of piercing one's nose was repugnant to her*). If your repugnance is extreme, go one step further and use **abhorrent** (*an abhorrent act that could not go unpunished*). Persons and things that are truly loathsome or terrifying can be called **abominable** (*an abominable act of desecration; the abominable snowman*), although this word is often used as an overstatement to mean "awful" (*abominable taste in clothes*).

offer verb 1 *Chris offered another suggestion* PUT FORWARD, proffer, provide, give, present, come up with, suggest, extend, recommend, propose, advance, submit, tender, render. ANTONYMS withdraw, withhold.

2 *she offered to help | if you're looking for assistance, I'm offering* VOLUNTEER, volunteer one's services, be at someone's disposal, be at someone's service, make oneself available, step/come forward.

3 *the product is offered at a competitive price* PUT UP FOR SALE, put on the market, sell, market, make available, put under the gavel/hammer; *Law* vend.

4 *he offered $200* BID, tender, put in a bid of, put in an offer of.

5 *a job offering good career prospects* PROVIDE, afford, supply, give, furnish, present, purvey, hold out.

6 *she offered no resistance* ATTEMPT, try, give, show, express; *formal* essay.

7 *birds were offered to the gods* SACRIFICE, offer up, immolate, give.

▸ noun 1 *a job offer | offers of help* PROPOSAL, proposition, suggestion, submission, approach, overture; *literary* proffer.

2 *the highest offer* BID, tender, bidding price.

offering noun 1 *you may place offerings in the basket* CONTRIBUTION, donation, gift, present, handout, charity; *formal* benefaction; *historical* alms.

2 *many offerings were made to the goddess* SACRIFICE, oblation, burnt offering, immolation, libation; peace offering, sin offering; *Hinduism* prasad, puja; *Judaism* Omer.

offhand adjective *an offhand manner* CASUAL, careless, uninterested, unconcerned, indifferent, cool, nonchalant, blasé, aloof, insouciant, cavalier, glib, perfunctory, cursory, unceremonious, ungracious, dismissive, discourteous, uncivil, impolite, terse, abrupt, curt; *informal* couldn't-care-less, take-it-or-leave-it.

▸ adverb *I can't think of a better answer offhand* ON THE SPUR OF THE MOMENT, without preparation, without consideration, extempore, impromptu, ad lib; extemporaneously, spontaneously; *Latin* ad libitum *informal* off the cuff, off the top of one's head, just like that. See note at SPONTANEOUS.

office noun 1 *her office on Union Street* PLACE OF WORK, place of business, workplace; headquarters, base; workroom, studio, workspace, cubicle.

2 *the newspaper's Paris office* BRANCH, division, section, bureau, department; agency.

3 *he assumed the office of mayor* POST, position, appointment, job, occupation, role, situation, station, function, capacity.

4 *he was saved by the good* ***offices*** *of his uncle* ASSISTANCE, help, aid, services, intervention, intercession, mediation, agency, support, backing, patronage, auspices, aegis.

5 *the offices of a nurse* DUTY, job, task, chore, obligation, assignment, responsibility, charge, commission.

officer noun 1 *an officer in the army* MILITARY OFFICER, commissioned officer, noncommissioned officer, NCO, commanding officer, CO.

2 *all the officers in this precinct carry guns* POLICE OFFICER, policeman, policewoman, officer of the law, law-enforcement officer/agent, peace officer, patrolman, trooper; *informal* cop, copper, flatfoot.

3 *the officers of the society* OFFICIAL, officeholder, committee member, board member; public servant, administrator, executive, functionary, bureaucrat; *derogatory* apparatchik.

4 *officers of the court* REPRESENTATIVE, deputy, agent, envoy.

official adjective 1 *an official inquiry* AUTHORIZED, approved, validated, authenticated, certified, accredited, endorsed, sanctioned, licensed, recognized, accepted, legitimate, legal, lawful, valid, bona fide, proper, ex cathedra; *informal* kosher. ANTONYMS unofficial, unauthorized.

2 *an official function* CEREMONIAL, formal, solemn, ceremonious; bureaucratic; *informal* stuffed-shirt. See note at OFFICIOUS. ANTONYM informal.

▸ noun *a union official* OFFICER, officeholder, administrator, executive, appointee, functionary; bureaucrat, mandarin; representative, agent; *derogatory* apparatchik.

officiate verb 1 *he officiated the game* PRESIDE OVER, be in charge of, take charge of, direct, head (up); oversee, superintend, supervise, conduct, run; referee, umpire, judge, adjudicate; emcee.

2 *Father Buckley* ***officiated at*** *the wedding service* CONDUCT, perform, celebrate, solemnize.

officious adjective *I try to avoid their officious salesclerks* SELF-IMPORTANT, bumptious, self-assertive, overbearing, overzealous, domineering, opinionated, interfering, intrusive, meddlesome, meddling; *informal* pushy, bossy. ANTONYM self-effacing.

EASILY CONFUSED WORDS **officious, official**

Officious individuals are excessively fond of asserting their authority. They behave in an annoyingly domineering fashion, especially in relation to trivial matters (*he was an officious teller who chastised us for not properly sorting our money by denomination*). **Official**, on the other hand, means 'relating to the responsibilities and authority of public office' (*her official duties in the White House*) or 'approved or issued by an authority' (*the official unemployment figures*). So, should you encounter an officious person who is acting in an official capacity, consider it an unfortunate coincidence, not a requisite circumstance.

offing PHRASE: **in the offing** *I knew that a significant change in my life was in the offing* ON THE WAY, coming (soon), (close) at hand, near, imminent, in prospect, on the horizon, in the wings, just around the corner, in the air, in the wind, brewing, upcoming, forthcoming; bound to happen, likely to happen; *informal* in the cards, coming down the pike.

off-key adjective **1** *an off-key rendition of a popular hymn* OUT OF TUNE, flat, tuneless, discordant, dissonant, unmusical, unharmonious. ANTONYM in tune.

2 *the cinematic effects are distractingly off-key* INCONGRUOUS, inappropriate, unsuitable, out of place, out of keeping, jarring, discordant, dissonant, inharmonious. ANTONYM harmonious.

off-kilter adjective **1** *positioned at off-kilter angles* OUT OF ALIGNMENT, off-center, crooked, askew, awry, out of line, at an angle, off-balance, lopsided, skewed; *informal* cockeyed, wonky. ANTONYMS aligned, straight, right.

2 *her sense of humor is a bit off-kilter* OFFBEAT, eccentric, zany, unconventional, unorthodox, bizarre, weird, strange, funny; *informal* wacky, kooky, off the wall. ANTONYM conventional.

offload verb **1** *the cargo was being offloaded* UNLOAD, remove, empty (out), tip (out); *archaic* unlade.

2 *he offloaded 5,000 shares* DISPOSE OF, dump, jettison, get rid of, transfer, shift; palm off, foist; *Brit.* fob off.

off-putting adjective **1** *an off-putting aroma* UNPLEASANT, unappealing, uninviting, unattractive, disagreeable, repellent, offensive, distasteful, unsavory, unpalatable, unappetizing, objectionable, nasty, disgusting; *informal* horrid, horrible.

2 *her manner was off-putting* UNINVITING, discouraging, disheartening, demoralizing, dispiriting, daunting, disconcerting, unnerving, unsettling; *formal* rebarbative.

offset verb *we were not able to offset our losses over the last quarter* COUNTERBALANCE, balance (out), cancel (out), even out/up, counteract, countervail, neutralize, compensate for, make up for, make good, redeem, indemnify; atone for, make amends for, make restitution for.

offshoot noun **1** *the plant's offshoots* SIDE SHOOT, shoot, sucker, tendril, runner, scion, slip, offset, stolon; twig, branch, bough, limb.

2 *an offshoot of Cromwell's line* DESCENDANT, scion, relation.

3 *rap music began as an underground offshoot of disco* OUTCOME, result, (side) effect, corollary, consequence, upshot, product, by-product, spin-off, development, outgrowth, fallout.

4 *the company now controls several offshoots* SUBSIDIARY, branch, adjunct, derivative.

offspring noun (usually as plural) *his offspring gathered to mourn his passing* CHILDREN, sons and daughters, progeny, family, youngsters, babies, brood; descendants, heirs, successors, scions; *Law* issue; *informal* kids; *derogatory* spawn; *archaic* fruit of one's loins.

often adverb *we go there often* FREQUENTLY, many times, many a time, on many/numerous occasions, a lot, as often as not, repeatedly, again and again, time and (time) again; all the time, regularly, routinely, usually, habitually, commonly, generally, in many cases/instances, ordinarily, oftentimes, recurrently; *informal* lots; *literary* oft, ofttimes. ANTONYMS seldom, never.

ogle verb *he never disguised his desire to ogle the young ladies* LEER AT, stare at, eye, make eyes at, check out; *informal* give someone the once-over, lech after, undress with one's eyes.

ogre noun **1** *an ogre with two heads* MONSTER, giant, troll.

2 *he is not the ogre he sometimes seems to be* BRUTE, fiend, monster, beast, barbarian, savage, animal, tyrant; *informal* bastard, swine, pig.

ogress noun **1** *a one-eyed ogress* MONSTER, giantess.

2 *the French teacher was a real ogress* HARRIDAN, tartar, termagant, gorgon, virago; *informal* battle-ax.

oil noun **1** *make sure the car has enough oil | we heat our house with oil* LUBRICANT, lubrication, grease; crude, crude oil, fuel oil, petroleum; *informal* black gold; *humorous* Texas tea.

2 *brown the beef in hot oil* COOKING OIL, vegetable oil; corn oil, olive oil, sunflower oil, safflower oil, canola oil, peanut oil.

3 *add some oil to the bath water* bath oil, essential oil, baby oil, scented oil, suntan oil.

▸ verb *I'll oil that gate for you* LUBRICATE, grease, smear/cover/rub with oil; *informal* lube.

oily adjective **1** *oily substances* GREASY, oleaginous, unctuous; *technical* sebaceous; *formal* pinguid.

2 *oily food* GREASY, fatty, buttery, swimming in oil/fat.

3 *he's an oily character* UNCTUOUS, ingratiating, fawning, smooth-talking, fulsome, flattering, obsequious, sycophantic, oleaginous; *informal* smarmy, slimy.

ointment noun *apply the ointment twice a day* LOTION, cream, salve, liniment, rub, gel, balm, emollient, unguent; *formal* embrocation; *technical* humectant; *proprietary* Vaseline.

OK, okay *informal* exclamation *OK, I'll go with him* ALL RIGHT, right, very well, very good, fine, fair enough; *informal* okey-doke, okey-dokey. ANTONYM no way.

▸ adjective **1** *the movie was okay* SATISFACTORY, all right, acceptable, competent; adequate, tolerable, passable, reasonable, fair, decent, good enough, not bad, average, middling, moderate, unremarkable, unexceptional; *informal* so-so, 'comme ci, comme ça,' fair-to-middling. ANTONYMS unsatisfactory, unacceptable.

2 *Jo's feeling OK now* FINE, all right, well, in good shape, in good health, fit, healthy, up to snuff; *informal* as fit as a fiddle, in the pink, as right as rain, hunky-dory. ANTONYMS ill, unwell.

3 *is it OK for me to come?* PERMISSIBLE, allowable, acceptable, all right, in order, permitted, fitting, suitable, appropriate, fine; *informal* kosher.

▸ adverb *everything seems to be going okay* ALL RIGHT, fine, well, well enough, satisfactorily, acceptably.

▸ noun *he's just given me his OK | we have to wait for **the OK*** AUTHORIZATION, approval, (the) seal of approval, agreement, consent, assent, permission, endorsement, ratification, sanction, approbation, confirmation, (the) blessing, leave; *informal* (the) go-ahead, (the) green light, (the) thumbs up, (the) say-so. ANTONYM refusal.

▸ verb *the move must be okayed by the president* AUTHORIZE, approve, agree to, consent to, sanction, pass, ratify, endorse, allow, give something the nod, rubber-stamp; *informal* give the go-ahead, give the green light, give the thumbs up; *formal* accede to. ANTONYMS refuse, veto.

old adjective **1** *old ladies* ELDERLY, aged, older, senior, advanced in years, up in years; venerable; in one's dotage, long in the tooth, gray-haired, grizzled, hoary; past one's prime, not as young as one was, ancient, decrepit, doddering, doddery, not long for this world, senescent, senile, superannuated; *informal* getting on, past it, over the hill, no spring chicken. ANTONYM young.

2 *that old barn is an eyesore* DILAPIDATED, broken-down, beat-up, run-down, tumbledown, ramshackle, decaying, crumbling, disintegrating. ANTONYMS new, modern.

3 *old clothes | an old sofa* WORN, worn out, shabby, threadbare, holey, torn, frayed, patched, tattered, moth-eaten, ragged; old-fashioned, out of date, outmoded, démodé; castoff, hand-me-down; *informal* tatty. ANTONYMS new, fashionable.

4 *a collector | of old cars the city's old architecture* ANTIQUE, historic, vintage, classic; veteran. ANTONYMS new, modern.

5 *she's old for her years* MATURE, wise, sensible, experienced, worldly-wise, knowledgeable. ANTONYMS young, inexperienced.

6 *in the old days* BYGONE, past, former, olden, of old, previous, early, earlier, earliest; medieval, ancient, classical, primeval, primordial, prehistoric, antediluvian. ANTONYMS modern, recent.

7 *the same old phrases* HACKNEYED, hack, banal, trite, overused, overworked, tired, worn out, stale, clichéd, platitudinous, unimaginative, pedestrian, stock, conventional; out of date, outdated, old-fashioned, outmoded, archaic, obsolete, antiquated, hoary; *informal* old hat, corny, played out. ANTONYMS fresh, innovative.

8 *an old girlfriend* FORMER, previous, ex-, one-time, erstwhile, once, then; *formal* quondam. ANTONYM new.

9 *the town has held tight to its old ways* TIME-HONORED, old-time, long-established, age-old; FAMILIAR, established; customary, usual, routine, habitual; historic, folk, ancestral, old-world. ANTONYMS modern, progressive.

PHRASES: **old age** *I was not prepared to deal with my father's old age* DECLINING YEARS, advanced years, age, agedness, oldness, winter/autumn of one's life, senescence, senility, dotage. ANTONYMS youth, childhood.

old person *the old people in this community deserve our support* SENIOR CITIZEN, senior, elder, retiree, geriatric, dotard, golden ager; crone; Methuselah; septuagenarian, octogenarian, nonagenarian, centenarian; *informal* old-timer, oldie, oldster, codger. ANTONYMS youngster, child.

THE RIGHT WORD

Almost no one likes to be thought of as **old**, which means having been in existence or use for a relatively long time (*an old washing machine*). But those who are **aged**, indicating a longer life span than *old* and usually referring to persons of very advanced years, are often proud of the fact that they have outlived most of their peers. Children may exaggerate and regard their parents as **ancient**, which means dating back to the remote past, often specifically the time before the end of the Roman Empire (*ancient history*), and their attitudes as **antediluvian**, which literally means dating back to the period before the biblical Great Flood and Noah's ark (*an antediluvian transportation system*). Some people seem older than they really are, simply because their ideas are **antiquated**, which means out of vogue or no longer practiced (*antiquated ideas about dating*). Things rather than people are usually described as **archaic**, which means having the characteristics of an earlier, sometimes primitive, period (*archaic words like "thou" and "thine"*). **Obsolete** also refers to things, implying that they have gone out of use or need to be replaced by something newer (*an obsolete textbook; a machine that will be obsolete within the decade*).

old-fashioned adjective *an old-fashioned hairstyle | old-fashioned thinking* OUT OF DATE, outdated, dated, out of fashion, outmoded, unfashionable, passé, démodé, frumpy; outworn, old, old-time, behind the times, archaic, obsolescent, downlevel, obsolete, ancient, antiquated, superannuated, defunct; medieval, prehistoric, antediluvian, old-fogeyish, old-fangled, conservative, backward-looking, quaint, anachronistic, fusty, moth-eaten, old-world, olde-worlde; *informal* old hat, square, not with it; horse-and-buggy, clunky, mossy. ANTONYMS modern, fashionable.

old-time adjective *we danced to Grandfather's old-time music | it's an old-time tradition* OLD-STYLE, former, past, bygone, old-fashioned, historic; traditional, folk, ancestral, classical, old-world, quaint. ANTONYM modern.

WORD NOTE **old-time**

Old-time, once a fond word meant to bring up happy, nostalgic feelings, has been so completely subsumed by the marketing hive-mind that it now brings forth only thoughts of ersatz lemonade produced in city-sized vats, hard candies labeled "Grandma's" but made exclusively by child laborers of the Third World, and "entertainment" of the animatronic kind. **—EM**

omen noun *the torrential rains on day one of their journey was an omen of things to come* PORTENT, sign, signal, token, forewarning, warning, foreshadowing, prediction, forecast, prophecy, harbinger, augury, auspice, presage; straw in the wind, (hand)writing on the wall, indication, hint; *literary* foretoken. See note at SIGN.

ominous adjective *ominous clouds* THREATENING, menacing, baleful, forbidding, sinister, inauspicious, unpropitious, unfavorable, unpromising; portentous, foreboding, fateful, premonitory; black, dark, gloomy; *formal* minatory; *literary* direful; *rare* minacious. ANTONYMS promising, auspicious.

THE RIGHT WORD

A sky filled with low, dark clouds might look **ominous**, but it probably wouldn't be considered **portentous**, even though the root words *omen* and *portent* are nearly synonymous. What is *ominous* is usually threatening and may imply impending disaster (*an ominous silence*), while *portentous* is more often used to describe something that provokes awe or amazement (*a portentous show of military strength*) or a very important outcome (*a portentous moment for the American people*). Like *ominous*, **foreboding** implies that something evil is coming (*foreboding words that sent shivers through us*), while **forbidding** suggests an unfriendly or threatening appearance (*a dark, forbidding castle*). **Fateful** and **premonitory** are less frightening words. What is *fateful* appears to have been inevitable or decreed by fate, with an emphasis on decisive importance (*a fateful meeting with her ex-boyfriend; a battle that would prove fateful*). Anything that serves to warn beforehand is **premonitory**, whether or not the warning concerns something negative (*a premonitory dream about her father's death; a premonitory feeling about the exam*).

---

omission noun **1** *we have read the report, and there seem to be several omissions* EXCLUSION, leaving out, exception; deletion, cut, excision, elimination, erasure; gap, blank, absence; oversight. ANTONYM inclusion.

2 *the damage was not caused by any omission on behalf of the carrier* NEGLIGENCE, neglect, neglectfulness, dereliction, forgetfulness, oversight, default, lapse, failure. ANTONYM conscientiousness.

omit verb **1** *they omitted his name from the list* LEAVE OUT, exclude, leave off, fail to mention, miss, pass over; take out, drop, cut, delete, eliminate, erase, rub out, cross out, expunge, strike out. ANTONYM include.

2 *I omitted to mention our guest lecturer* FORGET, neglect, fail; leave undone, overlook, ignore, skip. ANTONYM remember.

omnipotence noun *the omnipotence of God* ALL-POWERFULNESS, almightiness, supremacy, preeminence, supreme power, absolute power, unlimited power; invincibility. ANTONYM powerlessness.

omnipotent adjective *the worship of omnipotent deities* ALL-POWERFUL, almighty, supreme, preeminent, most high; invincible, unconquerable.

omnipresent adjective *she was omnipresent in her children's lives long after her death* UBIQUITOUS, all-pervasive, everywhere; boundless, infinite; rife, pervasive, prevalent, far-reaching.

omniscient adjective *he thought I was some kind of omniscient guru* ALL-KNOWING, all-wise, all-seeing.

omnivorous adjective **1** *most duck species are omnivorous* ABLE TO EAT ANYTHING, having a mixed/varied diet; *rare* omnivorant.

2 *an omnivorous reader* OF VARIED TASTES, undiscriminating, indiscriminate, unselective.

on preposition **1** *your purse is on the hood of my car* RESTING ON, supported by, resting atop, touching the (upper) surface of. ANTONYMS under, underneath.

2 *put the cushion on the chair* SO AS TO BE RESTING ON, on to, onto, to the (upper) surface.

▸ adjective *the computer's on* FUNCTIONING, in operation, working, in use, operating. ANTONYM off.

▸ adverb *the professor droned on.* See ON AND ON below.

PHRASES: **on and off** *they've been dating, on and off, for years.* See OFF AND ON at OFF. **on and on** *after a few drinks, he blabbers on and on* FOR A LONG TIME, for ages, for hours, at (great) length, incessantly, ceaselessly, constantly, continuously, continually, endlessly, unendingly, eternally, forever, interminably, unremittingly, relentlessly, indefatigably, without letup, without a pause/break, without cease.

once adverb **1** *I spoke to him only once* ON ONE OCCASION, one time, one single time. ANTONYMS twice, many times, often.

2 *he did not once help* EVER, at any time, on any occasion, at all, under any circumstances, on any account.

3 *they were friends once* FORMERLY, previously, in the past, at one time, at one point, once upon a time, time was when, in days/times gone by, in times past, in the (good) old days, long ago; *archaic* sometime, erstwhile, whilom; *literary* in days/times of yore, of yore. ANTONYMS now, currently.

▸ conjunction *he'll be all right once she's gone* AS SOON AS, when, after, the instant, the second, the minute, the moment.

PHRASES: **at once 1** *you must leave at once* IMMEDIATELY, right away, right now, this instant, this second, this minute, this moment, now, straightaway, instantly, directly, forthwith, promptly, without delay, without hesitation, without further ado; quickly, as fast as possible, as soon as possible, ASAP, speedily; *informal* like a shot, in a flash, pronto, in two shakes (of a lamb's tail). ANTONYMS later, in due course. **2** *all the guests arrived at once* AT THE SAME TIME, at one and the same time, (all) together, simultaneously; as a group, in unison, in concert, in chorus. ANTONYMS singly, in dribs and drabs.

once and for all *I've made up my mind, once and for all* CONCLUSIVELY, decisively, finally, positively, definitely, definitively, absolutely, irrevocably; for good, for always, forever, permanently; *informal* for keeps. **once in a while** *we go hiking once in a while* OCCASIONALLY, from time to time, (every) now and then/again, every so often, on occasion, at times, sometimes, off and on, at intervals, periodically, sporadically, intermittently.

oncoming adjective *the lights from the oncoming traffic* | *bracing for the oncoming storm* APPROACHING, advancing, nearing, onrushing; forthcoming, on the way, imminent, impending, looming, gathering, (close) at hand, about to happen, to come.

one cardinal number **1** *each one is loosely wrapped* UNIT, item; *technical* monad.

2 *only one person came* A SINGLE, a solitary, a sole, a lone.

3 *her one concern was her daughter* ONLY, single, solitary, sole, exclusive.

4 *they have now become one* UNITED, a unit, unitary, amalgamated, consolidated, integrated, combined, incorporated, allied, affiliated, linked, joined, unified, in league, in partnership; wedded, married.

5 *I'll get my big break one day* SOME, any.

▸ pronoun *one never knows what tomorrow may bring.* See note below.

USAGE NOTE one

One is used as a pronoun to mean 'anyone' or 'I (or me) and people in general,' as in *one must try one's best.* In modern English, it is generally used only in formal and written contexts. In informal and spoken contexts, the normal alternative is **you**, as in *you must try your best.*

Until quite recently, sentences in which **one** is followed by **his** or **him** were considered perfectly correct: *one must try his best.* These uses are now held to be less than perfectly grammatical (and possibly sexist as well).

onerous adjective *the job had become onerous* BURDENSOME, arduous, strenuous, difficult, hard, severe, heavy, back-breaking, oppressive, weighty, uphill, formidable, laborious, Herculean, exhausting, tiring, taxing, demanding, punishing, grueling, exacting, wearing, wearisome, fatiguing; *archaic* toilsome. ANTONYMS effortless, easy.

oneself PHRASE: **by oneself.** See BY.

one-sided adjective **1** *a one-sided account* BIASED, prejudiced, partisan, partial, preferential, discriminatory, slanted, colored, inequitable, unfair, unjust. ANTONYMS impartial, fair-minded.

2 *a one-sided game* UNEQUAL, uneven, unbalanced, lopsided.

one-time adjective *a one-time Little League coach* FORMER, ex-, old, previous, sometime, erstwhile; lapsed; *formal* quondam.

ongoing adjective **1** *negotiations are ongoing* IN PROGRESS, under way, going on, continuing, taking place, proceeding, progressing, advancing; unfinished. ANTONYMS stalled, finished.

2 *an ongoing struggle* CONTINUOUS, continuing, uninterrupted, unbroken, nonstop, constant, around/round-the-clock, ceaseless, unceasing, unending, endless, never-ending, unremitting, relentless, unfaltering. ANTONYM intermittent.

online adjective **1** *online shopping environments* INTERNET, virtual, digital, cyber-, e-.

2 *our computers are now online* WEB-ENABLED, wired, hooked up.

onlooker noun *onlookers lined the streets* EYEWITNESS, witness, observer, looker-on, fly on the wall, spectator, watcher, viewer, bystander; sightseer; *informal* rubberneck; *literary* beholder.

only adverb **1** *there was only enough for two* AT MOST, at best, (only) just, no/not more than; barely, scarcely, hardly, narrowly.

2 *she works only on one painting at a time* EXCLUSIVELY, solely, to the exclusion of everything else.

3 *you're only saying that* MERELY, simply, just.

▸ adjective *their only son* SOLE, single, one (and only), solitary, lone, unique; exclusive.

USAGE NOTE **only**

In normal, everyday English, the tendency is to place the word **only** as early as possible in the sentence, generally just before the verb, and the result is rarely ambiguous. Misunderstandings are possible, however, and grammarians have debated the matter for more than two hundred years. Advice varies, but in general, ambiguity is less likely if *only* is placed as close as is naturally possible to the word(s) to be modified or emphasized:

The wording *Bill ate* ***only the salad*** explains that the salad was the sole item that Bill ate. There is no doubt what the statement means. The clear implication is that Bill did not eat the ham, the dessert, or anything else that may have been available.

The wording *Bill* ***only ate*** *the salad* almost certainly means the same thing, but in a literal sense, there is indeed some doubt. The linking of *only* with *ate* could imply that what Bill did to the salad was simply eat it; he did not prepare it, or spill it, or throw it across the room, or anything else that one could imagine doing to a salad.

In normal conversation, the second statement would probably not be so misunderstood, but, especially when writing, it's never a mistake to favor the less ambiguous wording.

onomatopoeic adjective *several words that describe sounds are onomatopoeic, like 'hiss' and 'buzz'* IMITATIVE, echoic.

onset noun *they foolishly ignored the onset of his aggressive behavior* START, beginning, commencement, arrival, (first) appearance, inception, emergence, day one, outbreak, dawn, genesis. ANTONYM end.

onslaught noun *the battalion's onslaught was relentless* ASSAULT, attack, offensive, advance, charge, onrush, rush, storming, sortie, sally, raid, descent, incursion, invasion, foray, push, thrust, drive, blitz, bombardment, barrage, salvo; *historical* broadside.

onus noun *the onus of single parenting* BURDEN, responsibility, liability, obligation, duty, weight, load, charge, mantle, encumbrance; cross to bear, millstone round one's neck, albatross.

oops exclamation See WHOOPS.

ooze verb **1** *blood oozed from the wound* SEEP, discharge, flow, exude, trickle, drip, dribble, issue, filter, percolate, escape, leak, drain, empty, bleed, sweat, well; *Medicine* extravasate.

2 *she was positively oozing charm* EXUDE, gush, drip, pour forth, emanate, radiate.

▸ noun **1** *the ooze of blood* SEEPAGE, seeping, discharge, flow, exudation, trickle, drip, dribble, percolation, escape, leak, leakage, drainage; secretion, excretion; *Medicine* extravasation.

2 *the ooze on the ocean floor* MUD, slime, alluvium, silt, mire, sludge, muck, deposit.

opacity noun **1** *analyzing the opacity of their drinking water* CLOUDINESS, nontransparency, opaqueness, filminess, blurriness, blurredness, blur, haziness, haze. ANTONYMS transparency, translucence, clarity.

2 *the opacity of his arguments* OBSCURITY, lack of clarity, abstruseness, unclearness, unintelligibility, density, incomprehensibility. ANTONYM clarity.

opalescent adjective *opalescent sequins* IRIDESCENT, prismatic, rainbowlike, kaleidoscopic, multicolored, many-hued, lustrous, shimmering, glittering, sparkling, variegated, scintillating, shot, moiré, opaline, milky, pearly, nacreous.

opaque adjective **1** *opaque glass* NONTRANSPARENT, cloudy, filmy, blurred, smeared, smeary, misty, hazy; dirty, muddy, muddied, grimy. ANTONYMS transparent, translucent, clear.

2 *the technical jargon was opaque to him* OBSCURE, unclear, mysterious, puzzling, perplexing, baffling, mystifying, confusing, unfathomable, incomprehensible, unintelligible, ambiguous, Delphic, impenetrable, oblique, enigmatic, cryptic, hazy, foggy; *informal* as clear as mud. ANTONYM clear.

open adjective **1** *the door's open* NOT SHUT, not closed, unlocked, unbolted, unlatched, off the latch, unfastened, unsecured; ajar, gaping, wide open, yawning. ANTONYMS closed, shut.

2 *a blue silk shirt, open at the neck* UNFASTENED, not done up, undone, loose; unbuttoned, unzipped, unbuckled, untied, unlaced.

3 *the main roads are open* CLEAR, passable, navigable, unblocked, unobstructed. ANTONYMS blocked, impassable.

4 *open countryside | open spaces* UNENCLOSED, rolling, sweeping, extensive, wide open, unfenced, exposed, unsheltered; spacious, airy, uncrowded, uncluttered; undeveloped, unbuilt-up. ANTONYMS enclosed, developed.

5 *a map was open beside him* SPREAD OUT, unfolded, unfurled, unrolled; extended, stretched out. ANTONYMS closed (up), folded.

6 *the bank wasn't open* OPEN FOR BUSINESS, open to the public. ANTONYM closed.

7 *the position is still open* AVAILABLE, vacant, free, unfilled; *informal* up for grabs. ANTONYMS unavailable, filled.

8 *the system is **open to** abuse* VULNERABLE TO, subject to, susceptible to, liable to, exposed to, an easy target for, at risk of, permitting of. ANTONYM immune.

9 *she was open about her feelings* FRANK, candid, honest, forthcoming, communicative, forthright, direct, unreserved, plain-spoken, outspoken, straightforward, blunt, not afraid to call a spade a spade; *informal* upfront; *archaic* free-spoken. ANTONYMS secretive, withdrawn.

10 *open hostility* OVERT, obvious, patent, manifest, palpable, conspicuous, plain, undisguised, unconcealed, clear, apparent, evident; blatant, flagrant, barefaced, brazen. ANTONYM concealed.

11 *the case is still open* UNRESOLVED, undecided, unsettled, yet to be settled, up in the air; open to debate, open for discussion, arguable, debatable, moot. ANTONYMS resolved, concluded.

12 *an open mind* IMPARTIAL, unbiased, unprejudiced, objective, disinterested, nonpartisan, nondiscriminatory, neutral, dispassionate, detached. ANTONYMS biased, one-sided.

13 *I'm open to suggestions* RECEPTIVE, amenable, willing to listen, ready to listen, responsive.

14 *what other options are open to us?* AVAILABLE, accessible, on hand, obtainable.

15 *an open meeting* PUBLIC, general, unrestricted, nonexclusive, nonrestrictive. ANTONYM private.

▸ verb **1** *she opened the front door* UNFASTEN, unlatch, unlock, unbolt, unbar; throw wide. ANTONYMS close, shut.

2 *Katherine opened the parcel* UNWRAP, undo, untie, unseal. ANTONYMS wrap, seal.

3 *shall I open another bottle?* UNCORK, broach, crack (open). ANTONYMS seal, cork.

4 *Adam opened the map* SPREAD OUT, unfold, unfurl, unroll, straighten out; extend, stretch out. ANTONYMS close, fold up.

5 *he opened his heart to her* REVEAL, uncover, expose, lay bare, bare, pour out, disclose, divulge.

6 *we're hoping to open next month* OPEN FOR BUSINESS, start trading, set up shop; *informal* hang out one's shingle.

7 *Valerie opened the meeting* BEGIN, start, commence, initiate, set in motion, launch, get going, get underway, get the ball rolling, get off the ground; inaugurate; *informal* kick off, get the show on the road. ANTONYMS conclude, end.

8 *the lounge **opens on to** a balcony* GIVE ACCESS TO, lead to, be connected to, communicate with; face, overlook, command a view of.

▸ ***open***
begin
start
activate
initiate
commence
usher in
get going
bring into being
embark on
lay the foundations of
kick off
get underway
get the show on the road
launch
set in motion
get off the ground
get the ball rolling
introduce
inaugurate
institute
create
give rise to
promote
develop
evolve
unfold
mature
reach maturity
bring to fruition
fulfill
consummate
complete
wind up
wrap up
adjourn
dissolve
prorogue
suspend
intermit
halt
break off
discontinue
end
bring an end to
bring to an end
stop
finish
terminate
conclude
bring to a conclusion
close ◂

open-air adjective *an open-air market* OUTDOOR, out-of-doors, outside, alfresco, al fresco. ANTONYM indoor.

openhanded adjective *it was a much-appreciated openhanded contribution* GENEROUS, magnanimous, charitable, benevolent, beneficent, munificent, bountiful, liberal, unstinting; altruistic, philanthropic; *literary* bounteous. ANTONYMS tightfisted, stingy.

opening noun **1** *an opening in the center of the roof* HOLE, gap, aperture, orifice, vent; peephole; split, crack, fissure, cleft, crevice, chink, slit; perforation; *Anatomy* foramen.

2 *the opening in the wall* DOORWAY, gateway, portal, entrance, (means of) entry, entryway, way in, (means of) access; way out, exit, egress.

3 *their defensive lapse gave Torrez the opening he needed* OPPORTUNITY, chance, window (of opportunity), possibility; *informal* (lucky) break, shot.

4 *an opening in the sales department* VACANCY, position, job, opportunity.

5 *the opening of the session* BEGINNING, start, commencement, outset, inception; introduction, prefatory remarks, opening statement; *informal* kickoff; *formal* proem. ANTONYMS close, closure.

6 *a gallery opening* OPENING CEREMONY, official opening, launch, inauguration; opening night, premiere, first showing, first night; vernissage.

openly adverb 1 *drugs were openly on sale* PUBLICLY, for all to see, blatantly, flagrantly, brazenly, boldly, overtly, in full view; shamelessly, immodestly, wantonly. ANTONYMS secretly, covertly.

2 *the senator spoke openly of his drinking problems* FRANKLY, candidly, explicitly, honestly, sincerely, forthrightly, straightforwardly, bluntly, without constraint, without holding back, straight from the shoulder, straight from the hip. ANTONYMS allusively, indirectly.

open-minded adjective 1 *open-minded attitudes* UNBIASED, unprejudiced, nonpartisan, neutral, nonjudgmental, nondiscriminatory; objective, dispassionate, disinterested; tolerant, liberal, permissive, broad-minded. ANTONYMS prejudiced, judgmental.

2 *it was a progressive school that appealed to parents who were open-minded* RECEPTIVE, open to suggestions, open to new ideas, amenable, flexible, willing to change. ANTONYM narrow-minded.

open-mouthed adjective *Riley's friends stood frozen and open-mouthed when he confessed to being the arsonist* ASTOUNDED, amazed, in amazement, surprised, stunned, bowled over, staggered, thunderstruck, aghast, agape, stupefied, dazed, taken aback, shocked, in shock, speechless, dumbfounded, dumbstruck, at a loss for words; *informal* flabbergasted.

opera GRAND OPERA, light opera, musical, musical comedy, opéra bouffe, operetta.

WORD NOTE **opera**

Opera, contrary to a commonly held view, does not mean "a play sung through without speech," so cutting the dialogue doesn't make a musical an opera. Rather, *opera* is a musical theater style in which audience comprehension of the lyrics is subordinate to purity of vocal tone. Thus opera need not be translated to be sung abroad, whereas an untranslated musical would induce catatonia. *Operetta* is something in between: either a comic opera, which depends on understanding the words; or a very pretty musical, whose characters are usually opera singers, which excuses any difficulty in understanding what they say. —**SM**

operate verb 1 *he can operate the machine* WORK, run, make go, use, utilize, handle, control, manage; drive, steer, maneuver.

2 *the machine ceased to operate* FUNCTION, work, go, run, be in working/running order, be operative. ANTONYM break down.

3 *the way the law operates in practice* TAKE EFFECT, act, apply, be applied, function.

4 *he operated the mine until 1931* DIRECT, control, manage, run, govern, administer, superintend, head (up), supervise, oversee, preside over, be in control/charge of.

5 *doctors decided to operate* PERFORM SURGERY, do an operation; *informal* put under the knife.

operation noun 1 *the slide bars ensure smooth operation* FUNCTIONING, working, running, performance, action.

2 *the operation of the factory* MANAGEMENT, running, control, direction, governing, administration, supervision.

3 *a cardiologist from Atlanta will perform the operation* SURGERY, surgical procedure.

4 *a military operation* ACTION, activity, exercise, undertaking, enterprise, maneuver, campaign.

5 *their mining operation in Pennsylvania* BUSINESS, enterprise, company, organization, firm, concern; *informal* outfit, setup. PHRASE: **in operation** *only one of the automatic doors was in operation.* See OPERATIONAL.

operational adjective *the new conveyor belts will be operational by tomorrow* UP AND RUNNING, running, working, functioning, operative, in operation, in use, in action; in working order, workable, serviceable, functional, usable, ready for action. ANTONYMS out of order, broken.

operative adjective 1 *this piece of legislation is not yet operative* IN FORCE, in operation, in effect, valid. ANTONYM invalid.

2 *most of our antique machinery is operative.* See OPERATIONAL.

3 *when I say 'perhaps I'll go,' the operative word is 'perhaps'* KEY, significant, relevant, applicable, pertinent, apposite, germane, crucial, critical, pivotal, central, essential. ANTONYM irrelevant.

▸ noun 1 *the operatives clean the machines* MACHINIST, (machine) operator, mechanic, engineer, worker, workman, blue-collar worker.

2 *an operative of the CIA* AGENT, secret agent, undercover agent, spy, mole, plant, double agent; *informal* spook; *archaic* intelligencer.

3 *we hired our own operatives* DETECTIVE, private detective, investigator, private investigator, sleuth; *informal* private eye, bloodhound; *informal, dated* gumshoe, dick, private dick.

operator noun 1 *a machine operator* MACHINIST, mechanic, operative, engineer, driver, worker.

2 *a tour operator* CONTRACTOR, entrepreneur, promoter, arranger, fixer, dealer, outfitter, expediter.

3 *informal a ruthless operator* MANIPULATOR, maneuverer, mover and shaker, wheeler-dealer, hustler, wirepuller.

opiate noun *she refused to take the prescribed opiates* DRUG, narcotic, sedative, tranquilizer, depressant, soporific, anesthetic, painkiller, analgesic, anodyne; morphine, opium, codeine; *informal* dope; *Medicine* stupefacient.

opine verb *formal he opined that a relaxed dress code was inconsistent with the club's image* SUGGEST, say, declare, observe, comment, remark, submit, put forward; contend, be convinced; think, believe, consider, maintain, be of the opinion, imagine, reckon, guess, assume, presume, take it, suppose, reason; *informal* allow.

opinion noun *she did not share her husband's opinion* BELIEF, judgment, thought(s), (way of) thinking, mind, (point of) view, viewpoint, outlook, attitude, stance, position, perspective, persuasion, standpoint; sentiment, conception, conviction. PHRASES: **a matter of opinion** *whether his art is worthy of an exhibition is a matter of opinion* DEBATABLE, open to question, open to debate, a moot point, up to the individual. **be of the opinion** *we are of the opinion that his poetry lacks insight* BELIEVE, think, consider, maintain, reckon, estimate, feel, have a/the feeling, contend, be convinced; *informal* allow; *formal* opine. **in my opinion** *in my opinion, the green tiles clash with the yellow walls* AS I SEE IT, to my mind, (according) to my way of thinking, personally, in my estimation, if you ask me, for my money, in my book.

THE RIGHT WORD

When you give your **opinion** on something, you offer a conclusion or a judgment that, although it may be open to question, seems true or probable to you at the time (*she was known for her strong opinions on women in the workplace*). A **view** is an opinion that is affected by your personal feelings or biases (*his views on life were essentially optimistic*), while a **sentiment** is a more or less settled opinion that may still be colored by emotion (*her sentiments on aging were shared by many other women approaching fifty*). A **belief** differs from an opinion or a view in that it is not necessarily the creation of the person who holds it; the emphasis here is on the mental acceptance of an idea, a proposition, or a doctrine and on the assurance of its truth (*religious beliefs; his belief in the power of the body to heal itself*). A **conviction** is a firmly-held and unshakable belief whose truth is not doubted (*she could not be swayed in her convictions*), while a **persuasion** (in this sense) is a strong belief that is unshakable because you want to believe that it's true rather than because there is evidence proving it so (*she was of the persuasion that he was innocent*).

opinionated adjective *she got tired of listening to her opinionated boyfriend* DOGMATIC, of fixed views, dictatorial, pontifical, domineering, pompous, self-important, arrogant; inflexible, uncompromising, prejudiced, bigoted. ANTONYMS open-minded, flexible.

opponent noun **1** *his political opponent* RIVAL, adversary, opposer, (the) opposition, fellow contestant, (fellow) competitor, enemy, antagonist, combatant, contender, challenger; *literary* foe. ANTONYMS ally, partner.

2 *an opponent of the reforms* OPPOSER, objector, dissenter, dissident. ANTONYM supporter.

opportune adjective *it seemed like the most opportune occasion to make our announcement* AUSPICIOUS, propitious, favorable, advantageous, golden, felicitous; timely, convenient, suitable, appropriate, apt, fitting. ANTONYMS inopportune, disadvantageous. See note at TIMELY.

opportunism noun *she scaled the ladder of success with hard work and opportunism* EXPEDIENCY, pragmatism, exploitation, Machiavellianism, maneuvering; pushing (all) the right buttons striking while the iron is hot, making hay while the sun shines.

opportunity noun *this is your opportunity to move on* | *don't miss another opportunity* CHANCE, lucky chance, favorable time/occasion/moment, time, right set of circumstances, occasion, moment, opening, option, window (of opportunity), turn, go, possibility; *informal* shot, break, new lease on life.

oppose verb *most voters opposed the new school budget* BE AGAINST, object to, be hostile to, be in opposition to, disagree with, dislike, disapprove of; resist, take a stand against, put up a fight against, stand up to, fight, challenge; take issue with, dispute, argue with/against, quarrel with; *informal* be anti-; *formal* gainsay; *rare* controvert. ANTONYM support.

opposed adjective **1** *the residents are **opposed to** the building of a nuclear power plant* AGAINST, (dead) set against; in opposition to, averse to, hostile to, antagonistic to, antipathetic to, resistant to; *informal* anti. ANTONYM in favor of.

2 *their interests were opposed.* See OPPOSING sense 1. PHRASE: **as opposed to** *we use only steam, as opposed to chemical products, to clean our house* IN CONTRAST WITH, as against, as contrasted with, rather than, instead of, as an alternative to.

opposing adjective **1** *two opposing points of view* CONFLICTING, contrasting, opposite, incompatible, irreconcilable, contradictory, antithetical, differing, different, dissimilar clashing, at variance, at odds, divergent, opposed, poles apart, polar. ANTONYMS similar, in agreement, identical.

2 *opposing sides in the war* RIVAL, opposite, enemy, antagonistic. ANTONYM allied.

3 *the opposing page* OPPOSITE, facing.

opposite adjective **1** *the opposite page* FACING, opposing, reverse.

2 *opposite views* CONFLICTING, contrasting, incompatible, irreconcilable, antithetical, contradictory, clashing, contrary, at variance, at odds, different, differing, divergent, dissimilar, unalike, disagreeing, opposed, opposing, poles apart, polar. ANTONYMS similar, same, identical.

3 *opposite sides in a war* RIVAL, opposing, enemy. ANTONYM same.

▸ preposition *they sit opposite one another* FACING, face to face with, across from; *informal* eyeball to eyeball with; *archaic* fronting.

▸ noun *the opposite was also true* REVERSE, converse, antithesis, contrary, inverse, obverse, antipode; the other side of the coin; *informal* flip side.

THE RIGHT WORD

All of these adjectives are usually applied to abstractions and are used to describe ideas, statements, qualities, forces, etc., that are so far apart as to seem irreconcilable. **Opposite** refers to ideas or things that are symmetrically opposed in position, direction, or character—in other words, that are set against each other in such a way that the contrast or conflict between them is highlighted (*they sat opposite one another at the table*). **Contradictory** goes a little further, implying that if one of two opposing statements, propositions, or principles is true, the other must be false (*he assured us the fee would be under $500; his partner gave us contradictory information, saying costs could go as high as $800.*). Two contradictory elements are mutually exclusive; for example, *alive* and *dead* are contradictory terms because logically they cannot be applied to the same thing. **Antithetical** implies that the two things being contrasted are diametrically opposed—as far apart or as different from each other as is possible (*they debated the antithetical theories of creationism and evolution*). **Contrary** adds connotations of conflict or antagonism (*the group's discussion was hindered by his contrary remarks*). **Reverse** applies to that which moves or faces in the opposite direction (*he scribbled something on the reverse side of her business card*).

opposition noun **1** *the proposal met with opposition* RESISTANCE, hostility, antagonism, enmity, antipathy, objection, dissent, disapproval, criticism, demurral; defiance, noncompliance, obstruction.

2 *they beat the opposition* OPPONENTS, opposing side, other side, other team, competition, opposers, rivals, adversaries; enemies; *literary* foes.

3 *the opposition between the public and the private domains* CONFLICT, clash, disparity, antithesis, polarity.

oppress verb **1** *the invaders oppressed the people* PERSECUTE, abuse, maltreat, ill-treat, tyrannize, crush, repress, suppress, subjugate, subdue, keep down, grind down, ride roughshod over, rule with an iron fist/hand.

2 *the darkness of winter oppressed her* DEPRESS, make gloomy, make despondent, weigh down, weigh heavily on, cast down, dampen someone's spirits, dispirit, dishearten, discourage, sadden, get down, bring down; *archaic* deject.

oppressed adjective *talk of a revolution spread rapidly among the oppressed masses* PERSECUTED, downtrodden, abused, maltreated, ill-treated, subjugated, tyrannized, repressed, subdued, crushed, browbeaten; disadvantaged, underprivileged.

oppression noun *the young people in this country have known nothing but oppression* PERSECUTION, abuse, maltreatment, ill-treatment, tyranny, despotism repression, suppression, subjection, subjugation; cruelty, brutality, injustice, hardship, suffering, misery. ANTONYMS freedom, democracy.

oppressive adjective **1** *an oppressive dictatorship* HARSH, cruel, brutal, repressive, tyrannical, tyrannous, iron-fisted, autocratic, dictatorial, despotic, undemocratic; ruthless, merciless, pitiless, draconian. ANTONYMS lenient, humane.

2 *an oppressive sense of despair* OVERWHELMING, overpowering, unbearable, unendurable, intolerable, burdensome.

3 *it was gray and oppressive* MUGGY, close, heavy, hot, humid, sticky, steamy, airless, stuffy, stifling, suffocating, sultry. ANTONYMS airy, fresh.

oppressor noun *the rebels overthrew their oppressors in a bloody coup* PERSECUTOR, tyrant, despot, autocrat, dictator, subjugator, tormentor, slave driver, taskmaster.

opprobrious adjective *he was embarrassed by his father's opprobrious remarks* ABUSIVE, vituperative, derogatory, disparaging, denigratory, pejorative, deprecatory, insulting, offensive, defamatory, vitriolic, libelous, venomous; scornful, contemptuous, derisive; *informal* bitchy.

opprobrium noun **1** *the government endured months of opprobrium* VILIFICATION, abuse, vituperation, condemnation, criticism, censure, denunciation, defamation, denigration, castigation, disparagement, obloquy, derogation, slander, calumny, execration, lambasting, bad press, invective, libel, character assassination; *informal* flak, mudslinging, bad-mouthing, tongue-lashing; *formal* excoriation; *archaic* contumely; *rare* objurgation. ANTONYM praise.

2 *the opprobrium of being associated with thugs* DISGRACE, shame, dishonor, stigma, humiliation, discredit, loss of face, ignominy, obloquy, disrepute, infamy, notoriety, scandal; *rare* disesteem. ANTONYM honor.

opt verb **1** *I always **opt for** the better quality* CHOOSE, select, pick (out), decide on, go for, settle on, take.

2 *she's opted to stay in Richmond* CHOOSE, elect, decide, make/reach the decision, make up one's mind.

optimism noun *I wish I had your optimism* HOPEFULNESS, hope, confidence, buoyancy, cheer, cheerfulness, good cheer, sanguineness, positiveness, positive attitude. ANTONYM pessimism.

optimistic adjective **1** *she felt optimistic about the future* HOPEFUL, confident, positive, cheerful, cheery, sanguine, bright, buoyant, full of hope, bullish, Panglossian, Pollyannaish; *informal* upbeat; *dated* of good cheer. ANTONYMS pessimistic, hopeless.

2 *the forecast is optimistic* ENCOURAGING, promising, hopeful, reassuring, favorable, auspicious, propitious. ANTONYMS ominous, gloomy.

optimistic
hopeful
full of hope
confident
self-confident
self-assured
sanguine
positive
expecting the best
looking on the bright side
bright
cheery
cheerful
of good cheer
buoyant
bullish
upbeat
chirpy
sunny
glad
untroubled
without a care in the world
light-hearted
in good spirits
in high spirits
good-humored
good-natured
unworried
willing to go along
open-minded
having a wait-and-see attitude
uncommitted
indifferent
detached
unenthusiastic
unenthused
dispirited
disheartened
blue
down
down in the dumps
gloomy
gloom-ridden
glum
downbeat
negative
lugubrious
discouraged
lacking confidence
having lost heart
depressed
despairing
despondent
hopeless
pessimistic

optimum adjective *the team is in optimum health | this is the optimum gas-to-oil ratio* (THE) BEST, (the) best of(the) most favorable, (the) most advantageous, ideal, perfect, prime, optimal, model; top, (the) finest, peak, excellent; *informal* tip-top, top-notch, A1.

option noun **1** *leave quietly or be forcibly removed—it's your option* CHOICE, alternative, recourse, course of action; power to choose, right to choose.

2 *there are three options: beef, chicken, fish* CHOICE, selection, alternative, possibility, way to go; *informal* bet.

optional adjective *in senior year, phys ed is optional* VOLUNTARY, discretionary, not required, elective, noncompulsory, nonmandatory; *Law* permissive; *rare* discretional. ANTONYMS compulsory, mandatory, required.

opulence noun **1** *the opulence of the room* LUXURIOUSNESS, sumptuousness, lavishness, richness, luxury, luxuriance, splendor, magnificence, grandeur, splendidness; *informal* plushness, classiness, ritziness, poshness, swankiness. ANTONYMS simplicity, restraint.

2 *a display of opulence* WEALTH, affluence, wealthiness, richness, riches, prosperity, money. ANTONYM poverty.

opulent adjective **1** *his opulent home* LUXURIOUS, sumptuous, palatial, lavish, lavishly appointed, rich, splendid, magnificent, grand, grandiose, fancy; *informal* plush, classy, ritzy, posh, swanky, swank. ANTONYMS spartan, stark, ascetic.

2 *an opulent family* WEALTHY, rich, affluent, well off, well-to-do, moneyed, prosperous, of means, of substance; *informal* well-heeled, rolling in money/dough, rolling in it, loaded, stinking/filthy rich, made of money, in clover, (living) on easy street; *dated* in the chips. See note at WEALTHY. ANTONYMS penniless, poor, impoverished.

3 *her opulent red hair* COPIOUS, abundant, profuse, prolific, plentiful, luxuriant; *literary* plenteous. ANTONYMS sparse, thin.

opus noun *her latest opus is a critical success* COMPOSITION, work, work of art, oeuvre, piece, creation.

oracle noun **1** *the oracle of Apollo* PROPHET, PROPHETESS, sibyl, seer, augur, prognosticator, diviner, soothsayer, fortune teller, sage.

2 *our oracle on Africa* AUTHORITY, expert, specialist, pundit, mentor, adviser, guru.

oracular adjective **1** *his every utterance was given oracular significance* PROPHETIC, prophetical, sibylline, predictive, prescient, prognostic, divinatory, augural.

2 *oracular responses* ENIGMATIC, cryptic, abstruse, unclear, obscure, confusing, mystifying, baffling, puzzling, perplexing, mysterious, arcane; ambiguous, equivocal, Delphic. ANTONYMS clear, unambiguous.

oral adjective *an oral agreement* SPOKEN, verbal, unwritten, vocal, uttered, said, by mouth, viva voce. ANTONYM written.

▸ noun *studying for French orals* ORAL EXAMINATION; *Brit.* viva, viva voce.

orate verb *she orated with a contagious passion* DECLAIM, make a speech, hold forth, speak, discourse, pontificate, preach, sermonize, sound off, spout off, speechify; *informal* spiel; *formal* perorate, *humorous* bloviate.

WORD NOTE **bloviate**

Just what it sounds like, *bloviate* means "to pontificate or give a pompous speech," especially when the speaker is a self-promoting blowhard. It was used by (and probably about) Warren G. Harding, president from 1921 to 1923. Earlier examples date to the 1850s. **—JS**

oration noun *an oration given in memory of McKinley* SPEECH, address, lecture, talk, homily, sermon, discourse, declamation, valedictory, salutatory; *informal* spiel; *rare* allocution.

orator noun *Patrick Henry, the great orator* SPEAKER, public speaker, speech-maker, lecturer, declaimer, rhetorician, rhetor.

oratorical adjective *he imitated the oratorical style of Churchill* RHETORICAL, grandiloquent, magniloquent, high-flown, orotund, bombastic, grandiose, pompous, pretentious, overblown, declamatory, turgid, flowery, florid, Ciceronian; *informal,* silver-tongued; *rare* euphuistic, fustian. ANTONYMS plain-spoken, simple.

oratory noun *Dr. King was noted for his oratory* RHETORIC, eloquence, grandiloquence, magniloquence, public speaking, speech-making, declamation, way with words; *informal* (the) gift of gab, silver tongue.

orb noun *the hallway features a display of luminous orbs suspended at various lengths from the ceiling* SPHERE, globe, ball; spheroid, spherule; circle.

WORD NOTE **orbs**

Reeks of mawkish adolescent poetry in almost every one of its surviving usages, and now obsolete in its previously strong astrological sense—those concentric hollow spheres we once believed surrounded the earth and carried the planets and stars with them in their revolutions. It is never to be used as a synonym for *eyes,* particularly not in any attempts at feminine flattery unless hilarity is the desired result. Eyes are eyes. Circular and spherical forms are properly *orbs,* but there's rarely a compelling reason to call them such. **—ZS**

orbit noun **1** *the monthly orbit of the Moon* COURSE, path, circuit, track, trajectory, rotation, revolution, circle; *rare* circumgyration.

2 *the problem comes outside our orbit* SPHERE, sphere of influence, area of activity, range, scope, ambit, compass, jurisdiction, authority, domain, realm, province, territory, turf; *informal* bailiwick.

▸ verb *Mercury orbits the Sun* REVOLVE AROUND, circle around, go around, travel around.

orchestra noun *the orchestra needs another percussionist* ENSEMBLE; *informal* band. See table on page 638.

orchestrate verb **1** *the piece was orchestrated by Mozart* ARRANGE, adapt, score.

2 *orchestrating a campaign of civil disobedience* ORGANIZE, arrange, plan, set up, bring about, mobilize, mount, stage, stage-manage, mastermind, coordinate, direct, engineer, choreograph.

ordain verb **1** *the Church voted to ordain women* CONFER HOLY ORDERS ON, appoint, anoint, consecrate, install, invest, induct.

2 *the path ordained by fate* PREDETERMINE, predestine, preordain, destine, determine, prescribe, designate, will.

ORCHESTRAL INSTRUMENTS

bass clarinet	oboe
bass drum	piano
bassoon	piccolo
celesta/celeste	snare drum
cello	tam-tam
chimes	tambourine
clarinet	timpani
contrabassoon	triangle
cymbals/crash cymbals	trombone
double bass/string bass	trumpet
English horn/cor anglais	tuba/bass tuba
flute	tubular bells
French horn	viola
glockenspiel	violoncello
gong	violin
harp	xylophone
kettledrums	

3 *she ordained that anyone found hunting in the forest must pay a fine* DECREE, rule, order, command, enjoin, lay/set down, establish, dictate, legislate, prescribe, pronounce.

ordeal noun *the hostages survived the ordeal* UNPLEASANT EXPERIENCE, painful experience, trial, tribulation, nightmare, trauma, hell (on earth), misery, trouble, difficulty, torture, torment, agony.

order noun 1 *alphabetical order* SEQUENCE, arrangement, organization, disposition, system, series, succession; grouping, classification, categorization, codification, systematization.

2 *his tidy desk demonstrates his sense of order* TIDINESS, neatness, orderliness, organization, method, system; symmetry, uniformity, regularity; routine. ANTONYMS chaos, disarray.

3 *the police were needed to keep order* PEACE, control, law (and order), lawfulness, discipline, calm, (peace and) quiet, peacefulness, peaceableness.

4 *the equipment was in good order* CONDITION, state, repair, shape.

5 *I had to obey her orders* COMMAND, instruction, directive, direction, decree, edict, injunction, mandate, dictate, commandment, rescript; law, rule, regulation, diktat; demand, bidding, requirement, stipulation; *informal* say-so; *formal* ordinance; *literary* behest. ANTONYM suggestion.

6 *the company has won the order* COMMISSION, contract, purchase order, request, requisition; booking, reservation. ANTONYM chaos.

7 *the lower orders of society* CLASS, level, rank, grade, degree, position, category; *dated* station.

8 *the established social order* (CLASS) SYSTEM, hierarchy, pecking order, grading, ranking, scale.

9 *the higher orders of insects* TAXONOMIC GROUP, class, family, species, breed; taxon.

10 *a religious order* COMMUNITY, brotherhood, sisterhood, organization, association, society, fellowship, fraternity, confraternity, congregation, sodality, lodge, guild, league, union, club; sect.

11 *skills of a very high order* TYPE, kind, sort, nature, variety; quality, caliber, standard.

▸ verb 1 *he ordered me to return* INSTRUCT, command, direct, enjoin, tell, require, charge; *formal* adjure; *literary* bid.

2 *the judge ordered that their assets be confiscated* DECREE, ordain, rule, legislate, dictate, prescribe.

3 *you can order your tickets by phone* REQUEST, apply for, place an order for; book, reserve; *formal* bespeak.

4 *the messages are ordered chronologically* ORGANIZE, put in order, arrange, sort out, marshal, dispose, lay out; group, classify, categorize, catalog, codify, systematize, systemize.

PHRASES: **in order** 1 *list the dates in order* IN SEQUENCE, in series. 2 *he found everything in order* TIDY, neat, orderly, straight, trim, shipshape, in apple-pie order; in position, in place. 3 *I think it's in order for me to take the credit* APPROPRIATE, fitting, suitable, acceptable, (all) right, permissible, permitted, allowable; *informal* okay. **order about/around** *what makes him think he can just waltz in and start ordering us about?* TELL WHAT TO DO, give orders to, dictate to; lay down the law to; *informal* boss around, push around. **out of order** *the elevator's out of order* NOT WORKING, not in working order, not functioning, broken, broken-down, out of service, out of commission, faulty, defective, inoperative; down; *informal* conked out, bust, busted, (gone) kaput, on the fritz, on the blink, out of whack.

orderly adjective 1 *an orderly room* NEAT, tidy, well-ordered, in order, trim, in apple-pie order, spick-and-span, shipshape. ANTONYMS untidy, messy.

2 *the orderly presentation of information* (WELL) ORGANIZED, efficient, methodical, systematic, meticulous, punctilious; coherent, structured, logical, well-planned, well regulated, systematized. ANTONYM disorganized.

3 *the crowd was orderly* WELL-BEHAVED, law-abiding, disciplined, peaceful, peaceable, nonviolent. ANTONYM unruly.

ordinance noun *formal* 1 *the president issued an ordinance* EDICT, decree, law, injunction, fiat, command, order, rule, ruling, dictum, dictate, directive, mandate.

2 *religious ordinances* RITE, ritual, ceremony, sacrament, observance, service.

ordinarily adverb *he ordinarily worked from home* USUALLY, normally, as a (general) rule, generally, in general, for the most part, mainly, mostly, most of the time, typically, habitually, commonly, routinely.

ordinary adjective 1 *the ordinary course of events* USUAL, normal, standard, typical, common, customary, habitual, everyday, regular, routine, day-to-day. See note at NORMAL. See also word spectrum at ODD. ANTONYM abnormal.

2 *my life seemed very ordinary* AVERAGE, normal, run-of-the-mill, standard, typical, middle-of-the-road, conventional, unremarkable, unexceptional, workaday, undistinguished, nondescript, colorless, commonplace, humdrum, mundane, unmemorable, pedestrian, prosaic, quotidian, uninteresting, uneventful, dull, boring, bland, suburban, hackneyed, garden-variety; *informal* plain-vanilla, nothing to write home about, no great shakes. ANTONYMS unusual, exceptional.

PHRASE: **out of the ordinary** *nothing out of the ordinary happened* UNUSUAL, exceptional, remarkable, extraordinary, unexpected, surprising, unaccustomed, unfamiliar, abnormal, atypical, different, special, exciting, memorable, noteworthy, unique, singular, outstanding; unconventional, unorthodox, strange, peculiar, odd, queer, curious, bizarre, outlandish; *informal* offbeat.

ordnance noun *the disposal of WWI ordnance continues* GUNS, cannon, artillery, weapons, arms, ammunition; munitions, materiel.

ordure noun *neighbors complained about the ordure in the kennels* EXCREMENT, excreta, dung, manure, muck, droppings, feces, stools, night soil, sewage; *informal* poo, poop.

organ noun **1** *the internal organs* BODY PART, biological structure.

2 *the official organ of the Communist Party* NEWSPAPER, paper, journal, periodical, magazine, newsletter, gazette, publication, mouthpiece; *informal* rag.

organic adjective **1** *organic matter* LIVING, live, animate, biological, biotic.

2 *organic vegetables* PESTICIDE-FREE, additive-free, natural.

3 *the love scenes were an organic part of the drama* ESSENTIAL, fundamental, integral, intrinsic, vital, indispensable, inherent.

4 *a society is an organic whole* STRUCTURED, organized, coherent, integrated, coordinated, ordered, harmonious.

organism noun **1** *fish and other organisms* LIVING THING, being, creature, animal, plant, life form.

2 *a complex political organism* STRUCTURE, system, organization, entity.

organization noun **1** *the organization of conferences* PLANNING, arrangement, coordination, administration, organizing, running, management.

2 *the overall organization of the book* STRUCTURE, arrangement, plan, pattern, order, form, format, framework, composition, constitution.

3 *his lack of organization* EFFICIENCY, order, orderliness, planning.

4 *a large international organization* COMPANY, firm, corporation, institution, group, consortium, conglomerate, agency, association, society; *informal* outfit.

organize verb **1** *organizing and disseminating information* (PUT IN) ORDER, arrange, sort (out), assemble, marshal, put straight, group, classify, collocate, categorize, catalog, codify, systematize, systemize; *rare* methodize.

2 *they organized a search party* MAKE ARRANGEMENTS FOR, arrange, coordinate, sort out, put together, fix up, set up, orchestrate, take care of, see to/about, deal with, manage, conduct, administrate, mobilize; schedule, timetable, program; *formal* concert.

organized adjective *an organized campaign* (WELL) ORDERED, well run, well regulated, structured; orderly, efficient, neat, tidy, methodical; *informal* together. ANTONYM inefficient.

orgiastic adjective *their infamous orgiastic parties* DEBAUCHED, wild, riotous, wanton, dissolute, depraved.

orgy noun **1** *a drunken orgy* WILD PARTY, debauch, carousal, carouse, revel, revelry; *informal* binge, jag, bender, love-in, toot; *literary* bacchanal; *archaic* wassail.

2 *an orgy of violence* BOUT, excess, spree, surfeit; *informal* binge.

orient, orientate verb **1** *she paused at the intersection, trying to* ***orient herself*** GET/FIND ONE'S BEARINGS, establish one's location.

2 *you need to orientate yourself to your new way of life* ADAPT, adjust, familiarize, acclimatize, accustom, attune; acclimate.

3 *magazines oriented to the business community* AIM, direct, pitch, design, intend.

4 *the fires are oriented in line with the sunset* ALIGN, place, position, dispose.

oriental adjective *oriental cooking* EASTERN, Far Eastern, Asian, Asiatic; *literary* orient.

orientation noun **1** *the orientation of the radar station* POSITIONING, location, position, situation, placement, alignment.

2 *his orientation to his new way of life* ADAPTATION, adjustment, acclimatization.

3 *broadly Marxist in orientation* ATTITUDE, inclination.

4 *freshman orientation begins the week before school starts* INDUCTION, training, initiation, briefing.

orifice noun *the orifice must be kept free from debris* OPENING, hole, aperture, slot, slit, cleft.

origin noun **1** *the origin of life* BEGINNING, start, commencement, origination, genesis, birth, dawning, dawn, emergence, creation, birthplace, cradle; source, basis, cause, root(s); *formal* radix.

2 *the Latin origin of the word* SOURCE, derivation, root(s), provenance, etymology.

3 *her Scottish origin* DESCENT, ancestry, parentage, pedigree, lineage, line (of descent), heritage, birth, extraction, family, stock, blood, bloodline.

THE RIGHT WORD

The **origin** of something is the point from which it starts or sets out, or the person or thing from which it is ultimately derived (*the origin of the custom of carving pumpkins at Halloween; the origin of a word*). It often applies to causes that were in operation before the thing itself was brought into being. **Source**, on the other hand, applies to that which provides a first and continuous supply (*the source of the river; an ongoing source of inspiration and encouragement*). **Root**, more often than *source*, applies to what is regarded as the first or final cause of something; it suggests an origin so fundamental as to be the ultimate cause from which something stems (*money is the root of all evil*). **Inception** refers specifically to the beginning of an undertaking, project, institution, or practice (*she was in charge of the organization from its inception*). **Provenance** is similarly restricted in meaning, referring to the specific place, or sometimes the race or people, from which something is derived or by whom it was invented or constructed (*in digging, they uncovered an artifact of unknown provenance*).

original adjective **1** *the original inhabitants* INDIGENOUS, native, aboriginal, autochthonous; first, earliest, early.

2 *original Rembrandts* AUTHENTIC, genuine, actual, true, bona fide; *informal* kosher.

3 *the film is highly original* INNOVATIVE, creative, imaginative, inventive; new, novel, fresh, refreshing; unusual, unconventional, unorthodox, groundbreaking, pioneering, avant-garde, cutting-edge, unique, distinctive. See note at CREATIVE.

▸ noun **1** *a copy of the original* ARCHETYPE, prototype, source, master.

2 *he really is an original* INDIVIDUALIST, individual, eccentric, nonconformist, free spirit, maverick; *informal* character, oddball.

originality noun *their animated short won an award for its originality* INVENTIVENESS, ingenuity, creativeness, creativity, innovation, novelty, freshness, imagination, imaginativeness, individuality, unconventionality, uniqueness, distinctiveness.

originally adverb *the conference was originally scheduled for November* (AT) FIRST, in/at the beginning, to begin with, initially, in the first place, at the outset.

originate verb **1** *the disease originates in Africa* ARISE, have its origin, begin, start, stem, spring, emerge, emanate.

2 *Tom originated the idea* INVENT, create, initiate, devise, think up, dream up, conceive, formulate, form, develop, generate, engender, produce, mastermind, pioneer; *literary* beget.

originator noun *the originator of the Dixie cup* INVENTOR, creator, architect, author, father, mother, initiator, innovator, founder, pioneer, mastermind; *literary* begetter.

ornament noun **1** *small tables covered with ornaments* KNICKKNACK, trinket, bauble, bibelot, gewgaw, gimcrack, furbelow; *informal* whatnot, doodad, tchotchke.

2 *the dress had no ornament at all* DECORATION, adornment, embellishment, ornamentation, trimming, accessories.

▸ verb *the room was highly ornamented* DECORATE, adorn, embellish, trim, bedeck, deck (out), festoon; *literary* bedizen.

ornamental adjective *the ornamental trim above the doors gives the room a dramatic lift* DECORATIVE, fancy, ornate, ornamented.

ornamentation noun *he prefers furniture with very straight lines and little ornamentation* DECORATION, adornment, embellishment, ornament, trimming, accessories.

ornate adjective **1** *an ornate mirror* ELABORATE, decorated, embellished, adorned, ornamented, fancy, fussy, ostentatious, showy; *informal* flash, flashy. ANTONYM unadorned.

2 *ornate language* ELABORATE, flowery, florid; grandiose, pompous, pretentious, high-flown, orotund, magniloquent, grandiloquent, rhetorical, oratorical, bombastic, overwrought, overblown; *informal* highfalutin, purple. ANTONYMS plain, simple.

ornery adjective *they finally realized that his illness was what had made him so ornery* GROUCHY, grumpy, cranky, crotchety, cantankerous, bad-tempered, ill-tempered, dyspeptic, irascible, waspish; truculent, cussed, stubborn.

orotund adjective **1** *an orotund singing voice* DEEP, sonorous, strong, powerful, full, rich, resonant, loud, booming.

2 *the orotund rhetoric of his prose* POMPOUS, pretentious, affected, fulsome, grandiose, ornate, overblown, flowery, florid, high-flown, magniloquent, grandiloquent, rhetorical, oratorical; *informal* highfalutin, purple.

orthodox adjective **1** *orthodox views* CONVENTIONAL, mainstream, conformist, (well) established, traditional, traditionalist, prevalent, popular, conservative, unoriginal. ANTONYM unconventional.

2 *an orthodox Hindu* CONSERVATIVE, traditional, observant, devout, strict.

orthodoxy noun **1** *a pillar of orthodoxy* CONVENTIONALITY, conventionalism, conformism, conservatism, traditionalism, conformity.

2 *Christian orthodoxies* DOCTRINE, belief, conviction, creed, dogma, credo, theory, tenet, teaching.

oscillate verb **1** *the pendulum started to oscillate* SWING, swing back and forth, swing to and fro, sway; *informal* wigwag.

2 *oscillating between fear and bravery* WAVER, swing, fluctuate, alternate, seesaw, yo-yo, sway, vacillate, waffle, hover; *informal* wobble.

oscillation noun **1** *the oscillation of the pendulum* SWINGING, swinging to and fro, swing, swaying.

2 *his oscillation between commerce and art* WAVERING, swinging, fluctuation, seesawing, yo-yoing, vacillation.

ossify verb **1** *the cartilage may ossify* TURN INTO BONE, become bony, calcify, harden, solidify, rigidify, petrify.

2 *the old political institutions have ossified* BECOME INFLEXIBLE, become rigid, fossilize, calcify, rigidify, stagnate.

ostensible adjective *the ostensible star is Lana Turner, but it's Juanita Moore who makes the movie click* APPARENT, outward, superficial, professed, supposed, alleged, purported. ANTONYM genuine.

THE RIGHT WORD

The **apparent** reason for something is not necessarily the real reason. In this sense the word applies to what appears only on the surface, not to what is borne out by scientific investigation or an examination of the relevant facts and circumstances (*the apparent cause was only an illusion*). The **ostensible** reason for something is the reason that is expressed, declared, or avowed; but it implies that the truth is being concealed (*the ostensible purpose of the meeting was to give the two men a chance to get acquainted*). **Seeming** usually refers to the character of the thing observed rather than to a defect in the observation; it implies even more doubt than either *apparent* or *ostensible* (*her seeming innocence fooled no one*). That which is **illusory** is always deceptive; it has a character or appearance that doesn't really exist (*an illusory beauty that faded quickly in the bright light*).

ostensibly adverb *it is ostensibly a book about football* APPARENTLY, seemingly, on the face of it, to all intents and purposes, outwardly, superficially, allegedly, supposedly, purportedly.

ostentation noun *most car buyers are looking for a lot more than ostentation* SHOWINESS, show, pretentiousness, vulgarity, conspicuousness, display, flamboyance, gaudiness, brashness, extravagance, ornateness, exhibitionism; *informal* flashiness, glitz, glitziness, ritziness.

ostentatious adjective *an ostentatious display of wealth* SHOWY, pretentious, conspicuous, flamboyant, gaudy, brash, vulgar, loud, extravagant, fancy, ornate, overelaborate; *informal* flash, flashy, splashy, over the top, glitzy, ritzy, superfly. ANTONYM restrained.

ostracize verb *they were ostracized by their fellow workers* EXCLUDE, shun, spurn, cold-shoulder, reject, shut out, avoid, ignore, snub, cut dead, keep at arm's length, leave out in the cold; blackball, blacklist; *informal* freeze out. ANTONYM welcome.

other adjective **1** *these homes use other fuels* ALTERNATIVE, different, dissimilar, disparate, distinct, separate, contrasting.

2 *are there any other questions?* MORE, further, additional, extra, added, supplementary.

otherwise adverb **1** *hurry up, otherwise we'll be late* OR, or else, if not.

2 *she's exhausted, but otherwise she's fine* IN OTHER RESPECTS, apart from that.

3 *he could not have acted otherwise* IN ANY OTHER WAY, differently.

otherworldly adjective *the distant, otherworldly look on his face* ETHEREAL, dreamy, spiritual, mystic, mystical; unearthly, unworldly, supernatural. ANTONYM realistic.

ounce noun *it took every ounce of courage for her to board the plane* PARTICLE, scrap, bit, speck, iota, whit, jot, trace, atom, shred, crumb, fragment, grain, drop, soupçon, spot; *informal* smidgen.

oust verb *armed forces ousted the new coalition government* DRIVE OUT, expel, force out, throw out, remove (from office/power), eject, get rid of, depose, dethrone, topple, unseat, overthrow, bring down, overturn, dismiss, dislodge, displace; *informal* boot out, kick out. See note at EJECT.

out adjective & adverb **1** *she's out at the moment* NOT HERE, not at home, not in, (gone) away, elsewhere, absent. ANTONYM in.

2 *the secret was out* REVEALED, (out) in the open, common knowledge, public knowledge, known, disclosed, divulged. ANTONYM unknown.

3 *the roses are out* IN FLOWER, flowering, in (full) bloom, blooming, in blossom, blossoming, open.

4 *the book should be out soon* AVAILABLE, for sale, obtainable, in stores, published, in print.

5 *the fire was nearly out* EXTINGUISHED, no longer alight.

6 *informal* *grunge is out* UNFASHIONABLE, out of fashion, dated, outdated, passé; *informal* old hat, old school, not with it. ANTONYM fashionable.

7 *smoking and drinking are out* FORBIDDEN, not permitted, not allowed, proscribed, taboo, unacceptable. ANTONYMS permitted, OK.

▸ verb *informal* *it was not our intention to out him* EXPOSE, unmask.

PHRASE: **out cold** *one swift punch from Max, and Parnell was out cold* UNCONSCIOUS, knocked out, down/out for the count; *informal* KO'd, kayoed.

outage noun *the outage has left more than a million people in the dark* POWER FAILURE, brownout, blackout.

out-and-out adjective *he's an out-and-out chauvinist* UTTER, downright, thoroughgoing, absolute, complete, thorough, total, unmitigated, outright, full-bore, real, perfect, consummate. ANTONYM partial.

outbreak noun **1** *the latest outbreak of hostility* ERUPTION, flare-up, upsurge, groundswell, outburst, rash, wave, spate, flood, explosion, burst, flurry.

2 *on the outbreak of war* START, beginning, commencement, onset, outset.

outburst noun *a wild outburst of applause* ERUPTION, explosion, burst, outbreak, flare-up, access, rush, flood, storm, outpouring, surge, upsurge, outflowing.

outcast noun *his corrupt practices as an attorney had made him an outcast in the community* PARIAH, persona non grata, reject, black sheep, outsider, leper.

outclass verb *even in her freshman year, Taurasi outclassed most everyone on the team* SURPASS, be superior to, be better than, outshine, overshadow, eclipse, outdo, outplay, outmaneuver, outstrip, get the better of, upstage; top, cap, beat, defeat, exceed; *informal* be a cut above, be head and shoulders above, run rings around.

outcome noun *the future of the industry could hinge on the outcome of next month's election* RESULT, end result, consequence, net result, upshot, aftereffect, aftermath, conclusion, issue, end, end product.

outcry noun **1** *an outcry of passion* SHOUT, exclamation, cry, yell, howl, roar, scream; *informal* holler.

2 *public outcry* PROTEST(S), protestation(s), complaints, objections, furor, fuss, commotion, uproar, outbursts, opposition, dissent; *informal* hullabaloo, ballyhoo, ructions, stink.

outdated adjective *an outdated filing system* OLD-FASHIONED, out of date, outmoded, out of fashion, unfashionable, dated, passé, old, behind the times, behindhand, obsolete, antiquated; *informal* out, old hat, square, not with it, horse-and-buggy, clunky. ANTONYM modern.

outdistance verb **1** *the hare outdistanced the fox* OUTRUN, outstrip, outpace, leave behind, get (further) ahead of; overtake, pass.

2 *the mill outdistanced all its rivals* SURPASS, outshine, outclass, outdo, exceed, transcend, top, cap, beat, better, leave behind; *informal* leave standing.

outdo verb *every year, Hank and Oscar try to outdo each other in the triathlon* SURPASS, outshine, overshadow, eclipse, outclass, outmaneuver, get the better of, put in the shade, upstage; exceed, transcend, top, cap, beat, better, leave behind, get ahead of; *informal* be a cut above, be head and shoulders above, run rings around.

outdoor adjective *outdoor activities* OPEN-AIR, outdoors, outside, alfresco, field. ANTONYM indoor.

outer adjective **1** *the outer layer* OUTSIDE, outermost, outward, exterior, external, surface.

2 *outer areas of the city* OUTLYING, distant, remote, faraway, furthest, peripheral; suburban. ANTONYM inner.

outfit noun **1** *a new outfit* COSTUME, suit, uniform, ensemble, attire, clothes, clothing, dress, garb; *informal* getup, gear, togs, threads; *formal* apparel; *archaic* habit, raiment.

2 *a studio lighting outfit* KIT, equipment, tools, implements, tackle, apparatus, paraphernalia, things, stuff.

3 *a local manufacturing outfit* ORGANIZATION, setup, enterprise, company, firm, business; group, band, body, team.

▸ verb *enough swords to outfit an army* EQUIP, kit out, fit out/up, rig out, supply, arm; dress, attire, clothe, deck out; *archaic* apparel, invest, habit.

outfitter noun **1** *our outfitters planned the canoe route* supplier, grubstaker; guide.

2 *the studio has dozens of outfitters at its disposal* CLOTH-

IER, tailor, couturier, costumer, dressmaker, seamstress; *dated* modiste.

outflow noun *the outflow of waste materials is monitored continuously* DISCHARGE, outflowing, outpouring, rush, flood, deluge, issue, spurt, jet, cascade, stream, torrent, gush, outburst; flow, flux; *technical* efflux.

outgoing adjective **1** *outgoing children* EXTROVERT, uninhibited, unreserved, demonstrative, affectionate, warm, friendly, genial, cordial, affable, easygoing, sociable, convivial, lively, gregarious; communicative, responsive, open, forthcoming, frank. ANTONYM introverted.

2 *the outgoing president* DEPARTING, retiring, leaving. ANTONYM incoming.

outgrowth noun *the outgrowth on his back was benign* PROTUBERANCE, swelling, excrescence, growth, lump, bump, bulge; tumor, cancer, boil, carbuncle, pustule.

outhouse noun *dozens of these families still use outhouses* PRIVY, latrine, outdoor toilet.

outing noun **1** *family outings* (PLEASURE) TRIP, excursion, jaunt, expedition, day out, (mystery) tour, drive, ride, run; *informal* junket, spin.

2 *informal* *the outing of public figures* EXPOSURE, unmasking, revelation.

outlandish adjective *he gives the most outlandish excuses* WEIRD, queer, far out, quirky, zany, eccentric, idiosyncratic, unconventional, unorthodox, funny, bizarre, unusual, singular, extraordinary, strange, unfamiliar, peculiar, odd, curious; *informal* offbeat, off the wall, way-out, wacky, freaky, kooky, kinky, oddball, in left field. ANTONYM ordinary.

outlast verb *there were many times we thought we would never outlast the war* OUTLIVE, survive, live/last longer than; ride out, weather, withstand.

outlaw noun *bands of outlaws* FUGITIVE, (wanted) criminal, public enemy, outcast, exile, pariah; bandit, robber; *dated* desperado.

▸ verb **1** *they voted to outlaw the grizzly hunt* BAN, bar, prohibit, forbid, veto, make illegal, proscribe, interdict. ANTONYM permit.

2 *she feared she would be outlawed* BANISH, exile, expel.

outlay noun *the initial outlay of funds was within their means* EXPENDITURE, expenses, spending, cost, price, payment, investment. ANTONYM profit.

outlet noun **1** *a power outlet* SOCKET, receptacle, power bar, power source.

2 *the outlet of the drain* VENT, way out, egress; outfall, opening, channel, conduit, duct.

3 *an outlet for farm produce* STORE, market, marketplace, shop, source.

4 *an outlet for their creative energies* MEANS OF EXPRESSION, (means of) release, vent, avenue, channel.

outline noun **1** *the outline of the building* SILHOUETTE, profile, shape, contours, form, line, delineation; diagram, sketch; *literary* lineaments.

2 *an outline of expenditure for each department* ROUGH IDEA, thumbnail sketch, (quick) rundown, summary, synopsis, résumé, précis; essence, main/key points, gist, (bare) bones, draft, sketch.

▸ verb **1** *the plane was outlined against the sky* SILHOUETTE, define, demarcate; sketch, delineate, trace.

2 *she outlined the plan briefly* ROUGH OUT, sketch out, draft, give a rough idea of, summarize, précis.

outlive verb *that old tomcat has outlived at least six of our other pets* LIVE ON AFTER, live longer than, outlast, survive.

outlook noun **1** *the two men were wholly different in outlook* POINT OF VIEW, viewpoint, views, opinion, (way of) thinking, perspective, attitude, standpoint, stance, frame of mind.

2 *the outlook for the economy* PROSPECTS, expectations, hopes, future, lookout.

3 *a lovely open outlook* VIEW, vista, prospect, panorama, scene, aspect.

outlying adjective *people in the outlying areas had little interest in the politics of the city* DISTANT, remote, outer, out of the way, faraway, extrasolar, far-flung, inaccessible, off the beaten track/path.

outmaneuver verb **1** *the army was outmaneuvered* OUTFLANK, circumvent, bypass.

2 *he outmaneuvered his critics* OUTWIT, outsmart, outthink, outplay, steal a march on, trick, get the better of; *informal* outfox, put one over on, euchre.

outmoded adjective *the fax machine we got three years ago is already outmoded* OUT OF DATE, old-fashioned, out of fashion, outdated, dated, behind the times, antiquated, obsolete, passé, unstylish, untrendy, uncool; *informal* old hat, old school.

out of date adjective **1** *this design is out of date* OLD-FASHIONED, outmoded, out of fashion, unfashionable, frumpish, frumpy, outdated, dated, old, passé, behind the times, behindhand, obsolete, antiquated; *informal* out, old hat, square, not with it, horse-and-buggy, clunky. ANTONYMS fashionable, modern.

2 *many of the facts are out of date* SUPERSEDED, obsolete, expired, lapsed, invalid, (null and) void. ANTONYM current.

out of kilter See KILTER.

out-of-the-way adjective *an out-of-the-way campsite* OUTLYING, distant, remote, faraway, far-flung, isolated, lonely, godforsaken, inaccessible, off the beaten track/path. ANTONYM accessible.

out of work adjective *I'm an actor, currently out of work* UNEMPLOYED, jobless, out of a job; redundant, laid off, on welfare, on the dole; *euphemistic* between jobs.

outpouring noun *the defendant received an outpouring of public support* OUTFLOW, outflowing, rush, flood, deluge, discharge, issue, spurt, jet, cascade, stream, torrent, gush, outburst, niagara, flow, flux; *technical* efflux.

output noun *our output always increases at the end of summer* PRODUCTION, amount/quantity produced, yield, gross domestic product, works, writings.

outré adjective *I don't mind clothes that are a bit out of the ordinary, but that dress is positively outré* WEIRD, queer, outlandish, far out, freakish, quirky, zany, eccentric, off-center, unconventional, unorthodox, funny, bizarre, fantastic, unusual, singular, extraordinary, strange, unfamiliar, peculiar, odd, out of the way; *informal* way-out, wacky, freaky, kooky, oddball, off the wall, offbeat, (out) in left field.

outrage noun **1** *widespread public outrage* INDIGNATION, fury, anger, rage, disapproval, wrath, resentment.

2 *it is an outrage* SCANDAL, offense, insult, injustice, disgrace.

3 *the bomb outrage* ATROCITY, act of violence/wickedness, crime, wrong, barbarism, inhumane act.

▸ verb *his remarks outraged his parishioners* ENRAGE, infuriate, incense, anger, scandalize, offend, give offense to, affront, shock, horrify, disgust, appall.

outrageous adjective **1** *outrageous acts of cruelty* SHOCKING, disgraceful, scandalous, atrocious, appalling, monstrous, heinous; evil, wicked, abominable, terrible, horrendous, dreadful, foul, nauseating, sickening, vile, nasty, odious, loathsome, unspeakable; beastly.

2 *the politician's outrageous promises* FAR-FETCHED, (highly) unlikely, doubtful, dubious, questionable, implausible, unconvincing, unbelievable, incredible, preposterous, extravagant, excessive.

3 *outrageous clothes* EYE-CATCHING, flamboyant, showy, gaudy, ostentatious; shameless, brazen, shocking; *informal* saucy, flashy.

outright adverb **1** *he rejected the proposal outright* COMPLETELY, entirely, wholly, fully, totally, categorically, absolutely, utterly, flatly, unreservedly, in every respect.

2 *I told her outright* EXPLICITLY, directly, forthrightly, openly, frankly, candidly, honestly, sincerely, bluntly, plainly, in plain language, truthfully, to someone's face, straight from the shoulder, straight up, in no uncertain terms.

3 *they were killed outright* INSTANTLY, instantaneously, immediately, at once, straightaway, then and there, on the spot.

4 *paintings have to be bought outright* ALL AT ONCE, in one go.

▸ adjective **1** *an outright lie* OUT-AND-OUT, absolute, complete, downright, utter, sheer, categorical, unqualified, unmitigated, unconditional.

2 *the outright winner* DEFINITE, unequivocal, clear, unqualified, incontestable, unmistakable.

outrun verb *an antelope could easily outrun a lion* RUN FASTER THAN, outstrip, outdistance, outpace, leave behind, lose; *informal* leave standing.

outset noun *at the outset, we had nothing but problems* START, starting point, beginning, commencement, dawn, birth, origin, inception, opening, launch, inauguration; *informal* the word go. ANTONYM end.

outshine verb *watching Nadia outshine the other gymnasts was a thrill for viewers around the world* SURPASS, overshadow, eclipse, outclass, put in the shade, upstage, exceed, transcend, top, cap, beat, better; *informal* be a cut above, be head and shoulders above, run rings around.

outside noun *the outside of the building* OUTER/EXTERNAL SURFACE, exterior, outer side/layer, case, skin, shell, covering, facade.

▸ adjective **1** *outside lights* EXTERIOR, external, outer, outdoor, out-of-doors.

2 *outside contractors* INDEPENDENT, hired, temporary, freelance, casual, external, extramural.

3 *an outside chance* SLIGHT, slender, slim, small, tiny, faint, negligible, remote, vague.

▸ adverb *they went outside | shall we eat outside?* OUTDOORS, out of doors, alfresco. ANTONYM inside.

outsider noun *after six years, I still feel like an outsider in this town* STRANGER, visitor, nonmember; foreigner, alien, immigrant, emigrant, émigré; newcomer, parvenu.

outsize adjective **1** *her outsize handbag* HUGE, oversized, enormous, gigantic, very big/large, great, giant, colossal, massive, mammoth, vast, immense, tremendous, monumental, prodigious, mountainous, king-sized, economy-size(d); *informal* mega, monster, humongous, jumbo, bumper, ginormous.

2 *an outsize actor* VERY LARGE, big, massive, fat, corpulent, stout, heavy, plump, portly, ample, bulky; *informal* pudgy, tubby, zaftig.

outskirts plural noun *they live in the outskirts of Youngstown* OUTLYING DISTRICTS, edges, fringes, suburbs, suburbia, bedroom community, commutershed; purlieus, borders, environs.

outsmart verb *buyers and sellers attempt to outsmart each other* OUTWIT, outmaneuver, outplay, steal a march on, trick, get the better of; *informal* outfox, pull a fast one on, put one over on.

outsource verb *maintenance jobs are outsourced* CONTRACT OUT, farm out, subcontract, delegate.

outspoken adjective *an outspoken critic of the Reagan administration* FORTHRIGHT, direct, candid, frank, straightforward, honest, open, plain-spoken; blunt, abrupt, bluff, brusque.

outspread adjective *kestrels soaring with outspread wings* FULLY EXTENDED, outstretched, spread-eagled, spread out, fanned out, unfolded, unfurled, open, wide open, opened out.

outstanding adjective **1** *an outstanding painter* EXCELLENT, marvelous, magnificent, superb, fine, wonderful, superlative, exceptional, first-class, first-rate; *informal* great, terrific, tremendous, super, amazing, fantastic, sensational, fabulous, ace, neat, killer, crack, A1, mean, awesome, bang-up, skookum, out of this world; smashing, brilliant. ANTONYM mediocre.

2 *the outstanding decorative element in this presentation* REMARKABLE, extraordinary, exceptional, striking, eye-catching, arresting, impressive, distinctive, unforgettable, memorable, special, momentous, significant, notable, noteworthy; *informal* out of this world. See note at NOTICEABLE. ANTONYM unexceptional.

3 *how much work is still outstanding?* TO BE DONE, undone, unattended to, unfinished, incomplete, remaining, pending, ongoing. ANTONYM finished.

4 *outstanding debts* UNPAID, unsettled, owing, past due, owed, to be paid, payable, due, overdue, undischarged, delinquent. ANTONYM paid.

outstrip verb **1** *he outstripped the police cars* GO FASTER THAN, outrun, outdistance, outpace, leave behind, get (further) ahead of, lose; *informal* leave standing.

2 *demand far outstrips supply* SURPASS, exceed, be more than, top, eclipse.

outward adjective *his outward demeanor hides the pain he feels inside* EXTERNAL, outer, outside, exterior; surface, superficial, seeming, apparent, ostensible. ANTONYM inward.

outwardly adverb *outwardly, these two products are just* *about identical* EXTERNALLY, on the surface, superficially, on the face of it, to all intents and purposes, apparently, ostensibly, seemingly.

outweigh verb *the costs outweigh the benefits* BE GREATER THAN, exceed, be superior to, prevail over, have the edge on/over, override, supersede, offset, cancel out, (more than) make up for, outbalance, compensate for.

outwit verb *the murderers always thought they could outwit Columbo, but of course they couldn't* OUTSMART, outmaneuver, outplay, steal a march on, trick, gull, get the better of, euchre; *informal* outfox, pull a fast one on, put one over on.

oval adjective *an oval mirror* EGG-SHAPED, ovoid, ovate, oviform, elliptical.

ovation noun *what performer doesn't appreciate an ovation from the crowd?* ROUND OF APPLAUSE, applause, hand-clapping, clapping, cheering, cheers, bravos, acclaim, acclamation, tribute, standing ovation; *informal* (big) hand.

oven noun *the roast is in the oven* (kitchen) stove, microwave (oven), (kitchen) range; roaster; kiln.

over preposition **1** *there will be clouds over most of the state* ABOVE, on top of, higher (up) than, atop, covering. ANTONYM under.

2 *he walked over the grass* ACROSS, around, throughout.

3 *over 200,000 people live in the area* MORE THAN, above, in excess of, upwards of.

4 *lengthy discussions over what to do next* ON THE SUBJECT OF, about, concerning, apropos of, with reference to, regarding, relating to, in connection with, vis-à-vis.

▸ adverb **1** *a flock of geese flew over* OVERHEAD, on high, above, past, by.

2 *the relationship is over* AT AN END, finished, concluded, terminated, ended, no more, a thing of the past; *informal* kaput.

3 *he had some money left over* REMAINING, unused, surplus, in excess, in addition.

PHRASES: **over and above** *we will not pay any costs over and above the original quote* IN ADDITION TO, on top of, plus, as well as, besides, along with. **over and over** *he tells the same jokes over and over* REPEATEDLY, again and again, over and over again, time and (time) again, many times over, frequently, constantly, continually, persistently, ad nauseam.

overact verb *during dramatic scenes, she has a tendency to overact* EXAGGERATE, overdo it, overplay it; *informal* ham it up, camp it up.

overall adjective *the overall cost* ALL-INCLUSIVE, general, comprehensive, universal, all-embracing, gross, net, final, inclusive, total; wholesale, complete, across the board, global, worldwide.

▸ adverb *overall, things have improved* GENERALLY (SPEAKING), broadly, in general, altogether, all in all, on balance, on average, for the most part, in the main, on the whole, by and large, to a large extent.

overawe verb *Jane was overawed by her landlady* INTIMIDATE, daunt, cow, disconcert, unnerve, subdue, dismay, frighten, alarm, scare, terrify; *informal* psych out.

overbearing adjective *his overbearing wife* DOMINEERING, dominating, autocratic, tyrannical, despotic, oppressive, high-handed, bullying; *informal* bossy.

overblown adjective *an overblown piece of writing* OVERWRITTEN, florid, grandiose, pompous, overelaborate, flowery, overwrought, pretentious, high-flown, turgid, grandiloquent, magniloquent, orotund; *informal* highfalutin.

overcast adjective *she feared it was bad luck to be married on an overcast day* CLOUDY, clouded (over), sunless, darkened, dark, gray, black, leaden, heavy, dull, murky, dismal, dreary. ANTONYM bright.

overcharge verb **1** *clients are being overcharged* SWINDLE, charge too much, cheat, defraud, fleece, shortchange; *informal* rip off, sting, screw, rob, diddle, have, rook, gouge.

2 *the decoration is overcharged* OVERSTATE, overdo, exaggerate, overembroider, overembellish; overwrite, overdraw.

overcome verb **1** *we overcame the home team* DEFEAT, beat, conquer, trounce, thrash, rout, vanquish, overwhelm, overpower, get the better of, triumph over, prevail over, win over/against, outdo, outclass, worst, crush; *informal* drub, slaughter, clobber, hammer, lick, best, crucify, demolish, wipe the floor with, make mincemeat of, blow out of the water, take to the cleaners, shellac, skunk.

2 *they overcame their fear of flying* GET THE BETTER OF, prevail over, control, get/bring under control, master, conquer, defeat, beat; get over, get a grip on, curb, subdue; *informal* lick, best.

▸ adjective *I was overcome* OVERWHELMED, emotional, moved, affected, speechless.

overconfident adjective *her downfall came through being overconfident* COCKSURE, cocky, smug, conceited, self-assured, brash, blustering, overbearing, presumptuous, heading for a fall, riding for a fall; *informal* too big for one's britches/boots.

overcritical adjective *overcritical parents* FAULT-FINDING, hypercritical, captious, carping, caviling, quibbling, hair-splitting, overparticular; fussy, finicky, fastidious, pedantic, overscrupulous, punctilious; *informal* nitpicking, persnickety.

overcrowded adjective *an overcrowded bus* OVERFULL, overflowing, full to overflowing/bursting, crammed full, congested, overpopulated, overpeopled, crowded, swarming, teeming; *informal* bursting/bulging at the seams, full to the gunwales, jam-packed. ANTONYM empty.

overdo verb **1** *she overdoes the love scenes* EXAGGERATE, overstate, overemphasize, overplay, go overboard with, overdramatize; *informal* ham up, camp up. ANTONYM understate.

2 *don't overdo the desserts* OVERINDULGE IN, have/use/eat/drink too much of, have/use/eat/drink to excess.

3 *they overdid the beef* OVERCOOK, burn. PHRASE: **overdo it** *on your first day of an exercise program, you mustn't overdo it* WORK TOO HARD, overwork, do too much, burn the candle at both ends, overtax oneself, drive/push oneself too hard, work/run oneself into the ground, wear oneself out, bite off more than one can chew, strain oneself; *informal* kill oneself, knock oneself out.

overdone adjective **1** *the flattery was overdone* EXCESSIVE, too much, undue, immoderate, inordinate, disproportionate, inflated, overstated, overworked, exaggerated,

overweight adjective *the growing number of overweight children is a legitimate health crisis* FAT, obese, stout, full-figured, corpulent, gross, fleshy, plump, portly, chubby, rotund, paunchy, potbellied, flabby, well-upholstered, broad in the beam; *informal* porky, tubby, blubbery, pudgy. ANTONYM skinny.

overwhelm verb **1** *advancing sand dunes could overwhelm the village* SWAMP, submerge, engulf, bury, deluge, flood, inundate.

2 *Canada overwhelmed the U.S. in the hockey final* DEFEAT (UTTERLY/HEAVILY), trounce, rout, beat (hollow), conquer, vanquish, be victorious over, triumph over, worst, overcome, overthrow, crush; *informal* thrash, steamroller, lick, best, massacre, clobber, wipe the floor with.

3 *she was overwhelmed by a sense of tragedy* OVERCOME, move, stir, affect, touch, strike, dumbfound, shake, devastate, floor, leave speechless; *informal* bowl over, snow under.

overwhelming adjective **1** *an overwhelming number of players were unavailable* VERY LARGE, enormous, immense, inordinate, massive, huge.

2 *the overwhelming desire to laugh* VERY STRONG, forceful, uncontrollable, irrepressible, irresistible, overpowering, compelling.

overwork verb **1** *we should not overwork* WORK TOO HARD, work/run oneself into the ground, wear oneself to a shadow, work one's fingers to the bone, burn the candle at both ends, overtax oneself, burn oneself out, do too much, overdo it, strain oneself, overload oneself, drive/push oneself too hard; *informal* kill oneself, knock oneself out.

2 *my colleagues did not overwork me* DRIVE (TOO HARD), exploit, drive into the ground, tax, overtax, overburden, put upon, impose on.

overworked adjective **1** *overworked staff* STRESSED (OUT), stress-ridden, overtaxed, overburdened, overloaded, exhausted, worn out, burned out. ANTONYM relaxed.

2 *an overworked phrase* HACKNEYED, overused, worn out, tired, played out, clichéd, threadbare, stale, trite, banal, stock, unoriginal. ANTONYM original.

overwrought adjective **1** *she was too overwrought to listen* TENSE, agitated, nervous, on edge, edgy, keyed up, worked up, high-strung, neurotic, overexcited, beside oneself, distracted, distraught, frantic, hysterical; *informal* in a state, in a tizzy, uptight, wound up, het up, strung out. ANTONYM calm.

2 *the painting is overwrought* OVERELABORATE, overornate, overblown, overdone, contrived, overworked, strained. ANTONYM understated.

owe verb *I don't want to owe anyone* BE IN DEBT TO, be indebted to, be in arrears to, be under an obligation to.

owing adjective *the rent was owing* UNPAID, to be paid, payable, due, past due, overdue, undischarged, owed, outstanding, in arrears, delinquent. ANTONYM paid.

PHRASE: **owing to** *owing to the severity of the weather, tonight's concert will be postponed until next Tuesday* BECAUSE OF, as a result of, on account of, due to, as a consequence of, thanks to, in view of, by dint of; *formal* by reason of.

owl noun. See table at RAPTOR.

own adjective *he has his own reasons* PERSONAL, individual, particular, private, personalized, unique.

▸ verb **1** *I own this house* BE THE OWNER OF, possess, be the possessor of, have in one's possession, have (to one's name).

2 *she had to own that she agreed* ADMIT, concede, grant, accept, acknowledge, agree, confess.

PHRASES: **hold one's own** *Britain has begun to hold its own in world markets* STAND FIRM, stand one's ground, keep one's end up, keep one's head above water, compete, survive, cope, get on/along. **on one's own 1** *I live on my own* (ALL) ALONE, (all) by oneself, solitary, unaccompanied, companionless; *informal* by one's lonesome. **2** *she works well on her own* UNAIDED, unassisted, without help, without assistance, (all) by oneself, independently. **own up to** *in the long run, it's always better to own up to your mistakes* CONFESS, admit to, admit the guilt of, accept blame/responsibility for, tell the truth about, make a clean breast of; *informal* come clean about.

owner noun *the owner is no longer interested in selling* POSSESSOR, holder, proprietor/proprietress, homeowner, landowner, freeholder, landlord, landlady.

ownership noun *there is no question of ownership* POSSESSION, right of possession, freehold, proprietorship, proprietary rights, title.

ox noun *a team of oxen* bull, bullock, steer; *Farming* beef.

P

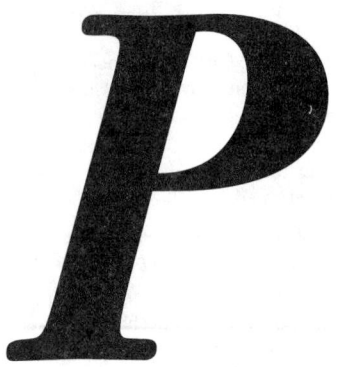

pace noun **1** *he stepped back a pace* STEP, stride.

2 *a slow, steady pace* GAIT, stride, walk, march.

3 *he drove home at a furious pace* SPEED, rate, velocity; *informal* clip, lick.

▸ verb *she paced up and down* WALK, stride, tread, march, pound, patrol.

pacific adjective **1** *a pacific community* PEACE-LOVING, peaceable, pacifist, nonviolent, nonaggressive, nonbelligerent, unwarlike. ANTONYMS aggressive, belligerent.

2 *their pacific intentions* CONCILIATORY, peacemaking, placatory, propitiatory, appeasing, mollifying, mediatory, dovish; *formal* irenic. ANTONYM warmongering.

3 *pacific waters* CALM, still, smooth, tranquil, placid, waveless, unruffled, like a millpond. ANTONYM stormy.

pacifism noun *he returned from Vietnam with a desire to promote pacifism* PEACEMAKING, conscientious objection(s), passive resistance, peace-mongering, nonviolence.

pacifist noun *you know, even pacifists can support their nation's armed forces* PEACE-LOVER, conscientious objector, passive resister, peacemaker, peace-monger, dove. ANTONYM warmonger.

pacify verb *go out there and try to pacify the passengers* PLACATE, appease, calm (down), conciliate, propitiate, assuage, mollify, soothe. ANTONYM enrage.

THE RIGHT WORD

You might try to **pacify** a crying baby, to **appease** a demanding boss, to **mollify** a friend whose feelings have been hurt, and to **placate** an angry crowd. While all of these verbs have something to do with quieting people who are upset, excited, or disturbed, each involves taking a slightly different approach. *Pacify* suggests soothing or calming (*the mother made soft cooing noises in an attempt to pacify her child*). *Appease* implies that you've given in to someone's demands or made concessions in order to please (*she said she would visit his mother just to appease him*), while *mollify* stresses minimizing anger or hurt feelings by taking positive action (*her flattery failed to mollify him*). *Placate* suggests changing a hostile or angry attitude to a friendly or favorable one, usually with a more complete or long-lasting effect than *appease* (*they were able to placate their enemies by offering to support them*). You can **propitiate** a superior or someone who has the power to injure you by allaying or forestalling their anger (*they were able to propitiate the trustees by holding a dinner party in their honor*). **Conciliate** implies the use of arbitration or compromise to settle a dispute or to win someone over (*the company made every effort to conciliate its angry competitor*).

pack noun **1** *a pack of cigarettes* PACKET, container, package, box, carton, parcel.

2 *with a pack on his back* BACKPACK, knapsack, rucksack, day pack, kit bag, bag.

3 *a pack of youngsters* CROWD, mob, group, band, troupe, troop, party, set, clique, gang, rabble, horde, herd, throng, huddle, mass, assembly, gathering, host; *informal* crew, bunch.

▸ verb **1** *she helped pack the picnic basket* FILL (UP), put things in, load.

2 *they packed their belongings* STOW, put away, store, box up.

3 *the glasses were packed in straw* WRAP (UP), package, parcel, swathe, swaddle, encase, enfold, envelop, bundle.

4 *Christmas shoppers packed the store* THRONG, crowd (into), fill (to overflowing), cram, jam, squash into, squeeze into.

5 *pack the cloth against the wall* COMPRESS, press, squash, squeeze, jam, tamp.

PHRASES: **pack off** *informal we packed our youngest son off to college just last week* SEND OFF, dispatch, bundle off. **pack up 1** *pack up your Legos* PUT AWAY, tidy up/away, clear up/away. **2** *informal it's time to pack up* STOP, call it a day, finish, cease; *informal* knock off, quit, pack it in.

package noun **1** *the delivery of a package* PARCEL, packet, container, box.

2 *a complete package of services* COLLECTION, bundle, combination.

▸ verb *goods packaged in recyclable materials* WRAP (UP), gift-wrap; pack (up), parcel (up), box, encase.

packaging noun *the outer packaging is crucial to consumer appeal* WRAPPING, wrappers, packing, covering.

packed adjective *the actors peeked from behind the curtain to see a packed house* CROWDED, full, filled (to capacity), crammed, jammed, solid, overcrowded, overfull, teeming, seething, swarming; *informal* jam-packed, chock-full, standing room only, chockablock, full to the gunwales, bursting/bulging at the seams.

packet noun *a small packet of jelly beans* PACK, carton, (cardboard) box, container, case, package.

pact noun *the pact was signed at the site of the surrender* AGREEMENT, treaty, entente, protocol, deal, settlement, concordat, accord; armistice, truce; *formal* concord.

pad[1] noun **1** *a pad over the eye* piece of cotton, dressing, pack, padding, wadding, wad.

2 *a seat pad* CUSHION, pillow.

3 *making notes on a pad* NOTEBOOK, notepad, writing pad, memo pad, sketch pad, steno pad, sketchbook, scratch pad.

▸ verb *a quilted jacket padded with goose down* STUFF, fill, pack, wad.

PHRASE: **pad out** *don't pad out your answer to make it seem impressive* EXPAND UNNECESSARILY, fill out, amplify, increase, flesh out, lengthen, spin out, overdo, elaborate.

pad[2] verb *he padded along toward the bedroom* WALK QUIETLY, tread warily, creep, tiptoe, steal, pussyfoot.

padding noun **1** *padding around the ankle* WADDING, cushioning, stuffing, packing, filling, lining.

2 *a concise style with no padding* VERBIAGE, verbosity, wordiness, prolixity, filler.

paddle[1] noun *use the paddles to row ashore* OAR, scull, blade.

▸ verb *we paddled around the bay* row gently, pull, scull, canoe, kayak.

paddle[2] verb *children were paddling in the water* SPLASH ABOUT, wade; dabble.

paddock noun *the horses got out of the paddock* FIELD, meadow, pasture; pen, pound, corral.

padlock verb *padlock the shed* LOCK (UP), fasten, secure.

padre noun *many of the soldiers requested time with the padre before shipping out* CHAPLAIN, priest, minister, pastor, father, parson, clergyman, cleric, ecclesiastic, man of the cloth, churchman, vicar, rector, curate, preacher; *informal* reverend, Holy Joe, sky pilot.

paean noun *a great paean of triumph* SONG OF PRAISE, hymn, alleluia; plaudit, glorification, eulogy, tribute, panegyric, accolade, acclamation; *formal* encomium.

pagan noun *pagans worshiped the sun* HEATHEN, infidel, idolater, idolatress; *archaic* paynim.

▸ adjective *the pagan festival* HEATHEN, ungodly, irreligious, infidel, idolatrous.

page[1] noun **1** *a book of 672 pages* FOLIO, sheet, side, leaf.

2 *a glorious page in her life* PERIOD, time, stage, phase, epoch, era, chapter; episode, event.

page[2] noun *she worked as a page at the state legislature* MESSENGER, errand boy/girl.

▸ verb *could you please page Mr. Johnson?* CALL (FOR), summon, send for, buzz.

pageant noun *people dress up their dogs in wild costumes for the annual pageant* PARADE, procession, cavalcade, tableau (vivant); spectacle, extravaganza, show.

pageantry noun *the pageantry of Diana's wedding* SPECTACLE, display, ceremony, magnificence, pomp, splendor, grandeur, show; *informal* razzle-dazzle, razzmatazz.

pain noun **1** *she endured great pain* SUFFERING, agony, torture, torment, discomfort.

2 *a pain in the stomach* ACHE, aching, soreness, throb, throbbing, sting, stinging, twinge, shooting pain, stab, pang, cramps; discomfort, irritation, tenderness.

3 *the pain of losing a loved one* SORROW, grief, heartache, heartbreak, sadness, unhappiness, distress, desolation, misery, wretchedness, despair; agony, torment, torture, via dolorosa.

4 *informal that child is a pain.* See NUISANCE.

5 (**pains**) *he took great pains to hide his feelings* CARE, effort, bother, trouble.

▸ verb **1** *her foot is still* ***paining her*** HURT, cause pain, be painful, be sore, be tender, ache, throb, sting, twinge, cause discomfort; *informal* kill one.

2 *the memory pains her* SADDEN, grieve, distress, trouble, perturb, oppress, cause anguish to.

pained adjective *it troubles us to see you so pained* UPSET, hurt, wounded, injured, insulted, offended, aggrieved, displeased, disgruntled, annoyed, angered, angry, cross, indignant, irritated, resentful; *informal* riled, miffed, aggravated, peeved, teed off, ticked off, sore.

painful adjective **1** *a painful arm* SORE, hurting, tender, aching, throbbing, angry.

2 *a painful experience* DISAGREEABLE, unpleasant, nasty, bitter, distressing, upsetting, traumatic, miserable, sad, heartbreaking, agonizing, harrowing.

painkiller noun *these painkillers will make you drowsy* ANALGESIC, pain reliever, anodyne, anesthetic, narcotic; palliative.

painless adjective **1** *any killing of animals should be painless* WITHOUT PAIN, pain-free. ANTONYM painful.

2 *getting rid of him proved to be painless* EASY, trouble-free, effortless, simple, plain sailing; *informal* as easy as pie, a piece of cake, child's play, a cinch. ANTONYM difficult.

painstaking adjective *painting these window frames is painstaking work* CAREFUL, meticulous, thorough, assiduous, sedulous, attentive, diligent, industrious, conscientious, punctilious, scrupulous, rigorous, particular; pedantic, fussy. ANTONYM slapdash.

paint noun *a gallon of white paint* COLORING, colorant, tint, dye, stain, pigment, color. See table on page 650.

▸ verb **1** *paint the ceiling* COLOR, apply paint to, decorate, whitewash, emulsion, gloss, spray-paint, airbrush.

2 *painting slogans on a wall* DAUB, smear, spray-paint, airbrush.

3 *Rembrandt painted his mother* PORTRAY, picture, paint a picture of, depict, represent.

4 *you paint a very stark picture of the suffering* TELL, recount, outline, sketch, describe, depict, evoke, conjure up.

PHRASE: **paint the town red** *informal we're taking the train into Albany, and we're gonna paint the town red* CELEBRATE, carouse, enjoy oneself, have a good/wild time, have a party; *informal* go out on the town, whoop it up, make whoopee, live it up, party, have a ball.

TYPES OF PAINT

acrylic	matte
color wash	oil
distemper	poster paint
eggshell	primer
emulsion	tempera
enamel	undercoat
gloss	watercolor
gouache	whitewash
latex	

painting noun *his paintings are so charming in their simplicity* PICTURE, illustration, portrayal, depiction, representation, image, artwork; oil (painting), watercolor, canvas.

pair noun **1** *a pair of gloves* SET (OF TWO), matching set, two of a kind.

2 *the pair were arrested* TWO, couple, duo, brace, twosome, duplet; twins.

3 *a pair of lines* COUPLET; *Prosody* distich.

4 *the happy pair* COUPLE, man/husband and wife.

▸ verb *a cardigan paired with a matching skirt* MATCH, put together, couple, twin.

PHRASE: **pair off/up** *Rachel paired up with Tommy* GET TOGETHER, team up, form a couple, make a twosome, hook up, marry.

WORD NOTE **hook up, hookup**

In the title essay of his book *Hooking Up,* Tom Wolfe wrote that to anyone over the age of 9 in the year 2000, the term always referred to a sexual experience, but that the "nature and extent" of the experience varied widely. Several twenty-something sources in 2004 report that the imprecision of the term is precisely the point. From California: "It makes space for everything from what another generation might have called *making out* right up to full-on intercourse—that ambiguity preserves a modicum of privacy in a largely privacy-free discourse. You can tell people you've hooked up with someone without giving away all the who-did-what-to-whom." A *hookup* is a casual encounter, no history, no obligations, but it can lead to something more serious. From New York: "My relationship with my girlfriend began with a hookup, since we'd never met before that night, and developed into a relationship. That didn't retrospectively make it not a hookup." **—JS**

pajamas noun *all comfy in my new flannel pajamas* PJS, jammies, sleeper; nightgown.

pal *informal* noun *my best pal.* See FRIEND sense 1.

palace noun *tourists are not allowed in the east wing of the palace* ROYAL/OFFICIAL RESIDENCE, castle, château, mansion, stately home, schloss.

palatable adjective **1** *palatable meals* EDIBLE, eatable, digestible, tasty, appetizing, flavorful; *formal* comestible. ANTONYMS tasteless, insipid.

2 *the truth is not always palatable* PLEASANT, acceptable, pleasing, agreeable, to one's liking. ANTONYMS disagreeable, unpleasant.

palate noun **1** *the tea burned her palate* ROOF OF THE MOUTH, hard/soft palate.

2 *menus to suit the tourist palate* (SENSE OF) TASTE, appetite, stomach.

3 *wine with a peachy palate* FLAVOR, savor, taste.

palatial adjective *a palatial estate on Long Island* LUXURIOUS, deluxe, magnificent, sumptuous, splendid, grand, opulent, lavish, stately, regal; fancy, upscale, upmarket; *informal* plush, swanky, posh, ritzy, swish. ANTONYM modest.

palaver *informal* noun *holy cow, what a palaver we caused in the girls' dormitory!* FUSS, commotion, trouble, rigmarole, folderol; *informal* song and dance, performance, to-do, carrying-on, hoo-ha, hullabaloo, ballyhoo.

pale[1] noun **1** *the pales of a fence* STAKE, post, pole, picket, upright.

2 *outside the pale of decency* BOUNDARY, confines, bounds, limits. PHRASE: **beyond the pale** *his behavior was beyond the pale* UNACCEPTABLE, unseemly, improper, unsuitable, unreasonable, unforgivable, intolerable, disgraceful, deplorable, outrageous, scandalous, shocking; *informal* not on, out of line; *formal* exceptionable.

pale[2] adjective **1** *she looked pale and drawn* WHITE, pallid, pasty, wan, colorless, anemic, bloodless, washed out, peaked, ashen, gray, whitish, white-faced, whey-faced, drained, sickly, sallow, as white as a sheet, deathly pale; milky, creamy, cream, ivory, milk-white, alabaster; *informal* like death warmed over. ANTONYMS rosy, flushed.

2 *pale colors* LIGHT, light-colored, pastel, muted, subtle, soft; faded, bleached, washed out.

3 *the pale light of morning* DIM, faint, weak, feeble. ANTONYMS dark, bright.

4 *a pale imitation* FEEBLE, weak, insipid, bland, poor, inadequate; uninspired, unimaginative, lackluster, spiritless, lifeless; *informal* pathetic.

▸ verb **1** *his face paled* GO/TURN WHITE, grow/turn pale, blanch, lose color.

2 *everything else pales by comparison* DECREASE IN IMPORTANCE, lose significance, pale into insignificance, fade into the background.

THE RIGHT WORD

Someone of fair complexion who usually stays indoors and spends little time in the sun is apt to be **pale**, referring to an unusually white or colorless complexion; one can also become *pale* out of fear or illness. Someone who has lost color from being ill or under stress may be described as **pallid**, which suggests a paleness that is the result of some abnormal condition (*she appeared pallid when she left the police station*). **Wan** also connotes an unhealthy condition or sickly paleness (*her wan face smiled at him from the hospital bed*). Someone who is **ashen** has skin the pale grayish color of ashes (*ashen with fear*), while **livid** can mean either bluish to describe loss of normal coloring (*the livid face of a drowned corpse*) or reddish or flushed (*livid with rage*).

palisade noun *sentries were posted along the palisade* FENCE, paling, barricade, stockade.

pall[1] noun **1** *a rich velvet pall* FUNERAL CLOTH, coffin covering.

2 *a pall of black smoke* CLOUD, covering, cloak, veil, shroud, layer, blanket. PHRASE: **cast a pall over** *the bad news from home cast a pall over our honeymoon* SPOIL, cast a shadow over, overshadow, cloud, put a damper on.

pall[2] verb *the high life was beginning to pall* BECOME/GROW TEDIOUS, become/grow boring, lose its/their interest, lose attraction, wear off; weary, sicken, nauseate; irritate, irk.

palliate verb **1** *the treatment works by palliating symptoms* ALLEVIATE, ease, relieve, soothe, take the edge off, assuage, moderate, temper, diminish, decrease, blunt, deaden.

2 *there is no way to palliate his dirty deed* DISGUISE, hide, gloss over, conceal, cover (up), camouflage, mask; excuse, justify, extenuate, mitigate.

palliative adjective *palliative medicine* SOOTHING, alleviating, sedative, calmative; for the terminally ill.

▸ noun *antibiotics and palliatives* PAINKILLER, analgesic, pain reliever, sedative, tranquilizer, anodyne, calmative, opiate, bromide.

pallid adjective 1 *a pallid child* PALE, white, pasty, wan, colorless, anemic, washed out, peaked, whey-faced, ashen, gray, whitish, drained, sickly, sallow; *informal* like death warmed over. See note at PALE[3].

2 *pallid watercolors* INSIPID, uninspired, colorless, uninteresting, unexciting, unimaginative, lifeless, spiritless, sterile, bland.

pallor noun *her dark hair accentuated her pallor* PALENESS, pallidness, lack of color, wanness, ashen hue, pastiness, grayness, sickliness, sallowness.

palm[1] PHRASES: **grease someone's palm** *informal my Uncle Duke would grease the commissioner's palm on Tuesday, and on Wednesday his speakeasy would be serving up booze by the barrel* BRIBE, buy (off), corrupt, suborn, give an inducement to; *informal* give a sweetener to. **have someone in the palm of one's hand** *can't you see that Dorrey has you in the palm of her hand?* HAVE CONTROL OVER, have influence over, have someone eating out of one's hand, have someone on a string, have someone in one's hip pocket, have someone wrapped around one's finger. **palm off** *you're not going to palm off that rusty old truck on me* FOIST, fob off, get rid of, dispose of, unload.

palm[2] noun *the palm of victory* PRIZE, trophy, award, crown, laurel wreath, laurels, bays.

palmistry noun *she practiced palmistry merely as an amusement* FORTUNE TELLING, palm-reading, clairvoyance, chiromancy.

palpable adjective 1 *a palpable bump* TANGIBLE, touchable, noticeable, detectable. See note at TANGIBLE. ANTONYM imperceptible.

2 *his reluctance was palpable* PERCEPTIBLE, perceivable, visible, noticeable, discernible, detectable, observable, tangible, unmistakable, transparent, self-evident; obvious, clear, plain (to see), evident, apparent, manifest, staring one in the face, written all over someone. ANTONYM imperceptible.

USAGE NOTE **palpable**

Palpable (literally, "touchable") = tangible; apparent. There is nothing wrong with using this word in figurative senses (*palpable weaknesses in the argument*), as it has been used since at least the fifteenth century. What is nonsensical, however, is to say that the *level* of frustration, tension, etc., is *palpable*—e.g.: "When they share a scene, the energy level is palpable [read *the energy is palpable*]." (*Daily News* [New York]; Sept. 24, 2002.) **—BG**

palpitate verb 1 *her heart began to palpitate* BEAT RAPIDLY, pound, throb, pulsate, pulse, thud, thump, hammer, race.

2 *palpitating with terror* TREMBLE, quiver, quake, shake (like a leaf).

paltry adjective 1 *a paltry sum of money* SMALL, meager, trifling, insignificant, negligible, inadequate, insufficient, derisory, pitiful, pathetic, miserable, niggardly, beggarly; *informal* measly, piddling; *formal* exiguous. ANTONYM considerable.

2 *naval glory struck him as paltry* WORTHLESS, petty, trivial, unimportant, insignificant, inconsequential, of little account. ANTONYM important.

pamper verb *Trevor's big sister pampered him* SPOIL, indulge, overindulge, cosset, mollycoddle, coddle, baby, wait on someone hand and foot.

pamphlet noun *there's some interesting information in this pamphlet* BROCHURE, leaflet, booklet, circular, flyer, fact sheet, handbill, mailer, folder.

pan[1] noun 1 *a heavy pan* SAUCEPAN, skillet, frying pan, pot, wok.

2 *salt pans* HOLLOW, pit, depression, dip, crater, concavity.

▸ verb 1 *informal the movie was panned by the critics.* See CRITICIZE.

2 *prospectors panned for gold* SIFT, search, look.

PHRASE: **pan out** 1 *Bob's idea hadn't panned out* SUCCEED, be successful, work (out), turn out well, come to fruition. 2 *the deal panned out badly* TURN OUT, work out, end (up), come out, fall out, evolve; *formal* eventuate.

pan[2] verb *the camera panned to the building* SWING (AROUND), sweep, move, turn, circle.

panacea noun *a panacea for the country's economic problems* UNIVERSAL CURE, cure-all, cure for all ills, universal remedy, elixir, wonder drug; *informal* magic bullet.

panache noun *the chorus line lacks panache* FLAMBOYANCE, confidence, self-assurance, style, flair, élan, dash, verve, zest, spirit, brio, éclat, vivacity, gusto, liveliness, vitality, energy; *informal* pizzazz, oomph, zip, zing.

pancake noun *a short stack of pancakes with maple syrup* hotcake, flapjack, griddle cake, crepe, blintz; latke, potato pancake.

pandemic adjective *the disease is pandemic in Africa* WIDESPREAD, prevalent, pervasive, rife, rampant. See note at EPIDEMIC.

pandemonium noun *we heard a bang and then there was complete pandemonium* BEDLAM, chaos, mayhem, uproar, turmoil, tumult, commotion, confusion, anarchy, furor, hubbub, rumpus; *informal* hullabaloo, hoopla. ANTONYM peace.

pander PHRASE: **pander to** *David was always there to pander to her every whim* INDULGE, gratify, satisfy, cater to, give in to, accommodate, comply with.

panegyric noun *the panegyric she delivered in Syd's memory brought tears to our eyes* EULOGY, speech of praise, paean, accolade, tribute.

panel noun 1 *a control panel* CONSOLE, instrument panel, dashboard; instruments, controls, dials.

2 *a panel of judges* GROUP, team, body, committee, board, jury.

pang noun 1 *hunger pangs* PAIN, sharp pain, shooting pain, twinge, stab, spasm.

2 *a pang of remorse* QUALM, twinge, prick.

panic noun *a wave of panic* ALARM, anxiety, nervousness, fear, fright, trepidation, dread, terror, agitation, hysteria, consternation, perturbation, dismay, apprehension; *informal* flap, fluster, cold sweat, funk, tizzy, swivet. ANTONYM calm.

▸ verb **1** *there's no need to panic* BE ALARMED, be scared, be nervous, be afraid, take fright, be agitated, be hysterical, lose one's nerve, get overwrought, get worked up; *informal* flap, get in a flap, lose one's cool, get into a tizzy, freak out, get in a stew, have kittens.

2 *talk of love panicked her* FRIGHTEN, alarm, scare, unnerve; *informal* throw into a tizzy, freak out.

panic-stricken adjective *panic-stricken workers fled the burning factory* ALARMED, frightened, scared (stiff), terrified, terror-stricken, petrified, horrified, horror-stricken, fearful, afraid, panicky, frantic, in a frenzy, nervous, agitated, hysterical, beside oneself, worked up, overwrought; *informal* in a cold sweat, in a flap, in a fluster, in a tizzy.

panoply noun **1** *the full panoply of U.S. military might* ARRAY, range, collection.

2 *all the panoply of religious liturgy* TRAPPINGS, regalia; splendor, spectacle, ceremony, ritual.

panorama noun **1** *he surveyed the panorama* VIEW, wide view, scenic view, vista, prospect, scene, scenery, landscape, seascape.

2 *a panorama of the art scene* OVERVIEW, survey, review, presentation, appraisal.

panoramic adjective **1** *a panoramic view* SWEEPING, wide, extensive, scenic, commanding.

2 *a panoramic look at the twentieth century* WIDE-RANGING, extensive, broad, far-reaching, comprehensive, all-embracing.

pant verb **1** *he was panting as they reached the top* BREATHE HEAVILY, breathe hard, puff, huff and puff, gasp, wheeze.

2 *it makes you* ***pant for*** *more* YEARN FOR, long for, crave, hanker after/for, ache for, hunger for, thirst for, be hungry for, be thirsty for, wish for, desire, want; *informal* itch for, be dying for.

panting adjective *all was quiet except for a ticking clock and Louise's panting dog* OUT OF BREATH, breathless, short of breath, puffing, huffing and puffing, gasping (for breath), wheezing, wheezy, hyperventilating.

pantry noun *we set out moth traps in the pantry* LARDER, store, storeroom; *archaic* spence.

pants plural noun *a cashmere sweater with khaki pants* TROUSERS, slacks, britches. See table.

pap noun **1** *a plateful of tasteless pap* SOFT FOOD, mush, slop, pulp, purée, mash, *trademark* Pablum; *informal* goo, goop, glop, gook.

2 *commercial pap* TRIVIA, pulp (fiction), garbage, rubbish, nonsense; *informal* dreck, drivel, trash, twaddle, pablum.

paper noun **1** *a sheet of paper* writing paper, notepaper, vellum.

2 *the local paper* NEWSPAPER, journal, gazette, periodical; tabloid, broadsheet, daily, weekly, evening paper; *informal* rag, tab.

3 *the paper was peeling off the walls* WALLPAPER, wallcovering.

4 *a three-hour paper* EXAM, examination, test, quiz.

5 *she has just published a paper* ESSAY, article, monograph, thesis, work, dissertation, treatise, study, report, analysis, tract, critique, exegesis, review, term paper, theme.

6 **(papers)** *personal papers* DOCUMENTS, certificates, letters, files, deeds, records, archives, paperwork, documentation; *Law* muniments.

7 **(papers)** *they asked us for our papers* IDENTIFICATION PAPERS/DOCUMENTS, identity card, ID, credentials.

▸ verb *we papered the walls* WALLPAPER, hang wallpaper on.

PHRASE: **on paper** **1** *he put his thoughts on paper* IN WRITING, in black and white, in print. **2** *the combatants were evenly matched on paper* IN THEORY, theoretically, supposedly.

papery adjective *papery leaves* THIN, paper-thin, flimsy, delicate, insubstantial, light, lightweight.

par PHRASES: **below par** **1** *their performances have been below par* SUBSTANDARD, inferior, not up to scratch, subpar, under par, below average, second-rate, mediocre, poor, undistinguished; *informal* not up to snuff, bush-league. **2** *I'm feeling below par* SLIGHTLY UNWELL, not (very) well, not oneself, out of sorts; ill, unwell, poorly, washed out, run-down, peaked, off; *informal* under the weather, not up to snuff, lousy, rough. **on a par with** *his voice is on a par with Tony Bennett* AS GOOD AS, comparable with, in the same class/league as, equivalent to, equal to, on a level with, of the same standard as. **par for the course** *long hours are par for the course in catering* NORMAL, typical, standard, usual, what one would expect. **up to par** *students whose grades are up to par* GOOD ENOUGH, up to the mark, satisfactory, acceptable, adequate, up to scratch; *informal* up to snuff.

parable noun *the parable of the prodigal son* ALLEGORY, moral story/tale, fable, exemplum.

PANTS AND TROUSERS

baggies	hot pants
bell-bottoms	jeans
Bermuda shorts	jodhpurs
bicycle shorts	khakis
bloomers	knee pants
blue jeans	knickers
breeches	overalls
britches	pajama pants
capri pants	palazzo pants
cargo pants	pantalets
chaps	pantaloons
chinos	pedal pushers
clamdiggers	rugby pants
cords	shorts
corduroys	ski pants
culottes	slacks
cutoffs	stirrup pants
dress pants	stretch pants
dungarees	sweatpants
flannels	tin pants
flares	toreador pants
galligaskins	track pants
gauchos	trousers
harem pants	tuxedo pants
hip-huggers	walking shorts

parade noun **1** *a Memorial Day parade* PROCESSION, march, cavalcade, motorcade, spectacle, display, pageant; review, dress parade, tattoo; march past.

2 *she made a great parade of doing the housework* EXHIBITION, show, display, performance, spectacle, fuss; *informal* hoo-ha, to-do.

▸ verb **1** *the teams paraded through the city* MARCH, process, file, troop.

2 *she paraded up and down* STRUT, swagger, stride.

3 *he was keen to parade his knowledge* DISPLAY, exhibit, make a show of, flaunt, show (off), demonstrate.

paradigm noun *why should your sets of values be the paradigm for the rest of us?* MODEL, pattern, example, exemplar, template, standard, prototype, archetype. See note at MODEL.

paradisal adjective *paradisal happiness* HEAVENLY, idyllic, blissful, divine, sublime, perfect.

paradise noun **1** *the souls in paradise* HEAVEN, the kingdom of heaven, the heavenly kingdom, Elysium, the Elysian Fields, Valhalla, Avalon. ANTONYM hell.

2 *Adam and Eve's expulsion from Paradise* THE GARDEN OF EDEN, Eden.

3 *a tropical paradise* UTOPIA, Shangri-La, heaven, idyll, nirvana.

4 *this is sheer paradise!* BLISS, heaven, ecstasy, delight, joy, happiness, nirvana, heaven on earth. ANTONYM hell.

paradox noun *the paradox of war is that you have to kill people in order to stop people from killing each other* CONTRADICTION, contradiction in terms, self-contradiction, inconsistency, incongruity; oxymoron; conflict, anomaly; enigma, puzzle, mystery, conundrum. See note at RIDDLE.

paradoxical adjective *I admit it seems paradoxical for a pacifist such as myself to be in favor of this military action* CONTRADICTORY, self-contradictory, inconsistent, incongruous, anomalous; illogical, puzzling, baffling, incomprehensible, inexplicable.

paragon noun *a paragon of cheerfulness* | *your cook is a paragon* PERFECT EXAMPLE, shining example, model, epitome, archetype, ideal, exemplar, nonpareil, embodiment, personification, quintessence, apotheosis, acme; jewel, gem, angel, treasure; *informal* one in a million, the tops; *archaic* a nonesuch.

paragraph noun **1** *the concluding paragraph* SECTION, subdivision, part, subsection, division, portion, segment, passage.

2 *a paragraph in the newspaper* REPORT, article, item, sidebar, piece, write-up, mention.

paralipsis noun See note below.

WORD NOTE **paralipsis, proslepsis**

Paralipsis is one of the most useful and most common of all the sneaky rhetorical devices. When you mention something by declaring your intention not to mention it, that's paralipsis: *I won't even talk about all the money he's borrowed from me.* When you go into even more detail, that's *proslepsis: Never mind the days of wild drinking, illegal drug use, traffic violations (including vehicular manslaughter), and overdue library books: those are beyond the scope of this profile.* Used too freely, though, paralipsis and proslepsis give your writing a gossipy and back-biting tone (and might quite possibly be actionable). Unless your goal is to be gossipy and backbiting, employ these devices with care. **—EM**

parallel adjective **1** *parallel lines* SIDE BY SIDE, aligned, collateral, equidistant.

2 *parallel careers* SIMILAR, analogous, comparable, corresponding, like, of a kind, akin, related, equivalent, matching, homologous.

3 *a parallel universe* COEXISTING, coexistent, concurrent; contemporaneous, simultaneous, synchronous. ANTONYM divergent.

▸ noun **1** *an exact parallel* COUNTERPART, analog, equivalent, likeness, match, twin, duplicate, mirror.

2 *there is an interesting parallel between these figures* SIMILARITY, likeness, resemblance, analogy, correspondence, equivalence, correlation, relation, symmetry, parity.

▸ verb **1** *his experiences parallel mine* RESEMBLE, be similar to, be like, bear a resemblance to; correspond to, be analogous to, be comparable/equivalent to, equate with/to, correlate with, imitate, echo, remind one of, duplicate, mirror, follow, match.

2 *her performance has never been paralleled* EQUAL, match, rival, emulate.

paralysis noun **1** *the disease can cause paralysis* IMMOBILITY, powerlessness, incapacity, debilitation; *Medicine* paraplegia, quadriplegia, tetraplegia, monoplegia, hemiplegia, diplegia, paresis, paraparesis.

2 *complete paralysis of the ports* SHUTDOWN, immobilization, stoppage.

paralytic adjective *her hands became paralytic* PARALYZED, crippled, disabled, incapacitated, powerless, immobilized, useless.

paralyze verb **1** *both of his legs were paralyzed* DISABLE, cripple, immobilize, incapacitate, debilitate; *formal* torpefy.

2 *Sally was paralyzed by the sight of him* IMMOBILIZE, transfix, become rooted to the spot, freeze, stun, render motionless.

3 *the capital was paralyzed by a general strike* BRING TO A STANDSTILL, immobilize, bring to a (grinding) halt, freeze, cripple, disable.

paralyzed adjective *paralyzed veterans* DISABLED, crippled, handicapped, incapacitated, paralytic, powerless, immobilized, useless; *Medicine* paraplegic, quadriplegic, tetraplegic, monoplegic, hemiplegic, paretic, paraparetic.

parameter noun *the parameters of the debate* FRAMEWORK, variable, limit, boundary, limitation, restriction, criterion, guideline.

WORD NOTE **parameter**

Parameter is a technical term for a variable or an arbitrary constant that appears in a mathematical equation—its value restricts or determines the specific form of the numerical expression. Lazily equating it with *perimeter,* the otherwise lexically correct deploy it to mean "boundary" or "limit," as in, *I'm checking out the parameters of the debate.* Stick with *perimeters,* or, in this example, *boundaries* or *terms.* **—JS**

paramount adjective *the safety of the staff is paramount* MOST IMPORTANT, of greatest/prime importance; uppermost, supreme, chief, overriding, predominant, foremost, prime, primary, principal, highest, main, key, central, leading, major, top; *informal* number-one.

paramour noun *archaic he was in love with his father's* *paramour* LOVER, significant other, inamorata; mistress, girlfriend, kept woman, other woman; boyfriend, main squeeze, other man, inamorato; *informal* toy boy, sugar daddy; *archaic* concubine, courtesan.

paranoia noun *her husband had concocted a cruel scheme to inflict her with paranoia* PERSECUTION COMPLEX, delusions, obsession, psychosis.

paranoid adjective *all the layoffs in my department have made me paranoid* OVERSUSPICIOUS, paranoiac, suspicious, mistrustful, fearful, insecure.

parapet noun **1** *Marian leaned over the parapet* BALUSTRADE, barrier, wall.

2 *the sandbags making up the parapet* BARRICADE, rampart, bulwark, bank, embankment, fortification, defense, earthwork, breastwork, bastion.

paraphernalia plural noun *they have a ton of camping paraphernalia* EQUIPMENT, stuff, things, apparatus, kit, implements, tools, utensils, material(s), appliances, accoutrements, appurtenances, odds and ends, bits and pieces; *informal* gear.

paraphrase verb *paraphrasing literary texts* REWORD, rephrase, put/express in other words, rewrite, gloss.

▸ noun *this paraphrase of Frye's words* REWORDING, rephrasing, rewriting, rewrite, rendition, rendering, gloss.

parasite noun *she longed to be free of the parasites in her family* HANGER-ON, cadger, leech, passenger; *informal* bloodsucker, sponger, bottom feeder, scrounger, freeloader, mooch.

parcel noun **1** *a parcel of clothes* PACKAGE, packet; pack, bundle, box, case, bale.

2 *a parcel of land* PLOT, piece, patch, tract, allotment, lot, plat.

▸ verb **1** *she* ***parceled up*** *the papers* PACK (UP), package, wrap (up), gift-wrap, tie up, bundle up.

2 ***parceling out*** *commercial farmland* DIVIDE UP, portion out, distribute, share out, allocate, allot, apportion, hand out, dole out, dish out; *informal* divvy up.

parched adjective **1** *the parched earth* (BONE) DRY, dried up/out, arid, desiccated, dehydrated, baked, burned, scorched; withered, shriveled. See note at DRY.

2 *informal* *I'm parched.* THIRSTY, longing for a drink, dry, dehydrated.

pardon noun **1** *pardon for your sins* FORGIVENESS, absolution, clemency, mercy, leniency, remission.

2 *he offered them a full pardon* REPRIEVE, free pardon, amnesty, exoneration, release, acquittal, discharge; *formal* exculpation.

▸ verb **1** *I know she will pardon me* FORGIVE, absolve, have mercy on; excuse, condone, overlook. ANTONYM blame.

2 *they were subsequently pardoned* EXONERATE, acquit, amnesty; reprieve, release, free; *informal* let off; *formal* exculpate. See note at ABSOLVE. ANTONYM punish.

▸ exclamation *Pardon?* WHAT DID YOU SAY, what, what's that, pardon me, I beg your pardon, sorry, excuse me; *informal* come again, say what.

pardonable adjective *a pardonable offense* EXCUSABLE, forgivable, condonable, understandable, minor, venial, slight. ANTONYM inexcusable.

pare verb **1** *pare the peel from the lemon* CUT (OFF), trim (off), peel (off), strip (off), skin; *technical* decorticate.

2 *domestic operations have been* ***pared down*** REDUCE, diminish, decrease, cut (back/down), trim, slim down, prune, curtail.

parent noun *you'll need the signed consent of a parent* MOTHER, FATHER, birth/biological parent, progenitor; adoptive parent, foster-parent, step-parent, guardian; *literary* begetter.

▸ verb *those who parent young children* RAISE, bring up, look after, take care of, rear.

parentage noun *Deedham was bound by tradition to marry only a woman of the finest parentage* ORIGINS, extraction, birth, family, ancestry, lineage, heritage, pedigree, descent, blood, stock, roots.

parenthetical adjective *parenthetical remarks* INCIDENTAL, supplementary, in brackets, in parentheses, parenthetic; explanatory, qualifying.

parenthetically adverb *and I should say parenthetically that the rental of Ryder trucks is incidental to his body shop* INCIDENTALLY, by the way, by the by(e), in passing, in parenthesis.

parenthood noun *parenthood is the toughest, most rewarding job you'll ever have* child-rearing, motherhood, fatherhood, child care, parenting.

pariah noun *they were treated as social pariahs* OUTCAST, persona non grata, black sheep, leper, undesirable, unperson, nonperson.

parings plural noun *throw all the parings into the compost bin* PEELINGS, clippings, peel, rind, cuttings, trimmings, shavings.

parish noun **1** *the municipal council of the parish of Oka* DISTRICT, community.

2 *the story scandalized the parish* PARISHIONERS, churchgoers, congregation, fold, flock, community.

parity noun *we strive for a parity of wages* EQUALITY, equivalence, uniformity, consistency, correspondence, congruity, levelness, unity, coequality.

park noun **1** *we were playing in the park* playground, play area, public garden, garden(s), green.

2 *a new national park* PARKLAND, wilderness area, protected area, nature reserve, game reserve.

▸ verb **1** *she parked her car* LEAVE, position; stop, pull up, pull over.

2 *informal* *park your bag by the door* PUT (DOWN), place, deposit, leave, stick, shove, dump; *informal* plonk.

PHRASE: **park oneself** *informal* *park yourself there and we'll be with you in a moment* SIT DOWN, seat oneself, settle (oneself), install oneself; *informal* plunk oneself.

parlance noun *for the character of Lyndsay-Ann, she uses her most annoying Valley girl parlance* JARGON, language, phraseology, talk, speech, argot, patois, cant; *informal* lingo, -ese, -speak.

parley noun *a peace parley* NEGOTIATION, talk(s), conference, summit, discussion, powwow; *informal* confab; *formal* colloquy, confabulation. See note at CONVERSATION.

▸ verb *the two parties were willing to parley* DISCUSS TERMS, talk, hold talks, negotiate, deliberate; *informal* powwow.

parliament noun *the Russian parliament* LEGISLATURE, legislative assembly, congress, senate, (upper/lower) house, (upper/lower) chamber, diet, assembly.

parliamentary adjective *parliamentary assemblies* LEGISLATIVE, lawmaking, governmental, congressional, senatorial, democratic, elected, representative.

parlous adjective *the parlous state of the industry* BAD, dire, dreadful, awful, terrible, grave, serious, desperate, precarious; sorry, poor, lamentable, hopeless; unsafe, perilous, dangerous, risky; *informal* dicey, hairy, woeful.

parochial adjective *she was constantly challenging their parochial approach to education* NARROW-MINDED, small-minded, provincial, narrow, small-town, conservative, illiberal, intolerant; *informal* jerkwater. ANTONYM broad-minded. See note at BIAS.

parochialism noun *the family crisis that now faced the Lemmons would cause them to question their own parochialism* NARROW-MINDEDNESS, provincialism, small-mindedness.

parody noun **1** *a parody of the Gothic novel* SATIRE, burlesque, lampoon, pastiche, caricature, imitation, mockery; *informal* spoof, takeoff, send-up. See note at CARICATURE.

2 *a parody of the truth* DISTORTION, travesty, caricature, misrepresentation, perversion, corruption, debasement.

▸ verb *parodying schoolgirl fiction* SATIRIZE, burlesque, lampoon, caricature, mimic, imitate, ape, copy, make fun of, travesty, take off; *informal* send up.

paroxysm noun *paroxysms of coughing* SPASM, attack, fit, burst, bout, convulsion, seizure, outburst, eruption, explosion, access.

parrot verb *they parroted slogans without appreciating their significance* REPEAT (MINDLESSLY), repeat mechanically, echo.

parry verb **1** *Alfonso parried the blow* WARD OFF, fend off; deflect, hold off, block, counter, repel, repulse.

2 *I parried her constant questions* EVADE, sidestep, avoid, dodge, answer evasively, field, fend off.

parsimonious adjective *Lou's parsimonious mother was horrified by his lavish spending* CHEAP, miserly, mean, niggardly, close-fisted, close, penny-pinching, ungenerous, Scroogelike; *informal* tightfisted, cheeseparing, tight, stingy, mingy; *formal* penurious. See note at ECONOMICAL. ANTONYM generous.

parsimony noun *the parsimony of her grandparents had embittered her against the elderly* CHEAPNESS, miserliness, meanness, parsimoniousness, niggardliness, close-fistedness, closeness, penny-pinching; *informal* stinginess, minginess, tightness, tightfistedness, cheeseparing; *formal* penuriousness.

parson noun *the new parson brings a youthful joy to the pulpit* VICAR, rector, clergyman, cleric, chaplain, pastor, curate, man of the cloth, ecclesiastic, minister, priest, preacher; *informal* reverend, padre.

part noun **1** *the last part of the cake* | *a large part of their life* BIT, slice, chunk, lump, hunk, wedge, fragment, scrap, piece; portion, proportion, percentage, fraction. See note at FRAGMENT. ANTONYM whole.

2 *car parts* COMPONENT, bit, constituent, element, module.

3 *body parts* PART OF THE BODY, organ, limb, member.

4 *the third part of the book* SECTION, division, volume, chapter, act, scene, installment.

5 *another part of the country* DISTRICT, neighborhood, quarter, section, area, region.

6 *the part of Juliet* (THEATRICAL) ROLE, character, persona.

7 *she's learning her part* LINES, words, script, speech; libretto, lyrics, score.

8 *he was jailed for his part in the affair* INVOLVEMENT, role, function, hand, work, responsibility, capacity, position, participation, contribution; *informal* bit.

▸ verb **1** *the curtains parted* SEPARATE, divide (in two), split (in two), move apart. ANTONYM join.

2 *we parted on bad terms* LEAVE, take one's leave, say goodbye/farewell, say one's goodbyes/farewells, go one's (separate) ways, split, go away, depart. ANTONYM meet.

▸ adjective *a part payment* INCOMPLETE, partial, half, semi-, limited, inadequate, insufficient, unfinished. ANTONYM complete.

▸ adverb *it is part finished* TO A CERTAIN EXTENT/DEGREE, to some extent/degree, partly, partially, in part, half, relatively, comparatively, (up) to a point, somewhat; not totally, not entirely, (very) nearly, almost, just about, all but. ANTONYM completely.

PHRASES: **for the most part.** See MOSTLY. **in part** *the water damage is due in part to the clogged gutters* TO A CERTAIN EXTENT/DEGREE, to some extent/degree, partly, partially, slightly, in some measure, (up) to a point. **on the part of** *there is increased interest in these coins on the part of collectors* (MADE/DONE) BY, carried out by, caused by, from. **part with** *Danielle could not part with her stuffed animals* GIVE UP/AWAY, relinquish, forgo, surrender, hand over, deliver up, dispose of. **take part** *anyone who cares to can take part* PARTICIPATE, join in, get involved, enter, play a part/role, be a participant, contribute, have a hand, help, assist, lend a hand; *informal* get in on the act. **take part in** *all students must take part in the CPR course before the end of junior year* PARTICIPATE IN, engage in, join in, get involved in, share in, play a part/role in, be a participant in, contribute to, be associated with, have a hand in.

partake verb **1** *only senior officers are allowed to **partake in** the negotiations* PARTICIPATE IN, take part in, engage in, join in, enter into, get involved in, share in, contribute to, play a part in, have a hand in, sit in on. ANTONYMS be excluded from, sit out.

2 *those averse to sushi can **partake of** the hot buffet* CONSUME, have, eat, drink, take, ingest, devour; *informal* wolf down, polish off, tuck into. ANTONYMS forgo, abstain from.

3 *the lyric essay **partakes of** the poem in its distillation of ideas and musicality of language* HAVE THE QUALITIES/ATTRIBUTES OF, suggest, evoke, be characterized by, hint at, manifest, evince.

partial adjective **1** *a partial recovery* INCOMPLETE, limited, qualified, imperfect, fragmentary, unfinished. ANTONYMS complete, total.

2 *a very partial view of the situation* BIASED, prejudiced, partisan, one-sided, slanted, skewed, colored, unbalanced. ANTONYM unbiased.

PHRASE: **be partial to** *I'm partial to hotdogs and beer* LIKE, love, enjoy, have a liking for, be fond of, be keen on, have a soft spot for, have a taste for, have a penchant for; *informal* adore, be mad about/for, have a thing about, be crazy about, be nutty about, cotton to.

partiality noun 1 *his partiality toward their cause* BIAS, prejudice, favoritism, favor, partisanship. See note at BIAS.

2 *her partiality for brandy* LIKING, love, fondness, taste, soft spot, predilection, penchant, passion.

partially adverb *the plan was only partially successful* TO A LIMITED EXTENT/DEGREE, to a certain extent/degree, partly, in part, not totally, not entirely, relatively, moderately, (up) to a point, somewhat, comparatively, slightly.

participant noun *the first 100 participants to sign up will get a free T-shirt* PARTICIPATOR, contributor, party, member; entrant, competitor, player, contestant, candidate.

participate verb *at least he's willing to* ***participate in*** *town events* TAKE PART IN, engage in, join in, get involved in, share in, play a part/role in, be a participant in, partake in, have a hand in, be associated with; cooperate in, help (out) with, assist in, lend a hand with/to.

participation noun *your participation is appreciated* INVOLVEMENT, part, contribution, association.

particle noun 1 *minute particles of rock* (TINY) BIT, (tiny) piece, speck, spot, fleck; fragment, sliver, splinter. See table.

2 *he never showed a particle of sympathy* IOTA, jot, whit, bit, scrap, shred, crumb, drop, hint, touch, trace, suggestion, whisper, suspicion, scintilla; *informal* smidgen.

SUBATOMIC PARTICLES

antiparticle	neutrino
baryon	neutron
boson	photon
electron	pion/pi meson
fermion	positron
gluon	proton
hadron	quark
hyperon	string
kaon	tau particle
lepton	triton
meson	WIMP
muon	

particular adjective 1 *a particular group of companies* SPECIFIC, certain, distinct, separate, discrete, definite, precise; single, individual. ANTONYM general.

2 *an issue of particular importance* (EXTRA) SPECIAL, especial, exceptional, unusual, singular, uncommon, notable, noteworthy, remarkable, unique; *formal* peculiar. ANTONYM ordinary.

3 *he was particular about what he ate* FUSSY, fastidious, finicky, meticulous, punctilious, discriminating, selective, painstaking, exacting, demanding; *informal* persnickety, choosy, picky. ANTONYM careless.

▸ noun *the same in every particular* DETAIL, item, point, specific, element, aspect, respect, regard, particularity, fact, feature.

PHRASE: **in particular** 1 *nothing in particular* SPECIFIC, special. 2 *the poor, in particular, were hit by rising prices* PARTICULARLY, specifically, especially, specially.

particularity noun 1 *the particularity of each human being* INDIVIDUALITY, distinctiveness, uniqueness, singularity, originality.

2 *a great degree of particularity* DETAIL, precision, accuracy, thoroughness, scrupulousness, meticulousness.

particularize verb *the indictment particularized several incidents* SPECIFY, detail, itemize, list, enumerate, spell out, cite, stipulate, instance.

particularly adverb 1 *the acoustics are particularly good* ESPECIALLY, specially, very, extremely, exceptionally, singularly, peculiarly, unusually, extraordinarily, remarkably, outstandingly, amazingly, incredibly, really, seriously.

2 *he particularly asked that I should help you* SPECIFICALLY, explicitly, expressly, in particular, especially, specially.

parting noun 1 *an emotional parting* FAREWELL, leave-taking, goodbye, adieu, departure; valediction.

2 *they kept their parting quiet* SEPARATION, breakup, split, divorce, rift, estrangement.

3 *the parting of the Red Sea* DIVISION, dividing, separation, separating, splitting, breaking up/apart, partition, partitioning.

▸ adjective *a parting kiss* FAREWELL, goodbye, last, final, valedictory.

partisan noun 1 *conservative partisans* SUPPORTER, follower, adherent, devotee, champion; fanatic, fan, enthusiast, stalwart, zealot, booster.

2 *the partisans opened fire from the woods* GUERRILLA, freedom fighter, resistance fighter, underground fighter, irregular (soldier).

▸ adjective *partisan attitudes* BIASED, prejudiced, one-sided, discriminatory, colored, partial, interested, sectarian, factional. ANTONYM unbiased.

partisanship noun *we are here to promote voter registration for everyone, not to promote any one person's partisanship* BIAS, prejudice, one-sidedness, discrimination, favor, favoritism, partiality, sectarianism, factionalism.

partition noun 1 *the partition of Palestine* DIVIDING UP, partitioning, separation, division, dividing, subdivision, splitting (up), breaking up, breakup.

2 *room partitions* SCREEN, (room) divider, (dividing) wall, barrier, panel.

▸ verb 1 *the resolution partitioned Poland* DIVIDE (UP), subdivide, separate, split (up), break up; share (out), parcel out.

2 *the huge hall was partitioned* SUBDIVIDE, divide (up); separate (off), section off, screen off.

partly adverb *I admit I am partly responsible* TO A CERTAIN EXTENT/DEGREE, to some extent/degree, in part, partially, a little, somewhat, not totally, not entirely, relatively, moderately, (up) to a point, in some measure, slightly. ANTONYM completely.

partner noun 1 *business partners* COLLEAGUE, associate, coworker, fellow worker, collaborator, comrade, teammate; *archaic* compeer.

2 *his partner in crime* ACCOMPLICE, confederate, accessory, collaborator, fellow conspirator, helper; *informal* sidekick.

3 *your relationship with your partner* SPOUSE, husband, wife, consort, life partner; lover, girlfriend, boyfriend, fiancé, fiancée, significant other, live-in lover, common-

law husband/wife, man, woman, mate; *informal* hubby, missus, old man, old lady/woman, better half, intended, other half, main squeeze.

partnership noun **1** *close partnership* COOPERATION, association, collaboration, coalition, alliance, union, affiliation, relationship, connection.

2 *thriving partnerships* COMPANY, firm, business, corporation, organization, association, consortium, syndicate.

parturition noun *formal* *even today, in many parts of the world, mortality associated with parturition is alarmingly high* CHILDBIRTH, birth, delivery, birthing, labor; *archaic* confinement, travail.

party noun **1** *150 people attended the party* (SOCIAL) GATHERING, (social) function, get-together, affair, celebration, festivity, reception, at-home; frolic, soiree, carousal, carouse, fête; *informal* bash, shindig, rave, do, shebang, bop, hop, blast, wingding. See table.

2 *a party of German tourists* GROUP, company, body, gang, band, crowd, pack, contingent; *informal* bunch, crew, load.

3 *the left-wing parties* FACTION, political party, group, grouping, cabal, junta, bloc, camp, caucus.

4 *don't mention a certain party* PERSON, individual, somebody, someone.

▸ verb *informal* *let's party!* CELEBRATE, have fun, enjoy oneself, have a party, have a good/wild time, go on a spree, rave it up, carouse, make merry; *informal* go out on the town, paint the town red, whoop it up, let one's hair down, make whoopee, live it up, have a ball.

PHRASE: **be a party to** *he refused to be a party to their vandalism* GET INVOLVED IN/WITH, be associated with, be a participant in.

party-pooper noun *informal* *don't be such a party pooper!* KILLJOY, spoilsport, wet blanket, sourpuss, damper (on the fun).

parvenu noun make way for our newest little hotshot parvenu UPSTART, social climber, arriviste.

pass[1] verb **1** *the traffic passing through the village* GO, proceed, move, progress, make one's way, travel. ANTONYM stop.

2 *a car passed him* OVERTAKE, go past/by, pull ahead of, overhaul, leave behind; *informal* leapfrog.

3 *time passed* ELAPSE, go by/past, advance, wear on, roll by, tick by.

4 *he passed the time writing letters* OCCUPY, spend, fill, use (up), employ, while away.

5 *pass me the salt* HAND (OVER), give, reach.

6 *Max passed the ball back* KICK, hit, throw, lob.

7 *her estate passed to her grandson* BE TRANSFERRED, go, be left, be bequeathed, be handed down/on, be passed on; *Law* devolve.

8 *his death passed almost unnoticed* HAPPEN, occur, take place, come about, transpire, come and go; *literary* befall.

9 *the storm passed* ABATE, fade (away), come to an end, blow over, run its course, die out, finish, end, cease, subside.

10 *nature's complexity passes all human understanding* SURPASS, exceed, transcend.

11 *he passed the exam* BE SUCCESSFUL IN, succeed in, gain a pass in, get through; *informal* sail through, scrape through. ANTONYM fail.

12 *the senate passed the bill* APPROVE, vote for, accept, ratify, adopt, agree to, authorize, endorse, legalize, enact; *informal* OK. ANTONYM reject.

13 *she could not let that comment pass* GO (UNNOTICED), stand, go unremarked, go undisputed.

14 *we should not pass judgment* DECLARE, pronounce, utter, express, deliver, issue.

15 *passing urine* DISCHARGE, excrete, evacuate, expel, emit, release.

▸ noun **1** *you must show your pass* PERMIT, warrant, authorization, license.

2 *a perfectly executed pass* KICK, hit, throw, cross, lateral (pass).

PHRASES: **come to pass** *literary* *it came to pass that Dorothy left Roberto* HAPPEN, come about, occur, transpire, arise; *literary* befall. **make a pass at** *are you accusing Mr. Allen of making a pass at you* MAKE (SEXUAL) ADVANCES TO, proposition; *informal* come on to, make a play for, hit on, make time with, put the make on. **pass away/on.** See DIE sense 1. **pass as/for** *I really think you could pass for an attorney* BE MISTAKEN FOR, be taken for, be accepted as. **pass off** *he tried to pass her off as his daughter* MISREPRESENT, falsely represent; disguise. **pass out** *this heat could make anyone pass out* FAINT, lose consciousness, black out. **pass over** *many a great movie has been passed over by the Academy* DISREGARD, overlook, ignore, pay no attention to, let pass, gloss over, take no notice of, pay no heed to, turn a blind eye to. **pass up** *I should never have passed up my chance to go to Rome* TURN DOWN, reject, refuse, decline, give up, forgo, let pass, miss (out on); *informal* give something a miss.

PARTIES AND SOCIAL EVENTS

anniversary party	housewarming
baby shower	jamboree
bachelor party	jubilee
ball	keg party
banquet	lawn party
barbecue	luau
barn dance	masquerade (party)
beach party	mixer
beer bash/blast/bust	office party
birthday party	pajama party
black-tie affair	party
block party	patio party
box social	picnic
bridal shower	potluck party
clambake	progressive dinner
class reunion	prom
cocktail party	reception
coffee klatch	reunion
cookout	roast
costume party	semiformal
dance	shower
dance party	sleepover
dinner party	slumber party
dinner dance	social
family reunion	stag party
fête champêtre	Super Bowl party
formal	surprise party
garden party	tailgate party
graduation party	tea party
hoedown	Tupperware party
holiday party	wedding shower
hootenanny	white-tie affair
hop	wine tasting
house party	

pass[2] noun *a pass through the mountains* ROUTE, way, road, passage, cut, gap, notch.

passable adjective **1** *the beer was passable* ADEQUATE, all right, fairly good, acceptable, satisfactory, moderately good, not (too) bad, average, tolerable, fair; mediocre, middling, ordinary, indifferent, unremarkable, unexceptional; *informal* OK, so-so, 'comme ci, comme ça', nothing to write home about.

2 *the road is still passable* NAVIGABLE, traversable, negotiable, unblocked, unobstructed, open, clear.

passably adverb *a passably good dinner* QUITE, rather, somewhat, fairly, reasonably, moderately, comparatively, relatively, tolerably; *informal* pretty.

passage noun **1** *their passage through the country* TRANSIT, progress, passing, movement, motion, traveling.

2 *the passage of time* PASSING, advance, course, march.

3 *a passage from the embassy* SAFE CONDUCT, warrant, visa; admission, access.

4 *the overnight passage* VOYAGE, crossing, trip, journey.

5 *clearing a passage to the front door* WAY (THROUGH), route, path.

6 *a passage to the kitchen.* See PASSAGEWAY sense 1.

7 *a passage between the buildings.* See PASSAGEWAY sense 2.

8 *the nasal passages* DUCT, orifice, opening, channel; inlet, outlet.

9 *the passage to democracy* TRANSITION, development, progress, move, change, shift.

10 *the passage of the bill* ENACTMENT, passing, ratification, royal assent, approval, adoption, authorization, legalization.

11 *a passage from "Macbeth"* EXTRACT, excerpt, quotation, quote, citation, reading, piece, selection.

passageway noun **1** *secret passageways* CORRIDOR, hall, passage, hallway, walkway, aisle.

2 *a narrow passageway off the main street* ALLEY, alleyway, passage, lane, path, pathway, footpath, track, thoroughfare.

passé adjective See OLD-FASHIONED.

passenger noun *rail passengers* TRAVELER, commuter, fare, rider.

passerby noun *several passersby confirmed his description of the collision* BYSTANDER, eyewitness, witness.

passing adjective **1** *of passing interest* FLEETING, transient, transitory, ephemeral, brief, short-lived, temporary, momentary; *literary* evanescent.

2 *a passing glance* HASTY, rapid, hurried, brief, quick; cursory, superficial, casual, perfunctory.

▸ noun **1** *the passing of time* PASSAGE, course, progress, advance.

2 *Jack's passing* DEATH, demise, passing away/on, end, loss, quietus; *formal* decease.

3 *the passing of the new bill* ENACTMENT, ratification, approval, adoption, authorization, legalization, endorsement.

PHRASE: **in passing** *in passing, let me add that the new membership directory will be available on Thursday* INCIDENTALLY, by the by/way, en passant.

passion noun **1** *the passion of activists* FERVOR, ardor, enthusiasm, eagerness, zeal, zealousness, vigor, fire, fieriness, energy, fervency, animation, spirit, spiritedness, fanaticism. ANTONYM apathy.

2 *he worked himself up into a passion* (BLIND) RAGE, fit of anger/temper, temper, towering rage, tantrum, fury, frenzy. See note at EMOTION.

3 *hot with passion* LOVE, (sexual) desire, lust, ardor, infatuation, lasciviousness, lustfulness.

4 *his passion for football* ENTHUSIASM, love, mania, fascination, obsession, fanaticism, fixation, compulsion, appetite, addiction; *informal* thing.

5 *French literature is my passion* OBSESSION, preoccupation, craze, mania, hobbyhorse.

6 *the Passion of Christ* CRUCIFIXION, suffering, agony, martyrdom.

passionate adjective **1** *a passionate entreaty* INTENSE, impassioned, ardent, fervent, vehement, heated, emotional, heartfelt, eager, excited, animated, adrenalized, spirited, energetic, fervid, frenzied, fiery, wild, consuming, violent; *literary* perfervid. ANTONYM apathetic.

2 *Elizabeth is **passionate about** sports* VERY KEEN ON, very enthusiastic about, addicted to; *informal* mad about, crazy about, hooked on, nuts about, nutso for.

3 *a passionate kiss* AMOROUS, ardent, hot-blooded, aroused, loving, sexy, sensual, erotic, lustful; *informal* steamy, hot, red-hot, turned on. ANTONYM cold.

4 *a passionate woman* EXCITABLE, emotional, fiery, volatile, mercurial, quick-tempered, high-strung, impulsive, temperamental. ANTONYM phlegmatic.

passionless adjective *a room full of passionless faces* UNEMOTIONAL, cold, cold-blooded, emotionless, frigid, cool, unfeeling, unloving, unresponsive, undemonstrative, impassive.

passive adjective **1** *a passive role* INACTIVE, nonactive, nonparticipative, uninvolved.

2 *passive victims* SUBMISSIVE, acquiescent, unresisting, unassertive, compliant, pliant, obedient, docile, tractable, malleable, pliable. ANTONYMS active, assertive.

3 *the woman's face was passive* EMOTIONLESS, impassive, unemotional, unmoved, dispassionate, passionless, detached, unresponsive, undemonstrative, apathetic, phlegmatic.

passport noun *qualifications are the passport to success* KEY, path, way, route, avenue, door, doorway.

past adjective **1** *memories of times past* GONE (BY), over (and done with), no more, done, bygone, former, (of) old, olden, long-ago; *literary* of yore.

2 *the past few months* LAST, recent, preceding.

3 *a past chairman* PREVIOUS, former, foregoing, erstwhile, one-time, sometime, ex-; *formal* quondam. ANTONYMS present, future.

▸ noun *details about her past* HISTORY, background, life (story).

▸ preposition **1** *she walked past the café* IN FRONT OF, by.

2 *he's past retirement age* BEYOND, in excess of.

▸ adverb *they hurried past* ALONG, by, on.

PHRASE: **in the past** *in the past, they did not allow women to sit in the bar* FORMERLY, previously, in days/years/times gone by, in former times, in the (good) old days, in days of old, in olden times, once (upon a time); *literary* in days of yore, in yesteryear.

pasta noun See table.

PASTA

acomo pepe	maruzzelle
anelli	mezze penne
angel hair	midollini
bavette	millerighe
bavettine	mostaccioli
bucatini	occhi di lupo
campanelle	orecchiette
cannaroni	orsetti
cannelloni	orzo
capelli d'Angelo	pansotti
capellini	pappardelle
cappelletti	pastina
casarecci	penne
cavatappi	pennette
cavatelli	perciatelli
conchiglie	pezzoccheri
conchiglioni	pipe rigate
coralli	pipette rigate
creste di galli	quadrefiore
ditali	quadrettini
ditalini	quadrucci
eliche	radiatore
elicodali	ravioli
farfalle	riccioli
fedelini	rigatoni
fettucce	riso
fettuccine	rotelle
fettucelle	rotelli
fideo	rotini
fischietti	ruote
fusilli	sedani rigati
fusilli col buco	sedanini rigati
garganelli	seme di mellone
gemelli	spaghetti
gigantoni	spaghettini
gigli	spiralini
gnocchetti	stelle
gnocchi	stellini
gramigna	strozzapreti
grattugiata	tagliarini
igomiti	tagliatelle
lasagne	tagliolini
linguine	tonnarelli
lumache	torchio
lumaconi	tortellini
macaroni	tortelloni
macceroni	tortiglioni
mafalda	trenne
malloreddus	trennette
maltagliati	tripolini
manicotti	troffiette
margherite	tubetti
margheritine	vermicelli
maruzze	ziti

See also table at NOODLE.

paste noun **1** *blend the ingredients to a paste* PURÉE, pulp, mush, mash, blend.

2 *wallpaper paste* ADHESIVE, glue, gum, fixative, mucilage.

▸ verb *a notice was pasted on the door* GLUE, stick, gum, fix, affix.

pastel adjective *we softened the look of the room with pastel paints and fabrics* PALE, soft, light, light-colored, muted, subtle, subdued, soft-hued. ANTONYMS dark, bright.

pastiche noun **1** *a pastiche of literary models* MIXTURE, blend, medley, mélange, miscellany, mixed bag, potpourri, mix, compound, composite, collection, assortment, conglomeration, jumble, ragbag, hodgepodge.

2 *a pastiche of eighteenth-century style* IMITATION, parody; *informal* takeoff.

pastime noun *two of my favorite pastimes are softball and street hockey* HOBBY, leisure activity/pursuit, sport, game, recreation, amusement, diversion, avocation, entertainment, interest, sideline.

past master noun *when it comes to interior design, Sheri is a past master* EXPERT, master, wizard, genius, old hand, veteran, maestro, connoisseur, authority, grandmaster; *informal* ace, pro, star, hotshot, maven, crackerjack.

pastor noun *our pastor is taking a group to Guatemala to help with disaster relief* MINISTER, clergyman, priest, parson, cleric, chaplain, padre, ecclesiastic, man of the cloth, churchman, vicar, rector, curate, preacher, imam; *informal* reverend.

pastoral adjective **1** *a pastoral scene* RURAL, country, countryside, rustic, agricultural, bucolic; *literary* sylvan, Arcadian. ANTONYM urban.

2 *his pastoral duties* PRIESTLY, clerical, ecclesiastical, ministerial.

pastry noun **1** *breakfast pastries* cake, doughnut, croissant, cruller, Danish (pastry), eclair, tart, tartlet, pie. See table.

2 *two layers of pastry* CRUST, piecrust, croute.

PASTRIES

almond horn	finanacier
baklava	frangipane
beggar's purse	kringle
cannoli	madeleine
cornet	mille-feuille
craquelin	napoleon
cream puff	pain au chocolat
croissant	pate a choux
croquembouche	petit four
crumpet	profiterole
danish	schnecken
eclair	sfogliatelle
elephant ear	strudel
feuilletee	vol-au-vent

See also tables at CAKE, CANDY, COOKIE, DOUGHNUT, and PIE.

pasture noun *the cows are in the pasture* GRAZING LAND, grassland, grass, pastureland, pasturage; *Brit.* ley; meadow, field; *literary* lea, mead, greensward.

pasty adjective *my complexion gets so pasty over the winter* PALE, pallid, wan, colorless, anemic, ashen, white, gray, pasty-faced, washed out, sallow.

pat[1] verb *Brian patted her on the shoulder* TAP, slap lightly, clap, touch.

▸ noun **1** *a pat on the cheek* TAP, light blow, clap, touch.

2 *a pat of butter* PIECE, dab, lump, portion, knob, mass, gobbet, ball, curl.

PHRASE: **pat on the back** *Lenny's fellow students were eager to pat him on the back for his amazing test scores* CONGRATULATE, praise, take one's hat off to; commend, compliment, applaud, acclaim.

pat[2] adjective *pat answers* GLIB, simplistic, facile, unconvincing.

▸ adverb *his reply came rather pat* OPPORTUNELY, conveniently, at just/exactly the right moment, expediently, favorably, appropriately, fittingly, auspiciously, providentially, felicitously, propitiously.

PHRASES: **down pat** *the understudy knew Lori's lines down pat* WORD-PERFECT, by heart, by rote, by memory. **get down pat** *I have to get these lyrics down pat within the next two hours* MEMORIZE, commit to memory, remember, learn by heart, learn (by rote).

patch noun **1** *a patch over one eye* COVER, eye patch, covering, pad.

2 *a reddish patch on her wrist* BLOTCH, mark, spot, smudge, speckle, smear, stain, streak, blemish; *informal* splotch.

3 *a patch of ground* PLOT, area, piece, strip, tract, parcel; bed, allotment, lot, plat.

4 *informal they are going through a difficult patch* PERIOD, time, spell, phase, stretch.

▸ verb *her jeans were neatly patched* MEND, repair, put a patch on, sew (up), stitch (up).

PHRASE: **patch up** *informal* **1** *the houses were being patched up* REPAIR, mend, fix hastily, do a makeshift repair on. **2** *he's trying to patch things up with his wife* RECONCILE, make up, settle, remedy, put to rights, rectify, clear up, set right, make good, resolve, square.

patchwork noun *the exhibit is essentially a patchwork of the students' favorite pieces* ASSORTMENT, miscellany, mixture, mélange, medley, blend, mixed bag, mix, collection, selection, assemblage, combination, potpourri, jumble, mishmash, bricolage, ragbag, hodgepodge.

patchy adjective **1** *their education has been patchy* UNEVEN, varying, variable, intermittent, fitful, sporadic, erratic, irregular, haphazard, hit-and-miss. ANTONYM uniform.

2 *patchy evidence* FRAGMENTARY, inadequate, insufficient, rudimentary, limited, sketchy. ANTONYM comprehensive.

patent noun *there is a patent on the drug* COPYRIGHT, license, legal protection, registered trademark.

▸ adjective **1** *patent nonsense* OBVIOUS, clear, plain, evident, manifest, self-evident, transparent, overt, conspicuous, blatant, downright, barefaced, flagrant, undisguised, unconcealed, unmistakable.

2 *patent medicines* PROPRIETARY, patented, licensed, branded.

paternal adjective **1** *his face showed paternal concern* FATHERLY, fatherlike, patriarchal; protective, solicitous, compassionate, sympathetic.

2 *his paternal grandfather* ON ONE'S FATHER'S SIDE, patrilineal. ANTONYM maternal.

paternity noun *the blood tests are used to determine paternity* FATHERHOOD.

path noun **1** *a path down to the beach* TRAIL, pathway, walkway, track, footpath, trackway, bridleway, bridle path, portage trail, lane, alley, alleyway, passage, passageway; sidewalk, bikeway.

2 *journalists blocked his path* ROUTE, way, course; direction, bearing, line; orbit, trajectory.

3 *the best path toward a settlement* COURSE OF ACTION, route, road, avenue, line, approach, tack, strategy, tactic.

pathetic adjective **1** *a pathetic groan* PITIFUL, pitiable, piteous, moving, touching, poignant, plaintive, distressing, upsetting, heartbreaking, heart-rending, harrowing, wretched, forlorn. See note at MOVING.

2 *informal a pathetic excuse* FEEBLE, woeful, sorry, poor, pitiful, lamentable, deplorable, contemptible, inadequate, paltry, insufficient, insubstantial, unsatisfactory.

pathfinder noun PIONEER, groundbreaker, trailblazer, trendsetter, leader, torchbearer, pacemaker.

pathological adjective **1** *a pathological condition* MORBID, diseased.

2 *informal a pathological liar* COMPULSIVE, obsessive, inveterate, habitual, persistent, chronic, hardened, confirmed.

pathos noun *the pathos of Antoine's predicament* POIGNANCY, tragedy, sadness, pitifulness, piteousness, pitiableness.

patience noun **1** *she tried everyone's patience* FORBEARANCE, tolerance, restraint, self-restraint, stoicism; calmness, composure, equanimity, serenity, tranquility, imperturbability, phlegm, understanding, indulgence.

2 *a task requiring patience* PERSEVERANCE, persistence, endurance, tenacity, assiduity, application, staying power, doggedness, determination, resolve, resolution, resoluteness.

patient adjective **1** *I must ask you to be patient* FORBEARING, uncomplaining, tolerant, resigned, stoical; calm, composed, even-tempered, imperturbable, unexcitable, accommodating, understanding, indulgent; *informal* unflappable, cool.

2 *a good deal of patient work* PERSEVERING, persistent, tenacious, indefatigable, dogged, determined, resolved, resolute, single-minded; *formal* pertinacious.

▸ noun *a doctor's patient* SICK PERSON, case; invalid, convalescent, outpatient, in-patient.

patio noun *we had cocktails on the patio* TERRACE, sundeck, deck; courtyard.

patois noun *he recognized the patois of New Orleans in her speech* VERNACULAR, (local) dialect, regional language; jargon, argot, cant; *informal* (local) lingo.

patriarch noun *as patriarch of this family, I am passing fiduciary control of the estate on to Derek* SENIOR FIGURE, father, paterfamilias, leader, elder.

patrician noun *the great patricians of the British Empire* ARISTOCRAT, grandee, noble, nobleman, noblewoman, lord, lady, peer, peeress; blue blood.

▸ adjective *patrician families* ARISTOCRATIC, noble, titled, blue-blooded, high-born, upper-class, landowning; *informal* upper-crust; *archaic* gentle.

patrimony noun *our cultural patrimony is in jeopardy* HERITAGE, inheritance, birthright; legacy, bequest, endowment.

patriot noun *would a true patriot abandon a comrade?* NATIONALIST, loyalist; chauvinist, jingoist, flag-waver.

patriotic adjective *a patriotic show of support* NATIONALIST, nationalistic, loyalist, loyal; chauvinistic, jingoistic, flag-waving. ANTONYM traitorous.

WORD NOTE **patriotic**

Patriotic and *unpatriotic* are words that carry so much emotional baggage that they should be used only after considerable reflection. A patriot loves his homeland and is willing to defend it against enemies. But these days *patriotic* often implies a blustery, unthinking, my country-right-or-wrong nationalism. As people used to say in the 1960s, the word has been co-opted and has become a crude means of provoking an almost Pavlovian twitch response: For example, if you don't agree with whatever the United States undertakes, especially in foreign affairs or military operations, you may be vilified as unpatriotic, i.e., cowardly, unworthy of being an American, and possibly traitorous. Yet turn around and the flag-wavingly patriotic are pitied as little more than dupes of the government or victims of jingoistic brainwashing. Furthering the confusion, every extremist cadre in the world employs the rhetoric of patriotism to recruit its members and maintain their allegiance. Thus, to some a patriot suggests a crude and belligerent fanatic, while to others he is a loyal-to-the-death defender of his country's traditions and values. Sometimes only God can distinguish the one from the other. Whatever the case, *patriotic* and *unpatriotic* are always fighting words, and usually bullying ones too. **—MD**

---

patrol noun **1** *an all-night patrol to protect the witness* VIGIL, guard, watch, monitoring, policing, patroling.

2 *the patrol stopped a suspect* SECURITY GUARD, sentry, sentinel, patrolman; scout, scouting party.

▸ verb *a security guard was patroling the neighborhood* KEEP GUARD (ON), guard, keep watch (on); police, make the rounds (of); stand guard (over), keep a vigil (on), defend, safeguard.

patron noun **1** *a patron of the arts* SPONSOR, backer, financier, benefactor, benefactress, contributor, subscriber, donor; philanthropist, promoter, friend, supporter; *informal* angel.

2 *club patrons* CUSTOMER, client, frequenter, consumer, user, visitor, guest; *informal* regular, habitué.

patronage noun **1** *art patronage* SPONSORSHIP, backing, funding, financing, promotion, assistance, support.

2 *political patronage* POWER OF APPOINTMENT, favoritism, nepotism, preferential treatment, cronyism, pork-barreling.

3 *thank you for your patronage* CUSTOM, trade, business.

patronize verb **1** *don't patronize me!* TREAT CONDESCENDINGLY, condescend to, look down on, talk down to, put down, treat like a child, treat with disdain.

2 *they patronized local merchants* DO BUSINESS WITH, buy from, shop at, be a customer of, be a client of, deal with, trade with, frequent, support.

3 *he patronized a national museum* SPONSOR, back, fund, finance, be a patron of, support, champion.

patronizing adjective *your patronizing mother just told me how "adequate" my dress is* CONDESCENDING, disdainful, supercilious, superior, imperious, scornful, contemptuous; *informal* uppity, high and mighty.

patter[1] verb **1** *raindrops pattered against the window* GO PITTER-PATTER, tap, drum, beat, pound, rat-a-tat, go pit-a-pat, thrum.

2 *she pattered across the floor* SCURRY, scuttle, skip, trip.

▸ noun *the patter of rain* PITTER-PATTER, tapping, pattering, drumming, beat, beating, pounding, rat-a-tat, pit-a-pat, clack, thrum, thrumming.

patter[2] noun **1** *this witty patter* PRATTLE, prating, blather, blither, drivel, chatter, jabber, babble; *informal* yabbering, yatter; *archaic* twaddle.

2 *the salesman's patter* (SALES) PITCH, sales talk; *informal* line, spiel.

3 *the local patter* SPEECH, language, parlance, dialect; *informal* lingo.

▸ verb *she pattered on incessantly* PRATTLE, prate, blather, drivel, chatter, jabber, babble; *informal* yabber, yatter.

pattern noun **1** *the pattern on the wallpaper* DESIGN, decoration, motif, marking, ornament, ornamentation. See table.

2 *the patterns of ant behavior* SYSTEM, order, arrangement, form, method, structure, scheme, plan, format, framework.

3 *this would set the pattern for a generation* MODEL, example, criterion, standard, basis, point of reference, gauge, norm, yardstick, touchstone, benchmark; blueprint, archetype, prototype. See note at MODEL.

4 *textile patterns* SAMPLE, specimen, swatch.

▸ verb *someone else is patterning my life* SHAPE, influence, model, fashion, mold, style, determine, control.

PATTERNS

argyle	moire
basketweave	oblique
bird's-eye	paisley
Black Watch	parquet
broken check	pinstripe
check	plaid
diaper	pointillé
dogtooth	polka dot
Fair Isle	stripe
figured	tartan
geometric	tattersall
glen plaid	tiling
houndstooth	twill
herringbone	waffle
labyrinth	zigzag

patterned adjective *patterned glassware* DECORATED, ornamented, fancy, adorned, embellished. ANTONYM plain.

paucity noun *a paucity of evidence* SCARCITY, sparseness, sparsity, dearth, shortage, poverty, insufficiency, deficiency, lack, want. ANTONYM abundance.

paunch noun *I love everything about him, even his cute little paunch* POTBELLY, beer belly, beer gut, spare tire, pot.

pauper noun *the story of a lowly pauper who rises to the top of a major crime syndicate* POOR PERSON, indigent, down-and-out; *informal* have-not.

pause noun *a pause in the conversation* STOP, cessation, break, halt, interruption, check, lull, respite, breathing space, discontinuation, hiatus, gap, interlude; adjournment, suspension, rest, wait, hesitation; *informal* letup, breather.

▸ verb *Hannah paused for a moment* STOP, cease, halt, discontinue, break off, take a break; adjourn, rest, wait, hesitate, falter, waver; *informal* take a breather, take five.

pave PHRASE: **pave the way for** *a document that could pave the way for legislation* PREPARE (THE WAY) FOR, make preparations for, get ready for, lay the foundations for, herald, precede.

paw noun *protect their paws from frostbite* FOOT, forepaw, hind paw.

▸ verb **1** *their offspring were pawing each other* HANDLE ROUGHLY, pull, grab, maul, manhandle.

2 *some Casanova tried to paw her* FONDLE, feel, maul, molest; *informal* grope, feel up, goose.

pawn verb *he pawned his watch* PLEDGE, put in pawn, give as security, use as collateral; *informal* hock, put in hock.

▸ noun *a pawn in the battle for the throne* PUPPET, dupe, hostage, tool, cat's paw, instrument.

pay verb **1** *I want to pay him for his work* REWARD, reimburse, recompense, give payment to, remunerate.

2 *Tom must pay a few more dollars* SPEND, expend, pay out, dish out, disburse; *informal* lay out, shell out, fork out, cough up; ante up, pony up.

3 *he paid his debts* DISCHARGE, settle, pay off, clear, liquidate.

4 *hard work will pay dividends* YIELD, return, produce.

5 *he made the buses pay* BE PROFITABLE, make money, make a profit.

6 *it doesn't pay to get involved* BE ADVANTAGEOUS, be of advantage, be beneficial, benefit.

7 *paying compliments* BESTOW, grant, give, offer.

8 *he will pay for his mistakes* SUFFER, suffer the consequences, be punished, atone, pay the penalty/price.

▸ noun *equal pay for women* SALARY, wages, payment; earnings, remuneration, reimbursement, income, revenue; *formal* emolument(s).

PHRASES: **pay back 1** *she has sworn to pay him back for his philandering* GET ONE'S REVENGE ON, be revenged on, avenge oneself on, get back at, get even with, settle accounts with, exact retribution on. **2** *they eventually paid back the money* REPAY, pay off, give back, return, reimburse, refund. **pay for** *I'll pay for dinner* FUND, finance, defray the cost of, settle up for, treat someone to; *informal* foot the bill for, shell out for, fork out for, cough up for, ante up for, pony up for. **pay off 1** *he was busted for trying to pay off a cop* BRIBE, suborn, buy (off); *informal* grease someone's palm. **2** *she paid off the car loan in less than a year* PAY (IN FULL), settle, discharge, clear, liquidate. **3** *his hard work paid off* MEET WITH SUCCESS, be successful, be effective, get results. **pay out** *how much did you have to pay out for that bike?* SPEND, expend, dish out, put up, part with, hand over; *informal* shell out, fork out/up, lay out, cough up. **pay up** *you have one more week to pay up* MAKE PAYMENT, settle up, pay (in full); *informal* cough up.

payable adjective *a notice of payable taxes* DUE, owed, owing, outstanding, unpaid, overdue, in arrears, delinquent.

payment noun **1** *discounts for early payment* REMITTANCE, settlement, discharge, clearance, liquidation.

2 *monthly payments* INSTALLMENT, premium.

3 *extra payment for good performance* SALARY, wages, pay, earnings, fee(s), remuneration, reimbursement, income; *formal* emolument(s).

payoff noun *informal* **1** *the lure of enormous payoffs* PAYMENT, payout, reward; bribe, inducement, incentive, payola; *informal* kickback, sweetener.

2 *a payoff of $160,000* RETURN (ON INVESTMENT), yield, payback, profit, gain, dividend.

3 *a dramatic payoff* OUTCOME, denouement, culmination, conclusion, development, result.

peace noun **1** *can't a man get any peace around here?* TRANQUILITY, calm, restfulness, peace and quiet, peacefulness, quiet, quietness; privacy, solitude. ANTONYM noise.

2 *peace of mind* SERENITY, peacefulness, tranquility, equanimity, calm, calmness, composure, ease, contentment, contentedness. ANTONYMS agitation, distress.

3 *we pray for peace* LAW AND ORDER, lawfulness, order, peacefulness, peaceableness, harmony, nonviolence; *formal* concord. ANTONYM conflict.

4 *a lasting peace* TREATY, truce, cease-fire, armistice, cessation/suspension of hostilities. ANTONYM war.

peaceable adjective **1** *a peaceable man* PEACE-LOVING, nonviolent, nonaggressive, easygoing, placid, gentle, inoffensive, good-natured, even-tempered, amiable, amicable, friendly, affable, genial, pacific, dovelike, dovish, unwarlike, pacifist; *formal* irenic. ANTONYMS aggressive, belligerent.

2 *a peaceable society* PEACEFUL, strife-free, harmonious; law-abiding, disciplined, orderly, civilized. ANTONYMS unruly, warring.

peaceful adjective **1** *everything was quiet and peaceful* TRANQUIL, calm, restful, quiet, still, relaxing, soothing, undisturbed, untroubled, private, secluded. See note at CALM. ANTONYMS noisy, bustling.

2 *his peaceful mood* SERENE, calm, tranquil, composed, placid, at ease, untroubled, unworried, content. ANTONYM agitated.

3 *peaceful relations* HARMONIOUS, at peace, peaceable, on good terms, amicable, friendly, cordial, nonviolent. ANTONYM hostile.

peacemaker noun *she was regarded as the great peacemaker of her people* ARBITRATOR, arbiter, mediator, negotiator, conciliator, go-between, intermediary, pacifier, appeaser, peace-monger, pacifist, peace-lover, dove; *informal* peacenik.

peak noun **1** *the peaks of the mountains* SUMMIT, top, crest, pinnacle, apex, crown, cap.

2 *the highest peak* MOUNTAIN, hill, height, mount, alp.

3 *the peak of a cap* BRIM, visor.

4 *the peak of his career* HEIGHT, high point/spot, pinnacle, summit, top, climax, culmination, apex, zenith, crowning point, acme, capstone, apogee, prime, heyday.

▸ verb *conservative support has peaked* REACH ITS HEIGHT, climax, reach a climax, come to a head.

▸ adjective *peak loads* MAXIMUM, top, greatest, highest; ultimate, best, optimum.

peaked adjective *Marjorie, my dear, you look so peaked* PALE, pasty, wan, drained, washed out, drawn, pallid, anemic, ashen, gray, pinched, sickly, sallow, ill, unwell, poorly, indisposed, run down, off; *informal* under the weather, rough, lousy.

peal noun **1** *a peal of bells* CHIME, carillon, ring, ringing, tintinnabulation.

2 *peals of laughter* SHRIEK, shout, scream, howl, gale, fit, roar, hoot.

3 *a peal of thunder* RUMBLE, roar, boom, crash, clap, crack.

▸ verb 1 *the bell pealed* RING (OUT), chime (out), clang, sound, ding, jingle.

2 *the thunder pealed* RUMBLE, roar, boom, crash, resound.

peasant noun 1 *peasants working the land* AGRICULTURAL WORKER, small farmer, rustic, swain, villein, serf, campesino; *historical* habitant.

2 *informal you peasants!* See BOOR.

peccadillo noun *I'm sure we can overlook a few peccadilloes* MISDEMEANOR, petty offense, indiscretion, lapse, misdeed.

peck verb 1 *the cockerel pecked my heel* BITE, nip, strike, hit, tap, rap, jab.

2 *he pecked her on the cheek* KISS, give a peck.

3 *informal she* ***pecked at*** *her food* NIBBLE (AT), pick at, take very small bites from, toy with, play with.

peculiar adjective 1 *something peculiar began to happen* STRANGE, unusual, odd, funny, curious, bizarre, weird, queer, unexpected, unfamiliar, abnormal, atypical, anomalous, out of the ordinary; exceptional, extraordinary, remarkable; puzzling, mystifying, mysterious, perplexing, baffling; suspicious, eerie, uncanny, unnatural; *informal* freaky, fishy, creepy, spooky. ANTONYM ordinary.

2 *peculiar behavior* BIZARRE, eccentric, strange, odd, weird, queer, funny, unusual, abnormal, idiosyncratic, unconventional, outlandish, quirky; *informal* wacky, freakish, oddball, offbeat, off the wall, wacko.

3 *mannerisms* ***peculiar to*** *the islanders* CHARACTERISTIC OF, typical of, representative of, indicative of, suggestive of, exclusive to, unique to.

4 *their own peculiar contribution* DISTINCTIVE, characteristic, distinct, individual, special, idiosyncratic, unique, personal.

peculiarity noun 1 *a legal peculiarity* ODDITY, anomaly, abnormality.

2 *a physical peculiarity* IDIOSYNCRASY, mannerism, quirk, foible.

3 *one of the peculiarities of the city* CHARACTERISTIC, feature, (essential) quality, property, trait, attribute, hallmark, trademark.

4 *the peculiarity of this notion* STRANGENESS, oddness, bizarreness, weirdness, queerness, unexpectedness, unfamiliarity, incongruity.

5 *there is a certain peculiarity about her appearance* OUTLANDISHNESS, bizarreness, unconventionality, idiosyncrasy, weirdness, oddness, eccentricity, unusualness, abnormality, queerness, strangeness, quirkiness; *informal* wackiness, freakiness.

pecuniary adjective *free from pecuniary anxieties* FINANCIAL, monetary, money, fiscal, economic. See note at FINANCIAL.

pedagogic adjective *Dr. Snow encouraged me in my pedagogic endeavors* EDUCATIONAL, educative, pedagogical, teaching, instructional, instructive, didactic; academic, scholastic.

pedagogue *formal* noun *her thirty-two years as a most beloved pedagogue* TEACHER, schoolteacher, schoolmaster, schoolmistress, master, mistress, tutor; lecturer, academic, don, professor, instructor, educator, educationist, educationalist.

pedant noun *pedants insist that the twenty-first century starts with 2001* DOGMATIST, purist, literalist, formalist, doctrinaire, perfectionist; quibbler, hair-splitter, casuist, sophist; *informal* nitpicker.

pedantic adjective *a pedantic interpretation of the rules* OVERSCRUPULOUS, scrupulous, precise, exact, perfectionist, punctilious, meticulous, fussy, fastidious, finicky; dogmatic, purist, literalist, literalistic, formalist; casuistic, casuistical, sophistic, sophistical; captious, hair-splitting, quibbling; *informal* nitpicking, persnickety.

pedantry noun *the pedantry in her argument has upset the flow of our discussion* DOGMATISM, purism, literalism, formalism; overscrupulousness, scrupulousness, perfectionism, fastidiousness, punctiliousness, meticulousness; captiousness, quibbling, hair-splitting, casuistry, sophistry; *informal* nitpicking. See note at KNOWLEDGE.

peddle verb 1 *they are peddling water filters* SELL, sell from door to door, hawk, tout, vend; trade (in), deal in, traffic in.

2 *peddling unorthodox views* ADVOCATE, champion, preach, put forward, proclaim, propound, promote, promulgate.

peddler noun 1 *a poor and lonesome peddler* TRAVELING SALESMAN/SALESPERSON, door-to-door salesman/salesperson; huckster; street trader, hawker; *archaic* chapman.

2 *a drug peddler* TRAFFICKER, dealer; *informal* pusher.

pedestal noun *a bust on a pedestal* PLINTH, base, support, mounting, stand, foundation, pillar, column, pier; *Architecture* socle. PHRASE: **put on a pedestal** *if you put me on a pedestal, I'll eventually disappoint you* IDEALIZE, lionize, look up to, respect, hold in high regard, think highly of, admire, esteem, revere, worship.

pedestrian noun *accidents involving pedestrians* WALKER, person on foot; **(pedestrians)** foot traffic. ANTONYM driver.

▸ adjective *pedestrian lives* DULL, boring, tedious, monotonous, uneventful, unremarkable, tiresome, wearisome, uninspired, unimaginative, unexciting, uninteresting; unvarying, unvaried, repetitive, routine, commonplace, workaday; ordinary, everyday, run-of-the-mill, mundane, humdrum; *informal* plain-vanilla. ANTONYM exciting.

pedigree noun *a long pedigree* ANCESTRY, descent, lineage, line (of descent), genealogy, family tree, extraction, derivation, origin(s), heritage, parentage, bloodline, background, roots.

▸ adjective *a pedigree cat* PURE-BRED, thoroughbred, pure-blooded.

pee verb *informal before we leave, does anyone have to pee?* URINATE, relieve oneself, pass water, make water; *informal* take a leak, piddle, tinkle, take a whiz/piss; *formal* micturate.

peek verb 1 *Hermione peeked from behind the curtains* (HAVE A) PEEP, have a peek, spy, take a sly/stealthy look, sneak a look/peek; *informal* take a gander.

2 *the deer's antlers* ***peeked out*** *from the trees* APPEAR (SLOWLY/PARTLY), show, come into view/sight, become visible, emerge, peep (out).

▸ noun *a peek at the map* SECRET LOOK, sly look, stealthy

look, sneaky look, peep, glance, glimpse, hurried/quick look; *informal* gander, squint.

peel verb **1** *peel and core the fruit* PARE, skin, take the skin/rind off; hull, shell, husk, shuck; *technical* decorticate.

2 *use a long knife to peel the veneer* TRIM (OFF), peel off, pare, strip (off), shave (off), remove.

3 *the wallpaper was peeling* FLAKE (OFF), peel off, come off in layers/strips.

▸ noun *orange peel* RIND, skin, covering, zest; hull, pod, integument, shuck.

PHRASE: **keep one's eyes peeled** *keep your eyes peeled for a light blue Pontiac* KEEP A (SHARP) LOOKOUT, look out, keep one's eyes open, keep watch, be watchful, be alert, be on the alert, be on the qui vive, be on guard.

peep[1] verb **1** *I peeped through the keyhole* LOOK QUICKLY, cast a brief look, take a secret look, sneak a look, (have a) peek, glance; *informal* take a gander.

2 *the moon peeped through the clouds* APPEAR (SLOWLY/PARTLY), show, come into view/sight, become visible, emerge, peek, peer out.

▸ noun *I'll just take a peep at it* QUICK LOOK, brief look, (sneak) peek, glance; *informal* gander, squint.

peep[2] noun **1** *I heard a quiet peep* CHEEP, chirp, chirrup, tweet, twitter, chirr, warble.

2 *there's been not a peep out of the children* SOUND, noise, cry, word.

3 *the painting was sold without a peep* COMPLAINT, grumble, mutter, murmur, grouse, objection, protest, protestation; *informal* moan, gripe, grouch.

peephole noun *just take a look through this peephole* OPENING, gap, cleft, slit, crack, chink, keyhole, knothole, squint.

peer[1] verb *he peered at the manuscript* LOOK CLOSELY, try to see, narrow one's eyes, screw up one's eyes, squint.

peer[2] noun **1** *his academic peers* EQUAL, coequal, fellow, confrere; contemporary; *formal* compeer.

2 *hereditary peers* ARISTOCRAT, lord, lady, peer of the realm, peeress, noble, nobleman, noblewoman, titled man/woman, patrician; duke/duchess, marquess/marchioness, earl/countess, viscount/viscountess, baron/baroness, marquis/marquise, count.

peerage noun *she claims to be related to British peerage* ARISTOCRACY, nobility, peers and peeresses, lords and ladies, patriciate; the House of Lords, the Lords.

peerless adjective *a peerless performance* INCOMPARABLE, matchless, unrivaled, inimitable, beyond compare/comparison, unparalleled, unequaled, without equal, second to none, unsurpassed, unsurpassable, nonpareil; unique, consummate, perfect, rare, transcendent, surpassing; *formal* unexampled.

peeve verb *informal it seems that everything I do peeves her* IRRITATE, annoy, vex, anger, exasperate, irk, gall, pique, nettle, put out, get on someone's nerves, try someone's patience, ruffle someone's feathers; rub the wrong way; *informal* aggravate, rile, needle, get to, bug, get someone's goat, get/put someone's back up, tee off, tick off.

peeved adjective *informal I left feeling frustrated and peeved* IRRITATED, annoyed, cross, angry, vexed, displeased, disgruntled, indignant, exasperated, galled, irked, put out, aggrieved, offended, affronted, piqued, nettled, in high dudgeon; *informal* aggravated, miffed, riled, teed off, ticked off, sore.

peevish adjective *he was embarrassed by his mother's peevish disposition* IRRITABLE, fractious, fretful, cross, petulant, querulous, pettish, crabby, crotchety, cantankerous, curmudgeonly, sullen, grumpy, bad-tempered, short-tempered, touchy, testy, tetchy, snappish, irascible, waspish, prickly, crusty, dyspeptic, splenetic, choleric; *informal* cranky, ornery. ANTONYM good-humored.

peewee adjective *we even have these baseball jerseys in peewee sizes, perfect for infants and toddlers* TINY, very small, baby, pint-sized, diminutive, miniature.

peg noun *the joints are secured by pegs* PIN, nail, dowel, skewer, spike, rivet, brad, screw, bolt, hook, spigot; *Mountaineering* piton; *Golf* tee.

▸ verb **1** *the tarp is pegged to the ground* FIX, pin, attach, fasten, secure, make fast.

2 *we decided to peg our prices* HOLD DOWN, keep down, fix, set, hold, freeze.

PHRASE: **take down a peg or two** *wouldn't I just love to take that Mr. Bigshot down a peg or two* HUMBLE, humiliate, mortify, bring down, shame, embarrass, abash, put someone in their place, chasten, subdue, squash, deflate, make someone eat humble pie; *informal* show up, settle someone's hash, cut down to size, make someone eat crow.

pejorative adjective *his remarks were considered too pejorative for daytime radio* DISPARAGING, derogatory, denigratory, deprecatory, defamatory, slanderous, libelous, abusive, insulting, slighting; *informal* bitchy. ANTONYM complimentary.

pellet noun **1** *a pellet of mud* LITTLE BALL, little piece.

2 *pellet wounds* BULLET, shot, lead shot, buckshot, slug.

3 *rabbit pellets* EXCREMENT, excreta, droppings, feces, dung, turd.

pell-mell adverb **1** *people streamed pell-mell from the building* HELTER-SKELTER, headlong, (at) full tilt, hotfoot, posthaste, hurriedly, hastily, recklessly, precipitately.

2 *the sacks' contents were thrown pell-mell to the ground* UNTIDILY, anyhow, in disarray, in a mess, in a muddle; *informal* all over the place, every which way, any old how, all over the map, all over the lot.

pellucid adjective **1** *the pellucid waters* TRANSLUCENT, transparent, clear, crystal clear, crystalline, glassy, limpid, unclouded, gin-clear.

2 *pellucid prose* LUCID, limpid, clear, crystal clear, articulate; coherent, comprehensible, understandable, intelligible, straightforward, simple, clean, well-constructed; *formal* perspicuous.

pelt[1] verb **1** *they pelted him with snowballs* BOMBARD, shower, attack, assail, pepper.

2 *they said we'd get some showers, but it's really **pelting down*** POUR (DOWN), come down, teem (down), stream down, rain cats and dogs, rain hard.

3 *informal they pelted into the factory* DASH, run, race, rush, sprint, bolt, dart, career, charge, shoot, hurtle, careen, fly, speed, zoom, streak; hasten, hurry; *informal* tear, belt, hotfoot it, scoot, leg it, go like a bat out of hell, bomb, hightail it.

pelt[2] noun *an animal's pelt* SKIN, hide, fleece, coat, fur.

pen[1] noun *you'll need a pen and paper* ballpoint (pen), fountain pen, rollerball; felt tip (pen); highlighter, marker (pen).

▸ verb *she penned a number of articles* WRITE, compose, draft, dash off; write down, jot down, set down, take down, scribble.

pen[2] noun *a sheep pen* ENCLOSURE, fold, sheepfold, pound, compound, stockade; sty, coop, corral.

▸ verb *the hostages had been penned up in a basement* CONFINE, coop (up), cage, shut in, box up/in, lock up/in, trap, imprison, incarcerate, immure.

penal adjective **1** *a penal institution* DISCIPLINARY, punitive, corrective, correctional.

2 *penal rates of interest* EXORBITANT, extortionate, excessive, outrageous, preposterous, unreasonable, inflated, sky-high.

penalize verb **1** *if you break the rules you will be penalized* PUNISH, discipline, inflict a penalty on. ANTONYM reward.

2 *people with certain medical conditions would be penalized* HANDICAP, disadvantage, put at a disadvantage, cause to suffer. ANTONYM favor.

penalty noun **1** *increased penalties for dumping oil at sea* PUNISHMENT, sanction, punitive action, retribution; fine, forfeit, sentence; penance; *formal* mulct. ANTONYM reward.

2 *a game full of penalties* FOUL, infraction.

3 *the penalties of old age* DISADVANTAGE, difficulty, drawback, handicap, downside, minus; trial, tribulation, bane, affliction, burden, trouble. ANTONYM advantage.

penance noun *true penance requires honest self-examination* ATONEMENT, expiation, self-punishment, self-mortification, self-abasement, amends; punishment, penalty.

penchant noun *I have a penchant for small dogs* LIKING, fondness, preference, taste, relish, appetite, partiality, soft spot, love, passion, desire, fancy, whim, weakness, inclination, bent, bias, proclivity, predilection, predisposition.

pencil noun **1** *a sharpened pencil* lead pencil, mechanical pencil, colored pencil; grease pencil; eyebrow pencil, lip pencil.

2 *a pencil of light* BEAM, ray, shaft, finger, gleam.

▸ verb **1** *he penciled his name inside the cover* WRITE, write down, jot down, scribble, note, take down.

2 *pencil a line along the top of the molding* DRAW, trace, sketch.

pendant noun *she wore an antique gold pendant around her neck* NECKLACE, locket, medallion.

pendent adjective *the tree's pendent catkins* HANGING, suspended, dangling, pendulous, pensile, pendant, drooping, droopy, trailing.

pending adjective **1** *nine cases were still pending* UNRESOLVED, undecided, unsettled, awaiting decision/action, undetermined, open, hanging fire, (up) in the air, on ice, ongoing, outstanding, not done, unfinished, incomplete; *informal* on the back burner.

2 *with a general election pending* IMMINENT, impending, about to happen, forthcoming, upcoming, on the way, coming, approaching, looming, gathering, near, nearing, close, close at hand, in the offing, to come.

▸ preposition *they were released on bail pending an appeal* AWAITING, until, till, until there is/are.

pendulous adjective *large, pendulous flowers* DROOPING, dangling, trailing, droopy, sagging, saggy, floppy; hanging, pendent, pensile.

penetrable adjective **1** *a penetrable subsoil* PERMEABLE, pervious, porous.

2 *books that are barely penetrable to anyone under 50* UNDERSTANDABLE, fathomable, comprehensible, intelligible.

penetrate verb **1** *the knife penetrated his lungs* PIERCE, puncture, make a hole in, perforate, stab, prick, gore, spike.

2 *they penetrated the enemy territory* INFILTRATE, slip into, sneak into, insinuate oneself into.

3 *fear penetrated her bones* PERMEATE, pervade, fill, spread throughout, suffuse, seep through.

4 *he seemed to have penetrated the mysteries of nature* UNDERSTAND, comprehend, apprehend, fathom, grasp, perceive, discern, get to the bottom of, solve, resolve, make sense of, interpret, puzzle out, work out, unravel, decipher, make head(s) or tail(s) of; *informal* crack, get, figure out.

5 *her words finally penetrated* REGISTER, sink in, be understood, be comprehended, become clear, fall into place; *informal* click.

penetrating adjective **1** *a penetrating wind* PIERCING, cutting, biting, stinging, keen, sharp, harsh, raw, freezing, chill, wintry, cold. ANTONYMS mild, gentle. See note at KEEN.

2 *a penetrating voice* SHRILL, strident, piercing, carrying, loud, high, high-pitched, piping, ear-splitting, screechy, intrusive. ANTONYMS mellow, soft.

3 *a penetrating smell* PUNGENT, pervasive, strong, powerful, sharp, acrid; heady, aromatic. ANTONYM mild.

4 *her penetrating gaze* OBSERVANT, searching, intent, alert, shrewd, perceptive, probing, piercing, sharp, keen.

5 *a penetrating analysis* PERCEPTIVE, insightful, keen, sharp, sharp-witted, intelligent, clever, smart, incisive, piercing, razor-edged, trenchant, astute, shrewd, clear, acute, percipient, perspicacious, discerning, sensitive, thoughtful, deep, profound. ANTONYM dull.

penetration noun **1** *skin penetration by infective larvae* PERFORATION, piercing, puncturing, puncture, stabbing, pricking.

2 *remarks of great penetration* INSIGHT, discernment, perception, perceptiveness, intelligence, sharp-wittedness, cleverness, incisiveness, keenness, sharpness, trenchancy, astuteness, shrewdness, acuteness, clarity, acuity, percipience, perspicacity, discrimination, sensitivity, thoughtfulness, profundity; *formal* perspicuity.

penguin noun *renowned ornithologist Roger Tory Peterson was especially fond of penguins.* See table on page 666.

peninsula noun *residents on the peninsula take these storm warnings very seriously* CAPE, promontory, point, head, headland, foreland, ness, horn, bill, bluff.

penitence noun *the writer prays to God in penitence* REPENTANCE, contrition, regret, remorse, remorsefulness, ruefulness, sorrow, sorrowfulness, pangs of conscience, self-reproach, shame, guilt, compunction; *archaic* rue.

PENGUINS

Adélie penguin	Humboldt penguin
African jackass penguin	king penguin
blue penguin	little penguin
chinstrap penguin	macaroni penguin
emperor penguin	Magellanic penguin
erect-crested penguin	Peruvian penguin
fairy penguin	rockhopper (penguin)
Fiordland crested penguin	royal penguin
Galapagos penguin	Snares Island penguin
gentoo (penguin)	yellow-eyed penguin

penitent adjective *she stood there looking like a penitent child* REPENTANT, contrite, remorseful, sorry, apologetic, regretful, conscience-stricken, rueful, ashamed, shamefaced, abject, in sackcloth and ashes. ANTONYM unrepentant.

pen name noun *her pen name was Annabelle Lord* PSEUDONYM, nom de plume, assumed name, alias, professional name.

pennant noun *pennants fly from the towers* FLAG, standard, ensign, color(s), banner, banderole, guidon; *Nautical* burgee.

penniless adjective *Van Gogh died penniless* DESTITUTE, poverty-stricken, impoverished, poor, indigent, impecunious, in penury, moneyless, necessitous, needy, bankrupt, insolvent, without a cent (to one's name), without a sou; *informal* (flat) broke, cleaned out, strapped for cash, bust; *formal* penurious. ANTONYM wealthy.

penny PHRASE: **a pretty penny** *informal I bet that boat cost you a pretty penny* A LOT OF MONEY, millions, billions, a king's ransom; *informal* a (small) fortune, lots/heaps of money, a mint, a killing, a bundle, a tidy sum, big money, big bucks, an arm and a leg.

penny-pincher noun *you expect to get a raise from that penny-pincher?* MISER, Scrooge; *informal* skinflint, money-grubber, cheapskate, tightwad. ANTONYM spendthrift.

penny-pinching adjective *Zane's penny-pinching aunt gave him five dollars as a wedding gift* MEAN, miserly, niggardly, parsimonious, close-fisted, cheeseparing, grasping, Scroogelike; *informal* stingy, mingy, tight, tightfisted, money-grubbing; *formal* penurious; *archaic* near. ANTONYM generous.

pension noun *I doubt I can live on my pension* retirement (benefits), superannuation; Social Security; allowance, benefit, support, welfare.

pensive adjective *sorry to interrupt your pensive mood, but we've got to leave* THOUGHTFUL, reflective, contemplative, musing, meditative, introspective, ruminative, absorbed, preoccupied, deep/lost in thought, in a brown study, brooding; *formal* cogitative.

pent-up adjective *pent-up anger will eventually explode* REPRESSED, suppressed, stifled, smothered, restrained, confined, bottled up, held in/back, unvented, kept in check, curbed, bridled.

penultimate adjective *the penultimate movie on my top-ten list is an animated feature* NEXT-TO-LAST, second-to-last, second-last.

USAGE NOTE **penultimate**

Penultimate (= next-to-last) is sometimes misused for *ultimate* or *quintessential*—e.g.: "As our cover story points out, data warehouses have been sold by many vendors as the penultimate [read *quintessential*] business solution." (*ComputerWorld*; Apr. 1, 1996.)

Sometimes, too, the word is misspelled *pentultimate* (perhaps through sound association with *pent-up*)—e.g.: "When Poole secured a 4–2 in the pentultimate [read *penultimate*] race the scores were level at 42–42." (*Birmingham Evening Mail* [UK]; Apr. 8, 2003.) —**BG**

penurious adjective *formal* **1** *a penurious student* POOR, poor as a church mouse, poverty-stricken, destitute, necessitous, impecunious, impoverished, indigent, needy, in need/want, badly off, in reduced/straitened circumstances, hard up, unable to make ends meet, penniless, without a cent (to one's name), without a sou; *informal* (flat) broke, strapped for cash. ANTONYM wealthy.

2 *a penurious old skinflint* MEAN, miserly, niggardly, parsimonious, penny-pinching, close-fisted, Scroogelike; *informal* stingy, mingy, tight, tightfisted, money-grubbing; *archaic* near. ANTONYM generous.

penury noun *Dylan was oblivious to his brother's wretched state of penury* EXTREME POVERTY, destitution, pennilessness, impecuniousness, impoverishment, indigence, pauperism, privation, beggary.

people noun **1** *crowds of people* HUMAN BEINGS, persons, individuals, humans, mortals, (living) souls, personages, 'men, women, and children'; *informal* folks. See note at PERSON.

2 *the American people* CITIZENS, subjects, electors, voters, taxpayers, residents, inhabitants, (general) public, citizenry, nation, population, populace.

3 *a man of the people* COMMON PEOPLE, proletariat, masses, populace, rank and file, commonality, third estate, plebeians; *derogatory* hoi polloi, common herd, great unwashed, proles, plebs.

4 *her people don't live far away* FAMILY, parents, relatives, relations, folks, kinsmen, kin, kith and kin, kinsfolk, flesh and blood, nearest and dearest.

5 *the peoples of Africa* RACE, (ethnic) group, tribe, clan. See note at PERSON.

▸ verb *the Beothuk who once peopled Newfoundland* POPULATE, settle (in), colonize, inhabit, live in, occupy; *formal* reside in, be domiciled in, dwell in.

pep *informal* noun *a performance full of pep* DYNAMISM, life, energy, spirit, liveliness, animation, bounce, sparkle, effervescence, verve, spiritedness, ebullience, high spirits, enthusiasm, vitality, vivacity, fire, dash, panache, élan, zest, exuberance, vigor, gusto, brio; *informal* feistiness, get-up-and-go, oomph, pizzazz, vim. PHRASE: **pep up** *why don't we pep up this gathering with some tunes?* ENLIVEN, animate, liven up, put some/new life into, invigorate, vitalize, revitalize, vivify, ginger up, energize, galvanize, put some spark into, stimulate, get something going, perk up; brighten up, cheer up; *informal* buck up.

pepper verb **1** *salt and pepper the potatoes* ADD PEPPER TO, season, flavor.

2 *stars peppered the desert skies* SPRINKLE, fleck, dot, spot, stipple; cover, fill.

3 *a burst of bullets peppered the tank* BOMBARD, pelt, shower, rain down on, attack, assail, batter, strafe, rake, blitz, hit.

peppery adjective **1** *a peppery sauce* SPICY, spiced, peppered, hot, highly seasoned, piquant, pungent, sharp. ANTONYMS mild, bland.

2 *a peppery old man* IRRITABLE, cantankerous, irascible, bad-tempered, ill-tempered, grumpy, grouchy, crotchety, short-tempered, tetchy, testy, crusty, crabby, curmudgeonly, peevish, cross, fractious, pettish, prickly, waspish; *informal* ornery, snappish, cranky. ANTONYM affable.

perceive verb 1 *I immediately perceived the flaws in her story* DISCERN, recognize, become aware of, see, distinguish, realize, grasp, understand, take in, make out, find, identify, hit on, comprehend, apprehend, appreciate, sense, divine; *informal* figure out; *Brit. informal* twig; *formal* become cognizant of.

2 *she perceived a twitch in his nose whenever he lied* SEE, discern, detect, catch sight of, spot, observe, notice.

3 *she was perceived as too negative* REGARD, look on, view, consider, think of, judge, deem, adjudge.

perceptible adjective *I am sure that the flaw in the upholstery is perceptible only to you, my dear* NOTICEABLE, perceivable, detectable, discernible, visible, observable, recognizable, appreciable; obvious, apparent, evident, manifest, patent, clear, distinct, plain, conspicuous. See note at TANGIBLE.

perception noun 1 *our perception of our own limitations* RECOGNITION, awareness, consciousness, appreciation, realization, knowledge, grasp, understanding, comprehension, apprehension; *formal* cognizance.

2 *popular perceptions of old age* IMPRESSION, idea, conception, notion, thought, belief, judgment, estimation.

3 *he talks with great perception* INSIGHT, perceptiveness, percipience, perspicacity, understanding, sharpness, sharp-wittedness, intelligence, intuition, cleverness, incisiveness, trenchancy, astuteness, shrewdness, acuteness, acuity, discernment, sensitivity, penetration, thoughtfulness, profundity; *formal* perspicuity.

perceptive adjective *children are usually more perceptive than their parents think* INSIGHTFUL, discerning, sensitive, intuitive, observant; piercing, penetrating, percipient, perspicacious, penetrative, clear-sighted, farsighted, intelligent, clever, canny, keen, sharp, sharp-witted, astute, shrewd, quick, smart, acute, discriminating; *informal* on the ball, right-brained, heads-up, with it. ANTONYM obtuse.

perch noun *the chicken's perch* POLE, rod, branch, roost, rest, resting place.

▸ verb 1 *three swallows perched on the telegraph wire* ROOST, sit, rest; alight, settle, land, come to rest.

2 *she perched her glasses on her nose* PUT, place, set, rest, balance.

3 *the church **is perched** on a hill* BE LOCATED, be situated, be positioned, be sited, stand.

perchance adverb *literary perchance we shall meet again* MAYBE, perhaps, possibly, for all one knows, it could be, it's possible, conceivably; *literary* peradventure.

percipient adjective See PERCEPTIVE.

percolate verb 1 *water percolated through the soil* FILTER, drain, drip, ooze, seep, trickle, dribble, leak, leach.

2 *these views began to percolate through society as a whole* SPREAD, be disseminated, filter, pass; permeate, pervade.

3 *he put some coffee on to percolate* BREW; *informal* perk.

perdition noun *I hope that lawyer goes to perdition!* DAMNATION, eternal punishment; hell, hellfire, doom.

peregrinations plural noun *archaic such fascinating peregrinations you've experienced, Mr. Soo* TRAVELS, wanderings, journeys, globe-trotting, voyages, expeditions, odysseys, trips, treks, excursions; *formal* perambulations.

peremptory adjective 1 *a peremptory reply* BRUSQUE, imperious, high-handed, brisk, abrupt, summary, commanding, dictatorial, autocratic, overbearing, dogmatic, arrogant, overweening, lordly, magisterial, authoritarian; emphatic, firm, insistent; *informal* bossy.

2 *a peremptory order of the court* IRREVERSIBLE, binding, absolute, final, conclusive, decisive, definitive, categorical, irrefutable, incontrovertible; *Law* unappealable.

perennial adjective *the perennial fascination with crime* ABIDING, enduring, lasting, everlasting, perpetual, eternal, continuing, unending, unceasing, never-ending, endless, undying, ceaseless, persisting, permanent, constant, continual, unfailing, unchanging, never-changing.

perfect adjective 1 *she strove to be the perfect wife* IDEAL, model, without fault, faultless, flawless, consummate, quintessential, exemplary, best, ultimate, copybook; unrivaled, unequaled, matchless, unparalleled, beyond compare, without equal, second to none, too good to be true, Utopian, incomparable, nonpareil, peerless, inimitable, unexcelled, unsurpassed, unsurpassable.

2 *a classic Les Paul guitar in perfect condition* FLAWLESS, mint, as good as new, pristine, impeccable, immaculate, superb, superlative, optimum, prime, optimal, peak, excellent, faultless, as sound as a bell, unspoiled, unblemished, undamaged, spotless, unmarred; *informal* tip-top, A1.

3 *a perfect copy* EXACT, precise, accurate, faithful, correct, unerring, inerrant, right, true, strict; *informal* on the money.

4 *the perfect Christmas present for golfers* IDEAL, just right, right, appropriate, fitting, fit, suitable, apt, made to order, tailor-made; very.

5 *she felt like a perfect idiot* ABSOLUTE, complete, total, real, out-and-out, thorough, thoroughgoing, downright, utter, sheer, arrant, unmitigated, unqualified, veritable, in every respect, unalloyed.

▸ verb *he's busy perfecting his bowling technique* IMPROVE, better, polish (up), hone, refine, put the finishing/final touches to, brush up, fine-tune.

perfection noun 1 *the perfection of her technique* IMPROVEMENT, betterment, refinement, refining, honing.

2 *for him, she was still perfection* THE IDEAL, a paragon, the ne plus ultra, a nonpareil, the crème de la crème, the last word, the ultimate, the best; *informal* one in a million, the tops, da bomb; *dated, informal* the bee's knees, the cat's meow/pajamas/whiskers.

perfectionist noun *the just-so placement of every little figurine and throw pillow immediately gave him away as a perfectionist* PURIST, stickler for perfection, idealist; pedant.

perfectly adverb 1 *a perfectly cooked meal* FAULTLESSLY, superbly, superlatively, excellently, flawlessly, to perfection, without fault, ideally, inimitably, incomparably, impeccably, immaculately, exquisitely, consummately; *informal* like a dream, to a T.

2 *I think we understand each other perfectly* ABSOLUTELY, utterly, completely, altogether, entirely, wholly, totally, thoroughly, fully, in every respect.

3 *you know perfectly well that is not what I meant* VERY, quite, full; *informal* damn, damned, darned, bloody.

perfidious adjective *literary a perfidious lover* TREACHEROUS, duplicitous, deceitful, disloyal, faithless, unfaithful, traitorous, treasonous, false, false-hearted, double-dealing, two-faced, untrustworthy. ANTONYM faithful.

perfidy noun *literary the perfidy of her husband* TREACHERY, duplicity, deceit, deceitfulness, disloyalty, infidelity, faithlessness, unfaithfulness, betrayal, treason, double-dealing, untrustworthiness, breach of trust; *literary* perfidiousness.

perforate verb *a shell fragment perforated his left lung* PIERCE, penetrate, enter, puncture, prick, bore through, riddle.

perforce adverb *formal amateurs, perforce, have to settle for less expensive solutions* NECESSARILY, of necessity, inevitably, unavoidably, by force of circumstances, needs must; *informal* like it or not; *formal* nolens volens.

perform verb **1** *I have my duties to perform* CARRY OUT, do, execute, discharge, bring about, bring off, accomplish, achieve, fulfill, complete, conduct, effect, dispatch, work, implement; *informal* pull off; *formal* effectuate; *archaic* acquit oneself of. ANTONYM neglect.

2 *a car that performs well at low speeds* FUNCTION, work, operate, run, go, respond, behave, act, acquit oneself/itself.

3 *the play has been performed in San Francisco* STAGE, put on, present, mount, enact, act, produce.

4 *the band performed live in Central Park* APPEAR, play, be on stage, sing, dance, act.

performance noun **1** *the evening performance* SHOW, production, showing, presentation, staging; concert, recital; *informal* gig.

2 *their performance of Mozart's concerto in E flat* RENDITION, rendering, interpretation, reading, playing, acting, representation.

3 *the continual performance of a single task* CARRYING OUT, execution, discharge, accomplishment, completion, fulfillment, dispatch, implementation; *formal* effectuation.

4 *the performance of the processor* FUNCTIONING, working, operation, running, behavior, capabilities, capability, capacity, power, potential.

5 *informal he made a great performance of telling her about it* FUSS, production, palaver, scene, business, pantomime; *informal* song and dance, big deal, to-do, hoo-ha.

performer noun *he began his career as a bit performer in B movies* ACTOR, ACTRESS, thespian, artiste, artist, entertainer, trouper, player, musician, singer, dancer, comic, comedian, comedienne.

WORD NOTE **artiste**

It is, of course, the French word for *artist,* and that's what it also appears to have meant at one time, in English. But it is rarely used anymore to mean a genuine or serious artist, but rather to signify something quite different—that is, someone with artistic pretensions, or even delusions. *The ballroom-dancing instructor in my home town was a regular artiste.* One wonders if the reason for its shift from the descriptive to the derogatory had something to do with its "continental" association, and if a French pronunciation (as opposed to a more plain, down-home American one) was sufficient to lend it the veneer of fakery and ostentation. **—FP**

perfume noun **1** *a bottle of perfume* FRAGRANCE, scent, eau de toilette, toilet water, eau de cologne, cologne, aftershave.

2 *the heady perfume of lilacs* SMELL, scent, fragrance, aroma, bouquet, redolence. See note at SMELL.

perfumed adjective *perfumed soap* SWEET-SMELLING, scented, fragrant, fragranced, perfumy, aromatic.

perfunctory adjective *a perfunctory review* CURSORY, desultory, quick, brief, hasty, hurried, rapid, fleeting, token, casual, superficial, careless, halfhearted, sketchy, mechanical, automatic, routine, offhand, inattentive. ANTONYMS careful, thorough.

perhaps adverb *perhaps they'll get married* MAYBE, for all one knows, it could be, it may be, it's possible, possibly, conceivably; *literary* peradventure, perchance.

peril noun *a situation fraught with peril* DANGER, jeopardy, risk, hazard, insecurity, uncertainty, menace, threat, perilousness; pitfall, problem.

perilous adjective *a perilous journey through the mountains* DANGEROUS, fraught with danger, hazardous, risky, unsafe, treacherous; precarious, vulnerable, uncertain, insecure, exposed, at risk, in jeopardy, in danger, touch-and-go; *informal* dicey. ANTONYM safe.

perimeter noun **1** *the perimeter of a circle* CIRCUMFERENCE, outside, outer edge.

2 *the perimeter of the vast estate* BOUNDARY, border, limits, bounds, confines, edge, margin, fringe(s), periphery, borderline, verge; *literary* bourn, marge.See note at PARAMETER.

period noun **1** *a six-week period* TIME, spell, interval, stretch, term, span, phase, bout, run, duration, chapter, stage; while, patch.

2 *the postwar period* ERA, age, epoch, time, days, years; *Geology* eon.

3 *a double math period* LESSON, class, session.

4 *women who suffer from painful periods* MENSTRUATION, menstrual flow, menses; *informal* the curse, time of the month, monthlies.

periodic adjective *Michael made periodic visits to the hospital* REGULAR, periodical, at fixed intervals, recurrent, recurring, repeated, cyclical, cyclic, seasonal; occasional, infrequent, intermittent, sporadic, spasmodic, odd.

periodical noun *he wrote for two periodicals* JOURNAL, publication, magazine, newspaper, paper, review, digest, gazette, newsletter, organ, quarterly, annual, weekly; *informal* mag, glossy.

peripatetic adjective *I could never get used to her peripatetic lifestyle* NOMADIC, itinerant, traveling, wandering, roving, roaming, migrant, migratory, unsettled.

peripheral adjective **1** *the city's peripheral subdivisions* OUTLYING, outer, on the edge/outskirts, surrounding.

2 *peripheral issues* SECONDARY, subsidiary, incidental, tangential, marginal, minor, unimportant, lesser, inessential, nonessential, immaterial, ancillary. ANTONYM central.

periphery noun *rambling estates on the periphery of the city* EDGE, outer edge, margin, fringe, boundary, border, perimeter, rim, verge, borderline; outskirts, outer limits/reaches, bounds; *literary* bourn, marge. ANTONYM center.

periphrastic adjective *the periphrastic nature of legal syntax* CIRCUMLOCUTORY, circuitous, roundabout, indirect, tautological, pleonastic, prolix, verbose, wordy, long-winded, rambling, wandering, tortuous, diffuse.

WORD NOTE **periphrastic**

A friend used to collect what he called middle-class circumlocutions—unnecessarily elongated phrases that English suburban bores once liked to employ to give them a friendlier, breezier tone than that for which they were normally known. So instead of asking for beer in the pub—*A pint of the amber fluid, my man!* Instead of calling for the bill—*What's the damage, old boy?* Rather than referring to *my wife*—please meet *the little woman,* or *my better half.* May I smoke in your house? Of course, dear fellow—*it's Liberty Hall here.* And this being Britain there were many self-deprecating versions of the form: of a brand-new car parked proudly on the gravel at the golf club—*Oh yes, not a bad little bus, gets you from A to B.* The term *circumlocution* for such a roundabout construction is a fair choice, of course; but technically the term in grammar is *periphrasis* (which merely derives from the Greek, while *circumlocution* is from the Latin), and *periphrastic,* so pleasantly complicated-sounding a word, is the adjective. It is vaguely similar in its sound, of course, to *paraphrase*—and since that word means "to expand in order to make clear," while *periphrase* in essence means "to expand in order to make slightly ridiculous," the close similarity in both sound and sense will serve to ensure that both uses are carefully chosen. Or so one hopes. **—SW**

perish verb **1** *millions of soldiers perished* DIE, lose one's life, be killed, fall, expire, meet one's death, be lost, lay down one's life, breathe one's last, pass away, go the way of all flesh, give up the ghost, go to glory, meet one's maker, cross the great divide; *informal* kick the bucket, turn up one's toes, shuffle off this mortal coil, buy it, croak, bite the big one, buy the farm; *archaic* decease, depart this life.

2 *must these hopes perish so soon?* COME TO AN END, die (away), disappear, vanish, fade, dissolve, evaporate, melt away, wither.

3 *the wood had perished* GO BAD, go off, spoil, rot, go moldy, molder, putrefy, decay, decompose.

perjure PHRASE: **perjure oneself** *he made the regrettable mistake of perjuring himself* LIE UNDER OATH, lie, commit perjury, give false evidence/testimony; *formal* forswear oneself, be forsworn.

perjury noun *she was found guilty of perjury* LYING UNDER OATH, giving false evidence/testimony, making false statements, willful falsehood.

perk[1] PHRASE: **perk up 1** *you seem to have perked up* CHEER UP, brighten up, liven up, take heart; *informal* buck up. **2** *the economy has been slow to perk up* RECOVER, rally, improve, revive, take a turn for the better, look up, pick up, bounce back. **3** *you could do with something to perk you up* CHEER UP, liven up, brighten up, raise someone's spirits, give someone a boost/lift, revitalize, invigorate, energize, enliven, ginger up, put new life/heart into, put some spark into, rejuvenate, refresh, vitalize; *informal* buck up, pep up.

perk[2] noun *a job with a lot of perks* FRINGE BENEFIT, additional benefit, benefit, advantage, bonus, extra, plus; *informal* freebie; *formal* perquisite.

perky adjective *a nice uninterrupted eight hours of sleep will make you as perky as ever* CHEERFUL, lively, vivacious, animated, bubbly, effervescent, bouncy, spirited, high-spirited, in high spirits, cheery, merry, buoyant, ebullient, exuberant, jaunty, frisky, sprightly, spry, bright, sunny, jolly, sparkly, pert; *informal* full of beans, bright-eyed and bushy-tailed, chipper, peppy.

permanence noun *the permanence of their relationship gives them a mutual sense of security* STABILITY, durability, permanency, fixity, fixedness, changelessness, immutability, endurance, constancy, continuity, immortality, indestructibility, perpetuity, endlessness.

permanent adjective **1** *permanent brain damage* LASTING, enduring, indefinite, continuing, perpetual, everlasting, eternal, abiding, constant, irreparable, irreversible, lifelong, indissoluble, indelible, standing, perennial, unending, endless, never-ending, immutable, undying, imperishable, indestructible, ineradicable; *literary* sempiternal, perdurable. ANTONYM temporary.

2 *a permanent job* LONG-TERM, stable, secure, durable. ANTONYM temporary.

permanently adverb **1** *the attack left her permanently disabled* FOR ALL TIME, forever, forevermore, for good, for always, for ever and ever, (for) evermore, until hell freezes over, in perpetuity, indelibly, immutably, until the end of time; *informal* for keeps, until the cows come home, until kingdom come; *archaic* for aye.

2 *I was permanently hungry* CONTINUALLY, constantly, perpetually, always.

permeable adjective *the innermost lining is permeable* POROUS, pervious, penetrable, absorbent, absorptive.

permeate verb **1** *the delicious smell permeated the entire apartment* PERVADE, spread through, fill, filter through, diffuse through, imbue, penetrate, pass through, percolate through, perfuse, charge, suffuse, steep, impregnate, inform.

2 *these resins are able to permeate the timber* SOAK THROUGH, penetrate, seep through, saturate, transfuse, percolate through, leach through.

permissible adjective *permissible levels of atmospheric pollution* PERMITTED, allowable, allowed, acceptable, legal, lawful, legitimate, admissible, licit, authorized, sanctioned, tolerated; *informal* legit, OK. ANTONYM forbidden.

permission noun *so, do I have permission to use the car?* AUTHORIZATION, consent, leave, authority, sanction, license, dispensation, assent, acquiescence, agreement, approval, seal/stamp of approval, approbation, endorsement, blessing, imprimatur, clearance, allowance, tolerance, sufferance, empowerment; *informal* the go-ahead, the thumbs up, the OK, the green light, say-so. See note at LIBERTY.

permissive adjective *our parents were far less permissive than we are* LIBERAL, broad-minded, open-minded, free, free and easy, easygoing, live-and-let-live, latitudinarian, laissez-faire, libertarian, tolerant, forbearing, indulgent, lenient; overindulgent, lax, soft. See note at LENIENT. ANTONYMS intolerant, strict.

permit verb *I cannot permit you to leave I cannot permit your leaving* ALLOW, authorize, give someone permission, sanction, grant, give someone the right, license, empower, enable, entitle, qualify; give one's blessing to, give the nod to; consent to, assent to, acquiesce in, agree to, tolerate, countenance; legalize, legitimate; *informal* give the go-ahead to, give the thumbs up to, OK, give the OK to, give the green light to; *formal* accede to; *archaic* suffer; (**permit someone to**), let. ANTONYMS ban, forbid.

▸ noun *I need to see your permit* AUTHORIZATION, license, pass, ticket, warrant, document, certification; passport, visa.

permutation noun *all the possible permutations were explored* ARRANGEMENT, form, version, configuration, incarnation, order, organization, selection.

pernicious adjective *a pernicious influence on society* HARMFUL, damaging, destructive, injurious, hurtful, detrimental, deleterious, dangerous, adverse, inimical, unhealthy, unfavorable, bad, evil, baleful, wicked, malign, malevolent, malignant, noxious, poisonous, corrupting; *literary* maleficent. ANTONYM beneficial.

perpendicular adjective **1** *the perpendicular stones* UPRIGHT, vertical, erect, plumb, straight (up and down), on end, standing, upended. ANTONYM horizontal.

2 *lines perpendicular to each other* AT RIGHT ANGLES, at 90 degrees.

3 *the perpendicular hillside* STEEP, sheer, precipitous, abrupt, bluff, vertiginous.

perpetrate verb *they perpetrated a series of armed robberies* COMMIT, carry out, perform, execute, do, effect, bring about, accomplish; be guilty of, be to blame for, be responsible for, inflict, wreak; *informal* pull off; *formal* effectuate.

perpetual adjective **1** *deep caves in perpetual darkness* EVERLASTING, never-ending, eternal, permanent, unending, endless, without end, lasting, long-lasting, constant, abiding, enduring, perennial, timeless, ageless, deathless, undying, immortal; unfailing, unchanging, never-changing, changeless, unfading; *rare* sempiternal, perdurable. ANTONYMS transitory, temporary.

2 *a perpetual state of fear* CONSTANT, permanent, uninterrupted, continuous, unremitting, unending, unceasing, persistent, unbroken. ANTONYM intermittent.

3 *her mother's perpetual nagging* INTERMINABLE, incessant, ceaseless, endless, without respite, relentless, unrelenting, persistent, continual, continuous, nonstop, never-ending, recurrent, repeated, unremitting, sustained, around/round-the-clock, chronic, unabating; *informal* eternal.

perpetuate verb *must you perpetuate these stupid myths?* KEEP ALIVE, keep going, preserve, conserve, sustain, maintain, continue, extend, carry on, keep up, prolong; immortalize, commemorate, memorialize, eternalize.

perpetuity PHRASE: **in perpetuity** *the archive will be preserved in perpetuity as a unified collection* FOREVER, forevermore, permanently, for always, for good, perpetually, for ever and ever, for all time, until the end of time, until hell freezes over, eternally, for eternity, everlastingly; *informal* for keeps; *archaic* for aye.

perplex verb *the bizarre notes left at each of these crime scenes perplexed us* PUZZLE, baffle, mystify, bemuse, bewilder, confound, confuse, disconcert, dumbfound, throw, throw/catch off balance, exercise, worry; *informal* flummox, be all Greek to, stump, bamboozle, floor, beat, faze, fox; *informal* discombobulate.

perplexing adjective *he was famous for solving the most perplexing cases* PUZZLING, baffling, mystifying, mysterious, bewildering, confusing, disconcerting, worrying, unaccountable, difficult to understand, beyond one, paradoxical, peculiar, funny, strange, weird, odd.

perplexity noun **1** *he scratched his head in perplexity* CONFUSION, bewilderment, puzzlement, bafflement, incomprehension, mystification, bemusement; *informal* bamboozlement, discombobulation.

2 *the perplexities of international relations* COMPLEXITY, complication, intricacy, problem, difficulty, mystery, puzzle, enigma, paradox.

perquisite noun *formal* See PERK².

per se adverb *possessing a knife was not per se an unlawful act* IN ITSELF, of itself, by itself, in and of itself, as such, intrinsically; by its very nature, in essence, by definition, essentially.

persecute verb **1** *they were persecuted for their religious beliefs* OPPRESS, abuse, victimize, ill-treat, mistreat, maltreat, tyrannize, torment, torture; martyr.

2 *she was persecuted by the press* HARASS, hound, plague, badger, harry, intimidate, pick on, pester, bother, devil, bully, victimize, terrorize; *informal* hassle, give someone a hard time, get on someone's case.

persecution noun **1** *victims of religious persecution* OPPRESSION, victimization, maltreatment, ill-treatment, mistreatment, abuse, ill-usage, discrimination, tyranny; *informal* witch hunt.

2 *the persecution she endured at school* HARASSMENT, hounding, intimidation, bullying.

perseverance noun *in a competitive environment, perseverance is an invaluable asset* PERSISTENCE, tenacity, determination, staying power, indefatigability, steadfastness, purposefulness; patience, endurance, application, diligence, dedication, commitment, doggedness, assiduity, tirelessness, stamina; intransigence, obstinacy; *informal* stick-to-it-iveness; *formal* pertinacity.

persevere verb *she will persevere regardless of the obstacles* PERSIST, continue, carry on, go on, keep on, keep going, struggle on, hammer away, be persistent, be determined, see/follow something through, keep at it, press on/ahead, not take no for an answer, be tenacious, stand one's ground, stand fast/firm, hold on, go the distance, stay the course, plod on, stop at nothing, leave no stone unturned; *informal* soldier on, hang on, plug away, stick to one's guns, stick it out, hang in there. ANTONYM give up.

persist verb **1** *Corbett persisted with his questioning.* See PERSEVERE.

2 *if dry weather persists, water the lawn thoroughly* CONTINUE, hold, carry on, last, keep on, keep up, remain, linger, stay, endure.

persistence noun See PERSEVERANCE.

persistent adjective **1** *a very persistent man* TENACIOUS, persevering, determined, resolute, purposeful, dogged, single-minded, tireless, indefatigable, patient, unflagging, untiring, insistent, importunate, relentless, unrelenting; stubborn, intransigent, obstinate, obdurate; *formal* pertinacious. ANTONYM irresolute.

2 *persistent rain* CONSTANT, continuous, continuing, continual, nonstop, never-ending, steady, uninterrupted, unbroken, interminable, incessant, unceasing, endless, unending, perpetual, unremitting, unrelenting, relentless, unrelieved, sustained. ANTONYMS occasional, intermittent.

3 *a persistent cough* CHRONIC, permanent, nagging, frequent; repeated, habitual.

persnickety adjective *informal my persnickety boss makes us disinfect the drawers in the cash register every night* FUSSY, difficult to please, difficult, finicky, overfastidious, fastidious, overparticular, particular, faddish, punctilious, hair-splitting, critical, overcritical; *informal* nitpicking, choosy, picky. ANTONYM easygoing.

person noun *that person over there is the one who called the police* HUMAN BEING, individual, man/woman, child, human, being, (living) soul, mortal, creature; personage, character, customer; *informal* type, sort, cookie; *informal, dated* body, dog; *archaic* wight. PHRASE: **in person** *I hope to talk to you in person before I leave Cleveland* PHYSICALLY, in the flesh, in propria persona, personally; oneself; *informal* as large as life.

EASILY CONFUSED WORDS **persons, people**

The words **people** and **persons** can both be used as the plural of **person**, but they are not used in exactly the same way. **People** is by far the more common of the two words and is used in most ordinary contexts: *a group of people*; *there were only about ten people*; *several thousand people have been rehoused*. **Persons**, on the other hand, tends now to be restricted to official or formal contexts, as in *this vehicle is authorized to carry twenty persons*; *no persons admitted without a pass*. In some contexts, **persons**, by pointing to the individual, may sound less friendly than **people**: *the number should not be disclosed to any unauthorized persons*.

persona noun *her stage persona is nothing like the real Muriel* IMAGE, face, public face, character, personality, identity, self; front, facade, guise, exterior, role, part.

personable adjective *I was blessed with the most personable in-laws* PLEASANT, agreeable, likable, nice, amiable, affable, charming, congenial, genial, simpatico, engaging, pleasing; attractive, presentable, good-looking, nice-looking, pretty, appealing; *Scottish* bonny. ANTONYMS disagreeable, unattractive.

personage noun *we always have a table for a personage such as yourself* IMPORTANT PERSON, VIP, luminary, celebrity, personality, name, famous name, household name, public figure, star, leading light, dignitary, notable, notability, worthy, panjandrum; person; *informal* celeb, somebody, big shot, big wheel, big kahuna, big cheese.

personal adjective **1** *a highly personal style* DISTINCTIVE, characteristic, unique, individual, one's own, particular, peculiar, idiosyncratic, individualized, personalized. ANTONYMS public, general.

2 *a personal appearance* IN PERSON, in the flesh, actual, live, physical.

3 *his personal life* PRIVATE, intimate; confidential, secret.

4 *a personal friend* INTIMATE, close, dear, great, bosom.

5 *I have personal knowledge of the family* DIRECT, empirical, firsthand, immediate, experiential.

6 *personal remarks* DEROGATORY, ad hominem; disparaging, belittling, insulting, critical, rude, slighting, disrespectful, offensive, pejorative.

personality noun **1** *her cheerful personality* CHARACTER, nature, disposition, temperament, makeup, persona, psyche.

2 *she had loads of personality* CHARISMA, magnetism, strength/force of personality, character, charm, presence.

3 *a famous personality* CELEBRITY, VIP, star, superstar, name, famous name, household name, big name, somebody, leading light, luminary, notable, personage, notability; *informal* celeb.

personalize verb **1** *products that can be personalized to your requirements* CUSTOMIZE, individualize.

2 *attempts to personalize God* PERSONIFY, humanize, anthropomorphize.

personally adverb **1** *I'd like to thank you personally* IN PERSON, oneself.

2 *personally, I think it's a good idea* FOR MY PART, for myself, to my way of thinking, to my mind, in my estimation, as far as I am concerned, in my view/opinion, from my point of view, from where I stand, as I see it, if you ask me, my sense is, for my money, in my book; privately. PHRASE: **take personally** *please don't take this personally, but I think the trim should be a shade darker* TAKE OFFENSE, take something amiss, be offended, be upset, be affronted, take umbrage, take exception, feel insulted, feel hurt.

personification noun *Foote is the personification of heroism* EMBODIMENT, incarnation, epitome, quintessence, essence, type, symbol, soul, model, exemplification, exemplar, image, representation.

personify verb *the picture on the label should personify good, wholesome American cooking* EPITOMIZE, embody, hypostatize, typify, exemplify, represent, symbolize, stand for, be the incarnation of, body forth, put a face on.

personnel noun *sales personnel* STAFF, employees, workforce, workers, labor force, human resources, manpower, wage labor; *informal* liveware.

perspective noun **1** *her perspective on things had changed* OUTLOOK, view, viewpoint, point of view, POV, standpoint, position, stand, stance, angle, slant, attitude, frame of mind, frame of reference, approach, way of looking, interpretation.

2 *a perspective of the whole valley* VIEW, vista, panorama, prospect, bird's-eye view, outlook, aspect.

perspicacious adjective *his perspicacious advisers recommended caution* DISCERNING, shrewd, perceptive, astute, penetrating, observant, percipient, sharp-witted, sharp, smart, alert, clear-sighted, farsighted, acute, clever, canny, intelligent, insightful, wise, sage, sensitive, intuitive, understanding, aware, discriminating; *informal* on the ball, heads-up, with it. See note at KEEN. ANTONYM stupid.

perspiration noun *you should avoid products that prevent normal perspiration* SWEAT, moisture; *Medicine* diaphoresis.

perspire verb *it's natural to perspire under these hot lights* SWEAT, be dripping/pouring with sweat, glow.

persuadable adjective *the kid wasn't nearly as persuadable as I had hoped* MALLEABLE, tractable, pliable, compliant, amenable, adaptable, accommodating, cooperative, flexible, acquiescent, yielding, biddable, complaisant, like putty in one's hands, suggestible.

persuade verb **1** *he tried to persuade her to come with him* PREVAIL ON, coax, convince, get, induce, win over, bring around, coerce, influence, sway, inveigle, entice, tempt, lure, cajole, wheedle; *Law* procure; *informal* sweet-talk, twist someone's arm; **(persuade someone to)** make. See note at CONVINCE. ANTONYMS dissuade, deter.

2 *a shortage of money persuaded them to abandon the scheme* CAUSE, lead, move, dispose, incline.

persuasion noun **1** *Monica needed plenty of persuasion* COAXING, persuading, coercion, inducement, convincing, blandishment, encouragement, urging, inveiglement, cajolery, enticement, wheedling; *informal* sweet-talking, arm-twisting; *formal* suasion.

2 *various political and religious persuasions* GROUP, grouping, sect, denomination, party, camp, side, faction, affiliation, school of thought, belief, creed, credo, faith, philosophy. See note at OPINION.

persuasive adjective *her argument is quite persuasive* CONVINCING, cogent, compelling, potent, forceful, powerful, eloquent, impressive, influential, sound, valid, strong, effective, winning, telling; plausible, credible. ANTONYM unconvincing.

pert adjective **1** *a pert little hat* JAUNTY, neat, chic, trim, stylish, smart, perky, rakish; *informal* natty, sassy.

2 *a young girl with a pert manner* IMPUDENT, impertinent, cheeky, irreverent, forward, insolent, disrespectful, flippant, familiar, presumptuous, bold, as bold as brass, brazen; *informal* fresh, saucy, sassy.

pertain verb **1** *developments **pertaining to** the economy* CONCERN, relate to, be related to, be connected with, be relevant to, regard, apply to, be pertinent to, refer to, have a bearing on, appertain to, bear on, affect, involve, touch on.

2 *the stock and assets **pertaining to** the business* BELONG TO, be a part of, be included in.

3 *the economic situation that pertained at that time* EXIST, be the order of the day, be the case, prevail; *formal* obtain.

pertinacious adjective *formal they were quite pertinacious in their demands* DETERMINED, tenacious, persistent, persevering, purposeful, resolute, dogged, indefatigable, insistent, single-minded, unrelenting, relentless, tireless, unshakable; stubborn, obstinate, inflexible, unbending. See note at STUBBORN. ANTONYMS irresolute, tentative.

pertinent adjective *he asked a lot of pertinent questions* RELEVANT, to the point, apposite, appropriate, suitable, fitting, fit, apt, applicable, material, germane, to the purpose, apropos; *formal* ad rem. ANTONYM irrelevant.

perturb verb *David's appearance perturbs his parents* WORRY, upset, unsettle, disturb, concern, trouble, disquiet; disconcert, discomfit, unnerve, alarm, bother, distress, dismay, gnaw at, agitate, fluster, ruffle, discountenance; *informal* rattle, throw. ANTONYM reassure.

perturbed adjective *our pets are perturbed by all the construction going on next door* UPSET, worried, unsettled, disturbed, concerned, troubled, anxious, ill at ease, uneasy, disquieted, fretful; disconcerted, discomposed, distressed, unnerved, alarmed, bothered, dismayed, agitated, flustered, ruffled, shaken, discountenanced; *informal* twitchy, rattled, fazed, unstrung; discombobulated. ANTONYM calm.

peruse verb *perusing the racing forms* READ, study, scrutinize, inspect, examine, wade through, look through; browse through, leaf through, scan, run one's eye over, glance through, flick through, skim through, thumb through, dip into.

pervade verb *the smell of floor polish pervaded the house* PERMEATE, spread through, fill, suffuse, be diffused through, imbue, penetrate, filter through, percolate through, infuse, perfuse, flow through; charge, steep, saturate, impregnate, inform.

pervasive adjective *the low-carb craze is pervasive* PREVALENT, pervading, permeating, extensive, ubiquitous, omnipresent, universal, rife, widespread, general.

perverse adjective **1** *he is being deliberately perverse* AWKWARD, contrary, difficult, unreasonable, uncooperative, unhelpful, obstructive, disobliging, recalcitrant, stubborn, obstinate, obdurate, mulish, pigheaded, bullheaded; *formal* refractory. ANTONYMS accommodating, cooperative. See note at STUBBORN.

2 *a verdict that is manifestly perverse* ILLOGICAL, irrational, unreasonable, wrong, wrong-headed. ANTONYM reasonable.

3 *an evil life dedicated to perverse pleasure* PERVERTED, depraved, unnatural, abnormal, deviant, degenerate, immoral, warped, twisted, corrupt; wicked, base, evil; *informal* kinky, sick, pervy.

perversion noun **1** *a twisted perversion of the truth* DISTORTION, misrepresentation, falsification, travesty, misinterpretation, misconstruction, twisting, corruption, subversion, misuse, misapplication, debasement.

2 *sexual perversion* DEVIANCE, abnormality; depravity, degeneracy, debauchery, corruption, vice, wickedness, immorality.

perversity noun **1** *out of sheer perversity, he refused* CONTRARINESS, awkwardness, recalcitrance, stubbornness, obstinacy, obduracy, mulishness, pigheadedness; *formal* refractoriness.

2 *the perversity of the decision* UNREASONABLENESS, irrationality, illogicality, wrong-headedness.

pervert verb **1** *people who attempt to pervert the rules* DISTORT, corrupt, subvert, twist, bend, abuse, misapply, misuse, misrepresent, misinterpret, falsify.

2 *men can be perverted by power* CORRUPT, lead astray, debase, warp, pollute, poison, deprave, debauch.

▸ noun *a sexual pervert* DEVIANT, degenerate; *informal* perv, dirty old man, sicko.

perverted adjective *I don't want to hear any more of your perverted stories* UNNATURAL, deviant, warped, corrupt, twisted, abnormal, unhealthy, depraved, perverse, aberrant, immoral, debauched, debased, degenerate, evil, wicked, vile, amoral, wrong, bad; *informal* sick, sicko, kinky, pervy. See note at DEPRAVED.

pessimism noun *Felicia has apparently drawn him out of his pessimism* DEFEATISM, negativity, doom and gloom, gloominess, cynicism, fatalism; hopelessness, depression, despair, despondency, angst.

pessimist noun *pessimists have been predicting the doom of the planet for thousands of years* DEFEATIST, fatalist, prophet of doom, cynic, doomsayer, doomster, Cassandra; skeptic, doubter, doubting Thomas; misery, killjoy, Job's comforter; *informal* doom (and gloom) merchant, wet blanket, Chicken Little, gloomy Gus. ANTONYMS optimist, Pollyanna.

pessimistic adjective *a pessimistic outlook on life*

GLOOMY, negative, defeatist, downbeat, cynical, bleak, fatalistic, dark, black, despairing, despondent, depressed, hopeless; suspicious, distrustful, doubting. See word spectrum at OPTIMISTIC. ANTONYM optimistic.

pest noun *Dan is dating the girl he used to think was such a pest* NUISANCE, annoyance, irritation, irritant, thorn in one's flesh/side, vexation, trial, the bane of one's life, menace, trouble, problem, worry, bother; *informal* pain (in the neck), aggravation, headache, nudnik.

pester verb *is there someplace I can study where no one will pester me?* BADGER, hound, harass, plague, annoy, bother, trouble, keep after, persecute, torment, bedevil, harry, worry, beleaguer, nag, hassle, bug, devil, get on someone's case.

pestilence noun *archaic* See PLAGUE noun sense 1.

pestilential adjective **1** *pestilential fever* PLAGUELIKE, infectious, contagious, communicable, epidemic, virulent; *informal* catching.

2 *informal you pestilential man!* ANNOYING, irritating, infuriating, exasperating, maddening, tiresome, troublesome, irksome, vexing, vexatious; *informal* aggravating, pesky, infernal.

pet noun *the teacher's pet* FAVORITE, darling, the apple of one's eye; *informal* fair-haired boy/girl.

▸ adjective **1** *a pet lamb* TAME, domesticated, domestic, housebroken, house-trained.

2 *his pet theory* FAVORITE, favored, cherished, dear to one's heart; particular, special, personal.

▸ verb **1** *the cats came to be petted* STROKE, caress, fondle, pat.

2 *she had always been petted by her parents* PAMPER, spoil, mollycoddle, coddle, cosset, baby, indulge, overindulge.

3 *couples were petting in their cars* KISS AND CUDDLE, kiss, cuddle, embrace, caress; *informal* make out, canoodle, neck, smooch, get it on.

PHRASE: **pet name** *'Cuddles' is a pet name John gave to me years ago* AFFECTIONATE NAME, term of endearment, endearment, nickname, diminutive; *rare* hypocoristic.

peter PHRASE: **peter out** *our enthusiasm eventually petered out* FIZZLE OUT, fade (away), die away/out, dwindle, diminish, taper off, tail off, trail away/off, wane, ebb, melt away, evaporate, disappear, come to an end, subside.

petite adjective *these dresses are designed for the more petite woman* SMALL, dainty, diminutive, slight, little, tiny, elfin, delicate, small-boned; *Scottish* wee; *informal* pint-sized. See note at SMALL.

petition noun **1** *more than 1,000 people signed the petition* APPEAL, round robin.

2 *petitions to Allah* ENTREATY, supplication, plea, prayer, appeal, request, invocation, suit; *archaic* orison.

▸ verb *they petitioned the governor to revoke the decision* APPEAL TO, request, ask, call on, entreat, beg, implore, plead with, apply to, press, urge; *formal* adjure; *literary* beseech. See note at BEG.

petrified adjective **1** *she looked petrified* TERRIFIED, terror-stricken, horrified, scared/frightened out of one's wits, scared/frightened to death.

2 *petrified remains of prehistoric animals* OSSIFIED, fossilized, calcified.

petrify verb *the thought of speaking in public petrified her* TERRIFY, horrify, frighten, scare, scare/frighten to death, scare/frighten the living daylights out of, scare/frighten the life out of, strike terror into, put the fear of God into; paralyze, transfix; *informal* scare the pants off, scare the bejesus out of.

petticoat noun *a starched white petticoat* SLIP, half-slip, undergarment; *archaic* kirtle; *historical* crinoline, farthing.

petty adjective **1** *petty regulations* TRIVIAL, trifling, minor, small, unimportant, insignificant, inconsequential, inconsiderable, negligible, paltry, footling, pettifogging; *informal* piffling, piddling, fiddling. ANTONYMS important, serious.

2 *a petty form of revenge* SMALL-MINDED, mean, ungenerous, shabby, spiteful. ANTONYM magnanimous.

petulant adjective *he's as petulant as a spoiled child* PEEVISH, bad-tempered, querulous, pettish, fretful, cross, irritable, sulky, snappish, crotchety, touchy, tetchy, testy, fractious, grumpy, disgruntled, crabby; *informal* grouchy, cranky. ANTONYM good-humored.

phantasmagorical adjective *phantasmagorical landscapes* DREAMLIKE, psychedelic, kaleidoscopic, surreal, unreal, hallucinatory, fantastic, fantastical, chimerical.

phantom noun **1** *a phantom who haunts lonely roads* GHOST, apparition, spirit, specter, wraith; *informal* spook; *literary* phantasm, shade.

2 *the phantoms of an overactive imagination* DELUSION, figment of the imagination, hallucination, illusion, chimera, vision, mirage.

phase noun **1** *the final phase of the campaign* STAGE, period, chapter, episode, part, step, point, time, juncture.

2 *he's going through a difficult phase* PERIOD, stage, time, spell, patch.

3 *the phases of the moon* ASPECT, shape, form, appearance, state, condition.

▸ verb See note at FAZE.

PHRASES: **phase in** *compliance with the new regulations will be phased in over a six-month period* INTRODUCE GRADUALLY, begin to use, ease in. **phase out** *we're going to phase out the cash-rebate program* WITHDRAW GRADUALLY, discontinue, stop using, run down, wind down.

phenomenal adjective *sales growth has been nothing short of phenomenal* REMARKABLE, exceptional, extraordinary, amazing, astonishing, astounding, sensational, stunning, incredible, unbelievable; marvelous, magnificent, wonderful, outstanding, singular, out of the ordinary, unusual, unprecedented; *informal* fantastic, terrific, tremendous, stupendous, awesome, out of this world; *literary* wondrous. ANTONYM ordinary.

phenomenon noun **1** *a rare phenomenon* OCCURRENCE, event, happening, fact, situation, circumstance, experience, case, incident, episode.

2 *the band was a pop phenomenon* MARVEL, sensation, wonder, prodigy, miracle, rarity, nonpareil; *informal* humdinger, phenom, stunner, doozy, ripsnorter.

philander verb *he had no time or inclination to philander* WOMANIZE, have affairs, flirt; *informal* play around, carry on, play the field, sleep around, fool around.

philanderer noun *everyone warned me he was a philanderer* WOMANIZER, Casanova, Don Juan, Lothario, flirt, ladies' man, playboy, rake, roué; *informal* stud, skirt-chaser, ladykiller, wolf.

philanthropic adjective *a philanthropic millionaire* CHARITABLE, generous, benevolent, humanitarian, public-spirited, altruistic, magnanimous, munificent, openhanded, bountiful, liberal, generous to a fault, beneficent, caring, compassionate, unselfish, kind, kind-hearted, bighearted; *formal* eleemosynary. ANTONYMS selfish, mean.

philanthropist noun *the trust was funded by an anonymous philanthropist* BENEFACTOR, benefactress, patron, patroness, donor, contributor, sponsor, backer, helper, good Samaritan; do-gooder, Lady Bountiful; *historical* almsgiver.

philanthropy noun *a family noted for its philanthropy* BENEVOLENCE, generosity, humanitarianism, public-spiritedness, altruism, social conscience, charity, charitableness, brotherly love, fellow feeling, magnanimity, munificence, liberality, largesse, openhandedness, bountifulness, beneficence, unselfishness, humanity, kindness, kindheartedness, compassion; *historical* almsgiving.

philippic noun *literary no publisher wanted to touch his scathing philippic* TIRADE, diatribe, harangue, lecture, attack, onslaught, denunciation, rant, polemic, broadside, fulmination, condemnation, criticism, censure; *informal* blast.

philistine adjective *my only mistake was thinking I could share something culturally uplifting with you philistines* UNCULTURED, lowbrow, anti-intellectual, uncultivated, uncivilized, uneducated, unenlightened, commercial, materialist, bourgeois; ignorant, crass, boorish, barbarian.

philosopher noun *when I was young, I failed to appreciate what an insightful philosopher my father was* THINKER, theorist, theorizer, theoretician, metaphysicist, metaphysician; scholar, intellectual, sage, wise man.

philosophical adjective **1** *a philosophical question* THEORETICAL, metaphysical.

2 *a philosophical mood* THOUGHTFUL, reflective, pensive, meditative, contemplative, introspective, ruminative; *formal* cogitative.

3 *he was philosophical about losing the contract* CALM, composed, cool, collected, 'calm, cool, and collected', self-possessed, serene, tranquil, stoical, impassive, dispassionate, phlegmatic, unperturbed, imperturbable, unruffled, patient, forbearing, long-suffering, resigned, rational, realistic.

philosophize verb *philosophizing on racial equality* THEORIZE, speculate; pontificate, preach, sermonize, moralize.

philosophy noun **1** *the philosophy of Aristotle* THINKING, thought, reasoning.

2 *her political philosophy* BELIEFS, credo, convictions, ideology, ideas, thinking, notions, theories, doctrine, tenets, principles, views, school of thought; *informal* ism.

phlegmatic adjective *I come from a very demonstrative, emotional Italian family—I can't remember one phlegmatic moment from my childhood* CALM, cool, composed, 'calm, cool, and collected', controlled, serene, tranquil, placid, impassive, imperturbable, unruffled, dispassionate, philosophical; stolid, dull, bland, unemotional, lifeless; *informal* unflappable. ANTONYM excitable.

WORD NOTE **phlegmatic**

Of the descriptions of human personality derived from the idea of bodily humors, *phlegmatic* seems to have been left behind. (We use *humorous* and *melancholy* all the time, of course, and even *bilious* and *choleric* are relatively familiar.) Just because it describes a personality type that is, by its nature, unemotional and self-effacing, refusing to draw attention to itself, doesn't mean the word itself should be overlooked. They are poorly represented on reality-TV shows, but lots of people—accountants, failed Democratic presidential candidates, Belgians—are phlegmatic. Speak up for them! **—DA**

phobia noun *fear of spiders is just one of his many phobias* FEAR, irrational fear, obsessive fear, dread, horror, terror, hatred, loathing, detestation, aversion, antipathy, revulsion; complex, neurosis; *informal* thing, hang-up.

phone noun *she tried to reach you on your phone* TELEPHONE, cell phone, cell, car phone, cordless phone, speakerphone; extension; *informal* blower, horn.

▸ verb *I'll phone you later* TELEPHONE, call, give someone a call; *informal* call up, give someone a buzz, get someone on the horn/blower.

phony *informal* adjective *a phony address* BOGUS, false, fake, fraudulent, spurious; counterfeit, forged, feigned; pseudo, imitation, sham, man-made, mock, ersatz, synthetic, artificial; simulated, pretended, contrived, affected, insincere, inauthentic; *informal* pretend, put-on. ANTONYM authentic.

▸ noun **1** *he's nothing but a phony* IMPOSTOR, sham, fake, fraud, charlatan; *informal* con artist.

2 *the diamond's a phony* FAKE, imitation, counterfeit, forgery.

photocopy noun *we kept a photocopy for our records* COPY, facsimile, duplicate, reproduction; *trademark* Xerox.

photograph noun *a photograph of her father* PICTURE, photo, snapshot, shot, image, likeness, print, slide, transparency, still, enlargement, snap; *informal* mug shot, head shot.

▸ verb *she was photographed leaving the castle* TAKE SOMEONE'S PICTURE/PHOTO, snap, shoot, film.

photographer noun *photographers hounded them all over Paris* SHUTTERBUG, paparazzo, photojournalist; lensman, cameraman.

USAGE NOTE **paparazzi**

Paparazzi (= photographers who follow celebrities, often aggressively, in hopes of snapping candid photos) is a plural; *paparazzo* is the singular. Originally Italian—invented for Federico Fellini's film *La Dolce Vita* (1960)—the term first surfaced in English in the mid-1960s. Unfortunately, because the singular form is so rare, some writers have begun using the misbegotten double plural *paparazzis*—e.g.: "The paparazzis [read *paparazzi*] even left the Clintons to find her [Princess Diana] on the Vineyard." (*Boston Herald*; Dec. 25, 1994.) On August 31, 1997, the day Diana died after a car crash while being chased by paparazzi, many television commentators used the incorrect form—no doubt spreading the mistake among millions of viewers. **—BG**

photographic adjective 1 *a photographic record* PICTORIAL, in photographs; cinematic, filmic.

2 *a photographic memory* DETAILED, graphic, exact, precise, accurate, vivid, picture-perfect.

phrase noun *familiar words and phrases* EXPRESSION, group of words, construction, locution, term, turn of phrase; idiom, idiomatic expression; saying, tag.

▸ verb *how could I phrase the question?* EXPRESS, put into words, put, word, style, formulate, couch, frame, articulate, verbalize.

phraseology noun *no phraseology is more endearing than that of Miss Sallie* WORDING, choice of words, phrasing, way of speaking/writing, usage, idiom, diction, parlance, words, language, vocabulary, terminology; jargon; *informal* lingo, -speak, -ese.

physical adjective 1 *physical pleasure* BODILY, corporeal, corporal, somatic; carnal, fleshly, nonspiritual. ANTONYMS mental, spiritual.

2 *hard physical work* MANUAL, laboring, labor-intensive, blue-collar. ANTONYMS intellectual, clerical.

3 *the physical universe* MATERIAL, concrete, tangible, palpable, solid, substantial, real, actual, visible. ANTONYMS intangible, abstract.

physician noun *consult your physician first* DOCTOR, doctor of medicine, MD, medical practitioner, general practitioner, GP, clinician, family doctor; specialist, consultant; *informal* doc, quack, medic, medico; intern, resident; *informal, dated* sawbones.

physiognomy noun *his physiognomy was European* FACE, features, countenance, expression, look, mien; *informal* mug, puss; *literary* visage, lineaments.

physique noun *the physique of an athlete* BODY, build, figure, frame, anatomy, shape, form, proportions; muscles, musculature; *informal* vital statistics, bod.

pick verb 1 *I got a job picking apples* HARVEST, gather (in), collect, pluck; *literary* cull.

2 *pick the time that suits you best* CHOOSE, select, pick out, single out, take, opt for, elect, decide on, settle on, fix on, sift out, sort out; name, nominate.

3 *Beth* ***picked at*** *her food* NIBBLE (AT), toy with, play with, eat like a bird.

4 *people were picking guitars and singing* STRUM, twang, thrum, pluck.

5 *he tried to pick a fight* PROVOKE, start, cause, incite, stir up, whip up, instigate, prompt, bring about.

▸ noun 1 *take your pick* CHOICE, selection, option, decision; preference, favorite.

2 *the pick of the crop* BEST, finest, top, choice, choicest, prime, cream, flower, prize, pearl, gem, jewel, jewel in the crown, crème de la crème, elite.

PHRASES: **pick on** *why don't you pick on somebody your own size?* BULLY, victimize, tyrannize, torment, persecute, criticize, harass, hound, taunt, tease; *informal* get at, have it in for, be down on, needle. **pick out** 1 *one painting was picked out for special mention* CHOOSE, select, single out, opt for, decide on, elect, settle on, fix on, sift out, sort out; name, nominate. 2 *she picked out Jessica in the crowd* SEE, make out, distinguish, discern, spot, perceive, detect, notice, recognize, identify, catch sight of, glimpse; *literary* espy, behold, descry. **pick up** 1 *business has really picked up* IMPROVE, recover, be on the road to recovery, rally, make a comeback, bounce back, perk up, look up, take a turn for the better, turn the/a corner, be on the mend, make headway, make progress. 2 *they teach you the proper way to pick up heavy boxes* LIFT, take up, raise, hoist, scoop up, gather up, snatch up. 3 *I'll pick you up after lunch* FETCH, collect, call for. 4 *informal she was picked up by the police* ARREST, apprehend, detain, take into custody, seize; *informal* nab, run in, bust. 5 *we picked it up at a thrift store* FIND, discover, come across, stumble across, happen on, chance on; acquire, obtain, come by, get, procure; purchase, buy; *informal* get hold of, get/lay one's hands on, get one's mitts on, bag, land. 6 *she picked up a virus* CATCH, contract, get, come down with. 7 *he told us the bits of gossip he'd picked up* HEAR, hear tell, get wind of, be told, learn; glean, garner. 8 *we're picking up a distress signal* RECEIVE, detect, get, hear.

picket noun 1 *forty pickets were arrested* STRIKER, demonstrator, protester, objector, picketer.

2 *fences made of cedar pickets* STAKE, post, paling; upright, stanchion, piling.

▸ verb *over 200 people picketed the factory* DEMONSTRATE AT, protest at, strike at, form a picket at, man the picket line at; blockade, shut off.

pickle noun *informal they got into a real pickle over this one* PLIGHT, predicament, mess, difficulty, trouble, dire/desperate straits, problem, quandary; *informal* tight corner, tight spot, jam, fix, scrape, bind, hole, hot water, fine kettle of fish.

▸ verb *fish pickled in brine* PRESERVE, souse, marinate, conserve.

pick-me-up noun 1 *a drink that's a good pick-me-up* TONIC, restorative, energizer, stimulant, refresher, reviver; *informal* bracer; *Medicine* analeptic.

2 *his winning goal was a perfect pick-me-up* BOOST, boost to the spirits, fillip, stimulant, stimulus; *informal* shot in the arm.

pickpocket noun *a crowded outdoor event is a pickpocket's playground* THIEF, petty thief, purse-snatcher, sneak thief; *archaic* cutpurse.

picnic noun 1 *a picnic on the beach* OUTDOOR MEAL, alfresco meal, cookout, barbecue.

2 *informal working for him was no picnic* EASY TASK/JOB, child's play, five-finger exercise, gift, walkover; *informal* piece of cake, cinch, breeze, kids' stuff, cakewalk, pushover, duck soup.

pictorial adjective *a pictorial essay on desegregation* ILLUSTRATED, in pictures, in picture form, in photographs, photographic, graphic. See note at GRAPHIC.

picture noun 1 *pictures in an art gallery* PAINTING, DRAWING, sketch, oil painting, watercolor, print, canvas, portrait, portrayal, illustration, artwork, depiction, likeness, representation, image, icon, miniature, landscape; fresco, mural, wall painting; *informal* oil.

2 *we were told not to take pictures* PHOTOGRAPH, photo, snap, snapshot, shot, print, slide, transparency, exposure, still, enlargement.

3 *do you have a picture of what your ideal home might look*

like? CONCEPT, idea, impression, view, (mental) image, vision, visualization, notion.

4 *the picture of health* PERSONIFICATION, embodiment, epitome, essence, quintessence, perfect example, soul, model.

5 *a picture starring Robert de Niro* MOVIE, film, motion picture, feature film; *informal* flick; *dated* moving picture.

▸ verb 1 *he was pictured with his guests* PHOTOGRAPH, take a photograph/photo of, snap, shoot, film.

2 *in the drawing they were pictured against a snowy background* PAINT, DRAW, sketch, depict, delineate, portray, show, illustrate.

3 *Anne still pictured Richard as he had been* VISUALIZE, see in one's mind's eye, conjure up a picture/image of, imagine, see, evoke.

PHRASE: **put in the picture** *please come in and sit down, and we'll put you in the picture* INFORM, fill in, explain the situation/circumstances to, bring up to date, update, brief, keep posted, clue in, bring up to speed.

picturesque adjective 1 *a picturesque village* ATTRACTIVE, pretty, beautiful, lovely, scenic, charming, quaint, pleasing, delightful, picture-perfect. ANTONYMS ugly, drab.

2 *a picturesque description* VIVID, graphic, colorful, impressive, striking. ANTONYM dull. See note at GRAPHIC.

piddling adjective *informal I'm tired of your piddling complaints* TRIVIAL, trifling, petty, footling, slight, small, insignificant, unimportant, inconsequential, inconsiderable, negligible; meager, inadequate, insufficient, paltry, scant, scanty, derisory, pitiful, miserable, puny, niggardly, beggarly, mere; *informal* measly, pathetic, piffling, mingy, nickel-and-dime.

pie noun *the enticing aroma of fresh-baked pies* PASTRY, tart, turnover. See table. PHRASE: **pie in the sky** *informal they thought her dream of fame was just pie in the sky* FALSE HOPE, illusion, delusion, fantasy, pipe dream, daydream, a castle in the air, a castle in Spain.

piebald adjective See PIED.

piece noun 1 *a piece of cheese* | *a piece of wood* BIT, slice, chunk, segment, section, lump, hunk, wedge, slab, block, cake, bar, cube, stick, length; offcut, sample, fragment, sliver, splinter, wafer, chip, crumb, scrap, remnant, shred, shard, snippet; mouthful, morsel. See note at FRAGMENT.

2 *the pieces of a clock* COMPONENT, part, bit, section, segment, constituent, element; unit, module.

3 *a piece of furniture* ITEM, article, specimen.

4 *a piece of the profit* SHARE, portion, slice, quota, part, bit, percentage, amount, quantity, ration, fraction, division; *informal* cut.

5 *pieces from his private collection* WORK (OF ART), creation, production; composition, opus.

6 *the reporter who wrote the piece* ARTICLE, item, story, report, essay, study, review, composition, column.

7 *the pieces on a game board* TOKEN, counter, man, disk, chip, marker. PHRASES: **in one piece** 1 *the camera was still in one piece* UNBROKEN, entire, whole, intact, undamaged, unharmed. 2 *I'll bring her back in one piece* UNHURT, uninjured, unscathed, safe, safe and sound. **in pieces** *the vase was in pieces* BROKEN, in bits, shattered, smashed, in smithereens; *informal* bust, busted. **go/fall to pieces** *he went to pieces when his wife died* HAVE A BREAKDOWN, break down, go out of one's mind, lose control, lose one's head, fall apart; *informal* crack up, lose it, come/fall apart at the seams, freak, freak out.

pièce de résistance noun *this scampi is Chef Gautier's pièce de résistance* MASTERPIECE, magnum opus, chef-d'œuvre, masterwork, tour de force, showpiece, prize, jewel in the crown.

piecemeal adverb *the reforms were implemented piecemeal* A LITTLE AT A TIME, piece by piece, bit by bit, gradually, slowly, in stages, in steps, step by step, little by little, by degrees, in/by fits and starts.

pied adjective *a lovely little pied pony* PARTI-COLORED, multicolored, variegated, black and white, brown and white, piebald, skewbald, dappled, brindle, spotted, mottled, speckled, flecked, pinto, calico, tabby.

pier noun 1 *a boat was tied to the pier* JETTY, quay, wharf, dock, levee, landing, landing stage.

2 *the piers of the bridge* SUPPORT, cutwater, pile, piling, abutment, buttress, stanchion, prop, stay, upright, pillar, post, column.

pierce verb 1 *the metal pierced his flesh* PENETRATE, puncture, perforate, prick, lance; stab, spike, stick, impale, transfix, bore through, drill through.

2 *his anguish pierced her very soul* HURT, wound, pain, sting, sear, grieve, distress, upset, trouble, harrow, afflict; affect, move.

PIES, TARTS, AND TURNOVERS

Pies	strudel
apple pie	sweet potato pie
banana cream pie	tarte au sucre
bierrock	tarte Tatin
bisteeya	tiropita
black bottom pie	torta
bridie	tourtiere
buttermilk pie	Washington pie
cherry pie	
chess pie	**Tarts**
coconut cream pie	Banbury tart
French silk pie	bitter tart
grasshopper pie	jam tart
key lime pie	onion tart
lemon chiffon pie	pasteis de nata
lemon meringue pie	
millionaire pie	**Turnovers**
mincemeat pie	borek
Mississippi mud pie	boureki
moon pie	calzone
pecan pie	Cornish pasty
pierogy/piroshki	dumpling
pot pie	empanada
pumpkin pie	mezzaluna
quesadilla	momo
quiche lorraine	pot sticker
ricotta pie	pyrizhky
runza	roly poly
shepherd's pie	rustici
shoofly pie	sambusak
spanakopita	samosa
steak and kidney pie	shu mai
strawberry rhubarb pie	wonton

See also tables at CAKE, CANDY, COOKIE, DOUGHNUT, and PASTRY.

piercing adjective **1** *a piercing shriek* SHRILL, ear-splitting, high-pitched, penetrating, strident, loud.

2 *the piercing wind* BITTER, biting, cutting, penetrating, sharp, keen, stinging, raw; freezing, frigid, glacial, arctic, chill.

3 *a piercing pain* INTENSE, excruciating, agonizing, sharp, stabbing, shooting, stinging, severe, extreme, fierce, searing, racking.

4 *his piercing gaze* SEARCHING, probing, penetrating, penetrative, shrewd, sharp, keen.

5 *his piercing intelligence* PERCEPTIVE, percipient, perspicacious, penetrating, discerning, discriminating, intelligent, quick-witted, sharp, sharp-witted, shrewd, insightful, keen, acute, astute, clever, smart, incisive, razor-edged, trenchant.

piety noun *the piety of a saint* DEVOUTNESS, devotion, piousness, religion, holiness, godliness, saintliness; veneration, reverence, faith, religious duty, spirituality, religious zeal, fervor; pietism, religiosity.

piffle noun *informal* See NONSENSE sense 1.

pig noun **1** *a herd of pigs* HOG, boar, sow, porker, swine, piglet; *children's word* piggy.

2 *informal* *he's such a pig, he'll eat us out of house and home* GLUTTON; *informal* hog, greedy guts.

pigeonhole verb **1** *they were pigeonholed as an indie guitar band* CATEGORIZE, compartmentalize, classify, characterize, label, brand, tag, typecast, ghettoize, designate.

2 *the plan was pigeonholed last year* POSTPONE, put off, put back, defer, shelve, hold over, put to one side, put on ice, mothball, put in cold storage; *informal* put on the back burner.

pigheaded adjective *you pigheaded old fool* OBSTINATE, stubborn (as a mule), mulish, bullheaded, obdurate, headstrong, self-willed, willful, perverse, contrary, recalcitrant, stiff-necked; uncooperative, inflexible, uncompromising, intractable, intransigent, unyielding, bloody-minded; *formal* refractory.

pigment noun *a chestnut brown pigment* COLORING MATTER, coloring, colorant, color, tint, dye, dyestuff.

pile[1] noun **1** *a pile of stones* HEAP, stack, mound, pyramid, mass, quantity; collection, accumulation, assemblage, store, stockpile, hoard.

2 *informal* *I've got a pile of work to do* GREAT DEAL, lot, large quantity/amount, mountain; abundance, cornucopia; *informal* load, heap, mass, slew, ocean, stack, ton.

3 *informal* *he'd made his pile in the fur trade* FORTUNE, millions, billions; *informal* small fortune, bundle, wad.

▸ verb **1** *she* ***piled up*** *the plates* HEAP (UP), stack (up).

2 *he piled his plate with fried eggs* LOAD, heap, fill (up), lade, stack, charge, stock.

3 *our debts were piling up* INCREASE, grow, mount up, escalate, soar, spiral, leap up, shoot up, rocket, climb, accumulate, accrue, build up, multiply.

4 *we piled into the car* CROWD, climb, pack, squeeze, push, shove.

PHRASE: **pile it on** *informal* *if you pile it on like that, no one will believe you* EXAGGERATE, overstate the case, make a mountain out of a molehill, overdo it, overplay it, overdramatize; *informal* lay it on thick.

pile[2] noun *a wall supported by timber piles* POST, stake, pillar, column, support, foundation, piling, abutment, pier, cutwater, buttress, stanchion, upright.

pile[3] noun *a carpet with a short pile* NAP, fibers, threads.

pileup noun *a terrible pileup on I-95* CRASH, multiple crash, collision, multiple collision, smash, accident, road accident, wreck; *informal* smash-up.

pilfer verb *the gun was part of a cache pilfered from the air force* STEAL, thieve, take, snatch, purloin, loot; *informal* swipe, rob, nab, rip off, lift, "liberate", "borrow", filch, snaffle; pinch, heist.

pilgrim noun *the destination of these weary pilgrims* worshiper, devotee, believer; traveler, crusader; *literary* wayfarer; *historical* palmer.

pilgrimage noun *an annual pilgrimage to the Holy City* RELIGIOUS JOURNEY, religious expedition, hajj, crusade, mission. See note at JOURNEY.

pill noun *take one pill at bedtime* TABLET, capsule, caplet, cap, gelcap, pellet, lozenge, pastille, horse pill; *Veterinary Medicine* bolus.

pillage verb **1** *the abbey was pillaged* RANSACK, rob, plunder, despoil, raid, loot; sack, devastate, lay waste, ravage, rape. See note at RAVAGE.

2 *columns pillaged from an ancient town* STEAL, pilfer, thieve, take, snatch, purloin, loot; *informal* swipe, rob, nab, rip off, lift, "liberate", "borrow", filch, snaffle, pinch, heist.

▸ noun *the rebels were intent on pillage* ROBBERY, robbing, raiding, plunder, looting, sacking, rape, marauding; *literary* rapine.

pillar noun **1** *stone pillars* COLUMN, post, support, upright, baluster, pier, pile, pilaster, stanchion, prop, newel; obelisk, monolith.

2 *a pillar of the community* STALWART, mainstay, bastion, rock; leading light, worthy, backbone, support, upholder, champion, tower of strength.

pillory noun *offenders were put in the pillory* STOCKS.

▸ verb **1** *he was pilloried by the press* ATTACK, criticize, censure, condemn, denigrate, lambaste, savage, stigmatize, denounce; *informal* knock, slam, pan, bash, crucify, hammer, pummel; *formal* excoriate.

2 *they were pilloried at school* RIDICULE, jeer at, sneer at, deride, mock, scorn, make fun of, poke fun at, laugh at, scoff at, tease, taunt; *informal* rib, josh, razz.

pillow noun *his head rested on the pillow* CUSHION, bolster, pad; headrest.

▸ verb *she pillowed her head on folded arms* CUSHION, cradle, rest, lay, support.

pilot noun **1** *a fighter pilot* AIRMAN/AIRWOMAN, flyer; captain, commander, co-pilot, wingman, first officer, bush pilot; *informal* skipper; *dated* aviator, aviatrix, aeronaut.

2 *a harbor pilot* NAVIGATOR, helmsman, steersman, coxswain.

3 *a pilot for his new TV series* TRIAL EPISODE; sample, experiment, trial run.

▸ adjective *a pilot project* EXPERIMENTAL, exploratory, trial, test, sample, speculative; preliminary.

▸ verb **1** *he piloted the jet to safety* NAVIGATE, guide, maneuver, steer, control, direct, captain, shepherd; fly, drive; sail; *informal* skipper.

2 *the questionnaire has been piloted* TEST, trial, try out; assess, investigate, examine, appraise, evaluate.

pimp noun *her pimp was a vicious heroin addict* PROCURER, procuress; brothel-keeper, pander, madam; *archaic* bawd.

pimple noun *the last thing you want on prom night is a pimple* ZIT, pustule, bleb, boil, swelling, eruption, blackhead, whitehead, carbuncle, blister, spot; *technical* comedo, papule; **(pimples)** acne, bad skin.

pin noun **1** *fasten the hem with a pin* TACK, safety pin, nail, staple, fastener.

2 *a broken pin in the machine* BOLT, peg, rivet, dowel, screw.

3 *souvenir pins* BADGE, brooch.

▸ verb **1** *she pinned the brooch to her dress* ATTACH, fasten, affix, fix, tack, clip; join, secure.

2 *they pinned him to the ground* HOLD, press, hold fast, hold down; restrain, pinion, immobilize.

3 *they **pinned** the crime **on** him* BLAME FOR, hold responsible for, attribute to, impute to, ascribe to; lay something at someone's door; *informal* stick on.

PHRASE: **pin down 1** *our troops can pin down the enemy* CONFINE, TRAP, hem in, corner, close in, shut in, hedge in, pen in, restrain, entangle, enmesh, immobilize. **2** *she tried to pin him down to a plan* CONSTRAIN, make someone commit themselves, pressure, tie down, nail down. **3** *it evoked a memory but he couldn't pin it down* DEFINE, put one's finger on, put into words, express, name, specify, identify, pinpoint, place.

pinch verb **1** *he pinched my arm* TWEAK, nip, squeeze, grasp.

2 *my new shoes pinch my toes* HURT, pain; squeeze, crush, cramp; be uncomfortable.

3 *I scraped and pinched to afford it* ECONOMIZE, scrimp (and save), be sparing, be frugal, cut back, tighten one's belt, retrench; *informal* be stingy, be tight.

4 *informal you pinched his baseball cards* STEAL, thieve, take, snatch, pilfer, purloin, loot; *informal* swipe, rob, nab, lift, "liberate", "borrow", filch, heist.

▸ noun **1** *he gave her arm a pinch* TWEAK, nip, squeeze.

2 *a pinch of salt* BIT, touch, dash, spot, trace, soupçon, speck, taste; *informal* smidgen, tad.

PHRASES: **feel the pinch** *many of our customers are feeling the pinch* SUFFER HARDSHIP, be short of money, be poor, be impoverished. **in a pinch** *there's room for four adults, five in a pinch* IF NECESSARY, if need be, in an emergency, just possibly, with difficulty.

pinched adjective *their pinched faces* STRAINED, stressed, fraught, tense, taut; tired, worn, drained, sapped; wan, peaked, pale, gray, blanched; thin, drawn, haggard, gaunt. ANTONYM healthy.

pine verb **1** *I am **pining away** from love* LANGUISH, decline, weaken, waste away, wilt, wither, fade, sicken, droop; brood, mope, moon.

2 *he was pining for his son* YEARN, long, ache, sigh, hunger, languish; miss, mourn, lament, grieve over, shed tears for, bemoan, rue, eat one's heart out over; *informal* itch.

pinion verb *the hostages were pinioned to each other* HOLD DOWN, pin down, restrain, hold fast, immobilize; tie, bind, truss (up), shackle, fetter, hobble, manacle, handcuff; *informal* cuff.

pink adjective *the meat should be slightly pink* ROSE, rosy, rosé, pale red, salmon, coral; flushed, blushing.

▸ noun *informal she's in the pink of condition* PRIME, perfection, best, finest, height; utmost, greatest, apex, zenith, acme, bloom.

PHRASE: **in the pink** *informal I'm finally in the pink again* IN GOOD HEALTH, very healthy, very well, hale and hearty; blooming, flourishing, thriving, vigorous, strong, lusty, robust, in fine fettle, (as) fit as a fiddle, in excellent shape.

pinnacle noun **1** *pinnacles of rock* PEAK, needle, crag, tor, aiguille, hoodoo; summit, crest, apex, tip.

2 *the pinnacles of the clock tower* TURRET, minaret, spire, finial, mirador.

3 *the pinnacle of the sport* HIGHEST LEVEL, peak, height, high point, top, capstone, apex, zenith, apogee, acme. ANTONYM nadir.

pinpoint noun *a pinpoint of light* POINT, spot, speck, dot, speckle.

▸ adjective *pinpoint accuracy* PRECISE, strict, exact, meticulous, scrupulous, punctilious, accurate, careful.

▸ verb *pinpoint the cause of the trouble* IDENTIFY, determine, distinguish, discover, find, locate, detect, track down, spot, diagnose, recognize, pin down, home in on, put one's finger on.

pioneer noun **1** *the pioneers of the Wild West* SETTLER, colonist, colonizer, frontiersman, frontierswoman, explorer, trailblazer, bushwhacker.

2 *an aviation pioneer* DEVELOPER, innovator, trailblazer, groundbreaker, spearhead; founder, founding father, architect, creator.

▸ verb *he pioneered the sale of insurance* INTRODUCE, develop, evolve, launch, instigate, initiate, spearhead, institute, establish, found, be the father/mother of, originate, set in motion, create; lay the groundwork, prepare the way, blaze a trail, break new ground.

pious adjective **1** *a pious family* RELIGIOUS, devout, God-fearing, churchgoing, spiritual, prayerful, holy, godly, saintly, dedicated, reverent, dutiful, righteous. ANTONYM irreligious.

2 *pious platitudes* SANCTIMONIOUS, hypocritical, insincere, self-righteous, holier-than-thou, pietistic, churchy; *informal* goody-goody. ANTONYM sincere.

3 *a pious hope* FORLORN, vain, doomed, hopeless, desperate; unlikely, unrealistic.

pip noun *apple pips* SEED, stone, pit.

pipe noun **1** *a water pipe* TUBE, conduit, hose, main, duct, line, channel, pipeline, drain; tubing, piping, siphon.

2 *he smokes a pipe* brier (pipe), meerschaum, chibouk; hookah, narghile, bong, churchwarden.

3 *she was playing a pipe* WHISTLE, pennywhistle, tin whistle, flute, recorder, fife; chanter.

4 *regimental pipes and drums* BAGPIPES, uillean pipes; pan pipes.

▸ verb **1** *the beer is piped into barrels* SIPHON, feed, channel, run, convey.

2 *television shows piped in from New York* TRANSMIT, feed, patch.

3 *he heard a tune being piped* PLAY ON A PIPE, tootle, whistle; *literary* flute.

4 *a curlew piped* CHIRP, cheep, chirrup, twitter, warble, trill, peep, sing, shrill.

PHRASE: **pipe down** *informal we had to ask that couple in the first row to pipe down* BE QUIET, be silent, hush, stop talking, hold one's tongue, settle down; *informal* shut up, shut one's mouth, zip it, button it, button one's lip, put a sock in it.

pipe dream noun *for most aspiring actors, that starring role is just a pipe dream* FANTASY, false hope, illusion, delusion, daydream, chimera; castle in the air, castle in Spain; *informal* pie in the sky.

pipeline noun *a gas pipeline* PIPE, conduit, main, line, duct, tube. PHRASE: **in the pipeline** *word of a layoff is in the pipeline* ON THE WAY, coming, forthcoming, upcoming, imminent, about to happen, near, close, brewing, in the offing, in the wind.

pipsqueak noun *informal we're not going to let some fresh-out-of-college pipsqueak give the orders around here* NOBODY, nonentity, insignificant person, no-name, nonperson, cipher, small fry; upstart, stripling; *informal* squirt, whippersnapper; picayune.

piquant adjective 1 *a piquant sauce* SPICY, tangy, peppery, hot; tasty, flavorful, appetizing, savory; pungent, sharp, tart, zesty, strong, salty. ANTONYM bland.

2 *a piquant story* INTRIGUING, stimulating, interesting, fascinating, colorful, exciting, lively; spicy, provocative, racy; *informal* juicy. ANTONYM dull.

pique noun *a fit of pique* IRRITATION, annoyance, resentment, anger, displeasure, indignation, petulance, ill humor, vexation, exasperation, disgruntlement, discontent; offense, umbrage.

▸ verb 1 *his curiosity was piqued* STIMULATE, arouse, rouse, provoke, whet, awaken, excite, kindle, stir, galvanize.

2 *she was piqued by his neglect* IRRITATE, annoy, bother, vex, displease, upset, offend, affront, anger, exasperate, infuriate, gall, irk, nettle; *informal* peeve, aggravate, miff, rile, bug, needle, get someone's back up, get someone's goat, tick off, tee off.

piracy noun 1 *piracy on the high seas* FREEBOOTING, robbery at sea; *archaic* buccaneering.

2 *software piracy* ILLEGAL COPYING, plagiarism, copyright infringement, bootlegging.

pirate noun 1 *pirates boarded the ship* FREEBOOTER, marauder, raider; *historical* privateer; *archaic* buccaneer, corsair.

2 *software pirates* COPYRIGHT INFRINGER, plagiarist, plagiarizer.

▸ verb *designers may pirate good ideas* STEAL, plagiarize, poach, copy illegally, reproduce illegally, appropriate, bootleg; *informal* crib, lift, rip off, pinch.

pirouette noun *she did a little pirouette* SPIN, twirl, whirl, turn, twizzle.

▸ verb *she pirouetted before the mirror* SPIN AROUND, twirl, whirl, turn around, revolve, pivot.

pistol noun *a concealed pistol* REVOLVER, gun, handgun, sidearm; automatic, six-shooter, thirty-eight, derringer; *informal* gat, piece; *trademark* Colt, Luger.

pit[1] noun 1 *a pit in the ground* HOLE, ditch, trench, trough, hollow, excavation, cavity, crater, pothole; shaft, mineshaft, sump.

2 *pit closures* COAL MINE, colliery, quarry.

3 *the pits in her skin* POCKMARK, pock, hollow, indentation, depression, dent, dimple.

▸ verb 1 *his skin had been pitted by acne* MARK, pockmark, scar, blemish, disfigure.

2 *raindrops pitted the bare earth* MAKE HOLES IN, make hollows in, dent, indent.

PHRASES: **pit against** *it's your chance to pit your wits against the world champions* SET AGAINST, match against, put in opposition to, put in competition with; compete with, contend with, vie with, wrestle with. **the pits** *informal this place is really the pits* HELL, the worst, the lowest of the low, a nightmare; rock-bottom, extremely bad, awful, terrible, dreadful, deplorable; *informal* appalling, lousy, abysmal.

pit[2] noun *cherry pits* STONE, pip, seed.

pitch[1] noun 1 *her voice rose in pitch* TONE, timbre, key, modulation, frequency.

2 *the pitch of the roof* GRADIENT, slope, slant, angle, steepness, tilt, incline, inclination.

3 *her anger reached such a pitch that she screamed* LEVEL, intensity, point, degree, height, extent.

4 *a pitch of the ball* THROW, fling, hurl, toss, lob; delivery; *informal* heave.

5 *his sales pitch* PATTER, talk; *informal* spiel, line.

▸ verb 1 *she pitched the crumpled note into the fire* THROW, toss, fling, hurl, cast, lob, flip, propel, bowl; *informal* chuck, sling, heave, peg.

2 *he pitched overboard* FALL, tumble, topple, plunge, plummet.

3 *they pitched their tents* PUT UP, set up, erect, raise.

4 *the boat pitched* LURCH, toss (about), plunge, roll, reel, sway, rock, keel, list, wallow, labor.

PHRASES: **make a pitch for** *we made a pitch for the Loman account, but we lost in the bidding* TRY TO OBTAIN, try to acquire, try to get, bid for, make a bid for. **pitch in** *if we all pitch in, we can be out of here in thirty minutes* HELP (OUT), assist, lend a hand, join in, participate, contribute, do one's bit, chip in, cooperate, collaborate.

pitch[2] noun *cement coated with pitch* bitumen, asphalt, tar.

pitch-black adjective *we ventured into the pitch-black tunnel* BLACK, dark, pitch-dark, inky, jet-black, coal-black, jet, ebony; starless, moonless; *literary* Stygian.

pitcher noun *a pitcher of beer* JUG, ewer, jar; creamer.

piteous adjective *a piteous cry* SAD, pitiful, pitiable, pathetic, heart-rending, heartbreaking, moving, touching; plaintive, poignant, forlorn; poor, wretched, miserable.

pitfall noun *home schooling has its pitfalls* HAZARD, danger, risk, peril, difficulty, catch, snag, stumbling block, drawback.

pith noun 1 *the pith of the argument* ESSENCE, main point, fundamentals, heart, substance, nub, core, quintessence, crux, gist, meat, kernel, marrow, burden; *informal* nitty-gritty.

2 *he writes with pith and exactitude* SUCCINCTNESS, conciseness, concision, pithiness, brevity; cogency, weight, depth, force.

pithy adjective *pithy comments* SUCCINCT, terse, concise, compact, short (and sweet), brief, condensed, to the point, epigrammatic, crisp, thumbnail; significant, meaningful, expressive, telling; *formal* compendious. See note at TERSE. ANTONYM verbose.

pitiful adjective 1 *a child in a pitiful state* DISTRESSING, sad, piteous, pitiable, pathetic, heart-rending, heartbreaking, moving, touching, tearjerking; plaintive, poignant, forlorn; poor, sorry, wretched, abject, miserable.

2 *a pitiful $500 a month* PALTRY, miserable, meager, insufficient, trifling, negligible, pitiable, derisory; *informal* pathetic, measly, piddling, mingy.

3 *his performance was pitiful* WOEFUL, deplorable, awful, terrible, lamentable, hopeless, poor, bad, feeble, pitiable, dreadful, inadequate, below par, laughable; *informal* pathetic, useless, appalling, lousy, abysmal, dire.

pitiless adjective *a pitiless executioner* MERCILESS, unmerciful, unpitying, ruthless, cruel, heartless, remorseless, hard-hearted, cold-hearted, harsh, callous, severe, unsparing, unforgiving, unfeeling, uncaring, unsympathetic, uncharitable, brutal, inhuman, inhumane, barbaric, sadistic. ANTONYM merciful.

pittance noun *the musicians were paid a pittance* A TINY AMOUNT, next to nothing, very little; *informal* peanuts, chicken feed, slave wages, chump change.

pitted adjective 1 *his skin was pitted* POCKMARKED, pocked, scarred, marked, blemished. ANTONYM smooth.

2 *the pitted lane* POTHOLED, rutted, rutty, holey, bumpy, rough, uneven.

pity noun 1 *a voice full of pity* COMPASSION, commiseration, condolence, sympathy, fellow feeling, understanding; sorrow, regret, sadness. ANTONYMS indifference, cruelty.

2 *it's a pity he never had children* SHAME, sad thing, bad luck, misfortune; *informal* crime, bummer, sin.

▸ verb *they pitied me* FEEL SORRY FOR, feel for, sympathize with, empathize with, commiserate with, take pity on, be moved by, grieve for.

PHRASES: **take pity on** *a better person would take pity on them* FEEL SORRY FOR, relent, be compassionate toward, be sympathetic toward, have mercy on, help (out), put someone out of their misery. **what a pity!** *Cameron lost by less than a tenth of a second? What a pity!* HOW SAD, what a shame, too bad, tant pis, oh dear, bummer.

pivot noun 1 *the machine turns on a pivot* FULCRUM, axis, axle, swivel; pin, shaft, hub, spindle, hinge, kingpin, gudgeon.

2 *the pivot of government policy* CENTER, focus, hub, heart, nucleus, crux, keystone, cornerstone, linchpin, kingpin.

▸ verb 1 *the panel pivots inward* ROTATE, turn, swivel, revolve, spin.

2 *it all pivoted on his response* DEPEND, hinge, turn, center, hang, rely, rest; revolve around.

pivotal adjective *Japan's pivotal role in the world economy* CENTRAL, crucial, vital, critical, focal, essential, key, decisive.

pixie noun *Loolah was a mischievous little pixie* ELF, fairy, sprite, imp, brownie, puck, leprechaun; *literary* faerie, fay.

placard noun *placards with antiwar slogans* NOTICE, poster, sign, bill, advertisement; banner; *informal* ad.

placate verb *John did his best to placate her* PACIFY, calm, appease, mollify, soothe, win over, conciliate, propitiate, make peace with, humor. See note at PACIFY. ANTONYM provoke.

place noun 1 *an ideal place for dinner* LOCATION, site, spot, setting, position, situation, area, region, locale; venue; *technical* locus.

2 *foreign places* COUNTRY, state, area, region, town, city; locality, district; *literary* clime.

3 *a place of her own* HOME, house, flat, apartment; accommodations, property, pied-à-terre; rooms, quarters; *informal* pad, digs; *formal* residence, abode, dwelling (place), domicile, habitation.

4 *if I were in your place, I'd sell now* SITUATION, position, circumstances; *informal* shoes.

5 *a place was reserved for her* SEAT, chair, space.

6 *I offered him a place in the company* JOB, position, post, appointment, situation, office; employment.

7 *I know my place* STATUS, position, standing, rank, niche; *dated* estate, station.

8 *it was not her place to sort it out* RESPONSIBILITY, duty, job, task, role, function, concern, affair, charge; right, privilege, prerogative.

▸ verb 1 *books were placed on the table* PUT (DOWN), set (down), lay, deposit, position, plant, rest, stand, station, situate, leave; *informal* stick, dump, park, plonk, pop, plunk.

2 *the trust you placed in me* PUT, lay, set, invest.

3 *a survey placed the company sixth* RANK, order, grade, class, classify, categorize; put, set, assign.

4 *Joe couldn't quite place her* IDENTIFY, recognize, remember, put a name to, pin down; locate, pinpoint.

5 *we were **placed with** foster parents* house with, billet to; allocate to, assign to, appoint to.

PHRASE: **in the first place** *in the first place, you're not old enough* INITIALLY, at first, at the start, at the outset, in/at the beginning, in the first instance, to begin with, to start with, originally.

PHRASES: **in place** 1 *the veil was held in place by pearls* IN POSITION, in situ. 2 *the plans are in place* READY, set up, all set, established, arranged, in order. **in place of** *in place of fresh flowers, use sprays of dried lavender* INSTEAD OF, rather than, as a substitute for, as a replacement for, in exchange for, in lieu of; in someone's stead. **out of place** 1 *she never had a hair out of place* OUT OF POSITION, out of order, in disarray, disarranged, in a mess, messy, topsy-turvy, muddled. 2 *he said something out of place* INAPPROPRIATE, unsuitable, unseemly, improper, untoward, out of keeping, unbecoming, wrong. 3 *she seemed out of place at the literary parties* INCONGRUOUS, out of one's element, like a fish out of water; uncomfortable, uneasy. **put someone in their place** *Marsha's father-in-law finally spoke up and put that hateful woman in her place* HUMILIATE, take down a peg or two, deflate, crush, squash, humble; *informal* cut down to size, settle someone's hash, make someone eat crow. **take place** *the site where the crash took place* HAPPEN, occur, come about, transpire, crop up, materialize, arise, go down; *literary* come to pass, befall, betide. **take the place of** *I know I'll never be able to take the place of your father* REPLACE, stand in for, substitute for, act for, fill in for, cover for, relieve.

placement noun **1** *the placement of the chairs* POSITIONING, placing, arrangement, position, deployment, location, disposition.

2 *teaching placements* JOB, post, assignment, posting, position, appointment, engagement.

placid adjective **1** *she's normally very placid* EVEN-TEMPERED, calm, tranquil, equable, unexcitable, serene, mild, 'calm, cool, and collected', composed, self-possessed, poised, easygoing, levelheaded, steady, unruffled, unperturbed, phlegmatic; *informal* unflappable. ANTONYM excitable. See note at CALM.

2 *a placid village* QUIET, calm, tranquil, still, peaceful, undisturbed, restful, sleepy. ANTONYM bustling.

plagiarism noun *accusations of plagiarism* COPYING, infringement of copyright, piracy, theft, stealing; *informal* cribbing.

plagiarize verb *he was fined for plagiarizing a song* COPY, infringe the copyright of, pirate, steal, poach, appropriate; *informal* rip off, crib, "borrow", pinch.

plague noun **1** *they died of the plague* BUBONIC PLAGUE, pneumonic plague, Black Death; disease, sickness, epidemic; *dated* contagion; *archaic* pestilence.

2 *a plague of fleas* INFESTATION, epidemic, invasion, swarm, multitude, host.

3 *theft is the plague of restaurants* BANE, curse, scourge, affliction, blight.

▸ verb **1** *he was plagued by poor health* AFFLICT, bedevil, torment, trouble, beset, dog, curse.

2 *he plagued her with questions* PESTER, harass, badger, bother, torment, persecute, bedevil, harry, hound, trouble, irritate, nag, annoy, vex, molest; *informal* hassle, bug, aggravate, devil.

plaid adjective *a white blouse with a green plaid skirt* CHECKERED, checked, tartan.

plain adjective **1** *it was plain that something was wrong* OBVIOUS, clear, crystal clear, evident, apparent, manifest, patent; discernible, perceptible, noticeable, recognizable, unmistakable, transparent; pronounced, marked, striking, conspicuous, self-evident, indisputable; writ large; *informal* standing/sticking out like a sore thumb.

2 *plain English* INTELLIGIBLE, comprehensible, clear, understandable, coherent, uncomplicated, lucid, unambiguous, simple, straightforward, user-friendly; *formal* perspicuous. ANTONYMS obscure, unclear.

3 *plain speaking* CANDID, frank, outspoken, forthright, direct, honest, truthful, blunt, bald, explicit, unequivocal; *informal* upfront.

4 *a plain dress* SIMPLE, ordinary, unadorned, unembellished, unornamented, unostentatious, unfussy, basic, modest, unsophisticated, without frills, homespun; restrained, muted; everyday, workaday. ANTONYMS elaborate, fancy.

5 *a plain girl* HOMELY, unattractive, unprepossessing, ugly, ill-favored, unlovely, ordinary; *informal* not much to look at. ANTONYM attractive.

6 *it was plain bad luck* SHEER, pure, downright, out-and-out, unmitigated. See word spectrum on page 681.

▸ adverb *this is just plain stupid* DOWNRIGHT, utterly, absolutely, completely, totally, really, thoroughly, positively, simply, unquestionably, undeniably; *informal* plumb.

▸ noun *the endless grassy plains* GRASSLAND, prairie, flatland, lowland, pasture, meadowland, savanna, steppe; tableland, tundra, pampas, veld.

plain-spoken adjective *he's not being rude, he's just plain-spoken* CANDID, frank, outspoken, forthright, direct, honest, truthful, open, blunt, straightforward, explicit, unequivocal, unambiguous, not afraid to call a spade a spade, tell-it-like-it-is; *informal* upfront. ANTONYM evasive.

plaintive adjective *a plaintive cry* MOURNFUL, sad, wistful, doleful, pathetic, pitiful, piteous, melancholy, sorrowful, unhappy, wretched, woeful, forlorn, woebegone; *literary* dolorous.

plan noun **1** *a plan for raising money* PROCEDURE, scheme, strategy, idea, proposal, proposition, suggestion; project, program, system, method, stratagem, formula, recipe; way, means, measure, tactic.

2 *her plan was to win a medal* INTENTION, aim, idea, intent, objective, object, goal, target, ambition.

3 *plans for the clubhouse* BLUEPRINT, drawing, diagram, sketch, layout; illustration, representation.

▸ verb **1** *plan your route in advance* ORGANIZE, arrange, work out, design, outline, map out, prepare, schedule, formulate, frame, develop, devise, concoct; plot, scheme, hatch, brew, slate.

2 *he plans to buy a house* INTEND, aim, propose, mean, hope, want, wish, desire, envisage; *formal* purpose. See note at INTEND.

3 *I'm planning a new garden* DESIGN, draw up, sketch out, map out.

plane[1] noun **1** *a horizontal plane* FLAT SURFACE, level surface; horizontal.

2 *a higher plane of achievement* LEVEL, degree, standard, stratum; position, rung, echelon.

▸ adjective *a plane surface* FLAT, level, horizontal, even; smooth, regular, uniform; *technical* planar.

▸ verb **1** *seagulls planed overhead* SOAR, glide, float, drift, wheel.

2 *boats planed across the water* SKIM, glide.

plane[2] noun *the plane took off* AIRCRAFT, airplane, airliner, jet, jumbo jet, jetliner, bush plane, float plane, seaplane, crop duster, water bomber; *dated* flying machine.

planet noun *which planets are visible to the naked eye?* CELESTIAL BODY, heavenly body, satellite, moon, earth, asteroid, planetoid; *literary* orb.

plangent adjective *literary a plangent moan from somewhere not too distant* MELANCHOLY, mournful, plaintive; sonorous, resonant, loud.

plank noun *rough wooden planks* BOARD, floorboard, timber, stave.

planning noun *how much planning has gone into this event?* PREPARATION(S), organization, arrangement, design; forethought, groundwork.

plain →
severe
chaste
spartan
austere
stark
bare
unembellished
unostentatious
unornamented
unpretentious
unadorned
unsophisticated
restrained
uncluttered
unfussy
muted
simple
basic
ordinary
without frills
modest
homely
homespun
workaday
penny plain
everyday
undecorated
unpatterned
patternless
of simple design
classic
elegant

aesthetic

decorative
decorated
ornamental
ornamented
embellished
snazzy
jazzy
ritzy
glitzy
showy
flashy
busy
fussy
gaudy
OTT
flamboyant
expensive
deluxe
prime
flash
posh
swish
classy
high-class
luxurious
superior
extravagant
lavish
sumptuous
over the top
elaborate
intricate
ornate
adorned
baroque
rococo
ostentatious
fancy ←

plant noun **1** *garden plants* flower, vegetable, herb, shrub, weed; (**plants**) vegetation, greenery, flora, herbage, verdure.

2 *the plant commenced production* FACTORY, works, foundry, mill, workshop, shop.

3 *a CIA plant* SPY, informant, informer, agent, secret agent, mole, infiltrator, operative; *informal* spook.

▸ verb **1** *plant the seeds this autumn* SOW, scatter, seed; bed out, transplant.

2 *he planted his feet on the ground* PLACE, put, set, position, situate, settle; *informal* plonk.

3 *she planted the idea in his mind* INSTILL, implant, impress, imprint, put, place, introduce, fix, establish, lodge.

4 *letters were planted to embarrass them* HIDE, conceal, secrete.

plaque noun *a plaque in her honor was place on the door to the auditorium* PLATE, tablet, panel, sign, cartouche, brass.

plaster noun **1** *the plaster covering the bricks* PLASTERWORK, stucco, pargeting.

2 *a statuette made of plaster* PLASTER OF PARIS, gypsum.

▸ verb **1** *bread plastered with butter* COVER THICKLY, smother, spread, smear, cake, coat, slather.

2 *his hair was* ***plastered down*** *with sweat* FLATTEN (DOWN), smooth down, slick down.

plastic adjective **1** *at high temperatures the rocks become plastic* MALLEABLE, moldable, pliable, pliant, ductile, flexible, soft, workable, bendable; *informal* bendy. ANTONYM rigid.

2 *the plastic minds of children* IMPRESSIONABLE, malleable, receptive, pliable, pliant, flexible; compliant, tractable, biddable, persuadable, susceptible, manipulable. ANTONYM intractable.

3 *a plastic smile* ARTIFICIAL, false, fake, superficial, pseudo, bogus, unnatural, insincere; *informal* phony, pretend. ANTONYM genuine.

plate noun **1** *a dinner plate* DISH, platter, salver, paten, charger; *historical* trencher.

2 *a plate of spaghetti* PLATEFUL, helping, portion, serving.

3 *steel plates* PANEL, sheet, layer, pane, slab.

4 *a brass plate on the door* PLAQUE, sign, tablet, cartouche.

5 *the book has color plates* PICTURE, print, illustration, photograph, photo.

▸ verb *the roof was plated with steel* COVER, coat, overlay, laminate, veneer; electroplate, galvanize, gild.

plateau noun **1** *a windswept plateau* UPLAND, tableland, plain, mesa, highland, coteau.

2 *prices reached a plateau* quiescent period; letup, respite, lull.

platform noun **1** *he made a speech from the platform* STAGE, dais, rostrum, podium, soapbox.

2 *the party's platform* POLICY, program, party line, manifesto, plan, principles, objectives, aims.

platitude noun *boring us with his platitudes* CLICHÉ, truism, commonplace, banality, old chestnut, bromide, inanity, banal/trite/hackneyed/stock phrase.

platitudinous adjective *platitudinous political sound bites* HACKNEYED, overworked, overused, clichéd, banal, trite, commonplace, well-worn, stale, tired, unoriginal; *informal* corny, old hat. ANTONYM original.

platonic adjective *the roommates' platonic relationship* NONSEXUAL, nonphysical, chaste; intellectual, friendly. ANTONYM sexual.

platoon noun *our platoon lost 200 men on that mission* UNIT, patrol, troop, squad, squadron, team, company, corps, outfit, detachment, contingent.

platter noun *a platter of broiled oysters* PLATE, dish, salver, paten, tray; *historical* trencher.

plaudits plural noun *the mayor won plaudits for his aggressive campaign against crime* PRAISE, acclaim, commendation, congratulations, accolades, compliments, cheers, applause, tributes, bouquets; a pat on the back; *informal* a (big) hand. ANTONYM criticism.

plausible adjective *a plausible explanation* CREDIBLE, reasonable, believable, likely, feasible, tenable, possible, conceivable, imaginable; convincing, persuasive, cogent, sound, rational, logical, thinkable. See note at BELIEVABLE. ANTONYM unlikely.

play verb **1** *Aidan and Robert were playing with their toys* AMUSE ONESELF, entertain oneself, enjoy oneself, have fun; relax, occupy oneself, divert oneself; frolic, frisk, romp, caper; *informal* mess around.

2 *I used to play hockey* TAKE PART IN, participate in, be involved in, compete in, do.

3 *St. Joseph's plays Boston on Sunday* COMPETE AGAINST, take on, challenge, vie with, face, go up against.

4 *he was to play Macbeth* ACT (THE PART OF), take the role of, appear as, portray, depict, impersonate, represent, render, perform, enact; *formal* personate.

5 *get your guitar and let's play* PERFORM, make music, jam.

6 *Bryanna played a note on the flute* MAKE, produce, reproduce; blow, toot; plunk, bang out; sound.

7 *the sunlight played on the water* DANCE, flit, ripple, touch; sparkle, glint.

▸ noun **1** *a balance between work and play* AMUSEMENT, entertainment, relaxation, recreation, diversion, distraction, leisure; enjoyment, pleasure, fun, games, fun and games; horseplay, merrymaking, revelry; *informal* living it up.

2 *a Shakespearean play* DRAMA, theatrical work; screenplay, comedy, tragedy; production, performance, show, sketch.

3 *a new tool came into play* ACTION, activity, operation, working, function; interaction, interplay.

4 *there is foul play afoot* BEHAVIOR, goings-on, activity, action, deed.

5 *there was a little play in the rope* MOVEMENT, slack, give; room to maneuver, scope, latitude.

PHRASES: **play around** *informal he's been playing around for years* WOMANIZE, philander, have affairs, flirt; *informal* carry on, mess around, play the field, sleep around, fool around. **play at being** *she just plays at being the caring one* PRETEND TO BE, pass oneself off as, masquerade as, profess to be, pose as, impersonate; fake, feign, simulate, affect; *informal* make like. **play ball** *informal if you play ball, I can help you* CO-OPERATE, collaborate, play the game, help, lend a hand, assist, contribute; *informal* pitch in. **play down** *officials tried to play down the extent of the damage* MAKE LIGHT OF, make little of, gloss over, de-emphasize, downplay, understate; soft-pedal, tone down, diminish, trivialize, underrate, underestimate, undervalue; disparage, belittle, scoff at, sneer at, shrug off; *informal* pooh-pooh. **play for time** *Nesmith's opponents accused him of playing for time in order to pull an election-year coup* STALL, temporize, delay, hold back, hang fire, procrastinate, drag one's feet. **play it by ear** *when a guest doesn't show up for live radio, you learn quickly how to play it by ear* IMPROVISE, extemporize, ad lib; *informal* wing it. **play on** *they play on our fears* EXPLOIT, take advantage of, use, turn to (one's) account, profit by, capitalize on, trade on, milk, abuse. **play the fool** *by the time she was ten, Ronnie knew it was her God-given job to play the fool* CLOWN AROUND, fool around, mess around, monkey around, joke; *informal* horse around. **play the game** *you find out early on who's willing to play the game, and that's the kind of person this company holds on to* PLAY FAIR, be fair, play by the rules, conform, be a good sport, toe the line. **play up** *his agents really play up the story of his rise from poverty* EMPHASIZE, accentuate, call attention to, point up, underline, highlight, spotlight, foreground, feature, stress, accent. **play up to** *wannabes who play up to the boss* INGRATIATE ONESELF WITH, curry favor with, court, fawn over, make up to, toady to, crawl to, pander to, flatter; *informal* soft-soap, suck up to, butter up, lick someone's boots.

playboy noun *he claims his days as a playboy are over* SOCIALITE, pleasure-seeker, sybarite; ladies' man, womanizer, philanderer, wolf, rake, roué; *informal* ladykiller.

player noun **1** *a tournament for young players* PARTICIPANT, contestant, competitor, contender; sportsman/woman, athlete.

2 *the players in the orchestra* MUSICIAN, performer, instrumentalist, soloist, virtuoso.

3 *the players at the Shaw Festival* ACTOR, actress, performer, thespian, entertainer, artist/artiste, trouper.

playful adjective **1** *a playful mood* FRISKY, jolly, lively, full of fun, frolicsome, sportive, high-spirited, exuberant, perky; mischievous, impish, clownish, kittenish, rascally, tricksy; *informal* full of beans; *formal* ludic. ANTONYM solemn.

2 *a playful remark* LIGHTHEARTED, in jest, joking, jokey, teasing, humorous, jocular, good-natured, tongue-in-cheek, facetious, frivolous, flippant, arch; *informal* waggish. ANTONYM serious.

playground noun *they need more supervision on the playground* PLAY AREA, park, playing field, recreation ground.

playmate noun *Stanley and a playmate were caught with a book of matches* FRIEND, companion.

plaything noun *a child's plaything* TOY, game.

playwright noun *we're reading the works of Simon and other modern playwrights* DRAMATIST, dramaturge, scriptwriter, screenwriter, writer, scenarist; tragedian.

plea noun **1** *a plea for aid* APPEAL, entreaty, supplication, petition, request, call, suit, solicitation.

2 *her plea of a headache was unconvincing* CLAIM, explanation, defense, justification; excuse, pretext.

plead verb **1** *he **pleaded with** her to stay* BEG, implore, entreat, appeal to, supplicate, importune, petition, request, ask, call on; *literary* beseech. See note at BEG.

2 *she pleaded ignorance* CLAIM, use as an excuse, assert, allege, argue, state.

pleasant adjective 1 *a pleasant evening* ENJOYABLE, pleasurable, nice, agreeable, pleasing, satisfying, gratifying, good; entertaining, amusing, delightful, charming; fine, balmy; *informal* lovely, great.

2 *the staff are pleasant* FRIENDLY, agreeable, amiable, nice, genial, cordial, likable, amicable, good-humored, good-natured, personable; hospitable, approachable, gracious, courteous, polite, obliging, helpful, considerate; charming, lovely, delightful, sweet, sympathetic, simpatico. ANTONYM disagreeable.

THE RIGHT WORD

One might have a **pleasant** smile and a **pleasing** personality, since the former suggests something that is naturally appealing while the latter suggests a conscious attempt to please. Something that is **enjoyable** is able to give enjoyment or pleasure (*a thoroughly enjoyable evening*), while **agreeable** describes something that is in harmony with one's personal mood or wishes (*an agreeable afternoon spent relaxing in the sun*). **Gratifying** is more intense, suggesting that deeper expectations or needs have been met (*the awards ceremony was particularly gratifying for parents*). Something that is **attractive** gives pleasure because of its appearance or manner (*an attractive house in a wooded setting*), while **congenial** has more to do with compatibility (*a congenial couple*).

pleasantry noun 1 *we exchanged pleasantries* BANTER, badinage; polite remark, casual remark.

2 *he laughed at his own pleasantry* JOKE, witticism, quip, jest, gag, bon mot; *informal* wisecrack, crack.

please verb 1 *he'd do anything to please her* MAKE HAPPY, give pleasure to, make someone feel good; delight, charm, amuse, entertain; satisfy, gratify, humor, oblige, content, suit. ANTONYM annoy.

2 *do as you please* LIKE, want, wish, desire, see fit, think fit, choose, will, prefer.

▸ adverb *please sit down* IF YOU PLEASE, if you wouldn't mind, if you would be so good; kindly, pray; *archaic* prithee.

pleased adjective *Edward seemed really pleased to see me* HAPPY, glad, delighted, gratified, grateful, thankful, content, contented, satisfied; thrilled, elated, overjoyed; *informal* over the moon, tickled pink, on cloud nine. ANTONYM unhappy.

pleasing adjective 1 *a pleasing day* NICE, agreeable, pleasant, pleasurable, satisfying, gratifying, good, enjoyable, entertaining, amusing, delightful; *informal* lovely, great; *Brit. informal* cushty. See note at PLEASANT.

2 *her pleasing manner* FRIENDLY, amiable, pleasant, agreeable, affable, nice, genial, likable, good-humored, charming, engaging, delightful; *informal* lovely, simpatico.

pleasurable adjective *a pleasurable visit to Aunt Mae's garden* PLEASANT, enjoyable, delightful, nice, pleasing, agreeable, gratifying; fun, entertaining, amusing, diverting; *informal* lovely, great; *Brit. informal* cushty.

pleasure noun 1 *she smiled with pleasure* HAPPINESS, delight, joy, gladness, glee, satisfaction, gratification, contentment, enjoyment, amusement.

2 *his greatest pleasures in life* JOY, amusement, diversion, recreation, pastime; treat, thrill.

3 *don't mix business and pleasure* ENJOYMENT, fun, entertainment; recreation, leisure, relaxation; *informal* jollies.

4 *a life of pleasure* HEDONISM, indulgence, self-indulgence, self-gratification, lotus-eating.

5 *what's your pleasure?* WISH, desire, preference, will, inclination, choice. PHRASES: **take pleasure in** *we're still healthy enough to take pleasure in our retirement years* ENJOY, delight in, love, like, adore, appreciate, relish, savor, revel in, glory in; *informal* get a kick out of, get a thrill out of. **with pleasure** *certainly I can give you a ride, with pleasure* GLADLY, willingly, happily, readily; by all means, of course; *archaic* fain.

pleat noun *a curtain pleat* FOLD, crease, gather, tuck, crimp; pucker.

▸ verb *the dress is pleated at the front* FOLD, crease, gather, tuck, crimp; pucker.

plebeian noun *plebeians and gentry lived together* PROLETARIAN, commoner, working-class person, worker; peasant; *informal* pleb, prole. ANTONYM aristocrat.

▸ adjective 1 *people of plebeian descent* LOWER-CLASS, working-class, proletarian, common, peasant; mean, humble, lowly. ANTONYM noble.

2 *plebeian tastes* UNCULTURED, uncultivated, unrefined, lowbrow, philistine, uneducated; coarse, uncouth, common, vulgar. ANTONYM refined.

plebiscite noun *a plebiscite for the approval of constitutional reforms* VOTE, referendum, ballot, poll.

pledge noun 1 *his election pledge* PROMISE, undertaking, vow, word, word of honor, commitment, assurance, oath, guarantee.

2 *he gave it as a pledge to a creditor* SURETY, bond, security, collateral, guarantee, deposit.

3 *a pledge of my sincerity* TOKEN, symbol, sign, earnest, mark, testimony, proof, evidence.

▸ verb 1 *he pledged to root out corruption* PROMISE, vow, swear, undertake, engage, commit oneself, declare, affirm, avow.

2 *they pledged $10 million* PROMISE (TO GIVE), donate, contribute, give, put up.

3 *his home is pledged as security against the loan* MORTGAGE, put up as collateral, guarantee, pawn.

plenary adjective 1 *the council has plenary powers in this matter* UNCONDITIONAL, unlimited, unrestricted, unqualified, absolute, sweeping, comprehensive; plenipotentiary.

2 *a plenary session of the parliament* FULL, complete, entire.

plenipotentiary noun *a plenipotentiary in Paris* DIPLOMAT, dignitary, ambassador, minister, emissary, chargé d'affaires, envoy.

▸ adjective *plenipotentiary powers.* See PLENARY sense 1.

plenitude noun *formal Lord, we are so thankful for this plenitude* ABUNDANCE, lot, wealth, profusion, cornucopia, superabundance; *informal* load, slew, heap, ton.

plenteous adjective *literary* See PLENTIFUL.

plentiful adjective *a plentiful supply of food* ABUNDANT, copious, ample, profuse, rich, lavish, generous, bountiful, large, great, bumper, superabundant, inexhaustible, prolific; *informal* galore; *literary* plenteous. See note at PREVALENT. ANTONYM scarce.

plenty noun *times of plenty* PROSPERITY, affluence, wealth, opulence, comfort, luxury; plentifulness, abundance; *literary* plenteousness.

▸ pronoun *there are* ***plenty of*** *books* A LOT OF, many, a great deal of, enough (and to spare), no lack of, sufficient, a wealth of; *informal* loads of, lots of, heaps of, stacks of, masses of, tons of, oodles of, scads of, a slew of.

plethora noun *a plethora of opinion polls* EXCESS, overabundance, superabundance, surplus, glut, superfluity, surfeit, profusion; **(a plethora of)**, too many, too much, enough and to spare; *informal* more —— than one can shake a stick at. ANTONYM dearth.

USAGE NOTE **plethora**

According to the *Oxford English Dictionary* (OED) and most other dictionaries, this word refers (and has always referred) to an overabundance, an overfullness, or an excess. The phrase *a plethora of* is essentially a highfalutin equivalent of *too many*—e.g.: "Our electoral politics now is beset with a plethora of [read *too many*] players and a confusing clutter of messages." (*Brookings Review*; Jan. 1, 2002.) But sometimes, when not preceded by the indefinite article, the word is genuinely useful—e.g.: "Critics say the plethora of scrip circulating in Argentina risks running out of control." (*Wall Street Journal*; Dec. 26, 2001.)

Unfortunately, through misunderstanding of the word's true sense, many writers use it as if it were equivalent to *plenty* or *many*. This meaning is unrecorded in the OED and in most other dictionaries. And it represents an unfortunate degeneration of sense—e.g.:

- "Buffalo may seem like a boring city, but we've managed to produce a plethora [read *plenty*] of famous people, the Goo Goo Dolls, Ani Difranco, David Boreanaz and now, Chad Murray." (*Buffalo News*; Jan. 8, 2002.)
- "The old policies did not anticipate a plethora [read *series* or *group* or *lot*] of suicide bombers." (*Orlando Sentinel*; Jan. 10, 2002.) (One suicide bomber is too many—so plethora doesn't work.)

Phrases such as *a whole plethora of* are likewise ill-considered—e.g.: "Then, once you get to the airport ticket counter, there's a whole plethora [read *a whole range* or *a wide variety*] of biometric identifiers you could use to tie the background checks you've done to the individuals who present themselves at the ticket counter." (*Boston Globe*; Jan. 6, 2002.)

The word is pronounced /**pleth**-er-uh/, not /pluh-**thor**-uh/. **—BG**

pliable adjective **1** *leather is pliable* FLEXIBLE, pliant, bendable, elastic, supple, malleable, workable, plastic, springy, ductile; *informal* bendy. See note at FLEXIBLE. ANTONYM rigid.

2 *pliable teenage minds* MALLEABLE, impressionable, flexible, adaptable, pliant, compliant, biddable, tractable, yielding, amenable, susceptible, suggestible, persuadable, manipulable, receptive. ANTONYM obdurate.

pliant adjective See PLIABLE senses 1, 2. See also note at FLEXIBLE.

plight noun *the plight of the homeless* PREDICAMENT, quandary, difficult situation, dire straits, trouble, difficulty, extremity, bind; *informal* dilemma, tight corner, tight spot, hole, pickle, jam, fix.

plod verb **1** *Mom plodded wearily upstairs* TRUDGE, walk heavily, clump, stomp, tramp, tromp, lumber, slog.

2 *I have to plod through the whole book* WADE, plow, trawl, toil, labor; *informal* slog.

plot noun **1** *a plot to overthrow him* CONSPIRACY, intrigue, secret plan; machinations.

2 *the plot of her novel* STORY LINE, story, scenario, action, thread; *formal* diegesis.

3 *a three-acre plot* PIECE OF GROUND, patch, area, tract, acreage, allotment, lot, plat, homesite.

▸ verb **1** *he plotted their downfall* PLAN, scheme, arrange, organize, hatch, concoct, devise, dream up; *informal* cook up.

2 *his brother was plotting against him* CONSPIRE, scheme, intrigue, collude, connive, machinate.

3 *the fifty-three sites were plotted* MARK, chart, map, represent, graph.

THE RIGHT WORD

If you come up with a secret plan to do something, especially with evil or mischievous intent, it's called a **plot** (*a plot to seize control of the company*). If you get other people or groups involved in your plot, it's called a **conspiracy** (*a conspiracy to overthrow the government*). **Cabal** usually applies to a small group of political conspirators (*a cabal of right-wing extremists*), while **machination** (usually plural) suggests deceit and cunning in devising a plot intended to harm someone (*the machinations of the would-be assassins*). An **intrigue** involves more complicated scheming or maneuvering than a plot and often employs underhanded methods in an attempt to gain one's own ends (*she had a passion for intrigue, particularly where romance was involved*).

plotter noun *his fellow plotter was a disgruntled former employee of the mill* CONSPIRATOR, schemer, intriguer, machinator; planner.

plow verb **1** *the fields were plowed* TILL, furrow, harrow, cultivate, work, break up.

2 *the streets haven't been plowed yet* CLEAR (OF SNOW), shovel.

3 *the car plowed into a telephone pole* CRASH, smash, career, plunge, bulldoze, hurtle, careen, cannon, run, drive, barrel.

4 *they plowed through deep snow* TRUDGE, plod, toil, wade; *informal* slog.

ploy noun *perhaps this had been a ploy to revive her husband's fading interest* RUSE, tactic, move, device, stratagem, scheme, trick, gambit, plan, maneuver, dodge, subterfuge, wile.

pluck verb **1** *he plucked a thread from his lapel* REMOVE, pick (off), pull (off/out), extract, take (off).

2 *she* ***plucked at*** *his T-shirt* PULL (AT), tug (at), clutch (at), snatch (at), grab, catch (at), tweak, jerk; *informal* yank.

3 *the turkeys have been plucked* DEPLUME, remove the feathers from.

4 *Jen plucked the guitar strings* STRUM, pick, plunk, thrum, twang; play pizzicato.

▸ noun *saying those things to her took a lot of pluck* COURAGE, bravery, nerve, backbone, spine, daring, spirit, intrepidity, fearlessness, mettle, grit, true grit, determination, fortitude, resolve, stout-heartedness, dauntlessness, valor, heroism, audacity; *informal* guts, spunk, gumption, moxie. See note at COURAGE.

plucky adjective *these plucky young players are still about* *the game, not about the money* BRAVE, courageous, bold, daring, fearless, intrepid, spirited, game, valiant, valorous, stouthearted, dauntless, resolute, determined, undaunted, unflinching, audacious, unafraid, doughty, mettlesome; *informal* gutsy, spunky. ANTONYM timid.

plug noun **1** *she pulled out the plug* STOPPER, bung, cork, seal, spile.

2 *a plug of tobacco* WAD, quid, twist, chew, cake, stick.

3 *informal a plug for her new book* ADVERTISEMENT, promotion, commercial, recommendation, mention, good word; *informal* hype, push, puff piece, ad, boost, ballyhoo.

▸ verb **1** *plug the holes* STOP (UP), seal (up/off), close (up/off), cork, stopper, bung, block (up/off), fill (up).

2 *informal she plugged her new film* PUBLICIZE, promote, advertise, mention, bang the drum for, draw attention to; *informal* hype (up), push, puff.

3 *informal don't move or I'll plug you* SHOOT, gun down; *informal* blast, fill/pump full of lead.

PHRASE: **plug away** *informal he plugged away at his novel, unaware of the day or the time* TOIL, labor, slave away, soldier on, persevere, persist, keep on; *informal* slog away, beaver away.

plum adjective *informal a plum job* EXCELLENT, very good, wonderful, marvelous, choice, first-class; *informal* great, terrific, cushy.

plumb verb *an attempt to plumb her psyche* EXPLORE, probe, delve into, search, examine, investigate, fathom, penetrate, understand.

▸ adverb **1** *informal it went plumb through the screen* RIGHT, exactly, precisely, directly, dead, straight; *informal* bang.

2 *informal I plumb forgot* COMPLETELY, absolutely, downright, totally, quite, thoroughly.

3 *the bell hangs plumb* VERTICALLY, perpendicularly, straight down.

▸ adjective *a plumb drop* VERTICAL, perpendicular, straight.

PHRASE: **plumb the depth of** *she had plumbed the depths of depravity* FIND, experience the extremes of, reach the lowest point of; reach rock bottom of.

plume noun *ostrich plumes* FEATHER, quill; *Ornithology* plumule, covert.

plummet verb **1** *the plane plummeted to the ground* PLUNGE, nosedive, dive, drop, fall, descend, hurtle.

2 *share prices plummeted* FALL STEEPLY, plunge, tumble, drop rapidly, go down, slump; *informal* crash, nosedive.

plump adjective *a plump child* CHUBBY, fat, stout, rotund, well padded, ample, full-figured, pillowy, round, chunky, portly, overweight, fleshy, paunchy, bulky, corpulent; *rare* pulvinate; *informal* tubby, roly-poly, pudgy, beefy, porky, zaftig, corn-fed. ANTONYM thin.

WORD NOTE pulvinate, pulvinated

When seeking adjectives for soft, rounded things—especially on a woman's body—we too often fall at the first hurdle and choose the very tired Mills and Boon favorite, *pillowy.* And yet there is a ready-made word for the occasion; Latinate, graceful, specifically intended for things that are cushiony and cushionlike, that swell and bulge. The *pulvinated* face of a drunk, the *pulvinate* curve of your lover's breast . . . Much better. **—ZS**

plunder verb **1** *they plundered the countryside* PILLAGE, loot, rob, raid, ransack, despoil, strip, ravage, lay waste, devastate, sack, rape. See note at RAVAGE.

2 *money plundered from pension funds* STEAL, purloin, thieve, seize, pillage; embezzle.

▸ noun **1** *the plunder of the villages* LOOTING, pillaging, plundering, raiding, ransacking, devastation, sacking; *literary* rapine.

2 *the army took huge quantities of plunder* BOOTY, loot, stolen goods, spoils, ill-gotten gains; *informal* swag.

plunge verb **1** *Joy plunged into the sea* DIVE, jump, throw oneself, launch oneself.

2 *the aircraft plunged to the ground* PLUMMET, nosedive, drop, fall, pitch, tumble, descend, dive-bomb.

3 *the car plunged down an alley* CHARGE, hurtle, career, plow, cannon, tear; *informal* barrel.

4 *oil prices plunged* FALL SHARPLY, plummet, drop, go down, tumble, slump; *informal* crash, nosedive.

5 *he plunged the dagger into her back* THRUST, jab, stab, sink, stick, ram, drive, push, shove, force.

6 *plunge the pears into boiling water* IMMERSE, submerge, dip, dunk.

7 *the room was plunged into darkness* THROW, cast, pitch.

▸ noun **1** *a plunge into the deep end* DIVE, jump, nosedive, fall, pitch, drop, plummet, descent.

2 *a plunge in profits* FALL, drop, slump; *informal* nosedive, crash.

PHRASE: **take the plunge** *she decided to take the plunge and headed for Hollywood* COMMIT ONESELF, go for it, do the deed, throw caution to the wind(s), risk it; *informal* jump in at the deep end, go for broke.

plurality noun **1** *a plurality of theories* WIDE VARIETY, diversity, range, lot, multitude, multiplicity, galaxy, wealth, profusion, abundance, host; *informal* load, stack, heap, mass.

2 *in the plurality of cases* PREPONDERANCE, bulk, largest number; majority.

plus preposition **1** *three plus three makes six* AND, added to. ANTONYM minus.

2 *he wrote four novels plus various poems* AS WELL AS, together with, along with, in addition to, and, not to mention, besides.

▸ noun *one of the pluses of the job* ADVANTAGE, good point, asset, pro, (fringe) benefit, bonus, extra, attraction; *informal* perk; *formal* perquisite. ANTONYM disadvantage.

plush adjective *informal the car's plush interior* LUXURIOUS, luxury, deluxe, sumptuous, palatial, lavish, opulent, magnificent, lush, rich, expensive, fancy, grand, upscale, upmarket; *informal* posh, ritzy, swanky, classy, swank. ANTONYM austere.

plutocrat noun *champagne-swilling plutocrats* RICH PERSON, magnate, millionaire, billionaire, multimillionaire; nouveau riche; *informal* fat cat, moneybags.

ply[1] verb **1** *the gondolier plied his oar* USE, wield, work, manipulate, handle, operate, utilize, employ.

2 *he plied a profitable trade* ENGAGE IN, carry on, pursue, conduct, practice; *archaic* prosecute.

3 *ferries ply between all lake resorts* GO REGULARLY, travel, shuttle, go back and forth.

4 *she plied me with chocolate chip cookies* PROVIDE, supply, lavish, shower, regale.

5 *he plied her with questions* BOMBARD, assail, beset, pester, plague, harass, importune; *informal* hassle, devil.

ply[2] noun *a three-ply tissue* LAYER, thickness, strand, sheet, leaf.

poach verb **1** *he's been poaching salmon* HUNT ILLEGALLY, catch illegally, jacklight, jack; steal.

2 *workers were poached by other firms* STEAL, appropriate, purloin, take, lure away; *informal* nab, swipe, pinch.

pocket noun **1** *a bag with two pockets* POUCH, compartment.

2 *these donors have deep pockets* MEANS, budget, resources, finances, funds, money, wherewithal, pocketbook.

3 *pockets of disaffection* AREA, patch, region, isolated area, island, cluster, center.

▸ adjective *a pocket dictionary* SMALL, little, miniature, mini, compact, concise, abridged, portable, vest-pocket.

▸ verb *he pocketed $900,000 of their money* STEAL, take, appropriate, thieve, purloin, misappropriate, embezzle; *informal* filch, swipe, pinch.

pockmark noun *did he have any distinguishing characteristics, such as facial pockmarks?* SCAR, pit, pock, mark, blemish.

pod noun *the seeds are formed inside a pod* SHELL, husk, hull, case; shuck; *Botany* pericarp, capsule.

podium noun *he was a natural-born speaker, in his glory up at the podium* PLATFORM, stage, dais, rostrum, stand, soapbox.

poem noun *Lydia saved every poem that Marshall wrote that year* VERSE, rhyme, piece of poetry, song.

poet noun *she has the soul of a poet* WRITER OF POETRY, versifier, rhymester, rhymer, sonneteer, lyricist, lyrist; laureate; *literary* bard; *derogatory* poetaster; *historical* troubadour, balladeer.

poetic adjective **1** *poetic compositions* POETICAL, verse, metrical, lyrical, lyric, elegiac.

2 *poetic language* EXPRESSIVE, figurative, symbolic, flowery, artistic, elegant, fine, beautiful; sensitive, imaginative, creative.

poetry noun *a book of Jimmy Carter's poetry* POEMS, verse, versification, metrical composition, rhymes, balladry; *archaic* poesy. See also table.

WORD NOTE **poetry**

Poetry and *prose* are supposed to be opposites. Poetry is to dancing as prose is to walking, wrote Paul Valéry. Poetry is gratuitously beautiful, prose is functional, utilitarian. Or poetry is patrician and prose plebeian, pedestrian. Poetry is special, prose is ordinary, with the proviso that poetry can, like the word *special,* itself become commonplace, as in the mass-produced verse on a birthday card.

Yet it is in the prosaic walks of life that the word *poetic* has done much of its duty, complimenting the oratory of a politician, the grace of an athlete, the drama of a big game or a fabled competition. On the eve of the decisive seventh game of the 2003 American League Championship Series, which pitted the Boston Red Sox against their bitter rivals the New York Yankees, Theo Epstein, the Boston team's general manager, said, "It's definitely appropriate, definitely meant to be, and certainly poetic."

Poetry in this sense is a quality that exists independent of the art form that it names. And just to make things a little more complicated, the field of poetry itself comprises two categories, *verse* and *prose.* Most poems are in verse, but the prose poem, a seeming oxymoron, has flourished in France since Charles Baudelaire initiated it in 1862 and has more recently caught on in the United States. There is really only one salient difference between prose and verse. Verse is in lines—the lengths and endings of which are determined by the author. Prose is in sentences, the print running to the end of the page. Prose proceeds; verse reverses.

Now, with the general recognition of the validity of the prose poem, the turn at the end of the line that is definitive of verse has turned out to be an adjunct of poetry, no more indispensable than rhyme and meter had been. Is that a good or a bad thing? In a permissive age, the prose poem becomes just one more option for the poet. But rhyme, meter, and verse forms retain their appeal and will continue to do so, in some periods with great force. How can I be so sure? I think of U.S. Poet Laureate Louise Glück admirably terse reply when asked why she felt confident that poetry would survive the age of electronic media. "It has lasted this long," she said. **—DL**

POETIC FORMS, METERS, AND FEET

alexandrine	iamb
anapest	iambic
aubade	idyll
ballad	lay
ballade	limerick
blank verse	lyric
choriamb	madrigal
choriambic	monody
dactyl	ode
dactylic	pastoral
decasyllable	pentameter
dimeter	Petrarchan sonnet
dirge	prothalamion
disyllable	rondeau
dithyramb	roundel
dramatic monologue	roundelay
eclogue	saga
elegy	sapphics
encomium	satire
epic	sestina
epigram	sonnet
epithalamium	spondee
epode	tanka
epyllion	tetrameter
free verse	threnody
georgic	trimeter
ghazal	triolet
haiku	trochaics
heptameter	trochee
heroic	virelay
hexameter	

pogrom noun *how is that every civilized nation has not formally denounced this pogrom?* MASSACRE, slaughter, mass murder, annihilation, extermination, decimation, carnage, bloodbath, bloodletting, butchery, genocide, holocaust, purge, ethnic cleansing.

poignancy noun *his imminent death gave his words a special poignancy* PATHOS, pitifulness, piteousness, sadness, sorrow, mournfulness, wretchedness, misery, tragedy.

poignant adjective *they read aloud the poignant letters written by the victims' children* TOUCHING, moving, sad, affecting, pitiful, piteous, pathetic, sorrowful, mournful, wretched, miserable, distressing, heart-rending, tearjerking, plaintive, tragic. See note at MOVING.

point[1] noun **1** *the point of a needle* TIP, (sharp) end, extremity; prong, spike, tine, nib, barb.

2 *points of light* PINPOINT, dot, spot, speck, fleck.

3 *a meeting point* PLACE, position, location, site, spot, area.

4 *this point in her life* TIME, stage, juncture, period, phase.

5 *the tension had reached such a high point* LEVEL, degree, stage, pitch, extent.

6 *an important point* DETAIL, item, fact, thing, argument, consideration, factor, element; subject, issue, topic, question, matter.

7 *get to the point* HEART OF THE MATTER, most important part, essence, nub, keynote, core, pith, crux; meaning, significance, gist, substance, thrust, bottom line, burden, relevance; *informal* brass tacks, nitty-gritty.

8 *what's the point of this?* PURPOSE, aim, object, objective, goal, intention; use, sense, value, advantage.

9 *he had his good points* ATTRIBUTE, characteristic, feature, trait, quality, property, aspect, side.

▸ verb **1** *she pointed the gun at him* AIM, direct, level, train.

2 *the evidence* ***pointed to*** *his guilt* INDICATE, suggest, evidence, signal, signify, denote, bespeak, reveal, manifest.

PHRASES: **beside the point** *those accusations are beside the point* IRRELEVANT, immaterial, unimportant, neither here nor there, inconsequential, incidental, out of place, unconnected, peripheral, tangential, extraneous. **in point of fact** *in point of fact, all three of these gentlemen have immaculate service records* IN FACT, as a matter of fact, actually, in actual fact, really, in reality, as it happens, in truth. **make a point of** *she made a point of letting us know she was recently divorced* MAKE AN EFFORT TO, go out of one's way to, put emphasis on. **on the point of** *we were on the point of quitting, but something kept us going* (JUST) ABOUT TO (BE), on the verge of, on the brink of, going to (be), all set to (be). **point of view** *we have different points of view* OPINION, view, belief, attitude, feeling, sentiment, thoughts; position, perspective, viewpoint, standpoint, outlook. **point out** *the flaws in the plan have already been pointed out* IDENTIFY, show, designate, draw attention to, indicate, specify, detail, mention. **point up** *it's as if he deliberately points up every negative aspect of our work* EMPHASIZE, highlight, draw attention to, accentuate, underline, spotlight, foreground, put emphasis on, stress, play up, accent, bring to the fore. **to the point** *his observations were concise and to the point* RELEVANT, pertinent, apposite, germane, applicable, apropos, appropriate, apt, fitting, suitable, material; *formal* ad rem. **up to a point** *I agree with you, but only up to a point* PARTLY, to some extent, to a certain degree, in part, somewhat, partially.

point[2] noun *the ship rounded the point* PROMONTORY, headland, foreland, cape, spit, peninsula, bluff, ness, horn.

point-blank adverb **1** *he fired the pistol point-blank* AT CLOSE RANGE, close up, close to.

2 *she couldn't say it point-blank* BLUNTLY, directly, straight, frankly, candidly, openly, explicitly, unequivocally, unambiguously, plainly, flatly, categorically, outright.

▸ adjective *a point-blank refusal* BLUNT, direct, straight, straightforward, frank, candid, forthright, explicit, unequivocal, plain, clear, flat, decisive, unqualified, categorical, outright.

pointed adjective **1** *a pointed stick* SHARP, tapering, tapered, conical, jagged, spiky, spiked, barbed; *informal* pointy.

2 *a pointed remark* CUTTING, trenchant, biting, incisive, acerbic, caustic, scathing, venomous, sarcastic; *informal* snarky.

pointer noun **1** *the pointer moved to 100 mph* INDICATOR, needle, arrow, hand.

2 *he used a pointer on the chart* STICK, rod, cane; cursor.

3 *a pointer to the outcome of the election* INDICATION, indicator, clue, hint, sign, signal, evidence, intimation, inkling, suggestion.

4 *I can give you a few pointers* TIP, hint, suggestion, guideline, recommendation.

pointless adjective *our attempts to help Ryan were pointless* SENSELESS, futile, hopeless, fruitless, useless, needless, in vain, unavailing, aimless, idle, worthless, valueless; absurd, insane, stupid, silly, foolish. ANTONYM valuable.

poise noun **1** *poise and good deportment* GRACE, gracefulness, elegance, balance, control.

2 *in spite of the setback she retained her poise* COMPOSURE, equanimity, self-possession, aplomb, presence of mind, self-assurance, self-control, nerve, calm, sangfroid, dignity; *informal* cool, unflappability.

▸ verb **1** *she was poised on one foot* BALANCE, hold (oneself) steady, be suspended, remain motionless, hang, hover.

2 *he was poised for action* PREPARE ONESELF, ready oneself, brace oneself, gear oneself up, stand by.

poison noun **1** *a deadly poison* TOXIN, toxicant, venom; *archaic* bane.

2 *Marianne would spread her poison* MALICE, ill will, hate, malevolence, bitterness, spite, spitefulness, venom, acrimony, rancor; bad influence, cancer, corruption, pollution.

▸ verb **1** *her mother poisoned her* GIVE POISON TO; murder.

2 *a blackmailer poisoning pet food* CONTAMINATE, put poison in, envenom, adulterate, spike, lace, doctor.

3 *the Amazon is being poisoned* POLLUTE, contaminate, taint, blight, spoil; *literary* befoul.

4 *they poisoned his mind* PREJUDICE, bias, jaundice, embitter, sour, envenom, warp, corrupt, subvert.

poisonous adjective **1** *a poisonous snake* VENOMOUS, deadly. ANTONYM harmless.

2 *a poisonous chemical* TOXIC, noxious, deadly, fatal, lethal, mortal, death-dealing. ANTONYMS harmless, nontoxic.

3 *a poisonous glance* MALICIOUS, malevolent, hostile, vicious, spiteful, bitter, venomous, vindictive, vitriolic, rancorous, malign, pernicious, mean, nasty; *informal* bitchy, catty. ANTONYM benevolent.

poke verb **1** *she poked him in the ribs* PROD, jab, dig, nudge, butt, shove, jolt, stab, stick.

2 *leave the cable* ***poking out*** STICK OUT, jut out, protrude, project, extend.

▸ noun *give him a poke* PROD, jab, dig, elbow, nudge, shove, stab.

PHRASES: **poke around/about** *we were just poking around some antique shops* SEARCH, hunt, rummage (around), forage, grub, root about/around, scavenge, nose around, ferret (about/around); sift through, rifle through, scour, comb, probe. **poke fun at** *I never meant to poke fun at you* MOCK, make fun of, ridicule, laugh at, jeer at, sneer at, deride, scorn, scoff at, pillory, lampoon, tease, taunt, chaff, jibe at; *informal* send up, kid, rib, goof on. **poke one's nose into** *maybe Barry should stop poking his nose into other people's lives* PRY INTO, interfere in, intrude on, butt into, meddle with; *informal* snoop into.

poker noun See table.

POKER

Poker Hands	Cincinnati
royal flush	cowpie
straight flush	double-draw
four of a kind	English stud
full house	five-card draw
flush	follow the queen
straight	guts
three of a kind	have a heart
two pairs	Howdy Doody
one pair	jacks to open, trips to win
high card	Lame Brain Pete
Poker Games	Mexican stud
all for one/one for all	Omaha hold 'em
anaconda	second hand high
auction	seven-card stud
baseball	spit in the ocean
Canadian stud	Texas hold 'em
Chicago	trees

poky adjective *his poky old horse.* See SLOW adjective sense 1.

polar adjective **1** *polar regions* ARCTIC, Antarctic, circumpolar, Nearctic.

2 *polar conditions* COLD, freezing, icy, glacial, chilly, gelid, hypothermic.

3 *polar opposites* OPPOSITE, opposed, dichotomous, extreme, contrary, contradictory, antithetical.

polarity noun *the marked polarity of their political positions* DIFFERENCE, dichotomy, separation, opposition, contradiction, antithesis, antagonism.

pole[1] noun *gulls like to perch atop the poles* POST, pillar; telephone pole, utility pole; stanchion, paling, stake, stick, support, prop, batten, bar, rail, rod, beam; staff, stave, cane, baton.

pole[2] noun *points of view at opposite poles* EXTREMITY, extreme, limit, antipode. PHRASE: **poles apart** *it would seem that our priorities are poles apart* COMPLETELY DIFFERENT, directly opposed, antithetical, incompatible, irreconcilable, worlds apart, at opposite extremes.

polemic noun **1** *a polemic against injustice* DIATRIBE, invective, rant, tirade, broadside, attack, harangue, condemnation, criticism, stricture, admonition, rebuke; abuse; *informal* blast; *formal* castigation; *literary* philippic.

2 **(polemics)** *he is skilled in polemics* ARGUMENTATION, argument, debate, contention, disputation, discussion, altercation; *formal* contestation.

▸ adjective *his famous polemic book.* See POLEMICAL.

polemical adjective *polemic essays from the Vietnam era* CRITICAL, hostile, bitter, polemic, virulent, vitriolic, venomous, caustic, trenchant, cutting, acerbic, sardonic, sarcastic, scathing, sharp, incisive, devastating.

police noun *we phoned the police as soon as we heard the collision* POLICE FORCE, police officers, policemen, policewomen, officers of the law, law officers, authorities, constabulary; *informal* COPS, fuzz, law, long arm of the law, boys/men in blue; coppers, force, heat.

▸ verb **1** *we must police the area* GUARD, watch over, protect, defend, patrol; control, regulate.

2 *the regulations will be policed by the ministry* ENFORCE, regulate, oversee, supervise, monitor, observe, check.

police officer noun *she ran out of the store, hoping to find a police officer nearby* POLICEMAN, POLICEWOMAN, officer, officer of the law, law officer, patrolman; constable, sergeant, inspector, corporal, captain, lieutenant, superintendent; *informal* COP, flatfoot, copper.

policy noun **1** *government policy* PLANS, strategy, stratagem, approach, code, system, guidelines, theory; line, position, stance, attitude.

2 *it's good policy to listen to your elders* PRACTICE, custom, idea, procedure, conduct, convention.

polish verb **1** *I polished his shoes* SHINE, wax, buff, rub up/down; gloss, burnish; varnish, oil, glaze, lacquer, japan, shellac.

2 ***polish up*** *your essay* PERFECT, refine, improve, hone, enhance; brush up, revise, edit, correct, rewrite, go over, touch up; *informal* clean up.

▸ noun **1** *furniture polish* WAX, glaze, varnish; lacquer, japan, shellac.

2 *a good surface polish* SHINE, gloss, luster, sheen, sparkle, patina, finish.

3 *his polish made him stand out* SOPHISTICATION, refinement, urbanity, suaveness, elegance, style, grace, finesse, cultivation, civility, gentility, breeding, courtesy, (good) manners; *informal* class.

PHRASE: **polish off** *informal* **1** *he polished off an apple pie* EAT, finish, consume, devour, guzzle, wolf down, down, bolt; drink up, drain, quaff, gulp (down), binge on, gorge on; *informal* stuff oneself with, put away, scoff, shovel down, pig out on, swill, knock back, scarf (down/up). **2** *the enemy tried to polish him off* DESTROY, finish off, dispatch, do away with, eliminate, kill, liquidate; *informal* bump off, knock off, do in, take out, dispose of; rub out. **3** *I'll polish off the last few pages* COMPLETE, finish, deal with, accomplish, discharge, do; end, conclude, close, finalize, round off, wind up; *informal* wrap up, sew up.

THE RIGHT WORD

All of these words refer to a smooth, shining, or bright surface that reflects light. If this surface is produced by rubbing or friction, the correct word is **polish** (*the car's mirror-like polish was the result of regular waxing and buffing*). **Gloss**, on the other hand, suggests the hard smoothness associated with lacquered, varnished, or enameled surfaces (*a high-gloss paint*). **Luster** is associated with the light reflected from the surfaces of certain materials, such as silk or pearl (*a green stone with a brilliant luster*). **Sheen** describes a glistening or radiant brightness that is also associated with specific materials (*her hair had a rich, velvety sheen*).

polished adjective **1** *a polished table* SHINY, glossy, gleaming, lustrous, glassy; waxed, buffed, burnished; varnished, glazed, lacquered, japanned, shellacked. ANTONYMS dull, tarnished.

2 *a polished performance* EXPERT, accomplished, masterly, masterful, skillful, adept, adroit, dexterous; impeccable, flawless, perfect, consummate, exquisite, outstanding, excellent, superb, superlative, first-rate, fine; *informal* ace. ANTONYM inexpert.

3 *polished manners* REFINED, cultivated, civilized, well-bred, polite, courteous, genteel, decorous, respectable, urbane, suave, sophisticated. ANTONYM gauche.

polite adjective **1** *a very polite girl* WELL-MANNERED, civil, courteous, mannerly, respectful, deferential, well-behaved, well-bred, gentlemanly, ladylike, genteel, gracious, urbane; tactful, diplomatic. See word spectrum on page 691. ANTONYM rude.

2 *polite society* CIVILIZED, refined, cultured, sophisticated, genteel, courtly. ANTONYM uncivilized.

politic adjective *I do not think it politic to express my reservations* WISE, prudent, sensible, judicious, canny, sagacious, shrewd, astute; recommended, advantageous, beneficial, profitable, desirable, advisable; appropriate, suitable, fitting, apt. ANTONYM unwise.

political adjective **1** *the political affairs of the nation* GOVERNMENTAL, government, constitutional, ministerial, parliamentary, diplomatic, legislative, administrative, bureaucratic; public, civic, state.

2 *he's a political man* POLITICALLY ACTIVE, party; militant, factional, partisan.

politician noun *campaigning politicians make more promises than they can keep* LEGISLATOR, elected official, statesman, stateswoman, public servant; senator, congressman, congresswoman; *informal* politico, pol.

politics noun **1** *a career in politics* GOVERNMENT, affairs of state, public affairs; diplomacy.

2 *she studies politics* POLITICAL SCIENCE, civics, statecraft.

3 *what are his politics?* POLITICAL VIEWS, political leanings, party politics.

4 *office politics* POWER STRUGGLE, machinations, maneuvering, opportunism, realpolitik.

poll noun **1** *a second-round poll* VOTE, ballot, show of hands, referendum, plebiscite; election.

2 *the poll was unduly low* VOTING FIGURES, vote, returns, count, tally.

3 *a poll to investigate holiday choices* SURVEY, opinion poll, straw poll, canvass, market research, census.

▸ verb **1** *most of those polled supported the vice president* CANVASS, survey, ask, question, interview, ballot.

2 *she polled 119 votes* GET, gain, register, record, return.

pollute verb **1** *fish farms will pollute the lake* CONTAMINATE, adulterate, taint, poison, foul, dirty, soil, infect; *literary* befoul. ANTONYM purify.

2 *propaganda polluted this nation* CORRUPT, poison, warp, pervert, deprave, defile, blight, sully; *literary* besmirch.

THE RIGHT WORD

When a factory pours harmful chemicals or wastes into the air or water, it is said to **pollute** the environment. But *pollute* may also refer to impairing the purity, integrity, or effectiveness of something (*a campaign polluted by allegations of sexual impropriety*). To **contaminate** is to spread harmful or undesirable impurities throughout something; unlike *pollute*, which suggests visible or noticeable impurities, **contaminate** is preferred where the change is unsuspected or not immediately noticeable (*milk contaminated by radioactive fallout from a nuclear plant accident*). **Adulterate** often refers to food products to which harmful, low-quality, or low-cost substances have been added in order to defraud the consumer (*cereal adulterated with sawdust*), although this word can apply to any mixture to which the inferior or harmful element is added deliberately and in the hope that no one will notice (*a report adulterated with false statistics*). To **defile** is to pollute something that should be kept pure or sacred (*a church defiled by vandals*), while **taint** implies that a trace of something toxic or corrupt has been introduced (*he contracted the disease from a tainted blood transfusion; the book is tainted by gratuitous violence*).

pollution noun **1** *air and water pollution* CONTAMINATION, adulteration, impurity; dirt, filth, toxins, infection; smog.

2 *the pollution of young minds* CORRUPTION, defilement, poisoning, warping, depravation, sullying, violation.

pomp noun *the pomp of a royal wedding* CEREMONY, ceremonial, solemnity, ritual, display, spectacle, pageantry; show, showiness, ostentation, splendor, grandeur, magnificence, majesty, stateliness, glory, opulence, brilliance, drama, resplendence, splendidness; *informal* razzmatazz.

pompous adjective *pompous officials* SELF-IMPORTANT, imperious, overbearing, domineering, magisterial, pontifical, sententious, grandiose, affected, pretentious, puffed up, arrogant, vain, haughty, proud, conceited, egotistic, supercilious, condescending, patronizing; *informal* snooty, uppity, uppish. See note at FORMAL. ANTONYM modest.

pond noun *snowy egrets visit our pond* POOL, waterhole, lake, tarn, reservoir, slough, beaver pond, lagoon.

ponder verb *she had time to* ***ponder over*** *the incident* THINK ABOUT, contemplate, consider, review, reflect on, mull over, meditate on, muse on, deliberate about, cogitate on, dwell on, brood on, ruminate on, chew over, puzzle over, turn over in one's mind.

ponderous adjective **1** *a ponderous dance* CLUMSY, heavy, awkward, lumbering, slow, cumbersome, ungainly, graceless, uncoordinated, blundering; *informal* clodhopping, clunky. See note at HEAVY. ANTONYMS light, graceful.

2 *his ponderous sentences* LABORED, laborious, awkward, clumsy, forced, stilted, unnatural, artificial; stodgy, lifeless, plodding, pedestrian, boring, dull, tedious, monotonous; overelaborate, convoluted, windy. ANTONYM lively.

pontifical adjective *such explanations were met with pontifical disdain* POMPOUS, cocksure, self-important, arrogant, superior; opinionated, dogmatic, doctrinaire, authoritarian, domineering; adamant, obstinate, stubborn, single-minded, inflexible. ANTONYM humble.

pontificate verb *he pontificated about life and art* HOLD FORTH, expound, declaim, preach, lay down the law, sound off, dogmatize, sermonize, moralize, lecture; *informal* preachify, mouth off.

pooh-pooh verb *informal an idea pooh-poohed by the scientific community* DISMISS, reject, spurn, rebuff, wave aside, disregard, discount; play down, make light of, belittle, deride, mock, scorn, scoff at, sneer at.

pool[1] noun **1** *pools of water* PUDDLE, pond, slough; *literary* plash.

2 *the hotel has a pool* SWIMMING POOL, baths, lap pool, natatorium.

rude
insolent
churlish
contumelious
ill-mannered
bad-mannered
offensive
insulting
abusive
derogatory
disparaging
underbred
malapert
ill-bred
ungallant
ungentlemanly
unladylike
unmannerly
uncouth
ungracious
graceless
impolite
crass
curt
brusque
brash
blunt
short
sharp
uncharitable
unchivalrous
unpleasant
disagreeable
discourteous
disrespectful
presumptuous
impertinent
impudent
cheeky
audacious
uncivil
uncomplimentary
tactless
mannerless
undiplomatic
offhand
conscientious
well behaved
thoughtful
tactful
discreet
civil
courteous
diplomatic
respectful
well-mannered
polished
considerate
deferential
proper
gracious
formal
refined
genteel
well brought up
well bred
mannerly
cultured
cultivated
sophisticated
urbane
elegant
courtly
ladylike
gentlemanly
chivalrous
gallant
polite

pool[2] noun **1** *a pool of skilled labor* SUPPLY, reserve(s), reservoir, fund; store, stock, accumulation, cache.

2 *a pool of money for emergencies* FUND, reserve, kitty, pot, bank, purse.

3 *the office hockey pool* LOTTERY, bet.

▸ verb *they pooled their skills* COMBINE, amalgamate, group, join, unite, merge; fuse, conglomerate, integrate; share.

poor adjective **1** *a poor family* POVERTY-STRICKEN, penniless, moneyless, impoverished, low-income, necessitous, impecunious, indigent, needy, destitute, pauperized, unable to make ends meet, without a sou; insolvent, in debt, without a cent (to one's name); *informal* (flat) broke, hard up, cleaned out, strapped; *formal* penurious. See word spectrum at RICH. ANTONYMS rich, wealthy.

2 *poor workmanship* SUBSTANDARD, below par, bad, deficient, defective, faulty, imperfect, inferior; appalling, abysmal, atrocious, awful, terrible, dreadful, unsatisfactory, second-rate, third-rate, tinpot, shoddy, crude, lamentable, deplorable, inadequate, unacceptable; *informal* crummy, lame, crappy, dismal, bum, rotten. ANTONYM superior.

3 *a poor crop* MEAGER, scanty, scant, paltry, disappointing, limited, reduced, modest, insufficient, inadequate, sparse, spare, deficient, insubstantial, skimpy, short, small, lean, slender; *informal* measly, stingy, pathetic, piddling; *formal* exiguous. ANTONYMS satisfactory, good.

4 *poor soil* UNPRODUCTIVE, barren, unyielding, unfruitful; arid, sterile. ANTONYMS fertile, productive.

5 *the waters are **poor in** nutrients* DEFICIENT IN, lacking in, wanting in, weak in; short of, low on.

6 *you poor thing!* UNFORTUNATE, unlucky, luckless, unhappy, hapless, ill-fated, ill-starred, pitiable, pitiful, wretched. ANTONYM lucky.

poorly adverb *the text is poorly written* BADLY, deficiently, defectively, imperfectly, incompetently; appallingly, abysmally, atrociously, awfully, dreadfully; crudely, shoddily, inadequately.

▸ adjective *she felt poorly* ILL, unwell, not (very) well, ailing, indisposed, out of sorts, under/below par, peaked; sick, queasy, nauseous; off; *informal* under the weather, funny, peculiar, lousy, rough.

pop verb **1** *champagne corks popped* GO BANG, go off; crack, snap, burst, explode.

2 *I'm just popping home* GO; drop in, stop by, visit.

3 *pop a lid over the pot* PUT, place, slip, slide, stick, set, lay, install, position, arrange.

▸ noun **1** *the balloons burst with a pop* BANG, crack, snap; explosion, report.

2 *informal a bottle of pop* SOFT DRINK, soda, carbonated drink. See table at SOFT DRINK.

PHRASE: **pop up** *you never know when a new problem is going to pop up* APPEAR (SUDDENLY), occur (suddenly), arrive, materialize, come along, happen, emerge, arise, crop up, turn up, present itself, come to light; *informal* show up.

pope noun *blessed by the pope* PONTIFF, Bishop of Rome, Holy Father, Vicar of Christ, His Holiness.

pop music noun *the legends of pop music* POP, popular music, Top 40, bubble gum music, chart music.

poppycock noun *informal their claims are poppycock* NON-

SENSE, rubbish, claptrap, balderdash, blather, moonshine, garbage; *informal* rot, tripe, jive, hogwash, baloney, drivel, bilge, bunk, eyewash, piffle, phooey, twaddle; *informal* bushwa, malarkey, gobbledygook, mumbo-jumbo; *informal, dated* bunkum, tommyrot. See note at NONSENSE.

populace noun *when the populace wants to, it can change the course of history* POPULATION, inhabitants, residents, natives; community, country, (general) public, people, nation; common people, man/woman in the street, masses, multitude, rank and file, commonalty, commonality, third estate, plebeians, proletariat; *informal* proles, plebs; *formal* denizens; *derogatory* hoi polloi, common herd, rabble, riffraff; **(the populace)** Joe Public, John Q. Public.

popular adjective **1** *the most popular restaurant in town* WELL-LIKED, favored, sought-after, in demand, desired, wanted; commercial, marketable, fashionable, trendy, in vogue, all the rage, hot; *informal* in, cool, big.

2 *popular science* NONSPECIALIST, nontechnical, amateur, lay person's, general, middle-of-the-road; accessible, simplified, plain, simple, easy, straightforward, understandable; mass-market, middlebrow, lowbrow, pop. ANTONYM highbrow.

3 *popular opinion* WIDESPREAD, general, common, current, prevalent, prevailing, standard, stock; ordinary, usual, accepted, established, acknowledged, conventional, orthodox.

4 *a popular movement for independence* MASS, general, communal, collective, social, collaborative, group, civil, public.

popularize verb **1** *tobacco was popularized by Sir Walter Raleigh* MAKE POPULAR, make fashionable; market, publicize; *informal* hype.

2 *he popularized the subject* SIMPLIFY, make accessible, give mass-market appeal to, universalize, vulgarize.

3 *the report popularized the unfounded notion* GIVE CURRENCY TO, spread, propagate, give credence to.

popularly adverb **1** *old age is popularly associated with illness* WIDELY, generally, universally, commonly, usually, customarily, habitually, conventionally, traditionally, as a rule.

2 *the bar was popularly known as "the May"* INFORMALLY, unofficially; by lay people.

3 *the president is popularly elected* DEMOCRATICALLY, by the people.

populate verb **1** *the town is populated by 40,000 people* INHABIT, occupy, people; live in, reside in.

2 *an attempt to populate the island* SETTLE, colonize, people, occupy, move into, make one's home in.

population noun *a new social agenda for the population of these emerging nations* INHABITANTS, residents, people, citizens, citizenry, public, community, populace, society, body politic, natives, occupants; *formal* denizens.

populous adjective *a populous island* DENSELY POPULATED, heavily populated, congested, crowded, packed, jammed, crammed, teeming, swarming, seething, crawling; *informal* jam-packed. ANTONYM deserted.

porch noun *the chair would be ideal for a porch or patio* VESTIBULE, foyer, entrance (hall), entry, portico, lobby; veranda, terrace; stoop; *Architecture* lanai, tambour, narthex.

pore[1] noun *pores in the skin* OPENING, orifice, aperture, hole, outlet, inlet, vent; *Biology* stoma, foramen.

pore[2] verb *they* ***pored over*** *the map* STUDY, read intently, peruse, scrutinize, scan, examine, go over.

pornographic adjective *pornographic magazines* OBSCENE, indecent, crude, lewd, dirty, vulgar, smutty, filthy; erotic, titillating, arousing, suggestive, sexy, risqué; off-color, adult, X-rated, hard-core, soft-core; *informal* porn, porno, blue, skin. ANTONYM wholesome.

pornography noun *selling pornography to minors* erotica, pornographic material, dirty books; smut, filth, vice; *informal* (hard/soft) porn, porno, girlie magazines, skin flicks.

porous adjective *porous fibers* PERMEABLE, penetrable, pervious, cellular, holey; absorbent, absorptive, spongy. ANTONYM impermeable.

port[1] noun **1** *the German port of Kiel* SEAPORT.

2 *shells exploded down by the port* HARBOR, dock(s), haven, marina; anchorage, moorage, harborage, roads.

port[2] noun *push the supply pipes into the ports* APERTURE, opening, outlet, inlet, socket, vent.

portable adjective *a portable tape recorder* TRANSPORTABLE, movable, mobile, travel; lightweight, compact, handy, convenient.

portal noun *the portals to the palace were heavily guarded* DOORWAY, gateway, entrance, exit, opening; door, gate, entryway; *formal* egress.

portend verb *the sight of a dead bird was believed to portend tragedy* PRESAGE, augur, foreshadow, foretell, prophesy; be a sign, warn, be an omen, indicate, herald, signal, bode, promise, threaten, signify, spell, denote; *literary* betoken, foretoken, forebode.

portent noun **1** *a portent of things to come* OMEN, sign, signal, token, forewarning, warning, foreshadowing, prediction, forecast, prophecy, harbinger, augury, auspice, presage; writing on the wall, indication, hint; *literary* foretoken.

2 *the word carries terrifying portent* SIGNIFICANCE, importance, import, consequence, meaning, weight; *formal* moment.

portentous adjective **1** *portentous signs* OMINOUS, warning, premonitory, threatening, menacing, ill-omened, foreboding, inauspicious, unfavorable. See note at OMINOUS.

2 *portentous dialogue* POMPOUS, bombastic, self-important, pontifical, solemn, sonorous, grandiloquent.

porter[1] noun *a porter helped with the bags* carrier, baggage clerk, redcap.

porter[2] noun *the college porter* DOORMAN, doorkeeper, commissionaire, gatekeeper.

portfolio noun **1** *an artist's portfolio* SAMPLES, examples, selection.

2 *your financial portfolio* INVESTMENTS, holdings, funds.

3 *he kept the papers in his portfolio* BRIEFCASE, case, valise, bag, attaché.

portion noun **1** *the upper portion of the chimney* PART, piece, bit, section, segment. See note at FRAGMENT.

2 *her portion of the allowance* SHARE, slice, quota, quantum, part, percentage, amount, quantity, ration, fraction, division, allocation, measure; *informal* cut.

3 *a portion of cake* HELPING, serving, amount, quantity; plateful, bowlful; slice, piece, chunk, wedge, slab, hunk.

4 *archaic poverty was certain to be his portion.* See DESTINY sense 1.

▸ verb *she* ***portioned out*** *the food* SHARE OUT, allocate, allot, apportion; distribute, hand out, deal out, dole out, give out, dispense, mete out; *informal* divvy up.

portly adjective *a portly gentleman showed us the way to the dining room* STOUT, plump, fat, overweight, heavy, corpulent, fleshy, paunchy, potbellied, well padded, rotund, stocky, heavyset, bulky; *informal* tubby, roly-poly, beefy, porky, pudgy; *informal* corn-fed. ANTONYM slim.

portrait noun 1 *a portrait of the first lady* PAINTING, picture, drawing, sketch, likeness, image, study, miniature; *informal* oil; *formal* portraiture.

2 *a vivid portrait of Italy* DESCRIPTION, portrayal, representation, depiction, impression, account; sketch, vignette, profile.

portray verb 1 *she portrays the older architecture of her province* PAINT, draw, sketch, picture, depict, represent, illustrate, render.

2 *the Newfoundland portrayed by Proulx* DESCRIBE, depict, characterize, represent, present, delineate, evoke, tell of.

3 *the actor portrays a spy* PLAY, act the part of, take the role of, represent, appear as; *formal* personate.

portrayal noun 1 *a portrayal of a parrot* PAINTING, picture, portrait, drawing, sketch, representation, depiction, study.

2 *her portrayal of adolescence* DESCRIPTION, representation, characterization, depiction, evocation.

3 *Brando's* ***portrayal of*** *Corleone* PERFORMANCE AS, representation of, interpretation of, rendering of, reading of; *formal* personation of.

pose verb 1 *pollution poses a threat to health* CONSTITUTE, present, create, cause, produce, be.

2 *the question posed earlier* RAISE, ask, put, set, submit, advance, propose, suggest, moot.

3 *she posed for the artist* MODEL, sit.

4 *he posed her on the sofa* POSITION, place, put, arrange, dispose, locate, situate.

5 *I wonder what poor sucker she's posing for tonight* BEHAVE AFFECTEDLY, strike a pose, posture, attitudinize, put on airs; *informal* show off.

▸ noun 1 *a sexy pose* POSTURE, position, stance, attitude, bearing.

2 *her pose of aggrieved innocence* PRETENSE, act, affectation, facade, show, front, display, masquerade, posture.

PHRASE: **pose as** *they pay us to pose as the celebrities we resemble* PRETEND TO BE, impersonate, pass oneself off as, masquerade as, profess to be, represent oneself as; *formal* personate.

poser[1] noun *this situation's a bit of a poser* DIFFICULT QUESTION, vexed question, awkward problem, tough one, puzzle, mystery, conundrum, puzzler, enigma, riddle; *informal* dilemma, toughie, stumper.

poser[2] noun *he's such a poser* EXHIBITIONIST, poseur, posturer, fake; *informal* show-off.

poseur noun See POSER[2].

posh adjective *a posh hotel* SMART, stylish, fancy, high-class, fashionable, chic, luxurious, luxury, deluxe, exclusive, opulent, lavish, grand, showy, upscale, upmarket; *informal* classy, swanky, snazzy, plush, ritzy, flash, la-di-da, fancy-dancy, fancy-schmancy, swank, tony.

posit verb *they posit a purely biological basis for this phenomenon* POSTULATE, put forward, advance, propound, submit, hypothesize, propose, assert.

position noun 1 *the aircraft's position* LOCATION, place, situation, spot, site, locality, setting, area; whereabouts, bearings, orientation; *technical* locus.

2 *a standing position* POSTURE, stance, attitude, pose.

3 *our financial position* SITUATION, state, condition, circumstances; predicament, plight, strait(s).

4 *the two parties jockeyed for position* ADVANTAGE, the upper hand, the edge, the whip hand, primacy; *informal* the catbird seat.

5 *their position in society* STATUS, place, level, rank, standing; stature, prestige, influence, reputation, importance, consequence, class; *dated* station.

6 *a secretarial position* JOB, post, situation, appointment, role, occupation, employment; office, capacity, duty, function; opening, vacancy, placement.

7 *the government's position on the matter* VIEWPOINT, opinion, outlook, attitude, stand, standpoint, stance, perspective, approach, slant, thinking, policy, feelings.

▸ verb *he positioned a chair between them* PUT, place, locate, situate, set, site, stand, station; plant, stick, install; arrange, dispose; *informal* park.

positive adjective 1 *a positive response* AFFIRMATIVE, favorable, good, approving, enthusiastic, supportive, encouraging. ANTONYM negative.

2 *do something positive* CONSTRUCTIVE, practical, useful, productive, helpful, worthwhile, beneficial, effective.

3 *she seems a lot more positive* OPTIMISTIC, hopeful, confident, cheerful, sanguine, buoyant; *informal* upbeat. ANTONYM pessimistic.

4 *positive economic signs* FAVORABLE, good, promising, encouraging, heartening, propitious, auspicious. ANTONYMS negative, unfavorable.

5 *positive proof* DEFINITE, conclusive, certain, categorical, unequivocal, incontrovertible, indisputable, undeniable, unmistakable, irrefutable, reliable, concrete, tangible, clear-cut, explicit, firm, decisive, real, actual. ANTONYM doubtful.

6 *I'm positive he's coming back* CERTAIN, sure, convinced, confident, satisfied, assured. ANTONYMS uncertain, unsure.

positively adverb 1 *I could not positively identify the voice* CONFIDENTLY, definitely, emphatically, categorically, with certainty, conclusively, unquestionably, undoubtedly, indisputably, unmistakably, assuredly.

2 *he was positively livid* ABSOLUTELY, really, downright, thoroughly, completely, utterly, totally, extremely, fairly; *informal* plain.

posse noun *Sheriff Munro assembled a posse of armed men to track down the train robbers* GANG, band, group, crowd, pack, horde, herd, throng, mob, swarm, troop, cluster; company, gathering; *informal* bunch, gaggle, load.

possess verb **1** *the only hat she possessed* OWN, have (to one's name), hold.

2 *he does not possess a sense of humor* HAVE, be blessed with, be endowed with; enjoy, boast.

3 *a supernatural force possessed him* TAKE CONTROL OF, take over, control, dominate, influence; bewitch, enchant, enthrall.

4 *she was possessed by a need to talk to him* OBSESS, haunt, preoccupy, consume; eat someone up, prey on one's mind.

possessed adjective *he was like a man possessed* MAD, demented, insane, crazed, berserk, out of one's mind; bewitched, enchanted, haunted, under a spell.

possession noun **1** *the estate came into their possession* OWNERSHIP, control, hands, keeping, care, custody, charge, hold, title, guardianship.

2 *her possession of the premises* OCCUPANCY, occupation, tenure, holding, tenancy.

3 *she packed her possessions* BELONGINGS, things, property, (worldly) goods, (personal) effects, assets, chattels, movables, valuables; stuff, bits and pieces; luggage, baggage; *informal* gear, junk.

4 *colonial possessions* COLONY, dependency, territory, holding, protectorate. PHRASE: **take possession of** *they were under orders to take possession of the house and all of its contents* SEIZE, appropriate, impound, expropriate, sequestrate, sequester, confiscate; take, get, acquire, obtain, procure, possess oneself of, get hold of, get one's hands on; capture, commandeer, requisition; *Law* distrain; *informal* get one's mitts on.

possessive adjective **1** *he was very possessive* PROPRIETORIAL, overprotective, controlling, dominating, jealous, clingy.

2 *kids are possessive of their own property* COVETOUS, selfish, unwilling to share; grasping, greedy, acquisitive, grabby.

possibility noun **1** *there is a possibility that he might be alive* CHANCE, likelihood, probability, hope; risk, hazard, danger, fear.

2 *they discussed the possibility of launching a new project* FEASIBILITY, practicability, chances, odds, probability.

3 *buying a smaller house is one possibility* OPTION, alternative, choice, course of action, solution.

4 **(possibilities)** *the idea has distinct possibilities* POTENTIAL, promise, prospects.

possible adjective **1** *it's not possible to check the figures* FEASIBLE, practicable, practical, viable, within the bounds/realms of possibility, attainable, achievable, workable; *informal* doable.

2 *a possible reason for his disappearance* CONCEIVABLE, plausible, imaginable, believable, likely, potential, probable, credible. ANTONYM unlikely.

3 *a possible future leader* POTENTIAL, prospective, likely, probable.

possibly adverb **1** *possibly he took the boy with him* PERHAPS, maybe, it is possible, for all one knows, very likely; *literary* peradventure, perchance, mayhap.

2 *you can't possibly refuse* CONCEIVABLY, under any circumstances, by any means.

3 *could you possibly help me?* PLEASE, kindly, be so good as to.

post[1] noun *wooden posts* POLE, stake, upright, longer, shaft, prop, support, picket, strut, pillar, pale, paling, stanchion; *historical* puncheon.

▸ verb **1** *the notice posted on the wall* AFFIX, attach, fasten, display, pin (up), put up, stick (up), tack (up).

2 *the group posted a net profit* ANNOUNCE, report, make known, publish.

post[2] noun *our federally regulated post* MAIL, postal service; airmail, surface mail, registered mail.

▸ verb **1** *post the order form today* MAIL, send (off), put in the mail.

2 *post the transaction in the second column* RECORD, write in, enter, register.

PHRASE: **keep posted** *we have no more news at this moment, but we'll keep you posted* KEEP INFORMED, keep up to date, keep in the picture, keep briefed, update, fill in; *informal* keep up to speed.

post[3] noun **1** *there were seventy candidates for the post* JOB, position, appointment, situation, place; vacancy, opening.

2 *back to your posts!* (ASSIGNED) POSITION, station, observation post.

▸ verb **1** *he'd been* ***posted to*** *Berlin* SEND TO, assign to a post in/at, dispatch to.

2 *armed guards were posted beside the exit* PUT ON DUTY, station, position, situate, locate.

poster noun *they put up posters all over town* NOTICE, placard, bill, sign, advertisement, playbill.

posterior adjective **1** *the posterior part of the skull* REAR, hind, back, hinder; *technical* dorsal, caudal. ANTONYM anterior.

2 *formal* *a date* ***posterior to*** *statehood* LATER THAN, subsequent to, following, after. ANTONYM previous.

▸ noun *informal* *her plump posterior.* See BUTTOCKS.

posterity noun *the names of those who died are recorded for posterity* FUTURE GENERATIONS, the future.

posthaste adverb *he departed posthaste for Venice* AS QUICKLY AS POSSIBLE, without delay, (very) quickly, speedily, without further/more ado, with all speed, promptly, immediately, at once, straightaway, right away; *informal* pronto, straight off.

postman, postwoman noun *the postman left a package on your porch* POSTAL WORKER, mailman, mail carrier, letter carrier.

postmodern adjective See notes below.

WORD NOTE postmodern

Postmodern is among the most widely employed critical terms of our time, mainly because it can mean just about anything. Moreover, it neatly suggests that its user is learned, widely read, up to date on the latest in literary theory, and, in general, really cool, not to say—ahem—edgy. In essence *postmodern* describes the kind of self-aware writing or painting that doesn't take itself completely seriously, that recognizes with a wink that it's just writing or painting. In some ways, postmodern is an offshoot of Brechtian drama's "alienation" effect, in which the actor may address the audience, move in and out of character, regard the entire play and his role in it with world-weary irony. Similarly, the postmodern author deliberately undercuts the smooth surface of his narrative and by somehow standing back and commenting on the action prevents the reader from "losing himself in the story." Unfortunately, this isn't really very new. Many classic novelists have done this, notably Cervantes and Sterne, not to mention such twentieth-century masters as James Joyce. Just as modernism has been called a variant of romanticism, so postmodernism may be simply a late form of modernism. Whatever the case, unless you're going to define it clearly, don't bandy the word about. **—MD**

WORD NOTE **postmodernism**

Postmodernism is modernism after the shock wore off. **—DL**

---

post-mortem noun **1** *the hospital carried out a postmortem* AUTOPSY, postmortem examination, necropsy.

2 *a postmortem of her failed relationship* ANALYSIS, evaluation, assessment, appraisal, examination, review.

postpone verb *sorry, we'll have to postpone the relay race* PUT OFF/BACK, delay, defer, reschedule, adjourn, shelve, put over, take a rain check on; *informal* put on ice, put on the back burner; *rare* remit. ANTONYM bring forward.

THE RIGHT WORD

All of these verbs have to do with putting things off. **Defer** is the broadest in meaning; it suggests putting something off until a later time (*defer payment; defer a discussion*). If you **postpone** an event or activity, you put it off intentionally, usually until a definite time in the future (*we postponed the party until the next weekend*). If you **adjourn** an activity, you postpone its completion until another day or place; *adjourn* is usually associated with meetings or other formal gatherings that are brought to an end and then resumed (*the judge adjourned the hearing until the following morning*). If you **delay** something, you postpone it because of obstacles (*delayed by severe thunderstorms and highway flooding*) or because you are reluctant to do it (*delay going to the dentist*). **Suspend** suggests stopping an activity for a while, usually for a reason (*forced to suspend work on the bridge until the holiday weekend was over*).

---

postponement noun *a further postponement of the trial* DEFERRAL, deferment, delay, putting off/back, rescheduling, adjournment, shelving.

postscript noun **1** *a handwritten postscript* AFTERTHOUGHT, PS, additional remark.

2 *he added postscripts of his own* ADDENDUM, supplement, appendix, codicil, afterword, addition.

postulate verb *a theory postulated by a respected scientist* PUT FORWARD, suggest, advance, posit, hypothesize, propose; assume, presuppose, presume, take for granted.

posture noun **1** *a kneeling posture* POSITION, pose, attitude, stance.

2 *good posture* BEARING, carriage, stance, comportment.

3 *the unions adopted a militant posture* ATTITUDE, stance, standpoint, point of view, opinion, position, frame of mind.

▸ verb *Keith postured, flexing his biceps* POSE, strike an attitude, strut.

posy noun *a posy of snowdrops and violets* BOUQUET, bunch (of flowers), spray, nosegay, corsage; boutonniere.

pot noun **1** *pots and pans* COOKING UTENSIL, pan, saucepan, casserole, stewpot, stockpot, kettle.

2 *earthenware pots* FLOWERPOT, planter, jardinière.

3 *Jim raked in half the pot* BANK, kitty, pool, purse, jackpot. PHRASE: **go to pot** *informal they've certainly let the old homestead go to pot* DETERIORATE, decline, degenerate, go to (rack and) ruin, go downhill, go to seed, become rundown; *informal* go to the dogs, go down the tubes, go haywire.

potable adjective *we were running low on potable water* DRINKABLE, palatable, fit to drink, pure, clean, safe, unpolluted, untainted, uncontaminated.

potbellied adjective *potbellied old men sitting on the benches eating saltines* PAUNCHY, beer-bellied, portly, rotund, corpulent, Falstaffian; *informal* tubby, roly-poly.

potbelly noun *he noticed the onset of a potbelly and decided to start exercising* PAUNCH, belly, beer belly; *informal* pot, spare tire, tummy, bay window; *dated, informal* corporation.

potency noun **1** *the potency of his words* FORCEFULNESS, force, effectiveness, persuasiveness, cogency, influence, strength, authoritativeness, authority, power, powerfulness; *literary* puissance.

2 *the potency of the drugs* STRENGTH, powerfulness, power, effectiveness; *formal* efficacy; efficaciousness.

potent adjective **1** *a potent political force* POWERFUL, strong, mighty, formidable, influential, dominant, forceful; *literary* puissant. ANTONYM weak.

2 *a potent argument* FORCEFUL, convincing, cogent, compelling, persuasive, powerful, strong.

3 *a potent drug* STRONG, powerful, effective; *formal* efficacious. ANTONYM weak.

potentate noun *diplomatic missions to foreign potentates* RULER, monarch, sovereign, king, queen, emperor, empress, sultan, shah, raja, pharaoh.

potential adjective *a potential source of conflict* POSSIBLE, likely, prospective, future, probable; latent, inherent, undeveloped. See note at LATENT.

▸ noun *economic potential* POSSIBILITIES, potentiality, prospects; promise, capability, capacity.

potion noun *people paid good money to sample her so-called magic potions* CONCOCTION, mixture, brew, elixir, philter, drink, decoction; medicine, tonic; *literary* draft.

potpourri noun *the book is a potpourri of curious animal stories* MIXTURE, assortment, collection, selection, assemblage, medley, miscellany, mix, mélange, variety, mixed bag, patchwork, bricolage; ragbag, mishmash, salmagundi, jumble, farrago, hodgepodge, gallimaufry.

pottery noun *a collection of antique pottery* CHINA, crockery, ceramics, earthenware, stoneware.

pouch noun **1** *a leather pouch* BAG, purse, sack, sac, pocket.

2 *a kangaroo's pouch* marsupium.

pounce verb *two men **pounced on** him* JUMP ON, spring on, leap on, dive on, lunge at, fall on, set on, attack suddenly; *informal* jump, mug.

▸ noun *a sudden pounce* LEAP, spring, jump, dive, lunge, bound.

pound[1] verb **1** *the two men pounded him with their fists*

BEAT, strike, hit, batter, thump, pummel, punch, rain blows on, belabor, hammer, thrash, set on, tear into; *informal* bash, clobber, wallop, beat the living daylights out of, whack, thwack, lay into, pitch into, light into, whale.

2 *waves pounded the seafront* BEAT AGAINST, crash against, batter, dash against, lash, buffet.

3 *gunships pounded the capital* BOMBARD, bomb, shell, fire on; *archaic* cannonade.

4 *pound the cloves with salt* CRUSH, grind, pulverize, mill, mash, pulp; *technical* triturate.

5 *I heard him pounding along the gangway* WALK/RUN HEAVILY, stomp, lumber, clomp, clump, tramp, tromp, trudge.

6 *her heart was pounding* THROB, thump, thud, hammer, pulse, race, go pit-a-pat; *literary* pant, thrill.

pound[2] noun *a dog pound* ENCLOSURE, compound, pen, yard, corral.

pour verb **1** *blood was pouring from his nose* STREAM, flow, run, gush, course, jet, spurt, surge, spill.

2 *Amy poured wine into his glass* TIP, let flow, splash, spill, decant; *informal* slosh, slop.

3 *it was pouring when we set out* RAIN HEAVILY/HARD, teem down, pelt down, come down in torrents/sheets, rain cats and dogs.

4 *people poured off the train* THRONG, crowd, swarm, stream, flood.

pout verb *Crystal pouted sullenly* LOOK PETULANT, pull a face, look sulky.

▸ noun *a childish pout* PETULANT EXPRESSION, sulky expression, moue.

poverty noun **1** *abject poverty* PENURY, destitution, pauperism, pauperdom, beggary, indigence, pennilessness, impoverishment, neediness, need, hardship, impecuniousness. ANTONYM wealth.

2 *the poverty of choice* SCARCITY, deficiency, dearth, shortage, paucity, insufficiency, absence, lack. ANTONYM abundance.

3 *the poverty of her imagination* INFERIORITY, mediocrity, poorness, sterility.

poverty-stricken adjective *I'm not poverty-stricken, but I could certainly use some assistance* EXTREMELY POOR, impoverished, destitute, penniless, as poor as a church mouse, in penury, impecunious, indigent, needy, in need/want, without a cent (to one's name); *informal* without two coins/cents to rub together; *formal* penurious.

powder noun *the residue was a pinkish powder* DUST, fine particles; talcum powder, talc.

▸ verb **1** *she powdered her face* DUST, sprinkle/cover with powder.

2 *the grains are powdered* CRUSH, grind, pulverize, pound, mill; *technical* comminute.

3 *powdered milk* dry, freeze-dry; *technical* lyophilize.

powdery adjective *a powdery substance floated through the air* FINE, dry, fine-grained, powder-like, dusty, chalky, floury, sandy, crumbly, friable.

power noun **1** *the power of speech* ABILITY, capacity, capability, potential, faculty, competence. ANTONYM inability.

2 *the unions wield enormous power* CONTROL, authority, influence, dominance, mastery, domination, dominion, sway, weight, leverage; *informal* clout, teeth, drag; *literary* puissance. See note at JURISDICTION.

3 *police have the power to stop and search* AUTHORITY, right, authorization, warrant, license.

4 *a major international power* STATE, country, nation.

5 *he hit the ball with as much power as he could* STRENGTH, powerfulness, might, force, forcefulness, vigor, energy; brawn, muscle; *informal* punch; *literary* thew.

6 *the power of his arguments* FORCEFULNESS, powerfulness, potency, strength, force, cogency, persuasiveness. ANTONYMS impotence, weakness.

7 *the new engine has more power* DRIVING FORCE, horsepower, h.p., acceleration; *informal* oomph.

8 *generating power from waste* ENERGY, electrical power.

9 *informal* *the time off did him **a power of** good* A GREAT DEAL OF, a lot of, much; *informal* lots of, loads of. PHRASES: **have someone in/under one's power** *I doubt that Roger will ever have Etta under his power* HAVE CONTROL OVER, have influence over, have under one's thumb, have at one's mercy, have in one's clutches, have in the palm of one's hand, have someone wrapped around one's little finger, have in one's hip pocket; *informal* have over a barrel. **the powers that be** *the powers that be did nothing to defuse the situation* THE AUTHORITIES, the people in charge, the government.

powerful adjective **1** *powerful shoulders* STRONG, muscular, muscly, sturdy, strapping, robust, brawny, burly, athletic, manly, well built, solid; *informal* beefy, hunky; *dated* stalwart; *literary* stark, thewy. ANTONYM weak.

2 *a powerful drink* INTOXICATING, hard, strong, stiff, industrial-strength; *formal* spirituous.

3 *a powerful blow* VIOLENT, forceful, hard, mighty. ANTONYM gentle.

4 *he felt a powerful desire to kiss her* INTENSE, keen, fierce, passionate, ardent, burning, strong, irresistible, overpowering, overwhelming.

5 *a powerful nation* INFLUENTIAL, strong, important, dominant, commanding, potent, forceful, formidable; *literary* puissant. ANTONYMS weak, powerless.

6 *a powerful critique* COGENT, compelling, convincing, persuasive, forceful; dramatic, graphic, vivid, moving. ANTONYM ineffective.

powerless adjective *the outgoing administrators are essentially powerless* IMPOTENT, helpless, ineffectual, ineffective, useless, defenseless, vulnerable; lame-duck; *literary* impuissant.

practicable adjective *what we need is a practicable solution* REALISTIC, feasible, possible, within the bounds/realms of possibility, viable, reasonable, sensible, workable, achievable; *informal* doable.

practical adjective **1** *practical experience* EMPIRICAL, hands-on, actual, active, applied, heuristic, experiential, evidence-based. ANTONYM theoretical.

2 *there are no practical alternatives* FEASIBLE, practicable, realistic, viable, workable, possible, reasonable, sensible; *informal* doable.

3 *practical clothes* FUNCTIONAL, sensible, utilitarian, workaday.

4 *try to be more practical* REALISTIC, sensible, down-to-earth, businesslike, commonsensical, grounded, hardheaded, no-nonsense; *informal* hard-nosed.

5 *a practical certainty* VIRTUAL, effective, near.

practicality noun 1 *the practicality of the proposal* FEASIBILITY, practicability, viability, workability.

2 *practicality of design* FUNCTIONALISM, functionality, serviceability, utility.

3 *his calm practicality* SENSE, common sense, realism, pragmatism.

4 **(practicalities)** *the practicalities of army life* PRACTICAL DETAILS; *informal* nitty-gritty, nuts and bolts.

practical joke noun *it was just a practical joke, but it got out of hand* TRICK, joke, prank, jape, hoax.

practically adverb 1 *the theater was practically empty* ALMOST, (very) nearly, virtually, just about, all but, more or less, as good as, to all intents and purposes, verging on, bordering on; *informal* pretty near, pretty well; *literary* well-nigh.

2 *"You can't afford it," he pointed out practically* REALISTICALLY, sensibly, reasonably.

practice verb 1 *he practiced the songs every day* REHEARSE, run through, go over/through, work on/at; polish, perfect.

2 *the performers were practicing* TRAIN, rehearse, prepare, go through one's paces.

3 *we still practice these rituals today* CARRY OUT, perform, observe.

4 *she practices medicine* WORK AT, pursue a career in.

▸ noun 1 *the practice of hypnosis* APPLICATION, exercise, use, operation, implementation, execution.

2 *common practice* CUSTOM, procedure, policy, convention, tradition; *formal* praxis.

3 *it takes lots of practice | the team's final practice* TRAINING, rehearsal, repetition, preparation; practice session, dummy run, run-through; *informal* dry run.

4 *the practice of medicine* PROFESSION, career, business, work.

5 *a small legal practice* BUSINESS, firm, office, company; *informal* outfit.

PHRASES: **in practice** *it seemed like a good idea, but in practice it just didn't work* IN REALITY, realistically, practically. **out of practice** *considering how out of practice she was, Elizabeth did very well on the balance beam* RUSTY, unpracticed. **put into practice** *it's time you put your teaching degree into practice* USE, make use of, put to use, utilize, apply.

practiced adjective *a practiced judge of character* EXPERT, experienced, seasoned, skilled, skillful, accomplished, proficient, talented, able, adept, consummate, master, masterly; *informal* crack, ace, mean, crackerjack.

pragmatic adjective *she remains pragmatic in the most emotional circumstances* PRACTICAL, matter of fact, sensible, down-to-earth, commonsensical, businesslike, having both/one's feet on the ground, hardheaded, no-nonsense; *informal* hard-nosed. ANTONYM impractical.

prairie noun *homesteaders were allotted substantial acreage on the prairie* PLAINS, grasslands.

praise verb 1 *the police praised Pauline for her courage* COMMEND, express admiration for, applaud, pay tribute to, speak highly of, eulogize, compliment, congratulate, sing the praises of, rave about, go into raptures about, heap praise on, wax lyrical about, make much of, pat on the back, take one's hat off to, lionize, admire, hail, ballyhoo; *formal* laud. See word spectrum on page 698. ANTONYMS criticize, condemn.

2 *we praise God* WORSHIP, glorify, honor, exalt, adore, pay tribute to, give thanks to, venerate, reverence; *formal* laud; *archaic* magnify.

▸ noun 1 *your praise means a great deal to us* APPROVAL, acclaim, admiration, approbation, acclamation, plaudits, congratulations, commendation; tribute, accolade, compliment, a pat on the back, eulogy, panegyric; *formal* encomium.

2 *give praise to God* HONOR, thanks, glory, worship, devotion, adoration, reverence.

THE RIGHT WORD

If your dog sits when you tell him to sit, you'll want to **praise** him for his obedience. *Praise* is a general term for expressing approval, esteem, or commendation that usually suggests the judgment of a superior (*the teacher's praise for her students*). If a salesperson goes out of his way to help you, you may want to **commend** him to his superior, which is a more formal, public way of praising someone, either verbally or in writing. If you're watching a performance and want to express your approval verbally or with applause, **acclaim** is the verb you're looking for. **Laud** and **extol** suggest the highest of praise, although *laud* may imply that the praise is excessive (*the accomplishments for which she was lauded were really nothing out of the ordinary*). *Extol*, which comes from the Latin meaning to raise up, suggests that you're trying to magnify whatever or whomever you're praising (*to extol her virtues so that everyone would vote for her*). If you want to praise someone who has died recently, you will **eulogize** him or her, which means to speak or write your praise for a special occasion, such as a funeral.

praiseworthy adjective *it was a praiseworthy effort* COMMENDABLE, admirable, laudable, worthy (of admiration), meritorious, estimable, exemplary.

prance verb *prancing around in his underpants* CAVORT, dance, jig, trip, caper, jump, leap, spring, bound, skip, hop, frisk, romp, frolic.

prank noun *it was just a stupid and childish prank* (PRACTICAL) JOKE, trick, piece of mischief, escapade, stunt, caper, jape, game, hoax, antic; *informal* lark.

prattle verb *he **prattled on** for ages.* See CHAT verb.

▸ noun *childish prattle.* See CHATTER noun.

pray verb 1 *let us pray* SAY ONE'S PRAYERS, make one's devotions, offer a prayer/prayers.

2 *she prayed God to forgive her* INVOKE, call on, implore, appeal to, entreat, beg, petition, supplicate; *literary* beseech.

prayer noun 1 *the priest's murmured prayers* INVOCATION, intercession, devotion; *archaic* orison.

2 *a quick prayer that she wouldn't bump into him* APPEAL, plea, entreaty, petition, supplication, invocation. PHRASE: **not have a prayer** *informal everyone thought this Minnesota team didn't have a prayer against Duke* HAVE NO HOPE, have/stand no chance, not have/stand (the ghost of) a chance; *informal* not have a hope in hell.

preach verb 1 *he preached to a large congregation* GIVE/DELIVER A SERMON, sermonize, address, speak.

praise
panegyrize
lionize
extol
vaunt
hymn
laud
eulogize
glorify
honor
hail
acclaim
salute
pay homage/tribute to
celebrate
ballyhoo
toast
admire
go into raptures about
flatter
big someone/something up
commend
cheer
clap
sing the praises of
rave about
wax lyrical about
compliment
make much of
speak highly of
pat on the back
congratulate
say nice things about
mention favorably
express approval of
make a remark about
pooh-pooh
look down one's nose at
run down
speak ill of
speak badly of
knock
depreciate
badmouth
pan
do a hatchet job on
bash
pull to pieces
deflate
belittle
dismiss
discredit
cast aspersions on
slam
slate
drag through the mud
slur
libel
defame
decry
deprecate
malign
criticize
denigrate
laugh/sneer/scoff at
mock
ridicule
deride
impugn
slander
revile
traduce
vilify
calumniate
disparage

2 *preaching the gospel* PROCLAIM, teach, spread, propagate, expound.

3 *they preach toleration* ADVOCATE, recommend, advise, urge, teach, counsel.

4 *who are you to preach at me?* MORALIZE, sermonize, pontificate, lecture, harangue; *informal* preachify.

preacher noun *the preacher counsels young couples about marital concerns* MINISTER, parson, clergyman, clergywoman, member of the clergy, priest, imam, rabbi, man/woman of the cloth, man/woman of God, cleric, churchman, churchwoman, evangelist; *informal* reverend, padre, Holy Joe, sky pilot.

preaching noun *I ain't got no use for your preaching* RELIGIOUS TEACHING, message, sermons; *informal* Bible-thumping.

preachy adjective *informal the key to successful preaching is not to be too preachy* MORALISTIC, moralizing, sanctimonious, self-righteous, holier-than-thou, sententious.

preamble noun *we memorized the preamble to the Constitution* INTRODUCTION, preface, prologue; foreword, prelude, front matter; *informal* intro, lead-in; *formal* exordium, proem, prolegomenon.

pre-arranged adjective *your travel particulars have been prearranged* ARRANGED BEFOREHAND, agreed in advance, predetermined, pre-established, preplanned.

precarious adjective *those steps look a bit precarious* UNCERTAIN, insecure, unpredictable, risky, parlous, hazardous, dangerous, unsafe; unsettled, unstable, unsteady, shaky; *informal* dicey, chancy, iffy. ANTONYM safe.

precaution noun *the guard rails are just a precaution* SAFEGUARD, preventative/preventive measure, safety measure, contingency (plan), insurance.

precautionary adjective *as a precautionary measure, don't re-enter the building for at least 24 hours* PREVENTATIVE, preventive, safety.

precede verb **1** *commercials preceded the movie* GO/COME BEFORE, lead (up) to, pave/prepare the way for, herald, introduce, usher in. ANTONYM follow.

2 *Catherine preceded him into the studio* GO AHEAD OF, go in front of, go before, go first, lead the way.

3 *he preceded the book with a poem* PREFACE, introduce, begin, open.

precedence noun *quarrels over precedence* PRIORITY, rank, seniority, superiority, primacy, preeminence, eminence. PHRASE: **take precedence over** *the children's needs take precedence over all the other concerns* TAKE PRIORITY OVER, outweigh, prevail over, come before.

precedent noun *there are few precedents for this type of legislation* MODEL, exemplar, example, pattern, previous case, prior instance/example; paradigm, criterion, yardstick, standard.

preceding adjective *refer to the preceding chart* FOREGOING, previous, prior, former, precedent, earlier, above, aforementioned, antecedent; *formal* anterior, prevenient.

precept noun **1** *the precepts of Orthodox Judaism* PRINCIPLE, rule, tenet, canon, doctrine, command, order, decree, dictate, dictum, injunction, commandment; *Judaism* mitzvah; *formal* prescript.

2 *precepts that her grandmother used to quote* MAXIM, saying, adage, axiom, aphorism, apophthegm.

precinct noun 1 *a pedestrian precinct* AREA, zone, sector.

2 (**precincts**) *within the precincts of the city* BOUNDS, boundaries, limits, confines.

3 *the cathedral precinct* ENCLOSURE, close, court.

4 *the friendliest cop of the 20th precinct* division.

precious adjective 1 *precious works of art* VALUABLE, costly, expensive; invaluable, priceless, beyond price.

2 *her most precious possession* VALUED, cherished, treasured, prized, favorite, dear, dearest, beloved, darling, adored, loved, special.

3 *his precious manners* AFFECTED, overrefined, pretentious; *informal* la-di-da.

precipice noun *it's amazing how these goats can scale such a precipice* CLIFF FACE, cliff, steep cliff, rock face, sheer drop, height, crag, bluff, escarpment, scarp; *literary* steep.

precipitate verb 1 *the incident precipitated a crisis* BRING ABOUT/ON, cause, lead to, give rise to, instigate, trigger, spark, touch off, provoke, hasten, accelerate, expedite.

2 *they were precipitated down the mountain* HURL, catapult, throw, plunge, launch, fling, propel.

▸ adjective 1 *their actions were precipitate* HASTY, overhasty, rash, hurried, rushed; impetuous, impulsive, spur-of-the-moment, precipitous, incautious, imprudent, injudicious, ill-advised, reckless, harum-scarum; *informal* previous; *literary* temerarious.

2 *a precipitate decline.* See PRECIPITOUS sense 2.

precipitous adjective 1 *a precipitous drop* STEEP, sheer, perpendicular, abrupt, sharp, vertical.

2 *his fall from power was precipitous* SUDDEN, rapid, swift, abrupt, headlong, speedy, quick, fast, precipitate.

3 *she was too precipitous.* See PRECIPITATE adjective sense 1.

précis noun *a précis of the report* SUMMARY, synopsis, résumé, abstract, outline, summarization, summation; abridgment, digest, overview, epitome, wrap-up.

▸ verb *précising a passage* SUMMARIZE, sum up, give a summary/précis of, give the main points of; abridge, condense, shorten, synopsize, abstract, outline, abbreviate; *archaic* epitomize.

precise adjective 1 *precise measurements* EXACT, accurate, correct, specific, detailed, explicit, unambiguous, definite. ANTONYM inaccurate.

2 *at that precise moment the car stopped* EXACT, particular, very, specific.

3 *the attention to detail is very precise* METICULOUS, careful, exact, scrupulous, punctilious, conscientious, particular, methodical, strict, rigorous. ANTONYM careless.

precisely adverb 1 *at 2 o'clock precisely* EXACTLY, sharp, promptly, prompt, dead on, on the stroke of; *informal* on the button, on the dot, on the nose.

2 *precisely the kind of man I am looking for* EXACTLY, absolutely, just, in all respects; *informal* to a T.

3 *fertilization can be timed precisely* ACCURATELY, exactly; clearly, distinctly, strictly.

4 *"So it's all done?" "Precisely."* YES, exactly, absolutely, (that's) right, quite so, indubitably, definitely; *informal* you bet, I'll say.

precision noun *tools crafted with precision* EXACTNESS, exactitude, accuracy, correctness, preciseness; care, carefulness, meticulousness, scrupulousness, punctiliousness, methodicalness, rigor, rigorousness.

preclude verb *his difficulties preclude him from leading a normal life* PREVENT, make it impossible for, rule out, stop, prohibit, debar, bar, hinder, impede, inhibit, exclude. See note at PROHIBIT.

precocious adjective *some of the boys were extremely precocious* ADVANCED FOR ONE'S AGE, forward, mature, gifted, talented, clever, intelligent, quick; *informal* smart. ANTONYM backward.

preconceived adjective *our preconceived notions about his latest CD were, much to our delight, quite wrong* PREDETERMINED, prejudged; prejudiced, biased.

preconception noun *it will be difficult to find jurors who have no preconceptions about this case* PRECONCEIVED IDEA/NOTION, presupposition, assumption, presumption, prejudgment; prejudice.

precondition noun *one of the preconditions is a spotless driving record* PREREQUISITE, (necessary/essential) condition, requirement, necessity, essential, imperative, sine qua non; *informal* must.

precursor noun 1 *a three-stringed precursor of the guitar* FORERUNNER, predecessor, forefather, father, antecedent, ancestor, forebear.

2 *a precursor of disasters to come* HARBINGER, herald, sign, indication, portent, omen.

precursory adjective *precursory seismic activity* PRELIMINARY, prior, previous, introductory, preparatory, prefatory; *formal* anterior, prevenient.

predatory adjective 1 *predatory birds* PREDACIOUS, carnivorous, hunting, raptorial; of prey.

2 *a predatory gleam in his eyes* EXPLOITATIVE, wolfish, rapacious, vulturine, vulturous.

predecessor noun 1 *the senator's predecessor* FORERUNNER, precursor, antecedent. ANTONYM successor.

2 *our Victorian predecessors* ANCESTOR, forefather, forebear, antecedent. ANTONYM descendant.

predestined adjective *I find it hard to believe that our lives are predestined* PREORDAINED, ordained, predetermined, destined, fated.

predetermined adjective 1 *a predetermined budget* PREARRANGED, established in advance, preset, set, fixed, agreed.

2 *our predetermined fate* PREDESTINED, preordained.

predicament noun *how did you ever get yourself into such a predicament* DIFFICULT SITUATION, mess, difficulty, plight, quandary, muddle, mare's nest; *informal* hole, fix, jam, pickle, scrape, bind, tight spot/corner, dilemma, can of worms.

predicate verb *our campaign is predicated on the assumption that people want affordable health insurance* BASE, be dependent, found, establish, rest, ground, premise.

predict verb *no one can predict the outcome* FORECAST, foretell, foresee, prophesy, anticipate, tell in advance, envision, envisage; *literary* previse; *archaic* augur, presage.

THE RIGHT WORD

While all of these words refer to telling something before it happens, **predict** is the most commonly used and applies to the widest variety of situations. It can mean anything from hazarding a guess (*they predicted he'd never survive the year*) to making an astute inference based on facts or statistical evidence (*predict that the Republicans would win the election*). When a meteorologist tells us whether it will rain or snow tomorrow, he or she is said to **forecast** the weather, a word that means *predict* but is used particularly in the context of weather and other phenomena that cannot be predicted easily by the general public (*statistics forecast an influx of women into the labor force*). **Divine** and **foreshadow** mean to suggest the future rather than to predict it, especially by giving or evaluating subtle hints or clues. To *divine* something is to perceive it through intuition or insight (*to divine in the current economic situation the disaster that lay ahead*), while *foreshadow* can apply to anyone or anything that gives an indication of what is to come (*her abrupt departure that night foreshadowed the breakdown in their relationship*). **Foretell**, like *foreshadow*, can refer to the clue rather than the person who gives it and is often used in reference to the past (*evidence that foretold the young girl's violent end*). **Augur** means to foreshadow a favorable or unfavorable outcome for something (*the turnout on opening night augured well for the play's success*). **Prophesy** connotes either inspired or mystical knowledge of the future and suggests more authoritative wisdom than *augur* (*a baseball fan for decades, he prophesied the young batter's rise to stardom*). Although anyone who has inside information or knowledge of signs and symptoms can **prognosticate**, it is usually a doctor who does so by looking at the symptoms of a disease to predict its future outcome.

---

predictable adjective *Guido's reaction was predictable* FORESEEABLE, (only) to be expected, anticipated, foreseen, unsurprising; *informal* inevitable.

prediction noun *seven months later, his prediction came true* FORECAST, prophecy, prognosis, prognostication, augury; projection, conjecture, guess.

predilection noun LIKING, fondness, preference, partiality, taste, penchant, weakness, soft spot, fancy, inclination, leaning, bias, propensity, bent, proclivity, predisposition, appetite. ANTONYM dislike.

predispose verb **1** *lack of exercise may predispose an individual to high blood pressure* MAKE SUSCEPTIBLE, make liable, make prone, make vulnerable, put at risk of.

2 *attitudes which predispose people to behave badly* LEAD, influence, sway, induce, prompt, dispose; bias, prejudice.

predisposed adjective INCLINED, prepared, ready, of a mind, disposed, minded, willing.

predisposition noun **1** *a predisposition to heart disease* SUSCEPTIBILITY, proneness, tendency, liability, inclination, disposition, vulnerability.

2 *their political predispositions* PREFERENCE, predilection, inclination, leaning.

predominance noun **1** *the predominance of women caregivers* PREVALENCE, dominance, preponderance.

2 *the superpower's military predominance* SUPREMACY, mastery, control, power, ascendancy, dominance, preeminence, superiority.

predominant adjective **1** *our predominant objectives* MAIN, chief, principal, most important, primary, prime, central, leading, foremost, key, paramount; *informal* number-one.

2 *the predominant political forces* CONTROLLING, dominant, predominating, more/most powerful, preeminent, ascendant, superior, in the ascendancy. ANTONYM subsidiary.

predominantly adverb MAINLY, mostly, for the most part, chiefly, principally, primarily, predominately, in the main, on the whole, largely, by and large, typically, generally, usually.

predominate verb **1** *small-scale producers predominate* BE IN THE MAJORITY, preponderate, be predominant, prevail, be most prominent.

2 *private interest predominates over the public good* PREVAIL, dominate, be dominant, carry most weight; override, outweigh.

preeminence noun SUPERIORITY, supremacy, greatness, excellence, distinction, prominence, predominance, eminence, importance, prestige, stature, fame, renown, celebrity.

preeminent adjective GREATEST, leading, foremost, best, finest, chief, outstanding, excellent, distinguished, prominent, eminent, important, top, famous, renowned, celebrated, illustrious, supreme, marquee. ANTONYM undistinguished.

preeminently adverb *she is preeminently qualified to teach biology* PRIMARILY, principally, above all, chiefly, mostly, mainly, in particular.

preempt verb **1** *his action may have preempted war* FORESTALL, prevent.

2 *many tables were already preempted by family parties* COMMANDEER, occupy, seize, arrogate, appropriate, take over, secure, reserve.

preen verb **1** *the robin preened its feathers* CLEAN, tidy, groom, smooth, arrange; *archaic* plume.

2 *she preened before the mirror* ADMIRE ONESELF, primp oneself, groom oneself, spruce oneself up; *informal* titivate oneself, doll oneself up, gussy oneself up.

preface noun *the preface to the novel* INTRODUCTION, foreword, preamble, prologue, prelude; front matter; *informal* prelims, intro, lead-in; *formal* exordium, proem, prolegomenon.

▸ verb *the chapter is prefaced by a poem* PRECEDE, introduce, begin, open, start.

prefatory adjective *prefatory text* INTRODUCTORY, preliminary, opening, initial, preparatory, initiatory, precursory. ANTONYM closing.

prefer verb **1** *I prefer white wine to red* LIKE BETTER, would rather (have), would sooner (have), favor, be more partial to; choose, select, pick, opt for, go for.

2 *formal do you want to prefer charges?* BRING, press, file, lodge, lay.

3 *archaic he was preferred to the post* PROMOTE, upgrade, raise, elevate.

preferable adjective *Dom sleeps on a foam pillow, but for me goose down is preferable* BETTER, best, more desirable, more suitable, advantageous, superior, preferred, recommended.

preferably adverb *we'd like a table by the window, preferably nonsmoking* IDEALLY, if possible, for preference, from choice.

preference noun **1** *her preference for boys' games* LIKING, partiality, predilection, proclivity, fondness, taste, inclination, leaning, bias, bent, penchant, predisposition.

2 *my preference is rock music* FAVORITE, (first) choice, selection; *informal* cup of tea, thing, druthers.

3 *preference will be given to applicants speaking Japanese* PRIORITY, favor, precedence, preferential treatment. PHRASE: **in preference to** *the thief chose their home in preference to others* RATHER THAN, instead of, in place of, sooner than.

WORD NOTE **druthers**

As in "if I had my druthers." As a way of indicating a preference this nonstandard word deserves to be used more widely in place of bland, overly corporate- or financial-sounding terms like *options.*

The only problem is that some people who know *druthers* from *Li'l Abner* think it is a mock-Southernism, and therefore condescending. I don't hear it that way, though, and it predates the comic strip. So use without fear. **—DA**

preferential adjective *we were not expecting this preferential treatment* SPECIAL, better, privileged, superior, favorable; partial, discriminatory, partisan, biased.

prefigure verb *his work prefigures that of the magic realists* FORESHADOW, presage, be a harbinger of, herald; *literary* foretoken.

pregnancy noun *how far along is she in the pregnancy?* gestation; *rare* parturiency, gravidity.

pregnant adjective 1 *she is pregnant* EXPECTING A BABY, expectant, carrying a child; *informal* expecting, in the family way, with a bun in the oven, knocked up; *chiefly Brit. informal* preggers; *informal, dated* in trouble; *archaic* with child; *technical* parturient, gravid.

2 *a ceremony pregnant with religious significance* FILLED, charged, heavy; full of.

3 *a pregnant pause* MEANINGFUL, significant, suggestive, expressive, charged.

prehistoric adjective 1 *prehistoric times* PRIMITIVE, primeval, primordial, primal, ancient, early, antediluvian.

2 *the special effects look prehistoric* OUT OF DATE, outdated, outmoded, old-fashioned, passé, antiquated, archaic, behind the times, primitive, antediluvian; *informal* horse-and-buggy, clunky. ANTONYM modern.

prejudice noun 1 *male prejudices about women* PRECONCEIVED IDEA, preconception, prejudgment.

2 *they are motivated by prejudice* BIGOTRY, bias, partisanship, partiality, intolerance, discrimination, unfairness, inequality. See note at BIAS.

3 *without prejudice to the interests of others* DETRIMENT, harm, damage, injury, hurt, loss.

▸ verb 1 *the article could prejudice the jury* BIAS, influence, sway, predispose, make biased, make partial, color.

2 *this could prejudice his chances of victory* DAMAGE, be detrimental to, be prejudicial to, injure, harm, hurt, spoil, impair, undermine, hinder, compromise.

prejudiced adjective *his prejudiced views* BIASED, bigoted, discriminatory, partisan, intolerant, narrow-minded, unfair, unjust, inequitable, colored. ANTONYM impartial.

prejudicial adjective *disclosure of the information would be prejudicial* DETRIMENTAL, damaging, injurious, harmful, disadvantageous, hurtful, deleterious. ANTONYM beneficial.

preliminary adjective *the discussions are still at a preliminary stage* PREPARATORY, introductory, initial, opening, prefatory, precursory; early, exploratory. ANTONYM final.

▸ noun 1 **(preliminaries)** *he began without any preliminaries* INTRODUCTION, preamble, opening/prefatory remarks, formalities.

2 *a preliminary to the resumption of war* PRELUDE, preparation, preparatory measure, preliminary action.

PHRASE: **preliminary to** *the geese gather in estuaries, preliminary to their flight southward* IN PREPARATION FOR, before, in advance of, prior to, preparatory to.

prelude noun 1 *the cease-fire was a prelude to peace negotiations* PRELIMINARY, overture, opening, preparation, introduction, start, commencement, beginning, lead-in, precursor.

2 *an orchestral prelude* OVERTURE, introductory movement, introduction, opening.

3 *the passage forms a prelude to Part III* INTRODUCTION, preface, prologue, foreword, preamble; *informal* intro, lead-in; *formal* exordium, proem, prolegomenon.

premature adjective 1 *his premature death* UNTIMELY, (too) early, unseasonable, before time. ANTONYM overdue.

2 *a premature baby* PRETERM. ANTONYM overdue.

3 *such a step would be premature* RASH, ill-considered, overhasty, hasty, precipitate, precipitous, impulsive, impetuous, inopportune; *informal* previous.

premeditated adjective *the premeditated murder of Lady Boswell* PLANNED, intentional, deliberate, preplanned, calculated, cold-blooded, conscious, prearranged. ANTONYM spontaneous.

premeditation noun *the prosecution is trying to prove premeditation* (ADVANCE) PLANNING, forethought, preplanning, (criminal) intent; *Law* malice aforethought.

premier adjective *a premier chef* LEADING, foremost, chief, principal, head, top-ranking, top, prime, primary, first, highest, preeminent, nonpareil, senior, outstanding, master, ranking; *informal* top-notch, blue-ribbon, blue-chip.

▸ noun *the Nova Scotian premier* LEADER, head of government, government leader; president, chancellor, prime minister, PM.

premiere noun *tickets for a Broadway premiere* FIRST PERFORMANCE, first night, opening night.

premise noun *the premise that human life consists of a series of choices* PROPOSITION, assumption, hypothesis, thesis, presupposition, postulation, postulate, supposition, presumption, surmise, conjecture, speculation, assertion, belief.

▸ verb *they premised that the cosmos is indestructible* POSTULATE, hypothesize, conjecture, posit, theorize, suppose, presuppose, surmise, assume.

premises plural noun *he was asked to leave the premises* BUILDING(S), property, site, office.

premium noun 1 *monthly premiums of $30* (REGULAR) PAYMENT, installment.

2 *you must pay a premium for organic fruit* SURCHARGE, additional payment, extra amount.

3 *a foreign service premium* BONUS, extra; incentive, inducement; *informal* perk; *formal* perquisite. PHRASES: **at a premium** *back then, sugar was at a premium* SCARCE, in great demand, hard to come by, in short supply, thin on

the ground. **put/place a premium on** 1 *I place a high premium on our relationship* VALUE GREATLY, attach great/special importance to, set great store by, put a high value on. 2 *the high price of oil put a premium on the coal industry* MAKE VALUABLE, make invaluable, make important.

premonition noun *we've learned to take her premonitions seriously* FOREBODING, presentiment, intuition, (funny) feeling, hunch, suspicion, feeling in one's bones; misgiving, apprehension, fear; *archaic* presage. See note at OMINOUS.

preoccupation noun 1 *an air of preoccupation* PENSIVENESS, concentration, engrossment, absorption, self-absorption, musing, thinking, deep thought, brown study, brooding; abstraction, absentmindedness, distraction, forgetfulness, inattentiveness, woolgathering, daydreaming.

2 *their main preoccupation was feeding their family* OBSESSION, concern; passion, enthusiasm, hobbyhorse.

preoccupied adjective 1 *officials preoccupied with their careers* OBSESSED, concerned, absorbed, engrossed, intent, involved, wrapped up.

2 *she looked preoccupied* LOST/DEEP IN THOUGHT, in a brown study, pensive, absentminded, distracted, abstracted.

preoccupy verb *the issues that preoccupy environmentalists* ENGROSS, concern, absorb, take up someone's attention, distract, obsess, occupy, prey on someone's mind.

preordain verb *he believes that everything we do is preordained* PREDESTINE, destine, foreordain, ordain, fate, predetermine, determine.

preparation noun 1 *the preparation of contingency plans* DEVISING, putting together, drawing up, construction, composition, production, getting ready, development.

2 **(preparations)** *preparations for the party* ARRANGEMENTS, planning, plans, preparatory measures.

3 *preparation for exams* INSTRUCTION, teaching, coaching, training, tutoring, drilling, priming.

4 *a preparation to kill off mites* MIXTURE, compound, concoction, solution, tincture, medicine, potion, cream, ointment, lotion.

preparatory adjective *preparatory work* PRELIMINARY, initial, introductory, prefatory, opening, preparative, precursory. PHRASE: **preparatory to** *we locked all the doors and windows preparatory to leaving* IN PREPARATION FOR, before, prior to, preliminary to.

prepare verb 1 *I want you to prepare a report* MAKE/GET READY, put together, draw up, produce, arrange, assemble, construct, compose, formulate.

2 *the meal was easy to prepare* COOK, make, get, put together, concoct; *informal* fix, rustle up.

3 *preparing for war* GET READY, make preparations, arrange things, make provision, get everything set.

4 *athletes preparing for the Olympics* TRAIN, get into shape, practice, get ready.

5 *I must prepare for my exams* STUDY, review.

6 *this course prepares students for their exams* INSTRUCT, coach, train, tutor, drill, prime.

7 *prepare yourself for a shock* BRACE, make ready, tense, steel, steady.

prepared adjective 1 *he needs to be prepared for the worst* READY, (all) set, equipped, primed; waiting, on hand, poised, in position.

2 *I'm not prepared to cut the price* WILLING, ready, disposed, predisposed, (favorably) inclined, of a mind, minded.

preponderance noun 1 *the preponderance of women among older people* PREVALENCE, predominance, dominance.

2 *the preponderance of the evidence* BULK, majority, larger part, best/better part.

3 *the preponderance of the unions* PREDOMINANCE, dominance, ascendancy, supremacy, power.

preponderant adjective *the preponderant presence of the U.S. military* DOMINANT, predominant, preeminent, in control, more/most powerful, superior, supreme, ascendant, in the ascendancy.

preponderate verb *young voters preponderate at these benefit concerts* BE IN THE MAJORITY, predominate, be predominant; be more/most important, prevail, dominate, reign.

prepossessing adjective *his prepossessing wife turned heads wherever they went* ATTRACTIVE, beautiful, pretty, handsome, good-looking, fetching, charming, delightful, enchanting, captivating; *archaic* fair. ANTONYM ugly.

preposterous adjective *at these sessions, no ideas are too preposterous to throw on the table* ABSURD, ridiculous, foolish, stupid, ludicrous, farcical, laughable, comical, risible, nonsensical, senseless, insane; outrageous, monstrous; *informal* crazy. See note at ABSURD. ANTONYM sensible.

prerequisite noun *a prerequisite for the course* (NECESSARY) CONDITION, precondition, essential, requirement, requisite, necessity, sine qua non; *informal* must.

▸ adjective *the prerequisite qualifications* NECESSARY, required, called for, essential, requisite, obligatory, compulsory. ANTONYM unnecessary.

prerogative noun *it's my prerogative to hold on to the farm* ENTITLEMENT, right, privilege, advantage, due, birthright.

presage verb *the owl's hooting presages death* PORTEND, augur, foreshadow, foretell, prophesy, be an omen of, herald, be a sign of, be the harbinger of, warn of, be a presage of, signal, bode, promise, threaten; *literary* betoken, foretoken, forebode.

▸ noun *a somber presage of his final illness* OMEN, sign, indication, portent, warning, forewarning, harbinger, augury, prophecy, foretoken.

prescience noun *the uncanny prescience of children* FARSIGHTEDNESS, foresight, foreknowledge; psychic powers, clairvoyance; prediction, prognostication, divination, prophecy, augury; insight, intuition, perception, percipience.

WORD NOTE **prescience**

What appeals to me about this word is how you can use it to describe a predictive knowledge of the future *(In retrospect, Kafka's novels strike us as having an almost eerie prescience)* without sounding as if you believe in ESP, or some other such hocus-pocus. *Clairvoyance* and *second-sightedness* are obviously quite different. Perhaps that's simply because *prescience* has "science" embedded in it.

The word, and how we use it, seems to me to imply that, without necessarily admitting it or making a big fuss, we understand that there are many occasions on which, without any rational explanation, we know what is going to happen. —FP

---

prescient adjective *the outcome was predicted in Leonard's prescient article* PROPHETIC, predictive, visionary; psychic, clairvoyant; farsighted, prognostic, divinatory; insightful, intuitive, perceptive, percipient.

prescribe verb 1 *the doctor prescribed antibiotics* WRITE A PRESCRIPTION FOR, authorize.

2 *traditional values prescribe a life of domesticity* ADVISE, recommend, advocate, suggest, endorse, champion, promote.

3 *rules prescribing your duty* STIPULATE, lay down, dictate, specify, determine, establish, fix.

prescription noun 1 *the doctor wrote a prescription* INSTRUCTION, authorization; *informal* scrip; *archaic* recipe.

2 *he fetched the prescription from the drug store* MEDICINE, drugs, medication.

3 *a painless prescription for improvement* METHOD, measure; recommendation, suggestion, recipe, formula.

prescriptive adjective *their instructions are too prescriptive* DICTATORIAL, narrow, rigid, authoritarian, arbitrary, repressive, dogmatic.

presence noun 1 *the presence of a train was indicated electrically* EXISTENCE, being there. ANTONYM absence.

2 *I requested the presence of a nurse* ATTENDANCE, appearance; company, companionship. ANTONYM absence.

3 *a woman of great presence* AURA, charisma, (strength/force of) personality; poise, self-assurance, self-confidence.

4 *she felt a presence in the castle* GHOST, spirit, specter, phantom, apparition, supernatural being; *informal* spook; *literary* shade. PHRASE: **presence of mind** *I didn't have the presence of mind to read his license plate* COMPOSURE, equanimity, self-possession, levelheadedness, self-assurance, calmness, sangfroid, imperturbability; alertness, quick-wittedness; *informal* cool, unflappability.

present[1] adjective 1 *a doctor must be present at the ringside* IN ATTENDANCE, here, there, near, nearby, (close/near) at hand, available. ANTONYM absent.

2 *organic compounds are present in the waste* IN EXISTENCE, existing, existent. See note at ABSENT. ANTONYM absent.

3 *the present economic climate* CURRENT, present-day, existing. ANTONYMS past, future.

▸ noun *forget the past and think about the present* NOW, today, the present time/moment, the here and now. ANTONYMS past, future.

PHRASES: **at present** *at present, we are offering free installation* AT THE MOMENT, just now, right now, at the present time, currently, at this moment in time. **for the present** *he can stay in the guest room, but only for the present* FOR THE TIME BEING, for now, for the moment, for a while, temporarily, pro tem.

present[2] verb 1 *the president presented a check to the winner* HAND OVER/OUT, give (out), confer, bestow, award, grant, accord.

2 *the committee presented its report* SUBMIT, set forth, put forward, proffer, offer, tender, table.

3 *may I present my wife?* INTRODUCE, make known, acquaint someone with.

4 *I called to present my warmest compliments* OFFER, give, express.

5 *they presented their new product last month* DEMONSTRATE, show, put on show/display, exhibit, display, launch, unveil.

6 *presenting good quality opera* STAGE, put on, produce, perform.

7 *she presents a TV show* HOST, introduce, be the presenter of, emcee.

8 *the authorities present him as a common criminal* REPRESENT, describe, portray, depict. PHRASE: **present oneself/itself** 1 *he presented himself at ten* BE PRESENT, make an appearance, appear, turn up, arrive. 2 *an opportunity that presented itself* OCCUR, arise, happen, come about/up, appear, crop up, turn up.

present[3] noun *a birthday present* GIFT, donation, offering, contribution; *informal* freebie; *formal* benefaction.

THE RIGHT WORD

What's the difference between a birthday **present** and a Christmas **gift**? Both words refer to something given as an expression of friendship, affection, esteem, etc. But *gift* is a more formal term, suggesting something of monetary value that is formally bestowed on an individual, group, or institution (*a gift to the university*). *Present*, on the other hand, implies something of less value that is an expression of goodwill (*a housewarming present; a present for the teacher*). **Largesse** is a somewhat pompous term for a very generous gift that is conferred in an ostentatious or condescending way, often on many recipients (*the king's largesse; the largesse of our government*). A **gratuity** is associated with tipping and other forms of voluntary compensation for special attention or service above and beyond what is included in a charge (*known for her generous gratuities, the duchess enjoyed watching the waiters compete with each other to serve her*), while a **lagniappe** is a Southern word, used chiefly in Louisiana and southeast Texas, for either a gratuity or a small gift given to a customer along with a purchase. If you give money or anything else as a gift to a philanthropic, charitable, or religious organization, it is known as a **donation** (*donations for the poor*). But if your employer gives you money at the end of the year in addition to your regular salary, it isn't a Christmas gift; it's a Christmas **bonus**.

---

presentable adjective 1 *I'm making the place look presentable* TIDY, neat, straight, clean, spick-and-span, in good order, shipshape.

2 *make yourself presentable* NICELY DRESSED, tidily dressed, smartly dressed, tidy, well-groomed, trim, spruce; *informal* natty.

3 *presentable videos* FAIRLY GOOD, passable, all right, satisfactory, moderately good, not (too) bad, average, fair; *informal* OK.

presentation noun 1 *the presentation of his certificate* AWARDING, presenting, giving, handing over/out, bestowal, granting, award.

2 *the presentation of food* APPEARANCE, arrangement, packaging, disposition, display, layout.

3 *the presentation of new proposals* SUBMISSION, proffering, offering, tendering, advancing, proposal, suggestion, mooting, tabling.

4 *a sales presentation* DEMONSTRATION, talk, lecture, address, speech, show, exhibition, display, introduction, launch, launching, unveiling.

5 *a presentation of his latest play* STAGING, production, performance, mounting, showing.

present-day adjective *present-day methods are more effective as well as time-saving* CURRENT, present, contemporary, latter-day, present-time, modern, twenty-first-century; up-to-date, up-to-the-minute, fashionable, trend-setting, the latest, new, newest, newfangled; *informal* trendy, now.

presentiment noun *a presentiment of disaster* PREMONITION, foreboding, intuition, (funny) feeling, hunch, feeling in one's bones, sixth sense; *archaic* presage.

presently adverb 1 *I shall see you presently* SOON, shortly, directly, quite soon, in a short time, in a little while, at any moment/minute/second, in next to no time, before long, momentarily; *informal* pretty soon, any moment now, in a jiffy, in two shakes of a lamb's tail; *literary* ere long.

2 *he is presently abroad* CURRENTLY, at present, at the/this moment, at the present moment/time, now, nowadays, these days.

preservation noun 1 *wood preservation* CONSERVATION, protection, care.

2 *the preservation of the status quo* CONTINUATION, conservation, maintenance, upholding, sustaining, perpetuation.

3 *the preservation of food* CONSERVING, bottling, canning, freezing, drying; curing, smoking, pickling.

preserve verb 1 *oil helps preserve wood* CONSERVE, protect, maintain, care for, look after.

2 *they wish to preserve the status quo* CONTINUE (WITH), conserve, keep going, maintain, uphold, sustain, perpetuate.

3 *preserving him from harassment* GUARD, protect, keep, defend, safeguard, shelter, shield.

4 *spices enable us to preserve food* CONSERVE, bottle, can, freeze, dry, freeze-dry; cure, smoke, pickle.

▸ noun 1 **(preserves)** *strawberry preserves* JAM, jelly, marmalade, conserve, fruit spread.

2 *the preserve of an educated middle-class* DOMAIN, area, field, sphere, orbit, realm, province, territory; *informal* turf, bailiwick.

3 *a game preserve* SANCTUARY, (game) reserve, reservation, protected area.

preside verb *Dorothy* ***presides at*** *the meeting* CHAIR, be chairman/chairwoman/chairperson of/at, officiate (at), conduct, lead. PHRASE: **preside over** *the chief financial officer should preside over these budget talks* BE IN CHARGE OF, be responsible for, be at the head/helm of, head, be head of, manage, administer, be in control of, control, direct, lead, govern, rule, command, supervise, oversee; *informal* head up, be boss of, be in the driver's seat of/at, be in the saddle of/at.

president noun 1 *terrorists assassinated the president* HEAD OF STATE, chief executive, premier, prime minister.

2 *the president of the society* HEAD, chief, director, leader, governor, principal, master; *informal* prez.

3 *the president of the company* CHAIRMAN, chairwoman, chief executive (officer), CEO; owner, managing director.

press verb 1 *press the paper down firmly* PUSH (DOWN), press down, depress, hold down, force, thrust, squeeze, compress.

2 *his shirt was pressed* SMOOTH (OUT), iron, remove creases from.

3 *we pressed the grapes* CRUSH, squeeze, squash, mash, pulp, pound, pulverize, macerate.

4 *she pressed the child to her bosom* CLASP, hold close, hug, cuddle, squeeze, clutch, grasp, embrace.

5 *Hillary pressed his hand* SQUEEZE, grip, clutch.

6 *the crowd pressed around* CLUSTER, gather, converge, congregate, flock, swarm, throng, crowd.

7 *the government pressed its claim* PLEAD, urge, advance insistently, present, submit, put forward.

8 *they pressed him to agree* URGE, put pressure on, force, push, coerce, dragoon, steamroller, browbeat; *informal* lean on, put the screws on, twist someone's arm, railroad, bulldoze.

9 *they pressed for a ban on the ivory trade* CALL, ask, advocate, clamor, push, campaign, demand, lobby.

▸ noun 1 *a small literary press* PUBLISHING HOUSE, publisher; printing house/company; printing press.

2 *the freedom of* ***the press*** THE MEDIA, the newspapers, the papers, the news media, the fourth estate; journalists, reporters, newspapermen/newspaperwomen, newsmen/newswomen, pressmen; *informal* journos, newshounds, newsies.

3 *the company had some bad press* (PRESS) REPORTS, press coverage, press articles, (press) reviews, media attention.

PHRASES: **be pressed for** *you shouldn't schedule an interview when you are pressed for time* HAVE TOO LITTLE, be short of, have insufficient, lack, be lacking (in), be deficient in, need, be/stand in need of; *informal* be strapped for. **press on** *the team regrouped and pressed on* PROCEED, keep going, continue, carry on, make progress, make headway, press ahead, forge on/ahead, soldier on, push on, keep on, struggle on, persevere, keep at it, stay with it, stick with it, plod on, plug away.

pressing adjective 1 *a pressing problem* URGENT, critical, crucial, acute, desperate, serious, grave, life-and-death.

2 *a pressing engagement* IMPORTANT, high-priority, critical, crucial, compelling, inescapable. See note at CRUCIAL.

pressure noun 1 *confined gas exerts a constant pressure* PHYSICAL FORCE, load, stress, thrust; compression, weight.

2 *they put pressure on us to borrow money* COERCION, force, compulsion, constraint, duress; pestering, harassment, nagging, badgering, intimidation, arm-twisting, persuasion.

3 *she had a lot of pressure from work* STRAIN, stress, tension, trouble, difficulty; *informal* hassle.

▸ verb *they pressured him into resigning* COERCE, pressure, put pressure on, press, push, persuade, force, bulldoze, hound, harass, nag, harry, badger, goad, pester, browbeat, bully, bludgeon, intimidate, dragoon, twist someone's arm, strong-arm; *informal* railroad, lean on, hustle.

prestige noun *she missed the prestige of the job, but not the ungodly hours of work* STATUS, standing, stature, reputation, repute, regard, fame, note, renown, honor, esteem, celebrity, importance, prominence, influence, eminence; kudos, cachet; *informal* clout.

prestigious adjective 1 *prestigious journals* REPUTABLE, distinguished, respected, esteemed, eminent, august, highly regarded, well-thought-of, acclaimed, authoritative, celebrated, illustrious, leading, renowned. ANTONYM obscure.

2 *a prestigious job* IMPRESSIVE, important, prominent, high-ranking, influential, affluential, powerful, glamorous; well paid, expensive, upmarket. ANTONYM minor.

presumably adverb *presumably, they'll want an ocean view* I PRESUME, I expect, I assume, I take it, I suppose, I imagine, I dare say, I guess, in all probability, probably, in all likelihood, as likely as not, doubtless, undoubtedly, no doubt.

presume verb 1 *I presumed that it had once been an attic* ASSUME, suppose, dare say, imagine, take it, expect, believe, think, surmise, guess, judge, conjecture, speculate, postulate, presuppose.

2 *let me presume to give you some advice* VENTURE, dare, have the audacity/effrontery, be so bold as. PHRASE: **presume on** *he was careful not to presume on their friendship* TAKE (UNFAIR) ADVANTAGE OF, exploit, take liberties with; count on, bank on, place reliance on.

presumption noun 1 *this presumption may be easily rebutted* ASSUMPTION, supposition, presupposition, belief, guess, judgment, surmise, conjecture, speculation, hypothesis, postulation, inference, deduction, conclusion.

2 *he apologized for his presumption* BRAZENNESS, audacity, boldness, audaciousness, temerity, arrogance, presumptuousness, forwardness; cockiness, insolence, impudence, bumptiousness, impertinence, effrontery, cheek, cheekiness; rudeness, impoliteness, disrespect, familiarity; *informal* nerve, chutzpah, sass, sassiness; *archaic* assumption.

presumptive adjective 1 *a presumptive diagnosis* CONJECTURAL, speculative, tentative; theoretical, unproven, unconfirmed.

2 *the heir presumptive* PROBABLE, likely, prospective, assumed, supposed, expected.

presumptuous adjective *that was quite a presumptuous remark* BRAZEN, overconfident, arrogant, bold, audacious, forward, familiar, impertinent, insolent, impudent, cocky; cheeky, rude, impolite, uncivil, bumptious; *informal* sassy. See note at BOLD.

presuppose verb 1 *this presupposes the existence of a policy-making group* REQUIRE, necessitate, imply, entail, mean, involve, assume.

2 *I had presupposed that theme parks make people happy* PRESUME, assume, take it for granted, take it as read, suppose, surmise, think, accept, consider.

presupposition noun *the presupposition that all enzymes are proteins* PRESUMPTION, assumption, preconception, supposition, hypothesis, surmise, thesis, theory, premise, belief, postulation.

pretend verb 1 *they just pretend to listen* MAKE AS IF, profess, affect; dissimulate, dissemble, put it on, put on a false front, go through the motions, sham, fake it.

2 *I'll **pretend to be** the dragon* PUT ON AN ACT AS, make believe one is, play at being, act (the part of), play-act (the part of), impersonate.

3 *it was useless to pretend innocence* FEIGN, sham, fake, simulate, put on, counterfeit, affect.

4 *he cannot **pretend to** sophistication* CLAIM, lay claim to, purport to have, profess to have.

▸ adjective *informal* *a pretend conversation* IMAGINARY, imagined, pretended, make-believe, made-up, fantasy, fantasized, dreamed-up, unreal, invented, fictitious, mythical, feigned, fake, mock, sham, simulated, artificial, ersatz, false, pseudo; *informal* phony.

pretended adjective *pretended tears* FAKE, faked, affected, assumed, professed, spurious, mock, imitation, simulated, make-believe, pseudo, sham, false, bogus; *informal* pretend, phony.

pretender noun *a pretender to the throne* CLAIMANT, aspirant.

pretense noun 1 *cease this pretense* MAKE-BELIEVE, putting on an act, acting, dissembling, shamming, faking, feigning, simulation, dissimulation, play-acting, posturing; deception, deceit, deceitfulness, fraud, fraudulence, duplicity, subterfuge, trickery, dishonesty, hypocrisy, falsity, lying, mendacity. ANTONYM honesty.

2 *he made a pretense of being unconcerned* (FALSE) SHOW, semblance, affectation, (false) appearance, outward appearance, impression, (false) front, guise, facade, display.

3 *she had dropped any pretense to faith* CLAIM, profession.

4 *he was absolutely without pretense* PRETENTIOUSNESS, display, ostentation, affectation, showiness, posturing, humbug.

pretension noun 1 *the author has no pretension to exhaustive coverage* ASPIRATION, claim, assertion, pretense, profession.

2 *she spoke without pretension* PRETENTIOUSNESS, affectation, ostentation, artificiality, airs, posing, posturing, show, flashiness; pomposity, pompousness, grandiosity, grandiloquence, magniloquence.

pretentious adjective *Clytemnestra is a pretentious name for a dog* AFFECTED, ostentatious, showy; overambitious, pompous, artificial, inflated, overblown, high-sounding, flowery, grandiose, elaborate, extravagant, flamboyant, ornate, grandiloquent, magniloquent, sophomoric; *informal* flashy, highfalutin, la-di-da, pseudo.

preternatural adjective *autumn had arrived with preternatural speed* EXTRAORDINARY, exceptional, unusual, uncommon, singular, unprecedented, remarkable, phenomenal, abnormal, inexplicable, unaccountable; strange, mysterious, fantastic.

pretext noun *he used the pretext of looking for his dog to come into our yard* EXCUSE, false excuse, ostensible reason, alleged reason; guise, ploy, pretense, ruse.

prettify verb *plans to prettify Main Street* BEAUTIFY, make attractive, make pretty, spruce up, adorn, ornament, decorate, smarten (up); *informal* doll up, do up, give something a facelift, titivate.

pretty adjective *a pretty child* ATTRACTIVE, lovely, good-looking, nice-looking, personable, fetching, prepossessing, appealing, charming, delightful, cute, as pretty as a picture; *Scottish* bonny; *informal* easy on the eye; *literary* beauteous; *archaic* fair, comely. ANTONYMS plain, ugly.

▸ adverb *a pretty large sum* QUITE, rather, somewhat, fairly, reasonably, comparatively, relatively.

▸ verb *she's **prettying** herself **up*** BEAUTIFY, make attractive, make pretty, prettify, adorn, ornament, smarten; *informal* do oneself up, titivate.

prevail verb **1** *common sense will prevail* WIN, win out/through, triumph, be victorious, carry the day, come out on top, succeed, prove superior, conquer, overcome; rule, reign.

2 *the conditions that prevailed in the 1950s* EXIST, be in existence, be present, be the case, occur, be prevalent, be current, be the order of the day, be customary, be common, be widespread, be in force/effect; *formal* obtain. PHRASE: **prevail on/upon** *they prevailed upon me to emcee their charity affair* PERSUADE, induce, coax, convince, get, urge, pressure, coerce; *informal* sweet-talk, soft-soap.

prevailing adjective *prevailing attitudes* CURRENT, existing, prevalent, usual, common, general, widespread. See note at PREVALENT.

prevalence noun *the prevalence of smoking among teenagers* COMMONNESS, currency, widespread presence, generality, popularity, pervasiveness, universality, extensiveness; rampancy, rifeness.

prevalent adjective *opposition to the war is prevalent* WIDESPREAD, prevailing, frequent, usual, common, current, popular, general, universal; endemic, rampant, rife. ANTONYM rare.

THE RIGHT WORD

Wildflowers might be **prevalent** in the mountains during the spring months, but a particular type of wildflower might be the **prevailing** one. *Prevalent*, in other words, implies widespread occurrence or acceptance in a particular place or time (*a prevalent belief during the nineteenth century*), while *prevailing* suggests that something exists in such quantity that it surpasses or leads all others in acceptance, usage, or belief (*the prevailing theory about the evolution of man*). Wildflowers might also be **abundant** in the valleys—a word that, unlike *prevalent* and *prevailing*, is largely restricted to observations about a place and may suggest oversupply (*an abundant harvest*; *indications of decay were abundant*). **Plentiful**, on the other hand, refers to a large or full supply without the connotations of oversupply (*a country where jobs were plentiful*). If wildflowers are **rife**, it means that they are not only *prevalent* but spreading rapidly (*speculation was rife among the soldiers*); if they're **copious**, it means they are being produced in such quantity that they constitute a rich or flowing abundance (*weep copious tears*). What often happens, with wildflowers as well as with other beautiful things, is that they become so abundant they are regarded as **common**, a word meaning usual or ordinary (*the common cold*). Like *prevalent*, *common* can apply to a time as well as a place (*an expression common during the Depression*). But neither *abundant* nor *common* connotes dominance as clearly as *prevalent* does.

prevaricate verb *you have prevaricated so often through this testimony that the truth has become unrecognizable* BE EVASIVE, beat around the bush, hedge, fence, shilly-shally, dodge (the issue), sidestep (the issue), equivocate, waffle; temporize, stall (for time); hem and haw; *rare* tergiversate. See note at LIE[1].

prevent verb *how can any one agency prevent drug trafficking?* STOP, put a stop to, avert, nip in the bud, fend off, stave off, ward off; hinder, impede, hamper, obstruct, balk, foil, thwart, forestall, counteract, inhibit, curb, restrain, preclude, preempt; disallow, prohibit, forbid, proscribe, exclude, debar, bar; *literary* stay. See note at HINDER. ANTONYM allow.

preventive adjective **1** *preventive maintenance* PREEMPTIVE, deterrent, precautionary, protective.

2 *preventive medicine* PROPHYLACTIC, disease-preventing.

▸ noun **1** *a preventive against crime* PRECAUTIONARY MEASURE, deterrent, safeguard, security, protection, defense.

2 *disease preventives* PROPHYLACTIC, prophylactic device, prophylactic medicine, preventive drug.

previous adjective *the previous commissioner retired after more than 40 years of service* FOREGOING, preceding, antecedent; old, earlier, prior, former, ex-, past, last, sometime, one-time, erstwhile; *formal* quondam, anterior. ANTONYM next.

PHRASE: **previous to** *previous to this, everything was fine* BEFORE, prior to, until, leading up to, up to, earlier than, preceding; *formal* anterior to.

previously adverb *previously, only the outermost doors were locked at night* FORMERLY, earlier, earlier on, before, hitherto, once, at one time, in the past, in days gone by, in times gone by, in bygone days, in times past, in former times; in advance, already, beforehand; *formal* heretofore.

prey noun **1** *the lions killed their prey* QUARRY, kill. ANTONYMS predator, hunter.

2 *she was Julia's easy prey* VICTIM, target, dupe, gull; *informal* sucker, soft touch, pushover, patsy, sap, schlemiel. PHRASE: **prey on 1** *certain larvae prey on aphids* HUNT, catch; eat, feed on, live on/off. **2** *they prey on the elderly* EXPLOIT, victimize, pick on, take advantage of; trick, swindle, cheat, hoodwink, fleece; *informal* con. **3** *the problem preyed on his mind* OPPRESS, weigh on, weigh heavily on, lie heavy on, gnaw at; trouble, worry, beset, disturb, distress, haunt, nag, torment, plague, obsess.

price noun **1** *the purchase price* COST, charge, fee, fare, levy, amount, sum; outlay, expense, expenditure; valuation, quotation, estimate, asking price; *informal, humorous* damage.

2 *spinsterhood was the price of her career* CONSEQUENCE, result, cost, penalty, sacrifice; downside, snag, drawback, disadvantage, minus.

3 *he had a price on his head* REWARD, bounty, premium.

▸ verb *we priced each ticket is at $5.00* FIX/SET THE PRICE OF,, value, rate cost; estimate.

priceless adjective **1** *priceless works of art* INVALUABLE, of incalculable value/worth, of immeasurable value/worth, beyond price; irreplaceable, incomparable, unparalleled. ANTONYMS worthless, cheap.

2 *informal that's priceless!* See HILARIOUS sense 1.

pricey adjective *informal* See EXPENSIVE.

prick verb **1** *prick the potatoes with a fork* PIERCE, puncture, make/put a hole in, stab, perforate, nick, jab.

2 *her conscience pricked her* TROUBLE, worry, distress, perturb, disturb, cause someone anguish, afflict, torment, plague, prey on, gnaw at.

3 *ambition pricked him on to greater effort* GOAD, prod, incite, provoke, urge, spur, stimulate, encourage, inspire, motivate, push, propel, impel.

4 *the horse* ***pricked up*** *its ears* RAISE, erect.

▸ noun 1 *it felt like the prick of a pin* JAB, sting, pinprick, prickle, stab.

2 *the prick of tears behind her eyelids* STING, stinging, smart, smarting, burning.

3 *the prick of conscience* PANG, twinge, stab.

PHRASE: **prick up one's ears** *we pricked up our ears when he mentioned the Christmas bonuses* LISTEN CAREFULLY, pay attention, become attentive, begin to take notice, attend; *informal* be all ears.

prickle noun 1 *the cactus is covered with prickles* THORN, needle, barb, spike, point, spine.

2 *Willie felt a cold prickle of fear* TINGLE, tingling, tingling sensation, prickling sensation, chill, thrill; *Medicine* paresthesia.

▸ verb *its tiny spikes prickled his skin* STING, prick.

prickly adjective 1 *a prickly hedgehog* SPIKY, spiked, thorny, barbed, spiny; briery, brambly; rough, scratchy; *technical* spiculate, spicular, aculeate, spinose.

2 *my skin feels prickly* TINGLY, tingling, prickling.

3 *a prickly character.* See IRRITABLE.

4 *the prickly question of the refugees* PROBLEMATIC, awkward, ticklish, tricky, delicate, sensitive, difficult, knotty, thorny, irksome, tough, troublesome, bothersome, vexatious.

pride noun 1 *their triumphs were a source of pride* SELF-ESTEEM, dignity, honor, self-respect, self-worth, self-regard, pride in oneself. ANTONYM shame.

2 *take pride in a good job well done* PLEASURE, joy, delight, gratification, fulfillment, satisfaction, a sense of achievement.

3 *he refused her offer out of pride* ARROGANCE, vanity, self-importance, hubris, conceit, conceitedness, self-love, self-adulation, self-admiration, narcissism, egotism, superciliousness, haughtiness, snobbery, snobbishness; *informal* big-headedness; *literary* vainglory. ANTONYMS modesty, humility.

4 *the bull is the pride of the herd* BEST, finest, top, cream, pick, choice, prize, glory, jewel in the crown. ANTONYM dregs.

5 *the rose-covered trellis was the pride of the gardener* SOURCE OF SATISFACTION, pride and joy, treasured possession, joy, delight. PHRASE: **pride oneself on** *Lucas prides himself on his knowledge of wine* BE PROUD OF, be proud of oneself for, take pride in, take satisfaction in, congratulate oneself on, pat oneself on the back for.

THE RIGHT WORD

If you take **pride** in yourself or your accomplishments, it means that you believe in your own worth, merit, or superiority—whether or not that belief is justified (*she took pride in her accomplishments*). When your opinion of yourself is exaggerated, you're showing **conceit**, a word that combines *pride* with self-obsession. If you like to be noticed and admired for your appearance or achievements, you're revealing your **vanity**, and if you show off or boast about your accomplishments, you're likely to be accused of **vainglory**, a somewhat literary term for a self-important display of power, skill, or influence. **Arrogance** is an overbearing pride combined with disdain for others (*his arrogance led him to assume that everyone else would obey his orders*), while **egotism** implies self-centeredness or an excessive preoccupation with yourself (*blinded by egotism to the suffering of others*). While no one wants to be accused of *arrogance* or *egotism*, there's a lot to be said for **self-esteem**, which may suggest undue pride but is more often used to describe a healthy belief in oneself and respect for one's worth as a person (*she suffered from low self-esteem*).

priest noun *he requested to see a priest.* See CLERGYMAN.

priestly adjective *his priestly robes* CLERICAL, pastoral, priestlike, ecclesiastical, sacerdotal, hieratic, rectorial.

prig noun *the notion that librarians are typically prigs is ridiculous* PRUDE, puritan, killjoy; *informal* goody-goody, goody two-shoes.

priggish adjective *Miss Sinclair couldn't possibly have been as priggish as she seemed way back then* SELF-RIGHTEOUS, moralistic, holier-than-thou, sanctimonious, prudish, puritanical, prim, straitlaced, stuffy, prissy, governessy, narrow-minded; *informal* goody-goody, starchy. ANTONYM broad-minded.

prim adjective *Reverend Cooke had two prim little maids for daughters and one wild little hellion for a son* DEMURE, proper, prim and proper, formal, stuffy, straitlaced, prudish; governessy, prissy, priggish, puritanical; *informal* starchy.

primacy noun *the primacy of industry over agriculture* GREATER IMPORTANCE, priority, precedence, preeminence, superiority, supremacy, ascendancy, dominance, dominion, leadership.

prima donna noun 1 LEADING SOPRANO, leading lady, diva, star, opera star, principal singer.

2 *a city council filled with prima donnas* EGO, self-important person, his nibs, temperamental person, princess, diva, pooh-bah.

primal adjective 1 *primal masculine instincts* BASIC, fundamental, essential, elemental, vital, central, intrinsic, inherent.

2 *the primal source of living things* ORIGINAL, initial, earliest, first, primitive, primeval.

primarily adverb 1 *the bishop was primarily a leader of the local community* FIRST AND FOREMOST, first, firstly, essentially, in essence, fundamentally, principally, predominantly, basically.

2 *such work is undertaken primarily for large institutions* MOSTLY, for the most part, chiefly, mainly, in the main, on the whole, largely, to a large extent, especially, generally, usually, typically, commonly, as a rule.

primary adjective 1 *our primary role* MAIN, chief, key, prime, central, principal, foremost, first, first-line, most important, predominant, paramount; *informal* number-one. ANTONYMS secondary, subordinate.

2 *the primary cause* ORIGINAL, earliest, initial, first; essential, fundamental, basic. ANTONYM secondary.

primate noun See table on page 708.

prime[1] adjective 1 *his prime reason for leaving* MAIN, chief, key, primary, central, principal, foremost, first, most important, paramount, major; *informal* number-one. ANTONYMS secondary, subordinate.

2 *the prime cause of flooding* FUNDAMENTAL, basic, essential, primary, central. ANTONYM secondary.

PRIMATES

ape	langur
aye-aye	lemur
baboon	loris
Barbary ape	macaque
bonobo	mandrill
bush baby	mangabey
capuchin	marmoset
chimpanzee	monkey
colobus	orangutan
douroucouli	proboscis monkey
drill	rhesus monkey
gelada	silverback
gibbon	spider monkey
gorilla	squirrel monkey
guenon	tamarin
hamadryas	tarsier
hanuman	titi
howler	vervet
indri	wanderoo

3 *prime agricultural land* TOP-QUALITY, top, best, first-class, first-rate, grade A, superior, supreme, choice, select, finest; excellent, superb, fine; *informal* tip-top, A1, top-notch, blue-ribbon. ANTONYM inferior.

4 *a prime example* ARCHETYPAL, prototypical, typical, classic, excellent, characteristic, quintessential.

▸ noun *he is in his prime* HEYDAY, best days, best years, prime of one's life; youth, salad days; peak, pinnacle, zenith.

prime[2] verb **1** *he primed the gun* PREPARE, load, get ready.

2 *Lucy had primed him carefully* BRIEF, fill in, prepare, put in the picture, inform, advise, instruct, coach, drill; *informal* clue in, give someone the lowdown.

primeval adjective **1** *primeval forest* ANCIENT, earliest, first, prehistoric, antediluvian, primordial; pristine, original, virgin.

2 *primeval fears* INSTINCTIVE, primitive, basic, primal, primordial, intuitive, inborn, innate, inherent.

primitive adjective **1** *primitive times* ANCIENT, earliest, first, prehistoric, antediluvian, primordial, primeval, primal. ANTONYMS modern, recent.

2 *primitive peoples* UNCIVILIZED, barbarian, barbaric, barbarous, savage, ignorant, uncultivated. ANTONYM civilized.

3 *primitive tools* CRUDE, simple, rough, rough and ready, basic, rudimentary, unrefined, unsophisticated, rude, makeshift. ANTONYMS sophisticated, advanced.

4 *primitive art* SIMPLE, natural, unsophisticated, unaffected, undeveloped, unpretentious. ANTONYMS sophisticated, refined.

primordial adjective **1** *the primordial oceans* ANCIENT, earliest, first, prehistoric, antediluvian, primeval.

2 *their primordial desires* INSTINCTIVE, primitive, basic, primal, primeval, intuitive, inborn, innate, inherent, visceral.

primp verb *students are encouraged to primp just before the photo session* GROOM, tidy, arrange, brush, comb; smarten (up), spruce up; *informal* titivate, doll up, tart up, gussy up.

prince noun *the young prince was the object of much media attention* RULER, sovereign, monarch, king, princeling; crown prince; emir, sheikh, sultan, maharaja, raja.

princely adjective **1** *princely buildings.* See SPLENDID sense 1.

2 *a princely sum.* See HANDSOME sense 3.

principal adjective *the principal cause of poor air quality* MAIN, chief, primary, leading, foremost, first, first-line, most important, predominant, dominant, (most) prominent; key, crucial, vital, essential, basic, prime, central, focal; premier, paramount, major, overriding, cardinal, preeminent, uppermost, highest, top, topmost; *informal* number-one. ANTONYM minor.

▸ noun **1** *the principal of the firm* CHIEF, chief executive (officer), CEO, president, chairman, chairwoman, director, managing director, manager, head; *informal* boss.

2 *the school's principal* headmaster, headmistress; dean, rector, chancellor, president, provost.

3 *a principal in a soap opera* LEADING ACTOR/ACTRESS, leading player/performer/dancer, leading role, lead, star.

4 *repayment of the principal* CAPITAL (SUM), debt, loan.

USAGE NOTE **principal, principle**

These two words, though often confused and used incorrectly and interchangeably, share no common definitions. Generally, it's enough to remember that *principal* (= chief, primary, most important) is usually an adjective and that *principle* (= a truth, rule, doctrine, or course of action) is virtually always a noun. Although *principle* is not a verb, we have *principled* as an adjective. But *principal* is sometimes a noun—an elliptical form of *principal official* (*Morgan is principal of the elementary school*) or *principal investment* (*principal and interest*).

Substituting *principal* for *principle* is a fairly common blunder—e.g.: "The Ways and Means bill approved today, after more than a month of deliberation and voting, preserves two of the central principals [read *principles*] put forth by the President: universal coverage and the requirement that employers assume 80 percent of its cost for their workers." (*New York Times*; July 1, 1994.)

Substituting *principle* for *principal* is perhaps even more common—e.g.: "Audio CDs are a principle [read *principal*] source of material for making music with samples." (*Electronic Musician*; June 1994.) **—BG**

principally adverb *the decline is principally due to overfishing* MAINLY, mostly, chiefly, for the most part, in the main, on the whole, largely, to a large extent, predominantly, basically, primarily.

principle noun **1** *elementary principles* TRUTH, proposition, concept, idea, theory, assumption, fundamental, essential, ground rule.

2 *the principle of laissez-faire* DOCTRINE, belief, creed, credo, (golden) rule, criterion, tenet, code, ethic, dictum, canon, law.

3 *a woman of principle* | *sticking to one's principles* MORALS, morality, (code of) ethics, beliefs, ideals, standards; integrity, uprightness, righteousness, virtue, probity, (sense of) honor, decency, conscience, scruples. PHRASE: **in principle 1** *there is no reason, in principle, why we couldn't work together* IN THEORY, theoretically, on paper. **2** *he has accepted the idea in principle* IN GENERAL, in essence, on the whole, in the main. See note at PRINCIPAL.

principled adjective *she is clearly the most principled* *among the candidates* MORAL, ethical, virtuous, righteous, upright, upstanding, high-minded, honorable, honest, incorruptible.

print verb **1** *the newspaper is printed just after midnight* SEND TO PRESS, set in print, run off, reprint.

2 *patterns were printed on the cloth* IMPRINT, impress, stamp, mark.

3 *they printed 30,000 copies* PUBLISH, issue, release, circulate.

4 *the incident is printed on her memory* REGISTER, record, impress, imprint, engrave, etch, stamp, mark.

▸ noun **1** *small print* TYPE, printing, letters, lettering, characters, type size, typeface, font.

2 *prints of his left hand* IMPRESSION, fingerprint, footprint.

3 *Rockwell prints are on sale in the lobby* PICTURE, design, engraving, etching, lithograph, linocut, woodcut.

4 *prints and negatives* PHOTOGRAPH, photo, snapshot, picture, still.

5 *soft floral prints* PRINTED CLOTH/FABRIC, patterned cloth/fabric, chintz.

PHRASES: **in print** *I noticed on Amazon.com that the book is still in print* PUBLISHED, printed, available in bookstores. **out of print** *they will help you track down editions that are out of print* NO LONGER AVAILABLE, unavailable, unobtainable, discontinued.

prior adjective *by prior arrangement* EARLIER, previous, preceding, foregoing, antecedent, advance; *formal* anterior. ANTONYM subsequent.

PHRASE: **prior to** *prior to bedtime, set the clocks back an hour* BEFORE, until, till, up to, previous to, earlier than, preceding, leading up to; *formal* anterior to.

prioritize verb **1** *we must prioritize pollution control* EMPHASIZE, concentrate on, put first, focus on, fast-track, expedite, make a priority.

2 *they prioritize patients according to need* RANK, order, hierarchize, triage; grade, class, categorize.

WORD NOTE **triage**

Triage is an excellent substitute for the overused and often deprecated *prioritize*. A metaphorical extension of an existing word, however overblown, somehow is easier for certain readers and listeners to swallow than what they see as a verbification of an unsuspecting noun. **—EM**

priority noun **1** *safety is our priority* PRIME CONCERN, most important consideration, primary issue.

2 *giving priority to elementary schools* PRECEDENCE, greater importance, preference, preeminence, predominance, primacy, first place.

3 *traffic in the right lane has priority* RIGHT OF WAY.

priory noun *the sisters of this priory are famous for their spinning and weaving* RELIGIOUS HOUSE, abbey, cloister; monastery, friary; convent, nunnery.

prison noun *the prisons upstate are just as crowded* JAIL, lockup, penal institution, detention center, jailhouse, penitentiary, correctional facility; *informal* clink, slammer, hoosegow, the big house, stir, jug, brig, can, pen, cooler, pokey, slam; **(be in prison)** *informal* be inside, be behind bars, do time.

prisoner noun **1** *a prisoner serving a life sentence* CONVICT, detainee, inmate; *informal* jailbird, con, lifer, yardbird.

2 *the army took many prisoners* CAPTIVE, internee, prisoner of war, POW.

prissy adjective *the family was stunned when prissy Aunt Trudy ran off with the tractor salesman* PRUDISH, priggish, prim, prim and proper, straitlaced, Victorian, oldmaidish, schoolmarmish; *informal* starchy.

pristine adjective *Lurene's clothes are always so pristine* IMMACULATE, perfect, in mint condition, as new, unspoiled, spotless, flawless, clean, fresh, new, virgin, pure, unused. ANTONYMS dirty, spoiled.

privacy noun *protecting one's privacy* SECLUSION, solitude, isolation, freedom from disturbance, freedom from interference.

private adjective **1** *his private plane* PERSONAL, own, individual, special, exclusive, privately owned. ANTONYM public.

2 *private talks* CONFIDENTIAL, secret, classified, unofficial, off the record, closet, in camera; backstage, privileged, one-on-one, tête-à-tête, sub rosa. ANTONYMS public, open.

3 *private thoughts* INTIMATE, personal, secret; innermost, undisclosed, unspoken, unvoiced.

4 *a very private man* RESERVED, introvert, introverted, self-contained, reticent, discreet, uncommunicative, unforthcoming, retiring, unsociable, withdrawn, solitary, reclusive, hermitic. ANTONYMS extrovert, extroverted.

5 *they found a private place in which to talk* SECLUDED, solitary, undisturbed, concealed, hidden, remote, isolated, out of the way, sequestered. ANTONYMS busy, crowded.

6 *we can be private here* UNDISTURBED, uninterrupted; alone, by ourselves.

7 *the governor attended in a private capacity* UNOFFICIAL, personal. ANTONYM official.

8 *private industry* INDEPENDENT; privatized, denationalized; commercial, private-enterprise. ANTONYMS public, nationalized.

▸ noun *a private in the army* PRIVATE SOLDIER, common soldier; trooper; sapper, gunner; enlisted personnel; *informal* GI.

PHRASE: **in private** *I'll tell you later, in private* IN SECRET, secretly, privately, behind closed doors, in camera; in confidence, confidentially, between ourselves, entre nous, off the record; *formal* sub rosa.

private detective noun *they hired a private detective to find their birth father* PRIVATE INVESTIGATOR; *informal* private eye, PI, sleuth, snoop, shamus, gumshoe; *informal, dated* private dick.

privately adverb **1** *we must talk privately* IN SECRET, secretly, in private, behind closed doors, in camera; in confidence, confidentially, between ourselves, entre nous, off the record; *formal* sub rosa. ANTONYM publicly.

2 *privately, I am glad* SECRETLY, inwardly, deep down, personally, unofficially.

3 *he lived very privately* OUT OF THE PUBLIC EYE, out of public view, in seclusion, in solitude, alone.

privation noun *years of rationing and privation* DEPRIVATION, hardship, destitution, impoverishment, want, need, neediness, austerity. See note at LACK. ANTONYMS plenty, luxury.

privilege noun **1** *senior students have certain privileges* ADVANTAGE, benefit; prerogative, entitlement, right; concession, freedom, liberty.

2 *it was a privilege to meet her* HONOR, pleasure.

3 *congressional privilege* IMMUNITY, exemption, dispensation.

WORD NOTE **privilege**

Even though some dictionaries OK it, the verb *to privilege* is currently used only in a particular English subdialect that might be called academese. Example: *The patriarchal Western canon privileges univocal discourse situated within established contexts over the polyphonic free play of decentered utterance.* (Yes: it's often that ghastly.) Contemporary academese originated in literary and social theory but has now metastasized throughout much of the humanities. There is exactly one rhetorical situation in which you'd want to use *to privilege, to situate, to interrogate* + some abstract noun phrase, or pretty much any transitivized-verb construction that's three times longer than it needs to be—this is in a university course taught by a professor so thoroughly cloistered, insecure, or stupid as to believe that academese constitutes intelligent writing. A required course, one that you can't switch out of. In any other situation, run very fast the other way. **—DFW**

privileged adjective **1** *a privileged background* WEALTHY, rich, affluent, prosperous; LUCKY, fortunate, elite, favored; (socially) advantaged. ANTONYMS underprivileged, disadvantaged.

2 *privileged information* CONFIDENTIAL, private, secret, restricted, classified, not for publication, off the record, inside; *informal* hush-hush. ANTONYM public.

3 *these foreign diplomats are privileged* IMMUNE (FROM PROSECUTION), protected, exempt, excepted. ANTONYM liable.

privy adjective *he was not* ***privy to*** *the discussions* IN THE KNOW ABOUT, acquainted with, in on, informed of, advised of, apprised of; *informal* wise to; *formal* cognizant of.

▸ noun *dated* *he went out to the privy.* See BATHROOM.

prize noun **1** *an art prize* AWARD, reward, premium, purse; trophy, medal; honor, accolade, crown, laurels, palm.

2 **(prizes)** *the prizes of war* SPOILS, booty, plunder, loot, pickings.

▸ adjective **1** *a prize bull* CHAMPION, award-winning, prizewinning, winning, top, best. ANTONYM second-rate.

2 *a prize example* OUTSTANDING, excellent, superlative, superb, supreme, very good, prime, fine, magnificent, marvelous, wonderful; *informal* great, terrific, tremendous, fantastic.

3 *a prize idiot* COMPLETE, utter, total, absolute, real, perfect, veritable.

▸ verb *many collectors prize his work* VALUE, set great store by, rate highly, attach great importance to, esteem, hold in high regard, think highly of, treasure, cherish. See note at ESTEEM.

prized adjective *his prized sheepdog* TREASURED, precious, cherished, much loved, beloved, valued, esteemed, highly regarded.

prizewinner noun *all of the regional prizewinners advance to the state competition* CHAMPION, winner, gold medalist, victor; *informal* champ, number one.

proactive adjective *you need to be more proactive about the causes you care about* ENTERPRISING, take-charge, energetic, driven, bold, dynamic, motivated, go-ahead.

probability noun **1** *the probability of winning* LIKELIHOOD, prospect, expectation, chance, chances, odds.

2 *relegation is a distinct probability* PROBABLE EVENT, prospect, possibility, good/fair/reasonable bet.

probable adjective *a recurrence of the symptoms is probable* LIKELY, most likely, odds-on, expected, anticipated, predictable, foreseeable, ten to one; *informal* in the cards, a good/fair/reasonable bet. ANTONYM unlikely.

probably adverb *I knew I would probably never see her again* IN ALL LIKELIHOOD, in all probability, as likely as not, (very/most) likely, ten to one, the chances are, doubtless, no doubt; *archaic* like enough.

probation noun *during your probation it is imperative that you miss no scheduled meetings* TRIAL PERIOD, test period, experimental period, trial. See note at NOVICE.

probe noun *a probe into the air crash* INVESTIGATION, inquiry, examination, inquest, exploration, study, analysis.

▸ verb **1** *alien hands probed his body* EXAMINE, feel, feel around, explore, prod, poke, check.

2 *police probed the tragedy* INVESTIGATE, inquire into, look into, study, examine, scrutinize, go into, carry out an inquest into.

probity noun *Rowland has demonstrated little probity in this matter* INTEGRITY, honesty, uprightness, decency, morality, rectitude, goodness, virtue, right-mindedness, trustworthiness, truthfulness, honor. See note at GOODNESS. ANTONYM untrustworthiness.

problem noun **1** *they ran into a problem* DIFFICULTY, trouble, worry, complication, difficult situation; snag, hitch, drawback, stumbling block, obstacle, hurdle, hiccup, setback, catch; predicament, plight; misfortune, mishap, misadventure; dilemma, quandary; *informal* headache, nightmare.

2 *I don't want to be a problem* NUISANCE, bother, pest, irritant, thorn in one's side/flesh, vexation; *informal* drag, pain, pain in the neck.

3 *mathematical problems* PUZZLE, question, poser, enigma, riddle, conundrum; *informal* teaser, brainteaser.

▸ adjective *a problem child* TROUBLESOME, difficult, unmanageable, unruly, disobedient, uncontrollable, recalcitrant, delinquent. ANTONYMS well-behaved, manageable.

problematic adjective *the pest control in this building has gotten very problematic* DIFFICULT, hard, taxing, troublesome, tricky, awkward, controversial, ticklish, complicated, complex, knotty, thorny, prickly, vexed; *informal* sticky. See note at DOUBTFUL. ANTONYMS easy, simple, straightforward.

problematize verb See note below.

WORD NOTE **problematize**

The blame for this awful neologism lies with academia, where the word serves no apparent purpose except to demonstrate one's mastery of obscurantist jargon. Some random titles from the Internet: "Problematizing Formalism: A Double-Cross of the Genre Boundaries"; "Problematizing reifications and naturalizations out of focus ..."; "Problematizing Said's Exilic Category." Equally horrible is the related noun, "the problematic." Then there's "to privilege" (q.v.). Corporate as well as academic culture bears a share of responsibility for this verb-ification of nouns, such as "to incentivize," or—worse—"to incent" (meaning, I guess, to provide motivation for), along with "to prioritize," "to reference," and "to impact." Some of these words have actually made it into the *New Oxford American Dictionary,* but that's no excuse for using them. **—JS**

---

procedure noun *once we establish a procedure, it must be followed* COURSE OF ACTION, plan of action, action plan, policy, series of steps, method, system, strategy, way, approach, formula, mechanism, methodology, MO (modus operandi), technique; routine, drill, practice, operation.

proceed verb **1** *she was uncertain how to proceed* BEGIN, make a start, get going, move, set something in motion; TAKE ACTION, act, go on, go ahead, make progress, make headway. ANTONYM stop.

2 *he proceeded down the road* GO, make one's way, advance, move, progress, carry on, press on, push on. ANTONYM stop.

3 *we should proceed with the talks* GO AHEAD, carry on, go on, continue, keep on, get on, get ahead; **(proceed with)** pursue, prosecute.

4 *there is not enough evidence to* ***proceed against*** *him* TAKE SOMEONE TO COURT, start/take proceedings against, start an action against, make a case against, sue.

5 *all power proceeds from God* ORIGINATE, spring, stem, come, derive, arise, issue, flow, emanate.

proceedings plural noun **1** *the evening's proceedings are underway* EVENTS, activities, happenings, goings-on, doings.

2 *they published the proceedings of the meeting* REPORT, transactions, minutes, account, record(s); annals, archives.

3 *legal proceedings* LEGAL ACTION, court/judicial proceedings, litigation; lawsuit, case, prosecution.

proceeds plural noun *most of the proceeds go to pay salaries* PROFITS, earnings, receipts, returns, takings, take, income, revenue, royalty; *Sports* gate (money/receipts).

process noun **1** *investigation is a long process* PROCEDURE, operation, action, activity, exercise, affair, business, job, task, undertaking.

2 *a new canning process* METHOD, system, technique, means, practice, way, approach, methodology.

▸ verb *applications are processed rapidly* DEAL WITH, attend to, see to, sort out, handle, take care of, action.

PHRASE: **in the process of** *we're in the process of updating our files* IN THE MIDDLE OF, in the course of, in the midst of, in the throes of, busy with, occupied in/with, taken up with/by, involved in.

procession noun *a procession of marching bands* PARADE, march, march past, cavalcade, motorcade, cortège; column, file, train.

proclaim verb **1** *messengers proclaimed the good news* DECLARE, announce, pronounce, state, make known, give out, advertise, publish, broadcast, promulgate, trumpet, blazon. See note at ANNOUNCE.

2 *the men proclaimed their innocence* ASSERT, declare, profess, maintain, protest.

3 *she proclaimed herself president* DECLARE, pronounce, announce.

4 *cheap paint soon proclaims its cheapness* DEMONSTRATE, indicate, show, reveal, manifest, betray, testify to, signify.

proclamation noun *the Church issued a proclamation denouncing the movie* DECLARATION, announcement, pronouncement, statement, notification, publication, broadcast, promulgation, blazoning; assertion, profession, protestation; DECREE, order, edict, ruling.

proclivity noun *his sexual proclivities are none of your business* INCLINATION, tendency, leaning, disposition, proneness, propensity, bent, bias, penchant, predisposition; predilection, partiality, liking, preference, taste, fondness, weakness.

procrastinate verb *fear of failure often causes people to procrastinate* DELAY, put off doing something, postpone action, defer action, be dilatory, use delaying tactics, stall, temporize, drag one's feet/heels, take one's time, play for time, play a waiting game.

procreate verb *the biological imperative to procrastinate* PRODUCE OFFSPRING, reproduce, multiply, propagate, breed.

procure verb **1** *he managed to procure a coat* OBTAIN, acquire, get, find, come by, secure, pick up; buy, purchase, engage; *informal* get hold of, get one's hands on. See note at GET.

2 *the police found that he was procuring* PIMP.

prod verb **1** *Cassie prodded him in the chest* POKE, jab, dig, elbow, butt, stab.

2 *they hoped to prod the government into action* SPUR, stimulate, stir, rouse, prompt, drive, galvanize; persuade, urge, chivvy; incite, goad, egg on, provoke.

▸ noun **1** *a prod in the ribs* POKE, jab, dig, elbow, butt, thrust.

2 *they need a prod to get them to act* STIMULUS, push, prompt, reminder, spur; incitement, goad.

prodigal adjective **1** *prodigal habits die hard* WASTEFUL, extravagant, spendthrift, profligate, improvident, imprudent. ANTONYM thrifty.

2 *a composer who is prodigal with his talents* GENEROUS, lavish, liberal, unstinting, unsparing; *literary* bounteous. ANTONYM mean.

3 *a dessert prodigal with whipped cream* ABOUNDING IN, abundant in, rich in, covered in, awash with, slathered with. See note at PROFUSE. ANTONYM deficient.

prodigious adjective *prodigious quantities of food* ENORMOUS, huge, colossal, immense, vast, great, massive, gigantic, mammoth, tremendous, inordinate, monumental; amazing, astonishing, astounding, staggering, stunning, remarkable, phenomenal, terrific, miraculous, impressive, striking, startling, sensational, spectacular, extraordinary, exceptional, breathtaking, incredible; *informal* humongous, stupendous, fantastic, fabulous, mega, awesome, ginormous; *literary* wondrous. ANTONYMS small, unexceptional.

prodigy noun **1** *a seven-year-old prodigy* GENIUS, mastermind, virtuoso, wunderkind, wonder child, boy wonder, girl wonder; *informal* whiz kid, whiz, wizard.

2 *Germany seemed a prodigy of industrial discipline*

MODEL, classic example, paragon, paradigm, epitome, exemplar, archetype.

produce verb 1 *the company produces furniture* MANUFACTURE, make, construct, build, fabricate, put together, assemble, turn out, create; mass-produce; *informal* churn out.

2 *the vineyards produce excellent wines* YIELD, grow, give, supply, provide, furnish, bear, bring forth.

3 *she produced ten puppies* GIVE BIRTH TO, bear, deliver, bring forth, bring into the world.

4 *he produced five novels* CREATE, originate, fashion, turn out; compose, write, pen; paint.

5 *she produced an ID card* PULL OUT, extract, fish out; present, offer, proffer, show.

6 *no evidence was produced* PRESENT, offer, provide, furnish, advance, put forward, bring forward, come up with.

7 *that will produce a reaction* GIVE RISE TO, bring about, cause, occasion, generate, engender, lead to, result in, effect, induce, set off; provoke, precipitate, breed, spark off, trigger; *literary* beget.

8 *James produced the play* STAGE, put on, mount, present.

▸ noun *fresh produce* FOOD, foodstuff(s), products; harvest, crops, fruit, vegetables, greens.

producer noun 1 *a car producer* MANUFACTURER, maker, builder, constructor, fabricator.

2 *coffee producers* GROWER, farmer.

3 *the producer of the show* IMPRESARIO, manager, administrator, promoter, regisseur.

product noun 1 *a household product* ARTIFACT, commodity, manufactured article; creation, invention; (**products**) goods, wares, merchandise, produce.

2 *his skill is a product of experience* RESULT, consequence, outcome, effect, upshot, fruit, by-product, spin-off.

production noun 1 *the production of washing machines* MANUFACTURE, making, construction, building, fabrication, assembly, creation; mass-production.

2 *the production of literary works* CREATION, origination, fashioning; composition, writing.

3 *literary productions* WORK, opus, creation; publication, composition, piece; work of art, painting, picture; *Law* intellectual property.

4 *agricultural production* OUTPUT, yield; productivity.

5 *admission only on production of a ticket* PRESENTATION, proffering, showing.

6 *a theater production* PERFORMANCE, staging, presentation, show, piece, play.

productive adjective 1 *a productive artist* PROLIFIC, inventive, creative; energetic.

2 *productive talks* USEFUL, constructive, profitable, fruitful, gainful, valuable, effective, worthwhile, helpful.

3 *productive land* FERTILE, fruitful, rich, fecund. ANTONYMS sterile, barren.

productivity noun 1 *workers have boosted productivity* EFFICIENCY, work rate; output, yield, production.

2 *the productivity of the soil* FRUITFULNESS, fertility, richness, fecundity. ANTONYMS sterility, barrenness.

profane adjective 1 *subjects both sacred and profane* SECULAR, lay, nonreligious, temporal; *formal* laic. ANTONYMS religious, sacred.

2 *a profane man* IRREVERENT, irreligious, ungodly, godless, unbelieving, impious, disrespectful, sacrilegious. ANTONYM reverent.

3 *profane language* OBSCENE, blasphemous, indecent, foul, vulgar, crude, filthy, dirty, smutty, coarse, rude, offensive, indecorous. ANTONYM decorous.

▸ verb *invaders profaned our sacred temples* DESECRATE, violate, defile, treat sacrilegiously.

profanity noun 1 *he hissed a profanity | an outburst of profanity* OATH, swear word, expletive, curse, obscenity, four-letter word, dirty word; blasphemy, swearing, foul language, bad language, cursing; *informal* cuss, cuss word; *formal* imprecation; *archaic* execration.

2 *some traditional festivals were tainted with profanity* SACRILEGE, blasphemy, irreligion, ungodliness, impiety, irreverence, disrespect.

profess verb 1 *he professed his love* DECLARE, announce, proclaim, assert, state, affirm, avow, maintain, protest; *formal* aver.

2 *she professed to loathe publicity* CLAIM, pretend, purport, affect; make out; *informal* let on.

3 *the emperor professed Christianity* AFFIRM ONE'S FAITH IN, affirm one's allegiance to, avow, confess.

professed adjective 1 *his professed ambition* CLAIMED, supposed, ostensible, self-styled, apparent, pretended, purported.

2 *a professed libertarian* DECLARED, self-acknowledged, self-confessed, confessed, sworn, avowed, confirmed.

profession noun 1 *his chosen profession of teaching* CAREER, occupation, calling, vocation, métier, line (of work), walk of life, job, business, trade, craft; *informal* racket.

2 *a profession of allegiance* DECLARATION, affirmation, statement, announcement, proclamation, assertion, avowal, vow, claim, protestation; *formal* averment.

professional adjective 1 *people in professional occupations* WHITE-COLLAR, nonmanual. ANTONYM blue-collar.

2 *a professional rugby player* PAID, salaried. ANTONYM amateur.

3 *a thoroughly professional performance* EXPERT, accomplished, skillful, masterly, masterful, fine, polished, skilled, proficient, competent, able, experienced, practiced, trained, seasoned, businesslike, deft; *informal* ace, crack, top-notch. ANTONYM amateurish.

4 *not a professional way to behave* APPROPRIATE, fitting, proper, honorable, ethical, correct, comme il faut. ANTONYMS inappropriate, unethical.

▸ noun 1 *affluent young professionals* WHITE-COLLAR WORKER, office worker. ANTONYM blue-collar worker.

2 *his first season as a professional* PROFESSIONAL PLAYER, paid player, salaried player; *informal* pro. ANTONYM amateur.

3 *she was a real professional on stage* EXPERT, virtuoso, old hand, master, maestro, past master; *informal* pro, ace, wizard, whiz, hotshot, maven, crackerjack. ANTONYM amateur.

professor noun *a number of our professors were Rhodes scholars* PROF, tenured faculty member, dean, full/assistant/associate professor, instructor, lecturer, doctor, scholar, academic.

proffer verb *Coleman proffered his resignation* OFFER,

tender, submit, extend, volunteer, suggest, propose, put forward; hold out. ANTONYMS refuse, withdraw.

proficiency noun *her proficiency was obvious to anyone who sailed with her* SKILL, expertise, experience, accomplishment, competence, mastery, prowess, professionalism, deftness, adroitness, dexterity, finesse, ability, facility; *informal* know-how. ANTONYM incompetence.

proficient adjective *a proficient equestrian* SKILLED, skillful, expert, experienced, accomplished, competent, masterly, adept, adroit, deft, dexterous, able, professional, consummate, complete, master; *informal* crack, ace, mean. ANTONYM incompetent.

profile noun **1** *his handsome profile* SIDE VIEW, outline, silhouette, contour, shape, form, figure, lines.

2 *she wrote a profile of the organization* DESCRIPTION, account, study, portrait, portrayal, depiction, rundown, sketch, outline.

▸ verb *he was profiled in the local paper* DESCRIBE, write about, give an account of, portray, depict, sketch, outline.

PHRASE: **keep a low profile** *in matters concerning his family, he managed to keep a low profile* LIE LOW, keep quiet, keep out of the public eye, avoid publicity, keep out of sight.

profit noun **1** *the firm made a profit* (FINANCIAL) GAIN, return(s), yield, proceeds, earnings, winnings, surplus, excess; *informal* pay dirt, bottom line. ANTONYM loss.

2 *we could gain no profit by continuing* ADVANTAGE, benefit, value, use, good, avail; *informal* mileage. ANTONYM disadvantage.

▸ verb **1** *this company must not profit from its wrongdoing* MAKE MONEY, make a profit; *informal* rake it in, clean up, make a killing, make a bundle, make big bucks, make a fast/quick buck. ANTONYM lose.

2 *how will that profit us?* BENEFIT, be beneficial to, be of benefit to, be advantageous to, be of advantage to, be of use to, be of value to, do someone good, help, be of service to, serve, assist, aid. ANTONYM disadvantage.

PHRASE: **profit by/from** *if you're smart, you'll profit from their mistakes* BENEFIT FROM, take advantage of, derive benefit from, capitalize on, make the most of, turn to one's advantage, put to good use, do well out of, exploit, gain from; *informal* cash in on.

profitable adjective **1** *a profitable company* MONEYMAKING, profit-making, commercial, successful, solvent, in the black, gainful, remunerative, financially rewarding, paying, lucrative, bankable. ANTONYM loss-making.

2 *profitable study* BENEFICIAL, useful, advantageous, valuable, productive, worthwhile; rewarding, fruitful, illuminating, informative, well-spent. ANTONYMS fruitless, useless.

profiteer verb *a store owner was charged with profiteering* OVERCHARGE, racketeer; cheat someone, fleece someone; *informal* rip someone off, rob someone.

▸ noun *he was a war profiteer* RACKETEER, exploiter, black marketeer; *informal* bloodsucker, vampire.

profligate adjective **1** *profligate local authorities* WASTEFUL, extravagant, spendthrift, improvident, prodigal. ANTONYMS thrifty, frugal.

2 *a profligate lifestyle* DISSOLUTE, degenerate, dissipated, debauched, corrupt, depraved; PROMISCUOUS, loose, wanton, licentious, libertine, decadent, abandoned, fast; SYBARITIC, voluptuary. ANTONYMS moral, upright.

▸ noun *he was an out-and-out profligate* LIBERTINE, debauchee, degenerate, dissolute, roué, rake, sybarite, voluptuary.

profound adjective **1** *profound relief* HEARTFELT, intense, keen, great, extreme, acute, severe, sincere, earnest, deep, deep-seated, overpowering, overwhelming, fervent, ardent. ANTONYMS superficial, mild.

2 *profound silence* COMPLETE, utter, total, absolute.

3 *a profound change* FAR-REACHING, radical, extensive, sweeping, exhaustive, thoroughgoing. ANTONYM slight.

4 *a profound analysis* WISE, learned, clever, intelligent, scholarly, sage, erudite, discerning, penetrating, perceptive, astute, thoughtful, insightful, percipient, perspicacious; *rare* sapient. ANTONYM superficial.

5 *profound truths* COMPLEX, abstract, deep, weighty, difficult, abstruse, recondite, esoteric. ANTONYM simple.

profoundly adverb **1** *she was profoundly grateful that none of her colleagues could see her* EXTREMELY, very, deeply, exceedingly, greatly, immensely, enormously, tremendously, intensely, heartily, keenly, acutely, painfully, from the bottom of one's heart, downright, thoroughly, sincerely, so; *informal* awfully, terribly, seriously, majorly, oh-so, mighty.

2 *he spoke profoundly on the subject* PENETRATINGLY, discerningly, wisely, sagaciously, thoughtfully, philosophically, weightily, seriously, learnedly, eruditely.

profuse adjective **1** *profuse apologies* COPIOUS, prolific, abundant, liberal, unstinting, fulsome, effusive, extravagant, lavish, gushing; *informal* over the top, gushy.

2 *profuse blooms* LUXURIANT, plentiful, copious, abundant, lush, rich, exuberant, riotous, teeming, rank, rampant; *informal* jungly. ANTONYMS meager, sparse.

THE RIGHT WORD

Something that is **profuse** is poured out or given freely, often to the point of exaggeration or excess (*profuse apologies*). **Extravagant** also suggests unreasonable excess, but with an emphasis on wasteful spending (*her gift was much too extravagant for the occasion*). Someone who is **prodigal** is so recklessly extravagant that his or her resources will ultimately be exhausted (*the prodigal heir to the family fortune*). Another way to end up impoverished is through **lavish** spending, a word that combines extravagance with generosity or a lack of moderation (*lavish praise; lavish furnishings*). While *lavish*, *extravagant* and *prodigal* are often used to describe human behavior, **lush** and **luxuriant** normally refer to things. What is *luxuriant* is produced in great quantity, suggesting that it is not only profuse but gorgeous (*luxuriant auburn hair*). Something described as *lush* is not only luxuriant but has reached a peak of perfection (*the lush summer grass*).

profusion noun *a profusion of crocuses covered the front lawn* ABUNDANCE, mass, host, cornucopia, riot, superabundance; *informal* sea, wealth; *formal* plenitude.

progenitor noun **1** *the progenitor of an illustrious family* ANCESTOR, forefather, forebear, parent, primogenitor; *Law* stirps; *archaic* begetter.

2 *the progenitor of modern jazz* ORIGINATOR, creator, founder, architect, inventor, pioneer.

progeny noun *genetic traits passed on from parent to*

progeny OFFSPRING, young, babies, children, sons and daughters, family, brood; DESCENDANTS, heirs, scions; *Law* issue; *archaic* seed, fruit of one's loins.

prognosis noun *it is difficult to make an accurate prognosis* FORECAST, prediction, prognostication, prophecy, divination, augury.

prognosticate verb *economists were prognosticating financial Armageddon* FORECAST, predict, prophesy, foretell, foresee, forewarn of. See note at PREDICT.

prognostication noun *their prognostications had proved remarkably accurate* PREDICTION, forecast, prophecy, prognosis, divination, augury.

program noun **1** *our program for the day* SCHEDULE, agenda, calendar, timetable; order of events, lineup.

2 *the government's reform program* plan of action, series of measures, strategy, scheme.

3 *a television program* BROADCAST, production, show, presentation, transmission, performance, telecast.

4 *a program of study* COURSE, syllabus, curriculum.

5 *a theater program* guide, list of performers, cast list, playbill.

▸ verb *they programmed the day well* ARRANGE, organize, schedule, plan, map out, timetable, line up, slate.

progress noun **1** *boulders made progress difficult* FORWARD MOVEMENT, advance, going, progression, headway, passage.

2 *scientific progress* DEVELOPMENT, advance, advancement, headway, step(s) forward; improvement, betterment, growth.

▸ verb **1** *they progressed slowly down the road* GO, make one's way, move, move forward, go forward, proceed, advance, go on, continue, make headway, work one's way.

2 *the school has progressed rapidly* DEVELOP, make progress, advance, make headway, take steps forward, move on, get on, gain ground; improve, get better, come on, come along, make strides; thrive, prosper, blossom, flourish; *informal* be getting there. ANTONYM regress.

PHRASE: **in progress** *the game was already in progress* UNDERWAY, going on, ongoing, happening, occurring, taking place, proceeding, continuing; unfinished, in the works.

progression noun **1** *progression to the next stage* PROGRESS, advancement, movement, passage, march; development, evolution, growth.

2 *a progression of peaks on the graph* SUCCESSION, series, sequence, string, stream, chain, concatenation, train, row, cycle.

progressive adjective **1** *progressive deterioration* CONTINUING, continuous, increasing, growing, developing, ongoing, accelerating, escalating; gradual, step-by-step, cumulative.

2 *progressive views* MODERN, liberal, advanced, forward-thinking, enlightened, enterprising, innovative, pioneering, dynamic, bold, avant-garde, reforming, reformist, radical; *informal* go-ahead. ANTONYMS conservative, reactionary.

▸ noun *he is very much a progressive* INNOVATOR, reformer, reformist, liberal, libertarian.

prohibit verb **1** *state law prohibits gambling* FORBID, ban, bar, interdict, proscribe, make illegal, embargo, outlaw, disallow, veto; *Law* enjoin. ANTONYMS permit, authorize.

2 *a cash shortage prohibited the visit* PREVENT, stop, rule out, preclude, make impossible. ANTONYMS facilitate, allow.

THE RIGHT WORD

There are a number of ways to prevent something from happening. You can prohibit it, which assumes that you have legal or other authority and are willing to back up your prohibition with force (prohibit smoking); or you can simply forbid it and hope that you've got the necessary clout (forbid teenagers to stay out after midnight). Ban carries a little more weight—both legal and moral—and interdict suggests that church or civil authorities are behind the idea. To enjoin (in this sense) is to prohibit by legal injunction (the truckers were enjoined from striking), which practically guarantees that you'll get what you want. A government or some other authority may disallow an act it might otherwise have permitted (the IRS disallowed the deduction), but anyone with a little gumption can hinder an activity by putting obstacles in its path (hinder the thief's getaway by tripping him on his way out the door). Of course, the easiest way to prohibit something is to preclude it, which means stopping it before it even gets started.

prohibited adjective *smoking is prohibited* ILLEGAL, illicit, taboo, against the law, verboten; *informal* out, no go; *formal* non licet. ANTONYM permitted.

prohibition noun **1** *the prohibition of marijuana* BANNING, forbidding, prohibiting, barring, debarment, vetoing, proscription, interdiction, outlawing.

2 *a prohibition was imposed* BAN, bar, interdict, veto, embargo, injunction, moratorium.

prohibitive adjective **1** *prohibitive costs* EXORBITANT, excessively high, sky-high, overinflated; out of the question, beyond one's means; extortionate, unreasonable; *informal* steep, criminal.

2 *prohibitive regulations* PROSCRIPTIVE, prohibitory, restrictive, repressive.

project noun **1** *an engineering project* PLAN, program, enterprise, undertaking, venture; proposal, idea, concept, scheme.

2 *a history project* ASSIGNMENT, piece of work, piece of research, task.

▸ verb **1** *profits are projected to rise* FORECAST, predict, expect, estimate, calculate, reckon.

2 *his projected book* INTEND, plan, propose, devise, design, outline.

3 *balconies projected over the lake* STICK OUT, jut (out), protrude, extend, stand out, bulge out, poke out, thrust out, cantilever. See note at BULGE.

4 *seeds are projected from the tree* PROPEL, discharge, launch, throw, cast, fling, hurl, shoot.

5 *the sun projected his shadow on the wall* CAST, throw, send, shed, shine.

6 *she tried to project a calm image* CONVEY, put across, put over, communicate, present, promote.

projectile noun *the cyclone sent pieces of the house flying like wild projectiles* MISSILE, rocket, bullets.

projecting adjective *a projecting bay window* STICKING OUT, protuberant, protruding, prominent, jutting, overhanging, beetling, proud, bulging. ANTONYMS sunken, flush.

projection noun **1** *a sales projection* FORECAST, prediction, prognosis, outlook, expectation, estimate.

2 *tiny projections on the cliff face* PROTUBERANCE, protrusion, prominence, eminence, outcrop, outgrowth, jut, jag, snag; overhang, ledge, shelf.

proletarian adjective *a proletarian background* WORKING-CLASS, plebeian, common, blue-collar. ANTONYM aristocratic.

▸ noun *disaffected proletarians* WORKING-CLASS PERSON, worker, blue-collar worker, plebeian, commoner, man/woman/person in the street; *derogatory* prole. ANTONYM aristocrat.

proletariat noun *the voice of* ***the proletariat*** THE WORKERS, working-class people, wage earners, the working classes, the common people, the lower classes, the masses, the rank and file, the third estate, the plebeians; *derogatory* the hoi polloi, the plebs, the proles, the great unwashed, the mob, the rabble. ANTONYM aristocracy.

proliferate verb *stories of her trial proliferated* INCREASE RAPIDLY, grow rapidly, multiply, rocket, mushroom, snowball, burgeon, run riot. ANTONYMS decrease, dwindle.

prolific adjective **1** *a prolific crop of tomatoes* PLENTIFUL, abundant, bountiful, profuse, copious, luxuriant, rich, lush; fruitful, fecund; *literary* plenteous, bounteous.

2 *a prolific composer* PRODUCTIVE, creative, inventive, fertile. See note at FERTILE.

prolix adjective *his prolix speeches* LONG-WINDED, verbose, wordy, pleonastic, discursive, rambling, long-drawn-out, overlong, lengthy, protracted, interminable; *informal* windy, waffly.

prologue noun *Davis wrote the prologue to her brother's autobiography* INTRODUCTION, foreword, preface, preamble, prelude; *informal* intro, lead-in; *formal* exordium, proem, prolegomenon. ANTONYM epilogue.

prolong verb *your bickering just prolongs these negotiations* LENGTHEN, extend, draw out, drag out, protract, spin out, stretch out, string out, elongate; carry on, continue, keep up, perpetuate. ANTONYM shorten.

promenade noun **1** *the tree-lined promenade* ESPLANADE, front, seafront, parade, walk, boulevard, avenue, boardwalk.

2 *our nightly promenade* WALK, stroll, turn, amble, airing; *dated* constitutional.

▸ verb *we promenaded in the park* WALK, stroll, saunter, wander, amble, stretch one's legs, take a turn.

prominence noun **1** *his rise to prominence* FAME, celebrity, eminence, preeminence, importance, distinction, greatness, note, notability, prestige, stature, standing, position, rank.

2 *the press gave prominence to the reports* GOOD COVERAGE, importance, precedence, weight, a high profile, top billing.

3 *a rocky prominence* HILLOCK, hill, hummock, mound; outcrop, crag, spur, rise; ridge, arête; peak, pinnacle; promontory, cliff, headland.

prominent adjective **1** *a prominent surgeon* IMPORTANT, well-known, leading, eminent, distinguished, notable, noteworthy, noted, illustrious, celebrated, famous, renowned, acclaimed, famed, influential, affluential, major-league. ANTONYMS unimportant, unknown.

2 *prominent cheekbones* PROTUBERANT, protruding, projecting, jutting (out), standing out, sticking out, proud, bulging, bulbous.

3 *a prominent feature of the landscape* CONSPICUOUS, noticeable, easily seen, obvious, front-and-center, unmistakable, eye-catching, pronounced, salient, striking, dominant; obtrusive. See note at NOTICEABLE. ANTONYM inconspicuous.

promiscuity noun *the promiscuity associated with the sixties and seventies* LICENTIOUSNESS, wantonness, immorality; *informal* sleeping around, sluttishness, whorishness; *dated* looseness. ANTONYMS chastity, virtue.

promiscuous adjective **1** *a promiscuous teenager* LICENTIOUS, sexually indiscriminate, wanton, immoral, fast; *informal* easy, swinging, sluttish, whorish, bed-hopping; *dated* loose, fallen. ANTONYMS chaste, virtuous.

2 *promiscuous reading* INDISCRIMINATE, undiscriminating, unselective, random, haphazard, irresponsible, unthinking, unconsidered. ANTONYM selective.

promise noun **1** *you broke your promise* WORD (OF HONOR), assurance, pledge, vow, guarantee, oath, bond, undertaking, agreement, commitment, contract, covenant.

2 *he shows promise* POTENTIAL, ability, aptitude, capability, capacity.

3 *the promise of fine weather* INDICATION, hint, suggestion, sign.

▸ verb **1** *she promised to go* GIVE ONE'S WORD, swear, pledge, vow, undertake, guarantee, contract, engage, give an assurance, commit oneself, bind oneself, swear/take an oath, covenant; *archaic* plight.

2 *the skies promised sunshine* INDICATE, lead one to expect, point to, denote, signify, be a sign of, be evidence of, give hope of, bespeak, presage, augur, herald, bode, portend; *literary* betoken, foretoken, forebode.

promising adjective **1** *a promising start* GOOD, encouraging, favorable, hopeful, full of promise, auspicious, propitious, bright, rosy, heartening, reassuring. ANTONYM unfavorable.

2 *a promising actor* WITH POTENTIAL, budding, up-and-coming, rising, coming, in the making.

promontory noun *a lone beacon shone from the promontory* HEADLAND, point, cape, head, foreland, horn, bill, peninsula.

promote verb **1** *she's been promoted at work* UPGRADE, give promotion to, elevate, advance, move up; *humorous* kick upstairs; *archaic* prefer. ANTONYM demote.

2 *an organization promoting justice* ENCOURAGE, advocate, further, advance, assist, aid, help, contribute to, foster, nurture, develop, boost, stimulate, forward, work for. ANTONYM obstruct.

3 *she is promoting her new film* ADVERTISE, publicize, give publicity to, beat/bang the drum for, market, merchandise; *informal* push, plug, hype, boost, ballyhoo. ANTONYM play down.

promoter noun *concert promoters* ADVOCATE, champion, supporter, backer, proponent, protagonist, campaigner, booster, publicist; impresario.

promotion noun 1 *her promotion at work* UPGRADING, preferment, elevation, advancement, step up (the ladder).

2 *the promotion of justice* ENCOURAGEMENT, advocacy, furtherance, furthering, advancement, assistance, aid, help, contribution to, fostering, boosting, stimulation, boosterism.

3 *the promotion of her new film* ADVERTISING, publicizing, marketing; publicity, campaign, propaganda; *informal* hard sell, blitz, plug, hype, ballyhoo.

prompt verb 1 *curiosity prompted him to look* INDUCE, make, move, motivate, lead, dispose, persuade, incline, encourage, stimulate, prod, impel, spur on, inspire. ANTONYM discourage.

2 *the statement prompted a hostile reaction* GIVE RISE TO, bring about, cause, occasion, result in, lead to, elicit, produce, bring on, engender, induce, precipitate, trigger, spark off, provoke. ANTONYM restrain.

3 *the actors needed prompting* REMIND, cue, feed, help out; jog someone's memory.

▸ adjective *a prompt reply* QUICK, swift, rapid, speedy, fast, direct, immediate, instant, expeditious, early, punctual, in good time, on time, timely. ANTONYMS slow, late.

▸ noun *the actor stopped, and Julia supplied a prompt* REMINDER, cue, feed.

promptly adverb 1 *William arrived promptly at 7:30* PUNCTUALLY, on time; *informal* bang on, on the button, on the dot, on the nose. ANTONYM late.

2 *I expect the matter to be dealt with promptly* WITHOUT DELAY, straightaway, right away, at once, immediately, now, as soon as possible; QUICKLY, swiftly, rapidly, speedily, fast, expeditiously, momentarily; *informal* pronto, ASAP, PDQ (pretty damn quick). ANTONYM slowly.

promulgate verb 1 *they promulgated their own views* MAKE KNOWN, make public, publicize, spread, communicate, propagate, disseminate, broadcast, promote, preach; *literary* bruit abroad. See note at ANNOUNCE.

2 *the law was promulgated in 1942* PUT INTO EFFECT, enact, implement, enforce.

prone adjective 1 *untreated wood is prone to rotting* | *prone to disease* SUSCEPTIBLE, vulnerable, subject, open, liable, given, predisposed, likely, disposed, inclined, apt; at risk of. ANTONYMS resistant, immune.

2 *his prone body* (LYING) FACE DOWN, face downward, on one's stomach/front; LYING FLAT/DOWN, horizontal, prostrate. ANTONYM upright.

prong noun *sharpening the prongs of the pitchfork* TINE, spike, point, tip, projection.

pronounce verb 1 *his name is difficult to pronounce* SAY, enunciate, articulate, utter, voice, sound, vocalize, get one's tongue around.

2 *the doctor pronounced that I had a virus* ANNOUNCE, proclaim, declare, affirm, assert; judge, rule, decree.

pronounced adjective *a pronounced German accent* NOTICEABLE, marked, strong, conspicuous, striking, distinct, prominent, unmistakable, obvious, recognizable, identifiable. ANTONYM slight.

pronouncement noun *we awaited an official pronouncement from Washington* ANNOUNCEMENT, proclamation, declaration, assertion; judgment, ruling, decree; *formal* ordinance.

pronunciation noun *the pronunciation of difficult words* ACCENT, manner of speaking, speech, diction, delivery, elocution, intonation; articulation, enunciation, voicing, vocalization, sounding.

proof noun 1 *proof of ownership* EVIDENCE, verification, corroboration, authentication, confirmation, certification, documentation, validation, attestation, substantiation.

2 *the proofs of a book* PAGE PROOF, galley proof, galley.

▸ adjective *no system is proof against theft* RESISTANT, immune, unaffected, invulnerable, impenetrable, impervious, repellent.

prop noun 1 *the roof is held up by props* POLE, post, support, upright, brace, buttress, stay, strut, stanchion, shore, pier, pillar, pile, piling, bolster, truss, column.

2 *a prop for the economy* MAINSTAY, pillar, anchor, backbone, support, foundation, cornerstone.

▸ verb 1 *she propped her bike against the wall* LEAN, rest, stand, balance, steady.

2 *this post is* ***propping*** *the wall* ***up*** HOLD UP, shore up, bolster up, buttress, support, brace, underpin.

3 *they* ***prop up*** *failing industries* SUBSIDIZE, underwrite, fund, finance.

propaganda noun *a so-called documentary that was really socialist propaganda* INFORMATION, promotion, advertising, publicity, spin; disinformation, counter-information; *historical* agitprop; *informal* info, hype, plugging; puff piece; the big lie.

propagandist noun *a propagandist for the government's reforms* PROMOTER, champion, supporter, proponent, advocate, campaigner, crusader, publicist, evangelist, apostle.

propagate verb 1 *an easy plant to propagate* BREED, grow, cultivate.

2 *these shrubs propagate easily* REPRODUCE, multiply, proliferate, increase, spread, self-seed, self-sow.

3 *they propagated socialist ideas* SPREAD, disseminate, communicate, make known, promulgate, circulate, broadcast, publicize, proclaim, preach, promote; *literary* bruit abroad.

propel verb 1 *a boat propelled by oars* MOVE, power, push, drive.

2 *he propelled the ball into the air* THROW, thrust, toss, fling, hurl, launch, pitch, project, send, shoot.

3 *confusion propelled her into action* SPUR, drive, prompt, precipitate, catapult, motivate, force, impel.

propeller noun *damage to the propeller cost us the race* ROTOR, screw (propeller); *informal* prop.

propensity noun *his propensity for giving long speeches* TENDENCY, inclination, predisposition, proneness, proclivity, readiness, liability, disposition, leaning, weakness.

proper adjective 1 *he's not a proper scientist* REAL, genuine, actual, true, bona fide; *informal* kosher. ANTONYM fake.

2 *the proper channels* RIGHT, correct, accepted, orthodox, conventional, established, official, formal, regular, acceptable, appropriate, de rigueur; *archaic* meet. ANTONYMS inappropriate, wrong.

3 *they were terribly proper* RESPECTABLE, decorous, seemly, decent, refined, ladylike, gentlemanly, genteel; for-

mal, conventional, correct, comme il faut, orthodox, polite, punctilious. ANTONYM unconventional. See note at FORMAL.

property noun 1 *lost property* POSSESSIONS, belongings, things, effects, stuff, gear, chattels, movables; resources, assets, valuables, fortune, capital, riches, wealth; *Law* personalty, goods and chattels.

2 *private property* BUILDING(S), premises, house(s), land, estates, realty, real estate.

3 *healing properties* QUALITY, attribute, characteristic, feature, power, trait, mark, hallmark.

prophecy noun 1 *her prophecy is coming true* PREDICTION, forecast, prognostication, prognosis, divination, augury.

2 *the gift of prophecy* DIVINATION, fortune telling, crystal-gazing, prediction, second sight, prognostication, augury, soothsaying.

prophesy verb *did those mystical sages ever prophesy anything other than calamity?* PREDICT, foretell, forecast, foresee, forewarn of, prognosticate. See note at PREDICT.

prophet, prophetess noun *the queen was disturbed by the prophet's interpretation of her dreams* SEER, soothsayer, fortune teller, clairvoyant, diviner; oracle, augur, sibyl. PHRASE: **prophet of doom** *if you want to listen to these prophets of doom, you may as well cash it in today* PESSIMIST, doom-monger, doomsayer, doomster, Cassandra, Jeremiah; *informal* Chicken Little.

prophetic adjective *his words proved prophetic—within a week he was dead* PRESCIENT, predictive, far-seeing, prognostic, divinatory, sibylline, apocalyptic; *rare* vatic.

prophylactic adjective *prophylactic measures* PREVENTIVE, preventative, precautionary, protective, inhibitory.

▸ noun 1 *a prophylactic against malaria* PREVENTIVE MEASURE, precaution, safeguard, safety measure; preventive medicine.

2 *prophylactic dispensers in public washrooms.* See CONDOM.

prophylaxis noun *our dental insurance covers twice-yearly prophylaxis* PREVENTIVE TREATMENT, prevention, protection, precaution.

propitiate verb *my attempts to propitiate you are useless* APPEASE, placate, mollify, pacify, make peace with, conciliate, make amends to, soothe, calm. See note at PACIFY. ANTONYM provoke.

propitious adjective *the timing for such a meeting seemed propitious* FAVORABLE, auspicious, promising, providential, advantageous, optimistic, bright, rosy, heaven-sent, hopeful; opportune, timely. See note at TIMELY. ANTONYMS inauspicious, unfortunate.

proponent noun *a proponent of the youth basketball program* ADVOCATE, champion, supporter, backer, promoter, protagonist, campaigner, booster, cheerleader.

proportion noun 1 *a small proportion of the land* PART, portion, amount, quantity, bit, piece, percentage, fraction, section, segment, share.

2 *the proportion of water to alcohol* RATIO, distribution, relative amount/number; relationship.

3 *the drawing is out of proportion* BALANCE, symmetry, harmony, correspondence, correlation, agreement.

4 **(proportions)** *men of huge proportions* SIZE, dimensions, magnitude, measurements; mass, volume, bulk; expanse, extent, width, breadth.

proportional adjective *a proportional increase in wages* CORRESPONDING, proportionate, comparable, in proportion, pro rata, commensurate, equivalent, consistent, relative, analogous. ANTONYM disproportionate.

proposal noun 1 *the proposal was rejected* PLAN, idea, scheme, project, program, manifesto, motion, proposition, suggestion, submission, trial balloon.

2 *the proposal of a new constitution* PUTTING FORWARD, proposing, suggesting, submitting. ANTONYM withdrawal.

propose verb 1 *he proposed a solution* PUT FORWARD, suggest, submit, advance, offer, present, move, come up with, lodge, table, nominate. ANTONYM withdraw.

2 *do you propose to go?* INTEND, mean, plan, have in mind/view, resolve, aim, purpose, think of, aspire, want. See note at INTEND.

3 *you've proposed to her!* ASK SOMEONE TO MARRY YOU, make an offer of marriage, offer marriage; *informal* pop the question; *dated* ask for someone's hand in marriage.

proposition noun 1 *the analysis derives from one proposition* THEORY, hypothesis, thesis, argument, premise, principle, theorem, concept, idea, statement.

2 *a business proposition* PROPOSAL, scheme, plan, project, idea, program, bid.

3 *doing it for real is a very different proposition* TASK, job, undertaking, venture, activity, affair, problem.

▸ verb *he never dared proposition her* PROPOSE SEX WITH, make sexual advances to, make an indecent proposal to, make an improper suggestion to; *informal* hit on.

propound verb *exactly what solution are you propounding?* PUT FORWARD, advance, offer, proffer, present, set forth, submit, tender, suggest, introduce, postulate, propose, pose, posit; advocate, promote, peddle, spread.

proprietary adjective *'Kleenex' is a proprietary name* COPYRIGHTED, trademarked, owned, private, registered, patented, exclusive.

proprietor, proprietress noun *the proprietor is thinking about selling this bar* OWNER, possessor, holder, master/mistress; landowner, landlord/landlady; innkeeper, hotel-keeper, hotelier, storekeeper.

propriety noun 1 *she behaves with the utmost propriety* DECORUM, respectability, decency, correctness, protocol, appropriateness, suitability, good manners, courtesy, politeness, rectitude, morality, civility, modesty, demureness; sobriety, refinement, discretion. ANTONYM indecorum.

2 **(proprieties)** *he was careful to preserve the proprieties in public* ETIQUETTE, convention(s), social grace(s), niceties, one's Ps and Qs, protocol, standards, civilities, formalities, accepted behavior, good form, the done thing, the thing to do, punctilio.

propulsion noun *these birds use their wings for propulsion under water* THRUST, motive force, impetus, impulse, drive, driving force, actuation, push, pressure, power.

prosaic adjective *a prosaic lecture that had us fighting to stay awake* ORDINARY, everyday, commonplace, conventional, straightforward, routine, run-of-the-mill, by-the-numbers, workaday; UNIMAGINATIVE, uninspired, uninspiring, matter-of-fact, dull, dry, dreary, tedious, boring, humdrum, mundane, pedestrian, tame, plodding;

bland, insipid, banal, trite, literal, factual, unpoetic, unemotional, unsentimental. ANTONYMS interesting, imaginative, inspired.

proscribe verb 1 *gambling was proscribed* FORBID, prohibit, ban, bar, interdict, make illegal, embargo, outlaw, disallow, veto; *Law* enjoin. ANTONYMS allow, permit.

2 *the book was proscribed by the Church* CONDEMN, denounce, attack, criticize, censure, damn, reject, taboo. ANTONYMS authorize, accept.

proscription noun 1 *the proscription of alcohol* BANNING, forbidding, prohibition, prohibiting, barring, debarment, vetoing, interdiction, outlawing. ANTONYM allowing.

2 *a proscription was imposed* BAN, prohibition, bar, interdict, veto, embargo, moratorium. ANTONYM authorization.

3 *the proscription of his literary works* CONDEMNATION, denunciation, attacking, criticism, censuring, damning, rejection. ANTONYM acceptance.

prosecute verb 1 *they prosecute offenders* TAKE TO COURT, bring/institute legal proceedings against, bring an action against, take legal action against, sue, try, impeach, bring to trial, put on trial, put in the dock, bring a suit against, indict, arraign. ANTONYMS defend, let off, pardon.

2 *they helped him prosecute the war* PURSUE, fight, wage, carry on, conduct, direct, engage in, proceed with, continue (with), keep on with. ANTONYM give up.

proselyte noun *proselytes are not spiritually mature enough to be counseling others in church matters* CONVERT, new believer, catechumen.

proselytize verb 1 *I'm not here to proselytize* EVANGELIZE, convert, save, redeem, win over, preach (to), recruit, act as a missionary.

2 *he wanted to proselytize his ideas* PROMOTE, advocate, champion, advance, further, spread, proclaim, peddle, preach, endorse, urge, recommend, boost.

proslepsis See note at PARALIPSIS.

prospect noun 1 *there is little prospect of success* LIKELIHOOD, hope, expectation, anticipation, (good/poor) chance, odds, probability, possibility, promise; fear, danger.

2 **(prospects)** *her job prospects* POSSIBILITIES, potential, promise, expectations, outlook.

3 *a daunting prospect* VISION, thought, idea; task, undertaking.

4 *Jack is an exciting prospect* CANDIDATE, possibility; *informal* catch.

5 *there is a pleasant prospect from the lounge* VIEW, vista, outlook, perspective, panorama, aspect, scene; picture, spectacle, sight.

▸ verb *they are prospecting for gold* SEARCH, look, explore, survey, scout, hunt, reconnoiter, examine, inspect.

prospective adjective *offering incentives to prospective buyers* POTENTIAL, possible, probable, likely, future, eventual, -to-be, soon-to-be, in the making; intending, aspiring, would-be; forthcoming, approaching, coming, imminent.

prospectus noun *nowhere in your prospectus do you list actual costs* BROCHURE, pamphlet, description, particulars, announcement, advertisement; syllabus, curriculum, catalog, program, list, fact sheet, scheme, schedule.

prosper verb *the family business continues to prosper* FLOURISH, thrive, do well, bloom, blossom, burgeon, progress, do all right for oneself, get ahead, get on (in the world), be successful; *informal* go places. ANTONYMS fail, flounder.

prosperity noun *she deserves all the prosperity she now enjoys* SUCCESS, profitability, affluence, wealth, opulence, luxury, the good life, milk and honey, (good) fortune, ease, plenty, comfort, security, well-being. ANTONYMS hardship, failure.

prosperous adjective *a prosperous shipping firm* THRIVING, flourishing, successful, strong, vigorous, profitable, lucrative, expanding, booming, burgeoning; AFFLUENT, wealthy, rich, moneyed, well off, well-to-do, opulent, substantial, in clover; *informal* on a roll, in the money. See note at WEALTHY. ANTONYMS ailing, poor.

prostitute noun *undercover cops posing as prostitutes* CALL GIRL, whore; *informal* HOOKER; working girl, lady of the evening, streetwalker, member of the oldest profession, tart, moll, fille de joie, escort, courtesan, hustler; ho; *dated* scarlet woman, camp follower, cocotte, strumpet, harlot, trollop, woman of ill repute, wench.

▸ verb *they prostituted their art* BETRAY, sacrifice, sell, sell out, debase, degrade, demean, devalue, cheapen, lower, shame, misuse, pervert; abandon one's principles (at the expense of).

prostitution noun *they claim that the casino industry only encourages prostitution in the area* THE SEX TRADE, the sex industry, whoring, streetwalking, sex tourism; *informal* the oldest profession, hooking, hustling; *dated* whoredom; *archaic* harlotry.

prostrate adjective 1 *the prostrate figure on the ground* PRONE, lying flat, lying down, stretched out, spread-eagled, sprawling, horizontal, recumbent; *rare* procumbent. ANTONYM upright.

2 *his wife was prostrate with shock* OVERWHELMED, overcome, overpowered, brought to one's knees, stunned, dazed; speechless, helpless.

3 *the fever left me prostrate* WORN OUT, exhausted, fatigued, tired out, sapped, dog-tired, spent, drained, debilitated, enervated, laid low; *informal* dead, dead beat, dead on one's feet, ready to drop, bushed, frazzled, worn to a frazzle, whacked, pooped. ANTONYM fresh.

▸ verb *she was prostrated by the tragedy* OVERWHELM, overcome, overpower, bring to one's knees, devastate, debilitate, weaken, enfeeble, enervate, lay low, wear out, exhaust, tire out, drain, sap, wash out, take it out of; *informal* frazzle, do in, poop.

PHRASE: **prostrate oneself** *he prostrated himself on the altar mat* THROW ONESELF FLAT/DOWN, lie down, stretch oneself out; throw oneself (at someone's feet).

prostration noun *prostration from the heat* COLLAPSE, weakness, debility, lassitude, exhaustion, fatigue, tiredness, enervation, emotional exhaustion.

protagonist noun 1 *the protagonist in the plot* CHIEF/CENTRAL/PRINCIPAL/MAIN/LEADING CHARACTER, chief/central/principal/main/leading participant, chief/central/principal/main/leading figure, chief/central/principal/main/leading player, principal, hero/heroine, leading man/lady, title role, lead.

2 *a protagonist of deregulation* CHAMPION, advocate, upholder, supporter, backer, promoter, proponent, expo-

nent, campaigner, fighter, crusader; apostle, apologist, booster. ANTONYM opponent.

protean adjective 1 *the protean nature of mental disorders* EVER-CHANGING, variable, changeable, mutable, kaleidoscopic, inconstant, inconsistent, unstable, shifting, unsettled, fluctuating, fluid, wavering, vacillating, mercurial, volatile; *technical* labile. ANTONYMS constant, consistent.

2 *a remarkably protean composer* VERSATILE, adaptable, flexible, all-around, multifaceted, multitalented, many-sided. ANTONYM limited.

protect verb *they fought to protect their homes and families* KEEP SAFE, keep from harm, save, safeguard, preserve, defend, shield, cushion, insulate, hedge, shelter, screen, secure, fortify, guard, watch over, look after, take care of, keep; inoculate. ANTONYMS expose, neglect, attack, harm.

protection noun 1 *protection against frost* DEFENSE, security, shielding, preservation, conservation, safekeeping, safeguarding, safety, sanctuary, shelter, refuge, lee, immunity, insurance, indemnity.

2 *under the protection of the Church* SAFEKEEPING, care, charge, keeping, protectorship, guidance, aegis, auspices, umbrella, guardianship, support, patronage, championship, providence.

3 *good protection against noise* BARRIER, buffer, shield, screen, hedge, cushion, preventative, armor, refuge, bulwark.

protective adjective 1 *protective clothing* PRESERVATIVE, protecting, safeguarding, shielding, defensive, safety, precautionary, preventive, preventative.

2 *he felt protective toward the dog* SOLICITOUS, caring, warm, paternal/maternal, fatherly/motherly, gallant, chivalrous; overprotective, possessive, jealous.

protector noun 1 *a protector of the environment* DEFENDER, preserver, guardian, guard, champion, watchdog, ombudsman, knight in shining armor, guardian angel, patron, chaperone, escort, keeper, custodian, bodyguard, minder; *informal* hired gun.

2 *ear protectors* GUARD, shield, buffer, cushion, pad, screen.

protégé noun *his protégé was a young pianist from Belgium* STUDENT, pupil, trainee, apprentice; disciple, follower; discovery, find, ward.

protest noun 1 *he resigned as a protest* OBJECTION, complaint, exception, disapproval, challenge, dissent, demurral, remonstration, fuss, outcry. ANTONYMS support, approval.

2 *women staged a protest* DEMONSTRATION, (protest) march, rally; sit-in, occupation; work-to-rule, industrial action, (work) stoppage, strike, walkout, mutiny, picket, boycott.

▸ verb 1 *residents protested against the plans* EXPRESS OPPOSITION, object, dissent, take issue, make/take a stand, put up a fight, kick, take exception, complain, express disapproval, disagree, demur, remonstrate, make a fuss; cry out, speak out, rail, inveigh, fulminate; *informal* kick up a fuss/stink.

2 *people protested outside the cathedral* DEMONSTRATE, march, hold a rally, sit in, occupy somewhere; work to rule, take industrial action, stop work, strike, go on strike, walk out, mutiny, picket; boycott something.

3 *he protested his innocence* INSIST ON, maintain, assert, affirm, announce, proclaim, declare, profess, contend, argue, claim, vow, swear (to), stress; *formal* aver.

protestation noun 1 *her protestations of innocence* DECLARATION, announcement, profession, assertion, insistence, claim, affirmation, assurance, oath, vow.

2 *we helped him despite his protestations* OBJECTION, protest, exception, complaint, disapproval, opposition, challenge, dissent, demurral, remonstration, fuss, outcry; *informal* stink.

protester noun *protesters gathers outside of the arena* DEMONSTRATOR, objector, opposer, opponent, complainant, complainer, dissenter, dissident, nonconformist, protest marcher; striker, picket.

protocol noun 1 *a stickler for protocol* ETIQUETTE, conventions, formalities, customs, rules of conduct, procedure, ritual, accepted behavior, propriety, proprieties, one's Ps and Qs, decorum, good form, the done thing, the thing to do, punctilio.

2 *the two countries signed a protocol* AGREEMENT, treaty, entente, concordat, convention, deal, pact, contract, compact; *formal* concord.

prototype noun 1 *a prototype of the weapon* ORIGINAL, first example/model, master, mold, template, framework, mock-up, pattern, sample; DESIGN, guide, blueprint. See note at MODEL.

2 *the prototype of an ideal wife* PARADIGM, typical example, archetype, exemplar, essence.

protract verb *the opposition will try to protract the discussion* PROLONG, lengthen, extend, draw out, drag out, spin out, stretch out, string out, elongate; carry on, continue, keep up, perpetuate. ANTONYMS curtail, shorten.

protracted adjective *weeks of protracted negotiations* PROLONGED, long-lasting, extended, long-drawn-out, spun out, dragged out, strung out, lengthy, long; *informal* marathon. ANTONYM short.

protrude verb *the emergency lever protrudes from the left side* STICK OUT, jut (out), project, extend, stand out, bulge out, poke out, thrust out, cantilever. See note at BULGE.

protruding adjective *protruding teeth* STICKING OUT, protuberant, projecting, prominent, jutting, overhanging, beetling, proud, bulging. ANTONYMS sunken, flush.

protrusion noun 1 *the neck vertebrae have short vertical protrusions* BUMP, lump, knob; protuberance, projection, prominence, swelling, eminence, outcrop, outgrowth, jut, jag, snag; ledge, shelf, ridge.

2 *protrusion of the lips* STICKING OUT, jutting, projection, obtrusion, prominence; swelling, bulging.

protuberance noun 1 *a protuberance can cause drag* BUMP, lump, knob, projection, protrusion, prominence, swelling, eminence, outcrop, outgrowth, jut, jag, snag; ledge, shelf, ridge. See note at BUMP.

2 *the protuberance of the incisors* STICKING OUT, jutting, projection, obtrusion, prominence; swelling, bulging.

protuberant adjective *his eyes are a little protuberant* STICKING OUT, protruding, projecting, prominent, jutting, overhanging, proud, bulging. ANTONYMS sunken, flush.

proud adjective 1 *the proud parents beamed* PLEASED, glad, happy, delighted, joyful, overjoyed, thrilled, satisfied, gratified, content. ANTONYM ashamed.

2 *a proud day* PLEASING, gratifying, satisfying, cheering, heartwarming; happy, good, glorious, memorable, notable, red-letter. ANTONYM shameful.

3 *they were poor but proud* SELF-RESPECTING, dignified, noble, worthy; independent. ANTONYM humble.

4 *I'm not too proud to admit I'm wrong* ARROGANT, conceited, vain, self-important, full of oneself, puffed up, jumped-up, smug, complacent, disdainful, condescending, scornful, supercilious, snobbish, imperious, pompous, overbearing, bumptious, haughty; *informal* big-headed, too big for one's britches/boots, high and mighty, stuck-up, Pooterish, uppity, snooty, highfalutin; *literary* vainglorious; *rare* hubristic. ANTONYMS humble, modest.

5 *the proud ships* MAGNIFICENT, splendid, resplendent, grand, noble, stately, imposing, dignified, striking, impressive, majestic, glorious, awe-inspiring, awesome, monumental. ANTONYM unimpressive.

prove verb 1 *that proves I'm right* SHOW (TO BE TRUE), demonstrate (the truth of), show beyond doubt, manifest, produce proof/evidence; witness to, give substance to, determine, substantiate, corroborate, verify, ratify, validate, authenticate, document, bear out, confirm; *formal* evince. ANTONYM disprove.

2 *the rumor proved to be correct* TURN OUT, be found, happen. PHRASE: **prove oneself** *I was happy to have the chance to prove myself* DEMONSTRATE ONE'S ABILITIES/QUALITIES, show one's (true) mettle, show what one is made of.

provenance noun *the provenance of the paintings* ORIGIN, source, place of origin; birthplace, fount, roots, pedigree, derivation, root, etymology; *formal* radix. See note at ORIGIN.

proverb noun *Mama didn't just recite proverbs about decency and good sense, she lived by them* SAYING, adage, saw, maxim, axiom, motto, bon mot, aphorism, apophthegm, epigram, gnome, dictum, precept; words of wisdom. See note at SAYING.

proverbial adjective *well, the proverbial bad son has returned at last* WELL-KNOWN, famous, famed, renowned, traditional, time-honored, legendary; notorious, infamous.

provide verb 1 *the foundation will provide funds* SUPPLY, give, issue, furnish, come up with, dispense, bestow, impart, produce, yield, bring forth, bear, deliver, donate, contribute, pledge, advance, spare, part with, allocate, distribute, allot, put up; *informal* fork out, lay out, ante up, pony up. ANTONYMS refuse, withhold.

2 *she was provided with enough tools* EQUIP, furnish, issue, supply, outfit; fit out, rig out, arm, provision; *informal* fix up. ANTONYM deprive.

3 *he had to **provide for** his family* FEED, nurture, nourish; SUPPORT, maintain, keep, sustain, provide sustenance for, fend for, finance, endow. ANTONYM neglect.

4 *the test may provide the answer* MAKE AVAILABLE, present, offer, afford, give, add, bring, yield, impart.

5 *we have provided for further restructuring* PREPARE, allow, make provision, be prepared, arrange, get ready, plan, cater.

6 *the banks have to provide against bad debts* TAKE PRECAUTIONS, take steps/measures, guard, forearm oneself.

7 *the legislation provides that factories must be kept clean* STIPULATE, lay down, make it a condition, require, order, ordain, demand, prescribe, state, specify.

provided conjunction *we'll take care of the horses, provided we can stay at your house while you'll gone* IF, on condition that, providing (that), provided that, presuming (that), assuming (that), on the assumption that, as long as, given (that), with the provision/proviso that, with/on the understanding that, contingent on.

providence noun 1 *a life mapped out by providence* FATE, destiny, nemesis, kismet, God's will, divine intervention, predestination, predetermination, the stars; one's lot (in life); *archaic* one's portion.

2 *he had a streak of providence* PRUDENCE, foresight, forethought, farsightedness, judiciousness, shrewdness, circumspection, wisdom, sagacity, common sense; careful budgeting, thrift, economy.

provident adjective *Kaye was provident enough to be able to buy her first home at age 24* PRUDENT, farsighted, judicious, shrewd, circumspect, forearmed, wise, sagacious, sensible; thrifty, economical. See note at ECONOMICAL. ANTONYM improvident.

providential adjective *we won with the aid of a providential wind* OPPORTUNE, advantageous, favorable, auspicious, propitious, heaven-sent, welcome, golden, lucky, happy, fortunate, felicitous, timely, well-timed, seasonable, convenient, expedient. ANTONYM inopportune.

provider noun 1 *a service provider* SUPPLIER, donor, giver, contributor, source.

2 *the family's provider* BREADWINNER, wage earner.

providing conjunction See PROVIDED.

province noun 1 *Canada's westernmost province* TERRITORY, region, state, department, canton, area, district, sector, zone, division.

2 *that's outside my province* RESPONSIBILITY, area of activity, area of interest, knowledge, department, sphere, world, realm, field, domain, territory, orbit, preserve; business, affair, concern; specialty, forte; jurisdiction, authority; *informal* bailiwick, turf.

provincial adjective 1 *the provincial government* REGIONAL, state, territorial, district; sectoral, zonal, cantonal. ANTONYM national.

2 *provincial areas* NONMETROPOLITAN, small-town, nonurban, outlying, rural, country, rustic, backwoods, backwater; *informal* one-horse, hick, jerkwater, freshwater. ANTONYMS national, metropolitan, cosmopolitan.

3 *provincial attitudes* UNSOPHISTICATED, narrow-minded, parochial, small-town, suburban, insular, bush-league, inward-looking, conservative; small-minded, blinkered, bigoted, prejudiced; *informal* jerkwater, corn-fed. ANTONYMS sophisticated, broad-minded. See note at BIAS.

▸ noun *they were dismissed as provincials* HILLBILLY, (country) bumpkin, country cousin, rustic, yokel, village idiot, peasant, hayseed, hick, rube, redneck. ANTONYM sophisticate.

provision noun 1 *the provision of weapons to guerrillas* SUPPLYING, supply, providing, giving, presentation, donation; equipping, furnishing.

2 *there has been limited provision for gifted children* FACILITIES, services, amenities, resource(s), arrangements; means, funds, benefits, assistance, allowance(s).

3 **(provisions)** *provisions for the trip* SUPPLIES, food and drink, stores, groceries, foodstuff(s), provender, rations; *informal* grub, vittles, eats, nosh; *formal* comestibles; *literary* viands; *dated* victuals.

4 *he made no provision for the future* PREPARATIONS, plans, arrangements, prearrangement, precautions, contingency.

5 *the provisions of the law* TERM, clause; requirement, specification, stipulation; proviso, condition, qualification, restriction, limitation.

provisional adjective *a provisional government* INTERIM, temporary, pro tem; transitional, changeover, stopgap, short-term, fill-in, acting, caretaker, subject to confirmation; penciled in, working, tentative, contingent. ANTONYMS permanent, definite.

provisionally adverb *she was appointed provisionally to the post of general manager* TEMPORARILY, short-term, pro tem, for the interim, for the present, for the time being, for now, for the nonce; subject to confirmation, conditionally, tentatively.

proviso noun *he could use the company car, with the proviso that he would pay for routine maintenance* CONDITION, stipulation, provision, clause, rider, qualification, restriction, caveat.

provocation noun 1 *he remained calm despite severe provocation* GOADING, prodding, egging on, incitement, pressure; ANNOYANCE, irritation, nettling; harassment, plaguing, molestation; teasing, taunting, torment; affront, insults; *informal* hassle, aggravation.

2 *without provocation, Bill punched Mr. Cartwright* JUSTIFICATION, excuse, pretext, occasion, call, motivation, motive, cause, grounds, reason, need; *formal* casus belli.

provocative adjective 1 *provocative remarks* ANNOYING, irritating, exasperating, infuriating, maddening, vexing, galling; insulting, offensive, inflammatory, incendiary, controversial; *informal* aggravating, in-your-face. ANTONYMS soothing, calming.

2 *a provocative pose* SEXY, sexually arousing, sexually exciting, alluring, seductive, suggestive, inviting, tantalizing, titillating; indecent, pornographic, indelicate, immodest, shameless; erotic, sensuous, slinky, coquettish, amorous, flirtatious; *informal* tarty, come-hither. ANTONYMS modest, decorous.

provoke verb 1 *the plan has provoked outrage* AROUSE, produce, evoke, cause, give rise to, occasion, call forth, elicit, induce, excite, spark off, touch off, kindle, generate, engender, instigate, result in, lead to, bring on, precipitate, prompt, trigger; *literary* beget. ANTONYM allay.

2 *she was provoked into replying* GOAD, spur, prick, sting, prod, egg on, incite, rouse, stir, move, stimulate, motivate, excite, inflame, work/fire up, impel. See note at INCITE. ANTONYM deter.

3 *he wouldn't be provoked* ANNOY, anger, incense, enrage, irritate, infuriate, exasperate, madden, nettle, get/take a rise out of, ruffle, ruffle someone's feathers, make someone's hackles rise; harass, harry, plague, molest; tease, taunt, torment; rub the wrong way; *informal* peeve, aggravate, hassle, miff, needle, rankle, ride, rile, get, bug, make someone's blood boil, get under someone's skin, get in someone's hair, get/put someone's back up, get someone's goat, wind up. ANTONYMS pacify, appease.

prow noun *the prow of the skiff* BOW(S), stem, front, nose, head, cutwater.

prowess noun 1 *his prowess as a winemaker* SKILL, expertise, mastery, facility, ability, capability, capacity, savoir faire, talent, genius, adeptness, aptitude, dexterity, deftness, competence, accomplishment, proficiency, finesse; *informal* know-how. ANTONYMS inability, ineptitude.

2 *the knight's prowess in battle* COURAGE, bravery, gallantry, valor, heroism, intrepidity, nerve, pluck, pluckiness, feistiness, boldness, daring, audacity, fearlessness; *informal* guts, spunk, moxie, grit, sand. ANTONYM cowardice.

prowl verb *they were seen prowling around the docks late at night* MOVE STEALTHILY, slink, skulk, steal, nose, pussyfoot, sneak, stalk, creep; *informal* snoop.

proximity noun *the proximity to her parents' home was a consideration* CLOSENESS, nearness, propinquity; accessibility, handiness; *archaic* vicinity.

proxy noun *I am here to vote as Mrs. Carlson's proxy* DEPUTY, representative, substitute, delegate, agent, surrogate, stand-in, attorney, go-between.

prude noun *I never knew a boy to be such a prude* PURITAN, prig, killjoy, moralist, pietist; *informal* goody-goody.

prudence noun 1 *you have gone beyond the bounds of prudence* WISDOM, judgment, good judgment, common sense, sense, sagacity, shrewdness, advisability. ANTONYMS folly, recklessness.

2 *financial prudence* CAUTION, care, providence, farsightedness, foresight, forethought, shrewdness, circumspection; thrift, economy. ANTONYM extravagance.

prudent adjective 1 *it is prudent to obtain consent* WISE, well judged, sensible, politic, judicious, sagacious, sage, shrewd, advisable, well-advised. ANTONYM unwise.

2 *a prudent approach to borrowing* CAUTIOUS, careful, provident, farsighted, judicious, shrewd, circumspect; thrifty, economical. See note at ECONOMICAL. ANTONYM reckless.

prudish adjective *it's unusual to find someone so young and yet so prudish* PURITANICAL, priggish, prim, prim and proper, moralistic, pietistic, sententious, censorious, straitlaced, Victorian, old-maidish, governessy, fussy, stuffy, strict; *informal* goody-goody, starchy. ANTONYM permissive.

prune verb 1 *I pruned the roses* CUT BACK, trim, thin, pinch back, clip, shear, top, dock.

2 *prune lateral shoots of wisteria* CUT OFF, lop (off), chop off, clip, snip (off), nip off, dock.

3 *staff numbers have been pruned* REDUCE, cut (back/down), pare (down), slim down, make reductions in, make cutbacks in, trim, decrease, diminish, downsize, ax, shrink; *informal* slash. ANTONYM increase.

prurient adjective *she was completely turned off by his prurient remarks* SALACIOUS, licentious, voyeuristic, lascivious, lecherous, lustful, lewd, libidinous, lubricious; *formal* concupiscent.

pry[1] verb *I'm not one to pry, but the goings-on at that house are very suspicious* INQUIRE IMPERTINENTLY, be inquisitive, be curious, poke around/about, ferret (about/around), spy, be a busybody; eavesdrop, listen in, tap someone's phone, intrude; *informal* stick/poke one's nose in/into, be nosy, nose, snoop. ANTONYM mind one's own business.

pry[2] verb 1 *I pried the lid off* LEVER, jimmy, prize; wrench, wrest, twist.

2 *he had to pry information from them* WRING, wrest, worm out; *Brit.* winkle out, screw, squeeze, extract, prize.

psalm noun *one of the psalms attributed to King David* SACRED SONG, religious song, hymn, song of praise; **(psalms)** psalmody, psalter.

pseudo adjective *her 'diamonds' are so pseudo* BOGUS, sham, phony, artificial, mock, ersatz, quasi-, fake, false, spurious, deceptive, misleading, assumed, contrived, affected, insincere; *informal* pretend, put-on. ANTONYM genuine.

pseudonym noun *Geisel was best known by the pseudonym 'Dr. Seuss'* PEN NAME, nom de plume, assumed name, false name, alias, professional name, sobriquet, stage name, nom de guerre.

psych *informal* PHRASES: **psych someone out** *she's trying to psych me out with that demonic stare of hers* INTIMIDATE, daunt, browbeat, bully, cow, tyrannize, scare, terrorize, frighten, dishearten, unnerve, subdue; *informal* bulldoze. **psych oneself up** *I've really psyched myself up for the marathon* NERVE ONESELF, steel oneself, brace oneself, summon one's courage, prepare oneself, gear oneself up, urge oneself on, gird (up) one's loins.

psyche noun *getting in touch with your own psyche* SOUL, spirit, (inner) self, ego, true being, inner man/woman, persona, subconscious, mind, intellect; *technical* anima. ANTONYM body.

psychedelic adjective **1** *a psychedelic experience* HALLUCINATORY, trippy, dream-like, mind-bending, mind-altering, mind-expanding, mind-blowing, bizarre, surreal.

2 *psychedelic design* COLORFUL, chromatic, multicolored, vivid, abstract.

psychiatrist noun *he's been seeing a psychiatrist for several years* PSYCHOTHERAPIST, psychoanalyst; *informal* shrink, head doctor.

psychic adjective **1** *psychic powers* SUPERNATURAL, paranormal, otherworldly, supernormal, preternatural, metaphysical, extrasensory, magic, magical, mystical, mystic, occult.

2 *I'm not psychic* CLAIRVOYANT, telepathic, having second sight, having a sixth sense.

3 *psychic development* EMOTIONAL, spiritual, inner; cognitive, psychological, intellectual, mental, psychiatric, psychogenic. ANTONYM physical.

▸ noun *she is a psychic* CLAIRVOYANT, fortune teller, crystal-gazer; medium, channeler, spiritualist; telepath, mind-reader, palmist, palm-reader.

psychological adjective **1** *his psychological state* MENTAL, emotional, intellectual, inner, cerebral, brain, rational, cognitive.

2 *her pain was psychological* (ALL) IN THE MIND, psychosomatic, emotional, irrational, subjective, subconscious, unconscious. ANTONYM physical.

psychology noun **1** *a degree in psychology* STUDY OF THE MIND, science of the mind.

2 *the psychology of the motorist* MINDSET, mind, mental processes, thought processes, way of thinking, cast of mind, mentality, persona, psyche, (mental) attitude(s), makeup, character; *informal* what makes someone tick.

psychopath noun *by definition, is every psychopath a danger to himself or others?* MADMAN, MADWOMAN, maniac, lunatic, psychotic, sociopath; *informal* loony, fruitcake, nutcase, nut, psycho, schizo, head case, sicko, screwball, crazy, kook, loon.

psychopathic adjective See MAD sense 1.

psychosomatic adjective *psychosomatic illnesses can produce very real physical symptoms* (ALL) IN THE MIND, psychological, irrational, stress-related, stress-induced, subjective, subconscious, unconscious.

psychotic adjective See MAD sense 1.

pub noun See BAR sense 4.

puberty noun *parents often forget how difficult going through puberty can be* ADOLESCENCE, pubescence, sexual maturity, growing up; youth, young adulthood, the/one's teenage years, the/one's teens, the awkward age; *formal* juvenescence.

public adjective **1** *public affairs* state, national, federal, government; constitutional, civic, civil, official, social, municipal, community, communal, local; nationalized. ANTONYM private.

2 *by public demand* POPULAR, general, common, communal, collective, shared, joint, universal, widespread.

3 *a public figure* PROMINENT, well-known, important, leading, eminent, distinguished, notable, noteworthy, noted, celebrated, household, famous, famed, influential, major-league. ANTONYMS obscure, unknown.

4 *public places* OPEN (TO THE PUBLIC), communal, accessible to all, available, free, unrestricted, community. ANTONYM restricted.

5 *the news became public* KNOWN, published, publicized, in circulation, exposed, overt, plain, obvious. ANTONYMS unknown, secret.

▸ noun **1** *the American public* PEOPLE, citizens, subjects, general public, electors, electorate, voters, taxpayers, residents, inhabitants, citizenry, population, populace, community, society, country, nation, world; everyone.

2 *his adoring public* AUDIENCE, spectators, followers, following, fans, devotees, aficionados, admirers; patrons, clientele, market, consumers, buyers, customers, readers, viewers, listeners.

PHRASE: **in public** *she didn't like it when he would kiss her in public* PUBLICLY, in full view of people, openly, in the open, for all to see, undisguisedly, blatantly, flagrantly, brazenly, overtly.

publication noun **1** *the author of this publication* BOOK, volume, title, work, tome, opus; newspaper, paper, magazine, periodical, newsletter, bulletin, journal, report; organ, booklet, chapbook, brochure, catalog; daily, weekly, monthly, quarterly, annual; *informal* rag, mag, 'zine.

2 *the publication of her new book* ISSUING, announcement, publishing, printing, notification, reporting, declaration, communication, proclamation, broadcasting, publicizing, advertising, distribution, spreading, dissemination, promulgation, issuance, appearance.

publicity noun **1** *the blaze of publicity* PUBLIC ATTENTION, public interest, public notice, media attention/interest, face time, exposure, glare, limelight.

2 *all this publicity should boost sales* PROMOTION, advertising, propaganda; boost, push; *informal* hype, ballyhoo, puffery, buildup, razzmatazz; plug.

publicize verb 1 *I never publicize the fact* MAKE KNOWN, make public, publish, announce, report, post, communicate, broadcast, issue, put out, distribute, spread, promulgate, disseminate, circulate, air; disclose, reveal, divulge, leak. ANTONYM conceal.

2 *she just wants to publicize her book* ADVERTISE, promote, build up, talk up, push, beat the drum for, boost; *informal* hype, plug, puff (up). ANTONYM suppress.

public-spirited adjective *tonight we acknowledge three of our community's most public-spirited citizens* COMMUNITY-MINDED, socially concerned, philanthropic, charitable; ALTRUISTIC, humanitarian, generous, unselfish.

publish verb 1 *we publish novels* ISSUE, bring out, produce, print.

2 *he ought to publish his views* MAKE KNOWN, make public, publicize, announce, report, post, communicate, broadcast, issue, put out, distribute, spread, promulgate, disseminate, circulate, air; disclose, reveal, divulge, leak. See note at ANNOUNCE.

pucker verb *she puckered her forehead* WRINKLE, crinkle, crease, furrow, crumple, rumple, ruck up, scrunch up, corrugate, ruffle, screw up, shrivel.

▸ noun *a pucker in the sewing* WRINKLE, crinkle, crumple, corrugation, furrow, line, fold.

puckish adjective *he gave her a puckish grin* MISCHIEVOUS, naughty, impish, roguish, playful, arch, prankish; *informal* waggish.

puddle noun *puppies and kids are drawn to puddles the way moths are drawn to light* POOL, spill, splash; *literary* plash.

pudgy adjective *informal the toddler's pudgy little hands* CHUBBY, plump, fat, stout, rotund, well-padded, ample, round, chunky, portly, overweight, fleshy, paunchy, bulky, corpulent; *informal* tubby, roly-poly, beefy, porky, blubbery, zaftig, corn-fed. ANTONYM thin.

puerile adjective *you're too old for these puerile outbursts* CHILDISH, immature, infantile, juvenile, babyish; silly, inane, fatuous, jejune, asinine, foolish, petty. See note at YOUTHFUL. ANTONYMS mature, sensible.

puff noun 1 *a puff of wind* GUST, blast, flurry, rush, draft, waft, breeze, breath.

2 *he took a puff at his cigar informal* DRAG, toke.

▸ verb 1 *she walked fast, puffing a little* BREATHE HEAVILY, pant, blow; gasp, fight for breath.

2 *she **puffed on** a cigarette* SMOKE, draw on, suck at/on.

PHRASE: **puff up** *the site of the incision may puff up slightly* BULGE, swell (up), stick out, distend, tumefy, balloon (up/out), expand, inflate, enlarge.

puffed-up adjective *his not so puffed-up since Mr. Barrett took the CapCo account from him* SELF-IMPORTANT, conceited, arrogant, bumptious, pompous, overbearing; affected, stiff, vain, vainglorious, proud; *informal* snooty, uppity, uppish, Pooterish.

puffy adjective *the doctor said his eyes were puffy because of allergies* SWOLLEN, puffed up, distended, enlarged, inflated, dilated, bloated, engorged, bulging, tumid, tumescent.

pugilist noun *dated in his neighborhood, guys pretty much had two career choices: drug dealer or pugilist* BOXER, fighter, prizefighter; *informal* bruiser, pug.

pugnacious adjective *this looks like the kind of dive that appeals to pugnacious patrons* COMBATIVE, aggressive, antagonistic, belligerent, bellicose, warlike, quarrelsome, argumentative, contentious, disputatious, hostile, threatening, truculent; fiery, hot-tempered. ANTONYM peaceable.

puke verb & noun *informal* See VOMIT.

pull verb 1 *he pulled the box toward him* TUG, haul, drag, draw, tow, heave, lug, jerk, wrench; *informal* yank. ANTONYM push.

2 *he pulled the bad tooth out* EXTRACT, take out, remove.

3 *she pulled a muscle* STRAIN, sprain, wrench, turn, tear; damage.

4 *race day pulled big crowds* ATTRACT, draw, bring in, pull in, lure, seduce, entice, tempt, beckon, interest, fascinate. ANTONYM repel.

▸ noun 1 *give the chain a pull* TUG, jerk, heave; *informal* yank.

2 *she felt the pull of the sea* ATTRACTION, draw, lure, allurement, enticement, magnetism, temptation, fascination, appeal.

3 *he has a lot of pull in finance* INFLUENCE, sway, power, authority, say, prestige, standing, weight, leverage, muscle, teeth, clout.

PHRASES: **pull apart** *they pulled apart the suitcase looking for hidden drugs* DISMANTLE, disassemble, take/pull to pieces, take/pull to bits, take apart, strip down; demolish, destroy, break up. **pull back** *the troops were ordered to pull back* WITHDRAW, retreat, fall back, back off; pull out, retire, disengage; flee, turn tail. **pull in** *pull in here, next to the Camaro* STOP, halt, come to a halt, pull over, pull up, draw up, brake, park. **pull someone's leg** *are we really getting a snowstorm, or are you pulling my leg?* TEASE, fool, play a trick on, rag, pull the wool over someone's eyes; *informal* kid, rib, take for a ride, have on. **pull off** *they pulled off a daring crime* ACHIEVE, fulfill, succeed in, accomplish, bring off, carry off, perform, discharge, complete, clinch, fix, effect, engineer. **pull out** *our forces have begun to pull out* WITHDRAW, resign, leave, retire, step down, bow out, back out, give up; *informal* quit. **pull through** *we're all praying that Steve will pull through* GET BETTER, get well again, improve, recover, rally, come through, recuperate. **pull oneself together** *it's just a movie, pull yourself together* REGAIN ONE'S COMPOSURE, recover, get a grip on oneself, get over it; *informal* snap out of it, get one's act together, buck up. **pull over.** See PULL IN.

pulp noun 1 *he kneaded it into a pulp* MUSH, mash, paste, purée, pomace, pap, slop, slush, mulch; *informal* gloop, goo, glop.

2 *the sweet pulp on cocoa seeds* FLESH, marrow, meat.

▸ verb *pulp the blueberries* MASH, purée, cream, crush, press, liquidize, liquefy, sieve, squash, pound, macerate, grind, mince.

▸ adjective *pulp fiction* TRASHY, cheap, sensational, lurid, tasteless; *informal* tacky, rubbishy.

pulpit noun *from the pulpit she would speak great and moving things from her heart* STAND, lectern, platform, podium, stage, dais, rostrum.

pulpy adjective *cook the rhubarb slowly until it is soft and pulpy* MUSHY, soft, semiliquid, slushy, sloppy, spongy, squashy, squishy; succulent, juicy, gooey.

pulsate verb *the alien pods continued to pulsate, as if at any moment writhing creatures would emerge* PALPITATE, pulse, throb, pump, undulate, surge, heave, rise and fall; beat, thump, drum, thrum; flutter, quiver.

pulse[1] noun **1** *the pulse in her neck* HEARTBEAT, pulsation, pulsing, throbbing, pounding.

2 *the pulse of the train wheels* RHYTHM, beat, tempo, cadence, pounding, thudding, drumming.

3 *pulses of ultrasound* BURST, blast, spurt, impulse, surge.

▸ verb *music pulsed through the building* THROB, pulsate, vibrate, beat, pound, thud, thump, drum, thrum, reverberate, echo.

pulse[2] noun *eat plenty of pulses* LEGUME, pea, bean, lentil.

pulverize verb **1** *the seeds are pulverized into flour* GRIND, crush, pound, powder, mill, crunch, squash, press, pulp, mash, sieve, mince, macerate; *technical* comminute.

2 *informal he pulverized the opposition.* See TROUNCE.

pummel verb *you can't just freak out and start pummeling people* BATTER, pound, belabor, drub, beat; punch, strike, hit, thump, thrash, cold-cock; *informal* clobber, wallop, bash, whack, beat the living daylights out of, give someone a (good) hiding, belt, lay into, lam, bust, slug; *literary* smite.

pump verb **1** *I pumped air out of the tube* FORCE, drive, push; suck, draw, tap, siphon, withdraw, expel, extract, bleed, drain.

2 *she* ***pumped up*** *the tire* INFLATE, aerate, blow up, fill up; swell, enlarge, distend, expand, dilate, puff up.

3 *blood was pumping from his leg* SPURT, spout, squirt, jet, surge, spew, gush, stream, flow, pour, spill, well, cascade, run, course.

4 *informal I pumped them for information* INTERROGATE, cross-examine, ask, question, quiz, probe, sound out, catechize, give someone the third degree; *informal* grill.

pun noun *"you can make your own antifreeze by stealing her blanket" is a pun guaranteed to get some groans* PLAY ON WORDS, wordplay, double entendre, innuendo, witticism, quip, bon mot.

punch[1] verb *Diana punched him in the face* HIT, strike, thump, jab, smash, welt, cuff, clip; batter, buffet, pound, pummel; *informal* sock, slug, bop, wallop, clobber, bash, whack, thwack, clout, whomp, cold-cock; *literary* smite.

▸ noun **1** *a punch on the nose* BLOW, hit, knock, thump, box, jab, clip, uppercut, hook; *informal* sock, slug, bop, wallop, bash, whack, clout, belt, knuckle sandwich; *dated* buffet.

2 *the soundtrack is full of punch* VIGOR, liveliness, vitality, drive, strength, zest, verve, enthusiasm; impact, bite, kick; *informal* oomph, zing, pep.

punch[2] verb *he punched her ticket* MAKE A HOLE IN, perforate, puncture, pierce, prick, hole, spike, skewer; *literary* transpierce.

punchy adjective *punchy dialogue* FORCEFUL, incisive, strong, powerful, vigorous, dynamic, peppy, effective, impressive, telling, compelling; dramatic, passionate, graphic, vivid, potent, authoritative, aggressive; *informal* in-your-face. ANTONYM ineffectual.

punctilio noun **1** *a stickler for punctilio* CONFORMITY, conscientiousness, punctiliousness; etiquette, protocol, conventions, formalities, propriety, decorum, manners, politesse, good form, the done thing. ANTONYM informality.

2 *the punctilios of court procedure* NICETY, detail, fine point, subtlety, nuance, refinement.

punctilious adjective *his punctilious implementation of orders* METICULOUS, conscientious, diligent, scrupulous, careful, painstaking, rigorous, perfectionist, methodical, particular, strict; fussy, fastidious, finicky, pedantic; *informal* nitpicking, persnickety. See note at FORMAL. ANTONYM careless.

punctual adjective *she liked her guests to be punctual* ON TIME, prompt, on schedule, in (good) time; *informal* on the dot. ANTONYM late.

punctuate verb **1** *how to punctuate direct speech* ADD PUNCTUATION TO, put punctuation marks in.

2 *slides were used to punctuate the talk* BREAK UP, interrupt, intersperse, pepper.

puncture noun **1** *the tire developed a puncture* HOLE, perforation, rupture; cut, slit; leak.

2 *my car has a puncture* FLAT TIRE; *informal* flat.

▸ verb **1** *he punctured the child's balloon* MAKE A HOLE IN, pierce, rupture, perforate, stab, cut, slit, prick, spike, stick, lance; deflate.

2 *she knows how to puncture his speeches* PUT AN END TO, cut short, deflate, reduce.

pundit noun *an economics pundit* EXPERT, authority, specialist, doyen(ne), master, guru, sage, savant, maven; *informal* buff, whiz.

pungent adjective **1** *a pungent marinade* STRONG, powerful, pervasive, penetrating; sharp, acid, sour, biting, bitter, tart, vinegary, tangy; highly flavored, aromatic, spicy, piquant, peppery, hot. ANTONYMS bland, mild.

2 *pungent remarks* CAUSTIC, biting, trenchant, cutting, acerbic, sardonic, sarcastic, scathing, acrimonious, barbed, sharp, tart, incisive, bitter, venomous, waspish. ANTONYMS bland, mild.

punish verb **1** *they punished their children* DISCIPLINE, teach someone a lesson; tan someone's hide; *informal* wallop, come down on (like a ton of bricks).

2 *higher charges would punish the poor* PENALIZE, unfairly disadvantage, handicap, hurt, wrong, ill-use, maltreat.

punishable adjective *an offense punishable by law* ILLEGAL, unlawful, illegitimate, criminal, felonious, actionable, indictable, penal; blameworthy, dishonest, fraudulent, unauthorized, outlawed, banned, forbidden, prohibited, interdicted, proscribed.

punishing adjective *a punishing schedule* ARDUOUS, demanding, taxing, onerous, burdensome, strenuous, rigorous, stressful, trying; hard, difficult, tough, exhausting, tiring, grueling, crippling, relentless; *informal* killing. ANTONYM easy.

punishment noun **1** *the punishment of the guilty* PENALIZING, punishing, disciplining; retribution; *dated* chastisement.

2 *the teacher imposed punishments* PENALTY, penance, sanction, sentence, one's just deserts; discipline, correction, vengeance, justice, judgment; *informal* comeuppance.

3 *both boxers took punishment* A BATTERING, a thrashing, a beating, a drubbing.

4 *the ovens take continual punishment* MALTREATMENT, mistreatment, abuse, ill-use, manhandling; damage, harm.

punitive adjective 1 *punitive measures* PENAL, disciplinary, corrective, correctional, retributive.

2 *punitive taxes* HARSH, severe, stiff, stringent, burdensome, demanding, crushing, crippling; high, sky-high, inflated, exorbitant, extortionate, excessive, inordinate, unreasonable.

puny adjective 1 *he had been a puny kid* UNDERSIZED, undernourished, underfed, stunted, slight, small, little; weak, feeble, sickly, delicate, frail, fragile; *informal* weedy, pint-sized. ANTONYM sturdy.

2 *puny efforts to save their homes* PITIFUL, pitiable, inadequate, insufficient, derisory, miserable, sorry, meager, paltry, trifling, inconsequential; *informal* pathetic, measly, piddling; *formal* exiguous. ANTONYM substantial.

pupil noun 1 *former pupils of the school* STUDENT, scholar; schoolchild, schoolboy, schoolgirl.

2 *the guru's pupils* DISCIPLE, follower, student, protégé, apprentice, trainee, novice.

puppet noun 1 *a show with puppets* MARIONETTE; hand puppet, finger puppet.

2 *a puppet of the government* PAWN, tool, instrument, cat's paw, creature, dupe; mouthpiece, minion, stooge.

purchase verb *we purchased the software* BUY, pay for, acquire, obtain, pick up, snap up, take, procure; invest in; *informal* get hold of, score. ANTONYM sell.

▸ noun 1 *he's happy with his purchase* ACQUISITION, buy, investment, order, bargain; shopping, goods. ANTONYM sale.

2 *he could get no purchase on the wall* GRIP, grasp, hold, foothold, toehold, anchorage, attachment, support; resistance, friction, leverage.

purchaser noun *the purchaser agrees to pay all shipping charges* BUYER, shopper, customer, consumer, patron; *Law* vendee.

pure adjective 1 *pure gold* UNADULTERATED, uncontaminated, unmixed, undiluted, unalloyed, unblended; sterling, solid, refined, one hundred percent; clarified, clear, filtered; flawless, perfect, genuine, real. ANTONYM adulterated.

2 *the air is so pure* CLEAN, clear, fresh, sparkling, unpolluted, uncontaminated, untainted; wholesome, natural, healthy; sanitary, uninfected, disinfected, germ-free, sterile, sterilized, aseptic. ANTONYMS dirty, polluted.

3 *pure in body and mind* VIRTUOUS, moral, ethical, good, righteous, saintly, honorable, reputable, wholesome, clean, honest, upright, upstanding, exemplary, irreproachable; chaste, virginal, maidenly; decent, worthy, noble, blameless, guiltless, spotless, unsullied, uncorrupted, undefiled; *informal* squeaky clean. ANTONYM immoral.

4 *pure math* THEORETICAL, abstract, conceptual, academic, hypothetical, speculative, conjectural. ANTONYM practical.

5 *three hours of pure magic* SHEER, utter, absolute, out-and-out, complete, total, perfect, unmitigated.

pure-bred adjective *a pure-bred Norwich terrier* PEDIGREE, thoroughbred, full-bred, blooded, pedigreed, pure. ANTONYM hybrid.

purely adverb *the mission of this weekend is purely recreational* ENTIRELY, completely, absolutely, wholly, exclusively, solely, only, just, merely.

purgative adjective *purgative medicine* LAXATIVE, evacuant; *Medicine* aperient.

▸ noun *orris root is a purgative* LAXATIVE, evacuant; *Medicine* aperient; *dated* purge.

purgatory noun *his internship was purgatory* TORMENT, torture, misery, suffering, affliction, anguish, agony, woe, hell; an ordeal, a nightmare. ANTONYM paradise.

purge verb 1 *he purged them of their doubt* CLEANSE, clear, purify, wash, shrive, absolve.

2 *lawbreakers were purged from the army* REMOVE, get rid of, expel, eject, exclude, dismiss, sack, oust, eradicate, clear out, weed out.

▸ noun *the purge of dissidents* REMOVAL, expulsion, ejection, exclusion, eviction, dismissal, sacking, ousting, eradication.

purify verb 1 *trees help to purify the air* CLEAN, cleanse, refine, decontaminate; filter, clarify, clear, freshen, deodorize; sanitize, disinfect, sterilize.

2 *they purify themselves before the ceremony* PURGE, cleanse, unburden, deliver; redeem, shrive, exorcise, sanctify.

purist noun *the quilting purist doesn't want to hear the words "sewing machine"* PEDANT, perfectionist, formalist, literalist, stickler, traditionalist, doctrinaire, quibbler, dogmatist; *informal* nitpicker.

puritanical adjective *by modern standards, his parents are considered puritanical* MORALISTIC, puritan, pietistic, straitlaced, stuffy, prudish, prim, priggish; narrow-minded, sententious, censorious; austere, severe, ascetic, abstemious; *informal* goody-goody, starchy. ANTONYM permissive.

purity noun 1 *the purity of our tap water* CLEANNESS, clearness, clarity, freshness; sterility, healthiness, safety.

2 *they sought purity in a foul world* VIRTUE, morality, goodness, righteousness, saintliness, piety, honor, honesty, integrity, decency, ethicality, impeccability; innocence, chastity.

purloin verb *formal* *the scoundrels who purloined our tractor* STEAL, thieve, rob, take, snatch, pilfer, loot, appropriate; *informal* swipe, nab, rip off, lift, "liberate", "borrow", filch, snaffle, pinch, heist.

purport verb *this work* ***purports to be*** *authoritative* CLAIM TO BE, profess to be, pretend to be; appear to be, seem to be; be ostensibly, pose as, impersonate, masquerade as, pass for.

▸ noun 1 *the purport of his remarks* GIST, substance, drift, implication, intention, meaning, significance, sense, essence, thrust, message.

2 *the purport of the attack* INTENTION, purpose, object, objective, aim, goal, target, end, design, idea.

purpose noun 1 *the purpose of his visit* MOTIVE, motivation, grounds, cause, occasion, reason, point, basis, justification.

2 *their purpose was to subvert the economy* INTENTION,

aim, object, objective, goal, end, plan, scheme, target; ambition, aspiration.

3 *I cannot see any purpose in it* ADVANTAGE, benefit, good, use, value, merit, worth, profit; *informal* mileage, percentage.

4 *the original purpose of the porch* FUNCTION, role, use.

5 *they started the game with purpose* DETERMINATION, resolution, resolve, steadfastness, backbone, drive, push, enthusiasm, ambition, motivation, commitment, conviction, dedication; *informal* get-up-and-go.

▸ verb *formal they purposed to reach the summit* INTEND, mean, aim, plan, design, have the intention; decide, resolve, determine, propose, aspire. See note at INTEND.

PHRASE: **on purpose** *we'd like to believe that she didn't start the fire on purpose* DELIBERATELY, intentionally, purposely, by design, willfully, knowingly, consciously, of one's own volition; expressly, specifically, especially, specially.

purposeful adjective *she'll need a more purposeful attitude if she wants to succeed in college* DETERMINED, resolute, steadfast, single-minded; enthusiastic, motivated, committed, dedicated, persistent, dogged, tenacious, unfaltering, unshakable. ANTONYM aimless.

purposely adverb See ON PURPOSE at PURPOSE.

purse noun **1** *a woman's purse.* See HANDBAG.

2 *the public purse* FUND(S), kitty, coffers, pool, bank, treasury, exchequer; money, finances, wealth, reserves, cash, capital, assets.

3 *the fight will net him a $75,000 purse* PRIZE, reward, award; winnings, stake(s).

▸ verb *she pursed her lips* PRESS TOGETHER, compress, tighten, pucker, pout.

pursue verb **1** *I pursued him through the garden* FOLLOW, run after, chase; hunt, stalk, track, trail, shadow, hound, course; *informal* tail. ANTONYM avoid.

2 *pursue the goal of political union* STRIVE FOR, work toward, seek, search for, aim at/for, aspire to. ANTONYM eschew.

3 *he had been pursuing her for weeks* CHASE, run after, go after; *informal* make up to; *dated* woo, court, romance.

4 *she pursued a political career* ENGAGE IN, be occupied in, practice, follow, prosecute, conduct, ply, take up, undertake, carry on. ANTONYM shun.

5 *we will not pursue the matter* INVESTIGATE, research, inquire into, look into, examine, scrutinize, analyze, delve into, probe.

pursuit noun **1** *the pursuit of profit* STRIVING TOWARD, quest after/for, search for; aim, goal, objective, dream.

2 *a worthwhile pursuit* ACTIVITY, hobby, pastime, diversion, recreation, relaxation, divertissement, amusement; occupation, trade, vocation, business, work, job, employment.

purvey verb *they traveled southward to purvey their furs* SELL, supply, provide, furnish, cater, retail, deal in, trade, stock, offer; peddle, hawk, traffic in; *informal* flog.

purveyor noun *a local purveyor of gourmet sandwiches* SELLER, vendor, retailer, supplier, trader, peddler, hawker.

pus noun *cleanse the wound twice daily until there is no longer any pus* SUPPURATION, matter; discharge, secretion.

push verb **1** *she tried to push him away* SHOVE, thrust, propel; send, drive, force, prod, poke, nudge, elbow, shoulder; sweep, bundle, hustle, manhandle. ANTONYM pull.

2 *she pushed her way into the apartment* FORCE, shove, thrust, squeeze, jostle, elbow, shoulder, bundle, hustle; work, inch.

3 *he pushed the panic button* PRESS, depress, bear down on, hold down, squeeze; operate, activate.

4 *don't push her to join in* URGE, press, pressure, force, impel, coerce, nag; prevail on; *informal* lean on, twist someone's arm, bulldoze.

5 *they push their own products* ADVERTISE, publicize, promote, bang the drum for; sell, market, merchandise; *informal* plug, hype (up), puff (up), flog, ballyhoo.

▸ noun **1** *I felt a push in the back* SHOVE, thrust, nudge, ram, bump, jolt, butt, prod, poke.

2 *the enemy's eastward push* ADVANCE, drive, thrust, charge, attack, assault, onslaught, onrush, offensive, sortie, sally, incursion.

PHRASES: **push around** *she wasn't used to being pushed around* BULLY, domineer, ride roughshod over, trample on, bulldoze, browbeat, tyrannize, intimidate, threaten, victimize, pick on; *informal* lean on, boss around. **push for** *the workers are pushing for flexible hours* DEMAND, call for, request, press for, campaign for, lobby for, speak up for; urge, promote, advocate, champion, espouse. **push off** *informal you're not welcome here, so push off* GO AWAY, depart, leave, get out; go, get moving, be off (with you), shoo; *informal* skedaddle, vamoose, split, scram, run along, beat it, get lost, shove off, buzz off, clear off, bug off, take a powder, take a hike; *literary* begone. **push on** *I decided to push on toward the coast* PRESS ON, continue one's journey, carry on, advance, proceed, go on, progress, make headway, forge ahead.

pushcart noun *he sells pretzels from a pushcart* HANDCART, cart, wheelbarrow.

pushover noun **1** *the teacher was a pushover* WEAKLING, feeble opponent, straw man, prey; *informal* soft touch.

2 *this course is no pushover* EASY TASK, walkover, laugher, five-finger exercise, gift; child's play, Mickey Mouse course; *informal* piece of cake, picnic, walk in the park, cinch, breeze, duck soup, snap.

pushy adjective *a pushy salesperson* ASSERTIVE, self-assertive, overbearing, domineering, aggressive, forceful, forward, bold, bumptious, officious; thrusting, ambitious, overconfident, cocky; *informal* bossy. ANTONYM submissive.

pusillanimous adjective *with the tough issues facing this city, the last thing we need is another pusillanimous mayor* TIMID, timorous, cowardly, fearful, faint-hearted, lily-livered, spineless, craven, shrinking; *informal* chicken, gutless, wimpy, wimpish, sissy, yellow, yellow-bellied. ANTONYM brave.

pussyfoot verb *when the subject is the prosecution of abusive parents, we can't* ***pussyfoot around*** EQUIVOCATE, tergiversate, be evasive, be noncommittal, sidestep the issue, prevaricate, quibble, hedge, waffle, beat around the bush, hem and haw; *informal* duck the question, sit on the fence, shilly-shally.

pustule noun *an infected pustule that began as an ingrown hair* PIMPLE, spot, bleb, boil, swelling, eruption, carbuncle, blister, abscess; *informal* whitehead, zit, blackhead; *technical* comedo, papule.

put verb **1** *she put the parcel on a chair* PLACE, set (down), lay (down), deposit, position, settle; leave, plant; *informal* stick, dump, park, plonk, plunk, pop.

2 *he didn't want to be* ***put in*** *a category* ASSIGN TO, consign to, allocate to, place in.

3 *don't* ***put*** *the blame* ***on*** *me* LAY ON, pin on, place on, fix on; attribute to, impute to, assign to, allocate to, ascribe to.

4 *the proposals put to the committee* SUBMIT, present, tender, offer, proffer, advance, suggest, propose, put forward.

5 *she put it bluntly* EXPRESS, word, phrase, frame, formulate, render, convey, couch; state, say, utter.

6 *he put the cost at $8,000* ESTIMATE, calculate, reckon, gauge, assess, evaluate, value, judge, measure, compute, fix, set, peg; *informal* guesstimate. PHRASES: **put about** *the ship put about* TURN AROUND, tack, come about, change course. **put across/over** *we need to put our message across more clearly* COMMUNICATE, convey, get across/over, explain, make clear, spell out, clarify; get through to someone. **put aside 1** *we've got a bit put aside in the bank* SAVE, put by, set aside, deposit, reserve, store, stockpile, hoard, stow, cache; *informal* salt away, squirrel away, stash away. **2** *they put aside their differences* DISREGARD, set aside, ignore, forget, discount, bury. **put away** *informal* **1** *they put him away for life* JAIL, imprison, put in prison, put behind bars, lock up, incarcerate. **2** *you should be put away!* CERTIFY, commit, institutionalize, hospitalize, consign to a psychiatric/mental hospital. **3** *I put away some money.* See PUT ASIDE sense 1. **4** *she never puts her toys away* REPLACE, put back, tidy up, clean up, clear away. **5** *informal he can put away a lot of pies.* See EAT sense 1. **put back 1** *he put the books back* REPLACE, return, restore, put away. **2** *they put back the film's release date.* See PUT OFF sense 2. **put down 1** *informal she often puts me down* CRITICIZE, belittle, disparage, deprecate, denigrate, slight, humiliate, shame, crush, squash, deflate; *informal* show up, cut down to size. **2** *I* ***put*** *him* ***down as*** *shy* CONSIDER TO BE, judge to be, reckon to be, take to be; regard as, have down as, take for. **3** *she put her ideas down on paper* WRITE DOWN, note down, jot down, take down, set down; list, record, register, log. **4** *they put down the rebellion* SUPPRESS, check, crush, quash, squash, quell, overthrow, stamp out, repress, subdue. **5** *the horse had to be put down* DESTROY, put to sleep, put out of its misery, put to death, kill, euthanize. **6** *put it down to inexperience* ATTRIBUTE, ascribe, chalk up, impute; blame on. **put forward.** See PUT sense 4. **put in for** *I've put in for the promotion* APPLY FOR, put in an application for, try for; request, seek, ask for. **put off 1** *you shouldn't let his bad attitude put you off* DETER, discourage, dissuade, daunt, unnerve, intimidate, scare off, repel, repulse; distract, disturb, divert, sidetrack; *informal* turn off. **2** *don't put off such important decisions* POSTPONE, defer, delay, put back, adjourn, hold over, reschedule, shelve, table; *informal* put on ice, put on the back burner. **put it on** *she may be really crying, but I think she's putting it on* PRETEND, play-act, make believe, fake it, fool, go through the motions. **put on 1** *she put on jeans* DRESS IN, don, pull on, throw on, slip into, change into; *informal* doll oneself up in. **2** *I put the light on* SWITCH ON, turn on, activate. **3** *they put on an extra train* PROVIDE, lay on, supply, make available. **4** *the museum put on an exhibition* ORGANIZE, stage, mount, present, produce. **5** *she put on a funny English accent* FEIGN, fake, simulate, mimic, affect, assume. **6** *she put ten dollars on Blue Bonnet to win* BET, gamble, stake, wager; place, lay; risk, chance, hazard. **put one over on** *informal* . See HOODWINK. **put out 1** *Maria was put out by the slur* ANNOY, anger, irritate, offend, affront, displease, irk, vex, pique, nettle, gall, upset; *informal* rile, miff, peeve. **2** *I don't want to put you out* INCONVENIENCE, trouble, bother, impose on, disoblige; *informal* put on the spot; *formal* discommode. **3** *firefighters put out the blaze* EXTINGUISH, quench, douse, smother; blow out, snuff out. **4** *he put out a press release* ISSUE, publish, release, bring out, circulate, publicize, post. **put up 1** *we can put him up for a few days* ACCOMMODATE, house, take in, lodge, quarter, billet; give a roof over someone's head. **2** *they put up a candidate* NOMINATE, propose, put forward, recommend. **3** *the building was put up 100 years ago* BUILD, construct, erect, raise. **4** *she put up a poster* DISPLAY, pin up, stick up, hang up, post. **5** *we put up alternative schemes* PROPOSE, put forward, present, submit, suggest, tender. **6** *he put up most of the funding* PROVIDE, supply, furnish, give, contribute, donate, pledge, pay; *informal* fork out, cough up, shell out, ante up, pony up. **put upon** *informal you allow yourself to be put upon* TAKE ADVANTAGE OF, impose on, exploit, use, misuse; *informal* walk all over. **put up to** *informal was drag racing your idea, or did someone put you up to it?* PERSUADE TO (DO), encourage to (do), urge to (do), egg on to (do), incite to (do), goad into. **put up with** *she put up with his nonsense for two years, and then she kicked him out* TOLERATE, take, stand (for), accept, stomach, swallow, endure, bear, support, take something lying down; *informal* abide, lump it; *formal* brook.

putative adjective *the putative cause of the brain damage was lead poisoning* SUPPOSED, assumed, presumed; accepted, recognized; commonly regarded, presumptive, alleged, reputed, reported, rumored.

put-down noun *informal he was still smarting from the put-down* SNUB, slight, affront, rebuff, sneer, disparagement, humiliation, barb, jibe, criticism; *informal* dig.

putonghua See note below.

WORD NOTE **putonghua**

Small wonder that today's Chinese are not overly keen to speak a language to which others have long given a name, *Mandarin.* Since they live in a country they call not China, but the Middle Kingdom, Jung Guo, it is entirely reasonable that their language—if there can be a national language prescribed for so widely spread and disparate a people—has a homegrown name also. For decades it was known as *kuo-yü,* or "the national tongue," but in the 1950s, once Mao Zedong's revolution had been firmly installed, the northern Chinese dialects of this tongue were assembled together into what was renamed *putonghua,* or "the common language," and it is this that is taught, and to a very large degree spoken, everywhere from Manchuria to Hainan Island, from Shanghai to the frontiers with Tibet. It is therefore quite wrong and even slightly insulting to seek to learn a language called *Mandarin,* unless you are planning to do so in Taiwan; the appropriate word is Mao's new invention, and not the word that the elitist Portuguese chose, and which meant "an official." What was spoken before was the language of the elite; what is written and spoken now is the language of the Chinese common man, and to employ the word describing it so, *putonghua,* is to be on the side of the angels, at least so far as the Middle Kingdom is concerned. **–SW**

---

putrefy verb *the carcasses will putrefy quickly in this heat* DECAY, rot, decompose, go bad, go off, spoil, fester, perish, deteriorate; molder.

putrid adjective *putrid meat* DECOMPOSING, decaying, rotting, rotten, bad, off, putrefied, putrescent, rancid, moldy; foul, fetid, rank.

puzzle verb **1** *her decision puzzled me* PERPLEX, confuse, bewilder, bemuse, baffle, mystify, confound; *informal* flummox, faze, stump, beat, discombobulate.

2 *she puzzled over the problem* THINK HARD ABOUT, mull over, muse over, ponder, contemplate, meditate on, consider, deliberate on, chew over, wonder about.

3 *she tried to* ***puzzle out*** *what he meant* WORK OUT, understand, comprehend, sort out, reason out, solve, make sense of, make head(s) or tail(s) of, unravel, decipher; *informal* figure out.

▸ noun *the poem has always been a puzzle* ENIGMA, mystery, paradox, conundrum, poser, riddle, problem, quandary; *informal* stumper. See note at RIDDLE.

puzzled adjective *a puzzled look on her face* PERPLEXED, confused, bewildered, bemused, baffled, mystified, confounded, nonplussed, at a loss, at sea; *informal* flummoxed, stumped, fazed, clueless, discombobulated.

puzzling adjective *his explanation was rather puzzling* BAFFLING, perplexing, bewildering, confusing, complicated, unclear, mysterious, enigmatic, ambiguous, obscure, abstruse, unfathomable, incomprehensible, impenetrable, cryptic. ANTONYM clear.

pygmy noun **1** *a Congo pygmy* DWARF, midget, very small person, homunculus, manikin; Lilliputian; *informal* shrimp.

2 *an intellectual pygmy* LIGHTWEIGHT, mediocrity, nonentity, nobody, no-name, cipher; small fry; *informal* pipsqueak, no-hoper, picayune. ANTONYM giant.

pyromaniac noun *the fire marshal has suggested it may be the work of a pyromaniac* ARSONIST, incendiary; *informal* firebug, pyro, torch.

Q

quack noun *a quack selling fake medicines* SWINDLER, charlatan, mountebank, trickster, fraud, fraudster, impostor, hoaxer; *informal* con man, snake oil salesman, shark, grifter.

THE RIGHT WORD

There are many different ways to describe a **fake**, a colloquial term for anyone who knowingly practices deception or misrepresentation. Someone who sells a special tonic that claims to do everything from curing the common cold to making hair grow on a bald man's head is called a **quack**, a term that refers to any fraudulent practitioner of medicine or law. **Mountebank** sometimes carries implications of quackery, but more often it refers to a self-promoting person who resorts to cheap tricks or undignified efforts to win attention (*political mountebanks*). A **charlatan** is usually a writer, speaker, preacher, professor, or some other "expert" who tries to conceal his or her lack of skill or knowledge by resorting to pretentious displays (*supposedly a leading authority in his field, he turned out to be nothing but a charlatan*). An individual who tries to pass himself or herself off as someone else is an **impostor** (*an impostor who bore a close physical resemblance to the king*), although this term can also refer to anyone who assumes a title or profession that is not his or her own. Although all of these deceivers are out to fool people, it is the **dissembler** who is primarily interested in concealing his or her true motives or evil purpose (*he is a dissembler who weaves a tangled web of lies*).

quadrangle noun *meet me in the quadrangle after your Latin class* COURTYARD, quad, court, cloister, precinct; square, plaza, piazza.

quaff verb *they quaffed a few beers before heading home* DRINK, swallow, gulp (down), guzzle, slurp, down, empty; imbibe, partake of, consume; *informal* kill, swig, swill, slug, knock back, toss off, chug, chugalug, scarf (down).

quagmire noun **1** *the field became a quagmire* SWAMP, morass, bog, marsh, muskeg, mire, slough; *archaic* quag.

2 *a judicial quagmire* MUDDLE, mix-up, mess, predicament, mare's nest, can of worms, quandary, tangle, imbroglio; trouble, confusion, difficulty; *informal* sticky situation, pickle, stew, dilemma, fix, bind.

quail verb *the sound of gunfire made us quail* COWER, cringe, flinch, shrink, recoil, shy (away), pull back; shiver, tremble, shake, quake, blench.

quaint adjective **1** *a quaint town* PICTURESQUE, charming, sweet, attractive, old-fashioned, old-world, cunning; *pseudoarchaic* olde, olde worlde. ANTONYMS ugly, modern.

2 *quaint customs* UNUSUAL, different, out of the ordinary, curious, eccentric, quirky, bizarre, whimsical, unconventional; *informal* offbeat. ANTONYMS normal, ordinary.

quake verb **1** *the ground quaked* SHAKE, tremble, quiver, shudder, sway, rock, wobble, move, heave, convulse. See note at SHAKE.

2 *we quaked when we saw the soldiers* TREMBLE, shake, quiver, shiver; blench, flinch, shrink, recoil, cower, cringe.

qualification noun **1** *a teaching qualification* CERTIFICATE, diploma, degree, license, document, warrant; eligibility, acceptability, adequacy; proficiency, skill, ability, capability, aptitude.

2 *I can't accept it without qualification* MODIFICATION, limitation, reservation, stipulation; alteration, amendment, revision, moderation, mitigation; condition, proviso, caveat.

qualified adjective *qualified mechanics* CERTIFIED, certificated, chartered, credentialed, licensed, professional; trained, fit, competent, accomplished, proficient, skilled, experienced, expert.

qualify verb **1** *I* ***qualify for*** *free prescriptions* BE ELIGIBLE FOR, meet the requirements for; be entitled to, be permitted.

2 *they qualify as refugees* COUNT, be considered, be designated, be eligible.

3 *she qualified as a doctor* BE CERTIFIED, be licensed; pass, graduate, make the grade, succeed, pass muster.

4 *the course qualified them to teach* AUTHORIZE, empower, allow, permit, license; equip, prepare, train, educate, teach.

5 *they qualified their findings* MODIFY, limit, restrict, make conditional; moderate, temper, modulate, mitigate.

quality noun **1** *the TV signal is of a poor quality* | *the quality of life* STANDARD, grade, class, caliber, condition, character, nature, form, rank, value, level; sort, type, kind, variety.

2 *work of such quality is rare* EXCELLENCE, superiority, merit, worth, value, virtue, caliber, eminence, distinction, incomparability; talent, skill, virtuosity, craftsmanship.

3 *her good qualities* FEATURE, trait, attribute, characteristic, point, aspect, facet, side, property.

▸ adjective *quality furniture* EXCELLENT, superior, valuable, distinctive, incomparable; well-crafted; *informal* top-notch.

qualms plural noun *I have no qualms about overseas travel* MISGIVINGS, doubts, reservations, second thoughts, worries, concerns, anxiety; hesitation, hesitance, hesitancy, demur, reluctance, disinclination, apprehension, trepidation, unease; scruples, remorse, compunction.

THE RIGHT WORD

To have **qualms** is to have an uneasy feeling that you have acted or are about to act against your better judgment (*she had qualms about leaving a nine-year-old in charge of an infant*). **Misgivings** are even stronger, implying a disturbed state of mind because you're no longer confident that what you're doing is right (*his misgivings about letting his 80-year-old mother drive herself home turned out to be justified*). **Compunction** implies a momentary pang of conscience because what you are doing or are about to do is unfair, improper, or wrong (*they showed no compunction in carrying out their devious plans*). **Scruples** suggest a more highly-developed conscience or sense of honor; it implies that you have principles, and that you would be deeply disturbed if you thought you were betraying them (*her scruples would not allow her to participate in what she considered antifeminist activities*). **Demur** connotes hesitation to the point of delay, but the delay is usually caused by objections or indecision rather than a sense of conscience (*they accepted his decision without demur*).

quandary noun *conflicting appointments left us in a quandary* PREDICAMENT, plight, difficult situation, awkward situation; trouble, muddle, mess, confusion, difficulty, dilemma, mare's nest; *informal* sticky situation, pickle, hole, stew, fix, bind, jam.

quantity noun **1** *the quantity of food collected* AMOUNT, total, aggregate, sum, quota, mass, weight, volume, bulk; quantum, proportion, portion, part.

2 *a quantity of ammunition* AMOUNT, lot, great deal, good deal, abundance, wealth, profusion; *informal* pile, ton, load, heap, mass, stack.

quarrel noun *they had a quarrel about money* ARGUMENT, disagreement, squabble, fight, dispute, wrangle, clash, altercation, feud, contretemps, disputation, falling-out, war of words, shouting match; *informal* tiff, run-in, hassle, blowup, row.

▸ verb *don't quarrel over it* ARGUE, fight, disagree, fall out; differ, be at odds; bicker, squabble, cross swords, lock horns, be at each other's throats; *archaic* altercate.

PHRASE: **quarrel with** *you can't quarrel with the verdict* FIND FAULT WITH, fault, criticize, object to, oppose, take exception to; attack, take issue with, impugn, contradict, dispute, controvert; *informal* knock; *formal* gainsay.

THE RIGHT WORD

Family feuds come in a variety of shapes and sizes. A husband and his wife may have a **quarrel**, which suggests a heated verbal argument, with hostility that may persist even after it is over (*it took them almost a week to patch up their quarrel*). Siblings tend to have **squabbles**, which are childlike disputes over trivial matters, although they are by no means confined to childhood (*frequent squabbles over who would pick up the check*). A **spat** is also a petty quarrel, but unlike *squabble*, it suggests an angry outburst followed by a quick ending without hard feelings (*another spat in an otherwise loving relationship*). A **row** is more serious, involving noisy quarreling and the potential for physical violence (*a row that woke the neighbors*). Neighbors are more likely to have an **altercation**, which is usually confined to verbal blows but may involve actual or threatened physical ones (*an altercation over the location of the fence*). A **dispute** is also a verbal argument, but one that is carried on over an extended period of time (*an ongoing dispute over who was responsible for taking out the garbage*). Two families who have been enemies for a long time are probably involved in a **feud**, which suggests a bitter quarrel that lasts for years or even generations (*the feud between the Hatfields and the McCoys*). There is no dignity at all in being involved in a **wrangle**, which is an angry, noisy, and often futile dispute in which both parties are unwilling to listen to the other's point of view.

quarrelsome adjective *his quarrelsome neighbors* ARGUMENTATIVE, disputatious, confrontational, captious, pugnacious, combative, antagonistic, contentious, bellicose, belligerent, cantankerous, choleric; *informal* scrappy. ANTONYM peaceable.

quarry noun *he would not allow his quarry to elude him* PREY, victim; object, goal, target; kill, game.

quarter noun **1** *the Italian quarter* DISTRICT, area, region, part, side, neighborhood, precinct, locality, sector, zone; ghetto, community, enclave, Little ——, —— town.

2 *help from an unexpected quarter* SOURCE, direction, place, location; person.

3 **(quarters)** *the servants' quarters* ACCOMMODATIONS, lodgings, rooms, chambers; home; *informal* pad, digs; *formal* abode, residence, domicile.

4 *the riot squads gave no quarter* MERCY, leniency, clemency, lenity, compassion, pity, charity, sympathy, tolerance.

▸ verb **1** *they were quartered in a villa* ACCOMMODATE, house, board, lodge, put up, take in, install, shelter; *Military* billet.

2 *I quartered the streets* PATROL, range over, tour, reconnoiter, traverse, survey, scout.

quash verb **1** *the judge may quash the sentence* CANCEL, reverse, rescind, repeal, revoke, retract, countermand, withdraw, overturn, overrule, veto, annul, nullify, invalidate, negate, void; *Law* vacate; *formal* abrogate. ANTONYM validate.

2 *we want to quash these rumors* PUT AN END TO, put a stop to, stamp out, crush, put down, check, curb, nip in the bud, squash, quell, subdue, suppress, extinguish, stifle; *informal* squelch, put the kibosh on, deep-six. ANTONYM bring about.

quasi- combining form **1** *quasi-scientific theories* SUPPOSEDLY, seemingly, apparently, allegedly, ostensibly, on the face of it, on the surface, to all intents and purposes, outwardly, superficially, purportedly, nominally; pseudo-.

2 *a quasi-autonomous organization* PARTLY, partially, part, to a certain extent, to some extent, half, relatively, comparatively, (up) to a point; almost, nearly, just about, all but.

quaver verb *Farnam's voice quavered with emotion* TREMBLE, waver, quiver, shake, vibrate, oscillate, fluctuate, falter, warble.

quay noun *searching for starfish along the quay* WHARF, pier, jetty, landing stage, berth; marina, dock, harbor.

queasy adjective *just the smell of shellfish makes him queasy* NAUSEOUS, nauseated, bilious, sick; ill, unwell, poorly, green around the gills.

queen noun **1** *the queen was crowned* MONARCH, sovereign, ruler, head of state; Her Majesty; king's consort, queen consort. See also table at RULER.

2 *informal the queen of country music* DOYENNE, star, superstar, leading light, big name, queen bee, prima donna, idol, heroine, favorite, darling, goddess.

queer adjective **1** *his diction is archaic and queer* ODD, strange, unusual, funny, peculiar, curious, bizarre, weird, uncanny, freakish, eerie, unnatural; unconventional, unorthodox, unexpected, unfamiliar, abnormal, anomalous, atypical, untypical, out of the ordinary, incongruous, irregular; puzzling, perplexing, baffling, unaccountable; *informal* fishy, spooky, bizarro, freaky. ANTONYM normal.

2 *queer culture.* See GAY adjective sense 1.

USAGE NOTE **queer**

The word **queer** was first used to mean 'homosexual' in the early 20th century: it was originally, and often still is, a deliberately offensive and aggressive term when used by heterosexual people. In recent years, however, many gay people have taken the word **queer** and deliberately used it in place of *gay* or *homosexual*, in an attempt, by using the word positively, to deprive it of its negative power. This use of **queer** is now well established and widely used among gay people (esp. as an adjective or noun modifier, as in *queer rights*; *queer theory*) and at present exists alongside the other, deliberately offensive, use. (This use is similar to the way in which a racial epithet may be used *within* a racial group, but not by outsiders.)

quell verb **1** *troops quelled the unrest* PUT AN END TO, put a stop to, end, crush, put down, check, crack down on, curb, nip in the bud, squash, quash, subdue, suppress, overcome; *informal* squelch.

2 *he quelled his misgivings* CALM, soothe, pacify, settle, quiet, silence, allay, assuage, mitigate, moderate; *literary* stay.

quench verb **1** *they quenched their thirst* SATISFY, slake, sate, satiate, gratify, relieve, assuage, take the edge off, indulge; lessen, reduce, diminish, check, suppress, extinguish, overcome.

2 *the flames were quenched* EXTINGUISH, put out, snuff out, smother, douse.

querulous adjective *even the most querulous patients failed to upset the young nurse* PETULANT, peevish, pettish, complaining, fractious, fretful, irritable, testy, tetchy, cross, snappish, crabby, crotchety, cantankerous, miserable, moody, grumpy, bad-tempered, sullen, sulky, sour, churlish; *informal* snappy, grouchy, cranky.

query noun **1** *we are happy to answer any queries* QUESTION, inquiry.

2 *there was a query as to who owned the hotel* DOUBT, uncertainty, question, reservation; skepticism.

▸ verb **1** *"Why do that?" queried Isobel* ASK, inquire, question.

2 *some folk may query his credentials* QUESTION, call into question, challenge, dispute, cast aspersions on, doubt, have suspicions about, have reservations about.

quest noun **1** *their quest for her killer* SEARCH, hunt.

2 *Sir Galahad's quest* EXPEDITION, journey, voyage, trek, travels, odyssey, adventure, exploration, search; crusade, mission, pilgrimage; *informal* Holy Grail. PHRASE: **in quest of** *thousands flocked north in quest of gold* IN SEARCH OF, in pursuit of, seeking, looking for, on the lookout for, after.

question noun **1** *please answer my question* INQUIRY, query; interrogation. ANTONYMS answer, response.

2 *there is no question that he is ill* DOUBT, dispute, argument, debate, uncertainty, dubiousness, reservation. ANTONYM certainty.

3 *the political questions of the day* ISSUE, matter, business, problem, concern, topic, theme, case; debate, argument, dispute, controversy.

▸ verb **1** *the lieutenant questions the suspect* INTERROGATE, cross-examine, cross-question, quiz, catechize; interview, debrief, examine, give the third degree to; *informal* grill, pump.

2 *she questioned his motives* QUERY, call into question, challenge, dispute, cast aspersions on, doubt, suspect, have suspicions about, have reservations about.

PHRASES: **beyond question 1** *her loyalty is beyond question* UNDOUBTED, beyond doubt, certain, indubitable, indisputable, incontrovertible, unquestionable, undeniable, clear, patent, manifest. **2** *the results demonstrated this beyond question* INDISPUTABLY, irrefutably, incontestably, incontrovertibly, unquestionably, undeniably, undoubtedly, beyond doubt, without doubt, clearly, patently, obviously. **in question** *the matter in question* AT ISSUE, under discussion, under consideration, on the agenda, to be decided. **out of the question** *changing the date of the wedding is out of the question* IMPOSSIBLE, impracticable, unfeasible, unworkable, inconceivable, unimaginable, unrealizable, unsuitable.

questionable adjective **1** *the premise to the argument remains questionable* CONTROVERSIAL, contentious, doubtful, dubious, uncertain, debatable, arguable; unverified, unprovable, unresolved, unconvincing, implausible, improbable; borderline, marginal, moot; *informal* iffy. ANTONYMS indisputable, certain. See note at DOUBTFUL.

2 *questionable financial dealings* SUSPICIOUS, suspect, dubious, irregular, odd, strange, murky, dark, unsavory, disreputable; *informal* funny, fishy, shady, iffy. ANTONYM trustworthy.

questionnaire noun *census officials report that close to 66 percent of Americans have returned their questionnaires* QUESTION SHEET, survey, opinion poll; test, exam, examination, quiz.

queue noun *a long queue of people* LINEUP, line, row, column, file, chain, string; procession, train, cavalcade. See note at CUE.

▸ verb *we queued for ice cream* LINE UP, wait in line, form a line, fall in, form a queue, queue up.

quibble noun *I have just one quibble* CRITICISM, objection, complaint, protest, argument, exception, grumble, grouse, cavil; *informal* beef, gripe, moan.

▸ verb *no one* ***quibbled with*** *the title* OBJECT TO, find fault with, complain about, cavil at; split hairs about; criticize, query, fault, pick holes in; *informal* nitpick; *archaic* pettifog.

quick adjective **1** *a quick pace* FAST, swift, rapid, speedy, high-speed, breakneck, expeditious, brisk, smart; *informal* zippy; *literary* fleet. ANTONYM slow.

2 *she took a quick trip down memory lane* HASTY, hurried, cursory, perfunctory, desultory, superficial, summary; brief, short, fleeting, transient, transitory, short-lived, lightning, momentary, whirlwind, whistle-stop. ANTONYMS careful, long.

3 *a quick end to the recession* SUDDEN, instantaneous, immediate, instant, abrupt, precipitate. ANTONYM gradual.

4 *she isn't quick enough to advance to the next level* INTELLIGENT, bright, clever, gifted, able, astute, quick-witted, sharp-witted, smart; observant, alert, sharp, perceptive; *informal* brainy, on the ball, quick on the uptake. ANTONYM dull-witted.

quicken verb **1** *she quickened her pace* SPEED UP, accelerate, step up, hasten, hurry (up).

2 *the film quickened his interest in nature* STIMULATE, excite, arouse, rouse, stir up, activate, galvanize, whet, inspire, kindle; invigorate, revive, revitalize.

THE RIGHT WORD

While all of these verbs mean to make alive or lively, **quicken** suggests the rousing or renewal of life, especially life that has been inert or suspended (*she felt the baby quicken during her second trimester of pregnancy*). **Animate** means to impart life, motion, or activity to something that previously lacked such a quality (*a discussion animated by the presence of so many young people*). **Stimulate** means to goad into activity from a state of inertia, inactivity, or lethargy (*the professor's constant questions stimulated her students to do more research*), while **enliven** refers to a stimulating influence that brightens or makes lively what was previously dull, depressed, or torpid (*a sudden change in the weather enlivened the group's activities*). **Invigorate** and **vitalize** both mean to fill with vigor or energy, but the former refers to physical energy (*invigorated by the climb up the mountain*), while the latter implies that energy has been imparted in a nonphysical sense (*to vitalize an otherwise dull meeting*).

quickly adverb **1** *he walked quickly* FAST, swiftly, briskly, rapidly, speedily, at the speed of light, at full tilt, as fast as one's legs can carry one, at a gallop, on the double, posthaste; *informal* PDQ (pretty damn quick), like lightning, like greased lightning, like mad, like blazes, like the wind, lickety-split; *literary* apace.

2 *you'd better leave quickly* IMMEDIATELY, directly, at once, now, straightaway, right away, instantly, forthwith, without delay, without further ado; soon, promptly, early, momentarily; *informal* like a shot, ASAP (as soon as possible), pronto, straight off.

3 *he quickly inspected it* BRIEFLY, fleetingly, briskly; hastily, hurriedly, cursorily, perfunctorily, superficially, desultorily.

quick-tempered adjective *they tend to be impulsive and quick-tempered* IRRITABLE, irascible, hot-tempered, short-tempered, snappish, fiery, touchy, volatile; cross, crabby, crotchety, cantankerous, grumpy, ill-tempered, bad-tempered, testy, tetchy, prickly, choleric; *informal* snappy, grouchy, cranky, on a short fuse. ANTONYM placid.

quick-witted adjective *Russell was always the quick-witted one in our circle* INTELLIGENT, bright, clever, gifted, able, astute, quick, smart, sharp-witted; observant, alert, sharp, perceptive; *informal* brainy, on the ball, quick on the uptake. ANTONYM slow.

quid pro quo noun *the latest agreement between labor and management is a textbook example of quid pro quo* EXCHANGE, trade, trade-off, swap, switch, barter, substitute, reciprocation, return; amends, compensation, recompense, restitution, reparation.

quiescent adjective *the volcano is in a quiescent state* INACTIVE, inert, idle, dormant, at rest, inoperative, deactivated, quiet; still, motionless, immobile, passive. See note at LATENT. ANTONYM active.

quiet adjective **1** *the whole pub went quiet* SILENT, still, hushed, noiseless, soundless; mute, dumb, speechless. ANTONYM noisy.

2 *a quiet voice* SOFT, low, muted, muffled, faint, indistinct, inaudible, hushed, whispered, suppressed. ANTONYM loud.

3 *a quiet village* PEACEFUL, sleepy, tranquil, calm, still, restful, undisturbed, untroubled; unfrequented. ANTONYMS busy, hectic.

4 *can I have a quiet word?* PRIVATE, confidential, secret, discreet, unofficial, off the record, between ourselves. ANTONYM public.

5 *quiet colors* UNOBTRUSIVE, restrained, muted, understated, subdued, subtle, low-key; soft, pale, pastel. ANTONYM loud.

6 *you can't keep it quiet for long* SECRET, confidential, classified, unrevealed, undisclosed, unknown, under wraps; *informal* hush-hush, mum; *formal* sub rosa. ANTONYM public.

7 *business is quiet* SLOW, stagnant, slack, sluggish, inactive, idle. ANTONYMS busy, active.

▸ noun *the quiet of the countryside* PEACEFULNESS, peace, restfulness, calm, tranquility, serenity; silence, quietness, stillness, still, quietude, hush, soundlessness.

quietly adverb **1** *she quietly entered the room* SILENTLY, in silence, noiselessly, soundlessly, inaudibly; mutely.

2 *he spoke quietly* SOFTLY, in a low voice, in a whisper, in a murmur, under one's breath, in an undertone, sotto voce, gently, faintly, weakly, feebly.

3 *some bonds were sold quietly* DISCREETLY, privately, confidentially, secretly, unofficially, off the record.

4 *she is quietly confident* CALMLY, patiently, placidly, serenely.

quilt noun DUVET, cover(s), coverlet, comforter; bedspread; *dated* counterpane.

quintessence noun **1** *it's the quintessence of the modern home* PERFECT EXAMPLE, exemplar, prototype, stereotype, picture, epitome, embodiment, ideal, apotheosis; best, pick, prime, acme, crème de la crème.

2 *brain scientists are investigating the quintessence of intelligence* ESSENCE, soul, spirit, nature, core, heart, crux, kernel, marrow, substance; *informal* nitty-gritty; *Philosophy* quiddity, esse.

quintessential adjective *Abbie was the quintessential flower child* TYPICAL, prototypical, stereotypical, archetypal, classic, model, standard, stock, representative, conventional; ideal, consummate, exemplary, definitive, best, ultimate.See note at PENULTIMATE.

quip noun *the quip provoked a smile* JOKE, witty remark, witticism, jest, pun, bon mot, sally, pleasantry; *informal* one-liner, gag, crack, wisecrack, funny.

▸ verb *"I think he got the point," quipped Sean* JOKE, jest, pun, sally; *informal* wisecrack.

quirk noun **1** *they all know his quirks* IDIOSYNCRASY, peculiarity, oddity, eccentricity, foible, whim, vagary, caprice, fancy, crotchet, habit, characteristic, trait, fad; *informal* hang-up.

2 *a quirk of fate* CHANCE, fluke, freak, anomaly, twist.

quirky adjective *her quirky outfits* ECCENTRIC, idiosyncratic, unconventional, unorthodox, unusual, strange, bizarre, peculiar, odd, outlandish, zany; *informal* wacky, freaky, kinky, way-out, far out, kooky, offbeat. ANTONYM conventional.

WORD NOTE **quirky**

Just as the British use *clever* as a backhanded insult, meaning "merely clever, not actually intelligent or thoughtful," *quirky* is often used to mean "mildly and harmlessly peculiar" with "and totally uninteresting" implied. I hate *quirky* and hate having it applied to my own writing. I would rather receive a negative review that didn't use this word than a rave that did. **—DA**

quisling noun *Duquette said the allegations that her ex-husband acted as a quisling on behalf of the Chinese were ludicrous* COLLABORATOR, colluder, sympathizer; traitor, turncoat, backstabber, double-crosser, defector, Judas, snake in the grass, fifth columnist.

quit verb **1** *she quit work at 12:30* LEAVE, vacate, exit, depart from, withdraw from; abandon, desert.

2 *he's decided to quit his job* RESIGN FROM, leave, give up, hand in one's notice, stand down from, relinquish, vacate, walk out on, retire from; *informal* chuck, pack in; pack it in, call it quits.

3 *informal quit living in the past* GIVE UP, stop, cease, discontinue, drop, break off, abandon, abstain from, desist from, refrain from, avoid, forgo.

quite adverb **1** *two quite different types* COMPLETELY, entirely, totally, wholly, absolutely, utterly, thoroughly, altogether.

2 *red hair was quite common in Rita's family* FAIRLY, rather, somewhat, slightly, relatively, comparatively, moderately, reasonably, to a certain extent; *informal* pretty, kind of, kinda, sort of.

WORD NOTE **quite**

Quite nicely illustrates the dictum that England and America are two nations separated by a common language. If someone in London says, "The play was quite good" (with a slight intake of breath on *quite*), he means it was only fairly good, or not very good at all, whereas someone in New York who says "The play was quite good" means it was very good indeed. According to the *Oxford English Dictionary, quite* (sense III.8) means "in a weakened sense: rather, to a moderate degree, fairly." Americans never use it that way. However, when I pointed the British and American usages out to an English friend he said, "I see what you mean: they're quite different"—thereby destroying the case. Most of the time, the American and British *quites* do have the same meaning—the irony in the British *quite good* resembles the American sarcasm in *oh, great,* or *yeah, right,* which mean not great or right at all. **—JS**

quiver verb **1** *I quivered with terror* TREMBLE, shake, shiver, quaver, quake, shudder. See note at SHIVER.

2 *the bird quivers its wings* FLUTTER, flap, beat, agitate, vibrate.

▸ noun *a quiver in her voice* TREMOR, tremble, shake, quaver, flutter, fluctuation, waver.

quixotic adjective *many dismissed his missionary work as imprudent and quixotic* IDEALISTIC, romantic, visionary, Utopian, extravagant, starry-eyed, unrealistic, unworldly; impractical, impracticable, unworkable, impossible.

quiz noun **1** *there may be a short quiz next class* EXAM, test, pop quiz.

2 *a music quiz on the radio* COMPETITION, game, game show.

▸ verb *a man was being quizzed by police* QUESTION, interrogate, cross-examine, cross-question, interview, sound out, give someone the third degree; test, examine; *informal* grill, pump.

quizzical adjective *a quizzical look on her face* INQUIRING, questioning, curious; puzzled, perplexed, baffled, mystified; amused, mocking, teasing.

quota noun *she rarely took her full quota of vacation time* ALLOCATION, share, allowance, limit, ration, portion, dispensation, slice (of the cake); percentage, commission; proportion, fraction, bit, amount, quantity; *informal* cut.

quotation noun *a quotation from Jefferson's first inaugural address* CITATION, quote, excerpt, extract, passage, line, paragraph, verse, phrase; reference, allusion.

quote verb **1** *he quoted a sentence from the book* RECITE, repeat, reproduce, retell, echo, parrot, iterate; take, extract.

2 *she quoted one case in which a girl died* CITE, mention, refer to, name, instance, specify, identify; relate, recount; allude to, point out, present, offer, advance.

▸ noun **1** *a Shakespearean quote.* See QUOTATION sense 1.

2 *a quote from the contractor* ESTIMATE, price, bid, costing, charge, figure, tender.

quotidian adjective **1** *the quotidian routine* DAILY, everyday, day-to-day, diurnal.

2 *her horribly quotidian furniture* ORDINARY, average, run-of-the-mill, everyday, standard, typical, middle-of-the-road, common, conventional, mainstream, unremarkable, unexceptional, workaday, commonplace, mundane, uninteresting; *informal* nothing to write home about, a dime a dozen. ANTONYM unusual.

R

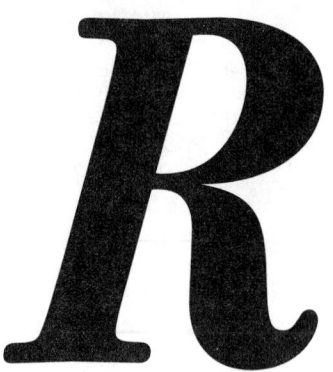

rabbit noun *hunting rabbits* buck, doe; cony; *informal* bunny.

rabble noun **1** *a rabble of noisy youths* MOB, crowd, throng, gang, swarm, horde, pack, mass, group.

2 *rule by the rabble* COMMON PEOPLE, masses, populace, multitude, rank and file, commonality, plebeians, proletariat, peasantry, hoi polloi, lower classes, riffraff; *informal* great unwashed, proles, plebs. ANTONYM nobility.

rabble-rouser noun *both the Republicans and the Democrats reluctantly have their own brand of rabble-rousers to contend with* AGITATOR, troublemaker, instigator, firebrand, revolutionary, insurgent, demagogue.

rabid adjective **1** *a rabid dog* rabies-infected, mad, hydrophobic.

2 *her rabid anti-immigration views | a mecca for rabid shoppers* EXTREME, fanatical, overzealous, extremist, maniacal, passionate, fervent, overkeen, diehard, uncompromising, illiberal; *informal* gung-ho, foaming at the mouth. ANTONYM moderate.

race[1] noun **1** *Sasha won the race* CONTEST, competition, event, heat, trial(s).

2 *the race for naval domination* COMPETITION, rivalry, contention; quest.

3 *the water in the race* CHANNEL, waterway, millrace, raceway, conduit, sluice, chute, spillway.

▸ verb **1** *he will race in the final* COMPETE, contend; run.

2 *Claire raced after him* HURRY, dash, rush, run, sprint, bolt, dart, gallop, career, charge, shoot, hurtle, careen, hare, fly, speed, scurry; *informal* tear, take off, belt, pelt, scoot, hotfoot it, leg it, hightail it.

3 *her heart was racing* POUND, beat rapidly, throb, pulsate, thud, thump, hammer, palpitate, flutter, pitter-patter, go pit-a-pat, quiver, pump.

race[2] noun **1** *students of many different races* ETHNIC GROUP, racial type, origin, ethnic origin, color.

2 *a bloodthirsty race* PEOPLE, nation.

racial adjective *racial pride* ETHNIC, ethnological, race-related; cultural, national, tribal.

racism noun *Aborigines are the main victims of racism is Australia* RACIAL DISCRIMINATION, racialism, racial prejudice, xenophobia, chauvinism, bigotry.

racist noun *he was exposed as a racist* RACIAL BIGOT, racialist, xenophobe, chauvinist, supremacist.

▸ adjective *a racist society* (RACIALLY) DISCRIMINATORY, racialist, prejudiced, bigoted.

rack noun *put the cake on a wire rack* FRAME, framework, stand, holder, trestle, support, shelf.

▸ verb *she was racked with guilt* TORMENT, afflict, torture, agonize, harrow; plague, bedevil, persecute, wrack, trouble, worry.

PHRASES: **on the rack** *these latest allegations are keeping the Church on the rack* UNDER PRESSURE, under stress, under a strain, in distress; in trouble, in difficulties, having problems. **rack one's brains** *I've racked my brain, but I still can't think of his name* THINK HARD, concentrate, try to remember; *informal* scratch one's head.

EASILY CONFUSED WORDS **rack, wrack**

The relationship between the forms **rack** and **wrack** is complicated. The most common noun sense of **rack**, 'a framework for holding and storing things,' is always spelled **rack**, never **wrack**. The figurative senses of the verb, deriving from the type of torture in which someone is stretched on a **rack**, can, however, be spelled either **rack** or **wrack**: thus, *racked with guilt* or *wracked with guilt*; *rack your brains* or *wrack your brains*. In addition, the phrase *rack and ruin* can also be spelled *wrack and ruin*.

racket noun **1** *the engine makes such a racket* NOISE, din, hubbub, clamor, uproar, tumult, commotion, rumpus, pandemonium, babel; *informal* hullabaloo.

2 *informal a gold-smuggling racket* SCHEME, fraud, swindle; *informal* rip-off, shakedown.

raconteur noun *an interviewer with his favorite raconteur, Studs Terkel* STORYTELLER, teller of tales, spinner of yarns, narrator; *rare* anecdotist, anecdotalist.

racy adjective *racy lingerie* RISQUÉ, suggestive, naughty, sexy, spicy, ribald; indecorous, indecent, immodest, off-color, dirty, rude, smutty, crude, salacious; *informal* raunchy, blue; *euphemistic* adult. ANTONYM prim.

radiance noun **1** *the radiance of the sun* LIGHT, brightness, brilliance, luminosity, beams, rays, illumination, blaze, glow, gleam, luster, glare; luminescence, incandescence.

2 *her face beamed with radiance* JOY, elation, jubilance, ecstasy, rapture, euphoria, delirium, happiness, delight, pleasure.

radiant adjective **1** *the radiant moon* SHINING, bright, illuminated, brilliant, gleaming, glowing, ablaze, luminous, luminescent, lustrous, incandescent, dazzling, shimmering, resplendent; *archaic* splendent. ANTONYMS dark, dull. See note at BRIGHT.

2 *she looked radiant* JOYFUL, elated, thrilled, overjoyed, jubilant, rapturous, ecstatic, euphoric, in seventh heaven, on cloud nine, delighted, very happy; *informal* on top of the world, over the moon. ANTONYM gloomy.

radiate verb **1** *the stars radiate energy* EMIT, give off, give out, discharge, diffuse; shed, cast.

2 *light radiated from the hall* SHINE, beam, emanate.

3 *their faces radiate hope* DISPLAY, show, exhibit; emanate, breathe, be a picture of.

4 *four spokes radiate from the hub* FAN OUT, spread out, branch out/off, extend, issue.

radical adjective **1** *radical reform* THOROUGHGOING, thorough, complete, total, comprehensive, exhaustive, sweeping, far-reaching, wide-ranging, extensive, across the board, profound, major, stringent, rigorous. ANTONYM superficial.

2 *radical differences between the two theories* FUNDAMENTAL, basic, essential, quintessential; structural, deep-seated, intrinsic, organic, constitutive. ANTONYM minor.

3 *a radical political movement* REVOLUTIONARY, progressive, reformist, revisionist, progressivist; extreme, extremist, fanatical, militant, diehard, hard-core. ANTONYMS reactionary, moderate, conservative.

▸ noun *the arrested man was a radical* REVOLUTIONARY, progressive, reformer, revisionist; militant, zealot, extremist, fanatic, diehard; *informal* ultra. ANTONYMS reactionary, moderate, conservative.

radio noun *a two-way radio* TRANSCEIVER, CB, walkie-talkie, ship-to-shore radio, radio phone; receiver, tuner.

raffish adjective *donning a raffish cap | her raffish, faithless husband* RAKISH, unconventional, Bohemian; devil-may-care, casual, careless; louche, disreputable, dissolute, decadent.

raffle noun *the winner of our raffle was Doris Toomey* LOTTERY, lotto, drawing, prize drawing, sweepstake(s).

rag noun **1** *an oily rag* CLOTH, scrap of cloth; *informal* schmatte.

2 **(rags)** *a man dressed in rags* TATTERS, torn clothing, old clothes; castoffs, hand-me-downs.

ragamuffin noun *I always got stuck playing the part of some Dickensian-type ragamuffin* URCHIN, waif, guttersnipe, street kid.

ragbag noun *the ideological ragbag of Milosevic opponents* JUMBLE, mishmash, mess, hash; assortment, mixture, miscellany, medley, mixed bag, mélange, variety, diversity, potpourri, hodgepodge.

rage noun **1** *his rage is due to frustration* FURY, anger, wrath, outrage, indignation, temper, spleen, resentment, pique, annoyance, vexation, displeasure; tantrum, bad mood; *literary* ire, choler.

2 *the current rage for home improvement* CRAZE, passion, fashion, taste, trend, vogue, fad, enthusiasm, obsession, compulsion, fixation, fetish, mania, preoccupation; *informal* thing.

▸ verb **1** *she raged silently* BE ANGRY, be furious, be enraged, be incensed, seethe, be beside oneself, rave, storm, fume, spit; *informal* be livid, be wild, foam at the mouth, have a fit, be steamed up.

2 *he **raged against** the reforms* PROTEST ABOUT, complain about, oppose, denounce; fulminate against, storm about, rail against.

3 *a storm was raging* THUNDER, rampage, be violent, be turbulent, be tempestuous.

PHRASE: **(all) the rage** *pocket-size digital cameras are all the rage* POPULAR, fashionable, in fashion, in vogue, the (latest) thing, in great demand, sought after, le dernier cri; *informal* in, the in thing, cool, big, trendy, red-hot, hip.

ragged adjective **1** *ragged jeans* TATTERED, in tatters, torn, ripped, holey, in holes, moth-eaten, frayed, worn, worn out, falling to pieces, threadbare, scruffy, shabby; *informal* tatty, raggedy-ass.

2 *a ragged child* SHABBY, scruffy, unkempt, dressed in rags.

3 *a ragged coastline* JAGGED, craggy, rugged, uneven, rough, irregular; serrated, sawtooth, sawtoothed, indented; *technical* crenulate, crenulated.

raging adjective **1** *a raging mob* ANGRY, furious, enraged, incensed, infuriated, irate, fuming, seething, ranting; *informal* livid, wild; *literary* wrathful; *informal* smash-mouth.

2 *raging seas* STORMY, violent, wild, turbulent, tempestuous.

3 *a raging headache* EXCRUCIATING, agonizing, painful, throbbing, acute, bad.

4 *her raging thirst* SEVERE, extreme, great, excessive.

raid noun **1** *the raid on Dieppe* ATTACK, assault, descent, blitz, incursion, sortie; onslaught, storming, charge, offensive, invasion, blitzkrieg.

2 *a police raid* SEARCH; *informal* bust, takedown, shakedown.

▸ verb **1** *they raided shipping in the harbor* ATTACK, assault, set upon, descend on, swoop on, blitz, assail, storm, rush.

2 *armed men raided the store* ROB, hold up, break into; plunder, steal from, pillage, loot, ransack, sack; *informal* stick up, heist.

raider noun *Kelley and his band of raiders* ROBBER, burglar, thief, housebreaker, plunderer, pillager, looter, marauder; attacker, assailant, invader.

rail verb *he **rails against** injustice* PROTEST (AGAINST), fulminate against, inveigh against, rage against, speak out against, make a stand against; expostulate about, criticize, denounce, condemn; object to, oppose, complain about, challenge; *informal* kick up a fuss about.

▸ noun *travel by rail* TRAIN, locomotive; *informal* iron horse.

railing noun *hold on to the railing* FENCE, fencing, rail(s), paling, palisade, balustrade, banister.

raillery noun *affectionate raillery* TEASING, mockery, chaff, ragging; banter, badinage; *informal* leg-pulling, joshing, ribbing, kidding.

rain noun **1** *the rain had stopped* RAINFALL, precipitation, raindrops, wet weather; drizzle, shower, rainstorm, cloudburst, torrent, downpour, deluge, storm.

2 *a rain of hot ash* SHOWER, deluge, flood, torrent, avalanche, flurry; storm, hail.

▸ verb 1 *it rained heavily* POUR, pour down, come down, pelt down, teem down, beat down, rain cats and dogs; fall, drizzle.

2 *bombs rained on the city* FALL, hail, drop, shower.

rainy adjective *rainy weather* WET, showery, drizzly, damp, inclement.

raise verb 1 *he raised a hand in greeting* LIFT, lift up, hold aloft, elevate, uplift, upraise, upthrust; hoist, haul up, hitch up. ANTONYM lower.

2 *he raised himself in the bed* SET UPRIGHT, set vertical; sit up, stand up. ANTONYMS lay down, knock over.

3 *they raised prices* INCREASE, put up, push up, up, mark up, escalate, inflate; *informal* hike (up), jack up, bump up. ANTONYMS lower, reduce.

4 *he raised his voice* AMPLIFY, louden, magnify, intensify, boost, lift, increase, heighten, augment. ANTONYM lower.

5 *the temple was raised in 900 BC* BUILD, construct, erect, assemble, put up. ANTONYMS raze, demolish.

6 *how will you raise the money?* GET, obtain, acquire; accumulate, amass, collect, fetch, net, make. ANTONYMS distribute, spend.

7 *the city raised troops to fight for them* RECRUIT, enlist, sign up, conscript, call up, mobilize, rally, assemble, draft. ANTONYMS demobilize, stand down.

8 *a tax raised on imports* LEVY, impose, exact, demand, charge.

9 *he raised several objections* BRING UP, air, ventilate; present, table, propose, submit, advance, suggest, moot, put forward. ANTONYMS withdraw, keep quiet about.

10 *the disaster raised doubts about safety* GIVE RISE TO, occasion, cause, produce, engender, elicit, create, result in, lead to, prompt, awaken, arouse, induce, kindle, incite, stir up, trigger, spark off, provoke, instigate, foment, whip up; *literary* beget. ANTONYMS allay, end.

11 *most parents try to raise their children well* BRING UP, rear, nurture, look after, care for, provide for, mother, parent, tend, cherish; educate, train.

12 *she raised cattle* BREED, rear, nurture, keep, tend; grow, farm, cultivate, produce.

13 *he was raised to a captaincy* PROMOTE, advance, upgrade, elevate, ennoble; *informal* kick upstairs. ANTONYM demote.

▸ noun *the workers wanted a raise* pay increase, increment.

PHRASE: **raise hell** *informal* See HELL.

raised adjective *an inscription in raised letters* EMBOSSED, relief, relievo, die-stamped.

rake[1] verb 1 *he raked the leaves into a pile* SCRAPE UP, collect, gather.

2 *she raked the gravel* SMOOTH, smooth out, level, even out, flatten, comb.

3 *the cat raked his arm with its claws* SCRATCH, lacerate, scrape, rasp, graze, grate; *Medicine* excoriate.

4 *she raked a hand through her hair* DRAG, pull, scrape, tug, comb.

5 *I raked through my pockets* RUMMAGE, search, hunt, sift, rifle.

6 *machine-gun fire raked the streets* SWEEP, enfilade, pepper, strafe. PHRASES: **rake something in** *informal his frozen yogurt business is raking in the dough* EARN, make, get, gain, garner, obtain, acquire, accumulate, bring in, pull in, pocket, realize, fetch, return, yield, raise, net, gross. **rake something up** *I guess I've raked up some bad memories* REMIND PEOPLE OF, recollect, remember, call to mind; drag up, dredge up.

rake[2] noun *he was something of a rake* PLAYBOY, libertine, profligate; degenerate, roué, debauchee; lecher, seducer, womanizer, philanderer, adulterer, Don Juan, Lothario, Casanova; *informal* ladykiller, ladies' man, lech.

rakish adjective *Felipe's snap-brimmed hat is always cocked at a rakish angle* DASHING, debonair, stylish, jaunty, devil-may-care; raffish, disreputable, louche; *informal* sharp.

rally verb 1 *the troops rallied and held their ground* REGROUP, reassemble, re-form, reunite. ANTONYM disperse.

2 *he rallied an army* MUSTER, marshal, mobilize, raise, call up, recruit, enlist, conscript; assemble, gather, round up, draft; *formal* convoke. ANTONYMS demobilize, disband.

3 *team owners rallied to denounce the rumors* GET TOGETHER, band together, assemble, join forces, unite, ally, collaborate, cooperate, pull together. ANTONYMS separate, split up.

4 *share prices rallied* RECOVER, improve, get better, pick up, revive, bounce back, perk up, look up, turn a corner. ANTONYMS deteriorate, slump.

▸ noun 1 *a rally in support of the strike* MEETING, mass meeting, gathering, assembly; demonstration, march, protest march, protest.

2 *a rally in oil prices* RECOVERY, upturn, improvement, comeback, resurgence. ANTONYM slump.

ram verb 1 *he rammed his sword into its sheath* FORCE, thrust, plunge, stab, push, sink, dig, stick, cram, jam, stuff, pack.

2 *a van rammed the police car* HIT, strike, crash into, collide with, impact, run into, smash into, smack into, bump (into), butt.

ramble verb 1 *we rambled around the village* WALK, hike, tramp, trek, backpack; wander, stroll, saunter, amble, roam, range, rove, traipse; *informal* mosey, tootle; *formal* perambulate.

2 *she does ramble* CHATTER, babble, prattle, prate, blather, jabber, twitter, maunder; *informal* jaw, gas, gab, yak, yabber.

▸ noun *a ramble in the hills* WALK, hike, trek; wander, stroll, saunter, amble, roam, traipse, jaunt, promenade; *informal* mosey, tootle; *formal* perambulation.

rambler noun *for two years, he and his dog were a pair of carefree ramblers* WALKER, hiker, backpacker, wanderer, rover; *literary* wayfarer.

rambling adjective 1 *a rambling speech* LONG-WINDED, verbose, wordy, prolix; digressive, maundering, roundabout, circuitous, tortuous, circumlocutory; disconnected, disjointed, incoherent. ANTONYM concise.

2 *rambling streets* WINDING, twisting, twisty, tortuous, labyrinthine; sprawling.

3 *a rambling rose* TRAILING, creeping, climbing, vining.

rambunctious adjective *rambunctious preschoolers* BOISTEROUS, rowdy, obstreperous, wild, turbulent, unruly, disorderly.

ramification noun *the Gulf War of 1991 had ramifications far beyond the Middle East* CONSEQUENCE, result, aftermath, outcome, effect, upshot; development, implication; product, by-product.

ramp noun *they wheeled the appliances down the ramp* SLOPE, bank, incline, gradient, tilt; rise, ascent, drop, descent, declivity.

rampage verb *mobs rampaged through the streets* RIOT, run riot, go on the rampage, run amok, go berserk; storm, charge, tear. PHRASE: **go on the rampage** *the prisoners have gone on a rampage* RIOT, go berserk, get out of control, run amok; *informal* go postal.

rampant adjective **1** *rampant inflation* UNCONTROLLED, unrestrained, unchecked, unbridled, widespread; out of control, out of hand, rife. ANTONYM controlled.

2 *rampant dislike* VEHEMENT, strong, violent, forceful, intense, passionate, fanatical. ANTONYM mild.

3 *rampant vegetation* LUXURIANT, exuberant, lush, rich, riotous, rank, profuse, vigorous; *informal* jungly.

rampart noun *the castle's stony ramparts* DEFENSIVE WALL, embankment, earthwork, parapet, breastwork, battlement, bulwark, outwork.

ramshackle adjective *their first home was a ramshackle cottage* TUMBLEDOWN, dilapidated, derelict, decrepit, neglected, run-down, gone to rack and ruin, beat-up, crumbling, decaying; rickety, shaky, unsound. ANTONYMS sound, sturdy.

rancid adjective *rancid bacon* SOUR, stale, overstored, turned, rank, putrid, foul, rotten, bad, off; gamy, high, fetid, stinking, malodorous, foul-smelling; *literary* noisome. ANTONYM fresh.

rancor noun *partisans on both sides have created much rancor* BITTERNESS, spite, hate, hatred, resentment, malice, ill will, malevolence, animosity, antipathy, enmity, hostility, acrimony, venom, vitriol.

rancorous adjective *California's rancorous recall campaign* BITTER, spiteful, hateful, resentful, acrimonious, malicious, malevolent, hostile, venomous, vindictive, baleful, vitriolic, vengeful, pernicious, mean, nasty; *informal* bitchy, catty. See note at VINDICTIVE. ANTONYM amicable.

random adjective *random spot checks* UNSYSTEMATIC, unmethodical, arbitrary, unplanned, undirected, casual, indiscriminate, nonspecific, haphazard, stray, erratic; chance, accidental. ANTONYM systematic.

PHRASE: **at random** *we chose the names at random* UNSYSTEMATICALLY, arbitrarily, randomly, unmethodically, haphazardly.

range noun **1** *his range of vision* SPAN, scope, compass, sweep, extent, area, field, orbit, ambit, horizon, latitude; limits, bounds, confines, parameters.

2 *a range of mountains* ROW, chain, sierra, ridge, massif; line, string, series.

3 *a range of quality foods* ASSORTMENT, variety, diversity, mixture, collection, array, selection, choice.

4 *she put the dish into the range* STOVE, oven.

5 *cows grazed on the open range* PASTURE, pasturage, pastureland, prairie, grass, grassland, grazing land, veld; *literary* greensward.

▸ verb **1** *interest charges range from 1% to 5%* VARY, fluctuate, differ; extend, stretch, reach, cover, go, run.

2 *they ranged over the sprawling hills* ROAM, rove, traverse, travel, journey, wander, drift, ramble, meander, stroll, traipse, walk, hike, trek.

THE RIGHT WORD

To say that someone has a wide **range** of interests implies that these interests are not only extensive but varied. Another way of expressing the same idea would be to say that the person's interests run the **gamut** from TV quiz shows to nuclear physics, a word that suggests a graduated scale or series running from one extreme to another. **Compass** implies a range of knowledge or activity that falls within very definite limits reminiscent of a circumference (*within the compass of her abilities*), while **sweep** suggests more of an arc-shaped range of motion or activity (*the sweep of the searchlight*) or a continuous extent or stretch (*a broad sweep of lawn*). **Latitude** and **scope** both emphasize the idea of freedom, although *scope* implies great freedom within prescribed limits (*the scope of the investigation*), while *latitude* means freedom from such limits (*she was granted more latitude than usual in interviewing the disaster victims*). Even someone who has a wide *range* of interests and a broad *scope* of authority, however, will sooner or later come up against something that is beyond his or her **reach**, which suggests the furthest limit of effectiveness or influence.

rangy adjective *their rangy gardener* LONG-LEGGED, long-limbed, leggy, tall; slender, slim, lean, thin, gangling, gangly, lanky, spindly, skinny, spare. ANTONYM squat.

rank[1] noun **1** *she was elevated to an administrative rank* POSITION, level, grade, echelon; class, status, standing; *dated* station.

2 *a family of rank* HIGH STANDING, blue blood, high birth, nobility, aristocracy; eminence, distinction, prestige; prominence, influence, consequence, power.

3 *a rank of riflemen* ROW, line, file, column, string, train, procession.

▸ verb **1** *this orchid is ranked as endangered* CLASSIFY, class, categorize, rate, grade, bracket, group, pigeonhole, designate; catalog, file, list.

2 *he ranked them in order of experience* PRIORITIZE, order, organize, arrange, list; triage.

3 *she ranked below the others* HAVE A RANK, be graded, have a status, be classed, be classified, be categorized; belong.

PHRASE: **rank and file 1** *the officers and the rank and file* OTHER RANKS, soldiers, NCOs, noncommissioned officers, lower ranks, enlisted personnel; men, troops; *informal* noncoms. **2** *a speech appealing to the rank and file* PEOPLE, common people, proletariat, masses, populace, commonality, third estate, plebeians; hoi polloi, rabble, riffraff, great unwashed; *informal* proles, plebs.

rank[2] adjective **1** *rank vegetation* ABUNDANT, lush, luxuriant, dense, profuse, vigorous, overgrown; *informal* jungly. ANTONYM sparse.

2 *a rank smell* OFFENSIVE, unpleasant, nasty, revolting, sickening, obnoxious, noxious; foul, fetid, smelly, stinking, reeking, high, off, rancid, putrid, malodorous; *literary* noisome; *Brit. informal* minging, pongy. ANTONYM pleasant.

3 *rank stupidity* DOWNRIGHT, utter, outright, out-and-out, absolute, complete, sheer, arrant, thoroughgoing, unqualified, unmitigated, positive, perfect, patent, pure, total; *archaic* arrant.

rankle verb *Rumsfeld's remarks rankled the Palestinians* CAUSE RESENTMENT TO, annoy, upset, anger, irritate, offend, affront, displease, provoke, irk, vex, pique, nettle, gall; *informal* rile, miff, peeve, aggravate, tick off.

ransack verb *Joonie's thugs ransacked Leon's apartment* PLUNDER, pillage, raid, rob, loot, sack, strip, despoil; ravage, devastate, turn upside down; scour, rifle, comb, search.

ransom noun *they demanded a huge ransom* PAYOFF, payment, sum, price.

▸ verb *the girl was ransomed for $4 million* RELEASE, free, deliver, liberate, rescue; exchange for a ransom, buy the freedom of.

rant verb *she ranted about the unfairness* FULMINATE, go on, hold forth, vociferate, sound off, spout, pontificate, bluster, declaim; shout, yell, bellow; *informal* mouth off.

▸ noun *he went into a rant about them* TIRADE, diatribe, broadside; *literary* philippic.

rap verb **1** *she rapped his fingers with a ruler* HIT, strike; *informal* whack, thwack, bash, wallop; *literary* smite.

2 *I rapped on the door* KNOCK, tap, bang, hammer, pound.

▸ noun **1** *a rap on the knuckles* BLOW, hit, knock, bang, crack; *informal* whack, thwack, bash, wallop.

2 *a rap at the door* KNOCK, tap, rat-tat, bang, hammering, pounding.

PHRASE: **take the rap** *informal why should I take the rap for what Clarence did?* BE PUNISHED, take the blame, suffer, suffer the consequences, pay, pay the price.

rapacious adjective *poor Tom has fallen for a rapacious gold digger* GRASPING, greedy, avaricious, acquisitive, covetous; mercenary, materialistic; insatiable, predatory; *informal* money-grubbing, grabby. See note at GREEDY. ANTONYM generous.

rape noun **1** *he was charged with rape* SEXUAL ASSAULT, sexual abuse, sexual interference; *archaic* ravishment, defilement.

2 *the rape of the rain forest* DESTRUCTION, violation, ravaging, pillaging, plundering, desecration, defilement, sacking, sack.

▸ verb **1** *he raped her at knifepoint* SEXUALLY ASSAULT, sexually abuse, violate, force oneself on; *literary* ravish; *archaic* defile.

2 *they raped our country* RAVAGE, violate, desecrate, defile, plunder, pillage, despoil; lay waste, ransack, sack.

rapid adjective *his rapid rise to stardom* QUICK, fast, swift, speedy, expeditious, express, brisk; lightning, meteoric, whirlwind; sudden, instantaneous, instant, immediate; hurried, hasty, precipitate; *informal* PDQ (pretty damn quick); *literary* fleet. ANTONYM slow.

rapidly adverb *a new computer worm spread rapidly through the Internet on Tuesday* QUICKLY, fast, swiftly, speedily, at the speed of light, posthaste, at full tilt, briskly; hurriedly, hastily, in haste, in a rush, precipitately; *informal* like a shot, PDQ (pretty damn quick), in a flash, on the double, like a bat out of hell, like lightning, like greased lightning, like mad, like the wind, lickety-split; *literary* apace. ANTONYM slowly.

rapport noun *board members fired him for failing to maintain good rapport with the trustees* AFFINITY, close relationship, understanding, mutual understanding, bond, empathy, sympathy, accord.

rapprochement noun *growing political and diplomatic rapprochement between the two countries* RECONCILIATION, increased understanding, détente, restoration of harmony, agreement, cooperation, harmonization, softening.

rapt adjective *a rapt teenage audience* FASCINATED, enthralled, spellbound, captivated, riveted, gripped, mesmerized, enchanted, entranced, bewitched, moonstruck; transported, enraptured, thrilled, ecstatic. ANTONYM inattentive.

raptor noun *this nest may belong to a hawk or an owl, or some other raptor.* See table.

BIRDS OF PREY

accipiter	kestrel
American eagle	kite
bald eagle	lammergeier
barn owl	lanner
barred owl	marsh harrier
boreal owl	marsh hawk
brown owl	merlin
burrowing owl	northern harrier
buteo	osprey
buzzard	owl
caracara	peregrine falcon
chicken hawk	pigeon hawk
condor	red-tailed hawk
eagle owl	ringtail
eagle	rough-legged hawk
falcon	saker
falconet	saw-whet owl
fish eagle	screech owl
fish hawk	sea eagle
golden eagle	sharp-shinned hawk
goshawk	sort-eared owl
great gray owl	snowy owl
great horned owl	sparrow hawk
gyrfalcon	spotted owl
harpy eagle	tawny eagle
harrier	tawny owl
hawk owl	tiercel
horned owl	

rapture noun *she gazed at him in rapture* ECSTASY, bliss, exaltation, euphoria, elation, joy, enchantment, delight, happiness, pleasure. PHRASE: **go into raptures** *the Cambodian crowd went into raptures over Carreras's rendition of "Some Enchanted Evening"* ENTHUSE, rhapsodize, rave, gush, wax lyrical; *informal* go wild/crazy/mad.

THE RIGHT WORD

Happiness is one thing; **bliss** is another, suggesting a state of utter joy and contentment (*marital bliss*). **Ecstasy** is even more extreme, describing a trancelike state in which one loses consciousness of one's surroundings (*the ecstasy of young love*). Although **rapture** originally referred to being raised or lifted out of oneself by divine power, nowadays it is used in much the same sense as *ecstasy* to describe an elevated sensation of bliss (*she listened in speechless rapture to her favorite soprano*). **Transport** applies to any powerful emotion by which one is carried away (*a transport of delight*). When happiness is carried to an extreme or crosses over into mania, it is called **euphoria**. *Euphoria* may outwardly resemble *ecstasy* or *rapture*;

but upon closer examination, it is usually found to be exaggerated and out of proportion (*the euphoria that came over him whenever he touched alcohol*).

---

rapturous adjective *Nelson Mandela received a rapturous welcome in London* ECSTATIC, joyful, elated, euphoric, enraptured, on cloud nine, in seventh heaven, transported, enchanted, blissful, happy; enthusiastic, delighted, thrilled, overjoyed, rapt; *informal* over the moon, on top of the world, blissed out.

rare adjective **1** *rare moments of privacy* INFREQUENT, scarce, sparse, few and far between, thin on the ground, like gold dust, as scarce as hen's teeth; occasional, limited, odd, isolated, unaccustomed, unwonted. ANTONYMS common, frequent.

2 *rare stamps* UNUSUAL, recherché, uncommon, unfamiliar, atypical, singular. ANTONYMS ordinary, commonplace.

3 *a man of rare talent* EXCEPTIONAL, outstanding, unparalleled, peerless, matchless, unique, unrivaled, inimitable, beyond compare, without equal, second to none, unsurpassed; consummate, superior, superlative, first-class; *informal* A1, top-notch. ANTONYMS common, everyday.

rare bird noun *even his fellow intellectuals call Stephenson a rare bird* RARITY, rara avis, wonder, marvel, nonpareil, nonesuch, one of a kind; curiosity, oddity, freak.

rarefied adjective *the rarefied legal circles in which he travels* ESOTERIC, exclusive, select; elevated, lofty.

rarely adverb *we rarely leave the house in the winter* SELDOM, infrequently, hardly ever, hardly, scarcely, not often; once in a while, now and then, occasionally; *informal* once in a blue moon. ANTONYM often.

raring adjective *the fully recovered Flaherty is raring to get back on the playing field* EAGER, keen, enthusiastic; impatient, longing, desperate; ready; *informal* dying, itching.

rarity noun **1** *the rarity of earthquakes in Vermont* INFREQUENCY, rareness, scarcity, unusualness, uncommonness.

2 *this book is a rarity* COLLECTOR'S ITEM, rare thing, rare bird, rara avis; wonder, nonpareil, one of a kind; curiosity, oddity.

rascal noun *the title character is a lovable rascal* SCALAWAG, imp, monkey, mischief-maker, wretch; *informal* scamp, tyke, horror, monster, varmint; *archaic* rapscallion.

rash[1] noun **1** *he broke out in **a rash*** SPOTS, a breakout, an eruption; hives; *Medicine* erythema, exanthema, urticaria.

2 *a rash of articles in the press* SERIES, succession, spate, wave, flood, deluge, torrent; outbreak, epidemic, flurry.

rash[2] adjective *a rash decision* RECKLESS, impulsive, impetuous, hasty, foolhardy, incautious, precipitate; careless, heedless, thoughtless, imprudent, foolish; ill-advised, injudicious, ill-judged, misguided, harebrained, trigger-happy; *literary* temerarious. See note at TEMERITY. ANTONYM prudent.

rasp verb **1** *tartar is rasped off the teeth* SCRAPE, rub, abrade, grate, grind, sand, file, scratch, scour; *Medicine* excoriate.

2 *"Help!" he rasped* CROAK, squawk, caw, say hoarsely.

rasping adjective *the rasping voice on the phone sounded familiar* HARSH, grating, jarring; raspy, scratchy, hoarse, rough, gravelly, croaky, gruff, husky, throaty, guttural.

rat *informal* noun **1** *rats in the basement.* See table at RODENT.

2 *her husband is a rat* SCOUNDREL, wretch, rogue; *informal* beast, pig, swine, creep, louse, lowlife, scumbag, scumbucket, scuzzball, sleazeball, sleazebag, heel, dog, weasel, ratfink.

3 *the most famous rat in mob history* INFORMER, betrayer, stool pigeon; *informal* snitch, squealer, fink, stoolie.
PHRASE: **rat on 1** *we don't rat on our friends* INFORM ON, betray, be unfaithful to, stab in the back; *informal* tell on, sell down the river, blow the whistle on, squeal on, rat out, finger. **2** *he ratted on his pledge* BREAK, renege on, go back on, welsh on.

rate noun **1** *a fixed rate of interest* PERCENTAGE, ratio, proportion; scale, standard, level.

2 *an hourly rate of $30* CHARGE, price, cost, tariff, fare, levy, toll; fee, remuneration, payment, wage, allowance.

3 *the rate of change* SPEED, pace, tempo, velocity, momentum.

▸ verb **1** *they rated his driving ability* ASSESS, evaluate, appraise, judge, estimate, calculate, gauge, measure, adjudge; grade, rank, classify, categorize.

2 *the scheme was rated effective* CONSIDER, judge, reckon, think, hold, deem, find; regard as, look on as, count as.

3 *he rated only a brief mention* MERIT, deserve, warrant, be worthy of, be deserving of.

PHRASE: **at any rate** *at any rate, we ask that you remember to vote* IN ANY CASE, anyhow, anyway, in any event, nevertheless; whatever happens, come what may, regardless, notwithstanding.

rather adverb **1** *I would rather stay home* SOONER, by preference, preferably, by choice.

2 *it's rather complicated* QUITE, a bit, a little, fairly, slightly, somewhat, relatively, to some degree, comparatively; *informal* pretty, sort of, kind of, kinda.

3 *her true feelings—or rather, lack of feelings* MORE PRECISELY, to be precise, to be exact, strictly speaking.

4 *she seemed sad rather than angry* MORE; as opposed to, instead of.

5 *it was not impulsive, but rather a considered decision* ON THE CONTRARY, au contraire, instead.

ratify verb *they failed to ratify the amendment* CONFIRM, approve, sanction, endorse, agree to, accept, uphold, authorize, formalize, validate, recognize; sign. See note at APPROVE. ANTONYM reject.

rating noun *the hotel's four-star rating* GRADE, grading, classification, ranking, rank, category, designation; assessment, evaluation, appraisal; mark, score.

ratio noun *the fat ratios in American diets are dangerously askew* PROPORTION, comparative number, correlation, relationship, correspondence; percentage, fraction, quotient.

ration noun **1** *a daily ration of chocolate* ALLOWANCE, allocation, quota, quantum, share, portion, helping; amount, quantity, measure, proportion, percentage.

2 **(rations)** *the garrison ran out of rations* SUPPLIES, provisions, food, foodstuffs, eatables, edibles, provender; stores; *informal* grub, eats, vittles; *formal* comestibles; *dated* victuals.

▸ verb *fuel supplies were rationed* CONTROL, limit, restrict; conserve.

rational adjective **1** *a rational approach* LOGICAL, reasoned, sensible, reasonable, cogent, intelligent, judicious, shrewd, common-sense, commonsensical, sound, prudent; down-to-earth, practical, pragmatic. See note at SENSIBLE. ANTONYM illogical.

2 *she was not rational at the time of signing* SANE, compos mentis, in one's right mind, of sound mind; normal, balanced, grounded, lucid, coherent; *informal* all there. ANTONYM insane.

3 *humans are rational beings* INTELLIGENT, thinking, reasoning; cerebral, logical, analytical; *formal* ratiocinative.

rationale noun *Bush outlined his rationale for a national missile defense plan* REASON(S), reasoning, thinking, logic, grounds, sense; principle, theory, argument, case; motive, motivation, explanation, justification, excuse; the whys and wherefores.

rationalize verb **1** *he tried to rationalize his behavior* JUSTIFY, explain, explain away, account for, defend, vindicate, excuse. See note at LIE[1].

2 *an attempt to rationalize the industry* STREAMLINE, reorganize, modernize, update; trim, hone, simplify, downsize, prune.

rattle verb **1** *hailstones rattled against the window* CLATTER, patter; clink, clunk.

2 *he rattled some coins* JINGLE, jangle, clink, tinkle.

3 *the bus rattled along* JOLT, bump, bounce, jounce, shake.

4 *the government was rattled by the strike* UNNERVE, disconcert, disturb, fluster, shake, perturb, discompose, discomfit, ruffle, throw; *informal* faze.

▸ noun **1** *the rattle of the bottles* CLATTER, clank, clink, clang; jingle, jangle.

2 *she gave the baby a rattle* NOISEMAKER, shaker, rain stick, maraca.

PHRASES: **rattle something off** *she can rattle off the complete list of Shakespeare's plays* REEL OFF, recite, list, fire off, run through, enumerate. **rattle on/away** *rattling on about her grandchildren* PRATTLE, babble, chatter, prate, go on, jabber, gibber, ramble; *informal* gab, yak, yap.

raucous adjective **1** *raucous laughter* HARSH, strident, screeching, piercing, shrill, grating, discordant, dissonant; noisy, loud, cacophonous. ANTONYMS soft, dulcet.

2 *a raucous party* ROWDY, noisy, boisterous, roisterous, wild. ANTONYMS restrained, quiet.

raunchy adjective *informal* See SEXY sense 2.

ravage verb *they ravaged the countryside* LAY WASTE, devastate, ruin, destroy, wreak havoc on, leave desolate; pillage, plunder, despoil, ransack, sack, loot, rape.

THE RIGHT WORD

Ravage, **pillage**, **sack**, and **plunder** are all verbs associated with the actions of a conquering army during wartime. *Ravage* implies violent destruction, usually in a series of raids or invasions over an extended period of time (*the invading forces ravaged the countryside*). *Plunder* refers to the roving of soldiers through recently conquered territory in search of money and goods (*they plundered the city and left its inhabitants destitute*), while *pillage* describes the act of stripping a conquered city or people of valuables (*churches pillaged by ruthless invaders*). *Sack* is even more extreme than *pillage*, implying not only the seizure of all valuables, but total destruction as well (*the army sacked every village along the coast*). **Despoil** also entails the stripping of valuables, but with less violence than *sack*; it is more common in nonmilitary contexts, where it describes a heedless or inadvertent destruction (*forests despoiled by logging companies*). **Devastate** emphasizes ruin and desolation, whether it happens to buildings, forests, or crops (*fields of corn devastated by flooding*). **Waste** comes close in meaning to *devastate*, but it suggests a less violent or more gradual destruction (*a region of the country wasted by years of drought and periodic fires*).

---

ravages plural noun **1** *the ravages of time* DAMAGING EFFECTS, ill effects.

2 *the ravages carried out by humanity* ACTS OF DESTRUCTION, destruction, damage, devastation, ruin, havoc, depredation(s).

rave verb **1** *he was raving about the fires of hell* TALK WILDLY, babble, jabber, talk incoherently.

2 *I raved and swore at them* RANT, rant and rave, rage, lose one's temper, storm, fulminate, fume; shout, roar, thunder, bellow; *informal* fly off the handle, blow one's top, hit the roof, flip one's wig.

3 *he **raved about** her singing* PRAISE ENTHUSIASTICALLY, go into raptures about/over, wax lyrical about, sing the praises of, rhapsodize over, enthuse about/over, acclaim, eulogize, extol; *informal* ballyhoo; *formal* laud; *archaic* panegyrize. ANTONYM criticize.

▸ noun *informal* **1** *the food won raves from the critics* ENTHUSIASTIC PRAISE, lavish praise, a rapturous reception, tribute, plaudits, acclaim. ANTONYM criticism.

2 *an all-night rave.* See PARTY noun sense 1.

▸ adjective *informal rave reviews* VERY ENTHUSIASTIC, rapturous, glowing, ecstatic, excellent, highly favorable.

raven adjective *raven hair* BLACK, jet-black, ebony; *literary* sable.

ravenous adjective **1** *I'm absolutely ravenous* VERY HUNGRY, starving, famished; *rare* esurient.

2 *her ravenous appetite* VORACIOUS, insatiable; greedy, gluttonous; *literary* insatiate.

ravine noun *the ravine that runs along Hubble Hollow Road* GORGE, canyon, gully, couloir; chasm, abyss, gulf, gulch, coulee.

raving adjective See MAD sense 1.

ravings plural noun *the ravings of a madman* GIBBERISH, rambling, babbling, wild talk, incoherent talk.

ravish verb **1** *literary he tried to ravish her* RAPE, sexually assault/abuse, violate, force oneself on, molest; *archaic* dishonor, defile.

2 *literary you will be ravished by this wine* ENRAPTURE, enchant, delight, charm, entrance, enthrall, captivate.

3 *archaic her child was ravished from her breast* SEIZE, snatch, carry off/away, steal, abduct.

ravishing adjective *you look utterly ravishing* VERY BEAUTIFUL, gorgeous, stunning, wonderful, lovely, striking, magnificent, dazzling, radiant, delightful, charming, enchanting; *informal* amazing, sensational, fantastic, fabulous, terrific, bodacious, hot, red-hot. ANTONYM hideous.

raw adjective **1** *raw carrot* UNCOOKED, fresh. ANTONYM cooked.

2 *raw materials* UNPROCESSED, untreated, unrefined, crude, natural; unedited, undigested, unprepared. ANTONYMS refined, processed.

3 *raw recruits* INEXPERIENCED, new, untrained, untried, untested, unseasoned; callow, immature, green, naive; *informal* wet behind the ears, raggedy-ass. ANTONYMS experienced, skilled.

4 *his skin is raw* SORE, red, painful, tender; abraded, chafed; *Medicine* excoriated.

5 *a raw morning* BLEAK, cold, chilly, bone-chilling, freezing, icy, icy-cold, wintry, bitter, biting; *informal* nippy. ANTONYMS warm, balmy.

6 *raw emotions* STRONG, intense, passionate, fervent, powerful, violent; undisguised, unconcealed, unrestrained, uninhibited.

7 *raw images of Latin America* REALISTIC, unembellished, unvarnished, brutal, harsh, gritty, graphic. ANTONYM idealized.

PHRASE: **in the raw** *informal . sleeping in the raw.* See NAKED sense 1.

rawboned adjective *the part called for a tall, rawboned teenager | a rawboned herd of spotted cows* THIN, lean, gaunt, bony, skinny, spare. ANTONYM plump.

ray noun 1 *rays of light* BEAM, shaft, streak, stream.

2 *a ray of hope* GLIMMER, flicker, spark, hint, suggestion, sign.

raze verb *the old library will be razed on Saturday* DESTROY, demolish, raze to the ground, tear down, pull down, knock down, level, flatten, bulldoze, wipe out, lay waste. See note at DESTROY.

re preposition *a memo re the new alarm system* ABOUT, concerning, regarding, with regard to, relating to, vis-à-vis, apropos (of), on the subject of, with respect to, with reference to, in connection with.

reach verb 1 *Travis **reached out** a hand* STRETCH OUT, hold out, extend, outstretch, thrust out, stick out.

2 *reach me that book* PASS, hand, give, let someone have.

3 *soon she reached Helen's house* ARRIVE AT, get to, come to; end up at; *informal* make.

4 *the temperature reached 32 degrees* ATTAIN, get to; rise to, climb to; fall to, sink to, drop to; *informal* hit.

5 *the leaders reached an agreement* ACHIEVE, attain, work out, draw up, put together, negotiate, thrash out, hammer out.

6 *I have been trying to reach you all day* GET IN TOUCH WITH, contact, get through to, get, speak to; *informal* get hold of.

7 *our concern is to reach more people* INFLUENCE, sway, get (through) to, make an impression on, have an impact on.

▸ noun 1 *Bobby moved out of her reach* GRASP, range. See note at RANGE.

2 *small goals within your reach* CAPABILITIES, capacity.

3 *beyond the reach of the law* JURISDICTION, authority, influence; scope, range, compass, ambit.

react verb 1 *how would he react if she told him the truth?* BEHAVE, act, take it, conduct oneself; respond, reply, answer.

2 *she **reacted against** the new regulations* REBEL AGAINST, oppose, rise up against.

reaction noun 1 *his reaction had bewildered her* RESPONSE, answer, reply, rejoinder, retort, riposte; *informal* comeback.

2 *a reaction against modernism* BACKLASH, counteraction.

reactionary adjective *a reactionary policy* RIGHT-WING, conservative, rightist, ultraconservative; traditionalist, conventional, old-fashioned, unprogressive; *informal* redneck. ANTONYM progressive.

▸ noun *an extreme reactionary* RIGHT-WINGER, conservative, rightist; traditionalist, conventionalist, dinosaur. ANTONYM radical.

read verb 1 *Nadine and Ian were reading the paper by the fireplace* PERUSE, study, scrutinize, look through; pore over, be absorbed in; run one's eye over, cast an eye over, leaf through, scan, flick through, skim through, thumb through.

2 *he read a passage of the letter* READ OUT/ALOUD, recite, declaim.

3 *I can't read my own writing* DECIPHER, make out, make sense of, interpret, understand.

4 *her remark could be read as a criticism* INTERPRET, take, take to mean, construe, see, understand.

5 *the dial read 70 mph* INDICATE, register, record, display, show.

▸ noun *have a read of this* PERUSAL, study, scan; look (at), browse (through).

PHRASES: **read something into something** *don't read too much into their statistics* INFER FROM, interpolate from, assume from, attribute to; read between the lines. **read up on** *we'll need to read up on Peruvian culture* STUDY, brush up on; *informal* bone up on.

readable adjective 1 *the inscription is perfectly readable* LEGIBLE, easy to read, decipherable, clear, intelligible, comprehensible, reader-friendly. ANTONYM illegible.

2 *her novels are immensely readable* ENJOYABLE, entertaining, interesting, absorbing, engaging, gripping, enthralling, engrossing, stimulating; *informal* unputdownable. ANTONYM boring.

readily adverb 1 *Durkin readily offered to drive him* WILLINGLY, without hesitation, unhesitatingly, ungrudgingly, gladly, happily, eagerly, promptly. ANTONYM reluctantly.

2 *the island is readily accessible* EASILY, with ease, without difficulty. ANTONYM with difficulty.

readiness noun 1 *their readiness to accept change* WILLINGNESS, enthusiasm, eagerness, keenness; promptness, quickness, alacrity.

2 *a state of readiness* PREPAREDNESS, preparation.

3 *the readiness of his reply* PROMPTNESS, quickness, rapidity, swiftness, speed, speediness. PHRASE: **in readiness** *there were candles in readiness* READY, at the ready, available, on hand, accessible, handy; prepared, primed, on standby, standing by, on full alert.

reading noun 1 *a cursory reading of the financial pages* PERUSAL, study, scan, scanning; browse (through), look (through), glance (through), leaf (through), skim (through).

2 *a man of wide reading* BOOK LEARNING, book learning, scholarship, education, erudition.

3 *readings from the Bible* PASSAGE, lesson; section, piece; recital, recitation.

4 *my reading of the situation* INTERPRETATION, construal, understanding, explanation, analysis.

5 *a meter reading* RECORD, figure, indication, measurement.

ready adjective **1** *are you ready?* PREPARED, set, all set, organized, primed; *informal* fit, psyched up, geared up.

2 *everything is ready* COMPLETED, finished, prepared, organized, done, arranged, fixed, in readiness.

3 *he's always ready to help* WILLING, prepared, pleased, inclined, disposed, predisposed; eager, keen, happy, glad; *informal* game.

4 *she looked* ***ready to*** *collapse* ABOUT TO, on the point of, on the verge of, close to, liable to, likely to.

5 *a ready supply of food* AVAILABLE, easily available, accessible; handy, close/near at hand, on hand, convenient, within reach, at the ready, near, at one's fingertips.

6 *a ready answer* PROMPT, quick, swift, speedy, fast, immediate, unhesitating; clever, sharp, astute, shrewd, keen, perceptive, discerning.

▸ verb *he needed time to ready himself* PREPARE, get/make ready, organize; gear oneself up; *informal* psych oneself up.

PHRASES: **at the ready** *the fire extinguishers are at the ready* IN POSITION, poised, ready for use/action, waiting, on deck. **make ready** *making ready for their departure* PREPARE, make preparations, get everything ready, gear up for.

ready-made adjective **1** *ready-made clothing* READY-TO-WEAR, off-the-rack, prêt-à-porter. ANTONYM tailor-made.

2 *ready-made meals* PRECOOKED, oven-ready, convenience, packaged. ANTONYM homemade.

real adjective **1** *is she a fictional character or a real person?* ACTUAL, nonfictional, factual, real-life; historical; material, physical, tangible, concrete, palpable. ANTONYM imaginary.

2 *real gold* GENUINE, authentic, bona fide; *informal* kosher, honest-to-goodness, honest-to-God. ANTONYMS imaginary, fake.

3 *my real name* TRUE, actual.

4 *tears of real grief* SINCERE, genuine, true, unfeigned, heartfelt, unaffected. ANTONYMS false, feigned.

5 *a real man* PROPER, true; *informal* regular.

6 *you're a real idiot* COMPLETE, utter, thorough, absolute, total, prize, perfect.

▸ adverb *informal that's real good of you.* See VERY adverb.

realism noun **1** *optimism tinged with realism* PRAGMATISM, practicality, common sense, levelheadedness.

2 *a degree of realism* AUTHENTICITY, fidelity, verisimilitude, truthfulness, faithfulness.

realistic adjective **1** *you've got to be realistic* PRACTICAL, pragmatic, matter-of-fact, down-to-earth, sensible, commonsensical, grounded; rational, reasonable, levelheaded, clear-sighted, businesslike; *informal* having both/one's feet on the ground, hard-nosed, no-nonsense. ANTONYM idealistic.

2 *a realistic aim* ACHIEVABLE, attainable, feasible, practicable, viable, reasonable, sensible, workable; *informal* doable. ANTONYM impracticable.

3 *a realistic portrayal of war* TRUE TO LIFE, lifelike, truthful, true, faithful, unidealized, real-life, naturalistic, graphic. ANTONYMS fictional, imaginative.

reality noun **1** *distinguishing fantasy from reality* THE REAL WORLD, real life, actuality; truth; physical existence. ANTONYM fantasy.

2 *the harsh realities of life* FACT, actuality, truth.

3 *the reality of Steinbeck's detail* VERISIMILITUDE, authenticity, realism, fidelity, faithfulness. ANTONYM idealism.

PHRASE: **in reality** *they got an invitation, but in reality they were not especially welcome* IN FACT, in actual fact, in point of fact, as a matter of fact, actually, really, in truth; in practice; *archaic* in sooth.

realization noun **1** *a growing realization of the danger* AWARENESS, understanding, comprehension, consciousness, appreciation, recognition, discernment; *formal* cognizance.

2 *the realization of our dreams* FULFILLMENT, achievement, accomplishment, attainment; *formal* effectuation.

realize verb **1** *he suddenly realized what she meant* REGISTER, perceive, discern, be/become aware of (the fact that), be/become conscious of (the fact that), notice; understand, grasp, comprehend, see, recognize, work out, fathom, apprehend; *informal* latch on to, savvy, figure out, get (the message); *Brit.* suss; *formal* be/become cognizant of.

2 *they realized their dream* FULFILL, achieve, accomplish, make a reality, make happen, bring to fruition, bring about/off, carry out/through; *formal* effectuate.

3 *the company realized significant profits* MAKE, clear, gain, earn, return, produce.

4 *the goods realized $3000* BE SOLD FOR, fetch, go for, make, net.

5 *he realized his assets* CASH IN, liquidate, capitalize.

really adverb **1** *he is really very wealthy* IN FACT, in actual fact, actually, in reality, in point of fact, as a matter of fact, in truth, to tell the truth; *archaic* in sooth.

2 *he really likes her* GENUINELY, truly, honestly; undoubtedly, without a doubt, indubitably, certainly, assuredly, unquestionably; *archaic* verily.

3 *they were really kind to me* VERY, extremely, thoroughly, decidedly, exceptionally, exceedingly, immensely, monumentally, tremendously, uncommonly, unbelievably, remarkably, eminently, extraordinarily, incredibly, most, downright, terrifically, awfully, so, ever so; *informal* totally, ultra, too —— for words, seriously, real, mighty, awful, plumb, powerful, way.

▸ exclamation *"They've split up." "Really?"* NO KIDDING, for real, is that so, is that a fact, is that right.

realm noun **1** *peace in the realm* KINGDOM, country, land, dominion, nation.

2 *the realm of academia* DOMAIN, sphere, area, field, world, province, territory.

realty noun *her holdings include vast amounts of realty* REAL ESTATE, property, land.

ream PHRASE: **ream out** *I got reamed out by the coach for being late.* See BERATE.

reap verb **1** *the grain has been reaped* HARVEST, garner, gather in, bring in.

2 *reaping the benefits* RECEIVE, obtain, get, acquire, secure, realize.

rear[1] verb **1** *I was reared on a farm* BRING UP, raise, care for, look after, nurture, parent; educate.

2 *he reared cattle* BREED, raise, keep, farm, ranch.

3 *laboratory-reared plants* GROW, cultivate.

4 *the bear reared its head* RAISE, lift (up), hold up, uplift.

5 *Mount Logan reared up before them* RISE, rise up, tower, soar, loom.

rear[2] noun **1** *the rear of the building* BACK, back part, hind part, back end; *Nautical* stern. ANTONYM front.

2 *we were standing near the rear of the line* END, tail, rear end, back end, tail, tag end. ANTONYM front.

3 *he slapped the horse on the rear.* See BUTTOCKS.

▸ adjective *the rear bumper* BACK, end, rearmost; hind, hinder, hindmost; *technical* posterior.

rearrange verb **1** *the furniture has been rearranged* REPOSITION, move around, change around, arrange differently.

2 *Tony had rearranged his schedule* REORGANIZE, alter, adjust, change, change around, reschedule, rejigger.

reason noun **1** *the main reason for his decision* CAUSE, ground(s), basis, rationale; motive, motivation, purpose, point, aim, intention, objective, goal; explanation, justification, argument, defense, vindication, excuse, pretext.

2 *postmodern voices railing against reason* RATIONALITY, logic, logical thought, reasoning, cognition; *formal* ratiocination.

3 *he was losing his reason* SANITY, mind, mental faculties; senses, wits; *informal* marbles.

4 *he continues, against reason, to love her* GOOD SENSE, good judgment, common sense, wisdom, sagacity, reasonableness.

▸ verb **1** *a young child is unable to reason* THINK RATIONALLY, think logically, use one's common sense, use one's head/brain; *formal* cogitate, ratiocinate.

2 *Scott reasoned that Annabel might be ill* CALCULATE, come to the conclusion, conclude, reckon, think, judge, deduce, infer, surmise; *informal* figure.

3 *she tried to* ***reason with*** *her husband* BRING AROUND, coax, persuade, prevail on, convince, make someone see the light.

PHRASES: **by reason of** *formal by reason of mental illness, Peterson will not be held in contempt of court* BECAUSE OF, on account of, as a result of, owing to, due to, by virtue of, thanks to. **reason something out** *we finally reasoned out the cryptic message in chapter twelve* WORK OUT, think through, make sense of, get to the bottom of, puzzle out; *informal* figure out. **with reason** *he was anxious, with reason, about his own political survival* JUSTIFIABLY, justly, legitimately, rightly, reasonably.

USAGE NOTE **reason is because**

This construction is loose because *reason* implies *because* and vice versa. As Robert W. Burchfield, the distinguished *Oxford English Dictionary* lexicographer, put it: "Though often defended by modern grammarians, the type 'the reason . . . is because' (instead of 'the reason . . . is that') aches with redundancy, and is still as inadmissible in Standard English as it was when H. W. Fowler objected to it in 1926." Points of View 116 (1992). After *reason is*, you'll need a noun phrase, a predicate adjective, or a clause introduced by *that*. The best cure for *reason is because* is to replace *because* with *that*—e.g.: "Marcello (Jean Reno) has one frantic mission in life: to keep anyone from dying in the small Italian village where he lives. The reason is because [read *reason is that*] there are only three plots left in the local cemetery and his terminally ill wife, Roseanna (Mercedes Ruehl), wishes only that she be buried next to their daughter." (*Star-Ledger* [Newark]; June 27, 1997.)

Variations such as *reason is due to* are no better—e.g.: "It's a challenge for any athlete to come back after four years of inactivity. The challenge is even greater when the reason is due to injury [read *the layoff is due to injury* or *injury is the cause*]." (*Tulsa Tribune & Tulsa World*; May 4, 1997.) **—BG**

reasonable adjective **1** *a reasonable man | a reasonable explanation* SENSIBLE, rational, logical, fair, fair-minded, just, equitable; intelligent, wise, levelheaded, practical, realistic; sound, reasoned, well-reasoned, valid, commonsensical; tenable, plausible, credible, believable.

2 *you must take all reasonable precautions* WITHIN REASON, practicable, sensible; appropriate, suitable.

3 *cars in reasonable condition* FAIRLY GOOD, acceptable, satisfactory, average, adequate, fair, all right, tolerable, passable; *informal* OK.

4 *reasonable prices* INEXPENSIVE, moderate, low, cheap, budget, bargain, downmarket; competitive.

reasoned adjective *you have drawn a reasoned conclusion* LOGICAL, rational, well-thought-out, clear, lucid, coherent, cogent, well-expressed, well-presented, considered, sensible.

reasoning noun *it is a neurological disorder that results in impaired memory and reasoning* THINKING, reason, thought, train of thought, thought process, logic, analysis, interpretation, explanation, rationalization; reasons, rationale, arguments; *formal* ratiocination.

reassure verb *officials hope to reassure tourists in the wake of these latest terrorist attacks* PUT/SET SOMEONE'S MIND AT REST, put someone at ease, encourage, inspirit, hearten, buoy up, cheer up; comfort, soothe. ANTONYM alarm.

rebate noun *a 20-percent rebate* REFUND, partial refund, repayment; discount, deduction, reduction, decrease.

rebel noun **1** *the rebels took control of the capital* REVOLUTIONARY, insurgent, revolutionist, mutineer, insurrectionist, insurrectionary, guerrilla, terrorist, freedom fighter.

2 *the concept of the artist as a rebel* NONCONFORMIST, dissenter, dissident, iconoclast, maverick.

▸ verb **1** *the citizens rebelled* REVOLT, mutiny, riot, rise up, take up arms, stage/mount a rebellion, be insubordinate.

2 *his stomach rebelled at the thought of food* RECOIL, show/feel repugnance.

3 *teenagers* ***rebelling against*** *their parents* DEFY, disobey, refuse to obey, kick against, challenge, oppose, resist. ANTONYM obey.

▸ adjective **1** *rebel troops* INSURGENT, revolutionary, mutinous, rebellious, insurrectionary, insurrectionist, renegade.

2 *rebel clergymen* REBELLIOUS, defiant, disobedient, insubordinate, subversive, resistant, recalcitrant; nonconformist, maverick, iconoclastic; *archaic* contumacious. ANTONYMS compliant, conformist.

rebellion noun **1** *troops suppressed the rebellion* UPRISING, revolt, insurrection, mutiny, revolution, insurgence, insurgency; rioting, riot, disorder, unrest. See note at UPRISING.

2 *an act of rebellion* DEFIANCE, disobedience, rebelliousness, insubordination, subversion, subversiveness, resistance.

rebellious adjective **1** *rebellious troops* REBEL, insurgent, mutinous, mutinying, rebelling, rioting, riotous, insurrectionary, insurrectionist, revolutionary.

2 *a rebellious adolescent* DEFIANT, disobedient, insubordinate, unruly, mutinous, wayward, obstreperous, recalcitrant, intractable; *formal* refractory; *archaic* contumacious.

rebirth noun *a residential rebirth in cities like Atlanta and Dallas* REVIVAL, renaissance, resurrection, reawakening, renewal, regeneration; revitalization, rejuvenation; *formal* renascence.

rebound verb **1** *the ball rebounded off the wall* BOUNCE, bounce back, spring back, ricochet, boomerang, carom.

2 *finally the dollar rebounded* RECOVER, rally, pick up, make a recovery.

3 *Thomas's tactics rebounded on him* BACKFIRE, boomerang, have unwelcome repercussions; come back to haunt; *archaic* redound on.

rebuff verb *his offer was rebuffed* REJECT, turn down, spurn, refuse, decline, repudiate; snub, slight, repulse, repel, dismiss, brush off, give someone the cold shoulder; *informal* give someone the brush-off, give someone the bum's rush, freeze out. ANTONYM accept.

▸ noun *the rebuff did little to dampen his ardor* REJECTION, snub, slight, repulse; refusal, spurning, cold-shouldering, discouragement; *informal* brush-off, kick in the teeth, slap in the face.

rebuild verb *rebuilding the barn* RECONSTRUCT, renovate, restore, remodel, remake, reassemble. ANTONYM demolish.

rebuke verb *she never rebuked him in front of others* REPRIMAND, reproach, scold, admonish, reprove, chastise, upbraid, berate, take to task, criticize, censure; *informal* tell off, give someone a talking-to, give someone a dressing-down, give someone an earful, chew out, ream out; *formal* castigate. ANTONYM praise.

▸ noun *Damian was silenced by the rebuke* REPRIMAND, reproach, reproof, scolding, admonishment, admonition, upbraiding; *informal* dressing-down; *formal* castigation. ANTONYM compliment.

THE RIGHT WORD

All of these verbs mean to criticize or express disapproval, but which one you use depends on how upset you are. If you want to go easy on someone, you can **admonish** or **reproach**, both of which indicate mild and sometimes kindly disapproval. To *admonish* is to warn or counsel someone, usually because a duty has been forgotten or might be forgotten in the future (*admonish her about leaving the key in the lock*), while *reproach* also suggests mild criticism aimed at correcting a fault or pattern of misbehavior (*he was reproved for his lack of attention in class*). If you want to express your disapproval formally or in public, use **censure** or **reprimand**. You can *censure* someone either directly or indirectly (*the judge censured the lawyer for violating courtroom procedures; a newspaper article that censured "deadbeat dads"*), while *reprimand* suggests a direct confrontation (*reprimanded by his parole officer for leaving town without reporting his whereabouts*). If you're irritated enough to want to express your disapproval quite harshly and at some length, you can **scold** (*to scold a child for jaywalking*). **Rebuke** is the harshest word of this group, meaning to criticize sharply or sternly, often in the midst of some action (*rebuke a carpenter for walking across an icy roof*).

rebut verb *you will have your opportunity to rebut the allegations* DENY, contradict, controvert, repudiate, counter, attempt to refute, attempt to discredit; *informal* poke holes in; *formal* gainsay. See note at REFUTE. ANTONYM confirm.

USAGE NOTE **rebut, refute**

Rebut means "attempt to refute." *Refute* means "defeat (countervailing arguments)." Thus one who *rebuts* certainly hopes to *refute*; it is immodest to assume, however, that one has *refuted* another's arguments. See also note at refute.

Rebut is sometimes wrongly written *rebutt*. **—BG**

rebuttal noun *now that you've heard the accusations, have you a rebuttal?* REFUTATION, denial, countering, invalidation, negation, contradiction. ANTONYM confirmation.

recalcitrant adjective *Amy was unprepared to deal with three recalcitrant stepchildren* UNCOOPERATIVE, intractable, obstreperous, truculent, insubordinate, defiant, rebellious, willful, wayward, headstrong, self-willed, contrary, perverse, difficult; *formal* refractory; *archaic* froward, contumacious. ANTONYM amenable.

recall verb **1** *he recalled his student days* REMEMBER, recollect, call to mind; think back on/to, look back on, reminisce about. ANTONYM forget.

2 *their exploits recall the days of chivalry* BRING TO MIND, call to mind, put one in mind of, call up, conjure up, evoke.

3 *the ambassador was recalled* SUMMON BACK, order back, call back. ANTONYM prorogue.

▸ noun **1** *the recall of the ambassador* SUMMONING BACK, ordering back, calling back.

2 *their recall of dreams* RECOLLECTION, remembrance, memory.

recant verb **1** *he was forced to recant his political beliefs* RENOUNCE, disavow, deny, repudiate, renege on; *formal* forswear, abjure.

2 *he refused to recant* CHANGE ONE'S MIND, be apostate; *rare* tergiversate.

3 *he recanted his testimony* RETRACT, take back, withdraw, unsay.

USAGE NOTE **recant, recount**

Recant = publicly repudiate a previous statement, belief, or accusation. *Recount* = narrate a past event, esp. from personal experience. *Recant* sometimes erroneously displaces the similar-sounding *recount*—e.g.: "Dressed in a top hat and tails, Garrett chats with his riders and recants [read *recounts*] tales of Weston's glory days." (*Des Moines Register*; May 19, 2002.) The *Oxford English Dictionary* does give "recount" as one sense of *recant* but labels it obsolete and rare. The most recent example is from 1611.

Recant is best reserved for use with personal statements and public positions (think *cant* = sing). Other words are better suited when the thing taken back is something other than words—e.g.:

• "The state's consumer counsel has asked state regulators to recant [read *reverse*] a recent decision under which she said Yankee Gas ratepayers would bear all of the costs of the company's proposed multimillion-dollar system expansion." (*Hartford Courant*; Feb. 14, 2002.)

• "Why do I feel like I'm listening to a deathbed confession by someone who's been a bastard all his life and suddenly, at the 11th hour, is terrified and wants to recant [read *make up for* or *renounce*?] his evil ways?" (*Daily News Leader* [Staunton, VA]; Mar. 5, 2002.)

Recant may be transitive (as in the first use in the following example) or intransitive (as in the second): "Police have a follow-up interview scheduled with Olowokandi's former girlfriend, Suzanne Ketcham, who says she plans to recant her original statements to them and a representative of the district attorney's special victims unit. 'It's not unusual for victims of domestic abuse to recant,' Nilsson said." (*Los Angeles Times*; Dec. 7, 2001.) **—BG**

---

recantation noun *an unconvincing recantation* RENUNCIATION, renouncement, disavowal, denial, repudiation, retraction, withdrawal.

recapitulate verb *I will recapitulate the main points* SUMMARIZE, sum up; restate, repeat, reiterate, go over, review; *informal* recap.

recede verb **1** *the floodwaters receded* RETREAT, go back, go down, move back, move away, withdraw, ebb, subside, abate. ANTONYMS advance, approach.

2 *the lights receded into the distance* DISAPPEAR FROM VIEW, fade, be lost to view, pass from sight.

3 *fears of violence have receded* DIMINISH, lessen, decrease, dwindle, fade, abate, subside, ebb, wane. ANTONYMS intensify, grow.

receipt noun **1** *the receipt of a letter* RECEIVING, getting, obtaining, gaining; arrival, delivery.

2 *make sure you get a receipt* PROOF OF PURCHASE, bill, bill of sale, invoice, sales ticket.

3 *receipts from house sales* PROCEEDS, takings, money/payment received, income, revenue, earnings; profits, return(s), financial return(s), take.

receive verb **1** *Toni received an award* | *they received $650 in damages* BE GIVEN, be presented with, be awarded, collect, garner; get, obtain, gain, acquire; win, be paid, earn, gross, net. ANTONYMS give, present.

2 *she received a letter* BE SENT, be in receipt of, accept delivery of, accept. ANTONYM send.

3 *Alec received the news on Monday* BE TOLD, be informed of, be notified of, hear, discover, find out (about), learn; *informal* get wind of.

4 *he received her suggestion with a complete lack of interest* HEAR, listen to; respond to, react to.

5 *she received a serious injury* EXPERIENCE, sustain, undergo, meet with; suffer, bear.

6 *they received their guests* GREET, welcome, say hello to.

7 *she's not receiving visitors* ENTERTAIN, see.

receiver noun **1** *the receiver of a gift* RECIPIENT, beneficiary, donee. ANTONYM donor.

2 *a telephone receiver* HANDSET.

recent adjective **1** *recent research* NEW, (the) latest, current, fresh, modern, contemporary, up-to-date, up-to-the-minute. ANTONYM old.

2 *his recent visit* NOT LONG PAST, occurring recently, just gone. ANTONYM former.

recently adverb *they recently installed a new flagpole* NOT LONG AGO, a short time ago, in the past few days/weeks/months, a little while back; lately, latterly, just now.

receptacle noun *a receptacle for recycling* CONTAINER, holder, repository; box, tin, bin, can, canister, case, bag.

reception noun **1** *the reception of the goods* RECEIPT, receiving, getting.

2 *the reception of foreign diplomats* GREETING, welcoming, entertaining.

3 *a chilly reception* RESPONSE, reaction, treatment.

4 *a wedding reception* (FORMAL) PARTY, function, social occasion, soiree, fête, levee; *informal* do, bash.

receptive adjective *a receptive audience* OPEN-MINDED, responsive, amenable, well-disposed, flexible, approachable, accessible; *archaic* susceptive. ANTONYM unresponsive.

recess noun **1** *two recesses fitted with bookshelves* ALCOVE, bay, niche, nook, corner, hollow, oriel.

2 **(recesses)** *the deepest recesses of the castle* INNERMOST PARTS/REACHES, remote places, secret places, heart, depths, bowels.

3 *the Christmas recess* ADJOURNMENT, break, interlude, interval, rest; vacation, holiday; *informal* breather.

▸ verb *let's recess for lunch* ADJOURN, take a recess, stop, pause, break, take a break; *informal* take five, take a time out.

recession noun *job losses are symptomatic of the recession* ECONOMIC DECLINE, downturn, depression, slump, slowdown. ANTONYM boom.

recherché adjective *most of the titles are recherché* OBSCURE, rare, esoteric, abstruse, arcane, recondite, exotic, strange, unusual, unfamiliar, out of the ordinary.

recipe noun **1** *a tasty recipe* cooking instructions/directions; *archaic* receipt.

2 *a recipe for success* MEANS/WAY OF ACHIEVING, prescription, formula, blueprint.

recipient noun *scholarship recipients* RECEIVER, beneficiary, legatee, donee. ANTONYM donor.

reciprocal adjective **1** *reciprocal love* GIVEN/FELT IN RETURN, requited, reciprocated.

2 *reciprocal obligations and duties* MUTUAL, common, shared, joint, corresponding, complementary.

reciprocate verb **1** *I was happy to reciprocate* DO THE SAME (IN RETURN), respond in kind, return the favor.

2 *love that was not reciprocated* REQUITE, return, give back; match, equal.

recital noun **1** *a piano recital* CONCERT, performance, musical performance, solo performance, solo; *informal* gig.

2 *her recital of Bob's failures* ENUMERATION, list, litany, catalog, listing, detailing; account, report, description, recapitulation, recounting.

3 *a recital of the Lord's Prayer.* See RECITATION sense 1.

recitation noun **1** *the recitation of his poem* RECITAL, saying aloud, declamation, rendering, rendition, delivery, performance.

2 *a recitation of her life story* ACCOUNT, description, narration, narrative, story.

3 *songs and recitations* READING, passage; poem, verse, monologue.

recite verb **1** *he began to recite verses of the Koran* REPEAT FROM MEMORY, say aloud, declaim, quote, deliver, render.

2 *he stood up and started reciting* GIVE A RECITATION, say a poem.

3 *Sir John recited the facts they knew* ENUMERATE, list, detail, reel off; recount, relate, describe, narrate, give an account of, recapitulate, repeat.

reckless adjective *reckless driving* RASH, careless, thoughtless, heedless, unheeding, hasty, overhasty, precipitate, precipitous, impetuous, impulsive, daredevil, devil-may-care; IRRESPONSIBLE, foolhardy, audacious, overadventurous; ill-advised, injudicious, madcap, imprudent, unwise, ill-considered; *informal* kamikaze; *literary* temerarious. ANTONYM careful.

reckon verb **1** *the cost was reckoned at $6,000* CALCULATE, compute, peg, work out, put a figure on, figure; count (up), add up, total; *chiefly Brit.* tot up.

2 *Anselm reckoned Hugh among his friends* INCLUDE, count, consider to be, regard as, look on as.

3 *informal I reckon I can manage that* BELIEVE, think, be of the opinion/view, be convinced, dare say, imagine, guess, suppose, consider, figure.

4 *it was reckoned a failure* REGARD AS, consider, judge, hold to be, think of as; deem, rate, gauge, count.

5 ***I reckon to*** *get good value for money* EXPECT TO, anticipate, hope to, be looking to; count on, rely on, depend on, bank on, figure on. PHRASES: **to be reckoned with** *the competition is indeed a force to be reckoned with* IMPORTANT, of considerable importance, significant; influential, estimable, powerful, strong, potent, formidable, redoubtable. **reckon with 1** *it's her mother you'll have to reckon with* DEAL WITH, contend with, face, face up to. **2** *they hadn't reckoned with her burning ambition* TAKE INTO ACCOUNT, take into consideration, bargain for/on, anticipate, foresee, be prepared for, consider.

reckoning noun **1** *by my reckoning, this comes to $2 million* CALCULATION, estimation, count, computation, working out, summation, addition.

2 *by her reckoning, the train was late* OPINION, view, judgment, evaluation, estimate, estimation.

3 *the terrible reckoning that he deserved* RETRIBUTION, fate, doom, nemesis, punishment. PHRASE: **day of reckoning** *I promise you, the enemy will remember this as their day of reckoning* JUDGMENT DAY, day of retribution, doomsday, D-Day.

reclaim verb **1** *traveling expenses can be reclaimed* GET BACK, recoup, claim back, recover, regain, retrieve. See note at RECOVER.

2 *Henrietta had reclaimed him from a life of despair* SAVE, rescue, redeem; reform.

recline verb *recline on the sofa* LIE, lie down, lie back, lean back; be recumbent; relax, repose, loll, lounge, sprawl, stretch out; *literary* couch.

recluse noun **1** *a religious recluse* HERMIT, ascetic, eremite, marabout; *historical* anchorite, anchoress.

2 *a natural recluse* LONER, solitary, lone wolf, troglodyte; misanthrope; *rare* solitudinarian, solitarian.

reclusive adjective *a reclusive life in the mountains* SOLITARY, secluded, isolated, hermitlike, hermitic, eremitic, eremitical, cloistered. ANTONYM gregarious.

recognition noun **1** *there was no sign of recognition on his face* IDENTIFICATION, recollection, remembrance.

2 *his recognition of his lack of experience* ACKNOWLEDGMENT, acceptance, admission; realization, awareness, consciousness, knowledge, appreciation; *formal* cognizance.

3 *the sport has finally received the recognition it deserves* OFFICIAL APPROVAL, certification, accreditation, endorsement, validation.

4 *you deserve recognition for the tremendous job you are doing* APPRECIATION, gratitude, thanks, congratulations, credit, commendation, acclaim, acknowledgment; *informal* bouquets.

recognizable adjective *he was recognizable only by his voice* IDENTIFIABLE, noticeable, perceptible, discernible, detectable, distinguishable, observable, perceivable; distinct, unmistakable, clear. ANTONYM imperceptible.

recognize verb **1** *Hannah recognized him at once* IDENTIFY, place, know, put a name to; remember, recall, recollect; know by sight.

2 *they recognized Alan's ability* ACKNOWLEDGE, accept, admit; realize, be aware of, be conscious of, perceive, discern, appreciate; *formal* be cognizant of.

3 *psychotherapists who are recognized* OFFICIALLY APPROVE, certify, accredit, endorse, sanction, validate.

4 *the board recognized their hard work* PAY TRIBUTE TO, show appreciation of/for, appreciate, be grateful for, acclaim, commend.

recoil verb **1** *she instinctively recoiled* DRAW BACK, jump back, pull back; flinch, shy away, shrink (back). See note at WINCE.

2 *he recoiled from the thought* FEEL REVULSION AT, feel disgust at, be unable to stomach, shrink from, balk at.

3 *her rifle recoiled* KICK (BACK), jerk back, spring back.

4 *this will eventually* ***recoil on*** *him* HAVE AN ADVERSE EFFECT ON, rebound on, affect badly, backfire on, boomerang on, come back to haunt; *archaic* redound on.

▸ noun *the recoil of the gun* KICKBACK, kick.

recollect verb *we recollected many events from our childhood* REMEMBER, recall, call to mind, think of; think back to, look back on, reminisce about. ANTONYM forget.

recollection noun *according to my recollection, he was wearing a striped necktie* MEMORY, remembrance, impression, reminiscence.

recommend verb **1** *her former employer recommended her for the post* ADVOCATE, endorse, commend, suggest, put forward, propose, nominate, put up; speak favorably of, speak well of, put in a good word for, vouch for; *informal* plug.

2 *the committee recommended a cautious approach* ADVISE, counsel, urge, exhort, enjoin, prescribe, argue for, back, support; suggest, advocate, propose.

3 *there was little to recommend her* HAVE IN ONE'S FAVOR, give an advantage to; *informal* have going for one.

recommendation noun **1** *the advisory group's recommendations* ADVICE, counsel, guidance, direction, suggestion, proposal.

2 *a personal recommendation* COMMENDATION, endorsement, good word, favorable mention, testimonial; suggestion, tip; *informal* plug.

3 *a place whose only recommendation is that it has few traffic problems* ADVANTAGE, good point/feature, benefit, asset, boon, attraction, appeal.

recompense verb 1 *offenders should recompense their victims* COMPENSATE, indemnify, repay, reimburse, make reparation to, make restitution to, make amends to.

2 *she wanted to recompense him* REWARD, pay back.

3 *nothing could recompense her loss* MAKE UP FOR, compensate for, make amends for, make restitution for, make reparation for, restore, redress, make good.

▸ noun *damages were paid in recompense* COMPENSATION, reparation, restitution, indemnification, indemnity; reimbursement, repayment, redress; *archaic* guerdon.

reconcilable adjective *the two sets of findings are reconcilable* COMPATIBLE, consistent, congruous, congruent, consilient.

reconcile verb 1 *the news reconciled us* REUNITE, bring (back) together (again), restore friendly relations between, make peace between; pacify, appease, placate, mollify; *formal* conciliate. ANTONYMS estrange, alienate.

2 *her divorced parents have reconciled* SETTLE ONE'S DIFFERENCES, make (one's) peace, make up, kiss and make up, bury the hatchet, declare a truce. ANTONYM quarrel.

3 *trying to reconcile his religious beliefs with his career* MAKE COMPATIBLE, harmonize, square, make congruent, balance; *rare* syncretize.

4 *the quarrel was reconciled* SETTLE, resolve, sort out, mend, remedy, heal, rectify; *informal* patch up.

5 *they had to* ***reconcile themselves to*** *drastic losses* ACCEPT, come to accept, resign oneself to, come to terms with, learn to live with, get used to.

reconciliation noun 1 *the reconciliation of the disputants* REUNITING, reunion, bringing together (again), conciliation, reconcilement, rapprochement, fence-mending; pacification, appeasement, placating, mollification.

2 *a reconciliation of their differences* RESOLUTION, settlement, settling, resolving, mending, remedying.

3 *there was little hope of reconciliation* AGREEMENT, compromise, understanding, peace; *formal* concord.

4 *the reconciliation of theory with practice* HARMONIZING, harmonization, squaring, balancing.

recondite adjective *the recondite realms of Semitic philology* OBSCURE, abstruse, arcane, esoteric, recherché, profound, difficult, complex, complicated, involved; incomprehensible, unfathomable, impenetrable, cryptic, opaque. See note at OBSCURE.

recondition verb *the engine has been completely reconditioned* OVERHAUL, rebuild, renovate, restore, repair, reconstruct, remodel, refurbish; *informal* do up, revamp.

reconnaissance noun *unfortunately, our latest reconnaissance has uncovered no new information* PRELIMINARY SURVEY, survey, exploration, observation, investigation, examination, inspection; patrol, search; reconnoitering; *informal* recon.

reconnoiter verb *two of our best pilots were sent in to reconnoiter the area* SURVEY, make a reconnaissance of, explore; investigate, examine, scrutinize, inspect, observe, take a look at; patrol; *informal* check out, scope out, recon.

reconsider verb *the plaintiff has asked an appeals court to reconsider its decision to order a new trial* RETHINK, review, revise, reexamine, reevaluate, reassess, reappraise; change, alter, modify; have second thoughts, change one's mind.

reconsideration noun *upon reconsideration, the council decided to allow the zoning variance* REVIEW, rethink, reexamination, reassessment, reevaluation, reappraisal.

reconstruct verb 1 *the building had to be reconstructed* REBUILD, restore, renovate, recreate, remake, reassemble, remodel, refashion, revamp, recondition, refurbish.

2 *reconstructing the events of that day* RECREATE, build up a picture/impression of, piece together, reenact.

record noun 1 *written records of the past* ACCOUNT(S), document(s), documentation, data, file(s), dossier(s), evidence, report(s); annal(s), archive(s), chronicle(s); minutes, transactions, proceedings, transcript(s); certificate(s), instrument(s), deed(s); register, log, logbook; *Law* muniment(s).

2 *listening to records* album, vinyl; *dated* phonograph record, LP, single, forty-five, seventy-eight.

3 *the judge weighed the factor of his good record* PREVIOUS CONDUCT/PERFORMANCE, track record, history, life history, reputation.

4 *she's got armed robbery on her record* CRIMINAL RECORD, police record; *informal* rap sheet.

5 *she won the race and set a new record* BEST PERFORMANCE, highest achievement; best time, fastest time; world record.

6 *a lasting record of what they have achieved* REMINDER, memorial, souvenir, memento, remembrance, testament.

▸ adjective *record profits* RECORD-BREAKING, best ever, unsurpassed, unparalleled, unequaled, second to none.

▸ verb 1 *the doctor recorded her blood pressure* WRITE DOWN, put in writing, take down, note, make a note of, jot down, put down on paper; document, put on record, enter, register, log; list, catalog.

2 *the thermometer recorded a high temperature* INDICATE, register, show, display.

3 *the team recorded their fourth win* ACHIEVE, accomplish, chalk up, notch up.

4 *the recital was recorded live* MAKE A RECORD/RECORDING OF, tape, tape-record; video-record, videotape, video.

PHRASE: **off the record** 1 *his comments were off the record* UNOFFICIAL, confidential, in (strict) confidence, not to be made public. 2 *they admitted, off the record, that they had made a mistake* UNOFFICIALLY, privately, in (strict) confidence, confidentially, between ourselves.

recorder noun 1 *he put a cassette in the recorder* tape recorder, cassette recorder; VCR, videocassette recorder, videotape recorder; DVD recorder, digital recorder.

2 *a recorder of rural life* RECORD KEEPER, archivist, annalist, diarist, chronicler, historian; *rare* chronologer, chronologist.

recount verb *Gretchen recounted everything she could remember about what happened that night* TELL, relate, narrate, give an account of, describe, report, outline, delineate, relay, convey, communicate, impart. See note at RECANT.

recoup verb *Andalusian health authorities bringing suit against tobacco giants in an attempt to recoup the cost of treating smokers* GET BACK, regain, recover, win back, retrieve, redeem. See note at RECOVER.

USAGE NOTE **recoup, recuperate**

Recoup, dating from the fifteenth century as an English word, is a transitive verb with two senses: (1) "get back (lost money, etc.)"; or (2) "pay back (money owed, etc.)." Although sense 2 is older, sense 1 is now predominant. *Recuperate*, dating from the mid-sixteenth century, is almost always an intransitive verb with the sense "get well; regain one's strength after a medical procedure or an illness." The misuse of *recoup* for *recuperate* is not uncommon—e.g.: "Still recouping [read *recuperating*] from foot surgery and planning to strike a long-term performance deal in Las Vegas for early next year, Cassidy kicked back and watched hours of rare footage of the Rats in action." (*Las Vegas Review-Journal*; July 23, 1999.)

A related mistake is the misspelling *recouperate*—e.g.: "Lance Diamond, the godfather of Buffalo soul, is in Mercy Hospital recouperating [read *recuperating*] from a flu-like illness." (*Buffalo News*; Nov. 30, 2000.)

Another error is the misuse of *recuperate* for *recoup*—e.g.:

• "The funeral provider would have to file a civil lawsuit to recuperate [read *recoup*] its money, Yabuno said." (*Press-Enterprise* [Riverside, CA]; July 19, 2000.)

• "They have demanded a jury trial in the hopes of recuperating [read *recouping*] losses they claim are a result of 'incompetence' by the attorneys they are suing." (*South Bend Tribune*; Aug. 4, 2000.) —**BG**

recourse noun *surgery may be the only recourse* OPTION, possibility, alternative, resort, way out, hope, remedy, choice, expedient. PHRASE: **have recourse to** *we had recourse to the national committee for additional funding* RESORT TO, make use of, avail oneself of, turn to, call on, look to, fall back on.

recover verb **1** *he's recovering from a heart attack* RECUPERATE, get better, convalesce, regain one's strength, get stronger, get back on one's feet; be on the mend, be on the road to recovery, pick up, rally, respond to treatment, improve, heal, pull through, bounce back. ANTONYM deteriorate.

2 *later, shares recovered* RALLY, improve, pick up, make a recovery, rebound, bounce back.

3 *the stolen material has been recovered* RETRIEVE, regain (possession of), get back, recoup, reclaim, repossess, redeem, recuperate, find (again), track down. ANTONYM lose.

4 *gold coins recovered from a wreck* SALVAGE, save, rescue, retrieve. PHRASE: **recover oneself** *as nervous as she was, she convincingly recovered herself* PULL ONESELF TOGETHER, regain one's composure, regain one's self-control; *informal* get a grip (on oneself).

THE RIGHT WORD

If you lose or let go of something and find it either by chance or with effort, you **recover** it (*recover the stolen artwork*). Although it is often used interchangeably with *recover*, **regain** puts more emphasis on the search or effort involved in getting back something you have been deprived of (*regain one's position as chairperson; regain one's eyesight*). **Recoup** refers to the recovery of something similar or equivalent to what has been lost, usually in the form of compensation (*he tried to recoup his gambling losses*). **Reclaim** and **restore** both involve bringing something back to its original condition or to a better or more useful state. *Reclaim* is usually associated with land (*reclaim neglected farmlands*), while *restore* is linked to buildings or objects of art (*restore an eighteenth-century house*). **Retrieve** implies that something has slipped beyond reach, and that a concerted effort or search is required to recover it (*her desperate efforts to retrieve the family dog from the flooded house*).

recovery noun **1** *her recovery may be slow* RECUPERATION, convalescence. ANTONYM relapse.

2 *the economy was showing signs of recovery* IMPROVEMENT, rallying, picking up, upturn, upswing. ANTONYM deterioration.

3 *the recovery of the stolen goods* RETRIEVAL, regaining, repossession, getting back, reclamation, recouping, redemption, recuperation. ANTONYM loss.

recreation noun **1** *she cycles for recreation* PLEASURE, leisure, relaxation, fun, enjoyment, entertainment, amusement; play, sport; *informal* R and R; *archaic* disport. ANTONYM work.

2 *his favorite recreations* PASTIME, hobby, leisure activity.

recrimination noun *this is not a time for recrimination, but a time to come together in solidarity* ACCUSATION(S), counteraccusation(s), countercharge(s), counterattack(s), retaliation(s).

recruit verb **1** *more soldiers were recruited* ENLIST, call up, conscript, draft, muster in; *archaic* levy.

2 *the king recruited an army* MUSTER, form, raise, mobilize. ANTONYM disband.

3 *the company is recruiting staff* HIRE, employ, take on; enroll, sign up, engage. ANTONYM dismiss.

▸ noun **1** *thousands of recruits were enlisted* CONSCRIPT, new soldier; draftee, yardbird.

2 *top-quality recruits* NEW MEMBER, new entrant, newcomer, initiate, beginner, novice, tenderfoot, hire; *informal* rookie, newbie, greenhorn.

rectify verb *Perry is willing to do anything to rectify the situation with his estranged grandfather* CORRECT, right, put right, put to rights, sort out, deal with, amend, remedy, repair, fix, make good, resolve, settle; *informal* patch up.

rectitude noun *not all of his colleagues share his personal frugality and public rectitude* RIGHTEOUSNESS, goodness, virtue, morality, honor, honorableness, integrity, principle, probity, honesty, trustworthiness, uprightness, decency, good character. See note at GOODNESS.

recumbent adjective *he stepped over Sadie's recumbent body* LYING, flat, horizontal, stretched out, sprawled (out), reclining, prone, prostrate, supine; lying down. ANTONYM upright.

recuperate verb **1** *Amanda went to Jackson Hole to recuperate* GET BETTER, recover, convalesce, get well, regain one's strength/health, get over something.

2 *he recuperated the money*. See note at RECOUP.

recur verb *we don't want the termite infestation to recur* HAPPEN AGAIN, reoccur, occur again, repeat (itself); come back (again), return, reappear, appear again.

recurrent adjective *a recurrent blood clot in his lung | patriotic feminism is a recurrent theme in her music* REPEATED, recurring, repetitive, periodic, cyclical, seasonal, perennial, regular, frequent; intermittent, sporadic, spasmodic.

recycle verb *the UPS Store will recycle those annoying styrofoam peanuts* REUSE, reprocess, reclaim, recover; salvage, save.

red adjective **1** *a red dress* scarlet, vermilion, crimson, ruby, cherry, cerise, cardinal, carmine, wine, blood-red; coral, cochineal, rose; brick-red, maroon, rufous; reddish; rusty, cinnamon, fulvous; *literary* damask, vermeil, sanguine.

2 *he was red in the face* FLUSHED, reddish, crimson, pink, pinkish, florid, rubicund; ruddy, rosy, glowing; burning, feverish; *literary* rubescent; *archaic* sanguine.

3 *his eyes were red* BLOODSHOT, sore.

4 *red hair* reddish, auburn, titian, chestnut, carroty, ginger, sandy. PHRASES: **in the red** *his account is still in the red* OVERDRAWN, in debt, in debit, in deficit, in arrears. **see red** *informal when Kate showed up drunk, Julian saw red* BECOME VERY ANGRY, become enraged, lose one's temper; *informal* go mad, go crazy, go wild, go bananas, hit the roof, fly off the handle, blow one's top, flip out, go ballistic, flip one's wig, blow one's stack.

WORD NOTE **fulvous**

This word describes the optical experience "reddish-yellow." A frequent color of the sun, many flowers, the dust found on the ground in some towns in the Caribbean, rust, a duck called the *fulvous whistling duck* native to East Africa, and more peaches than are actually accurately described by the shade "peach." For these and other reasons, it is a practical word for the travel writer—and other keen observers of the natural world—to have to hand. **—ZS**

red-blooded adjective *a red-blooded American boy* MANLY, masculine, virile, macho.

redden verb *the sleet reddened our faces | Sean could feel his cheeks redden* TURN RED, go red, make red, blush, flush, color, burn.

redeem verb **1** *the whimsical artwork redeems the book* SAVE, compensate for the defects of, vindicate.

2 *he fully redeemed himself in the next race* VINDICATE, free from blame, absolve.

3 *you cannot redeem their sins* ATONE FOR, make amends for, make restitution for.

4 *who shall redeem these sinners?* SAVE, deliver from sin, convert.

5 *Billy redeemed his drums from the pawnbrokers* RETRIEVE, regain, recover, get back, reclaim, repossess; buy back.

6 *this voucher can be redeemed at any branch* EXCHANGE, give in exchange, cash in, convert, trade in.

7 *they could not redeem their debts* PAY OFF/BACK, clear, discharge, honor.

8 *he made no effort to redeem his promise* FULFILL, carry out, discharge, make good; keep, keep to, stick to, hold to, adhere to, abide by, honor.

redeeming adjective *the critics are hard-pressed to find anything redeeming about Muzio's latest book* COMPENSATING, compensatory, extenuating, redemptive.

redemption noun **1** *God's redemption of his people* SAVING, freeing from sin, absolution.

2 *the redemption of their possessions* RETRIEVAL, recovery, reclamation, repossession, return.

3 *the redemption of credit vouchers* EXCHANGE, cashing in, conversion.

4 *the redemption of the mortgage* PAYING OFF, paying back, discharge, clearing, honoring.

5 *the redemption of his obligations* FULFILLMENT, carrying out, discharge, performing, honoring, meeting.

red-handed adjective, adverb *the thief was caught red-handed* IN THE ACT, with one's fingers/hand in the till, with one's hand in the cookie jar, in flagrante delicto; *informal* with one's pants down.

redneck *informal* noun *growing up, the only men she knew were church elders and rednecks* PROVINCIAL, yokel; conservative, reactionary; *informal* yahoo, hick, hayseed.

redolent adjective *their pubs bear names redolent of the monarchy* EVOCATIVE, suggestive, reminiscent.

redoubtable adjective *a redoubtable army commander* FORMIDABLE, awe-inspiring, fearsome, daunting; impressive, commanding, indomitable, invincible, doughty, mighty.

redound verb *formal such sanctions would not* ***redound to*** *their benefit internationally* CONTRIBUTE TO, be conducive to, result in, lead to, effect; *formal* conduce to.

redress verb **1** *we redressed the problem* RECTIFY, correct, right, put to rights, compensate for, amend, remedy, make good, resolve, settle.

2 *we aim to redress the balance* EVEN UP, regulate, equalize.

▸ noun *your best hope of redress* COMPENSATION, reparation, restitution, recompense, repayment, indemnity, indemnification, retribution, satisfaction; justice.

reduce verb **1** *the aim to reduce pollution* LESSEN, make smaller, lower, bring down, decrease, diminish, minimize; shrink, narrow, contract, shorten; ax, cut, cut back/down, make cutbacks in, trim, curtail, slim (down), prune; *informal* chop. ANTONYM increase.

2 *she* ***reduced*** *him* ***to*** *tears* BRING TO, bring to the point of, drive to.

3 *he was reduced to the ranks* DEMOTE, downgrade, bring low, lower, lower in rank. ANTONYM promote.

4 *Halloween items have been reduced* DISCOUNT, mark down, lower the price of, cut, cut in price, make cheaper, put on sale; *informal* slash, knock down. ANTONYM mark up.

PHRASE: **in reduced circumstances** *Quinlan was shocked to find his brother in reduced circumstances* IMPOVERISHED, broke, in straitened circumstances, ruined, bankrupted; poor, indigent, impecunious, in penury, poverty-stricken, destitute; needy, badly off, hard up; *informal* without two cents to rub together, strapped for cash; *formal* penurious.

reduction noun **1** *a reduction in pollution* LESSENING, lowering, decrease, diminution, fade-out.

2 *a staff reduction* CUTBACK, cut, downsizing, scaling down, trimming, pruning, axing, chopping.

3 *a reduction in inflationary pressure* EASING, lightening, moderation, alleviation.

4 *a reduction in status* DEMOTION, downgrading, lowering.

5 *substantial reductions* DISCOUNT, markdown, deduction, cut, price cut.

redundancy noun *redundancy in language* SUPERFLUITY, unnecessariness, excess.

redundant adjective *many churches are now redundant* UNNECESSARY, not required, inessential, unessential, needless, unneeded, uncalled for; surplus, superfluous. ANTONYMS essential, necessary.

reef noun *waves crashed over the reef* SHOAL, bar, sandbar, sandbank, spit; *Canadian & Scottish* skerry.

reek verb *the whole place reeked* STINK, smell, smell bad; stink to high heaven.

▸ noun *the reek of cattle dung* STINK, bad smell, stench, fetor, whiff; *literary* miasma.

reel verb 1 *he reeled as the ship began to roll* STAGGER, lurch, sway, rock, stumble, totter, wobble, falter.

2 *the room reeled* GO ROUND, go round and round, whirl, spin, revolve, swirl, twirl, turn, swim. PHRASES: **reel something off** *she can reel off all the U.S. vice presidents in less than a minute* RECITE, rattle off, list rapidly, run through, enumerate, detail, itemize. **reeling from** *we were reeling from the crisis* SHAKEN BY, stunned by, in shock from, shocked by, taken aback by, staggered by, aghast at, upset by.

refer verb 1 *he* ***referred to*** *errors in the article* MENTION, make reference to, allude to, touch on, speak of/about, talk of/about, write about, comment on, deal with, point out, call attention to.

2 *the matter has been referred to my insurers* PASS, hand over, hand, send on, transfer, remit, entrust, assign.

3 *these figures* ***refer to*** *only the year 2001* APPLY TO, be relevant to, concern, relate to, be connected with, pertain to, appertain to, be pertinent to, have a bearing on, cover.

4 *the name* ***refers to*** *a native village* DENOTE, describe, indicate, mean, signify, designate.

5 *the doctor* ***referred to*** *his notes* CONSULT, turn to, look at, have recourse to.

referee noun 1 *the referee blew his whistle* UMPIRE, judge, linesman; *informal* ref, ump.

2 *include the names of two referees* SUPPORTER, character witness, advocate.

▸ verb 1 *he refereed the game* UMPIRE, judge; *informal* ump.

2 *they asked him to referee in the dispute* ARBITRATE, mediate.

reference noun 1 *his journal contains many* ***references to*** *railroads* MENTION OF, allusion to, comment on, remark about.

2 *references are given in the bibliography* SOURCE, citation, authority, credit; bibliographical data.

3 *reference to a higher court* REFERRAL, transfer, remission.

4 *a glowing reference* TESTIMONIAL, character reference, recommendation; credentials. PHRASE: **with reference to** *with reference to your latest request for funding, the directors will submit their final decision on Friday* APROPOS TO, with regard to, regarding, with respect to, on the subject of, re; in relation to, relating to, vis-à-vis, in connection with.

referendum noun *he called for a referendum on the death penalty* POPULAR VOTE, vote, public vote, plebiscite, ballot, poll.

refine verb 1 *refining our cereal foods* PURIFY, process, treat.

2 *helping students to refine their language skills* IMPROVE, perfect, polish (up), hone, fine-tune.

refined adjective 1 *refined sugar* PURIFIED, processed, treated. ANTONYM crude.

2 *a refined lady* CULTIVATED, cultured, polished, stylish, elegant, sophisticated, urbane; polite, gracious, well-mannered, well-bred, gentlemanly, ladylike, genteel. ANTONYMS boorish, coarse.

3 *a person of refined taste* DISCRIMINATING, discerning, fastidious, exquisite, impeccable, fine.

refinement noun 1 *the refinement of sugar* PURIFICATION, refining, processing, treatment, treating.

2 *all writing needs endless refinement* IMPROVEMENT, polishing, honing, fine-tuning, touching up, finishing off, revision, editing, reworking.

3 *a woman of refinement* STYLE, elegance, finesse, polish, sophistication, urbanity; politeness, grace, graciousness, good manners, good breeding, gentility; cultivation, taste, discrimination.

reflect verb 1 *the snow reflects light* SEND BACK, throw back, cast back.

2 *their expressions reflected their feelings* INDICATE, show, display, demonstrate, be evidence of, register, reveal, betray, disclose; express, communicate; *formal* evince.

3 *he* ***reflected on*** *his responsibilities* THINK ABOUT, give thought to, consider, give consideration to, review, mull over, contemplate, cogitate about/on, meditate on, muse on, brood on/over, turn over in one's mind; *archaic* pore on. PHRASE: **reflect badly on** *stunts like these reflect badly on our school* DISCREDIT, disgrace, dishonor, shame, put in a bad light, damage, tarnish the reputation of, give a bad name to, bring into disrepute.

reflection noun 1 *the reflection of light* SENDING BACK, throwing back, casting back.

2 *her reflection in the pond* IMAGE, mirror image, likeness.

3 *your hands and nails are a reflection of your well-being* INDICATION, display, demonstration, manifestation; expression, evidence.

4 *a sad reflection on society* SLUR, aspersion, imputation, reproach, shame, criticism.

5 *after some reflection, he turned it down* THOUGHT, thinking, consideration, contemplation, deliberation, pondering, meditation, musing, rumination; *formal* cogitation.

6 *write down your reflections* OPINION, thought, view, belief, feeling, idea, impression, conclusion, assessment; comment, observation, remark.

reflex adjective *sneezing is a reflex action* INSTINCTIVE, automatic, involuntary, reflexive, impulsive, intuitive, spontaneous, unconscious, unconditioned, untaught, unlearned. ANTONYM conscious.

reform verb 1 *a plan to reform the system* IMPROVE, better, make better, ameliorate, refine; alter, make alterations to, change, adjust, make adjustments to, adapt, amend, revise, reshape, refashion, redesign, restyle, revamp, rebuild, reconstruct, remodel, reorganize.

2 *after his marriage he reformed* MEND ONE'S WAYS, change for the better, turn over a new leaf, improve.

▸ noun *the reform of the prison system* IMPROVEMENT, amelioration, refinement; alteration, change, adaptation, amendment, revision, reshaping, refashioning, redesigning, restyling, revamp, revamping, renovation, rebuilding, reconstruction, remodeling, reorganizing, reorganization.

refractory adjective *formal their refractory children* OBSTINATE, stubborn, mulish, pigheaded, obdurate, headstrong, self-willed, wayward, willful, perverse, contrary, recalcitrant, obstreperous, disobedient, difficult; *informal* balky; *archaic* contumacious, froward. ANTONYM obedient.

refrain verb *the demonstrators have promised to* ***refrain from*** *violent behavior* ABSTAIN FROM, desist from, hold back from, stop oneself from, forbear (from), avoid, eschew, shun, renounce; *informal* swear off; *formal* forswear, abjure.

refresh verb 1 *the cool air will refresh me* REINVIGORATE, revitalize, revive, restore, fortify, enliven, perk up, stimulate, freshen, energize, exhilarate, reanimate, wake up, revivify, inspirit; blow away the cobwebs; *informal* buck up, pep up. ANTONYM weary.

2 *let me refresh your memory* JOG, stimulate, prompt, prod.

3 *I refreshed his glass* REFILL, top up, replenish, recharge.

refreshing adjective 1 *a refreshing drink* INVIGORATING, revitalizing, reviving, restoring, bracing, fortifying, enlivening, inspiriting, stimulating, energizing, exhilarating.

2 *a refreshing change of direction* WELCOME, stimulating, fresh, imaginative, innovative, innovatory.

refreshment noun 1 **(refreshments)** *refreshments were available during the intermission* FOOD AND DRINK, sustenance, provender; snacks, tidbits, eatables; *informal* nibbles, eats, grub, nosh; *formal* comestibles; *literary* viands; *dated* victuals; *archaic* aliment.

2 *spiritual refreshment* INVIGORATION, revival, stimulation, reanimation, revivification, rejuvenation, regeneration, renewal.

refrigerate verb *don't refrigerate the bananas* KEEP COLD, cool, cool down, chill; freeze. ANTONYM heat.

refuge noun 1 *homeless people seeking refuge in subway stations* SHELTER, protection, safety, security, asylum, sanctuary.

2 *a refuge for mountain gorillas* SANCTUARY, shelter, place of safety, haven, safe haven, sanctum; retreat, hiding place, hideaway, hideout.

refugee noun *collecting blankets for the refugees* ÉMIGRÉ, fugitive, exile, displaced person, asylum seeker; **(refugees)** boat people.

refund verb 1 *we will refund your money if you're not satisfied* REPAY, give back, return, pay back.

2 *they refunded the subscribers* REIMBURSE, compensate, recompense, remunerate, indemnify.

▸ noun *a full refund* REPAYMENT, reimbursement, rebate.

refurbish verb *the airfield plans to refurbish its museum* RENOVATE, recondition, rehabilitate, revamp, overhaul, restore, renew, redevelop, rebuild, reconstruct; redecorate, spruce up, upgrade, refit, retrofit, bring up to code; *informal* do up, rehab.

refusal noun 1 *we had one refusal to our invitation* NONACCEPTANCE, no, dissent, demurral, negation, turndown; regrets.

2 *you can have first refusal* OPTION, choice, opportunity to purchase.

3 *the refusal of a zoning variance* WITHHOLDING, denial, turndown.

refuse[1] verb 1 *he refused their invitation* DECLINE, turn down, say no to; reject, spurn, rebuff, dismiss; send one's regrets; *informal* pass up. ANTONYM accept.

2 *the city refused planning permission* WITHHOLD, deny, refuse to grant; *informal* give thumbs down to. ANTONYM grant.

refuse[2] noun *piles of refuse* GARBAGE, trash, waste, debris, litter, detritus, dross; dregs, leftovers; *informal* junk.

refute verb *attempts to refute Einstein's theory* DISPROVE, prove wrong, prove false, debunk, discredit, invalidate; *informal* poke holes in; *formal* confute. See note at REBUT.

USAGE NOTE **refute, rebut, reject, confute**

Refute is not synonymous with *rebut* or *deny*. That is, it doesn't mean merely "counter an argument" but "disprove beyond doubt; prove a statement false." Yet the word is commonly misused for *rebut*—e.g.: "Ontario Hydro strongly refuted [read *rebutted* or *denied*] the charges, saying none of its actions violate the Power Corporations Act." (*Ottawa Citizen*; Apr. 25, 1997.) See also note at rebut.

Sometimes *refute* is misused for *reject*—e.g.: "Two-thirds of people refuted [read *rejected*] [Nicholas Ridley's] belief that European Monetary Union is a 'German racket to take over the whole of Europe.' " (*Sunday Telegraph* [UK]; July 15, 1990.)

Confute is essentially synonymous with *refute* in the sense "prove to be false or wrong." It's probably the stronger term, but it's much rarer. **—BG**

regain verb 1 *government troops regained the capital* RECOVER, get back, win back, recoup, retrieve, reclaim, repossess; take back, retake, recapture, reconquer. See note at RECOVER.

2 *they regained dry land* RETURN TO, get back to, reach again, rejoin.

regal adjective 1 *a regal feast.* See SPLENDID sense 1.

2 *his regal forebears* ROYAL, kingly, queenly, princely.

regale verb 1 *they were lavishly regaled* ENTERTAIN, wine and dine, fête, feast, serve, feed.

2 *he regaled her with colorful stories* ENTERTAIN, amuse, divert, delight, fascinate, captivate.

regard verb 1 *we regard these results as encouraging* CONSIDER, look on, view, see, think of, judge, deem, estimate, assess, reckon, adjudge, rate, gauge.

2 *he regarded her coldly* LOOK AT, contemplate, eye, gaze at, stare at; watch, observe, view, study, scrutinize; *literary* behold.

▸ noun 1 *she has no regard for human life* CONSIDERATION, care, concern, thought, notice, heed, attention.

2 *doctors are held in high regard* ESTEEM, respect, acclaim, admiration, approval, approbation, estimation. See note at ESTEEM.

3 **(regards)** *Jamie sends his regards* BEST WISHES, good

wishes, greetings, kind/kindest regards, felicitations, salutations, respects, compliments, best, love.

4 *his steady regard* LOOK, fixed look, gaze, stare; observation, contemplation, study, scrutiny.

5 *in this regard I disagree with you* RESPECT, aspect, point, item, particular, detail, specific; matter, issue, topic, question.

PHRASE: **with/in regard to.** See REGARDING.

USAGE NOTE **regard**

As a noun in *with regard to* and *in regard to*, the singular noun is correct. The plural form (as in with regards to and in regards to) is, to put it charitably, poor usage—e.g.: "Single men and women are overwhelmed and confused by a barrage of information and advice on what to do and what not to do in regards to [read *in regard to*] finding Mr. Right and Ms. Girl-of-My-Dreams." (*Ebony*; Dec. 1997.) The acceptable forms are best used as introductory phrases. But even these may be advantageously replaced by a single word such as *concerning*, *regarding*, or *considering*, or even *in*, *about*, or *for*.

The plural *regards* is acceptable in this sense only in the phrase *as regards*, a traditional literary idiom (though now a little old-fashioned). But some writers mistakenly use with *regards to*—e.g.: "He became furious at the mere mention of . . . the columnist who accused him recently of 'judicial exhibitionism' with regards to [read *with regard to*] his trade-agreement ruling." (*New York Times*; Sept. 17, 1993.)

The verb *regard* commonly appears in two combinations. The one phrase, *highly regarded*, is a vague expression of praise; the other, *widely regarded as*, usually leads to words of praise—though it would certainly be possible to say that someone is "widely regarded as beneath contempt." It's a mistake, however, to truncate the latter phrase—to say *widely regarded* in place of *highly regarded*: "Crotty has published four novels since leaving the newspaper, and he's widely regarded [read *highly regarded*] by both fiction writers and journalists." **—BG**

regarding preposition *the condo commission has called a special meeting regarding pet ownership* CONCERNING, as regards, with/in regard to, with respect to, with reference to, relating to, respecting, re, about, apropos, on the subject of, in connection with, vis-à-vis.

regardless adverb *he decided to go, regardless* ANYWAY, anyhow, in any case, nevertheless, nonetheless, despite everything, in spite of everything, even so, all the same, in any event, come what may; *informal* still and all, irregardless. PHRASE: **regardless of** *the race will be held on Saturday, regardless of the weather* IRRESPECTIVE OF, without regard to, without reference to, disregarding, without consideration of, discounting, ignoring, notwithstanding, no matter.

regenerate verb *Marion's daily walks really seem to regenerate her* REVIVE, revitalize, renew, restore, breathe new life into, revivify, rejuvenate, reanimate, resuscitate; *informal* give a shot in the arm to.

regime noun **1** *the former Communist regime* GOVERNMENT, system of government, authorities, rule, authority, control, command, administration, leadership.

2 *a health regime* SYSTEM, arrangement, order, pattern, method, procedure, routine, course, plan, program.

regiment noun *the regiment was fighting in Europe* UNIT, outfit, force, corps, division, brigade, battalion, squadron, company, platoon.

▸ verb *their life is strictly regimented* ORGANIZE, order, systematize, control, regulate, manage, discipline.

region noun *the western region of the country* DISTRICT, province, territory, division, area, section, sector, zone, belt, part, quarter; *informal* parts. PHRASE: **in the region of.** See APPROXIMATELY.

regional adjective **1** *regional variations* GEOGRAPHICAL, territorial; by region.

2 *a regional government* LOCAL, localized, provincial, district, parochial. ANTONYM national.

register noun **1** *the register of electors* OFFICIAL LIST, listing, roll, roster, index, directory, catalog, inventory.

2 *the parish register* RECORD, chronicle, log, logbook, ledger, archive; annals, files.

3 *the lower register of the piano* RANGE, reaches; notes, octaves.

▸ verb **1** *I wish to register a complaint* RECORD, put on record, enter, file, lodge, write down, put in writing, submit, report, note, log.

2 *it is not too late to register* ENROLL, put one's name down, enlist, sign on, sign up, apply.

3 *the dial registered a speed of 100 mph* INDICATE, read, record, show, display.

4 *her face registered anger* DISPLAY, show, express, exhibit, betray, evidence, reveal, manifest, demonstrate, bespeak; *formal* evince.

5 *the content of her statement did not register* MAKE AN IMPRESSION, get through, sink in, penetrate, have an effect, strike home.

regress verb *he regressed to his former state of madness* REVERT, retrogress, relapse, lapse, backslide, slip back; deteriorate, decline, worsen, degenerate, get worse; *informal* go downhill. ANTONYM progress.

regret verb **1** *they came to regret their decision* BE SORRY ABOUT, feel contrite about, feel remorse about/for, be remorseful about, rue, repent (of), feel repentant about, be regretful at/about. ANTONYMS welcome, applaud.

2 *regretting the passing of youth* MOURN, grieve for/over, feel grief at, weep over, sigh over, feel sad about, lament, sorrow for, deplore.

▸ noun **1** *both players later expressed regret* REMORSE, sorrow, contrition, contriteness, repentance, penitence, guilt, compunction, remorsefulness, ruefulness. ANTONYM satisfaction.

2 **(regrets)** *please give your grandmother my regrets* APOLOGY, apologies; refusal.

3 *they left with genuine regret* SADNESS, sorrow, disappointment, unhappiness, grief. ANTONYM happiness.

regretful adjective *when your abandoned children grow up, will they care that you claim to be regretful?* SORRY, remorseful, contrite, repentant, rueful, penitent, conscience-stricken, apologetic, guilt-ridden, ashamed, shamefaced. ANTONYM unrepentant.

regrettable adjective *a regrettable mistake* UNDESIRABLE, unfortunate, unwelcome, sorry, woeful, disappointing; deplorable, lamentable, shameful, disgraceful.

regular adjective **1** *plant them at regular intervals* UNIFORM, even, consistent, constant, unchanging, unvarying, fixed. ANTONYM erratic.

2 *a regular beat* RHYTHMIC, steady, even, uniform, constant, unchanging, unvarying. ANTONYM unsteady.

3 *the subject of regular protests* FREQUENT, repeated, continual, recurrent, periodic, constant, perpetual, numerous. ANTONYM occasional.

4 *regular methods of business* ESTABLISHED, conventional, orthodox, proper, official, approved, bona fide, standard, usual, traditional, tried and tested. ANTONYM experimental.

5 *a regular procedure* METHODICAL, systematic, structured, well-ordered, well-organized, orderly, efficient. See note at NORMAL. ANTONYM haphazard.

6 *his regular route to work* USUAL, normal, customary, habitual, routine, typical, accustomed, established. ANTONYM unusual.

regulate verb **1** *the flow of the river has been regulated* CONTROL, adjust, manage.

2 *a new act regulating businesses* SUPERVISE, police, monitor, check, check up on, be responsible for; control, manage, direct, guide, govern.

regulation noun **1** *they obey all the regulations* RULE, ruling, order, directive, act, law, bylaw, statute, edict, canon, pronouncement, dictate, dictum, decree, fiat, command, precept.

2 *the regulation of blood sugar* ADJUSTMENT, control, management, balancing.

3 *the regulation of financial services* SUPERVISION, policing, superintendence, monitoring, inspection; control, management, ordering.

▸ adjective *regulation dress* OFFICIAL, prescribed, set, fixed, mandatory, compulsory, obligatory, de rigueur. ANTONYM unofficial.

regurgitate verb **1** *a ruminant continually regurgitates food* DISGORGE, bring up.

2 *regurgitating facts* REPEAT, say again, restate, reiterate, recite, parrot.

rehabilitate verb **1** *efforts to rehabilitate patients* RESTORE TO NORMALITY, reintegrate, readapt; *informal* rehab.

2 *former dissidents were rehabilitated* REINSTATE, restore, bring back; pardon, absolve, exonerate, forgive; *formal* exculpate.

3 *rehabilitating vacant housing* RECONDITION, restore, renovate, refurbish, revamp, overhaul, redevelop, rebuild, reconstruct; redecorate, spruce up; upgrade, refit, modernize; *informal* do up, rehab.

rehearsal noun *our first concert rehearsal is Monday evening* PRACTICE, practice session, trial performance, read-through, run-through, walk-through; dress rehearsal; *informal* dry run.

rehearse verb **1** *I rehearsed the role* PREPARE, practice, read through, run through/over, go over.

2 *he rehearsed the Vienna Philharmonic* TRAIN, drill, prepare, coach, put someone through their paces.

3 *the document rehearsed all the arguments* ENUMERATE, list, itemize, detail, spell out, catalog, recite, rattle off; restate, repeat, reiterate, regurgitate, recapitulate, go over, run through; *informal* recap.

reign verb **1** *Robert II reigned for nineteen years* BE KING/QUEEN, be monarch, be sovereign, sit on the throne, wear the crown, rule.

2 *chaos reigned* PREVAIL, exist, be present, be the case, occur, be prevalent, be current, be rife, be rampant, be the order of the day, be in force, be in effect; *formal* obtain.

▸ noun **1** *during Henry's reign* RULE, sovereignty, monarchy. See note at REIN.

2 *his reign as manager* PERIOD IN OFFICE, incumbency, managership, leadership.

reigning adjective **1** *the reigning monarch* RULING, regnant; on the throne.

2 *the reigning world champion* INCUMBENT, current.

3 *the reigning legal conventions* PREVAILING, existing, current; usual, common, recognized, established, accepted, popular, widespread.

reimburse verb **1** *they will reimburse your travel costs* REPAY, refund, return, pay back.

2 *we'll reimburse you* COMPENSATE, recompense, repay.

rein noun *there is no rein on his behavior* RESTRAINT, check, curb, constraint, restriction, limitation, control, brake.See note at REIGN.

▸ verb *they* ***reined back*** *costs* RESTRAIN, check, curb, constrain, hold back/in, keep under control, regulate, restrict, control, curtail, limit.See note at REIGN.

PHRASES: **free rein** *the sponsors gave the writers free rein* FREEDOM, a free hand, leeway, latitude, flexibility, liberty, independence, free play, license, room to maneuver, carte blanche, a blank check.See note at REIGN. **keep a tight rein on** *he's a coach who likes to keep a tight rein on his players* EXERCISE STRICT CONTROL OVER, regulate, discipline, regiment, keep in line.See note at REIGN.

USAGE NOTE rein, reign

Like many homophones, these words are frequently mistaken for each other in print—but perhaps no other pair is confused in so many different ways. *Rein in*, not *reign in*, is the correct phrase for "check, restrain." The metaphorical image is of the rider pulling on the reins of the horse to slow down (i.e., "hold your horses")—e.g.: "With every disclosure it becomes clearer that Yeltsin is unwilling or unable to reign in [read *rein in*] his protégé." (*Times Magazine* [London]; Mar. 11, 1995.)

The error also occurs with the noun forms: one holds the *reins*, not the *reigns*—e.g.:

• "Ron Low has a hold of the Oilers' reigns [read *reins*] for now, but should he not work out, look for former Canucks and Flyers coach Bob McCammon to take over as coach next season." (*Tampa Tribune*; Apr. 16, 1995.)

• "In other cases, the computer recommended keeping tighter reign [read *rein*] on inventory, pressing the vendor for more discounts, or raising prices." (*New York Times*; May, 20, 2001.)

The opposite error (*rein* for *reign*) occurs as well—e.g.:

• "His rein [read *reign*] as Fort Meade's tobacco-chewing, play-calling leader ended abruptly in September 1993." (*Tampa Tribune*; Sept. 1, 1995.)

• "Confusion reined [read *reigned*] when everyone within a five-mile radius was asked to evacuate." (*Houston Chronicle*; Jan. 4, 2003.) **—BG**

reincarnation noun *she claims that she has intimate knowledge of events in the distant past as a result of her own reincarnation* REBIRTH, transmigration of the soul, metempsychosis; samsara; *rare* transanimation.

reinforce verb **1** *troops reinforced the dam* STRENGTHEN, fortify, bolster up, shore up, buttress, prop up, underpin, brace, support.

2 *reinforcing links between colleges and companies*

STRENGTHEN, fortify, support; cement, boost, promote, encourage, deepen, enrich, enhance, intensify, improve.

3 *the need to reinforce NATO troops* AUGMENT, increase, add to, supplement, boost, top up.

reinforcement noun 1 *the reinforcement of our defenses* STRENGTHENING, fortification, bolstering, shoring up, buttressing, bracing.

2 *reinforcement of the bomber force* AUGMENTATION, increase, supplementing, boosting, topping up.

3 *they returned later with reinforcements* ADDITIONAL TROOPS, fresh troops, auxiliaries, reserves; support, backup, help.

reinstate verb *the ousted president has been reinstated* RESTORE, return to power, put back, bring back, reinstitute, reinstall.

reiterate verb *he reiterated his concerns* REPEAT, say again, restate, retell, recapitulate, go over (and over), rehearse.

reject verb 1 *the loggers rejected the offer* TURN DOWN, refuse, decline, say no to, spurn; *informal* give the thumbs down to. See note at REFUTE. ANTONYM accept.

2 *Jamie rejected her* REBUFF, spurn, shun, snub, repudiate, cast off/aside, discard, abandon, desert, turn one's back on, have nothing (more) to do with, wash one's hands of; *informal* give someone the brush-off; *literary* forsake. ANTONYM welcome.

▸ noun 1 *a bin of factory rejects* SUBSTANDARD ARTICLE, discard, second.

2 *what a reject!* FAILURE, loser, incompetent.

rejection noun 1 *a rejection of the offer* REFUSAL, declining, turning down, dismissal, spurning.

2 *Madeleine's rejection of him* REPUDIATION, rebuff, spurning, abandonment, desertion; *informal* brush-off; *literary* forsaking.

rejoice verb 1 *they rejoiced when she returned* BE JOYFUL, be happy, be pleased, be glad, be delighted, be elated, be ecstatic, be euphoric, be overjoyed, be as pleased as punch, be jubilant, be in raptures, be beside oneself with joy, be delirious, be thrilled, be on cloud nine, be in seventh heaven; celebrate, make merry; *informal* be over the moon, be on top of the world; *literary* joy; *archaic* jubilate. ANTONYM mourn.

2 *he* ***rejoiced in*** *their success* TAKE DELIGHT IN, find/take pleasure in, feel satisfaction in, find joy in, enjoy, revel in, glory in, delight in, relish, savor.

rejoicing noun *news of the war's end unleashed a spectacle of rejoicing in the streets* HAPPINESS, pleasure, joy, gladness, delight, elation, jubilation, exuberance, exultation, celebration, revelry, merrymaking.

rejoin[1] verb *the path rejoins the main road further on* RETURN TO, be reunited with, join again, reach again, regain.

rejoin[2] verb *Eugene rejoined that you couldn't expect much* ANSWER, reply, respond, return, retort, riposte, counter.

rejoinder noun *what serious rejoinder could I possibly offer when you make such a ludicrous accusation?* ANSWER, reply, response, retort, riposte, counter; *informal* comeback.

rejuvenate verb *Gore's plan to rejuvenate Medicare* REVIVE, revitalize, regenerate, breathe new life into, revivify, reanimate, resuscitate, refresh, reawaken, put new life into; *informal* give a shot in the arm to, pep up, buck up.

relapse verb 1 *a few patients relapse* GET ILL/WORSE AGAIN, have/suffer a relapse, deteriorate, degenerate, take a turn for the worse. ANTONYM improve.

2 *she relapsed into silence* REVERT, lapse; regress, retrogress, slip back, slide back, degenerate.

▸ noun 1 *Dr. Bergdahl's pneumonia patient suffered a relapse* DETERIORATION, turn for the worse, setback.

2 *a relapse into alcoholism* DECLINE, lapse, deterioration, degeneration, reversion, regression, retrogression, fall, descent, slide.

relate verb 1 *he related many stories* TELL, recount, narrate, report, chronicle, outline, delineate, retail, recite, repeat, communicate, impart.

2 *suicide rates are* ***related to*** *unemployment levels* CONNECT TO/WITH, associate with, link to/with, correlate to/with, ally with, couple with.

3 *the charges* ***relate to*** *offenses committed in August* APPLY TO, be relevant to, concern, pertain to, be pertinent to, have a bearing on, appertain to, involve.

4 *she cannot* ***relate to*** *her stepfather* HAVE A RAPPORT WITH, get on (well) with, sympathize with, feel for, identify with, empathize with, understand; *informal* hit it off with.

related adjective 1 *related ideas* CONNECTED, interconnected, associated, linked, coupled, allied, affiliated, concomitant, corresponding, analogous, kindred, parallel, comparable, homologous, equivalent. ANTONYM unconnected.

2 *are you two related?* OF THE SAME FAMILY, kin, akin, kindred; *formal* cognate, consanguineous. ANTONYM unrelated.

relation noun 1 *the relation between church and state* CONNECTION, relationship, association, link, correlation, correspondence, parallel, alliance, bond, interrelation, interconnection.

2 *this had no relation to national security* RELEVANCE, applicability, reference, pertinence, bearing.

3 *are you a relation of his?* | *she has relations in Pennsylvania* RELATIVE, member of the family, kinsman, kinswoman; **(relations)** family, kin, kith and kin, kindred.

4 **(relations)** *improving relations with China* DEALINGS, communication, relationship, connections, contact, interaction.

5 *sexual relations.* See SEX sense 1.

relationship noun 1 *the relationship between diet and diabetes* CONNECTION, relation, association, link, correlation, correspondence, parallel, alliance, bond, interrelation, interconnection.

2 *evidence of their relationship to Buffalo Bill Cody* FAMILY TIES, family connections, blood ties, blood relationship, kinship, affinity, consanguinity, common ancestry, common lineage.

3 *the end of their relationship* ROMANCE, (love) affair, love, liaison, amour, partnership.

relative adjective 1 *the relative importance of each factor* COMPARATIVE, respective, comparable, correlative, parallel, corresponding.

2 *the food required is relative to body weight* PROPORTIONATE, proportional, in proportion, commensurate, corresponding.

3 *relative ease* MODERATE, reasonable, a fair degree of, considerable, comparative.

▸ noun *he's a relative of mine* RELATION, member of someone's/the family, kinsman, kinswoman; (**relatives**) family, kin, kith and kin, kindred, kinsfolk.

relatively adverb *today's puzzle is relatively easy* COMPARATIVELY, by comparison; quite, fairly, reasonably, rather, somewhat, to a (certain) degree, tolerably, passably; *informal* pretty, kind of, kinda, sort of.

relax verb **1** *yoga is helpful in learning to relax* UNWIND, loosen up, ease up/off, slow down, de-stress, unbend, rest, put one's feet up, take it easy; *informal* unbutton, hang loose, chill, chill out, take a load off. ANTONYM be tense.

2 *a leisurely walk will relax you* CALM, calm down, unwind, loosen up, make less tense/uptight, soothe, pacify, compose.

3 *he relaxed his grip* LOOSEN, loose, slacken, unclench, weaken, lessen. ANTONYM tighten.

4 *her muscles relaxed* BECOME LESS TENSE, loosen, slacken, unknot. ANTONYMS contract, tighten.

5 *they relaxed the restrictions* MODERATE, modify, temper, ease, ease up on, loosen, lighten, dilute, weaken, reduce, decrease; *informal* let up on. ANTONYM tighten up.

relaxation noun **1** *a state of relaxation* MENTAL REPOSE, repose, calm, tranquility, peacefulness, loosening up, unwinding.

2 *I just play for relaxation* RECREATION, enjoyment, amusement, entertainment, fun, pleasure, leisure; *informal* R and R, downtime.

3 *muscle relaxation* LOOSENING, slackening.

4 *relaxation of censorship rules* MODERATION, easing, loosening, lightening; alleviation, mitigation, dilution, weakening, reduction; *informal* letting up.

relay noun *a live relay of the performance* BROADCAST, transmission, showing.

▸ verb *relaying messages through a third party* PASS ON, hand on, transfer, repeat, communicate, send, transmit, disseminate, spread, circulate.

release verb **1** *all prisoners were released* FREE, set free, let go/out, allow to leave, liberate, set at liberty; *historical* manumit. ANTONYM imprison.

2 *Burke released the animal* UNTIE, undo, loose, let go, unleash, unfetter. ANTONYM tie up.

3 *this released staff for other duties* MAKE AVAILABLE, free, free up, put at someone's disposal, supply, furnish, provide. ANTONYM detain.

4 *she released Stephen from his promise* EXCUSE, exempt, discharge, deliver, absolve; *informal* let off.

5 *police released the news yesterday* MAKE PUBLIC, make known, issue, break, announce, declare, report, reveal, divulge, disclose, publish, broadcast, circulate, communicate, disseminate. ANTONYMS suppress, withhold.

6 *the film has been released on video* LAUNCH, put on the market, put on sale, bring out, make available.

▸ noun **1** *the release of political prisoners* FREEING, liberation, deliverance, bailout; freedom, liberty.

2 *the release of the news* ISSUING, announcement, declaration, reporting, revealing, divulging, disclosure, publication, communication, dissemination.

3 *a press release* ANNOUNCEMENT, bulletin, news flash, dispatch, proclamation.

4 *the hot new band's latest release* CD, album, single, record; video, film; book.

relegate verb *Islamic tradition and tribal custom relegate women to lives at home* DOWNGRADE, lower, lower in rank/status, put down, move down; demote, degrade. ANTONYM upgrade.

relent verb **1** *the government finally relented* CHANGE ONE'S MIND, backpedal, do a U-turn, back down, give way/in, capitulate; become merciful, become lenient, agree to something, allow something, concede something; *formal* accede.

2 *the rain has relented* EASE OFF/UP, slacken, let up, abate, drop, die down, lessen, decrease, subside, weaken.

relentless adjective **1** *their relentless pursuit of quality* PERSISTENT, continuing, constant, continual, continuous, nonstop, never-ending, unabating, interminable, incessant, unceasing, endless, unending, unremitting, unrelenting, unrelieved; unfaltering, unflagging, untiring, unwavering, dogged, tenacious, single-minded, tireless, indefatigable; *formal* pertinacious.

2 *a relentless taskmaster* HARSH, grim, cruel, severe, strict, remorseless, merciless, pitiless, ruthless, unmerciful, heartless, hard-hearted, unforgiving; inflexible, unbending, uncompromising, obdurate, unyielding.

relevant adjective *the relevant page numbers* PERTINENT, applicable, apposite, material, apropos, to the point, germane; connected, related, linked.

reliable adjective **1** *reliable evidence* DEPENDABLE, good, well-founded, authentic, valid, genuine, sound, true.

2 *a reliable friend* TRUSTWORTHY, dependable, good, true, faithful, devoted, steadfast, staunch, constant, loyal, trusty, dedicated, unfailing; truthful, honest. ANTONYM untrustworthy.

3 *reliable brakes* DEPENDABLE, safe, fail-safe.

4 *a reliable company* REPUTABLE, dependable, trustworthy, honest, responsible, established, proven. ANTONYM disreputable.

reliance noun **1** *reliance on the state* DEPENDENCE, dependency.

2 *reliance on his own judgment* TRUST, confidence, faith, belief, conviction.

relic noun **1** *a Viking relic* ARTIFACT, historical object, ancient object, antiquity, antique.

2 *a saint's relics* REMAINS, corpse, bones, *Medicine* cadaver.

relief noun **1** *it was such a relief to share my worries* REASSURANCE, consolation, comfort, solace.

2 *the relief of pain* ALLEVIATION, alleviating, relieving, assuagement, assuaging, palliation, allaying, soothing, easing, lessening, reduction. ANTONYM intensification.

3 *relief from her burden* FREEDOM, release, liberation, deliverance.

4 *a little light relief* RESPITE, amusement, diversion, entertainment, jollity, jollification, recreation. ANTONYM solemnity.

5 *bringing relief to the starving* HELP, aid, assistance, succor, sustenance, TLC; charity, gifts, donations.

6 *his relief arrived to take over* REPLACEMENT, substitute, deputy, reserve, cover, stand-in, supply, locum, locum tenens, understudy. PHRASE: **throw into relief** *we hope these photos will throw into relief the gravity of their plight* HIGHLIGHT, spotlight, give prominence to, point up, show up, emphasize, bring out, stress, accent, underline, underscore, accentuate.

relieve verb 1 *this helps relieve pain* ALLEVIATE, mitigate, assuage, ease, dull, reduce, lessen, diminish. See note at ALLEVIATE. ANTONYM aggravate.

2 *relieving the boredom* COUNTERACT, reduce, alleviate, mitigate; interrupt, vary, stop, dispel, prevent. ANTONYM exacerbate.

3 *the helpers relieved us* REPLACE, take over from, stand in for, fill in for, substitute for, deputize for, cover for.

4 *this relieves the teacher of a heavy load* FREE, set free, release, exempt, excuse, absolve, let off, discharge.

relieved adjective *I'll be relieved when it's over* GLAD, thankful, grateful, pleased, happy, easy/easier in one's mind, reassured. ANTONYM worried.

religion noun *the freedom to practice their own religion* FAITH, belief, worship, creed; sect, church, cult, denomination.

religious adjective 1 *a religious person* DEVOUT, pious, reverent, godly, God-fearing, churchgoing, faithful, devoted, committed. ANTONYMS atheistic, irreverent.

2 *religious beliefs* SPIRITUAL, theological, scriptural, doctrinal, ecclesiastical, church, faith-based, churchly, holy, divine, sacred. ANTONYM secular.

3 *religious attention to detail* SCRUPULOUS, conscientious, meticulous, sedulous, punctilious, strict, rigorous, close. ANTONYM slapdash.

relinquish verb 1 *he relinquished control of the company* RENOUNCE, give up/away, hand over, let go of. ANTONYMS retain, keep.

2 *she relinquished her post* LEAVE, resign from, stand down from, bow out of, give up; *informal* quit, chuck.

3 *he relinquished his pipe-smoking* DISCONTINUE, stop, cease, give up, desist from; *informal* quit, kick; *formal* forswear. ANTONYM continue.

4 *she relinquished her grip* LET GO OF, release, loose, loosen, relax.

THE RIGHT WORD

Of all these verbs meaning to let go or give up, **relinquish** is the most general. It can imply anything from simply releasing one's grasp (*she relinquished the wheel*) to giving up control or possession reluctantly (*after the defeat, he was forced to relinquish his command*). **Surrender** also implies giving up, but usually after a struggle or show of resistance (*the villagers were forced to surrender to the guerrillas*). **Yield** is a milder synonym for *surrender*, implying some concession, respect, or even affection on the part of the person who is surrendering (*she yielded to her mother's wishes and stayed home*). **Waive** means to give up voluntarily a right or claim to something (*she waived her right to have a lawyer present*), while **cede** is to give up by legal transfer or according to the terms of a treaty (*the French ceded the territory that is now Louisiana*). If one *relinquishes* something finally and completely, often because of weariness or discouragement, the correct word is **abandon** (*they were told to abandon all hope of being rescued*).

relish noun 1 *he dug into his food with relish* ENJOYMENT, gusto, delight, pleasure, glee, rapture, satisfaction, contentment, appreciation, enthusiasm, appetite; *humorous* delectation. ANTONYM dislike.

2 *a hot relish* CONDIMENT, sauce, dressing, flavoring, seasoning, dip, chutney, chili sauce.

▸ verb 1 *she was relishing her moment of glory* ENJOY, delight in, love, adore, take pleasure in, rejoice in, appreciate, savor, revel in, luxuriate in, glory in.

2 *I don't relish the drive* LOOK FORWARD TO, fancy, anticipate with pleasure.

relocate verb *we're relocating in June | the family relocated to Roseboom* MOVE, migrate; pull up stakes (and go).

reluctance noun *he said he was glad to go, but she sensed his reluctance* UNWILLINGNESS, disinclination; hesitation, wavering, vacillation; doubts, second thoughts, misgivings.

reluctant adjective 1 *when it came to trying something new, her parents were usually reluctant* UNWILLING, disinclined, unenthusiastic, resistant, resisting, opposed; hesitant. ANTONYMS willing, eager.

2 *a reluctant smile* SHY, bashful, coy, diffident, reserved, timid, timorous. ANTONYM eager.

3 *he was **reluctant to** leave* LOATH TO, unwilling to, disinclined to, indisposed to; not in favor of, against, opposed to. ANTONYMS willing, eager.

rely verb 1 *we can **rely on** his discretion* DEPEND ON, count on, bank on, place reliance on, reckon on; be confident of, be sure of, believe in, have faith in, trust in; *informal* swear by, figure on.

2 *we* rely on *government funding* BE DEPENDENT ON, depend on, be unable to manage without.

remain verb 1 *the problem will remain* CONTINUE TO EXIST, endure, last, abide, carry on, persist, stay, stay around, prevail, survive, live on.

2 *he remained in the hospital* STAY, stay behind, stay put, wait, wait around, be left, hang on; *informal* hang around.

3 *union leaders remain skeptical* CONTINUE TO BE, stay, keep, persist in being, carry on being.

4 *the few minutes that remain* BE LEFT, be left over, be still available, be unused; have not yet passed.

remainder noun *the remainder of the materials should be itemized on a separate list* RESIDUE, balance, remaining part/number, rest, others, those left, remnant(s), surplus, extra, excess, overflow; *technical* residuum.

remaining adjective 1 *the remaining workers* RESIDUAL, surviving, left over; extra, surplus, spare, superfluous, excess.

2 *his remaining jobs* UNSETTLED, outstanding, unfinished, incomplete, to be done, unattended to.

3 *my only remaining memories* SURVIVING, lasting, enduring, continuing, persisting, abiding, (still) existing.

remains plural noun 1 *the remains of her drink* REMAINDER, residue, remaining part/number, rest, remnant(s); *technical* residuum.

2 *Roman remains* ANTIQUITIES, relics.

3 *the saint's remains* CORPSE, body, dead body, carcass; bones, skeleton; *Medicine* cadaver. See note at BODY.

remark verb **1** *"You're quiet," he remarked* COMMENT, say, observe, mention, reflect, state, declare, announce, pronounce, assert; *formal* opine.

2 *many critics* ***remarked on*** *their rapport* COMMENT ON, mention, refer to, speak of, pass comment on.

3 *she remarked the absence of policemen* NOTE, notice, observe, take note of, perceive, discern.

▸ noun **1** *his remarks have been misinterpreted* COMMENT, statement, utterance, observation, declaration, pronouncement.

2 *worthy of remark* ATTENTION, notice, comment, mention, observation, acknowledgment.

remarkable adjective *a remarkable coincidence* EXTRAORDINARY, exceptional, amazing, astonishing, astounding, marvelous, wonderful, sensational, stunning, incredible, unbelievable, phenomenal, outstanding, momentous; out of the ordinary, unusual, uncommon, surprising; *informal* fantastic, terrific, tremendous, stupendous, awesome; *literary* wondrous. See note at NOTICEABLE. ANTONYM ordinary.

WORD NOTE **remarkable**

Should not be used as a synonym for *good. Remarkable* is value-neutral and means only "worth being remarked upon." Actually, what's really remarkable is how many words, like this one, have lost their specific meanings as they've been corralled into the sterile confinement pen of synonyms for *good: fabulous* (literally, like something in a fable), *fantastic* (like something in a fantasy), *wonderful* (fills you with wonder), *incredible* (not to be believed), etc. You help restore the richness of the language when you use these words in ways closer to their original meanings. **—DA**

remediable adjective *the unsafe features of the playground are all remediable* CURABLE, treatable, operable; solvable, reparable, rectifiable, resolvable. ANTONYM incurable.

remedy noun **1** *herbal remedies* TREATMENT, cure, medicine, medication, medicament, drug; *archaic* physic.

2 *a remedy for all kinds of problems* SOLUTION, answer, cure, antidote, curative, nostrum, panacea, cure-all; *informal* magic bullet.

▸ verb **1** *remedying the situation* PUT/SET RIGHT, put/set to rights, right, rectify, solve, sort out, straighten out, resolve, correct, repair, mend, make good.

2 *anemia can be remedied by iron pills* CURE, treat, heal, make better; relieve, ease, alleviate, palliate.

remember verb **1** *remembering happy times* RECALL, call to mind, recollect, think of; reminisce about, look back on; *archaic* bethink oneself of. ANTONYM forget.

2 *can you remember all that?* MEMORIZE, commit to memory, retain; learn by heart. ANTONYM forget.

3 *you must remember that she's only five* BEAR/KEEP IN MIND, be mindful of the fact; take into account, take into consideration. ANTONYM overlook.

4 *remember to feed the cat* BE SURE, be certain; mind that you, make sure that you. ANTONYM neglect.

5 ***remember me*** *to Alice* SEND ONE'S BEST WISHES, send one's regards, give one's love, send one's compliments, say hello.

6 *the nation remembered those who gave their lives* COMMEMORATE, pay tribute to, honor, salute, pay homage to.

7 *she remembered them in her will* BEQUEATH SOMETHING TO, leave something to, bestow something on.

remembrance noun **1** *an expression of remembrance* RECOLLECTION, reminiscence; remembering, recalling, recollecting, reminiscing.

2 *she smiled at the remembrance* MEMORY, recollection, reminiscence, thought.

3 *we sold poppies in remembrance* COMMEMORATION, memory, recognition.

4 *a remembrance of my father* MEMENTO, reminder, keepsake, souvenir, memorial, token.

remind verb **1** *I left a note to remind him* JOG SOMEONE'S MEMORY, help someone remember, prompt.

2 *the song* ***reminded me of*** *my sister* MAKE ONE THINK OF, cause one to remember, put one in mind of, bring/call to mind, evoke.

reminder noun *when the clock chimes, that'll be my reminder to get the mail* PROMPT, prompting, aide-mémoire, mental note, mnemonic.

reminisce verb *we reminisced about Freddy's first Christmas with us* REMEMBER, remember with pleasure, cast one's mind back to, look back on, be nostalgic about, recall, recollect, reflect on, call to mind.

reminiscences plural noun *her reminiscences of a wartime childhood* MEMORIES, recollections, reflections, remembrances.

reminiscent adjective *the smell of fresh apple pies was reminiscent of the aromas from Gramma's kitchen in Middlefield* SIMILAR TO, comparable with, evocative of, suggestive of, redolent of.

remiss adjective *I would be remiss if I did not thank my sister* NEGLIGENT, neglectful, irresponsible, careless, thoughtless, heedless, lax, slack, slipshod, lackadaisical, derelict; *informal* sloppy; *formal* delinquent. ANTONYM careful.

remission noun **1** *the remission of all fees* CANCELLATION, setting aside, suspension, revocation; *formal* abrogation.

2 *the cancer is in remission* RESPITE, abeyance.

3 *the wind howled without remission* RESPITE, lessening, abatement, easing, decrease, reduction, diminution, dying down, slackening, lull; *informal* letup.

4 *the remission of sins* FORGIVENESS, pardoning, absolution, exoneration; *formal* exculpation.

remit verb **1** *the fines were remitted* CANCEL, set aside, suspend, revoke; *formal* abrogate.

2 *remitting duties to the authorities* SEND, dispatch, forward, hand over; pay.

3 *the case was remitted to the Supreme Court* PASS (ON), refer, send (on), transfer.

4 rare *we remitted all further discussion* POSTPONE, defer, put off/back, shelve, delay, suspend, table; *informal* put on the back burner, put on ice.

5 *remitting their sins* PARDON, forgive; excuse.

remittance noun **1** *send the form with your remittance* PAYMENT, money, fee; check; *formal* monies.

2 *a monthly remittance* ALLOWANCE, sum of money.

remnant noun **1** *the remnants of the picnic* REMAINS, remainder, leftovers, residue, rest; *technical* residuum.

2 *remnants of cloth* SCRAP, piece, bit, fragment, shred, offcut, oddment. See note at TRACE.

remonstrate verb **1** *"I'm not a child!" he remonstrated* PROTEST, complain, expostulate; argue with, take issue with.

2 *we remonstrated against this proposal* OBJECT STRONGLY TO, complain vociferously about, protest against, argue against, oppose strongly, make a fuss about, challenge; deplore, condemn, denounce, criticize; *informal* kick up a fuss/stink about.

remorse noun *have you no remorse for what you did to your friends?* CONTRITION, deep regret, repentance, penitence, guilt, compunction, remorsefulness, ruefulness, contriteness; pangs of conscience, self-condemnation, self-reproach.

remorseful adjective *remorseful criminals* SORRY, full of regret, regretful, contrite, repentant, penitent, guilt-ridden, conscience-stricken, guilty, chastened. ANTONYM unrepentant.

remorseless adjective **1** *a remorseless terrorist* HEARTLESS, pitiless, merciless, ruthless, callous, cruel, hardhearted, inhumane, unmerciful, unforgiving, unfeeling. ANTONYM compassionate.

2 *remorseless cost-cutting* RELENTLESS, unrelenting, unremitting, unabating, inexorable, unstoppable.

remote adjective **1** *areas remote from hospitals* FARAWAY, distant, far, far off, far removed, extrasolar. ANTONYMS close, near.

2 *a remote mountain village* ISOLATED, out of the way, off the beaten track/path, secluded, lonely, in the back of beyond, godforsaken, inaccessible, far-flung, in the backwoods, lonesome; *informal* in the sticks, in the middle of nowhere. ANTONYM central.

3 *events **remote from** modern times* IRRELEVANT TO, unrelated to, unconnected to, unconcerned with, not pertinent to, immaterial to, unassociated with; foreign to, alien to. ANTONYM relevant.

4 *a remote possibility* UNLIKELY, improbable, implausible, doubtful, dubious; faint, slight, slim, small, slender. ANTONYMS likely, strong.

5 *she seems very remote* ALOOF, distant, detached, withdrawn, reserved, uncommunicative, unforthcoming, unapproachable, unresponsive, unfriendly, unsociable, introspective, introverted; *informal* standoffish. ANTONYMS friendly, approachable.

removal noun **1** *the removal of heavy artillery* TAKING AWAY, moving, carrying away. ANTONYM installation.

2 *his removal from office* DISMISSAL, ejection, expulsion, ousting, displacement, deposition, ouster; *informal* firing, sacking. ANTONYMS installation, appointment.

3 *the removal of customs barriers* WITHDRAWAL, elimination, taking away.

4 *the removal of errors in the copy* DELETION, elimination, erasing, effacing, obliteration.

5 *the removal of weeds* UPROOTING, eradication.

6 *the removal of old branches from the tree* CUTTING OFF, chopping off, hacking off.

7 *her removal to the West Coast* MOVE, transfer, relocation.

8 *the removal of a rival* DISPOSAL, elimination, killing, murder, dispatch; *informal* liquidation.

remove verb **1** *remove the plug* DETACH, unfasten; pull out, take out, disconnect. ANTONYM attach.

2 *she removed the lid* TAKE OFF, undo, unfasten. ANTONYM put on.

3 *he removed a twenty from his wallet* TAKE OUT, produce, bring out, get out, pull out, withdraw. ANTONYM insert.

4 *police removed boxes of documents* TAKE AWAY, carry away, move, transport; confiscate; *informal* cart off. ANTONYMS put back, replace.

5 *Sheila removed the mud* CLEAN OFF, wash off, wipe off, rinse off, scrub off, sponge out.

6 *Harry removed his coat* TAKE OFF, pull off, slip out of, peel off; *dated* doff. ANTONYMS put on, don.

7 *she was removed from her post* DISMISS, discharge, dislodge, displace, expel, oust, depose; *informal* fire, sack, kick out, boot out. ANTONYMS install, appoint.

8 *tax relief was removed* WITHDRAW, abolish, eliminate, get rid of, do away with, stop, cut; *informal* ax. ANTONYM introduce.

9 *Gabriel removed two words* DELETE, erase, rub out, cross out, strike out, obliterate; *informal* deep-six. ANTONYM add.

10 *weeds have to be removed* UPROOT, pull out, eradicate.

11 *removing branches* CUT OFF, chop off, lop off, hack off.

removed adjective *it's a fairy tale completely **removed from** reality* DISTANT FROM, remote from, disconnected from; unrelated to, unconnected to, alien to, foreign to, outside of.

remunerate verb *the painters were remunerated when the job was finished* PAY, reward, compensate, reimburse, recompense.

remuneration noun *you will receive adequate remuneration for the work you have done* PAYMENT, pay, salary, wages; earnings, fee(s), reward, compensation, recompense, reimbursement; *formal* emolument(s).

remunerative adjective *a remunerative position in his father's firm* LUCRATIVE, well-paid, financially rewarding; profitable.

renaissance noun *the renaissance of Byzantine art* REVIVAL, renewal, resurrection, reawakening, reemergence, rebirth, reappearance, resurgence, regeneration; *formal* renascence.

rend verb *a crisis threatened to rend the Atlantic alliance* TEAR/RIP APART, tear/rip in two, split, rupture, sever; *literary* tear/rip asunder, sunder; *rare* dissever.

render verb **1** *her fury rendered her speechless* MAKE, cause to be/become, leave.

2 *rendering assistance* GIVE, provide, supply, furnish, contribute; offer, proffer.

3 *the invoices rendered by the accountants* SEND IN, present, submit.

4 *the jury rendered its verdict* DELIVER, return, hand down, give, announce.

5 *paintings rendered in muted colors* PAINT, draw, depict, portray, represent, execute; *literary* limn.

6 *she rendered all three verses* PERFORM, sing.

7 *the characters are vividly rendered* ACT, perform, play, depict, interpret.

8 *the phrase was rendered into English* TRANSLATE, put, express, rephrase, reword.

9 *the fat can be rendered* MELT DOWN, clarify.

rendezvous noun *Eleanor was late for their rendezvous* MEETING, appointment, assignation; *informal* date; *literary* tryst.

▸ verb *the bar where they had agreed to rendezvous* MEET, come together, gather, assemble.

rendition noun **1** *our rendition of Beethoven's Fifth* PERFORMANCE, rendering, interpretation, presentation, execution, delivery.

2 *the artist's rendition of Adam and Eve* DEPICTION, portrayal, representation.

3 *an interpreter's rendition of the message* TRANSLATION, interpretation, version.

renegade noun **1** *he was denounced as a renegade* TRAITOR, defector, deserter, turncoat, rebel, mutineer.

2 *archaic a religious renegade* APOSTATE, heretic, dissenter.

▸ adjective **1** *renegade troops* TREACHEROUS, traitorous, disloyal, treasonous, rebel, mutinous. ANTONYM loyal.

2 *a renegade monk* APOSTATE, heretic, heretical, dissident.

renege verb *he reneged on his campaign promises* DEFAULT ON, fail to honor, go back on, break, back out of, withdraw from, retreat from, welsh on, backtrack on; break one's word/promise about. ANTONYM honor.

renew verb **1** *I renewed my search* RESUME, return to, take up again, come back to, begin again, start again, restart, recommence; continue (with), carry on (with).

2 *they renewed their vows* REAFFIRM, reassert; repeat, reiterate, restate.

3 *something to renew her interest in life* REVIVE, regenerate, revitalize, reinvigorate, restore, resuscitate, breathe new life into, rekindle.

4 *the hotel was completely renewed* RENOVATE, restore, refurbish, modernize, overhaul, redevelop, rebuild, reconstruct, remodel, bring something up to code; *informal* do up, rehab.

5 *they renewed Jackie's contract* EXTEND, prolong.

6 *I renewed my supply of toilet paper* REPLENISH, restock, resupply, top up, replace.

renewal noun **1** *the renewal of our friendship* RESUMPTION, recommencement, reestablishment; continuation.

2 *spiritual renewal* REGENERATION, revival, reinvigoration, revitalization.

3 *the renewal of urban areas* RENOVATION, restoration, modernization, reconditioning, overhauling, redevelopment, rebuilding, reconstruction.

renounce verb **1** *Edward renounced his claim to the throne* GIVE UP, relinquish, abandon, abdicate, surrender, waive, forego; *Law* disclaim; *formal* abnegate. ANTONYM assert.

2 *Hungary renounced the agreement* REJECT, refuse to abide by, repudiate. ANTONYMS abide by, accept.

3 *she renounced her family* REPUDIATE, deny, reject, abandon, wash one's hands of, turn one's back on, disown, spurn, shun; *literary* forsake. ANTONYM embrace.

4 *he renounced alcohol* ABSTAIN FROM, give up, desist from, refrain from, keep off, eschew; *informal* quit, pack in, lay off; *formal* forswear. ANTONYM turn to.

PHRASE: **renounce the world** *you can't just renounce the world* BECOME A RECLUSE, turn one's back on society, cloister oneself, hide oneself away.

renovate verb *the hotel has been renovated* MODERNIZE, restore, refurbish, revamp, recondition, rehabilitate, overhaul, redevelop; update, upgrade, refit, bring something up to code; *informal* do up, rehab.

renovation noun *funds have been allocated for the renovation of nine municipal structures* MODERNIZATION, restoration, redecoration, refurbishment, revamping, makeover, reconditioning, rehabilitation, overhauling, repair, redevelopment, rebuilding, reconstruction, remodeling, updating, improvement; gentrification, upgrading; refitting; *informal* facelift, reno.

renown noun *born to a family of political renown* FAME, distinction, eminence, preeminence, prominence, repute, reputation, prestige, acclaim, celebrity, notability.

renowned adjective *a renowned Indian filmmaker* FAMOUS, celebrated, famed, eminent, distinguished, acclaimed, illustrious, preeminent, prominent, great, esteemed, of note, of repute, well-known, well-thought-of. ANTONYM unknown.

rent[1] noun *I can't afford to pay the rent* RENTAL, fee, lease.

▸ verb **1** *she rented a car* lease, charter.

2 *why don't you **rent it out**?* LET (OUT), lease (out), hire (out); sublet, sublease.

rent[2] noun **1** *the rent in his pants* RIP, tear, split, hole, slash, slit.

2 *a vast rent in the mountains* GORGE, chasm, fault, rift, fissure, crevasse.

renunciation noun **1** *the queen's renunciation of her throne* RELINQUISHMENT, giving up, abandonment, abdication, surrender, waiving, foregoing; *Law* disclaimer; *rare* abnegation.

2 *his **renunciation of** luxury* ABSTENTION FROM, refraining from, going without, giving up, eschewal of; *formal* forswearing of.

3 *their renunciation of terrorism* REPUDIATION, rejection, abandonment; *rare* abjuration.

reorganize verb *the president's plan to reorganize foreign affairs agencies | the two banks are jointly discussing ways to reorganize* RESTRUCTURE, change, alter, adjust, transform, shake up, rationalize, rearrange, reshape, overhaul; *informal* clean house.

repair[1] verb **1** *the car was repaired* MEND, fix (up), put/set right, restore, restore to working order, overhaul, service; *informal* patch up.

2 *they repaired the costumes* MEND, darn; *informal* patch up.

3 *repairing relations with other countries* PUT/SET RIGHT, mend, fix, straighten out, smooth, improve, warm up; *informal* patch up.

4 *she sought to repair the wrong she had done* RECTIFY, make good, right, put right, correct, make up for, make amends for, make reparation for.

▸ noun **1** *in need of repair* RESTORATION, fixing (up), mending, renovation; *archaic* reparation.

2 *an invisible repair* MEND, darn.

3 *in good repair* CONDITION, working order, state, shape, fettle.

PHRASE: **beyond repair** *the front wheel is beyond repair | their marriage appears to be beyond repair* IRREPARABLE, irreversible, irretrievable, irremediable, irrecoverable, past hope.

repair[2] verb *formal we* ***repaired to*** *the sitting room* GO TO, head for, adjourn to, wend one's way to; *formal* remove to; *literary* betake oneself to.

reparable adjective *the situation is still reparable* RECTIFIABLE, remediable, curable, restorable, recoverable, retrievable, salvageable.

reparation noun *the victims are seeking reparation* AMENDS, restitution, redress, compensation, recompense, repayment, atonement.

repartee noun *an evening of wit and repartee* BANTER, badinage, bantering, raillery, witticism(s), ripostes, sallies, quips, joking, jesting; *formal* persiflage. See note at WIT.

repast noun *formal a sumptuous repast* MEAL, feast, banquet; *informal* spread, feed, bite, bite to eat; *formal* collation, refection.

repay verb **1** *they promised to repay customers who had been cheated* REIMBURSE, refund, pay back/off, recompense, compensate, indemnify.

2 *the grants have to be repaid* PAY BACK, return, refund, reimburse.

3 *I'd like to repay her generosity* RECIPROCATE, return, requite, recompense, reward.

repayment noun **1** *the repayment of tax* REFUND, reimbursement, paying back.

2 *repayment for all they have done* RECOMPENSE, reward, compensation.

repeal verb *the Eighteenth Amendment was repealed in 1933* REVOKE, rescind, cancel, reverse, annul, nullify, declare null and void, quash, abolish; *Law* vacate; *formal* abrogate; *archaic* recall. ANTONYM enact.

▸ noun *the repeal of the law* REVOCATION, rescinding, cancellation, reversal, annulment, nullification, quashing, abolition; *formal* abrogation; *archaic* recall.

repeat verb **1** *she repeated her story* SAY AGAIN, restate, reiterate, go/run through again, recapitulate; *informal* recap.

2 *children can repeat large chunks of text* RECITE, quote, parrot, regurgitate.

3 *Steele was invited to repeat his work* DO AGAIN, redo, replicate, rehash, duplicate.

4 *the episodes were repeated* REBROADCAST, rerun.

▸ noun **1** *a repeat of the previous year's final* REPETITION, duplication, replication, duplicate, rehash.

2 *repeats of the classic sitcom* RERUN, rebroadcast.

PHRASE: **repeat itself** REOCCUR, recur, occur again, happen again.

repeated adjective *his repeated complaints about the noise* RECURRENT, frequent, persistent, continual, incessant, constant; regular, periodic, numerous, many, very many. ANTONYM occasional.

repeatedly adverb *he tried repeatedly to hit that low note* FREQUENTLY, often, again and again, over and over (again), time and (time) again, time after time, many times, many a time; persistently, recurrently, constantly, continually, regularly, oftentimes; *literary* oft, ofttimes.

repel verb **1** *the rebels were repelled* FIGHT OFF, repulse, drive back/away, force back, beat back, push back; hold off, ward off, keep at bay; *archaic* rebut. See word spectrum at ATTRACT.

2 *the coating will repel water* BE IMPERVIOUS TO, be impermeable to, keep out, resist, be ——proof.

3 *the thought of kissing him repelled me* REVOLT, disgust, repulse, sicken, nauseate, turn someone's stomach, be repulsive, be distasteful, be repugnant; *informal* turn off, gross out.

repellent adjective **1** *a repellent stench* REVOLTING, repulsive, disgusting, repugnant, sickening, nauseating, stomach-turning, nauseous, vile, nasty, foul, horrible, awful, dreadful, terrible, obnoxious, loathsome, offensive, objectionable; abhorrent, despicable, reprehensible, contemptible, odious, hateful, execrable, vomitous; *informal* ghastly, horrid, gross, yucky, icky, funky; *literary* noisome. See note at REPULSIVE. ANTONYM delightful.

2 *a repellent coating* IMPERMEABLE, impervious, resistant; -proof.

repent verb *the senator claims to have repented* FEEL REMORSE, regret, be sorry, rue, reproach oneself, be ashamed, feel contrite; be penitent, be remorseful, be repentant.

repentance noun *her lack of repentance angered them* REMORSE, contrition, contriteness, penitence, regret, ruefulness, remorsefulness, shame, guilt.

repentant adjective *there are two repentant children in there waiting to talk to you* PENITENT, contrite, regretful, rueful, remorseful, apologetic, chastened, ashamed, shamefaced, guilt-ridden. ANTONYM impenitent.

repercussion noun (**repercussions**) *the political repercussions of the scandal* CONSEQUENCE(S), result(s), effect(s), outcome; reverberation(s), backlash, aftermath, fallout, tremors.

repertoire noun *the three tenors will fashion their repertoire to their audiences* COLLECTION, stock, range, repertory, reserve, store, repository, supply.

repetition noun **1** *the facts bear repetition* REITERATION, repeating, restatement, retelling.

2 *endless repetition of passages of poetry* REPEATING, echoing, parroting.

3 *a repetition of the scene in the kitchen* RECURRENCE, reoccurrence, rerun, repeat; *informal* déjà vu, instant replay.

4 *the author is guilty of repetition* REPETITIOUSNESS, repetitiveness, redundancy, tautology.

repetitious adjective *repetitious work.* See REPETITIVE.

repetitive adjective *repetitive tasks on the assembly line* MONOTONOUS, tedious, boring, humdrum, mundane, dreary, tiresome; unvaried, unchanging, unvarying, recurrent, recurring, repeated, repetitious, routine, mechanical, automatic.

rephrase verb *shall I rephrase that?* REWORD, recast, put in other words, express differently, paraphrase.

replace verb **1** *Eve replaced the receiver* PUT BACK, return, restore. ANTONYM remove.

2 *a new chairman came in to replace him* TAKE THE PLACE OF, succeed, take over from, supersede; stand in for, substitute for, deputize for, cover for, relieve; *informal* step into someone's shoes/boots.

3 *she replaced the spoon with a fork* SUBSTITUTE, exchange, change, swap.

THE RIGHT WORD

When a light bulb burns out, you **replace** it, meaning that you substitute something new or functioning for what is lost, destroyed, or worn out. If something that is obsolete or ineffective is replaced by something that is superior, more up-to-date, or more authoritative, the correct verb is **supersede** (*the computer superseded the electric typewriter*). In contrast, **displace** suggests that someone or something has been ousted or dislodged forcibly, without necessarily implying that it was inferior or ineffective (*a growing number of workers were being displaced by machines*). **Supplant** is more restricted in meaning; it suggests displacement by force, fraud, or innovation (*the democratic government had been supplanted by a power-hungry tyrant*). It can also mean to uproot or wipe out (*the English immigrants gradually supplanted the island's native inhabitants*).

replacement noun **1** *we have to find a replacement* SUCCESSOR; SUBSTITUTE, stand-in, locum, relief, cover.

2 *the wiring was in need of replacement* RENEWAL, replacing.

replenish verb **1** *she replenished their glasses* REFILL, top up, fill up, recharge, freshen. ANTONYM empty.

2 *their supplies were replenished* RESTOCK, stock up, restore, replace. ANTONYMS use up, exhaust.

replete adjective **1** *the guests were replete* WELL-FED, sated, satiated, full, full up; glutted, gorged; *informal* stuffed.

2 *a sumptuous environment replete with antiques* FILLED, full, well-stocked, well-supplied, crammed, packed, jammed, teeming, overflowing, bursting; *informal* jam-packed, chockablock, chock-full.

replica noun **1** *is it real or a replica?* COPY, carbon copy, model, duplicate, reproduction, replication; dummy, imitation, facsimile; *informal* knockoff.

2 *a replica of her mother* PERFECT LIKENESS, double, look-alike, mirror image, living image, picture, twin, clone, doppelgänger; *informal* spitting image, dead ringer, ringer.

replicate verb *the technology would be hard to replicate* COPY, reproduce, duplicate, recreate, repeat, perform again; clone.

reply verb *Rachel didn't bother to reply* ANSWER, respond, come back, write back, retort, riposte, counter.

▸ noun *"Why would we lie?" she replied* ANSWER, response, rejoinder, retort, riposte; *informal* comeback.

report verb **1** *the government reported a fall in inflation* ANNOUNCE, describe, give an account of, detail, outline, communicate, divulge, disclose, reveal, make public, publish, broadcast, proclaim, publicize.

2 *the newspapers* ***reported on*** *the scandal* COVER, write about, describe, give details of, commentate on; investigate, look into, inquire into.

3 *I reported him to the police* INFORM ON, tattle on; *informal* tell on, squeal on, rat on.

4 *Juliet reported for duty* PRESENT ONESELF, arrive, turn up, clock in, sign in, punch in; *informal* show up.

▸ noun **1** *a full report on the meeting* ACCOUNT, review, record, description, statement; transactions, proceedings, transcripts, minutes.

2 *reports of drug dealing* NEWS, information, word, intelligence; *literary* tidings.

3 *newspaper reports* STORY, account, article, piece, item, column, feature, bulletin, dispatch.

4 *a school report* ASSESSMENT, report card, evaluation, appraisal.

5 *reports of his imminent resignation* RUMOR, whisper; *informal* buzz; *archaic* bruit.

6 *the report of a gun* BANG, blast, crack, shot, gunshot, explosion, boom.

reporter noun *my client has been instructed not to talk to reporters* JOURNALIST, correspondent, newspaperman, newspaperwoman, newsman, newswoman, columnist, pressman; *informal* newshound, hack, stringer, journo, newsie.

repose noun **1** *a face in repose* REST, relaxation, inactivity; sleep, slumber.

2 *they found true repose* PEACE, peace and quiet, peacefulness, quiet, quietness, calm, tranquility.

3 *he lost his repose* COMPOSURE, serenity, equanimity, poise, self-possession, aplomb.

▸ verb **1** *the diamond reposed on a bed of velvet* LIE, rest, be placed, be situated.

2 *the trust he had reposed in her* PUT, place, invest, entrust.

3 *the beds where we reposed* LIE, lie down, recline, rest, sleep; *literary* slumber.

repository noun *a repository for nuclear fuel | he's a veritable repository of musical knowledge* STORE, storehouse, depository; reservoir, bank, cache, treasury, fund, mine.

reprehensible adjective *his conduct was reprehensible* DEPLORABLE, disgraceful, discreditable, despicable, blameworthy, culpable, wrong, bad, shameful, dishonorable, objectionable, opprobrious, repugnant, inexcusable, unforgivable, indefensible, unjustifiable; criminal, sinful, scandalous, iniquitous; *formal* exceptionable. ANTONYM praiseworthy.

represent verb **1** *a character representing a single quality* SYMBOLIZE, stand for, personify, epitomize, typify, embody, illustrate.

2 *the initials that represent her qualification* STAND FOR, designate, denote; *literary* betoken.

3 *Hathor is represented as a woman with cow's horns* DEPICT, portray, render, picture, delineate, show, illustrate; *literary* limn.

4 *he represented himself as the owner of the factory* DESCRIBE AS, present as, profess to be, claim to be, pass oneself off as, pose as, pretend to be.

5 *aging represents a threat to one's independence* CONSTITUTE, be, amount to, be regarded as.

6 *a panel representing a cross section of the public* BE A TYPICAL SAMPLE OF, be representative of, typify.

7 *her lawyer represented her in court* APPEAR FOR, act for, speak on behalf of; *informal* go to bat for.

8 *the governor general represented the royal family* DEPUTIZE FOR, substitute for, stand in for.

9 *formal I represented the case as I saw it* POINT OUT, state, present, put forward.

representation noun **1** *Rossetti's representation of women* PORTRAYAL, depiction, delineation, presentation, rendition.

2 *representations of the human form* LIKENESS, painting, drawing, picture, illustration, sketch, image, model, figure, figurine, statue, statuette.

3 *formal making representations to the council* STATEMENT, deposition, allegation, declaration, exposition, report, protestation.

representative adjective **1** *a representative sample* TYPICAL, prototypical, characteristic, illustrative, archetypal. ANTONYM atypical.

2 *the red maple leaf is representative of Canada* SYMBOLIC, emblematic, evocative.

3 *representative government* ELECTED, elective, chosen, democratic, popular. ANTONYM totalitarian.

▸ noun **1** *a representative of Greenpeace* SPOKESPERSON, spokesman, spokeswoman, agent, official, mouthpiece.

2 *one of our representatives will show you our new line of pop-up books* SALESPERSON, salesman, saleswoman, agent; *informal* rep.

3 *the Cambodian representative at the UN* DELEGATE, commissioner, ambassador, attaché, envoy, emissary, chargé d'affaires, deputy.

4 *contact your representatives and urge them to protect our wetlands* LEGISLATOR, lawmaker; senator, congressman, congresswoman, member of Congress, alderman, alderwoman, alderperson, selectman, selectwoman, lawmaker; voice.

5 *he acted as his father's representative* DEPUTY, substitute, stand-in, proxy.

6 *fossil representatives of lampreys* EXAMPLE, specimen, exemplar, exemplification.

repress verb **1** *the rebellion was repressed* SUPPRESS, quell, quash, subdue, put down, crush, extinguish, stamp out, defeat, conquer, rout, overwhelm, contain.

2 *the peasants were repressed* OPPRESS, subjugate, keep down, rule with a rod of iron, rule with an iron fist, intimidate, tyrannize, crush.

3 *these emotions may well be repressed* RESTRAIN, hold back/in, keep back, suppress, keep in check, control, keep under control, curb, stifle, bottle up; *informal* button up, keep the lid on.

repressed adjective **1** *a repressed country* OPPRESSED, subjugated, subdued, tyrannized. ANTONYMS democratic, free.

2 *repressed feelings* RESTRAINED, suppressed, held back/in, kept in check, stifled, pent up, bottled up, unvented. ANTONYMS overt, expressed.

3 *emotionally repressed* INHIBITED, frustrated, restrained; *informal* uptight, hung up. ANTONYMS relaxed, uninhibited.

repression noun **1** *the repression of the protests* SUPPRESSION, quashing, subduing, crushing, stamping out.

2 *political repression* OPPRESSION, subjugation, suppression, tyranny, despotism, authoritarianism.

3 *the repression of sexual urges* RESTRAINT, restraining, holding back, keeping back, suppression, keeping in check, control, keeping under control, stifling, bottling up.

repressive adjective *a repressive military regime* OPPRESSIVE, authoritarian, despotic, tyrannical, dictatorial, fascist, autocratic, totalitarian, undemocratic.

reprieve verb **1** *less than two hours ago the governor reprieved Edgerton* GRANT A STAY OF EXECUTION TO, pardon, spare, grant an amnesty to, amnesty; *informal* let off, let off the hook.

2 *the project has been reprieved* SAVE, rescue; *informal* take off the hit list.

▸ noun *a last-minute reprieve* STAY OF EXECUTION, remission, pardon, amnesty; *Law* continuance.

reprimand verb *was it really necessary to reprimand him in public?* REBUKE, admonish, chastise, chide, upbraid, reprove, reproach, scold, berate, take to task, lambaste, give someone a piece of one's mind, rake/haul over the coals, lecture, criticize, censure; *informal* come down on, give someone a talking-to, tell off, dress down, give someone a dressing-down, give someone an earful, give someone a roasting, rap over the knuckles, rap, slap someone's wrist, bawl out, lay into, lace into, blast, give someone what for, chew out, ream out; *formal* castigate. ANTONYM praise.

▸ noun *they received a severe reprimand* REBUKE, reproof, admonishment, admonition, reproach, scolding, upbraiding, censure; *informal* rap over the knuckles, slap on the wrist, dressing-down, talking-to, earful, roasting, tongue-lashing; *formal* castigation. See note at REBUKE. ANTONYM commendation.

reprisal noun *following the ethnic violence in Nigeria, the fear is of reprisal* RETALIATION, counterattack, comeback; revenge, vengeance, retribution, requital; *informal* a taste of one's own medicine.

reproach verb *Albert reproached him for being late.* See REPRIMAND verb. See also note at REBUKE.

▸ noun **1** *an expression of reproach.* See REPRIMAND noun.

2 *this party is a reproach to Canadian politics* DISGRACE, discredit, source of shame, blemish, stain, blot; *literary* smirch.

PHRASE: **beyond/above reproach** *I never claimed to be above reproach* PERFECT, blameless, above suspicion, without fault, faultless, flawless, irreproachable, exemplary, impeccable, immaculate, unblemished, spotless, untarnished, stainless, unsullied, whiter than white; *informal* squeaky clean.

reproachful adjective DISAPPROVING, reproving, critical, censorious, disparaging, withering, accusatory, admonitory. ANTONYM approving.

reprobate noun *a hardened reprobate* ROGUE, rascal, scoundrel, miscreant, good-for-nothing, villain, wretch, rake, degenerate, libertine, debauchee; *informal, dated* cad; *archaic* blackguard, knave, rapscallion.

▸ adjective *reprobate behavior* UNPRINCIPLED, bad, roguish, wicked, rakish, shameless, immoral, degenerate, dissipated, debauched, depraved; *archaic* knavish.

reproduce verb **1** *each piece of artwork is reproduced in color* COPY, duplicate, replicate; photocopy, xerox, print.

2 *this work has not been reproduced in other laboratories* REPEAT, replicate, recreate, redo; simulate, imitate, emulate, mirror, mimic.

3 *some animals reproduce prolifically* BREED, produce offspring, procreate, propagate, multiply.

reproduction noun **1** *color reproduction* COPYING, duplication, duplicating; photocopying, xeroxing, printing.

2 *a reproduction of the original* PRINT, copy, reprint, duplicate, facsimile, carbon copy, photocopy; *trademark* Xerox.

3 *the process of reproduction* BREEDING, procreation, multiplying, propagation.

reproductive adjective *reproductive organs* GENERATIVE, procreative, propagative; sexual, genital.

reproof noun *he muttered reproof* REBUKE, reprimand, reproach, admonishment, admonition; disapproval, censure, criticism, condemnation; *informal* dressing down.

reprove verb *was it necessary to reprove Vicki just for dropping a few crumbs?* REPRIMAND, rebuke, reproach, scold, admonish, chastise, chide, upbraid, berate, take to task, rake/haul over the coals, criticize, censure; *informal* tell off, give someone a talking-to, dress down, give someone a dressing-down, give someone an earful, give someone a roasting, rap over the knuckles, slap someone's wrist; *formal* castigate.

reptile noun See table.

REPTILES

alligator	green turtle
alligator snapping turtle	hawksbill
basilisk	horned toad
blindworm	iguana
box turtle	Komodo dragon
caiman	leatherback turtle
chameleon	lizard
chuckwalla	loggerhead turtle
crocodile	monitor lizard
diamondback	mugger
flying dragon	painted turtle
flying lizard	skink
frill lizard	slow-worm
galliwasp	snapping turtle
gecko	terrapin
gharial	tortoise
Gila monster	tuatara
glass lizard	turtle
goanna	

See also table at AMPHIBIAN.

reptilian adjective **1** *reptilian species* REPTILE, reptile-like, saurian; cold-blooded.

2 *a reptilian smirk* UNPLEASANT, distasteful, nasty, disagreeable, unattractive, off-putting, repulsive, horrible, horrid; unctuous, ingratiating, groveling, oily, oleaginous; *informal* smarmy, slimy, creepy.

repudiate verb **1** *she repudiated communism* REJECT, renounce, abandon, give up, turn one's back on, disown, cast off, lay aside; *formal* forswear, abjure; *literary* forsake. ANTONYM embrace.

2 *Hansen repudiated the allegations* DENY, contradict, controvert, rebut, dispute, dismiss, brush aside; *formal* gainsay. ANTONYMS acknowledge, confirm.

3 *Egypt repudiated the treaty* CANCEL, revoke, rescind, reverse, overrule, overturn, invalidate, nullify; disregard, flout, renege on; *Law* disaffirm; *formal* abrogate. ANTONYMS ratify, abide by.

repudiation noun **1** *the repudiation of one's religion* REJECTION, renunciation, abandonment, forswearing, giving up; *rare* abjuration.

2 *his repudiation of the allegations* DENIAL, refutation, rebuttal, rejection.

3 *a repudiation of the contract* CANCELLATION, revocation, reversal, invalidation, nullification; *formal* abrogation.

repugnance noun *a look of repugnance* REVULSION, disgust, abhorrence, repulsion, loathing, hatred, detestation, aversion, distaste, antipathy, contempt.

repugnant adjective **1** *the idea of cannibalism is repugnant* ABHORRENT, revolting, repulsive, repellent, disgusting, offensive, objectionable, cringeworthy, vile, foul, nasty, loathsome, sickening, nauseating, hateful, detestable, execrable, abominable, monstrous, appalling, insufferable, intolerable, unacceptable, contemptible, unsavory, unpalatable; *informal* ghastly, gross, horrible, horrid; *literary* noisome. See note at OFFENSIVE. ANTONYMS attractive, pleasant.

2 *formal* *the restriction is* ***repugnant to*** *the tenancy* INCOMPATIBLE WITH, in conflict with, contrary to, at variance with, inconsistent with.

repulse verb **1** *the rebels were repulsed* REPEL, drive back/away, fight back/off, put to flight, force back, beat off/back; ward off, hold off; *archaic* rebut.

2 *her advances were repulsed* REBUFF, reject, spurn, snub, cold-shoulder; *informal* give someone the brush-off, freeze out, give someone the bum's rush.

3 *his bid for the company was repulsed* REJECT, turn down, refuse, decline.

4 *the brutality repulsed her* REVOLT, disgust, repel, sicken, nauseate, turn someone's stomach, be repugnant to; *informal* turn off, gross out.

▸ noun **1** *the repulse of the attack* REPELLING, driving back; warding off, holding off.

2 *he was mortified by this repulse* REBUFF, rejection, snub, slight; *informal* brush-off.

repulsion noun *she shuddered with repulsion* DISGUST, revulsion, abhorrence, repugnance, nausea, horror, aversion, abomination, distaste.

repulsive adjective *their bathroom was repulsive* REVOLTING, disgusting, abhorrent, repellent, repugnant, offensive, objectionable, vile, foul, nasty, loathsome, sickening, nauseating, hateful, detestable, execrable, abominable, monstrous, noxious, horrendous, awful, terrible, dreadful, frightful, obnoxious, unsavory, unpleasant, disagreeable, distasteful; ugly, hideous, grotesque; *informal* ghastly, horrible, horrid, gross; *literary* noisome; *archaic* loathly. ANTONYM attractive.

THE RIGHT WORD

Repulsive and **repellent** are very close in meaning, but the former, perhaps because of its sound, is felt to express stronger feeling.

reputable adjective *a reputable talent scout* WELL-THOUGHT-OF, highly regarded, respected, well-respected, respectable, of (good) repute, prestigious, established;

reliable, dependable, trustworthy. ANTONYM untrustworthy.

reputation noun *your careless gossip has ruined my reputation in this town* NAME, GOOD NAME, character, repute, standing, stature, status, position, renown, esteem, prestige; *informal* rep, rap.

repute noun **1** *a woman of ill repute* REPUTATION, name, character.

2 *a firm of international repute* FAME, renown, celebrity, distinction, high standing, stature, prestige.

reputed adjective **1** *they are reputed to be very rich* THOUGHT, said, reported, rumored, believed, held, considered, regarded, deemed, alleged.

2 *his reputed father* SUPPOSED, putative.

3 *a reputed naturalist* WELL-THOUGHT-OF, respected, well-respected, highly regarded, of good repute.

reputedly adverb *this is reputedly the handwriting of Saddam's oldest son* SUPPOSEDLY, by all accounts, so I'm told, so people say, allegedly.

request noun **1** *requests for assistance* APPEAL, entreaty, plea, petition, application, demand, call; *formal* adjuration; *literary* behest.

2 *Charlotte spoke, at Ursula's request* BIDDING, entreaty, demand, insistence.

3 *indicate your requests on the form* REQUIREMENT, wish, desire; choice.

▸ verb **1** *the government requested military aid* ASK FOR, appeal for, call for, seek, solicit, plead for, apply for, demand; *formal* adjure.

2 *I requested him to help* CALL ON, beg, entreat, implore; *literary* beseech.

require verb **1** *the child required hospital treatment* NEED, be in need of.

2 *a situation requiring patience* NECESSITATE, demand, call for, involve, entail.

3 *unquestioning obedience is required* DEMAND, insist on, call for, ask for, expect.

4 *she was required to pay costs* ORDER, instruct, command, enjoin, oblige, compel, force.

5 *do you require anything else?* WANT, wish to have, desire; lack, be short of.

required adjective **1** *required reading* ESSENTIAL, vital, indispensable, necessary, compulsory, obligatory, mandatory, prescribed; *informal* must-have. ANTONYM optional.

2 *cut it to the required length* DESIRED, preferred, chosen; correct, proper, right.

requirement noun *good spelling is a requirement of the job* NEED, wish, demand, want, necessity, essential, prerequisite, stipulation.

requisite adjective *he lacks the requisite skills* NECESSARY, required, prerequisite, essential, indispensable, vital. See note at NECESSARY. ANTONYM optional.

▸ noun *a requisite for a successful career* NECESSITY, essential, essential requirement, prerequisite, precondition, sine qua non; *informal* must.

requisition noun **1** *we have submitted our requisition for additional staff* ORDER, request, call, application, claim, demand.

2 *the requisition of cultural treasures* APPROPRIATION, commandeering, seizure, confiscation, expropriation.

▸ verb **1** *their house was requisitioned by the army* COMMANDEER, appropriate, take over, take possession of, occupy, seize, confiscate, expropriate.

2 *she requisitioned statements* REQUEST, order, call for, demand.

requital noun **1** *in requital of your kindness* REPAYMENT, return, payment, recompense.

2 *personal requital* REVENGE, vengeance, retribution, redress.

requite verb **1** *requiting their hospitality* RETURN, reciprocate, repay.

2 *Drake had requited the wrongs inflicted on them* AVENGE, exact revenge for, revenge, pay someone back for; take reprisals for, get even for.

3 *she did not requite his love* RECIPROCATE, return.

rescind verb *the court can rescind a bankruptcy order* REVOKE, repeal, cancel, reverse, overturn, overrule, annul, nullify, void, invalidate, quash, abolish; *Law* vacate; *formal* abrogate. ANTONYM enforce.

rescission noun *formal the rescission of the contract* REVOCATION, repeal, annulment, nullification, invalidation, voiding; *formal* abrogation.

rescue verb **1** *an attempt to rescue the hostages* SAVE, save from danger, save the life of, come to the aid of; free, set free, release, liberate.

2 *Boyd rescued his papers* RETRIEVE, recover, salvage, get back.

▸ noun *the rescue of 10 crewmen* SAVING, rescuing; release, freeing, liberation, bailout, deliverance, redemption.

PHRASE: **come to someone's rescue** *we were stuck in the elevator until Marty came to our rescue* HELP, assist, lend a helping hand to, lend a hand to, bail out; *informal* save someone's bacon, save someone's neck, save someone's skin.

research noun **1** *medical research* INVESTIGATION, experimentation, testing, analysis, fact-finding, fieldwork, examination, scrutiny.

2 *he continued his research* EXPERIMENT(S), experimentation, test(s), testing, inquiry/inquiries, study/studies.

▸ verb **1** *the phenomenon has been widely researched* INVESTIGATE, study, inquire into, look into, probe, explore, analyze, examine, scrutinize, review.

2 *I researched all the available material* STUDY, read, read up on, sift through, look into; *informal* check out.

resemblance noun Sara says they're twins, but I don't see any resemblance SIMILARITY, likeness, similitude, correspondence, congruity, congruence, coincidence, conformity, agreement, equivalence, comparability, parallelism, uniformity, sameness. See note at LIKENESS.

resemble verb *don't you think he resembles Tom Cruise?* LOOK LIKE, be similar to, be like, bear a resemblance to, remind one of, take after, favor, have the look of; approximate to, smack of, have (all) the hallmarks of, correspond to, echo, mirror, parallel; *archaic* bear semblance to.

resent verb *she resented the models who got better assignments* BEGRUDGE, feel aggrieved at/about, feel bitter about, grudge, be annoyed at/about, be resentful of, dislike, take exception to, object to, take amiss, take offense at, take umbrage at, bear/harbor a grudge about. ANTONYM welcome.

resentful adjective *constant criticism will make your partner feel resentful* AGGRIEVED, indignant, irritated, piqued, put out, in high dudgeon, dissatisfied, disgruntled, discontented, offended, bitter, jaundiced; envious, jealous; brooding; *informal* miffed, peeved, sore.

resentment noun *the lingering Korean resentment of Japanese rule* BITTERNESS, indignation, irritation, pique, dissatisfaction, disgruntlement, discontentment, discontent, resentfulness, bad feelings, hard feelings, ill will, acrimony, rancor, animosity, jaundice; envy, jealousy.

reservation noun **1** **(reservations)** *grave reservations about traveling abroad* DOUBTS, qualms, scruples; misgivings, skepticism, unease, hesitation, objection.

2 *the reservation of the room* BOOKING, ordering, securing. PHRASE: **without reservation** *Mr. McNeill apologized without reservation* WHOLEHEARTEDLY, unreservedly, without qualification, fully, completely, totally, entirely, wholly, unconditionally.

reserve verb **1** *ask the library to reserve a copy for you* PUT TO ONE SIDE, put aside, set aside, keep, keep back, save, hold, put on hold, keep in reserve, earmark.

2 *he reserved a table* BOOK, make a reservation for, order, arrange for, secure; *formal* bespeak; *dated* engage.

3 *the management reserves the right to alter the program* RETAIN, maintain, keep, hold.

4 *reserve your judgment until you know him better* DEFER, postpone, put off, delay, withhold.

▸ noun **1** *reserves of gasoline* STOCK, store, supply, stockpile, pool, hoard, cache.

2 *the army is calling up reserves* REINFORCEMENTS, the militia, extras, auxiliaries.

3 *a nature reserve* NATIONAL PARK, sanctuary, preserve, conservation area, protected area, wildlife park.

4 *it was difficult to get past his reserve* RETICENCE, detachment, distance, remoteness, coolness, aloofness, constraint, formality; shyness, diffidence, timidity, taciturnity, inhibition; *informal* standoffishness.

5 *she trusted him without reserve* RESERVATION, qualification, condition, limitation, hesitation, doubt.

▸ adjective *a reserve goaltender* BACKUP, substitute, stand-in, relief, replacement, fallback, spare, extra.

PHRASE: **in reserve** *we have four generators in reserve* AVAILABLE, to/on hand, ready, in readiness, set aside, at one's disposal.

reserved adjective **1** *Rodney is rather reserved* RETICENT, quiet, private, uncommunicative, unforthcoming, undemonstrative, unsociable, formal, constrained, cool, aloof, detached, distant, remote, unapproachable, unfriendly, withdrawn, secretive, silent, taciturn; shy, retiring, diffident, timid, self-effacing, inhibited, introverted; *informal* buttoned-up, standoffish. ANTONYM outgoing.

2 *that table is reserved* BOOKED, taken, spoken for, prearranged; *dated* engaged; *formal* bespoken. ANTONYM free.

reservoir noun **1** *water pumped from the reservoir* pool, pond; water supply, water tower.

2 *an ink reservoir* RECEPTACLE, container, holder, repository, tank.

3 *the reservoir of managerial talent* STOCK, store, stockpile, reserve(s), supply, bank, pool, stable, fund.

reshuffle verb *the prime minister reshuffled her cabinet* REORGANIZE, restructure, rearrange, change, change around, shake up, shuffle.

▸ noun *a management reshuffle* REORGANIZATION, restructuring, change, rearrangement; *informal* shake-up, housecleaning, musical chairs.

reside verb **1** *most students **reside in** apartments* LIVE IN, occupy, inhabit, stay in, lodge in; *formal* dwell in, be domiciled in.

2 *the paintings reside in an air-conditioned vault* BE SITUATED, be found, be located, lie.

3 *executive power **resides in** the president* BE VESTED IN, be bestowed on, be conferred on, be in the hands of.

4 *the qualities that reside within each individual* BE INHERENT, be present, exist.

residence noun **1** *formal her private residence* HOME, house, place of residence, address; quarters, lodgings; *informal* pad, digs; *formal* dwelling, dwelling place, domicile, abode.

2 *the university residence* DORMITORY, dorm.

3 *his place of residence* OCCUPANCY, habitation, residency; *formal* abode.

resident noun *the residents of Ivoryton* INHABITANT, local, citizen, native; townsfolk, townspeople; householder, homeowner, occupier, tenant; *formal* denizen.

▸ adjective **1** *is he currently resident in New Brunswick?* LIVING, residing, in residence; *formal* dwelling.

2 *a resident nurse* LIVE-IN, living in.

residential adjective *residential neighborhoods* SUBURBAN, commuter; *rare* exurban.

residual adjective **1** *residual heat* REMAINING, leftover, unused, unconsumed.

2 *residual affection* LINGERING, enduring, abiding, surviving, vestigial.

residue noun *the residue of explosives found in the wreckage* REMAINDER, remaining part, rest, remnant(s); surplus, extra, excess; remains, leftovers; *technical* residuum.

resign verb **1** *the executive director resigned* LEAVE, hand in one's notice, give notice, stand down, step down; *informal* quit, jump ship.

2 *three state senators resigned their seats* GIVE UP, leave, vacate, stand down from; *informal* quit, pack in.

3 *he resigned his right to the title* RENOUNCE, relinquish, give up, abandon, surrender, forego, cede; *Law* disclaim; *literary* forsake.

4 *we **resigned ourselves to** a long wait* RECONCILE ONESELF TO, become resigned to, come to terms with, accept.

resignation noun **1** *his resignation from his post* DEPARTURE, leaving, standing down, stepping down; *informal* quitting.

2 *she handed in her resignation* NOTICE, notice to quit, letter of resignation.

3 *he accepted his fate with resignation* PATIENCE, forbearance, stoicism, fortitude, fatalism, acceptance, acquiescence, compliance, passivity.

resigned adjective *he gave a resigned sigh* PATIENT, long-suffering, uncomplaining, forbearing, stoical, philosophical, fatalistic, acquiescent, compliant, passive, submissive.

resilient adjective 1 *resilient materials* FLEXIBLE, pliable, supple; durable, hardwearing, stout, strong, sturdy, tough. See note at RESILIENT.

2 *young and resilient* STRONG, tough, hardy; quick to recover, buoyant, irrepressible.

resist verb 1 *built to resist cold winters* WITHSTAND, be proof against, combat, weather, endure, be resistant to, keep out. ANTONYMS be harmed by, be susceptible to.

2 *they resisted his attempts to change things* OPPOSE, fight against, refuse to accept, object to, defy, set one's face against, kick against; obstruct, impede, hinder, block, thwart, frustrate. ANTONYMS welcome, accept.

3 *I resisted the urge to retort* REFRAIN FROM, abstain from, forbear from, desist from, not give in to, restrain oneself from, stop oneself from. ANTONYMS succumb to, give in to.

4 *she tried to resist him* STRUGGLE WITH/AGAINST, fight (against), stand up to, withstand, hold off; fend off, ward off. ANTONYMS yield to, submit to.

PHRASE: **cannot resist** *I cannot resist a challenge* LOVE, adore, relish, have a weakness for, be very keen on, like, delight in, enjoy, take great pleasure in; *informal* be mad about, get a kick/thrill out of, cannot help wanting.

resistance noun 1 ***resistance to** change* OPPOSITION TO, hostility to, refusal to accept.

2 *a spirited resistance* OPPOSITION, fight, stand, struggle.

3 *the body's **resistance to** disease* ABILITY TO FIGHT OFF, immunity from, defenses against.

4 *the French resistance* RESISTANCE MOVEMENT, freedom fighters, underground, partisans.

resistant adjective 1 ***resistant to** water* IMPERVIOUS TO, unsusceptible to, immune, invulnerable to, proof against, unaffected by.

2 ***resistant to** change* OPPOSED TO, averse to, hostile to, inimical to, against; *informal* anti.

resolute adjective *Israelis and Palestinians held jittery but resolute hopes for peace* DETERMINED, purposeful, resolved, adamant, single-minded, firm, unswerving, unwavering, steadfast, staunch, stalwart, unfaltering, unhesitating, persistent, indefatigable, tenacious, strong-willed, unshakable; stubborn, dogged, obstinate, obdurate, inflexible, intransigent, implacable, unyielding, unrelenting; spirited, brave, bold, courageous, plucky, indomitable; *informal* gutsy, spunky, feisty; *formal* pertinacious. ANTONYM halfhearted.

THE RIGHT WORD

Any of the above adjectives might apply to you if you take a stand on something and stick to it, or show your loyalty to a person, country, or cause. If you show unswerving loyalty to someone or something you are tied to (as in marriage, friendship, etc.), you would be described as **faithful** (*a faithful wife; a faithful Republican*). **Constant** also implies a firm or steady attachment to someone or something, but with less emphasis on vows, pledges, and obligations; it is the opposite of fickleness rather than of unfaithfulness (*my grandfather's constant confidant*). To be described as **staunch** carries loyalty one step further, implying an unwillingness to be dissuaded or turned aside (*a staunch friend who refused to believe the rumors that were circulating*). To be called **resolute** means that you are both staunch and steadfast, but the emphasis here is on character and a firm adherence to your own goals and purposes rather than to those of others (*resolute in insisting upon her right to be heard*). **Determined** and **decisive** are less forceful words. You can be *decisive* in almost any situation, as long as you have a choice among alternatives and don't hesitate in taking a stand (*decisive as always, she barely glanced at the menu before ordering*). *Determined*, unlike *resolute*, suggests a stubborn will rather than a conscious adherence to goals or principles (*he was determined to be home before the holidays*).

---

resolution noun 1 *her resolution not to smoke* INTENTION, resolve, decision, intent, aim, plan; commitment, pledge, promise.

2 *the committee passed the resolution* MOTION, proposal, proposition, resolve.

3 *she handled the work with resolution* DETERMINATION, purpose, purposefulness, resolve, resoluteness, single-mindedness, firmness, firmness of purpose; steadfastness, staunchness, perseverance, persistence, indefatigability, tenacity, tenaciousness, staying power, dedication, commitment; stubbornness, doggedness, obstinacy, obduracy; boldness, spiritedness, braveness, bravery, courage, pluck, grit, courageousness; *informal* guts, spunk; *formal* pertinacity. See note at COURAGE.

4 *a satisfactory **resolution of** the problem* SOLUTION TO, answer to, end to, ending to, settlement of, conclusion to.

resolve verb 1 *this matter cannot be resolved overnight* SETTLE, sort out, solve, find a solution to, fix, straighten out, deal with, put right, put to rights, rectify; *informal* hammer out, thrash out, figure out.

2 *Bob resolved not to wait any longer* DETERMINE, decide, make up one's mind, make a decision.

3 *the committee resolved that the project should proceed* VOTE, pass a resolution, rule, decide formally, agree.

4 *the compounds were resolved into their active constituents* BREAK DOWN/UP, separate, reduce, divide.

5 *the ability to resolve facts into their legal categories* ANALYZE, dissect, break down, categorize.

6 *the gray smudge resolved into a sandy beach* TURN, change, be transformed, be converted.

▸ noun 1 *their intimidation merely strengthened his resolve.* See RESOLUTION sense 3.

2 *he made a resolve not to go there again* DECISION, resolution, commitment.

resolved adjective *he was resolved to marry her* DETERMINED, hell-bent, intent, set.

resonant adjective 1 *a resonant voice* DEEP, low, sonorous, full, full-bodied, vibrant, rich, clear, ringing; loud, booming, thunderous.

2 *valleys resonant with the sound of church bells* REVERBERATING, reverberant, resounding, echoing, filled.

3 *resonant words* EVOCATIVE, suggestive, expressive, redolent.

resort noun 1 *a seaside resort* VACATION SPOT, tourist center, vacationland; retreat; spa; *informal* tourist trap.

2 *settle the matter without **resort to** legal proceedings* RECOURSE TO, turning to, the use of, utilizing.

3 *strike action is our last resort* EXPEDIENT, measure, step, recourse, alternative, option, choice, possibility, hope.
PHRASE: **resort to** *I don't have to resort to such under-*

handed tricks HAVE RECOURSE TO, fall back on, turn to, make use of, use, employ, avail oneself of; stoop to, descend to, sink to.

resound verb **1** *the explosion resounded around the silent street* ECHO, re-echo, reverberate, ring out, boom, thunder, rumble.

2 *resounding with the clang of hammers* REVERBERATE, echo, re-echo, resonate, ring.

3 *nothing will resound like their earlier achievements* BE ACCLAIMED, be celebrated, be renowned, be famed, be glorified, be trumpeted.

resounding adjective **1** *a resounding voice* REVERBERANT, reverberating, resonant, resonating, echoing, ringing, sonorous, deep, full-throated, rich, clear; loud, booming.

2 *a resounding success* ENORMOUS, huge, very great, tremendous, terrific, colossal; emphatic, decisive, conclusive, outstanding, remarkable, phenomenal.

resource noun **1** **(resources)** *use your resources efficiently* ASSETS, funds, wealth, money, capital; staff; supplies, materials, raw materials, store(s), stock(s), reserve(s).

2 *your tutor is there as a resource* FACILITY, amenity, aid, help, support.

3 *tears were her only resource* EXPEDIENT, resort, course, scheme, stratagem; trick, ruse, device.

4 *a person of resource* INITIATIVE, resourcefulness, enterprise, ingenuity, inventiveness; talent, ability, capability; *informal* gumption.

resourceful adjective *a group of resourceful fifth graders came up with a workable plan to overhaul the town's inefficient recycling center* INGENIOUS, enterprising, inventive, creative; clever, talented, able, capable; *informal* clueful. See note at CREATIVE.

respect noun **1** *the respect due to a great artist* ESTEEM, regard, high opinion, admiration, reverence, deference, honor. ANTONYM contempt.

2 *he spoke to her with respect* DUE REGARD, politeness, courtesy, civility, deference. ANTONYM disrespect.

3 *paying one's respects* REGARDS, kind regards, compliments, greetings, best/good wishes, felicitations, salutations; *archaic* remembrances.

4 *the report was accurate in every respect* ASPECT, regard, facet, feature, way, sense, particular, point, detail.

▸ verb **1** *she is highly respected in the book industry* ESTEEM, admire, think highly of, have a high opinion of, hold in high regard, hold in (high) esteem, look up to, revere, reverence, honor. See note at ESTEEM. ANTONYM despise.

2 *they respected our privacy* SHOW CONSIDERATION FOR, have regard for, observe, be mindful of, be heedful of; *formal* take cognizance of. ANTONYM scorn.

3 *her father respected her wishes* ABIDE BY, comply with, follow, adhere to, conform to, act in accordance with, defer to, obey, observe, keep, keep to. ANTONYMS disregard, disobey.

PHRASE: **with respect to/in respect of** *with respect to the new town garage, the council has decided to accept contractors' bids through the end of the month* CONCERNING, regarding, in/with regard to, with reference to, respecting, re, about, apropos, on the subject of, in connection with, vis-à-vis.

respectable adjective **1** *a respectable middle-class background* REPUTABLE, of good repute, upright, honest, honorable, trustworthy, decent, good, well-bred, clean-living. ANTONYM disreputable.

2 *a respectable salary* FAIRLY GOOD, decent, fair, reasonable, moderately good; substantial, considerable, sizable. ANTONYM paltry.

respectful adjective *Mr. North had the reputation for turning a rowdy classroom into a group of respectful students* DEFERENTIAL, reverent, reverential, dutiful; polite, well-mannered, civil, courteous, gracious. ANTONYM rude.

respective adjective *please return to your respective classrooms* SEPARATE, personal, own, particular, individual, specific, special, appropriate, different, various.

respite noun **1** *a brief respite* REST, break, breathing space, interval, intermission, interlude, recess, lull, pause, time out; relief, relaxation, repose; *informal* breather, letup.

2 *respite from debts* POSTPONEMENT, deferment, delay, reprieve; *Law* continuance.

resplendent adjective *the general was resplendent in his uniform* SPLENDID, magnificent, brilliant, dazzling, glittering, gorgeous, impressive, imposing, spectacular, striking, stunning, majestic; *informal* splendiferous. See note at BRIGHT.

respond verb **1** *they do not* ***respond to*** *questions* ANSWER, reply to, make a response to, make a rejoinder to.

2 *"No," she responded* SAY IN RESPONSE, answer, reply, rejoin, retort, riposte, counter.

3 *they were slow to respond* REACT, make a response, reciprocate, retaliate.

response noun **1** *his response to the question* ANSWER, reply, rejoinder, retort, riposte; *informal* comeback.

2 *an angry response* REACTION, reply, retaliation, feedback; *informal* comeback.

responsibility noun **1** *it was his responsibility to find witnesses* DUTY, task, function, job, role, business.

2 *they denied responsibility for the bomb attack* BLAME, fault, guilt, culpability, liability.

3 *let's show some social responsibility* TRUSTWORTHINESS, common sense, sense, maturity, reliability, dependability.

4 *a job with greater responsibility* AUTHORITY, control, power, leadership.

responsible adjective **1** *who is* ***responsible for*** *the prisons?* IN CHARGE OF, in control of, at the helm of, accountable for, liable for.

2 *if an error's been made, I'm the one who's responsible* ACCOUNTABLE, answerable, to blame, guilty, culpable, blameworthy, at fault, in the wrong.

3 *a responsible job* IMPORTANT, powerful, executive.

4 *he is responsible to the president* ANSWERABLE, accountable.

5 *a responsible tenant* TRUSTWORTHY, sensible, mature, reliable, dependable.

THE RIGHT WORD

Responsible is an adjective that applies to anyone who is in charge of an endeavor or to whom a duty has been delegated, and who is subject to penalty or blame in case of default (*responsible for getting everyone out of the building in the event of a fire*). **Answerable** implies a legal or moral obligation for which one must answer (*the parents were held to be answerable for their children's behavior*). **Accountable** is more positive than *responsible* or *answerable*, suggesting that something has been entrusted to someone who will be called to account for how that trust has been carried out (*She was directly accountable to the department head for the funds that had been allocated to her group*). **Liable** is more restricted in scope than any of the foregoing words; it refers exclusively to the assignment of blame or the payment of monetary damages in the event of a mishap (*because he was responsible for the accident, he was held liable for damages*).

---

responsive adjective *several consumers said the company hasn't been* ***responsive to*** *their needs* QUICK TO REACT TO, reactive to, receptive to, open to suggestions about, amenable to, flexible to, sensitive to, sympathetic to; aware of.

rest[1] verb **1** *he needed to rest* RELAX, take a rest, ease up/off, let up, slow down, have/take a break, unbend, unwind, recharge one's batteries, be at leisure, take it easy, put one's feet up; lie down, go to bed, have/take a nap, catnap, doze, sleep; *informal* take five, have/take a breather, catch forty winks, get some shut-eye, take a load off, chill, chill out, catch some Zs.

2 *his hands rested on the rail* LIE, be laid, repose, be placed, be positioned, be supported by.

3 *she rested her basket on the ground* SUPPORT, prop (up), lean, lay, set, stand, position, place, put.

4 *the film script* ***rests on*** *an improbable premise* BE BASED ON, depend on, be dependent on, rely on, hinge on, turn on, be contingent on, revolve around, center on.

▸ noun **1** *get some rest* REPOSE, relaxation, leisure, respite, time off, breathing space, downtime; sleep, nap, doze; *informal* shut-eye, snooze, lie-down, forty winks.

2 *a short rest from work* BREAK, vacation, breathing space, interval, interlude, intermission, time off/out, holiday; *informal* breather.

3 *she took the poker from its rest* STAND, base, holder, support, rack, frame, shelf.

4 *passengers queried why the train had come to rest several miles before the next station* A STANDSTILL, a halt, a stop.

rest[2] noun *the rest of the board members are appointees* REMAINDER, residue, balance, remaining part/number/quantity, others, those left, remains, remnant(s), surplus, excess; *technical* residuum.

▸ verb *you may rest assured that he is there* REMAIN, continue to be, stay, keep, carry on being.

rest area noun REST STOP, picnic area, stopping place; *informal* pit stop.

restaurant noun See table.

restful adjective *a restful cruise* RELAXED, relaxing, quiet, calm, calming, tranquil, soothing, peaceful, placid, reposeful, leisurely, undisturbed, untroubled. ANTONYM exciting.

restitution noun **1** *restitution of the land seized* RETURN, restoration, handing back, surrender.

2 *restitution for the damage caused* COMPENSATION, recompense, reparation, damages, indemnification, indemnity, reimbursement, repayment, redress, remuneration.

restive adjective **1** *Edward is getting restive.* See RESTLESS sense 1.

2 *the militants are increasingly restive* UNRULY, disorderly, uncontrollable, unmanageable, willful, recalcitrant, insubordinate; *formal* refractory; *archaic* contumacious.

restless adjective **1** *Maria was restless throughout the meeting* UNEASY, ill at ease, restive, fidgety, edgy, on edge, tense, worked up, nervous, agitated, anxious, on tenterhooks, keyed up; *informal* jumpy, jittery, twitchy, uptight, antsy.

2 *a restless night* SLEEPLESS, wakeful; fitful, broken, disturbed, troubled, unsettled.

restlessness noun *an excess of the herb may cause headaches and restlessness* UNEASE, restiveness, edginess, tenseness, nervousness, agitation, anxiety, fretfulness, apprehension, disquiet; *informal* jitteriness.

restoration noun **1** *the restoration of democracy* REINSTATEMENT, reinstitution, reestablishment, reimposition, return.

2 *the restoration of derelict housing* REPAIR, repairing, fixing, mending, refurbishment, reconditioning, rehabilitation, rebuilding, reconstruction, overhaul, redevelopment, renovation; *informal* rehab.

restore verb **1** *the aim to restore democracy* REINSTATE, bring back, reinstitute, reimpose, reinstall, reestablish. See note at RECOVER. ANTONYM abolish.

2 *he restored it to its rightful owner* RETURN, give back, hand back.

3 *the building has been restored* REPAIR, fix, mend, refurbish, recondition, rehabilitate, rebuild, reconstruct, remodel, overhaul, redevelop, renovate; *informal* do up, rehab. ANTONYM neglect.

4 *a good sleep can restore you* REINVIGORATE, revitalize, revive, refresh, energize, fortify, revivify, regenerate, stimulate, freshen.

restrain verb **1** *Charles restrained his anger* CONTROL, keep under control, check, hold/keep in check, curb, suppress, repress, contain, dampen, subdue, smother, choke back, stifle, bottle up, rein back/in; *informal* keep the lid on.

RESTAURANTS

auberge	noodle shop
automat	osteria
bakery	oyster bar
bar	paninoteca
bar & grill	patisserie
barbecue	pizzeria
bistro	pub
brasserie	public house
buffet	rathskeller
café	raw bar
cafeteria	relais
charcuterie	sandwich shop
cantina	shabu-shabu
chophouse	sidewalk café
churrascaria	smorgasbord
coffee shop	snack bar
coffeehouse	steakhouse
delicatessen	supper club
diner	sushi bar
enoteca	sweet shop
fast food restaurant	tapas bar
gin joint	taqueria
greasy spoon	tavern
lunch counter	tea room
luncheonette	trattoria
malt shop	

2 *she could barely restrain herself from swearing* PREVENT, stop, keep, hold back.

3 *that beast ought to be restrained* TIE UP, bind, tether, chain (up), fetter, shackle, manacle, put in irons; *informal* hog-tie.

restrained adjective 1 *Julie was quite restrained* SELF-CONTROLLED, self-restrained, not given to excesses, sober, steady, unemotional, undemonstrative.

2 *restrained elegance* MUTED, soft, discreet, subtle, quiet, unobtrusive, unostentatious, understated, tasteful.

restraint noun 1 *a restraint on their impulsiveness* CONSTRAINT, check, control, restriction, limitation, curtailment; rein, bridle, brake, damper, impediment, obstacle.

2 *the protestors showed restraint* SELF-CONTROL, self-restraint, self-discipline, control, moderation, prudence, judiciousness, abstemiousness.

3 *the room has been decorated with restraint* SUBTLETY, understatedness, taste, tastefulness, discretion, discrimination.

4 *a child restraint* BELT, harness, strap.

restrict verb 1 *a busy working life restricted his leisure activities* LIMIT, keep within bounds, regulate, control, moderate, cut down.

2 *the cuff supports the ankle without restricting movement* HINDER, interfere with, impede, hamper, obstruct, block, check, curb, shackle.

3 *he restricted himself to a 15-minute speech* CONFINE, limit.

restricted adjective 1 *restricted space* CRAMPED, confined, constricted, small, narrow, tight. ANTONYM roomy.

2 *a restricted calorie intake* LIMITED, controlled, regulated, reduced, rangebound. ANTONYM unlimited.

3 *a restricted zone* OUT OF BOUNDS, off limits, private, exclusive. ANTONYM public.

4 *restricted information* SECRET, top secret, classified; *informal* hush-hush.

restriction noun 1 *there is no restriction on the number of places* LIMITATION, limit, constraint, control, check, curb; condition, proviso, qualification.

2 *the restriction of personal freedom* REDUCTION, limitation, diminution, curtailment.

3 *restriction of movement* HINDRANCE, impediment, slowing, reduction, limitation.

result noun 1 *stress is the result of overwork* CONSEQUENCE, outcome, product, upshot, sequel, effect, reaction, repercussion, ramification, conclusion, culmination. ANTONYM cause.

2 *having made the calculation, what is your result?* ANSWER, solution; sum, total, product.

3 *exam results* GRADE, score, mark.

4 *the result of the trial* VERDICT, decision, outcome, conclusion, judgment, findings, ruling.

▸ verb 1 *differences between species could* ***result from*** *their habitat* FOLLOW FROM, ensue from, develop from, stem from, spring from, arise from, derive from, evolve from, proceed from; occur from, happen from, take place from, come about from; be caused by, be brought about by, be produced by, originate in, be consequent on.

2 *the shooting* ***resulted in*** *five deaths* END IN, culminate in, finish in, terminate in, lead to, prompt, precipitate, trigger; cause, bring about, occasion, effect, give rise to, produce, engender, generate; *literary* beget.

resume verb 1 *the government resumed negotiations* RESTART, recommence, begin again, start again, reopen; renew, return to, continue with, carry on with. ANTONYMS suspend, abandon.

2 *the priest resumed his kneeling posture* RETURN TO, come back to, take up again, reoccupy. ANTONYM leave.

résumé noun 1 *give your résumé to the HR department* CURRICULUM VITAE, CV.

2 *a résumé of the course material* SUMMARY, précis, synopsis, abstract, outline, summarization, summation, epitome; abridgment, digest, condensation, abbreviation, overview, review.

resumption noun *they called for a* ***resumption of*** *negotiations* RESTART TO/OF, restarting of, recommencement of, reopening of; continuation of, carrying on of, renewal of, return to.

resurgence noun *the resurgence of jazz | green tea is enjoying a resurgence in popularity* RENEWAL, revival, recovery, comeback, reawakening, resurrection, reappearance, reemergence, regeneration; resumption, recommencement, continuation, renaissance.

resurrect verb 1 *we believe that Jesus was resurrected* RAISE FROM THE DEAD, restore to life, revive.

2 *resurrecting his career* REVIVE, restore, regenerate, revitalize, breathe new life into, bring back to life, reinvigorate, resuscitate, rejuvenate, stimulate, reestablish, relaunch.

resuscitate verb 1 *medics resuscitated him* BRING AROUND, revive, bring back to consciousness; give CPR (cardiopulmonary resuscitation) to, give the kiss of life to.

2 *measures to resuscitate the economy* REVIVE, resurrect, restore, regenerate, revitalize, breathe new life into, reinvigorate, rejuvenate, stimulate.

retain verb 1 *the government retained a share in the industries* KEEP, keep possession of, keep hold of, hold on to, hang on to. ANTONYM give up.

2 *existing footpaths are to be retained* MAINTAIN, keep, preserve, conserve. ANTONYM discontinue.

3 *some students retain facts easily* REMEMBER, memorize, keep in one's mind, keep in one's memory, store. ANTONYM forget.

4 *we have decided to retain a company lawyer* EMPLOY, contract, secure the services of, sign on, put on the payroll, keep on the payroll. ANTONYM dismiss.

retainer noun 1 *they're paid a retainer* RETAINING FEE, fee, periodic payment, advance, standing charge.

2 *a faithful retainer.* See SERVANT sense 1.

retaliate verb *the gang will look for an opportunity to retaliate* FIGHT BACK, hit back, respond, react, reply, reciprocate, counterattack, return like for like, get back at someone, give tit for tat, take reprisals, get even, get one's own back, pay someone back, give someone a taste of their own medicine; have/get/take one's revenge, be revenged, avenge oneself.

retaliation noun *the rebel forces awaited the government's retaliation* REVENGE, vengeance, reprisal, retribution, requital, recrimination, repayment; response, reaction, reply, counterattack.

retard verb *the process is retarded by bureaucratic red tape* DELAY, slow down, slow up, hold back, hold up, set back, postpone, put back, detain, decelerate; hinder, hamper, obstruct, inhibit, impede, check, restrain, restrict, trammel; *literary* stay. ANTONYM accelerate.

retch verb **1** *the sour taste made her retch* GAG, heave, almost vomit.

2 *he went into the bushes to retch.* See VOMIT verb sense 1.

reticence noun *security concerns may explain Taylor's reticence* RESERVE, restraint, inhibition, diffidence, shyness; unresponsiveness, quietness, taciturnity, secretiveness.

reticent adjective *Smith was reticent about his personal affairs* RESERVED, withdrawn, introverted, inhibited, diffident, shy; uncommunicative, unforthcoming, unresponsive, tight-lipped, buttoned-up, quiet, taciturn, silent, guarded, secretive. ANTONYM expansive.

retinue noun *the chancellor arrived with his retinue* ENTOURAGE, escort, company, court, staff, personnel, household, train, suite, following, bodyguard; aides, attendants, servants, retainers.

retire verb **1** *he has retired* GIVE UP WORK, stop working, stop work; pack it in, call it quits.

2 *we've retired him on full pension* force to retire, give someone the golden handshake/parachute.

3 *Gillian retired to her office* WITHDRAW, go away, take oneself off, decamp, shut oneself away; *formal* repair; *literary* betake oneself.

4 *their forces retired* RETREAT, withdraw, pull back, fall back, disengage, back off, give ground.

5 *everyone retired early* GO TO BED, call it a day, go to sleep; *informal* turn in, hit the hay, hit the sack.

retired adjective *a retired schoolteacher* FORMER, ex-, past, in retirement, superannuated.

▸ noun **(the retired)** *apartments for the retired* RETIRED PEOPLE, senior citizens, the elderly, seniors.

retiring adjective **1** *the retiring president* DEPARTING, outgoing. ANTONYM incoming.

2 *a retiring sort of man* SHY, diffident, self-effacing, unassuming, unassertive, reserved, reticent, quiet, timid, modest; private, secret, secretive, withdrawn, reclusive, unsociable. ANTONYM outgoing.

retort verb *"Oh, sure," she retorted* ANSWER, reply, respond, say in response, return, counter, rejoin, riposte, retaliate, snap back.

▸ noun *a sarcastic retort* ANSWER, reply, response, return, counter, rejoinder, riposte, retaliation; *informal* comeback.

retract verb **1** *the sea otter can retract its claws* PULL IN, draw in, pull back.

2 *she retracted her allegation* TAKE BACK, withdraw, recant, disavow, disclaim, repudiate, renounce, reverse, revoke, rescind, go back on, backtrack on, unsay; *formal* abjure.

retreat verb **1** *the army retreated* WITHDRAW, retire, draw back, pull back/out, fall back, give way, give ground, beat a retreat, beat a hasty retreat. ANTONYM advance.

2 *the tide was retreating* GO OUT, ebb, recede, fall, go down, wane.

3 *the government had to retreat* CHANGE ONE'S MIND, change one's plans; back down, climb down, do a U-turn, backtrack, backpedal, give in, concede defeat; *informal* pull a U-ey, do a one-eighty.

▸ noun **1** *the retreat of the army* WITHDRAWAL, pulling back.

2 *the president's retreat* ABOUT-FACE, U-turn; *informal* one-eighty.

3 *her rural retreat* REFUGE, haven, sanctuary; hideaway, hideout, hiding place, escape.

4 *a period of retreat from the world* SECLUSION, withdrawal, retirement, solitude, isolation, sanctuary.

retrench verb **1** *we have to retrench* ECONOMIZE, cut back, make cutbacks, make savings, make economies, reduce expenditure, be economical, be frugal, tighten one's belt.

2 *services have to be retrenched* REDUCE, cut, cut back, cut down, pare, pare down, slim down, make reductions in, make cutbacks in, trim, prune; shorten, abridge; *informal* slash.

retribution noun *officials condemned the suicide bombing and vowed retribution* PUNISHMENT, penalty, one's just deserts; revenge, reprisal, requital, retaliation, vengeance, an eye for an eye (and a tooth for a tooth), tit for tat, lex talionis; redress, reparation, restitution, recompense, repayment, atonement, indemnification, amends.

retrieve verb **1** *I retrieved our balls from their garden* GET BACK, bring back, recover, regain (possession of), recoup, reclaim, repossess, redeem, recuperate. See note at RECOVER.

2 *they were trying to retrieve the situation* PUT RIGHT, set right, rectify, remedy, restore, sort out, straighten out, resolve, save.

retrograde adjective **1** *a retrograde step* FOR THE WORSE, regressive, negative, downhill, unwelcome. ANTONYMS positive, forward-looking.

2 *retrograde motion* BACKWARD, backwards, reverse, rearward. ANTONYM forward.

retrospect PHRASE: **in retrospect** *in retrospect, we can see that more guards should have been installed at the front gate* LOOKING BACK, on reflection, on reexamination, in/with hindsight.

retrospective adjective *the government introduced retrospective legislation* BACKDATED, retroactive, ex post facto.

▸ noun *a two-hour retrospective on the Great Depression* LOOK BACK, reflection, review.

return verb **1** *he returned to Halifax* GO BACK, come back, come home. ANTONYM depart.

2 *the symptoms returned* RECUR, reoccur, occur again, repeat (itself); reappear, appear again. ANTONYM disappear.

3 *he returned the money* GIVE BACK, hand back; pay back, repay. ANTONYM keep.

4 *Peter returned the book to the shelf* RESTORE, put back, replace, reinstall.

5 *he returned the volley* HIT BACK, throw back. ANTONYM miss.

6 *she returned his kiss* RECIPROCATE, requite, give in return, respond to, repay, give back. ANTONYM ignore.

7 *"Later," returned Isabel* ANSWER, reply, respond, counter, rejoin, retort, come back.

8 *the jury returned a unanimous verdict* DELIVER, bring in, hand down.

9 *the club returned a profit* YIELD, earn, realize, net, gross, clear.

10 *the Green Party was returned* ELECT, vote in, choose, select.

▸ noun **1** *his return to Oregon* HOMECOMING. ANTONYM departure.

2 *the return of hard times* RECURRENCE, reoccurrence, repeat, repetition, reappearance, revival, resurrection, reemergence, resurgence, renaissance. ANTONYM disappearance.

3 *I requested the return of my books* GIVING BACK, handing back, replacement, restoration, reinstatement, restitution.

4 *a quick return on investments* YIELD, profit, gain, revenue, interest, dividend.

5 *a census return* STATEMENT, report, submission, record, dossier; document, form.

PHRASE: **in return for** *I'm authorized to show you some leniency in return for information about Sawyer* IN EXCHANGE FOR, as a reward for, as compensation for.

revamp verb *they plan to revamp the kitchen* RENOVATE, redecorate, refurbish, recondition, rehabilitate, overhaul, make over; upgrade, refit, re-equip; remodel, refashion, redesign, restyle; *informal* do up, give something a facelift, rehab.

reveal verb **1** *the police can't reveal his whereabouts* DIVULGE, disclose, tell, let slip, let drop, give away, give out, blurt (out), release, leak; make known, make public, broadcast, publicize, circulate, disseminate; *informal* let on. ANTONYMS hide, conceal.

2 *the screen moved back to reveal the new car* SHOW, display, exhibit, disclose, uncover, unveil; *literary* uncloak. ANTONYM hide.

3 *the data can reveal a good deal of information* BRING TO LIGHT, uncover, lay bare, unearth, expose; *formal* evince; *literary* uncloak.

revel verb **1** *they reveled all night* CELEBRATE, make merry, have a party, carouse, roister, go on a spree; *informal* party, live it up, whoop it up, make whoopee, rave, paint the town red.

2 *she* ***reveled in*** *the applause* ENJOY, delight in, love, like, adore, be pleased by, take pleasure in, appreciate, relish, lap up, savor; *informal* get a kick out of.

▸ noun *late-night revels* CELEBRATION, festivity, jollification, merrymaking, carousing, spree; party, jamboree, hedonism; *informal* rave, shindig, bash, wingding, blast.

revelation noun **1** *revelations about his personal life* DISCLOSURE, surprising fact, announcement, report; admission, confession.

2 *the revelation of a secret* DIVULGING, divulgence, disclosure, disclosing, letting slip, letting drop, giving away, giving out, leaking, leak, betrayal, unveiling, making known, making public, broadcasting, publicizing, dissemination, reporting, report, declaring, declaration.

reveler noun *the New Year's Eve revelers have poured into Times Square in record numbers* PARTYGOER, merrymaker, carouser, roisterer; *archaic* wassailer.

revenge noun **1** *she is seeking revenge* VENGEANCE, retribution, retaliation, reprisal, requital, recrimination, an eye for an eye (and a tooth for a tooth), redress, satisfaction.

2 *they were filled with revenge* VENGEFULNESS, vindictiveness, vitriol, spite, spitefulness, malice, maliciousness, malevolence, ill will, animosity, hate, hatred, rancor, bitterness; *literary* maleficence.

▸ verb *he revenged his brother's murder* AVENGE, take/exact revenge for, exact retribution for, take reprisals for, get redress for, get satisfaction for.

revenue noun *this month's revenue is up 5 percent from last month* INCOME, takings, receipts, proceeds, earnings, sales; profit(s). ANTONYM expenditure.

reverberate verb *Fred's voice reverberated across the room* RESOUND, echo, re-echo, resonate, ring, boom, rumble, vibrate.

reverberation noun **1** *natural reverberation* RESONANCE, echo, echoing, re-echoing, resounding, ringing, booming, rumbling.

2 *political reverberations* REPERCUSSIONS, ramifications, consequences, shock waves, tremors, vibrations; aftermath, fallout, backlash.

revere verb *she is revered as a national hero* RESPECT, admire, honor, think highly of, esteem, hold in high esteem, hold in high regard, look up to, put on a pedestal, lionize, reverence. ANTONYM despise.

THE RIGHT WORD

We might **admire** someone who walks a tightrope between two skyscrapers, **idolize** a rock star, **adore** our mothers, and **revere** a person like Martin Luther King, Jr. Each of these verbs conveys the idea of regarding someone or something with respect and honor, but they differ considerably in terms of the feelings they connote. *Admire* suggests a feeling of delight and enthusiastic appreciation (*admire the courage of the mountain climber*), while *adore* implies the tenderness and warmth of unquestioning love (*he adored babies*). *Idolize* is an extreme form of adoration, suggesting a slavish, helpless love, (*he idolized the older quarterback*). We *revere* individuals and institutions that command our respect for their accomplishments or attributes (*he revered his old English professor*). **Venerate** and **worship** are usually found in religious contexts (*venerate saints and worship God*) but both words may be used in other contexts as well. *Venerate* is usually associated with dignity and advanced age (*venerate the old man who had founded the company more than 50 years ago*), while *worship* connotes an excessive and uncritical respect (*the young girls who waited outside the stage door worshiped the ground he walked on*).

reverence noun *reverence for the countryside* HIGH ESTEEM, high regard, great respect, acclaim, admiration, appreciation, estimation, favor. See note at HONOR. ANTONYM scorn.

▸ verb *they reverence modern jazz.* See REVERE.

reverent adjective *a reverent silence* RESPECTFUL, reverential, admiring, devoted, devout, dutiful, awed, deferential.

reverie noun *startled out of her reverie by a loud crash* DAYDREAM, daydreaming, trance, musing; inattention, inattentiveness, woolgathering, preoccupation, absorption, abstraction, lack of concentration.

reversal noun **1** *there was no reversal on this issue* TURNAROUND, turnabout, about-face, volte-face, change of heart, U-turn, one-eighty, 180, backtracking; *rare* tergiversation.

2 *a reversal of roles* SWAP, exchange, change, swapping, interchange.

3 *the reversal of the decision* ALTERATION, changing; countermanding, undoing, overturning, overthrow, disallowing, overriding, overruling, veto, vetoing, revocation, repeal, rescinding, annulment, nullification, voiding, invalidation, abrogation.

4 *a very slow July was the only reversal we suffered during the entire fiscal year* SETBACK, reverse, upset, failure, misfortune, mishap, disaster, blow, disappointment, adversity, hardship, affliction, vicissitude, defeat; bad luck.

reverse verb 1 *the car reversed into a lamppost* BACK, back up, drive back/backward, move back/backward.

2 *reverse the bottle in the ice bucket* TURN UPSIDE DOWN, turn over, upend, upturn, invert.

3 *I reversed my jacket* TURN INSIDE OUT, turn outside in.

4 *reverse your roles* SWAP, change, change around, exchange, interchange, switch, switch around.

5 *the umpire reversed the decision* ALTER, change; overturn, overthrow, disallow, override, overrule, veto, revoke, repeal, rescind, annul, nullify, void, invalidate; *formal* abrogate.

▸ adjective 1 *in reverse order* BACKWARD, reversed, inverted, transposed.

2 *reverse racism* INVERSE, reversed, opposite, converse, contrary, counter, antithetical.

▸ noun 1 *the reverse is the case* OPPOSITE, contrary, converse, inverse, obverse, antithesis. See note at OPPOSITE.

2 *successes and reverses.* See REVERSAL sense 4.

3 *the reverse of the page* OTHER SIDE, reverse side, back, underside, wrong side, verso.

revert verb 1 *life will soon revert to normal* RETURN, go back, change back, default; fall back, regress, relapse.

2 *the property reverted to the landlord* BE RETURNED; *historical* escheat.

review noun 1 *the council undertook a review* ANALYSIS, evaluation, assessment, appraisal, examination, investigation, inquiry, probe, inspection, study.

2 *the rent is due for review* RECONSIDERATION, reassessment, reevaluation, reappraisal; change, alteration, modification, revision.

3 *book reviews* CRITICISM, critique, assessment, evaluation, commentary; *informal* take.

4 *a scientific review* JOURNAL, periodical, magazine, publication.

5 *their review of the economy* SURVEY, report, study, account, description, statement, overview, analysis.

6 *a military review* INSPECTION, parade, tattoo, procession, march past.

▸ verb 1 *I reviewed the evidence* SURVEY, study, research, consider, analyze, examine, scrutinize, explore, look into, probe, investigate, inspect, assess, appraise; *informal* size up.

2 *the referee reviewed his decision* RECONSIDER, reexamine, reassess, reevaluate, reappraise, rethink; change, alter, modify, revise.

3 *he reviewed the day* REMEMBER, recall, reflect on, think through, go over in one's mind, look back on.

4 *reviewing troops* INSPECT, view.

5 *she reviewed the play* COMMENT ON, evaluate, assess, appraise, judge, critique, criticize.

reviewer noun *a restaurant reviewer for the local paper* CRITIC, COMMENTATOR, judge, observer, pundit, analyst.

revile verb *reviled as a traitor* CRITICIZE, censure, condemn, attack, inveigh against, rail against, castigate, lambaste, denounce; slander, libel, malign, vilify, abuse; *informal* knock, slam, pan, crucify, roast, tear into, badmouth, dis, pummel; *formal* excoriate, calumniate. See note at SCOLD. ANTONYM praise.

revise verb 1 *she revised her opinion* RECONSIDER, review, reexamine, reassess, reevaluate, reappraise, rethink; change, alter, modify.

2 *the editor revised the text* AMEND, emend, correct, alter, change, edit, rewrite, redraft, rephrase, rework.

revision noun 1 *a revision of the fifth chapter* EMENDATION, correction, alteration, adaptation, editing, rewriting, redrafting.

2 *a new revision* VERSION, edition, rewrite.

3 *a major revision of the system* RECONSIDERATION, review, reexamination, reassessment, reevaluation, reappraisal, rethink; change, alteration, modification.

revitalize verb *the plan would revitalize the economy* REINVIGORATE, reenergize, boost, regenerate, revive, revivify, rejuvenate, reanimate, resuscitate, refresh, stimulate, breathe new life into; *informal* give a shot in the arm to, pep up, jump-start, buck up.

revival noun 1 *a revival in the economy* IMPROVEMENT, recovery, rallying, picking up, amelioration, turn for the better, upturn, upswing, resurgence. ANTONYM downturn.

2 *the revival of traditional crafts* COMEBACK, reestablishment, reintroduction, restoration, reappearance, resurrection, regeneration, renaissance, rejuvenation. ANTONYM disappearance.

revive verb 1 *attempts to revive her failed* RESUSCITATE, bring around, bring back to consciousness.

2 *the man soon revived* REGAIN CONSCIOUSNESS, come around, wake up.

3 *a cup of tea revived her* REINVIGORATE, revitalize, refresh, energize, reanimate, resuscitate, revivify, rejuvenate, regenerate, enliven, stimulate.

4 *reviving old traditions* REINTRODUCE, reestablish, restore, resurrect, bring back, regenerate, resuscitate, rekindle.

revoke verb *their liquor license was revoked* CANCEL, repeal, rescind, reverse, annul, nullify, void, invalidate, countermand, retract, withdraw, overrule, override; *Law* vacate; *formal* abrogate.

revolt verb 1 *the people revolted* REBEL, rise up, rise, take to the streets, riot, mutiny.

2 *the smell revolted him* DISGUST, sicken, nauseate, make nauseous, make someone sick, turn someone's stomach, be repugnant to, be repulsive to, put off, be offensive to, make someone's gorge rise; *informal* turn off, gross out.

▸ noun *an armed revolt* REBELLION, revolution, insurrection, mutiny, uprising, riot, rioting, insurgence, seizure of power, coup, coup d'état.

revolting adjective *a number of revolting items in their refrigerator* DISGUSTING, sickening, nauseating, stomach-turning, stomach-churning, repulsive, repellent, repugnant, appalling, abominable, hideous, horrible, awful, dreadful, terrible, obnoxious, vile, nasty, foul, loathsome, offensive, objectionable, off-putting, distasteful, disagreeable, vomitous; *informal* ghastly, putrid, horrid, gross, gut-churning, yucky, icky; *formal* rebarbative; *literary* noisome; *archaic* loathly. ANTONYMS attractive, pleasant, mouthwatering.

revolution noun **1** *the French aristocracy was ill-prepared to quell a revolution* REBELLION, revolt, insurrection, mutiny, uprising, riot, rioting, insurgence, seizure of power, coup (d'état). See note at UPRISING.

2 *a revolution in printing techniques* DRAMATIC CHANGE, radical alteration, sea change, metamorphosis, transformation, innovation, reorganization, restructuring; *informal* shake-up, shakedown.

3 *one revolution of a wheel* TURN, single turn, rotation, circle, spin; circuit, lap.

4 *the revolution of the earth* TURNING, rotation, circling; orbit.

revolutionary adjective **1** *revolutionary troops* REBELLIOUS, rebel, insurgent, rioting, mutinous, renegade, insurrectionary, insurrectionist, seditious, subversive, extremist.

2 *revolutionary change* THOROUGHGOING, thorough, complete, total, absolute, utter, comprehensive, sweeping, far-reaching, extensive, profound.

3 *a revolutionary kind of wheelchair* NEW, novel, original, unusual, unconventional, unorthodox, newfangled, innovative, modern, state-of-the-art, cutting-edge, futuristic, pioneering.

▸ noun *political revolutionaries* REBEL, insurgent, revolutionist, mutineer, insurrectionist, agitator, subversive.

revolutionize verb *aerial photography revolutionized archaeology* TRANSFORM, alter dramatically, shake up, turn upside down, restructure, reorganize, transmute, metamorphose; *humorous* transmogrify.

revolve verb **1** *a fan revolved slowly* GO AROUND, turn around, rotate, spin.

2 *the moon revolves around the earth* CIRCLE, travel, orbit.

3 *his life **revolves around** cars* BE CONCERNED WITH, be preoccupied with, focus on, center on/around.

revulsion noun *millions of peaceable Muslims regard the extremists' violence with revulsion* DISGUST, repulsion, abhorrence, repugnance, nausea, horror, aversion, abomination, distaste. ANTONYM delight.

reward noun *a reward for its safe return* RECOMPENSE, prize, award, honor, decoration, bonus, premium, bounty, present, gift, payment; *informal* payoff, perk; *formal* perquisite.

▸ verb *they were well rewarded* RECOMPENSE, pay, remunerate, make something worth someone's while; give an award to. ANTONYM punish.

rewarding adjective *working in Professor Ott's intern program has been a rewarding experience* SATISFYING, gratifying, pleasing, fulfilling, enriching, edifying, beneficial, illuminating, worthwhile, productive, fruitful.

reword verb *would you please reword that in language we can all understand?* REWRITE, rephrase, recast, put in other words, express differently, redraft, revise; paraphrase.

rewrite verb *the assignment is to rewrite the Gettysburg Address in modern vernacular* REVISE, recast, reword, rephrase, redraft.

rhetoric noun **1** *a form of rhetoric* ORATORY, eloquence, command of language, way with words.See note at PARALIPSIS.

2 *empty rhetoric* BOMBAST, turgidity, grandiloquence, magniloquence, pomposity, extravagant language, purple prose; wordiness, verbosity, prolixity; *informal* hot air; *rare* fustian.

USAGE NOTE **rhetoric**

Rhetoric = (1) the art of using language persuasively; the rules that help one achieve eloquence; (2) the persuasive use of language; (3) a treatise on persuasive language; (4) prose composition as a school subject. These are the main senses outlined in the *Oxford English Dictionary*. There should probably be added a new sense, related to but distinct from the first sense: (5) the bombastic or disingenuous use of language to manipulate people.

Older books defined *rhetoric* in line with sense 1:

- "Rhetoric is the Art of speaking suitably upon any Subject." (John Kirkby, *A New English Grammar*; 1746.)
- "Rhetoric is the art of adapting discourse, in harmony with its subject and occasion, to the requirements of a reader or hearer." (John F. Genung, *The Working Principles of Rhetoric*; 1902.)

But the slippage toward the pejorative sense 5 began early. In "Some Fruits of Solitude" (1693), William Penn suggested its iniquitous uses: "There is a Truth and Beauty in Rhetorick; but it oftener serves ill Turns than good ones." (Charles W. Eliot, ed., *Harvard Classics*; 1909.) By the twentieth century, some writers with a classical bent were trying hard to reclaim the word—e.g.: "No one who reads [ancient authors] can hold the puerile notions of rhetoric that prevail in our generation. The ancients would have made short work of the cult of the anti-social that lies behind the cult of mystification and the modern hatred of rhetoric. All the great literary ages have exalted the study of rhetoric." (Van Wyck Brooks, *Opinions of Oliver Allston*; 1941.) But T. S. Eliot probably had it right when he acknowledged that the word is essentially ambiguous today—generally pejorative but with flashes of a favorable sense: "The word [*rhetoric*] simply cannot be used as synonymous with bad writing. The meanings which it has been obliged to shoulder have been mostly opprobrious; but if a precise meaning can be found for it this meaning may occasionally represent a virtue." (" 'Rhetoric' and Poetic Drama," in *The Sacred Wood*, 7th ed.; 1950.) **—BG**

rhetorical adjective **1** *rhetorical devices* STYLISTIC, oratorical, linguistic, verbal. See table on page 774.

2 *rhetorical hyperbole* EXTRAVAGANT, grandiloquent, magniloquent, high-flown, orotund, bombastic, grandiose, pompous, pretentious, overblown, oratorical, turgid, flowery, florid; *informal* highfalutin; *rare* fustian.

rhyme noun an amusing rhyme by Ogden Nash POEM, piece of poetry, verse; **(rhymes)** poetry, doggerel.

WORD NOTE **rhyme**

An identity of vowels followed by different consonants in the final, or last accented, syllables of two or more words (or sometimes within the same word, e.g., *bandstand*). Rhyme in poetry is old-fashioned, and in pop music, anything goes (Madonna often eschews rhyme). It may be only in show tunes that strict rhyme is still necessary, and that's only because it's hard to tell what people are singing in the theater, but it's often essential for audience comprehension of plot points, and rhyme definitely helps. **—SM**

RHETORICAL DEVICES

allusion	hyperbole
amplification	hypocorisma
anacoluthon	hypophora
anadiplosis	hypotaxis
analogy	hysteron proteron
anaphora	kenning
antanagoge	litotes
anthimeria	malapropism
antimetabole	meiosis
antiphrasis	meronym
antithesis	metabasis
apophasis	metanoia
aporia	metaphor
aposiopesis	metonymy
apostrophe	onomatopoeia
appositive	oxymoron
assonance	paralipsis
asyndeton	parallelism
catachresis	parataxis
chiasmus	parenthesis
climax	paronomasia
conduplicatio	personification
diacope	pleonasm
dirimens copulatio	polysyndeton
distinctio	procatalepsis
dystmesis	prosopopoeia
ellipsis	rhetorical question
enthymeme	scesis onomaton
enumeratio	sententia
epanalepsis	simile
epimone	syllepsis
epistrophe	symploce
epithet	syncope
epizeuxis	synecdoche
eponym	tmesis
exemplum	trope
expletive	understatement
hendiadys	zeugma
hyperbaton	

rhythm noun **1** *the rhythm of the music* BEAT, cadence, tempo, time, pulse, throb, swing.

2 *poetic features such as rhythm* METER, measure, stress, accent, cadence.

3 *the rhythm of daily life* PATTERN, flow, tempo.

rhythmic adjective *rhythmic background music* RHYTHMICAL, with a steady pulse, measured, throbbing, beating, pulsating, regular, steady, even; *informal* foot-tapping.

ribald adjective See CRUDE sense 3.

ribbon noun *a hat decorated with red and white ribbons* STRIP, tape, band, cord.

rice noun See table at CEREAL.

rich adjective **1** *rich people* WEALTHY, affluent, moneyed, well off, well-to-do, prosperous, opulent, silk-stocking; *informal* rolling in money, rolling in it, rolling in (the) dough, in the money, loaded, flush, stinking rich, filthy rich, well-heeled, made of money. See note at WEALTHY. See also word spectrum on page 775. ANTONYM poor.

2 *rich furnishings* SUMPTUOUS, opulent, luxurious, luxury, deluxe, lavish, gorgeous, splendid, magnificent, costly, expensive, fancy; *informal* posh, plush, ritzy, swanky, classy, swank. ANTONYMS plain, austere.

3 *a garden* ***rich in*** *flowers* ABOUNDING IN, full of, well provided with, well stocked in/with, crammed with, packed with, teeming with, bursting with; *informal* jam-packed with, chockablock with, chock-full of.

4 *a rich supply of restaurants* PLENTIFUL, abundant, copious, ample, profuse, lavish, liberal, generous, bountiful; *literary* plenteous, bounteous. ANTONYMS poor, meager.

5 *rich soil* FERTILE, productive, fecund, fruitful. ANTONYM barren.

6 *a rich sauce* CREAMY, heavy, full-flavored, fatty. ANTONYMS delicate, light.

7 *a rich wine* FULL-BODIED, heavy, fruity. ANTONYM light.

8 *rich colors* STRONG, deep, full, intense, vivid, brilliant. ANTONYMS delicate, pastel.

9 *her rich voice* SONOROUS, full, resonant, deep, clear, mellow, mellifluous, full-throated. ANTONYMS thin, reedy.

riches plural noun **1** *his newfound riches* MONEY, wealth, funds, cash, (filthy) lucre, wherewithal, means, assets, liquid assets, capital, resources, reserves; opulence, affluence, prosperity; *informal* dough, bread, loot, shekels, moola, bucks, dinero, jack.

2 *a cache of underwater riches* RESOURCES, treasure(s), bounty; jewels, gems.

richly adverb **1** *the richly furnished chamber* SUMPTUOUSLY, opulently, luxuriously, lavishly, gorgeously, splendidly, magnificently; *informal* plushly, ritzily, swankily, classily. ANTONYMS meanly, shabbily.

2 *the joy she richly deserves* FULLY, thoroughly, in full measure, well, completely, wholly, totally, entirely, absolutely, amply, utterly.

rickety adjective *rickety stairs* SHAKY, unsteady, unsound, unsafe, tumbledown, broken-down, dilapidated, ramshackle.

rid verb *ridding the building of asbestos* CLEAR, free, purge, empty, strip. PHRASE: **get rid of 1** *we must get rid of some stuff* DISPOSE OF, throw away, throw out, clear out, discard, scrap, dump, jettison, divest oneself of; *informal* chuck, ditch, junk, trash, deep-six. **2** *the cats got rid of the rats* DESTROY, eliminate, annihilate, obliterate, wipe out, kill.

riddle[1] noun *an answer to the riddle* PUZZLE, conundrum, brainteaser, problem, unsolved problem, question, poser, enigma, mystery, quandary; *informal* stumper.

THE RIGHT WORD

All of these terms imply something baffling or challenging. A **mystery** is anything that is incomprehensible to human reason, particularly if it invites speculation (*the mystery surrounding her sudden disappearance*). An **enigma** is a statement whose meaning is hidden under obscure or ambiguous allusions, so that we can only guess at its significance; it can also refer to a person of puzzling or contradictory character (*he remained an enigma throughout his long career*). A **riddle** is a mystery involving contradictory statements, with a hidden meaning designed to be guessed at (*the old riddle about how many college graduates it takes to change a light bulb*). **Conundrum** applies specifically to a riddle phrased as a question, the answer to which usually involves a pun or a play on words, such as "What is black and white and read all over?"; conundrum can also refer to any puzzling or difficult situation. A **paradox** is a statement that seems self-contradictory or absurd, but in reality expresses a possible truth (*Francis Bacon's well-known paradox, "The most corrected copies are commonly the least correct"*). A **puzzle** is not necessarily a verbal statement, but it presents a problem with a particularly baffling solution or tests one's ingenuity or skill in coming up with a solution (*a crossword puzzle*).

► rich
wealthy
affluent
opulent
moneyed
propertied
substantial
prosperous
rolling in money
silk-stocking
loaded
rolling in it
made of money
in the money
stinking rich
filthy rich
flush
worth a packet
worth a bundle
on easy street
well-heeled
well-off
well-to-do
having money in the bank
thrifty
frugal
scrimping
counting one's pennies
in reduced circumstances
in straitened circumstances
badly off
short of money
a bit short
unable to make ends meet
broke
flat broke
strapped
cleaned out
skint
hard up
strapped for cash
without a penny (to one's name)
without two pennies to rub together
without a sou
without a red cent
as poor as a church mouse
stone broke
penniless
needy
needful
in need/want
underprivileged
deprived
poverty-stricken
moneyless
bust
in the red
in debt
bankrupt
insolvent
impecunious
impoverished
penurious
in penury
beggarly
beggared
indigent
destitute
pauperized
obolary
poor ◄

riddle[2] verb **1** *his car was riddled by gunfire* PERFORATE, pierce, puncture, pepper.

2 *he was riddled with cancer* PERMEATE, suffuse, fill, pervade, spread through, imbue, saturate, overrun, beset.

3 *the soil must be riddled* SIEVE, sift, strain, screen, filter.

ride verb **1** *she can ride a horse* SIT ON, mount, bestride; manage, handle, control.

2 *riding through the town on motorbikes* TRAVEL, move, proceed, make one's way; drive, cycle; trot, canter, gallop.

▸ noun *a ride in the new car* TRIP, journey, drive, run, excursion, outing, jaunt; lift; *informal* spin.

ridicule noun *she was subjected to ridicule* MOCKERY, derision, laughter, scorn, scoffing, contempt, jeering, sneering, sneers, jibes, jibing, teasing, taunts, taunting, badinage, chaffing, sarcasm, satire; *informal* kidding, ribbing, joshing, goofing, razzing. ANTONYM respect.

▸ verb *his theory was ridiculed* DERIDE, mock, laugh at, heap scorn on/upon, jeer at, jibe at, sneer at, treat with contempt, scorn, make fun of, poke fun at, scoff at, satirize, lampoon, burlesque, caricature, parody, tease, taunt, chaff; *informal* kid, rib, josh, razz.

ridiculous adjective **1** *she looked ridiculous in her dad's oversized shorts and striped socks* LAUGHABLE, absurd, comical, funny, hilarious, risible, droll, amusing, farcical, silly, ludicrous; *rare* derisible. ANTONYM serious.

2 *a ridiculous suggestion* SENSELESS, silly, foolish, foolhardy, stupid, inane, fatuous, childish, puerile, half-baked, harebrained, cockamamie, ill-thought-out, crackpot, idiotic. ANTONYM sensible.

3 *a ridiculous exaggeration* ABSURD, preposterous, ludicrous, risible, laughable, nonsensical, senseless, outrageous. See note at ABSURD. ANTONYM reasonable.

rife adjective **1** *violence is rife* WIDESPREAD, general, common, universal, extensive, ubiquitous, omnipresent, endemic, inescapable, insidious, prevalent. See note at PREVALENT. ANTONYMS scarce, unknown.

2 *the village was rife with gossip* OVERFLOWING, bursting, alive, teeming, abounding. ANTONYM devoid.

riffraff noun *this government considers its citizens riffraff and is quick to silence the mere whispers of dissent* RABBLE, scum, good-for-nothings, undesirables, lowlifes, hoi polloi, the lowest of the low; *informal* peasants. ANTONYM elite.

rifle verb **1** *she rifled through her closet* RUMMAGE, search, hunt, forage.

2 *a thief rifled her home* BURGLE, burglarize, rob, steal from, loot, raid, plunder, ransack.

▸ noun *he refused to register the rifle* FIREARM, gun, shotgun, 30-30; *trademark* Winchester.

rift noun **1** *a deep rift in the ice* CRACK, fault, flaw, split, break, breach, fissure, fracture, cleft, crevice, cavity, opening.

2 *the rift between them* BREACH, division, split; quarrel, squabble, disagreement, falling-out, row, argument, dispute, conflict, feud; estrangement; *informal* spat, scrap.

USAGE NOTE **riff, rift**

These two are sometimes confused. *Riff* is now largely confined to jazz and pop-music contexts. It refers to a melodic phrase, usually repeated and often played in unison by several instruments; sometimes it's a variation on a tune, and it may be either an accompaniment to a solo or the only melodic element—e.g.: "With guitar riffs so rudimentary they seem to have been made up on the spot, . . . the U.K. sextet played with rude ebullience." (*Chicago Tribune*; Sept. 29, 2000.) The term dates only from the mid-twentieth century—and has little discernible relation to the older, mostly obsolete senses of *riff* (= [1] a string of onions, [2] the diaphragm, or [3] the mange; an itchy rash). That's probably because this particular *riff* seems to have originated as a truncated form of the musical term *refrain*.

Rift arose in Middle English in the sense "a fissure or divide; a split or crack"—the meaning it still carries—e.g.: "Word out of Washington is that Bondra wants to change teams because of a rift with coach Ron Wilson." (*Boston Globe*; Oct. 1, 2000.) Occasionally the term also refers to the rapids formed by rocks protruding from the bed of a stream. It formerly also meant "a burp"—a sense long obsolete.

Although the *Oxford English Dictionary* records two early-seventeenth-century uses of *riff* in the obsolete sense "rift, chink," the modern use of the word in that sense appears to be nothing more than rank word-swapping resulting from sound association—e.g.: "The way he sees it, things aren't bad at all. No riffs [read *rifts*] between him and crew chief Todd Parrott." (*USA Today*; May 26, 2000.) **—BG**

---

rig[1] verb **1** *the boats were rigged with a single sail* EQUIP, fit out, supply, furnish, provide, arm.

2 *I* ***rigged*** *myself* ***out*** *in black* DRESS, clothe, attire, robe, garb, array, deck out, drape, accoutre, outfit, get up, trick out/up; *informal* doll up; *archaic* apparel.

3 *he will* ***rig up*** *a shelter* SET UP, erect, assemble, build; throw together, cobble together, put together, whip up, improvise, contrive.

▸ noun **1** *a CB radio rig* APPARATUS, appliance, machine, device, instrument, contraption, system; tackle, gear, kit, outfit.

2 *the rig of a Civil War cavalry officer* UNIFORM, costume, ensemble, outfit, livery, attire, clothes, clothing, garments, dress, garb, regalia, trappings; *informal* getup, gear, togs, kit; *formal* apparel; *archaic* raiment, vestments.

rig[2] verb *they rigged the election* MANIPULATE, engineer, distort, misrepresent, pervert, tamper with, doctor; falsify, fake, trump up; *informal* fix, fiddle with.

right adjective **1** *it wouldn't be right to do that* JUST, fair, proper, good, upright, righteous, virtuous, moral, ethical, honorable, honest; lawful, legal. See word spectrum on page 777. ANTONYMS wrong, unjust.

2 *Mr. Hubert had the right answer* CORRECT, accurate, exact, precise; proper, valid, conventional, established, official, formal. ANTONYMS wrong, inaccurate.

3 *the right person for the job* SUITABLE, appropriate, fitting, correct, proper, desirable, preferable, ideal; *archaic* meet. ANTONYMS wrong, unsuitable.

4 *you've come at the right time* OPPORTUNE, advantageous, favorable, propitious, good, lucky, happy, fortunate, providential, felicitous; timely, seasonable, convenient, expedient, suitable, appropriate. ANTONYMS wrong, inopportune.

5 *he's not right in the head* SANE, lucid, rational, balanced, together, compos mentis; healthy, well; *informal* all there. ANTONYMS non compos mentis, insane.

6 *my right hand* DEXTRAL. ANTONYM left.

▸ adverb **1** *she was right at the limit of her patience* COMPLETELY, fully, totally, absolutely, utterly, thoroughly, quite.

2 *right in the middle of the village* EXACTLY, precisely, directly, immediately, just, squarely, dead; *informal* bang, smack, plumb, smack dab.

3 *keep going right ahead* STRAIGHT, directly. ANTONYM indirectly.

4 *informal he'll be right down* STRAIGHT, immediately, instantly, at once, straightaway, now, right now, this minute, directly, forthwith, without further ado, promptly, quickly, as soon as possible, ASAP, in short order; *informal* straight off, PDQ (pretty damn quick), pronto, lickety-split. ANTONYMS sometime, later.

5 *I think I heard right* CORRECTLY, accurately, properly, precisely, aright, rightly, perfectly. ANTONYM wrong.

6 *make sure you're treated right by the authorities* WELL, properly, justly, fairly, nicely, equitably, impartially, honorably, lawfully, legally, ethically. ANTONYM unjustly.

7 *things will turn out right* WELL, for the best, favorably, happily, advantageously, profitably, providentially, luckily, conveniently. ANTONYM badly.

▸ noun **1** *the difference between right and wrong* GOODNESS, righteousness, virtue, integrity, rectitude, propriety, morality, truth, honesty, honor, justice, fairness, equity; lawfulness, legality. ANTONYM wrong.

2 *you have the right to say no* ENTITLEMENT, prerogative, privilege, advantage, due, birthright, liberty, authority, power, license, permission, dispensation, leave, sanction, freedom; *Law, historical* droit.

▸ verb **1** *the way to right a capsized dinghy* SET UPRIGHT, turn back over.

2 *we must right the situation* REMEDY, put right, rectify, retrieve, fix, resolve, sort out, settle, square; straighten out, correct, repair, mend, redress, make good, ameliorate, better.

PHRASES: **by rights** *by rights, these kids should have been offered a decent education* PROPERLY, correctly, technically, in fairness; legally, de jure. **in the right** *please explain why you think you're in the right* JUSTIFIED, vindicated. **put right.** See RIGHT verb sense 2. **right away** *we'll miss the bus if we don't leave right away* AT ONCE, straightaway, now, right now, this minute, this very minute, this instant, immediately, instantly, directly, forthwith, without further ado, promptly, quickly, without delay, as soon as possible, ASAP, in short order; *informal* straight off, PDQ (pretty damn quick), pronto, lickety-split. **within one's rights** *Mr. Barnes is within his rights to dispute the charges to his account* ENTITLED, permitted, allowed, at liberty, empowered, authorized, qualified, licensed, justified.

righteous adjective **1** *righteous living* GOOD, virtuous, upright, upstanding, decent; ethical, principled, moral, high-minded, law-abiding, honest, honorable, blameless, irreproachable, noble; saintly, angelic, pure. See note at MORAL. ANTONYM sinful.

2 *righteous anger* JUSTIFIABLE, justified, legitimate, defensible, supportable, rightful; admissible, allowable, understandable, excusable, acceptable, reasonable. ANTONYM unjustifiable.

rightful adjective **1** *the car's rightful owner* LEGAL, lawful, real, true, proper, correct, recognized, genuine, au-

right
exact
meet
authoritative
canonical
de règle
faultless
perfect
precise
meticulous
unerring
exact
official
orthodox
accurate
proper
correct
errorless
error-free
valid
word for word
unambiguous
on the money
on the mark
bang on
spot on
reliable
conventional
established
accepted
okay
passable
iffy
open to question
vague
unconvincing
implausible
dicey
dodgy
flimsy
shaky
weak
tenuous
unsupported
questionable
full of holes
unsound
doubtful
disreputable
suspect
distorted
garbled
mistaken
untrue
not true
not right
wide of the mark
out
off-target
flawed
faulty
fallible
inaccurate
unreliable
imperfect
inexact
imprecise
incorrect
erroneous
false
dubious
unsubstantiated
falsified
specious
fallacious
wrong

thentic, acknowledged, approved, licensed, valid, bona fide, de jure; *informal* legit, kosher.

2 *their rightful place in society* DESERVED, merited, due, just, right, fair, proper, fitting, appropriate, suitable.

right-wing adjective CONSERVATIVE, rightist, right-of-center, right-leaning, ultraconservative; blimpish, die-hard; reactionary, traditionalist, conventional, unprogressive; fascist. ANTONYM left-wing.

rigid adjective **1** *a rigid container* STIFF, hard, firm, inflexible, unbending, unyielding, inelastic. ANTONYM flexible.

2 *a rigid routine* FIXED, set, firm, inflexible, unalterable, unchangeable, immutable, unvarying, invariable, hard and fast, cast-iron, ironclad. ANTONYM flexible.

3 *a rigid approach to funding* STRICT, severe, stern, stringent, rigorous, inflexible, uncompromising, intransigent. ANTONYMS flexible, lenient.

rigmarole noun **1** *the rigmarole of dressing up* FUSS, bother, trouble, palaver, ado, pother, song and dance, performance, to-do, pantomime, hassle, folderol.

2 *that rigmarole about the house being haunted* TALE, saga, yarn, shaggy-dog story; *informal* spiel.

rigor noun **1** *a mine operated under conditions of rigor* STRICTNESS, severity, stringency, toughness, harshness, rigidity, inflexibility, intransigence.

2 *intellectual rigor* METICULOUSNESS, thoroughness, carefulness, diligence, scrupulousness, exactness, exactitude, precision, accuracy, correctness, strictness.

3 **(rigors)** *the rigors of the journey* HARDSHIP, harshness, severity, adversity; ordeal, misery, trial; discomfort, inconvenience, privation.

rigorous adjective **1** *rigorous attention to detail* METICULOUS, conscientious, punctilious, careful, diligent, attentive, scrupulous, painstaking, exact, precise, accurate, thorough, particular, strict, demanding, exacting; *informal* persnickety. ANTONYM slapdash.

2 *the rigorous enforcement of rules* STRICT, severe, stern, stringent, tough, harsh, rigid, relentless, unsparing, inflexible, draconian, intransigent, uncompromising, exacting. ANTONYM lax.

3 *rigorous yachting conditions* HARSH, severe, bad, bleak, extreme, inclement; unpleasant, disagreeable, foul, nasty, filthy; stormy, wild, tempestuous. ANTONYMS gentle, mild.

rile verb *informal* *she's easy to rile.* See ANNOY.

rim noun **1** *the rim of her cup* BRIM, edge, lip.

2 *the rim of the crater* EDGE, border, side, margin, brink, fringe, boundary, perimeter, limits, periphery. See note at BORDER.

rind noun *dried lemon rind* SKIN, peel, zest, integument; *Botany* pericarp.

ring[1] noun **1** *the rings around Saturn* CIRCLE, band, loop, hoop, halo, disk.

2 *she wore a ring* WEDDING RING, wedding band, band.

3 *a circus ring* ARENA, enclosure, field, ground; amphitheater, stadium.

4 *a ring of onlookers* CIRCLE, group, cluster, bunch, band, throng, crowd, flock, pack.

5 *a spy ring* GANG, syndicate, cartel, mob, band, circle, organization, association, society, alliance, league, coterie, cabal, cell.

▸ verb *police ringed the building* SURROUND, circle, encircle, encompass, girdle, enclose, hem in, confine, seal off.

ring[2] verb 1 *church bells rang all day* TOLL, sound, peal, chime, clang, bong, ding, jingle, tinkle; *literary* knell.

2 *the room rang with laughter* RESOUND, reverberate, resonate, echo.

▸ noun *the ring of a bell* CHIME, toll, peal, clang, clink, ding, jingle, tinkle, tintinnabulation, sound; *literary* knell.

PHRASE: **ring something in** *our biggest sale of the season will ring in the new year* HERALD, signal, announce, proclaim, usher in, introduce; mark, signify, indicate; *literary* betoken, knell.

rinse verb *the campers rinsed their socks and hung them near the fire* WASH, wash out, clean, cleanse, bathe; dip, drench, splash, hose down.

riot noun 1 *a riot in the capital* UPROAR, commotion, upheaval, disturbance, furor, tumult, melee, scuffle, fracas, fray, brawl, free-for-all; violence, fighting, vandalism, mayhem, turmoil, lawlessness, anarchy, violent protest.

2 *the garden was a riot of color* MASS, sea, splash, show, exhibition.

▸ verb *the miners rioted* RAMPAGE, go on the rampage, run riot, fight in the streets, run wild, run amok, go berserk; *informal* raise hell.

PHRASE: **run riot** 1 *the children ran riot* GO ON THE RAMPAGE, rampage, riot, run amok, go berserk, go out of control; *informal* raise hell. 2 *the vegetation has run riot* GROW PROFUSELY, spread uncontrolled, grow rapidly, spread like wildfire; burgeon, multiply, rocket, skyrocket.

riotous adjective 1 *the demonstration turned riotous* UNRULY, rowdy, disorderly, uncontrollable, unmanageable, undisciplined, uproarious, tumultuous; violent, wild, ugly, lawless, anarchic. ANTONYM peaceable.

2 *a riotous party* BOISTEROUS, lively, loud, noisy, unrestrained, uninhibited, uproarious, unruly, rollicking, knockabout; *informal* rambunctious. ANTONYM restrained.

rip verb 1 *he ripped the posters down* TEAR, wrench, wrest, pull, snatch, tug, pry, heave, drag, peel, pluck; *informal* yank.

2 *she ripped Leo's note into pieces* TEAR, claw, hack, slit, cut; *literary* rend.

▸ noun *a rip in my sleeve* TEAR, slit, split, rent, laceration, cut, gash, slash.

ripe adjective 1 *a ripe tomato* MATURE, ripened, full grown, ready to eat; luscious, juicy, tender, sweet. ANTONYM green.

2 *the dock is ripe for development* READY, fit, suitable, right. ANTONYMS unsuitable, unready.

3 *the ripe old age of ninety* ADVANCED, hoary, venerable, old.

4 *the time is ripe for his return* OPPORTUNE, advantageous, favorable, auspicious, propitious, promising, good, right, fortunate, benign, providential, felicitous, seasonable; convenient, suitable, appropriate, apt, fitting. ANTONYM unsuitable.

ripen verb *we let the grapes ripen on the vine* BECOME RIPE, mature, mellow. See note at MATURE.

rip-off noun *informal the insurance policy turned out to be a rip-off* FRAUD, cheat, deception, swindle, confidence trick; *informal* con, scam, flimflam, gyp, rip, gouge, shakedown, bunco.

riposte noun *an indignant riposte* RETORT, counter, rejoinder, sally, return, answer, reply, response; *informal* comeback.

▸ verb *"Heaven help you," riposted Alicia* RETORT, counter, rejoin, return, retaliate, hurl back, answer, reply, respond, come back.

ripple noun *he blew ripples in his coffee* WAVELET, wave, undulation, ripplet, ridge, ruffle.

▸ verb *a breeze rippled the lake* FORM RIPPLES ON, ruffle, wrinkle.

rise verb 1 *the sun rose* MOVE UP/UPWARDS, come up, make one's/its way up, arise, ascend, climb, mount, soar. ANTONYMS fall, descend, set.

2 *the mountains rising above us* LOOM, tower, soar, rise up, rear (up).

3 *prices rose* GO UP, increase, soar, shoot up, surge, leap, jump, rocket, escalate, spiral. ANTONYM drop.

4 *living standards have risen* IMPROVE, get better, advance, go up, soar, shoot up. ANTONYM worsen.

5 *her voice rose* GET HIGHER, grow, increase, become louder, swell, intensify. ANTONYM drop.

6 *he rose from his chair* STAND UP, get to one's feet, get up, jump up, leap up; *formal* arise. ANTONYM sit.

7 *she rises at dawn* GET UP, get out of bed, rouse oneself, stir, bestir oneself, be up and about; *informal* rise and shine, surface; *formal* arise. ANTONYMS retire, go to bed.

8 *the court rose at midday* ADJOURN, recess, be suspended, pause, take a break; *informal* knock off, take five. ANTONYMS resume, continue.

9 *he rose through the ranks* MAKE PROGRESS, climb, advance, get on, work one's way, be promoted.

10 *she wouldn't **rise to** the bait* REACT TO, respond to; take.

11 *on the third day, Christ rose* COME BACK TO LIFE, be resurrected, revive. ANTONYM die.

12 *the dough started to rise* SWELL, expand, enlarge, puff up.

13 *the nation rose against its oppressors* REBEL, revolt, mutiny, riot, take up arms. ANTONYM kowtow.

14 *the river **rises in** the mountains* ORIGINATE IN, begin in, start in, emerge in/from; issue from, spring from, flow from, emanate from.

15 *her spirits rose* BRIGHTEN, lift, cheer up, improve, pick up; *informal* buck up.

16 *the ground rose gently* SLOPE UPWARD, go uphill, incline, climb. ANTONYMS drop away, drop.

▸ noun 1 *a price rise* INCREASE, hike, leap, upsurge, upswing, climb, escalation.

2 *a rise in standards* IMPROVEMENT, amelioration, upturn, leap.

3 *her rise to power* PROGRESS, climb, promotion, elevation, aggrandizement.

4 *we walked up the rise* SLOPE, incline, hillock, hill; *formal* eminence.

risible adjective *a risible comedy routine from their old radio days* LAUGHABLE, ridiculous, absurd, comical, comic, amusing, funny, hilarious, humorous, droll, farcical, silly, ludicrous, hysterical; *informal* rib-tickling, priceless.

risk noun 1 *there is a certain amount of risk* CHANCE, uncertainty, unpredictability, precariousness, instability, insecurity, perilousness, riskiness. ANTONYM safety.

2 *the risk of fire* POSSIBILITY, chance, probability, likelihood, danger, peril, threat, menace, fear, prospect. ANTONYM impossibility.

▸ verb 1 *he risked his life to save them* ENDANGER, imperil, jeopardize, hazard, gamble, gamble with, chance; put on the line, put in jeopardy.

2 *you risk getting cold and wet* CHANCE, stand a chance of.

PHRASE: **at risk** *our soldiers are at risk every day* IN DANGER, in peril, in jeopardy, under threat.

risky adjective *risky sports* DANGEROUS, hazardous, perilous, high-risk, fraught with danger, unsafe, insecure, precarious, touch-and-go, treacherous, parlous; uncertain, unpredictable; *informal* chancy, dicey, hairy.

risqué adjective *risqué stories* RIBALD, rude, bawdy, racy, earthy, indecent, suggestive, improper, naughty, locker-room; vulgar, dirty, smutty, crude, coarse, obscene, lewd, X-rated; *informal* blue, raunchy; off-color.

rite noun *a religious rite practiced for thousands of years* CEREMONY, ritual, ceremonial; service, sacrament, liturgy, worship, office; act, practice, custom, tradition, convention, institution, procedure.

ritual noun *an elaborate civic ritual* CEREMONY, rite, ceremonial, observance; service, sacrament, liturgy, worship; act, practice, custom, tradition, convention, formality, procedure, protocol.

▸ adjective *a ritual burial* CEREMONIAL, ritualistic, prescribed, set, formal; sacramental, liturgical; traditional, conventional.

ritzy adjective *informal they're living in a ritzy apartment in Manhattan.* See POSH.

rival noun 1 *his rival for the nomination* OPPONENT, challenger, competitor, contender; adversary, antagonist, enemy; *literary* foe. ANTONYM ally.

2 *the tool has no rival* EQUAL, match, peer, equivalent, counterpart, like.

▸ verb *few countries can rival ours for natural resources* MATCH, compare with, compete with, vie with, equal, measure up to, be in the same league as, be on a par with, touch, challenge; *informal* hold a candle to.

▸ adjective *rival candidates* COMPETING, opposing, contending.

rivalry noun *a growing rivalry between the two groups* COMPETITIVENESS, competition, contention, vying; opposition, conflict, feuding, antagonism, friction, enmity.

riven adjective *a country riven by civil war* TORN APART, split, rent, severed; *literary* cleft, torn asunder.

river noun 1 *the old factories along the river* WATERCOURSE, waterway, tributary, stream, rivulet, brook, inlet, rill, runnel, freshet; bourn; creek.

2 *a river of molten lava* STREAM, torrent, flood, deluge, cascade. PHRASE: **sell down the river** *informal* . See DOUBLE-CROSS.

riveted adjective 1 *she just stood there, absolutely riveted* FIXED, rooted, frozen, unable to move; motionless, unmoving, immobile, stock-still.

2 *he was riveted by the newsreels* FASCINATED, engrossed, gripped, captivated, enthralled, spellbound, mesmerized, transfixed. ANTONYM bored.

3 *their eyes were riveted on the teacher* FIXED, fastened, focused, concentrated, locked.

riveting adjective *the final chapter was riveting* FASCINATING, gripping, engrossing, interesting, intriguing, absorbing, captivating, enthralling, compelling, spellbinding, mesmerizing; *informal* unputdownable. ANTONYM boring.

road noun 1 *the roads were crowded with traffic.* See table.

2 *a step on the road to recovery* WAY, path, route, course. PHRASE: **on the road** *the band will be on the road for two months* ON TOUR, touring, traveling.

ROADS

access road	interstate
avenue	lane
back road	lovers' land
beltway	one-way street
boulevard	overpass
broadway	parkway
bush road	pass
bylane	post road
bypass	ring road
byroad	roadway
byway	secondary road
causeway	service road
circle	shunpike
cloverleaf	side road
country road	speedway
crescent	street
cul-de-sac	surface road
dead-end street	thoroughfare
dirt road	thruway/throughway
drag strip	toll road
drive	tote road
expressway	trail
feeder road	turnpike
freeway	underpass
frontage road	walk
grid road	walkway
highway	

roadblock noun *the police have set up a roadblock just before the bridge* BARRIER, barricade, obstruction, checkpoint.

roam verb *he had roamed the countryside for nine years* WANDER, rove, ramble, drift, walk, traipse; range, travel, tramp, traverse, trek; *informal* cruise, mosey around/about; *formal* perambulate; *archaic* peregrinate.

roar noun 1 *the roars of the crowd* SHOUT, bellow, yell, cry, howl; clamor; *informal* holler.

2 *the roar of the sea* BOOM, crash, rumble, roll, thundering.

3 *roars of laughter* GUFFAW, howl, hoot, shriek, gale, peal.

▸ verb 1 *"Get out!" roared Angus* BELLOW, yell, shout, bawl, howl; *informal* holler.

2 *thunder roared* BOOM, rumble, crash, roll, thunder.

3 *the movie left them roaring* GUFFAW, laugh, hoot; *informal* split one's sides, be rolling in the aisles, be doubled up, crack up, be in stitches, die laughing.

4 *a motorbike roared past* SPEED, zoom, whiz, flash; belt, tear, zip, bomb.

roaring adjective 1 *a roaring fire* BLAZING, burning, flaming.

2 *informal* *a roaring success* ENORMOUS, huge, massive, great, very great, tremendous; complete, out-and-out, thorough; *informal* rip-roaring, whopping, fantastic.

roast verb 1 *potatoes roasted in olive oil* COOK, bake, grill, broil.

2 *informal* *they roasted him for wasting time.* See CRITICIZE.

roasting *informal* noun *the boss gave him a roasting.* See LECTURE noun sense 2.

rob verb 1 *the gang robbed the local bank* BURGLE, burglarize, steal from, hold up, break into; raid, loot, plunder, pillage; *informal* knock off, stick up.

2 *he robbed an old woman* STEAL FROM; *informal* mug, jump, roll.

3 *she was robbed of her savings* CHEAT (OUT), swindle (out), defraud (out); *informal* do out, con out, fleece (out); *informal* stiff (out).

4 *informal* *if you paid $300 for that watch, you were robbed* OVERCHARGE; *informal* rip off, sting, have, diddle, gouge.

5 *a dubious call robbed him of his championship title* DEPRIVE, strip, divest; deny.

robber noun *the robbers fled the scene in a blue Camaro* BURGLAR, thief, housebreaker, mugger, shoplifter, purse-snatcher; stealer, pilferer, raider, looter, plunderer, pillager; bandit; pirate; *informal* crook, yegg, second-story man; *literary* brigand, highwayman.

robbery noun 1 *they were arrested for the robbery* BURGLARY, theft, thievery, stealing, breaking and entering, housebreaking, larceny, shoplifting, purse-snatching; embezzlement, fraud; holdup, break-in, raid; *informal* mugging, stickup, heist.

2 *informal* *Six bucks? That's robbery!* A SWINDLE; *informal* a rip-off, a gyp, a con, a con job.

robe noun 1 *they put on their robes after swimming* BATHROBE, dressing gown, kimono, housecoat, kaftan, cover-up, wrapper.

2 *she wore a fur-trimmed red robe* CLOAK, wrap, mantle, cape.

3 **(robes)** *coronation robes* GARB, regalia, costume, finery; garments, clothes; *formal* apparel; *archaic* raiment, habiliments, vestments.

4 **(robes)** *priestly robes* VESTMENT, surplice, cassock, soutane, rochet, alb, dalmatic, chasuble, tunicle, Geneva gown; canonicals.

▸ verb *he robed for Mass* DRESS, vest, clothe oneself; *formal* enrobe.

robot noun *robots can perform certain tasks that are considered hazardous for humans* AUTOMATON, android, golem; *informal* bot, droid.

robust adjective 1 *a large, robust man* STRONG, vigorous, sturdy, tough, powerful, solid, muscular, sinewy, rugged, hardy, strapping, brawny, burly, husky; healthy, fit, fighting fit, hale and hearty, lusty, in fine fettle; *informal* beefy, hunky. ANTONYMS frail, weak.

2 *these knives are robust* DURABLE, resilient, tough, hard-wearing, long-lasting, sturdy, strong. ANTONYM fragile.

3 *a robust commodities market* STRONG, healthy, resilient, invulnerable; productive, profitable. ANTONYM vulnerable.

4 *a robust red wine* STRONG, full-bodied, flavorful, rich. ANTONYMS tasteless, insipid.

rock[1] verb 1 *the ship rocked on the water* MOVE TO AND FRO, move back and forth, sway, seesaw; roll, pitch, plunge, toss, lurch, reel, list; wobble, oscillate.

2 *the building began to rock* SHAKE, vibrate, quake, tremble.

3 *Wall Street was rocked by the news* STUN, shock, stagger, astonish, startle, surprise, shake, shake up, take aback, throw, unnerve, disconcert.

4 *informal* *this game totally rocks* BE IMPRESSIVE; *informal* kick butt, blow one away, blow one's mind, rock one's world, be cool, be on fire.

rock[2] noun 1 *a gully strewn with rocks* BOULDER, stone, pebble. See table.

2 *a castle built on a rock* CRAG, cliff, outcrop.

3 *Toni was the rock on which they relied* FOUNDATION, cornerstone, support, prop, mainstay; tower of strength, bulwark, anchor.

4 *informal* *she wore a massive rock on her finger* DIAMOND, jewel, precious stone. PHRASE: **on the rocks** *informal* 1 *her marriage is on the rocks* IN DIFFICULTY, in trouble, breaking up, over; in tatters, in ruins, ruined. 2 *a Scotch on the rocks* WITH ICE, on ice, over ice.

ROCKS

Metamorphic
amphibolite
blueschist
eclogite
epidiorite
epidosite
gneiss
granulite
hornfels
lazurite
marble
mica schist
mylonite
phyllite
psammite
pyroxenite
quartzite
schist
serpentinite
slate
verdite

Sedimentary
arenite
argillite
breccia
chalk
chert
claystone
coal
conglomerate
diatomite
dolomite
flint
ironstone
limestone
marl
mudstone
oil shale
oolite
pholphorite
pisolite
radiolarite
rag
rudite
sandstone
shale
siltstone
tillite

Igneous
andesite
anorthosite
aplite
basalt
diorite
dolerite
dunite
elvan
felsite
gabbro
granite
greenstone
kimberlite
lamprophyre
lava
monzonite
obsidian
ophiolite
pegmatite
peridotite
phonolite
picrite
porphyry
pumice
rhyolite
syenite
tephrite
tonalite
trachyte
trap rock
tuff
variolite
vitrophyre

rocket noun **1** *guerrillas fired rockets at them* MISSILE, projectile.

2 *they lit some colorful rockets* FIREWORK, firecracker, Roman candle.

▸ verb **1** *prices have rocketed* SHOOT UP, soar, increase, rise, escalate, spiral; *informal* go through the roof. ANTONYM plummet.

2 *they rocketed into the alley* SPEED, zoom, shoot, whiz, career; *informal* barrel, tear, bomb, hightail it.

rocky[1] adjective *a rocky path* STONY, pebbly, shingly; rough, bumpy; craggy, mountainous.

rocky[2] adjective **1** *that table's rocky* UNSTEADY, shaky, unstable, wobbly, tottery, rickety, flimsy. ANTONYMS steady, stable.

2 *a rocky marriage* DIFFICULT, problematic, precarious, unstable, unreliable, undependable; *informal* iffy, up and down. ANTONYMS solid, stable.

rococo adjective *rococo draperies* ORNATE, fancy, elaborate, extravagant, baroque; fussy, busy, ostentatious, showy; flowery, florid, flamboyant, high-flown, magniloquent, orotund, bombastic, overwrought, overblown, inflated, turgid; *informal* highfalutin. ANTONYM plain.

WORD NOTE **rococo, baroque**

In the complex, intricate, sometimes confusing and generally Byzantine world of choice and subtlety that is the English language, it is sometimes necessary to decide whether, in describing things that are similarly complex, intricate, and Byzantine, it is proper to employ the adjective *rococo* or *baroque.* Essentially the words have senses which are synonymous, though their etymologies (both have French origins) are not: *rococo* has something to do with ornate shell- or pebble-based decoration, while *baroque* may stem, oddly, from the very same root that gives us the far less appealing word *verruca,* the highly transmissible plantar wart to which the feet of summertime athletes are prone. In view of this displeasing association, *baroque* might seem to lean in a subtly pejorative direction—except that with the typical perversity of the language, usage suggests quite otherwise. *Rococo* has now come to mean tastelessly and tackily florid and ornate, while *baroque* is merely curlicued and frantically odd, but only whimsically so. Thus if it—whether by 'it' we mean a hairpiece, a chair leg, or a State of the Union address—is complicated, intricate, and vulgar, it is *rococo.* If it is merely endowed with flowery intricacy, but is more or less acceptable to a person of reasonable taste, it is best described simply as *baroque.* **–SW**

rod noun **1** *an iron rod* BAR, stick, pole, baton, staff; shaft, strut, rail, spoke.

2 *the ceremonial rod* STAFF, mace, scepter.

3 **(the rod)** *instruction was accompanied by the rod* CORPORAL PUNISHMENT, the cane, the lash, the birch; beating, flogging, caning, birching.

rodent noun See table.

rogue noun **1** *a rogue without ethics* SCOUNDREL, villain, miscreant, reprobate, rascal, good-for-nothing, ne'er-do-well, wretch; *informal* rat, dog, louse, crook; *dated* cad; *archaic* blackguard, picaroon, knave.

2 *your boy's a little rogue* RASCAL, imp, devil, monkey; *informal* scamp, scalawag, monster, horror, terror, hellion.

roguish adjective **1** *a roguish character* UNPRINCIPLED, dishonest, deceitful, unscrupulous, untrustworthy, shameless; wicked, villainous; *informal* shady, scoundrelly, rascally; *archaic* knavish.

2 *a roguish grin* MISCHIEVOUS, playful, teasing, naughty, cheeky, wicked, impish, devilish, arch; *informal* waggish.

roister verb *the mansions in which wealthy families had once roistered* ENJOY ONESELF, celebrate, revel, carouse, frolic, romp, have fun, make merry, rollick; *informal* party, live it up, whoop it up, have a ball, make whoopee.

role noun **1** *a small role in the film* PART; character, cameo.

2 *his role as class president* CAPACITY, position, job, post, office, duty, responsibility, mantle, place; function, part.

roll verb **1** *the bottle rolled down the table* TURN ROUND AND ROUND, go round and round, turn over and over, spin, rotate.

2 *waiters rolled in the trolleys* WHEEL, push, trundle.

3 *we rolled past fields* TRAVEL, go, move, pass, cruise, sweep.

4 *the months* ***rolled by*** PASS, pass by, go by, slip by, fly by, elapse, wear on, march on.

5 *tears rolled down her cheeks* FLOW, run, course, stream, pour, spill, trickle.

6 *the mist rolled in* BILLOW, undulate, tumble.

7 *he rolled his handkerchief into a ball* WIND, coil, fold, curl; twist.

8 ***roll out*** *the pastry* FLATTEN (OUT), level (out); even out.

9 *they rolled about with laughter* STAGGER, lurch, reel, totter, teeter, wobble.

10 *the ship began to roll* LURCH, toss, rock, pitch, plunge, sway, reel, list, keel.

11 *thunder rolled* RUMBLE, reverberate, echo, resound, boom, roar, grumble.

▸ noun **1** *a roll of wrapping paper* CYLINDER, tube, scroll; bolt.

2 *a roll of film* REEL, spool.

RODENTS

agouti	jerboa
Arctic ground squirrel	jumping mouse
bandicoot rat	kangaroo mouse
beaver	kangaroo rat
black squirrel	lemming
brown rat	marmot
bushy-tailed woodrat	mole rat
capybara	mouse
cavy	muskrat
chinchilla	Norway rat
chipmunk	paca
collared lemming	pack rat
coypu	pocket gopher
deer mouse	porcupine
dormouse	prairie dog
field mouse	rat
flying squirrel	red squirrel
gerbil	squirrel
golden hamster	suslik
gopher	viscacha
gray squirrel	vole
groundhog	water rat
ground squirrel	water vole
guinea pig	woodchuck
hamster	woodmouse
hoary marmot	wood rat
house mouse	

3 *a roll of $20 bills* WAD, bundle.

4 *a roll of the dice* THROW, toss, turn, spin.

5 *crusty rolls* BREAD ROLL, bun, bagel, hoagie, kaiser roll. See table at BREAD.

6 *the electoral roll* LIST, register, directory, record, file, index, catalog, inventory; census.

7 *a roll of thunder* RUMBLE, reverberation, echo, boom, clap, crack, roar, grumble.

PHRASES: **roll in** *informal* 1 *money has been rolling in* POUR IN, flood in, flow in. 2 *he rolled in at nine o'clock* ARRIVE, turn up, appear, show one's face; *informal* show up, blow in. **rolling in it** *informal*. See RICH sense 1. **roll something out** *she rolled out her towel* UNROLL, spread out, unfurl, unfold, open (out), unwind, uncoil. **roll something up** *they rolled up the sleeping bags* FOLD (UP), furl, wind up, coil (up), bundle up.

rollicking adjective *a rollicking party* LIVELY, boisterous, exuberant, spirited; riotous, noisy, wild, rowdy, roisterous, knockabout; *informal* rambunctious.

roly-poly adjective *informal a roly-poly couple played the Clauses for the Christmas skit* CHUBBY, plump, fat, stout, rotund, round, dumpy, chunky, portly, overweight, fleshy, paunchy, bulky, corpulent; *informal* tubby, pudgy, beefy, porky, blubbery, zaftig, corn-fed. ANTONYM skinny.

romance noun 1 *their romance blossomed* LOVE, passion, ardor, adoration, devotion; affection, fondness, attachment.

2 *he's had many romances* LOVE AFFAIR, relationship, liaison, courtship, attachment; flirtation, dalliance.

3 *an author of historical romances* LOVE STORY, novel; romantic fiction; *informal* tearjerker, bodice-ripper.

4 *the romance of the Far East* MYSTERY, glamour, excitement, exoticism, mystique; appeal, allure, charm. See note at ROMANTIC.

▸ verb 1 *dated he was romancing Carolyn* WOO, chase, pursue; go out with, seduce; *informal* see, go steady with, date; *dated* court, make love to.

2 *I am romancing the past* ROMANTICIZE, idealize, paint a rosy picture of.

WORD NOTE **romance**

There's an itch in one's pants versifiers treat of,
And *romance* rhymes with *dance*
Whereas *love* rhymes with . . . *glove* . . .
If it's more than a tryst
Let us call it *romance.*
It may not exist,
But it's better than *love.*
—SM

romantic adjective 1 *he's so romantic* LOVING, amorous, passionate, tender, affectionate; *informal* lovey-dovey.

2 *the book was a bit too romantic for my tastes* SENTIMENTAL, mawkish, saccharine, syrupy; *informal* mushy, schmaltzy, gooey, treacly, cheesy, corny, sappy, soppy, cornball. See note at SENTIMENTAL. ANTONYMS unsentimental, gritty.

3 *a romantic setting* IDYLLIC, picturesque, fairy-tale; beautiful, lovely, charming, pretty.

4 *romantic notions of life in rural communities* IDEALISTIC, idealized, romanticized, unrealistic, fanciful, impractical; head-in-the-clouds, starry-eyed, optimistic, hopeful, visionary, Utopian, fairy-tale. ANTONYMS practical, realistic.

▸ noun *an incurable romantic* IDEALIST, sentimentalist, romanticist; dreamer, visionary, Utopian, Don Quixote, fantasist, fantasizer; *archaic* fantast. ANTONYM realist.

WORD NOTE **romantic, romance**

Play Ella Fitzgerald's rendition of "Isn't it Romantic," the Rodgers and Hart standard, and get in the mood. For what? For romance—the romance of the words *romance* and *romantic. Romance* is a subgenre of fiction, a type of comic book, the element of doo-wop rock and roll. But the *romantic* is also the province of medieval chivalry, opera and musical comedy, jazz, swing, slow dancing, and moonlight. The dance of the sexes rhymes with *romance,* and when Freud wants to convey that there are ambiguous erotic edges to the relationships we have with our fathers and mothers, our sisters and brothers, he uses the phrase "family romance." Joseph Conrad speaks of the "romance of illusions," which is almost a redundancy. *Romance* is sex without the dirt, Eros without disease and old age. *Romance* is poetry; marriage and its aftermath is prose (the novel). *Romance* is one half of the truth, of which death is the other. Who among poets would not want to be a *romantic*—or even better a *Romantic*—poet? No matter how well you know that Keats, Shelley, Byron, and Coleridge were Romantic poets in a whole other and more complicated sense, a part of you persists in seeing in the sickly and sensual Keats, the dashing Byron, the political maverick Shelley, and the opium-tripping Coleridge, a quality of heroism that seems hot with the passion of youth—the quality of *romance.* **—DL**

Romeo noun *so, who's the Romeo with Angeline?* LADIES' MAN, Don Juan, Casanova, Lothario, womanizer, playboy, lover, seducer, philanderer, flirt; gigolo; *informal* ladykiller, stud, chick magnet, babe magnet.

romp verb 1 *two fox cubs romped playfully* PLAY, frolic, frisk, gambol, skip, prance, caper, cavort, rollick; *dated* sport.

2 *Pittsburgh romped to a win* SAIL, coast, sweep; win hands down, run away with it; *informal* win by a mile.

roof PHRASE: **hit the roof** *informal Anna's going to hit the roof when she sees her broken windshield* BE VERY ANGRY, be furious, lose one's temper; *informal* go mad, go crazy, go wild, freak out, go bananas, have a fit, blow one's top, go postal, go ballistic, go up the wall, go off the deep end, go ape, flip.

room noun 1 *there isn't much room* SPACE; headroom, legroom; area, expanse, extent; *informal* elbow room.

2 *room for improvement* CAPACITY, scope, leeway, latitude, freedom; opportunity, chance.

3 *she wandered around the room* CHAMBER. See table on page 783.

4 **(rooms)** *he had rooms at the Plaza* ACCOMMODATIONS, quarters, lodgings; a suite, an apartment, an efficiency unit; *informal* a pad, digs.

▸ verb *she roomed there in September* BOARD, lodge, live, stay; be quartered, be housed, be billeted; *formal* dwell, reside, sojourn.

roomy adjective *a roomy apartment* | *roomy pants* SPACIOUS, capacious, sizable, generous, big, large, extensive; voluminous, ample; *formal* commodious. ANTONYMS cramped, tight-fitting.

root noun 1 *a plant's roots* rootstock, tuber, rootlet; *Botany* rhizome, radicle.

2 *the root of the problem* SOURCE, origin, germ, beginning(s), genesis; cause, reason, basis, foundation, bottom, seat; core, heart, nub, essence; *informal* ground zero.

3 (**roots**) *he rejected his roots* ORIGINS, beginnings, family, ancestors, predecessors, heritage; birthplace, homeland. See note at ORIGIN.

▸ verb **1** *has the shoot rooted?* TAKE ROOT, grow roots, establish, strike, take.

TYPES OF ROOMS

anteroom	laundry room
antechamber	lavatory
armory	library
assembly room	living room
attic	lobby
backroom	locker room
ballroom	loft
barroom	lounge
basement	lunchroom
bathroom	maid's room
bedchamber	mailroom
bedroom	men's room
boardroom	morning room
boiler room	mud room
boudoir	newsroom
breakfast nook	nursery
cabin	office
cell	operating room
cellar	operations room
chamber	oratory
change room	panic room
chapel	pantry
checkroom	parlor
classroom	playroom
cloakroom	poolroom
coatroom	powder room
cold room	receiving room
common room	recovery room
control room	rec room
conference room	restroom
conservatory	rubber room
courtroom	rumpus room
crying room	salesroom
cubbyhole	salon
cutting room	schoolroom
darkroom	scullery
day room	showroom
den	sitting room
dining room	situation room
dormitory	smoking room
drawing room	solarium
dressing room	staff room
dungeon	state room
emergency room	stockroom
engine room	storeroom
family room	strongroom
fitting room	studio
Florida room	study
foyer	suite
front room	sunroom
game room	tack room
garret	throne room
great room	trophy room
green room	utility room
grotto	vestiary
guardroom	vestibule
guest room	waiting room
gunroom	wardroom
hall	war room
homeroom	washroom
keep	water closet
kitchen	weight room
kitchenette	women's room
ladies' room	workroom
larder	

2 *root the cuttings* PLANT, bed out, sow.

3 *he rooted around in the cupboard* RUMMAGE, hunt, search, rifle, delve, forage, dig, nose, poke.

PHRASES: **put down roots** *they married and put down roots in Yemen* SETTLE, establish oneself, make one's home, set up home. **root and branch 1** *the company's accounting department should be eradicated, root and branch* COMPLETELY, entirely, wholly, totally, thoroughly. **2** *a root-and-branch reform* COMPLETE, total, thorough, radical. **root for** *informal Mollie roots for the Broncos* CHEER, cheer on, applaud, support, encourage. **root out 1** *the hedge was rooted out* UPROOT, deracinate, pull up, grub out. **2** *root out corruption* ERADICATE, eliminate, weed out, destroy, wipe out, stamp out, extirpate, abolish, end, put a stop to. **3** *he rooted out a dark secret* UNEARTH, dig up, bring to light, uncover, discover, dredge up, ferret out, expose. **take root 1** *leave the plants to take root* GERMINATE, sprout, establish, strike, take. **2** *Christianity took root in Persia* BECOME ESTABLISHED, take hold; develop, thrive, flourish.

rooted adjective **1** *views rooted in Inuit culture* EMBEDDED, fixed, established, entrenched, ingrained.

2 *Neil was* rooted to *the spot* FROZEN TO, riveted to, paralyzed to, glued to, fixed to; stock-still at, motionless at, unmoving at.

rootless adjective *her rootless father made a surprise appearance at her wedding* ITINERANT, unsettled, drifting, roving, footloose; homeless, vagabond, of no fixed abode.

rope noun *secure the rope to the post* CORD, cable, line, hawser; string; lasso, lariat.

▸ verb *his feet were roped together* TIE, bind, lash, truss; secure, moor, fasten, attach; hitch, tether, lasso.

PHRASES: **know the ropes** *informal you'll spend your first day with someone who knows the ropes* KNOW WHAT TO DO, know the routine, know one's way around, know one's stuff, know what's what; be experienced; *informal* know the drill, know the score, be streetwise. **rope someone in/into** *why did you let Bruce rope you into this deal?* PERSUADE TO JOIN/PARTICIPATE IN, talk into, trap into, inveigle into; enlist in/into, engage in.

ropy adjective *ropy strands of lava* STRINGY, thready, fibrous, filamentous; viscous, sticky, mucilaginous, thick.

rose noun See note below.

WORD NOTE **rose**

Rose, when the language was young, was the most beautiful word, being the name of the flower with the sweetest scent and the dark crimson petals with drops of fresh rain glistening in the afternoon as the lovers walked by. It was enough then to compare your love to a red, red rose and everyone could see the redness of the rose. The tenor could conjure up the young man destined to have his heart broken by the thorns guarding the rose he loved on the meadow. But a hundred years went by, and with each bouquet a little of the red rubbed off. The lazy continued to compare their love to a rose, but the word was bloodless, the cup held water instead of wine. A crisis ensued. The poet declared the rose to be "obsolete." Then Gertrude Stein to the rescue rode declaring that "rose is a rose is a rose" and everyone laughed. She knew that people were making fun of her. "But I notice that you all know it," she said of her famous line. "I'm no fool; but I think that in that line the rose is red for the first time in English poetry for a hundred years."

Two more recent instances of the restoration of red to the rose occur to me. A schoolchild was given the assignment to imitate William Blake's interrogation of the brightly burning tyger in the forest of the night. The result was "Rose, where did you get that red?" Kenneth Koch liked the phrase so much he made it the title of one of his books on teaching poetry to children. The second instance was the cover tag on *Sports Illustrated* the week that Pete Rose was hired as manager of the Cincinnati Reds in 1984: "Rose is a Red." **—DL**

---

roster noun *check to see if your name's on the roster for tomorrow's game* SCHEDULE, list, listing, register, agenda, calendar, table.

rostrum noun *the speakers will be seated on either side of the rostrum* DAIS, platform, podium, stage; soapbox.

rosy adjective **1** *a rosy complexion* PINK, pinkish, roseate, reddish, peaches-and-cream; glowing, healthy, fresh, radiant, blooming; blushing, flushed; ruddy, high-colored, florid, rubicund; *rare* rubescent, erubescent. ANTONYMS pale, sallow.

2 *his future looks rosy* PROMISING, optimistic, auspicious, hopeful, encouraging, favorable, bright, golden; *informal* upbeat. ANTONYMS dismal, bleak.

rot verb **1** *the floorboards rotted* DECAY, decompose, become rotten; disintegrate, crumble, perish.

2 *the meat began to rot* GO BAD, spoil, go off; molder, putrefy, fester.

3 *poor neighborhoods have been left to rot* DETERIORATE, degenerate, decline, decay, go to rack and ruin, go to seed, go downhill; *informal* go to pot, go to the dogs. ANTONYMS improve, recover.

▸ noun **1** *the leaves turned black with rot* DECAY, decomposition, mold, mildew, blight, canker; putrefaction.

2 *traditionalists said the rot had set in* DETERIORATION, decline; corruption, cancer.

rotary adjective *rotary blades* ROTATING, rotational, revolving, turning, spinning, gyrating; *formal* rotatory.

rotate verb **1** *the wheels rotate continually* REVOLVE, go around, turn, turn around, spin, gyrate, whirl, twirl, swivel, circle, pivot.

2 *many nurses rotate jobs* ALTERNATE, take turns, change, switch, interchange, exchange, swap; move around.

rotation noun **1** *the rotation of the wheels* REVOLVING, turning, spinning, gyration, circling.

2 *a rotation of Jupiter* TURN, revolution, orbit, spin.

3 *each member is chair for six months in rotation* SEQUENCE, succession; alternation, cycle.

rote PHRASE: **by rote** *we learned our multiplication tables by rote* MECHANICALLY, automatically, unthinkingly, mindlessly; from memory, by heart.

rotten adjective **1** *rotten meat* DECAYING, rotting, bad, off, far gone, decomposing, putrid, putrescent, perished, moldy, moldering, mildewy, rancid, festering, fetid; maggoty, wormy. ANTONYM fresh.

2 *rotten teeth* DECAYING, decayed, carious, black; disintegrating, crumbling.

3 *he's rotten to the core* CORRUPT, unprincipled, dishonest, dishonorable, unscrupulous, untrustworthy, immoral; villainous, bad, wicked, evil, iniquitous, venal; *informal* crooked. ANTONYMS decent, honorable.

4 *informal a rotten thing to do* NASTY, unkind, unpleasant, obnoxious, vile, contemptible, despicable, shabby, loathsome; spiteful, mean, low, malicious, hateful, hurtful; unfair, uncharitable, uncalled for; *informal* dirty, lowdown. ANTONYMS nice, kind.

5 *informal he was a rotten singer* BAD, poor, dreadful, awful, terrible, frightful, atrocious, hopeless, inadequate, inferior, substandard; *informal* crummy, pathetic, useless, lousy, appalling, abysmal. ANTONYMS accomplished, good.

6 *informal she had a rotten time* UNPLEASANT, miserable, awful, dreadful, terrible, frightful, bad, horrible; disappointing, regrettable; *informal* crummy, lousy. ANTONYMS good, delightful.

7 *informal I feel rotten about it* GUILTY, conscience-stricken, remorseful, ashamed, shamefaced, chastened, contrite, sorry, regretful, repentant, penitent.

8 *informal I felt rotten with that cold.* See ILL adjective sense 1.

rotund adjective **1** *a small, rotund man* PLUMP, chubby, fat, stout, portly, dumpy, round, chunky, overweight, heavy, paunchy, ample; flabby, fleshy, bulky, heavyset, corpulent, obese; *informal* tubby, roly-poly, pudgy, porky, blubbery, zaftig, corn-fed. ANTONYM thin.

2 *rotund cauldrons* ROUND, bulbous, spherical, spheric.

3 *the tenor's splendidly rotund tones.* See ROUND adjective sense 3.

roué noun *Hattie never had the good sense to stay away from the roués who frequented the club* LIBERTINE, rake, rogue, debauchee, degenerate, profligate; lecher, seducer, womanizer, philanderer, adulterer, Don Juan, Casanova, Lothario; *informal* ladykiller, skirt-chaser, lech, dirty old man, goat.

rough adjective **1** *rough ground* UNEVEN, irregular, bumpy, lumpy, knobbly, stony, rocky, rugged, rutted, pitted, rutty. ANTONYMS smooth, flat.

2 *the terrier's rough coat* COARSE, bristly, scratchy, prickly; shaggy, hairy, bushy. ANTONYMS smooth, sleek.

3 *rough skin* DRY, leathery, weather-beaten; chapped, calloused, scaly, scabrous. ANTONYM smooth.

4 *his voice was rough* GRUFF, hoarse, harsh, rasping, raspy, croaking, croaky, husky, throaty, gravelly, guttural. ANTONYM soft.

5 *rough red wine* SHARP, sharp-tasting, sour, acidic, acid, vinegary, acidulous. ANTONYMS sweet, mellow.

6 *he gets rough when he's drunk* VIOLENT, brutal, vicious; AGGRESSIVE, belligerent, pugnacious, thuggish; boisterous, rowdy, disorderly, unruly, riotous. ANTONYMS gentle, passive.

7 *a machine that can take rough handling* CARELESS, clumsy, inept, unskillful. ANTONYM careful.

8 *rough manners* BOORISH, loutish, oafish, brutish, coarse, crude, uncouth, vulgar, unrefined, unladylike, ungentlemanly, uncultured; unmannerly, impolite, discourteous, uncivil, ungracious, rude. See note at RUDE. ANTONYMS cultured, refined, civilized.

9 *rough seas* TURBULENT, stormy, tempestuous, violent, heavy, heaving, choppy. ANTONYM calm.

10 *informal I've had a rough time* DIFFICULT, hard, tough, bad, unpleasant; demanding, arduous. ANTONYMS easy, pleasant.

11 *informal you were a bit **rough on** her* HARSH ON/TO, hard on, tough on, stern to, severe to, unfair to, unjust to; insensitive to, nasty to, cruel to, unkind to, unsympathetic to, brutal to, heartless to, merciless to. ANTONYMS gentle, kind.

12 *a rough draft* PRELIMINARY, hasty, quick, sketchy, cursory, basic, crude, rudimentary, raw, unpolished; incomplete, unfinished. ANTONYMS finished, perfected.

13 *a rough estimate* APPROXIMATE, inexact, imprecise, vague, estimated, hazy; *informal* ballpark. ANTONYMS exact, precise.

14 *the accommodations are rather rough* PLAIN, BASIC, simple, rough and ready, rude, crude, primitive, spartan. ANTONYM luxurious.

▸ noun *the artist's initial roughs* SKETCH, draft, outline, mock-up.

▸ verb *rough the surface with sandpaper* ROUGHEN, make rough.

PHRASES: **rough something out** *we roughed out a few drawings of the monument* DRAFT, sketch out, outline, block out, mock up. **rough someone up** *informal Berman's goons were sent to rough up Donatelli* BEAT UP, attack, assault, knock around/about, batter, manhandle; *informal* do over, beat the living daylights out of.

rough and ready adjective *the huts at our temporary encampments were rough and ready | a rough-and-ready plan* BASIC, simple, crude, unrefined, unsophisticated; makeshift, provisional, stopgap, improvised, extemporary, ad hoc; hurried, sketchy.

rough-and-tumble adjective *rough-and-tumble play* DISORDERLY, unruly, boisterous, rough, riotous, rowdy, knockabout, noisy, loud.

▸ noun *a political rough-and-tumble* SCUFFLE, fight, brawl, melee, free-for-all, fracas, rumpus; horseplay; *informal* scrap, dust-up, shindy, roughhouse.

roughly adverb 1 *he shoved her away roughly* VIOLENTLY, forcefully, forcibly, abruptly, unceremoniously.

2 *they treated him roughly* HARSHLY, unkindly, unsympathetically; brutally, savagely, mercilessly, cruelly, heartlessly.

3 *roughly $2.4 million* APPROXIMATELY, about, round/around about, around, circa, in the region of, something like, in the order of, or so, or thereabouts, more or less, give or take; nearly, close to, approaching.

roughneck noun *informal*. See RUFFIAN.

round adjective 1 *a round window* CIRCULAR, ring-shaped, disk-shaped, hoop-shaped; spherical, spheroidal, globular, globe-shaped, orb-shaped; cylindrical; bulbous, rounded, rotund; *technical* annular, discoid.

2 *round cheeks* PLUMP, chubby, fat, full. ANTONYM thin.

3 *his deep, round voice* SONOROUS, full-bodied, full-toned, rich, deep, mellow, resonant, reverberant; grandiloquent, magniloquent, rotund, orotund; pear-shaped; *rare* canorous. ANTONYMS thin, reedy.

4 *a round dozen* COMPLETE, entire, whole, full.

5 *datedshe berated him in round terms* CANDID, frank, direct, honest, truthful, straightforward, plain, blunt, forthright, bald, explicit, unequivocal, unmistakable, categorical. ANTONYM evasive.

▸ noun 1 *mold the dough into rounds* BALL, sphere, globe, orb, circle, disk, ring, hoop; *technical* annulus.

2 **(rounds)** *a policeman on his rounds* CIRCUIT, beat, route, tour.

3 *the first round of the tournament* STAGE, level; heat, game, bout, contest; go-round.

4 *an endless round of parties* SUCCESSION, sequence, series, cycle.

5 *the gun fires thirty rounds per second* BULLET, cartridge, shell, shot.

▸ verb *the ship rounded the point* GO AROUND, travel around, skirt, circumnavigate, orbit.

PHRASES: **round about** *the campsite is round about two miles from the main road.* See AROUND preposition sense 3. **round the bend** *this time, I think Gordon's really gone round the bend.* See MAD sense 1. **round the clock.** See AROUND THE CLOCK at AROUND. **round off** 1 *the square edges were rounded off* SMOOTH (OFF), plane (off), sand (off), blunt. 2 *the party rounded off a successful year* COMPLETE, finish off, crown, cap, top; conclude, close, end. **round up** *go round up your brothers for dinner* GATHER TOGETHER, herd together, muster, marshal, rally, assemble, collect, group, corral.

THE RIGHT WORD

What do a bicycle wheel, a basketball, and a barrel of oil have in common? All are considered to be **round**, an adjective that may be applied to anything shaped like a circle, a sphere, or a cylinder. But of these three objects, only a basketball is **spherical**, which means having a round body whose surface is equally distant from the center at all points. Something that is **globular** is shaped like a ball or a globe but is not necessarily a perfect sphere (*globular drops of oil leaking from the seam*). A wheel is *circular*, as is a Frisbee; in fact, anything with a round, flat surface in the shape of a ring or a disk may be described as *circular*—whether or not it corresponds to a perfect circle. But only the rings of a tree can be described as **annular**, a word that usually implies having a series of concentric ringlike forms or structures.

roundabout adjective 1 *a roundabout route* CIRCUITOUS, indirect, meandering, serpentine, tortuous. ANTONYMS direct, straight.

2 *I asked in a roundabout sort of way* INDIRECT, oblique, circuitous, circumlocutory, periphrastic, digressive, long-winded; evasive. ANTONYM direct.

roundly adverb 1 *he was roundly condemned* VEHEMENTLY, emphatically, fiercely, forcefully, severely; plainly, frankly, candidly.

2 *she was roundly defeated* UTTERLY, completely, thoroughly, decisively, conclusively, heavily, soundly.

roundup noun 1 *a cattle roundup* ASSEMBLY, muster, rally, rodeo.

2 *the sports roundup* SUMMARY, synopsis, overview, review, outline, digest, précis, wrap-up; *informal* recap.

rouse verb 1 *he roused Ralph at dawn* WAKE, wake up, awaken, arouse; *formal* waken.

2 *she roused and looked around* WAKE UP, awake, awaken, come to, get up, rise, bestir oneself; *formal* arise. ANTONYM go to sleep.

3 *he roused the crowd* STIR UP, excite, galvanize, electrify,

stimulate, inspire, inspirit, move, inflame, agitate, goad, provoke; incite, spur on, light a fire under. ANTONYM calm.

4 *he's got a temper when he's roused* PROVOKE, annoy, anger, infuriate, madden, incense, vex, irk; *informal* aggravate. ANTONYMS appease, pacify.

5 *her disappearance roused my suspicions* AROUSE, awaken, prompt, provoke, stimulate, pique, trigger, spark off, touch off, kindle, elicit. ANTONYM allay.

rousing adjective *rousing cheers from the audience* STIRRING, inspiring, exciting, stimulating, moving, electrifying, invigorating, energizing, exhilarating; enthusiastic, vigorous, spirited.

rout noun 1 *the army's ignominious rout* RETREAT, flight.

2 *the game was a rout for the Marlins* CRUSHING DEFEAT, trouncing, annihilation; debacle, fiasco; *informal* licking, hammering, thrashing, drubbing, massacre. ANTONYM victory.

▸ verb 1 *his army was routed* PUT TO FLIGHT, drive off, scatter; defeat, beat, conquer, vanquish, crush, overpower.

2 *he routed the defending champion.* See DEFEAT verb sense 1.

route noun *a different route to school* WAY, course, road, path, direction; passage, journey.

▸ verb *inquiries are routed to the relevant desk* DIRECT, send, convey, dispatch, forward.

routine noun 1 *his morning routine* PROCEDURE, practice, pattern, drill, regimen; program, schedule, plan; formula, method, system; customs, habits; wont.

2 *a stand-up routine* ACT, performance, number, turn, piece; *informal* spiel, patter, shtick.

▸ adjective *a routine safety inspection* STANDARD, regular, customary, normal, usual, ordinary, typical; everyday, common, commonplace, conventional, habitual, wonted. ANTONYM unusual.

rove verb *for ten years I roved about* WANDER, roam, ramble, drift, meander; range, travel.

rover noun *they spent their first summer after graduation as a couple of carefree rovers* WANDERER, traveler, globetrotter, drifter, roamer, itinerant, transient; nomad, gypsy, tramp, vagrant, vagabond, hobo.

row[1] noun 1 *rows of children* LINE, column, file, queue; procession, chain, string, succession.

2 *the middle row of seats* TIER, line, rank, bank. PHRASE: **in a row** *three days in a row* CONSECUTIVELY, in succession; running, straight.

row[2] *informal* noun *the siblings were having a row* ARGUMENT, quarrel, squabble, fight, contretemps, falling-out, disagreement, dispute, clash, altercation, shouting match; *informal* tiff, set-to, run-in, blowup, spat. See note at QUARREL.

rowdy adjective *rowdy youths* UNRULY, disorderly, obstreperous, riotous, undisciplined, uncontrollable, ungovernable, disruptive, out of control, rough, wild, lawless; boisterous, uproarious, noisy, loud, clamorous; *informal* rambunctious. ANTONYM peaceful.

▸ noun *the bar was full of rowdies* RUFFIAN, troublemaker, lout, hooligan, thug, hoodlum; *informal* tough, yahoo, punk.

royal adjective 1 *the royal prerogative* REGAL, kingly, queenly, princely; sovereign, monarchical.

2 *a royal welcome* EXCELLENT, fine, magnificent, splendid, superb, wonderful, first-rate, first-class; *informal* fantastic, great, tremendous.

3 *informal she's a royal pain in the neck* COMPLETE, utter, total, absolute, real, thorough.

rub verb 1 *Sally rubbed her arm* MASSAGE, knead; stroke, pat.

2 *he rubbed sunscreen on her back* APPLY, smear, spread, work in.

3 *my shoes rub badly* CHAFE, pinch; hurt, be painful.

▸ noun 1 *she gave his back a rub* MASSAGE, rubdown.

2 *I gave the countertop a rub* POLISH, wipe, clean.

3 *it's too complicated—that's the rub* PROBLEM, difficulty, trouble, drawback, hindrance, impediment; snag, hitch, catch.

PHRASES: **rub something down** *Jake and Pauline are in the stable, rubbing down the horses* CLEAN, sponge, wash; groom. **rub it in** *informal yes, I screwed up, but you don't have to rub it in* EMPHASIZE IT, stress it, underline it, highlight it; go on (and on) about it, harp on it; *informal* rub someone's nose in it. **rub off on** *we just don't want his bad habits rubbing off on you* BE TRANSFERRED TO, be passed on to, be transmitted to, be communicated to; affect, influence. **rub something out** *they promise to rub out your bad credit history* ERASE, delete, remove, efface, obliterate, expunge. **rub elbows** *it's our chance to rub elbows with the company execs* ASSOCIATE, mingle, fraternize, socialize, mix, keep company, consort; *informal* hang around/out, hobnob. **rub someone the wrong way** *Regina's roommates rub her boyfriend the wrong way* IRRITATE, annoy, irk, vex, provoke, displease, exasperate, infuriate, get on someone's nerves, put out, pique, upset, nettle, ruffle someone's feathers, make someone's hackles rise, try someone's patience, grate on; *informal* aggravate, get, get to, bug, miff, peeve, rile, needle, tick off, tee off, get under someone's skin, get in someone's hair, get/put someone's back up, get someone's goat, rankle, ride.

rubbish noun 1 *throw away that rubbish.* See GARBAGE sense 1.

2 *she's talking rubbish* NONSENSE, balderdash, gibberish, claptrap, blarney, moonshine, garbage; *informal* hogwash, baloney, jive, guff, tripe, drivel, bilge, bunk, BS, piffle, poppycock, hooey, twaddle, gobbledygook, flapdoodle; *dated* bunkum, tommyrot.

rubble noun *very few retrievable items were found in the rubble* DEBRIS, remains, ruins, wreckage.

ruckus noun *the kids are raising a ruckus | the ruckus over gun control* DISTURBANCE, noise, racket, din, commotion, hubbub, fuss, uproar, furor, hue and cry, rumpus, ruction, fracas; *informal* to-do, hullabaloo, hoo-ha, ballyhoo, stink, foofaraw.

ruddy adjective *a ruddy complexion* ROSY, red, pink, roseate, rubicund; healthy, glowing, fresh; flushed, blushing; florid, high-colored; *literary* rubescent. ANTONYM pale.

rude adjective 1 *a rude man rude remarks* ILL-MANNERED, bad-mannered, impolite, discourteous, uncivil, unmannerly, mannerless; impertinent, insolent, impudent, disrespectful, cheeky; churlish, curt, brusque, brash, offhand, short, sharp; offensive, insulting, derogatory, disparaging, abusive; tactless, undiplomatic, uncomplimentary. See note at OFFENSE. ANTONYMS polite, civil.

2 *rude jokes* VULGAR, coarse, smutty, dirty, filthy, crude, lewd, obscene, off-color, offensive, indelicate, tasteless; risqué, naughty, ribald, bawdy, racy; *informal* blue; *euphemistic* adult. ANTONYM clean.

3 *a rude awakening* ABRUPT, sudden, sharp, startling; unpleasant, nasty, harsh.

4 *dated a rude cabin* PRIMITIVE, crude, rudimentary, rough, simple, basic, makeshift. ANTONYMS classy, luxurious.

THE RIGHT WORD

Someone who lacks consideration for the feelings of others and who is deliberately insolent is **rude** (*It was rude of you not to introduce me to your friends*). **Ill-mannered** suggests that the person is ignorant of the rules of social behavior rather than deliberately rude (*an ill-mannered child*), while **uncivil** implies disregard for even the most basic rules of social behavior among civilized people (*his uncivil response resulted in his being kicked out of the classroom*). **Rough** is used to describe people who lack polish and refinement (*he was a rough but honest man*), while **crude** is a more negative term for individuals and behavior lacking culture, civility, and tact (*he made a crude gesture*). **Uncouth** describes what seems strange, awkward, or unmannerly rather than rude (*his uncouth behavior at the wedding*). Although individuals of any age may be rude, crude, ill-mannered, or uncouth, **callow** almost always applies to those who are young or immature; it suggests naïveté and lack of sophistication (*he was surprisingly callow for a man of almost 40*).

rudimentary adjective 1 *rudimentary carpentry skills* BASIC, elementary, primary, fundamental, essential. ANTONYM advanced.

2 *the equipment was rudimentary* PRIMITIVE, crude, simple, unsophisticated, rough, rough and ready, makeshift. ANTONYM sophisticated.

3 *a rudimentary thumb* VESTIGIAL, undeveloped, incomplete; *Biology* abortive, primitive. ANTONYM developed.

rudiments plural noun *the rudiments of sign language* BASICS, fundamentals, essentials, first principles, foundation; *informal* nuts and bolts, ABCs.

rue verb *she may live to rue this impetuous decision* REGRET, be sorry about, feel remorseful about, repent of, reproach oneself for; deplore, lament, bemoan, bewail. See note at MOURN.

rueful adjective *his rueful expression said it all* REGRETFUL, apologetic, sorry, remorseful, shamefaced, sheepish, abashed, hangdog, contrite, repentant, penitent, conscience-stricken, sorrowful, sad.

ruffian noun *a gang of young ruffians* THUG, lout, hooligan, hoodlum, vandal, delinquent, rowdy, scoundrel, villain, rogue, bully, brute; *informal* tough, roughneck, bruiser, heavy, yahoo, goon.

ruffle verb 1 *he ruffled her hair* DISARRANGE, tousle, dishevel, rumple, disorder, mess up, tangle; *informal* muss up. ANTONYM smooth.

2 *the wind ruffled the water* RIPPLE, riffle. ANTONYM smooth.

3 *don't let him ruffle you* ANNOY, irritate, vex, nettle, anger, exasperate; disconcert, unnerve, fluster, agitate, harass, upset, disturb, discomfit, put off, perturb, unsettle, bother, worry, trouble; *informal* rattle, faze, throw, get to, rile, needle, aggravate, bug, peeve. ANTONYMS calm, soothe.

▸ noun *a shirt with ruffles* FRILL, flounce, ruff, ruche, jabot, furbelow.

rug noun 1 *they sat on the rug* MAT, carpet, runner; hearth rug, floor cloth.

2 *informal who is he trying to fool with that rug?* TOUPEE, wig, hairpiece.

rugged adjective 1 *a rugged path* ROUGH, uneven, bumpy, rocky, stony, pitted, jagged, craggy. ANTONYM smooth.

2 *a rugged vehicle* DURABLE, sturdy, robust, strong, tough, resilient. ANTONYMS fragile, flimsy.

3 *rugged manly types* WELL-BUILT, burly, strong, muscular, muscly, brawny, strapping, husky, hulking; tough, hardy, robust, sturdy, lusty, solid; *informal* hunky, beefy. ANTONYMS frail, scrawny, weedy.

4 *his rugged features* STRONG, craggy, rough-hewn; manly, masculine; irregular, weathered. ANTONYM delicate.

5 *the rugged outdoor life* TOUGH, harsh, rigorous, arduous, onerous, exacting, difficult, hard; austere, spartan. ANTONYM easy.

6 *the author was captivated by the rugged individualism of these villagers* UNCOMPROMISING, unwavering, unflinching, firm, tenacious, resolute, determined. ANTONYMS feeble, ineffectual.

ruin noun 1 *the buildings were saved from ruin* DISINTEGRATION, decay, disrepair, dilapidation, ruination; destruction, demolition, wreckage. ANTONYMS preservation, reconstruction.

2 (**ruins**) *the ruins of a church* REMAINS, remnants, fragments, relics; rubble, debris, wreckage.

3 *he was careening toward his ruin* DOWNFALL, collapse, defeat, undoing, failure, breakdown, ruination; Waterloo. ANTONYMS success, triumph.

4 *local merchants are facing ruin* BANKRUPTCY, insolvency, penury, poverty, destitution, impoverishment, indigence; failure. ANTONYMS success, wealth.

▸ verb 1 *don't ruin my plans* WRECK, destroy, spoil, mar, blight, shatter, dash, torpedo, scotch, mess up; sabotage; *informal* screw up, foul up, put the kibosh on, nix, scupper, scuttle. ANTONYMS save, restore.

2 *the bank's collapse ruined them all* BANKRUPT, make insolvent, impoverish, pauperize, wipe out, break, cripple, devastate; bring someone to their knees.

3 *a country ruined by civil war* DESTROY, devastate, lay waste, ravage; raze, demolish, wreck, wipe out, flatten. ANTONYMS repair, rebuild.

PHRASE: **in ruins** 1 *the abbey is in ruins* DERELICT, ruined, in disrepair, falling to pieces, dilapidated, tumbledown, ramshackle, decrepit, decaying, ruinous.

2 *his career is in ruins* DESTROYED, ruined, in pieces, over, finished; *informal* in tatters, on the rocks, done for.

ruined adjective 1 *a ruined building* DERELICT, in ruins, dilapidated, ruinous, tumbledown, ramshackle, decrepit, falling to pieces, crumbling, decaying, disintegrating.

2 *he was financially ruined* DESTITUTE, impoverished, bankrupt, pauperized, wiped out, wrecked, cleaned out.

ruinous adjective **1** *a ruinous trade war* DISASTROUS, devastating, catastrophic, calamitous, crippling, crushing, damaging, destructive, harmful; costly.

2 *ruinous interest rates* EXTORTIONATE, exorbitant, excessive, sky-high, outrageous, inflated; *informal* criminal, steep.

rule noun **1** *health and safety rules* REGULATION, ruling, directive, order, act, law, statute, edict, canon, mandate, command, dictate, decree, fiat, injunction, commandment, stipulation, requirement, guideline, direction; *formal* ordinance.

2 *lateness was the general rule* PROCEDURE, practice, protocol, convention, norm, routine, custom, habit, wont; *formal* praxis.

3 *moderation is the golden rule* PRECEPT, principle, standard, axiom, truth, maxim.

4 *Punjab came under British rule* CONTROL, jurisdiction, command, power, dominion; government, administration, sovereignty, leadership, supremacy, authority.

▸ verb **1** *El Salvador was ruled by Spain* GOVERN, preside over, control, lead, dominate, run, head, administer, manage.

2 *Elizabeth has ruled for more than fifty years* BE IN POWER, be in control, be in command, be in charge, govern; reign, be monarch, be sovereign.

3 *the judge ruled that they be set free* DECREE, order, pronounce, judge, adjudge, ordain; decide, find, determine, resolve, settle.

4 *chaos ruled* PREVAIL, predominate, be the order of the day, reign supreme; *formal* obtain.

PHRASES: **as a rule** *as a rule, we eat in the kitchen* USUALLY, generally, in general, normally, ordinarily, customarily, for the most part, on the whole, by and large, in the main, mainly, mostly, commonly, typically. **rule something out** *the gold brocade isn't one of the top choices, but don't yet rule it out* EXCLUDE, eliminate, disregard; preclude, prohibit, prevent, disallow.

ruler noun *blessings on our fair ruler* LEADER, sovereign, monarch, potentate, king, queen, emperor, empress, prince, princess; crowned head, head of state, president, premier, governor; overlord, chief, chieftain, lord; dictator, autocrat. See table. ANTONYM subject.

RULERS

aga	prince
Caesar	princess
caliph	queen
emir	raja
emperor	rani
empress	regent
kaiser	satrap
king	shah
khan	sheikh
maharajah	shogun
mikado	sovereign
monarch	sultan
Negus	czar
pharaoh	viceroy

ruling noun *the judge's ruling* JUDGMENT, decision, adjudication, finding, verdict; pronouncement, resolution, decree, injunction.

▸ adjective **1** *the ruling class* GOVERNING, controlling, commanding, supreme, leading, dominant, ascendant, reigning.

2 *hockey was their ruling passion* MAIN, chief, principal, major, prime, dominating, foremost; predominant, central, focal; *informal* number-one.

rumble verb *the distant rumble of big rigs on the highway* BOOM, thunder, roll, roar, resound, reverberate, echo, grumble.

ruminate verb *we* ***ruminated on*** *the nature of existence* THINK ABOUT, contemplate, consider, meditate on, muse on, mull over, ponder on/over, deliberate about/on, chew on, puzzle over; *formal* cogitate about.

rummage verb *he* ***rummaged through*** *Stacey's bureau drawers* SEARCH (THROUGH), hunt through, root about/around (in), ferret about/around (in), fish about/around (in), poke around (in), dig through, delve through, go through, explore, sift through, rifle (through).

rumor noun *do you think the talk of her resignation is fact or just rumor? | the latest rumors say they're eloping* GOSSIP, hearsay, talk, tittle-tattle, speculation, word; **(rumors)** reports, stories, whispers, canards; *informal* grapevine, word on the street, buzz, dirt, scuttlebutt, loose lips.

rump noun **1** *a smack on the rump* REAR, rear end, backside, seat; buttocks, cheeks, bottom; *informal* behind; sit-upon, buns, derrière, butt, fanny, tush, tail, heinie, caboose; *chiefly Brit.* bum; *humorous* fundament, posterior, stern; *Anatomy* nates.

2 *the rump of the army* REMAINDER, rest, remnant, remains.

rumple verb **1** *the sheet was rumpled* CRUMPLE, crease, wrinkle, crinkle, scrunch up. ANTONYM smooth (out).

2 *Ian rumpled her hair* RUFFLE, disarrange, tousle, dishevel, mess up; *informal* muss up. ANTONYM smooth.

rumpus noun. See RUCKUS.

WORD NOTE **rumpus**

Certain authors have laid claim to certain words, for this and successive generations, and perhaps for all eternity. I cannot hear the word *rumpus* (and in truth I rarely do hear it) without thinking of Maurice Sendak's children's classic, *Where the Wild Things Are.* It's what the grinning, merry monsters say—"Let the wild rumpus start"—as they begin their joyous, abandoned merrymaking with the intrepid voyager, little Max. What's interesting, at least to me, is that the word instantly conjures up the accompanying image, and that the sound of it (a sound which, before I read the book, probably had no effect on me at all) inevitably fills me with the same giddy, heady, profound delight that I feel each time I look at Sendak's illustration. **—FP**

run verb **1** *she ran across the road* SPRINT, race, dart, rush, dash, hasten, hurry, scurry, scamper, bolt, fly, gallop, career, charge, shoot, hurtle, speed, zoom, go like lightning, go hell-bent for leather, go like the wind, go like a bat out of hell; jog, trot; *informal* tear, pelt, scoot, hotfoot it, leg it, belt, zip, whip, bomb, hightail it, barrel.

2 *the robbers turned and ran* FLEE, run away, run off, run for it, take flight, make off, take off, take to one's heels, make a break for it, bolt, make one's getaway, escape; *informal* beat it, clear off, clear out, vamoose, skedaddle, split, leg it, scram, light out, take a powder, make tracks.

3 *he ran in the marathon* COMPETE, take part, participate.

4 *a shiver ran down my spine* GO, pass, slide, move, travel.

5 *he ran his eye down the list* CAST, pass, skim, flick.

6 *the road runs the length of the valley* EXTEND, stretch, reach, continue.

7 *water ran from the eaves* FLOW, pour, stream, gush, flood, cascade, roll, course, spill, trickle, drip, dribble, leak.

8 *a bus runs to Sorrento* TRAVEL, go.

9 *I'll run you home* DRIVE, take, bring, ferry, chauffeur, give someone a ride/lift.

10 *he runs a mail-order company* BE IN CHARGE OF, manage, direct, control, head, govern, supervise, superintend, oversee; operate, conduct, own.

11 *it's expensive to run a car* MAINTAIN, keep, own, possess, have; drive.

12 *they ran some tests* CARRY OUT, do, perform, execute.

13 *he left the engine running* OPERATE, function, work, go; idle.

14 *the lease runs for twenty years* BE VALID, last, be in effect, be operative, continue, be effective.

15 *the show ran for two years* BE STAGED, be performed, be on, be mounted, be screened.

16 *he ran for president* BE A CANDIDATE FOR, stand for, be a contender for.

17 *the paper ran the story* PUBLISH, print, feature, carry, put out, release, issue.

18 *they run drugs* SMUGGLE, traffic in, deal in.

19 *they were run out of town* CHASE, drive, hound.

▸ noun **1** *his morning run* SPRINT, jog, dash, gallop, trot.

2 *she did the school run* ROUTE, journey; circuit, round, beat.

3 *an unbeaten run of victories* SERIES, succession, sequence, string, chain, streak, spell, stretch, spate.

4 *a **run on** umbrellas* DEMAND FOR, rush on.

5 *they had the **run of** the house* FREE USE OF, unrestricted access to.

6 *the usual run of movies* TYPE, kind, sort, variety, class.

7 *a dog run* ENCLOSURE, pen, coop.

8 *a toboggan run* SLOPE, track, piste, trail, slide.

9 *a run in her pantyhose* RIP, tear, snag, hole, pull; *Brit.* ladder.

PHRASES: **in the long run** *in the long run, the move to Spokane may be a really good thing* EVENTUALLY, in the end, ultimately, when all is said and done, in the fullness of time, over the long haul, at the end of the day. **on the run** *police report that Prentiss has been on the run since early this morning* ON THE LOOSE, at large, loose; running away, fleeing, fugitive; *informal* AWOL, on the lam. **run across** *we never expected to run across Mrs. Gundlach at the casino* MEET, meet by chance, come across, run into, chance on/upon, stumble on/upon, happen on/upon; *informal* bump into. **run after** *informal I have no intention of running after him* PURSUE, chase; make advances to, flirt with; *informal* come on to, be all over; *dated* set one's cap for/at. **run along** *informal it's time for you and your pesky little friends to run along* GO AWAY, be off (with you), shoo; *informal* scram, buzz off, skedaddle, scat, beat it, get lost, shove off, clear off; *literary* begone. **run around** *informal that creep's been running around since their honeymoon* BE UNFAITHFUL, have affairs, philander; *informal* play the field, sleep around, fool around. **run away** *her attacker ran away.* See RUN verb sense 2. **run away with** *she ran away with the championship* WIN EASILY, win hands down; *informal* win by a mile. **run down** *obviously, this barn didn't start running down yesterday* DECLINE, degenerate, go downhill, go to seed, decay, go to rack and ruin; *informal* go to pot, go to the dogs. **run someone down 1** *he was run down by a drunk driver* RUN OVER, knock down, knock over; hit, strike. **2** *she ran him down in front of other people* CRITICIZE, denigrate, belittle, disparage, deprecate, find fault with; *informal* put down, knock, badmouth, dis; *formal* derogate. **run for it** *they saw the cop car and ran for it.* See RUN verb sense 2. **run high** *feelings ran high* BE STRONG, be fervent, be passionate, be intense. **run in 1** *heart disease runs in the family* BE COMMON IN, be inherent in. **2** *informal you mean they actually ran him in for littering?* See ARREST verb sense 1. **run into 1** *a car ran into his van* COLLIDE WITH, hit, strike, crash into, smash into, plow into, ram, impact. **2** *I ran into Hugo the other day.* See RUN ACROSS. **3** *we ran into a problem* EXPERIENCE, encounter, meet with, be faced with, be confronted with. **4** *his debts run into six figures* REACH, extend to, be as much as. **run low** *supplies were running low* DWINDLE, diminish, become depleted, be used up, be in short supply, be tight. **run off** *the youths ran off.* See RUN verb sense 2. **run off with** *he ran off with her money.* See STEAL verb sense 1. **run something off 1** *would you run off that list for me?* COPY, photocopy, xerox, duplicate, print, reproduce. **2** *run off some of the excess water* DRAIN, bleed, draw off, pump out. **run on 1** *the call ran on for hours* CONTINUE, go on, carry on, last, keep going, stretch. **2** *your mother does run on* TALK INCESSANTLY, talk a lot, go on, chatter on, ramble on; *informal* yak, gab, run off at the mouth. **run out 1** *supplies ran out* BE USED UP, dry up, be exhausted, be finished, peter out. **2** *her contract ran out* EXPIRE, end, terminate, finish; lapse. **run out of** *they ran out of their cash* USE UP; be out of, consume, eat up; *informal* be fresh out of. **run out on** *informal she ran out on her husband.* See ABANDON verb sense 3. **run over 1** *the bathwater ran over* OVERFLOW, spill over, brim over. **2** *the project ran over budget* EXCEED, go over, overshoot, overreach. **3** *he quickly ran over the story* RECAPITULATE, repeat, run through, go over, reiterate, review; look over, read through; *informal* recap. **run someone over.** See RUN SOMEONE DOWN sense 1. **run the show** *informal Todd always tries to run the show* BE IN CHARGE, be in control, be at the helm, be in the driver's seat, be at the wheel; *informal* be the boss, call the shots. **run through 1** *they quickly ran through their money* SQUANDER, spend, fritter away, dissipate, waste, go through, consume, use up; *informal* blow. **2** *the attitude that runs through his writing* PERVADE, permeate, suffuse, imbue, inform. **3** *he ran through his notes.* See RUN OVER sense 3. **4** *let's run through scene three* REHEARSE, practice, go over, repeat; *informal* recap. **run someone through** *they hung an effigy of Bin Laden and ran it through with sharp sticks* STAB, pierce, transfix, impale. **run to 1** *the bill ran to $22,000* AMOUNT TO, add up to, total, come to, equal, reach, be as much as. **2** *he was running to fat* TEND TO, become, get, grow.

runaway noun *a teenage runaway* FUGITIVE, escapee; refugee; truant; absconder, deserter.

▸ adjective **1** *a runaway horse* OUT OF CONTROL, escaped, loose, on the loose.

2 *a runaway victory* EASY, effortless; *informal* as easy as pie.

3 *runaway inflation* RAMPANT, out of control, unchecked, unbridled.

rundown noun *here's the rundown on the latest digital gear* SUMMARY, synopsis, précis, run-through, summarization, summation, review, overview, briefing, sketch, outline; *informal* lowdown, recap.

run-down adjective 1 *a run-down area* DILAPIDATED, tumbledown, ramshackle, derelict, ruinous, in ruins, crumbling, beat-up; neglected, uncared-for, depressed, seedy, shabby, slummy, squalid, flea-bitten; *informal* crummy.

2 *she was feeling rather run-down* UNWELL, ill, poorly, unhealthy, peaked; tired, drained, exhausted, fatigued, worn out, below par, washed out; *informal* under the weather, off; *dated* seedy.

run-in noun *informal his latest run-in with the authorities* DISAGREEMENT, argument, dispute, altercation, confrontation, contretemps, quarrel; brush, encounter, tangle, blowup, fight, clash; *informal* spat, scrap, row.

runner noun 1 *the runners were limbering up* sprinter, hurdler, racer, jogger; athlete.

2 *a strawberry runner* SHOOT, offshoot, sprout, tendril; *Botany* stolon.

3 *he worked as a runner for the mob* MESSENGER, courier, errand boy; *informal* gofer.

running noun 1 *his running was particularly fast* SPRINTING, sprint, racing, jogging, jog.

2 *the running of the school* ADMINISTRATION, management, organization, coordination, orchestration, handling, direction, control, regulation, supervision.

3 *the smooth running of her department* OPERATION, working, function, performance.

▸ adjective 1 *running water* FLOWING, gushing, rushing, moving.

2 *a running argument* ONGOING, sustained, continuous, rolling, incessant, ceaseless, constant, perpetual; recurrent, recurring.

3 *she was late two days running* IN SUCCESSION, in a row, in sequence, consecutively; straight, together.

PHRASE: **in the running for** *he's in the running for a prize* LIKELY TO GET, a candidate for, in line for, on the short list for, up for.

running shoes plural noun athletic shoes, gym shoes, sneakers, cross-trainers, track shoes, joggers, tennis shoes.

runny adjective *the custard was too runny* LIQUEFIED, liquid, fluid, melted, molten; watery, thin. ANTONYM solid.

run-of-the-mill adjective *even the car he drives is run-of-the-mill* ORDINARY, average, middle-of-the-road, commonplace, humdrum, mundane, standard, nondescript, characterless, conventional; unremarkable, unexceptional, uninteresting, dull, boring, routine, bland, lackluster, garden-variety; *informal* nothing to write home about, nothing special, a dime a dozen. ANTONYM exceptional.

rupture noun 1 *pipeline ruptures* BREAK, fracture, crack, breach, burst, split, fissure.

2 *a rupture due to personal differences* RIFT, estrangement, falling-out, breakup, breach, split, separation, parting, division, schism; *informal* bust-up.

3 *an abdominal rupture* HERNIA.

▸ verb 1 *the reactor core might rupture* BREAK, fracture, crack, breach, burst, split; *informal* bust.

2 *the problem ruptured their relationships* SEVER, break off, breach, disrupt; *literary* sunder.

rural adjective *the rural backdrop was filmed in Georgia* COUNTRY, countryside, bucolic, rustic, pastoral; agricultural, agrarian; *literary* sylvan, georgic. ANTONYM urban.

ruse noun *his offer to help with my presentation was just a clever ruse* PLOY, stratagem, tactic, scheme, trick, gambit, cunning plan, dodge, subterfuge, machination, wile.

rush verb 1 *she rushed home* HURRY, dash, run, race, sprint, bolt, dart, gallop, career, charge, shoot, hurtle, careen, hare, fly, speed, zoom, scurry, scuttle, scamper, hasten; *informal* tear, belt, pelt, scoot, zip, whip, hotfoot it, leg it, bomb, hightail it.

2 *water rushed along gutters* FLOW, pour, gush, surge, stream, cascade, run, course.

3 *the legislation was rushed through both houses* PUSH, hurry, hasten, speed, hustle, press, force.

4 *the mob rushed the police* ATTACK, charge, run at, assail, storm.

▸ noun 1 *Tim made a rush for the exit* DASH, run, sprint, dart, bolt, charge, scramble, break.

2 *the lunch rush* HUSTLE AND BUSTLE, commotion, hubbub, stir; busy time.

3 *a last-minute rush for flights* DEMAND, clamor, call, request; run on.

4 *he was in no rush to leave* HURRY, haste, urgency.

5 *a rush of adrenaline* SURGE, flow, flood, spurt, stream; thrill, flash; *informal* charge, jolt, kick.

6 *a rush of cold air* GUST, blast, draft.

7 *I made a sudden rush at him* CHARGE, onslaught, attack, assault, onrush.

▸ adjective *a rush job* URGENT, high-priority, emergency; hurried, hasty, fast, quick, swift; *informal* hurry-up.

rushed adjective 1 *a rushed divorce* HASTY, fast, speedy, quick, swift, rapid, hurried.

2 *he was too rushed to enjoy his stay* PRESSED FOR TIME, busy, in a hurry, run off one's feet.

rust verb *the pipes have rusted* CORRODE, oxidize, become rusty, tarnish.

▸ noun *use a paint that will prevent rust from forming* CORROSION, oxidation.

rustic adjective 1 *a rustic setting* RURAL, country, countryside, countrified, pastoral, bucolic; agricultural, agrarian; *literary* sylvan, georgic. ANTONYM urban.

2 *rustic wooden tables* PLAIN, simple, homely, unsophisticated; rough, rude, crude. ANTONYMS fancy, ornate.

3 *rustic peasants* UNSOPHISTICATED, uncultured, unrefined, simple; artless, unassuming, guileless, naive, ingenuous; coarse, rough, uncouth, boorish; *informal* hillbilly, hick. ANTONYMS urbane, cultured, sophisticated.

▸ noun *the rustics were carousing* PEASANT, countryman, countrywoman, bumpkin, yokel, country cousin; *informal* hillbilly, hayseed, hick; *archaic* swain, cottier.

rustle verb 1 *her dress rustled as she moved* SWISH, whoosh, swoosh, whisper, sigh.

2 *he was rustling cattle* STEAL, thieve, take; abduct, kidnap; *informal* swipe.

▸ noun *the rustle of the leaves* SWISH, whisper, rustling; *literary* susurration, susurrus.

PHRASE: **rustle something up** *informal I'll rustle up some breakfast for us* PREPARE HASTILY, throw together, make; *informal* fix.

rusty adjective **1** *rusty wire* RUSTED, rust-covered, corroded, oxidized; tarnished, discolored.

2 *rusty hair* REDDISH-BROWN, rust-colored, chestnut, auburn, tawny, russet, coppery, copper, Titian, red, ginger, gingery.

3 *my French is a little rusty* OUT OF PRACTICE, below par; unpracticed, deficient, impaired, weak.

rut noun **1** *the car bumped across the ruts* FURROW, groove, trough, ditch, hollow, pothole, crater.

2 *he was stuck in a rut* BORING ROUTINE, humdrum existence, habit, dead end.

ruthless adjective *ruthless killers* MERCILESS, pitiless, cruel, heartless, hard-hearted, cold-hearted, cold-blooded, harsh, callous, unmerciful, unforgiving, uncaring, unsympathetic, uncharitable; remorseless, unbending, inflexible, implacable; brutal, inhuman, inhumane, barbarous, barbaric, savage, sadistic, vicious. ANTONYM merciful.

S

sable adjective *her long sable hair* BLACK, jet-black, pitch-black, ebony, raven, sooty, dusky, inky, coal-black.

sabotage noun *the fire may have been an act of sabotage* VANDALISM, wrecking, destruction, impairment, incapacitation, damage; subversion, obstruction, disruption, spoiling, undermining; *informal* a (monkey) wrench in the works.

▸ verb *they were hired to sabotage the competition* VANDALIZE, wreck, damage, destroy, cripple, impair, incapacitate; obstruct, disrupt, spoil, ruin, undermine, threaten, subvert.

saccharine adjective *saccharine love songs* SENTIMENTAL, sickly, mawkish, cloying, sugary, sickening, nauseating; *informal* mushy, sappy, schmaltzy, weepy, gooey, drippy, cheesy, corny, soppy, cornball.

sack[1] noun **1** *she carried her supplies in a sack* BAG, pouch, pack, satchel; knapsack, backpack, rucksack, packsack, day pack, bookbag, tote bag.

2 *informal work hard or you'll get* ***the sack*** A DISMISSAL, a discharge; *informal* the boot, the ax, the heave-ho, one's marching orders, a pink slip.

3 *informal she stayed in* ***the sack*** BED.

▸ verb *informal she was sacked for stealing* DISMISS, discharge, lay off, let go, terminate, get rid of; *Military* cashier; *Brit.* make redundant; *informal* fire, give the sack, give someone their marching orders, give someone the boot, show someone the door, send packing, pink-slip.

PHRASE: **hit the sack** *informal I'm hitting the sack early tonight* GO TO BED, retire, go to sleep; *informal* turn in, hit the hay.

sack[2] verb *raiders sacked the town* RAVAGE, lay waste, devastate, raid, ransack, strip, plunder, despoil, pillage, loot, rob. See note at RAVAGE.

sackcloth noun *artsy lamps made of castoff materials such as old chicken wire and sackcloth* HESSIAN, sacking, hopsack, burlap; gunny. PHRASE: **in/wearing sackcloth and ashes** *I never thought I'd live to see the day that Josie was wearing sackcloth and ashes* PENITENT, contrite, regretful, sorrowful, rueful, remorseful, apologetic, ashamed, guilt-ridden, chastened, shamefaced, guilty.

sacred adjective **1** *the priest entered the sacred place* HOLY, hallowed, blessed, consecrated, sanctified, venerated, revered; *archaic* blest. See note at DIVINE.

2 *sacred music* RELIGIOUS, spiritual, devotional, church, ecclesiastical. ANTONYMS secular, profane.

3 *the hill is sacred to the tribe* SACROSANCT, inviolable, inviolate, invulnerable, untouchable, protected, defended, secure.

sacrifice noun **1** *the sacrifice of animals* RITUAL SLAUGHTER, offering, oblation, immolation.

2 *the calf was a sacrifice* (VOTIVE) OFFERING, burnt offering, gift, oblation.

3 *the sacrifice of sovereignty* SURRENDER, giving up, abandonment, renunciation, forfeiture, relinquishment, resignation, abdication.

▸ verb **1** *two goats were sacrificed* OFFER UP, immolate, slaughter.

2 *he sacrificed his principles* GIVE UP, abandon, surrender, forgo, renounce, forfeit, relinquish, resign, abdicate; betray.

sacrificial adjective *the altar for sacrificial offerings* VOTIVE, expiatory, propitiatory.

sacrilege noun *any form of gambling on the church grounds, including bingo and raffles, would be sacrilege* DESECRATION, profanity, blasphemy, impiety, irreligion, unholiness, irreverence, disrespect, profanation. ANTONYM piety.

sacrilegious adjective *your vile language is sacrilegious* PROFANE, blasphemous, impious, sinful, irreverent, irreligious, unholy, disrespectful.

sacrosanct adjective *the separation of church and state is sacrosanct* SACRED, hallowed, respected, inviolable, inviolate, unimpeachable, invulnerable, untouchable, inalienable; protected, defended, secure, safe.

sad adjective **1** *we felt sad when we left* UNHAPPY, sorrowful, dejected, depressed, downcast, miserable, down, despondent, despairing, disconsolate, desolate, wretched, glum, gloomy, doleful, dismal, melancholy, mournful, woebegone, forlorn, crestfallen, heartbroken, inconsolable; *informal* blue, down in/at the mouth, down in the dumps, blah. ANTONYMS happy, cheerful.

2 *they knew her sad story* TRAGIC, unhappy, unfortunate, awful, miserable, wretched, sorry, pitiful, pathetic, traumatic, heartbreaking, heart-rending, harrowing. ANTONYM cheerful.

3 *a sad state of affairs* UNFORTUNATE, regrettable, sorry, deplorable, lamentable, pitiful, shameful, disgraceful. ANTONYM fortunate.

sadden verb *of course we all saddened by this tragic news* DEPRESS, dispirit, deject, dishearten, grieve, desolate, discourage, upset, get down, bring down, break someone's heart.

saddle verb *they were saddled with the children* BURDEN, encumber, land, charge; impose something on, thrust something on.

sadistic adjective *the heroine ends up going to prison for the murder of her sadistic father* CRUEL, barbarous, vicious, brutal, callous, fiendish, cold-blooded, inhuman, ruthless, heartless; perverted.

sadness noun *our sadness cannot be measured* UNHAPPINESS, sorrow, dejection, depression, misery, despondency, despair, desolation, wretchedness, gloom, gloominess, dolefulness, melancholy, mournfulness, woe, heartache, grief; *informal* the blues.

safe adjective **1** *the jewels are safe in the bank* SECURE, protected, shielded, sheltered, guarded, out of harm's way. ANTONYMS insecure, at risk.

2 *the lost children are all safe* UNHARMED, unhurt, uninjured, unscathed, all right, well, in one piece, out of danger, home free; *informal* OK. ANTONYM in danger.

3 *a safe place to hide* SECURE, sound, impregnable, unassailable, invulnerable. ANTONYM dangerous.

4 *a safe driver* CAUTIOUS, circumspect, prudent, attentive; unadventurous, conservative, unenterprising. ANTONYM reckless.

5 *the drug is safe* HARMLESS, innocuous, benign, nontoxic, nonpoisonous. ANTONYM harmful.

▸ noun *I keep the ring in a safe* STRONGBOX, safety-deposit box, safe-deposit box, coffer, strongroom, vault.

safeguard noun *a safeguard against terrorism* PROTECTION, defense, guard, screen, buffer, preventive, precaution, provision, security; surety, cover, insurance, indemnity.

▸ verb *the contract will safeguard 1,000 jobs* PROTECT, preserve, conserve, save, secure, shield, guard, keep safe. ANTONYM jeopardize.

safety noun **1** *the safety of the residents* WELFARE, well-being, protection, security.

2 *she worried about the safety of planes* SECURITY, soundness, dependability, reliability.

3 *we reached the safety of the shore* SHELTER, sanctuary, refuge.

sag verb **1** *she sagged in his arms* SINK, slump, loll, flop, crumple.

2 *the floors all sag* DIP, droop; bulge, bag.

3 *the markets sagged as the day wore on* DECLINE, fall, drop, slump, plummet; *informal* nosedive.

saga noun **1** *Celtic tribal sagas* EPIC, chronicle, legend, folk tale, romance, history, narrative, adventure, myth, fairy story.

2 *the saga of how they met* LONG STORY, rigmarole; chain of events; *informal* spiel.

sagacious adjective *they would all go to Granny Maywell, a sagacious old bird who could scare anyone into doing the right thing* WISE, clever, intelligent, knowledgeable, sensible, sage; discerning, judicious, canny, perceptive, astute, shrewd, prudent, thoughtful, insightful, perspicacious; *informal* streetwise, savvy; *formal* sapient. See note at SENSIBLE. ANTONYM foolish.

sage noun *the Chinese sage Confucius* WISE MAN/WOMAN, learned person, philosopher, thinker, scholar, savant; authority, expert, guru.

▸ adjective *some very sage comments* WISE, learned, clever, intelligent, having/showing great knowledge, knowledgeable, sensible, intellectual, scholarly, sagacious, erudite; discerning, judicious, canny, penetrating, perceptive, acute, astute, shrewd, prudent, politic, thoughtful, insightful, percipient, perspicacious, philosophical, profound, deep.

sail noun *the ship's sails* canvas, sailcloth.

▸ verb **1** *we sailed across the Atlantic* VOYAGE, travel by water, steam, navigate, cruise.

2 *you can learn to sail here* YACHT, boat, go sailing; crew, helm.

3 *we sail tonight* SET SAIL, put to sea, leave port, weigh anchor, shove off.

4 *he is sailing the ship* STEER, pilot, navigate, con, helm, captain; *informal* skipper.

5 *clouds were sailing past* GLIDE, drift, float, flow, sweep, skim, coast, flit.

6 *a pencil sailed past his ear* WHIZ, speed, streak, shoot, whip, buzz, zoom, flash; fly, wing, soar, zip.

PHRASE: **sail through** *she sailed through the exam* SUCCEED EASILY AT, pass easily, romp through, walk through.

sailing ship noun See table.

SAILING VESSELS

bark/barque	knockabout
barkentine	lateen
brig	longboat
brigantine	motorsailer
caique	sailboat
catamaran	schooner
catboat	skiff
clipper	skipjack
cutter	sloop
dhow	smack
felucca	tall ship
frigate	tartan
galleon	trimaran
gallery	windjammer
hoy	xebec
junk	yacht
ketch	yawl

See also tables at BOAT and SHIP.

sailor noun *his mentor at sea was a well-seasoned sailor named Coates* SEAMAN, seafarer, mariner; boatman, yachtsman, hand; *informal* (old) salt, sea dog, rating, bluejacket; *Brit.* matelot, shellback.

USAGE NOTE **sailor, sailer**

A *sailor* is one who sails—always in reference to a person. A *sailer* is a vessel or vehicle that sails, or that moves by the use of a sail—e.g.: "The second part of the project is to launch an operational solar sailer with eight sails to be tested in an 850-km. (528-mi.) circular orbit, also using a Volna rocket." (*Aviation Week & Space Technology*; July 16, 2001.) It isn't unusual to see *sailer* misused for *sailor*—e.g.: "The current exercises involve about 15,000 sailers [read *sailors*] and Marines, and include cruisers and destroyers, with nonexplosive bombs dropped from the air, according to the Associated Press." (*Chicago Sun-Times*; Apr. 30, 2001.) —**BG**

---

saintly adjective *he was a saintly but somewhat ineffective archbishop* HOLY, godly, pious, religious, devout, spiritual, prayerful; virtuous, righteous, good, moral, innocent, sinless, guiltless, irreproachable, spotless, uncorrupted, pure, angelic. ANTONYM ungodly.

sake noun **1** *this is simplified for the sake of clarity* PURPOSE, reason, aim, end, objective, object, goal, motive.

2 *she had to be brave for her daughter's sake* BENEFIT, advantage, good, well-being, welfare, interest, profit.

salacious adjective **1** *salacious writing* PORNOGRAPHIC, obscene, indecent, crude, lewd, vulgar, dirty, filthy; erotic, titillating, arousing, suggestive, sexy, risqué, ribald, smutty, bawdy; X-rated; *informal* porn, porno, blue, XXX; *euphemistic* adult.

2 *salacious women* LUSTFUL, lecherous, licentious, lascivious, libidinous, prurient, lewd; debauched, wanton, loose, fast, impure, unchaste, degenerate, sinful, depraved, promiscuous; *informal* randy, horny, hot to trot.

salary noun *a annual raise in his salary* PAY, wages, earnings, payment, remuneration, fee(s), stipend, income; *informal* take-home; *formal* emolument.

sale noun **1** *the sale of firearms* SELLING, vending; dealing, trading. ANTONYM purchase.

2 *they make a sale every minute* DEAL, transaction. ANTONYM purchase.

3 *there's a sale on* MARKDOWN, discount, blowout, clearance (sale), fire sale, liquidation (sale). PHRASE: **for sale** *is that picture for sale?* ON THE MARKET, on sale, available, purchasable, obtainable.

salesperson noun *salespersons who work on a commission* SALES ASSISTANT, sales associate, salesman, saleswoman, seller, agent, (sales) clerk; shopkeeper, trader, merchant, retailer, dealer, peddler, hawker, hustler; *informal* (sales) rep.

salient adjective *the most salient point is that the suggested cost is beyond our budget* IMPORTANT, main, principal, major, chief, primary; notable, noteworthy, outstanding, conspicuous, striking, noticeable, obvious, remarkable, prominent, predominant, dominant; key, crucial, vital, essential, pivotal, prime, central, paramount. ANTONYM minor.

saliva noun *now I've got dog saliva on my sleeve* SPIT, spittle, dribble, drool, slaver, slobber, gob, sputum.

sallow adjective *a disturbingly sallow complexion* YELLOWISH, jaundiced, pallid, wan, pale, anemic, bloodless, pasty; unhealthy, sickly, washed out; *informal* like death warmed over; *Medicine* icteric.

sally noun **1** *the garrison made a sally against us* SORTIE, charge, foray, thrust, drive, offensive, attack, assault, raid, incursion, invasion, onset, onslaught.

2 *a fruitless sally into the city* EXPEDITION, excursion, trip, outing, jaunt, visit.

3 *they exchanged amusing sallies* WITTICISM, smart remark, quip, barb, pleasantry; joke, pun, jest, bon mot; retort, riposte, counter, rejoinder; *informal* gag, wisecrack, comeback.

salon noun **1** *he works in an uptown salon* establishment, premises; boutique, store, shop; beauty parlor, beauty shop, hair salon; nail salon; tanning salon.

2 *the chateau's mirrored salon* DRAWING ROOM, sitting room, living room, lounge; *dated* parlor.

3 *he showed his artwork in a salon* EXHIBITION, (public) display, show, showing, showcase, exhibit.

saloon noun *historical* See TAVERN.

salt noun **1** *the potatoes need salt* SODIUM CHLORIDE, table salt, NaCl.

2 *literary he added salt to the conversation* ZEST, spice, piquancy, bite, edge; vitality, liveliness, spirit, sparkle; *informal* zing, punch.

▸ adjective *salt water* SALTY, salted, saline, briny, brackish.

PHRASES: **salt away** *informal Esther salted away most of her allowance* SAVE, put aside, put by, set aside, reserve, keep, store, stockpile, hoard, stow away; *informal* squirrel away, stash away. **with a grain of salt** *he's a spinner of tales, so take what he says with a grain of salt* WITH RESERVATIONS, with misgivings, skeptically, cynically, doubtfully, doubtingly, suspiciously, quizzically, incredulously.

salty adjective **1** *salty water* SALT, salted, saline, briny, brackish.

2 *a salty sense of humor* EARTHY, colorful, spicy, racy, risqué, naughty, vulgar, rude; piquant, biting.

salubrious adjective **1** *I found the climate salubrious* HEALTHY, health-giving, healthful, beneficial, wholesome; *archaic* salutary. See note at SANITARY. ANTONYM unhealthy.

2 *a salubrious Sunday afternoon* PLEASANT, agreeable, pleasing, enjoyable, pleasurable, nice, delightful; select, high-class, upscale, upmarket; *informal* posh, swanky, classy, swank; *Brit. informal* cushty. ANTONYM unpleasant.

salutary adjective **1** *a salutary lesson on the fragility of nature* BENEFICIAL, advantageous, good, profitable, productive, helpful, useful, valuable, worthwhile; timely.

2 *archaic the salutary Atlantic air.* See SALUBRIOUS sense 1.

salutation noun *his cheery salutations are a bit too much for a Monday morning* GREETING, salute, address, welcome.

salute noun **1** *he gave the captain a salute* GREETING, salutation, gesture of respect, obeisance, acknowledgment, welcome, address.

2 *she raised her hands in salutation* TRIBUTE, testimonial, homage, toast, honor, eulogy; celebration, acknowledgment.

▸ verb **1** *he saluted the ambassadors* GREET, address, hail, welcome, acknowledge, toast; make obeisance to.

2 *we salute a great photographer* PAY TRIBUTE TO, pay homage to, honor, celebrate, acknowledge, take one's hat off to.

salvage verb **1** *an attempt to salvage the vessel* RESCUE, save, recover, retrieve, raise, reclaim.

2 *he tried to salvage his reputation* RETAIN, preserve, conserve; regain, recoup, redeem, snatch.

▸ noun **1** *the salvage is taking place off the coast* RESCUE, recovery, reclamation.

2 *she sifted through the salvage* REMAINS, debris, wreckage, rubble, remnants, flotsam and jetsam, scrap.

salvation noun **1** *salvation by way of repentance* REDEMPTION, deliverance, reclamation. ANTONYM damnation.

2 *that conviction was her salvation* LIFELINE, preservation; means of escape, help, saving, savior.

salve noun *lip salve* OINTMENT, cream, balm, unguent, emollient; embrocation, liniment.

▸ verb *she did it to salve her conscience* SOOTHE, assuage, ease, allay, lighten, alleviate, comfort, mollify.

salver noun See TRAY.

same adjective **1** *we stayed at **the same** hotel* IDENTICAL, selfsame, very same, one and the same. ANTONYMS another, different.

2 *they had **the same** symptoms* MATCHING, identical, alike, duplicate, carbon copy, twin; indistinguishable, interchangeable, corresponding, equivalent, parallel, like, comparable, similar, congruent, concordant, consonant. ANTONYMS different, dissimilar.

3 *it happened that same month* SELFSAME; aforesaid, aforementioned.

4 *they provide **the same** menu worldwide* UNCHANGING, unvarying, unvaried, invariable, consistent, uniform, regular. ANTONYMS varying, different.

▸ noun *Louise said the same* SAME THING, aforementioned, aforesaid, above-mentioned.

PHRASE: **all the same 1** *I was frightened all the same* IN SPITE OF EVERYTHING, despite that, nevertheless, nonetheless, even so, however, but, still, yet, though, be that as it may, just the same, at the same time, in any event, notwithstanding, regardless, anyway, anyhow; *informal* still and all. **2** *it's all the same to me* IMMATERIAL, of no importance, of no consequence, inconsequential, unimportant, of little account, irrelevant, insignificant, trivial, petty.

THE RIGHT WORD

All of these adjectives describe something that is not significantly different from something else. **Same** may imply, and **selfsame** always implies, that what is referred to is one thing and not two or more distinct things (*they go to the same restaurant every Friday night; this is the selfsame house in which the family once lived*). In one sense, **identical** is synonymous with *selfsame* (*the identical place where we first met*); but it can also imply exact correspondence in quality, shape, and appearance (*wearing identical raincoats*). **Equivalent** describes things that are interchangeable or that amount to the same thing in value, force, or significance (*the equivalent of a free hotel room at a luxury resort*), while **equal** implies exact correspondence in quantity, value, or size (*equal portions of food*). **Tantamount** is used to describe one of a pair of things, usually intangible, that are in effect equivalent to each other (*her tears were tantamount to a confession of guilt*).

sample noun **1** *a sample of the fabric* SPECIMEN, example, bit, snippet, swatch, representative piece, exemplification; prototype, test piece, dummy, pilot, trial, taste, taster, tester.

2 *a sample of 10,000 people nationwide* CROSS SECTION, variety, sampling, test.

▸ verb *we sampled the culinary offerings* TRY (OUT), taste, test, put to the test, experiment with; appraise, evaluate, test drive; *informal* check out.

▸ adjective **1** *the sample group is small* REPRESENTATIVE, illustrative, selected, specimen, test, trial, typical.

2 *a sample copy can be obtained* SPECIMEN, test, trial, pilot, dummy.

sanatorium noun *by July of that year, the sanatorium was filled with tuberculosis patients* INFIRMARY, clinic, hospital, medical center, hospice; sick bay, sickroom.

sanctify verb **1** *he came to sanctify the site* CONSECRATE, bless, make holy, hallow, make sacred, dedicate to God.

2 *they sanctified themselves* PURIFY, cleanse, free from sin, absolve, unburden, redeem.

3 *we must not sanctify this outrage* APPROVE, sanction, condone, vindicate, endorse, support, back, permit, allow, authorize, legitimize.

sanctimonious adjective *no one wants to hear your sanctimonious hot air* SELF-RIGHTEOUS, holier-than-thou, pious, pietistic, churchy, moralizing, preachy, smug, superior, priggish, hypocritical, insincere; *informal* goody-goody. See note at MORAL.

sanction noun **1** *trade sanctions* PENALTY, punishment, deterrent; punitive action, discipline, restriction; embargo, ban, prohibition, boycott. ANTONYM reward.

2 *the scheme has the sanction of the court* AUTHORIZATION, consent, leave, permission, authority, warrant, license, dispensation, assent, acquiescence, agreement, approval, approbation, endorsement, accreditation, ratification, validation, blessing, imprimatur; *informal* go-ahead, OK, green light. ANTONYM prohibition.

▸ verb **1** *the rally was sanctioned by the government* AUTHORIZE, permit, allow, warrant, accredit, license, endorse, approve, accept, back, support; *informal* OK. See note at APPROVE. ANTONYM prohibit.

2 *the penalties available to sanction crime* PUNISH, discipline someone for.

WORD NOTE **sanction**

A rare Janus word that means both one thing and its opposite, or antonym. A *sanction* is the endorsement or approval of a course of action—*I sanction this plan*—and also (usually plural) coercive measures designed to oppose a course of action: *The UN imposed sanctions on Iraq.* Other examples of words with diametrically opposed meanings are *cleave*—to separate forcefully, and to adhere or cling to—and *oversight*—supervision, the act of watching over, and failure to notice, the act of overlooking. **—JS**

sanctity noun **1** *the sanctity of St. Francis* HOLINESS, godliness, blessedness, saintliness, spirituality, piety, piousness, devoutness, righteousness, goodness, virtue, purity; *formal* sanctitude.

2 *the sanctity of the family meal* INVIOLABILITY; importance, paramountcy.

sanctuary noun **1** *the sanctuary at Delphi.* See SANCTUM sense 1.

2 *the island is our sanctuary* REFUGE, haven, harbor, port in a storm, oasis, shelter, retreat, hideaway, hideout.

3 *he was given sanctuary in the embassy* SAFETY, protection, shelter, immunity, asylum.

4 *a bird sanctuary* RESERVE, park, reservation, preserve.

sanctum noun **1** *the sanctum in the temple* HOLY PLACE, shrine, sanctuary, temple, holy of holies, sanctum sanctorum.

2 *a private sanctum for the bar's regulars* REFUGE, retreat, hideout, hideaway, den.

sand noun *she ran across the sand* BEACH, sands, shore, seashore; (sand) dunes; *literary* strand.

sandwich noun See table.

SANDWICHES

arepa	hobo
bagel	hot brown
baguette	hot dog
barbecue beef	hot pastrami
BLT	meat loaf
boat	meatball
bologna	Monte Cristo
burrito	muffuletta
California club	open-faced
calzone	oyster loaf
canapé	pan bagnat
chicken salad	panino
chilaquile	PB & J
chili dog	peanut butter and jelly
chimichanga	Philly cheese steak
club	pig in a blanket
Coney Island	pinwheel
corn dog	pistolette
corned beef	pita pocket
Cornish pasty	poor boy
crepe	pocket
croissant	pulled pork
croque madame	quesadilla
croque monsieur	Rachel
Cuban	Reuben
cucumber	roast beef
Dagwood	sausage and pepper(s)
deviled ham	shawarma
eggplant parmigiana	sloppy joe
egg salad	smoked salmon
empanada	steak
enchilada	stromboli
fajita	sub
finger	submarine
flauta	taco
fluffernutter	tea
focaccia	tongue
french dip	torpedo
fried peanut butter and	torta
banana	triple-decker
gordita	tuna melt
grilled cheese	tuna salad
grinder	watercress
gyro	wedge
ham and cheese	Welsh rarebit/rabbit
hamburger	Western
hero	wrap
hoagie	

sane adjective **1** *the accused is presumed to be sane* OF SOUND MIND, in one's right mind, compos mentis, lucid, rational, balanced, stable, normal; *informal* all there, together. ANTONYM mad.

2 *it isn't sane to use nuclear weapons* SENSIBLE, practical, advisable, responsible, realistic, prudent, wise, reasonable, rational, levelheaded, commonsensical, judicious, politic. See note at SENSIBLE. ANTONYM foolish.

sang-froid noun *he recovered his usual sangfroid* COMPOSURE, equanimity, self-possession, equilibrium, aplomb, poise, self-assurance, self-control, nerve, calm, presence of mind; *informal* cool, unflappability.

sanguine adjective **1** *he is sanguine about the advance of technology* OPTIMISTIC, bullish, hopeful, buoyant, positive, confident, cheerful, cheery; *informal* upbeat. ANTONYM gloomy.

2 *archaic a sanguine complexion.* See FLORID sense 1.

sanitary adjective *improvements in health are also the result of more sanitary conditions* HYGIENIC, clean, antiseptic, aseptic, sterile, uninfected, disinfected, unpolluted, uncontaminated; salubrious, healthy, wholesome.

THE RIGHT WORD

Americans thrive on cleanliness and the eradication of germs. They try to keep their homes **sanitary**, a term that goes beyond cleanliness to imply that measures have been taken to guard against infections or disease. They demand that their communities provide schools and workplaces that are **hygienic**—in other words, that adhere to the rules or standards promoting public health. But it would be almost impossible to duplicate the conditions found in a hospital, where everything that comes in contact with patients must be **sterile** or free of germs entirely. Most Americans want to make their environment **healthful**, which means conducive to the health or soundness of the body, but they are not interested in making it **antiseptic**, a word that is similar in meaning to *sterile* but implies preventing infections by destroying germs that are already present (*an antiseptic solution*). Many Americans, as they grow older, choose to move to a more **salubrious** climate, a word that means health-giving and applies primarily to an air quality that is invigorating and that avoids harsh extremes.

sanitize verb **1** *the best way to sanitize a bottle* STERILIZE, disinfect, clean, cleanse, purify, fumigate, decontaminate.

2 *the diaries have not been sanitized* MAKE PRESENTABLE, make acceptable, make palatable, clean up; expurgate, bowdlerize, censor.

sanity noun **1** *she was losing her sanity* MENTAL HEALTH, faculties, reason, rationality, saneness, stability, lucidity; sense, wits, mind.

2 *sanity has prevailed* (COMMON) SENSE, wisdom, prudence, judiciousness, rationality, soundness, sensibleness.

sap[1] noun **1** *sap from the roots of trees* JUICE, secretion, fluid, liquid.

2 *they're full of youthful sap* VIGOR, energy, drive, dynamism, life, spirit, liveliness, sparkle, verve, ebullience, enthusiasm, gusto, vitality, vivacity, fire, zest, zeal, exuberance; *informal* get-up-and-go, oomph, vim.

▸ verb *they sapped the will of the troops* ERODE, wear away/down, deplete, reduce, lessen, attenuate, undermine, exhaust, drain, bleed.

sap[2] noun *informal he fell for it — what a sap!* See IDIOT.

sappy adjective See SACCHARINE.

sarcasm noun *well, it's easy to see that she got her biting sarcasm from her mother* DERISION, mockery, ridicule, scorn, sneering, scoffing; irony; cynicism. See note at WIT.

sarcastic adjective *I've had enough of your sarcastic comments* SARDONIC, ironic, ironical; derisive, snide, scornful, contemptuous, mocking, sneering, jeering; caustic, scathing, trenchant, cutting, biting, sharp, acerbic; *informal* smart-alecky.

sardonic adjective *his sardonic wit* MOCKING, satirical, sarcastic, ironical, ironic; cynical, scornful, contemptuous, derisive, derisory, sneering, jeering; scathing, caustic, trenchant, cutting, sharp, acerbic.

sash noun *the yellow sash looks dramatic with the black dress* BELT, cummerbund, waistband, girdle, obi; *literary* cincture.

sass noun *informal* See SAUCE sense 2.

Satan noun. See DEVIL sense 1.

satanic adjective *a series of satanic messages were written on the wall* DIABOLICAL, fiendish, devilish, demonic, demoniacal, ungodly, hellish, infernal, wicked, evil, sinful, iniquitous, nefarious, vile, foul, abominable, unspeakable, loathsome, monstrous, heinous, hideous, horrible, horrifying, shocking, appalling, dreadful, awful, terrible, ghastly, abhorrent, despicable, damnable.

sate verb See SATIATE.

satellite noun **1** *the satellite orbited the earth* SPACE STATION, space capsule, spacecraft; communications satellite, weather satellite.

2 *the two small satellites of Mars* MOON, secondary planet.

3 *Bulgaria was then a Russian satellite* BRANCH, colony, protectorate, puppet state, possession, holding; *historical* fief, vassal; *informal* offshoot.

▸ adjective *a satellite state* DEPENDENT, subordinate, subsidiary.

satiate verb *here, this stew should satiate you* FILL, satisfy, sate; slake, quench; gorge, stuff, surfeit, glut, cloy, sicken, nauseate.

satiny adjective *the paint dries to a nice satiny finish* SMOOTH, shiny, glossy, shining, gleaming, lustrous, sleek, silky.

satire noun **1** *a satire on Canadian politics* PARODY, burlesque, caricature, lampoon, skit; *informal* spoof, takeoff, sendup. See note at WIT.

2 *he has become the subject of satire* MOCKERY, ridicule, derision, scorn, caricature; irony, sarcasm.

satirical adjective *satirical essays about American politics* MOCKING, ironic, ironical, satiric, sarcastic, sardonic; caustic, trenchant, mordant, biting, cutting, stinging, acerbic; critical, irreverent, disparaging, disrespectful.

satirize verb *a comedy troupe that satirized the conservative establishment of the sixties* MOCK, ridicule, deride, make fun of, poke fun at, parody, lampoon, burlesque, caricature, take off; criticize; *informal* send up.

satisfaction noun **1** *he derived great satisfaction from his work* CONTENTMENT, pleasure, gratification, fulfillment, enjoyment, happiness, pride; self-satisfaction, smugness, complacency.

2 *the satisfaction of consumer needs* FULFILLMENT, gratification; appeasement, assuaging.

3 *investors turned to the courts for satisfaction* COMPENSATION, recompense, redress, reparation, restitution, repayment, payment, settlement, reimbursement, indemnification, indemnity.

satisfactory adjective *the work isn't extraordinary, but it is satisfactory* ADEQUATE, all right, acceptable, good enough, sufficient, reasonable, quite good, competent, fair, decent, average, passable; fine, in order, up to scratch, up to the mark, up to standard, up to par; *informal* OK, jake, hunky-dory, so-so, 'comme ci, comme ça'. ANTONYMS inadequate, poor.

satisfied adjective **1** *a satisfied smile* PLEASED, well pleased, content, contented, happy, proud, triumphant; smug, self-satisfied, pleased with oneself, complacent. ANTONYM unhappy.

2 *the pleasure of satisfied desire* FULFILLED, gratified. ANTONYM unfulfilled.

3 *I am satisfied that she understands* CONVINCED, certain, sure, positive, persuaded, easy in one's mind. ANTONYM unconvinced.

satisfy verb **1** *a last chance to satisfy his hunger for romance* FULFILL, gratify, meet, fill; indulge, cater to, pander to; appease, assuage; quench, slake, satiate, sate, take the edge off. ANTONYM frustrate.

2 *she satisfied herself that it had been an accident* CONVINCE, persuade, assure; reassure, put someone's mind at rest.

3 *products that satisfy the criteria* COMPLY WITH, meet, fulfill, answer, conform to; measure up to, come up to; suffice, be good enough, fit/fill the bill.

4 *there was insufficient collateral to satisfy the loan* REPAY, pay (off), settle, make good, discharge, square, liquidate, clear.

saturate verb **1** *heavy rain saturated the ground* SOAK, drench, waterlog, wet through; souse, steep, douse.

2 *the air was saturated with the stench of incense* PERMEATE, suffuse, imbue, pervade, charge, infuse, fill.

3 *the company has saturated the market* FLOOD, glut, oversupply, overload.

saturnine adjective **1** *a saturnine temperament* GLOOMY, somber, melancholy, moody, lugubrious, dour, glum, morose, unsmiling, humorless. See note at GLUM. ANTONYM cheerful.

2 *his saturnine good looks* SWARTHY, dark, dark-skinned, dark-complexioned; mysterious, mercurial, moody, brooding.

WORD NOTE saturnine

Saturnine, although it suffers some from romance-novel overuse, is much preferable to the slightly derogatory *swarthy,* if circumstances permit. Rochester (of *Jane Eyre*) is *saturnine* (possibly even the Platonic ideal of saturnine); Seth Starkadder (of *Cold Comfort Farm*) is *swarthy.* (It's never a good idea to use *swarthy* as a shorthand ethnic description.) **—EM**

sauce noun **1** *a piquant sauce* gravy; relish, condiment, salsa, ketchup; dip, dressing. See table on page 798.

2 *informal "I'll have less of your sauce," said Aunt Edie* IMPUDENCE, impertinence, cheek, cheekiness, sauciness, effrontery, forwardness, brazenness; insolence, rudeness, disrespect; *informal* mouth, lip, sass, sassiness.

3 *Uncle Reg was into the sauce again* ALCOHOL, drink, spirits, liquor; *informal* booze, hooch, hard stuff, firewater, rotgut, moonshine, grog, demon rum, bottle, juice.

saucepan noun *boil 2 cups of water in a saucepan* PAN, pot, casserole, skillet, stockpot, stewpot, Dutch oven, double boiler.

saucy adjective *informal* **1** *you saucy girl!* CHEEKY, impudent, impertinent, irreverent, forward, disrespectful, bold, as bold as brass, brazen, pert; *informal* fresh, lippy, mouthy, sassy. ANTONYMS demure, polite.

2 *the cap sat at a saucy angle* JAUNTY, rakish, sporty, raffish.

WORD NOTE **saucy**

Since it's difficult now to actually be *saucy*—lighthearted, flirtatious impudence is nonsensical in a society that produces *Girls Gone Wild* videos—I am nostalgic for this word. It could be revived, though. It doesn't have to be limited to the serving-wench context. Try switching genders—couldn't some men be usefully described as *saucy*? *(At the press conference, he responded with saucy evasions.)* Or used to anthropomorphize alluring inanimate objects? *(The stilettos lounged saucily in the display window.)* **—DA**

SAUCES, CONDIMENTS, AND DRESSINGS

alfredo	mole
applesauce	mornay
arrabbiata	mousseline
avgolemono	mustard
barbecue sauce	nam pla
Béarnaise	nuoc mam
béchamel	oyster sauce
beurre blanc	pesto
bolognese	piccalilli
bourguignon	piri piri
brandy butter	pistou
bread sauce	plum sauce
carbonara	ranch dressing
chili sauce	relish
chutney	rémoulade
coulis	Roquefort dressing
cream sauce	rouille
crème anglaise	Russian dressing
custard	salad dressing
dip	salsa
dressing	salsa verde
duxelles	sweet and sour sauce
fish sauce	tartar sauce (sauce tartare)
French dressing	skordalia
gravy	soy sauce
guacamole	Tabasco™
hard sauce	tahini
hoisin sauce	tamari
hollandaise	tapenade
horseradish	teriyaki
hot sauce	Thousand Island dressing
hummus	velouté
jus	vinaigrette
ketchup	white sauce
marinara	Worcestershire sauce
mayonnaise	
mint sauce	

saunter verb *they sauntered back to the car* STROLL, amble, wander, meander, drift, walk; stretch one's legs, take the air; *informal* mosey, tootle; *formal* promenade.

sausage noun See table.

SAUSAGES AND HOT DOGS

andouille	Genoa salami
banger	hard salami
bierwurst	kielbasa
blood sausage	knackwurst
black pudding	kolbassa
bratwurst	kubasa
bologna	liverwurst
chili dog	Polish sausage
chorizo	salami
chub	saveloy
cooked salami	summer sausage
corn dog	wiener
frankfurter	wurst

savage adjective **1** *savage dogs* FEROCIOUS, fierce; wild, untamed, untamable, undomesticated, feral. ANTONYM tame.

2 *a savage assault* VICIOUS, brutal, cruel, sadistic, ferocious, fierce, violent, bloody, murderous, homicidal, bloodthirsty; *literary* fell; *archaic* sanguinary; *informal* smash-mouth.

3 *a savage attack on free-trade policy* FIERCE, blistering, scathing, searing, stinging, devastating, mordant, trenchant, caustic, cutting, biting, withering, virulent, vitriolic. ANTONYM mild.

4 *a savage race* PRIMITIVE, uncivilized, unenlightened, nonliterate. ANTONYM civilized.

5 *a savage landscape* RUGGED, rough, wild, inhospitable, uninhabitable.

6 *a savage blow for the town* SEVERE, crushing, devastating, crippling, terrible, awful, dreadful, dire, catastrophic, calamitous, ruinous.

▸ noun **1** *she'd expected mud huts and savages* BARBARIAN, wild man, wild woman, primitive.

2 *she described her son's assailants as savages* BRUTE, beast, monster, barbarian, sadist, animal.

▸ verb **1** *he was savaged by a dog* MAUL, attack, tear to pieces, lacerate, claw, bite.

2 *critics savaged the film* CRITICIZE SEVERELY, attack, lambaste, condemn, denounce, pillory, revile; *informal* pan, tear to pieces, hammer, slam, do a hatchet job on, crucify, trash; *formal* excoriate.

savant noun *how out of place she was, a world-hungry young savant in a family of dull-witted couch potatoes* INTELLECTUAL, scholar, sage, philosopher, thinker, wise/learned person; guru, master, pandit. ANTONYM ignoramus.

save verb **1** *the captain was saved by his crew* RESCUE, come to someone's rescue, save someone's life; set free, free, liberate, deliver, extricate; bail out; *informal* save someone's bacon/neck/skin.

2 *the farmhouse has been saved from demolition* PRESERVE, keep safe, keep, protect, safeguard; salvage, retrieve, reclaim, rescue.

3 *start saving money* PUT ASIDE, set aside, put by, put to one side, save up, keep, retain, reserve, conserve, stockpile, store, hoard, save for a rainy day; *informal* salt away, squirrel away, stash away, hang on to.

4 *asking me first would have saved a lot of trouble* PREVENT, obviate, forestall, spare; stop; avoid, avert.

▸ preposition & conjunction *formal no one needed to know save herself* EXCEPT, apart from, but, other than, besides, aside from, bar, barring, excluding, leaving out, saving; *informal* outside of.

saving noun **1** *a considerable saving in development costs* REDUCTION, cut, decrease, economy.

2 **(savings)** *I'll have to use some of my savings* NEST EGG, money for a rainy day, life savings; capital, assets, funds, resources, reserves.

saving grace noun *the room's only saving grace was a spectacular view of the ocean* REDEEMING QUALITY, good point, thing in its/one's favor, advantage, asset, selling point.

savior noun *he was hailed as the country's savior* RESCUER, liberator, deliverer, emancipator; champion, knight in shining armor, friend in need, good Samaritan.

savoir faire noun *the French admired Franklin's wit and Jefferson's savoir faire* SOCIAL SKILL, social grace(s), urbanity, suavity, finesse, sophistication, poise, aplomb, adroitness, polish, style, smoothness, tact, tactfulness, diplomacy, discretion, delicacy, sensitivity; *informal* savvy. ANTONYM gaucheness.

savor verb **1** *she wanted to savor every moment* RELISH, enjoy (to the full), appreciate, delight in, revel in, luxuriate in, bask in.

2 *such a declaration* ***savored of*** *immodesty* SUGGEST, smack of, have the hallmarks of, seem like, have the air of, show signs of.

▸ noun **1** *the subtle savor of wood smoke* SMELL, aroma, fragrance, scent, perfume, bouquet; TASTE, flavor, tang, smack.

2 *a savor of bitterness seasoned my feelings for him* TRACE, hint, suggestion, touch, smack.

3 *her usual diversions had lost their savor* PIQUANCY, interest, attraction, flavor, spice, zest, excitement, enjoyment, shine; *informal* zing, pizzazz, sparkle.

savory adjective **1** *sweet or savory dishes* salty, spicy, piquant, tangy. ANTONYM sweet.

2 *a rich, savory aroma* APPETIZING, mouthwatering, delicious, delectable, luscious; tasty, flavorful, full of flavor, palatable, toothsome; *informal* scrumptious, finger-licking, lip-smacking, melt-in-your/the-mouth, yummy. ANTONYM unappetizing.

3 *one of the less savory aspects of the affair* ACCEPTABLE, pleasant, respectable, wholesome, honorable, proper, seemly. ANTONYMS unpleasant, unacceptable.

savvy *informal* noun *his political savvy* SHREWDNESS, astuteness, sharp-wittedness, sharpness, acuteness, acumen, acuity, intelligence, wit, canniness, common sense, discernment, insight, understanding, penetration, perception, perceptiveness, perspicacity, knowledge, sagacity; *informal* horse sense, know-how, (street) smarts; *rare* sapience.

▸ adjective *a savvy investor* SHREWD, astute, sharp-witted, sharp, acute, adroit, intelligent, clever, canny, perceptive, perspicacious, sagacious, sage, wise; *informal* on the ball, quick on the uptake, smart, streetwise, heads-up.

saw noun **1** *an old rusty saw.* See table.

2 *the old saw about when the going gets tough* SAYING, maxim, proverb, aphorism, axiom, adage, epigram.

TYPES OF SAW

backsaw	fretsaw
bandsaw	hacksaw
bench saw	handsaw
bow saw	jigsaw
bucksaw	miter saw
buzz saw	radial arm saw
chainsaw	ripsaw
circular saw	saber saw
compass saw	scroll saw
coping saw	slasher
crosscut saw	table saw
cylinder saw	whipsaw
dovetail saw	

say verb **1** *she felt her stomach flutter as he said her name* SPEAK, utter, voice, pronounce, give voice to, vocalize.

2 *"I must go," she said* DECLARE, state, announce, remark, observe, mention, comment, note, add; reply, respond, answer, rejoin; *informal* come out with.

3 *Newall says he's innocent* CLAIM, maintain, assert, hold, insist, contend; allege, profess; *formal* opine, aver.

4 *I can't conjure up the words to say how I feel* EXPRESS, put into words, phrase, articulate, communicate, make known, put/get across, convey, verbalize; reveal, divulge, impart, disclose; imply, suggest.

5 *they sang hymns and said a prayer* RECITE, repeat, utter, deliver, perform, declaim, orate.

6 *the clock said one twenty* INDICATE, show, read.

7 *I'd say it's about five miles* ESTIMATE, judge, guess, hazard a guess, predict, speculate, surmise, conjecture, venture; *informal* reckon.

8 *let's say you'd just won a million dollars* SUPPOSE, assume, imagine, presume, hypothesize, postulate, posit.

▸ noun **1** *everyone is entitled to their say* CHANCE TO SPEAK, turn to speak, opinion, view, voice; *informal* two cents, two cents' worth.

2 *don't I have any say in the matter?* INFLUENCE, sway, weight, voice, input, share, part.

PHRASES: **that is to say** *they're inquiring about Miss Leslie—that is to say, they want to know if she's safe and well.* IN OTHER WORDS, to put it another way; i.e., that is, to wit, viz., namely. **to say the least** *his performance was disappointing to say the least* TO PUT IT MILDLY, putting it mildly, without any exaggeration, at the very least.

WORD NOTE **said**

While most writing can be improved by choosing strong and precise nouns, adjectives, and verbs, this isn't always so. When reading a novel's dialogue, we should be paying attention to what the characters say, and learn about their feelings through their words. But too many young authors overstress the verbal markers of back-and-forth speech. So we read *Frank replied* or *Frank riposted* or even *Losing his temper, Frank violently expostulated.* Much of the time a careful writer can set up the rhythm of a conversation so that it's always clear who's speaking and with what degree of passion. If more precise identification is needed, a simple *Frank said* will usually suffice, the weak and common verb scarcely intruding on the give-and-take on the page. **—MD**

saying noun *you know the old saying about all work and no play?* PROVERB, maxim, aphorism, axiom, adage, saw, tag, motto, epigram, dictum, expression, phrase, formula; slogan, catchphrase, mantra; platitude, cliché, commonplace, truism, chestnut. PHRASE: **it goes without saying** *it goes without saying we'll need to rent a car when we get there* OF COURSE, naturally, needless to say, it's taken for granted, it's understood/assumed, it's taken as read, it's an accepted fact; obviously, self-evidently, manifestly; *informal* natch.

THE RIGHT WORD

"Once burned, twice shy" is an old **saying** about learning from your mistakes. In fact, *sayings*—a term used to describe any current or habitual expression of wisdom or truth—are a dime a dozen. **Proverbs**—sayings that are well known and often repeated, usually expressing metaphorically a truth based on common sense or practical experience—are just as plentiful (*her favorite proverb was "A stitch in time saves nine"*). An **adage** is a time-honored and widely known proverb, such as "Where's there's smoke, there's fire." A **maxim** offers a rule of conduct or action in the form of a proverb, such as "Neither a borrower nor a lender be." **Epigram** and **epigraph** are often confused, but their meanings are quite separate. An *epigram* is a terse, witty, or satirical statement that often relies on a paradox for its effect (*Oscar Wilde's well-known epigram that "The only way to get rid of temptation is to yield to it"*). An *epigraph*, on the other hand, is a brief quotation used to introduce a piece of writing (*he used a quote from T. S. Eliot as the epigraph to his new novel*). An **aphorism** requires a little more thought than an *epigram*, since it aims to be profound rather than witty (*she'd just finished reading a book of Mark Twain's aphorisms*). An **apothegm** is a pointed and often startling aphorism, such as Samuel Johnson's remark that "Patriotism is the last refuge of a scoundrel."

---

say-so noun *informal* **1** *they could not act without the senate's say-so* AUTHORIZATION, (seal of) approval, agreement, consent, assent, permission, endorsement, sanction, ratification, approbation, acquiescence, blessing, leave; *informal* OK, go-ahead, green light, thumbs up, rubber stamp. ANTONYMS refusal, denial.

2 *we wouldn't proceed merely on his say-so* ASSERTION, declaration, opinion.

scalawag noun *informal you scalawags get out of here!* RASCAL, scamp, monkey, imp, devil, rogue; *informal* hellion, rapscallion, monster, terror, horror, varmint.

scalding adjective *a pot of scalding water* EXTREMELY HOT, burning, blistering, searing, red-hot; piping hot; *informal* BOILING (HOT), sizzling. See note at BURN.

scale[1] noun **1** *reptiles have scales covering the skin* plate; *technical* lamella, lamina, squama, scute, scutum.

2 *the disease causes scales on the skin* FLAKE; **(scales)** scurf, dandruff; *technical* furfur.

3 *how can I remove the scale from my tea kettle?* BUILDUP, deposit, incrustation.

scale[2] noun **1** *the Richter scale* CALIBRATED SYSTEM, calibration, graduated system, system of measurement, measuring system.

2 *we are at opposite ends of the social scale* HIERARCHY, ladder, ranking, pecking order, order, spectrum, progression, succession, sequence, series.

3 *the scale of the map is too small to show details* RATIO, proportion, relative size.

4 *no one foresaw the scale of the disaster* EXTENT, size, scope, magnitude, dimensions, range, breadth, compass, degree, reach, spread, sweep.

▸ verb *thieves scaled the fence* CLIMB, ascend, go up, clamber up, scramble up, mount, shinny (up); *historical* escalade.

PHRASES: **scale down** *manufacturing capacity has been scaled down* REDUCE, cut down, cut back, cut, make cutbacks in, decrease, lessen, lower, trim, slim down, prune, curtail. **scale up** *the departments intend to scale up their activities* INCREASE, expand, augment, build up, add to; step up, boost, escalate.

scaly adjective **1** *the dragon's scaly hide technical* squamous, squamate, squamose, lamellate, lamellar, lamelliform, lamellose.

2 *scaly patches of dead skin* FLAKY, DRY, flaking, scurfy, peeling, rough, scabrous, mangy, scabious; *technical* furfuraceous.

scam noun *informal the scam involved a series of bogus investment deals* FRAUD, swindle, fraudulent scheme, racket, trick; *informal* con, hustle, flimflam, bunco, grift, gyp, shakedown.

▸ verb *Bennett was trying to scam the Vogelmans with phony insurance policies* SWINDLE, cheat, deceive, trick, dupe, hoodwink, double-cross, gull; *informal* rip off, con, fleece, shaft, hose, sting, bilk, diddle, rook, gyp, finagle, bamboozle, flimflam, put one over on, pull a fast one on, sucker, stiff, shake down, hornswoggle.

scamp noun *informal he was a scamp in his younger days* RASCAL, monkey, devil, imp, wretch, mischief-maker, troublemaker, prankster, rogue; *informal* scalawag, horror, monster, terror, holy terror, hellion, varmint, rapscallion; *archaic* scapegrace.

scamper verb *the boy scampered off | his dogs scampered around the yard* SCURRY, scuttle, dart, run, rush, race, dash, sprint, hurry, hasten, make haste, scoot; romp, skip, frolic, gambol; *Brit.* scutter.

scan verb **1** *Adam scanned the horizon* SCRUTINIZE, EXAMINE, study, inspect, survey, search, scour, sweep, look at, stare at, look someone/something up and down, gaze at, eye, watch; contemplate, regard, take stock of; *informal* check out, scope (out).

2 *I scanned the pages of his diary* GLANCE THROUGH/OVER, look through/over, have a look at, run/cast/pass one's eye over, skim (through), flick through, flip through, leaf through, thumb through, rifle through, read quickly, browse (through). ANTONYM pore over.

▸ noun **1** *a careful scan of the terrain* INSPECTION, scrutiny, examination, survey.

2 *a quick scan through the report* GLANCE, look, flick, browse, skim.

3 *a brain scan* EXAMINATION, screening, MRI, ultrasound.

scandal noun **1** *the sex scandal forced him to resign* (OUTRAGEOUS) WRONGDOING, impropriety, misconduct, immoral behavior, unethical behavior, discreditable behavior, outrageous behavior; shocking incident, shocking series of events; offense, transgression, crime, sin; skeleton in the closet; *informal* business, affair, -gate.

2 *unmarried motherhood at that time was fraught with scandal* SHAME, dishonor, disgrace, disrepute, discredit, infamy, ignominy, embarrassment; odium, opprobrium, censure, obloquy; stigma.

3 *it's a scandal that the disease is not adequately treated* DISGRACE, outrage, injustice; (crying) shame, pity; affront, insult, reproach.

4 *no scandal is attached to her name* MALICIOUS GOSSIP, malicious rumor(s), slander, libel, calumny, defamation, aspersions, muckraking, scandalmongering, smear campaign; *informal* dirt.

scandalize verb *the audience was scandalized by the speaker's racist remarks* SHOCK, appall, outrage, horrify, disgust, revolt, repel, sicken; offend, give offense to, affront, insult; cause raised eyebrows. ANTONYM impress.

scandalous adjective **1** *a scandalous waste of taxpayers' money* DISGRACEFUL, shocking, outrageous, monstrous, criminal, wicked, sinful, shameful, atrocious, appalling, dreadful, deplorable, reprehensible, inexcusable, intolerable, insupportable, unforgivable, unconscionable, unpardonable; *rare* egregious. ANTONYMS acceptable, praiseworthy.

2 *a series of scandalous liaisons* DISCREDITABLE, disreputable, dishonorable, improper, unseemly, sordid. ANTONYMS proper, seemly.

3 *scandalous rumors* SCURRILOUS, malicious, slanderous, libelous, defamatory; *rare* calumnious, calumniatory, aspersive.

scant adjective *there is only scant evidence to support this hypothesis* LITTLE, little or no, minimal, hardly (any), limited, negligible, barely sufficient, meager; insufficient, too little, inadequate, deficient; *formal* exiguous. ANTONYMS abundant, ample, sufficient.

scanty adjective **1** *their scanty wages details of his life are scanty* MEAGER, scant, minimal, limited, modest, restricted, sparse; tiny, small, paltry, negligible, insufficient, inadequate, deficient, too small/little/few, poor, sketchy, thin; scarce, in short supply, few and far between; *informal* measly, piddling, mingy, pathetic; *formal* exiguous. ANTONYMS ample, abundant, plentiful.

2 *scanty clothing* SKIMPY, revealing, short, brief; low, low-cut; indecent. ANTONYM modest.

scapegoat noun *find yourself another scapegoat* WHIPPING BOY; *informal* fall guy, patsy.

scar noun **1** *the scar on his left cheek* CICATRIX, mark, blemish, disfigurement, discoloration, defacement; pockmark, pock, pit; lesion, stigma; birthmark, nevus; **(scars)** stigmata.

2 *deep psychological scars* TRAUMA, damage, injury.

▸ verb **1** *the leg will heal, but he's likely to be scarred for life* DISFIGURE, mark, blemish, discolor; pockmark, pit; stigmatize.

2 *the landscape has been scarred by strip mining* DAMAGE, spoil, mar, deface, injure; *rare* disfeature.

3 *she was profoundly scarred by the incident* TRAUMATIZE, damage, injure, wound; distress, disturb, upset.

USAGE NOTE **scarify, scorify**

Scarify (from *scar*, but pronounced as if from *scare*) means (1) "make superficial marks or incisions in; cut off skin from"; (2) "break up the surface of (the ground) with a spiked machine [a scarifier] for loosening soil or building roads"; or (3) "pain by severe criticism."

Sense 1 is most common—e.g.: "Rub the seed across some sandpaper to weaken the hard seed coat or scarify it with a knife for better germination." (*Virginian-Pilot* [Norfolk]; Apr. 20, 1997.) This sense applies also to body adornment by cutting and scraping—e.g.: "Worse, once piercing becomes commonplace among people like, well, Leslie, the trendsetters up the ante with other forms of body alteration: cutting (scarification as adornment), branding (searing flesh with high heat in artistic patterns) and—please don't eat during this next sentence—tongue splitting, in which the tongue is cleaved nearly in half so as to cause it to fork like a lizard's." (*Washington Post*; Feb. 11, 2003.)

Sense 3 is also fairly common—e.g.: "With a combination of dazzling philosophical acumen and scarifying wit, Stove does for irrationalism in Karl Popper's philosophy . . . what the Romans did for Carthage in the Third Punic War." (*New Criterion*; Mar. 1997.)

An identically pronounced, but separate, *scarify*, based on the root word *scare*, dates from the late 18th century but remains mostly dialectal. It often carries a lighthearted connotation—e.g.: "The cost-of-living index had taken a scarifying new jump of 1.2 percent in February, to an annual rate of 15 percent." (*Newsweek*; Apr. 2, 1979.)

Scorify = reduce to dross or slag. The term surfaces most commonly in cognate forms, such as *scorifier*—e.g.: "Hanging adjacent to the furnace are the specialized tongs for handling crucibles, cupels and the dishlike ceramic containers called scorifiers." (*Bulletin* [Bend, OR]; Apr. 2, 1997.) —**BG**

scarce adjective **1** *food was scarce | scarce financial resources* IN SHORT SUPPLY, scant, scanty, meager, sparse, short, hard to find, hard to come by, too little, insufficient, deficient, inadequate, lacking, wanting; at a premium, paltry, negligible; *informal* rare/scarce as hen's teeth, rarer/scarcer than hen's teeth, not to be had for love or money; *formal* exiguous. ANTONYMS plentiful, abundant.

2 *birds that prefer dense forest are becoming scarce* RARE, few and far between; uncommon, unusual. ANTONYM common.

scarcely adverb **1** *she could scarcely hear what he was saying* HARDLY, barely, only just; almost not.

2 *I **scarcely ever** see him* RARELY, seldom, infrequently, not often, hardly ever, almost never, on rare occasions, every once in a while; *informal* once in a blue moon. ANTONYM often.

3 *this could scarcely be accidental* SURELY NOT, not, hardly, certainly not, definitely not, not at all, on no account, under no circumstances, by no means, in no way, noway, noways.

scarcity noun *the scarcity of affordable housing* SHORTAGE, dearth, lack, want, undersupply, insufficiency, paucity, scarceness, scantness, scantiness, meagerness, sparseness, poverty; deficiency, inadequacy; unavailability, absence; *rare* exiguity, exiguousness. ANTONYMS abundance, excess, surplus.

scare verb *stop it, you're scaring me* FRIGHTEN, startle, alarm, terrify, petrify, intimidate, terrorize, make afraid, make fearful, fill with fear, give someone a fright, panic, throw into a panic, shock, unnerve, cow; strike terror into, put the fear of God into, chill to the bone/marrow, make someone's blood run cold, scare/frighten to death, scare/frighten someone out of their wits, send into a cold sweat, scare/frighten the living daylights out of, scare/frighten the life out of, scare the hell out of, scare stiff, scare witless, make someone shake in their boots/shoes; *informal* scare the pants off, make someone's hair stand on end, make someone jump out of their skin, make someone's hair curl, spook, scarify, scare the bejesus out of, scare the bejabbers out of, give someone the heebie-jeebies; *vulgar slang* scare shitless, scare the shit out of. ANTONYM reassure.

▸ noun *you gave me a scare—how did you get here?* FRIGHT, shock, start, turn, jump; *informal* heart attack.

scared adjective *I've never been so scared in all my life* FRIGHTENED, afraid, fearful, startled, nervous, panicky, alarmed, intimidated; terrified, petrified, terrorized, horrified, unnerved, panic-stricken/-struck, terror-stricken/-struck, horror-stricken/-struck, with one's heart in one's mouth, scared stiff, scared/frightened out of one's wits, scared witless, scared/frightened to death, chilled to the bone/marrow, in a cold sweat; *informal* spooked, scarified; *vulgar slang* scared shitless.

scaremonger noun *the scaremongers want us to believe there is no safe produce in the grocery store* ALARMIST, prophet of doom, Cassandra, voice of doom, doom-monger; *informal* Chicken Little, doom-and-gloom merchant, merchant of doom and gloom, paranoia peddler, end-of-the-worlder.

scarf noun *she wore a scarf* MUFFLER, headscarf, mantilla, stole, tippet; kerchief, neckerchief, bandanna, babushka.

▸ verb *informal stop scarfing your food!* | *we* ***scarfed down*** *the entire batch of cookies* | *I can't believe how fast he* ***scarfed up*** *his dinner* GOBBLE UP/DOWN, eat greedily, eat hungrily, guzzle, bolt, gulp (down), devour, wolf (down), gorge (oneself) on; *informal* tuck into, put away, pack away, demolish, polish off, shovel in/down, stuff one's face (with), pig out (on); *informal* scoff (down/up), inhale; *rare* gluttonize, gourmandize, ingurgitate. ANTONYM nibble.

scary adjective *informal that movie is too scary for me* FRIGHTENING, alarming, terrifying, petrifying, hair-raising, spine-chilling, blood-curdling, bone-chilling, chilling, horrifying, nerve-racking, fearsome, unnerving; eerie, sinister; *informal* creepy, spine-tingling, spooky, hairy.

scathing adjective *another restaurant has fallen victim to one of her scathing reviews* DEVASTATING, extremely critical, blistering, searing, withering, scorching, fierce, ferocious, savage, severe, stinging, biting, cutting, mordant, trenchant, virulent, caustic, vitriolic, scornful, sharp, bitter, harsh, unsparing; *rare* mordacious. ANTONYMS mild, gentle; complimentary.

scatter verb **1** *the papers were scattered by the sudden breeze* | *scatter the seeds as evenly as possible* THROW, strew, toss, fling; SPRINKLE, spread, distribute, sow, broadcast, disseminate; *literary* bestrew. ANTONYM gather.

2 *the crowd scattered* | *onlookers were scattered in all directions* DISPERSE, break up, disband, separate, move/go in different directions, go separate ways; dissipate, dissolve; drive, send, put to flight, chase. ANTONYM assemble.

THE RIGHT WORD

If you **scatter** something, you throw it about in different directions, often using force (*the wind scattered leaves around the yard*). **Disperse** implies a scattering that completely breaks up a mass or assemblage and spreads the units far and wide (*the crowd dispersed as soon as the storm arrived; the ships were so widely dispersed that they couldn't see each other*). To **dispel** is to scatter or to drive away something that obscures, confuses, or bothers (*to dispel her fears*), while to **diffuse** is to lessen the intensity of something by spreading it out over a broader area (*the curtains diffused the bright sunlight pouring in the window*). **Dissipate** suggests that something has completely dissolved, disintegrated, or vanished (*early-morning mist dissipated by the sun*). **Broadcast** originally meant to scatter seed, but it is also used figuratively to mean make public (*The news of the president's defeat was broadcast the next morning*). **Disseminate** also means to publish or make public, but it implies a wider audience and usually a longer duration. You can spend a lifetime *disseminating* knowledge, in other words, but you would *broadcast* the news of the birth of your first grandchild.

scatterbrain noun *he's such a scatterbrain that he missed his own birthday* ABSENTMINDED PERSON; *informal* airhead, flake, ditz, space cadet.

scatterbrained adjective *my scatterbrained kids left their jackets on the bus* ABSENTMINDED, forgetful, disorganized; dreamy, with one's head in the clouds, with a mind/memory like a sieve, featherbrained, birdbrained, giddy; *informal* dizzy, dippy, ditzy, flaky, scatty, not with it, out to lunch.

scavenge verb *they scavenge for food in the restaurant's trash cans* FORAGE, rummage, search, hunt, look, root around/about, grub around/about.

scavenger *yesterday he ran the company, today he's a homeless scavenger* FORAGER, rummager, grubber; *historical* ragpicker; *rare* mudlark.

scenario noun **1** *Walt wrote scenarios for a major Hollywood studio* PLOT, outline, synopsis, story line, framework; screenplay, script, libretto; *formal* diegesis.

2 *every possible scenario must be explored* SEQUENCE OF EVENTS, course of events, chain of events, series of developments, situation.

3 *this film has a more contemporary scenario* SETTING, background, context, scene, milieu.

scene noun **1** *the scene of the accident* LOCATION, site, place, position, point, spot; locale, setting, whereabouts; *technical* locus.

2 *the scene is Montreal, in the late 1890s* BACKGROUND, setting, context, milieu, backdrop, mise en scène.

3 *terrible scenes of violence* INCIDENT, event, episode, happening, moment.

4 *an impressive mountain scene* VIEW, vista, outlook, panorama, sight; landscape, scenery; picture, tableau, spectacle.

5 *she created a scene outside the bank* FUSS, exhibition of oneself, performance, tantrum, outburst, commotion, disturbance, upset, furor, brouhaha, row, contretemps; *informal* song and dance, to-do.

6 *the political scene sorry, fishing just isn't my scene* ARENA, stage, sphere, world, milieu, realm, domain; area of interest, field, field of interest, specialty, province, preserve; *informal* thing.

7 *the last scene of the play* SUBDIVISION, division, section, segment.

8 *a scene from a Laurel and Hardy movie* CLIP, section, segment, part, sequence. PHRASES: **behind the scenes** adverb *informal discussions continued behind the scenes* SECRETLY, in secret, privately, in private, behind closed doors, surreptitiously, off the record; *informal* on the quiet, on the QT; *formal* sub rosa. **behind-the-scenes** adjective *a behind-the-scenes romance* SECRET, private, clandestine, surreptitious; confidential.

scenery noun **1** *the beautiful scenery of the Rockies* LANDSCAPE, countryside, country, terrain, topography, setting, surroundings, environment; view, vista, panorama; cityscape, townscape, roofscape; riverscape, seascape, waterscape, snowscape.

2 *we all helped with the scenery and costumes* STAGE SET, set, mise en scène, backdrop, drop curtain; setting, background, decor.

scenic adjective *countless miles of Route 1 are still quite scenic* PICTURESQUE, pretty, pleasing, attractive, lovely, beautiful, charming, pretty as a picture, easy on the eye; impressive, striking, spectacular, breathtaking; panoramic. ANTONYMS dreary, unattractive.

scent noun **1** *the scent of freshly cut hay* SMELL, fragrance, aroma, perfume, redolence, savor, odor, whiff; bouquet, nose. See note at SMELL.

2 *that's a lovely scent you're wearing* PERFUME, fragrance, cologne, toilet water.

3 *the hounds picked up the scent of a rabbit* SPOOR, trail, track; *Hunting* foil, wind.

4 *there was a scent of rain in the air* HINT, suggestion, trace, whiff.

▸ verb 1 *a shark can scent blood from over half a mile away* SMELL, detect the smell of, get a whiff of.

2 *Rose looked at him, scenting a threat* SENSE, become aware of, detect, discern, perceive, recognize, get wind of.

scented adjective *a hotel with private saunas and scented sheets* PERFUMED, fragranced, perfumy; sweet-smelling, fragrant, aromatic; *rare* aromatized.

schadenfreude noun See note below.

WORD NOTE **schadenfreude**

Derived from the German words for *trouble* and *pleasure,* it means the joy we sometimes cannot help but experience when we hear about another's misfortune. The downfall of an enemy, scandals involving our least favorite celebrities. *She felt a certain schadenfreude when she read the bad reviews of Madonna's children's book.* How thrilling that there should be a single word that not only describes a highly complex, uncharitable, and (one hopes) relatively rare psychological state, but also one which very few people will even admit to feeling. There should be more words like that. *Realestateenvy,* for one. **—FP**

schedule noun 1 *we need to draw up a production schedule* PLAN, program, timetable, scheme.

2 *I have a very busy schedule* TIMETABLE, agenda, diary, calendar, timeline; itinerary.

▸ verb *another meeting was scheduled for April 20* ARRANGE, organize, plan, program, timetable, set up, line up, slate.

PHRASE: **behind schedule** *the museum renovations are behind schedule* LATE, running late, overdue, behind time, behind, behindhand.

scheme noun 1 *crazy fundraising schemes* PLAN, project, plan of action, program, strategy, stratagem, tactic, game plan, course/line of action; system, procedure, design, formula, recipe.

2 *police uncovered a scheme to steal the paintings* PLOT, intrigue, conspiracy; ruse, ploy, stratagem, maneuver, subterfuge; machinations; *informal* game, racket, con, scam.

3 *the sonnet's rhyme scheme* ARRANGEMENT, system, organization, configuration, pattern, format; *technical* schema.

▸ verb *he schemed to bring about the collapse of the government* PLOT, hatch a plot, conspire, intrigue, connive, maneuver, plan.

scheming adjective *he finally saw his scheming wife for what she really was* CUNNING, crafty, calculating, devious, designing, conniving, wily, sly, tricky, artful, guileful, slippery, slick, manipulative, Machiavellian, unscrupulous, disingenuous; duplicitous, deceitful, underhanded, treacherous. ANTONYMS ingenuous, honest.

schism noun *the schism between her father and his brother* DIVISION, split, rift, breach, rupture, break, separation, severance; chasm, gulf; discord, disagreement, dissension.

schmaltzy adjective *informal schmaltzy lyrics.* See SENTIMENTAL sense 2.

schmooze verb *the party will give you a chance to schmooze* TALK, chat (up), converse, mingle, mix, hobnob, network; *informal* work the room.

scholar noun 1 *a leading biblical scholar* ACADEMIC, intellectual, learned person, man/woman of letters, mind, intellect, savant, polymath, highbrow, bluestocking; authority, expert; *informal* egghead.

2 *archaic the school had 28 scholars* STUDENT, pupil, schoolchild, schoolboy, schoolgirl.

scholarly adjective 1 *an earnest, scholarly man* LEARNED, erudite, academic, well-read, widely read, intellectual, literary, lettered, educated, knowledgeable, highbrow; studious, bookish, donnish, bluestocking, cerebral; *informal* pointy-headed. ANTONYMS uneducated, illiterate.

2 *a scholarly career* ACADEMIC, scholastic, pedagogic.

scholarship noun 1 *a center of medieval scholarship* LEARNING, book learning, knowledge, erudition, education, letters, culture, academic study, academic achievement. See note at KNOWLEDGE.

2 *a scholarship of $200 per semester* GRANT, award, endowment, payment, bursary.

scholastic adjective *their scholastic achievements* ACADEMIC, educational, school, scholarly.

school noun 1 *their children went to the local school* EDUCATIONAL INSTITUTION; academy, college, university; seminary; alma mater. See table on page 804.

2 *the university's School of Law* DEPARTMENT, faculty, division.

3 *the Barbizon school* GROUP, set, circle; followers, following, disciples, apostles, admirers, devotees, votaries; proponents, adherents.

4 *the school of linguistics associated with his ideas* WAY OF THINKING, persuasion, creed, credo, doctrine, belief, faith, opinion, point of view; approach, method, style.

5 *a school of fish* shoal; pod, gam.

▸ verb 1 *he was born in Paris and schooled in Lyon* EDUCATE, teach, instruct.

2 *he schooled her in horsemanship* TRAIN, teach, tutor, coach, instruct, drill, discipline, direct, guide, prepare, groom; prime, verse.

schooling noun 1 *his parents paid for his schooling* EDUCATION, teaching, tuition, instruction, tutoring, tutelage; lessons; (book) learning.

2 *the schooling of horses* TRAINING, coaching, instruction, drill, drilling, discipline, disciplining.

schoolteacher noun *until 1912, the town had in its employ just one schoolteacher* TEACHER, schoolmaster, schoolmistress, tutor, educationist; *informal* schoolmarm; *formal* pedagogue.

science noun 1 *he teaches science at the high school* physics, chemistry, biology; physical sciences, life sciences.

2 *the science of criminology* BRANCH OF KNOWLEDGE, body of knowledge/information, area of study, discipline, field.

scientific adjective 1 *scientific research* technological, technical; research-based, knowledge-based, empirical.

2 *you need to approach it in a more scientific way* SYSTEMATIC, methodical, organized, well-organized, ordered, orderly, meticulous, rigorous; exact, precise, accurate, mathematical; analytical, rational.

SCHOOLS

academy	library school
Bible school	lycée
boarding school	magnet school
charm school	middle school
charter school	Montessori school
cheder	night school
choir school	nursery school
church school	parochial school
college	prep school
community college	preparatory school
conservatory	preschool
convent school	private school
correspondence school	public school
day school	reform school
divinity school	residential school
elementary school	secondary school
finishing school	seminary
grade school	senior high school
graduate school	summer school
grammar school	Sunday school
high school	teachers' college
juku	technical school
junior college	university
junior high school	vocational school
kindergarten	yeshiva
law school	

scintilla noun *you haven't got a scintilla of evidence to back that up* PARTICLE, iota, jot, whit, atom, speck, bit, trace, ounce, shred, crumb, fragment, grain, drop, spot, modicum, hint, touch, suggestion, whisper, suspicion; *informal* smidgen, tad.

scintillating adjective **1** *a scintillating diamond necklace* SPARKLING, shining, bright, brilliant, gleaming, glittering, twinkling, shimmering, glistening; *literary* glistering. ANTONYM dull.

2 *a scintillating performance* BRILLIANT, dazzling, exciting, exhilarating, stimulating; sparkling, lively, buzzy, vivacious, vibrant, animated, ebullient, effervescent; witty, clever; *literary* coruscating. ANTONYMS dull, boring.

scion noun **1** *a scion of the tree* CUTTING, graft, slip; shoot, offshoot, twig.

2 *the scion of an aristocratic family* DESCENDANT; heir, successor; child, offspring; *Law* issue.

scoff verb *they **scoffed at** her article* MOCK, deride, ridicule, sneer at, jeer at, jibe at, taunt, make fun of, poke fun at, laugh at, scorn, laugh to scorn, dismiss, make light of, belittle; *informal* pooh-pooh.

scold verb *Mom took Anna away, scolding her for her bad behavior* REBUKE, reprimand, reproach, reprove, admonish, remonstrate with, chastise, chide, upbraid, berate, take to task, read someone the riot act, give someone a piece of one's mind, rake/haul someone over the coals; *informal* tell off, dress down, give someone an earful, rap over the knuckles, let someone have it, bawl out, give someone hell, give someone what for, chew out, ream (out), light into; *formal* castigate. See note at REBUKE. ANTONYM praise.

▸ noun *archaic she is turning into a scold* NAG, shrew, fishwife, harpy, termagant, harridan; complainer, moaner, grumbler; *informal* kvetch.

THE RIGHT WORD

A mother might **scold** a child who misbehaves, which means to rebuke in an angry, irritated, and often nagging way, whether or not such treatment is justified. **Chide** is a more formal term than *scold*, and it usually implies disapproval for specific failings (*she was chided by her teacher for using "less" instead of "fewer"*), while **berate** suggests a prolonged scolding, usually aimed at a pattern of behavior or way of life rather than a single misdeed and often combined with scorn or contempt for the person being criticized (*he berated his parents for being too protective and ruining his social life*). **Upbraid** also implies a lengthy expression of displeasure or criticism, but usually with more justification than scold and with an eye toward encouraging better behavior in the future (*the tennis coach upbraided her players for missing so many serves*). **Revile** and **vituperate** are reserved for very strong or even violent displays of anger. To *revile* is to use highly abusive and contemptuous language (*revile one's opponent in the press*), while **vituperate** connotes even more violence in the attack (*the angry hockey players were held apart by their teammates, but they continued to vituperate each other with the foulest possible language*).

scolding noun *I'll be in Mr. Kling's office getting my weekly scolding* REBUKE, reprimand, reproach, reproof, admonishment, remonstration, lecture, upbraiding; *informal* talking-to, rap over the knuckles, dressing-down, earful, roasting; *formal* castigation.

scoop noun **1** *a measuring scoop* SPOON, ladle, dipper; bailer.

2 *a scoop of vanilla ice cream* SPOONFUL, ladleful, portion, lump, ball; *informal* dollop.

3 *informal he got the scoop on the new CEO* EXCLUSIVE (STORY), inside story, exposé, revelation, information.

▸ verb **1** *a hole was **scooped out** in the floor* HOLLOW OUT, gouge out, dig, excavate, cut out.

2 *cut the tomatoes in half and **scoop out** the flesh* REMOVE, take out, spoon out, scrape out.

3 *she **scooped up** armfuls of clothes* PICK UP, gather up, lift, take up; snatch up, grab.

scoot verb *informal* See SCURRY verb.

scope noun **1** *the scope of the investigation* EXTENT, range, breadth, width, reach, sweep, purview, span, horizon; area, sphere, field, realm, compass, orbit, ambit, terms/field of reference, jurisdiction; confine, limit; gamut. See note at RANGE.

2 *the scope for change is limited by political realities* OPPORTUNITY, freedom, latitude, leeway, capacity, liberty, room (to maneuver), elbow room; possibility, chance.

scorch verb **1** *the buildings were scorched by the fire* BURN, sear, singe, char, blacken, discolor. See note at BURN.

2 *grass scorched by the sun* DRY UP, desiccate, parch, wither, shrivel; burn, bake.

scorching adjective **1** *the scorching July sun* EXTREMELY HOT, red-hot, blazing, flaming, fiery, burning, blistering, searing, sweltering, torrid, broiling; *informal* boiling (hot), baking (hot), sizzling. ANTONYM freezing.

2 *scorching criticism* FIERCE, savage, scathing, withering, blistering, searing, devastating, stringent, severe, harsh, stinging, biting, mordant, trenchant, caustic, virulent, vitriolic. ANTONYM mild.

score noun **1** *the final score was 4–3* RESULT, outcome; total, sum total, tally, count.

2 *an IQ score of 161* RATING, grade, mark, percentage.

3 *I've got a score to settle with you* GRIEVANCE, grudge, complaint; dispute, bone of contention; **(score to settle)** bone to pick, ax to grind.

4 *informal he knew* ***the score*** *before he got here* THE SITUATION, the position, the facts, the truth of the matter, the (true) state of affairs, the picture, how things stand, the lay of the land; *informal* what's what, what the deal is/was.

5 **(scores)** *scores of complaints* A GREAT MANY, a lot, a great/good deal, large quantities, plenty; *informal* lots, umpteen, a slew, loads, masses, stacks, scads, heaps, piles, bags, tons, oodles, dozens, hundreds, thousands, millions, billions, gazillions, a bunch.

▸ verb **1** *Lou's already scored 13 goals this season* NET, bag, rack up, chalk up, tally, notch, record; get, gain, achieve, make.

2 *informal his new movie really scored* BE SUCCESSFUL, be a success, triumph, make an impression, go down well; *informal* be a hit, be a winner, be a sellout.

3 *the piece was scored for flute and violin* ORCHESTRATE, arrange, set, adapt; write, compose.

4 *score the wood in crisscross patterns* SCRATCH, cut, notch, incise, scrape, nick, chip, gouge; mark.

5 *informal he was hoping to score on his date tonight* GET LUCKY, have sex, go all the way, do it.

PHRASE: **score points off** *he's obsessed with scoring points off everyone, even his best friends* GET THE BETTER OF, gain the advantage over, outdo, best, have the edge over; have the last laugh on, make a fool of, humiliate; *informal* get/be one up on, get one over on.

scorn noun *he was unable to hide the scorn in his voice* CONTEMPT, derision, contemptuousness, disdain, derisiveness, mockery, sneering. ANTONYMS admiration, respect.

▸ verb **1** *critics scorned the painting* DERIDE, hold in contempt, treat with contempt, pour/heap scorn on, look down on, look down one's nose at, disdain, curl one's lip at, mock, scoff at, sneer at, jeer at, laugh at, laugh out of court; disparage, slight; dismiss, thumb one's nose at; *informal* turn one's nose up at. See note at DESPISE. ANTONYMS admire, respect.

2 *"I am a woman scorned," she thought* SPURN, rebuff, reject, ignore, shun, snub.

scornful adjective *his scornful remarks* CONTEMPTUOUS, derisive, withering, mocking, scoffing, sneering, jeering, scathing, snide, disparaging, supercilious, disdainful, superior; *archaic* contumelious. ANTONYMS admiring, respectful.

scotch verb *the bad weather scotched our plans for a rematch* PUT AN END TO, put a stop to, nip in the bud, put the lid on; ruin, wreck, destroy, smash, shatter, demolish, frustrate, thwart; *informal* put paid to, put the kibosh on, scupper, scuttle.

scot-free adverb *the small-time dealers are behind bars, while the big bosses go scot-free* UNPUNISHED, without punishment; unscathed, unhurt, unharmed, without a scratch; safely.

scoundrel noun *the lying scoundrel* ROGUE, rascal, miscreant, good-for-nothing, reprobate; cheat, swindler, scam artist, fraudster, trickster, charlatan; *informal* villain, bastard, beast, son of a bitch, SOB, rat, louse, swine, dog, skunk, heel, snake (in the grass), wretch, scumbag, scumbucket, scuzzball, sleazeball, sleazebag, ratfink; *informal, dated* hound; *dated* cad; *archaic* blackguard, knave, varlet, whoreson, picaroon.

scour[1] verb *she scoured the oven and cleaned out the cupboards* SCRUB, rub, clean, wash, cleanse, wipe; polish, buff (up), shine, burnish; abrade.

scour[2] verb *Christine scoured the stores for a gift* SEARCH, comb, hunt through, rummage through, go through with a fine-tooth comb, root through, rake through, leave no stone unturned in, look high and low in; ransack, turn upside-down.

scourge noun **1** *historical he was beaten with a scourge* WHIP, horsewhip, lash, strap, birch, switch, bullwhip, rawhide; *historical* cat-o'-nine-tails.

2 *inflation was the scourge of the mid-1970s* AFFLICTION, bane, curse, plague, menace, evil, misfortune, burden, cross to bear; blight, cancer, canker. ANTONYMS blessing, godsend.

▸ verb **1** *historical he was publicly scourged* FLOG, whip, beat, horsewhip, lash, flagellate, strap, birch, cane, thrash, belt, leather; *informal* tan someone's hide, take a strap to.

2 *a disease that scourged North America* AFFLICT, plague, torment, torture, curse, oppress, burden, bedevil, beset.

scout noun **1** *scouts reported the enemy's position* LOOKOUT, outrider, advance guard, vanguard; spy.

2 *a lengthy scout around the area* RECONNAISSANCE, reconnoiter; exploration, search, expedition; *informal* recon.

3 *a scout for a major-league team* TALENT SPOTTER, talent scout; *informal* bird dog.

▸ verb **1** *I* ***scouted around*** *for some logs* SEARCH, look, hunt, ferret about/around, root around/about.

2 *a night patrol was sent to* ***scout out*** *the area* RECONNOITER, explore, make a reconnaissance of, inspect, investigate, spy out, survey; examine, scan, study, observe; *informal* check out, case.

scowl noun *the scowl on his face* FROWN, glower, glare, grimace, black look; *informal* dirty look.

▸ verb *she* ***scowled at*** *him* GLOWER AT, frown at, glare at, grimace at, lower at, look daggers at, give someone a black look; make a face at, pull a face, turn the corner's of one's mouth down at, pout at; *informal* give someone a dirty look. ANTONYMS smile, grin.

scrabble verb *they scrabbled around for the strewn coins* SCRATCH, grope, rummage, root, grub, scavenge, fumble, feel, clamber, scramble.

scraggy adjective *this scraggy mutt just wandered into our yard* SCRAWNY, thin, as thin as a rake, skinny, skin-and-bones, gaunt, bony, angular, gawky, rawboned. ANTONYM fat.

scram verb *informal scram or I'll call the police* GO AWAY, leave, get out; go, get moving, be off (with you), shoo; *informal* skedaddle, split, scat, run along, beat it, get lost, shove off, buzz off, push off, clear off, bug off, take a powder, take a hike; *literary* begone.

scramble verb **1** *we scrambled over the boulders* CLAMBER, climb, crawl, claw one's way, scrabble, grope one's way, struggle, shinny.

2 *children scrambled for the scattered coins* JOSTLE, scuffle, tussle, struggle, strive, compete, contend, vie, jockey.

3 *the alcohol has scrambled his brains* MUDDLE, confuse, mix up, jumble (up), disarrange, disorganize, disorder, disturb, mess up.

▸ noun **1** *a short scramble over the rocks* CLAMBER, climb, trek.

2 *I lost Tommy in the scramble for a seat* TUSSLE, jostle, scrimmage, scuffle, struggle, free-for-all, competition, contention, vying, jockeying; muddle, confusion, melee.

scrap[1] noun **1** *a scrap of paper* FRAGMENT, piece, bit, snippet, shred; offcut, oddment, remnant.

2 *there wasn't a scrap of evidence* BIT, speck, iota, particle, ounce, whit, jot, atom, shred, scintilla, tittle, jot or tittle; *informal* smidgen, tad.

3 *he slept in the streets and lived on scraps* LEFTOVERS, leavings, crumbs, scrapings, remains, remnants, residue, odds and ends, bits and pieces.

4 *the whole thing was made from scrap* WASTE, rubbish, refuse, litter, debris, detritus; flotsam and jetsam, garbage, trash; *informal* junk.

▸ verb **1** *old cars due to be scrapped* THROW AWAY, throw out, dispose of, get rid of, toss out, throw on the scrap heap, discard, remove, dispense with, lose, decommission, recycle, break up, demolish; *informal* chuck, ditch, dump, junk, trash, deep-six. ANTONYMS keep, preserve.

2 *campaigners called for the plans to be scrapped* ABANDON, drop, abolish, withdraw, throw out, do away with, put an end to, cancel, ax, jettison; *informal* ditch, dump, junk, can, scrub. ANTONYMS keep, restore.

scrap[2] *informal* noun *he and Joe had several scraps* QUARREL, argument, row, fight, disagreement, difference of opinion, falling-out, blowup, dispute, squabble, contretemps, clash, altercation, brawl, tussle, conflict, shouting match; *informal* tiff, set-to, run-in, spat, ruction.

▸ verb *the older boys started scrapping with me* QUARREL, argue, row, fight, squabble, brawl, bicker, spar, wrangle, lock horns.

scrape verb **1** *we scraped all the paint off the windows* ABRADE, grate, sand, sandpaper, scour, scratch, rub, file, rasp.

2 *their boots scraped along the floor* GRATE, creak, rasp, grind, scratch.

3 *she scraped her hair back behind her ears* RAKE, drag, pull, tug, draw.

4 *he scraped a hole in the ground* SCOOP OUT, hollow out, dig (out), excavate, gouge out.

5 *Ellen had scraped her shins on the wall* GRAZE, scratch, abrade, scuff, rasp, skin, rub raw, cut, lacerate, bark, chafe; *Medicine* excoriate.

▸ noun **1** *the scrape of her key in the lock* GRATING, creaking, grinding, rasp, rasping, scratch, scratching.

2 *there was a long scrape on his leg* GRAZE, scratch, abrasion, cut, laceration, wound.

3 *informal he's always getting into scrapes* PREDICAMENT, plight, tight corner/spot, ticklish/tricky situation, problem, crisis, mess, muddle; *informal* jam, fix, stew, bind, hole, hot water, a pretty/fine kettle of fish.

PHRASE: **scrape by** *when the money's not there, you learn how to scrape by* MANAGE, cope, survive, muddle through/along, make ends meet, get by/along, make do, keep the wolf from the door, keep one's head above water, eke out a living; *informal* make out.

scrappy adjective *a scrappy kid of sixteen* FEISTY, tenacious, determined, persistent, dogged, aggressive, forceful; argumentative, confrontational, combative, antagonistic, bellicose, belligerent, combative, pugnacious; *informal* spoiling for a fight.

scratch verb **1** *the paint was scratched* SCRAPE, abrade, score, scuff.

2 *thorns scratched her skin* GRAZE, scrape, abrade, skin, rub raw, cut, lacerate, bark, chafe; wound; *Medicine* excoriate.

3 *many names had been* ***scratched out*** CROSS OUT, strike out, score out, delete, erase, remove, eliminate, expunge, obliterate.

4 *she was forced to* ***scratch from*** *the race* WITHDRAW FROM, pull out of, back out of, bow out of, stand down from.

▸ noun **1** *he had two scratches on his cheek* GRAZE, scrape, abrasion, cut, laceration, wound.

2 *a scratch on the car door* SCRAPE, mark, line, score.

PHRASE: **up to scratch** *my housekeeper's work is nearly always up to scratch* GOOD ENOUGH, up to the mark, up to standard, up to par, satisfactory, acceptable, adequate, passable, sufficient, all right; *informal* OK, jake, up to snuff.

scrawl verb *he scrawled his name at the bottom of the page* SCRIBBLE, write hurriedly, write untidily, dash off.

▸ noun *his writing was a scrawl* SCRIBBLE, chicken scratch, squiggle(s), hieroglyphics.

scrawny adjective *scrawny teenage girls addicted to dieting* SKINNY, thin, lean, as thin as a rake, skin-and-bones, gaunt, bony, angular, gawky, scraggy, rawboned, anorexic. ANTONYM fat.

scream verb *he screamed in pain* SHRIEK, screech, yell, howl, shout, bellow, bawl, cry out, call out, yelp, squeal, wail, squawk; *informal* holler.

▸ noun **1** *a scream of pain* SHRIEK, screech, yell, howl, shout, bellow, bawl, cry, yelp, squeal, wail, squawk; *informal* holler.

2 *informal the whole thing's a scream* LAUGH, hoot; *informal* gas, giggle, riot, laff riot, bundle of fun/laughs, blast.

3 *informal he's an absolute scream* WIT, hoot, comedian, comic, entertainer, joker, clown, character; *informal* gas, riot; *informal, dated* caution, card.

screech verb See SCREAM verb.

screen noun **1** *he dressed hurriedly behind the screen* PARTITION, (room) divider.

2 *a computer with a 15-inch screen* DISPLAY, monitor, video display terminal, VDT, cathode-ray tube, CRT.

3 *the screen keeps out mosquitoes* MESH, net, netting.

4 *the hedge acts as a screen against the wind* BUFFER, protection, shield, shelter, guard, windbreak.

5 *sift the dirt through a screen* SIEVE, riddle, strainer, colander, filter.

▸ verb **1** *the end of the hall had been screened off* PARTITION, divide, separate, curtain.

2 *the cottage was screened by the trees* CONCEAL, hide, veil; shield, shelter, shade, protect, guard, safeguard.

3 *the prospective candidates will have to be screened* VET, check, check up on, investigate; *informal* check out.

4 *all donated blood is screened for the virus* CHECK, test, examine, investigate.

5 *coal used to be screened by hand* SIEVE, riddle, sift, strain, filter, winnow.

6 *the program is screened on Thursday evenings* SHOW, broadcast, transmit, air, televise, telecast, put on the air.

screw noun **1** *stainless steel screws* bolt, fastener; nail, pin, tack, spike, rivet, brad.

2 *the handle needs a couple of screws to tighten it* TURN, twist, wrench.

3 *the ship's twin screws* PROPELLER, rotor.

▸ verb **1** *he screwed the lid back on the jar* TIGHTEN, turn, twist, wind.

2 *the bracket was screwed in place* FASTEN, secure, fix, attach.

3 *informal she intended to screw money out of them* EXTORT, force, extract, wrest, wring, squeeze; *informal* bleed.

4 *informal he realized he had been screwed* CHEAT, trick, deceive, swindle, con, scam, dupe, fool; *informal* rip off, hose, gyp, bamboozle, stiff.

PHRASES: **put the screws on** *informal you don't pay up and my pal Bruno here will put the screws on you, see?* PRESSURE, put pressure on, coerce, browbeat, use strong-arm tactics on, strong-arm; hold a gun to someone's head; *informal* turn the heat on, lean on, bulldoze. **screw up 1** *Tina screwed up her face in disgust* WRINKLE (UP), pucker, crumple, crease, furrow, contort, distort, twist, purse. **2** *informal they'll screw up the whole economy* WRECK, ruin, destroy, wreak havoc on, damage, spoil, mar; dash, shatter, scotch, make a mess of, mess up; *informal* louse up, foul up, put the kibosh on, scupper, scuttle, do for, nix.

scribble verb *he scribbled a few lines on a piece of paper* SCRAWL, write hurriedly, write untidily, scratch, dash off, jot (down); doodle.

▸ noun *a page of scribble* SCRAWL, squiggle(s), jottings; doodle, doodlings.

scribe noun **1** *historical a medieval scribe* CLERK, secretary, copyist, transcriber, amanuensis; *historical* penman, scrivener.

2 *informal a local scribe* WRITER, author, penman; journalist, reporter; *informal* hack, pencil pusher.

scrimmage noun *a scrimmage broke out in the parking lot* FIGHT, tussle, brawl, struggle, fracas, free-for-all, rough-and-tumble; *informal* scrap, set-to, scrum, roughhouse.

scrimp verb *I used to criticize my mother for the way she would scrimp* ECONOMIZE, skimp, scrimp and save, save; be thrifty, be frugal, tighten one's belt, cut back, husband one's resources, watch one's pennies, pinch (the) pennies.

script noun **1** *her neat, tidy script* HANDWRITING, writing, hand, penmanship, calligraphy.

2 *the script of the play* TEXT, screenplay; libretto, score; lines, dialogue, words.

Scrooge noun *you're going to borrow money from that Scrooge?* MISER, penny-pincher, pinchpenny; *informal* skinflint, money-grubber, cheapskate, tightwad. ANTONYM spendthrift.

scrounge verb *they were always scrounging food from the tourists* BEG, borrow, cadge; *informal* sponge, bum, touch someone for, mooch.

scrounger noun *don't give your money to that scrounger* BEGGAR, borrower, parasite, cadger; *informal* sponger, freeloader, mooch, moocher, bum, bottom feeder, schnorrer.

scrub[1] verb **1** *he scrubbed the kitchen floor* SCOUR, rub; clean, cleanse, wash, wipe.

2 *informal the plans were scrubbed.* See SCRAP[1] verb sense 2.

scrub[2] noun *there the buildings ended and the scrub began* BRUSH, brushwood, scrubland, underbrush, undergrowth, krummholz.

scruffy adjective *dressed in scruffy clothes* SHABBY, worn, down-at-heel, down-at-the-heel(s), ragged, tattered, mangy, dirty; untidy, unkempt, bedraggled, messy, disheveled, ill-groomed; *informal* tatty, raggedy-ass, the worse for wear, ratty, raggedy, scuzzy. ANTONYMS smart, tidy.

scrumptious adjective *informal scrumptious desserts* DELICIOUS, delectable, mouthwatering, tasty, appetizing, rich, savory, flavorful, toothsome; succulent, luscious; *informal* yummy, lip-smacking, finger-licking, melt-in-your/the-mouth, nummy. ANTONYM unpalatable.

scrunch verb *he scrunches his face into the most hilarious expressions* CRUMPLE, crunch, crush, rumple, screw up, squash, squeeze, compress.

scruple verb *she would not **scruple to** ask them for money* HESITATE TO, be reluctant to, be loath to, have qualms about, have scruples about, have misgivings about, have reservations about, think twice about, balk to, demur to; recoil from, shrink from, shy away from, flinch from.

scruples plural noun *he had no scruples about eavesdropping* QUALMS, compunction, pangs/twinges of conscience, hesitation, reservations, second thoughts, doubt(s), misgivings, uneasiness, reluctance. See note at QUALMS.

scrupulous adjective **1** *scrupulous attention to detail* CAREFUL, meticulous, painstaking, thorough, assiduous, sedulous, attentive, conscientious, punctilious, searching, close, minute, rigorous, particular, strict. ANTONYM careless.

2 *a scrupulous man* HONEST, honorable, upright, upstanding, high-minded, right-minded, moral, ethical, good, virtuous, principled, incorruptible. ANTONYM dishonest.

scrutinize verb *it has become necessary for us to scrutinize the behavior of our staff toward the customers* EXAMINE, inspect, survey, study, look at, peruse; investigate, explore, probe, inquire into, go into, check; *informal* eyeball.

scrutiny noun *passengers can expect much more scrutiny at our terminals* EXAMINATION, inspection, survey, study, perusal; investigation, exploration, probe, inquiry; *informal* going-over.

scud verb *I wanted to be one of those guys scudding across the lake on their iceboats* SPEED, race, rush, sail, shoot, sweep, skim, whip, whiz, flash, fly, scurry, flit; *Brit.* scutter, scuttle.

WORD NOTE scud

Once I heard a teacher tell a seventh-grade class that this was precisely the sort of verb they should use to make their writing livelier and more interesting. The example she gave was: *The storm clouds scudded over the horizon.* In fact, this is precisely the sort of word—words that call unnecessary attention to themselves, that sound artificial and stop the reader in mid-sentence—that should not be used for that reason. Or for any reason. When in doubt, use a simpler and more everyday word, and try to make the content of the sentence livelier and more interesting, which is always a better idea. If you don't have anything fresh to report about the rapidly moving clouds, writing that they scudded won't help. **—FP**

---

scuff verb *my kids could scuff a brand new shoe before we even got out of the store* SCRAPE, scratch, rub, abrade; mark.

scuffle noun *there was a scuffle outside the pub* FIGHT, struggle, tussle, brawl, fracas, free-for-all, scrimmage; *informal* scrap, set-to, roughhouse.

▸ verb *demonstrators scuffled with police* FIGHT, struggle, tussle, exchange blows, come to blows, brawl, clash; *informal* scrap.

sculpt verb *figures sculpted by Lena's skilled hands* CARVE, model, chisel, sculpture, fashion, form, shape, cast, cut, hew.

sculpture noun *a bronze sculpture* MODEL, carving, statue, statuette, figure, figurine, effigy, bust, head, likeness.

▸ verb *the choir stalls were carefully sculptured.* See SCULPT.

scum noun **1** *the water was covered with a thick green scum* FILM, layer, covering, froth; filth, dross, dirt.

2 *informal drug dealers are scum* DESPICABLE PEOPLE, the lowest of the low, the dregs of society, vermin, riffraff, lowlifes; *informal* the scum of the earth, dirt.

scupper *chiefly Brit.* verb **1** *the captain decided to scupper the ship* SINK, scuttle, submerge, send to the bottom.

2 *informal he denied trying to scupper the agreement* RUIN, wreck, destroy, sabotage, torpedo, spoil, mess up; *informal* screw up, foul up, put the kibosh on; *archaic* bring to naught.

scurrilous adjective *such scurrilous language!* DEFAMATORY, slanderous, libelous, scandalous, insulting, offensive, gross; abusive, vituperative, malicious; *informal* bitchy.

scurry verb *pedestrians scurried for cover* HURRY, hasten, run, rush, dash; scamper, scuttle, scramble; *Brit.* scutter; *informal* scoot, beetle; *dated* make haste. ANTONYM amble.

▸ noun *there was a scurry to get out* RUSH, race, dash, run, hurry; scramble, bustle.

scuttle verb See SCURRY verb.

sea noun **1** *the sea sparkled in the sun* OCEAN; *informal* drink, briny, salt chuck; *literary* deep, main, foam.

2 (seas) *the boat overturned in the heavy seas* WAVES, swell, breakers, rollers, combers.

3 *a sea of roofs and turrets* EXPANSE, stretch, area, tract, sweep, blanket, sheet, carpet, mass; multitude, host, profusion, abundance.

▸ adjective *sea creatures* MARINE, ocean, oceanic; saltwater, seawater; oceangoing, seagoing, seafaring; maritime, naval, nautical; *technical* pelagic.

PHRASE: **at sea** *most of her calculus lectures left me completely at sea* CONFUSED, perplexed, puzzled, baffled, mystified, bemused, bewildered, nonplussed, disconcerted, disoriented, dumbfounded, at a loss, at sixes and sevens; *informal* flummoxed, bamboozled, fazed, discombobulated; *archaic* mazed.

seabird noun *she's been studying the breeding habits of Maine's seabirds.* See table.

SEABIRDS

ancient murrelet	little gull
Arctic tern	little tern
Atlantic puffin	Manx shearwater
auk	marbled murrelet
auklet	mew gull
baccalieu bird	Mother Carey's chicken
bawk	murre
black guillemot	murrelet
black skimmer	noddy
black tern	northern fulmar
black-footed albatross	northern gannet
Bonaparte's gull	parasitic jaeger
booby	pelagic cormorant
brown noddy	pelican
brown pelican	petrel
bull bird	pigeon guillemot
cahow	pomarine jaeger
Cassin's auklet	prion
common murre	puffin
cormorant	razorbill
crow duck	ring-billed gull
double-crested cormorant	roseate tern
dovekie	Ross's gull
Franklin's gull	Sabine's gull
frigate bird	sea pigeon
fulmar	sea swallow
gannet	seagull
glaucous gull	shag
greater shearwater	shearwater
guillemot	skimmer
gull	skua
gun-billed tern	sooty shearwater
herring gull	sooty tern
Iceland gull	storm petrel
jaeger	tern
kittiwake	ticklace
laughing gull	tropicbird
little auk	turr
	white pelican

See also tables at PENGUIN, SHOREBIRD, and WATERFOWL.

seafaring adjective *all of her children were seafaring men* MARITIME, nautical, naval, seagoing, sea.

seafood noun *a restaurant famous for its fresh seafood* FISH, SHELLFISH; clam(s), lobster, shrimp, crab(s), scallop(s), oyster(s), mussel(s), steamer(s), calamari, scungilli; scampi, clams casino, oysters Rockefeller, lobster thermidor, lobster Newburg, filet of sole, escargot; smoked salmon, lox, gravlax; (Maryland) crab cake(s), fish stick(s), clam fritter(s); bouillabaisse, cioppino, étouffée; caviar, roe. See tables at CRUSTACEAN, FISH, and MOLLUSK.

seal[1] noun **1** *the seal around the bathtub* SEALANT, sealer, adhesive, caulk, caulking.

2 *the king put his seal on the letter* EMBLEM, symbol, insignia, device, badge, crest, coat of arms, mark, monogram, stamp.

3 *the project cannot begin without the committee's seal* RATIFICATION, approval, seal of approval, blessing, consent, agreement, permission, sanction, endorsement, clearance.

▸ verb **1** *she quietly sealed the door behind her* FASTEN, secure, shut, close, lock, bolt.

2 *seal each bottle while it is hot* STOP UP, seal up, make airtight/watertight, cork, stopper, plug.

3 **(seal off)** *police sealed off the block* CLOSE OFF, shut off, cordon off, fence off, isolate.

4 *that seals it* CLINCH, secure, settle, conclude, determine, complete, establish, set the seal on, confirm, guarantee; *informal* sew up.

seal[2] noun *seals were basking in the water male* : bull; *female* : cow; *young* : calf, pup, whelp. See table.

SEALS

bearded seal	ringed seal
California sea lion	sea dog
common seal	sea elephant
elephant seal	sea lion
fur seal	square-flipper seal
gray seal	walrus
harp seal	bedlamer
hooded seal	blueback
northern sea lion	whitecoat

seam noun **1** *the seam was coming undone* JOIN, stitching; *Surgery* suture.

2 *a seam of coal* LAYER, stratum, vein, lode.

3 *the seams of his face* WRINKLE, line, crow's foot, furrow, crease, corrugation, crinkle, pucker, groove, ridge.

seaman noun *many a seaman lost his life on this reef* SAILOR, seafarer, mariner, boatman, hand; *informal* (old) salt, sea dog, bluejacket, shellback; *Brit.* rating, matelot. ANTONYM landlubber.

seamy adjective *Viper and his seamy friends were last seen at the bus station* SORDID, disreputable, degenerate, seedy, sleazy, squalid, insalubrious, unwholesome, unsavory, rough, unpleasant. ANTONYM salubrious.

sear verb **1** *the heat of the blast seared his face* SCORCH, burn, singe, char. See note at BURN.

2 *sear the meat before adding the other ingredients* FLASH-FRY, seal, brown.

3 *his betrayal had seared her terribly* HURT, wound, pain, cut to the quick, sting; distress, grieve, upset, trouble, harrow, torment, torture.

search verb **1** **(search for)** *I searched for the key in my handbag* HUNT (FOR), look for, seek, forage for, fish around/about for, look high and low for, ferret around/about for, root around/about for, rummage around/about for, cast around/about for.

2 *he searched every room in the house* LOOK THROUGH, hunt through, explore, scour, rifle through, go through, sift through, comb, go through with a fine-tooth comb; turn upside down, turn inside out, leave no stone unturned in.

3 *the guards searched him for weapons* EXAMINE, inspect, check, frisk.

▸ noun *the police continued their search* HUNT, look, quest; pursuit, manhunt.

PHRASES: **in search of** *they say they are in search of a silver flask with the monogram 'DLR'* SEARCHING FOR, hunting for, seeking, looking for, on the lookout for, in pursuit of. **search me** *informal "Where's my toolbox?" "Search me."* I DON'T KNOW, how should I know?, it's a mystery, I haven't a clue, I haven't the least/slightest idea, I've no idea, who knows; *informal* (I) dunno, don't ask me, I haven't the faintest/foggiest (idea/notion), (it) beats me, you got me.

searching adjective *they asked some very searching questions* PENETRATING, piercing, probing, penetrative, keen, shrewd, sharp, intent.

searing adjective **1** *the searing heat* SCORCHING, blistering, sweltering, blazing (hot), burning, fiery, torrid; *informal* boiling (hot), baking (hot), sizzling, roasting.

2 *searing pain* INTENSE, excruciating, agonizing, sharp, stabbing, shooting, stinging, severe, extreme, racking.

3 *a searing attack* FIERCE, savage, blistering, scathing, stinging, devastating, mordant, trenchant, caustic, cutting, biting, withering.

seaside noun *vacationing at the seaside* COAST, shore, seashore, waterside; beach; *literary* strand.

season noun *the rainy season* PERIOD, time, time of year, spell, term.

▸ verb **1** *season the casserole to taste* FLAVOR, add flavoring to, add salt (and pepper) to, spice.

2 *his answers were seasoned with wit* ENLIVEN, leaven, spice (up), liven up; *informal* pep up.

PHRASE: **in season** *we make gallons of sauce when the local tomatoes are in season* AVAILABLE, obtainable, to be had, on the market; plentiful, abundant.

seasonable adjective *the Northeast is enjoying seasonable temperatures* USUAL, expected, predictable, normal for the time of year. See note at TIMELY.

seasoned adjective *seasoned sportscasters* EXPERIENCED, practiced, well versed, knowledgeable, established, habituated, veteran, hardened, battle-scarred, battle-weary. ANTONYM inexperienced.

seasoning noun *we use a secret seasoning made from 12 herbs and spices* FLAVORING, salt (and pepper), herbs, spices, condiments.

seat noun **1** *a wooden seat* CHAIR, bench, stool, settle, stall; pew; **(seats)** seating.

2 *the seat of government* HEADQUARTERS, base, center, nerve center, hub, heart; location, site, whereabouts, place.

▸ verb **1** *they seated themselves around the table* POSITION, put, place; ensconce, install, settle; *informal* plonk, park.

2 *the hall seats 500* HAVE ROOM FOR, contain, take, sit, hold, accommodate.

seating noun *we have seating for 200* SEATS, room, places, chairs, accommodations.

secede verb *the southern states seceded from the Union, precipitating the Civil War* WITHDRAW FROM, break away from, break with, separate (oneself) from, leave, split with, split off from, disaffiliate from, resign from, pull out of; *informal* quit. ANTONYM join.

secluded adjective *a secluded little park* SHELTERED, private, concealed, hidden, unfrequented, sequestered, tucked away. ANTONYM busy.

seclusion noun *she enjoys the seclusion of her cabin* ISOLATION, solitude, retreat, privacy, retirement, withdrawal, concealment, hiding, secrecy.

second[1] adjective **1** *the second day of the trial* NEXT, following, subsequent, succeeding. ANTONYMS first, preceding.

2 *he keeps a second pair of glasses in his office* ADDITIONAL, extra, alternative, another, spare, backup, fallback, alternate. ANTONYM primary.

3 *he was demoted to the second level* SECONDARY, lower, subordinate, subsidiary, lesser, inferior. ANTONYMS first, top.

4 *the conflict could turn into a second Vietnam* ANOTHER, new; repeat of, copy of, carbon copy of. ANTONYM original.

▸ noun 1 *Eva had been working as his second.* See SECOND-IN-COMMAND.

2 *informal* (**seconds**) *he enjoyed the pie and asked for seconds* A SECOND HELPING, a further helping, more.

▸ verb *Hooper seconded the motion* FORMALLY SUPPORT, give one's support to, vote for, back, approve, endorse.

PHRASE: **second to none** *Lori's cheesecake is second to none* INCOMPARABLE, matchless, unrivaled, inimitable, beyond compare/comparison, unparalleled, without parallel, unequaled, without equal, in a class of its own, peerless, unsurpassed, unsurpassable, nonpareil, unique; perfect, consummate, transcendent, surpassing, superlative, supreme; *formal* unexampled.

second[2] noun *I'll only be gone for a second* MOMENT, bit, little while, short time, instant, split second, eyeblink, heartbeat; *informal* sec, jiffy, the blink of an eye. PHRASE: **in a second** *I can fix that lamp in a second* VERY SOON, in a minute, in a moment, in a trice, shortly, any minute (now), in the twinkling of an eye, in (less than) no time, in no time at all, momentarily; *informal* in a jiffy, in two shakes (of a lamb's tail), in the blink of an eye, in a snap; *literary* ere long.

second[3] verb *he was seconded to my department* ASSIGN TEMPORARILY, lend; transfer, move, shift, relocate, assign, reassign, send.

secondary adjective 1 *a secondary issue* LESS IMPORTANT, subordinate, lesser, minor, peripheral, incidental, ancillary, subsidiary, nonessential, inessential, of little account, unimportant. ANTONYM primary.

2 *secondary infections* ACCOMPANYING, attendant, concomitant, consequential, resulting, resultant. ANTONYM primary.

second-class adjective *we were treated like second-class citizens* SECOND-RATE, second-best, inferior, lesser, unimportant.

secondhand adjective 1 *secondhand clothes* USED, old, worn, preowned, handed-down, hand-me-down, castoff; *informal* preloved. ANTONYM new.

2 *secondhand information* INDIRECT, derivative; vicarious. ANTONYM direct.

▸ adverb *I ignore anything I hear secondhand* INDIRECTLY, at secondhand; *informal* on the grapevine. ANTONYM directly.

second-in-command noun *while Reade is recuperating, Dunlop will be my second-in-command* DEPUTY, number two, subordinate, right-hand man/woman, second; understudy; *informal* sidekick, second banana.

secondly adverb *in the first place you're too young, and secondly it's too dangerous* FURTHERMORE, also, moreover, likewise; second, in the second place, next; secondarily.

second-rate adjective *I would never buy second-rate shoes* INFERIOR, substandard, low-quality, below par, bad, poor, deficient, defective, faulty, imperfect, shoddy, chintzy, inadequate, insufficient, unacceptable; *informal* crummy, not up to scratch/snuff, rinky-dink. ANTONYMS first-rate, excellent.

secrecy noun 1 *the secrecy of the material* CONFIDENTIALITY, classified nature.

2 *a government that thrives on secrecy* SECRETIVENESS, covertness, furtiveness, surreptitiousness, stealth, stealthiness.

secret adjective 1 *a secret plan* CONFIDENTIAL, top secret, classified, undisclosed, unknown, private, under wraps; *informal* hush-hush; *formal* sub rosa. ANTONYMS public, known.

2 *a secret drawer in the table* HIDDEN, concealed, disguised; invisible. ANTONYM visible.

3 *a secret operation to infiltrate terrorist groups* CLANDESTINE, covert, undercover, underground, surreptitious, stealthy, furtive, cloak-and-dagger, hole-and-corner, closet; *informal* hush-hush. ANTONYM overt.

4 *a secret message* | *a secret code* CRYPTIC, encoded, coded; mysterious, abstruse, recondite, arcane, esoteric, Kabbalistic. ANTONYM open.

5 *a secret place* SECLUDED, private, concealed, hidden, unfrequented, out of the way, tucked away. ANTONYMS public, known about.

6 *a very secret person.* See SECRETIVE.

▸ noun 1 *he just can't keep a secret* CONFIDENTIAL MATTER, confidence, private affair; skeleton in the closet.

2 *the secrets of the universe* MYSTERY, enigma, paradox, puzzle, conundrum, poser, riddle.

3 *the secret of their success* RECIPE, (magic) formula, blueprint, key, answer, solution.

PHRASE: **in secret** *they met in secret throughout the month of July.* See SECRETLY sense 1.

THE RIGHT WORD

While all of these adjectives describe an attempt to do something without attracting attention or observation, **secret** is the most general term, implying that something is being concealed or kept from the knowledge of others (*a secret pact; a secret passageway*). **Covert** suggests that something is being done under cover, or concealed as if with a veil or disguise (*a covert attack; a covert threat*), while **clandestine** suggests that something illicit or immoral is being concealed (*a clandestine meeting between the two lovers*). Someone who is deliberately sneaking around and trying to do something without attracting notice is best described as **stealthy** (*the cat moved toward the bird with a slow, stealthy pace*), and **furtive** connotes even more slyness and watchfulness, as revealed not only by movements but by facial expressions (*a furtive glance; a furtive movement toward the door*). **Surreptitious** connotes guilt on the part of the individual who is acting in a stealthy or furtive manner (*a surreptitious attempt to hide the book before it was noticed*). **Underhanded** is the strongest of these words, implying fraud, deceit, or unfairness (*underhanded business dealings*).

secret agent noun *she had been a secret agent for the Soviet Union* SPY, double agent, counterspy, undercover agent, operative, plant, mole, sleeper, informant.

secretary noun *my secretary will call you about setting up an appointment* ASSISTANT, executive assistant, administrative assistant, personal assistant, clerical assistant, administrator, amanuensis, girl/gal/man Friday, clerk.

secrete[1] verb *a substance secreted by the prostate gland*

PRODUCE, discharge, emit, excrete, release, send out. ANTONYM absorb.

secrete[2] verb *we secreted ourselves in the bushes* CONCEAL, hide, cover up, veil, shroud, screen, stow away; bury, cache; *informal* stash away. ANTONYM reveal.

secretive adjective *I trusted you with this because you're the most secretive person I know* UNCOMMUNICATIVE, secret, unforthcoming, playing one's cards close to one's chest, reticent, reserved, silent, noncommunicative, quiet, tight-lipped, buttoned-up, close-mouthed, taciturn. ANTONYMS open, communicative.

secretly adverb **1** *they met secretly for a year* IN SECRET, in private, privately, behind closed doors, in camera, behind the scenes, under cover, under the counter, behind someone's back, furtively, stealthily, on the sly, on the quiet, conspiratorially, covertly, clandestinely, on the side; *informal* on the QT, off the record, hush-hush; *formal* sub rosa.

2 *he was secretly jealous of Bartholomew* PRIVATELY, in one's heart (of hearts), deep down.

sect noun *she had been duped into joining a sect of supposed do-gooders* (RELIGIOUS) CULT, religious group, denomination, persuasion, religious order; splinter group, faction.

sectarian adjective *a sectarian society of white supremacists* FACTIONAL, separatist, partisan, parti pris; doctrinaire, dogmatic, extreme, fanatical, rigid, inflexible, bigoted, hidebound, narrow-minded. ANTONYMS tolerant, liberal.

section noun **1** *the separate sections of a train* PART, piece, bit, segment, component, division, portion, element, unit, constituent. See note at FRAGMENT.

2 *the last section of the questionnaire* SUBDIVISION, part, subsection, division, portion, bit, chapter, passage, clause.

3 *the reference section of the library* DEPARTMENT, area, part, division.

4 *a residential section of the city.* See SECTOR sense 2.

sector adjective **1** *every sector of the industry is affected* PART, branch, arm, division, area, department, field, sphere.

2 *the northeastern sector of the town* DISTRICT, quarter, part, section, zone, region, area, belt.

secular adjective *secular music* NONRELIGIOUS, areligious, lay, temporal, worldly, earthly, profane; *formal* laic. ANTONYMS holy, religious.

secure adjective **1** *check to ensure that all bolts are secure* FASTENED, fixed, secured, done up; closed, shut, locked. ANTONYM loose.

2 *an environment in which children can feel secure* SAFE, protected from harm/danger, out of danger, sheltered, safe and sound, out of harm's way, in a safe place, in safe hands, invulnerable; at ease, unworried, relaxed, happy, confident. ANTONYM vulnerable.

3 *a secure investment* CERTAIN, assured, reliable, dependable, settled, fixed. ANTONYM uncertain.

▸ verb **1** *pins secure the handle to the main body* FIX, attach, fasten, affix, connect, couple.

2 *the doors had not been properly secured* FASTEN, close, shut, lock, bolt, chain, seal.

3 *he leapt out to secure the boat* TIE UP, moor, make fast; anchor.

4 *they sought to secure the country against attack* PROTECT, make safe, fortify, strengthen; undergird.

5 *a written constitution would secure the rights of the individual* ASSURE, ensure, guarantee, protect, confirm, establish.

6 *the division secured a major contract* OBTAIN, acquire, gain, get, get possession of; *informal* get hold of, land. See note at GET.

security noun **1** *the security of the nation's citizens* SAFETY, freedom from danger, protection, invulnerability. ANTONYMS vulnerability, danger.

2 *he could give her the security she needed* PEACE OF MIND, feeling of safety, stability, certainty, happiness, confidence. ANTONYM disquiet.

3 *security at the court was tight* SAFETY MEASURES, safeguards, surveillance, defense, protection.

4 *additional security for your loan may be required* GUARANTEE, collateral, surety, pledge, bond.

sedate[1] verb *the patient had to be sedated* TRANQUILIZE, put under sedation, drug.

sedate[2] adjective **1** *a sedate pace* SLOW, steady, dignified, unhurried, relaxed, measured, leisurely, slow-moving, easy, easygoing, gentle. ANTONYM fast.

2 *he had lived a sedate life* CALM, placid, tranquil, quiet, uneventful; boring, dull. ANTONYM exciting.

sedative adjective *sedative drugs* TRANQUILIZING, calming, calmative, relaxing, soporific, narcotic; depressant; *Medicine* neuroleptic.

▸ noun *the doctor gave him a sedative* TRANQUILIZER, calmative, sleeping pill, narcotic, opiate; depressant; *informal* trank, downer.

sedentary adjective *a sedentary job* SITTING, seated, desk-bound, stationary; inactive, lethargic, lazy, idle. ANTONYM active.

sediment noun *the sediment in the coffee pot* DREGS, lees, precipitate, deposit, grounds; residue, remains; silt, alluvium; *technical* residuum.

sedition noun *the on-campus protestors were charged with sedition* RABBLE-ROUSING, incitement to rebel, subversion, troublemaking, provocation; rebellion, insurrection, mutiny, insurgence, civil disorder.

seditious adjective *a seditious speech* RABBLE-ROUSING, provocative, inflammatory, subversive, troublemaking; rebellious, insurrectionist, mutinous, insurgent.

seduce verb **1** *he took her to his hotel room and tried to seduce her* PERSUADE TO HAVE SEX; *euphemistic* have one's way with, take advantage of; *dated* debauch.

2 *she was seduced by the smell of coffee* ATTRACT, allure, lure, tempt, entice, beguile, inveigle, maneuver. See note at TEMPT.

seducer noun *if you want to avoid seducers, why would come into this bar?* WOMANIZER, philanderer, Romeo, Don Juan, Lothario, Casanova, playboy, ladies' man; *informal* ladykiller, wolf, skirt-chaser.

seductive adjective *a seductive red dress* SEXY, alluring, tempting, irresistible, exciting, provocative, sultry, slinky; coquettish, flirtatious; *informal* vampish, come-hither.

seductress noun *she looks ridiculous trying to be the se-*

ductress TEMPTRESS, siren, femme fatale, Mata Hari, home wrecker, man-eater; flirt, coquette; *informal* vamp.

sedulous adjective *he picked the thorn from his leg with sedulous care* DILIGENT, careful, meticulous, thorough, assiduous, attentive, industrious, conscientious, ultracareful, punctilious, scrupulous, painstaking, minute, rigorous, particular. See note at BUSY.

see verb **1** *he saw her running across the road* DISCERN, spot, notice, catch sight of, glimpse, catch/get a glimpse of, make out, pick out, spy, distinguish, detect, perceive, note; *informal* lay/set eyes on; *literary* behold, descry, espy.

2 *I saw a documentary about it last week* WATCH, look at, view; catch.

3 *would you like to see the house?* INSPECT, view, look round, tour, survey, examine, scrutinize; *informal* give something a/the once-over.

4 *I finally saw what she meant* UNDERSTAND, grasp, comprehend, follow, take in, realize, appreciate, recognize, work out, get the drift of, perceive, fathom; *informal* get, latch on to, cotton on to, catch on to, savvy, figure out, get a fix on.

5 *I must go and see what Victor is up to* FIND OUT, discover, learn, ascertain, determine, establish.

6 *see that no harm comes to him* ENSURE, make sure/certain, see to it, take care, mind.

7 *I see trouble ahead* FORESEE, predict, forecast, prophesy, anticipate, envisage, picture, visualize.

8 *about a year later, I saw him in town* ENCOUNTER, meet, run into/across, come across, stumble on/across, happen on, chance on; *informal* bump into.

9 *they see each other from time to time* MEET, meet up with, get together with, socialize with.

10 *you'd better see a doctor* CONSULT, confer with, talk to, speak to, have recourse to, call on, call in, turn to, ask.

11 *he's seeing someone else now* GO OUT WITH, date, take out, be involved with; *informal* go steady with; *dated* court.

12 *he saw her to her car* ESCORT, accompany, show, walk, conduct, lead, take, usher, attend. PHRASES: **see through 1** *they can see through your dirty little plan* UNDERSTAND, get/have the measure of, read like a book; *informal* be wise to; have someone's number (about). **2** *Marlon saw us through these long, hard months* SUSTAIN, encourage, buoy up, keep going, support, be a tower of strength to, comfort, help (out), stand by, stick by. **3** *I'm tired of this campaign, but I promised I would see it through* PERSEVERE WITH, persist with, continue (with), carry on with, keep at, follow through, stay with; *informal* stick to, stick it out, hang in there (with/for). **see to** *I'll see to the dogs as soon as we finish lunch* ATTEND TO, deal with, see about, take care of, look after, sort out, fix, organize, arrange.

seed noun **1** *apple seeds* pip, stone, kernel; ovule. See table at NUT.

2 *each war contains within it the seeds of a fresh war* GENESIS, source, origin, root, starting point, germ, beginnings, potential (for); cause, reason, motivation, motive, grounds.

3 *Abraham and his seed* DESCENDANTS, heirs, successors, scions; offspring, children, sons and daughters, progeny, family; *Law* issue; *derogatory* spawn; *archaic* fruit of someone's loins. PHRASE: **go/run to seed** *in just two years, this hotel has really gone to seed* DETERIORATE, degenerate, decline, decay, fall into decay, go to rack and ruin, go downhill, molder, rot; *informal* go to pot, go to the dogs, go down the toilet.

seedy adjective **1** *the seedy world of prostitution* SORDID, disreputable, seamy, sleazy, squalid, unwholesome, unsavory. ANTONYM high-class.

2 *a seedy roadside diner* DILAPIDATED, tumbledown, ramshackle, falling to pieces, decrepit, gone to rack and ruin, run-down, down-at-heel, down-at-the-heel(s), shabby, dingy, slummy, insalubrious, squalid; *informal* crummy; scuzzy. ANTONYM classy.

seek verb **1** *they sought shelter from the winter snows* SEARCH FOR, try to find, look for, be on the lookout for, be after, hunt for, be in quest of.

2 *the company is seeking a judicial review of the decision* TRY TO OBTAIN, work toward, be intent on, aim at/for.

3 *he sought help from the police* ASK FOR, request, solicit, call for, entreat, beg for, petition for, appeal for, apply for, put in for.

4 *we constantly seek to improve the service* TRY, attempt, endeavor, strive, work, do one's best; *formal* essay.

seem verb *they seem friendly* APPEAR (TO BE), have the appearance/air of being, give the impression of being, look, look as though one is, show signs of being, look to be; come across as, strike someone as, sound.

seeming adjective *his seeming gentility* APPARENT, ostensible, supposed, outward, surface, superficial; pretended, feigned. See note at OSTENSIBLE. ANTONYMS actual, genuine.

seemingly adverb *the building was seemingly secure* APPARENTLY, on the face of it, to all appearances, as far as one can see/tell, on the surface, to all intents and purposes, outwardly, superficially, supposedly.

seemly adjective *we expect more seemly behavior at our dinner table* DECOROUS, proper, decent, becoming, fitting, suitable, appropriate, apt, apposite, in good taste, genteel, polite, the done thing, right, correct, acceptable, comme il faut. ANTONYMS unseemly, unbecoming.

seep verb *a brown substance is seeping into the basement* OOZE, trickle, exude, drip, dribble, flow, issue, escape, leak, drain, bleed, filter, percolate, soak.

seer noun *the woeful predictions of an ancient seer* SOOTHSAYER, oracle, prophet(ess), augur, prognosticator, diviner, visionary, fortune teller, crystal-gazer, clairvoyant, psychic, medium; *literary* sibyl.

seesaw verb *interest rates continue to seesaw* FLUCTUATE, swing, go up and down, rise and fall, oscillate, alternate, yo-yo, vary.

▸ noun *the seesaws on the playground* TEETER-TOTTER.

seethe verb **1** *the brew seethed* BOIL, bubble, simmer, foam, froth, fizz, effervesce.

2 *the water was seething with fish* TEEM, swarm, boil, swirl, churn, surge.

3 *I seethed at the injustice of it all* BE ANGRY, be furious, be enraged, be incensed, be beside oneself, boil, simmer, rage, rant, rave, storm, fume, smolder; *informal* be livid, be wild, foam at the mouth, be steamed up, be hot under the collar.

see-through adjective *a see-through blouse* TRANSPAR-

ENT, translucent, clear, limpid, pellucid; thin, lightweight, flimsy, sheer, diaphanous, filmy, gossamer, chiffony, gauzy. ANTONYM opaque.

segment noun **1** *orange segments* PIECE, bit, section, part, chunk, portion, division, slice; fragment, wedge, lump. See note at FRAGMENT.

2 *all segments of society* PART, section, sector, division, portion, constituent, element, unit, compartment; branch, wing.

▸ verb *they plan to segment their market share* DIVIDE (UP), subdivide, separate, split, cut up, carve up, slice up, break up; segregate, divorce, partition, section. ANTONYM amalgamate.

segregate verb *routes that will segregate passenger cars from tractor trailers* SEPARATE, set apart, keep apart, isolate, quarantine, closet; partition, divide, detach, disconnect, sever, dissociate; marginalize, ghettoize. ANTONYM amalgamate.

seize verb **1** *she seized the microphone* GRAB, grasp, snatch, take hold of, get one's hands on; grip, clutch; nab. ANTONYM let go of.

2 *rebels seized the air base* CAPTURE, take, overrun, occupy, conquer, take over. ANTONYMS relinquish, liberate.

3 *the drugs were seized by customs* CONFISCATE, impound, commandeer, requisition, appropriate, expropriate, take away; *Law* distrain. ANTONYM release.

4 *terrorists seized his wife* KIDNAP, abduct, take captive, take prisoner, take hostage, hold for ransom; *informal* snatch. ANTONYMS ransom, release.

PHRASE: **seize on** *they seized on the opportunity* TAKE ADVANTAGE OF, exploit, grasp with both hands, leap at, jump at, pounce on.

seizure noun **1** *Napoleon's seizure of Spain* CAPTURE, takeover, annexation, invasion, occupation, colonization.

2 *the seizure of property* CONFISCATION, appropriation, expropriation, sequestration; *Law* distraint.

3 *the seizure of UN staff by rebels* KIDNAPPING, kidnap, abduction.

4 *the baby suffered a seizure* CONVULSION, fit, spasm, paroxysm; *Medicine* ictus; *dated* apoplexy.

seldom adverb *we seldom use the dining room* RARELY, infrequently, hardly (ever), scarcely (ever), almost never; now and then, occasionally, sporadically; *informal* once in a blue moon. ANTONYM often.

select verb *select the correct tool for the job* CHOOSE, pick (out), single out, sort out, take; opt for, decide on, settle on, determine, nominate, appoint, elect.

▸ adjective **1** *a select group of players* CHOICE, hand-picked, prime, first-rate, first-class, superior, finest, best, top-class, blue-ribbon, supreme, superb, excellent; *informal* A1, top-notch. ANTONYM inferior.

2 *a select clientele* EXCLUSIVE, elite, favored, privileged; wealthy; *informal* posh. ANTONYM common.

selection noun **1** *Jim made his selection of toys* CHOICE, pick; option, preference.

2 *a wide selection of dishes* RANGE, array, diversity, variety, assortment, mixture.

3 *a selection of his poems* ANTHOLOGY, assortment, collection, assemblage, compilation; miscellany, medley, potpourri.

selective adjective *he's very selective about his coffee* DISCERNING, discriminating, discriminatory, critical, exacting, demanding, particular; fussy, fastidious; *informal* choosy, persnickety, picky, finicky.

self noun *listen to your inner self* EGO, I, oneself, persona, person, identity, character, personality, psyche, soul, spirit, mind, (inner) being. ANTONYM other.

self-assurance noun *you need to build up your self-assurance* SELF-CONFIDENCE, confidence, assertiveness, self-reliance, composure, self-possession, presence of mind, aplomb. ANTONYM diffidence.

self-assured adjective *a self-assured young woman, fresh out of law school* SELF-CONFIDENT, confident, assertive, assured, authoritative, commanding, self-reliant, self-possessed, poised.

self-centered adjective *he's too self-centered to care what his children do* EGOCENTRIC, egotistic, egotistical, egomaniacal, self-absorbed, self-obsessed, self-seeking, self-interested, self-serving; narcissistic, vain; inconsiderate, thoughtless; *informal* looking after number one.

self-confidence noun *they told Tom he lacked the self-confidence to make it as a singer* MORALE, confidence, self-assurance, assurance, assertiveness, self-reliance, self-possession, composure.

self-conscious adjective *he gave me a self-conscious grin* EMBARRASSED, uncomfortable, uneasy, nervous; unnatural, inhibited, gauche, awkward; modest, shy, diffident, bashful, retiring, shrinking. ANTONYM confident.

self-contained adjective **1** *each train was a self-contained unit* COMPLETE, independent, separate, free-standing, enclosed.

2 *a very self-contained child* INDEPENDENT, self-sufficient, self-reliant; introverted, quiet, private, aloof, insular, reserved, reticent, secretive.

self-control noun *I had more self-control when I was younger* SELF-DISCIPLINE, restraint, self-possession, willpower, composure, coolness; moderation, temperance, abstemiousness; *informal* cool.

self-denial noun *it took years of hard work and self-denial* SELF-SACRIFICE, selflessness, unselfishness; self-discipline, asceticism, self-deprivation, abstemiousness, abstinence, abstention; moderation, temperance. ANTONYM self-indulgence.

self-discipline noun *he lacks the self-discipline to stick to an exercise program* SELF-CONTROL; restraint, self-restraint; willpower, purposefulness, strong-mindedness, resolve, moral fiber; doggedness, persistence, determination, grit.

self-employed adjective *many of our articles come from self-employed contributors* FREELANCE, independent, casual; consultant, consulting; temporary, contract, visiting, outside, external, extramural.

self-esteem noun *the best thing I ever did for my self-esteem was to divorce Roger* SELF-RESPECT, pride, dignity, self-regard, faith in oneself; morale, self-confidence, confidence, self-assurance. See note at PRIDE.

self-evident adjective *the reasons he left are self-evident* OBVIOUS, clear, plain, evident, apparent, manifest, patent, axiomatic; distinct, transparent, overt, conspicuous, palpable, unmistakable, undeniable. ANTONYM unclear.

self-explanatory adjective *I thought the directions were* *self-explanatory* EASILY UNDERSTOOD, comprehensible, intelligible, straightforward, unambiguous, accessible, crystal clear, user-friendly, simple, self-evident, obvious. ANTONYM impenetrable.

self-government noun *the self-government of our island nation* INDEPENDENCE, self-rule, home rule, self-determination, sovereignty, autonomy, nonalignment, freedom. ANTONYMS hegemony, colonialism.

self-important adjective *why, you self-important little toad!* CONCEITED, arrogant, bumptious, full of oneself, puffed up, pompous, overbearing, opinionated, cocky, presumptuous, sententious, vain, overweening, proud, egotistical; *informal* snooty, uppity, uppish; *literary* Pooterish. ANTONYM humble.

self-indulgent adjective *the kids in that group are all rich and self-indulgent* HEDONISTIC, pleasure-seeking, sybaritic, indulgent, luxurious, lotus-eating, epicurean; intemperate, immoderate, overindulgent, excessive, extravagant, licentious, dissolute, decadent. ANTONYM abstemious.

self-interested adjective *if you weren't so self-interested, you would have noticed that Deanna was upset* SELF-SEEKING, self-serving, self-obsessed, self-absorbed, wrapped up in oneself, egocentric, egotistic, egotistical, egomaniacal, selfish; *informal* looking after number one.

selfish adjective *he is just selfish by nature* EGOCENTRIC, egotistic, egotistical, egomaniacal, self-centered, self-absorbed, self-obsessed, self-seeking, self-serving, wrapped up in oneself; inconsiderate, thoughtless, unthinking, uncaring, uncharitable; mean, miserly, grasping, greedy, mercenary, acquisitive, opportunistic; *informal* looking after number one. ANTONYM altruistic.

selfless adjective *it was very selfless of you to help out your ex-husband like that* UNSELFISH, altruistic, self-sacrificing, self-denying; considerate, compassionate, kind, noble, generous, magnanimous, ungrudging, charitable, benevolent, openhanded. ANTONYM inconsiderate.

self-possessed adjective *I'm usually pretty self-possessed during an interview* ASSURED, self-assured, calm, cool, composed, at ease, unperturbed, unruffled, confident, self-confident, poised, imperturbable; *informal* together, unfazed, nonplussed, unflappable. ANTONYM unsure.

self-possession noun *self-possession is an absolute must for any trial attorney* COMPOSURE, assurance, self-assurance, self-control, imperturbability, impassivity, equanimity, nonchalance, confidence, self-confidence, poise, aplomb, presence of mind, nerve, sangfroid; *informal* cool.

self-reliant adjective *after Linus died, I became surprisingly self-reliant* SELF-SUFFICIENT, self-supporting, self-sustaining, able to stand on one's own two feet; independent, autarkic.

self-respect noun *if you had any self-respect, you wouldn't be wasting your life in front of the television* SELF-ESTEEM, self-regard, amour propre, faith in oneself, pride, dignity, morale, self-confidence.

self-restraint noun *please exercise some self-restraint and don't start screaming when he gets here* SELF-CONTROL, restraint, self-discipline, self-possession, willpower, moderation, temperance, abstemiousness, abstention. ANTONYM self-indulgence.

self-righteous adjective *we listened to Mom because she wasn't as self-righteous as you* SANCTIMONIOUS, holier-than-thou, self-satisfied, smug, priggish, complacent, pious, moralizing, preachy, superior, hypocritical; *informal* goody-goody. ANTONYM humble.

self-sacrifice noun *the self-sacrifice of these young men and women is indeed admirable* SELF-DENIAL, selflessness, unselfishness; self-discipline, abstinence, asceticism, abnegation, self-deprivation, moderation, austerity, temperance, abstention.

self-satisfied adjective *she's such a self-satisfied Miss Perfect* COMPLACENT, self-congratulatory, smug, superior, puffed up, pleased with oneself; *informal* goody-goody.

self-seeking adjective *the self-seeking players would get humbled fast by Coach Higgins* SELF-INTERESTED, self-serving, selfish; egocentric, egotistic, egotistical, self-obsessed, self-absorbed; inconsiderate, thoughtless, unthinking; *informal* looking after number one. ANTONYM altruistic.

self-styled adjective *a self-styled poet* WOULD-BE, so-called, self-appointed, self-titled, professed, self-confessed, soi-disant.

self-sufficient adjective *you'll need to be more self-sufficient once you get to college* SELF-SUPPORTING, self-reliant, self-sustaining, able to stand on one's own two feet; independent, autarkic.

self-willed adjective *how can you reason with a self-willed teenager?* WILLFUL, contrary, perverse, uncooperative, wayward, headstrong, stubborn, obstinate, obdurate, pigheaded, mulish, intransigent, recalcitrant, intractable; *formal* refractory. ANTONYM biddable.

sell verb **1** *they are selling their house* PUT UP FOR SALE, offer for sale, put on sale, dispose of, vend, auction (off); trade, barter. See word spectrum at BUY. ANTONYM buy.

2 *he sells cakes* TRADE IN, deal in, traffic in, stock, carry, offer for sale, peddle, hawk, retail, market.

3 *the book should sell well* GO, be bought, be purchased; move, be in demand.

4 *it **sells for** $79.95* COST, be priced at, retail at, go for, be.

5 *he still has to sell his plan to management* PROMOTE; persuade someone to accept, talk someone into, bring someone around to, win someone over to, win approval for. PHRASES: **sell down the river** *informal* . *my own friends sold me down the river* BETRAY, inform on; be disloyal to, be unfaithful to, double-cross, break faith with, stab in the back, sell out; *informal* tell on, blow the whistle on, squeal on, finger. **sell out 1** *we **have sold out** of chocolate* HAVE NONE LEFT, be out of stock, have run out; *informal* be fresh out, be cleaned out. **2** *the edition sold out quickly* BE BOUGHT UP, be depleted, be exhausted. **3** *they say he has sold out as an artist* ABANDON ONE'S PRINCIPLES, prostitute oneself, sell one's soul, betray one's ideals, be untrue to oneself; debase oneself, degrade oneself, demean oneself. **4** *he never thought his own brother would sell him out.* See SELL DOWN THE RIVER above. **sell short** *she is always selling herself short* UNDERVALUE, underrate, underestimate, disparage, deprecate, belittle; *formal* derogate.

seller noun *the seller does not seem to know the real values of his antiques* VENDOR, retailer, purveyor, supplier, trader, merchant, dealer; shopkeeper, salesperson, salesman, saleswoman, sales assistant, sales associate, clerk, shop assistant, traveling salesperson, peddler, hawker; auctioneer.

semblance noun *there remained at least a semblance of discipline* (OUTWARD) APPEARANCE, air, show, facade, front, veneer, guise, pretense.

seminal adjective *her paper is a seminal work on the subject* INFLUENTIAL, formative, groundbreaking, pioneering, original, innovative; major, important.

seminar noun **1** *a seminar for education officials* CONFERENCE, symposium, meeting, convention, forum, summit, discussion, consultation.

2 *teaching in the form of seminars* STUDY GROUP, workshop, tutorial, class, lesson.

seminary noun *the students at our seminary were no more chaste than the students anywhere else* THEOLOGICAL COLLEGE, divinity school, rabbinical college, Talmudical college, Bible school/college; academy, training college, training institute, school.

send verb **1** *they sent a message to HQ* DISPATCH, post, mail, address, consign, direct, forward; transmit, convey, communicate; telephone, phone, broadcast, radio, fax, e-mail; *dated* telegraph, wire, cable. ANTONYM receive.

2 *we **sent for** a doctor* CALL FOR, summon, contact; ask for, request, order.

3 *the pump **sent out** a jet of steam* PROPEL, project, eject, deliver, discharge, spout, fire, shoot, release; throw, let fly; *informal* chuck.

send-off noun *we gave a Valerie a teary send-off* FAREWELL, goodbye, adieu, leave-taking, valediction; *archaic* vale. ANTONYM welcome.

send-up noun *informal Carvey does a hilarious sendup of the president* SATIRE, burlesque, lampoon, pastiche, caricature, imitation, impression, impersonation; mockery, mimicry, travesty; *informal* spoof, takeoff.

senile adjective *she's in her nineties, but she's not a bit senile* DODDERING, doddery, decrepit, senescent, declining, infirm, feeble; aged, long in the tooth, in one's dotage; mentally confused, having Alzheimer's (disease), having senile dementia; *informal* past it, gaga.

senior adjective **1** *the senior students can get parking permits* OLDER, elder. ANTONYM junior.

2 *a senior officer* SUPERIOR, higher-ranking, high-ranking, more important; top, chief, ranking. ANTONYMS junior, subordinate.

3 *Albert Stone, Senior* SR., the Elder, I. ANTONYMS Junior, Jr.

▸ noun **1** *Angela is a senior at Cal Tech | the seniors are sponsoring a concert* senior student, fourth-year student; (**seniors**) graduating class.

2 *the quilts are made by a group of seniors at our church.* See SENIOR CITIZEN.

WORD NOTE senior

Commencement

They're calling old people *seniors*
short for senior citizens but it's as though
they're still in college and can look forward
to graduate school at Purgatory State
or the University of the Damned and
I can see this poem is intent on being Catholic
though it started out agnostic
Maybe that's because I was talking
to Ed Webster on the phone tonight
and he described himself as an agnostic
who got a job teaching at a Catholic school
in the South Bronx or maybe because I was reading
the classifieds in the *Daily News* today
and several greeted dead ones in heaven
in any case I like seniors maybe the rest of us
are juniors and sophomores and we still have
the junior prom and all that romantic angst
to go through before we reach the holy land
—DL

senior citizen noun *affordable housing for senior citizens* retired person; old person, elderly person, senior, geriatric, dotard, Methuselah, retiree, golden ager; *informal* old-timer, oldie, oldster, geezer, blue-hair.

seniority noun *the promotions are based on seniority* RANK, superiority, standing, primacy, precedence, priority; age, experience.

sensation noun **1** *a sensation of light* FEELING, sense, awareness, consciousness, perception, impression.

2 *he caused a sensation by donating a million dollars* COMMOTION, stir, uproar, furor, scandal, impact; interest, excitement; *informal* splash, to-do, hullabaloo, hoopla.

3 *the movie became an instant sensation* TRIUMPH, success, sellout; talking point; *informal* smash (hit), hit, winner, crowd-pleaser, knockout, blockbuster.

sensational adjective **1** *a sensational murder trial* SHOCKING, scandalous, appalling; amazing, startling, astonishing, staggering; stirring, exciting, thrilling, electrifying, red-hot; fascinating, interesting, noteworthy, significant, remarkable, momentous, historic, newsworthy. ANTONYM run-of-the-mill.

2 *sensational stories* OVERDRAMATIZED, dramatic, melodramatic, exaggerated, sensationalist, sensationalistic; graphic, explicit, lurid; *informal* juicy. ANTONYMS dull, understated.

3 *informal she looked sensational* GORGEOUS, stunning, wonderful, exquisite, lovely, radiant, delightful, charming, enchanting, captivating; striking, spectacular, remarkable, outstanding, arresting, eye-catching; marvelous, superb, excellent, fine, first-class; *informal* great, terrific, tremendous, super, fantastic, fabulous, fab, heavenly, divine, knockout, hot, red-hot, delectable, scrumptious, awesome, magic, wicked, killer, out of this world, smashing, brilliant. ANTONYM unremarkable.

sense noun **1** *the sense of touch* SENSORY FACULTY, feeling, sensation, perception; sight, hearing, touch, taste, smell.

2 *a sense of guilt* FEELING, awareness, sensation, consciousness, recognition.

3 *a sense of humor* APPRECIATION, awareness, understanding, comprehension, discernment; *informal* nose.

4 *she had the sense to press the panic button* WISDOM, common sense, sagacity, discernment, perception; wit, intelligence, cleverness, shrewdness, judgment, reason, logic, brain(s); *informal* gumption, horse sense, savvy, (street) smarts. ANTONYM stupidity.

5 *I can't see the sense in this* PURPOSE, point, reason, object, motive; use, value, advantage, benefit.

6 *the different senses of "well"* MEANING, definition, import, signification, significance, purport, implication, nuance; drift, gist, thrust, tenor, message.

▸ verb *she sensed their hostility* DISCERN, feel, observe, notice, recognize, pick up (on), be aware of, distinguish, make out, identify; comprehend, apprehend, see, appreciate, realize; suspect, have a funny feeling about, have a hunch about, divine, intuit; *informal* catch on to.

senseless adjective **1** *they found him senseless on the floor* UNCONSCIOUS, stunned, insensible, insensate, comatose, knocked out, out cold, out for the count; numb; *informal* KO'd, dead to the world, passed out. ANTONYM conscious.

2 *a senseless waste* POINTLESS, futile, useless, needless, unavailing, in vain, purposeless, meaningless, unprofitable; absurd, foolish, insane, stupid, idiotic, ridiculous, ludicrous, mindless, illogical. ANTONYM wise.

sensibility noun **1** *develop your sensibility* SENSITIVITY, finer feelings, delicacy, taste, discrimination, discernment; understanding, insight, empathy, appreciation; feeling, intuition, responsiveness, receptiveness, perceptiveness, awareness.

2 (**sensibilities**) *the wording might offend their sensibilities* (FINER) FEELINGS, emotions, sensitivities, moral sense.

sensible adjective *isn't this the sensible thing to do? | a sensible young man* PRACTICAL, realistic, responsible, reasonable, commonsensical, rational, logical, sound, balanced, grounded, sober, no-nonsense, pragmatic, levelheaded, thoughtful, down-to-earth, wise, prudent, judicious, sagacious, shrewd. See note at TANGIBLE. ANTONYM foolish.

THE RIGHT WORD

A **sensible** person brings an umbrella when rain is forecast. A **rational** one studies the weather map, observes the movement of the clouds across the sky, listens to the forecast on the radio, and then decides whether or not an umbrella is necessary. *Sensible* implies the use of common sense and an appreciation of the value of experience (*a sensible decision not to travel until his injuries had healed*), while *rational* suggests the ability to reason logically and to draw conclusions from inferences (*a rational explanation for why she failed the exam*). **Lucid** and **sane**, like *rational*, are associated with coherent thinking. *Lucid* suggests a mind free of internal pressures or distortions (*lucid intervals during which he was able to recognize his wife and children*), while *sane* indicates freedom from psychosis or mental derangement (*judged to have been sane when she committed the crime*). *Sane* also has a meaning very close to that of *sensible* (*a sane approach to disciplining problem teenagers*). A **sagacious** person is an extremely shrewd one who is both discerning and practical. He or she can look out the window and tell whether it's going to rain by studying the facial expressions of passersby as they glance nervously at the sky.

sensitive adjective **1** *she's* ***sensitive to*** *changes in temperature* RESPONSIVE TO, reactive to, sentient of, sensitized to; aware of, conscious of, alive to; susceptible to, affected by, vulnerable to; attuned to. ANTONYMS impervious, unresponsive.

2 *sensitive skin* DELICATE, fragile; tender, sore, raw. ANTONYMS resilient, tough.

3 *the matter needs sensitive handling* TACTFUL, careful, thoughtful, diplomatic, delicate, subtle, kid-glove; sympathetic, compassionate, understanding, intuitive, responsive, insightful. ANTONYM clumsy.

4 *he's sensitive about his bald patch* TOUCHY, oversensitive, hypersensitive, easily offended, easily upset, easily hurt, thin-skinned, defensive; paranoid, neurotic; *informal* uptight. ANTONYM thick-skinned.

5 *a sensitive issue* DIFFICULT, delicate, tricky, awkward, problematic, ticklish, precarious; controversial, emotive; *informal* sticky. ANTONYM uncontroversial.

sensitivity noun **1** *the sensitivity of the skin* RESPONSIVENESS, sensitiveness, reactivity; susceptibility, vulnerability.

2 *the job calls for sensitivity* CONSIDERATION, care, thoughtfulness, tact, diplomacy, delicacy, subtlety, finer feelings; understanding, empathy, sensibility, feeling, intuition, responsiveness, receptiveness; perception, discernment, insight; savoir faire.

3 *her sensitivity on the subject of marriage* TOUCHINESS, oversensitivity, hypersensitivity, defensiveness.

4 *the sensitivity of the issue* DELICACY, trickiness, awkwardness, ticklishness.

sensual adjective **1** *sensual pleasure* PHYSICAL, carnal, bodily, fleshly, animal; hedonistic, epicurean, sybaritic, voluptuary. See note at SENSUOUS. ANTONYM spiritual.

2 *a beautiful, sensual woman* SEXUALLY ATTRACTIVE, sexy, voluptuous, sultry, seductive, passionate; sexually arousing, erotic, sexual. ANTONYM passionless.

sensuality noun *he seemed barely aware of his own sensuality* SEXINESS, sexual attractiveness, sultriness, seductiveness; sexuality, eroticism; physicality, carnality.

sensuous adjective **1** *they lived amid sensuous surroundings* AESTHETICALLY PLEASING, gratifying, rich, sumptuous, luxurious; sensory, sensorial.

2 *sensuous lips* SEXUALLY ATTRACTIVE, sexy, seductive, voluptuous, luscious, lush.

THE RIGHT WORD

Sensuous and **sensual** are often confused. *Sensuous* implies gratification of the senses for the sake of aesthetic pleasure, or delight in the color, sound, or form of something (*a dress made from a soft, sensuous fabric*), while **sensual** implies indulgence of the appetites or gratification of the senses as an end in itself (*he leads a life of sensual excess*). **Luxurious** implies indulgence in sensuous or sensual pleasures, especially those that induce a feeling of physical comfort or satisfaction (*a luxurious satin coverlet*), while **epicurean** refers to taking delight in the pleasures of eating and drinking (*the epicurean life of a king and his courtiers*). To be **voluptuous** is to give oneself up to the pleasures of the senses (*the symphony is voluptuous in its scoring*), but it carries a suggestion of sensual rather than sensuous enjoyment and can refer to a curvaceous and sexually attractive woman (*he was seen with a voluptuous blonde*). *Sybaritic* implies an overrefined luxuriousness, also suggesting indulgence in good food and drink and the presence of things designed to soothe and charm the senses (*he lived alone, in sybaritic splendor*).

sentence noun *the judge shortened his sentence to nine months* PRISON TERM, prison sentence; punishment; *informal* time, stretch, stint.

▸ verb *they were sentenced to death* PASS JUDGMENT ON, punish, convict; condemn, doom.

sententious adjective *your new churchy friends have certainly made you sententious* MORALISTIC, moralizing, sanctimonious, self-righteous, pietistic, pious, priggish, judgmental; pompous, pontifical, self-important; *informal* preachy.

sentient adjective *any sentient creature should have the good sense to avoid something so dangerous* (CAPABLE OF) FEELING, living, live; conscious, aware, responsive, reactive.

sentiment noun **1** *the comments echo my own sentiments* VIEW, feeling, attitude, thought, opinion, belief. See note at OPINION.

2 *there's no room for sentiment in this sport* SENTIMENTALITY, sentimentalism, mawkishness, emotionalism; emotion, sensibility, soft-heartedness, tenderheartedness; *informal* schmaltz, mush, slushiness, corniness, soppiness, sappiness. See note at EMOTION.

sentimental adjective **1** *she kept the vase for sentimental reasons* NOSTALGIC, tender, emotional, affectionate. ANTONYMS practical, dispassionate.

2 *the film is too sentimental* MAWKISH, overemotional, cloying, sickly, saccharine, sugary, oversweet; romantic, touching; *informal* slushy, mushy, weepy, tear-jerking, schmaltzy, lovey-dovey, gooey, drippy, cheesy, corny, cornball, sappy, hokey. ANTONYMS realistic, gritty.

3 *she is sentimental about animals* SOFTHEARTED, tenderhearted, soft.

THE RIGHT WORD

If you are moved to tears by a situation that does not really warrant such a response, you're likely to be called **sentimental**, an adjective used to describe a willingness to get emotional at the slightest prompting (*a sentimental man who kept his dog's ashes in an urn on the mantel*). **Effusive** applies to excessive or insincere displays of emotion, although it may be used in an approving sense (*effusive in her gratitude for the help she had received*). **Maudlin** derives from the name Mary Magdalene, who was often shown with her eyes swollen from weeping. It implies a lack of self-restraint, particularly in the form of excessive tearfulness. **Mawkish** carries sentimentality a step further, implying emotion so excessive that it provokes loathing or disgust (*mawkish attempts to win the audience over*). Although **romantic** at one time referred to an expression of deep feeling, nowadays it is often used disapprovingly to describe emotion that has little to do with the way things actually are and that is linked to an idealized vision of the way they should be (*she had a romantic notion of what it meant to be a "starving artist"*). **Mushy** suggests both excessive emotion or sentimentality and a contempt for romantic love (*a mushy love story*).

sentry noun *the sentry on the tower signaled to the gatekeeper* GUARD, sentinel, lookout, watch, watchman, patrol.

separable adjective *the hood on the sweatshirt is separable* DIVISIBLE, distinct, independent, distinguishable; detachable, removable, pull-off.

separate adjective **1** *his personal life was separate from his job* UNCONNECTED, unrelated, different, distinct, discrete; detached, divorced, disconnected, independent, autonomous. ANTONYMS linked, interdependent.

2 *the infirmary was separate from the school* SET APART, detached, fenced off, cut off, segregated, isolated; freestanding, self-contained. ANTONYM attached.

▸ verb **1** *they separated two rioting mobs* SPLIT (UP), break up, part, pull apart, divide; *literary* sunder. ANTONYMS unite, bring together.

2 *the connectors can be separated* DISCONNECT, detach, disengage, uncouple, unyoke, disunite, disjoin; split, divide, sever; disentangle. ANTONYMS join, connect, combine.

3 *the wall that separates the two properties* PARTITION, divide, come between, keep apart; bisect, intersect. ANTONYMS link, bridge.

4 *the south aisle was **separated off*** ISOLATE, partition off, section off; close off, shut off, cordon off, fence off, screen off.

5 *they separated at the airport* PART (COMPANY), go their separate ways, split up; say goodbye; disperse, disband, scatter. ANTONYM meet.

6 *the road separated* FORK, divide, branch, bifurcate, diverge. ANTONYMS merge, converge.

7 *her parents separated* SPLIT UP, break up, part, be estranged, divorce. ANTONYMS get together, marry.

8 *separate fact from fiction* ISOLATE, set apart, segregate; distinguish, differentiate, dissociate; sort out, sift out, filter out, remove, weed out.

9 *those who **separate themselves from** society* BREAK AWAY FROM, break with, secede from, withdraw from, leave, quit, dissociate oneself from, resign from, drop out of, repudiate, reject. ANTONYM join.

separately adverb *I'll have to interview you all separately* INDIVIDUALLY, one by one, one at a time, singly, severally; apart, independently, alone, by oneself, on one's own.

separation noun **1** *the separation of the two companies* DISCONNECTION, detachment, severance, dissociation, disunion, disaffiliation, segregation, partition.

2 *her parents' separation* BREAKUP, split, parting (of the ways), estrangement, rift, rupture, breach; divorce.

3 *the separation between art and life* DISTINCTION, difference, differentiation, division, dividing line; gulf, gap, chasm.

septic adjective *a septic finger* INFECTED, festering, suppurating, pus-filled, putrid, putrefying, poisoned, diseased; *Medicine* purulent.

sepulchral adjective *the sepulchral tone in their voices* GLOOMY, lugubrious, somber, melancholy, melancholic, sad, sorrowful, mournful, doleful, dismal; *literary* dolorous. ANTONYM cheerful.

sepulchre noun *an old family sepulcher on the grounds of the estate* TOMB, vault, burial chamber, mausoleum, crypt, undercroft, catacomb; grave.

sequel noun **1** *the film inspired a sequel* FOLLOW-UP, continuation.

2 *the immediate sequel to the coup was an armed uprising* CONSEQUENCE, result, upshot, outcome, development, issue, postscript; effect, aftereffect, aftermath, by-product; *informal* payoff.

sequence noun **1** *the sequence of events* SUCCESSION, order, course, series, chain, train, string, progression, chronology, timeline; pattern, flow; *formal* concatenation.

2 *a sequence from his film* EXCERPT, clip, extract, episode, section.

sequester verb **1** *he sequestered himself from the world* ISOLATE ONESELF, hide away, shut oneself away, seclude oneself, cut oneself off, segregate oneself; closet oneself, cloister oneself, withdraw, retire.

2 *the government sequestered his property* CONFISCATE, seize, sequestrate, take, appropriate, expropriate, impound, commandeer.

seraphic adjective *a look of seraphic contentment on his face* BLISSFUL, beatific, sublime, rapturous, ecstatic, joyful, rapt; serene, ethereal; cherubic, saintly, angelic.

serendipitous adjective *our meeting was purely serendipitous* CHANCE, accidental, coincidental; lucky, fluky, fortuitous; unexpected, unforeseen.

serendipity noun *the consequence of serendipity is sometimes a brilliant discovery* (HAPPY) CHANCE, (happy) accident, fluke; luck, good luck, good fortune, fortuity, providence; happy coincidence.

serene adjective **1** *on the surface she seemed serene* CALM, composed, tranquil, peaceful, untroubled, relaxed, at ease, unperturbed, unruffled, unworried; placid, equable, centered; *informal* together, unflappable. See note at CALM. ANTONYM agitated.

2 *serene valleys* PEACEFUL, tranquil, quiet, still, restful, relaxing, undisturbed. ANTONYM turbulent.

series noun **1** *a series of lectures* SUCCESSION, sequence, string, chain, run, round; spate, wave, rash; set, course, cycle; row, line; *formal* concatenation.

2 *a new TV series* SERIAL, program, show, drama; soap opera; *informal* soap, sitcom, miniseries.

serious adjective **1** *a serious expression* SOLEMN, earnest, grave, somber, sober, unsmiling, poker-faced, stern, grim, dour, humorless, stony-faced; thoughtful, preoccupied, pensive. ANTONYMS lighthearted, cheerful.

2 *serious decisions* IMPORTANT, significant, consequential, momentous, weighty, far-reaching, major, grave; urgent, pressing, crucial, critical, vital, life-and-death, high-priority. ANTONYMS unimportant, trivial.

3 *give serious consideration to this* CAREFUL, detailed, in-depth, deep, profound, meaningful. ANTONYM superficial.

4 *a serious play* INTELLECTUAL, highbrow, heavyweight, deep, profound, literary, learned, scholarly; *informal* heavy. ANTONYMS lowbrow, light.

5 *serious injuries* SEVERE, grave, bad, critical, acute, terrible, dire, dangerous, perilous, parlous; *formal* grievous. ANTONYMS minor, negligible.

6 *we're serious about equality* IN EARNEST, earnest, sincere, wholehearted, genuine; committed, resolute, determined. ANTONYM halfhearted.

seriously adverb **1** *Faye nodded seriously* SOLEMNLY, earnestly, gravely, soberly, somberly, sternly, grimly, dourly, humorlessly; pensively, thoughtfully.

2 *she was seriously injured* SEVERELY, gravely, badly, critically, acutely, dangerously; *formal* grievously.

3 *do you seriously expect me to come?* REALLY, actually, honestly.

4 *seriously, I'm very pleased* JOKING ASIDE, to be serious, honestly, truthfully, truly, I mean it; *informal* scout's honor.

5 *informal "I've resigned." "Seriously?"* REALLY?, is that so?, is that a fact?, you're joking, well I never, go on, you don't say; *informal* you're kidding.

6 *informal he was seriously rich.* See EXTREMELY.

sermon noun **1** *he preached a sermon* HOMILY, address, speech, talk, discourse, oration; lesson.

2 *her mother gave her a sermon on personal hygiene* LECTURE, tirade, harangue, diatribe; speech, disquisition, monologue; reprimand, reproach, reproof, admonishment, admonition, remonstration, criticism; *informal* talking-to, dressing-down, earful; *formal* castigation.

serpentine adjective **1** *a serpentine form* SERPENTLIKE, snakelike. ANTONYM straight.

2 *a serpentine path* WINDING, windy, zigzag, twisty, twisting and turning, labyrinthine, meandering, sinuous, snaky, tortuous. ANTONYM straight.

3 *serpentine sentences* COMPLICATED, complex, intricate, involved, tortuous, convoluted, elaborate, knotty, confusing, bewildering, baffling, impenetrable. ANTONYMS straightforward, simple.

serrated adjective *the serrated edge of the knife* JAGGED, sawtoothed, sawtooth, zigzag, notched, indented, toothed; *Botany* serrate; *technical* crenulated. ANTONYM smooth.

serried adjective *serried ranks of soldiers* CLOSE TOGETHER, packed together, close-set, dense, tight, compact.

servant noun **1** *servants were cleaning the hall* ATTENDANT, retainer; domestic (worker), (hired) help, cleaner; lackey, flunky, minion; maid, housemaid, footman, page (boy), valet, butler, manservant; housekeeper, steward; drudge, menial, slave, water boy; *archaic* scullion.

2 *a servant of the people* HELPER, supporter, follower.

serve verb **1** *they served their masters faithfully* WORK FOR, be in the service of, be employed by; obey.

2 *this job serves the community* BE OF SERVICE TO, be of use to, help, assist, aid, make a contribution to, do one's bit for, do something for, benefit.

3 *she **served on** the committee for years* BE A MEMBER OF, work on, be on, sit on, have a place on.

4 *he served his apprenticeship in Washington* CARRY OUT, perform, do, fulfill, complete, discharge; spend.

5 *serve the soup hot* DISH UP/OUT, give out, distribute; present, provide, supply.

6 *she served another customer* ATTEND TO, deal with, see to; ASSIST, help, look after.

7 *they **served** him **with** a writ* PRESENT WITH, deliver to, give (to), hand over to.

8 *a plate **serving as** an ashtray* ACT AS, function as, do the work of, be a substitute for.

9 *these three sizes of brush will serve for most paint jobs* SUFFICE, be adequate, be good enough, fit/fill the bill, do, answer, be useful, meet requirements, suit.

server noun WAITER/WAITRESS, attendant, garçon, waitperson; busboy; hostess, host, maître d'; wait staff.

service noun **1** *your conditions of service* WORK, employment, employ, labor.

2 *he has done us a service* FAVOR, kindness, good turn, helping hand; **(services)** ASSISTANCE, help, aid, offices, ministrations.

3 *the food and service were excellent* WAITING, waitressing, serving, attendance.

4 *products that give reliable service* USE, usage; functioning.

5 *the service on the Chevy cost $80* tune-up, maintenance check, servicing, overhaul.

6 *a marriage service* CEREMONY, ritual, rite, observance; liturgy, sacrament; *formal* ordinance.

7 *a range of local services* AMENITY, facility, resource, utility.

8 *soldiers leaving the service* ARMED FORCES, armed services, military; army, navy, air force, marines, coast guard.

▸ verb *the appliances are serviced regularly* check, go over, maintain, overhaul; repair, mend, recondition.

PHRASES: **be of service** *can I be of service to you?* HELP, assist, benefit, be of assistance, be beneficial, serve, be useful, be of use, be valuable; do someone a good turn. **out of service** *the candy machine is out of service* OUT OF ORDER, broken, broken-down, out of commission, unserviceable, faulty, defective, inoperative, in disrepair; down; *informal* conked out, bust, kaput, on the blink, on the fritz, acting up, shot.

serviceable adjective 1 *a serviceable heating system* IN WORKING ORDER, working, functioning, functional, operational, operative; usable, workable, viable. ANTONYM unusable.

2 *serviceable lace-up shoes* FUNCTIONAL, utilitarian, sensible, practical; HARDWEARING, durable, tough, robust. ANTONYM impractical.

service station noun *we dropped the Jeep off at Jimmy's service station* GAS STATION, garage, filling station, gasoline station, self-serve, truck stop.

servile adjective *here comes Mr. Archer and his servile assistant, Bradley* OBSEQUIOUS, sycophantic, deferential, subservient, fawning, ingratiating, unctuous, groveling, toadyish, slavish, humble, self-abasing; *informal* slimy, bootlicking, smarmy, sucky. See note at OBSEQUIOUS. ANTONYM assertive.

serving noun *you should have at least four servings of vegetables* PORTION, helping, plateful, plate, bowlful; amount, quantity, ration.

servitude noun *born into a life of servitude* SLAVERY, enslavement, bondage, subjugation, subjection, domination; *historical* serfdom. ANTONYM liberty.

session noun 1 *a special session of the committee* MEETING, sitting, *Law* assize, assembly, conclave, plenary; hearing; conference, discussion, forum, symposium, caucus.

2 *training sessions* PERIOD, time, spell, stretch, bout.

3 *the next session on campus begins in August* ACADEMIC YEAR, school year; term, semester.

set[1] verb 1 *Beth set the bag on the table* PUT (DOWN), place, lay, deposit, position, settle, leave, stand, plant, posit; *informal* stick, dump, park, plunk.

2 *the cottage is set on a hill* BE SITUATED, be located, lie, stand, be sited, be perched.

3 *the fence is set in concrete* FIX, embed, insert; mount.

4 *a ring set with precious stones* ADORN, ornament, decorate, embellish; *literary* bejewel.

5 *I'll go and set the table* LAY, prepare, arrange.

6 *we set them some easy tasks* ASSIGN, allocate, give, allot, prescribe.

7 *just set your mind to it* APPLY, address, direct, aim, turn, focus, concentrate.

8 *they set a date for the election* DECIDE ON, select, choose, arrange, schedule; fix (on), settle on, determine, designate, name, appoint, specify, stipulate.

9 *he set his horse toward her* DIRECT, steer, orient, orientate, point, aim, train.

10 *his jump set a national record* ESTABLISH, create, institute.

11 *he set his watch* ADJUST, regulate, synchronize; calibrate; put right, correct; program, activate, turn on.

12 *the adhesive will set in an hour* SOLIDIFY, harden, stiffen, thicken, jell, cake, congeal, coagulate, clot; freeze, crystallize. ANTONYM melt.

13 *the sun was setting* GO DOWN, sink, dip; vanish, disappear. ANTONYM rise.

PHRASES: **set about** *Mike set about raising $5,000* BEGIN, start, commence, go about, get to work on, get down to, embark on, tackle, address oneself to, undertake. **set against** *you deliberately set me against my family* ALIENATE FROM, estrange from, set at odds; drive a wedge between (one and another), sow dissension between (one and another). **set apart** 1 *the orchestral background sets this song apart from the rest* DISTINGUISH, differentiate, mark out, single out, separate, demarcate. 2 *one pew was set apart from the rest* ISOLATE, separate, segregate, put to one side. **set aside** 1 *set aside some money each month* SAVE, put by, put aside, put away, lay by, keep, reserve; store, stockpile, hoard, stow away, cache, withhold; *informal* salt away, squirrel away, stash away. 2 *he set aside his cup* PUT DOWN, cast aside, discard, abandon, dispense with. 3 *set aside your differences* DISREGARD, put aside, ignore, forget, discount, shrug off, bury. 4 *the Supreme Court set aside the decision* OVERRULE, overturn, reverse, revoke, countermand, nullify, annul, cancel, quash, dismiss, reject, repudiate; *Law* disaffirm; *formal* abrogate. **set back** *the rains have set back the work on the bridge* DELAY, hold up, hold back, slow down/up, retard, check, decelerate; hinder, impede, hobble, obstruct, hamper, inhibit, frustrate, thwart. **set down** 1 *he set down his thoughts* WRITE DOWN, put in writing, jot down, note down, make a note of; record, register, log. 2 *we set down some rules* FORMULATE, draw up, establish, frame; lay down, determine, fix, stipulate, specify, prescribe, impose, ordain. 3 *I set it down to the fact that he was drunk* ATTRIBUTE, put down, ascribe, assign, chalk up; blame on, impute. **set forth** *you have set forth a very credible argument* PRESENT, describe, set out, detail, delineate, explain, expound; state, declare, announce; submit, offer, put forward, advance, propose, propound. **set free** *the hostages were released just minutes ago* RELEASE, free, let go, turn loose, let out, liberate, deliver, emancipate. **set in** *bad weather set in* BEGIN, start, arrive, come, develop. **set off** 1 *they set off for America with nothing but the clothes on their backs* SET OUT, start out, sally forth, leave, depart, embark, set sail; *informal* hit the road. 2 *the bomb was set off* DETONATE, explode, blow up, touch off, trigger; ignite. 3 *it set off a wave of protest* GIVE RISE TO, cause, lead to, set in motion, occasion, bring about, initiate, precipitate, prompt, trigger (off), spark (off), touch off, provoke, incite. 4 *the blue dress set off her auburn hair* ENHANCE, bring out, emphasize, show off, throw into relief; complement. **set on/upon** *the relentless Cossacks set upon village after village* ATTACK, assail, assault, hit, strike, beat, thrash, pummel, wallop, set about, fall on; *informal* lay into, lace into, let someone have it, work over, rough up, knock about/around, have a go at, beat up on, light into. **set one's heart on** *I think she's set her heart on the orange kitten* WANT DESPERATELY, wish for, desire, long for, yearn for, hanker after, ache for, hunger for, thirst for, burn for; *informal* be itching for, be dying for. **set out 1** *he set out early.* See SET OFF sense 1 above. **2** *the gifts were set out on tables* ARRANGE, lay out, put out, array, dispose, display, exhibit. **3** *they set out some guidelines* PRESENT, set forth, detail; state, declare, announce; submit, put forward, advance, propose, propound. **4** *you've done what you set out to do* AIM, intend, mean, seek; hope, aspire, want. **set up 1** *his father set him up in business* ESTABLISH, finance, fund, back, subsidize. **2** *informal she set him up for Newley's murder* FALSELY INCRIMINATE, frame, entrap. **3** *a monument to her memory was set up* ERECT, put up, construct, build, raise, elevate. **4** *she set up her own business* ESTABLISH, start, begin, initiate, institute, found, create. **5** *set up a meeting* ARRANGE, organize, fix (up), schedule, timetable, line up. **6** *set up a committee* ESTABLISH, form.

WORD NOTE set

I include this simply as an *aide-mémoire:* there are more meanings for this innocent-looking trinity of letters than there are for any other word in the English language—fully 62 columns' worth in the complete *Oxford English Dictionary,* and which naturally include such obvious examples as: the condition of what the sun does each evening; a major part of a game of tennis; what one does if one embarks on a journey; what one does if one puts something down on a table; a collection of a number of items of a particular kind; and a further score, or more, of other disparate and unconnected things and actions. *Set* is a term in bowling; it is what a dog (especially a setter, of course) does when he is dealing with game; it is a grudge; what cement does when it dries; what Jell-O does when it doesn't dry; a form of power used by shipwrights; what a young woman does when she wants to secure a man's affections; the direction of a current at sea; the build of a person; a kind of underdeveloped fruit; the stake that is put down at dice . . . need I go on? In the search for a synonym it is worth pointing out, and only half in jest, that it is quite possible that one or other meanings for *set* might fit the bill, exactly, and will have you *all set,* semantically, and quite neatly, without nearly as much effort as you supposed. **—SW**

set[2] noun **1** *a set of color postcards* GROUP, collection, series; assortment, selection, compendium, batch, number; arrangement, array.

2 *the literary set* CLIQUE, coterie, circle, crowd, group, crew, band, company, ring, camp, fraternity, school, faction, league; *informal* gang, bunch.

3 *a chemistry set* KIT, apparatus, equipment, outfit.

4 *a set of china* SERVICE.

5 *the set of his shoulders* POSTURE, position, cast, attitude; bearing, carriage.

6 *a set for the play* SCENERY, setting, backdrop, flats; mise en scène.

7 *the band played two sets* SESSION, time; stretch, bout, round.

set[3] adjective **1** *a set routine* FIXED, established, predetermined, hard and fast, prearranged, prescribed, specified, defined; unvarying, unchanging, invariable, unvaried, rigid, inflexible, cast-iron, strict, ironclad, settled, predictable; routine, standard, customary, regular, usual, habitual, accustomed, wonted. ANTONYMS variable, changing.

2 *she had set ideas* INFLEXIBLE, rigid, fixed, firm, deep-rooted, deep-seated, ingrained, entrenched. ANTONYM flexible.

3 *he had a set speech for such occasions* STOCK, standard, routine, rehearsed, well-worn, formulaic, conventional. ANTONYMS original, fresh.

4 *I was all set for the evening* READY, prepared, organized, equipped, primed; *informal* geared up, psyched up. ANTONYM unprepared.

5 *he's* ***set on*** *marrying her* DETERMINED TO, intent on, bent on, hell-bent on, resolute about, insistent about. ANTONYM uncertain.

6 *you were dead* ***set against*** *the idea* OPPOSED TO, averse to, hostile to, resistant to, antipathetic to, unsympathetic to; *informal* anti.

setback noun *this is a team famous for surmounting every setback that fate sends their way* PROBLEM, difficulty, hitch, complication, upset, disappointment, misfortune, mishap, reversal; blow, stumbling block, hurdle, hindrance, impediment, obstruction; delay, holdup; *informal* glitch, hiccup. ANTONYM breakthrough.

settee noun *a new settee for the sun porch* SOFA, couch, divan, chaise longue, chesterfield, davenport, daybed.

setting noun **1** *a rural setting* SURROUNDINGS, position, situation, environment, background, backdrop, milieu, environs, habitat; spot, place, location, locale, site, scene; area, region, district.

2 *a garnet in a gold setting* MOUNT, fixture, surround.

settle verb **1** *they settled the dispute* RESOLVE, sort out, solve, clear up, end, fix, work out, iron out, straighten out, set right, rectify, remedy, reconcile; *informal* patch up. ANTONYM prolong.

2 *she settled their affairs* PUT IN ORDER, sort out, tidy up, arrange, organize, order, clear up.

3 *they* ***settled on*** *a date for the wedding* DECIDE ON, set, fix, agree on, name, establish, arrange, appoint, designate, assign; choose, select, pick.

4 *she went down to the lobby to settle her bill* PAY, settle up, square, clear, defray.

5 *they* ***settled for*** *a 4.2% raise* ACCEPT, agree to, assent to; *formal* accede to.

6 *he* ***settled in*** *Otsego County* MAKE ONE'S HOME IN, set up home in, take up residence in, put down roots in, establish oneself in; live in, move to, emigrate to.

7 *immigrants settled much of Australia* COLONIZE, occupy, inhabit, people, populate.

8 *Catherine* ***settled down to*** *her work* APPLY ONESELF TO, get down to, set about, attack; concentrate on, focus on, devote oneself to.

9 *the class wouldn't* ***settle down*** CALM DOWN, quiet down, be quiet, be still; *informal* shut up.

10 *a brandy will settle your nerves* CALM, quiet; *Brit.* quieten, soothe, pacify, quell; sedate, tranquilize. ANTONYMS agitate, disturb.

11 *he settled into an armchair* SIT DOWN, seat oneself, install oneself, ensconce oneself, plant oneself; *informal* park oneself, plunk oneself.

12 *a butterfly settled on the flower* LAND, come to rest, alight, descend, perch; *archaic* light.

13 *when the stirring stops, the sediment settles* SINK, subside, fall, gravitate. ANTONYM rise.

settlement noun 1 *a pay settlement* AGREEMENT, deal, arrangement, resolution, bargain, understanding, pact.

2 *the settlement of the dispute* RESOLUTION, settling, solution, reconciliation.

3 *a frontier settlement* COMMUNITY, colony, outpost, encampment, post; village, commune; *historical* plantation, clearing.

4 *the settlement of the area* COLONIZATION, settling, populating; *historical* plantation.

5 *the settlement of their debts* PAYMENT, discharge, liquidation, clearance.

settler noun *the settlers were ill-prepared for the severe winter ahead* COLONIST, colonizer, frontiersman, frontierswoman, pioneer, bushwhacker; immigrant, newcomer; *historical* homesteader. ANTONYM native.

set-up noun 1 *a complicated setup* SYSTEM, structure, organization, arrangement, framework, layout, configuration.

2 *a setup called Film International* ORGANIZATION, group, body, agency, association, operation; company, firm; *informal* outfit.

3 *informal the whole thing was a setup* TRICK, trap; conspiracy; *informal* put-up job, frame-up.

seven cardinal number *they're a silly seven, these girls from Wisconsin, and they're as lovely as they are funny* SEPTET, septuplets; *technical* heptad.

sever verb 1 *the head was severed from the body* CUT OFF, chop off, detach, disconnect, dissever, separate, part; amputate; *literary* sunder. ANTONYMS join, attach.

2 *a knife had severed the artery* CUT (THROUGH), rupture, split, pierce.

3 *they severed diplomatic relations* BREAK OFF, discontinue, suspend, end, terminate, cease, dissolve. ANTONYMS establish, maintain.

several adjective 1 *several people* SOME, a number of, a few; various, assorted, sundry, diverse; *literary* divers.

2 *they sorted out their several responsibilities* RESPECTIVE, individual, own, particular, specific; separate, different, disparate, distinct; various.

severe adjective 1 *severe injuries* ACUTE, very bad, serious, grave, critical, dreadful, terrible, awful; dangerous, parlous, life-threatening; *formal* grievous. ANTONYMS minor, negligible.

2 *severe storms* FIERCE, violent, strong, powerful, intense; tempestuous, turbulent. ANTONYM gentle.

3 *a severe winter* HARSH, bitter, cold, bleak, freezing, icy, arctic, extreme; *informal* brutal. ANTONYM mild.

4 *a severe headache* EXCRUCIATING, agonizing, intense, dreadful, awful, terrible, unbearable, intolerable; *informal* splitting, pounding, screaming. ANTONYM slight.

5 *a severe test of their stamina* DIFFICULT, demanding, tough, arduous, formidable, exacting, rigorous, punishing, onerous, grueling. ANTONYMS easy, simple.

6 *severe criticism* HARSH, scathing, sharp, strong, fierce, savage, scorching, devastating, trenchant, caustic, biting, withering. ANTONYM mild.

7 *severe tax penalties* EXTORTIONATE, excessive, unreasonable, inordinate, outrageous, sky-high, harsh, stiff; punitive.

8 *they received severe treatment* HARSH, stern, hard, inflexible, uncompromising, unrelenting, merciless, pitiless, ruthless, draconian, oppressive, repressive, punitive; brutal, cruel, savage. ANTONYMS lenient, lax.

9 *his severe expression* STERN, dour, grim, forbidding, disapproving, unsmiling, unfriendly, somber, grave, serious, stony, steely; cold, frosty. ANTONYMS friendly, genial.

10 *a severe style of architecture* PLAIN, simple, austere, unadorned, unembellished, unornamented, stark, spartan, ascetic; clinical, uncluttered. ANTONYMS fancy, ornate.

THE RIGHT WORD

A storm, a hairdo, and a punishment may all be described as **severe**, which means harsh or uncompromising, without a hint of softness, mildness, levity, or indulgence. **Austere**, on the other hand, primarily applies to people, their habits, their way of life, and the environments they create; it implies coldness, stark simplicity, and restraint (*an austere room with only a table and chair*). **Ascetic** implies extreme self-denial and self-discipline, in some cases to the point of choosing what is painful or disagreeable (*he had an ascetic approach to life and rejected all creature comforts*). **Strict** literally means bound or stretched tight; in extended use, it means strenuously exact (*a strict curfew; strict obedience*). **Stern** combines harshness and authority with strictness or severity (*a stern judge*). **Unmitigated** means unmodified and unsoftened in any way (*a streak of unmitigated bad luck*).

severely adjective 1 *he was severely injured* BADLY, seriously, critically; fatally; *formal* grievously.

2 *she was severely criticized* SHARPLY, roundly, soundly, fiercely, savagely.

3 *murderers should be treated more severely* HARSHLY, strictly, sternly, rigorously, mercilessly, pitilessly, roughly, sharply; with a rod of iron; brutally, cruelly, savagely.

4 *she looked severely at Harriet* STERNLY, grimly, dourly, disapprovingly; coldly, frostily.

5 *she dressed severely in black* PLAINLY, simply, austerely, starkly.

sew verb *she sewed the seams of the tunic* STITCH, tack, baste, seam, hem; embroider. PHRASE: **sew up** 1 *the tear was sewn up* DARN, mend, repair, patch. 2 *informal the company sewed up a deal with IBM* SECURE, clinch, pull off, bring off, settle, conclude, complete, finalize, tie up; *informal* swing.

sewing noun *her sewing is exceptional, as these blue ribbons would suggest* STITCHING, needlework, needlecraft, fancy-work. See table on page 822.

SEWING AND NEEDLEWORK TERMS

appliqué	needlepoint
backstitch	overcasting
Bargallo	overhand
bar tack	oversewing
basting	overstitch
binding	patchwork
blanket stitch	petit point
blind stitch	pin tuck
bobbin	pleating
braid	presser foot
broderie anglaise	quilting
buttonhole stitch	running stitch
casing	saddle stitch
catch stitch	satin stitch
chain stitch	seam
crewel work	seamstress
cross-stitch	selvage
cutwork	serger
darning	serging
drawn work	sewing machine
dressmaker	sewing silk
embroidery	shirring
fagoting	slip stitch
fancywork	smocking
feather stitch	stay stitching
fell	stitch
floss	straight stitch
French knot	tack
French seam	tent stitch
gros point	thimble
handstitch	thread
hemming	topstitch
hemstitch	trapunto
herringbone stitch	tucking
lock stitch	tufting
loop stitch	twist
mending	whipstitch
mitering	

sex noun **1** *they talked about sex* SEXUAL INTERCOURSE, intercourse, lovemaking, making love, sex act, (sexual) relations; mating, copulation; *informal* nooky, whoopee, bonking, boinking, boffing, a roll in the hay, quickie; *formal* fornication; *technical* coitus, coition; *dated* carnal knowledge.

2 *teach your children about sex* THE FACTS OF LIFE, reproduction; *informal* the birds and the bees.

3 *adults of both sexes* GENDER. See note at GENDER. PHRASE: **have sex with** *she had no interest in having sex with Richie* HAVE SEXUAL INTERCOURSE WITH, make love to/with, sleep with, go to bed with; mate with, copulate with; seduce; rape; *informal* do it with, go all the way with, know in the biblical sense; bonk, boink, boff, get it on with; *euphemistic* be intimate with; *literary* ravish; *formal* fornicate with.

sex appeal noun *central to these cigarette ads is sex appeal* SEXINESS, seductiveness, sexual attractiveness, desirability, sensuality, sexuality; *informal* it, SA.

sexism noun *your hiring practices have generated numerous complaints about sexism* SEXUAL DISCRIMINATION, chauvinism, gender prejudice, gender bias.

sexless adjective *their sexless marriage* ASEXUAL, nonsexual, neuter; androgynous, epicene.

sex symbol noun *sex symbols come and go, but Marilyn is forever* SEXUALLY ATTRACTIVE PERSON, sex object, sexpot, sex kitten.

sexual adjective **1** *the sexual organs* REPRODUCTIVE, genital, sex, procreative.

2 *sexual activity* CARNAL, erotic; *formal* venereal; *technical* coital.

sexual intercourse noun. See SEX sense 1.

sexuality noun **1** *she had a powerful sexuality* SENSUALITY, sexiness, seductiveness, desirability, eroticism, physicality; sexual appetite, passion, desire, lust.

2 *I'm open about my sexuality* SEXUAL ORIENTATION, sexual preference, leaning, persuasion; heterosexuality, homosexuality, lesbianism, bisexuality.

sexy adjective **1** *he's so sexy* SEXUALLY ATTRACTIVE, seductive, desirable, alluring, toothsome, sensual, sultry, slinky, provocative, tempting, tantalizing; nubile, voluptuous, luscious, lush, hot, beddable, foxy, cute; *informal* bootylicious.

2 *sexy videos* EROTIC, sexually explicit, arousing, exciting, stimulating, hot, titillating, racy, naughty, risqué, adult, X-rated; rude, pornographic, crude, lewd; *informal* raunchy, steamy, porno, blue, skin, XXX.

3 *they weren't feeling sexy* (SEXUALLY) AROUSED, sexually excited, amorous, lustful, passionate; *informal* horny, hot, turned on, sexed up.

4 *informal* *a sexy sales promotion* EXCITING, stimulating, interesting, appealing, intriguing, slick, red-hot.

WORD NOTE **sexy**

It's gratifying to be described as intelligent, witty, or well dressed, but the best possible compliment is to be called *sexy.* If you're sexy, you've got it all. However, be careful when using this revealing adjective: It allows others a peek into your unclothed psyche. Sexiness, after all, takes myriad forms—from a Victoria's Secret model wearing nothing but a come-hither smile and a few wisps of silk to the sullen James Dean wannabe in faded denim and snugly muscled T-shirt. Out in the world, power, money, and high social position are all sexy, but in the dark, so are submission, surrender, and obedience. The word works so powerfully because it shuttles constantly between the public and the private. What we label as *sexy* may be conventional and obvious, or it may hint at our own inner life, our unspoken, perhaps unspeakable desires. **—MD**

shabby adjective **1** *a shabby little bar* RUN-DOWN, down-at-heel, down-at-the-heel(s), scruffy, dilapidated, ramshackle, tumbledown; seedy, slummy, insalubrious, squalid, sordid, flea-bitten; *informal* crummy, scuzzy, raggedy-ass. ANTONYMS smart, upmarket.

2 *a shabby gray coat* SCRUFFY, old, worn out, threadbare, ragged, frayed, tattered, battered, faded, moth-eaten, mangy; *informal* tatty, ratty, the worse for wear, raggedy. ANTONYM new.

3 *her shabby treatment of Bill* CONTEMPTIBLE, despicable, dishonorable, discreditable, mean, low, dirty, hateful, shameful, sorry, ignoble, unfair, unworthy, unkind, shoddy, nasty; *informal* rotten, lowdown; beastly. ANTONYMS decent, honorable.

shack noun *they go off to their shack in the mountains every few months* HUT, chantey, cabin, lean-to, shed; hovel. PHRASE: **shack up with** *informal she's been shacking up with George for five years* COHABIT, live with; *informal, dated* live in sin.

shackle verb **1** *he was shackled to the wall* CHAIN, fetter, manacle; secure, tie (up), bind, tether, hobble; put in chains, clap in irons, handcuff.

2 *journalists were shackled by a new law* RESTRAIN, restrict, limit, constrain, handicap, hamstring, hamper, hinder, impede, obstruct, inhibit, check, curb.

shackles plural noun **1** *shackles of iron* CHAINS, fetters, irons, leg irons, manacles, handcuffs; bonds; *informal* cuffs, bracelets.

2 *the shackles of bureaucracy* RESTRICTIONS, restraints, constraints, impediments, hindrances, obstacles, barriers, obstructions, checks, curbs; *literary* trammels.

shade noun **1** *they sat in the shade* SHADOW(S), shadiness, shelter, cover; cool. ANTONYMS light, glare.

2 *shades of blue* COLOR, hue, tone, tint, tinge.

3 *shades of meaning* NUANCE, gradation, degree, difference, variation, variety; nicety, subtlety; undertone, overtone.

4 *her skirt was* ***a shade*** *too short* A LITTLE, a bit, a trace, a touch, a modicum, a tinge; slightly, rather, somewhat; *informal* a tad, a smidgen, a titch, a tinch, a hair.

5 *the window shade* BLIND, curtain, screen, cover, covering; awning, canopy.

6 *informal* **(shades)** *he was wearing shades* SUNGLASSES, dark glasses; *proprietary* Polaroids, Raybans.

▸ verb **1** *vines shaded the garden* CAST A SHADOW OVER, shadow, shelter, cover, screen; darken.

2 *she* ***shaded in*** *the picture* DARKEN, color in, pencil in, block in, fill in; cross-hatch.

3 *the sky shaded from turquoise to blue* CHANGE, transmute, turn, go; merge, blend, graduate.

PHRASES: **put in the shade** *Candi's clarinet solo puts mine in the shade* SURPASS, outshine, outclass, overshadow, eclipse, transcend, cap, top, outstrip, outdo, put to shame, beat, outperform, upstage; *informal* run rings around, be a cut above. **shades of** *this weekend has been perfectly romantic—you know, shades of our honeymoon* ECHOES OF, a reminder of, memories of, suggestions of, hints of.

shadow noun **1** *he saw her shadow in the doorway* SILHOUETTE, outline, shape, contour, profile.

2 **(shadows)** *he emerged from the shadows* SHADE, darkness, twilight; gloom, murkiness.

3 *the shadow of war* BLACK CLOUD, cloud, pall; gloom, blight; threat.

4 *she knew without any shadow of doubt* TRACE, scrap, shred, crumb, iota, scintilla, jot, whit, grain; *informal* smidgen, smidge, tad.

5 *a shadow of a smile* TRACE, hint, suggestion, suspicion, ghost, glimmer.

6 *he's a shadow of his former self* INFERIOR VERSION, poor imitation, apology, travesty; remnant.

7 *the dog became her shadow* CONSTANT COMPANION, alter ego, second self; close friend, bosom friend; *informal* Siamese twin, bosom buddy.

▸ verb **1** *the market is shadowed by the church* OVERSHADOW, shade; darken, dim.

2 *he is shadowing a poacher* FOLLOW, trail, track, stalk, pursue, hunt; *informal* tail, keep tabs on.

shadowy adjective **1** *a shadowy corridor* DARK, dim, gloomy, murky, crepuscular, shady, shaded; *literary* tenebrous. ANTONYM bright.

2 *a shadowy figure* INDISTINCT, hazy, indefinite, vague, nebulous, ill-defined, faint, blurred, blurry, unclear, indistinguishable, unrecognizable; ghostly, spectral, wraithlike. ANTONYM clear.

shady adjective **1** *a shady garden* SHADED, shadowy, dim, dark; sheltered, screened, shrouded; leafy; *literary* bosky, tenebrous. ANTONYMS bright, sunlit.

2 *informal shady deals* SUSPICIOUS, suspect, questionable, dubious, doubtful, disreputable, untrustworthy, dishonest, devious, dishonorable, underhanded, unscrupulous, irregular, unethical; *informal* fishy, murky. ANTONYMS reputable, honest.

shaft noun **1** *the shaft of a golf club* POLE, shank, stick, rod, staff; handle, hilt, stem.

2 *the shaft of a feather* QUILL; *Ornithology* rachis.

3 *shafts of sunlight* RAY, beam, gleam, streak, finger.

4 *a ventilation shaft* mineshaft, tunnel, passage, pit, adit, downcast, upcast; borehole, bore; duct, well, flue, vent.

▸ verb *I think we've just been shafted* DECEIVE, delude, trick, hoodwink, mislead, take in, dupe, fool, double-cross, cheat, defraud, swindle, fleece, catch out, gull, hoax, bamboozle, con, diddle, rook, put one over on, pull a fast one on, pull the wool over someone's eyes, take for a ride, shanghai, flimflam, sucker, snooker.

shaggy adjective *his shaggy beard* HAIRY, bushy, thick, woolly; tangled, tousled, unkempt, disheveled, untidy, matted; *formal* hirsute. ANTONYM sleek.

shake verb **1** *the whole building shook* VIBRATE, tremble, quiver, quake, shiver, shudder, jiggle, wobble, rock, sway; convulse.

2 *she shook the bottle* JIGGLE, joggle, agitate.

3 *he shook his stick at them* BRANDISH, wave, flourish, swing, wield.

4 *the look in his eyes really shook her* UPSET, distress, disturb, unsettle, disconcert, discompose, disquiet, unnerve, trouble, throw off balance, agitate, fluster; shock, alarm, frighten, scare, worry; *informal* rattle. ANTONYM soothe.

5 *this will shake their confidence* WEAKEN, undermine, damage, impair, harm; reduce, diminish, decrease. ANTONYM strengthen.

▸ noun **1** *he gave his coat a shake* JIGGLE, joggle.

2 *a shake of his fist* FLOURISH, brandish, wave.

3 **(shakes)** *it gives me the shakes* TREMORS, delirium tremens; *informal* DTs, jitters, the creeps, the shivers, willies, heebie-jeebies, the jim-jams.

PHRASES: **in two shakes (of a lamb's tail)** *informal I'll be there in two shakes.* See IN A MOMENT at MOMENT. **no great shakes** *informal that movie was no great shakes* NOT VERY GOOD, unexceptional, unmemorable, forgettable, uninspired, uninteresting, indifferent, unimpressive, lackluster; *informal* nothing to write home about, nothing special. **shake a leg** *informal c'mon, Ruthie, shake a leg.* See HURRY verb sense 1. **shake off 1** *I think we shook off that cop* GET AWAY FROM, escape, elude, dodge, lose, leave behind, get rid of, give someone the slip, throw off the scent. **2** *she can't seem to shake off this virus* RECOVER FROM, get over; get rid of, free oneself from. **shake up 1** *the accident shook him up.* See SHAKE verb sense 4. **2** *plans to shake up the legal profession* REORGANIZE, restructure, revolutionize, alter, change, transform, reform, overhaul.

THE RIGHT WORD

Does a cool breeze make you **shiver**, **quiver**, **shudder**, or **tremble**? All of these verbs describe vibrating, wavering, or oscillating movements that, in living creatures, are often involuntary expressions of strain or discomfort. **Shake**, which refers to abrupt forward-and-backward, side-to-side, or up-and-down movements, is different from the others in that it can be done to a person or object as well as by one (*shake a can of paint; shake visibly while lifting a heavy load*). *Tremble* applies specifically to the slight and rapid shaking motion the human body makes when it is nervous, frightened, or uneasy (*his hands trembled when he picked up the phone*). To *shiver* is to make a similar movement with the entire body, but the cause is usually cold or fear (*shiver in the draft from an open door*). *Quiver* suggests a rapid and almost imperceptible vibration resulting from disturbed or irregular surface tension; it refers more often to things (*the leaves quivered in the breeze*), although people may quiver when they're under emotional tension (*her lower lip quivered and her eyes were downcast*). *Shudder* suggests a more intense shaking, usually in response to something horrible or revolting (*shudder at the thought of eating uncooked meat*). **Quake** implies a violent upheaval or shaking, similar to what occurs during an earthquake (*the boy's heart quaked at his father's approach*).

shake-up noun *informal we've heard there's going to be a shake-up in the sales department* REORGANIZATION, restructuring, reshuffle, change, overhaul, makeover; upheaval, shakedown, housecleaning.

shaky adjective **1** *shaky legs* TREMBLING, shaking, tremulous, quivering, quivery, unsteady, wobbly, weak; tottering, tottery, teetering, doddery; *informal* trembly. ANTONYM steady.

2 *I feel a bit shaky* FAINT, dizzy, lightheaded, giddy; weak, wobbly, quivery, groggy, muzzy; *informal* trembly, woozy.

3 *a shaky table* UNSTEADY, unstable, wobbly, precarious, rocky, rickety, ramshackle. ANTONYM stable.

4 *the evidence is shaky* UNRELIABLE, untrustworthy, questionable, dubious, doubtful, tenuous, suspect, flimsy, weak, unsound, unsupported, unsubstantiated, unfounded; *informal* iffy. ANTONYM sound.

shallow adjective *a shallow analysis of contemporary society* SUPERFICIAL, facile, simplistic, oversimplified; flimsy, insubstantial, lightweight, empty, trivial, trifling; surface, skin-deep, two-dimensional; frivolous, foolish, silly, Mickey Mouse. See note at SUPERFICIAL. ANTONYM profound.

sham noun **1** *his tenderness had been a sham* PRETENSE, fake, act, fiction, simulation, fraud, feint, lie, counterfeit; humbug.

2 *the doctor was a sham* CHARLATAN, fake, fraud, impostor, pretender; quack, mountebank; *informal* phony.

▸ adjective *sham togetherness* FAKE, pretended, feigned, simulated, false, artificial, bogus, insincere, contrived, affected, make-believe, fictitious; imitation, mock, counterfeit, fraudulent; *informal* pretend, put-on, phony, pseudo. ANTONYM genuine.

shaman noun *several American doctors have consulted our shaman* medicine man/woman, healer, kahuna.

shamble verb *I hear Mr. Billings shambling down the hall* SHUFFLE, drag one's feet, lumber, totter, dodder; hobble, limp.

shambles plural noun **1** *we have to sort out this shambles* CHAOS, mess, muddle, confusion, disorder, havoc, mare's nest, dog's breakfast.

2 *the room was a shambles* MESS, pigsty; *informal* disaster area.

shame noun **1** *her face was scarlet with shame* HUMILIATION, mortification, chagrin, ignominy, embarrassment, indignity, discomfort. ANTONYM pride.

2 *I felt shame at telling a lie* GUILT, remorse, contrition, compunction. ANTONYM indifference.

3 *he brought shame on the family* DISGRACE, dishonor, discredit, degradation, ignominy, disrepute, infamy, scandal, opprobrium, contempt; *dated* disesteem. ANTONYMS glory, honor.

4 *it's a shame she never married* PITY, misfortune, sad thing; bad luck; *informal* bummer, crime, sin, crying shame.

▸ verb **1** *you shamed your family's name* DISGRACE, dishonor, discredit, degrade, debase; stigmatize, taint, sully, tarnish, besmirch, blacken, drag through the mud. ANTONYM honor.

2 *he was shamed in public* HUMILIATE, mortify, chagrin, embarrass, abash, chasten, humble, take down a peg or two, cut down to size; *informal* show up, make someone eat crow.

PHRASE: **put to shame** *these new materials put our old plastics to shame* OUTSHINE, outclass, eclipse, surpass, excel, outstrip, outdo, put in the shade, upstage; *informal* run rings around.

shamefaced adjective *Giles looked shamefaced* ASHAMED, abashed, sheepish, guilty, conscience-stricken, guilt-ridden, contrite, sorry, remorseful, repentant, penitent, regretful, rueful, apologetic; embarrassed, mortified, red-faced, chagrined, humiliated; *informal* with one's tail between one's legs. ANTONYM unrepentant.

shameful adjective **1** *shameful behavior* DISGRACEFUL, deplorable, despicable, contemptible, dishonorable, discreditable, reprehensible, low, unworthy, ignoble, shabby; shocking, scandalous, outrageous, abominable, atrocious, appalling, vile, odious, heinous, egregious, loathsome, bad; inexcusable, unforgivable; *informal* lowdown, hateful. ANTONYM admirable.

2 *a shameful secret* EMBARRASSING, mortifying, humiliating, degrading, ignominious.

shameless adjective *a shameless display of flirtation* FLAGRANT, blatant, barefaced, overt, brazen, brash, audacious, outrageous, undisguised, unconcealed, transparent; immodest, indecorous; unabashed, unashamed, unblushing, unrepentant. ANTONYM modest.

shanty noun *they stay in a little shanty by the lake* SHACK, hut, (log) cabin, lean-to, shed, hovel.

shape noun **1** *the shape of the dining table* FORM, appearance, configuration, formation, structure; figure, build, physique, body; contours, lines, outline, silhouette, profile.

2 *a spirit in the shape of a fox* GUISE, likeness, semblance, form, appearance, image.

3 *you're in pretty good shape* CONDITION, health, fettle, order.

▸ verb **1** *the metal is shaped into tools* FORM, fashion, make, mold, model, cast; sculpt, sculpture, carve, cut, whittle.

2 *attitudes were shaped by his report* DETERMINE, form, fashion, mold, define, develop; influence, affect.

PHRASES: **shape up** *her work is shaping up nicely* IMPROVE, get better, progress, show promise; develop, take shape, come on, come along. **take shape** *our remodeling plans were really starting to take shape* BECOME CLEAR, become definite, become tangible, crystallize, come together, fall into place.

shapeless adjective **1** *shapeless lumps* FORMLESS, amorphous, unformed, indefinite.

2 *a shapeless dress* BAGGY, saggy, ill-fitting, sacklike, oversized, unshapely, formless.

shapely adjective *the shapely models of the forties* WELL-PROPORTIONED, clean-limbed; curvaceous, voluptuous, Junoesque; attractive, sexy; *informal* curvy, bootylicious; *archaic* comely.

shard noun *a shard of glass in her heel* FRAGMENT, sliver, splinter, shiver, chip, piece, bit, particle.

share noun *her share of the profits* PORTION, part, division, quota, quantum, allowance, ration, allocation, measure, due; percentage, commission, dividend; helping, serving; *informal* cut, slice.

▸ verb **1** *we share the bills* SPLIT, divide, go halves on; *informal* go fifty-fifty on, go Dutch on.

2 *they* ***shared out*** *the bottles of water* APPORTION, divide up, allocate, portion out, ration out, parcel out, measure out; carve up, divvy up.

3 *we all* share in *the learning process* PARTICIPATE IN, take part in, play a part in, be involved in, contribute to, have a hand in, partake in.

WORD NOTE **share**

Try as I might, I will never be able to bring myself to use this word to mean "to tell a story" or "to make a confession." *Thank you for sharing that sad account of your most embarrassing moment.* In my view, the object of the verb should be a real or abstract commodity, not a narrative. *The king was deposed because he refused to share his wealth and power.* Perhaps it's because, in the more old-fashioned usage, sharing (and, by extension, whatever was being shared) was an inarguably good thing. *Children should be taught to share their toys.* But being invited to *share* our personal history can feel like an invasion of privacy, and when someone else *shares* in that way, it's possible that the process can turn out to be a burden or an imposition, rather than a desirable act of unselfishness and generosity. **—FP**

shark noun See table.

SHARKS

angel shark	monkfish
basking shark	nurse shark
blue shark	porbeagle
dogfish	requiem shark
great white shark	shovelhead
hammerhead	thresher shark
mackerel shark	tope
mako	whale shark

sharp adjective **1** *a sharp knife* KEEN, razor-edged; sharpened, honed. See note at KEEN. ANTONYM blunt.

2 *a sharp pain* EXCRUCIATING, agonizing, intense, stabbing, shooting, severe, acute, keen, fierce, searing; exquisite.

3 *a sharp taste* TANGY, piquant, strong; ACIDIC, acid, sour, tart, pungent, acrid, bitter, acidulous. ANTONYMS mild, mellow, bland.

4 *a sharp cry of pain* LOUD, piercing, shrill, high-pitched, penetrating, harsh, strident, ear-splitting, deafening. ANTONYMS soft, quiet.

5 *a sharp wind* COLD, chilly, chill, brisk, keen, penetrating, biting, icy, bitter, freezing, raw; *informal* nippy, wicked. ANTONYMS warm, balmy.

6 *sharp words* HARSH, bitter, cutting, scathing, caustic, barbed, trenchant, acrimonious, acerbic, sarcastic, sardonic, spiteful, venomous, malicious, vitriolic, vicious, hurtful, nasty, cruel, abrasive; *informal* bitchy, catty. ANTONYMS amicable, kind.

7 *a sharp sense of loss* INTENSE, acute, keen, strong, bitter, fierce, heartfelt, overwhelming.

8 *the lens brings it into sharp focus* DISTINCT, clear, crisp; stark, obvious, marked, definite, pronounced. ANTONYMS blurred, indistinct.

9 *a sharp increase* SUDDEN, abrupt, rapid; steep, precipitous. ANTONYM gradual.

10 *a sharp corner* HAIRPIN, tight.

11 *a sharp drop* STEEP, sheer, abrupt, precipitous, vertical. ANTONYMS gentle, gradual.

12 *sharp eyes* KEEN, perceptive, observant, acute, beady, hawklike. ANTONYM weak.

13 *she was sharp and witty* PERCEPTIVE, percipient, perspicacious, incisive, sensitive, keen, acute, quick-witted, clever, shrewd, canny, astute, intelligent, intuitive, bright, alert, smart, quick off the mark, insightful, knowing; *informal* on the ball, quick on the uptake, savvy, heads-up. ANTONYMS slow, dull, stupid.

14 *informal a sharp suit* SMART, stylish, fashionable, chic, modish, elegant; *informal* trendy, cool, hip, snazzy, classy, snappy, styling/stylin', natty, nifty, fly, spiffy. ANTONYM shabby.

▸ adverb **1** *nine o'clock sharp* PRECISELY, exactly, on the dot; promptly, prompt, punctually, dead on; *informal* on the nose, on the button. ANTONYM roughly.

2 *the recession pulled people up sharp* ABRUPTLY, suddenly, sharply, unexpectedly.

sharpen verb **1** *sharpen the carving knife* HONE, whet, strop, grind, file.

2 *the players are sharpening their skills* IMPROVE, brush up, polish up, better, enhance; hone, fine-tune, perfect.

sharp-eyed adjective *a sharp-eyed witness contacted the police* OBSERVANT, perceptive, eagle-eyed, hawk-eyed, gimlet-eyed; watchful, vigilant, alert, on the lookout; *informal* beady-eyed.

sharp-tongued adjective *Shakespeare's sharp-tongued Kate* SCOLDING, shrill, shrewish; harsh, cutting, caustic, abrasive; *literary* trenchant.

shatter verb **1** *the glasses shattered* SMASH, break, splinter, crack, fracture, fragment, disintegrate, shiver; *informal* bust.

2 *the announcement shattered their hopes* DESTROY,

wreck, ruin, dash, crush, devastate, demolish, torpedo, scotch; *informal* put the kibosh on, scuttle.

3 *we were shattered by the news* DEVASTATE, shock, stun, daze, traumatize, crush, distress.

shave verb 1 *he shaved his beard* CUT OFF, snip off; crop, trim, barber.

2 *shave off excess wood* PLANE, pare, whittle, scrape.

3 *they shaved the deficit by 4 percent* REDUCE, cut, lessen, decrease, pare down, shrink.

4 *the shot just shaved my arm* GRAZE, brush, touch, glance off, kiss.

sheaf noun *a sheaf of papers* BUNDLE, bunch, stack, pile, heap, mass.

sheath noun 1 *put the sword in its sheath* SCABBARD, case.

2 *the wire has a plastic sheath* COVERING, cover, case, casing, envelope, sleeve, wrapper, capsule.

3 *a contraceptive sheath.* See CONDOM.

shed[1] noun *the rabbit lives in the shed* HUT, lean-to, outhouse, outbuilding; shack; potting shed, woodshed, tool shed, garden shed.

shed[2] verb 1 *the trees shed their leaves* DROP, scatter, spill.

2 *the caterpillar shed its skin* SLOUGH OFF, cast off, molt.

3 *we shed our jackets* TAKE OFF, remove, shrug off, discard, doff, climb out of, slip out of, divest oneself of, peel off. ANTONYM don.

4 *much blood has been shed* SPILL, discharge.

5 *she shed 20 pounds* LOSE, get rid of, discard. ANTONYM put on.

6 *they must shed their illusions* DISCARD, get rid of, dispose of, do away with, drop, abandon, jettison, scrap, cast aside, dump, reject, repudiate; *informal* ditch, junk. ANTONYMS adopt, keep.

7 *the moon shed a watery light* CAST, radiate, diffuse, disperse, give out. PHRASE: **shed tears** *now, now, there's no need to shed tears* WEEP, cry, sob; lament, grieve, mourn; *informal* blubber, boo-hoo.

sheen noun *we were admiring the sheen of your dog's coat* SHINE, luster, gloss, patina, shininess, burnish, polish, shimmer, brilliance, radiance. See note at POLISH.

sheep noun *a herder of sheep* ram, ewe, lamb, wether, bellwether.

sheepish adjective *stop looking so sheepish and come on in* EMBARRASSED, uncomfortable, hangdog, self-conscious; shamefaced, ashamed, abashed, mortified, chastened, remorseful, contrite, apologetic, rueful, regretful, penitent, repentant.

sheer[1] adjective 1 *the sheer audacity of the plan* UTTER, complete, absolute, total, pure, downright, out-and-out, arrant, thorough, thoroughgoing, patent, veritable, unmitigated, plain.

2 *a sheer drop* PRECIPITOUS, steep, vertical, perpendicular, abrupt, bluff, sharp. ANTONYM gradual.

3 *a sheer dress* DIAPHANOUS, gauzy, filmy, floaty, gossamer, thin, translucent, transparent, see-through, insubstantial. ANTONYM thick.

sheer[2] verb 1 *the boat **sheered off** from the landing* SWERVE, veer, slew, skew, swing, change course.

2 *her mind **sheered away from** his image* TURN AWAY FROM, flinch from, recoil from, shy away from; avoid.

sheet noun 1 (often **sheets**) *she changed the sheets* BED LINEN, linen, bedclothes.

2 *a sheet of ice* LAYER, stratum, covering, blanket, coating, coat, film, skin.

3 *a sheet of glass* PANE, panel, piece, plate; slab.

4 *she put a fresh sheet in the typewriter* PIECE OF PAPER, leaf, page, folio.

5 *a sheet of water* EXPANSE, area, stretch, sweep.

shelf noun 1 *the plant on the shelf* LEDGE, sill, bracket, rack; mantelpiece; shelving.

2 *an ocean shelf* SANDBANK, sandbar, bank, bar, reef, shoal.

shell noun 1 *a crab shell* CARAPACE, exterior; armor; *Zoology* exoskeleton.

2 *peanut shells* POD, husk, hull, casing, case, covering, integument, shuck.

3 *shells passing overhead* PROJECTILE, bomb, explosive; grenade; bullet, cartridge.

4 *the metal shell of the car* FRAMEWORK, frame, chassis, skeleton; hull, exterior.

▸ verb 1 *they were shelling peas* HULL, pod, husk, shuck.

2 *rebel artillery shelled the city* BOMBARD, fire on, shoot at, attack, bomb, blitz, strafe.

PHRASE: **shell out** *informal how much did you shell out for those shoes?* See PAY verb sense 2.

shellfish noun *are you allergic to all types of shellfish?* See tables at CRUSTACEAN and MOLLUSK.

shelter noun 1 *the trees provide shelter for animals* PROTECTION, cover, screening, shade; safety, security, refuge, sanctuary, asylum. ANTONYM exposure.

2 *a shelter for abused women* SANCTUARY, refuge, home, haven, safe house; harbor, port in a storm.

▸ verb 1 *the hut sheltered him from the wind* PROTECT, shield, screen, cover, shade, save, safeguard, preserve, defend, cushion, guard, insulate. ANTONYM expose.

2 *the anchorage where the convoy sheltered* TAKE SHELTER, take refuge, seek sanctuary, take cover; *informal* hole up.

sheltered adjective 1 *a sheltered stretch of water* PROTECTED, screened, shielded, covered; shady; cozy.

2 *she led a sheltered life* SECLUDED, cloistered, isolated, protected, withdrawn, sequestered, reclusive; privileged, secure, safe, quiet.

shelve verb *plans to reopen the school have been shelved* POSTPONE, put off, delay, defer, put back, reschedule, hold over/off, put to one side, suspend, stay, keep in abeyance, mothball; abandon, drop, give up, stop, cancel, jettison, ax, put over, table, take a rain check on; *informal* put on ice, put on the back burner, put in cold storage, ditch, dump, junk. ANTONYM execute.

shepherd noun *he worked as a shepherd* herdsman, herder, shepherdess, sheepman.

▸ verb *we shepherded them away* USHER, steer, herd, lead, take, escort, guide, conduct, marshal, walk; show, see, chaperone.

shh exclamation *hey, you two, shh!* BE QUIET, keep quiet, quiet down, be silent, silence, stop talking, hold your tongue; *informal* shut up, hush (up), shut your mouth, shut your face, shut your trap, button your lip, pipe down, put a sock in it, give it a rest, save it, not another word.

shield noun **1** *he used his shield to fend off blows* *Heraldry* escutcheon; *historical* buckler, target.

2 *a shield against dirt* PROTECTION, guard, defense, cover, screen, security, shelter, safeguard, protector.

▸ verb *he shielded his eyes* PROTECT, cover, screen, shade; save, safeguard, preserve, defend, secure, guard; cushion, insulate. ANTONYM expose.

shift verb **1** *she shifted her position* CHANGE, alter, adjust, vary; modify, revise, reverse, retract; do a U-turn. ANTONYM keep.

2 *the cargo has shifted* MOVE, slide, slip, be displaced.

3 *the wind shifted* VEER, alter, change, turn, swing round.

▸ noun **1** *the southward shift of people* MOVEMENT, move, transference, transport, transposition, relocation.

2 *a shift in public opinion* CHANGE, alteration, adjustment, amendment, variation, modification, revision, reversal, retraction, U-turn.

3 *they worked three shifts* STINT, stretch, spell of work.

4 *the night shift went home* WORKERS, crew, gang, team, squad, patrol.

shiftless adjective *he thought the whole family shiftless and dishonest* LAZY, idle, indolent, slothful, lethargic, lackadaisical; spiritless, apathetic, feckless, good-for-nothing, worthless; unambitious, unenterprising.

shifty adjective *informal* *he had a shifty look about him* DEVIOUS, evasive, slippery, duplicitous, false, deceitful, underhanded, untrustworthy, dishonest, shady, wily, crafty, tricky, sneaky, treacherous, artful, sly, scheming, snide; *informal* hinky. ANTONYM honest.

shilly-shally verb *we must not tolerate leaders who shilly-shally over matters of national security* DITHER, be indecisive, be irresolute, vacillate, waver, hesitate, blow hot and cold, falter, drag one's feet, hem and haw; *informal* dilly-dally.

shimmer verb *the lake shimmered* GLINT, glisten, twinkle, sparkle, flash, scintillate, gleam, glow, glimmer, glitter, wink; *literary* coruscate.

▸ noun *the shimmer of lights from the traffic* GLINT, twinkle, sparkle, flash, gleam, glow, glimmer, luster, glitter; *literary* coruscation.

shindig noun *the annual Harvest Moon shindig* SOCIAL EVENT, party, social occasion, affair, function, gathering, reception, soiree, jamboree, gala, meet-and-greet, levee; *informal* do, bash.

shine verb **1** *the sun shone* EMIT LIGHT, beam, radiate, gleam, glow, glint, glimmer, sparkle, twinkle, glitter, glisten, shimmer, flash, flare, glare, fluoresce; *literary* glister, coruscate.

2 *she shone his shoes* POLISH, burnish, buff, wax, gloss.

3 *they shone at gymnastics* EXCEL, be outstanding, be brilliant, be successful, stand out.

▸ noun **1** *the shine of the moon on her face* LIGHT, brightness, gleam, glow, glint, glimmer, sparkle, twinkle, glitter, glisten, shimmer, beam, glare, radiance, illumination, luminescence, luminosity, incandescence.

2 *linseed oil restores the shine* POLISH, burnish, gleam, gloss, luster, sheen, patina.

shining adjective **1** *a shining expanse of water* GLEAMING, bright, brilliant, illuminated, lustrous, glowing, glinting, sparkling, twinkling, glittering, glistening, shimmering, dazzling, luminous, luminescent, incandescent; *literary* glistering, coruscating. See note at BRIGHT.

2 *a shining face* GLOWING, beaming, radiant, happy.

3 *shining chromium tubes* SHINY, bright, polished, gleaming, glossy, sheeny, lustrous. PHRASE: **a shining example** *a shining example of Yankee ingenuity* PARAGON, model, epitome, archetype, ideal, exemplar, nonpareil, paradigm, quintessence, beau ideal, acme, jewel, flower, treasure.

shinny verb **1** *she could* ***shinny up*** *that oak tree faster than any of the boys in our school* CLIMB (UP), clamber up, scramble up, go up; mount, ascend, scale.

2 *you'd better* ***shinny down*** *that pole before Mama sees you* CLIMB DOWN, scramble down, come down (from); dismount, descend.

shiny adjective *a shiny red apple* GLOSSY, glassy, bright, polished, gleaming, satiny, sheeny, lustrous. ANTONYM matte.

WORD NOTE **shiny**

Shiny is too marvelous a word to be restricted only to things that are reflective. I use it (overuse it, really) for anything bright, sparkling, polished, smooth—in the figurative meanings of these words, giving *shiny* a figurative meaning, too, by association. **—EM**

ship noun *they traveled by ship* BOAT, vessel, craft. See table.

▸ verb *he shipped me the package* SEND, post, mail, dispatch, courier, forward, express.

SHIPS

aircraft carrier	freighter
barge	frigate
battle cruiser	galleon
battleship	galley
bulk carrier	icebreaker
capital ship	laker
caravel	liner
cargo ship	merchant ship
carrack	oil tanker
coal ship	passenger ship
container ship	pirate ship
corvette	schooner
cruise ship	steamship
cutter	supertanker
destroyer	tall ship
dreadnought	tanker
factory ship	

See also tables at BOAT and SAILING SHIP.

shirk verb **1** *she didn't shirk any task* EVADE, dodge, avoid, get out of, sidestep, shrink from, shun, skip, miss; neglect; *informal* duck (out of), cop out of, cut.

2 *no one shirked* AVOID ONE'S DUTY, be remiss, be negligent, play truant, swing the lead, slack off; *informal* goof off, play hooky.

shirker noun *you'll find no shirkers in my crew* DODGER, truant, absentee, layabout, good-for-nothing, loafer, idler; *informal* slacker, bum, lazybones.

shirt noun See table.

SHIRTS AND TOPS

blouse	muscle shirt
boat neck	overblouse
button-down shirt	overshirt
camisole	Oxford shirt
cowl neck	polo shirt
dashiki	rugby shirt
dress shirt	shell
golf shirt	sports shirt
halter top	sweatshirt
Hawaiian shirt	tank top
jersey	T-shirt
kurta	tube top
lumberjack shirt	turtleneck
middy	twin set

shiver[1] verb *he was shivering with fear* TREMBLE, quiver, shake, shudder, quaver, quake. See note at SHAKE.

▸ noun *she gave a shiver as the door opened* TREMBLE, quiver, shake, shudder, quaver, quake, tremor, twitch.

shiver[2] noun *shivers of glass* SPLINTER, sliver, shard, fragment, chip, shaving, smithereen, particle, bit, piece.

▸ verb *the window shivered into thousands of pieces* SHATTER, splinter, smash, fragment, crack, break.

shivery adjective *she felt sick and shivery* TREMBLING, trembly, quivery, shaky, shuddering, shuddery, quavery, quaking; cold, chilly.

shoal noun *at low tide we go out on the shoal to look for fiddler crabs* SANDBANK, bank, mudbank, bar, sandbar, shelf, cay, key.

shock[1] noun **1** *the news came as a shock* BLOW, upset, disturbance; surprise, revelation, a bolt from the blue, thunderbolt, bombshell, rude awakening, eye-opener; *informal* whammy, wake-up call.

2 *you gave me a shock* FRIGHT, scare, jolt, start; *informal* turn.

3 *she was suffering from shock* TRAUMA, prostration; collapse, breakdown.

4 *the first shock of the earthquake* VIBRATION, reverberation, shake, jolt, jar, jerk; impact, blow.

▸ verb *the murder shocked the nation* APPALL, horrify, outrage, revolt, disgust, nauseate, sicken; traumatize, distress, upset, disturb, disquiet, unsettle; stun, rock, stagger, astound, astonish, amaze, startle, surprise, dumbfound, shake, take aback, throw, unnerve.

shock[2] noun *a shock of red hair* MASS, mane, mop, thatch, head, crop, bush, frizz, tangle, cascade, halo.

shocking adjective *the news from Cambodia was shocking* APPALLING, horrifying, horrific, dreadful, awful, frightful, terrible; scandalous, outrageous, disgraceful, vile, abominable, abhorrent, atrocious; odious, repugnant, disgusting, nauseating, sickening, loathsome; distressing, upsetting, disturbing, disquieting, unsettling; staggering, amazing, astonishing, startling, surprising; *informal* gut-wrenching.

shoddy adjective **1** *shoddy goods* POOR-QUALITY, inferior, second-rate, third-rate, tinpot, cheap, cheapjack, trashy, jerry-built; *informal* tacky, chintzy, rubbishy, junky, cheapo, cheesy, schlocky. ANTONYM quality.

2 *shoddy workmanship* CARELESS, slapdash, sloppy, slipshod, crude; negligent, cursory. ANTONYM careful.

shoe noun *he laced up his shoe* (**shoes**) footwear. See table.

SHOES AND OTHER FOOTWEAR

aerobic shoes	Louis heels
athletic shoes	low heels
ballerinas	Mary Janes
ballet flats	moccasins
ballet slippers	mules
bedroom slippers	open-toes
boat shoes	overshoes
booties/bootees	oxfords
boots	patent leather
bowling shoes	pattens
brogans	penny loafers
brogues	platform shoes
buckskins	pumps
buskins	running shoes
cleats	sabots
clodhoppers	saddle shoes
clogs	sandals
cross-trainers	sling-backs
Cuban heels	slip-ons
deck shoes	slippers
dress shoes	sneakers
elevator shoes	spectator pumps
espadrilles	spike heels
flip-flops	spikes
French heels	square-toed shoes
galoshes	stacked heels
ghillies	stiletto heels
golf shoes	tap shoes
gym shoes	tennis shoes
heels	thongs
high heels	Top-Siders™
high-lows	track shoes
high-tops	training shoes
hiking shoes	T-straps
huaraches	walking shoes
jazz shoes	wedge heels
jellies	wedgies
jogging shoes	white bucks
kilties	wing tips
loafers	

shoemaker noun *the shoemaker fixed her heel* COBBLER, bootmaker.

shoot verb **1** *they shot him in the street* GUN DOWN, mow down, hit, wound, injure; put a bullet in, pick off, bag, fell, kill; *informal* pot, blast, pump full of lead, plug.

2 *they shot at the enemy* FIRE, open fire, aim, snipe, let fly; bombard, shell.

3 *faster than a gun can shoot bullets* DISCHARGE, fire, launch, loose off, let fly, emit.

4 *a car shot past* RACE, speed, flash, dash, dart, rush, hurtle, careen, streak, whiz, go like lightning, go hell-bent for leather, zoom, charge; career, sweep, fly, wing; *informal* belt, scoot, scorch, tear, zip, whip, step on it, burn rubber, bomb, hightail it, barrel.

5 *the plant failed to shoot* SPROUT, bud, burgeon, germinate.

6 *the film was shot in Toronto* FILM, photograph, take, snap, capture, record, tape; videotape, video.

▸ noun *nip off the new shoots* SPROUT, bud, offshoot, scion, sucker, spear, runner, tendril, sprig.

shop noun **1** *a shop selling clothes* STORE, (retail) outlet, boutique, emporium, department store, big box store, supermarket, superstore, chain store, market, mart, minimart, convenience store, trading post.

2 *he works in the machine shop* WORKSHOP, workroom, plant, factory, works, mill, yard.

▸ verb *he was **shopping for** spices* BUY, purchase, get, acquire, obtain, pick up, snap up, procure, stock up on.

shopkeeper noun *the downtown shopkeepers keep their sidewalks spotless* STOREKEEPER, shop owner, vendor, retailer, dealer, seller, merchant, trader, wholesaler.

shopper noun *there is plenty of parking for shoppers* BUYER, purchaser, customer, consumer, client, patron; *Law* vendee.

shopping center noun *there's probably a jewelry store in the shopping center* (SHOPPING) MALL, shopping complex, plaza, megamall, mini-mall, strip mall, marketplace, galleria.

shore[1] noun *he swam out from the shore* SEASHORE, lakeshore, lakefront, bayfront, beach, foreshore, sand(s), shoreline, waterside, front, coast, seaboard; *literary* strand.

shore[2] verb *we had to **shore up** the building* PROP UP, hold up, bolster, support, brace, buttress, strengthen, fortify, reinforce, underpin.

shorebird noun *a well-protected refuge for herons, whooping cranes, and other shorebirds.* See table.

SHOREBIRDS

adjutant stork	marabou
American egret	moorhen
avocet	oystercatcher
Baird's sandpiper	pectoral sandpiper
beach bird	pewit
bittern	piping plover
brolga	plover
cattle egret	rail
coot	red knot sandpiper
crane	ringed plover
curlew	ruff/reeve
dotterel	sanderling
dowitcher	sandhill crane
dunlin	sandpiper
egret	snipe
flamingo	snowy egret
gallinule	sora
godwit	spoonbill
golden plover	stilt
great blue heron	stint
great white egret	stork
heron	tattler
ibis	turnstone
jabiru	waterhen
jacana	whimbrel
killdeer	whooping crane
lapwing	willet
least bittern	yellowlegs
limpkin	

See also tables at SEABIRD and WATERFOWL.

short adjective **1** *a short piece of string* SMALL, little, tiny; *informal* teeny. ANTONYM long.

2 *short people* SMALL, little, petite, tiny, diminutive, stubby, elfin, dwarfish, midget, pygmy, Lilliputian, minuscule, miniature; *informal* pint-sized, vertically challenged, teeny, knee-high to a grasshopper; *Scottish* wee. ANTONYM tall.

3 *a short report* CONCISE, brief, succinct, compact, summary, economical, crisp, pithy, epigrammatic, laconic, thumbnail, capsule, abridged, abbreviated, condensed, synoptic, summarized, contracted, truncated; *formal* compendious. ANTONYMS long, verbose.

4 *a short time* BRIEF, momentary, temporary, short-lived, impermanent, cursory, fleeting, passing, fugitive, lightning, transitory, transient, ephemeral, quick. ANTONYM long.

5 *money is a bit short* SCARCE, in short supply, scant, meager, sparse, insufficient, deficient, inadequate, lacking, wanting, tight; *rare* exiguous. ANTONYM plentiful.

6 *he was rather short with her* CURT, sharp, abrupt, blunt, brusque, terse, offhand, gruff, surly, testy, rude, uncivil; *informal* snappy, snappish. ANTONYMS patient, courteous.

▸ adverb *she stopped short* ABRUPTLY, suddenly, sharply, all of a sudden, all at once, unexpectedly, without warning, out of the blue.

PHRASES: **in short** *in short, we want you to leave* BRIEFLY, in a word, in a nutshell, in précis, in essence, to come to the point; in conclusion, in summary, to sum up. **short of 1** *we are short of nurses* DEFICIENT IN, lacking, wanting, in need of, low on, short on, missing; *informal* strapped for, pushed for, minus. **2** *short of searching everyone, there is nothing we can do* APART FROM, other than, aside from, besides, except (for), excepting, without, excluding, not counting, save (for).

shortage noun *the islanders are accustomed to a shortage of fresh water* SCARCITY, sparseness, sparsity, dearth, paucity, poverty, insufficiency, deficiency, inadequacy, famine, lack, want, deficit, shortfall, rarity. See note at LACK. ANTONYM abundance.

shortcoming noun *after forty years of marriage, he still claimed she had nary a shortcoming* DEFECT, fault, flaw, imperfection, deficiency, limitation, failing, drawback, weakness, weak point, foible, frailty, vice. See note at FAULT. ANTONYM strength.

shorten verb *shorten your essay to a three-paragraph summary | the drapes will have to be shortened* MAKE SHORTER, abbreviate, abridge, condense, précis, synopsize, contract, compress, reduce, shrink, diminish, cut (down); dock, trim, crop, pare down, prune; curtail, truncate. ANTONYM extend.

short-lived adjective *it was a short-lived romance* BRIEF, short, momentary, temporary, impermanent, cursory, fleeting, passing, fugitive, lightning, transitory, transient, ephemeral, quick.

shortly adverb **1** *she will be with you shortly* SOON, presently, momentarily, in a little while, at any moment, in a minute, in next to no time, before long, by and by; *informal* anon, any time now, pretty soon, in a jiffy; *dated* directly.

2 *"I know," he replied shortly* CURTLY, sharply, abruptly, bluntly, brusquely, tersely, gruffly, snappily, testily, rudely.

shortsighted adjective *shortsighted critics* NARROW-MINDED, unimaginative, small-minded, insular, parochial, provincial, improvident. ANTONYMS farsighted, imaginative.

short-staffed adjective *we're always short-staffed around the holidays* UNDERSTAFFED, short-handed, undermanned, below strength.

short-tempered adjective *don't get short-tempered with me, pal!* IRRITABLE, irascible, hot-tempered, quick-tempered, snappish, fiery, touchy, volatile; cross, crabby, crotchety, cantankerous, grumpy, ill-tempered, bad-tempered, testy, tetchy, prickly, choleric; *informal* snappy, grouchy, cranky, on a short fuse, bitchy. ANTONYM placid.

shot noun **1** *a shot rang out* report of a gun, crack, bang, blast; (**shots**) gunfire.

2 *the cannons have run out of shot* BULLETS, cannonballs, pellets, ammunition.

3 *the winning shot* STROKE, hit, strike; kick, throw, pitch, lob.

4 *Mike was an excellent shot* MARKSMAN, markswoman, shooter.

5 *a shot of us on holiday* PHOTOGRAPH, photo, snap, snapshot, picture, print, slide, still.

6 *informal it's nice to get a shot at driving* ATTEMPT, try; turn, chance, opportunity; *informal* go, stab, crack; *formal* essay.

7 *tetanus shots* INJECTION, inoculation, immunization, vaccination, booster; *informal* jab, needle. PHRASES: **a shot in the arm** *informal the new sidewalks and landscaping have been a shot in the arm to downtown commerce* BOOST, tonic, stimulus, spur, impetus, encouragement. **a shot in the dark** *my answer was just a shot in the dark* (WILD) GUESS, surmise, supposition, conjecture, speculation. **like a shot** *informal when they called his name he ran on to the stage like a shot* WITHOUT HESITATION, unhesitatingly, eagerly, enthusiastically; immediately, at once, right away/now, straightaway, instantly, instantaneously, without delay; *informal* in/like a flash. **not by a long shot** *he is not yet out of the woods, not by a long shot* BY NO (MANNER OF) MEANS, not at all, in no way, certainly not, absolutely not, definitely not.

shoulder verb **1** *he shouldered the burden* TAKE ON (ONESELF), undertake, accept, assume; bear, carry.

2 *another kid shouldered him aside* PUSH, shove, thrust, jostle, force, bulldoze, elbow. PHRASES: **give the cold shoulder** *ever since Deke's party, Linnie has been giving me the cold shoulder* SNUB, shun, ignore, rebuff, spurn, ostracize, cut out; *informal* freeze out. **put one's shoulder to the wheel** *it's time to stop talking and start putting your shoulder to the wheel* GET (DOWN) TO WORK, apply oneself, set to work, buckle down, roll up one's sleeves; work hard, be diligent, be industrious, exert oneself. **shoulder to shoulder** **1** *the regiment lined up shoulder to shoulder* SIDE BY SIDE, abreast, alongside (each other). **2** *he fought shoulder to shoulder with the others* UNITED, (working) together, jointly, in partnership, in collaboration, in cooperation, side by side, in alliance.

shout verb *"Help," he shouted* YELL, cry (out), call (out), roar, howl, bellow, bawl, call at the top of one's voice, clamor, shriek, scream; raise one's voice, vociferate; *informal* holler. ANTONYM whisper.

▸ noun *a shout of pain* YELL, cry, call, roar, howl, bellow, bawl, clamor, vociferation, shriek, scream; *informal* holler.

shove verb **1** *she shoved him back into the chair* PUSH, thrust, propel, drive, force, ram, knock, elbow, shoulder; jostle, hustle, manhandle.

2 *she shoved past him* PUSH (ONE'S WAY), force one's way, barge (one's way), elbow (one's way), shoulder one's way.

▸ noun *a hefty shove* PUSH, thrust, bump, jolt.

PHRASE: **shove off** *informal shove off, you little creep!* GO AWAY, get out (of my sight); get going, take oneself off, be off (with you), shoo; *informal* scram, make yourself scarce, be on your way, beat it, get lost, push off, buzz off, clear off, go (and) jump in the lake, bug off, take a hike; *literary* begone.

shovel noun *a pick and shovel* SPADE.

▸ verb *shoveling snow* SCOOP (UP), dig, excavate.

show verb **1** *the stitches do not show* BE VISIBLE, be seen, be in view, be obvious. ANTONYM be invisible.

2 *he wouldn't show the picture* DISPLAY, exhibit, put on show/display, put on view, parade, uncover, reveal. ANTONYM conceal.

3 *Frank showed his frustration* MANIFEST, exhibit, reveal, convey, communicate, make known; express, proclaim, make plain, make obvious, disclose, betray; *formal* evince. ANTONYM suppress.

4 *I'll show you how to make a daisy chain* DEMONSTRATE TO, explain to, describe to, illustrate to; teach, instruct, give instructions to.

5 *recent events show this to be true* PROVE, demonstrate, confirm, show beyond doubt; substantiate, corroborate, verify, establish, attest, certify, testify, bear out; *formal* evince.

6 *a young woman showed them to their seats* ESCORT, accompany, take, conduct, lead, usher, guide, direct, steer, shepherd.

7 *informal they never showed* APPEAR, arrive, come, get here/there, put in an appearance, materialize, turn up; *informal* show up.

▸ noun **1** *a spectacular show of fireworks* DISPLAY, array, exhibition, presentation, exposition, spectacle.

2 *the boat show* EXHIBITION, exposition, fair, extravaganza, spectacle, exhibit.

3 *they took in a show* (THEATRICAL) PERFORMANCE, musical, play, opera, ballet.

4 *she's only doing it for show* APPEARANCE, display, impression, ostentation, image.

5 *Drew made a show of looking busy* PRETENSE, outward appearance, (false) front, guise, semblance, pose, parade.

6 *informal I don't run the show* UNDERTAKING, affair, operation, proceedings, enterprise, business, venture.

PHRASES: **show off** *informal* **1** *he likes to show off when we have company* BEHAVE AFFECTEDLY, put on airs, put on an act, swagger around, swank, strut, strike an attitude, posture; draw attention to oneself; *informal* cop an attitude. **2** *that dress really shows off your green eyes* DISPLAY, show to advantage, exhibit, demonstrate, parade, draw attention to, flaunt. **show up** **1** *cancers show up on X-rays* BE VISIBLE, be obvious, be seen, be revealed. **2** *informal only two waitresses showed up.* See SHOW verb sense 7. **3** *the sun showed up the shabbiness of the room* EXPOSE, reveal, make visible, make obvious, highlight. **4** *informal they showed him up in front of his friends.* See HUMILIATE.

showdown noun *his girlfriend got into a showdown with his ex-wife* CONFRONTATION, clash, face-off.

shower noun **1** *a shower of rain* (LIGHT) FALL, drizzle, sprinkling, misting.

2 *a shower of arrows* VOLLEY, hail, salvo, bombardment, barrage, fusillade, cannonade.

3 *a shower of awards* AVALANCHE, deluge, flood, spate, flurry; profusion, abundance.

▸ verb 1 *confetti showered down on us* RAIN, fall, hail.

2 *she showered them with gifts* DELUGE, flood, inundate, swamp, engulf; overwhelm, overload, snow under.

3 *showering praise on his cronies* LAVISH, heap, bestow freely.

showing noun 1 *another showing of the series* PRESENTATION, broadcast, airing, televising, screening.

2 *the party's present showing* PERFORMANCE, (track) record, results, success, achievement.

showman noun 1 *a traveling showman* IMPRESARIO, stage manager; ringmaster, host, master of ceremonies, MC; presenter; *informal* emcee.

2 *Jack is a great showman* ENTERTAINER, performer, virtuoso.

show-off noun *informal* *no one minds that Amy's a show-off because she's just so funny* EXHIBITIONIST, extrovert, poser, poseur, peacock, swaggerer, self-publicist, braggart; *informal* showboat, blowhard, grandstander.

showy adjective *they spared no sequins or feathers in what may be the most showy finale ever seen on this stage* OSTENTATIOUS, conspicuous, pretentious, flamboyant, gaudy, garish, brash, vulgar, loud, extravagant, fancy, ornate, overelaborate, kitsch, kitschy; pyrotechnical; *informal* flash, flashy, glitzy, ritzy, swanky, fancy-dancy, fancy-schmancy. ANTONYM restrained.

WORD NOTE **pyrotechnical**

There is nothing properly wrong with describing a piece of writing or a vocal performance as *pyrotechnical.* The *Oxford English Dictionary* patiently lists this usage as the word's third figurative meaning: "Of wit, rhetoric, etc.: resembling or suggestive of fireworks; brilliant, sensational." No, there is nothing properly wrong here. But something dies in a piece of figurative language when it is used so frequently and debased so often, and becomes a kind of "fudging term," standing in for what would otherwise be a lengthier descriptive act. If you mean *showy* then say *showy,* and if you mean *complex* then say that, but if you want to unpick and understand the way a piece of rhetoric works, than *pyrotechnical* is a very weak adjective indeed. **—ZS**

shred noun 1 *her dress was torn to shreds* TATTER, scrap, strip, ribbon, rag, fragment, sliver, (tiny) bit/piece.

2 *not a shred of evidence* SCRAP, bit, speck, iota, particle, ounce, whit, jot, crumb, morsel, fragment, grain, drop, trace, scintilla, spot; *informal* smidgen.

▸ verb *shredding vegetables* CHOP FINELY, cut up, tear up, grate, mince, macerate, grind.

shrew noun *my brother has just married a despicable shrew* VIRAGO, dragon, termagant, fishwife, witch, tartar, hag; *informal* battle-ax, old bag, old bat; *archaic* scold.

shrewd adjective *a shrewd businessman would never have been so careless about keeping appointments* ASTUTE, sharp-witted, sharp, smart, acute, intelligent, clever, canny, perceptive, perspicacious, sagacious, wise; *informal* on the ball, savvy, heads-up; *formal* sapient. See note at KEEN. ANTONYM stupid.

shrewdness noun *he was never known for his shrewdness, but we never thought he could be that stupid* ASTUTENESS, sharp-wittedness, acuteness, acumen, acuity, intelligence, cleverness, smartness, wit, canniness, common sense, discernment, insight, understanding, perception, perceptiveness, perspicacity, discrimination, sagacity, sageness; *informal* horse sense, savvy, (street) smarts; *formal* sapience.

shrewish adjective *an unhappy marriage has made her bitter and shrewish* BAD-TEMPERED, quarrelsome, spiteful, sharp-tongued, scolding, nagging; venomous, rancorous, bitchy.

shriek verb *she shrieked with fear* SCREAM, screech, squeal, squawk, roar, howl, shout, yelp; *informal* holler.

▸ noun *a shriek of laughter* SCREAM, screech, squeal, squawk, roar, howl, shout, yelp; *informal* holler.

shrill adjective *that shrill voice gives me a headache* HIGH-PITCHED, piercing, high, sharp, ear-piercing, ear-splitting, penetrating, screeching, shrieking, screechy.

shrine noun 1 *the shrine of St. James* HOLY PLACE, temple, church, chapel, tabernacle, sanctuary, sanctum.

2 *a shrine to the Beatles* MEMORIAL, monument.

shrink verb 1 *the number of competitors shrank* GET SMALLER, become/grow smaller, contract, diminish, lessen, reduce, decrease, dwindle, decline, fall off, drop off. ANTONYMS expand, increase.

2 *he* ***shrank back*** *against the wall* DRAW BACK, recoil, back away, retreat, withdraw, cringe, cower, quail.

3 *he doesn't* ***shrink from*** *naming names* RECOIL FROM, shy away from, demur from, flinch from, have scruples about, have misgivings about, have qualms about, be loath to, be reluctant to, be unwilling to, be averse to, fight shy of, be hesitant to, be afraid to, hesitate to, balk at.

shrivel verb *the neglected plants shriveled in their pots* WITHER, shrink; wilt; dry up, desiccate, dehydrate, parch, frazzle.

shroud noun 1 *the shroud of Turin* WINDING SHEET; *historical* cerements.

2 *a shroud of mist | a shroud of secrecy* COVERING, cover, cloak, mantle, blanket, layer, cloud, veil.

▸ verb *a mist shrouded the shore* COVER, envelop, veil, cloak, blanket, screen, conceal, hide, mask, obscure; *literary* enshroud.

shrub noun *pruning the shrubs* BUSH, woody plant; hedge.

shrug PHRASE: **shrug off** *he just shrugged off all of my advice* DISREGARD, dismiss, take no notice of, ignore, pay no heed to, play down, make light of.

shudder verb *she shuddered at the thought* SHAKE, shiver, tremble, quiver, vibrate, palpitate. See note at SHAKE.

▸ noun *a shudder racked his body* SHAKE, shiver, tremor, tremble, trembling, quiver, quivering, vibration, palpitation, spasm.

shuffle verb 1 *they shuffled along the passage* SHAMBLE, drag one's feet, totter, dodder.

2 *she shuffled her feet* SCRAPE, drag, scuffle, scuff.

3 *he shuffled the cards* MIX (UP), mingle, rearrange, jumble.

shun verb *he shunned publicity* AVOID, evade, eschew,

steer clear of, shy away from, fight shy of, keep one's distance from, give a wide berth to, have nothing to do with; snub, give someone the cold shoulder, cold-shoulder, ignore, look right through; reject, rebuff, spurn, ostracize; *informal* give someone the brush-off, freeze out, give someone the bum's rush, give someone the brush off. ANTONYM welcome.

shut verb *please shut the door* CLOSE, pull/push to, slam, fasten; put the lid on, bar, lock, secure. ANTONYMS open, unlock.

PHRASES: **shut down** *the plant is shutting down in August* CEASE ACTIVITY, close (down), cease operating, cease trading, be shut (down); turn off, switch off; *informal* fold; power down. **shut in** *shut the goats in for the night* CONFINE, enclose, impound, shut up, pen (in/up), fence in, immure, lock up/in, cage, imprison, intern, incarcerate, corral. **shut out 1** *he shut me out of the house* LOCK OUT, keep out, refuse entrance to. **2** *she shut out the memories* BLOCK, suppress. **3** *the bamboo shut out the light* KEEP OUT, block out, screen, veil. **4** *they shut out the Blue Jays in three straight games* PREVENT FROM SCORING, blank. **shut up 1** *informal will you please shut up so we can hear the movie?* BE QUIET, keep quiet, hold one's tongue, keep one's lips sealed; stop talking, quiet (down); *informal* keep mum, button it, hush up, shut it, shut your face/mouth/trap, put a sock in it, give it a rest, save it. **2** *informal that should shut them up* QUIET (DOWN), silence, hush, shush, gag, muzzle. **3** *I haven't shut the hens up yet.* See SHUT IN.

shutdown noun *the shutdown of the plant has been a dark event for this community* CLOSURE, termination, closing down, winding up; turning off, switching off, powering down.

shuttle verb *they provided a bus to shuttle us to the mall* PLY, run, commute, go/travel back and forth, go/travel to and fro; ferry.

shy adjective *I was painfully shy* BASHFUL, diffident, farouche, timid, sheepish, reserved, reticent, introverted, retiring, self-effacing, withdrawn, timorous, mousy, nervous, insecure, unconfident, inhibited, repressed, self-conscious, embarrassed. ANTONYM confident.

PHRASE: **shy away from** *she shied away from success* FLINCH AT, demur at, recoil at, hang back from, have scruples about, have misgivings about, have qualms about, be chary of, be diffident toward, be bashful about, fight shy of, balk at.

shyness noun *Gerald's shyness was often mistaken for disinterest* BASHFULNESS, diffidence, sheepishness, reserve, reservedness, introversion, reticence, timidity, timidness, timorousness, mousiness, lack of confidence, self-consciousness, embarrassment, coyness, demureness.

sibling noun *he hasn't seen his siblings in eight years* brother, sister; sib.

sick adjective **1** *the children are sick* ILL, unwell, poorly, ailing, indisposed, not oneself; off; *informal* laid up, under the weather. ANTONYMS well, healthy.

2 *he was feeling sick* NAUSEOUS, nauseated, queasy, bilious, green around/at the gills; seasick, carsick, airsick, travel-sick; *informal* about to throw up.

3 *informal we're just sick about it* DISAPPOINTED, depressed, dejected, despondent, downcast, unhappy; angry, cross, annoyed, displeased, disgruntled, fed up. ANTONYM glad.

4 *I'm* ***sick of*** *this music* FED UP WITH, bored with, tired of, weary of. ANTONYM fond.

5 *informal a sick joke* MACABRE, black, ghoulish, morbid, perverted, gruesome, sadistic, cruel. PHRASE: **be sick** *I'm going to be sick* VOMIT, throw up, retch, heave, gag; *informal* hurl, puke, spew, spit up, barf, upchuck, toss one's cookies.

sicken verb **1** *the stench sickened him* CAUSE TO FEEL SICK/NAUSEOUS, make sick, turn someone's stomach, revolt, disgust; *informal* make someone want to throw up, gross out.

2 *she sickened and died* BECOME ILL, fall ill, be taken ill/sick, catch something. ANTONYM recover.

sickening adjective *ooh, that smell is sickening* NAUSEATING, stomach-turning, stomach-churning, repulsive, revolting, disgusting, repellent, repugnant, appalling, obnoxious, nauseous, vile, nasty, foul, loathsome, offensive, objectionable, off-putting, distasteful, obscene, gruesome, grisly, vomitous; *informal* gross; *formal* rebarbative.

sickly adjective **1** *a sickly child* UNHEALTHY, in poor health, delicate, frail, weak. ANTONYM healthy.

2 *sickly faces* PALE, wan, pasty, sallow, pallid, ashen, anemic. ANTONYM rosy.

3 *a sickly green* INSIPID, pale, light, light-colored, washed out, faded. ANTONYM deep.

4 *sickly love songs* SENTIMENTAL, mawkish, cloying, sugary, syrupy, saccharine; *informal* mushy, slushy, schmaltzy, weepy, lovey-dovey, corny, cornball, sappy, hokey, three-hankie.

sickness noun **1** *she was absent because of sickness* ILLNESS, disease, ailment, complaint, infection, malady, infirmity, indisposition; *informal* bug, virus.

2 *a wave of sickness* NAUSEA, biliousness, queasiness.

3 *he suffers this kind of sickness whenever we travel* VOMITING, retching, gagging; travel-sickness, seasickness, carsickness, airsickness, motion sickness; *informal* throwing up, puking, barfing.

side noun **1** *they were standing on the side of the road* EDGE, border, verge, boundary, margin, fringe(s), flank, bank, perimeter, extremity, periphery, (outer) limit, limits, bounds; *literary* marge, bourn. ANTONYM center.

2 *you're driving on the wrong side of the road* HALF, part; lane.

3 *the east side of the city* DISTRICT, quarter, area, region, part, neighborhood, sector, section, zone, ward.

4 *one side of the paper* SURFACE, face, plane.

5 *his side of the argument* POINT OF VIEW, viewpoint, perspective, opinion, way of thinking, standpoint, position, outlook, slant, angle.

6 *the losing side in the war* FACTION, camp, bloc, party, wing.

7 *the players on their side* TEAM, squad, lineup.

▸ adjective **1** *elaborate side pieces* LATERAL, wing, flanking. ANTONYM front.

2 *a side issue* SUBORDINATE, lesser, lower-level, secondary, minor, peripheral, incidental, ancillary, subsidiary, of little account, extraneous. ANTONYM central.

▸ verb ***siding with*** *the underdog.* See TAKE SOMEONE'S SIDE below.

PHRASES: **side by side** *they worked side by side* ALONGSIDE (EACH OTHER), beside each other, abreast, shoulder to shoulder, close together; in collaboration, in solidarity. **take someone's side** *I was surprised to see you taking Jack's side* SUPPORT, take someone's part, side with, be on someone's side, stand by, back, give someone one's backing, be loyal to, defend, champion, ally (oneself) with, sympathize with, favor.

sideline noun *he founded the company as a sideline* SECONDARY OCCUPATION, second job; hobby, leisure activity/pursuit, recreation.

▸ verb **1** *the injury sidelined their top reliever* REMOVE, take out, bench.

2 *we've sidelined plans to build a house* POSTPONE, suspend, delay, defer, shelve; *informal* put on the back burner.

PHRASE: **on the sidelines** *they attend the meetings, but they always stay on the sidelines* WITHOUT TAKING PART, without getting involved.

sidelong adjective *a sidelong glance* INDIRECT, oblique, sideways, sideward; surreptitious, furtive, covert, sly. ANTONYM overt.

▸ adverb *he looked sidelong at her* INDIRECTLY, obliquely, sideways, out of the corner of one's eye; surreptitiously, furtively, covertly, slyly.

side-splitting adjective *informal* See HILARIOUS.

sidestep verb *he neatly sidestepped the questions about crime* AVOID, evade, dodge, circumvent, skirt around, bypass; *informal* duck, pussyfoot around.

sidetrack verb *I'm easily sidetracked by things going on outside my office window* DISTRACT, divert, deflect, draw away.

sidewalk noun *shoveling the sidewalks* WALKWAY, walk, path.

sideways adverb **1** *I slid off sideways* TO THE SIDE, laterally.

2 *the expansion slots are mounted sideways* EDGEWISE, sideward/sidewards, side first, edgeways, end on, broadside.

3 *he looked sideways at her* OBLIQUELY, indirectly, sidelong; covertly, furtively, surreptitiously, slyly.

▸ adjective **1** *sideways force* LATERAL, sideward, on the side, side to side.

2 *a sideways look* OBLIQUE, indirect, sidelong; covert, furtive, sly, surreptitious.

siding noun *applying some new siding to the house* cladding, clapboard, board and batten, shiplap; vinyl siding; facade.

sidle verb *the sheriff sidled up to the window on the north side of the cabin* CREEP, sneak, slink, slip, slide, steal, edge, inch, move furtively.

siege noun *the siege of the fort lasted into the morning* BLOCKADE, encirclement. ANTONYM relief.

siesta noun *he's enjoying a siesta on the terrace* AFTERNOON SLEEP, nap, catnap, doze, rest; *informal* snooze, liedown, forty winks, bit of shut-eye.

sieve noun *use a sieve to strain the mixture* STRAINER, sifter, filter, riddle, screen.

▸ verb **1** *sieve the mixture into a bowl.* See SIFT sense 1.

2 *the coins were sieved from the ash* SEPARATE OUT, filter out, sift, sort out, isolate, part, extract, remove.

sift verb **1** *sift the flour into a large bowl* SIEVE, strain, screen, filter, riddle; *archaic* bolt.

2 *we **sift out** unsuitable applications* SEPARATE OUT, filter out, sort out, put to one side, weed out, get rid of, remove.

3 *investigators are **sifting through** the wreckage* SEARCH THROUGH, look through, examine, inspect, scrutinize, pore over, investigate, analyze, dissect, review.

sigh verb **1** *she sighed with relief* BREATHE OUT, exhale; groan, moan.

2 *the wind sighed in the trees* RUSTLE, whisper, murmur, sough.

3 *he **sighed for** younger days gone by* YEARN FOR, long for, pine for, ache for, grieve for, cry for/over, weep for/over, rue, miss, mourn, lament, hanker for/after.

sight noun **1** *she has excellent sight* EYESIGHT, vision, eyes, faculty of sight, visual perception.

2 *her first sight of it* VIEW, glimpse, glance, look.

3 *within sight of the enemy* RANGE OF VISION, field of vision, view.

4 *dated* *we are all equal in the sight of God* PERCEPTION, judgment, belief, opinion, point of view, view, viewpoint, mind, perspective, standpoint.

5 *historic sights* LANDMARK, place of interest, monument, spectacle, view, marvel, wonder.

6 *informal* *I must look a sight* EYESORE, spectacle, mess; *informal* fright.

▸ verb *one of the helicopters sighted wreckage* GLIMPSE, catch/get a glimpse of, catch sight of, see, spot, spy, notice, observe; *literary* espy, descry.

PHRASES: **catch sight of** *we caught sight of a dim flicker of light in the distance* GLIMPSE, catch/get a glimpse of, see, spot, spy, make out, pick out, have sight of; *literary* espy, descry. **set one's sights on** *she set her sights on a teaching career* ASPIRE TO, aim at/for, try for, strive for/toward, work toward.

sightseer noun *the view from our rooftop cafe is a favorite among sightseers* TOURIST, visitor, day tripper.

sign noun **1** *a sign of affection* INDICATION, signal, symptom, pointer, suggestion, intimation, mark, manifestation, demonstration, token, evidence; *literary* sigil.

2 *a sign of things to come* PORTENT, omen, warning, forewarning, augury, presage; promise, threat.

3 *at his sign the soldiers followed* GESTURE, signal, wave, gesticulation, cue, nod.

4 *he read the sign on the wall* NOTICE, signpost, signboard, warning sign, road sign, traffic sign, guidepost, marquee.

5 *the dancers were daubed with signs* SYMBOL, mark, cipher, letter, character, figure, hieroglyph, ideogram, rune, emblem, device, logo. See note at EMBLEM.

▸ verb **1** *he signed the letter* WRITE ONE'S NAME ON, autograph, endorse, initial, countersign, ink; *formal* subscribe.

2 *the government signed the agreement* ENDORSE, validate, certify, authenticate, sanction, authorize; agree to, approve, ratify, adopt, give one's approval to; *informal* give something the go-ahead, give something the green light, give something the thumbs up.

3 *he signed his name* WRITE, inscribe, pen.

4 *we have signed a new player* RECRUIT, hire, engage, employ, take on, appoint, sign on/up, enlist.

5 *she signed to Susan to leave.* See SIGNAL[1] verb sense 1.

PHRASES: **sign on/up 1** *I signed up with Will's committee to raise money for the school library* ENLIST, take a job, join (up), enroll, register, volunteer. **2** *the Yankees have signed on Rodriguez.* See SIGN verb sense 4. **sign over** *he signed over the business to his children* TRANSFER, make over, hand over, bequeath, pass on, transmit, cede; *Law* devolve, convey.

THE RIGHT WORD

What's the difference between a **sign** and a **signal**? The former (in this sense) is a general term for anything that gives evidence of an event, a mood, a quality of character, a mental or physical state, or a trace of something (*a sign of approaching rain; a sign of good breeding; a sign that someone has entered the house*). While a sign may be involuntary or even unconscious, a *signal* is always voluntary and is usually deliberate. A ship that shows signs of distress may or may not be in trouble; but one that sends a distress *signal* is definitely in need of help. **Indication**, like *sign*, is a comprehensive term for anything that serves to indicate or point out (*he gave no indication that he was lying*). A **manifestation** is an outward or perceptible indication of something (*the letter was a manifestation of his guilt*), and a **symptom** is an indication of a diseased condition (*a symptom of pneumonia*). An object that proves the existence of something abstract is called a **token** (*she gave him a locket as a token of her love*). **Omen** and **augury** both pertain to foretelling future events, with *augury* being the general term for a prediction of the future and *omen* being a definite sign foretelling good or evil (*they regarded the stormy weather as a bad omen*).

signal[1] noun **1** *a signal to stop* GESTURE, sign, wave, gesticulation, cue, indication, warning, motion.

2 *a clear signal that the company is in trouble* INDICATION, sign, symptom, hint, pointer, intimation, clue, demonstration, evidence, proof. See note at SIGN.

3 *the encroaching dark is a signal for people to emerge* CUE, prompt, impetus, stimulus; *informal* go-ahead.

▸ verb **1** *the driver signaled to her to cross* GESTURE, sign, give a sign to, direct, motion; wave, beckon, nod.

2 *they signaled displeasure by refusing to cooperate* INDICATE, show, express, communicate, proclaim, declare.

3 *his death signals the end of an era* MARK, signify, mean, be a sign of, be evidence of, herald; *literary* betoken, foretoken.

signal[2] adjective *a signal victory.* See SIGNIFICANT sense 1.

signature noun *is this your signature?* AUTOGRAPH, inscription; *informal* John Hancock.

significance noun **1** *a matter of considerable significance* IMPORTANCE, import, consequence, seriousness, gravity, weight, magnitude, momentousness; *formal* moment.

2 *the significance of his remarks* MEANING, sense, signification, import, thrust, drift, gist, implication, message, essence, substance, point.

significant adjective **1** *a significant increase* NOTABLE, noteworthy, worthy of attention, remarkable, important, of importance, of consequence, signal; serious, crucial, weighty, momentous, epoch-making, uncommon, unusual, rare, extraordinary, exceptional, special; *formal* of moment.

2 *a significant look* MEANINGFUL, expressive, eloquent, suggestive, knowing, telling.

significantly adverb **1** *significantly better* NOTABLY, remarkably, outstandingly, importantly, crucially, materially, appreciably; markedly, considerably, obviously, conspicuously, strikingly, signally.

2 *he paused significantly* MEANINGFULLY, expressively, eloquently, revealingly, suggestively, knowingly.

signify verb **1** *this signified a fundamental change* BE EVIDENCE OF, be a sign of, mark, signal, mean, spell, be symptomatic of, herald, indicate; *literary* betoken.

2 *the egg signifies life* MEAN, denote, designate, represent, symbolize, stand for; *literary* betoken.

3 *signify your agreement by signing below* EXPRESS, indicate, show, proclaim, declare.

4 *the locked door doesn't signify* MEAN ANYTHING, be of importance, be important, be significant, be of significance, be of account, count, matter, be relevant.

silence noun **1** *the silence of the night* QUIETNESS, quiet, quietude, still, stillness, hush, tranquility, noiselessness, soundlessness, peacefulness, peace (and quiet). ANTONYM sound.

2 *she was reduced to silence* SPEECHLESSNESS, wordlessness, dumbness, muteness, taciturnity. ANTONYMS speech, loquacity.

3 *the politicians kept their silence* SECRETIVENESS, secrecy, reticence, taciturnity, uncommunicativeness. ANTONYM communicativeness.

▸ verb **1** *he silenced her with a kiss* QUIET, hush, shush; gag, muzzle, censor.

2 *silencing outside noises* MUFFLE, deaden, soften, mute, smother, dampen, damp down, mask, suppress, reduce.

3 *this would silence their complaints* STOP, put an end to, put a stop to.

silent adjective **1** *the night was silent* COMPLETELY QUIET, still, hushed, inaudible, noiseless, soundless. ANTONYMS audible, noisy.

2 *the right to remain silent* SPEECHLESS, quiet, unspeaking, dumb, mute, taciturn, uncommunicative, tight-lipped; *informal* mum. ANTONYM loquacious.

3 *silent thanks* UNSPOKEN, wordless, unsaid, unexpressed, unvoiced, tacit, implicit, understood. ANTONYM spoken.

silently adverb **1** *Nancy crept silently up the stairs* QUIETLY, inaudibly, noiselessly, soundlessly, in silence. ANTONYMS audibly, noisily.

2 *they drove on silently* WITHOUT A WORD, saying nothing, in silence.

3 *I silently said goodbye* WITHOUT WORDS, wordlessly, in one's head, tacitly, implicitly. ANTONYMS aloud, out loud.

silhouette noun *the silhouette of the dome* OUTLINE, contour(s), profile, form, shape, figure, shadow.

▸ verb *the castle was silhouetted against the sky* OUTLINE, delineate, define; stand out.

silky adjective *her long, silky hair* SMOOTH, soft, sleek, fine, glossy, satiny, silken.

silly adjective 1 *don't be so silly* FOOLISH, stupid, unintelligent, idiotic, brainless, mindless, witless, imbecilic, doltish; imprudent, thoughtless, rash, reckless, foolhardy, irresponsible; mad, scatterbrained, featherbrained; frivolous, giddy, inane, immature, childish, puerile, empty-headed; *informal* crazy, dotty, scatty, loopy, wingy, ditzy, screwy, thick, thickheaded, birdbrained, pea-brained, dopey, dim, dimwitted, halfwitted, dippy, blockheaded, boneheaded, lamebrained; daft, chowderheaded; *dated* tomfool. ANTONYM sensible.

2 *that was a silly thing to do* UNWISE, imprudent, thoughtless, foolish, stupid, idiotic, senseless, mindless; rash, reckless, foolhardy, irresponsible, injudicious, misguided, irrational; *informal* crazy; daft. ANTONYM sensible.

3 *he would brood about silly things* TRIVIAL, trifling, frivolous, footling, petty, small, insignificant, unimportant; *informal* piffling, piddling, small-bore. ANTONYM important.

4 *he drank himself silly* SENSELESS, insensible, unconscious, stupid, into a stupor, into senselessness, stupefied.

▸ noun *informal you're such a silly!* See FOOL noun sense 1.

silt noun *the flooding brought more silt* SEDIMENT, deposit, alluvium, mud.

▸ verb *the harbor had* ***silted up*** BECOME BLOCKED, become clogged, fill up (with silt).

silver noun 1 *freshly polished silver* SILVERWARE, (silver) plate; cutlery, 'knives, forks, and spoons'.

2 *a handful of silver* COINS, coinage, specie; (small) change, loose change.

3 *she won three silvers* SILVER MEDAL, second prize.

▸ adjective 1 *silver hair* GRAY, grayish, white.

2 *the silver water* SILVERY, shining, lustrous, gleaming; *literary* argent.

silviculture noun See FORESTRY.

similar adjective 1 *you two are very similar* ALIKE, (much) the same, indistinguishable, almost identical, homogeneous, homologous; *informal* much of a muchness. ANTONYM different.

2 *northern India and similar areas* COMPARABLE, like, corresponding, homogeneous, equivalent, analogous. PHRASE: **be similar to** *other towns were similar to this one* BE LIKE, RESEMBLE, look like, have the appearance of, be much the same as, be comparable to.

similarity noun *the similarity between John and his daughter* RESEMBLANCE, likeness, sameness, similitude, comparability, correspondence, parallel, equivalence, homogeneity, indistinguishability, uniformity; *archaic* semblance. See note at LIKENESS.

similarly adverb *the two vases are similarly flawed at the base* LIKEWISE, in similar fashion, in like manner, comparably, correspondingly, uniformly, indistinguishably, analogously, homogeneously, equivalently, in the same way, the same, identically.

similitude noun *Conrad uses a range of constructions that imply similitude* RESEMBLANCE, similarity, likeness, sameness, similar nature, comparability, correspondence, comparison, analogy, parallel, parallelism, equivalence; interchangeability, closeness, nearness, affinity, homogeneity, agreement, indistinguishability, uniformity; community, kinship, relatedness; *archaic* semblance. See note at LIKENESS.

simmer verb 1 *the soup was simmering on the stove* BOIL GENTLY, cook gently, bubble, stew.

2 *she was simmering with resentment* BE FURIOUS, be enraged, be angry, be incensed, be infuriated, seethe, fume, brim, smolder; *informal* be steamed up, be hot under the collar, stew. PHRASE: **simmer down** *we're not going to discuss this until you simmer down* BECOME LESS ANGRY, cool off/down, be placated, control oneself, become calmer, calm down, become quieter, quiet down; *informal* chill out.

simper verb *she sat there simpering, knowing she would have the last laugh* SMILE AFFECTEDLY, smile coquettishly, look coy, smirk, giggle, titter. See note at SMILE.

simple adjective 1 *it's really simple* STRAIGHTFORWARD, easy, uncomplicated, uninvolved, effortless, painless, undemanding, elementary, child's play; *informal* as easy as pie, as easy as ABC, a piece of cake, a cinch, no sweat, a pushover, kids' stuff, a breeze, duck soup, a snap. See word spectrum at COMPLICATED. ANTONYMS difficult, hard, complicated.

2 *simple language* CLEAR, plain, straightforward, intelligible, comprehensible, uncomplicated, accessible; *informal* user-friendly. ANTONYM complex.

3 *a simple white blouse* PLAIN, unadorned, undecorated, unembellished, unornamented, unelaborate, basic, unsophisticated, no-frills; classic, understated, uncluttered, restrained. ANTONYMS fancy, elaborate.

4 *the simple truth* CANDID, frank, honest, sincere, plain, absolute, unqualified, bald, stark, unadorned, unvarnished, unembellished.

5 *simple country people* UNPRETENTIOUS, unsophisticated, ordinary, unaffected, unassuming, natural, honest-to-goodness, cracker-barrel. ANTONYMS pretentious, affected.

6 *he's a bit simple* HAVING LEARNING DIFFICULTIES, having special (educational) needs; of low intelligence, simpleminded, unintelligent, backward, (mentally) retarded. ANTONYM gifted.

7 *simple chemical substances* NONCOMPOUND, noncomplex, uncombined, unblended, unalloyed, pure, single. ANTONYM compound.

simpleton noun See FOOL noun sense 1.

simplicity noun 1 *the simplicity of the recipes* STRAIGHTFORWARDNESS, ease, easiness, simpleness, effortlessness.

2 *the simplicity of the language* CLARITY, clearness, plainness, simpleness, intelligibility, comprehensibility, understandability, accessibility, straightforwardness.

3 *the building's simplicity* PLAINNESS, lack/absence of adornment, lack/absence of decoration, austerity, spareness, clean lines.

4 *the simplicity of their lifestyle* UNPRETENTIOUSNESS, ordinariness, lack of sophistication, lack of affectation, naturalness.

simplify verb *please simplify your answer* MAKE SIMPLE/SIMPLER, make easy/easier to understand, make plainer, clarify, make more comprehensible/intelligible; paraphrase. ANTONYM complicate.

simplistic adjective *the proposed solutions are too simplistic* FACILE, superficial, oversimple, oversimplified; shallow, jejune, naive.

simply adverb **1** *he spoke simply and forcefully* STRAIGHTFORWARDLY, directly, clearly, plainly, intelligibly, lucidly, unambiguously.

2 *she was dressed simply* PLAINLY, without adornment, without decoration, without ornament/ornamentation, soberly, unfussily, unelaborately, classically.

3 *they lived simply* UNPRETENTIOUSLY, modestly, quietly.

4 *they are welcomed simply because they have plenty of money* MERELY, just, purely, solely, only.

5 *Mrs. Marks was simply livid* UTTERLY, absolutely, completely, positively, really; *informal* plain.

6 *it's simply the best thing ever written* WITHOUT DOUBT, unquestionably, undeniably, incontrovertibly, certainly, categorically.

simulate verb **1** *they simulated pleasure* FEIGN, pretend, fake, sham, affect, put on, give the appearance of.

2 *simulating conditions in space* IMITATE, reproduce, replicate, duplicate, mimic.

simulated adjective **1** *simulated fear* FEIGNED, fake, mock, affected, sham, insincere, false, bogus; *informal* pretend, put-on, phony. ANTONYM real.

2 *simulated leather* ARTIFICIAL, imitation, fake, mock, synthetic, man-made, ersatz. ANTONYM real.

simultaneous adjective *they carried out simultaneous raids at two houses* CONCURRENT, happening at the same time, contemporaneous, concomitant, coinciding, coincident, synchronous, synchronized.

simultaneously adverb *Alison and Frank spoke simultaneously* AT (ONE AND) THE SAME TIME, at the same instant/moment, at once, concurrently, concomitantly; (all) together, in unison, in concert, in chorus.

sin noun **1** *a sin in the eyes of God* IMMORAL ACT, wrong, wrongdoing, act of evil/wickedness, transgression, crime, offense, misdeed, misdemeanor; *archaic* trespass.

2 *the human capacity for sin* WICKEDNESS, wrongdoing, wrong, evil, evildoing, sinfulness, immorality, iniquity, vice, crime. ANTONYM virtue.

3 *informal they've cut the school music program—it's a sin* SCANDAL, crime, disgrace, outrage.

▸ verb *I have sinned* COMMIT A SIN, commit an offense, transgress, do wrong, commit a crime, break the law, misbehave, go astray; *archaic* trespass.

THE RIGHT WORD

If you've ever driven through a red light or chewed with your mouth open, you've committed an **offense**, which is a broad term covering any violation of the law or of standards of propriety and taste. A **sin**, on the other hand, is an act that specifically violates a religious, ethical, or moral standard (*to marry someone of another faith was considered a sin*). **Transgression** is a weightier and more serious word for *sin*, suggesting any violation of an agreed-upon set of rules (*their behavior was clearly a transgression of the terms set forth in the treaty*). A **crime** is any act forbidden by law and punishable upon conviction (*a crime for which he was sentenced to death*). A **vice** has less to do with violating the law and more to do with habits and practices that debase a person's character (*alcohol was her only vice*). **Fault** and **indiscretion** are gentler words, although they may be used as euphemisms for *sin* or *crime*. A *fault* is an unsatisfactory feature in someone's character (*she is exuberant to a fault*), while *indiscretion* refers to an unwise or improper action (*speaking to the media was an indiscretion for which she was chastised*). In recent years, however, *indiscretion* has become a euphemism for such sins as adultery, as if to excuse such behavior by attributing it to a momentary lapse of judgment (*his indiscretions were no secret*).

since conjunction *Larry's not coming since his back is acting up again* BECAUSE, as, inasmuch, for the reason that, seeing that/as.

sincere adjective **1** *our sincere gratitude* HEARTFELT, wholehearted, profound, deep; genuine, real, unfeigned, unaffected, true, honest, bona fide.

2 *a sincere person* HONEST, genuine, truthful, unhypocritical, straightforward, direct, frank, candid; *informal* straight, upfront, on the level, on the up and up.

sincerely adverb *we sincerely hope you'll be better soon* GENUINELY, honestly, really, truly, truthfully, wholeheartedly, earnestly, fervently.

sincerity noun *there's no reason to doubt her sincerity* HONESTY, genuineness, truthfulness, integrity, probity, trustworthiness; straightforwardness, openness, candor, candidness.

sinecure noun *mowing the Ortons' lawn is a sinecure* EASY JOB, cushy job, soft option; *informal* picnic, cinch, easy money, free ride, gravy train.

sinewy adjective *he was tall, blond, and sinewy* MUSCULAR, muscly, brawny, powerfully built, burly, strapping, sturdy, rugged, strong, powerful, athletic, muscle-bound, hard-bodied; *informal* hunky, beefy; *dated* stalwart; *literary* thewy. ANTONYM puny.

sinful adjective **1** *sinful conduct* IMMORAL, wicked, (morally) wrong, wrongful, evil, bad, iniquitous, corrupt, criminal, nefarious, depraved, degenerate. ANTONYM virtuous.

2 *a sinful waste of money* REPREHENSIBLE, scandalous, disgraceful, deplorable, shameful, criminal. ANTONYM admirable.

sinfulness noun *own up to your sinfulness and find the redemption you are seeking* IMMORALITY, wickedness, sin, wrongdoing, evil, evil-doing, iniquitousness, corruption, depravity, degeneracy, vice; *formal* turpitude. ANTONYM virtue.

sing verb **1** *the choir began to sing* croon, carol, trill, chant, intone, chorus; *informal* belt out.

2 *the birds were singing* WARBLE, trill, chirp, chirrup, cheep, peep.

3 *Rudy* ***sang out*** *a greeting* CALL (OUT), cry (out), shout, yell; *informal* holler.

4 *informal he's going to sing to the police* INFORM (ON SOMEONE), confess; *informal* squeal, rat on someone, blow the whistle on someone, snitch (on someone), narc (on someone), finger someone, fink on someone.

WORD NOTE **sing**

This word encompasses the unpitched guttural tones of death metal, the wailing of Screamin' Jay Hawkins (a trained opera singer), the speak-singing of Rex Harrison, and the extended vocal techniques of Joan LaBarbara. *Rapping* and *talking blues* are usually considered a separate musical activity, but *toasting,* the high-pitched rhythmic chant on one note associated with Jamaican pop, would qualify. The gray area is wide, and fertile. **—SM**

singe verb *the ends of my hair were singed when I leaned over the candle* SCORCH, burn, sear, char. See note at BURN.

singer noun *she's the lead singer* VOCALIST, soloist, songster, songstress, cantor, chorister, cantor; *informal* songbird, siren, diva, chanteuse, chansonnier; *literary* troubadour, minstrel.

single adjective **1** *a single red rose* ONE (ONLY), sole, lone, solitary, by itself/oneself, unaccompanied, alone. ANTONYM double.

2 *she wrote down every single word* INDIVIDUAL, separate, distinct, particular, last.

3 *is she single?* UNMARRIED, unwed, unwedded, unattached, free, a bachelor, a spinster; partnerless, husbandless, wifeless; separated, divorced, widowed; *informal* solo. ANTONYM married.

PHRASE: **single out** *her watercolors were singled out by the judges* SELECT, pick out, choose, decide on; target, earmark, mark out, separate out, set apart/aside.

single-handed adverb *I installed the alarm single-handed* BY ONESELF, alone, on one's own, solo, unaided, unassisted, without help.

single-minded adjective *I got where I am with hard work and single-minded determination* DETERMINED, committed, unswerving, unwavering, resolute, purposeful, devoted, dedicated, uncompromising, tireless, tenacious, persistent, indefatigable, dogged; *formal* pertinacious. ANTONYM halfhearted.

singly adverb *people, please entry singly into the hallway* ONE BY ONE, one at a time, one after the other, individually, separately, by oneself, on one's own. ANTONYM together.

singular adjective **1** *the gallery's singular capacity to attract sponsors* REMARKABLE, extraordinary, exceptional, outstanding, signal, notable, noteworthy; rare, unique, unparalleled, unprecedented, amazing, astonishing, phenomenal, astounding; *informal* fantastic, terrific.

2 *why was Betty behaving in so singular a fashion?* STRANGE, unusual, odd, peculiar, funny, curious, extraordinary, bizarre, eccentric, weird, queer, unexpected, unfamiliar, abnormal, atypical, unconventional, out of the ordinary, untypical, puzzling, mysterious, perplexing, baffling, unaccountable.

singularity noun **1** *the singularity of their concerns* UNIQUENESS, distinctiveness.

2 *his singularities* IDIOSYNCRASY, quirk, foible, peculiarity, oddity, eccentricity.

singularly adverb *you are singularly beautiful* REMARKABLY, extraordinarily, exceptionally, very, extremely, really, outstandingly, signally, particularly, incredibly, decidedly, supremely, distinctly, tremendously; *informal* awfully, terribly, terrifically, powerful.

sinister adjective **1** *there was a sinister undertone in his words* MENACING, threatening, ominous, forbidding, baleful, frightening, alarming, disturbing, disquieting, dark, black; *formal* minatory; *literary* direful.

2 *a sinister motive* EVIL, wicked, criminal, corrupt, nefarious, villainous, base, vile, malevolent, malicious; *informal* shady. ANTONYM innocent.

sink verb **1** *the coffin sank below the waves* BECOME SUBMERGED, be engulfed, go down, drop, fall, descend. ANTONYMS float, rise.

2 *the cruise liner sank yesterday* FOUNDER, go under, submerge.

3 *they sank their ships* SCUTTLE, send to the bottom; scupper.

4 *the announcement sank hopes of a recovery* DESTROY, ruin, wreck, put an end to, demolish, smash, shatter, dash; *informal* put the kibosh on, put paid to; *informal* scupper; *archaic* bring to naught.

5 *I sank myself in student life* IMMERSE, submerge, plunge, lose, bury.

6 *the plane sank toward the airstrip* DESCEND, drop, go down/downward. ANTONYM ascend.

7 *the sun was sinking* SET, go down/downward. ANTONYM rise.

8 *Loretta sank into an armchair* LOWER ONESELF, flop, collapse, fall, drop down, slump; *informal* plunk oneself.

9 *her voice sank to a whisper* FALL, drop, become/get quieter, become/get softer. ANTONYM rise.

10 *she would never sink to your level* STOOP, lower oneself, descend.

11 *he was sinking fast* DETERIORATE, decline, fade, grow weak, flag, waste away; be at death's door, be on one's deathbed, be slipping away; *informal* go downhill, be on one's last legs, be giving up the ghost. ANTONYMS recover, improve.

12 *sink the pots into the ground* EMBED, insert, drive, plant.

13 *sinking a gold mine* DIG, excavate, bore, drill.

14 *they sank their life savings into the company* INVEST, venture, risk.

▸ noun *he washed himself at the sink* BASIN, wash basin; *dated* lavabo.

PHRASE: **sink in** *bad news like this often takes time to sink in* REGISTER, be understood, be comprehended, be grasped, get through.

sinless adjective *who among us in sinless?* INNOCENT, pure, virtuous, as pure as the driven snow, uncorrupted, faultless, blameless, guiltless, immaculate. ANTONYM wicked.

sinner noun *on a mission to rescue these sinners from the darkness* WRONGDOER, evildoer, transgressor, miscreant, offender, criminal; *archaic* trespasser.

sinuous adjective **1** *a sinuous river* WINDING, windy, serpentine, curving, twisting, meandering, snaking, zigzag, curling, coiling.

2 *she moved with sinuous grace* LITHE, supple, agile, graceful, loose-limbed, limber, lissome.

sip verb *Amanda sipped her coffee* DRINK (SLOWLY).

▸ noun *a sip of whiskey* MOUTHFUL, swallow, drink, drop, dram, nip, taste; *informal* swig.

siren noun **1** *a fire engine's siren* ALARM (BELL), warning bell, danger signal; *archaic* tocsin.

2 *the siren's allure* SEDUCTRESS, temptress, tease, femme fatale; flirt, coquette; *informal* man-eater, home wrecker, vamp.

sissy *informal* noun *he's a real sissy* COWARD, weakling, milksop, namby-pamby, baby, wimp; *informal* softie, chicken, milquetoast; mama's boy, pantywaist, twinkie, crybaby, powder puff.

▸ adjective *sissy manners* effeminate, effete, unmanly.

sister noun **1** *my sister Martha* SIBLING; *informal* sis, sib.

2 *we are a united front of sisters* COMRADE, colleague, associate, partner, fellow, friend; *informal* pal, chum, mate.

3 *the sisters in the convent* NUN, novice, abbess, prioress.

sit verb 1 *here, sit on the comfy chair* TAKE A SEAT, seat oneself, be seated, perch, ensconce oneself, plump oneself, flop; *informal* take the load/weight off one's feet, plunk oneself, take a load off. ANTONYM stand.

2 *she sat the package on the table* PUT (DOWN), place, set (down), lay, deposit, rest, stand; *informal* stick, dump, park, plunk. ANTONYM lift.

3 *the church sat about 3,000 people* HOLD, seat, have seats for, have space/room for, accommodate.

4 *she sat for Picasso* POSE, model.

5 *a hotel sitting on the mountain* BE SITUATED, be located, be sited, stand.

6 *the committee sits on Saturday* BE IN SESSION, meet, be convened.

7 *women jurists* ***sit on*** *the tribunal* SERVE ON, have a seat on, be a member of.

8 *his shyness doesn't sit easily with Hollywood tradition* BE HARMONIOUS, go, fit in, harmonize.

9 *Mrs. Hillman will sit for us* BABYSIT. PHRASES: **sit back** *sit back and listen to the music* RELAX, unwind, lie back; *informal* let it all hang out, veg out, hang loose, chill (out), take a load off. **sit in for** *I'll be sitting in for Tim while he's away* STAND IN FOR, fill in for, cover for, substitute for; *informal* sub for. **sit in on** *you're welcome to sit in on any of your son's classes* ATTEND, be present at, be an observer at, observe, audit. **sit tight** *informal* 1 *just sit tight while I call your parents* STAY PUT, wait there, remain in one's place. 2 *we're advising our clients to sit tight* TAKE NO ACTION, wait, hold back, bide one's time; *informal* hold one's horses.

site noun *the site of the battle* LOCATION, place, position, situation, locality, whereabouts; *technical* locus.

▸ verb *garbage cans sited along the street* PLACE, put, position, situate, locate.

sitting noun *all-night sittings* SESSION, meeting, assembly; hearing.

▸ adjective *a sitting position* SEDENTARY, seated. ANTONYM standing.

sitting room noun *Jocelyn is waiting for you in the sitting room* LIVING ROOM, lounge, front room, drawing room, family room, den; *dated* parlor.

situate verb *the library is situated just west of the town hall* LOCATE, site, position, place, station, build.

situation noun 1 *their financial situation* CIRCUMSTANCES, (state of) affairs, state, condition.

2 *I'll fill you in on* ***the situation*** THE FACTS, how things stand, the lay of the land, what's going on; *informal* the score, the scoop.

3 *the hotel's pleasant situation* LOCATION, position, spot, site, setting, environment; *technical* locus.

4 *he was offered a situation in Canada* JOB, post, position, appointment; employment.

six cardinal number *these six are the pups of our champion stud* SEXTET, sextuplets; *technical* hexad.

sizable adjective *a sizable monthly allowance* FAIRLY LARGE, substantial, considerable, respectable, significant, largish, biggish, goodly. ANTONYM small.

size noun *the room was of medium size* DIMENSIONS, measurements, proportions, magnitude, largeness, bigness, area, expanse; breadth, width, length, height, depth; immensity, hugeness, vastness.

▸ verb *the drills are sized in millimeters* SORT, categorize, classify.

PHRASE: **size up** *informal having sized up the competition, I knew I would win* ASSESS, appraise, form an estimate of, take the measure of, judge, take stock of, evaluate.

sizzle verb *the sizzle of bacon in the skillet* CRACKLE, frizzle, sputter, spit.

sizzling adjective *informal* 1 *sizzling temperatures* EXTREMELY HOT, unbearably hot, blazing, burning, scorching, sweltering, broiling, blistering; *informal* boiling (hot), baking (hot). ANTONYM freezing.

2 *a sizzling affair* PASSIONATE, torrid, ardent, lustful, erotic; *informal* steamy, hot.

skedaddle verb *informal* See RUN verb sense 2.

skeletal adjective 1 *a skeletal man* EMACIATED, very thin, as thin as a rake, cadaverous, skin-and-bones, skinny, bony, gaunt; *informal* anorexic. ANTONYM fat.

2 *a skeletal account* LACKING IN DETAIL, incomplete, outline, fragmentary, sketchy; thumbnail. ANTONYM detailed.

skeleton noun 1 *the human skeleton* BONES.

2 *she was no more than a skeleton* SKIN AND BONE; *informal* bag of bones.

3 *a concrete skeleton* FRAMEWORK, frame, shell.

4 *the skeleton of a report* OUTLINE, (rough) draft, abstract, (bare) bones.

▸ adjective *a skeleton staff* MINIMUM, minimal, basic; essential.

skeptic noun 1 *skeptics said the marriage wouldn't last* CYNIC, doubter; pessimist, prophet of doom.

2 *skeptics who have found faith* AGNOSTIC, atheist, unbeliever, nonbeliever, disbeliever, doubting Thomas.

skeptical adjective *she was wisely skeptical about his get-rich-quick scheme* DUBIOUS, doubtful, taking something with a pinch of salt, doubting; cynical, distrustful, mistrustful, suspicious, disbelieving, unconvinced, incredulous, scoffing; pessimistic, defeatist. ANTONYMS certain, convinced.

skepticism noun 1 *his ideas were met with skepticism* DOUBT, doubtfulness, a pinch of salt; disbelief, cynicism, distrust, mistrust, suspicion, incredulity; pessimism, defeatism; *formal* dubiety. See note at UNCERTAINTY.

2 *he passed from skepticism to religious belief* AGNOSTICISM, doubt; atheism, unbelief, nonbelief.

sketch noun 1 *a sketch of the proposed design* (PRELIMINARY) DRAWING, outline; diagram, design, plan; *informal* rough.

2 *she gave a rough sketch of what had happened* OUTLINE, brief description, rundown, main points, thumbnail sketch, (bare) bones; summary, synopsis, summarization, précis, résumé, wrap-up.

3 *a biographical sketch* DESCRIPTION, portrait, profile, portrayal, depiction.

4 *a hilarious sketch* SKIT, scene, piece, act, item, routine.

▸ verb **1** *he sketched the garden* DRAW, make a drawing of, draw a picture of, pencil, rough out, outline.

2 *the company **sketched out** its plans* DESCRIBE, outline, give a brief idea of, rough out; summarize, précis.

sketchily adverb *investors will want to know more than this sketchily described plan* PERFUNCTORILY, cursorily, incompletely, patchily, vaguely, imprecisely; hastily, hurriedly.

sketchy adjective *we have only a sketchy description of the assailant* INCOMPLETE, patchy, fragmentary, cursory, perfunctory, scanty, vague, imprecise, imperfect; hurried, hasty. ANTONYM detailed.

skew verb *anyone can skew the data to their own advantage* DISTORT, misrepresent, pervert, twist, falsify, bias, alter, change; *informal* doctor, put a spin on.

skill noun **1** *his skill as a politician* EXPERTISE, skillfulness, expertness, adeptness, adroitness, deftness, dexterity, ability, prowess, mastery, competence, capability, aptitude, artistry, virtuosity, talent. ANTONYM incompetence.

2 *bringing up a family gives you many skills* ACCOMPLISHMENT, strength, gift.

skilled adjective *a skilled architect* EXPERIENCED, trained, qualified, credentialed, proficient, practiced, accomplished, expert, skillful, talented, gifted, adept, adroit, deft, dexterous, able, good, competent; *informal* crack, crackerjack. ANTONYM inexperienced.

skillful adjective *the work of a skillful shoemaker* EXPERT, accomplished, skilled, masterly, master, virtuoso, consummate, proficient, talented, gifted, adept, adroit, deft, dexterous, able, good, competent, capable, brilliant, handy; *informal* mean, wicked, crack, ace, wizard, crackerjack, pro.

skim verb **1** ***skim off** the scum* REMOVE, cream off, scoop off.

2 *the boat skimmed over the water* GLIDE, move lightly, slide, sail, skate, float.

3 *he skimmed the pebble across the water* THROW, toss, cast, pitch; bounce.

4 *she **skimmed through** the newspaper* GLANCE THROUGH, flick through, flip through, leaf through, riffle through, thumb through, read quickly, scan, run one's eye over.

5 *Hannah **skimmed over** this part of the story* MENTION BRIEFLY, pass over quickly, skate over, gloss over. ANTONYM elaborate on.

skimp verb **1** *don't **skimp on** the quantity* STINT ON, scrimp on, economize on, cut back on, be sparing with, be frugal with, be mean with, be parsimonious with, cut corners with; *informal* be stingy with, be mingy with, be tight with.

2 *the process cannot be skimped* DO HASTILY, do carelessly.

skimpy adjective **1** *a skimpy black dress* REVEALING, short, low, low-cut; flimsy, thin, see-through, indecent.

2 *my information is rather skimpy* MEAGER, scanty, sketchy, limited, paltry, deficient, sparse.

skin noun **1** *these chemicals could damage the skin* EPIDERMIS, dermis, derma.

2 *Mary's fair skin* COMPLEXION, coloring, skin color/tone, pigmentation.

3 *leopard skins* HIDE, pelt, fleece, *historical* plew; *archaic* fell.

4 *a banana skin* PEEL, rind, integument.

5 *milk with a skin on it* FILM, layer, membrane.

6 *the plane's skin was damaged* CASING, exterior.

▸ verb **1** *skin the tomatoes* PEEL, pare, hull; *technical* decorticate.

2 *he skinned his knee* GRAZE, scrape, abrade, bark, rub raw, chafe; *Medicine* excoriate.

PHRASES: **by the skin of one's teeth** *he won, but only by the skin of his teeth* (ONLY) JUST, narrowly, barely, by a hair's breadth, by a very small margin; *informal* by a whisker. **get under someone's skin** *informal* **1** *the children really got under my skin.* See IRRITATE sense 1. **2** *she got under my skin* OBSESS, intrigue, captivate, charm; enthrall, enchant, entrance. **it's no skin off my nose** *informal if you want to go swimming in that icy water, it's no skin off my nose* I DON'T CARE, I don't mind, I'm not bothered, it doesn't bother me, it doesn't matter to me; *informal* I don't give a damn, I couldn't/could care less. **skin alive** *informal Dad would skin me alive if I forgot it* PUNISH SEVERELY; *informal* murder, come down on (like a ton of bricks), give what for.

skin-deep adjective *her compassion for our cause proved to be skin-deep* SUPERFICIAL, (on the) surface, external, outward, shallow.

skinflint noun *informal Jodie has the charisma needed to pry those dollar bills from these skinflints' fists* MISER, penny-pincher, Scrooge, pinchpenny; *informal* money-grubber, cheapskate, tightwad, piker.

skinny adjective *his extreme height made him look especially skinny* THIN, scrawny, scraggy, bony, angular, rawboned, hollow-cheeked, gaunt, as thin as a rake, skin-and-bones, sticklike, emaciated, waiflike, skeletal, pinched, undernourished, underfed; SLIM, lean, slender, rangy; lanky, spindly, gangly, gangling, gawky; *informal* looking like a bag of bones, anorexic; *dated* spindle-shanked. See note at THIN.

▸ noun *informal everybody wants to know the skinny on Karen's divorce* GOSSIP, (inside) information, intelligence, news, inside story; *informal* lowdown, info, dope, dirt, scoop, poop.

skip verb **1** *skipping down the path* CAPER, prance, trip, dance, bound, bounce, gambol, frisk, romp, cavort.

2 *we skipped the boring stuff* OMIT, leave out, miss out, dispense with, pass over, skim over, disregard; *informal* give something a miss.

3 *I skipped school* PLAY TRUANT FROM, miss, cut; *informal* play hooky from, ditch.

4 *informal they **skipped off** again | first chance I get, I'm **skipping out*** RUN OFF/AWAY, take off; *informal* beat it, clear off, cut and run, light out, cut out.

skirmish noun **1** *the unit was caught up in a skirmish* FIGHT, battle, clash, conflict, encounter, engagement, fray, combat.

2 *there was a skirmish over the budget* ARGUMENT, quarrel, squabble, contretemps, disagreement, difference of opinion, falling-out, dispute, blowup, clash, altercation; *informal* tiff, spat; row.

▸ verb *they skirmished with enemy soldiers* FIGHT, (do) battle with, engage with, close with, combat, clash with.

skirt noun *a blue skirt with a white blouse.* See table.

▸ verb **1** *he skirted the city* GO AROUND, walk around, circle.

2 *the fields that skirt the highway* BORDER, edge, flank, line, lie alongside.

3 *he carefully skirted the subject* AVOID, evade, sidestep, dodge, pass over, gloss over; *informal* duck.

SKIRTS

A-line skirt	kilt
bias-cut skirt	miniskirt
circle skirt	overskirt
crinoline	petal skirt
dirndl (skirt)	petticoat
flared skirt	pleated skirt
gored skirt	poodle skirt
grass skirt	prairie skirt
half-circle skirt	sheath
hobble skirt	wraparound skirt
jeans skirt	

skit noun *we auditioned by acting out our own three-minute skits* COMEDY SKETCH, comedy act, parody, pastiche, burlesque, satire; *informal* spoof, takeoff, sendup.

skittish adjective *going to the dentist makes me skittish* NERVOUS, anxious, on edge, excitable, restive, skittery, jumpy, jittery, high-strung.

skulduggery noun *Yvonne found herself entangled in the skulduggery of Gregor's private business deals* TRICKERY, fraudulence, underhandedness, chicanery; *informal* shenanigans, funny business, monkey business, monkeyshines.

skulk verb *you're right, I think someone is skulking around behind those cars* LURK, loiter, hide; creep, sneak, slink, prowl, pussyfoot.

skull noun *examination of the skull revealed prior injuries* CRANIUM, braincase; *informal* brainpan.

sky noun *the sun was shining in the sky* the upper atmosphere; *literary* the heavens, the firmament, the blue, the (wide) blue yonder, the welkin, the azure, the empyrean. PHRASE: **to the skies** *he praised Lizzie to the skies* EFFUSIVELY, profusely, very highly, very enthusiastically, unreservedly, fervently, fulsomely, extravagantly.

slab noun *slabs of concrete* PIECE, block, hunk, chunk, lump; cake, tablet, brick.

slack adjective **1** *the rope went slack* LOOSE, limp, hanging, flexible. ANTONYMS tight, taut.

2 *slack skin* FLACCID, flabby, loose, sagging, saggy. ANTONYM taut.

3 *business is slack* SLUGGISH, slow, quiet, slow-moving, flat, depressed, stagnant. ANTONYMS thriving, busy.

4 *slack accounting procedures* LAX, negligent, remiss, careless, slapdash, slipshod, lackadaisical, inefficient, casual; *informal* sloppy, slaphappy. ANTONYM diligent.

▸ noun **1** *the rope had some slack in it* LOOSENESS, play, give.

2 *foreign demand will help pick up the slack* SURPLUS, excess, residue, spare capacity.

3 *a little slack in the daily routine* LULL, pause, respite, break, hiatus, breathing space; *informal* letup, breather.

▸ verb *informal no slacking!* IDLE, shirk, be lazy, be indolent, waste time, lounge about; *informal* goof off.

PHRASES: **slack off 1** *the rain has slacked off* DECREASE, subside, let up, ease off, abate, diminish, die down, fall off. **2** *you deserve to slack off a bit* RELAX, take things easy, let up, ease up/off, loosen up, slow down; *informal* hang loose, chill (out). **slack up** *he doesn't slack up until he gets there* SLOW (DOWN), decelerate, reduce speed.

WORD NOTE **slack**

Not as in *cut me some slack* or *slack off,* but as a synonym for "limp, loose." There's a wrongness in *slack* that isn't in *limp* or *loose;* a slack mouth is disturbing, revolting; a slack rope betides some terrible accident as yet unseen. *Slacks,* meaning "casual trousers," is of course one of the most disgusting words in English, and should be avoided both linguistically and sartorially. **—EM**

slacken verb **1** *he slackened his grip* LOOSEN, release, relax, loose, lessen, weaken. ANTONYM tighten.

2 *he slackened his pace* SLOW (DOWN), become/get/make slower, decelerate, slack (up). ANTONYM quicken.

3 *the rain is slackening* DECREASE, lessen, subside, ease up/off, let up, abate, slack off, diminish, die down.

slacker noun *informal all right, you slackers, let's get this cargo across the river before the sun sets* LAYABOUT, idler, shirker, malingerer, sluggard, laggard; *informal* lazybones, bum, goof-off.

slake verb *we longed for a mountain spring to slake our thirst* QUENCH, satisfy, sate, satiate, relieve, assuage.

slam verb **1** *he slammed the door behind him* BANG, shut/close with a bang, shut/close noisily, shut/close with force.

2 *the car* ***slammed into*** *a post* CRASH INTO, smash into, collide with, hit, strike, ram, plow into, run into, bump into, impact.

3 *informal he was slammed by the critics.* See CRITICIZE.

slander noun *he could sue us for slander* DEFAMATION (OF CHARACTER), character assassination, calumny, libel; scandalmongering, malicious gossip, disparagement, denigration, aspersions, vilification, traducement, obloquy; lie, slur, smear, false accusation; *informal* mudslinging, bad-mouthing; *archaic* contumely.

▸ verb *they were accused of slandering the minister* DEFAME (SOMEONE'S CHARACTER), blacken someone's name, tell lies about, speak ill/evil of, sully someone's reputation, libel, smear, cast aspersions on, spread scandal about, besmirch, tarnish, taint; malign, traduce, vilify, disparage, denigrate, run down, slur; *informal* badmouth, dis, trash; *formal* derogate. See note at MALIGN.

slanderous adjective *slanderous accusations* DEFAMATORY, denigratory, disparaging, libelous, pejorative, false, misrepresentative, scurrilous, scandalous, malicious, abusive, insulting; *informal* mudslinging. ANTONYM complimentary.

slang noun *the street slang was a bit rough for his uptown ears* INFORMAL LANGUAGE, colloquialisms, patois, argot, cant, jargon. See note at DIALECT.

slant verb **1** *the floor was slanting* SLOPE, tilt, incline, be at an angle, tip, cant, lean, dip, pitch, shelve, list, bank.

2 *their findings were slanted in our favor* BIAS, distort, twist, skew, weight, give a bias to.

▸ noun 1 *the slant of the roof* SLOPE, incline, tilt, gradient, pitch, angle, cant, camber, inclination.

2 *a feminist slant* POINT OF VIEW, viewpoint, standpoint, stance, angle, perspective, approach, view, attitude, position; bias, leaning.

slanting adjective *the slanting angle of the deck* OBLIQUE, sloping, at an angle, on an incline, inclined, tilting, tilted, slanted, aslant, diagonal, canted, cambered.

slap verb 1 *he slapped her hard* HIT, strike, smack, clout, cuff, thump, punch, spank; *informal* whack, thwack, wallop, bash, bop, slug, bust; *archaic* smite.

2 *he slapped down a $10 bill* FLING, throw, toss, slam, bang; *informal* plunk.

3 *slap on a coat of paint* DAUB, plaster, spread.

4 *informal they slapped a huge tax on imports* IMPOSE, levy, put.

▸ noun *a slap across the cheek* SMACK, blow, thump, cuff, clout, punch, spank; *informal* whack, thwack, wallop, clip, bash.

PHRASES: **a slap in the face** *your disloyalty was a brutal slap in the face* REBUFF, rejection, snub, insult, put-down, humiliation. **a slap on the back** *he was always trying to earn a slap on the back from his stepfather* CONGRATULATIONS, commendation, approbation, approval, accolades, compliments, tributes, a pat on the back, praise, acclaim, acclamation. **a slap on the wrist** *the judge let that bastard go free, with nothing more than a slap on the wrist* REPRIMAND, rebuke, reproof, scolding, admonishment; *informal* rap on/over the knuckles, dressing-down.

slapdash adjective *they did a slapdash job on the driveway* CARELESS, slipshod, hurried, haphazard, unsystematic, untidy, messy, hit-or-miss, negligent, neglectful, lax; *informal* sloppy, slaphappy, shambolic. See note at SUPERFICIAL. ANTONYM meticulous.

slap-happy adverb *informal* 1 *his slaphappy friend* HAPPY-GO-LUCKY, devil-may-care, carefree, easygoing, nonchalant, insouciant, blithe, airy, casual.

2 *slaphappy work.* See SLAPDASH.

3 *she's a bit slaphappy after such a narrow escape* DAZED, stupefied, punch-drunk.

slash verb 1 *her tires had been slashed* CUT (OPEN), gash, slit, split open, lacerate, knife, make an incision in.

2 *informal the company slashed prices* REDUCE, cut, lower, bring down, mark down.

3 *informal they have slashed 10,000 jobs* GET RID OF, ax, cut, shed, make redundant.

▸ noun 1 *a slash across his arm* CUT, gash, laceration, slit, incision; wound.

2 *sentence breaks are indicated by slashes* SOLIDUS, oblique, backslash.

slate verb *we've slated your speech for 2:10 on Thursday afternoon* PLAN, schedule, book; organize, arrange.

slatternly adjective *why would you bring that slatternly woman to our lovely dinner party?* SLOVENLY, untidy, messy, scruffy, unkempt, ill-groomed, disheveled, frowzy, bedraggled; *informal* raggedy, grubby, scuzzy.

slaughter verb 1 *the animals were slaughtered* KILL, butcher.

2 *innocent civilians are being slaughtered* MASSACRE, murder, butcher, kill (off), annihilate, exterminate, liquidate, eliminate, destroy, decimate, wipe out, put to death; *literary* slay. See note at KILL.

3 *informal their team was slaughtered.* See DEFEAT verb sense 1.

▸ noun 1 *the slaughter of 20 demonstrators* MASSACRE, murdering, (mass) murder, mass killing, mass execution, annihilation, extermination, liquidation, decimation, carnage, butchery, genocide; *literary* slaying.

2 *a scene of slaughter* CARNAGE, bloodshed, bloodletting, bloodbath.

3 *informal their electoral slaughter.* See DEFEAT noun sense 1.

slave noun 1 *the work was done by slaves historical* serf, vassal, thrall; *archaic* bondsman, bondswoman. ANTONYMS freeman, master.

2 *Anna was his willing slave* DRUDGE, servant, lackey, minion; *informal* gofer.

3 *a fashion slave* DEVOTEE, worshiper, adherent; fan, lover, aficionado; *informal* fanatic, freak, nut, addict.

▸ verb ***slaving away** for a pittance* TOIL, labor, grind away, sweat, work one's fingers to the bone, work like a Trojan/dog; *informal* kill oneself, sweat blood, slog away; *literary* travail; *archaic* drudge, moil.

slave-driver noun *Mr. Donegan is the first boss I've had who's not a slave driver* (HARD) TASKMASTER, (hard) taskmistress, tyrant, dictator.

slaver verb *her bloodhound loves to slaver on me* DROOL, slobber, dribble, salivate.

slavery noun 1 *thousands were sold into slavery* BONDAGE, enslavement, servitude, thralldom, thrall, serfdom, vassalage. ANTONYM freedom.

2 *this work is sheer slavery* DRUDGERY, toil, hard labor, grind; *literary* travail; *archaic* moil.

slavish adjective 1 *slavish lackeys of the government* SERVILE, subservient, fawning, obsequious, sycophantic, toadying, unctuous; *informal* bootlicking, forelock-tugging. See note at OBSEQUIOUS.

2 *slavish copying* UNORIGINAL, uninspired, unimaginative, uninventive, imitative.

slay verb 1 *literary 8,000 men were slain* KILL, murder, put to death, butcher, cut down, cut to pieces, slaughter, massacre, shoot down, gun down, mow down, eliminate, annihilate, exterminate, liquidate; *informal* wipe out, bump off, do in. See note at KILL.

2 *informal you slay me, you really do* AMUSE GREATLY, entertain greatly, make someone laugh; *informal* have people rolling in the aisles, kill, knock dead, be a hit with.

slaying noun *literary the slaying of political prisoners is a moral outrage* MURDER, killing, butchery, slaughter, massacre, extermination, liquidation.

sleazy adjective 1 *sleazy arms dealers* CORRUPT, immoral, unsavory, disreputable; *informal* shady, sleazoid. ANTONYM reputable.

2 *a sleazy bar* SQUALID, seedy, seamy, sordid, insalubrious, mean, cheap, low-class, run-down; *informal* scruffy, scuzzy, crummy, skanky, flea-bitten. ANTONYM upmarket.

3 *a sleazy outfit* REVEALING, skimpy; *informal* slutty, whorish.

sled noun *the snowy hills are alive with squealing children on their new Christmas sleds* toboggan, sledge, bobsled, luge, coaster; dogsled; sleigh, cutter; *Canadian* carriole, troika.

sleek adjective **1** *his sleek dark hair* SMOOTH, glossy, shiny, shining, lustrous, silken, silky.

2 *the car's sleek lines* STREAMLINED, trim, elegant, graceful.

3 *sleek young men in city suits* WELL-GROOMED, stylish, wealthy-looking, suave, sophisticated, debonair.

sleep noun *go and have a sleep* NAP, doze, siesta, catnap, beauty sleep; *informal* snooze, forty winks, bit of shut-eye, power nap; *literary* slumber.

▸ verb *she slept for about an hour* BE ASLEEP, doze, take a siesta, take a nap, catnap, sleep like a log; *informal* snooze, catch/snatch forty winks, get some shut-eye, put one's head down, catch some Zs; *humorous* be in the land of Nod, be in the arms of Morpheus; *literary* slumber. ANTONYM wake up.

PHRASES: **go to sleep** *I'm trying to go to sleep* FALL ASLEEP, get to sleep; *informal* drop off, nod off, drift off, crash out, sack out. **put an animal to sleep** *our beloved poodle Maxie had to be put to sleep* PUT DOWN, destroy, euthanize.

sleepiness noun *did you tell the doctor about your chronic sleepiness?* DROWSINESS, tiredness, somnolence, languor, languidness, doziness; lethargy, sluggishness, lassitude, enervation.

sleepless adjective *he lay sleepless until dawn* WAKEFUL, restless, without sleep, insomniac; (wide) awake, unsleeping, tossing and turning.

sleepwalker noun *Hansen was startled to learn he had become a sleepwalker* SOMNAMBULIST.

sleepy adjective **1** *she felt very sleepy* DROWSY, tired, somnolent, languid, languorous, heavy-eyed, asleep on one's feet; lethargic, sluggish, enervated, torpid; *informal* dopey; *literary* slumberous. ANTONYMS awake, alert.

2 *the sleepy heat of the afternoon* SOPORIFIC, sleep-inducing, somnolent. ANTONYM invigorating.

3 *a sleepy little village* QUIET, peaceful, tranquil, placid, slow-moving; dull, boring. ANTONYMS busy, bustling.

sleight of hand noun **1** *impressive sleight of hand* DEXTERITY, adroitness, deftness, skill.

2 *financial sleight of hand* DECEPTION, deceit, dissimulation, chicanery, trickery.

slender adjective **1** *her tall slender figure* SLIM, lean, willowy, sylphlike, svelte, lissome, graceful; slight, slightly built, thin, skinny. See note at THIN. ANTONYM plump.

2 *slender evidence* MEAGER, limited, slight, scanty, scant, sparse, paltry, insubstantial, insufficient, deficient, negligible; *formal* exiguous. ANTONYM considerable.

3 *we had a slender chance of making it* FAINT, remote, flimsy, tenuous, fragile, slim; unlikely, improbable. ANTONYM strong.

sleuth noun *informal I didn't have to be much of a sleuth to catch Irene stealing company funds* (PRIVATE) DETECTIVE, (private) investigator; *informal* private eye, snoop, shamus, gumshoe, (private) dick, PI.

slice noun **1** *a slice of fruitcake* PIECE, portion, slab, sliver, wafer, shaving.

2 *a huge slice of public spending* SHARE, part, portion, tranche, piece, proportion, allocation, percentage.

▸ verb **1** *slice the cheese thinly* CUT (UP), shave, carve, julienne, section.

2 *one man had his ear sliced off* CUT OFF, sever, chop off, shear off.

slick adjective **1** *a slick advertising campaign* EFFICIENT, smooth, smooth-running, polished, well-organized, well run, streamlined.

2 *his slick use of words* GLIB, smooth, fluent, plausible.

3 *a slick salesman* SUAVE, urbane, polished, assured, self-assured, smooth-talking, glib; *informal* smarmy.

4 *her slick brown hair* SHINY, glossy, shining, sleek, smooth, oiled.

5 *the sidewalks were slick with rain* SLIPPERY, wet, greasy; *informal* slippy.

▸ verb *his hair was slicked down* SMOOTH, sleek, grease, oil, gel.

slide verb **1** *the glass slid across the table* GLIDE, move smoothly, slip, slither, skim, skate; skid, slew.

2 *tears slid down her cheeks* TRICKLE, run, flow, pour, stream.

3 *four men slid out of the shadows* CREEP, steal, slink, slip, tiptoe, sidle.

4 *the country is sliding into recession* SINK, fall, drop, descend; decline, degenerate.

▸ noun **1** *the current slide in house prices* FALL, decline, drop, slump, downturn, downswing. ANTONYM rise.

2 *a slide show* TRANSPARENCY.

PHRASE: **let slide** *I guess I let things slide at the office during my wife's illness* NEGLECT, pay little/no attention to, not attend to, be remiss about, let something go downhill.

slight adjective **1** *the chance of success is slight* SMALL, modest, tiny, minute, inappreciable, negligible, insignificant, minimal, remote, slim, faint; *informal* minuscule; *formal* exiguous. ANTONYM considerable.

2 *the book is of slight consequence* MINOR, inconsequential, trivial, unimportant, lightweight, superficial, shallow. ANTONYM substantial.

3 *Elizabeth's slight figure* SLIM, slender, petite, diminutive, small, delicate, dainty. ANTONYM burly.

▸ verb *he had been slighted* INSULT, snub, rebuff, repulse, spurn, treat disrespectfully, give someone the cold shoulder, scorn; *informal* give someone the brush-off, freeze out. See note at NEGLECT. ANTONYM respect.

▸ noun *an unintended slight* INSULT, affront, snub, rebuff; *informal* put-down, dig. ANTONYM compliment.

slighting adjective *one more slighting remark from you and I'm walking out that door* INSULTING, disparaging, derogatory, disrespectful, denigratory, pejorative, abusive, offensive, defamatory, slanderous, scurrilous; disdainful, scornful, contemptuous; *archaic* contumelious.

slightly adverb *beat the egg whites until they're slightly stiff* A LITTLE, a bit, somewhat, rather, moderately, to a certain extent, faintly, vaguely, a shade, a touch. ANTONYM very.

slim adjective **1** *she was tall and slim* SLENDER, lean, thin, willowy, sylphlike, svelte, lissome, trim, slight, slightly built. ANTONYM plump.

2 *a slim silver bracelet* NARROW, slender, slimline. ANTONYM broad.

3 *a slim chance of escape* SLIGHT, small, slender, faint, poor, remote, unlikely, improbable. ANTONYM strong.

▸ verb **1** *I'm trying to* ***slim down*** LOSE WEIGHT, get thinner, lose some pounds/inches, diet, get into shape, slenderize.

2 *the number of staff had been* ***slimmed down*** REDUCE, cut (down/back), scale down, decrease, diminish, pare down.

slime noun *a greenish slime slowly dripped from the pipe* OOZE, sludge, muck, mud, mire; *informal* goo, gunk, gook, gloop, gunge, guck, glop; *humorous* ectoplasm.

slimy adjective **1** *the floor was slimy* SLIPPERY, greasy, muddy, mucky, sludgy, wet, sticky; *informal* slippy, gunky, gooey.

2 *informal her slimy press agent* OBSEQUIOUS, sycophantic, excessively deferential, subservient, fawning, toadying, ingratiating, unctuous, oily, oleaginous, greasy, toadyish, slavish; *informal* bootlicking, smarmy, forelock-tugging.

sling noun **1** *she had her arm in a sling* (SUPPORT) BANDAGE, support, strap.

2 *armed only with a sling* CATAPULT, slingshot.

▸ verb **1** *a hammock was slung between two trees* HANG, suspend, string, swing.

2 *informal she slung her jacket on the sofa.* See THROW verb sense 1.

slink verb *it's impossible to slink quietly across these squeaky floors* CREEP, sneak, steal, slip, slide, sidle, tiptoe, pussyfoot.

slinky adjective *informal a slinky black dress* TIGHT-FITTING, close-fitting, form-fitting, figure-hugging, sexy.

slip[1] verb **1** *she slipped on the ice* SLIDE, skid, glide; fall (over), lose one's balance, tumble.

2 *the envelope slipped through Luke's fingers* FALL, drop, slide.

3 *we slipped out by a back door* CREEP, steal, sneak, slide, sidle, slope, slink, tiptoe.

4 *standards have slipped* DECLINE, deteriorate, degenerate, worsen, get worse, fall (off), drop; *informal* go downhill, go to the dogs, go to pot.

5 *the stock index slipped 30 points* DROP, go down, sink, slump, decrease, depreciate.

6 *the hours* ***slipped by*** PASS, elapse, go by/past, roll by/past, fly by/past, tick by/past.

7 *she slipped the map into her pocket* PUT, tuck, shove; *informal* pop, stick, stuff.

8 *Sarah* ***slipped into*** *a black skirt* PUT ON, pull on, don, dress/clothe oneself in; change into.

9 *she* ***slipped out of*** *her clothes* TAKE OFF, remove, pull off, doff, peel off.

10 *he slipped the knot of his tie* UNTIE, unfasten, undo.

▸ noun **1** *a single slip could send them plummeting downward* FALSE STEP, misstep, slide, skid, fall, tumble.

2 *a careless slip* MISTAKE, error, blunder, gaffe, slip of the tongue/pen; oversight, omission, lapse, inaccuracy; *informal* slip-up, boo-boo, howler, goof, blooper. See note at MISTAKE.

3 *a silk slip* UNDERSKIRT, petticoat.

PHRASES: **give someone the slip** *informal we gave Murphy the slip and headed for the docks* ESCAPE FROM, get away from, evade, dodge, elude, lose, shake off, throw off (the scent), get clear of. **let something slip** *who let it slip that we were hiding here?* REVEAL, disclose, divulge, let out, give away, blurt out; give the game away; *informal* let on, blab, let the cat out of the bag, spill the beans. **slip away 1** *they managed to slip away* ESCAPE, get away, break free; *informal* fly the coop, take a powder. **2** *she slipped away in her sleep.* See DIE sense 1. **slip up** *informal Hennie slipped up and left the corral open* MAKE A MISTAKE, (make a) blunder, get something wrong, make an error, err; *informal* make a boo-boo, goof up.

slip[2] noun *they took slips from rare plants* CUTTING, graft; scion, shoot, offshoot. PHRASES: **a slip of a ——** *she's just a slip of a girl* SMALL, slender, slim, slight, slightly built, petite, little, tiny, diminutive; *informal* pint-sized. **slip of paper** *each person takes one slip of paper from the hat* PIECE OF PAPER, scrap of paper, sheet, note; *trademark* Post-it.

slipper noun *he pulled on his slippers* bedroom slipper, house shoe, slipper sock, moccasin; mule.

slippery adjective **1** *the roads are slippery* ICY, greasy, oily, glassy, smooth, slimy, wet; *informal* slippy.

2 *a slippery customer* EVASIVE, unreliable, unpredictable; devious, crafty, cunning, unscrupulous, wily, tricky, artful, slick, sly, sneaky, scheming, untrustworthy, deceitful, duplicitous, dishonest, treacherous, two-faced, snide; *informal* shady, shifty, hinky.

slipshod adjective *a slipshod sales presentation* CARELESS, lackadaisical, slapdash, disorganized, haphazard, hit-or-miss, untidy, messy, unsystematic, unmethodical, casual, negligent, neglectful, remiss, lax, slack; *informal* sloppy, slaphappy. ANTONYM meticulous.

slip-up noun *informal don't worry, everyone makes a slip-up or two* MISTAKE, slip, error, blunder, oversight, omission, gaffe, slip of the tongue/pen, inaccuracy; *informal* boo-boo, howler, goof, blooper, boner.

slit noun **1** *three diagonal slits* CUT, incision, split, slash, gash, laceration.

2 *a slit in the curtains* OPENING, gap, chink, crack, aperture, slot.

▸ verb *he threatened to slit her throat* CUT, slash, split open, slice open, gash, lacerate, make an incision in.

slither verb *the garter snake slithered under the shed* SLIDE, slip, glide, wriggle, crawl; skid.

sliver noun *slivers of glass | who wants this last sliver of cheesecake?* SPLINTER, shard, shiver, chip, flake, shred, scrap, shaving, paring, piece, fragment.

slob noun *informal her no-good slob of a husband* LAYABOUT, good-for-nothing, sluggard, laggard; *informal* slacker, lazybones, bum, couch potato; *archaic* sloven.

slobber verb *ooh, this mutt keeps slobbering on me* DROOL, slaver, dribble, salivate.

slog verb **1** *they were all* ***slogging away*** WORK HARD, toil, labor, work one's fingers to the bone, work like a Trojan/dog, exert oneself, grind, slave, grub, plow, plod, peg; *informal* beaver, plug, work one's guts out, put one's nose to the grindstone, sweat blood; *literary* travail; *archaic* drudge, moil. ANTONYM relax.

2 *they slogged around the streets* TRUDGE, tramp, tromp, traipse, toil, plod, trek, footslog.

▸ noun 1 *10 months' hard slog* HARD WORK, toil, toiling, labor, effort, exertion, grind, drudgery; *informal* sweat; *literary* travail; *archaic* moil. ANTONYM leisure.

2 *a steady uphill slog* TRUDGE, tramp, traipse, plod, trek, footslog.

slogan noun *familiar advertising slogans* CATCHPHRASE, jingle, byword, motto; *informal* tag line, buzzword, mantra.

slop verb *water slopped over the edge* SPILL, flow, overflow, run, slosh, splash.

slope noun 1 *the slope of the roof* GRADIENT, incline, angle, slant, inclination, pitch, decline, ascent, declivity, rise, fall, tilt, tip, downslope, upslope, grade, downgrade, upgrade.

2 *a grassy slope* HILL, hillside, hillock, bank, sidehill, escarpment, scarp; *literary* steep.

3 *the ski slopes* PISTE, run, trail.

▸ verb *the garden sloped down to a stream* SLANT, incline, tilt; drop away, fall away, decline, descend, shelve, lean; rise, ascend, climb.

sloping adjective *a sloping floor* AT A SLANT, on a slant, at an angle, slanting, slanted, leaning, inclining, inclined, angled, cambered, canted, tilting, tilted, dipping. ANTONYM level.

sloppy adjective 1 *their defense was sloppy* CARELESS, slapdash, slipshod, lackadaisical, haphazard, lax, slack, slovenly; *informal* slaphappy, shambolic.

2 *sloppy T-shirts* BAGGY, loose-fitting, loose, generously cut; shapeless, sacklike, oversized.

3 *a sloppy serving of cereal* RUNNY, watery, thin, liquid, semiliquid, mushy, gloppy.

4 *sloppy letters* SENTIMENTAL, mawkish, cloying, saccharine, sugary, syrupy; romantic; *informal* slushy, schmaltzy, lovey-dovey, soppy, cornball, corny, sappy, hokey, three-hankie.

slosh verb 1 *beer sloshed over the side of the glass* SPILL, slop, splash, flow, overflow.

2 *workers sloshed around in boots* SPLASH, squelch, wade; *informal* splosh.

3 *she sloshed more wine into her glass* POUR, slop, splash.

slot noun 1 *he slid a coin into the slot* APERTURE, slit, crack, hole, opening.

2 *I have an early time slot* SPOT, time, period, niche, space; *informal* window.

▸ verb *he slotted a cassette into the machine* INSERT, put, place, slide, slip.

sloth noun *who is responsible for the sloth of this department?* LAZINESS, idleness, indolence, slothfulness, inactivity, inertia, sluggishness, shiftlessness, apathy, acedia, listlessness, lassitude, lethargy, languor, torpidity; *literary* hebetude. ANTONYM industriousness.

slothful adjective *fatigue made him slothful* LAZY, idle, indolent, inactive, sluggish, apathetic, lethargic, listless, languid, torpid; *archaic* otiose.

slouch verb 1 *sit up straight—don't slouch!* SLUMP, hunch; loll, droop.

2 *he just slouched, pretending to work* LOUNGE, loaf, laze, loll, idle, do nothing.

▸ noun *she's no slouch* INCOMPETENT, amateur, bumbler, bungler.

slovenly adjective 1 *his slovenly appearance* SCRUFFY, untidy, messy, unkempt, ill-groomed, slatternly, disheveled, bedraggled, tousled, rumpled, frowzy; *informal* slobbish, slobby, raggedy, scuzzy. ANTONYM tidy.

2 *his work is slovenly* CARELESS, slapdash, slipshod, haphazard, hit-or-miss, untidy, messy, negligent, lax, lackadaisical, slack; *informal* sloppy, slaphappy. ANTONYM careful.

slow adjective 1 *during their walk home the donkey was annoyingly slow* UNHURRIED, leisurely, steady, sedate, slow-moving, downtempo, plodding, dawdling, sluggish, sluggardly, lead-footed, poky. ANTONYM fast.

2 *a slow process* LONG-DRAWN-OUT, time-consuming, lengthy, protracted, prolonged, gradual. ANTONYMS brief, short.

3 *he can be so slow* OBTUSE, stupid, unperceptive, insensitive, bovine, stolid, slow-witted, dull-witted, unintelligent, doltish, witless; *informal* dense, dim, dimwitted, thick, slow on the uptake, dumb, dopey, boneheaded, chowderheaded. See note at STUPID. ANTONYMS astute, bright.

4 *they were slow to voice their opinions* RELUCTANT, unwilling, disinclined, loath, hesitant, afraid, chary, shy.

5 *the slow season* SLUGGISH, slack, quiet, inactive, flat, depressed, stagnant, dead. ANTONYMS busy, hectic.

6 *a slow movie* DULL, boring, uninteresting, unexciting, uneventful, tedious, tiresome, wearisome, monotonous, dreary, lackluster. ANTONYM exciting.

▸ verb 1 *the traffic forced him to* ***slow down*** REDUCE SPEED, go slower, decelerate, brake. ANTONYM accelerate.

2 *you need to* ***slow down*** TAKE IT EASY, relax, ease up/off, take a break, slack off, let up; *informal* chill (out), hang loose.

3 *this would* ***slow up*** *our progress* HOLD BACK/UP, delay, retard, set back; restrict, check, curb, inhibit, impede, obstruct, hinder, hamper; *archaic* stay.

slowly adverb 1 *Tom walked off slowly* AT A SLOW PACE, without hurrying, unhurriedly, steadily, at a leisurely pace, at a snail's pace; *Music* adagio, lento, largo. ANTONYM quickly.

2 *her health is improving slowly* GRADUALLY, bit by bit, little by little, slowly but surely, step by step. ANTONYM by leaps and bounds.

sludge noun *they plodded through the cold sludge for nearly an hour* MUD, muck, mire, ooze, silt, alluvium; *informal* gunk, crud, gloop, gook, goo, gunge, guck, glop.

slug *informal* verb *he started slugging the other patrons.* See HIT verb sense 1.

▸ noun 1 *don't be such a slug.* See SLUGGARD.

2 *he put three slugs into him* BULLET, shot, cartridge.

sluggard noun *that sluggard attached to the sofa is my brother Lew* NE'ER-DO-WELL, layabout, do-nothing, idler, loafer, lounger, good-for-nothing, shirker, underachiever; *informal* slacker, slug, lazybones, bum, couch potato.

sluggish adjective 1 *Alex felt tired and sluggish* LETHARGIC, listless, lacking in energy, lifeless, inert, inactive, slow, torpid, languid, apathetic, weary, tired, fatigued, sleepy, drowsy, enervated; lazy, idle, indolent, slothful, sluggardly, logy; *Medicine* asthenic; *informal* dozy, dopey. ANTONYM vigorous.

2 *the economy is sluggish* INACTIVE, quiet, slow, slack, flat, depressed, stagnant. ANTONYM brisk.

sluice verb 1 *crews sluiced down the decks* WASH (DOWN), rinse, clean, cleanse.

2 *the water sluiced out* POUR, flow, run, gush, stream, course, flood, surge, spill.

slum noun *this is the slum we call home* HOVEL, rathole; (**slums**) ghetto, shantytown, skid row, shacktown.

slumber *literary* verb *the child slumbered fitfully.* See SLEEP verb.

▸ noun *an uneasy slumber.* See SLEEP noun.

slummy adjective *it was a slummy little bar down at the wharf* SEEDY, insalubrious, squalid, sleazy, run-down, down-at-heel, down-at-the-heel(s), shabby, dilapidated; *informal* scruffy, skanky, flea-bitten. ANTONYM upmarket.

slump verb 1 *he slumped into a chair* SIT HEAVILY, flop, flump, collapse, sink, fall; *informal* plunk oneself.

2 *housing prices slumped* FALL STEEPLY, plummet, tumble, drop, go down; *informal* crash, nosedive.

3 *reading standards have slumped* DECLINE, deteriorate, degenerate, worsen, slip; *informal* go downhill.

▸ noun 1 *a slump in profits* STEEP FALL, drop, tumble, downturn, downswing, slide, *informal* decline, decrease, nosedive. ANTONYM rise.

2 *an economic slump* RECESSION, economic decline, depression, slowdown, stagnation. ANTONYM boom.

slur verb *she was slurring her words* MUMBLE, speak unclearly, garble.

▸ noun *a gross slur* INSULT, slight, slander, slanderous statement, aspersion, smear, allegation.

slush noun 1 *he wiped the slush off his shoes* MELTING SNOW, wet snow, mush, sludge.

2 *informal the slush of romantic movies* SENTIMENTALITY, mawkishness, sentimentalism; *informal* schmaltz, mush, slushiness, corniness, soppiness, sappiness, hokeyness.

slut noun *she dressed like a slut and didn't act much better* PROMISCUOUS WOMAN, prostitute, whore; *informal* tart, floozy, tramp, hooker, hustler; *dated* scarlet woman, loose woman, hussy, trollop; *archaic* harlot, strumpet, wanton.

sly adjective 1 *she's rather sly* CUNNING, crafty, clever, wily, artful, guileful, tricky, scheming, devious, deceitful, duplicitous, dishonest, underhanded, sneaky; *archaic* subtle.

2 *a sly grin* ROGUISH, mischievous, impish, playful, wicked, arch, knowing.

3 *she took a sly sip of water* SURREPTITIOUS, furtive, stealthy, covert. PHRASE: **on the sly** *he's dating Peggy on the sly* IN SECRET, secretly, furtively, surreptitiously, covertly, clandestinely, on the quiet, behind someone's back; *informal* on the QT.

smack[1] noun 1 *she gave him a smack* SLAP, clout, cuff, blow, spank, rap, swat, crack, thump, punch, karate chop; *informal* whack, thwack, clip, wallop, swipe, bop, belt, bash, sock.

2 *the package landed with a smack* BANG, crash, crack, thud, thump.

3 *informal a smack on the lips* KISS, peck, smooch; *informal* smacker.

▸ verb 1 *he tried to smack her* SLAP, hit, strike, spank, cuff, clout, thump, punch, swat; box someone's ears; *informal* whack, clip, wallop, swipe, bop, belt, bash, sock, slug.

2 *the waiter smacked a plate down* BANG, slam, crash, thump; sling, fling; *informal* plunk.

▸ adverb *informal smack in the middle* EXACTLY, precisely, straight, right, directly, squarely, dead, plumb, point-blank; *informal* slap, bang, smack dab.

smack[2] noun 1 *the beer has a smack of hops* TASTE, flavor, savor.

2 *a smack of bitterness in his words* TRACE, tinge, touch, suggestion, hint, overtone, suspicion, whisper. PHRASE: **smack of** 1 *the tea smacked of tannin* TASTE OF, have the flavor of. 2 *the plan smacked of self-promotion* SUGGEST, hint at, have overtones of, give the impression of, have the stamp of, seem like; smell of, reek of.

smack[3] noun *informal they were shooting smack in the alley.* See HEROIN.

small adjective 1 *a small apartment* LITTLE, compact, bijou, tiny, miniature, mini; minute, microscopic, minuscule; toy, baby; poky, cramped, boxy; *informal* teeny, teensy, itsy-bitsy, itty-bitty, pocket-sized, half-pint, little-bitty; *Scottish* wee. ANTONYMS big, large.

2 *a very small man* SHORT, little, petite, diminutive, elfin, tiny; puny, undersized, stunted, dwarfish, midget, pygmy, Lilliputian; *Scottish* wee; *informal* teeny, pint-sized. ANTONYMS large, tall, heavily built.

3 *a few small changes* SLIGHT, minor, unimportant, trifling, trivial, insignificant, inconsequential, negligible, nugatory, infinitesimal; *informal* minuscule, piffling, piddling. ANTONYMS major, substantial.

4 *small helpings* INADEQUATE, meager, insufficient, ungenerous; *informal* measly, stingy, mingy, pathetic. ANTONYMS ample, generous.

5 *they made him feel small* FOOLISH, stupid, insignificant, unimportant; embarrassed, humiliated, uncomfortable, mortified, ashamed; crushed. ANTONYM proud.

6 *a small business* SMALL-SCALE, modest, unpretentious, humble. ANTONYMS big, large-scale, substantial.

THE RIGHT WORD

Why do we call a house **small** and a woman **petite**? *Small* and **little** are used interchangeably to describe people or things of reduced dimensions, but *small* is preferred when describing something concrete that is of less than the usual size, quantity, value, or importance (*a small matter to discuss; a small room; a small price to pay*). *Little* more often refers to concepts (*through little fault of his own; an issue of little importance*) or to a more drastic reduction in scale (*a little shopping cart just like the one her mother used*). **Diminutive** and *petite* intensify the meaning of *small*, particularly with reference to women's figures that are very trim and compact (*with her diminutive figure, she had to shop in stores that specialized in petite sizes*). **Tiny** is used to describe what is extremely small, often to the point where it can be seen only by looking closely (*a tiny flaw in the material; a tiny insect*), while **minute** not only describes what is seen with difficulty but may also refer to a very small amount of something (*minute traces of gunpowder on his glove*). **Miniature** applies specifically to a copy, a model, or a representation of something on a very small scale (*a child's mobile consisting of miniature farm animals*).

---

small change noun *check your pockets for small change* COINS, change, coppers, silver, cash, specie.

small-minded adjective *they were too small-minded to listen to our views on interracial marriage* NARROW-MINDED, petty, mean-spirited, uncharitable; close-minded, shortsighted, myopic, blinkered, inward-looking, unimaginative, parochial, provincial, insular, small-town; intolerant, illiberal, conservative, hidebound, dyed-in-the-wool, set in one's ways, inflexible; prejudiced, bigoted. ANTONYM tolerant.

small-time adjective *a small-time thief from New Haven* MINOR, small-scale; petty, unimportant, insignificant, inconsequential, minor-league; *informal* penny-ante, piddling, two-bit, bush-league, picayune. ANTONYM major.

smarmy adjective *informal his smarmy confessions make me sick* UNCTUOUS, ingratiating, slick, oily, greasy, obsequious, sycophantic, fawning; *informal* slimy, sucky.

smart adjective **1** *informal he's the smart one* CLEVER, bright, intelligent, sharp-witted, quick-witted, shrewd, astute, able; perceptive, percipient; *informal* brainy, savvy, quick on the uptake. ANTONYM stupid.

2 *you look very smart* WELL-DRESSED, stylish, chic, fashionable, modish, elegant, neat, spruce, trim, dapper; *informal* snazzy, natty, snappy, sharp, cool, spiffy, fly, kicky. ANTONYM scruffy.

3 *a smart restaurant* FASHIONABLE, stylish, high-class, exclusive, chic, fancy, upscale, upmarket, high-toned; *informal* trendy, posh, ritzy, plush, classy, swanky, glitzy, swank. ANTONYM downmarket.

4 *a smart pace* BRISK, quick, fast, rapid, swift, lively, spanking, energetic, vigorous; *informal* snappy, cracking. ANTONYM slow.

5 *a smart blow on the snout* SHARP, severe, forceful, violent. ANTONYM gentle.

▸ verb **1** *her eyes were smarting* STING, burn, tingle, prickle; hurt, ache.

2 *she smarted at the accusations* FEEL ANNOYED, feel upset, take offense, feel aggrieved, feel indignant, be put out, feel hurt.

smash verb **1** *he smashed a window* BREAK, shatter, splinter, crack, shiver; *informal* bust.

2 *she's smashed the car* CRASH, wreck, write off; *informal* total.

3 *they* ***smashed into*** *a wall* CRASH INTO, collide with, hit, strike, ram, smack into, slam into, plow into, run into, bump into, impact.

4 *Don smashed him over the head* HIT, strike, thump, punch, smack; *informal* whack, bash, bop, clout, wallop, crown, slug.

5 *he smashed their hopes of glory* DESTROY, wreck, ruin, shatter, dash, crush, devastate, demolish, overturn, scotch; *informal* put the kibosh on, scuttle.

▸ noun **1** *the smash of glass* BREAKING, shattering, crash.

2 *it was a terrible smash* CRASH, collision, accident, wreck; *informal* pileup, smash-up.

3 *informal a box-office smash* SUCCESS, sensation, sellout, triumph; *informal* (smash) hit, blockbuster, winner, knockout, wow, barn burner, biggie.

smattering noun *it's mostly modern, with a smattering of art deco* BIT, modicum, touch, soupçon; nodding acquaintance; *informal* smidgen, smidge, tad.

smear verb **1** *the table was smeared with grease* STREAK, smudge, mark, soil, dirty; *informal* splotch; *literary* besmear.

2 *smear the meat with olive oil* COVER, coat, grease; *literary* bedaub.

3 *she smeared sunblock on her skin* SPREAD, rub, daub, slap, slather, smother, plaster, slick; apply; *literary* besmear.

4 *they are trying to smear our reputation* SULLY, tarnish, blacken, drag through the mud, taint, damage, defame, discredit, malign, slander, libel, slur; *informal* do a hatchet job on; *formal* calumniate, impugn; *literary* besmirch.

▸ noun **1** *smears of blood* STREAK, smudge, daub, dab, spot, patch, blotch, mark; *informal* splotch.

2 *they printed smears about his closest aides* FALSE ACCUSATION, lie, untruth, slur, slander, libel, defamation, calumny.

smell noun *the smell of the kitchen* ODOR, aroma, fragrance, scent, perfume, redolence; bouquet, nose; stench, fetor, stink, reek, whiff; *informal* funk; *literary* miasma.

▸ verb **1** *he smelled her perfume* get a sniff of, scent, detect.

2 *the dogs smelled each other* SNIFF, nose.

3 *the cellar smells* STINK, reek, have a bad smell, whiff.

4 *it* ***smells like*** *a hoax to me* SMACK OF, have the hallmark(s) of, seem like, have the air of, suggest.

THE RIGHT WORD

Everyone appreciates the **fragrance** of fresh-cut flowers, but the **stench** from the paper mill across town is usually unwelcome. Both have a distinctive **smell**, which is the most general of these words for what is perceived through the nose, but there is a big difference between a pleasant smell and a foul one. An **odor** may be either pleasant or unpleasant, but it suggests a smell that is clearly recognizable and can usually be traced to a single source (*the pungent odor of onions*). An **aroma** is a pleasing and distinctive odor that is usually penetrating or pervasive (*the aroma of fresh-ground coffee*), while **bouquet** refers to a delicate aroma, such as that of a fine wine (*after swirling the wine around in her glass, she sniffed the bouquet*). A **scent** is usually delicate and pleasing, with an emphasis on the source rather than on an olfactory impression (*the scent of balsam associated with Christmas*). *Fragrance* and **perfume** are both associated with flowers, but *fragrance* is more delicate; a *perfume* may be so rich and strong that it is repulsive or overpowering (*the air was so dense with the perfume of lilacs that I had to go indoors*). *Stench* and **stink** are reserved for smells that are foul, strong, and pervasive, although *stink* implies a sharper sensation, while *stench* refers to a more sickening one (*the stink of sweaty gym clothes; the stench of a rotting animal*).

---

smelly adjective *get that smelly wet dog off the sofa* FOUL-SMELLING, stinking, reeking, fetid, malodorous, pungent, rank, noxious, mephitic; off, gamy, high; musty, fusty; *informal* stinky, humming, funky; *Brit. informal* minging, pongy; *literary* miasmic, noisome.

smile verb *he smiled at her* BEAM, grin (from ear to ear), dimple, twinkle; smirk, simper; leer. ANTONYM frown.

▸ noun *the smile on Sara's face* BEAM, grin, twinkle; smirk, simper; leer.

THE RIGHT WORD

The facial expression created by turning the corners of the mouth upward is commonly known as a **smile**. It can convey a wide range of emotion, from pleasure, approval, or amusement to insincerity and disinterest (*his complaint was met with a blank smile*). A **grin** is a wide smile that suggests spontaneous cheerfulness, warmth, pleasure, or amusement (*her teasing provoked an affectionate grin*). But *grin* may also describe a ferocious baring of the teeth or an angry grimace (*the grin of a skeleton*). A **simper**, on the other hand, is an expression of smugness and self-righteousness (*her simper of superiority*) as well as a silly or affected smile (*she curtsied with a girlish simper*). **Smirk** also implies an affected or self-conscious smile, but one that expresses derision or hostility (*to trick someone and then smirk as he makes a fool of himself*).

smirk verb *I hate the way they just sit there smirking* SMILE SMUGLY, simper, snicker, snigger; leer.

smite verb *literary* See HIT verb sense 1.

smitten adjective **1** *he was smitten with cholera* STRUCK DOWN, laid low, suffering, affected, afflicted, plagued, stricken.

2 *Jane's* ***smitten with*** *you* INFATUATED WITH, besotted with, in love with, obsessed with, head over heels; enamored of, attracted to, taken with; captivated by, enchanted by, under someone's spell, moonstruck by; *informal* bowled over by, swept off one's feet by, crazy about, mad about, keen on, hot on/for, gone on, sweet on, gaga for.

smog noun *the smog in LA is intolerable* FOG, haze; fumes, smoke, pollution.

smoke verb **1** *the fire was smoking* SMOLDER, emit smoke; *archaic* reek.

2 *he smoked his cigarette* PUFF ON, draw on, pull on; inhale; light; *informal* drag on, toke.

3 *they smoke their salmon* CURE, preserve, dry.

▸ noun *the smoke from the bonfire* FUMES, exhaust, gas, vapor; smog.

WORD NOTE **tabagie**

French, originally, meaning "a group of smokers who meet together in the manner of a club." It was just about to go the way of the dodo, but now suddenly a renaissance—in all of the major American cities one can find them once more, a *tabagie,* huddled together outside bars and workplaces and restaurants, united in suffering under the ban of their favorite activity. **–ZS**

smoky adjective **1** *the smoky atmosphere* SMOKE-FILLED, sooty, smoggy, hazy, foggy, murky, thick.

2 *her smoky eyes* GRAY, sooty, dark, black.

smolder verb **1** *the bonfire still smoldered* SMOKE, glow, burn.

2 *she was smoldering with resentment* SEETHE, boil, fume, burn, simmer, be boiling over, be beside oneself; *informal* be livid.

smooth adjective **1** *the smooth flat rocks* EVEN, level, flat, plane; unwrinkled, featureless; glassy, glossy, silky, polished. ANTONYMS uneven, rough.

2 *his face was smooth* CLEAN-SHAVEN, hairless. ANTONYMS rough, hairy.

3 *a smooth sauce* CREAMY, velvety, blended. ANTONYM lumpy.

4 *a smooth sea* CALM, still, tranquil, undisturbed, unruffled, even, flat, waveless, like a millpond. ANTONYMS rough, choppy.

5 *the smooth running of the equipment* STEADY, regular, uninterrupted, unbroken, fluid, fluent; straightforward, easy, effortless, trouble-free, seamless. ANTONYMS irregular, jerky.

6 *a smooth wine* MELLOW, mild, agreeable, pleasant. ANTONYMS harsh, bitter.

7 *the smooth tone of the clarinet* DULCET, soft, soothing, mellow, sweet, silvery, honeyed, mellifluous, melodious, lilting, lyrical, harmonious. ANTONYM raucous.

8 *a smooth, confident man* SUAVE, urbane, sophisticated, polished, debonair; courteous, gracious, glib, slick, ingratiating, unctuous; *informal* smarmy. ANTONYM gauche.

▸ verb **1** *she smoothed the soil* FLATTEN, level (out/off), even out/off; press, roll, steamroll, iron, plane.

2 *a plan to smooth the way for the agreement* EASE, facilitate, clear the way for, pave the way for, expedite, assist, aid, help, oil the wheels of, lubricate.

smoothly adverb **1** *her hair was combed smoothly back* EVENLY, level, flat, flush.

2 *the door closed smoothly* FLUIDLY, fluently, steadily, frictionlessly, easily; quietly.

3 *the plan had gone smoothly* WITHOUT A HITCH, like clockwork, without difficulty, easily, effortlessly, according to plan, swimmingly, satisfactorily, very well; *informal* like a dream.

smooth-talking adjective *informal a smooth-talking car salesman* PERSUASIVE, glib, plausible, silver-tongued, slick, eloquent, fast-talking; ingratiating, flattering, unctuous, obsequious, sycophantic; *informal* smarmy. ANTONYM blunt.

smother verb **1** *she tried to smother her baby* SUFFOCATE, asphyxiate, stifle, choke.

2 *we smothered the flames* EXTINGUISH, put out, snuff out, dampen, douse, stamp out, choke.

3 *we smothered ourselves with sunscreen* SMEAR, daub, spread, cover; *literary* besmear, bedaub.

4 *their granny always smothers them with affection* OVERWHELM, inundate, envelop, cocoon.

5 *she smothered a sigh* STIFLE, muffle, strangle, repress, suppress, hold back, fight back, bite back, swallow, contain, bottle up, conceal, hide; bite one's lip; *informal* keep a/the lid on.

smudge noun *a smudge of ink* STREAK, smear, mark, stain, blotch, stripe, blob, dab; *informal* splotch.

▸ verb **1** *her face was smudged with dust* STREAK, mark, dirty, soil, blotch, blacken, smear, blot, daub, stain; *informal* splotch; *literary* bedaub, besmirch.

2 *she smudged her makeup* SMEAR, streak, mess up.

smug adjective *he was feeling smug after his win* SELF-SATISFIED, self-congratulatory, complacent, superior, pleased with oneself, self-approving.

smuggle verb *they smuggled drugs across the border* IMPORT/EXPORT ILLEGALLY, traffic in, run, bootleg.

smuggler noun *it was a small uncharted island frequented by smugglers* TRAFFICKER, runner, courier; *informal* mule, moonshiner, rum-runner.

smutty adjective *he writes smutty articles for porn sites* VULGAR, rude, crude, dirty, filthy, salacious, coarse, obscene, lewd, pornographic, X-rated; risqué, racy, earthy, bawdy, suggestive, naughty, ribald, off-color; *informal* blue, raunchy, saucy; *euphemistic* adult.

snack noun *she made herself a snack* LIGHT MEAL, collation, treat, refreshments, lunch, nibbles, tidbit(s); *informal* bite (to eat).

▸ verb *don't snack on sugary foods* EAT BETWEEN MEALS, nibble, munch; *informal* graze, nosh.

snafu noun *the foreman got called in to explain this latest snafu* MUDDLE, mess, tangle, jumble, confusion; misunderstanding, misinterpretation, misconception; mistake, mix-up, bungle; *informal* hash, foul-up, screw-up.

snag noun **1** *the snag is that this might affect inflation* COMPLICATION, difficulty, catch, hitch, hiccup, obstacle, stumbling block, pitfall, problem, impediment, hindrance, inconvenience, setback, hurdle, disadvantage, downside, drawback.

2 *smooth rails with no snags* SHARP PROJECTION, jag; thorn, spur.

3 *a snag in her stocking* TEAR, rip, hole, gash, slash; run.

▸ verb **1** *she snagged her stockings* TEAR, rip.

2 *the zipper snagged on the fabric* CATCH, get caught, hook.

snake noun *the snake shed its skin* *literary* serpent; *Zoology* ophidian. See table.

▸ verb *the road snakes inland* TWIST, wind, meander, zigzag, curve.

PHRASE: **snake in the grass** *her Prince Charming turned out to be a snake in the grass* TRAITOR, turncoat, betrayer, informer, backstabber, double-crosser, quisling, Judas; fraudster, trickster, charlatan, scam artist; *informal* two-timer, rat.

SNAKES

adder	horned viper
anaconda	king cobra
asp	krait
boa	mamba
boa constrictor	massasauga
bull snake	milk snake
cobra	pit viper
constrictor	puff adder
copperhead	python
coral snake	rattlesnake
cottonmouth	rock python
death adder	sidewinder
diamondback	spitting cobra
fer-de-lance	taipan
garter snake	viper
grass snake	water moccasin
hamadryad	water snake
hognose snake	whip snake

snap verb **1** *the ruler snapped* BREAK, fracture, splinter, come apart, split, crack; *informal* bust.

2 *she snapped after years of violence* FLARE UP, lose one's self-control, freak out, go to pieces, get worked up; *informal* crack up, lose one's cool, blow one's top, fly off the handle.

3 *a dog was snapping at his heels* BITE; gnash its teeth.

4 *"Be quiet!" Anna snapped* SAY ROUGHLY, say brusquely, say abruptly, say angrily, bark, snarl, growl; retort, rejoin, retaliate; *informal* jump down someone's throat.

▸ noun **1** *she closed her purse with a snap* CLICK, crack, pop.

2 *a cold snap* PERIOD, spell, time, interval, stretch, patch.

3 *informal vacation snaps* PHOTOGRAPH, picture, photo, shot, snapshot, print, slide, frame, still; *informal* mug shot.

4 *it's **a snap** to put together* AN EASY TASK; *informal* a piece of cake, a cinch, a breeze, child's play, kid's stuff, duck soup.

PHRASES: **snap out of it** *informal you can't tell a clinically depressed person to just snap out of it* RECOVER, get a grip, pull oneself together, get over it, get better, cheer up, perk up; *informal* buck up. **snap up** *customers are snapping up these DVDs as fast as we can put them out* BUY EAGERLY, accept eagerly, jump at, take advantage of, grab, seize (on), grasp with both hands, pounce on.

snappy adjective *informal* **1** *a snappy catchphrase* CONCISE, succinct, memorable, catchy, neat, clever, crisp, pithy, witty, incisive, brief, short. ANTONYM long-winded.

2 *a snappy dresser* SMART, fashionable, stylish, chic, modish, elegant, neat, spruce, trim, dapper; *informal* snazzy, natty, sharp, nifty, cool, hip, styling, spiffy, fly. ANTONYM slovenly.

PHRASE: **make it snappy** *make it snappy, Trina, the Watsons will be here in five minutes* HURRY (UP), be quick (about it), get a move on, look lively, speed up; *informal* get cracking, step on it, move it, buck up, shake a leg; *dated* make haste.

snare noun **1** *the hare was caught in a snare* TRAP, gin, net, noose.

2 *avoid the snares of the new law* PITFALL, trap, catch, danger, hazard, peril; web, mesh.

▸ verb **1** *game birds were snared* TRAP, catch, net, bag, ensnare, entrap.

2 *he managed to snare an heiress* ENSNARE, catch, get hold of, bag, hook, land.

snarl[1] verb **1** *the wolves are snarling* GROWL, gnash one's teeth.

2 *"Shut up!" he snarled* SAY ROUGHLY, say brusquely, say nastily, bark, snap, growl; *informal* jump down someone's throat.

snarl[2] verb **1** *the rope got snarled up in a bush* TANGLE, entangle, entwine, enmesh, ravel, knot, foul.

2 *this case has snarled up the court process* COMPLICATE, confuse, muddle, jumble; *informal* mess up.

snatch verb **1** *she snatched the sandwich* GRAB, seize, take hold of, get one's hands on, take, pluck; grasp at, clutch at.

2 *informal someone snatched my bag.* See STEAL verb sense 1.

3 *informal she snatched the newborn from the hospital.* See ABDUCT.

4 *he snatched victory* SEIZE, pluck, wrest, achieve, secure, obtain; scrape.

▸ noun **1** *brief snatches of sleep* PERIOD, spell, time, fit, bout, interval, stretch.

2 *a snatch of conversation* FRAGMENT, snippet, bit, scrap, part, extract, excerpt, portion.

snazzy adjective *informal* See STYLISH.

sneak verb **1** *I sneaked out* CREEP, slink, steal, slip, slide, sidle, edge, move furtively, tiptoe, pussyfoot, pad, prowl.

2 *she sneaked a camera in* SMUGGLE, bring/take surreptitiously, bring/take secretly, bring/take illicitly, spirit, slip.

3 *he sneaked a doughnut* STEAL, take furtively, take surreptitiously; *informal* snatch.

▸ adjective **1** *a sneak attack* FURTIVE, secret, stealthy, sly, surreptitious, clandestine, covert.

2 *a sneak preview* EXCLUSIVE, private, quick.

sneaking adjective **1** *she had a sneaking admiration for him* SECRET, private, hidden, concealed, unvoiced, undisclosed, undeclared, unavowed.

2 *a sneaking feeling* NIGGLING, nagging, lurking, insidious, lingering, gnawing, persistent.

sneaky adjective *switching our place cards was a sneaky thing to do* SLY, crafty, cunning, wily, artful, scheming, devious, guileful, deceitful, duplicitous, underhanded, unscrupulous; furtive, secretive, secret, stealthy, surreptitious, clandestine, covert; *informal* foxy, shifty, dirty. ANTONYM honest.

sneer noun **1** *she had a sneer on her face* SMIRK, curl of the lip, disparaging smile, contemptuous smile, cruel smile.

2 *the sneers of others* JIBE, barb, jeer, taunt, insult, slight, affront, slur; *informal* dig.

▸ verb **1** *he looked at me and sneered* SMIRK, curl one's lip, smile disparagingly, smile contemptuously, smile cruelly.

2 *it is easy to* ***sneer at*** *them* SCOFF AT, scorn, disdain, mock, jeer at, hold in contempt, ridicule, deride, insult, slight, slur.

snicker verb *they all snickered at her* GIGGLE, titter, snigger, chortle, simper, laugh.

▸ noun *he could not suppress a snicker* GIGGLE, titter, snigger, chortle, simper.

snide adjective *at his final snide comment, she slapped him across the face* DISPARAGING, derogatory, deprecating, denigratory, insulting, contemptuous; mocking, taunting, sneering, scornful, derisive, sarcastic, spiteful, nasty, mean.

sniff verb **1** *she sniffed and blew her nose* INHALE, breathe in; snuffle.

2 *Sandra sniffed the socks and grimaced* SMELL, scent, get a whiff of.

▸ noun **1** *she gave a loud sniff* SNUFFLE, inhalation.

2 *a sniff of fresh air* SMELL, scent, whiff; lungful.

3 *informal* *the first sniff of trouble* INDICATION, hint, whiff, inkling, suggestion, whisper, trace, sign, suspicion.

PHRASES: **sniff at** *how dare you sniff at me just because I'm poor?* SCORN, disdain, hold in contempt, look down one's nose at, treat as inferior, look down on, sneer at, scoff at; *informal* turn one's nose up at. **sniff out** *informal* *McMahon and Romero were sent uptown to sniff out the source of these letters* DETECT, find, discover, bring to light, track down, dig up, hunt out, ferret out, root out, uncover, unearth.

snigger verb & noun See SNICKER.

snip verb **1** *an usher snipped our tickets* CUT, clip, slit, nick, notch.

2 ***snip off*** *the faded flowers* CUT OFF, trim (off), clip, prune, chop off, lop (off), dock, crop, sever, detach, remove, take off.

▸ noun **1** *make snips along the edge* CUT, slit, nick, notch, incision.

2 *snips of wallpaper* SCRAP, snippet, cutting, shred, remnant, fragment, sliver, bit, piece.

snippet noun *any snippet of information you can share would be appreciated* PIECE, bit, scrap, fragment, particle, shred; excerpt, extract.

snit noun *what's he in a snit about today?* STATE, temper, bad mood, fit of pique, huff, hissy fit.

snivel verb **1** *he slumped in a chair, sniveling* SNIFFLE, snuffle, whimper, whine, weep, cry; *informal* blubber, boohoo.

2 *don't snivel about what you get* COMPLAIN, mutter, grumble, grouse, groan, carp, bleat, whine; *informal* gripe, moan, grouch, beef, bellyache, whinge, sound off, kvetch.

snobbery noun *they were raised in an environment of complacent snobbery* AFFECTATION, pretension, pretentiousness, arrogance, haughtiness, airs and graces, elitism; disdain, condescension, superciliousness; *informal* snootiness, uppitiness.

snobbish adjective *the snobbish distinction between art and craft* ELITIST, snobby, superior, supercilious; arrogant, haughty, disdainful, condescending; pretentious, affected; *informal* snooty, uppity, high and mighty, la-di-da, stuck-up, hoity-toity, snotty.

WORD NOTE **elitist**

A dangerous (that is, dangerous to the culture) word to misuse. Make sure that you are really referring to a person or group that believes one sector of society is superior—smarter, richer, more aristocratic or sophisticated—to another, and therefore is more entitled to be taken seriously, listened to, assisted, and so forth. *Because of its elitist policies, the club only admitted white male millionaires.* Do not use *elitist* as a way of dismissing anything that has a contaminating association with intelligence, great literature, or high art—in other words, anything that demonstrates real quality, that upholds high standards, and that encourages us to think and to make valuable esthetic, moral, or intellectual distinctions. **—FP**

snoop *informal* verb **1** *don't* ***snoop into*** *our affairs* PRY INTO, inquire into/about, be inquisitive about/of, be curious about, poke about/around, be a busybody about, poke one's nose into; interfere in/with, meddle in/with, intrude on; *informal* be nosy about.

2 *they snooped around the building* INVESTIGATE, explore, search, nose, have a good look; prowl around.

▸ noun *he went for a snoop around* SEARCH, nose, look, prowl, ferret, poke, investigation.

snooper noun *a snooper hired by her ex-husband's lawyer* MEDDLER, busybody, eavesdropper; investigator, detective; *informal* snoop, private eye, PI, sleuth, Nosy Parker, gumshoe.

snooty adjective *informal* a dress shop that caters to snooty clientele ARROGANT, proud, haughty, conceited, aloof, superior, self-important, disdainful, supercilious, snobbish, snobby, patronizing, condescending; *informal* uppity, high and mighty, la-di-da, stuck-up, hoity-toity. ANTONYM modest.

snooze *informal* noun *a good place for a snooze* NAP, doze, sleep, rest, siesta, catnap; *informal* forty winks; *literary* slumber.

▸ verb *she gently snoozed* NAP, doze, sleep, rest, take a siesta, catnap, drop off; *informal* snatch forty winks, get some shut-eye, put one's head down, catch some Zs; *literary* slumber.

snout noun *the hound's long snout* MUZZLE, nose, proboscis, trunk.

snow noun SNOWFLAKES, flakes, snowfall, white stuff; snowdrift, snowbank, snowpack; avalanche. See table.

TYPES AND CONDITIONS OF SNOW

blizzard	packing snow
blowing snow	powder
corn snow	skiff
drift	sleet
dusting	slush
flurry/flurries	snow devil
freezing rain	snow squall
frozen granular snow	snowstorm
hard-packed snow	soft-packed snow
icy snow	wet granular snow
lake effect	wet-packed snow
loose granular snow	wet snow
machine-groomed snow	whiteout
névé	windblown snow
packed powder	

snub verb *they snubbed their hosts* REBUFF, spurn, repulse, cold-shoulder, brush off, give the cold shoulder to, keep at arm's length; ignore; insult, slight, affront, humiliate; *informal* freeze out, stiff.

▸ noun *a very public snub* REBUFF, repulse, slap in the face; humiliation, insult, slight, affront; *informal* brush-off, kiss-off, put-down.

snuff verb *snuff the candles before you leave* EXTINGUISH, put out, douse, smother, choke, blow out, quench, stub out.

snug adjective **1** *our tents were snug* COZY, comfortable, warm, welcoming, restful, reassuring, intimate, sheltered, secure; *informal* comfy. ANTONYMS bleak, unwelcoming.

2 *a snug dress* TIGHT, skintight, close-fitting, form-fitting, figure-hugging, slinky. ANTONYM loose.

snuggle verb *Kent and Maris snuggled by the fire* NESTLE, curl up, huddle (up), cuddle up, nuzzle, settle.

so See note below.

WORD NOTE **so**

This intensifying adverb, pronounced with verbal italics, has the effect of turning phrases and nouns into adjectives, as in: *I am so out of here,* or *Pashmina is so ten minutes ago,* or *I am so not interested in that movie.* The *Columbia Journalism Review's* CampaignDesk.org reported in February 2004 on blog coverage of the presidential election campaign: "[X] is still writing about WMDs or something, which is, like, so January." **—JS**

soak verb **1** *soak the beans in water* IMMERSE, steep, submerge, submerse, dip, dunk, bathe, douse, marinate, souse.

2 *we got soaked outside* DRENCH, wet through, saturate, waterlog, deluge, inundate, submerge, drown, swamp.

3 *the sweat **soaked through** his clothes* PERMEATE, penetrate, percolate, seep into, spread through, infuse, impregnate.

4 *use towels to **soak up** the water* ABSORB, suck up, blot (up), mop (up), sponge up, sop up.

soaking adjective *good Lord, look at these soaking children* DRENCHED, wet (through), soaked (through), sodden, soggy, waterlogged, saturated, sopping wet, dripping wet, wringing wet. ANTONYM parched.

soar verb **1** *the bird soared into the air* FLY, wing, ascend, climb, rise; take off, take flight. ANTONYM plummet.

2 *the gulls soared on the winds* GLIDE, plane, float, drift, wheel, hover.

3 *the cost of living soared* INCREASE, escalate, shoot up, rise, spiral; *informal* go through the roof, skyrocket.

sob verb *must she sob during every romantic scene?* WEEP, cry, shed tears, snivel, whimper; howl, bawl; *informal* blubber, boo-hoo.

sober adjective **1** *the driver was clearly sober* NOT DRUNK, clearheaded; teetotal, abstinent, abstemious, dry; *informal* on the wagon. ANTONYM drunk.

2 *a sober view of life* SERIOUS, solemn, sensible, thoughtful, grave, somber, staid, levelheaded, businesslike, down-to-earth, commonsensical, pragmatic, conservative; unemotional, dispassionate, objective, matter-of-fact, no-nonsense, rational, logical, straightforward. ANTONYM frivolous.

3 *a sober suit* SOMBER, subdued, severe; conventional, traditional, quiet, drab, plain. ANTONYM flamboyant.

▸ verb **1** *I ought to **sober up*** QUIT DRINKING, dry out, become sober.

2 *his expression sobered her* MAKE SERIOUS, subdue, calm down, quiet, steady; bring down to earth, make someone stop and think, give someone pause for thought.

sobriety noun **1** *she noted his sobriety* SOBERNESS, clearheadedness; abstinence, teetotalism, nonindulgence, abstemiousness, temperance.

2 *the mayor is a model of sobriety* SERIOUSNESS, solemnity, gravity, gravitas, dignity, levelheadedness, common sense, pragmatism, practicality, self-control, self-restraint, conservatism.

so-called adjective *your so-called dream date is hitting on our waitress* INAPPROPRIATELY NAMED, supposed, alleged, presumed, ostensible, reputed; nominal, titular, self-styled, professed, would-be, self-appointed, soi-disant.

sociable adjective *it was a sociable group, but he would rather have been with his own friends* FRIENDLY, affable, companionable, gregarious, convivial, amicable, cordial, warm, genial; communicative, responsive, forthcoming, open, outgoing, extrovert, hail-fellow-well-met, approachable; *informal* chummy, clubby. ANTONYM unfriendly.

social adjective **1** *a major social problem* COMMUNAL, community, collective, group, general, popular, civil, public, societal. ANTONYM individual.

2 *a social club* RECREATIONAL, leisure, entertainment, amusement.

3 *a uniquely social animal* GREGARIOUS, interactional; organized.

▸ noun *the club has a social once a month* PARTY, gathering, function, get-together, soiree; celebration, reunion, jamboree; *informal* bash, shindig, do. See table at PARTY.

socialism noun *my appreciation for certain aspects of socialism does not mean I'm a socialist* LEFTISM, welfarism; radicalism, progressivism, social democracy; communism, Marxism, labor movement.

socialist adjective *the socialist movement* LEFT-WING, progressive, leftist, labor, anti-corporate, antiglobalization; radical, revolutionary, militant; communist; *informal* lefty, red. ANTONYM conservative.

▸ noun *a well-known socialist* LEFT-WINGER, leftist, progressive, progressivist; radical, revolutionary; communist, Marxist; *informal* lefty, red. ANTONYM conservative.

socialize verb *these are not the type of people we want you socializing with* INTERACT, converse, be sociable, mix, mingle, get together, meet, fraternize, consort; entertain, go out; *informal* hobnob.

society noun **1** *a danger to society* THE COMMUNITY, the (general) public, the people, the population; civilization, humankind, mankind, humanity.

2 *an industrial society* CULTURE, community, civilization, nation, population.

3 *Sir Paul will help you enter society* HIGH SOCIETY, polite society, the upper classes, the elite, the smart set, the beautiful people, the beau monde, the haut monde; *informal* the upper crust, the top drawer.

4 *a local history society* ASSOCIATION, club, group, circle, fellowship, guild, lodge, fraternity, brotherhood, sisterhood, sorority, league, union, alliance.

5 *the society of others* COMPANY, companionship, fellowship, friendship, comradeship, camaraderie.

socket noun *she plugged the toaster into the wall socket* POWER OUTLET, jack, port; *informal* plug.

soda noun *a bottle of icy cold soda* POP, fizzy drink, soft drink; soda water, club soda. See table at SOFT DRINK.

sodden adjective **1** *his clothes were sodden* SOAKING, soaked (through), wet (through), saturated, drenched, sopping wet, wringing wet. ANTONYM dry.

2 *sodden fields* WATERLOGGED, soggy, saturated, boggy, swampy, miry, marshy; heavy, soft. ANTONYM arid.

sofa noun. *the sofas have been reupholstered with a more durable fabric* COUCH. See table.

SOFAS AND COUCHES

button-back sofa	futon
camelback sofa	loveseat
canapé	pullout
chaise longue	settee
chesterfield	sleeper
davenport	sofa bed
daybed	studio couch
divan	tête-à-tête

soft adjective **1** *soft fruit* MUSHY, squashy, pulpy, pappy, slushy, squishy, doughy; *informal* gooey. ANTONYM hard.

2 *soft ground* SWAMPY, marshy, boggy, miry, oozy; heavy, squelchy. ANTONYM firm.

3 *a soft cushion* SQUASHY, spongy, compressible, supple, springy, pliable, pliant, resilient, malleable. ANTONYM hard.

4 *soft fabric* VELVETY, smooth, fleecy, downy, furry, silky, silken, satiny. ANTONYMS rough, harsh.

5 *a soft wind* GENTLE, light, mild, moderate. ANTONYM strong.

6 *soft light* DIM, low, faint, subdued, muted, mellow. ANTONYM harsh.

7 *soft colors* PALE, pastel, muted, understated, restrained, subdued, subtle. ANTONYM lurid.

8 *soft voices* QUIET, low, faint, muted, subdued, muffled, hushed, whispered, stifled, murmured, gentle, dulcet; indistinct, inaudible. ANTONYMS strident, clear.

9 *soft outlines* BLURRED, vague, hazy, misty, foggy, nebulous, fuzzy, blurry, indistinct, unclear. ANTONYM sharp.

10 *he seduced her with soft words* KIND, gentle, sympathetic, soothing, tender, sensitive, affectionate, loving, amorous, warm, sweet, sentimental, pretty; *informal* mushy, slushy, schmaltzy, sappy. ANTONYM harsh.

11 *she's too soft with her students* LENIENT, easygoing, tolerant, forgiving, forbearing, indulgent, clement, permissive, liberal, lax. ANTONYM strict.

12 *informal* *he's soft in the head* FOOLISH, stupid, simple, brainless, mindless; mad, scatterbrained, featherbrained; slow, weak, feeble; *informal* dopey, dippy, scatty, loopy, flaky. ANTONYM sensible.

soft drink noun See table.

SOFT DRINKS AND OTHER NON-ALCOHOLIC BEVERAGES

ambrosia	kava
atole	kefir
batido	koumiss
birch beer	lemonade
bubble tea	lemon-lime
café au lait	lime rickey
café latte	limeade
cappuccino	malted
chai	maté
cherry cola	milkshake
chocolate milk	mineral water
cider	mochaccino
club soda	Mountain Dew™
Coca-Cola™	nectar
coconut milk	orangeade
coffee	orange soda
cola	Orangina™
cream soda	Pepsi™
diet	pop
Dr. Pepper™	refresco
egg cream	ristretto
eggnog	root beer
espresso	Russian tea
flip	sarsaparilla
float	seltzer
frappe	7-UP™
fruit juice	Shirley Temple
fruit punch	slush
ginger ale	smoothie
ginger beer	soy milk
grape soda	spritzer
green tea	tea
guarana	tisane
horchata	tonic water
iced coffee	wassail
iced tea	

soften verb **1** *she tried to soften the blow of new service cuts* ALLEVIATE, ease, relieve, soothe, take the edge off, assuage, cushion, moderate, mitigate, palliate, diminish, blunt, deaden.

2 *the winds softened* DIE DOWN, abate, subside, moderate, let up, calm, diminish, slacken, weaken. PHRASE: **soften up** *she knows how to soften up Dad just before reaching into his wallet* CHARM, win over, persuade, influence, weaken, disarm, sweeten, butter up, soft-soap.

soft-hearted adjective *he was too softhearted to give his children the discipline they needed* KIND, kindly, tenderhearted, tender, gentle, sympathetic, compassionate, humane; generous, indulgent, lenient, merciful, benevolent.

soft-pedal verb *the major candidates wish to soft-pedal the immigration issue* PLAY DOWN, make light of, make little/nothing of, set little/no store by, gloss over, deemphasize, underemphasize, downplay, understate, underplay, minimize, shrug off. ANTONYMS emphasize, exaggerate.

soggy adjective *the cushions are completely soggy from last night's rain* MUSHY, squashy, pulpy, slushy, squishy; swampy, marshy, boggy, miry; soaking, soaked through, wet, saturated, drenched.

soil[1] noun **1** *acid soil* EARTH, loam, dirt, clay, gumbo; ground.

2 *Canadian soil* TERRITORY, land, domain, dominion, region, country.

soil[2] verb **1** *he soiled his tie* DIRTY, stain, splash, spot, spatter, splatter, smear, smudge, sully, spoil, foul; *literary* begrime.

2 *our reputation is being soiled* DISHONOR, damage, sully, stain, blacken, tarnish, taint, blemish, defile, blot, smear, drag through the mud; *literary* besmirch.

sojourn *formal* noun *a sojourn in France* STAY, visit, stop, stopover; vacation.

▸ verb *they sojourned in the monastery* STAY, live, put up, stop (over), lodge, room, board; vacation.

solace noun *they found solace in each other* COMFORT, consolation, cheer, support, relief.

▸ verb *she was solaced with tea and sympathy* COMFORT, console, cheer, support, soothe, calm.

soldier noun *her daddy was a soldier in the Continental Army* FIGHTER, trooper, serviceman, servicewoman; warrior; GI; peacekeeper; *archaic* man-at-arms. PHRASE: **soldier on** *informal* . See PERSEVERE.

sole adjective *my sole excuse is that I once loved her* ONLY, one (and only), single, solitary, lone, unique, exclusive, isolated.

solecism noun **1** *a poem marred by solecisms* (GRAMMATICAL) MISTAKE, error, blunder; *informal* howler, blooper.

2 *it would have been a solecism to answer* FAUX PAS, gaffe, impropriety, social indiscretion, infelicity, slip, error, blunder, lapse; *informal* slip-up, boo-boo, goof, blooper, flub.

solely adverb *people are appointed solely on the basis of merit* ONLY, simply, just, merely, uniquely, exclusively, entirely, wholly; alone.

solemn adjective **1** *a solemn occasion* DIGNIFIED, ceremonious, ceremonial, stately, formal, courtly, majestic; imposing, awe-inspiring, splendid, magnificent, grand. ANTONYM frivolous.

2 *he looked very solemn* SERIOUS, grave, sober, somber, unsmiling, stern, grim, dour, humorless; pensive, meditative, thoughtful. ANTONYM lighthearted.

3 *a solemn promise* SINCERE, earnest, honest, genuine, firm, heartfelt, wholehearted, sworn. ANTONYM insincere.

solemnize verb *her baptism was solemnized at St. Patrick's Cathedral* PERFORM, celebrate; formalize, officiate at.

solicit verb **1** *Phil tried to solicit his help* ASK FOR, request, seek, apply for, put in for, call for, press for, beg, plead for. See note at BEG.

2 *they are solicited for their opinions* ASK, petition, importune, implore, plead with, entreat, appeal to, lobby, beg, supplicate, call on, press; *literary* beseech.

solicitous adjective *she was always solicitous about the welfare of her students* CONCERNED, caring, considerate, attentive, mindful, thoughtful, interested; anxious, worried.

solid adjective **1** *the ice cream was solid* HARD, rock-hard, rigid, firm, solidified, set, frozen, concrete. ANTONYMS liquid, gaseous.

2 *solid gold* PURE, 24-carat, unalloyed, unadulterated, genuine. ANTONYMS alloyed, plated, hollow.

3 *a solid line* CONTINUOUS, uninterrupted, unbroken, nonstop, undivided. ANTONYM broken.

4 *solid houses* WELL-BUILT, sound, substantial, strong, sturdy, durable. ANTONYM flimsy.

5 *a solid argument* WELL-FOUNDED, valid, sound, reasonable, logical, authoritative, convincing, cogent, plausible, credible, reliable. ANTONYMS untenable, incoherent.

6 *a solid friendship* DEPENDABLE, reliable, firm, unshakable, trustworthy, stable, steadfast, staunch, constant, rock-steady. ANTONYM unreliable.

7 *solid citizens* SENSIBLE, dependable, trustworthy, decent, law-abiding, upright, upstanding, worthy.

8 *the company is very solid* FINANCIALLY SOUND, secure, creditworthy, profit-making, solvent, in credit, in the black.

9 *solid support from their colleagues* UNANIMOUS, united, consistent, undivided, wholehearted. ANTONYM divided.

solidarity noun *our solidarity is what gives us the credibility and power to make changes* UNANIMITY, unity, likemindedness, agreement, accord, harmony, consensus, concurrence, cooperation, cohesion, fraternity, mutual support; *formal* concord.

solidify verb *the mixture will solidify in about nine hours at room temperature* HARDEN, set, freeze, thicken, stiffen, congeal, cake, dry, bake; ossify, calcify, fossilize, petrify. ANTONYM liquefy.

soliloquy noun *Viola ends the scene with a soliloquy* MONOLOGUE, speech, address, lecture, oration, sermon, homily, aside.

solitary adjective **1** *a solitary life* LONELY, companionless, unaccompanied, by oneself, on one's own, alone, friendless; antisocial, unsociable, withdrawn, reclusive, cloistered, hermitic, incommunicado, lonesome. ANTONYM sociable.

2 *solitary farmsteads* ISOLATED, remote, lonely, out of the way, in the back of beyond, outlying, off the beaten track/path, godforsaken, obscure, inaccessible, cutoff; secluded, private, sequestered, desolate, in the backwoods;

informal in the sticks, in the middle of nowhere, in the boondocks, in the back woods; *literary* lone. ANTONYM accessible.

3 *a solitary piece of evidence* SINGLE, lone, sole, unique; only, one, individual; odd.

solitude noun **1** *she savored her solitude* LONELINESS, solitariness, isolation, seclusion, sequestration, withdrawal, privacy, peace.

2 (**solitudes**) *solitudes in the north of the state* WILDERNESS, rural area, wilds, backwoods; desert, emptiness, wasteland; the bush, backcountry; *informal* the sticks, the boondocks.

THE RIGHT WORD

Loneliness, which refers to a lack of companionship and is often associated with unhappiness, should not be confused with **solitude**, which is the state of being alone or cut off from all human contact (*the solitude of the lighthouse keeper*). You can be in the midst of a crowd of people and still experience *loneliness*, but not *solitude*, since you are not physically alone. Similarly, if you enjoy being alone, you can have solitude without loneliness. **Lonesomeness** is more intense than *loneliness*, suggesting the downheartedness you may experience when a loved one is absent (*she experienced lonesomeness following the death of her dog*). **Desolation** is more intense still, referring to a state of being utterly alone or forsaken (*the widow's desolation*). *Desolation* can also indicate a state of ruin or barrenness (*the desolation of the volcanic islands*). **Alienation**, **disaffection**, and **estrangement** have less to do with being or feeling alone and more to do with emotions that change over time. *Alienation* is a word that suggests a feeling of unrelatedness, especially a feeling of distance from your social or intellectual environment (*alienation from society*). *Disaffection* suggests that you now feel indifference or even distaste toward someone of you were once fond of (*a wife's growing disaffection for her husband*), while *estrangement* is a voluntary disaffection that can result in complete separation and strong feelings of dislike or hatred (*a daughter's estrangement from her parents*).

solo adjective *a solo flight* UNACCOMPANIED, single-handed, companionless, unescorted, unattended, unchaperoned, independent, solitary; alone, on one's own, by oneself. ANTONYM accompanied.

▸ adverb *he went solo to the party* UNACCOMPANIED, alone, on one's own, single-handed(ly), by oneself, unescorted, unattended, unchaperoned, unaided, independently; *informal* stag. ANTONYM accompanied.

solution noun **1** *an easy solution to the problem* ANSWER, result, resolution, way out, fix, panacea; key, formula, explanation, interpretation.

2 *a solution of ammonia in water* MIXTURE, mix, blend, compound, suspension, tincture, infusion, emulsion.

solve verb *has anyone ever solved this riddle?* RESOLVE, answer, work out, find a solution to, find the key to, puzzle out, fathom, decipher, decode, clear up, straighten out, get to the bottom of, unravel, piece together, explain; *informal* figure out, crack.

solvent adjective *after years in debt, he finally knew what it meant to be solvent* FINANCIALLY SOUND, debt-free, in the black, in credit, creditworthy, solid, secure, profit-making; *Finance* unleveraged.

somber adjective **1** *somber clothes* DARK, drab, dull, dingy; restrained, subdued, sober, funereal. ANTONYM bright.

2 *a somber expression* SOLEMN, earnest, serious, grave, sober, unsmiling, stern, grim, dour, humorless; gloomy, depressed, sad, melancholy, dismal, doleful, mournful, lugubrious. ANTONYM cheerful.

somebody noun *she wanted to be a somebody* IMPORTANT PERSON, VIP, public figure, notable, dignitary, worthy; someone, (big/household) name, celebrity, star, superstar; grandee, luminary, leading light; *informal* celeb, bigwig, big shot, big cheese, hotshot, megastar. ANTONYMS nonentity, no-name.

someday adverb *someday I'll live in the countryside* SOMETIME, one (fine) day, one of these days, at a future date, sooner or later, by and by, in due course, in the fullness of time, in the long run. ANTONYM never.

somehow adverb *I knew that somehow I would find a way to buy that car* BY SOME MEANS, by any means, in some way, one way or another, no matter how, by fair means or foul, by hook or by crook, come what may.

sometime adverb **1** *I'll visit sometime* SOMEDAY, one day, one of these (fine) days, at a future date, sooner or later, by and by, in due course, in the fullness of time, in the long run. ANTONYM never.

2 *it happened sometime on Sunday* AT SOME TIME, at some point; during, in the course of.

▸ adjective *the sometime editor of the paper* FORMER, past, previous, prior, foregoing, late, erstwhile, one-time, ex-; *formal* quondam.

sometimes adverb *sometimes we have supper down on the beach* OCCASIONALLY, from time to time, now and then, every so often, once in a while, on occasion, at times, off and on, at intervals, periodically, sporadically, spasmodically, intermittently.

somewhat adverb **1** *matters have improved somewhat* A LITTLE, a bit, to some extent, (up) to a point, in some measure, rather, quite, some; *informal* kind of, kinda, sort of. ANTONYM greatly.

2 *a somewhat thicker book* SLIGHTLY, relatively, comparatively, moderately, fairly, rather, quite, marginally.

somnolent adjective **1** *he felt somnolent after lunch* SLEEPY, drowsy, tired, languid, dozy, groggy, lethargic, sluggish, enervated, torpid; *informal* snoozy, dopey, yawny; *literary* slumberous.

2 *a somnolent village* QUIET, restful, tranquil, calm, peaceful, relaxing, soothing, undisturbed, untroubled.

son noun *my oldest son is in the navy* MALE CHILD, boy, heir; descendant, offspring, scion; *informal* lad.

song noun **1** *a beautiful song* AIR, strain, ditty, melody, tune, number, track, anthem, hymn, chanty, chantey, ballad, aria.

2 *the song of the birds* CALL(S), chirping, cheeping, peeping, chirruping, warble(s), warbling, trilling, twitter; birdsong. PHRASE: **song and dance** *informal why does he have to make such a song and dance out of everything?*See FUSS noun sense 1.

songster, songstress noun *dozens of songsters turned out for the audition* SINGER, vocalist, soloist, crooner, chorister, choirboy, choirgirl, songbird, diva, chansonnier, chanteuse; alto, bass, basso profundo, baritone, contralto, tenor, soprano, mezzo (soprano); balladeer; *informal* warbler, popster, soulster, folkie; *historical* minstrel, troubadour; *archaic* melodist.

sonorous adjective **1** *a sonorous voice* RESONANT, rich, full, round, booming, deep, clear, mellow, orotund, fruity, strong, resounding, reverberant.

2 *sonorous words of condemnation* IMPRESSIVE, imposing, grandiloquent, magniloquent, high-flown, lofty, orotund, bombastic, grandiose, pompous, pretentious, overblown, turgid; oratorical, rhetorical; *informal* highfalutin.

soon adverb **1** *we'll be there soon* SHORTLY, presently, in the near future, before long, in a little while, in a minute, in a moment, in an instant, in a bit, in the twinkling of an eye, in no time, before you know it, any minute (now), any day (now), by and by; *informal* pronto, in a jiffy; *dated* directly, anon.

2 *how soon can you get here?* EARLY, quickly, promptly, speedily, punctually.

sooner adverb **1** *he should have done it sooner* EARLIER, before, beforehand, in advance, ahead of time; already.

2 *I would sooner stay* RATHER, preferably, by preference, by choice, more willingly, more readily.

WORD NOTE **Sooner or Later**

Sooner is sooner than *later,* yet "see you later" implies a reunion sooner than "see you soon." Go figure. **–DL**

soothe verb **1** *Rachel tried to soothe him* CALM (DOWN), pacify, comfort, hush, quiet, subdue, settle (down), lull, tranquilize; appease, conciliate, mollify. ANTONYM agitate.

2 *an anesthetic to soothe the pain* ALLEVIATE, ease, relieve, take the edge off, assuage, allay, lessen, palliate, diminish, decrease, dull, blunt, deaden. ANTONYM aggravate.

soothing adjective **1** *soothing music* RELAXING, restful, calm, calming, tranquil, peaceful, reposeful, tranquilizing, soporific.

2 *soothing ointment* PALLIATIVE, pain-relieving, analgesic, mild, calmative.

soothsayer noun *the most respected of the king's soothsayers* SEER, oracle, augur, prophet/prophetess, sage, prognosticator, diviner, fortune teller, crystal-gazer, clairvoyant, psychic; *literary* sibyl; *rare* haruspex.

WORD NOTE **haruspex**

In the age of bewilderment, when formal religions had not quite yet wholly seized the hearts and minds of the English-speaking people—roughly between the 12th and 16th centuries—much power was given to diviners of one kind or another, men and women who claimed to see signs—indications of future fortune—in a variety of commonplace objects and occurrences. *Pessomancers,* for example, looked for signs in the random arrangements of pebbles; *capnomancers* saw signs in smoke; *metopomancers* studied foreheads; *onychomancers* claimed to see heavenly indications in the growth of fingernails; and *tyromancers* found the future in pieces of cheese (for while *tyro* in Latin means "a young soldier" or more generally, "a beginner," in Greek it does indeed mean "cheese.") Ever eager that the language be littered with such words, both to keep the words themselves alive and the writings rich with color, I advocate rediscovering some of the more unusual of the breed, and *haruspex* fits the bill nicely. It is the kind of soothsayer who offers divinations and diagnoses from examining the entrails of animals: in rural Ecuador, for example, village *haruspices* (the plural ending follows the Latin) inspect the insides of dead guinea pigs, the better to cure the patients in their care. **–SW**

sophisticated adjective **1** *sophisticated techniques* ADVANCED, modern, state of the art, the latest, new, up-to-the-minute; innovative, trailblazing, revolutionary, futuristic, avant-garde; complex, complicated, intricate, highly evolved. ANTONYM crude.

2 *a sophisticated woman* WORLDLY, worldly-wise, experienced, enlightened, cosmopolitan, knowledgeable; urbane, cultured, cultivated, civilized, polished, refined; elegant, stylish; *informal* cool. See note at URBANE. ANTONYM naive.

sophistication noun *the shabbiest of work clothes could not disguise his sophistication* WORLDLINESS, experience; urbanity, culture, civilization, polish, refinement; elegance, style, poise, finesse, savoir faire; *informal* cool.

sophistry noun **1** *to claim this is pure sophistry* SPECIOUS REASONING, fallacy, sophism, casuistry.

2 *a speech full of sophistries* FALLACIOUS ARGUMENT, sophism, fallacy; *Logic* paralogism.

soporific adjective **1** *soporific drugs* SLEEP-INDUCING, sedative, somnolent, calmative, tranquilizing, narcotic, opiate; drowsy, sleepy, somniferous; *Medicine* hypnotic. ANTONYM invigorating.

2 *a soporific TV drama* BORING, tedious, tired, dreary, turgid, dry, mind-numbing.

▸ noun *she was given a soporific* SLEEPING PILL, sedative, calmative, tranquilizer, narcotic, opiate; *Medicine* hypnotic. ANTONYM stimulant.

soppy adjective *informal* . See SENTIMENTAL sense 2.

sorcerer, sorceress noun *he was convinced that a sorceress had cast an evil spell upon his household* WIZARD, witch, magician, warlock, enchanter, enchantress, magus; witch doctor; *archaic* mage.

sorcery noun *the practice of sorcery was strictly forbidden* (BLACK) MAGIC, the black arts, witchcraft, wizardry, enchantment, spells, incantation, witching, witchery, thaumaturgy.

sordid adjective **1** *a sordid love affair* SLEAZY, dirty, seedy, seamy, unsavory, tawdry, cheap, debased, degenerate, dishonorable, disreputable, discreditable, contemptible, ignominious, shameful, abhorrent. ANTONYM respectable.

2 *a sordid little street* SQUALID, slummy, insalubrious, dirty, filthy, mucky, grimy, shabby, messy, soiled, scummy, unclean; *informal* cruddy, grungy, crummy, scuzzy. ANTONYM immaculate.

WORD NOTE **sordid**

Sordid is a word now used more with a wink and nod than straightforwardly—there seems to be a disbelief that anything can really be sordid anymore. The primary meaning, "involving ignoble actions and motives," can certainly be found without too much looking; it's the second meaning, "arousing moral distaste and contempt" that gives us pause. **–EM**

sore adjective **1** *a sore leg* PAINFUL, hurting, hurt, aching, throbbing, smarting, stinging, agonizing, excruciating;

inflamed, sensitive, tender, raw, bruised, wounded, injured.

2 *we are in sore need of you* DIRE, urgent, pressing, desperate, parlous, critical, crucial, acute, grave, serious, drastic, extreme, life-and-death, great, terrible; *formal* exigent.

3 *informal they were sore at us* UPSET, angry, annoyed, cross, furious, vexed, displeased, disgruntled, dissatisfied, exasperated, irritated, galled, irked, put out, aggrieved, offended, affronted, piqued, nettled; *informal* aggravated, miffed, peeved, riled, teed off, ticked off.

▸ noun *a sore on his leg* INFLAMMATION, swelling, lesion; wound, scrape, abrasion, cut, laceration, graze, contusion, bruise; ulcer, boil, abscess, carbuncle.

sorrow noun 1 *he felt sorrow at her death* SADNESS, unhappiness, misery, despondency, regret, depression, despair, desolation, dejection, wretchedness, gloom, dolefulness, melancholy, woe, heartache, grief; *literary* dolor. ANTONYM joy.

2 *the sorrows of life* TROUBLE, difficulty, problem, adversity, misery, woe, affliction, trial, tribulation, misfortune, pain, setback, reverse, blow, failure, tragedy. ANTONYM joy.

▸ verb *they sorrowed over her grave* MOURN, lament, grieve, be sad, be miserable, be despondent, despair, suffer, ache, agonize, anguish, pine, weep, wail. See note at MOURN. ANTONYM rejoice.

sorrowful adjective 1 *sorrowful eyes* SAD, unhappy, dejected, regretful, downcast, miserable, downhearted, despondent, despairing, disconsolate, desolate, glum, gloomy, doleful, dismal, melancholy, mournful, woeful, woebegone, forlorn, crestfallen, heartbroken; *informal* blue, down in/at the mouth, down in the dumps.

2 *sorrowful news* TRAGIC, sad, unhappy, awful, miserable, sorry, pitiful; traumatic, upsetting, depressing, distressing, dispiriting, heartbreaking, harrowing; *formal* grievous.

sorry adjective 1 *I was sorry to hear about his accident* SAD, unhappy, sorrowful, distressed, upset, downcast, downhearted, disheartened, despondent; heartbroken, inconsolable, grief-stricken. ANTONYM glad.

2 *he felt sorry for her* FULL OF PITY, sympathetic, compassionate, moved, consoling, empathetic, concerned. ANTONYM unsympathetic.

3 *I'm sorry if I was brusque* REGRETFUL, remorseful, contrite, repentant, rueful, penitent, apologetic, abject, guilty, ashamed, sheepish, shamefaced. ANTONYM unrepentant.

4 *he looks a sorry sight* PITIFUL, pitiable, heart-rending, distressing; unfortunate, unhappy, wretched, unlucky, shameful, regrettable, awful.

▸ exclamation *"Hey, that's my foot!" "Sorry!"* APOLOGIES, excuse me, pardon me, forgive me, my mistake; *informal* my bad.

sort noun 1 *what sort of book is it?* TYPE, kind, nature, manner, variety, class, category, style; caliber, quality, form, group, set, bracket, genre, species, family, order, generation, vintage, make, model, brand, stamp, stripe, ilk, cast, grain, mold.

2 *informal he's a good sort* PERSON, individual, soul, creature, human being; character, customer; *informal* fellow, type.

▸ verb *they sorted things of similar size* CLASSIFY, class, categorize, catalog, grade, group; organize, arrange, order, marshal, assemble, systematize, systemize, pigeonhole, sort out.

PHRASES: **out of sorts** 1 *I'm feeling out of sorts* UNWELL, ill, poorly, sick, queasy, nauseous, peaked, run-down, below par; *informal* under the weather, funny, lousy, rotten, awful, crappy, off. 2 *he's out of sorts because she turned him down* GRUMPY, irritable, crabby; unhappy, sad, miserable, down, depressed, gloomy, glum, forlorn, low, in a blue funk; *informal* blue, down in the dumps. **sort of** *informal* 1 *you look sort of familiar* SLIGHTLY, faintly, remotely, vaguely; somewhat, moderately, quite, rather, fairly, reasonably, relatively; *informal* pretty, kind of, kinda. 2 *he sort of pirouetted* AS IT WERE, kind of, somehow. **sort out** *they must sort out their problems* RESOLVE, settle, solve, fix, work out, straighten out, deal with, put right, set right, rectify, iron out; answer, explain, fathom, unravel, clear up; *informal* sew up, hammer out, thrash out, patch up, figure out.

sortie noun 1 *a sortie against their besiegers* FORAY, sally, charge, offensive, attack, assault, onset, onslaught, thrust, drive.

2 *a bomber sortie* RAID, flight, mission, operation, op.

so-so adjective *informal the appetizers were exceptional, but the chowder was so-so* MEDIOCRE, indifferent, average, middle-of-the-road, middling, moderate, ordinary, adequate, fair; uninspired, undistinguished, unexceptional, unremarkable, run-of-the-mill, lackluster, 'comme ci, comme ça'; *informal* no great shakes, not up to much, okay.

soul noun 1 *seeing the soul through the eyes* SPIRIT, psyche, (inner) self, inner being, life force, vital force; individuality, makeup, subconscious, anima; *Philosophy* pneuma; *Hinduism* atman.

2 *he is the soul of discretion* EMBODIMENT, personification, incarnation, epitome, quintessence, essence; model, exemplification, exemplar, image, manifestation.

3 *not a soul in sight* PERSON, human being, individual, man, woman, mortal, creature.

4 *their music lacked soul* INSPIRATION, feeling, emotion, passion, animation, intensity, fervor, ardor, enthusiasm, warmth, energy, vitality, spirit.

soulful adjective *she gave him a soulful glance* EMOTIONAL, deep, profound, fervent, heartfelt, sincere, passionate; meaningful, significant, eloquent, expressive; moving, stirring; sad, mournful, doleful.

soulless adjective 1 *a soulless room* CHARACTERLESS, featureless, bland, dull, colorless, lackluster, dreary, drab, uninspiring, undistinguished, anemic, insipid.

2 *it was soulless work* BORING, dull, tedious, dreary, humdrum, tiresome, wearisome, uninteresting, uninspiring, unexciting, soul-destroying, mind-numbing, dry; monotonous, repetitive. ANTONYM exciting.

sound[1] noun 1 *the sound of the car* NOISE, note; din, racket, row, hubbub; resonance, reverberation. ANTONYM silence.

2 *she did not make a sound* UTTERANCE, cry, word, noise, peep.

3 *the sound of the flute* MUSIC, tone, notes.

4 *I don't like the sound of that* IDEA, thought, concept, prospect, description.

▸ verb **1** *the buzzer sounded* MAKE A NOISE, resonate, resound, reverberate, go off, blare; ring, chime, peal.

2 *drivers must sound their horns* BLOW, blast, toot, blare; operate, set off; ring.

3 *do you sound the "h"?* PRONOUNCE, verbalize, voice, enunciate, articulate, vocalize, say.

4 *she sounded a warning* UTTER, voice, deliver, express, speak, announce, pronounce.

5 *it **sounds like** a crazy idea* APPEAR, look (like), seem, strike someone as being, give every indication of being, come across as.

sound[2] adjective **1** *your heart is sound* HEALTHY, in good condition, in good shape, fit, hale and hearty, in fine fettle; undamaged, unimpaired. ANTONYM unhealthy.

2 *a sound building* WELL-BUILT, solid, substantial, strong, sturdy, durable, stable, intact, unimpaired. ANTONYMS unsafe, flimsy.

3 *sound advice* WELL-FOUNDED, valid, reasonable, logical, weighty, authoritative, reliable, well-grounded.

4 *a sound judge of character* RELIABLE, dependable, trustworthy, fair; good, sensible, wise, judicious, sagacious, shrewd, perceptive. ANTONYM unreliable.

5 *financially sound* SOLVENT, debt-free, in the black, in credit, creditworthy, secure, solid. ANTONYMS insolvent, light.

6 *a sound sleep* DEEP, undisturbed, uninterrupted, untroubled, peaceful. ANTONYM light.

sound[3] verb *sound the depth of the river* MEASURE, gauge, determine, test, investigate, survey, plumb, fathom, probe. PHRASE: **sound out** *if you'll just sound them out, you might learn something useful* INVESTIGATE, test, check, examine, probe, research, look into; canvass, survey, poll, question, interview, sample; *informal* pump.

sound[4] noun *an oil spill in the sound* CHANNEL, (sea) passage, strait(s), narrows, waterway; inlet, arm (of the sea), fjord, creek, bay; estuary.

soup noun *a cup of homemade soup* BROTH, potage, consommé, bouillon, chowder, bisque. See table.

SOUPS

alphabet soup	minestrone
bird's nest soup	miso soup
bisque	mock turtle soup
borscht	mulligatawny
bouillon	New England clam chowder
broth	oxtail
burgoo	pea soup
callaloo	pistou
chicken noodle soup	pot-au-feu
chowder	potage
cock-a-leekie	Scotch broth
congee	shchi
consommé	stracciatella
corn chowder	tomato soup
egg drop soup	turtle soup
gazpacho	vichyssoise
gumbo	won ton soup
hot and sour soup	zuppa
Manhattan clam chowder	

sour adjective **1** *sour wine* ACID, acidic, acidy, acidulated, tart, bitter, sharp, vinegary, pungent; *technical* acerbic. ANTONYM sweet.

2 *sour milk* BAD, off, turned, curdled, rancid, rank, foul, fetid; (of beer) skunky. ANTONYM fresh.

3 *a sour old man* EMBITTERED, resentful, rancorous, jaundiced, bitter; nasty, spiteful, irritable, peevish, fractious, cross, crabby, crotchety, cantankerous, disagreeable, petulant, querulous, grumpy, bad-tempered, ill-humored, sullen, surly, sulky, churlish; *informal* grouchy, cranky. ANTONYM amiable.

▸ verb **1** *the war had soured him* EMBITTER, disillusion, disenchant, poison, alienate; dissatisfy, frustrate.

2 *the dispute soured relations* SPOIL, mar, damage, harm, impair, wreck, upset, poison, blight, tarnish. ANTONYM improve.

source noun **1** *the source of the river* SPRING, origin, headspring, headwater(s); *literary* wellspring.

2 *the source of the rumor* ORIGIN, birthplace, spring, fountainhead, fount, starting point, ground zero; history, provenance, derivation, root, beginning, genesis, start, rise; author, originator, initiator, inventor. See note at ORIGIN.

3 *a historian uses primary and secondary sources* REFERENCE, authority, material, document, informant.

souse verb *a crunchy bruschetta soused in green olive oil* DRENCH, douse, soak, steep, saturate, plunge, immerse, submerge, dip, sink, dunk.

soused adjective **1** *a soused herring* PICKLED, marinated, soaked, steeped.

2 *informal he was truly soused.* See DRUNK adjective.

south adjective *refreshing south winds* SOUTHERN, southerly, meridional, austral.

souvenir noun *keep the key ring as a souvenir* MEMENTO, keepsake, reminder, remembrance, token, memorial; bomboniere; trophy, relic.

sovereign noun *the daughter of their beloved sovereign* RULER, monarch, crowned head, head of state, potentate, suzerain, overlord, dynast, leader; king, queen, emperor, empress, prince, princess, czar, royal duke, regent, mogul, emir, sheikh, sultan, maharaja, raja.

▸ adjective **1** *sovereign control* SUPREME, absolute, unlimited, unrestricted, boundless, ultimate, total, unconditional, full; principal, chief, dominant, predominant, ruling; royal, regal, monarchical.

2 *a sovereign state* INDEPENDENT, autonomous, self-governing, self-determining; nonaligned, free.

sovereignty noun **1** *their sovereignty over the islands* JURISDICTION, rule, supremacy, dominion, power, ascendancy, suzerainty, hegemony, domination, authority, control, influence. See note at JURISDICTION.

2 *the colony demanded full sovereignty* AUTONOMY, independence, self-government, self-rule, home rule, self-determination, freedom.

sow verb **1** *sow the seeds in rows* PLANT, scatter, spread, disperse, strew, disseminate, distribute, broadcast; drill, seed.

2 *the new policy has sown confusion* CAUSE, bring about, occasion, create, lead to, produce, spread, engender, generate, prompt, initiate, precipitate, trigger, provoke; culminate in, entail, necessitate; foster, foment; *literary* beget.

spa noun **1** *she spent her money at a luxury spa* HEALTH CLUB, health farm, beauty parlor.

2 *the healing waters of a spa in upstate New York* MINERAL SPRING, source; *literary* wellspring, fount.

space noun 1 *there was not enough space* ROOM, capacity, area, volume, expanse, extent, scope, latitude, margin, leeway, play, clearance.

2 *green spaces in the city* AREA, expanse, stretch, sweep, tract.

3 *the space between the timbers* GAP, interval, opening, aperture, cavity, cranny, fissure, crack, interstice, lacuna.

4 *write your name in the appropriate space* BLANK, gap, box; place.

5 *a space of seven years* PERIOD, span, time, duration, stretch, course, interval.

6 *the first woman in space* OUTER SPACE, deep space; the universe, the galaxy, the solar system; infinity.

▸ verb *the chairs were spaced widely* POSITION, arrange, range, array, dispose, lay out, locate, situate, set, stand.

spaceman, spacewoman noun *a hilarious short story about a spaceman who lands in a remote village in Kenya* ASTRONAUT, cosmonaut, space traveler.

spaceship noun *a televised report from the spaceship* SPACECRAFT, space shuttle, rocket ship.

spacious adjective *spacious accommodations* ROOMY, capacious, palatial, airy, sizable, generous, large, big, vast, immense; extensive, expansive, sweeping, rolling, rambling, open; *formal* commodious. ANTONYM cramped.

span noun 1 *a six-foot wing span* EXTENT, length, width, reach, stretch, spread, distance, range.

2 *the span of one working day* PERIOD, space, time, duration, course, interval.

▸ verb 1 *an arch spanned the stream* BRIDGE, cross, traverse, pass over.

2 *his career spanned twenty years* LAST, cover, extend, spread over, comprise.

spank verb *he would never dream of spanking his children* SMACK, slap, hit, cuff; *informal* wallop, belt, whack, tan someone's hide.

spar verb *they sparred over every little thing* QUARREL, argue, fight, disagree, differ, be at odds, be at variance, fall out, dispute, squabble, wrangle, bandy words, cross swords, lock horns, be at loggerheads; *informal* scrap, spat.

spare adjective 1 *a spare set of keys* EXTRA, supplementary, additional, second, other, alternative, alternate; emergency, reserve, backup, relief, fallback, substitute; fresh.

2 *they sold off the spare land* SURPLUS, superfluous, excessive, extra; redundant, unnecessary, inessential, unessential, unneeded, uncalled for, dispensable, disposable, expendable, unwanted; *informal* going begging.

3 *your spare time* FREE, leisure, own.

4 *a man of spare build.* See THIN adjective sense 3. See also note at THIN.

▸ verb 1 *sorry, I can't spare a quarter* AFFORD, do without, manage without, dispense with, part with, give, provide.

2 *their captors eventually spared them* PARDON, let off, forgive, reprieve, release, free; leave uninjured, leave unhurt; be merciful to, show mercy to, have mercy on, be lenient to, have pity on.

sparing adjective *a fiercely sparing man, he died rich and friendless* THRIFTY, economical, frugal, canny, careful, prudent, cautious; mean, miserly, niggardly, parsimonious, close-fisted, penny-pinching, ungenerous, close, grasping; *informal* stingy, cheap, tightfisted, tight, mingy, money-grubbing. See note at ECONOMICAL. ANTONYM lavish.

spark noun 1 *a spark of light* FLASH, glint, twinkle, flicker, flare, pinprick.

2 *not a spark of truth in the story* PARTICLE, iota, jot, whit, glimmer, atom, bit, trace, vestige, ounce, shred, crumb, grain, mite, hint, touch, suggestion, whisper, scintilla; *informal* smidgen, tad.

▸ verb *the trial sparked a furious debate* CAUSE, give rise to, lead to, occasion, bring about, start, initiate, precipitate, prompt, trigger (off), provoke, stimulate, stir up.

sparkle verb 1 *her earrings sparkled* GLITTER, glint, glisten, twinkle, flash, blink, wink, shimmer, shine, gleam; *literary* coruscate, glister.

2 *she sparkled as the hostess* BE LIVELY, be vivacious, be animated, be ebullient, be exuberant, be bubbly, be effervescent, be witty, be full of life.

▸ noun *the sparkle of the pool* GLITTER, glint, twinkle, flicker, shimmer, flash, shine, gleam; *literary* coruscation.

sparkling adjective 1 *sparkling wine* EFFERVESCENT, fizzy, carbonated, aerated, gassy, bubbly, frothy; spumante. ANTONYMS still, flat.

2 *a sparkling performance* BRILLIANT, dazzling, scintillating, exciting, exhilarating, stimulating, invigorating; vivacious, lively, vibrant, animated. ANTONYM dull.

sparse adjective *areas of sparse population* SCANT, scanty, scattered, scarce, infrequent, few and far between; meager, paltry, skimpy, limited, in short supply. ANTONYM abundant.

spartan adjective *the monk's spartan cell* AUSTERE, harsh, hard, frugal, stringent, rigorous, strict, stern, severe; ascetic, abstemious; bleak, joyless, grim, bare, stark, plain. ANTONYM luxurious.

spasm noun 1 *a muscle spasm* CONTRACTION, convulsion, cramp; twitch, jerk, tic, shudder, shiver, tremor.

2 *a spasm of coughing* FIT, paroxysm, attack, burst, bout, seizure, outburst, outbreak, access.

spasmodic adjective *the car chugged up the road with spasmodic lurches* INTERMITTENT, fitful, irregular, sporadic, erratic, occasional, infrequent, scattered, patchy, isolated, periodic, periodical, on and off; *informal* herky-jerky.

spate noun *a spate of interest in military memorabilia* SERIES, succession, run, cluster, string, rash, epidemic, outbreak, wave, flurry, rush, flood, deluge, torrent.

spatter verb *the curtains were spattered with champagne* SPLASH, bespatter, splatter, spray, sprinkle, shower, speck, speckle, fleck, mottle, blotch, mark, cover; *informal* splotch.

spawn verb *that one brief statement has spawned a blitz of criticism* GIVE RISE TO, bring about, occasion, generate, engender, originate; lead to, result in, effect, induce, initiate, start, set off, precipitate, trigger; breed, bear; *literary* beget.

speak verb 1 *she refused to speak about it* TALK, say anything/something; utter, state, declare, tell, voice, express, pronounce, articulate, enunciate, vocalize, verbalize.

2 *we spoke the other day* CONVERSE, have a conversation, talk, communicate, chat, pass the time of day, have a

word, gossip; *informal* have a confab, chew the fat; natter, shoot the breeze; *formal* confabulate.

3 *the minister spoke for two hours* GIVE A SPEECH, talk, lecture, hold forth, discourse, expound, expatiate, orate, sermonize, pontificate, declaim; *informal* spout, spiel, speechify, jaw, sound off.

4 *he was **spoken of** as a promising student* MENTION, talk about, discuss, refer to, remark on, allude to, describe.

5 *her expression spoke disbelief* INDICATE, show, display, register, reveal, betray, exhibit, manifest, express, convey, impart, bespeak, communicate, evidence; suggest, denote, reflect; *formal* evince.

6 *you must **speak to** him about his rudeness* REPRIMAND, rebuke, admonish, chastise, chide, upbraid, reprove, reproach, scold, remonstrate with, take to task; *informal* tell off, dress down, rap over the knuckles, come down on, give someone what for; *formal* castigate. PHRASES: **speak for** 1 *she speaks for the Arts Council* REPRESENT, act for, appear for, express the views of, be spokesperson for. 2 *I spoke for the motion* ADVOCATE, champion, uphold, defend, support, promote, recommend, back, endorse, sponsor, espouse. **speak out** *if you've got a grievance, then speak out* SPEAK PUBLICLY, speak openly, speak frankly, speak one's mind, sound off, stand up and be counted. **speak up** *speak up so we can hear you* SPEAK LOUDLY, speak clearly, raise one's voice; shout, yell, bellow; *informal* holler.

speaker noun *Reverend Graham is one of the guest speakers* SPEECHMAKER, lecturer, talker, speechifier, orator, declaimer, rhetorician; spokesperson, spokesman/woman, mouthpiece; reader, lector, commentator, broadcaster, narrator; *informal* spieler; *historical* demagogue, rhetor.

spear noun *a hand-carved ceremonial spear* JAVELIN, lance, assegai, harpoon, bayonet; gaff, leister; *historical* pike.

spearhead noun 1 *a Bronze Age spearhead* SPEAR TIP, spear point.

2 *the spearhead of the struggle against fascism* LEADER(S), driving force; forefront, front runner(s), front line, vanguard, van, cutting edge.

▸ verb *she spearheaded the campaign* LEAD, head, front; lead the way, be in the van, be in the vanguard.

special adjective 1 *a very special person* EXCEPTIONAL, unusual, singular, uncommon, notable, noteworthy, remarkable, outstanding, unique. ANTONYM ordinary.

2 *our town's special character* DISTINCTIVE, distinct, individual, particular, characteristic, specific, peculiar, idiosyncratic. ANTONYM general.

3 *a special occasion* MOMENTOUS, significant, memorable, signal, important, historic, festive, gala, red-letter.

4 *a special tool for cutting tiles* SPECIFIC, particular, purpose-built, tailor-made, custom-built/made.

WORD NOTE **special**

From a novel in progress: The boy no longer wanted to be special, or have a special treat, or enjoy anything special, from the time he realized that special in the sense of the Special Children's Center, where he had gone to nursery school, meant kids with cerebral palsy, muscular dystrophy, or other such ailments. **—DL**

specialist noun *he's an electronics specialist* EXPERT, authority, pundit, professional; connoisseur; master, maestro, adept, virtuoso; *informal* pro, buff, ace, whiz, hotshot, maven. ANTONYM amateur.

specialty noun 1 *his specialty was watercolors* FORTE, strong point, strength, métier, strong suit, talent, skill, bent, gift; *Brit.* speciality; *informal* bag, thing, cup of tea.

2 *a specialty of the region* DELICACY; *Brit.* speciality, fine food/product, traditional food/product.

species noun *there are several species of spadefoot toad* TYPE, kind, sort; genus, family, order, breed, strain, variety, class, classification, category, set, bracket; style, manner, form, genre; generation, vintage.

specific adjective 1 *a specific purpose* PARTICULAR, specified, fixed, set, determined, distinct, definite; single, individual, peculiar, discrete, express, precise. ANTONYM general.

2 *I gave specific instructions* DETAILED, explicit, express, clear-cut, unequivocal, precise, exact, meticulous, strict, definite. ANTONYM vague.

specification noun 1 *the clear specification of objectives* STATEMENT, identification, definition, description, setting out, framing, designation, detailing, enumeration; stipulation, prescription.

2 **(specifications)** *a shelter built to their specifications* INSTRUCTIONS, guidelines, parameters, stipulations, requirements, conditions, provisions, restrictions, order; description, details; *informal* specs.

specify verb *specify your color preferences* STATE, name, identify, define, describe, set out, frame, itemize, detail, list, spell out, enumerate, particularize, cite, instance; stipulate, prescribe.

specimen noun a specimen of his handwriting SAMPLE, example, instance, illustration, demonstration, exemplification; bit, snippet; model, prototype, pattern, dummy, pilot, trial, taster, tester.

specious adjective *specious reasoning* MISLEADING, deceptive, false, fallacious, unsound, spurious, casuistic, sophistic.

speck noun 1 *a mere speck in the distance* DOT, pinprick, spot, fleck, speckle.

2 *a speck of dust* PARTICLE, grain, atom, molecule; bit, trace.

speckled adjective *speckled eggs* FLECKED, speckly, specked, freckled, freckly, spotted, spotty, dotted, mottled, dappled.

spectacle noun 1 *a spectacle fit for a monarch* DISPLAY, show, pageant, parade, performance, exhibition, extravaganza, spectacular.

2 *they were rather an odd spectacle* SIGHT, vision, scene, prospect, vista, picture.

3 *don't make a spectacle of yourself* EXHIBITION, laughingstock, fool, curiosity.

spectacles plural noun *dated she broke the frames on her spectacles* EYEGLASSES, glasses, eyewear; *informal* specs; bifocals.

spectacular adjective 1 *a spectacular victory* IMPRESSIVE, magnificent, splendid, dazzling, sensational, dramatic, remarkable, outstanding, memorable, unforgettable. ANTONYM unimpressive.

2 *a spectacular view* STRIKING, picturesque, eye-catching,

breathtaking, arresting, glorious; *informal* out of this world. ANTONYMS unimpressive, dull.

spectator noun *the stands are brimming with eager spectators* WATCHER, viewer, observer, onlooker, looker-on, bystander, witness; commentator, reporter, monitor; *literary* beholder. ANTONYM participant.

specter noun 1 *the specters in the crypt* GHOST, phantom, apparition, spirit, wraith, shadow, presence; *informal* spook; *literary* phantasm, shade.

2 *the looming specter of war* THREAT, menace, shadow, cloud; prospect; danger, peril, fear, dread.

spectral adjective *a spectral figure darting about in a purplish fog* GHOSTLY, phantom, wraithlike, shadowy, incorporeal, insubstantial, disembodied, unearthly, otherworldly; *informal* spooky.

spectrum noun *a broad spectrum of opinion* RANGE, gamut, sweep, extent, scope, span; compass, orbit, ambit.

speculate verb 1 *they speculated about my private life* CONJECTURE, theorize, hypothesize, guess, surmise; think, wonder, muse.

2 *investors* ***speculate on*** *the stock market* GAMBLE ON, take a risk on, venture in, wager on; invest in, play.

speculative adjective 1 *any discussion is largely speculative* CONJECTURAL, suppositional, theoretical, hypothetical, putative, academic, notional, abstract; tentative, unproven, unfounded, groundless, unsubstantiated.

2 *a speculative investment* RISKY, hazardous, unsafe, uncertain, unpredictable; *informal* chancy, dicey, iffy.

speech noun 1 *he doesn't have the power of speech* SPEAKING, talking, verbal expression, verbal communication.

2 *her speech was slurred* DICTION, elocution, articulation, enunciation, pronunciation; utterance, words.

3 *an after-dinner speech* TALK, address, lecture, discourse, oration, disquisition, peroration, deliverance, presentation; sermon, homily; monologue, soliloquy; *informal* spiel.

4 *Spanish popular speech* LANGUAGE, tongue, parlance, idiom, dialect, vernacular, patois; *informal* lingo, patter, -speak, -ese.

speechless adjective *her talk of divorce left him speechless* LOST FOR WORDS, at a loss (for words), dumbstruck, dumbfounded, bereft of speech, tongue-tied, inarticulate, mute, dumb, voiceless, silent; *informal* mum. ANTONYM verbose.

speed noun 1 *the speed of their progress* RATE, pace, tempo, momentum.

2 *the speed with which they responded* RAPIDITY, swiftness, speediness, quickness, dispatch, promptness, immediacy, briskness, sharpness; haste, hurry, precipitateness; acceleration, velocity; *informal* lick, clip; *literary* celerity.

▸ verb 1 *I sped home* HURRY, rush, dash, run, race, sprint, bolt, dart, gallop, career, charge, shoot, hurtle, careen, hare, fly, zoom, scurry, scuttle, scamper, hasten; *informal* tear, belt, pelt, scoot, zip, zap, whip, hotfoot it, bomb, hightail it.

2 *he was caught speeding* DRIVE TOO FAST, exceed the speed limit.

3 *a holiday will speed his recovery* HASTEN, expedite, speed up, accelerate, advance, further, promote, boost, stimulate, aid, assist, facilitate. ANTONYMS slow, hinder.

speedily adverb *complaints are handled speedily* RAPIDLY, swiftly, quickly, fast, posthaste, at the speed of light, at full tilt; promptly, immediately, briskly; hastily, hurriedly, precipitately; *informal* PDQ (pretty damn quick), hell-bent for leather, on the double, like the wind, like (greased) lightning, lickety-split; *literary* apace.

speedy adjective 1 *a speedy reply* RAPID, swift, quick, fast; prompt, immediate, expeditious, express, brisk, sharp; whirlwind, lightning, meteoric; hasty, hurried, precipitate, breakneck, rushed; *informal* PDQ (pretty damn quick), snappy, quickie. ANTONYM slow.

2 *a speedy little car* FAST, high-speed; *informal* nippy, zippy, peppy; *literary* fleet. ANTONYM slow.

spell[1] verb *the drought spelled disaster for them* SIGNAL, signify, mean, amount to, add up to, constitute; portend, augur, herald, bode, promise; involve; *literary* betoken, foretoken, forebode. PHRASE: **spell out** *allow us to spell out the plan in detail* EXPLAIN, make clear, make plain, elucidate, clarify; specify, itemize, detail, enumerate, list, expound, particularize, catalog.

spell[2] noun 1 *the witch recited a spell* INCANTATION, charm, conjuration, formula; (**spells**) magic, sorcery, witchcraft, hex, curse.

2 *she surrendered to his spell* INFLUENCE, (animal) magnetism, charisma, allure, lure, charm, attraction, enticement; magic, romance, mystique. PHRASE: **cast a spell on** *it's as if this town cast a spell on me* BEWITCH, enchant, entrance; curse, jinx, witch, hex.

spell[3] noun 1 *a spell of dry weather* PERIOD, time, interval, season, stretch, run, course, streak, patch.

2 *a spell of dizziness* BOUT, fit, attack.

spellbinding adjective *a spellbinding tale set in the Far East* FASCINATING, enthralling, entrancing, bewitching, captivating, riveting, engrossing, gripping, absorbing, compelling, compulsive, mesmerizing, hypnotic; *informal* unputdownable. ANTONYM boring.

spellbound adjective *the audience was spellbound* ENTHRALLED, fascinated, rapt, riveted, transfixed, gripped, captivated, bewitched, enchanted, mesmerized, hypnotized; *informal* hooked.

spend verb 1 *she spent $185 on shoes* PAY OUT, dish out, expend, disburse; squander, waste, fritter away; lavish; *informal* fork out, lay out, shell out, cough up, drop, blow, splurge, pony up.

2 *the morning was spent gardening* PASS, occupy, fill, take up, while away.

3 *I've spent hours on this essay* PUT IN, devote; waste.

4 *the storm had spent its force* USE UP, consume, exhaust, deplete, drain.

spendthrift noun *he is such a spendthrift* PROFLIGATE, prodigal, squanderer, waster; *informal* big spender. ANTONYM miser.

▸ adjective *his spendthrift father* PROFLIGATE, improvident, thriftless, wasteful, extravagant, prodigal. ANTONYM frugal.

spent adjective 1 *a spent force* USED UP, consumed, exhausted, finished, depleted, drained; *informal* burnt out.

2 *that's enough—I'm spent* EXHAUSTED, tired (out), weary,

worn out, dog-tired, on one's last legs, drained, fatigued, ready to drop; *informal* done in, all in, dead on one's feet, dead beat, bushed, wiped out, frazzled, whacked, pooped, tuckered out.

spew verb *factories **spewed out** yellow smoke* EMIT, discharge, eject, expel, belch out, pour out, spout, gush, spurt, disgorge.

sphere noun **1** *a glass sphere* GLOBE, ball, orb, spheroid, globule, round; bubble.

2 *our sphere of influence* AREA, field, compass, orbit; range, scope, extent.

3 *the sphere of foreign affairs* DOMAIN, realm, province, field, area, territory, arena, department.

spherical adjective *a spherical Japanese lantern* ROUND, globular, globose, globoid, globe-shaped, spheroidal, spheric. See note at ROUND.

spic-and-span adjective *Joe's kitchen is always spick-and-span* NEAT, tidy, orderly, well-kept, shipshape, in apple-pie order; immaculate, uncluttered, trim, spruce; spotless. ANTONYM untidy.

spice noun **1** *the spices in curry powder* SEASONING, flavoring, condiment. See table.

2 *the risk added spice to their affair* EXCITEMENT, interest, color, piquancy, zest; an edge; *informal* a kick; *literary* salt.

PHRASE: **spice up** *they spiced up the party with some wild dancing* ENLIVEN, make more exciting, vitalize, perk up, put some life into, ginger up, galvanize, electrify, boost; *informal* pep up, jazz up, buck up.

SPICES

achiote	ginger
ajwain	grains of paradise
allspice	green peppercorn
angelica	horseradish
anise	juniper
aniseed	licorice
annatto	mace
arrowroot	mahaleb
asafetida	mastic
benne seed	mustard seed
berbere	nigella
black pepper	nutmeg
cacao	paprika
caraway seed	pepper
cardamom	pepper flakes
cassia	pickling spice
cayenne	pimento
celery seed	pomegranate
chicory	poppy seed
chili pepper	ras el hanout
chili powder	red pepper
cinnamon	safflower
cloves	saffron
coriander	sansho
cubeb	sassafras
cumin	sesame seed
curry powder	Sichuan pepper
dill seed	St John's bread
dukka	star anise
epazote	sumac
epices fines	tonka bean
fennel seed	turmeric
fenugreek	valerian
filé	vanilla
fingerroot	wasabi
finochio	white pepper
galangal	zahtar
garam masala	zedoary
garlic powder	

spicy adjective **1** *a spicy casserole* HOT, peppery, piquant, picante; spiced, seasoned; tasty, zesty, strong, pungent. ANTONYM bland.

2 *spicy stories* ENTERTAINING, colorful, lively, spirited, exciting, piquant, zesty; risqué, racy, scandalous, ribald, titillating, bawdy, naughty, salacious, dirty, smutty; *informal* raunchy, juicy, saucy. ANTONYM boring.

spider noun See table.

SPIDERS AND OTHER ARACHNIDS

Spiders	ray spider
American house spider	red widow
ant mimic	sac spider
argiope	shamrock spider
banana spider	sheetweb spider
barn spider	six-eyed crab spider
basilica spider	spitting spider
bird spider	star-bellied spider
black widow	tarantula
bolas spider	thick-jawed spider
bowl and doily spider	trapdoor spider
brown recluse	triangle spider
brown spider	wandering spider
brown widow	wolf spider
cave spider	wood spider
cellar spider	
cobweb weaver	**Other Arachnids**
combfooted spider	blue bug
crab spider	brown dog tick
cross spider	castor bean tick
dwarf spider	cattle tick
featherlegged spider	chigger
filmy dome spider	daddy longlegs
fishing spider	deer tick
folding-door spider	giant hairy hadrurus
funnel weaver	harvestman
furrow spider	harvest mite
garden spider	itch mite
giant crab spider	Lone Star tick
golden silk spider	mite
grass spider	pseudoscorpion
hairy mygalomorph	rabbit tick
hammock spider	scabies mite
jumping spider	schizomid
lattice spider	scorpion
lynx spider	spider mite
marbled spider	sun spider/scorpion
micrathena	tick
northern widow	velvet mite
nursery web spider	vinegarone/vinegaroon
orb weaver	water mite
ogre-faced spider	whip scorpion
orchard spider	wind scorpion
pirate spider	wood tick
platform spider	yellow vejovis
purseweb spider	

spiel noun *informal* *he launched into his spiel about life insurance* SPEECH, patter, (sales) pitch, blurb, talk; monologue; rigmarole, story, saga.

spiffy adjective *a spiffy new blazer* FASHIONABLE, well-dressed, elegant, trendy, stylish, chic, sharp, snazzy.

spike noun **1** *a metal spike* PRONG, barb, point; skewer, stake, spit; tine, pin; spur; *Mountaineering* piton.

2 *the spikes of a cactus* THORN, spine, prickle, bristle; *Zoology* spicule.

▸ verb **1** *she spiked an oyster* IMPALE, spear, skewer; pierce, penetrate, perforate, stab, stick, transfix; *literary* transpierce.

2 *informal* *his drink was spiked with drugs* ADULTERATE, contaminate, drug, lace; *informal* dope, doctor, cut.

spill verb **1** *Kevin spilled his drink* KNOCK OVER, tip over, upset, overturn.

2 *the bath water spilled onto the floor* OVERFLOW, flow, pour, run, slop, slosh, splash; leak, escape; *archaic* overbrim.

3 *students spilled out of the building* STREAM, pour, surge, swarm, flood, throng, crowd.

4 *the horse spilled its rider* UNSEAT, throw, dislodge, unhorse.

5 *informal he's spilling out his troubles to her* REVEAL, disclose, divulge, blurt out, babble, betray, tell; *informal* blab.

▸ noun **1** *an oil spill* SPILLAGE, leak, leakage, overflow, flood.

2 *she took a spill in the opening race* FALL, tumble; *informal* header, cropper, nosedive.

PHRASE: **spill the beans** *informal somebody spilled the beans about the surprise party* REVEAL ALL, tell all, give the game away, talk; *informal* let the cat out of the bag, blab, come clean.

spin verb **1** *the bike wheels are spinning* REVOLVE, rotate, turn, go round, whirl, gyrate, circle.

2 *she spun around to face him* WHIRL, wheel, twirl, turn, swing, twist, swivel, pirouette, pivot.

3 *her head was spinning* REEL, whirl, go around, swim.

4 *she spun an amusing yarn* TELL, recount, relate, narrate; weave, concoct, invent, fabricate, make up.

▸ noun **1** *a spin of the wheel* ROTATION, revolution, turn, whirl, twirl, gyration.

2 *a positive spin on the campaign* SLANT, angle, twist, bias.

3 *a quick spin to the grocery store* TRIP, jaunt, outing, excursion, journey; drive, ride, run, turn, airing, joyride.

PHRASE: **spin out** *the longer you can spin out the negotiations the better* PROLONG, protract, draw out, drag out, string out, extend, carry on, continue; fill out, pad out.

spindle noun *the spindle automatically rotates when the power is turned on* pivot, pin, rod, axle, capstan; axis.

spindly adjective **1** *he was pale and spindly* LANKY, thin, skinny, lean, spare, gangling, gangly, scrawny, bony, rangy, angular; *dated* spindle-shanked. ANTONYM stocky.

2 *spindly chairs* RICKETY, flimsy, wobbly, shaky.

spine noun **1** *he injured his spine* BACKBONE, spinal column, vertebral column; back; *technical* rachis.

2 *the spine of his philosophy* CORE, center, cornerstone, foundation, basis.

3 *the spines of a porcupine* NEEDLE, quill, bristle, barb, spike, prickle; thorn; *technical* spicule.

spine-chilling adjective *a spine-chilling ghost story* TERRIFYING, blood-curdling, petrifying, hair-raising, frightening, scaring, chilling, horrifying, fearsome; eerie, sinister, bone-chilling, ghostly; eldritch; *informal* scary, creepy, spooky. ANTONYMS comforting, reassuring.

spineless adjective *Flora could have smacked him for being so spineless* WEAK, weak-willed, weak-kneed, feeble, soft, ineffectual, irresolute, indecisive; COWARDLY, timid, timorous, fearful, faint-hearted, pusillanimous, craven, unmanly, namby-pamby, lily-livered, chicken-hearted; *informal* wimpish, wimpy, sissy, wussy, chicken, yellow, yellow-bellied, gutless. ANTONYMS bold, brave, strong-willed.

spiny adjective *spiny clumps of blackthorn* PRICKLY, spiky, thorny, bristly, bristled, spiked, barbed, scratchy, sharp; *technical* spinose, spinous.

spiral adjective *a spiral column of smoke* COILED, helical, corkscrew, curling, winding, twisting, whorled; *technical* voluted, helicoid, helicoidal.

▸ noun *a spiral of smoke* COIL, helix, corkscrew, curl, twist, gyre, whorl, scroll; *technical* volute, volution.

▸ verb **1** *smoke spiraled up* COIL, wind, swirl, twist, wreathe, snake, gyrate; *literary* gyre.

2 *prices spiraled* SOAR, shoot up, rocket, increase rapidly, rise rapidly, escalate, climb; *informal* skyrocket, go through the roof. ANTONYM fall.

3 *the economy is **spiraling downward*** DETERIORATE, decline, degenerate, worsen, get worse; *informal* go downhill, take a nosedive, go to pot, go to the dogs, hit the skids, go down the tubes. ANTONYM improve.

spire noun *the spire of a nearby church* STEEPLE, flèche.

spirit noun **1** *harmony between body and spirit* SOUL, psyche, (inner) self, inner being, inner man/woman, mind, ego, id; *Philosophy* pneuma. ANTONYMS body, flesh.

2 *a spirit haunts the island* GHOST, presence; *informal* spook. See table on page 862.

3 *that's the spirit* ATTITUDE, frame of mind, way of thinking, point of view, outlook, thoughts, ideas.

4 *she was in good spirits when I left* MOOD, frame of mind, state of mind, emotional state, humor, temper.

5 *team spirit* MORALE, esprit de corps.

6 *the spirit of the age* ETHOS, prevailing tendency, motivating force, essence, quintessence; atmosphere, mood, feeling, climate; attitudes, beliefs, principles, standards, ethics.

7 *his spirit never failed him* COURAGE, bravery, pluck, valor, strength of character, fortitude, backbone, mettle, stoutheartedness, determination, resolution, resolve, fight, grit; *informal* guts, spunk, sand, moxie.

8 *they played with great spirit* ENTHUSIASM, eagerness, keenness, liveliness, vivacity, vivaciousness, animation, energy, verve, vigor, dynamism, zest, dash, élan, panache, sparkle, exuberance, gusto, brio, pep, fervor, zeal, fire, passion; *informal* get-up-and-go.

9 *the spirit of the law* REAL/TRUE MEANING, true intention, essence, substance.

10 *he drinks spirits* STRONG LIQUOR/DRINK; *informal* hard stuff, firewater, hooch. See tables at LIQUOR and COCKTAIL. PHRASE: **spirit away** *they made up a story about having been spirited away by gypsies* WHISK AWAY/OFF, make off with, make disappear, run away with, abscond with, carry off, steal away, abduct, kidnap, snatch, seize.

WORD NOTE **ectoplasm**

I realize that this word does have a legitimate scientific usage—it's the part of the cell that lies just beneath the outer membrane—but the meaning that intrigues me has something (understandably vague and mysterious) to do with the spirits of the dead. It's the stuff ghosts are made of, or alternately, some substance that signals an active communication between spiritualist mediums and those who have, as the mediums themselves would say, passed over.

A trace of ectoplasm indicated that a ghost had visited the seance. It does make you wonder about the first moment when someone decided that there was a need for such a word, and that *ectoplasm* would do nicely. **–FP**

SPIRITS AND SPRITES

angel	jinn/jinni
apparition	kachina
banshee	kelpie
bogey/bogy	kobold
bogeyman	leprechaun
brownie	manes
cacodemon	manitou
daemon/daimon	naiad
demon	nature spirit
deva	Nereid
devil	nixie
djinn	numen
dryad	nymph
dybbuk	ogre
earth mother	ogress
eidolon	oread
elf	phantom
erlking	pixie
eudemon	poltergeist
fairy	puca
familiar spirit	puck
fiend	sea nymph
fay	shade
genie	sidh
ghost	specter
ghoul	succubus
gnome	sylph
goblin	sylvan
hamadryad	undine
hobgoblin	water sprite
imp	wraith
incubus	

spirited adjective *spirited young dancers* LIVELY, vivacious, vibrant, full of life, vital, animated, high-spirited, sparkling, sprightly, energetic, active, vigorous, dynamic, dashing, enthusiastic, passionate; determined, resolute, purposeful; *informal* feisty, spunky, take-charge, gutsy, peppy. ANTONYMS timid, apathetic, lifeless.

spiritless adjective *a spiritless performance* APATHETIC, passive, unenthusiastic, lifeless, listless, weak, feeble, spineless, languid, bloodless, insipid, characterless, submissive, meek, irresolute, indecisive; lackluster, flat, colorless, passionless, uninspired, wooden, dry, anemic, vapid, dull, boring, wishy-washy. ANTONYMS spirited, lively.

spiritual adjective **1** *your spiritual self* NONMATERIAL, incorporeal, intangible; inner, mental, psychological; transcendent, ethereal, otherworldly, mystic, mystical, metaphysical; *rare* extramundane. ANTONYM physical.

2 *spiritual writings* RELIGIOUS, sacred, divine, holy, nonsecular, church, ecclesiastical, faith-based, devotional. ANTONYM secular.

spit[1] verb **1** *Cranston coughed and spat* EXPECTORATE; *informal* hawk, gob.

2 *"Go to hell," she spat* SNAP, say angrily, hiss.

3 *the fat began to spit* SIZZLE, hiss; crackle, sputter.

▸ noun *I could just retch watching that tobaccoey spit run down his chin* SPITTLE, saliva, sputum, slobber, dribble, drool.

spit[2] noun *chicken cooked on a spit* SKEWER, brochette, rotisserie.

spite noun *he said it out of spite* MALICE, malevolence, ill will, vindictiveness, vengefulness, revenge, malignity, evil intentions, animus, enmity; *informal* bitchiness, cattiness; *literary* maleficence. ANTONYM benevolence.

▸ verb *he did it to spite me* UPSET, hurt, make miserable, grieve, distress, wound, pain, torment, injure. ANTONYM please.

PHRASE: **in spite of** *in spite of their mutual dislike, he had helped her* DESPITE, notwithstanding, regardless of, for all; undeterred by, in defiance of, in the face of; even though, although.

spiteful adjective *they made spiteful remarks about Paula* MALICIOUS, malevolent, evil-intentioned, vindictive, vengeful, malign, mean, nasty, hurtful, mischievous, wounding, cruel, unkind; *informal* bitchy, catty; *literary* malefic, maleficent. See note at VINDICTIVE. ANTONYM benevolent.

splash verb **1** *splash your face with cool water* SPRINKLE, spray, shower, splatter, slosh, slop, squirt; daub; wet.

2 *his boots were splashed with mud* SPATTER, bespatter, splatter, speck, speckle, blotch, smear, stain, mark; *informal* splotch.

3 *waves splashed against the pier* SWASH, wash, break, lap; dash, beat, lash, batter, crash, buffet; *literary* plash.

4 *children splashed in the water* PADDLE, wade, slosh; wallow; *informal* splosh; *rare* plash.

5 *the story was splashed across the front pages* BLAZON, display, spread, plaster, trumpet, publicize; *informal* splatter.

▸ noun **1** *a splash of grease on his shirt* SPOT, blob, dab, daub, smudge, smear, speck, fleck; mark, stain; *informal* splotch.

2 *a splash of soda water* DROP, dash, bit, spot, soupçon, dribble, driblet.

3 *a splash of color* PATCH, burst, streak.

PHRASE: **make a splash** *informal he always believed he would make a splash in Washington* CAUSE A SENSATION, cause a stir, attract attention, draw attention to oneself/itself, get noticed, make an impression, make an impact.

WORD NOTE **plash**

If it's good enough for Yeats, it's good enough for all of us. Familiar to basket-weavers as a synonym for *plait,* it has also this sweet secondary meaning of both "a small puddle" and "stepping into a small puddle." Gentler than a splash, and much more appealing. **–ZS**

splashy adjective *a splashy sequined gown* OSTENTATIOUS, sensational, attention-grabbing, showy, eye-catching, flashy, glitzy.

spleen noun *that doesn't give you the right to vent your spleen on me* BAD TEMPER, bad mood, ill temper, ill humor, anger, wrath, vexation, annoyance, irritation, displeasure, dissatisfaction, resentment, rancor; spite, ill feeling, malice, maliciousness, bitterness, animosity, antipathy, hostility, malevolence, venom, gall, malignance, malignity, acrimony, bile, hatred, hate; *literary* ire, choler. ANTONYM good humor.

splendid adjective **1** *splendid costumes* MAGNIFICENT, sumptuous, grand, impressive, imposing, superb, spectacular, resplendent, opulent, luxurious, deluxe, rich, fine, costly, expensive, lavish, ornate, gorgeous, glorious, dazzling, elegant, regal, handsome, beautiful; stately, majestic, princely, noble, proud, palatial; *informal* plush, posh, swanky, spiffy, ritzy, splendiferous, swank; *literary* brave. ANTONYM modest.

2 *informal* *we had a splendid holiday* EXCELLENT, wonderful, marvelous, superb, glorious, sublime, lovely, delightful, first-class, first-rate, blue-chip; *informal* super, great, amazing, fantastic, terrific, tremendous, phenomenal, sensational, heavenly, gorgeous, dreamy, grand, fabulous, fab, awesome, magic, ace, cool, mean, wicked, far out, A1, out of this world, killer; smashing, dandy, neat, divine, swell; *archaic* goodly. ANTONYM awful.

splendor noun *a wedding long remembered for its splendor* MAGNIFICENCE, sumptuousness, grandeur, impressiveness, resplendence, opulence, luxury, richness, fineness, lavishness, ornateness, glory, beauty, elegance; majesty, stateliness; *informal* ritziness, splendiferousness. ANTONYMS ordinariness, simplicity, modesty.

splenetic adjective *he wrote a characteristically splenetic article* BAD-TEMPERED, ill-tempered, angry, cross, peevish, petulant, pettish, irritable, irascible, choleric, dyspeptic, testy, tetchy, snappish, waspish, crotchety, crabby, querulous, resentful, rancorous, bilious; SPITEFUL, malicious, ill-natured, hostile, acrimonious, sour, bitter, malevolent, malignant, malign; *informal* bitchy. ANTONYM good-humored.

splice verb **1** *the ropes are spliced together* INTERWEAVE, braid, plait, entwine, intertwine, interlace, knit, mesh; *Nautical* marry.

2 *we had to splice the two sections* JOIN, attach, stick together, unite; blend, mix together.

splinter noun *a splinter of wood* SLIVER, shiver, chip, shard; fragment, piece, bit, shred; **(splinters)** matchwood, flinders.

▸ verb *the windshield splintered* SHATTER, break into tiny pieces, smash, smash into smithereens, fracture, split, crack, disintegrate, crumble.

split verb **1** *the ax split the wood* BREAK, chop, cut, hew, lop, cleave; snap, crack.

2 *the ice cracked and split* BREAK APART, fracture, rupture, fissure, snap, come apart, splinter.

3 *her dress was split* TEAR, rip, slash, slit; *literary* rend.

4 *the issue could split the party* DIVIDE, disunite, separate, sever; bisect, partition; *literary* tear asunder. ANTONYMS unite, unify.

5 *they split the money between them* SHARE (OUT), divide (up), apportion, allocate, allot, distribute, dole out, parcel out, measure out; carve up, slice up; *informal* divvy up.

6 *the path split* FORK, divide, bifurcate, diverge, branch. ANTONYMS converge, merge.

7 *they* ***split up*** *last year* BREAK UP, separate, part, part company, become estranged; divorce, get divorced. ANTONYMS get together, marry.

8 *informal* *let's split.* See LEAVE[1] sense 1.

▸ noun **1** *a split in the rock face* CRACK, fissure, cleft, crevice, break, fracture, breach.

2 *a split in the curtain* RIP, tear, cut, rent, slash, slit.

3 *a split in the governing party* DIVISION, rift, breach, schism, rupture, partition, separation, severance, scission, breakup.

4 *the acrimonious split with his wife* BREAKUP, split-up, separation, parting, estrangement, rift; divorce.

PHRASE: **split hairs** *while you're splitting hairs over who's the better parent, no one is watching the kids* QUIBBLE, cavil, carp, niggle, chop logic; *informal* nitpick; *archaic* pettifog.

spoil verb **1** *too much sun spoils the complexion* MAR, damage, impair, blemish, disfigure, blight, flaw, deface, scar, injure, harm; ruin, destroy, wreck; be a blot on the landscape. ANTONYMS improve, enhance.

2 *rain spoiled my plans* RUIN, wreck, destroy, upset, undo, mess up, make a mess of, dash, sabotage, scotch, torpedo; *informal* foul up, louse up, muck up, screw up, put the kibosh on, scuttle, do for, throw a (monkey) wrench in the works of, deep-six; *archaic* bring to naught. ANTONYMS further, help.

3 *his sisters spoil him* OVERINDULGE, pamper, indulge, mollycoddle, cosset, coddle, baby, wait on hand and foot, kill with kindness; nanny. ANTONYMS neglect, be strict with.

4 *stockpiled food may spoil* GO BAD, go off, go rancid, turn, go sour, go moldy, go rotten, rot, perish. ANTONYM keep.

PHRASE: **spoiling for** *it's obvious he's spoiling for a fight* EAGER FOR, itching for, looking for, keen to have, after, bent on, longing for.

spoils plural noun **1** *the spoils of war* BOOTY, loot, stolen goods, plunder, ill-gotten gains, haul, pickings; *informal* swag, boodle.

2 *the spoils of office* BENEFITS, advantages, perks, prize; *formal* perquisites.

spoilsport noun *what spoilsport turned down the music?* KILLJOY, misery, damper; *informal* wet blanket, party pooper.

spoken adjective *spoken communication* VERBAL, oral, vocal, viva voce, uttered, said, stated; unwritten; by word of mouth. ANTONYMS nonverbal, written.

PHRASE: **spoken for 1** *the money is spoken for* RESERVED, set aside, claimed, owned, booked. **2** *Claudine is spoken for* ATTACHED, going out with someone, in a relationship; *informal* going steady, taken.

spokesman, spokeswoman noun *he's the spokesman for our athletics program* SPOKESPERSON, representative, agent, mouthpiece, voice, official; *informal* spin doctor, PR person.

sponge verb **1** *I'll sponge your face* WASH, clean, wipe, swab; mop, rinse, sluice, swill.

2 *informal* *he lived by* ***sponging off*** *others* SCROUNGE OFF/FROM, be a parasite on, beg from; live off; *informal* freeload on, cadge from, bum off, mooch off.

sponger noun *informal* *Ida's good fortune brought out all the spongers in the family* PARASITE, hanger-on, leech, scrounger, beggar; *informal* freeloader, cadger, bum, bloodsucker, mooch, moocher, bottom feeder, schnorrer.

spongy adjective *a spongy layer of foam* SOFT, squashy, cushioned, cushiony, compressible, yielding; springy, resilient, elastic; porous, absorbent, permeable; *technical* spongiform. ANTONYMS hard, solid.

sponsor noun *the money came from sponsors* BACKER,

patron, promoter, benefactor, benefactress, supporter, partner, contributor, subscriber, friend, guarantor, underwriter; *informal* angel.

▸ verb *a bank sponsored the event* FINANCE, put up the money for, fund, subsidize, back, promote, support, contribute to, be a patron of, guarantee, underwrite; *informal* foot the bill for, pick up the tab for, bankroll.

sponsorship noun *corporate sponsorship saved the museum* BACKING, support, promotion, patronage, subsidy, funding, financing, aid, financial assistance.

spontaneous adjective **1** *a spontaneous display of affection* UNPLANNED, unpremeditated, unrehearsed, impulsive, impetuous, unstudied, impromptu, spur-of-the-moment, extempore, extemporaneous; unforced, voluntary, unconstrained, unprompted, unbidden, unsolicited; *informal* off-the-cuff. ANTONYMS planned, calculated.

2 *a spontaneous reaction to danger* REFLEX, automatic, mechanical, natural, knee-jerk, involuntary, unthinking, unconscious, instinctive, instinctual, visceral; *informal* gut. ANTONYMS conscious, voluntary.

3 *a spontaneous kind of person* NATURAL, uninhibited, relaxed, unselfconscious, unaffected, open, genuine, easy, free and easy; impulsive, impetuous. ANTONYM inhibited.

THE RIGHT WORD

If you're the kind of person who acts first and thinks about it later, your friends are likely to describe you as **spontaneous**, which means that you behave in a very natural way, without prompting or premeditation (*a spontaneous embrace*; a *spontaneous burst of applause*). Or they may call you **impulsive**, which has somewhat less positive connotations, suggesting someone who is governed by his or her own moods and whims without regard for others. Although *impulsive* behavior may be admirable (*his impulsive generosity prompted him to empty his pockets*), it is just as likely to be ugly or disruptive (*impulsive buying*; *an impulsive temper*). **Offhand** also has negative overtones, implying behavior that is spontaneous to the point of being cavalier or brusque (*her offhand remarks offended them*). **Unpremeditated** is a more formal term, often used in a legal context to describe an impulsive crime committed without forethought (*unpremeditated murder*). In the world of public speaking, an **extemporaneous** speech is one that is delivered without referring to a written text, although the speaker may have been aware that he or she would be called upon to speak, while an **impromptu** speech is one that the speaker was not expecting to give. **Improvised** is often used in the context of a musical or theatrical performance, suggesting a basic structure within which the performers are free to play in a spontaneous manner (*by its very nature, jazz is improvised*). But it has broader applications as well; in fact, anything that is devised on the spur of the moment may be described as *improvised*.

spontaneously adverb **1** *they applauded spontaneously* WITHOUT BEING ASKED, of one's own accord, voluntarily, on impulse, impulsively, on the spur of the moment, extempore, extemporaneously; *informal* off the cuff.

2 *he reacted spontaneously* WITHOUT THINKING, automatically, mechanically, unthinkingly, involuntarily, instinctively, naturally, by oneself/itself.

spooky adjective *informal* EERIE, sinister, ghostly, uncanny, weird, unearthly, mysterious; FRIGHTENING, spine-chilling, hair-raising; *informal* creepy, scary, spine-tingling.

spool noun *a spool of fishing filament* REEL, bobbin.

sporadic adjective *partly cloudy with sporadic showers* OCCASIONAL, infrequent, irregular, periodic, scattered, patchy, isolated, odd; intermittent, spasmodic, fitful, desultory, erratic, unpredictable. ANTONYMS frequent, steady, continuous.

sport noun **1** *we did a lot of sports* (COMPETITIVE) GAME(S), physical recreation, physical activity, physical exercise, athletics; pastime. See table at WINTER SPORTS.

2 *dated they were rogues out for a bit of sport* FUN, pleasure, enjoyment, entertainment, amusement, diversion.

▸ verb *he sported a beard* WEAR, have on, dress in; DISPLAY, exhibit, show off, flourish, parade, flaunt.

sporting adjective *they encourage sporting behavior among the boys* SPORTSMANLIKE, generous, gentlemanly, considerate; fair, just, honorable, decent. ANTONYMS dirty, unfair.

sporty adjective *informal* **1** *he's quite a sporty type* ATHLETIC, fit, active, energetic. ANTONYMS unfit, lazy.

2 *a sporty outfit* STYLISH, smart, jaunty; CASUAL, informal; *informal* trendy, cool, snazzy, sassy, spiffy. ANTONYMS formal, sloppy.

3 *a sporty car* FAST, speedy; *informal* nippy, zippy, peppy. ANTONYM slow.

spot noun **1** *a grease spot on the wall* MARK, patch, dot, fleck, smudge, smear, stain, blotch, blot, splash; *informal* splotch.

2 *a secluded spot* PLACE, location, site, position, point, situation, scene, setting, locale, locality, area, neighborhood, region; venue; *technical* locus.

3 *social policy has a regular spot on the agenda* POSITION, place, slot, space.

4 *informal in a tight spot* PREDICAMENT, mess, difficulty, trouble, plight, corner, quandary, dilemma; *informal* fix, jam, hole, sticky situation, can of worms, pickle, scrape, hot water, Catch-22.

▸ verb **1** *she spotted him in his car* NOTICE, see, observe, note, discern, detect, perceive, make out, recognize, identify, locate; catch sight of, glimpse; *literary* behold, espy.

2 *her clothes were spotted with grease* STAIN, mark, fleck, speckle, smudge, streak, splash, spatter; *informal* splotch.

PHRASE: **on the spot** *violators will be arrested on the spot* IMMEDIATELY, at once, right away, without delay, without hesitation, that instant, directly, there and then, then and there, forthwith, instantly, summarily, straightaway, in short order; *archaic* straightway.

spot check noun *drivers stopped at random spot checks* checkpoint, roadblock.

spotless adjective **1** *the kitchen was spotless* PERFECTLY CLEAN, ultra-clean, pristine, immaculate, shining, shiny, gleaming, spick-and-span. ANTONYM dirty.

2 *a spotless reputation* UNBLEMISHED, unsullied, untarnished, untainted, unstained, pure, whiter than white, innocent, impeccable, blameless, irreproachable, above reproach; *informal* squeaky clean, Teflon. ANTONYMS tarnished, impure.

spotlight noun *she was constantly in the spotlight* PUBLIC EYE, glare of publicity, limelight, center stage; focus of public/media attention.

▸ verb *this article spotlights the problem* FOCUS ATTENTION ON, highlight, point up, draw/call attention to, give prominence to, throw into relief, turn the spotlight on, bring to the fore.

spotted adjective **1** *spotted leaves* MOTTLED, dappled, speckled, flecked, freckled, freckly, dotted, stippled, brindle(d); *informal* splotchy. ANTONYM plain.

2 *a black-and-white spotted dress* POLKA-DOT, dotted. ANTONYM plain.

WORD NOTE stippled

Stippled, flecked, dappled, variegated, speckled, spotted, pied, larded, dominoed, polka-dotted, brindled, freckled—all the words suggesting a mixture of light and dark strike me as one-word poems. Gerard Manley Hopkins called his great lyric about dappled things "Pied Beauty," and to my ear such adjectives—and the condition they describe—seem homey, down to earth, essentially human. Nothing in our lives is pure and unalloyed; we love and we hate simultaneously, we act well and badly from one moment to the next. Our very souls are pieced together like old quilts or rag rugs. **—MD**

spotty adjective *their body of reasoning was spotty* PATCHY, uneven, inconsistent, erratic, fluctuating, irregular.

spouse noun *are spouses invited to the office party?* (LIFE) PARTNER, mate, consort; *informal* better half, other half. See also HUSBAND, WIFE.

spout verb **1** *lava was spouting from the crater* SPURT, gush, spew, erupt, shoot, squirt, spray; disgorge, discharge, emit, belch forth.

2 *there he is, **spouting off** about religion, as usual* HOLD FORTH, sound off, go on, talk at length, expatiate; *informal* mouth off, speechify, spiel.

▸ noun *a can with a spout* NOZZLE, lip.

sprawl verb **1** *he sprawled on a sofa* STRETCH OUT, lounge, loll, lie, recline, drape oneself, slump, flop, slouch.

2 *the town sprawled ahead of them* SPREAD, stretch, extend, be strung out, be scattered, straggle, spill.

spray[1] noun **1** *a spray of water* SHOWER, sprinkling, sprinkle, jet, mist, drizzle; spume, spindrift; foam, froth.

2 *a perfume spray* ATOMIZER, vaporizer, aerosol, sprinkler; nebulizer.

▸ verb **1** *water was sprayed around* SPRINKLE, shower, spatter; scatter, disperse, diffuse; mist; douche; *literary* besprinkle.

2 *water sprayed into the air* SPOUT, jet, gush, spurt, shoot, squirt.

spray[2] noun **1** *a spray of holly* SPRIG, twig.

2 *a spray of flowers* BOUQUET, bunch, posy, nosegay; corsage.

spread verb **1** *he spread the map out* LAY OUT, open out, unfurl, unroll, roll out; straighten out, fan out; stretch out, extend; *literary* outspread. ANTONYM fold up.

2 *the landscape **spread out** below* EXTEND, stretch (out), open out, be displayed, be exhibited, be on show; sprawl (out).

3 *papers were spread all over his desk* SCATTER, strew, disperse, distribute.

4 *he's been spreading rumors* DISSEMINATE, circulate, pass on, put about, communicate, diffuse, make public, make known, purvey, broadcast, publicize, propagate, promulgate; repeat; *literary* bruit about/abroad. ANTONYM suppress.

5 *she spread cold cream on her face* SMEAR, daub, plaster, slather, lather, apply, put; smooth, rub.

6 *he spread the toast with butter* COVER, coat, layer, daub; smother.

▸ noun **1** *the spread of learning* EXPANSION, proliferation, extension, growth; dissemination, diffusion, transmission, propagation.

2 *a spread of six feet* SPAN, width, extent, stretch, reach.

3 *the immense spread of the heavens* EXPANSE, area, sweep, stretch.

4 *a wide spread of subjects* RANGE, span, spectrum, sweep; variety.

5 *informal the caterers laid on a huge spread* LARGE/ELABORATE MEAL, feast, banquet; *informal* blowout, nosh.

spree noun *a spending spree* BINGE, bout, orgy, splurge, session.

sprig noun *a sprig of mistletoe* SMALL STEM, spray, twig.

sprightly adjective *sprightly Irish folk dancers* SPRY, lively, agile, nimble, energetic, active, full of energy, vigorous, spirited, animated, vivacious, frisky; *informal* full of vim and vigor. ANTONYMS doddery, lethargic.

spring verb **1** *the cat sprang off her lap* LEAP, jump, bound, vault, hop.

2 *the branch sprang back* FLY, whip, flick, whisk, kick, bounce.

3 *all art springs from feelings* ORIGINATE, derive, arise, stem, emanate, proceed, issue, evolve, come.

4 *fifty men sprang from nowhere* APPEAR SUDDENLY, appear unexpectedly, materialize, pop up, shoot up, sprout, develop quickly; proliferate, mushroom.

5 *he sprang the truth on me* ANNOUNCE SUDDENLY/UNEXPECTEDLY, reveal suddenly/unexpectedly, surprise someone with.

▸ noun **1** *with a sudden spring he leapt on to the table* LEAP, jump, bound, vault, hop; pounce.

2 *the mattress has lost its spring* SPRINGINESS, bounciness, bounce, resilience, elasticity, flexibility, stretch, stretchiness, give.

3 *there was a spring in his step* BUOYANCY, bounce, energy, liveliness, jauntiness, sprightliness, confidence.

4 *a mineral spring* SOURCE, geyser; *literary* wellspring, fount.

5 *the spring from which all her emotions poured* ORIGIN, source, fountainhead, root, roots, basis; *informal* ground zero.

springy adjective *the earth was springy beneath her feet* ELASTIC, stretchy, stretchable, tensile; flexible, pliant, pliable, whippy; bouncy, resilient, spongy. ANTONYMS rigid, squashy.

sprinkle verb **1** *he sprinkled water over the towel* SPLASH, trickle, spray, shower; spatter.

2 *sprinkle sesame seeds over the top* SCATTER, strew; drizzle, pepper.

3 *sprinkle the cake with powdered sugar* DREDGE, dust.

4 *the sky was sprinkled with stars* DOT, stipple, stud, fleck, speckle, spot, pepper; scatter, cover.

sprinkling noun **1** *a sprinkling of nutmeg* SCATTERING, sprinkle, scatter, dusting; pinch, dash.

2 *mainly women, but a sprinkling of men* FEW, one or two, couple, handful, small number, trickle, scattering.

sprint verb *the lead racers sprinted past our corner at about two o'clock* RUN, race, dart, rush, dash, hasten, hurry, scurry, scamper, hare, bolt, fly, gallop, career, charge, shoot, hurtle, speed, zoom, go like lightning, go hell-bent for leather, go like the wind; jog, trot; *informal* tear, pelt, scoot, hotfoot it, belt, zip, whip, bomb, hightail it, barrel. ANTONYM walk.

sprite noun *by light of moon the woodland sprites do dance and play* FAIRY, elf, pixie, imp, brownie, puck, peri, leprechaun; nymph, sylph, naiad. See table at SPIRIT.

sprout verb **1** *the weeds begin to sprout* GERMINATE, put/send out shoots, bud, burgeon.

2 *he had sprouted a beard* GROW, develop, put/send out.

3 *parsley sprouted from the pot* SPRING UP, shoot up, come up, grow, burgeon, develop, appear.

spruce adjective *the captain looked very spruce* NEAT, well-groomed, well-turned-out, well-dressed, smart, trim, dapper, elegant, chic; *informal* natty, snazzy, spiffy. ANTONYM untidy.

▸ verb **1** *the cottage had been* ***spruced up*** SMARTEN (UP), tidy, neaten, put in order, clean, upgrade, renovate; *informal* do up, gussy up.

2 *Sarah wanted to* ***spruce*** *herself* ***up*** GROOM, tidy, smarten (up), preen, primp; *informal* titivate, doll up.

spry adjective *isn't Aunt Helen spry for her age?* SPRIGHTLY, lively, agile, nimble, energetic, active, full of energy, full of vim and vigor, vigorous, spirited, animated, vivacious, frisky, peppy. ANTONYMS doddery, lethargic.

spume noun *the boat left a wake of white spume* FOAM, froth, surf, spindrift, bubbles.

spunk noun *informal it took a lot of spunk to blow the whistle on your own boss* COURAGE, bravery, valor, nerve, confidence, daring, audacity, pluck, spirit, grit, mettle, spine, backbone; *informal* guts, gumption, moxie; *dated, or humorous* derring-do.See note at DERRING-DO.

spur noun **1** *competition can be a spur* STIMULUS, incentive, encouragement, inducement, impetus, prod, motivation, inspiration, catalyst, springboard; *informal* kick up the backside, shot in the arm. ANTONYMS disincentive, discouragement.

2 *a spur of bone* PROJECTION, spike, point; *technical* process.

▸ verb *the thought spurred him into action* STIMULATE, encourage, prompt, propel, prod, induce, impel, motivate, move, galvanize, inspire, incentivize, urge, drive, egg on, stir; incite, goad, provoke, prick, sting, light a fire under. ANTONYM discourage.

PHRASE: **on the spur of the moment** *the decision had been made on the spur of the moment* IMPULSIVELY, on impulse, impetuously, without thinking, without premeditation, unpremeditatedly, impromptu, extempore, spontaneously; *informal* off the cuff.

spurious adjective *an attempt to be excused due to some spurious medical condition* BOGUS, fake, false, counterfeit, forged, fraudulent, sham, artificial, imitation, simulated, feigned, deceptive, misleading, specious; *informal* phony, pretend. ANTONYM genuine.

THE RIGHT WORD

These adjectives pertain to what is false or not what it appears to be, although not all have negative connotations. **Artificial** implies manmade, especially in imitation of something natural (*artificial flowers; artificial turf*). A **synthetic** substance or material is one produced by a chemical process and used as a substitute for the natural substance it resembles (*boots made from synthetic rubber*). Something that is **counterfeit** is an imitation of something else—usually something rarer, finer, or more valuable—and is intended to deceive or defraud (*counterfeit bills*). **Spurious** also means false rather than true or genuine, but it carries no strong implication of being an imitation (*spurious letters falsely attributed to Winston Churchill*). **Ersatz** refers to an artificial substitute that is usually inferior (*ersatz tea made from tree bark and herbs*). The meaning of **apocryphal**, however, is much more restricted. It applies to accounts of the past that are widely circulated but whose truth or accuracy are doubtful (*an apocryphal story about George Washington as a boy*).

spurn verb *he's been spurned by every woman he ever loved* REJECT, rebuff, scorn, turn down, treat with contempt, disdain, look down one's nose at, despise; snub, slight, jilt, dismiss, brush off, turn one's back on; give someone the cold shoulder, cold-shoulder; *informal* turn one's nose up at, give someone the brush-off, kick in the teeth, give someone the bum's rush. ANTONYMS welcome, accept.

spurt verb *water spurted from the tap* SQUIRT, shoot, jet, erupt, gush, pour, stream, pump, surge, spew, course, well, spring, burst; disgorge, discharge, emit, belch forth, expel, eject.

▸ noun **1** *a spurt of water* SQUIRT, jet, spout, gush, stream, rush, surge, flood, cascade, torrent.

2 *a spurt of courage* BURST, fit, bout, rush, spate, surge, attack, outburst, blaze.

3 *the sprinter put on a spurt* BURST OF SPEED, turn of speed, sprint, rush, burst of energy.

spy noun *a foreign spy* SECRET AGENT, intelligence agent, double agent, undercover agent, counterspy, mole, sleeper, plant, scout; *informal* snooper; *archaic* intelligencer.

▸ verb **1** *she spied for the West* BE A SPY, gather intelligence, work for the secret service; *informal* snoop.

2 *investigators* ***spied on*** *them* OBSERVE FURTIVELY, keep under surveillance/observation, watch, keep a watch on, keep an eye on.

3 *she spied a coffee shop* NOTICE, observe, see, spot, sight, catch sight of, glimpse, make out, discern, detect; *informal* clap/lay/set eyes on; *literary* espy, behold, descry.

spying noun *it will not be easy to walk away from a life of spying* ESPIONAGE, intelligence gathering, surveillance, infiltration, undercover work, cloak-and-dagger activities.

squabble noun *there was a squabble over which way they should go* QUARREL, disagreement, argument, contretemps, falling-out, dispute, clash, blowup, altercation, shouting match, row, exchange, war of words; *informal* tiff, set-to, run-in, spat, scrap, rhubarb. See note at QUARREL.

▸ verb *the boys were squabbling over a ball* QUARREL, argue, bicker, fall out, disagree, have words, dispute, spar, cross swords, lock horns, be at loggerheads; *informal* scrap.

squad noun **1** *an assassination squad* TEAM, crew, gang, band, cell, body, mob, outfit, force.

2 *a firing squad* DETACHMENT, detail, unit, platoon, battery, troop, patrol, squadron, cadre, commando.

squalid adjective **1** *a squalid prison* DIRTY, filthy, grubby, grimy, mucky, slummy, foul, vile, poor, sorry, wretched, miserable, mean, seedy, shabby, sordid, insalubrious; NEGLECTED, uncared-for, broken-down, run-down, down-at-heel, down-at-the-heel(s), depressed, dilapidated, ramshackle, tumbledown, gone to rack and ruin, crumbling, decaying; *informal* scruffy, crummy, ratty, flea-bitten. ANTONYMS clean, pleasant.

2 *a squalid deal with the opposition* IMPROPER, sordid, unseemly, unsavory, sleazy, seedy, seamy, shoddy, cheap, base, low, corrupt, dishonest, dishonorable, disreputable, despicable, discreditable, disgraceful, contemptible, shameful, underhanded. ANTONYMS proper, decent.

squall noun *the first squall we hit was just two hours after setting sail* GUST, storm, blast, flurry, shower, gale, blow, rush.

squally adjective *the squally conditions of the North Atlantic* STORMY, gusty, gusting, blustery, blustering, windy, blowy; wild, tempestuous, rough.

squalor noun *they lived in squalor* DIRT, filth, grubbiness, grime, muck, foulness, vileness, poverty, wretchedness, meanness, seediness, shabbiness, sordidness, sleaziness, NEGLECT, decay, dilapidation; *informal* scruffiness, crumminess, grunge, rattiness. ANTONYMS cleanliness, pleasantness, smartness.

squander verb *they squander their profits on expensive cars* WASTE, misspend, misuse, throw away, fritter away, spend recklessly, spend unwisely, spend like water; *informal* blow, go through, splurge, drop, pour down the drain. ANTONYMS manage, make good use of, save.

square noun **1** *a shop in the square* market square, marketplace, plaza, piazza.

2 *informal* *you're such a square!* (OLD) FOGEY, conservative, traditionalist, conformist, bourgeois, fossil; *informal* stick-in-the-mud, fuddy-duddy, prig, stuffed shirt. ANTONYM trendy.

▸ adjective **1** *a square table* QUADRILATERAL, rectangular, oblong, right-angled, at right angles, perpendicular; straight, level, parallel, horizontal, upright, vertical, true, plane. ANTONYMS crooked, uneven.

2 *the sides were square at halftime* LEVEL, even, drawn, equal, tied; neck and neck, nip and tuck, side by side, evenly matched; *informal* even-steven(s). ANTONYM uneven.

3 *I'm going to be square with you* FAIR, honest, just, equitable, straight, true, upright, aboveboard, ethical, decent, proper; *informal* on the level. ANTONYM underhanded.

4 *informal* *don't be square!* OLD-FASHIONED, behind the times, out of date, conservative, traditionalist, conventional, conformist, bourgeois, straitlaced, fogeyish, stuffy; *informal* stick-in-the-mud, fuddy-duddy. ANTONYM trendy.

▸ verb **1** *the theory does not square with the data* AGREE, tally, be in agreement, be consistent, match up, correspond, fit, coincide, accord, conform, be compatible.

2 *his goal squared the match 1–1* LEVEL, even, make equal.

3 *would you **square up** the bill?* PAY, settle, discharge, clear, meet.

4 *Bob squared things with his boss* RESOLVE, sort out, settle, clear up, work out, iron out, smooth over, straighten out, deal with, put right, set right, put to rights, rectify, remedy; *informal* patch up.

squash verb **1** *the fruit got squashed* CRUSH, squeeze, flatten, compress, press, smash, distort, pound, trample, stamp on; pulp, mash, cream, liquidize, beat, pulverize; *informal* squish, squoosh.

2 *she squashed her clothes inside the bag* FORCE, ram, thrust, push, cram, jam, stuff, pack, compress, squeeze, wedge, press.

3 *the proposal was immediately squashed* REJECT, block, cancel, scotch, frustrate, thwart, suppress, put a stop to, nip in the bud, put the lid on; *informal* put the kibosh on, stymie, scuttle, deep-six.

▸ noun *a side order of steamed squash* acorn squash, butternut squash, crookneck squash, Hubbard squash, scallop squash, spaghetti squash, summer squash, winter squash, zucchini, pumpkin, (vegetable) marrow.

squashy adjective **1** *a squashy pillow* SPRINGY, resilient, spongy, soft, pliant, pliable, yielding, elastic, cushiony, compressible. ANTONYMS firm, hard.

2 *squashy pears* MUSHY, pulpy, slushy, squelchy, squishy, oozy, doughy, soft. ANTONYMS firm, hard.

squat verb **1** *I was squatting on the floor* CROUCH (DOWN), hunker (down), sit on one's haunches, sit on one's heels.

2 *they are squatting on private land* OCCUPY ILLEGALLY, set up residence, dwell, settle, live.

▸ adjective *he was muscular and squat* STOCKY, thickset, dumpy, stubby, stumpy, short, small; *informal, humorous* vertically challenged.

▸ noun *informal* *they gave me squat.* See DIDDLY-SQUAT.

squawk verb & noun *a pheasant squawked | the gull gave a squawk* SCREECH, squeal, shriek, scream, croak, crow, caw, cluck, cackle, hoot, cry, call.

squeak noun & verb **1** *the vole's squeak | the rat squeaked* PEEP, cheep, pipe, piping, squeal, tweet, yelp, whimper.

2 *the squeak of the hinge | the hinges of the gate squeaked* SCREECH, creak, scrape, grate, rasp, jar, groan.

squeal noun *the harsh squeal of a fox* SCREECH, scream, shriek, squawk.

▸ verb **1** *a dog squealed* SCREECH, scream, shriek, squawk.

2 *the bookies only squealed because we beat them* COMPLAIN, protest, object, grouse, grumble, whine, wail, carp, squawk; *informal* kick up a fuss, gripe, grouch, bellyache, moan, bitch, beef, whinge.

3 *informal* *he **squealed on** the rest of the gang to the police* INFORM ON, tell tales on; report, give away, be disloyal to, sell out, stab in the back; *informal* rat on, rat out, snitch on, put the finger on, finger, sell down the river.

squeamish adjective **1** *I'm too squeamish to gut fish | are you squeamish about a little blood?* EASILY NAUSEATED, nervous; (**squeamish about**) PUT OFF BY, not able to stand the sight of.

2 *less squeamish nations will sell them arms* SCRUPULOUS, principled, fastidious, particular, punctilious, honorable, upright, upstanding, high-minded, righteous, right-minded, moral, ethical.

squeeze verb 1 *I squeezed the bottle* COMPRESS, press, crush, squash, pinch, nip, grasp, grip, clutch, flatten.

2 *squeeze the juice from both oranges* EXTRACT, press, force, express.

3 *Sally squeezed her feet into the sandals* FORCE, thrust, cram, ram, jam, stuff, pack, wedge, press, squash.

4 *we all squeezed into Steve's van* CROWD, crush, cram, pack, jam, squash, wedge oneself, shove, push, force one's way.

5 *he would squeeze more money out of Bill* EXTORT, force, extract, wrest, wring, milk; *informal* bleed.

▸ noun 1 *he gave her hand a squeeze* PRESS, pinch, nip; grasp, grip, clutch, hug, clasp; compression.

2 *it was a tight squeeze in the tiny hall* CRUSH, jam, squash, press, huddle; congestion.

3 *a squeeze of lemon juice* FEW DROPS, dash, splash, dribble, trickle, spot, hint, touch.

squiggle noun *their logo is the one with the two purple squiggles above the letter "Q"* WAVY LINE, doodle.

squint verb 1 *the sun made them squint* SCREW UP ONE'S EYES, narrow one's eyes, peer, blink.

2 *he has squinted from birth* BE CROSS-EYED, have a squint, suffer from strabismus.

▸ noun 1 *informal we must have another squint at his records* LOOK, glance, peep, peek, glimpse; view, examination, study, inspection, scan, sight; *informal* eyeful, gander, look-see, once-over.

2 *does he have **a squint**?* CROSS-EYES, strabismus.

squire noun 1 *the squire of the village* LANDOWNER, landholder, landlord, lord of the manor, country gentleman.

2 *historical his squire carried a banner* ATTENDANT, courtier, equerry, aide, steward, page boy.

squirm verb 1 *I tried to squirm away* WRIGGLE, wiggle, writhe, twist, slide, slither, turn, shift, fidget, jiggle, twitch, thresh, flounder, flail, toss and turn.

2 *he squirmed as everyone laughed* WINCE, shudder, feel embarrassed, feel ashamed.

squirrel noun. *prairie dogs share certain characteristics with their sciurine cousins, those familiar gray squirrels of park and patio.* See note below. See also table at RODENT. PHRASE: **squirrel away** *my intention was to squirrel away this money for a new car* SAVE, put aside, put by, lay by, set aside, lay aside, keep in reserve, stockpile, accumulate, stock up with/on, hoard; *informal* salt away, stash away.

WORD NOTE **sciurine**

Murine, porcine, feline, ursine . . . all perfectly nice. But the squirrel's nomenclature has a particular charm. From the Greek *skiouros* (*skia* shadow + *oura* tail), the description is not merely zoological, it is also poetic and descriptively sound. Also, the enjoyments that can be found nailing a human face to its animal double are multiplied with *sciurine.* Many men look *porcine,* and many women *feline,* so many that the description feels cloudy and general. However, a *sciurine* face is such a specific, singular, and fatal resemblance that the user may conjure up the entire physical character of a person with just this one word. **–ZS**

squirt verb 1 *a jet of ink squirted out of the tube* SPURT, shoot, spray, fountain, jet, erupt; gush, rush, pump, surge, stream, spew, well, spring, burst, issue, emanate; emit, belch forth, expel, eject.

2 *she squirted me with cologne* SPLASH, wet, spray, shower, spatter, splatter, sprinkle; *literary* besprinkle.

▸ noun 1 *a squirt of water* SPURT, jet, spray, fountain, gush, stream, surge.

2 *informal he was just a little squirt* IMPUDENT PERSON, insignificant person, gnat, insect; *informal* pipsqueak, whippersnapper, picayune.

stab verb 1 *a soldier stabbed the civilian* KNIFE, run through, skewer, spear, bayonet, gore, spike, stick, impale, transfix, pierce, prick, puncture; *literary* transpierce.

2 *she stabbed at the earth with a fork* LUNGE, thrust, jab, poke, prod, dig.

▸ noun 1 *a stab in the leg* KNIFE WOUND, puncture, incision, prick, cut, perforation.

2 *they made stabs into the air* LUNGE, thrust, jab, poke, prod, dig, punch.

3 *a stab of pain* TWINGE, pang, throb, spasm, cramp, dart, prick, flash, thrill.

4 *informal he took a stab at writing* ATTEMPT, try, effort, endeavor; guess; *informal* go, shot, crack, bash, whack; *formal* essay.

PHRASE: **stab in the back** *just two months after I got her hired, she stabbed me in the back* BETRAY, be disloyal to, be unfaithful to, desert, break one's promise to, double-cross, break faith with, sell out, play false, inform on/against; *informal* tell on, sell down the river, squeal on, rat out, finger.

stability noun 1 *the stability of playground equipment* FIRMNESS, solidity, steadiness, strength, security, safety.

2 *his mental stability* BALANCE OF MIND, mental health, sanity, normality, soundness, rationality, reason, sense.

3 *the stability of their relationship* STEADINESS, firmness, solidity, strength, durability, lasting nature, enduring nature, permanence, changelessness, invariability, immutability, indestructibility, reliability, dependability.

stable adjective 1 *a stable tent* FIRM, solid, steady, secure, fixed, fast, safe, moored, anchored, stuck down, immovable. ANTONYMS rickety, wobbly.

2 *a stable person* WELL-BALANCED, of sound mind, compos mentis, sane, normal, right in the head, rational, steady, reasonable, sensible, sober, down-to-earth, matter-of-fact, having both one's feet on the ground; *informal* all there. ANTONYM unbalanced.

3 *a stable relationship* SECURE, solid, strong, steady, firm, sure, steadfast, unwavering, unvarying, unfaltering, unfluctuating; established, abiding, durable, enduring, lasting, permanent, reliable, dependable. ANTONYMS rocky, changeable.

stack noun 1 *a stack of boxes* HEAP, pile, mound, mountain, pyramid, tower.

2 *a stack of hay* HAYSTACK, rick, hayrick, mow, shock, haycock; *dated* cock.

3 *informal a stack of money.* See LOT pronoun.

4 CHIMNEY, smokestack, funnel, exhaust pipe.

▸ verb 1 *Leo was stacking plates* HEAP (UP), pile (up), make a heap/pile/stack of; assemble, put together, collect, hoard, store, stockpile.

2 *they stacked the shelves* LOAD, fill (up), lade, pack, charge, stuff, cram; stock. ANTONYM empty.

stadium noun *many think the Expos play in the worst stadium in the majors* ARENA, field, ground; bowl, amphitheater, coliseum, ring, dome, manège; track, course, racetrack, racecourse, raceway, speedway, velodrome, sportsplex; *Brit.* pitch.

staff noun **1** *there is a reluctance to take on new staff* EMPLOYEES, workers, workforce, personnel, human resources, manpower, labor.

2 *he carried a wooden staff* STICK, stave, pole, crook.

3 *a staff of office* ROD, tipstaff, cane, mace, wand, scepter, crozier, verge; *Greek Mythology* caduceus.

▸ verb *the center is staffed by teachers* MAN, people, crew, work, operate, occupy.

stage noun **1** *this stage of the development* PHASE, period, juncture, step, point, time, moment, instant, level.

2 *the last stage of the race* PART, section, portion, stretch, leg, lap, circuit.

3 *a theater stage* PLATFORM, dais, stand, grandstand, staging, apron, rostrum, podium; bandstand, bandshell; catwalk.

4 *she has written for the stage* THEATER, drama, dramatics, dramatic arts, thespianism; *informal* boards.

5 *the political stage* SCENE, setting; context, frame, sphere, field, realm, arena, backdrop; affairs.

▸ verb **1** *they staged two plays* PUT ON, put before the public, present, produce, mount, direct; perform, act, give.

2 *workers staged a protest* ORGANIZE, arrange, coordinate, lay on, put together, get together, set up; orchestrate, choreograph, mastermind, engineer; take part in, participate in, join in.

stagger verb **1** *he staggered to the door* LURCH, walk unsteadily, reel, sway, teeter, totter, stumble, wobble.

2 *I was absolutely staggered* AMAZE, astound, astonish, surprise, startle, stun, confound, dumbfound, stupefy, daze, take aback, leave open-mouthed, leave aghast; *informal* flabbergast, bowl over.

3 *meetings are staggered throughout the day* SPREAD (OUT), space (out), time at intervals.

stagnant adjective **1** *stagnant water* STILL, motionless, static, stationary, standing, dead, slack; FOUL, stale, putrid, smelly. ANTONYMS flowing, fresh.

2 *a stagnant economy* INACTIVE, sluggish, slow-moving, lethargic, static, flat, depressed, declining, moribund, dying, dead, dormant. ANTONYMS active, vibrant.

stagnate verb **1** *obstructions allow water to stagnate* STOP FLOWING, become stagnant, become trapped; stand; become foul, become stale; fester, putrefy. ANTONYM flow.

2 *exports stagnated* LANGUISH, decline, deteriorate, fall, become stagnant, do nothing, stand still, tread water, be sluggish. ANTONYM boom.

staid adjective *I'm not some staid librarian, you know* SEDATE, respectable, quiet, serious, serious-minded, steady, conventional, traditional, unadventurous, unenterprising, set in one's ways, sober, proper, decorous, formal, stuffy, stiff, priggish; *informal* starchy, buttoned-down, stick-in-the-mud. ANTONYMS frivolous, daring, informal.

stain verb **1** *her clothing was stained with blood* DISCOLOR, blemish, soil, mark, muddy, spot, spatter, splatter, smear, splash, smudge, blotch, blacken; *literary* imbrue.

2 *the report stained his reputation* DAMAGE, injure, harm, sully, blacken, tarnish, taint, smear, bring discredit to, dishonor, drag through the mud; *literary* besmirch.

3 *the wood was stained* COLOR, tint, dye, tinge, pigment.

▸ noun **1** *a mud stain* MARK, spot, spatter, splatter, blotch, smudge, smear.

2 *a stain on his character* BLEMISH, injury, taint, blot, smear, discredit, dishonor; damage.

3 *dark wood stain* TINT, color, dye, tinge, pigment, colorant.

stake[1] noun *a stake in the ground* POST, pole, stick, spike, upright, support, prop, strut, pale, paling, picket, pile, piling, cane.

▸ verb **1** *the plants have to be staked* PROP UP, tie up, tether, support, hold up, brace, truss.

2 *he staked his claim* ASSERT, declare, proclaim, state, make, lay, put in.

PHRASE: **stake out 1** *builders staked out the plot* MARK OFF/OUT, demarcate, measure out, delimit, fence off, section off, close off, shut off, cordon off. **2** *informal the police staked out his apartment* OBSERVE, watch, keep an eye on, keep under observation, keep watch on, monitor, keep under surveillance, surveil; *informal* keep tabs on, keep a tab on, case.

stake[2] noun **1** *playing dice for high stakes* BET, wager, ante.

2 *they are racing for record stakes* PRIZE MONEY, purse, pot, winnings.

3 *low down in the popularity stakes* COMPETITION, contest, battle, challenge, rivalry, race, running, struggle, scramble.

4 *a 40-percent stake in the business* SHARE, interest, ownership, involvement.

▸ verb *he staked all his week's pay* BET, wager, lay, put on, gamble, chance, venture, risk, hazard.

stale adjective **1** *stale food* OLD, past its best, off, dry, hard, musty, rancid, overstored. ANTONYM fresh.

2 *stale air* STUFFY, close, musty, fusty, stagnant. ANTONYM fresh.

3 *stale beer* FLAT, turned, spoiled, off, insipid, tasteless.

4 *stale jokes* HACKNEYED, tired, worn out, overworked, threadbare, warmed-up, banal, trite, clichéd, platitudinous, unoriginal, unimaginative, uninspired, flat; out of date, outdated, outmoded, passé, archaic, obsolete; warmed-over; *informal* old hat, corny, unfunny, played out. ANTONYM original.

stalemate noun *the talks had reached a stalemate* DEADLOCK, impasse, standoff; draw, tie, dead heat.

stalk[1] noun *the stalk of a plant* STEM, shoot, trunk, stock, cane, bine, bent; *Brit.* haulm, straw, reed.

stalk[2] verb **1** *a cat was stalking a rabbit* CREEP UP ON, trail, follow, shadow, track down, go after, be after, course, hunt; *informal* tail, still-hunt.

2 *she stalked out* STRUT, stride, march, flounce, storm, stomp, sweep.

stall noun **1** *a market stall* STAND, table, counter, booth, kiosk.

2 *stalls for larger animals* PEN, coop, sty, corral, enclosure, compartment.

▸ verb **1** *the government has stalled the project* OBSTRUCT, impede, interfere with, hinder, hamper, block, interrupt, hold up, hold back, thwart, balk, sabotage, delay, stonewall, check, stop, halt, derail, put a brake on; *informal* stymie.

2 *the project has stalled* STOP, fizzle, flatline, die, reach an impasse, hit a roadblock.

3 *quit stalling* USE DELAYING TACTICS, play for time, temporize, gain time, procrastinate, hedge, beat around the bush, drag one's feet, delay, filibuster, stonewall, give someone the runaround.

4 *stall him for a bit* DELAY, divert, distract; HOLD OFF, stave off, fend off, keep off, ward off, keep at bay.

stalwart adjective *a stalwart supporter of the cause* STAUNCH, loyal, faithful, committed, devoted, dedicated, dependable, reliable, steady, constant, trusty, solid, hardworking, steadfast, redoubtable, unwavering. ANTONYMS disloyal, unfaithful, unreliable.

stamina noun *I felt my stamina weakening* ENDURANCE, staying power, tirelessness, fortitude, strength, energy, toughness, determination, tenacity, perseverance, grit.

stammer verb *he began to stammer* STUTTER, stumble over one's words, hesitate, falter, pause, halt, splutter.

▸ noun *he had a stammer* STUTTER, speech impediment, speech defect.

stamp verb **1** *he* ***stamped on*** *my toe* TRAMPLE (ON), step on, tread on, tramp on, stomp on; CRUSH, squash, flatten.

2 *John stamped off, muttering* STOMP, stump, clomp, clump.

3 *the name is stamped on the cover* IMPRINT, print, impress, punch, inscribe, emboss, brand, frank.

4 *his face was stamped on Martha's memory* FIX, inscribe, etch, carve, imprint, impress.

5 *his style stamps him as a player to watch* IDENTIFY, characterize, brand, distinguish, classify, mark out, set apart, single out.

▸ noun **1** *the stamp of authority* MARK, hallmark, indication, sign, seal, sure sign, telltale sign, quality, smack, smell, savor, air.

2 *he was of a very different stamp* TYPE, kind, sort, variety, class, category, classification, style, description, condition, caliber, status, quality, nature, ilk, kidney, cast, grain, mold, stripe.

PHRASE: **stamp out** *Miller's promise to stamp out crime on these streets is, at best, a naive fantasy* PUT AN END/STOP TO, end, stop, crush, put down, crack down on, curb, nip in the bud, scotch, squash, quash, quell, subdue, suppress, extinguish, stifle, abolish, get rid of, eliminate, eradicate, beat, overcome, defeat, destroy, wipe out; *informal* put the kibosh on, clean house.

stamp collecting noun *maybe stamp collecting would interest you* PHILATELY.

stampede noun *the noise caused a stampede* CHARGE, panic, rush, flight, rout.

▸ verb *the sheep stampeded* BOLT, charge, flee, take flight; race, rush, career, sweep, run.

stance noun **1** *a natural golfer's stance* POSTURE, body position, pose, attitude.

2 *a liberal stance* ATTITUDE, stand, point of view, viewpoint, opinion, way of thinking, outlook, standpoint, position, angle, perspective, approach, line, policy.

stand verb **1** *Lionel stood in the doorway* BE ON ONE'S FEET, be upright, be erect, be vertical. ANTONYMS sit, lie.

2 *the men* ***stood up*** RISE, get/rise to one's feet, get up, straighten up, pick oneself up, find one's feet, be upstanding; *formal* arise. ANTONYMS sit down, lie down.

3 *today a house stands on the site* BE, exist, be situated, be located, be positioned, be sited, have been built.

4 *he stood the book on the shelf* PUT, set, set up, erect, upend, place, position, locate, prop, lean, stick, install, arrange; *informal* park.

5 *my decision stands* REMAIN IN FORCE, remain valid/effective/operative, remain in operation, hold, hold good, apply, be the case, exist.

6 *her heart could not stand the strain* WITHSTAND, endure, bear, put up with, take, cope with, handle, sustain, resist, stand up to.

7 *informal I can't stand arrogance* ENDURE, tolerate, bear, put up with, take, abide, support, countenance; *informal* swallow, stomach; *formal* brook.

▸ noun **1** *the party's stand on immigration* ATTITUDE, stance, point of view, viewpoint, opinion, way of thinking, outlook, standpoint, position, approach, thinking, policy, line.

2 *a stand against tyranny* OPPOSITION, resistance, objection, hostility, animosity.

3 *a large mirror on a stand* BASE, support, mounting, platform, rest, plinth, bottom; tripod, rack, trivet.

4 *a beer stand* STALL, counter, booth, kiosk, tent.

5 *a taxi stand* stop, station, park, bay.

6 *the train drew to a stand* STOP, halt, standstill, dead stop.

7 *a stand of trees* COPSE, thicket, grove, bush, woodlot.

PHRASES: **stand by 1** *stand by for further instructions* WAIT, be prepared, be in (a state of) readiness, be ready for action, be on full alert, wait in the wings. **2** *she stood by her husband* REMAIN/BE LOYAL TO, stick with/by, remain/be true to, stand up for, support, back up, defend, stick up for. **3** *the government must stand by its pledges* ABIDE BY, keep (to), adhere to, hold to, stick to, observe, comply with. **stand down** *tell the troops to stand down* RELAX, stand easy, come off full alert. **stand for 1** *BC stands for British Columbia* MEAN, be an abbreviation of, represent, signify, denote, indicate, symbolize. **2** *informal I won't stand for any nonsense* PUT UP WITH, endure, tolerate, accept, take, abide, support, countenance; *informal* swallow, stomach; *formal* brook. **3** *we stand for animal welfare* ADVOCATE, champion, uphold, defend, stand up for, support, back, endorse, be in favor of, promote, recommend, urge. **stand in** *during Coach Clement's absence, Mr. Maynard will stand in* DEPUTIZE, act, act as deputy, substitute, fill in, sit in, do duty, take over, act as locum, be a proxy, cover, hold the fort, step into the breach; replace, relieve, take over from; *informal* sub, fill someone's shoes, step into someone's shoes, pinch-hit. **stand out 1** *his veins stood out* PROJECT, stick out, bulge (out), be proud, jut (out). **2** *she stood out in the crowd* BE NOTICEABLE, be visible, be obvious, be conspicuous, stick out, be striking, be distinctive, be prominent, attract attention, catch the eye, leap out, show up; *informal* stick/stand out like a sore thumb. **stand up** 1 *after 200 years, his theory still stands up* REMAIN/BE VALID, be sound, be plausible, hold water, hold up, stand questioning, survive investigation, bear examination, be verifiable. 2 *that creep Roger stood up his blind date* FAIL TO KEEP A DATE WITH, fail to meet, fail to keep an appointment with, jilt. **stand up for** *dozens of Mr. Merlin's students stood up for him at the hearing* SUPPORT, defend, back, back up, stick up for, champion, promote, uphold, take someone's part, take the side of, side with. **stand up to** 1 *she stood up to her parents* DEFY, confront, challenge, resist, take on, put up a fight against, argue with, take a stand against. 2 *the old house has stood up to the war* WITHSTAND, survive, come through (unscathed), outlast, outlive, weather, ride out, ward off.

standard noun 1 *the standard of her work* QUALITY, level, grade, caliber, merit, excellence.

2 *a safety standard* GUIDELINE, norm, yardstick, benchmark, measure, criterion, guide, touchstone, model, pattern, example, exemplar.

3 *a standard to live by* PRINCIPLE, ideal; (**standards**) code of behavior, code of honor, morals, scruples, ethics.

4 *the regiment's standard* FLAG, banner, pennant, ensign, color(s), banderole, guidon; *Nautical* burgee.

▸ adjective 1 *the standard way of doing it* NORMAL, usual, typical, stock, common, ordinary, customary, conventional, wonted, established, settled, set, fixed, traditional, prevailing. ANTONYMS unusual, special.

2 *the standard work on the subject* DEFINITIVE, established, classic, recognized, accepted, authoritative, most reliable, exhaustive.

standardize verb *teachers have been asked to standardize their final exams* SYSTEMATIZE, make consistent, make uniform, make comparable, regulate, normalize, bring into line, equalize, homogenize, regiment.

stand-in noun *a stand-in for the minister* SUBSTITUTE, replacement, deputy, surrogate, proxy, understudy, locum, supply, fill-in, cover, relief, stopgap; *informal* temp, pinch-hitter; (body) double, stuntman.

▸ adjective *a stand-in goaltender* SUBSTITUTE, replacement, deputy, fill-in, stopgap, supply, surrogate, relief, acting, temporary, provisional, caretaker; *informal* pinch-hitting.

standing noun 1 *his standing in the community* STATUS, rank, ranking, position; reputation, estimation, stature; *dated* station.

2 *a person of some standing* SENIORITY, rank, eminence, prominence, prestige, repute, stature, esteem, importance, account, consequence, influence, distinction; *informal* clout.

3 *a squabble of long standing* DURATION, existence, continuance, endurance, life, history.

▸ adjective 1 *standing stones* UPRIGHT, erect, vertical, plumb, upended, on end, perpendicular; on one's feet. ANTONYMS flat, lying down, seated.

2 *standing water* STAGNANT, still, motionless, static, stationary, dead, slack. ANTONYM flowing.

3 *a standing invitation* PERMANENT, perpetual, everlasting, continuing, abiding, indefinite, open-ended; regular, repeated. ANTONYMS temporary, occasional.

standoff noun *a nuclear standoff* DEADLOCK, stalemate, impasse; draw, tie, dead heat; suspension of hostilities, lull.

standoffish adjective *informal a standoffish prig* ALOOF, distant, remote, detached, withdrawn, reserved, uncommunicative, unforthcoming, unapproachable, unresponsive, unfriendly, unsociable, introspective, introverted. ANTONYMS friendly, approachable, sociable.

standpoint noun *she writes on religion from the standpoint of a believer* POINT OF VIEW, viewpoint, vantage point, attitude, stance, view, opinion, position, way of thinking, outlook, perspective.

standstill noun *negotiations have come to a standstill* HALT, stop, dead stop, stand, gridlock.

staple adjective *rice is their staple crop* MAIN, principal, chief, major, primary, leading, foremost, first, most important, predominant, dominant, (most) prominent, basic, standard, prime, premier; *informal* number-one.

star noun 1 *the sky was full of stars* CELESTIAL BODY, heavenly body, sun; asteroid, planet. See table at CONSTELLATION.

2 *the stars of the film* PRINCIPAL, leading lady/man, lead, female/male lead, hero, heroine. ANTONYMS extra, bit player.

3 *a star of the world of chess* CELEBRITY, superstar, big name, famous name, household name, someone, somebody, lion, leading light, VIP, personality, personage, luminary; *informal* celeb, big shot, megastar. See word spectrum on page 872. ANTONYM nobody.

▸ adjective 1 *a star pupil* BRILLIANT, talented, gifted, able, exceptional, outstanding, bright, clever, masterly, consummate, precocious, prodigious.

2 *the star attraction* TOP, leading, best, greatest, foremost, major, preeminent, champion. ANTONYMS poor, minor.

starchy adjective *informal compared to her starchy parents, Jon's mom was a wild bohemian.* See STAID.

stare verb *staring out the window* GAZE, gape, goggle, glare, ogle, peer; *informal* gawk, rubberneck.

stark adjective 1 *a stark silhouette* SHARP, sharply defined, well-focused, crisp, distinct, obvious, evident, clear, clear-cut, graphic, striking. ANTONYMS fuzzy, indistinct.

2 *a stark landscape* DESOLATE, bare, barren, arid, vacant, empty, forsaken, godforsaken, bleak, somber, depressing, cheerless, joyless; *literary* drear. ANTONYM pleasant.

3 *a stark room* AUSTERE, severe, bleak, plain, simple, bare, unadorned, unembellished, undecorated. ANTONYM ornate.

4 *stark terror* SHEER, utter, complete, absolute, total, pure, downright, out-and-out, outright; rank, thorough, consummate, unqualified, unmitigated, unalloyed.

5 *the stark facts* BLUNT, bald, bare, simple, basic, plain, unvarnished, harsh, grim. ANTONYM disguised.

▸ adverb *stark naked* COMPLETELY, totally, utterly, absolutely, downright, dead, entirely, wholly, fully, quite, altogether, thoroughly, truly, one hundred percent.

start verb 1 *the meeting starts at 7:45* BEGIN, commence, get underway, go ahead, get going; *informal* kick off. ANTONYM finish.

star
megastar
superstar
celebrity
somebody
luminary
leading light
celeb
big name
bigwig
big shot
big noise
big cheese
big fish
household name
dignitary
VIP
lion
high muckamuck
nob
macher
kahuna
personality
public figure
object of attention
target of criticism
disappointment
underachiever
write-off
no-hoper
nonstarter
ne'er-do-well
incompetent
nonachiever
flop
dud
washout
dead loss
born loser
loser
no one
nobody

2 *this was how her illness had started* ARISE, come into being, begin, commence, be born, come into existence, appear, arrive, come forth, establish oneself, emerge, erupt, burst out, originate, develop. ANTONYMS clear up, end.

3 *she started her own charity* ESTABLISH, set up, found, create, bring into being, institute, initiate, inaugurate, introduce, open, launch, float, kick-start, jump-start, get something off the ground, pioneer, organize, mastermind; *informal* kick something off. ANTONYM end.

4 *we had better start now if we want to finish the job* COMMENCE, make a start, begin, take the first step, make the first move, get going, go ahead, set things moving, start/get/set the ball rolling, buckle to/down, turn to; *informal* get moving, get cracking, get down to, get to it, get down to business, get the show on the road, take the plunge, kick off, get off one's backside, fire away. ANTONYMS stop, give up, procrastinate.

5 *he started across the field* SET OFF, set out, start out, set forth, begin one's journey, get on the road, depart, leave, get underway, make a start, sally forth, embark, sail; *informal* hit the road. ANTONYMS arrive, stay.

6 *you can start the machine* ACTIVATE, set in motion, switch on, start up, turn on, fire up; energize, actuate, set off, start off, set something going/moving. ANTONYMS stop, shut down, close down.

7 *the machine started* BEGIN WORKING, start up, get going, spring into life. ANTONYM stop.

8 *"Oh my!" she said, starting* FLINCH, jerk, jump, twitch, recoil, shy, shrink, blench, wince.

▸ noun **1** *the start of the event* BEGINNING, commencement, inception. ANTONYM end.

2 *the start of her illness* ONSET, commencement, emergence, (first) appearance, arrival, eruption, dawn, birth; *informal* square one.

3 *a quarter of an hour's start* LEAD, head start, advantage. ANTONYM handicap.

4 *a start in life* ADVANTAGEOUS BEGINNING, flying start, helping hand, lift, assistance, support, encouragement, boost, kick-start; *informal* break, leg up. ANTONYM handicap.

5 *she awoke with a start* JERK, twitch, flinch, wince, spasm, convulsion, jump.

startle verb *naturally their screaming startled me* SURPRISE, frighten, scare, alarm, give someone a shock/fright/jolt, make someone jump; PERTURB, unsettle, agitate, disturb, disconcert, disquiet; *informal* give someone a turn, make someone jump out of their skin, freak someone out. ANTONYM put at ease.

startling adjective *startling news awaited him at Naples* SURPRISING, astonishing, amazing, unexpected, unforeseen, staggering, shocking, stunning; extraordinary, remarkable, dramatic; disturbing, unsettling, perturbing, disconcerting, disquieting; frightening, alarming, scary. ANTONYMS predictable, ordinary.

starvation noun *half of the people here face starvation* EXTREME HUNGER, lack of food, famine, undernourishment, malnourishment, fasting; deprivation of food; death from lack of food.

starving adjective *the world's starving children* DYING OF HUNGER, deprived of food, undernourished, malnourished, starved, half-starved; very hungry, ravenous, famished, empty, hollow; fasting. ANTONYM full.

stash *informal* verb *he **stashed** his things **away*** STORE, stow, pack, load, cache, hide, conceal, secrete; hoard, save, stockpile; *informal* salt away, squirrel away.

▸ noun *a stash of money* CACHE, hoard, stock, stockpile, store, supply, accumulation, collection, reserve.

state[1] noun **1** *the state of the economy* CONDITION, shape, situation, circumstances, position; predicament, plight.

2 *informal don't get into a state* FLUSTER, frenzy, fever, fret, panic, state of agitation/anxiety; *informal* flap, tizzy, dither, stew, sweat.

3 *informal your room is in a state* MESS, chaos, disorder, disarray, confusion, muddle, heap, shambles; clutter, untidiness, disorganization, imbroglio.

4 *an autonomous state* COUNTRY, nation, land, sovereign state, nation state, kingdom, realm, power, republic, confederation, federation.

5 *the country is divided into thirty-two states* PROVINCE, federal state, region, territory, canton, department, county, district, shire.

6 *the power of the state* GOVERNMENT, parliament, administration, regime, authorities.

▸ adjective *a state visit to China* CEREMONIAL, official, formal, governmental, national, public. ANTONYMS unofficial, private, informal.

state[2] verb *I stated my views* EXPRESS, voice, utter, put into words, declare, affirm, assert, announce, make known, put across/over, communicate, air, reveal, disclose, divulge, proclaim, present, expound; set out, set down; *informal* come out with.

stated adjective *the stated aim of the program* SPECIFIED, fixed, settled, set, agreed, declared, designated, laid down. ANTONYMS undefined, irregular, tacit.

stately adjective *a stately mansion on the hill* DIGNIFIED, majestic, ceremonious, courtly, imposing, impressive, solemn, awe-inspiring, regal, elegant, grand, glorious, splendid, magnificent, resplendent; slow-moving, measured, deliberate.

statement noun *how do you respond to the president's statement about homeland security?* DECLARATION, expression of views/facts, affirmation, assertion, announcement, utterance, communication, proclamation, presentation, expounding; account, testimony, evidence, report, bulletin, communiqué.

state-of-the-art adjective *state-of-the-art recording equipment* MODERN, ultra-modern, the latest, new, the newest, up-to-the-minute, cutting-edge; advanced, highly developed, innovative, trailblazing, revolutionary; sophisticated.

statesman, stateswoman noun *Franklin was the great statesman of his day* SENIOR POLITICIAN, respected political figure, elder statesman, political leader, national leader.

static adjective **1** *static prices* UNCHANGED, fixed, stable, steady, unchanging, changeless, unvarying, invariable, constant, consistent. ANTONYM variable.

2 *a static display* STATIONARY, motionless, immobile, unmoving, still, stock-still, at a standstill, at rest, not moving a muscle, like a statue, rooted to the spot, frozen, inactive, inert, lifeless, inanimate. ANTONYMS mobile, active, dynamic.

station noun **1** *a train station* STOPPING PLACE, stop, halt, stage; terminus, terminal, depot.

2 *a research station* ESTABLISHMENT, base, camp; post, depot; mission; site, facility, installation, yard.

3 *a police station* OFFICE, depot, base, headquarters, precinct, station house, detachment; *informal* cop shop.

4 *a radio station* CHANNEL, broadcasting organization; wavelength.

5 *the watchman resumed his station* POST, position, place.

6 *dated* *Karen was getting ideas above her station* RANK, place, status, position in society, social class, stratum, level, grade; caste; *archaic* condition, degree.

▸ verb *the regiment was stationed at Camp Pendleton* PUT ON DUTY, post, position, place; establish, install; deploy, base, garrison.

stationary adjective **1** *a stationary car* STATIC, parked, stopped, motionless, immobile, unmoving, still, stock-still, at a standstill, at rest; not moving a muscle, like a statue, rooted to the spot, frozen, inactive, inert, lifeless, inanimate. ANTONYM moving.

2 *a stationary population* UNCHANGING, unvarying, invariable, constant, consistent, unchanged, changeless, fixed, stable, steady. ANTONYM shifting.

statistics noun *recent statistics show an increase in allergic reactions* DATA, facts and figures, numbers, information, details; *informal* stats.

statue noun *a statue of Alexander Hamilton* SCULPTURE, figure, effigy, statuette, figurine, idol; carving, bronze, graven image, model; bust, head.

statuesque adjective *statuesque beauty queens* TALL AND DIGNIFIED, imposing, striking, stately, majestic, noble, magnificent, splendid, impressive, regal.

stature noun **1** *she was small in stature* HEIGHT, tallness; size, build.

2 *an architect of international stature* REPUTATION, repute, standing, status, position, prestige, distinction, eminence, preeminence, prominence, importance, influence, note, fame, celebrity, renown, acclaim.

status noun **1** *the status of women* STANDING, rank, ranking, position, social position, level, place, estimation; *dated* station.

2 *wealth and status* PRESTIGE, kudos, cachet, standing, stature, regard, fame, note, renown, honor, esteem, image, importance, prominence, consequence, distinction, influence, authority, eminence.

3 *the current status of the project* STATE, position, condition, shape, stage.

statute noun *she built her case around an all but forgotten statute* LAW, regulation, enactment, act, bill, decree, edict, rule, ruling, resolution, dictum, command, order, directive, order-in-council, pronouncement, proclamation, dictate, fiat, bylaw, ordinance.

staunch[1] adjective *a staunch supporter* STALWART, loyal, faithful, committed, devoted, dedicated, dependable, reliable, steady, constant, trusty, hard-working, steadfast, redoubtable, unwavering, tireless. See note at RESOLUTE. ANTONYMS disloyal, unfaithful, unreliable.

staunch[2] verb *she tried to staunch the flow of blood* STEM, stop, halt, check, hold back, restrain, restrict, control, contain, curb; block, dam; slow, lessen, reduce, diminish, retard, stanch; *archaic* stay.

stave PHRASE: **stave off** *here, eat some crackers to stave off your hunger* AVERT, prevent, avoid, counter, preclude, forestall, nip in the bud; ward off, fend off, head off, keep off, keep at bay.

stay[1] verb **1** *he stayed where he was* REMAIN (BEHIND), stay behind, stay put; wait, linger, stick, be left, hold on, hang on, lodge; *informal* hang around; *archaic* bide, tarry. ANTONYM leave.

2 *they won't stay hidden* CONTINUE (TO BE), remain, keep, persist in being, carry on being, go on being.

3 *our aunt is staying with us* VISIT, spend time, put up, stop (off/over); lodge, room, board, have rooms, be housed, be accommodated, be quartered, be billeted, vacation; *formal* sojourn; *archaic* bide.

4 *legal proceedings were stayed* POSTPONE, put off, delay, defer, put back, hold over/off; adjourn, suspend, prorogue, put over, table, lay on the table, take a rain check on; *Law* continue; *informal* put on ice, put on the back burner. ANTONYM advance.

5 *literary* *we must stay the enemy's advance* DELAY, slow down/up, hold back/up, set back, keep back, put back, put a brake on, retard; hinder, hamper, obstruct, inhibit, impede, curb, check, restrain, restrict, arrest; *informal* throw a (monkey) wrench in the works of. ANTONYM promote.

▸ noun **1** *a stay at a hotel* VISIT, stop, stop-off, stopover, overnight, break, vacation; *formal* sojourn.

2 *a stay of judgment* POSTPONEMENT, putting off, delay, deferment, deferral, putting back; adjournment, suspension, prorogation, tabling.

stay[2] noun *the stays holding up the mast* STRUT, WIRE, brace, tether, guy, prop, rod, support, truss; *Nautical* shroud.

▸ verb *her masts were well stayed* BRACE, tether, strut, wire, guy, prop, support, truss.

steadfast adjective **1** *a steadfast friend* LOYAL, faithful, committed, devoted, dedicated, dependable, reliable, steady, true, constant, staunch, solid, trusty. ANTONYM disloyal.

2 *a steadfast policy* FIRM, determined, resolute, relentless, implacable, single-minded; unchanging, unwavering, unhesitating, unfaltering, unswerving, unyielding, unflinching, uncompromising. ANTONYM irresolute.

steady adjective **1** *the ladder must be steady* STABLE, firm, fixed, secure, fast, safe, immovable, unshakable, dependable; anchored, moored, jammed, rooted, braced. ANTONYMS unstable, loose.

2 *keep the camera steady* MOTIONLESS, still, unshaking, static, stationary, unmoving. ANTONYM shaky.

3 *a steady gaze* FIXED, intent, unwavering, unfaltering. ANTONYM darting.

4 *a steady young student* SENSIBLE, levelheaded, rational, settled, mature, down-to-earth, full of common sense, reliable, dependable, sound, sober, serious-minded, responsible, serious. ANTONYMS flighty, immature, impulsive.

5 *a steady income* CONSTANT, unchanging, regular, consistent, invariable; continuous, continual, unceasing, ceaseless, perpetual, unremitting, unwavering, unfaltering, unending, endless, around/round-the-clock, all-year-round. ANTONYMS fluctuating, sporadic.

6 *a steady boyfriend* REGULAR, usual, established, settled, firm, devoted, faithful. ANTONYM occasional.

▸ verb **1** *he steadied the rifle* STABILIZE, hold steady; brace, support; balance, poise; secure, fix, make fast.

2 *she needed to steady her nerves* CALM, soothe, quiet, compose, settle; subdue, quell, control, get a grip on.

steal verb **1** *the burglars stole a fax machine* PURLOIN, thieve, take, take for oneself, help oneself to, loot, pilfer, run off with, abscond with, carry off, shoplift; embezzle, misappropriate; *informal* walk off with, rob, swipe, snatch, nab, rip off, lift, "liberate", "borrow", filch, pinch, heist; *Brit. informal* nick; *formal* peculate.

2 *his work was stolen by his tutor* PLAGIARIZE, copy, pass off as one's own, pirate, poach, borrow; *informal* rip off, lift, pinch, crib; *Brit. informal* nick.

3 *he stole a kiss* SNATCH, sneak, get stealthily/surreptitiously.

4 *he stole out of the room* CREEP, sneak, slink, slip, slide, glide, tiptoe, sidle, edge.

▸ noun *informal at $30 it's a steal.* See BARGAIN noun sense 1.

WORD NOTE **filch**

The best advertisement for petty thievery is this lovely word, with *pilfer* a close second; it is not hard to imagine a mildly larcenous character in Dickens named Nick Filch. In J.K. Rowling's Harry Potter books, the creepy caretaker at Hogwarts School of Witchcraft and Wizardry is Argus Filch, a "squib" who does not have magical powers but tries to teach himself the basics from a correspondence course. **—JS**

stealing noun *he was convicted of stealing* THEFT, thieving, thievery, robbery, larceny, burglary, shoplifting, pilfering, pilferage, looting, misappropriation; embezzlement; *formal* peculation.

stealth noun *the stealth of a cat burglar* FURTIVENESS, secretiveness, secrecy, surreptitiousness, sneakiness, slyness. ANTONYM openness.

stealthy adjective she was a natural for such stealthy activities FURTIVE, secretive, secret, surreptitious, sneaking, sly, clandestine, covert, conspiratorial. See note at SECRET. ANTONYM open.

steam noun **1** *steam from the kettle* WATER VAPOR, condensation, mist, haze, fog, moisture.

2 *he ran out of steam* ENERGY, vigor, vitality, stamina, enthusiasm; MOMENTUM, impetus, force, strength, thrust, impulse, push, drive; speed, pace.

PHRASES: **steamed up** *informal* **1** *he got steamed up about forgetting his papers.* See AGITATED. **2** *they get steamed up about the media.* See ANGRY sense 1. **let/blow off steam** *informal you'll go nuts if you don't let off steam once in a while* GIVE VENT TO ONE'S FEELINGS, speak one's mind, speak out, sound off, lose one's inhibitions, let oneself go; use up surplus energy.

steamy adjective **1** *the steamy jungle* HUMID, muggy, sticky, dripping, moist, damp, clammy, sultry, sweaty, steaming.

2 *informal a steamy love scene.* See EROTIC.

3 *informal they had a steamy affair* PASSIONATE, torrid, amorous, ardent, lustful; *informal* sizzling, hot, red-hot.

steel PHRASE: **steel oneself** *the coach gives us tips on how to steel ourselves before a game* BRACE ONESELF, nerve oneself, summon (up) one's courage, screw up one's courage, gear oneself up, prepare oneself, get in the right frame of mind; fortify oneself, harden oneself; *informal* psych oneself up; *literary* gird (up) one's loins.

steely adjective **1** *steely light* BLUE-GRAY, gray, steel-colored, steel-gray, iron-gray.

2 *steely muscles* HARD, firm, toned, rigid, stiff, tense, tensed, taut. ANTONYM flabby.

3 *steely eyes* CRUEL, unfeeling, merciless, ruthless, pitiless, heartless, hard-hearted, hard, stony, cold-blooded, cold-hearted, harsh, callous, severe, unrelenting, unpitying, unforgiving, uncaring, unsympathetic; *literary* adamantine. ANTONYM kind.

4 *steely determination* RESOLUTE, firm, steadfast, dogged, single-minded; bitter, burning, ferocious, fanatical; ruthless, iron, grim, gritty; unquenchable, unflinching, unswerving, unfaltering, untiring, unwavering. ANTONYM halfhearted.

steep[1] adjective **1** *steep cliffs* PRECIPITOUS, sheer, abrupt, sharp, perpendicular, vertical, bluff, vertiginous. ANTONYM gentle.

2 *a steep increase* SHARP, sudden, precipitate, precipitous, rapid. ANTONYM gradual.

3 *informal steep prices* EXPENSIVE, costly, high, stiff; unreasonable, excessive, exorbitant, extortionate, outrageous, prohibitive, dear. ANTONYM reasonable.

steep[2] verb 1 *the ham is then steeped in brine* MARINADE, marinate, soak, souse, macerate; pickle.

2 *winding sheets were steeped in mercury sulfate* SOAK, saturate, immerse, wet through, drench; *technical* ret.

3 *a city steeped in history* IMBUE WITH, fill with, permeate with, pervade with, suffuse with, infuse with, soak in.

steeple noun *a solitary gull perched atop the church steeple* SPIRE, tower; bell tower, belfry, campanile; minaret.

steer verb 1 *he steered the boat* GUIDE, direct, maneuver, drive, pilot, navigate; *Nautical* con, helm.

2 *Luke steered her down the path* GUIDE, conduct, direct, lead, take, usher, shepherd, marshal, herd. PHRASE: **steer clear of** *mind my words and steer clear of that man* KEEP AWAY FROM, keep one's distance from, keep at arm's length, give a wide berth to, avoid, avoid dealing with, have nothing to do with, shun, eschew.

stellar adjective 1 *an estimate of stellar ages* ASTRAL, sidereal.

2 *a stellar cast* ALL-STAR, star-studded.

3 *a stellar performance* MARVELOUS, outstanding, superb, first-rate, out of this world, heavenly, dazzling.

stem[1] noun *a plant stem* STALK, shoot, trunk, stock, cane, bine. PHRASE: **stem from** *this type of behavior often stems from a childhood of abuse and neglect* HAVE ITS ORIGINS IN, arise from, originate from, spring from, derive from, come from, emanate from, flow from, proceed from; BE CAUSED BY, be brought on/about by, be produced by.

stem[2] verb *he stemmed the flow of blood* STAUNCH, stop, halt, check, hold back, restrict, control, contain, curb; block, dam; slow, lessen, reduce, diminish, stanch; *archaic* stay.

stench noun the stench from the basement was vile STINK, reek, whiff, fetor, funk; *literary* miasma. See note at SMELL.

stentorian adjective *his stentorian voice resonated throughout the theater* LOUD, thundering, thunderous, ear-splitting, deafening; powerful, strong, carrying; booming, resonant; strident. ANTONYMS quiet, soft.

step noun 1 *Frank took a step forward* PACE, stride.

2 *she heard a step on the stairs* FOOTSTEP, footfall, tread.

3 *she left the room with a springy step* GAIT, walk, tread.

4 *it is only a step to the river* SHORT DISTANCE, stone's throw, spitting distance; *informal* 'a hop, skip, and jump'.

5 *the top step* STAIR, tread; **(steps)** STAIRS, staircase, stairway.

6 *each step of the ladder* RUNG, tread.

7 *resigning is a very serious step* COURSE OF ACTION, measure, move, act, action, initiative, maneuver, operation, tactic.

8 *a significant step toward a cease-fire* ADVANCE, development, move, movement; breakthrough.

9 *the first step on the managerial ladder* STAGE, level, grade, rank, degree; notch, rung.

▸ verb 1 *she stepped gingerly through the snow* WALK, move, tread, pace, stride.

2 *the bull* ***stepped on*** *the farmer's foot* TREAD ON, stamp on, trample (on); squash, crush, flatten.

PHRASES: **in step** *he is in step with mainstream thinking* IN ACCORD, in accordance, in harmony, in agreement, in tune, in line, in keeping, in conformity, compatible. **mind/watch one's step** *just watch your step when Mrs. Kline gets here* BE CAREFUL, take care, step/tread carefully, exercise care/caution, mind how one goes, look out, watch out, be wary, be on one's guard, be on the qui vive. **out of step** *the paper was often out of step with public opinion* AT ODDS, at variance, in disagreement, out of tune, out of line, not in keeping, out of harmony. **step by step** *I followed the directions step by step* ONE STEP AT A TIME, bit by bit, gradually, in stages, by degrees, slowly, steadily. **step down** *it's time for Rowland to step down* RESIGN, quit, stand down, give up one's post/job, bow out, abdicate; pack it in, call it quits. **step in** 1 *nobody stepped in to save the bank* INTERVENE, intercede, involve oneself, become/get involved, take a hand. 2 *I stepped in for a sick colleague* STAND IN, sit in, fill in, cover, substitute, take over; replace, take someone's place; *informal* sub. **step on it** *informal if we don't step on it we'll miss the boat* HURRY UP, get a move on, speed up, go faster, be quick; *informal* get cracking, get moving, step on the gas; *dated* make haste. **step up** 1 *the army stepped up its offensive* INCREASE, intensify, strengthen, augment, escalate; *informal* up, crank up. 2 *I stepped up my pace* SPEED UP, increase, accelerate, quicken, hasten.

stereo noun *we bought a new stereo* SOUND SYSTEM, ghetto blaster, radio, CD player, tape deck, boom box, hi-fi.

stereotype noun *the stereotype of the rancher* STANDARD/CONVENTIONAL IMAGE, received idea, cliché, hackneyed idea, formula.

▸ verb *women in detective novels are often stereotyped as femmes fatales* TYPECAST, pigeonhole, conventionalize, categorize, label, tag.

stereotyped adjective *the stereotyped image of a stewardess* STOCK, conventional, stereotypical, standard, formulaic, predictable; hackneyed, clichéd, cliché-ridden, banal, trite, unoriginal; typecast; *informal* corny, old hat. ANTONYMS unconventional, original.

sterile adjective 1 *mules are sterile* INFERTILE, unable to reproduce/conceive, unable to have children/young; *archaic* barren. ANTONYMS fertile, fecund.

2 *sterile desert* UNPRODUCTIVE, infertile, unfruitful, uncultivatable, barren. ANTONYMS fertile, productive, rich.

3 *a sterile debate* POINTLESS, unproductive, unfruitful, unrewarding, useless, unprofitable, profitless, futile, vain, idle; *archaic* bootless. ANTONYM fruitful.

4 *sterile academicism* UNIMAGINATIVE, uninspired, uninspiring, unoriginal, stale, lifeless, musty, phlegmatic. ANTONYMS creative, original.

5 *sterile conditions* ASEPTIC, sterilized, germ-free, antiseptic, disinfected; uncontaminated, unpolluted, pure, clean; sanitary, hygienic. See note at SANITARY. ANTONYM septic.

sterilize verb 1 *the scalpel was first sterilized* DISINFECT, fumigate, decontaminate, sanitize; pasteurize; clean, cleanse, purify; *technical* autoclave. ANTONYM contaminate.

2 *over 6.5 million people were sterilized* MAKE UNABLE TO HAVE CHILDREN, make infertile, hysterectomize, vasectomize, have one's tubes tied, have a tubal ligation, have a salpingectomy.

3 *sterilizing domestic animals* NEUTER, castrate, spay, geld, cut, fix, desex, alter, doctor.

sterling adjective *this is a sterling example of the power of a positive attitude* EXCELLENT, first-rate, first-class, exceptional, outstanding, splendid, superlative, praiseworthy, laudable, commendable, admirable, valuable, worthy, deserving. ANTONYMS poor, unexceptional.

stern[1] adjective **1** *a stern expression* SERIOUS, unsmiling, frowning, severe, forbidding, grim, unfriendly, austere, dour, stony, flinty, steely, unrelenting, unforgiving, unbending, unsympathetic, disapproving. ANTONYMS genial, friendly.

2 *stern measures* STRICT, severe, stringent, harsh, drastic, hard, tough, extreme, rigid, ruthless, rigorous, exacting, demanding, uncompromising, unsparing, inflexible, authoritarian, draconian. See note at SEVERE. ANTONYMS lenient, lax.

stern[2] noun *the stern of the ship* REAR (END), back, after end, poop, transom, tail. ANTONYM bow.

stew noun **1** *we ate a hearty stew.* See table.

STEWS AND CASSEROLES

adobo	groundnut stew
baked ziti	gumbo
beef bourgignon	hasenpfeffer
beef en daube	hunter's stew
beef pilaf	Irish stew
beef stew	jager-eintopf
beef stroganoff	jambalaya
blanquette de veau	kedgeree
bobotie	kugel
bouillabaisse	lamb stew
Brunswick stew	lasagna/lasagne
burgoo	lobscouse
callaloo	lobster Newburg
carne guisada	macaroni and cheese
cassoulet	manicotti
chicken and dumplings	matelote
chicken cacciatore	Mongolian hot pot
chicken Marengo	moussaka
chicken paprika	mulligatawny
chili	olla podrida
cholent	oyster stew
chop suey	paella
choucroute garni	peperonata
cioppino	pepper pot
colcannon	potage
coquilles St. Jacques	pot-au-feu
curry	ragout
dhal	ratatouille
daube	rendang
eggplant parmigiana	Swedish meatballs
fricassee	tikka
frikadeller	tuna casserole
ful medames	vindaloo
goulash	waterzooi

2 *informal she's in a stew about that parking ticket* MOOD, flap, panic, fluster, fret, fuss, sweat, lather, tizzy, dither, twitter, state; *literary* pother.

▸ verb **1** *stew the meat for an hour* BRAISE, simmer, boil.

2 *informal there's no point stewing about it.* See WORRY verb sense 1.

3 *informal the girls sat stewing in the heat* SWELTER, be very hot, perspire, sweat; *informal* roast, bake, cook, be boiling.

steward noun **1** *an air steward* FLIGHT ATTENDANT, cabin attendant; stewardess, air hostess, purser.

2 *the race stewards* OFFICIAL, marshal, organizer.

3 *the steward of the estate* (ESTATE) MANAGER, agent, overseer, custodian, caretaker; *historical* reeve.

stick[1] noun **1** *a fire made of sticks* PIECE OF WOOD, twig, small branch.

2 *he walks with a stick* WALKING STICK, cane, staff, alpenstock, crook, crutch.

3 *the plants need supporting on sticks* CANE, pole, post, stake, upright.

4 *he beat me with a stick* CLUB, cudgel, bludgeon, shillelagh; truncheon, baton; cane, birch, switch, rod. PHRASE: **the sticks** *informal she didn't want him to know that she'd grown up in the sticks* THE COUNTRY, the countryside, rural areas; the backwoods, the back of beyond, the wilds, the hinterland, a backwater, the backcountry, the backland, the middle of nowhere, the boondocks, the boonies, hicksville.

stick[2] verb **1** *he stuck his fork into the sausage* THRUST, push, insert, jab, poke, dig, plunge.

2 *the bristles* **stuck into** *her skin* PIERCE, penetrate, puncture, prick, stab.

3 *the cup stuck to its saucer* ADHERE, cling, be fixed, be glued.

4 *stick the stamp there* AFFIX, attach, fasten, fix; paste, glue, gum, tape, Scotch-tape, pin, tack.

5 *the wheels stuck in the mud* BECOME TRAPPED, become jammed, jam, catch, become wedged, become lodged, become fixed, become embedded.

6 *that sticks in his mind* REMAIN, stay, linger, dwell, persist, continue, last, endure, burn.

7 *the charges won't stick* BE UPHELD, hold, be believed; *informal* hold water.

8 *informal just stick that sandwich on my desk* PUT (DOWN), place, set (down), lay (down), deposit, position; leave, stow; *informal* dump, park, pop, plunk. PHRASES: **stick at** *anything you stick at will eventually get done* PERSEVERE WITH, persist with, keep at, work at, continue with, carry on with, not give up with, hammer away at, stay with; go the distance, stay the course; *informal* soldier on with, hang in there. **stick by** *Rodney stuck by me when everyone else bailed out* BE LOYAL TO, be faithful to, be true to, stand by, keep faith with, keep one's promise to. **stick it out** *I think I can stick it out for another two weeks* PUT UP WITH IT, grin and bear it, keep at it, keep going, stay with it, see it through; persevere, persist, carry on, struggle on; *informal* hang in there, soldier on, tough it out, nail one's colors to the mast. **stick out 1** *his front teeth stuck out* PROTRUDE, jut (out), project, stand out, extend, poke out; bulge, overhang. **2** *they stuck out in their strange clothes* BE NOTICEABLE, be visible, be obvious, be conspicuous, stand out, be obtrusive, be prominent, attract attention, catch the eye, leap out, show up; *informal* stick/stand out like a sore thumb. **stick to** *he stuck to his promise* ABIDE BY, keep, adhere to, hold to, comply with, fulfill, make good, stand by. **stick up for** *after what she did, not even* *her family would stick up for her* SUPPORT, take someone's side, side with, be on the side of, stand by, stand up for, take someone's part, defend, come to the defense of, champion, speak up for, fight for.

sticker noun *read the warning on the sticker* LABEL, adhesive, decal, (price) tag.

stick-in-the-mud noun *informal her fun-loving boyfriend had become her stick-in-the-mud husband* (OLD) FOGEY, conservative, fossil, troglodyte, museum piece, fuddy-duddy, square, stuffed shirt, dinosaur, throwback.

stickler noun *there's no pleasing you if you're going to be such a stickler* PERFECTIONIST, pedant, nitpicker, purist, diehard, hard-liner, fanatic.

sticky adjective **1** *sticky tape* (SELF-)ADHESIVE, gummed, self-stick; *technical* adherent.

2 *sticky clay* GLUTINOUS, viscous, viscid, gluey, tacky, gummy, treacly, syrupy; mucilaginous; *informal* gooey, icky, gloppy. ANTONYM dry.

3 *sticky weather* HUMID, muggy, close, sultry, steamy, sweaty, oppressive, heavy. ANTONYMS fresh, cool.

4 *a sticky situation* AWKWARD, difficult, tricky, ticklish, problematic, delicate, touch-and-go, touchy, embarrassing, sensitive, uncomfortable; *informal* hairy. ANTONYM easy.

stiff adjective **1** *stiff cardboard* RIGID, hard, firm, inelastic, inflexible. ANTONYMS flexible, plastic, limp.

2 *a stiff paste* SEMISOLID, viscous, viscid, thick, stiffened, firm. ANTONYM runny.

3 *I'm stiff all over* ACHING, achy, painful; arthritic, rheumatic; *informal* creaky, rusty. ANTONYMS supple, limber.

4 *a rather stiff manner* FORMAL, reserved, unfriendly, chilly, cold, frigid, icy, austere, wooden, forced, strained, stilted; *informal* starchy, uptight, standoffish. ANTONYMS relaxed, informal.

5 *a stiff fine* HARSH, severe, heavy, crippling, punishing, stringent, drastic, draconian. ANTONYMS lenient, mild.

6 *stiff resistance* VIGOROUS, determined, full of determination, strong, spirited, resolute, tenacious, steely, foursquare, unflagging, unyielding, dogged, stubborn, obdurate, rock-ribbed. ANTONYM halfhearted.

7 *a stiff climb* DIFFICULT, hard, arduous, tough, strenuous, laborious, uphill, exacting, tiring, demanding, formidable, challenging, punishing, grueling; *informal* killing, hellish. ANTONYM easy.

8 *a stiff breeze* STRONG, fresh, brisk. ANTONYM gentle.

9 *a stiff drink* STRONG, potent, alcoholic. ANTONYM weak.

stiffen verb **1** *stir until the mixture stiffens* BECOME STIFF, thicken; set, become solid, solidify, harden, jell, congeal, coagulate, clot. ANTONYMS soften, liquefy.

2 *she stiffened her muscles | without exercise, joints will stiffen* MAKE/BECOME STIFF, tense (up), tighten, tauten. ANTONYM relax.

3 *intimidation stiffened their resolve* STRENGTHEN, harden, toughen, fortify, reinforce, give a boost to. ANTONYM weaken.

stifle verb **1** *she stifled him with a pillow* SUFFOCATE, choke, asphyxiate, smother, gag.

2 *Eleanor stifled a giggle* SUPPRESS, smother, restrain, fight back, choke back, gulp back, check, swallow, curb, silence. ANTONYM let out.

3 *cartels stifle competition* CONSTRAIN, hinder, hamper, impede, hold back, curb, check, restrain, prevent, inhibit, suppress. ANTONYM encourage.

stifling adjective *it's stifling and you've got no windows open* AIRLESS, suffocating, oppressive; very hot, sweltering; humid, close, muggy; *informal* boiling. ANTONYMS fresh, airy, cold.

stigma noun the stigma of bankruptcy SHAME, disgrace, dishonor, ignominy, opprobrium, humiliation, (bad) reputation. ANTONYMS honor, credit.

stigmatize verb *as foreign emissaries, we find it nearly impossible to help those who've been taught to stigmatize us* CONDEMN, denounce; brand, label, mark out; disparage, vilify, pillory, pour scorn on, defame.

still adjective **1** *the parrot lay still* MOTIONLESS, unmoving, not moving a muscle, stock-still, immobile, inanimate, like a statue, as if turned to stone, rooted to the spot, transfixed, static, stationary. ANTONYMS moving, active.

2 *a still night* QUIET, silent, hushed, soundless, noiseless, undisturbed; CALM, peaceful, serene, windless; *literary* stilly. ANTONYM noisy.

3 *the lake was still* CALM, flat, even, smooth, placid, tranquil, pacific, waveless, glassy, like a millpond, unruffled, stagnant. ANTONYMS rough, turbulent.

▸ noun *the still of the night* QUIETNESS, quiet, quietude, silence, stillness, hush, soundlessness; calm, tranquility, peace, serenity. ANTONYMS noise, disturbance, hubbub.

▸ adverb **1** *she's still running in circles* UP TO THIS TIME, up to the present time, until now, even now, yet.

2 *He's crazy. Still, he's good for dinner conversation* NEVERTHELESS, nonetheless, regardless, all the same, just the same, anyway, anyhow, even so, yet, but, however, notwithstanding, despite that, in spite of that, for all that, be that as it may, in any event, at any rate; *informal* still and all, anyhoo.

▸ verb **1** *she stilled the crowd* QUIET, silence, hush; calm, settle, pacify, soothe, lull, allay, subdue. ANTONYM stir up.

2 *the wind stilled* ABATE, die down, lessen, subside, ease up/off, let up, moderate, slacken, weaken. ANTONYM get stronger.

stilted adjective *a few minutes of stilted conversation* STRAINED, forced, contrived, constrained, labored, stiff, self-conscious, awkward, unnatural, wooden. ANTONYMS natural, effortless, spontaneous.

WORD NOTE stilted

As a synonym for *awkward, stilted* can itself occasionally be awkward. People can be naturally awkward, but if you want to use *stilted,* your subjects should be awkward only as the result of straining to be something other than what they naturally are. You're *awkward* when out of your depth; *stilted* only when you know you are but pretend you're not. **—EM**

stimulant noun **1** *caffeine is a stimulant* TONIC, restorative; antidepressant; *informal* pep pill, upper, pick-me-up, bracer, happy pill; *Medicine* analeptic. ANTONYMS sedative, downer.

2 *a stimulant to discussion* STIMULUS, incentive, encouragement, impetus, inducement, boost, spur, prompt; *informal* shot in the arm. ANTONYM deterrent.

stimulate verb *we're looking for ways to stimulate tourism* ENCOURAGE, act as a stimulus/incentive/impetus/spur to, prompt, prod, move, motivate, trigger, spark, spur on, galvanize, activate, kindle, fire, fire with enthusiasm, fuel, whet, nourish; inspire, incentivize, inspirit, rouse, excite, animate, electrify, jump-start, light a fire under. See notes at ENCOURAGE, QUICKEN. ANTONYM discourage.

stimulating adjective **1** *a stimulating effect on the circulation* RESTORATIVE, tonic, invigorating, bracing, energizing, reviving, refreshing, revitalizing, revivifying; *Medicine* analeptic. ANTONYM sedative.

2 *a stimulating lecture* THOUGHT-PROVOKING, interesting, fascinating, inspiring, inspirational, lively, sparkling, exciting, stirring, rousing, intriguing, giving one food for thought, refreshing; provocative, challenging; *informal* buzzy. ANTONYMS uninspiring, uninteresting, boring.

stimulus noun *this sports facility has been a stimulus to the economic restoration of our city* SPUR, stimulant, encouragement, impetus, boost, prompt, prod, incentive, inducement, inspiration; motivation, impulse; *informal* shot in the arm. ANTONYMS deterrent, discouragement.

sting noun **1** *a bee sting* PRICK, wound, injury, puncture.

2 *this cream will take the sting away* SMART, pricking; pain, soreness, hurt, irritation.

3 *the sting of his betrayal* HEARTACHE, heartbreak, agony, torture, torment, hurt, pain, anguish.

4 *there was a sting in her words* SHARPNESS, severity, bite, edge, pointedness, asperity; sarcasm, acrimony, malice, spite, venom.

5 *informal the victim of a sting* SWINDLE, fraud, deception; trickery, sharp practice; *informal* rip-off, con, fiddle, bunco.

▸ verb **1** *she was stung by a scorpion* PRICK, wound, bite; poison.

2 *the smoke made her eyes sting* SMART, burn, hurt, be irritated, be sore.

3 *the criticism stung her* UPSET, wound, cut to the quick, sear, grieve, hurt, pain, torment, mortify.

4 *he was stung into action* PROVOKE, goad, incite, spur, prick, prod, rouse, drive, galvanize. ANTONYM deter.

5 *informal they stung a bank for thousands* SWINDLE, defraud, cheat, fleece, gull; *informal* rip off, screw, shaft, bilk, do, rook, diddle, take for a ride, chisel, gouge.

stingy adjective *informal you can think I'm stingy all you want, I'm not giving you a penny* MEAN, miserly, niggardly, close-fisted, parsimonious, penny-pinching, cheeseparing, Scroogelike; *informal* tightfisted, cheap, tight, mingy, money-grubbing. ANTONYMS generous, liberal.

stink verb **1** *his clothes stank of sweat* REEK, smell (foul/bad/disgusting), stink/smell to high heaven.

2 *informal the idea stinks* BE VERY UNPLEASANT, be abhorrent, be despicable, be contemptible, be disgusting, be vile, be foul; *informal* suck.

3 *informal the whole affair stinks of a setup* SMACK, reek, give the impression, have all the hallmarks; strongly suggest.

▸ noun **1** *the stink of a dirty diaper* STENCH, reek, fetor, foul/bad smell; *informal* funk; *literary* miasma. See note at SMELL.

2 *informal a big stink about the new proposals* FUSS, commotion, rumpus, ruckus, trouble, outcry, uproar, brouhaha, furor; *informal* song and dance, to-do, hoo-ha.

stinking adjective **1** *stinking garbage* FOUL-SMELLING, smelly, reeking, fetid, malodorous, rank, putrid, noxious; *informal* stinky, humming, funky; *literary* miasmic, noisome. ANTONYMS sweet-smelling, aromatic.

2 *informal this stinking tax* HORRIBLE, nasty, foul, dreadful, awful, terrible, frightful, ghastly, vile, rotten.

stint verb *we saved by **stinting on** food* SKIMP ON, scrimp on, be economical with, economize on, be sparing with, hold back on, be frugal with; be mean with, be parsimonious with; limit, restrict; *informal* be stingy with, be mingy with, be tight with.

▸ noun *a two-week stint in the office* SPELL, stretch, turn, session, term, shift, tour of duty.

stipulate verb *the document stipulates certain conditions* SPECIFY, set down, set out, lay down; demand, require, insist on, make a condition of, prescribe, impose; *Law* provide.

stipulation noun *the foundation could use the Lynde name, with the stipulation that a Lynde would always sit on the board of directors* CONDITION, precondition, proviso, provision, prerequisite, specification; demand, requirement; rider, caveat, qualification.

stir verb **1** *stir the mixture well* MIX, blend, agitate; beat, whip, whisk, fold in.

2 *Travis stirred in his sleep* MOVE SLIGHTLY, change one's position, shift.

3 *a breeze stirred the leaves* DISTURB, rustle, shake, move, flutter, agitate.

4 *she finally stirred at ten o'clock* GET UP, get out of bed, rouse oneself, rise; WAKE (UP), awaken; *informal* rise and shine, surface, show signs of life; *formal* arise; *literary* waken. ANTONYMS go to bed, retire.

5 *I never stirred from here* MOVE, budge, make a move, shift, go away; leave. ANTONYMS stay, stay put.

6 *symbolism can stir the imagination* AROUSE, rouse, fire, kindle, inspire, stimulate, excite, awaken, quicken; *literary* waken. ANTONYM stultify.

7 *the war stirred him to action* SPUR, drive, rouse, prompt, propel, prod, motivate, encourage; urge, impel; provoke, goad, prick, sting, incite, light a fire under.

▸ noun *the news caused a stir* COMMOTION, disturbance, fuss, excitement, turmoil, sensation; *informal* to-do, hoo-ha, hullabaloo, flap, splash.

PHRASE: **stir up** *his remarks stirred up a furor* WHIP UP, work up, foment, fan the flames of, trigger, spark off, precipitate, excite, provoke, incite, ignite.

stirring adjective *a stirring portrait of his life as a missionary* EXCITING, thrilling, rousing, stimulating, moving, inspiring, inspirational, passionate, impassioned, emotional, heady. ANTONYMS boring, pedestrian.

stitch noun *he was panting and had a stitch* SHARP PAIN, stabbing pain, shooting pain, stab of pain, pang, twinge, spasm.

▸ verb *the seams are stitched by hand* SEW, baste, tack; seam, hem; darn.

stock noun **1** *the store carries little stock* MERCHANDISE, goods, wares, items/articles for sale, inventory.

2 *a stock of fuel* STORE, supply, stockpile, reserve, hoard, cache, bank, accumulation, quantity, collection.

3 *farm stock* ANIMALS, livestock, beasts; flocks, herds.

4 (**stocks**) *blue-chip stocks* SHARES, securities, equities, bonds.

5 *her stock is low with most voters* POPULARITY, favor, regard, estimation, standing, status, reputation, name, prestige.

6 *his mother was of French stock* DESCENT, ancestry, origin(s), parentage, pedigree, lineage, line (of descent), heritage, birth, extraction, family, blood, bloodline.

7 *chicken stock* BOUILLON, broth, consommé.

8 *the stock of a weapon* HANDLE, butt, haft, grip, shaft, shank.

▸ adjective 1 *a stock size* STANDARD, regular, normal, established, set; common, readily/widely available; staple. ANTONYM nonstandard.

2 *the stock response* USUAL, routine, predictable, set, standard, staple, customary, familiar, conventional, traditional, stereotyped, clichéd, hackneyed, unoriginal, formulaic. ANTONYMS original, unusual.

▸ verb 1 *we stock organic food* SELL, carry, keep (in stock), offer, have (for sale), retail, supply.

2 *the fridge was well stocked with milk* SUPPLY, provide, furnish, provision, equip, fill, load.

PHRASES: **in stock** *what brands of dog food do you have in stock?* FOR/ON SALE, (immediately) available, on the shelf. **stock up on/with** *people are stocking up on batteries and water* AMASS SUPPLIES OF, stockpile, hoard, cache, lay in, buy up/in, put away/by, put/set aside, collect, accumulate, save; *informal* squirrel away, salt away, stash away. **take stock of** *let's stock of our current situation* REVIEW, assess, appraise, evaluate; *informal* size up.

stockings plural noun *you'll need a pair of black stockings* NYLONS, pantyhose, tights; hosiery, hose, leotards; knee-highs.

stockpile noun *a stockpile of weapons* STOCK, store, supply, accumulation, collection, reserve, hoard, cache; *informal* stash.

▸ verb *food had been stockpiled* STORE UP, amass, accumulate, store (up), stock up on, hoard, cache, collect, lay in, put away, put/set aside, put by, put away for a rainy day, stow away, save; *informal* salt away, stash away.

stock-still adjective *two stock-still deer were not more than twenty feet away from us* MOTIONLESS, completely still, unmoving, not moving a muscle, immobile, like a statue/stone, rooted to the spot, transfixed, paralyzed, petrified, static, stationary. ANTONYMS moving, active.

stocky adjective *he was short but stocky, and his physical strength was amazing* THICKSET, sturdy, heavily built, chunky, burly, strapping, brawny, solid, heavy, heavyset, hefty, beefy, blocky. ANTONYMS slender, skinny.

stodgy adjective 1 *stodgy writing* BORING, dull, uninteresting, dreary, turgid, tedious, dry, unimaginative, uninspired, unexciting, unoriginal, monotonous, humdrum, prosaic, staid, heavy going; *informal* deadly, square. ANTONYMS interesting, lively.

2 *a stodgy pudding* SOLID, substantial, filling, hearty, heavy, starchy, indigestible. ANTONYM light.

stoic adjective *I had no intention of spending my life as the stoic spouse to that autocratic buffoon* LONG-SUFFERING, uncomplaining, patient, forbearing, accepting, tolerant, resigned, phlegmatic, philosophical. ANTONYMS complaining, intolerant.

stoicism noun *she accepted her sufferings with remarkable stoicism* PATIENCE, forbearance, resignation, fortitude, endurance, acceptance, tolerance, phlegm. ANTONYM intolerance.

stoke verb *we took turns stoking the fires throughout the night* ADD FUEL TO, keep burning, tend.

stolid adjective *her stolid facade is somewhat unnerving* IMPASSIVE, phlegmatic, unemotional, cool, calm, placid, unexcitable; dependable; unimaginative, dull. ANTONYMS emotional, lively, imaginative.

stomach noun 1 *a stomach pain* ABDOMEN, belly, gut, middle; *informal* tummy, insides.

2 *his fat stomach* PAUNCH, potbelly, beer belly, girth; *informal* beer gut, pot, tummy, spare tire, breadbasket, middle-aged spread.

3 *he had no stomach for it* APPETITE, taste, hunger, thirst; inclination, desire, relish, fancy.

▸ verb 1 *I can't stomach butter* DIGEST, keep down, manage to eat/consume, tolerate, take.

2 *they couldn't stomach the sight* TOLERATE, put up with, take, stand, endure, bear; *informal* hack, abide.

stomachache noun *he's in bed with a stomachache* INDIGESTION, dyspepsia; colic, gripe, cramps; *informal* bellyache, tummy ache.

stone noun 1 *someone threw a stone at me* ROCK, pebble, boulder.

2 *a commemorative stone* TABLET, monument, monolith, obelisk; gravestone, headstone, tombstone.

3 *paving stones* SLAB, flagstone, flag, cobble.

4 *what beautiful stones in her tiara* GEM, gemstone, jewel, semiprecious stone, brilliant; *informal* rock, sparkler.

5 *a peach stone* KERNEL, seed, pip, pit.

stony adjective 1 *a stony path* ROCKY, pebbly, gravelly, shingly; rough, hard. ANTONYM smooth.

2 *a stony stare* UNFRIENDLY, hostile, cold, chilly, frosty, icy; hard, flinty, steely, stern, severe; fixed, expressionless, blank, poker-faced, deadpan; unfeeling, uncaring, unsympathetic, indifferent, cold-hearted, callous, heartless, hard-hearted, stony-hearted, merciless, pitiless. ANTONYMS friendly, sympathetic.

stooge noun 1 *a government stooge* UNDERLING, minion, lackey, subordinate; henchman; PUPPET, pawn, cat's paw; *informal* sidekick.

2 *a comedian's stooge* BUTT, foil, straight man.

stoop verb 1 *she stooped to pick up the pen* BEND (OVER/DOWN), lean over/down, crouch (down).

2 *he stooped his head* LOWER, bend, incline, bow, duck.

3 *he stoops when he walks* HUNCH ONE'S SHOULDERS, walk with a stoop, be round-shouldered.

4 *Davis would stoop to committing a crime* LOWER ONESELF, sink, descend, resort; go as far as, sink as low as.

▸ noun 1 *a man with a stoop* HUNCH, round shoulders; curvature of the spine; *Medicine* kyphosis.

2 *we sat on the front stoop and watched the passers-by* PORCH, steps, platform, veranda, terrace.

stop verb 1 *we can't stop the decline* PUT AN END/STOP/HALT TO, bring to an end/stop/halt/close/standstill, end, halt; finish, terminate, discontinue, cut short, interrupt, nip in the bud; deactivate, shut down. ANTONYMS start, begin, continue.

2 *he stopped smoking* CEASE, discontinue, desist from, break off; give up, abandon, abstain from, cut out; *informal* quit, leave off, knock off, pack in, lay off, give over.

3 *the car stopped* PULL UP, draw up, come to a stop/halt, come to rest, pull in, pull over; park.

4 *the music stopped* CONCLUDE, come to an end/stop/standstill, cease, end, finish, draw to a close, be over, terminate; pause, break off; peter out, fade away.

5 *divers stopped the flow of oil* STEM, staunch, hold back, check, curb, block, dam; *archaic* stay.

6 *the police stopped her leaving* PREVENT, hinder, obstruct, impede, block, bar, preclude; dissuade from. ANTONYM encourage.

7 *the council stopped the housing project* THWART, balk, foil, frustrate, stand in the way of; scotch, derail; *informal* put paid to, put the kibosh on, put a stop to, do for, stymie, scuttle, deep-six. ANTONYM expedite.

8 *just stop the bottle with your thumb* BLOCK (UP), plug, close (up), fill (up); seal, caulk, bung up; *technical* occlude.

▸ noun 1 *all business came to a stop* HALT, end, finish, close, standstill; cessation, conclusion, stoppage, discontinuation. ANTONYMS start, beginning, continuation.

2 *a brief stop in the town* BREAK, stopover, stop-off, stay, visit; *formal* sojourn.

3 *the next stop is Central Park* STOPPING PLACE, halt, station.

PHRASES: **put a stop to.** *how can we put a stop to this senseless violence?* See STOP verb senses 1, 7. **stop off/over** *we decided to stop over in Denver* BREAK ONE'S JOURNEY, take a break, pause, linger; stay, remain, put up, lodge, rest; *formal* sojourn.

stopgap noun *that old plane was merely a stopgap* TEMPORARY SOLUTION/FIX, expedient, makeshift; substitute, stand-in, pinch-hitter.

▸ adjective *a stopgap measure* TEMPORARY, provisional, interim, pro tem, short-term, working, makeshift, emergency; caretaker, acting, stand-in, fill-in. ANTONYM permanent.

stopover noun *our stopover in Dallas lasted two weeks* BREAK, stop, stop-off, layover, overnight, visit, stay; *formal* sojourn.

stoppage noun 1 *the stoppage of production* DISCONTINUATION, stopping, halting, cessation, termination, end, finish; interruption, suspension, breaking off. ANTONYMS start, continuation.

2 *a stoppage of the blood supply* OBSTRUCTION, blocking, blockage, block; *Medicine* occlusion, stasis.

3 *a stoppage over pay* STRIKE, walkout; industrial action.

stopper noun *the stopper is not keeping the water from running out* PLUG, cork, bung, spigot, spile, seal.

store noun 1 *a store of money* STOCK, supply, stockpile, hoard, cache, reserve, bank, pool; *informal* war chest, pork barrel.

2 *a grain store* STOREROOM, storehouse, repository, depository, stockroom, depot, warehouse, magazine; *informal* lockup.

3 *ship's stores* SUPPLIES, provisions, stocks, necessities; food, rations, provender; materials, equipment, hardware; *Military* matériel, accoutrements; *Nautical* chandlery.

4 *a hardware store* SHOP, (retail) outlet, boutique, department store, chain store, emporium; supermarket, superstore, megastore.

▸ verb *rabbits don't store food* KEEP, keep in reserve, stockpile, lay in, put/set aside, put away/by, put away for a rainy day, save, collect, accumulate, hoard, cache; *informal* squirrel away, salt away, stash away. ANTONYMS use, discard.

PHRASE: **set (great) store by** *Gwen set great store by good manners* VALUE, attach great importance to, put a high value on, put a premium on; THINK HIGHLY OF, hold in (high) regard, have a high opinion of; *informal* rate.

storehouse noun *we have more furniture in our storehouse* WAREHOUSE, depository, repository, store, storeroom, depot, storage.

storm noun 1 *battered by a storm* WINDSTORM, tempest, whirlwind, gale, strong wind, high wind, squall; cyclone, tornado, twister, dust devil, dust storm; rainstorm, thunderstorm, thundershower; monsoon, typhoon, hurricane, tropical storm; hailstorm, snowstorm, blizzard.

2 *a storm of bullets* VOLLEY, salvo, fusillade, barrage, cannonade; shower, spray, hail, rain.

3 *there was a storm over his remarks* UPROAR, outcry, fuss, furor, brouhaha, rumpus, trouble, hue and cry, controversy; *informal* to-do, hoo-ha, hullabaloo, ballyhoo, stink, row.

4 *a storm of protest* OUTBURST, outbreak, explosion, eruption, outpouring, surge, blaze, flare-up, wave.

▸ verb 1 *she stormed out* STRIDE ANGRILY, stomp, march, stalk, flounce, stamp.

2 *his mother stormed at him* RANT, rave, shout, bellow, roar, thunder, rage.

3 *police stormed the building* ATTACK, charge, rush, assail, descend on, swoop on. See note at ATTACK.

stormy adjective 1 *stormy weather* BLUSTERY, squally, windy, gusty, blowy; rainy, thundery, snowy; wild, tempestuous, turbulent, violent, rough, foul. ANTONYMS calm, fine.

2 *a stormy debate* ANGRY, heated, fiery, fierce, furious, passionate, lively. ANTONYM peaceful.

story[1] noun 1 *a story about his summer in Hawaii* TALE, narrative, account, anecdote; *informal* yarn, spiel. See table on page 881.

2 *the novel has a good story* PLOT, story line, scenario, libretto.

3 *the story appeared in the papers* NEWS ITEM, news report, article, feature, piece.

4 *there have been a lot of stories going around* RUMOR, piece of gossip, whisper; speculation.

5 *Harper changed his story* TESTIMONY, statement, report, account, version.

6 *Ellie never told stories.* See FALSEHOOD sense 1.

story[2] noun *they're adding a story to their house* FLOOR, level, deck.

storyteller noun *my uncle was a great storyteller who*

would amuse us for hours NARRATOR, teller of tales, raconteur, raconteuse, fabulist, anecdotalist.

stout adjective **1** *a short stout man* FAT, plump, portly, rotund, dumpy, chunky, corpulent; stocky, burly, bulky, hefty, heavyset, solidly built, thickset; *informal* tubby, pudgy, zaftig, corn-fed. ANTONYMS thin, slender.

2 *stout leather shoes* STRONG, sturdy, solid, substantial, robust, tough, durable, hardwearing. ANTONYMS fragile, flimsy.

3 *stout resistance* DETERMINED, vigorous, forceful, spirited; staunch, steadfast, stalwart, firm, resolute, unyielding, dogged; brave, bold, courageous, valiant, valorous, gallant, fearless, doughty, intrepid; *informal* gutsy, spunky. ANTONYMS halfhearted, feeble.

stouthearted adjective *we stand in awe of these stouthearted heroes* BRAVE, determined, courageous, bold, plucky, spirited, valiant, valorous, gallant, fearless, doughty, intrepid, stalwart; *informal* gutsy, spunky.

stove noun *there's a pot of coffee on the stove* OVEN, range, wood stove, wood-burning stove, potbellied stove, Franklin stove; *trademark* Coleman stove.

stow verb *Barney stowed her bags in the trunk* PACK, load, store, place, put (away), deposit, stash. ANTONYM unload.

PHRASE: **stow away** *you'd better stow away until the air clears* HIDE, conceal oneself, travel secretly.

straddle verb **1** *she straddled the motorbike* SIT/STAND ASTRIDE, bestride, mount, get on.

2 *a mountain range straddling the border* LIE ON BOTH SIDES OF, extend across, span.

3 *he straddled the issue of taxes* BE EQUIVOCAL ABOUT, be undecided about, equivocate about, vacillate about, waver about, waffle on; *informal* sit on the fence regarding.

strafe verb *enemy aircraft strafed our carriers* BOMB, shell, bombard, fire on, machine-gun, rake with gunfire, enfilade; *archaic* fusillade.

straggle verb *we were straggling toward the end, but we weren't the last ones to cross the finish line* TRAIL, lag, dawdle, walk slowly, dally, lollygag; fall behind, bring up the rear.

straggly adjective *we'll have to do something about those straggly old clothes* UNTIDY, messy, unkempt, straggling, disheveled.

TYPES OF STORIES

adventure story	gothic novel
allegory	historical novel
bedtime story	horror story
black comedy	just-so story
cliffhanger	legend
cock-and-bull story	morality tale
comedy	mystery
conte	myth
crime story	parable
detective story	romance
epic	saga
exemplum	shaggy-dog story
fable	short story
farce	tearjerker
fairy tale	thriller
fantasy	tragedy
fish story	traveler's tale
folk tale	true story
ghost story	urban myth

straight adjective **1** *a long, straight road* UNSWERVING, undeviating, linear, as straight as an arrow, uncurving, unbending. ANTONYMS winding, zigzag.

2 *that picture isn't straight* LEVEL, even, in line, aligned, square; vertical, upright, perpendicular; horizontal. ANTONYMS askew, crooked.

3 *we must get the place straight* IN ORDER, (neat and) tidy, neat, shipshape, orderly, spick-and-span, organized, arranged, sorted out, straightened out. ANTONYMS untidy, messy.

4 *a straight answer* HONEST, direct, frank, candid, truthful, sincere, forthright, straightforward, plain-spoken, blunt, straight from the shoulder, unequivocal, unambiguous; *informal* upfront. ANTONYMS indirect, evasive.

5 *straight thinking* LOGICAL, rational, clear, lucid, sound, coherent. ANTONYMS irrational, illogical.

6 *three straight wins* SUCCESSIVE, in succession, consecutive, in a row, running.

7 *straight brandy* UNDILUTED, neat, pure, straight up. ANTONYM diluted.

8 *informal* *she's very straight* RESPECTABLE, conventional, conservative, traditional, old-fashioned, straitlaced; *informal* stuffy, square, fuddy-duddy.

▸ adverb **1** *he looked me straight in the eyes* RIGHT, directly, squarely, full; *informal* smack, bang, spang, smack dab.

2 *she drove straight home* DIRECTLY, right, by a direct route.

3 *I'll call you straight back* RIGHT AWAY, straightaway, immediately, directly, at once; *archaic* straightway.

4 *I told her straight* FRANKLY, directly, candidly, honestly, forthrightly, plainly, point-blank, bluntly, flatly, straight from the shoulder, without beating about the bush, without mincing words, unequivocally, unambiguously, in plain English, to someone's face, straight up.

5 *he can't think straight* LOGICALLY, rationally, clearly, lucidly, coherently, cogently.

PHRASES: **go straight** *maybe a few nights in jail will inspire him to go straight* REFORM, mend one's ways, turn over a new leaf, get back on the straight and narrow. **straight away** *I'll be there straightaway* AT ONCE, right away, (right) now, this/that (very) minute, this/that instant, immediately, instantly, directly, forthwith, without further/more ado, promptly, quickly, without delay, then and there, here and now, as soon as possible, ASAP, as quickly as possible, in short order; *informal* straight off, PDQ, pretty damn quick, pronto, lickety-split; *archaic* straightway. **straight from the shoulder** *I have to tell you the truth straight from the shoulder.* See STRAIGHT adverb sense 4.

straighten verb **1** *Rory straightened his tie* MAKE STRAIGHT, adjust, arrange, rearrange, (make) tidy, spruce up.

2 *we must straighten things out with Violet* PUT/SET RIGHT, sort out, clear up, settle, resolve, put in order, regularize, rectify, remedy; *informal* patch up.

3 *he straightened up* STAND UP (STRAIGHT), stand upright.

straightforward adjective **1** *the process was remarkably straightforward* UNCOMPLICATED, simple, easy, effortless, painless, undemanding, plain sailing, child's play; *informal* as easy as pie, a piece of cake, a cinch, a snip, a breeze, a cakewalk, duck soup, a snap. ANTONYM complicated.

2 *a straightforward man* HONEST, frank, candid, open, truthful, sincere, on the level; forthright, plain-speaking, direct, unambiguous; *informal* upfront, on the up and up. ANTONYM evasive.

strain[1] verb **1** *take care that you don't strain yourself* OVERTAX, overwork, overextend, overreach, drive too far; exhaust, wear out; overdo it; *informal* knock oneself out.

2 *you have strained a muscle* INJURE, damage, pull, wrench, twist, sprain.

3 *we strained to haul the guns up the slope* STRUGGLE, labor, toil, make every effort, try very hard, break one's back, push/drive oneself to the limit; *informal* pull out all the stops, go all out, bust a gut.

4 *the flood of refugees is straining the relief services* MAKE EXCESSIVE DEMANDS ON, overtax, be too much for, test, tax, put a strain on.

5 *the bear strained at the chain* PULL, tug, heave, haul, jerk; *informal* yank.

6 *archaic she strained the infant to her bosom* CLASP, press, clutch, hold tight; embrace, hug, enfold, envelop.

7 *strain the mixture* SIEVE, sift, filter, screen, riddle; *rare* filtrate.

▸ noun **1** *the rope snapped under the strain* TENSION, tightness, tautness.

2 *muscle strain* INJURY, sprain, wrench, twist.

3 *the strain of her job* PRESSURE, demands, burdens; stress; *informal* hassle.

4 *Nancy was showing signs of strain* STRESS, (nervous) tension; exhaustion, fatigue, pressure of work, overwork.

5 *the strains of Brahms's lullaby* SOUND, music; melody, tune.

strain[2] noun **1** *a different strain of flu* VARIETY, kind, type, sort; breed, genus.

2 *McCallum was of Puritan strain* DESCENT, ancestry, origin(s), parentage, lineage, extraction, family, roots.

3 *there was a strain of insanity in the family* TENDENCY, susceptibility, propensity, proneness; trait, disposition.

4 *a strain of solemnity* ELEMENT, strand, vein, note, trace, touch, suggestion, hint.

strained adjective **1** *relations between them were strained* AWKWARD, tense, uneasy, uncomfortable, edgy, difficult, troubled. ANTONYM friendly.

2 *Jean's strained face* DRAWN, careworn, worn, pinched, tired, exhausted, drained, haggard.

3 *a strained smile* FORCED, constrained, unnatural; artificial, insincere, false, affected, put-on. ANTONYM natural.

strainer noun *pour the noodles into a strainer* SIEVE, colander, filter, sifter, riddle, screen; *archaic* griddle.

strait noun **1** *a strait about six miles wide* CHANNEL, sound, inlet, stretch of water.

2 *the company is in desperate straits* A BAD/DIFFICULT SITUATION, difficulty, trouble, crisis, a mess, a predicament, a plight; *informal* hot/deep water, a jam, a hole, a bind, a fix, a scrape.

straitened adjective *our straitened circumstances improved once Desmond got his first teaching job* IMPOVERISHED, poverty-stricken, poor, destitute, penniless, as poor as a church mouse, in penury, impecunious, unable to make ends meet, in reduced circumstances; *informal* (flat) broke, strapped (for cash); *formal* penurious.

straitlaced adjective *our straitlaced relatives were horrified by Stacey's punk hairdo* PRIM (AND PROPER), prudish, puritanical, prissy, conservative, old-fashioned, stuffy, staid, narrow-minded; *informal* starchy, square, fuddy-duddy. ANTONYM broad-minded.

strand[1] noun **1** *strands of wool* THREAD, filament, fiber; length, ply.

2 *the various strands of the ecological movement* ELEMENT, component, factor, ingredient, aspect, feature, strain.

strand[2] noun *literary a walk along the strand* SEASHORE, shore, beach, sands, foreshore, shoreline, seaside, waterfront, front, waterside.

stranded adjective **1** *a stranded ship* BEACHED, grounded, run aground, high and dry; shipwrecked, wrecked, marooned.

2 *she was stranded in a strange city* HELPLESS, without resources, in difficulties; in the lurch, abandoned, deserted.

strange adjective **1** *strange things have been happening* UNUSUAL, odd, curious, peculiar, funny, bizarre, weird, uncanny, queer, unexpected, unfamiliar, atypical, anomalous, out of the ordinary, extraordinary, puzzling, mystifying, mysterious, perplexing, baffling, unaccountable, inexplicable, singular, freakish; suspicious, questionable; eerie, unnatural; *informal* fishy, bizarro, creepy, spooky. ANTONYMS ordinary, usual.

2 *strange clothes* WEIRD, eccentric, odd, peculiar, funny, bizarre, unusual; unconventional, outlandish, freakish, quirky, zany; *informal* wacky, way out, freaky, kooky, offbeat, off the wall, screwy, wacko. ANTONYMS normal, conventional.

3 *visiting a strange house* UNFAMILIAR, unknown, new. ANTONYM familiar.

4 *Jean was feeling strange* ILL, unwell, poorly, peaked; *informal* under the weather, funny, peculiar, lousy, off; *dated* queer. ANTONYM well.

5 *she felt strange with him* ILL AT EASE, uneasy, uncomfortable, awkward, self-conscious. ANTONYM relaxed.

strangeness noun *there was a strangeness about Wally that I couldn't quite explain* ODDITY, eccentricity, peculiarity, curiousness, bizarreness, weirdness, queerness, unusualness, abnormality, unaccountability, inexplicability, incongruousness, outlandishness, singularity.

stranger noun *they were taught to fear strangers* NEWCOMER, new arrival, visitor, outsider, newbie. PHRASE: **a stranger to** *I'm afraid I'm a stranger to these automated methods* UNACCUSTOMED TO, unfamiliar with, unused to, new to, fresh to, inexperienced in; *archaic* strange to.

strangle verb **1** *the victim was strangled with a scarf* THROTTLE, choke, garrote; *informal* strangulate.

2 *she strangled a sob* SUPPRESS, smother, stifle, repress, restrain, fight back, choke back.

3 *bureaucracy is strangling commercial activity* HAMPER, hinder, impede, restrict, inhibit, curb, check, constrain, squash, crush, suppress, repress.

strap noun *thick leather straps* THONG, tie, band, belt.

▸ verb **1** *a bag was strapped to the bicycle* FASTEN, secure, tie, bind, make fast, lash, truss.

2 *his knee was strapped up* BANDAGE, bind.

3 *his father strapped him.* See LASH verb sense 1.

strapping adjective *here comes Tom and his strapping son Leroy* BIG, strong, well-built, brawny, burly, broad-shouldered, muscular, hard-bodied, rugged; *informal* hunky, beefy; *dated* stalwart. ANTONYM weedy.

stratagem noun *Warren devised a series of stratagems to win their confidence* PLAN, scheme, tactic, maneuver, ploy, device, trick, ruse, plot, machination, dodge; subterfuge, artifice, wile; *archaic* shift.

USAGE NOTE **stratagem**

The mistaken spelling *strategem* (on the analogy of *strategy*) appears about 20% as often as the correct spelling *stratagem*. Though the words *stratagem* and *strategy* are etymologically related, they came into English by different routes, and their spellings diverged merely as a matter of long-standing convention. What happened is that the Latin *strategema* became *stratagema* in Romance languages such as French. (The *Century Dictionary* calls the Romance spelling "erroneous.") *Stratagem* came into English in the fifteenth century, through French. But it wasn't until the early nineteenth century that English and American writers borrowed *strategy* (originally a Greek term) from Latin. Hence our incongruous spellings today. **—BG**

strategic adjective *his lawyers were known for their strategic defense methods* PLANNED, calculated, tactical, politic, judicious, prudent, shrewd.

strategy noun **1** *the government's economic strategy* MASTER PLAN, grand design, game plan, plan (of action), action plan, policy, program; tactics.

2 *military strategy* THE ART OF WAR, (military) tactics.

stratum noun **1** *a stratum of flint* LAYER, vein, seam, lode, bed.

2 *this stratum of society* LEVEL, class, echelon, rank, grade, group, set; caste; *dated* station, estate.

stray verb **1** *the gazelle had strayed from the herd* WANDER OFF, go astray, get separated, get lost.

2 *we strayed from our original topic* DIGRESS, deviate, wander, get sidetracked, go off at a tangent, veer off; get off the subject.

3 *the young men were likely to stray* BE UNFAITHFUL, have affairs, cheat, philander; *informal* play around, play the field.

4 *forgive me, Father, for I have strayed* SIN, transgress, err, go astray; *archaic* trespass.

▸ adjective **1** *a stray dog* HOMELESS, lost, strayed, gone astray, abandoned.

2 *a stray bullet* RANDOM, chance, freak, unexpected, isolated, lone, single.

▸ noun *she adopted three strays* HOMELESS ANIMAL, stray dog/cat, waif.

streak noun **1** *a streak of orange light* BAND, line, strip, stripe, vein, slash, ray.

2 *green streaks on her legs* MARK, smear, smudge, stain, blotch; *informal* splotch.

3 *a streak of self-destructiveness* ELEMENT, vein, touch, strain; trait, characteristic.

4 *a winning streak* PERIOD, spell, stretch, run, patch.

▸ verb **1** *the sky was streaked with red* STRIPE, band, fleck.

2 *overalls streaked with paint* MARK, daub, smear; *informal* splotch.

stream noun **1** *a mountain stream* CREEK, river, rivulet, rill, runnel, streamlet, freshet; tributary; bourn; brook.

2 *a stream of boiling water* JET, flow, rush, gush, surge, torrent, flood, cascade, outpouring, outflow; *technical* efflux.

3 *a steady stream of visitors* SUCCESSION, flow, series, string.

▸ verb **1** *tears were streaming down her face* FLOW, pour, course, run, gush, surge, flood, cascade, spill.

2 *children streamed out of the classrooms* POUR, surge, charge, flood, swarm, pile, crowd.

3 *a flag streamed from the mast* FLUTTER, float, flap, fly, blow, waft, wave.

streamer noun *streamers fluttered from every post and pole along the parade route* PENNANT, pennon, flag, banderole, banner.

streamlined adjective **1** *streamlined cars* AERODYNAMIC, smooth, sleek.

2 *a streamlined organization* EFFICIENT, smooth-running, well run, slick; time-saving, labor-saving.

street noun *Amsterdam's narrow cobbled streets* ROAD, thoroughfare, avenue, drive, crescent, boulevard; side street/road, lane, highway. PHRASES: **the man/woman in the street** *they claim to be interested in what the man in the street has to say, but that hardly seems the case* AN ORDINARY PERSON, Mr./Ms. Average; *informal* Joe Public, John Q. Public, Joe Blow, Joe Schmo, schmo, John Doe, Joe Sixpack. **on the streets** *many of these teens have parents who don't care that their kids are on the streets* HOMELESS, down and out, of no fixed abode.

street smarts noun *Donna's the only one in their crowd with any street smarts* COMMON SENSE, acumen, savvy, shrewdness, wisdom, know-how, horse sense.

streetwise adjective *his mother had always tried to shield him from the more streetwise boys* WORLDLY, savvy, street smart, experienced, seasoned.

strength noun **1** *enormous physical strength* POWER, brawn, muscle, muscularity, burliness, sturdiness, robustness, toughness, hardiness; vigor, force, might; *informal* beef; *literary* thew. ANTONYMS weakness, frailty.

2 *Oliver began to regain his strength* HEALTH, fitness, vigor, stamina. ANTONYM infirmity.

3 *her great inner strength* FORTITUDE, resilience, spirit, backbone, strength of character; courage, bravery, pluck, pluckiness, courageousness, grit, mettle; *informal* guts, spunk. ANTONYM vulnerability.

4 *the strength of the retaining wall* ROBUSTNESS, sturdiness, firmness, toughness, soundness, solidity, durability. ANTONYM weakness.

5 *China's military strength* POWER, influence, dominance, ascendancy, supremacy; *informal* clout; *literary* puissance. ANTONYMS weakness, impotence.

6 *the strength of feeling against the president* INTENSITY, vehemence, force, forcefulness, depth, ardor, fervor. ANTONYM halfheartedness.

7 *the strength of their argument* COGENCY, forcefulness, force, weight, power, potency, persuasiveness, soundness, validity. ANTONYMS weakness, ineffectiveness.

8 *what are your strengths?* STRONG POINT, advantage, asset, forte, aptitude, talent, skill; specialty. ANTONYMS failing, flaw, limitation.

9 *the strength of the army* SIZE, extent, magnitude. ANTONYM weakness.

PHRASE: **on the strength of** *she got into Princeton on the strength of her essays* BECAUSE OF, by virtue of, on the basis of.

strengthen verb **1** *calcium strengthens growing bones* FORTIFY, make strong/stronger, build up, give strength to. ANTONYM weaken.

2 *engineers strengthened the walls* REINFORCE, make stronger, buttress, shore up, underpin.

3 *how does this process strengthen the glass?* TOUGHEN, temper, anneal.

4 *the wind had strengthened* BECOME STRONG/STRONGER, gain strength, intensify, pick up. ANTONYM die down.

5 *his insistence strengthened her determination* FORTIFY, bolster, make stronger, boost, reinforce, harden, stiffen, toughen, fuel. ANTONYM weaken.

6 *they strengthened their efforts* REDOUBLE, step up, increase, escalate; *informal* up, crank up, beef up. ANTONYMS relax, decrease.

7 *the argument is strengthened by this evidence* REINFORCE, lend more weight to; support, substantiate, back up, confirm, bear out, corroborate. ANTONYM undermine.

strenuous adjective **1** *a strenuous climb* ARDUOUS, difficult, hard, tough, taxing, demanding, exacting, exhausting, tiring, grueling, back-breaking; *informal* killing; *archaic* toilsome. ANTONYM easy.

2 *strenuous efforts* VIGOROUS, energetic, zealous, forceful, strong, spirited, intense, determined, resolute, tenacious, tireless, indefatigable, dogged; *formal* pertinacious. ANTONYM halfhearted.

stress noun **1** *he's under a lot of stress* STRAIN, pressure, (nervous) tension, worry, anxiety, trouble, difficulty; *informal* hassle.

2 *laying greater stress on education* EMPHASIS, importance, weight.

3 *the stress falls on the first syllable* EMPHASIS, accent, accentuation; beat; *Prosody* ictus.

4 *the stress is uniform across the bar* PRESSURE, tension, strain.

▸ verb **1** *they stressed the need for reform* EMPHASIZE, draw attention to, underline, underscore, point up, place emphasis on, lay stress on, highlight, accentuate, press home. ANTONYM play down.

2 *the last syllable is stressed* PLACE THE EMPHASIS ON, emphasize, place the accent on.

3 *all the staff were stressed* OVERSTRETCH, overtax, push to the limit, pressure, make tense, worry, harass; *informal* hassle.

stressful adjective *it had been a stressful day* DEMANDING, trying, taxing, difficult, hard, tough; fraught, traumatic, pressured, tense, frustrating. ANTONYM relaxing.

stretch verb **1** *this material stretches* BE ELASTIC, be stretchy, be tensile.

2 *he stretched the elastic* PULL (OUT), draw out, extend, lengthen, elongate, expand.

3 *stretch your weekend into a vacation* PROLONG, lengthen, make longer, extend, spin out. ANTONYM shorten.

4 *my budget won't* ***stretch to*** *a new car* BE SUFFICIENT FOR, be enough for, cover; afford, have the money for.

5 *the court case stretched their finances* PUT A STRAIN ON, overtax, overextend, drain, sap.

6 *stretching the truth* BEND, strain, distort, exaggerate, embellish.

7 *she* ***stretched out*** *her hand to him* REACH OUT, hold out, extend, outstretch, proffer; *literary* outreach. ANTONYM withdraw.

8 *he stretched his arms* EXTEND, straighten (out).

9 *she* ***stretched out*** *on the sofa* LIE DOWN, recline, lean back, be recumbent, sprawl, lounge, loll.

10 *the desert stretches for miles* EXTEND, spread, continue.

▸ noun **1** *magnificent stretches of forest* EXPANSE, area, tract, belt, sweep, extent.

2 *a four-hour stretch* PERIOD, time, spell, run, stint, session, shift.

3 *informal a ten-year stretch* (PRISON) SENTENCE, (prison) term, stint, rap.

▸ adjective *stretch fabrics* STRETCHY, stretchable, elastic.

strew verb *rose petals were strewn along the aisle* SCATTER, spread, disperse, litter, toss; *literary* bestrew.

stricken adjective *stricken with grief | she looked at Anne's stricken face* TROUBLED, (deeply) affected, afflicted, struck, hit.

strict adjective **1** *a strict interpretation of the law* PRECISE, exact, literal, faithful, accurate, rigorous, careful, meticulous, pedantic. ANTONYMS loose, imprecise.

2 *strict controls on spending* STRINGENT, rigorous, severe, harsh, hard, rigid, tough, ironclad. See note at SEVERE. ANTONYM liberal.

3 *strict parents* STERN, severe, harsh, uncompromising, authoritarian, governessy, firm, austere. ANTONYM lenient.

4 *this will be treated in strict confidence* ABSOLUTE, utter, complete, total.

5 *a strict Roman Catholic* ORTHODOX, devout, conscientious. ANTONYMS moderate, liberal.

strictness noun **1** *the strictness of the laws* SEVERITY, harshness, rigidity, rigidness, stringency, rigorousness, sternness. ANTONYM flexibility.

2 *the provision has been interpreted with strictness* PRECISION, preciseness, accuracy, exactness, faithfulness; meticulousness, scrupulousness. ANTONYM imprecision.

stricture noun **1** *the constant strictures of the nuns* CRITICISM, censure, condemnation, reproof, reproach, admonishment, animadversion. ANTONYM praise.

2 *the strictures on Victorian women* CONSTRAINT, restriction, limitation, restraint, curb, impediment, barrier, obstacle. ANTONYM freedom.

3 *an intestinal stricture* NARROWING, constriction.

stride verb *she came striding down the path* MARCH, pace, step.

▸ noun *long swinging strides* (LONG/LARGE) STEP, pace.

PHRASE: **take something in one's stride** *he seem to be tak-*

ing the news in his stride DEAL WITH EASILY, cope with easily, not bat an eyelid.

strident adjective *a strident voice interrupted the consultation* HARSH, raucous, rough, grating, rasping, jarring, loud, shrill, screeching, piercing, ear-piercing. See note at VOCIFEROUS. ANTONYM soft.

strife noun *these countries have been immersed in political strife for more than a hundred years* CONFLICT, friction, discord, disagreement, dissension, dispute, argument, quarreling, wrangling, bickering, controversy; ill/bad feeling, falling-out, bad blood, hostility, animosity. ANTONYM peace.

strike verb **1** *the teacher struck Mary* HIT, slap, smack, beat, thrash, spank, thump, punch, cuff; cane, lash, whip, club; *informal* clout, schmuck, wallop, belt, whack, thwack, bash, clobber, bop, cold-cock; *literary* smite.

2 *he struck the gong* BANG, beat, hit; *informal* bash, wallop.

3 *the car struck a tree* CRASH INTO, collide with, hit, run into, bump into, smash into, impact.

4 *Jennifer struck the ball* HIT, drive, propel; *informal* clout, wallop, swipe.

5 *he struck a match* IGNITE, light.

6 *she was asleep when the killer struck* ATTACK, set upon someone, fall on someone, assault someone.

7 *the disease is striking 3,000 people a year* AFFECT, afflict, attack, hit.

8 *striking a balance* ACHIEVE, reach, arrive at, find, attain, establish.

9 *we have struck a bargain* AGREE (ON), come to an agreement on, settle on; *informal* clinch.

10 *he struck a heroic pose* ASSUME, adopt, take on/up, affect, cop.

11 *they have struck oil* DISCOVER, find, come upon, hit.

12 *a thought struck her* OCCUR TO, come to (mind), dawn on one, hit, spring to mind, enter one's head.

13 *you strike me as intelligent* SEEM TO, appear to, come across to, give the impression to.

14 *drivers are striking* TAKE INDUSTRIAL ACTION, go on strike, down tools, walk out, hit the bricks.

15 *the commodore struck his flag* LOWER, take down, bring down.

16 *we should strike south* GO, make one's way, head, forge.

▸ noun **1** *a 48-hour strike* INDUSTRIAL ACTION, walkout, job action, stoppage.

2 *a military strike* (AIR) ATTACK, assault, bombing, raid.

3 *a gold strike* FIND, discovery.

PHRASES: **strike out** *strike out the old phone number* DELETE, cross out, erase, rub out. **strike up 1** *the band struck up another tune* BEGIN TO PLAY, start playing. **2** *we struck up a friendship* BEGIN, start, commence, embark on, establish.

striking adjective **1** *Lizzie bears a striking resemblance to her sister* NOTICEABLE, obvious, conspicuous, evident, marked, notable, unmistakable, strong; remarkable, extraordinary, incredible, amazing, astounding, astonishing, staggering. See note at NOTICEABLE. ANTONYM unremarkable.

2 *Kenya's striking landscape* IMPRESSIVE, imposing, grand, splendid, magnificent, spectacular, breathtaking, superb, marvelous, wonderful, stunning, staggering, sensational, dramatic. ANTONYM unimpressive.

3 *what a striking young couple* STUNNING, attractive, good-looking, beautiful, glamorous, gorgeous, prepossessing, ravishing, handsome, pretty; *informal* knockout, drop-dead gorgeous; *archaic* fair, comely. ANTONYMS unremarkable, unattractive.

string noun **1** *a knotted piece of string* TWINE, cord, yarn, thread, strand.

2 *a string of convenience stores* CHAIN, group, firm, company.

3 *a string of convictions* SERIES, succession, chain, sequence, run, streak.

4 *a string of wagons* LINE, train, procession, queue, file, column, convoy, cavalcade.

5 *a string of pearls* STRAND, rope, necklace.

6 *a guaranteed loan with no strings* CONDITION, qualification, provision, proviso, caveat, stipulation, rider, prerequisite, limitation, limit, constraint, restriction; *informal* catch.

▸ verb **1** *lights were strung across the promenade* HANG, suspend, sling, stretch, run; thread, loop, festoon.

2 *beads strung on a silver chain* THREAD, loop, link.

PHRASES: **string along 1** *must your sister always string along?* GO ALONG, come too, accompany someone, join someone. **2** *I think Daisy is just stringing poor Dave along* MISLEAD, deceive, take advantage of, dupe, hoax, fool, make a fool of, play with, toy with, dally with, trifle with; *informal* lead up the garden path, take for a ride. **string out 1** *stringing out a story* SPIN OUT, drag out, lengthen. **2** *airfields strung out along the Gulf* SPREAD OUT, space out, distribute, scatter. **string up** *informal Dawes and his boys went after Lucius, threatening to string him up* HANG, lynch, gibbet.

stringent adjective *stringent regulations* STRICT, firm, rigid, rigorous, severe, harsh, tough, tight, exacting, demanding, inflexible, hard and fast.

stringy adjective **1** *stringy hair* STRAGGLY, lank, thin.

2 *a stringy brunette* LANKY, gangling, gangly, rangy, wiry, bony, skinny, scrawny, thin, spare, gaunt.

3 *stringy meat* FIBROUS, gristly, sinewy, chewy, tough, leathery.

strip[1] verb **1** *he stripped and got into bed* UNDRESS, strip off, take one's clothes off, unclothe, disrobe, strip naked. ANTONYM dress.

2 ***stripping off** paint* PEEL (OFF), remove, take off, scrape (off), rub off, clean off.

3 *they **stripped her of** her doctorate* TAKE AWAY FROM SOMEONE, dispossess someone of, deprive someone of, confiscate, divest someone of, relieve someone of.

4 *they **stripped down** my engine* DISMANTLE, disassemble, take to bits/pieces, take apart. ANTONYM assemble.

5 *the house had been stripped* EMPTY, clear, clean out, plunder, rob, burgle, burglarize, loot, pillage, ransack, despoil, sack.

strip[2] noun *a strip of paper* (NARROW) PIECE, bit, band, belt, ribbon, slip, shred.

stripe noun *it's a red jacket with a white stripe down each sleeve* LINE, band, strip, belt, bar, streak, vein, flash, blaze; *technical* stria, striation.

striped adjective *a tropical plant with large striped leaves* barred, lined, banded, stripy; streaky, variegated; *technical* striated.

stripling noun *it's natural for these striplings to get into a bit of trouble now and then* YOUTH, adolescent, youngster, boy, schoolboy, lad, teenager, juvenile, minor, young man; *informal* kid, young 'un, whippersnapper, shaver.

stripper noun *she was a stripper in one of those exclusive clubs* EXOTIC DANCER, lap dancer, striptease artist; *informal* peeler; *humorous* ecdysiast.

strive verb **1** *I shall strive to be virtuous* TRY (HARD), attempt, endeavor, aim, venture, make an effort, exert oneself, do one's best, do all one can, do one's utmost, labor, work; *informal* go all out, give it one's best shot, pull out all the stops; *formal* essay.

2 *scholars must strive against bias* STRUGGLE, fight, battle, combat; campaign, crusade.

stroke noun **1** *five strokes of the ax* BLOW, hit, thump, punch, slap, smack, cuff, knock; *informal* wallop, clout, whack, thwack, bash, swipe; *archaic* smite.

2 *she hit the green in three strokes* SHOT, hit, strike.

3 *light upward strokes* MOVEMENT, action, motion.

4 *a stroke of genius* FEAT, accomplishment, achievement, master stroke.

5 *broad brush strokes* MARK, line.

6 *the budget was full of bold strokes* DETAIL, touch, point.

7 *he suffered a stroke* THROMBOSIS, seizure; *Medicine* ictus.

▸ verb *she stroked the cat* CARESS, fondle, pat, pet, touch, rub, massage, soothe.

stroll verb *they strolled along the river* SAUNTER, amble, wander, meander, ramble, promenade, walk, go for a walk, stretch one's legs, get some air; *informal* mosey; *formal* perambulate.

▸ noun *a stroll in the park* SAUNTER, amble, wander, walk, turn, promenade; *informal* mosey; *dated* constitutional; *formal* perambulation.

strong adjective **1** *Ben is a strong lad* POWERFUL, muscular, brawny, powerfully built, strapping, sturdy, burly, meaty, robust, athletic, tough, rugged, lusty, strong as an ox/horse; *informal* beefy, hunky, husky; *dated* stalwart. ANTONYMS weak, puny.

2 *a strong character* FORCEFUL, determined, spirited, self-assertive, tough, tenacious, indomitable, formidable, redoubtable, strong-minded; *informal* gutsy, feisty. ANTONYM weak.

3 *a strong fortress* SECURE, well-built, indestructible, well fortified, well protected, impregnable, solid.

4 *strong cotton bags* DURABLE, hardwearing, heavy-duty, industrial-strength, tough, sturdy, well-made, long-lasting. ANTONYMS weak, flimsy.

5 *the current is very strong* FORCEFUL, powerful, vigorous, fierce, intense. ANTONYM gentle.

6 *a strong interest in literature* KEEN, eager, passionate, fervent.

7 *strong feelings* INTENSE, forceful, passionate, ardent, fervent, fervid, deep-seated; *literary* perfervid.

8 *a strong supporter* KEEN, eager, enthusiastic, dedicated, staunch, loyal, steadfast.

9 *strong arguments* COMPELLING, cogent, forceful, powerful, potent, weighty, convincing, sound, valid, well-founded, persuasive, influential. ANTONYMS weak, unconvincing.

10 *a need for strong action* FIRM, forceful, drastic, extreme.

11 *she bore a very strong resemblance to Vera* MARKED, striking, noticeable, pronounced, distinct, definite, unmistakable, notable. ANTONYM slight.

12 *a strong voice* LOUD, powerful, forceful, resonant, sonorous, rich, deep, booming. ANTONYMS weak, quiet.

13 *strong language* BAD, foul, obscene, profane.

14 *a strong blue color* INTENSE, deep, rich, bright, brilliant, vivid. ANTONYM pale.

15 *strong lights* BRIGHT, brilliant, dazzling, glaring.

16 *strong black coffee* CONCENTRATED, undiluted, potent. ANTONYMS weak, mild.

17 *strong cheese* HIGHLY FLAVORED, flavorful, piquant, tangy, spicy. ANTONYM mild.

18 *strong drink* ALCOHOLIC, intoxicating, hard, stiff; *formal* spirituous. ANTONYMS soft, nonalcoholic.

strong-arm adjective *their strong-arm tactics won't work with me* AGGRESSIVE, forceful, bullying, coercive, threatening, intimidatory.

strongbox noun *there was nothing in the strongbox but some worthless old stocks* SAFE, safety deposit box, cash/money box.

stronghold noun **1** *the enemy stronghold* FORTRESS, fort, castle, citadel, garrison.

2 *a liberal stronghold* BASTION, center, hotbed, safe seat.

strong-minded adjective *a strong-minded social reformer* DETERMINED, firm, resolute, purposeful, strong-willed, uncompromising, unbending, forceful, persistent, tenacious, dogged; *informal* gutsy, spunky.

strong point noun *hiring the right people is her strong point* STRENGTH, strong suit, forte, specialty. ANTONYM weakness.

strong-willed adjective *you strong-willed recruits had better prepare yourselves to get broken* DETERMINED, resolute, stubborn, obstinate, willful, headstrong, strong-minded, self-willed, unbending, unyielding, intransigent, intractable, obdurate, recalcitrant; *formal* refractory.

structure noun **1** *a vast Gothic structure* BUILDING, edifice, construction, erection, pile.

2 *the structure of local government* CONSTRUCTION, form, formation, shape, composition, anatomy, makeup, constitution; organization, system, arrangement, design, framework, configuration, pattern.

▸ verb *the program is structured around periods of home study* ARRANGE, organize, design, shape, construct, build, put together.

struggle verb **1** *they struggled to do better* STRIVE, try hard, endeavor, make every effort, do one's best/utmost, bend over backwards, put oneself out; *informal* go all out, give it one's best shot; *formal* essay.

2 *James struggled with the intruders* FIGHT, grapple, wrestle, scuffle, brawl, spar; *informal* scrap.

3 *the teams struggled to be first* COMPETE, contend, vie, fight, battle, jockey.

4 *she struggled over the dunes* SCRAMBLE, flounder, stumble, fight/battle one's way, labor.

▸ noun **1** *the struggle for justice* ENDEAVOR, striving, effort, exertion, labor; campaign, battle, crusade, drive, push.

2 *they were arrested without a struggle* FIGHT, scuffle, brawl, tussle, wrestling bout, skirmish, fracas, melee; breach of the peace; *informal* scrap.

3 *many perished in the struggle* CONFLICT, fight, battle, confrontation, clash, skirmish; hostilities, fighting, war, warfare, campaign.

4 *a struggle within the leadership* CONTEST, competition, fight, clash; rivalry, friction, feuding, conflict, tug-of-war, turf war.

5 *life has been a struggle for me* EFFORT, trial, trouble, stress, strain, battle; *informal* grind, hassle.

strumpet noun *dated* See PROSTITUTE noun.

strut verb *he strutted around his vast office* SWAGGER, swank, parade, stride, sweep, sashay.

stub noun **1** *a cigarette stub* BUTT, (tail) end.

2 *a ticket stub* COUNTERFOIL, ticket slip, tab.

3 *a stub of pencil* STUMP, remnant, (tail) end.

stubble noun **1** *a field of stubble* STALKS, straw.

2 *gray stubble* BRISTLES, whiskers, facial hair; *informal* five o'clock shadow.

stubbly adjective *his stubbly face was not exactly kissable* BRISTLY, unshaven, whiskered; prickly, rough, coarse, scratchy.

stubborn adjective **1** *you're too stubborn to admit it* OBSTINATE, headstrong, willful, strong-willed, pigheaded, obdurate, difficult, contrary, perverse, recalcitrant, inflexible, iron-willed, uncompromising, unbending; *informal* stiff-necked, bloody-minded, balky; *formal* pertinacious, refractory, contumacious. ANTONYM compliant.

2 *stubborn stains* INDELIBLE, permanent, persistent, tenacious, resistant.

THE RIGHT WORD

If you're the kind of person who takes a stand and then refuses to back down, your friends might say you have a **stubborn** disposition, a word that implies an innate resistance to any attempt to change one's purpose, course, or opinion. People who are *stubborn* by nature exhibit this kind of behavior in most situations, but they might be **obstinate** in a particular instance (*a stubborn child, he was obstinate in his refusal to eat vegetables*). *Obstinate* implies sticking persistently to an opinion, purpose, or course of action, especially in the face of persuasion or attack. While *obstinate* is usually a negative term, **dogged** can be either positive or negative, implying both tenacious, often sullen, persistence (*dogged pursuit of a college degree, even though he knew he would end up in the family business*) and great determination (*dogged loyalty to a cause*). **Obdurate** usually connotes a stubborn resistance marked by harshness and lack of feeling (*obdurate in ignoring their pleas*), while **intractable** means stubborn in a headstrong sense and difficult for others to control or manage (*intractable pain*). No matter how stubborn you are, you probably don't want to be called **pertinacious**, which implies persistence to the point of being annoying or unreasonable (*a pertinacious panhandler*).

stubby adjective *a small stubby man with glasses* DUMPY, stocky, chunky, chubby, squat; short, stumpy, dwarfish; *informal* vertically challenged. ANTONYMS slender, tall.

stuck adjective **1** *a message was stuck to his screen* FIXED, fastened, attached, glued, pinned.

2 *the gate was stuck* IMMOVABLE, stuck fast, jammed.

3 *if you get stuck, leave a blank* BAFFLED, beaten, at a loss, at one's wits' end; *informal* stumped, bogged down, flummoxed, fazed, bamboozled. PHRASES: **stuck on** *informal no one knew that Kit was stuck on his brother's wife* INFATUATED WITH, besotted with, smitten with, (head over heels) in love with, obsessed with; *informal* crazy about, mad about, wild about, carrying a torch for. **stuck with** *she's always getting stuck with the neighbors' kids* LUMBERED WITH, left with, made responsible for.

stuck-up adjective *informal* See CONCEITED.

stud noun **1** *he's a real stud* HUNK, ladies' man, ladykiller, Romeo, Don Juan, Casanova, Lothario, womanizer, playboy, gigolo, lover, chick/babe magnet, studmuffin.

2 *a jacket with silver studs* BUTTON, fastener; knob, boss; ornament, jewel.

studded adjective *stone-washed jeans studded with rhinestones* DOTTED, scattered, sprinkled, covered, spangled; *literary* bespangled, bejeweled.

student noun **1** *a college student* SCHOLAR, undergraduate, graduate, grad student, postdoctoral fellow; freshman, sophomore, junior, senior.

2 *high school student* PUPIL, schoolchild, schoolboy, schoolgirl, scholar.

3 *a nursing student* TRAINEE, apprentice, probationer, recruit, intern, novice; *informal* rookie.

studied adjective the words were said with studied politeness DELIBERATE, careful, considered, conscious, calculated, intentional; affected, forced, strained, artificial.

studio noun *the artist's studio* WORKSHOP, workroom, atelier, workspace.

studious adjective **1** *a studious nature* SCHOLARLY, academic, bookish, intellectual, erudite, learned, donnish.

2 *studious attention* DILIGENT, careful, attentive, assiduous, painstaking, thorough, meticulous.

3 *his studious absence from public view* DELIBERATE, willful, conscious, intentional.

study noun **1** *two years of study* LEARNING, education, schooling, academic work, scholarship, tuition, research; *informal* cramming.

2 *a study of global warming* INVESTIGATION, inquiry, research, examination, analysis, review, survey.

3 *Father was in his study* OFFICE, workroom, studio.

4 *a critical study* ESSAY, article, work, review, paper, dissertation, disquisition.

▸ verb **1** *Anne studied hard* WORK, review; *informal* cram, hit the books.

2 *he studied electronics* LEARN, read, be taught.

3 *Thomas was studying child development* INVESTIGATE, inquire into, research, look into, examine, analyze, explore, review, appraise, conduct a survey of.

4 *she studied her friend thoughtfully* SCRUTINIZE, examine, inspect, consider, regard, look at, eye, observe, watch, survey; *informal* check out, eyeball.

PHRASE: **in a brown study** *you'll often catch a student in a brown study on a warm spring day like today* LOST IN THOUGHT, in a reverie, musing, ruminating, cogitating, dreaming, daydreaming; *informal* miles away.

stuff noun **1** *suede is tough stuff* MATERIAL, fabric, cloth, textile; matter, substance.

2 *first-aid stuff* ITEMS, articles, objects, goods, equipment; *informal* things, bits and pieces, odds and ends.

3 *all my stuff is in the suitcase* BELONGINGS, (personal) possessions, effects, goods (and chattels), paraphernalia; *informal* gear, things.

4 *he knows his stuff* FACTS, information, data, subject.

▸ verb **1** *stuffing pillows* FILL, pack, pad, upholster.

2 *Robyn stuffed her clothes into a bag* SHOVE, thrust, push, ram, cram, squeeze, force, jam, pack, pile, stick.

3 *informal they* ***stuffed themselves with*** *chocolate* FILL ONESELF WITH, gorge oneself with/on, overindulge oneself with; gobble, devour, wolf; *informal* pig out on, make a pig of oneself with/on.

4 *my nose was* ***stuffed up*** BLOCK (UP), congest, obstruct.

stuffing noun **1** *the stuffing is coming out of the armchair* PADDING, wadding, filling, upholstery, packing, filler.

2 *sage and onion stuffing* dressing, filling, forcemeat, salpicon. PHRASE: **knock the stuffing out of** *informal news of Pam's engagement knocked the stuffing out of Bob* DEVASTATE, shatter, crush, shock.

stuffy adjective **1** *a stuffy atmosphere* AIRLESS, close, musty, stale. ANTONYM airy.

2 *a stuffy young man* STAID, sedate, sober, prim, priggish, straitlaced, conformist, conservative, old-fashioned, governessy; *informal* square, straight, starchy, fuddy-duddy. ANTONYMS laid-back, modern.

3 *a stuffy nose* BLOCKED, stuffed up, congested. ANTONYM clear.

stultify verb **1** *social welfare was stultified by international trade regulations* HAMPER, impede, thwart, frustrate, foil, suppress, smother.

2 *he stultifies her with too much gentleness* BORE, make bored, dull, numb, benumb, stupefy.

stumble verb **1** *she stumbled and fell heavily* TRIP (OVER/UP), lose one's balance, lose/miss one's footing, slip.

2 *he stumbled back home* STAGGER, totter, teeter, dodder, blunder, hobble, move clumsily.

3 *she stumbled through her speech* STAMMER, stutter, hesitate, falter, speak haltingly; *informal* fluff/flub one's lines. PHRASE: **stumble across/on** *I stumbled across these old photographs in the attic* COME ACROSS/UPON, chance on, happen on, bump into, light on; discover, find, unearth, uncover; *informal* dig up.

stumbling block noun *Abel never let his deformity be a stumbling block* OBSTACLE, hurdle, barrier, bar, hindrance, impediment, handicap, disadvantage; snag, hitch, catch, drawback, difficulty, problem, weakness, defect, pitfall; *informal* fly in the ointment, hiccup.

stump verb *we could never stump Mr. Marlowe with our riddles* BAFFLE, perplex, puzzle, confuse, confound, defeat, put at a loss; *informal* flummox, throw, floor, discombobulate.

stumpy adjective *a stumpy and sturdy little dog* SHORT, stubby, squat, stocky, chunky. ANTONYMS long, thin.

stun verb **1** *a glancing blow stunned Gary* DAZE, stupefy, knock unconscious, knock out, lay out.

2 *she was stunned by the news* ASTOUND, amaze, astonish, dumbfound, stupefy, stagger, shock, take aback; *informal* flabbergast, bowl over.

stunning adjective **1** *a stunning win* REMARKABLE, extraordinary, staggering, incredible, outstanding, amazing, astonishing, marvelous, phenomenal, splendid; *informal* fabulous, fantastic, tremendous, jaw-dropping. ANTONYM ordinary.

2 *she was looking stunning.* See BEAUTIFUL.

WORD NOTE **stunning**

Stunning is probably the most overused synonym for "very good," especially in movie ads and book blurbs. When was the last time you went to a movie and saw a performance that actually "stunned" you—i.e., rendered you unconscious or semiconscious? Use of the word in this context has become not only an empty cliché but also annoyingly counterintuitive: wouldn't you be more likely to feel *stunned* by something bad than by something good? If you insist on using this word, try reversing the polarity and making it an insult. Lincoln, for example, knew how to use *stun* so that it really did retain the force of a blunt object—as when he contemptuously described General Rosecrans after a losing battle: "Confused and stunned, like a duck that's been hit on the head." **—DA**

stunt[1] verb *a disease that stunts growth* INHIBIT, impede, hamper, hinder, restrict, retard, slow, curb, check. ANTONYM encourage.

stunt[2] noun *acrobatic stunts* FEAT, exploit, trick.

stunted adjective *a stunted geranium* SMALL, undersize(d), diminutive.

stupefaction noun **1** *alcoholic stupefaction* OBLIVION, obliviousness, unconsciousness, insensibility, stupor, daze.

2 *Don shook his head in stupefaction* BEWILDERMENT, confusion, perplexity, wonder, amazement, astonishment.

stupefy verb **1** *the blow had stupefied her* STUN, daze, knock unconscious, knock out, lay out.

2 *they were stupefied from the wine* DRUG, sedate, tranquilize, intoxicate, inebriate; *informal* dope.

3 *the cost stupefied us* SHOCK, stun, astound, dumbfound, overwhelm, stagger, amaze, astonish, take aback, take someone's breath away; *informal* flabbergast, bowl over, floor.

stupendous adjective **1** *stupendous achievements* AMAZING, astounding, astonishing, extraordinary, remarkable, phenomenal, staggering, breathtaking; *informal* fantastic, mind-boggling, awesome; *literary* wondrous. ANTONYM ordinary.

2 *a building of stupendous size* COLOSSAL, immense, vast, gigantic, massive, mammoth, huge, enormous. ANTONYM minute.

stupid adjective **1** *they're rather stupid* UNINTELLIGENT, ignorant, dense, foolish, dull-witted, slow, simpleminded, vacuous, vapid, idiotic, imbecilic, imbecile, obtuse, doltish; *informal* thick, dim, dimwitted, dumb, dopey, dozy, moronic, cretinous, pea-brained, halfwitted, soft in the head, brain-dead, boneheaded, thickheaded, wooden-headed, muttonheaded, daft. ANTONYM intelligent.

2 *that was a really stupid thing to do* FOOLISH, silly, unintelligent, idiotic, scatterbrained, nonsensical, senseless, unthinking, ill-advised, ill-considered, unwise, injudicious; inane, absurd, ludicrous, ridiculous, laughable, risible, fatuous, asinine, mad, insane, lunatic; *informal* crazy, dopey, cracked, half-baked, dimwitted, cockeyed, harebrained, lamebrained, nutty, batty, cuckoo, loony, loopy. ANTONYM sensible.

3 *he drank himself stupid* INTO A STUPOR, into a daze, into oblivion; stupefied, dazed, unconscious. ANTONYM alert.

THE RIGHT WORD

If you want to impugn someone's intelligence, the options are almost limitless. You can call the person **stupid**, a term that implies a sluggish, slow-witted lack of intelligence. **Asinine** is a harsher word, implying asslike or foolish behavior rather than slow-wittedness (*a woman her age looked asinine in a miniskirt*). Calling someone **dumb** is risky, because it is not only an informal word (*you dumb bunny!*), but because it also means mute and is associated with the offensive expression "deaf and dumb," used to describe people who cannot hear or speak. **Dense** implies an inability to understand even simple facts or instructions (*too dense to get the joke*), while **dull** suggests a sluggishness of mind unrelieved by any hint of quickness, brightness, or liveliness (*a dull stare*). **Slow** also implies a lack of quickness in comprehension or reaction and is often used as a euphemistic substitute for *stupid* (*he was a little slow intellectually*). **Obtuse** is a more formal word for slow-wittedness, but with a strong undercurrent of scorn (*it almost seemed as though he were being deliberately obtuse*). You can't go wrong with a word like **unintelligent**, which is probably the most objective term for low mental ability and the least likely to provoke an angry response (*unintelligent answers to the teacher's questions*).

stupidity noun **1** *he cursed their stupidity* LACK OF INTELLIGENCE, foolishness, denseness, brainlessness, ignorance, dull-wittedness, slow-wittedness, doltishness, slowness; *informal* thickness, dimness, dopiness.

2 *the stupidity of the question* FOOLISHNESS, folly, silliness, idiocy, brainlessness, senselessness, injudiciousness, ineptitude, inaneness, inanity, absurdity, ludicrousness, ridiculousness, fatuousness, madness, insanity, lunacy; *informal* craziness.

stupor noun *they left him slumped in a drunken stupor* DAZE, state of unconsciousness, torpor, insensibility, oblivion.

sturdy adjective **1** *a sturdy lad* STRAPPING, well-built, muscular, athletic, strong, hefty, brawny, powerful, solid, burly, rugged, robust, tough, hardy, lusty; *informal* husky, beefy, meaty; *dated* stalwart; *literary* thewy. ANTONYMS puny, frail.

2 *sturdy boots* ROBUST, strong, strongly made, well built, solid, stout, tough, resilient, durable, long-lasting, hard-wearing. ANTONYMS weak, flimsy.

3 *sturdy resistance* VIGOROUS, strong, stalwart, firm, determined, resolute, staunch, steadfast. ANTONYM weak.

stutter verb *he stuttered over a word* STAMMER, stumble, falter.

▸ noun *a bad stutter* STAMMER, speech impediment, speech defect.

Stygian adjective *literary* See DARK adjective sense 1.

style noun **1** *differing styles of management* MANNER, way, technique, method, methodology, approach, system, mode, form, modus operandi; *informal* MO.

2 *a nondirective style of counseling* TYPE, kind, variety, sort, genre, school, brand, pattern, model.

3 *wearing clothes with style* FLAIR, stylishness, elegance, grace, gracefulness, poise, polish, suaveness, sophistication, urbanity, chic, dash, panache, élan; *informal* class, pizzazz.

4 *Laura traveled in style* COMFORT, luxury, elegance, opulence, lavishness.

5 *modern styles* FASHION, trend, vogue, mode.

▸ verb **1** *sportswear styled by Karl* DESIGN, fashion, tailor.

2 *men who were styled "knight"* CALL, name, title, entitle, dub, designate, term, label, tag, nickname; *formal* denominate.

WORD NOTE **style**

In the past, a writer's style was thought to reflect that person's character—thus Julius Caesar's masculine authority and decisiveness can be seen in any line of his commentaries on the Gallic Wars. What you read was the verbal expression of the man himself. But a style can also be a disguise or the expression of a secret self. Yeats maintained that to create art one needed to wear a mask. What, after all, is so common as the humorist revealed as sullen and melancholy in real life? Often to write well, an inner daemon must be allowed to break free. We put aside our staid daytime selves for a more swashbuckling or daring, bawdy, or ironic personality in print. Be wary then of drawing conclusions about writers from their diction. Murderers have been known to possess fancy prose styles, and the crisp, no-nonsense sentences of Hemingway are far more stoic and assured than the man who typed them. **—MD**

stylish adjective *a stylish raincoat* FASHIONABLE, modish, voguish, modern, up to date; smart, sophisticated, elegant, chic, dapper, dashing; *informal* trendy, natty, classy, nifty, ritzy, snazzy, fly, kicky, tony, spiffy. ANTONYM unfashionable.

stymie verb *informal* See HAMPER².

suave adjective *your clothes should show what a suave man you are* CHARMING, sophisticated, debonair, urbane, polished, refined, poised, self-possessed, dignified, civilized, gentlemanly, gallant; smooth, polite, well-mannered, civil, courteous, affable, tactful, diplomatic. See note at URBANE. ANTONYM unsophisticated.

suavity noun *the suavity of Cary Grant* CHARM, sophistication, polish, urbanity, suaveness, refinement, poise; politeness, courtesy, courteousness, civility, tact.

subconscious adjective *subconscious desires* UNCONSCIOUS, latent, suppressed, repressed, subliminal, dormant, underlying, innermost; *informal* bottled up.

▸ noun *the creative powers of the subconscious* (UNCONSCIOUS) MIND, imagination, inner(most) self, psyche.

subdue verb **1** *he subdued all his enemies* CONQUER, defeat, vanquish, overcome, overwhelm, crush, quash, beat, trounce, subjugate, suppress, bring someone to their knees; *informal* lick, thrash, hammer.

2 *she could not subdue her longing* CURB, restrain, hold back, constrain, contain, repress, suppress, stifle, smother, keep in check, rein in, control, master, quell; *informal* keep a/the lid on.

subdued adjective **1** *Lewis's subdued air* SOMBER, low-spirited, downcast, sad, dejected, depressed, gloomy, despondent, dispirited, disheartened, forlorn, woebegone; withdrawn, preoccupied; *informal* down in/at the mouth, down in the dumps, in the doldrums, in a blue funk. ANTONYMS cheerful, lively.

2 *subdued voices* HUSHED, muted, quiet, low, soft, faint, muffled, indistinct. ANTONYM loud.

3 *subdued light* DIM, muted, softened, soft, lowered, subtle. ANTONYM bright.

subject noun **1** *the subject of this chapter* THEME, subject matter, topic, issue, question, concern, point; substance, essence, gist.

2 *popular university subjects* BRANCH OF STUDY, discipline, field.

3 *six subjects did the trials* PARTICIPANT, volunteer; *informal* guinea pig.

4 *Her Majesty's subjects* CITIZEN, national; taxpayer, voter.

5 *a loyal subject* LIEGE, liegeman, vassal, henchman, follower.

▸ verb *they were* ***subjected to*** *violence* PUT THROUGH, treat with, expose to.

PHRASE: **subject to** **1** *it is subject to budgetary approval* CONDITIONAL ON, contingent on, dependent on. **2** *horses are subject to coughs* SUSCEPTIBLE TO, liable to, prone to, vulnerable to, predisposed to, at risk of. **3** *we are all subject to the law* BOUND BY, constrained by, accountable to.

subjection noun *the subjection of aboriginal peoples* SUBJUGATION, domination, oppression, mastery, repression, suppression.

subjective adjective *a subjective analysis* PERSONAL, individual, emotional, instinctive, intuitive. ANTONYM objective.

subjugate verb *the Normans had subjugated most of Ireland's Gaelic population* CONQUER, vanquish, defeat, crush, quash, bring someone to their knees, enslave, subdue, suppress. ANTONYM liberate.

sublimate verb *work can serve as a means of sublimating rage* CHANNEL, control, divert, transfer, redirect, convert.

sublime adjective **1** *sublime music* EXALTED, elevated, noble, lofty, awe-inspiring, majestic, magnificent, glorious, superb, wonderful, marvelous, splendid; *informal* fantastic, fabulous, terrific, heavenly, divine, out of this world.

2 *the sublime confidence of youth* SUPREME, total, complete, utter, consummate.

subliminal adjective *the screen flashed subliminal messages* SUBCONSCIOUS, unconscious; hidden, concealed. ANTONYM explicit.

submerge verb **1** *the U-boat submerged* GO UNDER WATER, dive, sink. ANTONYM surface.

2 *submerge the bowl in water* IMMERSE, plunge, sink.

3 *the farmland was submerged* FLOOD, inundate, deluge, swamp.

4 *she was submerged in work* OVERWHELM, inundate, deluge, swamp, bury, engulf, snow under.

submission noun **1** *submission to authority* YIELDING, capitulation, acceptance, consent, compliance. ANTONYM defiance.

2 *Tim raised his hands in submission* SURRENDER, capitulation, resignation, defeat.

3 *he wanted her total submission* COMPLIANCE, submissiveness, acquiescence, passivity, obedience, docility, deference, subservience, servility, subjection. ANTONYMS defiance, resistance.

4 *a report for submission to the Board* PRESENTATION, presenting, proffering, tendering, proposal, proposing.

5 *his original submission* PROPOSAL, suggestion, proposition, recommendation.

6 *the judge rejected her submission* ARGUMENT, assertion, contention, statement, claim, allegation.

submissive adjective *she's far from being a submissive woman* COMPLIANT, yielding, acquiescent, unassertive, passive, obedient, biddable, dutiful, docile, pliant; *informal* under someone's thumb.

submit verb **1** *she submitted under duress* GIVE IN/WAY, yield, back down, cave in, capitulate; surrender, knuckle under. ANTONYMS resist, defy.

2 *he refused to* ***submit to*** *their authority* BE GOVERNED BY, abide by, be regulated by, comply with, accept, adhere to, be subject to, agree to, consent to, conform to. ANTONYMS resist, defy.

3 *we submitted an unopposed bid* PUT FORWARD, present, offer, proffer, tender, propose, suggest, float; put in, send in, register. ANTONYM withdraw.

4 *they submitted that the judgment was inappropriate* CONTEND, assert, argue, state, claim, posit, postulate.

subnormal adjective *subnormal trade activity* BELOW AVERAGE, below normal, low, poor, subpar.

subordinate adjective **1** *subordinate staff* LOWER-RANKING, junior, lower, supporting. ANTONYM senior.

2 *a subordinate rule* SECONDARY, lesser, minor, subsidiary, subservient, ancillary, auxiliary, peripheral, marginal; supplementary, accessory. ANTONYM central.

▸ noun *the manager and his subordinates* JUNIOR, assistant, second (in command), number two, right-hand man/woman, deputy, aide, underling, minion; *informal* sidekick, second banana. ANTONYM superior.

subordination noun *a dismal life of subordination* INFERIORITY, subjection, subservience, submission, servitude.

sub rosa adverb *formal the committee operates sub rosa* IN SECRET, secretly, in private, privately, behind closed doors, in camera. ANTONYM openly.

subscribe verb **1** *we* ***subscribe to*** *several news magazines* PAY A SUBSCRIPTION FOR, have a subscription to, take, buy regularly.

2 *I subscribe to the ballet* HAVE SEASON TICKETS, have a subscription.

3 *I can't* ***subscribe to*** *that theory* AGREE WITH, accept, believe in, endorse, back, support, champion, buy into; *formal* accede to.

4 *formal he subscribed the document* SIGN, countersign, initial, autograph, witness.

subscriber noun *complaints from subscribers have prompted these changes* (regular) reader, member, patron, supporter, backer, contributor, season-ticket holder, subscription holder.

subscription noun **1** *the club's subscription* MEMBERSHIP FEE, dues, annual payment, charge.

2 *their subscription to capitalism* AGREEMENT, belief, endorsement, backing, support.

3 *formal* *the subscription was witnessed* SIGNATURE, initials; addition, appendage.

subsequent adjective *the subsequent months* FOLLOWING, ensuing, succeeding, later, future, coming, to come, next. ANTONYM previous.

PHRASE: **subsequent to** *tell us what happened in the hours subsequent to the shooting* FOLLOWING, after, at the close/end of.

subsequently adverb *we bought the house on the lake and subsequently added two room* LATER (ON), at a later date, afterward, in due course, following this/that, eventually; *informal* after a bit; *formal* thereafter.

subservient adjective **1** *subservient women* SUBMISSIVE, deferential, compliant, obedient, dutiful, biddable, docile, passive, unassertive, subdued, downtrodden; *informal* under someone's thumb. See note at OBSEQUIOUS. ANTONYM independent.

2 *individual rights are subservient to the interests of the state* SUBORDINATE, secondary, subsidiary, peripheral, ancillary, auxiliary, less important. ANTONYM superior.

subset noun *the quartet is a subset of our orchestral group* SUBCATEGORY, branch, subdivision, subsection, subsidiary.

subside verb **1** *wait until the storm subsides* ABATE, let up, quiet down, calm, slacken (off), ease (up), relent, die down, recede, lessen, soften, diminish, decline, dwindle, weaken, fade, wane, ebb. ANTONYM intensify.

2 *the floodwaters have subsided* RECEDE, ebb, fall, go down, get lower, abate. ANTONYM rise.

3 *the volcano is gradually subsiding* SINK, settle, cave in, collapse, crumple, give way.

subsidiary adjective *a subsidiary company* SUBORDINATE, secondary, ancillary, auxiliary, subservient, supplementary, peripheral. ANTONYM principal.

▸ noun *two major subsidiaries* SUBORDINATE COMPANY, branch, branch plant, division, subdivision, derivative, subset, offshoot.

subsidize verb *they have agreed to subsidize the after-school program* GIVE MONEY TO, pay a subsidy to, contribute to, invest in, sponsor, support, fund, finance, underwrite; *informal* shell out for, fork out for, cough up for; bankroll.

subsidy noun *the theater receives a subsidy of 1.7 million dollars a year* GRANT, allowance, endowment, contribution, donation, bursary, handout; backing, support, sponsorship, finance, funding; *formal* benefaction.

subsist verb **1** *he subsists on his pension* SURVIVE, live, stay alive, exist, eke out an existence; support oneself, manage, get along/by, make (both) ends meet.

2 *the tenant's rights of occupation subsist* CONTINUE, last, persist, endure, prevail, carry on, remain.

subsistence noun **1** *they depend on fish for subsistence* SURVIVAL, existence, living, life, sustenance, nourishment.

2 *the money needed for his subsistence* MAINTENANCE, keep, upkeep, livelihood, room and board, board, nourishment, food.

substance noun **1** *an organic substance* MATERIAL, matter, stuff.

2 *ghostly figures with no substance* SOLIDITY, body, corporeality; density, mass, weight, shape, structure.

3 *none of the objections has any substance* MEANINGFULNESS, significance, importance, import, validity, foundation; *formal* moment.

4 *the substance of the tale is very thin* CONTENT, subject matter, theme, message, essence.

5 *the Huskies are a team of substance* CHARACTER, backbone, mettle.

6 *independent men of substance* WEALTH, fortune, riches, affluence, prosperity, money, means.

substandard adjective *substandard school facilities* INFERIOR, second-rate, low-quality, poor, below par, subpar, imperfect, faulty, defective, shoddy, shabby, unsound, unsatisfactory, third-rate, crummy, lousy.

substantial adjective **1** *substantial beings* REAL, true, actual; physical, solid, material, concrete, corporeal.

2 *substantial progress had been made* CONSIDERABLE, real, significant, important, notable, major, valuable, useful.

3 *substantial damages* SIZABLE, considerable, significant, large, ample, appreciable, goodly.

4 *substantial oak beams* STURDY, solid, stout, thick, strong, well built, durable, long-lasting, hardwearing.

5 *rugby players with substantial builds* HEFTY, stout, sturdy, large, solid, bulky, burly, well built, portly.

6 *substantial landowners* SUCCESSFUL, profitable, prosperous, wealthy, affluent, moneyed, well-to-do, rich; *informal* loaded, stinking rich.

7 *substantial agreement* FUNDAMENTAL, essential, basic.

substantially adverb **1** *the cost has fallen substantially* CONSIDERABLY, significantly, to a great/large extent, greatly, markedly, appreciably. ANTONYM slightly.

2 *the draft was substantially accepted* LARGELY, for the most part, by and large, on the whole, in the main, mainly, in essence, basically, fundamentally, to all intents and purposes.

substantiate verb *can you substantiate your allegations?* PROVE, show to be true, give substance to, support, uphold, bear out, justify, vindicate, validate, corroborate, verify, authenticate, confirm, endorse, give credence to. ANTONYM disprove.

substitute noun *substitutes for permanent employees* REPLACEMENT, deputy, relief, proxy, reserve, surrogate, cover, stand-in, locum (tenens), understudy; *informal* sub, pinch-hitter.

▸ adjective *a substitute teacher* ACTING, supply, replacement, deputy, relief, reserve, surrogate, stand-in, temporary, caretaker, interim, provisional. ANTONYM permanent.

▸ verb **1** *cottage cheese can be substituted for yogurt* EXCHANGE, replace, use instead of, use as an alternative to, use in place of, swap.

2 *the senate was empowered to substitute for the president*

DEPUTIZE, act as deputy, act as a substitute, stand in, cover; replace, relieve, take over from; *informal* sub, fill someone's boots/shoes.

substitution noun *the substitution of color for black and white* EXCHANGE, change; replacement, replacing, swapping, switching; *informal* switcheroo.

subterfuge noun **1** *the use of subterfuge by journalists* TRICKERY, intrigue, deviousness, deceit, deception, dishonesty, cheating, duplicity, guile, cunning, craftiness, chicanery, pretense, fraud, fraudulence.

2 *a disreputable subterfuge* TRICK, hoax, ruse, wile, ploy, stratagem, artifice, dodge, bluff, pretense, deception, fraud, blind, smokescreen; *informal* con, scam.

subtext See note below.

WORD NOTE **subtext**

Alertness to the "hidden meanings" or unspoken assumptions of a text is necessary for anyone who hopes to read with understanding. Though abused by overuse in academic writing, *subtext* is nonetheless a useful term: Under its aegis lurk unreliable narration, irony, double-entendre, misdirection, and many of the other techniques that transform the artless into the artful. All mysteries, for instance, seek to discover the proper subtext of a narrative designed, by the murderer and the author, to mislead the detective and the reader. A classic of literary criticism like *Seven Types of Ambiguity* strips the veneer from numerous English poems to disclose unsuspected and multiple subtexts behind even the most seemingly pellucid lines. A novel like Nabokov's *Pale Fire* is almost nothing but subtext. Works of art are generally more than they seem at first sight, and only after a long, intent second glance do we start to detect the embedded symbolism, the secret messages and the deep structures that generate richness and complexity. **—MD**

subtle adjective **1** *subtle colors* UNDERSTATED, muted, subdued; delicate, faint, pale, soft, indistinct.

2 *subtle distinctions* FINE, fine-drawn, nice, hair-splitting.

3 *a subtle mind* ASTUTE, keen, quick, fine, acute, sharp, shrewd, perceptive, discerning, discriminating, penetrating, sagacious, wise, clever, intelligent.

4 *a subtle plan* INGENIOUS, clever, cunning, crafty, wily, artful, devious.

subtlety noun **1** *the subtlety of the flavor* DELICACY, delicateness, subtleness; understatedness, mutedness, softness.

2 *classification is fraught with subtlety* FINENESS, subtleness, niceness, nicety, nuance.

3 *the subtlety of the human mind* ASTUTENESS, keenness, acuteness, sharpness, canniness, shrewdness, perceptiveness, discernment, discrimination, percipience, perspicacity, wisdom, cleverness, intelligence.

4 *the subtlety of their tactics* INGENUITY, cleverness, skillfulness, adroitness, cunning, guile, craftiness, wiliness, artfulness, deviousness.

subtract verb *we'll subtract the cost of shipping* TAKE AWAY/OFF, deduct, debit, dock; *informal* knock off, minus. ANTONYM add.

suburb noun *a fast-growing suburb just west of Albany* | *you'll need a car if you move to the suburbs* RESIDENTIAL AREA, dormitory area, bedroom community, commutershed, commuter belt, exurb; (**suburbs**) suburbia, the burbs.

WORD NOTE **suburb**

An arbitrary selection of the hundreds of suburban labels:
edge city: urban facilities out of town; secondary city fragments
residential ring, bedroom community, commuter belt: wherefrom commuters come
sprawl: irregular exurban development, often connecting urban areas
slurb: a suburban slum
ribbon development: a thin layer of buildings encrusting the road out of town
streetcar suburb: development along public transportation routes
technoburb: full-service exurb based on technology centers
—SM

suburban adjective **1** *a suburban area* RESIDENTIAL, commuter, dormitory.

2 *her drab suburban existence* DULL, boring, uninteresting, conventional, ordinary, commonplace, unremarkable, unexceptional; provincial, unsophisticated, parochial, bourgeois, middle-class, white-picket-fence.

subversive adjective *subversive activities* DISRUPTIVE, troublemaking, inflammatory, insurrectionary; seditious, revolutionary, rebellious, rebel, renegade, dissident.

▸ noun *a dangerous subversive* TROUBLEMAKER, dissident, agitator, revolutionary, renegade, rebel.

subvert verb **1** *a plot to subvert the state* DESTABILIZE, unsettle, overthrow, overturn; bring down, topple, depose, oust; disrupt, wreak havoc on, sabotage, ruin, undermine, weaken, damage.

2 *attempts to subvert Soviet youth* CORRUPT, pervert, deprave, contaminate, poison, embitter.

subway noun *taking the subway to Yankee Stadium* underground (rail system), metro, train; *Brit. informal* tube.

succeed verb **1** *Darwin succeeded where others had failed* TRIUMPH, achieve success, be successful, do well, flourish, thrive; *informal* make it, make the grade, make a name for oneself. ANTONYM fail.

2 *the plan succeeded* BE SUCCESSFUL, turn out well, work (out), be effective; *informal* come off, pay off. ANTONYMS fail, flop.

3 *upon Taylor's death, his vice president, Millard Fillmore, succeeded him* REPLACE, take the place of, take over from, follow, supersede; *informal* step into someone's shoes. ANTONYM precede.

4 *he* ***succeeded to*** *the throne* INHERIT, assume, acquire, attain; *formal* accede to. ANTONYMS renounce, abdicate.

5 *embarrassment was succeeded by fear* FOLLOW, come after, follow after. ANTONYM precede.

succeeding adjective *strands of DNA are reproduced through succeeding generations* SUBSEQUENT, successive, following, ensuing, later, future, coming.

success noun **1** *the success of the scheme* FAVORABLE OUTCOME, successfulness, successful result, triumph. See word spectrum on page 893. ANTONYM failure.

2 *the trappings of success* PROSPERITY, affluence, wealth, riches, opulence. ANTONYM poverty.

3 *a box-office success* TRIUMPH, best seller, blockbuster, sellout; *informal* (smash) hit, megahit, winner. ANTONYMS failure, flop.

4 *an overnight success* STAR, superstar, celebrity, big name, household name; *informal* celeb, megastar. ANTONYM nobody.

success
triumph
coup
victory
smash hit
hit
smash
master stroke
winner
knockout
sensation
wow
crowd-puller
biggie
phenomenon
event
occasion
showcase
amateur night
dull fare
disappointment
damp squib
defeat
botch
hash
foul-up
blunder
vain attempt
screw-up
flop
snafu
clinker
washout
letdown
dead loss
dead duck
lead balloon
collapse
defeat
disaster
fiasco
fuck-up
debacle
catastrophe
failure

successful adjective **1** *what can we do to make this campaign successful?* VICTORIOUS, triumphant; fortunate, lucky; effective; *informal* socko, in like Flynn.

2 *a successful designer* PROSPEROUS, affluent, wealthy, rich; doing well, famous, eminent, top.

3 *successful companies* FLOURISHING, thriving, booming, buoyant, doing well, profitable, moneymaking, lucrative.

USAGE NOTE **in like Flynn**

This phrase, meaning "assured of success," first became widespread during World War II as an allusion to the actor Errol Flynn's legendary prowess in seducing women. (In 1942, Flynn was prosecuted for the statutory rape of two teenage girls—and was acquitted.) Today the phrase has generally lost any sexual connotation—e.g.: • "By these standards, Gore should be in like Flynn." (*Commercial Appeal* [Memphis]; Feb. 13, 2000.) • "Based on the results of our Triangle Census, you'll be in like Flynn." (*News & Observer* [Raleigh]; Mar. 27, 2000.) • "Follow the formula, and you're in like Flynn." (*BusinessWeek,* Aug. 7, 2000.) The phrase has been the subject of wordplay and consequent confusion. In 1966 appeared *Our Man Flint,* a film starring James Coburn and spoofing the James Bond series; the following year, its sequel, *In Like Flint,* was released. The popularity of these films—especially the latter with its pun on *in like Flynn*—sparked lingering confusion about what the proper phrase should be. Thus, during coverage of the 2000 Republican Convention, Mark Shields, a PBS commentator, said that George W. Bush might be "in like Flynn, or in like Flint—whatever we say" (PBS Convention Coverage, Aug. 3, 2000). This confusion had already surfaced in print—e.g.: "Yep, with my peacoat, I was in like Flint [read *Flynn*], I thought, able to hubbub with the highbrows or hang with the homeboys." (*News & Observer* [Raleigh]; Jan. 11, 1998) (in this example, *hubbub* should probably be *hobnob*). "If you want to be 'in like Flint [read *Flynn*],' there has to be a measure of exclusivity." Larry Lipson, (*Daily News* [L.A.]; Aug. 27, 1999.) "Finder praises Gawande as a quick learner. If he failed to incorporate advice initially, says Finder, 'the second time he was in like Flint [read *Flynn*].' (*Boston Globe,* Nov. 10, 1999.) Although this usage occasionally appears in tongue-in-cheek references to Flint, Michigan, and to flint as stone, it shouldn't appear in sentences such as those just quoted. Errol Flynn is reported to have resented the phrase, but it will always be linked etymologically to him. **—BG**

succession noun **1** *a succession of exciting events* SEQUENCE, series, progression, chain, cycle, round, string, train, line, run, flow, stream.

2 *his succession to the throne* ACCESSION, elevation, assumption. PHRASE: **in succession** *the next four houses went up in succession, in a matter of just a few months* ONE AFTER THE OTHER, in a row, consecutively, successively, in sequence.

successive adjective *three successive wins* CONSECUTIVE, in a row, straight, sequential, in succession, running.

successor noun *Mary was the rightful successor to the English throne* HEIR (APPARENT), inheritor, next-in-line. ANTONYM predecessor.

succinct adjective *what is your succinct appraisal of our situation?* CONCISE, short (and sweet), brief, compact, condensed, crisp, laconic, terse, to the point, pithy, epigrammatic, synoptic, gnomic; *formal* compendious. See note at TERSE. ANTONYM verbose.

succor noun *providing succor in times of need* AID, help, a helping hand, assistance; comfort, ease, relief, support, TLC.

▸ verb *the prisoners were succored* HELP, aid, bring aid to, give/render assistance to, assist, lend a (helping) hand to; minister to, care for, comfort, bring relief to, support, take care of, look after, attend to.

succulent adjective *succulent black grapes* JUICY, moist, luscious, soft, tender; choice, mouthwatering, appetizing, tasty, delicious; *informal* scrumptious. ANTONYM dry.

succumb verb **1** *she succumbed to temptation* YIELD, give in/way, submit, surrender, capitulate, cave in. See note at TERSE. ANTONYM resist.

2 *he **succumbed to** the disease* DIE FROM/OF; catch, develop, contract, fall ill with; *informal* come down with. ANTONYM withstand.

suck verb **1** *they sucked orange juice through straws* SIP, sup, siphon, slurp, draw, drink.

2 *Fran **sucked in** a deep breath* DRAW, breathe, gasp; inhale, inspire.

3 *they got **sucked into** petty crime* IMPLICATE IN, involve in, draw into; *informal* mix up in.

4 *informal the weather sucks* BE VERY BAD, be awful, be terrible, be dreadful, be horrible; *informal* stink. PHRASE: **suck up to** *informal they suck up to him, hanging on to his every word* GROVEL TO, creep to, toady to, be obsequious to, be sycophantic to, kowtow to, bow and scrape to, truckle to; fawn on; *informal* lick someone's boots, be all over, brown-nose.

suckle verb *the lioness suckled her cubs* BREAST-FEED, feed, nurse.

sudden adjective *a sudden change in plans* UNEXPECTED, unforeseen, unanticipated, unlooked-for; immediate, instantaneous, instant, precipitous, precipitate, abrupt, rapid, swift, quick.

suddenly adverb *suddenly the scene shifts to the year 1954* IMMEDIATELY, instantaneously, instantly, straightaway, all of a sudden, all at once, promptly, abruptly, swiftly; unexpectedly, without warning, without notice, out of the blue; *informal* straight off, in a flash, like a shot. ANTONYM gradually.

suds plural noun *a detergent low in suds* LATHER, foam, froth, bubbles, soap.

sue verb 1 *he sued the contractor for negligence* TAKE LEGAL ACTION AGAINST, take to court, bring an action/suit against, proceed against, prefer/bring charges against.

2 ***suing for** peace* APPEAL FOR, petition for, ask for, solicit (for), request, seek.

suffer verb 1 *I hate to see him suffer* HURT, ache, be in pain, feel pain; be in distress, be upset, be miserable.

2 *she **suffers from** asthma* BE AFFLICTED BY/WITH, be affected by, be troubled with, have.

3 *Brazil suffered a humiliating defeat* UNDERGO, experience, be subjected to, receive, endure, face.

4 *the school's reputation has suffered* BE IMPAIRED, be damaged, deteriorate, decline.

5 archaic *he was obliged to suffer her intimate proximity* TOLERATE, put up with, bear, stand, abide, endure; *formal* brook.

6 archaic *my conscience would not suffer me to accept* ALLOW, permit, let, give leave to, sanction.

suffering noun *the suffering of these refugees defied description* HARDSHIP, distress, misery, wretchedness, adversity, tribulation; pain, agony, anguish, trauma, torment, torture, hurt, affliction, sadness, unhappiness, sorrow, grief, woe, angst, heartache, heartbreak, stress; *literary* dolor.

suffice verb *a simple yes or no will suffice* BE ENOUGH, be sufficient, be adequate, do, serve, meet requirements, satisfy demands, answer/meet one's needs, answer/serve the purpose; *informal* fit/fill the bill.

sufficient adjective *there was sufficient evidence to justify a charge* ENOUGH, plenty of, ample; adequate, satisfactory. ANTONYM inadequate.

suffocate verb *it appears that the victim has been suffocated with a bed pillow* SMOTHER, asphyxiate, stifle; choke, strangle.

suffrage noun *suffrage for women is not yet a universal condition* FRANCHISE, right to vote, the vote, enfranchisement, ballot.

suffuse verb *the room was suffused with soft, pink light* PERMEATE, spread over, spread throughout, cover, bathe, pervade, wash, saturate, imbue.

sugar noun See table.

TYPES OF SUGAR

beet sugar	lactose
birch sugar	loaf sugar
blackstrap molasses	maltose
brown sugar	manna
cane sugar	maple sugar
caramel	molasses
confectioners' sugar	muscovado (sugar)
corn syrup	palm sugar
cube sugar	panela
dark brown sugar	piloncillo
demerara (sugar)	powdered sugar
dextrose	preserving sugar
fructose	raw sugar
galactose	sorghum
golden syrup	spun sugar
granulated sugar	sucrose
gur	superfine sugar
honey	treacle
icing	turbinado sugar
jaggery	

sugary adjective 1 *sugary snacks* SWEET, sugared, sugar-coated, candied. ANTONYM sour.

2 *sugary romance* SENTIMENTAL, mawkish, cloying, sickly (sweet), saccharine, syrupy; *informal* sappy, schmaltzy, slushy, mushy, sloppy, cutesy, corny.

suggest verb 1 *Ruth suggested a vacation* PROPOSE, put forward, recommend, advocate; advise, urge, encourage, counsel.

2 *evidence suggests that teenagers are responsive to price increases* INDICATE, lead to the belief, argue, demonstrate, show; *formal* evince.

3 *sources suggest that the prime minister will change his cabinet* HINT, insinuate, imply, intimate, indicate; *informal* put ideas into one's head.

4 *the seduction scenes suggest his guilt and her loneliness* CONVEY, express, communicate, impart, imply, intimate, smack of, evoke, conjure up; *formal* evince.

suggestion noun 1 *some suggestions for tackling this problem* PROPOSAL, proposition, motion, submission, recommendation; advice, counsel, hint, tip, clue, idea, trial balloon.

2 *the suggestion of a smirk* HINT, trace, touch, suspicion, dash, soupçon, tinge; ghost, semblance, shadow, glimmer, impression, whisper.

3 *there is no suggestion that he was party to a conspiracy* INSINUATION, hint, implication, intimation, innuendo, imputation.

suggestive adjective 1 *suggestive remarks* INDECENT, indelicate, improper, unseemly, sexual, sexy, smutty, dirty, ribald, bawdy, racy, risqué, lewd, vulgar, coarse, salacious.

2 *an odor suggestive of a brewery* REDOLENT, evocative, reminiscent; characteristic, indicative, typical.

suicide noun *was it suicide or murder?* SELF-DESTRUCTION, taking one's own life, killing oneself, self-murder.

suit noun 1 *a pinstriped suit* OUTFIT, set of clothes, ensemble.

2 *informal* *suits in faraway boardrooms* BUSINESSMAN, BUSINESSWOMAN, executive, bureaucrat, administrator, manager.

3 *a medical malpractice suit* LEGAL ACTION, lawsuit, (court) case, action, (legal/judicial) proceedings, litigation.

4 *they spurned his suit* ENTREATY, request, plea, appeal, petition, supplication, application.

5 *dated* *his suit came to nothing* COURTSHIP, wooing, attentions.

▸ verb 1 *blue really suits you* BECOME, work for, look good on, look attractive on, flatter.

2 *savings plans to suit all customers* BE CONVENIENT FOR, be acceptable to, be suitable for, meet the requirements of; *informal* fit the bill for.

3 *recipes ideally suited to students* MAKE APPROPRIATE TO/FOR, tailor, fashion, adjust, adapt, modify, fit, gear, design.

suitable adjective 1 *suitable employment opportunities* ACCEPTABLE, satisfactory, fitting; *informal* right up someone's alley. ANTONYM inappropriate.

2 *a drama suitable for all ages* APPROPRIATE, fitting, fit, acceptable, right. ANTONYM inappropriate.

3 *music* ***suitable for*** *a lively dinner party* APPROPRIATE TO/FOR, suited to, befitting, in keeping with; *informal* cut out for. ANTONYM unfit.

4 *they treated him with suitable respect* PROPER, seemly, decent, appropriate, fitting, befitting, correct, due.

5 *suitable candidates* WELL QUALIFIED, well-suited, appropriate, fitting. ANTONYM unfit.

suitcase noun *the old brown suitcase had survived two ocean voyages and more train and bus trips than she could ever calculate* TRAVEL BAG, traveling bag, case, valise, overnight case, portmanteau, vanity case, garment bag, backpack, duffel bag; (**suitcases**) luggage, baggage.

WORD NOTE **portmanteau**

The image is arresting: a room in a Days Inn beside some endless American highway, and a soft-sided carrying case flung onto the bed by the weary traveler. There are two potential uses here of the term *portmanteau*—one of them forgotten, the other, generally unknown. The suitcase provides the first: the word *portmanteau* comes initially from the title of the French servant who carried the princely mantle, the clothes or raiment that were to be worn on the morrow. From clothes-carrying servant to clothes-carrying bag the word then evolved, until by the middle of the sixteenth century it had assumed the meaning "a suitcase." Sadly for so pretty a word it is a form seldom used today, with the inelegant *garment bag* assuming its role in all but the most pretentious situations (one imagines Ritz-Carlton Hotels, one of whose slogans is "Ladies and Gentlemen Serving Ladies and Gentlemen," expected their guests to own portmanteaus, or even portmanteaux). The suitcase is not all, however: the very building that houses the aforesaid bedroom has an even less familiar association with the word. A Days Inn is technically what is called a *motel,* and this word, it is often forgotten, is a grammatical construction that welds two together two words—*motor* and *hotel*—to give us a wholly new word that is properly described as a *portmanteau* term. Lewis Carroll was the inventor of the genre, of words which, just like the suitcase, pack things up together—and he formed familiar constructions such as *slithy* (from *slimy* and *lithe*), and *mimsy* (from *flimsy* and *miserable*). Luggage becomes grammar, in one easy step. **—SW**

suite noun *we were quite comfortable in our suite at the Biltmore* APARTMENT, rooms, set of rooms; *Brit.* flat.

suitor noun *Rosie routinely rejected the suitors who sought her affections, until Laurence came along* ADMIRER, wooer, boyfriend, sweetheart, lover, beau; *literary* swain.

sulk verb *Dad was sulking* MOPE, brood, be sullen, have a long face, be in a bad mood, be in a huff, be grumpy, be moody; *informal* be down in the dumps.

▸ noun *she sank into a deep sulk* (BAD) MOOD, fit of ill humor, fit of pique, pet, huff, (bad) temper; the sulks, the blues.

sulky adjective *sulky faces* SULLEN, surly, moping, pouting, moody, sour, piqued, petulant, brooding, broody, disgruntled, ill-humored, in a bad mood, out of humor, fed up, put out; bad-tempered, grumpy, huffy, glum, gloomy, morose; *informal* grouchy, crabby, cranky. ANTONYM cheerful.

sullen adjective *a bunch of sullen, spoiled brats* SURLY, sulky, pouting, sour, morose, resentful, glum, moody, gloomy, grumpy, bad-tempered, ill-tempered; unresponsive, uncommunicative, farouche, uncivil, unfriendly. See note at GLUM. ANTONYM cheerful.

sully verb *he never sullied his lips with foul language* TAINT, defile, soil, tarnish, stain, blemish, pollute, spoil, mar; *literary* besmirch, befoul.

sultry adjective 1 *a sultry day* HUMID, close, airless, stifling, oppressive, muggy, sticky, sweltering, tropical, heavy; hot; *informal* boiling, roasting. ANTONYM refreshing.

2 *a sultry film star* PASSIONATE, attractive, sensual, sexy, voluptuous, erotic, seductive.

sum noun 1 *a large sum of money* AMOUNT, quantity, volume.

2 *just a small sum* AMOUNT OF MONEY, price, charge, fee, cost.

3 *the sum of two numbers* (SUM) TOTAL, grand total, tally, aggregate, summation. ANTONYM difference.

4 *the sum of his wisdom* ENTIRETY, totality, total, whole, aggregate, summation, beginning and end.

5 *we did sums at school* (ARITHMETICAL) PROBLEM, calculation; (**sums**) arithmetic, mathematics, math, computation. PHRASE: **sum up** 1 *one reviewer summed it up as "compelling"* EVALUATE, assess, appraise, rate, gauge, judge, deem, adjudge, estimate, form an opinion of. 2 *he summed up his reasons* SUMMARIZE, make/give a summary of, précis, outline, give an outline of, recapitulate, review; *informal* recap.

summarily adverb *accused of treason, he was summarily executed* IMMEDIATELY, instantly, right away, straightaway, at once, on the spot, promptly; speedily, swiftly, rapidly, without delay; arbitrarily, without formality, peremptorily, without due process.

summarize verb *he summarized these ideas in a single phrase* SUM UP, abridge, condense, encapsulate, outline, give an outline of, put in a nutshell, recapitulate, give/make a summary of, give a synopsis of, précis, synopsize, give the gist of; *informal* recap.

summary noun *a summary of the findings* SYNOPSIS, précis, résumé, abstract, digest, encapsulation, abbreviated version; outline, sketch, rundown, review, summing-up, overview, recapitulation, epitome; *informal* recap.

▸ adjective **1** *a summary financial statement* ABRIDGED, abbreviated, shortened, condensed, concise, capsule, succinct, short, brief, pithy; *formal* compendious.

2 *summary execution* IMMEDIATE, instant, instantaneous, on-the-spot; speedy, swift, rapid, without delay, sudden; arbitrary, without formality, peremptory.

summit noun **1** *the summit of Mount Washington* (MOUNTAIN) TOP, peak, crest, crown, apex, tip, cap, hilltop. ANTONYMS base, bottom.

2 *the summits of world literature* ACME, peak, height, pinnacle, zenith, climax, high point/spot, highlight, crowning glory, capstone, best, finest, nonpareil. ANTONYM nadir.

3 *the next superpower summit* MEETING, negotiation, conference, talk(s), discussion.

summon verb **1** *the embassy summoned her* SEND FOR, call for, request the presence of; ask, invite.

2 *they were summoned as witnesses* SERVE WITH A SUMMONS, summons, subpoena, cite, serve with a citation.

3 *the chair summoned a meeting* CONVENE, assemble, order, call, announce; *formal* convoke.

4 *he summoned the courage to move closer* MUSTER, gather, collect, rally, screw up.

5 ***summoning up*** *their memories of home* CALL TO MIND, call up/forth, conjure up, evoke, recall, revive, arouse, kindle, awaken, spark (off).

6 *they summoned spirits of the dead* CONJURE UP, call up, invoke.

summons noun **1** *the court issued a summons* WRIT, subpoena, warrant, court order; *Law* citation.

2 *a summons to go to the boss's office* ORDER, directive, command, instruction, demand, decree, injunction, edict, call, request.

▸ verb *he was summonsed to appear in court* SERVE WITH A SUMMONS, summon, subpoena, cite, serve with a citation.

sumptuous adjective *sumptuous brocade drapes* LAVISH, luxurious, opulent, magnificent, resplendent, gorgeous, splendid, grand, lavishly appointed, palatial, rich; *informal* plush, ritzy. ANTONYM plain.

sun noun *she could feel the sun on her face* SUNSHINE, sunlight, daylight, light, warmth; beams, rays. PHRASE: **sun oneself.** See SUNBATHE.

sunbathe verb *sunbathing on the deck of their sailboat* SUN ONESELF, bask, get a tan, tan; *informal* catch some rays.

sunburned adjective **1** *his sunburned shoulders* BURNED, burnt, sunburnt, red, scarlet.

2 *a handsome sunburned face* TANNED, suntanned, brown, bronzed, bronze. ANTONYM pale.

sunder verb *literary his father and he were sundered by religious differences* DIVIDE, split, cleave, separate, rend, sever, rive.

sundry adjective *wings, radiators, and sundry other items were sent out to various workshops* VARIOUS, varied, miscellaneous, assorted, mixed, diverse, diversified; several, numerous, many, manifold, multifarious, multitudinous; *literary* divers.

sunken adjective **1** *sunken eyes* HOLLOWED, hollow, depressed, deep-set, concave, indented.

2 *a sunken garden* BELOW GROUND LEVEL, at a lower level, lowered.

sunless adjective **1** *a cold sunless day* DARK, overcast, cloudy, gray, gloomy, dismal, murky, dull.

2 *the sunless side of the house* SHADY, shadowy, dark, gloomy.

sunlight noun *avoid sunlight when taking this medication* DAYLIGHT, (the) sun, sunshine, the sun's rays, (natural) light.

sunny adjective **1** *a sunny day* BRIGHT, sunshiny, sunlit, clear, fine, cloudless, without a cloud in the sky, sundrenched. ANTONYM cloudy.

2 *a sunny disposition* CHEERFUL, cheery, happy, lighthearted, bright, merry, joyful, bubbly, blithe, jolly, jovial, animated, buoyant, ebullient, upbeat, vivacious. ANTONYM miserable.

3 *look on the sunny side* OPTIMISTIC, rosy, bright, hopeful, auspicious, favorable. ANTONYMS sad, pessimistic.

sunrise noun *the infantry advanced at sunrise* DAWN, crack of dawn, daybreak, break of day, sun-up, first light, (early) morning, cock crow; *literary* aurora.

sunset noun the blossoms close at sunset SUNDOWN, nightfall, close of day, twilight, dusk, evening; *literary* eventide, gloaming.

sunshine noun **1** *relaxing in the sunshine* SUNLIGHT, sun, sun's rays, daylight, (natural) light.

2 *his smile was all sunshine* HAPPINESS, cheerfulness, cheer, gladness, laughter, gaiety, merriment, joy, joyfulness, blitheness, joviality, jollity.

super adjective *informal we had a super time at the water park* EXCELLENT, superb, superlative, first-class, outstanding, marvelous, magnificent, wonderful, splendid, glorious; *informal* great, fantastic, fabulous, terrific, ace, divine, A1, wicked, cool, killer; smashing, brilliant. ANTONYM rotten.

superannuated adjective **1** *a superannuated civil servant* PENSIONED (OFF), retired; elderly, old.

2 *superannuated computing equipment* OLD, old-fashioned, antiquated, out of date, outmoded, broken-down, obsolete, disused, defunct.

superb adjective **1** *he scored a superb goal* EXCELLENT, superlative, first-rate, first-class, outstanding, remarkable, marvelous, magnificent, wonderful, splendid, admirable, noteworthy, impressive, fine, exquisite, exceptional, glorious; *informal* great, fantastic, fabulous, terrific, super, awesome, ace, cool, A1, brilliant, killer. ANTONYMS poor, inferior.

2 *a superb diamond necklace* MAGNIFICENT, majestic, splendid, grand, impressive, imposing, awe-inspiring, breathtaking; gorgeous. ANTONYMS poor, inferior.

supercilious adjective *a supercilious young clerk* ARROGANT, haughty, conceited, disdainful, overbearing, pompous, condescending, superior, patronizing, imperious, proud, snobbish, snobby, smug, scornful, sneering; *informal* hoity-toity, high and mighty, uppity, snooty, stuck-up, snotty, snot-nosed, jumped up, too big for one's britches.

superficial adjective **1** *superficial burns* SURFACE, exterior, external, outer, outside, slight. ANTONYMS deep, thorough.

2 *a superficial friendship* SHALLOW, surface, skin-deep, artificial; empty, hollow, meaningless. ANTONYMS deep, significant.

3 *a superficial investigation* CURSORY, perfunctory, casual, sketchy, desultory, token, slapdash, offhand, rushed, hasty, hurried. ANTONYMS comprehensive, thorough.

4 *a superficial resemblance* APPARENT, seeming, outward, ostensible, cosmetic, slight. ANTONYMS genuine, authentic.

5 *a superficial analysis* TRIVIAL, lightweight, two-dimensional. ANTONYM profound.

6 *a superficial person* FACILE, shallow, flippant, empty-headed, trivial, frivolous, silly, inane. ANTONYMS deep, thoughtful.

THE RIGHT WORD

No one wants to be accused of being **superficial** or **shallow**, two adjectives that literally indicate a lack of depth (*a superficial wound; a shallow grave*). *Superficial* suggests too much concern with the surface or obvious aspects of something, and it is considered a derogatory term because it connotes a personality that is not genuine or sincere. *Shallow* is even more derogatory because it implies not only a refusal to explore something deeply but an inability to feel, sympathize, or understand. It is unlikely that a *shallow* person, in other words, will ever have more than superficial relationships with his or her peers. **Cursory**, which may or may not be a derogatory term, suggests a lack of thoroughness or attention to detail (*a cursory glance at the newspaper*), while **hasty** emphasizes a refusal or inability to spend the necessary time on something (*a hasty review of the facts*). If you are **slapdash** in your approach, it means that you are both careless and hasty (*a slapdash job of cleaning up*).

superficially adverb *some reptiles and amphibians are superficially alike* APPARENTLY, seemingly, ostensibly, outwardly, on the surface, on the face of it, at first glance, to the casual eye.

superfluity noun *California has always had a superfluity of fresh crab* SURPLUS, excess, overabundance, glut, surfeit, profusion, plethora. ANTONYM shortage.

superfluous adjective 1 *superfluous material* SURPLUS (TO REQUIREMENTS), nonessential, redundant, unneeded, excess, extra, (to) spare, remaining, unused, left over, in excess, waste. ANTONYMS necessary, essential.

2 *words seemed superfluous* UNNECESSARY, unneeded, redundant, uncalled for, unwarranted. ANTONYM necessary.

superhuman adjective 1 *a superhuman effort* EXTRAORDINARY, phenomenal, prodigious, stupendous, exceptional, remarkable, immense, heroic. ANTONYMS average, unremarkable.

2 *superhuman power* DIVINE, holy, heavenly.

3 *superhuman beings* SUPERNATURAL, preternatural, paranormal, otherworldly, unearthly; *rare* extramundane. ANTONYM mundane.

superintend verb *he was expected to superintend a grand banquet* SUPERVISE, oversee, be in charge of, be in control of, preside over, direct, administer, manage, run, be responsible for.

superintendent noun 1 *the superintendent of the museum* MANAGER, director, administrator, supervisor, overseer, controller, chief, head, governor; *informal* boss.

2 *the building's superintendent* CARETAKER, janitor, warden, porter.

superior adjective 1 *a superior officer* HIGHER-RANKING, higher-level, senior, higher, higher-up. ANTONYMS junior, inferior.

2 *the superior candidate* BETTER, more expert, more skillful; worthier, fitter, preferred. ANTONYMS worse, inferior.

3 *superior workmanship* HIGH-QUALITY; finer better, higher-grade, of higher quality, greater; accomplished, expert. ANTONYMS low-quality, inferior.

4 *superior chocolate* GOOD-QUALITY, high-quality, first-class, first-rate, top-quality; choice, select, exclusive, prime, prize, fine, excellent, best, choicest, finest. ANTONYMS low-quality, inferior.

5 *a superior hotel* HIGH-CLASS, upper-class, select, exclusive, upscale, upmarket, five-star; *informal* classy, posh. ANTONYMS downmarket, inferior.

6 *Hamish regarded her with superior amusement* CONDESCENDING, supercilious, patronizing, haughty, disdainful, pompous, snobbish; *informal* high and mighty, hoity-toity, snooty, stuck-up. ANTONYMS humble, modest.

▸ noun *my immediate superior* MANAGER, chief, supervisor, senior, controller, foreman; *informal* boss. ANTONYM subordinate.

superiority noun *the military superiority of the North* SUPREMACY, advantage, lead, dominance, primacy, ascendancy, eminence.

superlative adjective *a superlative photographer* EXCELLENT, magnificent, wonderful, marvelous, supreme, consummate, outstanding, remarkable, fine, choice, first-rate, first-class, premier, prime, unsurpassed, unequaled, unparalleled, unrivaled, preeminent; *informal* crack, ace, wicked, brilliant. ANTONYM mediocre.

supernatural adjective 1 *supernatural powers* PARANORMAL, psychic, magic, magical, occult, mystic, mystical, superhuman, supernormal; *rare* extramundane.

2 *a supernatural being* GHOSTLY, phantom, spectral, otherworldly, unearthly, unnatural.

supersede verb *I was superseded by much younger men* REPLACE, take the place of, take over from, succeed; supplant, displace, oust, overthrow, remove, unseat; *informal* fill someone's shoes/boots. See note at REPLACE.

superstition noun 1 *the old superstitions held by sailors* MYTH, belief, old wives' tale; legend, story.

2 *medicine was riddled with superstition* UNFOUNDED BELIEF, credulity, fallacy, delusion, illusion; magic, sorcery; *informal* humbug, hooey.

superstitious adjective 1 *superstitious beliefs* MYTHICAL, irrational, illusory, groundless, unfounded; traditional. ANTONYM factual.

2 *he's incredibly superstitious* CREDULOUS, naive, gullible. ANTONYM skeptical.

supervise verb 1 *he had to supervise the loading* OVERSEE, superintend, be in charge of, preside over, direct, manage, run, look after, be responsible for, govern, organize, handle, micromanage.

2 *you may need to supervise the patient* WATCH, oversee, keep an eye on, observe, monitor, mind; invigilate.

supervision noun 1 *the supervision of the banking system*

ADMINISTRATION, management, control, charge; superintendence, regulation, government, governance.

2 *keep your children under supervision* OBSERVATION, guidance, custody, charge, safekeeping, care, guardianship; control.

supervisor noun *the supervisor of sector B* MANAGER, director, overseer, controller, superintendent, governor, chief, head; steward, foreman; *informal* boss.

supine adjective 1 *she lay supine on the sand* FLAT ON ONE'S BACK, face upward, facing upward, flat, horizontal, recumbent, stretched out. ANTONYM prostrate.

2 *the supine media* WEAK, spineless, yielding, effete; docile, acquiescent, pliant, submissive, passive, inert, spiritless. ANTONYM strong.

supper noun *I had a bowl of chili for my supper* DINNER, evening meal, main meal; snack, mealtime; *formal* repast; *literary* refection.

supplant verb 1 *paved highways supplanted the network of dirt roads* REPLACE, supersede, displace, take over from, substitute for, override.

2 *the man he supplanted as prime minister* OUST, usurp, overthrow, remove, topple, unseat, depose, dethrone; succeed, come after; *informal* fill someone's shoes/boots.

supple adjective 1 *her supple body* LITHE, limber, lissome, willowy, flexible, loose-limbed, agile, acrobatic, nimble, double-jointed. See note at FLEXIBLE. ANTONYM stiff.

2 *supple leather* PLIANT, pliable, flexible, soft, bendable, workable, malleable, stretchy, elastic, springy, yielding, rubbery. ANTONYMS inflexible, rigid.

supplement noun 1 *a mouse is a keyboard supplement* ADDITION, accessory, supplementation, supplementary, extra, add-on, adjunct, appendage; *Computing* peripheral.

2 *a single room supplement* SURCHARGE, addition, increase.

3 *a supplement to the essay* APPENDIX, addendum, adhesion, end matter, tailpiece, codicil, postscript, addition, coda.

4 *a special supplement with today's paper* PULLOUT, insert, extra section.

▸ verb *they supplemented their incomes by waiting tables on weekends* AUGMENT, increase, add to, boost, swell, amplify, enlarge, top up.

supplementary adjective 1 *supplementary income* ADDITIONAL, supplemental, extra, more, further; add-on, subsidiary, auxiliary, ancillary.

2 *a supplementary index* APPENDED, attached, added, extra, accompanying.

suppliant noun *they were not mere suppliants* PETITIONER, supplicant, pleader, beggar, applicant.

▸ adjective *those around her were suppliant* PLEADING, begging, imploring, entreating, supplicating; on bended knee.

supplicate verb *he supplicated the governor for leniency* ENTREAT, beg, plead with, implore, petition, appeal to, call on, urge, enjoin, importune, sue, ask, request; *literary* beseech.

supply verb 1 *they supplied money to rebels* GIVE, contribute, provide, furnish, donate, bestow, grant, endow, impart; dispense, disburse, allocate, assign; *informal* fork out, shell out.

2 *the lake supplies the city with water* PROVIDE, furnish, endow, serve, confer; equip, arm.

3 *windmills supply their power needs* SATISFY, meet, fulfill, cater for.

▸ noun 1 *a limited supply of food* STOCK, store, reserve, reservoir, stockpile, hoard, cache; storehouse, repository; fund, mine, bank.

2 *the supply of liquor* PROVISION, dissemination, distribution, serving.

3 **(supplies)** *go to the grocery store for supplies* PROVISIONS, stores, stocks, rations, food, foodstuffs, eatables, produce, necessities; *informal* eats; *formal* comestibles.

support verb 1 *a roof supported by pillars* HOLD UP, bear, carry, prop up, keep up, brace, shore up, underpin, buttress, reinforce, undergird.

2 *he struggled to support his family* PROVIDE FOR, maintain, sustain, keep, take care of, look after.

3 *she supported him to the end* COMFORT, encourage, sustain, buoy up, hearten, fortify, console, solace, reassure; *informal* buck up. ANTONYMS neglect, abandon.

4 *evidence to support the argument* SUBSTANTIATE, back up, bear out, corroborate, confirm, attest to, verify, prove, validate, authenticate, endorse, ratify, undergird. ANTONYMS contradict, undermine.

5 *the money supports charitable projects* HELP, aid, assist; contribute to, back, subsidize, fund, finance; *informal* bankroll.

6 *an independent candidate supported by locals* BACK, champion, help, assist, aid, abet, favor, encourage; vote for, stand behind, defend; sponsor, second, promote, endorse, sanction; *informal* throw one's weight behind. ANTONYM oppose.

7 *they support human rights* ADVOCATE, promote, champion, back, espouse, be in favor of, recommend, defend, subscribe to.

▸ noun 1 *bridge supports* PILLAR, post, prop, upright, crutch, plinth, brace, buttress; base, substructure, foundation, underpinning.

2 *she pays support for her ex-husband* MAINTENANCE, keep, sustenance, subsistence; alimony.

3 *I was lucky to have their support* ENCOURAGEMENT, friendship, strength, consolation, solace, succor, relief.

4 *he was a great support* COMFORT, help, assistance, tower of strength, prop, mainstay.

5 *support for community services* CONTRIBUTIONS, backing, donations, money, subsidy, funding, funds, finance, capital.

6 *they voiced their support for him* BACKING, help, assistance, aid, endorsement, approval; votes, patronage.

7 *a surge in support for decentralization* ADVOCACY, backing, promotion, championship, espousal, defense, recommendation.

supporter noun 1 *supporters of gun control* ADVOCATE, backer, adherent, promoter, champion, defender, upholder, crusader, proponent, campaigner, apologist; *informal* cheerleader.

2 *Republican supporters* BACKER, helper, adherent, follower, ally, voter, disciple; member.

3 *the charity relies on its supporters* CONTRIBUTOR, donor, benefactor, sponsor, backer, patron, well-wisher.

4 *the team's supporters* FAN, follower, enthusiast, devotee, admirer; *informal* buff, addict, groupie.

supportive adjective 1 *a supportive teacher* ENCOURAGING, caring, sympathetic, reassuring, understanding, concerned, helpful, kind, kindly; *informal* boosterish

2 *we are supportive of the proposal* IN FAVOR OF, favorable to, pro, on the side of, sympathetic to, well-disposed to, receptive to.

suppose verb 1 *I suppose he's used to this* ASSUME, presume, expect, dare say, take it (as read); believe, think, fancy, suspect, sense, trust; guess, surmise, reckon, conjecture, deduce, infer, gather; *formal* opine.

2 *suppose you had a spacecraft* ASSUME, imagine, (let's) say; hypothesize, theorize, speculate.

3 *the theory supposes rational players* REQUIRE, presuppose, imply, assume; call for, need.

supposed adjective 1 *the supposed phenomena* APPARENT, ostensible, seeming, alleged, putative, reputed, rumored, claimed, purported; professed, declared, assumed, presumed.

2 *I'm supposed to meet him at 8:30* MEANT, intended, expected; required, obliged.

supposition noun *her supposition is based on previous results* BELIEF, surmise, idea, notion, suspicion, conjecture, speculation, inference, theory, hypothesis, postulation, guess, feeling, hunch, assumption, presumption.

suppress verb 1 *they could suppress the rebellion* SUBDUE, repress, crush, quell, quash, squash, stamp out; defeat, conquer, overpower, put down, crack down on; end, stop, terminate, halt. ANTONYMS incite, encourage.

2 *she suppressed her irritation* CONCEAL, restrain, stifle, smother, bottle up, hold back, control, check, curb, contain, bridle, inhibit, keep a rein on, put a lid on. ANTONYM express.

3 *the report was suppressed* CENSOR, keep secret, conceal, hide, hush up, gag, withhold, cover up, stifle; ban, proscribe, outlaw; sweep under the carpet. ANTONYMS disclose, publicize.

suppurate verb *the lesions are suppurating* FESTER, form pus, discharge, run, weep, become septic.

supremacy noun *the supremacy of oppressive leadership anywhere in the world is bad for everyone in the world* ASCENDANCY, predominance, primacy, dominion, hegemony, authority, mastery, control, power, rule, sovereignty, influence; dominance, superiority, advantage, the upper hand, the whip hand, the edge; distinction, greatness.

supreme adjective 1 *the supreme commander* HIGHEST RANKING, chief, head, top, foremost, principal, superior, premier, first, prime; greatest, dominant, predominant, preeminent. ANTONYMS subordinate, inferior.

2 *a supreme achievement* EXTRAORDINARY, remarkable, incredible, phenomenal, rare, exceptional, outstanding, great, incomparable, unparalleled, peerless. ANTONYM minimum.

3 *the supreme sacrifice* ULTIMATE, final, last; utmost, extreme, greatest, highest. ANTONYM insignificant.

sure adjective 1 *I am sure that they didn't know* CERTAIN, positive, convinced, confident, definite, assured, satisfied, persuaded; unhesitating, unwavering, unshakable. ANTONYMS uncertain, doubtful.

2 *someone was sure to be blamed* BOUND, likely, destined, fated. ANTONYM unlikely.

3 *a sure winner with the children* GUARANTEED, unfailing, infallible, unerring, assured, certain, inevitable; *informal* sure-fire. ANTONYMS uncertain, unlikely.

4 *he entered in the sure knowledge that he would win* UNQUESTIONABLE, indisputable, irrefutable, incontrovertible, undeniable, indubitable, undoubted, absolute, categorical, true, certain; obvious, evident, plain, clear, conclusive, definite.

5 *a sure sign that he's worried* RELIABLE, dependable, trustworthy, unfailing, infallible, certain, unambiguous, true, foolproof, established, effective; *informal* sure-fire; *formal* efficacious.

6 *the sure hand of the soloist* FIRM, steady, stable, secure, confident, steadfast, unfaltering, unwavering.

▸ exclamation *"Can I come too?" "Sure."* YES, all right, of course, indeed, certainly, absolutely, agreed; *informal* OK, yeah, yep, uh-huh, you bet, I'll say, sure thing.

PHRASES: **be sure to** *be sure to feed the cat* REMEMBER TO, don't forget to, see that you, mind that you, take care to, be certain to. **for sure** *informal I'll be there for sure* DEFINITELY, surely, certainly, without doubt, without question, undoubtedly, indubitably, absolutely, undeniably, unmistakably. **make sure** *make sure that all the doors are locked* CHECK, confirm, make certain, ensure, assure; verify, corroborate, substantiate.

surely adverb 1 *surely you remembered?* IT MUST BE THE CASE THAT, assuredly, without question.

2 *I will surely die* CERTAINLY, for sure, definitely, undoubtedly, without doubt, doubtless, indubitably, unquestionably, without fail, inevitably.

3 *slowly but surely manipulating the public* FIRMLY, steadily, confidently, assuredly, unhesitatingly, unfalteringly, unswervingly, determinedly, doggedly, tenaciously.

surety noun 1 *she's a surety for his obligations* GUARANTOR, sponsor.

2 *a $10,000 surety* PLEDGE, collateral, guaranty, guarantee, bond, assurance, insurance, deposit; security, indemnity, indemnification; earnest.

surface noun 1 *the surface of the door* OUTSIDE, exterior; top, side; finish, veneer. ANTONYMS inside, interior.

2 *the surface of police culture* OUTWARD APPEARANCE, facade.

3 *a floured surface* counter, table.

▸ adjective *surface appearances* SUPERFICIAL, external, exterior, outward, ostensible, apparent, cosmetic, skin deep. ANTONYM underlying.

▸ verb 1 *a submarine surfaced* COME TO THE SURFACE, come up, rise. ANTONYM dive.

2 *the idea first surfaced in the sixties* EMERGE, arise, appear, come to light, crop up, materialize, spring up.

3 *informal she eventually surfaces for breakfast* GET UP, get out of bed, rise, wake, awaken, appear.

PHRASE: **on the surface** *it sounded plausible enough on the surface* AT FIRST GLANCE, to the casual eye, outwardly, to all appearances, apparently, ostensibly, superficially, externally.

surfeit noun *a surfeit of apples* EXCESS, surplus, abundance, oversupply, superabundance, superfluity, glut, avalanche, deluge; overdose; *informal* bellyful. ANTONYM lack.

▸ verb *we'll all be surfeited with food* SATIATE, sate, gorge, overfeed, overfill, glut, cram, stuff, overindulge, fill; saturate.

surfer noun *a compendium of tech-support links judged most useful by surfers like yourselves* INTERNET USER, netizen, nethead.

surge noun **1** *a surge of water* GUSH, rush, outpouring, stream, flow.

2 *a surge in public support* INCREASE, rise, growth, upswing, upsurge, groundswell, escalation, leap.

3 *a sudden surge of anger* RUSH, uprush, storm, torrent, blaze, outburst, eruption.

4 *the surge of sea* SWELL, heaving, rolling, roll, swirling; tide.

▸ verb **1** *the water surged into people's homes* GUSH, rush, stream, flow, burst, pour, cascade, spill, overflow, sweep, roll.

2 *the stock surged 47.63 points* INCREASE, rise, grow, escalate, leap.

3 *the sea surged* SWELL, heave, rise, roll.

surly adjective *we've had complaints from customers about your surly disposition* SULLEN, sulky, moody, sour, unfriendly, unpleasant, scowling, unsmiling; bad-tempered, grumpy, crotchety, prickly, cantankerous, irascible, testy, short-tempered; abrupt, brusque, curt, gruff, churlish, ill-humored, crabby, cranky, uncivil; *informal* grouchy. See note at BRUSQUE. ANTONYM pleasant.

surmise verb *I can only surmise that they're plotting against me* GUESS, conjecture, suspect, deduce, infer, conclude, theorize, speculate, divine; assume, presume, suppose, understand, gather, feel, sense, think, believe, imagine, fancy, reckon; *formal* opine.

surmount verb **1** *his reputation surmounts language barriers* OVERCOME, conquer, prevail over, triumph over, beat, vanquish; clear, cross, pass over; resist, endure.

2 *they surmounted the ridge* CLIMB OVER, top, ascend, scale, mount. ANTONYM descend.

3 *the dome is surmounted by a statue* CAP, top, crown, finish.

surname noun *his real surname is MacNeil* FAMILY NAME, last name; patronymic.

surpass verb *Hanley has surpassed Rich in the polls* EXCEL, exceed, transcend; outdo, outshine, outstrip, outclass, overshadow, eclipse; improve on, top, trump, cap, beat, better, outperform; *informal* leapfrog.

surplus noun *a surplus of grain* EXCESS, surfeit, superabundance, superfluity, oversupply, glut, profusion, plethora; remainder, residue, remains, leftovers. ANTONYM dearth.

▸ adjective *surplus adhesive* EXCESS, leftover, unused, remaining, extra, additional, spare; superfluous, redundant, unwanted, unneeded, dispensable, expendable. ANTONYM insufficient.

surprise noun **1** *Kate looked at me in surprise* ASTONISHMENT, amazement, wonder, incredulity, bewilderment, stupefaction, disbelief.

2 *the test came as a big surprise* SHOCK, bolt from the blue, bombshell, revelation, rude awakening, eye-opener, wake-up call; *informal* shocker.

▸ verb **1** *I was so surprised that I dropped it* ASTONISH, amaze, startle, astound, stun, stagger, shock; leave open-mouthed, take someone's breath away, dumbfound, stupefy, daze, take aback, shake up; *informal* bowl over, floor, flabbergast.

2 *she surprised a burglar* TAKE BY SURPRISE, catch unawares, catch off guard, catch red-handed, catch in the act.

surprised adjective *Lenore's unexpected return surprised everyone* ASTONISHED, amazed, astounded, startled, stunned, staggered, nonplussed, shocked, taken aback, stupefied, dumbfounded, dumbstruck, speechless, thunderstruck, confounded, shaken up; *informal* bowled over, flabbergasted, floored, flummoxed.

surprising adjective *the results of the study were surprising* UNEXPECTED, unforeseen, unpredictable; astonishing, amazing, startling, astounding, staggering, incredible, extraordinary, breathtaking, remarkable; *informal* mind-blowing.

surreal adjective *a backdrop of surreal images* UNREAL, bizarre, unusual, weird, strange, freakish, unearthly, uncanny, dreamlike, phantasmagorical.

surrender verb **1** *the army surrendered* CAPITULATE, give in, give (oneself) up, give way, yield, concede (defeat), submit, climb down, back down, cave in, relent, crumble; lay down one's arms, raise the white flag, throw in the towel. ANTONYM resist.

2 *they surrendered power to the workers* GIVE UP, relinquish, renounce, forgo, forswear; cede, abdicate, waive, forfeit, sacrifice; hand over, turn over, yield, resign, transfer, grant. See note at RELINQUISH. ANTONYM seize.

3 *don't surrender all hope of changing things* ABANDON, give up, cast aside.

▸ noun *the ordeal ended with their peaceful surrender* CAPITULATION, submission, yielding, succumbing, acquiescence; fall, defeat, resignation.

surreptitious adjective *a surreptitious glance* SECRET, secretive, stealthy, clandestine, sneaky, sly, furtive; concealed, hidden, undercover, covert, veiled, cloak-and-dagger. See note at SECRET. ANTONYM blatant.

surrogate noun *even as a well-meaning surrogate, I could never replace their dad* SUBSTITUTE, proxy, replacement; deputy, representative, stand-in, standby, stopgap, relief, pinch-hitter, understudy.

surround verb *we were surrounded by cops* ENCIRCLE, enclose, encompass, ring; fence in, hem in, confine, bound, circumscribe, cut off; besiege, trap. See note at CIRCUMSCRIBE.

surrounding adjective *tenants in the surrounding buildings were evacuated as a precaution* NEIGHBORING, nearby, near, neighborhood, local; adjoining, adjacent, bordering, abutting; encircling, encompassing.

surroundings plural noun *the surroundings were unfamiliar* ENVIRONMENT, setting, milieu, background, backdrop; conditions, circumstances, situation, context; vicinity, locality, habitat.

surveillance noun *we learned later that we had been under surveillance* OBSERVATION, scrutiny, watch, view, inspection, supervision; spying, espionage, infiltration, reconnaissance; *informal* bugging, wiretapping, recon.

survey verb **1** *he surveyed his work* LOOK AT, look over, observe, view, contemplate, regard, gaze at, stare at, eye; scrutinize, examine, inspect, scan, study, consider, review, take stock of; *informal* size up; *literary* behold.

2 *they surveyed 4,000 drug users* INTERVIEW, question, canvass, poll, cross-examine, investigate, research, study, probe, sample.

▸ noun **1** *a survey of the current literature* STUDY, review, consideration, overview; scrutiny, examination, inspection, appraisal.

2 *a survey of sexual behavior* POLL, review, investigation, inquiry, study, probe, questionnaire, census, research.

survive verb **1** *he survived by escaping through a hole* REMAIN ALIVE, live, sustain oneself, pull through, get through, hold on/out, make it, keep body and soul together.

2 *the theater must survive* CONTINUE, remain, persist, endure, live on, persevere, abide, go on, carry on, be extant, exist.

3 *he **was survived by** his sons* OUTLIVE, outlast; live longer than.

susceptible adjective **1** *susceptible children* IMPRESSIONABLE, credulous, gullible, innocent, ingenuous, naive, easily led; defenseless, vulnerable; persuadable, tractable; sensitive, responsive, thin-skinned. ANTONYMS skeptical, streetwise.

2 *people **susceptible to** blackmail* OPEN TO, receptive to, vulnerable to; an easy target for.

3 *he is **susceptible to** ulcers* LIABLE TO, prone to, subject to, inclined to, predisposed to, disposed to, given to, at risk of. ANTONYMS immune, resistant.

sushi noun See table.

SUSHI

aji (horse mackerel)	masago (smelt roe)
ama-ebi (raw shrimp)	masu (trout)
anago (sea eel)	mekajiki (swordfish)
awabi (abalone)	mirugai (surf clam)
ebi (boiled shrimp)	saba (mackerel)
hamachi (yellowtail)	sake (salmon)
hamaguri (clam)	sawara (Spanish mackerel)
hamo (sea eel)	suzuki (sea bass)
hirame (flounder)	tai (sea bream)
hokkigai (surf clam)	tairagai (razor-shell clam)
hotategai (scallop)	tako (octopus)
ika (squid)	tamago (sweet egg omelet)
ikura (salmon roe)	tobiko (flying fish roe)
kaibashira (scallop)	toro (fatty tuna)
kajiki (swordfish)	unagi (freshwater eel)
kani (crab or surimi)	uni (sea urchin roe)
karei (flatfish)	
katsuo (bonito)	
kazunoko (herring roe)	
maguro (tuna)	

suspect verb **1** *I suspected she'd made a mistake* HAVE A SUSPICION, have a feeling, feel, (be inclined to) think, fancy, reckon, guess, surmise, conjecture, conclude, have a hunch; suppose, presume, deduce, infer, sense, imagine; fear.

2 *he had no reason to suspect my honesty* DOUBT, distrust, mistrust, have misgivings about, be skeptical about, have qualms about, be suspicious of, be wary of, harbor reservations about.

▸ noun *a murder suspect* SUSPECTED PERSON, accused, defendant.

▸ adjective *a suspect package* SUSPICIOUS, dubious, doubtful, untrustworthy; odd, queer; *informal* fishy, funny, shady.

suspend verb **1** *the court case was suspended* ADJOURN, interrupt, break off, postpone, delay, defer, shelve, put off, put on hold, intermit, prorogue, hold over, hold in abeyance; cut short, discontinue, dissolve, disband, terminate, table; *informal* put on ice, put on the back burner, mothball, take a rain check on. See note at POSTPONE.

2 *he was suspended from his duties* EXCLUDE, debar, remove, eliminate, expel, eject.

3 *lights were suspended from the ceiling* HANG, sling, string; swing, dangle.

suspenders plural noun *he looks snazzy with those bright red suspenders Brit.* braces; *dated* galluses.

suspense noun *I can't bear the suspense* TENSION, uncertainty, doubt, anticipation, expectation, expectancy, excitement, anxiety, apprehension, strain. PHRASE: **in suspense** *he left us waiting in suspense for hours* EAGERLY, agog, with bated breath, on tenterhooks; on edge, anxious, edgy, jumpy, keyed up, uneasy, antsy, uptight, jittery.

suspension noun **1** *the suspension of army operations* ADJOURNMENT, interruption, postponement, delay, deferral, deferment, stay, prorogation; armistice; cessation, end, halt, stoppage, dissolution, disbandment, termination.

2 *his suspension from school* EXCLUSION, debarment, removal, elimination, expulsion, ejection.

suspicion noun **1** *she had a suspicion that he didn't like her* INTUITION, feeling, impression, inkling, hunch, fancy, notion, supposition, belief, idea, theory; presentiment, premonition; *informal* gut feeling, sixth sense.

2 *I confronted him with my suspicions* MISGIVING, doubt, qualm, reservation, hesitation, question; skepticism, uncertainty, distrust, mistrust.

3 *wine with a suspicion of soda* TRACE, touch, suggestion, hint, soupçon, tinge, shade, whiff, bit, drop, dash, taste, jot, mite.

suspicious adjective **1** *she gave him a suspicious look* DOUBTFUL, unsure, dubious, wary, chary, skeptical, distrustful, mistrustful, disbelieving, cynical. ANTONYM trusting.

2 *a highly suspicious character* DISREPUTABLE, unsavory, dubious, suspect, dishonest-looking, funny-looking, slippery; *informal* shifty, shady. ANTONYMS upright, reputable.

3 *she disappeared in suspicious circumstances* QUESTIONABLE, odd, strange, dubious, irregular, queer, funny, doubtful, mysterious, murky; *informal* fishy. ANTONYM innocent.

sustain verb **1** *the balcony might not sustain the weight* BEAR, support, carry, stand, keep up, prop up, shore up, underpin.

2 *her memories sustained her* COMFORT, help, assist, encourage, succor, support, give strength to, buoy up, carry, cheer up, hearten; *informal* buck up.

3 *they were unable to sustain a coalition* CONTINUE, carry on, keep up, keep alive, maintain, preserve, conserve, perpetuate, retain.

4 *she had bread and cheese to sustain her* NOURISH, feed, nurture; maintain, preserve, keep alive, keep going, provide for.

5 *she sustained slight injuries* UNDERGO, experience, suffer, endure.

6 *the allegation was not sustained* UPHOLD, validate, ratify, vindicate, confirm, endorse; verify, corroborate, substantiate, bear out, prove, authenticate, back up, evidence, justify.

sustained adjective *her sustained battle against alcoholism* CONTINUOUS, ongoing, steady, continual, constant, prolonged, persistent, nonstop, perpetual, unabating, relentless, rolling, unrelieved, unbroken, never-ending, incessant, unceasing, ceaseless, around/round-the-clock. ANTONYM sporadic.

sustenance noun **1** *the creature needs sustenance* NOURISHMENT, food, nutriment, nutrition, provisions, provender, rations; *informal* grub, chow, vittles; *formal* comestibles; *literary* viands; *dated* victuals.

2 *the sustenance of his family* SUPPORT, maintenance, keep, living, livelihood, subsistence, income.

svelte adjective *svelte swimsuit models* SLENDER, slim, graceful, elegant, willowy, sylphlike. See note at THIN.

swagger verb **1** *we swaggered into the arena* STRUT, parade, stride; walk confidently; *informal* sashay.

2 *try to swagger less and instead show some humility* BOAST, brag, bluster, crow, gloat; strut, posture, blow one's own horn, lord it; *informal* show off, swank.

▸ noun **1** *a slight swagger in his stride* STRUT; confidence, arrogance, ostentation.

2 *he was full of swagger* BLUSTER, braggadocio, bumptiousness, vainglory; *informal* swank.

swallow verb **1** *she couldn't swallow anything* EAT, gulp down, consume, devour, put away; ingest, assimilate; drink, guzzle, quaff, imbibe, sup, slug; *informal* polish off, swig, chug, swill, down, scoff.

2 *I can't swallow any more of your insults* TOLERATE, endure, stand, put up with, bear, abide, countenance, stomach, take, accept; *informal* hack; *formal* brook.

3 *he swallowed my story* BELIEVE, credit, accept, trust; *informal* fall for, buy, go for, 'swallow hook, line, and sinker'.

4 *she swallowed her pride* RESTRAIN, repress, suppress, hold back, fight back; overcome, check, control, curb, rein in; silence, muffle, stifle, smother, hide, bottle up; *informal* keep a/the lid on. PHRASE: **swallow up 1** *the darkness swallowed them up* ENGULF, swamp, devour, overwhelm, overcome. **2** *the colleges were swallowed up by universities* TAKE OVER, engulf, absorb, assimilate, incorporate.

swamp noun *her horse got stuck in a swamp* MARSH, bog, muskeg, quagmire, mire, morass, fen; quicksand, bayou; *archaic* quag.

▸ verb **1** *the rain was swamping the dry roads* FLOOD, inundate, deluge, immerse; soak, drench, saturate.

2 *he was swamped by media attention* OVERWHELM, inundate, flood, deluge, engulf, snow under, overload, overpower, weigh down, besiege, beset.

swampy adjective *the swampy acreage behind the orchard* MARSHY, boggy, fenny, miry; soft, soggy, muddy, spongy, heavy, squelchy, waterlogged, sodden, wet; *archaic* quaggy.

swan noun *male* : cob; *female* : pen; *young* : cygnet. See table at WATERFOWL.

swap verb **1** *I swapped my stereo for some hockey equipment* EXCHANGE, trade, barter, interchange, bargain; switch, change, replace.

2 *we swapped jokes* BANDY, exchange, trade, reciprocate.

▸ noun *a job swap* EXCHANGE, interchange, trade, switch, trade-off, substitution; *informal* switcheroo.

swarm noun **1** *a swarm of bees* HIVE, flock, collection.

2 *a swarm of gendarmes* CROWD, multitude, horde, host, mob, gang, throng, mass, army, troop, herd, pack; *literary* myriad.

▸ verb *reporters were swarming all over the place* FLOCK, crowd, throng, surge, stream.

PHRASE: **be swarming with** *the woods were swarming with biting flies* BE CROWDED WITH, be thronged with, be overrun with, be full of, abound in, be teeming with, be aswarm with, bristle with, be alive with, be crawling with, be infested with, overflow with, be prolific in, be abundant in; *informal* be thick with.

swarthy adjective *his swarthy complexion* DARK-SKINNED, olive-skinned, dusky, tanned, saturnine, black; *archaic* swart. See note at SATURNINE. ANTONYM pale.

swashbuckling adjective *a swashbuckling hero of silent films* DARING, heroic, daredevil, dashing, adventurous, bold, valiant, valorous, fearless, lionhearted, dauntless, devil-may-care; gallant, chivalrous, romantic. ANTONYM timid.

swathe verb *his hands were swathed in bandages* WRAP, envelop, bind, swaddle, bandage, cover, shroud, drape, wind, enfold, sheathe.

sway verb **1** *the curtains swayed in the breeze* SWING, shake, oscillate, undulate, move to and fro, move back and forth.

2 *she swayed on her feet* STAGGER, wobble, rock, lurch, reel, roll, list, stumble, pitch.

3 *we are swayed by the media* INFLUENCE, affect, bias, persuade, win over; manipulate, bend, mold.

4 *you must not be swayed by emotion* RULE, govern, dominate, control, guide.

▸ noun **1** *the sway of her hips* SWING, roll, shake, oscillation, undulation.

2 *his opinions have a lot of sway* CLOUT, influence, power, weight, authority, control. See note at JURISDICTION.

PHRASE: **hold sway** *they had held sway in France for a quarter of a century* HOLD POWER, wield power, exercise power, have jurisdiction, have authority, have dominion, rule, be in control, predominate; have the upper hand, have the edge, have the whip hand, have mastery; *informal* run the show, be in the driver's seat, be in the saddle.

swear verb **1** *they swore to marry each other* PROMISE, vow, pledge, give one's word, take an oath, undertake, guarantee; *Law* depose; *formal* aver.

2 *she swore she would never go back* INSIST, avow, pronounce, declare, proclaim, assert, profess, maintain, contend, emphasize, stress; *formal* aver.

3 *Kate spilled wine and swore* CURSE, blaspheme, utter profanities, utter oaths, use bad language, take the Lord's name in vain; *informal* cuss; *archaic* execrate. PHRASES: **swear by** *informal we swear by these all-weather tires* EXPRESS CONFIDENCE IN, have faith in, trust, believe in; set store by, value; *informal* rate. **swear off** *informal I swore off hard liquor years ago* RENOUNCE, forswear, forgo, abstain from, go without, shun, avoid, eschew, steer clear of; give up, dispense with, stop, discontinue, drop; *informal* kick, quit.

swearing noun *they had to bleep out all the swearing* BAD LANGUAGE, strong language, cursing, blaspheming, blasphemy; profanities, obscenities, curses, oaths, expletives, swear words; *informal* cussing, four-letter words; *formal* imprecation.

sweat noun **1** *he was drenched with sweat* PERSPIRATION, moisture, dampness, wetness; *Medicine* diaphoresis.

2 *informal he got into such a sweat about that girl* FLUSTER, panic, frenzy, fever, pother; *informal* state, flap, tizzy, dither, stew, lather.

3 *informal the sweat of the working classes* LABOR, hard work, toil(s), effort(s), exertion(s), industry, drudgery, slog; *informal* grind, elbow grease.

▸ verb **1** *she was sweating heavily* PERSPIRE, swelter, glow; be damp, be wet; secrete.

2 *I've sweated over this for six months* WORK (HARD), work like a Trojan, labor, toil, slog, slave, work one's fingers to the bone; *informal* plug away; *archaic* drudge.

3 *he sweated over his mistakes* WORRY, agonize, fuss, panic, fret, lose sleep; *informal* be on pins and needles, be in a state, be in a flap, be in a stew, torture oneself, torment oneself.

sweaty adjective *his sweaty palms* PERSPIRING, sweating, clammy, sticky, glowing; moist, damp.

sweep verb **1** *she swept the floor* BRUSH, clean, scrub, wipe, mop, dust, scour; *informal* do.

2 *I swept the crumbs off* REMOVE, brush, clean, clear, whisk.

3 *he was swept out to sea* CARRY, pull, drag, tow.

4 *riots swept the country* ENGULF, overwhelm, flood.

5 *he swept down the stairs* GLIDE, sail, breeze, drift, flit, flounce; stride, stroll, swagger.

6 *a limousine swept past* GLIDE, sail, rush, race, streak, speed, fly, zoom, whiz, hurtle; *informal* tear, whip.

7 *police swept the conference room* SEARCH, probe, check, explore, go through, scour, comb.

▸ noun **1** *a great sweep of his hand* GESTURE, stroke, wave, movement.

2 *a security sweep* SEARCH, hunt, exploration, probe.

3 *a long sweep of golden sand* EXPANSE, tract, stretch, extent, plain.

4 *the broad sweep of our interests* RANGE, span, scope, compass, reach, spread, ambit, gamut, spectrum, extent. See note at RANGE.

PHRASES: **sweep aside** *you can't sweep aside these allegations forever* DISREGARD, ignore, take no notice of, dismiss, shrug off, forget about, brush aside. **sweep under the carpet** *their grievances could no longer be swept under the carpet* HIDE, conceal, suppress, hush up, keep quiet about, censor, gag, withhold, cover up, stifle.

sweeping adjective **1** *sweeping changes* EXTENSIVE, wide-ranging, global, broad, comprehensive, all-inclusive, all-embracing, far-reaching, across the board; thorough, radical; *informal* wall-to-wall. ANTONYMS limited, narrow.

2 *a sweeping victory* OVERWHELMING, decisive, thorough, complete, total, absolute, out-and-out, unqualified, landslide. ANTONYM narrow.

3 *sweeping statements* WHOLESALE, blanket, generalized, all-inclusive, unqualified, indiscriminate, universal, oversimplified, imprecise. ANTONYMS narrow, focused.

4 *sweeping banks of flowers* BROAD, extensive, expansive, vast, spacious, boundless, panoramic. ANTONYM small.

sweet adjective **1** *sweet cinnamon buns* SUGARY, sweetened, saccharine; sugared, honeyed, candied, glacé; sickly, cloying. ANTONYMS sour, savory.

2 *the sweet scent of roses* FRAGRANT, aromatic, perfumed; *literary* ambrosial.

3 *her sweet voice* DULCET, melodious, lyrical, mellifluous, musical, tuneful, soft, harmonious, silvery, honeyed, mellow, rich, golden. ANTONYMS harsh, discordant.

4 *life was still sweet* PLEASANT, pleasing, pleasurable, agreeable, delightful, nice, satisfying, gratifying, good, acceptable, fine; *informal* lovely, great. ANTONYMS harsh, disagreeable.

5 *the sweet April air* PURE, wholesome, fresh, clean, clear. ANTONYMS harsh, rotten.

6 *she has a sweet nature* LIKABLE, appealing, engaging, amiable, pleasant, agreeable, genial, friendly, nice, kind, thoughtful, considerate; charming, enchanting, captivating, delightful, lovely. ANTONYM nasty.

7 *she looks quite sweet* CUTE, lovable, adorable, endearing, charming, attractive, dear.

8 *my sweet Lydia* DEAR, dearest, darling, beloved, loved, cherished, precious, treasured.

▸ noun **1** **(sweets)** *trying to cut back on sweets* DESSERTS, treats, cakes, cookies, pastries. See table at CANDY.

2 *happy birthday, my sweet!* DEAR, darling, dearest, love, sweetheart, beloved, honey, hon, pet, treasure, angel.

PHRASE: **sweet on** *informal it's obvious that Sam is sweet on Joanie* FOND OF, taken with, attracted to, in love with, enamored of, captivated by, infatuated with, keen on, devoted to, smitten with, moonstruck by; *informal* mad about, bowled over by.

sweeten verb **1** *sweeten the milk with honey* MAKE SWEET, add sugar to, sugar, sugar-coat.

2 *he chewed gum to sweeten his breath* FRESHEN, refresh, purify, deodorize, perfume.

3 *try to sweeten the bad news* SOFTEN, ease, alleviate, mitigate, temper, cushion; embellish, embroider.

4 *informal a bigger dividend to sweeten shareholders* MOLLIFY, placate, soothe, soften up, pacify, appease, win over.

sweetheart noun **1** *you look lovely, sweetheart* DARLING, dear, dearest, love, beloved, sweet; *informal* honey, hon, sweetie, sugar, baby, babe.

2 *my high-school sweetheart* LOVER, love, girlfriend, boyfriend, beloved, significant other, lady love, loved one, suitor, admirer; *informal* steady, flame, main squeeze; valentine; *literary* swain; *dated* beau; *archaic* paramour.

swell verb **1** *her lip* ***swelled up*** EXPAND, bulge, distend, inflate, dilate, bloat, puff up, balloon, fatten, fill out, tumefy. ANTONYMS shrink, contract.

2 *the population swelled* GROW, enlarge, increase, expand, rise, escalate, multiply, proliferate, snowball, mushroom. ANTONYMS wane, decrease.

3 *she swelled with pride* BE FILLED, be bursting, brim, overflow.

4 *the program swelled enrollments* INCREASE, enlarge, augment, boost, top up, step up, multiply. ANTONYM decrease.

5 *the music swelled to fill the house* GROW LOUD, grow louder, amplify, crescendo, intensify, heighten. ANTONYM quiet.

▸ noun **1** *a brief swell in the volume* INCREASE, rise, escalation, surge, boost. ANTONYMS decrease, dip.

2 *a heavy swell on the sea* SURGE, wave, undulation, roll.

▸ adjective *informal, dated a swell idea* EXCELLENT, marvelous, wonderful, splendid, magnificent, superb; *informal* super, great, fantastic. ANTONYM bad.

WORD NOTE **swell**

There's a pleasure in using slightly dated slang. I have an unreasonable affection for the word *swell,* which in my boyhood was the preferred locution for when you wanted to express enthusiasm or praise something as really first-rate. It was as versatile as *terrific* or the more recent *cool* as an informal, all-purpose, thumbs-up conversational rejoinder. *Swell* derived from the slang word for a patrician or a dandy, an upper-crust fashion plate—what in Britain was known as a *toff.* Maybe that's why the word appealed so much to the smart set. I love the way the word appears in great American songs. *Swell,* in the Rodgers and Hart standard "Thou Swell," is followed by *witty, sweet,* and *grand* as adjectives for the beloved. The wit of the title lies in its conjoining of archaic diction *(thou)* and up-to-date vernacular *(swell).* The refrain in Cole Porter's "Well, Did You Evah!"—written as a duet for Bing Crosby and Frank Sinatra in the movie *High Society*—is, "What a swell party this is." The usage here is half ironic, half sincere, altogether jovial. As the song concludes, Porter swells the word *swell* to make it rhyme with elegant. It's a "swellagant, elegant party," the great baritones agree, drinking their bubbly. Now that's swell. **—DL**

swelling noun *use ice to reduce the swelling* BUMP, lump, bulge, protuberance, enlargement, distension, prominence, protrusion, node, nodule, tumescence; boil, blister, bunion, carbuncle.

sweltering adjective *a sweltering afternoon* HOT, stifling, humid, sultry, sticky, muggy, close, stuffy; tropical, torrid, searing, blistering; *informal* boiling (hot), baking, roasting, sizzling. ANTONYM freezing.

swerve verb *a car swerved into her path* VEER, deviate, skew, diverge, sheer, weave, zigzag, change direction; *Sailing* tack.

▸ noun *the bowler regulated his swerve* CURVE, curl, deviation, twist.

swift adjective **1** *a swift decision* PROMPT, rapid, sudden, immediate, instant, instantaneous; abrupt, hasty, hurried, precipitate, headlong. ANTONYM unhurried.

2 *swift runners* FAST, rapid, quick, speedy, high-speed, fast-paced, brisk, lively; express, breakneck; fleet-footed; *informal* nippy, supersonic. ANTONYMS slow, sluggish.

WORD NOTE **swift**

A lovely onomatopoeic synonym for *quick,* evoking the gust of wind whispering in the wake of the described rapidly moving object, animal, or person. Great for descriptions of athletes and races—see Ecclesiastes. ***—DA***

swill verb *informal she was swilling beers* DRINK, quaff, swallow, down, gulp, drain, imbibe, sup, slurp, consume, slug; *informal* swig, knock back, toss off, put away, chug, chugalug.

▸ noun **1** *informal she took a swill of coffee* GULP, swallow, drink, draft, mouthful, slug; *informal* swig.

2 *swill for the pigs* PIGSWILL, mash, slops, scraps, refuse, scourings, leftovers; *archaic* hogwash.

swim verb **1** *they swam in the pool* BATHE, take a dip, splash around; float, tread water, paddle.

2 *his food was **swimming in** gravy* BE SATURATED IN, be drenched in, be soaked in, be steeped in, be immersed in, be covered in, be drowning in, be full of.

swimming noun See table.

SWIMMING STROKES AND KICKS

Australian crawl	freestyle
backstroke	sidestroke
breaststroke	flutter kick
butterfly (stroke)	frog kick
crawl	scissor kick
dog paddle	whip kick
elementary backstroke	

swimmingly adverb *everything was going swimmingly* WELL, smoothly, easily, effortlessly, like clockwork, without a hitch, as planned, to plan; *informal* like a dream, like magic.

swimming pool noun *an indoor swimming pool* POOL, baths, lap pool, natatorium.

swimsuit noun *bring your swimsuit to the party* BATHING SUIT, (swim/swimming) trunks, bikini; swimwear.

swindle verb *I was swindled out of money | he's been swindling clients for years* DEFRAUD, cheat, trick, dupe, deceive, fool, hoax, hoodwink, bamboozle; *informal* fleece, con, bilk, sting, hose, diddle, rip off, take for a ride, pull a fast one on, put one over on, take to the cleaners, gull, stiff, euchre, hornswoggle; *literary* cozen.

▸ noun *an insurance swindle* FRAUD, trick, deception, deceit, cheat, sham, artifice, ruse, dodge, racket, wile; sharp practice; *informal* con, fiddle, diddle, rip-off, flimflam, bunco.

swindler noun *the guy collecting for the hospital fund was a swindler* FRAUDSTER, fraud, confidence man, confidence trickster, trickster, cheat, rogue, mountebank, charlatan, impostor, hoaxer; *informal* con man, con artist, scam artist, shyster, gonif, shark, sharp, hustler, phony, crook, snake oil salesman.

swing verb **1** *the sign swung in the wind* SWAY, oscillate, move back and forth, move to and fro, wave, wag, rock, flutter, flap.

2 *Helen swung the bottle* BRANDISH, wave, flourish, wield, shake, wag, twirl.

3 *this road swings off to the north* CURVE, bend, veer, turn, bear, wind, twist, deviate, slew, skew, drift, head.

4 *the balance swung from one party to the other* CHANGE, fluctuate, shift, alter, oscillate, waver, alternate, seesaw, yo-yo, vary.

5 *informal if we keep trying, we can swing this deal* ACCOMPLISH, achieve, obtain, acquire, get, secure, net, win, attain, bag, hook; *informal* wangle, land.

▸ noun **1** *a swing of the pendulum* OSCILLATION, sway, wave.

2 *a swing to the New Democrats in this constituency* CHANGE, move; turnaround, turnabout, reversal, about face, volte face, change of heart, U-turn, sea change.

3 *a swing toward plain food* TREND, tendency, drift, movement.

4 *a mood swing* FLUCTUATION, change, shift, variation, oscillation.

swipe *informal* verb **1** *he swiped at her head* SWING, lash out; strike, hit, slap, cuff; *informal* belt, wallop, sock, clout.

2 *they're always swiping candy* STEAL, thieve, take, pilfer, purloin, snatch, shoplift; *informal* filch, lift, rob, nab, pinch, glom.

▸ noun *she took a swipe at his face* SWING, stroke, strike, hit, slap, cuff, clip; *informal* belt, wallop.

swirl verb *the snow swirled around them* WHIRL, eddy, billow, spiral, circulate, revolve, spin, twist; flow, stream, surge, seethe.

switch noun **1** *the switch on top of the telephone* BUTTON, lever, control, dial, rocker.

2 *a switch from direct to indirect taxation* CHANGE, move, shift, transition, transformation; reversal, turnaround, U-turn, changeover, transfer, conversion; substitution, exchange.

3 *a switch of willow* BRANCH, twig, stick, rod.

▸ verb **1** *he switched sides* CHANGE, shift; reverse; *informal* chop and change.

2 *he managed to switch envelopes* EXCHANGE, swap, interchange, trade, substitute, replace, rotate.

PHRASES: **switch on** *switch on the air conditioning* TURN ON, put on, flick on, activate, start, power up, set going, set in motion, operate, initiate, actuate, initialize, energize; toggle, flip, throw. **switch off** *who switched off the fan?* TURN OFF, shut off, flick off, power down, stop, cut, halt, deactivate; toggle, flip.

swivel verb *the speaker swivels on a small base* TURN, rotate, revolve, pivot, swing; spin, twirl, whirl, wheel, gyrate, pirouette.

swollen adjective *the rivers are swollen | swollen glands* DISTENDED, expanded, enlarged, bulging, inflated, dilated, bloated, puffed up, puffy, tumescent, tumid; inflamed, varicose.

swoop verb **1** *pigeons swooped down after the grain* DIVE, descend, sweep, pounce, plunge, pitch, nosedive; rush, dart, speed, zoom.

2 *police **swooped on** the building* RAID, pounce on, attack, assault, assail, charge, bust. PHRASE: **in one fell swoop.** See FELL[2] .

sword noun *a ceremonial sword* BLADE, foil, broadsword, épée, cutlass, rapier, saber, scimitar; *literary* brand. PHRASE: **cross swords** *Larry is crossing swords with his brother-in-law again* QUARREL, disagree, dispute, wrangle, bicker, be at odds, be at loggerheads, lock horns; fight, contend; *informal* scrap.

sybarite noun *an exclusive resort that caters to wealthy sybarites* HEDONIST, sensualist, voluptuary, libertine, pleasure-seeker, epicure, bon vivant, bon viveur. ANTONYM puritan.

sybaritic adjective *she regretted having left her homespun past for this sybaritic life with Lanzo* LUXURIOUS, extravagant, lavish, self-indulgent, pleasure-seeking, sensual, voluptuous, hedonistic, epicurean, lotus-eating, libertine, debauched, decadent. See note at SENSUOUS. ANTONYM ascetic.

sycophant noun *I thought you wanted a competent assistant, not a nodding sycophant* YES-MAN, bootlicker, brown-noser, toady, lickspittle, flatterer, flunky, lackey, spaniel, doormat, stooge, cringer, suck, suck-up.

sycophantic adjective *his clique of sycophantic friends* OBSEQUIOUS, servile, subservient, deferential, groveling, toadying, fawning, flattering, ingratiating, cringing, unctuous, slavish; *informal* smarmy, bootlicking, brown-nosing.

syllabus noun *the Film History syllabus for next semester has been posted* CURRICULUM, course (of study), program of study, course outline; timetable, schedule, calendar.

symbol noun **1** *the lotus is the symbol of purity* EMBLEM, token, sign, representation, figure, image; metaphor, allegory; icon.

2 *the chemical symbol for helium* SIGN, character, mark, letter, ideogram.

3 *the Red Cross symbol* LOGO, emblem, badge, stamp, trademark, crest, insignia, coat of arms, seal, device, monogram, hallmark, flag, motif, icon. See note at EMBLEM.

symbolic adjective **1** *the Colosseum is symbolic of the Roman Empire* EMBLEMATIC, representative, typical, characteristic, symptomatic.

2 *symbolic language* FIGURATIVE, representative, illustrative, emblematic, metaphorical, allegorical, parabolic, allusive, suggestive; meaningful, significant. ANTONYM literal.

symbolize verb *the wheel symbolizes the power of peaceful change* REPRESENT, stand for, be a sign of, exemplify; denote, signify, mean, indicate, convey, express, imply, suggest, allude to; embody, epitomize, encapsulate, personify, typify; *literary* betoken.

symmetrical adjective *the two doves on the flag are symmetrical* evenly shaped, aligned, equal; mirror image; regular, uniform, consistent; balanced, proportional, even.

symmetry noun *the garden is laid out with perfect symmetry* REGULARITY, evenness, uniformity, consistency, conformity, correspondence, equality; balance, proportions; *formal* concord.

sympathetic adjective **1** *a sympathetic listener* COMPASSIONATE, caring, concerned, solicitous, empathetic, understanding, sensitive; commiserative, pitying, consoling, comforting, supportive, encouraging; considerate, kind, tenderhearted; *informal* boosterish. ANTONYM unfeeling.

2 *the most sympathetic character in the book* LIKABLE, pleasant, agreeable, congenial, friendly, genial, simpatico. ANTONYM unfriendly.

3 *I was **sympathetic to** his cause* IN FAVOR OF, in sympathy with, pro, on the side of, supportive of, encouraging of; well-disposed to, favorably disposed to, receptive to. ANTONYMS indifferent, opposed.

sympathize verb **1** *I do **sympathize with** the poor creature* PITY, feel sorry for, show compassion for, commiserate with, offer condolences to, feel for, show concern for, show interest for; console, comfort, solace, soothe, support, encourage; empathize with, identify with, understand, relate to.

2 *they* ***sympathize with*** *the critique* AGREE WITH, support, be in favor of, go along with, favor, approve of, back, side with.

sympathizer noun *his Confederate brothers accused him of being a Yankee sympathizer* SUPPORTER, backer, well-wisher, advocate, ally, partisan; collaborator, fraternizer, conspirator, quisling.

sympathy noun 1 *he shows sympathy for the poor* COMPASSION, caring, concern, solicitude, empathy; commiseration, pity, condolence, comfort, solace, support, encouragement; consideration, kindness. ANTONYM indifference.

2 *sympathy with a fellow journalist* RAPPORT, fellow feeling, affinity, empathy, harmony, accord, compatibility; fellowship, camaraderie. ANTONYM hostility.

3 *their sympathy with the Communists* AGREEMENT, favor, approval, approbation, support, encouragement, partiality; association, alignment, affiliation. ANTONYM disapproval.

symptom noun 1 *the symptoms of the disease* MANIFESTATION, indication, indicator, sign, mark, feature, trait; *Medicine* prodrome.

2 *a symptom of the country's present turmoil* EXPRESSION, sign, indication, mark, token, manifestation; portent, warning, clue, hint; testimony, evidence, proof; result, consequence, product. See note at SIGN.

symptomatic adjective *they worried that her lethargy was symptomatic of depression* INDICATIVE, characteristic, suggestive, typical, representative, symbolic.

syndrome noun *he is suffering from an inner-ear syndrome that is not uncommon among divers* CONDITION, illness, complex, disorder, affliction, sickness.

synergy, synergism *there's no synergy between the two, so no costs are saved* COOPERATIVE INTERACTION, cooperation, combined effort, give and take.

WORD NOTE **synergy**

Some words don't work. *Synergy* is one of them. Theoretically it makes sense. *Synergy* is a business term, corporate-speak for the advantages of amalgamating the operations of several different but related companies. When, for example, a book publisher merges with a movie studio, one reason given is that there are bound to be significant *synergies:* ways one branch of the new structure can feed the other. It turns out, however, that the concept is flawed; these mergers seldom go according to plan. And that is surely why you hear the word only in the business news, among executives and mouthpieces for whom hope springs eternal. —**DL**

synonym noun *'harsh' may be used as synonym for 'oppressive'* ALTERNATE, substitute, alternative, equivalent, euphemism.

synopsis noun *the synopsis was so intriguing that I just had to buy the book* SUMMARY, summarization, précis, abstract, outline, digest, rundown, roundup, abridgment.

synthesis noun *the synthesis of their diverse styles makes for a wonderful new sound in country music* COMBINATION, union, amalgam, blend, mixture, compound, fusion, composite, alloy; unification, amalgamation, marrying.

synthesizer noun *they were one of the first bands to use a synthesizer on stage* KEYBOARD, keys, synth, vocoder, sampler, MIDI device.

WORD NOTE **synthesizer**

A *synthesizer* is a sound-making electronic device allowing a large degree of control over sound output. A *vocoder* mixes two audio signals, one of which is usually a voice, to make special effects such as talking wind. A *sampler* records sounds (any sound, not just other people's records) and plays them back as different notes. A *MIDI device* is one using the Musical Instrument Digital Interface language to communicate with others, facilitating synchronization and exchange of musical information and playback. —**SM**

synthetic adjective *synthetic leather* ARTIFICIAL, fake, imitation, faux, mock, simulated, ersatz, substitute; pseudo, so-called; man-made, manufactured, fabricated; *informal* phony, pretend. See note at SPURIOUS. ANTONYM natural.

syrupy adjective 1 *syrupy medicine* OVERSWEET, sweet, sugary, treacly, honeyed, saccharine; thick, sticky, gluey, viscid, glutinous; *informal* gooey.

2 *syrupy romantic drivel* SENTIMENTAL, mawkish, cloying, sickly, saccharine, trite; *informal* soppy, schmaltzy, mushy, slushy, sloppy, lovey-dovey, cheesy, corny.

system noun 1 *a system of canals* STRUCTURE, organization, arrangement, complex, network; *informal* setup.

2 *a system for regulating sales* METHOD, methodology, technique, process, procedure, approach, practice; means, way, mode, framework, modus operandi; scheme, plan, policy, program, regimen, formula, routine.

3 *there was no system in his work* ORDER, method, orderliness, systematization, planning, logic, routine.

4 *youngsters have no faith in* ***the system*** THE ESTABLISHMENT, the administration, the authorities, the powers that be; bureaucracy, officialdom; the status quo.

systematic adjective *the systematic firing of one department head after another* STRUCTURED, methodical, organized, orderly, planned, systematized, regular, routine, standardized, standard; logical, coherent, consistent; efficient, businesslike, practical; *informal* left-brained. ANTONYM disorganized.

T

tab noun **1** *his name is on the tab of his jacket* TAG, label, flap.

2 *informal* *the company will pick up the tab* BILL, invoice, account, charge, check, expense, cost.

table noun **1** *put the plates on the table* bench, buffet, stand, counter, work surface; desk; bar.

2 *he provides an excellent table* MEAL, food, fare, menu, nourishment; eatables, provisions; *informal* spread, grub, chow, eats, nosh; *literary* viands; *dated* victuals.

3 *the report has numerous tables* CHART, diagram, figure, graph, plan; list, tabulation, index.

▸ verb *the council tabled the rezoning issue until April* POSTPONE, delay, defer, sideline, put on the back burner.

tableau noun **1** *mythic tableaux* PICTURE, painting, representation, illustration, image.

2 *the first act consists of a series of tableaux* PAGEANT, tableau vivant, parade, diorama, scene.

3 *a domestic tableau around the fireplace* SCENE, arrangement, grouping, group; picture, spectacle, image, vignette.

tablet noun **1** *a carved tablet* SLAB, stone, panel, plaque, plate, sign.

2 *a headache tablet* PILL, capsule, lozenge, caplet, pastille, drop, pilule; *informal* tab.

3 *a writing tablet* PAD, notepad, memo pad, notebook, scratchpad.

taboo noun *the taboo against healing on the Sabbath* PROHIBITION, proscription, veto, interdiction, interdict, ban, restriction.

▸ adjective *taboo subjects* FORBIDDEN, prohibited, banned, proscribed, interdicted, outlawed, illegal, illicit, unlawful, restricted, off limits; unmentionable, unspeakable, unutterable, unsayable, ineffable; rude, impolite. ANTONYM acceptable.

tabulate verb *we tabulate the phone-in pledges every twenty minutes* CHART, arrange, order, organize, systematize, systemize, catalog, list, index, classify, class, codify; compile, group, log, grade, rate.

tacit adjective *tacit promises* IMPLICIT, understood, implied, hinted, suggested; unspoken, unstated, unsaid, unexpressed, unvoiced; taken for granted, taken as read, inferred. ANTONYM explicit.

taciturn adjective *our taciturn daughter has suddenly become a little chatty* UNTALKATIVE, uncommunicative, reticent, unforthcoming, quiet, secretive, tight-lipped, buttoned-up, close-mouthed; silent, mute, dumb, inarticulate; reserved, withdrawn. ANTONYM talkative.

tack noun **1** *tacks held the carpet down* PIN, thumbtack, pushpin, nail, staple, rivet, stud.

2 *the boat bowled past on the opposite tack* HEADING, bearing, course, track, path, line.

3 *Mitchell wisely changed his tack* APPROACH, way, method; policy, procedure, technique, tactic, plan, strategy, stratagem; path, line, angle, direction, course.

▸ verb **1** *a photo tacked to the wall* PIN, nail, staple, fix, fasten, attach, secure, affix.

2 *the dress was roughly tacked together* STITCH, baste, sew, bind.

3 *the yachts tacked back and forth* ZIGZAG, change direction, change course, swerve, veer; *Nautical* go about, come about, beat.

4 *poems* ***tacked on*** *at the end of the book* ADD (ON), append, join, stick (on).

tackle noun **1** *fishing tackle* GEAR, equipment, apparatus, kit, hardware; implements, instruments, accoutrements, paraphernalia, trappings, appurtenances; *informal* things, stuff, bits and pieces; *archaic* equipage.

2 *lifting tackle* PULLEYS, gear, hoist, crane, winch, davit, windlass, sheave.

3 *a tackle by the linebacker* BLOCK, interception, challenge, attack.

▸ verb **1** *we must tackle environmental problems* COME TO GRIPS WITH, address, get to work on, set one's hand to, approach, take on, attend to, see to, try to sort out; deal with, take care of, handle, manage; *informal* have a crack at, have a go at.

2 *he tackled a masked intruder* CONFRONT, face up to, take on, contend with, challenge, attack; seize, grab, grapple with, intercept, block, stop; bring down, floor, fell; *informal* have a go at.

tacky[1] adjective *the paint was still tacky* STICKY, wet, gluey, gummy, adhesive, viscous, viscid, treacly; *informal* gooey.

tacky[2] adjective *a tacky game show* TAWDRY, TASTELESS, kitsch, kitschy, vulgar, crude, garish, gaudy, showy, trashy, cheesy, cheap, common, second-rate. ANTONYM tasteful.

WORD NOTE **tacky**

Tacky is used for anything aesthetically excessive:
corny: overly sentimental or countrified
hammy: overly theatrical, esp. of acting or singing
kitschy: grandiosely tasteless
pretentious: overreaching the boundaries of the medium or abilities of the creator
schmaltzy: excessively sweet or sentimental
self-indulgent: tastelessly expressive of concerns unique to the artist
—SM

tact noun *Dr. Porter has a lot to learn about timing and tact* DIPLOMACY, tactfulness, sensitivity, understanding, thoughtfulness, consideration, delicacy, discretion, prudence, judiciousness, subtlety, savoir faire; *informal* savvy.

tactful adjective *tactful criticism* DIPLOMATIC, discreet, considerate, sensitive, understanding, thoughtful, delicate, judicious, politic, perceptive, subtle; courteous, polite, decorous, respectful; *informal* savvy.

tactic noun **1** *a tax-saving tactic* STRATEGY, scheme, stratagem, plan, maneuver; method, expedient, gambit, move, approach, tack; device, trick, ploy, dodge, ruse, machination, contrivance; *informal* wangle; *archaic* shift.

2 *our fleet's superior tactics* STRATEGY, policy, campaign, battle plans, game plans, maneuvers, logistics; generalship, organization, planning, direction, orchestration.

tactical adjective *they met secretly to discuss their next tactical move* CALCULATED, planned, strategic; prudent, politic, diplomatic, judicious, shrewd, cunning, artful.

tactless adjective *it was a cruel, tactless thing to say* INSENSITIVE, inconsiderate, thoughtless, indelicate, undiplomatic, impolitic, indiscreet, unsubtle, clumsy, heavy-handed, graceless, awkward, inept, gauche; blunt, frank, outspoken, abrupt, gruff, rough, crude, coarse; imprudent, injudicious, unwise; rude, impolite, uncouth, discourteous, crass, tasteless, disrespectful, boorish.

tad noun *I'll have just a tad of whipped cream* BIT, whit, mite, touch, modicum, iota, hint, soupçon, fraction, titch, tinch.

tag noun **1** *a price tag* LABEL, ticket, badge, mark, marker, tab, sticker, stub, counterfoil, flag.

2 *he gained a "bad boy" tag* DESIGNATION, label, description, characterization, identity; nickname, name, epithet, title, sobriquet; *informal* handle, moniker; *formal* denomination, appellation.

3 *tags from Shakespeare* QUOTATION, quote, tag line, phrase, platitude, cliché, excerpt; saying, proverb, maxim, adage, aphorism, motto, epigram; slogan, catchphrase.

▸ verb **1** *bottles tagged with colored stickers* LABEL, mark, ticket, identify, flag, indicate.

2 *she is tagged as a "thinking" actor* LABEL, class, categorize, characterize, designate, describe, identify, classify; mark, stamp, brand, pigeonhole, stereotype, typecast, compartmentalize, typify; name, call, title, entitle, dub, term, style.

3 *a poem **tagged on** as an afterthought* ADD, tack on, join; attach, append, stick on.

4 *he was **tagging along** behind her* FOLLOW, trail; come after, go after, shadow, dog; accompany, attend, escort; *informal* tail.

tail noun **1** *the dog's tail* brush, scut, dock; tail feathers; hindquarters. ANTONYMS head, front.

2 *the tail of the plane* REAR, end, back, extremity; bottom. ANTONYMS head, front.

3 *the tail of the hunting season* CLOSE, end, conclusion, tail end. ANTONYMS beginning, start.

4 *informal put a tail on that suspect* DETECTIVE, investigator, shadow; *informal* sleuth, private eye, gumshoe.

▸ verb *informal the paparazzi tailed them* FOLLOW, shadow, stalk, trail, track, hunt, hound, dog, pursue, chase.

PHRASES: **on someone's tail** *a police car stayed on his tail* CLOSE BEHIND, following closely, (hard) on someone's heels. **tail off/away** *her voice tailed off* FADE, wane, ebb, dwindle, decrease, lessen, diminish, decline, subside, abate, drop off, peter out, taper off; let up, ease off, die away, die down, come to an end. **turn tail** *I was so shocked, I just turned tail* RUN AWAY, flee, bolt, make off, take to one's heels, cut and run, beat a (hasty) retreat; *informal* scram, skedaddle, vamoose.

tailor noun *the finest tailor in Memphis* OUTFITTER, dressmaker, couturier, fashion designer, designer; clothier, costumer, seamstress.

▸ verb *services can be tailored to customer requirements* CUSTOMIZE, adapt, adjust, modify, change, convert, alter, attune, mold, gear, fit, cut, shape, tune.

tailspin noun *the stock market went into a tailspin* NOSEDIVE, dive, plummet, plunge, fall, rapid descent, sharp decline.

taint noun *the taint of corruption* TRACE, touch, suggestion, hint, tinge; stain, blot, blemish, stigma, black mark, discredit, dishonor, disgrace, shame.

▸ verb **1** *the wilderness is tainted by pollution* CONTAMINATE, pollute, adulterate, infect, blight, spoil, soil, ruin, destroy; *literary* befoul. See note at POLLUTE. ANTONYM clean.

2 *those fraudsters taint the reputation of legitimate claimants* TARNISH, sully, blacken, stain, blot, blemish, stigmatize, mar, corrupt, defile, soil, muddy, damage, harm, hurt; drag through the mud; *literary* besmirch. ANTONYM improve.

take verb **1** *she took his hand* LAY HOLD OF, get hold of; grasp, grip, clasp, clutch, grab. ANTONYM give.

2 *he took an envelope from his pocket* REMOVE, pull, draw, withdraw, extract, fish. ANTONYM give.

3 *a passage taken from my book* EXTRACT, quote, cite, excerpt, derive, abstract, copy, cull.

4 *she took a little wine* DRINK, imbibe; consume, swallow, eat, ingest.

5 *many prisoners were taken* CAPTURE, seize, catch, arrest, apprehend, take into custody; carry off, abduct. ANTONYMS liberate, free.

6 *someone's taken my car* STEAL, remove, appropriate, make off with, pilfer, purloin; *informal* filch, swipe, snaffle, pinch. ANTONYMS give back, restore.

7 *take four from the total* SUBTRACT, deduct, remove; discount; *informal* knock off, minus. ANTONYM add.

8 *all the seats had been taken* OCCUPY, use, utilize, fill, hold; reserve, engage; *informal* bag.

9 *I have taken a room nearby* RENT, lease, hire, charter; reserve, book, engage.

10 *I took the job* ACCEPT, undertake, take on. ANTONYMS refuse, turn down.

11 *I'd take this over the other option* PICK, choose, select; prefer, favor, opt for, vote for. ANTONYMS refuse, turn down.

12 *take, for instance, Altoona* CONSIDER, contemplate, ponder, think about, mull over, examine, study, meditate over, ruminate about.

13 *she took his temperature* ASCERTAIN, determine, establish, measure, find out, discover; calculate, compute, evaluate, rate, assess, appraise, gauge.

14 *he took notes* WRITE, note (down), jot (down), scribble, scrawl, record, register, document, minute.

15 *I took the package to Wilmington* BRING, carry, bear, transport, convey, move, transfer, ferry; *informal* cart, tote.

16 *the police took her home* ESCORT, accompany, help, assist, show, lead, guide, see, usher, shepherd, convey.

17 *he took the train* TRAVEL ON/BY, journey on, go via; use.

18 *the town takes its name from the lake* DERIVE, get, obtain, come by, acquire, pick up.

19 *she took the prize for best speaker* RECEIVE, obtain, gain, get, acquire, collect, accept, be awarded; secure, come by, win, earn, pick up, carry off; *informal* land, bag, net, scoop.

20 *I took the chance to postpone it* ACT ON, take advantage of, capitalize on, use, exploit, make the most of, leap at, jump at, pounce on, seize, grasp, grab, accept. ANTONYMS ignore, miss.

21 *he took great pleasure in painting* DERIVE, draw, acquire, obtain, get, gain, extract, procure; experience, undergo, feel.

22 *Liz took the news badly* RECEIVE, respond to, react to, meet, greet; deal with, cope with.

23 *do you **take** me **for** a fool?* REGARD AS, consider to be, view as, see as, believe to be, reckon to be, imagine to be, deem to be.

24 *I **take it** that you are hungry* ASSUME, presume, suppose, imagine, expect, reckon, gather, dare say, trust, surmise, deduce, guess, conjecture, fancy, suspect.

25 *I take your point* UNDERSTAND, grasp, get, comprehend, apprehend, see, follow; accept, appreciate, acknowledge, sympathize with, agree with.

26 *Shirley was very taken with him* CAPTIVATE, enchant, charm, delight, attract, beguile, enthrall, entrance, infatuate, dazzle; amuse, divert, entertain; *informal* tickle someone's fancy.

27 *I can't take much more* ENDURE, bear, tolerate, stand, put up with, abide, stomach, accept, allow, countenance, support, shoulder; *formal* brook; *archaic* suffer.

28 *applicants must take a test* CARRY OUT, do, complete, write, conduct, perform, execute, discharge, accomplish, fulfill.

29 *I took drama, French, and art history* STUDY, learn, have lessons in; take up, pursue; *informal* do.

30 *the journey took six hours* LAST, continue for, go on for, carry on for; require, call for, need, necessitate, entail, involve.

31 *it would take an expert to know that* REQUIRE, need, necessitate, demand, call for, entail, involve.

32 *I take size six shoes* WEAR, use; require, need.

33 *the dye did not take* BE EFFECTIVE, take effect, hold, root, be productive, be effectual, be useful; work, operate, succeed, function; *formal* be efficacious.

▸ noun **1** *the whalers' commercial take* CATCH, haul, bag, yield, net.

2 *the state's tax take* REVENUE, income, gain, profit; takings, proceeds, returns, receipts, winnings, pickings, earnings, spoils; purse.

3 *a clapperboard for the start of each take* SCENE, sequence, film clip, clip.

4 *a fresh **take on** gender issues* VIEW OF, reading of, version of, interpretation of, understanding of, account of, analysis of, approach to.

PHRASES: **take after** *Sandy takes after his adventurous Uncle Lenny* RESEMBLE, look like; remind one of, make one think of, recall, conjure up, suggest, evoke; *informal* favor, be a chip off the old block. **take apart 1** *we took the machine apart* DISMANTLE, pull to pieces, pull apart, disassemble, break up; tear down, demolish, destroy, wreck. **2** *informal* *the scene was taken apart by the director.* See CRITICIZE. **take someone back 1** *the dream **took me back to** Vienna* EVOKE, remind one of, conjure up, summon up; echo, suggest. **2** *I will never take her back* BE RECONCILED (TO), forgive, pardon, excuse, exonerate, absolve; let bygones be bygones, bury the hatchet. **take something back 1** *I take back every word* RETRACT, withdraw, renounce, disclaim, unsay, disavow, recant, repudiate; *formal* abjure. **2** *I must take the keys back* RETURN, bring back, give back, restore. **take something down** *I took down everything she said* WRITE DOWN, note down, jot down, set down, record, commit to paper, register, draft, document, minute, pen. **take someone in 1** *she took in paying guests* ACCOMMODATE, board, house, feed, put up, admit, receive; harbor. **2** *you were taken in by a hoax* DECEIVE, delude, hoodwink, mislead, trick, dupe, fool, cheat, defraud, swindle, outwit, gull, hoax, bamboozle; *informal* con, put one over on. **take something in 1** *she could hardly take in the news* COMPREHEND, understand, grasp, follow, absorb; *informal* get. **2** *this route takes in some great scenery* INCLUDE, encompass, embrace, contain, comprise, cover, incorporate, comprehend, hold. **take someone in hand** *part of your job is to take young Master Jonathon in hand* CONTROL, be in charge of, dominate, master; reform, improve, correct, change, rehabilitate. **take something in hand** *are you willing to take this project in hand?* DEAL WITH, apply oneself to, come to grips with, set one's hand to, grapple with, take on, attend to, see to, sort out, take care of, handle, manage. **take it out of someone** *the final lap has taken it out of Johnson* EXHAUST, drain, enervate, tire, fatigue, wear out, weary, debilitate; *informal* poop. **take off 1** *the horse took off at great speed* RUN AWAY/OFF, flee, abscond, take flight, decamp, leave, go, depart, make off, bolt, take to one's heels, escape; *informal* split, clear off, skedaddle, vamoose. **2** *the plane took off* BECOME AIRBORNE, take to the air, take wing; lift off, blast off. **3** *the idea really took off* SUCCEED, do well, become popular, catch on, prosper, flourish, thrive, boom. **take someone on 1** *there was no* *challenger to take him on* COMPETE AGAINST, oppose, challenge, confront, face, fight, vie with, contend with, stand up to. **2** *we took on extra staff* ENGAGE, hire, employ, enroll, enlist, sign up; *informal* take on board. **take something on 1** *he took on more responsibility* UNDERTAKE, accept, assume, shoulder, acquire, carry, bear. **2** *the study took on political meaning* ACQUIRE, assume, come to have. **take one's time** *if the place were on fire, Mark would still take his time* GO SLOWLY, dally, dawdle, delay, linger, drag one's feet, waste time, kill time; *informal* dilly-dally, lollygag; *archaic* tarry. **take someone out 1** *he asked if he could take her out* GO OUT WITH, escort, partner, accompany, go with; romance; *informal* date, see, go steady with; *dated* court, woo. **2** *informal the sniper took them all out* KILL, murder, assassinate, dispatch, execute, finish off, eliminate, exterminate, terminate; *informal* do in, do away with, bump off, rub out, mow down. *literary* slay. **take something over** *the workers were stunned to learn that a rival corporation had taken over their company* ASSUME CONTROL OF, take charge of, take command of. **take to 1** *he took to carrying his money in his sock* MAKE A HABIT OF, resort to, turn to, have recourse to (start/begin); start, begin, commence. **2** *Ruth took to the cat instantly* LIKE, get on with, be friendly toward; *informal* take a shine to. **3** *the dog has really taken to racing* BECOME GOOD AT, develop an ability for; like, enjoy. **take something up 1** *she took up abstract painting* ENGAGE IN, practice; begin, start, commence. **2** *the meetings took up all her time* CONSUME, fill, absorb, use, occupy; waste, squander. **3** *her cousin took up the story* RESUME, recommence, restart, carry on, continue, pick up, return to. **4** *he took up their offer of a job* ACCEPT, say yes to, agree to, adopt; *formal* accede to. **5** *take the skirt up an inch* SHORTEN, turn up; raise, lift. **take up with** *Burt has taken up with the kids in the ski club* BECOME FRIENDS WITH, (begin to) go around with, fall in with, string along with, get involved with, start seeing; *informal* (begin to) hang out with.

takeoff noun **1** *the plane performed a safe takeoff* DEPARTURE, liftoff, launch, blastoff; ascent, flight. ANTONYM touchdown.

2 *informal a takeoff of a talent show* PARODY, pastiche, mockery, caricature, travesty, satire, lampoon, mimicry, imitation, impersonation, impression; *informal* sendup, spoof.

takeover noun *a corporate takeover* BUYOUT, merger, amalgamation; purchase, acquisition.

takings plural noun *his takings from the race were substantial* PROCEEDS, returns, receipts, earnings, winnings, pickings, spoils; profit, gain, income, revenue; gate, purse.

tale noun **1** *a tale of witches* STORY, narrative, anecdote, report, account, history; legend, fable, myth, parable, allegory, saga; *informal* yarn.

2 *she told tales to her mother* LIE, fib, falsehood, story, untruth, fabrication, fiction; *informal* tall story, fairy tale, fairy story, cock-and-bull story.

talent noun *a natural talent for dancing* FLAIR, aptitude, facility, gift, knack, technique, touch, bent, ability, expertise, capacity, faculty; strength, forte, genius, brilliance; dexterity, skill, artistry.

talented adjective *a talented sculptor* GIFTED, skillful, skilled, accomplished, brilliant, expert, consummate, masterly, adroit, dexterous, able, competent, apt, capable, deft, adept, proficient; *informal* crack, ace. ANTONYM inept.

talisman noun *this talisman has been in our family for more than twelve generations* LUCKY CHARM, charm, fetish, amulet, mascot, totem, juju.

talk verb **1** *I was talking to a friend* SPEAK, chat, chatter, gossip, prattle, babble, rattle on, blather; *informal* yak, gab, jaw, chew the fat, natter, rap.

2 *you're talking garbage* UTTER, speak, say, voice, express, articulate, pronounce, verbalize, vocalize.

3 *they were able to talk in peace* CONVERSE, communicate, speak, confer, consult; negotiate, parley; *informal* have a confab, chew the fat, rap; *formal* confabulate.

4 *he* ***talked of*** *suicide* MENTION, refer to, speak about, discuss.

5 *he learned to talk Cree* SPEAK (IN), talk in, communicate in, converse in, express oneself in; use.

6 *nothing would make her talk* CONFESS, speak out, speak up, reveal all, tell tales, give the game away, open one's mouth; *informal* come clean, blab, squeal, let the cat out of the bag, spill the beans, sing, rat.

7 *the others will talk* GOSSIP, pass comment, make remarks; criticize.

▸ noun **1** *he was bored with all this talk* CHATTER, gossip, prattle, jabbering, babbling, gabbling; *informal* yakking, gabbing, nattering.

2 *she needed a talk with Jim* CONVERSATION, chat, discussion, tête-à-tête, heart-to-heart, dialogue, parley, powwow, consultation, conference, meeting; *informal* confab, jaw, chitchat, gossip; *formal* colloquy, confabulation.

3 **(talks)** *peace talks* NEGOTIATIONS, discussions; conference, summit, meeting, consultation, dialogue, symposium, seminar, conclave, parley; mediation, arbitration; *informal* powwow.

4 *she gave a talk on her travels* LECTURE, speech, address, discourse, oration, presentation, report, sermon; *informal* spiel.

5 *there was talk of a takeover* GOSSIP, rumor, hearsay, tittle-tattle; news, report.

6 *informal he's all talk* BOASTING, bragging, idle talk, bombast, braggadocio; *informal* hot air, mouth.

7 *baby talk* SPEECH, language, slang, idiom, idiolect; words; *informal* lingo, -ese.

PHRASES: **talk back to** *nobody talks back to Mr. Lynde* ANSWER BACK (TO), be impertinent to, be cheeky to, be rude to; contradict, argue with, disagree with. **talk big** *informal*. See BOAST verb sense 1. **talk down to** *he routinely talks down to women* CONDESCEND TO, patronize, look down one's nose at, put down. **talk someone into something** *don't even try to talk me into giving you another loan* PERSUADE INTO, argue into, cajole into, coax into, bring around to, inveigle into, wheedle into, sweet-talk into, prevail on someone to; *informal* hustle into, fast-talk into.

talkative adjective *the talkative person in the seat next to mine* CHATTY, loquacious, garrulous, voluble, conversational, communicative; gossipy, babbling, blathering; long-winded, wordy, verbose, prolix; *informal* gabby, mouthy, motormouthed, talky. ANTONYM taciturn.

THE RIGHT WORD

Someone who likes to talk frequently or at length might be described as **talkative** (*He was the most talkative person I'd ever met*). This word implies a readiness to engage in talk, while **loquacious** implies an inclination to talk incessantly or to keep up a constant flow of chatter (*a loquacious woman who never seemed to tire of hearing her own voice*). **Glib** and **voluble** pertain to the ease with which someone is able to converse or speak, although *voluble* may be used in either an approving or a critical sense (*a voluble speaker who was in great demand; a voluble neighbor who could not keep a secret*). *Glib* is almost always negative, referring to a superficial or slick way of speaking (*the glib manner of a used-car salesperson*). **Garrulous** also has negative overtones, implying a tedious or rambling talkativeness, usually about trivial things (*a garrulous old man who bored everyone with his stories about "the old days"*).

talker noun *Sue's husband is a real talker* CONVERSATIONALIST, speaker, communicator; chatterbox, motormouth, gossip, flibbertigibbet.

talking-to noun *informal if you ask me, that kid needs a good talking-to.* See REPRIMAND noun.

tall adjective **1** *a tall man* BIG, large, huge, towering, colossal, gigantic, giant, monstrous; leggy; *informal* long. ANTONYMS short, small.

2 *tall buildings* HIGH, big, lofty, towering, elevated, sky-high; multistory. ANTONYM low.

3 *she's five feet tall* IN HEIGHT, high, from head to toe; from top to bottom. ANTONYM wide.

4 *a tall tale* UNLIKELY, improbable, exaggerated, farfetched, implausible, dubious, unbelievable, incredible, absurd, untrue; *informal* cock-and-bull. ANTONYMS credible, believable.

5 *a tall order* DEMANDING, exacting, difficult; unreasonable, impossible. ANTONYM easy.

tally noun **1** *he keeps a tally of the score* RUNNING TOTAL, count, record, reckoning, register, account, roll; census, poll.

2 *her tally of 22 victories* TOTAL, score, count, sum.

▸ verb **1** *these statistics* ***tally with*** *government figures* CORRESPOND WITH, agree with, accord with, concur with, coincide with, match, fit, be consistent with, conform to, equate with, harmonize with, be in tune with, dovetail, correlate with/to, parallel; *informal* square with, jibe with. ANTONYMS disagree, differ.

2 *votes were tallied with abacuses* COUNT, calculate, add up, total, compute; figure out, work out, reckon, measure, quantify, tot up; *formal* enumerate.

tame adjective **1** *a tame elephant* DOMESTICATED, domestic, docile, tamed, broken, trained; gentle, mild; pet, housebroken; *chiefly Brit.* house-trained. ANTONYMS wild, fierce.

2 *informal he has a tame lawyer* AMENABLE, biddable, cooperative, willing, obedient, tractable, acquiescent, docile, submissive, compliant, meek. ANTONYM uncooperative.

3 *it was a pretty tame affair* UNEXCITING, uninteresting, uninspiring, dull, bland, flat, insipid, spiritless, pedestrian, colorless, run-of-the-mill, mediocre, ordinary, humdrum, boring; harmless, safe, inoffensive. ANTONYM exciting.

▸ verb **1** *wild rabbits can be tamed* DOMESTICATE, break, train, master, subdue.

2 *she learned to tame her emotions* SUBDUE, curb, control, calm, master, moderate, overcome, discipline, suppress, repress, mellow, temper, soften, bridle, get a grip on; *informal* lick.

tamper verb **1** *she saw them* ***tampering with*** *her car* INTERFERE WITH, monkey around with, meddle with, tinker with, fiddle with, fool around with, play around with; doctor, alter, change, adjust, damage, deface, vandalize; *informal* mess around with.

2 *the defendant* ***tampered with*** *the jury* INFLUENCE, get at, rig, manipulate, bribe, corrupt, bias; *informal* fix.

tan adjective *a tan waistcoat* YELLOWISH-BROWN, light brown, pale brown, beige, tawny.

▸ verb **1** *use a sunscreen to help you tan* BECOME SUNTANNED, get a suntan, brown, go/get/become brown, bronze.

2 *informal I'll tan his hide.* See THRASH sense 1.

WORD NOTE **tan**

In Edward Albee's play *The American Dream,* there is a running gag about whether a hat is *beige, wheat,* or *cream.* Fine distinctions used to be made about gradations of racial makeup (*quadroon, octoroon,* etc.) and correlating skin tone *(chocolate, coffee, yellow, mocha, olive),* but in contemporary usage we seem to consider brown colors beneath precise description. **–SM**

tang noun *there's a lovely tang to the glaze* FLAVOR, taste, savor; sharpness, zest, bite, edge, smack, piquancy, spice; smell, odor, aroma, fragrance, perfume, redolence; *informal* kick, pep.

tangible adjective *I'd prefer a reward more tangible than praise—say, cash* TOUCHABLE, palpable, material, physical, real, substantial, corporeal, solid, concrete; visible, noticeable; actual, definite, clear, clear-cut, distinct, manifest, evident, unmistakable, perceptible, discernible. ANTONYM abstract.

THE RIGHT WORD

Anything that can be grasped, either with the hand or with the mind, is **tangible** (*tangible assets; tangible objects*). **Palpable**, like *tangible*, means capable of being touched or felt (*a palpable mist*), but it is often applied to whatever evokes a tactile response from the body (*a palpable chill in the room*). **Perceptible** is used to describe something that just crosses the border between invisibility and visibility or some other sense barrier (*a perceptible change in her tone of voice; a perceptible odor of garlic*). **Sensible** (in this sense) means that which can clearly be perceived through the senses or which makes a strong impression on the mind through the medium of sensations. In contrast to *perceptible*, something that is *sensible* is more obvious or immediately recognized (*a sensible shift in the tenor of the conversation*). **Corporeal** means bodily or material, in contrast to things that are immaterial or spiritual (*corporeal goods*). Something that is **appreciable** is large enough to be measured, valued, estimated, or considered significant. An *appreciable* change in temperature, for example, can be determined by looking at a thermometer; a *palpable* change in temperature may be slight, but still great enough to be felt; and a *perceptible* change in temperature might be so slight that it almost—but not quite—escapes notice.

---

tangle verb **1** *the wool got tangled* ENTANGLE, snarl, catch, entwine, twist, ravel, knot, enmesh, coil, mat, jumble, muddle.

2 *he tangled with his old rival* COME INTO CONFLICT, dispute, argue, quarrel, fight, wrangle, squabble, contend, cross swords, lock horns.

▸ noun **1** *a tangle of branches* SNARL, mass, knot, mesh, mishmash.

2 *the defense got into an awful tangle* MUDDLE, jumble, mix-up, confusion, shambles.

tangled adjective **1** *tangled hair* KNOTTED, knotty, raveled, entangled, snarled (up), twisted, matted, tangly, messy; tousled, unkempt; *informal* mussed up.

2 *a tangled bureaucratic mess* CONFUSED, jumbled, mixed up, messy, chaotic, complicated, involved, complex, intricate, knotty, tortuous. ANTONYMS simple, straightforward.

tangy adjective *a tangy cocktail sauce* ZESTY, sharp, acid, acidic, tart, sour, bitter, piquant, spicy, tasty, pungent. ANTONYM bland.

tank noun **1** *a hot water tank* CONTAINER, receptacle, vat, cistern, repository, reservoir, basin.

2 *a tank full of fish* AQUARIUM, bowl.

3 *the army's use of tanks* ARMORED VEHICLE, armored car, combat vehicle; panzer.

tanning noun *informal they gave him a tanning* BEATING, battering, thrashing, thumping, pounding, drubbing, pummeling, flogging, whipping, caning, spanking; *informal* licking, belting, bashing, pasting, walloping, whacking, clobbering, shellacking, going-over.

tantalize verb *Steve was tantalized by Liliana's exotic eyes* TEASE, torment, torture, bait; tempt, entice, lure, allure, beguile; excite, fascinate, titillate, intrigue.

tantamount adjective *this is **tantamount to** mutiny* EQUIVALENT TO, equal to, as good as, more or less, much the same as, comparable to, on a par with, commensurate with. See note at SAME.

tantrum noun *how can you tolerate his tantrums?* FIT OF TEMPER, fit of rage, fit, outburst, pet, paroxysm, frenzy, bad mood, mood, huff, scene; *informal* hissy fit.

tap[1] noun **1** *she turned the tap on* FAUCET, valve, stopcock, cock, spout, spigot, spile.

2 *a phone tap in the embassy* LISTENING DEVICE, wiretap, wire, bug, bugging device, (hidden) microphone, (hidden) mic, receiver.

▸ verb **1** *several barrels were tapped* DRAIN, bleed, milk; broach, open.

2 *butlers were tapping ale* POUR (OUT), draw off, siphon off, pump out, decant.

3 *their telephones are tapped* BUG, wiretap, monitor, overhear, eavesdrop on, spy on.

4 *the resources were to be tapped for our benefit* DRAW ON, exploit, milk, mine, use, utilize, turn to account.

PHRASE: **on tap** **1** *beers on tap* ON DRAFT, from barrels, cask-conditioned. **2** *informal trained staff are on tap* ON HAND, at hand, available, ready, handy, accessible, standing by.

tap[2] verb **1** *she tapped on the door* KNOCK, rap, strike, beat, drum.

2 *Dad tapped me on the knee* PAT, hit, strike, slap, jab, poke, dig.

▸ noun **1** *a sharp tap at the door* KNOCK, rap, drumming.

2 *a tap on the shoulder* PAT, blow, slap, jab, poke, dig.

tape noun **1** *a package tied with tape* BINDING, ribbon, string, braid.

2 *secure the bandage with tape* ADHESIVE TAPE, sticky tape, masking tape, duct tape; *trademark* Scotch Tape.

3 *they recorded the interview on tape* AUDIOCASSETTE/VIDEOCASSETTE, (a) reel, (a) spool; video, VHS.

▸ verb **1** *a card was taped to the box* BIND, stick, fix, fasten, secure, attach; tie, strap.

2 *they **taped off** the area* CORDON (OFF), seal (off), close (off), shut (off), mark (off), fence (off); isolate, segregate.

3 *police taped his confession* RECORD, tape-record, capture on tape; video.

4 *tape your ankle* BIND, wrap, bandage.

taper verb **1** *the leaves taper at the tip* NARROW, thin (out), come to a point, attenuate. ANTONYMS thicken, swell.

2 *the meetings soon **tapered off*** DECREASE, lessen, dwindle, diminish, reduce, decline, die down, peter out, wane, ebb, slacken (off), fall off, let up, thin out. ANTONYM increase.

taqueria noun See note below.

WORD NOTE **taqueria**

Every so often, a word seems to teeter on the very edge—the border, so to speak—between cultures. Consequently, it makes you wonder about how widely and closely those cultures have merged. When one of my fictional characters wanted some *tacos al pastor,* I sent him to a taqueria. Should I have written *Mexican taqueria?* Is that redundant? How many of my readers, outside certain geographical areas, will know what a *taqueria* is? It's an unlikely word to find in a thesaurus, since there is no other place quite like a café that specializes in soft, hand-rolled tacos, often featuring some unusual cut of meat or inventive stew. Though perhaps there might be similar entries in a Spanish, or preferably Mexican, thesaurus. **—FP**

---

tardy adjective *Professor Wainwright is tardy again* LATE, behind schedule, running late; behind, overdue, belated, delayed; slow, dilatory. ANTONYM punctual.

target noun **1** *targets at a range of 200 meters* MARK, bull's-eye, goal.

2 *eagles can spot their target from half a mile* PREY, quarry, game, kill.

3 *their profit target* OBJECTIVE, goal, aim, end; plan, intention, intent, design, aspiration, ambition, ideal, desire, wish.

4 *she was the target for a wave of abuse* VICTIM, butt, recipient, focus, object, subject.

▸ verb **1** *he was targeted by a gunman* PICK OUT, single out, earmark, fix on; attack, aim at, fire at.

2 *the product is **targeted at** a specific market* AIM AT, direct at, level at, intend for, focus on.

PHRASE: **on target** 1 *the shot was on target* ACCURATE, precise, unerring, sure, on the mark. 2 *the project was on target* ON SCHEDULE, on track, on course, on time.

tariff noun *the lower tariffs across the border* TAX, duty, toll, excise, levy, charge, rate, fee, countervail; price list.

tarnish verb 1 *gold does not tarnish easily* DISCOLOR, rust, oxidize, corrode, stain, dull, blacken. ANTONYMS polish, brighten.

2 *it tarnished his reputation* SULLY, blacken, stain, blemish, blot, taint, soil, ruin, disgrace, mar, damage, harm, hurt, undermine, dishonor, stigmatize; *literary* besmirch. ANTONYM enhance.

▸ noun 1 *the tarnish on the candlesticks* DISCOLORATION, oxidation, rust; film.

2 *the tarnish on his reputation* SMEAR, stain, blemish, blot, taint, stigma.

tarry verb *dated they tarried by the lake, prolonging their teary farewells* LINGER, loiter, procrastinate, delay, wait, dawdle; *informal* hang around. ANTONYM hurry.

tart[1] noun *a lemon tart* PASTRY, flan, tartlet, quiche, pie. See table at PIE.

tart[2] adjective 1 *a tart apple* SOUR, sharp, acid, acidic, zesty, tangy, piquant; lemony, acetic. ANTONYM sweet.

2 *a tart reply* ACERBIC, sharp, biting, cutting, astringent, caustic, trenchant, incisive, barbed, scathing, sarcastic, acrimonious, nasty, rude, vicious, spiteful, venomous. ANTONYM kind.

task noun *a daunting task* JOB, duty, chore, charge, assignment, detail, mission, engagement, occupation, undertaking, exercise, business, responsibility, burden, endeavor, enterprise, venture. PHRASE: **take someone to task** *Bryce took me to task for having "borrowed" his car* REBUKE, reprimand, reprove, reproach, remonstrate with, upbraid, scold, berate, castigate, lecture, censure, criticize, admonish, chide, chasten, arraign; *informal* tell off, bawl out, give someone a dressing-down.

taste noun 1 *a distinctive sharp taste* FLAVOR, savor, relish, tang, smack.

2 *he was dying for a taste of brandy* MOUTHFUL, drop, bit, sip, nip, swallow, touch, soupçon, dash, modicum.

3 *it's too sweet for my taste* PALATE, taste buds, appetite, stomach.

4 *a taste for adventure* LIKING, love, fondness, fancy, desire, preference, penchant, predilection, inclination, partiality; hankering, appetite, hunger, thirst, relish. ANTONYM dislike.

5 *my first **taste of** prison* EXPERIENCE OF/WITH, impression of; exposure to, contact with, involvement with.

6 *the house was furnished with taste* JUDGMENT, discrimination, discernment, tastefulness, refinement, finesse, elegance, grace, style. ANTONYMS tastelessness, tackiness.

7 *the photo was rejected on grounds of taste* DECORUM, propriety, etiquette, politeness, delicacy, nicety, sensitivity, discretion, tastefulness. ANTONYM dislike.

▸ verb 1 *Adam tasted the wine* SAMPLE, test, try, savor; sip, sup.

2 *he could taste blood on his lip* PERCEIVE, discern, make out, distinguish.

3 *a beer that **tasted of** pumpkin* HAVE A/THE FLAVOR OF, savor of, smack of, be reminiscent of; suggest.

4 *it'll be good to taste real coffee again* CONSUME, drink, partake of; eat, devour.

5 *he tasted defeat* EXPERIENCE, encounter, come face to face with, come up against, undergo; know.

tasteful adjective *the decor is simple and tasteful* AESTHETICALLY PLEASING, in good taste, refined, cultured, elegant, stylish, smart, chic, attractive, exquisite. ANTONYMS tasteless, tacky.

tasteless adjective 1 *the vegetables are tasteless* FLAVORLESS, bland, insipid, unappetizing, savorless, watery, weak. ANTONYMS tasty, appetizing.

2 *tasteless leather paneling* VULGAR, crude, tawdry, garish, gaudy, loud, trashy, showy, ostentatious, cheap, chintzy, kitschy, kitsch, inelegant; *informal* tacky. ANTONYMS refined, tasteful.

3 *a tasteless remark* CRUDE, vulgar, indelicate, uncouth, unseemly, crass, tactless, gauche, undiplomatic, indiscreet, inappropriate, offensive. ANTONYMS tasteful, seemly.

tasty adjective *a tasty meal* DELICIOUS, palatable, luscious, mouthwatering, delectable, ambrosial, toothsome, dainty, flavorful; appetizing, tempting; *informal* yummy, scrumptious, finger-licking, lip-smacking, melt-in-your/the-mouth. ANTONYMS bland, insipid.

tatters plural noun *the satin had frayed to tatters* RAGS, scraps, shreds, bits, pieces, ribbons. PHRASE: **in tatters** 1 *his clothes were in tatters* RAGGED, tattered, torn, ripped, frayed, in pieces, worn out, moth-eaten, falling to pieces, threadbare. 2 *her marriage is in tatters* IN RUINS, on the rocks, destroyed, finished, devastated.

tattle verb 1 *we were tattling about him* GOSSIP, chatter, chat, prattle, babble, jabber, gabble, rattle on; *informal* chinwag, jaw, yak, gab, natter, tittle-tattle, chitchat.

2 *I would tattle on her if I had evidence* INFORM; report, talk, tell all, spill the beans; *informal* squeal, sing, let the cat out of the bag.

▸ noun *tabloid tattle* GOSSIP, rumor, tittle-tattle, hearsay, scandal.

taunt noun *the taunts of his classmates* JEER, jibe, sneer, insult, barb, catcall; *informal* dig, put-down; (**taunts**) teasing, provocation, goading, derision, mockery.

▸ verb *she taunted him about his job* JEER AT, sneer at, scoff at, poke fun at, make fun of, get at, insult, tease, chaff, torment, goad, ridicule, deride, mock, heckle, ride; *informal* rib, needle.

taut adjective 1 *the rope was taut* TIGHT, stretched, rigid. ANTONYMS slack, loose.

2 *her muscles remained taut* FLEXED, tense, hard, solid, firm, rigid, stiff. ANTONYM relaxed.

3 *a taut expression* FRAUGHT, strained, stressed, tense; *informal* uptight.

tautology noun *avoid such tautology as "let's all work together, everyone, as a team" by saying simply "let's work together"* PLEONASM, repetition, reiteration, redundancy, superfluity, duplication.

tavern noun BAR, pub, cocktail lounge, lounge, taproom, nightclub, roadhouse, club; inn; rathskeller; *informal* gin mill, nineteenth hole, dive, watering hole *historical* saloon, alehouse, speakeasy, public house.

tawdry adjective *the tawdry rings she wore on her fingers* GAUDY, flashy, showy, garish, loud; tasteless, vulgar, trashy, junky, shoddy, shabby, gimcrack, chintzy; kitsch, kitschy; *informal* tacky, cheesy, schlocky. ANTONYM tasteful.

tax noun **1** *they have to pay tax on the interest* DUTY, tariff, excise, customs, dues; levy, toll, impost, tithe, charge, fee. ANTONYM rebate.

2 *a heavy tax on one's attention* BURDEN, load, weight, demand, strain, pressure, stress, drain, imposition.

▸ verb **1** *they tax foreign companies more harshly* CHARGE (DUTY ON), tithe; *formal* mulct.

2 *his whining taxed her patience* STRAIN, stretch, overburden, overload, encumber, push too far; overwhelm, try, wear out, exhaust, sap, drain, weary, weaken.

WORD NOTE **indiction**

There can be a sonorous magnificence to our language, episodes of phrasing which yearn to be spoken out loud, mantra-like. I particularly enjoy turning over in my mind, for example, the phrase *The Bombay, Baroda and Central India Railway Company*. I like imagining what goes on at *The Mendocino Triple Junction* (it is nothing to do with railways, as it happens, but all to do with geology). And I positively tremble with pleasure when, all too rarely for my money, I am reminded of something called *The Constantinopolitan Indiction,* a complex formula of 15-year tax cycles introduced in the fourth century and which, though falling out of favor in 1807, would give to the year of publication of this thesaurus an indiction of 12. (The formula for getting to this number is complicated indeed.) *Indiction* has three very distinct meanings: it is an alternative word for a declaration or a proclamation; it is a kind of tax assessment created by the Romans—a concept, in other words, that could well be used in a modern property tax office; and it is a 15-year period, such as that invented by the Emperor Constantine in AD 312. It is also the kind of word that, since it looks so very similar to the very different word *indication,* I like to use from time to time to keep readers alert and on their feet—and, because of its aforesaid sonorous magnificence, enjoying what they are reading. **—SW**

taxi noun *I'd rather walk than take a taxi such a short distance* CAB, taxicab, hack; rickshaw; *historical* calèche, trishaw, pedicab.

taxing adjective *restaurant work can be taxing* DEMANDING, exacting, challenging, burdensome, arduous, onerous, difficult, hard, tough, laborious, back-breaking, strenuous, rigorous, punishing; tiring, exhausting, enervating, wearing, stressful; *informal* murderous. ANTONYM easy.

tea noun See table.

teach verb **1** *Alison teaches small children* EDUCATE, instruct, school, tutor, coach, train; enlighten, illuminate, verse, edify, indoctrinate; drill, discipline.

2 *I taught yoga* GIVE LESSONS IN, lecture in, be a teacher of; demonstrate, instill, inculcate.

3 *she taught me how to love* TRAIN, show, guide, instruct, explain to, demonstrate to.

teacher noun *the new physics teacher used to be a nun* EDUCATOR, tutor, instructor, master, mistress, governess, educationist, preceptor; coach, trainer; lecturer, professor, don; guide, mentor, guru, counselor; substitute teacher, sub; *informal* teach; *formal* pedagogue; *historical* schoolman, schoolmarm.

team noun **1** *the sales team* GROUP, squad, company, party, crew, troupe, band, side, lineup, phalanx; *informal* bunch, gang, posse.

2 *a team of horses* PAIR, span, yoke, duo, set, tandem.

▸ verb **1** *the horses are teamed in pairs* HARNESS, yoke, hitch, couple.

2 *you could* ***team up*** *with another artist for an exhibition* JOIN (FORCES), collaborate, get together, work together; unite, combine, cooperate, link, ally, associate.

tear[1] verb **1** *I* ***tore up*** *the letter* RIP UP, rip in two, pull to pieces, shred.

2 *his flesh was torn* LACERATE, cut (open), gash, slash, scratch, hack, pierce, stab; injure, wound.

3 *the traumas* ***tore*** *her family* ***apart*** DIVIDE, split, sever, break up, disunite, rupture; *literary* rend, sunder, cleave. ANTONYM unite.

4 *Gina tore the book from his hands* SNATCH, grab, seize, rip, wrench, wrest, pull, pluck; *informal* yank.

5 *informal Jack tore down the street* SPRINT, race, run, dart, rush, dash, hasten, hurry, bolt, fly, career, charge, shoot, hurtle, careen, speed, whiz, zoom, go like lightning, go like the wind; *informal* pelt, scoot, hotfoot it, belt, zip, whip, bomb, hightail it. ANTONYMS stroll, amble.

▸ noun *a tear in her dress* RIP, hole, split, slash, slit; snag.

PHRASE: **tear down** *they tore down the old barn* DEMOLISH, knock down, raze, raze to the ground, flatten, level, bulldoze; dismantle, disassemble.

tear[2] noun *tears in her eyes* TEARDROP; drop, droplet. PHRASE: **in tears** *he was nearly in tears* CRYING, weeping, sobbing, wailing, howling, bawling, whimpering; tearful, upset; *informal* weepy, teary, blubbering.

TEAS

Assam	Irish breakfast
black	jasmine
black currant	Kashmiri
Caravan	Keemun
Ceylon	kukicha
chai	lapsang souchong
chamomile	matcha
chrysanthemum	Nilgiri
dragon well	oolong
Darjeeling	pearl
dragon phoenix	pekoe
Earl Grey	peppermint
English breakfast	pinhead
genmai	Pu-erh
ginseng	red
green	Rooibos
gunpowder	sage
Gyokuro Asahi	sencha
herbal	tisane
Hubei	white
Huo Mountain	Yunnan
infusion	Zhufeng

tearful adjective **1** *Bess was tearful* IN TEARS, with tears in one's eyes, choked up, crying, weeping, sobbing, sniveling; close to tears, emotional, upset, distressed, sad, unhappy; *informal* weepy, teary, misty-eyed; *formal* lachrymose. ANTONYMS laughing, smiling.

2 *a tearful farewell* EMOTIONAL, upsetting, distressing, sad, heartbreaking, sorrowful; poignant, moving, touching, tear-jerking; *literary* dolorous. ANTONYM cheerful.

tease verb *Larry's dentist is the dork he used to tease in sixth grade* MAKE FUN OF, poke fun at, laugh at, guy, make a monkey (out) of; taunt, bait, goad, pick on; deride, mock, ridicule; *informal* rib, josh, pull/yank someone's chain, razz.

teaser noun **1** *a difficult teaser to answer* QUESTION, problem, quandary, poser.

2 *teasers point readers to the main features* ADVERTISEMENT, hook, come-on.

technical adjective **1** *an important technical achievement* practical, scientific, technological, high-tech.

2 *this might seem very technical* SPECIALIST, specialized, scientific; complex, complicated, esoteric.

3 *a technical fault* MECHANICAL.

technique noun **1** *different techniques for solving the problem* METHOD, approach, procedure, system, modus operandi, MO, way; means, strategy, tack, tactic, line; routine, practice.

2 *I was impressed with his technique* SKILL, ability, proficiency, expertise, mastery, talent, genius, artistry, craftsmanship; aptitude, adroitness, deftness, dexterity, facility, competence; performance, delivery; *informal* know-how.

tedious adjective *work on the assembly line was tedious* BORING, dull, monotonous, repetitive, unrelieved, unvaried, uneventful; characterless, colorless, lifeless, insipid, uninteresting, unexciting, uninspiring, flat, bland, dry, stale, tired, lackluster, stodgy, dreary, mundane, monochrome; mind-numbing, soul-destroying, wearisome, tiring, tiresome, irksome, trying, frustrating; *informal* deadly, not up to much, humdrum, ho-hum, blah, dullsville, [same old, same old]. ANTONYM exciting.

tedium noun **1** *she loathed the tedium of housework* MONOTONY, boredom, ennui, uniformity, routine, dreariness, dryness, banality, vapidity, insipidity. ANTONYM variety.

2 *I dozed off during the tedium of the third act* TEDIOUS PASSAGE, tedious moments, tedious period of time, flatness, longueur.

WORD NOTE **longueur**

I find myself using this word more often than I probably should, to describe those boring stretches of a novel or play during which your attention drifts, and you catch yourself wondering what's in the refrigerator, or if there's anything good on TV. *The five-hundred word meditation on the author's dietary preferences certainly had its longueurs.* I would probably use it even more frequently were it not so difficult to spell. What I like is how the sound of it suggests a combination of *languor* and *length*—the languor produced by something that is unduly long—though I have learned that its derivation has to do with length rather than lassitude. **—FP**

teem[1] verb *the pond once* ***teemed with*** *fish* BE FULL OF, be filled with, be alive with, be brimming with, abound in, be swarming with, be aswarm with; be packed with, be crawling with, be overrun by, bristle with, seethe with, be thick with; be jam-packed with, be chock-full of.

teem[2] verb *the rain was* ***teeming down*** POUR (DOWN), (really) come down, pelt down, beat down; come down in torrents, come down in buckets, come down in sheets, rain cats and dogs.

teenage adjective *a teenage hairstyle* ADOLESCENT, teenaged, youthful, young, juvenile; *informal* teen.

teenager noun *he's been counseling teenagers for twenty years* ADOLESCENT, youth, young person, minor, juvenile; *informal* teen, teenybopper.

teeny adjective *informal a teeny green inchworm.* See TINY.

teeter verb **1** *Daisy teetered toward them* TOTTER, wobble, toddle, sway, stagger, stumble, reel, lurch, pitch.

2 *the situation teetered between tragedy and farce* SEESAW, veer, fluctuate, oscillate, swing, alternate, waver.

teetotal adjective *he's strictly teetotal these days* ABSTINENT, abstemious; sober, dry; *informal* on the wagon. ANTONYM alcoholic.

WORD NOTE **Rechabite**

The stern application of Prohibition was once known jokingly as *teetotalitarianism,* an example of a *portmanteau* form (q.v.) used to denote the practice of avoiding strong drink. From describing oneself as an *abstainer,* to being *on the wagon,* to counting oneself a *Friend of Bill* (which is the Masonically secret form used by members of Alcoholics Anonymous), there are scores of words used to describe, and usually euphemistically, this generally unusual practice. It is rare to see the word *Rechabite* in use: not only did this Jewish sect not drink, they also, for some unknown reason, declined to live in houses—and so Rechabites do not just abhor strong liquor, but also live in tents. The extent to which this might be employed as a synonym for an abstainer is thus limited: but it is the job of this volume to offer it up, and suggest when it might be appropriate. Describing a camping holiday involving a party of Mormons might be one occasion when the word, even if used allusively, might work. **—SW**

telegram noun *the message arrived by telegram* telex; *informal* wire; *dated* radiogram; *historical* cable, cablegram.

telepathic adjective *she convinced her friends that her sister Shawna was telepathic* PSYCHIC, clairvoyant.

telepathy noun *he claims he knew about Dylan's past through telepathy* MIND-READING, thought transference; extrasensory perception, ESP; clairvoyance, sixth sense; psychometry.

telephone noun *she picked up the telephone* PHONE, cell phone, cellular phone, cell; handset, receiver; *informal* blower, horn.

▸ verb *he telephoned me last night* PHONE, call, ring; get, reach; *dated* dial; *informal* call up, give someone a buzz, get on the blower to, get someone on the horn.

telescope noun *a pocket telescope* SPYGLASS, glass; *informal* scope.

▸ verb **1** *the front of the car was telescoped* CONCERTINA, compact, compress, crush, squash.

2 *his recent employment experience can be telescoped into a short paragraph* CONDENSE, shorten, reduce, abbreviate, abridge, summarize, précis, abstract, shrink, consolidate; truncate, curtail.

televise verb *the school concert was televised on a local channel* BROADCAST, screen, air, telecast; transmit, relay.

television noun *what's on television this evening?* TV; *informal* the small screen, the idiot box, the tube, the boob tube, the box.

tell verb **1** *why didn't you tell me before?* INFORM, notify, apprise, let know, make aware, acquaint with, advise, put in the picture, brief, fill in; alert, warn; *informal* clue in/up.

2 *she told the story slowly* RELATE, recount, narrate, unfold, report, recite, describe, sketch, weave, spin; utter, voice, state, declare, communicate, impart, divulge.

3 *she told him to leave* INSTRUCT, order, command, direct, charge, enjoin, call on, require; *literary* bid.

4 *I tell you, I did nothing wrong* ASSURE, promise, give one's word, swear, guarantee.

5 *the figures tell a different story* REVEAL, show, indicate, be evidence of, disclose, convey, signify.

6 *promise you won't tell?* GIVE THE GAME AWAY, talk, tell tales, tattle; *informal* spill the beans, let the cat out of the bag, blab.

7 *she was bound to **tell on** him* INFORM ON, tell tales on, give away, denounce, sell out; *informal* blow the whistle on, rat on, squeal on, finger.

8 *it was hard to tell what he said* ASCERTAIN, determine, work out, make out, deduce, discern, perceive, see, identify, recognize, understand, comprehend; *informal* figure out; *Brit. informal* suss out.

9 *he couldn't tell one from the other* DISTINGUISH, differentiate, discriminate.

10 *the strain began to **tell on** him* TAKE ITS TOLL, leave its mark; affect. PHRASE: **tell off** *informal oh, brother, did he ever tell you off.* See REPRIMAND verb.

teller noun **1** *a bank teller* CASHIER, clerk.

2 *a teller of tales* NARRATOR, raconteur; storyteller, anecdotalist.

telling adjective *a telling critique of the military mind* REVEALING, significant, weighty, important, meaningful, influential, striking, potent, powerful, compelling. ANTONYM insignificant.

telltale adjective *the telltale blush on her face* REVEALING, revelatory, suggestive, meaningful, significant, meaning; *informal* giveaway.

temerity noun *I doubt they'll have the temerity to print these accusations* AUDACITY, nerve, effrontery, impudence, impertinence, cheek, gall, presumption; daring; *informal* face, front, neck, chutzpah.

THE RIGHT WORD

The line that divides boldness from foolishness or stupidity is often a fine one. Someone who rushes hastily into a situation without thinking about the consequences might be accused of **rashness**, while **temerity** implies exposing oneself needlessly to danger while failing to estimate one's chances of success (*she had the temerity to criticize her teacher in front of the class*). **Audacity** describes a different kind of boldness, one that disregards moral standards or social conventions (*he had the audacity to ask her if she would mind paying for the trip*). Someone who behaves with **foolhardiness** is reckless or downright foolish (*climbing the mountain after dark was foolhardiness and everyone knew it*), while **impetuosity** describes an eager impulsiveness or behavior that is sudden, rash, and sometimes violent (*his impetuosity had landed him in trouble before*). **Gall** and **effrontery** are always derogatory terms. *Effrontery* is a more formal word for the flagrant disregard of the rules of propriety and courtesy (*she had the effrontery to call the president by his first name*), while *gall* is more colloquial and suggests outright insolence (*he was the only one who had the gall to tell the boss off*).

temper noun **1** *he walked out in a temper* FIT OF RAGE, rage, fury, fit of pique, tantrum, bad mood, mood, sulk, huff; *informal* grump, snit, hissy fit.

2 *a display of temper* ANGER, fury, rage, annoyance, vexation, irritation, irritability, ill humor, spleen, pique, petulance, testiness, tetchiness, touchiness, crabbiness; *literary* ire, choler.

3 *she struggled to keep her temper* COMPOSURE, equanimity, self-control, self-possession, sangfroid, calm, good humor; *informal* cool.

▸ verb **1** *the steel is tempered by heat* HARDEN, strengthen, toughen, fortify, anneal.

2 *their idealism is tempered with realism* MODERATE, modify, modulate, mitigate, alleviate, reduce, weaken, lighten, soften. See note at ALLEVIATE.

PHRASE: **lose one's temper** *calm down, there's no need to lose your temper* GET ANGRY, fly into a rage, erupt, lose control, go berserk, breathe fire, flare up, boil over; *informal* go mad, go crazy, go bananas, have a fit, see red, fly off the handle, blow one's top, hit the roof, go off the deep end, go ape, flip, freak out.

temperament noun *Haley's dog has the nicest temperament* DISPOSITION, nature, character, personality, makeup, constitution, mind, spirit; stamp, mettle, mold; mood, frame of mind, attitude, outlook, humor.

temperamental adjective **1** *a temperamental chef* VOLATILE, excitable, emotional, mercurial, capricious, erratic, unpredictable, changeable, inconsistent; hotheaded, fiery, quick-tempered, irritable, irascible, impatient; touchy, moody, sensitive, oversensitive, highstrung, neurotic, melodramatic. ANTONYM placid.

2 *a temperamental dislike of conflict* INHERENT, innate, natural, inborn, constitutional, deep-rooted, ingrained, congenital.

temperance noun *a strict advocate of temperance* TEETOTALISM, abstinence, abstention, sobriety, self-restraint; prohibition. See note at ABSTINENCE. ANTONYM alcoholism.

temperate adjective **1** *temperate climates* MILD, clement, benign, gentle, balmy. ANTONYM extreme.

2 *he was temperate in his consumption of food* SELF-RESTRAINED, restrained, moderate, self-controlled, disciplined; abstemious, self-denying, austere, ascetic; teetotal, abstinent. ANTONYM immoderate.

tempest noun *the skies opened and a tempest erupted* STORM, gale, hurricane; tornado, whirlwind, cyclone, typhoon.

tempestuous adjective **1** *the fair weather passed and the day became tempestuous* STORMY, blustery, squally, wild, turbulent, windy, gusty, blowy, rainy; foul, nasty, inclement. ANTONYMS calm, fine.

2 *the tempestuous political environment* TURBULENT, stormy, tumultuous, wild, lively, heated, explosive, feverish, frenetic, frenzied. ANTONYM peaceful.

3 *a tempestuous woman* EMOTIONAL, passionate, impassioned, fiery, intense; temperamental, volatile, excitable, mercurial, capricious, unpredictable, quick-tempered. ANTONYMS calm, placid.

template noun *trace the template* MODEL, example, guide, mold, blueprint, pattern.

temple noun *at the altar of the temple* HOUSE OF GOD, house of worship, shrine, sanctuary; church, cathedral, mosque, synagogue, shul; *archaic* fane.

tempo noun 1 *the tempo of the music* SPEED, cadence, rhythm, beat, time, pulse; measure, meter.

2 *the tempo of life in Western society* PACE, rate, speed, velocity.

temporal adjective *the temporal aspects of church government* SECULAR, nonspiritual, worldly, profane, material, mundane, earthly, terrestrial; nonreligious, areligious, lay. ANTONYM spiritual.

temporarily adverb 1 *the girl was temporarily placed with a foster family* FOR THE TIME BEING, for the moment, for now, for the present, in the interim, for the nonce, in/for the meantime, in the meanwhile; provisionally, pro tem; *informal* for the minute. ANTONYM permanently.

2 *he was temporarily blinded by the light* BRIEFLY, for a short time, momentarily, fleetingly. ANTONYM permanently.

temporary adjective 1 *temporary accommodations | the temporary captain* NONPERMANENT, short-term, interim; provisional, pro tem, makeshift, stopgap; acting, fill-in, stand-in, caretaker. ANTONYM permanent.

2 *a temporary loss of self-control* BRIEF, short-lived, momentary, fleeting, passing. ANTONYM lasting.

THE RIGHT WORD

Things that don't last long are called **temporary**, which emphasizes a measurable but limited duration (*a temporary appointment as chief of staff*). Something that is **fleeting** passes almost instantaneously and cannot be caught or held (*a fleeting thought; a fleeting glimpse*). **Transient** also applies to something that lasts or stays only a short time (*transient house guests*), while **transitory** refers to something that is destined to pass away or come to an end (*the transitory pleasure of eating*). **Evanescent** and **ephemeral** describe what is even more short-lived. *Ephemeral* literally means lasting for only a single day, but is often used to describe anything that is slight and perishable (*his fame was ephemeral*). *Evanescent* is a more lyrical word for whatever vanishes almost as soon as it appears. In other words, a job might be *temporary*, an emotion *fleeting*, a visitor *transient*, a woman's beauty *transitory*, and glory *ephemeral*, but the flash of a bird's wing across the sky would have to be called *evanescent*.

temporize verb *he temporized for weeks, hoping the problem would go away* EQUIVOCATE, procrastinate, play for time, play a waiting game, stall, use delaying tactics, give someone the runaround, delay, hang back, prevaricate, hem and haw; *rare* tergiversate.

tempt verb 1 *the manager tried to tempt him to stay* ENTICE, persuade, convince, inveigle, induce, cajole, coax, woo; *informal* sweet-talk. ANTONYMS discourage, deter.

2 *more customers are being tempted by credit* ALLURE, attract, appeal to, whet the appetite of; lure, seduce, beguile, tantalize, draw. ANTONYMS repel, put off.

THE RIGHT WORD

When we are under the influence of a powerful attraction, particularly to something that is wrong or unwise, we are **tempted. Entice** implies that a crafty or skillful person has attracted us by offering a reward or pleasure (*she was enticed into joining the group by a personal plea from its handsome leader*), while **inveigle** suggests that we are enticed through the use of deception or cajolery (*inveigled into supporting the plan*). If someone **lures** us, it suggests that we have been tempted or influenced for fraudulent or destructive purposes or attracted to something harmful or evil (*lured by gang members*). **Allure** may also suggest that we have been deliberately tempted against our will, but the connotations here are often sexual (*allured by her dark green eyes*). **Seduce** carries heavy sexual connotations (*seduced by an older woman*), although it can simply mean prompted to action against our will (*seduced by a clever sales pitch*). While **beguile** at one time referred exclusively to the use of deception to lead someone astray, nowadays it can also refer to the use of subtle devices to lead someone on (*a local festival designed to beguile the tourists*).

temptation noun 1 *Mary resisted the temptation to answer back* DESIRE, urge, itch, impulse, inclination.

2 *the temptations of Las Vegas* LURE, allurement, enticement, seduction, attraction, draw, pull; siren song.

3 *the temptation of travel to exotic locations* ALLURE, appeal, attraction, fascination.

tempting adjective 1 *a tempting opportunity* ENTICING, alluring, attractive, appealing, inviting, captivating, seductive, beguiling, fascinating, tantalizing; irresistible. ANTONYMS off-putting, uninviting.

2 *a plate of tempting cakes* APPETIZING, mouthwatering, delicious, toothsome; *informal* scrumptious, yummy, lip-smacking. ANTONYM unappetizing.

temptress noun *he was an easy target for the temptress who lived next door* SEDUCTRESS, siren, femme fatale; Mata Hari; *informal* vamp, home wrecker, man-eater.

ten cardinal number *the ten will perform a piece by Berlioz* DECADE; *Music* decad, decuplet; *rare* tensome.

tenable adjective *O'Leary's confession has certainly made Cohn's alibi more tenable* DEFENSIBLE, justifiable, supportable, sustainable, arguable, able to hold water, reasonable, sensible, rational, sound, viable, plausible, credible, believable, conceivable. ANTONYM indefensible.

tenacious adjective 1 *his tenacious grip* FIRM, tight, fast, clinging; strong, forceful, powerful, unshakable, immovable, iron. ANTONYMS weak, loose.

2 *a tenacious opponent* PERSEVERING, persistent, determined, dogged, strong-willed, tireless, indefatigable, resolute, patient, unflagging, staunch, steadfast, untiring, unwavering, unswerving, unshakable, unyielding, insistent; stubborn, intransigent, obstinate, obdurate, stiff-necked; rock-ribbed; pertinacious. ANTONYM irresolute.

tenacity noun *she practices her gymnastics routine with the tenacity of a bulldog* PERSISTENCE, determination, perseverance, doggedness, strength of purpose, tirelessness, indefatigability, resolution, resoluteness, resolve, firmness, patience, purposefulness, staunchness, steadfastness, staying power, endurance, stamina, stubbornness, intransigence, obstinacy, obduracy, pertinacity. See note at COURAGE.

tenant noun *the tenants' rent is due on the first of each month* OCCUPANT, resident, inhabitant; renter, leaseholder, lessee, lodger, roomer; squatter. ANTONYMS owner, freeholder.

tend[1] verb **1** *I tend to get very involved in my work* BE INCLINED, be apt, be disposed, be prone, be liable, have a tendency, have a propensity.

2 *some of the younger voters tended toward the tabloid press* INCLINE, lean, gravitate, move; prefer, favor, trend.

tend[2] verb *she tended her garden* LOOK AFTER, take care of, care for, minister to, attend to, see to, wait on; watch over, keep an eye on, mind, protect, watch, guard, supervise; nurse, nurture, cherish. ANTONYM neglect.

tendency noun **1** *his tendency to take the law into his own hands* PROPENSITY, proclivity, proneness, aptness, likelihood, inclination, disposition, predisposition, bent, leaning, penchant, predilection, susceptibility, liability; readiness; habit.

2 *this tendency toward cohabitation* TREND, movement, drift, swing, gravitation, direction, course; orientation, bias.

tender[1] adjective **1** *a gentle, tender man* CARING, kind, kindly, kindhearted, softhearted, tenderhearted, compassionate, sympathetic, warm, warmhearted, solicitous, fatherly, motherly, maternal, gentle, mild, benevolent, generous, giving, humane. ANTONYMS hard-hearted, callous.

2 *a tender kiss* AFFECTIONATE, fond, loving, emotional, warm, gentle, soft; amorous, adoring; *informal* lovey-dovey.

3 *simmer until the meat is tender* EASILY CHEWED, chewable, soft; succulent, juicy; tenderized, fork-tender. ANTONYM tough.

4 *tender plants* DELICATE, easily damaged, fragile, vulnerable. ANTONYM hardy.

5 *her ankle was swollen and tender* SORE, painful, sensitive, inflamed, raw, red, chafed, bruised, irritated; hurting, aching, throbbing, smarting.

6 *the tender age of fifteen* YOUNG, youthful, early; impressionable, inexperienced, immature, unseasoned, juvenile, callow, green, raw, unripe, wet behind the ears. ANTONYM advanced.

7 *the issue of conscription was a particularly tender one* DIFFICULT, delicate, touchy, tricky, awkward, problematic, troublesome, thorny, ticklish; controversial, emotive; *informal* sticky. ANTONYM straightforward.

tender[2] verb **1** *she tendered her resignation* OFFER, proffer, present, put forward, propose, suggest, advance, submit, extend, give, render; hand in.

2 *firms of interior decorators tendered for the work* PUT IN A BID, bid, quote, give an estimate.

▸ noun *six contractors were invited to submit tenders* BID, offer, quotation, quote, estimate, price; proposal, submission, pitch.

tenderhearted adjective See TENDER[1] sense 1.

tenderness noun **1** *I felt an enormous tenderness for her* AFFECTION, fondness, love, devotion, loving kindness, emotion, sentiment.

2 *with unexpected tenderness, he told her what had happened* KINDNESS, kindliness, kindheartedness, tenderheartedness, compassion, care, concern, sympathy, humanity, warmth, fatherliness, motherliness, gentleness, benevolence, generosity.

3 *abdominal tenderness* SORENESS, pain, inflammation, irritation, bruising; ache, aching, smarting, throbbing.

tenet noun *the fundamental tenet of Marxism* PRINCIPLE, belief, doctrine, precept, creed, credo, article of faith, axiom, dogma, canon; theory, thesis, premise, conviction, idea, view, opinion, position; (**tenets**) ideology, code of belief, teaching(s).

tennis noun See table.

TENNIS TERMS

ace	game point
advantage	grand slam
alley	grass court
backcourt	clay court
backhand	groundstroke
ball boy	half court
ball girl	half-volley
baseline	let
break	match point
break point	mixed doubles
chop	net
court	overhand
cross-court	passing shot
deuce	rally
double fault	serve
doubles	service break
drop shot	set
fault	set point
foot-fault	slice
forecourt	smash
forehand	topspin
game	volley

tenor noun **1** *the general tenor of his speech* SENSE, meaning, theme, drift, thread, import, purport, intent, intention, burden, thrust, significance, message; gist, tone, essence, substance, spirit, feel.

2 *the even tenor of life in the village* COURSE, direction, movement, drift, current, trend.

tense adjective **1** *the tense muscles of his neck* TAUT, tight, rigid, stretched, strained, stiff. ANTONYMS slack, loose.

2 *Loretta was feeling tense and irritable* ANXIOUS, nervous, on edge, edgy, antsy, strained, stressed, under pressure, agitated, ill at ease, fretful, uneasy, restless, strung out, worked up, wound up, keyed up, overwrought, jumpy, on tenterhooks, with one's stomach in knots, worried, apprehensive, panicky; *informal* uptight, het up, stressed out, jittery, twitchy, squirrelly, in a state, a bundle of nerves. ANTONYMS relaxed, calm.

3 *a tense moment* NERVE-RACKING, stressful, anxious, worrying, fraught, charged, strained, nail-biting, suspenseful, uneasy, difficult, uncomfortable; exciting, cliffhanging, knife-edge; *informal* hairy, white-knuckle. ANTONYM relaxing.

▸ verb *Hebden tensed his muscles* TIGHTEN, tauten, tense up, flex, contract, brace, stiffen; screw up, knot, strain, stretch, squinch up. ANTONYM relax.

tension noun **1** *the tension of the rope* TIGHTNESS, tautness, rigidity; pull, traction.

2 *the tension was unbearable* STRAIN, stress, anxiety, pressure; worry, apprehensiveness, apprehension, agitation, nerves, nervousness, jumpiness, edginess, restlessness; suspense, uncertainty, anticipation, excitement; *informal* heebie-jeebies, butterflies (in one's stomach), collywobbles.

3 *months of tension between the military and the govern-*

ment STRAINED RELATIONS, strain; ill feeling, friction, antagonism, antipathy, hostility, enmity.

tent noun *circus tents | our tent sleeps four* marquee, big top; dome tent, pup tent; teepee, wigwam.

tentative adjective **1** *tentative arrangements | a tentative conclusion* PROVISIONAL, unconfirmed, penciled in, iffy, preliminary, to be confirmed, subject to confirmation; speculative, conjectural, sketchy, untried, unproven, exploratory, experimental, trial, test, pilot. ANTONYM definite.

2 *he took a few tentative steps* HESITANT, uncertain, cautious, timid, hesitating, faltering, shaky, unsteady, halting; wavering, unsure. ANTONYM confident.

tenterhooks PHRASE: **on tenterhooks** *she's been on tenterhooks ever since the job interview* IN SUSPENSE, waiting with bated breath; anxious, nervous, apprehensive, worried, worried sick, on edge, edgy, antsy, tense, strained, stressed, agitated, restless, worked up, keyed up, jumpy, with one's stomach in knots, with one's heart in one's mouth; *informal* with butterflies in one's stomach, jittery, twitchy, in a state, uptight, het up; squirrelly.

tenuous adjective **1** *a tenuous connection* SLIGHT, insubstantial, meager, flimsy, weak, doubtful, dubious, questionable, suspect; vague, nebulous, hazy. ANTONYMS convincing, strong.

2 *a tenuous thread* FINE, thin, slender, delicate, wispy, gossamer, fragile. ANTONYMS thick, strong.

tenure noun *his tenure with the company* INCUMBENCY, term of office, term, period of/in office, time, time in office, stint.

tepid adjective **1** *tepid water* LUKEWARM, warmish, slightly warm; at room temperature. ANTONYMS hot, cold.

2 *a tepid response* UNENTHUSIASTIC, apathetic, muted, halfhearted, so-so, 'comme ci, comme ça,' indifferent, subdued, cool, lukewarm, uninterested, unenthused. ANTONYMS passionate, enthusiastic.

term noun **1** *scientific and technical terms* WORD, expression, phrase, turn of phrase, idiom, locution; name, title, designation, label, moniker; *formal* appellation, denomination, descriptor.

2 **(terms)** *a protest in the strongest terms* LANGUAGE, mode of expression, manner of speaking, phraseology, terminology; words, expressions.

3 **(terms)** *the terms of the contract* CONDITIONS, stipulations, specifications, provisions, provisos, qualifications, particulars, small print, details, points.

4 **(terms)** *a policy offering more favorable terms* RATES, prices, charges, costs, fees; tariff.

5 *the director is elected for a two-year term* PERIOD, period of time, time, length of time, spell, stint, duration; stretch, run; period of office, incumbency.

6 *archaic* *the whole term of your natural life* DURATION, length, span.

7 *the summer term* SESSION, semester, trimester, quarter; intersession.

▸ verb *he has been termed the father of modern theology* CALL, name, entitle, title, style, designate, describe as, dub, label, brand, tag, bill, nickname; *formal* denominate.

PHRASE: **come to terms** **1** *the two sides came to terms* REACH AN AGREEMENT/UNDERSTANDING, make a deal, reach a compromise, meet each other halfway. **2** *she eventually **came to terms with** her situation* ACCEPT, come to accept, reconcile oneself to, learn to live with, become resigned to, make the best of; face up to.

terminal adjective **1** *a terminal illness* INCURABLE, untreatable, inoperable; fatal, mortal, deadly; *Medicine* immedicable.

2 *terminal patients* INCURABLE, dying; near death, on one's deathbed, on one's last legs, with one foot in the grave.

3 *a terminal bonus may be payable when a policy matures* FINAL, last, concluding, closing, end.

▸ noun **1** *a railroad terminal* STATION, last stop, end of the line; depot; *chiefly Brit.* terminus.

2 *a computer terminal* WORKSTATION, VDT, visual display terminal.

terminate verb **1** *the project was terminated* BRING TO AN END, end, abort, curtail, bring to a close/conclusion, close, conclude, finish, stop, put an end to, wind up, wrap up, discontinue, cease, kill, cut short, ax; *informal* pull the plug on, can. ANTONYMS begin, start, continue.

2 *ten employees were terminated* FIRE, ax; downsize; *informal* can, cut. ANTONYM hire.

3 *this bus terminates at Granville Street* END ITS JOURNEY, finish up, stop.

termination noun *the termination of the after-school music program* ENDING, end, closing, close, conclusion, finish, stopping, winding up, discontinuance, discontinuation; cancellation, dissolution; *informal* windup. ANTONYMS start, beginning.

terminology noun *medical terminology* PHRASEOLOGY, terms, expressions, words, language, lexicon, parlance, vocabulary, wording, nomenclature; usage, idiom; jargon, cant, argot; *informal* lingo, -speak, -ese.

terrace noun *dinner on the terrace* PATIO, sundeck, platform, porch, stoop, veranda, balcony.

terrain noun *it's a stark and hostile terrain* LAND, ground, territory; topography, landscape, countryside, country.

terrestrial adjective *our terrestrial existence* EARTHLY, worldly, mundane, earthbound, land; *literary* sublunary.

terrible adjective **1** *a terrible crime | terrible injuries* DREADFUL, awful, appalling, horrific, horrifying, horrible, horrendous, atrocious, abominable, deplorable, egregious, abhorrent, frightful, shocking, hideous, ghastly, grim, dire, unspeakable, gruesome, monstrous, sickening, heinous, vile; serious, grave, acute; *formal* grievous. ANTONYMS minor, negligible.

2 *a terrible smell* REPULSIVE, disgusting, awful, dreadful, ghastly, horrid, horrible, vile, foul, abominable, frightful, loathsome, revolting, nasty, odious, nauseating, repellent, horrendous, hideous, appalling, offensive, objectionable, obnoxious, gruesome, putrid, noisome, yucky, godawful, gross. ANTONYMS nice, delightful, pleasant.

3 *he was in terrible pain* SEVERE, extreme, intense, acute, excruciating, agonizing, unbearable, intolerable, unendurable. ANTONYM slight.

4 *that's a terrible thing to say* UNKIND, nasty, unpleasant, foul, obnoxious, vile, contemptible, despicable, wretched, shabby; spiteful, mean, malicious, poisonous, mean-spirited, cruel, hateful, hurtful; unfair, uncharitable, uncalled for, below the belt, unwarranted. ANTONYMS kind, nice.

5 *the movie was terrible* VERY BAD, dreadful, awful, deplorable, atrocious, hopeless, worthless, useless, poor, pathetic, pitiful, lamentable, appalling, abysmal; *informal* lame, lousy, brutal, painful, crappy. ANTONYMS brilliant, excellent.

6 *I feel terrible. I've been in bed all day* ILL, sick, queasy, poorly, unwell, nauseous, nauseated, peaked, green around the gills; *dizzy,* groggy; *informal* under the weather, lousy, crummy, awful, dreadful, crappy; *rare* peakish. ANTONYM well.

7 *she still feels terrible about what she did to John* GUILTY, conscience-stricken, remorseful, guilt-ridden, ashamed, chastened, contrite, sorry, sick, bad, awful. ANTONYMS untroubled, unashamed.

terribly adverb **1** *she's not terribly upset* VERY, extremely, particularly, hugely, intensely, really, terrifically, tremendously, immensely, dreadfully, incredibly, remarkably, extraordinarily, seriously; *informal* real, mighty, awful, majorly.

2 *he played terribly* VERY BADLY, atrociously, deplorably, awfully, dreadfully, appallingly, execrably, abysmally, pitifully.

3 *I shall miss you terribly* VERY MUCH, greatly, a great deal, a lot; *informal* tons, loads, big time.

terrific adjective **1** *a terrific all-star cast* MARVELOUS, wonderful, sensational, outstanding, great, superb, excellent, first-rate, first-class, dazzling, out of this world, breathtaking; fantastic, fabulous, super, blue-ribbon, magic; *informal* cool, wicked, awesome, bang-up, dandy, mean.

2 *a terrific bang* TREMENDOUS, huge, massive, enormous, gigantic, colossal, mighty, great, prodigious, formidable, monstrous, sizable, considerable; intense, extreme, extraordinary; *informal* whopping, humongous; deafening.

terrify verb *that crazy driver terrified us* PETRIFY, horrify, frighten, scare, scare stiff, scare/frighten to death, scare/frighten the living daylights out of, scare/frighten the life out of, scare/frighten someone out of their wits, scare witless, strike terror into, put the fear of God into; terrorize, paralyze, transfix; *informal* scare the pants off, scare the bejesus out of.

territorial adjective **1** *the two nations have engaged in territorial disputes* GEOGRAPHICAL, jurisdictional, regional, land-related.

2 *she gets territorial about her clients* DEFENSIVE, possessive, protective, jealous.

territory noun **1** *the island is a U.S. territory* AREA, area of land, region, enclave; country, state, land, colony, dominion, protectorate, fief, dependency, possession, jurisdiction, holding; section, turf.

2 *mountainous territory* TERRAIN, land, ground, countryside.

3 *linguistic puzzles are Stina's territory* DOMAIN, area of concern/interest/knowledge, province, department, field, preserve, bailiwick, sphere, arena, realm, world.

terror noun **1** *she screamed in terror* EXTREME FEAR, dread, horror, fear and trembling, fright, alarm, panic.

2 *informal* *that child is a little terror* RASCAL, rogue, rapscallion, devil, imp, monkey, mischief-maker, troublemaker, scalawag, scamp; *informal* holy terror, horror, hellion, varmint; *archaic* scapegrace.

terrorist noun *the detainees are suspected terrorists* EXTREMIST, fanatic; revolutionary, radical, insurgent, guerrilla, anarchist, freedom fighter; bomber, gunman, assassin, hijacker, arsonist, incendiary.

terrorize verb *terrorized by racist thugs* PERSECUTE, victimize, torment, harass, tyrannize, intimidate, menace, threaten, bully, browbeat; scare, frighten, terrify, petrify.

terse adjective *we were offended by her terse answers* BRIEF, short, to the point, concise, succinct, crisp, pithy, incisive, trenchant, short and sweet, laconic, elliptical; BRUSQUE, abrupt, curt, clipped, blunt, pointed, ungracious, gruff. ANTONYMS long-winded, polite.

THE RIGHT WORD

If you don't like to mince words, you'll make every effort to be **concise** in both your writing and speaking, which means to remove all superfluous details (*a concise summary of everything that happened*). **Succinct** is very close in meaning to *concise*, although it emphasizes compression and compactness in addition to brevity (*succinct instructions for what to do in an emergency*). If you're **laconic**, you are brief to the point of being curt, brusque, or even uncommunicative (*his laconic reply left many questions unanswered*). **Terse** can also mean clipped or abrupt (*a terse command*), but it usually connotes something that is both concise and polished (*a terse style of writing that was much admired*). A **pithy** statement is not only succinct but full of substance and meaning (*a pithy argument that no one could counter*).

test noun **1** *a series of scientific tests* TRIAL, experiment, test case, case study, pilot study, trial run, tryout, dry run; check, examination, assessment, evaluation, appraisal, investigation, inspection, analysis, scrutiny, study, probe, exploration; screening; *technical* assay.

2 *candidates may be required to take a test* EXAM, examination, quiz.

▸ verb **1** *a small-scale prototype was tested* TRY OUT, put to the test, put through its paces, experiment with, pilot; check, examine, assess, evaluate, appraise, investigate, analyze, scrutinize, study, probe, explore, trial; sample; screen; *technical* assay.

2 *such behavior would test any marriage* PUT A STRAIN ON, strain, tax, try; make demands on, stretch, challenge.

testament noun *an achievement that is a testament to his professionalism and dedication* TESTIMONY, witness, evidence, proof, attestation; demonstration, indication, symbol, exemplification; monument, tribute.

testicles plural noun *the bull's testicles* gonads, testes; *informal* prairie oysters, mountain oysters, cojones, family jewels; *vulgar slang* BALLS, nuts, nads; *Brit.* bollocks.

testify verb **1** *you may be required to testify in court* GIVE EVIDENCE, bear witness, be a witness, give one's testimony, attest; *Law* make a deposition.

2 *he testified that he had been threatened by a fellow officer* ATTEST, swear, state on oath, state, declare, assert, affirm; allege, submit, claim; *Law* depose.

3 *the exhibits* ***testify to*** *the talents of the local sculptors* BE EVIDENCE/PROOF OF, attest to, confirm, prove, corroborate, substantiate, bear out; show, demonstrate, bear witness to, speak to, indicate, reveal, bespeak.

testimonial noun *a glowing testimonial* RECOMMENDATION, reference, character reference, letter of recommendation, commendation, endorsement, blurb.

testimony noun **1** *Smith was in court to hear her testimony* EVIDENCE, sworn statement, attestation, affidavit; statement, declaration, assertion, affirmation; allegation, submission, claim; *Law* deposition.

2 *the work is a* ***testimony to*** *his professional commitment* TESTAMENT TO, proof of, evidence of, attestation to, witness to; confirmation of, verification of, corroboration of; demonstration of, illustration of, indication of.

testy adjective *what's made you so testy today?* IRRITABLE, tetchy, cranky, ornery, cantankerous, irascible, bad-tempered, grumpy, grouchy, crotchety, petulant, crabby, crusty, curmudgeonly, ill-tempered, ill-humored, peevish, cross, fractious, pettish, prickly, short-fused, waspish, snappish, snippy. ANTONYM good-humored.

tetchy adjective See TESTY.

tête-à-tête noun *we enjoyed a private tête-à-tête on the patio* CONVERSATION, dialogue, chat, chitchat, talk, heart-to-heart, one-on-one, confab; *formal* confabulation. See note at CONVERSATION.

tether verb *the horse had been tethered to a post* TIE, tie up, hitch, rope, chain; fasten, bind, fetter, secure. ANTONYM unleash.

▸ noun *a dog on a tether* ROPE, chain, cord, leash, lead; restraint, fetter; halter.

text noun **1** *a text that explores pain and grief* BOOK, work, written work, printed work, document.

2 *the pictures are clear and relate well to the text* WORDS, wording, writing; content, body, main body; narrative, story.

3 *academic texts* TEXTBOOK, book, material.

4 *a text from the First Book of Samuel* PASSAGE, extract, excerpt, quotation, verse, line; reading.

textiles plural noun *a manufacturer of fine textiles* FABRICS, cloths, materials. See table at FABRIC.

texture noun *the texture of the burlap is coarse and nubby* FEEL, touch; appearance, finish, surface, grain; quality, consistency; weave, nap.

thank verb *the boss thanked us for our special effort* EXPRESS (ONE'S) GRATITUDE TO, express one's thanks to, offer/extend thanks to, say thank you to, show one's appreciation to, credit, recognize, bless.

thankful adjective *she was thankful that the evening was over* GRATEFUL, appreciative, filled with gratitude, relieved.

thankless adjective **1** *a thankless task* UNENVIABLE, difficult, unpleasant, unrewarding; unappreciated, unrecognized, unacknowledged. ANTONYM rewarding.

2 *her thankless children* UNGRATEFUL, unappreciative, unthankful, ingrate. ANTONYM grateful.

thanks plural noun *they expressed their thanks and wished her well* GRATITUDE, appreciation; acknowledgment, recognition, credit.

▸ exclamation *thanks for being so helpful* THANK YOU, many thanks, thanks very much, thanks a lot, thank you kindly, much obliged, much appreciated, bless you; *informal* thanks a million.

PHRASE: **thanks to** *thanks to the untiring support of my wife, I've gotten back on my feet* AS A RESULT OF, owing to, due to, because of, through, as a consequence of, on account of, by virtue of, by dint of, by reason of.

that pronoun See note below.

WORD NOTE that

There is widespread ignorance about how to use *that* as a relative pronoun, and two common *that*-errors are so severe that teachers, editors, and other high-end readers will make unkind judgments about you if you commit them. The first is to use *which* when you need *that.* Writers who do this usually think the two relative pronouns are interchangeable but that *which* makes you look smarter. They aren't, and it doesn't. For writers, the abstract rule that *that* introduces restrictive elements and *which* introduces nonrestrictive elements is probably less helpful than the following simple test: if there needs to be a comma before the relative pronoun, you need *which*; otherwise, you need *that.* *Examples: *We have a massive SUV that we purchased on credit last month*; *The massive SUV, which we purchased on credit last month, seats us ten feet above any other driver on the road.* The second error, even more common, is worse. It's using *that* when you really need *who* or *whom.* Examples: *She is the girl that he's always dreamed of*; *Daddy promised the air rifle to the first one of us that cleaned out the hog pen.* There's a basic rule: *who* and *whom* are the relative pronouns for people; *that* and *which* are the relative pronouns for everything else. It's true that there's a progressive-type linguistic argument to be made for the thesis that the supposed "error" of using *that* with people is in fact the first phase of our language evolving past the *who/that* distinction, since a universal *that* is simpler and would allow English to dispense with the whole subject-*who*-vs.-object-*whom* thing. This sort of argument is interesting in theory; ignore it in practice. The truth is that, as of 2004, misusing *that* for *who* or *whom,* whether in writing or speech, functions as a kind of class marker—it's the grammatical equivalent of wearing NASCAR paraphernalia or liking pro wrestling. If you think this last assertion too snooty or extreme, please be informed that the hideous old *PTL Club*'s initials actually stood for "People That Love."

*Bonus Factoid and Suggestion: It so happens that you can occupy a bright child for most of a very quiet morning by challenging her to use *that* five times in a row in a single coherent sentence, to which stumper the solution is all about the present distinction: *He said that that* that *that that writer used should really have been a* which. (You can up the challenge to six in a row if the kid is old enough to know about the medial-question-mark-in-sentence trick: *He said that? that that* that *that that writer used should have been a* which?) —**DFW**

thaw verb *allow the ice cream to thaw for about ten minutes before folding in the other ingredients* MELT, unfreeze, soften, liquefy, dissolve; defrost, warm. ANTONYM freeze.

▸ noun **1** *spring thaw* RUNOFF, debacle, ice-out.

2 *a thaw in relations* IMPROVEMENT, relaxation, coming-to-terms, rapprochement.

theater noun **1** *the local theater* PLAYHOUSE, auditorium, amphitheater; cinema, movie theater, movie house; *dated* nickelodeon.

2 *what made you want to go into* ***the theater****?* ACTING, performing, the stage; drama, the dramatic arts, dramaturgy, the thespian art; show business, Broadway; *informal* the boards, show biz.

3 *the lecture theater* HALL, room, auditorium.

4 *the Pacific theater of the war* SCENE, arena, field/sphere/place of action, setting, site.

theatrical adjective **1** *a theatrical career* STAGE, dramatic, thespian, dramaturgical; show-business; *informal* show-biz; *formal* histrionic.

2 *Henry looked over his shoulder with theatrical caution* EXAGGERATED, ostentatious, stagy, showy, melodramatic, overacted, overdone, histrionic, over-the-top, artificial, affected, mannered; *informal* hammy, ham, camp.

theft noun *the theft was reported on Thursday morning* ROBBERY, stealing, thieving, larceny, thievery, shoplifting, burglary, misappropriation, appropriation, embezzlement; raid, holdup; *informal* heist, stickup; five-finger discount, rip-off; *formal* peculation.

theme noun 1 *the theme of her speech* SUBJECT, topic, subject matter, matter, thesis, argument, text, burden, concern, thrust, message; thread, motif, keynote.

2 *the first violin takes up the theme* MELODY, tune, air; motif, leitmotif.

3 *the band played a medley of popular TV show themes* SONG, theme song, jingle.

then adverb 1 *I was living in Cairo then* AT THAT TIME, in those days; at that point (in time), at that moment, on that occasion.

2 *she won the first and then the second game* NEXT, after that, afterward/afterward, subsequently, later.

3 *and then there's another problem* IN ADDITION, also, besides, as well, additionally, on top of that, over and above that, moreover, furthermore, what's more, to boot; too.

4 *well, if that's what he wants, then he should leave* IN THAT CASE, that being so, it follows that.

theological adjective *theological writings* RELIGIOUS, scriptural, ecclesiastical, doctrinal; divine, holy.

theoretical adjective *it's just a theoretical situation* HYPOTHETICAL, abstract, conjectural, academic, suppositional, speculative, notional, postulatory, what-if, assumed, presumed, untested, unproven, unsubstantiated. ANTONYMS actual, real.

theorize verb *Darwin theorized that the atolls marked the sites of vanished volcanoes* SPECULATE, conjecture, hypothesize, philosophize, postulate, propose, posit, suppose.

theory noun 1 *I reckon that confirms my theory* HYPOTHESIS, thesis, conjecture, supposition, speculation, postulation, postulate, proposition, premise, surmise, assumption, presupposition; opinion, view, belief, contention.

2 *modern economic theory* PRINCIPLES, ideas, concepts; philosophy, ideology, system of ideas, science. PHRASE: **in theory** *in theory, your idea sounds great, but can it be practically applied?* IN PRINCIPLE, on paper, in the abstract, all things being equal, in an ideal world; hypothetically, theoretically, supposedly.

therapeutic adjective *the therapeutic effects of acupuncture* HEALING, curative, remedial, medicinal, restorative, salubrious, health-giving, tonic, reparative, corrective, beneficial, good, salutary. ANTONYM harmful.

therapist noun *events he would speak of only to his therapist* PSYCHOLOGIST, psychotherapist, analyst, counselor, psychoanalyst, psychiatrist; *informal* shrink.

therapy noun 1 *a wide range of complementary therapies* TREATMENT, remedy, cure.

2 *he's currently in therapy* PSYCHOTHERAPY, psychoanalysis, analysis, counseling.

there adverb See note below.

USAGE NOTE **there is, there are**

These phrases, though sometimes useful, can also be the enemies of a lean writing style, as several commentators have observed—e.g.:

- "The habit of beginning statements with the impersonal and usually vague *there is* or *there are* shoves the really significant verb into subordinate place instead of letting it stand vigorously on its own feet." (David Lambuth et al., *The Golden Book on Writing*; 1964.)
- "The *there* construction is not to be condemned out of hand; it is both idiomatic and common in the best literature; it is clumsy and to be avoided with a passive verb; and in view of the prejudice against it [for promoting wordiness], the writer who uses it discriminatingly should take heart and be prepared to defend himself, for defense is indeed possible." (Roy H. Copperud, *American Usage and Style: The Consensus*; 1980.)

When is the phrase *there is* defensible? When the writer is addressing the existence of something. That is, if the only real recourse is to use the verb *exist*, then *there is* is perfectly fine—e.g.: "There is unlimited competition for our entertainment dollars." (*Kansas City Star*; Sept. 21, 1997.) Otherwise, though, the phrase should typically be cut—e.g.: "There is wide support among congressional Republicans for a flat tax." (*Dallas Morning News*; Sept. 20, 1997.) (A possible revision: "Congressional Republicans tend to support a flat tax." Or: "Many congressional Republicans support a flat tax.") The phrase *there is wide support* has become a cliché among political commentators. And it robs the sentence of a good strong verb.

The number of the verb is controlled by whether the subject that follows the inverted verb is singular or plural. Mistakes are common—e.g.:

- "He said there is [read *there are*] several truckloads of nuclear waste." (*Knoxville News-Sentinel*; Apr. 18, 1996.)
- "There seems [read *there seem*] to be two key reasons for Capriati's renaissance." (*USA Today*; Jan. 26, 2000.)

Especially when followed by a negative, *there* has in many minds come to represent a single situation. It therefore often appears, though wrongly, with a singular verb—e.g.: " There wasn't [read *there weren't*] any other witnesses. " (*Austin American-Statesman*; Dec. 9, 1994.) —**BG**

thereabouts adverb 1 *the land thereabouts* NEAR THERE, around there, in that area.

2 *they sold it for five million* ***or thereabouts*** APPROXIMATELY, roughly, or so, give or take, plus or minus, in round numbers, in the ballpark of.

thereafter adverb *thereafter their fortunes suffered a deep decline* AFTER THAT, following that, afterward/afterward, subsequently, then, next.

therefore adverb *Rodriguez was injured and therefore unable to play* CONSEQUENTLY, so, as a result, hence, thus, accordingly, for that reason, ergo, that being the case, on that account; *formal* whence; *archaic* wherefore.

thesaurus noun *Oxford's newest thesaurus* WORDFINDER, wordbook, synonym dictionary; *rare* synonymy.

thesis noun 1 *the central thesis of his lecture* THEORY, contention, argument, line of argument, proposal, proposition, idea, claim, premise, assumption, hypothesis, postulation, supposition.

2 *a doctoral thesis* DISSERTATION, essay, paper, treatise, disquisition, composition, monograph, study.

they pronoun See note.

USAGE NOTE **they**

The word **they** (with its counterparts **them**, **their**, and **themselves**) as a singular pronoun to refer to a person of unspecified sex has been used since at least the sixteenth century. In the late twentieth century, as the traditional use of **he** to refer to a person of either sex came under scrutiny on the grounds of sexism, this use of **they** has become more common. It is now generally accepted in contexts where it follows an indefinite pronoun such as **anyone**, **no one**, **someone**, or **a person**: *anyone can join if they are a resident; each to their own*. In other contexts, coming after singular nouns, the use of **they** is now common, although less widely accepted, esp. in formal contexts. Sentences such as *ask a friend if they could help* are still criticized for being ungrammatical. Nevertheless, in view of the growing acceptance of **they** and its obvious practical advantages, **they** is used in this dictionary in many cases where **he** would have been used formerly.

thick adjective **1** *the walls are five feet thick* IN EXTENT/DIAMETER, across, wide, broad, deep.

2 *his short, thick legs* STOCKY, sturdy, stubby, chunky, blocky, hefty, thickset, burly, beefy, meaty, big, solid; fat, stout, plump. ANTONYMS thin, slender.

3 *a thick winter sweater* CHUNKY, bulky, heavy; cable-knit, woolly. ANTONYMS thin, lightweight.

4 *the arena was thick with skaters* CROWDED, swarming, filled, packed, teeming, seething, buzzing, crawling, crammed, solid, overflowing, choked, jammed, congested; *informal* jam-packed, chockablock, stuffed.

5 *the thick summer vegetation* PLENTIFUL, abundant, profuse, luxuriant, bushy, rich, riotous, exuberant; rank, rampant; dense, impenetrable, impassable; *informal* jungly. ANTONYMS meager, sparse.

6 *a thick paste* VISCOUS, gooey, syrupy, firm, stiff, heavy; clotted, coagulated, viscid, semisolid, gelatinous; concentrated. ANTONYMS runny, thin.

7 *thick fog* DENSE, heavy, opaque, impenetrable, soupy, murky. ANTONYM light.

8 *informal he's a bit thick.* See STUPID sense 1.

9 *Guy's voice was thick with desire* HUSKY, hoarse, throaty, guttural, gravelly, rough. ANTONYMS clear, shrill.

10 *a thick Scottish accent* OBVIOUS, pronounced, marked, broad, strong, rich, decided, distinct. ANTONYMS faint, vague.

▸ noun *in the thick of the crisis* MIDST, center, hub, middle, core, heart.

thicken verb *stir the sauce as it thickens* BECOME THICK/THICKER, stiffen, condense; solidify, firm up, set, jell, congeal, clot, coagulate, cake, inspissate.

thicket noun *rabbits taking refuge in the thicket* COPSE, coppice, grove, brake, covert, clump; wood, woodlot, bush.

thickness noun **1** *the wall is several feet in thickness* WIDTH, breadth, depth, diameter.

2 *several thicknesses of limestone* LAYER, stratum, stratification, seam, vein; sheet, lamina.

thickset adjective *a thickset Caucasian male in his thirties* STOCKY, sturdy, big-boned, heavily built, well-built, chunky, burly, strapping, brawny, solid, blocky, heavy, hefty, beefy, meaty. ANTONYM slight.

thick-skinned adjective *these guards have gotten pretty thick-skinned over the years* INSENSITIVE, unfeeling, tough, hardened, callous, case-hardened; *informal* hard-boiled. ANTONYM sensitive.

thief noun *the thief is at large* ROBBER, burglar, housebreaker, cat burglar, rustler, shoplifter, pickpocket, purse snatcher, sneak thief, mugger; embezzler, swindler, plunderer; criminal, villain; kleptomaniac; bandit, pirate, highwayman; *informal* crook; *literary* brigand.

thieve verb *before we were out of diapers, we were learning how to thieve anything that wasn't nailed down* STEAL, take, purloin, help oneself to, snatch, pilfer; embezzle, misappropriate; have one's fingers/hand in the till, rob; swipe, make off with, finagle, lift, "liberate", "borrow", filch, snaffle, pinch, heist; *formal* peculate.

thievery noun See THEFT.

thieving noun See THEFT.

thin adjective **1** *a thin white line* NARROW, fine, attenuated. ANTONYMS thick, broad.

2 *a thin cotton nightdress* LIGHTWEIGHT, light, fine, delicate, floaty, flimsy, diaphanous, gossamer, insubstantial; sheer, gauzy, filmy, transparent, see-through; paper-thin. ANTONYMS thick, heavy.

3 *a tall, thin woman* SLIM, lean, slender, rangy, willowy, svelte, sylphlike, spare, slight; SKINNY, underweight, scrawny, waiflike, scraggy, bony, angular, rawboned, hollow-cheeked, gaunt, skin-and-bones, emaciated, skeletal, wasted, pinched, undernourished, underfed; lanky, spindly, gangly, gangling, weedy; *informal* anorexic, like a bag of bones. ANTONYMS plump, overweight, fat.

4 *his thin gray hair* SPARSE, scanty, wispy, thinning. ANTONYMS thick, abundant.

5 *a bowl of thin soup* WATERY, weak, dilute, diluted; runny. ANTONYMS thick, hearty.

6 *her thin voice* WEAK, faint, feeble, small, soft; reedy. ANTONYMS strong, loud.

7 *the plot is very thin* INSUBSTANTIAL, flimsy, slight, feeble, lame, poor, weak, tenuous, inadequate, insufficient, unconvincing, unbelievable, implausible. ANTONYMS meaty, convincing.

▸ verb **1** *some paint must be* ***thinned down*** *before use* DILUTE, water down, weaken.

2 *the crowds were beginning to* ***thin out*** DISPERSE, dissipate, scatter; become less dense, become less in number, decrease, diminish, dwindle.

THE RIGHT WORD

You can't be too rich or too **thin**, but you can be too **skinny**. *Thin* describes someone whose weight is naturally low in proportion to his or her height, although it may also imply that the person is underweight (*she looked pale and thin after her operation*). *Skinny* is a more blunt and derogatory term for someone who is too thin, and it often implies underdevelopment (*a skinny little boy; a tall, skinny fashion model*). Most people would rather be called **slender**, which combines thinness with gracefulness and good proportions (*the slender legs of a Queen Anne table*), or better yet, **svelte**, a complimentary term that implies a slim, elegant figure (*after six months of dieting, she looked so svelte I hardly recognized her*). **Lean** and **spare** are used to describe people who are naturally thin, although *spare* suggests a more muscular leanness (*a tall, spare man who looked like Abraham Lincoln*). **Gaunt**, on the other hand, means so thin that the angularity of the bones can be seen beneath the skin (*looking gaunt after her latest bout with cancer*).

---

thing noun **1** *the room was full of strange things* OBJECT, article, item, artifact, commodity; device, gadget, instrument, utensil, tool, implement; entity, body; *informal* whatsit, whatchamacallit; *Brit.* thingummy, thingy, thingamabob, thingamajig, doohickey, doodad, dingus.

2 (**things**) *I'll come back tomorrow to collect my things* BELONGINGS, possessions, stuff, property, worldly goods, effects, personal effects, trappings, paraphernalia, bits and pieces, luggage, baggage, bags; *informal* gear, junk; *Law* goods and chattels.

3 (**things**) *his gardening things* EQUIPMENT, apparatus, gear, kit, tackle, stuff; implements, tools, utensils; accoutrements.

4 *I've got several things to do today* ACTIVITY, act, action, deed, undertaking, exploit, feat; task, job, chore.

5 *I've got other things on my mind just now* THOUGHT, notion, idea; concern, matter, worry, preoccupation.

6 *I keep remembering things he said* REMARK, statement, comment, utterance, observation, declaration, pronouncement.

7 *quite a few odd things happened* INCIDENT, episode, event, happening, occurrence, phenomenon.

8 (**things**) *how are things with you?* MATTERS, affairs, circumstances, conditions, relations; state of affairs, situation, life.

9 *one of the things I like about you is your optimism* CHARACTERISTIC, quality, attribute, property, trait, feature, point, aspect, facet, quirk.

10 *there's another thing you should know* FACT, piece of information, point, detail, particular, factor.

11 *the thing is, I'm not sure if it's what I want* FACT OF THE MATTER, fact, point, issue, problem.

12 *you lucky thing!* PERSON, soul, creature, wretch; *informal* devil, bastard.

13 *Twylla developed a* ***thing about*** *noise* PHOBIA OF/ABOUT, fear of, dislike of, aversion to, problem with; obsession with, fixation about; *informal* hang-up.

14 *she had a* ***thing about*** *men who wore glasses* PENCHANT FOR, preference for, taste for, inclination for, partiality for, predilection for, soft spot for, weakness for, fondness for, fancy for, liking for, love for; fetish for, obsession with, fixation on/with.

15 *books aren't really my thing* WHAT ONE LIKES, what interests one; *informal* one's cup of tea, one's bag, what turns one on.

16 *it's the latest thing* FASHION, trend, style, rage, fad.

think verb **1** *I think he's gone home* BELIEVE, be of the opinion, be of the view, be under the impression; expect, imagine, anticipate; surmise, suppose, conjecture, guess, fancy; conclude, determine, reason; *informal* reckon, figure; *formal* opine.

2 *his family was thought to be enormously rich* DEEM, judge, hold, reckon, consider, presume, estimate; regard (as), view (as).

3 *Jack thought for a moment* PONDER, reflect, deliberate, consider, meditate, contemplate, muse, ruminate, be lost in thought, be in a brown study, brood; concentrate, brainstorm, rack one's brains; put on one's thinking cap, sleep on it; *formal* cogitate.

4 *she* ***thought of*** *all the visits she had made to her father* RECALL, remember, recollect, call to mind, think back to.

5 *she forced herself to* ***think of*** *how he must be feeling* IMAGINE, picture, visualize, envisage, consider; dream about, fantasize about. PHRASES: **think better of** *Donnie was going to crash his ex-girlfriend's wedding, but he thought better of it* HAVE SECOND THOUGHTS ABOUT, think twice about, think again about, change one's mind about; reconsider, decide against; *informal* get cold feet about. **think over** *take a few days to think over the proposal* CONSIDER, contemplate, deliberate about, mull over, ponder, chew over, chew on, reflect on, muse on, ruminate on. **think up** *I'm sure by Friday we'll have thought up a great idea for the presentation* DEVISE, dream up, conjure up, come up with, invent, create, concoct, make up; hit on.

thinker noun *one of the most influential economic thinkers of the century* THEORIST, philosopher, scholar, savant, sage, intellectual, intellect, ideologist, ideologue; mind, brain, brainiac, genius.

thinking adjective *he seemed a thinking man* INTELLIGENT, sensible, reasonable, rational; logical, analytical; thoughtful, reflective, meditative, contemplative, pensive, shrewd, philosophical, sagacious. ANTONYMS stupid, irrational.

▸ noun *the thinking behind the campaign* REASONING, logic, idea(s), theory, line of thought, philosophy, beliefs; opinion(s), view(s), thoughts, position, judgment, assessment, evaluation.

thin-skinned adjective *you can't benefit from constructive criticism if you're going to be so thin-skinned* SENSITIVE, oversensitive, hypersensitive, easily offended, easily hurt, touchy, defensive. ANTONYMS insensitive, unfeeling.

third-rate adjective *a third-rate hotel* SUBSTANDARD, bad, inferior, poor, poor-quality, low-grade, inadequate, unsatisfactory, unacceptable, not up to snuff, not up to scratch; appalling, abysmal, atrocious, awful, terrible, dreadful, execrable, godawful, miserable, pitiful; jerry-built, shoddy, chintzy, tinpot, trashy; cheapjack; *informal* lousy, rotten, bum, crummy, crappy. ANTONYM excellent.

thirst noun **1** *I need a drink—I'm dying of thirst* THIRSTINESS, dryness; dehydration.

2 *his thirst for knowledge* CRAVING, desire, longing, yearning, hunger, hankering, keenness, eagerness, lust, appetite; *informal* yen, itch.

▸ verb *she* ***thirsted for*** *power* CRAVE, want, covet, desire, hunger for, burn for, lust after, hanker after, have one's heart set on; wish, long.

thirsty adjective **1** *the boys were hot and thirsty* LONGING FOR A DRINK, dry, dehydrated; *informal* parched, gasping.

2 *the thirsty soil* DRY, arid, dried up/out, bone-dry, parched, baked, desiccated.

3 *she was thirsty for power* EAGER, hungry, greedy, thirsting, craving, longing, yearning, lusting, burning, desirous, hankering; *informal* itching, dying.

thong noun *leather thongs fastened to the quiver* STRIP, band, cord, string, lash, tie, belt, strap, tape, rope, tether.

thorn noun *a thorn in her finger* PRICKLE, spike, barb, spine.

thorny adjective 1 *dense thorny undergrowth* PRICKLY, spiky, barbed, spiny, sharp; *technical* spinose, spinous.

2 *the thorny subject of confidentiality* PROBLEMATIC, tricky, ticklish, touchy, delicate, controversial, awkward, difficult, knotty, tough, taxing, trying, troublesome; complicated, complex, involved, intricate; vexed, sticky.

thorough adjective 1 *a thorough investigation* RIGOROUS, in-depth, exhaustive, thoroughgoing, minute, detailed, close, meticulous, methodical, careful, complete, comprehensive, full, extensive, widespread, sweeping, all-embracing, all-inclusive. ANTONYMS superficial, cursory, partial.

2 *he is slow but thorough* METICULOUS, scrupulous, assiduous, conscientious, painstaking, methodical, careful, diligent, industrious, hard-working. ANTONYM careless.

3 *the child is being a thorough nuisance* UTTER, downright, thoroughgoing, absolute, complete, total, out-and-out, arrant, real, perfect, sheer, unqualified, unmitigated.

thoroughbred adjective *thoroughbred horses* PUREBRED, pedigree, pure, pure-blooded, blooded.

thoroughfare noun *avoiding the busy thoroughfares* ROUTE, passageway, waterway, throughway; main road, highway, freeway, street, road, roadway, avenue, boulevard.

thoroughly adverb 1 *we will investigate all complaints thoroughly* RIGOROUSLY, in depth, exhaustively, minutely, closely, in detail, meticulously, scrupulously, assiduously, conscientiously, painstakingly, methodically, carefully, comprehensively, fully, from A to Z, from soup to nuts.

2 *she is thoroughly spoiled* UTTERLY, downright, absolutely, completely, totally, entirely, one-hundred-percent, really, perfectly, positively, in every respect, through and through; *informal* plain, to the hilt.

though conjunction *though she smiled bravely, she looked pale and tired* ALTHOUGH, even though/if, in spite of the fact that, despite the fact that, notwithstanding (the fact) that, for all that.

▸ adverb *it seems impossible, but you can try, though* NEVERTHELESS, nonetheless, even so, however, be that as it may, for all that, despite that, having said that; *informal* still and all.

thought noun 1 *what are your thoughts on the matter?* IDEA, notion, opinion, view, impression, feeling, theory; judgment, assessment, conclusion. See note at IDEA.

2 *he gave up any thought of getting a degree* HOPE, aspiration, ambition, dream; intention, idea, plan, design, aim.

3 *it only took a moment's thought* THINKING, contemplation, musing, pondering, consideration, reflection, introspection, deliberation, rumination, meditation, brooding, reverie, concentration; *formal* cogitation.

thoughtful adjective 1 *a thoughtful expression* PENSIVE, reflective, contemplative, musing, meditative, introspective, philosophical, ruminative, absorbed, engrossed, rapt, preoccupied, lost in thought, deep in thought, in a brown study, brooding; *formal* cogitative. ANTONYM vacant.

2 *how very thoughtful of you!* CONSIDERATE, caring, attentive, understanding, sympathetic, solicitous, concerned, helpful, obliging, neighborly, unselfish, kind, compassionate, charitable. ANTONYM inconsiderate.

thoughtless adjective 1 *I'm so sorry—how thoughtless of me* INCONSIDERATE, uncaring, insensitive, uncharitable, unkind, flippant, tactless, undiplomatic, indiscreet, remiss. ANTONYM considerate.

2 *a few minutes of thoughtless pleasure* UNTHINKING, heedless, careless, unmindful, unguarded, absentminded; injudicious, ill-advised, ill-considered, imprudent, unwise, foolish, frivolous, silly, stupid, reckless, rash, precipitate, negligent, neglectful. ANTONYM careful.

thought-provoking adjective *a thought-provoking lecture* INTERESTING, provocative, stimulating, intriguing, inspiring, meaty.

thousand cardinal number *I'll give you four thousand for the lot informal* grand, K, thou.

thrall noun *literary he held us in his evil thrall* POWER, clutches, hands, control, grip, yoke, tyranny. PHRASE: **in thrall** *they grew up in thrall to their repressive parents* ENSLAVED, subjected, subjugated.

thrash verb 1 *she thrashed him across the head and shoulders* HIT, beat, strike, batter, thump, hammer, pound, rain blows on; assault, attack; cudgel, club; *informal* wallop, belt, bash, whup, whack, thwack, clout, clobber, pummel, slug, tan, sock, beat the (living) daylights out of.

2 *he was thrashing around in pain* FLAIL, writhe, thresh, jerk, toss, twist, twitch. PHRASE: **thrash out** 1 *thrash out a problem* RESOLVE, settle, sort out, work out, straighten out, iron out, clear up; talk through, discuss, debate. 2 *thrash out an agreement* WORK OUT, negotiate, agree on, bring about, hammer out, hammer together, hash out, produce, effect.

WORD NOTE **whup**

A good-ol'-boy verb from the late nineteenth century, which sounds as if it originated in the South or West, meaning decisively to beat or whip (from which it derives): *Zeke, if you don't stop messin' with them pigeons your daddy's gonna whup your behind.* In fact, *whup* means "beat" in two other ways as well: "defeat" *(Boys, are we gonna whup the Tigers tomorrow? You're goddam right we are!)* and, as a past participle, "exhausted" (Southern guy walks into a bar, sits down, says, *Man, I'm whupped. Gimme some of that good beer*). **—JS**

thread noun 1 *a needle and thread* cotton, filament, fiber; yarn, string, twine.

2 *literary the Fraser was a thread of silver below them* STREAK, strand, stripe, line, strip, seam, vein.

3 *she lost the thread of the conversation* GIST, train of thought, drift, direction; theme, motif, tenor; story line, plot.

▸ verb 1 *he threaded the rope through a pulley* PASS, string, work, ease, push, poke.

2 *she threaded her way through the tables* WEAVE, inch, wind, squeeze, make.

threadbare adjective *a threadbare carpet* WORN, well-worn, old, thin, worn out, holey, moth-eaten, mangy, ragged, frayed, tattered, battered; decrepit, shabby, scruffy, unkempt; having seen better days, falling apart at the seams, falling to pieces, tatty, ratty, the worse for wear, raggedy, dog-eared; *informal* raggedy-ass.

threat noun 1 *Maggie ignored his threats* THREATENING REMARK, warning, ultimatum.

2 *a possible threat to aircraft* DANGER, peril, hazard, menace, risk.

3 *the company faces the threat of liquidation proceedings* POSSIBILITY, prospect, chance, probability, likelihood, risk.

threaten verb 1 *how dare you threaten me?* MENACE, intimidate, browbeat, bully, blackmail, terrorize; make/issue threats to.

2 *these events could threaten the stability of Europe* ENDANGER, be a danger to, be a threat to, jeopardize, imperil, put at risk, put in jeopardy.

3 *the gray skies threatened snow* FORESHADOW, bode, warn of, presage, augur, portend, herald, be a harbinger of, indicate, point to, be a sign of, signal, spell; *literary* foretoken.

4 *as rain threatened, the party moved indoors* SEEM LIKELY, seem imminent, be on the horizon, be brewing, be gathering, be looming, be on the way, be impending; hang over someone.

threatening adjective 1 *a threatening letter* MENACING, intimidating, bullying, frightening, hostile; *formal* minatory.

2 *banks of threatening clouds* OMINOUS, sinister, menacing, alarming, portentous, dark, black, thunderous.

three cardinal number *the three over there are the lounge singers* TRIO, threesome, triple, triad, trinity, troika, triumvirate, trilogy, triptych, trefoil, three-piece, triplets.

three-dimensional adjective 1 *three-dimensional art* SOLID, concrete, sculptural, perspectival, stereoscopic, stereographic, stereo-, pop-up. ANTONYM flat.

2 *three-dimensional characters* VIVID, realistic, rounded, concrete.

threesome noun *a talented threesome* TRIO, triumvirate, triad, trinity, troika; triplets.

threshold noun 1 *the threshold of the church* DOORSTEP, doorway, entrance, entry, door, gate, gateway, portal, doorsill.

2 *the threshold of a new era* START, beginning, commencement, brink, verge, cusp, dawn, inception, day one, opening, debut; *informal* kickoff.

3 *the human threshold of pain* LOWER LIMIT, minimum.

thrift noun *she learned her sense of thrift from her mother* FRUGALITY, economy, economizing, thriftiness, providence, prudence, good management, good husbandry, saving, scrimping and saving, abstemiousness; parsimony, penny-pinching, austerity. ANTONYM extravagance.

thrifty adjective *these kids have no idea what it means to be thrifty* FRUGAL, economical, sparing, careful with money, penny-wise, provident, prudent, abstemious; parsimonious, penny-pinching, cheap. See note at ECONOMICAL. ANTONYM extravagant.

thrill noun 1 *the thrill of jumping out of an airplane* EXCITEMENT, feeling of excitement, stimulation, adrenaline rush, pleasure, tingle; fun, enjoyment, amusement, delight, joy; *informal* buzz, high, rush, kick, charge.

2 *a thrill of excitement ran through her* WAVE, shiver, rush, surge, flash, blaze, tremor, quiver, flutter, shudder, frisson.

▸ verb 1 *his words thrilled her* EXCITE, stimulate, arouse, rouse, inspire, delight, exhilarate, intoxicate, stir, charge up, electrify, galvanize, move, fire (with enthusiasm), fire someone's imagination; *informal* give someone a buzz, give someone a kick, give someone a charge. ANTONYM bore.

2 *he thrilled at the sound of her voice* BE/FEEL EXCITED, tingle, quiver; *informal* get a buzz out of, get a kick out of, get a charge out of.

thrilling adjective *a thrilling race* EXCITING, stirring, action-packed, breathtaking, rip-roaring, spine-tingling, gripping, riveting, fascinating, dramatic, hair-raising, mind-blowing; rousing, stimulating, moving, inspiring, inspirational, electrifying, heady. ANTONYM boring.

thrive verb *the roses in the west garden are thriving | business generally thrives this time of year* FLOURISH, prosper, burgeon, bloom, blossom, mushroom, do well, advance, succeed, boom. ANTONYMS decline, wither.

thriving adjective *real estate continues to be a thriving industry* FLOURISHING, prosperous, prospering, growing, developing, burgeoning, blooming, healthy, successful, booming, mushrooming, profitable, expanding; *informal* going strong, going from strength to strength. ANTONYM moribund.

throat noun *an inflamed throat* GULLET, esophagus; windpipe, trachea, gorge; maw, neck, jowl.

throaty adjective *Ms. Diamond's throaty voice* GRAVELLY, husky, rough, guttural, deep, thick, smoky, gruff, growly, growling, hoarse, croaky, croaking; rasping, raspy. ANTONYMS pure, crystal-clear.

throb verb *her arms and legs throbbed with tiredness* PULSATE, beat, pulse, palpitate, pound, thud, thump, drum, thrum, pitter-patter, go pit-a-pat, quiver; *rare* quop.

▸ noun *the throb of the ship's engines* PULSATION, beat, beating, pulse, palpitation, pounding, thudding, thumping, drumming, thrumming.

throes plural noun *the throes of childbirth* AGONY, pain, pangs, spasms, torment, suffering, torture; *literary* travail. PHRASE: **in the throes of** *we're in the throes of hurricane preparations* IN THE MIDDLE OF, in the process of, in the midst of, busy with, occupied with, taken up with/by, involved in, dealing with; struggling with, wrestling with, grappling with.

throne noun *the czar risked losing his throne* SOVEREIGN POWER, sovereignty, rule, dominion.

throng noun *a throng of people blocked her way* CROWD, horde, mass, multitude, host, army, herd, flock, drove, swarm, mob, sea, troop, pack, crush; collection, company, gathering, assembly, congregation; *informal* gaggle, bunch, gang.

▸ verb 1 *people thronged to see the play* FLOCK, stream, swarm, troop, pour in.

2 *visitors thronged around him* CROWD, cluster, mill, swarm, surge, congregate, gather.

throttle verb 1 *he tried to throttle her* CHOKE, strangle, strangulate, garrote, gag.

2 *attempts to throttle the criminal supply of drugs* SUPPRESS, inhibit, stifle, control, restrain, check, contain, choke off, put a/the lid on; stop, put an end to, end, stamp out.

through preposition 1 *we drove through the tunnel* INTO AND OUT OF, to the other side of, to the far side of, from one side to the other of.

2 *he got the job through an advertisement* BY MEANS OF, by way of, by dint of, via, using, thanks to, by virtue of, as a result of, as a consequence of, on account of, owing to, because of.

3 *he worked through the night* THROUGHOUT, all through, for the whole of, for the duration of, until/to the end of.

▸ adverb *as soon as we opened the gate they came streaming through* FROM ONE SIDE TO THE OTHER, from one end to another, in and out the other side.

▸ adjective *a through train* DIRECT, nonstop.

PHRASE: **through and through** *he was a city kid through and through* IN EVERY RESPECT, to the core; thoroughly, utterly, absolutely, completely, totally, wholly, fully, entirely, unconditionally, unreservedly, altogether, out-and-out.

throughout preposition 1 *it had repercussions throughout the Middle East* ALL OVER, across, in every part of, everywhere in, all through, right through, all around.

2 *she remained fit throughout her life* ALL THROUGH, all, for the duration of, for the whole of, until the end of.

throw verb 1 *she threw the ball back* HURL, toss, fling, pitch, cast, lob, launch, catapult, project, propel; bowl; *informal* chuck, heave, sling, peg, let fly with.

2 *he threw another punch* DELIVER, give, land.

3 *she threw a withering glance at him* DIRECT, cast, send, dart, shoot.

4 *the horse threw its rider* UNSEAT, dislodge.

5 *her question threw me* DISCONCERT, unnerve, fluster, ruffle, agitate, discomfit, put off, throw off balance, discountenance, unsettle, confuse; *informal* rattle, faze, flummox, baffle, befuddle, discombobulate.

6 *he threw a farewell party for them* GIVE, host, hold, have, provide, put on, lay out, arrange, organize.

7 *books were thrown all over her desk* STREW, cast, scatter, disperse.

8 *he threw his keys on the table* TOSS, deposit, throw down, put down, dump, drop, plunk, plonk, plump.

▸ noun 1 *we were allowed two throws each* LOB, pitch; go, turn; bowl, ball.

2 *the loveseat was decorated with a red throw* BLANKET, afghan, covering, fabric; shawl.

PHRASES: **throw something away** 1 *she hated throwing old clothes away* DISCARD, throw out, dispose of, get rid of, do away with, toss out, scrap, clear out, dump, jettison; *informal* chuck (away/out), deep-six, ditch. 2 *the Tigers threw away a 3-0 lead* SQUANDER, waste, fritter away, fail to exploit, lose, let slip; *informal* blow. **throw someone out** *the duke and his family were thrown out* EXPEL, eject, evict, drive out, force out, oust, remove; get rid of, depose, topple, unseat, overthrow, bring down, overturn, dislodge, displace, supplant, show someone the door; banish, deport, exile; *informal* boot out, kick out, give someone the boot. **throw something out** 1 *throw out this moldy food.* See THROW SOMETHING AWAY sense 1. 2 *his case was thrown out* REJECT, dismiss, turn down, refuse, disallow, veto; *informal* give the thumbs down to. **throw up** *informal* . See VOMIT verb sense 1.

throwaway adjective 1 *throwaway packaging* DISPOSABLE, single-use, nonreturnable, unrecyclable.

2 *throwaway remarks* CASUAL, passing, careless, unthinking, unstudied, unconsidered, offhand; underemphasized.

thrust verb 1 *she thrust her hands into her pockets* SHOVE, push, force, plunge, stick, drive, propel, ram, poke, jam.

2 *fame had been thrust on him* FORCE, foist, impose, inflict.

3 *he thrust his way past her* PUSH, shove, force, elbow, shoulder, barge, bulldoze.

▸ noun 1 *a hard thrust* SHOVE, push, lunge, poke.

2 *a thrust led by Canadian forces* ADVANCE, push, drive, attack, assault, onslaught, offensive, charge, sortie, foray, raid, sally, invasion, incursion.

3 *only one engine is producing thrust* FORCE, propulsive force, propulsion, power, impetus, momentum.

4 *the thrust of the speech* GIST, substance, drift, burden, meaning, sense, theme, message, import, tenor.

thud noun & verb *it landed with a thud* | *bullets thudded into the ground* THUMP, thunk, clunk, clonk, crash, smack, bang; stomp, stamp, clump, clomp; *informal* wham, whump.

thug noun *one of Capone's thugs* RUFFIAN, hooligan, vandal, hoodlum, gangster, villain, criminal; *informal* tough, bruiser, goon, heavy, enforcer, hired gun, hood.

thumb noun *the thumb on his left hand* *technical* pollex, opposable digit.

▸ verb 1 *he thumbed through his notebook* LEAF, flick, flip, riffle, skim, browse, look.

2 *his dictionaries were thumbed and ink-stained* SOIL, mark, make dog-eared.

3 *he was thumbing his way across Mexico* HITCHHIKE; *informal* hitch, hitch/thumb a lift.

PHRASES: **all thumbs** *don't let Anthony carry the punch bowl—he's all thumbs* CLUMSY, klutzy, awkward, maladroit, inept, unskillful, heavy-handed, inexpert, butterfingered, ham-fisted. **thumbs down** *informal the budget increase has been given a thumbs down* REJECTION, refusal, veto, no, negation, rebuff; *informal* red light. **thumbs up** *informal we got the board's thumbs up for the land grant* APPROVAL, seal of approval, endorsement; permission, authorization, consent, yes, leave, authority, sanction, ratification, license, dispensation, nod, assent, blessing, rubber stamp, clearance; *informal* go-ahead, OK, A-OK, green light, say-so.

thumbnail adjective *a thumbnail sketch of the political climate* CONCISE, short, brief, succinct, to the point, compact, crisp, short and sweet, quick, rapid; miniature, mini, small.

thump verb 1 *the two men kicked and thumped him* HIT, strike, beat, batter, pound, knock, rap, smack, thwack, pummel, punch, thrash, cuff, box someone's ears; *informal* bash, bop, clout, clobber, sock, swipe, slug, lash, whack, wallop, beat the (living) daylights out of, belt, tan, lay into, let someone have it, whup; *literary* smite.

2 *her heart thumped with fright* THROB, pound, thud, hammer, pulsate, pulse, pump, palpitate, race, beat heavily.

▸ noun *she put the box down with a thump* THUD, thunk, clunk, clonk, crash, smack, bang.

thunder noun **1** *thunder and lightning* THUNDERCLAP, peal of thunder, roll of thunder, rumble of thunder, crack of thunder, crash of thunder; *literary* thunderbolt.

2 *the ceaseless thunder of the traffic* RUMBLE, rumbling, boom, booming, roar, roaring, pounding, thud, thudding, crash, crashing, reverberation.

▸ verb **1** *below me the surf thrashed and thundered* RUMBLE, boom, roar, pound, thud, thump, bang; resound, reverberate, beat.

2 *she **thundered against** the evils of the age* RAIL AGAINST, fulminate against, inveigh against, rage against/about, rant about; condemn, denounce.

3 *"Answer me!" he thundered* ROAR, bellow, bark, yell, shout, bawl; *informal* holler.

thundering adjective. See THUNDEROUS.

thunderous adjective *a thunderous noise* VERY LOUD, tumultuous, booming, roaring, resounding, reverberating, reverberant, ringing, deafening, ear-splitting, noisy, overloud, stentorian, thundering.

thunderstruck adjective *Charles was so thunderstruck that his voice was barely audible* ASTONISHED, amazed, astounded, staggered, surprised, startled, stunned, shocked, aghast, taken aback, dumbfounded, floored, blown away, dumbstruck, stupefied, dazed, speechless; *informal* flabbergasted.

thus adverb **1** *the studio handled production, thus cutting its costs* CONSEQUENTLY, as a consequence, in consequence, thereby, so, that being so, therefore, ergo, accordingly, hence, as a result, for that reason, ipso facto, because of that, on that account.

2 *all decent aristocrats act thus* LIKE THAT, in that way, so, like so. PHRASE: **thus far** *thus far, we've avoided any unanticipated expenditures* SO FAR, until now, up until now, up to now, up to this point, hitherto.

USAGE NOTE **thus**

There is never a need to expand the adverb **thus** to "thusly."

thwack noun *the plastic ruler made a loud thwack on the desk* SLAP, whack, smack, wallop.

▸ verb See THUMP verb sense 1.

thwart verb *their plans to attack the embassy were thwarted* FOIL, frustrate, stand in the way of, forestall, derail, dash; stop, check, block, stonewall, prevent, defeat, impede, hinder, obstruct; *informal* put a crimp in, put the kibosh on, scotch, scuttle, do for, stymie. ANTONYM facilitate.

THE RIGHT WORD

These verbs refer to the various ways in which we can outwit or overcome opposing forces. **Thwart** suggests using cleverness rather than force to bring about the defeat of an enemy or to block progress toward an objective (*thwart a rebellion; have one's goals thwarted by lack of education*). **Balk** also emphasizes setting up barriers (*a sudden reversal that balked their hopes for a speedy resolution*), but it is used more often as an intransitive verb meaning to stop at an obstacle and refuse to proceed (*he balked at appearing in front of the angry crowd*). To **baffle** is to cause defeat by bewildering or confusing (*the police were baffled by the lack of evidence*), while **foil** means to throw off course so as to discourage further effort (*her plan to arrive early was foiled by heavy traffic*). **Frustrate** implies rendering all attempts or efforts useless (*frustrated by the increasingly bad weather, they decided to work indoors*), while **inhibit** suggests forcing something into inaction (*to inhibit wage increases by raising corporate taxes*). Both *frustrate* and *inhibit* are used in a psychological context to suggest barriers that impede normal development or prevent the realization of natural desires (*he was both frustrated by her refusal to acknowledge his presence and inhibited by his own shyness*).

tic noun *a tick under his left eye* TWITCH, spasm, jerk, tremor; quirk.

tick noun **1** *the tick of his watch* TICKING, tick-tock, click, clicking, tap, tapping.

2 *put a tick against the item of your choice* CHECK MARK, check, stroke, mark.

▸ verb **1** *the clock ticks* CLICK, tock, tick-tock, tap.

2 *time is **ticking away*** PASS, elapse, go, continue, advance, wear on, roll on, fly, run out, vanish.

PHRASE: **tick off 1** *that really ticked me off* ANNOY, irritate, rile, rattle, anger, antagonize, make someone mad, get on someone's nerves, get to, get someone's back up. **2** *tick off a list* CHECK OFF; count off, cross off.

ticket noun *present your ticket at the gate* PASS, authorization, permit, token, coupon, voucher; transfer.

tickle noun *a tickle in her throat* TINGLE, itch, irritation.

▸ verb **1** *he tried to tickle her under the chin* STROKE, pet, tease, chuck.

2 *she found something that tickled her imagination* STIMULATE, interest, appeal to, arouse, titillate, excite.

PHRASE: **tickled pink** *the kids were tickled pink when we mentioned Disney World* DELIGHTED, thrilled, tickled to death, jumping for joy, high as a kite, pleased as punch, over the moon.

ticklish adjective *the issue has been made more ticklish since the factors of race and gender have entered the picture* DIFFICULT, problematic, tricky, touchy, delicate, sensitive, tender, awkward, prickly, thorny, tough; vexed, sticky.

tidbit noun **1** *a tidbit of information* MORSEL, piece, scrap, item, bit, nugget.

2 *tasty tidbits* DELICACY, dainty, snack, nibble, appetizer, hors d'oeuvre, goody, dipper, finger food, nibbly.

tide noun **1** *ships come up the river with the tide* TIDEWATER, ebb and flow, tidal flow.

2 *the tide of history* COURSE, movement, direction, trend, current, drift, run, turn, tendency, tenor. PHRASE: **tide someone over** *these canned goods should tide us over until the storm is over and the power is restored* SUSTAIN, keep someone going, keep someone afloat, keep someone's head above water, see someone through; keep the wolf from the door; help out, assist, aid.

tidings plural noun *literary what tidings do you bring us from across the wide ocean?* NEWS, information, intelligence, word, reports, dispatches, notification, communication, latest; *informal* info, scuttlebutt, lowdown, scoop.

tidy adjective **1** *a tidy room* NEAT, neat and tidy, orderly, well-ordered, in (good) order, well-kept, shipshape, in apple-pie order, immaculate, spick-and-span, uncluttered, straight, trim, spruce. ANTONYM messy.

2 *he's a very tidy person* NEAT, trim, spruce, dapper, well-groomed, organized, well-organized, methodical, meticulous; fastidious; *informal* natty. ANTONYMS scruffy, messy.

3 *informal* *a tidy sum* LARGE, sizable, considerable, substantial, generous, significant, appreciable, handsome, respectable, ample, decent, goodly. ANTONYMS small, paltry.

▸ verb 1 *I'd better* ***tidy up*** *the living room* PUT IN ORDER, clear up, sort out, straighten (up), clean up, spruce up.

2 *she* ***tidied herself up*** *in the bathroom* GROOM ONESELF, spruce oneself up, freshen oneself up, smarten oneself up; *informal* titivate oneself.

tie verb 1 *they tied Max to a chair* BIND, tie up, tether, hitch, strap, truss, fetter, rope, chain, make fast, moor, lash, attach, fasten, fix, secure, join, connect, link, couple.

2 *he bent to tie his shoelaces* DO UP, lace, knot.

3 *a bonus deal* ***tied to*** *a productivity agreement* LINK TO, connect to, couple to/with, relate to, join to, marry to; make conditional on, bind up with.

4 *they tied for second place* DRAW, be equal, be even, be neck and neck.

▸ noun 1 *he tightened the ties of his robe* LACE, string, cord, fastening, fastener.

2 *a collar and tie* NECKTIE, bow tie, string tie, bolo tie.

3 *family ties* BOND, connection, link, relationship, attachment, affiliation, allegiance, friendship; kinship, interdependence.

4 *there was a tie for first place* DRAW, dead heat, deadlock.

PHRASES: **tie someone down** *she was afraid of getting tied down* RESTRICT, restrain, limit, constrain, trammel, confine, cramp, hamper, handicap, hamstring, encumber, shackle, inhibit. **tie in** *how do these revisions tie in with the ultimate plan?* BE CONSISTENT, tally, agree, be in agreement, accord, concur, fit in, harmonize, be in tune, dovetail, correspond, match; square, jibe. **tie someone/something up** 1 *robbers tied her up and ransacked her home* BIND, bind hand and foot, truss (up), fetter, chain up. 2 *he is tied up in meetings all morning* OCCUPY, engage, keep busy. 3 *her capital is tied up in real estate* LOCK, bind up, trap; entangle.

tiebreaker noun *the fans are charged up for an inevitable tiebreaker* RUBBER MATCH, deciding game, deciding round, playoff; game-decider; overtime, OT, sudden death, sudden-death overtime.

tie-in noun 1 *a tie-in to the Expo theme* CONNECTION, link, association, correlation, relation, relationship; parallel, similarity.

2 *a movie tie-in* JOINT PROMOTION, spin-off.

tier noun 1 *tiers of empty seats* ROW, line; layer, level; balcony.

2 *the most senior tier of management* GRADE, gradation, echelon, rank, stratum, level, rung on the ladder.

tiff noun *informal* *her in-laws were always having a tiff* QUARREL, squabble, argument, disagreement, fight, falling-out, rift, difference of opinion, dispute, row, wrangle, altercation, contretemps, disputation, shouting match, blowup, duel; *informal* run-in, spat, scrap, set-to.

tight adjective 1 *a tight grip* FIRM, fast, secure, fixed, clenched. ANTONYM relaxed.

2 *the rope was tight* TAUT, rigid, stiff, tense, stretched, strained. ANTONYM slack.

3 *tight jeans* TIGHT-FITTING, close-fitting, form-fitting, narrow, figure-hugging, skintight; *informal* sprayed-on. ANTONYMS loose, baggy.

4 *a tight mass of fibers* COMPACT, compacted, compressed, dense, solid. ANTONYM loose.

5 *a tight space* SMALL, tiny, narrow, limited, restricted, confined, cramped, constricted, uncomfortable; *rare* incommodious. ANTONYMS roomy, generous.

6 *tight control over the family's finances* STRICT, rigorous, stringent, tough, rigid, firm, uncompromising. ANTONYM lax.

7 *a tight schedule* BUSY, rigorous, packed, nonstop. ANTONYM open.

8 *he's in a tight spot* DIFFICULT, tricky, delicate, awkward, problematic, worrying, precarious; *informal* sticky. ANTONYM problem-free.

9 *a tight piece of writing* SUCCINCT, concise, pithy, incisive, crisp, condensed, well structured, clean, to the point. ANTONYMS wordy, flowery.

10 *a tight race* CLOSE, even, evenly matched, well-matched; hard-fought, neck and neck. ANTONYM open.

11 *money is tight these days* LIMITED, restricted, in short supply, scarce, depleted, diminished, low, inadequate, insufficient. ANTONYMS plentiful, abundant.

12 *she is tight with the big movie stars* CLOSE, friendly, intimate, connected, close-knit, tight-knit, on good terms, buddy-buddy.

tighten verb 1 *she tightened the rope* PULL TAUT, tauten, pull tight, stretch, tense. ANTONYMS loosen, slacken.

2 *he tightened his lips* NARROW, constrict, contract, compress, screw up, pucker, purse, squinch up. ANTONYM relax.

3 *security in the area has been tightened* INCREASE, make stricter, toughen up, heighten, scale up. ANTONYM relax.

tight-fisted adjective *it hardly promotes your faith to be such a tightfisted Christian* CHEAP, miserly, parsimonious, niggardly, penny-pinching, cheeseparing, Scrooge-like, close; *informal* stingy, mingy, tight, mean; *formal* penurious. ANTONYM generous.

tight-lipped adjective *the company remains tight-lipped regarding the launch date* RETICENT, uncommunicative, unforthcoming, quiet, secretive, cagey, playing one's cards close to one's chest, close-mouthed, silent, taciturn; *informal* mum. ANTONYM forthcoming.

tightwad noun *informal* *her life as a tightwad had given her a handsome bank account and no one to share it with* MISER, cheapskate, penny-pincher, skinflint, Scrooge.

till[1] noun *she counted the money in the till* CASH REGISTER, cash drawer(s), cashbox, strongbox; checkout.

till[2] verb *he went back to tilling the land* CULTIVATE, work, farm, plow, dig, hoe, turn over, prepare.

till[3] preposition & conjunction 1 *he'll be in London till July* UNTIL, to, up to, through (to), up until, as late as.

2 *we didn't know about this till yesterday* BEFORE, prior to, previous to, up to, up until, earlier than.

USAGE NOTE till, until

Till is, like *until*, a bona fide preposition and conjunction. Though less formal than *until*, *till* is neither colloquial nor substandard. As Anthony Burgess put it, "In nonpoetic English we use 'till' and 'until' indifferently." (*A Mouthful of Air*; 1992.) It's especially common in British English—e.g.:

• "After the First World War, Hatay, named by Attaturk after the Hittites, fell into the hands of the French, who did not return it till 1939." (*Independent* [UK]; Apr. 1, 1995.)

• "He works from dawn till dusk, six days a week." (*Daily Telegraph* [UK]; Mar. 31, 1997.)

And it still occurs in American English—e.g.: "In medium skillet, sauté the garlic till golden. Add onion, wait till brown." (*Palm Beach Post*; Mar. 23, 1995.)

But the myth of the word's low standing persists. Some writers and editors mistakenly think that *till* deserves a bracketed *sic*—e.g.: " 'Trading in cotton futures was not practiced till [sic] after the close of the Civil War, spot cotton being quoted like other stocks in cents, halves, quarters, etc.' " (*School Science and Mathematics*; Apr. 1, 1997 [in which the *sic* appeared in the original source being quoted].)

If a form deserves a *sic*, it's the incorrect *'til*. Worse yet is *'till*, which is abominable—e.g.: "A month or two remain 'till [read *till*] you grab your dancing shoes, plus a crew of pals or that special date." (*Denver Post*; Mar. 21, 1997.) —**BG**

tilt verb *you'll have to tilt the sofa to fit it through the door* SLOPE, tip, lean, list, bank, slant, incline, pitch, cant, angle. PHRASE: **(at) full tilt** *our toboggans went down the icy slope at full tilt* (AT) FULL SPEED, at top speed, full bore, as fast as one's legs can carry one, at a gallop, helter-skelter, headlong, pell-mell, at breakneck speed, with great force, with full force; *informal* like crazy, like mad, hell-bent for leather, a mile a minute, like the wind, like a bat out of hell, like (greased) lightning, lickety-split, full blast, all out, with a vengeance; *literary* apace.

timber noun *some eighty acres of marketable timber | expertly milled timbers* WOOD, lumber, logs; trees, sawlogs; hardwood, softwood; beam, spar, plank, batten, lath, board, joist, rafter.

timbre noun *the timbre of the reeds* TONE, sound, sound quality, voice, voice quality, color, tone color, tonality, resonance.

time noun **1** *what time is it?* HOUR; *dated* o'clock.

2 *late at night was the best time to leave* MOMENT, point, point in time, occasion, hour, minute, second, instant, juncture, stage.

3 *he worked there for a time* WHILE, spell, stretch, stint, span, season, interval, period, period of time, length of time, duration, phase, stage, term, patch.

4 *the time of the dinosaurs* ERA, age, epoch, period, years, days; generation, date.

5 *I've known a lot of cats in my time* LIFETIME, life, life span, days, time on earth, existence.

6 *he had been a professional actor in his time* HEYDAY, day, best days, best years, glory days, prime, peak, Golden Age.

7 **(the times)** *the times are a-changing* CONDITIONS, circumstances; life, the state of affairs, the way of the world.

8 *tunes in waltz time* RHYTHM, tempo, beat; meter, measure, pattern.

▸ verb **1** *the events were timed perfectly* SCHEDULE, set, set up, arrange, organize, coordinate, fix, line up, slot in, prearrange, timetable, plan; slate.

2 *we timed ourselves to prepare for the race* MEASURE, clock, record one's time.

PHRASES: **ahead of time** *get to the airport ahead of time* EARLY, in good time, with time to spare, in advance. **ahead of one's/its time** *Leonardo was ahead of his time in almost all endeavors | a laser procedure that is ahead of its time* REVOLUTIONARY, avant-garde, futuristic, innovatory, innovative, trailblazing, pioneering, groundbreaking, advanced, cutting edge. **all the time** *their bleeping dog barks all the time* CONSTANTLY, the entire time, around/round the clock, day and night, night and day, [morning, noon, and night], [day in, day out], at all times, always, nonstop, without a break, ceaselessly, endlessly, unfailingly, incessantly, perpetually, permanently, interminably, continuously, continually, eternally, unremittingly, remorselessly, relentlessly, unrelentingly; *informal* 24-7; *archaic* without surcease. **at one time** *she was a nurse at one time* FORMERLY, previously, once, in the past, at one point, once upon a time, time was when, one fine day, in days/times gone by, in times past, in the (good) old days, long ago, back in the day; *literary* in days/times of yore; *archaic* erstwhile, whilom. **at the same time** **1** *they arrived at the same time* SIMULTANEOUSLY, at the same instant, at the same moment, together, all together, as a group, at once, at one and the same time; in unison, in concert, in chorus, in synchrony, as one, in tandem. **2** *Curt seems like a nice guy—at the same time I'm not sure I would trust him* NONETHELESS, even so, however, but, still, yet, though, on the other hand; in spite of that, despite that, be that as it may, for all that, that said; notwithstanding, regardless, anyway, anyhow, still and all. **at times** *she is at times cruel and ruthless* OCCASIONALLY, sometimes, from time to time, now and then, every so often, once in a while, on occasion, off and on, at intervals, periodically, sporadically. **behind the times** *the older I get, the less I think my parents are behind the times* OLD-FASHIONED, out of date, outmoded, outdated, dated, old, passé; *informal* square, not with it, old-school, horse-and-buggy, fusty. **for the time being** *we're living in the cottage for the time being* FOR NOW, for the moment, for the present, in the interim, for the nonce, in/for the meantime, in the meanwhile, for a short time, briefly; temporarily, provisionally, pro tem. **from time to time** See AT TIMES (above). **in no time** *I'll be dressed in no time* (VERY) SOON, in a second, in an instant, in a minute, in a moment, in a trice, in a flash, shortly, any second, any minute (now), momentarily; *informal* in a jiffy, in a sec, in two shakes of a lamb's tail, in a snap; *formal* directly. **in good time** *don't worry, Father will get here in good time* PUNCTUALLY, promptly, on time, early, with time to spare, ahead of time, ahead of schedule. **in time** **1** *I came back in time for the party* EARLY ENOUGH, in good time, punctually, on time, not too late, with time to spare, on schedule. **2** *in time, she'll forgot about it* EVENTUALLY, in the end, in due course, by and by, finally, after a while; one day, some day, sometime, sooner or later. **many a time** *many a time they had gone to bed hungry* FREQUENTLY, regularly, often, very often, all the time, habitually, customarily, routinely; again and again, time and again, over and over again, repeatedly, recurrently, continually, oftentimes; *literary* oft, ofttimes. **on time** *Rupert never gets to work on time* PUNCTUALLY, in good time, to/on schedule, when expected, on the dot. **time after time** *the camera produces excellent results time after time* REPEATEDLY, frequently, often, again and again, over and over (again), time and (time) again, many times, many a time; persistently, recurrently, constantly, continually, oftentimes; *literary* oft, ofttimes.

time-consuming adjective *Henry Ford carefully assessed each time-consuming task* LABORIOUS, tedious, drawn-out, prolonged, protracted, lengthy, labor-intensive, time-wasting.

time-honored adjective *our time-honored practice of slow brewing* TRADITIONAL, established, long-established, long-standing, long-lived, time-tested, age-old, enduring, lasting, tried and tested, tried and true.

timeless adjective *the timeless appeal of a well-crafted rocking chair* LASTING, enduring, classic, ageless, permanent, perennial, abiding, unfailing, unchanging, unvarying, never-changing, changeless, unfading, unending, undying, immortal, eternal, everlasting, immutable. ANTONYM ephemeral.

timely adjective *his refresher course on giving CPR proved to be very timely* OPPORTUNE, well-timed, at the right time, convenient, appropriate, expedient, seasonable, felicitous. See note at OPPORTUNE.

THE RIGHT WORD

Some people seem to have a knack for doing or saying the right thing at the right time. A **timely** act or remark is one that comes at a moment when it is of genuine value or service (*a timely interruption*), while an **opportune** one comes in the nick of time, as if by accident, and exactly meets the needs of the occasion (*a storm came up at an opportune moment, squelching enthusiasm for the fight*). **Seasonable** applies to whatever is suited to the season of the year or fits in with the needs of the moment or the character of the occasion (*seasonable weather; a seasonable menu for a cold winter day*). **Propitious** means presenting favorable conditions. In other words, while a warm day in December might not be *seasonable*, it might very well be *propitious* for the sailor setting off on a round-the-world cruise.

time out noun *let's have some time out before we head back to the cabins* PAUSE, break, rest; stoppage, intermission, recess.

timetable noun *a bus timetable | I have a very full timetable* SCHEDULE, program, agenda, calendar; list, itinerary, timeline.

timeworn adjective **1** *the carpet was old and timeworn* WORN OUT, worn, well-worn, old, threadbare, moth-eaten, tattered, battered, dog-eared, well-used, shabby, having seen better days, tatty, dilapidated; *informal* raggedy. ANTONYMS new, pristine.

2 *timeworn faces* OLD, aged, weathered, lined, wrinkled, hoary, bedraggled. ANTONYMS youthful, fresh.

3 *a timeworn aphorism* HACKNEYED, trite, banal, platitudinous, clichéd, stock, conventional, unoriginal, overused, overworked, tired, stale; antiquated, old hat. ANTONYMS imaginative, fresh.

timid adjective *I was too timid to ask for what I wanted* APPREHENSIVE, fearful, easily frightened, afraid, fainthearted, timorous, nervous, scared, frightened, cowardly, pusillanimous, spineless; shy, diffident, self-effacing; *informal* wimpish, wimpy, yellow, chicken, mousy, gutless, sissy, lily-livered, candy-assed, weak-kneed. ANTONYM bold.

timorous adjective See TIMID.

timpani plural noun See note below.

USAGE NOTE **timpani, tympani**

In modern print sources, the spelling *timpani* is more common than *tympani* by a 5-to-1 ratio. The latter ought to be rejected as a variant spelling. British English writers solve the problem by using the term *kettledrum*. (Another synonym, rarely used, is *timbal*.)

The word *timpani*—though borrowed into English as the plural form of the Italian singular *timpano*—has become interchangeably singular or plural. Most commonly the word is plural—e.g.: "The Jefferson Symphony Orchestra has been awarded a $14,110 grant by the Bonfils-Stanton Foundation for a set of four new timpani." (*Rocky Mountain News* [Denver]; Oct. 3, 1996.) But it's often singular as well. Even professional musicians commonly refer to a *timpani*, not a *timpano*—e.g.: "[It is an opera] house where Mozart's double-bass or timpani is heard as clearly as the soprano." (*New York Times*; July 11, 1994.)

The phrase *timpani drum* is a redundancy—e.g.:

• "The pit . . . is made up of 14 people on xylophones, marimbas, chimes, gongs, tympani drums [read *timpani* or *kettledrums*], glockenspiels, bells, triangles, tambourines and more." (*Boston Globe*; Aug. 17, 1994.)

• "A timpani drum [read *timpani* or *kettledrum*], its head torn, . . . was serving as a trash can." (*Florida Times-Union*; Aug. 28, 1996.) **—BG**

tin noun *a tin of butter cookies* CONTAINER, metal container, box, can, tin can.

tincture noun **1** *tincture of iodine* SOLUTION, suspension, infusion, elixir.

2 *a tincture of bitterness.* See TINGE noun sense 2.

tinderbox noun *the issue became a political tinderbox* POWDER KEG, time bomb, ticking bomb, explosive situation, flash point, minefield, disaster waiting to happen, can of worms.

tinge verb **1** *a mass of white blossom tinged with pink* TINT, color, stain, shade, wash.

2 *his optimism is tinged with realism* INFLUENCE, affect, touch, flavor, color, modify; taint.

▸ noun **1** *the light had a blue tinge to it* TINT, color, shade, tone, hue.

2 *a tinge of cynicism* TRACE, note, touch, suggestion, hint, bit, scintilla, savor, flavor, element, modicum, streak, vein, suspicion, soupçon, tincture.

tingle verb *her flesh still tingled from the shock* PRICKLE, sting; tremble, quiver, shiver.

▸ noun *she felt a tingle of anticipation* THRILL, buzz, quiver, shiver, tingling, sting, stinging; tremor.

tinker verb *a mechanic was **tinkering with** the engine* FIDDLE WITH, adjust, fix, try to mend, play about with, fool with, futz with; tamper with, interfere with, mess about with, meddle with.

tinkle verb **1** *the bell tinkled* RING, jingle, jangle, chime, peal, ding, ping.

2 *cool water tinkled in the stone fountain* SPLASH, purl, babble, burble; *literary* plash.

▸ noun *the tinkle of sleigh bells* RING, chime, ding, ping, jingle, jangle, tintinnabulation.

tinnitus noun See note below.

WORD NOTE **tinnitus**

A disease you probably already have, whose environmental causes are not limited to: loud tinny music, the subway, telephones, construction sites, headphones, other people yelling; in short, modern life, plus being older than 12 or so. A nasty variety is *recruitment,* in which ordinary sound levels seem louder and louder and more distorted in a vicious feedback loop, ending of course in misery and despair. **—SM**

tinny adjective *I don't like the wind chimes that make a tinny sound* JANGLY, jangling, jingling, jingly; thin, metallic.

tinsel noun *the tinsel of Hollywood* OSTENTATION, showiness, show, glitter, flamboyance, gaudiness; attractiveness, glamour; *informal* flashiness, ritz, glitz, garishness, razzle-dazzle, razzmatazz, eye candy.

tint noun **1** *the sky was taking on an apricot tint* SHADE, color, tone, hue, pigmentation, tinge, cast, tincture, flush, blush, wash.

2 *a hair tint* DYE, coloring, rinse, highlights, lowlights.

tiny adjective *what are these tiny red insects on my houseplants?* MINUTE, minuscule, microscopic, nanoscale, infinitesimal, very small, little, mini, diminutive, miniature, scaled down, baby, toy, dwarf, pygmy, peewee, Lilliputian; *informal* teeny, teeny-weeny, teensy, teensy-weensy, itty-bitty, itsy-bitsy, eensy, eensy-weensy, little-bitty; bite-sized, pint-sized; *chiefly Scottish* wee. See note at SMALL. ANTONYM huge.

tip[1] noun *the swords we use in the play have blunt tips | the tip of the iceberg* POINT, end, extremity, head, sharp end, spike, prong, tine, nib; top, summit, apex, cusp, crown, crest, pinnacle, vertex.

tip[2] verb **1** *the boat tipped over* OVERTURN, turn over, topple (over), fall (over); keel over, capsize, flip, turn turtle; *Nautical* pitchpole.

2 *a whale could tip over a small boat* UPSET, overturn, topple over, turn over, knock over, push over, upend, capsize, roll, flip.

3 *the car tipped to one side* LEAN, tilt, list, slope, bank, slant, incline, pitch, cant, heel, careen.

tip[3] noun **1** *a generous tip* GRATUITY, baksheesh; present, gift, reward.

2 *useful tips* PIECE OF ADVICE, suggestion, word of advice, pointer, recommendation; clue, hint, steer, tip-off; word to the wise.

tip-off noun *police have received an anonymous tip-off* PIECE OF INFORMATION, warning, lead, forewarning; hint, clue; advice, information, notification.

tipsy adjective *you're too tipsy to be driving home* MERRY, half-drunk, lightheaded, woozy, mellow, slightly drunk, lubricated. See note at DRUNK. ANTONYM sober.

tirade noun *both attorneys were stunned when the judge launched into a tirade* DIATRIBE, harangue, rant, onslaught, attack, polemic, denunciation, broadside, fulmination, condemnation, censure, invective, criticism, tongue-lashing; blast; lecture; *literary* philippic.

tire verb **1** *he began to tire as the ascent grew steeper* WEAKEN, grow weak, flag, wilt, droop; deteriorate.

2 *the journey had tired her* FATIGUE, tire out, exhaust, wear out, drain, weary, frazzle, overtire, enervate; *informal* knock out, do in, wear to a frazzle.

3 *we **are tired of** your difficult behavior* WEARY OF, get fed up with, get sick of, get bored with, get impatient with; *informal* have had it up to here with, have had enough of.

tired adjective **1** *you're just tired from traveling* EXHAUSTED, worn out, weary, fatigued, dog-tired, dead beat, bone-tired, ready to drop, drained, zonked, wasted, enervated, jaded; *informal* done in, bushed, whipped, bagged, knocked out, wiped out, pooped, tuckered out. ANTONYMS energetic, wide awake, fresh.

2 *are you **tired of** having him here?* FED UP WITH, weary of, bored with/by, sick (to death) of; *informal* up to here with.

3 *tired jokes* HACKNEYED, overused, overworked, worn out, stale, clichéd, hoary, stock, stereotyped, predictable, unimaginative, unoriginal, uninspired, dull, boring, routine; *informal* old hat, corny. ANTONYMS lively, fresh.

WORD NOTE **tired**

Tired is the perfect example of how language can illuminate the murkier corners of the psyche, and raise delicate questions of etiquette, sensibility, and intention. Of course, the word has many obvious, simple, and appropriate usages. *After running the marathon and swimming the English Channel, I felt a bit tired.* But in my opinion, it should never be used to convey one's sympathy with someone else's overtaxed physical or psychological state. *Oh you poor thing, you look so terribly tired!* It is less likely to make the *tired* person feel like the recipient of tender solicitude than like the victim of some deforming and previously undiagnosed wasting illness. Told we look tired, we are less apt to feel that our hard work is being appreciated than that we should immediately run to the mirror to check out the damage—and to wonder, with good reason, if the person whose sympathies we have aroused was actually expressing some sort of covert hostility. **—FP**

THE RIGHT WORD

Tired is what you are after you've cleaned the house, spent two hours reading a dull report, or trained for a marathon; it means that you are drained of your strength and energy, without giving any indication of degree. **Weary**, on the other hand, is how you feel after you've had to interrupt your dinner five or six times to answer the phone. It implies not only a depletion of energy but also the vexation that accompanies having to put up with something that is, or has become, disagreeable. **Exhausted** means that you are totally drained of strength and energy, a condition that may even be irreversible (*exhausted by battling a terminal disease*). **Fatigued** is a more precise word than either *tired* or *weary*; it implies a loss of energy through strain, illness, or overwork to the point where rest or sleep is essential (*fatigued after working a 24-hour shift*). **Tuckered** is an informal word that comes close in meaning to *fatigued* or *exhausted*, but often carries the suggestion of loss of breath (*tuckered out after running up six flights of stairs*).

tiredness noun *her eyes were heavy with tiredness* FATIGUE, weariness, exhaustion, burnout, enervation, inertia; sleepiness, drowsiness, somnolence. ANTONYM energy.

tireless adjective *their tireless efforts to reclaim the Hudson have given us a remarkably cleaner river* INDEFATIGABLE, energetic, vigorous, industrious, hard-working, determined, enthusiastic, keen, zealous, spirited, dynamic, dogged, tenacious, persevering, untiring, unwearying, unremitting, unflagging, indomitable. ANTONYM lazy.

tiresome adjective *the word is that she just couldn't stand one more day of his tiresome obsession with computer games* BORING, dull, tedious, insipid, wearisome, wearing, uninteresting, uneventful, humdrum, monotonous, mind-numbing; annoying, irritating, trying, irksome, vexing, troublesome, bothersome, nettlesome; *informal* aggravating, pesky. ANTONYMS interesting, pleasant.

tiring adjective *it was very tiring work* EXHAUSTING, wearying, taxing, fatiguing, wearing, enervating, draining; hard, heavy, arduous, strenuous, onerous, uphill, demanding, grueling; *informal* murderous.

tissue noun **1** *living tissue* MATTER, material, substance; flesh.

2 *a box of tissues* FACIAL TISSUE; *trademark* Kleenex.

titanic adjective *he told a titanic lie to his parole officer* HUGE, great, enormous, gigantic, massive, colossal, monumental, mammoth, immense, tremendous, mighty, stupendous, prodigious, gargantuan, Herculean; *informal* humongous, ginormous, whopping.

tit for tat noun *if they want to play dirty, we can give them tit for tat* RETALIATION, reprisal, counterattack, comeback; revenge; vengeance, retribution, an eye for an eye, a tooth for a tooth, payback; *informal* a taste of someone's own medicine; *Latin* lex talionis, quid pro quo.

titillate verb *the dancers titillated the audience* AROUSE, excite, tantalize, stimulate, stir, thrill, interest, attract, fascinate; *informal* turn on. ANTONYM bore.

titillating adjective *a titillating rendition of "Baby, It's Cold Outside"* AROUSING, exciting, stimulating, sexy, thrilling, provocative, tantalizing, interesting, fascinating; suggestive, salacious, erotic. ANTONYM boring.

titivate verb *informal she titivated herself in front of the hall mirror* GROOM, smarten (up), spruce up, freshen up, preen, primp, tidy, arrange, gussy up, doll up.

title noun **1** *the title of the work* NAME, heading, legend, label, caption, inscription.

2 *the company publishes 400 titles a year* PUBLICATION, work, book, newspaper, paper, magazine, periodical.

3 *the title of governor general* DESIGNATION, name, form of address, honorific; epithet, rank, office, position, job title; *informal* moniker, handle, tag; *formal* appellation, denomination; sobriquet.

4 *an Olympic title* CHAMPIONSHIP, crown, first place; laurels, palm.

5 *the landlord is obliged to prove his* ***title to*** *the land* OWNERSHIP OF, proprietorship of, possession of, holding of, freehold of, entitlement to, right to, claim to.

▸ verb *a paper titled "Immigration Today"* CALL, entitle, name, dub, designate, style, term; *formal* denominate.

titmouse noun See note below.

USAGE NOTE **titmouse**

Titmouse (= a small songbird) is also known as a *tit*, but only serious birdwatchers use the shortened form (because of the vulgar homonym). The vastly predominant plural (and the one recognized by dictionaries) is *titmice*, not *titmouses*—e.g.: "In recent days chickadees, titmice, robins, cardinals, and white-breasted nuthatches seemed to celebrate the return of blue skies and sunshine." (*Pittsburgh Post-Gazette*; Mar. 16, 2003.) The form *titmouses*, though perhaps logical (since it's not a mouse at all), occurs so infrequently as to be ill-advised—e.g.: "Other visitors to the Gibbs' yard Monday were cardinals, white-throated sparrows, . . . titmouses [read *titmice*], chickadees, juncos, Carolina wrens, bluebirds and goldfinches." (*Augusta Chronicle* [GA]; Jan. 24, 2003.) **—BG**

titter verb & noun *she caused a few titters | the people at out table started to titter* GIGGLE, snicker, twitter, tee-hee, chuckle, laugh, chortle.

tittle-tattle noun See GOSSIP.

titular adjective **1** *the titular head of a university* NOMINAL, in title only, in name only, ceremonial, honorary, so-called; token, puppet.

2 *the book's titular hero* EPONYMOUS, identifying.

tizzy noun *informal what's put Glenn in such a tizzy?* FRENZY, state of anxiety, state of agitation, nervous state, panic, fret, hysteria; *informal* flap, state, sweat.

toady noun *a conniving little toady* SYCOPHANT, brownnoser, lickspittle, flatterer, flunky, lackey, trained seal, doormat, stooge, cringer; *informal* bootlicker, suck-up, yes-man; *vulgar slang* kiss-ass, ass-kisser.

▸ verb *she imagined him* ***toadying to*** *his rich clients* GROVEL TO, ingratiate oneself with, be obsequious to, kowtow to, pander to, crawl to, truckle to, bow and scrape to, curry favor with, make up to, fawn on/over, slaver over, flatter, adulate, suck up to, lick the boots of, butter up.

toast noun **1** *he raised his glass in a toast* TRIBUTE, salute, salutation; *archaic* pledge.

2 *he was the toast of Toledo* DARLING, favorite, pet, heroine, hero; talk; fair-haired boy/girl.

▸ verb **1** *she toasted her hands in front of the fire* WARM, warm up, heat, heat up.

2 *we toasted the couple with champagne* DRINK (TO) THE HEALTH OF, drink to, salute, honor, pay tribute to.

today adverb **1** *the work must be finished today* THIS DAY, this very day, this morning, this afternoon, this evening.

2 *the complex tasks demanded of computers today* NOWADAYS, these days, at the present time, in these times, in this day and age, now, currently, at the moment, at present, at this moment in time; in the present climate, presently.

toddle verb **1** *the child toddled toward him* TOTTER, teeter, wobble, falter, waddle, stumble.

2 *informal I toddled down to the quay* AMBLE, wander, meander, stroll, saunter; *informal* mosey, toodle, tootle, putter.

toddler noun *a play center for toddlers* SMALL CHILD, infant, tot, preschooler; *informal* moppet, munchkin, tyke, rug rat, young 'un.

to-do noun *informal the to-do in the street finally prompted a call to the police* COMMOTION, fuss, ado, excitement, agitation, stir, palaver, confusion, disturbance, brouhaha, fracas, uproar, furor, tempest in a teapot, much ado about nothing; *informal* hoo-ha, ballyhoo, hullabaloo; *Brit. informal* kerfuffle.

toehold noun *they soon gained a toehold in the cosmetics industry* FOOTHOLD, foot in the door, jumping-off point; beachhead.

together adverb **1** *friends who work together* WITH EACH OTHER, in conjunction, jointly, in cooperation, in collaboration, in partnership, in combination, in league, in tandem, side by side, hand in hand, shoulder to shoulder, cheek by jowl; in collusion, hand in glove; *informal* in cahoots. ANTONYM separately.

2 *they both spoke together* SIMULTANEOUSLY, at the same time, at one and the same time, at once, all together, as a group, in unison, in concert, in chorus, as one, with one accord. ANTONYM separately.

▸ adjective *informal a very together young woman.* See LEVELHEADED.

togetherness noun *the camp inspired togetherness* COHESION, cohesiveness, harmony, fellowship, camaraderie, close bond(s).

toil verb **1** *she toiled all night* WORK HARD, labor, exert oneself, slave (away), grind away, strive, work one's fingers to the bone, put one's nose to the grindstone; *informal* slog away, plug away, beaver away, work one's butt off, sweat blood; *literary* travail; *archaic* drudge, moil. See note at LABOR. ANTONYMS rest, relax.

2 *she began to toil up the cliff path* STRUGGLE, trudge, tramp, tromp, traipse, slog, plod, trek, drag oneself; *informal* schlep.

▸ noun *a life of toil* HARD WORK, labor, exertion, slaving, drudgery, effort, industry, [blood, sweat, and tears]; slogging, elbow grease; *literary* travail; *archaic* moil.

toilet noun *he left to use the toilet.* See BATHROOM.

toke noun & verb *informal have another toke, man | if you ain't gonna toke it, pass it on* DRAG, puff, smoke.

token noun **1** *a token of our appreciation* SYMBOL, sign, emblem, badge, representation, indication, mark, manifestation, expression, pledge, demonstration, recognition; evidence, proof. See note at SIGN.

2 *he kept the menu as a token of their wedding anniversary* MEMENTO, souvenir, keepsake, reminder, remembrance, memorial. See note at EMBLEM.

▸ adjective *token resistance* SYMBOLIC, emblematic; perfunctory, slight, nominal, minimal, minor, mild, superficial, inconsequential.

tolerable adjective **1** *a tolerable noise level* BEARABLE, endurable, supportable, acceptable. ANTONYM intolerable.

2 *he had a tolerable voice* FAIRLY GOOD, passable, adequate, all right, acceptable, satisfactory, not (too) bad, average, fair; mediocre, middling, ordinary, indifferent, unremarkable, unexceptional; *informal* OK, so-so, 'comme ci, comme ça,' nothing to write home about, no great shakes. ANTONYMS unacceptable, exceptional.

tolerance noun **1** *an attitude of tolerance toward other people* ACCEPTANCE, toleration; open-mindedness, broad-mindedness, forbearance, liberality, liberalism; patience, charity, indulgence, understanding.

2 *she has a low* ***tolerance to*** *alcohol* ENDURANCE OF, RESISTANCE TO, resilience to, resistance to, immunity to.

WORD NOTE **tolerance**

The various usages of this word promise, perhaps falsely, to reveal some hidden truth about what has become its most common use—that is, the freedom from racial and ethnic prejudice, the willingness to accept the differences between ourselves and our neighbors. How does this relate to the meaning that conveys endurance or forbearance *(His tolerance for pain—or for large quantities of the experimental drug—was impressive)* or the sense, employed in architecture and engineering, of allowable deviance from a standard? I've also heard the word used, informally, as a measure of physical space, most often narrow. *The tolerance between the car and the walls of the alley was minuscule.* Is this a helpful reminder that *tolerance* (in the sense of open-mindedness) may require a certain amount of flinty endurance, that it is unusual, and that it has something to do with how much room we have, with the space we are obliged to share with the neighbor whose differences we must learn to tolerate? **—FP**

tolerant adjective *a tolerant attitude toward other religions* OPEN-MINDED, forbearing, broad-minded, liberal, unprejudiced, unbiased; patient, long-suffering, understanding, forgiving, charitable, lenient, indulgent, permissive, easygoing, lax; *informal* laid-back. ANTONYM intolerant.

tolerate verb **1** *a regime unwilling to tolerate dissent* ALLOW, permit, condone, accept, swallow, countenance; *formal* brook; *archaic* suffer.

2 *he couldn't tolerate her mood swings any longer* ENDURE, put up with, bear, take, stand, support, stomach, deal with; abide.

toleration noun *her father demonstrated little toleration where her boyfriends were concerned* ACCEPTANCE, tolerance, endurance; forbearance, sufferance, liberality, open-mindedness, broad-mindedness, liberalism; patience, charity, indulgence, understanding.

toll[1] noun **1** *a highway toll* CHARGE, fee, payment, levy, tariff, tax.

2 *the toll of dead and injured* NUMBER, count, tally, total, sum total, grand total, sum; record, list.

3 *the toll on the environment has been high* ADVERSE EFFECT(S), detriment, harm, damage, injury, impact, hurt; cost, price, loss, disadvantage, suffering, penalty.

toll[2] verb *I heard the bell toll* RING (OUT), chime, strike, peal; sound, ding, dong, clang, bong, resound, reverberate; *literary* knell.

tomb noun *the tomb of old Mr. Momphreys* BURIAL CHAMBER, sepulcher, mausoleum, vault, crypt, catacomb; last/final resting place, grave, barrow, burial mound; *historical* charnel house.

tombstone noun *the writing on the tombstone* GRAVESTONE, headstone, stone; memorial, monument.

tome noun *he expects us to read this tome by Monday* VOLUME, book, work, opus, publication, title.

tomfoolery noun *Mrs. Marks had no patience for tomfoolery* SILLINESS, fooling around, clowning, shenanigans, capers, antics, pranks, tricks, buffoonery, skylarking, nonsense, horseplay, monkey business, mischief, foolishness, foolery, fandango.

tone noun **1** *the tone of the tuba* TIMBRE, sound, sound quality, voice, voice quality, color, tonality.

2 *the somewhat impatient tone of his letter* MOOD, air, spirit, feel, sound, flavor, note, attitude, character, nature, manner, temper; tenor, vein, drift, gist.

3 *a dial tone* NOTE, signal, beep, bleep.

4 *tones of burgundy and firebrick red* SHADE, color, hue, tint, tinge. PHRASE: **tone down** *the pastels in the upholstery will help to tone down the color scheme* SOFTEN, lighten, mute, subdue, mellow; MODERATE, modify, modulate, mitigate, temper, dampen.

tongue noun **1** *a foreign tongue* LANGUAGE, dialect, patois, vernacular, mother tongue, native tongue, heritage language, lingua franca; *informal* lingo.

2 *her sharp tongue* WAY/MANNER OF SPEAKING, speech, choice of words, parlance.

tongue-tied adjective *he was tongue-tied with strangers* LOST FOR WORDS, speechless, unable to get a word out, struck dumb, dumbstruck; mute, dumb, silent; *informal* mum. ANTONYM loquacious.

tonic noun **1** *ginseng can be used as a natural tonic* STIMULANT, restorative, refresher, medicine; *informal* pick-me-up; *Medicine* analeptic.

2 *we found the change of scene a tonic* STIMULANT, boost, fillip; *informal* shot in the arm, pick-me-up.

tony adjective *a tony young man in his designer duds* STYLISH, fashionable, high-class, uptown, posh; salubrious.

too adverb **1** *invasion would be too risky* EXCESSIVELY, overly, over, unduly, immoderately, inordinately, unreasonably, extremely, exorbitantly, very; *informal* too-too.

2 *he was unhappy, too, you know* ALSO, as well, in addition, additionally, into the bargain, besides, furthermore, moreover, on top of that, to boot, likewise.

tool noun **1** *garden tools* IMPLEMENT, utensil, instrument, device, apparatus, gadget, appliance, machine, contrivance, contraption; *informal* gizmo.

2 *the beautiful Estella is Miss Havisham's tool* PUPPET, pawn, creature, cat's paw; minion, lackey, instrument, organ; *informal* stooge.

▸ verb *tool leather into a saddle* WORK, fashion, shape, cut; ornament, embellish, decorate, chase.

THE RIGHT WORD

A wrench is a **tool**, meaning that it is a device held in and manipulated by the hand and used by a mechanic, plumber, carpenter, or other laborer to work, shape, move, or transform material (*he couldn't fix the drawer without the right tools*). An **implement** is a broader term referring to any tool or mechanical device used for a particular purpose (*agricultural implements*). A washing machine is an **appliance**, which refers to a mechanical or power-driven device, especially for household use (*the newly-married couple went shopping for appliances*). A **utensil** is a hand-held implement for domestic use (*eating utensils*), while an **instrument** is used for scientific or artistic purposes (*musical instrument; surgical instrument*). **Apparatus** refers to a collection of distinct instruments, tools, or other devices that are used in connection or combination with one another for a certain purpose (*the gym was open, but the exercise apparatus had not been set up*).

toot verb *on the count of three, toot the whistles* BLOW, sound. PHRASE: **toot one's own horn** *I want to tell you about Roberto, because he's never one to toot his own horn* BOAST, brag, sing one's own praises, show off, congratulate oneself.

tooth noun *the teeth of an extinct fish* FANG, tusk, molar, incisor; *Zoology* denticle; *informal* pearly white; **(teeth)** *informal* choppers.

toothsome adjective *a toothsome lemon tart* TASTY, delicious, luscious, mouthwatering, delectable, succulent; tempting, appetizing, inviting; *informal* scrumptious, yummy, nummy, finger-licking, melt-in-your-mouth, lip-smacking.

top noun **1** *the top of the cliff* SUMMIT, peak, pinnacle, crest, crown, brow, head, tip, apex, vertex. ANTONYMS bottom, base.

2 *the top of the table* UPPER PART, upper surface, upper layer.

3 *the carrots' green tops* LEAVES, shoots, stem, stalk. ANTONYMS root, tuber.

4 *the top of the coffee jar* LID, cap, cover, stopper, cork.

5 *a short-sleeved top* SHIRT, jersey, sweatshirt, sweater, pullover, vest; T-shirt, tank top; blouse. See table at SHIRT.

6 *by 1981 he was at the top of his profession* HIGH POINT, height, peak, pinnacle, zenith, acme, culmination, climax, prime. ANTONYM low point.

▸ adjective **1** *the top floor* HIGHEST, topmost, uppermost. ANTONYMS bottom, lowest.

2 *the world's top scientists* FOREMOST, leading, principal, preeminent, greatest, best, finest, elite; *informal* top-notch, number one, blue-ribbon, blue-chip.

3 *the organization's top management* UPPER, chief, principal, main, leading, highest, highest-ranking, ruling, commanding, most powerful, most important.

4 *a top Paris hotel* PRIME, excellent, superb, superior, choice, select, top-quality, top-grade, first-rate, first-class, grade A, best, finest, premier, superlative, second to none, nonpareil; *informal* A1, top-notch, blue-ribbon, blue-chip, number one. ANTONYMS mediocre, inferior.

5 *they are traveling at top speed* MAXIMUM, maximal, greatest, utmost. ANTONYMS lowest, minimum.

▸ verb **1** *sales are expected to top $1.3 billion* EXCEED, surpass, go beyond, better, best, beat, outstrip, outdo, outshine, eclipse, go one better than, cap.

2 *their debut CD is currently topping the charts* LEAD, head, be at the top of.

3 *chocolate mousse topped with whipped cream* COVER, cap, coat, smother; finish, garnish.

PHRASES: **over the top** *the lavish dessert buffet after that meal was simply over the top* EXCESSIVE, immoderate, inordinate, extreme, exaggerated, extravagant, overblown, too much, unreasonable, hyperbolic, disproportionate, undue, unwarranted, uncalled for, unnecessary, going too far. **top up** *remember to top up your gas tank before heading back to Houston* FILL, refill, refresh, freshen, replenish, recharge, resupply; supplement, add to, augment.

topic noun *today's topic is skin care* SUBJECT, subject matter, theme, issue, matter, point, talking point, question, concern, argument, thesis, text, keynote.

topical adjective *let's stick to topical issues* CURRENT, up-to-date, up-to-the-minute, contemporary, recent, relevant; newsworthy, in the news. ANTONYM out-of-date.

topless adjective *topless sunbathers* HALF-NAKED, bare-breasted, bare-chested, semi-nude, shirtless.

topmost adjective See UPPERMOST sense 1.

top-notch adjective *informal Rebecca is one of our top-notch salespeople* FIRST-CLASS, first-rate, top-quality, five-star; superior, prime, premier, premium, grade A, blue-chip, blue-ribbon, superlative, best, finest, select, exclusive, excellent, superb, outstanding, unbeatable, splendid, of the highest order, top-of-the-line, top-flight, top-grade; *informal* bang-up, A1.

topple verb **1** *she* ***toppled over*** FALL, fall over, tumble, overturn, tip over, keel over, collapse; lose one's balance.

2 *protesters toppled a huge statue* KNOCK OVER, upset, push over, tip over, fell, upend.

3 *a plot to topple the government* OVERTHROW, oust, unseat, overturn, bring down, defeat, get rid of, dislodge, eject.

topsy-turvy adjective **1** *a topsy-turvy flag* UPSIDE DOWN, wrong side up, inverted, reversed, upset; *informal* bass-ackward, ass-backward. ANTONYM right side up.

2 *everything in the apartment was topsy-turvy* IN DISARRAY, in a mess, in a muddle, in disorder, disordered, jumbled, in chaos, chaotic, disorganized, awry, upside down, at sixes and sevens; *informal* every which way, higgledy-piggledy. ANTONYMS neat, ordered.

torch noun *a torch at each turret* LIGHT, flame; *historical* cresset, flambeau, lantern.

▸ verb *informal one of the stores had been torched* BURN, set fire to, set on fire, set alight, incinerate, put a match to.

torment noun **1** *months of mental and emotional torment* AGONY, suffering, torture, pain, anguish, misery, distress, affliction, trauma, wretchedness; hell, purgatory.

2 *it was a torment to see him like that* ORDEAL, affliction, scourge, curse, plague, bane, thorn in someone's side/flesh, cross to bear; sorrow, tribulation, trouble.

▸ verb **1** *she was tormented by shame* TORTURE, afflict, rack, harrow, plague, haunt, bedevil, distress, agonize.

2 *she began to torment the two younger boys* TEASE, taunt, bait, harass, provoke, goad, plague, bother, trouble, persecute; *informal* needle.

torn adjective **1** *a torn shirt* RIPPED, rent, cut, slit; ragged, tattered, in tatters, in ribbons.

2 *she was torn between the two options* WAVERING, vacillating, irresolute, dithering, uncertain, unsure, undecided, split, of two minds.

tornado noun See STORM noun sense 1.

torpid adjective *torpid tourists traveled tired through the tropics* LETHARGIC, sluggish, inert, inactive, slow, lifeless; languid, listless, lazy, idle, indolent, slothful, supine, passive, apathetic, phlegmatic, somnolent, sleepy, weary, tired. ANTONYM energetic.

WORD NOTE **torpid**

When I hear this word, I picture a hippo lolling around in shallow river water, steam rising from his stinking flesh, indolent, indifferent to the flies clinging to him, inert and contemptible. The word is therefore extremely useful for describing, say, a writer sitting around sending e-mail or playing video games when he ought to be working; and as a self-rebuke and spur to creative activity for that writer. **—DA**

torpor noun *the feeling of torpor lingered for weeks* LETHARGY, sluggishness, inertia, inactivity, lifelessness, listlessness, languor, lassitude, laziness, idleness, indolence, sloth, acedia, passivity, somnolence, weariness, sleepiness.

torrent noun **1** *a torrent of water* FLOOD, deluge, inundation, spate, cascade, cataract, rush, stream, current, flow, overflow, tide.

2 *a torrent of abuse* OUTBURST, outpouring, stream, flood, volley, barrage, tide, spate. ANTONYM trickle.

torrential adjective *he would never forget the misery associated with those torrential rains in Nam* COPIOUS, heavy, teeming, pelting, severe, relentless, violent.

torrid adjective **1** *a torrid summer* HOT, dry, scorching, searing, blazing, blistering, sweltering, burning, sultry; *informal* boiling (hot), baking (hot), sizzling. ANTONYMS cold, wet.

2 *a torrid affair* PASSIONATE, ardent, lustful, amorous; *informal* steamy, sultry, sizzling, hot. ANTONYM passionless.

torso noun *a clay figure of his torso* BODY, upper body, trunk, chest.

tortuous adjective **1** *a tortuous route* TWISTING, twisty, twisting and turning, winding, windy, zigzag, sinuous, snaky, serpentine, meandering, circuitous. ANTONYM straight.

2 *a tortuous argument* CONVOLUTED, complicated, complex, labyrinthine, tangled, tangly, involved, confusing, difficult to follow, involuted, lengthy, overlong, circuitous. ANTONYM straightforward.

torture noun **1** *acts of torture* INFLICTION OF PAIN, abuse, ill-treatment, maltreatment, persecution; sadism.

2 *the torture of losing a loved one* TORMENT, agony, suffering, pain, anguish, misery, distress, heartbreak, affliction, scourge, trauma, wretchedness; hell, purgatory.

▸ verb **1** *the security forces routinely tortured suspects* INFLICT PAIN ON, ill-treat, abuse, mistreat, maltreat, persecute.

2 *he was tortured by grief* TORMENT, rack, afflict, harrow, plague, agonize, scourge, crucify.

toss verb **1** *he tossed the ball over the fence* THROW, hurl, fling, sling, cast, pitch, lob, project; *informal* heave, chuck.

2 *he tossed a coin and it landed heads* FLIP, flick.

3 *the ship tossed about on the waves* PITCH, lurch, rock, roll, plunge, reel, list, keel, sway, wallow, flounder.

4 *she tossed about in her sleep* THRASH, squirm, wriggle, writhe, fidget, turn.

5 *toss the salad ingredients together* SHAKE, stir, turn, mix, combine.

total adjective **1** *the total cost* ENTIRE, complete, whole, full, comprehensive, combined, aggregate, gross, overall, final. ANTONYM partial.

2 *a total success* COMPLETE, utter, absolute, thorough, out-and-out, outright, all-out, sheer, perfect, consummate, arrant, positive, rank, unmitigated, unqualified, unreserved, categorical. ANTONYM partial.

▸ noun *a total of $160,000* SUM, sum total, grand total, aggregate, result; whole, entirety, totality.

▸ verb **1** *the prize money totaled $33,050* ADD UP TO, amount to, come to, run to, make, work out to.

2 *she totaled up her score* ADD (UP), count, reckon, tot up, tally, compute, work out.

totalitarian adjective *Saddam's totalitarian regime* AUTOCRATIC, undemocratic, one-party, dictatorial, tyrannical, despotic, fascist, oppressive, repressive, illiberal; authoritarian, autarchic, absolute, absolutist; dystopian. ANTONYM democratic.

totality noun *the concept is difficult to grasp in its totality*

ENTIRETY, wholeness, fullness, completeness; whole, total, aggregate, sum, sum total; all, everything.

totally adverb *the decor is totally pink* COMPLETELY, entirely, wholly, thoroughly, fully, utterly, absolutely, perfectly, unreservedly, unconditionally, quite, altogether, downright; in every way, in every respect, one hundred percent, every inch, to the hilt; *informal* flat out, to the max. ANTONYM partly.

tote verb *they were sent with buckets to tote water from the river* CARRY, move, take, bring, bear, lug, fetch, cart.

totter verb **1** *arm in arm, they tottered across the lawn* TEETER, dodder, walk unsteadily, stagger, wobble, stumble, shuffle, shamble, toddle; reel, sway, roll, lurch.

2 *the foundations began to heave and totter* SHAKE, sway, tremble, quiver, teeter, shudder, rock, quake; *chiefly Brit.* judder.

touch verb **1** *his shoes were touching the end of the bed* BE IN CONTACT WITH, come into contact with, meet, join, connect with, converge with, be contiguous with, be against.

2 *he touched her cheek* PRESS LIGHTLY, tap, pat; feel, stroke, fondle, caress, pet; brush, graze, put a hand to.

3 *nobody can touch her when she's on her game* COMPARE WITH, rival, compete with, come/get close to, be on a par with, equal, match, be a match for, be in the same class/league as, measure up to; better, beat; *informal* hold a candle to.

4 *you're not supposed to touch the computer* HANDLE, hold, pick up, move; meddle with, play about with, fiddle with, interfere with, tamper with, disturb, lay a finger on; use, employ, make use of.

5 *people whose lives have been touched by the recession* AFFECT, impact, have an effect on, have an impact on, make a difference to, change.

6 *years later she wrote to tell them how much their kindnesses had touched her* AFFECT, move, tug at someone's heartstrings; leave an impression on, have an effect on.

▸ noun **1** *he felt her touch on his shoulder* TAP, pat; stroke, caress; brush, graze; hand.

2 *his political touch* SKILL, skillfulness, expertise, dexterity, deftness, adroitness, adeptness, ability, talent, flair, facility, proficiency, mastery, knack, technique, approach, style.

3 *a touch of sadness* TRACE, bit, grain, hint, suggestion, suspicion, scintilla, tinge, overtone, undertone, note; dash, taste, drop, dab, dribble, pinch, speck, soupçon.

4 *the oil lamps are a nice touch* DETAIL, feature, point; addition, accessory.

5 *have you been in touch with him?* CONTACT, communication, correspondence; connection, association, interaction.

PHRASES: **touch down** *the plane is expected to touch down in San Juan* LAND, alight, come down, put down, arrive. **touch off** *the action touched off a string of protests* CAUSE, spark, trigger, start, set in motion, ignite, stir up, provoke, give rise to, lead to, generate, set off. **touch on/upon** *his speech is sure to touch on the subject of school vouchers* REFER TO, mention, comment on, speak on, remark on, bring up, raise, broach, allude to; cover, deal with. **touch something up 1** *these paints are handy for touching up small areas* REPAINT, retouch, patch, fix; renovate, refurbish, revamp. **2** *the editor touched up my prose* IMPROVE, enhance, make better, refine, give the finishing touches to; *informal* tweak.

touch-and-go adjective *his recovery is touch-and-go* UNCERTAIN, precarious, risky, chancy, hazardous, dangerous, critical, suspenseful, cliffhanging, hanging by a thread; *informal* dicey. ANTONYM certain.

touching adjective *a touching tribute to their mother* MOVING, affecting, heartwarming, emotional, emotive, tender, sentimental; poignant, sad, tearjerker, tearjerking. See note at MOVING.

touchstone noun *the declaration was considered a touchstone for Soviet dissidents* CRITERION, standard, yardstick, benchmark, barometer, bellwether, litmus test; measure, point of reference, norm, gauge, test, guide, exemplar, model, pattern.

touchy adjective **1** *Arnie can be so touchy* SENSITIVE, oversensitive, hypersensitive, easily offended, thin-skinned, high-strung, tense; irritable, dyspeptic, tetchy, testy, crotchety, peevish, waspish, querulous, bad-tempered, petulant, pettish, cranky, fractious, choleric. ANTONYMS affable, good-humored.

2 *a touchy subject* DELICATE, sensitive, tricky, ticklish, thorny, prickly, embarrassing, awkward, difficult; contentious, controversial.

touchy-feely adjective *informal* **1** *a touchy-feely person* DEMONSTRATIVE, affectionate, tender; *informal* huggy, huggy-kissy.

2 *a touchy-feely political initiative* FEEL-GOOD, sentimental, softhearted, saccharine; ingratiating, toadying; *informal* warm and fuzzy.

tough adjective **1** *tough leather gloves* DURABLE, strong, resilient, sturdy, rugged, solid, stout, long-lasting, heavy-duty, industrial-strength, well-built, made to last. ANTONYMS soft, flimsy, fragile.

2 *the steak was tough* CHEWY, leathery, gristly, stringy, fibrous. ANTONYM tender.

3 *she'll survive—she's tough* ROBUST, resilient, strong, hardy, rugged, flinty, fit; stalwart, tough as nails. ANTONYM weak.

4 *another tough report from the auditor* STRICT, stern, severe, stringent, rigorous, hard, firm, hard-hitting, uncompromising; unsentimental, unsympathetic. ANTONYMS soft, light, lenient.

5 *that exercise sure was tough* ARDUOUS, onerous, strenuous, grueling, exacting, difficult, demanding, hard, taxing, tiring, exhausting, punishing, laborious, stressful, backbreaking, Herculean; *archaic* toilsome. ANTONYM easy.

6 *these are tough questions* DIFFICULT, hard, baffling, knotty, thorny, tricky. ANTONYM easy.

▸ noun *a gang of toughs* RUFFIAN, thug, goon, hoodlum, hooligan; *informal* roughneck, hood, heavy, bruiser, yahoo.

toughen verb **1** *the process toughens the wood fibers* STRENGTHEN, fortify, reinforce, harden, temper, anneal.

2 *measures to* ***toughen up*** *prison discipline* MAKE STRICTER, make more severe, stiffen, tighten up; *informal* beef up.

tour noun **1** *we enjoyed a two-week* ***tour of*** *Italy* TRIP TO/THROUGH, excursion to/through, journey to/

through, expedition to/through, jaunt to/through, outing to/through; trek to/through, safari to/through; *archaic* peregrination to/through.

2 *a tour of the factory* VISIT, inspection, guided tour.

▸ verb **1** *this hotel is well placed for touring the Cariboo* TRAVEL AROUND, explore, discover, vacation in, visit.

2 *the governor toured the factory* VISIT, go around/through, walk around/through, inspect; *informal* check out.

PHRASE: **tour of duty** *his tour of duty in Afghanistan* STINT, stretch, spell, turn, assignment, period of service.

tour de force noun *Carrey's latest comedic tour de force* TRIUMPH, masterpiece, achievement, success, masterful performance, magnum opus.

tourist noun *the islands teem with tourists* VACATIONER, traveler, sightseer, visitor, backpacker, globetrotter, day tripper, out-of-towner. ANTONYM local.

tournament noun **1** *a golf tournament* COMPETITION, contest, championship, meeting, tourney, meet, event, match, round robin.

2 *historical a knight preparing for a tournament* JOUST, tilt; the lists.

tousled adjective *tousled hair* UNTIDY, disheveled, windblown, messy, disordered, disarranged, messed up, rumpled, uncombed, ungroomed, tangled, wild, unkempt; *informal* mussed up. ANTONYMS neat, tidy.

tout verb **1** *street merchants were touting their wares* PEDDLE, sell, hawk, offer for sale, promote.

2 *cab drivers were* ***touting for*** *business* SOLICIT, seek, drum up; ask for, petition for, appeal for,

3 *she's being touted as the next party leader* RECOMMEND, speak of, extol, advocate, talk of; predict.

tow verb *the car was towed back to the garage* PULL, haul, drag, draw, tug, lug. PHRASE: **in tow** *he arrived with his new girlfriend in tow* IN ATTENDANCE, by one's side, alongside, in one's charge; accompanying, following, tagging along.

toward, towards preposition **1** *they were driving toward her apartment* IN THE DIRECTION OF, to; on the way to, on the road to, en route to.

2 *toward evening, dark clouds gathered* JUST BEFORE, shortly before, near, around, approaching, close to, coming to, getting on for.

3 *her attitude toward politics* WITH REGARD TO, as regards, regarding, in/with regard to, respecting, in relation to, concerning, about, apropos, vis-à-vis.

4 *some money toward the cost of a new house* AS A CONTRIBUTION TO, for, to help with.

WORD NOTE toward, as

It might seem pedantic to point out that *toward* is the correct U.S. spelling and *towards* is British. On the other hand, so many writers at all levels seem ignorant of the difference that always using *toward* is a costless, unpretentious way to signal your fluency in American English. It's the same with *gray* (U.S.) and *grey* (Brit.), though many Americans have been using these two interchangeably for so long that some U.S. dictionaries now list *grey* as a passable variant. This is not likely to happen with *toward/towards,* though—at least not in our lifetimes. Nor will it happen with using *as* to mean *since* or *because,* which a lot of U.S. students like to do because they think it makes their prose look classier (*As Dostoevsky is so firmly opposed to nihilism, it should come as no surprise that he often presents his novels' protagonists with moral dilemmas*). For really knowledgeable readers, the causal *as* is acceptable only in British English, and even there it's OK only if the dependent *as*-clause comes at the start of the sentence, since if it comes in the middle the *as* can look temporal and cause confusion (e.g., *I declined her offer as I was on my way to the bank already*). **—DFW**

tower noun *a church tower* STEEPLE, spire; minaret; turret; bell tower, belfry, campanile; skyscraper, high-rise, edifice; transmission tower.

▸ verb **1** *snow-capped peaks towered over the valley* SOAR, rise, rear, loom; overshadow, overhang, hang over, dominate.

2 *she* ***towered over*** *most other theologians of her generation* ECLIPSE, overshadow, outshine, outclass, surpass, dominate, be head and shoulders above, put someone/something in the shade.

towering adjective **1** *a towering skyscraper* HIGH, tall, lofty, soaring, sky-high, multistory; giant, gigantic, enormous, huge, massive; *informal* ginormous.

2 *a towering intellect* OUTSTANDING, preeminent, leading, foremost, finest, top, surpassing, supreme, great, incomparable, unrivaled, unsurpassed, peerless.

town noun *they live in a town just outside Milwaukee* MUNICIPALITY, township, conurbation, urban area; city, capital, metropolis, megalopolis, megacity, burg; small town, whistle-stop.

toxic adjective *toxic houseplants* POISONOUS, virulent, noxious, deadly, dangerous, harmful, injurious, pernicious. ANTONYM harmless.

toy noun *Santa left a bundle of toys* PLAYTHING, game; gadget, device; trinket, knickknack, gizmo.

▸ adjective **1** *a toy gun* MODEL, imitation, replica, fake; miniature.

2 *a toy poodle* MINIATURE, small, tiny, diminutive, dwarf, midget, pygmy.

PHRASE: **toy with 1** *I was toying with the idea of writing a book* THINK ABOUT, consider, flirt with, entertain the possibility of; kick around. **2** *Adam toyed with his glasses* FIDDLE WITH, play with, fidget with, twiddle; finger. **3** *she toyed with her food* NIBBLE, pick at, peck at, eat listlessly, eat like a bird. **4** *you are toying with my emotions* TRIFLE WITH, play with, play havoc with, amuse oneself with, mess with, be flippant with.

trace verb **1** *police hope to trace the owner of the vehicle* TRACK DOWN, find, discover, detect, unearth, turn up, hunt down, ferret out.

2 *she traced a pattern in the sand with her toe* DRAW, outline, mark, sketch.

3 *the analysis traces the origins of cowboy poetry* OUTLINE, map out, follow, sketch out, delineate, depict, show, indicate.

▸ noun **1** *no trace had been found of the runaways* VESTIGE, sign, mark, indication, evidence, clue; trail, tracks, marks, prints, footprints, spoor; remains, remnant, relic.

2 *a trace of bitterness crept into her voice* BIT, touch, hint, suggestion, suspicion, shadow, whiff; drop, dash, tinge, speck, shred, iota; smidgen, tad.

THE RIGHT WORD

You can follow the **track** of a deer in the snow, the **trace** of a sleigh, or the **trail** of someone who has just cut down a Christmas tree and is dragging it back to the car. A *track* is a line or a series of marks left by the passage of something or someone; it often refers specifically to a line of footprints or a path worn into the ground by the feet (*to follow the track of a grizzly bear*). **Trace** may refer to a line or a rut made by someone or something that has been present or passed by; it may also refer to a mark serving as evidence that something has happened or been there (*traces of mud throughout the house; the telephoto shots have a trace of a camera shake*). **Trail** may refer to the track created by the passage of animals or people, or to the mark or marks left by something being dragged along a surface (*they followed the trail of the injured dog*). **Vestige** and **remnant** come closer in meaning to *trace*, as they refer to what remains after something has passed away. A *vestige* is always slight when compared to what it recalls (*the last vestiges of a great civilization*), while a *remnant* is a fragment or scrap of something (*all that remained of the historic tapestry after the fire was a few scorched remnants*).

track noun **1** *a gravel track* PATH, pathway, footpath, lane, trail, route, way, course.

2 *the final lap of the track* COURSE, racetrack, raceway; velodrome.

3 (**tracks**) *he found the tracks of a wolverine* TRACES, marks, prints, footprints, trail, spoor.

4 *we followed the track of the hurricane* COURSE, path, line, route, way, trajectory, wake.

5 *railroad tracks* RAIL, line.

6 *the album's title track* SONG, recording, number, piece.

▸ verb *he tracked a bear for 40 miles* FOLLOW, trail, trace, pursue, shadow, stalk, keep an eye on, keep in sight; *informal* tail.

PHRASES: **keep track of** *the electronic log keeps track of your blood-glucose readings* MONITOR, follow, keep up with, keep an eye on; keep in touch with, keep up to date with; *informal* keep tabs on. **track down** *Captain Pearce vowed that they would track down the killer* DISCOVER, find, detect, hunt down/out, unearth, uncover, turn up, dig up, ferret out, bring to light. **on track** *the fund-raising is on track* ON COURSE, on an even keel, on schedule.

track and field noun See table.

TRACK AND FIELD EVENTS

biathlon	marathon
cross-country run	modern pentathlon
decathlon	pole vault
discus throw	relay
hammer throw	shot put
heptathlon	steeplechase
high jump	triathlon
hurdles	triple jump
javelin throw	walk
long jump	

tract[1] noun *large tracts of land* AREA, region, expanse, sweep, stretch, extent, belt, swathe, zone.

tract[2] noun *a political tract* TREATISE, essay, article, paper, work, monograph, disquisition, dissertation, thesis, homily, tractate; pamphlet, booklet, chapbook, leaflet.

tractable adjective *our preschool teachers disagree with the statement that children are becoming less tractable every year* MALLEABLE, manageable, amenable, pliable, governable, yielding, complaisant, compliant, game, persuadable, accommodating, docile, biddable, obliging, obedient, submissive, meek. ANTONYM recalcitrant.

traction noun *new tires with improved traction* GRIP, purchase, friction, adhesion.

trade noun **1** *the illicit trade in stolen cattle* COMMERCE, buying and selling, dealing, traffic, trafficking, business, marketing, merchandising; dealings, transactions, dealmaking.

2 *we shook hands as we made the trade* EXCHANGE, transaction, swap, trade-off; *archaic* truck.

3 *the glazier's trade* CRAFT, occupation, job, career, profession, business, line of work, line, métier, vocation, calling, walk of life, field; work, employment, livelihood.

▸ verb **1** *he made his fortune* ***trading in*** *beaver pelts* DEAL (IN), buy and sell, traffic (in), market, merchandise, peddle, vend; *informal* hawk, run.

2 *the business is trading at a loss* OPERATE, run, do business.

3 *I traded the old machine for a newer model* SWAP, exchange, switch; barter, trade in.

PHRASE: **trade on** *he trades on his friendship with powerful people* EXPLOIT, take advantage of, capitalize on, profit from, use, make use of; milk; *informal* cash in on.

trademark noun **1** *the company's trademark* LOGO, brand, emblem, sign, mark, stamp, symbol, badge, crest, monogram, colophon; brand name, trade name, proprietary name.

2 *it had all the trademarks of a Mafia hit* CHARACTERISTIC, hallmark, calling card, sign, trait, quality, attribute, feature, peculiarity, idiosyncrasy, quirk.

trader noun *a commodities trader* DEALER, merchant, buyer, seller, buyer and seller, marketeer, merchandiser, broker, agent; distributor, vendor, purveyor, monger, supplier, trafficker; retailer, wholesaler; storekeeper, shopkeeper; wheeler-dealer.

tradesman, tradeswoman noun *a qualified tradesman* CRAFTSMAN, craftsperson, workman, artisan.

tradition noun **1** *during a maiden speech, by tradition, everyone keeps absolutely silent* HISTORICAL CONVENTION, unwritten law, mores; oral history, lore, folklore.

2 *an age-old tradition* CUSTOM, practice, convention, ritual, observance, way, usage, habit, institution; *formal* praxis.

traditional adjective **1** *traditional Christmas fare* LONG-ESTABLISHED, customary, time-honored, established, classic, accustomed, standard, regular, normal, conventional, usual, orthodox, habitual, set, fixed, routine, ritual; old, age-old, ancestral.

2 *traditional beliefs* HANDED-DOWN, folk, unwritten, oral.

traduce verb *you dare to traduce my family?* DEFAME, slander, speak ill of, misrepresent, malign, vilify, denigrate, disparage, slur, impugn, smear, besmirch, run down, blacken the name of, cast aspersions on; *informal* badmouth, dis.

traffic noun **1** *the bridge is not open to traffic* VEHICLES; cars, trucks.

2 *they might be stuck in traffic* A TRAFFIC JAM, congestion, a gridlock, a holdup, a bottleneck, a tie-up; *informal* a snarl-up, a logjam.

3 *the illegal traffic in stolen art* TRADE, trading, trafficking, dealing, commerce, business, buying and selling; smuggling, bootlegging, black market; dealings, transactions.

▸ verb *he confessed to* ***trafficking in*** *narcotics* TRADE (IN), deal (in), do business in, buy and sell; smuggle, bootleg; *informal* run, push.

tragedy noun *the flood was the worst tragedy in the city's history* DISASTER, calamity, catastrophe, cataclysm, misfortune, mishap, blow, trial, tribulation, affliction, adversity.

tragic adjective **1** *a tragic accident* DISASTROUS, calamitous, catastrophic, cataclysmic, devastating, terrible, dreadful, awful, appalling, dismal, horrendous; fatal, deadly, mortal, lethal. ANTONYMS fortunate, lucky.

2 *a tragic tale* SAD, unhappy, pathetic, moving, distressing, depressing, painful, harrowing, heart-rending, piteous, wretched, sorry; melancholy, doleful, mournful, miserable, gut-wrenching. ANTONYMS joyful, happy.

3 *a tragic waste of talent* REGRETTABLE, shameful, terrible, horrible, awful, deplorable, lamentable, piteous, dreadful, grievous.

trail noun **1** *he left a trail of clues | a trail of devastation* SERIES, string, chain, succession, sequence; aftermath, wake. See note at TRACE.

2 *wolves on the trail of their prey* TRACK, spoor, path, scent; traces, marks, signs, prints, footprints.

3 *the airplane's vapor trail* WAKE, contrail, tail, stream.

4 *a trail of ants* LINE, column, train, file, procession, string, chain, convoy; lineup.

5 *provincial parks with nature trails* PATH, pathway, way, footpath, walk, track, course, route.

▸ verb **1** *her robe trailed along the ground* DRAG, sweep, swish, be drawn; dangle, hang (down), droop.

2 *the roses grew wild, their stems trailing over the banks* HANG, droop, fall, spill, cascade.

3 *Filteau suspected that they were trailing him* FOLLOW, pursue, track, shadow, stalk, hunt (down); *informal* tail.

4 *the defending champions were trailing 3–1 in the second period* LOSE, be down, be behind, lag behind.

5 *her voice trailed off* FADE, tail off/away, grow faint, die away, dwindle, taper off, subside, peter out, fizzle out.

trailblazer noun *a trailblazer in the automotive industry* PIONEER, innovator, groundbreaker, spearhead, trendsetter; explorer, bushwhacker.

trailblazing adjective *their trailblazing designs for handicapped housing* INNOVATIVE, cutting-edge, leading-edge, groundbreaking, pioneering, state-of-the-art, avant-garde, trendsetting, unprecedented, experimental, original, inventive, new.

train verb **1** *an engineer trained in remote-sensing techniques* INSTRUCT, teach, coach, tutor, school, educate, prime, drill, ground; inculcate, indoctrinate, initiate, break in.

2 *she's training to be a hairdresser* STUDY, learn, prepare, take instruction.

3 *with the Olympics in mind, athletes are training hard* EXERCISE, do exercises, work out, get into shape, practice, prepare.

4 *she trained the gun on his chest* AIM, point, direct, level, focus; zero in.

▸ noun **1** *the train for Youngstown* locomotive, subway, monorail; *informal* iron horse; *baby talk* choo choo.

2 *a minister and his train of attendants* RETINUE, entourage, cortège, following, staff, household.

3 *a train of elephants* PROCESSION, line, file, column, convoy, cavalcade, caravan, string, succession, trail.

4 *a bizarre train of events* CHAIN, string, series, sequence, succession, set, course, cycle, concatenation.

trainee noun *two trainees will be starting this afternoon* APPRENTICE, new employee, new hire, intern; cadet, novice, student; *informal* rookie, newbie.

trainer noun *my personal trainer at the gym* COACH, instructor, teacher, tutor; handler.

training noun **1** *in-house training for staff* INSTRUCTION, teaching, coaching, tuition, tutoring, guidance, schooling, education, orientation; indoctrination, inculcation, initiation.

2 *four months' hard training before the tournament* EXERCISE, exercises, working out, conditioning; practice, preparation.

traipse verb *I haven't the time to go traipsing around art galleries* TRUDGE, trek, tramp, tromp, trail, plod, drag oneself, slog, schlep.

trait noun *elaborating on the truth is just one of her personality traits* CHARACTERISTIC, attribute, feature, quality, property; habit, custom, mannerism, idiosyncrasy, peculiarity, quirk, oddity, foible.

traitor noun *convicted traitors will be executed* BETRAYER, backstabber, double-crosser, renegade, fifth columnist; turncoat, defector, deserter; collaborator, informer, mole, snitch, double agent; Judas, Benedict Arnold, quisling; *informal* snake in the grass, two-timer, rat, scab, fink.

traitorous adjective *his dealings with a traitorous party* TREACHEROUS, disloyal, treasonous, renegade, backstabbing; double-crossing, double-dealing, faithless, unfaithful, two-faced, duplicitous, deceitful, false; *informal* two-timing; *literary* perfidious. ANTONYM loyal.

trajectory noun *the missile's trajectory* COURSE, path, route, track, line, orbit.

trammel *literary* noun *the trammels of domesticity* RESTRAINT, constraint, curb, check, impediment, obstacle, barrier, handicap, bar, hindrance, encumbrance, disadvantage, drawback, shackles, fetters, bonds.

▸ verb *those less trammeled by convention than himself* RESTRICT, restrain, constrain, hamper, confine, hinder, handicap, obstruct, impede, hold back, tie down, hamstring, shackle, fetter.

tramp verb *we tramped across France* TRUDGE, tromp, plod, galumph, stamp, trample, lumber, clump, clomp, stump, stomp; trek, slog, schlep, drag oneself, walk, hike, march, traipse.

▸ noun **1** *a wandering old tramp* VAGRANT, vagabond, street person, hobo, homeless person, down-and-out; traveler, drifter, derelict, beggar, mendicant, bag lady, bum.

2 *the regular tramp of the sentry's boots* FOOTSTEP, tromp, step, footfall, tread, stamp, stomp.

trample verb **1** *someone had trampled on the tulips* TREAD, tramp, stamp, stomp, walk over; squash, crush, flatten.

2 *we do nothing but* ***trample over*** *their feelings* TREAT WITH CONTEMPT, disregard, show no consideration for, abuse; encroach on, infringe (on).

trance noun *he pretended to be in a trance* DAZE, stupor, hypnotic state, half-conscious state, dream, reverie, fugue state.

tranquil adjective **1** *the lake's tranquil waters* PEACEFUL, calm, calming, still, serene, placid, restful, quiet, relaxing, undisturbed, limpid, pacific. ANTONYM disturbed.

2 *Martha smiled, perfectly tranquil* CALM, serene, relaxed, unruffled, unperturbed, unflustered, untroubled, composed, 'calm, cool, and collected'; equable, even-tempered, placid, unflappable. See note at CALM. ANTONYM excitable.

tranquility noun **1** *the tranquility of the countryside* PEACE, peacefulness, restfulness, repose, calm, calmness, quiet, quietness, stillness.

2 *the incident jolted her out of her tranquility* COMPOSURE, calmness, serenity, peace; equanimity, equability, placidity; *informal* cool, unflappability.

tranquilize verb *the horse was tranquilized* SEDATE, put under sedation, narcotize, anesthetize, etherize, drug.

tranquilizer noun *don't have any wine if you're taking tranquilizers* SEDATIVE, barbiturate, calmative, sleeping pill, depressant, narcotic, opiate; *informal* downer. ANTONYM stimulant.

transact verb *no business will be transacted on the day after Christmas* CONDUCT, carry out, negotiate, do, perform, execute, take care of, discharge; settle, conclude, finish, accomplish.

transaction noun **1** *property transactions* DEAL, business deal, undertaking, arrangement, bargain, negotiation, agreement, settlement; proceedings.

2 *the bank statement records your transactions* DEBIT, credit, deposit, withdrawal.

3 *the transaction of government business* CONDUCT, carrying out, negotiation, performance, execution.

transcend verb **1** *an issue that transcended party politics* GO BEYOND, rise above, cut across.

2 *his exploits far transcended those of his predecessors* SURPASS, exceed, beat, cap, tower above, outdo, outclass, outstrip, leave behind, outshine, eclipse, overshadow, throw into the shade, upstage, top.

transcendence, transcendency noun *the transcendence of love over the coercions of the church* EXCELLENCE, supremacy, incomparability, matchlessness, peerlessness, magnificence; *rare* paramountcy.

transcendent adjective **1** *the search for a transcendent level of knowledge* MYSTICAL, mystic, transcendental, spiritual, divine; metaphysical.

2 *a transcendent genius* INCOMPARABLE, matchless, peerless, unrivaled, inimitable, beyond compare/comparison, unparalleled, unequaled, without equal, second to none, unsurpassed, unsurpassable, nonpareil; exceptional, consummate, unique, perfect, rare, surpassing, magnificent.

transcendental adjective See TRANSCENDENT sense 1.

transcribe verb **1** *each interview was taped and transcribed* WRITE OUT, write down, copy down, put in writing, put on paper, render.

2 *a person who can take and transcribe shorthand* TRANSLITERATE, interpret, translate.

transcript noun **1** *a radio transcript* WRITTEN VERSION, printed version, script, text, transliteration, record, reproduction.

2 *university transcript* STUDENT RECORD, grades, report card.

transfer verb **1** *the hostages were transferred to a safe house* MOVE, convey, take, bring, shift, remove, carry, transport; transplant, relocate, resettle.

2 *the property was transferred to his wife* HAND OVER, pass on, make over, turn over, sign over, consign, devolve, assign, delegate.

▸ noun **1** *he died shortly after his transfer to hospital* MOVE, conveyance, transferral, transference, shift, relocation, removal, switch, transplantation.

2 *keep your bus transfer in your pocket* TICKET, pass; receipt, proof of purchase.

transfigure verb *the glow of the sunrise transfigured the whole landscape* TRANSFORM, transmute, change, alter, metamorphose; *informal* transmogrify.

transfix verb **1** *she was transfixed by the images on the screen* MESMERIZE, hypnotize, spellbind, bewitch, captivate, entrance, enthrall, fascinate, absorb, enrapture, grip, hook, rivet, paralyze.

2 *a field mouse is transfixed by the owl's curved talons* IMPALE, stab, spear, pierce, spike, skewer, gore, stick, run through.

transform verb *the old inn has been transformed into an outpatient medical facility* CHANGE, alter, convert, metamorphose, transfigure, transmute, mutate; revolutionize, overhaul; remodel, reshape, redo, reconstruct, rebuild, reorganize, rearrange, rework, renew, revamp, remake, retool; *informal* transmogrify, morph.

transformation noun *the transformation of the sales department has been dramatic* CHANGE, alteration, mutation, conversion, metamorphosis, transfiguration, transmutation, sea change; revolution, overhaul; remodeling, reshaping, redoing, reconstruction, rebuilding, reorganization, rearrangement, reworking, renewal, revamp, remaking, remake; *informal* transmogrification, morphing.

transgress verb **1** *if they transgress, the punishment is harsh* MISBEHAVE, behave badly, break the law, err, fall from grace, stray from the straight and narrow, sin, do wrong, go astray; *archaic* trespass.

2 *she had transgressed an unwritten social law* INFRINGE, breach, contravene, disobey, defy, violate, break, flout.

transgression noun **1** *a punishment for past transgressions* OFFENSE, crime, sin, wrong, wrongdoing, misdemeanor, impropriety, infraction, misdeed, lawbreaking; error, lapse, peccadillo, fault; *archaic* trespass.

2 *Adam's transgression of God's law* INFRINGEMENT, breach, contravention, violation, defiance, disobedience, nonobservance. See note at SIN.

transgressor noun *grant these transgressors forgiveness*

OFFENDER, miscreant, lawbreaker, criminal, villain, felon, malefactor, guilty party, culprit; sinner, evildoer; *archaic* trespasser, miscreant.

transient adjective *our interest in the environment must not be transient* TRANSITORY, temporary, short-lived, short-term, ephemeral, impermanent, brief, short, momentary, fleeting, passing, here today and gone tomorrow; *literary* evanescent, fugitive. See note at TEMPORARY. ANTONYM permanent.

▸ noun *the plight of poor transients* HOBO, vagrant, vagabond, street person, homeless person, down-and-out; traveler, drifter, derelict.

transit noun **1** *public transit* TRANSPORTATION, transport, mass transit, bus system, subway system.

2 *the transit of goods between states* TRANSPORTATION, transport, movement, flow, conveyance, shipping, shipment, trucking, carriage, transfer. PHRASE: **in transit** *the building supplies are in transit* EN ROUTE, on the journey, on the way, on the road.

transition noun *the transition from school to work* CHANGE, passage, move, transformation, conversion, metamorphosis, alteration, handover, changeover; segue, shift, switch, jump, leap, progression; progress, development, evolution, flux.

transitional adjective **1** *a transitional period* CHANGEOVER, interim; changing, fluid, in flux, unsettled, intermediate, liminal.

2 *the transitional government* INTERIM, temporary, provisional, pro tem, acting, caretaker.

transitory adjective *transitory fashions* TRANSIENT, temporary, brief, short, short-lived, short-term, impermanent, ephemeral, momentary, fleeting, passing, here today and gone tomorrow; *literary* evanescent, fugitive. See note at TEMPORARY. ANTONYM permanent.

translate verb **1** *the German original had been translated into English* RENDER, put, express, convert, change; transcribe, transliterate.

2 *be prepared to translate plenty of jargon* RENDER, paraphrase, reword, rephrase, convert, decipher, decode, gloss, explain.

3 *interesting ideas cannot always be translated into effective movies* ADAPT, change, convert, transform, alter, turn, transmute; *informal* transmogrify, morph.

translation noun *the translation of the Bible into English* RENDITION, rendering, conversion; transcription, transliteration.

translucent adjective *a mantle of translucent ice* SEMITRANSPARENT, semiopaque, pellucid, limpid, clear; diaphanous, gossamer, sheer. ANTONYM opaque.

transmission noun **1** *the transmission of ideas* SPREAD, transferral, communication, conveyance; dissemination, circulation, transference.

2 *a live transmission* BROADCAST, program, show, airing.

3 *her car had a faulty transmission* POWER TRAIN, drivetrain.

transmit verb **1** *the use of computers to transmit information* TRANSFER, pass on, hand on, communicate, convey, impart, channel, carry, relay, forward, dispatch; disseminate, spread, circulate.

2 *the program will be transmitted on Sunday* BROADCAST, relay, send out, air, televise.

transmute verb *the books were transmuted into workable scripts* CHANGE, alter, adapt, transform, convert, metamorphose, morph, translate; *humorous* transmogrify.

transparency noun **1** *the transparency of the glass* TRANSLUCENCY, limpidity, clearness, clarity.

2 *color transparencies* SLIDE, acetate.

3 *the new government aims for better transparency* OPENNESS, accountability, straightforwardness, candor.

transparent adjective **1** *transparent blue water* CLEAR, crystal clear, see-through, translucent, pellucid, limpid, glassy, vitreous. ANTONYMS opaque, cloudy.

2 *fine transparent fabrics* SEE-THROUGH, sheer, filmy, gauzy, diaphanous, translucent. ANTONYM thick.

3 *a transparent attempt to win favor* OBVIOUS, evident, self-evident, undisguised, unconcealed, conspicuous, patent, clear, crystal clear, plain, (as) plain as the nose on your face, apparent, unmistakable, easily discerned, manifest, palpable, indisputable, unambiguous, unequivocal. ANTONYMS ambiguous, obscure.

transpire verb **1** *it transpired that her family had moved away* BECOME KNOWN, emerge, come to light, be revealed, turn out, come out, be discovered, prove to be the case, unfold.

2 *I'm going to find out exactly what transpired* HAPPEN, occur, take place, arise, come about, materialize, turn up, chance, befall, ensue; *literary* come to pass. See note at HAPPEN.

USAGE NOTE **transpire**

The common use of **transpire** to mean 'occur, happen' (*I'm going to find out exactly what transpired*) is a loose extension of an earlier meaning, 'come to be known' (*it transpired that Mark had been baptized a Catholic).* This loose sense of 'happen,' which is now more common in American usage than the sense of 'come to be known,' was first recorded in American English toward the end of the eighteenth century and has been listed in American dictionaries from the nineteenth century. Careful writers should note, however, that in cases where *occur* or *happen* would do just as well, the use of **transpire** may strike readers as an affectation or as jargon.

transplant verb **1** *our headquarters will be transplanted to Pennsylvania* TRANSFER, move, remove, shift, relocate, take.

2 *the seedlings should be transplanted in larger pots* REPLANT, repot, relocate.

3 *kidneys must be transplanted within 48 hours of removal* TRANSFER, implant.

transport verb *barges transport the lumber from the mill* CONVEY, carry, take, transfer, move, shift, send, deliver, bear, ship, ferry, haul; *informal* cart. See note at RAPTURE.

▸ noun *alternative forms of transport.* See TRANSPORTATION sense 1.

transportation noun **1** *alternative forms of transportation* TRANSIT, transport, conveyance, travel, getting around; vehicle, car, truck, train.

2 *the transportation of crude oil* TRANSPORT, conveyance, movement, carriage, haulage, freight, shipment, shipping.

transpose verb **1** *the blue and black plates were transposed* INTERCHANGE, exchange, switch, swap (around), reverse, invert, flip.

2 *the themes are transposed from the sphere of love to that of work* TRANSFER, shift, relocate, transplant, move, displace.

transsexual noun *a transsexual from Transylvania* HERMAPHRODITE, androgyne, epicene, intersex, transgendered person; *informal* gender-bender, trannie.

transverse adjective *a transverse bar* CROSSWISE, crossways, cross, horizontal, diagonal, oblique, slanted.

transvestite noun *the revue featured a hilarious transvestite with an amazing singing voice* DRAG QUEEN, cross-dresser, female impersonator; *informal* gender-bender, trannie.

trap noun **1** *an animal caught in a trap* SNARE, net, mesh, deadfall, leghold (trap), pitfall.

2 *the question was set as a trap* TRICK, ploy, ruse, deception, subterfuge; booby trap, ambush, setup.

3 *informal shut your trap!* See MOUTH noun sense 1.

▸ verb **1** *police trapped the two men and arrested them* SNARE, entrap, ensnare, lay a trap for; capture, catch, bag, corner, ambush.

2 *a rat trapped in a barn* CONFINE, cut off, corner, shut in, pen in, hem in; imprison, hold captive.

3 *I hoped to trap him into an admission* TRICK, dupe, deceive, lure, inveigle, beguile, fool, hoodwink; catch, trip up.

trappings plural noun *surrounded by the trappings of royalty* ACCESSORIES, accoutrements, appurtenances, trimmings, frills, accompaniments, extras, ornamentation, adornment, decoration; regalia, panoply, paraphernalia, apparatus, finery, equipment, gear, effects, things, bits and pieces.

trash noun **1** *the subway entrance was blocked with trash* GARBAGE, refuse, waste, litter, junk, debris, detritus, rubbish.

2 *if they read at all, they read trash* JUNK, dross, dreck, drivel, nonsense, trivia, pulp, pulp fiction, pap, garbage, rubbish; *informal* crap, schlock.

3 *informal that family is trash* SCUM, vermin, the dregs of society, the lowest of the low; *informal* the scum of the earth, dirt, riffraff.

▸ verb **1** *the apartment had been totally trashed* WRECK, ruin, destroy, wreak havoc on, devastate; vandalize, tear up, bust up, smash; *informal* total.

2 *his play was trashed by the critics* CRITICIZE, LAMBASTE, censure, attack, insult, abuse, malign, give a bad press to, condemn, flay, savage, pan, knock, take to pieces, take/pull apart, crucify, hammer, slam, bash, trash talk, roast, maul, rubbish, pummel; *informal* bad-mouth, bitch about.

trashy adjective **1** *a trashy roadhouse on Route 42.* See THIRD-RATE.

2 *reading trashy novels was one of her secret pleasures.* See LOWBROW.

trauma noun **1** *the trauma of divorce* SHOCK, upheaval, distress, stress, strain, pain, anguish, suffering, upset, agony, misery, sorrow, grief, heartache, heartbreak, torture; ordeal, trial, tribulation, trouble, worry, anxiety; nightmare, hell, hellishness.

2 *the trauma to the liver* INJURY, damage, wound; cut, laceration, lesion, abrasion, contusion.

traumatic adjective *the enduring pain of this traumatic event* DISTURBING, shocking, distressing, upsetting, heartbreaking, painful, scarring, jolting, agonizing, hurtful, stressful, damaging, injurious, harmful, awful, terrible, devastating, harrowing.

travail *literary* noun *the travails of the migrant worker* ORDEAL, trial, tribulation, trial and tribulation, trouble, hardship, privation, stress; drudgery, toil, slog, effort, exertion, labor, work, endeavor, sweat, struggle. See note at LABOR.

travel verb **1** *Tim spent much of his time traveling abroad* JOURNEY, tour, take a trip, voyage, explore, go sightseeing, globe-trot, backpack, gallivant; *archaic* peregrinate.

2 *we traveled the length and breadth of the island* JOURNEY THROUGH, cross, traverse, cover; roam, wander, rove, range, trek.

3 *light travels faster than sound* MOVE, be transmitted.

▸ noun (**travels**) *she amassed great wealth during her travels* JOURNEYS, expeditions, trips, tours, excursions, voyages, treks, safaris, explorations, wanderings, odysseys, pilgrimages, jaunts, junkets; traveling, touring, sightseeing, backpacking, globe-trotting, gallivanting; *archaic* peregrinations.

traveler noun *thousands of travelers were left stranded* TOURIST, vacationer, sightseer, visitor, globe-trotter, backpacker; pilgrim, wanderer, drifter, nomad, migrant; passenger, commuter, fare.

traveling adjective *in those days, many a tired traveling man would stop at Aunt Dilly's for some hot soup and a warm bath* NOMADIC, itinerant, peripatetic, wandering, roaming, roving, wayfaring, migrant, vagrant, of no fixed address.

traverse verb **1** *he traversed the deserts of Iran* TRAVEL OVER/ACROSS, cross, journey over/across, pass over; cover; ply; wander, roam, range.

2 *a ditch traversed by a wooden bridge* CROSS, bridge, span; extend across, lie across, stretch across.

travesty noun *a* ***travesty of*** *justice* PERVERSION OF, distortion of, corruption of, misrepresentation of, poor imitation of, poor substitute for, mockery of, parody of, caricature of; farce of, charade of, pantomime of, sham of, spoof of; *informal* apology for, (poor) excuse for. See note at CARICATURE.

trawl verb *they trawl for shrimp every morning* FISH, seine, drag a net; sift, troll; hunt, search, look.

tray noun *a tray of imported cheeses* PLATTER, salver, plate, dish, box, basket.

treacherous adjective **1** *her treacherous brother betrayed her* TRAITOROUS, disloyal, faithless, unfaithful, duplicitous, deceitful, deceptive, false, backstabbing, double-crossing, double-dealing, two-faced, weaselly, untrustworthy, unreliable; apostate, renegade, two-timing; *literary* perfidious. ANTONYMS loyal, faithful.

2 *treacherous driving conditions* DANGEROUS, hazardous, perilous, unsafe, precarious, risky, deceptive, unreliable; *informal* dicey, hairy. ANTONYMS safe, reliable.

treachery noun *Myrna never forgave Warren his treachery* BETRAYAL, disloyalty, faithlessness, unfaithfulness, infidelity, breach of trust, duplicity, dirty tricks, deceit, deception, chicanery, stab in the back, backstabbing, double-dealing, untrustworthiness; treason, two-timing; *literary* perfidy.

tread verb **1** *he trod purposefully down the hall* WALK, step, stride, pace, go; march, tramp, plod, thump, stomp, trudge.

2 *the snow had been* ***trodden down*** *by the horses* CRUSH, flatten, press down, squash; trample on, tramp on, stamp on, stomp on.

▸ noun *we heard her heavy tread on the stairs* STEP, footstep, footfall, tramp, thump; clip-clop.

treason noun *the treason of Benedict Arnold will be recounted for centuries* TREACHERY, disloyalty, betrayal, faithlessness; sedition, subversion, mutiny, rebellion; high treason, lèse-majesté; apostasy; *literary* perfidy. ANTONYMS allegiance, loyalty.

treasonable adjective *treasonable offenses against the king* TRAITOROUS, treasonous, treacherous, disloyal; seditious, subversive, mutinous, rebellious; *literary* perfidious. ANTONYM loyal.

treasure noun **1** *a casket of treasure* RICHES, valuables, jewels, gems, gold, silver, precious metals, money, cash; wealth, fortune; treasure trove.

2 *art treasures* VALUABLE OBJECT, valuable, work of art, masterpiece, precious item.

3 *informal she's a real treasure* PARAGON, gem, angel, find, star, one of a kind, one in a million.

▸ verb *I treasure the photographs I took of Jack* CHERISH, hold dear, prize, value greatly; adore, dote on, love, be devoted to, worship, venerate.

treasury noun **1** *the club treasury* COFFERS, purse, finance department; bank, revenues, finances, funds, moneys.

2 *the area is a treasury of early fossils* RICH SOURCE, repository, storehouse, treasure house; fund, mine, bank, treasure trove.

3 *a treasury of stories* ANTHOLOGY, collection, miscellany, compilation, compendium.

treat verb **1** *Charlotte treated him very badly* BEHAVE TOWARD, act toward; deal with, handle; *literary* use.

2 *police are treating the fires as arson* REGARD, consider, view, look upon, think of.

3 *the book treats its subject with insight and responsibility* TACKLE, deal with, handle, discuss, present, explore, investigate, approach; consider, study, analyze.

4 *she was treated at St. Paul's Hospital* GIVE MEDICAL CARE (TO), nurse, care for, tend (to), help, give treatment (to), attend (to), administer (to); medicate.

5 *the plants may prove useful in treating cancer* CURE, heal, remedy; fight, combat.

6 *she* ***treated him to*** *an expensive meal* BUY (FOR) SOMEONE, take someone out for, give (to) someone; pay for (for someone); foot the bill for, pick up the tab for.

7 *delegates were* ***treated to*** *an Indonesian dance show* REGALE WITH, entertain with/by, fête with, amuse with, divert with.

▸ noun **1** *a birthday treat* CELEBRATION, entertainment, amusement; surprise; party, excursion, outing, special event.

2 *I bought you some chocolate as a treat* PRESENT, gift; delicacy, luxury, indulgence, extravagance, guilty pleasure; *informal* goodie.

3 *it was a real treat to see them* PLEASURE, delight, boon, thrill, joy.

treatise noun *a treatise on the principles of democracy* DISQUISITION, essay, paper, work, exposition, discourse, dissertation, thesis, monograph, opus, oeuvre, study, critique; tract, pamphlet, account.

treatment noun **1** *the company's treatment of its workers* BEHAVIOR TOWARD, conduct toward; handling of, dealings with, management of.

2 *she's responding well to treatment* MEDICAL CARE, therapy, nursing, ministrations; medication, drugs, medicaments; cure, remedy.

3 *her treatment of the topic* DISCUSSION, handling, investigation, exploration, consideration, study, analysis, critique; approach, methodology.

treaty noun *several terms of the treaty were casually violated* AGREEMENT, settlement, pact, deal, entente, concordat, accord, protocol, convention, contract, covenant, bargain, pledge; concord, compact.

tree noun sapling, conifer, evergreen. See table.

TREES OF NORTH AMERICA

acacia	horse chestnut
alder	ironwood
allthorn	Joshua tree
apple	juneberry
apricot	juniper
arbor vitae	kidneywood
ash	larch
aspen	laurel
bald cypress	leadtree
basswood	lemon
bayberry	lime
beech	linden
birch	magnolia
blackhaw	maple
bladdernut	moosewood
buckeye	mulberry
buckthorn	oak
bumelia	palmetto
butternut	peach
camphor tree	pear
cascara (buckthorn)	pecan
catalpa	persimmon
cedar	pine
cherry	pistachio
chestnut	plum
chinaberry	poplar
chinquapin/chinkapin	red bay
chokecherry	redbud
cholla	redshank
cliffrose	redwood
cottonwood	Russian olive
crab apple	sassafras
cypress	sequoia
dogwood	service tree
Douglas fir	sourgum
elephant tree	sourwood
elm	spruce
eucalyptus	sumac
fig	sweet gum
fir	sycamore
ginkgo	tamarack
grapefruit	Texas ebony
hackberry	torreya
hawthorn	toyon
hazel	tulip tree
hemlock	tupelo
hickory	wahoo
hog plum	walnut
holly	willow
honey locust	yew
hornbeam	yucca

trek noun *a three-day trek across the desert* JOURNEY, trip, expedition, safari, odyssey, voyage; hike, march, slog, tramp, walk; long haul.

▸ verb *we trekked through the jungle* HIKE, tramp, march, slog, footslog, trudge, traipse, walk; travel, journey; *informal* hoof it.

trellis noun *rambling roses scrambled up the trellis* LATTICE, framework, espalier, arbor; network, mesh; grille, grid, grating; latticework; *technical* reticulation.

tremble verb 1 *Joe's hands were trembling* SHAKE, shake like a leaf, quiver, twitch, jerk; quaver, waver. See note at SHAKE.

2 *the entire building trembled* SHAKE, shudder, quake, wobble, rock, vibrate, move, sway, totter, teeter; *chiefly Brit.* judder.

3 *she trembled at the thought of what he had in store for her* BE AFRAID, be frightened, be apprehensive, worry, shake in one's boots; quail, quake, shrink, blench.

▸ noun *the slight tremble in her hands* TREMOR, shake, shakiness, trembling, quiver, quaking, twitch, vibration, unsteadiness. ANTONYM steadiness.

tremendous adjective 1 *tremendous sums of money* HUGE, enormous, immense, colossal, massive, prodigious, stupendous, monumental, mammoth, vast, gigantic, giant, mighty, epic, titanic, towering, king-size(d), jumbo, gargantuan, Herculean; substantial, considerable, Brobdingnagian; *informal* whopping, astronomical, humongous, ginormous. ANTONYMS tiny, small, slight.

2 *a tremendous explosion* VERY LOUD, deafening, ear-splitting, booming, thundering, thunderous, resounding. ANTONYM soft.

3 *informal I've seen him play and he's tremendous* EXCELLENT, splendid, wonderful, marvelous, magnificent, superb, sublime, lovely, delightful, too good to be true; *informal* super, great, amazing, fantastic, terrific, sensational, heavenly, divine, fabulous, awesome, to die for, magic, wicked, mind-blowing, splendiferous, far out, out of this world, brilliant, boss, swell. ANTONYMS bad, poor.

tremor noun 1 *the sudden tremor of her hands* TREMBLING, shaking, shakiness, tremble, shake, quivering, quiver, twitching, twitch, tic; quavering, quaver, quake, palpitation.

2 *a tremor of fear ran through her* SHIVER, frisson, spasm, thrill, tingle, stab, dart, wave, surge, rush, ripple.

3 *the epicenter of the tremor* EARTHQUAKE, earth tremor, shock; *informal* quake.

tremulous adjective 1 *a tremulous voice* SHAKY, trembling, shaking, unsteady, quavering, wavering, quivering, quivery, quaking, weak, warbly, trembly. ANTONYM steady.

2 *a tremulous smile* TIMID, diffident, shy, hesitant, uncertain, nervous, jittery, timorous, frightened, scared, anxious, apprehensive. ANTONYM confident.

trench noun *Chechen fighters steel themselves in their trenches around the city* DITCH, channel, trough, excavation, furrow, rut, conduit, cut, drain, duct, waterway, watercourse; entrenchment, moat; *Archaeology* fosse.

trenchant adjective *trenchant criticism of her leadership* INCISIVE, penetrating, sharp, keen, insightful, acute, focused, shrewd, razor-sharp, piercing; vigorous, forceful, strong, potent, telling, emphatic, forthright; mordant, cutting, biting, acerbic, pungent. ANTONYM vague.

trend noun 1 *an upward trend in unemployment* TENDENCY, movement, drift, swing, shift, course, current, direction, progression, inclination, leaning; bias, bent.

2 *the latest trend in dance music* FASHION, vogue, style, mode, craze, mania, rage; *informal* fad, thing, flavor of the month.

▸ verb *interest rates are trending up* MOVE, go, head, drift, gravitate, swing, shift, turn, incline, tend, lean, veer.

trendoid noun *informal Garth took his inheritance, moved uptown, and became a trendoid* TRENDSETTER, slave to fashion, fashion victim, fop.

▸ adjective See TRENDY.

trendy adjective *trendy teens vying for modeling jobs | trendy hairstyles* FASHIONABLE, in fashion, in vogue, popular, up-to-date, au courant, modern, all the rage, du jour, modish, à la mode, trendsetting; stylish, chic, designer; *informal* cool, funky, in, the in thing, hot, big, hip, now, happening, sharp, groovy, snazzy, with it, trendoid, tony, fly. ANTONYM unfashionable.

trepidation noun *he sat in the waiting room, full of trepidation* FEAR, apprehension, dread, fearfulness, fright, agitation, anxiety, worry, nervousness, tension, misgivings, unease, uneasiness, foreboding, disquiet, dismay, consternation, alarm, panic; *informal* butterflies (in one's stomach), jitteriness, the jitters, the creeps, the shivers, a cold sweat, the heebie-jeebies, the willies, the shakes, jim-jams, collywobbles, cold feet. ANTONYMS equanimity, composure.

trespass verb 1 *there is no excuse for* ***trespassing on*** *railroad property* INTRUDE ON, encroach on, enter without permission, invade.

2 *I must not* ***trespass on*** *your good nature* TAKE ADVANTAGE OF, impose on, play on, exploit, abuse; encroach on, infringe on.

3 *archaic he would be the last among us to trespass* SIN, transgress, offend, do wrong, err, go astray, fall from grace, stray from the straight and narrow.

▸ noun 1 *his alleged trespass on private land* UNLAWFUL ENTRY, intrusion, encroachment, invasion.

2 *archaic he asked forgiveness for his trespasses* SIN, wrong, wrongdoing, transgression, crime, offense, misdeed, misdemeanor, error, lapse, fall from grace.

trespasser noun *trespassers will be prosecuted* INTRUDER, interloper, unwelcome visitor, encroacher.

tresses plural noun *her strawberry blonde tresses* HAIR, head of hair, mane, mop of hair, shock of hair, shag of hair; locks, curls, ringlets.

trial noun 1 *the trial is expected to last several weeks* COURT CASE, case, assize, lawsuit, suit, hearing, inquiry, tribunal, litigation, legal proceedings, judicial proceedings, proceedings, legal action; court-martial; appeal, retrial.

2 *the product is undergoing clinical trials* TEST, tryout, experiment, pilot study; examination, check, assessment, evaluation, appraisal; trial/test period, trial/test run, beta test, dry run.

3 *she could be a bit of a trial at times* NUISANCE, pest, irritant, problem, ordeal, inconvenience, plague, thorn in one's side, one's cross to bear; bore; *informal* pain, pain in the neck, pain in the butt, headache, drag, bother, nightmare, albatross; nudnik, burr under someone's saddle.

4 *a long account of her trials and tribulations* TROUBLE, anxiety, worry, burden, affliction, ordeal, tribulation, adversity, hardship, trying time, tragedy, trauma, setback, difficulty, problem, misfortune, bad luck, mishap, misadventure; *informal* hassle; *literary* travails.

▸ adjective *a three-month trial period* TEST, experimental, pilot, exploratory, probationary, provisional.

tribalism noun *the latest waves of violence were blamed on tribalism* SECTARIANISM, chauvinism; esprit de corps.

tribe noun *nomadic tribes of the Sahara* ETHNIC GROUP, people, band, nation; family, dynasty, house, clan, sept.

tribulation noun **1** *the tribulations of her personal life* TROUBLE, difficulty, problem, worry, anxiety, burden, cross to bear, ordeal, trial, adversity, hardship, tragedy, sorrow, trauma, affliction; setback, blow; *informal* hassle; *literary* travail.

2 *his time of tribulation was just beginning* SUFFERING, distress, trouble, misery, wretchedness, unhappiness, sadness, heartache, woe, grief, sorrow, pain, anguish, agony; *literary* travail.

tribunal noun *they awaited the decision of the tribunal* ARBITRATION BOARD/PANEL, board, panel, committee, jury, forum; COURT, court of justice, court of law.

tributary noun *the countless tributaries of the mighty Mississippi* HEADWATER, creek, branch, fork, feeder, side stream, side channel, snye.

tribute noun **1** *tributes flooded in from friends and colleagues* ACCOLADE, praise, commendation, salute, testimonial, homage, eulogy, paean, panegyric; congratulations, compliments, plaudits, appreciation; gift, present, offering; bouquet; *formal* encomium. ANTONYMS criticism, condemnation.

2 *it is a tribute to his courage that he ever played again* TESTIMONY, indication, manifestation, testament, evidence, proof, attestation. PHRASE: **pay tribute to** *the players on both teams paid tribute to the retiring Ripken* PRAISE, sing the praises of, speak highly of, commend, acclaim, tip one's hat to, applaud, salute, honor, show appreciation of, recognize, acknowledge, pay homage to, extol; *formal* laud.

trice PHRASE: **in a trice** *the medics will be here in a trice* VERY SOON, in a moment, in a second, in an instant, shortly, ASAP, as soon as possible, pronto, any minute (now), in a short time, in no time, in less than no time, in a flash, before you know it, before long; momentarily, directly; *informal* in a jiffy, in the twinkling of an eye, in two shakes, in two shakes of a lamb's tail, in a snap; *dated* anon; *formal* forthwith.

trick noun **1** *he's capable of any mean trick | their clever little trick cost us $500* STRATAGEM, ploy, ruse, scheme, device, maneuver, contrivance, machination, artifice, wile, dodge; deceit, deception, trickery, subterfuge, chicanery, swindle, hoax, fraud, confidence trick; *informal* con, setup, rip-off, game, scam, sting, flimflam, bunco; *archaic* shift, fetch, rig.

2 *I think she's playing a trick on us* PRACTICAL JOKE, joke, prank, jape, spoof, gag, put-on.

3 *conjuring tricks* FEAT, stunt; **(tricks)** SLEIGHT OF HAND, legerdemain, prestidigitation; magic.

4 **(tricks)** *the tricks of the trade* KNACK, art, skills, techniques; secrets, shortcuts.

▸ verb *many people have been tricked by con artists with fake IDs* DECEIVE, delude, hoodwink, mislead, take in, dupe, fool, double-cross, cheat, defraud, swindle, gull, hoax, bamboozle, entrap; *informal* con, bilk, diddle, rook, put one over on, pull a fast one on, pull the wool over someone's eyes, take for a ride, shaft, flimflam, sucker, snooker; *literary* cozen, illude; *archaic* chicane.

PHRASES: **do the trick** *informal here, these two aspirins should do the trick* BE EFFECTIVE, work, solve the problem, fill/fit the bill. **trick of the light** *it was probably just a trick of the light* ILLUSION, optical illusion, figment of the imagination; mirage.

trickery noun *she suspects me of trickery* DECEPTION, deceit, dishonesty, cheating, duplicity, double-dealing, legerdemain, sleight of hand, guile, craftiness, deviousness, subterfuge, skulduggery, chicanery, fraud, fraudulence, swindling; *formal* pettifoggery; *informal* monkey business, funny business. ANTONYM honesty.

trickle verb *blood was trickling from two cuts in his lip* DRIP, dribble, ooze, leak, seep, percolate, spill. ANTONYMS pour, gush.

▸ noun *trickles of water* DRIBBLE, drip, thin stream, rivulet.

trickster noun *she spent her whole life loving and protecting a brother who was never better than the lowest of tricksters* SWINDLER, cheat, fraud, fraudster; charlatan, mountebank, quack, impostor, sham, hoaxer; rogue, villain, shyster, scoundrel; *informal* con man, con artist, sharp, shark, flimflammer, grifter, scam artist, bunco artist, chiseler.

tricky adjective **1** *a tricky situation* DIFFICULT, awkward, problematic, delicate, ticklish, sensitive, embarrassing, touchy; risky, uncertain, precarious, touch-and-go; thorny, knotty, complex, complicated; *informal* sticky, hairy, dicey. ANTONYMS straightforward, uncomplicated.

2 *a tricky and unscrupulous politician* CUNNING, crafty, wily, guileful, artful, devious, sly, scheming, slippery, slick, calculating, designing, sharp, shrewd, astute, canny; duplicitous, dishonest, deceitful. ANTONYM honest.

tried and true adjective *we rely on methods that are tried and true | a tried-and-true air purifier* RELIABLE, dependable, trustworthy, trusted, certain, sure; proven, tested, tried and tested, established, traditional, good old-fashioned, fail-safe; reputable.

trifle noun **1** *we needn't bother the principal over such trifles* UNIMPORTANT THING, trivial thing, triviality, thing of no importance, thing of no consequence, bagatelle, inessential, nothing; technicality, nonissue; **(trifles)** trivia, minutiae, flummery, small potatoes.

2 *we wrapped up a few trifles as party favors* BAUBLE, trinket, knickknack, gimcrack, gewgaw, toy; *informal* whatnot

3 *he bought it for* ***a trifle*** NEXT TO NOTHING, a very small amount; a pittance; *informal* peanuts, chump change. PHRASES: **a trifle** *Candace is a trifle miffed at Brad* A LITTLE, a bit, somewhat, a touch, a mite, a whit; *informal* a tad. **trifle with** *you should never have trifled with her emotions* PLAY WITH, amuse oneself with, toy with, dally with, be flippant with, flirt with, play fast and loose with, mess about with; *dated* sport with.

trifling adjective *a trifling matter* TRIVIAL, unimportant, insignificant, inconsequential, petty, minor, of little/no account, of little/no consequence, footling, pettifogging, incidental; silly, idle, insipid, superficial, small, tiny, inconsiderable, nominal, negligible, nugatory; *informal* piddling; *formal* exiguous. ANTONYM important.

trigger verb **1** *the incident triggered an acrimonious debate* PRECIPITATE, prompt, elicit, trigger off, set off, spark (off), touch off, provoke, stir up; cause, give rise to, launch, lead to, set in motion, occasion, bring about, generate, engender, begin, start, initiate; *literary* enkindle.

2 *thieves triggered the alarm* ACTIVATE, set off, set going, trip.

trill verb *songbirds trill their sweet music* WARBLE, sing, chirp, chirrup, tweet, twitter, cheep, peep.

trim verb **1** *his hair had been washed and trimmed* CUT, crop, bob, shorten, clip, snip, shear, barber; neaten, shape, tidy up.

2 ***trim off*** *the lower leaves using a sharp knife* CUT OFF, remove, take off, chop off, lop off; prune.

3 *production costs need to be trimmed* REDUCE, decrease, cut down, cut back on, scale down, prune, slim down, pare down, dock.

4 *the story was severely trimmed for the movie version* SHORTEN, abridge, condense, abbreviate, telescope, truncate.

5 *a pair of black leather gloves trimmed with fake fur* DECORATE, adorn, ornament, embellish; edge, pipe, border, hem, fringe.

▸ noun **1** *white curtains with a tasteful blue trim* DECORATION, trimming, ornamentation, adornment, embellishment; border, edging, piping, rickrack, hem, fringe, frill, frippery.

2 *an unruly mop in need of a trim* HAIRCUT, cut, barbering, clip, snip; pruning, tidying up.

▸ adjective **1** *a trim little villa* NEAT, tidy, neat and tidy, orderly, in (good) order, uncluttered, well-kept, well-maintained, shipshape, spruce, in apple-pie order, immaculate, spick-and-span. ANTONYMS untidy, messy.

2 *she does Pilates to stay trim* SLIM, in shape, slender, lean, sleek, willowy, lissome, svelte; streamlined. ANTONYM fat.

trimming noun **1** *a black dress with lace trimming.* See TRIM noun sense 1.

2 **(trimmings)** *roast turkey with all the trimmings* ACCOMPANIMENTS, extras, frills, fixings, accessories, accoutrements, trappings, paraphernalia; garnishing, garnish.

trinket noun *he brought back some lovely little trinkets from the South Seas* KNICKKNACK, bauble, ornament, bibelot, curio, trifle, gimcrack, gewgaw, toy, novelty; *informal* whatnot, doohickey, tchotchke; *dated* kickshaw.

trio noun *a talented trio from East Orange will sing the closing hymn* THREESOME, triumvirate, triad, trinity, troika; triplets.

trip verb **1** *he tripped on the loose stones* STUMBLE, lose one's footing, catch one's foot, slip, lose one's balance, fall, fall down, tumble, topple, take a spill, wipe out.

2 *students often* ***trip up*** *by forgetting to add a bibliography* MAKE A MISTAKE, miscalculate, make a blunder, blunder, go wrong, make an error, err; *informal* slip up, screw up, make a boo-boo, goof up, mess up, fluff.

3 *the question was intended to* trip *him* ***up*** CATCH OUT, trick, outwit, outsmart; throw off balance, disconcert, unsettle, discountenance, discomfit, throw, wrong-foot.

4 *they tripped merrily along the path* SKIP, run, dance, prance, bound, spring, scamper.

5 *Hoffman tripped the alarm* SET OFF, activate, trigger; turn on.

▸ noun **1** *a trip to Oahu* EXCURSION, outing, jaunt; VACATION, visit, tour, journey, expedition, voyage; drive, run, day out, day trip, road trip, cruise, junket, spin; *rare* peregrination. See note at JOURNEY.

2 *a trip down icy front steps can be a devastating accident* STUMBLE, slip, misstep, false step; fall, tumble, spill.

triple adjective **1** *a triple alliance* THREE-WAY, tripartite; threefold, trifold.

2 *they paid her triple the standard fee* THREE TIMES, treble.

trite adjective *critics were put off by the trite dialogue* BANAL, hackneyed, clichéd, platitudinous, vapid, commonplace, stock, conventional, stereotyped, overused, overdone, overworked, stale, worn out, timeworn, tired, hoary, hack, unimaginative, unoriginal, uninteresting, dull; *informal* old hat, corny, cornball, cheesy, boilerplate. ANTONYMS original, imaginative.

triumph noun **1** *Gretzky's many triumphs* VICTORY, win, conquest, success; achievement, feat, accomplishment. ANTONYM defeat.

2 *his eyes shone with triumph* JUBILATION, exultation, elation, delight, joy, happiness, glee, pride, satisfaction. ANTONYM disappointment.

3 *a triumph of their ingenuity* TOUR DE FORCE, masterpiece, coup, wonder, sensation, master stroke, feat. ANTONYM failure.

▸ verb **1** *she triumphed in the tournament* WIN, succeed, come first, clinch first place, be victorious, carry the day, prevail, take the honors, come out on top. ANTONYMS lose, fail.

2 *they had no chance of* ***triumphing over*** *the Democrats in the third district* DEFEAT, beat, conquer, trounce, vanquish, overcome, overpower, overwhelm, get the better of; bring someone to their knees, prevail against, subdue, subjugate; *informal* lick, best.

triumphant adjective **1** *the triumphant Swedish team* VICTORIOUS, successful, winning, conquering, all-conquering; undefeated, unbeaten. ANTONYMS unsuccessful, defeated.

2 *a triumphant expression* JUBILANT, exultant, elated, rejoicing, joyful, joyous, delighted, gleeful, proud, gloating. ANTONYMS disappointed, despondent.

trivia plural noun *his head is overflowing with obscure trivia* MINUTIAE, minor details, petty detail, niceties, technicalities, trivialities, trifles, trumpery, nonessentials, ephemera; *informal* small potatoes, peanuts.

trivial adjective **1** *trivial problems* UNIMPORTANT, banal, trite, commonplace, insignificant, inconsequential, minor, of no account, of no consequence, of no importance; incidental, inessential, nonessential, petty, trifling, trumpery, pettifogging, footling, small, slight, little, inconsiderable, negligible, paltry, nugatory; *informal* piddling, picayune, nickel-and-dime, penny-ante; *trademark* Mickey Mouse. ANTONYMS important, significant, life-and-death.

2 *I used to be quite a trivial person* FRIVOLOUS, superficial, shallow, unthinking, airheaded, featherbrained, lightweight, foolish, silly, trite. ANTONYMS profound, serious.

triviality noun **1** *the triviality of the subject matter* UNIMPORTANCE, insignificance, inconsequence, inconsequentiality, pettiness, banality.

2 *he need not concern himself with such trivialities* MINOR DETAIL, thing of no importance/consequence, trifle, nonessential, nothing; technicality; **(trivialities)** trivia, minutiae.

trivialize verb *I would appreciate it if you would not trivialize my problems* TREAT AS UNIMPORTANT, minimize, play down, underestimate, make light of, treat lightly, dismiss, underplay, downplay, diminish, belittle; *informal* pooh-pooh.

troll noun *the storybook trolls who live under the bridge* GOBLIN, hobgoblin, gnome, demon, monster, bugaboo, ogre. See also table at MONSTER.

troop noun **(troops)** *Ethiopian troops were stationed there* SOLDIERS, armed forces, servicemen, servicewomen, infantry; peacekeepers; guards, escorts; the services, the army, the military.

▸ verb *we trooped out of the hall* WALK, march, file, proceed; flock, crowd, throng, stream, swarm, surge, spill.

trophy noun **1** *a swimming trophy* CUP, medal; prize, award.

2 *a cabinet full of trophies from his travels* SOUVENIR, memento, keepsake; spoils, booty.

tropical adjective *tropical weather* VERY HOT, sweltering, boiling, scorching, humid, sultry, steamy, sticky, oppressive, stifling, suffocating, heavy, equatorial. ANTONYMS cold, arctic.

trot verb *the Scottie dog trotted across the patio* RUN, jog; scuttle, scurry, bustle, scamper.

troubadour noun *historical* *a band of wandering troubadours* MINSTREL, singer, balladeer, poet, bard; *historical* jongleur.

trouble noun **1** *you've caused enough trouble already* PROBLEMS, difficulty, bother, inconvenience, worry, concern, anxiety, distress, stress, strife, agitation, harassment, hassle, unpleasantness.

2 *she poured out all her troubles* PROBLEM, misfortune, difficulty, trial, tribulation, trauma, burden, pain, woe, grief, heartache, misery, affliction, vexation, suffering.

3 *he's gone to a lot of trouble to help you* EFFORT, inconvenience, fuss, bother, exertion, work, labor; pains, care, attention, thought.

4 *Rodney has been no trouble at all* NUISANCE, bother, inconvenience, irritation, irritant, problem, trial, pest, thorn in someone's flesh/side, headache, pain, pain in the neck/backside, drag; *informal* pain in the butt, burr under someone's saddle, nudnik.

5 *you're too gullible, that's your trouble* SHORTCOMING, flaw, weakness, weak point, failing, fault, imperfection, defect, blemish; problem, difficulty.

6 *he had a history of heart trouble* DISEASE, illness, sickness, ailments, complaints, problems; disorder, disability.

7 *the crash was due to engine trouble* MALFUNCTION, dysfunction, failure, breakdown.

8 *a game marred by serious crowd trouble* DISTURBANCE, disorder, unrest, unruliness, fighting, fracas, breach of the peace.

▸ verb **1** *this matter had been troubling her for some time* WORRY, bother, concern, disturb, upset, agitate, distress, perturb, annoy, irritate, vex, irk, nag, niggle, prey on someone's mind, weigh down, burden; *informal* bug.

2 *he **was troubled by** bouts of ill health* BE AFFLICTED BY, be burdened with; suffer from, be cursed with, be plagued by.

3 *there is nothing you need trouble about* WORRY, upset oneself, fret, be anxious, be concerned, concern oneself.

4 *don't trouble to see me out* BOTHER, take the trouble, go to the trouble, exert oneself, go out of one's way.

5 *I'm sorry to trouble you* INCONVENIENCE, bother, impose on, disturb, put out, pester, hassle; *formal* discommode.

PHRASE: **in trouble** *he comes to visit only when he's in trouble* IN DIFFICULTY, in difficulties, in a mess, in a bad way, in a predicament, in dire straits; *informal* in a fix, in a pickle, in a tight corner/spot, in a hole, in hot water, up a tree, up a/the creek, up against it.

troubled adjective **1** *Joanna looked troubled* ANXIOUS, worried, concerned, perturbed, disturbed, bothered, ill at ease, uneasy, unsettled, agitated; distressed, upset, dismayed, haunted.

2 *we live in troubled times* DIFFICULT, problematic, full of problems, unsettled, hard, tough, stressful, dark.

troublemaker noun *I have little use for my former friends, who were, for the most part, troublemakers* RABBLE-ROUSER, rogue, scourge, agitator, agent provocateur, ringleader; incendiary, firebrand, demagogue; scandalmonger, gossipmonger, meddler, nuisance, mischief-maker, hell raiser; *informal* badass.

troubleshooting noun *among our techies, Zach is the best at troubleshooting* FIXING, problem-solving, repairing, debugging, technical support; crisis management.

troublesome adjective **1** *a troublesome problem* ANNOYING, irritating, exasperating, maddening, infuriating, irksome, pesky, vexatious, vexing, bothersome, nettlesome, tiresome, worrying, worrisome, disturbing, upsetting, niggling, nagging; difficult, awkward, problematic, taxing; *informal* aggravating. ANTONYMS simple, straightforward.

2 *a troublesome child* DIFFICULT, awkward, trying, demanding, uncooperative, rebellious, unmanageable, unruly, obstreperous, disruptive, badly behaved, disobedient, naughty, recalcitrant, high-maintenance; *formal* refractory. ANTONYMS obedient, cooperative.

trough noun **1** *a large feeding trough* MANGER, feeder, bunk, rack, crib, feed box; waterer.

2 *a thirty-foot trough* CHANNEL, conduit, trench, ditch, gully, drain, culvert, cut, flume, gutter; rain gutter.

trounce verb *Turner scored a season-high 19 points when the UConn women trounced St. Joseph's 87–34* DEFEAT CONVINCINGLY, rout, crush, overwhelm; *informal* hammer, clobber, thrash, whip, drub, shellac, cream, skunk, pulverize, massacre, crucify, demolish, destroy, blow away, annihilate, make mincemeat of, wipe the floor with, walk all over, murder.

troupe noun *our theater troupe is on tour* GROUP, company, band, ensemble, set; cast.

trousers plural noun See PANTS. See also table at PANTS.

truancy noun *the Board of Ed wants to know why truancy in the high school is at an all-time high* ABSENTEEISM, nonattendance, playing truant, truanting; *informal* playing hooky, skipping; booking out.

truant noun *the truants were sent to Mr. Maurer's office* ABSENTEE, runaway. PHRASE: **play truant** *more than half of the freshman class staged a protest by playing truant on Monday* stay away from school; *informal* skip school, skip, play hooky; book out.

truce noun *news of the truce spread quickly among the locals* CEASE-FIRE, armistice, suspension of hostilities, peace, entente; respite, lull; *informal* letup.

truck noun *a heavily laden truck* RIG, eighteen-wheeler, transport, transport truck, tractor-trailer, flatbed; pickup, pickup truck, van; *Brit.* lorry.

trucker noun *the truckers always left her the most generous tips* TRUCK DRIVER, teamster.

truckle verb *an ambitious woman who* ***truckled to*** *no man* KOWTOW TO, submit to, defer to, yield to, back down to, bow and scrape to, be obsequious to, be subordinate to, pander to, toady to, prostrate oneself to, grovel to; dance attendance on, curry favor with, ingratiate oneself with; *informal* suck up to, crawl to, lick the boots of.

truculent adjective *a number of staffers have complained that Wilson is too truculent to work with* DEFIANT, aggressive, antagonistic, combative, belligerent, pugnacious, confrontational, ready for a fight, obstreperous, argumentative, quarrelsome, uncooperative; bad-tempered, ornery, short-tempered, cross, snappish, cranky; feisty, spoiling for a fight. ANTONYMS cooperative, amiable.

trudge verb *they trudged through two miles of wet snow* PLOD, tramp, tromp, drag oneself, walk heavily, walk slowly, plow, slog, toil, trek; *informal* traipse, galumph.

true adjective **1** *you'll see that what I say is true* CORRECT, accurate, right, verifiable, in accordance with the facts, what actually/really happened, well-documented, the case, so; literal, factual, unelaborated, unvarnished. ANTONYMS untrue, false, fallacious.

2 *people are still willing to pay for true craftsmanship* GENUINE, authentic, real, actual, bona fide, proper; honest-to-goodness, kosher, legit, the real McCoy. ANTONYMS bogus, phony.

3 *the true owner of the goods* RIGHTFUL, legitimate, legal, lawful, authorized, bona fide, de jure. ANTONYM de facto.

4 *the necessity for true repentance* SINCERE, genuine, real, unfeigned, heartfelt, hearty, from the heart. ANTONYMS insincere, feigned.

5 *a true friend* LOYAL, faithful, constant, devoted, staunch, steadfast, true-blue, unswerving, unwavering; trustworthy, trusty, reliable, dependable. ANTONYMS disloyal, faithless.

6 *a true reflection of life in the 50s* ACCURATE, true to life, faithful, telling it like it is, fact-based, realistic, close, lifelike. ANTONYM inaccurate.

true-blue adjective *my parents were God-fearing, true-blue Democrats* STAUNCH, loyal, faithful, stalwart, committed, card-carrying, confirmed, dyed-in-the-wool, devoted, dedicated, firm, steadfast, unswerving, unwavering, unfaltering.

truism noun *"look before you leap" is a truism that Sharon has rarely heeded* PLATITUDE, commonplace, cliché, stock phrase, banality, (old) chestnut, (old) saw, axiom, bromide.

truly adverb **1** *tell me truly what you want* TRUTHFULLY, honestly, frankly, sincerely, candidly, openly, to someone's face, laying one's cards on the table; *informal* pulling no punches.

2 *I'm truly grateful to them* SINCERELY, genuinely, really, indeed, from the bottom of one's heart, heartily, profoundly; very, surely, extremely, immensely, thoroughly, positively, completely, tremendously, totally, incredibly, awfully; *formal* most; *informal* sure.

3 *this is truly a miracle* WITHOUT (A) DOUBT, unquestionably, undoubtedly, certainly, surely, definitely, beyond doubt, beyond question, indubitably, undeniably, beyond the shadow of a doubt; in truth, really, in reality, actually, in fact; *archaic* forsooth, verily.

4 *exams do not truly reflect children's abilities* ACCURATELY, correctly, exactly, precisely, faithfully; *informal* to a T.

trump verb *by wearing the simplest of dresses, she had trumped them all* OUTSHINE, outclass, upstage, put in the shade, eclipse, surpass, outdo, outperform; beat, better, top, cap; *informal* be a cut above, be head and shoulders above, leave standing.

trumped-up adjective *they held him on trumped-up charges of theft and drug possession* BOGUS, spurious, specious, false, fabricated, invented, manufactured, contrived, made-up, falsified, fake, factitious; *informal* phony, cooked-up. ANTONYM genuine.

trumpet verb **1** *the elephant trumpeted* call out, bellow, roar, yell, cry out, toot, bugle, holler.

2 *companies trumpeted their success* PROCLAIM, announce, declare, herald, celebrate, shout from the rooftops.

truncate verb *the program may need to be truncated* SHORTEN, cut, cut short, curtail, bring to an untimely end; abbreviate, condense, reduce, prune. ANTONYMS lengthen, extend.

truncheon noun See BLUDGEON noun.

trunk noun **1** *the trunk of a tree* MAIN STEM, bole.

2 *the trunk of her car* LUGGAGE COMPARTMENT, back.

3 *his powerful trunk* TORSO, body, upper body.

4 *an elephant's trunk* PROBOSCIS, nose, snout.

5 *a steamer trunk* CHEST, box, crate, coffer; case.

truss noun *three steel trusses* SUPPORT, buttress, joist, brace, beam, prop, strut, stay, stanchion, pier.

▸ verb *she taught us how to truss the hens before roasting* TIE UP, bind, chain up; pinion, fetter, tether, secure; swaddle, wrap.

trust noun **1** *good relationships are built on trust* CONFIDENCE, belief, faith, certainty, assurance, conviction, credence; reliance. ANTONYMS distrust, mistrust, doubt.

2 *a position of trust* RESPONSIBILITY, duty, obligation.

3 *the money is to be held in trust for his son* SAFEKEEPING, protection, charge, care, custody; trusteeship.

▸ verb **1** *I should never have trusted her* PUT ONE'S TRUST IN, have faith in, have (every) confidence in, believe in, pin one's hopes/faith on, confide in. ANTONYMS distrust, mistrust, doubt.

2 *he can be trusted to carry out an impartial investigation* RELY ON, depend on, bank on, count on, be sure of.

3 *I trust we shall meet again* HOPE, expect, take it, assume, presume, suppose.

4 *they don't like to trust their money to anyone outside the family* ENTRUST, consign, commit, give, hand over, turn over, assign.

trustee noun *Uncle Harris was appointed trustee of Esther's estate* ADMINISTRATOR, agent; custodian, keeper, steward, depositary; executor, executrix; board member; *Law* fiduciary.

trusting adjective *her experiences with David have made her far less trusting* TRUSTFUL, unsuspecting, unquestioning, unguarded, unwary; naive, innocent, childlike, ingenuous, wide-eyed, credulous, gullible, easily taken in. See note at GULLIBLE. ANTONYMS distrustful, suspicious.

trustworthy adjective *a trustworthy citizen* RELIABLE, dependable, honest, honorable, upright, principled, true, truthful, as good as one's word, ethical, virtuous, incorruptible, unimpeachable, above suspicion; responsible, sensible, levelheaded; loyal, faithful, staunch, steadfast, trusty; safe, sound, reputable, discreet; *informal* on the level, straight-up. ANTONYM unreliable.

trusty adjective *a cowboy and his trusty horse* RELIABLE, dependable, trustworthy, unfailing, fail-safe, trusted, tried and true; loyal, faithful, true, staunch, steadfast, constant, unswerving, unwavering. ANTONYM unreliable.

truth noun **1** *he doubted the truth of her statement* VERACITY, truthfulness, verity, sincerity, candor, honesty; accuracy, correctness, validity, factuality, authenticity. ANTONYMS dishonesty, falseness.

2 *it's **the truth**, I swear* WHAT ACTUALLY HAPPENED, the case, so; the gospel (truth), the honest truth. ANTONYM lies.

3 *truth is stranger than fiction* FACT(S), reality, real life, actuality. ANTONYM fiction.

4 *scientific truths* FACT, verity, certainty, certitude; law, principle. ANTONYMS lie, falsehood.

PHRASE: **in truth** *in truth, their marriage was rocky from the start* IN FACT, in actual fact, as it happens, in point of fact, in reality, really, actually, to tell the truth, if truth be told.

truthful adjective **1** *truthful behavior* HONEST, sincere, trustworthy, genuine; candid, frank, straight-shooting, open, forthright, straight, upfront, on the level, on the up and up. ANTONYMS deceitful, deceptive.

2 *a truthful account* TRUE, accurate, correct, factual, faithful, reliable; unvarnished, unembellished, unidealized; *formal* veracious, veridical. ANTONYMS inaccurate, untrue.

try verb **1** *try to help him* ATTEMPT, endeavor, venture, make an effort, exert oneself, strive, do one's best, do one's utmost, move heaven and earth; undertake, aim, take it upon oneself; *informal* have a go, give it one's best shot, bend over backwards, bust a gut, do one's damnedest, pull out all the stops, go all out, knock oneself out; *formal* essay.

2 *try it and see what you think* TEST, put to the test, sample, taste, inspect, investigate, examine, appraise, evaluate, assess; *informal* check out, give something a whirl, test drive.

3 *Mary tried everyone's patience* TAX, strain, test, stretch, sap, drain, exhaust, wear out.

4 *the case is to be tried by a jury* ADJUDICATE, consider, hear, adjudge, examine.

▸ noun *I'll have one last try* ATTEMPT, effort, endeavor; *informal* go, shot, crack, stab; *formal* essay.

PHRASE: **try something out** *they volunteered to try out the*

→ ***trustworthy***
honorable
reputable
upright
honest
faithful
conscientious
industrious
capable
competent
dependable
trusty
responsible
reliable
wise
sane
rational
reasonable
sensible
mature
adult
discreet
stable
sensible
adult
levelheaded
reliable
practical
experienced
hard-working
studious
willing to learn
untrained
inexpert
inexperienced
immature
flighty
giddy
bull-in-a-china-shop
scatterbrained
harebrained
featherbrained
harum-scarum
slap-happy
naive
foolish
careless
fickle
capricious
mutable
erratic
undependable
irresponsible
unpredictable
irregular
undependable
unreliable
inconstant
untrue
reckless
untrustworthy
faithless
negligent
unreliable ←

new system TEST, trial, experiment with, pilot; put through its paces; assess, evaluate.

trying adjective **1** *a trying day* STRESSFUL, taxing, demanding, difficult, tough, hard, pressured, frustrating, fraught; arduous, grueling, tiring, exhausting; *informal* hellish. See note at HARD. ANTONYMS easy, painless.

2 *Steve was very trying* ANNOYING, irritating, exasperating, maddening, infuriating; tiresome, irksome, troublesome, bothersome, vexing; *informal* aggravating. ANTONYM accommodating.

tryout noun *the tryouts begin on Thursday* TRIAL, audition, training camp, test.

tryst noun *a secret tryst known only to Mamie and her lover* MEETING, rendezvous, date, appointment, assignation; love affair.

tub noun **1** *a wooden tub* CONTAINER, barrel, cask, drum, keg.

2 *a tub of yogurt* CONTAINER, carton, cup.

3 *a soak in the tub* BATH, bathtub; hot tub, Jacuzzi.

tubby adjective *informal* See CHUBBY.

tube noun *the fluid travels through the tube* CYLINDER, pipe, piping, conduit, line, flue, hose, cannula, catheter, siphon, pipette, funnel, duct, pipeline, drain.

tuck verb **1** *he tucked his shirt into his pants* PUSH, insert, slip, fold; thrust, stuff, stick, cram.

2 *the dress was tucked all over* PLEAT, gather, fold, ruffle.

3 *he tucked the knife behind his seat* HIDE, conceal, secrete; store, stow, stash.

▸ noun *a dress with tucks* PLEAT, gather, fold, ruffle.

PHRASE: **tuck in** *Toby tucked the children in after reading them a story* PUT TO BED, settle down, cover up; make comfortable.

tuft noun *tufts of grass | a tuft of hair* CLUMP, bunch, knot, cluster, tussock, tuffet; lock, wisp; crest, topknot; tassel.

tug verb **1** *Ben* ***tugged at*** *her sleeve* PULL (AT), pluck, tweak, twitch, jerk, wrench; catch hold of, yank (at).

2 *she tugged him toward the door* DRAG, pull, lug, draw, haul, heave, tow.

▸ noun *one good tug would loosen it* PULL, jerk, wrench, heave, yank.

tug-of-war noun *the ongoing tug-of-war between rival drug czars* STRUGGLE, battle, conflict, fight, altercation, duel, tussle, wrangle, dispute, rivalry.

tuition noun **1** *students go broke paying the increased tuition* FEES, charges, bill.

2 *her skill improved with tuition* INSTRUCTION, teaching, coaching, tutoring, tutelage, lessons, education, schooling; training, drill, preparation, guidance.

tumble verb **1** *he* ***tumbled over*** FALL (OVER), fall down, topple over, lose one's balance, keel over, take a spill, go headlong, go head over heels, trip, stumble; *informal* come a cropper.

2 *they all tumbled from the room* HURRY, rush, scramble, scurry, bound, pile, bundle.

3 *a creek tumbled over the rocks* CASCADE, fall, flow, pour, spill, stream.

4 *oil prices tumbled* PLUMMET, plunge, fall, dive, nosedive, drop, slump, slide, decrease, decline, crash. ANTONYM rise.

▸ noun **1** *I took a tumble in the bushes* FALL, trip, spill; *informal* nosedive.

2 *a tumble in share prices* DROP, fall, plunge, dive, nosedive, slump, decline, collapse; *informal* crash. ANTONYM rise.

tumbledown adjective *a tumbledown shack in the woods* DILAPIDATED, ramshackle, decrepit, neglected, beat-up, run-down, falling to pieces, decaying, derelict, crumbling; rickety, shaky.

tummy noun *informal a nice firm and flat tummy* STOMACH, abdomen, belly, gut, middle, midriff, paunch, breadbasket; *informal* insides.

tumor noun *a biopsy of the tumor* CANCEROUS GROWTH, malignant growth, cancer, malignancy; lump, growth, swelling, fibroid; *Medicine* carcinoma, sarcoma.

tumult noun **1** *she added her voice to the tumult* CLAMOR, din, noise, racket, uproar, hue and cry, commotion, ruckus, maelstrom, rumpus, hubbub, pandemonium, babel, bedlam, brouhaha, furor, fracas, melee, frenzy; *informal* hullabaloo. ANTONYM silence.

2 *years of political tumult* TURMOIL, confusion, disorder, disarray, unrest, chaos, turbulence, mayhem, maelstrom, havoc, upheaval, ferment, agitation, trouble. ANTONYM tranquility.

tumultuous adjective **1** *tumultuous applause* LOUD, deafening, thunderous, uproarious, noisy, clamorous, vociferous, vehement. ANTONYM soft.

2 *their tumultuous relationship* TEMPESTUOUS, stormy, turbulent, passionate, intense, explosive, violent, volatile, full of ups and downs, roller-coaster. ANTONYMS peaceful, uneventful.

3 *a tumultuous crowd* DISORDERLY, unruly, rowdy, turbulent, boisterous, excited, agitated, restless, wild, riotous, frenzied. ANTONYM orderly.

tune noun *she hummed a cheerful tune* MELODY, air, strain, theme; song, jingle, ditty.

▸ verb **1** *they tuned their guitars* ADJUST, fine-tune, tune up.

2 *a body clock tuned to the lunar cycle* ATTUNE, adapt, adjust, fine-tune; regulate, modulate.

PHRASES: **change one's tune** *our "Bachelor Bob" seems to have changed his tune about settling down and raising a family* CHANGE ONE'S MIND, do a U-turn, have a change of heart; do an about-face; *informal* do a one-eighty, pull a U-ey. **in tune** *are any of the candidates really in tune with the voters?* IN ACCORD, in keeping, in accordance, in agreement, in harmony, in step, in line, in sympathy, compatible. **tune up** *most of these old cash registers just need to be tuned up a bit* TWEAK, adjust, fine-tune, calibrate, maintain, improve, ameliorate, enhance.

tuneful adjective *an evening of tuneful songs* MELODIOUS, melodic, musical, mellifluous, dulcet, euphonious, harmonious, lyrical, lilting, sweet. ANTONYM discordant.

tuneless adjective *his tuneless whistling* DISCORDANT, unmelodious, dissonant, harsh, cacophonous; monotonous, dull. ANTONYM melodious.

tune-up noun *all of our vehicles have regular tune-ups* SERVICE, servicing, maintenance, repairs, fine-tuning, tweaking.

tunnel noun *a tunnel under the hills* UNDERGROUND PASSAGE, underpass, subway; shaft; burrow, hole; *historical* mine.

▸ verb *he tunneled under the fence* DIG, burrow, mine, bore, drill.

tunnel vision noun *without the tunnel vision that exasperated their friends and family, this team of inventors would never have made their mark in history* NARROW FOCUS, concentration, fixation, narrow-mindedness, single-mindedness, closed-mindedness.

turbid adjective *turbid waters* MURKY, opaque, cloudy, unclear, muddy, thick, milky, roily. ANTONYM clear.

EASILY CONFUSED WORDS **turbid, turgid**

Is it **turbid** or **turgid**? **Turbid** is used of a liquid or color to mean 'muddy, not clear': *turbid water*. **Turgid** means 'swollen, inflated, enlarged': *turgid veins*. Both **turbid** and **turgid** can also be used to describe language or literary style: as such, **turbid** means 'confused' (*the turbid utterances of Carlyle)*, and **turgid** means 'pompous, bombastic' (*a turgid and pretentious essay*).

turbulent adjective **1** *the country's turbulent past* TEMPESTUOUS, stormy, unstable, unsettled, tumultuous, chaotic; violent, anarchic, lawless. ANTONYM peaceful.

2 *turbulent seas* ROUGH, stormy, tempestuous, storm-tossed, heavy, violent, wild, roiling, raging, seething, choppy, agitated, boisterous. ANTONYM calm.

turd noun *informal golfers are complaining about the goose turds* STOOL, dung, scat, dropping; excrement, feces, fecal matter; *informal* poo, doo-doo.

turf noun **1** *they walked over a patch of turf* GRASS, lawn, sod.

2 *she was keen to protect her turf* TERRITORY, domain, province, preserve, sphere of influence; stomping ground, stamping ground; bailiwick.

turgid adjective **1** *his turgid prose* BOMBASTIC, pompous, overblown, inflated, tumid, high-flown, puffed up, affected, pretentious, grandiose, florid, ornate, grandiloquent, orotund; *informal* highfalutin, purple. ANTONYM simple.

2 *the tissues become turgid* SWOLLEN, distended, tumescent, engorged, bloated, tumid. See note at TURBID.

turmoil noun *political turmoil* CONFUSION, upheaval, turbulence, tumult, disorder, disturbance, agitation, ferment, unrest, disquiet, trouble, disruption, chaos, mayhem; uncertainty. ANTONYM peace.

PHRASE: **in turmoil** *Michel's sudden death left the family in turmoil* CONFUSED, chaotic, in chaos, topsy-turvy, at sixes and sevens; reeling, disorientated; *informal* all over the place.

turn verb **1** *the wheels were still turning* GO AROUND, revolve, rotate, spin, roll, circle, wheel, whirl, twirl, gyrate, swivel, pivot.

2 *I turned and headed back* CHANGE DIRECTION, change course, make a U-turn, about-face, turn around/about; *informal* pull a U-ey, do a one-eighty.

3 *the car turned the corner* GO AROUND, round, negotiate, take.

4 *the path turned to right and left* BEND, curve, wind, veer, twist, meander, snake, zigzag.

5 *he **turned** his gun **on** Lenny* AIM AT, point at, level at, direct at, train on.

6 *he turned his ankle* SPRAIN, twist, wrench; hurt.

7 *their honeymoon **turned into** a nightmare* BECOME, develop into, turn out to be; be transformed into, metamorphose into, descend into, grow into.

8 *Emma turned red* BECOME, go, grow, get.

9 *he turned the house into apartments* CONVERT, change, transform, make; adapt, modify, rebuild, reconstruct.

10 *I've just turned forty* REACH, get to, become, hit.

11 *she **turned to** politics* TAKE UP, become involved in, go into, enter, undertake.

12 *we can now **turn to** another topic* MOVE ON TO, go on to, proceed to, consider, attend to, address; take up, switch to.

▸ noun **1** *a turn of the wheel* ROTATION, revolution, spin, whirl, gyration, swivel.

2 *a turn to the left* CHANGE OF DIRECTION, veer, divergence.

3 *we're approaching the turn* BEND, corner, turning, turn-off, junction, crossroads.

4 *you'll get your turn in a minute* OPPORTUNITY, chance, say; stint, time; try; *informal* go, shot, stab, crack.

5 *she did me some good turns* SERVICE, deed, act; favor, kindness.

PHRASES: **at every turn** *her name seemed to come up at every turn* REPEATEDLY, recurrently, all the time, always, constantly, again and again. **in turn** *let's consider these three points in turn* ONE AFTER THE OTHER, one by one, one at a time, in succession, successively, sequentially. **take a turn for the better** *his luck took a turn for the better* IMPROVE, pick up, look up, perk up, rally, turn the corner; recover, revive. **take a turn for the worse** *even the doctors were surprised when Richie took a turn for the worse* DETERIORATE, worsen, decline; *informal* go downhill. **turn against** *after his father died, Bruce turned against his stepmother* BECOME HOSTILE TO, take a dislike to, betray, double-cross. **turn away** *I know you're hurt, but please don't turn us away* SEND AWAY, reject, rebuff, repel, cold-shoulder; *informal* send packing. **turn back** *just before boarding the ferry, Clint changed his mind and turned back* RETRACE ONE'S STEPS, go back, return; retreat. **turn down 1** *his novel was turned down* REJECT, refuse, decline, spurn, rebuff. **2** *Pete turned the volume down* REDUCE, lower, decrease, lessen; muffle, mute. **turn in 1** *he turned in his brother to the police* BETRAY, inform on, denounce, sell out, stab someone in the back; blow the whistle on, rat on, squeal on, finger. **2** *we turned in the entrance forms just in time* HAND IN/OVER/BACK, give in, submit, surrender, give up; deliver, return. **3** *I usually turn in before 10 o'clock* GO TO BED, retire, go to sleep, call it a day; *informal* hit the hay, hit the sack. **turn of events** *she was unprepared for this turn of events* DEVELOPMENT, incident, occurrence, happening, circumstance, surprise. **turn of phrase** *a clever turn of phrase* EXPRESSION, idiom, phrase, term, word, aphorism. **turn off 1** *his so-called jokes really turn me off* PUT OFF, leave cold, repel, disgust, revolt, offend; disenchant, alienate; bore, gross out. **2** *please turn off the garage lights* SWITCH OFF, shut off, turn out; extinguish; deactivate; *informal* kill, cut, power down. **turn on 1** *the decision turned on the law* DEPEND ON, rest on, hinge on, be contingent on, be decided by. **2** *okay, I admit it—his green eyes turn me on.* See AROUSE sense 3. **3** *I'll turn on the generator* SWITCH ON, start up, activate, trip, power up. **4** *it began as a simple disagreement, but then he turned on us like a mad dog* ATTACK, set on, fall on, let fly at, lash out at, hit out at; *informal* lay into, tear into, let someone have it, bite someone's head off, jump down someone's throat; light into. **turn on to** *Christie has turned me on to the health benefits of yoga* INTRODUCE SOMEONE TO, get someone into, pique someone's interest in. **turn out 1** *a huge crowd turned out* COME, be present, attend, appear, turn up, arrive; assemble, gather, show up. **2** *it turned out that she had been abroad* TRANSPIRE, emerge, come to light, become apparent, become clear. **3** *things didn't turn out as I'd intended* HAPPEN, occur, come about; develop, proceed; work out, come out, end up, pan out, result; *formal* eventuate. **4** *it's about time she turned out that bum of a boyfriend* THROW OUT, eject, evict, expel, oust, drum out, banish; *informal* kick out, send packing, boot out, show someone the door. **5** *turn out the light.* See TURN OFF (above) sense 2. **6** *they turn out a million engines a year* PRODUCE, make, manufacture, fabricate, generate, put out, churn out. **turn over 1** *the crate fell off the back of the truck and turned over* OVERTURN, upturn, capsize, keel over, flip, turn turtle, be upended, tip. **2** *I turned over a few pages* FLIP OVER, flick through, leaf through. **3** *she turned the proposal over in her mind* THINK ABOUT, think over, consider, ponder, contemplate, reflect on, chew over, mull over, muse on, ruminate on. **4** *he turned over the business to his brother* TRANSFER, hand over, pass on, consign, commit. **turn someone's stomach** *the sight of blood turns my stomach* NAUSEATE SOMEONE, sicken someone, make someone sick. **turn to** *I always had my grandparents to turn to* SEEK HELP FROM, have recourse to, approach, apply to, appeal to; take to, resort to. **turn up 1** *the missing documents turned up* BE FOUND, be discovered, be located, reappear. **2** *the police turned up* ARRIVE, appear, present oneself, show up, show, show one's face. **3** *something better will turn up* PRESENT ITSELF, offer itself, occur, happen, crop up, appear. **4** *she turned up the treble* INCREASE, raise, amplify, intensify. **5** *they turned up lots of information* DISCOVER, uncover, unearth, find, dig up, ferret out, root out, expose.

turnaround noun *has any character's turnaround been as celebrated as Scrooge's?* REVERSAL, change, sea change, turnabout, volte-face, about-face, one-eighty.

turncoat noun *the Dunlaps were wrongly accused of harboring turncoats during the war* TRAITOR, renegade, defector, deserter, betrayer; Judas, Benedict Arnold; fifth columnist, quisling; *informal* rat, fink.

turning point noun *the turning point in their relationship* CROSSROADS, critical moment, decisive moment, moment of truth, watershed, crisis, landmark.

turnoff noun **1** *I missed my turnoff* TURN, exit, junction, off-ramp, turning.

2 *informal narrow-mindedness is a real turnoff for me* PEEVE, bugbear, bête noire, disincentive; *informal* no-no, gross-out.

turn-on noun *informal good manners are a definite turn-on* ATTRACTION, aphrodisiac, thrill, stimulant, rush, inducement, incentive.

turnout noun *the producers were overjoyed with the turnout* ATTENDANCE, audience, crowd, gathering, showing, throng, assembly, assemblage, congregation, number; participation.

turnover noun **1** *an annual turnover of $2.25 million* (GROSS) REVENUE, income, yield; sales, gross.

2 *a high turnover of staff* rate of replacement, change, movement.

3 See table at PIE.

turpitude noun *formal* See DEPRAVITY.

tussle noun *his glasses were smashed in the tussle* SCUFFLE, fight, struggle, skirmish, brawl, scrum, rough-and-tumble, free-for-all, fracas, fray, rumpus, melee; *informal* spat, scrap, roughhouse, tug-of-war.

▸ verb *demonstrators tussled with police* SCUFFLE, fight, struggle, brawl, grapple, wrestle, clash; *informal* scrap, roughhouse.

tutor noun *a history tutor* TEACHER, instructor, educator, lecturer, trainer, mentor; *formal* pedagogue.

▸ verb *he was tutored at home* TEACH, instruct, educate, school, coach, train, drill.

tutorial noun *Clarence will give a tutorial for those unfamiliar with our new spreadsheet* LESSON, class, seminar, training session.

tuxedo noun *Aaron looks handsome in his tuxedo* FORMAL WEAR; *informal* penguin suit, monkey suit, tux.

TV noun See TELEVISION.

twaddle noun *informal* See NONSENSE sense 1. See note at NONSENSE.

tweak verb **1** *she tweaked his nose* PULL, jerk, tug, twist, twitch, pinch, squeeze.

2 *the product can be tweaked to suit your needs* ADJUST, modify, alter, change, adapt; refine.

▸ noun **1** *he gave her hair a tweak* PULL, jerk, tug, twist, pinch, twitch, squeeze.

2 *a few minor tweaks were required* ADJUSTMENT, modification, alteration, change; refinement.

tweet verb See CHIRP.

tweeze verb *tweezing her eyebrows* PLUCK, tweezer, pinch, extract.

tweezers noun *before using, dip the tweezers in alcohol* PINCERS; pliers, needle-nose pliers.

twerp noun *informal* See FOOL noun sense 1.

twiddle verb *she twiddled the dials* TURN, twist, swivel, twirl; adjust, move, jiggle; fiddle with, play with. PHRASE: **twiddle one's thumbs** *don't just sit there twiddling your thumbs* BE IDLE, do nothing, kill time, waste time, hang around, stand/sit around; *informal* futz around.

twig noun *leafy twigs* STICK, sprig, shoot, stem, branchlet.

twilight noun **1** *we arrived at twilight* DUSK, sunset, sundown, nightfall, evening, close of day, day's end; *literary* eventide, gloaming. ANTONYMS dawn, daybreak.

2 *it was scarcely visible in the twilight* HALF-LIGHT, semidarkness, gloom.

3 *the twilight of his career* DECLINE, waning, ebb; autumn, final years, tail end. ANTONYMS dawn, peak, height.

▸ adjective *a twilight world* SHADOWY, dark, shady, dim, gloomy, obscure, crepuscular, twilit.

twin noun *a bedroom that was the twin of her own* DUPLICATE, double, carbon copy, exact likeness, mirror image, replica, look-alike, doppelgänger, clone; counterpart, match, pair; *informal* dead ringer, spitting image.

▸ adjective **1** *twin peaks* MATCHING, identical, matched, paired.

2 *the twin aims of conservation and recreation* TWOFOLD, double, dual; related, linked, connected; corresponding, parallel, complementary, equivalent.

▸ verb *the company twinned its brewing with distilling* COMBINE, join, link, couple, pair.

twine noun *a ball of twine* STRING, cord, thread, yarn.

▸ verb **1** *she twined her arms around him* WIND, entwine, wrap, wreathe.

2 *ivy twined around the tree* ENTWINE (ITSELF), coil, loop, twist, spiral, curl; weave, interlace, intertwine, braid.

twinge noun **1** *twinges in her stomach* PAIN, spasm, ache, throb; cramp, stitch.

2 *a twinge of guilt* PANG, prick, qualm, scruple, misgiving.

twinkle noun & verb *a twinkle in her eye | the lights of the city twinkled below me* GLITTER, sparkle, shine, glimmer, shimmer, glint, gleam, flicker, flash, wink; *literary* glister.

twinkling adjective *twinkling white lights graced the gazebo* SPARKLING, glistening, glittering, glimmering, glinting, gleaming, flickering, winking, shining, scintillating, lambent; *literary* coruscating.

twirl verb **1** *he twirled the gun around* SPIN, whirl, turn, pivot, swivel, twist, revolve, rotate.

2 *she twirled her hair around her finger* WIND, twist, coil, curl, wrap.

▸ noun *she did a quick twirl* PIROUETTE, spin, whirl, turn, twist, rotation, revolution, gyration, twizzle.

twist verb **1** *the impact twisted the chassis* CRUMPLE, crush, buckle, mangle, warp, deform, distort.

2 *her face twisted with rage* CONTORT, screw up.

3 *Ma anxiously twisted a handkerchief* WRING, squeeze.

4 *he twisted around in his seat* TURN (AROUND), swivel (around), spin (around), pivot, rotate, revolve.

5 *she twisted out of his grasp* WRIGGLE, squirm, worm one's way, wiggle.

6 *I twisted my ankle* SPRAIN, wrench, turn.

7 *you are twisting my words* DISTORT, misrepresent, change, alter, pervert, falsify, warp, skew, misinterpret, misconstrue, misstate, misquote; garble.

8 *he twisted the radio knob* TWIDDLE, adjust, turn, rotate, swivel.

9 *she twisted her hair around her finger* WIND, twirl, coil, curl, wrap.

10 *the wires were twisted together* INTERTWINE, twine, interlace, weave, plait, braid, coil, wind.

11 *the road twisted and turned* WIND, bend, curve, turn, meander, weave, zigzag, swerve, snake.

▸ noun **1** *a twist of the wrist* TURN, twirl, spin, rotation; flick.

2 *the twists of the road* BEND, curve, turn, zigzag, kink.

3 *the twists of the plot* CONVOLUTION, complication, complexity, intricacy; surprise, revelation.

4 *a modern twist on an old theme* INTERPRETATION, slant, outlook, angle, approach, treatment; variation, change, difference.

PHRASE: **twist someone's arm** *I didn't want to go with them, but Hazel twisted my arm* PRESSURIZE SOMEONE, coerce someone, force someone; persuade someone; *informal* lean on someone, browbeat someone, strong-arm someone, bulldoze someone, railroad someone, put the screws to/on someone.

twisted adjective **1** *twisted metal* CRUMPLED, bent, crushed, buckled, warped, misshapen, distorted, deformed.

2 *his twisted mind* PERVERTED, warped, deviant, depraved, corrupt, abnormal, unhealthy, aberrant, distorted, corrupted, debauched, debased, disturbed; *informal* sick, kinky.

twisty adjective *the river gets very twisty just south of the old ironworks* WINDING, windy, twisting, bendy, zigzag, meandering, curving, sinuous, snaky. ANTONYM straight.

twit noun *informal* See FOOL noun sense 1.

twitch verb *he twitched and then lay still* JERK, convulse, have a spasm, quiver, tremble, shiver, shudder.

▸ noun **1** *a twitch of her lips* SPASM, convulsion, quiver, tremor, shiver, shudder, small movement; tic.

2 *he gave a twitch at his mustache* PULL, tug, tweak, yank, jerk.

3 *he felt a twitch in his left side* PANG, twinge, dart, stab, prick.

twitter verb **1** *sparrows twittered under the eaves* CHIRP, chirrup, cheep, tweet, peep, chatter, trill, warble, sing.

2 *stop twittering about Francis* BLATHER, jabber, blabber, chatter, chitter, gabble, go on, blab, rattle, yap, prattle, babble, blither, ramble; *informal* yak, quack, yabber, talk someone's ear off.

▸ noun **1** *a bird's twitter* CHIRP, chirrup, cheep, tweet, peep, trill, warble, song.

2 *her nonstop twitter* PRATTLE, chatter, babble, talk, gabble, blabber; *informal* yakking.

two cardinal number *the last two on the dance floor will win the grand prize* PAIR, duo, duet, double, dyad, duplet, tandem; *archaic* twain.

two-faced adjective *her two-faced ex* DECEITFUL, insincere, double-dealing, hypocritical, backstabbing, false, fickle, untrustworthy, duplicitous, deceiving, dissembling, dishonest; disloyal, treacherous, faithless, traitorous, cheating, lying, weaselly; *literary* perfidious. ANTONYM sincere.

twosome noun *this year's hottest celebrity twosome* COUPLE, pair, duo.

two-timing adjective *several people heard the threats she made to her two-timing husband* ADULTEROUS, unfaithful, untrue, unchaste, inconstant, fickle; cheating, philandering.

tycoon noun *a newspaper tycoon* MAGNATE, mogul, industrialist, businessman, financier, entrepreneur, captain of industry, millionaire, multimillionaire, merchant prince; *informal* big shot, bigwig, honcho, supremo, big wheel, kahuna; *derogatory* fat cat, robber baron.

tyke noun *informal the tykes on the playground* CHILD, toddler, tot, small child, young child; infant; *informal* moppet, young 'un, munchkin, rug rat, ankle-biter.

type noun **1** *a pastor of the old-fashioned type* KIND, sort, variety, class, category, set, genre, species, order, breed, race; style, nature, manner, rank; generation, vintage; stamp, ilk, cast, grain, mold, stripe, brand, flavor. See note at EMBLEM.

2 *sporty types* PERSON, individual, character, sort.

3 *italic type* PRINT, font, typeface, face, characters, lettering, letters.

typecast verb *she will always be typecast as the ditzy blonde* LABEL, tag; characterize, style; stereotype, pigeonhole.

typhoon noun. See STORM noun sense 1.

typical adjective **1** *a typical example of art deco* REPRESENTATIVE, classic, quintessential, archetypal, model, prototypical, stereotypical, paradigmatic. ANTONYMS atypical, unusual, abnormal.

2 *a fairly typical day* NORMAL, average, ordinary, standard, regular, routine, run-of-the-mill, conventional, unremarkable, unsurprising, unexceptional; *informal* blah. ANTONYMS atypical, unusual, exceptional. See note at NORMAL.

3 *it's typical of him to forget* CHARACTERISTIC, in keeping, usual, normal, par for the course, predictable, true to form; customary, habitual. ANTONYM uncharacteristic.

typify verb *the girls basketball team typifies the school spirit of our student body* EPITOMIZE, exemplify, characterize, be representative of; personify, embody, be emblematic of.

tyrannical adjective *a tyrannical government* DICTATORIAL, despotic, autocratic, oppressive, repressive, totalitarian, undemocratic, illiberal; authoritarian, high-handed, imperious, harsh, strict, iron-handed, iron-fisted, severe, cruel, brutal, ruthless. ANTONYM liberal.

tyrannize verb *she tyrannized her daughter-in-law* DOMINATE, dictate to, browbeat, intimidate, bully, lord it over; persecute, victimize, torment, terrorize; oppress, repress, crush, subjugate; *informal* push around.

tyranny noun *they will not soon forget the brutal tyranny of Amin* DESPOTISM, absolute power, autocracy, dictatorship, totalitarianism, Fascism; oppression, repression, subjugation, enslavement; authoritarianism, bullying, severity, cruelty, brutality, ruthlessness.

tyrant noun *dare we envision a world free from tyrants?* DICTATOR, despot, autocrat, authoritarian, oppressor; slave driver, martinet, bully, megalomaniac.

tyro noun *in 1925, he was a Capitol Hill tyro* NOVICE, beginner, learner, neophyte, newcomer, initiate, fledgling; apprentice, trainee, probationer, tenderfoot; *informal* rookie, newbie, greenhorn. ANTONYM veteran.

U

ubiquitous adjective *the ubiquitous golden arches of burgerdom* OMNIPRESENT, ever-present, everywhere, all over the place, pervasive, universal, worldwide, global; rife, prevalent, far-reaching, inescapable. ANTONYM rare.

UFO noun *the Phoenix police received sixteen calls about the sighting of a UFO last night* FLYING SAUCER, alien spacecraft/spaceship, unidentified flying object.

ugly adjective **1** *an ugly face* UNATTRACTIVE, unappealing, unpleasant, hideous, unlovely, unprepossessing, unsightly, horrible, frightful, awful, ghastly, vile, revolting, repellent, repulsive, repugnant; grotesque, disgusting, monstrous, reptilian, misshapen, deformed, disfigured, plug-ugly, butt-ugly; homely, plain, not much to look at. See word spectrum at BEAUTIFUL. ANTONYM beautiful.

2 *things got pretty ugly* UNPLEASANT, nasty, disagreeable, alarming, tense, charged, serious, grave; dangerous, perilous, threatening, menacing, hostile, ominous, sinister. ANTONYM pleasant.

3 *an ugly rumor* HORRIBLE, despicable, reprehensible, nasty, appalling, objectionable, offensive, obnoxious, vile, dishonorable, rotten, vicious, spiteful.

uh-oh exclamation *uh-oh, the cat got out!* YIKES, oh dear, cripes, mercy, holy moly, alas, dear me, 'oh me, oh my,' whoops.

ulcer noun *something to soothe the ulcers in his mouth* SORE, ulceration, abscess, boil, carbuncle, blister, gumboil, cyst; *Medicine* aphtha, chancre, furuncle.

ulterior adjective *his ulterior objectives were disguised by feigned concern* UNDERLYING, undisclosed, undivulged, concealed, hidden, covert, secret, personal, private, selfish. ANTONYM overt.

ultimate adjective **1** *the ultimate collapse of their empire* EVENTUAL, final, concluding, terminal, end; resulting, ensuing, consequent, subsequent.

2 *ultimate truths about civilization* FUNDAMENTAL, basic, primary, elementary, elemental, absolute, central, key, crucial, essential, pivotal.

3 *the ultimate gift for cat lovers* BEST, ideal, perfect, greatest, supreme, paramount, superlative, highest, utmost, optimum, quintessential.See note at PENULTIMATE.

▸ noun *the ultimate in Bohemian chic* UTMOST, optimum, last word, height, epitome, peak, pinnacle, acme, zenith, nonpareil, dernier cri, ne plus ultra; **(the ultimate)** *informal* da bomb; *dated, informal* the bee's knees, the cat's pajamas/whiskers/meow.

ultimately adverb **1** *the money will ultimately belong to us* EVENTUALLY, in the end, in the long run, at length, finally, sooner or later, in time, in the fullness of time, when all is said and done, one day, some day, sometime, over the long haul; *informal* when push comes to shove.

2 *two ultimately contradictory reasons* FUNDAMENTALLY, basically, primarily, essentially, at heart, deep down.

ultimatum noun *he gave me an ultimatum, basically I pay him by Thursday or he calls the cops* FINAL OFFER, final demand, take-it-or-leave-it deal; threat.

ultra- combining form *an ultraconservative view* EXTREMELY, exceedingly, excessively, immensely, especially, exceptionally; über-, over-; *informal* mega, mucho, majorly, oh-so, real, mighty, awful, powerful, way.

WORD NOTE über, ur

There is on occasion a small degree of confusion over these two Germanic words, not least because both begin with the same letter, both are short, both are used only as prefixes, and both confer a kind of mittel-European sophistication, not warranted if they are employed in error, on the user. *Über,* with the diacritic firmly in place, suggests "over-" or "bigger"—so an *Übermensch,* taken from the German, is a kind of superman. It is generally complimentary, although the first line of the German national anthem, *Deutschland über alles,* has an unpleasant connotation if, wrongly, it is taken to mean "Germany Supreme." (It in fact reflects Germans' supposed affection for Germany Above All Others, which is rather different.) The shorter prefix *ur-* denotes origin and originality—Leonardo da Vinci designed, for example, what might be described as an ur-tank and an ur-helicopter. Confusion over the use of the two words can thus be easily avoided; but the overuse of them as prefixes can lead to accusations of pretentiousness. Far better than the other use of *ur*—which, like *er,* suggests an unwonted hesitancy at the beginning of a sentence. **—SW**

ultrasound noun *the ultrasound shows a healthy fetus* SONOGRAM, echocardiogram; tomography.

umbrage PHRASE: **take umbrage** *I would take umbrage at that if I thought you were serious* TAKE OFFENSE, take exception, be aggrieved, be affronted, be annoyed, be angry, be indignant, be put out, be insulted, be hurt, be piqued, be resentful, be disgruntled, go into a huff, be miffed, have one's nose put out of joint, chafe.

umbrella noun 1 *they huddled under the umbrella* parasol, sunshade.

2 *the groups worked under the umbrella of the Communist Party* AEGIS, auspices, patronage, protection, guardianship, support, backing, agency, guidance, care, charge, responsibility, cover.

umpire noun *the umpire reversed his decision* REFEREE, linesman, adjudicator, arbitrator, judge, moderator, official; ref, ump.

▸ verb *he umpired a boat race* REFEREE, adjudicate, arbitrate, judge, moderate, oversee, officiate; *informal* ref, ump.

umpteen adjective See COUNTLESS.

unabashed adjective *her unabashed relationship with a convicted felon* UNASHAMED, shameless, unembarrassed, brazen, audacious, blatant, flagrant, bold, barefaced, cocky, unrepentant, undaunted, unconcerned, fearless. ANTONYM sheepish.

unable adjective *I'm unable to fix the leak* POWERLESS, impotent, at a loss, inadequate, incompetent, unfit, unqualified, incapable.

unabridged adjective the unabridged version is in two volumes COMPLETE, entire, whole, full-length, intact, uncut, unshortened, unexpurgated.

unacceptable adjective *the repair job on the gutters was unacceptable* INTOLERABLE, insufferable, unsatisfactory, inadmissible, inappropriate, unsuitable, undesirable, unreasonable, insupportable; offensive, obnoxious, disagreeable, disgraceful, deplorable, beyond the pale, bad; a bit much, too much, not on. ANTONYM satisfactory.

unaccompanied adjective *when Howard arrived at the dance he was unaccompanied* ALONE, on one's own, by oneself, solo, lone, solitary, single-handed; unescorted, unattended, unchaperoned; *informal* by one's lonesome.

unaccountable adjective 1 *for some unaccountable reason, the dogs have been pacing the floor all evening* INEXPLICABLE, insoluble, incomprehensible, unfathomable, impenetrable, puzzling, perplexing, baffling, bewildering, mystifying, mysterious, inscrutable, peculiar, strange, queer, odd, obscure; *informal* weird, freaky.

2 *a private company unaccountable to voters* NOT ANSWERABLE, not liable, not responsible; free, exempt, immune; unsupervised.

unaccustomed adjective 1 *she was **unaccustomed to** being bossed around* UNUSED TO, new to, fresh to; unfamiliar with, inexperienced in, unconversant with, unacquainted with. ANTONYM habitual.

2 *he showed unaccustomed emotion* UNUSUAL, unfamiliar, uncommon, unwonted, exceptional, unprecedented, extraordinary, rare, surprising, abnormal, atypical. ANTONYM habitual.

unacknowledged adjective *he made several unacknowledged contributions to the production* UNSUNG, unstated, uncelebrated, unrewarded, neglected, unrecognized, unheeded, overlooked, forgotten, ignored; uncredited.

unacquainted adjective *I'm **unacquainted with** Indian food* UNFAMILIAR WITH, unaccustomed to, unused to; inexperienced with, ignorant of, uninformed of, unenlightened about, not conversant with; *informal* in the dark about. ANTONYM familiar.

unadorned adjective *she preferred the feel of an uncluttered, unadorned room* UNEMBELLISHED, unornamented, undecorated, unvarnished, unfussy, no-nonsense, no-frills; plain, basic, restrained; bare, simple, austere, stark, spartan, clinical, chaste. ANTONYM ornate.

unadulterated adjective *the unadulterated truth* PURE, unalloyed, unsullied, untainted, virgin, untouched; absolute, downright, solid, utter.

unadventurous adjective *I've been quite happy with my predictable, unadventurous life* CAUTIOUS, careful, circumspect, wary, hesitant, timid; conservative, conventional, unenterprising, unexciting, unimaginative, myopic; boring, straitlaced, stuffy, narrow-minded; *informal* square, straight, stick-in-the-mud. ANTONYM enterprising.

unaffected adjective 1 *they are **unaffected by** the change in command* UNCHANGED BY, unaltered by, uninfluenced by; untouched by, unmoved by, unresponsive to; proof against, impervious to, immune to. ANTONYM influenced.

2 *his manner was unaffected* UNASSUMING, unpretentious, down-to-earth, natural, easy, uninhibited, open, artless, guileless, ingenuous, unsophisticated, genuine, real, sincere, honest, earnest, wholehearted, heartfelt, true, bona fide, frank; *informal* upfront. ANTONYMS pretentious, false.

unafraid adjective *he remembered how, in the toughest of times, his mother had been strong and unafraid* UNDAUNTED, unabashed, fearless, brave, courageous, plucky, intrepid, stouthearted, bold, valiant, daring, confident, audacious, unshrinking; *informal* gutsy, spunky. ANTONYM timid.

unalterable adjective See UNCHANGEABLE.

unanimous adjective 1 *doctors were unanimous about the effects* UNITED, in agreement, in accord, of one mind, of the same mind, in harmony, concordant, undivided, as one. ANTONYM divided.

2 *a unanimous vote* UNIFORM, consistent, united, concerted, congruent.

unanswerable adjective 1 *an unanswerable case* IRREFUTABLE, indisputable, undeniable, incontestable, incontrovertible, irrefragable; conclusive, absolute, positive. ANTONYMS weak, flawed.

2 *unanswerable questions* INSOLUBLE, unsolvable, inexplicable, unexplainable. ANTONYM obvious.

unanswered adjective *there were a number of unanswered questions* UNRESOLVED, undecided, unsettled, undetermined; pending, open to question, up in the air, doubtful, disputed.

unappetizing adjective *a platter of unappetizing leftovers* UNPALATABLE, uninviting, unappealing, unpleasant, off-putting, disagreeable, distasteful, unsavory, insipid, tasteless, flavorless, dull; inedible, uneatable, revolting; *informal* yucky, gross. ANTONYM tempting.

unappreciated adjective *Luann has been unappreciated for too long* UNACKNOWLEDGED, unthanked, uncredited, unrecognized, taken for granted, overlooked; undervalued, underpaid.

unapproachable adjective 1 *unapproachable islands* INACCESSIBLE, unreachable, remote, out of the way, isolated, far-flung, off the beaten track/path; *informal* in the middle of nowhere, in the sticks, in the boondocks. ANTONYM accessible.

2 *her boss appeared unapproachable* ALOOF, distant, remote, detached, reserved, withdrawn, uncommunicative, guarded, unresponsive, unforthcoming, unfriendly, unsympathetic, unsociable; cool, cold, frosty, stiff, haughty, superior, formal, intimidating; *informal* standoffish, stuck-up. ANTONYM friendly.

unarmed adjective *they fired into a crowd of unarmed civilians* DEFENSELESS, weaponless; unprotected, undefended, unguarded, unshielded, vulnerable, exposed, assailable, open to attack.

unassailable adjective 1 *an unassailable fortress* IMPREGNABLE, invulnerable, impenetrable, inviolable, invincible, unconquerable; secure, safe, strong, indestructible. ANTONYM defenseless.

2 *his logic was unassailable* INDISPUTABLE, undeniable, unquestionable, incontestable, incontrovertible, irrefutable, indubitable, watertight, sound, rock-solid, good, sure, manifest, patent, obvious.

unassertive adjective *we felt we couldn't fill the position with someone as unassertive as Jim* PASSIVE, retiring, submissive, unassuming, self-effacing, modest, humble, meek, unconfident, diffident, shy, timid, feeble, insecure; *informal* mousy. ANTONYM bold.

unassisted adjective *an unassisted effort* INDIVIDUAL, unaided, unsupported, single-handed, lone, solo.

▸ adverb *she achieved it all unassisted* ALONE, individually, single-handedly, by oneself, on one's own, without help.

unassuming adjective *she's not quite the unassuming ingenue she seems to be* MODEST, self-effacing, humble, meek, bashful, reserved, diffident; unobtrusive, unostentatious, low-key, unpretentious, unaffected, natural, artless, ingenuous.

unattached adjective 1 *they were both unattached* SINGLE, unmarried, unwed, uncommitted, available, at large, footloose and fancy free, on one's own; unloved. ANTONYM married.

2 *we are unattached to any organization* UNAFFILIATED, unallied; autonomous, independent, nonaligned, self-governing, neutral, separate, unconnected, detached. ANTONYM affiliated.

unattended adjective 1 *his cries went unattended* IGNORED, disregarded, neglected, passed over, unheeded.

2 *an unattended vehicle* UNGUARDED, unwatched, alone, solitary; abandoned.

3 *she had to walk there unattended* UNACCOMPANIED, unescorted, partnerless, unchaperoned, alone, on one's own, by oneself, solo; *informal* by one's lonesome.

unattractive adjective *there were only a few unattractive dresses left on the rack* PLAIN, ugly, unappealing, unpleasant, hideous, unlovely, unprepossessing, unsightly, ghastly, revolting, repellent, repulsive, repugnant; grotesque, disgusting, misshapen, plug-ugly; homely, not much to look at. ANTONYM beautiful.

unauthorized adjective *you can't hold an unauthorized meeting in a town building* UNOFFICIAL, unsanctioned, unaccredited, unlicensed, unwarranted, unapproved, bootleg, pirated; wildcat; disallowed, prohibited, out of bounds, banned, barred, forbidden, outlawed, illegal, illegitimate, illicit, proscribed. ANTONYM official.

unavoidable adjective *it was an unavoidable mishap* INESCAPABLE, inevitable, inexorable, assured, certain, predestined, predetermined, fated, ineluctable; necessary, compulsory, required, obligatory, mandatory.

unaware adjective *the vice president claimed to unaware of the arms deal* IGNORANT, unknowing, unconscious, heedless, unmindful, oblivious, incognizant, unsuspecting, uninformed, unenlightened, unwitting, innocent; inattentive, unobservant, unperceptive, blind; *informal* in the dark; *literary* nescient. ANTONYM conscious.

unawares adverb 1 *brigands caught them unawares* BY SURPRISE, unexpectedly, without warning, suddenly, abruptly, unprepared, off-guard; *informal* with one's pants down, napping. ANTONYM prepared.

2 *the chipmunk, unawares, approached the waiting cat* UNKNOWINGLY, unwittingly, unconsciously; unintentionally, inadvertently, accidentally, by mistake. ANTONYM knowingly.

unbalanced adjective 1 *he is unbalanced and dangerous* UNSTABLE, mentally ill, deranged, demented, disturbed, unhinged, insane, mad, out of one's mind; *informal* crazy, loopy, loony, nuts, nutso, nutty, cracked, bushed, screwy, batty, dotty, cuckoo, bonkers, squirrelly; *dated* touched. ANTONYM sane.

2 *a most unbalanced article* BIASED, prejudiced, one-sided, partisan, inequitable, unjust, unfair, parti pris. ANTONYM unbiased.

unbearable adjective *the cold made the waiting even more unbearable* INTOLERABLE, insufferable, insupportable, unendurable, unacceptable, unmanageable, overpowering; *informal* too much. ANTONYM tolerable.

unbeatable adjective *the Cubs were unbeatable in April* INVINCIBLE, unstoppable, unassailable, indomitable, unconquerable, unsurpassable, matchless, peerless, nonpareil; supreme.

unbeaten adjective *the Lady Vols are unbeaten so far this season* UNDEFEATED, unconquered, unsurpassed, unequaled, unrivaled; triumphant, victorious, supreme, second to none.

unbecoming adjective 1 *an unbecoming sundress* UNFLATTERING, unattractive, unsightly, plain, ugly, homely, hideous; unsuitable, ill-fitting. ANTONYM flattering.

2 *as a representative of this state, your conduct was unbecoming* INAPPROPRIATE, unfitting, unbefitting, unsuitable, unsuited, inapt, indecorous, out of keeping, untoward, incorrect, unacceptable; unworthy, improper, unseemly, undignified. ANTONYM appropriate.

unbelievable adjective *an unbelievable story | the grandeur of this casino is unbelievable* INCREDIBLE, beyond belief, inconceivable, unthinkable, unimaginable; unconvincing, far-fetched, dubious, implausible, improbable, unrealistic; *informal* hard to swallow. ANTONYM credible.

unbeliever noun *a Holy War against the unbelievers* INFIDEL, heretic, heathen, nonbeliever, atheist, agnostic, pagan, nihilist, apostate, freethinker, dissenter, nonconformist; disbeliever, skeptic, cynic, doubter, doubting Thomas, questioner, scoffer. ANTONYM believer.

unbending adjective *she resented the demands of her unbending father* INFLEXIBLE, rigid, strict, austere, stern, tough, firm, uncompromising, unyielding, hard line, resolute, determined, unrelenting, relentless, inexorable, intransigent, immovable; unfeeling, unemotional, stiff, forbidding, unfriendly.

unbiased adjective *we need an unbiased opinion* IMPARTIAL, unprejudiced, neutral, nonpartisan, disinterested, detached, dispassionate, objective, value-free, open-minded, equitable, evenhanded, fair. ANTONYM prejudiced.

unblemished adjective *it's a shame that this incident has to mar your unblemished record* IMPECCABLE, flawless, faultless, perfect, pure, virgin, clean, spotless, immaculate, unsullied, unspoiled, undefiled, untouched, untarnished, unpolluted; guiltless, sinless, innocent, blameless; *informal* squeaky clean. ANTONYM flawed.

unborn adjective *smoking can be harmful to your unborn child* EMBRYONIC, fetal, in utero; expected.

unbounded adjective *unbounded enthusiasm* UNLIMITED, boundless, limitless, illimitable; unrestrained, unrestricted, unconstrained, uncontrolled, unchecked, unbridled, rampant; untold, immeasurable, endless, unending, interminable, everlasting, infinite, inexhaustible. ANTONYM limited.

unbreakable adjective *unbreakable dishes* INDESTRUCTIBLE, shatterproof, durable, long-lasting; reinforced, sturdy, tough, stout, resistant, infrangible, heavy-duty, industrial-strength. ANTONYM fragile.

unbridled adjective *the unbridled spirit in these young players is very contagious* UNRESTRAINED, unconstrained, uncontrolled, uninhibited, unrestricted, unchecked, unmufflered, uncurbed, rampant, runaway, irrepressible, unstoppable, intemperate, immoderate. ANTONYM restrained.

unbroken adjective **1** *the last unbroken window* UNDAMAGED, unimpaired, unharmed, unscathed, untouched, sound, intact, whole, perfect.

2 *an unbroken horse* UNTAMED, undomesticated, untrained, wild, feral.

3 *an unbroken chain of victories* UNINTERRUPTED, continuous, endless, constant, unremitting, perpetual; unobstructed.

4 *his record is still unbroken* UNBEATEN, undefeated, unsurpassed, unrivaled, unmatched, supreme, intact.

unburden verb *she had a sudden wish to* ***unburden herself*** OPEN ONE'S HEART, confess, confide, tell all; *informal* come clean, fess up, spill one's guts, let it all out.

uncalled PHRASE: **uncalled for** *those vicious remarks were completely uncalled for* GRATUITOUS, unnecessary, needless, inessential; undeserved, unmerited, unwarranted, unjustified, unreasonable, unfair, inappropriate, inapt, pointless; unasked, unsolicited, unrequested, unprompted, unprovoked, unwelcome.

uncanny adjective **1** *the silence was uncanny* EERIE, unnatural, unearthly, preternatural, supernatural, otherworldly, ghostly, mysterious, strange, unsettling, abnormal, weird, bizarre, surreal, eldritch; *informal* creepy, spooky, freakish, freaky.

2 *an uncanny resemblance* STRIKING, remarkable, extraordinary, exceptional, incredible, noteworthy, notable, arresting.

unceasing adjective *with unceasing determination she reached her fitness goals in less than ten months* INCESSANT, ceaseless, constant, continual, unabating, interminable, endless, unending, never-ending, everlasting, eternal, perpetual, continuous, nonstop, uninterrupted, unbroken, unremitting, persistent, relentless, unrelenting, unrelieved, sustained.

uncensored adjective *this version of the movie is supposedly uncensored* UNCUT, complete, raw, whole, unexpurgated, unedited.

unceremonious adjective **1** *an unceremonious dismissal* ABRUPT, sudden, hasty, hurried, summary, perfunctory, undignified; rude, impolite, discourteous, offhand.

2 *an unceremonious man* INFORMAL, casual, relaxed, easygoing, familiar, natural, laid-back. ANTONYM formal.

uncertain adjective **1** *the outcome is uncertain* UNKNOWN, debatable, open to question, in doubt, undetermined, unsure, in the balance, up in the air; unpredictable, unforeseeable, incalculable; risky, chancy, dicey; *informal* iffy. ANTONYMS predictable, settled.

2 *its origin is uncertain* VAGUE, unclear, fuzzy, ambiguous, unknown, unascertainable, obscure, arcane.

3 *uncertain weather* CHANGEABLE, variable, irregular, unpredictable, unreliable, unsettled, erratic, fluctuating.

4 *Ed was uncertain about what to do* UNSURE, doubtful, dubious, undecided, irresolute, hesitant, blowing hot and cold, vacillating, vague, unclear, ambivalent, of two minds. ANTONYM sure.

5 *an uncertain smile* HESITANT, tentative, faltering, unsure, unconfident. ANTONYM confident.

uncertainty noun **1** *the uncertainty of the stock market* UNPREDICTABILITY, unreliability, riskiness, chanciness, precariousness, changeability, variability, inconstancy, fickleness, caprice. ANTONYM predictability.

2 *uncertainty about the future is always bad for morale* DOUBT, lack of certainty, indecision, irresolution, hesitancy, unsureness, doubtfulness, wavering, vacillation, equivocation, vagueness, haziness, ambivalence, lack of conviction, disquiet, wariness, chariness, leeriness, skepticism; queries, questions; *formal* dubiety.

3 *she pushed the anxious uncertainties out of her mind* DOUBT, qualm, misgiving, apprehension, quandary, reservation, scruple, second thought, query, question, question mark, suspicion.

4 *there was uncertainty in his voice* HESITANCY, hesitation, tentativeness, unsureness, lack of confidence, diffidence, doubtfulness, doubt. ANTONYM confidence.

THE RIGHT WORD

If you're not sure about something, you're probably experiencing a degree of **uncertainty**, which is a general term covering everything from a mere lack of absolute certainty (*uncertainty about the time of the dinner party*) to an almost complete lack of knowledge that makes it impossible to do more than guess at the result or outcome (*uncertainty about the country's future*). **Doubt** implies both uncertainty and an inability to make a decision because the evidence is insufficient (*considerable doubt as to her innocence*). **Dubiety** comes closer in meaning to *uncertainty* than to *doubt*, because it stresses a lack of sureness rather than an inability to reach a decision; but unlike *uncertainty*, it connotes wavering or fluctuating between one conclusion and another (*no one could fail to notice the dubiety in his voice*). If you exhibit **skepticism**, you are not so much uncertain as unwilling to believe. It usually refers to an habitual state of mind or to a customary reaction (*she always listened to his excuses with skepticism*).

---

unchangeable adjective *the political climate in this town is unchangeable* UNALTERABLE, immutable, invariable, changeless, fixed, hard and fast, cast-iron, ironclad, set/cast/carved in stone, dyed-in-the-wool, established, permanent, enduring, abiding, lasting, indestructible, ineradicable, irreversible. ANTONYM variable.

unchanging adjective *they followed the same unchanging routine for almost forty years* CONSISTENT, constant, regular, unvarying, predictable, stable, steady, fixed, rigid, abiding, permanent, perpetual, eternal, enduring; sustained, lasting, persistent.

uncharitable adjective *in the end, the uncharitable old miser has a change of heart and becomes the benevolent hero* MEAN, mean-spirited, unkind, selfish, self-centered, inconsiderate, thoughtless, insensitive, unfriendly, unsympathetic, hard-hearted, uncaring, unfeeling, ungenerous, ungracious, unfair.

uncharted adjective *they approached the uncharted territory with some trepidation* UNEXPLORED, undiscovered, unmapped, untraveled, unfamiliar, untrodden, unplumbed, unknown.

uncivil adjective *she apologized to her family for Rusty's uncivil words* IMPOLITE, rude, discourteous, disrespectful, unmannerly, bad-mannered, impertinent, impudent, ungracious; brusque, sharp, curt, offhand, gruff, churlish, snippy. See note at RUDE. ANTONYM polite.

uncivilized adjective *we had been taught that working-class people were inferior and uncivilized* UNCOUTH, coarse, rough, boorish, vulgar, philistine, uneducated, uncultured, uncultivated, benighted, unsophisticated, unpolished; ill-bred, ill-mannered, thuggish, loutish, redneck; barbarian, primitive, savage, brutish; *archaic* rude.

unclean adjective **1** *unclean premises* DIRTY, filthy, grubby, grimy, mucky, foul, impure, tainted, grungy, sullied, soiled, unwashed; polluted, contaminated, infected, unsanitary, unhygienic, unhealthy, disease-ridden. ANTONYMS pure, clean.

2 *an unclean meat* IMPURE; forbidden, taboo. ANTONYM kosher.

unclear adjective *his reason for being here is unclear* UNCERTAIN, unsure, unsettled, up in the air, debatable, open to question, in doubt, doubtful; ambiguous, equivocal, indefinite, vague, mysterious, obscure, hazy, foggy, nebulous; *informal* iffy. ANTONYM evident.

unclothed adjective *I hope you weren't unclothed when she walked in* NAKED, bare, nude, stripped, undressed, undraped, unclad; *informal* in one's birthday suit, in the buff, in the raw, in the altogether, au naturel, buck-naked, butt-naked, mother-naked, buck; *Brit. informal* starkers. ANTONYM dressed.

uncomfortable adjective **1** *an uncomfortable chair* PAINFUL, disagreeable, intolerable, unbearable, confining, cramped.

2 *I felt uncomfortable in her presence* UNEASY, awkward, nervous, tense, ill-at-ease, strained, edgy, restless, embarrassed, troubled, worried, anxious, fraught, rattled, twitchy, discombobulated, antsy. ANTONYM relaxed.

uncommitted adjective **1** *uncommitted voters* FLOATING, undecided, nonpartisan, unaffiliated, neutral, nonaligned, impartial, independent, undeclared, uncertain; *informal* sitting on the fence. ANTONYM aligned.

2 *the uncommitted male* UNMARRIED, unattached, unwed, partnerless; footloose and fancy free, available, single, lone. ANTONYM attached.

uncommon adjective **1** *an uncommon occurrence* UNUSUAL, abnormal, rare, atypical, unconventional, unfamiliar, strange, odd, curious, extraordinary, outlandish, novel, singular, peculiar, bizarre; alien, weird, oddball, offbeat; scarce, few and far between, exceptional, isolated, infrequent, irregular, seldom seen.

2 *an uncommon capacity for hard work* REMARKABLE, extraordinary, exceptional, singular, particular, marked, outstanding, noteworthy, significant, especial, special, signal, superior, unique, unparalleled, prodigious, unearthly; *informal* mind-boggling.

uncommonly adverb *the cherry blossoms are uncommonly magnificent this year* UNUSUALLY, remarkably, extraordinarily, exceptionally, singularly, particularly, especially, decidedly, notably, eminently, extremely, very.

uncommunicative adjective *their uncommunicative dinner guests made the evening seem terribly long* TACITURN, quiet, unforthcoming, reserved, reticent, laconic, tongue-tied, mute, silent, tight-lipped, close-mouthed; guarded, secretive, close, private; distant, remote, aloof, curt, withdrawn, unsociable, farouche; *informal* mum, standoffish. ANTONYM talkative.

uncomplicated adjective *the software installation is genuinely uncomplicated* SIMPLE, straightforward, clear, accessible, basic, undemanding, unchallenging, unsophisticated, trouble-free, painless, effortless, easy, elementary, foolproof, idiot-proof, goof-proof; *informal* a piece of cake, child's play, a cinch, a breeze. ANTONYM complex.

uncompromising adjective *two uncompromising parties will never reach a common ground* INFLEXIBLE, unbending, unyielding, unshakable, resolute, rigid, hard-line, immovable, intractable, inexorable, firm, determined, obstinate, stubborn, adamant, obdurate, intransigent, headstrong, stiff-necked, pigheaded, single-minded, bloody-minded. ANTONYM flexible.

unconcerned adjective **1** *she is unconcerned about their responses* INDIFFERENT, unmoved, apathetic, uninterested, incurious, dispassionate, heedless, impassive, unmindful. ANTONYM interested.

2 *he tried to look unconcerned* UNTROUBLED, unworried, unruffled, insouciant, nonchalant, blasé, carefree, casual, blithe, relaxed, at ease, 'calm, cool, and collected'; *informal* laid-back, poker-faced. ANTONYM anxious.

unconditional adjective *they gave their mom's new husband an unconditional welcome* WHOLEHEARTED, unqualified, unreserved, unlimited, unrestricted, unmitigated, unquestioning; complete, total, entire, full, absolute, out-and-out, unequivocal.

unconnected adjective **1** *the ground wire was unconnected* DETACHED, disconnected, loose. ANTONYM attached.

2 *unconnected tasks* UNRELATED, dissociated, separate, independent, distinct, different, disparate, discrete. ANTONYM related.

3 *unconnected chains of thought* DISJOINTED, incoherent, disconnected, rambling, wandering, diffuse, disorderly, haphazard, disorganized, garbled, mixed, muddled, aimless. ANTONYM coherent.

unconscionable adjective 1 *the unconscionable use of test animals* UNETHICAL, amoral, immoral, unprincipled, indefensible, unforgivable, wrong; unscrupulous, unfair, underhanded, dishonorable. ANTONYM ethical.

2 *we waited an unconscionable length of time* EXCESSIVE, unreasonable, unwarranted, uncalled for, unfair, inordinate, immoderate, undue, inexcusable, unforgivable, unnecessary, needless; *informal* over the top. ANTONYM acceptable.

WORD NOTE **unconscionable**

Unconscionable is a much stronger word than *unthinkable.* Something that is unthinkable is not to be considered; something that is unconscionable is against all reason, not just thought. However, *unconscionable* is a little trickier to spell, which probably accounts for *unthinkable's* unthinkably greater popularity. **—EM**

unconscious adjective 1 *she made sure he was unconscious* INSENSIBLE, senseless, insentient, insensate, comatose, inert, knocked out, stunned; motionless, immobile, prostrate; *informal* out cold, out like a light, out of it, down for the count, passed out, dead to the world.

2 *she was **unconscious of** the pain* HEEDLESS OF, unmindful of, disregarding of, oblivious to, insensible to, impervious to, unaffected by, unconcerned by, indifferent to; unaware of, unknowing of, ignorant of, incognizant of. ANTONYM aware.

3 *an unconscious desire* SUBCONSCIOUS, latent, suppressed, subliminal, sleeping, dormant, inherent, instinctive, involuntary, uncontrolled, spontaneous; unintentional, unthinking, unwitting, inadvertent; *informal* gut. ANTONYM voluntary.

▸ noun *fantasies raging in the unconscious* SUBCONSCIOUS, psyche, ego, id, inner self.

WORD NOTE **unconscious**

George Bernard Shaw wrote that the "unconscious self is the real genius. Your breathing goes wrong the moment your conscious self meddles with it." In this maxim, Shaw articulated the rationale behind the use of the word *unconscious* to describe, in basketball, a player whose every shot seems miraculously to go into the basket. **—DL**

uncontrollable adjective 1 *the crowds were uncontrollable* UNMANAGEABLE, out of control, ungovernable, wild, unruly, disorderly, recalcitrant, turbulent, disobedient, delinquent, defiant, undisciplined; *formal* refractory. ANTONYM compliant.

2 *an uncontrollable rage* UNSTOPPABLE, irrepressible, ungovernable, unquenchable; wild, violent, frenzied, furious, mad, hysterical, passionate, out of control.

unconventional adjective *her unconventional sense of humor didn't sit well with some of the audience* UNUSUAL, irregular, unorthodox, unfamiliar, uncommon, unwonted, out of the ordinary, atypical, singular, alternative, different; new, novel, innovative, groundbreaking, pioneering, original, unprecedented; eccentric, idiosyncratic, quirky, odd, strange, bizarre, weird, outlandish, curious; abnormal, anomalous, aberrant, extraordinary; nonconformist, Bohemian, avant-garde; *informal* far out, offbeat, off the wall, wacky, madcap, oddball, zany, hippie, kooky, wacko. ANTONYM orthodox.

unconvincing adjective *he had a plausible though highly unconvincing story* IMPROBABLE, unlikely, implausible, incredible, unbelievable, questionable, dubious, doubtful; strained, labored, far-fetched, unrealistic, fanciful, fantastic; feeble, flimsy, weak, transparent, poor, lame, ineffectual, half-baked; *informal* hard to swallow. ANTONYM persuasive.

uncool adjective 1 *those shoes are uncool* SQUARE, unhip, boring, unfashionable, unstylish, untrendy, behind the times; conformist, straitlaced, goody-goody.

2 *it was so uncool of her to pick on Smitty* LAME, unpleasant, unfair, unimpressive; *informal* sucky, crappy.

uncooperative adjective *the authorities were inclined to be uncooperative* UNHELPFUL, awkward, recalcitrant, perverse, contrary, stubborn, stiff-necked, unyielding, unbending, inflexible, immovable, obstructive, difficult, obstreperous, cussed, disobedient, disobliging, bloody-minded. ANTONYM obliging.

uncoordinated adjective *you'd be surprised how many uncoordinated hopefuls show up for these dance auditions* CLUMSY, awkward, blundering, bumbling, lumbering, flat-footed, heavy-handed, graceless, gawky, ungainly, ungraceful; inept, unhandy, unskillful, inexpert, maladroit, bungling; *informal* klutzy, butterfingered, hamfisted, ham-handed, all thumbs. ANTONYM dexterous.

uncouth adjective *I was hoping you'd be less uncouth in public* UNCIVILIZED, uncultured, uncultivated, unrefined, unpolished, unsophisticated, bush-league, common, plebeian, low, rough, rough-hewn, coarse, loutish, boorish, oafish, troglodyte; churlish, uncivil, rude, impolite, discourteous, disrespectful, unmannerly, bad-mannered, ill-bred, indecorous, crass, indelicate; vulgar, crude, raunchy. See note at RUDE. ANTONYM refined.

uncover verb 1 *she uncovered the new artwork* EXPOSE, reveal, lay bare; unwrap, unveil; strip, denude.

2 *they uncovered a money-laundering plot* DETECT, discover, come across, stumble on, chance on, find, turn up, unearth, dig up; expose, unveil, unmask, disclose, reveal, lay bare, make known, make public, bring to light, blow the lid off, blow the whistle on, pull the plug on.

unctuous adjective *she sees through his unctuous manners* SYCOPHANTIC, ingratiating, obsequious, fawning, servile, groveling, subservient, cringing, humble, hypocritical, insincere, gushing, effusive; glib, smooth, slick, slippery, oily, greasy; smarmy, slimy.

undaunted adjective *through all our crises, Cal has been the undaunted one* UNAFRAID, undismayed, unflinching, unshrinking, unabashed, fearless, dauntless, intrepid, bold, valiant, brave, courageous, plucky, gritty, indomitable, confident, audacious, daring; *informal* gutsy, spunky. ANTONYM fearful.

undead noun *eerie tales of the undead* LIVING DEAD, zombies, vampires.

undecided adjective *Gavin is hoping to win over the majority of undecided voters* UNRESOLVED, uncertain, unsure, unclear, unsettled, indefinite, undetermined, unknown, in the balance, up in the air, debatable, arguable, moot, open to question, doubtful, dubious, borderline, ambiguous, vague; indecisive, irresolute, hesitant, tentative, wavering, vacillating, uncommitted, ambivalent, of two minds, torn, fence-sitting, on the fence; *informal* iffy, wishy-washy. ANTONYM certain.

undefined adjective 1 *some matters are still undefined* UNSPECIFIED, unexplained, unspecific, indeterminate, unsettled; unclear, woolly, imprecise, inexact, indefinite, vague, fuzzy. ANTONYMS definite, specific.

2 *undefined shapes* INDISTINCT, indefinite, formless, indistinguishable, vague, amorphous, hazy, misty, shadowy, nebulous, blurred, blurry. ANTONYMS clear, distinct.

undemanding adjective *it's an undemanding job that can get pretty boring* EASY, accessible, manageable, straightforward, painless, unchallenging; easygoing, obliging, low-maintenance.

undeniable adjective *her willingness to work is undeniable* INDISPUTABLE, indubitable, unquestionable, beyond doubt, beyond question, undebatable, incontrovertible, incontestable, irrefutable, unassailable; certain, sure, definite, positive, conclusive, plain, obvious, unmistakable, self-evident, patent, emphatic, categorical, unequivocal. ANTONYM questionable.

under preposition 1 *they hid under a bush* BENEATH, below, underneath. ANTONYMS above, over.

2 *the rent is under $450* LESS THAN, lower than, below. ANTONYMS more than, over.

3 *branch managers are under the retail director* SUBORDINATE TO, junior to, inferior to, subservient to, answerable to, responsible to, subject to, controlled by. ANTONYMS above, over.

4 *the town was under water* FLOODED BY, immersed in, submerged by, sunk in, engulfed by, inundated by. ANTONYM above.

5 *forty homes are under construction* UNDERGOING, in the process of.

6 *our finances are under pressure* SUBJECT TO, liable to, at the mercy of.

▸ adverb *coughing and spluttering she went under* DOWN, lower, below, underneath, beneath; underwater.

underachiever noun *these underachievers are very intelligent and yet have no interest in their own potential* UNDERPERFORMER, slacker, disappointment, failure, loser.

underarm noun *swollen nodes in her left underarm* ARMPIT, pit; *technical* axilla.

undercooked adjective *I can't eat asparagus if it's undercooked* UNDERDONE, half-cooked, half-baked, uncooked; rare, raw.

undercover adjective *she does undercover work for the insurance company* COVERT, secret, clandestine, incognito, underground, surreptitious, furtive, cloak-and-dagger, stealthy, hidden, concealed, backstairs, closet; *informal* hush-hush, sneaky, on the QT. ANTONYM overt.

undercurrent noun 1 *dangerous undercurrents in the cove* UNDERTOW, underflow; riptide.

2 *the undercurrent of despair in his words* UNDERTONE, overtone, suggestion, connotation, intimation, hint, nuance, trace, suspicion, whisper, tinge; feeling, atmosphere, aura, echo; *informal* vibes.

undercut verb 1 *the firm undercut their rivals* CHARGE LESS THAN, undersell, underprice, underbid.

2 *his authority was being undercut* UNDERMINE, weaken, impair, sap, threaten, subvert, sabotage, ruin, destabilize, wreck.

underdog noun *yesterday's underdog is today's champion* LONG SHOT, dark horse, weaker one, little guy, David; downtrodden, victim, loser, fall guy.

underestimate verb *underestimating the opposition was our biggest mistake* UNDERRATE, undervalue, lowball, do an injustice to, be wrong about, sell short, play down, understate; minimize, de-emphasize, underemphasize, diminish, gloss over, trivialize; miscalculate, misjudge, misconstrue, misread. ANTONYM exaggerate.

underfoot adverb *it was very muddy underfoot* UNDERNEATH, beneath one's feet, on the ground.

underfunded adjective *the reality is that many of these underfunded programs have to shut down* UNDERCAPITALIZED, cash-starved, starved for funds, neglected.

undergarment noun See table at UNDERWEAR.

undergo verb *she underwent a lengthy cross-examination* GO THROUGH, experience, undertake, face, submit to, be subjected to, come in for, receive, sustain, endure, brave, bear, tolerate, stand, withstand, weather.

undergraduate noun *most of my students are undergraduates* STUDENT, undergrad, scholar, freshman; *informal* frosh.

underground adjective 1 *an underground parking garage* SUBTERRANEAN, buried, sunken, subsurface, basement.

2 *underground trade* CLANDESTINE, secret, surreptitious, covert, undercover, closet, cloak-and-dagger, back-alley, backstairs, black-market, hidden, sneaky, furtive; resistance, subversive; *informal* hush-hush.

3 *the underground art scene* ALTERNATIVE, radical, revolutionary, unconventional, unorthodox, avant-garde, counterculture, experimental, innovative.

▸ adverb 1 *the insects live underground* BELOW GROUND, in the earth, subterraneously.

2 *the rebels went underground* INTO HIDING, into seclusion, undercover, to earth, to ground.

undergrowth noun *the undergrowth is a habitat for various small mammals and certain birds* SHRUBBERY, vegetation, underbrush, greenery, ground cover, underwood, brushwood, brush, scrub, bush, covert, thicket, copse; bushes, plants, brambles, herbage; *technical* herbaceous layer.

underhanded adjective *lying about knowing their son was just one of the underhanded things he did* DECEITFUL, deceptive, dishonest, dishonorable, disreputable, unethical, unprincipled, immoral, unscrupulous, fraudulent, dubious, unfair, snide; treacherous, lowdown, duplicitous, double-dealing; devious, artful, crooked, shady, crafty, conniving, scheming, sly, wily, not aboveboard; clandestine, backstairs, secret, surreptitious, sneaky, furtive, covert, cloak-and-dagger. See note at SECRET. ANTONYM honest.

underline verb 1 *she underlined a phrase* UNDERSCORE, mark, pick out, emphasize, highlight.

2 *the program underlines the benefits of exercise* EMPHASIZE, stress, highlight, accentuate, accent, focus on, spotlight, point up, play up.

underling noun *he dishes out orders to his underlings* SUBORDINATE, inferior, junior, minion, lackey, subaltern, flunky, menial, vassal, subject, hireling, servant, henchman, factotum; *informal* gofer. ANTONYM boss.

underlying adjective **1** *the underlying aims of the research* FUNDAMENTAL, basic, primary, prime, central, principal, root, chief, cardinal, key, elementary, intrinsic, essential.

2 *an underlying feeling of irritation* LATENT, repressed, suppressed, unrevealed, undisclosed, unexpressed, concealed, hidden, masked.

undermine verb **1** *their integrity is being undermined* SUBVERT, undercut, sabotage, threaten, weaken, compromise, diminish, reduce, impair, mar, spoil, ruin, damage, hurt, injure, cripple, sap, shake; *informal* drag through the mud. ANTONYMS strengthen, enhance.

2 *rivers undermined their banks* ERODE, wear away, eat away at.

underneath adjective & adverb *the underneath suitcase is mine | the woodchuck burrowed underneath the garage* BELOW, beneath, under, underfoot, lower down.

underpants plural noun See table at UNDERWEAR.

underpin verb See REINFORCE sense 1.

underprivileged adjective *he spends his summers backpacking with underprivileged children from his hometown* NEEDY, deprived, disadvantaged, poor, destitute, in need, in straitened circumstances, impoverished, poverty-stricken, on the poverty line, indigent, lower-class; *formal* penurious. ANTONYM wealthy.

underrate verb *for years the girls' athletic program was underrated* UNDERVALUE, underestimate, do an injustice to, sell short, play down, understate, minimize, diminish, downgrade, trivialize. ANTONYM exaggerate.

undersized adjective *the lack of nutrients will result in undersized tomatoes* UNDERDEVELOPED, stunted, small, short, little, tiny, petite, slight, compact, miniature, mini, diminutive, dwarfish, pygmy, pint-sized, pocket-sized, baby, teeny-weeny, itsy-bitsy, itty-bitty, vertically challenged. ANTONYM overgrown.

understand verb **1** *he couldn't understand anything we said* COMPREHEND, grasp, take in, see, apprehend, follow, make sense of, fathom; unravel, decipher, interpret; *informal* figure out, work out, make head(s) or tail(s) of, get one's head around, get the drift of, catch on to, get; *Brit. informal* twig.

2 *she understood how hard he'd worked* APPRECIATE, recognize, realize, acknowledge, know, be aware of, be conscious of; *informal* be wise to; *formal* be cognizant of.

3 *I understand that you wish to go* BELIEVE, gather, take it, hear (tell), notice, see, learn; conclude, infer, assume, surmise, fancy.

▸ exclamation *I want out, understand?* get it, get the picture, see, right, know what I mean, get my drift, capisce, comprende.

understandable adjective **1** *make it understandable to the beginner* COMPREHENSIBLE, intelligible, coherent, clear, explicit, unambiguous, transparent, plain, straightforward, digestible, accessible, user-friendly.

2 *an understandable desire to be happy* UNSURPRISING, expected, predictable, inevitable; reasonable, acceptable, logical, rational, normal, natural; justifiable, justified, defensible, excusable, pardonable, forgivable.

understanding noun **1** *test your understanding of the language* COMPREHENSION, apprehension, grasp, mastery, appreciation, assimilation, absorption; knowledge, awareness, insight, skill, expertise, proficiency; *informal* know-how; *formal* cognizance. ANTONYM ignorance.

2 *it was my understanding that this was free* BELIEF, perception, view, conviction, feeling, opinion, intuition, impression, assumption, supposition, inference, interpretation.

3 *she treated me with understanding* COMPASSION, sympathy, pity, feeling, concern, consideration, kindness, sensitivity, decency, humanity, charity, goodwill, mercy, tolerance. ANTONYM indifference.

4 *we had a tacit understanding* AGREEMENT, arrangement, deal, bargain, settlement, pledge, pact, compact, contract, covenant, bond, meeting of minds.

▸ adjective *an understanding friend* COMPASSIONATE, sympathetic, sensitive, considerate, tender, kind, thoughtful, tolerant, patient, forbearing, lenient, merciful, forgiving, humane; approachable, supportive, perceptive.

understate verb *let's not understate the importance of the coaching staff* PLAY DOWN, downplay, underrate, underplay, de-emphasize, trivialize, minimize, diminish, downgrade, brush aside, gloss over, put it mildly; *informal* soft-pedal, sell short. ANTONYM exaggerate.

understatement noun *calling this event unfortunate is a gross understatement* MINIMIZATION, trivialization, euphemism; understatedness, restraint, reserve, underplaying, underemphasis; subtlety, delicacy; *technical* litotes, meiosis. ANTONYMS overstatement, exaggeration.

understood adjective *I thought these rules were understood* ACCEPTED, agreed-upon, acknowledged, assumed, established, unwritten, unspoken, taken for granted, tacit.

understudy noun *Mark's understudy got better reviews than Mark* STAND-IN, substitute, replacement, reserve, fill-in, locum, proxy, backup, relief, standby, stopgap; *informal* sub, pinch-hitter.

undertake verb *are you ready to undertake this challenge?* TACKLE, take on, assume, shoulder, handle, manage, deal with, be responsible for; engage in, take part in, go about, set about, get down to, come to grips with, embark on; attempt, try, endeavor; *informal* have a go at; *formal* essay.

undertaker noun *in those days, an epidemic of the flu would have the undertaker working around the clock* FUNERAL DIRECTOR, mortician.

undertaking noun **1** *a risky undertaking* ENTERPRISE, venture, project, campaign, scheme, plan, operation, endeavor, effort, task, deed, activity, pursuit, exploit, business, affair, procedure; mission, quest.

2 *make an undertaking to comply with the rules* PLEDGE, agreement, promise, oath, covenant, vow, commitment, guarantee, assurance, contract.

undertone noun **1** *he said something in an undertone* LOW VOICE, murmur, whisper, mutter.

2 *the story's dark undertones* UNDERCURRENT, overtone, suggestion, nuance, vein, atmosphere, aura, tenor, flavor, tinge; vibrations.

undervalue verb *I didn't mean to undervalue your contributions* UNDERRATE, underestimate, play down, understate, underemphasize, diminish, minimize, downgrade, reduce, brush aside, gloss over, trivialize, underprice; *informal* sell short.

underwater adjective *an underwater laboratory* SUBMERGED, immersed, sunken, subaqueous, subsurface; undersea, subsea, submarine.

underwear noun *he always managed to leave half of his underwear at camp* undergarment(s), underthings, underclothes, lingerie; foundation garment(s); *informal* undies, drawers, skivvies. See table.

UNDERWEAR

bikini briefs	shorts
bloomers	slip
boxers/boxer shorts	snuggies
bra	sports bra
brassiere	tanga briefs
briefs	tap pants
camisole	teddy
chemise	thermals/thermal underwear
corset	thong
girdle	tighty-whities
Jockey shorts™	underpants
long johns	undershirt
long underwear	undershorts
panties	union suit
petticoat	

underworld noun **1** *Osiris, god of* ***the underworld*** THE NETHERWORLD, the nether regions, hell, the abyss; eternal damnation; Sheol, Hades, Gehenna, Tophet; *informal* the other place; *literary* the pit. ANTONYM heaven.

2 *the city's violent underworld* CRIMINAL WORLD, gangland; criminals, gangsters; *informal* mobsters.

underwrite verb *a local businesswoman has agreed to underwrite our charter* SPONSOR, support, back, insure, guarantee, indemnify, subsidize, pay for, finance, fund; *informal* foot the bill for, bankroll.

undesirable adjective **1** *undesirable side effects* UNPLEASANT, disagreeable, objectionable, nasty, unwelcome, unwanted, unfortunate, inconvenient, infelicitous. ANTONYM pleasant.

2 *some very undesirable people* UNPLEASANT, disagreeable, obnoxious, nasty, vile, unsavory, awful, repulsive, repellent, objectionable, abhorrent, loathsome, hateful, detestable, deplorable, appalling, insufferable, intolerable, despicable, contemptible, odious, terrible, dreadful, frightful, ghastly, horrible, horrid. ANTONYMS pleasant, agreeable.

▸ noun *the bar was full of undesirables* OUTCAST, lowlife, misfit, deviant, unsavory character, pariah, leper, untouchable, freak.

undetectable adjective *there may have been an undetectable amount of poison in the tea* UNNOTICEABLE, imperceptible, invisible, inaudible, odorless, subtle, faint, obscure; tiny, minute, infinitesimal.

undignified adjective *an undignified scramble for seats* UNSEEMLY, demeaning, unbecoming, unworthy, unbefitting, degrading, shameful, dishonorable, ignominious, discreditable, ignoble, untoward, unsuitable; scandalous, disgraceful, indelicate, indecent, low, base.

undisciplined adjective *you've never seen such a bunch of undisciplined kids and pets under one roof* UNRULY, disorderly, disobedient, badly behaved, recalcitrant, restive, wayward, delinquent, rebellious, refractory, insubordinate, disruptive, errant, out of control, uncontrollable, wild, naughty; disorganized, unsystematic, unmethodical, lax, slapdash, slipshod, sloppy.

undisguised adjective *he regarded her with undisguised affection* OBVIOUS, evident, patent, manifest, transparent, overt, unconcealed, unhidden, unmistakable, undeniable, plain, clear, clear-cut, explicit, naked, visible; blatant, flagrant, glaring, bold.

undisputed adjective *his military preeminence was undisputed* UNCONTESTED, indubitable, undoubted, incontestable, unchallenged, incontrovertible, unequivocal, undeniable, irrefutable, unmistakable, sure, certain, definite, accepted, acknowledged, recognized. ANTONYM doubtful.

undistinguished adjective *an undistinguished career as a claims adjuster* UNEXCEPTIONAL, indifferent, run-of-the-mill, middle-of-the-road, ordinary, average, commonplace, mediocre, humdrum, lackluster, forgettable, uninspired, uneventful, unremarkable, inconsequential, featureless, nondescript, middling, moderate; *informal* garden-variety, by-the-numbers, nothing special, no great shakes, nothing to write home about, OK, so-so, 'comme ci, comme ça', bush-league, blah, plain-vanilla. ANTONYM extraordinary.

undivided adjective *I need your undivided attention* COMPLETE, full, total, whole, entire, absolute, wholehearted, unqualified, unreserved, unmitigated, unbroken, consistent, thorough, exclusive, dedicated; focused, engrossed, absorbed, attentive, committed.

undo verb **1** *he undid another button* UNFASTEN, unbutton, unhook, untie, unlace; unlock, unbolt; loosen, disentangle, extricate, release, detach, free, open; disconnect, disengage, separate. ANTONYM fasten.

2 *they will undo a decision by the superior court* REVOKE, overrule, overturn, repeal, rescind, reverse, retract, countermand, cancel, annul, nullify, invalidate, void, negate; *Law* vacate; *formal* abrogate. ANTONYM ratify.

3 *she undid much of the good work done* RUIN, undermine, subvert, overturn, scotch, sabotage, spoil, impair, mar, destroy, wreck, eradicate, obliterate; cancel out, neutralize, thwart, foil, frustrate, hamper, hinder, obstruct; *informal* blow, put the kibosh on, foul up, scuttle. ANTONYM enhance.

undoing noun **1** *she plotted the emperor's undoing* DOWNFALL, defeat, conquest, deposition, overthrow, ruin, ruination, elimination, end, collapse, failure, fall, fall from grace, debasement; Waterloo.

2 *their complacency was their undoing* FATAL FLAW, Achilles heel, weakness, weak point, failing, nemesis, affliction, curse.

undone adjective **1** *some work was left undone* UNFINISHED, incomplete, half-done, unaccomplished, unfulfilled, unconcluded; omitted, neglected, disregarded, ignored; remaining, outstanding, deferred, pending, on ice; *informal* on the back burner. ANTONYM finished.

2 *formal she had lost and was utterly undone* DONE FOR, finished, ruined, destroyed, doomed, lost, defeated, beaten; *informal* washed up, toast. ANTONYM successful.

undoubted adjective *their undoubted friendship* UNDISPUTED, unchallenged, unquestioned, indubitable, incontrovertible, irrefutable, incontestable, sure, certain, unmistakable; definite, accepted, acknowledged, recognized.

undoubtedly adverb *they are undoubtedly guilty* DOUBTLESS, indubitably, doubtlessly, no doubt, without (a) doubt, unquestionably, without question, indisputably, undeniably, incontrovertibly, clearly, obviously, patently, certainly, definitely, surely, of course, indeed.See note at CLEARLY.

undress verb *he undressed and got into bed* STRIP (OFF), disrobe, take off one's clothes, peel down. PHRASE: **in a state of undress** *she waltzed in while I was in a state of undress* NAKED, (in the) nude, bare, stripped, unclothed, undressed, unclad; *informal* in one's birthday suit, in the raw, in the buff, au naturel, buck-naked, butt-naked, mother-naked.

undue adjective *we didn't intend to add undue stress to your situation* EXCESSIVE, immoderate, intemperate, inordinate, disproportionate; uncalled for, unneeded, unnecessary, needless, unwarranted, unjustified, unreasonable; inappropriate, unmerited, unsuitable, improper. ANTONYM appropriate.

undulate verb *she watched the waves undulating from her stateroom window* RISE AND FALL, surge, swell, heave, ripple, billow, flow, roll; wind, wobble, oscillate, fluctuate.

unduly adverb See EXCESSIVELY.

undying adjective *his undying devotion to Aunt Myrna* ABIDING, lasting, enduring, permanent, constant, infinite; unceasing, perpetual, ceaseless, incessant, unending, never-ending, unfading, amaranthine; immortal, eternal, deathless.

unearth verb **1** *workers unearthed an artillery shell* DIG UP, excavate, exhume, disinter, root out, unbury.

2 *I unearthed an interesting fact* DISCOVER, uncover, find, come across, stumble upon, hit on, bring to light, expose, turn up, hunt out.

unearthly adjective *an unearthly chill in the air* OTHERWORLDLY, supernatural, preternatural, alien; ghostly, spectral, phantom, mysterious, spine-chilling, hair-raising; uncanny, eerie, strange, weird, unnatural, bizarre, surreal; eldritch; *informal* spooky, creepy, scary. ANTONYM normal.

uneasy adjective **1** *the doctor made him feel uneasy* WORRIED, anxious, troubled, disturbed, agitated, rattled, nervous, tense, overwrought, edgy, jumpy, apprehensive, restless, discomfited, perturbed, fearful, uncomfortable, unsettled; *informal* jittery, antsy. ANTONYMS calm, at ease.

2 *he had an uneasy feeling* WORRYING, disturbing, troubling, alarming, disquieting, unsettling, disconcerting, upsetting, nagging, niggling.

3 *the victory ensured an uneasy peace* TENSE, awkward, strained, fraught; precarious, unstable, insecure. ANTONYM stable.

uneconomic, uneconomical adjective *these measures are impractical and uneconomic for middle-class taxpayers* UNPROFITABLE, uncommercial, money-losing, not viable, unviable, unsustainable, worthless; wasteful, inefficient, improvident.

uneducated adjective *uneducated laborers* UNTAUGHT, unschooled, untutored, untrained, unread, unscholarly, illiterate, unlettered, ignorant, ill-informed, uninformed; uncouth, unsophisticated, uncultured, unaccomplished, unenlightened, philistine, benighted, backward, redneck. See note at IGNORANT. ANTONYM learned.

unemotional adjective *an effective clinician must remain unemotional when the patient is most out of control* RESERVED, undemonstrative, sober, restrained, passionless, perfunctory, emotionless, unsentimental, unexcitable, impassive, apathetic, phlegmatic, stoical, equable; cool, cold, frigid, unfeeling, callous.

unemployed adjective *most of my former colleagues are still unemployed* JOBLESS, out-of-work, between jobs, unwaged, unoccupied, laid off, idle; on welfare; *Brit.* redundant.

unending adjective *the unending noise from that construction site is making us crazy* ENDLESS, never-ending, interminable, perpetual, eternal, amaranthine, ceaseless, incessant, unceasing, nonstop, uninterrupted, continuous, continual, constant, persistent, recurring, unbroken, unabating, unremitting, relentless. See note at ETERNAL.

unendurable adjective *the pain was unendurable* INTOLERABLE, unbearable, insufferable, insupportable, too much to bear.

unenthusiastic adjective *they were unenthusiastic about the script* INDIFFERENT, apathetic, halfhearted, lukewarm, tepid, casual, cool, lackluster, subdued, unmoved; cursory, perfunctory; *informal* so-so, 'comme ci, comme ça.' ANTONYM keen.

unenviable adjective DISAGREEABLE, nasty, unpleasant, undesirable, unfortunate, unlucky, horrible, thankless; unwanted.

unequal adjective **1** *they are unequal in length* DIFFERENT, dissimilar, unalike, unlike, disparate, unmatched, uneven, irregular, varying, variable, asymmetrical. ANTONYM identical.

2 *the unequal distribution of wealth* UNFAIR, unjust, disproportionate, inequitable, biased, askew. ANTONYM fair.

3 *an unequal contest* ONE-SIDED, uneven, unfair, ill-matched, unbalanced, lopsided, skewed. ANTONYMS evenly balanced, fair.

4 *she felt **unequal to** the task* INADEQUATE FOR, incapable of, unqualified for, unsuited to, incompetent at, not up to; *informal* not cut out for. ANTONYM competent.

unequaled adjective UNBEATEN, matchless, unmatched, unrivaled, unsurpassed, unparalleled, peerless, incomparable, inimitable, unique, second to none, in a class of its/one's own.

unequivocal adjective *the report's advice was unequivocal* UNAMBIGUOUS, unmistakable, indisputable, incontrovertible, indubitable, undeniable; clear, clear-cut, plain, plain-spoken, explicit, specific, categorical, straightforward, blunt, candid, emphatic, manifest. ANTONYM ambiguous.

unerring adjective UNFAILING, infallible, perfect, flawless, faultless, error-free, impeccable, unimpeachable; sure, accurate, true, assured, sure-fire, sure-footed; *Theology* inerrant.

unethical adjective IMMORAL, amoral, unprincipled, unscrupulous, dishonorable, dishonest, wrong, deceitful, unconscionable, unfair, fraudulent, underhanded, wicked, evil, sneaky, corrupt; unprofessional, improper.

uneven adjective **1** *uneven ground* BUMPY, rough, lumpy, stony, rocky, rugged, potholed, rutted, pitted, jagged. ANTONYMS flat, smooth.

2 *uneven teeth* IRREGULAR, unequal, unbalanced, misaligned, lopsided, askew, crooked, asymmetrical, unsymmetrical. ANTONYM regular.

3 *uneven quality* INCONSISTENT, variable, varying, fluctuating, irregular, erratic, patchy; choppy, unsteady. ANTONYM consistent.

4 *an uneven contest* ONE-SIDED, unequal, unfair, unjust, inequitable, ill-matched, unbalanced, David and Goliath. ANTONYM fair.

uneventful adjective *our flight was, thankfully, quite uneventful* UNEXCITING, uninteresting, monotonous, boring, dull, tedious, humdrum, routine, unvaried, ordinary, run-of-the-mill, pedestrian, mundane, predictable; *informal* blah. ANTONYM exciting.

unexceptional adjective *an adequate but unexceptional hotel* ORDINARY, average, typical, everyday, mediocre, run-of-the-mill, middle-of-the-road, indifferent; *informal* OK, blah, so-so, 'comme ci, comme ça', nothing special, no great shakes, fair-to-middling.

unexpected adjective *an unexpected change in plans* UNFORESEEN, unanticipated, unpredicted, unlooked-for, sudden, abrupt, surprising, unannounced.

unexpectedly adverb *Darren unexpectedly announced he was getting married* OUT OF THE BLUE, out of nowhere, out of left field, without warning, unannounced, surprisingly.

unfailing adjective *he hits the target with unfailing accuracy* CONSTANT, reliable, dependable, steadfast, steady; endless, undying, unfading, inexhaustible, indefatigable, boundless, tireless, ceaseless.

unfair adjective **1** *the trial was unfair* UNJUST, inequitable, prejudiced, biased, discriminatory; one-sided, unequal, uneven, unbalanced, partisan, partial, skewed. ANTONYM just.

2 *his comments were unfair* UNDESERVED, unmerited, uncalled for, unreasonable, unjustified. ANTONYM justified.

3 *unfair play* UNSPORTSMANLIKE, unsporting, dirty, below the belt, underhanded, dishonorable. ANTONYM sporting.

4 *you're being very unfair* INCONSIDERATE, thoughtless, insensitive, selfish, spiteful, mean, unkind, unreasonable; hypercritical, overcritical.

unfaithful adjective **1** *her husband had been unfaithful* ADULTEROUS, faithless, fickle, untrue, inconstant; unchaste, cheating, philandering, two-timing.

2 *an unfaithful friend* DISLOYAL, treacherous, traitorous, untrustworthy, unreliable, undependable, fair-weather, false, two-faced, double-crossing, deceitful; *literary* perfidious. ANTONYM loyal.

unfaltering adjective *her unfaltering patience* STEADY, resolute, resolved, firm, steadfast, fixed, decided, unswerving, unwavering, tireless, indefatigable, persistent, unyielding, relentless, unremitting, unrelenting, rock-steady. ANTONYM unsteady.

unfamiliar adjective **1** *an unfamiliar part of the city* UNKNOWN, new, strange, foreign, alien; unexplored, uncharted.

2 *the unfamiliar sounds* UNUSUAL, uncommon, unconventional, novel, different, exotic, unorthodox, odd, peculiar, curious, uncharacteristic, anomalous, abnormal, out of the ordinary.

3 *investors* ***unfamiliar with*** *the stock market* UNACQUAINTED WITH, unused to, unaccustomed to, unconversant with, unversed in, inexperienced in, uninformed of, unschooled in, unenlightened of, ignorant of, not cognizant of, new to, a stranger to.

unfashionable adjective *a pair of unfashionable shoes will ruin the whole look* OUT, out of date, outdated, old-fashioned, outmoded, out of style, dated, unstylish, passé, démodé, unhip, uncool, nerdy, dowdy, frumpy, lame, unsexy, old hat, square.

unfasten verb *Ron unfastened his belt* UNDO, open, disconnect, remove, untie, unbutton, unzip, unlash, loose, loosen, free, unlock, unbolt.

unfathomable adjective *unfathomable mysteries* INSCRUTABLE, incomprehensible, enigmatic, indecipherable, impenetrable, obscure, esoteric, mysterious, mystifying, deep, profound. ANTONYM penetrable.

unfavorable adjective **1** *unfavorable comments* ADVERSE, critical, hostile, inimical, unfriendly, unsympathetic, negative, scathing; discouraging, disapproving, uncomplimentary, unflattering. ANTONYM positive.

2 *the unfavorable economic climate* GLOOMY, adverse, inauspicious, unpropitious, disadvantageous; unsuitable, inappropriate, inopportune. ANTONYM advantageous.

unfazed adjective *we thought the news would upset him, but he seemed unfazed* CALM, unruffled, unperturbed, untroubled, poised, relaxed, self-possessed, nonplussed, together, laid-back.

unfeeling adjective *humiliating Don in front of his children was an unfeeling thing to do* UNCARING, unsympathetic, unemotional, uncharitable; heartless, hard-hearted, hard, harsh, austere, cold, cold-hearted, cold-blooded, insensitive, callous. ANTONYM compassionate.

unfeigned adjective *he looked at his wife with unfeigned admiration* SINCERE, genuine, real, true, honest, unaffected, unforced, heartfelt, wholehearted, bona fide. ANTONYM insincere.

unfettered adjective *the choice between a planned economy and an unfettered market* UNRESTRAINED, unrestricted, unconstrained, uninhibited, free, rampant, unbridled, unchecked, unmufflered, uncontrolled. ANTONYM restricted.

unfinished adjective **1** *an unfinished essay* INCOMPLETE, uncompleted; partial, undone, half-done, in progress; imperfect, unpolished, unrefined, sketchy, fragmentary, rough. ANTONYM complete.

2 *the door can be supplied unfinished* UNPAINTED, unvarnished, untreated. ANTONYMS painted, varnished.

unfit adjective **1** *that party is* ***unfit to*** *govern* | ***unfit for*** *service* UNQUALIFIED, unsuitable, unsuited, inappropriate, unequipped, inadequate, not designed; incapable of, unable to, not up to, not equal to, unworthy of; *informal* not cut out for, not up to scratch. ANTONYM suitable.

2 *unfit and overweight children* UNHEALTHY, out of shape, in poor condition/shape. ANTONYM (physically) fit.

unflagging adjective *an unflagging commitment to the ideals of peace* TIRELESS, persistent, dogged, tenacious, determined, indefatigable, resolute, steadfast, staunch, single-minded, unrelenting, unfaltering, unfailing. ANTONYM inconstant.

unflappable adjective *informal a crack team of unflappable medics* IMPERTURBABLE, unexcitable, cool, calm, 'calm, cool, and collected', self-controlled, coolheaded, levelheaded; *informal* laid-back, Type-B. ANTONYM excitable.

unflattering adjective **1** *an unflattering review* UNFAVORABLE, uncomplimentary, harsh, unsympathetic, critical, negative, hostile, scathing. ANTONYM complimentary.

2 *an unflattering dress* UNATTRACTIVE, unbecoming, unsightly, ugly, homely, plain, ill-fitting. ANTONYM becoming.

unflinching adjective *they stood together in unflinching determination* RESOLUTE, determined, single-minded, dogged, steadfast, solid, resolved, firm, committed, steady, unwavering, unflagging, unswerving, unfaltering, untiring, undaunted, fearless.

unfold verb **1** *May unfolded the map* OPEN OUT, spread out, flatten, straighten out, unroll, unfurl.

2 *I watched the events unfold* DEVELOP, evolve, happen, take place, occur, transpire, progress, play out.

unforeseen adjective *the problems with the bus were, of course, unforeseen* UNPREDICTED, unexpected, unanticipated, unplanned, not bargained for, surprising. ANTONYM expected.

unforgettable adjective *the trip to Indonesia was unforgettable* MEMORABLE, not/never to be forgotten, haunting, catchy; striking, impressive, outstanding, extraordinary, exceptional. ANTONYM unexceptional.

unforgivable adjective *he had committed the unforgivable sin—he had informed on his friends* INEXCUSABLE, unpardonable, unjustifiable, indefensible. ANTONYM venial.

unfortunate adjective **1** *unfortunate people* UNLUCKY, hapless, jinxed, out of luck, luckless, wretched, miserable, forlorn, poor, pitiful; *informal* down on one's luck.See note at HAPLESS. ANTONYM lucky.

2 *an unfortunate start to our vacation* ADVERSE, disadvantageous, unfavorable, unlucky, unwelcome, unpromising, inauspicious, unpropitious, bad; *formal* grievous. ANTONYM auspicious.

3 *an unfortunate remark* REGRETTABLE, inappropriate, unsuitable, infelicitous, unbecoming, inopportune, tactless, injudicious. ANTONYMS tactful, appropriate.

unfortunately adverb *unfortunately, Mr. Hillman will not be joining us tonight* UNLUCKILY, sadly, regrettably, unhappily, alas, sad to say; *informal* worse luck.

unfounded adjective *unfounded speculation* GROUNDLESS, baseless, unsubstantiated, unproven, unsupported, uncorroborated, unconfirmed, unverified, unattested, unjustified, without basis, without foundation; specious, speculative, conjectural, idle; false, untrue. ANTONYM proven.

unfriendly adjective **1** *an unfriendly look* HOSTILE, disagreeable, antagonistic, aggressive; ill-natured, unpleasant, surly, sour, uncongenial; inhospitable, unneighborly, unwelcoming, unkind, unsympathetic; unsociable, antisocial; aloof, stiff, cold, cool, frosty, distant, unapproachable; *informal* standoffish, starchy. ANTONYM amiable.

2 *an unfriendly wind* UNFAVORABLE, unhelpful, disadvantageous, unpropitious, inauspicious, hostile. ANTONYM favorable.

3 *environmentally unfriendly* HARMFUL, damaging, destructive, disrespectful.

unfunny adjective *it was an unfunny practical joke* UNAMUSING, bad, lame, stupid, pathetic, stale, flat.

ungainly adjective *they were as ungainly as fifth-grade boys taking dance lessons in a foot of snow* AWKWARD, clumsy, klutzy, ungraceful, graceless, inelegant, gawky, maladroit, gauche, uncoordinated; *archaic* lubberly. ANTONYM graceful.

ungodly adjective **1** *ungodly behavior* UNHOLY, godless, irreligious, impious, blasphemous, sacrilegious, profane; immoral, corrupt, depraved, sinful, wicked, evil, iniquitous.

2 *he called at an ungodly hour* UNREASONABLE, unsocial, antisocial, unearthly, godforsaken.

ungovernable adjective *Lisa had not yet met the boss's ungovernable children* UNCONTROLLABLE, unmanageable, anarchic, intractable; unruly, disorderly, rebellious, riotous, restive, refractory, wild, mutinous, undisciplined.

ungracious adjective *our ungracious host didn't even stay through the end of the meal* RUDE, impolite, uncivil, discourteous, ill-mannered, bad-mannered, curt, brusque, uncouth, disrespectful, insolent, impertinent, offhand. ANTONYM polite.

ungrateful adjective *she's been so generous to those ungrateful children* UNAPPRECIATIVE, unthankful, thankless, ungracious, churlish. ANTONYM thankful.

unguarded adjective **1** *an unguarded frontier* UNDEFENDED, unprotected, unfortified; vulnerable, insecure, open to attack.

2 *an unguarded remark* CARELESS, indiscreet, incautious, thoughtless, rash, reckless, foolhardy, foolish, imprudent, injudicious, ill-considered, ill-judged, insensitive; unwary, inattentive, off guard, distracted, absentminded; candid, open; *literary* temerarious.

unhappiness noun *the poetry of her later years was largely a testament of unhappiness* SADNESS, sorrow, dejection, depression, misery, wretchedness, despondency, despair, desolation, glumness, gloom, gloominess, dolefulness; melancholy, low spirits, mournfulness, woe, malaise, heartache, distress, chagrin, grief, pain, agony, anguish, torment, suffering, tribulation; *informal* the blues.

unhappy adjective **1** *the unhappy boy cried all night* SAD, miserable, sorrowful, dejected, despondent, disconsolate, morose, broken-hearted, heartbroken, hurting, down, downcast, dispirited, downhearted, depressed, melancholy, mournful, gloomy, glum, lugubrious, despairing, doleful, forlorn, woebegone, woeful, long-faced, joyless, cheerless; *informal* down in the dumps, down in/at the mouth, blue. ANTONYM cheerful.

2 *in the unhappy event of litigation* UNFORTUNATE, unlucky, luckless; ill-starred, ill-fated, doomed; regrettable, lamentable; *informal* jinxed; *literary* star-crossed.

3 *I was unhappy with the service I received* DISSATISFIED, displeased, discontented, disappointed, disgruntled, angry; *informal* PO'd.

unharmed adjective *the painting was returned unharmed* UNINJURED, unhurt, unscathed, safe (and sound), alive and well, in one piece, without a scratch; undamaged, unbroken, unmarred, unspoiled, unsullied, unmarked; sound, intact, perfect, unblemished, pristine. ANTONYMS injured, damaged.

unhealthy adjective **1** *an unhealthy lifestyle* HARMFUL, detrimental, destructive, injurious, damaging, deleterious; malign, noxious, poisonous, insalubrious, baleful.

2 *an unhealthy pallor* SICKLY, ill, unwell, in poor health, ailing, sick, indisposed, weak, wan, sallow, frail, delicate, infirm, washed out, run-down.

3 *an unhealthy obsession with toenails* UNWHOLESOME, morbid, macabre, twisted, abnormal, warped, depraved, unnatural; *informal* sick, wrong.

unheard of adjective *these medical procedures were unheard of just ten years ago* UNPRECEDENTED, exceptional, extraordinary, out of the ordinary, unthought of, undreamed of, unbelievable, inconceivable, unimaginable, unthinkable; UNKNOWN, unfamiliar, new. ANTONYMS common, well-known.

unheeded adjective *he was soon reminded of his parents' unheeded warnings* DISREGARDED, ignored, neglected, overlooked, unnoted, unrecognized.

unheralded adjective *tonight, an unheralded young playwright has become a lion* OVERLOOKED, unhyped, unannounced, unnoticed, unsung, underrated, underestimated, disregarded.

unhinged adjective *he was completely unhinged just because we were a few minutes late* DERANGED, demented, unbalanced, unglued, crazed, mad, insane, disturbed, out of one's mind, out of one's tree; *informal* crazy, mental, nutso, bonkers, batty, loopy, loco, postal, bananas, touched. ANTONYM sane.

unholy adjective **1** *a grin of unholy amusement* UNGODLY, godless, irreligious, impious, blasphemous, sacrilegious, profane, irreverent; wicked, evil, immoral, corrupt, depraved, sinful.

2 *an unholy alliance* UNNATURAL, unusual, improbable, made in Hell.

unhurried adjective *we live at an unhurried pace around here* LEISURELY, easy, easygoing, relaxed, slow, deliberate, measured, calm. ANTONYM hasty.

unhygienic adjective *the medical facilities were appallingly unhygienic* UNSANITARY, dirty, filthy, contaminated, unhealthy, unwholesome, insalubrious, polluted, foul. ANTONYM sanitary.

unidentified adjective *an unidentified caller said he knew the whereabouts of Lyle* UNKNOWN, unnamed, anonymous, incognito, nameless, unfamiliar, strange, mysterious. ANTONYM known.

unification noun *the costs of German unification* UNION, merger, fusion, fusing, amalgamation, coalition, combination, confederation, federation, synthesis, joining.

uniform adjective **1** *a uniform temperature* CONSTANT, consistent, steady, invariable, unvarying, unfluctuating, unchanging, stable, static, regular, fixed, even, equal. ANTONYM variable.

2 *pieces of uniform size* IDENTICAL, matching, similar, equal; same, like, homogeneous, consistent. ANTONYM varied.

▸ noun *a soldier in uniform* COSTUME, livery, regalia, suit, ensemble, outfit; colors; *informal* getup, monkey suit, rig, gear; *archaic* habit.

uniformity noun **1** *uniformity in tax law* CONSTANCY, consistency, conformity, invariability, stability, regularity, evenness, homogeneity, equality, harmony. ANTONYM variation.

2 *a dull uniformity* MONOTONY, tedium, tediousness, dullness, dreariness, flatness, sameness. ANTONYM variety.

unify verb *he unified the confederacy into a powerful entity* UNITE, bring together, join (together), marry, merge, fuse, amalgamate, integrate, coalesce, combine, blend, mix, meld, bind, consolidate. ANTONYM separate.

unilateral adjective *no one on this board has the authority to make a unilateral decision* INDEPENDENT, autonomous, solitary, solo, go-it-alone, single-handed, self-determined, maverick, isolationist.

unimaginable adjective *the phone bills have been unimaginable* UNTHINKABLE, inconceivable, indescribable, incredible, unbelievable, unheard of, unthought of, untold, mind-boggling, undreamed of, beyond one's wildest dreams.

unimaginative adjective *the biggest letdown is the dessert menu, which is quite unimaginative* UNINSPIRED, uninventive, unoriginal, uncreative, commonplace, pedestrian, mundane, institutional, ordinary, routine, matter-of-fact, humdrum, workaday, run-of-the-mill, by-the-numbers, hackneyed, trite, hoary.

unimpeachable adjective *Carruthers is an unimpeachable source of information* TRUSTWORTHY, reliable, dependable, above suspicion, irreproachable; *informal* squeaky clean, Teflon. ANTONYM unreliable.

unimpeded adjective *a unimpeded view* UNRESTRICTED, unhindered, unblocked, unhampered, free, clear.

unimportant adjective *the details are unimportant at this stage* INSIGNIFICANT, inconsequential, insubstantial, immaterial, trivial, minor, venial, trifling, of little/no importance, of little/no consequence, of no account, no-account, irrelevant, peripheral, extraneous, petty, paltry, derisory, weightless, small; *informal* piddling.

uninhabited adjective *most of the village has been uninhabited since the epidemic in the seventies* UNPOPULATED, unpeopled, unsettled, vacant, empty, unoccupied; unlived-in, untenanted.

uninhibited adjective **1** *uninhibited dancing* UNRESTRAINED, unrepressed, abandoned, wild, reckless; unrestricted, unmufflered, uncontrolled, unchecked, intemperate, wanton, loose; *informal* gung-ho. ANTONYM controlled.

2 *I'm pretty uninhibited* UNRESERVED, unrepressed, liberated, unselfconscious, free and easy, free-spirited, relaxed, informal, open, outgoing, extrovert, outspoken, candid, frank, forthright; *informal* upfront, jiggy. ANTONYM repressed.

uninitiated adjective *the uninitiated volunteers go through a two-day orientation* UNTRAINED, uninstructed, unschooled, untaught, untutored, uneducated, unknowledgeable, unprepared, unfamiliar.

▸ noun *most of this literature was written for the benefit of the uninitiated* OUTSIDERS, beginners, novices, newcomers, neophytes, newbies.

uninspired adjective *pages and pages of uninspired verse* UNIMAGINATIVE, uninventive, pedestrian, mundane, unoriginal, commonplace, ordinary, routine, humdrum, run-of-the-mill, hackneyed, trite; spiritless, passionless, stolid, prosaic.

uninspiring adjective *an uninspiring political force* BORING, dull, dreary, unexciting, unstimulating; dry, colorless, bland, lackluster, tedious, flaccid, formulaic, humdrum, run-of-the-mill, by-the-numbers.

unintelligent adjective *I'd say he was more lazy than unintelligent* STUPID, ignorant, dense, brainless, mindless, slow, dull-witted, feebleminded, simpleminded, vacuous, obtuse, vapid, irrational, idiotic; *informal* thick, knuckleheaded, bubbleheaded, lunkheaded, dim, dumb, dopey, halfwitted, dozy. See note at STUPID.

unintelligible adjective **1** *unintelligible sounds* INCOMPREHENSIBLE, indiscernible, mumbled, indistinct, unclear, slurred, inarticulate, incoherent, garbled.

2 *unintelligible logic* IMPENETRABLE, baffling, perplexing, inscrutable, opaque, cryptic, abstruse, unfathomable, incoherent, incomprehensible, as clear as mud, impossible to follow.

3 *unintelligible graffiti* ILLEGIBLE, indecipherable, unreadable, hieroglyphic.

unintentional adjective *I assure you, the insult was unintentional* UNINTENDED, accidental, inadvertent, involuntary, unwitting, unthinking, unpremeditated, unconscious; random, fortuitous, serendipitous, fluky. ANTONYM deliberate.

uninterested adjective *I couldn't live with someone* ***uninterested in*** *world affairs* INDIFFERENT TO, unconcerned with, incurious about, uninvolved with/in, apathetic to, lukewarm about, unenthusiastic about, bored with. See notes at DISINTERESTED.

uninteresting adjective *an uninteresting book about genealogy* UNEXCITING, boring, dull, tiresome, wearisome, soporific, tedious, jejune, lifeless, lackluster, humdrum, colorless, soulless, bland, insipid, banal, dry, dreary, drab, pedestrian, lacking; *informal* blah, samey. ANTONYM exciting.

uninterrupted adjective *an uninterrupted 55 minutes of your favorite music* UNBROKEN, continuous, continual, constant, nonstop, ceaseless; undisturbed, untroubled. ANTONYM intermittent.

uninvited adjective **1** *an uninvited guest* UNASKED, unexpected; unwelcome, unwanted.

2 *uninvited suggestions* UNSOLICITED, unrequested, unsought.

uninviting adjective *the bed looked cold and uninviting* UNAPPEALING, unattractive, unappetizing, off-putting; bleak, cheerless, dreary, dismal, depressing, grim, inhospitable, forbidding. ANTONYM tempting.

union noun **1** *the union of art and nature* UNIFICATION, uniting, joining, merging, merger, fusion, fusing, amalgamation, coalition, combination, synthesis, blend, blending, mingling; MARRIAGE, wedding, alliance; coupling. ANTONYMS separation, parting.

2 *the workers joined a union* ASSOCIATION, labor union, trade union, league, guild, confederation, federation, brotherhood, organization.

unionize verb *they made several failed attempts to unionize the assembly crew* ORGANIZE, unite; join forces, band together, gang up.

unique adjective **1** *each site is unique* DISTINCTIVE, distinct, individual, special, idiosyncratic; single, sole, lone, unrepeated, unrepeatable, solitary, exclusive, rare, uncommon, unusual, sui generis; *informal* one-off, one-of-a-kind, once-in-a-lifetime, one-shot.

2 *a unique insight* REMARKABLE, special, singular, noteworthy, notable, extraordinary; unequaled, unparalleled, unmatched, unsurpassed, unrivaled, peerless, nonpareil, incomparable; *formal* unexampled.

3 *species unique to the island* PECULIAR, specific, limited.

WORD NOTE **unique**

This is one of a class of adjectives, sometimes called uncomparables, that present special problems. Among other uncomparables are *precise, exact, correct, whole, accurate, preferable, inevitable, possible, false;* there are probably two dozen in all. These adjectives all describe absolute, non-negotiable states: something is either false or it's not; something is either whole or it's not. Many writers, though, get careless and try to modify uncomparables with comparatives like *more* and *less* or intensives like *very.* If you really think about them, the core assertions in sentences like *War is becoming increasingly inevitable as Middle East tensions rise, Their cost estimate was more accurate than the other firms',* and *As a mortician, he has a very unique attitude* make no sense. If something is inevitable, it is bound to happen; it cannot be bound to happen and then somehow even more bound to happen. *Unique* already means one-of-a-kind, so the adjective phrase *very unique* is at best redundant and at worst stupid, like *audible to the ear* or *rectangular in shape.* Uncomparable-type boners can be easily fixed—*War is looking increasingly inevitable*; *Their estimate was more nearly accurate*; *He has a unique attitude*—but for writers the hard part is noticing such errors in the first place. You can blame the culture of marketing for some of this difficulty. As the number and rhetorical volume of U.S. ads increase, we become inured to hyperbolic language, which then forces marketers to load superlatives and uncomparables with high-octane modifiers (special→very special→Super-Special!→***Mega-Special!!***). So, a deeper issue implicit in the problem of uncomparables concerns the dissimilarities between Standard Written English and the language of advertising. Today's "Advertising English," which probably deserves to be studied as its own dialect, operates under very different syntactic rules than SWE, primarily because Advertising English's goals and assumptions are different. Sentences like *We offer a totally unique dining experience, Come on down and receive your free gift,* and *Save up to fifty percent and more!* are perfectly OK in Advertising English, but this is because AE is aimed at people who are not paying close attention. If your audience is by definition involuntary, distracted, and numbed, then *free gift* and *totally unique* stand a better chance of penetrating their awareness—and simple penetration is what Advertising English is all about. The goals and assumptions of Standard Written English are obviously far more complex, but one axiom of SWE is that your reader is paying close attention and will expect you to have done the same. **—DFW**

USAGE NOTE **unique**

Strictly speaking, *unique* means "being one of a kind," not "unusual." Hence the phrases *very unique, quite unique, how unique*, and the like are slovenly. *The Oxford English Dictionary* notes that this tendency to hyperbole—to use *unique* when all that is meant is "uncommon, unusual, remarkable"—began in the nineteenth century. However old it is, the tendency is worth resisting.

Unless the thing is the only one of its kind, rarity does not make it unique. For instance, if a thing is one in a million, logically there would be two things in two million. Rare indeed but not unique. Who can demand responsible use of the language from an ad writer who is reckless enough to say, in a national advertisement, that a certain luxury sedan is "so unique, it's capable of thought"? And what are we to make of the following examples?

- "This year the consensus among the development executives seems to be that there are some fantastically funny, very exciting, very, very unique talents here." (*Time*; Aug. 16, 1993.)

• "Residents of college basketball's most unique unincorporated village were in place yesterday afternoon, the day before their Blue Devils will face North Carolina." (*New York Times*; Feb. 2, 1995.)

Arguably, our modern culture lacks and does not want absolutes, in intellectual life or in language. But stick with the uncomparable *unique*, and you may stand out as almost unique. *—BG*

---

unisex adjective *unisex jackets* | *a unisex sailing team* GENDER-NEUTRAL, androgynous, epicene; coed, mixed.

unison PHRASE: **in unison** *they lifted their arms in unison* SIMULTANEOUSLY, at (one and) the same time, (all) at once, (all) together.

unit noun **1** *the family is the fundamental unit of society* COMPONENT, element, building block, constituent; subdivision.

2 *a unit of currency* QUANTITY, measure, denomination.

3 *a guerrilla unit* DETACHMENT, contingent, division, company, squadron, corps, regiment, brigade, platoon, battalion; cell, faction.

unite verb **1** *uniting the municipalities* UNIFY, join, link, connect, combine, amalgamate, fuse, weld, bond, wed, marry, bring together, knit together, splice. See note at JOIN. ANTONYM divide.

2 *environmentalists and union activists united to demand changes* JOIN TOGETHER, join forces, combine, band together, ally, cooperate, collaborate, work together, pull together, team up, hitch up, hook up, twin. ANTONYM split.

united adjective **1** *a united Germany* UNIFIED, integrated, amalgamated, joined, merged; federal, confederate.

2 *a united response* COMMON, shared, joint, combined, communal, cooperative, collective, collaborative, concerted; *Brit. informal* joined-up.

3 *they were united in their views* UNANIMOUS, in agreement, agreed, in unison, of the same opinion, like-minded, as one, in accord, in harmony, in unity.

United States of America noun *Sasha's tour of duty in Afghanistan made her appreciate everyday life in the United States of America* USA, U.S., US, America; *informal* the States, the U.S. of A., the US of A, Uncle Sam.

WORD NOTE **Made in the USA**

Akin to the theoretical pleasure of explaining the rules of baseball to an Oxford don is the perpetuation of sentences composed of neologisms made in the USA: "The G-man, clad in tuxedo and T-shirt, played strip poker with the terrorist wannabe before wasting him at a unisex boutique." Try explaining that to anyone caught in a 1928 time-warp. Why 1928? Because that year the last part of the *Oxford English Dictionary* was published. It is now "updated" (itself a term unknown in 1928) online quarterly, but the first revision was edited by Robert Burchfield, who completed *A Supplement to the Oxford English Dictionary* in 1986. The final volume of the supplement includes the nouns *sit-com, sit-in, teenager, touchdown, transistor,* and the adjective *user-friendly,* and one might write a sestina using precisely these as the six recurrent endwords on which the sestina as a form is based. "The center of gravity for the English language is no longer Britain," Burchfield observed in 1986. "American English is the greatest influence on English everywhere." *—DL*

---

unity noun **1** *European unity* UNION, unification, integration, amalgamation; coalition, federation, confederation. ANTONYM division.

2 *unity between alliance members* HARMONY, accord, cooperation, collaboration, agreement, consensus, solidarity; *formal* concord, concordance. ANTONYMS strife, discord.

3 *the organic unity of the universe* ONENESS, singleness, wholeness, uniformity, homogeneity.

universal adjective *the universal features of language* GENERAL, ubiquitous, comprehensive, common, omnipresent, all-inclusive, all-embracing, across-the-board; global, worldwide, international, widespread; *formal* catholic.

THE RIGHT WORD

Something that is **universal** applies to every case or individual in a class or category (*a universal practice among aboriginal tribesmen; a universal truth*). **General**, on the other hand, is less precise; it implies applicability to all or most of a group or class, whether the members of that group are clearly defined or only casually associated (*a drug that has come into general use among women but has not yet won the universal acceptance of doctors*). **Generic** is often used in place of *general* when referring to every member of a genus or clearly-defined scientific category (*a generic characteristic of insects*); with reference to language, it means referring to both men and women (*a generic pronoun*). **Common** implies participation or sharing by all members of a class (*a common interest in French culture*) or frequently occurring (*a common complaint*). **Catholic** implies a wide-ranging or inclusive attitude (*known for his catholic tastes in music*), while **ecumenical** means pertaining to the whole Christian church or promoting unity among religious groups or divisions (*an ecumenical marriage ceremony*).

---

universally adverb *it was universally accepted that no man married merely for love* GENERALLY, widely, commonly, across the board, all over.

universe noun **1** *the physical universe* COSMOS, macrocosm, totality; infinity, all existence, Creation; space, outer space, firmament.

2 *the universe of computer hardware* WORLD, sphere, domain, preserve, milieu, province.

university noun *the oldest university in New England* COLLEGE, school, academy, institute, polytechnic, alma mater, graduate school.

unjust adjective **1** *the assessment was unjust* UNFAIR, prejudiced, prejudicial, biased, inequitable, discriminatory, partisan, partial, one-sided, jaundiced. ANTONYM fair.

2 *an unjust attack* WRONGFUL, unfair, undeserved, unmerited, unwarranted, uncalled for, unreasonable, unjustifiable, undue, gratuitous. ANTONYMS fair, reasonable.

unjustifiable adjective **1** *an unjustifiable extravagance* INDEFENSIBLE, inexcusable, unforgivable, unpardonable, uncalled for, gratuitous, without justification, unwarrantable; excessive, immoderate. ANTONYM reasonable.

2 *an unjustifiable slur on his character* GROUNDLESS, unfounded, baseless, unsubstantiated, unconfirmed, uncorroborated, indefensible, irrational.

unkempt adjective *unkempt hair* UNTIDY, messy, scruffy, straggly, disordered, disheveled, disarranged, rumpled, wind-blown, ungroomed, bedraggled, in a mess, mussed, messed up; tousled, uncombed. ANTONYM tidy.

WORD NOTE **kempt**

Kempt and *couth* belong to a set of orphan positives: they are words that are more commonly heard in the negative. It's entertaining to use words that fall a little further into this set: *crepit* (instead of *decrepit*), *advertent* (instead of *inadvertent*), (and on the sillier side) *combobulated* and *chalant* (instead of *discombobulated* and *nonchalant*). These (like any joke) can be annoying and cloying if used too often, but once in a while I like to remind readers and myself that even long-cemented prefixes can be wrenched away from their stems. You can also do this with words that don't even, strictly speaking, have prefixes—only parts that look like prefixes. My favorite is *livious*—although it's hard to use this one since there are so few opportunities to employ it, compared with its parent, *oblivious*. **—EM**

unkind adjective *everyone was being rude and unkind to him* UNCHARITABLE, unpleasant, disagreeable, nasty, mean, mean-spirited, cruel, vindictive, vicious, spiteful, malicious, callous, unsympathetic, unfeeling, uncaring, unsparing, hurtful, ill-natured, hard-hearted, cold-hearted; unfriendly, uncivil, inconsiderate, insensitive, hostile; *informal* bitchy, catty.

unknown adjective **1** *the future is unknown* UNCERTAIN, undisclosed, unrevealed, secret; undetermined, undecided, unresolved, unsettled, unsure, unascertained. ANTONYM decided.

2 *unknown country* UNEXPLORED, uncharted, unmapped, untraveled, undiscovered, unfamiliar, unheard of, new, novel, strange. ANTONYM familiar.

3 *persons unknown* UNIDENTIFIED, anonymous, unnamed, nameless; faceless, hidden. ANTONYMS identified, named.

4 *unknown artists* OBSCURE, unrecognized, unheard of, unsung, overlooked, unheralded, minor, insignificant, unimportant. ANTONYM familiar.

▸ noun *the overseas ballots are a big unknown* MYSTERY, unknown quantity, uncertainty, ambiguity, variable, anyone's guess; *informal* crapshoot.

unlawful adjective *unlawful imports of drugs* ILLEGAL, illicit, illegitimate, against the law; criminal, felonious; prohibited, banned, outlawed, proscribed, forbidden. ANTONYM legal.

unleash verb *we are asking that you not unleash your reporters until the children have been safely escorted to a secured location* LET LOOSE, release, (set) free, unloose, untie, unchain.

unlettered adjective *the unlettered foundry workers* ILLITERATE, uneducated, poorly educated, unschooled, unlearned, untutored, ignorant. See note at IGNORANT. ANTONYM educated.

unlike preposition **1** *the familiar artichoke is totally unlike a Jerusalem artichoke* DIFFERENT FROM, dissimilar to. ANTONYM similar to.

2 *unlike Bob, Regis enjoyed swing dancing* IN CONTRAST TO, as opposed to. ANTONYM similarly to.

▸ adjective *a meeting of unlike minds* DISSIMILAR, unalike, disparate, contrasting, antithetical, different, diverse, incongruous, heterogeneous, mismatched, divergent, at variance, varying, at odds; *informal* poles apart, like night and day, like apples and oranges.

unlikely adjective **1** *it is unlikely they will ever recover* IMPROBABLE, doubtful, dubious. ANTONYM probable.

2 *an unlikely story* IMPLAUSIBLE, improbable, questionable, unconvincing, far-fetched, unrealistic, incredible, unbelievable, inconceivable, unimaginable; absurd, preposterous; *informal* tall. ANTONYM believable.

unlimited adjective **1** *unlimited supplies of water* INEXHAUSTIBLE, limitless, illimitable, boundless, immeasurable, incalculable, untold, infinite, endless, bottomless, never-ending. ANTONYM finite.

2 *unlimited travel* UNRESTRICTED, unconstrained, unrestrained, unchecked, unbridled, uncurbed. ANTONYM restricted.

3 *unlimited power* TOTAL, unqualified, unconditional, unrestricted, absolute, supreme. ANTONYMS conditional, restricted.

unload verb **1** *we unloaded the van* UNPACK, empty.

2 *they unloaded the cases from the truck* REMOVE, offload, discharge.

3 *the government unloaded its 20 percent stake* SELL, discard, jettison, offload, get rid of, dispose of; palm something off (on someone), foist something (on someone), fob something off (on someone); *informal* dump, ditch, get shut of.

4 *she unloaded her troubles* DIVULGE, talk about, open up about, pour out, vent, give vent to, get something off one's chest.

unlock verb *I unlocked the door and led the way in* UNBOLT, unlatch, unbar, unfasten, open.

unloved adjective *Melanie felt lonely and unloved* UNWANTED, uncared-for, friendless, unvalued; rejected, unwelcome, shunned, spurned, neglected, abandoned.

unlucky adjective **1** *he was unlucky not to score* UNFORTUNATE, luckless, out of luck, jinxed, hapless, ill-fated, ill-starred, unhappy; *informal* down on one's luck; *literary* star-crossed. See note at LUCKY. ANTONYM fortunate.

2 *an unlucky number* UNFAVORABLE, inauspicious, unpropitious, ominous, cursed, ill-fated, ill-omened, disadvantageous, unfortunate. ANTONYM favorable.

unmanageable adjective **1** *the huge project was unmanageable* TROUBLESOME, awkward, inconvenient; cumbersome, bulky, unwieldy.

2 *his behavior was becoming unmanageable* UNCONTROLLABLE, ungovernable, unruly, disorderly, out of hand, difficult, disruptive, undisciplined, wayward, refractory, restive; *archaic* contumacious.

unmanly adjective *he was on the verge of tears, but did not wish to appear unmanly* EFFEMINATE, effete, unmasculine, womanish, epicene; weak, limp-wristed, soft, timid, timorous; *informal* sissy, swishy, wimpish, wimpy, nancy, pansy, camp. ANTONYM virile.

unmanned adjective **1** *an unmanned spacecraft* AUTOMATIC, computerized, remote-controlled, robotic.

2 *he was unmanned by her response* TAKEN ABACK; *Brit. informal* gobsmacked, shell-shocked, devastated.

unmarried adjective *all of my siblings are happily unmarried* SINGLE, unwed, unwedded; spinster, bachelor; unattached, available, eligible, free.

unmask verb *they unmasked the bronze bust of Dr. Peters* *in front of a cheering crowd of students and alumni* REVEAL, uncover, expose, bring to light, lay bare.

unmatched adjective *his oratory skills are unmatched* UNEQUALED, unrivaled, unparalleled, unsurpassed, peerless, matchless, without equal, nonpareil, without parallel, incomparable, inimitable, superlative, second to none, in a class of its own.

unmentionable adjective *sex was the unmentionable subject* TABOO, censored, forbidden, banned, proscribed, prohibited, not to be spoken of, ineffable, unspeakable, unutterable, unprintable, off limits; *informal* no go.

unmercifully adjective *she treated her poor little nephews unmercifully* RUTHLESSLY, cruelly, harshly, mercilessly, pitilessly, cold-bloodedly, hard-heartedly, callously, brutally, severely, unforgivingly, inhumanely, inhumanly, heartlessly, unsympathetically, unfeelingly, unsparingly.

unmistakable adjective *the taste of ginger is unmistakable* DISTINCTIVE, distinct, telltale, indisputable, indubitable, undoubted, unambiguous, unequivocal; plain, clear, clear-cut, definite, obvious, unmissable, evident, self-evident, manifest, patent, pronounced, as plain as the nose on your face, as clear as day.

unmitigated adjective the raid was an unmitigated disaster ABSOLUTE, unqualified, categorical, complete, total, downright, outright, utter, out-and-out, undiluted, unequivocal, untempered, veritable, perfect, consummate, pure, sheer. See note at SEVERE.

unmoved adjective **1** *he was totally unmoved by her outburst* UNAFFECTED, untouched, unimpressed, aloof, cool, cold, dry-eyed; unconcerned, uncaring, unsympathetic, unreceptive, indifferent, impassive, unemotional, stoical, phlegmatic, equable, nonchalant; impervious (to), oblivious (to), heedless (of), deaf to.

2 *he remained unmoved on the crucial issues* STEADFAST, firm, unwavering, unswerving, resolved, resolute, decided, unswayed, uninfluenced, inflexible, unbending, intransigent, implacable, adamant.

unnatural adjective **1** *the life of a circus bear is completely unnatural* ABNORMAL, unusual, uncommon, extraordinary, strange, odd, peculiar, unorthodox, exceptional, irregular, atypical, untypical; freakish, freaky, uncanny. ANTONYM normal.

2 *a flash of unnatural color* ARTIFICIAL, man-made, synthetic, manufactured, inorganic, genetically engineered. ANTONYM genuine.

3 *unnatural vice* PERVERTED, warped, aberrant, twisted, deviant, depraved, degenerate; *informal* kinky, sick.

4 *her voice sounded unnatural* AFFECTED, artificial, mannered, stilted, forced, labored, strained, false, fake, theatrical, insincere, ersatz; *informal* put on, phony.

unnecessary adjective *extra blankets are unnecessary* UNNEEDED, nonessential, inessential, not required, uncalled for, useless, unwarranted, unwanted, undesired, dispensable, unimportant, optional, extraneous, gratuitous, expendable, noncore, disposable, redundant, pointless, purposeless. ANTONYM essential.

unnerve verb *the bleakness of his gaze unnerved her* DEMORALIZE, discourage, dishearten, dispirit, daunt, alarm, frighten, dismay, disconcert, discompose, perturb, upset, discomfit, take aback, unsettle, disquiet, fluster, agitate, shake, ruffle, throw off balance; *informal* rattle, faze, shake up, discombobulate. ANTONYM hearten.

unobtrusive adjective *she was unobtrusive and shy* INCONSPICUOUS, unnoticeable, low-key, discreet, circumspect, understated, unostentatious. ANTONYMS extrovert, conspicuous.

unoccupied adjective **1** *an unoccupied house* VACANT, empty, uninhabited, unlived-in, untenanted, abandoned; free, available. ANTONYM inhabited.

2 *an unoccupied territory* UNINHABITED, unpopulated, unpeopled, unsettled. ANTONYMS inhabited, populated.

3 *many young people were unoccupied* AT LEISURE, idle, free, with time on one's hands, at a loose end; unemployed, without work. ANTONYM busy.

unofficial adjective **1** *unofficial figures* UNCONFIRMED, unauthenticated, uncorroborated, unsubstantiated, provisional, off the record. ANTONYM confirmed.

2 *an unofficial committee* INFORMAL, casual; unauthorized, unsanctioned, unaccredited. ANTONYM formal.

unoriginal adjective *the characters were somewhat interesting, but the story itself was unoriginal* CONVENTIONAL, uninspired, overdone, tired, clichéd, hackneyed; recycled, stock, paint-by-number.

unorthodox adjective *Hobson's unorthodox views denied him an academic career* UNCONVENTIONAL, unusual, radical, nonconformist, avant-garde, eccentric, maverick, strange, idiosyncratic; heterodox, heretical, dissenting; *informal* off-the-wall, way out, offbeat, kooky. ANTONYM conventional.

unpaid adjective **1** *unpaid bills* UNSETTLED, outstanding, due, overdue, owing, owed, payable, undischarged, delinquent, past due.

2 *unpaid charity work* VOLUNTARY, volunteer, honorary, unsalaried, unremunerative, unwaged, pro bono (publico).

unpalatable adjective **1** *unpalatable food* UNAPPETIZING, unappealing, unsavory, inedible, uneatable; disgusting, rancid, revolting, nauseating, tasteless, flavorless, gross. ANTONYM tasty.

2 *the unpalatable truth* DISAGREEABLE, unpleasant, regrettable, unwelcome, lamentable, hard to swallow, hard to take.

unparalleled adjective *an unparalleled opportunity to change society* EXCEPTIONAL, unique, singular, rare, unequaled, unprecedented, without parallel, without equal, nonpareil, matchless, peerless, unrivaled, unsurpassed, unexcelled, incomparable, second to none; *formal* unexampled.

unperturbed adjective *Daniel was unperturbed by the outburst* UNTROUBLED, undisturbed, unworried, unconcerned, unmoved, unflustered, unruffled, undismayed, impassive; calm, composed, cool, collected, unemotional, self-possessed, self-assured, levelheaded, unfazed, nonplussed, laid-back.

unplanned adjective *an unplanned pregnancy would change the course of their lives* UNPREMEDITATED, unscheduled, accidental, unexpected, surprise; spontaneous, impromptu, impulsive, sudden.

unpleasant adjective **1** *a very unpleasant situation* DISAGREEABLE, irksome, troublesome, annoying, irritating, vexatious, displeasing, distressing, nasty, horrible, terrible, awful, dreadful, hateful, miserable, invidious, objectionable, offensive, obnoxious, repugnant, repulsive, repellent, revolting, disgusting, distasteful, nauseating, unsavory. ANTONYM agreeable.

2 *an unpleasant man* UNLIKABLE, unlovable, disagreeable; unfriendly, rude, impolite, obnoxious, nasty, spiteful, mean, mean-spirited; insufferable, unbearable, annoying, irritating. ANTONYM likable.

unpolished adjective 1 *unpolished wood* UNVARNISHED, unfinished, untreated, natural. ANTONYM varnished.

2 *his unpolished ways* UNSOPHISTICATED, unrefined, uncultured, uncultivated, inelegant, coarse, vulgar, crude, rough (and ready), awkward, clumsy, gauche. ANTONYM sophisticated.

3 *an unpolished performance* SLIPSHOD, rough, loose, crude, uneven; amateurish; unprepared, unrehearsed, inchoate.

unpopular adjective *he was unpopular at school* DISLIKED, friendless, unliked, unloved, loathed, despised; unwelcome, avoided, ignored, rejected, outcast, shunned, spurned, cold-shouldered, ostracized; unfashionable, unhip, out.

unprecedented adjective *warfare on an unprecedented scale* UNHEARD OF, unknown, new, novel, groundbreaking, revolutionary, pioneering, epoch-making; unparalleled, unequaled, unmatched, unrivaled, without parallel, without equal, out of the ordinary, unusual, exceptional, singular, unique; *formal* unexampled.

unpredictable adjective 1 *unpredictable results* UNFORESEEABLE, uncertain, unsure, doubtful, dubious, iffy, dicey, in the balance, up in the air.

2 *unpredictable behavior* ERRATIC, moody, volatile, unstable, capricious, temperamental, mercurial, changeable, variable; 'on-again, off-again'.

unprejudiced adjective 1 *unprejudiced observation* OBJECTIVE, impartial, unbiased, neutral, value-free, nonpartisan, detached, disinterested. ANTONYM partisan.

2 *unprejudiced attitudes* UNBIASED, tolerant, nondiscriminatory, politically correct, liberal, broad-minded. ANTONYM intolerant.

WORD NOTE **politically correct**

The tediously overworked phrase *politically correct* can be used only with a smile, whether of irony or slightly embarrassed affection. Originally, the politically correct were those who ardently championed the rights of women, people of color, homosexuals, and other long-marginalized groups. But *politically correct* rapidly came to be associated with adherents who were overscrupulous in these observances, in short, zealots. Today most people recognize the fundamental justice of many, if not all, the legal and social advances linked to political correctness, but no one really cares to be called *P.C.* The fight has largely been won, at least *de jure* if not always *de facto,* and so the term now sounds a bit old-fashioned, and usually carries an undertone of mild vexation or benign indulgence: *Oh, Joan, she's so politically correct!* —**MD**

unpremeditated adjective *she later regretted her unpremeditated response* UNPLANNED, spontaneous, unprepared, impromptu, spur-of-the-moment, unrehearsed, ad lib, improvised, extemporaneous; *informal* off-the-cuff, off the top of one's head. See note at SPONTANEOUS. ANTONYM planned.

unprepared adjective 1 *we were unprepared for the rate hike* UNREADY, (caught) off (one's) guard, surprised, taken aback; caught napping, caught flat-footed, caught with one's pants down. ANTONYM ready.

2 *they are unprepared to support the reforms* UNWILLING, disinclined, loath, reluctant, resistant, opposed. ANTONYM willing.

3 *the pianist's recital sounded unprepared.* See UNPOLISHED sense 3.

unpretentious adjective 1 *he was thoroughly unpretentious* UNAFFECTED, modest, unassuming, without airs, natural, straightforward, open, honest, sincere, frank, ingenuous.

2 *an unpretentious hotel* SIMPLE, plain, modest, humble, unostentatious, unsophisticated, folksy, no-frills.

unprincipled adjective *he is an unprincipled opportunist* IMMORAL, unethical, amoral, unscrupulous, Machiavellian, dishonorable, dishonest, deceitful, devious, corrupt, crooked, wicked, evil, villainous, shameless, base, low; libertine, licentious. ANTONYM ethical.

unproductive adjective 1 *unproductive soil* INFERTILE, sterile, barren, arid, unfruitful, poor. ANTONYM fertile.

2 *unproductive meetings* FRUITLESS, futile, vain, idle, useless, worthless, valueless, pointless, ineffective, ineffectual, unprofitable, unrewarding. ANTONYM fruitful.

unprofessional adjective 1 *unprofessional conduct* IMPROPER, unethical, unprincipled, unscrupulous, dishonorable, disreputable, unseemly, unbecoming, indecorous.

2 *you don't want to hire unprofessional roofers* AMATEURISH, amateur, unskilled, unskillful, inexpert, unqualified, inexperienced, incompetent, second-rate, inefficient.

unpromising adjective *they were not deterred by this unpromising start* INAUSPICIOUS, unfavorable, unpropitious, discouraging, disheartening, gloomy, bleak, black, portentous, ominous, ill-omened. ANTONYM auspicious.

unprotected adjective *our left flank was unprotected* VULNERABLE, defenseless, undefended, unguarded, helpless, wide open, exposed.

unqualified adjective 1 *an unqualified accountant* UNTRAINED, inexperienced; unlicensed, quack.

2 *those unqualified to look after children* UNSUITABLE, unsuited, unfit, ineligible, incompetent, unable, incapable, unprepared, ill-equipped, ill-prepared.

3 *unqualified support* UNCONDITIONAL, unreserved, unlimited, without reservations, categorical, unequivocal, unambiguous, wholehearted; complete, absolute, downright, undivided, total, utter.

unquestionable adjective *the sincerity of his beliefs is unquestionable* INDUBITABLE, undoubted, beyond question, beyond doubt, indisputable, undeniable, irrefutable, incontestable, incontrovertible, unequivocal; certain, sure, definite, self-evident, evident, manifest, obvious, apparent, patent.

unravel verb 1 *he unraveled the strands* UNTANGLE, disentangle, separate out, unwind, untwist, unsnarl, unthread. ANTONYM entangle.

2 *detectives are trying to unravel the mystery* SOLVE, resolve, clear up, puzzle out, unscramble, get to the bottom of, explain, clarify, make head(s) or tail(s) of; figure out, dope out. ANTONYM complicate.

3 *society is starting to unravel* FALL APART, fail, collapse,

go wrong, deteriorate, go downhill, fray. ANTONYM succeed.

unreadable adjective **1** *unreadable writing* ILLEGIBLE, hard to read, indecipherable, unintelligible, hieroglyphic, scrawled, crabbed, chicken-scratchy. ANTONYM legible.

2 *heavy, unreadable novels* DULL, tedious, boring, uninteresting, dry, wearisome, stodgy, turgid, difficult, indigestible, impenetrable, heavy, ponderous. ANTONYM accessible.

3 *Tyler's expression was unreadable* INSCRUTABLE, enigmatic, impenetrable, cryptic, mysterious, deadpan; *informal* poker-faced. ANTONYM transparent.

unready adjective See UNPREPARED sense 1.

unreal adjective **1** *an unreal world of monsters and fairies* IMAGINARY, fictitious, pretend, make-believe, made-up, dreamed-up, mock, false, illusory, chimerical, mythical, fanciful; hypothetical, theoretical; *informal* phony.

2 *informal that roller coaster was totally unreal* INCREDIBLE, fantastic, unbelievable, out of this world.

unrealistic adjective **1** *unrealistic expectations* IMPRACTICAL, impracticable, unfeasible, nonviable; unreasonable, irrational, illogical, senseless, silly, foolish, fanciful, idealistic, quixotic, romantic, starry-eyed, blue-sky, pie in the sky; *chiefly Brit. informal* airy-fairy. ANTONYM pragmatic.

2 *unrealistic images* UNLIFELIKE, nonrealistic, unnatural, nonrepresentational, abstract; unbelievable, implausible. ANTONYM lifelike.

unreasonable adjective **1** *an unreasonable officer* UNCOOPERATIVE, unhelpful, disobliging, unaccommodating, awkward, contrary, difficult; obstinate, obdurate, willful, headstrong, pigheaded, cussed, intractable, intransigent, inflexible; irrational, illogical, prejudiced, intolerant.

2 *unreasonable demands* UNACCEPTABLE, preposterous, outrageous, ridiculous; excessive, impossible, immoderate, disproportionate, undue, inordinate, intolerable, unjustified, unwarranted, uncalled for. See note at ABSURD.

unrecognizable adjective *with the beard, Steven was practically unrecognizable* UNIDENTIFIABLE, unknowable; disguised, beyond recognition.

unrefined adjective **1** *unrefined clay* UNPROCESSED, untreated, crude, raw, natural, unprepared, unfinished. ANTONYM processed.

2 *unrefined people* UNCULTURED, uncultivated, uncivilized, uneducated, unsophisticated; boorish, lumpen, oafish, loutish, coarse, vulgar, rude, rough, uncouth. ANTONYM cultured.

unrelated adjective **1** *unrelated incidents* SEPARATE, unconnected, independent, unassociated, distinct, discrete, disparate, random.

2 *a reason unrelated to my work* IRRELEVANT, immaterial, inapplicable, extraneous, unconcerned, off the topic, beside the point, not pertinent, not germane.

unrelenting adjective **1** *the unrelenting heat* CONTINUAL, constant, continuous, relentless, unremitting, unabating, unflagging, uninterrupted, unrelieved, incessant, unceasing, ceaseless, endless, unending, persistent, nonstop. ANTONYM intermittent.

2 *an unrelenting opponent* IMPLACABLE, inflexible, uncompromising, unyielding, unbending, relentless, determined, dogged, tenacious, steadfast, tireless, indefatigable, unflagging, unshakable, unswerving, unwavering.

unreliable adjective **1** *unreliable volunteers* UNDEPENDABLE, untrustworthy, irresponsible, fickle, fair-weather, capricious, erratic, unpredictable, inconstant, faithless, temperamental; *informal* hinky. See note at TRUSTWORTHY.

2 *an unreliable indicator* QUESTIONABLE, open to doubt, doubtful, dubious, suspect, unsound, tenuous, uncertain, fallible; risky, chancy, inaccurate; *informal* iffy, dicey.

unremitting adjective *the unremitting rain* RELENTLESS, incessant, unrelenting, continual, constant, continuous, unabating, uninterrupted, unbroken, unrelieved, sustained, unshakable, unceasing, ceaseless, endless, unending, persistent, perpetual, interminable; merciless.

unrepentant adjective *how can you expect to be forgiven if you're unrepentant?* REMORSELESS, unrepenting, impenitent, unashamed, shameless, unapologetic, unabashed.

unreported adjective See UNTOLD sense 2.

unrequited adjective *his unrequited affection for Daniel* UNRECIPROCATED, unreturned; vain, spurned, rejected, unsatisfied.

unreserved adjective **1** *unreserved support* UNCONDITIONAL, unqualified, without reservations, unlimited, categorical, unequivocal, unambiguous; absolute, complete, thorough, wholehearted, full, total, utter, undivided. ANTONYM qualified.

2 *unreserved seats* NOT BOOKED, unallocated, unoccupied, free, empty, vacant, available. ANTONYM booked.

unresolved adjective *as long as this issue is unresolved we cannot move ahead* UNDECIDED, unsettled, undetermined, uncertain, open, pending, open to debate/question, moot, doubtful, on the table, in play, in doubt, up in the air. ANTONYM decided.

unrest noun *social unrest* DISRUPTION, disturbance, trouble, turmoil, turbulence, disorder, chaos, anarchy; discord, disquiet, dissension, dissent, strife, protest, rebellion, uprising, rioting. ANTONYM peace.

unrestrained adjective *unrestrained laughter* UNCONTROLLED, rampant, runaway, unconstrained, unrestricted, unreserved, unchecked, unbridled, unlimited, unfettered, uninhibited, full on, unbounded, unmuffered, undisciplined.

unrestricted adjective *this area is reserved for unrestricted play* UNLIMITED, open, free, freewheeling, clear, unhindered, unimpeded, unhampered, unchecked, unqualified, unrestrained, unconstrained, unblocked, unbounded, unconfined, rampant. ANTONYM limited.

unripe adjective *the peaches on the tree are unripe* IMMATURE, unready, green, sour; incipient, in development.

unrivaled adjective *an unrivaled collection of rare coins* UNEQUALED, without equal, unparalleled, without parallel, unmatched, unsurpassed, unexcelled, incomparable, beyond compare, inimitable, second to none, nonpareil.

unruffled adjective *Julius replied in an unruffled tone* CALM, composed, self-controlled, self-possessed, untroubled, unperturbed, at ease, relaxed, serene, cool, poised, placid, coolheaded, unemotional, equanimous, equable, stoical; *informal* unfazed, nonplussed, laid-back, loosey-goosey.

unruly adjective *I can't take care of your unruly brats* DISORDERLY, rowdy, wild, unmanageable, uncontrollable, disobedient, disruptive, undisciplined, restive, wayward, willful, headstrong, irrepressible, obstreperous, difficult, intractable, out of hand, recalcitrant; boisterous, lively, rambunctious, refractory; *archaic* contumacious. ANTONYM disciplined.

unsafe adjective **1** *the building was unsafe* DANGEROUS, risky, perilous, hazardous, life-threatening, high-risk, treacherous, hairy, insecure, unsound; harmful, injurious, toxic, contaminated. ANTONYMS safe, secure.

2 *an unsafe assumption* UNRELIABLE, insecure, unsound, questionable, open to question/doubt, doubtful, dubious, suspect, fallible; *informal* iffy. ANTONYM reliable.

unsaid adjective *our unsaid feelings for one another* UNSPOKEN, unuttered, unstated, unexpressed, unvoiced, suppressed; tacit, implicit, not spelled out, implied; understood, inferred.

unsanitary adjective *the unsanitary conditions in this kitchen* UNHYGIENIC, unhealthy, contaminated, germ-ridden, disease-ridden, unclean, insalubrious, squalid, dirty, filthy, polluted, unsafe; *informal* germy.

unsatisfactory adjective *the results of your test were unsatisfactory* DISAPPOINTING, dissatisfying, undesirable, disagreeable, displeasing; inadequate, unacceptable, poor, bad, substandard, weak, mediocre, no good, not good enough, lacking, wanting, subpar, defective, deficient, insufficient, imperfect, inferior; *informal* leaving a lot to be desired, no great shakes.

unsavory adjective **1** *unsavory portions of food* UNPALATABLE, unappetizing, distasteful, disagreeable, unappealing, repugnant, off-putting, unattractive; inedible, uneatable, disgusting, revolting, nauseating, sickening, foul, raunchy, nasty, vile; tasteless, bland, flavorless; *informal* yucky. ANTONYMS tasty, appetizing.

2 *an unsavory character* DISREPUTABLE, unpleasant, undesirable, disagreeable, nasty, mean, rough; immoral, degenerate, dishonorable, dishonest, unprincipled, unscrupulous, low, villainous; *informal* shady, crooked. ANTONYM reputable.

unscathed adjective *remarkably, the passengers were unscathed* UNHARMED, unhurt, uninjured, undamaged, in one piece, intact, safe (and sound), unmarked, untouched, without a scratch. ANTONYMS harmed, injured.

unscrupulous adjective *we didn't want to believe that someone in our group could be that unscrupulous* UNPRINCIPLED, unethical, immoral, conscienceless, shameless, reprobate, exploitative, corrupt, dishonest, dishonorable, deceitful, devious, underhanded, unsavory, disreputable, evil, wicked, villainous, Machiavellian; *informal* crooked, shady, hinky; *dated* dastardly.

unseat verb **1** *the horse unseated his rider* DISLODGE, throw, dismount, upset, unhorse.

2 *an attempt to unseat the party leader* DEPOSE, oust, remove from office, topple, overthrow, bring down, overturn, eject, dislodge, supplant; usurp.

unseemly adjective *their unseemly behavior at Donna's baby shower* IMPROPER, unbecoming, unfitting, unbefitting, unworthy, undignified, indiscreet, indelicate, indecorous, ungentlemanly, unladylike. ANTONYM decorous.

unseen adjective *an unseen sniper* HIDDEN, concealed, obscured, camouflaged, out of sight, invisible, imperceptible, undetectable, unnoticeable, unnoticed, unobserved; mysterious.

unselfish adjective *his unselfish motives* ALTRUISTIC, selfless, self-denying, self-sacrificing; generous, giving, magnanimous, philanthropic, public-spirited, charitable, benevolent, caring, kind, considerate, thoughtful, noble.

unsettle verb *all this talk of death was unsettling him* UNNERVE, upset, disturb, disquiet, perturb, discomfit, disconcert, alarm, dismay, trouble, bother, agitate, fluster, ruffle, shake (up), throw, unbalance, destabilize; *informal* rattle, faze, pull the rug (out) from under.

unsettled adjective **1** *an unsettled life* AIMLESS, directionless, purposeless, without purpose; rootless, nomadic.

2 *an unsettled child* RESTLESS, restive, fidgety, anxious, worried, troubled, fretful; agitated, ruffled, uneasy, disconcerted, discomposed, unnerved, ill at ease, edgy, on edge, tense, nervous, apprehensive, disturbed, perturbed, unstrung; *informal* rattled, fazed.

3 *unsettled weather* CHANGEABLE, changing, variable, varying, inconstant, inconsistent, ever-changing, erratic, unstable, undependable, unreliable, uncertain, unpredictable, protean.

4 *the question is still unsettled* UNDECIDED, to be decided, unresolved, undetermined, moot, uncertain, open to debate, doubtful, in doubt, up in the air, in a state of uncertainty.

5 *the debt remains unsettled* UNPAID, payable, outstanding, owing, owed, to be paid, due, undischarged, delinquent, past due.

6 *unsettled areas* UNINHABITED, unpopulated, unpeopled, unoccupied, desolate, lonely.

unshakable adjective *she finally came to trust Hal's unshakable love* STEADFAST, resolute, staunch, firm, decided, determined, unswerving, unwavering; unyielding, inflexible, dogged, obstinate, obdurate, tenacious, persistent, indefatigable, tireless, unflagging, unremitting, unrelenting, relentless.

unsightly adjective *unsightly stains on the wall* UGLY, unattractive, unprepossessing, unlovely, disagreeable, displeasing, hideous, horrible, repulsive, revolting, offensive, grotesque, monstrous, gross, ghastly. ANTONYM attractive.

unskilled adjective *the unskilled workforce* UNTRAINED, unqualified; manual, blue-collar, laboring, menial; inexpert, inexperienced, unpracticed, amateurish, unprofessional.

unskillful adjective *these are the repairs of an unskillful hand* INEXPERT, incompetent, inept, unskilled, amateurish, hack, unprofessional, inexperienced, untrained, unpracticed; uncoordinated; *informal* ham-fisted, ham-handed.

unsociable adjective *we found him to be stiff and unsociable* UNFRIENDLY, uncongenial, unneighborly, unapproachable, introverted, reticent, reserved, withdrawn, aloof, distant, remote, detached, unsocial, antisocial, asocial, taciturn, silent, quiet; *informal* standoffish. ANTONYM friendly.

EASILY CONFUSED WORDS **unsociable, unsocial, antisocial**

There is some overlap in the use of the adjectives **unsociable, unsocial**, and **antisocial**, but they also have distinct core meanings. Generally speaking, **unsociable** means 'not enjoying, or avoiding, the company of others':

Terry was grumpy and unsociable. **Antisocial** can be used as a synonym for **unsociable**, but can further be used to mean 'contrary to the laws and customs of a society': *aggressive and antisocial behavior.* **Unsocial** can be used as a synonym for *unsociable* as well, but it may also denote a preference for solitude and not hostility toward company: *Ben's feeling a little tired and unsocial tonight.*

---

unsolicited adjective *their unsolicited opinions* UNINVITED, unsought, unasked-for, unrequested.

unsophisticated adjective **1** *she seemed a bit unsophisticated* UNWORLDLY, naive, unrefined, simple, innocent, ignorant, green, immature, callow, inexperienced, childlike, artless, guileless, ingenuous, natural, unaffected, unassuming, unpretentious; *informal* cheesy. See note at GULLIBLE.

2 *unsophisticated software* SIMPLE, crude, low-tech, basic, rudimentary, primitive, rough and ready, homespun, bush-league; straightforward, uncomplicated, uninvolved.

unsound adjective **1** *structurally unsound* WEAK, rickety, flimsy, wobbly, unstable, crumbling, damaged, rotten, ramshackle, shoddy, insubstantial, unsafe, dangerous. ANTONYM strong.

2 *this plan appears unsound* UNTENABLE, flawed, defective, faulty, ill-founded, flimsy, unreliable, questionable, dubious, tenuous, suspect, fallacious, fallible; *informal* iffy.

3 *of unsound mind* DISORDERED, deranged, disturbed, demented, unstable, unbalanced, unhinged, addled, insane. ANTONYM sane.

unsparing adjective **1** *he is unsparing in his criticism* MERCILESS, pitiless, ruthless, relentless, remorseless, unmerciful, unforgiving, implacable, uncompromising; stern, strict, severe, harsh, tough, rigorous.

2 *unsparing approval* UNGRUDGING, unstinting, willingly given, free, ready; lavish, liberal, generous, magnanimous, openhanded.

unspeakable adjective **1** *unspeakable delights* INDESCRIBABLE, beyond description, inexpressible, unutterable, indefinable, unimaginable, inconceivable.

2 *an unspeakable crime* HORRIFIC, awful, appalling, dreadful, horrifying, horrendous, abominable, frightful, fearful, shocking, ghastly, gruesome, monstrous, heinous, egregious, deplorable, despicable, execrable, vile.

unspecified adjective *she has agreed to write the book for an unspecified amount of money* UNNAMED, unstated, unidentified, undesignated, undefined, unfixed, undecided, undetermined, uncertain; nameless, unknown, indefinite, indeterminate, vague, t.b.a.

unspectacular adjective *an unspectacular parade* UNREMARKABLE, unexceptional, undistinguished, unmemorable; ordinary, average, commonplace, mediocre, run-of-the-mill, indifferent. ANTONYM remarkable.

unspoiled adjective *the unspoiled landscape* IMMACULATE, perfect, pristine, virgin, unimpaired, unblemished, unharmed, unflawed, undamaged, untouched, unmarked, untainted, as good as new/before.

unspoken adjective *they had an unspoken understanding* UNSTATED, unexpressed, unuttered, unsaid, unvoiced, unarticulated, undeclared, not spelt out; tacit, implicit, implied, understood, unwritten. ANTONYM explicit.

unsportsmanlike adjective *Dickerson and Ponti were suspended for unsportsmanlike behavior in the clubhouse* DISHONORABLE, unfair, underhanded, below the belt, improper, unseemly, foul, mean.

unstable adjective **1** *that old ladder looks unstable* UNSTEADY, rocky, wobbly, tippy; rickety, shaky, unsafe, insecure, precarious. ANTONYM steady.

2 *unstable coffee prices* CHANGEABLE, volatile, variable, fluctuating, irregular, unpredictable, capricious, erratic, 'on-again, off-again'. ANTONYMS fixed, firm.

3 *he was mentally unstable* UNBALANCED, of unsound mind, mentally ill, deranged, demented, disturbed, unhinged, volatile; *informal* kooky. ANTONYMS balanced, of sound mind.

unsteady adjective **1** *she was unsteady on her feet* UNSTABLE, rocky, wobbly, rickety, shaky, tottery, doddery, insecure. ANTONYM stable.

2 *an unsteady flow* IRREGULAR, uneven, varying, variable, erratic, spasmodic, changeable, changing, fluctuating, inconstant, intermittent, fitful, stop-and-go; *informal* herky-jerky. ANTONYM regular.

unstinting adjective *her unstinting charity work* UNGRUDGING, unsparing, free, ready, benevolent, big-hearted, kind-hearted, kind, unselfish; lavish, liberal, generous, magnanimous, openhanded, freely given, munificent, beneficent, bountiful; profuse, abundant, ample, gushing; *literary* plenteous, bounteous.

unstoppable adjective *an unstoppable sales force* INDOMITABLE, unbeatable, invincible, supreme; *informal* on fire; irrepressible, inextinguishable, inexorable, uncontrollable.

unstudied adjective *his unstudied grace* NATURAL, easy, spontaneous, unaffected, unforced, uncontrived, unstilted, unpretentious, ingenuous, without airs, artless.

unsubstantiated adjective *unsubstantiated rumors* UNCONFIRMED, unsupported, uncorroborated, unverified, unattested, unproven; unfounded, groundless, baseless, without foundation, unjustified.

unsuccessful adjective **1** *an unsuccessful attempt* FAILED, ineffective, fruitless, profitless, unproductive, abortive; vain, futile, useless, pointless, worthless, luckless.

2 *an unsuccessful business* UNPROFITABLE, loss-making.

3 *an unsuccessful candidate* FAILED, losing, beaten; unlucky, out of luck; *informal* losingest.

unsuitable adjective **1** *the product is unsuitable for your needs* INAPPROPRIATE, unsuited, wrong, ill-suited, inapt, inapplicable, unacceptable, unfitting, unbefitting, incompatible, out of place, out of keeping, misplaced; *formal* inapposite. ANTONYM appropriate.

2 *an unsuitable moment for belching* INOPPORTUNE, infelicitous, inappropriate, wrong, unfortunate; *formal* malapropos. ANTONYM opportune.

unsullied adjective *his unsullied reputation* SPOTLESS, untarnished, unblemished, unspoiled, untainted, impeccable, undamaged, unimpaired, stainless, immaculate, flawless, unflawed. ANTONYM tarnished.

unsung adjective *no victory is without its unsung heroes* UNACKNOWLEDGED, uncelebrated, unacclaimed, unapplauded, unhailed, unheralded; neglected, unrecognized, overlooked, forgotten. ANTONYM celebrated.

unsure adjective **1** *she felt very unsure* UNCONFIDENT, unassertive, insecure, hesitant, diffident, anxious, apprehensive. ANTONYM confident.

2 *Sally was unsure what to do* UNDECIDED, irresolute, dithering, equivocating, vacillating, of two minds, wishy-washy, in a quandary. ANTONYM decided.

3 *some teachers are unsure about the proposed strike* DUBIOUS, doubtful, skeptical, uncertain, unconvinced. ANTONYM convinced.

4 *the date is unsure* NOT FIXED, undecided, uncertain. ANTONYM fixed.

unsurpassed adjective Lubell is unsurpassed in season wins UNMATCHED, unrivaled, unparalleled, unequaled, matchless, peerless, without equal, nonpareil, inimitable, incomparable, unsurpassable; *formal* unexampled.

unsurprising adjective *in an unsurprising move, Hyde's attorney filed for a continuance* PREDICTABLE, foreseeable, to be expected, foreseen, anticipated, routine, par for the course; *informal* inevitable, in the cards.

unsuspecting adjective *it's a trap deliberately set for unsuspecting first-time buyers* UNSUSPICIOUS, unwary, unaware, unconscious, ignorant, unwitting; trusting, gullible, credulous, ingenuous, naive, wide-eyed. ANTONYM wary.

unswerving adjective *your unswerving belief in me has made all the difference* UNWAVERING, unfaltering, steadfast, unshakable, staunch, firm, resolute, stalwart, dedicated, committed, constant, single-minded, dogged, indefatigable, unyielding, unbending, indomitable.

unsympathetic adjective 1 *unsympathetic staff* UNCARING, unconcerned, unfriendly, unfeeling, apathetic, insensitive, indifferent, unkind, pitiless, thoughtless, heartless, hard-hearted, stony, callous. ANTONYM caring.

2 *the government was* ***unsympathetic to*** *these views* OPPOSED TO, against, (dead) set against, antagonistic to, ill-disposed to; *informal* anti.

3 *an unsympathetic character* UNLIKABLE, dislikable, disagreeable, unpleasant, unappealing, off-putting, objectionable, unsavory; unfriendly. ANTONYM likable.

unsystematic adjective *how this unsystematic approach works for him is beyond me* UNMETHODICAL, uncoordinated, disorganized, unplanned, indiscriminate; random, inconsistent, irregular, erratic, casual, haphazard, chaotic.

untamed adjective *untamed horses* WILD, feral, undomesticated, unbroken.

untangle verb 1 *I untangled the fishing tackle* DISENTANGLE, unravel, unsnarl, straighten out, untwist, untwine, unknot.

2 *untangling a mystery* SOLVE, find the/an answer to, resolve, puzzle out, work out, fathom, clear up, clarify, get to the bottom of; *informal* figure out.

untarnished adjective *the untarnished truth* UNSULLIED, unblemished, untainted, impeccable, undamaged, unspoiled, unimpaired, spotless, stainless, pristine, perfect; *informal* squeaky clean.

untenable adjective *these untenable explanations are not helping your case* INDEFENSIBLE, insupportable, unsustainable, unjustified, unjustifiable, flimsy, weak, shaky.

untested adjective See UNTRIED.

unthinkable adjective *winning the lottery is just too unthinkable* UNIMAGINABLE, inconceivable, unbelievable, incredible, beyond belief, implausible, preposterous.

unthinking adjective 1 *an unthinking lout* THOUGHTLESS, inconsiderate, insensitive; tactless, undiplomatic, indiscreet. ANTONYM thoughtful.

2 *an unthinking remark* ABSENTMINDED, heedless, thoughtless, careless, injudicious, imprudent, unwise, foolish, reckless, rash, precipitate; involuntary, inadvertent, unintentional, spontaneous, impulsive, unpremeditated. ANTONYM intentional.

untidy adjective 1 *untidy hair* SCRUFFY, tousled, disheveled, unkempt, messy, disordered, disarranged, messed up, rumpled, bedraggled, uncombed, ungroomed, straggly, ruffled, tangled, matted, wind-blown, raddled; *informal* mussed up, raggedy. ANTONYM neat.

2 *the room was untidy* DISORDERED, messy, in a mess, disorderly, disorganized, in disorder, cluttered, in a muddle, muddled, in chaos, chaotic, haywire, topsy-turvy, in disarray, at sixes and sevens; *informal* higgledy-piggledy. ANTONYMS neat, orderly.

untie verb *untie the team of horses* UNDO, unknot, unbind, unfasten, unlace, untether, unhitch, unmoor; (turn) loose, (set) free, release, let go, unshackle.

until preposition & conjunction 1 *I work until Thursday* (UP) TILL, to, up to, through (to), up until, as late as. See note at TILL[3].

2 *this did not happen until 1998* BEFORE, prior to, previous to, up to, up until, (up) till, earlier than. See note at TILL[3].

untimely adjective 1 *an untimely interruption* ILL-TIMED, badly timed, mistimed; inopportune, inappropriate, unseasonable; inconvenient, unwelcome, infelicitous; *formal* malapropos. ANTONYM opportune.

2 *his untimely death* PREMATURE, (too) early, too soon, before time, unexpected. ANTONYM expected.

untiring adjective *these kids have been untiring in their efforts to get to the championship* VIGOROUS, energetic, determined, resolute, enthusiastic, keen, zealous, spirited, dogged, tenacious, persistent, persevering, staunch; tireless, unflagging, unfailing, unfaltering, unwavering, indefatigable, unrelenting, unswerving; *formal* pertinacious.

untold adjective 1 *untold quantities* BOUNDLESS, immeasurable, incalculable, limitless, unlimited, infinite, measureless; countless, innumerable, endless, numberless, uncountable; numerous, many, multiple; *literary* multitudinous, myriad. ANTONYM limited.

2 *the untold story* UNREPORTED, overlooked, ignored; hidden, secret, unrecounted, unrevealed, undisclosed, undivulged, unpublished.

untouched adjective 1 *the food was untouched* UNEATEN, unconsumed, undrunk, untasted; ignored.

2 *one of the few untouched areas* UNSPOILED, unmarked, unblemished, unsullied, undefiled, undamaged, unharmed; pristine, natural, immaculate, virgin, in perfect condition, unaffected, unchanged, unaltered.

untoward adjective 1 *an untoward occurrence* INCONVENIENT, unlucky, unexpected, unforeseen, surprising, unusual; unwelcome, unfavorable, adverse, unfortunate, infelicitous; *formal* malapropos.

2 *untoward behavior* IMPROPER, unseemly; perverse.

untrained adjective *there are many available positions for untrained workers* UNSKILLED, untaught, unschooled, untutored, unpracticed, uninitiated, inexperienced, ill-equipped, ill-prepared; unqualified, unlicensed, amateur, nonprofessional.

untried adjective *these are largely untried methods* UNTESTED, unestablished, new, experimental, unattempted, trial, test, pilot, unproven. ANTONYM established.

untroubled adjective *they all thought I was untroubled, but I was really falling to pieces* UNWORRIED, unperturbed, unconcerned, unruffled, undismayed, unbothered, unalarmed, unflustered; insouciant, nonchalant, composed, blasé, carefree, calm, serene, tranquil, relaxed, halcyon, comfortable, at ease, happy-go-lucky, blissful, laid-back, mellow; *informal* supercool.

untrue adjective **1** *these suggestions are totally untrue* FALSE, untruthful, fabricated, made up, invented, concocted, trumped up; erroneous, wrong, incorrect, inaccurate; fallacious, fictitious, unsound, unfounded, baseless, misguided. ANTONYM correct.

2 *he was untrue to his friends* UNFAITHFUL, disloyal, faithless, false, treacherous, traitorous, deceitful, deceiving, duplicitous, double-dealing, insincere, unreliable, undependable, inconstant; *informal* two-timing; *literary* perfidious. ANTONYM faithful.

untrustworthy adjective *the group's untrustworthy treasurer* DISHONEST, deceitful, double-dealing, treacherous, traitorous, two-faced, duplicitous, mendacious, dishonorable, unprincipled, unscrupulous, corrupt, slippery; unreliable, undependable, fly-by-night, capricious, fickle; *informal* hinky. ANTONYM reliable.

untruth noun **1** *a patent untruth* LIE, falsehood, fib, fabrication, invention, falsification, half-truth, exaggeration; story, myth, piece of fiction; *informal* tall story, fairy tale, cock-and-bull story, whopper.

2 *the total untruth of the story* FALSITY, falsehood, falseness, untruthfulness, fictitiousness; fabrication, dishonesty, deceit, deceitfulness, inaccuracy, unreliability.

untruthful adjective **1** *the answers may be untruthful* FALSE, untrue, fabricated, made up, invented, trumped up; erroneous, wrong, incorrect, inaccurate, fallacious, fictitious.

2 *an untruthful person* LYING, mendacious, dishonest, deceitful, duplicitous, false, double-dealing, two-faced, untrustworthy, dishonorable; *informal* crooked; *literary* perfidious. ANTONYM honest.

untutored adjective *it will make little sense to the untutored reader* UNEDUCATED, untaught, unschooled, ignorant, unsophisticated, uncultured, unenlightened, unlettered, uninitiated. See note at IGNORANT. ANTONYM educated.

untwist verb *untwist the raffia to make grand bows for your packages* UNDO, untwine, disentangle, unravel, unsnarl, unwind, unroll, uncoil, unfurl, open (out), straighten (out).

unused adjective **1** *unused supplies* UNUTILIZED, unemployed, unexploited, spare, surplus; left over, extra, untouched, remaining, uneaten, unopened, unconsumed, unneeded, not required, not in service.

2 *he was **unused to** such directness* UNACCUSTOMED TO, new to, unfamiliar with, unconversant with, unacquainted with; a stranger to. ANTONYM accustomed.

unusual adjective *an unusual color for a marigold* UNCOMMON, abnormal, atypical, unexpected, surprising, unfamiliar, different; strange, odd, curious, out of the ordinary, extraordinary, unorthodox, unconventional, outlandish, singular, special, unique, peculiar, bizarre; rare, scarce, few and far between, thin on the ground, exceptional, isolated, occasional, infrequent; *informal* weird, offbeat, out there, freaky. ANTONYM common.

unutterable adjective See UNSPEAKABLE.

unvarnished adjective **1** *unvarnished wood* BARE, plain, unpainted, unpolished, unfinished, untreated.

2 *the unvarnished truth* STRAIGHTFORWARD, plain, simple, stark, blunt, straight-up, raw, undiluted; truthful, realistic, candid, honest, frank, forthright, direct.

unveil verb *this afternoon they are unveiling the details of yesterday's invasion* REVEAL, present, display, show, exhibit, put on display; release, launch, bring out; disclose, divulge, make known, make public, publish, broadcast, communicate.

unwanted adjective **1** *an unwanted development* UNWELCOME, undesirable, undesired, unpopular; unpleasant, disagreeable, displeasing, distasteful, objectionable; regrettable, deplorable, lamentable; unacceptable, intolerable, awful. ANTONYM welcome.

2 *an unwanted guest* UNINVITED, unbidden, unasked, unrequested, unsolicited. ANTONYM invited.

3 *many people feel unwanted* FRIENDLESS, unloved, uncared-for, forsaken, rejected, shunned, ostracized; superfluous, useless, unnecessary, unneeded. ANTONYM loved.

4 *unwanted food* UNUSED, left over, surplus, excess, uneaten, unconsumed, untouched.

unwarranted adjective **1** *the criticism is unwarranted* UNJUSTIFIED, uncalled for, unnecessary, unreasonable, unjust, groundless, excessive, gratuitous, immoderate, disproportionate, undue, unconscionable, unjustifiable, indefensible, inexcusable, unforgivable, unpardonable. ANTONYM justified.

2 *an unwarranted invasion of privacy* UNAUTHORIZED, unsanctioned, unapproved, uncertified, unlicensed; illegal, unlawful, illicit, illegitimate. ANTONYM legal.

unwary adjective *an unwary tourist is the pickpocket's blessing* INCAUTIOUS, careless, thoughtless, heedless, inattentive, unwatchful, off one's guard.

unwavering adjective *their unwavering devotion to each other* STEADY, fixed, resolute, resolved, firm, constant, steadfast, enduring, abiding, unswerving, unfaltering, untiring, tireless, indefatigable, unyielding, relentless, unremitting, unrelenting, sustained. ANTONYM unsteady.

unwelcome adjective **1** *I was made to feel unwelcome* UNWANTED, uninvited, unaccepted, excluded, rejected.

2 *even a small increase is unwelcome* UNDESIRABLE, undesired, unpopular, unfortunate, disappointing, upsetting, distressing, disagreeable, displeasing; regrettable, deplorable, objectionable, lamentable.

unwell adjective *I felt unwell as soon as we hit the open sea* ILL, sick, indisposed, ailing, not (very) well, not too good, lousy, bad, rough, not oneself, under/below par, groggy, peaked, queasy, woozy, nauseous, nauseated; off, poorly, wretched, dead; under the weather; funny, weird; *informal* crappy, pukey.

unwholesome adjective **1** *unwholesome air* UNHEALTHY, noxious, poisonous; insalubrious, unhygienic, unsanitary; harmful, injurious, detrimental, destructive, damaging, deleterious, baleful. ANTONYM healthy.

2 *unwholesome Web sites* IMPROPER, immoral, indecent, depraved, corrupting, salacious. ANTONYM seemly.

unwieldy adjective *an unwieldy trunk full of old clothes* CUMBERSOME, unmanageable, unmaneuverable; awkward, clumsy, massive, heavy, hefty, ponderous, bulky, weighty. ANTONYM manageable.

unwilling adjective 1 *unwilling conscripts* RELUCTANT, unenthusiastic, hesitant, resistant, grudging, involuntary, forced. ANTONYM keen.

2 *he was unwilling to take on that responsibility* DISINCLINED, reluctant, averse, loath; (**be unwilling to do something**) not have the heart to, balk at, refuse to, demur at, shy away from, flinch from, shrink from, have qualms about, have misgivings about, have reservations about. ANTONYM keen.

unwillingness adjective *their unwillingness to subsidize a school lunch program* DISINCLINATION, reluctance, hesitation, diffidence, wavering, vacillation, resistance, foot-dragging, objection, opposition, doubts, second thoughts, scruples, qualms, misgivings.

unwind verb 1 *Ella unwound the scarf from her neck* UNROLL, uncoil, unravel, untwine, untwist, disentangle, open (out), straighten (out).

2 *he liked to unwind after work* RELAX, loosen up, ease up/off, slow down, de-stress, unbend, rest, put one's feet up, sit back, take it easy, take a load off; *informal* wind down, mellow (out), let it all hang out, veg, hang loose, chill (out).

unwise adjective *it would have been unwise to argue* INJUDICIOUS, ill-advised, ill-judged, imprudent, inexpedient, foolish, silly, inadvisable, impolitic, misguided, foolhardy, irresponsible, impetuous, rash, hasty, overhasty, reckless. ANTONYM sensible.

unwitting adjective 1 *an unwitting accomplice* UNKNOWING, unconscious, unsuspecting, oblivious, unaware, innocent, in the dark. ANTONYM knowing.

2 *an unwitting mistake* UNINTENTIONAL, unintended, inadvertent, involuntary, unconscious, accidental. ANTONYM conscious.

unworkable adjective *the new production schedule is unworkable* IMPRACTICABLE, unfeasible, nonviable, unrealizable, impossible.

unworldly adjective 1 *a gauche, unworldly girl* NAIVE, simple, inexperienced, innocent, green, raw, callow, immature, ignorant, gullible, ingenuous, artless, guileless, childlike, trusting, credulous; nonmaterialistic.

2 *unworldly beauty* UNEARTHLY, otherworldly, ethereal, ghostly, preternatural, supernatural, paranormal, mystical.

unworthy adjective 1 *he was unworthy of trust* UNDESERVING, ineligible, unqualified, unfit. ANTONYM deserving.

2 *unworthy behavior* UNBECOMING, unsuitable, inappropriate, unbefitting, unfitting, unseemly, improper; discreditable, shameful, dishonorable, despicable, ignoble, contemptible, reprehensible. ANTONYM becoming.

unwritten adjective *I thought we had an unwritten understanding* TACIT, implicit, unvoiced, taken for granted, accepted, recognized, understood; traditional, customary, conventional; oral, verbal, spoken, vocal, word-of-mouth.

unyielding adjective 1 *an unyielding oak door* STIFF, inflexible, unbending, rigid, firm, hard, solid, tough, tight, compact, compressed, dense.

2 *an unyielding taskmaster* RESOLUTE, inflexible, uncompromising, unbending, unshakable, unwavering, immovable, intractable, intransigent, rigid, stiff, firm, determined, dogged, iron, obstinate, stubborn, adamant, obdurate, tenacious, insistent, relentless, implacable, single-minded; *formal* pertinacious.

up adverb See UPWARD.

▸ adjective 1 *she was up early today* AWAKE, wide awake, out of bed, about, conscious, alert, functioning.

2 *he was up for some fun* READY, eager, willing, open, prepared.

3 *I'm not up on the latest news* INFORMED, up-to-date, versed, cognizant, familiar, briefed, in touch, plugged in, savvy.

USAGE NOTE **up to off and more**

This bit of illogic crops up fairly often in print ads and store signs. At a sale touted as offering "up to 50% off and more," for example, all we know is that the sale price is (1) less than 50% off, (2) 50% off, or (3) more than 50% off. The number itself, then, is meaningless and serves only as bait in big, bold type. The small type, as usual, taketh away. Versions of the phrase appear in places other than signs announcing sales—e.g.:

• "Some lakes and forests devastated by acid rain will likely take up to 70 years or more to recover." (*Post-Standard* [Syracuse]; Mar. 26, 2001.) (A possible revision: "Some lakes and forests devastated by acid rain could take 70 years or more to recover.")

• "Use live bait or cut bait for yellow perch up to 1½ pounds or more." (*Richmond Times-Dispatch*; Mar. 30, 2001.) —**BG**

---

up-and-coming adjective *up-and-coming young players* PROMISING, budding, emerging, rising, with potential, to watch, upwardly-mobile; talented, gifted, able.

upbeat adjective *it's nice to read an upbeat story for a change* OPTIMISTIC, cheerful, cheery, positive, confident, hopeful, sanguine, bullish, buoyant, gung-ho. ANTONYMS pessimistic, negative.

upbraid verb *we were upbraided for leaving the back door unlocked* REPRIMAND, rebuke, admonish, chastise, chide, reprove, reproach, scold, berate, take to task, lambaste, give someone a piece of one's mind, give someone a tongue-lashing, rake/haul over the coals, lecture; *informal* tell off, give someone a talking-to, tear a strip off (of), dress down, give someone an earful, rap over the knuckles, bawl out, lay into, chew out, ream out; *formal* castigate; *rare* reprehend. See note at SCOLD.

upbringing noun *tell us a little about your upbringing* CHILDHOOD, early life, formative years, teaching, education, instruction, tutelage, care, rearing, raising, breeding.

upcoming adjective *Jonah's story will be in our upcoming newsletter* FORTHCOMING, coming, impending, future, imminent, approaching, looming, ahead, in the pipeline, in the offing, on the horizon, coming down the pike.

update verb 1 *security measures are continually updated* MODERNIZE, upgrade, bring up to date, improve, overhaul.

2 *I'll update him on today's developments* BRIEF, bring up to date, inform, fill in, tell, notify, apprise, keep posted; *informal* clue in, put in the picture, bring/keep up to speed.

upend verb *the table was upended in the struggle* OVERTURN, invert, turn over, turn upside down; capsize, flip, tip, keel over, turn turtle; trip, take the legs out from under.

upfront adjective *you should have been upfront with me from the beginning* FRANK, open, honest, candid, forthright, plain-spoken, direct, unequivocal.

upgrade verb 1 *there are plans to upgrade the rail system* IMPROVE, modernize, update, bring up to date, make better, ameliorate, reform; rehabilitate, recondition, refurbish, spruce up, renovate, rejuvenate, overhaul; bring up to code. ANTONYM downgrade.

2 *he was upgraded to a seat in the cabinet* PROMOTE, give promotion to, elevate, move up, raise. ANTONYM demote.

upheaval noun *the upheaval caused by wartime evacuation* DISRUPTION, disturbance, trouble, turbulence, disorder, confusion, turmoil, pandemonium, chaos, mayhem, cataclysm, shakeup, debacle; revolution, change, craziness.

uphill adjective 1 *an uphill path* UPWARD, rising, ascending, climbing. ANTONYM downhill.

2 *an uphill struggle* ARDUOUS, difficult, hard, tough, taxing, demanding, exacting, stiff, formidable, exhausting, tiring, wearisome, laborious, grueling, back-breaking, punishing, burdensome, onerous, Herculean; *informal* no picnic, killing; *archaic* toilsome. ANTONYM easy.

uphold verb 1 *the court upheld his claim for damages* CONFIRM, endorse, sustain, approve, agree to, support; champion, defend. ANTONYMS overturn, oppose.

2 *they've a tradition to uphold* MAINTAIN, sustain, continue, preserve, protect, champion, defend, keep, hold to, keep alive, keep going, back (up), stand by. ANTONYM abandon.

upkeep noun *the upkeep of the kennel can be quite expensive* MAINTENANCE, repair(s), service, servicing, preservation, conservation; running; care, support, keep, subsistence.

uplift verb *she needs something to uplift her spirits* BOOST, raise, buoy up, lift, cheer up, perk up, enliven, brighten up, lighten, stimulate, inspire, revive, restore; *informal* buck up.

uplifted adjective *his uplifted hand signaled us to stop* RAISED, upraised, elevated, upthrust; held high, erect, proud.

uplifting adjective *an uplifting story about surviving cancer* INSPIRING, stirring, inspirational, rousing, moving, touching, affecting, cheering, heartening, heartwarming, encouraging; *formal* numinous.

upload verb *upload the revised data* TRANSFER, send, transmit.

upper adjective 1 *the upper floor* HIGHER, superior; top; *informal* nosebleed. ANTONYM lower.

2 *the upper echelons of the party* SENIOR, superior, higher-level, higher-ranking, top, loftier. ANTONYMS junior, inferior.

PHRASE: **the upper hand** *it remains to be seen which party will have the upper hand in this election* AN ADVANTAGE, the edge, the whip hand, a lead, a head start, ascendancy, superiority, supremacy, sway, control, power, mastery, dominance, command, leverage.

upper-class adjective *our upper-class relations look down on us* ARISTOCRATIC, noble, of noble birth, patrician, titled, blue-blooded, high-born, well-born, elite, born with a silver spoon in one's mouth; rich, wealthy; upscale, upmarket, upper-crust, high-class, tony, top-drawer, classy, posh, uptown; landowning, landed; *archaic* gentle, of gentle birth.

uppermost adjective 1 *the uppermost branches* HIGHEST, top, topmost.

2 *their own problems remained uppermost in their minds* PREDOMINANT, of greatest importance, to the fore, foremost, first, primary, dominant, principal, chief, main, paramount, supreme, preponderant, major.

uppity adjective *getting that modeling job has made Quinn too uppity to bear* ARROGANT, snobbish, hoity-toity, snooty, pretentious, bumptious, full of oneself, puffed up, conceited, pompous, self-assertive, overbearing, cocky, cocksure, impertinent, haughty, self-important, superior, presumptuous, overweening, uppish, high and mighty; too big for one's britches/boots.

upright adjective 1 *an upright position* VERTICAL, perpendicular, plumb, straight (up), straight up and down, standing, bolt upright, erect, on end; on one's feet. ANTONYM horizontal.

2 *an upright member of the community* HONEST, honorable, upstanding, respectable, high-minded, law-abiding, right-minded, worthy, moral, ethical, righteous, decent, scrupulous, conscientious, good, virtuous, principled, of principle, noble, incorruptible. ANTONYM dishonorable.

uprising noun *the uprising was put down by government forces* REBELLION, revolt, insurrection, mutiny, revolution, insurgence, intifada, rioting, riot; civil disobedience, unrest, anarchy, coup, coup d'état, putsch.

THE RIGHT WORD

There are a number of ways to defy the established order or overthrow a government. You can stage an **uprising**, which is a broad term referring to a small and usually unsuccessful act of popular resistance (*uprisings among angry workers all over the country*). An uprising is often the first sign of a general or widespread **rebellion**, which is an act of armed resistance against a government or authority; this term is usually applied after the fact to describe an act of resistance that has failed (*a rebellion against the landowners*). If it is successful, however, a rebellion may become a **revolution**, which often implies a war or an outbreak of violence (*the American Revolution*). Although a *revolution* usually involves the overthrow of a government or political system by the people, it can also be used to describe any drastic change in ideas, economic institutions, or moral values (*the sexual revolution*). An **insurrection** is an organized effort to seize power, especially political power, while an **insurgency** is usually aided by foreign powers. If you're on a ship, you can stage a **mutiny**, which is an insurrection against military or naval authority. But if you're relying on speed and surprise to catch the authorities off guard, you'll want to stage a **putsch**, which is a small, popular uprising or planned attempt to seize power.

uproar noun 1 *the uproar in the kitchen continued for some time* TURMOIL, disorder, confusion, chaos, commotion, disturbance, rumpus, ruckus, tumult, turbulence, mayhem, pandemonium, bedlam, noise, din, clamor, hubbub, racket; shouting, yelling, babel; *informal* hullabaloo, hoo-ha, brouhaha. ANTONYM calm.

2 *there was an uproar when she was dismissed* OUTCRY, furor, protest; fuss, reaction, backlash, commotion, hue and cry; *informal* hullabaloo, stink, rhubarb, firestorm. ANTONYM acquiescence.

uproarious adjective **1** *an uproarious party* RIOTOUS, rowdy, noisy, loud, wild, unrestrained, unruly, rip-roaring, rollicking, boisterous, rambunctious, knockabout. ANTONYM quiet.

2 *an uproarious joke* HILARIOUS, hysterical, rib-tickling, gut-busting, priceless, side-splitting, knee-slapping, thigh-slapping. ANTONYM solemn.

uproot verb **1** *don't uproot the flowers* PULL UP, root out, rip out; *literary* deracinate. ANTONYM plant.

2 *hundreds of families were uprooted* DISPLACE, expel, drive out, evict, deport. ANTONYM establish.

upscale adjective *we can't afford this upscale furniture* DELUXE, posh, ritzy, upper-class, classy, chi-chi; high-end, expensive, high-priced.

upset verb **1** *the accusation upset her* DISTRESS, trouble, perturb, dismay, disturb, discompose, unsettle, disconcert, disquiet, worry, bother, agitate, fluster, throw, ruffle, unnerve, shake; hurt, sadden, grieve.

2 *he upset a tureen of soup* KNOCK OVER, overturn, upend, tip over, flip, topple (over); spill.

3 *the dam will upset the ecological balance* DISRUPT, interfere with, disturb, throw out, throw into confusion, throw off balance, mess with/up.

4 *the Indians upset the Angels 9-0* DEFEAT, beat, topple; surprise, embarrass.

▸ noun **1** *a stomach upset* COMPLAINT, disorder, ailment, illness, sickness, malady; *informal* bug.

2 *the Oilers' victory was a remarkable upset* SURPRISE WIN, shocker.

▸ adjective **1** *the loss made Jane upset* DISTRESSED, troubled, perturbed, dismayed, disturbed, unsettled, disconcerted, worried, bothered, anxious, agitated, flustered, ruffled, unnerved, shaken, unstrung; hurt, saddened, grieved; *informal* cut up, choked. ANTONYMS unperturbed, calm.

2 *an upset stomach* DISTURBED, unsettled, queasy, bad, hurting, poorly.

upshot noun *the upshot of this conflict of interests was a compromise* RESULT, end result, consequence, outcome, conclusion; effect, repercussion, reverberations, ramification, aftereffect, payoff. ANTONYM cause.

upside down adjective *an upside-down canoe* UPTURNED, upended, inverted, wrong side up, overturned; capsized, flipped. PHRASE: **turned upside down** *the apartment was turned upside down* IN DISARRAY, in disorder, jumbled up, in a mess, in a muddle, untidy, disorganized, chaotic, all over the place, in chaos, in confusion, topsy-turvy, at sixes and sevens; *informal* higgledy-piggledy.

upstage verb *she is now upstaging the very person who brought her into the company* OUTSHINE, outclass, eclipse, overshadow, trump, put someone in the shade, put to shame.

upstanding adjective *an upstanding citizen* HONEST, honorable, upright, respectable, high-minded, law-abiding, right-minded, worthy, trustworthy, moral, ethical, righteous, decent, good, virtuous, principled, of principle, noble, incorruptible, straightforward. ANTONYM dishonorable.

upstart noun *these upstarts, they don't know their place* PARVENU, arriviste, nouveau riche, status seeker, social climber, a jumped-up ——, johnny-come-lately.

upswing noun See SURGE sense 2.

uptight adjective *the wait wouldn't have been so bad if that uptight Felix hadn't been with us* TENSE, nervous, anxious, on edge, high-strung, hypersensitive, defensive, worked up, impatient, angry; strait-laced, rigid, prim, priggish, anal-retentive, anal.

up to date adjective **1** *up-to-date equipment* MODERN, contemporary, the latest, state-of-the-art, cutting-edge, leading-edge, new, present-day, up-to-the-minute; advanced; mod. ANTONYMS out of date, old-fashioned.

2 *the newsletter will keep you up to date* INFORMED, up to speed, in the picture, in touch, au fait, au courant, conversant, familiar, knowledgeable, acquainted, aware, clued in.

upturn noun *we've enjoyed an upturn in sales this quarter* IMPROVEMENT, upswing, turn for the better; recovery, revival, rally, resurgence, increase, rise, hike, jump, leap, upsurge, boost, escalation. ANTONYMS fall, slump.

upward adjective *an upward trend* RISING, on the rise, ascending, climbing, mounting; uphill. ANTONYM downward.

▸ adverb (also **upwards**) *the smoke drifts upward | he inched his way upwards* UP, upward, higher, uphill, upslope; to the top, skyward, heavenward. ANTONYM downward.

PHRASE: **upward(s) of** *he makes upwards of $500 per session* MORE THAN, above, over, in excess of, exceeding, beyond, greater than.

urban adjective *crimes rates are significantly higher in urban areas* TOWN, city, municipal, civic, metropolitan, built-up, inner-city, downtown, suburban; urbanized, citified, townie. ANTONYM rural.

urbane adjective *the urbane English professor* SUAVE, sophisticated, debonair, worldly, cultivated, cultured, civilized, cosmopolitan; smooth, polished, refined, self-possessed; courteous, polite, well-mannered, mannerly, civil, charming, gentlemanly, gallant. ANTONYMS uncouth, unsophisticated.

THE RIGHT WORD

In his long career as a film star, Cary Grant was known for playing **urbane**, **sophisticated** roles. *Urbane* in this context suggests the social poise and polished manner of someone who is well-traveled and well-bred, while *sophisticated* means worldly-wise as opposed to naïve (*a sophisticated young girl who had spent her childhood in Paris and London*). **Cosmopolitan** describes someone who is at home anywhere in the world and is free from provincial attitudes (*a cosmopolitan man who could charm women of all ages and nationalities*), while **suave** suggests the gracious social behavior of *urbane* combined with a certain glibness or superficial politeness (*she was taken in by his expensive clothes and suave manner*). At one time **genteel** meant well-bred or refined, but nowadays it has connotations of self-consciousness or pretentiousness (*too genteel to drink wine from a juice glass*).

urchin noun *Mrs. Duffy made frequent complaints about the urchins who played stickball on her street* RAGAMUFFIN, waif, stray; imp, rascal, street urchin; *derogatory* guttersnipe; scapegrace; *dated* gamin.

urge verb **1** *she urged him to try again* ENCOURAGE, exhort, enjoin, press, entreat, implore, call on, appeal to, beg, plead with, coax; egg on, prod, prompt, spur, goad, incite, push, pressure, pressurize; *formal* adjure; *literary* beseech.

2 *she urged her horse down the lane* SPUR (ON), force, drive, impel, propel.

3 *I urge caution in interpreting these results* ADVISE, counsel, advocate, recommend, suggest, advance.

▸ noun *his urge to travel* DESIRE, wish, need, compulsion, longing, yearning, hankering, craving, appetite, hunger, thirst; fancy, impulse, impetus; *informal* yen, itch.

urgent adjective **1** *the urgent need for more funding* ACUTE, pressing, dire, desperate, critical, serious, grave, intense, crying, burning, compelling, extreme, exigent, high-priority, top-priority; life-and-death. See note at CRUCIAL.

2 *an urgent whisper* INSISTENT, persistent, importunate, earnest, pleading, begging.

urinate verb *it was a bit of a culture shock to see men urinating out on the street* relieve oneself, pass water, make water; *informal* pee, take a leak, piddle, tinkle, (take a) whiz, piss; *formal* micturate.

URL noun *this one catalog company has several URLs* ADDRESS, IP address, link, alias.

usability noun *all of our office furniture is designed for usability* ERGONOMICS, ease of use, user-friendliness, accessibility, convenience, intuitiveness.

usable adjective *the postage meter on the third floor will not be usable until further notice* READY/FIT FOR USE, able to be used, at someone's disposal, disposable; working, in working order, functioning, functional, serviceable, operational, up and running, accessible.

usage noun **1** *energy usage* USE, consumption, utilization.

2 *the usage of equipment* USE, utilization, operation, manipulation, running, handling.

3 *the intricacies of English usage* PHRASEOLOGY, parlance, idiom, way of speaking/writing, mode of expression, style; idiolect.

4 *the usages of polite society* CUSTOM, practice, habit, tradition, convention, rule, observance; way, procedure, form, wont; *formal* praxis; **(usages)** mores.

EASILY CONFUSED WORDS **usage, use**

Usage means 'manner of use, practice,' while **use** means 'the act of employing.' In discussions of writing, **usage** is the term for normal or prescribed practice: *standard usage calls for a plural*. In describing particular examples, however, employ **use**: *the use of the plural with this noun is incorrect*.

use verb **1** *she used her key to open the front door* UTILIZE, make use of, avail oneself of, employ, work, operate, wield, ply, apply, maneuver, manipulate, put to use, put/press into service.

2 *the court will use its discretion in making an order* EXERCISE, employ, bring into play, practice, apply, exert, bring to bear.

3 *he just felt used* TAKE ADVANTAGE OF, exploit, manipulate, take liberties with, impose on, abuse; capitalize on, profit from, trade on, milk; *informal* walk all over.

4 *we have used all the available funds* CONSUME, get/go through, exhaust, deplete, expend, spend; waste, fritter away, squander, dissipate, run out of.

▸ noun **1** *the use of such weapons* UTILIZATION, usage, application, employment, operation, manipulation.

2 *what is the use of that?* ADVANTAGE, benefit, service, utility, usefulness, help, good, gain, avail, profit, value, worth, point, object, purpose, sense, reason.

3 *composers have not found much use for the device* NEED, necessity, call, demand, requirement.See note at USE.

used adjective *a used car* SECONDHAND, preowned, nearly new, old; worn, hand-me-down, castoff, recycled, warmed-over; *informal* preloved. ANTONYM new.

PHRASE: **used to** *I'm not used to such fine dining* ACCUSTOMED TO, no stranger to, familiar with, at home with, in the habit of, an old hand at, experienced in, versed in, conversant with, acquainted with.

useful adjective **1** *a useful multipurpose tool* FUNCTIONAL, practical, handy, convenient, utilitarian, serviceable, of use, of service. ANTONYM useless.

2 *a useful experience* BENEFICIAL, advantageous, helpful, worthwhile, profitable, rewarding, productive, constructive, valuable, fruitful. ANTONYM disadvantageous.

useless adjective **1** *useless attempts* FUTILE, to no avail, (in) vain, pointless, to no purpose, unavailing, hopeless, ineffectual, ineffective, to no effect, fruitless, unprofitable, profitless, unproductive; *archaic* bootless. ANTONYMS useful, beneficial.

2 *useless machines* UNUSABLE, broken, kaput, defunct, dud, faulty.

3 *informal he was a useless worker* INCOMPETENT, inept, ineffective, incapable, unemployable, inadequate, hopeless, no-account, bad; *informal* pathetic. ANTONYM competent.

user noun *the instructions are too complicated for the typical user to follow* CUSTOMER, consumer, client; operator.

user-defined adjective *user-defined functions* ADJUSTABLE, changeable, editable, customizable.

user-friendly adjective *user-friendly manuals* EASY-TO-USE, accessible, intuitive, usable, practical, ergonomic, simple, idiot-proof, goof-proof.

usher verb *she ushered him to a window seat* ESCORT, accompany, take, show, see, lead, conduct, guide, steer, shepherd, marshal.

▸ noun *ushers showed them to their seats* GUIDE, attendant, escort, sidesman.

PHRASE: **usher in** *Henry Ford' assembly line ushered in an era of unprecedented productivity* HERALD, mark the start of, signal, ring in, show in, set the scene for, pave the way for; start, begin, introduce, open the door to, get going, set in motion, get underway, kick off, launch.

usual adjective *meatloaf is their usual Wednesday special* HABITUAL, customary, accustomed, wonted, normal, routine, regular, standard, typical, established, set, settled, stock, conventional, traditional, expected, predictable, familiar; average, general, ordinary, everyday. See note at NORMAL. ANTONYM exceptional.

usually adverb *he usually arrived home about one o'clock* NORMALLY, generally, habitually, customarily, routinely, typically, ordinarily, commonly, conventionally, traditionally; as a rule, in general, more often than not, in the main, mainly, mostly, for the most part, nine times out of ten.

usurp verb **1** *Richard usurped the throne* SEIZE, take over, take possession of, take, commandeer, wrest, assume, expropriate.

2 *the Hanoverian dynasty had usurped the Stuarts* OUST, overthrow, remove, topple, unseat, depose, dethrone; supplant, replace.

utensil noun *kitchen utensils* IMPLEMENT, tool, instrument, device, apparatus, gadget, appliance, contrivance, contraption, aid; *informal* gizmo. See note at TOOL.

utilitarian adjective *she traded in her sporty little coupe for a utilitarian station wagon* PRACTICAL, functional, pragmatic, serviceable, useful, sensible, efficient, utility, workaday, no-frills; plain, unadorned, undecorative. ANTONYM decorative.

utility noun **1** *we have increased the machine's utility* USEFULNESS, use, benefit, value, advantage, advantageousness, help, helpfulness, effectiveness, avail; *formal* efficacy.

2 *an important public utility* SERVICE, service provider, organization, corporation, institution.

utilize verb *the foam pellets are utilized to make lightweight insulation* USE, make use of, put to use, employ, avail oneself of, bring/press into service, bring into play, deploy, draw on, exploit, harness.

WORD NOTE **utilize**

This is a puff-word. Since it does nothing that good old *use* doesn't do, its extra letters and syllables don't make a writer seem smarter. Rather, using *utilize* makes you seem like either a pompous twit or someone so insecure that he'll use pointlessly big words in an attempt to look smart. The same is true for the noun *utilization,* for *vehicle* as used for *car,* for *residence* as used for *home,* for *indicate* as used for *say,* for *presently, at present, at this time,* and *at the present time* as used for *now,* and so on. What's worth remembering about puff-words is something that good writing teachers spend a lot of time drumming into undergrads: "Formal writing" does not mean gratuitously fancy writing; it means clean, clear, maximally considerate writing. **—DFW**

utmost adjective *a matter of the utmost importance* GREATEST, highest, maximum, most, uttermost; extreme, supreme, paramount.

▸ noun *a plot that stretches credulity to the utmost* MAXIMUM, uttermost, limit; *informal* max.

Utopia noun *it may be your idea of Utopia, but it's not mine* PARADISE, heaven (on earth), Eden, Garden of Eden, Shangri-La, Elysium; idyll, nirvana, God's country; *literary* Arcadia.

Utopian adjective *a Utopian vision of world peace* IDEALISTIC, visionary, romantic, starry-eyed, fanciful, unrealistic, pie-in-the-sky; ideal, perfect, paradisal, heavenly, idyllic, blissful, Elysian; *literary* Arcadian.

utter[1] adjective *that's utter garbage* COMPLETE, total, absolute, thorough, perfect, downright, out-and-out, outright, thoroughgoing, all-out, sheer, arrant, wholesale, rank, pure, real, veritable, consummate, categorical, unmitigated, unqualified, unadulterated, unalloyed.

utter[2] verb **1** *he uttered an exasperated snort* EMIT, let out, give, produce.

2 *he hardly uttered a word* SAY, speak, voice, express, articulate, pronounce, enunciate, verbalize, vocalize.

utterance noun *your snide utterances are not appreciated* REMARK, comment, word, statement, observation, declaration, pronouncement; exclamation, assertion.

utterly adverb *this is utterly ridiculous* COMPLETELY, totally, absolutely, entirely, wholly, fully, thoroughly, quite, altogether, one hundred percent, downright, outright, in all respects, unconditionally, perfectly, really, to the hilt, to the core; dead.

uttermost adjective & noun See UTMOST.

U-turn noun *a complete U-turn in economic policy* ABOUT-FACE, turnaround, volte-face, reversal, shift, change of heart, change of mind, backtracking, change of plan, flip-flop; one-eighty, U-ey.

V

vacancy noun **1** *there are vacancies for computer technicians* OPENING, position, post, job, opportunity, place.

2 *a hotel vacancy* ROOM AVAILABLE, space for rent.

vacant adjective **1** *a vacant house* EMPTY, unoccupied, available, not in use, free, unfilled; uninhabited, untenanted. ANTONYMS full, occupied.

2 *a vacant look* BLANK, expressionless, unresponsive, emotionless, impassive, uninterested, vacuous, empty, absent, glazed, glassy; unintelligent, dull-witted, dense, brainless, empty-headed; *informal* zombified, lobotomized. ANTONYM expressive.

vacate verb **1** *he was forced to vacate the premises* LEAVE, move out of, evacuate, quit, depart from; abandon, desert. ANTONYMS occupy, inhabit.

2 *he will be vacating his post next year* RESIGN FROM, leave, stand down from, give up, bow out of, relinquish, retire from, quit. ANTONYM take up.

vacation noun *their summer vacations in Hawaii* BREAK, time off, recess, leave, leave of absence, furlough, sabbatical; TRIP, tour; *chiefly Brit.* holiday; *formal* sojourn.

▸ verb *I was vacationing in Europe with my family* TRAVEL, tour, stay, visit, stop over; *formal* sojourn.

vaccination noun *polio vaccination* INOCULATION, immunization; vaccine; injection; *informal* jab, shot.

vacillate verb *I vacillated between teaching and journalism* DITHER, waver, be indecisive, be undecided, be ambivalent, hesitate, be of two minds, blow hot and cold, keep changing one's mind, be conflicted; fluctuate, oscillate, hem and haw; *informal* dilly-dally, shilly-shally.

vacuous adjective *that vacuous laugh of his drives me nuts* SILLY, inane, unintelligent, insipid, foolish, stupid, fatuous, idiotic, brainless, witless, vapid, vacant, empty-headed; *informal* dumb, moronic, brain-dead, fluffy, fluffball. ANTONYM intelligent.

vacuum noun **1** *people longing to fill the spiritual vacuum in their lives* EMPTINESS, void, nothingness, vacancy, absence, black hole.

2 *the political vacuum left by the emperor's death* GAP, space, lacuna, void.

3 *informal I need to replace the bag in the vacuum* VACUUM CLEANER, vac; *trademark* Dustbuster, Hoover.

vagabond noun & adjective See VAGRANT noun.

vagary noun *the vagaries of the weather* CHANGE, fluctuation, variation, quirk, peculiarity, oddity, eccentricity, unpredictability, caprice, foible, whim, whimsy, fancy.

vagrant noun *a temporary home for vagrants* STREET PERSON, homeless person, tramp, hobo, drifter, down-and-out, derelict, beggar; itinerant, wanderer, nomad, traveler, vagabond, transient; *informal* bag lady, bum; *literary* wayfarer.

▸ adjective *vagrant beggars* HOMELESS, drifting, transient, roving, roaming, itinerant, wandering, nomadic, traveling, vagabond, rootless, of no fixed address/abode *archaic* errant.

vague adjective **1** *a vague shape* INDISTINCT, indefinite, indeterminate, unclear, ill-defined; hazy, fuzzy, misty, blurred, blurry, out of focus, faint, shadowy, dim, obscure, nebulous, amorphous, diaphanous. ANTONYMS clear, precise.

2 *a vague description* IMPRECISE, rough, approximate, inexact, nonspecific, generalized, ambiguous, equivocal, hazy, woolly. ANTONYMS clear, precise.

3 *they had only vague plans* HAZY, uncertain, undecided, unsure, unclear, unsettled, indefinite, indeterminate, unconfirmed, up in the air, speculative, sketchy. ANTONYM firm.

4 *she was so vague in everyday life* ABSENTMINDED, forgetful, dreamy, abstracted, with one's head in the clouds, scatty, scattered, not with it. ANTONYMS organized, together.

vaguely adverb **1** *she looks vaguely familiar* SLIGHTLY, a little, a bit, somewhat, rather, in a way; faintly, obscurely; *informal* sort of, kind of, kinda. ANTONYM very.

2 *he fired his rifle vaguely in our direction* ROUGHLY, more or less, approximately. ANTONYM exactly.

3 *he smiled vaguely* ABSENTMINDEDLY, abstractedly, vacantly.

vain adjective **1** *he was vain about his looks* CONCEITED, narcissistic, self-loving, in love with oneself, self-admiring, self-regarding, self-obsessed, egocentric, egotistic, egotistical; proud, arrogant, boastful, cocky, cocksure, immodest, swaggering; *informal* big-headed; *literary* vainglorious. ANTONYM modest.

2 *a vain attempt* FUTILE, useless, pointless, to no purpose, hopeless, in vain; ineffective, ineffectual, inefficacious, impotent, unavailing, to no avail, fruitless, profitless, unrewarding, unproductive, unsuccessful, failed, abortive, for nothing; thwarted, frustrated, foiled; *archaic* bootless. ANTONYM successful.

PHRASE: **in vain** 1 *they tried in vain to save him* UNSUCCESSFULLY, without success, to no avail, to no purpose, fruitlessly. 2 *his efforts were in vain.* See VAIN sense 2. 3 *she took the Lord's name in vain* IRREVERENTLY, casually, disrespectfully, flippantly.

valediction noun *he departed without a valediction* FAREWELL, goodbye, adieu, leave-taking; parting words.

valedictory noun *at their fifty-year reunion, Estelle Carver read the valedictory that she had delivered in 1954* SPEECH, address, lecture, declamation.

▸ adjective *a valedictory message* FAREWELL, goodbye, leaving, parting; last, final.

valet noun *his personal valet makes all the travel arrangements* MANSERVANT, man, personal attendant, personal servant, page, servant, flunky; hotel attendant, parking attendant, concierge.

valiant adjective *a valiant warrior | her valiant efforts* BRAVE, courageous, valorous, intrepid, heroic, gallant, lionhearted, bold, fearless, daring, audacious; unflinching, unshrinking, unafraid, dauntless, undaunted, doughty, tough, indomitable, mettlesome, stouthearted, spirited, plucky; *informal* game, gutsy, spunky. ANTONYM cowardly.

valid adjective 1 *a valid criticism* WELL-FOUNDED, sound, reasonable, rational, logical, justifiable, defensible, viable, bona fide; cogent, effective, powerful, potent, convincing, credible, forceful, strong, solid, weighty. See note at BELIEVABLE.

2 *a valid contract* LEGALLY BINDING, lawful, legal, legitimate, official, signed and sealed, contractual; in force, current, in effect, effective; *informal* legit.

3 *valid information* LEGITIMATE, authentic, authoritative, reliable, bona fide.

validate verb 1 *clinical trials now exist to validate this claim* PROVE, substantiate, corroborate, verify, support, back up, bear out, lend force to, confirm, justify, vindicate, authenticate. ANTONYM disprove.

2 *250 certificates need to be validated* RATIFY, endorse, approve, agree to, accept, authorize, legalize, legitimize, warrant, license, certify, recognize. ANTONYMS reject, revoke.

valley noun *the homes in the valley are subject to mudslides* DALE, vale; hollow, basin, gully, gorge, ravine, coulee, trough, canyon, rift; glen; *literary* dell.

valor noun *medals awarded for acts of valor* BRAVERY, courage, pluck, nerve, daring, fearlessness, audacity, boldness, dauntlessness, stout-heartedness, heroism, backbone, spirit; *informal* guts, true grit, spunk; moxie. ANTONYM cowardice.

valuable adjective 1 *a valuable watch* PRECIOUS, costly, pricey, expensive, dear, high-priced, high-cost, high-end, upscale, big-ticket; worth its weight in gold, priceless. ANTONYMS cheap, worthless.

2 *a valuable contribution* USEFUL, helpful, beneficial, invaluable, crucial, productive, constructive, effective, advantageous, worthwhile, worthy, important. ANTONYM useless.

valuation noun *get an insurance valuation on that painting* PRICE, evaluation, assessment, appraisal, costing, quotation, estimate.

value noun 1 *houses exceeding $250,000 in value* PRICE, cost, worth; market price, monetary value, face value.

2 *the value of adequate preparation cannot be understated* WORTH, usefulness, advantage, benefit, gain, profit, good, help, merit, helpfulness, avail; importance, significance.

3 *society's values are passed on to us as children* PRINCIPLES, ethics, moral code, morals, standards, code of behavior.

▸ verb 1 *his estate was valued at $345,000* EVALUATE, assess, estimate, appraise, price, put/set a price on.

2 *she valued his opinion* THINK HIGHLY OF, have a high opinion of, hold in high regard, rate highly, esteem, set (great) store by, put stock in, appreciate, respect; prize, cherish, treasure.

valued adjective *this is my most valued piece of crystal* CHERISHED, treasured, dear, prized; esteemed, respected, highly regarded, appreciated, important.

valueless adjective *this box of rusty old hardware is valueless* WORTHLESS, of no value, useless, to no purpose, (of) no use, profitless, futile, pointless, vain, in vain, to no avail, to no effect, fruitless, unproductive, idle, meretricious, ineffective, unavailing; *archaic* bootless.

valve noun *the valve on the tank needs to be replaced* FLAP, gate, inlet, tap, faucet, stopcock.

vamoose verb *informal* See BUZZ OFF at BUZZ.

vamp noun *informal a tawny-haired vamp* SEDUCTRESS, temptress, siren, femme fatale, sex kitten, trollop, home wrecker, man-eater; flirt, coquette, tease.

vandal noun *vandals defaced the front steps of the church* HOODLUM, barbarian, thug, hooligan, delinquent, despoiler, desecrator, saboteur.

vandalize verb *several parked cars have been vandalized on this street in the past three months* DESTROY, desecrate, despoil, deface, disfigure, mutilate, damage, sabotage, wreck, ruin.

vanguard noun *she was in the vanguard of the labor movement | they were destined to become the vanguard of space exploration* FOREFRONT, advance guard, spearhead, front, front line, fore, van, lead, cutting edge; avant-garde, leaders, founders, founding fathers, pioneers, trailblazers, trendsetters, innovators, groundbreakers. ANTONYMS rear, followers.

vanish verb 1 *he vanished without a trace* DISAPPEAR, be lost to sight/view, become invisible, vanish into thin air, recede from view, dematerialize. ANTONYMS appear, materialize.

2 *all hope of freedom vanished* FADE, fade away, evaporate, vaporize, melt away, come to an end, end, cease to exist, pass away, die out, be no more. ANTONYMS endure, materialize.

vanity noun 1 *she had none of the vanity often associated with beautiful women* CONCEIT, narcissism, self-love, self-admiration, self-absorption, self-regard, egotism; pride, arrogance, boastfulness, cockiness, swagger, rodomontade; *informal* big-headedness; *literary* vainglory. See notes at EGOTISM, PRIDE. ANTONYM modesty.

2 *the vanity of all desires of the will* FUTILITY, uselessness, pointlessness, worthlessness, fruitlessness.

vanquish verb *I promise you, we shall vanquish our enemy and reclaim what is rightfully ours* CONQUER, defeat, beat, trounce, rout, triumph over, be victorious over, get the better of, worst, upset; overcome, overwhelm, overpower, overthrow, subdue, subjugate, quell, quash, crush, bring someone to their knees, tear someone apart; *informal* lick, hammer, clobber, thrash, smash, demolish, wipe the floor with, make mincemeat of, massacre, slaughter, annihilate, cream, skunk, shellac.

vapid adjective *a tuneful but vapid musical comedy* INSIPID, uninspired, colorless, uninteresting, feeble, flat, dull, boring, tedious, tired, unexciting, uninspiring, unimaginative, lifeless, tame, vacuous, bland, trite, jejune. ANTONYMS lively, colorful.

vapor noun *bluish vapor rose from the basement window* HAZE, mist, steam, condensation, moisture; fumes, exhalation, fog, smog, smoke.

variable adjective *the weather on the shoreline is known for being variable* CHANGEABLE, changing, varying, shifting, fluctuating, irregular, inconstant, inconsistent, fluid, unsteady, unstable, unsettled, fitful, mutable, protean, wavering, vacillating, capricious, fickle, volatile, unpredictable, mercurial, unreliable; *informal* up and down. ANTONYM constant.

▸ noun *there are other variables to consider* FACTOR, element, ingredient, quantity, unknown quantity, condition.

variance noun *the variance between the two groups is slight* DIFFERENCE, variation, discrepancy, dissimilarity, disagreement, conflict, divergence, deviation, contrast, contradiction, imbalance, incongruity. PHRASE: **at variance** 1 *his recollections were* ***at variance with*** *documentary evidence* INCONSISTENT, at odds, not in keeping, out of keeping, out of line, out of step, in conflict, in disagreement. 2 *science and religion need not be at variance* CONFLICTING, in conflict, in disagreement, in opposition; different, differing, divergent, discrepant, dissimilar, contrary, incompatible, contradictory, irreconcilable, incongruous; at cross purposes, at loggerheads, in dispute.

variant noun *there are a number of variants of the same idea* VARIATION, form, alternative, adaptation, alteration, modification, permutation, version, analog.

▸ adjective *a variant spelling* ALTERNATIVE, other, different, substitute, divergent, derived, modified.

variation noun 1 *regional variations in farming practice* DIFFERENCE, dissimilarity; disparity, contrast, discrepancy, imbalance; *technical* differential.

2 *opening times are subject to variation* CHANGE, alteration, modification; diversification.

3 *there was very little variation from an understood pattern* DEVIATION, variance, divergence, departure, fluctuation.

4 *hurling is an Irish variation of field hockey* VARIANT, form, alternative form; development, adaptation, alteration, mutation, transformation, diversification, modification.

varied adjective *her varied interests keep her extremely busy* DIVERSE, assorted, miscellaneous, mixed, sundry, heterogeneous, wide-ranging, manifold, multifarious; disparate, motley.

variegated adjective *variegated leaves* MULTICOLORED, multicolor, many-colored, many-hued, polychromatic, varicolored, colorful, prismatic, rainbow, kaleidoscopic; mottled, striated, marbled, streaked, speckled, flecked, dappled; *informal* splotchy. ANTONYMS plain, monochrome.

variety noun 1 *the lack of variety in the curriculum* DIVERSITY, variation, diversification, heterogeneity, multifariousness, change, choice, difference. ANTONYM uniformity.

2 *a wide variety of flowers and shrubs* ASSORTMENT, miscellany, range, array, collection, selection, mixture, medley, multiplicity; mixed bag, motley collection, potpourri, hodgepodge.

3 *fifty varieties of pasta* SORT, kind, type, class, category, style, form; make, model, brand; strain, breed, genus.

various adjective *there are various styles to choose from* DIVERSE, different, differing, varied, varying, a variety of, assorted, mixed, myriad, sundry, miscellaneous, heterogeneous, disparate, motley; several, a number of, an assortment of; *literary* divers.

varnish noun & verb *two coats of varnish | she varnished the woodwork* LACQUER, shellac, finish, japan, enamel, glaze; polish, wax.

vary verb 1 *estimates of the development cost vary* DIFFER, be different, be dissimilar, conflict.

2 *rates of interest can vary over time* FLUCTUATE, rise and fall, go up and down, change, alter, shift, swing, deviate, differ.

3 *the diaphragm is used for varying the aperture of the lens* MODIFY, change, alter, transform, adjust, regulate, control, set; diversify, reshape; *informal* tweak.

vase noun *a decorative antique vase* VESSEL, urn, amphora, jar.

vassal noun *historical he was born an English vassal* SERF, dependent, servant, slave, subject, bondsman, thrall, villein; *historical* vavasour, helot.

vast adjective *a vast holding of farmland* HUGE, extensive, expansive, broad, wide, sweeping, boundless, immeasurable, limitless, infinite; enormous, immense, great, massive, colossal, tremendous, mighty, prodigious, gigantic, gargantuan, mammoth, monumental; giant, towering, mountainous, titanic, Brobdingnagian; *informal* jumbo, mega, monster, whopping, humongous, astronomical, ginormous. ANTONYM tiny.

vat noun *a vat of molasses* TUB, tank, cistern, barrel, cask, tun, drum, basin; vessel, receptacle, container, holder, reservoir.

vault[1] noun 1 *the highest Gothic vault in Europe* ARCHED ROOF, dome, arch.

2 *the vault under the church* CELLAR, basement, underground chamber; crypt, catacomb, burial chamber.

3 *valuables stored in the vault* SAFE, safety deposit box, repository, coffer, strongroom.

vault[2] verb *he* ***vaulted over*** *the gate* JUMP OVER, leap over, spring over, bound over; hurdle, clear.

vaunt verb *their much vaunted record of accuracy* BOAST ABOUT, brag about, make much of, crow about, parade, flaunt; acclaim, trumpet, praise, extol, celebrate; *informal* show off about, hype; *formal* laud.

veer verb *we then saw the car veer suddenly to the right* TURN, swerve, curve, swing, sheer, career, weave, wheel; change direction, change course, go off course, deviate.

veg verb *informal I just want to veg in front of the TV* RELAX, do nothing, unwind, de-stress, unbend, rest, put one's feet up, take a load off, take it easy; *informal* mellow (out), chill (out), let it all hang out, veg out, hang loose.

vegetable noun See table.

VEGETABLES

- acorn squash
- agave
- ancho pepper
- artichoke
- arugula
- ash gourd
- asparagus
- asparagus bean
- avocado
- bamboo shoot
- banana pepper
- banana squash
- basil
- bean sprout
- beet
- beet green
- bell pepper
- bibb lettuce
- bitter gourd
- bok choy
- Boston lettuce
- bottle gourd
- brinjal
- broad bean
- broccoflower
- broccoli
- broccoli rabe
- broccolini
- Brussels sprout
- burdock
- butternut squash
- cabbage
- caper
- carrot
- cassava
- cayenne pepper
- celeriac
- celery
- chard
- cherry pepper
- chicory
- chili pepper
- Chinese cabbage
- chive
- cilantro
- cluster bean
- collard green
- colocasia
- corn
- cress
- cubanelle pepper
- cucumber
- curry leaf
- daikon
- dandelion green
- delicata squash
- dill
- edamame
- eggplant
- endive
- epazote
- escarole
- fava bean
- fennel
- fenugreek
- fiddlehead
- frisée
- galangal
- gherkin
- ginger root
- gourd
- green bean
- green pea
- Habanero pepper
- haricot vert
- horseradish
- Hubbard squash
- iceberg lettuce
- jalapeño pepper
- Jerusalem artichoke
- jicama
- kabocha squash
- kale
- kencur
- kohlrabi
- leek
- lemon grass
- lima bean
- lotus root
- mache
- marrow
- mesclun
- mizuna
- mung bean
- mushroom
- mustard green
- napa cabbage
- nopal
- okra
- onion
- pandan leaf
- parsley
- parsnip
- pasilla pepper
- pea
- pea pod
- petit pois
- plantain
- potato
- pumpkin
- purslane
- radicchio
- radish
- ramp
- rhubarb
- ridge gourd
- romaine lettuce
- runner bean
- rutabaga
- salsify
- scallion
- sea kale
- Serrano pepper
- shallot
- shiso
- snake gourd
- snow pea
- sorrel
- spaghetti squash
- spinach
- spring onion
- sugar snap pea
- summer squash
- sweet potato
- Swiss chard
- taro
- Thai chili pepper
- tomatillo
- turnip
- wakame
- water chestnut
- watercress
- wax bean
- winged bean
- winter melon
- yam
- yard-long bean
- yellow squash
- zucchini

See also table at BEAN.

vegetarian adjective *vegetarian food* MEATLESS, meat-free, no-meat; vegan; *informal* veggie.

vegetate verb *ever since school ended, he just vegetates* DO NOTHING, relax, rest, idle, languish, laze, lounge, loll; stagnate; *informal* veg, bum around, hang out, zone out, lollygag.

vegetation noun *lush tropical vegetation* PLANTS, flora; greenery, foliage, herbage, verdure.

vehemence noun *the recruiters were talk to speak with unwavering vehemence* PASSION, force, forcefulness, ardor, fervor, violence, urgency, strength, vigor, intensity, keenness, feeling, enthusiasm, zeal.

vehement adjective *her vehement arguments persuaded them to save the housing project* PASSIONATE, forceful, ardent, impassioned, heated, spirited, urgent, fervent, violent, fierce, fiery, strong, forcible, powerful, emphatic, vigorous, intense, earnest, keen, enthusiastic, zealous. ANTONYMS mild, apathetic.

vehicle noun **1** *a stolen vehicle* MEANS OF TRANSPORT, conveyance, motor vehicle. See table at CAR.

2 *a vehicle for the communication of original ideas* CHANNEL, medium, conduit, means, means of expression, agency, agent, instrument, mechanism, organ, apparatus.

veil noun **1** *a thin veil of high cloud made the sun hazy* COVERING, cover, screen, curtain, mantle, cloak, mask, blanket, shroud, canopy, cloud, pall.

2 *the women wore black veils* MASK, scarf, kerchief, head covering, headdress; dupatta, purdah, mantilla, chador, hijab, yashmak.

▸ verb *the peak was veiled in mist* ENVELOP, surround, swathe, enfold, cover, conceal, hide, screen, shield, cloak, blanket, shroud; obscure; *literary* enshroud, mantle.

veiled adjective *veiled threats* DISGUISED, camouflaged, masked, covert, hidden, concealed, suppressed, underlying, implicit, implied, indirect. ANTONYM overt.

vein noun **1** *a vein in his neck pulsed* BLOOD VESSEL.

2 *the mineral veins in the rock* LAYER, lode, seam, stratum, stratification, deposit, pipe.

3 *white marble with gray veins* STREAK, marking, mark, line, stripe, strip, band, thread, strand; *technical* stria, striation.

4 *he closes the article in a humorous vein* MOOD, frame of mind, temper, disposition, attitude, tenor, tone, key, spirit, character, fashion, feel, flavor, quality, atmosphere, humor; manner, mode, way, style.

velocity noun *light travels at a constant velocity* SPEED, pace, rate, tempo, momentum, impetus; swiftness, rapidity; *literary* fleetness, celerity.

velvety adjective *the puppy's velvety coat* SOFT, furry, downy, fleecy, creamy; velvet; strokable.

venal adjective *they ran the town according to their own venal system of 'law and order'* CORRUPT, corruptible, bribable, open to bribery; dishonest, dishonorable, untrustworthy, unscrupulous, unprincipled; mercenary, greedy; *informal* crooked. ANTONYMS honorable, honest.

EASILY CONFUSED WORDS **venal, venial**

Venal and **venial** are sometimes confused. **Venal** means 'corrupt, able to be bribed, or involving bribery': *local customs officials are notoriously venal, and smuggling thrives.* **Venial** is used to describe a sin or offense that is 'pardonable, excusable, not mortal': *in our high school, smoking cigarettes was a venial sin.*

vend verb See SELL sense 1.

vendetta noun *the vendetta between our families is older than our grandparents* FEUD, blood feud, quarrel, argument, falling-out, dispute, fight, war; bad blood, enmity, rivalry, conflict, strife.

vendor noun *most of the vendors on Main Street are participating in Saturday's sidewalk sales* RETAILER, seller, dealer, trader, purveyor, storekeeper, shopkeeper, merchant; salesperson, supplier, peddler, hawker; scalper, huckster, trafficker.

veneer noun **1** *American cherry wood with a maple veneer* SURFACE, lamination, layer, overlay, facing, covering, finish, exterior, cladding, laminate.

2 *a veneer of sophistication* FACADE, front, false front, show, outward display, appearance, impression, semblance, guise, disguise, mask, masquerade, pretense, camouflage, cover, window dressing.

venerable adjective *the venerable Martin Steed joined our faculty in 1962* RESPECTED, venerated, revered, honored, esteemed, hallowed, august, distinguished, eminent, great, grand.

venerate verb *Dr. Browne is venerated by the poor mining families in this valley* REVERE, regard highly, reverence, worship, hallow, hold sacred, exalt, vaunt, adore, honor, respect, esteem. See note at REVERE.

vengeance noun *your appetite for vengeance has destroyed your life* REVENGE, retribution, retaliation, payback, requital, reprisal, satisfaction, an eye for an eye (and a tooth for a tooth). PHRASE: **with a vengeance** *she returned to the stage with a vengeance* VIGOROUSLY, strenuously, energetically, with a will, with all the stops out, for all one is worth, all out, flat out, at full tilt; *informal* hammer and tongs, like crazy, like mad, like gangbusters.

vengeful adjective *they worship a vengeful god* VINDICTIVE, revengeful, out for revenge, unforgiving, on the warpath. See note at VINDICTIVE. ANTONYM forgiving.

venial adjective *the venial indiscretions of my youth* FORGIVABLE, pardonable, excusable, allowable, permissible; slight, minor, unimportant, insignificant, trivial, trifling. See note at VENAL. ANTONYMS unforgivable, mortal.

venom noun **1** *snake venom* POISON, toxin; *archaic* bane.

2 *his voice was full of venom* RANCOR, malevolence, vitriol, spite, vindictiveness, malice, maliciousness, ill will, acrimony, animosity, animus, bitterness, antagonism, hostility, bile, hate, hatred; *informal* bitchiness, cattiness.

venomous adjective **1** *a venomous snake | the spider's venomous bite* POISONOUS, toxic; dangerous, deadly, lethal, fatal, mortal. ANTONYM harmless.

2 *venomous remarks* VICIOUS, spiteful, rancorous, malevolent, vitriolic, vindictive, malicious, poisonous, virulent, bitter, acidic, acrimonious, caustic, antagonistic, hostile, cruel; *informal* bitchy, catty; *literary* malefic, maleficent. See note at VINDICTIVE. ANTONYMS kind, benevolent.

vent noun *an air vent* DUCT, flue, shaft, well, passage, airway; outlet, inlet, opening, aperture, hole, gap, orifice.

▸ verb *the crowd vented their fury on the police* RELEASE, air, give vent to, give free rein to, let out, pour out, express, give expression to, voice, give voice to, verbalize, ventilate, discuss, talk over, communicate.

ventilate verb *ventilate all work areas* AIR, aerate, air out, oxygenate, air-condition, fan; freshen, cool.

venture noun *a business venture* ENTERPRISE, undertaking, project, initiative, scheme, operation, endeavor, speculation, plunge, gamble, gambit, experiment.

▸ verb **1** *we ventured across the country* SET OUT, go, travel, journey.

2 *may I venture an opinion?* PUT FORWARD, advance, proffer, offer, volunteer, air, suggest, submit, propose, moot,

3 *I ventured to ask her to come and dine with me* DARE, be/make so bold as, presume; take the liberty of, stick one's neck out, go out on a limb.

veracious adjective *formal* See TRUTHFUL sense 2.

veracity noun *we do not question the veracity of your story* TRUTHFULNESS, truth, accuracy, correctness, faithfulness, fidelity; reputability, honesty, sincerity, trustworthiness, reliability, dependability, scrupulousness, ethics, morality, righteousness, virtuousness, decency, straightforwardness, goodness, probity.

veranda noun *we'll have our coffee on the veranda* PORCH, gallery, balcony, lanai, sun porch, stoop.

verbal adjective *a verbal agreement* ORAL, spoken, stated, said, verbalized, expressed; unwritten, word-of-mouth.

verbatim adverb *I memorized his monologue verbatim* WORD FOR WORD, letter for letter, line for line, to the letter, literally, exactly, precisely, accurately, closely, faithfully.

verbiage noun *Professor Chin's verbiage is tiresome* VERBOSITY, wordiness, prolixity, long-windedness, loquacity, rigmarole, circumlocution, superfluity, periphrasis.

verbose adjective *try not to be so verbose when you're being interviewed* WORDY, loquacious, garrulous, talkative, voluble; long-winded, flatulent, lengthy, prolix, tautological, pleonastic, periphrastic, circumlocutory, circuitous, wandering, discursive, digressive, rambling; *informal* mouthy, gabby, chatty, motormouthed. ANTONYMS succinct, laconic.

verdant adjective *the verdant spring mosses* GREEN, leafy, grassy; lush, rich; *literary* verdurous.

verdict noun *the judge's verdict is final* JUDGMENT, adjudication, decision, finding, ruling, decree, resolution, pronouncement, conclusion, opinion; *Law* determination.

verge noun **1** *the verge of the lake* EDGE, border, margin, side, brink, rim, lip; fringe, boundary, perimeter, outskirts; *literary* skirt. See note at BORDER.

2 *Spain was on the verge of an economic crisis* BRINK, threshold, edge, point.

▸ verb *a degree of caution that* ***verged on*** *the obsessive* APPROACH, border on, come close/near to, be tantamount to; tend toward, approximate to, resemble.

verification noun *they may require further verification* CONFIRMATION, substantiation, proof, corroboration, support, attestation, validation, authentication, endorsement.

verify verb **1** *the evidence verifies my claim* SUBSTANTIATE, confirm, prove, corroborate, back up, bear out, justify, support, uphold, attest to, testify to, validate, authenticate, endorse, certify. ANTONYM refute.

2 *we need to verify those figures* TEST, double-check, check out, establish the truth of.

verisimilitude noun *the verisimilitude of her performance is gripping* REALISM, believability, plausibility, authenticity, credibility, lifelikeness.

veritable adjective *a veritable price explosion* REAL, bona fide, authentic, genuine, indubitable, utter; *informal* sure as shootin'. See note at GENUINE.

vermin plural noun *an apartment crawling with vermin | the vermin who deal drugs in broad daylight* PESTS, parasites; infestations; undesirables, lowlifes.

vernacular noun **1** *he wrote in* ***the vernacular*** *to reach a wider audience* EVERYDAY LANGUAGE, colloquial language, conversational language, common parlance, demotic, lay terms.

2 *informal the preppy vernacular of Orange County* LANGUAGE, dialect, regional language, regionalisms, patois, parlance; idiom, slang, jargon; *informal* lingo, -speak, -ese. See note at DIALECT.

versatile adjective *she's our most versatile player* ADAPTABLE, flexible, all-around, multifaceted, multitalented, resourceful; adjustable, multipurpose, all-purpose, handy; *rare* polytropic.

verse noun **1** *Elizabethan verse* POETRY, versification, poetic form; poems, balladry, lyrics, lines, doggerel; *literary* poesy. See also the table at POETRY. ANTONYM prose.

2 *a verse he'd composed for our anniversary* POEM, lyric, ballad, sonnet, ode, limerick, rhyme, ditty, lay.

3 *a poem with sixty verses* STANZA, canto, couplet; strophe.

WORD NOTE verse

In contemporary pop music, the *verse* is the section of a song that changes lyrics, whereas the *chorus* stays the same. In classic pop, the verse was a prologue, considered optional, and the *refrain* was the body of the song. A few people still use *refrain* when they mean *chorus*. **—SM**

versed adjective See INFORMED.

version noun **1** *his version of events* ACCOUNT, report, statement, description, record, story, rendering, interpretation, explanation, understanding, reading, impression, side, take.

2 *the Japanese version will be published next year* EDITION, translation, impression.

3 *they replaced coal-burning furnaces with gas versions* FORM, sort, kind, type, variety, variant, model.

versus preposition *it's essentially an examination of self-interest versus self-sacrifice* AGAINST, facing, confronting, v., vs.; as opposed to, in contrast with.

vertex noun *a line drawn from the vertex of the figure to the base* APEX, peak, pinnacle, zenith, crown, crest, tip, top.

vertical adjective *workers enter through a vertical shaft* UPRIGHT, erect, perpendicular, plumb, straight up and down, on end, standing, upstanding, bolt upright. ANTONYM horizontal.

vertigo noun *the steep narrow stairs give me vertigo* DIZZINESS, giddiness, lightheadedness, loss of balance.

verve noun *the kids performed with joyful verve* ENTHUSIASM, vigor, energy, pep, dynamism, élan, vitality, vivacity, buoyancy, liveliness, animation, zest, sparkle, charisma, spirit, ebullience, exuberance, life, brio, gusto, eagerness, keenness, passion, zeal, relish, feeling, ardor, fire; *informal* zing, zip, vim, pizzazz, oomph, get-up-and-go.

very adverb *that's very kind of you* EXTREMELY, exceedingly, exceptionally, extraordinarily, tremendously, immensely, hugely, intensely, acutely, abundantly, singularly, uncommonly, decidedly, particularly, supremely, highly, remarkably, really, truly, mightily, ever so; *informal* terrifically, awfully, fearfully, terribly, devilishly, majorly, seriously, mega, ultra, damn, damned; dead, real, way, mighty, awful, darned; *archaic* exceeding. ANTONYM slightly.

▸ adjective **1** *those were his very words* EXACT, actual, precise.

2 *the very thought of food made her feel ill* MERE, simple, pure; sheer.

WORD NOTE very

Early on we are taught to be leery of *very* and similar intensives *(exceptionally, especially)*. Indeed, if writers had to do without one of the eight parts of speech, the adverbs would probably be least missed. Yet *very* is among the few words that gains in effectiveness when repeated. *There was definitely something moving around the darkened room. Frightened, Mildred turned the doorknob very, very quietly.* The doubling of *very* slows the sentence down, and conveys a more palpable sense of Mildred's trepidation. Nevertheless, be very, very cautious about using this common adverb, and do so only after thinking twice. **—MD**

vessel noun **1** *a fishing vessel* BOAT, ship, craft, watercraft; *literary* bark/barque.

2 *pour the mixture into a heatproof vessel* CONTAINER, receptacle; basin, bowl, pan, pot; urn, tank, cask, barrel, drum, vat.

vest verb *executive power is* ***vested in*** *the president* CONFER ON, entrust to, invest in, bestow on, grant to, give to, put in the hands of; endow in, lodge in, lay on, place on.

vestibule noun *brochures are available in the vestibule* ENTRANCE HALL, hall, hallway, entrance, porch, portico, foyer, lobby, anteroom, narthex, antechamber, waiting room.

vestige noun 1 *the last vestiges of colonialism* REMNANT, fragment, relic, echo, indication, sign, trace, residue, mark, legacy, reminder; remains. See note at TRACE.

2 *she showed no vestige of emotion* BIT, touch, hint, suggestion, suspicion, shadow, scrap, tinge, speck, shred, jot, iota, whit, scintilla, glimmer; *informal* smidgen, tad, titch, tinch.

vestigial adjective 1 *vestigial limbs* RUDIMENTARY, undeveloped; nonfunctional; *Biology* primitive.

2 *he felt a vestigial flicker of anger from last night* REMAINING, surviving, residual, leftover, lingering.

vet verb *press releases are vetted by an executive council* CHECK, examine, scrutinize, investigate, inspect, look over, screen, assess, evaluate, appraise; *informal* check out.

▸ noun *I took the cat to the vet* VETERINARIAN, animal doctor, horse doctor.

veteran noun *a veteran of 16 political campaigns* OLD HAND, past master, doyen, vet; *informal* old-timer, old stager, old warhorse. ANTONYM novice.

▸ adjective *a veteran diplomat* LONG-SERVING, seasoned, old, hardened; adept, expert, well trained, practiced, experienced, senior; *informal* battle-scarred.

veto noun *the president's right of veto* REJECTION, dismissal; prohibition, proscription, embargo, ban, interdict, check; *informal* thumbs down, red light. ANTONYM approval.

▸ verb *China vetoed the proposal* REJECT, turn down, throw out, dismiss; prohibit, forbid, interdict, proscribe, disallow, embargo, ban, rule out, say no to; *informal* kill, put the kibosh on, give the thumbs down to, give the red light to. ANTONYM approve.

vex verb *Alice was vexed by his remarks* ANNOY, irritate, anger, infuriate, exasperate, irk, gall, pique, put out, antagonize, nettle, get on someone's nerves, ruffle someone's feathers, rattle someone's cage, make someone's hackles rise, rub the wrong way; *informal* aggravate, peeve, miff, rile, needle, get (to), bug, get someone's goat, get someone's back up, get someone's dander up, tee off, tick off, burn up, rankle.

vexation noun *she stamped her foot in vexation* ANNOYANCE, irritation, exasperation, indignation, anger, crossness, displeasure, pique, bile, disgruntlement, bad mood; *informal* aggravation.

vexed adjective 1 *a vexed expression* ANNOYED, irritated, cross, angry, infuriated, exasperated, irked, piqued, nettled, displeased, put out, disgruntled; *informal* aggravated, peeved, miffed, riled, hacked off, hot under the collar, teed off, ticked off, sore, bent out of shape; PO'd; *archaic* wroth.

2 *the vexed issue of immigration* DISPUTED, in dispute, contested, in contention, contentious, debated, at issue, controversial, moot; problematic, difficult, knotty, thorny, ticklish, tense.

via preposition *enjoy the opera via your own television* THROUGH, by way of; by means of, with the aid of, by virtue of.

viable adjective *it doesn't sound like a viable solution* FEASIBLE, workable, practicable, practical, usable, possible, realistic, achievable, attainable, realizable; *informal* doable. ANTONYM impracticable.

vibe noun *informal I get a good vibe from her parents* FEELING, vibration, atmosphere, sensation, energy.

vibrant adjective 1 *a vibrant and passionate woman* SPIRITED, lively, full of life, energetic, vigorous, vital, full of vim and vigor, animated, sparkling, effervescent, vivacious, dynamic, stimulating, exciting, passionate, fiery; *informal* peppy, feisty. ANTONYMS listless, dull.

2 *vibrant colors* VIVID, bright, striking, brilliant, strong, rich, colorful, bold. ANTONYMS washed out, pale.

3 *his vibrant voice* RESONANT, sonorous, reverberant, resounding, ringing, echoing; strong, rich, full, round. ANTONYMS soft, feeble.

vibrate verb 1 *the floor beneath them vibrated* QUIVER, shake, tremble, shiver, shudder, throb, pulsate, rattle; rock, wobble, oscillate, waver, swing, sway, move to and fro; *chiefly Brit.* judder.

2 *a low rumbling sound began to vibrate through the car* REVERBERATE, resonate, resound, ring, echo.

vibration noun *loose bolts are causing the vibration* TREMOR, shaking, quivering, quaking, shuddering, throb, throbbing, pulsation; *chiefly Brit.* judder, juddering.

vicarious adjective *I had the vicarious thrill of knowing my wife was to be named the next university president* INDIRECT, secondhand, secondary, derivative, derived, surrogate, substitute; empathetic, empathic.

vice noun 1 *youngsters driven to vice* IMMORALITY, wrongdoing, wickedness, badness, evil, iniquity, villainy, corruption, misconduct, misdeeds; sin, sinfulness, ungodliness; depravity, degeneracy, dissolution, dissipation, debauchery, decadence, lechery, perversion; crime, transgression; *formal* turpitude; *archaic* trespass. See note at SIN. ANTONYM virtue.

2 *smoking is my only vice* SHORTCOMING, failing, flaw, fault, bad habit, defect, weakness, deficiency, limitation, imperfection, blemish, foible, frailty. ANTONYM virtue.

viceroy noun *his grandfather served as viceroy during the island's last few years of colonial rule* GOVERNOR, deputy, representative, proconsul; regent, steward.

vice versa adverb *dancers can teach actors a lot and vice versa* CONVERSELY, inversely, contrariwise; reciprocally, the other way around/round.

vicinity noun *many female artists and writers live in the vicinity* NEIGHBORHOOD, surrounding area, locality, locale, area, local area, district, region, quarter, zone; environs, surroundings, precincts; *informal* neck of the woods. PHRASE: **in the vicinity of** *his fortune is in the vicinity of four billion dollars* AROUND, about, nearly, circa, approaching, roughly, approximating, approximately, something like, more or less; in the region of, in the neighborhood of, near to, close to.

vicious adjective 1 *a vicious killer* BRUTAL, ferocious, savage, violent, dangerous, ruthless, remorseless, merciless, heartless, callous, cruel, harsh, cold-blooded, inhuman, fierce, barbarous, barbaric, brutish, bloodthirsty, fiendish, sadistic, monstrous, murderous, homicidal *informal* smash-mouth. ANTONYM gentle.

2 *a vicious hate campaign* MALICIOUS, malevolent, malignant, malign, spiteful, hateful, vindictive, venomous, poisonous, rancorous, mean, cruel, bitter, cutting, acrimonious, hostile, nasty; defamatory, slanderous; *informal* catty. ANTONYMS benevolent, kindly.

vicious circle noun *but if I bring Mr. Raines the foods he asks for, he blames me for not serving healthier meals—it's a vicious circle* DILEMMA, vicious cycle, downward spiral, vortex, no-win situation, catch-22, chicken-and-egg situation.

vicissitude noun *the vicissitude of our love* CHANGE, alteration, shift, reversal, twist, turn, downturn, variation; inconstancy, instability, uncertainty, chanciness, unpredictability, fickleness, variability, changeability, fluctuation, vacillation; ups and downs.

victim noun **1** *a victim of crime* SUFFERER, injured party, casualty; fatality, loss; loser.

2 *the victim of a con game* TARGET, object, subject, focus, recipient, butt.

3 *a born victim* LOSER, prey, stooge, dupe, sucker, quarry, fool, fall guy, chump; *informal* patsy, sap.

4 *he offered himself as a victim* SACRIFICE, offering, burnt offering, scapegoat. PHRASE: **fall victim to** *they fell victim to the flu* FALL ILL WITH, be stricken with, catch, develop, contract, pick up; succumb to.

victimize verb *a government that victimizes the most needy and defenseless* PERSECUTE, pick on, push around, bully, abuse, discriminate against, ill-treat, mistreat, maltreat, terrorize, hector; exploit, prey on, take advantage of, dupe, cheat, double-cross, get at, have it in for, give someone a hard time, hassle, lean on, gang up on.

victor verb *to the victors go all the sponsorship opportunities* WINNER, champion, conqueror, conquering hero, vanquisher, hero; prize winner, gold medalist; *informal* champ, top dog. ANTONYM loser.

victorious adjective *the victorious Romanians brought home the gold* TRIUMPHANT, conquering, vanquishing, winning, champion, successful, top, first.

victory noun *after a season of tough losses, this year's opening-game victory was extra sweet* SUCCESS, triumph, conquest, win, favorable result; landslide, coup; mastery, superiority, supremacy; *informal* walkover, thrashing, trouncing. ANTONYM defeat.

victuals plural noun *dated* See FOOD sense 1.

video noun *we recorded it on video* TAPE, videotape, DVD, *trademark* VHS.

vie verb *the brothers had always vied for favoritism* COMPETE, contend, contest, struggle, fight, battle, cross swords, lock horns, buck, jockey; war, feud.

view noun **1** *the view from her apartment* OUTLOOK, prospect, panorama, vista, scene, aspect, perspective, spectacle, sight; scenery, landscape.

2 *we agree with this view* OPINION, point of view, viewpoint, belief, judgment, thinking, notion, idea, conviction, persuasion, attitude, feeling, sentiment, concept, hypothesis, theory; stance, standpoint, philosophy, doctrine, dogma, approach, take. See note at OPINION.

3 *the church came into view* SIGHT, perspective, vision, visibility.

▸ verb **1** *they viewed the landscape* LOOK AT, eye, observe, gaze at, stare at, ogle, contemplate, watch, scan, regard, take in, survey, inspect, scrutinize; *informal* check out, get a load of, eyeball; *literary* espy, behold.

2 *the law was viewed as a last resort* CONSIDER, regard, look upon, see, perceive, judge, deem, reckon.

PHRASES: **in view of** *in view of this new evidence, we would like to reconsider our decision* CONSIDERING, bearing in mind, taking into account, on account of, in (the) light of, owing to, because of, as a result of, given. **on view** *the Garbo memorabilia will be on view until Thursday* ON DISPLAY, on exhibition, on show.

viewer noun *one of our lucky viewers will win a trip to Mexico* WATCHER, spectator, onlooker, looker-on, observer, member of the audience; (**viewers**) audience, crowd; *literary* beholder.

viewpoint noun *I understand your viewpoint.* See VIEW noun sense 2.

vigilant adjective *we've become more vigilant since the neighbors were robbed* WATCHFUL, observant, attentive, alert, eagle-eyed, hawk-eyed, on the lookout, on one's toes, on the qui vive; wide awake, wakeful, unwinking, on one's guard, cautious, wary, circumspect, heedful, mindful; *informal* beady-eyed. ANTONYM inattentive.

THE RIGHT WORD

All of these adjectives connote being on the lookout for danger or opportunity. Watchful is the most general term, meaning closely observant (a watchful young man who noticed everything). If you're vigilant, you are watchful for a purpose (to be vigilant in the presence of one's enemies), and wary suggests being on the lookout for treachery or trickery (wary of his neighbor's motives in offering to move the fence). If you're alert, you are quick to apprehend a danger, an opportunity, or an emergency (she was much more alert after a good night's sleep), and if you're careful, you may be able to avoid danger or error altogether. Cautious and circumspect also emphasize the avoidance of danger or unpleasant situations. To be circumspect is to be watchful in all directions and with regard to all possible consequences (these journalists have to be circumspect, not criticizing anyone too harshly); to be cautious is to guard against contingencies (a cautious approach to treating illness).

vigor noun *they ran with great vigor* ROBUSTNESS, health, hardiness, strength, sturdiness, toughness; bloom, radiance, energy, life, vitality, virility, verve, spirit; zeal, passion, determination, dynamism, zest, pep, drive, force; *informal* oomph, get-up-and-go, zing, piss and vinegar. ANTONYM lethargy.

vigorous adjective **1** *the child was vigorous* ROBUST, healthy, hale and hearty, strong, sturdy, fit; hardy, tough, athletic; bouncing, thriving, flourishing, blooming; energetic, lively, active, perky, spirited, vibrant, vital, zestful; *informal* peppy, bouncy, in the pink. ANTONYMS weak, frail.

2 *a vigorous defense of policy* STRENUOUS, powerful, forceful, spirited, mettlesome, determined, aggressive, two-fisted, driving, eager, zealous, ardent, fervent, vehement, passionate; tough, robust, thorough, blunt, hard-hitting; *informal* punchy. ANTONYMS weak, feeble.

vigorously adverb *she pedaled vigorously* STRENUOUSLY, strongly, powerfully, forcefully, energetically, heartily, vehemently, for dear life, for all one is worth, all out, fiercely, hard; *informal* like mad, like crazy, like gangbusters.

vile adjective *a vile smell | his vile crimes* FOUL, nasty, unpleasant, bad, disagreeable, horrid, horrible, dreadful, abominable, atrocious, offensive, obnoxious, odious, unsavory, repulsive, disgusting, distasteful, loathsome, hateful, nauseating, sickening; disgraceful, appalling, shocking, sorry, shabby, shameful, dishonorable, execrable, heinous, abhorrent, deplorable, monstrous, wicked, evil, iniquitous, nefarious, depraved, debased; contemptible, despicable, reprehensible; *informal* gross, godawful, lowdown, lousy; *archaic* scurvy. See note at DEPRAVED. ANTONYM pleasant.

vilify verb *the press has eagerly vilified Smith and her attorneys* DISPARAGE, denigrate, defame, run down, revile, abuse, speak ill of, criticize, condemn, denounce; malign, slander, libel, slur; *informal* tear apart/into, lay into, slam, badmouth, dis, crucify; *formal* derogate, calumniate. See note at MALIGN. ANTONYM commend.

village noun *the village of Cooperstown* SMALL TOWN, hamlet; settlement, community; whistle-stop.

villain noun *my favorite Disney villain was Cruella* CRIMINAL, lawbreaker, offender, felon, convict, malefactor, wrongdoer; gangster, gunman, thief, robber; rogue, reprobate, ruffian, hoodlum; miscreant, scoundrel; *Law* malfeasant; *informal* crook, con, bad guy, baddy, lowlife; *dated* cad, knave; *archaic* blackguard.

villainous adjective *a taut thriller in which the hero makes a subtle shift from virtuous to villainous* WICKED, evil, iniquitous, sinful, nefarious, vile, foul, monstrous, outrageous, atrocious, abominable, reprehensible, hateful, odious, contemptible, horrible, heinous, egregious, diabolical, flagitious, fiendish, vicious, murderous; criminal, illicit, unlawful, illegal, lawless; immoral, corrupt, degenerate, sordid, depraved, dishonest, dishonorable, unscrupulous, unprincipled; *informal* crooked, bent, lowdown, dirty, shady; *dated* dastardly. ANTONYM virtuous.

vindicate verb **1** *he was vindicated by the jury* ACQUIT, clear, absolve, exonerate; discharge, liberate, free; *informal* let off, let off the hook; *formal* exculpate. See note at ABSOLVE.

2 *I had fully vindicated my contention* JUSTIFY, warrant, substantiate, ratify, authenticate, verify, confirm, corroborate, prove, defend, support, back up, bear out, evidence, endorse.

vindictive adjective *in her memoirs she revealed that Drake had been a vindictive ex-lover* VENGEFUL, revengeful, unforgiving, resentful, acrimonious, bitter; spiteful, mean, rancorous, venomous, malicious, malevolent, nasty, mean-spirited, cruel, unkind; *informal* catty. ANTONYM forgiving.

THE RIGHT WORD

Someone who is motivated by a desire to get even might be described as **vindictive**, a word that suggests harboring grudges for imagined wrongs (*a vindictive person who had alienated friends and neighbors alike*). **Spiteful** is a stronger term, implying a bitter or vicious vindictiveness (*a spiteful child who broke the toy she had been forced to share*). **Vengeful** implies a strong urge to actually seek vengeance (*vengeful after losing her husband in hit-and-run accident*). Someone who is **rancorous** suffers from a deep-seated and lasting bitterness, although it does not imply a desire to hurt or to be vindictive (*his rancorous nature made him difficult to befriend*). **Venomous** takes its meaning from "venom" referring to someone or something of a spiteful, malignant nature and suggesting a poisonous sting (*a critic's venomous attack on the author's first novel*).

vine noun *after years of neglect, the vines had choked the old pear tree* CLIMBING PLANT, trailing plant, trailer; creeper, climber, rambler.

vineyard noun *the vineyards of Napa Valley* VINERY, domaine, cru; winery, microwinery.

vintage noun **1** *1986 was a classic vintage for the Cabernet Sauvignon* YEAR.

2 *furniture of Louis XV vintage* PERIOD, era, epoch, time, origin; genre, style, kind, sort, type.

▸ adjective **1** *vintage French wine* HIGH-QUALITY, quality, choice, select, prime, superior, best.

2 *vintage automobiles* CLASSIC, ageless, timeless; old, antique, heritage, historic.

3 *his reaction was vintage Bush* CHARACTERISTIC, typical, pure, prime, trademark.

violate verb **1** *this violates fundamental human rights* CONTRAVENE, breach, infringe, break, transgress, overstep, disobey, defy, flout; disregard, ignore, trample on. ANTONYM comply with.

2 *they felt their privacy had been violated* INVADE, trespass upon, encroach upon, intrude upon; disrespect. ANTONYM respect.

3 *the tomb was violated* DESECRATE, profane, defile, degrade, debase; damage, vandalize, deface, destroy.

4 *he drugged and then violated her* RAPE, sexually assault, assault, force oneself on, abuse, attack, molest, interfere with; *archaic* defile, deflower, dishonor, ruin; *literary* ravish.

violence noun **1** *violence against women* BRUTALITY, brute force, ferocity, savagery, cruelty, sadism, barbarity, brutishness.

2 *the protest ended in violence* FIGHTING, fights, bloodshed, brawling, disorder, rioting, hostility, turbulence, mayhem.

3 *the violence of the blow* FORCEFULNESS, force, power, strength, might, savagery, ferocity, brutality.

4 *the violence of his passion* INTENSITY, severity, strength, force, vehemence, power, potency, fervency, ferocity, fury, fire.

violent adjective **1** *he gets violent when drunk* BRUTAL, vicious, savage, rough, aggressive, abusive, physically abusive, threatening, fierce, physical, wild, ferocious; barbarous, barbaric, thuggish, pugnacious, cutthroat, smash-mouth, homicidal, murderous, cruel. ANTONYM gentle.

2 *a violent blow* POWERFUL, forceful, hard, sharp, smart, strong, vigorous, mighty, hefty; savage, ferocious, brutal, vicious. ANTONYM weak.

3 *violent jealousy* INTENSE, extreme, strong, powerful, vehement, intemperate, unbridled, uncontrollable, ungovernable, inordinate, consuming, passionate. ANTONYM mild.

4 *a violent movie* GORY, gruesome, grisly, full of violence.

VIP noun *they treat all their guests like VIPs* CELEBRITY, famous person, very important person, personality, big name, star, superstar; dignitary, luminary, leading light, worthy, grandee, lion, notable, personage; *informal* heavyweight, celeb, bigwig, big shot, big cheese, honcho, top dog, megastar, big wheel, big kahuna, mucky-muck, high muckamuck.

virago noun *she unfairly labeled her sister-in-law a backstabbing virago* HARRIDAN, shrew, dragon, termagant, vixen; fishwife, witch, hellcat, she-devil, tartar, martinet, ogress; *informal* battle-ax; *archaic* scold.

virgin noun *she remained a virgin* chaste woman/man, celibate; *literary* maiden, maid, vestal, ingenue.

▸ adjective **1** *virgin forest* UNTOUCHED, unspoiled, untainted, immaculate, pristine, flawless; spotless, unsullied, unpolluted, undefiled, perfect; unchanged, intact; unexplored, uncharted, unmapped.

2 *virgin girls* CHASTE, virginal, celibate, abstinent; maiden, maidenly; pure, uncorrupted, undefiled, unsullied, innocent; *literary* vestal.

virginal adjective See VIRGIN adjective sense 2.

virginity noun *the sleazy tabloids speculated on the loss of her virginity* CHASTITY, maidenhood, maidenhead, honor, purity, innocence; celibacy, abstinence; *informal, dated* cherry; *archaic* virtue.

virile adjective *the strong, virile hero* MANLY, masculine, male; strong, tough, vigorous, robust, muscular, muscly, brawny, rugged, sturdy, lusty, husky; red-blooded, fertile; *informal* macho, butch, beefy, hunky. See note at MALE. ANTONYM effeminate.

virtual adjective **1** *a virtual guarantee* EFFECTIVE, in effect, near, near enough, essential, practical, to all intents and purposes.

2 *a virtual shopping environment* SIMULATED, artificial, imitation, make-believe; computer-generated, online, virtual reality.

virtually adverb *the building is virtually empty* EFFECTIVELY, in effect, all but, more or less, practically, almost, nearly, close to, verging on, just about, as good as, essentially, to all intents and purposes, roughly, approximately; *informal* pretty much, pretty well; *literary* well-nigh, nigh on.

virtue noun **1** *the simple virtue of farm life* GOODNESS, virtuousness, righteousness, morality, integrity, dignity, rectitude, honor, decency, respectability, nobility, worthiness, purity; principles, ethics. See note at GOODNESS. ANTONYMS vice, iniquity.

2 *promptness was not one of his virtues* STRONG POINT, good point, good quality, asset, forte, attribute, strength, talent, feature. ANTONYM failing.

3 *archaic she lost her virtue in the city.* See VIRGINITY.

4 *I can see no virtue in this* MERIT, advantage, benefit, usefulness, strength, efficacy, plus, point. ANTONYM disadvantage.

PHRASE: **by virtue of** *they hold the posts by virtue of family connections* BECAUSE OF, on account of, by dint of, by means of, by way of, via, through, as a result of, as a consequence of, on the strength of, owing to, thanks to, due to, by reason of.

virtuosity noun *the architect's virtuosity* SKILL, skillfulness, mastery, expertise, prowess, proficiency, ability, aptitude; excellence, brilliance, talent, genius, artistry, flair, panache, finesse, wizardry; *informal* know-how, chops.

virtuoso noun *the pianist is clearly a virtuoso* GENIUS, expert, master, past master, maestro, artist, prodigy, marvel, adept, professional, doyen, veteran; star, champion; *informal* hotshot, wizard, magician, pro, ace. ANTONYM beginner.

▸ adjective *a virtuoso violinist* SKILLFUL, expert, accomplished, masterly, master, consummate, proficient, talented, gifted, adept, good, capable; impressive, outstanding, exceptional, magnificent, supreme, first-rate, stellar, brilliant, excellent; *informal* superb, mean, ace. ANTONYM incompetent.

virtuous adjective *they were entirely virtuous in their endeavors* RIGHTEOUS, good, pure, whiter than white, saintly, angelic, moral, ethical, upright, upstanding, high-minded, principled, exemplary; law-abiding, irreproachable, blameless, guiltless, unimpeachable, immaculate, honest, honorable, reputable, laudable, decent, respectable, noble, worthy, meritorious; See note at MORAL. *informal* squeaky clean.

virulent adjective **1** *virulent herbicides* POISONOUS, toxic, venomous, noxious, deadly, lethal, fatal, dangerous, harmful, injurious, pernicious, damaging, destructive; *literary* deathly. ANTONYMS harmless, nontoxic.

2 *a virulent epidemic* INFECTIOUS, infective, contagious, communicable, transmittable, transmissible, spreading, pestilential; *informal* catching. ANTONYM noncontagious.

3 *a virulent attack on morals* VITRIOLIC, malicious, malevolent, hostile, spiteful, venomous, vicious, vindictive, bitter, sharp, rancorous, acrimonious, scathing, caustic, withering, nasty, savage, harsh. ANTONYMS benevolent, amicable.

virus noun **1** *the child caught a virus* DISEASE, bug, infection; *dated* contagion.

2 *a computer virus* WORM, Trojan Horse.

visage noun *a visage marked by years of depression* FACE, countenance, look, (facial) features, (facial) expression.

vis-à-vis preposition *we need to discuss our test results vis-à-vis the national standards* REGARDING, concerning, apropos to, toward, relating to, compared with, with respect to; *informal* re.

visceral adjective *a visceral fear of change* INSTINCTIVE, instinctual, gut, deep-down, deep-seated, deep-rooted, inward; emotional; animal.

viscosity noun *the viscosity of motor oil* THICKNESS, gooeyness, viscidity; consistency, texture.

viscous adjective *it's impossible to clean up this viscous substance with water* GLUTINOUS, gelatinous, thick, viscid, mucous, mucoid, mucilaginous, gummy, gluey, adhesive, tacky, adherent, treacly, syrupy; *technical* viscoelastic; *informal* gooey, gloppy.

visible adjective *there are no visible scratches* PERCEPTIBLE, perceivable, seeable, observable, noticeable, detectable, discernible; in sight, in/on view, on display; evident, apparent, manifest, transparent, plain, clear, conspicuous, front-and-center, obvious, patent, unmistakable, unconcealed, undisguised, prominent, salient, striking, glaring.

vision noun **1** *her vision was blurred by tears* EYESIGHT, sight, observation, (visual) perception; eyes; view, perspective.

2 *the psychic was troubled by visions of the dead* APPARITION, hallucination, illusion, mirage, specter, phantom, ghost, wraith, manifestation; *literary* phantasm, shade.

3 *visions of a better future* DREAM, daydream, reverie; plan, hope; fantasy, pipe dream, delusion.

4 *his speech lacked vision* IMAGINATION, creativity, inventiveness, innovation, inspiration, intuition, perception, insight, foresight, prescience.

5 *Melissa was a vision in lilac* BEAUTIFUL SIGHT, feast for the eyes, pleasure to behold, delight, dream, beauty, picture, joy, marvel; *informal* sight for sore eyes, stunner, knockout, looker, eye-catcher, peach.

visionary adjective **1** *a visionary person* INSPIRED, imaginative, creative, inventive, ingenious, enterprising, innovative; insightful, perceptive, intuitive, prescient, discerning, shrewd, wise, clever, resourceful; idealistic, romantic, quixotic, dreamy; *informal* starry-eyed.

2 *archaic a visionary image.* See IMAGINARY.

▸ noun *a visionary pictured him in hell* SEER, mystic, oracle, prophet/prophetess, soothsayer, augur, diviner, clairvoyant, crystal-gazer, medium; *literary* sibyl.

visit verb **1** *I visited my dear uncle* CALL ON, pay a visit to, go to see, look in on; stay with; stop by, drop by; *informal* go see; pop in on, drop in on, look up.

2 *she never visits* STOP BY, drop by, pay a visit, call; *informal* pop in, drop in.

3 *Alex was visiting the Yukon* STAY IN, stop over in, spend time in, vacation in; tour, explore, see.

▸ noun **1** *she paid a visit to her mom* CALL, social call, visitation.

2 *a **visit to** the museum* TRIP TO, tour of, look around; stopover at, stay at; vacation at; *formal* sojourn at.

visitation noun **1** *the bishop's visitations* VISIT, official, tour of inspection, survey, examination.

2 *a visitation from God* APPARITION, vision, appearance, manifestation, materialization.

3 *Jehovah punished them by visitations* AFFLICTION, scourge, bane, curse, plague, blight, disaster, tragedy, catastrophe; punishment, retribution, vengeance.

visitor noun **1** *I am expecting a visitor* GUEST, caller, house guest; company; *archaic* visitant.

2 *the monument attracts thousands of visitors each month* TOURIST, traveler, vacationer, day tripper, sightseer; pilgrim, habitué; foreigner, outsider, stranger, alien.

visor noun *a blue cap with a red visor* BRIM, peak, eyeshade; bill.

vista noun *a marvelous vista from the hotel balcony* VIEW, prospect, panorama, aspect, perspective, spectacle, sight, outlook; scenery, landscape.

visual adjective **1** *visual defects* OPTICAL, optic, ocular, eye; vision, sight.

2 *a visual indication that the alarm works* VISIBLE, perceptible, perceivable, discernible.

▸ noun *the speaker used excellent visuals* GRAPHIC, visual aid, image, illustration, diagram, display; show and tell.

visualize verb *Grampa's colorful tales made it easy to visualize his childhood adventures* ENVISAGE, envision, conjure up, picture, call to mind, see, imagine, evoke, dream up, fantasize about, conceptualize, contemplate, conceive of.

vital adjective **1** *it is vital that action be taken soon* ESSENTIAL, of the essence, critical, crucial, key, indispensable, integral, all-important, imperative, mandatory, requisite, urgent, pressing, burning, compelling, high-priority, life-and-death. ANTONYMS unimportant, peripheral.

2 *the vital organs* MAJOR, main, chief; essential, necessary. ANTONYMS minor, dispensable.

3 *he is young and vital* LIVELY, energetic, active, sprightly, spry, spirited, vivacious, exuberant, bouncy, enthusiastic, vibrant, zestful, sparkling, dynamic, virile, vigorous, lusty, hale and hearty; *informal* peppy, spunky, full of beans, bright-eyed and bushy-tailed. See note at ALIVE. ANTONYM listless.

vitality noun *the bright weather has revived my vitality* LIVELINESS, life, energy, spirit, vivacity, exuberance, buoyancy, bounce, élan, verve, vim, pep, brio, zest, sparkle, dynamism, passion, fire, vigor, drive, punch; getup-and-go.

vitriolic adjective *a vitriolic attack on the government* ACRIMONIOUS, rancorous, bitter, caustic, mordant, acerbic, trenchant, virulent, spiteful, savage, venomous, poisonous, malicious, splenetic; nasty, mean, cruel, unkind, harsh, hostile, vindictive, vicious, scathing, barbed, wounding, sharp, cutting, withering, sarcastic; *informal* bitchy, catty.

vituperation noun *in public he hid well the vituperation he dispensed at home* INVECTIVE, condemnation, opprobrium, scolding, criticism, disapprobation, fault-finding; blame, abuse, insults, vilification, denunciation, obloquy, denigration, disparagement, slander, libel, defamation, slurs, aspersions; vitriol, venom; *informal* flak; *formal* castigation. See note at SCOLD. ANTONYM praise.

vivacious adjective *their vivacious daughter had become moody and morose* LIVELY, spirited, bubbly, ebullient, buoyant, sparkling, lighthearted, jaunty, merry, happy, jolly, full of fun, cheery, cheerful, perky, sunny, breezy, enthusiastic, irrepressible, vibrant, vital, zestful, energetic, effervescent, dynamic; *informal* peppy, bouncy, upbeat, chirpy. ANTONYM dull.

vivid adjective **1** *a vivid blue sea* BRIGHT, colorful, brilliant, radiant, vibrant, glaring, strong, bold, deep, intense, rich, warm. ANTONYM dull.

2 *a vivid account of urban poverty* GRAPHIC, evocative, realistic, lifelike, faithful, authentic, clear, detailed, lucid, eloquent, striking, arresting, impressive, colorful, rich, dramatic, lively, stimulating, interesting, fascinating, scintillating; memorable, powerful, stirring, moving, telling, haunting. See note at GRAPHIC. ANTONYM vague.

viz. adverb *article one sets out its purpose, viz. to ensure the continuation of farming* NAMELY, that is to say, in other words, to wit, specifically, i.e.; *formal* videlicet.

vocabulary noun **1** *technical vocabulary* LANGUAGE, lexicon, lexis, words; diction, terminology, phraseology, nomenclature, terms, expressions, parlance, idiom, jargon, vernacular, argot, cant; *informal* vocab, lingo, -speak, -ese.

2 *she is improving her vocabulary* WORD POWER, lexicon, command of language; *informal* vocab.

vocal adjective **1** *vocal sounds* VOCALIZED, voiced, uttered, articulated, oral; spoken, viva voce, said.

2 *a vocal critic of the government* VOCIFEROUS, outspoken, forthright, plain-spoken, expressive, blunt, frank, candid, open; vehement, strident, vigorous, emphatic, insistent, forceful, zealous, clamorous, loudmouthed.

▸ **(vocals)** plural noun *we'll record the vocals later* VOICES, singing; harmonies.

vocal cords plural noun VOICE BOX, vocal folds, larynx; *informal* pipes.

vocalist noun *the featured vocalist in their choir* SINGER, songster; diva, songbird, prima donna, chanteuse, chansonnier; melodist.

vocation noun *forestry is my vocation* CALLING, life's

work, mission, purpose, function; profession, occupation, career, job, employment, trade, craft, business, line, line of work, métier.

vociferous adjective See VOCAL sense 2.

THE RIGHT WORD

An angry crowd might be **vociferous**, which implies loud and unrestrained shouting or crying out (*a vociferous argument*). A happy crowd might be **boisterous**, which implies noisy exuberance or high-spirited rowdiness (*a boisterous celebration of spring*). A crowd that wants something is likely to be **clamorous**, which suggests an urgent or insistent vociferousness in demanding or protesting something. If people's demands are not met, they might become **obstreperous**, which means noisy in an unruly and aggressive way, usually in defiance of authority (*an obstreperous child*). **Strident** suggests a harsh, grating loudness that is particularly distressing to the ear (*her strident voice could be heard throughout the building*).

vogue noun *retro accessories are enjoying a new vogue* FASHION, trend, fad, craze, rage, enthusiasm, passion, obsession, mania; fashionableness, popularity, currency, favor; *informal* trendiness. PHRASE: **in vogue** *denim's been in vogue my whole lifetime* FASHIONABLE, voguish, stylish, modish, up-to-date, up-to-the-minute, du jour, modern, current; prevalent, popular, in favor, in demand, sought-after, all the rage; chic, chi-chi, smart, tony, kicky, le dernier cri; trendy, hip, cool, big, happening, now, in, with it.

voice noun **1** *she lost her voice* POWER OF SPEECH.

2 *he gave voice to his anger* EXPRESSION, utterance, verbalization, vocalization.

3 *we speak with one voice* OPINION, view, feeling, wish, desire, will; (**voice of the people**) vox populi; *informal* vox pop.

4 *citizens must have a voice in this* SAY, influence, vote, input, role, representation, seat at the table.

5 *a powerful voice for conservation* SPOKESPERSON, speaker, champion, representative, mouthpiece, intermediary; forum, vehicle, instrument, channel, organ, agent.

▸ verb *they voiced their opposition* EXPRESS, vocalize, communicate, articulate, declare, state, assert, reveal, proclaim, announce, publish, publicize, make public, make known, table, air, vent; utter, say, speak; *informal* come out with.

void noun *the void of space* VACUUM, emptiness, nothingness, nullity, blankness, vacuity; empty space, blank space, space, gap, cavity, chasm, abyss, gulf, pit, black hole.

▸ verb *the contract was voided* INVALIDATE, annul, nullify; negate, quash, cancel, countermand, repeal, revoke, rescind, retract, withdraw, reverse, undo, abolish; *Law* vacate; *formal* abrogate. ANTONYM validate.

▸ adjective **1** *vast void spaces* EMPTY, vacant, blank, bare, clear, free, unfilled, unoccupied, uninhabited. ANTONYM full.

2 *a country **void of** man or beast* DEVOID OF, empty of, vacant of, bereft of, free from; lacking, wanting, without, with nary a. ANTONYM occupied.

3 *the election was void* INVALID, null, ineffective, nonviable, useless, worthless, nugatory. ANTONYM valid.

THE RIGHT WORD

To **void** a check, to **invalidate** a claim, to **abrogate** a law, and to **annul** a marriage all refer to the same basic activity, which is putting an end to something or depriving it of validity, force, or authority. But these verbs are not always interchangeable. *Annul* is the most general term, meaning to end something that exists or to declare that it never really existed (*the charter was annulled before it could be challenged*). *Abrogate* implies the exercise of legal authority (*Congress abrogated the treaty between the two warring factions*), while **nullify** means to deprive something of its value or effectiveness (*nullify the enemy's attempt to establish communications*). *Void* and *invalidate* are often used interchangeably as they both mean to make null or worthless (*void a legal document by tearing it up; invalidate a check by putting the wrong date on it*). **Negate** means to prove an assertion false (*her version of the story negated everything her brother had said*) or to nullify or make something ineffective (*the study's findings were negated by its author's arrest for fraud*).

voilà exclamation *all you do is add a new drawer pull and—voilà!—a whole new look to the nightstand* ta-da, presto, look; here you are, here you go.

volatile adjective **1** *a volatile personality* UNPREDICTABLE, changeable, variable, inconstant, inconsistent, erratic, irregular, unstable, turbulent, blowing hot and cold, varying, shifting, fluctuating, fluid, mutable; mercurial, capricious, whimsical, fickle, flighty, impulsive, temperamental, high-strung, excitable, emotional, fiery, moody, tempestuous. ANTONYMS stable, constant.

2 *the atmosphere is too volatile for an election* TENSE, strained, fraught, uneasy, uncomfortable, charged, explosive, inflammatory, turbulent; *informal* nail-biting, ready to blow. ANTONYMS stable, calm.

3 *a volatile organic compound* EVAPORATIVE, vaporous; explosive, inflammable; unstable, labile. ANTONYM stable.

volition PHRASE: **of one's own volition** *I joined the army of my own volition* OF ONE'S OWN FREE WILL, of one's own accord, by choice, by preference; voluntarily, willingly, readily, freely, intentionally, consciously, deliberately, on purpose, purposely; gladly, with pleasure.

volley noun *a volley of rifle shots* BARRAGE, cannonade, battery, bombardment, salvo, discharge, fusillade; storm, hail, shower, deluge, torrent; *historical* broadside.

volte-face noun See ABOUT-FACE.

voluble adjective *she was as voluble as her husband was silent* TALKATIVE, loquacious, garrulous, verbose, wordy, chatty, gossipy, effusive, gushing, forthcoming, conversational, communicative, expansive; articulate, fluent; *informal* mouthy, motormouthed, gabby, gassy, windy, talky. See note at TALKATIVE. ANTONYM taciturn.

volume noun **1** *a volume from the library* BOOK, publication, tome, hardback, paperback, title; manual, almanac, compendium.

2 *a glass syringe of known volume* CAPACITY, cubic measure, size, magnitude, mass, bulk, extent; dimensions, proportions, measurements.

3 *a huge volume of water* QUANTITY, amount, proportion, measure, mass, bulk.

4 *she turned the volume down* LOUDNESS, sound, amplification; *informal* decibels.

voluminous adjective *the clown's voluminous trousers*

CAPACIOUS, roomy, spacious, ample, full, big, large, bulky, extensive, sizable, generous; billowing, baggy, loose-fitting; *formal* commodious.

voluntarily adverb *they agreed to leave the country voluntarily* FREELY, of one's own free will, of one's own accord, of one's own volition, by choice, by preference; willingly, readily, intentionally, deliberately, on purpose, purposely, spontaneously; gladly, with pleasure.

voluntary adjective **1** *attendance is voluntary* OPTIONAL, discretionary, elective, noncompulsory, volitional; *Law* permissive. ANTONYMS compulsory, obligatory.

2 *voluntary work* UNPAID, unsalaried, unwaged, for free, without charge, for nothing; honorary, volunteer; *Law* pro bono (publico). ANTONYM paid.

volunteer verb **1** *I volunteered my services* OFFER, tender, proffer, put forward, put up, venture.

2 *he volunteered as a driver* OFFER ONE'S SERVICES, present oneself, make oneself available, sign up.

▸ noun *each volunteer was tested three times* SUBJECT, participant, case, patient; *informal* guinea pig.

voluptuous adjective **1** *a voluptuous model* CURVACEOUS, shapely, ample, buxom, full-figured; seductive, alluring, comely, sultry, sensuous, sexy, womanly; Junoesque, Rubenesque; *informal* bodacious, curvy, busty, stacked, built, slinky. See note at SENSUOUS. ANTONYM scrawny.

2 *she was voluptuous by nature* HEDONISTIC, sybaritic, epicurean, pleasure-loving, self-indulgent; decadent, intemperate, immoderate, dissolute, sensual, licentious. ANTONYM ascetic.

vomit verb **1** *he needed to vomit* BE SICK, spew, heave, retch, gag, get sick; *informal* throw up, puke, purge, hurl, barf, upchuck, ralph.

2 *I vomited my breakfast* REGURGITATE, bring up, spew up, cough up, lose; *informal* throw up, puke, spit up.

▸ noun *a coat stained with vomit* VOMITUS; *informal* puke, spew, barf.

voodoo noun *the elders still practice voodoo* WITCHCRAFT, magic, black magic, sorcery, wizardry, dark arts, devilry, hoodoo, necromancy, mojo.

voracious adjective *her voracious appetite* INSATIABLE, unquenchable, unappeasable, prodigious, uncontrollable, compulsive, gluttonous, greedy, rapacious; enthusiastic, eager, keen, avid, desirous, hungry, ravenous; *informal* piggish; *rare* esurient.

vortex noun *a whirling vortex of smoke* WHIRLWIND, cyclone, whirlpool, gyre, maelstrom, eddy, swirl, spiral; black hole.

vote noun **1** *a rigged vote* BALLOT, poll, election, referendum, plebiscite; show of hands.

2 *women finally got the vote* SUFFRAGE, voting rights, franchise, enfranchisement; voice, say.

▸ verb **1** *only half of them voted* GO TO THE POLLS, cast one's vote, cast one's ballot.

2 *he was **voted in** as secretary* ELECT, return, select, choose, pick, adopt, appoint, designate, opt for, decide on.

3 *I vote we have one more game* SUGGEST, propose, recommend, advocate, move, submit.

vouch PHRASE: **vouch for** *I can vouch for his honesty* ATTEST TO, confirm, affirm, verify, swear to, testify to, bear out, back up, support, stick up for, go to bat for, corroborate, substantiate, prove, uphold, sponsor, give credence to, endorse, certify, warrant, validate.

voucher noun *present your voucher to the attendant at the front door* COUPON, token, ticket, license, permit, pass; chit, slip, stub; *informal* ducat, comp.

vow noun *a vow of silence* OATH, pledge, promise, bond, covenant, commitment, avowal, profession, affirmation, attestation, assurance, guarantee; word, word of honor; *formal* troth.

▸ verb *I vowed to do better* SWEAR, pledge, promise, avow, undertake, engage, make a commitment, give one's word, guarantee; *archaic* plight.

voyage noun *the voyage lasted 120 days* JOURNEY, trip, expedition, excursion, tour; hike, trek, travels; pilgrimage, quest, crusade, odyssey; cruise, passage, flight, drive, road trip. See note at JOURNEY.

▸ verb *he voyaged through Peru* TRAVEL, journey, tour, globe-trot; sail, steam, cruise, fly, drive; *informal* gallivant; *archaic* peregrinate.

voyeur noun *the neighbors accused him of being a voyeur* PEEPING TOM, pervert, watcher; *informal* perv.

vulgar adjective **1** *a vulgar joke* RUDE, indecent, indelicate, offensive, distasteful, coarse, crude, ribald, risqué, naughty, suggestive, racy, earthy, off-color, bawdy, obscene, profane, lewd, salacious, smutty, dirty, filthy, pornographic, X-rated; *informal* sleazy, raunchy, blue, locker-room; saucy, salty; *euphemistic* adult. ANTONYMS decent, inoffensive.

2 *the decor was lavish but vulgar* TASTELESS, crass, tawdry, ostentatious, flamboyant, overdone, showy, gaudy, garish, brassy, kitsch, kitschy, tinselly, loud; *informal* flash, flashy, tacky. ANTONYMS tasteful, restrained.

3 *it is vulgar to belch in public* IMPOLITE, ill-mannered, unmannerly, rude, indecorous, unseemly, ill-bred, boorish, uncouth, crude, rough; unsophisticated, unrefined, common, low-minded; unladylike, ungentlemanly. ANTONYMS genteel, decorous.

vulture noun *these ambulance chasers are vultures* PREDATOR, shark, vampire, bloodsucker, profiteer, racketeer, opportunist, extortionist.

W

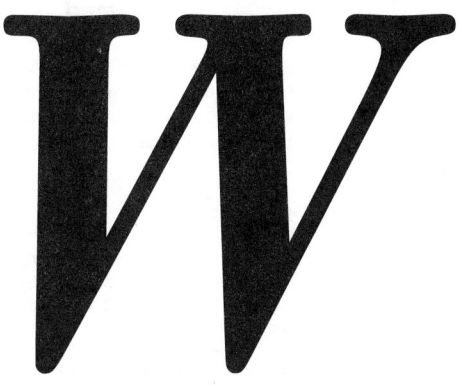

wacky adjective *informal* See ECCENTRIC adjective.

wad noun **1** *a wad of cotton* LUMP, clump, mass, pad, swab, hunk, wedge, ball, cake, nugget; bit, piece, plug.

2 *a wad of $20 bills* BUNDLE, roll, pile, stack, sheaf, bankroll.

3 *a wad of tobacco* QUID, twist, plug, chew, chaw.

▸ verb *he wadded up his napkin* CRUMPLE, stuff, press, gather, pack, wrap.

wadding noun *the wadding in the quilt is all lumpy* STUFFING, filling, filler, packing, padding, cushioning, quilting; (cotton) batting, (cotton) batten.

waddle verb *after seven weeks in a hospital bed, it's normal to waddle a bit* TODDLE, dodder, totter, wobble, shuffle; duckwalk.

wade verb **1** *they waded in the icy water* PADDLE, wallow, dabble; *informal* splosh.

2 *I had to wade through some hefty documents* PLOW, plod, trawl, labor, toil; study, browse; *informal* splash, slog.

waffle verb *faced with this commitment, she waffled* WAVER, vacillate, equivocate, sit on the fence.

waft verb **1** *smoke wafted through the air* DRIFT, float, glide, whirl, travel.

2 *a breeze wafted the smell toward us* CONVEY, carry, transport, bear; blow, puff.

wag[1] verb **1** *the dog's tail wagged frantically* SWING, swish, switch, sway, shake, quiver, twitch, whip, bob; *informal* waggle.

2 *he wagged his stick at them* SHAKE, wave, wiggle, waggle, flourish, brandish.

wag[2] noun *he's a bit of a wag.* See JOKER.

wage noun **1** (usu. **wages**) *the farm workers' wages a fair wage* PAY, payment, remuneration, salary, stipend, fee, honorarium; income, revenue; profit, gain, reward; earnings, paycheck; *Brit.* pay packet; *formal* emolument.

2 (**wages**) *the wages of sin is death* REWARD, recompense, retribution; returns, deserts.

▸ verb *they waged war on the guerrillas* ENGAGE IN, carry on, conduct, execute, pursue, prosecute, proceed with.

wager noun *a wager of $100* BET, gamble, speculation; stake, pledge, ante.

▸ verb *I'll wager ten bucks on the home team* BET, gamble, lay odds, put money on; stake, pledge, risk, venture, hazard, chance.

waggle verb *informal* See WAG[1] verb senses 1, 2.

wagon noun See table at CARRIAGE.

waif noun *a homeless waif* RAGAMUFFIN, urchin; foundling, orphan, stray; *derogatory* guttersnipe; *dated* gamin.

wail noun *a wail of anguish* HOWL, bawl, yowl, cry, moan, groan; shriek, scream, holler, yelp.

▸ verb *the children began to wail* HOWL, weep, cry, sob, moan, groan, keen, lament, yowl, snivel, whimper, whine, bawl, shriek, scream, yelp, caterwaul; *informal* blubber.

waist noun *tie a pink sash around the waist* MIDDLE, midriff, abdomen, waistline.

wait verb **1** *Jill waited while Jack fetched the water* STAY (PUT), remain, rest, stop, halt, pause; linger, loiter, dally; *informal* stick around, hang out, hang around, kill time, waste time, kick one's heels, twiddle one's thumbs; *archaic* tarry.

2 *Joey waited until she nodded* HOLD ON, hold back, bide one's time, hang fire, mark time, stand by, sit tight, hold one's horses.

3 *they were waiting for the kettle to boil* AWAIT; anticipate, look forward, long, pine, yearn, expect, be ready.

4 *the movie will have to wait* BE POSTPONED, be delayed, be put off, be deferred; *informal* be put on the back burner, be put on ice.

▸ noun *a long wait* DELAY, holdup, interval, interlude, intermission, pause, break, stay, cessation, suspension, stoppage, halt, interruption, lull, respite, recess, moratorium, hiatus, gap, rest.

PHRASES: **wait on** *he waits on her as if he were a paid servant* SERVE, attend to, tend (to), cater for/to; minister to, take care of, look after, see to. **wait up 1** *she waited up for him every night* STAY AWAKE, stay up, keep vigil. **2** *hey, wait up!* STOP, slow down, hold on, wait for me.

waiter, waitress noun *ask the waiter for some butter* SERVER, stewardess, steward, attendant, garçon, waitperson; busboy; hostess, host, maître d'; butler, servant, page; carhop; wait staff.

waive verb **1** *he waived his right to a hearing* RELINQUISH, renounce, give up, abandon, surrender, cede, sign away, yield, reject, dispense with, abdicate, sacrifice, refuse, turn down, spurn. See note at RELINQUISH.

2 *the manager waived the rules* DISREGARD, ignore, overlook, set aside, forgo, drop.

wake[1] verb **1** *at 4:30 am Mark woke up* AWAKE, waken, awaken, rouse oneself, stir, come to, come round, bestir oneself; get up, get out of bed; *formal* arise. ANTONYM sleep.

2 *she woke her husband* ROUSE, arouse, waken.

3 *a shock woke him up a bit* ACTIVATE, stimulate, galvanize, enliven, animate, stir up, spur on, buoy, invigorate, revitalize; *informal* perk up, pep up.

4 *they **woke up to** what we were saying* REALIZE, become aware of, become conscious of, become mindful of, clue in to.

5 *the name woke an old memory* EVOKE, conjure up, rouse, stir, revive, awaken, rekindle, rejuvenate, stimulate. ANTONYM suppress.

▸ noun *a mourner at a wake* VIGIL, watch; funeral.

wake[2] noun *the cruiser's wake* BACKWASH, wash, slipstream, trail, path. PHRASE: **in the wake of** IN THE AFTERMATH OF, after, subsequent to, following, as a result of, as a consequence of, on account of, because of, owing to.

wakeful adjective **1** *he had been wakeful all night* AWAKE, restless, restive, tossing and turning. ANTONYM asleep.

2 *I was suddenly wakeful* ALERT, watchful, vigilant, on the lookout, on one's guard, attentive, heedful, wary. ANTONYM inattentive.

waken verb See WAKE[1] verb senses 1, 2.

walk verb **1** *they walked along the road* STROLL, saunter, amble, trudge, plod, dawdle, hike, tramp, tromp, slog, stomp, trek, march, stride, sashay, glide, troop, patrol, wander, ramble, tread, prowl, promenade, roam, traipse; stretch one's legs; *informal* mosey, hoof it; *formal* perambulate.

2 *he walked her home* ACCOMPANY, escort, guide, show, see, usher, take, chaperone, steer, shepherd.

▸ noun **1** *their country walks* STROLL, saunter, amble, promenade; ramble, hike, tramp, march; turn; *dated* constitutional.

2 *the map shows several nature walks.* See TRAIL noun sense 5.

3 *he shoveled the front walk* PATH, pathway, walkway, sidewalk.

4 *her elegant walk* GAIT, step, stride, tread.

PHRASES: **walk all over** *informal* **1** *be firm or he'll walk all over you* TAKE ADVANTAGE OF, impose on, exploit, use, abuse, misuse, manipulate, take liberties with; *informal* take for a ride, run rings around. **2** *we walked all over the home team.* See TROUNCE. **walk off/away with 1** *informal she walked off with my wallet.* See STEAL verb sense 1. **2** *he walked off with four awards* WIN EASILY, win hands down, attain, earn, gain, garner, receive, acquire, secure, collect, pick up, net; *informal* bag. **walk of life** *we come from different walks of life* CLASS, status, rank, caste, sphere, arena; profession, career, vocation, job, occupation, employment, business, trade, craft; province, field. **walk out 1** *he walked out in a temper* LEAVE, depart, get up and go, storm off/out, flounce out, absent oneself; *informal* take off. **2** *teachers walked out in protest* (GO ON) STRIKE, stop work; protest, mutiny, revolt. **walk out on** *did you hear that Sierra walked out on Curt?* DESERT, abandon, leave, betray, throw over, jilt, run out on; *informal* dump, ditch.

WORD NOTE traipse

No other synonym for *walk* conveys a value judgment. *Amble, stroll, saunter, mosey* all refer, more or less neutrally, to velocity (or, in a stretch, rhythm). Only *traipse* is morally loaded: it hints at disapproval, even contempt for the ambler's lazy, aimless ways. Superficially innocent words that let you get in a dig below the radar should be treasured. **—DA**

walker noun *a vigorous walker* HIKER, rambler, traveler, roamer, rover, pedestrian; *literary* wayfarer.

walkout noun *workers staged a walkout at 10:45 this morning* STRIKE, stoppage, industrial action, job action, revolt, rebellion.

walkover noun *after yesterday's walkover, today's tight game was especially exciting* EASY VICTORY, rout, landslide; *informal* piece of cake, pushover, cinch, breeze, picnic, laugher, whitewash; *informal* duck soup.

wall noun **1** *brick walls* BARRIER, partition, enclosure, screen, panel, divider; bulkhead.

2 *an ancient city wall* FORTIFICATION, rampart, barricade, bulwark, stockade.

3 *break down the walls that stop world trade* OBSTACLE, barrier, fence; impediment, hindrance, block, roadblock, check.

▸ verb **1** *tenements **walled in** the courtyard* ENCLOSE, bound, encircle, confine, hem, close in, shut in, fence in.

2 *the doorway had been **walled up*** BLOCK, seal, close, brick up.

PHRASES: **go to the wall for** *informal I never asked you to go the wall for me* RISK EVERYTHING FOR, do anything for, put one's life on the line for. **off the wall** *informal his outfits are really off the wall.* See UNCONVENTIONAL.

wallet noun *I've got maybe two or three dollars in my wallet* PURSE, change purse; billfold, pocketbook, fanny pack.

wallop verb *informal*. See THUMP verb sense 1.

wallow verb **1** *pigs wallow in the mud* LOLL ABOUT/AROUND, roll about/around, lie about/around, splash about/around; slosh, wade, paddle; *informal* splosh.

2 *a ship wallowing in stormy seas* ROLL, lurch, toss, plunge, pitch, reel, rock, flounder, keel, list; labor.

3 *she seems to wallow in self-pity* LUXURIATE, bask, take pleasure, take satisfaction, indulge (oneself), delight, revel, glory; enjoy, like, love, relish, savor; *informal* get a kick out of, get off on.

wan adjective **1** *she looked so wan and frail* PALE, pallid, ashen, white, gray; anemic, colorless, bloodless, waxen, chalky, pasty, peaked, sickly, washed out, drained, drawn, ghostly. See note at PALE[2]. ANTONYM flushed.

2 *the wan light of the moon* DIM, faint, weak, feeble, pale, watery, washy. ANTONYM bright.

wand noun *the magician's wand* BATON, stick, staff, bar, dowel, rod; twig, cane, birch, switch; *historical* caduceus.

wander verb 1 *I wandered around the mansion* STROLL, amble, saunter, walk, dawdle, potter, ramble, meander; roam, rove, range, drift, prowl; *informal* traipse, mosey, tootle, mooch.

2 *we are wandering from the point* STRAY, depart, diverge, veer, swerve, deviate, digress, drift, get sidetracked.

wanderer noun *a wanderer in the wilderness* TRAVELER, rambler, hiker, migrant, globetrotter, roamer, rover; itinerant, rolling stone, nomad; tramp, transient, drifter, vagabond, vagrant; *informal* hobo, bum; *literary* wayfarer.

wane verb *time-lapse photography shows the moon waning* DECLINE, diminish, decrease, dwindle, shrink, tail off, ebb, fade (away), lessen, peter out, fall off, recede, slump, flag, weaken, give way, wither, crumble, evaporate, disintegrate, die out; *literary* evanesce. ANTONYMS wax, grow.

wangle verb *informal*. See CONTRIVE.

want verb 1 *do you want more coffee?* DESIRE, wish for, hope for, aspire to, fancy, care for, like; long for, yearn for, crave, hanker after, hunger for, thirst for, cry out for, covet; need; *informal* have a yen for, have a jones for, be dying for.

2 *informal* *you **want to** be more careful* SHOULD, ought to, need to, must.

3 *this mollycoddled generation **wants for** nothing* LACK, be without, have need of, be devoid of, be bereft of, be missing. See note at LACK.

▸ noun 1 *his want of vigilance* LACK, absence, nonexistence, unavailability; dearth, deficiency, inadequacy, insufficiency, paucity, shortage, scarcity, deficit.

2 *a time of want* NEED, neediness, austerity, privation, deprivation, poverty, impoverishment, penury, destitution; famine, drought.

3 *all her wants would be taken care of* WISH, desire, demand, longing, yearning, fancy, craving, hankering; need, requirement; *informal* yen.

wanting adjective 1 *the defenses were found wanting* DEFICIENT, inadequate, lacking, insufficient, imperfect, unacceptable, unsatisfactory, flawed, faulty, defective, unsound, substandard, inferior, second-rate, poor, shoddy. ANTONYM sufficient.

2 *millions were left* wanting *for food* WITHOUT, lacking, deprived of, devoid of, bereft of, in need of, out of; deficient in, short on; *informal* minus.

wanton adjective 1 *wanton destruction* DELIBERATE, willful, malicious, spiteful, wicked, cruel; gratuitous, unprovoked, motiveless, arbitrary, groundless, unjustifiable, needless, unnecessary, uncalled for, senseless, pointless, purposeless, meaningless, empty, random; capricious. ANTONYM justifiable.

2 *a wanton seductress* PROMISCUOUS, immoral, immodest, indecent, shameless, unchaste, fast, loose, impure, abandoned, lustful, lecherous, lascivious, libidinous, licentious, dissolute, debauched, degenerate, corrupt, whorish, disreputable. ANTONYM chaste.

war noun 1 *the Napoleonic wars* CONFLICT, warfare, combat, fighting, (military) action, bloodshed, struggle; battle, skirmish, fight, clash, engagement, encounter; offensive, attack, campaign; hostilities; jihad, crusade. ANTONYM peace.

2 *the war against drugs* CAMPAIGN, crusade, battle, fight, struggle, movement, drive.

▸ verb *rival empires **warred against** each other* FIGHT (AGAINST), battle (against), combat (against), wage war against, take up arms against; feud with, quarrel with, struggle with/against, contend with, wrangle with, cross swords with; attack, engage (against), take on, skirmish with.

warble verb *larks warbled in the sky* TRILL, sing, chirp, chirrup, cheep, twitter, tweet, chatter, peep, call.

ward noun 1 *the surgical ward* ROOM, department, unit, area, wing.

2 *the majority of voters in our ward are Democrats* DISTRICT, constituency, division, quarter, zone, parish.

3 *the boy is my ward* DEPENDENT, charge, protégé. PHRASE: **ward off** 1 *we use this lotion to ward off gnats* FEND OFF, repel, repulse, beat back, chase away; *informal* send packing. 2 *she warded off the blow* PARRY, avert, deflect, block; evade, avoid, dodge. 3 *garlic is worn to ward off evil spirits* REBUFF, avert, keep at bay, fend off, stave off, turn away, repel, resist, prevent, obstruct, foil, frustrate, thwart, check, stop.

warden noun 1 *a park warden* RANGER; custodian, keeper, guardian, protector; superintendent, caretaker, supervisor.

2 *his behavior was reported to the warden* GOVERNOR, executive, president, official; jailer, keeper; *informal* screw.

wardrobe noun 1 *she bought new shirts to expand his wardrobe* COLLECTION OF CLOTHES; garments, attire, outfits; trousseau.

2 *chiefly Brit.* *she opened the wardrobe* (CLOTHES) CLOSET, armoire, locker, cupboard, cabinet.

warehouse noun *twelve DVD players were stolen from the warehouse* DEPOT, distribution center, storehouse, store, storeroom, depository, storage, entrepôt, stockroom; granary; *Military* magazine.

wares plural noun *on Saturdays, the weaver would come into town with his wares* MERCHANDISE, goods, products, produce, stock, commodities; lines, range; *informal* stuff.

warfare noun *neither side seems ready to end this warfare* FIGHTING, war, combat, conflict, (military) action, hostilities; bloodshed, battles, skirmishes.

warlike adjective *warlike leaders* AGGRESSIVE, belligerent, warring, bellicose, pugnacious, combative, bloodthirsty, jingoistic, hostile, threatening, quarrelsome; militaristic, militant, warmongering.

warlock noun *Samantha's father, the warlock Maurice* SORCERER, wizard, magus, (black) magician, enchanter; *archaic* mage.

warm adjective 1 *a warm kitchen* HOT, cozy, snug; *informal* toasty. ANTONYMS cold, cool.

2 *a warm day in spring* BALMY, summery, sultry, hot, mild, temperate; sunny, fine. ANTONYMS cold, chilly.

3 *warm water* HEATED, tepid, lukewarm. ANTONYMS cold, chilled.

4 *a warm sweater* THICK, thermal, winter, woolly, fleecy, chunky. ANTONYMS light, summery.

5 *a warm welcome* FRIENDLY, cordial, amiable, genial, kind, pleasant, fond; welcoming, hospitable, benevolent,

benign, charitable; sincere, genuine, wholehearted, heartfelt, enthusiastic, eager, hearty. ANTONYMS unfriendly, hostile.

▸ verb *warm the soup in that pan* HEAT (UP), reheat, cook; thaw (out), melt, warm up, microwave; *informal* zap, nuke. ANTONYM chill.

PHRASES: **warm to 1** *everyone warmed to him* LIKE, take to, get on (well) with, hit it off with, be on good terms with. **2** *he couldn't warm to the notion* BE ENTHUSIASTIC ABOUT, be supportive of, be excited about, get into. **warm up 1** *I run in place a bit just to warm up* LIMBER UP, loosen up, stretch, work out, exercise; prepare, rehearse. **2** *the emcee warmed up the crowd* ENLIVEN, liven, stimulate, animate, rouse, stir, excite; *informal* get going.

WORD NOTE warm

In music, *warm* refers to sound rich in mid-range tones, or pleasantly distorted. In spoken language, open vowels are synesthetically cooling and thinner vowels warming, for both speaker and auditor. I have a theory: Music from hot climates sounds cooling—'ooo' sounds, often metallic, like steel drums, marimba, thumb piano, pedal steel guitar—and music from cold climates warms you up with hotter 'zzz' timbres, often from wooden instruments, like distorted electric guitar, hurdy-gurdy, and bowed strings. The 'zzz' sounds are made by continuous friction, which heats the instrument and requires more exertion form the performer (producing heat). Even analog circuits heat up and produce correspondingly warm sounds valued by musicians and listeners. **—SM**

warm-blooded adjective **1** *mammals are warm-blooded* HOMEOTHERMIC, homeothermal. ANTONYM poikilothermic.

2 *a warm-blooded woman* PASSIONATE, ardent, red-blooded, emotional, intense, impetuous, lively, lusty, spirited, fiery, tempestuous. ANTONYM reserved.

warm-hearted adjective *the boundless comfort of her warmhearted embrace* KIND, warm, big-hearted, tender-hearted, tender, loving, caring, feeling, unselfish, selfless, benevolent, humane, good-natured; friendly, sympathetic, understanding, compassionate, charitable, generous.

warmonger noun *the president's critics were quick to label him a warmonger* MILITARIST, hawk, jingoist, aggressor, belligerent.

warmth noun **1** *the warmth of the fire* HEAT, warmness, hotness, fieriness; coziness.

2 *the warmth of their welcome* FRIENDLINESS, amiability, geniality, cordiality, kindness, tenderness, fondness; benevolence, charity; enthusiasm, eagerness, ardor, fervor, energy, effusiveness.

warn verb **1** *David warned her about the cat* NOTIFY, alert, apprise, inform, tell, make someone aware, forewarn, remind, give notice; *informal* tip off.

2 *police are warning galleries to be alert* ADVISE, exhort, urge, counsel, caution.

warning noun **1** *the earthquake came without warning* (ADVANCE) NOTICE, forewarning, alert; hint, signal, sign, alarm bells; *informal* tip-off, heads-up, red flag.

2 *a health warning* CAUTION, advisory, notification, information; exhortation, injunction; advice.

3 *a warning of things to come* OMEN, premonition, foreboding, prophecy, prediction, forecast, token, portent, signal, sign; *literary* foretoken.

4 *his sentence is a warning to other drunk drivers* EXAMPLE, deterrent, lesson, caution, exemplar, message, moral.

5 *a written warning* ADMONITION, remonstrance, reprimand, censure, caution; *informal* dressing-down, talking-to.

warp verb **1** *lumber that is too dry will warp* BUCKLE, twist, bend, distort, deform, misshape, skew, curve, bow, contort. ANTONYM straighten.

2 *he warped the mind of her child* CORRUPT, twist, pervert, deprave, lead astray.

warrant noun **1** *a warrant for his arrest* AUTHORIZATION, order, license, permit, document; writ, summons, subpoena; mandate, decree, fiat, edict.

2 *a travel warrant* VOUCHER, slip, ticket, coupon, pass.

▸ verb **1** *the charges warranted a severe sentence* JUSTIFY, vindicate, call for, sanction, validate; permit, authorize; deserve, excuse, account for, legitimize; support, license, approve of; merit, qualify for, rate, be worthy of, be deserving of.

2 *we warrant that the texts do not infringe copyright* GUARANTEE, affirm, swear, promise, vow, pledge, undertake, state, assert, declare, profess, attest; vouch, testify, bear witness; *formal* aver.

warranty noun *a three-year warranty* GUARANTEE, assurance, promise, covenant, commitment, agreement.

warring adjective *warring tribes* OPPOSING, conflicting, at war, fighting, battling, quarreling; competing, hostile, rival.

warrior noun *fearsome warriors* FIGHTER, soldier, serviceman, combatant, mercenary.

wart noun a painful wart on her foot GROWTH, lump, swelling, protuberance, carbuncle, boil, blister, verruca, corn, tumor, excrescence, blemish.

war-torn adjective *Vu had grown up in war-torn South Vietnam* WAR-RAVAGED, war-weary, devastated, racked.

wary adjective **1** *he was trained to be wary* CAUTIOUS, careful, circumspect, on one's guard, chary, alert, on the lookout, on one's toes, on the qui vive; attentive, heedful, watchful, vigilant, observant; *informal* wide awake. See note at VIGILANT. ANTONYM inattentive.

2 *we are wary of strangers* SUSPICIOUS, chary, leery, careful, distrustful, mistrustful, skeptical, doubtful, dubious. ANTONYM trustful.

wash verb **1** *he is washing in the guest bathroom* CLEAN ONESELF; bathe, take a bath, shower, soak, freshen up; *formal* perform one's ablutions.

2 *he washed her socks* CLEAN, cleanse, rinse, launder, scour; shampoo, lather, sponge, scrub, wipe; sluice, douse, swab, disinfect; *literary* lave. ANTONYM soil.

3 *waves washed against the hull* SPLASH, lap, splosh, dash, crash, break, beat, surge, ripple, roll.

4 *the wreckage was washed downriver* SWEEP, carry, convey, transport.

5 *it washed up on my front lawn* LAND, come to rest, be deposited, be beached.

6 *guilt **washed over** her* SURGE THROUGH, rush through, course through, flood over, flow over; affect, overcome.

7 *informal* *this story just won't wash* BE ACCEPTED, be acceptable, be plausible, be convincing, hold up, hold water, stand up, bear scrutiny; do.

▸ noun **1** *she needs a wash* CLEAN, shower, dip, bath, soak; *formal* ablutions.

2 *that shirt should go in the wash* LAUNDRY, washing.

3 *antiseptic skin wash* LOTION, salve, preparation, rinse, liquid; liniment.

4 *the wash of the boat* BACKWASH, wake, trail, path.

5 *the wash of the waves on the beach* SURGE, flow, swell, sweep, rise and fall, roll, splash.

6 *a light watercolor wash* PAINT, stain, film, coat, coating; tint, glaze.

PHRASES: **wash one's hands of** *I'm going to wash my hands of the whole business* DISOWN, renounce, reject, forswear, disavow, give up on, turn one's back on, cast aside, abandon; *formal* abjure. **wash up** *you kids can wash up after dinner* WASH THE DISHES, do the dishes, clean up.

washed out adjective **1** *a washed-out denim jacket* FADED, bleached, decolorized, stonewashed; pale, light, drab, muted. ANTONYM bold.

2 *he looked washed out after his exams* EXHAUSTED, tired, worn out, weary, fatigued, spent, drained, enervated, rundown; *informal* done in, dog-tired, bushed, beat, zonked, pooped, tuckered out. ANTONYM energetic.

washout noun *informal*. See FAILURE sense 2.

washroom noun See BATHROOM.

waspish adjective *he's a waspish old geezer* IRRITABLE, touchy, testy, cross, snappish, cantankerous, splenetic, short-tempered, bad-tempered, moody, ornery, crotchety, crabby; *informal* grouchy.

waste verb **1** *he doesn't like to waste money* SQUANDER, misspend, misuse, fritter away, throw away, lavish, dissipate, throw around; *informal* blow, splurge. ANTONYM conserve.

2 *these children are **wasting away** in the streets* GROW WEAK, grow thin, shrink, decline, wilt, fade, flag, deteriorate, degenerate, languish. ANTONYMS flourish, thrive.

3 *the disease wasted his legs* EMACIATE, atrophy, wither, debilitate, shrivel, shrink, weaken, enfeeble. See note at RAVAGE.

4 *informal* *I saw them waste the guy*. See MURDER verb sense 1.

▸ adjective **1** *waste material* UNWANTED, excess, superfluous, left over, scrap, useless, worthless; unusable, unprofitable.

2 *waste ground* UNCULTIVATED, barren, desert, arid, bare; desolate, void, uninhabited, unpopulated; wild.

▸ noun **1** *a waste of money* MISUSE, misapplication, misemployment, abuse; extravagance, wastefulness, lavishness.

2 *household waste* GARBAGE, rubbish, trash, refuse, litter, debris, flotsam and jetsam, dross, junk, detritus, scrap; dregs, scraps; sewage, effluent.

3 (usu. **wastes**) *the frozen wastes of the Arctic* DESERT, wasteland, wilderness, wilds, emptiness.

PHRASE: **lay waste** See LAY[1].

wasted adjective **1** *a wasted effort* SQUANDERED, misspent, misdirected, misused, dissipated; pointless, useless, needless, unnecessary; vain, fruitless.

2 *a wasted opportunity* MISSED, lost, forfeited, neglected, squandered, bungled; *informal* down the drain.

3 *I'm **wasted in** this job* UNDEREMPLOYED IN/FOR, underused in, too good for, above.

4 *his wasted legs* EMACIATED, atrophied, withered, shriveled, weak, frail, shrunken, skeletal, rickety, scrawny, wizened.

5 *informal* *everybody at the party was wasted*. See DRUNK.

wasteful adjective *a wasteful use of fuel* PRODIGAL, profligate, uneconomical, inefficient, extravagant, lavish, excessive, imprudent, improvident, intemperate; thriftless, spendthrift; needless, useless. ANTONYM frugal.

wasteland noun *a desolate wasteland* WILDERNESS, desert; wilds, wastes, badlands.

wastrel noun See DEADBEAT.

watch verb **1** *she watched him as he spoke* OBSERVE, view, look at, eye, gaze at, stare at, gape at, peer at; contemplate, survey, keep an eye on; inspect, scrutinize, scan, examine, study, ogle, gawk at, regard, mark; *informal* check out, get a load of, eyeball; *literary* behold. ANTONYM ignore.

2 *he was being watched by the police* SPY ON, keep in sight, track, monitor, survey, follow, keep under surveillance; *informal* keep tabs on, stake out.

3 *will you watch the kids?* LOOK AFTER, mind, keep an eye on, take care of, supervise, tend, attend to; guard, safeguard, protect, babysit. ANTONYM neglect.

4 *we stayed to watch the boat* GUARD, protect, shield, defend, safeguard; cover, patrol, police.

5 *watch what you say* BE CAREFUL, mind, be aware of, pay attention to, consider, pay heed to.

▸ noun **1** *Bill looked at his watch* TIMEPIECE, chronometer; wristwatch, pocket watch, stopwatch.

2 *we kept watch on the yacht* GUARD, vigil, lookout, an eye; observation, surveillance, vigilance.

PHRASE: **watch out/it/yourself** *watch it, Bob, or you'll go over the edge | hey, you kids, watch yourselves!* BE CAREFUL, be watchful, be on your guard, beware, be wary, be cautious, look out, pay attention, take heed, take care, keep an eye open/out, keep one's eyes peeled, be vigilant.

watchdog noun **1** *they use watchdogs to ward off trespassers* GUARD DOG.

2 *a consumer watchdog* OMBUDSMAN, monitor, scrutineer, inspector, supervisor; custodian, guardian, protector.

watcher noun *the crime scene brought out your typical collection of watchers* ONLOOKER, spectator, observer, viewer, fly on the wall; witness, bystander, looker-on; spy; *informal* rubberneck; *literary* beholder.

watchful adjective *the watchful eye of their mother* OBSERVANT, alert, vigilant, attentive, awake, aware, heedful, sharp-eyed, eagle-eyed, hawk-eyed; on the lookout, on the qui vive, wary, cautious, careful, canny, chary. See note at VIGILANT.

watchman noun *the morning watchman comes on duty at half past five* SECURITY GUARD, custodian, warden; sentry, guard, patrolman, lookout, sentinel, scout, watch.

watchword noun Quality First is the watchword of our company GUIDING PRINCIPLE, motto, slogan, maxim, mantra, catchphrase, byword, shibboleth; *informal* buzzword.

water noun **1** *a glass of water* H_2O; *dated* Adam's ale.

2 *a house down by the water* SEA, ocean; lake, river; drink.

▸ verb **1** *water the plants* SPRINKLE, moisten, dampen, wet, spray, splash; soak, douse, souse, drench, saturate; hose (down).

2 *my mouth watered* MOISTEN, become wet, salivate; *informal* drool.

PHRASES: **hold water** *your story just doesn't hold water* BE TENABLE, ring true, bear scrutiny, make sense, stand up, hold up, be convincing, be plausible, be sound. **water down 1** *staff had watered down the drinks* DILUTE, thin (out), weaken; adulterate, doctor, mix; *informal* cut. **2** *the proposals were watered down* MODERATE, temper, mitigate, tone down, soften, tame; understate, play down, soft-pedal.

waterfall noun *a family of otters was frolicking in the waterfall* CASCADE, cataract, falls, chute.

waterfowl plural noun See table.

WATERFOWL

Ducks	Geese
baldpate	barnacle goose
black duck	blue goose
bufflehead	brant
canvasback	Canada goose
common eider	gray goose
common merganser	graylag
common pintail	Ross's goose
eider	snow goose
fulvous whistling duck	white-fronted goose
gadwall	
garganey	**Swans**
goldeneye	black swan
harlequin duck	mute swan
hooded merganser	trumpeter swan
king eider	tundra swan
mallard	whistling swan
mandarin duck	whooper
merganser	
mottled duck	**Loons**
Muscovy duck	Arctic loon
oldsquaw	common loon
pintail	Pacific loon
red-breasted merganser	red-throated loon
redhead	yellow-billed loon
ring-necked duck	
ruddy duck	**Grebes**
sawbill	eared grebe
scaup	helldiver
scoter	horned grebe
shoveler	pied-billed grebe
smew	red-necked grebe
surf scoter	Western grebe
teal	
white-winged scoter	
wigeon	
wood duck	

See also tables at SEABIRD and SHOREBIRD.

waterfront noun *the homes along the waterfront are quite stately* SHORE, lakefront, lakeshore, harborfront, riverfront, riverside, esplanade, docks, quay, beach, foreshore, shoreline, embankment.

waterlogged adjective *the floorboards are waterlogged* SATURATED, sodden, soaked, soggy, wet through.

waterproof adjective *a waterproof jacket* WATERTIGHT, water-repellent, water-resistant, weathertight, rainproof, impermeable, impervious; rubberized, waxed.

watershed noun **1** *the Mackenzie River watershed* divide.

2 *a watershed in the party's history* turning point, milestone, landmark.

watertight adjective **1** *a watertight container* IMPERMEABLE, impervious, (hermetically) sealed; waterproof, water-repellent, water-resistant. ANTONYM leaky.

2 *a watertight alibi* INDISPUTABLE, unquestionable, incontrovertible, irrefutable, unassailable, impregnable; foolproof, sound, flawless, airtight, bulletproof, conclusive. ANTONYM flawed.

waterway noun *environmental measures to clean up these waterways* CHANNEL, water route, watercourse, canal, river, seaway.

watery adjective **1** *a watery discharge* LIQUID, fluid, aqueous; *technical* hydrous. ANTONYMS solid, thick.

2 *a watery meadow* WET, damp, moist, sodden, soggy, squelchy, slushy, soft; saturated, waterlogged; boggy, marshy, swampy, miry, muddy. ANTONYM dry.

3 *watery soup* THIN, runny, weak, sloppy, dilute, diluted; tasteless, flavorless, insipid, bland. ANTONYMS thick, hearty.

4 *the light was watery and gray* PALE, wan, faint, weak, feeble; *informal* wishy-washy, washy. ANTONYM bright.

5 *watery eyes* TEARFUL, teary, weepy, moist, rheumy; *formal* lachrymose. ANTONYM dry.

wave verb **1** *he waved his flag in triumph* BRANDISH, shake, swish, move to and fro, move up and down, wag, sweep, swing, flourish, wield; flick, flutter.

2 *the grass waved in the breeze* RIPPLE, flutter, undulate, stir, flap, sway, billow, shake, quiver, move.

3 *the waiter waved them closer* GESTURE, gesticulate, signal, beckon, motion.

▸ noun **1** *she gave him a friendly wave* GESTURE, gesticulation; signal, sign, motion; salute.

2 *he surfs the Malibu waves* BREAKER, roller, comber, boomer, ripple, white horse, bore, big kahuna; **(waves)** swell, surf, froth; backwash.

3 *a wave of emigration* FLOW, rush, surge, flood, stream, tide, deluge, spate.

4 *a wave of self-pity* SURGE, rush, stab, dart, upsurge, groundswell; thrill, frisson; feeling.

5 *his hair grew in thick waves* CURL, kink, corkscrew, twist, ringlet, coil.

6 *electromagnetic waves* ripple, vibration, oscillation.

PHRASES: **make waves** *informal just be quiet and don't make waves* CAUSE TROUBLE, be disruptive, be troublesome; make an impression, get noticed. **wave aside** *he waved aside her protest* DISMISS, reject, brush aside, shrug off, disregard, ignore, discount, play down; *informal* pooh-pooh. **wave down** *she had no luck waving down a cab* FLAG DOWN, hail, stop, summon, call, accost.

waver verb **1** *the candlelight wavered in the draft* FLICKER, quiver, twinkle, glimmer, wink, blink.

2 *his voice wavered* FALTER, wobble, tremble, quaver, shake.

3 *he wavered between the choices* BE UNDECIDED, be irresolute, hesitate, dither, equivocate, vacillate, waffle, fluctuate; think twice, change one's mind, blow hot and cold; *informal* shilly-shally, sit on the fence.

wavy adjective *wavy hair* | *a screen filled with wavy lines* CURLY, curvy, curved, undulating, squiggly, rippled, crinkly, kinked, zigzag.

wax verb *the moon is waxing* GET BIGGER, increase, enlarge. ANTONYM wane.

PHRASE: **wax lyrical** *sorry, I didn't mean to wax lyrical about the good old days* BE ENTHUSIASTIC, enthuse, eulogize, rave, gush, get carried away.

waxen adjective *the prisoner's waxen complexion* PALLID, pale, pasty, wan, ashen, colorless, anemic, bloodless, washed out, white, gray, whitish, waxy, drained, sickly. ANTONYM ruddy.

waxy adjective See WAXEN.

way noun **1** *a way of reducing the damage* METHOD, process, procedure, technique, system; plan, strategy, scheme; means, mechanism, approach.

2 *she kissed him in her brisk way* MANNER, style, fashion, mode; modus operandi, MO.

3 *I've changed my ways* PRACTICE, wont, habit, custom, policy, procedure, convention, routine, modus vivendi; trait, attribute, peculiarity, idiosyncrasy; conduct, behavior, manner, style, nature, personality, temperament, disposition, character.

4 *which way leads home?* ROUTE, course, direction; road, street, track, path.

5 *I'll go out the back way* DOOR, gate, exit, entrance, entry; route.

6 *a short way downstream* DISTANCE, length, stretch, journey; space, interval, span.

7 *April is a long way away* TIME, stretch, term, span, duration.

8 *a car coming the other way* DIRECTION, bearing, course, orientation, line, tack.

9 *in some ways, he may be better off* RESPECT, regard, aspect, facet, sense, angle; detail, point, particular.

10 *the country is in a bad way* STATE, condition, situation, circumstances, position; predicament, plight; *informal* shape. PHRASES: **by the way** *by the way, Roy is back in town* INCIDENTALLY, by the by, in passing, en passant, as an aside. **give way 1** *the government gave way and passed the bill* YIELD, back down, surrender, capitulate, concede defeat, give in, submit, succumb; acquiesce, agree, assent; *informal* throw in the towel/sponge, cave in. **2** *the door gave way* COLLAPSE, give, cave in, fall in, come apart, crumple, buckle. **3** *grief* ***gave way to*** *guilt* BE REPLACED BY, be succeeded by, be followed by, be supplanted by. **on the way** *help is on the way* COMING, imminent, forthcoming, approaching, impending, close, near, on us; proceeding, en route, in transit.

wayfarer noun *literary* See WANDERER.

waylay verb **1** *we were waylaid and robbed* AMBUSH, hold up, attack, assail, rob; *informal* mug, stick up.

2 *several people waylaid her for an interview* ACCOST, detain, intercept, take aside, pounce on, importune; *informal* buttonhole.

way-out adjective *informal a way-out ideology* UNCONVENTIONAL, avant-garde, outlandish, eccentric, quirky, unusual, bizarre, strange, peculiar, odd, uncommon, offbeat; *informal* far-out, oddball, off the wall. ANTONYM ordinary.

wayward adjective *a wayward child* WILLFUL, headstrong, stubborn, obstinate, obdurate, perverse, contrary, disobedient, insubordinate, undisciplined; rebellious, defiant, uncooperative, recalcitrant, unruly, wild, unmanageable, erratic; difficult, impossible; *formal* refractory. ANTONYM docile.

weak adjective **1** *they are too weak to move* FRAIL, feeble, delicate, fragile; infirm, sick, sickly, debilitated, incapacitated, ailing, indisposed, decrepit; tired, fatigued, exhausted, anemic; *informal* weedy. ANTONYM strong.

2 *weak eyesight* INADEQUATE, poor, feeble; defective, faulty, deficient, imperfect, substandard. ANTONYMS strong, powerful, convincing, resolute, bright, loud.

3 *a weak excuse* UNCONVINCING, untenable, tenuous, implausible, unsatisfactory, poor, inadequate, feeble, flimsy, lame, hollow; *informal* pathetic. ANTONYMS strong, powerful.

4 *I was too weak to be a rebel* SPINELESS, craven, cowardly, pusillanimous, timid; irresolute, indecisive, ineffectual, inept, effete, meek, tame, ineffective, impotent, soft, fainthearted; *informal* yellow, weak-kneed, gutless, chicken. ANTONYMS strong, resolute.

5 *a weak light* DIM, pale, wan, faint, feeble, muted. ANTONYMS strong, bright.

6 *a weak voice* INDISTINCT, muffled, muted, hushed, low, faint, thready, thin. ANTONYMS strong, loud.

7 *weak coffee* WATERY, diluted, dilute, watered down, thin, tasteless, flavorless, bland, insipid, wishy-washy. ANTONYMS strong, powerful.

8 *a weak smile* UNENTHUSIASTIC, feeble, halfhearted, lame.

THE RIGHT WORD

Someone who is **weak** lacks physical, mental, or moral strength (*a weak heart; a weak excuse; too weak to resist temptation*). But there's nothing to suggest what the cause of this lack of strength might be. Someone who is **frail**, on the other hand, is weak because he or she has a slight build or delicate constitution (*a small, frail man*). Calling someone **feeble** implies that his or her weakness is pitiable (*too feeble to get out of bed*); when applied to things, *feeble* means faint or inadequate (*a feeble light*). **Infirm** suggests a loss of soundness, as from aging or illness (*poverty and illness had made him infirm*). **Debilitated** and **decrepit** also suggest that strength once present has been lost. But while someone who is young may be *debilitated* by disease, *decrepit* specifically refers to a loss of strength due to advanced age or long use (*a decrepit old woman who seldom left her house; a decrepit building that would soon be torn down*).

weaken verb **1** *the virus weakened him terribly* ENFEEBLE, debilitate, incapacitate, sap, enervate, tire, exhaust, wear out; wither, cripple, disable, emasculate.

2 *she tried to weaken the blow for him* REDUCE, decrease, diminish, soften, lessen, moderate, temper, dilute, blunt, mitigate.

3 *our morale weakened* DECREASE, dwindle, diminish, wane, ebb, subside, peter out, fizzle out, tail off, decline, falter.

4 *the move weakened her authority* IMPAIR, undermine,

erode, eat away at, compromise; invalidate, negate, discredit.

weakling noun *a ninety-pound weakling* PUSHOVER, namby-pamby, coward, milksop; *informal* wimp, weed, sissy, twinkie, drip, softie, doormat, chicken, yellow-belly, scaredy-cat, wuss.

weakness noun **1** *with old age came weakness* FRAILTY, feebleness, enfeeblement, fragility, delicacy; infirmity, sickness, sickliness, debility, incapacity, impotence, indisposition, decrepitude, vulnerability.

2 *he has worked on his weaknesses* FAULT, flaw, defect, deficiency, weak point, failing, shortcoming, weak link, imperfection, Achilles heel, foible.

3 *a weakness for champagne* FONDNESS, liking, partiality, preference, love, penchant, soft spot, predilection, inclination, taste, eye; enthusiasm, appetite; susceptibility.

4 *the president was accused of weakness* TIMIDITY, cowardliness, pusillanimity; indecision, irresolution, ineffectuality, ineptitude, impotence, meekness, powerlessness, ineffectiveness.

5 *the weakness of this argument* UNTENABILITY, implausibility, poverty, inadequacy, transparency; flimsiness, hollowness.

6 *the weakness of the sound* INDISTINCTNESS, mutedness, faintness, feebleness, lowness; dimness, paleness.

weak-willed adjective *you're too weak-willed to ask for a raise* SPINELESS, weak, irresolute, indecisive, weak-minded; impressionable, persuadable, submissive, unassertive, compliant, pusillanimous; *informal* wimpish, chicken.

wealth noun **1** *a gentleman of wealth* AFFLUENCE, prosperity, riches, means, substance, fortune; money, cash, lucre, capital, treasure, finance; assets, possessions, resources, funds; property, stock, reserves, securities, holdings; *informal* wherewithal, dough, moola. ANTONYM poverty.

2 *a wealth of information* ABUNDANCE, profusion, mine, store, treasury, bounty, bonanza, cornucopia, myriad; *informal* lot, load, heap, mass, mountain, stack, ton; *formal* plenitude. ANTONYM dearth.

wealthy adjective *our wealthy neighbors have an indoor swimming pool* RICH, affluent, moneyed, well off, well-to-do, prosperous, comfortable, propertied; of substance; *informal* well-heeled, rolling in it, in the money, made of money, filthy rich, stinking rich, loaded, flush. ANTONYM poor.

THE RIGHT WORD

If you have an abundance of money, you are **rich**. Another term for *rich* is **wealthy**, which may further imply that you are an established and prominent member of the community whose lifestyle is in keeping with your income (*a wealthy family whose influence on public opinion could not be ignored*). **Affluent** comes from the Latin word meaning to flow, and it connotes a generous income (*an affluent neighborhood*), while **opulent** suggests lavish spending or an ostentatious display of wealth (*an opulent mansion with every imaginable luxury*). One may come from an *affluent* family, in other words, and not have a particularly *opulent* lifestyle. If you're **prosperous**, you are thriving or flourishing (*a prosperous merchant; a prosperous business*). While *prosperous* suggests an economic situation that is on the rise, **flush** means having plenty of money on hand at a particular time (*she was feeling flush after receiving her first paycheck*). **Well-to-do** implies a generous income, enough to support comfortable living but not necessarily enough to be considered rich (*they were known as a well-to-do family with a strong commitment to educating their children*).

wean verb **1** *they weaned him off the habit* DISENGAGE; accustom, train; guide, encourage.

2 *she was weaned on sitcoms* RAISE, fed, nourish.

wear verb **1** *he wore a suit* DRESS IN, be clothed in, have on, sport, model; put on, don.

2 *Barbara wore a smile* BEAR, have (on one's face), show, display, exhibit; give, put on, assume.

3 *the bricks have been* ***worn down*** ERODE, abrade, rub away, grind away, wash away, crumble (away), wear down; corrode, eat away (at), dissolve.

4 *the tires are wearing well* LAST, endure, hold up, bear up, prove durable.

▸ noun **1** *you won't get much wear out of that* USE, wearing, service, utility, value; *informal* mileage.

2 *evening wear* CLOTHES, clothing, garments, dress, attire, garb, wardrobe; *informal* getup, gear, togs, duds; *formal* apparel; *literary* array.

3 *the varnish will withstand wear* DAMAGE, friction, erosion, attrition, abrasion; weathering.

PHRASES: **wear down** *he wore down her resistance* GRADUALLY OVERCOME, slowly reduce, erode, wear away, exhaust, undermine. **wear off** *the novelty soon wore off* FADE, diminish, lessen, dwindle, decrease, wane, ebb, peter out, fizzle out, pall, disappear, run out. **wear on** *the afternoon wore on* PASS, elapse, proceed, advance, progress, go by, roll by, march on, slip by/away, fly by/past. **wear out 1** *the fabric will eventually wear out* DETERIORATE, become worn, wear thin, fray, become threadbare, wear through. **2** *the grandkids wore me out* FATIGUE, tire out, weary, exhaust, drain, sap, overtax, enervate, debilitate, jade, prostrate; *informal* poop, frazzle, do in.

wearing adjective See WEARISOME.

wearisome adjective *the wearisome job of shingling the roof* TIRING, exhausting, wearying, fatiguing, enervating, draining, sapping, stressful, wearing, crushing; demanding, exacting, taxing, trying, challenging, burdensome, arduous, grueling, punishing, grinding, onerous, difficult, hard, tough, heavy, laborious, back-breaking, crippling, strenuous, rigorous, uphill; tiresome, irksome, weary, boring, dull, tedious, monotonous, humdrum, prosaic, unexciting, uninteresting.

weary adjective **1** *he was weary after cycling* TIRED, worn out, exhausted, fatigued, sapped, burnt-out, dog-tired, spent, drained, prostrate, enervated; *informal* all in, done in, beat, ready to drop, bushed, worn to a frazzle, pooped, tuckered out. ANTONYMS fresh, energetic. See note at TIRED.

2 *she was* ***weary of*** *the arguments* TIRED OF, fed up with, bored by, sick of, burnt-out on; *informal* have had it up to here with. ANTONYM enthusiastic.

3 *a weary journey* TIRING, exhausting, wearying, fatiguing, enervating, draining, sapping, wearing, trying, demanding, taxing, arduous, grueling, difficult, hard, tough. ANTONYM refreshing.

wearying adjective See WEARISOME.

weasel noun *he was a double-crossing weasel* SCOUN-

DREL, wretch, rogue; *informal* swine, bastard, creep, louse, rat, ratfink, toad, snake, snake in the grass, serpent, viper, skunk, dog, cur, scumbag, scumbucket, scuzzball, sleazeball, sleazebag, slimeball, sneak, backstabber, heel, nogoodnik, nasty piece of work; *dated* cad; *archaic* blackguard, knave, varlet.

weather noun *what's the weather like?* FORECAST, outlook; meteorological conditions, climate, atmospheric pressure, temperature; elements.

▸ verb *we weathered the recession* SURVIVE, come through, ride out, pull through; withstand, endure, rise above, surmount, overcome, resist, brave; *informal* stick out.

PHRASE: **under the weather** *informal we were sorry to hear that Dottie's been under the weather.* See ILL adjective sense 1.

weathered adjective *the weathered face of an old seaman* WEATHER-BEATEN, worn; tanned, bronzed; lined, creased, wrinkled, gnarled, gnarly.

weave verb **1** *flowers were woven into their hair* ENTWINE, lace, twist, knit, intertwine, braid, plait, loop.

2 *he weaves colorful plots* INVENT, make up, fabricate, construct, create, contrive, spin; tell, recount, relate.

3 *he had to weave his way through the crowds* THREAD, wind, wend; dodge, zigzag.

web noun **1** *a spider's web* MESH, net, lattice, latticework, lacework, webbing; gauze, gossamer.

2 *a web of friendships* NETWORK, nexus, complex, set, chain; tissue.

3 *visit us on the Web* INTERNET, World Wide Web, Net, information superhighway, Infobahn, cyberspace.

▸ adjective *a web environment* ONLINE, Internet, virtual, digital, cyber, web-based, e-.

weblog noun *your personal weblog* BLOG, online journal/diary.

Web page noun *what's the URL for that Web page?* WEBSITE, home page, hypertext document.

wed verb **1** *they are old enough to wed* MARRY, get married, become husband and wife; *informal* tie the knot, walk down the aisle, get hitched, take the plunge. ANTONYMS divorce, separate.

2 *he will wed his girlfriend* MARRY, take as one's wife/husband, lead to the altar; *informal* make an honest woman of; *archaic* espouse. ANTONYMS divorce, jilt.

3 *she wedded the two forms of spirituality* UNITE, unify, join, combine, amalgamate, fuse, integrate, bond, merge, meld, splice.

wedded adjective **1** *wedded bliss* MARRIED, matrimonial, marital, conjugal, nuptial; *Law* spousal; *literary* connubial.

2 *she is **wedded to** her work* DEDICATED TO, devoted to, attached to, fixated on, single-minded about.

wedding noun *a noon wedding at St. Mark's* MARRIAGE (SERVICE/CEREMONY/RITES), nuptials, union, commitment ceremony; *archaic* espousal.

wedge noun **1** *the door was secured by a wedge* DOORSTOP, chock, block, stop.

2 *a wedge of cheese* HUNK, segment, triangle, slice, section; chunk, lump, slab, block, piece.

▸ verb *she wedged her case between two bags* SQUEEZE, cram, jam, ram, force, push, shove; *informal* stuff.

wedlock noun *are you truly ready to enter into wedlock?* MARRIAGE, (holy) matrimony, married state, union, conjugal bond.

wee adjective See LITTLE adjective sense 1.

weed PHRASE: **weed out** *first we weed out the unqualified candidates* ISOLATE, separate out, sort out, sift out, winnow out, filter out, set apart, segregate; eliminate, get rid of, remove, cut, chop; *informal* lose.

weedy adjective *informal I'm surprised to see such a weedy little thing carrying all those heavy boxes* PUNY, feeble, weak, frail, undersized, slight, skinny; *informal* pint-sized, pantywaist.

weekly adjective *weekly installments* ONCE A WEEK; lasting a week; *formal* hebdomadal.

▸ adverb *the directors meet weekly* ONCE A WEEK, every week, each week, on a weekly basis; by the week, per week, a week.

weep verb *even the toughest soldiers wept* CRY, shed tears, sob, snivel, whimper, whine, wail, bawl; *informal* boo-hoo, blubber.

weepy adjective *there were a lot a weepy people in the audience* TEARFUL, close to tears, upset, distressed, sad, unhappy; in tears, crying, weeping, sniveling; *informal* teary, misty-eyed, choked-up; *formal* lachrymose.

weigh verb **1** *she weighs the fruit* MEASURE THE WEIGHT OF, put on the scales; heft.

2 *he weighed 170 lbs* HAVE A WEIGHT OF, tip the scales at, weigh in at.

3 *the situation **weighed** heavily **on** him* OPPRESS, lie heavy on, burden, hang over, gnaw at, prey on (one's mind); trouble, worry, bother, disturb, get down, depress, haunt, nag, torment, plague.

4 *he has to weigh his options* CONSIDER, contemplate, think about, mull over, chew over, reflect on, ruminate about, muse on; assess, appraise, analyze, investigate, inquire into, look into, examine, review, explore, take stock of.

5 *they need to weigh benefit against risk* BALANCE, evaluate, compare, juxtapose, contrast, measure. PHRASE: **weigh down** *my fishing gear weighed me down* BURDEN, saddle, overload, overburden, encumber, hamper, handicap.

weight noun **1** *the weight of the book* HEAVINESS, mass, load, burden, pressure, force; poundage, tonnage.

2 *his recommendation will carry great weight* INFLUENCE, force, leverage, sway, pull, importance, significance, consequence, value, substance, power, authority; *informal* clout.

3 *a weight off her mind* BURDEN, load, millstone, albatross, encumbrance; trouble, worry, pressure, strain.

4 *the weight of the evidence is against him* PREPONDERANCE, majority, bulk, body, lion's share, predominance; most, almost all.

weighty adjective **1** *a weighty tome* HEAVY, thick, bulky, hefty, cumbersome, ponderous. See note at HEAVY. ANTONYM light.

2 *a weighty subject* IMPORTANT, significant, momentous, consequential, far-reaching, key, major, big, vital, critical, crucial; serious, grave, solemn. ANTONYMS unimportant, trivial.

3 *a weighty responsibility* BURDENSOME, onerous, heavy, oppressive, taxing, troublesome, solemn.

4 *weighty arguments* COMPELLING, cogent, strong, forceful, powerful, beefy, potent, effective, sound, valid, telling; impressive, persuasive, convincing, influential, authoritative. ANTONYM weak.

weird adjective **1** *weird apparitions* UNCANNY, eerie, unnatural, supernatural, unearthly, otherworldly, ghostly, mysterious, strange, abnormal, unusual; eldritch; *informal* creepy, spooky, freaky. ANTONYM normal.

2 *a weird sense of humor* BIZARRE, quirky, outlandish, eccentric, unconventional, unorthodox, idiosyncratic, surreal, crazy, peculiar, odd, strange, queer, freakish, zany, madcap, outré; *informal* bizarro, wacky, freaky, way-out, offbeat, off the wall, wacko. ANTONYM conventional.

PHRASE: **weird out** *I'm a little weirded out by his spiky blue hair* DISTURB, freak out, unnerve, unsettle, alarm, alienate.

weirdo noun *informal* See ECCENTRIC noun.

welcome noun *I appreciate the welcome I got from your parents* GREETING, salutation; reception, hospitality; red carpet (treatment).

▸ verb **1** *welcome your guests in their own language* GREET, salute, receive, meet, usher in.

2 *we welcomed their decision* BE PLEASED BY, be glad about, approve of, appreciate, embrace; *informal* give the thumbs up to.

▸ adjective *welcome news* PLEASING, agreeable, encouraging, gratifying, heartening, promising, favorable, pleasant, refreshing; gladly received, wanted, appreciated, popular, desirable.

weld verb *the handle is then welded to the top of the box* FUSE, bond, stick, join, attach, seal, splice, melt, solder, cement.

welfare noun **1** *the welfare of children* WELL-BEING, health, comfort, security, safety, protection, prosperity, success, fortune; interest, good.

2 *we cannot claim welfare* social security, social assistance, benefit, public assistance; pension, credit, support; sick pay, unemployment benefit; *informal* the dole.

well[1] adverb **1** *he behaves well* SATISFACTORILY, nicely, correctly, properly, fittingly, suitably, appropriately; decently, fairly, kindly, generously, honestly. ANTONYM badly.

2 *they get along well* HARMONIOUSLY, agreeably, pleasantly, nicely, happily, amicably, amiably, peaceably; *informal* famously. ANTONYM badly.

3 *he plays the piano well* SKILLFULLY, ably, competently, proficiently, adeptly, deftly, expertly, admirably, excellently. ANTONYM poorly.

4 *I know her well* INTIMATELY, thoroughly, deeply, profoundly, personally. ANTONYM barely.

5 *they studied the recipe well* CAREFULLY, closely, attentively, rigorously, in depth, exhaustively, in detail, meticulously, scrupulously, conscientiously, methodically, completely, comprehensively, fully, extensively, thoroughly, effectively. ANTONYM negligently.

6 *they speak well of him* ADMIRINGLY, highly, approvingly, favorably, appreciatively, warmly, enthusiastically, positively, glowingly. ANTONYM disparagingly.

7 *she makes enough money to live well* COMFORTABLY, in (the lap of) luxury, prosperously.

8 *you may well be right* QUITE POSSIBLY, conceivably, probably; undoubtedly, certainly, unquestionably.

9 *he is well over forty* CONSIDERABLY, very much, a great deal, substantially, easily, comfortably, significantly. ANTONYM barely.

10 *she could well afford it* EASILY, comfortably, readily, effortlessly. ANTONYM barely.

▸ adjective **1** *she was completely well again* HEALTHY, fine, fit, robust, strong, vigorous, blooming, thriving, hale and hearty, in good shape, in good condition, in fine fettle; *informal* in the pink. ANTONYM ill.

2 *all is not well* SATISFACTORY, all right, fine, in order, as it should be, acceptable; *informal* OK, hunky-dory, jake. ANTONYM unsatisfactory.

3 *it would be well to tell us in advance* ADVISABLE, sensible, prudent, politic, commonsensical, wise, judicious, expedient, recommended, advantageous, beneficial, profitable, desirable; a good idea. ANTONYM inadvisable.

PHRASES: **as well** *I'll have the shrimp cocktail as well* TOO, also, in addition, additionally, into the bargain, besides, furthermore, moreover, likewise, to boot. **as well as** *we sell books as well as newspapers* TOGETHER WITH, along with, besides, plus, and, with, on top of, not to mention, to say nothing of, let alone. **well done** *well done, Robbie, your voice has never been better* CONGRATULATIONS, bravo, right on, congrats, my compliments, good work, three cheers, felicitations.

well[2] noun **1** *she drew water from the well* borehole, bore, spring, waterhole.

2 *he's a bottomless well of forgiveness* SOURCE, supply, fount, reservoir, wellspring, mine, fund, treasury.

▸ verb *tears welled from her eyes* FLOW, spill, stream, run, rush, gush, roll, cascade, flood, spout; seep, trickle; burst, issue, upwell.

well-advised adjective *I'm not sure this is a well-advised investment* WISE, prudent, sensible.

well-balanced adjective See BALANCED senses 1, 2.

well-behaved adjective *it takes only one little brat to ruin it for all the well-behaved children* ORDERLY, obedient, disciplined, peaceable, docile, controlled, restrained, cooperative, compliant, law-abiding; mannerly, polite, civil, courteous, respectful, proper, decorous, refined, polished. ANTONYM naughty.

well-being noun See WELFARE sense 1.

well-bred adjective *a well-bred youngster such as yourself should not be cavorting with people of their station* WELL BROUGHT UP, polite, civil, mannerly, courteous, respectful; ladylike, gentlemanly, genteel, cultivated, urbane, proper, refined, patrician, polished, well-behaved.

well-built adjective *we need a couple of well-built guys to move these bookcases* STURDY, strapping, brawny, burly, hefty, muscular, muscly, strong, rugged, lusty, Herculean; *informal* hunky, beefy, husky, hulking. ANTONYM puny.

well-dressed adjective *a well-dressed man really stands out in this place* SMART, fashionable, stylish, chic, chi-chi, modish, elegant, neat, spruce, trim, dapper; snazzy, natty, snappy, sharp, spiffy, fly, preppy. ANTONYM scruffy.

well-founded adjective *her suspicions were well-founded*

JUSTIFIABLE, justified, warranted, legitimate, defensible, valid, admissible, allowable, understandable, excusable, acceptable, reasonable, sensible, sound, well-grounded. ANTONYM groundless.

well-heeled adjective *informal* See WEALTHY.

well-known adjective **1** *well-known principles* FAMILIAR, widely known, popular, common, everyday, established. ANTONYM abstruse.

2 *a well-known family of architects* FAMOUS, famed, prominent, notable, renowned, distinguished, eminent, illustrious, celebrated, acclaimed, recognized, important; notorious. ANTONYM obscure.

well-mannered adjective *we were quite impressed by the well-mannered students who met us in the library* POLITE, courteous, civil, mannerly, genteel, decorous, debonair, respectful, refined, polished, civilized, urbane, well-behaved, well-bred.

well-nigh adverb *enforcing the recycling ordinance is well-nigh impossible* ALMOST, nearly, just about, more or less, practically, virtually, all but, as good as, nearing, close to, approaching; roughly, approximately; *informal* pretty much, nigh on.

well off adjective **1** *her family's very well off.* See WELL-TO-DO.

2 *the prisoners were relatively well off* FORTUNATE, lucky, comfortable; *informal* sitting pretty.

3 *the island is not* ***well off for*** *harbors* WELL SUPPLIED WITH, well stocked with, well furnished with, well equipped with; well situated for.

well-read adjective *a well-read history professor* KNOWLEDGEABLE, well-informed, well versed, erudite, scholarly, literate, educated, cultured, bookish, studious; *dated* lettered. ANTONYM ignorant.

well-spoken adjective *what a bright, well-spoken young man* ARTICULATE, eloquent, coherent, nicely spoken; refined, polite.

well-to-do adjective *her well-to-do Uncle Leroy* WEALTHY, rich, affluent, moneyed, well off, prosperous, comfortable, propertied; *informal* rolling in it, in the money, loaded, well-heeled, flush, made of money, on easy street. See note at WEALTHY.

welt noun *the lashing left a nasty welt* SWELLING, lump, bump; mark, pimple, blister, bruise, contusion, *Medicine* bleb.

welter noun *the notebook was a welter of half-finished stories* CONFUSION, jumble, tangle, mess, hodgepodge, mishmash, mass; *informal* rat's nest.

wend verb *they* ***wended their way*** *across the city* MEANDER, wind one's way, wander, amble, stroll, saunter, drift, roam, traipse, walk; journey, travel; *informal* mosey, tootle.

west adjective *a west wind* WESTERN, westerly, occidental; Pacific.

▸ noun *commercialism in the West* OCCIDENT, Western nations.

wet adjective **1** *wet clothes* DAMP, moist, soaked, drenched, saturated, sopping, dripping, soggy; waterlogged. ANTONYM dry.

2 *it was cold and wet* RAINY, raining, pouring, teeming, inclement, showery, drizzly, drizzling; damp; humid, muggy. ANTONYM dry.

3 *the paint is still wet* STICKY, tacky; fresh. ANTONYM dry.

4 *a wet mortar mix* AQUEOUS, watery, sloppy. ANTONYM dry.

▸ verb *wet the clothes before ironing them* DAMPEN, damp, moisten; sprinkle, spray, splash, spritz; soak, saturate, flood, douse, souse, drench. ANTONYM dry.

▸ noun **1** *the wet of his tears* WETNESS, damp, moisture, moistness, sogginess; wateriness.

2 *the race was held in the wet* RAIN, drizzle, precipitation; spray, dew, damp.

wetland noun the wetland here is protected from the hands of developers MARSH; *Brit.* bogland, bog, swamp, morass, quagmire, muskeg, slough, fen, fenland, bayou.

whack *informal* verb *she whacked him on the head.* See STRIKE verb sense 1.

▸ noun *he got a whack with a stick.* See BLOW noun sense 1.

whale noun *watching whales from our cruise ship* CETACEAN, leviathan. See table.

WHALES, DOLPHINS, AND PORPOISES

Whales	killer whale
beaked whale	pilot whale
beluga	right whale dolphin
blue whale	rough-toothed dolphin
bottlenose whale	spinner dolphin
bowhead	spotted dolphin
finback (whale)	striped dolphin
gray whale	tucuxi
humpback (whale)	white-beaked dolphin
minke (whale)	white-sided dolphin
narwhal	
right whale	**Porpoises**
rorqual	Burmeister's porpoise
sei whale	cochito
sperm whale	Dall's porpoise
strap-toothed whale	finless porpoise
white whale	harbor porpoise
	spectacled porpoise
Dolphins	dolphin
black dolphin	finback
bottlenose dolphin	grampus
common dolphin	orca
dusky dolphin	porpoise
hourglass dolphin	pothead
humpbacked dolphin	
Irrawaddy dolphin	

wharf noun *there are no available boat slips at this wharf* QUAY, pier, dock, berth, landing, jetty; harbor, dockyard, marina.

what-if noun *the idea is just a what-if, but it may be worth thinking about* SPECULATION, conjecture, fancy, thought experiment.

▸ adjective the last thing we need is another what-if solution HYPOTHETICAL, speculative, theoretical, notional; imagined.

whatsit noun *informal just connect the blue knob to the whatsit* THING, so-and-so, whatever it's called; *informal* whatnot, whatchamacallit, whatchacallit, what-d'you-call-it, what's-its-name, thingy; *Brit.* thingummy, thingamabob, thingamajig, doodad, doohickey.

whatsoever adjective *I have no intention whatsoever of going with you* AT ALL, of any kind, whatever, in the least, 'in any way, shape or form.'

wheat noun cracked wheat, whole wheat. See table at CEREAL.

wheedle verb *she wheedled us into hiring her brother* COAX, cajole, inveigle, induce, entice, charm, tempt, beguile, blandish, flatter, persuade, influence, win someone over, bring someone around, convince, prevail on, get around; *informal* sweet-talk, soft-soap.

wheel noun *a wagon wheel* disk, hoop, ring, circle.

▸ verb 1 *she wheeled the trolley away* PUSH, trundle, roll.

2 *the flock of doves wheeled around* TURN, go around, circle, orbit.

PHRASE: **at/behind the wheel** *were you at the wheel when the accident occurred?* DRIVING, steering, in the driver's seat.

wheelbarrow noun a wheelbarrow full of grass clippings CART, barrow.

wheeze verb *even with that terrible wheezing, she won't quit smoking* BREATHE NOISILY, gasp, whistle, hiss, rasp, croak, pant, cough.

whereabouts plural noun his whereabouts remain secret LOCATION, position, site, place, situation, spot, point, vicinity; home, address, locale, neighborhood; bearings, orientation.

wherewithal noun he has the wherewithal to start up his own business MONEY, cash, capital, finance(s), funds; resources, means, ability, capability; *informal* dough, loot, necessary, boodle, bucks.

whet verb 1 *he whetted his knife on a stone* SHARPEN, hone, strop, grind, file. ANTONYM blunt.

2 *something to whet your appetite* STIMULATE, excite, arouse, rouse, kindle, trigger, spark, quicken, stir, inspire, animate, waken, fuel, fire, activate, tempt, galvanize. ANTONYMS dull, spoil.

whether conjunction See note at IF.

whew exclamation *whew, we got out just in the nick of time* PHEW, thank goodness, thank God, what a relief.

whiff noun 1 *I caught a whiff of perfume* FAINT SMELL, trace, sniff, scent, odor, aroma.

2 *the faintest whiff of irony* TRACE, hint, suggestion, impression, suspicion, soupçon, smidgen, nuance, intimation, tinge, vein, shred, whisper, air, element, overtone.

3 *whiffs of smoke from the boiler* PUFF, gust, flurry, breath, draft, waft.

while noun *we chatted for a while* TIME, spell, stretch, stint, span, interval, period; duration, phase, patch.

▸ verb *tennis helped to while away the time* PASS, spend, occupy, use up, fritter, kill.

whim noun 1 *she bought it on a whim* IMPULSE, urge, notion, fancy, foible, caprice, conceit, vagary, inclination, megrim.

2 *human whim* CAPRICIOUSNESS, whimsy, caprice, volatility, fickleness, idiosyncrasy.

whimper noun & verb *we heard her whimpers from downstairs | why is he whimpering?* WHINE, cry, sob, moan, snivel, wail, groan; mewl, bleat.

whimsical adjective 1 *a whimsical sense of humor* FANCIFUL, playful, mischievous, waggish, quaint, quizzical, curious, droll; eccentric, quirky, idiosyncratic, unconventional, outlandish, queer, fey; *informal* offbeat, freaky. See note at FEY.

2 *the whimsical arbitrariness of autocracy* VOLATILE, capricious, fickle, changeable, unpredictable, variable, erratic, mercurial, mutable, inconstant, inconsistent, unstable, protean.

whine noun & verb 1 *a whine from the kennel | she heard an animal whine* WHIMPER, cry, mewl, howl, yowl.

2 *the motor's whine the motor whined* HUM, drone.

3 *his latest whine was about the long hours | stop whining!* COMPLAINT [noun], COMPLAIN [verb], grouse, grumble, murmur; *informal* gripe, moan, grouch, whinge, bellyache, beef.

WORD NOTE **whinge**

An invaluable term for persistent complaining, whining, generally making such a peevish fuss as to cause a listener to cringe. **—JS**

whip noun *he would use a whip on his dogs* LASH, scourge, strap, belt, rod, bullwhip; *historical* cat-o'-nine-tails.

▸ verb 1 *he whipped the boy* FLOG, scourge, flagellate, lash, strap, belt, thrash, beat, tan someone's hide.

2 *whip the cream* WHISK, beat.

3 *she whipped her listeners into a frenzy* ROUSE, stir up, excite, galvanize, electrify, stimulate, inspire, fire up, get someone going, inflame, agitate, goad, provoke.

4 *informal* *he whipped around the corner.* See DASH verb sense 1.

5 *informal* *then she whipped out a revolver* PULL, whisk, pluck, jerk.

WORD NOTE **whipper**

From *As You Like It*, Act III, Scene ii. Rosalind: "Love is merely a madness, and, I tell you, deserves as well a dark house and a whip as madmen do; and the reason why they are not so punish'd and cured is, that the lunacy is so ordinary that the whippers are in love too."

Shakespeare coined about half the words in modern English, why not add one more? I propose using *whipper* to mean "someone helplessly implicated in the irrationality of love." **—DA**

whippersnapper noun *informal* *listen, you little whippersnapper, I'm still in charge here* UPSTART, stripling; *informal* pipsqueak, squirt.

whirl verb 1 *leaves whirled in eddies* ROTATE, circle, wheel, turn, revolve, orbit, spin, twirl.

2 *they whirled past* HURRY, race, dash, rush, run, sprint, bolt, dart, gallop, career, charge, shoot, hurtle, fly, speed, scurry; *informal* tear, belt, pelt, scoot, bomb, hightail it.

3 *his mind was whirling* SPIN, reel, swim.

▸ noun 1 *a whirl of dust* SWIRL, flurry, eddy.

2 *the mad social whirl* HURLY-BURLY, activity, bustle, rush, flurry, fuss, turmoil, merry-go-round.

3 *Laura's mind was in a whirl* SPIN, daze, stupor, muddle, jumble; confusion; *informal* dither.

whirlpool noun 1 *a river full of whirlpools* EDDY, vortex, maelstrom.

2 *the health club has a whirlpool* HOT TUB; *trademark* Jacuzzi.

whirlwind noun 1 *the building was hit by a whirlwind*

TORNADO, hurricane, typhoon, cyclone, vortex, twister, dust devil.

2 *a whirlwind of activity* MAELSTROM, welter, bedlam, mayhem, babel, swirl, tumult, hurly-burly, commotion, confusion; *informal* madhouse, three-ring circus.

▸ adjective *a whirlwind romance* RAPID, lightning, headlong, impulsive, breakneck, meteoric, sudden, swift, fast, quick, speedy, dizzying; *informal* quickie.

whisk verb 1 *the cable car will whisk you to the top* SPEED, hurry, rush, sweep, hurtle, shoot.

2 *she whisked the cloth away* PULL, snatch, pluck, tug, jerk; *informal* whip, yank.

3 *he whisked out of sight* DASH, rush, race, bolt, dart, gallop, career, charge, shoot, hurtle, fly, speed, zoom, scurry, scuttle, scamper; *informal* tear, belt, pelt, scoot, zip, whip.

4 *she whisked the hair from her face* FLICK, brush, sweep, wave.

5 *whisk the egg yolks* WHIP, beat, mix.

whisker noun *his graying whiskers* FACIAL HAIR, mustache, beard, mustachios, goatee, mutton chop; stubble, five o'clock shadow.

whisper verb 1 *Alison whispered in his ear* MURMUR, mutter, mumble, speak softly, breathe; hiss; *formal* susurrate. ANTONYM shout.

2 *literary the wind whispered in the grass* RUSTLE, murmur, sigh, moan, whoosh, whir, swish, blow, breathe. ANTONYM roar.

▸ noun 1 *she spoke in a whisper* MURMUR, mutter, mumble, low voice, undertone; *rare* sibilation, susurration.

2 *literary the wind died to a whisper* RUSTLE, murmur, sigh, whoosh, swish.

3 *I heard the whisper that he's left town* RUMOR, story, report, speculation, insinuation, suggestion, hint; *informal* buzz.

4 *not a whisper of interest.* See WHIT.

whit noun *they gave him not a whit of consideration* SCRAP, bit, speck, iota, jot, atom, crumb, shred, grain, mite, touch, trace, shadow, suggestion, whisper, suspicion, scintilla, modicum; *informal* smidgen, smidge.

white adjective 1 *a clean white bandage* COLORLESS, unpigmented, bleached, natural; snowy, milky, chalky, ivory.

2 *her face was white with fear* PALE, pallid, wan, ashen, bloodless, waxen, chalky, pasty, washed out, drained, drawn, ghostly, deathly.

3 *white hair* SNOWY, gray, silver, silvery, hoary, grizzled.

4 *the early white settlers* CAUCASIAN, European.

white-collar adjective *white-collar workers* CLERICAL, administrative, professional, executive, salaried, office.

whiten verb *the sun has whitened the pink towels* MAKE WHITE, make pale, bleach, blanch, lighten, fade.

whitewash noun 1 *the report was a whitewash* COVER-UP, camouflage, deception, facade, veneer, pretext. ANTONYM exposé.

2 *informal a four-game whitewash* WALKOVER, rout, landslide; *informal* pushover, cinch, breeze.

▸ verb *don't whitewash what happened* COVER UP, sweep under the carpet, hush up, suppress, draw a veil over, conceal, veil, obscure, keep secret; gloss over, downplay, soft-pedal. ANTONYM expose.

whittle verb 1 *he sat whittling a piece of wood* PARE, shave, trim, carve, shape, model.

2 *his powers were* ***whittled away*** ERODE, wear away, eat away, reduce, diminish, undermine, weaken, subvert, compromise, impair, impede, hinder, cripple, disable, enfeeble, sap.

3 *the ten teams have been* ***whittled down*** *to six* REDUCE, cut down, cut back, prune, trim, slim down, pare down, shrink, decrease, diminish.

whiz noun *Carlton's a whiz on the sax* GENIUS, virtuoso, ace, master, prodigy, hotshot, wizard, magician.

▸ verb *four emergency vehicles whizzed past us on Glenwood* ZOOM, flash, zip, whip, hurtle, fly.

who pronoun See note below.

USAGE NOTE **who, whom**

Edward Sapir, the philosopher of language, prophesied that "within a couple of hundred years from to-day not even the most learned jurist will be saying 'Whom did you see?' By that time the *whom* will be as delightfully archaic as the Elizabethan *his* for *its*. No logical or historical argument will avail to save this hapless *whom*." (*Language*; 1921.) A safer bet might be that no one will be spelling *to-day* with a hyphen. In any event, writers in the twenty-first century ought to understand how the words *who* and *whom* are correctly used.

Who, the nominative pronoun, is used (1) as the subject of a verb (*it was Kate who rescued the dog*); and (2) as the complement of a linking verb, i.e., as a predicate nominative (*they know who you are*). *Whom*, the objective pronoun, is used (1) as the object of a verb (*whom did you see?*); and (2) as the object of a preposition (*the person to whom we're indebted*).

It's true that in certain contexts, *whom* is stilted. That has long been so: "Every sensible English speaker on both sides of the Atlantic says *Who were you talking to?* [—not *Whom*—] and the sooner we begin to write it the better." (J. Y. T. Greig, *Breaking Priscian's Head*; ca. 1930.) But there are other constructions in which *whom* remains strong—and more so in American English than in British English. Although writers have announced the demise of *whom*, it persists in American English—e.g.:

• "Susan McDonough's classroom is filled with primary-school children of different ages, all of whom are lagging behind in reading skills." (*Washington Post*; Sept. 28, 1997.)

• "He was implicated in the murder of a man whom his workers caught tampering with some stone blocks." (*SmartMoney*; Oct. 1, 1997.) (In this sentence, *that* might work more naturally than *whom*.)

The correct uses of *who* are sometimes tricky. But if the pronoun acts as the subject of a clause, it must be *who*, never *whom*—e.g.: "Alan Alda, who you quickly realize is sorely missed on TV, stars as Dan Cutler, a type-A personality advertising executive." (*Sun-Sentinel* [Fort Lauderdale]; May 20, 1994.) (*Who* is the subject of *is*.)

While the subject of a finite verb is nominative (*I know she is good*), the subject of an infinitive is in the objective case (*I know her to be good*). The same is true of *who* and *whom*. Strictly, *whom* is always either the object of a verb or preposition, or else the subject of an infinitive—e.g.: "Do all you can to develop your intuition—this will help you to know when to act and when to wait, whom to be cautious about and whom to trust." (*Washington Times*; July 9, 1997.)

But often journalists don't get it right, perhaps because they consider the word stuffy—e.g.:

• "And he [nominee Stephen G. Breyer] promised, following the admonition of the late Justice Arthur Goldberg, who [read *whom*] he served as a law clerk 30 years ago, to do his best to avoid footnotes." (*Washington Post*; May 17, 1994.)

• "A polite, helpful 11-year-old who [read *whom*] everybody called Jake was fatally shot in his bedroom in this small rural town on Thursday, and a 13-year-old friend was charged hours later with killing him." (*New York Times*; Sept. 3, 1994.), at 1. (Replacing *who* with *that* would also work naturally here.)

• "Those friends include Myra Guarino, 62, of Valdosta, who [read *whom*] Mrs. Helms represents in a suit against the manufacturer of silicone breast implants." (*New York Times*; July 7, 1995.)

In the citations just listed, *who* is defensible in informal contexts. But the objective *who* is not idiomatically normal after a preposition. For example, *one of whom* is something of a set phrase—e.g.: "Parents proudly whooped it up for the players, not one of who [read *one of whom*] wore shoulder pads." (*USA Today*; Jan. 27, 2003.)

Among the toughest contexts in which to get the pronouns right are those involving linking verbs. We say, for example, *who it is* for the same reason we say *this is he*, but some very good writers have nodded. In any event, *whom* shouldn't be used as the subject of any finite verb—e.g.:

• "The distinguished political and social philosopher Russell Kirk used the word 'energumen' to describe . . . whom [read *who*] it is I agitate against." (William F. Buckley, *The Jeweler's Eye*; 1969.) (*Who* is needed as the inverted subject of *is*: *it is who*, as in *it is he*.)

• "Police went to several addresses looking for a 17-year-old whom [read *who*] they thought was staying with his aunt." (*San Francisco Chronicle*; Apr. 20, 1994.) (*Who* is needed as the subject of *was*.)

• "In the other corner are the anti-Stratfordians, the heretics and conspiracy theorists of literature, most of them devoted amateurs whose dogged sleuthing and amassing of evidence (albeit mostly circumstantial) continues to enlarge the body of contention that Shakespeare wasn't himself. But if not he, then whom [read *who*]?" (*Washington Post*; May 17, 1994.) (*Who* is needed in a parallel phrasing with *he*.)

• "But Beck ought to serve as an inspiration for a host of other superb golfers whom [read *who*] naysayers claim 'can't win the big ones.' " (*Sky*; Sept. 1995.) (*Who* is needed as the subject of *can't win*.)

• "Sam divorced in 1969, and is survived by his son, Sam III, his wife, Angela, and their daughter, Samantha, of Clarksville, Tennessee; his daughter, Marguerite; the mother of Matthew and Grace, whom [read *who*] all lived with Sam in Austin." (*Austin American-Statesman*; Feb. 10, 1996.) (*Who* is needed as the subject of *lived*.)

William Safire takes an interesting approach for those who fear seeming pedantic (by using *whom*) or being incorrect (by using *who* for *whom*): "When *whom* is correct, recast the sentence." (*New York Times*; Oct. 4, 1992.) Thus "Whom do you trust?" becomes, in a political campaign, "Which candidate do you trust?" The relative pronoun *that* can also substitute in many situations. But one commentator, Steven Pinker, calls Safire's suggestion an "unacceptable pseudo-compromise." And Pinker has a point: "Telling people to avoid a problematic construction sounds like common sense, but in the case of object questions with *who*, it demands an intolerable sacrifice. People ask questions about the objects of verbs and prepositions a lot." (*The Language Instinct*; 1994.) Moreover, a phrase such as *which person* is wordier and slightly narrower than *who* or *whom*. Perhaps the most sensible approach was the one taken by Robert C. Pooley in 1974: "Considering the importance some people place on mastery of [the textbook rules for *whom*], the schoolbooks may be justified in distinguishing the case forms for the relative pronouns for literary usage. But to insist that these literary and formal distinctions be made in informal writing and speech as necessary to achieve 'correctness' is to do violence to the readily observed facts of current usage." (*The Teaching of English Usage*, 2d ed.; 1974.)

Who is the relative pronoun for human beings (though *that* is also acceptable); *that* and *which* are the relative pronouns for anything other than humans, including entities created by humans. But writers too often forget this elementary point—e.g.: "The best borrowers are grabbed by the banks and financial institutions who [read *that*] are in a position now to offer finer rates." (*Business Standard*; Oct. 25, 1997.)

Some inattentive writers use *which* in referring to human beings—e.g.: "The bakery employs 11 people, two of which [read *whom*] are English (non-Amish) women, and one who is a salesman." (*Plain Dealer* [Cleveland]; June 13, 1995.)

That, of course, is permissible when referring to humans: "the people that were present" or "the people who were present." Editors tend, however, to prefer the latter phrasing. **—BG**

---

whoa exclamation **1** *whoa, boy!* STOP, easy, slow down, hold your horses.

2 *whoa—look at that!* See WOW.

whole adjective **1** *the whole report* ENTIRE, complete, full, unabridged, uncut. ANTONYM incomplete.

2 *they unearthed a whole humanoid skull* INTACT, in one piece, unbroken; undamaged, unmarked, perfect.

▸ noun **1** *a single whole* ENTITY, unit, body, discrete item, ensemble.

2 ***the whole** of the year* ALL, every part, the lot, the sum, the sum total, the entirety.

PHRASE: **on the whole** *on the whole, they lived peaceably* OVERALL, all in all, all things considered, for the most part, in the main, in general, generally, generally speaking, as a rule, as a general rule, by and large; normally, usually, more often than not, almost always, most of the time, typically, ordinarily.

wholehearted adjective *you have my wholehearted support* COMMITTED, positive, emphatic, devoted, dedicated, enthusiastic, unshakable, unswerving; unqualified, unstinting, unreserved, without reservations, unconditional, unequivocal, unmitigated; complete, full, total, absolute. ANTONYM halfhearted.

wholesale adverb *the images were removed wholesale* EXTENSIVELY, on a large scale, comprehensively; indiscriminately, without exception, across the board. ANTONYM selectively.

▸ adjective *wholesale destruction* EXTENSIVE, widespread, large-scale, wide-ranging, comprehensive, total, mass; indiscriminate. ANTONYM partial.

wholesome adjective **1** *wholesome food* HEALTHY, health-giving, healthful, good (for one), nutritious, nourishing; natural, uncontaminated, organic.

2 *wholesome fun* GOOD, ethical, moral, clean, virtuous, pure, innocent, chaste; uplifting, edifying, proper, correct, decent, harmless; *informal* squeaky clean.

wholly adverb **1** *the measures were wholly inadequate* COMPLETELY, totally, absolutely, entirely, fully, thoroughly, utterly, quite, perfectly, downright, in every respect, in all respects; *informal* one hundred percent, 'lock, stock, and barrel'.

2 *they rely wholly on you* EXCLUSIVELY, only, solely, purely, alone.

whoop noun & verb *whoops of delight* | *he whooped for joy*

SHOUT, cry, call, yell, roar, scream, shriek, screech, cheer, hoot; *informal* holler.

whoop-de-do exclamation *sarcastic* *the Yankees are going to the playoffs?—whoop-de-do* BIG DEAL, big whoop, whoopee, stop the presses; so what, so, who cares, and . . . ?.

whoops exclamation *whoops! I dropped the butter* OOPS, oh dear, oh no, eek, ack, yikes, uh-oh, sorry, silly me, doh, damn, darn, aargh, whoopsy, oopsy-daisy.

whopper noun *informal* **1** *among the prehistoric land creatures, T. rex was quite a whopper!* GIANT, monster, colossus, mammoth, monstrosity, brute; *informal* jumbo.

2 *Joseph's story is a whopper.* See LIE[1].

whopping adjective *informal* See HUGE.

whore noun *the whores on the street.* See PROSTITUTE.

▸ verb **1** *she spent her life whoring* WORK AS A PROSTITUTE, sell one's body, sell oneself, be on the streets.

2 *the men whored and drank* USE PROSTITUTES; *archaic* wench.

whorehouse noun See BROTHEL.

whorl noun *elegant whorls of wrought iron* LOOP, coil, hoop, ring, curl, twirl, twist, spiral, helix, arabesque.

why adverb *I know you're quitting school, but why?* HOW COME, for what reason, for what purpose, what for, to what end; *archaic* wherefore.

wicked adjective **1** *wicked deeds* EVIL, sinful, immoral, wrong, morally wrong, wrongful, bad, iniquitous, corrupt, base, mean, vile; villainous, nefarious, erring, foul, monstrous, shocking, outrageous, atrocious, abominable, depraved, reprehensible, hateful, detestable, despicable, odious, contemptible, horrible, heinous, egregious, execrable, fiendish, vicious, murderous, black-hearted, barbarous; criminal, illicit, unlawful, illegal, lawless, felonious, dishonest, unscrupulous; *Law* malfeasant; *informal* crooked; *dated* dastardly. ANTONYM virtuous.

2 *the wind was wicked* NASTY, harsh, formidable, unpleasant, foul, bad, disagreeable, irksome, troublesome, displeasing, uncomfortable, annoying, irritating, hateful, detestable. ANTONYM agreeable.

3 *a wicked sense of humor* MISCHIEVOUS, playful, naughty, impish, roguish, arch, puckish, cheeky.

4 *informal* *Sophie makes wicked cakes.* See EXCELLENT.

wickedness noun *they spoke of Stalin's wickedness* EVIL, sin, evildoing, sinfulness, iniquity, vileness, baseness, badness, wrongdoing, dishonesty, unscrupulousness, roguery, villainy, viciousness, degeneracy, depravity, immorality, vice, corruption, corruptness, devilry, fiendishness; *Law* malfeasance; *informal* crookedness; *formal* turpitude.

wide adjective **1** *a wide river* BROAD, extensive, spacious, vast, spread out. ANTONYM narrow.

2 *their eyes were wide with shock* FULLY OPEN, dilated, gaping, staring, wide open. ANTONYM closed.

3 *a wide range of opinion* COMPREHENSIVE, broad, extensive, diverse, full, ample, large, large-scale, wide-ranging, exhaustive, general, all-inclusive. ANTONYMS limited, restricted.

4 *her shot was wide* OFF TARGET, off the mark, inaccurate. ANTONYM on target.

▸ adverb **1** *he opened his eyes wide* FULLY, to the fullest/furthest extent, as far/much as possible, all the way, completely.

2 *he shot wide* OFF TARGET, inaccurately.

PHRASE: **wide open 1** *their mouths were wide open* AGAPE, yawning, open wide, fully open. **2** *the championship is wide open* UNDECIDED, unpredictable, uncertain, unsure, in the balance, up in the air; *informal* anyone's/anybody's guess. **3** *they were **wide open to** attacks* VULNERABLE TO, exposed to, unprotected from, undefended from, at risk of, in danger of.

wide-eyed adjective **1** *the onlookers were wide-eyed as the spaceship descended* SURPRISED, flabbergasted, amazed, astonished, astounded, stunned, staggered, goggle-eyed, pop-eyed, open-mouthed, dumbstruck; enthralled, fascinated, gripped.

2 *a wide-eyed youth in a wicked world* INNOCENT, naive, impressionable, ingenuous, childlike, credulous, trusting, unquestioning, unsophisticated, gullible.

widen verb **1** *a proposal to widen the highway* BROADEN, make/become wider, open up/out, expand, extend, enlarge.

2 *the organization must widen its support* INCREASE, augment, boost, swell, enlarge.

widespread adjective *widespread starvation* GENERAL, extensive, universal, common, global, worldwide, international, omnipresent, ubiquitous, across the board, blanket, sweeping, wholesale; predominant, prevalent, rife, broad, rampant, pervasive. ANTONYM limited.

width noun **1** *the width of the river* BREADTH, broadness, wideness, thickness, span, diameter, girth. ANTONYM length.

2 *the width of experience required* RANGE, breadth, compass, scope, span, spectrum, scale, extent, extensiveness, comprehensiveness. ANTONYM narrowness.

wield verb **1** *he was wielding a sword* BRANDISH, flourish, wave, swing; use, employ, handle.

2 *he has wielded power since 1972* EXERCISE, exert, hold, maintain, command, control.

wiener noun See table at SAUSAGE.

wife noun *after seventeen years, he was still madly in love with his wife* SPOUSE, partner, life partner, mate, consort, woman, helpmate, helpmeet, bride; *informal* old lady, wifey, better half, other half, missus, ball and chain, significant other.

wiggle verb *she wiggled her toes | the dancers wiggled across the stage* JIGGLE, wriggle, twitch, shimmy, joggle, wag, wobble, shake, twist, squirm, writhe; *informal* bump and grind.

wild adjective **1** *wild animals* UNTAMED, undomesticated, feral; fierce, ferocious, savage, untamable. ANTONYM tame.

2 *wild flowers* UNCULTIVATED, native, indigenous. ANTONYM cultivated.

3 *wild tribes* PRIMITIVE, uncivilized, uncultured; savage, barbarous, barbaric. ANTONYM civilized.

4 *wild country* UNINHABITED, unpopulated, uncultivated; rugged, rough, inhospitable, desolate, barren.

5 *wild weather* STORMY, squally, tempestuous, turbulent. ANTONYM calm.

6 *her wild black hair* DISHEVELED, tousled, tangled, windswept, untidy, unkempt, mussed up. ANTONYM tidy.

7 *wild behavior* UNCONTROLLED, unrestrained, out of control, undisciplined, unruly, rowdy, disorderly, riotous, corybantic. ANTONYMS self-disciplined, disciplined.

8 *wild with excitement* VERY EXCITED, delirious, in a frenzy; tumultuous, passionate, vehement, unrestrained. ANTONYM calm.

9 *informal I was wild with jealousy* DISTRAUGHT, frantic, beside oneself, in a frenzy, hysterical, deranged, berserk; *informal* mad, crazy.

10 *informal Hank went wild when he found out.* See FURIOUS sense 1.

11 *informal his family wasn't* ***wild about*** *me* ENAMORED OF, (very) enthusiastic about, (very) keen on, infatuated with, smitten with; *informal* crazy about, blown away by, mad about, nuts about. ANTONYMS indifferent, unenthusiastic.

12 *Bill's wild schemes* MADCAP, ridiculous, ludicrous, foolish, rash, stupid, foolhardy, idiotic, absurd, silly, ill-considered, senseless, nonsensical; impractical, impracticable, unworkable; *informal* crazy, crackpot, cockeyed, harebrained, cockamamie, loopy. ANTONYMS sensible, practical.

13 *a wild guess* RANDOM, arbitrary, haphazard, hit-or-miss, uninformed. ANTONYM considered.

PHRASE: **run wild 1** *the children are running wild* RUN AMOK, run riot, get out of control, be undisciplined. **2** *the garden had run wild* GROW UNCHECKED, grow profusely, run riot, ramble.

wilderness noun **1** *the Siberian wilderness* WILDS, wastes, bush, bush country, bushland, inhospitable region; desert, backcountry, outback, great outdoors; *informal* boondocks, boonies.

2 *the urban wilderness* WASTELAND, no man's land; *informal* wilds.

▸ adjective *wilderness activities* OUTDOOR RECREATION, ecotourism, adventure, backcountry.

wildlife noun *the wildlife of Southeast Asia* (WILD) ANIMALS, fauna, flora and fauna.

wilds plural noun See WILDERNESS.

wiles plural noun *it's just amazing how many women have fallen for his wiles* TRICKS, ruses, ploys, schemes, dodges, maneuvers, subterfuges, shenanigans, artifices; guile, artfulness, cunning, craftiness.

will[1] verb *accidents will happen* TEND TO, have a tendency to, are bound to, do, are going to, must.

will[2] noun **1** *the will to succeed* DETERMINATION, willpower, strength of character, resolution, resolve, resoluteness, single-mindedness, purposefulness, drive, commitment, dedication, doggedness, tenacity, tenaciousness, staying power.

2 *they stayed against their will* DESIRE, wish, preference, inclination, intention, intent, volition.

3 *God's will* WISH, desire, decision, choice; decree, command.

4 *the dead man's will* TESTAMENT, last will and testament, bequest.

▸ verb **1** *do what you will* WANT, wish, please, see/think fit, think best, like, choose, prefer.

2 *God willed it* DECREE, order, ordain, command.

3 *she willed the money to her husband* BEQUEATH, leave, hand down, pass on, settle on; *Law* devise.

PHRASE: **at will** *he thought he could walk in and out of my life at will* AS ONE PLEASES, as one thinks fit, to suit oneself, at whim.

willful adjective **1** *willful destruction* DELIBERATE, intentional, done on purpose, premeditated, planned, conscious. ANTONYMS accidental, unintentional.

2 *a willful child* HEADSTRONG, strong-willed, obstinate, stubborn, pigheaded, recalcitrant, uncooperative, obstreperous, ungovernable, unmanageable; balky; *formal* refractory, contumacious. ANTONYMS biddable, amenable.

willing adjective **1** *I'm willing to give it a try* READY, prepared, disposed, inclined, of a mind, minded; happy, glad, pleased, agreeable, amenable; *informal* game. ANTONYMS reluctant, disinclined.

2 *willing help* READILY GIVEN, willingly given, ungrudging, volunteered. ANTONYM grudging.

willingly adverb *I willingly agreed to make a donation* VOLUNTARILY, of one's own free will, of one's own accord; readily, without reluctance, ungrudgingly, cheerfully, happily, gladly, with pleasure.

willingness noun *we appreciate your willingness to help* READINESS, inclination, will, wish, desire, alacrity.

willowy adjective *as willowy as a young Doris Day* TALL, SLIM, slender, svelte, lissome, sylphlike, long-limbed, graceful, lithe; *informal* slinky.

willpower noun See WILL[2] noun sense 1.

willy-nilly adverb *cars were parked willy-nilly* HAPHAZARDLY, at random, randomly, every which way, here and there, all over the place, in no apparent order.

wilt verb **1** *the roses had begun to wilt* DROOP, sag, become limp, flop; wither, shrivel (up). ANTONYMS flourish, thrive.

2 *we wilted in the heat* LANGUISH, flag, droop, become listless, tire, wane. ANTONYM perk up.

wily adjective *a wily old rascal* SHREWD, clever, sharp, sharp-witted, astute, canny, smart; crafty, cunning, artful, sly, scheming, calculating, devious; *informal* clueful, tricky, foxy; *archaic* subtle. ANTONYM naive.

wimp noun *informal she was ashamed of her husband, who had shown himself to be a cowering wimp* COWARD, namby-pamby, pantywaist, milksop, weakling, milquetoast; *informal* sissy, wuss, pansy, candy-ass, scaredy-cat, chicken, twinkie, cupcake; *archaic* poltroon.

win verb **1** *he won the race* TAKE, be the victor in, be the winner of, come first in, take first prize in, triumph in, be successful in. ANTONYM lose.

2 *Claire knew he would win* BE THE WINNER, come in first, be victorious, carry the day, win the day, come out on top, succeed, triumph, prevail. ANTONYM lose.

3 *he won a cash prize* SECURE, gain, garner, collect, pick up, walk away/off with, carry off; *informal* land, net, bag, scoop.

4 *she won his heart* CAPTIVATE, steal, snare, capture.

▸ noun *a 1–0 win* VICTORY, triumph, conquest. ANTONYM defeat.

PHRASE: **win over** *do you really believe that flowers and* *jewelry are enough to win her over?* PERSUADE, convince, sway, prevail on; seduce.

wince verb *he winced at the pain* GRIMACE, make a face, flinch, blanch, start.

▸ noun *a wince of pain* GRIMACE, flinch, start.

THE RIGHT WORD

The same individual might **wince** when receiving a flu shot, **flinch** from a difficult task, and **cower** in fear at the approach of a tornado. All of these verbs mean to draw back in alarm, disgust, faintheartedness, or servility, but there are subtle differences among them. To *wince* is to make a slight recoiling movement, often an involuntary contraction of the facial features, in response to pain or discomfort (*to wince when a singer misses a high note*), while *flinch* may imply a similar drawing-back motion or, more abstractly, a reluctance or avoidance (*to tackle the job without flinching*). *Cower* and **cringe** both refer to stooped postures, although *cower* is usually associated with fearful trembling (*he cowered in the doorway*) while *cringe* is usually linked to servile, cowardly, or fawning behavior (*she cringed before her father's authority*). More than any of the other verbs here, **recoil** suggests a physical movement away from something (*recoil at the sight of a poisonous snake*), although that movement may also be psychological (*recoil at the very thought of a family reunion*).

wind[1] noun **1** *the trees were swaying in the wind* BREEZE, current of air; gale, hurricane; *literary* zephyr.

2 *Jez got his wind back* BREATH.

3 *the discomfort of holding back one's wind* FLATULENCE, gas; *informal* fart(s), farting; *formal* flatus. PHRASES: **get wind of** *informal White House officials got wind of the plan* HEAR ABOUT/OF, learn about/of, find out about, pick up on, be told about/of, be informed of; *informal* hear (about) through the grapevine. **in the wind** *we fear that civil war is in the wind* ON THE WAY, coming, about to happen, in the offing, in the air, on the horizon, approaching, looming, brewing, afoot; *informal* in the cards.

wind[2] verb **1** *this road winds dangerously* TWIST AND TURN, twist, bend, curve, loop, zigzag, weave, snake.

2 *she wound a towel around her waist* WRAP, furl, entwine, lace, loop.

3 *he wound the yarn into a ball* COIL, roll, twist, twine. PHRASES: **wind down 1** *informalthey needed to wind down* RELAX, unwind, calm down, cool down/off, ease up/off, take it easy, rest, put one's feet up; *informal* take a load off, hang loose, chill, chill out, kick back. **2** *the summer was winding down* DRAW TO A CLOSE, come to an end, tail off, taper off, slack off, slacken off, slow down, die, die down. **wind up 1** *let's wind up this meeting and go to lunch* CONCLUDE, bring to an end/close, end, terminate; *informal* wrap up. **2** *informal I never thought that Jerry would wind up in real estate* END UP, finish up, find oneself.

winded adjective *he is winded just from walking up the stairs* OUT OF BREATH, breathless, gasping for breath, panting, hyperventilating; *informal* huffing and puffing.

windfall noun *the inheritance from Uncle Larry was an unexpected windfall* BONANZA, jackpot, pennies from heaven, stroke/piece of luck, godsend, manna from heaven.

winding noun *the windings of the stream* TWIST, turn, turning, bend, loop, curve, zigzag, meander.

▸ adjective *the winding country roads* TWISTING AND TURNING, meandering, windy, twisty, bending, curving, zigzag, zigzagging, serpentine, sinuous, snaking, tortuous; *rare* flexuous. ANTONYM straight.

window noun *there are two small windows on the south side* opening, aperture. See table.

WINDOWS

awning window	jalousie
barred window	loop window
bay window	Palladian window
bow window	picture window
bull's-eye	porthole
casement	projected window
Chicago window	ribbon window
cottage window	rose window
dormer	sash window
double-glazed window	sidelight
double-hung window	single-hung window
drop window	stained glass window
fanlight	store window
fan window	storm window
French window	transom window
gable window	Venetian window
hopper casement	wheel window

windpipe noun *a blockage in the windpipe* TRACHEA, pharynx; throat.

windswept adjective **1** *the windswept prairies* EXPOSED, bleak, bare, desolate.

2 *his windswept hair* DISHEVELED, tousled, unkempt, wind-blown, untidy, mussed up.

windy adjective **1** *a windy day* BREEZY, blowy, blustery, gusty; wild, stormy, squally, tempestuous, boisterous. ANTONYM still.

2 *a windy hillside* WINDSWEPT, exposed, open to the elements, bare, bleak. ANTONYM sheltered.

wine noun *informal* VINO, the grape; *literary* vintage. See table. See also note at MERITAGE.

WINES AND WINE GRAPES

Aglianco	Cabernet
Albariño	Cabernet Franc
Alicante Bouschet	Cabernet Sauvignon
Amarone	Carignane
Amontillado	Carnelian
Ardeche	Cava
Arneis	Chablis
Asti Spumante	Chambertin
Barbaresco	Chambourcin
Barbera	Champagne
Barolo	Charbono
Barsac	Chardonnay
Beaujolais	Château Pétrus
Beaujolais-Villages	Chenas
Beaune	Chenin Blanc
blanc de blancs	Chianti
blanc de noirs	Chianti Classico
blush	Chianti Ruffina
Bordeaux	Chiroubles
Bordeaux Blanc	Claret
Bordeaux Rouge	Classico
Bourgogne Blanc	Concord
Brouilly	Condrieu
Brunello	Corvina
brut	Côte de Brouilly
Bual	demi sec
Burger	Dolcetto
Burgundy	doux

Durif	Palomino
Eiswein	Pauillac
extra dry	Pedro Ximénez
extra sec	Petite Syrah
Fino	Petite Verdot
Fleurie	Piesporter
Flor	Pinot
Flora	Pinot Bianco
Folle Blanche	Pinot Blanc
fortified	Pinot Grigio
Frascati	Pinot Gris
French Colombard	Pinot Noir
Frontignac	Pinotage
Fumé Blanc	Pomerol
Gamay	Port
Garnacha	Pouilly-Fumé
Gattinara	Premier Cru
Gewürztraminer	Prosecco
Ghemme	Régnié
Grand Cru	Retsina
Graves	Rhenish
Grenache	Riesling
Grignolino	Rioja
Haut-Medoc	Riserva
Hermitage	Rosé
Heuriger	Roussanne
ice wine	Ruby Port
Johannisberg Riesling	Saint-Amour
Johannisberger	Saint-Émilion
Juliènas	Saint-EstÈphe
Kabinett	sake
Labrusca	Sancerre
Lambrusco	Sangiovese
Liebfraumilch	Sauternes
Madiera	Sauvgnon Blanc
Málaga	Sauvignon
Malbec	Scheurebe
Malmsey	sec
Malvasia	sekt
Malvasia Blanca	Sémillon
Malvoisie	semisweet
Manzanilla	Sercial
Margaux	sherry
Marichal Foch	Shiraz
Marsanne	Soave
Mataro	Solera
Medoc	Souzao
Melon	Spatlese
Meritage™	Spumante
Merlot	Sylvaner
Meursault	Symphony
Monastrell	Syrah
Montepulciano	table wine
Montilla	Taurasi
Montrachet	Tavel
Morgon	Tawny Port
Moscato	Tempranillo
Moselle	Toscana
Moulin-à-Vent	Traminer
Mourvedre	Trebbiano
Mousseux	Trockenbeerenauslese
Muscadel	Valpolicella
Muscadelle	Vendange
Muscadet	Verdelho
Muscadine	Verdicchio
Muscat	Vermouth
Muscatel	Vernaccia
Nebbiolo	vin de pays
Negra Mole	vin de table
Negro Amaro	vin ordinaire
Niersteiner	vinho verde
nonvintage	vino
off-dry	Vino Nobile
Oloroso	vintage
Orvieto	Vintage Port
Viognier	White Zinfandel
Vouvray	Zinfandel

See also tables at BEER, COCKTAIL, and LIQUOR.

wing noun **1** *a bird's wings literary* pinion.

2 *the east wing of the house* PART, section, side; annex, extension, ell.

3 *the radical wing of the party* FACTION, camp, arm, branch, group, section, set, coterie, cabal; side, end.

▸ verb **1** *a seagull winged its way over the sea* FLY, glide, soar.

2 *the bomb winged past* HURTLE, speed, shoot, whiz, zoom, streak, fly.

3 *the hunter only winged the hawk* WOUND, graze, hit.

PHRASE: **wing it** *informal if you don't know all the words, just wing it* IMPROVISE, play it by ear, extemporize, ad lib, fly by the seat of one's pants, fake it.

wink verb **1** *he winked an eye at her* BLINK, flutter, bat.

2 *the diamond winked in the moonlight* SPARKLE, twinkle, flash, glitter, gleam, shine, scintillate. PHRASE: **wink at** *too many people on the payroll were willing to wink at the corruption in high places* TURN A BLIND EYE TO, close one's eyes to, ignore, overlook, disregard; connive at, condone, tolerate.

winner noun *the winners receive trophies at the closing ceremony* VICTOR, champion, conqueror, vanquisher, hero; medalist; *informal* champ, top dog, world-beater. ANTONYM loser.

winning adjective **1** *the winning team* VICTORIOUS, successful, triumphant, vanquishing, conquering; first, first-place, top, leading.

2 *a winning smile* ENGAGING, charming, appealing, endearing, sweet, cute, winsome, attractive, pretty, prepossessing, fetching, lovely, lovable, adorable, delightful, disarming, captivating, bewitching.

winnings plural noun *he put all his winnings into a college fund* PRIZE MONEY, gains, prize, booty, spoils, loot; proceeds, profits, earnings, takings, purse.

winnow verb *the chaff is winnowed from the grain* SEPARATE (OUT), divide, segregate, sort out, sift out, filter out; isolate, narrow down; remove, get rid of.

winsome adjective See WINNING sense 2.

winter sports noun See table.

WINTER SPORTS

alpine skiing	luge
biathlon	moguls
bobsled	Nordic combined
cross-country skiing	skating
curling	skeleton
dog racing	ski jumping
downhill skiing	slalom
figure skating	snowboarding
freestyle skiing	speed skating
giant slalom	super-G
hockey	

wintry adjective **1** *wintry weather* BLEAK, cold, chilly, chill, frosty, freezing, icy, snowy, blizzardy, arctic, glacial, bitter, raw, hypothermic; *informal* nippy. ANTONYMS summery, hot.

2 *a wintry smile* UNFRIENDLY, unwelcoming, cool, cold, frosty, frigid, dismal, cheerless. ANTONYMS friendly, warm.

wipe verb 1 *Beth wiped the table* RUB, mop, sponge, swab; clean, dry, polish, towel.

2 *he **wiped** the marks **off** the window* RUB OFF, clean off, remove from, get rid of from, take off from, erase from, efface from.

3 *she wiped the memory from her mind* OBLITERATE, expunge, erase, blot out.

▸ noun *he gave the table a wipe* RUB, mop, sponge, swab; clean, polish.

PHRASE: **wipe out** 1 *the influenza of 1918 wiped out entire families* DESTROY, annihilate, eradicate, eliminate; slaughter, massacre, kill, exterminate; demolish, raze to the ground; *informal* take out, zap, waste; *literary* slay. 2 *I wiped out the file accidentally* ERASE, delete, trash, zap, kill, nuke.

wire noun *the wires will be run under the ground* CABLE, lead, cord; power line; filament.

wired adjective 1 *she's totally wired* HYPER, buzzing, excited, adrenalized, high, manic, tense, strung out, antsy.

2 *get your company wired* ONLINE, hooked up, connected, web-enabled.

wiry adjective 1 *a wiry man* SINEWY, athletic, strong; lean, spare, thin, stringy, skinny. ANTONYMS flabby, frail.

2 *wiry hair* COARSE, rough, stiff; curly, wavy. ANTONYMS straight, smooth.

wisdom noun 1 *we questioned the wisdom of the decision* SAGACITY, intelligence, sense, common sense, shrewdness, astuteness, smartness, judiciousness, judgment, prudence, circumspection; logic, rationale, rationality, soundness, advisability. ANTONYMS folly, stupidity.

2 *the wisdom of the East* KNOWLEDGE, learning, erudition, sophistication, scholarship, philosophy; lore. See note at KNOWLEDGE.

wise adjective 1 *a wise old man* SAGE, sagacious, intelligent, clever, learned, knowledgeable, enlightened; astute, smart, shrewd, sharp-witted, canny, knowing; sensible, prudent, discerning, discriminating, sophisticated, judicious, perceptive, insightful, perspicacious; rational, logical, sound, sane; *formal* sapient. ANTONYM foolish.

2 *wise course of action.* See SENSIBLE. PHRASE: **wise to** *informal countless generations of local fishermen have been wise to these riptides* AWARE OF, familiar with, acquainted with; *formal* cognizant of.

wisecrack noun *informal her parents were not amused by Lenny's wisecracks* JOKE, witticism, quip, jest, sally; pun, bon mot; *informal* crack, gag, funny, one-liner, zinger.

wish verb 1 *I **wished for** power* DESIRE, want, hope for, covet, dream of, long for, yearn for, crave, hunger for, lust after; aspire to, be desirous of, set one's heart on, seek, fancy, hanker after; *informal* have a yen for, itch for.

2 *they can do as they wish* WANT, desire, feel inclined, feel like, care; choose, please, think fit.

3 *I wish you to send them a message* WANT, desire, require.

4 *I wished him farewell* BID.

▸ noun 1 *his wish to own a Mercedes* DESIRE, longing, yearning, inclination, urge, whim, craving, hunger; hope, aspiration, aim, ambition, dream; *informal* hankering, yen, itch.

2 *her parents' wishes* REQUEST, requirement, bidding, instruction, direction, demand, entreaty, order, command; want, desire; will; *literary* behest.

wishy-washy adjective 1 *he's so wishy-washy* FEEBLE, ineffectual, weak, vapid, effete, gutless, spineless, limp, namby-pamby, spiritless, indecisive, characterless; pathetic. ANTONYMS strong, decisive.

2 *wishy-washy soup* WATERY, weak, thin; tasteless, flavorless, insipid. ANTONYM tasty.

3 *a wishy-washy color* PALE, insipid, pallid, muted, pastel. ANTONYM vibrant.

wisp noun *a stray wisp of hair* STRAND, tendril, lock; scrap, shred, thread.

wispy adjective *the seeds are borne on wispy silken tufts* THIN, fine, feathery, flyaway.

wistful adjective *the old photos gave me a wistful feeling* NOSTALGIC, yearning, longing; plaintive, regretful, rueful, melancholy, mournful, elegiac; pensive, reflective, contemplative.

wit noun 1 (**wits**) *he needed all his wits to escape* INTELLIGENCE, shrewdness, astuteness, cleverness, canniness, sense, common sense, wisdom, sagacity, judgment, acumen, insight; brains, mind; *informal* gumption, savvy, horse sense, smarts, street smarts.

2 *my sparkling wit* WITTINESS, humor, funniness, drollery, esprit; repartee, badinage, banter, wordplay; jokes, witticisms, quips, puns.

3 *she's such a wit* COMEDIAN, humorist, comic, joker, jokester; *informal* wag, card, funnyman.

THE RIGHT WORD

If you're good at perceiving analogies between dissimilar things and expressing them in quick, sharp, spontaneous observations or remarks, you have **wit. Humor**, on the other hand, is the ability to perceive what is comical, ridiculous, or ludicrous in a situation or character, and to express it in a way that makes others see or feel the same thing. It suggests more sympathy, tolerance, and kindliness than *wit* (*she maintained a sense of humor in the midst of trying circumstances*). **Irony** is the implicit humor in the contradiction between what is meant and what is expressed, or in the discrepancy between appearance and reality. An example would be to shout, in the midst of a hurricane, "What a perfect day for a wedding!" Although **sarcasm** may take the form of irony, it is less subtle and is often used harshly or bitterly to wound or ridicule someone. Unlike irony, however, *sarcasm* depends on tone of voice for its effect (*"a fine friend you turned out to be!" he said, with obvious sarcasm*). **Satire** usually implies the use of sarcasm or irony for the purpose of ridicule or criticism, often directed at institutions or political figures (*she wrote political satire for the comedy team*). If you are good at making quick, witty replies, you will be known for your **repartee**, which is the art of responding pointedly and skillfully with wit or humor in a conversational exchange (*no one could compete with her witty repartee*).

witch noun 1 *the witch cast a spell* SORCERESS, enchantress, necromancer; Wiccan; *archaic* pythoness.

2 *informal she's a nasty old witch* HAG, crone, harpy, harridan, she-devil; *informal* battle-ax.

witchcraft noun *they've practiced witchcraft on this island for centuries* SORCERY, black magic, white magic, magic, witching, witchery, wizardry; spells, incantations; Wicca; *rare* thaumaturgy.

with preposition **1** *Sharon is the one with Ike* ACCOMPANIED BY, escorted by, in the company of.

2 *I'll have a salad with the steak* IN ADDITION TO, as well as, alongside.

withdraw verb **1** *she withdrew her hand from his* REMOVE, extract, pull out, take out; take back, take away. ANTONYM insert.

2 *the ban on advertising was withdrawn* ABOLISH, cancel, lift, set aside, end, stop, remove, reverse, revoke, rescind, repeal, annul, void. ANTONYM introduce.

3 *she withdrew the allegation* RETRACT, take back, go back on, recant, disavow, disclaim, repudiate, renounce, abjure; back down, climb down, backtrack, backpedal, do a U-turn, eat one's words. ANTONYM put forward.

4 *the troops **withdrew from** the city* LEAVE, pull out of, evacuate, quit, (beat a) retreat from. ANTONYM enter.

5 *his partner **withdrew from** the project* PULL OUT OF, back out of, bow out of; get cold feet.

6 *they withdrew to their rooms* RETIRE, retreat, adjourn, decamp; leave, depart, absent oneself; *formal* repair; *dated* remove; *literary* betake oneself.

withdrawal noun **1** *the withdrawal of subsidies* REMOVAL, abolition, cancellation, discontinuation, termination, elimination.

2 *the withdrawal of the troops* DEPARTURE, pullout, exit, exodus, evacuation, retreat.

3 *she's suffering the effects of withdrawal* DETOXIFICATION; *informal* detox, (going) cold turkey.

withdrawn adjective *Kate has become so withdrawn since Lucius left for the Gulf* INTROVERTED, unsociable, inhibited, uncommunicative, unforthcoming, quiet, taciturn, reticent, reserved, retiring, private, reclusive; shy, timid; aloof, indrawn; *informal* standoffish. ANTONYM outgoing.

wither verb **1** *the flowers withered in the sun* SHRIVEL (UP), dry up; wilt, droop, go limp, fade, perish; shrink, waste away, atrophy. ANTONYMS thrive, flourish.

2 *her confidence withered* DIMINISH, dwindle, shrink, lessen, fade, ebb, wane; evaporate, disappear. ANTONYM grow.

withering adjective *a withering look | withering remarks* SCORNFUL, contemptuous, scathing, stinging, devastating; humiliating, mortifying. ANTONYM admiring.

withhold verb **1** *he withheld the information* HOLD BACK, keep back, refuse to give; retain, hold on to; hide, conceal, keep secret; *informal* sit on.

2 *she could not withhold her tears* SUPPRESS, repress, hold back, fight back, choke back, control, check, restrain, contain.

within preposition **1** *within the prison walls* INSIDE, in, enclosed by, surrounded by; within the bounds of, within the confines of. ANTONYM outside.

2 *within a few hours* IN LESS THAN, in under, in no more than, after only.

without preposition **1** *thousands were without food* LACKING, short of, deprived of, in need of, wanting, needing, requiring.

2 *I don't want to go without you* UNACCOMPANIED BY, unescorted by; in the absence of; *informal* sans, minus.

withstand verb *it was a miracle that they were able to withstand the brutal winter* RESIST, weather, survive, endure, cope with, stand, tolerate, bear, stomach, defy, brave, hold out against, tough out, bear up against; stand up to, face, confront.

witless adjective *another one of his witless ideas* FOOLISH, stupid, unintelligent, idiotic, brainless, mindless; fatuous, inane, half-baked, empty-headed, slow-witted; *informal* thick, birdbrained, pea-brained, dopey, doltish, dim, dimwitted, halfwitted, dippy, dumb-ass, lamebrained, wooden-headed, daft.

witness noun **1** *witnesses claimed that he started the fight* OBSERVER, onlooker, eyewitness, spectator, viewer, watcher; bystander, passerby.

2 *she cross-examined the witness* DEPONENT, testifier.

▸ verb **1** *who witnessed the incident?* SEE, observe, watch, view, notice, spot; be present at, attend; *literary* behold; *informal* get a look at.

2 *Canada witnessed a cultural explosion* UNDERGO, experience, go through, see; enjoy; suffer.

3 *the will is correctly witnessed* COUNTERSIGN, sign, endorse, validate; notarize. PHRASE: **bear witness to** *his diary bears witness to his lifelong struggle with depression* ATTEST TO, testify to, confirm, evidence, prove, verify, corroborate, substantiate; show, demonstrate, indicate, reveal, bespeak.

witticism noun *the publisher asked her to put some of her witticisms in a weekly feature* JOKE, quip, jest, pun, play on words, bon mot; *informal* one-liner, gag, funny, crack, wisecrack, zinger.

witty adjective *it was a pleasure to sit and listen to their witty conversations* HUMOROUS, amusing, droll, funny, comic, comical; jocular, facetious, waggish, tongue-in-cheek; sparkling, scintillating, entertaining; clever, quick-witted.

wizard noun **1** *the wizard cast a spell over them* SORCERER, warlock, magus, (black) magician, necromancer, enchanter; *archaic* mage.

2 *a financial wizard* GENIUS, expert, master, virtuoso, maestro, marvel, Wunderkind, guru; *informal* hotshot, demon, whiz kid, buff, pro, ace; maven.

wizardry noun *the lonely retreat where Muzzwell practiced his wizardry* SORCERY, witchcraft, witchery, witching, magic, black magic, enchantment; spells, charms.

wizened adjective *their wizened faces said much about the hard lives they had endured* WRINKLED, lined, creased, shriveled (up), withered, weather-beaten, shrunken, gnarled, aged.

wobble verb **1** *the table wobbled* ROCK, teeter, jiggle, sway, seesaw, shake.

2 *he wobbled across to the door* TEETER, totter, stagger; lurch.

3 *her voice wobbled* TREMBLE, shake, quiver, quaver, waver.

▸ noun **1** *she stood up with a wobble* TOTTER, teeter, sway.

2 *the operatic wobble in her voice* TREMOR, quiver, quaver, trembling, vibrato.

wobbly adjective **1** *a wobbly table* UNSTEADY, unstable, shaky, rocky, rickety; unsafe, precarious; uneven, unbalanced; *informal* wonky. ANTONYMS stable, steady.

2 *her legs were a bit wobbly* SHAKY, quivery, weak, unsteady; *informal* trembly, like jelly. ANTONYM steady.

woe noun **1** *a tale of woe* MISERY, sorrow, distress, wretchedness, sadness, unhappiness, heartache, heartbreak, despondency, despair, depression, regret, gloom, melancholy; adversity, misfortune, disaster, suffering, hardship; *literary* dolor. ANTONYMS joy, happiness.

2 *financial woes* TROUBLE, difficulty, problem, trial, tribulation, misfortune, setback, reverse.

woebegone adjective *we were not prepared to find Thom in such a woebegone condition* SAD, unhappy, miserable, dejected, disconsolate, forlorn, crestfallen, downcast, glum, gloomy, doleful, downhearted, heavy-hearted, despondent, melancholy, sorrowful, mournful, woeful, plaintive, depressed, wretched, desolate; *informal* down in/at the mouth, down in the dumps, blue. ANTONYM cheerful.

woeful adjective **1** *her face was woeful.* See WOEBEGONE.

2 *a woeful ballad* TRAGIC, sad, miserable, cheerless, gloomy, sorry, pitiful, pathetic, traumatic, depressing, heartbreaking, heart-rending, tear-jerking, gut-wrenching. ANTONYMS cheerful, uplifting.

3 *the team's woeful performance* LAMENTABLE, awful, terrible, atrocious, disgraceful, deplorable, shameful, hopeless, dreadful; substandard, poor, inadequate, inferior, unsatisfactory; *informal* rotten, appalling, crummy, pathetic, pitiful, lousy, abysmal, dire, crappy, lame, brutal. ANTONYM excellent.

wolf noun **1** *a pack of wolves.* See table.

2 *informal he's a bit of a wolf.* See WOMANIZER.

▸ verb *he **wolfed down** his breakfast* DEVOUR, gobble (up), guzzle, gulp down, bolt (down); *informal* put away, demolish, shovel in/down, scoff (down), scarf (up).

WILD DOGS

Arctic fox	jackal
Arctic wolf	prairie wolf
brush wolf	red fox
coyote	silver fox
cross fox	swift fox
dingo	timber wolf
fox	tundra wolf
gray wolf	wolf

wolfish adjective *informal her wolfish brother gave me the creeps* LASCIVIOUS, lecherous, lustful; predatory, rapacious.

woman noun **1** *a woman got out of the car* LADY, girl, female; matron; *Scottish* lass, lassie; *informal* chick, girlie, sister, dame, broad, gal; grrrl; *literary* maid, maiden, damsel; *archaic* wench, gentlewoman; **(women)** womenfolk.

2 *he found himself a new woman* GIRLFRIEND, sweetheart, partner, significant other, inamorata, lover, mistress; fiancée; wife, spouse; *informal* missus, better half, main squeeze, squeeze, babe, baby; *dated* lady friend, lady love.

WORD NOTE **female**

There's nothing like a *dame.* Unless it's a hot *babe* or a shy young *maiden.* Whether one regards the abundance of nouns for the human female as a sign of a phallocratic culture or an indication of woman's infinite variety (or both), there's no denying the rude poetry of *chick, broad,* and *minx* or the provincial charm of *lass, colleen,* and *demoiselle.* A Damon Runyon might refer to a *doll* or a *skirt,* a Nabokov linger over a *nymphet,* C.S. Lewis address a *daughter of Eve,* Sir Lancelot rescue a *damsel,* and Falstaff call for a *wench.* In rap songs a woman may be reduced to her sexual parts and in romantic poetry find herself a *goddess* or a "belle dame sans merci." So many possibilities! One can suggest an entire mind-set or social stratum by choosing just the right synonym. Is your companion a formidable *dowager* or just a *nice bit of fluff?* The Queen of Sheba speaks for her sex when she reminds us, in Flaubert's novel *The Temptation of St. Anthony,* "I am not a woman, I am a world." —**MD**

womanish adjective *Andrew's first stage role was that of a womanish baker from Brooklyn* EFFEMINATE, girlish, girly, unmanly, unmasculine, epicene. ANTONYM manly.

womanizer noun *informal her friends tried to warn her about his reputation as a womanizer* PHILANDERER, Don Juan, Casanova, Romeo, Lothario, playboy, ladies' man, flirt, seducer, rake, roué, lecher, libertine, debauchee; *informal* skirt-chaser, wolf, ladykiller, lech.

womankind noun *we are mindful of the plight of womankind throughout the world* WOMEN; woman, the female sex, womenkind, womanhood, womenfolk; *informal* the gentler sex.

womanly adjective **1** *womanly virtues* FEMININE, female; *archaic* feminal. ANTONYM masculine.

2 *her womanly figure* VOLUPTUOUS, curvaceous, shapely, ample, buxom, full-figured; Junoesque, Rubenesque; *informal* curvy, busty. ANTONYM boyish.

wonder noun **1** *she was speechless with wonder* AWE, admiration, wonderment, fascination; surprise, astonishment, stupefaction, amazement.

2 *the wonders of nature* MARVEL, miracle, phenomenon, sensation, spectacle, beauty; curiosity; *informal* humdinger.

▸ verb **1** *I wondered what was on her mind* PONDER, think about, meditate on, reflect on, muse on, puzzle over, speculate about, conjecture; be curious about.

2 *people wondered at such bravery* MARVEL, be amazed, be astonished, stand in awe, be dumbfounded, gape, goggle; *informal* be flabbergasted.

wonderful adjective *a wonderful vacation in Europe* MARVELOUS, magnificent, superb, glorious, sublime, lovely, delightful; *informal* super, great, fantastic, terrific, tremendous, sensational, incredible, fabulous, fab, out of this world, awesome, magic, wicked, far out, killer, brilliant, peachy, dandy, neat, swell. ANTONYM awful.

wonky adjective *informal* **1** *a wonky picture.* See CROOKED sense 3.

2 *wonky stools.* See WOBBLY sense 1.

wont adjective *he was wont to arise at 5:30* ACCUSTOMED, used, given, inclined.

▸ noun *Paul drove fast, as was his wont* CUSTOM, habit, way, practice, convention, rule.

wonted adjective *he retreated to his wonted solitude* CUSTOMARY, habitual, usual, accustomed, familiar, normal, conventional, routine, common.

woo verb *dated* **1** *Richard wooed Joan all through their college years* ROMANTICALLY PURSUE, pursue, chase (after); *dated* court, pay court to, romance, seek the hand of, set one's cap for/at, make love to.

2 *the party wooed voters with promises* SEEK, pursue, curry favor with, try to win, try to attract, try to cultivate.

3 *an attempt to woo him out of retirement* ENTICE, tempt, coax, persuade, wheedle; *informal* sweet-talk.

WORD NOTE **woo**

There are plenty of synonyms for sex, not enough for flirtation and romantic pursuit, for the work of winning someone over. *Make love* used to refer to the process toward, with a little useful ambiguity; now it strictly denotes the act. *Court* sounds too aristocratic and medieval; *seduce* is overly limited to the carnal objective. That leaves *woo.* It's true that *woo* sounds a little goofy, but that might be ameliorated by more frequent use, or could even be considered a useful bonus connotation in a word for an activity that can put anybody in danger of making a fool of themselves. —**DA**

wood noun 1 *there should be enough wood left over to make a small shelf* LUMBER, timber, planks, planking; logs, sawlogs.

2 (usu. **woods**) *a walk through the woods* FOREST, woodland, trees; copse, coppice, grove, bush, woodlot.

wooded adjective *the wooded area behind the library* FORESTED, treed, tree-covered, woody; *literary* sylvan.

wooden adjective 1 *a wooden door* WOOD, timber, woody; ligneous.

2 *his wooden posture* STILTED, stiff, unnatural, awkward, leaden; dry, flat, stodgy, lifeless, passionless, spiritless, soulless.

3 *her face was wooden* EXPRESSIONLESS, impassive, poker-faced, emotionless, blank, vacant, unresponsive.

woodland noun *they've cleared part of the woodland to build a cabin* WOODS, wood, forest, trees; *archaic* greenwood.

woof noun & verb *a little dog with a big woof* | *her dogs woofed at the slightest sound* BARK, yap, yelp, bay.

wool noun 1 *sheep's wool* FLEECE, hair, coat; floccus.

2 *a sweater made of cream wool* YARN. PHRASE: **pull the wool over someone's eyes** *informal he was never very good at pulling the wool over Mom's eyes* DECEIVE, fool, trick, hoodwink, dupe, delude; *informal* lead up the garden path, put one over on, bamboozle, con.

woolgathering noun *lost in her daily woolgathering* DAYDREAMING, reverie, dreaming, musing, abstraction, preoccupation; absentmindedness, forgetfulness.

woolly adjective 1 *a woolly hat* WOOLEN, wool, fleecy.

2 *a sheep's woolly coat* FLEECY, shaggy, hairy, fluffy, flocculent.

3 *woolly generalizations* VAGUE, ill-defined, hazy, unclear, fuzzy, blurry, foggy, nebulous, imprecise, inexact, indefinite; confused, muddled.

woozy adjective *informal*. See GROGGY.

word noun 1 *the Italian word for "ham"* TERM, name, expression, designation, locution, vocable; *formal* appellation.

2 *his words were meant kindly* REMARK, comment, observation, statement, utterance, pronouncement.

3 (**words**) *I've got three weeks to learn the words* SCRIPT, lyrics, libretto.

4 *I give you my word* PROMISE, word of honor, assurance, guarantee, undertaking; pledge, vow, oath, bond; *formal* troth.

5 *I want a word with you* TALK, conversation, chat, tête-à-tête, heart-to-heart, one-to-one, man-to-man; discussion, consultation; *informal* confab, powwow; *formal* confabulation.

6 *there's no word from the hospital* NEWS, information, communication, intelligence; message, report, communiqué, dispatch, bulletin; *informal* info, dope; *literary* tidings.

7 *word has it he's turned over a new leaf* RUMOR, hearsay, talk, gossip; *informal* the grapevine, the word on the street.

8 *I'm waiting for the word from HQ* INSTRUCTION, order, command; signal, prompt, cue, tip-off; *informal* go-ahead, thumbs up, green light.

9 *Heather's word was law* COMMAND, order, decree, edict; bidding, will.

10 *our word now must be success* MOTTO, watchword, slogan, catchword, buzzword.

▸ verb *the question was carefully worded* PHRASE, express, put, couch, frame, formulate, style; say, utter.

PHRASES: **have words** *we had words, and Jason walked out* QUARREL, argue, disagree, squabble, bicker, fight, wrangle, dispute, fall out, clash, row. **in a word** *in a word, it was a miserable day for sailing* BRIEFLY, to be brief, in short, in a nutshell, to come to the point, to cut a long story short, not to put too fine a point on it; to sum up, to summarize, in summary. **word for word** 1 *they took down the speeches word for word* VERBATIM, letter for letter, to the letter; exactly, faithfully. 2 *a word-for-word translation* VERBATIM, literal, exact, direct, accurate, faithful; unadulterated, unabridged.

wording noun *the wording of the question was ambiguous* PHRASING, words, phraseology, language, expression, terminology.

wordplay noun *her verses are often cryptic and usually contain some clever wordplay* PUNNING, puns, play on words; wit, witticisms, repartee.

wordy adjective *a wordy sermon* LONG-WINDED, verbose, prolix, lengthy, protracted, long-drawn-out, overlong, rambling, circumlocutory, periphrastic, pleonastic; loquacious, garrulous, voluble; *informal* windy. ANTONYM succinct.

work noun 1 *a day's work in the fields* LABOR, toil, slog, drudgery, exertion, effort, industry, service; *informal* grind, sweat, elbow grease; *literary* travail. ANTONYMS leisure, rest. See note at LABOR.

2 *I'm looking for work* EMPLOYMENT, a job, a position, a situation, a post; an occupation, a profession, a career, a vocation, a calling; wage labor; tasks, jobs, duties, assignments, projects; chores. ANTONYMS unemployment, retirement.

3 *works of literature* COMPOSITION, piece, creation; opus, oeuvre.

4 (**works**) *the complete works of Shakespeare* WRITINGS, oeuvre, canon, output.

5 *this is the work of a radical faction* HANDIWORK, doing, act, deed.

6 (**works**) *a lifetime spent doing good works* DEEDS, acts, actions.

7 *informal* (**the works**) *for only $60 you can get the works* EVERYTHING, the full treatment; *informal* the lot, the whole shebang, the full nine yards, the whole kit and kaboodle, the whole ball of wax.

▸ verb 1 *staff worked late into the night* TOIL, labor, exert oneself, slave (away); keep at it, put one's nose to the grindstone; *informal* slog (away), plug away, put one's back into it, knock oneself out, sweat blood; *literary* travail. ANTONYMS rest, play.

2 *he worked in education for years* BE EMPLOYED, have a job, earn one's living, do business.

3 *farmers worked the land* CULTIVATE, farm, till, plow.

4 *his car was working perfectly* FUNCTION, go, run, operate; *informal* behave.

5 *how do I work this machine?* OPERATE, use, handle, control, manipulate, run.

6 *their ploy worked* SUCCEED, work out, turn out well, go as planned, get results, be effective; *informal* come off, pay off, do/turn the trick. ANTONYM fail.

7 *makeup can work miracles* BRING ABOUT, accomplish, achieve, produce, perform, create, engender, contrive, effect.

8 *informal can you* ***work it*** *so I can get in for free?* ARRANGE IT/THINGS, manipulate it/things, contrive it; pull strings, fix it, swing it, wangle it.

9 *he worked the crowd into a frenzy* STIR (UP), excite, drive, move, rouse, fire, galvanize; whip up, agitate.

10 *work the mixture into a paste* KNEAD, squeeze, form; mix, stir, blend. See note at WROUGHT.

11 *he worked the blade into the padlock* MANEUVER, manipulate, guide, edge.

12 *her mouth worked furiously* TWITCH, quiver, convulse.

13 *he worked his way through the crowd* MANEUVER, make, thread, wind, weave, wend.

PHRASES: **work on** *leave Hank to me—I'll work on him* PERSUADE, manipulate, influence; coax, cajole, wheedle, soften up, sweet-talk; *informal* twist someone's arm, lean on. **work out** 1 *the bill works out to $50* AMOUNT TO, add up to, come to, total. 2 *my idea worked out.* See WORK verb sense 6. 3 *things didn't work out the way she planned* END UP, turn out, go, come out, develop; happen, occur; *informal* pan out. 4 *he works out at the local gym* EXERCISE, train. 5 *work out what you can afford* CALCULATE, compute, determine, reckon (up). 6 *I'm trying to work out what she meant* UNDERSTAND, comprehend, sort out, make sense of, get to the bottom of, make head(s) or tail(s) of, unravel, decipher, decode, puzzle out; *informal* figure out. 7 *they worked out a plan* DEVISE, formulate, draw up, put together, develop, construct, arrange, organize, contrive, concoct; hammer out, negotiate. **work up** *he couldn't work up any enthusiasm* STIMULATE, rouse, raise, arouse, awaken, excite.

workable adjective *a workable household budget* PRACTICABLE, feasible, viable, possible, achievable; realistic, reasonable, sensible, practical; *informal* doable. ANTONYM impracticable.

workaday adjective *workaday prose | our workaday lives* ORDINARY, average, run-of-the-mill, middle-of-the-road, conventional, unremarkable, unexceptional, humdrum, undistinguished, commonplace, mundane, pedestrian; routine, everyday, day-to-day, garden-variety, standard; *informal* nothing to write home about, dime a dozen. ANTONYM exceptional.

worker noun 1 *a strike by 500 workers* EMPLOYEE, member of staff; workman, laborer, hand, operative, operator; proletarian; artisan, craftsman, craftswoman; wage earner, breadwinner.

2 *informal I have a reputation for being a worker* HARD WORKER, toiler, workhorse; *informal* busy bee, eager beaver, workaholic, wheelhorse.

workforce noun *management must now justify its actions to the workforce* EMPLOYEES, staff, personnel, workers, labor force, human resources, manpower.

working adjective 1 *working mothers* EMPLOYED, in (gainful) employment, in work, waged. ANTONYMS unemployed, out of work.

2 *a working windmill* FUNCTIONING, operating, running, active, operational, functional, serviceable; *informal* up and running. ANTONYMS broken, faulty.

3 *a working knowledge of contract law* SUFFICIENT, adequate, viable; useful, effective.

▸ noun 1 *the working of a carburetor* FUNCTIONING, operation, running, action, performance.

2 (**workings**) *the workings of a watch* MECHANISM, machinery, parts, movement, action, works; *informal* insides.

workman noun *the workmen are on their lunch break* WORKER, laborer, hand, operative, operator; employee; journeyman, artisan.

workmanship noun *the workmanship evidenced in these chairs is superb* CRAFTSMANSHIP, artistry, craft, art, artisanship, handiwork; skill, expertise, technique.

workout noun *cool down gradually after your workout* EXERCISE SESSION, training session, drill; warm-up; exercises, aerobics, isometrics, calisthenics.

workshop noun 1 *the craftsmen had a chilly workshop* WORKROOM, studio, atelier; factory, plant.

2 *a workshop on combating stress* STUDY GROUP, discussion group, seminar, class; support group.

world noun 1 *he traveled the world* EARTH, globe, planet, sphere.

2 *life on other worlds* PLANET, moon, star, heavenly body, orb.

3 *the academic world* SPHERE, society, circle, arena, milieu, province, domain, orbit, preserve, realm, field, discipline, area, sector.

4 *she would show* ***the world*** *that she was strong* EVERYONE, everybody, people, mankind, humankind, humanity, the (general) public, the population, the populace, all and sundry, 'every Tom, Dick, and Harry.'

5 *a world of difference* HUGE AMOUNT, good deal, great deal, abundance, wealth, profusion, mountain; *informal* heap, lot, load, ton.

6 *she renounced* ***the world*** SOCIETY, material things, secular interests, temporal concerns, earthly concerns. PHRASES: **on top of the world** *informal at age twenty, I was*

on top of the world. See OVERJOYED. **out of this world** *informal the scampi at Vinnie's is out of this world.* See WONDERFUL.

WORD NOTE **world**

As an adjective, *world* has the following meanings:
World music: any music culturally or linguistically exotic to the official culture of the contiguous United States and its major trading partners
World cinema: any movie not in English, French, or German
World literature: any book in Spanish from South America
World sports: soccer
—SM

worldly adjective **1** *his youth was wasted on worldly pursuits* EARTHLY, terrestrial, temporal, mundane; mortal, human, material, materialistic, physical, carnal, fleshly, bodily, corporeal, sensual. ANTONYM spiritual.

2 *a worldly woman* SOPHISTICATED, experienced, worldly-wise, knowledgeable, knowing, enlightened, shrewd, mature, seasoned, cosmopolitan, streetwise, street-smart, urbane, cultivated, cultured. ANTONYMS unsophisticated, naive.

worldly-wise adjective See WORLDLY sense 2.

worldwide adjective *a worldwide effort to combat AIDS* GLOBAL, international, intercontinental, universal; ubiquitous, extensive, widespread, far-reaching, wide-ranging, all-embracing. ANTONYM local.

worn adjective **1** *his hat was worn* SHABBY, worn out, threadbare, tattered, in tatters, holey, falling to pieces, ragged, frayed, well-used, moth-eaten, scruffy, having seen better days; *informal* tatty, ratty, the worse for wear, raggedy, dog-eared. ANTONYMS smart, new.

2 *her face looked worn.* See WORN OUT sense 2.

worn out adjective **1** *a worn-out shirt.* See WORN sense 1.

2 *by evening they were worn out* EXHAUSTED, fatigued, tired (out), weary, drained, worn, drawn, wan, sapped, spent, burned out; careworn, haggard, hollow-eyed, pale, peaked; *informal* all in, done in, dog-tired, dead beat, fit to drop, pooped, tuckered out. ANTONYMS energetic, fresh.

3 *worn-out ideas* OBSOLETE, antiquated, stale, hackneyed, trite, tired, old, hoary, overused, overworked, clichéd, unoriginal, commonplace, pedestrian, prosaic, stock, conventional; old hat. ANTONYM fresh.

worried adjective *Father Douglas came to sit with the worried parents* ANXIOUS, perturbed, troubled, bothered, concerned, upset, distressed, distraught, disquieted, uneasy, fretful, agitated, nervous, edgy, on edge, tense, overwrought, worked up, keyed up, jumpy, stressed, strung out; apprehensive, fearful, afraid, frightened, scared; *informal* uptight, a bundle of nerves, on tenterhooks, jittery, twitchy, in a stew, in a sweat, het up, rattled, antsy, squirrelly. ANTONYMS carefree, unconcerned.

worrisome adjective *their financial situation was worrisome* ALARMING, worrying, daunting, perturbing, niggling, nagging, bothersome, troublesome, unsettling, nerve-racking; distressing, disquieting, upsetting, traumatic, problematic; *informal* scary, hairy.

worry verb **1** *she worries about his health* FRET, be concerned, be anxious, agonize, brood, panic, lose sleep, get worked up, get stressed, get in a state, stew, torment oneself.

2 *is something worrying you?* TROUBLE, bother, make anxious, disturb, distress, upset, concern, disquiet, fret, agitate, unsettle, perturb, scare, fluster, stress, tax, torment, plague, bedevil; prey on one's mind, weigh down, gnaw at, rattle; *informal* bug, get to, dig at, nag.

▸ noun **1** *I'm beside myself with worry* ANXIETY, perturbation, distress, concern, uneasiness, unease, disquiet, fretfulness, restlessness, nervousness, nerves, agitation, edginess, tension, stress; apprehension, fear, dread, trepidation, misgiving, angst; *informal* butterflies (in the stomach), the willies, the heebie-jeebies.

2 *the rats are a worry* PROBLEM, cause for concern, issue; nuisance, pest, plague, trial, trouble, vexation, bane, bugbear; *informal* pain, pain in the neck, headache, hassle, stress.

worrying adjective See WORRISOME.

worsen verb **1** *insomnia can worsen a patient's distress* AGGRAVATE, exacerbate, compound, add to, intensify, increase, magnify, heighten, inflame, augment; *informal* add fuel to the fire of. ANTONYM improve.

2 *the recession worsened* DETERIORATE, degenerate, decline, regress; *informal* go downhill, go to pot, go to the dogs, hit the skids, nosedive. ANTONYMS improve, recover.

worship noun **1** *the worship of idols* REVERENCE, veneration, adoration, glorification, glory, exaltation; devotion, praise, thanksgiving, homage, honor; *archaic* magnification.

2 *morning worship* SERVICE, religious rite, prayer, praise, devotion, religious observance.

3 *he contemplated her with worship* ADMIRATION, adulation, idolization, lionization, hero-worship.

▸ verb *they worship pagan gods* REVERE, reverence, venerate, pay homage to, honor, adore, praise, pray to, glorify, exalt, extol; hold dear, cherish, treasure, esteem, adulate, idolize, deify, hero-worship, lionize; follow, look up to; *informal* put on a pedestal; *formal* laud; *archaic* magnify. See note at REVERE.

worst verb *they were worsted by the Czechs in the first round* DEFEAT, beat, prevail over, triumph over, trounce, rout, vanquish, conquer, master, overcome, overwhelm, overpower, crush; outdo, outclass, outstrip, surpass; *informal* thrash, smash, lick, best, clobber, drub, slaughter, murder, wipe out, crucify, demolish, wipe the floor with, take to the cleaners, walk all over, make mincemeat of, shellac, cream, whup.

worth noun **1** *evidence of the rug's worth* VALUE, price, cost; valuation, quotation, estimate.

2 *the intrinsic worth of education* BENEFIT, advantage, use, value, virtue, utility, service, profit, help, aid; desirability, appeal; significance, sense; *informal* mileage, percentage; *archaic* behoof.

3 *a sense of personal worth* WORTHINESS, merit, value, excellence, caliber, quality, stature, eminence, consequence, importance, significance, distinction.

worthless adjective **1** *the item was worthless* VALUELESS; poor quality, inferior, second-rate, third-rate, low-grade, cheap, shoddy, tawdry, cheesy; *informal* crummy, nickel-and-dime. ANTONYMS valuable, precious.

2 *his conclusions are worthless* USELESS, (of) no use, ineffective, ineffectual, fruitless, unproductive, unavailing, pointless, nugatory, valueless, inadequate, deficient, meaningless, senseless, insubstantial, empty, hollow, trifling, petty, inconsequential, lame, paltry, pathetic, no-account. ANTONYM useful.

3 *his worthless son* GOOD-FOR-NOTHING, ne'er-do-well, useless, despicable, contemptible, low, ignominious, corrupt, villainous, degenerate, shiftless, feckless; *informal* no-good, lousy, no-account.

worthwhile adjective *a worthwhile expenditure of time* VALUABLE, useful, of use, of service, beneficial, rewarding, advantageous, positive, helpful, profitable, gainful, fruitful, productive, lucrative, constructive, effective, effectual, meaningful, worthy.

worthy adjective *a worthy citizen* VIRTUOUS, righteous, good, moral, ethical, upright, upstanding, high-minded, principled, exemplary; law-abiding, irreproachable, blameless, guiltless, unimpeachable, honest, honorable, reputable, decent, respectable, noble, meritorious; pure, saintly, angelic; *informal* squeaky clean. ANTONYM disreputable.

▸ noun *local worthies* DIGNITARY, personage, VIP, notable, notability, pillar of society, luminary, leading light, big name, grandee; *informal* heavyweight, bigwig, top dog, big shot, big cheese, big wheel, big kahuna. ANTONYM nobody.

PHRASE: **be worthy of** *your opinions are worthy of our consideration* DESERVE, merit, warrant, rate, justify, earn, be entitled to, qualify for.

would-be adjective *would-be actors* ASPIRING, budding, promising, prospective, potential, hopeful, keen, eager, ambitious; *informal* wannabe.

wound noun **1** *a chest wound* INJURY, lesion, cut, gash, laceration, tear, slash; graze, scratch, abrasion; bruise, contusion; *Medicine* trauma.

2 *the wounds inflicted by the media* INSULT, blow, slight, offense, affront; hurt, damage, injury, pain, distress, grief, anguish, torment.

▸ verb **1** *he was critically wounded* INJURE, hurt, harm; maim, mutilate, disable, incapacitate, cripple; lacerate, cut, graze, gash, stab, slash.

2 *her words had wounded him* HURT, scar, damage, injure; insult, slight, offend, affront, distress, disturb, upset, trouble; grieve, sadden, pain, cut, sting, shock, traumatize, torment.

wow exclamation *Wow! Did you see that?* HOLY COW, holy mackerel, holy moly, whoa; cool, amazing, awesome, far out, hot damn; *dated* golly, gosh, ye gods, gadzooks

wrack verb See note at RACK.

wraith noun *from a gray and billowy fog the wraith did appear* GHOST, specter, spirit, phantom, apparition, manifestation; *informal* spook; *literary* shade, phantasm.

wrangle noun *a wrangle over money* ARGUMENT, dispute, disagreement, quarrel, falling-out, fight, squabble, turf war, altercation, war of words, shouting match, tiff, tug-of-war; *informal* set-to, run-in, row. See note at QUARREL.

▸ verb *we wrangled over the details* ARGUE, quarrel, bicker, squabble, fall out, have words, disagree, be at odds, fight, battle, feud, clash; *informal* scrap.

wrap verb **1** *she wrapped herself in a towel* SWATHE, bundle, swaddle, muffle, cloak, enfold, envelop, encase, cover, fold, wind.

2 *I wrapped the vase carefully* PACKAGE, pack, pack up, bundle, bundle up; gift-wrap.

▸ noun *he put a wrap around her* SHAWL, stole, cloak, cape, mantle, scarf, poncho, serape, pelisse.

PHRASES: **wrap up** *wrap up well—it's cold* DRESS WARMLY, bundle up. **wrap something up** *informal our objective is to wrap up the Pendleton case by the end of the month* CONCLUDE, finish, end, wind up, terminate, stop, cease, finalize, complete, tie up; *informal* sew up.

wrapper noun *a candy wrapper* WRAPPING, wrap, packaging, paper, cover, covering; jacket, sheath.

wrath noun *I refuse to subject myself any longer to her wrath* ANGER, rage, fury, outrage, spleen, vexation, (high) dudgeon, crossness, displeasure, annoyance, irritation; *literary* ire, choler. ANTONYM happiness.

wreak verb *the damage this storm has wreaked is inestimable* INFLICT, bestow, mete out, administer, deliver, impose, exact, create, cause, result in, effect, engender, bring about, perpetrate, unleash, let loose, vent; *formal* effectuate. See note at WROUGHT.

wreath noun *a wreath of dried flowers* GARLAND, circlet, chaplet, crown, festoon, lei; ring, loop, circle.

wreathe verb **1** *a pulpit wreathed in holly* FESTOON, garland, drape, cover, bedeck, deck, decorate, ornament, adorn.

2 *blue smoke wreathed upward* SPIRAL, coil, loop, wind, curl, twist, snake, curve.

wreck noun **1** *salvage teams landed on the wreck* SHIPWRECK, sunken ship, derelict; shell, hull; wreckage.

2 *the wreck of a stolen car* WRECKAGE, debris, remainder, ruins, remains.

▸ verb **1** *he had wrecked her car* DEMOLISH, crash, smash up, damage, destroy; vandalize, deface, desecrate; *informal* trash, total.

2 *his ship was wrecked* SHIPWRECK, sink, capsize, run aground.

3 *the crisis wrecked his plans* RUIN, spoil, disrupt, undo, put a stop to, frustrate, blight, crush, quash, dash, destroy, scotch, shatter, devastate, sabotage; *informal* mess up, screw up, foul up, put paid to, scupper, scuttle, stymie, put the kibosh on, nix.

wreckage noun See WRECK noun senses 1, 2.

wrench noun **1** *she felt a wrench on her shoulders* TUG, pull, jerk, jolt, heave; *informal* yank.

2 *hold the piston with a wrench* monkey wrench.

3 *leaving was an immense wrench* TRAUMATIC EVENT, painful parting; pang, trauma.

▸ verb **1** *he wrenched the gun from her hand* TUG, pull, jerk, wrest, heave, twist, pluck, grab, seize, snatch, force, pry, jimmy; *informal* yank.

2 *she wrenched her ankle* SPRAIN, twist, turn, strain, pull; injure, hurt.

wrest verb *he wrested the broom from Angela's grasp* WRENCH, snatch, seize, grab, pry, pluck, tug, pull, jerk, dislodge, remove; *informal* yank.

wrestle verb *words were exchanged, and then they began wrestling | she wrestled with her conscience* GRAPPLE, fight, struggle, contend, vie, battle, wrangle; scuffle, tussle, brawl; *informal* scrap, wrassle, rassle.

wretch noun **1** *the wretches killed themselves* POOR CREATURE, poor soul, poor thing, poor unfortunate; *informal* poor devil.

2 *I wouldn't trust the old wretch* SCOUNDREL, villain, ruffian, rogue, rascal, reprobate, criminal, miscreant, good-for-nothing; *informal* heel, creep, louse, rat, swine, dog, lowlife, scumbag, scumbucket, scuzzball, sleazeball, sleazebag; *informal, archaic* blackguard, picaroon.

wretched adjective **1** *I felt so wretched without you* MISERABLE, unhappy, sad, heartbroken, grief-stricken, sorrowful, sorry for oneself, distressed, desolate, devastated, despairing, disconsolate, downcast, dejected, crestfallen, cheerless, depressed, melancholy, morose, gloomy, mournful, doleful, dismal, forlorn, woebegone; *informal* blue; *literary* dolorous. ANTONYM cheerful.

2 *I feel wretched* ILL, unwell, poorly, sick, below par; *informal* under the weather, out of sorts. ANTONYM well.

3 *their living conditions are wretched* HARSH, hard, grim, stark, difficult; poor, impoverished; pitiful, pathetic, miserable, cheerless, sordid, shabby, seedy, unhealthy, insalubrious, dilapidated; *informal* scummy. ANTONYMS comfortable, luxurious.

4 *the wretched dweller in the chantey town* UNFORTUNATE, unlucky, luckless, ill-starred, blighted, hapless, poor, pitiable, downtrodden, oppressed; *literary* star-crossed. ANTONYMS cheerful, well, comfortable, fortunate, excellent.

5 *he's a wretched coward* DESPICABLE, contemptible, reprehensible, base, vile, loathsome, hateful, detestable, odious, ignoble, shameful, shabby, worthless; *informal* dirty, rotten, lowdown, lousy. ANTONYM fortunate.

6 *wretched weather* TERRIBLE, awful, dire, atrocious, dreadful, bad, poor, lamentable, deplorable; *informal* godawful. ANTONYM excellent.

7 *I don't want the wretched money* *informal* DAMN, damned, blessed, cursed, flaming, confounded, rotten, blasted, bloody.

wriggle verb **1** *she tried to hug him but he wriggled* SQUIRM, writhe, wiggle, jiggle, jerk, thresh, flounder, flail, twitch, twist and turn; snake, worm, slither.

2 *he* ***wriggled out of*** *his responsibilities* AVOID, shirk, dodge, evade, elude, sidestep; escape from; *informal* duck.

wring verb **1** ***wring out*** *the clothes* TWIST, squeeze, screw, scrunch, knead, press, mangle.

2 *concessions were wrung from the government* EXTRACT, elicit, force, exact, wrest, wrench, squeeze, milk; *informal* bleed.

3 *his expression wrung her heart* REND, tear at, harrow, pierce, stab, wound, rack; distress, pain, hurt.

wrinkle noun **1** *fine wrinkles around her mouth* CREASE, fold, pucker, line, crinkle, furrow, ridge, groove; *informal* crow's feet, laugh line.

2 *the project has some wrinkles to iron out* DIFFICULTY, snag, hitch, drawback, imperfection, problem.

▸ verb *his coattails* ***wrinkled up*** CREASE, pucker, gather, crinkle, crimp, crumple, rumple, scrunch up.

writ noun *they were served with a writ* SUMMONS, subpoena, warrant, arraignment, indictment, citation, court order.

write verb **1** *he wrote her name in the book* PUT IN WRITING, write down, jot down, put down, note, take down, record, register, log, list; inscribe, sign, scribble, scrawl, pencil.

2 *Jacqueline wrote a poem* COMPOSE, draft, think up, formulate, compile, pen, dash off, produce.

3 *he had her address and promised to write* CORRESPOND, write a letter, communicate, get/stay in touch, keep in contact, e-mail; *informal* drop someone a line. PHRASE: **write off 1** *they have had to write off loans* FORGET ABOUT, disregard, give up on, cancel, annul. **2** *she wrote off the cost of the computer* DEDUCT, claim. **3** *who would write off a player of his stature?* DISREGARD, dismiss, ignore.

writer noun *my favorite American writer* AUTHOR, wordsmith, man/woman of letters, penman; novelist, essayist, biographer; journalist, columnist, correspondent; scriptwriter, playwright, dramatist, dramaturge, tragedian; poet; *informal* scribbler, scribe, hack.

writhe verb *she writhed about in pain* SQUIRM, wriggle, thrash, flail, toss, toss and turn, twist, twist and turn, struggle.

writing noun **1** *I can't read his writing* HANDWRITING, script, print, hand; penmanship, calligraphy, chirography; *informal* scribble, scrawl, chicken scratch.

2 **(writings)** *the writings of Woodrow Wilson* WORKS, compositions, books, publications, oeuvre; papers, articles, essays.

wrong adjective **1** *the wrong answer* INCORRECT, mistaken, in error, erroneous, inaccurate, inexact, imprecise, fallacious, wide of the mark, off target, unsound, faulty; *informal* out. See note at RIGHT. ANTONYMS right, correct.

2 *he knew he had said the wrong thing* INAPPROPRIATE, unsuitable, inapt, inapposite, undesirable; ill-advised, ill-considered, ill-judged, impolitic, injudicious, infelicitous, unfitting, out of keeping, improper; *informal* out of order. ANTONYM appropriate.

3 *I've done nothing wrong* ILLEGAL, unlawful, illicit, criminal, dishonest, dishonorable, corrupt; unethical, immoral, bad, wicked, sinful, iniquitous, nefarious, blameworthy, reprehensible; *informal* crooked. ANTONYMS ethical, legal.

4 *there's something wrong with the engine* AMISS, awry, out of order, not right, faulty, flawed, defective.

▸ adverb *she guessed wrong* INCORRECTLY, wrongly, inaccurately, erroneously, mistakenly, in error.

▸ noun **1** *the difference between right and wrong* IMMORALITY, sin, sinfulness, wickedness, evil; unlawfulness, crime, corruption, villainy, dishonesty, injustice, wrongdoing, misconduct, transgression. ANTONYMS right, virtue.

2 *an attempt to make up for past wrongs* MISDEED, offense, injury, crime, transgression, violation, peccadillo, sin; injustice, outrage, atrocity; *Law* tort; *archaic* trespass.

▸ verb **1** *she was determined to forget the man who had wronged her* ILL-USE, mistreat, do an injustice to, do wrong to, ill-treat, abuse, harm, hurt, injure.

2 *perhaps I am wronging him* MALIGN, misrepresent, do a disservice to, impugn, defame, slander, libel.

PHRASES: **get wrong** *don't get me wrong, I usually like Italian food* MISUNDERSTAND, misinterpret, misconstrue, mistake, misread, take amiss; get the wrong idea/impression; *informal* be barking up the wrong tree. **go wrong 1** *I've gone wrong somewhere* MAKE A MISTAKE, make an error, make a blunder, blunder, miscalculate, trip up; *informal* slip up, goof, screw up, make a boo-boo, fluff, flub. **2** *their plans went wrong* GO AWRY, go amiss, go off course, fail, be unsuccessful, fall through, come to nothing; backfire, misfire, rebound; *informal* come to grief, come a cropper, go up in smoke, go adrift. **3** *the radio's gone wrong* BREAK DOWN, malfunction, fail, stop working, crash, give out; *informal* be on the blink, conk out, go kaput, go on the fritz. **in the wrong** *just admit that you're in the wrong* TO BLAME, blameworthy, at fault, reprehensible, responsible, culpable, answerable, guilty; *archaic* peccant.

wrongdoer noun *the wrongdoers in our neighborhood were essentially harmless until the Hanovers moved in* OFFENDER, lawbreaker, criminal, felon, delinquent, villain, culprit, evildoer, sinner, transgressor, malefactor, miscreant, rogue, scoundrel; *informal* crook, *Law* malfeasant; *archaic* trespasser.

wrongdoing noun *are you accusing me of some kind of wrongdoing?* CRIME, lawbreaking, lawlessness, criminality, misconduct, misbehavior, malpractice, corruption, immorality, sin, sinfulness, wickedness, evil, vice, iniquity, villainy; offense, felony, wrong, misdeed, misdemeanor, fault, peccadillo, transgression; *Law* malfeasance, tort; *formal* malversation; *archaic* trespass.

wrongful adjective *a wrongful arrest* UNJUSTIFIED, unwarranted, unjust, unfair, undue, undeserved, unreasonable, groundless, indefensible, inappropriate, improper, unlawful, illegal, illegitimate. ANTONYMS rightful, fair.

wrought adjective *skillfully wrought works of art* MADE, created, built, crafted, fashioned, worked, molded, formed, manufactured. PHRASE: **wrought up** *she was obviously wrought up over something* AGITATED, tense, stressed, overwrought, nervous, on edge, edgy, keyed up, worked up, jumpy, antsy, anxious, flustered, fretful, upset; *informal* in a state, in a stew, het up, wound up, uptight, in a tizzy, squirrelly.

USAGE NOTE wrought

In the phrase **wrought havoc**, as in *they wrought havoc on the countryside*, **wrought** is an archaic past tense of **work**. It is not, as is sometimes assumed, a past tense of **wreak**.

wry adjective **1** *his wry humor* IRONIC, sardonic, satirical, mocking, sarcastic; dry, droll, witty, humorous.

2 *a wry expression* UNIMPRESSED, displeased, annoyed, irritated, irked, vexed, piqued, disgruntled, dissatisfied; *informal* peeved.

XYZ

xenophobic adjective *in eastern Germany, unemployment and lack of exposure to foreigners has fueled xenophobic sentiment* ULTRANATIONALISTIC, ULTRANATIONALIST, nationalistic, nationalist, isolationist, jingoistic; parochial, insular; ethnocentric, ethnocentrist, racist, racialist; prejudiced, bigoted, intolerant.

X-rated adjective *X-rated videos* ADULT, hard-core, pornographic, blue, triple-X, XXX.

X-ray noun *the X-ray shows a clean break* RADIOGRAPH, radiogram, X-ray image/picture/photograph, roentgenogram.

xylophone noun See note below.

WORD NOTE **xylophone**

The xylophone is a member of the ideophone family of instruments having tuned bars on a frame, played with mallets. The xylophone has wooden bars; African versions are the *marimba* and the *balaphone,* which has a gourd resonator hanging under each bar. Any ideophone with metal bars is a *metallophone:* one with only a few bars is a *chime;* more bars makes it a *glockenspiel;* a big one with mechanical vibrato is a *vibraphone,* or *vibes.* **—SM**

yahoo noun *informal her brother married into a family of yahoos* REDNECK, boor, lout, oaf; barbarian, Neanderthal, brute, thug; *informal* clod, roughneck.

▸ exclamation *Yahoo! We won!* WAHOO, yippee, hooray, hurrah, hallelujah, bravo, hot dog, whoopee, yay, yee-haw.

y'all See note below.

USAGE NOTE **y'all**

This sturdy Southernism is most logically *y'all*, not *ya'll*. Only the *you* of *you all* is contracted. And in modern print sources, *y'all* is ten times as common. So *ya'll* (which misleadingly resembles *he'll*, *she'll*, and *we'll*) deserves an edit—e.g.: " 'Ya'll [read *Y'all*] have got to help me a lot,' Bentley, a registered nurse at Chalmette Medical Centers, told the students about class planning." (*Times-Picayune* [New Orleans]; Feb. 25, 1997.) In the late twentieth century, some writers began spelling the term without an apostrophe: *yall*. This spelling is not yet widespread (and not recommended). Why has the spelling been so much trouble? *Y'all* is the only contraction in English in which a stressed form is contracted to an unstressed one.

Although the traditional use of *y'all* is plural, and although many Southerners have stoutly rejected the idea that it's ever used as a singular, there does seem to be strong evidence that it can refer to a single person—for example, "See y'all later" spoken to someone without a companion. One possibility is that the speaker means "you and anyone else who may be with you" or "you and anyone else who comes along." Another possibility is that *y'all* may in fact refer to one person. Getting at the truth depends on understanding the speaker's state of mind.

Many speakers in the South and Southwest, even highly educated ones, use the uncontracted *you all* as the plural form of *you*. This is a convenient usage, since *you* alone can be either singular or plural—and therefore is sometimes ambiguous. True, *you all* is unlikely to spread beyond regional usage. But speakers who grew up with the phrase won't be easily dispossessed of it. It's handy, and it's less susceptible to raised eyebrows than *y'all*. There is, however, a noticeable tendency in urban areas to replace this phrase with *you guys*. This may have resulted from the great influx of a geographically diverse population in major cities such as Dallas throughout the 1980s and 1990s, coupled with a growing sense among natives that *you all* and *y'all* signal provincialism. **—BG**

yank verb *informal give the rope a quick yank* JERK, pull, tug, wrench; snatch, seize.

yap verb **1** *the dogs yapped at his heels* BARK, woof, yelp, yip.

2 *informal what are they yapping about now?* See BABBLE verb sense 1.

yard noun **1** *they kicked a soccer ball around the yard* BACKYARD, lawn, grounds; courtyard, court, quadrangle, enclosure, cloister, quad.

2 *a boat-building yard* WORKSHOP, works, factory, garage, plant, foundry, mill, shipyard; *archaic* manufactory.

yardstick noun *many of the financial yardsticks known to our grandparents are simply not appropriate for today's investors* STANDARD, measure, gauge, scale, guide, guideline, indicator, test, touchstone, barometer, criterion, benchmark, point of reference, model, pattern, template.

yarn noun **1** *you need to use a fine yarn* THREAD, cotton, wool, fiber, filament; ply.

2 *informal a far-fetched yarn* STORY, tale, anecdote, saga, narrative; *informal* tall tale, tall story, fish story, cock-and-bull story, shaggy-dog story, spiel.

yawning adjective *a yawning hole where the door once was* GAPING, wide open, wide, cavernous, deep; huge, great, big.

year noun *he held the office for one year* TWELVE-MONTH PERIOD, twelve-month session, annum; calendar year, fiscal year, FY; *archaic* twelvemonth. PHRASE: **year in, year out** *we hear the same excuses, year in, year out* REPEATEDLY, again and again, time and (time) again, time after time, over and over (again); 'week in, week out', 'day in, day out', inexorably, recurrently; continuously, continually, constantly, nonstop, habitually, regularly, without a break, unfailingly, always.

yearly adjective *a yearly payment* ANNUAL, once a year, every year, each year, per annum.

▸ adverb *the guide is published yearly* ANNUALLY, once a year, per annum, by the year, every year, each year.

yearn verb *he **yearned for** a second chance* LONG FOR, pine for, crave, desire, want, wish for, hanker for, covet, lust after/for, pant for, hunger for, burn for, thirst for, ache for, eat one's heart out for, have one's heart set on; *informal* have a yen for, itch for.

yearning noun *a yearning for the mountains* LONGING, craving, desire, want, wish, hankering, urge, hunger, thirst, appetite, lust, ache; *informal* yen, itch.

yell verb *he yelled in agony* CRY OUT, call out, shout, howl, yowl, wail, scream, shriek, screech, yelp, squeal; roar, bawl; *informal* holler.

▸ noun *a yell of rage* CRY, shout, howl, yowl, scream, shriek, screech, yelp, squeal; roar; *informal* holler.

yellow adjective **1** *yellow hair* | *a yellow shirt* FLAXEN, golden, gold, blond/blonde, fair; lemon, cadmium yellow, daffodil, mustard, primrose yellow; tawny, fulvous.See note at YELLOW.

2 *informal he'll have to prove he's not yellow.* See COWARDLY.

yelp verb *the dogs were yelping* SQUEAL, shriek, howl, yowl, yell, cry, shout; bark, bay, woof; *informal* holler.

▸ noun *we heard a yelp from the neighbor's backyard* SQUEAL, shriek, howl, yowl, yell, cry, shout; bark, woof; *informal* holler.

yen noun *informal I've got a yen for chocolate cake* HANKERING, yearning, longing, craving, urge, desire, want, wish, hunger, thirst, lust, appetite, ache; fancy, inclination; *informal* itch.

yes exclamation *yes, I'll come to your party* ALL RIGHT, very well, of course, by all means, sure, certainly, absolutely, indeed, right, affirmative, in the affirmative, agreed, roger; *Nautical* aye aye; *informal* yeah, yep, yup, ya, uh-huh, okay, OK, okey-dokey, okey-doke; *archaic* yea, aye. ANTONYM no.

yes-man noun *informal a Hollywood yes-man* SYCOPHANT, toady, fawner, flatterer, lickspittle, minion, puppet, cat's paw, doormat, trained seal; stooge; *informal* bootlicker, suck-up, brown-noser.

yet adverb **1** *he hasn't made up his mind yet* SO FAR, thus far, as yet, up till/to now, until now.

2 *don't celebrate just yet* NOW, right now, at this time; already, so soon.

3 *he was doing nothing, yet he appeared purposeful* NEVERTHELESS, nonetheless, even so, but, however, still, notwithstanding, despite that, in spite of that, for all that, all the same, just the same, at the same time, be that as it may; *archaic* natheless.

4 *he supplied yet more unsolicited advice* EVEN, still, further, in addition, additionally, besides, into the bargain, to boot, on top (of that).

Yggdrasil See note below.

WORD NOTE **Yggdrasil**

For some curious reason—a holiday in Cornwall when I was small, perhaps; they talk a lot about Yggdrasil in the valleys down in this corner of Southwest England—I have always liked this word, which is very ancient and denotes the all-spreading Tree of Life. Its origins are obscure, its roots (linguistic and metaphoric) are everywhere and nowhere, and its canopy spreads above everything. It is the immense ash tree that is the symbol of everything, and any time I can employ it, usually allusively of course, in a sentence which speaks of such profundities, I try to do so. To be candid I think I have managed to use it but once in an entire lifetime (twice, with this entry), and yet I remain certain that sooner or later I will be able to slip it, with pleasing literary consequences, into a sentence somewhere. I wish all potential users good fortune with it too. A lovely word, rich with associations of antiquity and mystery. **–SW**

yield verb **1** *too many projects yield poor returns* PRODUCE, bear, give, supply, provide, afford, return, bring in, earn, realize, generate, deliver, offer, pay out; *informal* rake in.

2 *the nobility yielded power to the capitalists* RELINQUISH, surrender, cede, remit, part with, hand over; make over, bequeath, leave. See note at RELINQUISH. ANTONYMS withhold, retain.

3 *the duke was forced to yield* SURRENDER, capitulate, submit, relent, admit defeat, back down, climb down, give in, give up the struggle, lay down one's arms, raise/show the white flag; *informal* throw in the towel, cave in.

4 *he **yielded to** her demands* GIVE IN TO, give way to, submit to, bow down to, comply with, agree to, consent to, go along with; grant, permit, allow; *informal* cave in to; *formal* accede to. ANTONYMS resist, defy.

5 *the floorboards yielded underfoot* BEND, give, give way.

▸ noun *risky investments usually have higher yields* PROFIT, gain, return, dividend, earnings.

yoke noun **1** *the horses were loosened from the yoke* HARNESS, collar, coupling.

2 *countries struggling under the yoke of imperialism* TYRANNY, oppression, domination, hegemony, enslavement, servitude, subjugation, subjection, bondage, thrall; bonds, chains, fetters, shackles.

3 *the yoke of marriage* BOND, tie, connection, link.

▸ verb **1** *a pair of oxen were yoked together* HARNESS, hitch, couple, tether, fasten, attach, join.

2 *their aim of yoking biology and mechanics* UNITE, join, marry, link, connect; tie, bind, bond.

yokel noun *unless you want trouble, don't mess with the local yokels* BUMPKIN, peasant, provincial, rustic, country cousin, countryman, countrywoman; *informal* hayseed, hillbilly, hick, rube, clodhopper, yahoo.

young adjective **1** *young people* YOUTHFUL, juvenile; junior, adolescent, teenage; in the springtime of life, in one's salad days. ANTONYMS old, elderly, mature.

2 *she's very young for her age* IMMATURE, childish, inexperienced, unsophisticated, naive, unworldly; *informal* wet behind the ears. ANTONYMS old, elderly, mature.

3 *the young microbrewery industry* FLEDGLING, developing, budding, in its infancy, emerging. ANTONYMS old, elderly, mature.

▸ noun **1** *a robin feeding its young* OFFSPRING, progeny, family, babies.

2 **(the young)** *the young don't care nowadays* YOUNG PEOPLE, children, boys and girls, youngsters, youth, the younger generation, juveniles, minors; *informal* young 'uns, kids.

youngster noun *a new magazine for youngsters* CHILD, teenager, adolescent, youth, juvenile, minor, junior; boy, girl; lass, lad; whippersnapper, stripling; *informal* kid, young 'un, teen.

youth noun **1** *he had been a keen sportsman in his youth* EARLY YEARS, young days, salad days, teens, teenage years, adolescence, boyhood, girlhood, childhood; minority; *formal* juvenescence. ANTONYMS adulthood, old age.

2 *she had kept her youth and beauty* YOUTHFULNESS, freshness, bloom, vigor, energy. ANTONYM maturity.

3 *local youths* YOUNG PERSON/MAN/WOMAN, boy, girl, juvenile, teenager, adolescent, junior, minor; *informal* teen, kid.

4 *the youth of the nation* YOUNG PEOPLE, young, younger generation, next generation. ANTONYM elderly.

youthful adjective *a youthful new leader* YOUNG-LOOKING, spry, sprightly, vigorous, active; young, boyish, girlish; fresh-faced, in the springtime of life, in one's salad days. ANTONYMS old, elderly.

THE RIGHT WORD

Everyone wants to look **youthful**, an adjective that means possessing, or appearing to possess, the qualities associated with youth (*a youthful enthusiasm for the job*). But no one wants to be called **immature**, which means childish or emotionally underdeveloped and usually pertains to behavior and attitudes rather than to physical appearance (*still immature despite the fact that he was almost thirty*). **Juvenile** suggests immaturity of mind or body and is applied especially to things that are designed for boys and girls in their early teens (*juvenile books*), while **adolescent** applies to the period between puberty and maturity and suggests the physical awkwardness and emotional instability associated with the teenage years (*an adolescent response to criticism*). Young men in particular are often described as **callow**, which means immature in terms of experience (*a callow youth who had never lived away from his family*). Of all these words, **puerile** is probably the most insulting, because it is so often used to describe adults who display the immature behavior of a child (*a puerile piece of writing; a puerile revolt against his aging parents*).

yuck exclamation *Yuck! What is this slimy green stuff?* ICK, ugh, yech, blech, phew, eeew, gross.

yump See note below.

WORD NOTE **yump**

For those who like to provide a commentary to their television viewing, here is a useful, neglected term for that moment when the goodies' car hits a ramp at speed and improbably takes off into the air, thus putting a convenient distance between them and the baddies. Instead of simply saying "Whoa!," why not try: "That was an amazing *yump!*" **–ZS**

zany adjective *the zany humor of the Marx Brothers* ECCENTRIC, peculiar, odd, unconventional, strange, bizarre, weird; mad, crazy, comic, madcap, funny, quirky, idiosyncratic; *informal* wacky, screwy, nutty, oddball, off the wall; daft; kooky, wacko, bizarro. ANTONYMS conventional, sensible.

zap verb *informal* **1** *they were zapped by antiradar missiles.* See DESTROY sense 5.

2 *racecars zapped past.* See SPEED verb sense 1.

3 *she zapped a chicken burger for lunch* NUKE, microwave.

zeal noun *Ross's zeal for football* PASSION, ardor, love, fervor, fire, avidity, devotion, enthusiasm, eagerness, keenness, appetite, relish, gusto, vigor, energy, intensity; fanaticism. ANTONYMS apathy, indifference.

zealot noun *York was too much of a zealot for the party to endorse seriously* FANATIC, enthusiast, extremist, radical, young Turk, diehard, true believer, activist, militant; bigot, dogmatist, sectarian, partisan; *informal* fiend, maniac, ultra, nut; eager beaver.

THE RIGHT WORD

An **enthusiast** displays an intense and eager interest in something (*a sky-diving enthusiast*). A **fanatic** is not only intense and eager but possibly irrational in his or her enthusiasm; *fanatic* suggests extreme devotion and a willingness to go to any length to maintain or carry out one's beliefs (*a fly-fishing fanatic who hired a helicopter to reach his favorite stream*). A **zealot** exhibits not only extreme devotion but vehement activity in support of a cause or goal (*a feminist zealot who spent most of her time campaigning for women's rights*). An **extremist** is a supporter of extreme doctrines or practices, particularly in a political context (*a paramilitary extremist who anticipated the overthrow of the government*). But it is the **bigot** who causes the most trouble, exhibiting obstinate and often blind devotion to his or her beliefs and opinions. In contrast to *fanatic* and *zealot*, the term *bigot* implies intolerance and contempt for those who do not agree (*a bigot who could not accept his daughter's decision to marry outside her religion*).

zealous adjective *a zealous worker* FERVENT, ardent, fervid, fanatical, passionate, impassioned, devout, devoted, committed, dedicated, hard-core, enthusiastic, eager, keen, overkeen, avid, card-carrying, vigorous, energetic, intense, fierce; *literary* perfervid. See note at EAGER. ANTONYMS apathetic, indifferent.

zenith noun *at the zenith of his power* | *the view from the mountain's zenith* HIGHEST POINT, high point, crowning point, height, top, acme, peak, pinnacle, apex, apogee, crown, crest, summit, climax, culmination, prime, meridian. ANTONYM nadir.

zero noun *I rated my chances at zero* NOTHING, nothing at all, nil, none, naught/nought; *informal* zilch, nix, zip, nada, diddly-squat. PHRASE: **zero in on** *each study group will zero in on a different aspect of the ecosystem* FOCUS ON, focus attention on, center on, concentrate on, home in on, fix on, pinpoint, highlight, spotlight; *informal* zoom in on.

zero hour noun *as zero hour approached, thirty ships*

swung into position THE APPOINTED TIME, the critical moment, the moment of truth, the point/moment of decision, the Rubicon, the crux; *informal* the crunch.

zest noun **1** *she had a great zest for life* ENTHUSIASM, gusto, relish, appetite, eagerness, keenness, avidity, zeal, fervor, ardor, passion; verve, vigor, liveliness, sparkle, fire, animation, vitality, dynamism, energy, brio, pep, spirit, exuberance, high spirits, joie de vivre; *informal* zing, zip, oomph, vim, pizzazz, get-up-and-go. ANTONYMS apathy, indifference.

2 *the lemon pepper and cilantro will add zest to the sauce | he wanted to put some zest to his life* PIQUANCY, tang, flavor, savor, taste, spice, spiciness, relish, bite; excitement, interest, an edge; *informal* kick, punch, zing, oomph. ANTONYM blandness.

3 *the grated zest of an orange* RIND, peel, skin.

zigzag adjective *the zigzag patterns of erosion* TWISTING, twisty, full of twists and turns, serpentine, meandering, snaking, snaky, winding, crooked. ANTONYM straight.

zing noun *informal* See ZEST sense 1.

zinger *informal* noun *Yost got us with a few good zingers* WITTICISM, quip, joke; criticism, dig, poke.

zip *informal* noun *he's full of zip.* See ENERGY.

▸ verb *I zipped along the highway.* See SPEED verb sense 1.

zombie noun *why is walking around like a zombie?* LIVING DEAD, undead, walking dead, soulless corpse.

zone noun *the search continued in the zone south of the river* AREA, sector, section, belt, stretch, region, territory, district, quarter, precinct, locality, neighborhood, province.

zonked *informal* adjective See EXHAUSTED.

zoo noun **1** *observing apes at the zoo* PARK, menagerie, game farm, wildlife park, safari park, zoological park.

2 *informal* *it's an absolute zoo in here* CIRCUS, madhouse, maelstrom, hullabaloo, free-for-all; pandemonium, chaos, bedlam.

zoom verb *informal* *a lone car zoomed across the desert road* WHIZ, zip, whip, buzz, hurtle, speed, rush, streak, shoot, race, bolt, dash, run, flash, blast, charge, fly, careen, career, go like the wind; *informal* belt, scoot, tear, go like a bat out of hell, bomb, hightail, clip. PHRASE: **zoom in on** *zoom in on the rabbit in the background* ENLARGE, magnify, close in on, focus in on.

Writer's Reference

Language Guide

Rules of English: Understanding Grammar

Grammar is the system and structure of a language. It embodies all the principles by which the language works. All good writing begins with an understanding of the fundamentals of grammar:

- parts of speech
- parts of sentences
- sentence structures
- sentence functions

PARTS OF SPEECH

Noun

A **noun** is a word that identifies or names a person, place, thing, action, or quality. There are two types of nouns: proper and common.

PROPER NOUNS

A noun that names a particular person, place, or thing is a **proper noun**. It always begins with a capital letter:

Benito Mussolini
Cairo
the Chrysler Building
Jell-O
Mount Everest

COMMON NOUNS

A noun that names a type of person, place, or thing is a **common noun**. There are three kinds of common nouns: concrete, abstract, and collective.

A **concrete noun** names someone or something that you can see or touch:

arm
giraffe
hamburger
lake
stapler

An **abstract noun** names something intangible (that is, something that can neither be seen nor touched):

assistance
bravery
disappointment
flavor
wit

A **collective noun** names a group of persons or things:

audience
colony
herd
platoon
set

Singular and Plural Nouns

A noun that names one person, place, or thing is **singular**. A noun that names more than one person, place, or thing is **plural**. The spelling of a singular noun almost always changes when it becomes a plural. Most plurals can be formed by adding *s* or *es*, but many nouns do not follow this format.

beach/beaches
bean/beans
hairbrush/hairbrushes
leaf/leaves
mouse/mice
party/parties
school/schools
woman/women

If the spelling of a plural noun is in doubt, it is always advisable to consult a dictionary.

Appositives

An **appositive** is a noun (or a unit of words that acts as a noun) whose meaning is a direct copy or extension of the meaning of the preceding noun in the sentence. In other words, the appositive and the preceding noun refer to the same person, place, or thing. The appositive helps to characterize or elaborate on the preceding noun in a specific way.

The wedding cake, a chocolate masterpiece, was the hit of the reception.
[The noun *cake* and the appositive *masterpiece* are the same thing.]

His primary objective, to write the great American novel, was never realized.
[The noun *objective* and the appositive *to write the great American novel* are the same thing.]

Eleanor's math teacher, Mrs. Kennedy, is retiring next year.
[The noun *teacher* and the appositive *Mrs. Kennedy* are the same person.]

Possessives

A **possessive** is a noun whose form has changed in order to show possession. Certain rules can be followed to determine how the form should change for any given noun.

In the case of a singular noun, add an apostrophe and an *s*:

Lincoln's inaugural address
the baby's favorite blanket

Exception: Most singular nouns that end in *s* follow the preceding rule with no difficulty (e.g., *Chris's*, *Dickens's*), but some singular nouns that end in *s* may be exempted from the rule because the pronunciation of the plural is less awkward with just an apostrophe and no final *s*:

Ramses' dynasty
Aristophanes' great comedic works

In the case of a plural noun that ends in *s*, add just an apostrophe:

the Lincolns' summer home
our babies' double stroller

In the case of a plural noun that does not end in *s*, add an apostrophe and an *s*:

men's footwear
the fungi's rapid reproduction

In the case of a compound noun (a noun made of more than one word), only the last word takes the possessive form:

my sister-in-law's house
the commander in chief's personal staff

In the case of joint possession (that is, two or more nouns possess the same thing together), only the last of the possessing nouns takes the possessive form:

Ryan and Saul's nickel collection
[There is only one nickel collection, and *both* Ryan and Saul own it *together*.]

Gramma and Grampa's photo albums
[However many photo albums there may be, they all belong to *both* Gramma and Grampa *together*.]

In the case of individual possession by two or more nouns (that is, two or more nouns possess the same type of thing, but separately and distinctly), each of the possessing nouns takes the possessive form:

Lenny's and Suzanne's footprints on the beach
[Lenny and Suzanne *each* left *their own distinct* footprints on the beach.]

Strauss's and Khachaturian's waltzes
[Strauss and Khachaturian *each* composed *their own distinct* waltzes.]

Pronoun

A **pronoun** is a word that represents a person or thing without giving the specific name of the person or thing. There are five classes of pronouns: personal, relative, demonstrative, indefinite, and interrogative.

A **personal pronoun** is used to refer to the person speaking (first person), the person spoken to (second person), or the person or thing spoken about (third person). A pronoun formed from certain personal pronouns by adding the suffix *-self* (singular) or *-selves* (plural) is called "reflexive."

PERSON	SINGULAR	PLURAL	REFLEXIVE SINGULAR	REFLEXIVE PLURAL
first person	*I*	*we*	—	—
	my	*our*	*myself*	*ourselves*
	mine	*ours*	—	—
	me	*us*	—	—
second person	*you*	*you*	—	—
	your	*your*	*yourself*	*yourselves*
	yours	*yours*	—	—
	you	*you*	—	—
third person masculine	*he*	*they*	—	—
	his	*their*	—	—
	his	*theirs*	—	—
	him	*them*	*himself*	*themselves*
third person feminine	*she*	*they*	—	—
	her	*their*	—	—
	hers	*theirs*	—	—
	her	*them*	*herself*	*themselves*
third person neuter	*it*	*they*	—	—
	its	*their*	—	—
	its	*theirs*	—	—
	it	*them*	*itself*	*themselves*

Note that the gender designations of masculine, feminine, and neuter apply only to the third person singular.

Reflexive personal pronouns are so-called because they reflect the action of the verb back to the subject. It is incorrect to use a reflexive pronoun by itself; there must be a subject to which it refers.

incorrect: Denise and myself will fix the car.
[The reflexive pronoun *myself* has no subject to refer to; the wording should be "Denise and I."]

correct: I will fix the car myself.
[The reflexive pronoun *myself* refers to the subject *I*.]

A reflexive pronoun that adds force or emphasis to a noun or another pronoun is called "intensive":

You yourself must return the ladder.
Terri and Phil want to wallpaper the kitchen themselves.

A **relative pronoun** introduces a descriptive clause. The relative pronouns are *which*, *that*, *who*, *whoever*, *whose*, *whom*, and *whomever*.

Wendy was the pianist who won the scholarship.
Is Mr. Leonard the teacher whose book was just published?
Whoever wrote the speech is a genius.
I attended the morning meeting, which lasted for three hours.

A **demonstrative pronoun** is specific. It is used to point out particular persons, places, or things. The demonstrative pronouns are *this*, *that*, *these*, and *those*.

These are the finest fabrics available.
I'll look at those first.
What is this?

An **indefinite pronoun** is nonspecific. It is used to refer to persons, places, or things without particular identification. There are numerous indefinite pronouns, including the following:

all	everyone	none
any	everything	no one
anybody	few	other
anyone	little	others
anything	many	several
both	most	some
each	much	somebody
either	neither	someone
everybody	nobody	something

George brought two desserts, but I didn't try either.
Many are called, but few are chosen.
Can somebody please answer the phone?

An **interrogative pronoun** is used to ask a question. The interrogative pronouns are *who*, *which*, and *what*.

Who wants to buy a raffle ticket?
Which of the two applicants has more practical experience?
What is the purpose of another debate?

PRONOUN CASES

The case of a pronoun is what determines its relation to the other words in the sentence. There are three pronoun cases: nominative, objective, and possessive.

Nominative case

The nominative pronouns are *I*, *we*, *you*, *he*, *she*, *it*, *they*, *who*, and *whoever*.

A pronoun that is the subject (or part of the subject) of a sentence is in the nominative case:

> They loved the movie.
> Mark and I are going to the Bahamas.

A pronoun that is a predicate is in the nominative case:

> It was she who wrote the poem.
> The winner will probably be you.

Objective case

The objective pronouns are *me*, *us*, *you*, *him*, *her*, *it*, *them*, *whom*, and *whomever*.

A pronoun that is the direct object of a verb is in the objective case:

> Stephen already invited them.
> Should we keep it?

A pronoun that is the indirect object of a verb is in the objective case:

> Captain Mackenzie told us many seafaring tales.
> I'll give you the recipe tomorrow.

A pronoun that is the object of a preposition is in the objective case:

> Does she think this job is beneath her?
> To whom was it addressed?

Possessive case

A possessive pronoun shows ownership.

The possessive pronouns used as predicate nominatives are *mine*, *ours*, *yours*, *his*, *hers*, *its*, *theirs*, and *whose*.

> The blue station wagon is mine.
> None of the cash was theirs.

The possessive pronouns used as adjectives are *my*, *our*, *your*, *his*, *her*, *its*, *their*, and *whose*.

> Whose test scores were the highest?
> I believe this is your package.

TIP

A possessive pronoun never has an apostrophe. Remember, the word *it's* is the contraction of *it is* or *it has*—not the possessive form of *it*.

- possessive: Life has its ups and downs.
- contraction: It's good to see you.

SINGULAR AND PLURAL AGREEMENT

It is important to identify a pronoun as singular or plural and to make certain that the associated verb form is in agreement. The pronouns that tend to cause the most problems for writers and speakers are the indefinite pronouns.

Some indefinite pronouns are always singular and therefore always require a singular verb. These include *everybody*, *everyone*, *somebody*, *someone*, *nobody*, *one*, *either*, and *neither*.

> Nobody wants to leave.
> Don't get up unless someone knocks on the door.
> Either of these two colors is fine.

Other indefinite pronouns may be singular or plural, depending on the particular reference. These include *any*, *all*, *some*, *most*, and *none*.

> If <u>any</u> of these marbles <u>are</u> yours, let me know.
> [The noun *marbles* is plural.]
>
> If <u>any</u> of this cake <u>is</u> yours, let me know.
> [The noun *cake* is singular.]
>
> <u>Most</u> of the potatoes <u>are</u> already gone.
> [The noun *potatoes* is plural.]
>
> <u>Most</u> of the evening <u>is</u> already gone.
> [The noun *evening* is singular.]

Verb

A **verb** is a word that expresses an action or a state of being.

An **action verb** expresses a physical or mental action:

break
eat
intercept
operate
unveil
wish

A **state of being verb** expresses a condition or state of being:

be
become
is
lack
seem
smell

TRANSITIVE VERBS

A **transitive verb** expresses an action that is performed on someone or something. The someone or something is the **direct object.** Notice in each of the following examples that the direct object receives the action of the verb.

> Ingrid <u>restores</u> antique <u>furniture</u>.
> [transitive verb: *restores*; direct object: *furniture*]
>
> Hernandez <u>pitched</u> the <u>ball</u>.
> [transitive verb: *pitched*; direct object: *ball*]
>
> Did you <u>feed</u> the <u>animals</u>?
> [transitive verb: *feed*; direct object: *animals*]

Sometimes a transitive verb has both a direct object and an indirect object. An **indirect object** is the person or thing to whom or for whom the verb's action is being performed. Notice in each of the following examples that the direct object receives the action of the verb, while the indirect object identifies who or what the action affected.

> The captain <u>handed</u> <u>us</u> our <u>orders</u>.
> [transitive verb: *handed*; direct object: *orders*; indirect object: *us*]
>
> Did you <u>give</u> the <u>plants</u> some <u>water</u>?
> [transitive verb: *give*; direct object: *water*; indirect object: *plants*]

I tossed a pen to Herman.
[transitive verb: *tossed*; direct object: *pen*; indirect object: *Herman*]

TIP

Remember: A direct object answers *what?* An indirect object answers *to whom?* (or *to what?*) or *for whom?* (or *for what?*).

direct objects:	*What* does Ingrid restore?	furniture
	What did Hernandez pitch?	ball
	Did you feed *what*?	animals
	What did the captain hand?	orders
	Did you give *what*?	water
	What did I toss?	pen
indirect objects:	*To whom* did the captain hand orders?	us
	Did you give water *to what*?	plants
	To whom did I toss a pen?	Herman

INTRANSITIVE VERBS

An **intransitive verb** does not have an object. Notice in each of the following examples that the verb expresses an action that occurs without needing to be received.

We marched in the parade.
The tea kettle whistled.
Heidi sleeps on the third floor.

TIP

Remember: Because an intransitive verb does not have an object, the question *what?* will be unanswerable.

What did we march?
What did the kettle whistle?
What does Heidi sleep?

These questions simply cannot be answered; therefore the verbs are intransitive.

LINKING VERBS

A **linking verb** joins a word (or unit of words) that names a person or thing to another word (or unit of words) that renames or describes the person or thing. It is always intransitive and always expresses a state of being. The most common linking verbs are *to be* and all the forms of *to be*, which include *am*, *are*, *is*, *was*, and *were*. Other common linking verbs include the following:

act	feel	remain	sound
appear	grow	seem	taste
become	look	smell	turn

The air seemed humid yesterday.
What smells so good?
The days grow shorter.

I am a registered voter.
Kim remains a devout Catholic.
Butch and Sundance were the title characters.

Predicate adjectives and nominatives

The word (or unit of words) that a linking verb joins to the subject can be either an adjective or a noun, but its function is always the same: to tell something about the subject. An adjective that follows a linking verb is a **predicate adjective**. A noun that follows a linking verb is a **predicate nominative**.

predicate adjective: The air seemed humid yesterday.
What smells so good?
The days grow shorter.

predicate nominative: I am a registered voter.
Kim remains a devout Catholic.
Butch and Sundance were the title characters.

VOICE

The subject of a transitive verb either performs or receives the action. A verb whose subject performs is said to be in the **active voice**. A verb whose subject receives is said to be in the **passive voice**.

active voice: Brainerd & Sons built the storage shed.
[The subject *Brainerd & Sons* performed the action of building.]

Lydia will curry the horses.
[The subject *Lydia* will perform the action of currying.]

passive voice: The storage shed was built by Brainerd & Sons.
[The subject *shed* received the action of building.]

The horses will be curried by Lydia.
[The subject *horses* will receive the action of currying.]

MOOD

Verbs have a quality that shows the attitude or purpose of the speaker. This quality is called the **mood**. There are three verb moods: indicative, imperative, and subjunctive.

The **indicative mood** shows a statement or question of fact:

Does Paula know the combination to the safe?
Dr. Sliva is my dentist.

The **imperative mood** shows a command or request:

Make the most of your situation.
Proceed to the third traffic light.

The **subjunctive mood** shows a condition of doubtfulness, possibility, desirability, improbability, or unreality:

Should you decide to return the blouse, you will need the receipt.
If I were rich, I'd quit my job.

PERSON AND NUMBER

The **person** (first, second, or third) of a verb depends on to whom or to what the verb refers: the person speaking (first person), the person spoken to (second person), or the person or thing spoken about (third person).

The **number** (singular or plural) of a verb depends on whether the verb refers to a singular subject or a plural subject.

For nearly all verbs, the form of the verb changes only in the third person singular.

PERSON	SINGULAR	PLURAL
first person	I *know*	we *know*
second person	you *know*	you *know*
third person	he *knows* she *knows* it *knows*	they *know* they *know* they *know*
	Chris *knows* Mrs. Hansen *knows* God *knows* the teacher *knows* the heart *knows*	Chris and Pat *know* the Hansens *know* the gods *know* the teachers *know* our hearts *know*

TENSE

The **tense** of a verb shows the time of the verb's action. There are six verb tenses: present, present perfect, past, past perfect, future, and future perfect.

The **present tense** shows action occurring in the present:

I smell fresh coffee.

The present tense can also show the following:

action that is typical or habitual:	I design greenhouses. Stuart daydreams during math class.
action that will occur:	Lynne retires in six months. Our plane lands at midnight.
facts and beliefs:	March follows February. Greed destroys the spirit.

TIP

Yet another function of the present tense is what is called the **historical present**. This usage allows the writer or speaker to relate past actions in a present tone, which may enhance the descriptive flow of the text.

The United States acquires the Oklahoma Territory from France in 1803 as part of the Louisiana Purchase. Following the War of 1812, the U.S. government begins a relocation program, forcing Indian tribes from the eastern United States to move into certain unsettled western areas, including Oklahoma. Because of their opposition to the U.S. government, most of these native people lend their support to the Confederate South during the American Civil War. In 1865, the war ends in utter defeat for the Confederacy, and all of the Oklahoma Territory soon falls under U.S. military rule.

When using the historical present, writers and speakers must be careful not to lapse into the past tense. For example, it would be an incorrect mix of tenses to say, "In 1865, the war ended in utter defeat for the Confederacy, and all of the Oklahoma Territory soon falls under U.S. military rule."

The **present perfect tense** is formed with the word *has* or *have*. It shows action begun in the past and completed by the time of the present:

James has checked the air in the tires at least three times.
I have read the book you're talking about.

The **past tense** shows action that occurred in the past:

Greg memorized his speech.
The mouse scurried across the room.

The **past perfect tense** is formed with the word *had*. It shows action that occurred in the past, prior to another past action:

Eugene had finished his story by the time we got to the airport.
The parrot had flown into another room long before we noticed an empty cage.

The **future tense** is formed with the word *will*. It shows action that is expected to occur in the future:

The president will address the nation this evening.
Tempers will flare when the truth comes out.

The **future perfect tense** is formed with the words *will have*. It shows action that is expected to occur in the future, prior to another future or expected action:

Noreen will have finished painting by the time we're ready to lay the carpet.
The candidates will have traveled thousands of miles before this campaign is over.

VERBALS

A verb form that acts as a part of speech other than a verb is a **verbal**. There are three types of verbals: infinitives, participles, and gerunds.

An **infinitive** is a verb form that can act as a noun, an adjective, or an adverb. It is preceded by the preposition *to*.

noun: To steal is a crime.
[The infinitive *to steal* is the subject.]

Our original plan, to elope, was never discovered.
[The infinitive *to elope* is an appositive.]

adjective: Those are words to remember.
[The infinitive *to remember* modifies the noun *words*.]

adverb: The hill was too icy to climb.
[The infinitive *to climb* modifies the predicate adjective *icy*.]

He lived to golf.
[The infinitive *to golf* modifies the verb *lived*.]

A **participle** is a verb form that has one of two uses: to make a verb phrase ("they were trying"; "the car has died") or to act as an adjective. A participle is a verbal only when it acts as an adjective.

A **present participle** always ends in *-ing*:

catching
laughing
winding

A **past participle** usually ends in *-ed*, *-en*, or *-t*:

given
lost
toasted

In the following examples, each participle acts as an adjective and is therefore a verbal:

Does the zoo have a laughing hyena?
We live on a winding road.

It was a lost opportunity.
Add a cup of toasted coconut.

A **gerund** is a verb form that acts as a noun. It always ends in *–ing*:

Reading is my favorite pastime.
The next step, varnishing, should be done in a well-ventilated area.
The doctor suggested guidelines for sensible dieting.

TIP

Remember: Both gerunds and present participles always end in *–ing*, but their functions are quite distinct. Also remember that a present participle is only a verbal when it acts as an adjective, *not* when it acts as a verb phrase.

verbal:	Her singing has improved this year. [Used as a noun, *singing* is a gerund, which is always a verbal.]
	Peterson hired the singing cowboys. [Used as an adjective, *singing* is a present participle that is also a verbal.]
not a verbal:	The birds are singing. [Used to form a verb phrase, *singing* is a present participle, but not a verbal]

Adjective

An **adjective** is a word that modifies a noun. There are two basic types of adjectives: descriptive and limiting.

Descriptive adjectives

A **descriptive adjective** describes a noun. That is, it shows a quality or condition of a noun:

She is an upstanding citizen.
Josh has invited his zany friends.
That was a mighty clap of thunder.
I prefer the white shirt with the long sleeves.

Limiting adjectives

A **limiting adjective** shows the limits of a noun. That is, it indicates the number or quantity of a noun, or it points out a certain specificity of a noun. There are three types of limiting adjectives: numerical adjectives, pronominal adjectives, and articles.

A **numerical adjective** is a number. It may be cardinal ("how many") or ordinal ("in what order"):

cardinal:	We have served one million customers. There are three prizes. After Arizona was admitted, there were forty-eight states.
ordinal:	You are the one millionth customer. We won third prize. Arizona was the forty-eighth state to be admitted.

A **pronominal adjective** is a pronoun that acts as an adjective. A pronominal adjective may be personal (*my, our, your, his, her, their, its*), demonstrative (*this, that, these, those*), indefinite (*all, any, few, other, several, some*), or interrogative (*which, what*).

personal:	We loved her goulash. The squirrel returned to its nest.
demonstrative:	Those directions are too complicated. This window is broken.
indefinite:	Pick any card from the deck. All luggage will be inspected.
interrogative:	Which radios are on sale? What color is the upholstery?

There are three **articles** in English: *a*, *an*, and *the*. Articles are classified as either indefinite (*a, an*) or definite (*the*).

indefinite:	At dawn, a helicopter broke the silence. An usher seated us.
definite:	The paintings lacked imagination.

Comparison of adjectives

Descriptive adjectives are able to indicate qualities and conditions by three degrees of comparison: positive, comparative, and superlative. Adjectives may be compared in downward or upward order.

For **downward comparisons**, all adjectives use the words *less* (comparative) and *least* (superlative).

Downward Comparisons

positive (the quality or condition)	**comparative** (a degree lower than the positive)	**superlative** (the lowest degree of the positive)
intelligent	less intelligent	least intelligent
kind	less kind	least kind
salty	less salty	least salty

For **upward comparisons**, there are three different formats:

Upward Comparisons

positive (the quality or condition)	**comparative** (a degree higher than the positive)	**superlative** (the highest degree of the positive)
1. Almost all one-syllable adjectives use the endings *-er* (comparative) and *-est* (superlative). Some adjectives with two or more syllables follow this format as well.		
kind	kinder	kindest
straight	straighter	straightest
salty	saltier	saltiest
2. Most adjectives with two or more syllables use the words *more* (comparative) and *most* (superlative). Most one-syllable adjectives may use this format as an optional alternative to using *-er* and *-est.*		
harmonious	more harmonious	most harmonious
impatient	more impatient	most impatient
talkative	more talkative	most talkative
kind	more kind	most kind

3. Some adjectives have irregular forms.

bad/ill	worse	worst
good/well	better	best
far	farther/further	farthest/furthest
little	less	least
many	more	most

TIP

Never "double compare" an adjective. Remember:

- Sometimes a descriptive adjective may use either *-er* or *more*, but it never uses both.

  correct: The red grapes are sweeter than the green ones.
  The red grapes are more sweet than the green ones.

  incorrect: The red grapes are more sweeter than the green ones.

- Sometimes a descriptive adjective may use either *-est* or *most*, but it never uses both.

  correct: Samson is the friendliest dog in the building.
  Samson is the most friendly dog in the building.

  incorrect: Samson is the most friendliest dog in the building.

Adverb

An **adverb** is a word that modifies a verb, an adjective, or another adverb.

ADVERB MEANINGS

An adverb usually describes how, where, when, or to what extent something happens.

An **adverb of manner** describes *how*:

They argued loudly.

An **adverb of place** describes *where*:

Please sit near me.

An **adverb of time** describes *when*:

I'll call you later.

An **adverb of degree** describes *to what extent*:

The laundry is somewhat damp.

ADVERB FUNCTIONS

A **relative adverb** introduces a subordinate clause:

I'll be out on the veranda when the clock strikes twelve.

A **conjunctive adverb** (also called a **transitional adverb**) joins two independent clauses:

Dinner is ready; however, you may have to heat it up.

An **interrogative adverb** introduces a question:

Where did Lisa go?

TIP

A great number of adverbs are created by adding the suffix *–ly* to an adjective:

hesitant + *-ly* = hesitantly
strong + *-ly* = strongly

This does not mean, however, that all adverbs end in *–ly*.

adverbs: fast, seldom, now

Nor does it mean that all words ending in *–ly* are adverbs.

adjectives: friendly, homely, dastardly

The way to determine if a word is an adverb or an adjective is to see how it is used in the sentence:

- If it modifies a noun, it is an adjective.
- If it modifies a verb, an adjective, or another adverb, it is an adverb.

An **independent adverb** functions independently from the rest of the sentence. That is, the meaning and grammatical correctness of the sentence would not change if the independent adverb were removed:

<u>Besides</u>, I never liked living in the city.

COMPARISON OF ADVERBS

Like adjectives, adverbs of manner may be compared in three degrees: positive, comparative, and superlative.

Most adverbs, especially those that end in *–ly*, take on the upward comparing words *more* and *most*.

positive	**comparative**	**superlative**
nicely	more nicely	most nicely
diligently	more diligently	most diligently

Some adverbs take on the upward comparing suffixes *–er* and *–est*:

positive	**comparative**	**superlative**
early	earlier	earliest
soon	sooner	soonest
close	closer	closest

Some adverbs have irregular upward comparisons.

positive	**comparative**	**superlative**
much	more	most
little	less	least
badly	worse	worst
well	better	best
far	farther	farthest
far	further	furthest

Almost all adverbs take on the downward comparing words *less* and *least*:

positive	**comparative**	**superlative**
nicely	less nicely	least nicely
diligently	less diligently	least diligently
early	less early	least early
soon	less soon	least soon
close	less close	least close

Preposition

A **preposition** is a word or group of words that governs a noun or pronoun by expressing its relationship to another word in the clause.

> The suspects landed in jail.
> [The relationship between the noun *jail* and the verb *landed* is shown by the preposition *in*.]
>
> Please hide the packages under the bed.
> [The relationship between the noun *bed* and the noun *packages* is shown by the preposition *under*.]
>
> The guitarist playing with our band is Samantha's uncle.
> [The relationship between the noun *band* and the participle *playing* is shown by the preposition *with*.]
>
> I already knew about it.
> [The relationship between the pronoun *it* and the verb *knew* is shown by the preposition *about*.]

TIP

Many words used as prepositions may be used as other parts of speech as well.

The closest village is over that hill.	[preposition]
He leaned over and whispered in my ear.	[adverb]
I told no one but Corinne.	[preposition]
We played our best, but the other team won.	[conjunction]
She is but a shadow of her former self.	[adverb]

Common prepositions

aboard
about
above
according to
across
after
against
ahead
along
along with
amid
around
as
as far as
as for
as to
aside from
at
because of
before
behind
below
beneath
beside
besides
between
beyond
but
but for
by
by means of
by way of
concerning
contrary to
despite
down
during
except
for
from
in
in addition to
in back of
in case of
in front of
in lieu of
in place of
in regard to
in spite of
inside
instead of
into
like
near
next to
of
off
on
on account of
on behalf of
onto
opposite
out
out of
outside
over
past
per
prior to
regarding
round
since
thanks to
through
throughout
till
to
toward
under
underneath
unlike
until
up
upon
up to
with
within
without

Conjunction

A **conjunction** is a word (or unit of words) that connects words, phrases, clauses, or sentences. There are three kinds of conjunctions: coordinating, subordinating, and correlative.

Coordinating conjunctions

A **coordinating conjunction** connects elements that have the same grammatical rank—that is, it connects words to words (nouns to nouns, verbs to verbs, etc.), phrases to phrases, clauses to clauses, sentences to sentences. A coordinating conjunction is almost always one of these seven words: *and, but, for, nor, or, so, yet.*

> Would you prefer rice or potatoes?
> [The coordinating conjunction *or* connects the two nouns *rice* and *potatoes.*]

> I have seen and heard enough.
> [The coordinating conjunction *and* connects the two verbs *seen* and *heard.*]

> Vinnie's cat lay on the chair purring softly yet twitching its tail.
> [The coordinating conjunction *yet* connects the two participial phrases *purring softly* and *twitching its tail.*]

> O'Donnell is the reporter whose name is on the story but who denies having written it.
> [The coordinating conjunction *but* connects the two subordinate clauses *whose name is on the story* and *who denies having written it.*]

> We wanted to see batting practice, so we got to the stadium early.
> [The coordinating conjunction *so* connects the two sentences *We wanted to see batting practice* and *We got to the stadium early*, creating one sentence. Notice that a comma precedes the conjunction when two sentences are joined.]

Subordinating conjunctions

A **subordinating conjunction** belongs to a subordinate clause. It connects the subordinate clause to a main clause.

> I could get there on time if only the ferry were still running.
> [The subordinating conjunction *if only* connects the subordinate clause *if only the ferry were still running* to the main clause *I could get there on time.*]

TIP

A noun clause or an adjective clause may or may not be introduced by a subordinating conjunction, but an adverb clause is always introduced by a subordinating conjunction.

- noun clause introduced by subordinating conjunction:
  Jack asked the question even though he knew the answer.
- noun clause with no subordinating conjunction:
  We gave every single detail our fullest attention.
- adjective clause introduced by subordinating conjunction:
  This is the farm where we boarded our horses.
- adjective clause with no subordinating conjunction:
  The people we met last night are Hungarian.
- adverb clause with subordinating conjunction (as is always the case):
  I will speak as soon as the crowd quiets down.

Common subordinating conjunctions

after	but	since	until
although	even if	so	when
as	even though	so that	whenever
as if	how	than	where
as long as	if	that	whereas
as though	if only	though	wherever
because	in order that	till	while
before	rather than	unless	why

CORRELATIVE CONJUNCTIONS

Two coordinating conjunctions that function together are called a pair of **correlative conjunctions**. These are the most common pairs of correlative conjunctions:

both . . . and
either . . . or
neither . . . nor
not only . . . but
not only . . . but also
whether . . . or

The site in Denver offers the potential for both security and expansion.
[The pair of correlative conjunctions *both . . . and* connects the two nouns *security* and *expansion*.]

I'm running in tomorrow's race whether it is sunny or rainy.
[The pair of correlative conjunctions *whether . . . or* connects the two adjectives *sunny* and *rainy*.]

TIP

It would be incorrect to say:

Their dog is neither quiet nor obeys simple commands.

Why? Because the pair of correlative conjunctions *neither . . . nor* is being used to connect the adjective *quiet* to the verb phrase *obeys simple commands*. This is not a grammatically valid connection.

Remember: A pair of correlative conjunctions is comprised of two coordinating conjunctions, and a coordinating conjunction must connect elements that have the same grammatical rank—that is, it must connect words to words (nouns to nouns, verbs to verbs, etc.), phrases to phrases, clauses to clauses, sentences to sentences.

Therefore, the sentence must be reworded to make the grammatical ranks match. Here are two such corrected versions:

Their dog is neither quiet nor obedient.
[The adjective *quiet* is connected to the adjective *obedient*.]

Their dog neither stays quiet nor obeys simple commands.
[The verb phrase *stays quiet* is connected to the verb phrase *obeys simple commands*.]

Interjection

An interjection is a word or phrase that expresses emotion, typically in an abrupt or emphatic way. It is not connected grammatically to the rest of the sentence. When the emotion expressed is very strong, the interjection is followed by an exclamation point. Otherwise it is followed by a comma:

Stop! I can't let you in here.
Yeah! Dempsey has won another fight.

Ah, that was a wonderful meal.
Oh no, I left my sweater on the train.

TIP

Interjections occur more often in speech than in writing. It is not wrong to use interjections in writing, but writers should do so sparingly. Remember, an interjection is essentially an interruption, and too many may disrupt the flow of the text.

PHRASES, CLAUSES, SENTENCES, AND PARAGRAPHS

Phrases

A **phrase** is a unit of words that acts as a single part of speech.

Noun phrases

A phrase made up of a noun and its modifiers is a **noun phrase**:

The biggest pumpkin won a blue ribbon.
A magnificent whooping crane flew overhead.

Most noun phrases can be replaced with a pronoun:

Give the tickets to the tall, dark-haired gentleman.
Give the tickets to him.

Verb phrases

A phrase made up of a main verb and its auxiliaries is a **verb phrase** (also called a **complete verb**):

We have been waiting for three hours.
What type of music do you prefer?

Adjective phrases

A phrase made up of a participle and its related words is an **adjective phrase** (also called an **adjectival phrase** or a **participial phrase**). Acting as a single adjective, it modifies a noun or pronoun:

Awakened by the siren, we escaped to safety.
[The adjective phrase *Awakened by the siren* modifies the pronoun *we*.]

Following his grandmother's directions, Harry baked a beautiful apple pie.
[The adjective phrase *Following his grandmother's directions* modifies the noun *Harry*.]

Prepositional phrases

A phrase that begins with a preposition is a **prepositional phrase**. It can act as an adjective or an adverb:

adjective: The car with the sunroof is mine.
[The noun *car* is modified by the prepositional phrase *with the sunroof*.]

adverb: After the storm, we gathered the fallen branches.
[The verb *gathered* is modified by the prepositional phrase *After the storm*.]

Clauses

A clause is a unit of words that contains a subject and a predicate.

INDEPENDENT CLAUSES

A clause that can stand by itself as a complete thought is an **independent clause**. Any independent clause can stand alone as a complete sentence:

The Milwaukee Brewers joined the National League in November 1997.
It is snowing.
Vitus is the patron saint of actors.
Bob called.
The Celts were highly ritualistic.
Read what child development experts have to say.

SUBORDINATE CLAUSES

A clause that cannot stand by itself as a complete thought is a **subordinate clause** (also called a **dependent clause**). It cannot be a part of a sentence unless it is related by meaning to the independent clause. Essentially, it exists to build upon the information conveyed by the independent clause. A subordinate clause can relate to the independent clause as an adjective, an adverb, or a noun:

adjective:	The Milwaukee Brewers, who play at Miller Park, joined the National League in November 1997.
adverb:	Bob called when you were at the store.
noun:	Read what child development experts have to say about the virtues and drawbacks of homeschooling.

ELLIPTICAL CLAUSES

An **elliptical clause** deviates from the rule that states "a clause contains a subject and a predicate." What an elliptical clause does is *imply* both a subject and a predicate, even though both elements do not in fact appear in the clause:

While vacationing in Spain, Jo received word of her promotion.
[The elliptical clause implies the subject "she" and the predicate "was vacationing"—that is, it implies "While she was vacationing in Spain."]

Myers arrived on Saturday the 12th; Anderson, the following Monday.
[The elliptical clause implies the predicate "arrived the following Monday"—that is it implies "Anderson arrived the following Monday."]

Elliptical clauses are valuable devices, as they allow the writer to avoid excessive wordiness, preserve a sense of variety, and enhance the rhythm of the text.

RESTRICTIVE CLAUSES

A clause that is essential to the meaning of the sentence—that is, it *restricts* the meaning of the sentence—is a **restrictive clause**. The content of a restrictive clause identifies a particular person, place, or thing. If the restrictive clause were to be removed, the meaning of the sentence would change. A restrictive clause begins with the relative pronoun *that*, *who*, or *whom*. It should never be set off with commas.

I'm returning the coat that I bought last week.
[The identification of the coat is important. It's not just any coat. It's specifically the one and only coat "that I bought last week." Without the restrictive clause, the identification would be lost.]

The president who authorized the Louisiana Purchase was Thomas Jefferson.
[The point of this sentence is to identify specifically the one and only president responsible for the Louisiana Purchase. Without the restrictive clause, the point of the sentence would be lost.]

NONRESTRICTIVE CLAUSES

A clause that is not essential to the meaning of the sentence—that is, it does *not restrict* the meaning of the sentence—is a **nonrestrictive clause.** The content of a nonrestrictive clause adds information to what has already been identified. If the nonrestrictive clause were to be removed, the meaning of the sentence would not change. A nonrestrictive clause begins with the relative pronoun *which*, *who*, or *whom*. It should always be set off with commas.

I'm returning my new coat, which doesn't fit.

President Jefferson, who authorized the Louisiana Purchase, was the third U.S. president.

[The clauses *which doesn't fit* and *who authorized the Louisiana Purchase* are informative but not necessary. Without them, the meaning of each sentence is still clear.]

Sentences

Properly constructed sentences are integral to good communication. By definition, a sentence is "a set of words that is complete in itself, typically containing a subject and predicate, conveying a statement, question, exclamation, or command, and consisting of a main clause and sometimes one or more subordinate clauses." Simply put, a sentence is a group of words that expresses a complete thought.

SUBJECT AND PREDICATE

The primary building blocks of a sentence are the subject and the predicate.

The **subject** (usually a noun or pronoun) is the part that the sentence is telling about. A **simple subject** is simply the person, place, or thing being discussed. A **complete subject** is the simple subject along with all the words directly associated with it:

The large tropical plant in my office has bloomed every summer.
[Here, the simple subject is *plant*. The complete subject is *The large tropical plant in my office.*]

Two or more subjects that belong to the same verb comprise what is called a **compound subject:**

Stan Garrison and the rest of the department are relocating next week.
[Here, the compound subject consists of *Stan Garrison* and *the rest of the department*. They share the verb phrase *are relocating.*]

The **predicate** (a verb) is the "action" or "being" part of the sentence—the part that tells something about the subject. A **simple predicate** is simply the main verb and its auxiliaries. A **complete predicate** is the simple predicate along with all the words directly associated with it:

The setting sun has cast a scarlet glow across the skyline.
[Here, the simple predicate is *has cast.* The complete predicate is *has cast a scarlet glow across the skyline.*]

Two or more predicates that have the same subject comprise what is called a **compound predicate:**

I wanted to buy some art but left empty-handed.
[Here, the compound predicate consists of *wanted to buy some art* and *left empty-handed.* They share the subject *I.*]

FOUR SENTENCE STRUCTURES

A **simple sentence** contains one independent clause. Its subject and/or predicate may or may not be compound, but its one and only clause is always independent:

Paula rode her bicycle. [subject + predicate]
Honus Wagner and Nap Lajoie are enshrined in the Baseball Hall of Fame. [compound subject + predicate]
The correspondents traveled across the desert and slept in makeshift shelters. [subject + compound predicate]

Lunch and dinner are discounted on Sunday but are full price on Monday. [compound subject + compound predicate]

A **compound sentence** contains two or more independent clauses. The following examples show the various ways that coordinating conjunctions (e.g., *and*, *but*, *yet*), conjunctive adverbs (e.g., *however*, *therefore*), and punctuation may be used to join the clauses in a compound sentence:

Ken made the phone calls and Maria addressed the envelopes.
The war lasted for two years, but the effects of its devastation will last for decades.
Judges and other officials should sign in by noon; exhibitors will start arriving at 2:00.
I have decided to remain on the East Coast; however, I am willing to attend the monthly meetings in Dallas.
FDR initiated the New Deal, JFK embraced the New Frontier, and LBJ envisioned the Great Society.

A **complex sentence** contains one independent clause and one or more subordinate clauses:

Even though I majored in English, I was hired to teach applied physics.
We can have the party indoors if it gets too windy.
Before I agree, I have to read the final report that you drafted.
[The independent clauses are *I was hired to teach applied physics; We can have the party indoors; I have to read the final report.* The subordinate clauses are *Even though I majored in English; if it gets too windy; Before I agree; that you drafted.*]

A **compound-complex sentence** contains two or more independent clauses and one or more subordinate clauses:

Because the candidates have been so argumentative, some voters are confused and many have become disinterested.
We will begin painting tomorrow if the weather's nice; if it rains, we will start on Thursday.
[The independent clauses are *some voters are confused; many have become disinterested; We will begin painting tomorrow, we will start on Thursday.* The subordinate clauses are *Because the candidates have been so argumentative; if the weather's nice, if it rains.*]

FOUR SENTENCE FUNCTIONS

A **declarative sentence** states a fact, an assertion, an impression, or a feeling. It ends with a period:

Florence is a beautiful city.
Lewis Carroll died in 1898.
I'm sorry I missed the end of your speech.

An **interrogative sentence** asks a question. It ends with a question mark:

Did you read the article about migrating geese patterns?
How do spell your last name?
Mr. Young owns a kennel?

An **imperative sentence** makes a request or gives an order. It typically ends with a period but occasionally may end with an exclamation point:

Please lock the doors.
Do not throw trash in the recycling bins.
Think before you speak!

An **exclamatory sentence** expresses surprise, shock, or strong feeling. It ends with an exclamation point:

Look at this mess!
I can't believe how great this is!
I lost my purse!

Paragraphs

A paragraph is a series of sentences that conveys a single theme. Paragraphs help writers organize thoughts, actions, and descriptions into readable units of information. The paragraph, as a unit of text, may have one of several functions. It may be descriptive, giving certain details or impressions about a person, thing, or event. It may be instructive, explaining a method or procedure. It may be conceptual, stating thoughts, feelings, or opinions.

Every paragraph should contain a sentence that states the main idea of the paragraph. This is called the **topic sentence**. The other sentences in the paragraph are the **supporting sentences**, and their function is just that—to support or elaborate on the idea set forth in the topic sentence. Most paragraphs begin with the topic sentence, as in the following example:

> Each Thanksgiving we make place cards decorated with pressed autumn leaves. After gathering the smallest and most colorful leaves from the maples and oaks in our backyard, we place the leaves between sheets of blotter paper, which we then cover with a large, heavy book. In just a day or two, the leaves are ready to be mounted on cards. We use plain index cards, folded in half. Using clear adhesive paper, we put one leaf on each card, leaving room for the guest's name.

Try reading the preceding paragraph without the topic sentence (the first sentence). The supporting information becomes less unified because it has no main idea to support. Now imagine adding to the paragraph the following sentence:

> Last year, three of our guests were snowed in at the airport.

This would be a misplaced addition to the paragraph, as it is unrelated to the topic sentence (that is, it has nothing to do with making Thanksgiving place cards). Because it introduces a new and distinct idea, it should become the topic sentence for a new and distinct paragraph.

SENTENCE DEVELOPMENT: AVOIDING PROBLEMS

Sentence style

Getting one's ideas across in words is the core of communication. Sentences provide the means to arrange ideas in a coherent way. Certainly, the rules of grammar should be observed when constructing a sentence, but the general rhythm of the sentence is also important. Sentences may be categorized into three general types: loose, periodic, and balanced. Good writers typically use a combination of these styles in order to create a flow of ideas that will hold the reader's interest.

A **loose sentence** gets to the main point quickly. It begins with a basic and complete statement, which is followed by additional information:

> The power went out, plunging us into darkness, silencing the drone of the television, leaving our dinner half-cooked.
> [The basic statement is *The power went out*. Everything that follows is additional information.]

A **periodic sentence** ends with the main point. It begins with additional information, thus imposing a delay before the basic statement is given:

> With no warning, like a herd of stampeding bison, a mob of fans crashed through the gate.
> The basic statement is *a mob of fans crashed through the gate*. Everything that precedes is additional information.

A **balanced sentence** is comprised of grammatically equal or similar structures. The ideas in the sentence are linked by comparison or contrast:

> To visit their island villa is to sample nirvana.

As writers become more comfortable with the basic rules of grammar and the general patterns of sentence structure, they are able to remain compliant with the rules while getting more creative with the patterns. Many well-constructed sentences will not agree precisely with any of the three preceding examples, but they should always evoke an answer of "yes" to two fundamental questions:

- Is the sentence grammatically correct?
- Will the meaning of the sentence be clear to the reader?

Flawed sentences

Three types of "flawed sentences" are sentence fragments, run-on sentences, and sentences with improperly positioned modifiers.

SENTENCE FRAGMENTS

A **sentence fragment** is simply an incomplete sentence. Fundamental to every sentence is a complete thought that is able to stand on its own. Because a phrase or subordinate clause is not an independent thought, it cannot stand on its own as a sentence. To be a part of a sentence, it must either be connected to an independent clause or be reworded to become an independent clause. Consider this sentence fragment:

My English guest who stayed on for Christmas.

Here are three possible ways to create a proper sentence from that fragment:

Everyone left on Tuesday except Dan, my English guest who stayed on for Christmas.
[The fragment is added to the independent clause *Everyone left on Tuesday except Dan.*]

My English guest stayed on for Christmas.
[The fragment becomes an independent clause by removing the word *who.*]

Dan was my English guest who stayed on for Christmas.
[The fragment becomes an independent clause by adding the words *Dan was.*]

RUN-ON SENTENCES

A **run-on sentence** results when two or more sentences are improperly united into one sentence. Characteristic of a run-on sentence is the absence of punctuation between the independent clauses or the use of incorrect punctuation (typically a comma) between the independent clauses:

Our flight was canceled we had to spend the night in Boston.
Our flight was canceled, we had to spend the night in Boston.

Here are three possible ways to correct the preceding run-on sentences:

Our flight was canceled; we had to spend the night in Boston.
[A semicolon provides a properly punctuated separation of the two independent clauses.]

Our flight was canceled, so we had to spend the night in Boston.
[A comma followed by a conjunction (*so*) provides a properly worded and punctuated separation of the two independent clauses.]

Our flight was canceled. We had to spend the night in Boston.
[The creation of two distinct sentences provides an absolute separation of the two independent clauses.]

MODIFIER PROBLEMS

The improper placement of modifying words, phrases, and clauses is a common mistake. The result is a sentence in which the modifier unintentionally refers to the wrong person or thing. The three principal culprits are dangling modifiers, misplaced modifiers, and squinting modifiers. Writers must be careful to avoid these troublesome errors in sentence construction. Review the following examples to see how an improperly placed modifier can be confusing to the reader. It is important to recognize the subtle differences between the incorrect sentences and their corrected versions.

A **dangling modifier** is an adjectival phrase or clause that lacks a proper connection because the word it is supposed to modify is missing.

dangling: While waiting for my son, a cat jumped onto the hood of my car.
[This wrongly implies that "a cat was waiting for my son."]

correct: While I was waiting for my son, a cat jumped onto the hood of my car.
While waiting for my son, I saw a cat jump onto the hood of my car.
A cat jumped onto the hood of my car while I was waiting for my son.
[The word that was missing is "I."]

dangling: At age seven, her grandfather died of diphtheria.
[This wrongly implies that "her grandfather died when he was seven."]

correct: When she was seven, her grandfather died of diphtheria.
Her grandfather died of diphtheria when she was seven.
At age seven, she lost her grandfather when he died of diphtheria.
[The word that was missing is "she."]

A **misplaced modifier** is a phrase or clause that is not positioned close enough to the word it is supposed to modify. It will seem to the reader that a different word is being modified.

misplaced: There was an outbreak in our school of chicken pox.
[This wrongly implies that there is "a school of chicken pox."]

correct: There was an outbreak of chicken pox in our school.
In our school there was an outbreak of chicken pox.
Our school experienced an outbreak of chicken pox.

misplaced: I was stopped by a policeman without a driver's license.
[This wrongly implies that there was "a policeman without a driver's license."]

correct: Driving without a license, I was stopped by a policeman.
I was stopped by a policeman, and I did not have a driver's license.

A **squinting modifier** is an adverb placed between two verbs. For the reader, it is often difficult to determine which verb the adverb is supposed to modify.

squinting: The stack of chairs she had arranged carefully collapsed in the wind.
[Was the stack of chairs "arranged carefully" or did it "carefully collapse"?]

correct: The stack of chairs she had carefully arranged collapsed in the wind.
[Of the two possible meanings, this is only one that makes sense.]

squinting: The stack of chairs she had arranged quickly collapsed in the wind.
[Was the stack of chairs "arranged quickly" or did it "quickly collapse"?]

correct: The stack of chairs she had quickly arranged collapsed in the wind.
The stack of chairs she had arranged collapsed quickly in the wind.
[Either meaning could make sense, so only the writer would know which version is correct.]

Guide to Spelling

Any reader or writer knows that spelling is an important component of writing. Some individuals seem to have little or no trouble spelling words correctly, while others seem to struggle with spelling, often misspelling the same words over and over.

For those who have experienced the struggle, it is important to remember that spelling is a skill that improves with practice. Regular reading and writing, accompanied by a dictionary for consultation, are the best methods for improving one's spelling. Anyone who has encountered trouble with spelling knows that the English language contains numerous irregularities. Even so, there are basic spelling rules that can be followed in most cases.

[For spelling guidelines for plural nouns and possessive nouns, refer to the "Noun" section under "Parts of Speech."]

TIP

Keep a list of words that you find difficult to spell. Use a dictionary to confirm the correct spellings. Add to your list whenever you encounter a troublesome word. Refer to your list often, and quiz yourself. Make up sentences that include words from the list, writing them without going back and forth to double-check the spelling. Compare the words in your sentences to the words on your list. Make a note of the words that continue to give you trouble, and write these words in sentences every day until you have learned to spell them.

COMPOUND ADJECTIVES AND NOUNS

A compound adjective or noun is a single term formed from two or more distinct words. There are three spelling formats for compounds: open, hyphenated, and closed.

In an **open compound**, the component words are separate, with no hyphen (*well fed; wagon train*).
In a **hyphenated compound**, the component words are joined by a hyphen (*half-baked; city-state*).
In a **closed compound**, the component words are joined into a single word (*hardheaded; campfire*).

Compound Adjectives

For most cases of open compound adjectives, there is a general rule of thumb: the compound is left open when it is not followed by the modified noun; the compound is hyphenated when it is followed by the modified noun:

<u>She</u> was <u>well known</u> in the South for her poetry.
[The compound *well known* is open because it is not followed by the modified noun *She*.]

In the South, she was a <u>well-known poet</u>.
[The compound *well-known* is hyphenated because it is followed by the modified noun *poet*.]

A notable exception occurs when the first part of the compound adjective is an adverb that ends in *-ly*. In this case, the compound remains open, even when it is followed by the noun:

The <u>woman</u> who met us in the lobby was <u>beautifully dressed</u>.
A <u>beautifully dressed woman</u> met us in the lobby.

Compound Nouns

For spellers, the least troublesome compound nouns are familiar closed compounds:

briefcase
cupcake
downstairs
fireplace

Other compound nouns can be troublesome. Although certain ones, such as *mother-in-law*, are always hyphenated, many compound nouns commonly occur in more than one acceptable format, such as *ice cap* or *icecap* and *vice president* or *vice-president*. For most spelling questions, the best resource is a dictionary; for questions pertaining specifically to compounds, an unabridged edition is recommended.

> **TIP**
>
> Different dictionaries often disagree on the preferred spelling formats for a number of compounds, so writers are well advised to consult just one dictionary when establishing a spelling style.

PREFIXES

A prefix is a group of letters added to the beginning of a word to adjust its meaning.

In most cases, prefixes are affixed to the root word without hyphenation:

antibacterial
postwar
semicircle

Often, however, a hyphen is customary, necessary, or preferable.

Certain prefixes almost always take a hyphen: *all-*, *ex-*, *full-*, *quasi-*, *self-*:

all-encompassing
ex-partner
full-bodied
quasi-liberal
self-confidence

When the root word begins with a capital letter, the prefix takes a hyphen:

anti-American
pre-Conquest

Sometimes, without a hyphen, a word could be easily confused with another:

We recovered our furniture.

Does this mean we *found* our *missing* furniture? Or did we *put new coverings on* our furniture? If the latter is meant, a hyphen would have avoided confusion:

We re-covered our furniture.

Sometimes, a hyphen is not necessary but preferable. Without it, the word may look awkward. One such circumstance is when the last letter of the prefix and the first letter of the root word are both vowels, or when an awkward double consonant is created. For each of the following pairs of words, either spelling is acceptable:

antiknock / anti-knock
preadapt / pre-adapt
semiindependent / semi-independent
nonnegative / non-negative

> **TIP**
>
> Regarding the use of optional hyphens, the writer should establish a preferred style. Keeping a running list of hyphenated terms can help writers keep track of which spellings they have already used in their text, thus making the style consistent.

SUFFIXES

A suffix is a group of letters added to the end of a word to create a derivative of the word. There are exceptions to the following guidelines on how to spell with suffixes, but in most cases these rules apply:

A root word that ends in *e* drops the *e* when the suffix begins with a vowel:

rehearse / rehearsing

However, most words that end in *ce* or *ge* keep the *e* when the suffix begins with *a* or *o*:

service / serviceable
advantage / advantageous

A root word that ends in *e* keeps the *e* when the suffix begins with a consonant:

wise / wisely

A root word that ends in a *y* preceded by a consonant changes the *y* to *i* when the suffix begins with any letter other than *i*:

satisfy / satisfies / satisfying

A root word that ends in *ie* changes the *ie* to *y* when the suffix is *–ing*:

lie / lying

A root word that ends in *oe* keeps the *e* when the suffix begins with a vowel, unless the vowel is *e*:

toe / toeing / toed

A one-syllable root word that ends in a single consonant preceded by a single vowel doubles the consonant when the suffix is *–ed*, *–er*, or *–ing*. This rule also applies to root words with two or more syllables if the accent is on the last syllable.

stir / stirred
refer / referring

WORD DIVISION

Sometimes it is necessary to "break" a word when the line on the page has run out of space. Dividing a word at the end of a line is perfectly acceptable, as long as two conditions are met: the word must be divisible, and the division must be made in the right place.

When a word is properly divided, a hyphen is attached to its first part, so that the hyphen is at the end of the line:

At the conclusion of the interview, I had two minutes to summarize my management experiences.

What words are never divisible?	*for example:*
• one-syllable words	catch; flutes; strange; through
• contractions	didn't; doesn't; wouldn't; you're
• abbreviations	Calif.; NASCAR; RSVP; YMCA
• numbers written as numerals	1776; $2,800; 9:45; 0.137

Where is a correct place to divide a word?	*good break:*	*bad break:*
• after a prefix	inter-national	interna-tional
• before a suffix that has more than two letters	govern-ment	gov-ernment
• between the main parts of a closed compound	nut-cracker	nutcrack-er
• at the hyphen of a hyphenated compound	gender-neutral	gen-der-neutral
• after double consonants if the root word ends in the double consonants	address-ing	addres-sing
• otherwise, between double consonants	rib-bon	ribb-on
• in general (for words that don't fall into the previous categories), between syllables	whis-per	whi-sper

Where is an incorrect place to divide a word?	*good break:*	*bad break:*
• before a two-letter suffix	——	odd-ly
• after the first syllable if it has only one letter	Ameri-can	A-merican
• before the last syllable if it has only one letter	nu-tria	nutri-a
• before the ending *-ed* if the *-ed* is not pronounced	——	abash-ed

TIP

When dividing a word at the end of a line, it is always a good idea to use a dictionary to verify the word's proper syllabification.

NUMBERS

Numbers are an important part of everyday communication, yet they often cause a writer to stumble, particularly over questions of spelling and style. The guidelines on *how* to spell out a number are fairly straightforward. The guidelines on *when* to spell out a number are not so precise.

How to Spell Out Numbers

CARDINAL NUMBERS

The most common problem associated with the spelling of whole cardinal numbers is punctuation. The rules are actually quite simple: Numeric amounts that fall between twenty and one hundred are always hyphenated. No other punctuation should appear in a spelled-out whole number, regardless of its size.

26	twenty-six
411	four hundred eleven
758	seven hundred fifty-eight
6,500	six thousand five hundred
33,003	thirty-three thousand three
972,923	nine hundred seventy-two thousand nine hundred twenty-three

Note: The word *and* does not belong in the spelling of a number. For example, "758" should not be spelled "seven hundred and fifty-eight."

ORDINAL NUMBERS

The punctuation of spelled-out ordinal numbers typically follows the rules for cardinal numbers.

> What should we do for their fifty-fifth anniversary?
> He graduated two hundred twenty-ninth out of a class of two hundred thirty.

When ordinal numbers appear as numerals, they are affixed with *–th*, with the exception of those ending with the ordinal *first*, *second*, or *third*.

1st	581st
2nd	32nd
3rd	73rd
4th	907th

Note: Sometimes 2nd is written as 2d, and 3rd as 3d.

FRACTIONS

A fraction can appear in a number of formats, as shown here:

$\frac{3}{8}$	case fraction (or split fraction)
3/8	fraction with solidus
0.375	decimal fraction
three-eighths	spelled-out fraction

When acting as an adjective, a spelled-out fraction should always be hyphenated.

> The Serbian democrats have won a two-thirds majority.

When acting as a noun, a spelled-out fraction may or may not be hyphenated, according to the writer's or publisher's preferred style.

> At least four-fifths of the supply has been depleted.
> *or*
> At least four fifths of the supply has been depleted.

When to Spell Out Numbers

When to spell out a number, whole or fractional, is as much a matter of sense as of style. Text that is heavy with numbers, such as scientific or statistical material, could become virtually unreadable if the numbers were all spelled out. Conversely, conventional prose that occasionally makes mention of a quantity may look unbalanced with an occasional numeral here and there.

Often, the decision to spell or not to spell comes down to simple clarity:

> Our standard paper size is 8½ by 11.
> Our standard paper size is 8 1/2 by 11.
> Our standard paper size is eight and a half by eleven.
> Our standard paper size is eight and one-half by eleven.

The preceding four sentences say exactly the same thing, but the best choice for readability is the first.

TIP

Numerals and other symbols should never begin a sentence. If the symbol should not or cannot be spelled out, the sentence needs to be reworded.

> 19 students have become mentors.
> *should be:*
> Nineteen students have become mentors.
>
> 2006 is the year we plan to get married.
> *should be:*
> We plan to get married in 2006.
>
> $10 was found on the stairs.
> *should be:*
> Ten dollars was found on the stairs.
>
> 6:00 is the earliest I can leave.
> *should be:*
> Six o'clock is the earliest I can leave.
> *or:*
> The earliest I can leave is 6:00.
>
> $y = 2x + 1$ is a line with a slope of 2.
> *should be:*
> The line $y = 2x + 1$ has a slope of 2.

Even the most comprehensive books of style and usage do not dictate absolute rules regarding the style of numbers in text. When writing, it is most important to be as consistent as possible with a style once one has been established. For example, some writers or publishers may adopt a policy of spelling out the numbers zero through ten. Others may prefer to spell out the numbers zero through ninety-nine. Either style is perfectly acceptable, as long as the style is followed throughout the written work.

Sometimes, even after adopting a basic number style, the writer may wish to incorporate certain style allowances and exceptions. Perhaps the decision has been made by the writer to spell out only the numbers zero though ninety-nine. But in one paragraph, a sentence reads, "There must have been more than 1,000,000 people there." In this case, it may be better to write, "There must have been more than a million people there."

SYMBOLS

In most contexts of formal writing, the use of symbols should be strictly limited, but there are occasions when a symbol may be a better choice than a word. Text that deals largely with commerce, for instance, may rely on the use of various monetary symbols to keep the text organized and readable. In any text, mathematical equations and scientific formulas are much easier to read if written with symbols rather than words. Also, it is usually appropriate to use symbols within tables and charts; as symbols conserve space, they prevent a "cluttered look."

Here are some of the most common symbols found in print:

@	at	/	per *or* solidus
c/o	care of	%	percent
$	dollar	°	degree
¢	cent	+	plus
Can$	Canadian dollar	–	minus
£	pound sterling	÷	divided by
¥	yen	×	times
#	number *or* pound	±	plus *or* minus

=	equals	©	copyright
≈	is approximately equal to	®	registered
≠	is not equal to	™	trademark
<	is less than	¶	paragraph
>	is greater than	§	section
⩽	is less than or equal to	*	asterisk
⩾	is greater than or equal to	†	dagger
√‾	square root	‡	double dagger
∞	infinity	‖	parallels *or* pipes

Symbols are sometimes used to point out note references to the reader. In a table or chart, for instance, the writer may wish to indicate that an item is further explained or identified elsewhere on the page. A symbol placed with the item signals the reader to look for an identical symbol, which precedes the additional information. Sometimes, numerals are the symbols of choice, but if the material within the table or chart consists of numerals, it is probably better to use non-numeric symbols for the note references. The conventional set of symbols used for this purpose, in the conventional sequence in which to use them, is *, †, ‡, §, ‖, #.

COMMONLY MISSPELLED WORDS

abbreviated
absence
absolutely
acceptance
accessible
accidentally
accommodate
accompany
accuracy
ache
achieve
achievement
acquaintance
acquire
acre
across
actually
administration
admittance
adolescent
advantageous
advertisement
advisable
affectionate
affidavit
aficionado
afraid
again
aggravate
aghast
aisle
allege
allotment
ally
amateur
analysis
analyze
anesthetic
angel
angle
annihilation
annually
answer
anticipate
anxiety
apartheid
aperitif
apology
apparatus
apparent
appearance
appetite
appreciate
approach
appropriate
approximately
argue
argument
arithmetic
arrangement
ascend
ascertain
assistant
athletic
attendance
authority
auxiliary
available
awkward
bachelor
because
beggar
beginning
behavior
believe
benefit
benefited
bicycle
bouillon
boundary
bulletin
bureau
buried
business
cafeteria
calendar
campaign
cancellation
captain
carburetor
career
ceiling
cemetery
census
certificate
chamois

changeable
character
characteristic
chauffeur
chic
chief
chocolate
choice
choose
chose
Christian
clothes
collateral
colonel
color
column
commercial
commission
committee
community
compel
competitor
completely
conceivable
concentrate
condemn
confidence
confidential
confusion
connoisseur
conscience
conscious
continuous
controlled
controversial
conversant
convertible
cooperate
copyright
corps
correspondence
counterfeit
courageous
courteous
criticism
criticize
cruelly
curiosity
curious
cylinder
dealt
debtor
deceive
decision
definite
dependent
describe
despair
desperate
despise
develop
difference
dilemma
diphthong
disappearance
disappoint
disastrous
discipline
discrepancy
disease
diuretic
doctor
duplicate
easily
ecclesiastical
ecstasy
effect
efficient
eighth
elementary
eligible
embarrass
eminent
emphasize
encouragement
encumbrances
enforceable
entirely
entourage
envelope
environment
equipped
escape
especially
essential
et cetera (*abbreviated* etc.)
exaggerate
excellent
exciting
exercise
exhilarating
exhort
existence
expense
experience
experiment
extraordinary
extremely
facsimile
familiar
fantasy
fascinate
fashionable
fasten
fatal
favorite
February
field
fiery
finally
financial
fluorescent
forehead
foreign
forfeit
fortunately
forty
forward
fourth
freight
friend
fulfill
further
gauge
genius
gourmet
government
governor
gracious
grammar
guarantee
guerrilla
guess
guidance
gymnasium
gypsy
handsome
hangar
hanger
happened
happiness
harass
Hawaii

Commonly Misspelled Words (*cont.*)

heavily
height
heinous
heroine
hors d'oeuvre
hospital
humor
humorous
hungrily
hygiene
hypocrisy
hypocrite
hysterical
ignorance
illiterate
imagine
immediately
impossible
incidentally
increase
indefinite
independent
indictment
indispensable
individually
inevitable
influence
ingredient
innocence
inoculate
insurance
intelligence
intelligent
interference
interrupt
iridescent
irrelevant
itinerary
jealous
jewelry
knowledge
laboratory
laborer
laid
legitimate
leisure
liaison
library
license
lieutenant
lightning
likely
liquefy
liquidate
listener
literature
livelihood
lively
loneliness
luxury
magazine
magnificent
maintenance
maneuver
manufacturer
marriage
marvelous
mathematics
meant
mechanic
medical
medicine
melancholy
merchandise
millionaire
miniature
minimum
minuscule
minute
miscellaneous
mischief
mischievous
Massachusetts
misspell
mortgage
muscle
mysterious
narrative
naturally
necessary
nickel
niece
ninety
noisily
non sequitur
noticeable
obstacle
occasionally
occurrence
offensive
official
often
omission
omit
omitted
once
operate
opponent
opportunity
optimistic
orchestra
ordinarily
organization
originally
outrageous
pageant
paid
parallel
paralleled
paralyze
parliament
particular
pastime
peaceful
peculiar
performance
permanent
perseverance
personality
personnel
perspiration
persuade
pessimistic
phenomenal
Philippines
philosophy
physical
picnicking
pleasant
politician
Portuguese
possession
possibility
practically
practice
prairie
preferred
prejudice
preparation
presence

pressure
pretension
privilege
probably
procedure
proceed
procure
professor
proffered
promissory
pronunciation
propaganda
psychic
psychology
pumpkin
punctual
punctuation
pursuit
questionnaire
quiet
quite
quotient
raspberry
realize
really
realtor
realty
receipt
recipe
recognize
recommend
referred
reign
relevant
relieve
religious
removal
rendezvous
repertoire
repetition
rescind
reservoir
resistance
resource
responsibility
restaurant
rheumatism
rhythm
ridiculous
roommate
sachet
sacrifice
sacrilegious
safety
satisfied
scarcely
scarcity
scene
schedule
scholar
scissors
scurrilous
seance
secretary
seize
semester
separate
sergeant
shepherd
siege
similar
sincerely
skein
skiing
skillful
sophomore
soufflé
source
souvenir
specialty
specifically
specimen
sponsor
statistics
straight
strength
stretch
strictly
stubborn
substitute
subtle
succeed
successful
suede
sufficient
summary
superintendent
supersede
surgeon
surprise
susceptible
suspense
swimming
sympathetic
synonym
temperamental
temperature
tendency
therefore
thorough
though
thoughtful
tomorrow
tragedy
transferred
traveled
tremendous
truly
twelfth
typical
unanimous
unnecessary
useful
useless
usually
vacillate
vacuum
vague
valuable
variety
various
vegetable
vengeance
vilify
villain
warrant
weather
Wednesday
weird
whether
whole
yacht
yield

FOREIGN TERMS

Foreign words and phrases that are likely to be unfamiliar to the reader should be set in italics. When such terms are to be included in writing or speech, a dictionary should be consulted by the writer to insure proper placement of accents and other diacritical marks and by the speaker to insure correct pronunciations. Each of the following sample terms gives the literal translation, the English-usage definition, and an example sentence.

annus mirabilis: [Latin, 'wonderful year'] a remarkable or auspicious year.
This has been our team's *annus mirabilis.*

cause célèbre: [French, 'famous case'] a controversial issue that attracts a great deal of public attention.
The trial of Lizzie Borden became a *cause célèbre* throughout New England.

Weltschmerz: [German, 'world pain'] a feeling of melancholy and world-weariness.
A sense of *Weltschmerz* permeated his later works of art.
[Note that it is correct to capitalize a German noun.]

Familiar Foreign Terms

Many foreign terms have become so familiar and well-established in standard English usage that it is not necessary to put them in italic type. For most of these words, it is also not necessary to use accents and other diacritical marks, but in certain cases the inclusion of diacritics remains customary. There are, however, no absolute rules regarding when to italicize and when not to italicize, when to use diacritics and when not to use diacritics. Some foreign words may be more familiar to one group of readers than to another; therefore, targeted readership should be considered. Often, the style adopted is a matter of preference. As always, it is important for the writer to be consistent once this preference has been introduced.

Some familiar foreign terms:

ad absurdum
ad hoc
ad infinitum
ad interim
ad lib
ad nauseam
aficionado
à la carte (*or* a la carte)
à la king (*or* a la king)
à la mode (*or* a la mode)
al fresco
alter ego
annus mirabilis
Anno Domini
apartheid
aperitif
a priori
apropos
au contraire
au courant
au fait
au fond
au gratin
au jus
au naturel
au pair
avant-garde
ballet
basmati
bas-relief
baton
beau
beau monde
belle
bête noire
billet doux
bona fide
bonbon
bon mot
bon vivant
bouclé
boudoir
bouffant
bouillabaisse
bouillon
bouquet
bouquet garni
bourgeois
bric-a-brac
burka (*or* burkha)
burrito
cabaret
café (*or* cafe)
camisole
canapé
capo
carafe
carpe diem
carte blanche
cause célèbre
chaise longue
chalet
chamois
chapeau
chateau (*or* château)
chauffeur
chic
ciao
cognac
coiffeur
connoisseur
consommé

contretemps
corps
crepe (*or* crêpe)
croquette
cul-de-sac
de facto
déjà vu
de jure
de rigeur
dolce vita
doppelgänger
élan
elite
enchilada
enfant terrible
en masse
en route
entourage
entrée (*or* entree)
entre nous
eureka
ex cathedra
ex post facto
fait accompli
fajita
faux
faux pas
fiancé (*or* fiance)
fiancée (*or* fiancee)
fiesta
flagrante delicto
glasnost
gourmand
gourmet
hacienda
haute cuisine
hoi polloi
hors d'oeuvre
incognito
ingénue
in loco parentis
in re
in situ
in toto
in vitro
in vivo
jabot
judo
julienne
karma
karate
kasha
kibitz
kitsch
laissez-faire
lanai
lèse-majesté
loco
lorgnette
madame
mademoiselle
maître d' (*or* maitre d')
mañana
masseur
masseuse
materiel (*or* matériel)
mea culpa
modus operandi
monsieur
mot juste
née
ne plus ultra
nom de guerre
nom de plume
non sequitur
nota bene
nouveau riche
objet d'art
objet trouvé
pace
par excellence
pasha
pâté de foie gras
patio
per capita
persona non grata
pièce de résistance
pied-à-terre
piccolo
poncho
portière (*or* portiere)
post mortem
prima donna
prima facie
pro bono
pro forma
pronto
protégé (*or* protege)
purée (*or* puree)
quid pro quo
qui vive
raison d'être
re
rendezvous
repertoire
résumé (*or* resume)
revue
roué
roulette
sachet
salsa
samovar
samurai
sangfroid
sans souci
savoir faire
seance
serape
siesta
sine die
sine qua non
sombrero
soufflé
status quo
sub judice
suede
tableau
table d'hôte
tabula rasa
taco
tango
terra incognita
tête-à-tête
tour de force
tout le monde
trompe l'oeil
trousseau
verboten
vice versa
villa
viva voce
viz.
vox populi
Wanderjahr
Weltanschauung
Weltschmerz
yin/yang
yoga
Zeitgeist

Guide to Capitalization and Punctuation

CAPITALIZATION

Beginnings

The first word in a sentence is capitalized:

> <u>Dozens</u> of spectators lined the street.

The first word in a direct quotation is capitalized:

> Andy stood by the window and remarked, "<u>The</u> view from here is spectacular."

If a colon introduces more than one sentence, the first word after the colon is capitalized:

> We went over our findings, one piece of evidence at a time: <u>The</u> custodian had discovered the body just before midnight. The keys to the victim's office were found in the stairwell. In the adjoining office, three file cabinets had been overturned.

If a colon introduces a formal and distinct statement, the first word after the colon is capitalized:

> All my years on the basketball court have taught me one thing: <u>Winning</u> is more of a process than an outcome.

If a colon introduces a complete statement that is merely an extension of the statement preceding the colon, the first word after the colon is usually lowercased:

> Everything in the house was a shade of pink: <u>the</u> sofa was carnation blush, the tiles were misty mauve, and the carpet was dusty rose.

If a colon introduces an incomplete statement, the first word after the colon is lowercased:

> The caterer provided three choices: <u>chicken</u>, beef, and shrimp.

Proper Names

Proper names are capitalized. This is true of all proper names, including those of persons, places, structures, organizations, vessels, vehicles, brands, etc. Notice from the following examples that when a properly named entity is referred to in a "non-named" general sense, the general sense is almost always lowercased:

> Eleanor Roosevelt
> J. D. Salinger
> Carson City / a city in Nevada
> Ural Mountains / a view of the mountains
> New York Public Library / borrowing books from the public library
> Washington Monument / our photos of the monument
> Calvin Leete Elementary School / the rear entrance of the school
> Amherst Historical Society / when the society last met
> Boeing 747
> USS *Missouri* [note that the names of specific ships, aircraft, spacecraft, etc., are italicized]
> Chevy Malibu
> Slinky

Titles

The titles of works are capitalized. Titled works include:

- written material (books, periodicals, screenplays, etc.)
- components of written material (chapters, sections, etc.)
- filmed and/or broadcast works (movies, television shows, radio programs, etc.)
- works of art (paintings, sculptures, etc.)
- musical compositions (songs, operas, oratorios, etc.)

There are certain rules of convention regarding which words in the titles are capitalized.

Capitalize:

- first word in the title
- last word in the title
- nouns and pronouns
- adjectives
- verbs
- adverbs
- subordinating conjunctions (*although*, *as*, *because*, *if*, *since*, *that*, *whenever*, etc.)

Do not capitalize (unless they are first or last words in the title):

- articles (*a, an, the*)
- coordinating conjunctions (*and, but, for, nor, or, so, yet*)
- prepositions (although some guides suggest capitalizing prepositions of more than four letters)
- the word *to* in infinitives

The King, the Sword, and the Golden Lantern
A Room within a Room (*or* A Room Within a Room)
Seventy Ways to Make Easy Money from Your Home
The Stars Will Shine Because You Are Mine

If a subtitle is included, it typically follows a colon. It follows the capitalization rules of the main title, thus its first word is always capitalized:

Aftermath Explored: The Confessions of a Nuclear Physicist

The first element in a hyphenated compound is always capitalized. The subsequent elements are capitalized unless they are articles, prepositions, or coordinating conjunctions. But if the compound is the last word in the title, its final element is always capitalized, regardless of its part of speech:

Nineteenth-Century Poets
Over-the-Top Desserts
The Love-in of a Lifetime
The Year of the Love-In

An element that follows a hyphenated prefix is capitalized only if it is a proper noun or adjective:

Pre-Columbian Artifacts
Memoirs of a Semi-independent Child

Education

An academic title is capitalized (whether it is spelled out or abbreviated) when it directly accompanies a personal name. Otherwise, it is lowercased:

Professor Sarah McDonald
Assoc. Prof. Brown
my chemistry professor

An academic degree or honor is capitalized (whether it is spelled out or abbreviated) when it directly accompanies a personal name. Otherwise, it is lowercased:

> Harold L. Fox, Ph.D.
> Charles Gustafson, Fellow of the Geological Society
> working toward her master's degree

Academic years are lowercased:

> the senior prom
> he's a sophomore
> the fourth grade

The course name of a particular school subject is capitalized. A general field of study is lowercased (unless the word is normally capitalized, such as "English"):

> Astronomy 101
> Algebra II
> taking classes in psychology, French literature, and chemistry

Calendar Terms and Time

The names of the days of the week and months of the year are capitalized:

Sunday	September
Monday	October
Tuesday	November

The names of the four seasons are lowercased:

winter	summer
spring	fall *or* autumn

TIP

Which titles should be set in italics, and which should be set off by quotation marks? In printed material, the distinction can be significant. Here's a handy list of the most common categories of titles and their standard treatments in type:

italics:

- books
  Crossroads of Freedom: Antietam, by James M. McPherson
- pamphlets
  Thomas Paine's *Common Sense*
- magazines
  Popular Mechanics
- newspapers
  USA Today
- movies
  One Flew Over the Cuckoo's Nest
- television or radio series
  This Week in Baseball
- plays
  Neil Simon's *Lost in Yonkers*
- long poems
  Beowulf

The names of holidays (religious and secular) and periods of religious observance are capitalized:

Arbor Day
Easter
Halloween
Lent
Memorial Day
Ramadan

The names of time zones and the time systems they designate are lowercased (except for any words that are proper names). Their abbreviations are capitalized:

eastern daylight time (EDT)
Greenwich mean time (GMT)
Pacific standard time (PST)

Legislation, Treaties, etc.

The formal name of a policy, treaty, piece of legislation, or similar agreement is capitalized. A general reference to such is lowercased:

Volstead Act
the act sponsored by Congressman Volstead
Treaty of Versailles
the treaty at Versailles
Bottle Bill
Articles of Confederation
Connecticut Constitution
Connecticut's constitution
North American Free Trade Agreement

- collections of poems and other anthologies
  The Collected Poems of Emily Dickinson
- operas, oratorios, and other long musical compositions
  Madame Butterfly
- painting, sculptures, and other works of art
  Thomas Cole's *Mount Etna from Taormina*

quotation marks:

- articles
  "How to Remove Wallpaper"
- chapters
  "Betsy Saves the Day"
- short stories
  "The Pit and the Pendulum," by Edgar Allan Poe
- short poems
  "Tree at My Window," by Robert Frost
- essays
  Emerson's "Spiritual Laws"
- television or radio episodes
  "Lucy Does a TV Commercial"
- songs and other short musical compositions
  "Are You Lonesome Tonight?"

Military Service

A military title or rank is capitalized (whether it is spelled out or abbreviated) when it directly accompanies a personal name. Otherwise, it is lowercased:

Gen. George Patton
Ensign Irene Mahoney
promoted to admiral
James Kirk, captain of the USS *Enterprise*

There are two significant exceptions to the preceding rule: the U.S. military titles "Fleet Admiral" and "General of the Army" should always be capitalized, even when not directly accompanying a personal name:

became General of the Army in 1950
a visit from the Fleet Admiral

The full official name of a military group or force is capitalized. A general reference to a military group or force is lowercased:

the Royal Air Force
the British air force
the Army Corps of Engineers
the Third Battalion
our battalion
the U.S. Navy
joined the navy

The full name of a battle or war is capitalized. A general reference to a battle or war is lowercased:

the Russian Revolution
fought in the revolution
the Spanish-American War
the war in Vietnam
the Battle of the Bulge
the first battle of the campaign
the Norman Conquest

The official name of a military award or medal is capitalized:

the Purple Heart
the Silver Star
the Victoria Cross
the Congressional Medal of Honor

Science

The capitalization rules governing scientific terminology cover a wide range of categories and applications. Some of the basic rules are discussed here.

Taxonomic nomenclature—that is, the scientific classification of plants and animals—follows specific rules for both capitalization and italics.

The names of the phylum, class, order, and family of a plant or animal are capitalized and set in roman type. This format also applies to the intermediate groupings (suborder, subfamily, etc.) within these divisions:

The North American river otter belongs to the phylum Chordata, the subphylum Vertebrata, the class Mammalia, the order Carnivora, and the family Mustelidae.

The divisions lower than family—that is, genus, species, and subspecies—are set in italic type. Of these, only the genus is capitalized. When a plant or animal is identified by its "scientific name" or "Latin name," the name given is the genus and species (and, when applicable, the subspecies):

The scientific name of the river otter is *Lutra canadensis*.
The Manitoban elk (*Cervus elaphus manitobensis*) is a subspecies of the North American elk.

The common names of plants and animals, as well as their hybrids, varieties, and breeds, are lowercased and set in roman type. A part of the name may be capitalized if that part is a term normally capitalized (that is, a proper name). If there is doubt, a dictionary should be consulted.

Alaskan malamute
Christmas cactus
Johnny-jump-up
maidenhair fern
rainbow trout
rose-breasted grosbeak
Swainson's hawk
Vietnamese potbellied pig

The names of astronomical entities, such as planets, stars, constellations, and galaxies, are capitalized:

Alpha Centauri
Canis Major
Crab Nebula
Ganymede
Mercury
Milky Way
Orion
Sirius

TIP

The names *sun*, *moon*, and *earth* are frequently lowercased. It is customary to capitalize them only when they are being referred to as components of the solar system. Also noteworthy is the fact that, in any context, the words *sun* and *moon* typically are preceded by the definite article, *the*. In non-astronomical contexts, the word *earth* often is preceded by *the*, but it is never preceded by *the* when used specifically as the name of a planet. Hence, *the Earth* would not be an appropriate use of capitalization.

We enjoyed the warmth of <u>the sun</u>.
The glow of <u>the moon</u> has inspired poets for centuries.
Countless species inhabit <u>the earth</u>.
What on <u>earth</u> are you doing?
In size, Venus is comparable to <u>Earth</u>.
The eclipse of <u>the Moon</u> will be visible from the night side of <u>Earth</u>.
They made observations of Neptune's orbit around <u>the Sun</u>.

The names of geological eras, periods, epochs, etc., are capitalized. When included with the name, the words *era*, *period*, *epoch*, etc., are lowercased.

Mesozoic era
Quaternary period
Oligocene epoch
Upper Jurassic

Abbreviations

Although the use of abbreviations in formal writing should be limited, abbreviations are legitimate components of the language and deserve the same attention to spelling as do other words. Certain capitalization

> **TIP**
>
> If the name of an entity such as an organization, institution, or movement is to be abbreviated, its full name should be identified. Upon first mention, both abbreviation and full name should appear together, with either one being set within parentheses. (Usually the lesser known format goes in the parentheses.) Thereafter in the text, only the abbreviation need appear:
>
> In February 1909, a group of activists founded what would become the NAACP (National Association for the Advancement of Colored People). For more than ninety years, the NAACP has persevered to honor its founders' vision of racial equality and social justice.
>
> Plans to rebuild at the site of the World Trade Center (WTC) are being discussed today. Various designs for new office space are expected to be considered. Thousands of suggestions for a WTC memorial have already been submitted.

guidelines for a few types of abbreviations are given below. Because the possible variations are numerous, a standard dictionary should be consulted for more thorough guidance on the spelling, capitalization, and punctuation of a specific abbreviation.

When a capitalized term is abbreviated, the abbreviation is capitalized. If the abbreviation is comprised of initials, all the initials are capitalized:

Professor J. Leggett / Prof. J. Leggett
Sergeant David Potter / Sgt. David Potter
Master of Business Administration / MBA
United States Marine Corps / USMC

When a lowercased term is abbreviated as a simple shortening, the abbreviation is usually lowercased. But if the abbreviation is comprised of initials, all the initials are usually capitalized. When there is a compound word in the term, the initials may include the first letter of the root word:

especially / esp.
teaspoon / tsp.
deoxyribonucleic acid / DNA
monosodium glutamate / MSG
most favored nation / MFN

Usually, an abbreviation that ends in a capital letter is not followed by a period. An abbreviation that ends in a lowercase letter usually is followed by a period, although the period may be optional, depending on the prevailing style of the particular piece of writing.

One group of abbreviations that never ends with a period is the set of chemical symbols. Also, these abbreviations are always initially capitalized even though the terms they represent are lowercased:

Ar	argon	Na	sodium
Dy	dysprosium	Sb	antimony
H	hydrogen	Sn	tin
Kr	krypton	U	uranium
Lr	lawrencium	Xe	xenon

Note that some chemical symbols appear to be straightforward abbreviations (*Ca* for *calcium*) while others seem unrelated to their corresponding terms (*Au* for *gold*). In fact, these symbols are abbreviations of the official scientific, or Latin, names (*Au* for *aurum*, which is Latin for *gold*).

PUNCTUATION

Punctuation is an essential element of good writing because it makes the author's meaning clear to the reader. Although precise punctuation styles may vary somewhat among published sources, there are a number of fundamental principles worthy of consideration. Discussed below are these punctuation marks used in English:

comma	apostrophe
semicolon	quotation marks
colon	parentheses
period	dash
question mark	hyphen
exclamation point	

Comma

The **comma** is the most used mark of punctuation in the English language. It signals to the reader a pause, which generally clarifies the author's meaning and establishes a sensible order to the elements of written language. Among the most typical functions of the comma are the following:

1. It can separate the clauses of a compound sentence when there are two independent clauses joined by a conjunction, especially when the clauses are not very short:

   It never occurred to me to look in the attic, and I'm sure it didn't occur to Rachel either.

   The Nelsons wanted to see the Grand Canyon at sunrise, but they overslept that morning.

2. It can separate the clauses of a compound sentence when there is a series of independent clauses, the last two of which are joined by a conjunction:

   The bus ride to the campsite was very uncomfortable, the cabins were not ready for us when we got there, the cook had forgotten to start dinner, and the rain was torrential.

3. It is used to precede or set off, and therefore indicate, a nonrestrictive dependent clause (a clause that could be omitted without changing the meaning of the main clause):

   I read her autobiography, which was published last July.

   They showed up at midnight, after most of the guests had gone home.

   The coffee, which is freshly brewed, is in the kitchen.

4. It can follow an introductory phrase:

   Having enjoyed the movie so much, he agreed to see it again.

   Born and raised in Paris, she had never lost her French accent.

   In the beginning, they had very little money to invest.

5. It can set off words used in direct address:

   Listen, people, you have no choice in the matter.

   Yes, Mrs. Greene, I will be happy to feed your cat.

6. It can separate two or more coordinate adjectives (adjectives that could otherwise be joined with *and*) that modify one noun:

   The cruise turned out to be the most entertaining, fun, and relaxing vacation I've ever had.

   The horse was tall, lean, and sleek.

   Note that cumulative adjectives (those not able to be joined with *and*) are not separated by a comma:

   She wore bright yellow rubber boots.

7. It is used to separate three or more items in a series or list:

   Charlie, Melissa, Stan, and Mark will be this year's soloists in the spring concert.

We need furniture, toys, clothes, books, tools, housewares, and other useful merchandise for the benefit auction.

Note that the comma between the last two items in a series is sometimes omitted in less precise style:

The most popular foods served in the cafeteria are pizza, hamburgers and nachos.

8. It is used to separate and set off the elements in an address or other geographical designation:

   My new house is at 1657 Nighthawk Circle, South Kingsbury, Michigan.

   We arrived in Pamplona, Spain, on Thursday.

9. It is used to set off direct quotations (note the placement or absence of commas with other punctuation):

   "Kim forgot her gloves," he said, "but we have a pair she can borrow."

   There was a long silence before Jack blurted out, "This must be the world's ugliest painting."

   "What are you talking about?" she asked in a puzzled manner.

   "Happy New Year!" everyone shouted.

10. It is used to set off titles after a person's name:

    Katherine Bentley, M.D.

    Martin Luther King, Jr., delivered the sermon.

Semicolon

The **semicolon** has two basic functions:

1. It can separate two main clauses, particularly when these clauses are of equal importance:

   The crowds gathered outside the museum hours before the doors were opened; this was one exhibit no one wanted to miss.

   She always complained when her relatives stayed for the weekend; even so, she usually was a little sad when they left.

2. It can be used as a comma is used to separate such elements as clauses or items in a series or list, particularly when one or more of the elements already includes a comma:

   The path took us through the deep, dark woods; across a small meadow into a cold, wet cave; and up a hillside overlooking the lake.

   Listed for sale in the ad were two bicycles; a battery-powered, leaf-mulching lawn mower; and a maple bookcase.

Colon

The **colon** has five basic functions:

1. It can introduce something, especially a list of items:

   In the basket were three pieces of mail: a postcard, a catalog, and a wedding invitation.

   Students should have the following items: backpack, loose-leaf notebook, pens and pencils, pencil sharpener, and ruler.

2. It can separate two clauses in a sentence when the second clause is being used to explain or illustrate the first clause:

   We finally understood why she would never go sailing with us: she had a deep fear of the water.

   Most of the dogs in our neighborhood are quite large: two of them are St. Bernards.

3. It can introduce a statement or a quotation:

   His parents say the most important rule is this: Always tell the truth.

   We repeated the final words of his poem: "And such is the plight of fools like me."

4. It can be used to follow the greeting in a formal or business letter:

   Dear Ms. Daniels:

   Dear Sir or Madam:

5. It is used in the United States to separate minutes from hours, and seconds from minutes, in showing time of day and measured length of time:

   Please be at the restaurant before 6:45.

   Her best running time so far has been 00:12:35.

Period

The **period** has two basic functions:

1. It is used to mark the end of a sentence:

   It was reported that there is a shortage of nurses at the hospital. Several of the patients have expressed concern about this problem.

2. It is often used at the end of an abbreviation:

   On Fri., Sept. 12, Dr. Brophy noted that the patient's weight was 168 lb. and that his height was 6 ft. 2 in.

   (Note that another period is not added to the end of the sentence when the last word is an abbreviation.)

Question Mark and Exclamation Point

The only sentences that do not end in a period are those that end in either a question mark or an exclamation point.

Question marks are used to mark the end of a sentence that asks a direct question (generally, a question that expects an answer):

Is there any reason for us to bring more than a few dollars?

Who is your science teacher?

Exclamation points are used to mark the end of a sentence that expresses a strong feeling, typically surprise, joy, or anger:

I want you to leave and never come back!

What a beautiful view this is!

Apostrophe

The **apostrophe** has two basic functions:

1. It is used to show where a letter or letters are missing in a contraction.

   The directions are cont'd [continued] *on the next page.*
   We've [we have] *decided that if she can't* [cannot] *go, then we aren't* [are not] *going either.*

2. It can be used to show possession:

   The possessive of a singular noun or an irregular plural noun is created by adding an apostrophe and an *s*:

the pilot's uniform
Mrs. Mendoza's house
a tomato's bright red color
the oxen's yoke

The possessive of a regular plural noun is created by adding just an apostrophe:

the pilots' uniforms [referring to more than one pilot]
the Mendozas' house [referring to the Mendoza family]
the tomatoes' bright red color [referring to more than one tomato]

Quotation Marks

Quotation marks have two basic functions:

1. They are used to set off direct quotations (an exact rendering of someone's spoken or written words):

   "I think the new library is wonderful," she remarked to David.

   We were somewhat lost, so we asked, "Are we anywhere near the gallery?"

   In his letter he had written, "The nights here are quiet and starry. It seems like a hundred years since I've been wakened by the noise of city traffic and squabbling neighbors."

   Note that indirect quotes (which often are preceded by *that*, *if*, or *whether*) are not set off by quotation marks:

   He told me that he went to school in Boston.

   We asked if we could still get tickets to the game.

2. They can be used to set off words or phrases that have specific technical usage, or to set off meanings of words, or to indicate words that are being used in a special way in a sentence:

   The part of the flower that bears the pollen is the "stamen."

   When I said "plain," I meant "flat land," not "ordinary."

   Oddly enough, in the theater, the statement "break a leg" is meant as an expression of good luck.

   What you call "hoagies," we call "grinders" or "submarine sandwiches."

   He will never be a responsible adult until he outgrows his "Peter Pan" behavior.

   Note that sometimes single quotation marks, rather than double quotation marks, may be used to set off words or phrases:

   The part of the flower that bears the pollen is the 'stamen.'

   What is most important is to be consistent in such usage. Single quotation marks are also used to set off words or phrases within material already in double quotation marks, as:

   "I want the sign to say 'Ellen's Bed and Breakfast' in large gold letters," she explained.

Parentheses

Parentheses are used, in pairs, to enclose information that gives extra detail or explanation to the regular text. Parentheses are used in two basic ways:

1. They can separate a word or words in a sentence from the rest of the sentence:

   On our way to school, we walk past the Turner Farm (the oldest dairy farm in town) and watch the cows being fed.

   The stores were filled with holiday shoppers (even more so than last year).

Note that the period goes outside the parentheses, because the words in the parentheses are only part of the sentence.

2. They can form a separate complete sentence:

Please bring a dessert to the dinner party. (It can be something very simple.) I look forward to seeing you there.

Note that the period goes inside the parentheses, because the words in the parentheses are a complete and independent sentence.

Dash

A **dash** is used most commonly to replace the usage of parentheses within sentences. If the information being set off is in the middle of the sentence, a pair of long (or "em") dashes is used; if it is at the end of the sentence, just one long dash is used:

On our way to school, we walk past the Turner Farm—the oldest dairy farm in town—and watch the cows being fed.

The stores were filled with holiday shoppers—even more so than last year.

Hyphen

A **hyphen** has three basic functions:

1. It can join two or more words to make a compound, especially when doing so makes the meaning more clear to the reader:

We met to discuss long-range planning.

There were six four-month-old piglets at the fair.

That old stove was quite a coal-burner.

2. It can replace the word "to" when a span or range of data is given. This kind of hyphen is sometimes keyed as a short (or "en") dash:

John Adams was president of the United States 1797–1801.

Today we will look for proper nouns in the L–N section of the dictionary.

The ideal weight for that breed of dog would be 75–85 pounds.

3. It can indicate a word break at the end of a line. The break must always be between syllables:

It is important for any writer to know that there are numerous punctuation principles that are consid-ered standard and proper, but there is also flexibility regarding acceptable punctuation. Having learned the basic "rules" of good punctuation, the writer will be able to adopt a specific and consistent style of punc-tuation that best suits the material he or she is writing.

WORDS: MAKING THE RIGHT CHOICES

The building blocks of written or spoken communication are, of course, words. When we speak informally to one another throughout the day, we use our familiar vocabulary and patterns of expression without giving the individual words much thought. When our communication is more formal—as in a letter, an article, or a speech—our choice of words becomes more important.

Synonyms

Knowing which words to choose depends largely on knowing how to use synonyms. A **synonym** is a term that means exactly or nearly the same as another term in the same language. For example, *glad* is a synonym of *pleased*. By exploring synonym choices, writers are likely to keep their writing fresh and interesting.

Thoughtfully selected words not only convey the writer's message, they can enhance readability and demonstrate the writer's competency. It is usually well worth the writer's time to be guided by such resources as thesauruses and synonym studies.

USING THESAURUSES

A thesaurus, essentially a book of synonyms, can be an indispensable tool for the writer. There are two conventional types of thesauruses: one arranges the material by theme; the other arranges the headwords in an A-to-Z format, much like a dictionary. Most modern thesauruses are compiled in the latter format.

There are several reasons that one might consult a thesaurus. Perhaps "the right word" is somewhere in the writer's mind, but it just isn't coming to the writer at that moment. The writer thinks, "The word means something like *to pause*." When the writer looks up *pause* in the thesaurus, there in a list of synonyms is the very word! The writer is relieved and thinks, "Yes, that's what I was thinking of—the word *hesitate*."

Another valuable function of a thesaurus is to help the writer avoid repetition. Using the same word over and over again can be monotonous to the reader and may suggest weak vocabulary skills on the part of the writer. Consider the following paragraph:

> The movie we saw last night was very exciting. It started with an exciting car chase, and it just got more and more exciting as the plot developed. There were many moments that had me on the edge of my seat, but the scene in the train station was definitely the most exciting part of the story.

The writer risks losing the reader's attention because the reader may be thinking, "Doesn't this person know any word other than *exciting*?" If the writer were to consult a thesaurus, the paragraph could be greatly improved. One such revision might read as follows:

> The movie we saw last night was very <u>exciting</u>. It started with a <u>sensational</u> car chase, and it just got more and more <u>thrilling</u> as the plot developed. There were many moments that had me on the edge of my seat, but the scene in the train station was definitely the most <u>electrifying</u> part of the story.

A thesaurus can expand a writer's use of vocabulary and perk up a piece of writing, but it is the writer's responsibility to make certain that the words chosen are appropriate for the intended context. If a writer is not certain of the precise meaning or correct usage of a term listed in a thesaurus, a dictionary should be consulted as well.

Using synonym studies

Many dictionaries feature synonym studies, which expound on the usage of synonyms for selected terms. They offer an analytical treatment of the nuances of meaning that distinguish a set of closely related synonyms. If a synonym study were to appear at the dictionary entry for *distinguish*, for example, it might look like this:

> SYNONYM STUDY: **distinguish**
> DESCRY, DIFFERENTIATE, DISCERN, DISCRIMINATE. What we **discern**, we see apart from all other objects (*to discern the lighthouse beaming on the far shore*). **Descry** puts even more emphasis on the distant or unclear nature of what we're seeing (*the lookout was barely able to descry a man approaching*). To **discriminate** is to perceive the differences between or among things that are very similar; it may suggest that some aesthetic evaluation is involved (*to discriminate between two singers' styles*). **Distinguish** requires making even finer distinctions among things that resemble each other even more closely (*unable to distinguish the shadowy figures moving through the forest*). *Distinguish* can also mean recognizing by some special mark or outward sign (*the sheriff could be distinguished by his badge*). **Differentiate**, on the other hand, suggests the ability to perceive differences between things that are easily confused. In contrast to *distinguish*, *differentiate* suggests subtle differences that must be compared in some detail (*the color of the first paint sample was difficult to differentiate from the third sample*).

Clichés

A **cliché** is a worn-out expression. It was once fresh and meaningful, but it has lost its original impact through overuse. Numerous clichés have become so familiar that it would be virtually impossible to eradicate them from one's vocabulary. However, writers and speakers should make the effort to avoid using them, especially in formal material.

Common clichés to avoid

above and beyond the call of duty
accident waiting to happen
acid test
add insult to injury
after all is said and done
all hands on deck
all in all
all wet
all's well that ends well
almighty dollar
along the same lines
A-OK
as luck would have it
at a loss for words
at arm's length
avoid like the plague
back in the saddle
back on track
backseat driver
ball is in your court
barking up the wrong tree
be your own worst enemy
beat a dead horse
beat around the bush
been there, done that
beggars can't be choosers
be an open book
believe me
better late than never
between a rock and a hard place
between you, me, and the lamppost
big picture
big spender
bigger fish to fry
bird's-eye view
bitter end
bone of contention
born and bred
both sides of the coin
brain trust
bring home the bacon
broad spectrum
broaden one's horizons
bundle of nerves
bury the hatchet
busy as a bee
buy into
by leaps and bounds
by the skin of one's teeth
call her bluff
can't judge a book by its cover
can't take a joke
cast the net
catbird seat
catch as catch can
center of attention
cheat death
chew the fat
clear as a bell
clear as mud
cloak and dagger
coast is clear
cold as ice
cold shoulder
come full circle
come to no good
come up for air
conspicuous by their absence
cool it
cop out
could eat a horse
counting on you
count your blessings
cover all the bases
crazy like a fox
cream of the crop
creature of habit
crossing the line
cut me some slack
cut to the chase
dead in the water
dead wrong
dog-eat-dog
done deal
done to death
don't know him from Adam
down and dirty
down and out
down in the dumps
down in the mouth
dressed to the nines
due in large measure to

duly noted
dumb luck
easier said than done
easy come, easy go
easy mark
easy target
eat crow
end of discussion
every fiber of my being
face the music
fair and square
fall from grace
fall through the cracks
far and away
feast or famine
few and far between
fighting the tide
fill the bill
find it in your heart
fit as a fiddle
fit to be tied
fits like an old shoe
flat as a pancake
fly in the ointment
fly off the handle
for all intents and purposes
for love or money
for your information
fork it over
free as a bird
from the frying pan into the fire
from time immemorial
game plan
get behind the eight ball
get down to brass tacks
get off scot-free
get our ducks in a row
get the lead out
get the show on the road
get to the bottom of it
give a damn
give rise to
go for the kill
go it alone
go the distance
go the extra mile
go to pieces
go with the flow
goes without saying
good for nothing
goodly number
grass is always greener
green with envy
grist for the mill
hammer out the details
handwriting on the wall
hang in there
has a screw loose
have your heart in your mouth
head over heels
heated argument
his bark is worse than his bite
hit or miss
hit the ceiling
hit the ground running
hit the nail on the head
hold that thought
holding back the tide
hook, line, and sinker
hour of need
I wasn't born yesterday
icing on the cake
if looks could kill
if the price is right
I'm all over it
I'm speechless
in a nutshell
in due course
in hot water
in layman's terms
in one fell swoop
in over their heads
in seventh heaven
in the bag
in the ballpark
in the driver's seat
in the event that
in the final analysis
in the groove
in the near future
in the neighborhood of
in the nick of time
in the same boat
in the zone
in this day and age
irons in the fire
it could be worse
it stands to reason
it takes all kinds
it takes guts
it's your baby
join the club
keep your fingers crossed
keep the home fires burning
keeping score
kill the fatted calf

kiss of death
knock on wood
knock the socks off of
know the ropes
last but not least
last straw
lay an egg
learning curve
leave no stone unturned
left to his own devices
lend me an ear
let the cat out of the bag
let your hair down
letter perfect
lie low
light of day
like a bull in a china shop
like a bump on a log
like greased lightning
like rolling off a log
little does he know
live it up
lock, stock, and barrel
look like a million bucks
low man on the totem pole
make ends meet
make tracks
makes her blood boil
method in (*or* to) my madness
millstone around your neck
mince words
misery loves company
moment of truth
Monday-morning quarterback
monkey on your back
more money than God
more than meets the eye
more than you could shake a stick at
nail to the wall
naked truth
nearing the finish line
needle in a haystack
needs no introduction
never a dull moment
nip and tuck
nip in the bud
no harm, no foul
no skin off my nose
no strings attached
no-brainer
none the worse for wear
nose to the grindstone
not one red cent
nothing new under the sun
off the cuff
old as the hills
old hat
old soldiers never die
older than dirt
on cloud nine
on the one hand/on the other hand
on the road
on the same page
on the same track
on the wagon
on top of the world
out of my league
out of the woods
over a barrel
pan out
par for the course
pass the buck
pay the piper
perish the thought
piece of cake
playing for keeps
powers that be
practice makes perfect
proud as a peacock
pulling my leg
pulling no punches
put faces to names
put on hold
put the bite on
put words in one's mouth
put your money where your mouth is
quick and dirty
rags to riches
rant and rave
reading me like a book
real McCoy
red as a beet
regret to inform you
reign supreme
rings a bell
ripe old age
rise and shine
rolling over in his grave
rub elbows
rule the roost
run circles around
run it up the flagpole
run off at the mouth
sadder but wiser
safe to say
salt of the earth

scarce as hen's teeth
sea of faces
see the forest for the trees
sell like hotcakes
set in stone
shake a leg
sharp as a tack
ships that pass in the night
shoot the breeze
shooting himself in the foot
shot in the arm
shot to hell
sight for sore eyes
sitting duck
skeleton in the closet
skin alive
sleep on it
smells fishy
smooth sailing
snake in the grass
spill the beans
stay in the loop
steal the limelight
stem the tide
stick to your guns
stick your neck out
straight from the horse's mouth
strange bedfellows
strike a balance
strong as an ox
stubborn as a mule
sturdy as an oak
suffice it to say
sweating bullets
take a breather
take into consideration
take on board
take one's word for
take pleasure in
take the bitter with the sweet
take the easy way out
take the liberty of
talk shop
talk the talk
talk through your hat
talk your ear off
that's all she wrote
the die is cast
they'll be sorry
thick as thieves
thin as a rail
think outside the box
think tank
those are the breaks
through thick and thin
throw caution to the wind
thrown to the wolves
tighten our belts
time is money
time marches on
time waits for no man
to each his own
to your heart's content
too funny for words
took the words right out of my mouth
touch base
turn the other cheek
turn up your nose
two peas in a pod
ugly as sin
under the wire
up a creek
upset the applecart
venture a guess
vicious circle
waiting for the other shoe to drop
walk the walk
walking encyclopedia
walking on air
welcome with open arms
when the cows come home
where angels fear to tread
where there's smoke, there's fire
whole nine yards
wild-goose chase
wipe the slate clean
wishful thinking
with bated breath
without further ado
without further delay
wonders never cease
words fail me
wreak havoc
yada, yada, yada
you said a mouthful
you'll never know if you don't try

Redundant Expressions

A redundant expression is a group of words (usually a pair) in which at least one word is superfluous—that is, unnecessary. The superfluous element can be removed without affecting the meaning of the expression. In formal speech or writing, redundant expressions should be strictly avoided.

In the following list of common redundant expressions, the superfluous elements have been crossed out.

~~absolute~~ guarantee
~~absolutely~~ certain
~~absolutely~~ essential
~~absolutely~~ necessary
AC ~~current~~
~~actual~~ fact
~~actual~~ truth
add ~~an additional~~
adding ~~together~~
~~advance~~ reservations
~~advance~~ warning
after ~~the end of~~
all meet ~~together~~
alongside ~~of~~
~~already~~ existing
~~and~~ moreover
~~annoying~~ pest
ATM ~~machine~~
~~awkward~~ predicament
bald-~~headed~~
~~basic~~ essentials
~~basic~~ fundamentals
blend ~~together~~
~~brief~~ moment
~~but~~ however
~~but~~ nevertheless
came ~~at a time~~ when
cancel ~~out~~
~~chief~~ protagonist
~~clearly~~ obvious
climb ~~up~~
~~close~~ proximity
~~close~~ scrutiny
collaborate ~~together~~
combine ~~into one~~
commute ~~back and forth~~
~~complete~~ monopoly
~~completely~~ destroyed
~~completely~~ eliminated
~~completely~~ empty
~~completely~~ filled
~~completely~~ random
consensus ~~of opinion~~
continue ~~on~~
~~continue to~~ remain
cooperate ~~together~~
currently ~~today~~
DC ~~current~~
~~decorative~~ garnish
~~deep~~ chasm
~~definitely~~ decided
descend ~~down~~
~~different~~ varieties
~~difficult~~ dilemma
~~direct~~ confrontation
drop ~~down~~
during ~~the course of~~
dwindled ~~down~~
each ~~and every~~
earlier ~~in time~~
~~empty~~ space
~~end~~ result
enter ~~in~~
equal ~~to one another~~
~~established~~ fact
estimated at ~~about~~
estimated ~~roughly~~ at
~~every~~ now and then
~~evil~~ fiend
~~exact~~ duplicate
~~exact~~ opposites
~~fake~~ copy
~~false~~ pretenses
~~fellow~~ classmates
~~fellow~~ teammates
few ~~in number~~
filled ~~to capacity~~
~~final~~ conclusion
~~final~~ outcome
first ~~and foremost~~
~~first~~ began
~~first~~ introduction
first ~~of all~~
~~first~~ started
follow ~~after~~
for ~~a period of~~ six months
for ~~the purpose of~~
~~foreign~~ exports
~~foreign~~ imports
forever ~~and ever~~
foundered ~~and sank~~
~~free~~ gift
~~free~~ pass
~~future~~ prospects

gather ~~together~~
gave birth to a ~~baby~~ girl/boy
~~glowing~~ ember
~~good~~ bargain
~~good~~ benefits
had done ~~previously~~
~~harmful~~ injury
HIV ~~virus~~
~~honest~~ truth
~~hopeful~~ optimism
~~hot~~ water heater
I ~~myself personally~~
if ~~and when~~
~~important~~ breakthrough
in ~~close~~ proximity
~~intense~~ fury
introduced ~~for the first time~~
~~invited~~ guests
ISBN ~~number~~
joined ~~together~~
~~just~~ recently
kneel ~~down~~
last ~~of all~~
lift ~~up~~
look back ~~in retrospect~~
~~major~~ breakthrough
may ~~possibly~~
~~mental~~ telepathy
merged ~~together~~
meshed ~~together~~
~~midway~~ between
might ~~possibly~~
mix ~~together~~
~~mutual~~ cooperation
~~natural~~ instinct
never ~~at any time~~
~~new~~ beginning
~~new~~ bride
~~new~~ innovation
~~new~~ recruit
nine A.M. ~~in the morning~~
no trespassing ~~allowed~~
none ~~at all~~
~~now~~ pending
null ~~and void~~
~~old~~ cliché
~~old~~ proverb
~~opening~~ introduction
~~originally~~ created
over ~~and done with~~
~~over~~exaggerate
~~pair of~~ twins
parched ~~dry~~
~~passing~~ fad
~~past~~ experiences
~~past~~ history
~~past~~ memories
~~past~~ records
penetrate ~~into~~
~~perfect~~ ideal
permeate ~~throughout~~
~~personal~~ friend
~~personal~~ opinion
~~personally~~ believes
PIN ~~number~~
plan ~~in advance~~
~~poisonous~~ venom
~~positively~~ true
~~possibly~~ might
postponed ~~until a later time~~
~~pre~~recorded
~~present~~ incumbent
probed ~~into~~
proceed ~~ahead~~
protest ~~against~~
protrude ~~out~~
~~proven~~ facts
raise ~~up~~
reason ~~why~~
refer ~~back~~
reflect ~~back~~
repeat ~~again~~
reply ~~back~~
revert ~~back~~
Rio Grande ~~River~~
~~sad~~ tragedy
same ~~identical~~
seemed ~~to be~~
share ~~together~~
short ~~in length~~
since ~~the time when~~
~~sincerely~~ mean it
skipped ~~over~~
~~solemn~~ vow
spelled out ~~in detail~~
stacked ~~on top of each other~~
~~still~~ continues
~~still~~ persists
~~still~~ remains
strangled ~~to death~~
~~stupid~~ fool
~~suddenly~~ exploded
sufficient ~~enough~~
~~sum~~ total
summer ~~season~~
~~sworn~~ affidavit

~~temporary~~ recess
~~temporary~~ reprieve
~~terrible~~ tragedy
~~thoughtful~~ contemplation
~~thoughtful~~ deliberation
~~totally~~ eliminated
~~true~~ fact
~~twelve~~ midnight
~~twelve~~ noon
~~two~~ twins
~~ultimate~~ conclusion
~~unexpected~~ surprise
~~unintentional~~ mistake
~~uninvited~~ party crashers
UPC ~~code~~
~~usual~~ custom
~~utter~~ annihilation
~~very~~ unique
ways ~~and means~~
~~well-known old~~ adage
when ~~and if~~
whether ~~or not~~
widow ~~woman~~
written ~~down~~

Proofreader's Marks

- delete
- delete and close up
- delete and leave space
- insert
- space
- period
- comma
- semicolon
- colon
- apostrophe
- quotation marks
- parentheses
- square brackets
- hyphen
- em-dash
- en-dash
- new paragraph
- break line or word
- set as superscript
- set as subscript
- transpose
- transpose (note in margin)
- spell out
- spell out (note in margin)
- capitalize
- set as capitals (note in margin)
- make lower case
- set in lower case (note in margin)
- make boldface
- set in boldface (note in margin)
- make italic
- set in italic (note in margin)
- small caps
- set in small caps (note in margin)
- lightface (note in margin)
- set in roman (note in margin)

Writing Prompts

A writing prompt is an exercise to stretch your writing muscles before you begin your serious writing work-out. They're a good way to jump-start your flow of words when you feel stuck, unmotivated, or frustrated with your writing.

Writing prompts tend to ask the traditional questions: who? what? when? where? how? They often ask for personal, emotional responses rather than supporting facts and evidence.

Don't feel that you must complete an answer to a writing prompt. Write until you feel ready and able to tackle your main work—don't polish and buff up your prompt work until you have no energy for the writing you intended to do! You may want to try to write "drabbles" (short pieces of exactly 100 words) in response to prompts, both to keep your answers short and to teach yourself to be economical and concise.

Choose a writing prompt that you feel you can give a quick, personal, fluid answer to—if you're already blocked, choosing a difficult or remote topic will not make it any easier for you to get words on the page.

Here are a dozen basic writing prompts. If you need more, a quick Internet search will turn up pages and pages of possibilities.

1. Describe the room you're sitting in right now. What would you change if you could? What have you never noticed before?

2. What did you have for breakfast? What's the best breakfast you've ever had? What have you never eaten for breakfast?

3. When was the last time you were really furious, happy, or excited? What made you feel that way?

4. Who was the first person you ever hated? loved? worked for? Who was your first neighbor?

5. Write about a word that turned out not to mean what you thought it meant.

6. Imagine what your life would have been like fifty, a hundred, or two hundred years ago. What would you like about living then, and what could you not stand?

7. Did anyone ever pay you an unexpected compliment? What did they say, and when?

8. Describe a book that you would like to read that doesn't exist.

9. Take a familiar object (such as a toothbrush or a fork) and describe it in detail. How would you describe it to someone who has never seen one?

10. Describe exactly how you do something that you excel at. How do you make your famous apple pie? How do you hit the ball off the tee?

11. If you were asked to tell a stranger about the most emotionally significant moment of your life, what would you say? Would it be truthful, or would you not want to talk about it?

12. Write a conversation between two people who: are having an argument; are meeting for the first time; are old friends.

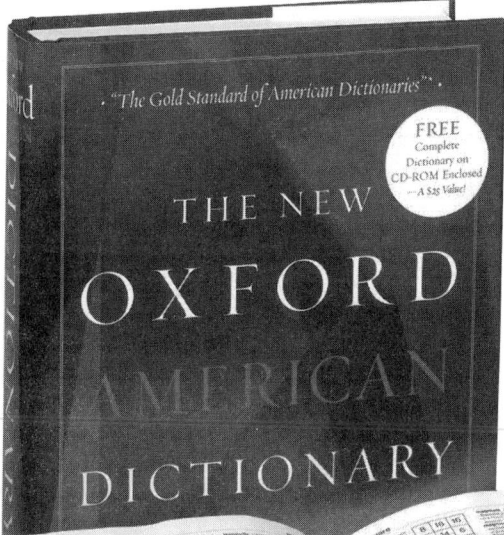